# THE OXFORD ENGLISH DICTIONARY

SECOND EDITION

# THE OXFORD ENGLISH DICTIONARY

*First Edited by*

JAMES A. H. MURRAY, HENRY BRADLEY, W. A. CRAIGIE
*and* C. T. ONIONS

COMBINED WITH

# A SUPPLEMENT TO THE OXFORD ENGLISH DICTIONARY

*Edited by*

R. W. BURCHFIELD

AND RESET WITH CORRECTIONS, REVISIONS
AND ADDITIONAL VOCABULARY

# THE OXFORD ENGLISH DICTIONARY

SECOND EDITION

*Prepared by*

J. A. SIMPSON *and* E. S. C. WEINER

VOLUME XV

Ser–Soosy

CLARENDON PRESS · OXFORD

*Oxford University Press, Great Clarendon Street, Oxford OX2 6DP*
*Oxford New York*
*Athens Auckland Bangkok Bogotá Buenos Aires Calcutta*
*Cape Town Chennai Dar es Salaam Delhi Florence Hong Kong Istanbul*
*Karachi Kuala Lumpur Madrid Melbourne Mexico City Mumbai*
*Nairobi Paris São Paulo Singapore Taipei Tokyo Toronto Warsaw*
*and associated companies in*
*Berlin Ibadan*

*Oxford is a registered trade mark of Oxford University Press*



*First published 1989*
*Reprinted 1991 (with corrections), 1998*



*British Library Cataloguing in Publication Data*
*Oxford English dictionary.—2nd ed.*
*1. English language—Dictionaries*
*I. Simpson, J. A. (John Andrew), 1953–*
*II. Weiner, Edmund S. C., 1950–*
*423*
*ISBN 0-19-861227-3 (vol. XV)*
*ISBN 0-19-861186-2 (set)*

*Library of Congress Cataloging-in-Publication Data*
*The Oxford English dictionary.—2nd ed.*
*prepared by J. A. Simpson and E. S. C. Weiner*
*Bibliography: p.*
*ISBN 0-19-861227-3 (vol. XV)*
*ISBN 0-19-861186-2 (set)*
*1. English language—Dictionaries. I. Simpson, J. A.*
*II. Weiner, E. S. C. III. Oxford University Press.*
*PE1625.087 1989*
*423—dc19 88-5330*

*Data capture by ICC, Fort Washington, Pa.*
*Text-processing by Oxford University Press*
*Typesetting by Pindar Graphics Origination, Scarborough, N. Yorks.*
*Manufactured in the United States of America by*
*World Color Book Services, Taunton, Mass.*

# KEY TO THE PRONUNCIATION

THE pronunciations given are those in use in the educated speech of southern England (the so-called 'Received Standard'), and the keywords given are to be understood as pronounced in such speech.

## I. *Consonants*

b, d, f, k, l, m, n, p, t, v, z *have their usual English values*

g as in *go* (gəʊ)
h ... *ho!* (həʊ)
r ... *run* (rʌn), *terrier* ('tɛrɪə(r))
(r) ... *her* (hɜː(r))
s ... *see* (siː), *success* (sək'sɛs)
w ... *wear* (wɛə(r))
hw ... *when* (hwɛn)
j ... *yes* (jɛs)

θ as in *thin* (θɪn), *bath* (bɑːθ)
ð ... *then* (ðɛn), *bathe* (beɪð)
ʃ ... *shop* (ʃɒp), *dish* (dɪʃ)
tʃ ... *chop* (tʃɒp), *ditch* (dɪtʃ)
ʒ ... *vision* ('vɪʒən), *déjeuner* (deʒøne)
dʒ ... *judge* (dʒʌdʒ)
ŋ ... *singing* ('sɪŋɪŋ), *think* (θiŋk)
ŋg ... *finger* ('fɪŋgə(r))

(FOREIGN AND NON-SOUTHERN)

ʎ as in It. *serraglio* (ser'raʎo)
ɲ ... Fr. *cognac* (kɔɲak)
x ... Ger. *ach* (ax), Sc. *loch* (lɒx), Sp. *frijoles* (fri'xoles)
ç ... Ger. *ich* (ɪç), Sc. *nicht* (nɪçt)
ɣ ... North Ger. *sagen* ('zaːɣən)
c ... Afrikaans *baardmannetjie* ('baːrtmanəci)
ɥ ... Fr. *cuisine* (kɥizin)

Symbols in parentheses are used to denote elements that may be omitted either by individual speakers or in particular phonetic contexts: e.g. *bottle* ('bɒt(ə)l), *Mercian* ('mɜːʃ(ɪ)ən), *suit* (s(j)uːt), *impromptu* (ɪm'prɒm(p)tjuː), *father* ('fɑːðə(r)).

## II. *Vowels and Diphthongs*

SHORT

ɪ as in *pit* (pɪt), *-ness*, (-nɪs)
ɛ ... *pet* (pɛt), Fr. *sept* (sɛt)
æ ... *pat* (pæt)
ʌ ... *putt* (pʌt)
ɒ ... *pot* (pɒt)
ʊ ... *put* (pʊt)
ə ... *another* (ə'nʌðə(r))
(ə) ... *beaten* ('biːt(ə)n)
i ... Fr. *si* (si)
e ... Fr. *bébé* (bebe)
a ... Fr. *mari* (mari)
ɑ ... Fr. *bâtiment* (bɑtimɑ̃)
ɔ ... Fr. *homme* (ɔm)
o ... Fr. *eau* (o)
ø ... Fr. *peu* (pø)
œ ... Fr. *boeuf* (bœf) *coeur* (kœr)
u ... Fr. *douce* (dus)
ʏ ... Ger. *Müller* ('mʏlər)
y ... Fr. *du* (dy)

LONG

iː as in *bean* (biːn)
ɑː ... *barn* (bɑːn)
ɔː ... *born* (bɔːn)
uː ... *boon* (buːn)
ɜː ... *burn* (bɜːn)
eː ... Ger. *Schnee* (ʃneː)
ɛː ... Ger. *Fähre* ('fɛːrə)
aː ... Ger. *Tag* (taːk)
oː ... Ger. *Sohn* (zoːn)
øː ... Ger. *Goethe* ('gøːtə)
yː ... Ger. *grün* (gryːn)

NASAL

ɛ̃, æ̃ as in Fr. *fin* (fɛ̃, fæ̃)
ɑ̃ ... Fr. *franc* (frɑ̃)
ɔ̃ ... Fr. *bon* (bɔ̃)
œ̃ ... Fr. *un* (œ̃)

DIPHTHONGS, etc.

eɪ as in *bay* (beɪ)
aɪ ... *buy* (baɪ)
ɔɪ ... *boy* (bɔɪ)
əʊ ... *no* (nəʊ)
aʊ ... *now* (naʊ)
ɪə ... *peer* (pɪə(r))
ɛə ... *pair* (pɛə(r))
ʊə ... *tour* (tʊə(r))
ɔə ... *boar* (bɔə(r))

aɪə as in *fiery* ('faɪərɪ)
aʊə ... *sour* (saʊə(r))

The incidence of main stress is shown by a superior stress mark (') preceding the stressed syllable, and a secondary stress by an inferior stress mark (ˌ), e.g. *pronunciation* (prəˌnʌnsɪ'eɪʃ(ə)n).

For further explanation of the transcription used, see *General Explanations*, Volume I.

# LIST OF ABBREVIATIONS, SIGNS, ETC.

Some abbreviations listed here in italics are also in certain cases printed in roman type, and vice versa.

| | |
|---|---|
| a. (in Etym.) | adoption of, adopted from |
| *a* (as *a* 1850) | *ante*, 'before', 'not later than' |
| a. | adjective |
| abbrev. | abbreviation (of) |
| abl. | ablative |
| *absol.* | absolute, -ly |
| *Abstr.* | (in titles) *Abstract, -s* |
| acc. | accusative |
| *Acct.* | (in titles) *Account* |
| A.D. | *Anno Domini* |
| ad. (in Etym.) | adaptation of |
| Add. | Addenda |
| *adj.* | adjective |
| *Adv.* | (in titles) *Advance, -d, -s* |
| *adv.* | adverb |
| advb. | adverbial, -ly |
| Advt. | advertisement |
| *Aeronaut.* | (as label) in Aeronautics; (in titles) *Aeronautic, -al, -s* |
| AF., AFr. | Anglo-French |
| Afr. | Africa, -n |
| *Agric.* | (as label) in Agriculture; (in titles) *Agriculture, -al* |
| Alb. | Albanian |
| *Amer.* | American |
| Amer. Ind. | American Indian |
| *Anat.* | (as label) in Anatomy; (in titles) *Anatomy, -ical* |
| *Anc.* | (in titles) *Ancient* |
| Anglo-Ind. | Anglo-Indian |
| Anglo-Ir. | Anglo-Irish |
| Ann. | Annals |
| *Anthrop., Anthropol.* | (as label) in Anthropology; (in titles) *Anthropology, -ical* |
| *Antiq.* | (as label) in Antiquities; (in titles) *Antiquity* |
| aphet. | aphetic, aphetized |
| app. | apparently |
| *Appl.* | (in titles) *Applied* |
| *Applic.* | (in titles) *Application, -s* |
| appos. | appositive, -ly |
| Arab. | Arabic |
| Aram. | Aramaic |
| *Arch.* | in Architecture |
| *arch.* | archaic |
| *Archæol.* | in Archæology |
| *Archit.* | (as label) in Architecture; (in titles) *Architecture, -al* |
| Arm. | Armenian |
| assoc. | association |
| *Astr.* | in Astronomy |
| *Astrol.* | in Astrology |
| *Astron.* | (in titles) *Astronomy, -ical* |
| *Astronaut.* | (in titles) *Astronautic, -s* |
| *attrib.* | attributive, -ly |
| *Austral.* | Australian |
| *Autobiogr.* | (in titles) *Autobiography, -ical* |
| A.V. | Authorized Version |
| B.C. | Before Christ |
| B.C. | (in titles) British Columbia |
| bef. | before |
| *Bibliogr.* | (as label) in Bibliography; (in titles) *Bibliography, -ical* |
| *Biochem.* | (as label) in Biochemistry; (in titles) *Biochemistry, -ical* |
| *Biol.* | (as label) in Biology; (in titles) *Biology, -ical* |
| *Bk.* | *Book* |
| *Bot.* | (as label) in Botany; (in titles) *Botany, -ical* |
| Bp. | Bishop |
| *Brit.* | (in titles) *Britain, British* |
| Bulg. | Bulgarian |
| *Bull.* | (in titles) *Bulletin* |
| *c* (as *c* 1700) | *circa*, 'about' |
| c. (as 19th c.) | century |
| *Cal.* | (in titles) *Calendar* |
| *Cambr.* | (in titles) *Cambridge* |
| *Canad.* | Canadian |
| Cat. | Catalan |
| *catachr.* | catachrestically |
| *Catal.* | (in titles) *Catalogue* |
| Celt. | Celtic |
| *Cent.* | (in titles) *Century, Central* |
| *Cent. Dict.* | *Century Dictionary* |
| Cf., cf. | *confer*, 'compare' |
| *Ch.* | Church |
| *Chem.* | (as label) in Chemistry; (in titles) *Chemistry, -ical* |
| *Chr.* | (in titles) *Christian* |
| *Chron.* | (in titles) *Chronicle* |
| *Chronol.* | (in titles) *Chronology, -ical* |
| *Cinemat., Cinematogr.* | in Cinematography |
| *Clin.* | (in titles) *Clinical* |
| cl. L. | classical Latin |
| cogn. w. | cognate with |
| *Col.* | (in titles) *Colonel, Colony* |
| *Coll.* | (in titles) *Collection* |
| *collect.* | collective, -ly |
| *colloq.* | colloquial, -ly |
| comb. | combined, -ing |
| *Comb.* | Combinations |
| *Comm.* | in Commercial usage |
| *Communic.* | in Communications |
| comp. | compound, composition |
| *Compan.* | (in titles) *Companion* |
| compar. | comparative |
| compl. | complement |
| *Compl.* | (in titles) *Complete* |
| *Conc.* | (in titles) *Concise* |
| *Conch.* | in Conchology |
| *concr.* | concrete, -ly |
| *Conf.* | (in titles) *Conference* |
| *Congr.* | (in titles) *Congress* |
| *conj.* | conjunction |
| cons. | consonant |
| const. | construction, construed with |
| contr. | contrast (with) |
| *Contrib.* | (in titles) *Contribution* |
| *Corr.* | (in titles) *Correspondence* |
| corresp. | corresponding (to) |
| Cotgr. | R. Cotgrave, *Dictionarie of the French and English Tongues* |
| cpd. | compound |
| *Crit.* | (in titles) *Criticism, Critical* |
| *Cryst.* | in Crystallography |
| *Cycl.* | (in titles) *Cyclopædia, -ic* |
| *Cytol.* | (in titles) *Cytology, -ical* |
| Da. | Danish |
| D.A. | *Dictionary of Americanisms* |
| D.A.E. | *Dictionary of American English* |
| dat. | dative |
| D.C. | District of Columbia |
| *Deb.* | (in titles) *Debate, -s* |
| def. | definite, -ition |
| dem. | demonstrative |
| deriv. | derivative, -ation |
| derog. | derogatory |
| *Descr.* | (in titles) *Description, -tive* |
| *Devel.* | (in titles) *Development, -al* |
| *Diagn.* | (in titles) *Diagnosis, Diagnostic* |
| *dial.* | dialect, -al |
| Dict. | Dictionary; *spec.*, the *Oxford English Dictionary* |
| dim. | diminutive |
| *Dis.* | (in titles) *Disease* |
| *Diss.* | (in titles) *Dissertation* |
| D.O.S.T. | *Dictionary of the Older Scottish Tongue* |
| Du. | Dutch |
| E. | East |
| *Eccl.* | (as label) in Ecclesiastical usage; (in titles) *Ecclesiastical* |
| *Ecol.* | in Ecology |
| *Econ.* | (as label) in Economics; (in titles) *Economy, -ics* |
| ed. | edition |
| E.D.D. | *English Dialect Dictionary* |
| *Edin.* | (in titles) *Edinburgh* |
| *Educ.* | (as label) in Education; (in titles) *Education, -al* |
| EE. | Early English |
| e.g. | *exempli gratia*, 'for example' |
| *Electr.* | (as label) in Electricity; (in titles) *Electricity, -ical* |
| *Electron.* | (in titles) *Electronic, -s* |
| *Elem.* | (in titles) *Element, -ary* |
| *ellipt.* | elliptical, -ly |
| *Embryol.* | in Embryology |
| e.midl. | east midland (dialect) |
| *Encycl.* | (in titles) *Encyclopædia, -ic* |
| Eng. | England, English |
| *Engin.* | in Engineering |
| *Ent.* | in Entomology |
| *Entomol.* | (in titles) *Entomology, -logical* |
| erron. | erroneous, -ly |
| *esp.* | especially |
| *Ess.* | (in titles) *Essay, -s* |
| et al. | *et alii*, 'and others' |
| etc. | et cetera |
| *Ethnol.* | in Ethnology |
| etym. | etymology |
| *euphem.* | euphemistically |
| *Exam.* | (in titles) *Examination* |
| exc. | except |
| *Exerc.* | (in titles) *Exercise, -s* |
| *Exper.* | (in titles) *Experiment, -al* |
| *Explor.* | (in titles) *Exploration, -s* |
| f. | feminine |
| f. (in Etym.) | formed on |
| f. (in subordinate entries) | form of |
| F. | French |
| *fem.* (*rarely* f.) | feminine |
| *fig.* | figurative, -ly |
| Finn. | Finnish |
| fl. | *floruit*, 'flourished' |
| *Found.* | (in titles) *Foundation, -s* |
| Fr. | French |
| freq. | frequent, -ly |
| Fris. | Frisian |
| *Fund.* | (in titles) *Fundamental, -s* |
| *Funk* or *Funk's Stand. Dict.* | *Funk and Wagnalls Standard Dictionary* |
| G. | German |
| Gael. | Gaelic |
| *Gaz.* | (in titles) *Gazette* |
| gen. | genitive |
| *gen.* | general, -ly |
| *Geogr.* | (as label) in Geography; (in titles) *Geography, -ical* |

| | |
|---|---|
| *Geol.* | (as label) in Geology; (in titles) *Geology, -ical* |
| *Geom.* | in Geometry |
| *Geomorphol.* | in Geomorphology |
| Ger. | German |
| Gloss. | Glossary |
| Gmc. | Germanic |
| Godef. | F. Godefroy, *Dictionnaire de l'ancienne langue française* |
| Goth. | Gothic |
| *Govt.* | (in titles) *Government* |
| Gr. | Greek |
| *Gram.* | (as label) in Grammar; (in titles) *Grammar, -tical* |
| Gt. | Great |
| Heb. | Hebrew |
| *Her.* | in Heraldry |
| *Herb.* | among herbalists |
| Hind. | Hindustani |
| *Hist.* | (as label) in History; (in titles) *History, -ical* |
| hist. | historical |
| *Histol.* | (in titles) *Histology, -ical* |
| *Hort.* | in Horticulture |
| *Househ.* | (in titles) *Household* |
| *Housek.* | (in titles) *Housekeeping* |
| *Ibid.* | *Ibidem*, 'in the same book or passage' |
| Icel. | Icelandic |
| *Ichthyol.* | in Ichthyology |
| *id.* | *idem*, 'the same' |
| i.e. | *id est*, 'that is' |
| IE. | Indo-European |
| *Illustr.* | (in titles) *Illustration, -ted* |
| imit. | imitative |
| *Immunol.* | in Immunology |
| imp. | imperative |
| *impers.* | impersonal |
| impf. | imperfect |
| ind. | indicative |
| indef. | indefinite |
| *Industr.* | (in titles) *Industry, -ial* |
| inf. | infinitive |
| infl. | influenced |
| *Inorg.* | (in titles) *Inorganic* |
| *Ins.* | (in titles) *Insurance* |
| *Inst.* | (in titles) *Institute, -tion* |
| *int.* | interjection |
| *intr.* | intransitive |
| *Introd.* | (in titles) *Introduction* |
| Ir. | Irish |
| irreg. | irregular, -ly |
| It. | Italian |
| J., (J.) | (quoted from) Johnson's *Dictionary* |
| (Jam.) | Jamieson, *Scottish Dict.* |
| Jap. | Japanese |
| joc. | jocular, -ly |
| *Jrnl.* | (in titles) *Journal* |
| *Jun.* | (in titles) *Junior* |
| *Knowl.* | (in titles) *Knowledge* |
| l. | line |
| L. | Latin |
| lang. | language |
| *Lect.* | (in titles) *Lecture, -s* |
| *Less.* | (in titles) *Lesson, -s* |
| *Let., Lett.* | letter, letters |
| LG. | Low German |
| lit. | literal, -ly |
| *Lit.* | Literary |
| Lith. | Lithuanian |
| LXX | Septuagint |
| m. | masculine |
| *Mag.* | (in titles) *Magazine* |
| *Magn.* | (in titles) *Magnetic, -ism* |
| Mal. | Malay, Malayan |
| *Man.* | (in titles) *Manual* |
| *Managem.* | (in titles) *Management* |
| *Manch.* | (in titles) *Manchester* |
| *Manuf.* | in Manufacture, -ing |
| *Mar.* | (in titles) *Marine* |
| masc. (*rarely* m.) | masculine |
| *Math.* | (as label) in Mathematics; (in titles) *Mathematics, -al* |
| MDu. | Middle Dutch |
| ME. | Middle English |
| *Mech.* | (as label) in Mechanics; (in titles) *Mechanics, -al* |
| *Med.* | (as label) in Medicine; (in titles) *Medicine, -ical* |
| med.L. | medieval Latin |
| *Mem.* | (in titles) *Memoir, -s* |
| *Metaph.* | in Metaphysics |
| *Meteorol.* | (as label) in Meteorology; (in titles) *Meteorology, -ical* |
| MHG. | Middle High German |
| midl. | midland (dialect) |
| *Mil.* | in military usage |
| *Min.* | (as label) in Mineralogy; (in titles) *Ministry* |
| *Mineral.* | (in titles) *Mineralogy, -ical* |
| MLG. | Middle Low German |
| *Misc.* | (in titles) *Miscellany, -eous* |
| mod. | modern |
| mod.L | modern Latin |
| (Morris), | (quoted from) E. E. Morris's *Austral English* |
| *Mus.* | (as label) in Music; (in titles) *Music, -al; Museum* |
| *Myst.* | (in titles) *Mystery* |
| *Mythol.* | in Mythology |
| N. | North |
| n. | neuter |
| *N. Amer.* | North America, -n |
| *N. & Q.* | *Notes and Queries* |
| *Narr.* | (in titles) *Narrative* |
| *Nat.* | (in titles) *Natural* |
| *Nat. Hist.* | in Natural History |
| *Naut.* | in nautical language |
| N.E. | North East |
| *N.E.D.* | *New English Dictionary*, original title of the *Oxford English Dictionary* (first edition) |
| *Neurol.* | in Neurology |
| neut. (*rarely* n.) | neuter |
| NF., NFr. | Northern French |
| No. | Number |
| nom. | nominative |
| north. | northern (dialect) |
| Norw. | Norwegian |
| n.q. | no quotations |
| N.T. | New Testament |
| *Nucl.* | Nuclear |
| *Numism.* | in Numismatics |
| N.W. | North West |
| *N.Z.* | New Zealand |
| obj. | object |
| obl. | oblique |
| *Obs., obs.* | obsolete |
| *Obstetr.* | (in titles) *Obstetrics* |
| occas. | occasionally |
| OE. | Old English (= Anglo-Saxon) |
| OF., OFr. | Old French |
| OFris. | Old Frisian |
| OHG. | Old High German |
| OIr. | Old Irish |
| ON. | Old Norse |
| ONF. | Old Northern French |
| *Ophthalm.* | in Ophthalmology |
| opp. | opposed (to), the opposite (of) |
| *Opt.* | in Optics |
| *Org.* | (in titles) *Organic* |
| orig. | origin, -al, -ally |
| *Ornith.* | (as label) in Ornithology; (in titles) *Ornithology, -ical* |
| OS. | Old Saxon |
| OSl. | Old (Church) Slavonic |
| O.T. | Old Testament |
| *Outl.* | (in titles) *Outline* |
| *Oxf.* | (in titles) *Oxford* |
| p. | page |
| *Palæogr.* | in Palæography |
| *Palæont.* | (as label) in Palæontology; (in titles) *Palæontology, -ical* |
| pa. pple. | passive participle, past participle |
| (Partridge), | (quoted from) E. Partridge's *Dictionary of Slang and Unconventional English* |
| *pass.* | passive, -ly |
| pa.t. | past tense |
| *Path.* | (as label) in Pathology; (in titles) *Pathology, -ical* |
| perh. | perhaps |
| Pers. | Persian |
| *pers.* | person, -al |
| *Petrogr.* | in Petrography |
| *Petrol.* | (as label) in Petrology; (in titles) *Petrology, -ical* |
| (Pettman), | (quoted from) C. Pettman's *Africanderisms* |
| pf. | perfect |
| Pg. | Portuguese |
| *Pharm.* | in Pharmacology |
| *Philol.* | (as label) in Philology; (in titles) *Philology, -ical* |
| *Philos.* | (as label) in Philosophy; (in titles) *Philosophy, -ic* |
| phonet. | phonetic, -ally |
| *Photogr.* | (as label) in Photography; (in titles) *Photography, -ical* |
| *phr.* | phrase |
| *Phys.* | physical; (*rarely*) in Physiology |
| *Physiol.* | (as label) in Physiology; (in titles) *Physiology, -ical* |
| *Pict.* | (in titles) *Picture, Pictorial* |
| pl., plur. | plural |
| *poet.* | poetic, -al |
| Pol. | Polish |
| *Pol.* | (as label) in Politics; (in titles) *Politics, -al* |
| *Pol. Econ.* | in Political Economy |
| *Polit.* | (in titles) *Politics, -al* |
| pop. | popular, -ly |
| *Porc.* | (in titles) *Porcelain* |
| poss. | possessive |
| *Pott.* | (in titles) *Pottery* |
| *ppl. a.*, pple. adj. | participial adjective |
| pple. | participle |
| Pr. | Provençal |
| pr. | present |
| *Pract.* | (in titles) *Practice, -al* |
| prec. | preceding (word or article) |
| *pred.* | predicative |
| *pref.* | prefix |
| pref., Pref. | preface |
| *prep.* | preposition |
| *pres.* | present |
| *Princ.* | (in titles) *Principle, -s* |
| priv. | privative |
| prob. | probably |
| *Probl.* | (in titles) *Problem* |
| *Proc.* | (in titles) *Proceedings* |
| *pron.* | pronoun |
| pronunc. | pronunciation |
| prop. | properly |
| *Pros.* | in Prosody |
| Prov. | Provençal |
| pr. pple. | present participle |
| *Psych.* | in Psychology |
| *Psychol.* | (as label) in Psychology; (in titles) *Psychology, -ical* |
| *Publ.* | (in titles) *Publications* |
| *Q.* | (in titles) *Quarterly* |
| quot(s). | quotation(s) |
| q.v. | *quod vide*, 'which see' |
| *R.* | (in titles) *Royal* |
| *Radiol.* | in Radiology |
| R.C.Ch. | Roman Catholic Church |
| *Rec.* | (in titles) *Record* |
| redupl. | reduplicating |
| *Ref.* | (in titles) *Reference* |
| refash. | refashioned, -ing |
| refl. | reflexive |
| *Reg.* | (in titles) *Register* |

| | |
|---|---|
| reg. | regular |
| rel. | related to |
| *Reminisc.* | (in titles) *Reminiscence, -s* |
| *Rep.* | (in titles) *Report, -s* |
| repr. | representative, representing |
| *Res.* | (in titles) *Research* |
| *Rev.* | (in titles) *Review* |
| rev. | revised |
| *Rhet.* | in Rhetoric |
| Rom. | Roman, -ce, -ic |
| Rum. | Rumanian |
| Russ. | Russian |
| S. | South |
| *S.Afr.* | South Africa, -n |
| *sb.* | substantive |
| *sc.* | *scilicet*, 'understand' or 'supply' |
| *Sc., Scot.* | Scottish |
| *Scand.* | (in titles) *Scandinavia, -n* |
| *Sch.* | (in titles) *School* |
| *Sc. Nat. Dict.* | *Scottish National Dictionary* |
| *Scotl.* | (in titles) *Scotland* |
| *Sel.* | (in titles) *Selection, -s* |
| Ser. | Series |
| sing. | singular |
| *Sk.* | (in titles) *Sketch* |
| Skr. | Sanskrit |
| Slav. | Slavonic |
| S.N.D. | *Scottish National Dictionary* |
| *Soc.* | (in titles) *Society* |
| *Sociol.* | (as label) in Sociology; (in titles) *Sociology, -ical* |
| Sp. | Spanish |
| *Sp.* | (in titles) *Speech, -es* |
| sp. | spelling |
| *spec.* | specifically |
| *Spec.* | (in titles) *Specimen* |
| St. | Saint |
| *Stand.* | (in titles) *Standard* |
| *Stanf.* | (quoted from) *Stanford Dictionary of Anglicised Words & Phrases* |
| str. | strong |
| *Struct.* | (in titles) *Structure, -al* |
| *Stud.* | (in titles) *Studies* |
| subj. | subject |
| *subord. cl.* | subordinate clause |
| subseq. | subsequent, -ly |
| subst. | substantively |
| *suff.* | suffix |
| superl. | superlative |
| Suppl. | Supplement |
| *Surg.* | (as label) in Surgery; (in titles) *Surgery, Surgical* |
| s.v. | *sub voce*, 'under the word' |
| Sw. | Swedish |
| s.w. | south-western (dialect) |
| *Syd. Soc. Lex.* | Sydenham Society, *Lexicon of Medicine & Allied Sciences* |
| syll. | syllable |
| Syr. | Syrian |
| *Syst.* | (in titles) *System, -atic* |
| *Taxon.* | (in titles) *Taxonomy, -ical* |
| *techn.* | technical, -ly |
| *Technol.* | (in titles) *Technology, -ical* |
| *Telegr.* | in Telegraphy |
| *Teleph.* | in Telephony |
| (Th.), | (quoted from) Thornton's *American Glossary* |
| *Theatr.* | in the Theatre, theatrical |
| *Theol.* | (as label) in Theology; (in titles) *Theology, -ical* |
| *Theoret.* | (in titles) *Theoretical* |
| Tokh. | Tokharian |
| tr., transl. | translated, translation |
| *Trans.* | (in titles) *Transactions* |
| *trans.* | transitive |
| *transf.* | transferred sense |
| *Trav.* | (in titles) *Travel(s)* |
| *Treas.* | (in titles) *Treasury* |
| *Treat.* | (in titles) *Treatise* |
| *Treatm.* | (in titles) *Treatment* |
| *Trig.* | in Trigonometry |
| *Trop.* | (in titles) *Tropical* |
| Turk. | Turkish |
| *Typog., Typogr.* | in Typography |
| ult. | ultimately |
| *Univ.* | (in titles) *University* |
| unkn. | unknown |
| *U.S.* | United States |
| U.S.S.R. | Union of Soviet Socialist Republics |
| usu. | usually |
| *v.*, vb. | verb |
| var(r)., vars. | variant(s) of |
| *vbl. sb.* | verbal substantive |
| *Vertebr.* | (in titles) *Vertebrate, -s* |
| *Vet.* | (as label) in Veterinary Science; (in titles) *Veterinary* |
| *Vet. Sci.* | in Veterinary Science |
| viz. | *videlicet*, 'namely' |
| *Voy.* | (in titles) *Voyage, -s* |
| *v.str.* | strong verb |
| *vulg.* | vulgar |
| *v.w.* | weak verb |
| W. | Welsh; West |
| wd. | word |
| Webster | *Webster's (New International) Dictionary* |
| *Westm.* | (in titles) *Westminster* |
| WGmc. | West Germanic |
| *Wks.* | (in titles) *Works* |
| w.midl. | west midland (dialect) |
| WS. | West Saxon |
| (Y.), | (quoted from) Yule & Burnell's *Hobson-Jobson* |
| *Yrs.* | (in titles) *Years* |
| *Zoogeogr.* | in Zoogeography |
| *Zool.* | (as label) in Zoology; (in titles) *Zoology, -ical* |

## *Signs and Other Conventions*

Before a word or sense

† = obsolete
‖ = not naturalized, alien
¶ = catachrestic and erroneous uses

In the listing of Forms

1 = before 1100
2 = 12th c. (1100 to 1200)
3 = 13th c. (1200 to 1300), etc.
5–7 = 15th to 17th century
20 = 20th century

In the etymologies

* indicates a word or form not actually found, but of which the existence is inferred
:— = normal development of

The printing of a word in SMALL CAPITALS indicates that further information will be found under the word so referred to.

.. indicates an omitted part of a quotation.

- (in a quotation) indicates a hyphen doubtfully present in the original; (in other text) indicates a hyphen inserted only for the sake of a line-break.

# PROPRIETARY NAMES

THIS Dictionary includes some words which are or are asserted to be proprietary names or trade marks. Their inclusion does not imply that they have acquired for legal purposes a non-proprietary or general significance nor any other judgement concerning their legal status. In cases where the editorial staff have established in the records of the Patent Offices of the United Kingdom and of the United States that a word is registered as a proprietary name or trade mark this is indicated, but no judgement concerning the legal status of such words is made or implied thereby.

**ser**, obs. form of SEAR *v.*

**1482** *Cely Papers* (Camden) 122 Lette hym [a horse] ron in a parke tyll Hallowtyd and then take hym wpe and ser hym and lette hym stand in the dede of whynter.

**ser**, obs. f. SEAR *a.*, SIR; obs. Sc. f. SORE *adv.*; var. SEER[2].

**ser.**, abbreviation of SERIES.

†**sera.** *Mil. Obs.* [? a. It. *serra* a tight place, vbl. sb. f. *serrāre* to shut up, press.] ***at the sera***: at close quarters.

**1591** *Garrard's Art Warre* 7 Which at the Sera and close is very necessarie.

**sera**, obs. form of SEER[2], SERAI.

‖**serab** (sɛˈrɑːb). Also **sirab**. [ad. Arab. *sarāb*.] A mirage.

*a* **1835** F. D. HEMANS *Wks.* (1844) III. 87 Suns of blasting light perchance illume The glistening Serab which illudes his eye. **1839** *Penny Cycl.* XV. 261/2 This kind of mirage is not peculiar to Egypt; it is known in Persia also, where it is called *Serab* or *Sir-ab* (miraculous water). **1883** *Encycl. Brit.* XVI. 50/2 When the soil is parched up the appearance of the mirage (serâb) is very common.

**Serabend**, var. SARABAND[2].

**Serabite**, obs. form of SARABAITE.

**serac** (səˈræk). Also ‖**sérac**. [a. Swiss-Fr. *sérac*, orig. the name of a kind of white cheese; the transferred application was doubtless suggested by similitude of form.] (See quot. 1898.)

**1860** TYNDALL *Glac.* I. vii. 51 These ridges are often cleft by fissures..thus forming detached towers of ice..*Footnote.* To such towers the name *Séracs* is applied. **1891** G. F. WRIGHT *Ice Age N. Amer.* 8 Fissures and seracs where the glacier moves down the steeper portion of its incline. **1898** *Encycl. Sports* II. 54/1 (Mountaineering) *Serac*, a tower of ice on a glacier, formed by the intersection of crevasses. **1900** *Proc. Boston Soc. Nat. Hist.* XXIX. 295 Weathering occurs where variations of external temperature penetrate to the bed-rock, as is particularly the case between the séracs of glacial cascades. **1933** J. BUCHAN *Prince of Captivity* I. iii. 92 They came on ice-fields..and mountainous seracs which would have puzzled an Alpine climber. **1936** M. ROBERTS *Poems* 36 The snow falls, and the séracs; and the green glacier-ice Moves down. **1963** G. CARR *Lewker in Norway* vi. 124 On the further side of the right-hand ridge he could just see the upper *séracs* of the Bojumsbre. **1979** C. KILIAN *Icequake* vi. 86 Huge fields of seracs—the topographical nightmare caused by intersecting crevasses.

**serace, seraff**, variant forms of SERAI, SARAF.

**seradeh**, obs. var. SHRADDHA, SRADDHA.

**seraffin(e**, var. ff. SERAPHIN *Obs.* (a coin).

**serafic**, obs. form of SERAPHIC.

**serafile**, variant of SERREFILE.

**serafin**, var. SERAPHIN *Obs.* (a coin); SERAPHIM.

**seraglio** (sɛˈrɑːljəʊ). Also 6 **sarralia, seralyo, serraqlio**, 7 **seraglia, seralia, seralio, serraglio, serralia, surralia, -ya, zereglia**, *Pl.* **seragli**. [a. It. *serraglio*:—popular L. **serrāculum* enclosure, place of confinement (cf. med.L. *serrāculum* fastening of a door), f. **serrāre* (whence It. *serrare*, F. *serrer*, Sp. *cerrar*) for *serāre* to lock up, close, f. *sera* lock or bolt. The It. word was, from similarity of sound, used to render the Turkish *serāī* lodging, palace (see SERAI[1]). The applications of the word which have been adopted in Eng. all relate to Turkey and the East, but some of them represent merely the etymological sense of the It. word, while others owe their meaning wholly or partly to the Turkish word. Cf. SERAI[1], SERAIL.]

I. Enclosure, place of confinement.

**1.** The part of a Muslim dwelling-house (esp. of the palace of a sovereign or great noble) in which the women are secluded; the apartments reserved for wives and concubines; a harem.

**1581** RICH *Farew.* P j, The kyng of Tunise..caused her to be put in the Cube, whiche is a place where he keepeth his Concubines (as the Turke doeth his in his Serraqlio [*sic*].) **1588** HICKOCK tr. *C. Frederick's Voy.* 30 One principall wife, which is kept in a Seralyo. **1610** B. JONSON *Alch.* II. ii, Thou shalt be the master Of my seraglia. **1624** MASSINGER *Renegado* I. i, Can I know my sister Mewde vp in his Serraglio..and not haste to send him To the Deuill his tutor? **1625** PURCHAS *Pilgrims* I. 553 A kinswoman of his, liuing in the Zereglia. **1653** RAMESEY *Astrol. Restored* 145 In this our age we build more Serralias then Churches. **1788** *Gentl. Mag.* LVIII. I. 100/2 Shutting up women in seraglios, and degrading them into an inferior class of beings. **1879** FARRAR *St. Paul* (1883) 233 The secrecy of Oriental seraglios.

**b.** The inmates of the harem; a polygamous household.

**1634** SIR T. HERBERT *Trav.* 115 Each house top spred with Carpets, wheron slept a man and his peculiar Seralio. **1847** C. BRONTË *Jane Eyre* xxiv, I would not exchange this one little English girl for the grand Turk's whole seraglio.

**c.** *transf.* and *fig.*

**1672** DRYDEN *Assignation* IV. i, This Key will admit me into the *Seraglio* of the Godly [*sc.* the Nunnery]. **1691** *Comedy, Win Her & Take Her* II. i. 15 He'le make the Drawing-Room his Seraglio. **1709** *Tatler* No. 50 ⁋1 Woman was his mistress; and the whole Sex his Seraglio. *a* **1711** KEN *Urania* Poet. Wks. 1721 IV. 478 There I a whole Seraglio met Of flatt'ring Lusts, which me beset. **1773** WILKES *Corr.* (1805) IV. 141 One grand-signior cock, with a seraglio of seven hens. **1820** SCOTT *Monast.* i, The mighty bull moved at the head of his seraglio and their followers. **1860** MOTLEY *Netherl.* ii. (1868) I. 48 A seraglio of maids of honour ministered to Henry's pleasures. **1881** H. W. ELLIOTT *Seal Isl. Alaska* (1884) 38 The same indifference is also exhibited by the male [fur-seal] to all that may take place..outside of the boundary of his seraglio.

†**2.** *gen.* An enclosure; a place of confinement.

*a* **1668** LASSELS *Voy. Italy* (1698) I. 136 Near to the Stables stands the Seraglio where the wild beasts are kept. *a* **1700** EVELYN *Diary* 15 Jan. 1645, I went to the Ghetto, where the Jewes dwell as in a suburbe by themselues... I passed by the Piazza Judea, where their Seraglio begins.

**II.** = SERAI[1].

**3.** A Turkish palace, *esp.* the palace of the Sultan at Constantinople. Now *Hist.*

**1599** HAKLUYT *Voy.* II. I. 290 The..dayly paiments..by the Grand Signior..to the Officers of his Seraglio or Court. **1600** DALLAM in *Early Voy. Levant* (Hakluyt Soc. 1893) 57 The surralia..which doth joyne close to the Cittie. *Ibid.* 61 The Grand Sinyors Courte, Called the surralya. **1630** R. JOHNSON *Kingd. & Commw.* 559 The pleasantest of any Palace on the face of the earth, termed by them the Port, or Seraglio. **1682** WHELER *Journ. Greece* I. 80 All about these parts are the Serraglioes, or Countrey-houses of the great Men among the Turks. **1728** ELIZA HEYWOOD tr. *Mme. de Somez's Belle A.* (1732) II. 251 He was immediately order'd to come to the Seraglio, where he was receiv'd by the Grand Visier with all imaginable tokens of Friendship and Esteem. **1877** *Encycl. Brit.* VI. 304/2 The remains of the Seraglio, former palace of the Ottoman sultans.

†**4.** A place of accommodation for travellers.

**1617** PURCHAS *Pilgrimage* (ed. 3) 606 At euery tenth course a Seraglia or Place of lodging for Man and Horse. **1659** EVELYN *Let. to R. Boyle* 3 Sept., At the other back front a plot walled in of a competent square for the common seraglio disposed into a garden.

†**5.** A warehouse. *Obs.*

**1628** in Foster *Eng. Factories India* (1909) III. 230 Depositing those intended for Cambay and Ahmadabad in the 'seraglia'. **1676** COVEL in *Early Voy. Levant* (Hakluyt Soc.) 168 On the shoar towardes the factory seraglio is a fair large fountain. **1682** WHELER *Journ. Greece* I. 42 The Currans..are..put into Ware-houses they call Seraglio's. **1712** tr. *Pomet's Hist. Drugs* I. 160 They are thrown thorow a Hole into the great Magazine, call'd the Seraglio.

†**6.** ? A barrack for a particular corps of the Turkish army; hence, a corps or grade of Turkish soldiers. *Obs.*

**1600** PORY *Leo's Africa*, etc. 386 They are called home againe to the Seraglios of the Zamoglans (for so are they termed, till they be enrolled among the Ianissaries). **1613** WOTTON *Let. to Sir E. Bacon* 21 Mar., The Turk..having made a leavy..of 5000 youths out of the Seragli. **1656** EARL MONM. tr. *Boccalini's Advts. fr. Parnass.* I. xxxii. 57 To give the command of Armies..to men of the first or second Seraglio.

**III. 7.** *attrib.* and *Comb.*: ***seraglio-guard***, ***lady***, ***window***; **seraglio cake**, a name given to a kind of fancy bread.

**1842** MERLE *Dom. Dict.* 46 *Seraglio Cake. **1821** SHELLEY *Hellas* 114 Man the *Seraglio-guard! **1717** LADY M. W. MONTAGU *Lett.* (1893) I. 294 This is the chief guardian of the *seraglio ladies. *Ibid.* 323 The Grand Signior was at the *seraglio window.

‖**serai**[1] (səˈraɪ). Forms: 7 **sarray, sera, seraw(e, serray, suray, surroie**, 7, 9 **sarai, -ay**, 8 **serauee**, 9 **seraee, seray, -oy**, 8- **serai**. [a. Turkish (orig. Persian) *serāī* lodging, residence, palace. Cf. SERAGLIO, SERAIL.]

**1.** In various Eastern countries, A building for the accommodation of travellers; a caravanserai.

**1609** W. FINCH in Purchas *Pilgrims* (1625) I. 434 By it the great Saray, besides which are diuers others..wherein diuers neate lodgings are to be let. *c* **1616** *Ibid.* 520 Euery fiue or sixe Course, there are Seraes built..for the..entertainment of Trauellers. **1782** G. FORSTER *Journ.* (1798) I. 74 The stationary tenants of the serauee..approach the traveller on his entrance. **1793** W. HODGES *Trav. India* 32 The lodgings of the traveller in India are the serais, or caravanserais,..as they are called in Europe. **1800** *Asiatic Ann. Reg.* 281/1 A handsome seray built of stone. **1848** MILL *Pol. Econ.* Prel. Rem. (1876) 8 The seraees for travellers..owe their existence to the enlightened self-interest of the better order of princes. **1879** W. WAKEFIELD *Happy Valley* 35 These serais..generally consist of a large square stone building. **1895** *Outing* (U.S) XXVI. 467/2 A 'Serai' covers a space about 150 feet square or larger, and is built around a quadrangular court with a continuous veranda.

†**b.** ? A warehouse. = SERAGLIO 5. *Obs.*

**1619** in Foster *Eng. Factories Ind.* (1906) 103 The goods have since been taken to Bershanpur, and placed in the common 'sera'.

**2.** A Turkish palace; esp. the palace of the Sultan at Constantinople.

**1617** MORYSON *Itin.* III. 68 The Sultans or Emperours Pallace (vulgarly called *Saray*, and by the Italians *Seraglio*). **1665** SIR T. HERBERT *Trav.* (1677) 117 Nothing more observable in the Town than the Serrays and [etc.]. **1812** BYRON *Ch. Har.* II. lxxvii, The Serai's impenetrable tower. **1869** TOZER *Highl. Turkey* I. 230 Having sent..to the Pasha to ask for horses, we thought it right to pay him a visit in his serai.

¶**3.** Misused for SERAGLIO 1: A harem.

**1813** BYRON *Giaour* 444 Not thus was Hassan wont to fly When Leila dwelt in his Serai.

‖**serai**[2] (səˈraɪ). Also 7 **sou-, sowray**, 9 **surahee, -hi, surai, suraiee**. [Anglo-Indian, repr. Urdu (orig. Arab.) *çurāhī*.] 'A long-necked earthenware (or metal) flagon for water' (Yule).

**1672** tr. *Bernier's Hist. Rev. Emp. Gt. Mogol* IV. 10 A Souray of the water of Ganges... Sowray is that Tin-flagon full of water, which the Servant that marcheth on foot before the Gentleman on horseback, carrieth in his hand. **1808** ELPHINSTONE in Colebrooke *Life* (1884) I. 199 We had..two surahees of water [etc.]. **1825-9** MRS. SHERWOOD *Lady of Manor* V. xxix. 47 She broke a serai of water. **1859** LANG *Wand. India* 145 Hold hard, syce, and give me the suraiee (water-bottle). **1874** H. H. COLE *Catal. Ind. Art S. Kens. Mus.* 144 A surai..with a long neck and flat bulged base.

**serail** (səˈreɪl). Now *rare*. Forms: 6 **sarail, sarell**, 7 **serail(l)e, serraill, serrayle**, 7- **serail**. [a. F. *sérail*, ad. It. *serraglio*: see SERAGLIO. Cf. Sp. *serrallo*.]

**1.** = SERAGLIO 1.

**1585** T. WASHINGTON tr. *Nicholay's Voy.* II. xxii. 59 b, [The women's] priuate bathes, which for the most part they haue..within their houses or Sarails. **1587** MARLOWE *1st Pt. Tamburl.* III. iii. 1176 He shall be made a chast and lustlesse Eunuke, And in my Sarell tend my Concubines. **1603** FLORIO *Montaigne* I. xlii. 143 What longing-lust would not be alaide, to see three hundred women at his dispose and pleasure, as hath the Grand Turke in his Seraille? **1628** LE GRYS tr. *Barclay's Argenis* III. 244 Thou wouldest haue said, that she was brought vp in the warres; they bred in a Serrayle of Women. **1786** tr. *Beckford's Vathek* (1883) 65 They consigned them with good commendations to the surgeons of the serail. **1808** E. S. BARRETT *Miss-led General* 161 A numerous serail must be attended with vast expence. **1844** KINGLAKE *Eothen* iii. 42 Venice..is the bowing slave of the Sultan..she watches the walls of his Serail. **1853** KINGSLEY *Hypatia* xxx, The purest monotheism, they discovered, was perfectly compatible with bigotry and ferocity, luxury and tyranny, serails and bowstrings.

†**2.** = SERAGLIO 3, SERAI[1] 2. *Obs.*

**1585** T. WASHINGTON tr. *Nicholay's Voy.* IV. xxv. 140 b, Selim builded there for a dwelling place, a fayre and sumptuous Sarail. **1603** KNOLLES *Hist. Turks* (1621) 1311 The embassador went himself to the serrail. **1687** *Lond. Gaz.* No. 2307/3 The other report is, That the Grand Signior is only kept a close Prisoner in the Serail. **1782** J. SCOTT *Poet. Wks.* 231 And from his high serail the sultan hears The wide Propontis' beating waves resound.

†**3.** A barrack for Turkish soldiers; = SERAGLIO 6.

**1585** T. WASHINGTON tr. *Nicholay's Voy.* IV. xxv. 140 b, There is besides another Sarail, for the lodging of the Azamoglans or Ianissaries.

**serain(e**, obs. forms of SERENE *sb.*[1], SIREN.

**seral** (ˈsɪərəl), *a.*[1] (and *sb.*) *Geol.* [f. L. *sēr-us* late + -AL[1]: see quot.] **a.** *adj.* Used by H. D. Rogers to designate the Millstone Grit formation of the Pennsylvanian Coal-measures. **b.** *absol.* or *sb.* Used as a name for this formation.

**1858** H. D. ROGERS *Geol. Pennsylv.* I. 109 Seral series, or Coal strata. Seral Conglomerate (or Lowest Division of the Coal-Measures). *Ibid.* II. II. 1027 Seral..a synonym for the coal-formation expressing the period of the nightfall or late twilight of the Appalachian Palæozoic day.

**seral** (ˈsɪərəl), *a.*[2] *Ecol.* [f. SERE *sb.*[2] + -AL.] Of or pertaining to a sere; being a member of a sere other than its climax.

**1916** F. E. CLEMENTS *Plant Succession* ix. 184 In lowland and montane regions examples of priseres are often more numerous than those of subseres, and such regions are of the first importance for seral investigations. **1926** TANSLEY & CHIPP *Study of Vegetation* ii. 18 We have a special technical term for the developmental series of communities... We apply the adjective *seral*, as opposed to *climax*, to such communities. **1932** *Forestry* VI. 190 The principal seral stages in natural succession from grassland or heath to beechwood are shortly described for certain soil types. **1955** P. A. BUXTON *Nat. Hist. Tsetse Flies* ix. 278 It appears to be generally true that the grassland is seral and that it is prevented from developing into bush or woodland by annual fires. **1973** P. A. COLINVAUX, *Introd. Ecol.* vi. 77 The communities are..classified into a number of subordinate communities, the seral stages, and the generic taxon, the *Beech-maple climax community*.

**seralbumen, -in** (ˌsɪəræl'bjuːmɛn, -ɪn). *Chem.* Also **sero-albumen.** [f. SER-UM + ALBUMEN.] The albumen of the blood. Hence **seral'buminous** (ˌsero-al'buminous) *a.*, composed of or containing seralbumen.

**1835-6** *Todd's Cycl. Anat.* I. 63/1 An orange-yellow coloured sero-albuminous fluid. *Ibid.* 89/2 When coagulated seralbumen is digested in acetic acid, it becomes soft and transparent. **1857** [see OVALBUMEN]. **1873** RALFE *Phys. Chem.* 28 Ovo-albumin is distinguished from sero-albumin by the following characteristics. **1878** KINGZETT *Anim. Chem.* 124 Chyle contains potassium-albumin, casein, and seralbumin.

‖**serang** (səˈræŋ). *Anglo-Indian.* Also **sarang, syrang.** [a. Pers. *sarhang* commander.] A native boatswain or captain of a Lascar crew.

**1799** *Hull Advert.* 21 Dec. 4/1 Seringapatam Prize-money ..first dividend. Commandant Subadars, and Serangs of Gun Lascars. **1806** *Naval Chron.* XV. 469 The sarang, or principal native. **1817** in R. G. Wallace *Fifteen Yrs. India* (1822) 256 The syrangs..exerted their powerful influence over the seamen. **1891** KIPLING *Life's Handicap* 297 Pambé, the Serang or head man of the Lascar sailors.

**seranine** ('sɛrənaɪn). (See quot.)

1889 CUNDILL *Dict. Explosives* 61 Seranine is a mixture of nitro-glycerine and chlorate of potash. 1890 EISSLER *Mod. Explosives* 38.

**serapah**, obs. form of SEERPAW.

**serape** (‖se'rape, sɛ'rɑːpeɪ). Also **sarape**, 9 *U.S.* **zarape**. [Mexican Sp. *serape, sarape*.] A shawl or plaid worn by Spanish-Americans.

1834 A. PIKE *Prose Sk. & Poems* 138 The men with..the zarape or blanket of striped red and white. 1836 [see RANCHERO]. 1847 RUXTON *Adv. Mexico*, etc. xxiv. 210, I..knew that I had seen the last..of civilized man under the garb of a Mexican sarape. 1850 MAYNE REID *Rifle Rangers* xi, The ranchero..is never seen without the 'serapé'. *a* 1883 —— *Lost Mtn.* xv. 147 Keeping the rain off with waterproof serapes. 1888 MARY E. BLAKE in *Lit. World* (U.S.) 18 Aug. 262/1 The men, with wide-rimmed sombrero and gay zarape. 1892 *Dial. Notes* I. 194 *Serápe*, a Mexican blanket, generally woven by hand by Indian women, with stripes of variegated colors. The *serape* has no opening or slit for the head, like the *poncho*, but is worn by men only, thrown across the shoulders. 1916 'B. M. BOWER' *Phantom Herd* 68 He had finished with an old Mexican serape draped around his person for warmth. 1950 *Chicago Tribune* 1 Mar. 20/3 The feminine counterpart of the serape is the rebozo. 1979 *United States 1980/81* (Penguin Travel Guides) 49 Mexican, Indian, and 'Old West' items are especially good buys. Serapes..and wool rebozos..make nice gifts.

**Serapeum** (sɛrə'piːəm). *Egyptology* and *Anc. Hist.* Also **Serapeion** (-'aɪɒn), **Serapeium**; pl. **Serapeia**. [a. late L., ad. Gr. *Σεραπεῖον*, f. *Σέραπις* Serapis.] A temple of Serapis; *spec.* the great precinct near Memphis, where the sacred Apis bulls were buried, and a temple in Alexandria.

1841 *Penny Cycl.* XXI. 260/2 He had temples (Serapeia) in several parts of Egypt. 1847 J. LEITCH tr. *Müller's Anc. Art* 243 The Serapeum was at the same time a sanatory institution. 1877 A. B. EDWARDS *Thousand Miles up Nile* iv. 86 According to one of these precious Serapeum tablets, the wounded bull did not die till the fourth year of the reign of Darius. 1927 TARN & GRIFFITH *Hellenistic Civiliz.* x. 294 The Serapeum at Delos has revealed that the triad who were so to influence Hellenism were..Isis, Sarapis, and Anubis. 1928 *Daily Tel.* 11 Dec. 13/4 It was suggested that the so-called Greek Serapeum was in truth nothing but the resting-place of the mother cows of Egyptian Apis. 1961 A. GARDINER *Egypt of Pharaohs* xii. 326 Not a single inscription of Dyn. XXI was found in the Serapeum [at Memphis]. 1972 P. M. FRASER *Ptolemaic Alexandria* I. v. 271 The Serapeum on Rhacotis Hill [in Alexandria] was within the Ptolemaic and Roman city-walls.

**seraph**[1] ('sɛrəf). [Back-formation from the plural SERAPHIM, SERAPHIN (on the analogy of *cherubim*, *-in* and *cherub*). (Perh. first used by Milton.)

Cf. G. *seraph*, in mod. use perh. from Eng., though Luther had in one passage used *seraph* (as a plural). Certain mediæval commentators on Pseudo-Dionysius, followed by many glossaries down to the *Ortus Vocabulorum* (1518), give *seraph* (genitive *seraphis*) as the sing. corresponding to the pl. *seraphin*; but the form appears to have had no actual currency in med. Latin.]

**1. a.** One of the SERAPHIM.

1667 MILTON *P.L.* III. 667 Brightest Seraph tell In which of all these shining Orbes hath Man His fixed seat. 1691 NORRIS *Pract. Disc.* (1716) II. 171 Who sees Darkness even in the Angels of Light, and charges the loftiest Seraph with Folly! *a* 1711 KEN *Hymns Evang.* Poet. Wks. 1721 I. 184 The Seraphs who of all love Godhead most Had near the Throne the honourable Post. 1786 COLERIDGE *Genevieve* 4 Sweet your voice, as Seraph's song. 1816 BYRON (*1st*) *Stanzas to Augusta* iv, Oh! blest be thine unbroken light, That watch'd me as a seraph's eye. 1842 TENNYSON *St. Simeon Styl.* 166 That Pontius and Iscariot by my side Show'd like fair seraphs.

**b.** *fig.* A seraphic person, an 'angel'.

1853 C. BRONTE *Villette* xxi, I knew another of these seraphs..she was [etc.].

**2.** *Geol.* A fossil shell. Cf. SERAPHIM 4.

1822 PARKINSON *Outl. Oryctol.* 153 *Seraphs*, a convoluted, elongated, univalved shell. 1851 WOODWARD *Mollusca* I. 106.

**3.** *attrib.* and *Comb.* (sometimes quasi-adj. = seraphic), as ***seraph-arrival***, ***-band***, ***-bard***, ***-cloud***, ***fire***, ***-man***, ***note***, ***-sense***, ***song***, ***way***, ***-wing***; ***seraph-bright***, ***-haunted***, ***-sent***, ***-winged*** adjs. Also **seraph-tide** *Anglo-Irish*, Michaelmas.

1876 G. M. HOPKINS *Wr. Deutschland* xxiii, in *Poems* (1967) 59 With the gnarl of the nails in thee,..his Lovescape crucified And seal of his *seraph-arrival. 1786 BURNS '*O Thou dread Power*' v, The beauteous, *seraph Sister-band. 1798 COLERIDGE *Anc. Mar.* VI. xx, This seraph-band, each waved his hand. 1729 SAVAGE *Wanderer* v. 379 Then, as yon *Seraph-Bard fram'd Hearts below, Each sees him here transcendant Knowledge show. 1949 BLUNDEN *After Bombing* 49 Marbles, mosaics, carvings, *seraph-bright Paintings of wall and window. 1928 —— *Japanese Garland* 30 Their mysteries luring that young *seraph-cloud Swan-like between the mountain and the moon. 1803 HEBER *Palestine* 32 One faint spark of Milton's *seraph fire. 1958 G. BARKER *Two Plays* 52 Lie dreaming on that *seraph-haunted shore. 1798 COLERIDGE *Anc. Mar.* VI. xix, A man all light, a *seraph-man On every corse there stood. 1814 BOWDLER *Hymn*, '*Sing to the Lord*', Israel's shepherds heard amazed The *seraph notes of peace and love. 1928 BLUNDEN *Retreat* 65 Her touch is *seraph sense. 1932 —— *Face of England* 126 They sparkled free In *seraph-sent lucidity. 1801 SOUTHEY *Thalaba* XII. iv, Or liker the first sound of *seraph song And Angel greeting. *a* 1849 MAR. EDGEWORTH *White Pigeon*, You promised to make me a compliment of it last *Seraph-tide was twelvemonth. 1818 BYRON *Juan* I. lxxxv, For he would learn the rudiments of love, I mean the *seraph way of those above. 1754 GRAY *Progr. Poesy* III. ii, He, that rode sublime Upon the *seraph-wings of Extasy. 1821 SHELLEY *Hellas* 448 A *seraph-winged Victory.

‖'**seraph**[2]. *Obs.* [a. F. †*seraph*, corruptly a. Turkish *sharīf*: see SHARIFFE. Cf. It. †*saraffo*.] A Turkish gold coin; a sequin.

1576 EDEN *Hist. Trav.* (1577) 364 Three thousande Saraphes of golde. 1653 URQUHART *Rabelais* II. xiv, I will give thee my Codpiece:..there are six hundred Seraphs in it, and some fine Diamonds. 1656 BLOUNT *Glossogr.*, *Seraph*, a Turkish coyn of fine gold, worth about a French crown.

**seraph**, obs. variant of GIRAFFE.

1607 TOPSELL *Four-f. Beasts* 4 Their nourishment goeth more forward then backward, like the best horses, and the Arabian Seraph, which are higher before then behinde.

**seraphic** (sə'ræfɪk), *a.* and *sb.* Also 7 **seraphique**, 7–8 **seraphick**, 8 **serafic**. [a. eccl. L. *seraphicus*, f. *seraph-im*: see SERAPHIM. Cf. F. *séraphique*, Sp. *seráfico*, Pg. *seraphico*, It. *serafico*.]

**A.** *adj.*

**1.** Of or pertaining to the seraphim.

1632 MASSINGER *Maid of Hon.* V. i, Seraphique Angells Clap their celestiall wings in heavenly plaudits. 1667 MILTON *P.L.* I. 794 The great Seraphic Lords and Cherubim In close recess and secret conclave sat. 1727 DE FOE *Syst. Magic* I. iii. (1840) 81 This supposition..places him [the Devil] beneath the dignity of his seraphic original. 1755 YOUNG *Centaur* vi. (1757) IV. 275 A being big with..hope..of adding melody to seraphic choirs, in ceaseless Hallelujahs to their Eternal King. 1850 MRS. JAMESON *Leg. Monast. Ord.* (1863) 238 Seven beautiful seraphic or allegorical figures.

**2.** Of attributes: Resembling what pertains to the seraphim; worthy of a seraph; ecstatically adoring.

1659 BOYLE *Some Motives Love of God* 9 This Love I have taken the freedome to style Seraphick Love, borrowing the name from..those nobler Spirits of the Cælestiall Hierarchie, whose Name..expresses them to be of a flaming Nature. 1683 NORRIS *Idea Happin.* 35 There is a more peculiar Acceptation of the Love of God proper to this place. And it is that which we call Seraphic. By which I understand..that Love of God which is the effect of an intense Contemplation of him. 1695 BLACKMORE *Pr. Arth.* I. 44 Nor did his Arts in vain weak Man assail, His false Seraphick Tongue and Charms prevail. *a* 1711 KEN *Hymns Festiv.* Poet. Wks. 1821 II. 191 Seraphick Ardour dwelling in each Vein, The Majestatick Presence in the Brain. 1778 WARNER in Jesse *Selwyn & Contemp.* (1844) III. 336 Mr. Mudge..had a most seraphic finger for the harpsichord. 1831 CARLYLE *Sart. Res.* II. viii, On the thick Hyperborean, cherubic reasoning, seraphic eloquence were lost. 1846 DE QUINCEY *Shelley* in *Tait's Mag.* Jan. 29 Many people remarked something seraphic in the expression of his features. 1850 TENNYSON *In Mem.* cix, Seraphic intellect and force To seize and throw the doubts of man. 1859 GEO. ELIOT *Adam Bede* vi, Dinah's seraphic gentleness of expression. 1872 CALVERLEY *Fly Leaves* (1884) 97 Her voice was sweet..Her singing quite seraphic. 1884 W. S. LILLY in *Contemp. Rev.* Feb. 263 That religious romanticism which paints for us a mediæval period full of seraphic sweetness.

†**b.** ? Concerned with sublime objects. *Obs.*

*a* 1697 AUBREY *Brief Lives*, *Dunstan* (1898) I. 243 Meredith Lloyd tells me that, three or 400 yeares ago, chymistry was in a greater perfection, much, then now; their proces was then more seraphique and universall: now they looke only after medicines.

**3.** Resembling a seraph, either in beauty or in fervour of exalted devotion.

1762–71 H. WALPOLE *Vertue's Anecd. Paint.* (1786) III. 121 That seraphic dame, Mrs. Rowe, also painted. 1807 CRABBE *Sir Eustace Grey* 71 Her morals [show'd] the seraphic saint. 1845 DISRAELI *Sybil* IV. x, That seraphic being, whose lustre even now haunts my vision. 1870 —— *Lothair* xiii, Seraphic saints, and gorgeous scenes by Tintoret.

**b.** Of discourse, actions, appearance: Showing ecstasy of devout contemplation.

*a* 1668 DAVENANT *Play-ho.* I. (1673) 76 A spiritual Musician too With his seraphick Colloquies exprest In stilo recitativo. 1668 PEPYS *Diary* 24 May, A very good and seraphic kind of sermon, too good for an ordinary congregation. 1884 *Punch* 18 Oct. 191/1 The seraphic look of personal affection that mantled his brow.

**4.** Special collocations: **Seraphic Doctor**, a title given to St. Bonaventura (in Spain also popularly to St. Teresa); **Seraphic Father**, a title given to St. Francis; **seraphic friar**, a Franciscan, hence ***seraphic habit***, ***order***; **seraphic hymn**, the Sanctus (see Isa. vi. 3).

1728 CHAMBERS *Cycl.* s.v., In the Schools, St. Bonaventure is call'd *The *Seraphic Doctor*, from his abundant Zeal and Fervour. 1834 K. H. DIGBY *Mores Cath.* V. v. 153 The seraphic doctor observes that [etc.]. 1894 MRS. G. C. GRAHAM *S. Teresa* I. iv. 179 *note*, Teresa, by a definitive decree of the Tribunal of the Rota, is formally declared a Doctor of the Church. The 'seraphic doctor', the antonomasia by which she is as often as not referred to in Spain, relates to this, and not to the Doctor's degree bestowed upon her, after her death, by the University of Salamanca. 1728 CHAMBERS *Cycl.* s.v., St. Francis, the Founder of the Cordeliers and Franciscans, is called the **Seraphic Father*, in Memory of a Vision he saw on Mount Alverna,..when..he saw a Seraph glide rapidly from Heaven upon him; which impress'd on him certain Stigmata or Marks. 1884 *Tablet* 11 Oct. 592/1 The Feast of the Seraphic Father St. Francis was celebrated with great solemnity. 1826 SOUTHEY *Lett. to Butler* 514 The *Seraphic and Cherubic friars. 1662 J. DAVIES tr. *Olearius' Voy. Ambass.* 143 Those who take that habit, which they call *Seraphick, are not to be numbered among Men, but are become Angels. 1796 SOUTHEY *Lett. Spain* (1799) 418 Of the Mendicants the most numerous is the *Serafic, or Franciscan order.

**B.** *sb.*

†**1. a.** [= eccl. L. *seraphicus*.] A Franciscan friar. **b.** Allusively applied in the sense of zealot.

1659 GAUDEN *Tears Ch.* II. xxxii. 256 Many high Seraphicks and supercilious Separatists. 1699 R. L'ESTRANGE *Erasm. Colloq.* (1725) 265 They are commanded to wear the Coat and Hood (for so say the Seraphicks).

**2.** ***seraphics***: rapturous moods or discourses.

1709 SWIFT & ADDISON *Tatler* No. 32 ¶2 To hear her talk Seraphicks, and run over Norris, and Moor, and Milton. 1789 CHARL. SMITH *Ethelinde* (1814) I. 182 And the angel will descend from her seraphics.

Hence **se'raphicness**. *rare*.

1727 BAILEY vol. II, *Seraphickness*, the being of the seraphick Nature. 1888 LIGHTHALL *Young Seigneur* 71 No romantic seraphicness glowed upon her features.

**seraphical** (sə'ræfɪkəl), *a.* Now *rare*. [f. eccl. L. *seraphic-us* SERAPHIC *a.* + -AL[1].] = SERAPHIC *a.*

**1.** Pertaining to the seraphim; = SERAPHIC 1.

1568 T. NEWTON in Farr *S.P. Eliz.* (1845) 553 The troupes seraphicall. 1633 T. ADAMS *Exp. 2 Pet.* ii. 13 Some of the hairs that fell from the seraphical angel.

**2.** Resembling what pertains to the seraphim; rapturous, ecstatically devout.

1581 J. BELL *Haddon's Answ. Osor.* 304 Let us take a test of this your Seraphicall obedience. 1593 G. HARVEY *New Letter* Wks. (Grosart) I. 274 In the profoundest traunce of rapt Seraphicall Zeale. 1596 NASHE *Saffron-Walden* G 4, My Seraphicall visions in Queene Poetrie. 1648 J. GOODWIN *Yongling Elder* 2 A man of such Seraphicall parts and learning. 1674 BP. CROFT *Let. Pop. Idol.* (1679) 13 St. Francis,..and many others, in their Seraphical Meditations, have been rapt up into the third Heaven. 1742–3 *Observ. Methodists* 17 Together with a mixture of Seemingly Seraphical Flights and extravagant Allusions.

†**b.** Of ideas, etc.: Lofty, sublime. Cf. SERAPHIC *a.* 2 b. (In quot. *ironical*.) *Obs.*

1656 CROMWELL *Sp.* in *Burton's Diary* (1828) I. Introd. 161 Now we would be loth to tell you of notions more seraphical.

**3.** Of persons: Resembling the seraphim; characterized by ecstatic fervour of devotion. In the 17th c. often *ironical*, applied to fanatical religionists or to impassioned orators.

1596 NASHE *Saffron-Walden* G 4 b, Graue Heliconists, seraphicall Omniscians. 1616 BULLOKAR *Eng. Expos.*, *Seraphicall*, inflamed with diuine loue like a Seraphin. 1644 VICARS *God in Mount* (1844) 44 Such like rare seraphical rhetoritians. 1691 WOOD *Ath. Oxon.* II. 18 The most florid and seraphical Teacher in the University. 1692 SOUTH *12 Sermons* (1697) V. 33 The most Seraphical *Illuminati*, and the highest Puritan Perfectionists. *a* 1714 ABP. J. SHARP *Serm.* Wks. 1754 III. 218 Thus some very seraphical men do talk.

†**4.** In ***seraphical doctor***, ***order***: see SERAPHIC 4.

*a* 1540 BARNES *Wks.* (1573) 278 For these thinges bee geuen vnto them peculiar names, as subtile and seraphicall, and irrefrigable Doctours. 1561 DAUS tr. *Bullinger on Apoc.* (1573) 116 b, The Seraphicall order of S. Fraunces. 1640 HOWELL *Dodona's Gr.* 80 These Seraphicall Fathers doe so under value all other Orders, that [etc.]. 1674 HICKMAN *Hist. Quinquart.* (ed. 2) 69 Bonaventure..called generally the Seraphical Doctor. 1721 *Constitutions Blue Nuns* x, Let them keep the Octave of the Seraphicall Father S. Francis.

Hence †**se'raphicalist**, one who pretends to 'seraphic' excellence; †**se'raphicalness**.

1659 *Clarke Papers* (Camden) IV. 301 It's strange to see these seraphiclists [*sic*] can act without law, against Parliaments and against morality. 1727 BAILEY vol. II, *Seraphicalness*, the being of the seraphick Nature.

**seraphically** (sə'ræfɪkəlɪ), *adv.* [f. SERAPHICAL + -LY[2].] In a seraphic manner.

1678 NORRIS *Misc.* (1699) 260 Till I ascend in Spirit to the Element of Love, where I shall know thee more clearly, and love thee more Seraphically. 1891 'J. S. WINTER' *Lumley* xiv, He is so seraphically happy. 1909 *Nation* 3 Apr. 14/1 He was smiling seraphically.

†**se'raphicism**. *Obs.* [f. SERAPHIC *a.* + -ISM.] Pretence of 'seraphic' raptures.

1676 CUDWORTH *Serm.* (1 Cor. xv. 57) 87 Such are a self-chosen holiness..high-flown enthusiasm and Seraphicism.

**seraphim** ('sɛrəfɪm), †'**seraphin**. Forms: 1, 3–7, 9 *arch.* **seraphin**, 3 **serafin**, 4 **serafyn**, 5 **ceraphin**, **secheraphym**, **-phyn**, **seraphyn**, **-en**, **serophyn**, **syraphyn**, 6–7 **seraphine**, 1, 6– **seraphim**. [a. late L. *seraphim* (Vulg.), in MSS. often *seraphin* (= Gr. *σεραφίμ*, *σεραφείμ*, LXX.), a. Heb. *s[e]rāphīm* (only in Isa. vi), pl. of **sārāph*, which is not recorded in the Bible, unless it be identical with the formally coincident word denoting a kind of venomous serpent, which occurs as quasi-adj. or in apposition with *nāḥāsh* serpent in Num. xxi. and Deut. viii. (Eng. Bible 'fiery serpents', after Vulg. *ignitos serpentes*, *serpens adurens*; LXX *ὄφεις θανατοῦντας*, *ὄφις δάκνων*), and in Isa. xiv. 29 and xxx. 6 with the epithet 'flying' (Eng. Bible 'fiery flying serpent').

Some scholars assume the identity of the word occurring in Isa. vi. with that found in the other passages. On this view the 'seraphim' seen by Isaiah flying above the throne of God represent a mythic or symbolic conception which must originally have had the form of a 'fiery flying serpent', though in the vision this appears considerably modified.

The word *sārāph*, as the name of a kind of serpent, may belong to the root *sāraph* to burn, in allusion to the effect of the bite (cf. Gr. πρηστήρ). This etymology has given rise to a conjecture that the celestial 'seraphim' originally symbolized the lightning. Of those who reject the identity of *sārāph* 'seraph' with *sārāph* 'fiery serpent', some refer the former to the root of the Arabic *sharafa* to be lofty or illustrious. Phonologically this is unobjectionable, but on other grounds it is now generally abandoned. Various suggestions of non-Hebrew (Egyptian, Assyrian, etc.) etymology have been made, but have not found wide acceptance.

The L. form *seraphin*, which is found in many MSS. of the Vulgate, and is the source of all the forms used in Eng. down to the 16th c. (as well as of those in the Rom. langs.), coincides with the Aramaic *s'rāphīn*, but it is very doubtful whether it is more than a scribal error or a euphonic alteration. Cf. F. *séraphin* (*serafin*, 12th c.), Pr. *serafi*, Sp. *serafin*, Pg. *seraphim*, It. *serafino* (all masc. sing.).

In the Latin liturgical passages from which the word first became widely known, it was prob. originally apprehended correctly as a plural, and readers of the Latin Bible would be guided aright by the syntax of Isa. vi. 2; but there is evidence that 'Cherubim and Seraphim' were often supposed to be the names of two individual angels. From the 15th to the 18th c. the English plural ending was often appended, but *seraphin* as a sing. = 'one of the seraphim' does not appear in Eng. till late in the 16th c. (the form *seraphim* in this use not till the 17th c.). After the introduction (perh. by Milton) of the form SERAPH, the misuse of the plural forms in singular sense gradually became rare, and it is now obsolete.]

**1.** In Biblical use: The living creatures with six wings, hands and feet, and a (presumably) human voice, seen in Isaiah's vision as hovering above the throne of God.

**1382** WYCLIF *Isa.* vi. 2 Serafyn stoden up on it. [**1535** (Coverdale), **1537**, **1539**, **1551** the Seraphins; **1540** Seraphins; **1560** (Geneva), **1611** the Seraphims; **1568**, **1609** (Douay) Seraphims; **1884** (Revised) the seraphim.]

**2.** By Christian interpreters the seraphim were from an early period supposed to be a class of angels, and the name, associated with that of the cherubim, was introduced in the Eucharistic preface and subsequently in the *Te Deum*, and thus became extensively known. The presumed derivation of the word from a Heb. root meaning 'to burn' (see above) led to the view that the seraphim are specially distinguished by fervour of love (while the cherubim excel in knowledge), and to the symbolic use of red as the colour appropriate to the seraphim in artistic representations. In the system of the Pseudo-Dionysius, the chief source of later angelology, the seraphim are the highest, and the cherubim the second, of the nine orders of angels.

**a.** *seraphin* (*obs.* exc. *poet.* as *nonce-use*), *seraphim*, used as *plural*. (Some of the early examples are ambiguous, and may belong to b.)

α. *a* **900** CYNEWULF *Elene* 754 Syndon tu..þe man Seraphin be naman hateð. *a* **1240** *Ureisun* in *Cott. Hom.* 191 Heih is þi kinestol onuppe cherubine, Biuoren ðine leoue sune wiðinnen seraphine. *c* **1250** *Meid. Maregrete* lxxv, Cherubin ant serafin, a þousend þer were. **13..** *Ipotis* 92 (Vernon MS.) in Horstm. *Altengl. Leg.* (1881) 342 Þe furste ordre is Cherubin And þat oþer Seraphin. **1362** LANGL. *P. Pl.* A. I. 104 Cherubin and Seraphin an al þe foure [*the B and C texts have* nine] ordres. **1398** TREVISA *Barth. De P.R.* II. viii. (1495) 34 Seraphyn is a multytude of angellis that is to vnderstonde: brennynge other settynge a fyre..and the propre offyce of thyse angels is to brenne in theymselfe and to moeue other to brenne in the loue of god. *c* **1400** *Prymer* (1891) 21 To thee cherubyn and seraphyn cryeth with uoys with owten ceessynge. *c* **1425** *St. Mary of Oignies* I. vii. in *Anglia* VIII. 140/3 She sawe oon of Seraphyn, þat is a brennynge aungel. **1486** *Bk. St. Albans, Her.* a iv b, The iiii. Tronli [orders of angels] be theys Principatus Trony Cherubyn and Seraphyn. **1549** *Bk. Com. Prayer, Te deum*, Cherubin, and Seraphin. **1642** R. WATSON *Serm. Schisme* 32 The first place or degree is given to the Angels of love, which are termed Seraphin. **1691** NORRIS *Pract. Disc.* 289 What is it that makes the Seraphin burn and flame above the rest of the Angelical Orders? **1897** F. THOMPSON *New Poems* 74 You shall..ay, press in Where faint the fledge-foot seraphin.

β. *a* **1000** *Andreas* 719 (Gr.) Cheruphim et Seraphim þa on sweȝeldreamum syndon nemned. *a* **1500** *Adrian & Epotys* 92 in *Brome Bk.* 28 The secund ordyr is secheraphym. **16..** MILTON *At a Solemn Music* 10 Where the bright Seraphim in burning row Their loud up-lifted Angel trumpets blow. *a* **1680** CHARNOCK *Attrib. God* (1834) II. 146 The angels..are here called Seraphim, from burning or fiery spirits. **1827** HEBER *Hymn, 'Thou art gone to the grave'*, The sound which thou heard'st was the Seraphim's song! **1829** COLERIDGE *Monody Chatterton* (later version) 24 Thou..The triumph of redeeming Love dost hymn..to harps of Seraphim. **1864** PUSEY *Lect. Daniel* ix. (1876) 533 Like the Seraphim, they are seen in adoring love, about His throne. **1871** ROSSETTI *Poems, Ave* 104 And from between the seraphim The glory issues for a hymn.

†**b.** Taken as the name of an angel.

*a* **1300** *Cursor M.* 22600 Þan sal quak sant cherubin, And alsua sal do seraphin. *a* **1400** *Relig. Pieces fr. Thornton MS.* 37 Michaell and Gabrielle and Raphaelle, cherubyn and seraphyn, and all þe oþer angells and archangells.

**c.** Plural. †*seraphins*, *seraphims* (now *rare*).

α. *a* **1400–50** *Wars Alex.* 9415 Þe silloure full of Seraphens & othire sere halows. *c* **1420** *Virgin's Compl.* 88 in *Pol. Rel. & L. Poems* (1903) 241, I sawe angelis with gret lithe of seraphynnys order adowne gan sende. **1490** CAXTON *How to die* 22 The cherubyns and the syraphyns come to thyne helpe. **1566** *Pasquine in Traunce* 73 These were their names, ..Angels, Arch-angels,..Powers, Cherubines, and Seraphines. **1596** SPENSER *Hymn Heav. Beauty* 94 Those eternall burning Seraphins, Which from their faces dart out fierie light. *a* **1610** PARSONS *Leicester's Ghost* (1641) 24 Know that the Prince of Heavenly Seraphines..Was tumbled downe for his presumptuous sinne. **1635** A. STAFFORD *Fem. Glory*, Panegyr. e 7, All the strings Of Seraphins tun'd high, lowd Hymnes did play. **1649** LOVELACE *Elegy on Princ. Katherine* 51 Clap wings with Seraphins before the Throne. **1659** H. L'ESTRANGE *Alliance Div. Off.* 76 The Seraphins resound it.

β. [**1560**, **1568**, **1609**, **1611**: see 1.] *a* **1627** SIR J. BEAUMONT *Epiphany* 38 Who..trie our actions in that searching fire By which the seraphims our lips inspire. **1653** JER. TAYLOR *Serm. for Yr.* ii. 16 The joy is so great that it runs over and wets the fair brows and beauteous locks of Cherubims and Seraphims. **1675** ABP. J. SHARP *Serm.* ii. Wks. 1754 I. 58 To know and be known by angels, arch-angels, and seraphims. *a* **1711** KEN *Hymnotheo* Poet. Wks. 1721 III. 201 Seraphims, whose Mold is heav'nly Love, Who nearest to the Godhead wait above. **1756–9** A. BUTLER *Lives Saints, S. Ludger*, God, in whose presence the highest seraphims annihilate themselves. **1924** E. SITWELL *Sleeping Beauty* iv. 23 From flowers as white as seraphims' breath.

**d.** *seraphin*, *seraphim* as a sing. = one of the seraphim, a seraph.

α. **1579** W. WILKINSON *Confut. Fam. Love* B ij, The Seraphin with his fiery sword not being taken away. *c* **1610** MIDDLETON *Witch* IV. ii. 111 No, he that would soul's sacred comfort win Must burn in pure love, like a seraphin. *c* **1645** HOWELL *Lett.* (1650) II. 35 She would have every thing divine That would befitt a Seraphin.

β. *a* **1649** CRASHAW *Carmen Deo Nostro* 74 We will pledge this Seraphim [*viz.* St. Teresa] Bowles full of richer blood [etc.]. *a* **1674** TRAHERNE *Poet. Wks.* (1903) 104 While we see What every Seraphim above admires! **1700** ASTRY tr. *Saavedra-Faxardo* I. 168 God gave not the flaming Sword, which guarded Paradise, to a Seraphim. **1802** MRS. WEST *Infidel Father* II. 85 Or had you..blended the service of the Deity with the idolatrous worship of a seraphim. **1920** 'K. MANSFIELD' *Let.* Nov. (1928) II. 80 A cherubim and a seraphim come winging their way towards me. **1974** *Times Lit. Suppl.* 29 Mar. 314/3 Lamartine is content to be a seraphim.

**3.** *Her.* †**a.** In Sir John Ferne's fanciful method of blazoning by 'spirits', the equivalent of Argent.

**1586** FERNE *Blaz. Gentrie* 144 A fosse waynee between the two starres artick and antiartick seraphines.

**b.** The representation of a seraph.

Usually, a child's head with two wings above, two below, and one on each side.

**1828–40** BERRY *Encycl. Her.* s.v. *Carruthers*, Crest, a seraphim, volant, ppr.

**4.** A Swedish order of knighthood. (See quot.)

**1784** H. CLARK *Hist. Knighthood* II. 213 Sweden. The Order of the Seraphim, or of Jesus..first instituted by Magnus the IId, in the year 1334... It..lay dormant, until February 1748, when it was revived..by Frederick the First.

**5.** *Geol. sing.* and *collect.* A fossil crustacean of the genus *Pterygotus*.

**1839** MURCHISON *Silur. Syst.* 606 Fig. 4 and 5 belong undoubtedly to the same animal as the Seraphim of the Old Red Sandstone. **1863** H. WOODWARD in *Intell. Observ.* IV. 229 The 'Seraphim', a fossil found in 'the Arbroath paving-stone' of Forfarshire, which from the wing-like form of some parts of the shell, and the scale or feather-like markings upon its surface, has given rise to this angelic title among the natives. **1894** *Q. Rev.* July 191 The giant crustaceans or arachnids known to the Scotch quarrymen as 'Seraphim'.

**6.** A moth of the genus *Lobophora*. Also ***seraphim-moth***.

**1832** J. RENNIE *Butterfl. & Moths* 132 The Seraphim (*Lobophora hexapterata*, Curtis) appears in June... The small Seraphim (*Lobophora sexalisata*, Curtis) appears in June and August. **1882** *Cassell's Nat. Hist.* VI. 67 In ..*Lobophoræ* there is so large an additional lobe to the hind wing as to give them the appearance of having six wings, whence they are called 'Seraphims' by collectors. *Ibid.*, Index to Popular Names, Seraphim Moths.

‖**'seraphin.** *Obs.* Forms: 6 **seraffine, serafyne, seraphine, xeraphin,** 7 **serafin, seraffin, zeraphin,** 8 **seraphyn, xerapheen,** 9 **zeraphim.** [a. Pg. *xerafim*, *xarafim*, a. Arab. *sharīfī*, orig. the name of a gold coin. Cf. SERAPH[2].] A silver coin formerly current in India; for its value, see quot. 1727.

**1582** N. LICHEFIELD tr. *Castanheda's Conq. E. Ind.* 56 b, He must give him 600 Serafynes. **1584** R. BARRET in *Hakluyt's Voy.* (1599) II. i. 273 There is also stamped in Ormuz a seraphine of gold, which is litle and round. **1588** HICKOCK tr. *C. Frederick's Voy.* 37, I lost my 800 Seraffines or duckets. *a* **1613** W. HAWKINS in Purchas *Pilgrims* (1625) I. 217 *Inprimis*, of Seraffins *Ecberi*, which be ten Rupias a piece, there are sixtie Leckes. **1698** FRYER *Acc. E. India & P.* 207 The Cruzado of Gold, 12 Zeraphins. **1704** *Churchill's Collect. Voy. & Trav.* III. 772/2 A *Candil* of Rice was sold ..for 2500 *Seraphyns*, or Gilders. **1727** A. HAMILTON *New Acc. E. Ind.* I. xxi. 249 Their Soldiers Pay [at Goa] is very small... They have but six Xerapheens per Month,..a Xerapheen is worth about sixteen Pence half Peny Ster. **1858** SIMMONDS *Dict. Trade*, *Zeraphim*, a former money of account of Goa, of 240 Portugese reis.

**seraphine** ('sɛrəfiːn). Also **seraphina**. [f. SERAPH + -INE.] A musical instrument of the reed kind, invented by John Green in 1833.

**1839** *Civ. Engin. & Arch. Jrnl.* II. 318/2 Certain improvements in the construction of certain musical instruments..of the kind commonly called seraphines. **1845** GRESLEY *Frank's First Trip* 201 Six or eight women..were singing a plaintive hymn, accompanied by a seraphine. **1879** A. J. HIPKINS in *Grove's Dict. Mus.* I. 667 In England keyboard harmonicas with bellows were known by the name of Seraphine, which was not an harmonium. **1900** *Westm. Gaz.* 7 June 8/1 In most Boer houses of the better class there is an American organ or 'seraphine'.

**'seraphism.** *rare.* [f. SERAPH[1] + -ISM.] Ecstatic devotion.

**1846** C. MAITLAND *Ch. Catacombs* 212 That religion.. presents..a joyful serenity, worth all..the proud seraphism of the Thebaid.

†**se'raphium.** *Obs.*$^{-1}$ ? = SERAPINE.

**1583** *Rates Custom ho.* E iij b, Seraphium the pound.

‖**Serapias** (sə'reɪpɪæs). [L. *serāpias*, f. the name of the Egyptian god *Serāpis*.] Formerly, a book-name for various orchids, and for the dried roots of these as used in pharmacy. Now only mod. Latin (*Bot.*) as the name of an orchidaceous genus.

**1597** GERARDE *Herbal* I. civ. 173 We haue called these kindes Serapias stones, or Orchis Serapiades,..taking the name as it were from Serapias the god of the Citizens of Alexandria... It is also called..in English Satyrion, and finger Orchis. **1640** PARKINSON *Theat. Bot.* 1354 The properties of these Serapiaes. **1706** PHILLIPS (ed. Kersey), *Serapias*, (Gr.) an Herb call'd Dog-stones, or Rag-wort. **1753** *Chambers's Cycl.* Suppl., *Serapias*, in the materia medica, the officinal name of the dried root, called *salep*.

**serapic** (sə'ræpɪk), *a.* [f. *Serap-is* + -IC.] Of or pertaining to the Egyptian god *Serapis*.

**1888** *Pop. Sci. Monthly* XXXII. 560 (Cent.) They include various types of the god Abraxas, Cnuphic and Serapic emblems, Egyptian types.

†**serapin(e.** *Obs.* Also in Latin form. [ad. med.L. *serapīnum*; of obscure origin; perh. this and SAGAPENUM represent some Oriental word.]

**1.** = SAGAPENUM.

α. *c* **1400** *Lanfranc's Cirurg.* (1894) 43 Azafetida is best medicyn if þou make of him emplastre, serapinum, & þe fecis of a litil wex. **1543** TRAHERON *Vigo's Chirurg.* Interpr., Sagapenum commonly called Serapinum droppeth out of the stalke of ferula. *a* **1618** *Rates Marchandizes* F 2 b, Gum Serapinum.

β. **1526** *Grete Herball* ccclxxx. (1529) X ij, Serapyn is..the gomme of a tre that groweth beyonde the see and in Grece. *c* **1550** LLOYD *Treas. Health* G ij, Serapine stampte and put into the hollow tooth taketh awai y^e^ paines therof. **1555** EDEN *Decades* (Arb.) 269 Gumme Serapine. **1714** *Fr. Bk. Rates* 92 Gum Serapin per 100 Weight 06 05.

**2.** The tree that produces sagapenum.

**1585** T. WASHINGTON tr. *Nicholay's Voy.* II. x. 43 Al maner of trees, as pinetrees, Serapins, Cypres, Terebinths [etc.].

‖**seraskier** (sɛræ'skɪə(r)). *Hist.* Also **seraskur, serasquier.** [repr. Turkish pronunciation of Pers. *serʿasker* head of the army, f. *ser* head + Arab. *ʿaskar* army.] The title of the Turkish Minister of War, who was also commander in chief of the army.

**1684** *Lond. Gaz.* No. 1952/2 The Turkish Officer, who is known by the Title of Serasquier. **1717** LADY M. W. MONTAGU *Let. to Pope* 12 Feb., A very numerous garrison of their bravest janissaries, commanded by a pasha seraskièr (i.e. general). **1803** WITTMAN *Trav. Turkey* 237 The title of Seraskier corresponds with that of our commander in chief of the army. **1876** A. J. EVANS *Through Bosnia* vi. 261 The Seraskier at Stamboul..had persisted in withdrawing the regulars stationed in the province.

‖**Seraskierate** (sɛræ'skɪərət). Also **seraskarat, -kerat, -keriat(e, -kierat.** [f. prec. + -ATE[1].] The War Office at Constantinople.

**1876** *Illustr. Lond. News* 8 July 43/2 The execution..took place..in the open square of the Seraskierate or War Office. **1877** *Encycl. Brit.* VI. 307 The great tower of Galata, like that of the Seraskierat (War Office) on the opposite height in Stamboul, is used as a fire-tower. **1891** *Athenæum* 26 Dec. 868/3 They are instructed to send all local details as to situation to the Seraskierate.

†**serate.** *Obs.*$^{-1}$ [a. F. †(*laict*) *serat* (Cotgr.).] (See quot.)

**1600** SURFLET *Country Farm* I. xiv. 90 The Normans do boile milke with garlicke and onions, and keepe it in vessels for their vse, calling it sowre milke or Serate.

**serauee, seraw(e, seray,** obs. ff. SERAI[1].

**Serax** ('sɛræks). *Pharm.* A proprietary name in Canada and the U.S. for OXAZEPAM.

**1957** *Official Gaz.* (U.S. Patent Office) 27 Aug. TM 148/2 American Home Products Corporaton... *Serax*. For ataractic. First use Feb. 4, 1957. **1968** *Jrnl. Pharmaceut. Sci.* LVII. 312/2 Oxazepam is a psychotropic agent. [*Note*] Marketed as Serax by Wyeth Laboratories, Philadelphia, Pa. **1974** M. C. GERALD *Pharmacol.* xvi. 309 The benzodiazepine derivatives include..oxazepam (Serax). **1977** *Rolling Stone* 30 June 81/3, I..reached into my shirt pocket, removed two ·30 mg. Serax capsules, popped them into my mouth, and washed them down with the drink.

**seraya** (sɛ'raɪə). [Mal.] A forest tree of the genus *Shorea* or *Parashorea*, belonging to the family Dipterocarpaceæ and native to south-east Asia; also, the hardwood timber produced by a tree of this kind. Cf. LAUAN, MERANTI.

**1893** G. KING in *Jrnl. Asiatic Soc. Bengal* LXII. II. 112 Its vernacular name in Penang is *Seraya*. **1916** *Bull. Dept. Forestry Brit. N. Borneo* No. 1. 19 The better coloured and figured pieces of Seriah make very acceptable substitutes for Mahogany, in panels, veneers, etc. **1920** A. L. HOWARD *Man. Timbers World* 256 The wood has been called by a variety of names such as East Indian mahogany and East Indian cedar, as well as by its proper name of serayah. **1940** E. J. H. CORNER *Wayside Trees Malaya* I. 213 The *Seraya* ..is perhaps the only forest-tree that can be identified from afar by its pale, outstanding crown. **1956** *Handbk. of Hardwoods* (Forest Prod. Res. Lab.) 153 Red seraya or light red seraya..may be described as the North Borneo equivalent of light red meranti. *Ibid.* 212 White seraya grows to an average height of 120 ft. **1962** J. C. S. Brough *Timbers for Woodwork* (rev. ed.) xvi. 174 Seraya..ranges from straw to reddish-brown. **1965** R. McKie *Company of Animals* i. 36 We stopped high on the ridge in light jungle topped by seraya trees. **1971** [see lauan].

**serayn(e**, obs. forms of siren.

**Serb** (sɜːb), *sb.* and *a.* Also 9 **Syrbe**. [a. Serbian *Srb, Serb.* Cf. F. *Serbe.*] **A.** *sb.*

**1.** † **a.** A Wend of Lusatia. (Cf. Sorb.) *Obs.* **b.** A native of Serbia, a Serbian.

**1813** *Q. Rev.* X. 283 The Serbs or Wends came about the same time into the countries between the Saal and the Oder. **1842** *Penny Cycl.* XXII. 103/2 The Syrbes or Wends, who inhabit Lusatia. **1861** Mill *Repr. Govt.* xvi. 292 The population of Hungary is composed of Magyars, Slovacks, Croats, Serbs, Roumans, and in some districts, Germans. **1866** *Chamb. Encycl.* VIII. 629/2 (art. *Servia*) Every Serb carries arms. **1883** Morfill *Slav. Lit.* ii. 33 The Serbs have, unlike the Russians and other Slavs, kept their old name.

**2.** The Serbian language.

**1886** *Fortn. Rev.* Jan. 146 Serb became a proscribed tongue. **1905** *Macm. Mag.* Nov. 40 Everyone, whether Christian or Moslem, speaks Serb only.

**B.** *adj.* Serbian.

**1876** A. J. Evans *Through Bosnia* i. 16 The barbarous Serb races who settled in the Danubian basin in the fifth and succeeding centuries.

**Serbian** (ˈsɜːbɪən), *a.* and *sb.* [f. Serb + -ian.] **A.** *adj.* Of or belonging to Serbia, a constituent republic of Yugoslavia, occupied by a Slavonic people.

The Slavonic kingdom of Serbia was conquered by the Turks in 1389; the country remained a principality tributary to Turkey until 1878, when the kingdom was revived. It was absorbed into Yugoslavia after the end of the First World War.

**1876** A. J. Evans *Through Bosnia* i. 7 The headdress of the Serbian women. **1883** Morfill *Slav. Lit.* i. 8 The Serbian chieftain, Vouk Brankovitch.

**B.** *sb.* **a.** A native or an inhabitant of Serbia.

**1848** C. Bunsen in *Rep. Brit. Assoc. Advancem. Sci. 1847* 267 The sixth family is that of the Slavonic nations in their two great branches;..the western, the languages of the Tschechs (Bohemians), Slovaks, Poles, and Serbians. **1862** Denton *Servia & Servians* 11 About the middle of the seventh century the Serbians, a Sclavonic tribe, entered Mœsia.

**b.** The Serbian language.

**1867** Misses Mackenzie & Irby *Turks, Greeks & Slavons* 412 We asked, in Serbian, if they would kindly show us their books. **1876** A. J. Evans *Through Bosnia* i. 26 Besides my native tongue..I know Serbian. **1887** Morfill (*title*) Simplified grammar of Serbian.

**ˈSerbo-**, combining form of Serb, as ***Serbo-Croat***, ***-Croatian***; ***Serbo-Bulgarian***, ***-Greek***, ***-Italian*** adjs. Cf. Servo-.

**1923** G. Buchanan *My Mission to Russia* I. vi. 69 The so-called *Serbo-Bulgarian Customs Union Treaty, negotiated in 1905, was never ratified by the Skuptschina. **1905** *Contemp. Rev.* Apr. 598 The *Serbo-Croat language. **1931** *Times Lit. Suppl.* 29 Jan. 82/3 Translations..from the Russian,..Judaeo-Spanish and Serbo-Croat. **1976** W. H. Canaway *Willow-Pattern War* vii. 78 Petar was bilingual in Serbo-Croat and Albanian. **1883** Morfill *Slav. Lit.* i. 8 The..extent of the territory over which *Serbo-Croatian and its dialects..are spoken. **1958** *Everyman's Encycl.* XI. 234/1 Later there were attempts to replace the decaying Byzantine empire by a *Serbo-Greek empire. **1972** D. Dakin *Unification of Greece* ix. 126 The Serbo-Greek alliance of 1867. **1876** A. J. Evans *Through Bosnia* ix. 389 Her *Serbo-Italian neighbours.

**Serbonian** (sɜːˈbəʊnɪən), *a.* [f. Gr. Σερβωνί-ς (λίμνη) + -an.] ***Serbonian bog***: Milton's name for Lake Serbonis in Lower Egypt, a marshy tract (now dry) covered with shifting sand. Hence used allusively.

**1667** Milton *P.L.* ii. 592 A gulf profound as that Serbonian Bog Betwixt Damiata and mount Casius old, Where Armies whole have sunk. **1790** Burke *Fr. Rev.* Sel. Wks. II. 231 In the 'Serbonian bog' of this base oligarchy they are all absorbed, sunk, and lost for ever. **1903** Morley *Gladstone* viii. vii. III. 121 The Serbonian bog of Egyptian finance.

**serc**, obs. form of sark.

**serce**, obs. Sc. form of search *v.*

**serce, sercer**, obs. ff. searce, searcer.

**sercell**, var. sarcel *Obs.* (hawk's feather).

**sercenett**, obs. form of sarsenet.

†**serch.** *Obs. rare.* Also 5 **seergh**. [Of obscure origin.] ? Some kind of worked stone for building purposes.

**1416-17** in Willis & Clark *Cambridge* (1886) II. 442 Pro lviij pedibus de lapid' vocat' seerghys ijˢ. vᵈ. *c* **1429** *Ibid.* II. 445 Pro..xxiij pedibus de serchis.

**serch(e**, obs. forms of search *sb.* and *v.*

**sercial** (ˈsɜːsɪəl). A kind of Madeira wine.

**1818** Accum *Chem. Tests* 190. **1851** Redding *Mod. Wines* (ed. 3) 265 The sercial is said to be the product of the hock grape, transplanted to the island. **1873** *St. Pauls Mag.* June 637 A glass of his favourite old Sercial. **1882** Ellen M. Taylor *Madeira* 75 The principal varieties of wine-making grapes are the following: Malvasia, Bual, Sercial [etc.].

**sercil**, var. sarcel.

**sercle**, obs. form of circle.

**serclet(t**, obs. forms of circlet.

**1530** Palsgr. 269/2 Serclet for a brides heed, *cedre.*

**sercote**, obs. form of surcoat.

**sercute**, obs. form of circuit *sb.*

**1506** *Kal. Sheph.* (Sommer) 125 The mone maketh one turnyng or one sercute..within xxvii. dayes or there about.

**serd**, var. sard *v.* and obs. pa. t. of serve.

‖**serdab** (sɜːˈdɑːb). Also **serdaub, sirdab**. [Pers. (hence Arab.) *serdāb* grotto, ice-house, cellar.] **a.** In Western Asia, a cellar or underground chamber. **b.** In Egypt, a secret passage or chamber in an ancient tomb.

**a. 1842** W. F. Ainsworth *Trav. Asia Minor*, etc. II. 331 The foundations, cellars, or serdaubs,..were generally all that remained. **1842** J. B. Fraser *Mesopot. & Assyria* i. 25 When the inhabitants of Bagdad are panting in their *sirdabs*, or cellars under ground, whither they retire to avoid the rays of the sun.

**b. 1877** Miss A. B. Edwards *Up Nile* iv. 92 This tomb.. also contains a secret passage of the kind that M. Mariette calls a serdab. These serdabs are constructed in the thickness of the walls and have no entrances. **1897** *Daily News* 5 July 8/3 In the serdab, or statue-chamber, of one of the principal tombs, a very fine statue..was found.

**serdar**, obs. form of sirdar.

**serdge**, obs. form of cierge, wax candle.

**1538** *Test. Ebor.* (Surtees) VI. 84 The other xii serdges to be burned in like manner.

†**serdoner.** *Obs. rare*⁻¹.

*a* **1550** *Image Ipocr.* ii. in *Skelton's Wks.* (1843) II. 429 Thou arte..The syre of serdoners, And prince of pardoners.

†**sere**, *sb.*¹ *Obs.* Also 7 **seere, serre, sear(e.** [a. OF. *serre*, vbl. n. f. *serre-r* to hold fast, shut:—pop.L. *serrāre*, altered form of late L. *serāre*, f. *sera* bolt, bar. Cf. sear *sb.*¹] A claw, talon.

**1606** Sylvester *Du Bartas* ii. iv. i. *Tropheis* 136 A paire of busie chattering Pies, Seeing some hardie Tercell from the skies To stoop with rav'nous seres, feel a chill fear. **1618** Chapman *Hesiod's Georg.* i. 318 The Hauke once, hauing trust vp in his Seres, The sweet-tun'd Nightingale. **1683** *Lond. Gaz.* No. 1799/4 Lost near Cadnam.., a thorough mewed Falcon, the Feet and Sear very yellow. **1864** Lowell *McClellan's Rep.* Wks. 1890 V. 94 Every excuse was invented..except the true one, that our chicken was no eagle after all. He was hardening his seres, he was waiting for his wings to grow [etc.].

**sere** (sɪə(r)), *sb.*² *Ecol.* [f. L. *serĕ-re* to join in a series.] A series of plant communities, each naturally succeeding the previous one.

**1916** F. E. Clements *Plant Succession* i. 4 A sere is a unit succession. It comprises the development of a formation from the appearance of the first pioneers through the final or climax stage. **1940** *Geogr. Jrnl.* XCVI. 8 The seres which follow the destruction of climax vegetation in the alpine region [of the Himalayas] vary. **1960** N. Polunin *Introd. Plant Geogr.* xi. 323 Such is succession, the developmental series of communities constituting a sere and leading up to a state of relative stability and permanence known as the climax.

**sere, sear** (sɪə(r)), *a.*¹ Forms: 1 **séar, síere**, 4-7 **seare, seere**, 4-8 **seer**, 5 **seyr**, 6 **seyre**, 7 **seir(e**, 7-9 (*dial.*) **sare**, 4- **sere**, 6- **sear**. [OE. *séar* corresponds to MLG. *sôr* (LG. *soor*), Du. *zoor*:—OTeut. **sauzo-*:—Indogermanic **sausó-*, whence Lith. *saũsas*, OSl. *suxŭ*, Gr. αὖος dry, Skr. *çôsha* drying up, withering.

OE. seems to have had also a synonymous derivative *síere* (:—**sauzjo-*), which in later Eng. would be represented by the same form as *séar*.]

**1. a.** Dry, withered. Now *poet.* or *rhetorical.*

**824** *Grant* in Birch *Cartul. Sax.* I. 515 Hit stent on þam sieran boc haȝan. *a* **1000** *Gloss. Prudent.* in *Germania* (1878) XI. 402 *Steriles*, seare. **13..** *K. Alis.* 4425 (Bodl. MS.) Þe spere crakeþ also þicke So on hegge sere stykke. *c* **1425** *Found. St. Bartholomew's* (E.E.T.S.) 28 Seyr and drye membyrs. **1526** *Pilgr. Perf.* (W. de W. 1531) 47 b, And that appereth in the tree of nature whiche..in wynter..semeth seyre, drye, & in maner as deed. **1590** Shaks. *Com. Err.* iv. ii. 19 He is deformed, crooked, old, and sere. **1620** Quarles *Feast for Wormes* C 4, Will greene wood burne, when so vnapt's the seire? **1725** *Bradley's Fam. Dict.* s.v. *Thatching*, When they [Withs] are grown Sear they will fly and break. **1805** Wordsw. *Prelude* i. 84 Now here, now there, an acorn, from its cup Dislodged, through sere leaves rustled. **1901** H. Trench *Deirdre Wed* 12 Aghast, the woman Fumbled at her sere breast, and wept.

**b.** *transf.* and *fig.*, and in fig. context.

**1530** Tindale *Gen.* xlvii. 21 *marg.* To sucke out yᵉ iuce of them with their poetrye, till all be seer bowes and no thinge greene save their awne comenwelth. **1567** Turberv. *Ovid's Ep.* 93 b, Receyue me to thy carelesse couch in sere and silent night. **1605** Shaks. *Macb.* v. iii. 25, I haue liu'd long enough, my way of life Is falne into the Seare, the yellow Leafe. **1633** T. Adams *Exp. 2 Pet.* ii. 13 The house that grows sere, needs supporters. **1795** Coleridge *Sonnet to Southey*, Till sickly Passion's drooping Myrtles sear Blossom anew. **1837** Card. Wiseman *St. Eliz. of Hungary* in *Ess.* (1853) III. 226 The rude materialities of life in this sear generation. **1880** O. W. Holmes *Shadows* 18 Some locks had got silvered, some lives had grown sere.

**c.** *absol.* (Cf. quot. 1605 in 1 b.)

**1791** W. Taylor tr. *Lessing's Nathan* iv. (1886) 133 In my sear of life An Assad blossoms for me. **1890** J. Watson *Conf. Poacher* (1893) 74 By the third week of October, the yellow and sere of the year has come.

†**2.** Of textile fabrics: Thin, worn. *Obs.*

**1523** *Rec. St. Mary at Hill* (1904) 35 An Olde Seer dyapur Towell. **1591** Percivall *Sp. Dict.*, *Raça de panno*, the place where cloth is seere or thinne. *a* **1631** Donne *Elegies* i. Poems (1633) 44 If swolne with poyson, hee lay in his last bed, His body with a sere-barke covered. **1736** Pegge *Kenticisms* (E.D.S.) 45 My coat is very sare. **1798** Coleridge *Anc. Mar.* v. v, A roaring wind..shook the sails That were so thin and sere.

**3.** *Comb.* **a.** Forming parasynthetic adjectives, as ***sere-coloured***, ***sere-leaved***, † ***sere-souled***. Also † **sere-dried** *pa. pple.*, dried to excess.

**1901** *Westm. Gaz.* 29 May 2/1 The background of *sere-coloured autumn foliage suggests the passing of a glorious summer day. **1657** G. Starkey *Helmont's Vind.* 62 Hay, which if *sear-dryed in the Sun, is half in half damnified. **1870** D. Lindsay in *Poets Ayrsh.* (1910) 254 *Sear leaved decay does o'er the woodland steal. **1659** H. M. *Pair Spectacles for Nation* 4 Tell us you *Sear-soul'd men that will swear *pro* and *con*, tell me what an oath is?

†**b.** in syntactical combinations formerly often hyphened or written as single words: ***sere tree***, ***wood***; also **sere month**, a name for August. *Obs.*

**1686-7** Aubrey *Rem. Gentilisme* (1881) 123 Proverbs.. Item, *Good to cut Briars in the *Sere month* (*i*) August. ? *a* **1616** Beaum. & Fl. *Wit without Money* iii. i, Old age like *Seer-trees, is seldom seen affected. *c* **1611** Chapman *Iliad* i. 449 The Priest, with small *sere wood Did sacrifice. **1700** Dryden *Flower & Leaf* 414 The Lawrel-Champions.. Sere-wood from the rotten Hedges took. **1784** Cullum *Hist. Hawsted* 173 The wood-stealers always tell you they never take any but sear wood.

**c. sereward** *adv.*, towards decay (*rare*⁻¹).

**1902** T. Hardy *Poems of Past & Present* 142 The sun and shadows wheel, Season and season sereward steal.

†**sere**, *adv.* and *a.*² *Obs.* (? exc. *dial.*). Forms: 3-5 **ser**, 3-6 **seir**, 3-6, 8 (*dial.*) **sere**, 4 **seyr, schere**, 4, 7, 9 (*dial.*) **seer**, 5-6 **seyr**, 5, 7 **seere**, 6 **seare**. [a. ON. *sér*, orig. dative of the refl. pron. (accus. *sik*, gen. *sin*); the sense 'for oneself' gave rise in ON. to the advb. meaning 'separately, apart' (also in compounds, e.g. *sérdeilis* partly, *sérligr* particular); the further development into an adj. is peculiar to English. Cf. Da. *sær* singular, Da. *især*, Sw. *sär* particularly.]

**A.** *adv.* Separately, severally. ***sere twice***, on two separate occasions.

*a* **1300** *Cursor M.* 4231 His oþer suns com ilkan sere For to mend þair fader chere. **13..** *Gaw. & Gr. Knt.* 1522, I haf seten by your-self here sere twyes, Ȝet herde I neuer of your hed helde no wordez þat euer longed to luf. *c* **1440** *York Myst.* ii. 20 Þe water I will be set to flowe bothe fare and nere, And þan þe firmament, in mydis to set þame sere.

**b.** ? 'All told', in all.

? *a* **1600** *Flodden F.* iii. (1664) 30 The number did but mount To six and twenty thousand seere.

**B.** *adj.*

**1.** Separate, distinct; each in particular, single.

*c* **1200** Ormin 18653 Forr ser iss Sune, & Faderr ser, & ser iss þe33re baþre Allmahhti3 Gast. *a* **1300** *Cursor M.* 5461 His suns blessed he on rau, He gaue ilkan seir benissun. **1340** Hampole *Pr. Consc.* 5894 Men sal alswa yhelde rekkenynges sere Of al gudes þat God has gefen þam here. *a* **1400** *Rel. Pieces fr. Thornton MS.* v. 64 Jhesu, joyne þi lufe in my thoghte, Swa þat þay neuer be sere. **1545** Ascham *Toxoph.* ii. (Arb.) 107 Instrumentes for euery sere archer to brynge with him, proper for his own vse. **1565** Calfhill *Answ. Martiall* v. 130 b, Traditions in euery age with euery sere byshop [haue] varied.

**2.** Divers, various, sundry.

*a* **1300** *Cursor M.* 2 And romans red on maneres sere. *Ibid.* 6840 Your land yee sal sau seuen yeir, And scer þar-of your corns seir. *a* **1340** Hampole *Ps.* cl. 4 Orgyns þat is made as a toure of sere whistils. *c* **1375** *Lay Folks Mass-bk.* (MS.B.) 70, I have synned largely, In mony synnes sere. *c* **1450** *Bk. Curtasye* 262 in *Babees Bk.*, Þe boke hym calles a chorle of chere, That vylany spekes be wemen sere. **1585** Jas. I *Ess. Poesie* (Arb.) 18 That your vertewis singuler and seir May wholly all in them be also found. **1691** Ray *N.C. Words* (E.D.S.). **1703** Thoresby *Let. to Ray* s.v. **1829** Brockett *N.C. Gloss.* (ed. 2) 261.

**3.** *Comb.*, as **sere-coloured**, parti-coloured; **(on) sere-wise** *adv.*, in divers ways.

*c* **1425** *St. Mary of Oignies* ii. i. in *Anglia* VIII. 151/5 A cote *sere-colerd comynge to þe helys. **1340** Hampole *Pr. Consc.* 3261 Þus sal þai on *sere-wyse pyned be, Sum many wynter for þair syn. *c* **1375** *Sc. Leg. Saints* xxviii. (*Margaret*) 515, & hyre prayere quhen scho had ser-wyse to god deuotely mad, a licht of hewine rathly schane.

**sere**, var. cere *sb.* and *v.*, sear *v.*; obs. f. sir *sb.*

**serea**, obs. form of sirrah.

†ˈ**Serean**, *a.* and *sb.* *Obs.* [f. L. *Sēr-es* (see Seres) + -ean. Cf. Serian, Seric.] **a.** *adj.* Of or pertaining to the Seres; silken. **b.** *sb. pl.* = seres.

**1606** Sylvester *Du Bartas* ii. iv. ii. *Magnif.* 316 That hath soft Sereans yellow Spoyls. **1633** Drumm. of Hawth. *Poems* (1656) 160 Here are no Serean Fleeces.

**serefe**, obs. Sc. form of SHERIFF.

**sereiaunt**, obs. form of SERGEANT.

‖**serein** (sərɛ̃). *Meteorology.* [Fr.: see SERENE *sb.*[1]] A fine rain falling from a cloudless sky.
**1870** TYNDALL *Heat* §495 Whose condensation produces the *serein.* **1878** HUXLEY *Physiogr.* 41.

**sereine**, variant of SERENE *sb.*[1]

†**'serekin(s**, *a. Obs.* Forms: 3 sirekin, serekines, serekens, 3–4 serekin, 3–5 serkin. [f. SERE *a.*[2] + KIN *sb.*[1] (6 b).] Of several kinds.
*a* **1300** *Cursor M.* 2654 Abraham.. þis nam sua mikel es to rede Als fader o mani serkyn lede. *Ibid.* 7407 Dauid cuth on sere-kin [*Gött.* serkin] note Bath he cuth on harpe and rote. *Ibid.* 10218 Ilkan þan to þe temple broght Sirekin gift after þai moght. *c* **1400** *Langland's P. Pl.* C. (Ilchester MS.), in Skeat III. Pref. 36 On serkyn wys þes seculers it certefiez also, Lewed men by labour lyue and lordez go to hunt In frith and in forest.

†**'serelepes**, *adv.* (*a.*). *Obs.* Also 3 *Ormin* serlepess, 4 -lypez. [f. SERE *a.*[2] + *-lep-* (as in ONLEPY) + advb. *-es, -s.*] Separately.
*c* **1200** ORMIN 513, & iwhillc an serlepess off þa fowwre & twennti3 hirdess Was nemmnedd affterr an mann off þa fowre & twennti3 prestess. **13..** *Gaw. & Gr. Knt.* 501 For-þi þis 3ol ouer-3ede, & þe 3ere after, & vche sesoun serlepes sued after oþer. **1377** LANGL. *P. Pl.* B. XVII. 164 That thre þinges bilongeth in owre lorde of heuene, And aren serelepes by hem-self asondry were neure.
**b.** as *adj.* Separate, distinct; sundry, various.
**13..** *E.E. Allit. P.* A. 994 Vch tabelment was a serlypez ston. *a* **1400–50** *Wars Alex.* 4893 Seuenty wyndows beside of serelepis werkes.

†**'serelepy**, *a. Obs.* [f. SERE *a.*[2] + *-lepy* (as in ONLEPY).] Separate; with pl. sb., sundry, various.
*a* **1400–50** *Wars Alex.* 605 3it ware þai sett vn-samen of serelypy hewys. *Ibid.* 4440 Sere-lepy kyndis. *Ibid.* 4521 Sacrifice to ilk a segge a sere-lepy gifte.

†**'serely**, *adv. Obs.* Forms: 4 serelych, serliche, 4–5 ser(e)ly. [a. ON. *sérliga*: see SERE *a.*[2] and -LY[2].] Particularly, separately.
*c* **1350** *Will. Palerne* 2149 þei sou3t alle so serliche þurh cites & smale townes,.. þat no seg.. schuld haue schapit. *c* **1375** *Lay-Folks Mass-Bk.* B. 465 For hore soules, I pray derly, þate I shall neuen serly. **13..** *E.E. Allit. P.* C. 193 Sone haf þay her sortes sette & serelych deled. *c* **1440** *York Myst.* xliv. 24 It nedis we vs avise, þat we saye no3t serely.

**serement**, var. SERMENT *Obs.*, oath.

**seremon(y**, obs. forms of CEREMONY.

†**se'rena.** *Obs. rare.* [It. (Neapolitan); cf. Sp. *sereno* in the same sense.] = SERENE *sb.*[1]
**1594** NASHE *Terrors Nt.* H 1 b, It hath caused such a thicke fulsome Serena to descend on my braine. *a* **1600** R. DUDLEY in *Hakluyt's Voy.* III. 575 The most infectious serenas or dewes that fall all along these coasts of Africa. **1713** *Gentl. Instructed* I. Suppl. iii. (ed. 5) 14 They had.. armed themselves against the *Serena* with a Caudle.

**serenade** (sɛrɪˈneɪd), *sb.* Also 7 serenate, 8 seranade. [a. F. *sérénade* (16th c. in Hatz.-Darm.), app. ad. It. *serenata*: see SERENATA.]
**1.** A performance of vocal or instrumental music given at night in the open air, esp. such a performance given by a lover under the window of his lady.
**1656** BLOUNT *Glossogr.* **1662** J. DAVIES tr. *Olearius' Voy. Ambass.* 236 They go and give the Governour a Serenade. **1667** MILTON *P.L.* IV. 768 Serenate, which the starv'd Lover sings To his proud fair. **1712** ARBUTHNOT *John Bull* II. v, The Musick and Serenades that were given her, sounded more ungratefully in her Ears, than the Noise of a Screech Owl. **1835** LYTTON *Rienzi* III. iii, My voice awaked the stillness of the waving sedges with a soldier's serenade. **1884** F. M. CRAWFORD *Roman Singer* I. 163 A serenade is an every-day affair.
**b.** *transf.* and *fig.*
**1649** LOVELACE *Lucasta, To a Lady Madam A. L.* 118 Or the soft Serenades above In calme of Night, when Cats make Love. **1656** COWLEY *Misc., Swallow* 3 Foolish Prater, what do'st thou So early at my window do With thy tuneless Serenade? **1695** J. EDWARDS *Author. O. & N. Test.* III. 27 We are enabled to.. entertain our selves with the serenades of a good conscience. **1843–54** SURTEES *Handley Cross* lix, When I will finish wot I've left unsung, as the tom-cat said when the brick-bat cut short his serenade. **1871** FORSYTH *Highl. Central India* 391, I listened one night to the most remarkable serenade of tigers I ever heard.
†**2.** A poem suitable for a serenade. *Obs.*
**1710** *Tatler* No. 222 ¶4 Horace's tenth Ode of the third book was originally a Serenade.
**3.** *Mus.* A piece of music suitable or specially composed for singing or playing in the open air as a complimentary performance.
**1728** CHAMBERS *Cycl.* s.v., The Pieces compos'd or play'd on these Occasions, are also call'd Serenades. **1794** MRS. RADCLIFFE *Myst. Udolpho* xvi, Some of their servants.. were performing a simple serenade. **1883** ROCKSTRO in *Grove's Dict. Mus.* III. 467/2 The most delicious example of this that we possess is the Serenade in Sterndale Bennett's Chamber Trio in A, Op. 27. *a* **1897** tr. *Riemann's Dict. Mus.* s.v., The only thing retained from the past in serenades is that they have more movements than is usual in a sonata or symphony.
**4.** *attrib.* and *Comb.*
**1908** ROCKSTRO in *Grove's Dict. Mus.* IV. 418/2 The two Serenade trios of Beethoven. **1911** *Encycl. Brit.* XXIV. 663/1 The six-movement scheme (though without the serenade style) was adopted by Beethoven in.. the string quartet in B flat. *Ibid.*, The classics of the serenade forms are among the works of Mozart and Haydn.

**serenade** (sɛrɪˈneɪd), *v.* [f. the sb.]
**1.** *trans.* To entertain (a person) with a serenade.
**1672** WYCHERLEY *Love in Wood* II. i, I intend to serenade the whole Park to-night. **1691** *Comedy, Win Her & Take Her* I. ii. 5 A fourth [would] make verses upon you; treat, present, and Serenade you. **1727** SEWALL *Diary* 15 Apr., Last night three musicians serenaded me under my chamber window. **1842** MRS. KIRKLAND *Forest Life* I. 253 It's only a parcel of fellers gone to serenade an old widower that's been a-marrying of a young girl. **1887** FENN *Master Cerem.* vi, I am going to beg our guests to come with us and serenade a lady whose name I will not mention.
**b.** *transf.* and *fig.*
**1749** FIELDING *Tom Jones* V. ii, From serenading his patient every hunting morning with the horn under his window, it was impossible to withhold him. **1774** G. WHITE *Selborne, To Barrington* 28 Sept., In hot mornings several [swifts].. dash round the steeples and churches, squeaking as they go in a very clamorous manner: these.. are supposed to be males serenading their sitting hens. **1825** SELBY *Illustr. Brit. Ornith.* 240 The male bird.. uttering the singular but unmusical notes with which he serenades his mate during incubation.
**2.** *intr.* (or *absol.*) To perform a serenade.
**1668** DRYDEN *Even. Love* II. i. 29 When I go a Serenading again with 'em, I'll give 'em leave to make Fiddle-strings of my small-guts. **1710** *Tatler* No. 222 ¶13 Our honest countrymen.. seldom begin to sing until they are drunk; which also is usually the time when they are most disposed to Serenade. **1832** W. IRVING *Alhambra* I. 299, I'll warrant, these cavaliers have their loves among the Spanish beauties.. and will soon be serenading under their balconies.
Hence **sere'nading** *vbl. sb.* and *ppl. a.*
**1673** DRYDEN *Assign.* II. iii. 19 Where is this Serenading Rascall? **1705** J. TAYLOR *Journ. Edin.* (1903) 90 We caus'd 3 Serenading Tunes to be particularly plai'd at Sir Lothian Blackets, Enamoretta's and Astraca's houses. **1797** T. HOLCROFT tr. *Stolberg's Trav.* III. lxxxviii. (ed. 2) 449 The custom of serenading.. ever will prevail.

**serenader** (sɛrɪˈneɪdə(r)). [f. SERENADE *v.* + -ER[1].] One who serenades.
**1676** DURFEY *Mad. Fickle* III. iii, That an impertinent Serenader.. shou'd have the impudence to talk thus. **1797** MRS. RADCLIFFE *Italian* xvii, The music of serenaders. **1883** FR. M. PEARD *Contrad.* I. 29 A barca with serenaders was slowly approaching.

‖**serenata** (sereˈnata). *Mus.* [a. It. *serenata* an evening song (whence Sp., Pg. *serenata*, F. *sérénade* SERENADE *sb.*), app. f. *sereno* the open air, subst. use of *sereno* SERENE *a.* (Pr. had *serena* in the sense of 'serenade').)]
**1.** A song or form of cantata suitable for performance in the open air.
**1743** BOYCE (*title*) Solomon, a Serenata. **1834** BECKFORD *Italy* II. 261 Having been a mighty reader of operas, serenatas, sonnets, and romances. **1862** SPENCER *First Princ.* II. ii. 173 From the ballad up to the serenata.
**2.** A piece of instrumental music, developed from the orchestral suite, and usually composed of a march, and a minuet interposed between two movements of another kind.
**1883** ROCKSTRO in *Grove's Dict. Mus.* III. 468/2 Haydn also wrote Serenatas, but seems to have taken less kindly to the style than Mozart.

†**'serenate**, *v. Obs. rare*[−1]. [f. SERENE *a.* + -ATE[3]; cf. It. *serenare.*] *trans.* To render serene.
**1654** FLECKNOE *Ten Years Trav.* 169 Then for serenating the mind,.. Where in lowd cities shall you find A recollection like to this?

**serenate**, obs. form of SERENADE *sb.*

**serendibite** (səˈrɛndɪbaɪt, sɛrənˈdɪbaɪt). *Min.* [f. *Serendib, Serendip*, a former name for Sri Lanka + -ITE[1].] A borosilicate of aluminium, calcium, and magnesium, $(Ca,Mg)_5Al_5BSi_3O_{20}$, found as bluish triclinic crystals in which iron often replaces some of the aluminium and magnesium.
**1902** *Nature* 20 Feb. 383/2 Messrs. G. T. Prior and A. K. Coomára-Swámy gave an account of the mode of occurrence and characters of 'serendibite', a new boro-silicate from Ceylon. **1978** W. A. DEER et al. *Rock-Forming Minerals* (ed. 2) IIA. 661 A number of serendibite.. occurrences in spinel-diopside skarns have been described from the Tayezhnoye iron ore localities of southern Yakutia... Serendibite is also found with sinhalite, warwickite and tourmaline.. in the skarns of Handemi district, Tanzania.

**serendipitous** (sɛrənˈdɪpɪtəs), *a.* [f. SERENDIPIT(Y + -OUS.] **a.** Of persons: having the faculty of making happy and unexpected discoveries by accident.
**1958** *Times Lit. Suppl.* 22 Aug. 468/4 In the matter of adventure Miss de Banke was serendipitous to the *n*th degree. **1968** 'E. MCBAIN' *Fuzz* ix. 146 La Brisca seemed to be a serendipitous type who led them on a jolly excursion halfway across the city. **1975** *Reader's Digest* Oct. 150/2 And all for the best, too, as serendipitous San Diegans gladly tell you.
**b.** (The more usual sense.) Applied to discoveries, meetings, etc., of this kind.
**1965** J. WAKEFIELD *Death the Sure Physician* 50 It's rather fortunate that I should come across a chap with similar interests... distinctly serendipitous, in fact. **1971** *Nature* 20 Aug. 538/2 This suggestion was confirmed by the isolation of a stable tricarbonyliron complex of tetraphenylbutadiene by a serendipitous method (many of the best discoveries in the field have been made by chance). **1979** *Amer. Speech* 1978 LIII. 272 As among these three systems, the girls couldn't have cared less, Yerke's suggestion was serendipitous.
Hence **seren'dipitously** *adv.*
**1969** C. C. WINTER *Pract. Urol.* vii. 211 Prostatitis is one of the most common of urologic disorders. It may be symptomless and discovered serendipitously in a routine, two glass urinalysis in which the first specimen shows some white blood cells or a few more than in the second glass. **1974** *Daily Tel.* (Colour Suppl.) 29 Nov. 16/3 We can imagine Hodder meeting Stoughton.. and their discovering, serendipitously, a mutual interest in books. **1980** *Times Lit. Suppl.* 14 Nov. 1275/4 He had the knack of always being serendipitously on hand when a tenement caught fire.

**serendipity** (sɛrənˈdɪpɪtɪ). [f. *Serendip*, a former name for Sri Lanka + -ITY.
A word coined by Horace Walpole, who says (Let. to Mann, 28 Jan. 1754) that he had formed it upon the title of the fairy-tale '*The Three Princes of Serendip*', the heroes of which 'were always making discoveries, by accidents and sagacity, of things they were not in quest of'.]
The faculty of making happy and unexpected discoveries by accident. Also, the fact or an instance of such a discovery.
Formerly rare, this word and its derivatives have had wide currency in the 20th century.
**1754** H. WALPOLE *Let. to Mann* 28 Jan., This discovery, indeed, is almost of that kind which I call Serendipity. **1880** E. SOLLY *Index Titles of Honour* Pref. 5 The inquirer was at fault, and it was not till some weeks later, when by the aid of *Serendipity*, as Horace Walpole called it—that is, looking for one thing and finding another—that the explanation was accidentally found. **1926** E. MEYNELL *Life of Francis Thompson* xiii. 221 To the Serendipity Shop—the venture of a friend in Westbourne Grove—he would often go. **1955** *Sci. Amer.* Apr. 92/1 Our story has as its critical episode one of those coincidences that show how discovery often depends on chance, or rather on what has been called 'serendipity'—the chance observation falling on a receptive eye. **1971** S. E. MORISON *European Discovery Amer.: Northern Voy.* i. 3 Columbus and Cabot.. (by the greatest serendipity of history) discovered America instead of reaching the Indies. **1980** *TWA Ambassador* Oct. 47/2 It becomes a glum bureaucracy, instead of the serendipity of 30 people putting out a magazine.
Hence **seren'dipitist.**
**1939** JOYCE *Finnegans Wake* 191 You.. semisemitic serendipitist, you (thanks, I think that describes you) Europasianised Afferyank! **1968** *Punch* 13 Nov. 684/1 There are the financial serendipitists, the men blessed monetarily by a fortunate law.

†**serene**, *sb.*[1] *Obs.* Forms: 6–7 seren, 7 serene, -eine, -ain(e, syren(e, 8 serein. See also SERENA and SEREIN. [a. F. *serein* of the same meaning (OF. *serain, sierain* evening) = Pg. *serão* :—popular L. **sērānum*, f. *sēr-um* (F. *soir*) evening, subst. use of neut. of L. *sērus* late.
The word seems to have been confused in Fr. with *serein* SERENE *a.* The Sp. *sereno* SERENA may be from Fr.]
A light fall of moisture or fine rain after sunset in hot countries (see SEREIN), formerly regarded as a noxious dew or mist.
**1591** FLORIO *2nd Fruites* 153 The Seren neuer hurts a man in these colde countries. **1605** B. JONSON *Volpone* III. vii, Some serene blast mee, or dire lightning strike This my offending face. **1616** BULLOKAR *Eng. Expos., Seraine*, a foggy mist or dampish vapour falling in Italie about sunne set, at which time it is vnwholesome to be abroad especially bareheaded. **1617** MORYSON *Itin.* I. 219 When the Syren or dew falls at night, they keepe themselves within dores till it be dried up. **1622** F. MARKHAM *Bk. War* III. vii. 105 Which not to acknowledge, would hang as a Sereine or rotting Mildew vpon any thankfull nature. **1636** G. SANDYS *Paraphr. Ps.* cxxi. 205 Nor unwholsome Serene shall From the Moons moyst influence fall. *c* **1645** HOWELL *Lett.* (1650) II. 7 Have a care of your health, take heed of the seren's. **1682** *Phil. Collect.* XII. 148 To preserve the Brain from the Serenes that fall in hot Countries. [**1706** PHILLIPS (ed. Kersey), *Serein* (Fr.), a dampish and unwholesome Vapour, that falls after Sun-set in hot Countries; a kind of Mildew.]

**serene** (sɪˈriːn), *a.* and *sb.*[2] [ad. L. *serēn-us* clear, fair, calm (of weather, etc.). Cf. OF. *seri, serin, serain*, mod.F. *serein*, Sp., Pg., It. *sereno.*]
**A.** *adj.*
**1.** Of the weather, air, sky: Clear, fine, and calm (without cloud or rain or wind).
**1508** DUNBAR *Gold. Targe* 108 Quhill loud resownyt the firmament serene. *a* **1513** FABYAN *Chron.* VI. ccxviii. 238 To perce the heuyns that beeth so serene. **1621** BURTON *Anat. Mel.* I. i. I. v, As the heauen it selfe is, so is our life, sometimes faire, sometimes ouercast, tempestious, and serene. **1634** MILTON *Comus* 4 Where those immortal shapes Of bright aëreal Spirits live insphear'd In Regions milde of calm and serene Ayr. **1660** R. COKE *Power & Subj.* 108 Whether it will be serene, or stormy weather. *a* **1771** GRAY *Song* 9 Western gales and skies serene Speak not always winter past. **1829** *Chapters Phys. Sci.* 200 Timely alternatives of serene and rainy days. **1867** H. MACMILLAN *Bible Teach.* v. (1870) 91 So pure and serene is the air that.. the faintest far-off sounds are heard with surprising distinctness.
**b.** Of the heavenly bodies: Shining with a clear and tranquil light.
**1704** POPE *Winter* 6 The moon, serene in glory, mounts the sky. **1744** AKENSIDE *Pleas. Imag.* I. 61 Ere the radiant sun

Sprung from the east, or 'mid the vault of night The moon suspended her serener lamp. **1817** SHELLEY *Pr. Athanase* I. 61 Through which his soul, like Vesper's serene beam.. Shone, softly burning.

**c.** Hence as a poetic epithet of colour: Pure, clear, bright. Also (cf. 2 b), Quiet, sober.

**1750** GRAY *Elegy* 53 Full many a gem of purest ray serene. **1846** LANDOR *Pentameron* Wks. II. 343 Serener colours are pleasanter to our eyes and more becoming to our character.

**2.** Of other natural phenomena (e.g. the sea): Calm, tranquil.

**1812** J. WILSON *Isle of Palms* III. 397 And gazed where inland waters lay Serene as night. **1816** SHELLEY *Mont Blanc* 61 Mont Blanc appears—still, snowy, and serene. **1821** —— *Hellas* 1067 A brighter Hellas rears its mountains From waves serener far. **1870** O'SHAUGHNESSY *Epic of Women* 76 Through each shock of sound that shivers The serene palms to their height.

**b.** *transf.* Restful to the eye, expressive or suggestive of repose.

**1849** RUSKIN *Sev. Lamps* ii. §8. 36 The magnificent and serene constructions of the early Gothic. *Ibid.* iii. §21. 88 Laws as inviolable and serene as those of nature herself.

**3.** Of a person, his mind, circumstances, etc.: Calm, tranquil, untroubled, unperturbed. Of the countenance: Expressive of inward calm, unruffled.

*a* **1635** [see SERENITY 2]. **1640** FULLER *Abel Rediv., Huss* (1867) I. 19 Stokes, an Englishman then present at the council, his serene antagonist. **1647** CLARENDON *Hist. Reb.* I. §67 The duke heard him without the least commotion, and with a countenance serene enough. *a* **1687** PETTY *Pol. Arith.* vii. (1691) 103 The ordinary charge of the Government, in times of deep and serene Peace. **1712** STEELE *Spect.* No. 282 ¶5 He who resigns the World.. is in constant Possession of a serene Mind. **1818** BYRON *Juan* I. lxxxiii, A quiet conscience makes one so serene! **1849** MACAULAY *Hist. Eng.* iv. I. 460 His serene intrepidity distinguished him among thousands of brave soldiers. **1870** E. PEACOCK *Ralf Skirl.* III. 144 A great event in her serene life. **1911** *Athenæum* 8 July 35/1 Mr. Austin surveys his mental development with serene satisfaction.

**b.** ***all serene***, a slang phr. for 'all's well', 'all right'. Also jocularly ***all sereno***.

**1856** K. H. DIGBY *Lover's Seat* I. vi. 161 Well I never, all serene, stunning,..and such like phrases. **1859** *Hotten's Slang Dict., Serene*, all right; 'its all serene', a street phrase of very modern adoption, the burden of a song. **1873** *Routledge's Ev. Boy's Ann.* 378/1 'All serene, Ben', was the general reply. **1901** F. HUME *Golden Wang-ho* i, 'All sereno!' sung out Teddy.

**4.** An honorific epithet given to a reigning prince (esp. of Germany), formerly also to a member of a royal house, etc.; sometimes jocularly applied to anything appertaining to a person so designated. Also ***most serene*** = med.L. *serenissimus*, It. *serenissimo*, F. *sérénissime*. Cf. SERENITY 4.

**1503** DUNBAR *Poems* lxxxix. 11 Borne of a princes most serene. **1552** LYNDESAY *Monarche* 3074 And send one Message to the Quene, Prayand hir Maiestie serene That scho wald [etc.]. **1629** MASSINGER *Picture* I. ii, You are like me a subiect. Her more then serene Maiesty being present. **1660** *Trial Regic.* 17 A Warrant for the Execution of His late Sacred and Serene Majesty. **1673** OGILBY *Asia* Ded., To His Most Serene, and Most Excellent Majesty, Charles II. **1711** *Act 10 Anne* c. 4 The most serene Elector of Brunswick-Lunenburgh. **1740** GRAY *Let.* 20 May, Poems (1775) 83 His Highness the Duke of Modena..laid his most serene commands upon me to write to Mr. West. **1745** H. WALPOLE *Let. to Mann* 24 June, The Duke of Saxe Weissenfels..is not of so serene a house but that he might have known something of the motions of the Prussians. **1746** —— *Let. to G. Montagu* 17 June, The Serene Hessian is gone. **1772** *Ann. Reg.* 153/2 Genoa, Dec. 26. On the 22d instant..died..the serene John Baptist Cambiaso, Doge of this republic. **1860** THACKERAY *Four Georges* i. (1861) 26 There were 600 horses in the Serene stables. *Ibid.* 29 The lovely sisters..journeyed to Hanover, and became favourites of the serene house there reigning. **1879** BARING-GOULD *Germany* I. 29 Princes to whom the predicate of durchlaucht ('your serene highness') is accorded.

**5.** ***drop serene***: Milton's rendering of mod.L. *gutta serena* amaurosis: see GUTTA[1] 1 b. Hence allusively (quot. 1843).

**1667** MILTON *P.L.* III. 25 So thick a drop serene hath quencht thir Orbs. **1843** CARLYLE *Past & Pr.* I. ii, Thick serene opacity, thicker than amaurosis, veiled those smiling eyes of his to Truth.

**6.** quasi-*adv.*

**1655** FANSHAWE tr. *Camoens' Lusiad* III. lv. 57 Her pleasant Vale..Which Thou, sweet Tagus, waterst so serene. **1728** YOUNG *Love Fame* ii. 43 Serene quoth Adam, 'Lo! 'twas crush'd by me'. **1769** GRAY *Install. Ode* 93 The Star of Brunswick smiles serene. **1847** EMERSON *Poems, Threnody* Wks. (Bohn) I. 488 Gentlest guardians marked serene His early hope, his liberal mien.

**B.** *sb.* (absol. use of the adj.). [Similarly L. *serēnum* (neut.), It. *sereno*, OF. *seri*, *serain*.] Now *rare* or *Obs.* **a.** A condition of fine quiet weather.

**1644** DERING *Prop. Sacr.* Pref. b 2, It is indeed the present issue of thunder and tempest, but was begotten in a quiet serene. **1760–72** H. BROOKE *Fool of Qual.* (1859) I. 220 No more than ye can see the gloom of last winter in the smiling serene of a summer's evening.

**b.** The unruffled expanse of clear sky or calm sea.

**1769** SIR W. JONES *Palace Fortune* Poems (1777) 28 And twinkling stars emblaz'd the blue serene. **1781** COWPER *Charity* 132 The bark that plows the deep serene. **1812** BYRON *Ch. Har.* II. lxx, As winds come whispering lightly from the west, Kissing, not ruffling, the blue deep's serene. **1834** MAR. EDGEWORTH *Helen* I. xiii. 279 Not a cloud obscured the deep serene. **1870** O'SHAUGHNESSY *Epic of Women* 172 And some have..through the blue serene Gone up to heaven and been lost.

**c.** Calm brightness, quiet radiance.

**1821** SHELLEY *Epipsych.* 506 With moonlight patches..Or fragments of the day's intense serene. **1863** I. WILLIAMS *Baptistery* II. xxiii. (1874) 84 Upon the dark and ruin'd scene Throwing a beautiful serene.

**d.** Serenity, tranquillity (of mind, conditions, etc.).

**1742** YOUNG *Nt. Th.* VII. 40 Deep in rich pasture will thy flocks complain? Not so; but to their master is deny'd To share their sweet serene. **1760–72** H. BROOKE *Fool of Qual.* (1809) IV. 107 The serene of heart-felt happiness has little of adventure in it. **1762–9** FALCONER *Shipwr.* I. 127 The calm domestic scene Had o'er his temper breathed a gay serene. **1851** MRS. BROWNING *Casa Guidi Wind.* II. 335 Behold, the people waits, Like God. As He, in His serene of might, So they, in their endurance of long straits.

**serene** (sɪ'riːn), *v.* Now *rare* or *Obs.* [ad. L. *serēnāre*, f. *serēn-us* SERENE *a.* Cf. 16th c. F. *serener* (Ronsard).] *trans.* To make serene.

**1.** To make (the sky, air) clear, bright, and tranquil. †Also, to clear *from* (cloud). Also *fig.*

**1613** J. DAVIES *Muses Teares* (Grosart) 15/1 Then let Fates Snuffes and Puffes as winds of Grace, Serene the Heauen of your Maiestick Face. **1639** SALTMARSHE *Pract. Policy* 4 If your businesse be perplexed and obscure..the best course heere for clearing and serening, is to divide the parts that are mingled and more obscure. **1655** FANSHAWE tr. *Camoens' Lusiad* IX. xxiv. 178 She, where she passes, makes the Wind to lye With gentle motion, and serenes the skye. *a* **1711** KEN *Edmund* Poet. Wks. 1721 II. 322 Heav'n which before in Rivulets ran down, Its Face seren'd, clear from all cloudy Frown. **1747** MALLET *Amyntor & Theodora* III. 42 As Reason thus the mental storm seren'd. **1828** *Blackw. Mag.* XXIII. 486 Homer and Shakspeare..so far from being unfit for the gross atmosphere of human nature, ..soared through it like eagles,..serened it like a calm.

†**b.** To clarify, make clear and bright (a liquid).

**1708** J. PHILIPS *Cyder* II. 68 The hoary Frosts and Northern Blasts take care Thy muddy Bev'rage to serene, and drive Præcipitant the baser, ropy Lees.

†**c.** To expose to the air (articles suspected of infection). *Obs.*

[Littré has F. *sérénage* for the action of doing this.]

*c* **1750** M. MACKENZIE *Plague* in *Phil. Trans.* XLVII. 385 To what purpose..keep ships in Sandgate-Creek for weeks, and even months, without landing and serening the goods?

**2.** To make (a person, his mind, etc.) calm and tranquil. †Also, to render free *from* (anything that perturbs).

**1654** WHITLOCK *Zootomia* 226 This temper Serenes the Soule from Passion. **1707** NORRIS *Treat. Humility* viii. 339 It calms and serenes the regions of the breast. **1742** YOUNG *Nt. Th.* VII. 1465 Hope, like a cordial,..Man's heart, at once, inspirits, and serenes. **1854** BAILEY *Festus* (ed. 5) 164 Thus serened, speak on.

*absol.* **1830** *Blackw. Mag.* XXVIII. 886 Something that serenes or troubles, soothes or jars.

**b.** To make (the countenance, brow) calm, unruffled, or cheerful.

**1648–99** J. BEAUMONT *Psyche* XV. ccxvii. (1702) 237 When he seren'd his Father's gloomy Frown. **1718** POPE *Iliad* XV. 178 While a Smile serenes his awful Brow. **1813** T. BUSBY *Lucretius* III. 316 While Air, all calm and gentle, soothes the breast, Serenes the face, and lulls the soul to rest.

**serene**, obs. form of SIREN.

**serenely** (sɪ'riːnlɪ), *adv.* [f. SERENE *a.* + -LY[2].] In a serene manner.

**1690** LOCKE *Hum. Und.* I. iii. §13 It being impossible, that Men should, without Shame or Fear, confidently and serenely break a Rule, which they could not but evidently know, that God had set up. **1704–9** POPE *Autumn* 13 Now setting Phœbus shone serenely bright. **1837** CARLYLE *Fr. Rev.* I. VII. xi, She..stands alone, her hands serenely crossed on her breast. **1880** 'OUIDA' *Moths* I. 9 Lady Dolly smiled serenely on the person who glided to her elbow.

**sereneness** (sɪ'riːnnɪs). *rare.* [-NESS.] The quality of being serene; serenity.

**1628** FELTHAM *Resolves* I. v. 11 A man that..labours to approue himselfe in the sereneness of a healthful Conscience. **1721** R. KEITH tr. *T. à Kempis, Solil. Soul* xvi. 233 But now in the Sereneness of my Mind, and in the Quiet of Solitude, I was in a Capacity to see and reflect. **1876** BLACKIE *Songs Relig.* 9 With a smile of cold sereneness, Came the Sadducee.

†**b.** as a title = SERENITY 4. *Obs.*

**1728** CHAMBERS *Cycl.* s.v. *Serene*, The Emperor,..in treating with them, uses *Electoral Sereneness* or *Serenity* to the Electors; and *Ducal Sereneness* to the other Princes.

†**'sereness**[1]. *Obs.* In 4 ser(e)nes. [f. SERE *a.*[2] + -NESS.] Diversity, variety.

*a* **1300** *Cursor M.* 368 Þe werld i call wit min entens þe mater of þe four elements, þat yeit was tan o forme mischapen, Quar of was serenes siþen scapen. *a* **1300** *E.E. Psalter* xliv. 11 Vmgiuen with sernes gode [Vulg. *circumdata varietate*]. *a* **1340** HAMPOLE *Psalter* xliv. 15 Vmcled in sernesis [Vulg. *circumamicta varietatibus*].

**'sereness**[2]. [f. SERE *a.*[1] + -NESS.] The quality of being sere, or dry and withered.

*c* **1440** *Promp. Parv.* 453/2 Seernesse [*v.r.* sernesse], or up-dryynge of treys or herbis, *ariditas, marcor.* **1530** PALSGR. 269/2 Serenesse drinesse, *sechevr.* **1611** SPEED *Hist. Gt. Brit.* IX. xii. §141 Wherin he seemed to forget the searnesse of his body, and the greennesse of his Grandchild yong Richard. **1660** HEXHAM II, *Dorheydt ofte Dorrigheydt*, Drienesse, Searenesse, or Witherednesse.

†**se'renify**, *v.* *Obs.* *rare*[−1]. [ad. med.L. *serēnificāre* to make serene: see SERENE *a.* and -FY.] *intr.* To become serene.

**1612** tr. *Benvenuto's Passenger* I. iv. 243 It's now the faire, virmilion, pleasant spring, When meadowes laugh, and heaven serenefies.

‖**sere'nissime**, *a.* and *sb.* *rare.* [a. F. *sérénissime* (15th c.), ad. It. *serenissimo* or L. *serēnissimus*, superl. of It. *sereno*, L. *serēnus* SERENE *a.*] 'Most serene'; an honorific epithet bestowed on certain princes. Also *sb.*, one so entitled.

**1624** *Brief Inform. Palatinate* 5 The Serenissime Prince and Lord Lewis King of Hungary. **1881** LARWOOD *Lond. Parks* xvi. 328 He showed his prowess to..foreign princes and German serenissimes.

‖**sere'nissimo**, *a.* and *sb.* *Obs.* Pl. -i, also -o's. [It.: see prec.] = prec.

**1665** SIR T. HERBERT *Trav.* (1677) 140 The Tiara which was worn by Serenissimo's. **1672** tr. *Nieremberg's Temporal & Eternal* III. vi. 272 (Stanf.) How many are called Serenissimi, who have their understanding darkened.

†**sere'nissimous**, *a.* *Obs.* *rare.* [f. L. *serēnissim-us* (see above) + -OUS.] = SERENISSIME *a.*

**1623** COCKERAM I, *Serenissimous*, most famous, a terme applyed to Kings. **1629** B. JONSON *New Inn* II. ii, Maiestique Pru, and Serenissimous Pru.

†**se'renitude.** *Obs.* *rare*[−1]. [f. L. *serēn-us* SERENE *a.* + -TUDE.] Serenity.

**1672** *Wotton's Reliq., Educ.* 79 From which..I am wont to hope..will flow a future quietude and serenitude [(1651) 325 and (1654) 294 Serenity] in the Affections.

**serenity** (sɪ'rɛnɪtɪ). Also 6 -yte, 6–7 -itie. [a. F. *sérénité*, ad. L. *serēnitās*, f. *serēn-us*: see SERENE *a.* and -ITY.]

**1.** Clear, fair and calm weather; clearness and stillness of air and sky.

**1538** STARKEY *England* 64 The sone communyth hys perfectyon at al tymys to thes inferyor thyngys..as wel in cloudys as in serenyte. **1594** ASHLEY tr. *Loys Le Roy* 42 In Syria, and Egipt, where by the serenitie of the summer season, almost all the starres are cleerely seen. **1669** STURMY *Mariner's Mag.* v. v. 19 There is never no Rain, Dew, Hail, Snow, or Wind, but still a clear serenity. **1748** *Anson's Voy.* I. viii. 108 The serenity of the sky was suddenly changed. **1820** W. IRVING *Sketch Bk.* I. 15 One of those sudden storms that will sometimes break in upon the serenity of a summer voyage. **1860** TYNDALL *Glac.* I. v. 40 No breath disturbed the perfect serenity of the night.

**2.** Tranquillity, peacefulness (of conditions, etc.). Sometimes with express reference to sense 1.

*a* **1635** NAUNTON *Fragm. Reg.* (Arb.) 32 Untill the tenth of her reign her times were calm and serene, though sometimes a little over-cast... For the clouds of Spain, and vapours of the Holy League, began then to disperse and threaten her serenity. **1657** CLARENDON *Hist. Reb.* I. §173 There being now so great a serenity in all his dominions. **1820** SCOTT *Monast.* xxx, 'The serenity of Heaven', she said, 'is above me; the sounds which are around are but those of earth and earthly passion.' **1867** H. MACMILLAN *Bible Teach.* iv. (1870) 65 The weary, careworn spirit bathes in the serenity of the silence.

**b.** *transf.* Appearance of reposefulness.

**1849** RUSKIN *Sev. Lamps* iii. §17. 83 The desirableness of serenity in plane surfaces.

**3.** Cheerful tranquillity (of mind, temper, countenance, etc.).

**1599** *Life Sir T. More* in Wordsw. *Eccl. Biog.* (1853) II. 77 His serenitie of mind was alwayes alike. *a* **1631** DONNE *Serm.* lvi. (1640) 566 This..is that *Serenitas Conscientiæ*,.. that calme and serenity, that acquiescence, and security of the Conscience. **1647** CLARENDON *Hist. Reb.* I. §9 By degrees he lost that temper and serenity of mind he had been before master of. **1690** LOCKE *Hum. Und.* I. iii. §9, I cannot see how any Men, should ever transgress those Moral Rules, with Confidence, and Serenity, were they innate, and stamped upon their Minds. **1794** MRS. RADCLIFFE *Myst. Udolpho* iii, When he returned, his countenance had recovered its usual serenity. **1855** BREWSTER *Newton* I. xii. 310 Though ruffled for a moment, Newton's excellent temper soon recovered its serenity. **1899** DOYLE *Duet* (1909) 123/1 She faced the future with a sweet serenity.

**4.** A title of honour given to reigning princes and other dignitaries. (So L. *Serenitas*, applied to the Roman emperor, the Pope, bishops, etc., F. *Sérénité*.)

*c* **1450** HOLLAND *Howlat* 379 Next the souerane signe was sekirly sene, That seruit his serenite euer seruable. **1596** DALRYMPLE *Leslie's Hist. Scot.* I. 296 Quhilk gif ȝour Serenitie plesandlie accepte. **1613** B. CARIER in *Buccleuch MSS.* (Hist. MSS. Comm.) I. 142 Do such good offices with her Serenity as the Catholics may continue that good hope of her. **1693** *Lond. Gaz.* No. 2878/2 His Serenity [the Doge of Venice] continues still at the Lido. **1707** J. STEVENS tr. *Quevedo's Com. Wks.* (1709) 452 They could..acquaint his Serenity [the Duke of Genoa]. **1848** THACKERAY *Van. Fair* lxiii, The army was exhausted in providing guards of honour for the Highnesses, Serenities, and Excellencies who arrived from all quarters. **1865** *Daily Tel.* 7 Nov. 6/4 The discreet policy adopted by their Serenities the Doges of Venice. **1880** DISRAELI *Endym.* I. v. 50 A German Serenity was her delight.

**serenize**, *v.* *rare.* [f. SERENE *a.* + -IZE. Stressed *'serenize* or *se'renize.*] *trans.* To make serene. Hence **serenizing** *ppl. a.*

**1598** TOFTE *Alba* (1880) 66 This my Icarian soaring (boue my reach) (Through Beautie, serenising fals my Hart). **1612** J. DAVIES *Muse's Sacrif.* (Grosart) 33/1 And being Grace and Goodnesse most abstract, How can I, wanting both, serenize thee? **1865** *Reader* 11 Feb. 157/3 The sweet, serenizing scenery of the Thames.

‖**sereno** (se'reno). [Sp.] A Spanish night-watchman.

**1897** *Outing* (U.S.) XXIX. 593/1 The foot-falls of the faithful *sereno* still lingered, echoing down the solitary street. **1904** W. CHURCHILL *Crossing* III. vii. 493 A sereno.. was crying the hour.

†**serenous,** *a. Obs. rare*⁻¹. [f. L. *serēn-us* SERENE *a.* + -OUS.] = SERENE *a.* 1.

*c* **1440** *Pallad. on Husb.* III. 67 In lond plesaunt & serenous they cheue In euery kynde.

‖**Seres** ('sɪəriːz), *pl.* [L. *Sērēs* (Gr. Σῆρες), whence *sēricum* SILK.] The name of a people anciently inhabiting some part of Eastern Asia (prob. China), whose country was believed to be the original home of silk. Hence †*the Seres' wool*, silk.

*a* **1400-50** *Wars Alex.* 3956 A sertane folke was in þat soile þat Serres ere callid, And all þe lyndis in þat land with leves as wolle. **1580** LYLY *Euphues* (Arb.) 388 Yet often-times the softnesse of Wooll, which the Seres sende, sticketh so fast to the skinne, that.. it fetcheth bloud. **1587** GREENE *Euphues' Censure* (1634) C 4 b, A worme that fretteth like the Seres woole. **1697** DRYDEN *Virg. Georg.* II. 169 How the Seres spin Their fleecy forests in a slender twine. **1842** *Smith's Dict. Grk. & Rom. Antiq.* s.v. *Sericum*, Many of those [silks] produced by the industry and taste of the Seres.

†'**seresith.** [f. SERE *a.*² + SITHE *sb.*¹] Several times.

*a* **1300** *Cursor M.* 7066 Þar was slain o þam.. Aght hundret sith sexti sexti and ten, O thusands seresith o þair men.

†'**serety.** *Obs. rare*⁻¹. In quot. seer-. [f. SERE *a.*² + -TY.] Variety.

*a* **1400-50** *Wars Alex.* 4654 For many seerties we seet [? *read* he set] þat sysed all þe werde.

**sereu(h)ful,** obs. forms of SORROWFUL.

**se-reverence,** variant of SIR-REVERENCE.

†**se'rew(e.** *Farriery. Obs.* [a. F. *suros*, †*surot* (13th c. *souros*), f. *sur* upon + *os* bone.] A bony excrescence on the leg of a horse.

**1523** FITZHERB. *Husb.* §96 A serewe is an yll soraunce, and is lyke a splent, but it is a lyttell longer and more, and lyeth vppe to the knee on the inner syde. And some horses haue a throughe serewe on bothe sydes of the legge. **1610** MARKHAM *Maister-Peece* II. lxiv. 326 Of the Serew, or therrow Splent. Although diuers of our Farriers do distinguish.. betwixt a serew and a splent, saying, that the serew is euer of the out-side of the leg, as the splent is of the inside; yet.. the disease.. is all of one. [Echoed by later writers.]

**serewe, sereyn,** obs. ff. SORROW, SIREN.

**serf** (sɜːf). [a. OF. *serf*:—L. *serv-um* slave; cf. Sp. *siervo*, Pg., It. *servo*.]

Not in Johnson. Todd 1818 has '*Serf*, a slave. Not in use', with quot. from Hume 1761 (see 2 b).

†**1.** A slave, bondman. Also *fig. Obs.*

**1483** CAXTON *Golden Leg.* 101/2 Who so loueth the rychessys of thys world he is.. bonde and serf in kepyng the rychesse. *Ibid.* 243/2 There was a yong man which was serf and bonde to a yonge lady. **1484** —— *Chivalry* 15 Yf thou be wycked thou aughtest to be put under a serf or bonde man.

**2.** A person in a condition of servitude or modified slavery, distinguished from what is properly called 'slavery' in that the services due to the master, and his power of disposal of his 'serf', are more or less limited by law or custom.

In most of the typical examples of serfdom, the serf was 'attached to the soil' (*adscriptus glebæ*), i.e. he could not be removed (except by manumission) from the lord's land, and was transferred with it when it passed to another owner. This feature is often assigned as the distinctive mark of 'serfdom' as opposed to 'slavery', and is popularly apprehended as an essential part of the notion.

**a.** In the 17-18th c. used (after Fr. example) with reference to the contemporary condition of the lower class of cultivators of the soil in various countries of Europe, esp. in parts of Germany, in Denmark, Poland, and Russia. Now used *Hist.* with the same application; chiefly with reference to Russia, where the serfs were not emancipated until 1861, while elsewhere in Europe serfdom ceased to exist early in the 19th century.

**1611** R. JOHNSON *Kingd. & Commw.* 75 [France], As for Serfes, Slaues or Villaines, they are Domesticke, and serue vppon baser condition, for Wages and Victuals. *Ibid.* 76 Neither the Subiect nor the Serf are bound to go to the warres, but only the vassall. **1761** HUME *Hist. Eng.* (1762) I. App. i. 151 There were two kinds of slaves among the Anglo-Saxons; household slaves,.. and prædial or rustic.. These latter resembled the serfs, which are at present met with in Poland, Denmark and some places in Germany. **1784** W. COXE *Trav.* I. viii. I. 129 The peasants in Poland, as in all feudal governments, are serfs or slaves. **1797** *Encycl. Brit.* (ed. 3) XVI. 571 The subordination of ranks was more complete [among the Russians] than in any other European nation; but with this simplicity peculiar to them and the Poles, that they had but three ranks, the sovereign, the noblesse or gentry, and the serfs. **1845** DISRAELI *Sybil* IV. v, Lower than the Portuguese or the Poles, the serfs of Russia, or the lazzaroni of Naples. **1861** BRIGHT *Sp., Amer.* 4 Dec. (1876) 90 [In Russia] twenty-three millions of human beings, lately serfs, little better than real slaves, have been raised to the ranks of freedom. **1880** 'OUIDA' *Moths* II. 381 You have no serfs now, even in Russia.

**b.** Used by modern writers with reference to mediæval Europe.

In English Law Latin the terms corresponding to the modern use of *serf* were *nativus* (NATIVE *sb.* 1, NEIF), *villanus* (VILLEIN), and occasionally *servus*. The OE. THEOW, and the *servus* of Domesday Book, are usually rendered 'slave'.

**1761** HUME *Hist. Eng.* (1762) I. App. ii. 404 A great part of them were serfs, and lived in a state of absolute slavery or villainage. **1805** SCOTT *Last Minstr.* IV. v, A half-clothed serf was all their train. **1874** GREEN *Short Hist.* v. §4. 240 By this entire detachment of the serf from actual dependence on the land, the manorial system was even more radically changed than by the rise of the serf into a copyholder. **1895** W. J. CORBETT in *Soc. Eng.* v. (1902) II. 140 As the tone of society became gentler, the lords naturally had a tendency to free their serfs;.. in the eyes of the law the villeins remained serfs.

**c.** *gen.*

**1908** G. A. SMITH in *Expositor* Sept. 268 The people they [the Israelites] conquered became their serfs.

**d.** *transf.* and *fig.*

**1847** HELPS *Friends in C.* I. ii. 22 The serf to custom points his finger at the slave to fashion. **1854** LOWELL *Keats* Wks. 1890 I. 245 As soon as we have discovered the word for our joy or sorrow we are no longer its serfs, but its lords.

**3.** *attrib.* and *Comb.*, simple attrib. and appositive, as *serf-class*, *-girl*, *-population*, *-system*, *-tenant*; objective, as *serf-emancipation*, *-owner*.

**1860** FORSTER *Gr. Remonstr.* 43 The rebellion of the *serf-class. **1887** *Encycl. Brit.* XXII. 143 The chief committee for peasant affairs to study the subject of *serf-emancipation. **1878** M. A. BROWN tr. *Runeberg's Nadeschda* 1, Then.. would I Brightly hide the *serf-girl's sombre garb. **1860** GEN. P. THOMPSON *Audi Alt.* III. clxxvii. 213 The mortifications and sufferings which might have been brought on aristocratic *serf-owners. **1852** GROTE *Greece* II. lxxiv. IX. 423 The *serf-population which tilled the fields. **1885** MABEL COLLINS *Prettiest Woman* v, There are still the remains of the *serf system. **1887** *Encycl. Brit.* XXII. 136/2 Under the developed regime of feudalism,.. the *serf-tenant has become simply a tributary under various appellations.

**serf,** obs. form of SERVE *v.*¹

**serfage** ('sɜːfɪdʒ). [f. SERF + -AGE; cf. SERVAGE.]

**1.** = SERFDOM.

**1775** DE LOLME *Eng. Const.* I. ii. (1784) 27 When the English villeins were freed from serfage. **1816** SOUTHEY in *Life* (1849) IV. 204, I am now in a manner attached to the soil by a sort of moral and intellectual serfage. **1868** ROGERS *Pol. Econ.* ix. (1876) 87 Serfage was extinguished, and an influential class of yeomanry.. arose. **1884** *Manch. Exam.* 14 July 6/1 The political serfage of long generations. **1903** COLLINS in *Camb. Mod. Hist.* II. xvii. 601 In Denmark they [the peasants] were obliged to have recourse to the practice of commendation, which ended.. in a widespread system of serfage.

**2.** The body of serfs collectively, the serf-class.

**1864** BURTON *Scot Abr.* I. i. 34 The wretched serfage who were driven into the field.

**serfdom** ('sɜːfdəm). [f. SERF + -DOM.] The state or condition of a serf, bondage.

**1850** MRS. BROWNING *H. Powers's Grk. Slave* 10 Break up ere long The serfdom of this world! **1856** FROUDE *Hist. Eng.* I. 13 Thus serfdom had merged into free servitude. **1861** BRIGHT *Sp., Amer.* 4 Dec. (1876) 90 The present Emperor of Russia.. has insisted upon the abolition of serfdom in that empire. **1866** GEO. ELIOT *F. Holt* iii, The Tories were far from being all oppressors, disposed to grind down the working classes into serfdom. **1899** *Westm. Gaz.* 12 June 8/1 Exactly one hundred years ago (June 13, 1799) the last survival of serfdom in the United Kingdom was swept away by the Act which declared the colliers 'in that part of Great Britain called Scotland' free from the servile yoke under which for several centuries they had groaned.

**b.** *fig.*

**1875** JOWETT *Plato* (ed. 2) III. 470 His soul is full of meanness and serfdom—the best elements in him are enslaved. **1876** MELLOR *Priesthood* ii, At length the laity sank into the most abject spiritual serfdom.

**serfe, serff,** obs. forms of SERVE *v.*¹

**serfhood** ('sɜːfhʊd). [f. SERF + -HOOD.] The collective body of serfs.

**1841** *Blackw. Mag.* L. 550 The Serfhood of Russia is a remarkable feature in her constitution. **1848** MRS. JAMESON *Sacr. & Leg. Art* (1850) 266 While knighthood had its St. George, serfhood had its St. Nicholas.

**serfice,** obs. form of SERVICE.

**serfish** ('sɜːfɪʃ), *a.* [f. SERF + -ISH¹.] Having the (debasing) qualities of one in a servile condition; characteristic of a serf. Hence '**serfishness**.

**1879** *Echo* 18 Apr. 1/4 The negroes, either through serfish instincts, from intimidation, or from a not unfounded belief that their interests are identical, are voting with their old masters. **1906** MACKINNON *Hist. Mod. Liberty* I. 145 There is no spirit of self-assertion in these serfish centuries to aspire to self-government. **1906** *Athenæum* 5 May 539/1 The absence of allusion to 'serfishness' in the second volume [of Mackinnon].

'**serfism.** *rare.* [f. SERF + -ISM.] The state of things characterized by the existence of serfs.

**1849** *Blackw. Mag.* LXVI. 592 No man.. can possibly sympathise with despotism, serfism, and that enormous stretch of feudal power which is given to a privileged class.

**serfship** ('sɜːfʃɪp). [f. SERF + -SHIP.] Serfdom.

**1830** GALT in *Fraser's Mag.* II. 446 In those countries where serfship exists—in Russia, for instance. **1854** H. MILLER *Sch. & Schm.* xiv. 305 *note*, [Scotch colliers.] Their slavery seems not to have been derived from the ancient times of general serfship, but to have originated in comparatively modern acts of the Scottish Parliament.

**serg,** var. SARGE².

**sergancie, -gant(e** :see SERGEANCY, SERGEANT.

**sergans, -gantz, -ganz,** obs. pl. ff. SERGEANT.

**serge** (sɜːdʒ). Forms: 4-6, 8 sarge, 6 surge, 7 searge, sierge, serg, sharge, 6- serge. [a. OF. *serge*, *sarge* (mod.F. *serge*) = Pr. *serga*, *sargua*, Pg., Catal. *sarja*, Sp. *sarga*, Rumanian *sàrică*:—popular L. **sārica* = class.L. *sērica* (*lāna*): see SERIC *a.* and SILK. From Fr. the word has passed into all the Teut. langs.: G. *sarsche*, *serge*, Du. *sargie*, Da. *sars*, *sarge*, Sw. *sars*.

The material originally designated by the name must have been silk, though there is no evidence of this in the early English (and app. not in the Romanic) uses of the word. But names of textile fabrics often come to be applied to materials cheaper and coarser than those which they originally designated.]

**1.** A woollen fabric, the nature of which has probably differed considerably at different periods. Before the 16th c. it is mentioned chiefly as material for hangings, bed-covers, and the like; afterwards it is often referred to as worn by the poorer classes (both men and women), perh. rather on account of its durability than of its price, which seems not to have been extremely low. The name now denotes a very durable twilled cloth of worsted, or with the warp of worsted and the woof of wool, extensively used for clothing and for other purposes.

Certain imported varieties were formerly known by French designations indicating the place of manufacture, as *serge de Ghent*, *s. de Nismes*, *s. de Ro(h)an*, *s. de Shaloon*.

*c* **1386** CHAUCER *Knt.'s T.* 1710 The Citee large, Hanged with clooth of gold, and nat with sarge. **1491** *Acta Domin. Concil.* (1839) 228/2, xxij coveringis of beddis of sarge, price x li. **1585** T. WASHINGTON tr. *Nicholay's Voy.* I. viii. 8 Som peece of a white sarge or blanket. **1620** *Reg. Privy Council Scot.* XII. 339 Seargeis Double and Single. **1631** T. POWELL *Tom of All Trades* 14 Where one is ready to take his rise out of Sierge into Sattin, out of Parsonage.. into a Deanarie. **1648** in Magrath *Flemings Oxf.* (O.H.S.) I. 391 For 8 ya. & halfe of serge de roan for sute.. 02 11 00. **1649** J. MASTER in *Archæol. Cant.* XV. 182 For 3 ya. 3 quar. of serge de shaloon at 6ˢ ye yard. **1683** *Repr. Advantages Manuf. Woollen-cloath* 4 That sort of Serges called Stirling Serges. *Ibid.* 5 Mixt Searges, Cloath-Searges, and these called in France Searge de Nismes. **1695** MOTTEUX tr. *St. Olon's Morocco* 138 Serges de Nismes, Fustians and Dimities of Montpelier. **1728** CHAMBERS *Cycl.*, *Serge*,.. a Woollen cross'd Stuff, manufactured on a Loom with four Treddles, after the Manner of Rateens, and other cross'd Stuffs. **1757** DYER *Fleece* III. 576 The Dune and Rother, who have won The serge and kersie to their blanching streams. **1835** LYTTON *Rienzi* I. i, The long loose gown and the plain tunic, both of dark-grey serge. **1861** *Our Engl. Home* 174 The walls [of a bedroom, temp. Q. Eliz.] were hung with say, or the scarlet serge of Ghent. **1882** MISS BRADDON *Mt. Royal* II. x. 221 Mopsy and Dopsy were dressed in home-made gowns of dark brown serge. **1882** CAULFEILD & SAWARD *Dict. Needlework* 443 There are a great many varieties of cloth known as Serge, viz. French Flannel Serge..; the Serge de Berri,.. Witney Serges,.. and Pompadour Flannel Serges. **1888** [see *navy blue* NAVY¹ 6].

**b.** A garment made of serge.

**1583** STOCKER *Civ. Warres Lowe C.* III. 93 They slewe two of the watch, hauing gotten for their paines, three cloaks, one Cushin and a Sarge. **1899** F. T. BULLEN *Way Navy* 43 Many of them tore off their serges and cast themselves recklessly overside. **1906** *Daily Chron.* 17 Oct. 6/6 'Serges'—as the loose-fitting jacket is termed in the [police] force.

**c.** *transf.* and *fig.*

**1599** B. JONSON *Cynthia's Rev.* III. ii, I wonder at nothing more then our gentlemen-ushers that will suffer a piece of serge, or *perpetuana*, to come into the presence. **1654** WHITLOCK *Zootomia* 320 Let your black Serge pore on Books, it is not for Scarlet Boyes, to task themselves to such serious spendings of their time.

¶**2.** Used to translate L. *sagum*, in Vulg. with the sense of curtain. Cf. SAY *sb.*¹ 2.

**1382** WYCLIF *Exod.* xxvi. 8 The lengthe of the too sarge shal haue thretti cubitis, and the brede foure; euen mesure shal be of alle the sarges [*MS. E. pr. m.* say.. says].

**3.** *silk serge*: a silk fabric twilled in the manner of serge, used for linings of coats, and formerly for mantles. Also †*serge du soy* (= Fr. *serge de soie*).

**1844** *Ladies' Hand-bk. Haberdashery* 15 Serge.. is of various colors and qualities; it is known by its being a stout silk with a very fine twill. **1853** PERKINS *Haberdashery* (ed. 8) 112 Serge is a stout twilled silk.. usually sold for lining the skirts, cuffs, and padded parts of coats. **1876** PLANCHÉ *Cycl. Costume* I. 450 A silken stuff called 'sergedusoy' was used in the last century for coats by the commonalty.

**4.** *attrib.* passing into *adj.* Made of serge.

**1608** MIDDLETON *Trick to catch Old One* I. iv, He in the uneven beard and serge cloak. **1685** *Rec. Scott. Cloth Manuf. New Mills* (S.H.S.) 105 Ane searge justicoat. **1690** CHILD *Disc. Trade* (1698) 10 Let us ask.. whether gentlewomen in those days would not esteem themselves well cloathed in a Serge gown, which a chamber maid now will be ashamed to be seen in. **1863** GEO. ELIOT *Romola* xiv, A serge covering.. concealed the contents of the basket. **1880** 'OUIDA' *Moths* I. 60 A white serge frock.

*humorous.* **1593** SHAKS. *2 Hen VI*, IV. vii. 27 Ah thou Say, thou Surge, nay thou Buckram Lord.

**5.** *Comb.*, as ***serge-cloth***, ***-clothier***, ***-maker***, ***manufacture***, ***-market***, ***-weaver***. Also † **serge-wale**, ? a striped serge (see WALE *sb.*).

*c* **1430** LYDG. *Min. Poems* (Percy Soc.) 201 Lych a *seerge-cloth hire nekke is clene. **1829** LAMB *Let. to Gillman* 30 Nov., A fall in serge cloth was expected. **1707** *Lond. Gaz.* No. 4377/4 William Crooke,.. *Serge-Clothier. **1689** *Ibid.* No. 2420/4 Richard Richardson..had a Box of *Serge Makers Paper sent by his Wagoner. **1822** LYSONS *Magna Brit.* VI. Devonsh. p. cccii, At Honiton there is only one serge-maker. **1742** *De Foe's Tour Gt. Brit.* (ed. 3) I. 310 Here we see the first of the *Serge-manufacture of Devonshire. *Ibid.* 324 The *Serge-market held here every Week. **1682** *Lond. Gaz.* No. 1762/4 Stolen..several Pieces of Rich Silk Druggets, *Serge-Wale, Thred Druggets. **1703** *Ibid.* No. 3920/4 Tho. Noble,..a *Serge-Weaver by Trade.

**serge**: see CIERGE, SEARCE *v.*, SEARCH *sb.*$^{1}$ and *v.*

**sergeancy, serjeancy** (ˈsɑːdʒənsɪ). *Hist.* Forms: 4 **sargeancie, serjancy, sergancie,** 7 **sergeancy, serjeancy,** (9 less correctly **sergeantcy**). [a. AF. *sergeancie*, graphic variant of *sergeantie* SERGEANTY. In later use a new formation on SERGEANT + -CY.]

†**1.** The body of sergeants in a country, the sergeant-class. *Obs.*

*c* **1330** R. BRUNNE *Chron. Wace* (Rolls) 13391 *note*, þe seriauntz [*v.r.* sargeancie] & þe archers, & oþere noble arbalasters. **1338** —— *Chron.* (1725) 83 Knyght & sergeancie als how mykelle þei helde.

†**2.** The district or province held by or under the government of a sergeant. *Obs.*

**1371** *Rolls of Parlt.* II. 306/1 Touz les Hundrez,.. Serjancies, & Fraunchises. **1464** *Ibid.* V. 547/2 Eny Graunte ..to be had..of the Sergancie withynne our Counties of Not' and Berk'.

†**3.** = SERGEANTY I. *Obs.*

**1602** FULBECKE *1st Pt. Parall.* 21 *Grand sergeancy*, is where a man holdeth his lands or tenements..by doing some speciall seruice to the king in person. *Ibid.*, *Petite Sergeancy*, is where a man holdeth his land of the king, paying yearely vnto him a bow, or a speare, or a dagger, or a launce, or a spurre of gold &c. *c* **1630** RISDON *Surv. Devon* §296 (1810) 306 Lord Martin held this land..by serjeancy.

**4.** The office of a sergeant or a serjeant in various senses; e.g. an appointment by writ or patent of the crown as serjeant-at-law; also the commission of sergeant in the army.

*a* **1670** HACKET *Abp. Williams* I. (1693) 110 Lord Keeper ..congratulated their Adoption unto that Title of Serjeancy. **1814** SCOTT *Wav.* vii, Some sly petitions for sergeantcies and corporalships. **1865** CARLYLE *Fredk. Gt.* XII. ix. (1872) IV. 205 He did reward them by present, by promotion to sergeantcy.

**sergeant, serjeant** (ˈsɑːdʒənt), *sb.* Forms: α. 3–5 **sergeaunte,** 3–6 **sergant(e,** 4 **sergiaunt, -gond, -gont(e,** 4–5 **sergaunt(e, seregeaun,** 4–6 **sarg(e)ante, -iant, sergeaunt,** 5 **sargeande, sergend, -gyaunte,** 5–6 **sargantt, -eaunt(e, -ent, sergeand,** 6 **schargant, sergeante, -ent, -iand, -iaunte,** 6–7 **s(e)argeant, sergiant,** 4– **sergeant.** β. 3–6 **seriaunt,** 3–7 **seriant,** 4 **seriont,** 4–5 **seriaunte,** 4–6 **sariant, serieaunt,** 5 **ceriawnt, sariand, -aunt, seriauntte, seriawnt(e, serja(u)nte,** 5–6 **seriand, -ante,** 6 **sereiaunt, serjeaunt(e,** 6–7 **serieant, serjand, -ant,** 7 **sarient, sarjant, sarriant,** 5– **serjeant.** (Down to the 15th c. the *t* was often omitted in the plural, which therefore ended in -ns, -nz, -nce.) [a. OF. *sergent*, *serjant* (mod.F. *sergent*) = Pr. *serven-s*, Sp. *sirviente*, Pg., It. *servente* servant:—L. *servientem*, pr. pple. of *servīre* SERVE *v.*$^{1}$ The Fr. word has been adopted into other Rom. langs.: It. *sergente*, Sp., Pg. *sargento* sergeant, Sp. *sergente*, Pg. *sargente* catchpoll.

Down to the 19th c. the α and β forms were used indiscriminately. In recent times, however, the spelling *serjeant* has come to be generally adopted as the correct form when the word is the designation of a member of the legal profession, while *sergeant* is the prevailing form in the other surviving senses, and in most of them the only form in use.]

†**1. a.** A serving-man, attendant, servant. *Obs.*

*c* **1200** *Trin. Coll. Hom.* 177 þe senden here sergantes to bringen iuele tiðinges. *c* **1250** *Kent. Serm.* in *O.E. Misc.* 29 Hac hye spac to þo serganz þet seruede of þo wyne. *c* **1290** *Beket* 687 in *S. Eng. Leg.* 126 On of is seriaunz sat a niȝt þe ȝwile þat men woke. *a* **1300** *Floriz & Bl.* 665 þer ben seriauns in þe stage, þat serue þe maidenes of parage. *a* **1300** *Cursor M.* 2516 He [*sc.* Abram] did to-geder samen his men, Thre hundret aght sariants and ten [Vulg. *vernaculos*, Gen. xiv. 14]. *Ibid.* 3221 A sargiant call þan comand he þat mast wist of his priuete. *c* **1300** *Havelok* 2066 Cum now forth with me..And þine seriaunz al þre. **1303** R. BRUNNE *Handl. Synne* 2361 ȝyf þou be a seriaunt And take more þan þy cunnaunt..Y rede þat þou þer-of lete. *c* **1330** *Arth. & Merl.* 2522 (Kölbing) On þe gate loude þai bete, Seriaunce com & hem in lete. **1340** *Ayenb.* 33 And þis is þe sixte vice of þe kueade sergonte. þet he fayleþ er þan he come..to his terme. **1377** LANGL. *P. Pl.* B. III. 216 Seruantz [*v.r.* Sergauntz] for her seruise..Taken Mede of here maistre. *c* **1450** LOVELICH *Grail* xii. 323 An Old Serjaunt he gan to calle, And there him Comaunded... The Cristene to kepen with ful gret honour. *c* **1450** *Mirour Saluacioun* (Roxb.) 133 Sho qwitte hym of awayt of hire ffaders sergeantz and lete him out at a wyndowe.

†**b.** *transf.* A servant (of God, of Satan). *Obs.*

*c* **1290** *Matheu* 64 in *S. Eng. Leg.* 79 'Nai certes', quath þis holie man; 'god nam ich nouȝt Ake godes seriaunt'. **14..** *Alexius* (Laud MS. 622) in *Archiv Stud. neu. Spr.* LIX. 104 Alexis hys sone..sayd, Sergeaunte of god haue pyte of me that am a poure pylgryme. **1483** CAXTON *G. de la Tour* h ij, Which [Raab] god wold haue saued by cause she had saued his mynystres and sergeans. **1513** BRADSHAW *St. Werburge* I. 1024 The minister of myschef & sergeaunt of sathanas. **1570** *Satir. Poems Reform.* xix. 78 That Apostat, that Feyndis awin Seriand.

†**2. a.** A common soldier. *Obs.*

[Cf. Cotgr. '*Sergent*..in old French, a footman, or souldier that serues on foot.']

*c* **1300** *Havelok* 2361 With hem fiue thusand gode Sergaunz, þat weren to fyht wode. *c* **1330** R. BRUNNE *Chron. Wace* (Rolls) 895 Seuen þousand now we are Of knyghtes to bataille ȝare, Wyþoute seriauntz & oþer pytaille. *a* **1352** MINOT *Poems* (ed. Hall) v. 22 He hasted him to þe Swin with sergantes snell. *c* **1450** *Merlin* 113 And the barons..were well viij$^{ml}$ knyghtes, with-outen seriantz and arblastis. **1456** SIR G. HAYE *Law Arms* (S.T.S.) 47 Sevin thousand knychtis, four score of thousandis of sergendis. **1490** CAXTON *Sonnes of Aymon* xxii. 478 He wythdrewe his arme, & gaff to one of the sergauntes suche a stroke wyth it in to y$^{e}$ forhede that [etc.].

†**b.** In alliterative verse used for: A man. *Obs.*

Perh. with a pun on *geaunt*, giant.

?*a* **1400** *Morte Arth.* 1173 Be sekere of this sergeaunt [*sc.* the giant], he has me sore greuede! **15..** *Droichis Play* in *Dunbar's Poems* (1893) 314 Se ȝe not quha is cum now?.. A sergeand out of Sowdoun land A gyane strang for to stand.

†**3.** A tenant by military service under the rank of a knight; esp. one of this class attending on a knight in the field. *Obs.*

App. nearly equivalent to ESQUIRE, though 'squires' and 'sergeants' are often mentioned together in a way that suggests that there was some difference of meaning in the terms. Cf. F. *sergent noble*.

*c* **1290** *Beket* 2427 in *S. Eng. Leg.* 176 For to honouri þis holi man þer cam folk i-novȝ;..Of Eorles and of barones and manie kniȝtes heom to; Of seriaunz and of squiers. **13..** *Coer de L.* 1259 To Londoun, to hys somouns, Come erl, bysschop, and barouns,..and manye bachelers, Serjaunts, and every freeholdande. **13..** *Seuyn Sag.* 253 Som squier or som seriant nice, Had i-told th'emperice Al of th'emperoures sone. **13..** *K. Alis.* 3464 Mony baron, mony sergant, Mony strong knyght and géant. *c* **1314** *Guy Warw.* 7000 On ich side he seye come kniȝtes, Burieys, and seriaunce redi to fiȝtes. *c* **1330** R. BRUNNE *Chron. Wace* (Rolls) 7210 Of hym [*sc.* the king] hauy no lond ne rent So þat y may not holde to me Fourty squiers [*Petyt MS.* sergeanz; Wace *sergans*] on al my fe. *c* **1400** *Ywaine & Gaw.* 1872 Knightes, serjantes, and swiers. *c* **1425** WYNTOUN *Chron.* VIII. xxix. 431 Off sergeandis þar and kynchtis keyn He gat a gret company.

†**4. a.** An officer whose duty is to enforce the judgements of a tribunal or the commands of a person in authority; one who is charged with the arrest of offenders or the summoning of persons to appear before the court. *Obs.*

*a* **1300** *Cursor M.* 17293 þai send sergantz for to nym Both sir nichodem & him. *a* **1330** *Roland & V.* 413 Seriaunce þe bodi souȝt. *c* **1386** CHAUCER *Clerk's T.* 519 A maner sergeant [Petrarch *satelles*] was this prince man. —— *Sec. Nun's T.* 361 The sergeantz of the toun of Rome hem soghte And hem biforn Almache the Prefect broghte. **1388** WYCLIF *1 Sam.* xix. 14 Saul sente sergeauntis [Vulg. *apparitores*], that schulden rauysche Dauid. **14..** *Nom.* in Wr.-Wülcker 684/5 *Hic lictor*, a sargent. **1433** *Rolls of Parlt.* IV. 477/1 That the Baylyffs..make 11 Sergeauntes of the seid Town. *c* **1440** *Promp. Parv.* 67/1 Ceriawnt, *indagator*. *Ibid.* 453/2 Seriawnt, undyr a domys mann, for to a-rest menn, or a catche-pol. *c* **1450** *Brut* II. 570 He..after sent forth sergeauntes, and arestit dyuers Constables and vinteners. **1455–6** *Cal. Anc. Rec. Dublin* (1889) 290 He schold assingne one of hys serjauntys to arest the Mayre. **1479–81** *Rec. St. Mary at Hill* (1904) 111 Item, payd to a sergeaunte for the arrest of our tenaunte þat dyd vs wronge, viij d. **1490** *Acc. Ld. High Treas. Scot.* I. 174 To the sergeandis of the towne ix s. **1496** *Ibid.* 302 To the seriand of Leith, to rest the avnaris of the Cukow to the court ij s. **1533** BELLENDEN *Livy* I. xi. (S.T.S.) I. 66 And quhen þe seriandis [orig. *præcones*] had with þare noyiss and hohas warnit in speciall þe albanis to here þe kingis concioun [etc.]. *Ibid.* III. xv. II. 5 Assembil þarefore now all þe seriandis and burreois of thy collegis [orig. *omnes collegarum lictores*], armit, as þare custome is, with wandis and axis. **1549** COVERDALE, etc. *Erasm. Par. 2 Cor.* xi. 21–30 Thryse was I beaten with sargeauntes roddes. **1557** N. T. (Genev.) *Matt.* v. 25 Agre with thin aduersarie quickely..least..thy iudge deliuer thee to the seargeant. **1590** SHAKS. *Com. Err.* IV. ii. 56 Oh yes, if any houre meete a Serieant, a turnes backe for verie feare. **1606** BP. HALL *Heaven upon Earth* §6 When..thy conscience, like a stern Sergeant, shall catch thee by the throat, and arrest thee vpon Gods debt. **1611** BIBLE *Acts* xvi. 35. **1617** MORYSON *Itin.* III. 244 Foure Serjeants attired in red gownes attend the Senate and summon men to appeare. **1621** J. TAYLOR (Water-P.) *Praise Beggery* B 2, He's free from shoulder-clapping Sergeants clawes. **1633** MARMION *Fine Comp.* II. vi. D 4 b, He may..consort with wits and sword-men, bee afraid of Sergeants, and spend more for his Protection then would pay the debt. **1648** HEXHAM II, *Een Schade-beletter*, A Sargeant to save one from Harme. **1673** *Aberdeen Reg.* (1872) IV. 286 The toun serjands of this brughe. **1680** C. NESSE *Ch. Hist.* 378 They were put into the serjeants ward.

**b.** *transf.* and *fig.*

**1413** *Pilgr. Sowle* (Caxton) I. xxii. (1859) 24 Thylke dethes sergeaunt, maladye, She hath arest, and haldyth the now in hande. **1593** G. HARVEY *Pierces Super.* 163 He shall finde it one of their speciall Priuiledges, to be exempted from the arrest of the sixfooted Sergeant, a continuall haunter of other hairy beastes, and onely fauorable to the good Asse, and the gentle Sheepe. **1600** TOURNEUR *Transf. Metam.* xli, One day? Nay sure a twelve-months' time t'will be, Ere seriant death will call me at my doore. **1602** SHAKS. *Ham.* V. ii. 347 Had I but time (as this fell Sergeant death Is strick'd in his arrest) oh I could tell you. **1618** BP. HALL *Contempl. N.T.*, *Widow's Son*, Our decrepit age both expects death and sollicites it; but vigorous youth, lookes strangely upon that grim sergeant of God. **1646** JENKYN *Remora* 12 You shall not be able to intoxicate this Sergeant of God [conscience]. **1681** FLAVEL *Meth. Grace* xxxv. 594 If ever God send forth those two grim sergeants, his Law and thine own conscience, to arrest thee for thy sins.

†**c.** More fully ***sergeant of* (*the*) *peace***. *Obs.*

**1357** in Blount *Law Dict.* (1691) s.v., Et etiam habere ibidem sex Servientes qui vocantur Serjeants of peace, qui servient Cur. Manerii prædicti, & facient Attach[iamenta] [etc.]. **1464** *Rolls of Parlt.* V. 541/2 Th'Office of Sergeant to the pees of alle oure Countees, in alle oure Lordship. **1485** *Ibid.* VI. 380/2 The Offices of Sergeaunt of Peas..in the Lordship of Denbygh.

**d.** ***King's sergeant*** (Guernsey): see quot.

**1682** WARBURTON *Hist. Guernsey* (1822) 58 The King's Sergeant... To his office it belongs to proclaim and publish all orders of the governor or of the Court.

**5. sergeant** (or **serjeant**) **at arms**. (Also †*sergeant of arms*.) †**a.** In early use *gen.*, an armed officer in the service of a lord (cf. sense 1); *spec.* one of a body of men of knightly rank, originally 24 in number, who were required to be in immediate attendance on the king's person, to arrest traitors and other offenders. **b.** An officer of each of the two Houses of Parliament, who is charged with the duty of enforcing the commands of the House, the arrest of offenders, etc. Hence, an officer having corresponding duties under certain other legislative assemblies, as the U.S. Senate and House of Representatives.

**1377** LANGL. *P. Pl.* B. XIX. 335 Now is Pieres to þe plow & pruyde it aspyde, And gadered hym a grete oest..And sente forth surquydous his seriaunt of armes. ?*a* **1400** *Morte Arth.* 632 He sendez furthe sodaynly sergeantes of armes. **1449** *Rolls of Parlt.* V. 159/1 One of the Sargeauntes of Armes of our Soverayne Lord the Kyng. *c* **1460** J. RUSSELL *Bk. Nurture* in *Babees Bk.* (1868) 71 A yeman of þe crowne Sargeaunt of armes with mace. **1462** *Paston Lett.* II. 87 Ther bode not with hym [a bishop] over xij persones atte the most, with his serjaunt of armes; whiche serjaunt was fayn to lay doun his mase. **1470–85** MALORY *Arthur* X. lxxxviii. 569 Thre sergeauntes of armes. **1473** *Rolls of Parlt.* VI. 84/1 His Office of oone of oure Sergeauntes at Armes. **1481** *Cov. Leet-bk.* 496 Ric. Shawe was arrested be þe seriaunt of armes þat brought þe writyng & caried vp to Wodstok vnto þe kyng. **1491** *Act 7 Hen. VII*, c. 2. §8 Serjauntes of Armes that be purposely ordeyned for the personall attendaunce of the ..King. **1556** *Chron. Grey Friars* (Camden) 45 A sergant at harmes of the parlament howse. **1565** COOPER *Thesaurus*, *Apparitor regis*, a serieaunt at armes. **1633** T. STAFFORD *Pac. Hib.* I. i. 7 A Serjeant at Armes, who shall beare the Mace of the Queenes Majesties Armes before him. **1710** J. CHAMBERLAYNE *St. Gt. Brit.* I. II. xiii. (ed. 23) 96 Knocking at the Door of the House of Commons, which thereupon is by the Serjeant at Arms attending the House opened. **1769** BLACKSTONE *Comm.* IV. xix. 259 The lord high steward directs a precept to a serjeant at arms, to summon the lords to attend and try the indicted peer. **1827** HALLAM *Const. Hist.* (1876) III. xiii. 25 Four counsel..were taken into custody of the Sergeant-at-arms by the speaker's warrant. **1886** C. E. PASCOE *London of To-day* viii. (ed. 3) 89 Seats for this space are in the gift of the Sergeant-at-Arms.

**6.** As a title borne by a lawyer. (Now always written **serjeant**.) **a.** A member of a superior order of barristers (abolished in 1880), from which, until 1873, the Common Law judges were always chosen (hence a serjeant was always called by a judge 'my brother So-and-so'). More explicitly, ***serjeant at* (†*the*) *law***, †***serjeant of* (*the*) *law***. Sometimes called ***serjeant of the coif***: see COIF *sb.* 3 b.

The title represents the law Latin *serviens ad legem*, which may be rendered 'one who serves (the king) in matters of law'.

**1297** R. GLOUC. (Rolls) 8833 Mid is wisdom þat was so muche he hom out drou & false serians of assise & dude hom ssame ynon. **1340** HAMPOLE *Pr. Consc.* 6084 þai sal þan na help gett Of sergeaunt, ne auturne, ne avoket. **1362** LANGL. *P. Pl.* A. III. 276 Schal no seriaunt for þat seruise were a selk houue. *c* **1386** CHAUCER *Prol.* 309 A Sergeant of the Lawe war and wys. **1404** *Rolls of Parlt.* III. 549/1 The Kynges entent is, to assigne..alle his Justices, and his Sergeantz. *c* **1435** in Kingsford *Chron. London* (1905) 57 Markham the Justice and Gascoigne Seriaunt of lawe. **1486** *Bk. St. Albans* f vj b, A sotelty of sergeauntis. **1501** in *Plumpton Corr.* (Camden) 152 *note*, John Yaxley, Sergent at the Law. **1503** *Privy Purse Exp. Eliz. York* (1830) 101 Item to John Mordant Sargeant at Lawe xl s. *c* **1530** HEYWOOD *Love* 808 (Brandl) Nowe am I a iudge and neuer was seriaunt. **1540** PALSGR. *Acolastus* II. iii. L j b, To Poules crosse, or to the barre, where sergeantes plede in westmister hall. **1552** EDW. VI *Jrnl.* Lit. Rem. (Roxb.) 415 Also ther ware appointed eight sergeants of the law against Michelmas next comming. **1597** HOOKER *Eccl. Pol.* V. lxvi. §9 A linnen Coife,..an ornament which only Sergeants at law doe weare. **1602** J. CHAMBERLAIN *Lett.* (Camden) 132 One Pelham, a lawyer, was made sergeant to be sent Cheife Baron into Ireland. **1656** BLOUNT *Glossogr.*, *Sergeant* at Law (or of the Coyf) is the highest degree, taken in that profession, as a Doctor of the Civil Law. **1697** DRYDEN *Ded. Æneis* Ess. (Ker) II. 162 A judge upon the bench..does not willingly commend his brother serjeant at the bar, especially when he controuls his law. **1710** J. CHAMBERLAYNE *St. Gt. Brit.* I. II. xv. (ed. 23) 122 None may be Judge in this Court, unless he be a Sergeant of the Degree of the Coif. **1711** ADDISON *Spect.* No. 89 ¶1 At present he is a Serjeant at Law. **1712** ARBUTHNOT *John Bull* III. viii, Serjeant such a one has a Silver Tongue at the Bar. **1764** *Oxf. Sausage* 172 Marking grave Serjeants cite each wise Report. **1819** TAUNTON *Rep. Cases Comm. Pleas* VII. 183 Lens and Vaughan, Serjts. now shewed cause against this rule. **1829** *Encycl. Metrop.* (1845) XX. 762/2 Three Inns have belonged from very early times to the Judges and Sergeants at Law. **1841** *Penny Cycl.* XXI. 272/1 A paper endorsed with..the words 'Mr. Serjeant A (or 'Mr. B'), retainer for the plaintiff' (or for the defendant). **1846** McCulloch *Acc. Brit. Empire* (1854) II. 155 Serjeants are sworn to do their duty to their clients. **1873** *Act 36 & 37 Vict.* c. 66 §8 Provided, that no person appointed a Judge of either of the said Courts shall henceforth be required to take, or have taken, the degree of Serjeant-at-Law.

*transf.* (*jocular*) **1663** Butler *Hud.* I. iii. 1164 By black caps underlaid with white, Give certain guess at inward light; Which Serjeants at the Gospel wear, To make the Spiritual Calling clear.

**b.** ***the King's*** (or ***Queen's***) ***Serjeant***: a title given to a limited number of the serjeants-at-law, appointed by patent.

The king's serjeants were supposed to be charged with the duty of pleading in the courts on behalf of the crown; but from an early period it had ceased to be more than an honorary distinction. The senior in rank of the king's serjeants was designated 'the King's Serjeant', and the second 'The King's Ancient Serjeant'.

**1423** *Rolls of Parlt.* IV. 201/2 The King' Sergeant to be sworne..to yeve the poor Man..Counsaill. **1454** *Ibid.* V. 240/1 Oon of the Kynges Sergeauntz atte lawe. **1482** *Ibid.* VI. 207/1 Richard Pygot, and Roger Townessend, the Kyng's Sergeants of the Lawe. **1512** *Act 4 Hen. VIII*, c. 11 Lews Pollard the Kynges serjeaunt at the Lawe. **1602** Coke *Rep.* III. To Rdr. D iv b, Out of these the King electeth one, two, or three as please him to be his Serieants, which are called the *Kings Serieants.* **1710** J. Chamberlayne *St. Gt. Brit.* II. III. xxx. (ed. 23) 576 The Queens Serjeants at Law. **1825** *Encycl. Metrop.* (1845) XVII. 308/2 The King's Serjeant, so constituted by special patent; the King's Ancient Serjeant. **1882** Serj. Ballantine *Exper.* I. 209 A post filled at that time by Mr. Serjeant Manning, Queen's ancient serjeant. **1886** *Encycl. Brit.* XXI. 682/2 Until 1814 the two senior King's serjeants had precedence of even the attorney-general and solicitor-general.

**c.** ***prime serjeant***: the title given until 1805 to the first in rank of the three (earlier two) serjeants-at-law in Ireland. (Afterwards called ***first serjeant***.)

**1666** in *Cal. St. Papers Irel.* 1666–9 (1908) 73 Sir Audley Mervin, Prime Sergeant at Law. **1733** Berkeley *Let.* Wks. 1871 IV. 205 The prime serjeant, Singleton, may probably be a means of assisting you to get light in these particulars. *a* **1797** H. Howard in *3rd Rep. Hist. MSS. Comm.* 434/1 John Hely Hutchinson, Prime Serjt at law, ye vainest man alive, set his heart upon ye place. *c* **1799** Sir L. Parsons in *Charlemont MSS.* (Hist. MSS. Comm. 1894) II. 404 There is no end of the turnings-out talked of,..——lord Carhampton, the prime serjeant,..and even Toler. The prime serjeant is, I believe, certain. **1806** Duncan *Nelson's Funeral* 31 Prime Serjeant.

**d.** **Common Serjeant (at Law).** A judicial officer appointed by the Corporation of London as an assistant to the Recorder.

[**1419** *Liber Albus* (Rolls) I. 47 Le..Commune Sergeaunt de ley, qui autrement est dit 'Commune Countour'.] **1556** *Chron. Grey Friars* (Camden) 64 It was proclamyd opynly with the kynges shreffe & two harraldes & two pursevanttes & a trumpet, with the comyne sargant of the citte of London. **1680** *Lex Londin.* 55 The Common Serjeant of the City is the only person intrusted by the Court of Aldermen to take all Inventories and Accompts of freemens' estates. **1797** *Encycl. Brit.* (ed. 3) XVII. 292/2 Common Sergeant, an officer..who attends the lord mayor..on court days. **1844** Ld. Brougham *Brit. Const.* xvi. (1862) 366 So high judicial functionaries as the Recorder of London and the Common Sergeant are elected. **1861** [see countour 2]. **1887** *Times* 27 Aug. 11/4 The three City Judges (the Recorder, the Common Serjeant, and Mr. Commissioner Kerr). **1890** *Ibid.* 28 Apr. 11/6 The Common Serjeant sentenced the prisoner to two years' hard labour.

**7.** (Now commonly written **sergeant**; in some uses **serjeant** appears to be officially adopted.) In the titles of certain officers of the Royal Household. **a.** The head of a specified department, as ***sergeant of the cellar***, of the ***saucery***, of the ***vestry***. †Also ***s. of the bears***, a bearward; ***s. of the minstrels***; ***s. of the surgeons***, ***of the trumpets*** = sergeant-surgeon, sergeant-trumpeter.

**1450** *Rolls of Parlt.* V. 192/1 William Pecke Clerke of oure Spicerye, Ric' Ludlowe Sergeant of oure Seler. *Ibid.*, Robert Broune Sergeant of oure Saucerye. *Ibid.*, Sergeant of oure Chaundelerye. **1464** [see masonry A. 3]. **1526** in *Househ. Ord.* (1790) 140 The Serjeant of the bake-house. *Ibid.* 141 The Serjeant of the chaundry... The Serjeant of the ewry. *Ibid.* 142 The Serjeant of the larder. *Ibid.* 143 The Serjeant of the squillery. *Ibid.* 169 Serjeant of the Mynstrills. **1539** Cromwell *Let.* 24 Apr. in Strype *Eccl. Mem.* (1733) I. II. 272 Jenyngs, Sergeant to your Graces Pastery House. **1541** in *Vicary's Anat.* (1888) App. ii. 109 Thomas Sperin and his son sergiantes of the beres. **1561** Vicary *Will* in *Anat.* (1888) App. vi. 187, I, Thomas Vicars, Seriante of the Suriantes vnto our saide soueraigne ladie the quenes maiestie. **1710** J. Chamberlayne *St. Gt. Brit.* I. II. xiv. (ed. 23) 120–1 The Serjeant of the King's Wood-Yard. .. The Serjeant of the Ewry... The Serjeant of the Larder. *Ibid.* II. III. xvii. 534 H. Parker, Esq; Serj. of the Vestry. **1721** Strype *Eccl. Mem.* II. I. i. 2 The Sergeants of the Trumpets.

**b.** Prefixed appositively to certain designations of office, as ***sergeant-cater***, ***-farrier*** (***-ferrour***), ***-footman***, ***-painter***, ***-plumber***, ***-porter***, ***-squiller***, ***-surgeon*** (†***chirurgeon***), ***-tailor***, ***-trumpet***, ***-trumpeter***.

Many other similar designations, adopted from Anglo-French, and not proved to have been used in English, will be found in F. Tate, *Household Ord. Edw. II*, 1601 (new ed. 1876).

**1614** Gentleman *Engl. Way to Wealth* 25 His Maiesties *Seriant Cater. *a* **1529** Skelton *Dyuers Balettys* Wks. 1843 I. 24 Haue in *sergeaunt ferrour, myne horse behynde is bare. **1710** J. Chamberlayne *St. Gt. Brit.* II. III. xx. (ed. 23) 549 Serjeant Farrier, John Willis, Esq. **1901** *Westm. Gaz.* 9 May 7/3 *Sergeant-footman Boswell. **1548** in Kempe *Losely MSS.* (1836) 81 To Anthony Toto, *sergeante payntor, in rewarde for his paynes takyng..in drawyng of patrons for the masks 20s. **1720** *Lond. Gaz.* No. 5848/3 His Majesty's Serjeant-Painter. **1887** Pater *Imag. Portr.* 146 The sergeant-painter and deputy sergeant-painter were conventional performers enough. **1533** in *Hampton Crt. Accts.*, The Kynges *sergeaunt plumber. **1663** Gerbier *Counsel* 58 The Serjeant Plumber calling his workmen to caste in his presence a Leaden Medal. **1450** *Rolls of Parlt.* V. 192/2 John Stok *Sergeant porter of oure Gate. **1710** J. Chamberlayne *St. Gt. Brit.* II. III. xix. (ed. 23) 545 To the Serjeant Porter. **1821** Scott *Kenilw.* xv, One of the sergeant porters told them they could not at present enter. **1901** *Whitaker's Almanack* 87 Sergeant State Porter. *a* **1483** *Liber Niger* in *Househ. Ord.* (1790) 81 He rescevethe..all the plates of peautyr by the pourveyaunce of the *sergeaunt-squylloure. **1710** J. Chamberlayne *St. Gt. Brit.* II. III. xix. (ed. 23) 545 *Serjeant skinner. **1565** J. Halle *Hist. Expost.* 19 Maister Vicary, late *sargeant chyrurgien to the queenes highnes. **1749** Fielding *Tom Jones* VIII. xiii, Serjeant-surgeon to the King. **1812** *Lond. Gaz.* No. 16663. 2189/1 Serjeant-Surgeon to His Majesty. **1901** *Whitaker's Almanack* 88 Sergeant Surgeon, Lord Lister. **1480** *Wardrobe Acc. Edw. IV* in *Privy Purse Exp. Eliz. York*, etc. (1830) 155 George Lufkyn *Sergeant taillour of the grete Warderobe of the Kynge. **1588** Deloney in *Roxb. Ball.* (1887) VI. 391 The *Sergeant trumpet with his mace, and nyne with trumpets after him, Bare headed went before her grace. **1708** *Lond. Gaz.* No. 4416/4 Her Majesty has appointed John Shore, Esq; Serjeant-Trumpet of Great Britain. **1603** *Rep. Hist. MSS. Comm.*, *Var. Coll.* III. 164 *Serjeant trumpeter. **1700** Luttrell *Brief Rel.* (1857) I. 413 Gervas Price esq., serjeant trumpeter to his majestie, died lately. **1901** *Whitaker's Almanack* 87 Sergeant Trumpeter.

**8. a.** In the titles of certain inferior officers employed by the Corporation of the City of London, and by other municipal bodies.

**1423** *Cov. Leet-Bk.* 43 þer schall no beestys be pynnyd at the comen pynfold by the comien seriante. **1672** Cave *Prim. Chr.* III. v. 359 Satan as the Common Serjeant and Jaylor seized upon them. **1710** J. Chamberlayne *St. Gt. Brit.* II. III. xliv (ed. 23) 631 Serjeant-Carvers... Serjeants of the Chamber or Mace... Moses Griffith, Serjeant of the Channel. **1720** [see taker 2 g]. **1766** Entick *Lond.* III. 307 The officers belonging to the lord-mayor,..are..the three serjeant carvers; three serjeants of the chamber; a serjeant of the channel [etc.]. **1835** *App. Munic. Corpor. Rep.* IV. 2345 [At Lincoln.] Four Serjeants of the Key or Bailiffs. *Ibid.* II. 998 (Hastings) The Mayor's Serjeant..serves process; attends the corporation meetings with a mace; and is sworn in as a constable... The Common Serjeant, who is also a serjeant at mace,..has the same salary and clothing as the mayor's serjeant.

**b.** ***sergeant at*** (†***the***) ***mace***, † ***of*** (***the***) ***mace***: an inferior executive officer (cf. sense 4), carrying a mace as a badge of office.

*c* **1420** *Anturs of Arth.* 64 The king..folowed fast one þe tras, Withe many Sergeant of mas. *Ibid.* 498 þe lordes bylyue hom to list ledes With many seriant of mace, as was þe manere. *c* **1440** *Promp. Parv.* 67/1 Ceriawnt of mace, *apparitor*. **1474** *Rolls of Parlt.* VI. 103/1 Henry Neuton, oon of the Sergeants at Mace of Robert Billesdon, oon of the Shirrefs of the Cite of London. **1510** *Sel. Cases Star Chamb.* (Selden) II. 70 The meyer..sent oon John Yong sergeaunt att the mace within the seid Towne to the seid Priour. **1556** *Chron. Grey Friars* (Camden) 43 For arest of Robert Taylor sergant of maysse. **1680** in *10th Rep. Hist. MSS. Comm.* App. v. 506 If the Sergeants-at-Mace shall neglect theire duty in not summoning every member of the Council [etc.]. **1715** *Lond. Gaz.* No. 5394/4 Cesar Grist, Serjeant at Mace to the Bailiffs of the Corporation of Welsh Poole. **1761** in Entick *London* (1766) IV. 369 The serjeants at mace for the city to arrest for debt in the Borough. **1797** *Encycl. Brit.* (ed. 3) XVII. 292 Sergeants of the mace of an inferior kind. **1835** [see 8]. **1901** *Whitaker's Almanack* 178 [Lord Mayor's Court.] Sergeant at Mace.

*transf.* **1745** P. Thomas *Jrnl. Anson's Voy.* 211 A hundred Soldiers..follow'd with a hundred Serjeants at Mace. **1790** Burke *Fr. Rev.* Wks. 1808 V. 356 He appears to be nothing more than a chief of bumbailiffs, serjeants at mace, catchpoles, jailers and hangmen.

†**c.** *Sc.* An officer of a guild. *Obs.*

**1557** *Baxter-bks. St. Andrews* (1903) 10, viii d to thomas demster, yair schargant.

**9.** *Mil.* **a.** (Now always written **sergeant**.) In modern use, a non-commissioned officer of the grade above that of corporal. In the 16th c. the title, more explicitly † ***sergeant of a band*** [= F. *sergent de bande*], appears, like many other military titles, to have indicated a much higher rank than in later times. See also colour-sergeant, drill-*sergeant*, recruiting-*sergeant*, sergeant-major.

**1548** Patten *Exped. Scot.* H vij b, Sargeauntes of the band to the forewarde. **1579** Digges *Stratiot.* 86 This Serjeant ought perfectly by memorie to know every Souldiour within the Bande. **1590** Sir R. Williams *Brief Disc. War* 26 The least Serieant of a Band, being a naturall Spaniard, will seeme to command the greatest man of qualitie of anie other Nation. **1593** Sutcliffe *Pract. & Law Arms* 61 The officers of companies, namely lieutenants, ensignes, sergiants, corporals, are chosen by the captaines of companies. **1624** W. G. *Count Mansfield's Direct. Warre* 11 If all the three fore-named Officers [Captain, Lieutenant, and Ensign] be out of the way by any accident, then the eldest Sergiant is to command the Company as next in place. **1690** Mackenzie *Siege Londonderry* 47/2 Serjeants, Corporals, Drummers, and private Men 2d. per diem each, besides Bread. **1709** Steele *Tatler* No. 87 ¶1 The Epistle is from one Serjeant Hall of the Foot-Guards. **1833** Marryat *P. Simple* xi, All disputed points were settled by the sergeant of marines with a party, who divided their antagonists from the Jews. **1898** Steevens *With Kitchener to Khartum* 274 'Fall out, sergeant, you're wounded,' said the subaltern of his troop.

**b.** Prefixed appositively to various designations of offices in which sergeants are employed, as ***sergeant armourer***, ***bugler***, ***clerk***, ***compounder***, ***cook***, ***drummer***, ***farrier***, ***instructor***, ***master tailor***, ***-pilot***, ***saddler***, ***schoolmaster***, ***tailor***, ***trumpeter***.

**1810** Wellington in Gurw. *Desp.* (1838) VI. 308 *Serjeant armourers and serjeant saddlers' implements. **1901** *Whitaker's Almanack* 220 *Sergt. Bugler. **1895** *Outing* (U.S.) XXVII. 252/1 It changes the title of the brigade sergeant-major to that of *sergeant-clerk. **1901** *Whitaker's Almanack* 220 *Sergeant Cook. **1899** *Westm. Gaz.* 27 June 1/2 A *sergeant-drummer in each battalion of the Grenadier, Coldstream, and Scots Guards. **1876** Voyle & Stevenson *Milit. Dict.*, *Sergeant instructor. **1865** *Army Clothing Warrant* 30 The *Sergeant Master Tailor. **1919** J. T. B. McCudden *Five Years in R.F.C.* III. iii. 86 About the end of August, 1915, a *Serjeant-Pilot named Watts arrived for duty. *a* **1963** J. Lusby in 'B. James' *Austral. Short Stories* (1963) 221 The new boys comprised Australians, Englishmen, and Canadians... Most were sergeant-pilots, and in age retired school-boys. **1837** *King's Regul. Army* 239 The *Serjeant-Schoolmasters. **1900** *Westm. Gaz.* 12 Dec. 4/2 The Secretary of State..is causing inquiries to be made on the feasibility of having officers' uniforms made by the *sergeant-tailors of their regiments.

**10.** (Now always written **sergeant**.) A police officer, of higher rank than a simple constable; in Great Britain ranking next below an inspector.

**1839** Hood *Lost Heir* 36 Oh serjeant McFarlane! you have not come across my poor little boy, have you, in your beat? **1856** A. Wynter *Curios. Civiliz.* 469 The force consists of three inspectors, nine sergeants, and a body of police termed 'plain-clothes men'.

**11.** Comb. **Sergeant Baker** *Australian*, a fish of New South Wales, *Aulopus purpurissatus*; †**sergeant corn** *Sc.*, ? some feudal impost paid in corn; **sergeant-fish**, a name applied to various fishes having marks like the stripes on the sleeve of a sergeant's uniform, esp. *Rachycentron canadum*, the cobia, a large game fish found in tropical and subtropical seas; †**sergeant-loaf**, some kind of bread; †**serjeant's ring**, one of the rings which a newly appointed serjeant-at-law was required by custom to present to various persons of high rank or official position.

**1882** Tenison-Woods *Fish N.S. Wales* 82 The *Sergeant Baker in all probability..was called after a sergeant of that name. **1581** *Reg. Mag. Sig. Scot.* 107/2 Lie *serjand-corne. **1873** *Forest & Stream* I. 258/1 *Sergeant Fish..derives its trivial name from a black stripe running along its silvery sides..like that on the trowsers of a sergeant. **1884** Goode, etc. *Nat. Hist. Aquatic Anim.* 444 The name 'Sergeant-fish' refers to its peculiar coloration, several stripes of brown and gray being visible on the sides of the body. **1947** K. H. Barnard *Dict. Guide S. Afr. Fishes* 112 Sergeant-fish... A somewhat rare fish, of elongate shape,..occasionally caught at Port Elizabeth and Natal. **1958** *Washington Post* 24 Sept. 1/2 An unusually fine run of cobia (the sergeant fish)..has caused big game fishermen to toss caution to the gods of Izaak Walton. **1341** *Secretum Abb. Glastonie* (MS. Wood empt. 1) lf. 146b, Unum panem uocatum Priketlof, et alterum panem uocatum Bastardlof et tercium panem uocatum *seriauntlof de Panetria predicti abbatis. **1690** *Lond. Gaz.* No. 2613/4 They offered to sell or pawn.., one Gold *Serjeants Ring, and one pair of Gold Lockets.

†**'sergeant**, *a.* *Obs. rare*−1. [Back-formation from sergeanty.] In ***grand***, ***petit sergeant***, said of a tenure by grand or petit serjeanty respectively.

**1513** Bradshaw *St. Werburge* II. 1771 Many helde their landes..By tenure grand-seriante..Some by petit-seriant.

†**'sergeant**, *v.* *Obs.*−1 [a. OF. *sergenter*, f. *sergent* sergeant *sb.*] *intr.* To act as a sergeant.

*c* **1430** *Pilgr. Lyf Manhode* IV. xxi. (1869) 187 After þat þat þe matere is..ordeyned, þer after j shal sergeaunte [orig. *use de ma commission*] and werche diuerseliche.

†**'sergeantess.** *Obs.*−1 [f. sergeant *sb.* + -ess.] A female sergeant.

*c* **1430** *Pilgr. Lyf Manhode* IV. xix. (1869) 185 And for oure mootiere þou art and oure sergeantesse we senden þee and comitte þee þat þou go bi alle houses, and [etc.].

†**sergeant-general.** *Obs.* [f. sergeant *sb.* + general *a.*] = sergeant-major 1 b. (In the later examples ***sergeant-general of battle***, as a title of high rank in certain foreign armies.)

**1579** Digges *Stratiot.* 93 To sende his serjeant to the Serjeant general. **1685** *Lond. Gaz.* No. 2028/3 Being a Sergeant-General of Batalia in the Service of his Catholick Majesty. **1693** *Mem. Count Teckely* IV. 55 The Prince of Auguste of Hanover, Serjeant General of Battle.

**'sergeant-'major.** [f. sergeant *sb.* + major *a.*; in Fr. *sergent-major*.]

†**1.** In the 16–17th c., a military title variously applied to officers widely differing in rank and function. **a.** A field officer, one in each regiment, next in rank to the lieutenant-colonel, and corresponding partly to the 'major', partly to the 'adjutant', of the modern army.

Ordinarily referred to as superior to the captains, but in many instances a 'captain' is said to be also 'sergeant-major'.

**1573** Whithorne *Briefe Tables* H j b, Maister of the Campe, or Seargeant Maier, or Capitaine. **1591** Sir J. Smythe *Instr. Milit.* (1595) 36 The Sergeant Maior must command all the Captaines or their Lieutenants. **1598** Barret *Theor. Warres* II. i. 15 Euery Regiment hath this Sergeant Maior. **1598** B. Jonson *Ev. Man in Hum.* III. v, He might haue beene Serieant-Maior, if not Lieutenant-

Coronell to the regiment. **1604** E. GRIMSTON *Siege Ostend* 20 An English Captaine who was also Sargent Maior. **1624** W. G. *Count Mansfield's Direct. Warre* 13 The eldest Sergeant..is also to fetch the Word from the Sergeant Maior of the Regiment. **1633** *Swed. Intelligencer* IV. 127 The Sergeant-Major over these 5 companies, was Captaine Thomas Grove, who now commanded them. **1642** (*title*) A List of the Names of the severall Colonells.. with the Leivtenant Colonells, Serieant Maiors, and Captaines and Lievtenants appointed by the Committee, for the ordering of the Militia of this Honourable City of London. **1642** *Declar. Lords & Comm. for Rais. Forces* 22 Dec. 7 Serjeant-Major of the sayd Regiment. **1683** TURNER *Pallas Armata* xi. 225 The Swedes of a long time allowed him [*sc.* the Major] no company, yet allow'd him the command over Captains, but it is now many years ago since they were permitted to have companies; hence perhaps it is that when they have no companies, they may be called Serjeant-Majors, as when they have companies, the Germans call them Captain-Majors, but the English use frequently the words of Serjeant Major and Serjeant-Major General, none of them are used either by German, Swede, or Dane. **1704** *Milit. Dict.* (ed. 2).

†**b.** A general officer, corresponding to the modern major-general. Also ***sergeant-major major, sergeant-major general***. *Obs.*

**1591** SIR J. SMYTHE *Instr. Milit.* (1595) 60 If a Lord Marshall or a Sergeant Maior Maior, haue..10000 or more or fewer piquers to reduce into one bodie of squadron, hee may [etc.]. *c* **1595** MAYNARDE *Drake's Voy.* (Hakl. Soc.) 14 We buried Captaine Arnolde Baskerville, our serjant-major generall. **1599** J. CHAMBERLAIN *Lett.* (Camden) 38 Sir Ferdinando Gorge is named to be Sergeant Major [of the army in Ireland]. **1625** G. M. *Souldier's Accid.* 62 The Serieant-Maior of the Horse, which in some discipline is called the Commissary-generall. **1633** T. STAFFORD *Pac. Hib.* II. xvii. 222 The Sergeant Major, being the second Commander to Don Iohn. **1642** *List Army Earl Essex* 1 His Excellencie Robert Earle of Essex, Capt. Generall. Sir Iohn Merrick, Serjeant Major Generall, and President of the Councell of Warre. **1644** SYMONDS *Diary* (Camden) 50 Lord Wentworth was Serjeant Major of the Horse. **1646** EARL MONM. tr. *Biondi's Civil Warres* VIII. 147 [Richard III] Went himselfe in Person in the head of his Army.. executing Himselfe the duty of a Sergeant Major. **1647** CLARENDON *Hist. Reb.* VII. §26 Philip Skippon..was now made sergeant-major-general of the army by the absolute power of the two houses.

**2.** A non-commissioned officer of the highest grade.

The ***regimental sergeant-major*** (who is, strictly speaking, not a 'non-commissioned officer', but a 'warrant officer'), is an assistant to the adjutant. There is also a sergeant-major belonging to each squadron of cavalry and each battery of artillery.

**1802** JAMES *Milit. Dict.* s.v., In most regiments the serjeant-major, under the direction of the adjutant, is directed to drill every young officer who comes into the regiment. **1816** SCOTT *Old Mort.* xxxiv, Claverhouse.. called for his serjeant-major. **1837** *King's Regul. Army* 170 The Troop Serjeant-Majors... The Regimental Serjeant-Major.

*transf.* **1897** *Daily News* 15 June 3/4 They were members of the Salvation Army, one of them, a woman, describing herself as the sergeant-major.

**3.** An American fish, the cow-pilot, *Pomacentrus saxatilis*.

**1876** GOODE *Fishes of Bermudas* 38 *Glyphidodon saxatilis*, ..Cow-pilot; Sergeant-major. **1885** LADY BRASSEY *The Trades* 407 Fine little black and white 'serjeant-majors' as they are called, because of their many stripes.

**4.** *Mil. slang.* Used *attrib.* to designate (*a*) coffee with cream or milk and sugar (*U.S.*); (*b*) strong sweet tea; tea with rum; also in the possessive and *ellipt*.

**1923** T. BOYD *Through Wheat* viii. 131 'Bring your canteen cups. Sergeant-major coffee.'.. 'Coffee, hot! And milk and sugar in it!' **1925** FRASER & GIBBONS *Soldier & Sailor Words* 254 *Sergeant Major's Tea*, tea with sugar and milk, or a dash of rum, in it. **1929** J. L. HODSON *Grey Dawn—Red Night* II. v. 210 Two of them got up before the rest and made a fire and produced 'sergeant-major's tea' and bacon done to a turn. **1929** J. B. PRIESTLEY *Good Compan.* I. iv. 115 I'd like a drop o' tea with some rum in it, good old sergeant-major's. **1939** JOYCE *Finnegans Wake* 331 Pointing up to skyless heaven like the spoon out of sergeantmajor's tay. **1948** PARTRIDGE *Dict. Forces' Slang 1939–1945* 164 *Sergeant-major's*, a Samson-strong, love-sweet brew of tea, popularly supposed to be the perquisite of holders of that rank. **1981** J. WAINWRIGHT *Urge for Justice* I. v. 30 This tea ..it damn near dissolved the spoon. A real 'sergeant major' brew. The way tea *should* be made.

Hence as *v. trans.*, to order or shout in a brusque and stentorian manner; **sergeant-majorish, -majorly** *adjs.*, characteristic of or resembling a sergeant-major; **sergeant-majorship**.

**1892** *Athenæum* 1 Oct. 448/2 [*c* 1630] The king gave him [Fabert] another company vacant by death, again permitting his retention of the sergeant-majorship. **1925** G. W. DEEPING *Sorrell & Son* viii. 77 Moreover, he might pocket a sergeant-majorly share of the tips. **1926** A. BENNETT *Lord Raingo* xxxvi. 168 'Bow,' said the sergeant-majorish official behind him, in a no-nonsense voice. **1931** E. A. ROBERTSON *Four Frightened People* ii. 77 Then we heard the voice of Mrs. Mardick sergeant-majoring the truant few. *a* **1935** T. E. LAWRENCE *Mint* (1955) II. iii. 108 Cursing fellows forbidden to look resentful..is a sergeant-majorish trick which good corporals would not allow themselves. **1962** M. DUFFY *That's how It Was* iv. 43 'She'll soon learn,' the voice sergeant-majored high above me.

†'**sergeantry, serjeantry.** *Obs.* Also 5 sergawntry, seriauntrie, -rye, seryauntre, 7 *Sc.* serjandrie. [a. OF. *sergenterie* (cf. Anglo-L. *sergenteria*, *c* 1200 in *Rot. Chart.*, ed. 1837, p. 56/2), f. *sergent*: see SERGEANT and -ERY.]

**1.** = SERGEANTY 1.

*c* **1400** *Brut* I. 242, Y ȝelde vp, Sir, now vnto ȝow my homage,..for ham alle þat holden by seriauntrye [**1480** CAXTON seryauntre]. **1778** *Eng. Gazetteer* (ed. 2) s.v. *Scrivelsby*, This manor is held by grand serjeantry. *Ibid.* s.v. *Pitchley, Northamp...* The ancient lords of this manor held it of the King by petit serjeantry, *i.e.* to furnish dogs, at their own cost, to destroy the wolves, foxes, polecats, and other vermin, in the counties of Northampton, Rutland, Oxford, Essex, and Bucks. **1795** BURKE *Abridgm. Eng. Hist.* Wks. 1842 II. 550 If the tenant was in an office about the king's person, this gave rise to sergeantry. **1830** SCOTT *Ayrsh. Trag.* I. i, We'll not suffer A word of sergeantry, or halberd-staff. **1837** BARHAM *Ingol. Leg.* Ser. I. *Spect. Tappington*, These lands were held in grand serjeantry by the presentation of three white owls. **1830** JAMES *Darnley* vii, To hold his land by sergeantry, as it had been held by Lord Fitzbernard.

**2.** The office of sergeant or serjeant.

**1426** LYDG. *De Guil. Pilgr.* 16221 [Tribulation *loq.*] And thus vsynge myn Sergawntry, I kan werke dyuersly; Wherffore I rede be war off me, For I anoon shal smyte the. **1669** *Sc. Acts Chas. II* (1820) VII. 588/2 All and haill the office of Serjandrie of the lands & Lordship of Methven.

**3.** *nonce-use.* Skill as a serjeant-at-law.

**1830** LAMB *Album Verses, In Autograph Bk. Mrs. Serjeant W——*, These should moot cases in your book, and vie To show their reading and their Serjeantry.

**sergeantship, serjeantship** ('sɑːdʒənt-ʃɪp). [f. SERGEANT, SERJEANT *sb.* + -SHIP.] The office of a sergeant or a serjeant, in various senses.

**1450** *Rolls of Parlt.* V. 197/2 Theyre Fees of Serjauntship atte armes. **1495** *Act 11 Hen. VII*, c. 33 §11 The offices of Sergeauntshippe of the Pese and [etc.]. **1584** in *10th Rep. Hist. MSS. Comm.* App. v. 436 The office of Sariantship. **1825** HONE *Every-day Bk.* I. 157 His serjeantship being denoted by the *Coif*. **1909** *Essex Rev.* XVIII. 71 The persons they thought of appointing to serjeantship or corporalship.

**sergeanty, serjeanty** ('sɑːdʒəntɪ). *Hist.* Forms: α. 5–7 sergeantie (5 sergeaunte), 6 sergeauntie, sergentie, 7– sergeanty. β. 4–5 seriauntye, 5 serjantie, (*pl.* serjaunteez), 7 seriantie, serieanty, serjeantie, 7– serjeanty. [a. OF. *serjantie*, *sergentie*, f. *serjant*, *sergent*: see SERGEANT *sb.* and -Y.] (The usual spelling is now **serjeanty**.)

**1.** A form of feudal tenure on condition of rendering some specified personal service to the king.

**1467** *Rolls of Parlt.* V. 595/2 The rent of the Sergeantie, and of the small parcellz of Serjaunteez of oure Counteez of Notyngh' and Derb'. **1468** *Ibid.* 605/2 Other fermes to us of Serjanties or otherwise. **1477** *Ibid.* VI. 171/1 Smale parcells of Serjantie in diverse parcells,..thre Roodes of Serjantie. **1610** HOLLAND *Camden's Brit.* I. 464 Baldwin Le Pettour.. held certaine lands, by Serjeanty. **1643** BAKER *Chron., Rich. II* 1 John Wiltshire Citizen of London, by reason of a Moyitie of the Manour of Heydon, holden in Sergeantie, claimed to hold a towell for the King to wipe with when he went to meat. **1880** HARTING *Extinct Brit. Anim.* I. 82 Several grants of land..held by the serjeanty of keeping.. boar-hounds. **1906** *Athenæum* 18 Sept. 269/1 A little criticism is perhaps invited by the interesting list of serjeanties with which the volume closes.

**b.** Distinguished as ***grand*** and ***petit*** (or ***petty***) ***serjeanty***.

In their AF. form, these terms occur in the 13th c. According to *Britton* (*c* 1292), *grand serjeanty* obliges the tenant to a service 'touching the defence of the country', such as acting as marshal, putting an army in the field, or finding a horseman and his equipment for the army, while *petit serjeanty* binds him to a service 'amounting to half a mark or less', such a carrying to the king a bag, a brooch, an arrow, or a bow without string, etc. Later writers give more or less differing accounts: see quots. The Latin of Magna Carta (1215) has *occasione parvarum sergantisarum* (v.r. *parvæ sergenteriæ*).

(*a*) **1449** *Rolls of Parlt.* V. 167/2 His Auncestres..have holden..the Manoir..by Graunte Sergeaunte. **1523** [see (*b*) below]. *a* **1625** SIR H. FINCH *Law* (1636) 154 Euery grand Serieanty is a tenure in chiefe, being of none but of the King, to doe vnto him a more speciall seruice whatsoeuer by the person of a man, as to beare his Banner or Lance, to lead his horse, to carry the sword before him at his coronation [etc.]. **1695** GIBSON *Camden's Brit.* 55 Brienston..was held in Grand Sergeanty by a pretty odd jocular tenure. **1766** BLACKSTONE *Comm.* II. v. 73 Such was the tenure by grand serjeanty, *per magnum servitium*, whereby the tenant was bound, instead of serving the king generally in his wars, to do some special honorary service to the king in person; as to carry his banner, his sword, or the like; or to be his butler, champion, or other officer at his coronation. **1818** CRUISE *Digest* (ed. 2) III. 118 The office of High Steward was originally annexed to the manor of Hinckley in Leicestershire, and held in grand serjeanty. **1875** STUBBS *Const. Hist.* I. xi. 344 These [offices] had become.. hereditary grand serjeanties.

(*b*) **1523** FITZHERB. *Surv.* 12 And all these tenauntes maye holde their landes by dyuers tenures..as by..graunt sergentie, petyte sergentie, franke almoyne. **1544** tr. *Littleton's Tenures* 37 b, Tenure by Petyte sergeauntye. **1616** BULLOKAR *Eng. Expos.*, *Pettie Sergeantie*, a tenure of lands, holden of the king, by yeilding to him, a Buckler, Arrow, Bow, or such like seruice. **1875** DIGBY *Real Prop.* i. (1876) 49 When land was held of the king not by military service, but under the obligation to render some small thing 'belonging to war', as, for instance, to 'yield to him yearly a bow or a sword, or a dagger, or a knife, or a pair of gilt spurs, or an arrow or divers arrows', this was called tenure by petit serjeanty.

†**2.** 'Sergeants' or squires collectively. *Obs.*

*c* **1330** R. BRUNNE *Chron. Wace* (Rolls) 11979 Alle armed men,..Wyþoute fotmen & seriauntye [*v.r.* sargeancie].

†**sergelim.** *Obs.* Also 6 zerzelnie, 6–7 zerzeline, 7 schirgelim, sergelin. [a. Pg. *gergelim*, *zirgelin*, a. Arab. *juljulī*, also *juljulān*.] = SESAMUM.

**1588** HICKOCK tr. *C. Frederick's Voy.* 22 b, Mirabolany.. long Pepper, Oyle of Zerzeline. **1698** PETIVER in *Phil. Trans.* XX. 314 Mixt with the Oyl Sergelin it stops pissing of Blood. *Ibid.* 322 Oyl of Schirgelim. **1707** SLOANE *Jamaica* I. 126 The Root boil'd in Sergelim Oil..takes away freckles or spots.

**sergend, -ent,** obs. forms of SERGEANT.

**sergette** (sɜːˈdʒɛt). [a. F. *sergette*, dim. of *serge*.] See quot.

**1858** SIMMONDS *Dict. Trade*, *Sergette*, a thin and slight serge.

**sergiand, -iant, -iaunt(e, sergond, -ont(e,** obs. ff. SERGEANT.

**sergre(i)ant**: see SERGEANT *Her*.

**seri,** var. SIRIH.

**seri,** obs. form of SORRY.

**serial** ('sɪərɪəl), *a.* and *sb.* [ad. mod.L. *seriālis*, f. *seri-ēs*: see SERIES and -AL[1]. Cf. F. *sérial* (1861), *sériel* (1874).] **A.** *adj.* **a.** Belonging to, forming part of, or consisting of a series; taking place or occurring in a regular succession.

**1840** A. BRISBANE tr. *Fourier's Social Destiny* xxiv. 344 Industry was developed sufficiently..to admit of the application of the Serial mechanism to it. **1854** *Fairholt's Dict. Terms Art* s.v., Serial Pictures are of that order in which a story is carried on consecutively, such as the four seasons, the four ages, &c. **1855** SPENCER *Princ. Psychol.* (1872) II. 16 A thinking of the three in serial order—first, second, third. **1864** *Realm* 6 July 8 The last performances of all the great serial concerts.

**b.** *spec.* of the publication of a literary work, *esp.* a story, in successive instalments (as in a periodical magazine or newspaper). Also of a radio play: broadcast in (usu. weekly) episodes.

***serial rights***, rights attaching to the publication of a story in serial form.

**1841** F. VESEY *Decl. Eng. Lang.* 86 Serial publication. **1867** E. YATES *Black Sheep* xxxi, She..had set herself to read the serial story. **1874** *Athenæum* 28 Feb. 293/1 After contributing to the newspapers and the magazines, [he] became a serial novelist. **1879** *19th Cent.* 997 Country journals,..instead of using an inferior article, will often purchase the 'serial right', as it is called, of stories which have already appeared elsewhere. **1890** [see RIGHT *sb.*[1] 9 f]. **1903** J. LONDON *Let.* 10 Mar. (1966) 150 The serial right has passed out of my hands. **1933** *B.B.C. Year-Bk. 1934* 213 Serial plays were a popular innovation: and their exciting episodes seemed to have appealed to..as many grown-ups as youngsters. **1944** *R.A.F. Jrnl.* Aug. 290 The American market..still offers big money for serial rights. **1955** *Radio Times* 22 Apr. 42/1 A new serial play in six parts written for broadcasting. **1960** *B.B.C. Handbk.* 68 An increased output of serial plays and characterized documentaries. **1970** [see *film rights* s.v. FILM *sb.* 7 c].

**c.** In scientific use; *esp.* applied to the disposition of the parts of an organism in a straight line or longitudinal succession. ***serial section***, each of a series of sections through tissue made in successive parallel planes; hence ***serial-section*** vb. trans., ***serial sectioning*** vbl. sb. ***serial temperatures***, temperatures taken at different successive depths between the bottom and the surface of water. In Computing = SEQUENTIAL *a.* 2 b.

**1855** T. WILLIAMS in *Ann. & Mag. Nat. Hist.* Ser. II. XVI. 405 The serial history of any given structural element of any given complex organ. **1857** A. GRAY *First Less. Bot.* (1866) Gloss., *Serial*, or *Seriate*, in rows. **1868** SPENCER *Princ. Psychol.* (1872) I. 16 They preserve a serial arrangement: their aggregation is little more than that of close linear succession. **1872** HUMPHRY *Myology* 9 The transverse septa, a serial continuation of those in the tail, are directed from the median line above. **1872** MIVART *Elem. Anat.* 10 Serial symmetry may be much less and much more developed than we find it to be in man. **1877** THOMSON *Voy. Challenger* I. 11 Taking bottom and serial temperatures. **1884** BOWER & SCOTT *De Bary's Phaner.* 109 The serial arrangement of the elements of the cork perpendicular to the surface is always very regularly preserved. **1885** A. B. LEE *Microtomist's Vade-Mecum* xxiv. 203 (*heading*) Serial section mounting. **1897** M. L. HUGHES *Mediterranean Fever* iii. 136 The qualitative alterations are both nodal and serial. **1908** *Q. Jrnl. Exper. Physiol.* I. 129 Where the epithelium persists ..serial sections show that the cleft is completely closed by it. **1948** *Gloss. Computer Terms* (U.S. Office of Naval Res. Special Devices Center: M.I.T. Servomechanisms Lab. Rep. R-138) 10 *Serial programming*, execution of complete arithmetic operations one at a time. Coding is simpler and easier to organize where simultaneous arithmetic operations are avoided. Serial programming is possible with either parallel or serial digit transmission. **1960** GREGORY & VAN HORN *Automatic Data-Processing Systems* viii. 248 Latency time for instructions stored in serial-access memories can increase program running time enough to warrant using other arrangements for storing instructions. **1961** *Lancet* 2 Sept. 523/1 The hypothalami..were embedded in celloidin and serial-sectioned. **1964** G. H. HAGGIS et al. *Introd. Molecular Biol.* v. 113 Consideration of the confusion which would result from the examination of fifty serial-section electron microscope pictures placed on top of each other. **1969** P. B. JORDAIN *Condensed Computer Encycl.* 449 In character-oriented memory computers, serial addition permits forming sums with inexpensive hardware... In faster, word-organized computers, parallel addition is used. **1977** *Sci. Amer.* Sept. 130/1 Serial-access and block-access memories have access times that depend on the storage location selected. **1979** *Nature* 22 Feb. 596/2 Here was a man who had pioneered .. the technique of serial sectioning, which enabled palaeontologists to examine the internal structures of fossils that would never have been accessible for study.

**d.** *Biol.* Involving or produced by the propagation of a micro-organism or tissue by means of a series of cultures, each grown from material derived from the previous one.

**1904** *Proc. Amer. Acad. Arts & Sci.* XL. 277 In investigating the persistence of the (+) and (−) characters in the individual strains, the writer has begun a number of serial cultures. **1947** *Ann. Rev. Microbiol.* I. 26 During the early period of study the original culture on serial plating continued to produce colonies about 5 per cent of which contained only $z_{30}$ and 95 per cent contained $z_{30}z_{31}$. **1970** L. T. MORTON *Med. Bibliogr.* (ed. 3) 609 Laveran and Mesnil discovered that trypanosomes could be maintained indefinitely in rats and mice by serial passage.

**e.** *Educ.* and *Psychol.*: ***serial learning***, the learning of words, numbers, etc., as a series so that each item acts as a stimulus for the next; ***serial position***, the position of items in a serial test studied for its effect on learning; hence *attrib.* as ***serial-position curve, effect***; ***serial test***, a test of ability that makes use of items in serial arrangement; hence ***serial testing***. Also ***serial reproduction***.

**1926** H. HEAD *Aphasia* I. II. i. 149 The order in which these serial tests are applied must be varied to suit the circumstances of the case. **1926** *Jrnl. Exper. Psychol.* IX. 195 (*title*) Specific serial learning; a study of backward association. **1926** *Amer. Jrnl. Psychol.* XXXVII. 538 It is apparent .. that the effects of serial position upon memorization still constitute something of an issue. **1932** F. C. BARTLETT *Remembering* vii. 173 There is some suggestion that material treated by way of serial reproduction may gain a kind of group stamp or character. **1948** E. R. HILGARD *Theories of Learning* iv. 97 (*caption*) Serial position effect in the memorization of a list of 15 nonsense syllables. **1952** McGEOCH & IRION *Psychol. Hum. Learning* iv. 115 (*heading*) Learning as a function of serial position. *Ibid.* x. 369 The results of one series of experiments by the method of serial reproduction .. are important for their bearing upon the social diffusion of information. **1962** E. R. HILGARD *Introd. Psychol.* (ed. 3) ix. 273/2 Serial learning is easier than paired-associates learning. **1971** *Jrnl. Gen. Psychol.* LXXXV. 100 RFT performance was not found to be stable .. but rather changed in the direction of greater field dependence on serial testing. **1972** *Jrnl. Social Psychol.* LXXXVI. 106 For both liked and disliked names the typical serial position curve was noted with most errors occurring in the middle of the lists. **1979** A. C. CATANIA *Learning* x. 243 Another variety of intraverbal relation occurs in serial learning, the learning of a list of items in a particular order.

**f.** In grammatical terminology; *spec.* in certain West African languages, designating a construction consisting of a series of verbs.

**1933** L. BLOOMFIELD *Language* xii. 195 Endocentric constructions are of two kinds, *co-ordinative* (or *serial*) and *subordinative* (or *attributive*). **1957** S. POTTER *Mod. Linguistics* v. 114 It [*sc.* the phrase *good men*] is a subordinate or attributive construction as opposed to such a phrase as *men and women*, which is said to be co-ordinate or serial. **1963** *Jrnl. Afr. Languages* II. II. 145 One .. feature of the syntax of Twi and many other West African languages which seems to have escaped the notice of the grammar-writers is that the only possible position for an object pronoun is immediately after a verb... It is necessary to introduce an extra verb to take the extra object pronoun... This introduction of an extra verb in this way results in a *serial verbal construction*. **1971** G. ANSRE in J. Spencer *Eng. Lang. W. Afr.* 157 Many of them [*sc.* the languages of West Africa] exhibit similarities in their grammatical patterning, such as the occurrence of a sequence of verbal forms within the same sentence which has come to be known as 'serial verbal construction'. **1977** E. A. GREGERSEN *Lang. in Afr.* v. 49 A distinctive feature of many West African languages is a multiple verb construction, known in the literature as serial verbs.

**g.** ***serial number***, a number assigned to a person, item, etc., indicating position in a series; *spec.* a number printed on a banknote or manufactured article by which it can be identified.

**1935** F. W. CROFT *Crime at Guildford* xiv. 201 All these high-class cameras bore a serial number. **1938** L. M. HARROD *Librarians' Gloss.* 135 *Serial Number*, the number indicating the order of publication in a series. **1959** *Ibid.* (ed. 2) 246 *Serial Number*... 2. One of the consecutive numbers appearing in front of an entry in a bibliography or catalogue. **1960** *Bedside 'Guardian'* IX. 135 It shows a willingness to surrender but a refusal to reveal one's serial number. **1962** L. DEIGHTON *Ipcress File* i. 11 People posted to him .. were .. given a new serial number from the batch .. reserved for Civil Servants seconded to military duties. **1968** 'R. SIMONS' *Death on Display* iv. 55 Crow .. took himself off to check on the serial numbers of the five-pound notes. **1971** R. K. SMITH *Ransom* (1972) III. 121 Very good field glasses for a kid... Probably stolen. He typed the serial number on the form. **1976** J. CROSBY *Snake* (1977) xxiv. 129 She paid cash with bills that had been carefully laundered... Elf doubted whether the Feds had the serial numbers on her bills but she was taking no chances.

**h.** *Mus.* Applied to a type of composition which takes as its starting-point an arrangement of the twelve tones of the chromatic scale. Cf. DODECAPHONIC *a.*, SERIES 20; *twelve-note, -tone* s.v. TWELVE *numeral a.* and *sb.* III. c.

**1947** H. SEARLE in *Penguin Music Mag.* Dec. 22 Fartein Valen, whose *Sonetto di Michelangelo* .. uses a serial technique derived from Berg. **1958** *Times* 6 June 4/4 Reti considers a number of alternatives to serial tonality, which is what dodecaphonists now practise in default of the milk of the word of Schönberg. **1963** *Times Lit. Suppl.* 3 May 320/4 Most of us reserve the term 'series' for an ordered succession of notes, as in the works of Schoenberg, but do not apply it to a collection of pitches such as are found in the works of Scriabine or Debussy. Mr. Perle extends 'serial composition' to both classes of music. **1978** P. GRIFFITHS *Conc. Hist. Mod. Music* vii. 88 The plate opposite shows the opening of his [*sc.* Webern's] Symphony (1928), arranged to display the serial structure. **1982** *Sunday Times* 25 July 41/6 In his [*sc.* Eisler's] film music he made bold use of the technique of montage, juxtaposing elements from jazz, cabaret and serial polyphony.

**B.** *sb.* **a.** A serial or periodical publication, *esp.* a novel published in serial (as opposed to *book*) form.

**1846** *Athenæum* 5 Dec. 1237/1 A fresh serial from the prolific pen of Dickens. **1859** *Jrnl. Soc. Arts* 25 Feb. 213/2 How valuable would be some of our serials with all their advertisements—The *Gentleman's Magazine*, for instance. **1882** A. W. WARD *Dickens* ii. 20 When the popularity of the serial was once established, it grew with extraordinary rapidity.

*attrib.* **1872** LOWELL *Milton* Wks. 1890 IV. 59 A practised serial writer.

**b.** A film shown in a number of episodes; a radio or television play broadcast in (usu.) weekly episodes.

**1914** R. GRAU *Theatre of Science* xi. 245 The latter arranged with the late Thomas W. Hanshew .. to prepare a serial. **1939** *BBC Handbk.* 20 An interesting aspect of the year's radio-dramatic work was the development of serial plays. The serial feature, which is the backbone of American radio, had made comparatively few appearances here before 1938... Publishers .. found that the 'Monte Cristo' serial caused a great demand for the novel. **1950** G. WEBB *Inside Story of Dick Barton* i. 13 One certain way of arousing interest and gaining an audience was through the medium of the radio serial. **1955** *Radio Times* 22 Apr. 21/1 *Counterspy*, the six-part serial which begins in Children's Hour on Friday. **1964** K. C. LAHUE (*title*) Continued next week: a history of the moving picture serial. **1974** *Broadcast* 22 July 14/1 There is abundant evidence that the serial, or its twin brother the series, is a popular form of TV programming. People seem to like stories in which the same characters appear and reappear.

Hence **seriality** (sɪərɪˈælɪtɪ), serial arrangement.

**1855** SPENCER *Princ. Psychol.* IV. i. 500 The advance of the correspondence of itself necessitates a growing seriality in the psychical changes.

**serial**, variant of CERRIAL *a. Obs.*

**serialism** (ˈsɪərɪəlɪz(ə)m). [f. SERIAL *a.* + -ISM: cf. next.] **1.** The name given by J. W. Dunne (1875–1949) to a theory of the serial nature of time, which he evolved to account for the phenomenon of precognition, esp. in dreams (see quots.).

**1927** J. W. DUNNE *Exper. with Time* xxi. 153 The serialism of the fields of presentation. *Ibid.* xxvi. 206 Serialism as a theory of the Universe. **1934** *Discovery* Aug. 239/1 His theory that in dreams the dreamer appears sometimes to move out of one dimension of time into another. Serialism, as Mr. Dunne terms his main principle, is a fascinating idea. **1937** *Mind* XLVI. 165 The novelty of Serialism lies in this: in a Serial Universe it is permissible to rotate the geometrically mapped-out axis of a time-dimension ($T_2$) until its divisions coincide with those of a time ($T_1$) one dimension lower. **1974** *Country Life* 7 Feb. 233/1 J. W. Dunne's theory of Serialism .. that we may discover the future in our dreams.

**2.** A belief or assumption that every process takes place in a regular succession.

**1943** C. S. LEWIS *Abolition of Man* iii. 39 Such a reply springs from the fatal serialism of the modern imagination —the image of infinite unilinear progression which so haunts our minds... We tend to think of every process as if it must be like the numeral series.

**3.** *Mus.* The practice or principles of serial composition.

**1958** [see ATONAL *a.*]. **1967** *Spectator* 18 Aug. 200/1 If we are to assume that atonality refers to the idiom characterising Schoenberg's works prior to his adoption of serialism .. then Penderecki's Passion .. does not come into this category. **1977** P. JOHNSON *Enemies of Society* xvii. 228 Serialism does not provide a workable order, at least for most listeners, because the structure is mathematical rather than aural.

**serialist** (ˈsɪərɪəlɪst). [f. SERIAL *a.* + -IST.]

**1.** A writer of serials.

**1846** *Blackw. Mag.* LX. 594 The characters depicted by some of our later serialists. **1902** A. BENNETT *Truth about Author* xii, in *Academy* 5 July 44/2, I found an outlet .. more remunerative than the concoction of serials; and I am a serialist no longer.

**2.** One who holds views that accord with a serial theory; *spec.* one who learns by studying items arranged in a series.

**1936** *Mind* XLV. 31 The controversy between substrativists and serialists is one of long standing. **1975** G. PASK *Conversation, Cognition & Learning* 561 Serialists learn, remember and recapitulate a body of information in small, well-defined and sequentially-ordered segments.

**3.** *Mus.* A composer or advocate of serial music.

**1959** *Atlantic Monthly* Feb. 88/2, I do believe, however, that success will not wholly pass by the rhythmic experimenters and the 100 per cent serialists. **1962** *Times* 26 Feb. 14/7 The two pieces .. illustrated the difference of outlook between the newest generation of English serialists and their predecessors. **1980** *Early Music* Apr. 253/3 Many of these works are characterized by a degree of formal organization which would delight serialists.

**4.** *attrib.* or as *adj.*

**1936** *Mind* XLV. 31 The serialist hypothesis .. seems to me beset with difficulties and obscurities. **1959** *Times* 13 Feb. 13/4 The Institute of Contemporary Arts is presenting a whole serialist programme. **1975** G. PASK *Conversation, Cognition & Learning* iv. 108 The respondent is free to learn in any way and is found to adopt a holist or serialist approach.

**serialization.** [-IZATION.] **1.** Publication in serial form; also, the broadcasting on radio or television, in serial form, of a dramatized novel etc.

**1892** *Author* July 49/1 It is desirable that authors should understand the difficulties with which serialisation is surrounded. **1965** *Radio Times* 18 Feb. 15/1 *The Mill on the Floss*, of which a four-part serialisation .. begins tonight. **1972** *Daily Tel.* 31 Jan. 7/2 This serialisation may well prove such compulsive viewing as to create new interest in this neglected German liberal.

**2.** *gen.* The action or state of forming a series.

**1857** H. CLAPP tr. *Fourier's Social Destiny* I. iv. 37 The Administrative unity of the Globe is nothing more nor less than the Serialization of the general interests, operations and relations of the Human Race. **1962** *Listener* 22 Mar. 513/1 The fate of man is now 'serialization'. We lose our individuality and our capacity for action by being turned into merely one term in a series which could equally well be replaced by any other term. **1966** A. MANSER *Sartre* xiii. 214 Sartre, in demanding the abolition of serialisation, seems to be asking for an impossible Utopia.

**3.** *Mus.* The composition of serial music.

**1959** *Observer* 23 Aug 7/3 This group [of composers] practices a technique of *total serialisation*, whereby not merely notes but all elements of music (pitch, instrumentation, rhythm, volume, etc.) are used in row formation, i.e., in regular patterns. **1966** F. HOYLE *October First is too Late* xi. 126 The style of this Greek music was more akin to the key system than to the modern serialization. **1976** P. STADLEN in D. Villiers *Next Year in Jerusalem* 328 Stravinsky .. turned into a serial convert in his old age... In total serialization, the individual note no longer functions as part of a musical thought.

**serialize,** *v.* [-IZE.] **a.** To publish in serial form. Also, to broadcast serially; to publish the work of (an author) in serial form.

**1892** *Author* July 48/2 If a story is *serialized* in England and is not serialized simultaneously in the States, the American copyright is of course seriously jeopardised. **1893** *Athenæum* 11 Nov. 663/3 The serializing of fiction. **1923** S. HOCKING *My Book of Memory* xiii. 186, I submitted it to other editors who had serialized my stories, but with the same result. *a* **1965** A. CHRISTIE *Autobiogr.* (1977) VIII. 414, I was beginning to be serialised in America... The money .. [was] far larger than anything I ever made from serial rights in Britain. **1971** *Guardian* 2 Mar. 9/3 The paperback sales of Compton Mackenzie's 'Sinister Street' jumped from a steady annual 2,000 to 16,000 when BBC-2 serialised the book.

**b.** To arrange in a series.

**1857** H. CLAPP tr. *Fourier's Social Destiny* I. i. 8 These three Faculties or Forces serialize the play and action of the other Motors of the Soul. **1907** W. JAMES *Pragmatism* v. 172 To frame some system of concepts mentally classified, serialized, or connected in some intellectual way.

**c.** *Mus.* To compose according to a serial technique.

**1959** *Listener* 8 Oct. 564/1 The fashionable Webernites went on to serialize not only the notes themselves, but the silences, the durations, the dynamic indications .. all by the number twelve. **1960** *Twentieth Century* Nov. 460 A note was said .. to exist in a *field* determined by the possible error of the performer. This element was immediately serialized.

Hence **ˈserialized, ˈserializing** *ppl. adjs.*

**1857** H. CLAPP tr. *Fourier's Social Destiny* I. iv. 32 The primary functions of the three Regulative or Serializing Faculties. **1921** *Public Opinion* 26 Aug. 204/2 Take the average short story, or serialised novel, and test it for the real wisdom involved. **1976** A. SHERIDAN-SMITH tr. *Sartre's Critique of Dialectical Reason* I. iv. 312 This serialised antagonism .. constitutes an initial structure of alterity. **1976** M. SPARK *Takeover* xi. 154 The theme of Hubert had become one of Mary's favourite serialized entertainments.

**serially** (ˈsɪərɪəlɪ), *adv.* [f. SERIAL *a.* + -LY[2].] **a.** In a series, in series, in serial arrangement; **b.** in serial form, as a serial.

**1854** OWEN in *Orr's Circ. Sci., Org. Nat.* I. 203 A supplementary costal piece, serially homologous with the appendage to the proper pleurapophysis. **1870** *Daily Tel.* 22 Sept., Small parties of the sparse artillerists hurrying along behind the wall from gun to gun, firing progressively and serially. **1872** *Athenæum* 1 June 681/1 However 'Middlemarch' may appear, it is clear that it has not been written, although published, serially. **1884** BOWER & SCOTT *De Bary's Phaner.* 163 Round bordered pits, arranged in left-handed oblique series, with the inner apertures serially coalescent into long slits.

†**ˈSerian,** *a. Obs. rare.* [f. SER-ES + -IAN.] ***Serian worm***, silkworm. (Cf. SEREAN, SERIC.)

**1633** P. FLETCHER *Purple Isl.* XII. iii, No Serian worms .. that with their threed Draw out their silken lives.

**seriand, -ant, -antie,** etc.: see SERGEANT, -Y.

**seriary** (ˈsɪərɪərɪ), *a. rare.* [f. SERI-ES + -ARY[1]. Cf. F. *sériaire*, Sp. *seriario.*] Serial.

**1900** DENIKER *Races of Man* 65 The characters called seriary, to which we have recourse in order to compare man with animals which bear the closest resemblance to him.

**seriate** (ˈsɪərɪət), *a.* Chiefly *Zool.* and *Bot.* [ad. mod.L. **seriāt-us*, f. SERIES.] Arranged or occurring in one or more series or rows.

**1846** DANA *Zooph.* (1848) 139 Tubercles small, .. vertically seriate. **1857** [see SERIAL A. c]. **1870** HOOKER *Stud. Flora* 137 Sedum acre .. leaves obscurely 6-seriate. **1874** T. HARDY *Far fr. Mad. Crowd* xxvi, The remainder was a mere question of time and natural seriate changes.

So 'seriated *a.*; hence 'seriately *adv.*, in series.
**1846** DANA *Zooph.* (1848) 266 Disks seriately and reticulately budding. **1872** H. C. WOOD *Fresh-w. Algæ* 227 The gelatinous tubes or sheaths in which the cells are seriated are very obvious. **1874** LEWES *Probl. Life & Mind* Ser. I. I. 120 Vitality and Sensibility may be said to rest on seriated Change.

**seriate** ('sɪərɪeɪt), *v.* [Back-formation from SERIATION.] *trans.* To arrange (items) in a sequence according to prescribed criteria.
**1944** *Genetics* XXIX. 526 We shall refer to these and other genes in the series, requiring testers to distinguish them and to seriate them, as iso-alleles. **1968** D. L. CLARKE *Analytical Archæol.* II. xi. 453 Initially, the matrix technique was devised for seriating assemblages in terms of their proportions of component types. **1972** *Computers & Humanities* VI. 179 The program constructs a classification of objects and seriates the classes by minimizing the distance according to the Brainerd Robinson model of seriation.

‖**seriatim** (sɪərɪ'eɪtɪm), *adv.* (and *a.*) [med.L., f. L. *seri-ēs* after GRADATIM, LITERATIM.] One after another, one by one in succession.
**1680** C. HATTON *Corr.* (Camden) I. 225 Ye judges did every one of them seriatim declare yt that board was a proper place of judicature of state affaires. *a* **1734** NORTH *Exam.* I. ii. §80 (1740) 72 The Judges thought fit to give their Judgments, *seriatim*, after solemn Argument had. **1815** KIRBY & SP. *Entomol.* x. I. 303 If not content with taking them [*sc.* spiders] seriatim you should feel desirous of eating them by handfulls. **1838** DICKENS *Nich. Nick.* xv, Mr. and Mrs. Kenwigs thanked every lady and gentleman, *seriatim*, for the favour of their company. **1871** SPENCER *Princ. Psychol.* (1872) II. 343 This question subdivides into several questions, which we will consider *seriatim*.
**b.** as *adj.* Following one after the other. *rare.*
**1871** EARLE *Philol. Eng. Tongue* x. 497 There are places where force would be lost by dividing it into two or three successive and *seriatim* sentences.

**seriation** (sɪərɪ'eɪʃən). [ad. mod.L. **seriātiōn-em*, f. *seri-ēs*: see SERIES and -ATION.] Succession in series, serial succession; formation of or into a series. In mod. use, esp. in *Archæol.*, the action or result of arranging items in a sequence according to prescribed criteria.
**1658** J. ROBINSON *Endoxa* iv. 30 Where there is no fear of enormity, there may be a secure seriation of supremacy. **1866** ODLING *Anim. Chem.* 47 The acids of these two series presented..a marked parallelism in their constitution, seriation, and properties. **1874** LEWES *Probl. Life & Mind* Ser. I. I. 144 The demonstration that thinking is seriation. **1887** *Athenæum* 3 Sept. 299/3 In the seriation of the [chemical] elements certain gaps occur. **1917** *Anthrop. Papers Amer. Mus. Nat. Hist.* XVIII. 283 We have found that another seriation based on the percentages of redware yields a cheaper result. **1944** *Genetics* XXIX. 534 The test indicated that the males carried bobbed alleles capable of seriation when in combination with the testes. But in homozygous condition several of these seriated alleles produced identical maximum bristle types. **1951** G. W. BRAINERD in *Amer. Antiq.* XVI. 304/1 If a series of collections comes from a culture changing through time, their placement on the time axis is a function of their similarity... This..allows a 'seriation' or ordering of collections to be formed which, if time be the only factor involved, must truly represent the temporal placing of the collections. *Ibid.* 311/2, I believe that..seriations formed by this technique will allow refinements in chronology greater than those currently possible. **1966** *Amer. Anthropologist* LXVIII. 1449 When the data are very reliable.., then both ordering criteria produce the same seriation of collections. Confidence in the resulting seriation is therefore high. **1971** *World Archaeol.* III. 197 The established sequence of changing settlements also corresponded with that reached by seriation of the pottery collections from the relevant sites.

†'**seriatly**, *adv. Obs.* Also 5 seryatt-, ceriat-, 6 seryat-. [Partial anglicization of med.L. SERIATIM.] In succession, seriatim.
*c* **1450** *Cov. Myst.* (Shaks. Soc.) 273 Now I wyl fede ȝow alle with awngellys mete, Wherfore to reseyve it come fforth seryattly. *c* **1475** *Partenay* 1836 Thai..With-out tariyng to wash ther handes went; After went to sitte ther ceriatly. *c* **1520** BARCLAY *Jugurth* 37 b, To write of the besynesse and dedes of both the parties seriatly and dystincly. **1540** *St. Papers Hen. VIII*, III. 200 We have receyuid Your Graces most gracius letters..the contents wherof we have seriatly redde.

**seriaun, -auns, -aunt(e**, etc.: see SERGEANT.

**seriba**, variant of ZAREBA.

**Seric** ('sɛrɪk), *a. rare.* [ad. L. *sēric-us*, (1) belonging to the Seres, (2) of silk (neut. *sēricum* as sb., silk), = Gr. σηρικός (neut. σηρικόν silk), f. Σῆρες: see SERES.]
**1.** Chinese.
**1842** TUPPER *Proverb. Philos.* Ser. II. Introd., Unclean meats as of the clean hang upon my Seric shambles. **1840** *New Monthly Mag.* LX. 310 The pure concoction of the seric herb [= tea].
**2.** Silken.
**1886** *Edin. Rev.* July 155 The manufacture of seric stuffs.

**sericate** ('sɛrɪkeɪt). *Chem.* [f. SERIC-IC + -ATE[2].] A salt of sericic acid.
**1841** *Turner's Elem. Chem., Org.* 1084 Sericate of oxide of ethule is a colourless mobile liquid.

'**sericated**, *a. rare*[—0]. [f. L. *sēricāt-us* (f. *sēric-um* silk: see SERIC) + -ED[1].] †Clothed in silk; also = SERICEOUS.
**1623** in COCKERAM. **1860** WORCESTER, *Serricated* [sic].

**sericeo-** (sɪ'rɪʃɪəʊ), used as comb. form of L. *sēriceus* (see next) = silky and...
**1841** *Penny Cycl.* XX. 359/2 Ovaries sericeo-tomentose.

**sericeous** (sɪ'rɪʃəs), *a. Zool.* and *Bot.* [f. L. *sērice-us*, f. *sēric-um* silk (see SERIC): see -EOUS.] Silky, covered with silky down.
**1777** ROBSON *Brit. Flora* 15 *Sericeous*, covered with a down of extremely fine texture. **1819** SAMOUELLE *Entomol. Compend.* 282 Hylæus... Lip lanceolate, little sericeous. **1847** HARDY in *Proc. Berw. Nat. Club* II. No. v. 236 Shining yellow sericeous down. **1885** H. O. FORBES *Nat. Wand.* IV. App. 376 The sericeous brand on the male.

**sericic** (sɪ'rɪsɪk), *a. Chem.* [f. L. *sēric-um* silk (see SERIC) + -IC.] = MYRISTIC.
**1841** *Turner's Elem. Chem., Org.* 1083 Sericic Acid. Syn. Myristic Acid. Discovered by Playfair.

**sericiculture** ('sɛrɪsɪˌkʌltjʊə(r), -tʃə(r)). [ad. F. *sériciculture*, f. L. *sēric-um* (see SERIC) + *cultūra* CULTURE.]
= SERICULTURE. Hence ˌ**serici'cultural** *a.*, ˌ**serici'culturist**.
**1892** CROOKES tr. *Wagner's Man. Chem. Technol.* 803 Sericiculture.—Varieties of Silkworms. *Ibid.* 804 Sericiculturists become sufficiently adepts..to be able to select a sufficient number of cocoons of each sex.

**sericin** ('sɛrɪsɪn). *Chem.* Also -ine. [Formed as SERICIC + -IN[1].]
**1.** = MYRISTIN.
**1841** *Turner's Elem. Chem., Org.* 1083 Sericate of oxide of glycerule (sericine or myristine).
**2.** The gelatinous constituent of silk.
**1868** BLOXAM *Chem.* §446. **1886** tr. *Benedikt's Chem. Coal-tar Colours* 39 Both fibroine and sericine (silk-glue) consist of carbon, nitrogen, hydrogen and oxygen.

**sericipary** (sɛrɪ'sɪpərɪ), *a. rare.* [f. L. *sēricum* silk + *-par-us* (-PAROUS) + -Y.] Producing silk.
**1869** *Eng. Mech.* 24 Dec. 350/3 A double apparatus.. situated on either side of the intestinal canal, and below it, called the sericipary gland.

**sericite** ('sɛrɪsaɪt). *Min.* [ad. G. *sericit* (1852), f. L. *sēric-um* silk: see SERIC and -ITE[1] 2 b.] A fibrous variety of muscovite.
**1854** DANA *Syst. Min.* (ed. 4) II. 223 Sericite of K. List, is regarded by him as near Damourite. **1866** LAWRENCE tr. *Cotta's Rocks Classified* 23 Sericite, a green mineral, of silky lustre.
**b.** *attrib.* = SERICITIC.
**1879** RUTLEY *Study of Rocks* 296 *Sericite-Schist.*—This is a schistose rock closely allied to the porphyroids, and consists of sericite, fragments of quartz [etc.]. **1884** *Nature* 13 Nov. 35/1 Sericite mica.
Hence **sericitic** (sɛrɪ'sɪtɪk) *a.*, containing or having the character of sericite.
**1814** *Nature* 13 Nov. 34/1 A slight development of sericitic mica.

**sericitization.** [f. prec.: see -IZATION.] Conversion into, or replacement by, sericite.
**1893** GEIKIE *Text-bk. Geol.* IV. VIII. ii. (ed. 3) 617 Where the silky unctuous sericite has been developed from orthoclase (sericitization). **1908** *Trans. N.Z. Inst.* XLI. 69 These figures show..that the type of rock-alteration may be regarded as partial sericitization. **1962** W. A. DEER et al. *Rock-Forming Minerals* III. 24 This sericitization may begin, and be complete, at an early stage of the metamorphism.
Hence '**sericitized** *ppl. a.*, converted into (a form containing) sericite.
**1935** *Geol. Mag.* LXXII. 276 Plagioclase..occurs as large sericitized laths. **1965** G. J. WILLIAMS *Econ. Geol. N.Z.* xiii. 195/2 The wall-rocks are sericitized and chloritized.

†**sericon.** *Alch. Obs.* [a. med.L. *sericon* (indeclinable).
In *Turbæ Philosophorum alterum exemplar*, printed in *Artis Auriferæ quam Chemiam vocant volumen primum* (Basileæ 1593) 138, 'sericon' is mentioned (in connexion with 'magnesia': see MAGNESIA 1) as 'a composition which is called by ten names', and which is one of the ingredients in 'the ferment of gold'. That the word originally stood for some real chemical substance is not improbable, but its proper meaning and etymology (perh. Arabic: ? cf. ZIRCON) are obscure. There is no ground for identifying it with mod.L. *sericum* (prob. merely a use of L. *sēricum* silk) cited by writers of the 18th c. as a name for the flowers of zinc. On the other hand, '*Sericum*, an old name for minium', in some modern dictionaries, may represent a conjecture as to the meaning of the alchemical term.]
A substance supposed to be concerned in the transmutation of inferior metals into gold.
The explanation given in Gifford's note on the Jonson passage, 'the red tincture', appears to be an unauthorized conjecture.
?**15..** in Ashmole *Theat. Chem.* (1652) 428 This centrall Earth who can it take, It and *Sercion* [sic] do our Maistry make. **1610** B. JONSON *Alch.* II. v, Both *Sericon*, and *Bufo* shall be lost.

‖**sericterium** (sɛrɪk'tɪərɪəm). *Entom.* Pl. -eria (-'ɪərɪə). Also anglicized serictery (sɪ'rɪktərɪ). [mod.L., irreg. f. Gr. σηρικόν silk (see SERIC) + -τηριον, after *sialisterium* (σιαλιστήριον) salivary gland of insects.] A glandular apparatus in silkworms for the production of silk; a silk or spinning gland.
**1826** KIRBY & SP. *Entomol.* xli. (1828) IV. 137 In the sericterium the fluid that produces it [*sc.* silk] is sometimes white or grey. **1875** BLAKE *Zool.* 287 The two fine filaments from the sericteria are glued together by another secretion from a small gland. **1898** PACKARD *Text-bk. Entomol.* 337 In the imago the sericteries revert to their primitive shape and use as salivary glands.

**sericultural** (sɛrɪ'kʌltjʊərəl, -tʃ-), *a.* [f. next + -AL[1].] Pertaining to or engaged in sericulture.
**1864** *Q. Jrnl. Sci.* I. 515 The sericultural departments of France. **1886** WARDLE *Catal. India Silk Culture* 28 Aids to Sericultural Study.

**sericulture** ('sɛrɪkʌltjʊə(r), -tʃə(r)). [Shortened ad. F. *sériciculture*: see SERICICULTURE.] The production of raw silk and the rearing of silkworms for the purpose.
**1851–4** *Tomlinson's Cycl. Useful Arts* (1867) II. 520/2 The Central Society of Sericulture of France. **1863** *All Year Round* 11 July 467/1 Model silkworm houses..would greatly tend to popularise this new branch of sericulture. **1881** WARDLE *Wild Silks of India* 53 Eria sericulture plantations.
Hence **seri'culturist**, one engaged in sericulture, a silk-grower.
**1864** *Q. Jrnl. Sci.* I. 515 He recommends the sericulturist to separate his dark worms from the general stock.

**seridclath**, northern f. *cered cloth*: see CERED.
**1438–9** *Durham Acc. Rolls* (Surtees) 408 In 22 virgis panni linei empt. pro le Seridclath pro vestimentis.

†**serie.** *Obs.* [app. ad. L. *seriēs*: see SERIES.] Succession of points in an argument.
*c* **1386** CHAUCER *Knt.'s T.* 2209 What may I concluden of this long serye, But after wo I rede vs to be merye?

**seriea(u)nt, -y**, obs. forms of SERGEANT, -Y.

**seriema** (sɛrɪ'iːmə), **çariama, cariama** (sæ-, kærɪ'ɑːmə). Also siriema. [mod.L. *seriema* (A. de St. Hilaire, 1830), *cariama* (Brisson, 1760), a. Tupi *siriema*, *sariama*, *çariama*, explained by Ruiz de Montaya as = crested. The erroneous form *cariama* (without cedilla) comes down from Marcgrav, *Hist. Nat. Brasil.* 1648.] A large long-legged crested bird, *Cariama cristata*, inhabiting parts of Brazil; the crested screamer.
**1836** *Proc. Zool. Soc.* 30 Though the Çariama, in its osseous structure, exhibits but little resemblance to the Birds of the Raptorial order. **1860** *Ibid.* 334 A New Form of Grallatorial Bird nearly allied to the Cariama. **1869** R. F. BURTON *Highl. Brazil* II. 26 The Siriéma, that hunted the serpents from our path. **1870** *Proc. Zool. Soc.* 666 Burmeister's Cariama. **1895** *Pop. Sci. Monthly* XLVI. 770 The far-famed seriema (*Dicholophus cristatus*), a form that has puzzled the best of taxonomers since the middle of the seventeenth century.

**series** ('sɪəriːz, formerly 'sɪərɪiːz). Pl. (8–) series, (7–8, *rare* in 9) serieses, (7–8) series's. [a. L. *seriēs* row, chain, series, f. *ser-ĕre* to join, connect. Cf. F. *série*, It., Sp., Pg. *serie*.]
**I.** General senses.
**1.** A number or set *of* material things of one kind ranged in a line, either contiguously or at more or less regular intervals; a range or continued spatial succession of similar objects; †in early use applied to a row of building.
**1611** CORYAT *Crudities* 454 A very faire architectonical Machine..in which are three degrees, whereof each contayneth a faire Statue... At the very toppe of this rowe or *series* of worke is erected a most excellent effigies of a Cocke. *Ibid.* 636 A faire front of building... Which front or *series* extendeth it selfe in a goodly length. **1638** SIR T. HERBERT *Trav.* (ed. 2) 163 For five hundred paces it every way gives a *series* of all sorts of Persian fruits and flowers. **1812** MISS MITFORD in L'Estrange *Life* (1870) I. 191 In Oxfordshire, where I saw a landscape, or rather a series of landscapes, of singular beauty. **1856** EMERSON *Eng. Traits, Aristocracy* Wks. (Bohn) II. 81 The series of squares called Belgravia. **1872** H. C. WOOD *Fresh-w. Algæ* 68 Cells mostly arranged in a simple or double series in the filament.
**2. a.** A number *of* things of one kind (chiefly immaterial, as events, actions, conditions, periods of time) following one another in temporal succession, or in the order of discourse or reasoning.
**1618** CHAPMAN *Hesiod's Georg.* II. 455 The noisome gales, ..that incense the seas And raise together in one *series* Ioues Autumne dashes. **1646** HOWELL *Lewis XIII*, 20 So was his whole life attended with a series of good successes. **1656** tr. *Hobbes' Elem. Philos.* I All men can reason to some degree, ..but where there is need of a long series of Reasons, there most men wander out of the way. **1663** POWER *Exp. Philos.* II. 122 The Series and Chain of our former Experiments. **1709** FELTON *Diss. Classics* (1718) 188 The worst Province an Historian can fall upon, is a Series of barren Times, in which nothing remarkable happeneth. **1765** W. WARD *Grammar* IV. iv. 167 Several participles cannot conveniently be used so as to affect every part of long serieses of words immediately. **1797** *Encycl. Brit.* (ed. 3) XVIII. 514/1 These different heights of tide are observed to succeed each other in a regular series... This series is completed in about 15 days... Two serieses are completed in the exact time of a lunation. **1837** CARLYLE *Fr. Rev.* II. I. vi, What a hoping People he had, judge by the fact, and series of facts, now to be noted. **1871** R. W. DALE *Commandm.* x. 242 These Commandments occupy a great place in a series of Divine revelations. **1886** *Act 49 & 50 Vict.* c. 44 §13 That the repayment of the money to be borrowed should be spread over a series of years.
*with pl. concord.* **1864** BABBAGE *Passages* 46 Another series of experiments were..made. **1871** MORLEY *Carlyle* in *Crit. Misc.* Ser. I. 245 A complex series of historic facts do not usually fit so neatly into the moral formula.

**b.** A number *of* persons in succession holding the same office or having some characteristic in common. †Also, a succession of persons in descent, a family line.

**1625** T. GODWIN *Moses & Aaron* I. v. 15 Aaron, and those that issued from his loynes, (in whom the series of Priests was continued). **1638** NABBES *Totenham Court* II. i, To make the series of their Families Spread in so many glorious divisions. **1656** BLOUNT *Glossogr.*, *Series*..an issue or descent of kindred. **1665** G. HAVERS *P. della Valle's Trav. E. India* 26 Teimùr Lenk, though extracted from the noblest blood of the Kings, yet remote from the Royal Stock by a long series. **1712** ADDISON *Spect.* No. 287 ¶6 Look into the Historian I have mentioned, or into any Series of Absolute Princes. **1776** JOHNSON in *Boswell* 16 Mar., Entails are good, because it is good to preserve in a country serieses of men, to whom the people are accustomed to look up as to their leaders. **1865** G. GROTE *Plato* I. iv. 134 Speusippus succeeded him..as teacher,..being succeeded..by Polemon, Krantor..and others in uninterrupted series.

†**c.** A catalogue, list. *Obs.*

**1656** EARL MONM. tr. *Boccalini's Advts. fr. Parnass.* I. lxxx. (1674) 108 [They] made a long and exact Series of many abuses which reigned in that State. **1660** R. COKE *Power & Subj.* 60 It is not my purpose to relate a series and catalogue of all the British Kings to the Saxon Monarchs.

†**3. a.** A succession, sequence, or continued course (*of* action or conduct, *of* time, life, etc.). *Obs.*

**1652** GAULE *Magastrom.* 152 The *series* both of fate, and of fortune. **1660** INGELO *Bentiv. & Ur.* II. (1682) 138 To devote the Series of their whole Life to the Divine honour. **1684** T. BURNET *Th. Earth* II. vii. 251 The Series of Providence that was to follow in this Earth. *Ibid.* xi. 316 No long Series's of Providence. **1690** CHILD *Disc. Trade* 190 After such a long series of time. **1725** POPE *Odyss.* III. 140 How trace the tedious series of our fate? **1772** BURKE *Corr.* (1844) I. 373 A more decent..and prudent series of proceeding. **1805** T. LINDLEY *Voy. Brazil* 11 His life had been a series of industry. **1815** JANE AUSTEN *Emma* xxii, After a series of what had appeared to him strong encouragement.

†**b.** A continued state or spell. *Obs.*

**1748** *Anson's Voy.* I. x. 98 We had a series of as favourable weather, as could well be expected. *Ibid.* II. i. 111 Those.. who have endured a long series of thirst. **1793** SMEATON *Edystone L.* §149 A series of unsettled weather.

†**4.** The connected sequence (*of* discourse, writing, thought). *Obs.*

**1631** BRATHWAIT *Whimzies* Ep. Ded., As the conceit may neither taste of too much lightnesse..nor the whole passage or *series* incline to too much dulnesse. **1646** CRASHAW *Steps to Temple, Delights Muses* 104 The plyant Series of her slippery song. **1661** BOYLE *Physiol. Ess.* (1669) 31 Not to look upon any thing as my Opinion or Assertion that is not deliver'd in the entire Series of my own Words. **1667-8** S. WARD *Infidelity* (1670) 5 Reflecting..upon the Text as it lies in the Series of the Epistle. **1696** PHILLIPS, *Series*,..a continuation of Discourse. **1712** ADDISON *Spect.* No. 549 ¶1, I am engaged in this Series of Thought by a Discourse which I had..with..Sir Andrew Freeport.

†**5.** Order of succession; sequence. *Obs.*

**1611** SPEED *Hist. Gt. Brit.* VII. xii. 312 Wee haue shewed the ancient Coines of the Britaines, and obserued a series thorow the Romanes succession. **1651** N. BACON *Disc. Gov. Eng.* II. xxviii. 223 Nor [are] they good Historians, that will tell you the bare journall of Action without the *Series* of occasion. **1662** STILLINGFL. *Orig. Sacræ* II. iii. §2 It seems impossible that any thing should really alter the *series* of things, without the same power which at first produced them. **1779** JOHNSON *L.P.*, *Watts* (1868) 450 The series of his works I am not able to deduce.

**6.** A number of magnitudes, degrees of some attribute, or the like, viewed as capable of being enumerated in a progressive order. Also, a set of objects of one kind, differing progressively in size or in some other respect, or having a recognized order of enumeration.

**1786-8** (*title*) A Series of [64] points of ancient history. **1818** ACCUM *Chem. Tests* (ed. 2) 61 *note*, A series of these [test] tubes should be always ready at hand. **1859** DARWIN *Orig. Spec.* ii. (1873) 41 These differences blend into each other by an insensible series.

**II.** Technical senses.

**7.** *Math.* A set of terms in succession (finite or infinite in number) the value of each of which is determined by its ordinal position according to a definite rule known as the *law* of the series; *esp.* a set of such terms continuously added together.

See ARITHMETICAL, GEOMETRICAL, RECURRING, etc.

**1671** J. GREGORY in Rigaud *Corr. Sci. Men* (1841) II. 224 Reducing all of them [*sc.* equations] to infinite serieses. **1736** *Gentl. Mag.* VI. 739/1 Any one who is conversant in Series. **1750** *Phil. Trans.* XLVII. 20 The operation, by having two or more series's to multiply into one another, becomes very troublesome. **1791** *Ibid.* LXXXI. 148 The serieses deduced should converge. **1839** R. MURPHY *Algebr. Equat.* 92 Recurring Series have been much used..in the solution of algebraical equations. **1874** GROSS *Algebra* II. 153 Summation of Series.

*allusively.* **1836** J. GILBERT *Chr. Atonem.* ii. 59 To examine in detail the series, of which the computed sum betrays at once somewhere in the calculation so gross an error. **1853** [WHEWELL] *Plural. Worlds* v. 76 We have here to build a theory without materials;—to sum a series of which every term, so far as we know, is nothing.

**8.** A set of coins, medals, etc. belonging to a particular epoch, locality, dynasty, or government. Also, a set of postage stamps, bank notes, etc., of a particular issue.

**1697** tr. *Jobert's Knowl. Medals* 28 A Gold or Silver series of Medals. **1697** EVELYN *Numismata* 26 We begin with Heads, as best determining and guiding the Series. **1730** A. GORDON *Maffei's Amphith.* 128 Among the many and particular Series's collected by him, he has 800 Medals of Colony's, 1500 Greek Coins, and 1200 Egyptian. **1808** PINKERTON *Ess. Medals* I. 3 Serieses of Roman coins. **1867** *Philatelist* I. 23/1 New series, 4 annas, light green. *Ibid.* 129/2 The stamps which were immediately adopted for the empire [*sc.* Mexico] were the 'eagle' series. **1876** MATHEWS *Coinage of World* Introd. p. iii, A recently discovered series of Bactrian coins. **1879** H. PHILLIPS, jr. *Addit. Notes upon Coins* 3 The present medal is one of a series struck to commemorate this occurrence. **1907** *Lancet* 16 Feb. 471/1 A fresh series of 5-franc notes is about to be issued.

**9. a.** A set of literary compositions having certain features in common, published successively or intended to be read in sequence; a succession of volumes or fascicules (of a periodical, the publications of a society, etc.) forming a set by itself (distinguished as *first*, *second*, etc. *series*). Also, in recent use, a succession of books issued by one publisher in a common form and having some similarity of subject or purpose; usually with a general title, as 'the Clarendon Press Series', 'the Men of Letters Series'.

**1711** ADDISON *Spect.* No. 106 ¶6 [The Chaplain] has digested them [*sc.* Sermons] into such a Series, that they follow one another naturally. (?) **1791** (*title*) A Series of original papers on that great National Subject, The improvement of the art of Ship-building. **1813** BRYDGES (*title*) The Ruminator: containing a series of moral, critical and sentimental essays. **1832** SCOTT *Betrothed* Introd., The Tales of the Crusaders was determined upon as the title of the following series of these Novels. **1889** *Pall Mall Gaz.* 3 Aug. 1/1 Of all these *serieses* the 'Men of Letters' has, I suppose, been the most popular.

**b.** A set of radio or television programmes concerned with the same theme or having the same range of characters and broadcast in sequence.

**1949** *Radio Times* 15 July 15/1 Fifth talk in the series devoted to English and French writings on art. **1962** *Listener* 11 Oct. 581/2 A series, *Zero One*, opened with an episode called *Stone Face.* **1974** *Radio Times* 14 Mar. 18/1 Series consultant Charlie Gillett.

**10.** *Nat. Sci.* A group of individuals exhibiting similar characteristics or a constant relation between successive members: see quots.

**1823** H. T. BROOKE *Crystallogr.* 100 When the sets of new planes..are so much extended as entirely to efface the primary planes, a *series* of entirely new solids will result. **1851** MANTELL *Petrifactions* ii. §3. 116 The entire series of phalangeals with the corresponding metatarsal of a..species of Dinornis. **1857** A. GRAY *First Less. Bot.* (1866) 177 The upper Series or grade of Flowering or Phænogamous Plants, which have their counterpart in the lower Series of Flowerless or Cryptogamous Plants. *Ibid.*, The following schedule..comprises all that are generally used in a natural classification,..Series, Class, Subclass [etc.]. **1857** [see ISOLOGOUS]. **1869**, **1876** [see HOMOLOGOUS 3]. **1878** DALLINGER in *Nature* 23 May 102/2 A hitherto unrecorded organism belonging to the septic series.

**11.** *Geol.* **a.** †(i) A set of successive deposits or group of successive formations having certain common fossil or mineral features. Also used for any assemblage of successive, usu. conformable, strata (without regard to the rank of the assemblage: cf. next sense). Now *Obs.*

**1822** CONYBEARE *Outl. Geol.* II. iii. §2. 181 A zone of argilleo-calcareous beds belonging to the Purbeck series. **1827** *Trans. Geol. Soc.* II. 293 The strata..were in fact the equivalent of the oolitic series. **1836** W. BUCKLAND *Geol. & Mineral.* I. ix. 76 The Tertiary Series introduces a system of new phenomena, presenting formations in which the remains of animal and vegetable life approach gradually nearer to species of our own epoch. **1839** DE LA BECHE *Rep. Geol. Cornwall*, etc. iii. 59 The series having been slightly overlapped. **1877** HUXLEY *Physiogr.* 197 A curious series of deposits may thus be produced. **1882** A. GEIKIE *Text-bk. Geol.* 648 The rocks of the Cambrian series present great uniformity of lithological character over the globe.

(ii) *Stratigraphy.* The primary subdivision of a system, composed of a number of stages and corresponding to an epoch in time; the rocks deposited during any specific epoch.

At the 1881 meeting of the International Geological Congress, a scheme of nomenclature was adopted in which the stratigraphical terms *group, system, series, stage* in decreasing order of comprehensiveness correspond to the terms *era, period, epoch, age* for time intervals. The *system* and its subdivisions are now regarded as the primary time-stratigraphical terms, and the use of *group* in this sense is deprecated.

**1881** *Geol. Mag.* Decade II. VIII. 558 The final result of the discussions was the adoption of terms in the following order, the most comprehensive being placed first:..Series.. Epoch... As equivalents of *Series*, the terms *Section* or *Abtheilung* may be used... According to this scheme, we would speak of the Palæozoic Group or Era, the Silurian System or Period, the Ludlow Series or Epoch, and the Aymestry Stage or Age. **1898** *Jrnl. Geol.* VI. 355 The faunas of the Trenton limestone, the Utica and Hudson River shales are very intimately related, and that relation should be indicated by grouping the three together as stages of a single series. **1931** *Bull. Geol. Soc. Amer.* XLII. 426 The Pleistocene or Glacial Period will be divided into epochs and ages, and the Pleistocene or Glacial system into corresponding rock terms, series and stages. **1931** GREGORY & BARRETT *General Stratigr.* x. 155 In Scotland the Upper Estuarine Series includes the Brora Coal seam, of which the roof is Callovian. **1961** *Bull. Amer. Assoc. Petroleum Geologists* XLV. 658 The term 'series' is not restricted to stratified rocks, but may be applied to intrusive rocks in the same time-stratigraphic sense. **1976** H. D. HEDBERG *Internat. Stratigr. Guide* vii. 72 The series is a unit in the conventional chrono-stratigraphic hierarchy, ranking above a stage and below a system. The geochronologic equivalent of a series is an epoch. A series is always a subdivision of a system; it is usually but not always broken up into stages.

**b.** Any group of (usu. igneous) rocks having similar forms of occurrence and petrographical characteristics.

**1844** C. DARWIN *Volcanic Islands* vi. 123 Is it not more probable, that these dikes have been formed by fissures penetrating into partially cooled rocks of the granitic and metamorphic series, and by their more fluid parts,..oozing out, and being sucked into such fissures? **1892-94** *Bull. Philos. Soc. Washington* XII. 178 Since neighboring centers may be erupting different phases of the rock series at one and the same time,..the same kinds of rock may occur in different parts of the whole complex series representing the order of eruption of the rocks in one region. **1909** J. P. IDDINGS *Igneous Rocks* I. II. iii. 408 The term series should be applied to groups of rocks characterized by similarity of certain chemical or mineral constituents and by variations in others; the rocks being members of one family. Series may traverse the general system of classification in various directions. **1975** A. E. KINGWOOD *Composition & Petrology of Earth's Mantle* vii. 243 The behaviour of the orogenic series is fundamentally different from that of the tholeiitic and alkalic series.

**12.** *Electr.* and *Magn.* **a.** A number of wires of different metals each connected with the preceding. Chiefly as ***in series***: in *Electr.* also said of circuit components connected together so as to form a single electrical path between two points (also *transf.*); const. *with.*

**1873** F. JENKIN *Electr. & Magn.* ii. §21 (1881) 43 Any series of metallic conductors thus placed in contact. **1884** *Jrnl. Soc. Telegr.-Engineers* XIII. 498 If you couple two such alternate-current machines in series, they will so control each others phase as to nullify each other. **1885** WATSON & BURBURY *Math. Th. Electr. Magn.* I. 229 If any number of wires of different metals $M_1$, $M_2$, $M_3$, $M_4$ are joined together in series,..the wire of metal $M_1$ beginning and ending the series. **1922** *Proc. IRE* X. 249 It was necessary to use a two-electrode tube in series with the auxiliary emf. **1943** C. L. BOLTZ *Basic Radio* viii. 132 When a condenser and resistor are in series in a circuit, the charging current when a D.C. supply is switched on causes a p.d. across the resistor for a fraction of a second. **1960** *Practical Wireless* XXXVI. 412/1 In series with the key jack is filled a potentiometer VR1 which provides a useful variation of the oscillator tone. **1968** *Brit. Med. Bull.* XXIV. 250/1 Each tissue consists of two compartments connected in series. **1975** G. J. KING *Audio Handbk.* iv. 84 The two transistors are connected in series across the supply.

**b.** *attrib.* or as *adj.* = (*a*) arranged or connected in series; (*b*) short for ***series-wound***, i.e. wound in series, or so that the coils on the field-magnets are placed in series with the outer circuit. Also more generally, pertaining to or involving connection in series. Also *Comb.*

**1884** C. G. W. LOCK *Workshop Rec.* Ser. III. 125/1 The ordinary or series dynamo. **1888** *Scribner's Mag.* Aug. 194/2 The 'series' system..may be likened to the arrangement of disks on the chain of a chain-pump. **1891** *Lightning* 19 Nov. 107 Series-wound dynamo-machine. **1893** SLOANE *Electr. Dict.*, *Series*, arranged in succession as opposed to parallel ..[e.g.] Series Connection. *Ibid.*, *Series-multiple*, arrangement of electric apparatus, in which the parts are grouped in sets in parallel and these sets are connected in series. **1920** *Whittaker's Electr. Engineer's Pocket-bk.* (ed. 4) 227 A motor has a series characteristic when the exciting or main flux is produced by the load current (or by part of it). **1926** R. W. HUTCHINSON *Wireless* vi. 101 In the above example of resonance the capacity and inductance were in series and such a case is often referred to as series resonance. **1950** *Engineering* 6 Jan. 8/2 The noise limiter..employs a series-diode circuit. **1957** *Practical Wireless* XXXII. 379/1 (Advt.), It is essential to use mains primary types with T.V. receivers having series-connected heaters. **1961** *Amateur Radio Handbk.* (ed. 3) ix. 257/2 Valves such as the 807 can be used in both positions in a series-modulation system from a 1000 volts supply. **1962** G. A. T. BURDETT *Automatic Control Handbk.* i. 26 The outstanding characteristic of the d.c. series motor is powerful torque at starting and also at low speeds. **1970** J. SHEPHERD et al. *Higher Electr. Engin.* (ed. 2) ix. 265 In Fig. 9.5(*a*) two mutually coupled coils are connected in series. The connexion is called series aiding, since current enters the dotted ends of the coils, which thus produce aiding fluxes. **1974** HARVEY & BOHLMAN *Stereo F.M. Radio Handbk.* iii. 51 The attenuation produced by the series insertion of a crystal into a circuit operating at a variable frequency. **1975** D. G. FINK *Electronics Engineers' Handbk.* XIII. 80 The two series-connected windings in series with the load are called gate windings.

**13. a.** *Philol.* (tr. G. *reihe.*) In the Indo-germanic languages, a set of vowels, or of diphthongs and vowels or sonants, which are mutually related by ablaut.

**1888** WRIGHT *OHG. Primer* 61 The vowels vary within certain series of related vowels, called ablaut-series. There are in OHG. six such series.

**b.** *Phonology.* (See quot. 1952.)

**1952** A. MARTINET in *Word* VIII. 13 A number of consonantal phonemes characterized by one and the same articulation will be said to form a 'series' if their other characteristic articulations can be located at different points along the air channel. Thus in English /p/, /t/, /č/, /k/,..will form a series, and so will /b/, /d/, /ǧ/, /g/. **1956** E. STANKIEWICZ *Phonemic Patterns of Polish Dialects* in *For Roman Jakobson* 521 This reduction resulted in the fusion of alveolars and palatals into a single series (ś, ź, ć, ʒ́). **1969** C. A. M. BALTAXE tr. *Trubetzkoy's Princ. Phonol.* I. iv. 125 Many languages have two apical series, one characterized by the tip of the tongue pointed upward, the other by the tip of the tongue pointed downward, instead of a single series characterized by the participation of the tip of the tongue.

**14.** A parcel of rough diamonds of assorted qualities.

*a* **1912** (In recent Dicts.)

**15. a.** *Chem.* A set of related elements or compounds, esp. a group or period of the periodic table, or a number of compounds differing successively in composition by a fixed amount; a set of elements or compounds arranged in order of magnitude of some property.

**1849** *Q. Jrnl. Chem. Soc.* II. 297 (*heading*) On a new series of organic bodies containing metals and phosphorus. **1869, 1876** [see HOMOLOGOUS *a.* 3]. **1922** [see GROUP *sb.* 3 c (ii)]. **1943** [see *electro-chemical* adj. s.v. ELECTRO-]. **1958**, etc. [see NEPHELAUXETIC *a.*]. **1962** Cotton & Wilkinson *Adv. Inorg. Chem.* xxiv. 495 For practical purposes.. the third transition series begins with hafnium.. and embraces the elements Ta, W, Re, Os, Ir, Pt and Au. **1964** N. G. Clark *Mod. Org. Chem.* ii. 12 Members of the series may be represented by a general molecular formula, and each member differs from the next by $CH_2$; the paraffins have the general formula $C_nH_{2n+2}$. **1972** Cotton & Wilkinson *Adv. Inorg. Chem.* (ed. 3) xiii. 373 The stability of these hydrides falls rapidly along the series, so that $SbH_3$ and $BiH_3$ are very unstable thermally.

**b.** = *radioactive series* s.v. RADIOACTIVE *a.* 4.

**1904** [see DISINTEGRATION a]. **1926** R. W. Lawson tr. *Hevesy & Paneth's Man. Radioactivity* xxiv. 180 The resulting end-product of the uranium-radium series does not emit rays, and is hence stable. **1949** F. Soddy *Story of Atomic Energy* v. 50/2 The RaE changes to Radium F,.. the last radio-element in the main uranium series. **1974** *Encycl. Brit. Macropædia* I. 67/2 The mass numbers of all isotopes of the so-called thorium series.. turn out to be multiples of four, and the series is known as the 4n series.

**16.** A set of alloys or minerals having the same chemical composition except for the relative proportions of two elements that can replace one another.

**1855** *Phil. Mag.* X. 249 We.. prepared a series of alloys in which copper predominated. **1859** *Phil. Trans. R. Soc.* CXLVIII. 357 The alloys of a series such as those of 2 equivalents of bismuth and 1 of lead, 3 Bi and 1 Pb, 4 Bi and 1 Pb, 5 Bi and 1 Pb, all conduct the same, viz. about 1·9, the various increasing quantities of lead exercising no influence on the conductibility of the alloys. **1911** *Encycl. Brit.* XVIII. 512/2 In other groups [of minerals] the replacement may be indefinite in extent, and between the ends of the series the different members may vary indefinitely in composition. **1914** C. H. Desch *Intermediate Compounds* vi. 50 The compound $Mg_3Bi_2$ has a conductivity very near that of bismuth, and the two series Mg–$Mg_3Bi_2$ and $Mg_3Bi_2$–Bi are simple conglomerates. **1971** I. G. Gass et al. *Understanding Earth* i. 17/1 The plagioclase feldspars show a slightly more complex type of ionic replacement and form the series $NaAlSi_3O_8$ (albite)–$CaAl_2Si_2O_8$ (anorthite).

**17. a.** *Baseball.* A set of games played on successive days between two teams. Also ***World Series***: see WORLD *sb.*

**1862** *Sunday Mercury* (N.Y.) 13 July 6/3 This last game ended the series, and the players were to return this.. morning. **1906** *World* (N.Y.) 26 July 8/4 To wind up their series with the Western teams, the hilltop boys gave the Michiganders a double drubbing. **1960** *Time* 3 Oct. 67/2 The Yankees have.. individual stars who can rouse themselves to greatness and win a short series by themselves. **1973** *Internat. Herald Tribune* 15 June 15/4 It was the first time in almost a month that the Mets had won two straight. And it was the first time in exactly a month that they had captured a series.

**b.** *Cricket.* A set of Test matches between two sides on any one tour.

**1912** A. A. Lilley *Twenty-Four Years Cricket* xiv. 195 The only Test match of the tour that had a definite conclusion was the second of the series. **1935** *Wisden* II. 1 The Australian team of 1934 arrived in this country with the knowledge that during the previous series of Test Matches in Australia they had been beaten four times. **1966** J. Arlott in B. Johnston *Armchair Cricket 1966* 12 The fifth —Oval—Test of that series was the first scheduled for regular eye-witness accounts on each day. **1976** *0–10 Cricket Scene* (Austral.) 5/2 Ian Chappell and Ian Redpath both gave away Test cricket, and with Edwards leaving the scene on a series before, Australia had lost their three most consistent, fighting batsmen.

**18.** *Physics.* A set of lines in a spectrum whose frequencies are mathematically related in a fairly simple way.

**1890** *Jrnl. Chem. Soc.* LVIII. II. 674 The corresponding components of the pairs form series whose wave-numbers are functions of the successive natural numbers. **1922** [see LYMAN]. **1952** R. W. Ditchburn *Light* xvii. 543 These formulæ suggest that the wave numbers of all these series may be expressed as differences of a set of wave numbers which are known as spectroscopic 'terms'. **1966** Williams & Fleming *Spectrosc. Methods in Org. Chem.* ii. 21 When more than two triple bonds are conjugated, the spectrum shows a characteristic series of low intensity bands.. at intervals of 2300 $cm^{-1}$.. and high intensity bands.. at intervals of 2600 $cm^{-1}$. **1978** E. P. Bertin *Introd. X-Ray Spectrometric Analysis* i. 37 X-ray spectral lines are grouped in series *K, L, M, N*; all lines in a series result from electron transitions from various higher orbitals to the indicated shell.

**19.** *Soil Sci.* A group of soils which are derived from the same parent material and are similar in profile, though not necessarily in the texture of the surface horizon; = *soil series* s.v. SOIL *sb.*[1] 10.

**1904** *Ann. Rep. U.S. Dept. Agric. 1903–4* 269 These types have been arranged in 31 series, in which the soils are related in point of origin. **1913** *U.S. Bureau of Soils Bull.* No. 96. 8 A soil series is named from some town, village, county, or natural feature existing in the area when it was first encountered. **1917** Mosier & Gustafson *Soil Physics & Management* viii. 79 The Cecil series include the most important and widely distributed soils of the Piedmont Plateau. **1952** L. M. Thompson *Soils & Soil Fertility* vi. 86 Several of the great soil groups of the United States include hundreds of series. **1970** E. M. Bridges *World Soils* v. 34/2 The Ettrick Association derived from Silurian greywackes and shales has six component series in the Jedburgh and Morebattle district.

**20.** *Mus.* The arrangement of the twelve-tone chromatic scale which is used as the starting-point of a piece of SERIAL music; = *tone-row* s.v. TONE *sb.* 11.

**1930** *Mod. Music* VII. IV. 5 The tonal material of a composition [by Schönberg] is a *series* of Twelve tones, borrowed from the chromatic scale and grouped in a special arrangement... The word 'series' is by no means identical with the idea of 'theme'... The series is to be considered rather as a tone-complex, whose successions and intervalic relations always recur. **1940** E. Křenek *Studies in Counterpoint* p. viii, The primary function of the series is that of a sort of 'store of motifs' out of which all the individual elements of the composition are to be developed. **1959** *Observer* 23 Aug. 7/3 According to this new system [of musical composition], a fixed *series* or succession of the twelve notes of the chromatic scale forms a framework which is the basis of the composition. **1978** P. Griffiths *Conc. Hist. Mod. Music* vii. 88 The music is.. constructed as a four-part canon, each part of which begins with a statement of the series in a different form.

**21.** *Eccl.* With a specifying number: a designation of one of the alternative experimental forms of service used within the Church of England since 1965.

These rites were replaced in 1980 by those printed in the *Alternative Service Book*.

**1965** (*title*) Alternative Services: First Series. **1965** (*title*) Alternative Services: Second Series. **1967** *Church Quarterly Rev.* CLXVIII. 442 It is undoubtedly the rite of Series 2 which points the way forward. *Ibid.* 449 It is appropriate here to look at the third form of Series 1 in which the self-oblation is omitted from the Canon. **1971** *Churchman* LXXXV. 212 The amended text.. has now been published as *Holy Communion: Series 3.* **1973** *Franciscan* XV. 169 In our worship at S. Bene't's we have moved.. from Series II to Series III, using John Rutter's setting. **1977** B. Pym *Quartet in Autumn* i. 15 What would be the reaction of the congregation if Father G. tried to introduce Series Three? **1981** Barton & Halliburton in *Believing in Church* iv. 107 The Durham book, which had in fact proposed that form of invitation which became the invitation to confession in Series 2 Communion.

**22.** Special Comb. **series-parallel** *Electr.*, used *attrib.* with reference to combinations of series and parallel connection, esp. to denote a method of control of sets of electric traction motors in which the motors work in series on starting and are switched to parallel working when a certain speed is reached; **series spectrum**, a spectrum consisting of a series (sense 18) of lines.

**1894** K. Hedges *Amer. Electr. Street Railways* vi. 68 In the *series parallel method of control, the motors are first connected in 'series'. **1903** *Trans. Inst. Naval Archit.* XLV. 182 A voltage of 220, the motors to have series parallel control. **1957** *Railway Mag.* June 427/2 The operating voltage is 500 volts d.c., with orthodox series-parallel control for the four-motor equipments. **1968** *Radio Communications Handbk.* (ed. 4) i. 13/2 This is the value of the equivalent inductance of the four coils in this series-parallel arrangement. **1922** A. D. Udden tr. *Bohr's Theory of Spectra* II. ii. 29 Although the *series spectra of the elements of higher atomic number have a more complicated structure than the hydrogen spectrum, simple laws have been discovered showing a remarkable analogy to the Balmer formula. **1974** G. Reece tr. *Hund's Hist. Quantum Theory* vii. 100 With the aid of the *n, l, j* scheme it was possible to understand the multiplicity of the terms in the optical series spectra for atoms with one, two or three external electrons.

**serif** ('sɛrɪf). *Typogr.* Also **seriff**; (formerly) **ceriph, seriph, -yph, surryph**: see SANSERIF. [Of obscure origin.] One of the fine cross-strokes at the top and bottom of a letter. Also used loosely as in quot. 1894. Hence **'serifed, seriffed** *a.*

**1841** Savage *Dict. Printing* 163 The fine lines, and the cross strokes at the tops and bottoms of letters, are termed by the letter founders ceriphs. **1869** *N. & Q.* Ser. IV. III. 381 The word *serif*, used by printers and type-founders. **1885** De Vinne in *Trans. Grolier Club* I. 36 The bracketed serifs of Van Dyke and Garamond. **1894** Kipling in *My First Bk.* 94 Even a Hindoo does not like to find the serifs of his f's cut away to make long s's. **1936** *Geogr. Jrnl.* LXXXVII. 571 Any criticism.. should be directed towards the lettering, particularly to the large serifed capitals indicating principal settlements. **1957** S. Morison *Aspects of Authority & Freedom* 12 It is not impossible that seriffed letters were considered more suitable for a revered text than unseriffed ones. **1980** B. Crutchley *To be Printer* 134 Hence the danger that seriffed forms will be passed over when they could do a job as well or better and at the same time enhance our aesthetic enjoyment.

**seriff**, variant of SHEREEF.

**serific** (sɪ'rɪfɪk), *a. rare.* [irreg. f. L. *sēric-um* silk (see Seric) + -FIC.] Producing silk.

**1895** Sedgwick *Peripatus* x. (Cambr. Nat. Hist.) 246 There are a large number of 'serific glands' of two kinds in the female [of the Mantidæ].

**Seriform** ('sɪərɪfɔːm), *a. rare.* [f. L. SER-ES + -FORM.] Applied to a division of the Asian races comprising the Chinese, Thais, etc., and to the group of languages spoken by these peoples.

**1849–52** W. B. Carpenter in *Todd's Cycl. Anat.* IV. 1347/2 The Seriform, or Indo-Chinese [languages], which are spoken by the people of South-Eastern Asia. *Ibid.* 1364/2 The Seriform stock of Southern Asia. **1850** Latham *Var. Man* 15 Altaic Mongolidæ... Seriform Stock.

**serigala** (sə'riːgələ). [Mal.] The Malaysian wild dog, *Cuon alpinus*. Cf. *red dog* s.v. RED *a.* 17 a; DHOLE.

**1903** J. L. Bonhote in Annandale & Robinson *Fasciculi Malayenses: Zool.* I. 12 There are two species of *srîgâla* not uncommon in the Jarum district. **1945** C. L. B. Hubbard *Observer's Bk. Dogs* 212 Serigala. The larger variety of Malayan Wild Dog... Long-coated, red-and-tan, with thick tail. **1965** C. Shuttleworth *Malayan Safari* v. 70 The serigala is related to the dhole of India. **1978** Ld. Medway *Wild Mammals Malaysia* (ed. 2) 84/1 Serigala.. occurring on the mainland wherever extensive tracts of tall forest remain, though nowhere abundant.

**serigraph** ('sɛrɪgrɑːf, -æ-). [irreg. f. L. *sēricum* silk (see Seric) + -GRAPH.] **1.** An instrument for testing the uniformity of raw silk.

**1887** *Encycl. Brit.* XXII. 62/2 A most ingenious American invention, the serigraph.

**2.** An original print produced by serigraphy. orig. *U.S.*

**1941** C. Zigrosser in *Print Collector's Q.* XXVIII. 455 A number of leading practitioners of the art.. have adopted the word 'Serigraph' for silk screen stencil prints. **1959** *Information Bull. Libr. Congr.* 25 May 284 Henry Miller.. has presented 7 rare ephemera to the Library. Two of them are promotional pamphlets for his *Into the Night Life* (1947), a serigraph or silk-screen creation. **1961** C. Zigrosser in *What is Original Print?* (Print Council of Amer.) 24 A number of artists who make original prints in the medium [*sc.* silk-screen printing] have decided to call them *serigraphs* to distinguish them from commercial silk screen reproductions. **1971** M. Turk *Buried Life* vi. 90 Sister Corita, I.H.M., one of the great contemporary printmakers whose own 'blabs & scrawls & squiggles' (otherwise known as serigraphs) hang in over forty museums. **1978** *New York* 3 Apr. 30/3 Pure color and shape in serigraphs.

So **serimeter** (sɪ'rɪmɪtə(r)), an instrument for testing the strength of silk thread.

**serigraphy** (sɛ'rɪgrafɪ). orig. *U.S.* Also **Serigraphy**. [Irreg. f. L. *sēricum* silk (see Seric *a.*) + -GRAPHY; cf. F. *sérigraphie*, G. *serigraphie*.] The art or process of printing original designs by means of the silk-screen method.

**1940** *Parnassus* Dec. 31 Serigraphy, or the silk screen process, is a comparative newcomer among the graphic arts. **1946** H. Shokler *Artists Man. Silk Screen Print Making* iv. 68 The explorations in Serigraphy have comprehended much more than simply textures and color. **1952** *Print* (N.Y.) VII. 4/2 In serigraphy there is no need to reverse the image. The artist draws directly on the silk. **1965** Zigrosser & Gaehde *Guide Coll. Orig. Prints* iv. 55 Serigraphy is specially adapted for color work, although Ben Shahn has used it effectively just with black lines... Serigraphy is part of the general method of silk-screen printing.., but the name serves to differentiate original artists' prints from commercial productions. **1977** *Crafts* Nov./Dec. 67/3 Serigraphy—The art of silk screen printing. Summer courses in West Cornwall.

Hence **se'rigrapher**, one who practises serigraphy; **seri'graphic** *a.*, of or pertaining to serigraphy.

**1944** *Canadian Art* Oct.-Nov. 8/2 Only the most experienced serigrapher can do this without the danger of muddling up his original artistic conception. **1946** H. Shokler *Artists Man. Silk Screen Print Making* i. 25 Paper is to the serigrapher what canvas is to the painter. **1957** *Screen Printer & Display Producer* July 12 (*caption*) A general view of the serigraphic exhibition. *Ibid.* 16/1 Any screen process stencil which is the result of writing, drawing or painting directly upon the screen is now generally known as a 'serigraphic' stencil.

**serimonie, -y**, obs. forms of CEREMONY.

**serin**[1] ('sɛrɪn). Also 6 **seryne, -ene**. [a. F. *serin* canary, of disputed origin; cf. Pr. *serin*.]

**1.** In early examples perh. the canary (*Serinus canarius*); in modern ornithology, a bird of the genus *Serinus*.

**1530** Palsgr. 269/2 Seryne a byrde, *serin*. **1549** *Compl. Scotl.* vi. 39 The grene serene sang sueit. **1894** R. B. Sharpe *Hand-bk. Birds Gt. Brit.* I. 53 A small Serin (*S. pusillus*) with a red forehead.

**2.** In full, ***serin finch***: the finch *S. serinus* (*S. hortulanus*), a native of central Europe.

*a* **1672** Willughby *Ornith.* (1678) 265 It [*sc.* the Citril] differs from the Siskin and Serin, 1. In its ash-coloured Neck [etc.]. **1783** Latham *Gen. Syn. Birds* II. I. 296 Serin F[inch]. **1836** *Partington's Brit. Cycl. Nat. Hist.* II. 540 The Serin.. is.. remarkable for its small and very short bill. **1871–81** Dresser *Birds Eur.* IV. Pl. 25 The call-note of the Serin Finch. **1882** Yarrell *Brit. Birds* (ed. 4) II. 113 The Serin is a very popular cage-bird on the continent.

**serin**[2] ('sɛrɪn). Also **serine**. [f. SERUM + -IN[1], -INE[5].]

**1.** *Chem.* **a.** Serum albumin. **b.** Amido-glycerol.

**1876** tr. *Schützenberger's Fermentation* 84 It is not the serine which is active in this case. **1898** *Daily News* 28 Feb. 6/4 The only hot drink we prepared was a kind of toddy made of lime juice tablets, or serine powder.

**2.** (See quot.)

**1898** Johansen in *Windsor Mag.* Sept. 436/2 'Serin', or whey powder... This is really nothing else than pulverised whey, which we mixed with boiling water.

**serine** (ˈsɛriːn). *Chem.* Formerly also **-in**. [ad. G. *serin* (E. Cramer 1865, in *Jrnl. für prakt. Chem.* XCVI. 93), f. L. *sēr-icum* silk: see -INE[5].]

**a.** A colourless, crystalline amino-acid, $CH_2OH{\cdot}CHNH_2{\cdot}COOH$, which is widely distributed in animal proteins.

**1880** *Jrnl. Chem. Soc.* XXXVIII. 713 Cramer's..serine is isomeric with amidohydroxypropionic acid. **1882** *Ibid.* XLII. 38 It..agrees in all its properties with Cramer's serin from silk, except that it is less soluble in water. **1908** HALL & DEFREN tr. *Abderhalden's Text-bk. Physiol. Chem.* viii. 149 Serine as it occurs in nature is lævo-rotatory. **1957** FOX & FOSTER *Introd. Protein Chem.* vii. 122 Serine is convertible to glycine in mammals, a capability that explains also its convertibility to heme. **1975** D. A. BENDER *Amino Acid Metabolism* (1978) iii. 59 Both serine and threonine have hydrophilic side-chains and therefore contribute to the hydrophilicity of proteins when they are in exposed regions of the chain.

**b.** *Comb.* In names of various enzymes which catalyse reactions of serine or serine residues, or reactions yielding serine.

**1938** *Biochem. Jrnl.* XXXII. 403 The decay of *dl*-serine deaminase appears to be due to a loss from the cell by diffusion of some substance or substances acting as coenzyme. **1943** *Jrnl. Biol. Chem.* CL. 262 The desulfurase and serine dehydrase of mammalian tissue were found to be similar to those of the microorganisms. **1956** *Ibid.* CCXX. 775 Since the reaction we have studied mainly is the formation of serine, and because of the similarity to aldol type reactions, we propose the name serine aldolase for this enzyme system. **1967** *New Scientist* 17 Aug. 353/1 Organophosphorus pesticides..are known to act as competitive inhibitors of the 'serine esterase' group of enzymes. **1974** *Sci. Amer.* July 74/2 Serine proteases participate in digestion, in the formation and dissolution of blood clots, in the immune reaction to foreign cells and organisms, in the fertilization of the ovum by the spermatozoon.

‖**serinette** (sɛriˈnɛt). [Fr., f. *serin* canary: see -ETTE.] A bird organ.

**1858** *Lond. Jrnl.* 27 Feb. 408/3 There are puppet-shows, and performances on the accordion, and the serinette in the subterranean passage.

**sering**, obs. form of SYRINGE.

**sering(e**, variant of CERING *vbl. sb.*

**1558** in Feuillerat *Revels Q. Eliz.* (1908) 88 Seringe candell. **1571** *Ibid.* 142 Other lightes Seringcandle Corde.

**seringa** (səˈrɪŋgə). [a. F. *seringa* (formerly also *seringat*) = Pg. *seringa*, ad. L. SYRINGA.]

**1.** Any of the shrubs of the genus *Philadelphus*, esp. *P. coronarius*, common in gardens; the mock-orange, SYRINGA. (Also †seringo.)

**1740** C'TESS HARTFORD *Let. to C'tess Pomfret* 17 Apr., Arbours interwoven with lilacs, woodbines, seringas, and laurels. *a* **1785** T. POTTER *Moralist* II. 144 'Twas then a Black-bird and its mate In a seringo built their nest. **1840** MISS MITFORD in L'Estrange *Life* (1870) III. 109 The rich perfume of the seringas and acacias. **1876** MISS BRADDON *J. Haggard's Dau.* x, A dark-brown jug of roses and seringa on the window-sill.

‖**2.** The Portuguese name for Brazilian plants of the genus *Hevea* (*Siphonia*), yielding india-rubber.

**1866** *Treas. Bot.* s.v. *Siphonia*, They [species of *Siphonia*] are called Seringa-trees by the Brazilians. **1880** C. R. MARKHAM *Peruv. Bark* 455 In Brazil the name is *seringa*, and the collectors are *seringueiros*.

Hence **seˈringahood** *nonce-wd.*, the condition of abounding in seringa bloom; **seˈringous** *a.*, resembling that of seringa.

**1754** H. WALPOLE *Let. to G. Montagu* 8 June, [Strawberry Hill] is now in the height of its greenth, blueth, gloomth, honeysuckle and seringahood. **1887** A. M. BROWN *Anim. Alkal.* 32 An almost cloudless liquid of slightly oleaginous consistence, of a seringous odour.

**seringe**, obs. form of SYRINGE.

**seringue.** = SERINGA 2.

**1866** *Treas. Bot.*, *Seringue*, a South American name for the caoutchouc-yielding Siphonia.

‖**seringueiro** (sɛrɪŋˈgeru). Also (*erron.*) seringero. [Pg., f. SERINGA.] In Brazil: a person employed to gather rubber.

**1860** MAYNE REID *Odd People* 82 The 'seringero' has provided a large quantity of palm-nuts, with which he intends to make a fire for smoking the caoutchouc. **1880** [see SERINGA 2]. **1913** [see ESTRADA]. **1934** *Times Lit. Suppl.* 15 Nov. 797/1 A Portuguese novelist, perhaps the only literary man who has ever actually worked as a *seringueiro*. **1968** R. E. POPPINO *Brazil* iv. 141 The rubber worker—known as a *seringueiro*—..also prepared his own crude shelter. **1970** E. B. BURNS *Hist. Brazil* v. 240 The dwindling number of Indians was pressed into service as *seringueiros*... The isolated, difficult life of the exploited *seringueiro* explained the recruitment problem.

**serio**, short for SERIO-COMIC *sb.*

**1894** *Yellow Bk.* I. 76 Coming after all those sly serios.. Miss Cissy Loftus had the charm which things of another period often do possess. **1908** *Daily Chron.* 3 Aug. 4/4 'As if a serio had anything to do with anything serious!'

**serio-** (ˈsɪərɪəʊ), used as comb. form (see -O-) of SERIOUS, = partly serious and partly...

**1902** *Academy* 12 Apr. 387/2 The *serio-grotesque headlines of the New York *Journal*. **1811** [E. NARES] (*title*) Thinks-I-to-Myself. A *serio-ludicro, tragico-comico tale. *a* **1834** LAMB *Guy Faux* Misc. Wks. (1871) 373 It is familiarized to us in a kind of *serio-ludicrous way. **1835** DICKENS *Sk. Boz, Mr. J. Dounce*, The young lady..went through various other *serio-pantomimic fascinations. **1866** CARLYLE *Remin.* (1881) I. 85 What a fantastic..*serio-ridiculous set these road companions of his mostly were.

**ˌserio-ˈcomedy.** [f. next.] A serio-comic piece. Also *transf.*

**1884** *Pall Mall Gaz.* 30 Apr. 4/1 The libretto of 'The Canterbury Pilgrims' is no ordinary work;..its story is..told tunefully and gaily, as befits a serio-comedy. **1891** M. WILLIAMS *Later Leaves* xix. 226 Nothing will ever come near him in *The Roused Lion*, which..was serio-comedy. **1929** BLUNDEN *Nature in Eng. Lit.* v. 125 From this serio-comedy of the strawyard the [farmer's] boy raises his face to the setting Sun and..gets to bed. **1936** H. A. L. FISHER *Hist. Europe* II. xviii. 634 The fashionable ladies who played so active a part in this serio-comedy.

**ˌserio-ˈcomic**, *a.* (*sb.*) [f. SERIO- + COMIC *a.*]

**a.** Partly serious and partly comic; (of an actor, vocalist, etc. or his performance) presenting a comic plot, situation, etc. under a serious form.

**1783** COLMAN *Prose Sev. Occas.* (1787) III. 147, I was almost confounded in the serio-comick scenes of the Satyrick Piece. **1787** KEATE (*title*) The Distressed Poet, a serio-comic poem. **1826** F. REYNOLDS *Life & Times* II. 321 Lewis, by a striking display of serio-comic talent,..proved, that..he could excite tears as abundantly as smiles. **1858** H. MORLEY *Jrnl. Lond. Playgoer* (1866) 227 The production at the Olympic of a 'new serio-comic drama'. **1877** MRS. FORRESTER *Mignon* ii, 'Good Heavens!' interrupts Fred, regarding him with serio-comic horror—'*young* did you say?'

**b.** as *sb.* (also **-comique**). A serio-comic actor, vocalist, etc.

**1895** [see *male impersonator* s.v. MALE *sb.* 4]. **1907** H. WYNDHAM *Flaire of Footlights* xxxi, Miss Constance Plantagenet, the Favourite Serio-Comique.

So **ˌserio-ˈcomical** *a.*; **ˌserio-ˈcomically** *adv.*

**1749** SMOLLETT *Gil Blas* VII. viii. (1782) III. 67 My serio-comical reception behind the scenes. **1872** *Punch* 18 May 202/1 The Ministry..were defeated only three times this week—once comically, once seriously, and once serio-comically. **1873** B. HARTE *Fiddletown* 11 Her hair..was tumbled serio-comically about her forehead.

†**seriol.** *Obs. rare*[−1]. [ad. L. *sēriola*, dim. of *sēria* jar.] A small jar.

*c* **1440** *Pallad. on Husb.* IV. 393 Ek whelue a seriol therout that haue Grauel vp to the myddes.

**serion, -iont**, obs. ff. SURGEON, SERGEANT.

**seriosity** (sɪərɪˈɒsɪtɪ). [ad. late L. *sēriōsitās*, f. *sēriōsus* SERIOUS. Cf. SERIOUSTE.] Seriousness.

**1637** BASTWICK *Letany* I. 6 It would..move laughter to men though disposed otherwise to seriosity. **1693** *Humours Town* 20 The grave starch'd seriosity of a Sylogistical Argumentation. **1837** *Fraser's Mag.* XVI. 284 If I may claim from my reader a moment's seriosity, I will explain. **1903** *Academy* 21 Feb. 168/1 Laugh! Few things are worthy of seriosity.

**b.** A serious saying, a piece of seriousness.

**1893** LELAND *Mem.* I. 288 Painfully elaborating jocosities or seriosities for the million.

**serious** (ˈsɪərɪəs), *a.* Forms: 5 sery-, ceryows, 5–6 seryous, 6 seryouse, -iouse, 6–7 -eous, (7 *superl.* seriousest, serioust), 6– serious. [ad. F. *sérieux* (14th c.) or its source, late L. *sēriōsus*, f. L. *sērius* (whence Sp., Pg., It. *serio*). Cf. It. *serioso*.]

**1. a.** Of persons, their actions, etc.: Having, involving, expressing, or arising from earnest purpose or thought; of grave or solemn disposition or intention; having depth or solidity of character, not light or superficial; now often, concerned with the grave and earnest sides of life as opposed to amusement or pleasure-seeking.

*c* **1440** *Promp. Parv.* 453/2 Seryows, sad and feythefulle, *seriosus*. **1530** PALSGR. 324/1 Seryouse ernest, *serieux*. **1532** MORE *Confut. Tindale* Wks. 480/2 Saint Paule woulde not haue made so serious and earnest remembrance of the putting vpon of the handes..if [etc.]. **1597** HOOKER *Eccl. Pol.* v. lxii. (1611) 329 All that belongeth to the mysticall perfection of baptisme outwardly, is the element, the word, and the serious application of both vnto him which receiueth both. **1611** BEAUM. & FL. *King & No K.* III. iii, The King is serious, And cannot now admit your vanities. *c* **1640** A. STAFFORD *Just Apol. Fem. Glory* (1869) p. xcii, The faire serious Prince wee are now blest in. **1663** MARVELL *Corr.* Wks. (Grosart) II. 95, I do hereby, with my last and seriousest thoughts, salute you. **1710** STEELE *Tatler* No. 222 ¶2 I have taken that Matter into my serious Consideration. **1712** ARBUTHNOT *John Bull* II. xii, Shaking off his old serious friends, and keeping company with buffoons and pick-pockets. **1823** SCOTT *Quentin D.* Introd., I was..glad to see that she took a serious thought of any kind. **1838–9** KEMBLE *Resid. in Georgia* (1863) 20, I really entertain serious thoughts of learning to use a gun. **1849** MACAULAY *Hist. Eng.* iii. I. 320 His chief serious employment was the care of his property. **1882** MOZLEY *Remin.* (ed. 2) I. 64 He was too serious to smile; indeed, I cannot remember him ever smiling except sadly. **1897** *Allbutt's Syst. Med.* IV. 619 Such a dietary, adapted for an adult man, is little irksome to any serious patient.

†**b.** Earnestly bent or applied (to the pursuit of something); keen. *Obs.*

**1567** MAPLET *Gr. Forest* A 5 Julius Cæsar,..serious after the inquisition of good Discipline. **1576** FLEMING *Panopl. Epist.* 178 If I should seeme serious, in doing seruice to the aduauncement of mine owne wit. *Ibid.* 186 They assaulted me with more serious supplications, not holding me.. excusable. **1671** MILTON *P.R.* I. 203 All my mind was set Serious to learn and know.

†**c.** Staid, steady, reliable. *Obs.*

**1693** J. CLAYTON in *Misc. Curiosa* (1708) III. 291, I have been told by very serious Planters, that 30 or 40 Years since, ..the Thunder was more fierce.

**2. a.** Earnest about the things of religion; religious.

**1796** SIMEON in Carus *Life* (1847) 117, I could wish..that the custom of drinking toasts was banished from the tables of the serious, because it tends to excess. **1838** DICKENS *Nich. Nick.* xvi, Pleasant Place, Finsbury. Wages, twelve guineas. No tea, no sugar. Serious family. **1840** NEWMAN *Lett.* (1891) II. 311 Such a general feeling exists amongst serious people of the need of religious communities.

**b.** Cited as a canting expression.

**1809** KENDALL *Trav.* I. xxxiii. 323 His sons death brought him to God—he grew serious [*note*, Serious has the cant acceptation of religious]. **1819** SHELLEY *Peter Bell 3rd* I. i, And Peter Bell, when he had been With fresh-imported Hell-fire warmed, Grew serious. **1885** 'F. ANSTEY' *Tinted Venus* x, No one knows the power that a single serious hairdresser might effect with worldly customers.

**3.** Dealing with or regarding a matter on its grave side; not jesting, trifling, or playful; in earnest. Hence, of theatrical compositions or actors, not jocular or comic. Also *spec.* of music and literature (in contrast with 'light').

[**1590**: see 4.] **1712–13** SWIFT *Jrnl. to Stella* 17 Jan., I was going to be serious, because it was seriously put; but I turned it to a jest. **1762–71** H. WALPOLE *Vertue's Anecd. Paint.* (1786) IV. 224 Magnificent serious pantomimes. **1796** OULTON *Theatres Lond.* II. 107 Orpheus and Euridice, a grand serious Opera, translated from the Italian. **1797** *Encycl. Brit.* (ed. 3) XII. 497/1 Gaetano Guadagni..had been in this country..as serious-man in a burletta troop of singers. **1825** T. HOOK *Sayings* Ser. II. *Passion & Princ.* viii. III. 104 A note of enquiry, half serious, half waggish. **1864** H. MORLEY *Jrnl. Lond. Playgoer* (1866) 339 A play which demands alternation of serious and comic acting. **1875** JOWETT *Plato* (ed. 2) I. 201 The gentlemen are not serious, but are only playing with you. **1901** G. B. SHAW *Three Plays for Puritans* p. xxiv, The Diabolonian position is new to the London playgoer of today, but not to lovers of serious literature. **1934** S. R. NELSON *All about Jazz* i. 14 To compare modern syncopation with serious music as an art form is manifestly ridiculous. **1942** H. HAYCRAFT *Murder for Pleasure* xii. 265 Many 'serious' writers manage to support their solider endeavours by turning their talents to occasional short magazine fiction. **1960** L. P. HARTLEY *Facial Justice* xxiii. 200 But to return to classical, or 'serious' music. **1971** 'E. CANDY' *Words for Murder Perhaps* ii. 25 You open a detective story in the mood in which you might attend a sherry party... But you approach a serious novel as you go to meet someone you greatly care for. **1974** *Country Life* 26 Dec. 1989/1 The BBC's serious and light music departments function as separate..entities.

**4. a.** Requiring earnest thought, consideration, or application; performed with earnestness of purpose.

**1531** ELYOT *Gov.* I. xx. (1537) 76b, Socrates..was not ashamed to account daunsynge amonge the seriouse disciplines. **1590** SHAKS. *Com. Err.* II. ii. 29 Your sawcinesse will iest vpon my loue, And make a Common of my serious howres. **1607** CHAPMAN *Bussy d'Ambois* II. ii, And never My fruitless love shall let your serious honour. *a* **1625** BEAUM. & FL. *Woman's Prize* III. iv, *Row.* She made a puppy of me... *Bya.* She must doe so sometimes, and oftentimes: Love were too serious else. **1706** E. WARD *Wooden World Diss.* (1708) 35 He makes Cards and Dice his serious Entertainment. **1825** LAMB *Elia* II. *Barbara S——*, I have played at serious whist with Mr. Liston. **1884** *Manch. Exam.* 26 May 6/2 Perhaps more serious reading would then dethrone the eternal novel. **1886** RUSKIN *Præterita* I. vi. 196 Knowing of sorrow only just so much as to make life serious to me.

†**b.** Used for purposes of business. *rare.*

**1621** QUARLES *Argalus & P.* (1678) 32 The treacherous Lady stept aside Into her serious closet.

**5. a.** Of grave demeanour or aspect.

**1613** SHAKS. *Hen. VIII*, Prol. 2 A weighty and a serious brow. *a* **1661** FULLER *Worthies, Staffs.* (1662) III. 47 Queen Elizabeth was serious (I dare not say sullen) and out of good humour. **1688** EVELYN *Diary* 18 Dec., He is very stately, serious and reserv'd. **1781** COWPER *Conversat.* 297 A shallow brain behind a serious mask. **1838** DICKENS *Nich. Nick.* x, A good portrait..must be either serious or smirking, or it's no portrait at all. **1859** MEREDITH *R. Feverel* ii, White smocks, and slate, surmounted by hats of a serious brim. **1877** MRS. OLIPHANT *Makers Flor.* iii. 82 His aspect was grave and quiet, and his dress seemly and serious.

**b.** Inducing or associated with grave or solemn thoughts.

**1822** LAMB *Elia* II. *Bks. & Reading*, I should not care to be caught in the serious avenues of some cathedral alone, and reading *Candide*. **1849** RUSKIN *Seven Lamps* vi. §1 It would be difficult to conceive a scene less dependent upon any other interest than that of its own secluded and serious beauty.

**6. a.** Weighty, important, grave; (of quantity or degree) considerable, not trifling.

**1584** B. R. tr. *Herodotus* I. 11 Ether permit me to..make one in yᵉ voiage, or alleage some more wayghty & seryous reason why you retayne me. **1687** A. LOVELL tr. *Thevenot's Trav.* I. b 2 b, So many different Employments..have not at all diverted him from the study of the most serious and difficult matters. **1782** WARTON *Ess. Pope* II. xii. 380 Swift was always reading lectures of œconomy..to his poetical friends. A shilling, says he, is a serious thing. **1793** SMEATON *Edystone L.* §103 To level the Sugar-Loaf to its base, would of itself be a serious work. **1810** CRABBE *Borough* xiii. 28 Serious sums in healing misery spent. **1835** ALISON *Hist. Eur.* IV. xxx. 336 The light infantry of the enemy, which was..making serious progress. **1861** F. A. PALEY *Æschylus* (ed. 2) *Prometh.* 433 *note*, In the epodus..it is probable that serious corruptions exist. **1875** JOWETT *Plato* (ed. 2) III. 13 Of the numerous company, three only take any serious part in the discussion. **1884** *Pall Mall G.* 11 Sept. 1/2 All vessels of serious tonnage must lie at the anchorage, about twelve miles by river from the city. **1884** *Times* 27 June 4 The damage is not thought to be serious.

**b.** Attended with danger; giving cause for anxiety.

**1800** MRS. HERVEY *Mourtray Fam.* IV. 260 As well as she had ever been since her serious illness. **1891** *Daily News* 21 Nov. 3/5 He was badly thrown... It is feared that his condition is serious.

**7.** quasi-sb. ***the serious***: that which is serious; the serious side of life, etc.

*c* **1730** RAMSAY *Some Contents* ii, Dunbar does..in the serious schyne. **1749** FIELDING *Tom Jones* v. i. *heading*, Of the serious in writing, and for what purpose it is introduced. **1897** FLANDRAU *Harvard Episodes* 71 You have found out how seriously he objects to the serious.

**8.** *Comb.* ***serious-minded*** adj., ***-mindedly*** adv.

**1825** HOOD *To Sylv. Urban* i, A sober age made serious drunk by thee. **1837** CARLYLE *Fr. Rev.* III. IV. iii, It was piercing and fearful, and a most serious-looking thing. **1845** S. AUSTIN *Ranke's Hist. Ref.* I. 489 The thinking and serious-minded among his contemporaries. **1894** BARING-GOULD *Queen of Love* v, He had been brought up in the straightest sect of serious-mindedness. **1921** A. HUXLEY *Crome Yellow* vii. 71, I sometimes wonder whether Denis is altogether serious-minded, whether he isn't rather a dilettante. **1965** H. GOLD *Man who was not with It* xxxii. 310, I had a serious-minded mother. **1966** 'W. COOPER' *Memoirs of New Man* I. v. 64, I heard two people serious-mindedly handing them to and fro.

**'seriously**, *adv.*[1] Also 4-5 **ceryous-, -ious-**. [Rendering of med.L. *seriōsē*, used as adv. of *seri-ēs* SERIES; cf. SERIATIM, SERIATLY.] In due order or sequence; from beginning to end; one after another, seriatim. *Obs.*

*c* **1386** CHAUCER *Man of Law's T.* 87 Thise Marchantz han hym toold of dame Custance So greet noblesse in ernest ceriously. *c* **1407** LYDG. *Reson & Sens.* 5442 There namys by and by Be rehersed ceriously. **1412-20** —— *Chron. Troy* I. 1449 Whan þe kyng had herd ceryously þentent of Iason. **1463** ASHRY *Prisoner's Refl.* 313 Redyng thys tretyse ceryously. **1513** *Life Hen. V* (1911) 79 And 6 Earles w[th] 470 speares, and 1420 archers, whose names seriouslie hereafter ensewe. **1531** ELYOT *Gov.* II. viii, Nowe will I procede seriously, and in a due forme to speke more particulerly of these thre vertues. *c* **1611** CHAPMAN *Iliad* x. 361 And this (said Dolon) too (my Lords) Ile seriously unfold.

**seriously** ('sɪərɪəslɪ), *adv.*[2] [f. SERIOUS *a.* + -LY[2].] In a serious manner.

**1.** With earnest thought or application; with serious intent; in earnest, earnestly; with gravity; not lightly, superficially, or jocosely.

Sometimes *ellipt.* introducing a qualifying statement or a question = to speak seriously.

**1509** FISHER *Funl. Serm. C'tess Richm.* Wks. (1876) 294 Tho dayes that by the chirche were appoynted she kept them diligently & sereously. *a* **1548** HALL *Chron., Edw. IV* 225 Kyng Edward and his counsaill tooke the matter in great earnest, and seriously wrote to Duke Charles, that [etc.]. **1576** FLEMING *Panopl. Epist.* 62 By the remembrance and thinking vpon the same seriously. **1601** SHAKS. *All's Well* II. i. 84 If seriously I may conuay my thoughts In this my light deliuerance. **1617** MORYSON *Itin.* I. 242 This I beleeved not, till..the English Merchants..seriously affirmed the same to be true. **1624** GATAKER *Transubst.* 15 It is absurd..to call a thing seriously (for in mockery indeed sometime we doe) by the name of some other thing. **1644** SYMONDS *Diary* (Camden) 67 Except here and there an officer, (and seriously I saw not above three or four that looked like a gentleman). **1650** BAXTER *Saint's R.* III. vi. 368 If one fall down in a swoun..how seriously will you run to relieve..them. **1706** E. WARD *Wooden World Diss.* (1708) 27 When he's sober again, he seriously curses the Freedom of his Tongue. **1711** ADDISON *Spect.* No. 89 ¶4, I would have them seriously think on the Shortness of their Time. **1818** SCOTT *Hrt. Midl.* xxxiv, As you seem to be a seriously disposed young woman, you may attend family worship in the hall this evening. **1849** MACAULAY *Hist. Eng.* ii. I. 165 Seriously impressed by religious convictions. **1872** RUSKIN *Eagle's N.* §104 Quite seriously, all the vital functions..rise and set with the sun. **1907** H. WYNDHAM *Flare of Footlights* xxiii, Seriously, though, what ought I to do?

**b.** Phr. *to take seriously* (cf. TAKE *v.* 42): to be serious in one's dealings with, or attitude towards.

**1782** MISS BURNEY *Cecilia* IV. xi, 'Dear Mrs. Delvile', cried Lady Honoria, giddily, 'you take me too seriously'. 'And dear Lady Honoria', said Mrs. Delvile, 'I would it were possible to make you take yourself seriously'. **1889** *Cornh. Mag.* Dec. 573 It is really time..that you took things more seriously.

**2.** To a serious extent.

**1765** R. RIGBY in Jesse *Selwyn & Contemp.* (1843) I. 365, I should be seriously sorry that March should suffer for want of attention to his master. **1825** SCOTT *Talism.* iii, 'Help, Nazarene!' cried Sheerkohf, now seriously alarmed. **1868** E. EDWARDS *Ralegh* I. iv. 59 The Earl fell more seriously than before under the Queen's anger. **1886** *Act 49 & 50 Vict.* c. 55 *Preamble*, The health of many young persons employed in shops and warehouses is seriously injured by reason of the length of the period of employment.

**seriousness** ('sɪərɪəsnɪs). [f. SERIOUS *a.* + -NESS.] The quality or condition of being serious; gravity or earnestness of purpose, thought, or conduct; importance, weightiness. † ***in seriousness***, seriously.

**1530** PALSGR. 269/2 Seriousnesse, *serieuseté*. **1598** MARSTON *Sco. Villanie* Prol. B 2 b, Where I but striue in honest seriousnes, To scourge some soule-poluting beastlines. **1607** FLETCHER *Woman Hater* I. iii, Sister, in seriousnesse you yet are young And faire. **1662** *Bk. Com. Prayer, Visit. Sick*, That the sense of his weakness may add ..seriousness to his repentance. **1700** T. BROWN tr. *Fresny's Amusem.* 3 Seriousness and Merriment are near Neighbours. **1725** DE FOE *Voy. round World* (1840) 153 The utmost gravity, seriousness, and solemnity in his countenance. **1837** CARLYLE *Fr. Rev.* I. III. ii, Nay, in seriousness, let no man say that Calonne had not genius. **1844** S. G. OSBORNE *Let.* 23 July (1891) I. 13 Now, Sir, one word in all sober seriousness. **1874** GREEN *Short Hist.* vii. §7. 417 The seriousness of his [Spenser's] poetic tone reflects the seriousness of his poetic purpose. **1895** *Law Times* XCVIII. 280/1 Plaintiff's counsel dwelt forcibly on the seriousness of the injury, as blighting the plaintiff's whole future career.

†**seriouste.** *Obs. rare*$^{-0}$. In 5 **cery-, -owste.** [f. SERIOUS + *-te*, -TY.] Seriousness.

**1440** *Promp. Parv.* 142/1 Ernest, ceryowste, *seriositas*. *c* **1490** *Ibid.* 453/2 Seriowste, *seriositas*.

**seriowre**, obs. form of SEARCHER.

**seriph**, variant of SERIF, SHEREEF.

**seripositor** (sɛrɪ'pɒzɪtə(r)). [f. L. *sēricum* silk (see SERIC) + POSITOR.]

**1881** WARDLE *Wild Silks of India* 28, I propose..to change the word 'spinnaret', which conveys an inaccurate impression, and substitute for it that of 'seripositor'. **1887** *Encycl. Brit.* XXII. 58/1.

**serir** (sə'rɪə(r)). *Physical Geogr.* Pl. serir, serirs. [Arab. *serir* dry.] In Libya and Egypt: a flat area of desert strewn with rounded pebbles and boulders. Cf. REG[2].

**1886** *Encycl. Brit.* XXI. 149/2 Nearly all the rest of the Sahara consists in the main of undulating surfaces of rock.., vast tracts of water-worn pebbles (*serir*), and regions of sandy dunes. **1925** W. F. HUME *Geol. Egypt* I. iv. 88 The same undulating 'serir' pebble-strewn country extends to the west of the Nile Valley, forming low undulations which are nevertheless sufficiently developed for whole camel parties to become rapidly lost to sight. **1942** O. D. VON ENGELN *Geomorphol.* xviii. 411 In the Libyan Sahara similar surface sheets, there composed of coarse rounded pebbles, a pebble armor, are known as serir; in the western Sahara smaller rounded pebbles, tightly packed, constitute the reg. **1974** *Encycl. Brit. Micropædia* III. 486/2 Evaporation of capillary water may cause the precipitation of calcium carbonate, gypsum, and other salts that cement the pebbles together to form a desert conglomerate. In the western Sahara such a surface is known as a reg.., whereas in the eastern Sahara it is called a serir.

†**'serish**, *a. Obs. rare*$^{-0}$. In 7 **searish.** [f. SERE *a.* + -ISH.] Dryish.

**1648** HEXHAM II, *Dorachtigh*, Dryish, or Searish.

**serius**, obs. form of SIRIUS.

**serjand, -jaunt**, etc.: see SERGEANT.

**serk(e**, obs. forms of SARK.

**serkel(l, serkle, serkill**, etc., obs. ff. CIRCLE.

**serkelet**, obs. form of CIRCLET.

**serly**: see SIRLY, SERELY, SURLY.

†**'serment.** *Obs.* Also 5 **serement.** [a. OF. *ser(e)ment, sairement*:—L. *sacrāmentum.*] An oath.

*a* **1325** tr. *Stat. Westm.* II. xlvii. (MS. Rawl. B 520, lf. 27), Ant te lord king aioinez to alle his Iustises in fei and in serment..þat [etc.]. **1387-8** T. USK *Test. Love* I. vii. (Skeat) l. 52 To make a trewe serment. **1422** YONGE tr. *Secreta Secret.* xv. 143 Kepe thy feyth, thyn vndyrtakynges, and thy Serementz. **1494** *Act 11 Hen. VII*, c. 21 If..it be found, that the Pety Jury have given a false Serement. **1549** *Compl. Scot.* xv. 136 This serment vas veil maid & bettir kepit.

**serment**, obs. form of SERMON.

**ser'mocinate**, *v. rare*$^{-0}$. [f. L. *sermōcinat-*, pa. ppl. stem of *sermōcinārī*, f. *sermo* (see SERMON).] *intr.* To talk.

**1623** COCKERAM I, *Sermocinate*, to talke, to commune.

†**sermocination.** *Obs.* Also 7 **cerm-.** [ad. L. *sermōcinātiōn-em*, n. of action f. *sermōcinārī* to SERMOCINATE.]

**1.** Talk, conversation; a discourse, sermon.

**1514** *Fruyte of Redempcyon* (W. de W.) A iij b, Every oryson, every tonge, and sermocynacyon. **1623** COCKERAM II, A Talking together... *Cermocination*. **1645** PAGITT *Heresiogr.* 53 Barrow and Greenwood were possessed with a spirit of railing and scoffing, terming..preaching preachment and sermocination. **1646** BP. HALL *Three Tract., Free Prisoner* §2 No sermocinations of Ironmongers, Feltmakers, Coblers. **1662** PHILLIPS Pref., Whatever kind of sermocination is generally used in any Country, may very properly be termed a Language. **1674** SIR W. PETTY *Disc. Royal Soc.* Ep. Ded., Falsity..cannot be rectified by any sermocinations.

**2.** *Rhet.* A form of prosopopœia in which the speaker, having made a remark or put a question, immediately answers it.

**1753** *Chambers's Cycl.* Supp., *Sermocination*,..in rhetoric, denotes discourse in general, whether held by a person alone, or in company, and is the same with what is called dialogism.

So †**sermocinator**, a talker, speaker; †**sermocinatrix**, a female talker.

**1623** COCKERAM I, *Sermocinator*, hee which talketh. *Ibid.*, *Cermocinatrix*, shee that instructed to speake. *Ibid.*, *Sermocinatrix*, she which talketh. **1640** HOWELL *Dodona's Gr.* 214 These obstreperous Sermocinators..make easie impressions upon the minds of the vulgar. **1657** [W. SANCROFT] *Mod. Policies* iv. (ed. 7) D 5 b, These Clancular Sermocinators bear as great sway in popular minds..as the Loyolists do.

**sermon** ('sɜːmən), *sb.* Forms: α. 3-4 **sermun**, 3-5 **sarmun**, 3-6 **sarmon, sermoun**, 4-5 **sarmoun(e, sermown(e**, 4-6 **sermone**, 4- **sermon.** β. 5-6 **sermond(e**, 6 **serment, sarmond**, 7 **searmond**, 8 *vulgar* **sarmant.** [a. AF. *sermun* = OF. *sermon* (= Pr. *sermo(n*, It. *sermone*, Sp. *sermon*, Pg. *sermão*), ad. L. *sermōnem, sermo* talk, discourse, speech.]

†**1.** Something that is said; talk, discourse. *Obs.*

***to make sermon***: to speak. ***to make (a) long sermon***: to speak at great length.

*c* **1275** *Serving Christ* 53 in *O.E. Misc.* 92 þureh his sely sermun sorewe him wes by-þouht. *a* **1300** *Cursor M.* 13245 To þe Iues..In his louing he made sermon. *Ibid.* 13494 Quat sal i sai yow lang sermun? *c* **1330** R. BRUNNE *Chron. Wace* (Rolls) 9240 Arme vs swyþe, & go we doun, Wyþoute any more sarmoun! **13..** *E.E. Allit. P.* A. 1185 If hit be ueray & soth sermoun. *c* **1430** LYDG. *Min. Poems* (Percy Soc.) 40 Withoute more sermone, Thei drouhe handes, as weddynge askethe of rihte. **1536** BELLENDEN *Cron. Scot.* (1821) II. 177 Thair wes na sermone amang thaim how thair army suld be arrayit. **1592** GREENE *Disput.* 16 When any of you come to your confession at Tyborne, what is your last sermon that you make. **1594** *2nd Rep. Faustus* in Thoms *Prose Rom.* (1858) III. 404 Desiring Don Infeligo with very mild sermon to be friends with Medesimo again.

†**b.** In particularized use: A speech, discourse; *pl.* in collective sense, words, talk. *Obs.*

α. *a* **1300** *Cursor M.* 22219 Sant Paule þus sais in his sarmuns To þe folk of þe tessaluns. *c* **1385** CHAUCER *L.G.W.* 2025 What shuld I langer sermone off it make? *c* **1386** —— *Man of Law's Prol.* 87 He..Nolde neuere write in none of his sermons Of swyche vnkynde abomynacions. **1447** BOKENHAM *Seyntys, Agnes* 189 The prefect..made hir a sermoun ful of flatery. *c* **1500** KENNEDY *Passion of Christ* 1509 Quhilk ar þe sarmonis quhilk ȝe at oþer speir? **1535** COVERDALE *Jer.* i. 1 These are the Sermons of Ieremy the sonne of Helchia the prest.

β. *c* **1400** *Destr. Troy* 11491 He said in his sermond, þat sothely the grekes Were of pepull & pouer plaintius mony. *a* **1533** LD. BERNERS *Huon* lxxxi. 246 It is not nedefull that I sholde make a longe sermonde. **1533** BELLENDEN *Livy* v. xi. (S.T.S.) II. 186 He ceissit nocht with sic playis, sermondis & exerciciouns..to draw þame.

†**c.** *pl.* The satires (*sermones*) of Horace.

**1540** PALSGR. *Acolastus* II. i. I j, As Horace witnesseth in his .ii. boke of sermons, the .iii. Satyre. **1601** B. JONSON *Poetaster* III. i, Good Horace..I am for your odes or your sermons, or any thing indeed. **1671** H. M. tr. *Erasm. Colloq.* 438 Again Horace in his Odes... Likewise in his Sermons.

**2.** A discourse, usually delivered from a pulpit and based upon a text of Scripture, for the purpose of giving religious instruction or exhortation. Phr. ***to preach***, † ***do***, † ***make***, † ***say a sermon***.

α. *a* **1200** *Vices & Virtues* 35 He wisseð ðes mannes iðang ..oðer ðurh haliȝe writes oðer ðurh hali sermuns. *a* **1225** *Ancr. R.* 312 Weope we, cweð þe holi mon in 'Uitas Patrum', þo me hefde longe iȝeied on him efter sarmun. **1340** *Ayenb.* 20 Ine þet þou ne hest..y-hyerd his seruise ne y-zed his benes ne yhyerd sermons. *c* **1386** CHAUCER *Sompn. T.* 81, I have to day been at youre chirche at messe, And seyd a sermoun after my symple wit. *a* **1400** *Relig. Pieces fr. Thornton MS.* 1 Here begynnes a Sermon..þe whilke teches how scrifte es to be made. **1474** CAXTON *Chesse* 65 He herde in a sermone that deth spareth none. *c* **1511** *1st Eng. Bk. Amer.* Introd. (Arb.) 35/1 He comyth bod[i]ly euery yere in his chirche & doth a sermon. **1597** HOOKER *Eccl. Pol.* v. xxi. 38 Sermons are not the onely preaching which doth saue soules. **1692** T. WATSON *Body Divinity* 342 Which is worse, to stay from a Sermon, or sleep at a Sermon? **1712** ADDISON *Spect.* No. 269 ¶5 The Sunday before he had made a most incomparable sermon out of Dr. Barrow. **1828** WHATELY in *Encycl. Metrop.* (1845) I. 263/1 Sermons not unfrequently prove popular, which consist avowedly and almost exclusively of Exhortation. **1869** ARNOLD *Cult. & Anarchy* 29 A life of jealousy of the Establishment, disputes, tea meetings, openings of chapels, sermons.

β. *c* **1500** *God spede the Plough* 62 Preching dayly Sermondys inough With good Examples full graciously. **1564** in *Three 15th Cent. Chron.* (Camden) 130 Y[e] Byshope of London went to the pulpyt and prechyd a sermond. **1599** in W. Kelly *Notices illustr. Drama* (1865) 230 [He] further said the preacher was a Liar, for that, in his sermond, he said [etc.].

**b.** as an institution connected with a particular church or pulpit or particular season.

**1479** in *Eng. Gilds* (1870) 426 The Maire and Shiref of Bristowe shall..kepe theire Aduent sermondes. **1550** WRIOTHSLEY *Chron.* (1877) II. 40 Allso this yeare the sermons at Whitsontyde was kept at Pawles Crosse. **1556** *Chron. Gr. Friars* (Camden) 57 Thys yere on sent Martyns day begane the sarmond at the crosse agayne. **1646** PRYNNE *Canterb. Doome* 378 Concerning the Sermon weekly on Wednesday in Saint James Chappell in Brackley. **1765** FOOTE *Commiss.* I. i, Never misses the sarmant on Sundays.

**c.** as a written or published work.

**1422** YONGE *Secreta Secret.* xxxii. 183, I fynde In a Sermonde writte, that an extorcionere is wors than the deuyll. **1547** (*title*) Certain Sermons, or Homilies, appoynted by the Kynges Maiestie, to be declared and redde, by all Persones. **1657** *Crooke's Div. Char.* To Rdr. A 2 b, Certain select Sermons..licensed by the Vice-chancellor of Oxford, to be printed there. *a* **1721** PRIOR *Turtle & Sparrow* 193 And Sermons are less read than Tales. **1862** J. F. STEPHEN *Def. Rowland Williams* 150 In Bishop Horsley's Sermons.

**d.** without article.

***at, after sermon*** = at, after church.

*a* **1470** GREGORY *Chron.* in *Hist. Coll. Cit. London* (Camden) 239 Whyle men were at sarmonys the Sonday aftyr noon. **1582-8** *Hist. Jas. VI* (1804) 106 Imediatlie he past to the kirk, and .. maid sermon as thogh he had done na sic thing. **1597** HOOKER *Eccl. Pol.* v. xxii. 49 Those places which euery day for the most part are at sermons as the flowing Sea. **1666** EVELYN *Diary* 4 July, After sermon I waited on my Lord Abp. of Canterbury. **1773** ANNE GRANT *Lett. Mountains* (1809) I. vii. 53 Kilmore, where we heard sermon, is four miles off. **1815** SCOTT *Guy M.* xi, The young Laird of Hazlewood rides hame half the road wi' her after sermon. **1837** CARLYLE *Fr. Rev.* I. IV. iv, To march in procession to Notre-Dame, and hear sermon.

**e.** Applied to the discourses of our Lord and the Apostles.

***Sermon on the Mount***, the discourse recorded in Matt. v-vii and introduced by the words 'he went up into a mountain ..and taught them, saying'.

*c* **1250** *Kent. Serm.* in *O.E. Misc.* 31 He hedde i-yne þo newe laghe in one montayne and hedde i-maked þet formeste sarmun þet euerte made in erþe. **1340** *Ayenb.* 138 Oure lord ate biginnynge of his uayre sermon zayþ þet yblyssed byeþ þe poure. *c* **1520** NISBET *N.T. in Scots* I. 13 The serment of Petir befor the congregratioun at Jerusalem. **1533** GAU *Richt Vay* 82 Quhen he prechit the sueit sermond to thaym apone the montane. **1582** *N. T.* (Rhem.) Matt. v. *margin*, The sermon of Christ vpon the Mount. **1597** HOOKER *Eccl. Pol.* v. xxii. 45 Hearers of the Apostles Sermons. **1645** HAMMOND *Of Conscience* 26 Christs improvements of the Law in the Sermon on the Mount. **1875** MANNING *Mission Holy Ghost* xii. 339 The Sermon on the Mount is the law of perfection given to the Christian people of the world. **1897** *Ch. Times* 20 Aug. 186/4 In spite of the Sermon on the Mount, men expect a deanery or a comfortable competency to be the sequel to a life of work for God.

**3.** *transf.* and *fig.* **a.** A discourse (spoken or written) on a serious subject, containing instruction or exhortation. Also *contemptuously*, a long or tedious discourse or harangue.

**1596** SHAKS. *Tam. Shr.* IV. i. 186 Making a sermon of continencie to her. **1786** BURNS *Ep. Yng. Friend* i, Perhaps it may turn out a Sang; Perhaps, turn out a Sermon. **1816** [see LAY *a.* (and *sb.*[1]) 2]. **1841** THACKERAY *Gt. Hoggarty Diam.* xii, And now let's go to business, gentlemen, and excuse this sermon. **1870** DICKENS *E. Drood* vii, I will not repay your confidence with a sermon. **1872** CALVERLEY *Fly Leaves* (1903) 62 They do not make their woes the text Of sermons in the *Times*.

**b.** Something that affords instruction or example.

**1600** SHAKS. *A.Y.L.* II. i. 17 Bookes in the running brookes, Sermons in stones. **1700** DRYDEN *Char. Gd. Parson* 78 His preaching much, but more his practice wrought; (A living sermon of the truths he taught).

**4.** *attrib.* and *Comb.*, as ***sermon book***, ***-head***, ***note***, ***-pamphlet***, ***-style***, ***-time***, †***while***; objective, as ***sermon-actor***, ***-borrower***, ***-hunter***, ***-hunting***, ***-maker***, ***-monger***, ***-slighter***, ***-taster***, ***-writer***; adverbial, as ***sermon-goer***, ***-proof*** adj., ***-shaken*** †***-trodden*** pa. pples., ***-wise*** adv.; **sermon-bell**, a bell rung to give notice of a sermon; **sermon case**, a cover for the protection of a sermon in manuscript; **sermon class**, a class for instruction in preaching sermons; **sermon paper**, writing paper of foolscap 4to size; †**sermon-prayer**, a prayer said by the preacher before his sermon; †**sermon-sick**, temporarily 'upset' by the hearing of a sermon; so **sermon-sickness**; **sermon-week** *Sc.*, the week passed in preparation for receiving the Sacrament.

**1642** MILTON *Apol. Smect.* 46 The finicall goosery of your neat *Sermon-actor. **1646** TRAPP *Comm. John* i. 41 Do the office of the *sermon-bell at least, we know not what God may there do for them. **1687** *Churchw. Acc. Pittington*, etc. (Surtees) 255 They shall..ring the great bell for the Searmond bell. **1807** CRABBE *Par. Reg.* I. 569 Of them not one Shall court our view on the sepulchral stone;.. Or keep the sexton from the sermon-bell. **1772** NUGENT *Hist. Fr. Gerund* II. 9 He might meet in any *sermon-book, with abundant field to forage in. **1653** WALTON *Angler* iv. 106 Which the *Sermon Borrower complained of to the Lender of it. **1853** *Hodson's Booksellers' Directory* Advt., *Sermon Cases, Black Roan, 2*s.* **1847** CARUS *Life C. Simeon* iv. 62 He would .. encourage the least hopeful of his *sermon-class by telling them, that with his example before them none need despair. **1612** T. TAYLOR *Comm. Titus* iii. 578 Hypocrites, dissemblers, holy brethren, *sermon-goers, Puritans. **1647** TRAPP *Comm. Mark* i. 15 These were foure of our Saviours *Sermon-heads. **1886** H. F. LESTER *Under two Fig Trees* 186 The fashionable *Sermon-hunters. **1768-74** TUCKER *Lt. Nat.* (1834) II. 208 Psalm-singing, *sermon-hunting, ejaculating. **1552** HULOET, *Sermon maker, *concionator*. **1850** THOMSON *Owen's Wks.* I. Life p. cvi, No one .. will refuse to him the praise of a great sermon-maker. **1673** HICKERINGILL *Greg., Fr. Greybeard* 231 These modern orthodox-juglers and *sermon-mongers. **1705** —— *Priest-cr.* II. ii. 22, I have found more Honesty [amongst the naked Indians in America] .. in one Day, than amongst those Sermon-mongers in a Year. **1691** WOOD *Ath. Oxon.* I. 269 He .. had .. taken *Sermon notes by his most dextrous and incomparable faculty in short-writing. **1716** M. DAVIES *Athen. Brit.* II. 69 Latin *Sermon-Pamphlets. **1855** *Hodson's Booksellers' Directory* Advt., Ralph's *Sermon Paper. **1637** C. DOW *Answ. to Burton* 161 If *Sermon-prayers shall bee used as libels. **1624** DONNE *Serm.* xlvi. (1640) 466 It is a fearfull obduration to be *Sermon-proofe. **1769** WESLEY *Wks.* (1872) III. 367, I am afraid many of them are sermon-proof. *a* **1656** VINES *Lord's Supper* (1657) 364 Sometimes a man is *Sermon-shaken, and his heart begins to tremble. **1607** HIERON *Wks.* I. 216 Many may be said to be *sermon-sicke, as there are some said to be sea-sick. *a* **1665** J. GOODWIN *Filled with Spirit* (1670) 38 That which some call a *Sermon-sickness, when the Conscience of a man is only troubled .. with the dreadful concernment of the things he hears. **1646** SALTMARSHE *Groans for Liberty* 29 That the Parliament are *Sermon sleighters. *a* **1704** T. BROWN *Wks.* (1711) IV. 191 Let 'em by N——'s *Sermon-Stile refine Their English Prose. **1709** *Female Tatler* No. 7/3 A Sett o' Gentlemen .. that are call'd *Sermon-Tasters, they peep in at twenty different Churches in a Service. **1534** *Chron.* in *Songs, Carols*, etc. (E.E.T.S.) 163, & þer stod on a skaffold, all þe *sermond tyme, þe holy maid of Kent. **1749** FIELDING *Tom Jones* VIII. xii, A set of wicked wretches, who were at play during Sermon-time. **1848** THACKERAY *Van. Fair* ix, He always took his nap during sermon-time. **1647** TRAPP *Comm. Matt.* xiii. 19 People are now so *Sermon-trodden .. that their hearts .. grow hard by the Word. **1794** SCOTT *Let.* in *Lockhart* (1837) I. 223 This being *sermon week .. we are looking very religious and very sour at home. **1583** STOCKER *Civ. Warres Lowe C.* IV. 546 On which date in the *Sermon while. **1646** PRYNNE *Canterb. Doome* 378 That it was a Catechizing *Sermon-wise, and as bad as preaching. **1796** CHARLOTTE SMITH *Marchmont* IV. 423 The first head of his argument, which he divided sermon-wise. **1788** V. KNOX *Winter Even.* (1790) I. xxxviii. 329 The quaintness of the old *sermon writers.

**sermon** ('sɜːmən), *v.* *rare* in mod. use. Also 3 **sarmoni, sermonye**, 4-5 **sar-, sermone, -oun, -un**, 5 **sermowne**. [a. AF. *sarmuner* = OF. *sermouner* (mod.F. *sermonner*), f. *sermon* (see prec.). In mod. use a new formation on SERMON *sb.*]

**1.** *trans.* To preach to (a person). *lit.* and *fig.*

*c* **1175** *Lamb. Hom.* 81 þis monne me mei sermonen mid godes worde. *Ibid.*, þes ilke Mon is strong to sermonen. **1607** SHAKS. *Timon* II. ii. 181 Come sermon me no further. **1863** R. F. BURTON *W. Africa* II. 185 He once .. gathered energy to sermon me upon the subject of over-curiosity.

**2.** *intr.* †**a.** To preach (*of* a thing).

*c* **1275** *Sinners Beware* 161 in *O.E. Misc.* 77 þeos prude leuedies .. Nulleþ here sermonye Of none gode þinge. *c* **1290** *S. Eng. Leg.* I. 466/158 Crist hire hauede a-boute i-sent to sarmoni and to preche. *a* **1300** *Cursor M.* 19320 'þe men þat yee did in prisun', He said, 'in temple þai sermon'. [*a* **1300-1657**: see SERMONING *vbl. sb.*]

**b.** To preach (*at* a person).

**1819** KEATS *King Stephen* I. iv. 16, I would be .. Spoken to in clear, plain, and open terms, Not side-ways sermon'd at.

†**3.** *intr.* To speak (*of* a thing). *Obs.*

*a* **1300** *Cursor M.* 18666 Wit þam he lenged fourti dais, And sermond .. Of heuen blis. **1303** R. BRUNNE *Handl. Synne* 6955 Seynt Ihon to Troyle bygan to sermun with ensamples of gode resun. *c* **1386** CHAUCER *Pard. T.* 551 What nedeth it to sermone of it more? *c* **1430** *Pilgr. Lyf Manhode* II. xciii. (1869) 109 Whan þe olde hadde þus spoken, and sermowned of hire craft. *c* **1440** *York Myst.* xxx. 302 And þerfore sermones you no more. **1586** J. HOOKER *Descr. Irel.* 28 in *Holinshed*, You sermon to vs of a dungeon appointed for offendors and miscredents. **1606** S. GARDINER *Bk. Angling* 25 And when Saul came himselfe, hee sermoned in such sort.

†**4.** *trans.* To speak, utter, declare. *Obs.*

**1382** WYCLIF *Wisdom* viii. 12 And me sermounende manye thingis [orig. *me sermocinante*]. **1590** SPENSER *F.Q.*, *Let. to Raleigh*, Good discipline deliuered plainly in way of precepts, or sermoned at large.

†'**sermonary**, *a.* *Obs.* [f. SERMON *sb.* + -ARY.] Of the nature of a sermon.

**1657** J. SERGEANT *Schism Dispach't* 338 Who never .. knew what it was to make any notions cohere at all save onely in a loose sermonary way. **1666** —— *Let. Thanks* 28 Loose sermonary Discourses.

**sermond(e, -one**, obs. forms of SERMON.

†**sermo'neer**. *Obs. rare.* [f. SERMON *sb.* + -EER[1].] A preacher.

*a* **1637** B. JONSON *Underwoods* lxvii. 39 The wits will leave you, if they once perceive You cling to Lords, and Lords, if them you leave For sermoneeres.

**sermoner** ('sɜːmənə(r)). *rare.* [f. SERMON + -ER[1]; in ME. after AF. *sarmuner* = OF. *sermounier* (f. *sermoun* SERMON *sb.*).] A preacher of sermons.

*c* **1325** *Metr. Hom.* 147 Quen he sendes his messageres, That es at sai, thir sarmouneres, That clenses man of gastli wede, And schawes in him Goddes sede. **1547** *Will of H. Marwood* in *C. Worthy's Devonshire Wills* (1896) 3 The sayde s[r]moner to have of my executryxe for hys stypent .. syxe shyllyngs and eghtypens. **1855** THACKERAY *Newcomes* x, Guarded by cordons of sentinels, sermoners, old aunts. **1895** *Westm. Gaz.* 15 May 2/2 Without hireling singers, sermoners, or supplicators.

**sermonesque** (sɜːmə'nɛsk), *a.* [f. SERMON *sb.* + -ESQUE.] Of the nature or style of a sermon: with depreciatory force.

**1859** HELPS *Friends in C.* Ser. II. II. vi. 117 This essay of Durnford's is not a bad essay, though somewhat sermonesque. **1883** *Pall Mall G.* 7 Sept. 3/2 These sermonesque platitudes.

**sermonette** (sɜːmə'nɛt). Also **-et**. [f. SERMON *sb.* + -ETTE (-ET).] A short sermon. Also *transf.* and *fig.*

**1814** H. & L. M. HAWKINS (*title*) Sermonets addressed to those who have not yet acquired .. the inclination to apply the power of attention to compositions of a higher kind. **1848** *Blackw. Mag.* Mar. 289 Each sermonette was succeeded by a prayer. **1895** S. R. HOLE *Tour Amer.* 241 He thrust in a sermonette, an impressive little moral deduction. **1943** E. GILLETT *Lit. of Eng.* xiv. 223 The tendency to allow digressions and sermonettes to swamp the main purpose of the novel. **1975** *Publishers Weekly* 23 June 72/3 Gavin is sincere and interesting, but too often he digresses into sermonettes that sound like echoes of the *National Review*. **1978** *Listener* 26 Jan. 110/2, I feel I should be issuing at least a sermonette from the mount.

Hence ˌ**sermone'ttino**, a diminutive sermon; **sermo'nettist**, a preacher of sermonettes.

**1818** LADY MORGAN *Flor. Macarthy* II. 17 Sermonettinos or religious Bagatelles. **1873** M. COLLINS *Squire Silchester* xxxii, Farmer Giles, continued our pretty sermonettist, is asked his opinion on free trade and protection.

**sermonic** (sɜː'mɒnɪk), *a.* [f. SERMON *sb.* + -IC.] Of the form or nature of a sermon; resembling (that of) a sermon. Somewhat *depreciatory*.

**1761** HURD in *Warburton & H.'s Lett.* (1809) 330 The sermonic cast of this sentence. *a* **1849** POE *Predicament* Wks. 1864 IV. 247 The grateful sermonic harangues of Dr. Ollapod. **1856** BAGEHOT *Biogr. Studies* (1881) 27 His tone is a trifle sermonic. **1892** *Bookman* Oct. 5/2 The book is introduced by a sermonic preface from the Committee of the Religious Tract Society.

**b.** *sb. pl.* Sermonizing. *rare.*

**1804** *Something Odd* III. 82, I have not troubled myself .. to transcribe the letter, well assured that .. you have no taste for sermonics.

So **ser'monical** *a.*; hence **ser'monically** *adv.*, after the fashion of a sermon.

**1782** V. KNOX *Ess.* clxiv. II. 324 First then of the first (forgive my sermonical style), namely, of the Fine Man. **1829** *Censor* 87 The egregious lecture .. half sermonical, half theatrical. **1844** *Fraser's Mag.* XXIX. 77 Sermonically speaking, I cannot conclude without a piece of advice.

**sermonies, -ys**, obs. pl. of CEREMONY.

†'**sermoning**, *vbl. sb.* *Obs.* [f. SERMON *v.*]

**1.** Preaching; also, a sermon.

*a* **1300** *Cursor M.* 1829 þai for-soke his sermoning And toke his word al til hething. *Ibid.* 21123 Matheu, a-postil and wangeliste, .. For sarmoning of gods word, Men sais he stiked was wit suord. *c* **1430** *Pilgr. Lyf Manhode* I. xxvii. (1869) 18 Sermonynge and prechinge maketh men many times leue sinne. **1554** PHILPOT tr. *Curio's Def.* Ded., Wks. (Parker Soc.) 323 The divelish hypocrisy hath been .. vanquished .. both by reasoning, sermoning and writing. **1642** MILTON *Apol. Smect.* 5 Quaint Sermonings interlin'd with barbarous Latin. **1657** J. WATTS *Scribe, Pharisee*, etc. Pref. Ep. 11 To break out unto preaching and sermoning in the pulpits of others.

**2.** Talk, discourse, conversation. ***to make sermoning of***, to speak of.

*c* **1330** R. BRUNNE *Chron. Wace* (Rolls) 8824 þe stones to Bretaigne for to brynge, þat Merlyn made of sermonynge. *c* **1375** *Sc. Leg. Saints* xxvii. (*Machor*) 1100 þan held þai wele lang sermonyng of .. hewinlik thing. *c* **1385** CHAUCER *L.G.W.* 1184 Herof was so longe a sermonynge. **1513** DOUGLAS *Æneis* v. xii. 98 With sic wordis and prudent sermonyng Of his wise agit freynd. **1535** STEWART *Cron. Scot.* II. 7 Thair he hes maid, with richt lang sermoning, Ane sair complaint.

So '**sermoning** *ppl. a.*, preaching.

**1677** *2nd Pacquet Advices* 57 The whole Posse of Sermoning Matrons (the chief Garison of the Presbyterian Clergie).

**sermonish** ('sɜːmənɪʃ), *a.* [f. SERMON *sb.* + -ISH.]

**1.** Inclined for a sermon.

**1858** BAILEY *Age* 113 When once a man feels sermonish or psalmy.

**2.** = SERMONIC *a.*

**1847-54** WEBSTER, *Sermonish*, resembling a sermon. **1880** *Academy* 16 Oct. 272 A sermonish restatement of what is very much better said in Canon Farrar's *Seekers after God*. **1889** *Advance* (Chicago) 25 Apr., A very prosaic and sermonish letter.

**sermonist** ('sɜːmənɪst). [f. SERMON + -IST.] A preacher, sermonizer.

**1630** WIDDOWES *Schysmat. Puritan* B 2 b, The factious Sermonist, is he, whose purenes is, to serue God with sermons, and extemporary praiers made according to his supposititious inspiration. **1632** LUPTON *Lond. Carbonadoed* 82 [Players] do as some wandring Sermonists, make one Sermon trauaile and serue twenty Churches. **1816** MISS MITFORD in L'Estrange *Life* (1870) I. 331 What a contrast between him and our dramatic sermonists. **1844** *Fraser's Mag.* XXIX. 292 We were together looking over the ponderous sermonist.

**sermonize** ('sɜːmənaɪz), *v.* [f. SERMON *sb.* + -IZE.]

**1.** *intr.* To deliver or compose a sermon; = PREACH *v.* 1. Chiefly *depreciatory*.

**1635** [see SERMONIZING *vbl. sb.*]. **1651** JANE *Εικων Ακλαστος* 214 Its like his preachers pray and sermonize without premeditation. **1772** *Town & Country Mag.* 35 To go and hear this black-gown lover sermonize. **1887** F. W. MACDONALD *Life W. M. Punshon* ii. 37 He sermonised with ease. **1893** JESSOPP *Stud. Recluse* vii. 229 Like a young curate sermonising.

**b.** To give serious exhortation, talk seriously; = PREACH *v.* 1 b. Also with *it*.

**1753** E. MOORE *Gamester* IV. (ed. 3) 55 If they should laugh at you, fly to my Lord, and sermonize it there. **1788** BURNS *Let. to R. Ainslie* 30 June, You see how I preach. You used occasionally to sermonize too. **1864** TENNYSON *Enoch Arden* 204 In sailor fashion roughly sermonizing On providence and trust in Heaven. **1874** SYMONDS *Sk. Italy & Greece* (1898) I. ii. 34 To allegorise and sermonise is out of place here.

**2.** *trans.* To preach a sermon to (*rare*); to talk seriously or earnestly to, 'preach' to, 'lecture'.

**1802** MARIAN MOORE *Lascelles* II. 60, I do not intend .. to sermonize you about coquetry. **1848** THACKERAY *Van. Fair* xiii, I won't be always sermonised by you because you're five years my senior. **1860** MRS. BYRNE *Undercurrents* II. 307 A preacher of the time of Charles II., .. being called upon to sermonize royalty. **1890** *Blackw. Mag.* CXLVIII. 173/1 Fined and sermonised by the magistrates at Bow Street.

**3.** To 'preach' upon (a subject). *rare.*

**1789** *Poetry* in *Ann. Reg.* 158 To .. sermonize the follies of the age.

**4.** To bring into a specified condition by preaching.

**1768** W. LIVINGSTON *Let. to Bp. Landaff* 15 People.. may be mendicated or sermonized out of their money. **1824** LANDOR *Imag. Conv.* Wks. 1853 I. 7/1 Which of us shall sing or sermonize the other fast asleep. **1868** HELPS *Realmah* xiv, I should have claimativeness written, talked, educated, and sermonized down.

**sermonizer** ('sɜːmənaɪzə(r)). [f. prec. + -ER.] One who sermonizes or preaches.

**1651** JANE *Εικων Ακλαστος* 46 The Rebellion, perjury and Atheisme, that hath followed such sermonizers. **1788** V. KNOX *Winter Even.* (1790) I. xxxviii. 324 The method which the old sermonizers pursued to eke out their sermons. **1863** 'OUIDA' *Held in Bondage* vi, What the deuce, Colonel! you turning sermonizer? **1868** DORAN *Saints & Sinners* I. 296 One of the heaviest and longest sermonizers of the seventeenth century was.. Dr. Manton.

**'sermonizing,** *vbl. sb.* [f. SERMONIZE + -ING[1].] Delivery or composition of sermons; preaching (*lit.* and *fig.*).

**1635** F. WHITE *Sabbath* Ep. Ded. 14 Concerning their owne ecclesiasticall sermonizing. **1761** HURD in *Warburton & H.'s Lett.* (1809) 331 The common way of sermonizing is most wretched: neither sense, nor eloquence. **1796** MRS. M. ROBINSON *Angelina* II. 245 There was something so awful in the old gentleman's sermonizing, that I could not immediately answer him. **1830** COLERIDGE *Table-t.* 27 May, Any whining or sermonizing would have.. confirmed me in my absurdity. **1890** *Spectator* 13 Sept., Dr. Liddon had early realised that preaching does not come by nature;.. that amateur sermonising is no better than amateur acting.

So **'sermonizing** *ppl. a.* (or *vbl. sb.* used *attrib.*).

**1714** MANDEVILLE *Fab. Bees* I. (1723) 12 Whom d'ye think The Sermonizing Rascal chid? A Glover that sold Lamb for Kid. **1740–87** *Lett. of Miss Talbot* (1808) 43 You see I am in a sermonizing humour. **1808** E. SLEATH *Bristol Heiress* III. 131 Tired of her sermonizing conversation. **1877** OWEN in Marq. Wellesley *Desp.* Introd. p. xxxvii, The sermonizing and inquisitorial passage from the Directors' own Despatch.

**'sermonless,** *a.* [-LESS.] Without a sermon.

**1869** LANDRETH *Adam Thomson* iii. 147 A sermonless Sabbath. *a* **1876** M. COLLINS *Pen Sk.* (1879) I. 20 A sermonless Sunday seems rather in the nature of a holiday.

**sermonoid** ('sɜːmənɔɪd). *rare.* [-OID.] Something of the nature of a sermon.

*a* **1849** POE *Marginalia* Wks. 1864 III. 489 For the want of merely a comma, it often occurs that an axiom appears a paradox, or that a sarcasm is converted into a sermonoid. **1886** *Tinsley's Mag.* Sept. 288, I will not turn more of my reminiscences into sermonoids.

**sermo'nolatry.** Excessive devotion to sermons.

**1859** F. E. PAGET *Curate of Cumberworth* 149 The rampant sermonolatry—(forgive so barbarous a word!) of the day.

**sermo'nology.** [-(O)LOGY.] Sermonizing; sermons collectively.

**1854** E. G. HOLLAND *Mem. Jos. Badger* viii. 141 The sermonology that then passed for the Word of Life. **1864** KIDDER *Homiletics* iii. 86 The opportunity of investigating ..the sermonology of ancient and medieval as well as of modern times. **1897** TALMAGE in *Chr. Herald* (N.Y.) 24 Nov. 884/1 The old styles of sermonology.

†**sermonward:** see -WARD.

*c* **1513** MORE *Rich. III*, Wks. 61/1 Nowe was it before deuised, that.. the protector should haue comen in among y[e] people to y[e] sermonwarde.

**sermonyal,** obs. form of CEREMONIAL.

*c* **1380** WYCLIF *Wks.* (1880) 285 Sermonyalis of þe oolde lawe.

†**sermountain.** *Obs.* [a. OF. *sermontain* (also *sel-*, *seur-*), *sermontaygne*, ad. med.L. *siler montanum*, lit. mountain willow.] The umbelliferous plant *Laserpitium Siler*. (Cf. HARTWORT 1.)

*c* **1450** *Alphita* (Anecd. Oxon.) 169 *Sifula*..gallice et anglice sermontaygne. *Ibid.* 169 *Siseleos uel siselenum*.. gall. et angl. sermontayne. **1640** PARKINSON *Theat. Bot.* 909 *Ligusticum verum sive Siler montanum.* Libisticke or Sermountaine of Liguria. **1768** W. LEWIS *Mat. Med.* (ed. 2) 541 *Seseli*.. Hartwort or Sermountain.

**sermuncle** ('sɜːrmʌŋk(ə)l). [ad. L. *sermunculus*, dim. of *sermo* SERMON.] A sermonette.

**1886** *Ch. Times* 2 Apr. 253/3 The essence of this devotion is a series of sermuncles, meditations, hymns, or prayers.

**Sernyl** ('sɜːnɪl). *Pharm.* Also **sernyl.** A proprietary name for PHENCYCLIDINE.

**1958** *Official Gaz.* (U.S. Patent Office) 9 Sept. TM 52/1 Parke, Davis & Company... *Sernyl*... For psycho-pharmacologic agents with anesthetic and analgesic properties. First use Nov. 22, 1957. **1959** *Antibiotic Med. & Clin. Therapy* VI. 79 Recently, laboratory observations indicated that phencyclidine (Sernyl) possessed central nervous system depressant properties associated with improvement in mood. **1964** C. WILLOCK *Enormous Zoo* vi. 107 Drugs so far used include.. Sernyl. **1970** PASSMORE & ROBSON *Compan. Med. Stud.* II. v. 28/2 Phencyclidene (sernyl) was introduced as an analgesic agent, but has been found to produce psychotomimetic effects. **1974** [see PHENCYCLIDINE].

†**sero.** *Obs.* [L., adv. of *sērus* late.] Late; also, a late boy (at school).

**1682** *Rec. Scott. Cloth Manuf. New Mills* (S.H.S.) 17 And if the clerk be *sero* or absent to pay the double. **1734** T. WATT *Vocab., Lang. School* 8 What will you do to me? I'll set you up Amongst the Sero's.

**sero-** ('sɪərəʊ), used as comb. form of SERUM in the senses: (*a*) of or pertaining to serum, as ***sero-diagnosis*** (hence ***-diagnostic*** adj.), ***-phthisis***; (*b*) pertaining to, consisting of, or involving serum (and something else), as ***sero-albuminous***, ***-fibrinous***, ***-fibrous***, ***-gelatinous***, ***-lactescent***, ***-membranous***, ***-mucous***, ***-puriform***, ***-purulent***, ***-sanguineous***, ***-sanguinolent***, ***-synovial*** adjs.; (*c*) characterized by serous effusion or infiltration, or involving a serous membrane (cf. SEROUS 1 b), as ***sero-colitis***, ***-cyst***, ***-cystic*** adj., ***-dermatosis***, ***-dermitis***, ***-enteritis***, ***hæmorrhagic*** adj., ***-hepatitis***, ***-synovitis***. Also **ˌseroaggluti'nation**, agglutination of the cultured cells of a micro-organism by an antiserum, as showing the serological identity of the micro-organism with the one that gave rise to the antiserum; **ˌsero-amni'otic** *a.*, pertaining to the serosa and the amnion; **'serodeme** *Biol.* [DEME *sb.*[2]], an immunologically distinct strain of organisms; **ˌserodifferenti'ation**, differentiation between micro-organisms by serological means; **ˌseroepidemi'ology**, the serological study of the prevalence and distribution of a pathogen in a population; so **ˌseroepidemio'logic, -'logical** *adjs.*; **'serogroup**, a group of serotypes with similar but distinguishable serological reactions; hence as *v. trans.*, to assign to a particular serogroup; **'serogrouping** *vbl. sb.*; **'sero-immunity**, immunity conferred by the administration of antiserum; **sero'mucoid** *Physiol.* [ad. It. *sieromucoide* (C. U. Zanetti 1903, in *Gazz. chim. ital.* XXXIII. I. 160)], a mucoprotein found in blood serum; **sero'negative** *a.*, opp. next; **sero'positive** *a.*, showing or accompanied by the presence of a characteristic serological reaction; hence **ˌsero-posi'tivity**; **sero-pus**, serous pus; **sero-serous** *a.*, pertaining to two or more serous membranes jointly; **ˌserota'xonomy**, the use of the serological reactions and structural similarities of proteins from different animals to provide information about their taxonomic relationship; hence **ˌserotaxo'nomic** *a.*; **sero'therapy**, treatment of disease or infection by serums, serum-therapy; hence **ˌsero-thera'peutic** *a.*, **sero'therapist**.

**1910** *Jrnl. Amer. Med. Assoc.* 12 Feb. 573/2 (*heading*) *Seroagglutination of *Sporothrix schenkii*. **1975** *Jrnl. Clin. Microbiol.* II. 268 (*heading*) Seroagglutination test for identification of *Mycobacterium paratuberculosis*. **1890** K. MITSUKURI in *Anatomischer Anzeiger* V. 512 A connection —quite elongated and definite in later stages—between the amnion and the serous envelope separates them [*sc.* the extra-embryonic coelomic cavities of the two moieties of the amnion] to the very end of the development... The connection I propose to call the *sero-amniotic connection. **1958** B. M. PATTEN *Found. Embryol.* xi. 183 The cavity between serosa and amnion (sero-amniotic cavity) is part of the extra-embryonic coelom. **1855** DUNGLISON *Med. Lex.* s.v. *Colitis*, Inflammation of the peritoneal.. membrane of the colon.. is termed *Sero-colitis. **1872** T. BRYANT *Pract. Surg.* 765 The simple *sero-cyst is usually found single in the mammary gland. **1846** SIR B. BRODIE *Lect. Pathol. & Surg.* vii. 156, I would suggest 'the *sero-cystic tumor of the breast' as being an appropriate appellation. **1875** H. WALTON *Dis. Eye* (ed. 3) 166 Sero-cystic sarcoma within the orbit. **1966** C. A. HOARE in *Ergebnisse der Mikrobiol. und Immunitätsforsch.* XXXIX. 55 A more suitable term [than 'type'] is 'deme'.., which denotes a population.. within a specified taxon.., and may be combined with an appropriate prefix... *T. evansi*.. contains immunologically distinct strains, which.. represent *serodemes. **1978** *Nature* 25 May 300/2 We have transmitted through *Glossina morsitans morsitans* trypanosomes of the AnTat serodeme. **1897** *Lippincott's Med. Dict.*, **Sero-dermatosis*, cutaneous disease with serous effusion into the skin. *Ibid.*, **Serodermitis*, dermitis with serous infiltration. **1896** *Lancet* 24 Oct. 1157/1 *Sero-diagnostic Test for Typhoid Fever. *Ibid.* 1157/2 *Sero-diagnosis of Typhoid Fever according to Widal's Method. **1960** *Virology* X. 376 (*heading*) A simple test for *serodifferentiation of poliovirus strains within the same type. **1974** *Bull. World Health Organization* L. 479 This heterogeneous immune response permits the preparation of specific antisera for intratypic serodifferentiation. **1876** *Dunglison's Med. Lex.* s.v. *Enteritis*, The inflammation of the serous coat, *Seroënteritis. **1958** *Jrnl. Amer. Med. Assoc.* 31 May 541/1 This paper will report *seroepidemiologic results associating the increase in influenza-pneumonia mortality.. with the influenza virus. **1978** *Ibid.* 16 Jan. 210/1 To define the epidemiologic features of occupationally acquired hepatitis B infection among physicians, we conducted a sero-epidemiologic survey of physicians attending three American Medical Association conventions. **1959** *Amer. Jrnl. Public Health* XLIX. 847 (*heading*) A laboratory analysis of the 1957–1958 influenza outbreak in New York City. II. A *seroepidemiological study. **1975** *Nature* 1 May 12/2 Limited seroepidemiological studies have shown that most individuals of a low socio-economic level had hepatitis antibodies. **1967** *Bull. World Health Organization* XXXVII. 79 (*heading*) WHO collaborative study on the *sero-epidemiology of Rubella. **1977** *Lancet* 12 Nov. 1038/2 The seroepidemiology of herpes simplex virus (H.S.V.) type 2 infection in man has been hampered by difficulties in demonstrating antibodies specific for H.S.V. type 2 in sera with cross-reacting H.S.V. type 1 antibodies. **1873** T. H. GREEN *Introd. Pathol.* (ed. 2) 215 The meshes of the pia mater become infiltrated with a *sero-fibrinous liquid. **1896** WHITNEY in *20 Cent. Pract.* VII. 10 Serofibrinous pleurisy. **1834** J. FORBES *Laennec's Dis. Chest* (ed. 4) 107 *Sero-fibrous adhesions. **1894** *Foster's Med. Dict.* s.v., **Sero-gelatinous*, partaking of the nature of both serum and gelatin. **1954** WOLFF & BROOM in *Documenta Med. Geogr. & Tropica* VI. 92 When two or more serotypes show marked similarities in their serological reactions.. it is convenient to assemble them into groups, which we suggest should be known as '*serogroups' (serological groups). **1962** *Austral. Jrnl. Exper. Biol. & Med. Sci.* XL. 84 We.. propose that strain 'Robinson' be recognized as a new serotype in the *pyrogenes* serogroup with the designation *Leptospira robinsoni*. **1963** *Jrnl. Clin. Investigation* XLII. 989/2 *Serogrouping of *E. coli* permitted the recognition of 25 instances of recurrent infection with a different serogroup.. and 24 instances of recurrence with the same serogroup. **1977** *Lancet* 29 Jan. 257/1 None of the other serogroups of streptococci (A, C, D, G and F) produce any pigment. **1977** *Jrnl. Clinical Path.* XXX. 834 (*heading*) Use of antiserum agar plates for serogrouping of meningococci. *Ibid.* 836 The meningococcal strains were serogrouped by slide-agglutination. **1898** *Allbutt's Syst. Med.* V. 569 *Serohæmorrhagic extravasations. **1839** *Lond. Med. Gaz.* XXIII. 570/1 By *sero-hepatitis is meant inflammation of the serous or peritoneal tunic of the liver. **1855** DUNGLISON *Med. Lex., Hepatitis*, It may be seated.. in the peritoneal covering, Sero-hepatitis. **1907** *Jrnl. Amer. Med. Assoc.* 6 Apr. 1219/1 *Sero-immunity to bile salts. **1975** *Amer. Jrnl. Epidemiol.* CI. 333/1 Most reports on sero-immunity have dealt with small children, following vaccine programs with very little information on maintenance of artificially induced antibody. **1857** BULLOCK tr. *Cazeaux' Midwifery* 130 A serous, or *sero-lactescent liquid. **1931** *Biochem. Jrnl.* XXV. 1064 It is considered unlikely that the carbohydrate isolated from serum-albumin and globulin preparations was in reality derived from admixed *seromucoid. **1955** *Methods Biochem. Anal.* II. 281 It is appropriate to replace the term plasma mucoprotein with the established term seromucoid. **1894** *Foster's Med. Dict.*, **Sero-mucous*, partaking of the nature of both serum and mucus. **1932** SCHAMBER & WRIGHT *Treatm. Syphilis* xxv. 404 (*table*) Two to 3 courses of combined therapy usually suffice for *seronegative primary syphilis. **1977** *Lancet* 9 Apr. 811/2 A seronegative donor showed no response at any concentration of antigen. **1932** SCHAMBER & WRIGHT *Treatm. Syphilis* xxv. 417 The treatment of seronegative primary syphilis should continue for two years and for *seropositive primary syphilis.. for from two to three years. **1975** *Nature* 12 June 546/1 Seronegative and seropositive squirrels were housed in an isolated room in different cages, usually in groups of six. **1969** *Acta Path. & Microbiol. Scandinavica* LXXVII. 278 The numbers of sero-positive experimental mice are expressed as ratios of the numbers surviving because this gives a more accurate impression of the *sero-positivity of each group. **1901** *Lancet* 2 Feb. 317/2 Some *sero-puriform fluid escaped. **1835–6** *Todd's Cycl. Anat.* I. 61/2 The inflammation.. producing *sero-purulent suppuration. **1873** RALFE *Phys. Chem.* 168 In ichorous, muco-, or *sero-pus. **1834** J. FORBES *Laennec's Dis. Chest* (ed. 4) 81 A *sero-sanguineous congestion of the pulmonary texture. **1874** VAN BUREN *Dis. Genit. Organs* 90 To.. change the discharge into a *sero-sanguinolent one. **1894** *Foster's Med. Dict.*, **Sero-serous*, pertaining to two or more serous membranes jointly. *Ibid.*, **Sero-synovial*, partaking of the nature of both serum and synovia. **1888** *Buck's Handbk. Med. Sci.* VI. 703/2 Acute serous synovitis,.. *sero-synovitis. **1967** *Nature* 9 Sept. 1213/1 Systematics Association... Symposium on 'Chemotaxonomy and *Serotaxonomy'. **1968** P. G. H. GELL in J. G. Hawkes *Chemotaxonomy & Serotaxonomy* vii. 74 The evidence that the heavy chains of other immunoglobulins were involved in the same evolutionary process comes from work on the allotypes. Here we return to studies rather closer to serotaxonomy. **1968** HAWKES & TUCKER in *Ibid.* viii. 77 The first stage of a serotaxonomic revision of the family Solanaceae is described in which seeds have been used as the source of saline soluble protein. **1971** *Nature* 9 Apr. 412/2 He is rather cautiously optimistic about the future possibilities of protein and DNA studies and of serotaxonomy. **1902** *Encycl. Brit.* XXX. 486 Experiments in immunizing by *sero-therapeutic methods have not as yet met with success. **1901** *Daily Chron.* 31 Aug. 5/6 The medical puffery of the *serotherapists. **1894** *Brit. Med. Jrnl.* 3 Nov. 1008 The series of discoveries which finally led to that of the *serotherapy.

**sero-albumen:** see SERALBUMEN.

**serocco,** obs. form of SIROCCO *sb.*

**seroconversion** (ˌsɪərəʊkən'vɜːʃən). *Biol.* and *Med.* [f. SERO- + CONVERSION.] A change from a seronegative to a seropositive state.

**1964** *Jrnl. Amer. Med. Assoc.* 18 May 639 (*heading*) Poliovirus shedding and seroconversion. **1968** *New Scientist* 28 Nov. 500/2 Successive tests then showed that there were nine seroconversions... Illnesses that suggested viral infection preceded seroconversion in four of the children. **1977** *Lancet* 15 Oct. 811/1 Vaccination of children in the first 6 months of life was unsuccessful—only 1 seroconversion in 58.

Hence **serocon'vert** *v. intr.*, to acquire such sensitivity.

**1969** *Amer. Jrnl. Dis. Children* CXVIII. 331/1 Antibody was slower to appear, titers were lower, one of the animals failed to seroconvert, and SN antibody was not detected. **1977** *Lancet* 18 June 1314/2 Of these [patients],.. 1 sero-converted to positive anti-$HB_8$.

**seroid** ('sɪərɔɪd), *a.* [f. SER-UM + -OID.] 'Resembling a serous membrane' (*Dunglison's Med. Lex.* 1876).

**serolin** (ˈsɪərəlɪn). Also -ine. [ad. F. *séroline* (Boudet), f. *sérum* SERUM, L. *oleum* oil + *ine* -IN.] A fatty substance found in blood serum.

**1835–6** *Todd's Cycl. Anat.* I. 411/1. **1845** W. GREGORY *Outl. Chem.* II. 556 A peculiar fat called seroline.

**serologic** (sɪərəˈlɒdʒɪk), *a.* [f. SEROLOG(Y + -IC.] = next.

**1910** *Jrnl. Amer. Med. Assoc.* 2 July 94/1 (*heading*) Vacuum bottles as aid in bacteriologic and serologic work. **1978** *Jrnl. R. Soc. Med.* LXXI. 362 By retrospective diagnosis on clinical and serologic grounds other episodes of LD have come to light.

**serological** (sɪərəˈlɒdʒɪkəl), *a.* [f. SERO- + -LOGICAL.] Pertaining to, by means of, or involving serology; (of strains of micro-organism) distinguishable by serology.

**1911** *Lancet* 4 Feb. 319/2 Serological tests for blood. **1917** *Lancet* 8 Dec. 847/1 Arkwright..was unable by serological methods to establish any specific differences between epidemic and sporadic strains of the meningococcus. **1931** *Times Lit. Suppl.* 31 Dec. 1054/4 Serological diagnosis of cancer. **1946** *Nature* 14 Dec. 879/2 The very similar chemical and physical properties and behaviour of the specific blood-group factors..forced one to rely on serological techniques for their differentiation. **1955** *New Biol.* XIX. 9 Pneumococci are classified into various serological types on the basis of the polysaccharides which form their capsules. **1966** *Punch* 7 Dec. 863/2 Recently the British Veterinary Association were given figures which showed how much sub-clinical ill-health may perhaps be due to *brucella*. Of three hundred and nine vets examined sixty-three per cent had serological evidence of infection. **1977** *Dædalus* Summer 165 It took a great deal of time, and work, before it could be understood that..there were more than forty different serological types of the principal streptococcal species responsible for human disease.

Hence **seroˈlogically** *adv.*

**1913** *Jrnl. Amer. Med. Assoc.* 6 Sept. 808/2 Serologically all nervous diseases are divided into two general and easily distinguishable classes, the negative and positive types. **1976** *Ann. Rev. Microbiol.* XXX. 107 Each fungus contains two serologically unrelated and electrophoretically distinguishable viruses.

**serologist** (sɪəˈrɒlədʒɪst). [f. next + -IST.] A student or practitioner of serology.

**1914** *Lancet* 25 Apr. 1216/2 (*heading*) Appointment of serologist in Calcutta. **1939** *Jrnl. Amer. Med. Assoc.* 1 Apr. 1245/1 The physical condition of the patient was not known to the serologist at the time the blood studies were made. **1959** M. BURNET *Clonal Selection Theory of Acquired Immunity* iii. 30 As every serologist knows, absorption of the serum with a series of more or less closely related bacterial suspensions will leave behind antibody solutions of quite distinct functional character. **1976** 'J. ROSS' *I know what it's like to Die* xxx. 199 'Is there any news about the blood in the Ford?'.. 'Sorry... The serologist was out.'

**serology** (sɪəˈrɒlədʒɪ). [f. SERO- + -LOGY.] The study of blood serum; *spec.* the study of pathogens and other potential antigens by means of the immune responses which they induce as evidenced in blood serum; also, the serological characteristics *of* a disease or individual.

**1909** *Jrnl. Amer. Med. Assoc.* 11 Sept. 891/2 (*heading*) Serology of syphilis. **1921** *Glasgow Herald* 22 Feb. 7 Medicine, surgery, and prevention of infectious diseases had been utterly revolutionised since bacteriology and serology were developed. **1948** *Nature* 20 Mar. 428/1 The studies in systematic serology which have been conducted at Rutgers University since 1925. **1956** *Jrnl. Mammalogy* XXXVII. 11 (*heading*) Comparative serology of carnivores. **1977** *Blut* XXXV. 165 (*heading*) Erythrocyte serology of some malignant diseases.

**seron** (ˈsɪərən, sɪˈruːn). Also 6, 9 **serone**, 9 **seroon**; see also CEROON. [ad. Sp. *seron* hamper, crate (f. *sera* large basket), partly through F. *serron* (spelt also *céron*).] A bale or package (of exotic products, e.g. almonds, medicinal bark, cocoa) made up in an animal's hide.

**1545** *Rates Custom ho.* d vij, A cheste of suger... A serone of sope... A barrell of pepper. **1577** HELLOWES *Gueuara's Chron.* 213 An olde Seron, wherein the slaues did beare out the ordure of the stable. **1640** in *Northouck's Lond.* (1773) 841/2 For a bag or sack 4*d*. For a seron 3*d*. **1706** PHILLIPS (ed. Kersey), *Seron of Almonds*, the Quantity of Two Hundred Weight: Of Anis-seeds from 3 to 4 C: Of Castle-Soap from 2¼ C to 3¾ C. **1745** *Lond. Even. Post* 5 Mar. 1/2 Having on board 800 Serons of Cacoa. **1748** *Anson's Voy.* II. iv. 164 Twenty-three serons of dollars, each weighing upwards of 200 *l.* averdupois. **1821** J. SMYTH *Pract. Customs* 103 [Horse Hair] In Serons or Bales from South America.. usually weighing from 18 to 24 lbs. each. **1833** M. SCOTT *Tom Cringle* ix, Forty seroons of cochineal. **1890** *Chamb. Jrnl.* 11 Jan. 22 The bulk of medicinal barks are imported in bales and serons.

‖**seroot** (səˈruːt). Also **serut**. [African.] A tabanid fly of the genus *Pangonia*, which inhabits the region of the upper Nile.

**1867** BAKER *Nile Trib.* viii. 189 The seroot fly was teasing them. **1903** in *Allbutt's Syst. Med.* (1907) II. II. 181 The first serut met with going south is at Goz-abu-Gooma.

**serop**, obs. f. SYRUP.

**serophyn**, obs. f. SERAPHIM.

**seropis**, obs. f. SERAPIS.

**serosa** (sɪˈrəʊsə). *Anat.* and *Med.* [f. mod.L. *membrāna serōsa* serous membrane.] A serous membrane; *spec.* (*a*) those lining the peritoneal, pleural, and pericardial sacs; †(*b*) the chorion of a bird embryo.

**1890** BILLINGS *Med. Dict., Serosa.* 1. The membrane of the bird embryo corresponding to the mammalian chorion. 2. Serous membrane. **1898** A. S. PACKARD *Text-bk. Entomol.* 533 The *serosa*..forms a closed sac which covers the whole surface of the egg. **1921** B. M. PATTEN *Early Embryol. of Chick* xi. 87 The albumen-sac..is surrounded by folds of serosa, and the allantois after its establishment develops within the serosa, between it and the amnion. Thus the serosa eventually encompasses the embryo itself and all the other extra-embryonic members. **1964** *Urologia Internationalis* XVII. 14 Reconstruction of the urinary bladder was done after subtotal vesicosectomy. One method employed Teflon lined by serosa.

**serosal** (sɪˈrəʊsəl), *a.* *Anat.* and *Med.* [f. L. *serōs-us*, f. *ser-um* SERUM + -AL.] Of or pertaining to serosa or serum.

**1949** *Jrnl. Physiol.* CX. 40 The serosal surface of the intestine. **1958** B. M. PATTEN *Found. Embryol.* xi. 187 There is thus formed a double layer of mesoderm, the serosal component of which is somatic mesoderm and the allantoic component of which is splanchnic mesoderm. **1968** [see MESOTHELIAL *a.*]. **1976** *Path. Ann.* XI. 4 (*caption*) Colonic wall with full-thickness ischemic necrosis. The inflammatory infiltrate is situated in the serosal region.

†**ˈserose**, *a.* *Obs. rare.* [ad. mod.L. *serōsus*, f. SERUM.] = SEROUS.

**1563** T. GALE *Antidot.* II. 9 It doeth much repell serose humors. **1653** H. MORE *Antid. Ath.* II. ii. §11 (1712) 46 Pressing out the milky and serose Humour in the Butter. **1707** FLOYER *Physic. Pulse-Watch* 70 They have a softer Habit of Body, their Bloods are more serose.

**serositis** (sɪərəʊˈsaɪtɪs). *Path.* [f. L. *serōs-us* serous + -ITIS.] Inflammation of serous membrane.

**1892** F. P. FOSTER *Illustr. Encycl. Med. Dict.* IV. 2788/1 Serositis. *Ibid.*, *Multiple serositis*, simultaneous inflammatory effusion into several serous sacs. **1905** H. A. HARE *Text-bk. Pract. of Med.* 465 The pericardium suffers from a chronic hyperplastic or fibroid inflammatory process, which likewise affects the serous membranes elsewhere, whence the name 'multiple serositis'. **1926** *Jrnl. Amer. Med. Assoc.* 24 Apr. 1323/2 (*heading*) Lipiodol in diagnosis and treatment of tuberculous serositis. **1961** R. D. BAKER *Essent. Path.* v. 92 Wherever an infarct extends to a serous surface it produces serositis.

**serosity** (sɪˈrɒsɪtɪ). [ad. F. *sérosité* (16th c.) or mod.L. *serōsitās*, f. *serōsus* SEROSE.]

**1.** Watery fluid in an animal body; the serous or watery part of blood or milk, serum; freq. *pl.* in 17–18th c. = watery humours.

**1601** HOLLAND *Pliny* II. Catal. Words Art, Serosities, or Serous humours, bee the thinner parts of the masse of bloud, answering to the whey in milke. **1646** SIR T. BROWNE *Pseud. Ep.* III. iii. 110 The salt and lixiviated serosity with some portion of choler, is divided betweene the guts and bladder. **1685** J. CHAMBERLAYNE *Coffee, Tea, & Chocolate* 66 The Cheese, which hinders and stops the flux of the Belly, the serosity or Cream which is purgative. **1753** N. TORRIANO *Gangr. Sore Throat* 16 From the two Nostrils there dropt a very sharp and corrosive Serosity (i.e. Ichor). **1771** T. PERCIVAL *Ess.* (1777) I. 243 By the seasonable discharge of the serosities, the fever..is..moderated. **1834** J. FORBES *Laennec's Dis. Chest* (ed. 4) 107 A bloody serosity. **1873** T. H. GREEN *Introd. Pathol.* (ed. 2) 216 The lateral ventricles..become distended with serosity (acute hydrocephalus). **1899** *Allbutt's Syst. Med.* VIII. 481 The eruption consists of papules infiltrated with serosity.

**b.** A yellowish alkaline liquid produced when serum is heated.

**1807** J. MURRAY *Syst. Chem.* IV. 531 If the coagulated mixture, obtained by the action of heat on serum, be gently pressed, there flows from it a liquor somewhat turbid, named the Serosity. **1836** BRANDE *Chem.* 1137.

**2.** The condition of being serous. *rare.*

**1743** tr. *Heister's Surg.* 232 The too great Serosity or Viscidity of the Blood. **1834** *Good's Study Med.* (ed. 4) IV. 365 The mass of the blood..is too copiously dissolved into a state of serosity. **1898** P. MANSON *Trop. Diseases* xii. 207 Deficient serosity of the blood from excessive sweating.

**serotinal** (sɪˈrəʊtɪnəl), *a.* *Biol.* [f. as SEROTINE *a.* and *sb.*[2] + -AL.] Autumnal, serotine.

**1898** *Minnesota Bot. Stud.* II. 19 The psoraleas, prairie clovers and blazing stars would probably occur to all as among the most abundant of the secondary species in the vernal, estival and serotinal aspects of the prairies respectively. **1959** *Insectes Sociaux* I. 103 Serotinal workers showed least success, callow workers produced an intermediate group of larvae, and vernal workers produced the best growth and development.

**serotine** (ˈsɛrətaɪn), *sb.*[1] [ad. F. *sérotine* (Buffon), ad. fem. of L. *serōtinus*, f. *serō*, adv. of *sērus* late.] A small brown bat belonging to the genus *Eptesicus*, esp. the European *E. serotinus*. Also *attrib.*, as ***serotine bat***.

**1771** PENNANT *Syn. Quadrupeds* 370 Serotine... Bat with a longish nose. **1800** SHAW *Gen. Zool.* I. 142 Great Serotine Bat. **1837** T. BELL *Brit. Quadrupeds* 34 The Serotine..was mistaken for the Noctule by Geoffroy. **1903** H. JOHNSTON *Brit. Mammals* 86 It has been named the 'serotine' bat from its habit of only making its appearance late in the evening. **1910** G. H. BARRETT-HAMILTON *Hist. Brit. Mammals* 131 In the British Isles the Serotine is entirely confined to the south of England. **1934** G. C. SHORTRIDGE *Mammals S.W. Afr.* I. 62 On first appearing Serotine Bats usually fly backwards and forwards with comparative regularity. **1965** D. R. ROSEVERE *Bats W. Afr.* 246 The Serotine Bats are widespread throughout Africa, Europe, Asia, America and Australia. **1971** L. H. MATTHEWS *Life Mammals* II. iii. 104 The most familiar members of it [*sc.* the genus *Eptesicus*] are the big brown bat..of North America, and the Serotine..of Europe and Asia..and west Africa.

**serotine** (ˈsɛrətaɪn), *a.* and *sb.*[2] [ad. L. *sērōtinus* (see prec.).] Late in occurrence or development; chiefly of plants late-flowering. Also *sb.*, a late-flowering plant or species.

**1597** A. M. tr. *Guillemeau's Fr. Chirurg.* 53/3 To serotine doth Doctour then beginne When the disease to deepe is rooted in. **1656** BLOUNT *Glossogr.* **1660** SHARROCK *Vegetables* 27, I find he [Ferrarius] makes but two sorts; Præcoces and Serotin's [*printed* Serolin's]. **1786** ABERCROMBIE *Arr.* in *Gard. Assist.* 76 Serotine, or late flowering, white autumnal narcissus. **1868** LONGF. *Dante, Purg.* xv. 141 As far as ever eye could stretch Against the sunbeams serotine and lucent.

**serotinous** (sɪˈrɒtɪnəs), *a.* [f. L. *sērōtinus*: see SEROTINE *sb.*[1]] **1.** = prec. adj.

**1656** BLOUNT *Glossogr.*, *Serotine, Serotinous*, that is in the evening, late, lateward. *a* **1682** SIR T. BROWNE *Misc. Tracts* (1684) 54 The Vulgar and Septuagint [signify] that it was serotinous or late, and our old Translation that it was late sown. **1857** A. GRAY *First Less. Bot.* (1866) Gloss., *Serotinous*, happening late in the season. **1900** *Jrnl. Quekett Microsc. Club* Apr. 260 The bulk of the Radiolaria belong to the latter or serotinous division.

**2.** *Bot.* Of a cone: remaining long unopened, slow to release seed.

**1880** *Bot. Gaz.* V. 54 How long pine seeds retain their vitality when enclosed in serotinous cones which sometimes occur on certain species has probably never been very carefully noted. **1911** *Forestry Q.* IX. 9 Cones may persist on the branches from 10 to 25 years, or even longer, and are serotinous. **1942** H. I. BALDWIN *Forest Tree Seed* vi. 83 McIntyre suggests that the seed is well preserved in the cones of the so-called serotinous pines because fungi are excluded. **1970** *Canad. Jrnl. Bot.* XLVIII. 1805/2 Genetic control of cone serotiny has been demonstrated in jack pine ..where the serotinous cone class was suggested to be homozygous recessive.

Hence **seˈrotiny**, the property or state of being serotinous.

**1960** *Forest Sci.* VI. 194 Jack pine is one of the ten North American pines whose cones exhibit some measure of serotiny. **1970** [see above]. **1977** J. L. HARPER *Population Biol. of Plants* xx. 629 The evolution of serotiny in pines ensures that seed is stored in cones on the tree and only released to germinate after a fire.

**serotonergic** (sɪərətəʊˈnɜːdʒɪk), *a.* *Physiol.* [f. next + Gr. ἔργ-ον work + -IC: cf. ADRENERGIC, CHOLINERGIC *adjs.*] Of a nerve ending: that liberates, and is stimulated by, serotonin. Also ˌ**serotoniˈnergic** *a.* in the same sense.

**1957** *Ann. N.Y. Acad. Sci.* LXVI. 598 They see mental disturbance as an imbalance between adrenergic or 'serotonergic' inhibition and cholinergic excitation in the more susceptible cerebral synapses. **1967** *Activitas Nervosa Superior* IX. 207 (*heading*) Integrated effect of psychotropic drugs on the balance of cholino-, adreno-, and serotoninergic processes in the brain. **1974** *Sci. Amer.* Feb. 84/2 There is no escaping the conclusion that nutrient intake does alter the amount of serotonin present in the serotoninergic neurons of the brain. **1977** *Lancet* 9 Apr. 812/2 The results suggest that in the first period of head injury, patients with a frontotemporal-lobe contusion show a decreased cerebral dopaminergic activity as well as a decreased serotonergic activity.

**serotonin** (sɪərəˈtəʊnɪn). *Biochem.* [f. SERO- + TON(IC *a.* and *sb.* + -IN[1].] 5-Hydroxytryptamine; a monoamine neurotransmitter, $C_{10}H_{12}N_2O$, active in the production of vasoconstriction and anaphylactic shock, and in the regulation of cycles of body temperature and sleep.

**1948** M. M. RAPPORT et al. in *Science* 24 Sept. 329 The general behaviour of the crystalline substance is suggestive of its homogeneity. We would like provisionally to name it *serotonin*, which indicates that its source is serum and its activity is one of causing constriction. **1949** *Jrnl. Biol. Chem.* CLXXX. 969 A recommendation has been made to reserve the name serotonin for the indole amine rather than the previously isolated complex. **1955** *Sci. News Let.* 19 Mar. 179/3 Serotonin has a chemical structure something like LSD-25. **1970** *Times* 4 May 11/8 The profound changes exerted by PCPA [*sc.* parachlorophenylalanine] on the cats' activities indicate the pervasive role played by serotonin in regulating the animals' drive and behaviour. **1974** M. C. GERALD *Pharmacol.* xvii. 324 There is a large body of evidence that links LSD's actions to its effects at serotonin receptor sites in the central nervous system. **1980** *Brit. Med. Jrnl.* 29 Mar. 939/3 There is also the question whether all the serotonin taken up by platelets in such an experiment is ..incorporated into the same pool as endogenous serotonin.

**serotype** (ˈsɪərəʊtaɪp), *sb.* *Microbiol.* [f. SERO- + TYPE *sb.*[1]] A serologically distinguishable strain of a micro-organism.

**1954** WOLFF & BROOM in *Documenta de Medicina Geographica et Tropica* VI. 82 They differed from authentic strains of *L*[*eptospira*] *icterohaemorrhagiae* and from all the other serotypes. *Ibid.* 85 We suggest the term 'serotype' (serological type)..should be adopted to designate the basic taxon of a serological classification based on the agglutinogens of the leptospires. **1963** *Lancet* 12 Jan. 92/2 Antibodies against all three serotypes are found in many samples of human and animal serum. **1976** *Ann. Rev. Microbiol.* XXX. 160 The serotypes of the sweet potato pathogens were similar but quantitatively distinct from the stone fruit tree pathogens.

So **seroˈtypic** *a.*, of or pertaining to serotypes.

**1953** *Jrnl. Immunol.* LXXI. 232 (*heading*) Serotypic recombination in *Salmonella*. **1973** *Infection & Immunity* VII. 499 Some recent isolates had different serotypic behaviour before and after purification, and..the widely distributed prototype strain T960 was composed of at least two different serotypes.

**serotype** ('sɪərəʊtaɪp), *v. Microbiol.* [f. prec.] *trans.* To assign to a particular serotype. So **'serotyping** *vbl. sb.*

**1968** *Manch. Guardian Weekly* 29 Aug. 9 In recent years Portsmouth has seen 331 cases of a particular Salmonella infection: of these 271 have been traced by serotyping through the abattoir and back to the farm. **1970** *Nature* 28 Nov. 827/1 The serotyping of histo-compatibility antigens relies heavily on complement-dependent serologic reactions. **1975** *Jrnl. Clinical Microbiol.* I. 469 A rapid and economical micromethod for serotyping strains of *Mycobacterium avium* is described. **1976** *Ann. Rev. Microbiol.* XXX. 183 Most investigators involved in the investigation of the role of T-strain mycoplasmas in nongonococcal urethritis..have..made no attempt to serotype the ureaplasmas isolated. **1977** *Lancet* 8 Oct. 774/1 Serotyping and biotyping indicated that all 8 isolates were unrelated.

**serous** ('sɪərəs), *a.* [ad. F. *séreux* (16th c.), ad. L. *serōsus*, f. *ser-um* SERUM.]

**1.** Of or pertaining to serum; consisting of or containing serum; of the nature of serum.

**1594** T. B. *La Primaud. Fr. Acad.* II. Ep. Rdr. A 8 b, The sucking veines serue to purge the blood from the serous substaunce of it. **1618** W. BARCLAY *Well at King-horne* A vj b, For the croudy part bindeth some, and the serous or wheyish part louseth others. **1638** BURTON *Anat. Mel.* I. i. III. iii, Ichores and those serious [ed. 1651 serous] matters. **1683–4** BOYLE *Mem. Nat. Hist. Hum. Blood* 13 The Differences between the Serous and the Red part of Humane Blood. **1735** SOMERVILLE *Chace* I. 345 The serous Particles evade Thro' th' open Pores. **1815** J. SMITH *Panorama Sci. & Art* II. 501 Ass's, mare's, and woman's milk, are the most saline and serous. **1876** tr. *Wagner's Gen. Pathol.* 334 Serous infiltration occurs in cells.

**b.** *Path.* Involving or characterized by an effusion of serum.

**1779** JOHNSON *Let. to Mrs. Thrale* 5 Oct., Mr. Thrale's disorder whether grumous or serous. **1879** P. SMITH *Glaucoma* 19 Serous Iritis. **1893** W. R. GOWERS *Man. Dis. Nerv. Syst.* (ed. 2) II. 407 The so-called 'serous apoplexy'. **1895** *Brit. Med. Jrnl.* 14 Dec. 1492/1 Serous cysts.

**2.** *Anat.* Secreting or moistened with serum, as a membrane.

**1732** ARBUTHNOT *Rules of Diet* iv. in *Aliments*, etc. (1735) 395 This Disease [dropsy] may happen wherever there are serous Vessels. **1813** J. THOMSON *Lect. Inflam.* 143 The external surface of the stomach is covered by a membrane, the peritoneum, denominated serous. **1869** *Eng. Mech.* 3 Dec. 271/2 The back layer of the cornea and the front of the iris are what anatomists call serous membranes. **1873** MIVART *Elem. Anat.* 462 The proper serous sac of the thorax.

**serow** ('sɛrəʊ). Also saraw, sarau, surow, se(e)rou. [Native name.] Any of the Asiatic antelopes of the genus *Nemorhædus* (*Capricornis*), esp. *N. thar* (*N. bubalinus*), the THAR.

**1847** HODGSON in *Jrnl. Asiatic Soc. Bengal* XVI. II. 697 Genus Nemorhædus. Vel Capricornis... The Thar or Saraw. **1848** tr. *Hoffmeister's Trav. Ceylon*, etc. viii. 295 Two species of antelopes (*Antilope Ghoral* and *A. Thar*), one called '*Ghoral*', and the other '*Surow*'. **1865** MATHIAS *Sport in Himalayas* 52 Returning to camp, I came across a serow, the first that I have seen. **1900** LYDEKKER *Gt. & Small Game India* 128 The Sumatran Serow (*Nemorhædus sumatrensis*). *Ibid.*, It appears preferable to call them by the name by which they are commonly known in the North-West Himalaya, viz. serow, or, correctly, sarao. **1908** *Times* 17 Aug. 11/3 A fine young serow..from Perak.

**seroy**, obs. f. SERAI.

**serozem**, var. SIEROZEM.

**Serpa**, obs. var. SHERPA.

**Serpasil** ('sɜːpəsɪl). *Pharm.* [f. RE)SERP(INE.] A proprietary name for reserpine.

**1953** *Trade Marks Jrnl.* 29 Apr. 358/2 *Serpasil*... Ciba Limited... Switzerland. **1953** *Official Gaz.* (U.S. Patent Office) 20 Oct. 564/2 Ciba Pharmaceutical Products, Inc... *Serpasil*. For sedative, hypotensive, and spasmolytic agent. .. Claims use since Mar. 17, 1953. **1954** *Jrnl. Pharmacol. & Exper. Therapeutics* CX. 205 This alkaloid, Serpasil (formerly known as Reserpine), produces a prolonged central nervous system depression in laboratory animals. **1963** *Times* 31 May 19/5 Among the anti-hypertensives doctors showed great interest in Serpasil. **1967** H. BECKMAN *Dilemmas in Drug Therapy* 175/1 Usual dosages of the Rauwolfia preparations employed in treating hypertension are as follows:..reserpine (Reserpoid, Serpasil, etc.), orally, 0·25–1·0 mg. daily in two or three divided doses.

**serpaw**, var. SEERPAW.

**serpe**, var. SARPE[2] *Obs.*, collar.

**1438** *E.E. Wills* (1882) 110 Item to Robert Greyndoor, squyer, my Serpe of siluer and my cheyne of goold.

**ser'pedinous**, *a. rare.* [f. med.L. *serpēdin-*, *serpēdo*, synon. of SERPIGO.] Serpiginous.

**1616** T. ADAMS *Soul's Sickness* 63 The Itch is a corrupt humour betweene the skin and the flesh, running with a serpedinous course.

**serpe(e)-cloth**, var. SARP-CLOTH, sarplier, *Obs.*

**serpent** ('sɜːpənt), *sb.* Also 6 sarpent; 4–6 *pl. Sc.* serpens. [a. OF. (mod.F.) *serpent* = Pr. *sarpent*, Sp. *serpiente*, It., Pg. *serpente*:—L. *serpent-em*, *serpens* creeping thing (e.g. a louse), serpent, properly pres. pple. of *serpĕre* to creep, cogn. with Gr. ἕρπειν to creep, Skr. *sṛp* to creep, crawl, *sarpa* creeping, crawling, snake.]

**1. a.** Any of the scaly limbless reptiles regarded as having the properties of hissing and 'stinging'; *Zool.* a reptile of the group OPHIDIA; a snake; now, in ordinary use, applied chiefly to the larger and more venomous species; otherwise only *rhetorical* (e.g. in contexts suggesting senses 2 and 3), or with reference to serpent-worship.

*c* **1305** *Land Cokayne* 157 Þer nis serpent, wolf no fox. *c* **1374** CHAUCER *Troylus* v. 1497 She told eek..of the holy serpent, and the welle. *c* **1386** —— *Manciple's T.* 5 He slowe phiton þe serpent. **1390** GOWER *Conf.* I. 57 A Serpent, which that Aspidis Is cleped. **1447** BOKENHAM *Seyntys* III. 835 (Horstm.) Julyan..clepyd to hym oon wych had cunnyng Serpentys to charm. **1475** *Bk. Noblesse* (Roxb.) 21 He slow the serpent clepit Ydra. **1549** *Compl. Scot.* i. 20 It is desolat, ande inhabit be serpens. **1592** SHAKS. *Ven. & Ad.* 17 Here come and sit, where neuer serpent hisses. **1606** —— *Ant. & Cl.* II. vii. 29 Your Serpent of Egypt, is bred now of your mud by the operation of your Sun. **1727–46** THOMSON *Summer* 895 The green serpent, from his dark abode,..At noon forth-issuing. **1834** MCMURTRIE *Cuvier's Anim. Kingd.* 181 The true Serpents..comprise the genera without a sternum, and in which there is no vestige of a shoulder. **1854** OWEN in *Orr's Circ. Sci., Org. Nat.* I. 198 The serpent has no limbs, yet it can outclimb the monkey, outswim the fish, outleap the jerboa. **1867** AUGUSTA WILSON *Vashti* xix, I trust neither men nor women, nor even the angels in heaven; for one of them turned serpent. **1889** RUSKIN *Præterita* III. 75 There used to be..harmless water serpents in the Swiss waters.

†**b.** A creeping thing or reptile, *esp.* one of a venomous or noxious kind. *Obs.*

**1440** [see 5]. **1553** EDEN *Treat. Newe Ind.* (Arb.) 27 The Serpente called Salamandra, which lyueth in the fyre wythoute any hurte. **1584** B. R. tr. *Herodotus* II. 77 b, Very hydeous and terrible serpents called Crocodyles. **1608** TOPSELL *Serpents* 10 By Serpents we vnderstand in this discourse all venomous Beasts, whether creeping without legges, as Adders and Snakes, or with legges, as Crocodiles and Lizards, or more neerely compacted bodies, as Toades, Spiders, and Bees; following heerein the warrant of the best ancient Latinists. **1691** EVELYN *Diary* 30 Dec., Mr. Charlton's collection of spiders, birds, scorpions, and other serpents.

**c.** Applied to serpent-like animals inhabiting the sea; cf. SEA-SERPENT.

**1608** TOPSELL *Serpents* 235 In the Germaine-Ocean there is found a Serpent about the bignesse of a mans legge. **1616** T. ADAMS *Soul's Sickness* 65 One knaue guls him, hee innumerable fooles, with the strange Fish at Yarmouth, or the Serpent in Sussex. **1697** DRYDEN *Æneid* II. 272 We spy'd Two Serpents rank'd abreast, the Seas divide. **1859** GRATTAN *Civilized Amer.* I. iv. 54 She saw..a huge serpent, gliding gracefully through the waves, having evidently performed the action of turning round.

**d.** In proverbial and allusive phr. referring to the serpent's guile, treachery, or malignancy. †*the serpent's tongue*, vulgarly supposed to be the 'sting'; allusively used for 'venomous' speech; also (*nonce-use*) for hissing.

*c* **1386** CHAUCER *Sompn. T.* 286 Þe serpent þat so slyly crepith Vndyr þe gres & styngith subtyly. **1388** WYCLIF *Gen.* xlix. 17 Dan be maad a serpent in the weie, and cerastes in the path. **1481** CAXTON *Godfrey* li. 93 This fals greek whiche counseylled them allewey to theyr dammage And was alway as the serpent emonge the elis. **1508** DUNBAR *Flyting* 75 Dissaitfull tyrand, with serpentis tung. **1584** LODGE *Alarum* 10 The Gentleman surprised with this sodaine ioye, and vnacquainted good speaches (not dreading that the Serpent laye hidden in the grasse)..assented. **1590** SHAKS. *Mids. N.* v. i. 440 Now to scape the Serpents tongue, We will make amends ere long. **1595** —— *John* III. iii. 61 He is a very serpent in my way. **1605** —— *Macb.* I. v. 67 Looke like th' innocent flower, But be the Serpent vnder't. **1647** COWLEY *Mistress, Heart-breaking* ii, The mighty Serpent Love, Cut by this chance in pieces small, In all still liv'd, and still it stung in all.

**e.** A pale green fashion shade.

**1895** *Montgomery Ward Catal.* Spring & Summer 12/1 Plain colored Gros Grain Silk... Colors: Green, prune,.. mode, serpent, tan. **1927** *Daily Express* 5 Apr. 6 Navy, Ash, Serpent, Pink.

**2.** The serpent, 'more subtil than any beast of the field', that tempted Eve (Gen. iii. 1–5); the Tempter, the Devil, Satan. Also, *the Old Serpent* (after Rev. xii. 9).

*a* **1300** *Fall & Passion* 26 in *E.E.P.* (1862) 13 A serpent he [þe deuil] com þroȝ felonie an makid eue chonge hir þoȝt. **1382** WYCLIF *Rev.* xii. 9 The greet olde serpent, that is clepid the Deuel. **1420–2** LYDG. *Thebes* 4663 Lucyfer, fader of Envie, The olde Serpent, he levyathan. **14..** —— *Serp. Div.* (1911) 50 The contagious Serpent of Division eclipsed and appalled theire worthines. **1534** in *Norwich Pageants* (1856) 17 It. to Edm[d] Thurston playeng y[e] Serpent, 4[d]. **1555** EDEN *Decades* (Arb.) 50 The oulde serpente who hath so longe had them in hys possession. **1622** MABBE tr. *Aleman's Guzman d'Alf.* I. 243 Being put into such a Paradise of Conserues, the Serpent of the flesh might tempt me to eate of this forbidden fruit. **1657** TRAPP *Comm. Ps.* xvi. 4 It was the Serpents grammar that first taught men to decline God in the plurall number. **1667** MILTON *P.L.* XII. 454 The Serpent, Prince of aire. *a* **1720** SEWELL *Hist. Quakers* (1722) 31 Some Men have the Nature of the Serpent (that old Adversary) to sting, envenom and poison. **1859** TENNYSON *Geraint & Enid* 638 Some, whose souls the old serpent long had drawn Down.

**3.** *fig.* **a.** As a symbol of envy, jealousy, malice, or wiliness.

*c* **1374** CHAUCER *Troylus* III. 837 Thou wikked serpent Ialousye. **1412–20** LYDG. *Chron. Troy* II. 1066 *rubric*, Howe Kynge Priamus..by þe serpente Of Envye was stirede. **1513** MORE in Grafton *Chron.* (1568) II. 760 Such a pestilent Serpent is ambition. **1609** TUVILL *Vade-mecum* (1629) 127 Here is Policie without Iustice, a Serpent without a Doue. **1854** T. T. LYNCH *Lett. to Scattered* (1872) 409 Error is a siren and a serpent.

**b.** A treacherous, deceitful, or malicious person.

[**1382** WYCLIF *Matt.* xxiii. 33 ȝee sarpentis, fruytis, or buriownyngus, of eddris,..hou shulen ȝee flee fro the dom of helle?] **1590** SHAKS. *Mids. N.* III. ii. 73 With doubler tongue Then thine (thou serpent) neuer Adder stung. **1605** —— *Lear* v. iii. 84 Edmund, I arrest thee On capitall Treason; and in thy arrest, This guilded Serpent. **1837** DICKENS *Pickw.* xviii, Mr. Pott..ground his teeth..and exclaimed, in a saw-like voice,—'Serpent!' **1884** *Chr. World* 15 May 366/1 The *Times* degraded itself..by patting these unmannerly serpents [*viz.* hissers] on the back.

**4.** A representation of a serpent, esp. as a symbol or an ornament.

***brazen serpent*** has been used allusively in reference to Num. xxi. 9.—The figure of a serpent with its tail in its mouth is a symbol of eternity.

**13..** *Coer de L.* 5728 In his blasoun..Was i-paynted a serpent. **1388** WYCLIF *Num.* xxi. 8 Make thou a serpent of bras. and sette thou it for a signe. **1388** —— *2 Kings* xviii. 4 He brak the brasun serpent, whom Moyses hadde maad. *c* **1400** MAUNDEV. (1839) xx. 217 At 4 Corners of the Mountour, ben 4 Serpentes of Gold. *c* **1440** *Alphabet of Tales* 434 Hym happend on a tyme to lose a sakett and a thowsand talentis þerin and a serpent of gold. **1577–8** *New Yrs. Gifts* in Nichols *Progr. Eliz.* (1823) II. 79 A sarpent of ophall with a ruby pendant. **1644** EVELYN *Diary* 7 Mar., A fountaine of serpents twisting about a globe. **1655** R. FARNWORTH (*title*) The Brazen Serpent lifted up on high, or Truth cleared and above the deceit exalted. **1730** BAILEY (folio), *Serpents*, (in Hieroglyphicks) were used to represent Hereticks. **1831** CARLYLE *Sartor Res.* II. x, Mistaking the ill-cut Serpent-of-Eternity for a common poisonous Reptile. **1867** AUGUSTA WILSON *Vashti* xi, The..daintily rounded wrist encircled by the jet serpent.

**5.** *Astron.* †**a.** The sign of Scorpio (? *nonce-use*). †**b.** The southern constellation *Hydra*. **c.** The northern constellation *Serpens*.

[*c* **1440** *Astron. Cal.* (MS. Ashm. 391), Whan þe moone is in Scorpio þ[t] is the signe of a serpent.] **1551** RECORDE *Cast. Knowl.* (1556) 269 The great Serpent whiche is called of the greekes and latines Hydra: it containeth 25 starres. **1599** T. HILL *Sch. Skil* 22 The Serpent hath 11. stars. **1674** MOXON *Tutor Astron.* I. iii. §10 (ed. 3) 19 The Southern Serpent. **1868** LOCKYER *Guillemin's Heavens* (ed. 3) 328 Above the Scorpion, Ophiuchus and the Serpent are..visible.

**6.** A kind of firework which burns with a serpentine motion or flame.

**1634** J. B[ATE] *Myst. Nat.* 61 The Composition for middle sized Rockets may serve for Serpents. **1666** PEPYS *Diary* 6 June, Mrs. Mercer's son had provided a great many serpents, and so I made the women all fire some serpents. **1697–8** *Act 9 Will. III*, c. 7 §1 Whereas much Mischief hath lately happened by throwing casting and fireing of Squibbs Serpentes Rockettes and other Fire-workes. **1763** COLMAN *Prose Sev. Occas.* (1787) I. 122 Some queer old gentleman may be alarmed at the..serpents hissing at his tail. *a* **1845** HOOD *To Vauxhall* 13 Wheels whiz—smash crackers—serpents twist. **1869** ALDRICH *Story of Bad Boy* viii, The smaller sort of fireworks, such as pin-wheels, serpents, double-headers.

**7.** A bass wind instrument of deep tone, about 8 feet long, made of wood covered with leather and formed with three U-shaped turns. (The instrument, once disused, has been revived in the performance of early music.) Also, an organ-stop of similar tone.

**1730** BAILEY (folio), *Serpent*, a Kind of musical Instrument, serving as a Bass to the Cornet or small Shawm. **1775** J. JEKYLL *Corr.* (1894) 16 High mass..was accompanied with a variety of instruments, among which the Serpent supplies a good bass. **1838** G. F. GRAHAM *Mus. Comp.* 12/1 The serpent is chiefly used in military music. **1852** SEIDEL *Organ* 105 Serpent is a reed-register seldom to be met with. **1861** THACKERAY *Leaf out of Sk. Bk.* Wks. 1900 XIII. 644 There is a great braying and bellowing of serpents and bassoons. **1872** T. HARDY *Under Greenw. Tree* I. iv, They should have stuck to strings as we did..and done away with serpents. **1928** *Punch* 2 May 485/1 The Serpent is a bass wind-instrument of wood, so-called from its shape. **1976** *Early Music* Oct. 477/2 We learn how Boosey and Hawkes bend brass tubes, but not why, or how, the cornett and serpent are bent.

**8.** Miscellaneous transferred uses: A candle of spiral form; a 'rope' of hair; the crank-shaft in a weaving-machine. ***Pharaoh's serpent***: see PHARAOH 4.

**1802** FOSBROOKE *Brit. Monachism* I. 33 On the Sunday the same ceremony followed..respecting the serpent. **1869** BROWNING *Ring & Bk.* XI. 1365 Had I enjoined 'Cut off the hair!'..at once a yard or so Had fluttered in black serpents to the floor. **1870** O'SHAUGHNESSY *Epic of Women* 120 Through the swift mesh'd serpents of her hair. **1878** BARLOW *Weaving* 230 The crankshaft is called a 'serpent'.

**9.** *Hist.* = SERPENTINE *sb.* 2.

**1830** D. BOOTH *Analyt. Dict.* 137 Smaller machines, having the names of Dragons, Serpents, Scorpions, War-wolves. **1895** OMAN in *Traill's Soc. Eng.* III. 75 A couple of hundred gunners, with ten or twelve 'serpents' or 'bombards'.

**10.** *attrib.* and *Comb.*: **a.** simple attrib., as ***serpent-bite***, ***breed***, ***-coil***, ***emblem***, ***enemy***, ***-poison***, ***-race*** (see OPHIOGENES), ***skin***, ***-slime***, ***symbol***, ***-tail***, ***-train***, ***tribe***; (with reference to the snake-like hair of the Furies) ***serpent-braid***, ***-fury***, ***-tress***; **b.** objective, as ***serpent-bruiser***, ***-charmer***, ***-eating*** adj., ***-killer***, ***slayer***, ***-worship***,

***-worshipper***; c. similative (cf. 12), as ***serpent-footed, -haired, -hearted, -rooted, -throated*** adjs., also ***serpent-green, -wise*** adjs.; **d.** instrumental, as ***serpent-bitten, -cinctured, -circled, -stung*** ppl. adjs.

**1837** Carlyle *Fr. Rev.* I. v. i, A miraculous Brazen Serpent..whereon whosoever looks..shall be healed of all woes and *serpent-bites. **1629** H. Burton *Truth's Tri.* 63 The *serpent-bitten-man looked, and liued. **1813** Byron *Giaour* 880 The sablest of the *serpent-braid That o'er her fearful forehead stray'd. **1774** J. Bryant *Anc. Mythol.* (1775) I. 481 *Οφιογενεις*, or the *serpent-breed. **1738** Wesley *Hymns, Jesu God of our Salvation* iv, Jesu! Help, thou *Serpent-Bruiser. **1861** Gosse *Rom. Nat. Hist.* Ser. II. 289 The poor *serpent-charmer never came to life again. *Ibid.* 279 [Hasselquist] records his judgment that there is no delusion in *serpent-charming. **1820** Shelley *Prometh. Unb.* I. 324 A *serpent-cinctured wand [*sc.* the caduceus]. **1896** A. E. Housman *Shropshire Lad* xlii, With..feet that fly on feathers, And *serpent-circled wand. **1833** L. Ritchie *Wand. Loire* 83 The *serpent-coil of Laocoon. **1596** Fitz-Geffrey *Sir F. Drake* C I Foule *serpent-eating envies loathsome cottage. **1887** G. Salmon in *W. Smith & Wace's Dict. Chr. Biog.* IV. 80 A religious use of the *serpent emblem was common to the Phoenicians with the Egyptians. **1848** R. I. Wilberforce *Doctr. Incarnation* ii. 18 That by the woman's seed her *serpent enemy should finally be subjugated. **1621** G. Sandys *Ovid's Met.* I. (1626) 5 The *Serpent-footed Giants. **1849** Aytoun *Lays Scott. Cavaliers* (ed. 2) 219 The *serpent-furies Coiled around the maddening brain. **1897** Mary Kingsley *W. Africa* 13 A *serpent-green sky. **1837** Carlyle *Fr. Rev.* III. III. viii, These *serpent-haired Extreme She-Patriots. **1850** F. Mason *Nat. Product. Burmah* 329 *Serpent-hearted eel. **1647** R. Stapylton *Juvenal* xv. Annot. 279 The *Serpent-killer, Ibis. **1774** Goldsm. *Nat. Hist.* VII. 200 The potency of the *serpent poison. **1774** J. Bryant *Anc. Mythol.* (1775) I. 484 The natives of Thebes in Bœotia..esteemed themselves of the *serpent race. **1855** Tennyson *Brook* 135 Seated on a *serpent-rooted beech. *c* **1440** *Pallad. on Husb.* XII. 125 A *serpent skyn. **1818** Keats *Endym.* III. 239 Where go, When I have cast this serpent-skin of woe? **1598** Sylvester *Du Bartas* II. ii. IV. *Columnes* 508 That stout *Serpent-slayer, His Satan-taming Son. **1844** Mrs. Browning *Drama of Exile* 651 Bring no *serpent-slime Athwart this path. **1855** Bailey *Mystic*, etc. 118 His bright bride Though *serpent-stung. **1851** Squier (*title*) The *Serpent Symbol, and the worship of the reciprocal principles of Nature in America. **1847** Tennyson *Princess* v. 243 The blast and bray of the long horn And *serpent-throated bugle. **1769** Gray *Installat. Ode* 8 Let painted Flatt'ry hide her *serpent-train in flowers. **1791** Darwin *Bot. Gard.* I. 217 With bright wreath of *serpent-tresses crown'd,..young Medusa frown'd. **1841** *Penny Cycl.* XXI. 279/2 The *serpent tribe. **1933** W. de la Mare *Fleeting* 144 Her eyes Stirred not a hair's breadth, *serpent-wise. **1774** J. Bryant *Anc. Mythol.* (1775) I. 425 Mount Lebanon, and Hermon..where *serpent-worship particularly prevailed. **1871** Tylor *Prim. Culture* II. 218 The old Prussian serpent-worship and offering of food to the household snakes. *Ibid.*, Legends of serpent-races who turn out to be simply *serpent-worshippers. *a* **1875** Kingsley in C. K. Paul *Memories* (1899) 160 I've always thought that the serpent [in Genesis] was a *serpent-worshipping black tribe.

**e.** ***serpent-tail*** vb. (nonce-wd.), to link up. (Cf. serpentine *a.* 1 b.)

**1872** Ruskin *Fors Clav.* xxiv. 12 It is necessary to serpent-tail this pit with the upper hell by a district for insanity without deed.

**f.** ***serpent-wise*** adv.

**1927** E. Sitwell *Rustic Elegies* 40 The wicked knife flashed serpent-wise.

**11. a.** Special comb.: **serpent-bearer** = Ophiuchus; **serpent bird**, a bird of the family *Plotidæ* = darter 4 a; **serpent-boat**, a canoe of great length used on the Malabar coast (Ogilvie, 1882); **serpent cucumber**, a cucumber of the genus *Trichosanthes*, having long serpent-like fruit, esp. *T. colubrina*; **serpent deity** = *serpent-god*; **serpent eagle**, a bird of prey of the genus *Spilornis*; **serpent-eater**, (*a*) the secretary bird; (*b*) the markhor; **serpent-eel**, a marine animal of the genus *Ophichthys*; **serpent-fence**, 'a zigzag fence made by placing the ends of the rails upon each other' (Ogilvie); **serpent-fish**, the red snake-fish, *Cepola rubescens*; **serpent-god**, a serpent worshipped as a god; the object of worship of the Ophites; **serpent-king**, a name given to Cecrops, who is represented with a body terminating in a serpent form; **serpent-lizard** = seps 2; **serpent melon** = *serpent cucumber*; **serpent paper** [= F. *papier* (*à la*) *serpente*], a very thin transparent paper having a serpent for the water-mark; **serpent-star**, an ophiuran; †**serpent-tongue**, a jeweller's ornament in the shape of a snake's tongue; **serpent-wand**, the caduceus; **serpent-withe**, *Aristolochia odoratissima*; †**serpent-wood**, the wood of *Strychnos colubrina* or some related plant.

**1551** Recorde *Cast. Knowl.* (1556) 264 Serpentarius, that is the manne with the Serpente, or *Serpent bearer. **1841** *Penny Cycl.* XXI. 273/1 *Serpens*..astronomically distinguished from Ophiuchus, but not mythologically, being the serpent carried by the Serpent-bearer. **1870** Gillmore tr. *Figuier's Reptiles & Birds* 263 The Darter..in the United States..has received the name of the *Serpent Bird. **1760** J. Lee *Introd. Bot.* App. 326 *Serpent Cucumber, *Trichosanthes.* **1774** J. Bryant *Anc. Mythol.* (1775) I. 428 When the Greeks understood that in these temples people worshiped a *serpent Deity, they concluded that Trachon was a serpent. **187.** *Cassell's Nat. Hist.* III. 284 The Indian *Serpent Eagle (*Spilornis cheela*). **1731** Medley *Kolben's Cape Good Hope* II. 142 The Cape Europeans call this Bird the *Serpent-Eater. **1819** Stephens in *Shaw's Gen. Zool.* XI. 193 Hoatzin Serpent-Eater. **1840** Vigne *Narr. Visit Afghanistan* 86, I procured a good skin of the markhur, or serpent-eater. **1896** *Lydekker's Roy. Nat. Hist.* v. 449 *Serpent-eels are represented by a great number of species. **1753** *Chambers' Cycl.* Suppl., *Serpens rubescens*, the red *serpent fish,..properly of the tænia kind. **1816** Kirby & Sp. *Entomol.* xxii. (1818) II. 273 Their wonder would have been diminished, and their *serpent-gods undeified. **1873** Miss R. H. Busk *Sagas fr. Far East* 18 A pool where lived two Serpent-gods, who had command of the water. **1855** Kingsley *Heroes, Theseus* I, Kekrops the *serpent-king. **1802** Shaw *Gen. Zool.* III. 307 *Serpent Lizard. **1778** *Ann. Reg., Chron.* 192 There is now growing ..in Lancashire a *serpent melon which measures in length five feet two inches and an half. **1797** *Encycl. Brit.* (ed. 3) XIII. 715/2 The manner of preparing this [oiled] paper is to take that which is thin and smooth, known commonly by the name of *serpent paper. **1851** Mantell *Petrifactions* ii. §1. 82 Asteridæ (named *Ophiura* or *Serpent-stars). **1488** *Acc. Ld. High Treas. Scot.* I. 81 A grete *serpent toung set with gold, perle and precious stanis. **1849** Aytoun *Lays Scott. Cavaliers* (ed. 2) 277, I have seen the robes of Hermes glisten —Seen him wave afar his *serpent-wand. **1864** Grisebach *Flora W. Ind. Islands* 787 *Serpent-withe. **1681** Grew *Musæum* II. §i. i. 180 A piece of *Serpent-Wood. *Lignum Colubrinum.*

**b.** Combinations with *serpent's*: **serpent's beard**, *Ophiopogon japonicus* (Treas. Bot. 1874); **serpent's head, skull**, names for species of cowry; **serpent's tongue**, †(*a*) = adder's tongue; (*b*) the fossil tooth of a shark.

**1815** S. Brookes *Conchol.* 156 *Serpents Head. *Cypræa Caput serpentis.* **1795** tr. *Thunberg's Trav.* (ed. 2) II. 82 Small shells, called *serpents skulls (*Cypræa moneta*). **1578** Lyte *Dodoens* I. xciii. 135 [Ophioglosson] is now called..in English, Adders tongue, & *Serpents tonge. **1607** Topsell *Four-f. Beasts* 720 A kind of stone called the serpents toong. **1835** D. Booth *Analyt. Dict.* 284 The fossil bodies called *Glossopetræ* (petrified tongues) and Serpents' Tongues.

**12.** quasi-*adj.* **a.** Resembling a serpent or that of a serpent, serpent-like, serpentiform, serpentine.

**1592** Shaks. *Rom. & Jul.* III. ii. 73 O Serpent heart, hid with a flowring face. **1633** P. Fletcher *Purple Isl.* II. ix, Their serpent windings. **1667** Milton *P.L.* VII. 302 With Serpent errour wandring. *a* **1718** Parnell *Hesiod* 101 Back roll'd her azure veil with serpent fold. **1725** Pope *Odyss.* IV. 342 He, whose practis'd wit Knew all the serpent-mazes of deceit. **1820** Shelley *Prometh. Unb.* III. iii. 135 It feeds the quick growth of the serpent vine. **1835** Lytton *Rienzi* II. v, The serpent smile is your countrymen's proper distinction. **1837** Carlyle *Fr. Rev.* I. v. iv, Shaking their serpent-hair. **1869** Browning *Ring & Bk.* XI. 1611 All the way down the serpent-stair to hell! **1872** Tennyson *Gareth & Lynette* 884 Those long loops Wherethro' the serpent river coil'd.

**b.** *Antiq.* of temples, etc. having the supposed symbolical form of a serpent.

**1774** J. Bryant *Anc. Mythol.* (1775) I. 464 Tor-Opus, the serpent-hill, or temple. **1830** Deane *Worship Serp.* vi. 341 The erection of a serpent-temple, like that of Abury. **1897** *Saga-Bk. Viking Club* Jan. 256 Whether any old serpent-mounds had been found in Iceland.

†**'serpent**, *a.* *Obs.* [ad. L. *serpent-em*, pres. pple. of *serpĕre* to creep.] Of an ulcer: Spreading.

**1541** R. Copland *Galyen's Terap.* G ij, Serpent vlceres & other affections y$^{t}$ maketh the vlceres long in healyng.

**'serpent**, *v.* Now *rare.* [ad. F. *serpenter* (14th c.), f. *serpent* serpent *sb.*]

**1.** *intr.* To move in a serpentine manner; to follow a tortuous course; to wind.

**1606** Sylvester *Du Bartas* II. iv. I. *Tropheis* 1038 The Banks of Forth (Whose forceful stream runs smoothly serpenting). **1679** Evelyn *Sylva* (ed. 3) 78 [Poplars] in Italy, for their Vines to serpent on. *a* **1706** —— *Hist. Relig.* (1850) I. 28 Rivers and larger streams; made to serpent in meandering crooks. **1746** *Phil. Trans.* XLIV. 58 One sees a Light serpenting all along the Tube. **1818** Keats *Endym.* III. 500 Shapes, wizard and brute, Laughing and wailing, groveling, serpenting.

*fig.* **1841** Lever *Charles O'Malley* xvii. 93 So did Mr. Webber tread his way, serpenting through the statute-book.

**b.** To make (one's way) tortuously.

**1891** *Sat. Rev.* 23 May 620/2 Serpenting their way through the dry grass.

†**2.** *trans.* To entwine. *Obs.*

*a* **1700** Evelyn *Diary* 30 Jan. 1645, Fruit-trees, whose boles are serpented with excellent vines.

‖**serpentaria** (sɜːpən'tɛərɪə). [late L. *serpentāria* (scil. *planta*), fem. of *serpentārius*, f. *serpent-*, *serpens* serpent *sb.*: see -ary.] = serpentary 2.

**1803** *Med. Jrnl.* IX. 100 A clyster made of a strong decoction of bark and serpentaria. **1811** A. T. Thomson *Lond. Disp.* (1818) 45 Dried serpentaria root is imported into this country in bales. **1874** Garrod & Baxter *Mat. Med.* 493 Serpentaria (in powder).

**b.** *Chem.* An alkaloid obtained from serpentary.

**1831** J. Davies *Man. Mat. Med.* 168 Dr. C. Conwell has lately discovered in this root, a new alkali, which he has called serpentaria... The hydrochlorate of serpentaria forms brilliant plumose fibrils.

**'serpentarin.** *Chem.* Also -ine. [f. late L. *serpentāria* serpentary *sb.* 1 + -in.] A bitter substance obtained from serpentary root.

**1847** *Turner's Elem. Chem.* (ed. 8) 1166.

‖**Serpentarius** (sɜːpən'tɛərɪəs). [mod.L.: see next.]

**1.** *Astron.* = Ophiuchus.

**1728** Chambers *Cycl.* s.v., The Stars in the Constellation Serpentarius in Ptolomy's Catalogue are 29. **1795** T. Maurice *Hindostan* I. I. x. 339 Serpentarius..is one of the forty-eight old constellations, and a very near neighbour of the Scorpion. **1868** Lockyer *Guillemin's Heavens* (ed. 3) 366 Since the observation of Tycho Brahé, many temporary stars have been seen in the constellations of Serpentarius and Cygnus.

**2.** *Ornith.* The serpent-eater or secretary-bird.

**1893** *Public Opin.* 10 Nov. 590.

**serpentary** ('sɜːpəntərɪ), *sb.* Also 5 -ory. [ad. late and med.L. *serpentāria* (in sense 1, scil. *retorta*, in sense 2 *planta*), fem. of *serpentārius*: see next.]

†**1.** A kind of retort or still. *Obs.* (Cf. serpent *sb.*)

*c* **1450** *M.E. Med. Bk.* (Heinrich) 183 On þe morowe dystylle hem þorow a serpentory. **1615** Markham *Eng. Housew.* 31 Take Saxifrage..two gallonds of good wine, or else wine lees, and put it into a slerpentary [*sic*].

**2.** The plant Virginian Snake-root, *Aristolochia Serpentaria*; the root of this (in full, Serpentary Root = *Serpentariæ Radix*) used medicinally.

**1658** Phillips, *Serpentary*, a kind of herb called Vipers-grasse. **1706** —— (ed. Kersey), *Serpentary-Wood*, a kind of Wood that grows in Malabar,..and is commended for its Virtue in expelling Poison. **1837** T. Castle *Pharmacopœia Lond.* 170 Infusion of Serpentary... Diaphoretic, diuretic, stimulant. **1871** Garrod *Mat. Med.* (ed. 3) 308 *Serpentariæ Radix.* Serpentary Root. *Ibid.* 309 Serpentary contains a volatile oil and resin.

**'serpentary,** *a.* *rare*$^{-1}$. [ad. med.L. *serpentārius*, f. *serpent-em* serpent *sb.*: see -ary.] = serpentine *a.*

**1681** Jordan *London's Joy* 10 Suppress Pamphlet-Contentions, for they are The Serpentary Seeds of Civil War.

**'serpentcleide** (-klaɪd). *Mus.* [f. serpent *sb.* + *-cleide* of ophicleide.] A form of the ophicleide with a body of wood instead of brass.

**1851** *Catal. Gt. Exhib.* I. 469/1 Newly-invented euphonic serpentcleide. **1882** in Grove *Dict. Mus.* III. 470.

†**'serpenter.** *Obs.* [app. f. serpent *v.* + -er$^{1}$.] A serpentine line.

**1598** Sylvester *Du Bartas* II. ii. IV. *Columnes* 170 Other, whose Tracts never directly slide, As with the Snayl, the crooked Serpenter [orig. *Comme la limaceuse auec la serpentee*].

†**'serpentess.** *Obs.* *rare*$^{-1}$. [f. serpent *sb.* + -ess.] A female serpent.

**1621** Molle *Camerar. Liv. Libr.* IV. xii. 273 Apollodorus saith, that Sphinx was engendred of Typhon and of a great Serpentesse [*ex Echidna & Typhone parentibus ortam*].

†**'serpentful,** *a.* *Obs.* *rare*$^{-1}$. [-ful.] Teeming with serpents.

**1557** Phaer *Æneid* VII. T 3, So serpentfull she seemes, and ouer all begrowen with snakes.

**Ser'pentian.** App. error for Serpentinian.

**1841** Murdock & Soames tr. *Mosheim's Eccl. Hist.* I. Cent. II. II. v. §19 The Ophites or Serpentians..of which one Euphrates is said to be the father.

†**serpentic,** *a.* *Obs.* *rare*$^{-1}$. [f. serpent *sb.* + -ic.] Serpent-like, serpentine.

**1661** Morgan *Sph. Gentry* I. v. 56 So also were the heroes of ancient time [honoured] for destroying of Serpentick kind of men.

†**ser'pentical,** *a.* *Obs.* *rare*$^{-1}$. [f. serpent *sb.* + -ical.] = prec.

**1546** *Supplic. Poore Commons* (E.E.T.S.) 74 O diuelish subtiltie, more then serpentical!

**serpenti'cidal,** *a.* [Formed as next + -al$^{1}$.] Serpent-slaying.

**1817** G. S. Faber *Eight Dissert.* (1845) I. 348 Their serpenticidal Chrishna. **1819** —— *Disp.* (1823) I. p. xx, The serpenticidal and virgin-born God.

**serpenticide$^{1}$** (sɜː'pɛntɪsaɪd). [f. serpent *sb.*: see -cide$^{1}$.] A slayer of serpents.

**1801** G. S. Faber *Horæ Mosaicæ* (1818) II. 294 *note*, Vishnu, much of whose character has been borrowed from old tradition respecting the predicted Serpenticide. **1817** S. R. Maitland *Dissertation* 31, I have before mentioned Apollo as a king: I must now say something of him as a Serpenticide.

**ser'penticide$^{2}$.** [f. serpent *sb.*: see -cide$^{2}$.] Killing of serpents.

**1882** *Field* 3 June 733, I think we must acquit the gentle deer of this charge of habitual serpenticide.

**serpenticone** (sɜː'pɛntɪkəʊn). *Palæont.* [f. *serpenti-*, comb. form of serpent *sb.* (see -i-) + cone *sb.*$^{1}$] An ammonoid in which the whorls are slender and overlap very little, so that the shell resembles a coiled snake.

**1923** H. H. Swinnerton *Outl. Palæont.* x. 214 The forms assumed by these derivatives [of cadicones] were determined mainly by modification of the whorl shape in two directions. In the one the venter and dorsum became arched; the outer consequently embraced the inner whorls and the umbilicus became narrower and even disappeared. The shell thus produced was globose in shape and is described as a sphærocone... In the other modification the whorl increased in height..; the effect of this was to produce a shell with a widely open umbilicus and having the appearance of a coiled snake. The descriptive term serpenticone is therefore applied to this type of shell. **1970** R. M. BLACK *Elements Palaeont.* viii. 87 *Dactylioceras*..has an evolute shell with a wide, shallow umbilicus; the whorl section is oval. It is a typical serpenticone.

**serpentiferous** (sɜːpən'tɪfərəs), *a.* *rare.* [f. SERPENT *sb.* + -FEROUS. Cf. L. *serpentifer.*]

**1.** Bearing or containing a serpent.

**1743** STUKELEY *Abury* 62 This sacred figure of the alate and serpentiferous circle.

**2.** Abounding in serpents.

**1905** GEIL *Yankee in Pigmy Land* iv. 45 This road was emphatically serpentine, if not serpentiferous.

**serpentiform** (sɜː'pɛntɪfɔːm). [ad. mod.L. *serpentiform-is*: see SERPENT *sb.* and -FORM. Cf. F. *serpentiforme.*] Having the form of a serpent; serpentine in shape.

**1777** PENNANT *Brit. Zool.* IV. 53 Asterias... Five-Rayed, with slender or serpentiform rays. **1819** SAMOUELLE *Entomol. Compend.* 114 Julus... Body serpentiform, cylindric. **1877** HUXLEY & MARTIN *Elem. Biol.* 26 A wriggling or serpentiform motion.

**serpen'tigenous,** *a.* *rare*$^{-0}$. [f. L. *serpentigena*, f. *serpent-* SERPENT *sb.* + *gen-* to produce.] See quot. So **serpen'tigerous** [L. *serpentiger*: see -GEROUS].

**1730** BAILEY (folio), *Serpentigenous*, ingender'd..of a Serpent. *Ibid.*, *Serpentigerous*, bearing or carrying Serpents.

**serpentile** ('sɜːpəntaɪl), *a.* *rare.* [f. SERPENT *sb.* + -ILE.] = SERPENTINE.

**1795** T. MAURICE *Hindostan* I. I. i. 68 This profound veneration of the serpentile tribe. **1857** MUNDY *Antipodes* 14 A serpentile [*ed.* 1852 serpentine] line of demolished rocks and gum-trees.

‖**serpentin** (sɛrpɑ̃tɛ̃). [F.: see next.] A long coloured paper ribbon which is unrolled and thrown into the air at times of rejoicing.

**1894** *Nation* 22 Mar. 215/2 They shouted unmusical songs, threw confetti, serpentins, and paper darts among the ladies. **1905** J. K. JEROME *Idle Ideas* iii, The 'serpentin' is a feature of the Belgian Carnival.

**serpentine** ('sɜːpəntaɪn), *sb.* Also 4–6 **serpentyn,** 5–6 **-yne,** (5, 7 **sarp-**, 5 **-ene,** 6–8 **-in,** 6 *Sc.* **scharpentyn**). [a. OF. *serpentin* and *serpentine*, ad. med.L. *serpentīnum* and *serpentīna*, absol. uses of the neut. and fem. sing. respectively of *serpentīnus* (see next).]

**1.** A name for certain plants reputed to contain an antidote to the poison of serpents; e.g. dragonwort, fenugreek.

*a* **1400** *Stockholm Med. MS.* ii. 651 in *Anglia* XVIII. 323 Dragaunce & serpentyn in same And nedderistonge, alle on be name. **1526** *Grete Herball* ccccx. (1529) Y iij, Powdre of serpentyne put alone in to yᵉ eye is good to clense the eye of the pynne & webbe. **1552** HULOET, Serpentine [*ed.* 1572 *adds* or serpentarie,..*dracuntium*..*Vulgo Serpentaria*]. **1608** TOPSELL *Four-f. Beasts* 611 Fænegreek..is called also Serpentine, because when Snakes..are hurt therewith, they recouer their woundes by eating therof.

**2.** A kind of cannon; in the 15th and 16th cent. used largely as a ship's gun. Now only *Hist.*

*c* **1450** *Brut* ccl. 505 Many other gret gonnes & serpentines. **1485** *Cely Papers* (1900) 177, iiij small sarpentynus with vij chamburs of on mackyng. **1513** *Acc. Ld. High. Treas. Scot.* IV. 484 For iij scharpentynnis..to the greit schip. **1627** CAPT. SMITH *Seaman's Gram.* xiv. 70 A Sarpentine. Height [= bore] in Inches 1½. **1824** MEYRICK *Ant. Armour* II. 201 In the year 1474 King Edward the Fourth directed all the bombs, cannons, culverines, fowlers, serpentines..to be taken and provided for his use. **1863** KIRK *Hist. Chas. Bold* II. 451 The battering-train consisted of thirty bombards and fifty large serpentines.

**3.** A rock or mineral, consisting mainly of hydrous magnesium silicate, of a dull green colour with markings resembling those of a serpent's skin. Also, an ornamental stone made of this.

The purest kind is called 'noble' or 'precious serpentine'. The impure or 'common serpentine' occurs in rock-masses and is worked as serpentine marble.

**1426** in *Somerset Med. Wills* (1901) 118 [My best covered cup of silver and gilt, with one] serpentyn [in the bottom (*in fundo*) of the said cup]. *c* **1450** METHAM *Wks.* (E.E.T.S.) 47/1256 A ston ys ther, That the serpent may noght hym noght dere. The name off home serpentyne ys. **1561–2** *New Yrs. Gifts* in Nichols *Progr. Eliz.* (1823) I. 114 A small coller of serpentyne garneshed with silver gilt. **1615** G. SANDYS *Trav.* 181 In the bottome of this manger, and just in the middle a round Serpentine is set. **1644** EVELYN *Mem.* (1857) I. 97 Four pillars of a kind of serpentine. **1756–7** tr. *Keysler's Trav.* (1760) IV. 288 The seats of the chairs in this apartment are made of serpentine. **1816** J. SMITH *Panorama Sci. & Art* II. 466 Serpentine..is either compact, granulated, scaly, lamellated, or fibrous. **1874** RAYMOND *Statist. Mines & Mining* 380 The main ridge seems to be made up of a series of metamorphic slates, sandstones, and serpentines.

†**4.** = SERPENT *sb.* 4. *Obs.*

*c* **1440** *Alphabet of Tales* 434 This sakett and þis gold is not þine, for þou says þou lost ij serpentynys and here-in is bod one.

**5.** The coiled pipe or worm of a distilling apparatus. *Obs.* exc. as representing F. *serpentin.*

**1519** in Noake *Mon. & Cath. Worc.* (1866) 185 A limbeke with a serpentyn closed both on oun. **1584** COGAN *Haven Health* ccxxii. (1636) 227 Distill it with a Limbecke or Serpentine. **1611** FLORIO, *Serpentina*,..a kind of winding limbecke called a Serpentine or doubble ss. **1694** SALMON *Bate's Dispens.* 34/2 Then distil twenty four hours, and distil through a Serpentine or Worm. **1725** *Bradley's Fam. Dict.* Qq 4/2 A Canal made of Tin,..very long, and winding..; For which Reason they have given it the Name of Serpentine. **1885** *Forestry* 209 This is subjected to a cooling process, in this case a serpentine of cold water.

†**6.** The cock of the harquebus. *Obs.*

**1590** SIR J. SMYTHE *Cert. Discourses* 21 b, If Harquebuziers in putting their matches into their serpentines do faile to set them of a conuenient length. **1611** FLORIO, *Serpentina*, an iron at the end of a Gunners Linstocke called a cocke or serpentine. [**1881** GREENER *Gun* 45 The serpentin is hung upon a pivot passing through the stock and continued past the pivot, forming a lever.]

†**7.** A serpiginous disease. *Obs.*

**1639** T. DE GRAY *Compl. Horsem.* 94 Pin and web, dragons, serpentines, and such numberlesse sorances. **1700** RYCAUT *Hist. Turks* III. 134 He was afflicted with a Distemper called a Serpentine or Cancer, which some Years since was caused by an Erysipelas.

†**8.** [after Pg. *serpentina.*] A kind of hammock.

**1767** *Byron's Voy. round World* 15 The rich [at Salvador, Brazil] cause themselves to be carried about in a kind of cotton hammocks called serpentines.

†**9. a.** A malicious action. **b.** A wily, cunning person. *Obs.*

*c* **1510** MORE *Picus* Wks. 3/2 When thei perceiued, that thei coulde not against his connyng any thing openly preuaile: thei brought forth the serpentines of false crime. *a* **1533** LD. BERNERS *Gold. Bk. M. Aurel.* vii. (1537) 11 When our senate fayllethe of meke and wyse Senatours, and multyplieth with these serpentines.

**10. a.** A winding path or line.

**1885** *Pall Mall G.* 20 Mar. 6/1 The narrow-gauge line can ..wind down mountains, with a number of quick turns and serpentines. **1886** *Field* 13 Mar. 310/1 (Skating) The more sedate delineator of 3's, 8's, Q's, serpentines, and what not. **1893** R. F. BURTON in Lady Burton *Life* I. 269 The yellow ..Wazegura wilderness, traversed by a serpentine of trees.

**b.** *Math.* A cubic curve to which the equation is $y\ (a^2 + x^2) = abx$. (In recent Dicts.)

**c.** A lake or canal of a winding shape, esp. the one constructed in Hyde Park in 1730.

**1837** W. TAYLER *Jrnl.* 2 Jan. in J. Burnett *Useful Toil* (1974) II. 176 Went round Hyde Park, saw some thousands of people sliding and skaiting on the Serpentine. **1853** GEO. ELIOT *Let.* 22 Oct. (1954) II. 120, I am hoping for a row.. on the Serpentine, which is really almost as good as a lake. **1885** C. M. YONGE *Nuttie's Father* II. xiii. 157 He said he'd take him to the Serpentine to sail his ship. **1971** *Country Life* 2 Sept. 546/2 By 1747 he [*sc.* George Anson of Shugborough] had erected a Chinese house on a little island formed by a new canal or serpentine. **1977** P. WILLIS *Charles Bridgeman* iv. 96 When Bridgeman's widow in her Petition to the Lords of the Treasury asks for money for making 'the lake in Hyde Park' she is obviously referring to the Serpentine.

**11.** *attrib.* **a.** Consisting of, containing, or made of serpentine (sense 3), as ***serpentine knife, porphyry, pillar, rock, tankard, -wacke.***

**1463** *Will of J. Baret* in *Bury Wills* (Camden) 35 My serpentyn knyves. **1582** HESTER *Secr. Phiorav.* I. lxv. 78 A rounde Corrall like vnto the Serpentine Purphire. **1781** GIBBON *Decl. & F.* xvii. II. 16 *note*, The serpentine pillar of the Hippodrome. **1799** W. TOOKE *View Russian Emp.* I. 120 The principal mountains of these parts [*sc.* Lapland], consist of granite..and probably likewise of porphyry and serpentine-wake. **1838** W. F. AINSWORTH *Res. Assyria*, etc. 336 Serpentine rocks. **1875** J. W. DAWSON *Dawn of Life* vi. 144 Serpentine-limestone or ophicalcite.

**b.** (sense 2) ***serpentine cart, gun.***

**1471** *Coventry Leet Bk.* 363 Delyuered to Rob. Onley a serpentyne gun & a staffe gun. **1496** *Acc. Ld. High Treas. Scot.* I. 291 The feys and schethis to the serpentyn cartis.

**serpentine** ('sɜːpəntaɪn), *a.* Also 5–6 **-yn(e,** 6–7 **-in.** [a. F. *serpentin* (12th cent.), ad. L. *serpentīnus*, f. *serpent-*, SERPENT *sb.* + *-īnus* -INE[1].]

**1. a.** Of or pertaining to a serpent or serpents; of the form of or resembling a serpent, or that of a serpent.

*c* **1420** ? LYDG. *Assembly of Gods* 616 Wyngys had hit serpentyne and a long tayll. *Ibid.* 968 Vice..On hys steede serpentyn. **1509** HAWES *Past. Pleas.* XXXVI. xi, The sorceresse..Of the best, made the head serpentyne. **1608** TOPSELL *Serpents* 235, I will not expresly define whether this may be called a Sea-Serpent, or a Serpentine-fish. **1664** H. MORE *Myst. Iniq.* I. viii. 250 That notorious Serpentine shape which deceived Adam and Eve. **1667** MILTON *P.L.* x. 870 Thy shape..and colour Serpentine. **1774** J. BRYANT *Anc. Mythol.* I. 428 Servius, who distributes the serpentine species into three tribes. **1834** *Good's Study Med.* (ed. 4) II. 80 The most active and malignant of all the serpentine poisons is that of the rattlesnake. **1880** *W. Smith & Cheetham's Dict. Chr. Antiq.* II. 1889/2 Continual use is made of the serpentine or lacertine form in Irish and Anglo-Saxon ornament. **1896** CROCKETT *Cleg Kelly* vii, Once more he protruded his head in that monstrously serpentine manner round the corner of the low shop-door.

**b.** In allusion to the representation of a serpent with its tail in its mouth. ***serpentine verse***, a metrical line beginning and ending with the same word.

**1605** CAMDEN *Rem.*, *Rythmes* 26 Our Poets hath their knacks..as Ecchos, Achrostiches, Serpentine verses,..&c. **1656** BLOUNT *Glossogr.*, *Serpentine verses*, are those which do, as it were, run into themselves, as we see Serpents pictured with tail in mouth.

**c.** *Surg.* (See quot.)

**1753** *Chambers's Cycl.* Suppl. s.v. *Bandage*, These creeping, or as we sometimes call them serpentine bandages.

**d.** ***serpentine pot***: a potters' utensil for colouring or ornamenting common stoneware.

**1839** URE *Dict. Arts* 1017 The serpentine or snake pots.. are made..in three compartments, each containing a different colour... On inclining the vessel, the three colours flow out at once..; whereby curious serpent-like ornaments may be readily obtained.

†**e.** Caused by serpents. *Obs. rare.*

**1446** LYDG. *Two Nightingale Poems* II. 315 Receyved.. medicyne Of al theyr hurtis, that were serpentyne.

**2.** Having the evil qualities of the serpent; pertaining to the Serpent as the tempter of mankind; diabolical, Satanic; devilishly wily or cunning.

In early use often with retention of literal phraseology.

**1387–8** T. USK *Test. Love* I. vii. (Skeat) l. 40 Enemyes.. wol seche privy serpentynes queintyses, to quenche..by venim of many besinesses, the light of truthe. *c* **1422** HOCCLEVE *Min. Poems* (1892) 236 This serpentyn womman ..shee That had him terned with false deceitis. **1491** CAXTON *Vitas Patr.* (W. de W. 1495) I. xl. 58 b, An euyll and serpentyne tongue full of venyme. *a* **1550** *Image Ipocr.* in *Skelton's Wks.* (1843) II. 426 Sectes serpentyne. **1599** SANDYS *Europæ Spec.* (1632) 96 A serpentine generation, wholly made of fraud, of policies and practises. **1637** DOW *Answ. to H. Burton* 25 The poysoned shafts of his serpentine tongue. **1663** BOYLE *Usef. Exp. Nat. Philos.* I. ii. 31 A serpentine warinesse in declining dangers. **1752** LAW *Spirit of Love* II. (1816) 125 All that is earthly, serpentine, and devilish in every man. **1830** *Westm. Rev.* XIII. 84 In De Foe's time the serpentine temptation consisted in laced shoes instead of leathern. **1873** DIXON *Two Queens* XIV. vi. III. 99 With serpentine deceit, she said the King was cheerful in his trials.

**3. a.** Having a direction or following a course resembling that of a serpent in motion; tortuous, sinuous, winding. Also, esp. in reference to canals or lakes.

**1615** CROOKE *Body of Man* 26 The Serpentine and writhen Meanders of the Veynes. *Ibid.* 603 A Serpentine Still. *c* **1645** HOWELL *Lett.* I. I. xvi, The branching and serpentin cours of the River Seine. **1696** PHILLIPS (ed. 5), *Serpentine Line*, a crooked winding, that incloses itself continually, as a Serpent wraps himself up in Folds. **1730** *London Jrnl.* 26 Sept. 2/3 Next Monday they begin upon the Serpentine River and Royal Mansion in Hyde-Park. **1754** SMEATON in *Phil. Trans.* XLVIII. 535 Upon the serpentine river in Hyde-park. **1796** WITHERING *Brit. Plants* (ed. 3) I. 81 (Dict. Terms), *Serpentine* (*repandus*), the edge of some leaves is formed like a serpentine line; without any angles or corners. **1809** PINKNEY *Trav. France* 127 The road was..so serpentine as never to be visible beyond an hundred yards. **1824** J. C. LOUDON *Encycl. Gardening* (ed. 2) III. iv. 1011 Those wavy serpentine canals..are never mistaken for natural scenes. **1829** *Good's Study Med.* (ed. 3) I. 379 When the stools were examined, they were found..to be serpentine or twisted. **1868** BAIN *Ment. & Mor. Sci.* III. xiii. §18. 307 The most beautiful line is the serpentine line, called by Hogarth, the Line of Grace. **1888** MISS BRADDON *Fatal Three* I. v, A broad gravel path led in a serpentine sweep towards the stables. **1948** C. HUSSEY in M. Jourdain *Work of William Kent* 23 The most famous Serpentine Lake, that in Hyde Park, was ordered by Queen Caroline and is probably due to Bridgeman.

**b.** In various technical uses (see quots.). ***serpentine temple*** = serpent temple (see SERPENT *sb.* 12).

**1743** STUKELEY *Abury* 9 Those with the form of a snake annext, as that of Abury, I call serpentine temples, or *Dracontia*, by which they were denominated of old. **1797** *Encycl. Brit.* (ed. 3) XVII. 311 A horse is said to have a serpentine tongue, if it is always frisking and moving, and sometimes passing over the bit. **1851** SQUIER *Serpent Symbol* 137 Ancient serpentine structures of the United States. **1860** C. R. M. TALBOT tr. *Newton's Lines 3rd Order* 12 We shall call..that which cuts the asymptote in contrary flexures, having on both sides contrary branches, the serpentine hyperbola. *Ibid.* 17 Where the serpentine curve does not pass through the intersection of the asymptotes. **1867** *Philatelist* I. 99/2 The peculiarity of the serpentine perforation is that no paper is taken away by the machine; it is simply a serpentine cut, with twelve waves to the base of the stamp on one, eighteen on the other. **1884** KNIGHT *Dict. Mech.* Suppl., *Serpentine Molding Machine*, one for carving parlor frames, lounge, sofa, and chair backs, and other crooked work [etc.].

**4.** *Comb.*, as ***serpentine-like*** adj.; **serpentine superphosphate** *N.Z.*, a mixture of superphosphate and crushed serpentinite, used as a fertilizer.

**1603** KNOLLES *Hist. Turks* (1621) 249 All that intestine and serpentine-like tragedie. **1867** *Philatelist* I. 103/1 This, which has been called serpentine-pierced, is found..on the ..stamps of Finland. **1887** P. M'NEILL *Blawearie* 93 The gentle serpentine-like curvings of the wall-sides. **1941** ELLIOTT & LYNCH in *N.Z. Jrnl. Agric.* 15 Sept. 179/1 The name serpentine superphosphate will be used in future in place of 'silico superphosphate', as it is a more accurate description of the material. It is made by mixing three parts of hot, newly-made superphosphate with one part of ground serpentine and allowing the mixture to 'mature' in heaps for several days. **1965** G. J. WILLIAMS *Econ. Geol. N.Z.* x. 143/1 Serpentinite is quarried in considerable quantity in New Zealand for the manufacture of 'serpentine-superphosphate'.

**'serpentine,** *v.* [f. prec.]

**1.** *intr.* To move in a serpentine manner; to pursue a serpentine or tortuous path; to wind.

*a* **1774** HARTE *Vis. Death* 2 In those fair vales..Where Guadalquiver serpentines with ease. **1797** T. HOLCROFT tr.

*Stolberg's Trav.* III. lxxi. (ed. 2) 83 Garlands of flowers serpentine with a free..air. **1802** COLMAN *Broad Grins, Elder Bro.* (1804) 120 Toby [who was drunk]..Went serpentining home. **1886** RUSKIN *Præterita* I. 289 Permitting the road to serpentine and zigzag up the cliff terraces.

**b.** *trans.* To pursue (one's way) with a winding motion.

**1837** T. HOOK *Jack Brag* viii, He was merely serpentining his way to the part of the details.

**2.** To cause to take a serpentine direction; to wind. Also, to bring into a condition by serpentine behaviour.

**1850** DICKENS *Dav. Copp.* xxxv, If you're an eel, Sir, conduct yourself like one... I am not going to be serpentined and corkscrewed out of my senses! **1870** THORNBURY *Tour Eng.* I. i. 25 He serpentined water through the gardens, and built two bridges. **1883** D. C. MURRAY *Val Strange* III. xxiv. 243 'My dear,' said Hiram, serpentining his long arm about her.

**'serpentinely**, *adv.* [f. SERPENTINE *a.* + -LY².] In a serpentine manner; in a serpentine path.

**1656** S. H. *Golden Law* 23 So would my Excepter do, if in their place, Serpentinely save his head. **1762** tr. *Busching's Syst. Geog.* III. 77 The great canal..serpentinely flows through the city. **1877** RUSLING *Great West* 87 Down this [bed] the wild little creek shoots very serpentinely. **1906** M. CHOLMONDELEY *Prisoners* iv, Perhaps..he might have serpentinely glided through into the next room without her perceiving him.

**serpentine marble.** [= med.L. *marmor serpentīnum*; cf. F. *marbre serpentin.*] The mineral serpentine in massive form.

**1601** HOLLAND *Pliny* xxxvi. vii. II. 573 The Serpentine marble called Ophites. **1657** [see OPHITICAL]. **1660** F. BROOKE tr. *Le Blanc's Trav.* 278 A Sphinx wrought in Numidian or Serpentine marble extraordinary hard. **1865** W. B. CARPENTER in *Reader* 8 July 45 The Serpentine marble of Canada. **1875** J. W. DAWSON *Dawn of Life* vi. 147 A beautiful variety of ophicalcite or serpentine-marble.

**serpentine powder.** [See SERPENTINE *sb.* 2.] Gunpowder for use with the serpentine; gunpowder in fine meal as distinguished from the corned or granulated kind.

**1497** *Naval Acc. Hen. VII* (1896) 129 Serpentine poudre with ij barelles brent in the botom. **1588** GREENE *Alcida* (1617) G 2 b, What though the Serpentine powder is quickly kindled, and quickly out. **1598** BARRET *Theor. Warres* v. iv. 137 Powder both serpentine and corne powder. *a* **1642** SIR W. MONSON *Naval Tracts* III. (1704) 344/1 Serpentine Powder..is weak, and will not keep at Sea. **1787** *Act 27 Geo. III*, c. 13 (Sched. A, Rates Inwards) Gunpowder, Serpentine Powder.

**serpentine stone.** [= med.L. *lapis serpentīnus*, rendering Gr. λίθος ὀφίτης: cf. OPHITE¹.] = SERPENTINE *sb.* 3.

**1662** MERRETT *Neri's Art of Glass* 259 This stone most commonly partakes of a light Green, like the Serpentine stone. **1726** LEONI *Alberti's Archit.* I. 33/1 The green, or Serpentine-stone mightily resists the Fire.

†**serpenting**, *vbl. sb. Obs.* [f. SERPENT *v.* + -ING¹.] Winding.

**1677** EVELYN *Diary* 12 Oct., This place is exceeding sharp in the winter, by reason of the serpenting of the hills. **1679** *Ibid.* 23 July, A circular view..which with the serpenting of the Thames is admirable.

So †**serpenting** *ppl. a.*, winding.

**1614** DRUMM. OF HAWTH. *Poems*, This Moone, that Sunne,..Be but the same which vnder Saturnes Raigne, Did the serpenting [*ed.* 1711 serpentine] Seasons interchaine. *a* **1649** —— *Flowers of Sion* Wks. (1711) 26 Her Floods and pratling Brooks,..with serpenting [*ed.* 1630 maz-like] Crooks.

**Serpentinian** (-'ɪnɪən). [f. L. *Serpentīnus* (see SERPENTINE *a.* and *sb.*) + -IAN.] = OPHITE².

**1758** MACLAINE tr. *Mosheim's Eccl. Hist.* I. Cent. II. II. v. §19 The Ophites, or Serpentinians, a ridiculous sort of heretics, who had for their leader a man called Euphrates.

**serpen'tinic**, *a.* [f. SERPENTINE *sb.* + -IC.] Of or pertaining to serpentine.

**1883** *Science* I. 75/2 The chloritic and serpentinic series. **1887** *Geol. Mag.* Jan. 23 A serpentinic substance containing bronzite, ilmenite [etc.].

**'serpentining**, *ppl. a.* [f. SERPENTINE *v.* + -ING².] Winding or coiling like a serpent; winding, sinuous, tortuous.

**1799** SOUTHEY *Let. to John May* Aug. *Life* (1850) II. 22 Ascending from Lynmouth up a road of serpentining perpendicularity. **1855** BROWNING *Men & Women, Andrea del Sarto* 26 My serpentining beauty, rounds on rounds! **1888** *Punch* 4 Feb. 60/2 The gnarled serpentining root of yonder..elm.

Hence **'serpentiningly** *adv.*, windingly.

**1871** BROWNING *Balaust.* 355 Though they leap all the way the pillar leads,..And serpentiningly enrich the roof.

**serpentinite** ('sɜːpəntɪnaɪt). *Petrogr.* [f. SERPENTINE *sb.* + -ITE¹.] A rock consisting largely of serpentine or related minerals.

**1936** G. C. SELFRIDGE in *Amer. Mineralogist* XXI. 463 The term serpentinite is suggested for rocks composed of serpentine or antigorite or a mixture of both. **1956** *Amer. Jrnl. Sci.* CCLIV. 201 Bare *roches moutonées* of serpentinite stand out from the heather. **1965** [see *serpentine superphosphate* s.v. SERPENTINE *a.* 11 a]. **1977** A. HALLAM *Planet Earth* 137 Serpentinites are rocks originally very rich in olivine that has been entirely converted to serpentine.

Hence **serpenti'nitic** *a.*

**1975** *Nature* 25 Dec. 701/2 The ubiquitous association of ultrabasic (mostly serpentinitic) rocks with glaucophane-schists may be represented here by the serpentinite-dunite of Gibbs Island and the glaucophane-schists of Smith Island.

**serpentinization** (ˌsɜːpəntɪnaɪ'zeɪʃən). *Geol.* [f. SERPENTINE *sb.* + -IZATION.] Conversion into serpentine.

**1885** JUDD in *Q. Jrnl. Geol. Soc.* XLI. 382 The results are, in this case, not complicated by serpentinization.

**serpentinize** ('sɜːpəntɪnaɪz), *v.* [f. SERPENTINE *sb.* or *a.* + -IZE.]

**1.** *intr.* = SERPENTINE *v.* 1.

**1791** NEWTE *Tour Eng. & Scot.* 248 The venerable beauties of Innerpaffray, fronting Castle Drummond, in a concavity of the serpentinizing Ern. **1798** W. MAVOR *Brit. Tourists* V. 18 Extensive lawns through which a river serpentinizes.

**2.** *trans.* (*Geol.*) To convert into serpentine.

**1886** [see PERIDOTITIC *a.*]. **1889** *Amer. Nat.* Nov. 1007 Scyelite..consists of serpentinized olivine, altered augite, bleached mica. **1899** *Nat. Sci.* XV. 173 The ferro-magnesian minerals are more or less serpentinised.

**'serpentinoid**, *a.* [f. SERPENTINE *sb.* + -OID.] Having the characters of the mineral serpentine.

**1888** *Encycl. Brit.* XXIII. 801/1 Serpentines and obscure serpentinoid rocks.

**serpentinous** ('sɜːpəntaɪnəs), *a.* [f. SERPENTINE *sb.* or *a.* + -OUS.]

**1.** Of the nature of or consisting of serpentine.

**1833-4** *Encycl. Metrop.* (1845) VI. 764/2 The serpentinous masses in the Northern Apennines. **1856** PAGE *Adv. Text-bk. Geol.* (1876) 157 The..serpentinous limestones of Canada.

**2.** Serpentine, winding.

**1882** GEIKIE *Text-bk. Geol.* IV. III. 511 Causes the outcrop to describe a widely serpentinous course.

†**serpentinously**, *adv. Obs.* [f. **serpentinous* (a. OF. *serpentineux*, f. *serpentin* SERPENTINE *a.*) + -LY².] With serpentine or diabolical action.

**1502** *Ord. Crysten Men* (W. de W.) II. xii. L ij, The deuyll the whiche by the meane of the tonge serpentynously putteth all humayne lygnage vnto perdycyon.

†**serpentive**, *a. Obs.* [f. SERPENT *sb.* + -IVE.] = SERPENTINE *a.* 2.

**1635** SHIRLEY *Traitor* III. i, Finding this serpentive treason broken in the shell. **1645** *City Alarum* 17 The Serpentive abuse that hath devoured the memory of all other. **1649** *Shute's Sarah & Hagar* Table b iij b, The serpentive motion of sin.

**serpentivorous** (sɜːpən'tɪvərəs), *a.* [f. L. *serpent-em* SERPENT + -VOROUS.] Serpent-eating.

**1882** *Nature* No. 642. 378 The lightning 'dabs' of a serpentivorous bird.

**serpentize** ('sɜːpəntaɪz), *v.* Now *rare.* [f. SERPENT *sb.* + -IZE.]

**1.** *intr.* = SERPENTINE *v.* 1.

**1699** GARTH *Dispens.* VI. 75 Where living Floods of Merc'ry serpentize. **1718** OZELL tr. *Tournefort's Voy.* II. 202 The Euphrates serpentizes among wonderful plants. **1755** *Gentl. Mag.* XXV. 128 The colour of this shell is the purest white; its canalures or ribs, which serpentize, are crossed by circular lines. **1834** BECKFORD *Italy* I. 23 How happy I was, when I had duly serpentized over his garden, to find myself once more in the grand avenue. **1865** CARLYLE *Fredk. Gt.* XVIII. ii. V. 32 The miserablest Brook in nature, which takes to oozing and serpentising forward thereabouts.

**2.** *trans.* To cause to take a serpentine shape, motion, or course.

**1762** MRS. MONTAGU in Doran *Lady Last Cent.* (1873) 117, I dare say his Grace of Newcastle will fall to serpentizing rivers. **1808** *Europ. Mag.* LIII. 253, I would teach them a circumbendibus; I would serpentize them.

Hence **'serpentizing** *ppl. a.*, winding, tortuous.

**1629** LE GRYS tr. *Barclay's Argenis* 266 A Cabinet..inlaid ..with siluer Plates, wrought in a serpentizing manner. **1739** H. BROOKE *Gustavus Vasa* II. i, I know thou hast a serpentizing genius, Canst wind the subtlest mazes of the soul. **1855** SINGLETON *Virgil* II. 455 A glen there is with serpentizing bend.

**serpent-like**, *a.* and *adv.* [-LIKE.]

**A.** *adj.* Like a serpent; = SERPENTINE *a.*

*a* **1586** SIDNEY *Arcadia* I. (1622) 93 A creeping serpent-like of mortall woe. **1629** H. BURTON *Truth's Tri.* 307 His serpent-like gate. *a* **1649** DRUMM. OF HAWTH. *Wks.* (1711) 4/1 Serpent-like Meander. **1774** GOLDSM. *Nat. Hist.* (1825) III. 159 Its serpent-like figure. **1890** 'R. BOLDREWOOD' *Miner's Right* xxv, I re-read the serpent-like scroll which had been cast into my Eden of love and faith.

**B.** *adv.* With serpentine motion, habit, disposition, etc.; †malignantly, treacherously.

**1605** SHAKS. *Lear* II. iv. 163 She hath..Look'd blacke vpon me, strooke me with her Tongue Most Serpent-like, vpon the very Heart. **1682** LISTER *Gœdart Of Insects* 109 These Insects did put off their skins, Serpent like. *a* **1699** J. BEAUMONT *Psyche* I. clxvi. (1702) 10 Where, Serpent-like, in Paradise, she over Her foul Design spread this fair-faced cover. **1825** SCOTT *Talism.* xxi, The marabout..glided on.. serpent-like, or rather snail-like.

**'serpently**, *adv.* [f. SERPENT *sb.* + -LY².] = prec. adv.

**1402** *Pol. Poems* (Rolls) II. 49 Jak, thou seist·ful serpentli. *c* **1530** *Calisto & Melib.* A ij, Semyng to be shepe and serpently shrewd. **1842** *Tait's Mag.* IX. 374 Stealthily, serpently, he slimed his way.

†**'serpentous**, *a. Obs. rare*⁻¹. [f. SERPENT *sb.* + -OUS.] = SERPENTINE *a.* 1.

*c* **1500** *Melusine* 320 On the basse stone of the wyndowe apereth at this day themprynte of her foote serpentous.

**serpentry** ('sɜːpəntrɪ). [f. SERPENT *sb.* + -RY.]

**1.** Serpents or serpentine creatures collectively.

**1818** KEATS *Endym.* I. 821 To..wipe away all slime Left by men-slugs and human serpentry. **1869** RUSKIN *Q. of Air* §87 There is an Æsculapian as well as an evil serpentry among the Draconidæ. **1869** BROWNING *Ring & Bk.* XII. 561 For egg turned snake needs fear no serpentry.

**2.** A place where serpents are kept and reared.

**1846** MRS. GORE *Engl. Char.* Introd. 12 A serpentry for improving the domestic breed of rattlesnakes [etc.].

**3.** A winding like that of a serpent.

**1848** in WEBSTER; and in later Dicts.

**serpent-stone.**

**1.** = AMMONITE 1. Now *Obs.* or *local.*

**1681** GREW *Musæum* III. §i. i. 261 The Helick Serpent. Stone, *Ophites Ammoneus.* **1807** VANCOUVER *Agric. Devon* (1813) 73 The serpent-stone, or *cornu ammonis.* **1851** *N. & Q.* Ser. I. IV. 261 At Whitby, where these fine fossils of the Lias are called 'St. Hilda's Serpent-stones'.

**2.** An artificial 'stone' used as a remedy for the poison of serpents. Also = BEZOAR 2 a.

**1681** GREW *Musæum* I. §iii. 52 The Serpentstone. Said by some, to be factitious. *c* **1711** PETIVER *Gazophyl.* vii. 62 East India Serpent Stone..much esteemed in the Indies as a certain Remedy for the Bite of the Cobra de Capello or Hooded Snake, out of whose Head some affirm this to be taken; but it's more probable..that it's factitious and said to be composed of burnt Elephant's Bones. **1731** MEDLEY *Kolben's Cape Gd. Hope* II. 167 The artificial Serpent-Stone ..is shap'd like a Bean. **1774** PENNANT *Tour Scot. in* 1772, 297 The *Glain naidr* or Druidical bead..is..made of glass, marked with figures of serpents coiled up. The common people in Wales and in Scotland..call it by the name of Serpent-stone. **1861** HULME tr. *Moquin-Tandon* II. III. 68 Bezoars:..(serpent stone, cobra de capello).

**3.** ? = SERPENTINE STONE.

**1757** tr. *Henckel's Pyritologia* 361 Ophites or serpent-stone.

†**serpet.** *Obs. rare*⁻¹. [error for Turkish *sepet* wicker basket.] A kind of basket. In 18th c. dicts. (by misinterpretation of quot. 1678), a kind of rush.

**1615** G. SANDYS *Trav.* 67 After them are carried in Serpets (a kind of baskets) their presents. **1678** PHILLIPS, *Serpet*, probably from *Scirpus* a sort of Rush, of which is made a kind of Basket. **1726** *Dict. Rust.* (ed. 3), *Serpet*, a sort of Rush of which Baskets are made.

**serpierite** ('sɜːpɪəraɪt). *Min.* [a. F. *serpierite* (A. des Cloizeaux 1881, in *Bull. de la Soc. min. de France* IV. 92), f. the name of J. B. *Serpieri*, 19th-cent. Italian engineer: see -ITE¹.] A hydrated basic sulphate of copper, zinc, and calcium found as crusts or aggregates of small pale blue orthorhombic crystals.

**1892** E. S. DANA *Dana's Syst. Min.* (ed. 6) 963 Serpierite. .. Crystals minute... Occurs on smithsonite at the zinc mines of Laurium, Greece. **1927** *Mineral. Mag.* XXI. 387 Smithsonite ($ZnCO_3$) is also tolerably abundant..and it is in cavities of this smithsonite that the serpierite occurs. **1964** *Amer. Mineralogist* XLIX. 1145 Devillite and serpierite were identified on the basis of morphology, optics, and microchemical tests.

**serpiginous** (sɜː'pɪdʒɪnəs), *a.* [ad. mod.L. **serpīginōsus*, f. *serpīgin-*, SERPIGO. Cf. F. *serpigineux.*] Of the nature of serpigo; (of skin diseases) creeping from one part to another.

**1676** WISEMAN *Chirurg. Treat.* I. xxv. 139 A dry white Scurf, under which the serpiginous circles lay covered. **1753** R. RUSSELL *Diss. Sea Water* 143 Many Diseases of the serpiginous Kind. **1771** SMOLLETT *Humph. Cl.* 18 Apr., A serpiginous eruption, or rather a pocky itch. **1861** BUMSTEAD *Ven. Dis.* (1879) 387 Serpiginous chancroids. **1876** BRISTOWE *Theory & Pract. Med.* 633 Deep ulcers.. spreading..in a serpiginous manner. **1899** *Allbutt's Syst. Med.* VI. 590 Senile gangrene..tends to be serpiginous.

Hence **ser'piginously** *adv.*, in a serpiginous manner or form. After the manner of serpigo.

**1897** *Allbutt's Syst. Med.* II. 51 Individual spots may increase greatly in size, or neighbouring ones may coalesce into large serpiginously bordered tracts.

‖**serpigo** (sɜː'paɪgəʊ). Pl. **serpigines** (sɜː'pɪdʒɪniːz), **serpigoes.** Also 6-7 **sarpego,** 7 **sapego.** [med.L. *serpīgo*, f. *serpĕre* to creep; cf. *herpes.*] A general term (cf. HERPES) for creeping or spreading skin diseases; *spec.* ringworm.

[**1398** TREVISA *Barth. De P.R.* VII. lxiii (1495) 278 Serpigo is a drye scabbe.] *c* **1400** *Lanfranc's Cirurg.* 194 Serpigo is a scharpnes of a mannes skyn, & it is clepid serpigo, for it passiþ fro place to place. **1527** ANDREW *Brunswyke's Distyll. Waters* L ij b, The..Serpigines that is drye and small scabbes and spottys. **1603** SHAKS. *Meas. for M.* III. i. 31 The Gowt, Sapego, and the Rheume. **1607** TOPSELL *Four-f. Beasts* 651 Carbuncles, Tetters, Serpigoes, and such like. **1637** HEYWOOD *Royall King* III. xi, Be all his body..with the Sarpego dry'd. **1694** SALMON *Bate's Dispens.* 677 Ulcers, Serpigines, Scall'd-Heads. **1799** UNDERWOOD *Dis. Childhood* (ed. 4) II. 25 *Herpes Exedens*, or Serpigo.

†**serpille.** *Obs. rare.* [ad. It. *serpillo*, ad. L. *serpyllum* (see SERPOL).] Wild thyme. Also †*serpyne* [?].

**1558** WARDE tr. *Alexis' Secr.* 45 b, Jasemyn, Maioram, Sauourye, Serpyne, or Serpille, called wilde Time [orig. *gelsomino, maggiorana, serpillo, saturegia*].

**serpils,** obs. form of SURPLICE.

**serpitant.** Blundered f. SERPENTINE *sb.* (2).

*a* **1578** LINDESAY (Pitscottie) *Chron. Scot.* (S.T.S.) I. 251 Serpitantis and doubill doggis witht hagbut and cullvering.

**serpivolant** (sə'pɪvələnt). [ad. It. *serpe volante* (pl. *serpi volanti*) flying serpent.] The figure of a flying serpent.

**1866** G. MACDONALD *Ann. Q. Neighb.* ix. (1878) 138 Under the outstretched neck of one of those serpivolants on the gate.

**serplaith, -ath(e,** Sc. variants of SARPLIER.

†**serpol.** *Obs. rare.* In 5 sorpol, 7 serpoile. [a. OF. *serpol, -oul*, = Sp., Pg. *serpol*:—L. *serpullum, -yllum*, repr. Gr. ἕρπυλλον.] = next 1.

*c* **1400** *Master of Game* (MS. Digby 182) fol. 7 b, Whan þei pasture of ij herbes, þat one is clepid Sorpol, and þat other puligin, þei be.. fastrennynge. **1646** SIR T. BROWNE *Pseud. Ep.* III. xvii. 147 The mutation of Mint into Cresses, Basill into Serpoile, and Turneps into Radishes.

**serpolet** ('sɜːpəlɛt). [ad. F. *serpolet*, a. Pr. *serpolet*, dim. of *serpol*:—L. *serpullum* (see prec.).]

†**1.** Thyme; wild thyme. *Obs.*

*a* **1693** *Urquhart's Rabelais* III. l. 407 [Called] Serpolet, because it creepeth along the ground. **1853** LANDOR *Imag. Conv., Achilles & Helena*, Pleasant the short slender grass, ..interrupted..by little troops of serpolet running in disorder here and there.

**2.** In full ***serpolet oil***: see quot.

**1866** *Treas. Bot.* s.v., *Serpolet*, an essential perfumery oil obtained from *Thymus Serpyllum*. **1897** *Lippincott's Med. Dict.*, *Serpolet oil*.

**serpoloid** ('sɜːpəlɔɪd). [f. L. *serpĕre* to creep, *serpens* SERPENT + POLOID.] = HERPOLHODE.

**1862** CAYLEY *Math. Papers* (1891) IV. 572 A curve called 'the Serpoloid', which is the locus of the points with which the several points of the poloid come successively in contact with the tangent plane, and is a species of undulating curve.

**serpow,** variant of SEERPAW.

**serppelys,** obs. form of SURPLICE.

‖**serpula** ('sɜːpjʊlə). *Zool.* Pl. serpulæ (-iː). [mod.L. use of late L. *serpula* small serpent.] A marine annelid which inhabits a tortuous calcareous tube.

**1767** *Phil. Trans.* LVII. 432 The Serpula, or Worm-shell. **1834** MCMURTRIE *Cuvier's Anim. Kingd.* 256 Bent like the tubes of a Serpula. **1855** KINGSLEY *Glaucus* 124 The tubes of serpulæ and other annelidæ. **1881-2** SAVILLE KENT *Man. Infusoria* II. 778 Flashing out of sight after the manner of a serpula with the rapidity of lightning.

Hence **serpu'lacean, ser'pulean, 'serpulid,** an annelid belonging to a group or family of which *Serpula* is a typical genus; also *attrib.* or as *adj.*; **ser'pulidan, 'serpuline** *sbs.*; **'serpulite** *Geol.*, a fossil serpula; also, a formation containing these; attrib. ***serpulite-grit***; **'serpuloid** *a.*, resembling or characteristic of the serpulæ.

**1841** *Penny Cycl.* XXI. 182/1 *Serpulaceans. Under this division Lamarck arranges the genera *Spirorbis Serpula, Vermilia, Galeolaria*, and *Magilus*. **1835** KIRBY *Hab. & Inst. Anim.* I. xii. 334 The second [Order] he [Savigny] names *Serpuleans. **1883** *Science* I. 344/2 A new species of *serpulid, belonging, apparently, to the Sabellidæ. **1888** ROLLESTON & JACKSON *Anim. Life* 608 *note*, A Serpulid *Placostegus benthalianus*. **1935** *Discovery* Apr. 98/2 The only growths..are..two species of serpulid worms. **1963** R. P. DALES *Annelids* 15 The most specialized tube-dwellers are the sabellid and serpulid fan-worms. **1980** *Nature* 29 May 323/1 The coarse and medium sand fractions consist of rock and pelecypod fragments, aragonitic and calcitic algae, serpulid tubes and peneroplid Foraminifera. **1835** KIRBY *Hab. & Inst. Anim.* I. xii. 344 The *Serpulidans, in general, imitate the spiral structure of the Trachelipod and other Molluscans. **1882** *Cassell's Nat. Hist.* VI. 240 *Ditrupa subulata*, one of the *Serpulines. **1828-32** WEBSTER, **Serpulite*, petrified shells or fossil remains of the genus Serpula. **1856** PAGE *Adv. Text-bk. Geol.* x. 118 We rank provisionally under the head *annelida* such organisms as serpulites (so called from their resemblance to the serpula of existing seas). **1880** J. F. BLAKE in *Q. Jrnl. Geol. Soc.* XXXVI. 192 The lower part is so full of *Serpula gordialis* as to almost merit the title of Serpulite. **1884** *Nature* 13 Nov. 34/1 Fucoid-shales, Serpulite-grit, and limestone. *a* **1843** *Encycl. Metrop.* (1845) VII. 272/1 The *Serpuloid, Lumbricoid, and Hirudinoid orders have no head.

†**serr,** *v. Obs.* Also serre. [ad. F. *serrer* = It. *serrare* (used intr. to close up the ranks):—pop. L. **serrāre*, for class. L. *serāre*, f. *sera* lock, bolt.] *refl.*, *pass.*, and *intr.* To press close *together*; esp. to serry the ranks, form a serried company.

**1562** J. SHUTE tr. *Cambini's Turk. Wars* 31 b, The Christians serred them selues and charged them. **1603** KNOLLES *Hist. Turks* (1621) 33 Let vs, serred together, forcibly breake into the riuer. **1623** BINGHAM *Xenophon* 18 His Troope of 600 Horse close serred. **1626** BACON *Sylva* §82 The more grosse of the Tangible Parts doe contract and serre themselues together. **1683** SIR JAS. TURNER *Pallas Armata* 22 They were oblig'd to serr together as close as they could. *Ibid.* 43 Some Tribunes..found the Gauls serr'd together in a Testudo. **1747** CARTE *Hist. Eng.* I. 88 His own men were..hardly able though serred together to stand the shock.

‖**serra**[1] ('sɛrə). Pl. serræ. [L. = saw, saw-fish.]

**1. a.** A fabulous marine monster.

The first quot. is doubtful.

*c* **1450** METHAM *Wks.* (E.E.T.S.) 44/1177 The qwyche dragan, serra men calle. *c* **1520** ANDREW *Noble Lyfe* III. lxxii. in *Babees Bk.*, Serra is a fysshe with great tethe, and on his backe he hathe sharpe fynnes lyke the combe of a cocke and iagged lyke a sawe. **1845** *Archæol. Album* (ed. T. Wright) 183 Among the monsters of the deep one of the most remarkable was the serra or serre... When a serre sees a ship, the bestiaries tell us, it flies up.

**b.** A saw-fish.

**1854** BADHAM *Halieut.* 418 The larger and fiercer the adversary, the more ardently does the serra desire to join battle.

**c.** The fish *Alepisaurus serra*, found on the coast of California.

**1896** JORDAN & EVERMANN *Fishes N. & Middle Amer.* I. 597.

**2.** Dentation resembling the teeth of a saw, as of the edge of a leaf, the sutures of the skull; *pl.* the 'teeth' of a serrated edge.

**1800** *Phil. Trans.* XC. 435 This has a serrated edge; but the serrae are confined to the soft part, not extending to the membrane covering the bone. **1866** *Treas. Bot.*, *Serra, Serratures*, the saw-toothings at the edge of leaves and similar bodies. **1898** JORDAN & EVERMANN *Fishes N. & Middle Amer.* II. 1285 Serræ of preopercle at angle blunt.

‖**serra**[2] ('sɛra). [Pg.:—L. *serra* saw. Cf. SIERRA.] A ridge of mountains or hills (in Portuguese territory).

**1830** *Portugal; or Yng. Travellers* 152 The burra-drivers kept shouting vociferously, to deter, they said, the wolves from coming down the serra. **1846** G. GARDNER *Brazil* 308 The storm..passing over a high Serra..again altered its course. **1853** A. R. WALLACE *Amazon & Rio Negro* 147 The great marsh which extends from the Amazon to the serras.

‖**serradilla** (sɛrə'dɪlə). Also -ella. [Pg., dim. f. *serrado* SERRATE. Cf. F. *serradelle*.] A kind of clover used as a fodder-plant.

**1846** LINDLEY *Veget. Kingd.* 547 Clover, Medick, Lucerne, Trefoil, &c., are well-known fodder-plants, as are also Saint-foin, Ornithopus or Serradilla. **1880** CRAWFURD *Portugal* 181 Cutting serradella, clover, and plantain for stall-feeding.

**serrafdom,** obs. form of SHERIFFDOM.

**serraglio, -aill, -alia,** obs. ff. SERAGLIO, SERAIL.

**serran** ('sɛrən). *Ichth.* [ad. mod.L. *serrānus*, f. *serra*: see SERRA and -AN.] A fish of the genus *Serranus* or the family *Serranidæ*, which includes many food fishes, as the black sea-bass.

**1803** SHAW *Gen. Zool.* IV. 439 Serran Sparus. **1841** KITTO *Palestine: Phys. Geog.* viii. 416 The Brazen Serran. **1851** GOSSE *Nat. Hist., Fishes* 57 The Serrans (*Serranina*), a very numerous sub-family [of the *Percadæ*].

Hence **'serranoid** *a.* and *sb.*, belonging to, a fish of, the family *Serranidæ*.

**1884** GOODE, etc. *Nat. Hist. Aquatic Anim.* 413 The Seranoid Fishes of the Pacific Coast.

**Serrano** (sɛ'rɑːnəʊ). Also serrano; †Serano. [a. Sp. *serrano* of the mountains; a highlander.] (A member of) an Indian people of southern California; the Uzo-Aztecan language of these Indians, a component of the Takic branch.

**1858** *San Francisco Bull.* 5 Nov., The true native Americans of the wild forests—such as the Yumas,.. Mohaves and Serranos—predominate. **1876** *Ann. Rep. U.S. Geogr. Surveys West of 100th Meridian* III. 553 Case-inflection is formed here..by adding to nouns post-positions as suffixes:..tumuet, in Serrano, mountain. **1896** F. BOAS in *Proc. Amer. Assoc. Advancem. Sci. 1895* XLIV. 261 The Serano call themselves Mā'ringayam. *Ibid.* 262 The Serano is less closely related to the other Shoshonean dialects than these are among themselves. **1907** A. L. KROEBER *Shoshonean Dialects Calif.* I. 69 The Gitanemuk.. vocabulary was..obtained at Tule river reservation... The vocabulary is the first that has been printed of this dialect, although it differs but little from Serrano, which has been known for years. **1921** *Glasgow Herald* 17 May 3/8 In due time he will become a 'Serrano' as the inhabitants of the highland regions are contemptuously styled by the dwellers in the cities of the coast. **1927** D. H. LAWRENCE *Mornings in Mexico* 84 The serranos, the Indians from the hills, wearing their little conical black felt hats. **1946** C. MCWILLIAMS *Southern Calif. Country* 26 The Serranos and the Gabrieleno were associated with the Mission San Gabriel. **1969** J. MANDER *Static Soc.* vi. 158 The *serranos* are pure Indian. They are the direct descendants of the Incas, and of the tribes subjugated by the Incas; and they speak Quechua in preference to Spanish. **1974** *Encycl. Brit. Micropædia* IX. 73/2 In the early 1970s, there were fewer than 400 Serrano proper remaining. **1977** *Language* LIII. 459 The Serrano element which L gives as *-nuk*, base /-nowk(i-)/, shows up as *-nuk* only in 3sg. *pi-nuk*.

**serrasalmonoid** (sɛrə'sælmənɔɪd). *Ichth.* [f. mod.L. *serrasalmon-, -salmo-*, irreg. f. *serra* saw + *salmo* SALMON: see -OID.] A fish of the South American genus *Serrasalmo*.

**1880** GÜNTHER *Fishes* 111 The voracious Serrasalmonoids of the South American rivers.

**serrate** ('sɛreɪt), *a.* Chiefly *Nat. Hist.* [ad. L. *serrāt-us*, f. *serra* saw: see -ATE[2].] Having or forming a row of small projections resembling the teeth of a saw; jagged or notched like a saw. ***serrate leaf***: see quot. 1866.

**1668** WILKINS *Real Char.* II. iv. §3. 109 Oblong shining serrate leaves. **1691** RAY *Creation* I. (1692) 145 All [Birds] that have serrate Teeth are carnivorous. **1713** DERHAM *Phys.-Theol.* IV. xv. (1727) 256 *note*, Strong hooked Talons, (one of which is remarkably serrate on the Edge) the better to hold their Prey. **1861** BENTLEY *Man. Bot.* 158 The leaf is serrate, as in the common Nettles. **1866** *Treas. Bot.*, *Serrate*, having sharp straight-edged teeth pointing to the apex. When these are themselves serrate, they are biserrate or duplicato-serrate.

**b.** *Comb.*, as ***serrate-spined, -toothed*** adjs.; also = SERRATO-.

**1793** MARTYN *Lang. Bot.*, *Serrato-ciliatum folium*, a Serrate-ciliate leaf. *Ibid.*, *Serrato-dentatum folium*, a Serrate-toothed leaf. **1850** F. MASON *Burmah* 323 Serrate-spined Cat-fish.

**'serrate,** *v.* [f. L. *serrāt-*, ppl. stem of *serrāre*, f. *serra* saw.]

**1.** *intr.* To saw. Only in vbl. sb.

**1597** A. M. tr. *Guillemeau's Fr. Chirurg.* 38/1 The membrane Periostium..which also in serratinge or sawinge might be some hinderance.

**2.** *trans.* To make serrated or saw-toothed, jag the edge of; to impress in a serrated form.

**1750** *Phil. Trans.* XLVII. 41 This mark..is found.. impress'd or serrated on the new shell. **1865** *Morn. Star* 4 Oct., This corner of Ireland is absolutely serrated with bays. **1877** *Encycl. Brit.* VI. 32/1 If you make any rude sketch.. of a pair of wheels acting together, and serrate the edges of the teeth. **1893** 'Q.' *Delect. Duchy* 47 The larches and Scotch firs that serrate the long ridge above.

**serrated** ('sɛreɪtɪd, sɛ'reɪtɪd), *a.* Chiefly scientific. [f. L. *serrāt-us* SERRATE + -ED.] = SERRATE *a.*

**1703** DAMPIER *Voy. New Holland* 156 The Leaves are.. like the top Leaves of *Bardana major*... In the Figure they are represented too stiff and too much serrated. **1768** PENNANT *Brit. Zool.* (1776) II. 469 The bill is..finely toothed, or serrated. **1802** SHAW *Gen. Zool.* III. 72 Serrated Tortoise. **1825** SCOTT *Talism.* xxviii, A serrated and rocky mountain. **1839-47** *Todd's Cycl. Anat.* III. 645/2 The *ligamentum dentatum* (serrated membrane of Gordon). **1851** MAYNE REID *Scalp Hunters* xi, That white spheroidal mass, with its grinning rows and serrated sutures, that is a human skull. **1878** H. M. STANLEY *Dark Cont.* I. xvi. 430 Bare and serrated hilly ridges.

**serratic** (sɛ'rætɪk), *a. Path.* [f. L. *serrāt-us* SERRATE *a.* + -IC.] Resembling or suggesting the motion of a saw or the sound of sawing; = SERRATILE. (Cf. SAWING *ppl. a.* 2.)

**1753** N. TORRIANO *Gangr. Sore Throat* 102 The Pulse was always small, *serratic*, or like a Saw, hard and unequal. **1859** SEMPLE *Diphtheria* 296 When the respiration is frequent and *serratic*, that is to say, imitating the noise of a saw cutting a stone.

**serratiform** (sɛ'reɪtɪfɔːm), *a.* [f. L. *serrāt-us* SERRATE *a.* + -FORM.] Saw-shaped, serriform.

**1821** W. P. C. BARTON *Flora N. Amer.* I. 59 The margin ..marked by about four serratiform indentures.

†**'serratile,** *a. Obs.* Also 6 sarratylle. [a. F. *serratile*, ad. mod.L. *serrātilis*, f. *serrāt-us* SERRATE *a.*: see -ILE.] Saw-like; serrate; serratic.

**1541** R. COPLAND *Guydon's Quest. Cyrurg.* D iv, The commyssures [of the skull] called sarratylles seames endented as tethe of a sawe. **1707** FLOYER *Physic. Pulse-Watch* 105 The Pulse in most Inflammations is hard and serratile.

**serration** (sɛ'reɪʃən). [ad. mod.L. *serrātiōnem*, f. *serrāre* (see SERRATE *v.*).]

**1.** *Surg.* The operation of sawing. *rare*$^{-0}$.

**1706** PHILLIPS (ed. Kersey).

**2.** The condition of being serrated; indentation like that of a saw; chiefly *concr.* and *pl.*, saw-like indentations, the teeth of a serrated edge or surface.

**1842** PRICHARD *Nat. Hist. Man* 101 The serrations are found to result from a structure resembling a series of inverted cones, encircling a central stem. **1849** D. J. BROWNE *Amer. Poultry Yd.* (1855) 38 The comb..is low, thick, destitute of serrations. **1851** RUSKIN *Stones Ven.* I. xiii. §8 The eye which has once been habituated to the continual serration of the pine forest. **1870** HOOKER *Stud. Flora* 122 Differing in pubescence and amount of double serration of the leaflets. **1872** C. KING *Sierra Nevada* vii. 141 Dim serrations of Coast Range loom indistinctly on the hazy air. **1897** P. WARUNG *Tales Old Regime* 123 As the saw refused..to 'bite', and he had to withdraw it to feel, with his tongue, if the serration was still perfect.

**serratirostral** (sɛreɪtɪ'rɒstrəl), *a. Ornith.* [f. L. *serrātus* SERRATE + *rostrum* beak + -AL[1].] = SAW-BILLED.

**serrato-,** used as comb. form (see -O-) of L. *serrātus* SERRATE *a.* in the senses 'serrate and...', 'in a serrate manner, with serrate indentation', as ***serrato-crenate, -dentate, -glandulous, -spinose*** adjs.

**1857** T. MOORE *Handbk. Brit. Ferns* (ed. 3) 40 [Pinnules] *serrato-crenate. **1846** DANA *Zooph.* (1848) 177 Lamellæ thin, regularly *serrato-dentate. **1775** J. JENKINSON *Brit. Plants* Gloss., **Serrato-glandulous*, bearing glands and partly serrated. **1822** J. PARKINSON *Outl. Oryctol.* 218 *Serrato-spinose before, and crenato-squamous in the hinder part.

**serrature** (ˈsɛrətjʊə(r), -tʃə(r)). [ad. L. *serrātūra*, f. *serrātus*: see SERRATE *a.* and -URE.] = SERRATION.

**1541** R. COPLAND *Guydon's Quest. Cyrurg.* F j b, In the top of euery of the other extremytees in cuttynge is a bowed sarrature which is composed with an addycion very subtylly made and bred there. *a* **1725** WOODWARD *Catal. For. Fossils* II. 25 The Serratures towards the Point are wanting in this Tooth. **1760** J. LEE *Introd. Bot.* III. v. (1765) 181 *Duplicato-serrate*,..when there is a twofold Serrature, the less upon the greater. **1802** BINGLEY *Anim. Biog.* (1813) II. 319 The edges of the mandibles are marked with sharp serratures. **1863** M. J. BERKELEY *Brit. Mosses* iii. 15 The serratures consisting..merely of cells projecting beyond their neighbours. **1880** GÜNTHER *Fishes* 115 In Petromyzon this serrature is absent, or but faintly indicated.

‖**serratus** (sɛˈreɪtəs). *Anat.* [mod.L. use of L. *serrātus* SERRATE.] Any of certain muscles which are inserted into the vertebral or costal region in such a way as to suggest a serrated border; *esp.* short for *serratus magnus*, which connects the eight upper ribs and the vertebral border of the shoulder-blade.

**1881** MIVART *Cat* 279 Where it [posterior thoracic nerve] lies upon the serratus muscle. **1899** *Allbutt's Syst. Med.* VII. 210 The posterior border of the scapula projects like a wing owing to paralysis of the serratus.

**serray**, obs. form of SERAI, SIRRAH.

**serrayle**, obs. form of SERAIL.

‖**serre** (sɛr), *sb.* [F., vbl. sb. f. *serrer*, ad. pop. L. **serrāre*: see SERR.] A greenhouse.

**1819** [H. BUSK] *Banquet* III. 147 Lock'd in my *serres*, from hail-engendering blast, Exotic fruits from spring to spring shall last.

‖**serré** (sɛre), *a.* [Fr., pa. pple. of *serrer* to close together.] Compact, logical; constricted by grief or emotion.

*a* **1854** J. S. MILL *Early Draft Autobiogr.* (1961) 115 Our debates..habitually consisted of the strongest arguments & most philosophic principles which either side was able to produce, thrown often into close & *serré* confutations of one another. **1908** D. H. LAWRENCE *Let.* 9 Oct. (1962) I. 28 My heart is '*serré*'—I shall soon have nothing inside my chest but the spent fragments of my organ of affection. **1931** T. S. ELIOT *Sel. Essays* (1932) VII. 448 Whether the transition is cogent or not, is merely a question of whether the mind is *serré* or *dolié*.

**serre.** Anglicized form of SERRA[1] (1 a).

**serre**, obs. form of SEER *sb.*[2]

‖**serre-**, stem of F. *serrer* to tighten, constrict, forming the first element in compounds denoting surgical instruments used for constricting ligatures, as **serre-nœud, serre-pédicule** (see quots.).

**1846** BRITTAN tr. *Malgaigne's Man. Oper. Surg.* 19 The '*Serre nœud' (Knot-tightener) of Graefe, an imitation of the tourniquet of Petit. *Ibid.* 326 The two ends of the ligature should be passed into a *serre-nœud*, and the polypus strangled to the required degree. **1881** *Trans. Obstet. Soc. Lond.* XXII. 160 Koeberle's serre-nœud. **1898** *Syd. Soc. Lex.*, **Serre-pedicule*, a clamp used for constricting a pedicule.

**serrefile** (ˈsɛrəfaɪl). *Mil.* Also **serafile**. [ad. F. *serrefile*, f. *serre-r* (see SERR) + *file* FILE *sb.*[2] Cf. Pg. *serrafila*.] *pl.* The line of supernumerary and non-commissioned officers placed in the rear of a squadron or troop; *sing.* one of these.

**1796** *Instr. & Reg. Cavalry* (1813) 19 In the filings of the squadron, the serrefiles take their place in the rear of the files. **1875** KINGLAKE *Crimea* (1877) V. 117 The serre-files were Boyd, Nugent, and..Prendergast. **1896** BADEN-POWELL *Matabele Campaign* xvi, Being now a sort of 'serrefile' or hanger-on to the column. **1906** *Daily Chron.* 15 Nov. 3/4 Sergeant-Major Harrison..bade me mount a grey mare he led as he rode serafile.

*attrib.* **1796** *Instr. & Reg. Cavalry* (1813) 219 The serre-file rank remains closed to the right. **1833** *Reg. & Instr. Cavalry* I. 35 The Serrefile Officers pass through the intervals and cover to the right.

‖**serre-fine** (sɛrfin). [F. *serre fine*, fine clamp.] (See quot.)

**1875** KNIGHT *Dict. Mech.*, *Serre-fine*, a small clip used to compress a severed artery pending the farther conduct of the operation. **1895** *Arnold's Catal. Surg. Instr.* 30 Serre-fines, Silver, straight or curved.

**serreli**, var. SIRLY *a. Obs.*

**serrey**, obs. f. SERRY.

**serrha**, obs. f. SIRRAH.

**serrhfull**, obs. f. SORROWFUL.

**serrial(l**, obs. ff. CERRIAL.

**serricorn** (ˈsɛrɪkɔːn), *a.* and *sb.* [ad. mod.L. *serricorn-is* (through F. *serricorne*), f. *serra* saw + *cornū* horn.] **A.** *adj.* Of beetles: Having serrated antennæ. **B.** *sb.* A beetle of this class.

[**1834** MCMURTRIE *Cuvier's Anim. Kingd.* 348 Those Sericornes, in which the posterior extremity of the præsternum is not similarly prolonged.] **1842** BRANDE *Dict. Sci.*, etc. *Serricorns*,..a family of Coleopterous insects. **1862** T. W. HARRIS *Insects Injur. Veget.* (ed. 3) 45 One great tribe, named serricorn or saw-horned beetles.

**serried** (ˈsɛrɪd), *ppl. a.* [app. f. SERRY + -ED[1]; but perhaps a graphic representation of *serred*, pa. pple. of SERR, pronounced as a disyllable. The modern currency of the word is app. due to Scott.] Of files or ranks of armed men: Pressed close together, shoulder to shoulder, in close order.

**1667** MILTON *P.L.* I. 548 Thronging Helms Appear'd, and serried Shields in thick array. *Ibid.* VI. 599 Nor serv'd it to relax thir serried files. **1757** W. WILKIE *Epigoniad* II. 39 The Theban chief survey'd The close-compacted ranks.. To find where least the serried orb could bear The strong impression of a pointed war. *a* **1785** GLOVER *Athenaid* II. 226 No engine..To man destructive, like his own fell hand In serried fight. **1808** SCOTT *Marm.* VI. xxxiv, Linked in the serried phalanx tight. **1814** —— *Ld. of Isles* V. xv, Shield compact and serried spear. **1828** TYTLER *Hist. Scot.* I. 164 To present a serried front to the enemy. **1859** JEPHSON *Brittany* xii. 192 The French ranks were so serried that.. you could not throw an apple but it would fall upon a helmet or a lance. **1879** GREEN *Readings Eng. Hist.* xv. 74 The Norman horsemen, in serried line and with lances at rest.

**b.** Of things likened to ranks of soldiers.

**1834** LYTTON *Pompeii* III. ix, The dark ranks of the serried clouds. **1857** GOSSE *Omphalos* iii. 57 An enormous Frog (*Labyrinthodon*),..apparently allied, in its serried teeth,..to the Crocodiles. **1858** LONGF. *M. Standish* v. 13 The serried billows, advancing. **1883** 'OUIDA' *Wanda* I. 31 The gorges, dark with the serried pines.

**c.** Of argument, etc.: Closely reasoned, compact in expression.

**1899** *Blackw. Mag.* No. 1001. 511 To follow a long or serried argument. **1910** *Edin. Rev.* Jan. 93 His composition is lucid, logical, serried.

¶ Misused for SERRATED.

**1848** B. WEBB *Cont. Ecclesiol.* 173 The bleak crags are serried by the numerous torrents which fall straight into the lake. ? **186.** B. HARTE *Friar Pedro's Ride* in *Fiddletown*, etc. (1873) 111 The morning came above the serried coast.

**serriform** (ˈsɛrɪfɔːm), *a.* Also erron. **serræ-**. [f. L. *serra* saw: see -FORM.] Saw-shaped, serrate.

**1822** J. PARKINSON *Outl. Oryctol.* 218 Thirty ribs, with serræform teeth. **1895** A. H. COOKE *Molluscs* (Camb. Nat. Hist. III.) 235 Marginals much pectinated and serriform.

†**ˈserrine**, *a. Obs. rare.* [f. L. *serra* saw + -INE[1].] Of the pulse: = SERRATIC.

**1707** FLOYER *Physic. Pulse-Watch* 136 In most Inflammations the Pulse is hard, and serrine.

†**ˈserring**, *vbl. sb.* [f. SERR *v.* + -ING[1].] Arraying in close order.

**1626** BACON *Sylva* §714 Grinding of the Teeth is caused (likewise) by a Gathering and Serring of the Spirits together to resist.

**serring**, obs. form of SYRINGE.

**ˈserriped(e**, *a.* [ad. mod.L. *serriped-*, *-pēs*, f. L. *serra* saw + *pēs* foot.] Having serrations on the feet.

**1858** MAYNE *Expos. Lex.* s.v. *Serripes*.

**serriˈrostrate**, *a.* [f. mod.L. *serrirostris*, f. L. *serra* saw + *rostrum* beak.] Having a serrated beak.

†**ˈserrous**, *a. Obs. rare*[−1]. [f. L. *serra* saw + -OUS.] Resembling the action of a saw, saw-like. (Cf. SERRATIC, SERRINE.)

**1646** SIR T. BROWNE *Pseud. Ep.* III. xxv. 176 A serrous or jarring motion like that which happeneth while we blow on the teeth of a combe through paper.

**serrulate** (ˈsɛrjʊleɪt), *a. Nat. Hist.* [ad. mod.L. *serrulātus*, f. late L. *serrula*, dim. of L. *serra* saw.] Finely or minutely serrated; having small serrations.

**1793** MARTYN *Lang. Bot.*, *Serrulatum folium*, a serrulate leaf. **1810** *Encycl. Lond.* I. 683/1 Leaves oval,..obsoletely serrulate. **1841** *Proc. Berw. Nat. Club* I. No. 9. 268 The penis of the male is..serrulate on the outer side.

**serrulated** (ˈsɛrjʊleɪtɪd), *a.* [Formed as prec. + -ED.] = prec.

**1796** WITHERING *Brit. Plants* (ed. 3) II. 126 Calyx, husks equal, both serrulated on the keel. **1851** WOODWARD *Mollusca* 133 Uncini, 2, the inner broad and serrulated.

**serrulation** (sɛrjʊˈleɪʃən). [f. prec.: see -ATION.] The condition of being serrulated; a fine or minute serration.

**1821** W. P. C. BARTON *Flora N. Amer.* I. 59 The margin ..in the older leaves..marked by about four serratiform indentures, scarcely deserving the appellation of serrulations. **1881** *Jrnl. Bot.* X. 115 The serrulation on the back of the nerve was also continued lower down.

**serry** (ˈsɛrɪ), *v.* Also 6 sar(r)ie, serrey, serrie. [As a military term in the 16th cent., app. f. F. *serré*, †*sarré*, pa. pple. of *serrer* (see SERR), already adopted in ME. as SARRAY (see also SARRALY). In recent use, a back-formation from SERRIED.]

**1.** *intr.* To press close *together* in the ranks; to stand or move in close or serried order.

**1581** STYWARD *Mart. Discipl.* I. 71 First, to cause your pikes to sarie close together, then to traile their pikes with the sharpe ende toward the enimie. *Ibid.* II. 102 They must sarrie close together, and not disseuer to followe or flie. **1598** BARRET *Theor. Warres* I. i. 4 When men come to the..push of the Pike, they sarrie close together. *Ibid.* III. i. 36 Being brought into a Ring, and serreying close shoulder to shoulder.

**1888** HENLEY *Bk. Verses* 18 High shoulders, low shoulders broad shoulders, narrow ones, Round, square and angular, serry and shove.

**2.** *trans.* To cause to stand in close order, to close up (the ranks).

**1635** BARRIFF *Milit. Discipl.* vi. (1643) 25 Close order is onely usefull for your files of Pike-men, so they may..stand the stronger, by so much as they are the closer serried together.

**1821** BYRON *Sardanap.* III. i. 259 Serry your ranks—stand firm. **1843** PRESCOTT *Mexico* III. ii. (1804) 143 The courageous band of warriors, serried together. **1887** BOWEN *Virg. Æneid* IV. 407 Others serry the ranks.

**serry**, obs. and dial. f. SORRY.

**sers(s**, obs. ff. SEARCH *v.*

**serse**, obs. f. SEARCE, SEARCH *sb.*[1]

**sersour**, obs. Sc. f. SEARCHER.

†**sert.** *Obs.* [Aphetic of DESERT *sb.*[1]] Desert, merit; phr. *for sert of*, for the sake of.

*c* **1375** *Sc. Leg. Saints* xxviii. (*Margaret*) 645 Nocht for my sert, bot þi gudnes. *a* **1400** *Pistil of Susan* 223 For sert of hire souereyn and for hire owne sake.

**sert-**: see CERT-.

‖**sertão** (ˈsɛrtɐ̃u). *Geogr.* Also †**Sertam; sertao, Sertão.** Pl. **sertãos, sertões** (ˈsɛrtõiʃ). [Pg.] The name of an arid, barren region, characterized by caatinga, in the interior of Pernambuco and neighbouring states in NE Brazil; also applied to other areas in Brazil of similar character. Also, more widely, the remote interior or outback of Brazil.

**1816** H. KOSTER *Trav. in Brazil* vi. 77 The trees had mostly lost their leaves. I had now entered upon the Sertam, and surely it deserves the name. **1851** *Illustr. Catal. Gt. Exhib.* v. 1429/2 The cap is made in the Sertaô (the interior) of the province of Pernambuco. **1876** *Encycl. Brit.* IV. 226/1 Except on the loftiest mountains, and on the wide *sertãos*, the vegetation of Brazil is luxuriant beyond description. **1903** W. R. FISHER tr. *A. F. W. Schimper's Plant-Geogr.* III. iii. 275 In contrast with its southern portion, the middle part of Central Brazil, the so-called Sertão district, possesses a xerophilous woodland climate. **1926** R. NASH *Conquest of Brazil* iv. 144 This Negro-Indian cross was considerable only in the lawless sertões of Matto Grosso. **1930** C. F. JONES *S. Amer.* xxxiii. 471 The physical landscape of Northeast Brazil consists of three major divisions: marginal lowlands; *sertão*, parched uplands of brushwood and grasses ..; *serra*, elevated mountain zones. **1950** E. G. ASHTON *S. Amer.* iv. 51 With a rather more generous rainfall on the *sertãos*..the characteristic vegetation resembles the savanna of the Matto Grosso. **1961** *Times* 8 Aug. 9/7 President Kubitschek's decision to move the capital from Rio to the heart of the undeveloped *sertao*. **1966** K. WEBB tr. *Pohl & Zepp's Latin Amer.* ii. 43 A particular vegetation type of these drier lands is the *caatinga* of the north-east, the *sertão*. This region of semi-desert has a vegetation cover made up of sparse thorn forest... *Sertão* in this sense means a particular place—the dry interior of north-east Brazil; in a more general usage *Sertão* means the sparsely inhabited backlands of the interior of Brazil. It is the equivalent of the Australian 'outback'. **1971** P. C. C. GARNHAM *Progress in Parasitology* ix. 191 The scene is laid in the sertão and its wide empty spaces in northern Minas Gerais.

Hence **sertanista** (-aˈnista), one engaged in activity in the *sertão*; one knowledgeable about the *sertão* and its inhabitants.

**1944** S. PUTNAM tr. *E. da Cunha's Rebellion in Backlands* i. 45 The northern *sertanistas*..were fully a match for the bandeirantes of the south. **1973** *Daily Colonist* (Victoria, B.C.) 22 June 5/2 Francisco Meireles and the two other sertanistas (Indian experts),..flew from Belem.

†**serte.** *Obs.* [a. OF. *serte* fem. (also *sert* masc., cf. *desert*, *deserte* DESERT *sb.*[1]):—pop. L. **servita* for **servīta*, noun of action f. *servire* to SERVE.] Service due from a servant to his lord.

*a* **1400** *Morte Arth.* 513 By sertes thow was my sandes, and senatour of Rome. *Ibid.* 2926 We for-sake þe to-daye be serte of owre lorde.

**Sertoli** (sɜːˈtəʊlɪ). *Anat.* The name of Enrico *Sertoli* (1842–1910), Italian histologist, used *attrib.*, with *of*, and in the possessive, to designate a type of somatic cell described by him, found in the walls of the seminiferous tubules.

**1880** E. KLEIN *Atlas of Histol.* xxxi. 270 Inside this *membrana propria* are several layers of epithelial cells, the seminal cells... They correspond to the germ-cells of Sertoli. **1888** *Buck's Handbk. Med. Sci.* VI. 522/2 Next to the tunica comes a layer... This layer contains two kinds of cells: First, the large Sertoli's cells, as they may be called after their discoverer. **1901** *Gray's Anat.* (ed. 15) 1004 The supporting cells, or cells of Sertoli. **1930** W. BLOOM *A. A. Maximow's Text-bk. Histol.* xxxi. 595 The Sertoli cells in a seminiferous tubule with active spermatogenesis are very infrequent in comparison with the number of spermatogenic cells. *Ibid.*, The sustentacular cells or the cells of Sertoli. **1965** LEE & KNOWLES *Animal Hormones* iii. 65 In many vertebrates oestrogens are secreted by the testis, probably by the Sertoli cells, but whether this hormone has a physiological action is still in doubt.

‖**sertularia** (sɜːtjʊˈlɛərɪə). *Zool.* Pl. **-æ, -as.** [mod.L., f. L. *sertula*, dim. of *serta* garland.] One of a genus of branching hydroids having small sessile hydrothecæ; the genus itself.

**1767** *Phil. Trans.* LVII. 434 A great many zoophytes, which were formerly called Corallines, now Sertularias and Cellularias. **1833** MANTELL *Wonders Geol.* (1838) 474 The elegant arborescent forms of the Sertulariæ. **1876** *Van Beneden's Anim. Parasites* 62 One of these Halodactyles spreads itself upon the stalk of a Sertularia.

Hence **sertu'larian** *a.*, of or belonging to the genus *Sertularia* or the family *Sertularidæ* of hydroids; *sb.* a sertularian hydroid; so **'sertularid**, in the same sense.

**1847-9** *Todd's Cycl. Anat.* IV. 47/1 The Sertularian Polypes. *Ibid.* 49/1 The stem of the Sertularian is composed of two layers. **1861** J. R. GREENE *Man. Anim. Kingd., Cœlent.* 90 For no example of a Sertularid has yet been recorded in which the hydrosoma exhibits but a single polypite.

‖**sertulum** (ˈsɜːtjʊləm). *Bot.* Also anglicized **'sertule.** [mod.L., dim. of *sertum*, assumed sing. of *serta* n. pl., garlands.] A simple umbel.

**1831** MACGILLIVRAY tr. *Richard's Elem. Bot.* 420 Small flowers, either solitary or disposed in a spike or sertule. **1866** *Treas. Bot., Sertulum*, a simple umbel.

‖**serula** (ˈsɛrjʊlə). [See quot. 1678.] The red-breasted merganser, *Merganser serrator.*

[**1678** RAY *Willughby's Ornith.* 336 The Bird called at Venice, *Serula*: *Mergus cirratus fuscus.*] **1802** MONTAGU *Ornith. Dict.*, Merganser-red-breasted... Red-breasted Goosander. Lesser-toothed Diver. Serula.

**serum** (ˈsɪərəm). Pl. **sera** (ˈsɪərə), **serums** (ˈsɪərəmz) [L. = whey, watery fluid.]

**1. a.** Watery animal fluid, normal or morbid; *spec.* blood-serum, the greenish yellow liquid which separates from the clot when blood coagulates.

**1672** WISEMAN *Treat. Wounds* I. 59 That morning I let her bloud, taking away about 10. ounces with a rotten *Serum* upon it. **1678** J. BROWN *Disc. Wounds* 272 Being as the Hearts *Marsupium*, it being wounded, it loseth its store of *Serum*, whereby the Heart is kept moyst. **1701** J. PETER *Truth* 36 Every Body useth the Salt.. to purge the Serum off, about the finishing of their Water-drinking. **1707** FLOYER *Physic. Pulse-Watch* 202 All Pains are to be Cured by removing of the Cause, as Inflammations, Sizy Serum. **1793** BEDDOES *Obs. Calculus* 230 The blood.. coagulated immediately... A small quantity of greenish serum was separated. **1813** J. THOMSON *Lect. Inflam.* 401 This swelling depends partly.. on the effusion of serum into the interstices of the cellular membrane. **1865** LIVINGSTONE *Zambesi* iii. 83 It brought out serum as black as porter, as if the blood had been impregnated with bile. **1872** T. BRYANT *Pract. Surg.* 444 The epidermis is raised by a small quantity of purulent serum.

**b.** *Therapeutics.* The blood serum of an animal used as a therapeutic or diagnostic agent.

**1895** *Brit. Med. Jrnl.* 20 July 181/1 The antitoxic serums prepared at the Pasteur Institute in Paris. *Ibid.* 16 Nov. 1253/1 The physiological action of the serums of tuberculised sheep is remarkably different in guinea-pigs and rabbits. **1910** *Lancet* 26 Mar. 861/2 The sera employed included anti-streptococcic serum, anti-diphtheritic serum, anti-tetanic serum.

**2. a.** *attrib.* (of 1), as ***serum albumin*** (cf. SERALBUMEN), ***-globulin.***

**1876** tr. *Wagner's Gen. Pathol.* 526 Leube has noticed the appearance of albumen and even of serum-albumen in the sweat of four patients. **1896** *Allbutt's Syst. Med.* I. 825 Of the various forms of albumin, serumalbumin is constantly found. **1897** *Ibid.* IV. 303 Serum albumin and globulin being also present. **1904** *Brit. Med. Jrnl.* 10 Sept. 562 Hahn could find no difference between the serum and histon blood. *Ibid.* 566, 0.24 and 0.48 mg. of acid reduce the serum agglutinability to one thirty-third of its normal value.

**b.** *attrib.* and *Comb.* (of 1 b); esp. applied to treatment by means of serum. ***serum jaundice, rash, urticaria;*** **serum broth** *Bacteriology*, a broth (BROTH *sb.* 1 c) containing added serum.

**1886** CROOKSHANK *Pract. Bacteriol.* 29 Serum-steriliser. *Ibid.* 30 Serum Inspissator. **1893** *Lancet* 21 Oct. 1036/2 Serum Injections in Tetanus. **1894** *Ibid.* 17 Nov. 1189/2 The Serum Treatment of Diphtheria in Russia. **1895** *Brit. Med. Jrnl.* 16 Nov. 1253/1 Serumtherapy in Tuberculosis. **1897** *Trans. Amer. Pediatric Soc.* IX. 44 A bacteriological diagnosis of diphtheria.. by means of the incubator and Loeffler serum tube. **1898** J. HUTCHINSON in *Archives Surg.* IX. 328 A serum-injection treatment. **1905** *Practitioner* May 665 The duration of serum urticaria varies within somewhat wide limits. **1908** *Glasgow Med. Jrnl.* LXIX. 277 The most obvious and constant features of the symptom-complex are the skin eruptions, or serum rash. **1934** L. E. H. WHITBY *Med. Bacteriol.* (ed. 2) ix. 109 Salicin serum broth .. is an excellent selective medium for *Streptococcus pyogenes.* **1945** *Jrnl. Amer. Med. Assoc.* 28 July 911/1 (*heading*) Transmission experiments in serum jaundice and infectious hepatitis. **1979** H. MCLEAVE *Borderline Case* v. 53 The tubes of serum broth and tissue culture supplied by WHO.

**c.** Used *attrib.* (with or without a following hyphen) to denote (the concentration of) substances in the serum.

**1958** J. B. MIALE *Lab. Med.—Hematol.* viii. 372 When the iron deficiency is caused by inadequate utilization of iron a *decreased* serum iron concentration and *increased* storage of iron in the tissues are usually seen. **1959** *Jrnl. Physiol.* CXLVI. 353 All the serum proteins are capable of binding thyroxine to some extent. **1960** LEAVELL & THORUP *Clin. Hematol.* iv. 187 The normal level of serum bilirubin on cord blood is considered to be from 0·8 to 2·6 mg. per 100 ml. **1961** *Lancet* 26 Aug. 492/2 Treatment of atherosclerosis .. may best be directed towards improving fat tolerance as well as reducing specific serum-lipid fractions. *Ibid.* 2 Sept. 499/1 The associations of high serum-cholesterol levels with coronary heart-disease do not necessarily indicate any *causal* relationship. **1962** *Ibid.* 22 Dec. 1293/1 There was no correlation on admission between the degree of weight deficit and the serum-transaminase levels. **1977** J. F. FIXX *Compl. Bk. Running* i. 5 In Southern California not long ago, fifty-eight doctors were given physical exams... More than half had high serum lipid levels.

**d.** Special Combs.: **serum agglutination**, agglutination of antigens by components of serum; **serum disease**, serum sickness; **serum hepatitis**, a viral hepatitis transmitted by injections of blood serum; **serum reaction**, serum sickness; **serum sickness** [tr. G. *serumkrankheit* (C. von Pirquet 1903, in *Wiener klin. Wochenschr.* XVI. 1244/2)], anaphylactic reaction to injected foreign serum.

**1914** *Jrnl. Hygiene* XIV. 264 In order to be able to observe *serum agglutination and acid agglutination with the same bacterial extract the bacilli from a 24 to 48 hrs. agar slope were washed off with 10 c.c. of distilled water and the resulting emulsion was centrifuged. **1970** W. H. PARKER *Health & Dis. in Farm Animals* xii. 161 An infected cow will give a positive reaction to the serum agglutination test. **1908** *Glasgow Med. Jrnl.* LXIX. 277 (*heading*) The *serum disease in man after single and repeated doses. **1951** Serum disease [see *serum sickness* below]. **1943** *Lancet* 16 Jan. 83/1 (*heading*) Measles serum hepatitis. **1946** *Med. Clinics N. Amer.* XXX. 1408 'Virus hepatitis'.. includes both infectious hepatitis.. and homologous *serum hepatitis. **1971** *New Scientist* 25 Mar. 676/1 This work promises a screening method which should help eliminate the danger of serum hepatitis developing after blood transfusions. **1905** *Practitioner* May 664 In cases of relapse, or of a second attack of diphtheria, the *serum reaction may be very marked. **1916** *Arch. Internal Med.* XVIII. 497 Most of the cases of *serum sickness occurred during convalescence from pneumonia. **1951** B. SCHICK tr. *von Pirquet & Schick's Serum Sickness* i. 5 We have abandoned the expression 'serum exanthema'... In its place we have proposed the name 'serum disease' or 'serum sickness'. **1970** W. H. PARKER *Health & Dis. in Farm Animals* xxi. 289 The most important practical significance of anaphylaxis in farm animals is that in the treatment of disease 'serum sickness' may follow the repeated use of serum from another species.

**serup**, obs. form of SYRUP.

**serurgien, -erie**, etc.: see CHIRURGEON, SURGEON, and CHIRURGERY, SURGERY.

**seruse**, obs. form of CERUSE.

†**'servable**, *a.*[1] *Sc. Obs.* Also 6 **serveabill.** [a. OF. *servable*, f. *servir* SERVE *v.*[1]: see -ABLE. Cf. SERVIABLE.] Ready to serve.

*c* **1450** HOLLAND *Howlat* 379 Next the souerane signe was sekirly sene, That seruit his serenite euer seruable, The armes of the Dowglass. *a* **1578** LINDESAY (Pitscottie) *Chron. Scot.* (S.T.S.) I. 50 He promist to [be] allis serueabill as ony man wnto this realme. **1626** J. HAIG in J. Russell *Haigs* (1881) 178, I rest, Your loving and servable brother.

†**'servable**, *a.*[2] *Obs.*$^{-0}$ [f. SERVE *v.*[2] + -ABLE.] That may be kept or preserved.

**1623** COCKERAM I. **1656** BLOUNT *Glossogr.* **1721** BAILEY.

**servable** (ˈsɜːvəb(ə)l), *a.*[3] [f. SERVE *v.*[1] + -ABLE.] That may be served, worthy to be served.

**1855** OGILVIE Suppl., *Servable*, capable of being served. **1881** F. HARRISON in *19th Cent.* Mar. 462 If we seek to love and serve the greatest loveable and serveable thing on this earth.

**servage** (ˈsɜːvɪdʒ). Also 6 **sarvage**, 7 **servadge.** [a. OF. *servage* (in med.L. *servāgium*):—L. type **servāticum*, f. *servus* slave, SERF: see -AGE. Cf. Pr. *servage, servagi*, It. *servaggio.*]

†**1.** Servitude, bondage, slavery. *Obs.*

*c* **1290** *Beket* 1999 in *S. Eng. Leg.* 164 Nov wolde ȝe holi churche In grete seruage do. *a* **1300** *Cursor M.* 4193 Þar was ioseph in seruage sald, For tuenti besands. *c* **1386** CHAUCER *Clerk's T.* 426 It is greet shame.. to been in seruage To thee, that born art of a smal village. *c* **1440** *Knt. de la Tour* (1868) 111 Thei were in seruage as prisoners in Egipte. *a* **1533** LD. BERNERS *Huon* cxxviii. 468 The emperour of Almayne who hath.. slayne my men, and some kepethe in saruage. **1536** *Ir. Acts 28 Hen. VIII*, c. 3 (1621) 97 The Kings enemies haue them in servadge. **1586** A. DAY *Eng. Secretary* II. (1625) 109 Scanderbeg declaring his wearisomenes of captivitie and servage.

*attrib.* **1567** TURBERV. *Ovid's Ep.* H iij, The selfe same man had Iole made in seruage yoke to toyle.

**b.** *fig.*

*c* **1380** WYCLIF *Wks.* (1880) 122 Coueitise & glotonye ben seruage of maumetrie. *c* **1450** tr. *De Imitatione* III. xi. 79 O þe holy state of religiose seruage [L. *famulatus*].

†**2.** Feudal homage, allegiance. *Obs.*

**1297** R. GLOUC. (Rolls) 1059 Is noble seruage Dude to þe heye emperour. *c* **1369** CHAUCER *Dethe Blaunche* 769 Al this I put in his seruage As to my lorde, and dyd homage. *a* **1400-50** *Wars Alex.* 918 (Dubl. MS.) This freke of all þe fraunches of kyng philop haldes,..& seruage hym awght. *a* **1533** LD. BERNERS *Huon* xxxiii. 105 He doth me yerely seruage by the seruyce of a rynge of gold.

†**3.** A service, or its equivalent in money or kind, due from a serf to his lord. *Obs.*

**1414** *Rolls of Parlt.* IV. 58/1 The forseide.. Chanons hav cleymed.. bonde servages and custumes. *c* **1460** *Oseney Reg.* 122, I, Henry of Saunder, clerck, ȝafe.. all my londe.. with all seruices and seruages, men [etc.].. of the same londe. *a* **1513** FABYAN *Chron.* VII. (1811) 645 The Kyng, yᵉ which yerely oppressyth his subiectys with taskys and other greuouse seruagys. **1563-87** FOXE *A. & M.* (1596) 122/2 Ethelwulfe.. gaue to them.. libertie and freedome from all servage and civill charges.

**4.** Serfage, serfdom.

**1848** MILL *Pol. Econ.* II. v. I. 298, I speak of negro slavery, not of the servage of the Slavonic nations.

**servagerous**, var. SAVAGEROUS *a.*

†**'servagery.** *Obs. rare.* [f. SERVAGE + -ERY.] = SERVAGE 2.

*c* **1400** *Laud Troy Bk.* 140 Polleus hadde wel gret envye That men dede him [Jason] suche seruagery. *Ibid.* 11494 He was not worthi To haue of hem suche seruageri.

**serval** (ˈsɜːvəl). Also **serval cat.** [a. mod.L. *serval*, F. *serval* (Buffon, 1765), a. Pg. (*lobo*) *cerval* lynx (cf. F. *loup-cervier*).] †**a.** A name applied (after Buffon) to some Asiatic wild cat or lynx; also to an American animal resembling this. *Obs.* **b.** A carnivorous quadruped, *Felis serval*, native of S. Africa, having a tawny coat spotted with black, a short tail and large ears; the *bush-cat* (BUSH *sb.*[1] 11).

**1771** PENNANT *Syn. Quadrupeds* 186 Called by the natives of Malabar, the Maraputé; by the Portuguese, the Serval. **1800** SHAW *Gen. Zool.* I. 369 The Serval is a native of India and Tibet and is an extremely fierce and rapacious animal. *Ibid.* 370 American Serval.. inhabits North America.. is considered as a mild and gentle animal. **1865** LUBBOCK *Prehist. Times* viii. 262 In the Genista Cave at Gibraltar ..[they] have discovered.. the leopard, lynx, serval [etc.]. **1899** F. V. KIRBY *Sport E.C. Africa* 321 The serval is a tireless hunter, and runs down its prey. **1919** F. W. FITZSIMONS *Nat. Hist. S. Afr.: Mammals* I. 142 These Serval Cats often break cover. **1933** N. DOUGLAS *Looking Back* II. 340 Somebody shot a serval cat.

**serval**, obs. Sc. form of SERVILE.

**'servaline**, *a. Zool.* [a. mod.L. specific name of *Felis servalina* (W. Ogilby 1839, in *Proc. Zool. Soc.* 94), f. SERVAL + -INE[1].] Resembling the serval: used to designate a serval in a darker colour phase than usual, with less obvious markings, once considered a separate species. Also as *sb.*

**1876** *Proc. Zool. Soc.* 413 A collection of Angolian animals... Servaline Cat. *Felis Servalina.* From River Kwanza. **1915** G. AYLMER in *Proc. Zool. Soc.* 154 The differences between the Servals and the Servaline Cats are of no systematic importance. **1964** L. S. CRANDALL *Managem. Wild Mammals in Captivity* 364 Specimens with markings reduced almost to dots were once distinguished under the name of servaline cat. **1970** DORST & DANDELOT *Field Guide Larger Mammals Afr.* 138 The servaline is a mere colour phase.

**servant** (ˈsɜːvənt), *sb.* Forms: α. 3-7 **servand**, 4 **servon, serfaunt**, 4-5 **servaund, -ond, sirvand**, 4-6 **servande, -ante, serwand, sirvant**, 4-7 **servaunt(e**, 5 **servaunth, -awnt, -onde, -unt, serwaunt, siervaunt, cervawnte**, 5-6 **serwant**, 6 **servont, -ent, serwonde, serviand, scherv-, scherw-, schirwand**, 3- **servant**; (pl. forms 3-4 **servanz**, 4 **-ans**); β. 4 **sarvaunte**, 4-5 **sarvande**, 4, 7, 9 *dial.* **sarvant**, 5-6 **sarvaunt**, 6 **sarvand, -ante.** [a. F. *servant*, subst. use of pr. pple. of *servir* SERVE *v.*[1]

In mod.Fr. only the fem. *servante* has survived in this sense. In OF. the pr. pple. had the same form in both genders; hence the Eng. word has always been applied both to males and females, without any distinction of form.]

A person of either sex who is in the service of a master or mistress; one who is under obligation to work for the benefit of a superior, and to obey his (or her) commands.

**1.** A personal or domestic attendant; one whose duty is to wait upon his master or mistress, or do certain work in his or her household. (The usual sense when no other is indicated by the context; sometimes with defining word, as ***domestic servant.***)

***upper servant***, a domestic servant of superior grade of employment, as a butler or a housekeeper. ***general servant*** (see GENERAL *a.* 6), ***servant of all work***: a female servant who does all kinds of housework. ***servants' hall***: an apartment for use as a common room by the servants in a large house.

α. *a* **1225** *Ancr. R.* 428 Non ancre seruant ne ouhte, mid rihte, uorto asken i-sette huire. *a* **1300** *Cursor M.* 2560 Child haue i self nan, Bot mi seruand sun allan þat serues me, eleazar [cf. *Gen.* xv. 2, Vulg.: *filius procuratoris domus meæ*]. *c* **1386** CHAUCER *Prol.* 101 A Yeman hadde he and seruantz namo. **1433** in *10th Rep. Hist. MSS. Comm.* App. v. 295 No citsaine herafter.. shall not bake ne brewe.. but only by his wif or siervaunt. **1447** *Shillingford Lett.* (Camden) 10 Alle men of habite servantis familiars knawed without any fraude generally. **1509** FISHER *Funeral Serm. C'tess Richmond* Wks. (1876) 296 The housholde seruauntes muste be put in some good ordre. **1611** SHAKS. *Cymb.* III. v, That man of hers, Pisanio, her old Seruant. *c* **1702** C. FIENNES, *Journeys* (1947) I. 55 Just behind the hall is the Servants hall. **1728** MRS. DELANY *Life & Corr.* (1861) I. 183, I am in great concern at your being without a servant. **1780** *Mirror* No. 96 We.. keep a good number of servants. **1785** G. WASHINGTON *Diaries* 12 Mar. (1925) II. 349 In a line with the East end of my Kitchen, and Servants' Hall. **1813** *Examiner* 8 Feb. 89/1 The ethics of the kitchen and servants'-hall. **1819** *Morning Post* 14 Jan. 1 (Advt.), Wanted immediately, a servant of all-work, where others are kept for the children. **1835** DICKENS *Sk. Boz, Scenes* vii, The intense delight with which 'a servant of all work', who is sent for a coach, deposits herself inside. **1843** WORDSWORTH in Chr. Wordsw. *Mem.* (1851) II. 76 A stranger.. asked of one of the female servants..

permission to see her master's study. **1881** *A Chequered Career* 285 Let us peep into the servants'-hall. **1908** R. BAGOT *A. Cuthbert* xxiii. 293 She had evidently learned the language from servants and was, therefore, not quite at home with her *h*'s.

*β. c* **1400** *Rule of St. Benet* (Verse) 54 And put vs vn-to pyen for þi, Als wykkyd saruandes er worthy. *c* **1500** *God Speed the Plough* 19 Our sarvauntys we Moste nedis paye. **1599** DALLAM in *Early Voy. Levant* (Hakl. Soc.) 41 John Knill, sarvante to Mr. Wyseman, marchante. *a* **1699** LADY HALKETT *Autobiog.* (1875) 29 One of his sarvants came and told mee that [etc.].

**2. a.** In wider sense: One who is under the obligation to render certain services to, and to obey the orders of, a person or a body of persons, esp. in return for wages or salary.

**1433** *Rolls of Parlt.* IV. 475/1 How that late he sende into Bretayn Wauter Trenchevyle, his Servant, Factour and Attournay, to Marchandise ther. **1683** W. HEDGES *Diary* (Hakl. Soc.) I. 85 Ye Honble Company's Servants. **1704** HEARNE *Duct. Hist.* (1714) I. 172 Polydore Virgil.. Servant to the Pope in the Time of K. Henry VIII. **1783** BURKE *Rep. Aff. India* Wks. 1842 II. 6 One provision, indeed, was made for restraining the servants [of the E. Ind. Comp.]. **1848** *Times* 6 Nov. 4/4 Every attention was paid by the servants of the [railway] company to the deceased.

**b.** *fig.* Applied to things (chiefly with more or less of personification).

*c* **1350** *Will. Palerne* 467 Mi siȝt is seruant to mi hert. **1390** GOWER *Conf.* III. 100 As it is in Phisique write Of livere, of lunge, of galle, of splen, Thei alle unto the herte ben Servantz. **1639** J. CLARKE *Parœmiologia* 206 Fire and water be good servants, but bad masters. **1688** HOLME *Armoury* III. 320/2 A Shovel.. is a Servant for several uses about the Lady Ceres. **1745** *Life Bampfylde-Moore Carew* 17 Disposing therefore of his faithful Servants, his Horse and Asses in Bridgwater. **1900** *Daily News* 19 Feb. 6/3 They knew that the Empire was the best servant that mankind had ever had.

†**c.** Used for SERGEANT, SERJEANT, in various senses. *Obs.*

**13..** *Coer de L.* 1641 Hys knyghtes weren dyght, al redy, Servauntes off armes, and squyers. **1340** *Ayenb.* 37 Þe ontrewe reuen prouos and bedeles and seruons, þet steleþ þe amendes, and wyþdraȝeþ þe rentes of hire lhordes. **1511** *Chron.* in *Songs, Carols*, etc. (1907) 156 This yer ix. seruantis of þe coyff made. **1513** *Bk. Keruynge* A 4 b, in *Babees Bk.*, Also yf marshall, squyers and seruauntes of armes be there. **1561–2** *New Yrs. Gifts* in Nichols *Progr. Eliz.* (1823) I. 127 To John Betts, Servent of the Pastrye, twoo guilt spoones.

†**d.** One who assists a workman. Cf. SERVE *v.*[1] 36. *Obs.*

**1554–5** in *Extracts Edin. Burgh Rec.* (1871) II. 313 Item, to David Grahame, masoun, for his oulk's wage xxiiijs. Item, to Laurence Paterson, his servand viijs.

**e.** Applied occas. to any state official, as expressing his relation to the Sovereign. Similarly, ***servant of the state, public servant***, etc. See also CIVIL SERVANT.

**1570** BUCHANAN *Admonitioun* Wks. (1892) 33 Being ane gude sruand to ye croun. **1607** SHAKS. *Cor.* II. iii. 186 When he had no Power, Butt was a pettie seruant to the State. *c* **1645** HOWELL *Lett.* (1650) I. 112 Besides Scots and Swissers, there are divers of the King's servants that are protestants. **1676** HOBBES *Iliad* I. 307 Talthybius and Eurybates.. Two public servants of the king were these. **1787** W. THOMSON *Cunningham's Hist. Gt. Brit.* I. Introd. 16 King William was wont to observe, that he got more truth from Argyle than from all the rest of his servants in Scotland. **1845** *Gen. Index Parl. Papers* 1832–44, 632 Public Servants voting at Elections. **1849** MACAULAY *Hist. Eng.* ii. I. 273 The chief servants of the crown form one body. **1888** 'R. BOLDREWOOD' *Robbery under Arms* xxxiv, We hadn't been used to firing on the Queen's servants.

**f.** In the 16th c., certain companies of actors were permitted to describe themselves as the 'servants' of some noble patron, and in the 17th c. similar privileges were granted by the sovereign. Hence in mod. use ***His*** (or ***Her***) ***Majesty's servants*** sometimes appears as a jocular designation for the theatrical profession.

**1559** EARL LEICESTER *Let. to E. Shrewsbury* in Collier *Northbrooke's Dicing* (Shaks. Soc.) Introd. 7 Where my servauntes.. be suche as ar plaiers of interludes, and for the same haue the licence.. to plaie in diverse shieres within the realme. **1603** in Rymer *Fœdera* XVI. 505 James by the Grace of God &c... Knowe ye that Wee.. doe licence and authorize theise our Servantes, Laurence Fletcher, William Shakespeare,.. And the rest of their Assosiates, Freely to use and exercise the Arte and Faculty of playing Comedies, Tragedies [etc.]. **1609** in *Shaks. Soc. Papers* (1849) IV. 45 Thomas Greene [and others].. Servants to our most deerely beloved wiefe, Queene Anne. **1696** J. DRYDEN, jun. (*title*), The Husband his own Cuckold. A Comedy, As it is Acted.. by His Majesty's Servants. **1864** DORAN (*title*) 'Their Majesties' Servants.' Annals of the English Stage.

**3. a.** In the 14th and 15th c. often used to render the L. *servus* slave. In all the Bible translations from Wyclif to the Revised Version of 1880–4, the word very often represents the Heb. *ʿébed* or the Gr. δοῦλος, which correspond to *slave*, though this term as applied to Israelitish conditions would perh. be misleading. *servant of servants*: a Hebraism for one in the most degrading bondage.

**1375** BARBOUR *Bruce* III. 220 Serwandis and threllis mad he fre. **1382** WYCLIF *Ezek.* xxvii. 13 Thei, thi biers, brouȝten seruauntis [1388 boonde men] and brasen vessels to thi puple. **1388** —— *Gen.* ix. 25 Cursid be the child Canaan, he schal be seruant of seruantis [so the later versions] to hise britheren. **1483** *Cath. Angl.* 330/2 To make a Servande, *mansipare*. *c* **1520** NISBET *N.T.*, *Gal.* iv. 30 The sonn of the seruand sall nocht be aire with the sonn of the fre wife. *fig.* **1474** CAXTON *Chesse* II. iii. (1883) 38 For he is seruant & bonde vnto money and not lord therof.

**b.** In the North American colonies in the 17–18th c., and subsequently in the United States, ***servant*** was the usual designation for a slave.

**1643** *Virginia Stat. at Large* (1823) I. 253 If any such runnaway servants or hired freemen shall produce a certificate [etc.]. **1784** *Acts & Laws of Conn.* (1784) 103 Apprentices under Age and Servants bought for Time excepted. **1809** KENDALL *Trav.* II. 272 Servant, in the statute book of Connecticut.. is put for slave. **1852** MRS. STOWE *Uncle Tom's C.* xxi. 223 Why don't we teach our servants to read?

**4.** In various transferred uses. †**a.** One who owes feudal service to his overlord, a vassal. *Obs.*

*c* **1330** R. BRUNNE *Chron. Wace* (Rolls) 11505 Þou frolle, our baroun [*v.r.* seruant], slow, ffrance & ffIaundres from vs þou drow. **1471** CAXTON *Recuyell* (Sommer) II. 525 O right noble kynge as I am your trewe seruant and vassale. **1527** *Caldwell Papers* (Maitland Club) I. 58 Me Johne Mure.. grants me and myne airs ppetualie, to bekum man and servand till Hew Erle of Eglingtone, and till his airs ppetualie.

†**b.** A professed lover; one who is devoted to the service of a lady. (Cf. MISTRESS 10.) Also, in bad sense, a paramour, gallant. *Obs.*

*c* **1368** CHAUCER *Compl. Pite* 60 Sheweth vnto youre rialle excellence Youre servaunt, yf I durst me so calle, Hys mortal harme. **1508** DUNBAR *Tua Mariit Wemen* 466, I have ane secrete seruand,.. That me supportis of sic nedis. **1598** B. JONSON *Ev. Man in Hum.* IV. ii, Servant (in troth) you are too prodigall Of your wits treasure, thus to powre it forth Upon .. my worth. **1614** W. BROWNE *Sheph. Pipe* vii. F 1 b, Nor hath her seruants nor her fauorites That waite her husbands issuing at dore. **1629** FORD *Lover's Mel.* I. iii, For your reward, Henceforth Ile call you Seruant. **1666–7** PEPYS *Diary* 4 Jan., Pegg, and her servant, Mr. Lowther. *a* **1700** SEDLEY *Poems* Wks. 1778 I. 54 Some caution yet I'd have thee use, Whene'er thou dost a servant chuse: Men are not all for lovers fit.

**c.** With religious signification.

***Servant of the servants of God*** (*servus servorum Dei*): a title assumed by the Popes (first by Gregory the Great).

*a* **1300** *Cursor M.* 3118 Herkens o godd þat all weldand, How he wald faand his lel seruand. *a* **1340** HAMPOLE *Pr. Consc.* 1082 Þe world here, es þe devels servand, þat brynges his servauntes til his hand. *a* **1340** —— *Ps.* lxv. 5 Þai ere saruauntes til þaire godes. *c* **1380** WYCLIF *Wks.* (1880) 362 It bylongiþ to þe godheed of criste.. to rewarde his trewe saruandis. *c* **1386** CHAUCER *Parson's T.* 699 The Pope calleth hym-self seruant of the seruantz of god. **1447** BOKENHAM *Seyntys* ix. 904 She seruaunth was To Cryst in heuene. **1574** *Wills & Inv. N.C.* (Surtees) I. 405 Lawrence dunccane serwand to the church of god and Minister at the church of belford. **1655** (*title*) A true Testimony of what was done concerning the servants of the Lord, at the Generall Assizes at Northampton. *a* **1770** JORTIN *Serm.* (1771) VII. ii. 19 Christians.. must not draw back and become the servants of sin. **1823** SCOTT *Quentin D.* xvi, The good Bishop labours night and day to preserve peace, as well becometh a servant of the altar. **1871** J. ELLERTON *Hymn*, '*Now the labourer's task is o'er*' i, Father, in Thy gracious keeping Leave we now Thy servant sleeping.

**d. *your*** (***humble, obedient***) ***servant***: one of the customary modes of subscribing a letter, or of addressing a patron in the dedication of a book. †(***your***) ***servant***: a mode of expressing submission to another's opinion, often equivalent to 'there is nothing more to be said upon the subject'; a form of greeting or leave-taking.

*a.* [**1444** *Paston Lett.* I. 48 Wretyn right simply.. By your most symple servaunt Jamys Gresham.] **1474** CAXTON *Chesse* Ded., Your most humble servant william Caxton amonge other of your seruantes sendes unto yow peas. *c* **1550** BALE *K. Johan* 1139 Yowr servont and Umfrey! of trewthe, father, I am he. **1601** J. DONNE in Kempe *Losely MSS.* (1836) 333 Yor L'ps most dejected and poore servant, J. Donne. **1649** LOVELACE *Being treated to Ellinda*, But now to close all I must switch-hard. Servant ever; *Lovelace Richard.* **1672** WYCHERLEY *Love in Wood* I. ii, Your Servant, —your Servant.—Mr. Ranger. **1687** PRIOR *Hind & P. Transversed* Wks. (1907) 9 Nay Gentlemen, if you question my skill in the Language, I'm your humble Servant. **1705** [T. WALKER] *Wit of a Woman* II. 21 Enter Boastwit. *Boast.* So, Sir, your Servant, your Servant, Captain. **1752** FOOTE *Taste* II. (1781) 27 As to Sculpture, I am his very humble Servant. A Man must know damn'd little of Statuary, that dislikes a Bust for want of a Nose. **1770** —— *Lame Lover* III. Wks. 1799 II. 89 Oh! if you are angry, your servant—I thought that the news would have pleased you. **1806–7** J. BERESFORD *Miseries Hum. Life* (1826) VI. 116 *Sen.* I shall be content with a few selections.. *Tes.* O, your servant!—those you shall have without demur. **1845** [MACRAY] *Man. Brit. Hist.* Ded., To the Rev. Bulkeley Bandinel,.. this volume is ..dedicated, by his obedient and obliged servant. **1851** LYTTON *Not so bad* II. i. 33 Enter Wilmot and Softhead. Wilmot. Your servant, ladies;—Sir Geoffrey, your servant. **1896** CROCKETT *Cleg Kelly* vii, 'Servant, m'am!' said he, putting his pipe behind him as he came into the shop.

*β.* **1680–1** MARLBOROUGH in Wolseley *Life* I. 237, I am your.. faithful frend and sarvant. **1859** HUGHES *Scouring Wh. Horse* vii. 169 The old farmer.. came and sat down at the table. 'Your sarvant, gen'l'men,' said he, taking off his broad-brimmed beaver.

**5.** *attrib.* and *appositive*, as ***servant-boy, -class***, †***-gentleman, -lass, -maid, -man, -problem***, †***-train, -trouble***, †***-wench, -wife, -woman***; ***servant-like*** adj. and adv. Also SERVANT-GIRL.

**1832** HT. MARTINEAU *Hill & Valley* vi, Her *servant-boy .. now came up. **1876** C. M. YONGE *Womankind* xxvii. 236 To raise the notions of the *servant and factory-classes about marriage. **1920** 'O. DOUGLAS' *Penny Plain* xiii. 134 Mawson.. belonged to that fast disappearing body, the real servant class. **1604** in *T. Pont's Topogr. Acc. Cunningham* (Maitland Club) 183 To Thomas Blair, his *servand-gentilman of fie, xl lib. **1694** *Aberdeen Reg.* (1872) IV. 315 That.. noe *servant lass goe in to the pews of either churches. **1848** THACKERAY *Van. Fair* xxvi, The Irish servant-lass rushed up from the kitchen. **1616** T. SCOT *Philomythie* I. (ed. 2) H 5 b, When thou most *seruant-like thy head dost beare Downe to the ground. **1853** HICKIE tr. *Aristoph.* (1872) II. 567 This is a servant-like act which you have openly done. **1661–2** in Swayne *Churchw. Acc. Sarum* (1896) 236 For the *servant maid of W. Hayter, 6s. **1782** COWPER *Let. to Hill* Wks. 1837 XV. 113 As servant maids, and such sort of folks. **1880** MCKAY *Hist. Kilmarnock* (ed. 4) 160 With his wife, eight children, and a servant-maid he then set out for London. **1379** *Poll-tax W. Riding* in *Yorks. Archæol. Jrnl.* VI. 12 Robertus *seruantman, iiijd. **1815** *Ann. Reg.*, *Chron.* 17 The wife of Mr. Metters,.. was murdered by her servant man. **1916** A. BENNETT *These Twain* III. xvii. 361 The *servant problem had been growing acute. **1973** R. LEWIS *Blood Money* viii. 117, I suppose you see it as somewhat anachronistic—a young girl 'in service'. .. But you won't be here to discuss the servant problem, Inspector Crow. **1725** POPE *Odyss.* IV. 906 Must my *servant train Th' allotted labours of the day refrain? **1859** GEO. ELIOT *Let.* 26 Feb. (1954) III. 26 The *servant-trouble seems less mountainous to me than it did the other day. **1977** A. WILSON *Strange Ride of Rudyard Kipling* vi. 272 Carrie Kipling['s].. diaries are entirely mundane.. financial transactions.. servant troubles. **1768** TUCKER *Lt. Nat.* (1834) I. 128 A *servant wench in London. **1812** *Ann. Reg.*, *Chron.* 37 The servant-wench, who slept in the next room. **1906** J. JOYCE *Let.* 3 Dec. (1966) II. 199 *Servant-wife blows her nose in the letter and lawyer confronts the mistress. **1379** *Poll-tax W. Riding* in *Yorks. Archæol. Jrnl.* VI. 23 Elena *Seruantwoman iiijd. **1842** AITON *Domest. Econ.* (1857) 126 The servant-women in the manse are nearly unexceptionable.

†**'servant**, *a. Obs. rare.* [a. F. *servant*, pr. pple. of *servir* to SERVE; cf. SERVANT *sb.*] Serving, ministering; serviceable, useful; servant-like.

**1531** TINDALE *Exp. John* (1537) 6 They.. haue promysed ..to waxe euer lower and lower, and euery daye more seruant then another. **1614–15** BOYS *Wks.* (1629) 758 He that in Christs Church is most seruant is the greatest, and he that is most lordly the least.

†**'servant**, *v. Obs. rare.* [f. SERVANT *sb.*]

**1.** *trans.* To put in subjection *to*.

**1607** SHAKS. *Cor.* V. ii. 89 My affaires Are Seruanted to others.

**2.** *pa. pple.* Provided with a servant.

**1631** J. DONE *Polydoron* (1650) 133 Hee is ill servanted that hears his mayde before hee sees her.

**3.** *intr.* ***to servant it***, to act as a servant.

**1656** S. H. *Golden Law* 68 He mated.. not only his Master, but his Masters also,.. by servanting it to them all in his administrations and services.. for their good.

**servantdom** ('sɜːvəntdəm). [f. SERVANT *sb.* + -DOM.] Servants as a class.

**1883** T. WRIGHT in *19th Cent.* Feb. 285 The point of the saying, 'No man is a hero to his valet' extends in practice to all servant-dom. **1884** MRS. BANKS *Sybilla* III. 88 Mrs. Price was holding forth on the subject of servantdom.

‖**servante** (sɛrvɑ̃t). [F. *servante* side table.] An extra table or concealed shelf used in conjuring.

**1872** *Routledge's Ev. Boy's Ann.* 344/1 The servante, or hidden shelf. **1878** tr. *Houdin's Secr. Conjuring* 66 The *gibecière* or *servante*, as it is now more generally called.

†**'servantess.** *Obs. rare*[−1]. [f. SERVANT *sb.* + -ESS[1].] A female servant.

**1388** WYCLIF *Gen.* xvi. 2 Entre thou to my seruantesse. *Ibid.* xxxii. 22 He took hise twei wyues, and so many seruantessis.. and passide the forthe of Jaboth.

**servant-girl.** A young female servant.

**1834** MRS. CARLYLE *Lett.* I. 10 The very servant-girls wear bustles. **1853** *Punch* XXIV. 98/1 *Servant Gal*... I a'int a going to stop in sarvice no longer.

*attrib.* **1894** MISS E. L. BANKS *Campaigns Curios.* 15, I sat down on the hat-rack in orthodox servant-girl fashion.

Hence **servantgirldom, servantgirlism.**

**1853** *Punch* XXIV. 98/1 Servantgalism; or, what's to become of the missuses? **1896** *Daily News* 6 Apr. 3/4 The Sunday afternoon attire of servant girldom in the East-end.

**servantless** ('sɜːvəntlɪs), *a.* [-LESS.] Having no servant (in various senses of the sb.).

**1669** COKAINE *Poems* 158 One of less beauty and.. Servant-less, sooner should my heart command. **1883** STEVENSON *Silverado Sq.* (1895) II. 306 We must go to our mountain servantless. **1889** G. GISSING *Nether World* III. xiii. 295 Bessie was just now servantless.

†**'servantly**, *a. Obs.* [f. SERVANT *sb.* + -LY[1].] Having the qualities appropriate to a servant.

**1561** DAUS tr. *Bullinger on Apoc.* (1573) 259 b, He would therfore haue worshipped and honoured the Angel wyth seruauntly worshyppe as they terme it [*dulia*]. *a* **1603** T. CARTWRIGHT *Confut. Rhem. N.T.* (1618) 78 You call the Pope the most seruantlie seruant of the Church.

**'servantry.** *rare.* [f. SERVANT *sb.* + -RY.] The servants of a household or estate considered collectively.

**1860** W. H. RUSSELL *Diary India* II. 205 The male servantry summoned to do homage by the blast of the cows' horns. **1891** HARDY *Tess* v, It was evidently the gentleman's wish not to be disturbed.. by the servantry.

**servantship** ('sɜːvəntʃɪp). [f. SERVANT *sb.* + -SHIP.] The state or condition of being a servant.

**1579** W. WILKINSON *Confut. Fam. Love* b i b, Supposed euen so that his seruaunt (that is his seruauntship out of the law) should be his heire. **1583** GOLDING *Calvin on Deut.* lxiv. 391 That seruantship bare no sway in him by the space of those fortie dayes. **1776–80** BENTHAM *Introd. Princ. Mor. & Legisl.* xvi. (1789) 263 Usurpation of servantship [coincides] with usurpation of mastership. **1803** JANE PORTER *Thaddeus* xxi, I suppose the appellation mistress put her in mind of her ci-devant servantship. **1876** BATHGATE *Deep Things* v. 87 Any man who treated his neighbour, either in servantship or mastership, as he should be treated.

†**ser'vation.** *Obs. rare*$^{-1}$. [ad. L. *servātiōnem*, n. of action f. *servāre* to preserve.] Preservation.
**1521** WOLSEY *Let.* in Strype *Eccl. Mem.* (1733) I. I. 32 For the Servation of themselves, and Surety of their Goods.

†**ser'vator.** *Obs. rare*$^{-1}$. [a. L. *servātor*, f. L. *servāre* to preserve.] A preserver.
**1502** ARNOLDE *Chron.* 60 b/1 Abdalazys Soldan of babilon ..seruator and defensor of the lordes of assia.

**servator(e, servatour,** erron. ff. SERVITOR.

†**'servatory.** *Obs.* [ad. med.L. *servātōrium* magazine, f. L. *servāre* to preserve: see -ORY[1].]
**1.** A reservoir or tank for water.
*c* **1450** *Godstow Reg.* 301 The cowrte, and all the bildyngis, with the gardeyne, and seruatory.
**2.** A safeguard, preservative (see quot.).
**1613** PURCHAS *Pilgrimage* (1614) 141 Their Phylacteries or Seruatories, Defensiues..(so the word signifieth)..they vsed as Preseruatiues, or Remembrancers of the law.

**servatour,** variant of SERVITER *Sc.*

†**serve,** *sb.*[1] *Obs. rare.* [OE. *syrfe* wk. fem.:—prehistoric **surƀjōn-*, a. popular L. **sorbea*, f. *sorb-us* SERVICE *sb.*[2]]
**1.** = SERVICE *sb.*[2]
**940** in Birch *Cartul. Sax.* II. 490 Of wulfa leaȝe to cawel dene. of cawel dene to þære syrfan. *c* **1440** *Pallad. on Husb.* II. 227 In Iane, in ffeueryeer and Marche in coold Erthe, October and Nouember in hoot Erthe, is settyng of seruys nobul hold. *Ibid.* III. 877 In serue & peche, in plane & populer, In wilous may this melis graffid be.
**2.** The fruit of the service-tree.
**1621** BURTON *Anat. Mel.* I. ii. II. i. 92 Nuts, Medlers, Serues, &c.

**serve** (sɜːv), *sb.*[2] [f. SERVE *v.*[1]]
†**1.** ? Service, adoration. *Obs. rare*$^{-1}$.
*c* **1440** *Rel. Pieces fr. Thornton MS.* 73 Þou gyffe me grace the serue to paye.
**2.** *Tennis.* An act of serving, a service.
**1688** HOLME *Armoury* III. 264/2 (Tennis) Serve, is the first casting out of the Ball upon the Pent-House, for him on the contrary side to strike at. **1905** *Westm. Gaz.* 17 Mar. 3/1 This is the serve, and to be a good one it has to come off the wall into the right court. The serve is then taken by one of the opposing party. **1909** *Ibid.* 7 Aug. 2/1 He is the most difficult of all the bowlers who have applied to cricket the American serve at tennis.
**3.** In fig. phr. *to give* (someone) *a serve*: to deal roughly with; to criticize or reprimand sharply. *Austral. slang.*
**1974** STACKPOLE & TRENGROVE *Not just for Openers* 104, I continued to give Snow a bit of a serve. **1977** *Australian* 1 June 3 He was glad to be leaving and he would be giving the country a serve in an unnamed English newspaper if it was willing to pay enough for his views. **1980** *Daily Tel.* 25 June 17/3 He debunks the fashionable diets but also criticises doctors for not speaking out about bad eating habits. 'I give them a little serve,' he said, using an Australian expression.

†**serve,** *sb.*[3] *Obs. rare*$^{-1}$. [a. F. *serve* (:—L. *serva*), fem. of *serf*. SERF.] A female slave.
**1480** CAXTON *Ovid's Met.* XI. v, And helde her as hys serve & paramour.

**serve** (sɜːv), *v.*[1] Forms: α. 2–3 (*Ormin*) serrfenn, serrvenn, 3 servie, sarvi, 3–4 servi, 2–5 serven, 3–5 servy, 3–6 serf, 3–5, 7 serfe, 3, 5–9 (*now vulgar*) sarve, 4 servin, 4–7 *Sc.* serwe, 5 cervyn, servyn(ne, 5–6 *Sc.* serff, (6 *Sc.* scherve, 7 searve, searfe, serv), 2– serve. β. 3 sarevy, 5 seryf(f, -iff, serof, serryff, sarif, -yf, sarofe. γ. *Sc.* and *dial.* 5, 6, 8 ser, 5–6, 9 sar, 5, 8– sair; 9 sarrow, sarra (see Eng. Dial. Dict.). [a. OF. (and F.) *serv-ir*:—L. *servīre* to be a servant or slave, to serve, f. *serv-us* slave, servant. Cf. Pr. *servir, sirvir*, Sp., Pg. *servir*, It. *servire*.

In Latin the verb was intransitive, often followed by a dative. In Fr. (as other Rom. langs.) the intransitive use has remained, but by the side of it there has been from an early period a transitive use, resulting from the conversion of the indirect into a direct object. In ME. both uses were common; in mod.Eng. the vb. is felt as primarily transitive, the intransitive senses which survive having blended with the absolute uses.]

**I.** To be a servant (to), render service (to).

**1. a.** *intr.* To be a servant; to perform the duties of a servant.
**1303** R. BRUNNE *Handl. Synne* 835 Þe seruyng man, þat seruyþ yn þe ȝere. **1338** —— *Chron.* (1810) 33 Whilom he serued in his panterie. *c* **1400** *Rule of St. Benet* (prose) xxxv. 26 Þe vassels þat tay serue wid [orig. *vasa ministerii sui*]. **1591** SHAKS. *Two Gent.* III. i. 270 She is her Masters maid, and serues for wages. *c* **1655** MILTON *Sonn.*, '*When I consider*', They also serve who only stand and waite. **1667** —— *P.L.* I. 263 Better to reign in Hell, then serve in Heav'n. **1664** R. CODRINGTON *Prov.* in *Youths Behav.* II. 200 He that serves well needs not fear to ask his wages. **1729** SWIFT *Direct. Serv., Cook* (1745) 37 Whether you serve in Town or Country. **1764** BURN *Poor Laws* 215 From the highest subject to the lowest, no man chuses to serve for nothing. **1800** WORDSW. *Farmer Tilsbury Vale* 50 All trades, as need was, did old Adam assume,—Served as stable-boy, errand-boy, porter, and groom. **1859** TENNYSON *Enid* 453 The men who served About my person. **1894** BARING-GOULD *Deserts S. France* II. 246 He served some time as a waiter in an eating-house.

†**b.** To be a slave or bondman; to be in bondage; to labour as a bondman. Also with cognate object. (A latinism.) *Obs.*
**1382** WYCLIF *Isa.* xiv. 3 Thin harde seruage, that thou beforn seruedist. **1382** —— *Gal.* iv. 3 So and we, whanne we weren litile, weren seruynge [**1388** we serueden] vndir the elementis of the world. **1611** BIBLE *Exod.* i. 13 The Egyptians made the children of Israel to serue with rigour. *Ibid.*, *Ezek.* xxix. 18 Nebuchad-rezzar..caused his armie to serue a great seruice against Tyrus. **1671** MILTON *P.R.* III. 378–9 Serving as of old Thir Fathers in the land of Egypt serv'd.

**2. a.** To go through or perform a term of service under a master. Usu. with advb. accus. denoting the period, as ***to serve one's time, to serve an apprenticeship*** (*to* a trade, etc.). Also with *out*.
[**1382** WYCLIF *Gen.* xxix. 20 Thanne Jacob serued for Rachel seuen ȝeer.] **1562** in W. H. Turner *Select. Rec. Oxford* 293 He served his apprentycehode. **1562–3** *Act 5 Eliz.* c. 4 §21 To serve as Apprentice..to any suche Arte Misterye or Manuell Occupacion. *c* **1570** *Saparton's Alarum* in *B. L. Ball. & Broadsides* (1867) 118 If euer warlike wighte Hath serued his time in vaine. **1608** SHAKS. *Per.* IV. vi. 187 (Qo.) Serue by indenture to the common hang-man. **1700** S. L. tr. *Fryke's Voy. E. Ind.* 110 Those who had served out their time [*sc.* as soldiers]. **1712** ARBUTHNOT *John Bull* I. iv, Lewis Baboon had taken up the Trade of Clothier and Draper, without serving his Time, or purchasing his Freedom. **1835** *App. Munic. Corpor. Rep.* III. 1667 A person bound to a free mariner..for seven years, and having served during that period. **1848** THACKERAY *Van. Fair* lvii, Having served his full time in India..he was free to come home and stay with a good pension. **1863** *Rep. Sea Fisheries Comm.* (1865) II. 418/1, I served my time to trawling.

**b.** *fig.*
**1553** R. ASCHAM in *Lett. Lit. Men* (Camden) 16 Som reason I have, to be made free and jorneyman in lernyng, whan I have allready served out three prentyships at Cambrige. **1593** SHAKS. *Rich II*, I. iii. 271 (Qo.) Must I not serue a long apprenticehood To forreine passages. **1603** DEKKER, etc. *Patient Grissill* IV. ii. 2132 When a quarrell enters into a trade, it serues seauen yeares before it be free. **1648** [see PRENTICEHOOD]. **1685** DRYDEN *Albion & Alb.* Pref. (b) 2 As if I had not serv'd out my time in Poetry, but was bound 'Prentice to some doggrel Rhymer. **1693** *Hum. Town* 107 Some old nonsensical Translations which have serv'd a Patriarch's age to the Library of Moore-fields. **1837** CARLYLE *Fr. Rev.* I. IV. iii, Or shall we say: Insurrection has now served its Apprenticeship.

**c.** *trans.* To go through, work out (a term of imprisonment, a penal sentence). Also with *out*. Also ellipt. ***to serve time*** and simply ***to serve***.
**1873** GREENWOOD *In Strange Comp.* 57 One lad..laid claim to have 'served' both in Maidstone gaol and the prison at Wandsworth. *Ibid.* 288 The virago who has just 'served' three months for a murderous assault. **1885** *Encycl. Brit.* XIX. 756/2 The obligation to return to a convict prison to serve out the unexpired term of penal servitude. **1886** *Science* 24 Sept. 287 Every unfortunate or miscreant who has once 'served time'.

**3. a.** To be a servant to; to work for, be employed in the personal service of (a master or mistress).

In the early instances the obj. may possibly be *dative*.

*a* **1225** *Ancr. R.* 422 Helpeð mid ower owune swinke,..to schruden ou suluen and þeo þet ou serueð. *c* **1250** *Gen. & Ex.* 1670 Ic sal, for rachel, Seruen ðe seuene winter wel. *c* **1325** *Chron. Eng.* 518 in Ritson *Metr. Rom.* II. 291 That on partie he [Alfred] yef hem That in ys court serveden hym. **1362** LANGL. *P. Pl.* A. v. 115 For sum tyme I Seruede Simme atte noke, And was his pliht prentys. **1584** COGAN *Haven Health* ii. 17 Plautus..was faine for his liuing to serue a baker. **1601** SHAKS. *All's Well* III. v. 54 A Gentleman that serues the Count. **1611** BIBLE *Exod.* xxi. 6 His master shall boare his eare through with an aule, and he shall serue him for euer. **1661** in *12th Rep. Hist. MSS. Comm.* App. v. 6 Gervise Lucas served George Earle of Rutland as gentleman of his horse some yeares. **1740** [? DE FOE] *Mrs. Chr. Davies* (1741) 10 Richard Welsh, a young Fellow who had served my Aunt. **1819** SCOTT *Ivanhoe* xxxvii, My two brethren, who serve the rich Rabbi. **1828** J. WILSON *Noct. Ambr.* Wks. 1856 II. 49 That is the lot o' the puirest herd callant, wha, ha'in na pawrents, is glad to sair a hard master, withooten ony wage.

**b.** *fig.* To be the slave of (sin, one's lower nature, etc.). *Obs.* or *arch.*
**1390** GOWER *Conf.* III. 3 It is the cuppe whom he serveth. *c* **1400** *Pety Job* in *26 Pol. Poems* 127, I seruyd syn, and was hys knaue. **1535** COVERDALE *Tit.* iii. 3 For we oure selues also were..seruynge lustes [**1382** WYCL. seruynge to desyris]. **1542** UDALL *Erasm. Apoph.* 135 Suche persones as serven onely the throte & the bealye.

**c.** *rarely* of a beast made to work for his master.
**1692** R. L'ESTRANGE *Fables* ccviii. 178 A Certain Ass that serv'd a Gard'ner.

**d.** To work for (a body of persons, a company) as a paid servant.
**1844** H. H. WILSON *Brit. India* III. 8 His retirement from public duty on account of failing health..called forth..a deserved tribute of acknowledgment from those whom he had long faithfully and ably served. **1876** GLADSTONE *Glean.* (1879) II. 296 Another term of four years brought him back, the least Indian..of all the civilians who had ever served the Company.

**4. a.** To attend upon (as a servant does); to wait upon, minister to the comfort of.
*c* **1250** *Owl & N.* 1579 Þat gode wif..serueþ [*Jesus MS.* saruep] him to bedde & to borde mid faire dede & faire worde. *c* **1275** *Passion our Lord* 40 in *O.E. Misc.* 38 And þer comen engles hym to seruy. *a* **1300** *Floriz & Bl.* 978 (Hausknecht), Ehc moretid þer moste come Two maidenes ut of hire bure, To serven him up in þe ture. *a* **1300** *Cursor M.* 20120 To fere and seke ai did scho bote, And serued taim till hand and fote. *c* **1450** *Merlin* xiv. 225 Whan the kynges doughter hadde serued the thre kynges, than she serued hir fader. **1617** MORYSON *Itin.* I. 251 He presently fell sicke, and not able to serve himselfe, could not..doe me any service. **1794** [see GRANNY 2]. **1852** THACKERAY *Esmond* III. iii, His health was still shattered; and he took a lodging near to his mistresses, at Kensington, glad enough to be served by them. **1859** TENNYSON *Enid* 379 The good house..Endures not that her guest should serve himself.
β. *c* **1440** *Alphabet of Tales* 80 What is he þis at syttis att supper & I holde candell vnto and dure such serves? what am I þat I sulde seryff hym þis? *c* **1450** *St. Cuthbert* (Surtees) 4347 All bot he and his wyfe, And a seruand þaim to sarofe.

**b.** *to be* (*well* or *ill*) *served*. (Cf. branch V.)
**1687** A. LOVELL tr. *Thevenot's Trav.* I. 32 The common price of the Bagnio, is two Aspres to the Master; and they who would be well served, give as much to the Man. **1779** WARNER in Jesse *Selwyn & Contemp.* (1844) IV. 283 Never were people worse served than we are in this country. **1858** LONGF. *M. Standish* i, Serve yourself, would you be well served, is an excellent adage. **1869** MISS ALCOTT *Gd. Wives* i, The mistress of a house, however splendid, should know how work *ought* to be done, if she wishes to be well and honestly served.

**5.** To assist (a priest) *at* (or †*to*) mass as server. Also *absol.*, to act as server. Also ***to serve mass*** (= F. *servir la messe*).
**1393** LANGL. *P. Pl.* C. VI. 12 'Canstow seruen,' he seide 'oþer syngen in a churche.' **1595** in J. H. Pollen *Acts Eng. Martyrs* vi. (1892) 108 It was proved he had served a priest to Mass some three days before this happened. **1667** in *Cath. Rec. Soc. Publ.* III. 62 There was nothing more gratefull vnto him then to serue Masse, nor any more welcome to the Priest he serued. **1706** J. STEVENS *Sp. Dict.*, *Missario*, or *Missero*, a Boy that serves at Mass. **1753** CHALLONER *Cath. Chr. Instr.* 153 [The] Acolyth, whose Function is to serve at Mass. **1844** A. P. DE LISLE in E. Purcell *Life* (1900) I. 122 Arno and Everard served the Mass. **1889** PATER *G. de Latour* (1896) 39 At the great ecclesiastical seasons..Gaston and his fellows 'served' Monseigneur.

**6. a.** (In the earliest use, with obj. in dative.) To be (officially) a servant of (God, a heathen deity); to take official part in the worship of.
*c* **1175** in Assmann *Ags. Hom.* 118/2 He sealde..oðerne del þæm þe gode ane seruedæn [*OE. orig.* þeowodon]. *c* **1200** ORMIN 615 Annd illc an hird wel wisste inoh Whillc lott badd hise prestess I Godess temmple serrfenn Godd. **1819** SHELLEY *Cenci* II. ii. 76 A priest who has forsworn the God he serves.

†**b.** *intr.* To officiate as a minister of God, to perform divine service. *Obs.*
*c* **1200** ORMIN 506 Þatt illc an shollde witenn wel Whillc lott himm shollde reȝȝsenn, To cumenn inntill Ȝerrsalæm, To serrvenn i þe temmple. *c* **1250** *Gen. & Ex.* 3634 Aaron bissop, oðere of ðat kin, Sette he hem for to seruen ðor-in. *a* **1330** *Rouland & V.* 358 Wiþ an hundred chanouns & her priour,..For to serui þere. *c* **1380** WYCLIF *Sel. Wks.* III. 346 Ȝif Apostlis weren now alyve, and sawen þus preestis serve in þe Chirche. **1435** in *Laing Charters* (1899) 30 [Granting to the] Lady Awter off the parissche kyrk of North Berwyk and tyll Schir Androw Ferour thare serwand. **1537** [see CLERK *sb.* 2]. **1568** *Peebles Burgh Rec.* (1872) 74 Being found qualifiit to serf and mak ministratioun in the kirk of God. **1691** *Galliæ Notitia* 68 There are eight Chaplains that serve quarterly..Who are to say every day (excepting the High-Mass dayes) a low Mass before the King.

**7.** †**a.** *trans.* To worship (God, a deity) with religious rites; to offer praise and prayer to, give divine honour to. *Obs.*
*a* **1300** *X Commandm.* 26 in *E.E.P.* (1862) 16 Sundai wel þat ȝe holde, to serue god þilk dai wis boþe ȝung and eke olde. **1340** *Ayenb.* 225 Ine holy stede..þet byeþ aproped uor god to bidde and hym seruy. *c* **1450** *Mirk's Festial* ii. 6 Þe whech dey ȝe schull come to þe chyrch to serue God, and forto worschip the holy apostoll for þe speciall uertues þat he hade. **1577** KENDALL *Flowers of Epigr.* 8 First serud on knees, the Maiestie deuine. **1587** GOLDING *De Mornay* xxiii. (1617) 377 The Spirits which were serued in Stockes and Images..were vncleane and mischieuous Spirits. *a* **1700** EVELYN *Diary* 17 Oct. 1686, Shewing the costome of the primitive Saints in serving God with Hymns. **1702** LUTTRELL *Brief Rel.* (1857) V. 221, 500 protestants in Languedock met in a wood to serve God.

**b.** To render habitual obedience to, to do the will of (God, a heathen deity, Satan).
*c* **1175** *Lamb. Hom.* 81 Hu me sulde godalmihti serue and his wille wurche in orðe. *c* **1200** *Vices & Virtues* 43 Ðo ðe ðese swikele woreld habbeð forlaten And seruið ure drihten on religiun. **1340** HAMPOLE *Pr. Consc.* 1080–1 Þas þat þe world serves and loves, Serves þe devel. **1340–70** *Alex. & Dind.* 632 Ȝe..serue sory idolus þat ȝou in sinne brynge. *c* **1400** *Rule of St. Benet* (prose) Prol. 1 To seryf our lorde Iesu criste. **1435** MISYN *Fire of Love* I. v. 10 God with-outen doutte we lufe noȝt, forsoth hym not sarifand. **1490** CAXTON *Eneydos* iv. 19, I swere to the, by the goddis whom thou seruest. **1535** COVERDALE *Ps.* cxlviii. 14 The children of Israel, euen the people that serueth him. **1566** PAINTER *Pal. Pleas.* I. lvi. (1890) II. 89 Now make accompt of your pilgrimage here, and serue no more such Saînctes. **1597** in *Spalding Club Misc.* (1841) I. 157 The Devill thy maister, quhome thow seruis. **1598** SHAKS. *Merry W.* IV. v. 130 Sure, one of you do's not serue heauen well, that you are so cross'd. *c* **1655** MILTON *Sonnet*, '*When I consider*' 11 Who best Bear his milde yoak, they serve him best. **1810** S. GREEN *Reformist* I. 186, I did not think that London was yet such a sink of depravity, as to openly serve God and Satan on the same day. **1850–1** LONGF. *Gold. Leg.* II, For a whole century Had he been there, Serving God in prayer.

**8. a.** To render obedience and service to, to fulfil one's duty to (a feudal superior, a sovereign).
*c* **1275** LAY. 4855 He saruede [*earlier version* herde] þan kinge mid halle his mihte. **13..** *Guy Warw.* 123 His lord he

serued treweliche In al þing manschipeliche. **1362** LANGL. *P. Pl.* A. III. 203 Hit bicomeþ For a kyng.. To ȝiue meede to men þat mekeliche him seruen. *c* **1470** HENRY *Wallace* I. 397 We serff a lord; thir fysche sall till him gang. **1528** ROY *Rede me* (Arb.) 92 To serve the kynge in warre and peace. **1611** BIBLE *Gen.* xiv. 4 Twelue yeeres they serued Chedorlaomer, and in the thirteenth yeere they rebelled. **1765** H. WALPOLE in *Lett. C'tess Suffolk* (1824) II. 299 Serving a tyrant, who does not allow me many holiday-minutes, I am forced to seize the first that offer. **1830** D'ISRAELI *Chas. I*, III. viii. 164 Northumberland was serving a master for whose service he felt no zeal.

†**b.** *intr.* Of land: To pay feudal service to a lord. [tr. L. *servīre.*] *Obs.*

**1652** NEEDHAM tr. *Selden's Mare Cl.* 272 At Excester when hee [the King] made any Expedition by Land or by Sea, this Citie served after the rate of V. Hides of Land.

†**c.** *trans.* To be obedient to (parents). *Obs.*

*c* **1200** ORMIN 9072 To cwemenn ure faderr wel & ure moderr baþe, To lutenn hemm, to lefftenn hemm, To serrfenn hemm well ȝerrne.

**d.** To be the 'servant' or lover of (a lady).

*c* **1374** CHAUCER *Troilus* IV. 448 But as hir man I wol ay live and sterve, And never other creature serve. **1390** GOWER *Conf.* I. 160 Mi ladi that I serve. **1562** A. BROOKE *Romeus & Iuliet* 78 What booteth me to loue and serue a fell vnthankfull one? **1590** SPENSER *F.Q.* III. vii. 53 That gentle Lady, whom I loue and serue. **1611** SIR W. MURE *Misc. P., Elegie* 24 Still sall I hir adoir and serwe. **1781** COWPER *Anti-Thelyph.* 119 Can he that serves the Fair do less? **1819** BYRON *To Murray* 29 June, A Neapolitan Prince.. serves the wife of the Gonfaloniere.

†**9.** *intr.* (with const.). To render service or obedience *to, unto* (God, Satan, a feudal lord, etc.: see 7, 8). *Obs.*

*a* **1300** *E.E. Psalter* xcix. 1 Serues to lauerd in fainenes [Vulg. *servite Domino in laetitia*]. *a* **1340** HAMPOLE *Psalter* Cant. 504 All vnrightwismen, þat seruys till þe deuyll as his trew knyghtis. *c* **1374** CHAUCER *Troil.* I. 458 Good goodly, to whom serve I and laboure As I best can. **1375** BARBOUR *Bruce* I. 436 For he Ay lely has serwyt to me. **1382** WYCLIF *Heb.* viii. 5 The whiche seruen to [**1611** Who serue vnto] the saumpler and schadewe of heuenly thingis. **1390** GOWER *Conf.* I. 322 And thus thi will is cause of Sinne, And is thi lord, to whom thou servest. **1590** SPENSER *F.Q.* II. viii. 1 But O th' exceeding grace Of highest God, that loues his creatures so.. That blessed Angels he sends to and fro, To serue to wicked man, to serue his wicked foe.

†**10. a.** *trans.* To obey (a person's will): to fulfil, execute (a command, etc.).

**1310** *St. Brendan* (Bälz) 24 Þer he miȝte alone be to servy godes wille. **13..** *Coer de L.* 1180 Gretes wel,.. Bothe myn erchebysschopys tway, And so ye doo the chaunceler, To serve the lettre in all maner, In no maner the lettre fayle. *a* **1400–50** *Wars Alex.* 2410 Þ at þai with-sitt suld his saȝes & serue noȝt his pistill. *c* **1400** MAUNDEV. (1839) xxii. 244 And thus rennethe on to other.. tille the Emperours entent be served. **1602** WARNER *Alb. Eng.* x. lix. (1612) 262 The King commands he there be slaine, Which Warrant did Banaiah serue. *a* **1639** SIR H. WOTTON *Char. Happy Life* 2 How happy is he born and taught, That serveth not an others will? **1822** SHELLEY *With Guitar* 34 Ariel still Has tracked your steps, and served your will.

**b.** To gratify, furnish means for satisfying (desire); to minister to, satisfy (one's need).

**1390** GOWER *Conf.* III. 23 For bot his lust be fully served, Ther hath no wiht his thonk deserved. **1500–20** DUNBAR *Poems* lxxxiv. 21 Sic is thair weird, thairfoir quha sould thame wyte To serue thair beistlie lust and appatite. **1585** T. WASHINGTON tr. *Nicholay's Voy.* IV. xxxvi. 159 To serue their insatiable and damnable auarice. **1597** SHAKS. *Lover's Compl.* 135 Many there were that did his picture gette To serue their eies. **1605** —— *Lear* III. iv. 89 A Seruingman.. that seru'd the Lust of my Mistris heart. **1697** PRIDEAUX *Mahomet* (1716) 131 It appears how much he made his Imposture serve his Lust. **1715** POPE *Iliad* III. 374 May all their Consorts serve promiscuous Lust! **1784** COWPER *Task* II. 138 The very elements, though each be meant The minister of man, to serve his wants, Conspire against him.

**c.** To comply with the request of (a person); to fulfil the wishes of, give (one) his wish.

*a* **1400–50** *Wars Alex.* 1685 Quod Alexander belyue, 'all þis I graunt, And els any othire thing aske & be serued'. **1500–20** DUNBAR *Poems* xxii. 31 Quhen seruit is all vdir man, .. Na thing I get, na conquest than.

†**d.** ? To give way to (the sea). *Obs. rare*$^{-1}$.

**1614** GORGES *Lucan* v. 200 To guide the helme the maister dreads: To port, to weare, or serue the seas, The labouring ship he cannot ease [v. 645–6 *nescitque magister Quam frangat, cui cedat aquae*].

**11.** ***to serve the time***: to shape one's conduct in self-interested conformity to the views that happen to be in favour at the time. [L. *tempori servire.*] Cf. TIMESERVING.

**1560** DAUS tr. *Sleidane's Comm.* 441 Those, whome it best became to remeadye it, partlye wincked therat, partly seruing the time [orig. *obsecundantes tempori*], had a respect more to their priuate commoditye. **1594** HOOKER *Eccl. Pol.* I. i. §1 Who thinke that herein we serue the time, and speake in fauour of the present state, because thereby we eyther holde or seeke preferment. **1604** R. CAWDREY *Table Alph.* (1613), *Temporise*, to serve the time. **1823** BYRON *Juan* XIII. xviii, Be wary, watch the time, and always serve it. **1852** TENNYSON *Ode Death Wellington* 179 Who never sold the truth to serve the hour.

**12. a.** To render active service to (a king or commander) in the army or navy; to fight for, 'to obey in military actions' (J.).

**1518** SIR J. STILE in Ellis *Orig. Lett.* Ser. III. I. 193 For otherwise he [the gunner] wol go to serve the King of Portugale. **1710** SWIFT *Jrnl. to Stella* 18 Nov., He had two hundred thousand men ready to serve her [*sc.* the queen] in the war. **1764** BURN *Poor Laws* 179 Let them be forced to serve the king in his fleet. **1786** BURNS *Ep. to J. Rankine* vi, I'd better gaen an' sair't the king, At Bunker's hill. **1821** SCOTT *Kenilw.* i, I have learned to be dangerous upon points of honour ever since I served the Spaniard. **1887** A. E. HOUSMAN *Shropsh. Lad* i, We pledge in peace by farm and town The Queen they served in war.

¶**b.** In the phrase ***to serve one's country*** the meaning of the vb. fluctuates between 'to labour for, be in the service of' and 'to benefit, do good offices to' (see 16).

**1600** SIR W. CORNWALLIS *Ess.* I. iii. D1, He serued his country for his countries sake. **1651** HOBBES *Leviathan* II. xxviii. 166 Men have no lawfull remedy, when they be commanded to quit their private businesse, to serve the publique, without Reward, or Salary. **1671** MILTON *Samson* 564 To what can I be useful, wherein serve My Nation. **1837** CARLYLE *Fr. Rev.* II. v. vi, War-Minister Narbonne.. threatens.. to 'take his sword',.. and go serve his country with that. **1868** RUSKIN *Pol. Econ. Art* Add. 196 A labourer serves his country with his spade, just as a man in the middle ranks of life serves it with his sword, pen, or lancet. **1875** JOWETT *Plato* (ed. 2) V. 527 Those who serve their country ought to serve without receiving gifts.

**13. a.** *intr.* To take one's part in war under a sovereign or commander; to be a soldier or man-of-war's-man. Said also of a ship.

**1518** SIR J. STILE in Ellis *Orig. Lett.* Ser. III. I. 192 The said Master George gonner,.. wol not in no wise serve any lenger here. **1523** BP. FOX *Ibid.* 323 Souldyers.. contynually attendante and servinge in the werre uppon the said borders. **1573** *Satir. Poems Reform.* xxxix. 158 The Suddartis swarfit, and said they wold not sar. **1585** T. WASHINGTON tr. *Nicholay's Voy.* I. xvii. 19b, [He] sent his gally.. to serue in the warres. **1599** SHAKS. *Hen. V*, IV. vii. 154 Who seru'st thou under? *Will.* Vnder Captaine Gower, my Liege. **1601** R. JOHNSON *Kingd. & Commw.* (1603) 95 The Ianizers, who serve with muskettes of longer and bigger bore then those of the germans. **1632** MASSINGER *Maid of Honour* I. i, You are S[r] A knight of Malta, and as I have heard, Have serv'd against the Turke. *a* **1700** EVELYN *Diary* 26 Apr. 1689, People being generally disaffected.. so that the sea and land men would scarce serve without compulsion. **1744** BIRCH *Life Boyle* 201 He.. then went to Scotland, where he served in the army till 1655. **1849** MACAULAY *Hist. Eng.* iii. I. 301 In 1666, John Sheffield, Earl of Mulgrave,.. volunteered to serve at sea against the Dutch. **1855** G. C. LEWIS *Credib. Rom. Hist.* II. 298 Pay had been introduced, in order to overcome the reluctance of the citizens to serve. **1869** E. A. PARKES *Pract. Hygiene* (ed. 3) 268 The 84th Regiment, in which I formerly served.

†**b.** Phr. ***to see and serve***: cf. *to see service* (SERVICE 12d). *Obs.*

**1590** SIR J. SMYTHE *Disc. Weapons* Ded. 1b, That haue seene and serued in the well ordered warres of Emperours or Kings. **1602** SHAKS. *Ham.* IV. vii. 84 I'ue seene my selfe, and seru'd against the French.

**c.** To be employed as a sailor in the mercantile marine.

**1864** TENNYSON *En. Arden* 52 [He had] served a year On board a merchantman, and made himself Full sailor. *Ibid.* 120 The master of that ship Enoch had served in.

**14. a.** *trans.* To perform the duties of (an office, cure of souls, etc.). Also, to go through a tenure of (a terminal office).

? **1404–8** *26 Pol. Poems* v. 46 Let eche man serue his charge in skylle. **1500–20** DUNBAR *Poems* lxxxi. 97 The ballance gois vnevin, That thow allace to serff hes kirkis sevin. **1557** in Warden *Burgh Laws Dundee*, etc. (1872) 335 Albeit he hes not seruit dewtie in all poyntis as become him of ye Craft. **1571** *Act 13 Eliz.* c. 20 §2 His Curat.. that shall there serve the Cure for hym. **1603** SHAKS. *Meas. for M.* II. i. 281 They do you wrong to put you so oft vpon't. Are there not men in your Ward sufficient to serue it? **1711** *Act 10 Anne*, c. 14 (*title*) For exempting Apothecaries from serving Parish and Ward-Offices. **1786** BURNS *To Gavin Hamilton* i, As lief then I'd have then, Your clerkship he should sair. **1824** G. CHALMERS *Caledonia* III. II. viii. 164 A Vicarage was established for serving the Cure. **1885** *Act 48 & 49 Vict.* c. 54 §9 The whole of the stipends to the curates serving any such benefice shall not exceed [etc.]. **1886** C. E. PASCOE *London of To-day* xxvi. (ed. 3) 240 The Lord Mayor.. must have served the office of sheriff.

**b.** To work for, assist at, take part in (a function); to take part in the service of (an institution); esp. to minister, discharge religious functions in (a church) or at (an altar).

**1477–9** *Rec. St. Mary at Hill* 80 Paid to John Modley, for servyng the quere for þe termez of Mydsomer & Mighelmasse. **1565** ALLEN *Defence Purg.* II. x. (1886) 299 Such as would profess the truth and serve the Altar. **1573** in Feuillerat *Revels Q. Eliz.* (1908) 218 For the children that served the Mask. **1673** CAVE *Prim. Chr.* III. ii. 253 A Gentile Player that served the Theatre. **1840** K. H. DIGBY *Mores Cath.* x. ii. (1847) III. 240/1 His monasteries were served by priests from without. **1868** FREEMAN *Norm. Conq.* II. x. 458 He found his church small, poor, served only by four or five canons. **1892** J. H. POLLEN *Acts Engl. Martyrs* 358 In the following year he came on the English Mission, which he served for seven years.

**c.** To attend (an auction).

**1854** W. CHAMBERS *Things in Amer.* 282 One migratory company.. serving all the slave-auctions in the place.

**15. a.** *intr.* To perform official duties, hold office (e.g. as sheriff or M.P., or on a jury). Formerly with sb. as direct complement, ***to serve church-warden***, etc.

**1477–9** *Rec. St. Mary at Hill* 80 To the same Iohn.. seruyng as a paressh Clerke, for his wages, xiijs iiijd. **1632** Serving in juries [see JURY 1]. **1676** *Rector's Bk. Clayworth* (1910) 19 Mr. Dickonson promisd me to serve Church warden next year if I would excuse him this. **1696** PRIDEAUX *Lett.* (1875) 174 A very fitt person to serve in parliament. **1698** *Laws Nevis* xvii. (1740) 16 Several Gentlemen of this Island have heretofore refused to serve as Assemblymen. **1721** BAILEY, *Burgess*,.. one that serves for a Borough in Parliament. **1818** CRUISE *Digest* (ed. 2) III. 180 The Crown's having power to compel a subject to be a sheriff; and to fine him for refusing to serve. **1834** MACAULAY *Ess.*, *Pitt* ¶10 When Parliament met in 1735, Thomas made his election to serve for Oakhampton. **1851** *Gentl. Mag.* Apr. 419 Members returned to serve in Parliament. **1880** *Encycl. Brit.* XIII. 786/1 The class of persons entitled and liable to serve on special juries.

†**b.** Of a serjeant: ***to serve at the bar***. *Obs.*

**1362** LANGL. *P. Pl.* A. Prol. 85 Þer houeþ an Hundret In Houues of selk, Seriauns hit semeþ to seruen atte Barre.

†**c.** To have the office *to do* something. *Obs.*

**1390** GOWER *Conf.* III. 271 Asmod, which was a fend of helle, And serveth, as the bokes telle, To tempte a man of such a wise.

**16. a.** *trans.* To render useful service to, do good offices to (a person); to work for or assist *in* any matter.

**1638** MARQ. HAMILTON *Let.* 1 Dec. in *H. Papers* (Camden) 64 Thinking my self most miserabill, in thatt I haue nat beine abill to serfe you as I uoold. **1658** W. DUGDALE *Let. to Sir T. Browne* 9 Nov., I.. shall rest At your Commands wherein I may serve you, W. Dugdale. **1727** LADY M. W. MONTAGU *Let. to C'tess Mar* June (1893) I. 507, I am sure whatever I can serve my poor nieces and nephews in, shall not be wanting on my part. **1748** SMOLLETT *R. Random* ii, In all his calamities, they never discovered the least inclination to serve him. **1802** MAR. EDGEWORTH *Moral T.* (1816) I. xiii. 106 He ardently desired to serve his fellow-creatures. **1828** MACAULAY *Ess.*, *Hallam* ¶29 Cranmer rose into favour by serving Henry in the disgraceful affair of his first divorce. **1866** G. MACDONALD *Ann. Q. Neighb.* xiii. (1878) 270 The lad thinks you were the ladies in serving whom he got into trouble.

**b.** To render service to (a person's memory); to labour for (a cause).

**1711** SWIFT *Jrnl. to Stella* 25 Dec., Which is all I can do to serve her memory. **1847** MARRYAT *Childr. N. Forest* viii, A tradesman or outlaw, who has served the cause.

**II.** (Chiefly of things, primarily as a fig. use of senses in branch I.) To be subordinate, serviceable, or useful (to); to answer a purpose.

**17.** Of a thing: To be subordinate or subsidiary to (another).

*a* **1225** *Ancr. R.* 6 Þe vttre riwle, ðet ich þuften cleopede, & is monnes findles, nis for noþing elles istald bute forte seruie ðe inre. *c* **1440** *Jacob's Well* 194 Fastyng was made to serue prayere, & noȝt prayere to serue fastyng. Þerfore, prayere, þe heued, goth be-forn & þe handyll, fastyng, folowyth after him to be redy to seruyn hym, as þe heued of þe schouele is be-fore, & þe handyl þer-of is be-hynde to serue þe heued. **1667** MILTON *P.L.* v. 101 In the Soule Are many lesser Faculties that serve Reason as chief. *Ibid.* VIII. 87 That Bodies bright and greater should not serve The less not bright.

†**18.** *intr.* To be serviceable *to* (a person); be subsidiary *to* (a thing). *Obs.*

*c* **1375** *Sc. Leg. Saints* v. (*Johannes*) 196 Al creatur to be commone settis þare cur, as sone, mone, sternis al smal, presis þam to serwe til all. *c* **1450** *St. Cuthbert* (Surtees) 4114 Bot or he partyd þat pelfe he proued first in him selfe Whatkyn vertu it was of; To him full wele it serof. **1669** HOLDER *Elem. Speech* 8 As was said of the Senses, to which they [the tongue and pen] serve.

**19. a.** *trans.* To be useful or advantageous to; to answer the requirements of; to be used by. Const. inf. of purpose. With negative expressed or implied: To avail or profit (one) nothing.

*a* **1300** *Cursor M.* 3545 For-birth, he said, quat serues me? **13..** *Coer de L.* 1550 Off froyt here is gret plente! Fyggys, raysyns, in frayel, And notes may serve us fol wel. **1393** LANGL. *P. Pl.* C. xx. 173 A flaume.. That serueþ þese swynkeres to seo by a nyghtes. *a* **1400–50** *Wars Alex.* 1364 If he cuthe seke any sleȝt þat him serue wald. **1540** PALSGR. *Acolastus* Ep. Ded. b ij, He hath maystered the latinitie, and forced it to serue hym, to set forthe to all clerkes his intent and purpose. **1565** ALLEN *Defence Purg.* xvii. 283 Which forme of argument serued the Arians against the consubstantiall vnitye of God the father, and his son our sauiour. **1596** SHAKS. *Merch. V.* IV. i. 444 That scuse serues many men to saue their gifts. **1604** E. G[RIMSTONE] *D'Acosta's Hist. Indies* II. vi. 94 It brings forth a great aboundance of reedes.. which serves them to a thousand vses. **1662** J. DAVIES tr. *Olearius' Voy. Ambass.* 405 We knew the Convoy he intended us, would serve us in no stead. **1779** WARNER in Jesse *Selwyn & Contemp.* (1844) IV. 178 If my going to Milan, or going anywhere, would serve you, I would joyfully go directly. **1818** SCOTT *Br. Lamm.* xxxv, May your penitence avail you before God; with me it shall serve you nothing. **1852** DICKENS *Bleak Ho.* iii, I had youth and hope. I believe, beauty... Neither of the three served, or saved me. **1861** PALEY *Æschylus* (ed. 2) *Agam.* 72 *note*, The readings of the MSS... may be made to serve both sides of the question.

**b.** To be used in common by (a number of persons).

**1418** *E.E. Wills* 32 That than the forsaide ij. vestmentes shull remayne & duelle still alwey in the forsaide Chaunterie to serue the prestes of the same Chaunterie. **1563** *Knaresb. Wills* (Surtees) I. 93 A graie stoned horse to serve the towneshippe. **1612–13** *Aberd. Acc.* in *Spalding Club Miscell.* V. 92 Item,.. for ane quheil barrou to serue the toune, 12s. **1749** SMOLLETT *Gil Blas* II. vii. (1782) I. 166 A wretched flock-bed, covered with a doubled sheet, which had served an hundred different travellers, at least, since the last washing. **1774** WARTON *Hist. Poetry* I. Diss. II. a 3 b, At the beginning of the tenth century books were so scarce in Spain, that one and the same copy of the bible.. often served several different monasteries.

**c.** Of a bodily faculty or organ: To render its normal service to (the owner). Also const. inf.

*c* **1350** *Will. Palerne* 463 Min eiȝen sorly aren sogettes to serue min hert, & buxum ben to his bidding as boie to his master. **1553** T. WILSON *Rhet.* (1580) 214 And yet his tongue serued hym well otherwise, to vtter what soeuer came in his hedde. **1668** R. L'ESTRANGE *Vis. Quev.* II. (1702) 58 Will your Teeth serve you now to fetch out the Marrow of this Prophesy? *a* **1700** EVELYN *Diary* 8 Mar. 1681, Her eyes serving her as well as ever. **1818** SCOTT *Hrt. Midl.* xviii,

'And where are the two women?' said Sharpitlaw. 'Both made their heels serve them, I suspect.'

**d.** Of a thing: To supply the need or contribute to the working of (another thing).

**1580** BLUNDEVIL *Cur. Horses Dis.* xcv. 42 b, *Tenasmus*..is an vlcer in the right gut seruing the fundament. **1601** HOLLAND *Pliny* xxx. iv. II. 378 As touching the cricks of the nerues or sinews that serve the nape of the necke. **1668** CULPEPER & COLE *Barthol. Anat.* III. ii. 325 The third [branch of a nerve] by the Cavity of the Nostrils serves the coat of the said Nostrils. **1669** STURMY *Mariner's Mag.* v. xii. 49 Two Screws fitted to serve the four holes. **1878** STEVENSON *Inland Voy.* 4 Here and there a flight of steps to serve a ferry.

**20.** *intr.* To have a definite use or function, answer a purpose, effect or conduce to an end; to admit of being used for some end. With negative expressed or implied = to be of no use, not to avail.

†**a.** const. *of* (a purpose). [= F. *servir de.*]

*a* **1300** *Cursor M.* 9687 For quar-of serues ani a-sise Of sothfastnes, or of iustise, Bot for to yeme þe pes in land, Dom es þar-for sett to stand. *c* **1386** CHAUCER *Manciple's T.* 235 Wost thou wherof a racle tonge serueth? **1399** LANGL. *Rich. Redeles* II. 45 Than was it ffoly..To sette siluer signes þat of nouȝt serued. **1477** EARL RIVERS (Caxton) *Dictes* 8 b, An enuious man serueth of noght but to dispravse alle other. **1550** *Reg. Privy Council Scot.* I. 90 The fortis..be cassin doun becaus tha serve of na thing in tyme of pece.

†**b.** const. *to* (a purpose). *Obs.*

*c* **1305** *Land Cokayne* 47 Watir seruiþ þer to no þing Bot to siȝt and to waiissing. **1340** HAMPOLE *Pr. Consc.* 2775 Penaunce to thole here with gude wille, Serves here til twa thynges by skille. **1579** GOSSON *Sch. Abuse* (Arb.) 51 As to the body, there are many members, seruing to seuerall vses. **1662** STILLINGFL. *Orig. Sacræ* II. iii. § 6 To what end do these miracles serve? **1690** LOCKE *Hum. Und.* III. vi. §28 Every Man's Words being intelligible only to himself, would no longer serve to Conversation. **1737** WATERLAND *Eucharist* 124 The Uses which they serve to. **1749** FIELDING *Tom Jones* I. viii, This served to many good purposes. **1853** LYTTON *My Novel* x. xiii, How far his reasonings and patience served to his ends, remains yet to be seen. **1863** —— *Caxtoniana* I. xi. 195 The times in which they were composed, and the purposes to which they served.

**c.** const. *for* (a purpose).

**1390** GOWER *Conf.* III. 380 And ther fore servith scheld and spere. *c* **1470** HENRY *Wallace* II. 73 Gud ordinance, that serd for his estate, His cusyng maid at all tyme. **1576** FLEMING tr. *Caius' Dogs* II. (1880) 14 Such Dogges as serue for fowling. **1599** E. WRIGHT *Err. Navig.* F 2, These numbers..serue only for the finding out of the degrees and minutes of latitude. **1646** SIR T. BROWNE *Pseud. Ep.* III. xxi. 161 Unto others it [*sc.* water] performs the common office of ayre, and serves for refrigeration of the heart. **1669** HOLDER *Elem. Speech* 32 The Organs which serve for Articulation. **1831** SCOTT *Ct. Robt.* xxxii, To clear a convenient part of the seats..that it might serve for the accommodation of Prince Tancred's followers. **1844** S. TYLER *Baconian Philos.* I. (1846) 51 (Funk) The nerve of vision..can never serve for hearing. **1845** J. MARTINEAU *Ess.* (1869) II. 20 This, however, though of very wide application, will not serve for the solution of every problem.

**d.** const. inf. (expressing purpose or use).

*a* **1300** [see a]. **1340–70** *Alex. & Dind.* 797 Alle þe godus þat ȝe geten..Seruen for to sustaine ȝour vnsely wombe. **1477** [see a]. **1560** DAUS tr. *Sleidane's Comm.* 20 b, They will serve well to confute their Errours. **1604** E. G[RIMSTONE] *D'Acosta's Hist. Indies* IV. xxxii. 296 The grape ripens not well..so as they serve only to eate. **1634** SIR T. HERBERT *Trav.* 211 [The dodo's wings] serue only to proue her Bird. **1700** DRYDEN *Sigism. & Guisc.* 84 This little Brand will serve to light your Fire. **1768** GOLDSM. *Good-n. Man* I, I'm sorry they taught him any philosophy at all; it has only served to spoil him. **1850** TENNYSON *In Mem.* lxxvi[i]. 7 These..lullabies..May serve to curl a maiden's locks. **1871** B. STEWART *Heat* §91 The great latent heat of water serves to retard the melting of snow.

**e.** without const. Often with negative, or in rhetorical question, as ***what serves it?*** = what is the use of it?

**13..** *E.E. Allit. P.* A. 331 What seruez tresor, bot garez men grete When he hit schal efte with tenez tyne? *a* **1400–50** *Wars Alex.* 2374 (Dubl. MS.) What seruyd ȝitte all þar sapience & sleghtes of were? *a* **1530** HEYWOOD *Play of Wether* 716 (Brandl) Nother of them both that hath wyt nor grace To perceyue that both myllys may serue in place. **1566** GASCOIGNE *Supposes* I. ii, But this lighte serueth not very well, I will beholde it an other day, when the ayre is clearer. *a* **1586** SIDNEY *Ps.* xxx. ix, What serves, alas, the blood of me When I with in the pitt doe bide? **1785** BURNS *Epist. to J. Lapraik* xi, If honest Nature made you fools, What sairs your Grammars? **1793** SMEATON *Edystone L.* §209 It makes however excellent water mortar,..and will very well serve in those parts of the kingdom. **1815** J. SMITH *Panorama Sci. & Art* II. 343 If the manganese that has been once used, be exposed for some time to the air, it will serve again. **1820** SHELLEY *Hymn Merc.* liii, When no evasion Served—for the cunning one his match had found. **1837** CARLYLE *Fr. Rev.* I. VII. x, Barricading serves not.

**f.** To be usable or available *for*.

**1528** ROY *Rede me* II. (Arb.) 98 For the best meate awaye they carve, Which for their harlottis must serve, With wother frendes of their kynne. **1614** GORGES *Lucan* IX. 385 Then they vnto that Temple came, That serues for all the Libian name. **1639** FULLER *Holy War* II. iii. (1640) 46 This vision, though calculated for this one Bishop, did generally serve for all the non-residents which posted hither. **1662** CHARLETON *Myst. Vintners* (1675) 181 The same Parell serves also for White Wines upon the Frett. **1671** E. CHAMBERLAYNE *St. Eng.* II. 79 Besides these Courts serving for the whole Province, every Bishop hath his Court held in the Cathedral of his Diocess.

**21.** *trans.* To help to fulfil or bring about (an end, purpose, etc.); to be a means to, contribute or conduce to, tend to promote.

*a* **1568** ASCHAM *Scholem.* I. (Arb.) 82 They make Christ and his Gospell, onelie serue Ciuill pollicie. **1596** SPENSER *F.Q.* VI. x. 36 He had no weapon, but his shepheards hooke, To serue the vengeaunce of his wrathfull will. **1607** SHAKS. *Cor.* I. i. 94 Since it serues my purpose. **1667** MILTON *P.L.* IV. 398 As thir shape servd best his end. **1680** MOXON *Mech. Exerc.* x. 178 Turners have commonly two or three pair of Puppets to fit one Lathe, and always strive to use the shortest they can to serve their Work. **1736** BUTLER *Anal.* II. i. Wks. 1874 I. 156 Christianity served these ends and purposes, when it was first published. **1778** MISS BURNEY *Evelina* xxxii, Neither do I know another human being who could serve any interest by such a deception. **1819** SHELLEY *Cenci* II. ii. 107 It fortunately serves my close designs. **1884** *Manch. Examiner* 20 Feb. 5/1 Diatribes so blind and furious can do no good to the cause they are meant to serve. **1893** J. A. HODGES *Elem. Photogr.* (1907) 19 It would serve no useful purpose. **1895** *Law Times* XCIX. 545/2 We best serve our own interests in studying the interests of those for whom we act.

**22.** To discharge a specified function; to take the place of some specified agency.

**a.** *intr.* To be of use, admit of being used *as*, *for*, *instead of* (some means, agency, or the like).

**1387** HIGDEN *Trevisa* (Rolls) V. 171 And anon his mouþ bycom his ers, and servede aftirward in stede of his neþer ende. **1566** PAINTER *Pal. Pleas.* I. 135 A naturall abashmente and shame, which with the vaile of honor doth serue, or ought to serue for a bridle. **1590** SHAKS. *Mids. N.* II. ii. 41 One turfe shall serue as pillow for vs both. **1606** KNOLLES tr. *Bodin's Commw.* I. v. 35 Let one example serue for many. **1642** FULLER *Holy & Prof. St.* II. xvi. 111 Those may make excellent merchants and mechanicks which will not serve for Scholars. **1651** HOBBES *Leviath.* III. xxxiv. 212 The Cloud served as a sign of God's presence. **1765** A. DICKSON *Treat. Agric.* (ed. 2) 280 When the land is wet, the furrows serve for drains. **1820** SHELLEY *Œdip.* I. 87 He'll serve instead of riot money. **1856** HAWTHORNE *Eng. Note-bks.* (1870) II. 145 Mr. Hall, being familiar with the localities, served admirably as a guide. **1861** M. PATTISON *Ess.* (1889) I. 44 The Great Hall, serving for a council-chamber on days of general convocation, and as a banqueting-room for the oft-recurring festivities. **1910** *Encycl. Brit.* II. 28/1 A grasshopper or almost any large fly will serve for bait.

†**b.** With omission of *as*. *Obs.*

**1601** SHAKS. *All's Well* I. ii. 15 It [*sc.* the Tuscan Servia] well may serue A nursserie to our Gentrie, who are sicke For breathing, and exploit. **1654** Z. COKE *Logick* Pref., Nor could the Monuments of these Whirlegigs serve Muniments to their expiring glories.

**c.** *trans.* To be of use to (a person or thing) in the way specified; const. as in a.

**1593** SHAKS. *Rich. II*, II. i. 47 This precious stone, set in the siluer sea, Which serues it in the office of a wall, Or as a Moate defensiue to a house. **1595** DANIEL *Civ. Wars* III. xix. 48 So that a talke of tumult and a breath Would serue him as his passing-bell to death. **1614** GORGES *Lucan* VIII. 329 Vntill..Babylon they had throwne downe To serue the Crassi for their tombe. **1731–8** SWIFT *Pol. Conversat.* 112 My Stomach serves me instead of a Clock. **1818** BYRON *Juan* I. vi, Some..paradise or cavern, Which serves the happy couple for a tavern. **1845** J. COULTER *Adv. in Pacific* viii. 95 There was plenty of long grass about... This served me well for a bed.

¶**d.** ***to serve the place*** or ***stead of***: app. for 'to serve in place of' (cf. a).

**1827** SCOTT *Highl. Widow* v, She lighted..a splinter of bog pine which was to serve the place of a candle. **1837** C. LOFFT *Self-formation* I. 199 They may serve the stead of presence of mind, to a certain point at least.

†**23. a.** Of one's courage, conscience, inclination, etc.: To prompt, encourage (one), *to do* something; (with negative expressed or implied) to permit, suffer.

*c* **1380** *Sir Ferumb.* 255 Ys herte was god & sykerly serued him to do þat dede. *c* **1460** FORTESCUE *Abs. & Lim. Mon.* xiii. (1885) 142 But þer hartes serue hem not to take a manys gode, while he is present, and woll defende it. **1463** *Bury Wills* (Camden) 33, I grawunte my executours ful pover to do to hire as ther discrecyon wyl serve hem to doo. **1521** BP. LONGLAND in Ellis *Orig. Lett.* Ser. III. I. 252, I mynystred as my weykenes wold serve, in pontificalibus. *a* **1530** HEYWOOD *Play of Wether* 871 (Brandl) Yf your appetyte serue you so to do. **1534** MORE *Comf. agst. Trib.* II. Wks. 1185/1 My conscience can not serue me..to praise her calfe aboue twoo pence. **1540** PALSGR. *Acolastus* I. ii. F j, Go safely thyther as thy harte or courage serueth the. **1576** in J. Morris *Troubles Cath. Forefathers* (1877) 249 He cometh not to the church because his conscience will not serve him so to do. **1596** SHAKS. *Tam. Shr.* I. i. 38 The Mathematickes, and the Metaphysickes Fall to them as you finde your stomacke serues you. **1596** —— *Merch. V.* II. ii. 1 Certainely, my conscience will serue me to run from this Iew my Maister. **1597** MORLEY *Introd. Mus.* 100 Do so if your mind serue you.

**b.** *intr.*

**1591** SHAKS. *1 Hen. VI*, V. iv. 164 And therefore take this compact of a Truce, Although you breake it, when your pleasure serues.

**24.** Of the wind, weather, tide, etc.:

†**a.** *trans.* To favour, be favourable to. *Obs.*

**13..** *Coer de L.* 56 Anon the sayl up thay drowgh, The wynd hem servyd wel inowgh. *c* **1400** *Sowdone Bab.* 143 The wynde hem served, it was ful goode. **1483** *Act 1 Rich. III*, c. 9 §6 As soon as Wind and Weather will serve them after the said Two Months. **1585** T. WASHINGTON tr. *Nicholay's Voy.* II. i. 31 [We] found the wind to be at Northwest, which serued vs so wel, that..we sayled that night 60. miles. **1604** E. G[RIMSTONE] *D'Acosta's Hist. Indies* III. iv. 131 They come from the East, where the Easterly or Northerne windes do serve them.

**b.** *intr.* To be favourable or suitable.

**1443** *Acts Privy Council* (1835) V. 239 Yif winde & weder wol serve. **1540** *Act 32 Hen. VIII*, c. 14 To make..their departur from the said port..as soone as wynde and wether wyl serue. **1599** DALLAM in *Early Voy. Levant* (Hakl. Soc.) 5 Thare we came to an anker, for the wynde sarved not to pass by Dover. **1601** SHAKS. *Jul. C.* IV. iii. 223 On such a full Sea are we now a-float, And we must take the current when it serues, Or loose our Ventures. **1682** *Lond. Gaz.* No. 1740/4 The Tide serving early. **1760** C. JOHNSTON *Chrysal* (1822) II. 73 The wind and tide served for us. **1793** SMEATON *Edystone L.* §225 The weather serving at intervals, ..the first course..was finished. **1815** SCOTT *Guy M.* xxi, I propose to make a farther excursion through this country while this fine frosty weather serves. **1827** —— *Surg. Dau.* Pref., Leaving to the atmosphere to bring forth the young, or otherwise, as the climate shall serve. **1894** ASTLEY *50 Yrs. Life* II. 247 As the tide did not serve, the anchor was let go.

**25.** Of time, occasion, or the like: To be opportune, convenient, or favourable (to). Of one's leisure: To afford (one) occasion or opportunity, to be at one's disposal. Also const. inf. of purpose.

**a.** *trans.*

**1570** T. WILSON tr. *Demosth. Orat.* iv. 38 There is no let in your way to passe into his country, when occasion shal serue you. **1593** SHAKS. *3 Hen. VI*, IV. vii. 78 If fortune serue me, Ile requite this kindnesse. **1596** —— *Merch. V.* IV. i. 405, I am sorry that your leysure serues you not. **1621** G. SANDYS *Ovid's Met.* v. (1626) 97 But, ours perhaps to heare, Nor leasure serues you, nor is't worth your eare. **1818** SCOTT *Br. Lamm.* xxxiii, Tell Colonel Ashton..I shall be found at Wolf's Crag when his leisure serves him.

**b.** *intr.*

**1410** *26 Pol. Poems* ix. 146 And ȝe in batayle haue maystrie, And fortune serue, and god ȝow spede. **1540** PALSGR. *Acolastus* III. iii. P ij, While the tyme dyd beare .i. whyle the tyme serued. **1562** WINȜET *Cert. Tractates* I. Wks. (S.T.S.) I. 8 Tyme seruis not to schaw. **1579** LYLY *Euphues* (Arb.) 194 And as occasion shall serue I will requite thee. **1584** A. MUNDAY *Fidele & Fortunio* 711 in *Archiv Stud. neu. Spr.* CXXIII. 62 My leasure serues, and I will stand. **1599** *George a Greene* C 3 b, In spight of thee they now shall feede their fill, And eate vntill our leasures serue to goe. **1607** SHAKS. *Cor.* IV. iii. 32 The day serues well for them now. **1681** DRYDEN *Span. Friar* IV. iii. 62 Read that, 'Tis with the Royal Signet sign'd, And given me by the King when time shou'd serve To be perus'd by you. **1821** SCOTT *Kenilw.* xxiii, The large boughs which had been left on the ground till time served to make them into fagots and billets. **1879** G. A. SALA in *Daily Tel.* 21 July, At eating and drinking London I shall arrive, should occasion serve by-and-bye. **1879** SPENCER *Princ. Sociol.* §349 II. 36 The sportsman, narrating his feats when opportunity serves.

**26.** Of the memory: To assist or prompt its owner, be at his call, not to fail him. **a.** *trans.*

**1634** in *Fasti Aberd.* (1854) 398 The subprincipall..testifiet that since the twalt day of Marche last, as his memorie serwes him, the said principall did [etc.]. **1641** MILTON *Reform. Eng.* II. 70 You have now at length this question..as my memory would best serve me in such a copious, and vast theme, fully handl'd. **1695** *New Light Chirurg. put Out* 54 The Doctor's either Modesty or Memory hath not served him to insert [etc.]. **1861** S. BROOKS *Silver Cord* viii. (1865) 44 Or perhaps your memory don't serve you as well as it did. **1862** MRS. H. WOOD *Channings* lv, I think I did tell you so, Hamish, if my memory serves me right. **1895** BUDD in *Law Times* XCIX. 543/2 If my memory serves me, the late Sir Henry Jackson ..brought a Bill into Parliament on the subject.

**b.** *intr.*

**1660** F. BROOKE tr. *Le Blanc's Trav.* 31, I will content my self to discover a view of the country, as faithfully, and exactly as my memory will serve. **1911** SAINTSBURY in *Cambr. Hist. Eng. Lit.* VII. v. 104 So far as memory serves, there is not any passage in his entire work which [etc.].

**27. a.** *trans.* To suffice (a person) in regard to some need or requirement. Const. inf., or *for* (a purpose). Also, to last (one) *for* a specified time.

**1450** HEN. VI in *Rep. Hist. MSS. Comm.* Var. Coll. IV. 85 There vitailes ben not suffisant to serue them for iij wekes at the farrest. **1500–20** DUNBAR *Poems* xv. 24 Few wordis may serve the wyis. *a* **1530** HEYWOOD *Play of Wether* 692, I say we nede no water mylles at all For wyndmylles be suffycyent to serue all. **1562** TURNER *Herbal* II. 52 b, A romishe acre of it [medick fodder]..will serue iii. horses for an hole yere. **1599** SHAKS. *Hen. V*, IV. viii. 74 It will serue you to mend your shooes. **1662** J. DAVIES tr. *Olearius' Voy. Ambass.* 303 They provide Ice enough to serve them all Summer. **1697** DAMPIER *Voy.* I. 146 The 21st day we sent out our Moskito Strikers for Turtle, who brought aboard enough to serve both Ships Companies. **1711** ADDISON *Spect.* No. 119 ⁋3 A polite Country 'Squire shall make you as many Bows in half an Hour, as would serve a Courtier for a Week. **1734** POPE *Hor. Sat.* II. ii. 53 One half-pint bottle serves them both to dine. **1777** SHERIDAN *Sch. Scand.* v. ii, Never let me hear you utter any thing like a sentiment; I have had enough of them to serve me the rest of my life. **1821** SCOTT *Kenilw.* iii, Private apartments..bedizened fine enough to serve the Queen.

**b.** In sentences containing a negative: To satisfy, content, meet the wishes or demands of. Esp. in forms like 'nothing would serve him but..'.

**1634** SIR T. HERBERT *Trav.* 140 No other water would serue their pallat. **1684** BUNYAN *Pilgr.* II. (1900) 168 Nothing will serve me but going on Pilgrimage. **1809** MALKIN *Gil Blas* III. i. (Rtldg.) 76 He took such a fancy to me that nothing would serve him but I must be his guest at Segovia. **1821** SCOTT *Kenilw.* xxv, With those whom such reasons did not serve, they dealt more rudely. **1861** HUGHES *Tom Brown at Oxf.* vi, Nothing would serve him but that we should turn off for Hungerford at once.

**c.** To be sufficient for, furnish what is requisite for (a thing). Also, †to be a sufficient account of, be applicable to.

**1566** PAINTER *Pal. Pleas.* I. xliii. (1890) I. 248 Not suffring so much straw, as would serve the couche of two dogges, to be left vnconsumed. **1615** W. LAWSON *Country Housew. Gard.* (1626) 9 Lesse fencing serues six acres together, than three in seuerall inclosures. **1660** SHARROCK *Vegetables* 96 About twelve or fourteen quarter of lime serves an acre. **1662** PLAYFORD *Skill Mus.* II. (1674) 99 These Directions for the Bass-Viol do also serve the Treble-Viol. **1705** tr.

*Bosman's Guinea* 476 What hath been said of the Habits, Cattle and Fruit of the former, may also serve them.

**28. a.** *intr.* To suffice, meet the needs of the case; to be adequate or sufficient. Also, to last for a given period. Const. *for* or inf.

**1496–7** *Act 12 Hen. VII*, c. 13 §1 As mych of the goodez ..as shall serve for the payment of suche somme. **1523** FITZHERB. *Husb.* §126 Reed wethy is beste in marsshe grounde; asshe, maple, hasel, and whyte-thorne wyl serue for a time. **1549** *Bk. Comm. Prayer, Commun.*, Puttyng yᵉ wyne into the Chalice, or else in some faire or conueniente cup, prepared for that use (if the Chalice will not serue). **1592** SHAKS. *Rom. & Jul.* III. i. 101 'Tis not so deepe as a well, nor so wide as a Church doore, but 'tis inough, 'twill serue. *c* **1610** BEAUM. & FL. *Philaster* IV. ii, Bestow on me.. so much as may serve To keep that little piece I hold of life From cold and hunger. **1662** STILLINGFL. *Orig. Sacræ* II. iv. 4 Thus much may serve concerning the originall and institution of these Schools of the Prophets. **1699** DAMPIER *Voy.* II. ii. 119 The Indians make use of no more Land than serves to maintain their Families in Maiz; and to pay their Taxes. **1700** S. L. tr. *Fryke's Voy. E. Ind.* 9 Which [provision] a man must husband as he thinks best; it is to serve for the whole week. **1801** H. K. WHITE *Let.* Apr. *Life & Rem.* (1850) 256 My father generally gives me one coat in a year, and I make two serve. **1808** SCOTT *Marm.* VI. xxiv, Short greeting serves in time of strife. **1879** G. MACDONALD *Sir Gibbie* lxii, *Laverock* III, A hert for the micht o' 't Wad sair for nine men.

**b.** (Chiefly in certain negative forms.) To satisfy, be considered satisfactory, meet people's wishes or demands.

**1712** ARBUTHNOT *John Bull* II. xiii, 'Will nothing less than Hanging serve' (quoth Jack)? **1837** CARLYLE *Fr. Rev.* II. III. ii, Nothing will serve but you must gather your way-worn limbs and thoughts, and speak to the multitudes.

†**29.** To be valid, hold good; to be available *for*; to be satisfactory, pass muster. Of coin: To pass current, be accepted. *Obs.*

*a* **1467** GREGORY *Chron.* in *Hist. Coll. Cit. London* (Camden) 230 But þe prevelege wolde not serve that tyme for noo cause of eresy. **1526** *Pilgr. Perf.* (W. de W. 1531), 26 The coyne of one countre wyll not serue ne be admytted or receyued in an other countre. **1568** GRAFTON *Chron.* II. 774 Serueth this libertie for my person onely, or for my goods to? **1588** SHAKS. *L.L.L.* I. ii. 119 The world was very guilty of such a Ballet some three ages since, but I thinke now 'tis not to be found: or if it were, it would neither serue for the writing, nor the tune. **1726** AYLIFFE *Parergon* 123 A Bishop may prove himself to be a Bishop several ways... First, By the Bulls or Letters of his Election: but then this only serves in the Romish Countries.

**30.** *trans.* To suit, fit. (Chiefly of clothes.) *Obs.* exc. *Sc.*

**1540** W. G. *Answ. to Maister Smyth* vii. (Huth), Although a shypmans hose wyll serue all sortes of legges. **1553** T. WILSON *Rhet.* (1580) 154 Demonedes hauing crooked feete ..made his praier to God, that his shoone might serue his feete, that had stolne them awaie. **1591** SHAKS. *Two Gent.* IV. iv. 167, I was trim'd in Madam Iulias gowne, Which serued me as fit, by all mens iudgements, As if the garment had bin made for me. **1611** —— *Cymb.* IV. i. 3 How fit his Garments serue me! **1749** SMOLLETT *Gil Blas* II. iii. (1782) I. 136 With a doublet and breeches which would have served a man four times as big as me. **1790** SCOTT *Let.* 6 Aug. in *Lockhart* (1837) I. vi. 167 This character.. would serve most of them. **1808** JAMIESON, *To Sair*,.. to fit, to be large enough. The coat does na sair him, i.e. it is too little. **1879** 'SARAH TYTLER' *Bride's Pass.* v. in *Good Words* 198 I've no quarrel with his appearance; unless that I think it would better serve a pinging lassie than a bold lad.

**III.** To minister to a person at table; hence, to supply, furnish, present *with* (a commodity).

**31. a.** [Cf. sense 4 above.] To wait upon (a person) at table; hence, to set food before, help (a person) to food.

***to serve in*** (later ***on***) ***silver***, etc.: to give (a person) his food in vessels of silver, etc.

*c* **1250** *Kent. Serm.* in *O.E. Misc.* 29 Architriclin, þat was se þet ferst was i-serued. *c* **1275** LAY. 22776 þe hehȝe ibore men þane mete beare.. ech man þare sareuede his freonde. **13..** *K. Alis.* 1156 He dude serve Olimpias In gold and seolver, in bras, in glas. **1388** WYCLIF *Luke* xvii. 8 Girde thee, and serue me [1382 mynystre to me, Vulg. *ministra mihi*], while Y ete and drynke. *c* **1400** MAUNDEV. (Roxb.) xxxiv. 153 He has fyfty damyselles þat seruez him ilk a day at his mete. *a* **1533** LD. BERNERS *Huon* lxvi. 226 They.. sat down to supper, where as they were rychely seruyd. **1600** HAKLUYT *Voy.* III. 370 All the vessels wherein they are serued,.. were of golde. **1731–8** SWIFT *Pol. Conversat.* 22 Let your Betters be serv'd before you. **1766** GOLDSM. *Vic. W.* v, Our two little ones.. were regularly served after we had done. **1823** SCOTT *Quentin D.* xxvi, When I was only a refugee.. I was served upon gold plate by order of the same Charles. **1848** THACKERAY *Van. Fair* lxiii, There is a servant in scarlet and lace to attend upon every four, and every one is served on silver.

**b.** Const. *with*, †*of*: To supply (one) with food at a meal, to help (one) to food.

**13..** *K. Alis.* 539 To the mete they weoren y-set, No myghte men beo served bet, Neither of mete no of drynke. *c* **1386** CHAUCER *Prol.* 749 And to the soper sette he vs anon And serued vs with vitaille at the beste. *c* **1400** *Anturs of Arth.* xxxvi, In siluer sa semly þai serue þame of the beste. **1474** CAXTON *Chesse* II. iv. (1883) 51 Whan they had seruyd Alexander in vayssell of gold and siluer with dyuerce metes. **1717** LADY M. W. MONTAGU *Let. to C'tess Mar* 18 Apr., I was very sorry I could not eat of as many [ragouts] as the good lady would have had me, who was very earnest in serving me of every thing. **1781** COWPER *Conversat.* 335 Serve him with ven'son, and he chooses fish. **1864** MRS. H. WOOD *Trevlyn Hold* xxix, How many are there to serve with pie still?

†**c.** ***to serve*** (a person) ***forth*** or ***in***: to set his food before him. (Cf. 43.) *Obs.*

**1513** *Bk. Kervynge* in *Meals & Manners* (E.E.T.S.) 156 Than serue forth your souerayne withouten blame. **1629** WADSWORTH *Pilgr.* iii. 16 Now let vs come to the Collegiates or Students, and their diet: First they are serued in by seuen of their owne rancke Weekely and in Course.

**d.** Proverbs. ***to serve with*** (or †***of***) ***the same sauce***: see SAUCE *sb.* 3 a. ***first come, first served*** (also used with reference to sense 35).

**1523–**: see SAUCE *sb.* 3 a. **1545–**: see FIRST *adv.* 1 b. **1583** GOLDING *Calvin on Deut.* cxv. 707 That hee which hath gone about to do his neighbour harme shall be serued of the same sawce himselfe. *a* **1722** FOUNTAINHALL *Decis.* (1759) I. 9 They must wait their tour..; and he that's first ready must be first served. **1837** CARLYLE *Fr. Rev.* I. VI. iv, Their long strings of purchasers, arranged *in tail*, so that the first come be the first served,—were the shop once open!

**32.** *absol.* [Cf. sense 1.] To wait at table; to present or hand food to guests. †Formerly const. *of* (meat or drink); also *to* (a person).

*c* **1250** *Kent. Serm.* in *O.E. Misc.* 29 Hye spac to þo serganz þat seruede of þo wyne. **1297** R. GLOUC. (Rolls) 3950 Kay king of aungeo a þousend kniȝtes nom.. Of o sywte & seruede at þis feste anon. *a* **1300** *K. Horn* 234 Tech him.. Biuore me to kerue & of þe cupe serue. ? *a* **1400** *Morte Arth.* 892 He calles sir Cayous that of the cowpe serfede. *c* **1440** *Ipomydon* 57 He taught hym.. to serve in halle, Bothe to grete and to smalle. **1526** TINDALE *Luke* xxii. 27 For whether is greater, he that sitteth at meate: or he that serveth? **1528** ROY *Rede me* II. (Arb.) 93 Knyghtes and squyres honorable, Are fayne to serve at their table As vnto Dukes excellent. *a* **1700** EVELYN *Diary* 11 Apr. 1645, [The Pope] serves at their table.

**33.** *trans.* To set food on (the table), to spread *with* food.

The expression *to serve tables*, in *Acts* vi. 2 applied with reference to the administration of the alms of the church, is now sometimes allusively used with reference to the secular functions attached to the office of the clergy, viewed as encroaching on the time available for their more spiritual work.

*c* **1386** CHAUCER *Nun's Pr. T.* 23 Hir bord was servyd most with whit and blak. **1539** BIBLE (Great) *Acts* vi. 2 It is not mete yᵗ we shuld leaue yᵉ worde of God, & serue tables [Gr. διακονεῖν τραπέζαις, **1526** TINDALE, serve at the tables]. **1557** F. S[EAGER] *Sch. Vertue* iii. (heading), Howe to behaue thi selfe in seruynge the table. **1621** G. SANDYS *Ovid's Met.* VI. (1626) 120 The boards are princely seru'd. *c* **1850** *Arab. Nts.* (Rtldg.) 107 As soon as the guests were all arrived, the table was served, and they sat down to eat.

*fig.* **1884** L. A. TOLLEMACHE *Safe Studies* 359 The violent recoil against materialism which.. has induced many good ..persons to sell their scientific birthright and to serve tables. **1906** F. POLLOCK *Let.* 28 Dec. in *Pollock-Holmes Lett.* (1942) I. 136 Such men should not be put to serve the tables of university routine.

**34.** To set food before, feed (animals). Const. *with*, †*of*. †Of meat: To be food for.

**1523** FITZHERB. *Husb.* §146 Serue thy swyne bothe mornyng and euenynge. *a* **1533** LD. BERNERS *Huon* lii. 177, I can.. serue the houndes of theyr ryghtes. *c* **1566** *Merie Tales of Skelton* in *S.'s Wks.* (1843) I. p. lxiv, Well, sayd Skelton, for this once, serue my mare wyth horse bread. *c* **1586** C'TESS PEMBROKE *Ps.* LXXIX. ii, The livelesse carcasses of those That liv'd thy servants, serve the crowes. **1602** J. CHAMBERLAIN *Lett.* (Camden) 148 Wherein you served two pigeons with one beane. **1625** BACON *Apophth.* §278. 304 This Lady.. called to one of her Maids, that lookt to the Swine, and askt; Is the piggy serued? **1680** O. HEYWOOD *Diaries* (1881) II. 298 Mathew Midleborough's wife serving a swine. **1781** BECKFORD *Hunting* 199 No, master, I have not seen him [the fox]; but I smelt him here this morning, when I came to serve my sheep.

**35. a.** To attend to the request of (a customer in a shop). Hence, to supply (a customer) *with* a commodity which he has come to purchase.

**1362** LANGL. *P. Pl.* A. II. 190 Marchaundes.. Bi-souȝten him in heore schoppes to sullen heore ware, Apparayleden him as a prentis þe Peple for to serue. **1556** BP. BROOKS *Injunct. Gloucester* § 20 All tavernes.. and vitlinge houses to be shutte up at the time of Divine Service, and non to be served there at those times, but passingers onlie. **1727** *De Foe's Compl. Eng. Tradesman* (1732) I. xii. 147 If I am at any other part of the shop, and see him serving a customer, I never interrupt them. **1831** LAMB *Elia* II. *Ellistoniana* ¶ 2, E ...was serving in person two damsels fair, who had come into the shop ostensibly to inquire for some new publication. **1838** DICKENS *Nich. Nick.* xxxviii. [Squeers *loq.*] You came to the right shop for mercy when you came to me, and thank your stars that it is me as has got to serve you with the article. **1851** *Beck's Florist* 181 My wife told me she noticed the shopkeeper served other people before her, though she came first. **1901** W. W. JACOBS *Light Freights, A Marked Man* (init.), Knocking on the mantelpiece all night with twopence and wanting to know why he wasn't being served.

**b.** ***to serve the shop***: to attend to customers.

**1849** CUPPLES *Green Hand* iii. (1856) 34 The old salt had been rocking the cradle, with.. a line made fast to keep it in play when he served the shop.

**c.** *intr.* To attend to customers in a shop.

**1825** HONE *Every-day Bk.* I. 49 All the pastrycooks always try to get handsome ladies to serve in the shop! **1860** MRS. GASKELL *Sylvia's Lovers* vii, Is na' this Hester, as serves in Foster's shop? **1881** *A Chequered Career* 279 This young man serves behind a counter in a grocer's shop.

**d.** Phr. ***serve-yourself***, used *attrib.* of a shop, restaurant, etc., where the customer serves himself.

**1937** M. HILLIS *Orchids on your Budget* iii. 50 Those serve-yourself emporiums.. often have simple ones [*sc.* evening wraps].. which.. won't look very different from the costly one on your neighbor. **1949** E. S. GARDNER *Reluctant Witness* in *Case of Crying Swallow* (1974) 166 Mugs handed him a photograph. It showed a young woman standing in a serve-yourself grocery store. **1971** *Guardian* 2 Jan. 8/5 There are plans for.. bold new excursions into what some experts see as the coming serve-yourself hotel era.

**36.** *trans.* To assist (a workman) by handing him materials; to 'feed' *with* material for work.

**1525** in Gage *Hengrave* (1822) 46 Paide to John Haddenham for sarving of the mason for ij days.. viijd. **1547** in *Archæologia* XXV. 562 To Dingle for iiij dayes thackinge xvj d... To Dingles sonne for servinge him iiij dayes viij d. **1601** *Shuttleworths' Acc.* (Chetham Soc.) 137 A laborer, for iij days sarving the wallers, le day ijᵈ ob., vijᵈ ob. **1676** *Poor Robin's Intell.* 9–16 May 1/2 A Magistrate.. received a Letter.. as he was thatching a Hogsty, which being with much difficulty read by the Clark of the Parish that was serving him with Straw [etc.]. **1816** *Cheshire Gloss.* s.v. *Sarve*, The assistant who hands the straw up to the thatcher, or bricks and mortar to the bricklayer, is always said to 'sarve' him.

**37.** To give alms to, relieve (a beggar). *dial.*

**1765** J. BROWN *Chr. Jrnl.* 205 How extremely impudent is this beggar! I served him as I went in; and yet now he bawls for more. *a* **1800** PEGGE *Suppl. Grose*, *Serve*, to relieve a beggar. Derb. **1822** GALT *Provost* xiii. 106 Two bonny bairns.. going from house to house, like the hungry babes in the wood;.. as I was seeing them served myself at our door, I spoke to them. **1825** JAMIESON s.v. *Sair.*

**38.** *gen.* (Said of persons and things.) To supply, provide, or furnish with something necessary or requisite. Also, to furnish (a person, town, etc.) with a regular or continuous supply.

†**a.** const. *of* (something).

*a* **1300** *Cursor M.* 22508 þe sun þat es sa bright, And seruis al þis werld o light. **1362** LANGL. *P. Pl.* A. I. 17 He hihte þe eorþe to seruen ow vchone Of wollene, Of linnene. *c* **1400** MAUNDEV. (Roxb.) xxxii. 145 Oure land seruez vs of twa thinges, þat es to say of oure lyflade,.. and of sepulture. *c* **1440** *Alphabet of Tales* 334 He.. serryffed seke folk of swilk as þaim nedud. **1483** *Act 1 Rich. III*, c. 6 §1 The Commons ..be worse served of such Stuff and Merchandise as else should come to the said Fairs. **1500–20** DUNBAR *Poems* xxvii. 64 Quhen thay wer serwit of thair speiris. **1594** NASHE *Unfort. Trav.* L iij, She appoynted.. her to.. serue mee of such necessaryes as I lacked. **1600** HOLLAND *Livy* XXXVIII. 1002 That.. they might.. be served of a mart-towne for vent.

**b.** const. *with*.

*c* **1470** HENRY *Wallace* x. 320 Serwyt thai war with gud speris enow. **1515** *Sel. Cases Star Chamb.* (Selden Soc.) II. 97 The said dauy serued my lord darcy house in Berwyke with hooppis. *c* **1553** CHANCELOR in *Hakluyt's Voy.* (1599) I. 252 Colmagro serues all the Countrey about it with salt, and salt fish. **1615** G. SANDYS *Trav.* IV. (1658) 202 Naples is.. served with water by fountains and conduits. *a* **1700** EVELYN *Diary* (Chandos) 18 Dorking, which serves it abundantly with provisions. **1726–31** WALDRON *Descr. Isle of Man* (1865) 32 A woman who.. used to serve my family with butter. **1784** COWPER *Task* IV. 758 These [plants] serve him with a hint That nature lives.

**c.** without const.

**1511** *Guylforde's Pilgr.* (Camden) 22 Which condyttes serue all the Cytie in euery place. **1531** *Dunfermline Reg.* (Bannatyne Club) 363 Giff þe said abbot.. desyris ony pan wod of my lord of sanct andr' coill thay sall be seruit befor ony vþeris. **1617** MORYSON *Itin.* I. 4 A Conduit of water, which serves all the Towne. **1712** ARBUTHNOT *John Bull* I. ii, Besides, the Rascal has good Ware, and will serve him as cheap as any Body in that Case. **1868** *Chamb. Encycl.* X. 104/1 The distributing reservoir.. must therefore be higher than the highest house to be served. **1892** KIPLING *Barrack-r. Ballads* 79 The thatch of the byres will serve their fires when all the cattle are slain.

**d.** To supply with means of transit and conveyance: esp. of railways.

**1866** *Roy. Comm. Railways, Min. Evid.* 601/1 He said that we [the company] had really served Rochdale well with trains and accommodation. **1892** TURRELL & GRAVES *Roads Oxf.* 38 The country described in this book is served almost entirely by the Great Western Railway.

†**39. a.** *refl.* To make use *of*, avail oneself *of*. Also const. *with*, in the same sense. [After F. *se servir de.*] *Obs.*

In quot. 1560 = 'to make use *of* as slaves'; the choice of expression was suggested by the Heb. original.

**1560** BIBLE (Geneva) *Jer.* xxv. 14 Many nacions and great Kings shal euen serue them selues of them [so **1611** and **1884**]. **1594** R. ASHLEY tr. *Loys le Roy* 56 Seruing himselfe with meane fellowes. **1600** HOLLAND *Livy* XXXVII. 960 Intending.. to serve himselfe of the provision prepared for the enemie. **1648** tr. *Senault's Paraphr. Job* 6 God.. serves himself sometimes with criminals to execute his designes. **1655** JER. TAYLOR *Golden Grove* 53 It were well if they would serve themselves of this form set down at the end of this Diary. **1714** MRS. MANLEY *Adv. Rivella* 114 She had serv'd her self with Romantick Names, and a feign'd Scene of Action. **1750** WARBURTON in W. & Hurd *Lett.* (1809) 58 You may serve yourself of the following hints. **1846** TRENCH *Mirac.* vi. (1862) 189 *note*, In the intercourse of ordinary life our Lord served Himself, as was natural, of the popular Aramaic.

†**b.** *intr.* (? for *refl.*). To make use *of*. *Obs.*

*c* **1380** WYCLIF *Wks.* (1880) 79 þes feyned þeues seruen of þis, to forbede men to do goddis seruyce.

**40.** *transf.* (*trans.*) To ply, assail *with* (hostile weapons). *rare.* (So F. *servir.*)

**1375** BARBOUR *Bruce* XVI. 451 And with suerdis that scharply schar Thai seruit thame full egyrly. *Ibid.* 454. **1837** CARLYLE *Fr. Rev.* II. I. ii, Then to read or mumble something about the King's peace; and, after certain pauses, serve any undispersing Assemblage with musket-shot, or whatever shot will disperse it.

**41.** *Sc.* To satisfy or content *with* (food, etc.). (Cf. sense 27 b.) Hence, to give (one) a glut *of*, weary *of*.

**1768** ROSS *Helenore* (1789) 30 The squire.. Says cannily, I'm sure ye are not saird; Here's fouth of meat, eat on and do not spair't. *Ibid.* 47 It seems ye are na sair'd wi' what ye got. **1806** A. DOUGLAS *Poems* 148 (E.D.D.) Whan sair'd o' beef, they get a roast O' dainty rare sweet mutton. *a* **1819** A. WATSON in W. Walker *Bards Bon-Accord* (1887) 328 They saired them o' fighting wi' very few blows. **1886** WILLOCK

*Rosetty Ends* xii. (1887) 93 Dauvit tried nae mair experiments in galvanism. Ae dose o'it saired him.

**IV.** (Inversion of the construction in branch III. Cf. the converse development of sense in PRESENT *v.* 11–13.) To dish up (food); to deal out, present (a commodity).

**42. a.** To set (meat or drink) on the table or before a person; to bring in or dish up (a meal). †Also const. *to* or *into* (the table). Also (*is*) ***serving*** = (is) being served.

**13..** *E.E. Allit. P.* B. 997 Ho [Lot's wife] serued at þe soper salt bifore dryȝtyn. *a* **1400** *Sir Cleges* 382 The cheryse were servyd thorowe the hall. **1513** *Bk. Kervynge* in *Meals & Manners* (E.E.T.S.) 160 Fyrste on that daye [Easter] he shall serue a calfe soden and blessyd. **1560** DAUS tr. *Sleidane's Comm.* 25 A piece whereof is served to the Emperours table. **1597** BEARD *Theatre God's Judgem.* (1612) 268 A fishes head of great bignesse being served into the table. **1640** tr. *Verdere's Rom. of Rom.* III. ii. 7 Having fed heartily on a kid, that was served into the table. **1726** SWIFT *Gulliver* III. ii. 188 They cut up the joints that were served to his majesty's table. **1781** COWPER *Truth* 213 The dinner serv'd, Charles takes his stand, Watches your eye, anticipates command. **1836** MARRYAT *Midsh. Easy* xxxviii, But dinner is serving, go into the after-cabin. **1856** KANE *Arctic Explor.* II. vi. 74 He cooked and served our breakfast-meal. **1877** MISS A. B. EDWARDS *Up Nile* xviii. 487 After luncheon..coffee was served. **1885** *Truth* 2 July 2/1 It was getting on for two before supper was served.

*absol.* **1697** VANBRUGH *Prov. Wife* II. ii, *Cor.* Will your ladyship please to dine yet? *Lady Fan.* Yes, let 'em serve. **1709** MRS. MANLEY *Secret Mem.* (1720) III. 241, I see my People coming to tell us they have served: *Allons*..refresh yourself at Dinner. **1905** R. BAGOT *Passport* xxiv. 256 The men-servants were already bringing in the coffee, and Monsieur d'Antin was constrained to wait until they had served and retired.

**b.** const. *to* (a person) or dative. Hence also in indirect passive. Also in phr. ***serve-yourself***, used *attrib.* of foods or meals which one serves to oneself.

**1596** SHAKS. *Tam. Shr.* IV. i. 167 How durst you villaines bring it from the dresser And serue it thus to me? **1717** LADY M. W. MONTAGU *Let. to C'tess Mar* 18 Apr., After this they served me coffee upon their knees in the finest japan china. **1743** BULKELEY & CUMMINS *Voy. S. Seas* 88 This afternoon the People insisted to be serv'd Brandy out of the Casks that were buried Under-ground; accordingly they were serv'd half a Pint each Man. **1848** THACKERAY *Van. Fair* liii, The Colonel's breakfast was served to him in the same dingy.. plated ware. **1859** TENNYSON *Enid* 304 So that ye do not serve me sparrow-hawks For supper. **1971** M. LEE *Dying for Fun* ii. 19 His host, left to himself, would have taken him to a little piece of America in London, with serve-yourself fried chicken. **1976** *Newmarket Jrnl.* 16 Dec., A serve-yourself buffet with a choice of several hot and cold dishes is the ideal solution to entertaining over the festive season.

**c.** To dish up or send to the table in a specified manner or *with* some other edible.

*c* **1430** *Two Cookery-bks.* I. 6 As men seruyth furmenty wyth venyson. *c* **1450** *Ibid.* II. 83 And so serue hit hote. **1747** MRS. GLASSE *Cookery* ii. 50 Bake them [Larks] in a gentle Oven, serve them without Sauce. **1849** M. ARNOLD *Sick King Bokhara* 287 Cherries served in drifts of snow. **1864** *Englishw. in India* 145 Boil these gently together and serve on toast. **1884** HOWELLS in *Harper's Mag.* Dec. 111/2 Everything is served *à la Russe*.

**d.** To hand out (food) in portions; = HELP *v.* 8 b.

**1682** G. ROSE *Sch. Instruct. Officers Mouth* 24 They ought to serve the Sweetmeats with a Fork, but the Dragee, or small Seeds of Sugar with a Spoon.

**43. a.** With adverbs, †*away*, †*forth*, †*forth in*, *in* (? obs.), *up*, in the same sense as in 42.

*c* **1430** *Two Cookery-bks.* I. 5 Serue it forth. *Ibid.* 13 þanne serue it forth ynne. *c* **1440** LYDG. *Hors, Shepe & G.* 208 (Harl. MS.) A fatt goos..Is served vp at the kyngis table. *c* **1530** *Doctrynall Gd. Servauntes* in *Anc. Poet. Tracts* (Percy Soc.) 8 Fyrste serue ye in the potage, And than eche meet after his degre. **1592** SHAKS. *Rom. & Jul.* I. iii. 101 Madam, the guests are come, supper seru'd vp. **1617** MORYSON *Itin.* III. 83 At supper they served in a peece of roasted beefe hot. **1667** MILTON *P.L.* IX. 38 Marshal'd Feast Serv'd up in Hall with Sewers, and Seneshals. **1711** ADDISON *Spect.* No. 108 ¶5 The Gentleman..had the Pleasure of seeing the huge Jack, he had caught, served up for the first Dish. **1747** MRS. GLASSE *Cookery* xi. 123 Put in the Meat again..and let it boil; then serve it away. **1775** S. J. PRATT *Liberal Opin.* lvi. (1783) II. 164 The dinner was serving up as I entered the dining-parlour. **1827** in Scott *Chron. Canongate* Introd. App., The dinner was very handsome (though slowly served in). **1878** W. S. GILBERT *H.M.S. Pinafore* II, And dinner served up in a pudding basin!

*absol.* *c* **1430** *Two Cookery-bks.* I. 7 Let boyle to-gederys, an serue in. *Ibid.* 8 Sette hem on þe dysshe, an serue forth.

**b.** *transf.* and *fig.* (Cf. *dish up.*)

**1390** GOWER *Conf.* I. 296 The beste wordes wolde I pike ..And serve hem forth in stede of chese. **1576** FLEMING tr. *Caius' Dogs* To Rdr., If I serue in their meat with wrong sawce. **1596** SHAKS. *Tam. Shr.* III. i. 14 Then giue me leaue to read Philosophy, And while I pause, serue in your harmony. **1633** G. HERBERT *Temple, Priesth.* v, Th' holy men of God such vessels are, As serve him up, who all the world commands. **1656** EARL MONM. tr. *Boccalini's Advts. fr. Parnass.* II. xiv. 243 History is meat not only well seasoned..but substantially and magnificently served in to please the curious pallat. **1711** *Medley* No. 23. 267 The Examiner utters Falshoods that are altogether stale and exploded; whereas Abel serves them up fresh and fresh. **1712** ADDISON *Spect.* No. 488 ¶2 Provided the *Spectator* might be served up to them every Morning as usual. **1848** BARTLETT *Dict. Amer.*, *To Serve up*, to expose to ridicule; to expose. **1875** MANNING *Mission Holy Ghost* xiii. 371 You serve them up to us like new articles of science.

**c.** ***to serve out***, to distribute or deal out (food, ammunition, etc.) in portions. Also jocularly (chiefly *Naut.*), to mete out or administer (corporal punishment); cf. 46.

**1793** J. MACDONELL *Jrnl.* 15 Aug. in *Five Fur-Traders of Northw.* (1933) 101 Our Bourgeois came up with us and ordered each man a dram, which I served out to them. **1802** RICHARDSON in *Naval Chron.* VII. 54 My grog was served out. **1819** SCOTT *Ivanhoe* xl, To preside over the stock-fish and ale, which was just serving out for the friars' breakfast. **1827** O. W. ROBERTS *Voy. Centr. Amer.* 67, I served out some kegs of gunpowder. **1867** SMYTH *Sailor's Word-bk.*, *Serving out slops*, distributing clothing, &c. Also, a cant term to denote punishment at the gangway. **1884** SIR S. ST. JOHN *Hayti* iii. 81 On many of the large estates, a certain number of lashes was served out every morning as regularly as the rations. **1887** F. FRANCIS *Saddle & Mocassin* xi. 207 The short measures of flour which 'Rowdy Jack', one of their fellow-men, served out.

†**44. a.** *gen.* To supply, furnish (a commodity); to yield a regular or continuous supply of. Of the earth: To yield, bring forth. Const. *to*. *Obs.*

**1575** GASCOIGNE *Kenelworth Castle* Wks. 1910 II. 129 What fruits this soyle may serve. **1590** SHAKS. *Com. Err.* IV. iv. 14 *Ant.* Fiue hundred Duckets villaine for a rope? *E. Dro.* Ile serue you sir fiue hundred at the rate. **1677** YARRANTON *Eng. Improv.* 102 Our People too, with this Money, make Cloth, and serve it cheap in all places where we send our Cloth. *a* **1700** EVELYN *Diary* 25 Oct. 1695, The pump he had erected that serves water to his garden.

**b.** *intr.* (? for *refl.*) Of a commodity: To yield a supply, to be forthcoming. *rare.*

**1575** GASCOIGNE *Fruits of Warre* cxxxvii, Three dayes wee fought, as long as water served. **1893–4** *Northumbld. Gloss.* s.v., Gas is said to *serve* when it issues more or less regularly from a fault, slip, etc., in a coal mine.

**45.** *trans.* (in *fig.* uses). †To deliver or deal *blows* or the like (*obs.*; cf. 43 c); †to play (one) a *trick*; to do (one) a (good or bad) *turn*.

**1591** SHAKS. *Two Gent.* IV. iv. 38, I remember the tricke you seru'd me, when I tooke my leaue of Madam Siluia. **1607** —— *Timon* I. ii. 237 What a coiles heere, seruing of beckes, and iutting out of bummes. **1794** MRS. RADCLIFFE *Myst. Udolpho* xxvii, It would have been serving you a good turn, ma'amselle, as well as myself. **1887** W. E. NORRIS *Major & Minor* III. 249 You never in your life served me a worse turn than when you prevented me from hitting that man.

**46.** To hand (a commodity) to a customer in a shop. (Cf. sense 35.)

**1862** MRS. H. WOOD *Mrs. Hallib.* III. vi, Ben Tyrrett's wife says will you let her have a gill of vinegar? Be I to serve it?

**V.** To treat in a specified manner. [Developed from the use of *to serve well*, *ill*, etc., in the senses of branch I. Cf. esp. sense 4 b.]

**47. a.** To treat in a specified (usually unpleasant or unfair) manner. Now chiefly *colloquial*.

*c* **1275** LAY. 9206 He lette smite him of þat heued..and þus he ȝam sareuede euerechone. **1297** R. GLOUC. (Rolls) 624 ȝif alle luþer holers were iserued so Me ssolde vinde þe les such spousbruche do. *c* **1386** CHAUCER *Clerk's T.* 584–5 As I his suster serued by nyghte Right so thenke I to serue hym pryuely. *c* **1412** HOCCLEVE *De Reg. Princ.* 3853 Allas! þat drynke so man serue schal! **1526** *Pilgr. Perf.* (W. de W. 1531) 49 The tree that bryngeth forth no good fruyte shall be serued in lyke wyse. **1589** PUTTENHAM *Eng. Poesie* I. xxviii. (Arb.) 71 Or else be locked into the Church by the Sexten as I my selfe was once serued reading an Epitaph in a certain cathedrall Church of England. **1611** SHAKS. *Cymb.* V. v. 248 She is seru'd, As I would serue a Rat. **1693** DRYDEN *Ded. to 3rd Misc.* Ess. (1900) II. 10 And no better than thus has Ovid been served by the so-much-admired Sandys. **1727** GAY *Fables* v. 7 All cowards should be serv'd like you. **1847** MARRYAT *Childr. N. Forest* xiii, If I served you as you deserve, I should now put my bullet into you. **1860** TYNDALL *Glac.* I. xvii. 119 On swerving a little..the mass turned over, and let me into the lake. I tried a second one, which served me in the same manner. **1870** *Murray's Handbk. Essex*, etc. 200 The nave piers have unfortunately been covered with a yellow wash, which..has been removed from some in the S. aisle with very good result. It is much to be wished that all the piers were so served.

**b.** ***to serve*** (a person) ***right***: to treat (an offender) as he deserves. Now chiefly in phr. ***it serves*** (me, you, etc.) ***right***; also colloq. ***serves*** (you, etc.) ***right***, (***and***) ***serve*** (you, etc.) ***right***, an exclamation of satisfaction at seeing a person punished for his folly or wrong-doing; also as *attrib. phr.*

**1587** HIGGINS *Mirr. Mag.*, *Iago* Lenvoy iii, This sleeper.. Which for his slouthfull sinne was serued right. *c* **1640** H. BELL *Luther's Colloq. Mens.* (1652) 303 The wretch (said Luther) was served right. **1705** tr. *Bosman's Guinea* 419 What think you, Sir, Were not these Villains right served? **1728** VANBR. & CIB. *Prov. Husb.* II. 31 They serv'd you right enough! will you never have done with your Horse-play? **1837** DICKENS *Pickw.* xlii, Natural death—..workhouse funeral—serve him right—all over. **1839** THACKERAY *Fatal Boots* Mar., But papa was stern for once, and vowed that I had been served quite right. **1841** BARHAM *Ingol. Leg.* Ser. II. *Misadvent. at Margate*, 'He's stolen my things and run away!!'—Says she, 'And sarve you right!!' **1885** J. PAYN *Talk of Town* I. 99 Confound the fellow!..it would serve him right if they tossed him. **1889** A. LANG *Prince Prigio* vi. 45 Everyone had heard of his disgrace, and almost everyone cried 'Serve him right!' **1935** H. STRAUMANN *Newspaper Headlines* i. 29 Lastly there is the *Daily Worker*, the Communist paper, with its serve-him-right attitude. **1946** N. E. ORCHARD in W. S. Knickerbocker *Twentieth Cent. Eng.* 164 Another little girl was sent off by herself when she needed punishment and made to read the family genealogy. Today when she visits the cemetery where her forebears lie, ..she walks between the tombstones, a 'serves-you-right' expression on her face. **1977** *New Yorker* 15 Aug. 66/2 The widespread serves-them-right judgment that greeted New York's misfortune.

†**48.** *Thieves' slang.* **a.** To rob. **b.** To maim, wound. ***to serve out and out***, to kill (cf. next). *Obs.*

**1812** J. H. VAUX *Flash Dict.*, *Serve*, to serve a person, or place, is to rob them; as I *serv'd* him *for* his *thimble*, I rob'd him of his watch; that crib has been *served* before, that shop has been already robbed, &c. To *serve* a man, also sometimes signifies to maim, wound, or do him some bodily hurt, and to *serve* him *out and out* is to kill him.

**49.** ***to serve out***: to punish, take revenge on; to retaliate on (one) *for* something objectionable. *colloq.* (orig. pugilistic slang). Also (*Hunting slang*), to 'punish' or smash (a fence).

**1817** *Sporting Mag.* L. 18 The butcher was so completely served out, that he resigned all pretensions to victory. **1819** MOORE *Tom Crib's Memor.* (ed. 3) 34 And whosoe'er grew unpolite, The well-bred Champion serv'd him out. **1836** COL. HAWKER *Diary* (1893) II. 113 I'll serve him out for it. **1862** H. H. DIXON *Scott & Sebright* 398 This was the third or fourth flight of rails that Cognac, who was very fresh after a frost,..had served out that day. **1863** KINGSLEY *Water-Bab.* 183 I'll serve you out for telling the salmon where I was. **1891** MRS. RIDDELL *Mad Tour* 9 He set his mind to work to consider how he could best serve me out.

**VI.** Technical senses (with various const.).

**50.** *Law.* **a.** To make legal delivery of (a process or writ). Const. *on* or *upon* (a person).

**1442** *Rolls of Parlt.* V. 43/2 If any Processe of suche Appell ..be awardet or servet in othir wyse. **1494** *Acc. Ld. High Treas. Scot.* I. 238 To the seruing of the breif of ydeotrye vpone the Erle of Suddirland in Inuerness. **1570–6** LAMBARDE *Peramb. Kent* (1826) 240 To serve the processe of that suite upon him. **1585** *Act 27 Eliz.* c. 3 §5 The same Privie Seale was duely served..upon the person of the same Heire. **1612** N. FIELD *Woman Weathercock* III. i, You are come to serue a warrant, or a Scitation. **1776** *Trial Nundocomar* 24/2 Has any notice been served upon you by Mr. Jarut? **1798** DALLAS *Amer. Law Rep.* II. 335 An attachment must be served by the marshall. **1896** *Law Times* C. 488/1 The vestry served a notice on the respondent, calling upon him to repair the drain.

*fig.* **1593** SHAKS. *Lucr.* 1780 The deepe vexation of his inward soule, Hath seru'd a dumbe arrest vpon his tongue. **1842** LOVER *Handy Andy* xxi, Some frank..girl would have been the only one likely to serve a writ on the jovial attorney's heart. **1847** DE QUINCEY *Sp. Mil. Nun* x. (1853) 22 Notice to quit was now served pretty liberally.

**b.** To present (a person) *with* a writ. Also, ***to serve in*** (cf. 31 c).

**1575** in D. King *Vale-Royal* (1656) I. 88 For which cause, he was served by a Pursevant from York. **1630** *Banquet of Jests* 135 A Waiting Gentlewoman being summoned into a Court to take an Oath (for she was serued in with a *sub pœna*) The Examiner asked how [etc.]. **1655** FULLER *Ch. Hist.* IV. 137 Never before was the Bishops served with such a prohibition. **1839** DE QUINCEY *Recoll. Lakes* Wks. 1862 II. 199 The holder of that place or fortune was immediately served with a summons to surrender it.

**c.** *Scots Law.* To declare (a person) heir to an estate, by the affirmative verdict of an 'inquest' or jury appointed to adjudicate the claim. Const. †*of* (an estate); now only with compl., ***to serve*** (a person) ***heir to***.

? An erroneous shortening of the phr. *to serve and retour*: see RETOUR *v.* 3.

**1506** *Reg. Privy Seal Scot.* I. 174 The inquest that servit him of his breif of the said vi merkis worth of land. **1533** *Acc. Ld. High Treas. Scot.* VI. 138 Ane inquest that servit Richert, umquhile lord Inuermeith, of..the landis of Inuermeith. **1582** *Reg. Privy Council Scot.* III. 558 He sall entir and obtene himself servit air as use is within the space of thrie termes. **1637** RUTHERFORD *Lett.* (1664) 54 O that he would..serve himself Heir to the poor mean portion I have. **1693** STAIR *Inst. Law Scot.* III. iv. (ed. 2) 449 Other Heirs.. cannot be served Heirs, but by a special Service, serving them to such particulars, whereunto they succeed, by Infeftment or Provision. **1815** SCOTT *Guy M.* l, We must pass over his father, and serve him heir to his grandfather Lewis. **1854** H. MILLER *Sch. & Schm.* xvi. (1857) 356 After getting myself served heir to my father before the Court of the Canongate. **1893** STEVENSON *Catriona* i, To-day I was served heir to my position in life.

*absol.* **1597** SKENE *De Verb. Sign.* s.v. *Breve de morte antecessoris*, Gif the persones of inquest..deliveris and servis *Negative*, in favoures of the defender.

**51.** *Tennis* (and similar games). †**a.** *intr.* To act as assistant or marker. Also ? *trans.* (see quot. 1611).

**1531** in *Privy Purse Exp. Hen. VIII* (1827) 180 Paid to one that served on the kinges side at Tennes at hampton-courte, in Rewarde, v[s]. *c* **1532** DU WES *Introd. Fr.* in Palsgr. 951 *Nacqueter*, to serve at tennes. **1611** COTGR., *Naquet*, the boy that serues, or stops the ball after the first bound, to make a better chace, at Tennis. *Naqueter*, to serue (or stop) a ball at Tennis.

**b.** *intr.* To start play by striking the ball into the opposite court.

**1585** HIGINS *Junius' Nomencl.* 296 *Datatim ludere*..to serue or to tosse from hand to hand. **1611** COTGR., *Blouse*, a close Tennis court,..hauing a house on either side to serue on. **1878** J. MARSHALL *Ann. Tennis* 162 The server continues to serve until two chases be made.

**c.** *trans.* To put (the ball) in play.

**1696** R. H. *Sch. Recreation* 97 Love is the Court, Hope is the House, And Favour serves the Ball. **1837** D. WALKER *Games & Sports* 255 The player who commences..must serve the first ball over a red line marked upon the wall. **1878** J. MARSHALL *Ann. Tennis* 161 The ball served must be struck with the racket.

**d.** To strike the ball to (one's opponent); to 'feed' *with* the ball. Also *fig.*

**1647** N. Bacon *Disc. Govt. Eng.* I. xliii. 111 And as at Tenis the Dane and Bishop served each other with the fond Countrey man. **1849** *Boy's Own Bk.* 29 (Rounders) Another in-player takes up the bat, and is served or fed with the ball.

**52.** Of a male animal: To cover (the female); esp. of stallions, bulls, etc. kept and hired out for the purpose. Also *absol.*

**1577** B. Googe *Heresbach's Husb.* III. (1586) 148b, At halfe a yeere old they [boars] are able to serue a sowe. **1621** *Shuttleworths' Acc.* (Chetham Soc.) 248 Given to Sir Raphe's man, when the little black mare was served at the Abbie, ij^s vj^d. **1714** Gay *Sheph. Week* Tuesd. 106 Then saw the cow well serv'd, and took a groat. **1837** Youatt *Sheep* 317 Ewes to be served by more than one ram. **1885** *Bell's Life* 15 June 1/2 Camballo will serve a limited number of mares at 70 sovs. each. **1909** *Ruff's Guide to Turf* IV. 145 List of principal stallions serving in 1909.

**53. a.** *Falconry.* To drive out game into the view of (the hawk). Said of the falconer or of the dog.

**1576** Fleming tr. *Caius' Dogs* II. (1880) 14 Of gentle Dogges seruing the hauke. **1891** Harting *Bibl. Accipitr.* 229 *Serving a hawk*, helping to put out the quarry from covert. **1897** *Encycl. Sport* I. 373/2 (Falconry) *Serve* (of the falconer), to put out the quarry from the cover for the falcon waiting overhead.

**b.** *Coursing.* (See quot. 1897.)

**1576** Turberv. *Venerie* 249 If there be no Cotes gyuen betwene a brase of Greyhounds, but the one of them serueth the other at turnyng. *a* **1600** in Markham *Country Contentm.* I. vii. (1615) 105 If one dogge turne the Hare, serue himselfe, and turne her againe, those two turnes shall be as much as a coate. **1897** *Encycl. Sport* I. 210/1 (Coursing) When a dog turns his hare, and keeps his place for another turn, he serves himself; or, losing his place, serves his opponent.

**54.** Chiefly *Naut.* [Formerly often in form *sarve.*] **a.** To bind (a rope, rod, etc.) with small cord or the like, so as to protect or strengthen.

**1627** Capt. Smith *Seaman's Gram.* v. 25 To sarue any rope with plats or Sinnet, is..to lay Sinnet, Spun yarne, Rope yarne, or a peece of Canuas vpon the rope, and then rowle it fast to keepe the rope from galling. **1669** Sturmy *Mariner's Mag.* v. xii. 64 Ropes..served close..with Yarn. **1775** Falck *Day's Diving Vessel* 54 The eyes, as well as the splice by which they were bent, were also served with inch rope. **1875** Bedford *Sailor's Pocket Bk.* x. (ed. 2) 360 Two men can worm and serve seven fathoms of 3½ inch rope in an hour. **1876** Preece & Sivewright *Telegraphy* 232 It [the copper conductor] is then served with a covering of tape which has been well soaked in Stockholm tar. **1895** 'J. Bickerdyke' *Sea Fishing* 60 For the simpler binding, intended merely to act as a protection.., we say we 'serve' the line rather than 'whip' it.

**b.** To wrap (a rope, bandage) round an object.

*a* **1586** Sidney *Arcadia* III. (Sommer) 295 Parthenia laid his head in her lap, tearing of her linnen sleeues & partlet, to serue about his wounds. **1806** A. Duncan *Life Nelson* 43 Her hull had long been kept together by cables served round. **1870** *Eng. Mech.* 11 Mar. 625/3 Over which a tarred rope..is 'served' or wrapped.

**55.** *Mil.* **a.** To operate, keep in play or action (a gun, battery, etc.).

**1706** Phillips (ed. Kersey), To *Serve a Battery*..is to see that the Guns play well. **1747** *Gentl. Mag.* 344 A constant fire of a numerous and well serv'd artillery. **1849** Macaulay *Hist. Eng.* v. I. 611 The cannon,..though ill served, brought the engagement to a speedy close. **1852** Thackeray *Esmond* III. i, The enemy's cannonade, which was very hot and well served. **1876** Doubleday *Forts Sumter & Moultrie* 163 An artillery-man, serving his gun.

**b.** *to serve the vent*: to close the vent of a muzzle-loading gun while it is being loaded.

**1828** Spearman *Brit. Gunner* (ed. 2) 175 Number..2, sponges; 3, loads; 4, serves the vent and primes.

**VII. 56.** *Comb.*: †**serve-image**, an idolater.

**1530** Tindale *Answ. More* Wks. (1573) 272/1 So art thou an Idolater, that is to say in Englishe, a serue Image.

☛ For *to serve one's* (*a, the*) *turn* (in various senses), see turn *sb.*

Hence **served** *ppl. a.* (chiefly with prefixed adverb).

**1747** [see 55]. **1884** Ruskin *Bible of Amiens* i. 1 At this halting-place in mid-journey there is a well-served buffet. **1907** Wyndham *Flare of Footlights* i, The well-chosen and perfectly served dinner.

†**serve**, *v.*² *Obs.* Chiefly *Sc.* and *north.* Also 3 sareve, 4–6 (chiefly *Sc.*) serf, *Sc.* serwe, 5 sarve. [App. aphetic a. OF. *deservir* deserve *v.* It may, however, be a use of serve *v.*¹, as the sense 'to gain by serving' may have been developed in the simple vb.; cf. It. *servire* to merit, deserve.]

**1.** *trans.* To earn or acquire a right to; to become, or to be, worthy of (reward or punishment, praise or blame); to merit; = deserve *v.* 1, 2.

*c* **1250** *Gen. & Ex.* 1686 Oc serf me seuene oðer ȝer, If ðu salt rachel seruen her. *a* **1300** *Cursor M.* 15849 Forsoth i neuer serued it, in dede ne yeitt in sau. **13..** *E.E. Allit. P.* A. 553 More haf we serued..Þat suffred han þe dayez hete. *c* **1375** *Sc. Leg. Saints* vi. (*Thomas*) 573 Þar-for, me think, I serwe no blame quhen I say: god luffis [etc.]. ? *a* **1400** *Morte Arth.* 1315 My lorde meruailles hym mekylle,..Why thow morthires his mene, that no mysse serues. *c* **1400** *Rule of St. Benet* (verse) 614 Vn-to hell we suld take hede, And were vs euer with al our mayn Fro filth of sin, þat sarues payn. *c* **1430** *Chev. Assigne* 194 For þe sauynge of hem þanke þou hast seruethe. **1456** Sir G. Haye *Law Arms* (S.T.S.) 298 Quhat blame serve we now..that brekis Goddis bidding. **1513** Douglas *Æneis* I. Prol. 78 Quhar I offend, the les repreif serf I. *a* **1578** Lindesay (Pitscottie) *Chron. Scot.* (S.T.S.) I. 195 It is tyme to seik your reward quhan ye haue serwed it. **1721** Kelly *Scot. Prov.* 319 They give you less wite than you serve.

**b.** with *inf.* or *clause* as obj.

*a* **1300** *Cursor M.* 9089 Sin i haf serued to haue þe scam, Gis me mi scrift, o godds name! *c* **1330** *Arth. & Merl.* 951 (Kölbing) Þei sche haue serued to be spilt, Þe child þer of haþ no gilt. *c* **1330** R. Brunne *Chron. Wace* (Rolls) 4900, Y serued neuere he scholde so do! *c* **1400** *Apol. Loll.* (Camden) 26 In þis maner of curse þat men curse man iustli for his misdede, was Crist not cursid, for He seruid not to be cursid. **1500–20** Dunbar *Poems* xxv. 81 And how nane servis to haif sweitness That nevir taistit bitterness. *c* **1550** Rolland *Crt. Venus* II. 335 Thow seruis weill on Rakkis to be rent.

**2.** *intr.* or *absol.* = deserve *v.* 3.

*c* **1275** Lay. 24154 And he þare eche cnihtes he ȝef alle hire rihtes, ech one he ȝaf heahte ase hii i-sareued [*c* 1205 ærned] hadde. *c* **1400** *Destr. Troy* 550 Þat ȝe me faith make, In dede for to do as I desyre wille, And my wille for to wirke, if I wele serue. *c* **1440** *York Myst.* ii. (*Playsterers*) 8 To suffir sorowe on soght, syne þai haue seruid so. *c* **1450** *St. Cuthbert* (Surtees) 866 As we haue serued, gif vs our mede. *c* **1550** Rolland *Crt. Venus* II. 361 Sayand, curst knaif thow sall haif afflictioun As thow did serue, rise, and resaif thy bill. **1575** *Mirr. Mag., Manlius* xiv, We either are rewarded, as we serue; Or else are plaged, as our deedes deserue.

†**serve**, *v.*³ *Obs. rare.* [ad. L. *servāre*, or aphetic form of preserve *v.*] *trans.* To preserve.

*c* **1386** Chaucer *Sqr.'s T.* 513 And in this wise he serued his entente That saue the feend noon wiste what he mente. **1470–85** Malory *Arthur* VI. xv. 207 Thenne wold I haue baumed hit [thy body] and serued hit and soo haue kepte it my lyfe dayes. **1559** Morwyng *Evonym.* 304 Whiche gathered diligently thou shalt serve in a phyall of glas.

**serveable**, variant of servable.

**serveiour**, obs. form of surveyor.

**serventism** (sɜːˈvɛntɪz(ə)m). Also **serventeism**. [f. It. *servente* (in *cavaliere servente*: see cavalier *sb.* 5) + -ism.] The system which countenances the devotion of a man to the service of a married woman; cicisbeism.

**1833** *New Monthly Mag.* XXXVIII. 151 The slavery of serventism. **1839** Darley *Introd. to Beaum. & Fl. Wks.* I. 29 Cicisbeism and serventeism were mentioned with no less complacency than if the dramatists themselves had been Italians. **1841** W. Spalding *Italy & It. Isl.* III. 277 We may still see serventeism ludicrously caricatured among the middle classes, where a domestic sometimes has to dress for the evening, and attend his mistress as a companion to the theatre or the promenade. **1843** *Penny Cycl.* XXV. 308/2 The cicisbeism or serventism of Italy and Spain.

**server** (ˈsɜːvə(r)). Forms: 4–5 **servere**, 6 **servar**, 5– **server**. See also servier. [f. serve *v.* + -er¹.]

**1.** One who serves or ministers to the requirements of another. Now *rare.* Also, †a servant.

*c* **1380** Wyclif *Sel. Wks.* I. 386 But Crist is among hem as a good servere. *c* **1440** *Alphabet of Tales* 60 Lo! yonder is his server. **1554** *Dyer's Acc.* in Sharp *Cov. Myst.* (1825) 186 Payd to ij servers of the cressets iiij d. **1868** Morris *Earthly Par., Man born to be King* 1277, I, who then Was but a server of poor men Outside our Abbey walls.

**b.** An attendant at a meal, one who serves food and drink to those sitting at table.

? **1460** *Bk. Curtasye* 532 in *Babees Bk.*, þe seruer hit next of alle kyn men Mays way and stondes by syde. **1545** *Ludlow Churchw. Acc.* (Camden) 21 Payde to the servars of wyne on Easter day. **1622** Mabbe tr. *Aleman's Guzman d'Alf.* II. 67 The Napkin where-with hee seru'd as Seruer. ? **1784** *Scot. Piper's Queries* 18 For one article having eggs the server of the table, as usual, laid the cloth on every one's knee, wherewith to hold their egg in when hot. **1868** Morris *Earthly Par., Land E. of Sun* 3065 While the servers bore Unto the guests rich meats and drink.

†**c.** An artisan's assistant. *Obs.*

**1481–90** *Howard Househ. Bks.* (Roxb.) 382 Item, to Iohn Hege, his server, for iij. dayes iiij.d. ob. **1514** *MS. Acc. St. John's Hosp., Canterb.*, Payd to ij tyllars & ij seruars ij days. **1605** Willet *Hexapla Gen.* 140 The seruer bringing one thing when the builder called for another. **1747** Hooson *Miner's Dict.* S ij, This Server likewise carries away the Wash-Ore, to the Ore-Place, it being their Business.

**d.** With religious signification. Now *arch.*

[**1530** Tindale *Answ. More* Wks. (1573) 282/1, I..am an image seruer & walke after myne own imagination & not after Gods word.] **1600** Palfreyman *Baldwin's Mor. Philos.* (ed. 4) 64 He cannot bee a true seruer of God, which serueth him not in the spirit of his minde, and in truth. **1678** Cudworth *Intell. Syst.* 446 Jupiter..made gods to be the curators of men, and he made men to be the worshippers and servers of those gods. **1900** *Pilot* 3 Nov. 551/1 The servers of icons..demonstrated that the doctrine of their opponents led to Judaism and Manichæism.

**e.** *Eccl.* An assistant at Mass who arranges the altar and makes the responses.

**1853** Dale tr. *Baldeschi's Cerem.* 292 Before leaving the sacristy with the Priest, the Server will light the candles on the Altar. **1879** Baring-Gould *Germany* II. 145 Two servers in surplices kneel before the altar in silence. **1894** *Westm. Gaz.* 20 Sept. 2/1 Working men generally act as servers at the early daily celebrations.

**f.** In various games: The player who serves or puts the ball in play.

**1585** Higins *Junius' Nomencl.* 296 *Dator*,..a player or seruer: he that in playeng casteth the ball. **1868** *Routledge's Ev. Boy's Bk.* 269 (Rackets) In a close-court game, the 'server' who serves the ball properly above the line [etc.]. **1875** 'Stonehenge' *Brit. Sports* III. I. v. §4. 690 The server [at lawn-tennis] then has to return the ball again, and so on till one player fails. **1897** *Encycl. Sport* I. 399/1 (Fives) The Server. A who begins serving, is bound to give C..the sort of service which he prefers.

**g.** *Anglo-Irish.* = process-*server*.

**1842** Lover *Handy Andy* xiv, To..harry a bum, Or 'clip a server' [*Footnote*, Cutting off the ears of a process-server].

**2.** Something which serves or is used for serving.

†**a.** A conduit or pipe for conveying water. *Obs.*

**1610** Holland *Camden's Brit.* I. 248 The Citizens likewise..deriued rilles and servers of waters into euery street.

**b.** = salver².

**1686** *Churchw. Acc. Pittington*, etc. (Surtees) 208 One silver server or a patten with a foot to screw on and a leather case. **1727** in W. Macgill *Old Ross-sh.* (1909) 133 Pewter spoons, server, basone, and potinger. **1816** Scott *Antiq.* iii, A little bit of diet-cake, on a small silver server of exquisite old workmanship. **1821** Galt *Ann. Parish* xii. (1895) 87 He took them [letters] both in to her ladyship on the silver server. **1894** Latto *Tam. Bodkin* xxv, My share o' the tea was brocht to me on a server.

**c.** *pl.* A spoon and fork for serving salad.

**1884** *Cyclist* 13 Feb. 243/1 Salad bowls and servers.

**servery** (ˈsɜːvərɪ). [f. serve *v.*¹ + -ery, after *pantry.*] A room from which meals, etc. are served. Also, = *serving-hatch* s.v. serving *vbl. sb.* 3.

**1893** *Builder* 11 Feb. 112 Kitchen... Servery... Pantry. **1899** *Athenæum* 15 Apr. 450/3 Chambers to let, unfurnished... Three Rooms, Bath-room, and Servery. **1942** G. Mitchell *Laurels are Poison* vi. 54 Kitty returned ..to get her own tea from the Servery. **1960** E. W. Hildick *Jim Starling & Colonel* ix. 75 They finally lined up in front of the servery. **1974** *Times* 3 May 11/3 The dividing unit acts as a servery, with drawers on the dining side for cutlery and linen.

**serves**, obs. form of service *sb.*¹ and *sb.*²

**servet**, obs. form of sherbet, serviette.

**Servetian** (sɜːˈviːʃən), *a.* (and *sb.*). *Eccl. Hist.* [f. *Servetus* + -ian.] **A.** *adj.* Of or pertaining to Michael Servetus (Miguel Servede), a Spanish heresiarch of semi-pantheistic opinions, who was burned at Geneva in 1553.

**1655** J. Owen *Vind. Evang.* Pref. 11 Every Heretical blasphemy,..whether it be Arian, Servetian, Eunomian [etc.].

**B.** *sb.* A follower of Servetus.

[**1564** Harding *Answ. Jewel* xv. 158 Anabaptistæ, Seruetiani, Antinomi.] **1645** Pagitt *Heresiogr.* (ed. 2) 35 *Servetians.* **1764** tr. *Mosheim's Eccl. Hist.* Cent. xvi. II. iv. §6 (1833) 531. **1874** *Blunt's Dict. Sects*, Servetians.

Hence **Serˈvetianism**, the heresy of Servetus.

**1655** J. Owen *Vind. Evang.* Pref. 12 A man..wholy infected with Servetianisme.

ˈ**serveting.** *Sc. Obs.* [f. *servet*, serviette + -ing¹.] Material for table-napkins.

**1612** *Sc. Bk. Rates* in *Halyburton's Ledger* (1867) 319 Linning cloth..Towelling and serveitting of Holland making the eln xxvi. s. vii. d. *Ibid.* 321 Servitting.

†**Serˈvetist.** *Eccl. Hist. Obs.* [f. as prec. + -ist.] A follower of Servetus (see Servetian).

**1621** Lodge *Summary Du Bartas* I. 9 The ancient and moderne Diuines, who haue disputed against the Arians, and Seruetists. **1728** Chambers *Cycl.* **1887** *Cassell's Encycl. Dict.*

**servi**, obs. form of serve *v.*¹

ˈ**serviable**, *a. Obs.* [a. OF. *serviable*, irreg. f. *servir* to serve; see -able.]

**1.** Willing to serve, complaisant, obedient.

*c* **1386** Chaucer *Clerk's T.* 979 (Camb. MS.) And sche þe moste seruyable of alle Hath euery chambre arayed and his halle. *c* **1400** *Rom. Rose* 6004 They..been, in good feith, more stable and trewer, and more serviable. *a* **1475** Ashby *Active Policy* 472 Also chese your servantes of goode draught, That wol attente and be seruiable. **1513** Douglas *Æneis* XII. ii. 88 The byssy knaipis..About thame stud, full ȝaip and seruyabill. **1638** W. Haig in Russell *Haigs* (1881) 219 Your loving and servyable friend.

**2.** Belonging to the servant class.

**1612** *Acts & Stat. Lawting, Sheriff, & Justice Courts* (Maitl. Club 1840) 160 Act for Servandis.—Item Forsamekill as thair is monie serviable persones that mareyis and takis up housis nocht haveing whervpone to live [etc.].

Hence ˈ**serviableness.**

**1530** Palsgr. 269/2 Servyablenesse, *seruiableté.*

**servial, -all**, obs. forms of servile.

**Servian** (ˈsɜːvɪən), *a.*¹ and *sb.* [f. *Servia* (properly *Serbia*: see Serbian *a.* and *sb.*) + -an.]

**A.** *adj.* = Serbian *a.*

**1808** C. Stower *Printer's Gram.*, Index, Servian alphabet. **1827** Bowring *Servian Pop. Poetry* Introd. 38 'Fair as the mountain Vila,' is the highest compliment to a Servian lady. **1879** Freeman *Hist. Ess.* Ser. III. 273 Had the Servian Czar entered Constantinople in the fourteenth century.

**B.** *sb.* **a.** = Serbian *sb.* a.

**1788** Gibbon *Decl. & F.* lv. V. 543 The language of the Dalmatians, Bosnians, Servians [etc.]. **1835** *Penny Cycl.* III. 328/1 A stronghold to the Servians in their wars with the Turks. **1878** *N. Amer. Rev.* CXXVII. 402 Christian volunteers from Russia helping the belligerent Servian.

**b.** = Serbian *sb.* b.

**1808** C. Stower *Printer's Gram.* 287 (*heading above the alphabet*) Servian. **1842** *Penny Cycl.* XXII. 127/2 The Servian was employed as a written language for the first time by Dositheus Obradovich. **1885** [see Croatian *sb.* and *a.*]. **1900** H. H. Chadwick in *Indogerman. Forsch.* XI. 168 The *-ā-* was probably accented, as in Servian.

**Servian** ('sɜːvɪən), *a.*² *Roman Hist.* [a. L. *Serviānus*, f. *Servius*: see -AN.] Of or pertaining to Servius Tullius, the sixth king of Rome, who is said to have organized the plebs into thirty local 'tribes', and to have encircled the city with a wall, of which extensive remains still exist.

**1839** *Dublin Rev.* Aug. 87 This method of election was a manifest reaction and encroachment upon the Servian constitution. **1843** *Penny Cycl.* XXV. 201 The probability is in favour of five tribunes, so that one was taken from each of the five Servian classes. **1855** LIDDELL *Hist. Rome* I. I. iii. 56 A person who once belonged either to a Romulian Tribe of birth or a Servian Tribe of place, always remained a member of that Tribe. **1886** PELHAM in *Encycl. Brit.* XX. 734/2 Only Etruscan builders..could have built..the Servian wall.

[**serviant.** A spurious word, due to Berners' having misread the F. *serment* oath as *seruiant.*

In the first quot. Berners seems to have taken the word as an adj. (cf. SERVIENT *a.*).

**1525** LD. BERNERS *Froiss.* II. clii. 167 b, There all the companyons made them seruyaunt to Aleyne Roux. *Ibid.* II. clxxiii. 210 No man myght entre in to that..company, without he make seruyaunt or othe, neuer to beare armoure agaynste the crowne of Englande.]

**service** ('sɜːvɪs), *sb.*¹ Forms: 1 serfise, 2-5 servise, 3 serviz, 3-4 serveis, 3-6 servyse, 3-7 servis, 4 servijs, servyss, *Sc.* serwise, 4-5 servese, serveys(e, 4-6 servyce, servys, 4-6 (8) serves, 5 cervyce, saryse, servysse, serwyse, 5-6 sarvys, 5-6 (8-9 *vulgar*) sarvice, 5-7 *Sc.* serwice, 6 sarves, servicie, *Sc.* schervice, scherwyce, servyiss, servyss, serwyce, 6-7 servies, 6-8 *dial.* sarvis, 7 cervis, 9 *Sc.* sairvice, 3- service. *Pl.* 7 service. [a. OF. *servise, service*, also *servige, serviche* (mod.F. *service*), ad. L. *servitium*, f. *servus* slave. Cf. Pr. *servizi, servis*, Sp. *servicio*, Pg. *serviço*, It. *servizio, servigio.*

The word in English, as also in the Romanic langs., has supplied the place of a noun of action to the cognate SERVE *v.*¹, and its sense-development appears to have been materially influenced by association with the verb.]

**I.** The condition of being a servant; the fact of serving a master.

**1.** The condition, station, or occupation of being a servant. (In mod. use almost exclusively *spec.* = *domestic service.*) **a.** In phrases with preps. † ***at, in,*** †***into,*** †***on, out of service; to go to, put to, set to service; to go into, put into, take into service; to place out at service.***

**1320-30** *Horn Ch.* 644 Icham comen to fand, For to win gold & fe, In seruise wiþ ȝour king to be. *c* **1400** *Destr. Troy* 4400 He ordant angels after his deuyse, And set hom in seruice hym seluyn to honour. *c* **1400** *Apol. Loll.* (Camden) 4 If a man haue an hired plowman in to serueys to dwel wiþ him. **1426** *E.E. Wills* (1882) 71 And I woll and pray ȝow þat Phelippe be kept on seruice stille. **1495** *Coventry Leet Bk.* 568 þat euery Maide & sole woman.. take a Chambre within an honest persone..or els to go to seruice. **1543-4** *Act 35 Hen. VIII*, c. 1 Persons..that shall haue any offyce ..or shalbe receyued in saruice with his grace. *a* **1548** HALL *Chron., Hen. VII*, 49 b, The sayde Barlo set me with a merchaunt of Middelboroughe too seruyce. *c* **1550** N. SMYTH tr. *Herodian* I. 10 The same beynge put to seruice in the Emperours house. **1557** *Order Hospitalls* F 5, Whether the same Childe be..in the Howse, or at Nurse; at Service, or els dead. **1592** *Soliman & Pers.* II. ii. 76 Least my maister turne me out of seruice. **1610** SHAKS. *Temp.* I. ii. 286 Caliban Whom now I keepe in seruice. **1749** SMOLLETT *Gil Blas* I. xvii. (1782) I. 104, I resolved to go to service, and hired myself to a great woollen-draper. **1771** —— *Humph. Cl.* 29 May, They..swarm up to London, in hopes of getting into service. **1798** O'KEEFFE *Wild Oats* II. ii, I place her out at sarvice. **1833** HT. MARTINEAU *Vanderput & S.* i. 12 All this is less than many a maid has that has been at service a shorter time. **1841** THACKERAY *Gt. Hoggarty Diam.* vii, He had put two of his daughters into service. **1881** O'SHAUGHNESSY *Songs of Worker* 176 Not even the fretting when the eldest girl In service far away forgot to write.

*fig.* **1600** SHAKS. *A.Y.L.* I. iii. 26 But turning these iests out of seruice, let vs talke in good earnest.

**b.** In other constructions.

*c* **1420** *Sir Amadace* (Camden) sc. i, Alle that ther wold seruyse haue, Knyȝte squiere, ȝoman and knaue. *a* **1450** *Knt. de la Tour* lxv. (1906) 86 The whiche Amon was Seneschall of the king,..and became riche by his seruice. **1525** in *Reg. Mag. Sig. Scot.* an. 1527 (1883) 97 Gif ony freman of the said craft pass furth of the toun or his band of his service be worne furth. **1567** PAINTER *Pal. Pleas.* II. xi. (1890) II. 268 [She] determined therefore..to seeke seruice in that house, counterfaytinge the kynde and habite of a Page. **1768** STERNE *Sent. Journ.* (1778) II. 124 (*Le Dimanche*), The sons and daughters of service part with liberty, but not with nature in their contracts. **1785** PALEY *Mor. Philos.* III. I. xi, Service in this country is, as it ought to be, voluntary, and by contract. **1870-2** LIDDON *Elem. Relig.* iv. §1 (1904) 137 Holy Scripture..speaks of sin as a service, the wages of which is death. **1876** HARDY *Ethelberta* xxx, I wish you could have given up service by this time. **1886** HERFORD *Lit. Rel. Eng. & Germany* 310 Grumshall.. goes to take service with Bartervile, a well-reputed Naples merchant. **1891** KIPLING *Light that Failed* ix. (1900) 157 'When did you leave service?'..'How did you know I was in service?..I was. General servant.'

*Proverb. c* **1412** HOCCLEVE *De Reg. Princ.* 841 Seruyse, I wot wel, is non heritage. **1631** BRATHWAIT *Whimzies, Undersheriff* 98 But service is no inheritance;..therefore.. hee beginnes now in his summer, to store up against winter. **1729** SWIFT *Direct. Serv.* Gen. Direct., Answer, that..a poor servant is not to be blamed if he strives to better himself; that service is no inheritance.

†**c.** Servitude, slavery. *Obs.*

**1340-70** *Alisaunder* 935 On weies & women awrak hee his teene And solde them too seruise in sorowe too liue.

**2. a.** Const. *of* or possessive: The condition of being a servant of a particular master.

*c* **1290** *St. Cristofer* 39 in *S. Eng. Leg.* 272 Ich am a man opon mi seruiz [*Harl. MS.* in mie seruise] and noman serui i nelle Bote mi louerd þat ich seche. *Ibid.* 59 Daþeit þanne, Cristofre seide, þat leng beo in þine seruise. *a* **1300** *Cursor M.* 9485 Nu has him sathanas in wald,..Quils he es thralled in his seruis He ne mai be fre on nakins wis. **1382** WYCLIF *2 Kings* v. 3 A lytill chyld woman caytife, that was in the seruyce [Vulg. *in obsequio*] of the wiyf of Naaman. *c* **1400** *Rom. Rose* 4594, I am so sore bounde him til, From his servyse I may not fleen. **1536** CROMWELL in Merriman *Life & Lett.* (1902) II. 5 For my sake to accept this berer salisbury again into your seruice. **1596** SHAKS. *Merch. V.* II. ii. 156 To leaue a rich Iewes seruice. **1716** HAWKINS *Pleas Crown* I. 130 If a Parent in a reasonable Manner chastise his child, or a Master his Servant, being actually in his Service at the Time. **1835** DICKENS *Sk. Boz, Mr. Watkins Tottle* i, That's the very housemaid... She went into Fanny's service when we were first married, and has been with us ever since. **1841** THACKERAY *Gt. Hoggarty Diam.* xii, You will hardly fancy that I..knew anything of the concerns of the Company into whose service I entered as twentieth clerk. **1881** BESANT & RICE *Chapl. Fleet* I. 26, I do not ask thee to enter my service, or to receive wages.

**b.** In religious use: The condition or fact of being a servant (of God). Cf. 13. †***to end in God's service***: to die in the faith.

*c* **1230** *Hali Meid.* 28 þe selie godes spuses, þe..in his anes seruise hare lif leadeð. **1297** R. GLOUC. (Rolls) 2277 Constance is eldoste sone in godes seruice Monek he made at winchestre. *a* **1300** *Cursor M.* 5482 Siþen him deid ioseph, þat wis, And endid in our lauerd seruis. *c* **1325** *Prov. Hendyng* 11 in Böddeker *Alteng. Dicht.* (1878) 288 Leue vs alle to ben wys, Ant to ende in his seruys. *c* **1450** tr. *De Imitatione* III. xi. [x.] 79 O þe acceptable & þe iocunde seruice of god. **1549** *Bk. Comm. Prayer, Morn. Prayer*, 2nd Collect, O God..whose seruice is perfect fredome.

†**c.** The condition of being the 'servant' (of Love, of one's lady). *Obs.* (Cf. 10.)

*c* **1374** CHAUCER *Compl. Mars* 189 For this day in hir seruise shal I dye. *c* **1386** —— *Squire's T.* 272 He moste han knowen loue and his seruyse. *a* **1450** MYRC 57 Wymmones serues thow most forsake. **1500-20** DUNBAR *Poems* xlvi. 8 This wes hir sentens sueit and delectable, A lusty lyfe in luves scheruice bene. **1588** SHAKS. *L.L.L.* v. ii. 276 And Longauill was for my seruice borne. **16..** MURE *Sonn. to Marg.* ii. 12 Gif I be thyne, no greiff can death impairt Sall mak me seime thy service to deny.

†**d.** A particular ministerial office or charge.

*c* **1250** *Gen. & Ex.* 3754 He [*sc.* Korah and his company] seiden he weren wurði bet to ðat seruise to ben set. *c* **1380** WYCLIF *Sel. Wks.* II. 247 þe sixte servise takeþ he þat is above in bysynesse..In þe sevenþe servyse is he þat haþ mercy in gladnes. **1382** —— *2 Cor.* v. 18 God..ȝaf to vs the mynisterie, or seruyse, of reconcilinge.

**3.** †**a.** A situation or place as servant (*obs.*). **b.** A particular employ; the serving of a certain master or household.

**1469** *Paston Lett.* II. 387 Whedyr that they shall sek hem newe servysys or not. **1505** in *Extracts Burgh. Rec. Edin.* (1869) I. 107 Ony maner of vagabounds, young fallowis or young husis, haffand na prettik nor seruice to life vpon. **1564** *Child-Marr.* 126 John Jackson came to this deponent, and willed to have a Service for a maide. **1596** SHAKS. *Merch. V.* II. ii. 165, I cannot get a seruice, no, I haue nere a tongue in my head. **1634** MILTON *Comus* 85 And take the Weeds and likenes of a Swain, That to the service of this house belongs. **1719** D'URFEY *Pills* (1872) III. 248 And doubtless for so small abuse, a young man may his Service lose. **1767** A. YOUNG *Farmer's Lett. to People* 181 The children..were put into the world in services. **1779** WARNER in Jesse *Selwyn & Contemp.* (1844) IV. 53 Her mother, who is now reduced to wish a service [as French governess] in a foreign land. **1818** SCOTT *Rob Roy* vi, It seems to me..that you might have found a service where they eat less, and are more orthodox in their worship. **1850** TENNYSON *In Mem.* xx, 'It will be hard' they say 'to find Another service such as this'.

**4. a.** The condition or employment of a public servant (of a sovereign or state). ***in the British, French,*** etc. ***service***: (chiefly of a soldier or sailor).

**1297** R. GLOUC. (Rolls) 2418 & hii ssolle be such þat no prince ne dorre hom vorsake Ac vor hor prowesse gladliche in to hor seruise hom take. **13..** *Guy Warw.* 704 & wiþ him felawes tventi,..þat wiþ þerl Rohaud hadde ben long, In his seruise armes to vnder-fong. **1396-7** *XII Concl. Lollards* vi. in *Eng. Hist. Rev.* (1907) XXII. 299 A kyng and a bisschop al in o persone,..a curat and an officer in worldly seruise, makin euery reme out of god reule. **1585** T. WASHINGTON tr. *Nicholay's Voy.* I. xvii. 19 b, He being in seruice of his most Christian Maiesty. *a* **1763** W. KING *Polit. & Lit. Anecd.* (1819) 55 My Lord Taaffe of Ireland, a general officer in the Austrian service. **1779** WARNER in Jesse *Selwyn & Contemp.* (1844) IV. 95 Charles Fox has made his motion for the removal of Lord Sandwich from his Majesty's service and counsels. **1839** THACKERAY *Fatal Boots* Jan., I have borne the commission of lieutenant in the service of King George. **1849** MACAULAY *Hist. Eng.* v. I. 594 That the three English regiments in the Dutch service might be sent to the Thames. **1897** CONSTANTINE *Mar. Engin.* vi. 51 Blasco de Garay, an officer in the Spanish naval service.

†**b.** ***horse of service***, a war-horse or charger.

**1577-86** STANYHURST *Descr. Irel.* ii. 20/1 in *Holinshed*, Of the horsse of seruice they make great store. **1585** T. WASHINGTON tr. *Nicholay's Voy.* IV. xxxiii. 155 b, Those whiche..might maintaine a horse of seruice, were..called knights. **1606** *Choice, Chance*, etc. (1881) 48 To see a horse of seruice drawe in a doung-carte. **1679** BLOUNT *Anc. Tenures* 116 That the said Robert ought to come armed upon his Horse of service, with twenty men at Armes [etc.].

**c.** ***to take service***: to enlist under a military commander, join a fighting force.

**1847** MARRYAT *Childr. N. Forest* xxvii, Recollect, that, whatever general you take service under, you will follow him. **1878** SIMPSON *Sch. Shaks.* I. 78 He.. had gone to Spain to take service against the Moors.

**5. a.** A branch of public employment, or a body of public servants, concerned with some particular kind of work or the supply of some particular need, as in ***the consular service, the customs service, the diplomatic service, the excise service, the*** CIVIL SERVICE.

**1685** W. HEDGES *Diary* (Hakl. Soc.) I. 176 Fearing Agent Beard and Councill at Hugly might be soe displeased with him for shewing any kindness to me, as to turne him out of yᵉ Service. **1776** MICKLE tr. *Camoens' Lusiad* Introd. 153 Thomas Pearson, Esq.; of the East India Company's Service. **1801** SURR *Splendid Misery* II. 194 A Neapolitan pirate originally, but who took to the land service afterwards. **1815** SCOTT *Guy M.* x, Francis Kennedy, of his majesty's excise service. **1835** *Act 5 & 6 Will. IV*, c. 19 §45 To prevent any Seaman..from entering or being received into the Naval Service of His Majesty. **1860** MRS. GASKELL *Sylvia's Lovers* xxiii, The commanding officer of the impress service. **1901** SKRINE *Sir W. Hunter* 308 With a small Service which has a few splendid prizes and many blanks, it is inevitable that [etc.].

**b.** ***the service***: the Army or Navy (according to the implication in the context) considered as a sphere of duty or occupation, or as a profession. Also, the Air Force and intelligence departments. So ***the*** (***United***) ***Services***, the Army and Navy.

For *the senior service* (the Navy), see SENIOR *a.* 2.

**1706** FARQUHAR *Recruit. Officer* IV. i, Sir, I wou'd qualifie my self for the Service. **1714** *Spect.* No. 566 ¶3 A Man has scarce the Face to make his Court to a Lady, without some Credentials from the Service to recommend him. **1777** EARL CARLISLE in Jesse *Selwyn & Contemp.* (1844) III. 208 No domestic reasons can be strong enough to justify a man in quitting the service at the opening of a campaign. **1833** MARRYAT *P. Simple* xxviii, I wish Mr. Harrison would stay on shore with his wife altogether,—it's really trifling with the service. **1842** BURN *Nav. & Mil. Techn. Fr. Dict.* Pref. (1852), My brother officers, or those of the Sister Service. **1845** STOCQUELER *Brit. India* (1854) 381 The merchants and others not connected with 'the services' could only be admitted by ballot. **1862** G. H. KINGSLEY *Sport & Trav.* (1900) 362 Every morning there is a small row of the United Services standing just abaft of the mainmast. **1872** *Routledge's Ev. Boy's Ann.* 185/1 The Service is going to the dogs.

**II.** The work or duty of a servant; the action of serving a master.

**6. a.** Performance of the duties of a servant; attendance of servants; work done in obedience to and for the benefit of a master. ***to do,*** †***bear*** (one) ***service***, to serve, attend on (a master); now *rare* exc. *poet.*

*a* **1200** *Vices & Virtues* 33 Ȝewerȝed bie ðe man..þe want his herte..more to mannes seruise ðanne te godes. *a* **1300** *Cursor M.* 28283 Ouer slaw i was for þam to ris, Reckeles to do þam þair seruise. **13..** *K. Alis.* 3138 Threo hundrod to-fore him stode, Flombardynges, knyghtis gode,..Redy to the kyngis servys. **1362** LANGL. *P. Pl.* A. III. 210 Seruauns for heore seruise..Takeþ Meede of heore Maystres. **1390** GOWER *Conf.* III. 145 Thre ther were That most service unto him bere. **1470-85** MALORY *Arthur* VII. xxiv. 251 Bothe I and these fyue honderd knyghtes shal alweyes be at your somons to doo you seruyse. **1586** *Shuttleworths' Acc.* (Chetham Soc.) 32 Margerie Heselden for tene wykes servies iijˢ vjᵈ. **1607** SHAKS. *Cor.* IV. v. 1 Wine, Wine, Wine: What seruice is heere? I thinke our Fellowes are asleepe. **1610** —— *Temp.* I. ii. 247 Remember I haue done thee worthy seruice. **1822** *S. Carolina Stat.* (1840) VII. 462 In case any male slave or slaves be so permitted..to hire out their own time, labor or service. **1845** S. FOX *Monks & Monast.* xiii. 147 He [the porter] was allowed the service of a boy. **1859** TENNYSON *Geraint & Enid* 405 Then tending her rough lord,..In silence, did him service as a squire. **1878** MANN *Dom. Econ.* 351 When there is a parlour-maid in the establishment her share of the service is the parlour and pantry work, and waiting at table.

*fig.* (of things). **1340** HAMPOLE *Pr. Consc.* 6389 What nede war þat þa creatures þan Shewed swilk servyse mare for man. **1535** COVERDALE *2 Esdras* vi. 46 The starres didest thou sett in ordre, and gauest them a charge, to do seruyce euen vnto man [Vulg. *ut deservirent homini*].

**b.** An act of serving; a duty or piece of work done for a master or superior.

*a* **1300** *Cursor M.* 15333 [Christ washing the disciples' feet.] þe seruis al i yow ha don. **1390** GOWER *Conf.* III. 156 Thus scholde every worthi king Take of his knihtes knowleching, Whan that he syh thei hadden nede, For every service axeth mede. **1600** SHAKS. *Sonn.* lvii. 4, I haue no precious time at al to spend, Nor seruices to doe til you require. **1610** —— *Temp.* IV. i. 35 Thou, and thy meaner fellowes, your last seruice Did worthily performe.

†**c.** ***the flesh's service***, sexual intercourse. Also ***the service of Venus. Obs.***

*c* **1315** SHOREHAM I. 1960 Ȝef þer ne mey noþere kendelyche Do þe flesches seruyse. *Ibid.* 1975 And þaȝ þat seruyse be foul, Ȝet hyt hys tokne of gode. **1398** TREVISA *Barth. De P.R.* XVII. iii. (1495) 605 The swete almonde.. kyndlyth the seruyce of Venus [orig. *venerem accendit*].

†**7.** The use of the sb. (in sense 6) as obj. to verbs of ambiguous meaning like ***pay, yield***, led to the development of the sense: Reward for service, wages, payment. (Cf. SERVE *v.*²) *Obs.*

*a* **1300** *K. Horn* 990 King þe wise, ȝeld me mi seruise. *a* **1300** *Cursor M.* 28397 Myn hird-men and als oþer maa Haf i þaire seruis halden fra. **13..** *Ibid.* 12390 (Gött.) Trein beddes was he wont to make, And þar-for his seruis to take. *c* **1325** *Song of Merci* 102 in *E.E.P.* (1862) 121 But ȝe þat hated cristendame..Ȝour seruise schal be endeles schame. *c* **1425** *Cast. Persev.* 846 in *Macro Plays* 102 Pay not þi serwauntys here serwyse! *c* **1430** *Chev. Assigne* 178 She.. delyuered hym his seruyse & he out of cowrte wendes. **1533** GAU *Richt Vay* (1888) 17 Thay that wil noth help thair nichtburs in thair necessite and wil notht len to thayme in thair mister without okker mony or seruice or raward.

**8.** In feudal use. †**a.** Feudal allegiance, fealty; profession of allegiance, homage. *Obs.*

**1297** R. Glouc. (Rolls) 3865 Þe king wende þo to parys ..& alle þe heye men of the lond þuder come ywis. Hor omage of hom & hor seruise he nom. **1390** Gower *Conf.* I. 259 But he [the king of France], that wiste nothing why He scholde do so gret servise After the world in such a wise, Withstod the wrong of that demande. *a* **1400–50** *Wars Alex.* 918 Þis freke all his franche of Ph[ilip] he haldis, And was a suget to himself & serues him aȝt. *c* **1489** Caxton *Sonnes of Aymon* xiv. 325 And I shall holde you quyte of all the servyse that ye owe me & your eyres also, for evermore. **1538** Starkey *England* 55 Gyuyng..to theyr pryncys and lordys al humbul seruyce and meke obedyence. **1595** Shaks. *John* v. i. 23 Vpon your oath of seruice to the Pope. *Ibid.* 34 Your Nobles will not heare you, but are gone To offer seruice to your enemy.

*fig.* **1523** Skelton *Garl. Laurel* 425 O noble Chaucer.. bounde ar we with all deu reuerence..To owe to yow our seruyce.

**b.** A duty (whether a payment in money or kind, a definite amount of forced labour, or some act useful or complimentary) which a tenant is bound to render periodically to his lord. Cf. ***knight-service*** 1.

**1338** R. Brunne *Chron.* (1810) 290 Þe barons..said, þei suld not so, Suilk a new seruise to reise ne to do. *c* **1380** Wyclif *Wks.* (1880) 26 Vpon þis seruyces þei han þes heiȝe statis & lordischipis. *c* **1450** *St. Cuthbert* (Surtees) 7984 Þe monkes possessiouns made he Fra all seruice and customes fre. **1491** *Act 7 Hen. VII* c. 19 Kyng Edward the fourthe.. graunted the Lordshippe..to Griseld..to have and hold to hir and to hir heires..by the service of a redde rose yerely. **1549** *Registr. Aberdon.* (Maitland Club) I. 434 Payand heir for ȝeirlie..ten penneis for bundage arrage or carrage and vthir dew seruice vsit and wont. **1651** Hobbes *Leviath.* II. xxiv. 129 Divers services reserved on the Land he gave his Subjects. *a* **1700** Evelyn *Diary* 11 Apr. 1689, When the King and Queen had din'd, the ceremonie of the Champion, and other services by tenure were perform'd. **1801** *Farmer's Mag.* Nov. 404 Landlords would soon find their advantage in converting all these services into a fixed rent. **1818** Cruise *Digest* (ed. 2) V. 611 The Duke of Bridgwater..granted the said premises to the said W. Murhall..freed and enfranchised from all services. **1883** R. W. Dixon *Mano* I. v. 13 The peasants groan..Weighed down by tolls, by services and dues, Which to their mighty lords they ever owe.

**c.** ***to hold in service*** [tr. AF. *tenir en service* (Britton), law Latin *tenere in servitio*]: To hold (land) not in one's own occupation ('in demesne') but in that of a sub-tenant. See demesne 1.

†**d.** A feudal holding. *Obs.*

**1362** Langl. *P. Pl.* A. II. 69 In al þe seruyse of Slouþe I sese hem to-gedere.

**9.** *transf.* **a.** In complimentary expressions: Respect, 'duty'. ***my service to you***: a phrase accompanying the drinking to a person. In epistolary use, ***give my service to*** = remember me respectfully to (a third person). ***to pay, present one's service (to)***, to pay a call of ceremony. Now *rare* or *Obs.*

**1601** Shaks. *Twel. N.* III. i. 106 My dutie Madam, and most humble seruice! **1606** —— *Tr. & Cr.* v. v. 3 Fellow, commend my seruice to her beauty. **1625** Massinger *New Way* I. ii, He will in person first present his seruice. **1646** Endecott in Hutchinson *Collect. Papers Massachusetts Bay* (1769) 158 [P.S.] My wife desires to have her service remembred to Mrs. Winthrop. **1679** Lady R. Russell *Lett.* I. i. 9 My kindest service to all the dear young ones. **1693** Congreve *Old Bach.* I. i. 4 It lies convenient for us to pay our Afternoon Service to our Mistresses. **1711** Swift *Jrnl. to Stella* 4 Apr., Give my hearty service to Stoyte and Catherine. *c* **1751** Chatham *Lett. Nephew* i. (1805) 3 Pray shew him this letter, with my service to him. **1773** Goldsm. *She Stoops* II, Sir, my service to you. **1778** Miss Burney *Evelina* xxi, Call..and give my service to him. **1816** Scott *Old Mort.* xxxiv, 'My service to you, Mr. Morton', he said, filling one horn of ale for himself, and handing another to his prisoner.

†**b.** *pl.* in the same sense. *Obs.*

**1605** Shaks. *Lear* I. i. 29 My seruices to your Lordship. **1614** J. Donne in Kempe *Losely MSS.* (1836) 345 My errand ys onely to deliver my thanks and services..to yo^r selfe, and all y^r good company. **1723** Atterbury *Let. to Pope* 10 Apr., Give my faithful services to Dr. Arbuthnot, and thanks for what he sent me.

**c.** ***at*** (a person's) ***service***: ready to obey his commands. (Cf. sense 25.) †***at your service***: used *ellipt.* as a phrase of politeness. Also †***yours to do you service.***

**1554** in Ellis *Orig. Lett.* Ser. III. III. 315 Youres to do yow service, as I am most bounden, duering lief Frauncis Yaxley. **1601** Shaks. *Twel. N.* I. v. 318 What hoa, Maluolio. *Mal.* Heere Madam, at your seruice. **1600** Sir W. Cornwallis *Ess.* I. xxiv. N 3, *At your seruice*, hath beene so conuersant, as one asking, what's a Clock? **1712** Addison *Spect.* No. 269 ¶5 The Knight told me..his Chaplain was very well, and much at my Seruice. **1771** Smollett *Humph. Cl.* 13 July (1815) 230 My name is Matthew Bramble, at your service. **1905** R. Bagot *Passport* xxxv. 408 'Ask me anything', Silvio replied. 'I am entirely at your service'.

**10.** The devotion or suit of a lover; professed love. *arch.* (Cf. 2 c.)

*c* **1374** Chaucer *Compl. Mars* 167, I yaf my trewe seruise and my thoght For evermore..To hir. *Ibid.* 183 What wonder is then, thogh that I besette My seruise on suche oon. **1500–20** Dunbar *Poems* xliv. 34 All wemen of ws suld haif honoring, Serwice and luve, aboif all vthir thing. **1596** Spenser *F.Q.* VI. x. 38 So well he wood her, and so well he wrought her, With humble service, and with daily sute. **1600** Shaks. *A.Y.L.* v. ii. 95 *Phe.* Good shepheard, tell this youth what 'tis to loue... *Sil.* It is to be all made of faith and seruice. **1611** —— *Cymb.* I. vi. 140 Let me my seruice tender on your lippes. **1859** Tennyson *Elaine* 119 Yourself, Now weary of my service and devoir.

**11.** The serving the sovereign or the state in an official capacity; the duties or work of public servants. ***On His*** (or ***Her***) ***Majesty's Service***: a formula (often abbreviated O.H.M.S.) printed on the cover of a letter to indicate that it is official (and therefore exempt from postage). ***secret service***: see secret *a.* 4 c.

**1389** in *Eng. Gilds* (1870) 30 Yat no man schal ben excusyd of absence at yat messe, but it be for ye kyngges seruise. **1536** *Cal. Anc. Rec. Dublin* (1889) 497 One that dyd good and trewe sarvys to owre soveren lord the kyng. **1568** in H. Campbell *Love Lett. Mary Q. Scot.* (1824) App. 27 You, taryying behynd, wold furder us in this her Majesties sarvys. **1617** Moryson *Itin.* II. 15 The Lords..because they so judged it best for her Majesties service, sent over Sir John Norreys. **1709** Swift *Project Adv. Relig.* Misc. (1711) 226 Men of great Abilities would then endeavour to excel in the Duties of a religious Life, in order to qualify themselves for publick Service. *a* **1713** Ellwood *Hist. Life* (1714) 12, [I] seldom went afterwards, upon those publick Services, without a loaded Pistol in my Pocket. **1829** Scott *Anne of G.* xxvii, 'And I,' said his father, 'have no wish to detain him on the service in which he is now employed'. **1837** Carlyle *Fr. Rev.* II. v. v, All Public Service lies slack and waste. **1874** Whyte Melville *Uncle John* xiv. II. 89 Three letters.. marked 'On Her Majesty's Service'.

**12. a.** The duty of a soldier or sailor; the performance of this duty. Often, actual participation in warfare; more fully ***active service.***

***piece*** (or †***parcel***) ***of service***: a military achievement or exploit. (In Shaks. used *ironically*.)

**1590** Sir J. Smythe *Disc. Weapons* 6 Our trained Low Countrie Captaines..some of them more hungrie after charge, spoyle and gaine, than skilfull to do anie great seruice. **1590** Barwick *Disc. Weapons* 7 And so dooth the matter fall out, if a parcell of seruice should be doon, where 500. [men] should be imployed therunto. **1593** Shaks. *2 Hen. VI*, v. i. 155 And such a peece of seruice will you do, If [etc.]. **1599** —— *Hen. V*, III. ii. 49. **1599** —— *Much Ado* I. i. 48 He hath done good seruice Lady in these wars. **1632** Massinger *Maid of Hon.* I. i. B 2 b, Pray you shew vs The difference betweene the city valour And service in the field. **1702** *Propos. Effectual War in Amer.* 9 When they [*sc.* the Companies] form a Battalion or go upon Service, the Eldest or Senior Officer should command. **1799** *Times* 1 June 3/2 General Moreau..caused the administrations that were unfit for the active service of the war..to be removed back towards France. **1828** *Sporting Mag.* XXII. 248 When I was a soldier we were on service together. **1829** W. Irving *Granada* lxvii. II. 160 It was evident, from the warlike character of El Zagal, that there would be abundance of active service and hard fighting. **1889** Gunter *That Frenchman* i. 10 Then I volunteered for service in Mexico, and fought my way to..a captaincy.

**b.** A military or naval operation in which a soldier or a regiment serves (often *pl.*); an expedition or engagement.

**1590** Barwick *Disc. Weapons* 7 The Countie of Creance had in the seruice against Charles the 5. the charge of 600. footmen. *c* **1594** Capt. Wyatt *R. Dudley's Voy. W. Ind.* (Hakl. Soc.) 4 Who made us this answear..that they came from the service of Brest, and withall delivered the truth of that honorable, allthough blooddy, service theare accomplished by our Englishmen. **1605** Bacon *Adv. Learn.* I. viii. §1. 41 b, Alexander..when hee receiued Letters out of Greece, of some fights and seruices there. **1647** Clarendon *Hist. Reb.* VI. §135 Then the King's forces entered the town after a very warm service, the chief officers and many soldiers of the other side being killed. **1748** Smollett *Rod. Rand.* xxxii, The captain..swore he would confine Mackshane as soon as the service should be over. **1760** *Ann. Reg.* 13 The late service..affords very little matter of improvement in the art of reducing or defending strong places. **1834** Medwin *Angler in Wales* II. 55 Nothing could be more harassing than that service. Driven from one stockade, they entrenched themselves behind another. **1844** *Asiatic Jrnl.* Ser. III. III. 407 The loss of the European Regiment during the foregoing services is stated as having been very severe.

†**c.** A manner of serving in warfare (e.g. mounted or on foot, with some specified weapon); a branch of the service (= arm *sb.*[2] 9). *Obs.*

**1610** Rich *Descr. Irel.* 37 The Galloglas succeedeth the Horsman..: his seruice in the field, is neither good against horsmen, nor able to endure an encounter of pikes. **1735** Johnson *Lobo's Abyssinia, Descr.* vii. 84 His force consisting only of Foot, and the Galles entirely of Horse, a Service at which they are very expert.

**d. to see service.** Of a soldier: To have experience of warfare. Hence (in perfect tense) of a thing, to have been much used or worn.

**1601** Shaks. *All's Well* I. ii. 14 Our Gentlemen that meane to see The Tuscan seruice. **1611** —— *Wint. T.* IV. iii. 71 If this bee a horsemans Coate, it hath seene very hot seruice. **1778** T. Townshend in Jesse *Selwyn & Contemp.* (1844) III. 304 He has an ardent desire to see service. **1794** Mrs. Radcliffe *Myst. Udolpho* xxxiv, There, take it—it has seen service, though it could do little in defending the castle. **1827** Scott *Chron. Canongate* iii, My face has seen service, but there is still a good set of teeth [etc.]. **1838** Mill *A. de Vigny* Diss. & Disc. (1859) I. 298 Fourteen years a soldier without seeing any service. **1891** A. H. Craufurd *Gen. Craufurd* 74 Many soldiers who had seen a good deal of active service.

†**e. man of service**: a veteran soldier. *Obs.*

**1590** Sir J. Smythe *Disc. Weapons* 6 b, Besides that, by the imployment of such a number of trained Captaines, the regiment..should bee the more full of men of seruice and skill. **1825** Carlyle *Schiller* III. 202 That rude tumultuous host which Wallenstein presided over... In this ludicrous doggrel..these men of service paint their hopes and doings.

**f.** *pl.* (See quot.)

**1802** C. James *Milit. Dict.*, *Services*, pecuniary disbursements, or payments which are made for military purposes.

**III.** In religious uses. (See also 2 b.)

**13.** The serving (God) by obedience, piety, and good works. Phrase, †***to do God's service.***

*c* **1175** *Lamb. Hom.* 155 Dauid..deþ us to understonden on hwiche wise þe halie Men hersumden ure drihten ine þisse liue, and hwiche mede heo sculen habben for hore feire seruise. *c* **1275** *Duty of Christians* 35 in *O.E. Misc.* 142 If we ..luuyeþ vre dryhte And doþ his seruyse myd al vre myhte. *a* **1340** Hampole *Psalter* xvii. 22 He..lufid vs in his goednes, noght for oure seruys. *c* **1380** Wyclif *Wks.* (1880) 6 þei don not goddis seruyce in hem selfe but drawen oþere men þerfro. **1521** Fisher *Serm. agst. Luther* iv. Wks. (1876) 343 He weneth that in so doyng he pleaseth god & dothe a specyall seruyce vnto god. **1552** Abp. Hamilton *Catech.* (1884) 39 Quharin standis the trew and principal service quhilk we aucht to God. **1563** *Homilies* II. *Almsdeeds* III. 180 Wyll he see vs lacke necessaries when we do hym true seruice? **1614** *Life & Death Geninges* 91 A Virgin who had wholy dedicated her selfe to the seruice of God. **1662** *Bk. Com. Prayer* General Thanksgiving By giving up ourselves to thy service. **1667** Milton *P.L.* v. 529 Our voluntarie service he requires. **1846** Ruskin *Mod. Paint.* II. III. i. xv. §12 There will come a time when the service of God shall be the beholding of him.

**14.** Worship; esp. public worship according to form and order. Now *rare* or *Obs.* exc. in ***divine service.*** †Formerly often, ***God's service, public service, common service.***

*c* **1205** Lay. 8071 Þe king bi-gon seruise on ælches cunnes wise æfter þan heðene laȝen. *a* **1300** *Cursor M.* 28251 In kyrk i wroght oft syth vn-ro Quen goddis seruis was to do. *a* **1340** Hampole *Psalter* 4 (Prol.) Þis boke of all haly writ is mast oysed in halykyrke seruys. **1340** —— *Pr. Consc.* 3455 When þe lyst slepe and wil noght ryse, And comes overlate tyl Goddes servise. *c* **1386** Chaucer *2nd Nun's T.* 553 Hir hous the chirche of seinte Cecilie highte..In which, in to this day, in noble wyse Men doon to Crist and to his seinte seruyse. **1534** More *Comf. agst. Trib.* I. Wks. 1146/2 Toward this purpose, are expresely praied many deuout orasons in the comon seruice of our mother holy church. **1597** Hooker *Eccl. Pol.* v. xi. §1 Solemne duties of publique seruice to be done vnto God must haue their places set and prepared. *Ibid.* v. xxix. §1 The attyre which the Minister of God is by order to vse at times of diuine seruice. **1629** Milton *Hymn Nativ.* xxi, A drear and dying sound Affrights the Flamins at their service quaint. **1749** *Minutes Method. Conf.* (1812) 41 Exhort those, who were brought up in the Church, constantly to attend its service.

**15.** A celebration of public worship.

Often without the article, where a particular occasion is indicated by the context.

*c* **1374** Chaucer *Troylus* I. 315 On other thing his look som-tyme he caste, And eft on hir, whyl that servyse laste. *c* **1440** *Alphabet of Tales* 144 When serves was done, he went vnto þe bysshopp & shrafe hym. **1470–85** Malory *Arthur* I. iii–v. 41 So vpon newe yeresday whan the seruyce was done, the barons rode vnto the feld. **1585** T. Washington tr. *Nicholay's Voy.* III. xxi. 110 b, The houre of seruice being come, the Maizins beginne to cry vppon the towres. **1597** Hooker *Eccl. Pol.* v. xxviii. §3 So that, according to this forme of theirs, it must stand for a rule, No Sermon, no seruice. **1599** Dallam in *Early Voy. Levant* (Hakl. Soc.) 23 Sarvis beinge ended, we Departed out of the chapell. **1600** *Weakest goeth to Wall* H 4, Then the Parish is like to haue no seruice to day. **1770** Goldsm. *Des. Vill.* 181 The service past, around the pious man, With steady zeal, each honest rustic ran. **1859** Jephson *Brittany* viii. 121, I looked into the church, where service was going on. **1882** Mozley *Remin.* (ed. 2) I. 55 He preached once at St. Mary's, and occasionally assisted in services.

**16. a.** A ritual or series of words and ceremonies prescribed for public worship, or for some particular occasion or ministration. Often with defining word, as ***baptismal, burial, communion, marriage service*** (none of these are so entitled in the Prayer-book). †***altar-service***, the Communion. †***book of service*** = ***service-book*** (see 38).

Phrases, *to read, say, sing service.*

? *a* **1100** *O.E. Chron.* an. 1070 (Parker MS.) Þa ȝewrað ede hine se arcebiscop Landfranc & bebead þam biscopan ðe þar cumene wæran..þa serfise to donde & eallan þan munecan þæt hi scoldan hi unscrydan. *c* **1305** *Oxf. Student* 63 in *E.E.P.* (1862) 42 Þo come þe maistres..þe seruise for to do. And þo hit was to ende ibrouȝt and þe bodi ibured [etc.]. *c* **1350** *Will. Palerne* 5059 Whan þe seruise was seid as it schold bene, þat fel to a mariage be-maked at cherche. *c* **1386** Chaucer *Knt.'s T.* 2054 To do the office of funeral seruyse. **1393** Langl. *P. Pl.* C. x. 227 And vp-on sonedays..godes seruyce to huyre, Boþe matyns and messe. **1396–7** *XII Concl. Lollards* iv. in *Eng. Hist. Rev.* (1907) XXII. 297 Þe seruise of Corpus Christi imad be frere Thomas. *c* **1400** *Ywaine & Gaw.* 2355 Sir Ywayn to the Kyrk yede, Or he did any other dede; He herd the servise of the day. **1418** *E.E. Wills* 31 To fynde Twey honestes prestes to singe goddys seruice for my soule..be vij ȝere next folwyng after my desese. *c* **1440** *Promp. Parv.* 454/1 Servyce, don for dede menn and women, *exequie.* *c* **1450** *Brut* 425 The Erchebisshop of Caunturburi..and othir Engelisshe Bisshoppis..diden this solempne seruyce there, and weddid hem togederis. **1543** in Rymer *Foedera* XIV. 766 Thies Bookes of Divine Service, that is to sey, the Masse Booke, the Graill, the Antyphoner, the Himptuall [*sic*], the Portans, and the Prymer, bothe in Latyn and in Englyshe of Sarum use. **1548–9** *Rec. St. Mary at Hill* (1904) 388 Paide for ij bookes of y^e new service, vijs. vjd. **1566** *Eng. Ch. Furniture* (Peacock 1866) 84 A mass booke portas wythe all other bookes of saruys. *c* **1585** [R. Browne] *Answ. Cartwright* 49 The dumbe ministers may be heard reading service. **1602** Shaks. *Ham.* v. i. 259 We should prophane the seruice of the dead, To sing sage Requiem, and such rest to her As to peace-parted Soules. **1635** Brereton *Trav.* (Chetham Soc.)

72 Here is only a curate maintained to say service. **1721** A. CAMPBELL *Doctr. Middle State* Pref. 7 Upon this bottom also were the Ten Commandments introduced into the Altar Service, for the first time. **1726–1857** [see BURIAL 5]. **1844** LINGARD *Anglo-Sax. Ch.* (1858) I. i. 14 The service of their church was performed in the Latin tongue. *Ibid.* I. ii. 90 This washing of feet formed part of the public service of the day. **1849** MACAULAY *Hist. Eng.* ii. I. 159 A baptismal service in which the sign of the cross might be used or omitted at discretion. **1883** J. GILMOUR *Mongols* xxvi. 317 A service consisting of the chanting of prayers and the blowing of trumpets is gone through.

†**b.** *spec.* The daily office or hours of the breviary (= OFFICE *sb.* 6 a); more fully ***divine service***. ***Our Lady service***, the Little Office of the Virgin Mary. *Obs.*

*a* **1225** *Ancr. R.* 8 Iðe ereste dole of ower boc, of ower seruise. *c* **1386** CHAUCER *Prol.* 122 Ful weel she soong the seruice dyuyne, Entuned in hir nose ful semeely. **1398** TREVISA *Barth. De P.R.* IX. xxix. (1495) 364 In fastyng tyme we reherse ofte the lj psalme in the seruyse of the daye. *c* **1440** *Alphabet of Tales* 166 Sho sufferd all þis becauce þe space of v wekis sho nowder hard dyvyne serves nor mes. *Ibid.* 250 A yong monk þat was passand devowte in saying of our Ladie serves & hur howres. **1450–1530** *Myrr. our Ladye* 11 How and why goddes seruyce is sayde, eche daye in .vii. howres. **1513** BRADSHAW *St. Werburge* I. 2548 Or that her systers came to the oratory To say dyuyne seruyce. **1516** BP. FOX *Rule of seynt Benet* F j, The .xlvii. chapiter treteth of thappoyntment of the houre of diuine seruice. **1547** *Injunctions given by Edw. VI* xxiv. c j b, People neuerthelesse perswadyng themselfes, sufficiently to honor God on that daie, if thei heare Masse & seruice. **1549** *Bk. Comm. Prayer* Pref., The common prayers in the Churche, commonlye called diuine seruice. **1583** in Foley *Rec. Eng. Prov. S.J.* (1880) VI. 714 He was made prest and beneficed in Queen Mary's time. He saith service with me daily.

†**c.** ***common service***, the 'Common Prayer' of the Prayer-book. *Obs.*

**1561** BP. PARKHURST *Injunctions* A iv, Whether the parsons, vicare, curate or reader doth reade the common seruice with a lowde, distinct and treatable voyce. **1565** *Aduertisments* 25 Jan. A iii, The booke of Common seruice.

†**d.** ***to give*** (*one*) ***service***: to have the service of the church performed over a dead man. *Obs.*

**1470–85** MALORY *Arthur* XVII. xviii. 716 And on the morne he gaf hym seruyse and putte hym in the erthe afore the hyghe Aulter.

†**e.** Used *transf.* of the singing of birds. *Obs.*

?*a* **1366** CHAUCER *Rom. Rose* 669 By note made fair serwyse These briddes..; They songe hir song as faire and wel As angels doon espiritueel. *c* **1369** —— *Dethe Blaunche* 302 [The birds] songen, euerich in his wyse, The moste solempne seruyse By note, that euer man, I trowe, Had herd.

**17.** A musical setting of those portions of the church-offices which are sung; esp. the music for the canticles at Morning and Evening Prayer.

**1691** WOOD *Ath. Oxon.* I. 815 Joh. Tomkins..a composer of certain Church Services and Anthems. **1782** MASON *Collect. Anthems, Ess. Cathedr. Mus.* p. xix, The Service which Thomas Tallis composed in the reign of Queen Elizabeth. *Ibid.* p. xlii, Those Hymns which Church Musicians call by the technical term of Services, by which they mean the *Te Deum, Magnificat*, &c. **1789** *J. Lewis' Mem. Dk. Glocester* 83 *note*, A very ingenious service of his, formerly performed at the King's Chapel. **1883** STAINER in *Grove's Dict. Mus.* III. 471 A Service may be defined as a collection of musical settings of the canticles and other portions of the liturgy which are by usage allowed to be set to free composition.

**18.** A SERVICE-BOOK. Now only, a volume containing the Book of Common Prayer together with the daily lessons; = CHURCH-SERVICE 3.

*a* **1700** EVELYN *Diary* 31 Aug. 1654, A vast old song book or service. **1860** SALA *Lady Chesterfield* v. 76 Young lasses.. with big velvet and gold-clasped Services in their hands.

**IV.** Help, benefit, advantage, use.

**19. a.** The action of serving, helping, or benefiting; conduct tending to the welfare or advantage of another. Chiefly in ***to do, render service*** (cf. 6).

**1582** N. LICHEFIELD tr. *Castenheda's Conq. E. Ind.* ii. 4 b, A man experimented in matters of the Sea, and of Navigation, wherein he had done to this kingdome great service. **1601** HAKLUYT *Galvano's Discov. World* 30 Christopher Columbus..who first had offered his seruice for a western discouerie vnto king Iohn of Portugall. **1605** BACON *Adv. Learn.* I. vi. §15. 31 We see..what notable seruice and reparation they [the Jesuits] haue done to the Romane Sea. **1663** S. PATRICK *Parab. Pilgr.* viii. (1687) 39, I intend to do you service by revealing to you my very heart. **1779** *Mirror* No. 35 Professions of friendship and regard will lead to expectations of service that cannot be answered. **1853** W. F. AINSWORTH *W. B. Barker's Lares & Penates* Introd. Pref. 3 During the campaign of the French in Syria he also rendered good service to our old ally the Porte. **1883** *Manch. Guard.* 4 Oct. 5/2 The Howard Association is doing good service by its persistent watchfulness in all matters relating to the treatment of crime.

**b.** An act of helping or benefiting; an instance of beneficial or friendly action; a useful office. Also in phr. ***for services rendered*** (orig. *Mil.*).

*a* **1533** LD. BERNERS *Huon* lvi. 189 The grete seruyce that he hathe done to me shall be euen ryght well rewarded. **1603** SHAKS. *Meas. for M.* I. ii. 181, I pre'thee (Lucio) doe me this kinde seruice. *a* **1700** EVELYN *Diary* 19 Sept. 1667, If they esteem'd it a service to the University (of which I had been a member). **1770** LANGHORNE *Plutarch, Pompey* (Rtldg.) 434/1 In the Mithridatic war they [the Pirates] assumed new confidence and courage, on account of some services they had rendered the king. **1817** JAS. MILL *Brit. India* II. v. iii. 406 He..mentioned two services by which the co-operation of that Prince might be ensured. **1855** MACAULAY *Hist. Eng.* xxi. IV. 567 While Mary lived, it might well be doubted whether the murder of her husband would really be a service to the Jacobite cause. **1862** MAURICE *Mod. Philos.* 604 In so far as Bentham brought these contradictions before the face of those who were committing them we conceive he was doing a service. [**1916** *Times* 24 July 9/4 The King has approved the issue of a silver badge to..men..who on account of age or..wounds or sickness caused by military service have..been discharged from the Army... The badge is in the form of a circle... The circle bears the words 'For King and Empire—Services rendered', and circumscribes the Imperial cipher.] **1933** *Radio Times* 14 Apr. 75/2 The war was newly over... Everywhere you saw the little silver badge 'For Services Rendered'. **1938** M. ALLINGHAM *Fashion in Shrouds* xx. 378 That's where Mazarini used to pay his thugs for services rendered on the race-course. **1976** W. H. CANAWAY *Willow-Pattern War* xviii. 189 As a *quid pro quo* for services rendered in another context, the Americans made their information available to Bonn.

**c.** *collect. pl.* Friendly or professional assistance.

**1832** HT. MARTINEAU *Life in Wilds* iii. 40 Seeing that greater strength of finger was what they wanted, he offered his services. **1848** THACKERAY *Van. Fair* xiv, I think we shall be able to help each other,..and shall have no need of Mr. Bowls's kind services. **1887** GUNTER *Mr. Barnes* xxiv. 192 Edwin said..that he would hand me over to you as his fee for your medical services.

†**20.** With *of* or possessive: A person's interest or advantage. *Obs.*

**14..** *26 Pol. Poems* v. 44 Loke how goddis lawe ȝe vse; Whom ȝe refuse, and whiche auaunce, ffor goddis loue, or ȝoure owen seruyce. *c* **1643** LD. HERBERT *Autobiog.* (1824) 227 The Queen of Bohemia, whose service they desired to advance. **1654** H. L'ESTRANGE *Chas. I* (1655) 26 He hath been sedulous in promoving the service and contentment of your house. **1713** JOHNSON *Guardian* No. 1 ¶5, I shall find enough to do to give Orders proper for their Service, to whom I am by Will of their Parents Guardian. **1768–74** TUCKER *Lt. Nat.* (1834) I. 266 If we have..a reasonable prospect of promoting her service in the long run.

**21. a.** Assistance or benefit afforded by an animal or thing (or by a person as involuntary agent); the work which an animal or thing is made to do. Phr. ***to do service***.

*c* **1470** HENRY *Wallace* IX. 1310 Thai..brak the bait, quhen thai war landyt thair; Serwice off it Sotheroun mycht haiff no mayr. **1523** FITZHERB. *Husb.* §146 The churle hempe..is nat so good as the female hempe, but yet it wyll do good seruice. **1598** SHAKS. *Merry W.* IV. ii. 218 Ile haue the cudgell hallow'd, and hung ore the Altar, it hath done meritorious seruice. **1604** N. F. *Fruiterers Secrets* 10 If they bee gathered afore, they will shrinke, wither, and eate tough, and doe no seruice. **1715** DE FOE *Fam. Instr.* I. i. (1766) I. 13 He..has given them to you for Food and Service. Don't you see that we eat them, ride upon them, and the like. **1749** SMOLLETT *Gil Blas* I. vi. ¶2 (1782) I. 36, I bore their discourse with patience, because to fret myself would have done me no service. **1816** SCOTT *Antiq.* i, He certainly would not..have suffered the coachman to proceed while the horse was unfit for service. **1882** FROUDE in *Longman's Mag.* I. 205, I passed the rod to X——, in whose hands it did better service. **1886** C. E. PASCOE *Lond. To-day* xxxv. (ed. 3) 311 Excursionists..press into service every vehicle which can carry them away from town.

**b.** Of the limbs: Function, office.

**1749** SMOLLETT *Gil Blas* II. i. (1782) I. 117 Though his hand shook, it did not refuse its service, but went and came with great expedition. *Ibid.* X. x. IV. 73 After having walked about two hours, my little legs began to refuse their service.

†**22. a.** The purpose or use to which a thing is put.

**1600** J. PORY tr. *Leo's Africa* II. 50 They know not what seruice to put their waxe vnto. **16..** SPELMAN (J.), All the vessels of the king's house are not for use of honour, some be common stuff, and for mean services, yet profitable. **1793** SMEATON *Edystone L.* §129 The Neptune..would be..a store-vessel for the service of rebuilding the Lighthouse. **1805** SKENE *Let.* in Lockhart *Scott* (1896) 130 A new kitchen range (as..the grate for that service is technically called).

†**b.** ***to stand*** (a person) ***in no service***: to be of no use to. *Obs.*

**1542** UDALL *Erasm. Apoph.* 12 b, He refused yᵉ gift whiche should stand hym in no service [orig. *munus inutile*].

**23.** Supply of the needs *of* (persons, occas. of things).

*a* **1325** *Prose Psalter* ciii. 15 Þou art bryngand forþe hay to meres and grasse to seruice of men [Vulg. *et herbam servituti hominum*]. *c* **1450** tr. *De Imitatione* III. xi. [x.] 78 Hevene & erþe, þat þou hast made unto mannes seruice [L. *in ministerium hominis*]. **1585** T. WASHINGTON tr. *Nicholay's Voy.* I. vi. 4 b, A great fountain for the common seruice of the house. **1781** GIBBON *Decl. & F.* xxxi. III. 214 The baths of Antoninus Caracalla, which were open, at stated hours, for the indiscriminate service of the senators and the people. **1886** STEVENSON *Kidnapped* v, On the south shore they have built a pier for the service of the Ferry.

**24. a.** Serviceableness, utility. Now *rare*.

**1679** PENN *Addr. Prot.* (1692) Pref., It may be objected by some, that much of the Service of it is over. **1691** T. H[ALE] *Acc. New Invent.* 103 The usefulness and service of the said Lead. **1910** *Expositor* Apr. 371 The system has its service in showing how impossible it is to get rid of Sin as a tragedy in the universe.

**b.** ***of service*** (predicatively): of use or assistance, useful, helpful. Const. *to*.

**1709** FELTON *Diss. Classics* (1718) 3 If I am of any Service to Your Lordship. **1729** BUTLER *Serm.* Wks. 1874 II. 132 Even the bearing of this rule in their thoughts may be of some service. **1756** BURKE *Subl. & B.* Pref., In this pursuit, whether we take or whether we lose our game, the chace is certainly of service. **1779** STORER in Jesse *Selwyn & Contemp.* (1844) IV. 295 This paper war will not be of much service to us. **1839** T. MITCHELL *Frogs of Aristoph.* Introd. 93 *note*, The reader who wishes to work this out for himself, will find the following references of service. **1860** TYNDALL *Glac.* I. xxii. 152, I found him of some service to me. **1867** BAKER *Nile Tribut.* viii. 196 The long tails of the giraffes.. would be of little service against..the seroot.

**25.** ***at one's service***, at one's disposal, ready or available for one to use. Cf. 9 c.

**1669** DAVENANT *Man's the Master* III. 47 *Tod.* Lead'em a Dance, I'll have a Dance. *D. John.* My feet are at your service, Sir. **1683** W. HEDGES *Diary* (Hakl. Soc.) I. 132, I told him the last time he was here..I promised him a Persian Horse; I had now one at his Service, which he accepted with some ceremony. **1837** CARLYLE *Fr. Rev.* III. II. ii, My whole strength..is, day and night, at the service of my fellow-Citizens. **1875** JOWETT *Plato* (ed. 2) I. 385 My means, which are certainly ample, are at your service.

†**26.** Permission to use; the loan *of* a thing for use.

**1810** SCOTT *Lady of L.* II. xxxvii, Tell Roderick Dhu I owed him naught, Not the poor service of a boat, To waft me to yon mountain-side. **1821** —— *Kenilw.* xiii, Wayland, obtaining from the cook the service of a mortar,..mixed, pounded, and amalgamated the drugs which he had bought.

**V.** Waiting at table, supply of food; hence, supply of commodities, etc.

**27. a.** The act of waiting at table or dishing up food; the manner in which this is done. Phrase, ***the service of the table*** (now *arch.*).

**13..** *E.E. Allit. P.* B. 1401 When alle segges were þer set, þen seruyse bygynnes. *c* **1386** CHAUCER *Squire's T.* 58 And eek it nedeth nat for to deuyse At euery cours the ordre of hire seruyse. **1412–20** LYDG. *Chron. Troy* II. 4187 Þe straunge metis, þe manere of þe seruyse. **1528** ROY *Rede me* II. (Arb.) 93 Whose prowde service to beholde, In plate of silver and golde, It passeth a mans witt. **1585** T. WASHINGTON tr. *Nicholay's Voy.* I. xxi. 27 He was..serued with al magnificence..and superfluity of meates.., and this seruice was done..by officers in number. **1588** KYD *Househ. Phil.* Wks. (1901) 275 Necessary implements, not onely for the vse of the Kitchin but seruice of the Table. **1632** MASSINGER *City Madam* I. i, You may want, though, A dish or two when the service ends. **1674** T. P., etc. *Eng. & Fr. Cook* 431 Bills of Fare, as well for great Feasts as ordinary Services through the whole year. **1815** SCOTT *Guy M.* xlix, More pretty things were said on both sides during the service of the tea-table than we have leisure to repeat. **1848** THACKERAY *Van. Fair* xlix, He described..the service of the table..enumerated the dishes and wines served. **1887** *Cassell's Encycl. Dict.*, *Service*, waiting at table: as, The service was good *or* indifferent.

**b.** That which is served up or placed on the table for a meal; the food set before a person; an allowance or portion of food. Now *rare*.

*a* **1300** *Cursor M.* 13990 A man þat hight symon leprus, At ete he praid him til his hus... Ful fair seruis symon him dight. **13..** *Coer de L.* 1504 Anon they wer to borde sette, And fayr servyse byfore hem sette. *c* **1400** *Rule St. Benet* (Verse) 1584 Þat euer-ilkon wil of hir laue þe third part til hir sopper saue, And to þe celerer wil it seme Swilk seruys for to saf & ȝeme. *c* **1430** *Stans Puer ad Mensam* 26 in *Meals & Manners* 278 And whanne þou seest afore þee þi service, be not to hasti upon breed to bite. *a* **1483** *Liber Niger* in *Househ. Ord.* (1790) 24 The servyce of his table and of his cupborde to be dayly recorded into the King's countyng-house. **1557** F. SEAGER *Sch. Vertue* 342 Disshes with measure thou oughtest to fyll, Els mayste thou happen thy seruyce to spyll. **1598–9** B. JONSON *Case Altered* I. i, Gods lid man, seruice is ready to go vp man, you must slip on your coate and come in, we lacke waiters pittyfully. **1607** TOPSELL *Four-f. Beasts* 81 In the Summer let them haue their first meate in the morning, and their second seruice at noone. **1610** HEYWOOD *Gold. Age* II. i. *Stage Direct.*, A banquet brought in, with the limbes of a Man in the seruice. **1700** [E. WARD] *Lond. Spy* XVII. 14 A Service of Sweet-meats, which every Gossip carry'd away in her Hankerchief. **1839** LANE *Arab. Nts.* I. 86 Services of food were then spread before them. *c* **1880** R. H. STODDARD *Sqr. Low Degree* (Cent.) I'll spread your service by the door, That when you eat you may behold The knights at play where the bowls are rolled.

†**c.** A division of a meal served up at one time, a course. Also, a particular 'dish' or kind of food.

*a* **1536** *Songs, Carols* etc. (E.E.T.S.) 33 The boris hede, I vnderstond, Ys cheff seruyce in all this londe. **1601** HOLLAND *Pliny* XVI. v. I. 458 Even at this day throughout Spaine, the manner is to serve up acorns and mast to the table for a second service. **1607** DEKKER & WEBSTER *Westw. Hoe* I. ii, An excellent pickeld Goose, a new seruice. *c* **1643** LD. HERBERT *Autobiog.* (1824) 152 One of the most sumptuous Feasts that ever I saw, being but of nine dishes, in three several services. **1662** J. DAVIES tr. *Olearius' Voy. Ambass.* 278 Certain services of Paste and Sugar, according to the German fashion, which were brought to the Table, rather to divert the Eye, than to sharpen the Appetite. **1715** *Lond. Gaz.* No. 5336/2 The Entertainments..consist only of one Service. **1707** *Curios. in Husb.* 47 Fruits..are still the most agreeable Service of Tables. **1765** in *Priv. Lett. Ld. Malmesbury* (1870) I. 137 His dinner—four services.

**d.** In the restaurant-car of a railway train, on a ship, etc.: the serving of a meal at one of a number of separate sittings, as ***first service***, etc.

**1914** KIPLING in *Nash's Mag.* July 484/1 Here is a fragment from the restaurant-car... 'I will give you the number, sar, at the time—for places at the first service.' **1926** E. HEMINGWAY *Sun also Rises* 86 Leaving the dining-car I asked the conductor for tickets for the first service. **1932** G. GREENE *Stamboul Train* III. ii. 140 Late for the last service Dr. Czinner came down the restaurant-car.

**28. a.** The furniture of the table; esp. a set of dishes and other utensils required for serving a particular meal. Often with defining word, as ***dinner, dessert, breakfast, tea service***.

**1669** R. MONTAGU in *Buccleuch MSS.* (Hist. MSS. Comm.) I. 445 A very pretty service of gilt plate. **1710** LUTTRELL *Brief Rel.* (1857) VI. 597 A magnificent service of plate, consisting of many large silver dishes, stands, plates,

&c. **1788** Ld. Auckland *Corr.* (1862) III. 67 The service of Sèvres china arrived all safe. **1851** *Beck's Florist* 266 A handsome silver tea and coffee service. **1882** Ogilvie, *Service*, an assortment of table-linen. **1885** *Law Times* LXXIX. 175/1 A service of plate bequeathed by a baronet. **1890** 'R. Boldrewood' *Col. Reformer* (1891) 345 The damsel..completed the clearing off and washing up of the various articles of the service.

**b.** Similarly: A set of vessels for the altar, for the toilet, etc.

*a* **1700** Evelyn *Diary* 25 Jan. 1645, The compleate service of the purest chrystal for the altar of the Chapell. **1851** Mayhew *Lond. Labour* I. 368/1 A green and white chamber service all complete, with soap trays and brush trays. **1867** C. T. Newton *Blacas Coll. Antiq. Brit. Mus.* 24 Silver toilet service of a Roman bride.

**29.** An administration or application (*of* something).

**1632** Lithgow *Trav.* x. 465 From whence carrying a pot full of water..hee did powre it in my bellie..The first and second seruices I gladly receaued, such was the scorching drouth of my tormenting payne. **1700** [E. Ward] *Lond. Spy* xvii. 10 The next piece of Lip-Exercise my Part'ner set me, was to make a Regular Service of Kisses round the Room. **1839** Ure *Dict. Arts* 1143 In France a small quantity of solution of sulphate of iron is added during the boiling of the soap, or rather with the first service of the lyes.

**30. a.** The supply or laying-on of gas, water, etc., through pipes from a reservoir; the apparatus of pipes, etc., by which this is done. Also applied to other facilities, such as electricity, waste disposal, etc., esp. provided for domestic use. Freq. *pl.*

**1879** W. Young *Town & Country Mansions* 41 From one of the cisterns a separate service of pipes should be carried to the water-closets. **1895** *Outing* XXVII. 254/1 Sinks were constructed, and the city water-service was introduced. **1963** *Ann. Reg. 1962* 450 Both make use of clusters of towers, mostly containing services, to give vertical emphasis and to free interior space. **1963** *Gloss. Gen. Building Terms* (*B.S.I.*) 24 *Services*, installations for (1) the introduction into and distribution within a building or structure of water, air, gas, liquid fuel, electricity, heat or other source of energy (2) the disposal of waste from a building or structure or (3) fire-fighting within a building or structure. **1979** *Nature* 1 Feb. p. xiii/2 The overhead service booms may provide such services as gas/electricity/water/vacuum/lighting.

**b.** *attrib.*, as ***service-box, -pipe***, etc.

**1819** Peckston *Gas-Lighting* 299 He must prepare to bring the gas into the houses by laying the service-pipes. **1862** *Catal. Internat. Exhib.* II. x. 44 Improved service-box for supplying water-closets. *Ibid.*, To be connected either with the service-pipe direct from the main, or with the supply-pipe from the cistern. **1868** *Chamb. Encycl.* X. 103/2 The distributing or service reservoirs should be roofed.

**c.** = *service-pipe* (see b).

**1865** S. Hughes *Gas-works* (ed. 2) 233 The pipes which convey gas or water through the different streets are called main pipes or mains; and the small pipes which convey the fluid therefrom to the houses are called services. **1877** W. Richards *Manuf. Coal Gas* 271 Services should be of course always laid with a slight incline to the main.

**31. a.** Provision (of labour, material appliances, etc.) for the carrying out of some work for which there is a constant public demand.

**1853** Papworth *Museums*, etc. 15 Regulations as to admission into public museums..the porter not to allow the entrance of any person out of the hours of public service. **1886** C. E. Pascoe *Lond. To-day* (ed. 3) 320 St. Bartholomew's Hospital..has a service of 710 beds. **1892** *Post Office Notice*, The object of the new Post Office Express Service is to secure the immediate delivery of Messages, Letters and Parcels by Special Messenger. **1904** G. B. Shaw *Common-sense Munic. Trading* vi. (1908) 48 There is, however, one very important difference between a telegraph and a telephone service.

**b.** Expert advice or assistance given by manufacturers and dealers to secure satisfactory results from goods made or supplied by them; *spec.*, the provision of maintenance or repair work to ensure the efficient running of a motor vehicle, etc.; a routine operation of examination and maintenance performed on a motor vehicle, etc.

**1919** W. H. Berry *New Motoring* xxiv. 183 The need of a better service system for motorists has often been emphasised... There is ample room for a big development of a scheme for rendering practical car service. **1925** *Morris Owner's Man.* 93 (*caption*) Whenever you see this hanging sign you know that it denotes an establishment where Morris Service can be obtained. **1930** *Economist* 6 Sept. 454/2 There are obviously wide undeveloped markets, of which Britain should be able to secure at least a proportion ..if English manufacturers can compete with those of America in the matter of 'service'. **1947** *E. African Ann. 1946–7* 24 'Service After Sales' is as much a Ford feature here as it is in other parts of the world. **1960** I. Jefferies *Dignity & Purity* iii. 44 The flat was paid up and the car never needed any service at all. **1974** 'J. le Carré' *Tinker, Tailor, Soldier, Spy* xx. 168 Take your car in for a service at your local garage. **1977** *Western Morning News* 30 Aug. 10/4 (Advt.), Backed by our largest combine stores and skilled after-sales service.

**c.** *Broadcasting.* The supply of programmes by a particular broadcasting station.

**1927** *B.B.C. Handbk. 1928* 32 Broadcasting Service. By 'service' is meant providing this public..with at least one programme a day. **1933** *B.B.C. Year-bk. 1934* 167 In August last the West Regional, the fourth of the new Regional Stations, began radiating a full programme service. **1949** *Radio Times* 15 July 9/1 *Variety Fanfare* returns to the air... Bowker Andrews first introduced this show in the North of England Home Service. **1957** [see carry *v.* 40 b]. **1977** *Church Times* 9 Dec. 8/3 Now that the 7.30 half-hour on Radio Four has been taken over for other things, there is a gap from 10.15 a.m. until 11 p.m. on Sunday on this service without a word being said about religion.

**d.** pl. *Econ.* The section of the economy that supplies needs of the consumer but produces no tangible goods.

**1936** *Discovery* Nov. 355/2 The distinction between capital goods and current goods is, of course, one of the most important in the whole of economics, but the remarkable growth in the number of those engaged in 'services', now estimated at 40 per cent. of the working population, is not so generally realised. **1941** *Economist* 22 Feb. 235/1 The British public spent almost £900 millions in 1937 on services, excluding entertainments, rent, rates and taxes. The largest constituents of the total were travel, domestic service, public utilities, hotels and restaurants. **1948** [see *current goods*]. **1965** *McGraw-Hill Dict. Mod. Econ.* 466 *Services*, the component of the gross national product that measures the output of intangible items. Services include such items as telephone service, railway, bus, and air transportation, private education, and radio and television repair. **1972** *Accountant* 17 Aug. 211/2 Manufacturing costs are of diminishing importance in an economy in which services are a major part of the whole.

**e.** *pl.* The provision of petrol, refreshments, etc., for motorists in buildings constructed near to or beside a motorway or other major road; the group of buildings themselves.

**1967** *Autocar* 28 Dec. 6/2 It was a relief to see the 'Services 1 mile' sign. **1968** *Listener* 1 Aug. 134/3 We drove back on Sunday night along the endless M1, punctuated only by almost identical airport-international-style 'Services'. **1975** C. Storr *Chinese Egg* xxix. 193 She was passing the Heston Services, she'd be at the Henley exit in another quarter of an hour.

**32.** Accommodation for conveyance or transit afforded by vehicles plying regularly on a route.

**1854** *N. & Q.* 1st Ser. IX. 355/1 *Service*..is of very late importation from the French, within three years, as applied to the lines of steamers, or traffic of railways. **1865** *Cassell's Handy Guide Sea-side* (ed. 2) 103 There is a very fine service of steamboats between Douglas, Ramsey, and Liverpool thrice a week in the winter. **1866** *Roy. Comm. Railways, Min. Evid.* 519/1 The London and North-western Company running a very good service between London and Birmingham. **1870** Dickens *E. Drood* vi, A short squat omnibus..which was then the daily service between Cloisterham and external mankind. **1885** *Law Times* LXXX. 111/1 The right of the railway company to suspend the ordinary service of trains on occasions of great and exceptional pressure. **1904** G. B. Shaw *Common-sense Munic. Trading* v. (1908) 40 London is at present helplessly at the mercy of a cab service which [etc.].

**VI.** Action of serving, in technical senses.

**33.** *Law.* **a.** The action or an act of serving (a writ, notice, etc.) upon a person.

*to accept service* (of a writ): see accept *v.* 3.

**1429** *Rolls of Parlt.* IV. 346/1 Touching the retourne, servise, and all executions of the Writtes, Processe and Juggementz, in and of the saide actions. **1837** Dickens *Pickw.* xxx, 'Beg your pardon, Mr. Pickwick', said Mr. Jackson... 'But personal service, by clerk or agent, in these cases, you know, Mr. Pickwick—eh, Sir?' **1863** Le Fanu *Ho. Churchyard* III. 7 I'll permit the services of the notices.

**b.** *Scots Law.* The procedure for ascertaining and declaring the heir to a person deceased. A ***general service*** determines generally who is heir to another; a ***special service*** determines who is heir to a special estate.

**1597** Skene *De Verb. Sign.* s.v. *Breve de morte antecessoris*, Be the auld law of this Realme, the Justice-generall and his deputes..was judge competent to the service of this breve. **1693** Stair *Inst. Law Scot.* iii. v. (ed. 2) 467 The general Service is a compleat establishing of the Right in the Person of the Heir. **1815** Scott *Guy M.* lviii, [We have] got our youngster's special service retoured into Chancery. **1847** *Act 10 & 11 Vict.* c. 47 §1 The Practice of issuing Brieves from Chancery for the Service of Heirs shall cease.

**34.** *Tennis* (and kindred games). The act of 'serving' the ball or starting it in play; a particular player's manner of doing this; the ball served.

**1611** Cotgr., *Grebonde*, a seruice at Tennice, wherein the ball runs not along on the house, but bounds on the side thereof. **1797** *Encycl. Brit.* XVIII. 380/2 (*Tennis*) When the player gives his service at the beginning of a set, his adversary is supposed to return the ball. **1819** *Examiner* 7 Feb. in *Hazlitt's Table-talk* ix. (1821) 203, 204 His service was tremendous. He once..made seven and twenty aces following by services alone. **1894** *Times* 6 Mar. 7/3 Mr. Young's service and return were very severe in the third game. **1897** *Encycl. Sport* I. 402/1 (Fives) If he fails to return the 'service' above the 'line' no stroke is counted.

**b.** *attrib.*, as ***service-box, -court, -line, -side, -wall.***

**1797** *Encycl. Brit.* XVIII. 380/1 (*Tennis*) Over this long gallery..is a covering, called the pent-house, on which they play the ball from the service-side. **1875** 'Stonehenge' *Brit. Sports* 690 If the service drops in the wrong court, or beyond the service line, it is a fault. **1878** J. Marshall *Ann. Tennis* 159 *Service court*, that part of the floor which is contained between the service-line, the pass-line, the grille-wall, and the gallery-wall and battery. *Ibid.* 160 *Service-wall*, the wall above the side-pent-house. **1898** *Encycl. Sport* II. 244/2 (Rackets), *Service-box*, the square (marked out on each side of the floor) from which the service must be delivered. **1898** [see *half-court* s.v. half- II. i]. **1963** *Times* 13 May 3/5 Lawrence's policy of holding the service-side at all costs, often using the side galleries to achieve the change of ends.

**35.** *Naut.* Small cord, or the like, wound about a rope to protect it. (Cf. serve *v.*[1] 54.)

**1729** Capt. W. Wriglesworth *MS. Log-bk. of the 'Lyell'* 24 Nov., Veered out the best bower Cable on the Flood, and claped on the moaring Service. **1748** *Anson's Voy.* iii. ii. 318 The cables..armed with the chains..were besides cackled ..seven fathom from the service. **1793** Smeaton *Edystone L.* §137 Not only the service and worming were cut, but the cable itself was..injured by the sharpness of the rocks. **1840** R. H. Dana *Bef. Mast* iii, This chafing gear consists of worming,..battens, and service of all kinds. **1899** F. T. Bullen *Log of Sea-waif* 323 We could not..repair the 'service' where chafed out aloft.

**36.** The action of covering a female animal. (Cf. serve *v.* 52.)

**1822** M. McSwiney *Let.* 6 Jan. (1972) II. 348 This debt I understand was due for the service of a *bull.* **1844** H. Stephens *Bk. Farm* III. 845 He is often so much fatigued when brought to the mare..as to be quite unfit for effective service. **1885** *Bazaar* 30 Mar. 1260/3 With each pup a written guarantee of a service from a pedigree St. Bernard dog will be given. **1911** *Kingsbridge* (Devon) *Gaz.* 26 Mar. 2/4 For service—a Pedigree Large Black Boar.

**VII.** *attrib.* and *Comb.* (See also 30 b, 34 b.)

**37.** Simple attrib., passing into adj.

**a.** Belonging to the army, navy, or Air Force; military (opp. civilian); esp., employed on active service, as ***service ammunition, bullet, charge, company, rifle***, etc. Also in *pl.*

**1828** J. M. Spearman *Brit. Gunner* (ed. 2) 124 The service charges in the above table [required for cartridges]. **1837** *King's Regul. Army* 153 Regiments on Foreign Stations are formed into Six Service Companies and Four Depôt Companies. **1844** *Queen's Regul. Army* 111 All Regiments are to have, in the constant possession of each Man, Ten Rounds of Service Ammunition. **1860** *All Year Round* No. 73. 546 The ordinary unrifled service gun. **1875** Bedford *Sailor's Pocket Bk.* vi. (ed. 2) 236 By service rigs, is to be understood the rig that boats use when on service. **1898** *Times* 28 June 13/6 The new service bullet..fits all the service rifles and machine guns in use by the British Army. **1901** *Scotsman* 4 Mar. 8/2 He wished the members of the service company God-speed. *Ibid.* 2 Mar. 10/1 Dressed in their service khaki. **1909** Col. Egerton in *Westm. Gaz.* 4 Mar. 3/1 Match-rifle conditions..are directly opposed to service-rifle shooting and training for war. **1917** *Times* 1 Nov. 3/5 The Services Club, 19, Stratford-place, W., have just acquired an adjoining house. **1926** E. Hemingway *Sun also Rises* xvii. 212 Always slept with a loaded service revolver. **1929** *Star* 21 Aug. 9/1 Private and even Service pilots have appeared near to the station at prohibited times. **1933** *Radio Times* 14 Apr. 75/2 The slang of the hour was Service slang. **1937** A. Christie *Dumb Witness* i. 13 Emily Arundell's people..were what is known as 'all service people'. **1945** *Manch. Guardian Weekly* 21 Dec. 323/3 There was an all-night Services canteen at Victoria station. **1945** *Tee Emm* (Air Ministry) V. 35 The Service scale of Tropical Kit, issued to airmen. **1954** *Economist* 11 Sept. 3/1 A trained test pilot is less likely to come to harm in a new and temperamental machine than an enthusiastic service flyer. **1958** *Listener* 6 Nov. 719/2 In 1947 Montgomery became Chief of the Imperial General Staff... He had to co-operate on equal terms with the Service Chiefs of the other two fighting services. **1973** J. Rossiter *Manipulators* iv. 48, I was so horribly humiliated—my service career finished. **1977** *R.A.F. News* 22 June–5 July 18 (*caption*) Alan won trophies for both rapid and snap shooting using the service-issue self-loading rifle. **1980** C. Smith *Cut-Out* xiii. 92 Photographs of her husband in service dress and holding a swagger cane.

**b.** Belonging to household service, the serving of meals, etc.

**1864** R. Kerr *Gentl. Ho.* 247 Butler's Service-room, its position, uses, and fittings. **1878** F. S. Williams *Midl. Railw.* 351 The ventilation of the kitchens is conducted up the 'service' staircase and shaft. **1885** in Willis & Clark *Cambridge* II. 774 While each man has a small service-room of his own, there are on each staircase two larger gyp-rooms. **1899** *Daily News* 18 Apr. 7/7 The fire originated in the service-lift. **1902** A. Bennett *Grand Babylon Hotel* i. 13 Jules walked to the service-door. **1907** *Daily Chron.* 25 June 3/4 In all the club rooms there are what are called 'service-hatches', which will supply food or drink in infinite variety. **1909** H. G. Wells *Tono-Bungay* i. i. 28 One came down the main service stairs..and..one went through a red baize door. **1919** *Chambers's Jrnl.* Jan. 57/2 What is known as the 'service' door..is likely to become popular for hotels, if not for private houses, all over the world. **1933** *Archit. Rev.* LXXIII. 24/2 (*caption*) The service-bay between the kitchen and the restaurant. **1950** T. S. Eliot *Cocktail Party* i. iii. 65, I shall take the precaution Of leaving by the service staircase. **1955** W. Gaddis *Recognitions* ii. viii. 653 A transmitter? Mr. Inononu demanded at the head of the service stairs. **1956** H. Kurnitz *Invasion of Privacy* xiv. 92 She went out the back, through the service entrance. **1961** M. W. Barley *Eng. Farmhouse & Cottage* ii. i. 64 His home consisted of a hall with a chamber over it, a ground floor chamber in which he slept, and four service-rooms, kitchen, buttery, milkhouse and cheese-house. **1976** H. Nielsen *Brink of Murder* xii. 106 The manager conceded that there was a service door and..accompanied them upstairs on the service stairway. **1976** *Washington Post* 19 Apr. c20/1 (Advt.), Eat in kitchen with service bar. **1978** R. Ludlum *Holcroft Covenant* xxxix. 452, I could say that someone fitting his description was seen leaving by the service entrance. **1979** M. Soames *Clementine Churchill* xxiv. 395 A service-lift to the floor below.

**c.** Of or pertaining to services (sense 31 d), as ***service industry, occupation, sector, trade.***

**1941** *Economist* 18 Jan. 65/2 The very considerable increase in the standard of living..explains the growth of the 'service', as distinct from the 'productive' industries since the last war. **1959** *Times* 5 Sept. 10/3 The rapid expansion of service occupations—administration, the professions, retailing, entertainment and numerous health and welfare services. **1966** *Listener* 5 May 642/2 There is to be a selective employments tax to help get workers out of service industries into the factories. **1970** S. L. Barraclough in I. L. Horowitz *Masses in Lat. Amer.* iv. 150 This is reflected in the rapid increase of employment in the 'service' sector. **1970** G. Jackson *Let.* 17 Apr. in *Soledad Brother* (1971) 221 The new slavery..places the victim..in the case of most blacks in support roles inside and around the factory system (service trades), working for a wage. **1979** G. WAGNER *Barnado* ii. 18 All the service industries took on extra labour at the beginning of the season.

**38.** Special combinations: **service alley**, a road or passage giving access to the back of a row of houses; **service area**, (*a*) the area in which broadcast transmissions can be received distinctly; (*b*) a space adjoining a house for the accommodation of dustbins, etc.; (*c*) an area providing petrol, refreshments, etc., for motorists; **service-book**, a book containing one or more forms of divine service (in the 17th c. often applied to the Book of Common Prayer); **service car** *Austral.* and *N.Z.*, a small motor-coach for public transport; **service ceiling** *Aeronaut.* (see CEILING *vbl. sb.* 6b); **service charge**, a charge made (additional to that for the food, etc.) for services rendered, esp. for service in a hotel or restaurant; **service club** *N. Amer.*, an association of business or professional people which seeks to promote community welfare and goodwill; **service contract**, a contract of employment; a business agreement between contractor and customer, normally one guaranteeing the maintenance and servicing of equipment; **service engineer**, an engineer engaged on the maintenance and servicing of equipment; **service flat**, a flat in which domestic service and other facilities are provided at a charge included in the rent; hence **service flatlet**; **service mark** orig. *U.S.*, a name or designation, protected by law, used by a commercial undertaking to distinguish a service offered by it from the services of competitors; **service measure, metre**, the 14-syllable line which is the equivalent of a couplet of common metre; also used = common metre (see COMMON *a.* 19b); **service module** *Astronautics*, a separable section of a spacecraft, esp. one in the U.S. Apollo series, containing the main engine and other supporting equipment; **service paste**, a porcelain-paste prepared to serve for all ordinary work; **service plate** *U.S.*, a large ornate plate which marks a place at table and on which dining plates, etc., are set during the first courses; **service record**, the record of service of a soldier, employee, etc.; **service reservoir**, a (usu. small) reservoir filled from an impounding reservoir at times of low demand to supplement the supply to the local area at time of high demand, so as to reduce the necessary capacity of the conduits from the impounding reservoir; **service road**, a subsidiary road giving access to houses, shops, etc., away from a main road; †**service-room**, a music-room or song-school in a religious house; **service routine** *Computers*, = *utility routine* s.v. UTILITY *sb.*; **service station**, an establishment providing service and maintenance for motor vehicles; more recently, merely = *filling-station* s.v. FILLING *vbl. sb.* 4; **service-time**, †**-while**, the time of divine service.

**1922** J. HERGESHEIMER *Bright Shawl* 11 The street outside was narrow..once no more than a *service alley for the larger dwellings back of which it ran. **1974** P. MCCUTCHAN *Call for Simon Shard* xi. 98 You take the back, Alan. There'll be a service alley. **1927** *B.B.C. Handbk. 1928* 62 Rival schemes can be compared as between those which base themselves upon very high power and believe that *service areas can be over 100 miles radius, and those which cover the country from more centres and with therefore somewhat less power. **1956** *Good Housek. Home Encyl.* (ed. 4) 327/2 The service area behind or at the side of the house. **1958** *News Chron.* 25 Nov. 7/4 The great London—Birmingham Motorway... A road remarkably straight, soaring over 150 specially built bridges; with flyovers, flyunders; with service and eating areas every 12 miles. **1970** J. EARL *Tuners & Amplifiers* iii. 74 If you have in mind trying for more distant stations..outside the normal service area, then you will certainly need a tuner of top sensitivity. **1971** M. MCCARTHY *Birds of Amer.* 76 The yard in back of their house was all flagged, with..a 'service area' containing garbage cans. **1980** J. MCNEIL *Spy Game* xiv. 141 They careered into the narrow, curving entrance to a service area. .. He cruised the crowded car park. **1580** HOLLYBAND *Treas. Fr. Tong*, *Breviaire*, the *service booke of priestes of the church of Rome. **1638** LAUD *Diary* 29 Apr., The tumults in Scotland, about the Service-Book offered to be brought in. *c* **1680** BEVERIDGE *Serm.* (1729) I. 558 The book of Lamentations seems to have been a kind of service-book or office. **1846** MASKELL *Mon. Rit.* I. p. lxxxi, The revision of the service-books of the Western Church which followed the council of Trent. **1924** R. REES *April's Sowing* ii. 19 I'd have gone in the *service car. **1933** *Bulletin* (Sydney) 26 July 20/1 The drivers of service cars Outback. **1948** V. PALMER *Golconda* xxi. 173 He piled his traps into the dusty service-car and climbed up beside the driver. **1965** S. T. OLLIVIER *Petticoat Farm* xii. 166 The road was open, they knew, because the service cars were running through. **1920** *Flight* XII. 980/2 Principal characteristics of the Martin torpedo 'plane are:—*Service ceiling..12,000 ft. **1944** H. F. BROWNE *Aeroplane Flight* vi. 97 At the service ceiling the aeroplane can fly only at speeds between 180 m.p.h. and 240 m.p.h. **1978** J. D. ANDERSON *Introd. to Flight* vi. 237 The service ceiling represents the practical upper limit of steady, level flight. **1929** *Post Office Guide* July 157 Any sum not exceeding £10 may be withdrawn by telegraph if the depositor pays the cost of the telegrams and a *service charge of one shilling. **1955** R. CHANDLER *Let.* 7 Feb. (1981) 382, I paid a service charge on the bill... This service charge is supposed to take the place of tipping. **1977** B. BAINBRIDGE *Injury Time* ii. 23 She looked at the bill and was astonished at the service charge. **1926** *Daily Colonist* (Victoria, B.C.) 16 July 2/5 He intended this time to take a party of executive officers of *service clubs. **1978** J. L. HENSLEY *Killing in Gold* (1979) v. 65 He'd joined..one of the service clubs, Lions, Rotary, or Kiwanis. **1948** *Rep. Native Laws Commission 1946–48* (Dept. Native Affairs, S. Afr.) 26/1 The *service contract duplicate, which is issued to a Native in urban areas where registration of service contracts in terms of the Natives (Urban Areas) Consolidation Act is in force, is likewise regarded by them as a pass. **1958** *Listener* 20 Nov. 824/1 It would be wrong to abandon altogether the distinction between service contracts and other types of contract. **1975** *Petroleum Economist* Aug. 299/2 In 1968, a service contract was agreed with Elf/ERAP by which the French company would have a share of any production which resulted. **1958** *Practical Wireless* XXXIV. 67/1, I do feel pity for the poor *service engineer. **1980** *West Lancs. Even. Gaz.* 28 Nov. 25 Sweda International..has vacancies for Service Engineers to service and maintain their range of electro-mechanical and electronic machines. **1922** W. J. LOCKE *Tale of Triona* iv. 38 She found herself the lucky tenant of a little suite in a set of *service flats in Victoria Street. **1973** 'E. FERRARS' *Foot in Grave* iv. 70 Being solitary in my service flat suits me, and that's how I'm going on. **1960** M. SPARK *Bachelors* x. 141 Those who were conducting love affairs in *service flatlets found it convenient that the maids did not come in with their vacuum cleaners on Sundays. **1945** *Business Week* 30 June 86/2 A separate register would be authorized for '*service' marks to identify services rather than merchandise. This register would include 'names, symbols, titles, designations, slogans, character names, and distinctive features of radio or other advertising used in commerce'. **1949** H. BENNETT *Trade-Marks* 130 Under the Lanham act service marks will be registrable for the first time. The new law thus gives great protection to a category of names and designations whose trade importance was not recognized under the old law. **1959** *Listener* 31 Dec. 1147/1 Trade marks, trade names, the so-called 'service-marks' of organizations such as transport undertakings and radio stations. **1973** S. A. DIAMOND *Trademark Problems & how to avoid Them* i. 2 Trademarks are not limited to goods; they may be used for services, like transportation, insurance, entertainments and advertising. Strictly speaking, they are then called 'service marks'. **1841** LATHAM *Eng. Lang.* v. 382 *Poulterer's Measure.*—Alexandrines and *Service Measures alternately... It will be seen that a couplet of Ballad Metre is equivalent to a line of *Service Metre. **1886** MEIKLEJOHN *Eng. Lang.* 182 Iambic Tetrameter with Iambic Trimeter in alternate lines—the second and fourth rhyming—is called Ballad Metre. When used, as it often is, in hymns, it is called Service Metre. **1961** *Space Technol.* Oct. 41 (*caption*) *Service module. **1962** *Manned Space Flight Program of N.A.S.A.* (U.S. Congress Senate Comm. on Aeronaut. & Space Sci.) 131 The service module..will contain the propulsion used for midcourse guidance corrections, for emergency abort situations, and for lunar takeoff. **1968** *Times* 16 Dec. 7/4 Before reentry, the command module holding the astronauts will separate from what is called the service module, the section of the spacecraft containing the main engine and power supplies. **1974** Service module [see RETROFIRE *sb.*]. **1839** URE *Dict. Arts* 1022 The following composition has been adopted for the *service paste of the royal manufactory of Sèvres. **1929** *Woman's Home Compan.* Apr. 67/2 The *service plate has been removed and a..fish plate has taken its place. (The individual place..is never left without a plate before it.) **1934** J. B. PRIESTLEY *Eng. Journey* vii. 223 A very queer American custom, that of having what are known as 'service plates', which are never loaded with food but are placed before guests between courses, to be looked at and admired... These luxury plates were usually very ornate and would be specially made, here in the Potteries, for each customer. Some Americans liked to have a picture of their college on their plates. **1977** H. FAST *Immigrants* I. 49 A maid placed a plate of crab meat and mayonnaise on his service plate. **1918** E. S. FARROW *Dict. Mil. Terms* s.v., When an enlisted man is detached from his company, his *service record will be forwarded by endorsement to his new commanding officer. **1923** J. D. HACKETT *Labor Terms in Managem. Engin.* May, *Service Record*, a summary of all the facts necessary for appraising the worth of an individual to an employer. **1981** J. B. HILTON *Playground of Death* x. 123 There's his service record... He was a brave man. **1869** *Bradshaw's Railway Man.* XXI. 266 The *service reservoir of the Ashton water-works. **1967** J. H. STEPHENS *Water & Waste* iii. 49 The purpose of the service reservoir, and its close relative, the water tower, is to allow for the peaks in demand. **1921** H. FOSTON *At Front* 16 Unmetalled portions of the '*service' road. **1935** *Times* 30 Dec. 13/6 There are signs in this neighbourhood that the future development will be the right one of groups of houses set back and approached by service roads. **1976** *Southern Even. Echo* (Southampton) 12 Nov. (Advt. Suppl.) 7/6 In quiet and well screened service road, a most attractive and compact 3-bedroom bungalow. **1669** WOODHEAD *St. Teresa* II. 276 The Nuns, then in the *Service-room. **1954** *Computers & Automation* Dec. 21/1 **Service routine*,..a routine designed to assist in the actual operation of the computer. **1969** P. B. JORDAIN *Condensed Computer Encycl.* 451 The most common service routines are the input/output programs... Other service routines perform such services as program loading, common calculations.., tracing, memory dumps, tape dumps, and the like. **1921** *Sci. Amer.* Dec. 135/3 Each..pipe at the *service station is provided with a plug... Each automobile comes into the service station charged with static. **1925** *Morris Owner's Man.* 61 Do not forget that Messrs. Lucas have for your benefit, Service Stations in the following towns. **1935** *Economist* 7 Dec. 1132/2 The tendency..for manufacturing companies to transfer their service stations away from the centre of London..has..lessened the convenience to the..motorist of running his car direct to the maker's service station for minor repairs. **1940** R. CHANDLER *Farewell, my Lovely* vii. 52 He gassed up there and the service station kid recognized him. **1977** *Lubricants Business* (Shell Internat. Petroleum Co.) 7 Supermarkets are increasingly competing with service stations for motor oil sales. *c* **1440** *Alphabet of Tales* 144 He..happend þat day.. to be assigned be þe bisshopp to be his dekyn in *serves tyme & rede þe pistle. **1582** in W. H. Turner *Select. Rec. Oxford* (1880) 420 Uppon the Soundaye..owt of service tyme. **1818** SCOTT *Hrt. Midl.* xviii, She had never seen Robertson since his remarkable escape during service-time. **1573** *Nottingham Rec.* IV. 154 Hyr gesse compyng in *sarves wylle. **1673** [R. LEIGH] *Transpr. Reh.* 83 A citizens sitting bare-headed all service-while.

**service** ('sɜːvɪs), *sb.*[2] Forms: α. 6 servis(se, serves, servyse, 6–7 cervise, cervice, 6–8 servise, 6– service; β. 6 sarves, 9 *U.S.* sarvice; γ. 7 sorvise, sorveise, sorvice. [orig. *serves*, pl. of SERVE *sb.*[1]]

**1.** A tree, *Pyrus* (*Sorbus* L., *Cormus* Spach) *domestica*, native in continental Europe and cultivated in the British Isles, bearing small pear-shaped or round fruit edible when in an over-ripe condition; see CORM[1] 1, SERVICE-TREE, SORB.

**1530** PALSGR. 265/1 Sarves, tree, *alisier*. *Ibid.* 269/2 Servyse, tree, *alisier*. **1577** B. GOOGE *Heresbach's Husb.* (1586) 72 Upon the same stock are graffed..the Medler, and the Servisse. **1601** HOLLAND *Pliny* xv. xiii. I. 437 The fruit Sebesten..beeing graffed vpon Sorvices. **1664** EVELYN *Kal. Hort.* (1679) 38 Catalogue of Fruit-trees... Services or Chequers. **1767** ABERCROMBIE *Ev. Man his own Gard.* (1803) 40 Plant fruit trees..quinces, medlars, mulberries, filberts, services, &c. **1906** *Westm. Gaz.* 27 Sept. 10/1 The service is of slow growth, seldom fruiting until sixty years old.

†**2.** The fruit of this tree. *Obs.*

**1530** PALSGR. 265/1 Sarves, frute, *alise*. *c* **1532** DU WES *Introd. Fr.* in Palsgr. 1073 Walnuttes, cervyse, medlers, aples. **1542** BOORDE *Dyetary* xxi. (1870) 283 Ceruyces be in maner of lyke operacyon. **1594** MARLOWE & NASHE *Dido* IV. v. N.'s Wks. (Grosart) VI. 64 Browne Almonds, Seruises, ripe Figs and Dates. **1601** HOLLAND *Pliny* XIX. v. II. 18 Divers there be, who after another sort make a confection thereof, namely with Quinces, with Sorvises, or Plums. **1612** PEACHAM *Gentl. Exerc.* II. vii. (1634) 126 A basket of Servises, Medlers and Chestnuts. **1682** WHELER *Journ. Greece* VI. 452 A Fruit,..not much bigger than Cervices. **1780** COXE *Russ. Discov.* 56 They also feed upon several species of roots and berries, namely, cloud-berries,..and services. **1796** C. MARSHALL *Garden.* xvii. (1813) 287 Service, (sweet) or sorb apple, is rarely cultivated for fruit, as it requires a warmer climate than England to ripen it.

**3.** ***wild service***: a bush or low tree (*Pyrus torminalis*) bearing harsh bitter fruit.

**1741** *Compl. Fam.-Piece* II. iii. 374 There are several other Trees and Shrubs which are now in Flower, as..wild Service or Quickbeam. **1852** G. W. JOHNSON *Gard. Dict.* 758 *Pyrus torminalis.* Wild-service.

**4.** *attrib.*, as †***service-apple***; **service-berry**, †(*a*) the fruit of the Service (*Pyrus domestica*); (*b*) a N. American tree or shrub of the genus *Amelanchier*, belonging to the family Rosaceæ and bearing clusters of white flowers followed by small, dark-coloured berries; also, the fruit of this tree or shrub; (*c*) the fruit of the white-beam, *Pyrus Aria* (*Cent. Dict.*).

**1820** T. MITCHELL *Aristoph.* I. 122 The baskets which held the cheeses, chesnuts, and dried *service-apples. **1578** LYTE *Dodoens* VI. lii. 727 The Sorbe Apples or *Seruice beries. **1807** P. GASS *Jrnl.* 136, I saw service-berry bushes hanging full of fruit. **1784** F. ASBURY *Jrnl.* 31 July (1821) I. 370 The child he fed with..sawice berries. **1847** RUXTON *Adv. Mexico* xxiv. 206 A shrub which produces a fruit called by the mountaineers service-berries. **1894** *Outing* July 306/1 The undergrowth was poplar, sarvice-berry bushes and other shrubs.

**service** ('sɜːvɪs), *v.* [f. SERVICE *sb.*[1]] **1.** *trans.* To be of service to; to serve; to provide with a service.

**1893** R. L. STEVENSON *Catriona* I. xvi. 178 If I am to service ye the way that you propose, I'll lose my lifelihood. **1948** J. STEINBECK *Russian Jrnl.* (1949) 15 Airports are so far from the cities they supposedly service. **1955** *News of North* (Yellowknife, N.W.T.) 18 Nov. 1/5 A new town house, available to water and sewer service, would be assessed at a much higher rate than duplicate property in a part of the town not serviced this way. **1969** D. WIDGERY in Cockburn & Blackburn *Student Power* 139 It is unlikely that a radical Executive would be able to..service the entirely different attitude of the apolitical small colleges. **1974** R. ADAMS *Shardik* lviii. 518 How many permanent camps or staging-forts would be needed to service a regular trade-route?

**2.** To perform routine maintenance or repair work on (a motor vehicle or other piece of equipment). orig. *U.S.*

**1926** *Amer. Speech* II. 112/2 The automobile dealer says: 'Run the new car five hundred miles at twenty or less an hour, then have it thoroughly serviced with grease and oil.' **1930** *Bookman* Dec. 398 Probably the greatest cost in Television will be that expended for servicing the equipment. **1935** A. P. HERBERT in *Punch* 27 Feb. 236/1, I denounce, Comrades, the foul new verb 'to service', an invention, I believe, of someone in the motor-trade. **1949** 'G. ORWELL' *Nineteen Eighty-Four* II. 131 She enjoyed her work, which consisted chiefly in running and servicing a powerful but tricky electric motor. **1958** *Listener* 23 Oct. 655/2 Vehicles—whether moving, parked, unloading or being serviced—have already taken charge of the present ground level. **1978** R. LEWIS *Uncertain Sound* vi. 154 Your car was serviced on the Thursday.

**3.** To pay interest on (a debt).

**1942** *Sun* (Baltimore) 15 Jan. 2/1 Secretary of Interior Ickes announced today that interest payments on outstanding bonds of the Philippine Government would continue to be met and serviced through the United States Treasury. **1952** *Times* 1 Aug. 9/2 Nobody oversea will ever accept the idea that a company which has all the pesetas it could want should be bankrupted in Spain..because the Spanish Government has not allowed it to buy sterling to service a sterling debt. **1975** *Daily Tel.* 21 Oct. 17/7 Unless there is a huge Federal loan guarantee by the end of next month the city will not be able to meet its payroll, let alone service its debts.

**4.** = SERVE *v.*[1] 52; also of a man, to have sexual intercourse with (a woman).

**1961** in WEBSTER. **1966** [see *post coitum* s.v. POST *Latin preposition*]. **1973** W. H. CANAWAY *Harry doing Good* II. v. 188, I knew a feller that married a twin. Identical. He was getting worn out..till he found out he was servicing both of these twins. **1976** T. HEALD *Let Sleeping Dogs Die* iv. 78 One dog could presumably service several bitches in a day.

**5. a.** To supply (a person) *with* something. **b.** To process.

**1969** *Daily Tel.* 6 Oct. 9/6 It is a proper function of local theatres to service their audiences with the latest in world taste. **1971** *Ibid.* 27 May 14/8 We'll be able to service the retailer with merchandise much faster than it can possibly be shipped in from overseas. **1971** D. POTTER *Brit. Eliz. Stamps* vi. 70 A Post Office First-Day Cover service was available, and no charge was made if the envelope carried sufficient postage. The complete set was serviced for the cost of the envelope and the stamps. **1973** *Daily Tel.* 16 Apr. 2/2 This year building societies have been without funds to service all the mortgages required, and sales are being cancelled.

Hence **'serviced** *ppl. a.*, provided with service or services; maintained.

**1938** C. HIMES *Headwaiter* in *Black on Black* (1973) 150 Over by the elevator where the room service was stationed, a waiter lounged indolently by a serviced table. **1968** *Globe & Mail* (Toronto) 13 Feb. 31/6 (Advt.), Serviced industrial land Northwest Metro bargain price. **1978** R. V. JONES *Most Secret War* xliv. 419 Each pilot could draw a serviced aircraft, probably a different one from that which he last flew, for each new operation.

**serviceability** (ˌsɜːvɪsə'bɪlɪtɪ). [f. next + -ITY.] Capability or readiness for service; usefulness. Also of machinery: the capacity to be maintained or repaired; reliability.

**1834** *Tait's Mag.* I. 531 Her kind-heartedness, her serviceability, and naiveté of mind, rendered her..a welcome guest. **1898** GREGORY *Side Lights Meth.* 13 The basis of his character was seriousness and an indomitable serviceability. **1913** *Chambers's Jrnl.* June 478/1 The claims of reliability, serviceability, and efficiency have been established. **1942** *R.A.F. Jrnl.* 3 Oct. 25 He looks at the Situation Map, the serviceability blackboard, and other items of visual intelligence. **1946** *Happy Landings* July 3/3 Drills connected with the serviceability of the engine..are clearing the supercharger gears and exercising propellers in flight. **1961** B. FERGUSSON *Watery Maze* xiii. 319 It had been calculated at Quadrant that the 'serviceability rate'—that is, the number which one could actually count on for use on D-Day—would be 90 per cent for LSTs and 85 per cent for the rest. **1981** S. DUNMORE *Ace* II. ii. 162 The shortages affected serviceability..damaged aircraft had to be cannibalized to provide spares.

**serviceable** ('sɜːvɪsəb(ə)l), *a.* Forms: α. 4 servisabylle, -abul, serviseable, 4 servicable, 4–6 servisable, 5 servesabill, cervysable, servysabill, 6 servychable, 6– serviceable; β. 4 servisiable, 4–5 serviciable, 5 cervycyable. [a. OF. *serviçable, -isable*, f. *service* SERVICE *sb.*[1]: see -ABLE. With the β forms cf. med.L. *serviciābilis* (Du Cange).]

**1.** Ready to do service; prepared to minister, willing to be of service; active or diligent in service. Now *rare*.

α. *c* **1330** R. BRUNNE *Chron.* (Rolls) 3139 He..was plesaunt & seruisable. *c* **1380** WYCLIF *Sel. Wks.* I. 40 þe Pope shulde be..moost servysable and most pore. *c* **1386** CHAUCER *Prol.* 99 Curteis he was, lowely, and seruysable, And carf biforn his fader at the table. *c* **1430** *Syr Gener.* (Roxb.) 36 Thei wer..ful seruiceable in al wise. *c* **1450** *Merlin* 100 Arthur was goode and seruisable, and seide, 'With gode will'. **1534** MORE *Picus* Wks. 32 Thirdelye of reason bee we seruisable..To suche as haue done muche for vs before. **1561** DAUS tr. *Bullinger on Apoc.* (1573) 80 Are they not all seruisable spirites sent forth to doe seruice for their sakes which are heyres of saluation. **1605** SHAKS. *Lear* IV. vi. 257 A seruiceable Villaine, As duteous to the vices of thy Mistris, As badnesse would desire. **1859** TENNYSON *Marr. Geraint* 393 Seeing her [Enid] so sweet and serviceable. **1890** *Spectator* 11 Jan., Her loyal and serviceable friend.

β. *c* **1386** CHAUCER *Clerk's T.* (Lansd.) 979 And sche þe most seruisiable of all Haþe euery chambre arraide. *c* **1440** *Alphabet of Tales* I. 223 Sho was seruyciable to euerilk creatur. *c* **1440** *Promp. Parv.* 67/1 Ceruycyable, or redy alle waye, *obsequiosus*. **1483** *Cath. Angl.* 331/1 Servysiable.

†**b.** Of actions or conditions: Involving or expressing readiness to serve. *Obs.*

*a* **1586** SIDNEY *Arcadia* II. (Sommer) 172 b, Once Zelmane could not stirre, but that..Basilius with seruiceable steppes, ..would follow her. **1608** D. T[UVILL] *Ess. Pol. & Mor.* A 3, My seruiceable affection towards your Honour. **1629** MILTON *Christ's Nativ.* xxvii, And all about the Courtly Stable, Bright-harnest Angels sit in order serviceable.

†**c.** Subservient. *Obs. rare.*

**1613** HAYWARD *Will. I* 88 He was..sottishly seruiceable both to pleasure and sloath. **1849** JAMES *Woodman* iii, Thou hireling, serviceable knave.

†**2.** Suitable to be served (as food). *Obs. rare.*

**1398** TREVISA *Barth. De P.R.* XVII. xcvi. (1495) 663 Lens lentis is a manere of coddeware: and is seruysable to potage. *c* **1460** J. RUSSELL *Bk. Nurture* 798 in *Babees Bk.*, Beef or moton stewed seruysable.

**3. a.** Of persons: Profitable, useful.

**1660** F. BROOKE tr. *Le Blanc's Trav.* 280 A dead man is often more serviceable to the living, than the living themselves. **1691** NORRIS *Pract. Disc.* 133 What makes you Good and Religious here, serves also to make you useful and serviceable hereafter. **1704** DE FOE in *15th Rep. Hist. MSS. Comm.* App. IV. 83 Wishing..that you may find this neglected fellow serviceable or at least make him so. **1794** S. WILLIAMS *Vermont* 263 In what manner the people of Vermont could be the most serviceable to the British government. **1866** GEO. ELIOT *F. Holt* xxix, Johnson was a most serviceable subordinate. **1881** BESANT & RICE *Chapl. Fleet* I. 129 'She will, I trust, be serviceable to you', said the doctor.

**b.** Of things: Capable of being applied to an appropriate purpose, or to the performance of a proper function.

**1390** GOWER *Conf.* II. 153 For thelementz ben servicable To man. **1577** B. GOOGE *Heresbach's Husb.* III. (1586) 126 b, The Camel..some suppose to be the seruiceablest cattell for man that is. **1590** SIR J. SMYTH *Disc. Weapons* Ded. 1 b, To suppresse and extinguishe the exercise and seruiceable vse of Long-bowes. **1601** R. JOHNSON *Kingd. & Commw.* (1603) 51 To find so and so many seruiceable horse for the war. **1668** HALE *Pref. to Rolle's Abridgm.* 8 He shall never be able to carry on a distinct serviceable Memory at all..without helps of Use or Method. **1708** SWIFT *Sacram. Test* Wks. 1755 II. I. 123 The most serviceable treatise that could have been published at such a juncture. **1774** GOLDSM. *Nat. Hist.* (1776) I. 306 The barometer..is also serviceable in measuring the heights of mountains. **1816** SCOTT *Antiq.* xxxv, His museum..contained nothing that could be serviceable on the present or any other occasion. **1857** RUSKIN *Pol. Econ. Art* 7 To procure him large intervals of healthful rest and serviceable leisure. **1880** ZAEHNSDORF *Bookbinding* 93 The work is as strong and serviceable as in a whole-bound book. **1894** K. GRAHAME *Pagan P.* 4 Past farmsteads where man and beast..learn pleasant and serviceable lessons each of the other.

**serviceableness** ('sɜːvɪsəb(ə)lnɪs). [f. SERVICEABLE + -NESS.] The quality of being serviceable.

**1.** Readiness for service, helpfulness. Now *rare*.

**1564** HAWARD *Eutropius* x. R iij b, He estemed him greatly for the earnest trauaile and payns which he sustained in the battail..& for other seruiceablenesse & good endeuor, which he apperceiued to be in him. **1578** J. JONES *Preserv. Bodie & Soule* I. xlv. 120 All godlinesse,..seruisablenesse, stayednesse, temperance. **1655** FULLER *Ch. Hist.* II. 77 Contending by laudable means, which shall surpasse other in their Serviceablenesse to God. **1702** C. MATHER *Magn. Chr.* II. ix. (1852) 154 Having always but low expectations, after he had merited as highly as possible by his universal serviceableness. **1878** FR. A. KEMBLE *Rec. Girlhood* II. vi. 196 His serviceableness to his friends was unwearied. **1886** HERFORD *Lit. Rel. Eng. & Germany* 317 The polished urbanity of King Alphonso's guest, the ironical serviceableness of the merchant's clerk.

**2.** Usefulness, ability to render service or to promote the interests of another.

**1653** H. MORE *Antid. Ath.* App. I. xi. (1712) 210 Those long and subordinate concatenations of instrumental serviceableness of such things, say they, is but our fancy, no design of any First Cause. **1721** DE FOE *Mem. Cavalier* (1840) 268 The serviceableness of these small bodies of firemen. **1851** RUSKIN *Sheepfolds* 46 There is no fear that the civil officer should underrate the dignity or shorten the serviceableness of the minister. **1870** J. H. NEWMAN *Gram. Assent* II. x. 421 Not undervaluing the force and serviceableness of his argument.

**'serviceably**, *adv.* [f. SERVICEABLE + -LY[2].]

†**1.** With a disposition to serve, obediently. *Obs.*

**1538** ELYOT *Dict.*, *Famulanter*, humbly, seruysably. **1579** G. HARVEY *Letter-bk.* (Camden) 64, I most humblye serviceablelye after my dutifull manner take my leave of your Excellencyes feete.

**2.** Usefully.

**1665** PEPYS *Diary* 16 June, My Lord Sandwich..hath done most honourably and serviceably. **1857** RUSKIN *Pol. Econ. Art* 15 She would know in an instant what part of to-morrow's work might be most serviceably forwarded.

†**'serviceage.** *Obs.* [f. SERVICE *sb.*[1] + -AGE.]

**1.** Bondage, servage.

**1594** CAREW *Tasso* (1881) 62 If but such sixe were mongst our enemies, Ere now had Syria stoupt to seruiceage. **1600** FAIRFAX *Tasso* VIII. lxxxiii, He..obaies the raine Of thraldome base, and seruiceage, though loth.

**2.** ? Feudal military service.

**1602** FULBECKE *1st Pt. Parall.* 24 The seruiceage is suspended vntill the maturitie of his age.

**'serviceless**, *a.* [f. SERVICE *sb.*[1] + -LESS.]

†**1.** ? Without reward or pay (cf. SERVICE *sb.*[1] 7).

**14..** *Langland's P. Pl.* B. (MS. O.) xv. 119 Many a prest ..Schulden go synge seruyseles wiþ sire philip þe sparwe.

**2.** Of no service; without usefulness, useless.

**1879** MEREDITH *Egoist* II. 93 They [truisms] will not be serviceless in their admonitions to your understanding. **1906** *Hibbert Jrnl.* Apr. 595 The intestine appendix..now is serviceless and a perpetual menace to health and life.

Hence **'servicelessness.**

**1876** MEREDITH *Beauch. Career* I. xv. 236 The elegant vessel..an image..of a beautiful servicelessness.

**'serviceman.** Also with capital initial, hyphened, and as two words. [SERVICE *sb.*[1]]

**1.** A man who serves, or has served, in the armed forces.

**1899** (*title*) Constitution of the Service men of the Spanish war (Columbus, Ga.). **1917** *Hansard Commons* 4 May 608 (*heading*) Disabled service men. **1918** *Sheffield Daily Tel.* 18 Sept. 2/6 Discharged soldiers should be represented on all committees that have to deal with the training of discharged service men. **1945** *Daily Express* 14 Aug. 3/7 Duty-Free cigarettes sent to Service men in Europe may be officially rationed soon. **1959** *Listener* 23 July 119/2, I go about a good deal, talking to trade unionists and to work-people generally, to managers, to civil servants, to servicemen, and to students and teachers of all kinds. **1976** M. GREEN *Children of Sun* (1977) viii. 366 Only 750 Old Etonian servicemen died in this war... In the first one..1,150 died.

**2.** A man who maintains and repairs equipment (SERVICE *sb.*[1] 31 b).

**1961** in WEBSTER. **1969** D. E. WESTLAKE *Up your Banners* xxviii. 195 Our serviceman wouldn't make the installation at night, sir. **1970** *Which?* May 143/2 All except the Bendix needed at least one visit from a serviceman before they were working properly. **1974** *Sci. Amer.* Jan. 120/3 Beginners will find that neighboring radio hams and television servicemen can pass along useful construction tips.

Similarly **'servicewoman.**

**1945** *Observer* 21 Oct. 6/1 (Advt.), For thousands of Service men and women the order is 'carry on'. **1972** J. WILLIAMS *Home Fronts* v. xv. 255 The historic Norfolk House in St James's Square was given over to service-women from overseas.

**servicer** ('sɜːvɪsə(r)). [f. SERVICE *v.* + -ER[1].] One who services.

**1973** *Houston* (Texas) *Chron.* (Suppl.) 14 Oct. 8/2 A better way to collect the oil from driveway auto servicers is being sought. *a* **1974** R. CROSSMAN *Diaries* (1976) II. 406 Many of the owners are people of substance who have servicers for their vehicles, chauffeurs so to speak, who look after them as a whole-time occupation.

**service-tree.** [f. SERVICE *sb.*[2] + TREE *sb.*]

**1.** = SERVICE *sb.*[2] 1.

**1600** SURFLET *Country Farm* III. xl. 507 Such is the force of the ceruise tree, to raise vp, renew and reuiue a qualified and appeased madnes. **1749** LADY LUXBOROUGH *Let. to Shenstone* 23 Mar., The walk which is bordered by service-trees. **1857** MILLER *Elem. Chem., Org.* (1862) 410 An acid derived from the berries of the service-tree. **1910** *Blackw. Mag.* Aug. 181/1 The..wood of the small service-tree.

**b.** The wood of this tree used in the arts.

**1545** ASCHAM *Toxoph.* II. (Arb.) 124 Steles be made of dyuerse woodes as..seruis tree. **1703** *Art's Improv.* I. 33 By this Method, the Violet Wood which Dyers use, will be Stained Black as Ebony;..Pear-Tree and Service-Tree will be of Reddish Colour.

**2.** *wild service-tree.* = SERVICE *sb.*[2] 3.

**1639** HORN & ROB. *Gate Lang. Unl.* xi. §122 The bay-tree, the maple and wild service-tree beare berries. **1796** WITHERING *Brit. Plants* (ed. 3) II. 458 Wild Service-tree, or Sorb. **1832** *Planting* 103 in *Libr. Usef. Knowl., Husb.* III, The wild service-tree (torminalis). **1859** W. S. COLEMAN *Our Woodlands* (1862) 55 In the Southern parts of the kingdom, we may often meet with the Wild Service Tree.

**3.** †*narrow-leaved, Fowler's service-tree*: names for the Mountain Ash, *Pyrus* (*Sorbus*) *Aucuparia*.

**1793** *Statist. Acc. Scot.* IX. 328 They fixed branches of mountain ash, or narrow leaved service-tree above the stakes of their cattle, to preserve them from the evil effects of elves and witches. **1859** W. S. COLEMAN *Our Woodlands* (1862) 59 The Mountain Ash is often called the Fowler's Service-tree.

**4.** The N. American service-berry (SERVICE *sb.*[2] 4).

**1884** SARGENT *Rep. Forests N. Amer.* 84 *Amelanchier Canadensis*... June berry. Shad bush. Service tree.

**servicie**, obs. form of SERVICE *sb.*[1]

**servicing** ('sɜːvɪsɪŋ), *vbl. sb.* [-ING[1].] **1.** The action of maintaining or repairing a motor vehicle, etc. Also *fig.*

**1935** *Economist* 7 Dec. 1131/2 Recognised dealers with facilities for the..'servicing' of the vehicles sold. **1956** *Good Housek. Home Encycl.* (ed. 4) 143/2 Servicing and repairs which can be carried out by the handyman of the house. **1959** I. JEFFERIES *Thirteen Days* x. 156 'Where's the bint, John?'.. 'I left her at the hospital for servicing and overhaul.' **1970** *Motoring Which?* July 91/1 All three needed routine servicing every 3,000 miles. **1978** D. DEVINE *Sunk without Trace* 253 There was the car... Why did she put it in for servicing that particular week?

**2.** The action of paying interest on a debt.

**1939** *Times* 2 Mar. 13/2 Financial circles hope that an arrangement will be reached in the meantime for the continued servicing of foreign loans. **1946** *Sun* (Baltimore) 7 Oct. 5/2 Servicing of these two issues has required $647,507.50 a year.

**3.** The action of providing a service.

**1944** *Ann. Reg. 1943* 90 Most of their reciprocal aid..had therefore been 'servicing', taking the form of providing transportation, accommodation, airfields,..local supplies to American forces. **1946** J. S. HUXLEY *Unesco* ii. 58 The general educational servicing of the public in the fields of science and culture.

**4.** *attrib.* and *Comb.*

**1930** *Economist* 31 May 1207/1 The unclassified group of trades—which includes road transport and most of what Americans term 'servicing' industries—contributed 20.08 per cent. **1944** *R.A.F. Jrnl.* Aug. 256, I joined the Servicing Commando unit at the Transit Camp. **1955** *Univ. of Virginia News Let.* 15 June 1/5 Growth of the servicing-type industries, such as retail and wholesale trade, utilities, business and repair services. **1968** [see POISSON 1]. **1978** R. V. JONES *Most Secret War* xxxix. 360 At Zempin we hoped to have the aircraft and its servicing installations isolated.

†**ser'vicious**, *a. Obs.* [ad. med.L. *servitiōs-us*, f. L. *servitium* service; see -OUS.] = SERVICEABLE.

**1460** *Promp. Parv.* (Winch.) 408 Servycyows, or seruicyable, *obsequiosus*.

**servie**, obs. form of SERVE *v.*[1]

**servient** ('sɜːvɪənt), *a.* [ad. L. *servient-em*, pr. pple. of *servīre* to serve.]

**1.** Subordinate, subject to rule. *rare.* †Also, performing service, serving.

**1647** COWLEY *Mistress, The Soul* i, My Soul..in another's Breast does lye, That neither Is, nor will be I, As a Form Servient and Assisting there. **1650** T. BAYLY *Herba Parietis* 3 A liberall fountaine, which was no lesse servient to the grotts for waterworks, then to the house for use. **1724** WATERLAND *Farther Vind.* 120 This celebrated Father is full and express, in his famous Creed, against any thing created, or servient, in the Trinity. **1892** T. WATTS in *Athenæum* 2 Apr. 436/2 She..endows men..with two different kinds of personality, the dominant and the servient.

†**b.** *absol. Obs. rare.*

*c***1615** BOYS *Wks.* (1629) 436 But in generall onely you se that Angels are seruients vnto God, and his people.

**2.** Law. ***servient land, tenement***: a land or tenement over which a servitude has been granted or acquired in favour of a dominant land or tenement. ***servient proprietor***: the tenant of a servient land or tenement.

**1681** STAIR *Inst. Law Scot.* II. vii. (1693) 284 The Servitude of Support, whereby the servient Tenement is lyable to bear any Burden for the use of the Dominant. *Ibid.* 287 A Watergang is a Servitude, of conveying Water thorow the servient Ground, for the use of the Dominant. **1754** ERSKINE *Princ. Law Scot.* (1809) 221 The owner of the servient tenement is not obliged, in a servitude of support, to repair it, unless [etc.]. **1838** W. BELL *Dict. Law Scot.* 864 This class of servitudes imports no obligation on the servient proprietor to maintain the road. **1871-4** MARKBY *Elem. Law* §371 English lawyers call..the land over which it [an easement] is exercised the servient land.

*transf.* **1864** BLACKMORE *Clara Vaughan* lxvii, His great fear was, that the..Della Croce estates should become a servient tenement to the frozen fields of the North.

†**ser'viential**, *a. Obs. rare*$^{-1}$. [f. SERVIENT *a.* + -IAL.] Pertaining to service.

**1897** F. W. MAITLAND *Domesday Bk.* 162 The relation between thegn and lord is no longer conceived as a menial, 'serviential' or ministerial relation.

†'**servier.** *Obs. rare.* Also 5 **sarueyere.** [irreg. f. SERVE *v.*[1]] = SERVER 1.

*a***1475** ASHBY *Poems* (1899) 26 And euer remembre olde Sarueyeres. **1530** *Fabric Rolls York Minster* (Surtees) 135 For a servyer to ye said maysons, 2s. 8d.

**serviette** (sɜːvɪ'ɛt). Forms: *α. Sc.* 5–7 **serviot,** 6 **serviat;** *β. Sc.* 6–7 **servit,** 8 **servite,** 6, 9 **servet;** *γ.* 6–7 *Sc.* **serviet,** 9 **serviette.** [a. F. *serviette* a towel, table-napkin, of obscure formation, connected with *servir* SERVE *v.*[1]

The older use of the word was exclusively Sc. In the 19th c. it was re-introduced with the French spelling (at first only as a foreign term). It may now be regarded as naturalized, but latterly has come to be considered vulgar.]

A table-napkin; also, †a slip-cloth.

*α.* **1489** *Acta Dom. Concil.* (1839) 131/2, xij cuschingis.. and xij seruiotis of dornewik. **1501** *Acc. Ld. High Treas. Scot.* II. 28 Item, for serviotis to the same [King's burd] vij elne lang and iij quartaris braid. **1560** *Stirling Burgh Rec.* (1887) I. 72 Ane hand towall, ane serviat [etc.]. *c***1575** *Balfour's Practicks* (1754) 235 The air sall have..twelf servettis and ane buird-claith of dornique. **1619** *Reg. Privy Council Scot.* XII. 761 Tua dusane of dornik serviottis.

*β.* **1588** *Cal. Laing Charters* (1899) 289 [Twenty-four] linteolum lie seruittis [at 18s. the dozen]. **1601** in *T. Pont's Topogr. Acc. Cunningham* (Maitland Club) 179 Ten small seruittis, twentie round seruittis. *a***1670** SPALDING *Troub. Chas. I* (Bannatyne Cl.) I. 108 The generall himselfe..and souldiers, sat doun..and of their own provision, with ane servitt on their knee, took their breakfast. **1719** in W. Macgill *Old Ross-sh.* (1909) 131 Table cloths and servites of damask and dornick and hagabag servites, sheets, &c. **1821** JOANNA BAILLIE *Metr. Leg., Lady G. Baillie* xxxi, Her hands ..Unfolding spread the servet white.

*γ.* **1513** DOUGLAS *Æneis* I. xi. 17 With soft serviettis to mak thair handis clene. **1587-8** in *Extracts Burgh Rec. Edin.* (1882) IV. 515 Thai sall nocht..be sene in the streits with thair aiprunes and seruiets. **1612** in A. M'Kay *Kilmarnock* 308 Saxteine seruietis of damais. **1818** LADY MORGAN *Autobiog.* (1859) 114 A dirty coarse canvas *serviette*. **1864** SALA *Quite alone* I. viii. 133 At table d'hôte time he..carried a serviette in lieu of a feather broom under his arm. **1889** ROY TELLET *Pr. Maskiloff* 167 Mordaunt and Scarnell.. always spoke of napkins as serviettes. **1906** H. BLAND *Lett. Daughter* 53, I think..she was the sort who would call a table napkin a serviette.

**servigrous** (sɜː'vaɪgrəs), *a. U.S. dial.* Also **savigrous, sevigrous, survigrous.** [Orig. unknown: freq. associated with a dial. pronunc. of *vigorous*, and cf. SAVAGEROUS *a.*] Fierce, severe, tough, vigorous. Hence **ser'vigrously** *adv.*

**1835** A. B. LONGSTREET *Georgia Scenes* 227 'Pretty *sevigrous*, but nothing killing yet,' said Billy Curlew, as he learned the place of Spivey's ball. **1888** 'C. E. CRADDOCK' *Keedon Bluffs* 88 He's a servigrous jumper, sure! *Ibid.* 215 The mos' servigrous singer they hed. **1890** T. N. PAGE in *Harper's New Monthly Mag.* Dec. 114/1 She so savigrous I tolt her I 'ain' nuver had nobody to prevaricate nuttin' 'bout me. **1901** *Nashville* (Tenn.) *Banner* 28 Oct. 4/3 The New York Sun..employs that expressive provincialism of the Southern mountaineer, 'servigrous'... The Sun says Mr. William Travis Jerome is 'servigrous' in the kind of oratory he uses. **1913** H. KEPHART *Our Southern Highlanders* xiii. 294 Survigrous (ser-*vi*-grus) is a superlative of vigorous (here pronounced *vi*-grus, with long *i*): as 'a survigrous baby', 'a most survigrous cusser'. **1928** M. CHAPMAN *Happy Mountain* vii. 70 The Preacher must have been a rip-snorting and most survigrous young-un before he caught religion. **1938** C. H. MATSCHAT *Suwannee River* 81 Ary fowkses knows as how onion juice, rubbed in servigerously, sprouts hair like weeds after a rain, iffen so be ye stand in the sun.

**servile** ('sɜːvaɪl, 'sɜːvɪl), *a.* and *sb.* Forms: 4, 6 **servyle,** (5 **servylle, serval, -all),** 6–7 **servil,** (6 *Sc.* **serviall,** 7 **servial),** 7 **servill,** 5– **servile.** [ad. L. *servīlis*, f. *serv-us* slave: see -ILE. Cf. F. *servile* (14th c. in *œvre servile*: see 1 b), Pr., Sp., Pg. *servil*, It. *servile*.] **A.** *adj.*

**1.** Of, belonging to or proper to a slave or slaves.

***servile habit*** was formerly sometimes applied *transf.* to the dress of a labourer or a poor man. ***servile war, insurrection***: one raised by slaves against their masters.

*c***1450** *Mirour Saluacioun* 2666 Thay knewe noght the king in his servylle habite. **1542** BECON *Potat. Lent* I v, The bearynge of Olyues shewethe that we are..delyuered oute of seruile captiuite. **1591** SAVILE *Tacitus, Hist.* IV. v. 176 Asiaticus, for his lewde credit vnder his master, made satisfaction now as a freed-man with a seruile death. **1607** CHAPMAN *Bussy d' Ambois* III. i. 28 Like a monster Kept only to show men for servile money. **1617** MORYSON *Itin.* I. 40 A Doctor..thinking my servile habit not fit for contemplation, commanded mee to draw water for his horse. **1770** LANGHORNE *Plutarch, Crassus* III. 430 He thought he could easily rekindle the Servile war, which had but lately been smothered. **1840** THIRLWALL *Greece* lix. VII. 325 Demetrius was of very low, if not of servile origin. **1841** ELPHINSTONE *Hist. India* I. 383 The total extinction of the servile condition of the Súdras is..an improvement. **1884** *Manch. Exam.* 7 Oct. 5/4 A well-known..device..for securing servile labour without the name of slavery. **1885** W. PATER *Marius* I. iv. I. 53 This lad of servile birth.

**b.** Of arts, employments, labour: Befitting a slave; unworthy of a free man; hence, 'mechanical' as opposed to *liberal*.

**1514** BARCLAY *Cyt. & Uplondyshm.* Wks. (1570) D iij b, Thus began honour and thus began bondage,..And seruile labour first in the worlde began. **1535** STEWART *Cron. Scot.* (Rolls) II. 444 Bot vse his office as ane man of kirk, No seruiall werkis with his handis wirk. *c***1590** MARLOWE *Faust* (1631) i, This study fits a mercenary drudge, Who aymes at nothing but externall trash, Too seruile and illiberall for me. **1679** BLOUNT *Anc. Tenures* 3 Each of which Bond-men was ..to Plow, reap, make the Lords Malt, and do other servile work. **1784** COWPER *Task* III. 406 No works indeed That ask robust tough sinews, bred to toil, Servile employ. **1838** ARNOLD *Hist. Rome* I. 81 [Tarquinius] employed the great bulk of them [*sc.* the people] in servile works, in the building of the circus [etc.]. **1868** RUSKIN *Time & Tide* xviii. (ed. 2) 109 A great number of quite necessary employments are, in the accuratest sense, 'servile,' that is, they sink a man to the condition of a serf, or unthinking worker.

**c.** ***servile work*** [after L. *opus servile* (Vulg.), a literal rendering of Heb. *m*[e]*léketh ‛ăbōdāh*]: in religious use applied *spec.* to laborious or mechanical work forbidden to be done on the Sabbath and hence on the festivals of the Church.

**1382** WYCLIF *Lev.* xxiii. 21 And ȝe shulen clepe this day.. moost holi; al seruyle werk ȝe shulen not do in it. *c***1430** *Hymns Virg.* 104 Haue mynde to helewe þin holi day,.. Leue seruile werkis & nyce aray. **1449** *Rolls of Parlt.* V. 152/1 Yt yer be no Merketts in thy places,..ne oyer servile werkes don uppon Sondays. **1637** GILLESPIE *Eng. Pop. Cerem.* IV. iii. 7 To doe servile worke upon the sixe dayes of labour is good. **1884** ADDIS & ARNOLD *Cath. Dict.* (1897) 218/1 To keep the Sundays and holidays of obligation holy, by hearing Mass and resting from servile works.

**2.** Of a person: Subject as a slave or serf to a master or owner; living in servitude. Of a class, etc.: Composed of slaves or serfs.

**1565** COOPER *Thesaurus* s.v. *Seruilis, Capita seruilia*, Liuius. Seruile persons. **1695** KENNETT *Paroch. Antiq.* Gloss. s.v. *Coterellus*, Spelman and Du Fresne make cotarius and coterellus to be both the servile inhabitants. **1704** POPE *Windsor For.* 365 Let barb'rous Ganges arm a servile train. **1776** GIBBON *Decl. & F.* xiii. I. 356 A distinct line of separation was hitherto preserved between the free and the servile part of mankind. **1784** CULLUM *Hist. Hawsted* iii. 95 To this manor belonged two *nativi*, or servants born of servile tenants. **1874** STUBBS *Const. Hist.* xxi. (1896) III. 624 Possibly these [*sc.* bondmen on some manors] were the survivors of the peasant population which had been servile before the Conquest. **1906** MACKINNON *Hist. Mod. Liberty* I. 285 During the three centuries following the Conquest, the condition of the servile class undoubtedly improved.

†**b.** In wider sense: Belonging to the serving class or to the lower orders; engaged in 'servile' or mechanical occupations. *Obs.*

**1447** BOKENHAM *Seyntys* xi. 163 If þou þan..be a ientyl wumman, A serual persone why shewyst the In maners & condycyouns for to be? **1588** SHAKS. *Tit. A.* v. ii. 55, I will ..by the Waggon wheele, Trot like a Seruile footeman all day long. **1599** *George-a-Greene* D 3, Ile..take that seruile pinner George a Greene, And butcher him. **1612** *Acts & Stat. Lawting, Sheriff & Justice Courts* (Maitl. Club 1840) 160 That it sall not be lesum to seruile persones not worth ..lxxij li Scottis to tak vp housis. **1628** BURTON *Anat. Mel.* I. ii. IV. i. (ed. 3) 136 The mother will be more carefull..then any seruile woman or such hired creatures. **1727** GAY *Begg. Op.* III. xliv, Of all mechanicks, of all servile handicraftsmen, a gamester is the vilest.

**3.** Of a person: That behaves like a slave; slavish, meanly submissive, 'cringing, fawning' (J.); destitute of independence in thought and action; slavishly deferential or obedient *to*.

**1605** SHAKS. *Lear* III. ii. 21 *Lear.* Heere I stand your Slaue, ..But yet I call you Seruile Ministers, That [etc.]. **1655** FULLER *Ch. Hist.* IV. 166 King Henry the fourth, who though curteous, was not servial to the Pope. **1725** WATTS *Logic* II. iii. §4 Others..give themselves up in too servile a manner to the Opinion and Authority of other Masters. **1728** POPE *Dunc.* II. 356 A low-born, cell-bred, selfish, servile band..who fight for any God, or Man. **1751** JOHNSON *Rambler* No. 96 ¶4 Those who are neither servile nor timorous are yet desirous to bestow pleasure. **1843** LYTTON *Last Bar.* II. i, Be courteous to all men, servile to none. **1840** KINGSLEY *Lett.* (1878) I. 49, I was servile to the opinions of the very persons I despised. **1860** EMERSON *Cond. Life* iv. Wks. (Bohn) II. 373 A supple, glib-tongued tribe, who live for show, servile to public opinion. **1849** MACAULAY *Hist. Eng.* ix. II. 418 A tribunal..where established principles of law could not be utterly disregarded even by the most servile judges. **1865** SEELEY *Ecce Homo* v. (ed. 8) 44 This magnanimous self-restraint saved him from false friends and mercenary or servile flatterers.

*absol.* **1665** EVELYN *Let. to Sir W. Coventry* 2 Oct., If you can believe I retaine so much of servile in me, as to informe you of tales.

†**b.** Slavishly devoted *to* (an object). *Obs.*

**1619** FLETCHER & MASSINGER *False One* IV. ii, He is..a meere wandring Merchant Servile to gaine.

**c.** Of personal attributes and action: Befitting, or characteristic of a slave or a state of servitude; slavish, ignoble. ***servile fear*** (Theol.): see FEAR 3 d.

**1526** *Pilgr. Perf.* (W. de W. 1531) 73 He that feareth god onely for this cause, his feare is called seruyle feare. **1601** SHAKS. *Jul. C.* I. i. 80 [Cæsar] Who else would soare aboue the view of men, And keepe vs all in seruile fearefulnesse. **1618** BOLTON *Florus* III. xxi. (1636) 243 Marius by servill flight saved himselfe. *a***1626** BACON *Ess., Riches* (Arb.) 239 Riches..when they are gotten by Flattery, Feeding Humours, and other Seruile Conditions. **1647** CLARENDON *Hist. Reb.* VII. §225 For as he [Falkland] had a full appetite of fame by just and generous actions, so he had an equal contempt of it by any servile expedients. **1667** MILTON *P.L.* XII. 305 Disciplin'd..from servil fear To filial. **1697** DRYDEN *Virg. Georg.* IV. 307 Besides, not Egypt, India, Media more With servile Awe their Idol King adore. **1699** SHAFTESB. *Inq. Virtue* I. iii. *Charac.* (1711) II. 55 The Obedience is servile, and all that is done thro it, merely servile. **1705** STANHOPE *Paraphr.* I. 37 The..Servile Fears usual in those of a mean depending Condition. **1720** POPE *Ep. to Craggs* 10 Then scorn to gain a Friend by servile ways. **1817** SHELLEY *To Ld. Chancellor* xii, By..The servile arts in which thou hast grown old. *a***1862** BUCKLE *Civiliz.* (1873) III. i. 2 It encourages that blind and servile respect which men are apt to feel for those who are above them. **1862** GLADSTONE *Gleanings* (1879) I. i. 6 In a presumptuous or in a servile spirit.

**4.** Of a people, state, its condition, etc.: Politically enslaved; subject to despotic or oppressive government or to foreign dominion. Const. *to*. Now *rare* or *Obs.*

**1547** J. HARRISON *Exhort. Scottes* 229 Wee could finde in our hartes to become seruile..to a forrein nacion. **1577** HOLINSHED *Chron.* (1586) III. 2/1 They..declared to them ..the pride and insolencie of the Normans, and the hardnesse and griefe of bondage and seruile estate. **1609** DANIEL *Civ. Wars* IV. xxxviii, What? haue we hands, and shall we seruile bee? Why were swordes made? but, to preserue men free. **1654** VILVAIN *Epit. Ess.* IV. xiv. 85 But Claudius since that Nation servil made. **1661** WEBSTER & ROWLEY *Thrac. Wonder* IV. i, His Subjects..shall servile be to Turks and Infidels. **1703** POPE *Thebais* I. 241 O servile land, Where exil'd tyrants still by turns command! **1727-46** THOMSON *Summer* 957 And all the green delights Ausonia pours When for them she must bend the servile knee. **1821** BYRON *Mar. Fal.* II. i, When wicked men wax mighty, and a state Turns servile. **1873** C. ROBINSON *N.S. Wales* 6 A despotic Government and a servile people never can prosper.

*absol.* **1753** JOHNSON *Adventurer* No. 69 ¶4 The day is always coming to the servile in which they shall be powerful.

†**b.** Of government: Exercised over slaves, oppressive, despotic. *Obs.*

**1603** KNOLLES *Hist. Turks* (1621) 57 Under whose servile government it was holden of long time. **1644** H. PARKER *Jus Pop.* 28 Servile power is tolerated because it tends to the good of him that is subject to it.

†**5.** Of immaterial things: Subject *to* the control of something else; not free. *Obs.*

**1581** J. BELL *Haddon's Answ. Osor.* 167 b, Agayne whether offence be committed through free or seruile choyse of will. **1603** SHAKS. *Meas. for M.* III. i. 9 Reason thus with life:..a breath thou art, Servile to all the skyie-influences. **1805** FOSTER *Ess.* (1806) I. I. iii. 51 Even should the attention be awake, and opinions be formed, the faculty which forms them is very servile to the other parts of the human constitution. *Ibid.* I. II. ii. 141 His judgment is not servile to the mood of his feelings.

**6.** Of imitation (esp. in literature and art), translation, etc.: Unintelligently close to the exemplar or original; 'slavish'. Hence of a person as agent.

After Hor. Ep. I. xix. 19 *O imitatores, servum pecus.*

**1605** BACON *Adv. Learn.* I. §2. 2 Speech that is framed after the imitation of some patterne of eloquence, though neuer so excellent: All this hath somewhat seruile, and holding of the subiect. **1638** JUNIUS *Paint. Ancients* 29 How unprofitable..it is that we should tie our endeavours to a kinde of servile Imitation. *c***1647** DENHAM *To Sir R. Fanshawe* Poems (1668) 120 That servile path thou nobly dost decline, Of tracing word by word, and line by line. **1680** DRYDEN *Pref. Ovid's Epist.* (1716) a 2, A servile, litteral Translation. **1781** COWPER *Table-T.* 666 While servile trick and imitative knack Confine the million in the beaten track. **1806** *Med. & Phys. Jrnl.* XV. 363 The idle conceits of the chemists, of which our modern quacks are the servile imitators. **1837** WHEWELL *Hist. Induct. Sci.* I. IV. ii. §3. 271 The commentators or disciples of the great philosophers did not assume at once their servile character. **1879** FARRAR *St. Paul* I. i. 11 If..a minute and servile record had preserved for us every hasty expression.

7. *Philol.* **a.** Of words: Expressing mere grammatical relations; auxiliary.

**1668** WILKINS *Real Char.* IV. iv. 419 The more servile Particles are of three kinds; Articles, Modes, Tenses. **1885** J. AVERY in *Trans. Amer. Philol. Assoc.* XVI. App. 17 Case relations are denoted by added syllables, some of which retain their form and sense as independent words, and others have been degraded into servile particles.

**b.** *Semitic Gram.* Of a letter: Not belonging to the root of the word in which it occurs; serving to express a derivative or flexional element. Hence applied to those letters of the alphabet (in Heb. the eleven grouped mnemonically in the words איתן משה וכלב) which represent sounds that may be used in derivation or flexion. Opposed to *radical*.

**1653** W. ROBERTSON *Gate to Holy Tongue* 7 These servile letters are eleven in number. *Ibid.* 9 These servile letters are so called, not because they are always servile, for all of them do make up roots by themselves,..but because they are often servile..; the other eleven, being always radicall. **1776** J. RICHARDSON *Arab. Gram.* 17 *note*, The *Alif of union* is always servile. **1843** *Proc. Philol. Soc.* I. 138 [Berber] has a distinction of letters..into servile and non-servile, nearly identical with that of Hebrew and Arabic.

**c.** Of a letter: 'Not itself sounded, but serving to lengthen the preceding vowel, as *e* in *tune*.'

**1864** WEBSTER.

**d.** Of sounds: Subject to euphonic change.

**1879** WHITNEY *Skr. Gram.* 23 Certain nasals in Sanskrit are of servile character, always to be assimilated to a following consonant.

**B.** *sb.* (elliptical or absolute uses of the adj.).

**1.** A servile person.

**1830** FONBLANQUE *Eng. under 7 Administr.* (1837) II. 17 They have been distinguished by the King's favour, and nothing else—quacks, serviles, sycophants, and buffoons. **1830** *Westm. Rev.* XIII. 476 Swarms of anti-national serviles, the relics of bygone days. **1831** E. ELLIOTT *Poet. Wks.* (1840) 108/2 Self-robb'd servile! sold, not bought, For the shadow of a groat! **1880** L. WALLACE *Ben-Hur* 19 The Sudra, or serviles, doomed to menial duties.

**2.** *Sp. Hist.* A hostile designation applied (in 1820 and later) by Spanish Liberals to the royalists.

**1822** *Gentl. Mag.* XCII. I. 75 The Lapidas, or constitutional pillars, set up in the different towns of Spain are sometimes, during the night, defaced or bemired by the Serviles. **1840** NAPIER *Penins. War* VI. XXII. vi. 312 And always the serviles yielded under the dread of personal violence. **1887** *Encycl. Brit.* XXII. 345/2 The royalists or serviles, as they were called, were dismissed from office.

**3.** *Philol.* **a.** A servile particle. See A. 7 a.

**1668** WILKINS *Real Char.* III. vii. 343 Both these may contribute to the Abbreviating of Language, when they are compounded as serviles.

**b.** *Hebr. Gram.* A servile letter. See A. 7 b.

**1738** R. GREY *New Meth. Hebr.* p. ii, The Letters are divided into an equal Number of Radicals and Serviles. **1773** BAYLY *Gram. Hebr.* p. xxvii, The principal use of the Letters יהוא is with the other Serviles to form Number, Gender, Moods, Tenses and Derivatives.

**servilely** ('sɜːvaɪllɪ), *adv.* Also 6-7 **servilly**, (7 -llye), 7-8 **servily**. [f. SERVILE *a.* + -LY[2].] In a servile manner.

**1.** In the spirit of a slave; with servile fear or submission; cringingly.

**1550** VERON *Godly Sayings* Ep. Ded. A 5 b, Seruillye.. worshipping..the signes, for the thinges, whiche by the signes are signified. **1596** *Edw. III*, I. i, *Ed.* I meane to visit him as he requests; But how? not seruilely disposd to bend, But like a conquerer to make him bowe. **1660** COKE *Power & Subj.* 72 He who rigorously executes his power will be hated, and servilely feared. **1667** MILTON *P.L.* IV. 959 Who more then thou Once fawn'd, and cring'd, and servilly ador'd Heav'ns awful Monarch? *a* **1677** MANTON *Serm. Ps. cxix.* 167 This is not true Obedience, that is done servilely and by constraint. **1727** [DORRINGTON] *Philip Quarll* (1816) 84 The docile beast most servilely obeys. **1849-50** ALISON *Hist. Europe* VIII. l. §74. 199 The senate joyfully and servilely registered his decrees. **1878** SPURGEON *Treas. Dav.* Ps. cxiii. 2 Not quarreling with his justice..nor servilely dreading his power.

**b.** With servile adherence to rules or conformity to an exemplar or original.

**1668** DRYDEN *Def. Ess. Dram. Poesy* Ess. (ed. Ker) I. 130, I say not this with the least design of limiting the stage too servilely to twenty-four hours. **1711** ADDISON *Spect.* No. 29 ¶8 An English composer should not follow the Italian recitative too servilely, but make use of many gentle deviations from it. **1748** HARTLEY *Observ. Man.* II. iii. 299 This Method of Reasoning has been adopted too servilely. **1852** H. ROGERS *Ecl. Faith* 43 Or how can you ascertain that these men meant what you mean, when you thus servilely copy their language? **1890** GROSS *Gild Merch.* I. 109 Most English writers servilely follow Brentano.

**2.** In or as if in a state of servitude or slavery; as a slave. Now *rare* or *Obs.*

**1561** T. NORTON *Calvin's Inst.* IV. (1562) 12 So many being seruilely born and brought vp, do wythout douting boast themselues to be the children of God. **1579** TWYNE *Phisicke agst. Fort.* II. vii. 171 b, I was seruylely borne. **1592** SHAKS. *Ven. & Ad.* 392 How like a iade he stood tied to the tree, Seruilly maisterd with a leatherne raine. **1617** MORYSON *Itin.* III. 220 The Germans are very churlish to their wives and keep them servily at home. **1681** GLANVILL *Sadducismus* I. (1726) 21 Who inveigle Children..and carry them away to the Plantations of America, to be servilely employ'd there. **1825** SCOTT *Talism.* xxv, Is it indeed you,.. gallant Sir Kenneth of Scotland..thus servilely disguised?

**servileness** ('sɜːvaɪlnɪs). *rare.* [f. SERVILE *a.* + -NESS.] Servility.

**1673** *Lady's Call.* I. ii. §4 To be thus yielding, is not a meekness but servileness of understanding. **1707** NORRIS *Treat. Humility* vi. 243 Humility will despise no man..for the servileness of his condition in being our slave or servant. **1755** in JOHNSON. In recent Dicts.

**servilism** ('sɜːvɪlɪz(ə)m). [f. SERVILE *a.* + -ISM. Cf. F. *servilisme*.]

**1.** Systematic servility.

**1831** *Fraser's Mag.* IV. 140 [That journal's] truckling, and trimming, and shifting, and debasing servilism to mob opinions. **1831** *Westm. Rev.* XV. 93 But we are not aware that servilism, and sycophancy,..ought to be considered as essential recommendations in an historian. **1845** *Foreign Q. Rev.* XXXIV. 277 Twenty years residence in Russia had encrusted Cobenzl with a coating of submissiveness (servilism), that was at times almost comical.

**2.** The doctrine which advocates political 'slavery'.

A hostile designation for anti-Liberal opinions. Cf. SERVILE *sb.* 1.

**1831** CARLYLE *Misc.* (1840) III. 242 Though calling himself Philosopher, Mr. Taylor..still painfully struggles in the questions of Naturalism and Supernaturalism, Liberalism and Servilism. **1841** *Fraser's Mag.* XXIII. 146 He who refutes servilism proves nothing for liberalism.

**3.** The social system based on the existence of slaves.

**1880** *Congregationalist* (U.S.) 17 Nov. (Cent.), The remnants of domination and of servilism [in the southern United States] will soon take themselves hence.

**servility** (sɜː'vɪlɪtɪ). [f. SERVILE *a.* + -ITY. Cf. F. *servilité* (18th c. in Hatz.-Darm.).]

†**1.** Servile condition; the quality or status of being a slave; the condition of being in bondage.

**1591** SAVILE *Tacitus, Agricola* 238 As our ancestours attained..the highest pitch and perfection of liberty, so we of servility. **1613** T. JACKSON *Eternal Truth Script.* I. II. §3. ix. 167 Such seruilitie as the Iewes suffered vnder the Greeks & Asiaticks. **1615** RICH *Honestie of Age* 47 The Pride of this age is growne to that height, that..who is able by the outward shew, to discerne betweene Nobility and Seruility, to know a Lord from a Lowt? **1645** MILTON *Colast.* 15 How should hee a Servingman..know..what the meaning is of gentle... Who could have devis'd to give us more breifly a better description of his own Servility?

quasi-*concr.* **1667** MILTON *P.L.* VI. 169 Such hast thou arm'd, the Minstrelsie of Heav'n, Servilitie with freedom to contend.

*fig.* **1581** J. BELL *Haddon's Answ. Osor.* 255 Shall the will be therfore not wicked in doyng wickedly, bycause it is not free, but enforced to yield to a necessary Servilitie?

**2.** Servile disposition or conduct.

†**a.** Illiberality, meanness. *Obs.*

*a* **1610** HEALEY *Theophrastus* (1616) 77 Illiberality, or Servility, is too great a contempt of glorie, proceeding from the like desire to spare expence.

**b.** Mean submissiveness, degradingly obsequious demeanour, cringing. (The prevailing sense.)

**1573** G. HARVEY *Common-pl. Bk.* (1884) 15 He tould me ..that it was mi flatteri and Serviliti (for so it pleasd him now to term it) that bewitchid him. **1674** *Govt. Tongue* viii. 135 Lying, Servility, and Treachery..make up a loathsome Monstrous guilt. **1797** HT. LEE *Canterb. T.* (1799) I. 374 The domestics..had an air of servility and constraint. **1841** ELPHINSTONE *Hist. India* I. 465 The ceremonial of the kings, however, had not the servility since introduced by the Mussulmans. **1856** FROUDE *Hist. Eng.* (1858) I. ii. 185 The servility with which she addressed the cardinal so long as he was in power. **1874** GREEN *Short Hist.* vii. §1. 341 The success of such a system depended wholly on the absolute servility of Parliament. **1909** GWATKIN *Early Ch. Hist.* I. iii. 50 Servility to Rome and armed resistance were alike impossible.

*personified.* **1781** COWPER *Table-T.* 127 Servility with supple knees, Whose trade it is to smile, to crouch, to please.

**c.** Lack of independence in opinion or action; undue subjection or deference *to* some person or influence.

**1674** *Govt. Tongue* vi. 94 For what besides this unhappy servility to custome, can possibly reconcile men that own Christianity, to a practice widely distant from it? **1849** MACAULAY *Hist. Eng.* iii. I. 398 In our island there was less of this servility than on the Continent... Yet even here homage was paid..to the literary supremacy of our neighbours.

**d.** Of imitation, translation, etc.: The quality of being servile or unduly close to the original.

**1782** MISS BURNEY *Cecilia* VIII. v, Servility of imitation.

†'**servilize**, *v.* *Obs.* *rare*[−2]. [f. SERVILE *a.* + -IZE.] *trans.* To make servile.

**1619** A. NEWMAN *Pleas. Vis.* etc. C 7, Know I must dye, That all the Land may mourne for me, That, seruilizd, first made it free. **1741** WARBURTON *Div. Legat.* v. App., Wks. 1788 III. 192 Lord Shaftesbury..pretended that every motive regarding self tended to servilize virtue.

**serving** ('sɜːvɪŋ), *vbl. sb.* [f. SERVE *v.*[1] + -ING[1].]

**1. a.** The action of the verb SERVE in various senses; an instance of this. Also comb. with advs., as ***serving-up***.

*c* **1205** LAY. 8097 þa þe seruuinge wes idon þat hit to þe mete com. *Ibid.* 8114 Hit wes al isomned & þere sereuunge. *a* **1310** in Wright *Lyric P.* xxv. 69 Jhesu,..Thou ne askesd me non other thing, Bot trewe love ant eke servyng. **1463** in *Acts Parlt. Scot.* (1874) XII. 28/2 And þat ȝe mak na ger mak na stoping to me in þe serving of thame [breves]. **1526** *Pilgr. Perf.* (W. de W. 1531) 65 As stacyons, inclynacyons, gestures, turnynges, wesshynge, seruynge at meet and in other places..and suche other. **1542-3** *Act 34 & 35 Hen. VIII*, c. 27 §79 The shirefe shall haue..for the seruing of euery writ of haberi fac. seisinam, syx shillinges eyght pence. **1656** *Artif. Handsom.* 52 Nor are [they] to be called crossings or opposings of his will; but rather they are servings and obeyings of it. **1757** CHALLONER *Garden of the Soul* (ed. 7), Method of Serving at Mass. **1816** J. SCOTT *Vis. Paris* (ed. 5) 127 Here [at restaurants] both the supply and the serving-up are of the most elegant description. **1857** J. H. WALSH *Man. Dom. Econ.* 240 The Serving at Dinner commences by taking in the first course, after which dinner is announced. **1863** MRS. GASKELL *Sylvia's L.* xvii, While Hester and me is left i' t' shop for t' bear t' brunt o' t' serving.

¶ The part or character 'served' by (a disguise).

**1611** SHAKS. *Cymb.* III. iv. 173, I haue already fit.. Doublet, Hat, Hose, all That answer to the them: Would you in their seruing,..fore Noble Lucius Present your selfe.

**b.** *concr.* A helping (of food, etc.); also *Sc.* as much as 'serves' or satisfies one.

**1769** ROSS *Helenore* 10 You cou'd na look your sairing at her face. **1818** SCOTT *Rob Roy* xxv, I hae been waur mistrysted than if I were set to gie ye baith your ser'ing o't. **1843** J. BALLANTINE *Gaberlunzie's Wallet* iv. 113 Baith beast an' bodie aye gat their full sairin. **1864** MRS. H. WOOD *Trevlyn Hold* xxix, Nora immediately drew an apple-pie before her, and began to cut unlimited servings from it. **1871** W. ALEXANDER *Johnny Gibb* xxi. 159 An' he gae far that road they'll seen get their sairin o' him.

**c.** *Cornwall.* 'A supply of tin ready for smelting'.

**1778** PRYCE *Min. Cornub.* 326. **1880** D. C. DAVIES *Metall. Min.* 420.

**2.** The action of winding 'service' round a rope, etc. Also the material so used.

*a* **1625** [see PUDDING *sb.* 4]. **1688** HOLME *Armoury* III. xv. (Roxb.) 30/1. **1769** FALCONER *Dict. Marine* (1780) s.v. **1833** MARRYAT *P. Simple* xvi, The captain of the maintop reports the breast backstay much chafed in the serving. **1860** H. STUART *Seaman's Catech.* 27 The parcelling is put on with the lay, and the serving against the lay. **1890** *Scribner's Mag.* Oct. 403 The core [of a submarine cable] travels through another set of machines which first wrap it with a thick serving of tarred jute.

**3.** *Comb.*, as ***serving-hatch***, ***-main***, ***-valve***, etc.; (in sense 2) ***serving-board***, ***-mallet*** (also *transf.*), ***spoon***; **serving cart** *U.S.*, a small trolley from which food and drink may be served.

**1794** *Rigging & Seamanship* I. 160 *Serving board is a tapering thin piece of board, with a small score gouged at the end and sides. It is used for serving small ropes. **1840** R. H. DANA *Bef. Mast* xxxiv, I balled up my yarns, took my serving-board in my hand. **1969** *Sears Catal.* Spring/Summer 9/2 *Serving cart... Removable tray. **1978** *Neiman Marcus Christmas Bk.* 98 'Le Gourmand' is a serving cart and more. Made of solid maple with butcher block top that slides back to reveal a stainless well for ice or storage. **1881** EDIS *Decor. & Furniture* 114 *Serving hatches. **1904** GASQUET *Eng. Monastic Life* ii. 23 A screen pierced with doors would probably have somewhat veiled the serving-hatch, the dresser, and the passages to the butteries, cellars, and pantry. **1823** P. NICHOLSON *Pract. Build.* 408 The Forcing-pump consists of a working-barrel, a suction-pipe and *serving-main, or raising-pipe. **1750** BLANCKLEY *Nav. Expositor* s.v. *Mallet*, *Serving Mallets. **1850** H. MELVILLE *White Jacket* II. xliv. 296 Ten of us Waisters mean to club together, and buy a serving-mallet boat. **1897** F. T. BULLEN *Cruise of 'Cachalot'* 371 Magnificent clipper ships..who seemed to turn up their splendid noses at the squat, dumpy, antiquated old serving-mallet that dared to mingle with so august a crowd. **1864** R. KERR *Gentl. Ho.* 248 To place the Butler's-Pantry in intercommunication with the *Serving-room. **1895** *Pall Mall Gaz.* 4 Feb. 8/1 A lift carries the joints up to the serving-room [from the kitchen]. **1960** M. SPARK *Bachelors* x. 155 'What!' said Marlene, holding the cold peas in the *serving-spoon suspended. **1978** M. RUSSELL *Daylight Robbery* xix. 184 Mrs Braithwaite dropped the serving spoon upon her plate with a clatter. **1797** *Monthly Mag.* III. 464 The small cylinder, which contains the *serving valve.

**serving** ('sɜːvɪŋ), *ppl. a.* [f. SERVE *v.*[1] + -ING[2].]

**1.** That serves, or does service to, another; that acts as a servant. Often hyphened to the qualified sb. as in ***serving-maid***, SERVING-MAN, -WOMAN.

**1303** [see SERVING-MAN]. **1382** WYCLIF *Heb.* i. 14 Seruyng spiritis, sent into mynysterie for hem that [etc.]. *a* **1450** [see SERVING-WOMAN]. **1592** *Arden of Feversham* IV. i. 67 To keepe her from the Painter. *Cla.* Why more from a Painter then from a seruing creature like your selfe? **1592** SHAKS. *Rom. & Jul.* IV. v. 119 Then will I lay the seruing Creatures Dagger on your pate. **1610** in *T. Pont's Topogr. Acc. Cunninghame* (Maitland Club) 185 To Johne Birsbane, his serveing gentilman, of fie the said zeir, threttie thrie pund vj s. viij d. **1688** DURFEY in *Roxb. Ball.* (1891) VII. 364 If I were but her Serving-Loon, I'd never ask for wages. **1693** G. STEPNEY *Dryden's Juvenal* VIII. *note* 43 Oriculana, whom Juvenal calls a Serving-Maid. **1818** SCOTT *Hrt. Midl.* xxviii, A tight serving-maiden entered the room. *c* **1820** S. ROGERS *Italy, A Funeral* (1838) 154 None were near, None save her serving-boy, who knelt and wept. **1851** SIR F. PALGRAVE *Norm. & Eng.* I. 267 The wanton serving wench. **1870** DICKENS *E. Drood* iv, His serving-maid entering, and announcing 'Mr. Jasper is come, sir'.

**b.** That acts as server at Mass.

**1885** (*title*), Server's Missal. A Practical Guide for Serving Boys at Mass.

**2.** Of a soldier, etc.: That is on service.

*c* **1570** *Saparton's Alarum* in B.L. *Ball. & Broadsides* (1867) 118 Al Mars his men..Sit downe a while, and harken heere,..A seruinge souldiers case. **1900** *Daily News* 21 Sept. 3/2 The whole of the home-serving troops. **1908** *Westm. Gaz.* 5 Mar. 9/1 Serving Yeomen and Volunteers who wish to enter the Territorial Force need not attest before June 30.

†**3.** Of things: Subsidiary. *Obs.*

*a* **1586** SIDNEY *Apol. Poetrie* (Arb.) 30 All these are but seruing Sciences, which..are..all directed to the highest end of the mistres Knowledge. **1594** Carew *Huarte's Exam. Wits* (1616) 87 For this sort of wisedome, the cold and drie of Melancholie is a seruing instrument.

**'serving-ˌman.** Now *arch.* [serving *ppl. a.*]

**1.** A man who serves; a male servant or attendant. (Common in 16th and 17th centuries.)

**1303** R. Brunne *Handl. Synne* 835 þe seruyng man, þat seruyþ yn þe ȝere, Oweþ to come [to church on Sunday] when he haþ leysere. **1538** Starkey *England* I. iii. 78 Of thos sortys be ouermany, and specyally of them wych we cal seruyng men, wych lyue in seruyce to gentylmen, lordys, and other of the nobylyte. **1581** W. Stafford *Exam. Compl.* ii. (1876) 64 For now a dayes Seruingmen goe more costely in apparell,.. then their maisters were wont to doe in times past. **1605** Shaks. *Lear* III. iv. 87. **1677** Mrs. Behn *Debauchee* I. i. 7 You know the serving-man is always allow'd to break his fast upon his master's leavings. **1818** Scott *Br. Lamm.* xviii 'The mercy of Heaven forbid!' said the old serving-man. **1872** Tennyson *Gareth & Lyn.* 781 There brake a serving-man Flying from out of the black wood, and crying, 'They have bound my lord to cast him in the mere.' **1888** J. Payn *Myst. Mirbridge* xx, Save these two serving-men, there was not a menial at the Court who [etc.].

*Comb.* **1667** Dryden & Dk. Newcastle *Sir M. Mar-all* IV. i, Or, Serving-man like, ready to carry up the hot meat for your Master.

†**2.** ***serving-man's joy***: a name for Rue. *Obs.*$^{-0}$

**1671** Phillips (ed. 3), *Rue*, a Solar herb,.. it is otherwise called Herb-grace, or serving-mans joy. **1721** Bailey, *Serving-man's joy*, the Herb Rue.

Hence †**serving-manned** *pa. pple.* (*nonce-wd.*).

**1609** Rowlands *Knave of Clubs* (1612) B 1, Yes sir (said she) I pray come in, Thus was she seruing-mand.

**'serving-ˌwoman.** Now *arch.* [serving *ppl. a.*] A female servant or attendant.

*a* **1450** *Knt. de la Tour* xxi. (1906) 31 There is a maner now amonge seruyng women of lowe astate, the whiche is comen, for thei furre her colers. **1633** Massinger *Guardian* IV. ii, One of those Ambitious Serving-women who [etc.]. **1849** James *Woodman* iv, One of the elder sisters soon appeared, followed by two stout serving women.

**servitary** ('sɜːvɪtərɪ). *local.* = servitor 5.

**1883** *B'ham Daily Post* 11 Oct., Servitary Wanted, for Gas Globes.

**Servite** ('sɜːvaɪt), *sb.* and *a.* [ad. med.L. *Servītæ* pl., f. L. *serv-us* servant (in *Servi Beatæ Mariæ*, the formal name of the order): see -ite$^1$.]

**A.** *sb.* A friar or nun of the order of 'Servants of Blessed Mary', founded in 1233.

*a* **1550** *Image Ipocr.* iv. 180 in *Skelton's Wks.* (1843) II. 441/1 Servi and Servytes, And sondry Jacobites. **1607** Sir H. Wotton *Let.* 13 Sept. *Lett.* (1907) I. 399 A very true picture.. of Maestro Paolo the Servite. **1768** Boswell *Corsica* iii. (ed. 2) 175 There are two colleges of Jesuits, two convents of Dominicans, five of Servites. **1857** F. W. Faber *Foot of the Cross* Pref., It is now twelve years since the Author became a tertiary of the ancient order of the Servites. **1884** Addis & Arnold *Cath. Dict.* (1897) 840/1 The habit finally adopted by the Servites was black, with a leather girdle, a scapulary, and a cope.

**B.** *adj.* Of or pertaining to this order.

**1756-7** tr. *Keysler's Trav.* (1760) III. 88 Poggibonzo of Tuscany, who was a Servite monk in the convent. **1862** Howells *Venet. Life* xv. (1866) 208 The old Servite Convent.. associated with the great name of Paolo Sarpi. **1884** Addis & Arnold *Cath. Dict.* (1897) 840/1 In England there is a flourishing Servite community established in the Fulham Road, London,.. also three convents of Servite nuns.

**'serviter.** *Sc. rare.* Forms: 6 **servatour, servitor,** 9 **serviter.** [app. alteration of *servet* serviette, perh. by association with L. *servātor* preserver.] A table napkin.

**1530** in A. Laing *Lindores Abb.* (1876) 489 Item xxxij hayll seruatours for my lords bourd. **1530** J. Symsoun *Inv.* in *Liber S. Marie de Lundoris* (Abbotsf. Club) 32, vij seruitors of dornyth werk. **1858-61** Ramsay *Remin.* vi. (1870) 246 Serviter, Napkin.

**servitial** (sɜː'vɪʃəl), *a. Hist.* [ad. med.L. *servitiālis*, f. L. *servitium* service *sb.*$^1$: see -al$^1$.] ***servitial nobility***, those ennobled by service in the king's household.

**1874** Stubbs *Const. Hist.* vi. §66 I. 160 In the laws of Canute.. the earl.. is included in the servitial nobility.

**servitor** ('sɜːvɪtə(r)). Forms: 4-5 **servytour,** 4-6 **servitur, -oure,** 4-8 **servitour,** 5 **servytor,** (**servertor, servitieure**), 5-6 **servytoure,** 6 **servyture, serveture, serviteure, -uir,** (**sarvytor**), *Sc.* **schervitour, servatour,** 6-8 **serviture, -eur,** 7 **serviter, servatore,** 5- **servitor.** [a. OF. *servitor* (mod.F. *serviteur*), a. late L. *servītor*, agent-n. f. *servīre* serve *v.*$^1$ Cf. Pr., Sp., Pg. *servidor*, It. *servitore*.]

**1.** A (male) personal or domestic attendant (in early use chiefly, one who waits at table); a man-servant. Now *arch.*

*c* **1330** R. Brunne *Chron. Wace* (Rolls) 11300 þat ilke vsage was at þer feste,.. þe wommen wyþoute men schuld be, But seruiturs of here meyne. **1338** —— *Chron.* (1810) 165 Statin his stiward spak to þe Emperoure, Als his mete he sat, & was his seruitoure. *c* **1400** Maundev. (1839) xxii. 239 He hathe in his Court many Barouns, as Servytoures, that ben Cristene. *c* **1460** J. Russell *Bk. Nurture* 682 in *Babees Bk.*, And se þat ye haue seruytours semely þe disches for to bere. **1466** *Paston Lett.* II. 267 To the prest that cam with the cors from London, iiis. iiii*d.* To servytors that awaytyd upon hym.. xxi*d.*.. To lxx. servertors, eche of them iii*d.*, xviii*s.* vi*d.* **1473** *Exch. Rolls Scot.* VIII. 157 *note*, Our lovete familiare servitieure of houshaulde Johnne of Wardelaw. **1549** *Compl. Scot.* xiv. 117 He hed ane domestik seruitour. **1573** Tusser *Husb.* (1878) 189 One diligent seruiture, skilfull to waight, more comelieth thy table than other some eight. **1582** *N.T.* (Rhem.) *Matt.* xxiii. 11 He that is the greater of you, shal be your seruiteur [Vulg. *minister*]. *a* **1617** Bayne *On Eph.* i. (1618) 7 We see in earthly seruiters, their glory is so much the greater, by how much their Lords and masters are in greater præeminencie. **1725** *Bradley's Fam. Dict.* s.v. *Pains*, It must be set on the Table by a neat handed Servitor, lest it should be broken as it is serving up. **1821** Scott *Kenilw.* xix, The least servitor of the favourite Earl. **1837** Dickens *Pickw.* xxx, That favoured servitor entered his bed-chamber. **1877** 'Rita' *Vivienne* III. vii, The old servitor left him alone with the dead.

**b.** *gen.* A servant. Also *transf.* and *fig.*

**1450-80** tr. *Secreta Secret.* Prol. 3, I that am servitoure of the kyng, haue put in execucioun his comaundement, and travaylid forto gete the book of good thewes to him. *a* **1500-34** *Coventry Corpus Chr. Plays* ii. 128 And so this stare wasse a serveture And vnto iij kyngis a playn cundeture Vnto the mancion of a virgin pure. **1543** Traheron tr. *Vigo's Chirurg.* 35/2 Nature sendeth bloude or cholere, and spirytes as seruitoures to succour the hurted place. **1563-87** Foxe *A. & M.* (1596) 7/2 The office of a Bishop or servitour ecclesiasticall, was in the old law to offer sacrifice. **1570** *Homilies* II. *Agst. Rebell.* IV. (1574) 586 Achitophel.. for lacke of an hangman, a conuenient seruitour for suche a traytour, went and hanged vp hym selfe. **1580** *Second & Third Blast Plays & Theatres* 109 Neede and flatterie are two brothers, and the eldest seruitors in the Court. **1594** Hooker *Eccl. Pol.* I. iii. §4 This workman [God], whose seruitor nature is, being in truth but only one. **1594** Shaks. *Lucr.* 285. **1616** Hieron *Three Serm.* 10 b, Surely the spirite of Christ Iesus is not in mee;.. I am yet a limme of the kingdome of darknesse, a seruitour of the prince of darknes. **1621** G. Sandys *Ovid's Met.* VIII. (1626) 156 A Bore: Dian's reuenge, and horrid Seruatore [orig. *famulus*]. **1641** Milton *Ch. Govt.* I. iv. 13 To the performance of w$^{ch}$ [office] the Levits were but as servitors & Deacons. **1654** H. L'Estrange *Chas. I* (1655) 5 And though he was an universall Scholar, yet did he make other sciences.. but drudges and serviteurs to Divinity. **1866** J. Martineau *Ess.* I. 126 The grandest.. are thus but servitors of a grander than themselves. **1874** Spurgeon *Treas. Dav.* Ps. xcvi. 9 Holiness is the royal apparel of his servitors.

†**c.** An attendant or caretaker in a church. *Obs.*

**1593** *Rites of Durham* (Surtees 1903) 38 Alwaies provyded w$^{th}$ fresh water.. by two of y$^e$ bell Ringers or servitors of y$^e$ church.

†**d.** *Sc.* A person in a subordinate office or employment; an assistant in a school; an apprentice, *spec.* a lawyer's apprentice or clerk. *Obs.*

**1486** *Aberd. Reg.* in *Spalding Club Miscell.* V. 30 Thome Gray, tailzour.. and in likuiss, gif ony seruitor of his be fundin conuikit in sic faltis [etc.]. **1598** *Reg. Mag. Sig. Scot.* 1588, 547/2 Patrik Glesfurde and Geo. M$^c$Cartnay schervitouris to the said Wil., Thomas Home schervitour to Mr. Jhone Prestoun advocat. **1601-2** *Aberd. Acc.* in *Spalding Club Miscell.* V. 129 Item, to Mr. George Mackie, servitor of the grammer school, for his panis in attending on the school, fra the deceis of the maister thairof till the new maisteris wer admittit.. 10 lib. **1814** Scott *Wav.* lxvi, The Bailie was in search of his apprentice (a servitor, as he was called Sixty Years since), Jock Scriever.

*attrib.* **1583** *Exch. Rolls Scot.* XXI. 559 James Bonar, servitour clerk of the schirefdome of Forfair.

**e.** An official or semi-official title of certain officers, e.g. of the Royal Household, or municipal bodies. † ***servitor of bills***, a tipstaff of the court of King's Bench.

**1543** tr. *Act 2 Hen. IV*, c. 23 No seruytour of bylles that bereth a staffe of the same courte shall [etc.]. **1597** in Feuillerat *Revels Q. Eliz.* (1908) 417 A petition of the Creditors & Servitors of the Revels. **1658** Fanshaw *Pract. Exch. Crt.* 48 All Officers, Ministers and Servitors of the Exchequer. **1671** Jordan *London's Resurr.* 2 The two City-Marshals, riding each of them on Horse-back, with six Servitors to attend them, with Scarfs and Colours of the Companies. **1683** Moxon *Mech. Exerc., Printing* 363 Four Whifflers (as Servitures) by two and two walking before with White Staves in their Hands.

**f.** A military attendant, a squire or page. *rare.*

*a* **1513** Fabyan *Chron.* VII. (1533) 124 b/2 They agreed to puruey at theyr propre costes .v. C. men of armys, wyth a seruyture to eueryche spere. **1839** Mrs. Browning *Romaunt of Page* xxiv, She.. followed him she wed before, Disguised as his true servitor, To the very battle-place.

**g.** A lover; = servant *sb.* 4 b. *rare.*

**1500-20** Dunbar *Poems* lxxxiv. 16 The lustiast ladie that nature can devyne, Thocht scho have mony semelie scheruitour, ȝit [etc.]. *a* **1529** Skelton *Calliope* 20 Yet is she fayne Voyde of disdayn, Me to retayne Her seruiture. *c* **1560** A. Scott *Poems* (S.T.S.) x. 39 Is no$^t$ in erd I cure, Bot pleiss my lady pure, Syne be hir scheruiture Vnto I de. *a* **1850** Rossetti *Dante & Circle* I. (1874) 145 Till, turning, I beheld the servitor Of Lady Lagia.

†**2.** Used in expressions of humility or politeness. = servant *sb.* 4 d. *Obs.*

*c* **1386** Chaucer *Sompn. T.* 477 'Now, maister', quod this lord, 'I yow biseke'. 'No maister, sir', quod he, 'but servitour, Though I have had in scole such honour'. **1470-85** Malory *Arthur* x. xxvii. 457, I am a poure knyght and a seruytour vnto yow and to alle good knyghtes. **1562** O. Rowe in Ellis *Orig. Lett.* Ser. III. III. 339 Your Honors pore sarvytor. **1580** J. Hay *Demandes* Ded. in *Cath. Tractates* (S.T.S.) 34 Yours most humble and obedient Seruiteure, Iohne Hay. **1593** Shaks. *3 Hen. VI*, III. iii. 196 *War*[*wick*]... My Noble Queene, let former grudges passe, And henceforth, I am thy true Seruitour. *c* **1645** Howell *Lett.* (1655) I. II. vi. 76 Your truly devoted Servitor, J. H.

‖**b.** In Fr. form *serviteur*. *Obs.*

**1664** Etherege *Com. Revenge* I. ii, Your most humble *Serviteur*, my Lord. **1697** Vanbrugh *2nd Pt. Æsop* (end), There's a Tale for your Tale, Old Dad; and so—*Serviteur*. [Exit.] **1702** —— *False Friend* I. 9, I like your Daughter very well; but for Marrying her—*Serviteur*.

**3.** One who serves in war; a soldier; *spec.* one of a class of persons to whom lands were assigned in Ulster in the reign of James I, as having served in a military or civil office in Ireland. *Obs.* exc. *Hist.* in the specific use.

**1561** Awdeley *Frat. Vacab.* (1869) 3 A Ruffeler goeth wyth a weapon to seeke seruice, saying he hath bene a Seruitor in the wars, and beggeth for his reliefe. **1587** T. Sanders *Voy. Tripoli* B ij b, A Spaniard called Sebastian, which had beene an old seruitor in Flanders. **1591** Shaks. *1 Hen. VI*, II. i. 5 *Sen*[*tinel*]. Thus are poore Seruitors.. Constrain'd to watch in darknesse, raine, and cold. **1598** Barret *Theor. Warres* IV. ii. 107 Among our English seruitours in the Low Countreis. **1610** Holland *Camden's Brit.* I. 422 The.. most venterous Mariners and servitours at sea. **1612** Davies *Why Ireland*, etc. 127 Our Norman Conqueror.. gaue away to his seruitors, the Lands and possessions of such, as did oppose his first inuasion. **1618** *Carew Papers* in *Roy. Engin. Jrnl.* Aug. (1909) 126 To survey and make a return of the proceedings and performances of conditions of the undertakers, servitors and natives planted [in Armagh, etc.]. **1634** *Ir. Act 10 Chas. I* Sess. II. c. 3 (*title*) The estates of the undertakers, servitors, natives, and others holding lands.. in.. the plantations. **1640** Yorke *Union Hon.* 20 A valiant servitour in sundry wars beyond sea. **1827** Hallam *Const. Hist.* (1876) III. xviii. 380 Sir Arthur Chichester.. advised that the lands should be assigned,.. partly to servitors of the crown, as they were called.

**4.** *Oxford University.* In certain colleges, one of a class of undergraduate members (later with change of title: see quot. 1852) who received their lodging and most of their board free, and were excused lecture fees.

Originally the servitors acted as servants to the fellows, and although the requirement of menial services from them gradually fell into disuse, they continued to be regarded as socially the inferiors of the commoners. The last mention in the Oxford University Calendar of servitors as an existing class (at Christ Church) is in 1867; in the following year the same persons are called 'exhibitioners'. In most of the colleges the funds originally used for servitorships are now used for 'exhibitions', but at Balliol for scholarships. The scholars of Balliol appear in 1507 as 'scholastici sive servitores'.

**1642** *Let. Stud. at Oxford, & Answ.* 2 My Servitor hath brought mee in the tidings. **1656** Blount *Glossogr.* s.v. *Serviteur*, Wee use the word *Servitor* in our Universities, where the poor or meaner sort of Schollars.. execute the office of a Servitor or attendant to those of greater wealth and quality. **1691** Wood *Ath. Oxon.* I. 305 Whether he was at his first coming a Servitour, or Scholar, I know not. **1731** *Gentl. Mag.* I. 118 The Bishop, in this case, must take some raw young Man, perhaps a Servitor in a College. **1745** Mrs. Delany *Life & Corr.* (1861) II. 377 The Dean said if his parents would consent to his entering the college of Dublin as a sizer (which in Oxford and Cambridge are called servitors) he would take care he was treated with a particular regard. **1754** Johnson *Let.* 28 Nov. in *Boswell*, Let a servitour transcribe the quotations. **1787** Sir J. Hawkins *Johnson* 12 It was the practice in his time, for a servitor, by order of the master, to go round to the rooms of the young men, and knocking at the door, to enquire if they were within, and if no answer was returned, to report them absent. **1848** Thackeray *Bk. of Snobs* xiii, The unlucky boys who have no tassels to their caps, are called sizars—*servitors* at Oxford. **1852** *Rep. Oxf. Univ. Comm.* 135 Servitors are found, under that name, only at Christchurch, where they used within the last twenty years to bring the first dish into the Hall; but now they differ from other Students of that Society in little, except in academic dues. In some other colleges the class of Servitors are represented by Clerks or Bible-Clerks, of whom there are about forty in the University. **1858** [J. C. Thomson] *Almæ Matres* 86 Christchurch.. is the only College which preserves the odious distinction of servitors, or as they call them, 'scrivs.'

**b.** *Eton.* (See quot.)

**1865** W. L. C. *Etoniana* viii. 138 At the college dinner three lower boys (called *servitors*) wait to hand the plates and pour out beer; their dinner is half an hour later, with the 'upper servitor'—one of the higher boys, who superintends the hall economy.

**5.** *Glassmaking.* †**a.** An assistant to a master workman (*obs.*). **b.** Now *spec.* as the designation of the second of the men composing a 'chair': see quots. Also servitary.

**1662** Merrett tr. *Neri's Art of Glass* 242 [Of the Furnaces.] *Boccarellas*, one on each side of the *Bocca*,.. out of these the Servitors take coloured or finer Metall from the piling pot. *Ibid.* 244, 246, 247. **1849** Pellatt *Curios. Glass-making* 89 [A 'chair' consists of] first, a gaffer, or workman; the second, a servitor; and the third, a foot-maker; the latter usually earns about half the wages paid to the chief, and the servitor receives an intermediate amount. **1887** *Rep. Patent Cases* IV. 273 Shaw was his servitor—the servitor being the man who made the feet of the wine glasses. **1897** *Worc. County Express* 3 Apr., There were ten chairs at the works each occupied by a glassmaker, servitor, and footmaker.

**servitorial** (sɜːvɪ'tɔərɪəl), *a. rare.* [f. prec. + -ial.] Of or pertaining to a servitor (in any sense).

**1843** *Blackw. Mag.* LIII. 386 Your cherry-cheeked friend and another.. do the servitorial offices of the table. **1866** Tyerman *Life S. Wesley* 81 His servitorial services [at Oxford] might obtain him bread. **1871** Meredith *H. Richmond* (1886) 4 The squire was diverted from his objurgations against this piece of servitorial defiance.

**servitorship** ('sɜːvɪtəʃɪp). [f. SERVITOR + -SHIP.] **a.** The position, state, or duties of a servitor at an Oxford college. *Obs.* exc. *Hist.*

**1785** BOSWELL *Tour Hebrides* 130 *note*, Dr. Johnson.. by his interest with the Rev. Dr. Adams, master of Pembroke College, Oxford,..obtained a servitorship for young M'Aulay. **1820** SOUTHEY *Wesley* I. 52 Servitorships are more in the spirit of a Roman Catholic than of an English establishment. **1868** M. PATTISON *Academ. Org.* 73 It is not so much we that have abolished servitorships, as time and manners that have made the position untenable. **1897** FAIRBAIRN *Catholicism* (1899) 445 The evil system and associations of the old servitorship left for life their ignoble stamp on the soul of Whitefield.

**b.** The condition of being a servitor or servant.

**1824** *Blackw. Mag.* XV. 254 Postmen, beadles, scavengers, chimney-sweeps—the whole *pecus* of parochial servitorship was at my gate.

**servitress** ('sɜːvɪtrɪs). [See SERVITOR and -TRESS.] A female servant or attendant.

**1860** J. P. KENNEDY *Rob of the Bowl* xii. 125 [She] now attended him as his servitress and only domestic. **1873** M. COLLINS *Miranda* II. 100 Tom Jones had fitted up a buffet ..and put some servitresses behind it. **1877** KINGLAKE *Crimea* VI. xi. 439 An obedient servitress attending hospital sick-beds.

†**servitrice.** *Sc. Obs.* Also 7 servetrice. [ad. med.L. *servītrīce-m*, acc. of *servītrix*.] = next.

**1477** *Exch. Rolls Scot.* IX. 101 *note*, Oure lovete familiare servitrice Margret Sandelandis. **1561** *Reg. Privy Council Scot.* I. 170, I, your servitrice and pure wedo. **1633** *Sc. Acts Chas. I* (1870) V. 124/1 Maistres Margaret Wincester servetrice to his Majesties said vmq[uhi]l darrest mother.

†**servitrix.** *Sc. Obs.* [a. med.L. *servītrix* (Diefenbach), fem. of L. *servītor*: see SERVITOR.] A female servant.

**1566** in *Maitl. Club Misc.* (1840) I. 43 Marie Betoune familiar servitrix to our said souerane lady. **1615** in Ritchie *Churches of St. Baldred* (1880) 136 Janet Shortus, servitrix to Mr. Alexander Knowis. *c* **1775** in McDowall *Hist. Dumfries* xlvii. (1867) 680 [Janet Watson] a servitrix [at the very farm].

**servitude** ('sɜːvɪtjuːd). Also 5-6 servytude, 6 *Sc.* schervitude. [a. F. *servitude*, ad. late L. *servitūdo*, f. *serv-us* slave, SERF: see -TUDE.]

**1.** The condition of being a slave or a serf, or of being the property of another person; absence of personal freedom. Often, and now usually, with additional notion of subjection to the necessity of excessive labour. Also, a (more or less rigorous) state of slavery or serfdom.

**1471** CAXTON *Recuyell* (Sommer) II. 611 Or that we shall be ledde in seruytude & bondage in to strange contreyes. *a* **1533** LD. BERNERS *Huon* xliii. 144, I had rather to be in seruitude there than to pay .iiii. drams to this Gyaunt. **1584** B. R. tr. *Herodotus* II. 107 Whiles shee abode in Ægypt, shee was redeemed and acquit of her seruitude by one Charaxus, who purchased her libertie by a great summe of money. **1687** A. LOVELL tr. *Thevenot's Trav.* I. 25 All the rest are shaved as a mark of their servitude. **1776** GIBBON *Decl. & F.* xiii. I. 270 The greatest part of the nation was gradually reduced into a state of servitude. **1832** HT. MARTINEAU *Homes Abroad* iv. 59 There was a probability of the woman marrying as soon as she could obtain remission of her servitude. **1845** SARAH AUSTIN *Ranke's Hist. Ref.* IV. iv. II. 457 It enabled them to reduce the peasantry to a still harder state of servitude. **1910** *Encycl. Brit.* XII. 40/1 In Hungary ..the abolition of servitude in 1781–1782 carried with it the freedom of the Gipsies.

*personified.* **1769** GRAY *Install. Ode* 6 Servitude that hugs her chain.

**b.** With reference to animals: Subjection to mankind. Now *rare* or *Obs.*

**1697** DRYDEN *Virg. Georg.* III. 268 For his soft Neck, a supple Collar make Of bending Osiers; and (with Time and Care Enur'd that easy Servitude to bear) Thy flatt'ring Method on the Youth pursue. **1774** GOLDSM. *Nat. Hist.* (1776) II. 376 The wild ass is even more asinine..than that bred in a state of domestic servitude.

**c.** The condition of being politically enslaved; subjection to a foreign power or to oppressive rule. †With *of* (or possessive): The state of being under the yoke *of* (a tyrant, a conqueror).

**1471** CAXTON *Recuyell* (Sommer) I. 276 For hit is the destyne that Troye shall neuer be quyte of this right harde seruytude and thraldom vnto the tyme that [etc.]. **1477** EARL RIVERS *Dictes* (Caxton) 10 b, Al be it that they be in his seruitude yet ought he to his power to kepe them in fraunchyse and liberte. **1584** *Leycesters Commw.* (1641) 5 The feare of servitude under forraine nations, may restraine them from such attempts. **1585** T. WASHINGTON tr. *Nicholay's Voy.* IV. xxxvi. 160 b, These wretched Græcians are left vnder the miserable seruitude of these miscreated Mahometists. **1598** BACON *Ess., Of Hon. & Reput.* (Arb.) 72 Such as..deliuer their Countries from seruitude of strangers or tyrants. **1660** R. COKE *Power & Subj.* 53 Nebuchadnezzar..carried the Jews themselves into most miserable servitude. **1716** ADDISON *Freeholder* No. 43 ¶2 A disturbed Liberty is better than a quiet servitude. *a* **1727** NEWTON *Chronol. Amended* ii. (1728) 217 Sesostris.. reduced Judæa into servitude. **1904** H. PAUL *Hist. Mod. Eng.* II. 244 One wanted the liberation of Italy and the other her servitude.

**d.** *transf.* and *fig.* A condition resembling slavery; a state of degrading or burdensome subjection.

**1474** CAXTON *Chesse* III. i. (1883) 80 For the debilite and feblenes of corage that is broken in conscience by pryde Enuye or by couetyse is ryght seruytude. **1532** MORE *Confut. Tindale* Wks. 429/1 He lamenteth the miserable seruitude of the symple soules the poore sely women, because men will not suffer them to say masse. *Ibid.* 556/1 The deadly synne in the time of his fall, and of the seruitude and thraldom that he lyeth in. *c* **1560** A. SCOTT *Poems* (S.T.S.) vii. 18 Thoᵗ this belappit body heir Be bound to scheruitude and thrall, My fathfull hairt is fre inteir And mynd to serf my lady at all. *a* **1586** SIDNEY *Arcadia* III. (Sommer) 265 b, So did she..with the tribute of gifts, seeke to bring her mind into seruitude. **1667** MILTON *P.L.* VI. 178 This is servitude, To serve th'unwise, or him who hath rebelld Against his worthier. **1685** BAXTER *Paraphr. N.T.* 2 Tim. i. 9 Who hath saved us from our servitude to sin and Satan, and called us out of the World to be a Holy people. *a* **1700** EVELYN *Diary* 29 May 1677, This business being now at an end and myself deliver'd from that intolerable servitude and correspondence, I [etc.]. **1837** WHEWELL *Hist. Induct. Sci.* I. IV. ii. §4. 276 The Arabians..tamely adopted the intellectual servitude of the nation which they conquered by their arms. *a* **1862** BUCKLE *Civiliz.* III. iv. (1869) 192 The religious servitude into which the Scotch fell ..was a willing servitude.

†**e.** *concr.* Slaves or servants collectively. *Obs.*

**1667** MILTON *P.L.* XII. 132 After him [Abraham] a cumbrous Train Of Herds, and Flocks, and numerous servitude.

**2.** The condition of being a servant, service; esp. domestic service. Now *rare* or *Obs.* (exc. as a contextual application of 1 d).

**1651** tr. *Life Sarpi* (1676) 10 He had likewise a very near familiarity with the Father Inquisitor,..with whom he continued servitude till his death. **1782** ELIZ. BLOWER *Geo. Bateman* II. 89 The longer Cecilia lived upon a footing.. with people of fortune, the more irksome Servitude would appear to her. **1792** G. WAKEFIELD *Mem.* (1804) I. 532 You would have been led into a more healthy situation, and might have procured, after a short servitude, some comfortable preferment. **1807** SOUTHEY *Spec. Eng. Poets* II. 234 At the age of 24, married, in servitude, with little leisure, and no money or books, he set about his plan of improvement. **1817** *Salisb. & Winch. Jrnl.* 29 Sept., A servant girl..was found drowned... She had been missing from her place of servitude since the preceding Thursday. **1822** GALT *Provost* xxxviii, He sentenced her to be dismissed from her servitude with no more than the wage she had actually earned.

**3.** Apprenticeship. ? *Obs.*

**1791** in Langford *Cent. B'ham Life* (1868) I. 368 At the Expiration of the Servitude of these..Apprentices. **1799** *Hull Advert.* 12 Oct. 2/4 John Brown..lately enticed.. apprentices..from their servitude. **1805** W. TAYLOR in *Ann. Rev.* III. 323 The duration of apprenticeship in this country is excessive. Five years ought to confer all the privileges of servitude. **1835** *App. Munic. Corpor. Rep.* III. 1667 Admission to the company [*sc.* Trinity House, Newcastle-on-Tyne] is acquired, 1st, by Birth; 2d, by Servitude; 3d, by Gift.

**4.** A person's (period of) service (in the Navy).

**1818** *Tuckey's Narr. Exped. R. Zaire* Introd. p. xlix, Though wanting eighteen months for the completion of his servitude to qualify him for a lieutenant's commission. **1836** MARRYAT *Three Cutters* ii, During my servitude as first lieutenant.

**5.** Compulsory labour as a punishment for criminals. Chiefly ***penal servitude***: see PENAL *a.*[1] 1 c.

***free by servitude*** (Austral.): see quot. 1889.

**1828** P. CUNNINGHAM *N.S. Wales* (ed. 3) II. 129 Those who have become free by servitude. **1889** *19th Cent.* Nov. 765 When you were a little familiar with colonial phraseology you at once understood that..Giles..was what was called a 'free by servitude man', i.e., a convict whose sentence of transportation had expired.

†**6.** Feudal or ecclesiastical subjection; vassalage, subordination. *Obs.*

*c* **1500** *Melusine* lix. 359 Thou holdest me for thy subget & woldest hold me in seruitude and thou hast therof nothing to shew. **1631** WEEVER *Anc. Funeral Mon.* 559 S. Albans exempted from the iurisdiction of Lincoln... Robert was the next Abbot..and deliuered his Monastery from the seruitude of the Bishop of Lincolne.

†**b.** Feudal homage or service. *Obs.*

**1498** *Coventry Leet Bk.* 594 Of all maner Toll, pontage, pykage,..kayage and all oþer Imposicions, charges & seruitudes. *c* **1500** *Melusine* xxxvi. 249 For yf he escape grete shame shal be to vs in an euyl heure is he come in to oure land for to demande seruytude of vs. **1809** PINKNEY *Trav. France* 26 But there are some instances of personal service, and which are held to be legal..provided they relate to husbandry, and not to any servitude or attendance upon the person of the landlord.

**7.** In *Civil Law* (= L. *servitus*), and hence in *Scots Law*: a subjection or subserviency of property either: (1) to some definite person other than its owner ('personal servitude'), or (2) to some definite property other than that of its owner for the benefit of the dominant property ('prædial servitude'). In *Scots Law* the term is now in practice restricted to prædial servitude, which includes both the 'easement' and the 'profit à prendre' of English Law; it has been sometimes used by English lawyers to include both these kinds of rights.

A personal servitude (of which usufruct is an example) could be constituted either over movables or immovables; a prædial servitude (e.g. a right of way) could only be constituted over an immovable in favour of another immovable.

**1592** *Sc. Acts Jas. VI* (1814) III. 609/2 And siclyk exceptand and reservand the seruitude altius edes non tollendj prospectui et luminibus non officiendj constitute and imposit vpon ane tenement of land now pertening to mʳ Johnne nicolsoun aduocat. *Ibid.*, And all vther servitude quhatsumeuer. **1652** NEEDHAM tr. *Selden's Mare Cl.* 133 Hereupon Servitudes have been imposed, against the rearing of Houses higher then ordinary. **1681** STAIR *Inst. Law Scot.* II. vii. (1693) 282 Servitudes are distinguished in Real and Personal, though neither of them be personal Rights; yet these Servitudes whereby one Tenement is subservient to another Tenement, and to persons only as having Right to, and for the use of that Tenement, are called Real Servitudes, as not being subservient directly to Persons, but to Things: And the other are called Personal; because thereby the Tenement is subservient directly to Persons, and not with respect to any other thing, as Life-rents, &c. *Ibid.* 287 Watering is a Servitude of taking Water, proper to one ground for the use of another. **1754** ERSKINE *Princ. Law Sc.* (1809) 221 The owner of the servient tenement is not obliged, in a servitude of support, to repair it, unless the servitude be expressly so constituted. **1765-8** —— *Inst. Law Scot.* II. ix. §12 The chief rural servitudes of the Roman law are, *iter, actus, via, aquæductus, aquæhaustus,* and *jus pascendi pecoris.* **1799** J. ROBERTSON *Agric. Perth* 558 One great obstacle to improvements in agriculture is the Servitude of Thirlage. **1816** G. J. BELL *Comm. Laws Scot.* (1826) I. 757 Servitudes, when of a positive nature, require possession to complete them; but negative servitudes are effectual without possession or registration. **1842** J. AITON *Dom. Econ.* (1857) 321 Ministers have frequently servitudes of peat, of feal, and divot, and of pasturage on particular estates or farms. **1872** W. GUTHRIE *G. J. Bell's Princ. Law Scot.* (ed. 6) §981 Servitudes have been classed as Prædial and Personal... But, practically, the only servitudes in Scotland are Prædial. **1888** W. D. EDWARDS *Law Property in Land* II. vi. 271 Easements resemble rights of common appendant and appurtenant, in that they are annexed to the ownership of land for its benefit. They are, therefore, sometimes classed with such rights of common, under the name of 'servitudes'. **1900** *Act 63 & 64 Vict.* c. 93 *title*, To acquire lands and servitudes for the purposes of such water supply.

*fig.* **1720** E. ERSKINE *Serm.* Wks. (1791) 59/2 This earthly house, it lies under many servitudes, and the believer..pays a dear mail or rent for his quarters.

**b.** *attrib.*

**1838** W. BELL *Dict. Law Scot.* s.v. *Road*, A public-road may be used by all the Queen's subjects, whereas a servitude-road can be legally used only by the dominant proprietor and his family. **1884** WATSON in *Law Times Rep.* LI. 802/1 Servitude rights burdening the corporeal lands taken by the company.

†**servi'tudinous,** *a. Obs. rare*⁻¹. [f. L. *servitūdin-*, *servitūdo* (see prec.) + -OUS.] Of the nature of, or characterized by servitude.

**1647** *Maids Petit.* 1 Wee the Mayd-servants in generall of the City of London, and in behalfe of the universall sisterhood of the same servitudinous ranke and quality.

†**serviture.** *Obs. rare.* Also 6 *Sc.* scherviture. [ad. med.L. *servitūra*, f. L. *servīre* to SERVE: see -TURE.]

**1.** Service, servitude.

**1500–20** DUNBAR *Poems* xlv. 8 Scho haldis with continwance No scheruiture.

**2.** The whole body of servants in a family.

*a* **1667** MILTON in *Prose Wks.* (1738) I. p. xliv, The Chorus of Shepherds præpare resistance in thire Maister's Defence, calling the rest of the serviture.

**serviture**, obs. form of SERVITOR.

†**servitute.** *Obs.* Also 4, 6 servitut, 5-6 servytute. [a. OF. *servitute*, *-uit*, or ad. L. *servitūt-em* (*servitūs*), f. *serv-us* slave.] Servitude, slavery. *lit.* and *fig.*

*c* **1375** *Sc. Leg. Saints* ii. (*Paulus*) 866 Seruitut or thrildome. *c* **1386** CHAUCER *Clerk's T.* 742 In gret lordshipe, if I wel avyse, Ther is gret servitute in sondry wyse. **1390** GOWER *Conf.* II. 182 Bot Pharao with wrong hem ladde In servitute ayein the pes. **1432–50** tr. *Higden* (Rolls) VII. 51 Ynglonde was redacte iiij. tymes into servitute. **1526** *Pilgr. Perf.* (W. de W.) 83 Whan virginite is vnder the seruytute or bondage of elacyon or pryde. **1533** GAU *Richt Vay* (1888) 95 Giff vsz grace to dant our bodis and to subiect thayme in seruitut. **1546** BALE *1st Exam. Askew* 40, A verye servitute of Ægipte is it, to be in daunger of these papystyck Byshoppes.

**servo** ('sɜːvəʊ), *sb.* [The first element of SERVO-MOTOR (and SERVO-MECHANISM) used substantively.] **1. a.** A servo-mechanism or servo-motor.

**1910** *Engineering* 14 Jan. 56/2 A patent 'Servo' regulator valve is fitted in the dome [of the boiler]. **1924** *Motor* 7 Oct. 448/3 The servo actually trebles the braking effect usually obtainable for a given pedal pressure. **1948** I. A. GREENWOOD in I. A. Greenwood et al. *Electronic Instruments* viii. 220 A convenient classification of servos may be made in accordance with their uses, the principal examples of which are 'position servos' and 'velocity servos'. **1959** *Times* 1 Sept. 12/2 The..company have now introduced a vacuum-hydraulic brake servo which can be fitted easily to cars and light motor vehicles and is claimed to make a vast improvement in braking. **1966** *Electronics* 17 Oct. 108 To test a servo that controls a radar antenna, the antenna must be moved. **1971** *Sci. Amer.* July 120/3 The first truly automatic servo..was the fantail, a small windwheel mounted at right angles to the main sails and geared to turn the entire top of the windmill. **1976** B. JACKSON *Flameout* (1977) iv. 28, I put electronic sensors on the wing tips and tail to respond to phugoid oscillations and dampen yaw. The control servos respond to the input from the sensors.

**b.** *transf.* = SERVO-MECHANISM b.

**1953** P. A. MERTON in G. E. W. Wolstenholme *Spinal Cord* (Ciba Foundation Symp.) 249 The stretch reflex servo, which is so obviously concerned with maintaining length and not tension, must necessarily have receptors which record length. **1969** *Proc. Roy. Soc.* B. CLXXIII. 156 Voluntary movement could be initiated by the α route without sacrificing the advantages of a servo.

**2.** *attrib.* and *Comb.*, as ***servo actuation***, ***-actuator***, ***assistance***, ***loop***; ***servo-actuated***, ***-assisted***, ***-driven***, ***-operated*** adjs.; **servo-'amplifier**, the part of a servo-mechanism that responds to the small error signal and delivers a corresponding large signal to drive the servo-motor; **servo brake**, (*a*) a vehicle brake whose application is assisted by the momentum of the vehicle; (*b*) a brake that is operated by a servo-mechanism; hence **servo-braking** *vbl. sb.*; **servo flap** *Aeronaut.* = *servo tab* below; **servohy'draulic** *a.*, both servo-controlled and hydraulic; **servo-'multiplier**, a device for separately multiplying each of several voltages by a single voltage, the former being applied to a set of potentiometers on the same shaft as a potentiometer controlled by a servomotor receiving the latter voltage; **servo system** = SERVO-MECHANISM a; also *transf.*; **servo tab** *Aeronaut.*, a tab, operated directly by the pilot, which gives rise to aerodynamic forces that assist in moving the main flap.

**1961** *Hovering Craft & Hydrofoil* Oct. 18/2 The ultimate *servo-actuated mechanical device may take ten years. **1959** K. HENNEY *Radio Engin. Handbk.* (ed. 5) xxv. 9 Deviations of the airplane about the yaw axis result in rotation of the heading stator with respect to the rotor and a signal to the rudder servoamplifier, causing *servo-actuation of the rudder surface and the servo loop action described above. **1970** *Times* 4 Sept. (Aviation Suppl.) p. iv/4 Savings will also accrue from the replacement of the common mechanically coupled control systems in the aircraft by electronic systems with electro-hydraulic *servo-actuators operating various aircraft control surfaces. **1946** *Radar: Summary Rep. & Harp Project* (U.S. Nat. Defense Res. Comm., Div. 14) 143/2 **Servo-amplifier*, the amplifier of power impulses in a servo system. **1947** *Electronic Engin.* July 215/1 In a characteristic arrangement, a valve circuit, known as the 'servo amplifier', controls the rotation of an electric motor. **1959** K. HENNEY *Radio Engin. Handbk.* (ed. 5) xxv. 8 The signal from the servoamplifier is applied to the elevator servo-motor which actuates and drives the elevator surface. **1966** *McGraw-Hill Encycl. Sci. & Technol.* XII. 199/2 The servoamplifier is often electronic but may be a magnetic amplifier, a relay type of amplifier, or any combination of these types. **1929** *Times* 2 Nov. 4/7 A pedal applies the rearmost Euro [brakes] with vacuum *servo assistance. **1972** *Guardian* 28 Jan. 3/4 (Advt.), To stop, there's a dual circuit four-disc system with servo assistance. **1951** *Automobile Engineer* May 199/1 (*heading*) *Servo-assisted hydraulic brakes. **1976** *Field* 18 Nov. 1021 (Advt.), All four alloy wheels enjoy servo-assisted disc brakes. **1924** A. W. JUDGE et al. *Mod. Motor Cars* II. vii. 118 The Hispano-Suiza *servo-brake controls are shown in perspective arrangement. **1926** *Encycl. Brit.* II. 980/2 This led to the development of so-called servo brakes, in which the momentum of the car was utilised to reinforce the effort of the driver in applying the brake. **1951** *Automobile Engineer* Feb. 60/1 (*heading*) Duo servo brakes. **1924** *Motor* 28 Oct. 707/1 We are now able..to give the first complete description of the *servo-braking system adopted. **1947** *Proc. IRE* XXXV. 450/2 It is possible to divide one voltage by another using a *servodriven potentiometer. **1966** M. WOODHOUSE *Tree Frog* xxi. 153 One small directional dish [antenna] which..I guessed was servo-driven. **1929** *Rep. & Mem. Aeronaut. Res. Comm.* No. 1262. 2 The control column is attached directly to the *servo flap by means of wires. **1935** *Aircraft Engin.* VII. 303/1 During the past year or so there has been a growing tendency towards the use of small servo flaps on elevators and rudders either for trimming or for balancing. **1972** *Physics Bull.* Aug. 492/2 Fulmer Research Institute has recently installed a Mand *servohydraulic testing facility to meet the increasing demand for testing larger specimens under widely varying rates of loading. **1980** *Jrnl. R. Soc. Arts* May 319/2 Facilities include a £350,000 Schenk servo hydraulic rig for testing structural fabrications to destruction. **1946** *Radar: Summary Rep. & Harp Project* (U.S. Nat. Defense Res. Comm., Div. 14) 143/2 **Servo loop*, that collection of elements in a servomechanism which measures the error in the quantity to be controlled and applies a correction tending to reduce that error to zero. **1953** P. A. MERTON in G. E. W. Wolstenholme *Spinal Cord* (Ciba Foundation Symp.) 247 The stretch reflex is a feedback or servo loop, the feedback being negative. **1978** R. JANSSON *News Caper* 10 Even with all the damping in the servo loops the controls leaped out of my hands... We flopped around the sky. **1952** G. A. & T. M. KORN *Electronic Analog Computers* vi. 245 In the case of *servomultipliers, probably the best solution..is to make sure that the follow-up and multiplying potentiometers are all loaded by equal resistances. **1965** A. W. LANGILL *Automatic Control Systems Engin.* II. xviii. 503 Although the servomultiplier is normally employed to form the product of two analog voltages, the system is also used extensively in the generation of arbitrary functions. **1928** *Rep. & Mem. Aeronaut. Res. Comm.* No. 1171. 9 (*heading*) Theory for aerofoil R.A.F. 28 with *servo operated flap. **1947** *Proc. IRE* XXXV. 444/1 Servo-operated torque amplifier. **1946** *Radar: Summary Rep. & Harp Project* (U.S. Nat. Defense Res. Comm., Div. 14) 143/2 **Servo system*, a mechanical, frequently electromechanical, system for transmitting accurate mechanical position from one point to another by electrical or other means. The position is corrected by feeding back an error signal. **1947** *Electronic Engin.* July 215/2 All quantities may be converted to a consistent electrical basis by employing a servo system. **1964** *Language* XL. 219 The fact that some sort of neurological servosystem does monitor encoding cannot be doubted. **1971** *Engineering* Apr. 45/2 A servo-system can be used to restore the balance after change of displacement. **1939** F. K. TEICHMANN *Airplane Design Man.* xiii. 207 If the tab can be controlled from the cockpit, it may be used to operate the larger surface and is then called a control-tab or a *servo-tab. **1975** L. J. CLANCY *Aerodynamics* xvi. 551 Another related device is the so-called servo-tab, which is designed to provide all the hinge movement required to deflect the control.

Hence as *v. trans.*, to control or operate by a servo-mechanism; **'servoed** *ppl. a.*

**1971** *New Scientist* 12 Aug. 359/2 Ferguson solved this problem with their ingenious double-sided vacuum servo, which servos the brakes on and servos them (and the driver's foot) off. **1978** *Nature* 20 Apr. 704/2 The mapping operation was achieved by driving the telescope in declination at the maximum servoed rate of 130′ $min^{-1}$ back and forth across the galactic plane.

**Servo-** ('sɜːvəʊ), combining form of SERVIAN, as *Servo-Croat, -Croatian.* Also *Servo-Turkish* adj.

**1887** MORFILL in *Encycl. Brit.* XXII. 145/1 Servo-Croats, including those of Servia, Montenegro, the southern part of Hungary. *Ibid.* 148/2 Servo-Croatian, Slovenish, Slovakish, and Bohemian possess the vocal *r.* **1896** KEANE *Ethnol.* 412 Slavic Branch..Servo-Croatian. **1897** E. A. BARTLETT *Battlefields of Thessaly* iii. 72 The last Servo-Turkish campaign, that of 1876. **1914** W. G. LAWRENCE in *Home Lett. T. E. Lawrence* (1954) 509 The Servo-Turkish war.

**servo control.** [f. SERVO *sb.*] **1.** †**a.** *Aeronaut.* An aircraft control using a servo tab (see SERVO *sb.* 2). *Obs.* **b.** *gen.* = SERVO-MECHANISM a.

**1928** *Rep. & Mem. Advisory Comm. Aeronaut.* No. 1187.4 There is no spring force on the servo control. **1934** *Jrnl. Aeronaut. Sci.* I. 155/1 The device now known as the servo control flap is a development of the 'Flettner Rudder' which was invented by the designer of the rotor ships. **1947** *Jrnl. Inst. Electr. Engineers* XCIV. IIA. 184/2 No output is produced in the bearing channel, and the feed to the corresponding servo control is consequently zero. **1951** *Instruments* XXIV. 650/1 Servocontrols for the steel industry require..relatively high power level. **1977** *Proc. R. Soc. Med.* LXX. 208/2 As with all tools, the servo-control incubator is only as good as the persons who use it.

**2.** The use of a servo-mechanism to assist with the control of a system; the action or practice of controlling a system by means of a servo-mechanism.

**1929** *Rep. & Mem. Aeronaut. Res. Comm.* No. 1262. 1 If no limit be set to the force which a pilot can exert then the maximum rolling moment possible with servo control is always less than that without it. **1953** P. A. MERTON in G. E. W. Wolstenholme *Spinal Cord* (Ciba Foundation Symp.) 247 (*heading*) Speculations on the servo-control of movement. **1977** *Proc. R. Soc. Med.* LXX. 207/1 The principle of servo-control is that the instrument senses the baby's temperature and adjusts the thermal environment automatically.

Hence **'servo-control** *v. trans.*, **'servo-controlled** *ppl. a.*

**1935** *Rep. & Mem. Aeronaut. Res. Comm.* No. 1652. 1 There have been several occurrences of flutter of servo-controlled rudders. **1948** I. A. GREENWOOD in I. A. Greenwood et al. *Electronic Instruments* viii. 217 Practically all heavy antiaircraft artillery..is servo-controlled by the output of some type of computer. **1972** *Physics Bull.* Apr. 232/2 The gratings are ruled in a very uniform layer of aluminium deposited on to an optically flat substrate..using a large precision ruling engine servocontrolled by laser interferometers. **1977** *Proc. R. Soc. Med.* LXX. 207/2 The disadvantage of a servo-controlled incubator is that the temperature of the baby as a clinical guide to serious conditions..is lost.

†**servoice.** *Obs. rare*$^{-1}$. [a. F. *cervoise*:—L. *cerevisia*.] Ale.

*a* **1483** *Liber Niger* in *Househ. Ord.* (1790) 32 One gallon servoice. *Ibid.* 35 A quart wyne, one gallon servoice.

**'servo-,mechanism.** Also without hyphen and as two words. [f. SERVO *sb.* + MECHANISM.]

**a.** A powered mechanism in which a controlled motion is produced at a high energy or power level in response to an input motion at a lower energy level; *esp.* one in which feedback is employed to make the control automatic, and generally comprising a measuring device, a servo-amplifier, and a servo-motor.

**1926** *Encycl. Brit.* II. 980/2 Some cars..were fitted with an hydraulic servo mechanism. **1935** *Jrnl. R. Aeronaut. Soc.* XXXIX. 794 The [de-icing] device..comprises two essentials, the ice detector and the servo-mechanism which controls the supply of alcohol. **1959** *Times Lit. Suppl.* 24 Apr. 245/2 All self-regulating machines are servo-mechanisms, in which one part of the machine regulates the operation of the other. **1960** *Times* 29 Jan. 3/1 (Advt.), The applicant should have a good knowledge of servomechanism theory. **1973** *Sci. Amer.* Nov. 129/1 Our seismographs and tiltmeters operate in tunnels several hundred feet underground and are provided with servomechanisms that automatically compensate for temperature changes. **1977** D. FRY *Homo Loquens* vii. 91 For centuries firearms..operated on the ballistic principle of the boy who throws the ball; in the last decades, feedback control has been introduced into this area by the employment of servo-mechanisms.

**b.** *transf.* A non-mechanical system that is characterized by self-regulating feedback, esp. in *Genetics* and *Physiol.* Also *fig.*

**1953** J. S. HUXLEY *Evolution in Action* ii. 46 Natural selection..provided a genetic servo-mechanism to regulate the mutant back towards normality in its effects. **1958** *Times Lit. Suppl.* 17 Jan. 34/3 The human or animal body is a remarkable example of servo-mechanisms, in which the expenditure of a small amount of energy is used to release a large amount of energy, and in which a balance..is maintained by 'feed-back' processes. **1964** M. MCLUHAN *Understanding Media* I. iv. 41 This extension of himself by mirror numbed his perceptions until he became the servomechanism of his own extended or repeated image. **1971** *Nature* 10 Dec. 325/1 Natural selection is not a chance process but a feedback servo-mechanism between the gene pool and the environment. **1976** *New Yorker* 15 Nov. 157/1 Their basic assumption is that speech can best be understood as the output of a servomechanism—that is, a device with built-in feedback loops which continuously monitors its own performance and modifies its activity accordingly.

Hence **servo-me'chanical** *a.*

**1947** *Proc. IRE* XXXV. 770/2 The..servomechanical type of control may be preferable where slow drifts over long periods of time are encountered. **1966** S. BEER *Decision & Control* xvi. 418 In this servomechanical model there is a special facility for identifying precisely what is self-regulating about the system. **1977** *Lancet* 5 Nov. 955/2 The finding of only partial suppression of A.C.T.H. with normal levels of cortisol is difficult to understand in conventional servomechanical concepts.

**servo-motor.** Also **servomotor, servo motor.** [ad. F. *servo-moteur* (1873 in Littré *Suppl.*), f. L. *servus* slave + F. *moteur* MOTOR.

In the official notice of the prize awarded in 1875 to the inventor, M. Farcot, the apparatus is called 'servo-moteur ou moteur asservi'.]

An auxiliary motor, e.g. one used for directing the rudders of a Whitehead torpedo, or the reversing gear of a large marine engine. More widely, any device used as the motive element in a servo-mechanism.

**1889** SLEEMAN *Torpedoes* (ed. 2) 184 The servo-motor is the air-engine from which is derived the power to move the horizontal or diving rudders. **1902** BODMER *Hydraulic Motors* (ed. 3) 504 [In turbines] a so-called indirect-acting governor is almost invariably necessary, that is, a governor acting on the regulator through a relay, or as it is sometimes called, a 'servo-motor'. **1932** *Jrnl. Iron & Steel Inst.* CXXV. 642 The apparatus..makes use of the dilatations of the test bar to regulate the temperature of the furnace by means of a servo-motor. **1933** *Electrician* 16 June 796/2 The servo-motor for controlling the vanes is located between the turbine and generator shafts, so that the coupling flanges of the respective machines form the lower and upper servo-motor covers. **1951** *Automobile Engineer* May 199/1 A mechanically operated transmission brake functions as a servo-motor to apply pressure to the master cylinder of a hydraulic braking system. **1976** *Gramophone* Sept. 510/1 A DC servo motor powers the movement of the arm.

†**'servulate,** *v. Obs. rare*$^{-1}$. [f. L. *servus* slave; ? after *adulate*.] *intr.* To be servile.

*a* **1625** FLETCHER *Elder Bro.* I. ii, *Br.* I embrace their loves. *Egr.* Which wee'l repay with servulating.

‖**servus** ('zɛrvʊs), *int.* [Ger., a. L. *servus* servant.] An informal greeting or farewell used in Austria and southern Germany.

**1893** E. R. PENNELL *To Gipsyland* ii. 33 All..drank to me in the wine of their country, and cried aloud their '*Servus! Viva! Eljeu!*' **1966** R. E. PICKERING *Himself Again* iv. 33 'Servus,' he said shortly. I ordered a coffee. **1978** H. MCINNES *Prelude to Terror* viii. 89 As for her hotel in Vienna ..the Sacher..everyone tugging a forelock and saying '*Servus!*'

**serwand,** obs. form of SERVANT *sb.*

**serwe,** obs. Sc. form of SERVE *v.*[1], SORROW.

**seryauntre,** variant of SERGEANTRY.

**seryf(f,** obs. forms of SERVE *v.*[1]

**serymonie, -y(e,** obs. forms of CEREMONY.

**seryne,** obs. Sc. form of SIREN *sb.*

**ses:** see CEASE, SAY *v.*[1], SEE, SESS.

**sesame** ('sɛsəmiː, *formerly* 'sɛsəm, 'siːsəm). Forms: 5 **sysane,** 6–7 **sesama,** 7 **sesami, sesamo, sesamy,** 7– **sesame,** (9 **-é**), 6– **sesam.** [In early use, a. or ad. L. *sēsamum* (see SESAMUM), also *sīsamum*, and *sēsama, -ima* = Gr. σήσαμον, σησάμη, prob. of oriental origin, but the relation to the Semitic forms (Syriac *shūshmâ*, Jewish Aramaic *shumshᵉmā*, Arab. *simsim*) is not clear. Some of the earlier forms represent It. *sesamo*, or mod.Gr. σησάμι (= earlier σησάμιον, dim.). The mod. currency and form of the word are due to translations of the Arabian Nights from Fr. (*sésame*), and the trisyllabic pronunciation to association with Gr. σησάμη.] **a.** A widely cultivated East Indian plant, *Sesamum indicum* (N.O. *Pedaliaceæ*). Also, the seeds of this plant, from which an oil is expressed.

*c* **1440** *Pallad. on Husb.* x. 67 Sysane in faat soil & grauel is sowe. **1551** TURNER *Herbal* I. P vj b, Euonymus..hath coddes lyke vnto sesam. **1562** *Ibid.* II. 134 No beast will eat sesama when it is grene. **1600** J. PORY tr. *Leo's Africa* VIII. 324 This little citie built vpon the riuer of Nilus,.. aboundeth greatly with the graine or seed called Sesama. **1601** HOLLAND *Pliny* XXII. XXV. II. 140 Sesama stamped or beaten into pouder, and so taken in wine, restraineth immoderat vomits. **1682** WHELER *Journ. Greece* I. 67 Sesami (of which they make Oyl). **1736** AINSWORTH *Lat.-Eng. Dict.*, *Sesama*, a white grain or corn growing in India,..sesame. **1744** in *6th Rep. Dep. Kpr.* App. II. 121 A vegetable (called Sesamo) extraordinary productive of oyl of a sweet taste. **1785** MARTYN *Rousseau's Bot.* xiii. (1794) 148 Wheat, Barley, Vetches, Sesame, &c., are said by Berosus to be wild in Babylonia. **1877** C. GEIKIE *Christ* xlvi. (1879) 547 Wheat fields alternated with fields of barley, sesame and rice. **1897** [see GINGILI].

**b.** The word used as a charm to open and shut the door of the robbers' den in the tale of 'Ali Baba and the Forty Thieves'; hence, a magic password, something which acts like magic in obtaining admission; = OPEN SESAME.

**1785** *Arab. Nts. Entert.* 562 Their captain..pronounced these words distinctly: 'Sesame' (which is a sort of corn), 'open.' *Ibid.*, Then Ali Baba heard him bid the door shut, by pronouncing these words—'Shut, Sesame'. *Ibid.*, Ali Baba ..perceiving the door,..said—'Open, Sesame'. **1831** LYTTON *Godolphin* xxii, No Tory, however wise,..could.. have obtained the *sesame* to those apartments. **1862** CALVERLEY *Verses & Transl.* (1894) 96 Thy name shall be a Sesame, at which the doors of the great shall fly open. **1894** K. GRAHAME *Pagan P.* 89 'Open, open, green hill!'—you needed no more recondite sesame than that.

**c.** *attrib.*, as ***sesame grain, oil, -seed; sesame cake; sesame grass*** = GAMA GRASS.

**1601** HOLLAND *Pliny* XV. vii. I. 434 The Sesame-seed doth yeeld an oile. **1745** tr. *Columella's Husb.* XI. ii, In the provinces beyond the sea some sow their sesam-seeds either in this or the following month. **1758** J. S. *Le Dran's Observ. Surg.* (1771) Dict. Cc 8b, *Sesamoidea Ossa*, several small Bones..resembling Sesamy-Seed. **1846–50** A. WOOD *Class-bk. Bot.* 623 *Tripsacum dactylöides.* Sesame Grass. **1867** BAKER *Nile Trib.* ii. (1872) 35 The sésamé grain. **1870** YEATS *Nat. Hist. Comm.* II. (1872) 207 Sesame oil..is frequently used for the adulteration of balsams and volatile oils. **1876** *Crace-Calvert's Dyeing* 111 The fabric is steeped in an emulsion of sesam oil. **1883** *Jrnl. Chem. Soc.* XLIV. 360 Albuminoids in Peach Kernels and Sesame Cake. **1972** *House & Garden* Feb. 98/2 Swiss fondue..Sesame seed sticks..make a happy accompaniment. **1973** *Time Out* 2–8 Mar. 27/4 They also have..sesame seed rolls with really thick fillings for around 13p. **1978** *Nagel's Encycl.-Guide: China* 380 Rolls covered with sesame seeds are eaten at the same time.

†**sesamine**, *a.* and *sb.* *Obs.* [ad. L. *sēsamin-us*, a. Gr. σησάμινος, f. σήσαμον SESAMUM.] **A.** *adj.*

**1.** Pertaining to, or obtained from sesame.

**1608** TOPSELL *Serpents* 214 A Sesamyne seede. **1613** PURCHAS *Pilgrimage* (1614) 454 They were annointed with Sesamine oyle.

**2.** = SESAMOID.

**1578** BANISTER *Hist. Man* I. 31 The Sesamine Ossicles.

**B.** *sb.* = SESAME.

**1607** TOPSELL *Four-f. Beasts* 133 A vomit made of Butter, Annise, and oyle of Sesamine. **1608** —— *Serpents* 212 Drinke also two drammes of the roote of Centaury, or Hartwort, Nosewort, or Gentian, or Sesamine.

**sesamoid** ('sɛsəmɔɪd), *a.* and *sb.* [ad. L. *sēsamoīdēs*, a. Gr. σησαμοειδής, f. σήσαμον SESAMUM: see -OID.]

**A.** *adj.* Shaped like a sesame-seed; applied in *Anat.* to certain small bones and cartilages formed in tendinous structures.

**1696** PHILLIPS (ed. 5), *Sesamoide*, Sixteen, Nineteen, Twenty, and sometimes more little Bones..which are found in the Joynts of the Hands and Feet. **1718** *Phil. Trans.* XXX. 891 Sesamoide Bones in the Fingers and Toes. **1808** BARCLAY *Muscular Motions* 404 A sesamoid bone belonging to the tendon of the *ulnaris internus.* **1846** BRITTAN tr. *Malgaigne's Man. Oper. Surg.* 247 Dissect the skin from the sole of the foot, leaving the sesamoid bones on the phalangeal articulation. **1854** *Orr's Circ. Sci., Org. Nat.* I. 234 A sesamoid ossicle.

**B.** *sb.* A sesamoid bone or cartilage.

**1854** *Orr's Circ. Sci., Org. Nat.* I. 256 The wrist has nine bones,..besides supplementary sesamoids. **1886** W. N. PARKER *Wiedersheim's Anat. Vertebr.* 113 Wherever a marked friction occurs, ossifications (sesamoids) may become developed in the course of a muscle or tendon.

So **sesa'moidal** *a.* (in recent Dicts.); **sesa'moideal** *a.* [mod.L. *sēsamoīdeus*] = SESAMOID *a.*

**1869** FITZWYGRAM *Horses & Stables* §678. 439 The superior Sesamoideal Ligament.

‖**sesamum** ('sɛsəməm). [L., ad. Gr. σήσαμον.] = SESAME.

**1577** B. GOOGE *Heresbach's Husb.* I. (1586) 32 b, What say you to Sesamum, that was greatly in vse in the olde tyme. **1600** SURFLET *Country Farm* II. xl. 251 You must steepe your seedes in the oile of Sesamum, otherwise called Turkie millet. **1796** MORSE *Amer. Geog.* II. 551 Rice, sugar-canes, corn, sesamum. **1822** *Hortus Anglicus* II. 133 Common Sesamum, or Oily Grain. **1884** A. LANG *Custom & Myth* 93 The girl performs no magic feat, but merely throws sesamum on the ground to delay the cannibals.

**b.** *attrib.*, as ***sesamum-cake, -oil, -plant, -seed.***

**1597** GERARDE *Herbal* II. ccccxcix. 1054 Columella saith, that Sesamum seedes must be sowen after Autumne Æquinoctiall. **1696** PHILLIPS (ed. 5) s.v. *Sesamoide*, Sesamum Seeds. **1850** F. MASON *Nat. Product. Burmah* 176 The sesamum plant is largely cultivated by the Karens. **1863** R. F. BURTON *Abeokuta* I. 132 Sesamum oil. **1891** *Daily News* 16 May 5/4 Sesamum cake..is..mixed with both Persian and Indian opium.

†**sesamus.** *Obs.* [mod.L., ad. Gr. σήσαμος = σήσαμον SESAMUM.] Sesame, sesame oil.

**1601** R. JOHNSON *Kingd. & Commw.* (1603) 205 Their sinewes and ioyntes are..annointed with the oyle Sesamus. **1813** J. C. HOBHOUSE *Journey* (ed. 2) 667 The plain of the Cayster..is cultivated with cotton and tobacco plants, with sesamus and a little barley.

**sesban** ('sɛsbæn). [ad. F. *sesban*, ultimately ad. Pers. *sīsabān.*] Any leguminous plant of the genus *Sesbania*, esp. *S. ægyptiaca* and *aculeata* (which yields rope fibre).

**1860** *Sir Rohan's Ghost* vi, Orange-colored sesban. **1864** GRISEBACH *Flora W. Ind. Islands* 787.

**sesce**, obs. form of CEASE.

**sescuple** ('sɛskju:p(ə)l), *a.* Now *rare.* [ad. L. *sescuplus* or *sescuplex*, var. *sesquiplus, -plex*, f. *sesqui-* SESQUI- + *-plus, -plex* -FOLD.] = SESQUIALTER *a.*

**1694** W. WOTTON *Anc. & Mod. Learn.* (1697) 100, 9 is in a Sescuple Proportion to 6. **1774** MITFORD *Ess. Harmony Lang.* 13 Rhythmus is either even, as in the dactyl, which has one long syllable equal to two short ones,..or it is sescuple, as in the pæon, composed of one long syllable and three short ones. **1846** *Penny Cycl.* Suppl. II. 369 Superparticular ratio..: its varieties are sescuple or sesquialter, sesquitertius, sesquiquartus, &c.

**sese**: see CEASE, CESS, SEE, SEIZE.

**seseli** ('sɛsɪlɪ). Also 6 -y. [med.L. *seseli, -is* (also *seseleos*), a. Gr. σέσελι, var. of σέσελις. Cf. F. *séséli* (16th c.), It., etc. *seseli*, and CICELY.]

**a.** = HARTWORT. **b.** A plant of the umbelliferous genus *Seseli.*

**1578** LYTE *Dodoens* 6 If it be drunken with Annis seede or Sesely. **1597** GERARDE *Herbal* II. ccccviii. 893 Of Seselios, or Harte woorts of Candie. *Ibid.* 894 *Seseli Creticum.* Seseleos of Candie. **1601** HOLLAND *Pliny* VIII. xxxii. I. 213 The hearbe Seselis or Siler-mountaine. **1605** TIMME *Quersit.* III. 172 Take..of the seedes peony, of seseli or comin, of each two ounces. **1753** *Chambers' Cycl.* Suppl., *Seseli seed*, in the materia medica, the name of the seed of a plant, called also by some *libanotis.* **1834** *Good's Study Med.* (ed. 4) I. 43 The root of several of the seselis.

**seser**, variant of SISER, cider.

†'**seskyn.** *Obs.* Also **suskyn.** [a. MDu. *seskijn*, f. *ses* six + dim. suffix *-kijn* = -KIN.] A Dutch coin of the value of 6 mites.

**1413** *Act 3 Hen. V*, c. 1 §2 Les Galyhalpens & la Moneie appelle Seskyn & Doydekyn. *Ibid.*, Galyhalpens, Seskyns ou Doykyns. **1423** *Rolls of Parlt.* IV. 255/1 Le moneie appelle Galihalpenys, Suskyns & Dodekyns. **14..** in *Athenæum* (1867) 7 Dec. 768, vi mytis is a seskyn.

**sesora**, variant of SISERARY.

**17..** *Ballad* in H. Walpole *Let. to Percy* 5 Feb. 1765, They [the bells] rung with a Sesora.

**Sesotho** (sɛ'su:tu:). Also **Sesuto, Sesutu.** [Bantu, = 'language of the Sotho'.] A south-eastern Bantu language spoken by members of the SOTHO people. Also *attrib.* or as *adj.*

**1846** J. C. BROWN tr. *Arbousset & Daumas's Narr. Tour N.-E. of Cape Good Hope* xxiii. 251, I spoke Sesuto, a dialect which the chief of the place.., also understood. **1871** J. MACKENZIE *Ten Years North of Orange River* 492 They [*sc.* clicks] are found in other African languages, as in Zulu and Kaffir, and a few words in Sesuto. **1894**, etc. [see *kitchen Dutch* s.v. KITCHEN *sb.* 7]. **1916** J. BUCHAN *Greenmantle* ix. 120, I spoke rapidly in Sesutu, for I was afraid the captain might know Dutch. **1939** tr. *E. N. Marais's My Friends the Baboons* vii. 81 From the struggling mass there arose constant laughter, mingled with Sesutu curses of the grossest kind. **1953** P. LANHAM *Blanket Boy's Moon* IV. iii. 208, I am a Mosotho; I love Lesotho; I love my language Sesotho. **1975** J. MCCLURE *Snake* x. 138 Marais made a point of thanking her in Sesotho, the only Bantu language he spoke. **1980** —— *Blood of Englishman* ix. 86 Zondi was fluent in Afrikaans..and Sesuto.

**sesours**, obs. form of SCISSORS.

**sesperal**, obs. variant of SUSPIRAL.

**Sesquesahamock**, obs. var. SUSQUEHANNOCK.

**sesqui-** ('sɛskwɪ), a Latin prefix [L. *sesqui-*, also *sesque-*, contraction of **sēmis-que* a half in addition; cf. *sestertius*:—**sēmis-tertius*], expressing a superparticular ratio.

**1. a.** With designations of measure or amount, denoting one-and-a-half times the unit; as *sesquihōra* an hour and a half; *sesquipēs* a foot and a half (see SESQUIPEDALIAN); so †**sesqui'horal** *a.*, lasting an hour and a half; ,**sesquio'cellus** *Ent.* (see SESQUIALTEROUS); †'**sesquitone** *Mus.*, an interval consisting of a tone and a semitone, a minor third; also used loosely in †**sesqui'decuman** *a.*, consisting of fifteen; †**sesqui'decury**, a set of fifteen.

**1650** *Descr. Future Hist. Eur.* 31 Merlin prophesied to him, 'That within lesse then a *sesquidecumane period of time, the Eagles head should be cloven in two.' **1650** RAVIS (*title*) A generall Grammer for the ready attaining of the Ebrew... Also a *Sesquidecury, or a number of Fifteene Adoptive Epistles..concerning care of the Orientall Tongues to be promoted. **1652** URQUHART *Jewel* Wks. (1834) 279 Their tedious pharisaical prayers before supper, and *sesquihoral graces upon a dish of skink and leg of mutton. **1694** W. HOLDER *Harmony* 80 The Third Minor, Trihemitone, or *Sesquitone, as consisting of three half Tones (or rather of a Tone and half a Tone).

**b.** *Chem.* In the names of salts, expressing a proportion of 3 to 2 between the constituents, *viz.* a combination of 3 atoms or equivalents of the substance denoted by the word to which it is prefixed with 2 atoms of another element or radical; e.g. ***sesquibromide***, a bromide containing 3 atoms of bromine for 2 of another substance; similarly **sesqui'basic** [see BASIC *a.*], having 3 equivalents of the base for 2 of the acid; '**sesqui,compound**, '**sesqui,salt**, a compound, a salt having its constituents in these proportions; **sesqui'terpene, -'terpenoid**, any terpene having the formula $C_{15}H_{24}$; any simple derivative of such a compound.

This terminology was introduced into English by T. Thomson in his *First Principles of Chemistry* 1825, and *System of Chemistry* 1831, where many terms, not illustrated here, are to be found.

**1849** D. CAMPBELL *Inorg. Chem.* 208 The *Sesquibasic acetate of lead, $3PbO,2(C_4H_3O)$ + Aq. **1831** T. THOMSON *Syst. Chem.* (ed. 7) II. 388 *Sesquiborate of ammonia. *Ibid.* I. 324 The *sesquibromide of arsenic. **1825** —— *1st Princ. Chem.* II. App. 515 *Sesquicarbonate of ammonia. **1883** HARDWICH *Photogr. Chem.* (ed. 9) 38 When first formed it has nearly the composition of a Sesquicarbonate, but by exposure to the air neutral Carbonate of Ammonia escapes, and a white powder is left, which is a Bicarbonate. **1871** *Jrnl. Chem. Soc.* XXIV. 1012 *Sesquicarbonyl Chloroplatinite, $C_3O_3Pt_2Cl_4$. **1825** T. THOMSON *1st Princ. Chem.* II. App. 515 *Sesquichloride of iron. **1857** MILLER *Elem. Chem., Org.* (1862) 218 Aluminum forms a *sesqui-compound $(Al_2(C_4H_5)_3)$ corresponding to its oxide $Al_2O_3$. **1839** *Penny Cycl.* XIII. 32/2 The ferrocyanide of potassium also gives a deep blue, but the *sesquiferrocyanide gives none at all. **1831** T. THOMSON *Syst. Chem.* (ed. 7) II. 452 *Sesquihydrated carbonate of soda. **1887** *Jrnl. Chem. Soc.* LII. I. 558 The formula of the fibrous alum, $3MgO,SO_3$ + $2Al_2O_3,3SO_3$ + $53H_2O$, represents a *sesqui-magnesia alum. **1849** D. CAMPBELL *Inorg. Chem.* 186 *Sesquinitrate of iron, $Fe_2O_{33}NO_5$. **1839** *Penny Cycl.* XIII. 32/1 Sulphate of Peroxide of Iron, or *Sesquipersulphate of Iron. *Ibid.*, [Pernitrate of iron] is..a *sesquisalt. **1825** T. THOMSON *1st Princ. Chem.* II. App. 515 *Sesquisulphate of uranium. *Ibid.*, *Sesquisulphuret of arsenic. **1890** *Westm. Gaz.* 1 Mar. 6/1 It has been found that sesqui-sulphuret of phosphorus ..melts only at 142 deg. **1838** T. THOMSON *Chem. Org. Bodies* 176 *Sesquitartrovinate of copper. **1888** *Jrnl. Chem. Soc.* LIV. 377 *Sesquiterpene, $C_{15}H_{24}$. **1922** *Nature* 16 Feb. 226/2 The principal constituents identified are safral, camphor, pinene, sesquiterpenes, eugenol, and alcoholic bodies. **1966** *New Scientist* 8 Dec. 576/2 The substance..is derived from farnesol, one of the basic sesquiterpenes, vegetable substances..which imitate the function of the juvenile hormone. **1976** *Nature* 5 Aug. 487/2 The essential oils D-bornyl acetate, α- and β-santalol and several plant sesquiterpene hydrocarbons have been shown to induce sexual excitement in male American cockroaches. **1951** *Jrnl. Chem. Soc.* 2988 (*heading*) *Sesquiterpenoids... Evidence for a nine-membered ring in caryophyllene. **1976** *Nature* 5 Aug. 488/2 Cadinol, a sesquiterpenoid biogenetically related to germacrene D, has been isolated from a plant and shown to be a stimulant for both male and female cockroaches.

**c.** In *Astrology*, **sesquiquadrate, -quartile**, denoting an aspect of planets when 135° from one another; **sesquiquintile**, when 108° from one another; **sesqui-square** = *sesquiquadrate.*

*c* **1610** SIR C. HEYDON *Astrol. Disc.* (1650) 95 The *Sesquiquadrate [aspect] of 135 degr. **1647** LILLY *Chr. Astrol.* c. 512. **1674** JEAKE *Arith.* (1696) 11 Aspects ..*Sesquiquartil. **1647** LILLY *Chr. Astrol.* c. 512 *Sesquiquintil [consists of degrees] 108. **1861** 'ZADKIEL' *Hand-bk. Astrol.* I. 8 The new aspects are semi-square, 45°; quintile, 72°; *sesqui-square, 135°.

†**d.** Prefixed to words descriptive of forms of religious belief, = extreme(ly), excessive(ly), ultra-; e.g. ***sesqui-conformist, -deist, -heretic, -Jesuit, separation***; also ***sesqui-superlative*** adj. *Obs.*

*a* **1661** FULLER *Worthies, Glouc.* (1662) I. 360 Some pressed super-Canonical Ceremonies, and such *Sesqui-Conformists made Mr. Workman turn first but a Semi-Conformist, and then by degrees to renounce all Conformity. **1880** F. HALL *Doctor Indoctus* 52 If he invented a brand-new form of allotheism, and came out a *sesquideist, or a quaternitarian. **1627** DONNE *Serm.* i. (1649) II. 5 They are *se[s]qui-Heretiks in this, that they countenance Incontinency, and Fornication, which those very heretiks abhorred. *a* **1631** —— *Serm.* xii. (1640) 113 A Jesuit, or a Semi-Jesuit, a practising Papist, or a *Sesqui-Jesuit, a Jesuited Lady. **1653** R. BAILLIE *Dissuas. Vind.* (1655) 9 Why..do the Independents..runne beyond it..to a *sesqui-separation? **1611** DONNE *Poems, Upon Coryat's Crudities* 2 Oh, to what height will love of greatness drive Thy learned spirit, *sesqui-superlative!

**2. a.** With an ordinal numeral adjective, denoting the proportion $1 + \frac{1}{n}:1$, *i.e.* $n + 1:n$, where n is the corresponding cardinal number, as *sesquioctāvus*, bearing the ratio $1\frac{1}{8}:1$, *i.e.* 9:8; so SESQUIALTER, -ALTERA, etc., SESQUITERTIA, etc.; †,**sesquibi'tertial**, involving a proportion of 5:3; †,**sesqui'decimal**, of 11:10; **sesqui'nonal**, of 10:9; ,**sesquioc'taval, -'octave**, of 9:8; ,**sesqui'quartal, -quartan**, of 5:4; ,**sesqui'septimal**, of 8:7.

*a* **1696** SCARBURGH *Euclid* (1705) 228 Sextuple proportion is by addition of the Antecedents made of Sesquitertial, *Sesquibitertial, and Triple proportions. *Ibid.* 180 If above the exact Multiple of the Consequent, there remains in the Antecedent any Quotal part of the Consequent, as an half, a third, a fourth, or a tenth part of the Consequent, (or otherwise thus named, a Sesquialteral, a Sesquitertial, a Sesquiquartal, a *Sesquidecimal part, &c.). **1787** HAWKINS *Life of Johnson* 375 The proportion of a column is taken from that of the human figure, which..is in a man sesquioctave of the head, and in a woman *sesquinonal. *a* **1696** SCARBURGH *Euclid* (1705) 182 The Exponent of their proportions is the common Quotient $1\frac{1}{8}$, which shews the proportion to be ..*Sesquioctaval. **1603** HOLLAND *Plutarch's Mor.* Explan. Words, **Sesqui-octave*, that which compriseth the whole and one 8 part; as 9 to 8. 18 to 16. **1726** LEONI *Alberti's Archit.* II. 30/2 Its proportion will be as eight to nine, which the Latins call a Sesquioctave. *a* **1696** SCARBURGH *Euclid* (1705) 180 This proportion is named triple *Sesquiquartal, and is noted thus $3\frac{1}{4}$. **1715** tr. *Gregory's Astron.* (1726) I. p. xi, The same Tension upon a sub-sesquialteran Chord acts in a double *sesquiquartan Ratio. **1726** LEONI *Alberti's Archit.* II. 30/2 Seven to eight,..the proportion which the Latins call *Sesquiseptimal.

**b.** in *Music*, after SESQUIALTERA and SESQUITERTIA; **sesquiquarta, -quinta, -sexta, -octava (-octave), -nona**, applied (i) to harmonic intervals producible by sounding four-fifths, five-sixths, etc. of a given string; (ii) rhythmic combinations of four notes against five, five against six, etc.

1597 MORLEY *Introd. Mus.* 54 If they would make fiue crotchets to one semibreefe, then must they set downe *Sesquiquarta* proportion thus $\frac{5}{4}$, wherein fiue semibriefes or their value make vp the time of foure semibriefes or strokes. 1694 W. HOLDER *Harmony* 153 To divide a Sesquioctave Tone (9 to 8) by dupling the Terms of the Ration thereof, into 2 Hemitones. 1698 WALLIS in *Phil. Trans.* XX. 81 We assign to a Fifth..the Sesqui-alter Proportion..And to a Tone..The Sesqui-octave (or that of 9 to 8). 1776 HAWKINS *Hist. Mus.* I. 74 The ditone he had demonstrated to be in sesquiquarta proportion, as 5 to 4. *Ibid.* 75 The greater or sesquioctave tone, 9 to 8, and the lesser or sesquinonal tone, 10 to 9. *Ibid.* The semiditone is sesquiquinta. 1883 ROCKSTRO in *Grove's Dict. Mus.* III. 475/1.

‖**sesquialter** (sɛskwɪˈæltə(r)), *a.* (*sb.*). [L., f. *sesqui-* (see prec.) + *alter* second. For the formation cf. ON. *hálfr annarr*, OE. *óþer healf*, G. *anderthalb*.]

**1.** Of a proportion: That is as $1\frac{1}{2}$ is to 1. Of an object: Proportionate *to* another object as $1\frac{1}{2}$ is to 1; that is such a multiple *of*.

1570 DEE *Math. Pref.* c j b, A Cylinder, whose heith, and Diameter of his base, is æquall to the Diameter of the Sphære, is Sesquialter to the same Sphære. 1598 FLORIO, *Hemiolio*, an arithmeticall proportion called Sesquialter or Sesquiplex, which is so much, and halfe so much againe. 1641 H. L'ESTRANGE *God's Sabbath* 119 This would by sesquialter proportion exceed all the rest. 1660 BARROW *Euclid* IV. xi. Schol., Isosceles triangle, whose angles at the base are multiples sesquialter of those at the top. 1698 *Phil. Trans.* XX. 81 We assign to a Fifth..the Sesquialter Proportion (or that of 3 to 2). 1711 H. NEEDLER in J. Duncombe *Lett.* (1773) I. 90, 6 is only sesquialter of 4. 1715 CHEYNE *Philos. Princ.* I. 222 In all the Revolutions of the Planets about the Sun,..the periodical Times is [*sic*] in a Sesquialter Proportion to the middle Distances. 1784 J. KEEBLE *Harmonics* 29 The sesquialter chromatic. 1846 *Penny Cycl.* Suppl. II. 369/2 The following ratios are super-particular: 15 to 10, which is sesquialter.

†**b.** *Mus.* = SESQUIALTERA 1 b.

1704 J. HARRIS *Lex. Techn.* s.v. *Time*, *Sesquialter Proportion*, which signifies a Triple Measure of three Notes, to two such like Notes of the Common Time.

**2.** = SESQUIALTERA 2.

1841 *Penny Cycl.* XXI. 293/2 Sometimes the Mixture stop is considered as part of the Sesquialter. 1846 *Ibid.* Suppl. II. 369/2 The sesquialter stop of an organ.

‖**sesquialtera** (sɛskwɪˈæltərə), *a.* (*sb.*). [L., fem. (sc. *ratio*) of *sesquialter* (see prec.).]

†**1.** = SESQUIALTER *a.* Also as *sb.*, a sesquialteral proportion. *Obs.*

1609 J. DOWLAND *Ornith. Microl.* 62 Now as of Duples you make Sesquialteraes, so of Triples you may make sesquitertiaes. 1650 BULWER *Anthropomet.* 150 If you onely contemplate the Diameters of longitude and latitude of a mans Face, you shall find a Sesquialtera proportion.

**b.** *Mus.* (See quots. and cf. SESQUI- 2 b.)

1501 DOUGLAS *Pal. Hon.* I. xli, Proportionis..Duplat, triplat, diatesseriall, Sesqui altera, and decupla resortis. 1597 MORLEY *Introd. Mus.* 32 *Phi.* Come then to Sesquialtera, what is it? *Ma.* It is when three notes are sung to two of the same kinde. *Ibid.* 92 The manner of singing *Sesquialtra* proportion. 1667 C. SIMPSON *Compend. Pract. Mus.* 34 Figures set thus $\frac{3}{2}$ called Sesquialtera proportion, which signifies a Tripla Measure of three Notes to two such like Notes of the Common Time. 1776 HAWKINS *Hist. Mus.* I. 67 If the fourth chord was to be..sesquialtera. 1883 ROCKSTRO in *Grove's Dict. Mus.* III. 475/1 Sesquialtera expresses the Proportion of two to three, and therefore represents the Perfect Fifth, which is produced by sounding two-thirds of a given string. *Ibid.*, In rhythmic combinations, Sesquialtera is used as the general symbol of Triple Time. The term Sesquialtera is also applied to passages of three notes sung against two.

**2.** The name of an organ stop, consisting of several ranks of pipes, of a brilliant tone. Usually *absol.* as *sb.*

1688 in Hopkins *Organ* (1870) 453 Ecchos... Sesquialtera ..105 pipes. 1798 HARGROVE *Hist. Knaresboro* (ed. 5) 53 The organ hath ten stops, viz. two diapasons,..one susquialtra [etc.]. 1801 BUSBY *Dict. Mus.* s.v. *Stop*, *Sesquialtera Stop*, a mixed stop running through the scale of the instrument, and consisting of three, four, and sometimes five ranks of pipes, tuned in thirds, fifths, and eighths. 1883 STAINER in *Grove's Dict. Mus.* III. 475/1 The Sesquialtera organ stop.

**sesquialteral** (sɛskwɪˈæltərəl), *a.* [f. L. *sesquialter*: see prec.] = SESQUIALTER 1.

1603 HOLLAND *Plutarch's Mor.* 1358 The proportion..of Diapente, [is] Hemiolios or Sesquialterall, that is to say, the whole and halfe as much more. 1692 BENTLEY *Boyle Lect.* viii. (1693) 10 As the six Primary Planets revolve about Him, so the Secondary ones are moved about Them..in the same Sesquialteral proportion of their Periodical motions to their Orbs. *a* 1696 SCARBURGH *Euclid* (1705) 180, 10 to 4 is in Multiple superparticular proportion duple Sesquialteral $2\frac{2}{4}$, that is $2\frac{1}{2}$. 1729 SHELVOCKE *Artillery* II. 148 The proportion of Coal to Sulphur, shall be either Sesquialteral or Double, or Triple, or sometimes Equal. 1817 H. T. COLEBROOKE *Algebra*, etc. 287.

**b.** *Bot.* and *Ent.* (See quots.)

1793 MARTYN *Lang. Bot.*, *Sesquialter flosculus*, a Sesquialteral floret. When a large fertile floret is accompanied by a small abortive one. 1806 TURTON tr. *Linn. Syst. Nat.* VII. Expl. Terms, *Sesquialteral*... In entomology it means occupying a third part of the wing, or including a smaller band or spot within a larger one. [1856 HENSLOW *Dict. Bot. Terms*, *Sesqui-alter*... Where the stamens are one half as many as the petals or sepals.]

†**sesquiˈalteran**, *a.* *Obs.* [Formed as prec. + -AN.] = SESQUIALTER 1.

1653 R. SANDERS *Physiogn.* 271 Here you may finde the Double proportion, the sesquialteran, the sesquitertian. 1715 tr. *Gregory's Astron.* (1726) I. 137 That the Periodic Times of the Planets will be exactly in the Sesquialteran Proportion of their Orbits or Circles.

**sesquialterate** (sɛskwɪˈæltərət), *a.* [Formed as prec. + -ATE[2].] = SESQUIALTER 1. Hence †**sesquialterate** *v.* (see quot. 1609).

1609 DOWLAND *Ornith. Microl.* 64 There be, which adde the colour to the figures which are made sesquialterate by the Caracters of the numbers: and contrarily sesquialterating the sesquialteraes. 1653 R. SANDERS *Physiogn.* 270 These all..bear a sesquialternate [*sic*] part to the former proportion. 1728 CHAMBERS *Cycl.* s.v. *Lime*, The Marks of a well-burnt Lime..are, that its Weight is to that of the Stone in a sesquialterate Proportion. 1776 BURNEY *Hist. Mus.* (1789) I. vi. 67 Time..of odd numbers or sesquialterate proportion is more proper to excite commotion. 1817 H. T. COLEBROOKE *Algebra*, etc. 287 In what time will my principal be raised to the sesquialterate amount? 1907 OMOND *Eng. Metrists* 14 Feet of sesquialterate ratio (3:2 or 2:3) 'answer to the Diapente or fifth in Music'.

**b.** (See quot. and SESQUIALTERA 1 b.)

1801 BUSBY *Dict. Mus.*, *Sesqui-Alterate*, *The greater Perfect*... A triple in the old music, in which the breve is three measures, or semibreves.

**sesquialterous** (sɛskwɪˈæltərəs), *a.* *Ent.* [Formed as prec. + -OUS.] See quots. and cf. SESQUIALTERAL b.

1826 KIRBY & SP. *Entomol.* xlvi. IV. 288 Sesquialterous Ocellus (*Ocellus sesquialterus*). An ocellus with a smaller near it, called also *Sesquiocellus*. *Ibid.* 289 Sesquialterous Fascia (*Fascia sesquialtera*). When both wings are traversed by a continued band, and either the primary or secondary by another. *Ibid.* 342 Sesquialterous (*Sesquialteræ*). When a minute areolet is appended to a large one.

**sesquicentenary** (ˌsɛskwɪsɛnˈtiːnərɪ). [f. SESQUI- + CENTENARY *sb.*] A one-hundred-and-fiftieth anniversary, a festival celebrating this; = SESQUICENTENNIAL *sb.*

1961 in WEBSTER. 1969 *New Scientist* 20 Nov. 389/1 The Cambridge Philosophical Society has just celebrated its sesquicentenary. 1978 *Times* 9 Jan. 9/7 This weekend's two 'Mainly Schubert' concerts..were of a kind to make one wish that his centenary celebrations, this year is the sesquicentenary of his death, came around more often.

**sesquicentennial** (ˌsɛskwɪsɛnˈtɛnɪəl), *a.* and *sb.* Chiefly *U.S.* [f. SESQUI- + CENTENNIAL.]

**A.** *adj.* Pertaining to a celebration of a hundred-and-fiftieth anniversary.

1888 *Advance* (Chicago) 9 Aug., The sesquicentennial celebration of the church. 1896 *Academy* 6 June 468/2 The sesquicentennial celebration of the University of Princeton, New Jersey.

**B.** *sb.* Such a celebration or anniversary.

1880 *Lond. & Prov. Mus. Trades Rev.* 15 Nov. 3/1 The Sesqui-centennial of Baltimore was celebrated during the second week of October. 1931 [see RED *sb.*[1] 1 g]. 1976 *Times Lit. Suppl.* 12 Mar. 278/2 In 1926 the sesquicentennial [of Adam Smith's *Wealth of Nations*] was celebrated more modestly with a series of lectures given in the new home of economic orthodoxy, the London School of Economics. 1978 *Nature* 8 June 421/2 This year is the sesquicentennial of the announcement by Wöhler that marked the birth of synthetic organic chemistry.

**sesquiduple** (ˈsɛskwɪˌdjuːp(ə)l), *a.* [f. SESQUI- + DUPLE, to express the meaning 'two and a half' (on a false analogy), after *sesquialteral*.] Involving a ratio of $2\frac{1}{2}$ to 1. So **sesquiˈduplicate** *a.*

1775 ASH, *Sesquiduplicate*, belonging to the ratio of five to two. 1842 BRANDE *Dict. Sci.*, etc. s.v. *Sesqui*, Sesquiduplicate..sometimes occurs in modern treatises. 1850 OGILVIE, *Sesquiduple*, is sometimes used in the same manner as *sesquiduplicate*.

**sesquioxide** (sɛskwɪˈɒksaɪd). *Chem.* Also †**sesquoxide.** [See SESQUI- 1 b.] An oxide containing three equivalents of oxygen to two of another element or radical.

1831 T. THOMSON *Syst. Chem.* (ed. 7) I. 515 When the native binoxide of manganese is exposed to a low red-heat it is converted into sesquoxide. *Ibid.* II. 818 Muriated sesquioxide of manganese. 1848 NORMANDY tr. *Rose's Chem. Analysis* I. 159 Sesquioxyde of Iridium, $Ir_2O_3$. 1880 BASTIAN *Brain* i. 5 The sesquioxides of chromium and iron.

Hence ˌ**sesquioxiˈdation**, conversion into a sesquioxide; ˌ**sesquioˈxidic** *a.*; ˌ**sesquiˈoxidized** *pa. pple.*, converted into a sesquioxide.

1849 D. CAMPBELL *Inorg. Chem.* 27 The amount of iron sesquioxidized. *Ibid.* 142 A complete sesquioxidation of the iron salt. 1906 *Proc. R. Inst.* XVII. 102 Sesquioxydic mordants. 1932 [see *red loam* s.v. RED *a.* 17 e].

**sesquipedal** (səsˈkwɪpɪdəl), ˈsɛskwɪpɛdəl), *a.* and *sb.* [ad. L. *sesquipedāl-is*, f. SESQUI- + *ped-*, *pēs* foot: cf. PEDAL.] **A.** *adj.* = SESQUIPEDALIAN.

1611 R. BADLEY in *Coryat's Crudities* k 2b, The sesquipedale belly of thy Tome. 1624 BURTON *Anat. Mel.* III. iv. II. vi, Fustian, big, sesquipedal words. 1802 SYD. SMITH *Wks.* (1869) 4 Dr. Parr seems to think that eloquence consists..in a studious arrangement of sonorous, exotic, and sesquipedal words. 1829 *Blackw. Mag.* XXVI. 917 Admirable dissertations on old chamber-pots are poured into ears sesquipedal. 1891 M. MURIEL DOWIE *Girl in Karp.* ix, Some lovely sesquipedal adverb.

**B.** *sb.* A thing a foot and a half in length: cf. next B. 1. (In quot. used jocularly.)

1713 *Guardian* No. 108 ¶4, I am but a Sesquipedal, having only six Feet and a half of Stature.

**sesquipedalian** (ˌsɛskwɪpɪˈdeɪlɪən), *a.* and *sb.* [f. L. *sesquipedālis*: see SESQUIPEDAL and -IAN.]

**A.** *adj.* **1.** Of words and expressions (after Horace's *sesquipedalia verba* 'words a foot and a half long', A.P. 97): Of many syllables.

1656 BLOUNT *Glossogr.* s.v., Sesquipedalian words (*verba sesquipedalia*) used by Horace for great, stout, and lofty words; words that are very long, consisting of many Syllables. 1661 K. W. *Conf. Char.*, *Courtier* (1860) 20 Noddle puzzling sesquepedalian words. 1791 BOSWELL *Johnson* an. 1776 (1831) III. 407 Finding one of his sesquipedalian words hang fire. 1793 W. ROBERTS *Looker-on* No. 80 (1794) III. 276 A set of sesquipedalian exclamations. 1807 SOUTHEY *Spec. Eng. Poets* I. Pref. p. xviii, The verses of Stephen Hawes are as full of barbarous sesquipedalian Latinisms, as the prose of the Rambler. 1861 MAX MÜLLER *Sci. Lang.* Ser. I. viii. (1864) 338 In these sesquipedalian compounds the significative root remains distinct. 1886 R. F. BURTON *Arab. Nts.* (abr. ed.) I. Forew. p. xii, Sesquipedalian un-English words.

**b.** *transf.* Given to using long words.

1853 MRS. GASKELL *Cranford* v, Towards the end of her letter Miss Jenkyns used to become quite sesquipedalian.

¶ Used for 'very tall or big'.

1857 TROLLOPE *Barchester T.* xxv, This [half-crown] she sacrificed to the avarice of Mrs. Proudie's metropolitan sesquipedalian serving-man.

**2.** Half a yard high or long.

*c* 1714 ARBUTHNOT, etc. *Mem. M. Scribl.* I. xiv. (1741) 48 Hast thou ever measur'd the gigantick Ethiopian, whose stature is above eight cubits high, or the sesquipedalian Pigmey?

**B.** *sb.* **1.** A person or thing that is a foot and a half in height or length.

1615 *Curry-Combe for Coxe-Combe* iii. 113 He thought fit by his variety, to make you knowne for a viperous Sesquipedalian in euery coast. 1656 BLOUNT *Glossogr.*

**2.** A sesquipedalian word.

1830 *Fraser's Mag.* I. 350 What an amazing power in writing down hard names and sesquipedalians does not the following passage manifest! 1894 *Nat. Observer* 6 Jan. 194/2 His sesquipedalians recall the utterances of another Doctor.

Hence ˌ**sesquipeˈdalianism**, style characterized by the use of long words; lengthiness; so **sesquiˈpedalism**; ˌ**sesquipeˈdality**, sesquipedalian quality; *transf.* great length, lengthiness; also, 'the practice of using long words' (Ogilvie, 1882).

1863 *Sat. Rev.* 440 How dear to his heart must be that marvellous *sesquipedalianism in which he ordinarily revels. 1887 W. C. RUSSELL *Bk. for Hammock* (1893) 120 Everything must be done quickly at sea: there is no time for sesquipedalianism. 1873 F. HALL *Mod. Eng.* 148 The era of galvanized *sesquipedalism and sonorous cadences. 1759 STERNE *Tr. Shandy* II. ix, With a breadth of back, and a *sesquipedality of belly, which might have done honour to a serjeant in the horse-guards. 1850 *Fraser's Mag.* XLI. 654 There is certainly some sesquipedality in the word. 1855 *Ibid.* LI. 63 A most wonderful topknotted cock with a sesquipedality of wattle.

**sesquiplane** (ˈsɛskwɪpleɪn). Now *Hist.* Also ‖**sesquiplan.** [ad. F. *sesquiplan*, f. *sesqui-* SESQUI- + *plan* PLANE *sb.*[3]] A biplane having one wing of surface area not more than half that of the other.

1921 *Flight* 29 Sept. 650/2 The Nieuport-Delage 'Sesquiplans' are to all intents and purposes monoplanes, but with a small plane covering-in the wheel axle as in some of the German Fokkers. 1921 *Aeroplane* 5 Oct. 293/2 Why the machine is called the 'Sesquiplan' is even a greater mystery than the name of the 'Bamel'. *Ibid.* 19 Oct. 348/2 (*heading*) What is a sesquiplane? 1930 *Flight* 17 Jan. 115/2 Its most unusual feature was that, although a *sesquiplane*, its top wing was smaller in span and chord than the lower wing. 1939 C. H. L. NEEDHAM *Aircraft Design* I. vi. 74 The sesquiplane arrangement, in which one wing, generally the top, has roughly twice the area of the lower wing, is a compromise which enables the advantages of the biplane structure to be combined with somewhat improved aerodynamic characteristics. 1960 C. H. GIBBS-SMITH *Aeroplane* II. 220 The Coanda sesquiplane of 1910. There has recently arisen some controversy about this machine... Until recently it has been accepted as an all-wood sesquiplane, with cantilever wings, powered by a 50-h.p. Clerget engine driving a 'turbo-propulseur' in the form of a large but simple ducted air-fan. 1981 ANDREWS & MORGAN *Supermarine Aircraft since 1914* 174 The superstructure was of sesquiplane form, that is with the lower wing only one third the area of the top wing.

**sesquiplicate** (sɛsˈkwɪplɪkət), *a.* [ad. mod.L. *sesquiplicātus*, f. SESQUI- + *plicātus* folded, PLICATE, to express the meaning 'subduplicate of the triplicate'. (L. *sesquiplex* = taken once and a half.)] Bearing or involving the ratio of the square roots of the cubes of the terms of a certain ratio.

Thus, $a$ is to $a'$ in the sesquiduplicate ratio of $b$ to $b'$, when $a{:}a'{::}\sqrt{b^3}{:}\sqrt{b'^3}$.

1714 DERHAM *Astrol. Theol.* (1769) 22 Their motions round the Sun, are in sesquiplicate proportion to their distances from him. 1728 tr. *Newton's Syst. World* 12 The periodic times of the satellits of Jupiter are, one to another, in the sesquiplicate proportion of their distances from the center of this planet. 1841 *Penny Cycl.* XIX. 309/2 Sesquiplicate ratio of A to B. 1873 PROCTOR *Expanse of Heaven* 108.

‖**sesquitertia** (sɛskwɪˈtɜːʃə). *Mus.* [L., fem. (sc. *ratio*) of *sesquitertius*, f. SESQUI- + *tertius* third.] Denoting a ratio of $1\frac{1}{3}$ to 1, *i.e.* 4 to 3; chiefly *Mus.* denoting (i) an interval having this ratio, viz. the perfect fourth, (ii) a rhythm of three notes against four.

**1597** MORLEY *Introd. Mus.* 33 Sesquitercia is when foure notes are sung to three of the same kinde. **1650** BULWER *Anthropomet.* 149 Wherefore the latitude of the Face compared with the longitude..should be in a sesquitertia proportion. **1776** HAWKINS *Hist. Mus.* I. 64 GB is sesquitertia to DB. *Ibid.* 68 The number 256, sesquitertia of 192. **1801** BUSBY *Dict. Mus.* **1883** ROCKSTRO in *Grove's Dict. Mus.* s.v. *Sesqui.*

**sesquitertial** (sɛskwɪˈtɜːʃəl), *a.* ? *Obs.* [f. prec. + -AL$^1$.] Expressing a ratio of 4:3. Cf. prec.

**1603** HOLLAND *Plutarch's Mor.* 1358 The proportion of the Musicke or Symphonie Diatessaron, is Epitritos or Sesquitertiall, that is to say, the whole and a third part over. **1658** ROWLAND tr. *Moufet's Theat. Ins.* II. xiii. 1066 These legs also are made in a sesquitertiall proportion. *a* **1696** SCARBURGH *Euclid* (1705) 180 As 40 to 12 is $3\frac{4}{12}$ or $3\frac{1}{3}$, Triple Sesquitertial.

**b.** *transf.* (See quot.)

**1806** TURTON tr. *Linn. Syst. Nat.* VII. Expl. Terms, *Sesquitertial*, occupying the fourth part.

**sesquitertian** (sɛskwɪˈtɜːʃən), *a.* ? *Obs.* [Formed as prec. + -AN.] = SESQUITERTIAL.

**1603** HOLLAND *Plutarch's Mor.* Explan. Words, *Sesquitertian*, a proportion, whereby is understood as much as comprehendeth the whole, and one third part, as 12. to 9. **1658** SIR T. BROWNE *Gard. Cyrus* iii. 58 The legs of Spiders are made after a sesquitertian proportion. **1698** *Phil. Trans.* XX. 81 We assign to a Fifth..the Sesqui-alter Proportion.. And, to a Fourth..the Sesquitertian. **1760** STILES in *Phil. Trans.* LI. 717 If the interval diatessaron, or sesquitertian ratio, should be assigned for the limitation of the extreme tones. **1774** J. DUNCOMBE *New Arithm. Dict.*

So †**sesquiˈtertianal** *a. Obs.*

**1704** J. HARRIS *Lex. Techn.* I, *Sesquitertianal Proportion*, is when any..Quantity contains another once and one third.

**sesquitertious** (sɛskwɪˈtɜːʃəs), *a. Ent.* [Formed as prec. + -OUS.] (See quot. and cf. SESQUIALTEROUS.)

**1826** KIRBY & SP. *Entomol.* xlvi. IV. 290 Sesquitertious Fascia (*Fascia sesquitertia*). When both wings are traversed by a continued band, and more than half of either the primary or secondary by another; or, when a wing or elytrum contains a band and the third of a band.

**sess**, *sb.*$^1$ Also 7 sesse. [Aphetic f. ASSESS *sb.*: see CESS *sb.*$^1$]

**1.** An assessment, impost. Now only *dial.* and in Ireland, a local rate; = CESS *sb.*$^1$ 1 a (which is more usual).

**1580** [see CESS *sb.* 1 a]. **1673** *Acct. Bk. W. Wray* in *Antiquary* XXXII. 119 Paid to Richerd Bell for the sesse, 8*d.* **1708** *Lond. Gaz.* No. 4442/4 They intend to make Sale of the Lands of such Persons.., who refuse to pay the Sesses laid upon them. **1840** BARHAM *Ingol. Leg.* Ser. II. *Row in Omnibus*, There's the rent, and the rates, and the sesses, and taxes.

†**2.** *Ireland.* = CESS *sb.*$^1$ 2. *Obs.*

**1571** CAMPION *Hist. Irel.* II. x. (1633) 126 The abuses whereof with sesse and Souldiours, doe so impouerish and alienate the needie Farmers from us. **1586** [see ASSESS *sb.*]. **1612** [see CESS *sb.* 2]. *a* **1661** FULLER *Worthies, Kent* (1662) II. 75 Sir Henry Sidney..established the Composition of the Pale, in lieu of Purveyance and Sesse of Souldiers.

**sess** (sɛs), *sb.*$^2$ *Soap-manuf.* [Origin obscure.] Each of the sections composing the frame or mould into which the soap is thrown to cool and solidify after the process of fitting (see FITTING *vbl. sb.* 4).

**1854** *Tomlinson's Cycl. Useful Arts* (1867) II. 539/1 The semi-fluid mass is ladled out from the precipitated ley into rectangular frames, or sesses, as they are called in Liverpool.

†**sess**, *v. Obs.* Forms: 5 ses, sese, 6 seasse, seise, 6–7 sease, seaze, sesse, 7 seize. [Aphetic f. ASSESS *v.*; see CESS *v.*$^1$

For the variation in the length of the vowel, cf. CEASE *v.*]

**1.** *trans.* To assess or determine officially the amount of (a tax, contribution, wages, or prices); = CESS *v.*$^1$ 1.

**1467** in *Eng. Gilds* (1870) 382 That the price of ale be sessed at euery lawday by the gret enquest. **1484** *Coventry Leet Bk.* 519 Wheruppon they were commytte to warde, and their ffyn sessed be þe seid Maire..at xx li. **1533–4** *Act 25 Hen. VIII*, c. 8 The saide maire and the aldermen maie haue power..to sesse fines by their discreasions. **1563** GOLDING *Cæsar* v. 108 b, When the hostages were brought in by the day limitted, he appointed dayesmen betwene the Cities to consyder of the matter in variance, and to sesse the penalty. **1620** J. WILKINSON *Coroners & Sherifes* 60 The Coroners ought to be there to sesse the wages. **1640** *Archdeaconry of Essex Min.* (MS.) 1638–40, 195 Not paying iis vid which he was seast for bread and wyne and diverse other necessary expences. **1656** EARL MONM. tr. *Boccalini's Advts. fr. Parnass.* II. lxxxii. 365 Those [taxes] which were at first sessed but for a limited time.

**2.** To impose (a tax, fine, etc.) *upon* a person or community; = CESS *v.*$^1$ 2.

**1465** *Paston Lett.* II. 199 There putte into the Kynges pryson by cawse of the fyn which was sessed upon the forsaid John Smyth, John Hopton, and me. **1551** in W. H. Turner *Select. Rec. Oxford* (1880) 207 Suche taxe and tallenge as shall be uppon hym taxed and sessyd. **1561** in *Rec. Caernarvon* (1838) 298 That you giue likewise in chardge to the said Jury to taske and sease such severalle fines vppon the severall offenders. **1633** T. STAFFORD *Pac. Hib.* I. i. 16 Any person, upon whom any such Fines shalbe so seased. **1764** [see CESS *v.*$^1$ 1].

**3.** To fix the amount of payment due from (a person, a community, a property); to impose a tax upon, tax: const. *at*, *to*, *unto*; also with indirect question as second object. = CESS *v.*$^1$ 4.

**1475** *Rolls of Parlt.* VI. 139/2 Henry Bodrugan..sessed the people of the said Shire to grete notable sommes. *c* **1488** *Plumpton Corr.* (Camden) 61 As for our land, we pay our dymes therfore, and trust in you that ye will not ses none thereof, wherby we should have cause to make further labor; for it is not the Kyngs mynd to ses no dymeable land. **1530** PALSGR. 710/1, I sesse, as a kynges officers do a kynges subjectes what they shall paye, *je taille.* **1542** in W. H. Turner *Select. Rec. Oxford* (1880) 166, ij persons shalbe chosen to sesse and tax..the inhabytaunts. *a* **1548** HALL *Chron., Hen. IV*, 29 For which cause the Kyng..seassed and fined her at a great some of money. **1577** HANMER *Anc. Eccl. Hist., Socrates* III. xi. 306 So that euery one rateably was seased [**1619** seised] at a certaine summe. **1600** J. PORY tr. *Leo's Africa* I. 43 At last the bird was sessed to pay. **1610** B. JONSON *Alch.* III. iv, That was with the griefe Thou took'st for being sess'd at eighteene pence, For the waterworke. **1611** SPEED *Hist. Gt. Brit.* VI. ix. 49 Cæsar..seized them at forty hostages, with sufficiency of graine for his whole army. **1643** BAKER *Chron., Will. I*, 32 Likewise he Sessed all Bishops and Abbotts what number of souldiers they should finde. **1643** PRYNNE *Sov. Power Parl.* App. 26 The Clergy and Lords then refusing to pay any more then they were first sessed unto. **1698** FRYER *Acc. E. India & P.* 166 Causing his Coin to be stamped with his Master's Inscription, his Subjects Mulcted and Sessed by his Impositions.

**sess**, *int. Obs.* exc. *dial.* (see Eng. Dial. Dict.). Also 7 ses. A call to a dog when giving him food.

**1606** SYLVESTER *Du Bartas* II. iv. IV. *Decay* 216 Ses, ses, here Dogs.

**sess**, variant of CESS *sb.*$^5$

**1887** HALL CAINE *Deemster* xxviii, Bad sess to the women, the idle shoulderin' craythurs.

**sess(e**, obs. forms of CEASE *v.*

†ˈ**sessa**, *int. Obs.* [perh. var. of SA, SA, or possibly a. F. *cessez* 'cease!'

It is not certain that modern editors are right in inserting the form *sessa* in all the passages; the word may not be the same in the three places.]

An exclamation of uncertain meaning.

**1596** SHAKS. *Tam. Shr.* Induct. i. 6 Looke in the Chronicles, we came in with Richard Conqueror: therefore *Paucas pallabris*, let the world slide: Sessa. **1605** —— *Lear* III. iv. 104 Dolphin my Boy, Boy Sesey [*Q1* caese; *Q2* cease; *Q3* ceas; *Malone* sessa!]: let him trot by. *Ibid.* III. vi. 77 Dogs leapt the hatch, and all are fled. Do, de, de, de: sese [*Malone* Sessa!]: Come, march to Wakes and Fayres.

†**sesse**$^1$. *Obs. rare*$^{-1}$. [a. F. *sesse*, a. Arab. *shāsh*: see SASH *sb.*$^1$] = SASH *sb.*$^1$

**1718** OZELL tr. *Tournefort's Voy.* II. 356 They are distinguished by the White Sesse [orig. *la sesse blanche*] of their turbants.

†**sesse**$^2$. *Obs.* Aphetic form of *dissesse*, DECEASE *sb.*; = CESS *sb.*$^2$

**1417–8** *E.E. Wills* (1882) 39/3 Also it ys my wyll þat..all þat sche schele haue, after þe sesse of her, þat it be sold.

**sesse**, obs. form of CEASE *sb.*

*c* **1330** R. BRUNNE *Chron. Wace* (Rolls) 15893 Þen com þe folk wyþouten sesse Aboute Brian for to presse.

**sessile** (ˈsɛsaɪl, ˈsɛsɪl), *a.* [a. L. *sessilis* sitting down, dwarfed, stunted, f. *sess-*, ppl. stem of *sedēre* to sit: see -ILE.]

**1.** Having no footstalk. **a.** *Bot.* Of leaves, fruits, flowers, or other organs: Immediately attached by the base; not having a peduncle, pedicel, or the like. Hence of a species or variety (e.g. of oak) bearing sessile fruits: opposed to *pedunculated.*

**1753** *Chambers' Cycl.* Suppl. s.v. *Leaf*, *Sessile Leaf*, one which rises immediately from the stalk without any pedicle. **1756** *Phil. Trans.* XLIX. 835 The leaves..[are] generally quite sessile, or close to the stalk. **1785** MARTYN *Rousseau's Bot.* vi. (1794) 70 In the whole compound class the seed is always sessile, that is, it bears immediately upon the receptacle without any intermediate pedicle. **1861** S. THOMSON *Wild Fl.* I. (ed. 4) 71 Seed-vessel of common Poppy, showing the *rayed stigma*..placed close down, or *sessile* upon the ovary. **1875** *Lyell's Princ. Geol.* II. III. xliv. 507 Prostrate trunks of the Sessile Variety of the Common oak occur. **1879** A. GRAY *Struct. Bot.* vi. §6. 251 The filament, being only a stalk or support, may be very short or wholly wanting; the anther is then sessile. **1882** VINES *Sachs' Bot.* 565 In Piperaceæ however the stigma, which is sessile on the apex of the ovary, is often placed obliquely or divided into several lobes.

**b.** *Zool.* Of limbs or organs: Immediately in contact with the structure to which they are attached; having no connecting neck or footstalk. Also of certain animals.

**1777** PENNANT *Brit. Zool.* IV. 61 The shell..fixed by a stem: or sessil. **1834** MCMURTRIE *Cuvier's Anim. Kingd.* 298 The Læmodipoda are the only Malacostraca with sessile eyes. **1840** F. D. BENNETT *Whaling Voy.* II. 248 A sessile spur on the heel. **1851** DARWIN *Monogr. Cirripedia* I. (Ray Soc.) 4 The more important valves..being common to the pedunculated and sessile Cirripedes. **1870** ROLLESTON *Anim. Life* Introd. 65 The cerebral hemispheres always contain a lateral ventricle, which is prolonged into the interior of the sessile olfactory lobes.

**c.** *Path.* Of morbid growths, warts, etc.: Adhering close to the surface.

**1725** HUXHAM in *Phil. Trans.* XXXIII. 380 During the Suppuration, the Pox would become very sessile, and the coherent kind would enlarge their Bases exceedingly. **1822–29** *Good's Study Med.* (ed. 3) V. 670 Simple Wart, Simple and distinct: sessile or pensile. **1899** *Allbutt's Syst. Med.* VIII. 891 The skin..in many cases 'peppered' with warts, both sessile and pedunculated.

**2.** Of certain animals: Sedentary, fixed to one spot; not ambulatory. Of cells: Immobile. Also in extended use.

**1860** WRAXALL *Life in Sea* x. 242 They [Serpulariæ, etc.] are, therefore, nothing further than sessile nurses, just as the Siphonophoræ are nurses swimming about freely. **1871** E. D. COPE *Orig. Fittest* (1887) 193 It is now important to observe that great numbers of centrifugal animals are sedentary or sessile; while the longitudinal are vagrant, moving from place to place. **1879** G. ALLEN *Colour-Sense* iii. 23 Sessile or sedentary animals, as a rule, do not possess any form of visual organ. **1880** E. R. LANKESTER *Degeneration* 39 We may now proceed to look at some sessile or immobile animals which are not usually regarded as degenerate. **1904** *Brit. Med. Jrnl.* 10 Sept. 586/1 Certain cells which are normally fixed or sessile cells. **1917** M. WEBB *Gone to Earth* xiii. 118 People remained in a sessile state over tea for a long time. **1926** T. E. LAWRENCE *Seven Pillars* (1935) 7 The current of tribal movements..sessile or nomad. **1930** AUDEN *Poems* 56 No chattering valves of laughter emphasised Nor the swept gown ends of a gesture stirred The sessile hush. **1971** *Guinness Bk. Records* (ed. 18) 169/2 The longest recorded push of a normally sessile object is of 411 miles in the case of a wheeled hospital bed.

**3.** *Cryst.* Of a dislocation in a crystal: unable to migrate through the lattice; fixed.

**1949** F. C. FRANK in *Proc. Physical Soc.* A. LXII. 202 Glide is prevented by a large restoring force... Such a dislocation will be called 'sessile', in contrast with 'glissile' dislocations—those which are capable of glide. **1966** C. R. TOTTLE *Sci. Engin. Materials* iv. 101 Frank described one form of sessile dislocation, in which an aggregate of vacant lattice sites collapses to form a loop of dislocation surrounding a disk of stacking fault. **1973** J. G. TWEEDDALE *Materials Technol.* I. v. 111 In the latter case they lock together (forming a sessile dislocation) and become very difficult to separate.

**4.** *Comb.*, as ***sessile-eyed, -flowered, -fruited, -leaved*** adjs.; **sessile oak**, *Quercus petræa*, which has stalkless acorns; = DURMAST.

**1854** A. ADAMS, etc. *Man. Nat. Hist.* 294 *Sessile-eyed Crustaceans (Edriophthalmata). **1796** C. MARSHALL *Gardening* xix. (1813) 372 Herb-true-love, nodding, and *sessile flowered. **1846** KEIGHTLEY *Notes Virg.* Flora 391 The *Quercus sessiliflora*, or *sessile-fruited oak. **1822** *Hortus Anglicus* II. 356 *Sessile-leaved Eupatorium. [**1838** J. C. LOUDON *Arboretum et Fruticetum Britannicum* III. 1736 (*heading*) The sessile-flowered Oak.] **1906** ELWES & HENRY *Trees Gt. Brit.* II. 291 *Sessile or Durmast Oak... More regular branching, resulting in a denser crown of foliage. **1971** *Country Life* 23 Dec. 1772/1 The lighter soils and hills were covered by the sessile oak, with acorns pressed against the twigs, and leaves on long stalks.

ˈ**sessiliflore**, *a. Bot. rare*$^{-1}$. [ad. mod.L. *sessiliflōrus* (f. L. *sessili-s* SESSILE *a.* + *flōr-*, *flōs* flower).] Sessile-flowered: specific name of a kind of oak.

**1842** J. B. FRASER *Mesopot. & Assyria* xv. 354 Quercus sessiliflora..Sessiliflore oak.

†ˈ**sessing**, *vbl. sb. Obs.* [f. SESS *v.* + -ING$^1$.] = ASSESSING.

**1481** *Coventry Leet Bk.* 480 This concideracion to be taken in their sessyng, that such persones as ware ouercharged in theire wardes at þe vij li. etc. aforeseid to be eased nowe. *a* **1500** *Chron. London* (Kingsford 1905) 186 This yere was a greate Sessyng of all lordes landes thrugh England. **1513** in W. H. Turner *Select. Rec. Oxford* (1880) 11 Ye sesseing of ye subsidy. **1522–3** *Rec. St. Mary at Hill* 316 Item, paid for brede, drink and ffire at þe Newe sessing of þe clarkes bill. **1530** PALSGR. 269/2 Sessyng that a prince setteth in a countrey, *imposition.* **1612** DAVIES *Why Ireland* 177 Irish exactions..namely..Sessings of the Kerne, of his family,..of his Horses,..and the like. **1622** MABBE tr. *Aleman's Guzman d'Alf.* II. 107 There was a certaine sessing to be set in a ratable proportion, vpon the Towne-dwellers ..for some publike peece of worke.

*attrib.* **1610** HOLLAND *Camden's Brit.* I. 153 Angliæ commentarios Censuales, that is, The Taxe register, or Sessing booke of England.

**session** (ˈsɛʃən), *sb.* Forms: 4–6 sessioun, 5 cessiown, sessyone, 5 cessione, 5–6 cession, sessyon, 6 cessioun, cecion, cessyon. [a. F. *session* (= Sp. *sesion*, Pg. *sessão*, It. *sessione*), ad. L. *sessiōnem* (*sessio*), n. of action f. *sedēre* to sit.]

**1. a.** The action or an act of sitting; the state or posture of being seated; occupation of a seat in an assembly or the like; also a manner of sitting. Now *rare.*

**1615** CROOKE *Body of Man* 996 On the foreside it is gibbous, and that is profitable..for Session and sitting. **1635** PAGITT *Christianogr.* I. ii. (1636) 65 To the Bishop whereof was assigned the next place of session in councell after the Bishop of Hierusalem. **1670** MARVELL *Corr.* Wks. (Grosart) II. 325 The King has ever since continued his session among them, and says it is better than going to a play. **1695** J. EDWARDS *Author. O. & N. Test.* III. 133 The antientest heroes used session not discumbiture. **1704** SWIFT *Mech. Operat. Spirit* 297 The Art of See-saw on a Beam, and swinging by Session upon a Cord. **1859** TENNYSON *Vivien* 693 Vivien..Leapt from her session on his lap. **1859** F. E. PAGET *Curate Cumberworth* iv. 34 Whether Mrs. Crakanthorpe had indulged herself during her decline by session or recumbency thereon [*sc.* on a settee] there is, unfortunately, no evidence to show.

**b.** *spec.* The 'sitting' of Christ at the right hand of God.

*c* **1557** ABP. PARKER *Ps.* cx. Collect, Where, by the session of the ryghte hande of thy father, thou subduest thy enemies. **1605** BP. ANDREWES *Serm.* (1629) 369 His Passion and his Session. **1706** STANHOPE *Paraphr.* III. 85 This Ascent, and Session of our Blessed Master at God's Right Hand. **1894** SWETE *Apostles' Creed* vi. 64 Some of the oldest accounts, which place the Session immediately after the Resurrection.

†**c.** A place for sitting. *Obs. rare*$^{-1}$.

**1412-20** LYDG. *Chron. Troy* II. 1003 And al aboue, reysed was a se, .. þat callid was .. Of þe regne þe sete moste royal. .. And sessions wer made on euery syde, Only þe statis by ordre to deuyde.

**2. a.** The sitting together of a number of persons (esp. of a court, a legislative, administrative, or deliberative body) for conference or the transaction of business. Also (now somewhat *rarely*), a single continuous sitting of persons assembled for conference or business. Also, a business period on the Stock Exchange and other commercial markets.

**1444** *Rolls of Parlt.* V. 122/1 To eny Baillif or Baillifs, Lieutenauntz, Deputez or eny othur, in her Sessions and assembleez. **1564** HAWARD *Eutrop.* VI. 60 When Cesar on a daye wyth the reste of the Senate, were at theyr sessyon in the councell house. **1577-87** HOLINSHED *Chron.* I. 121/1 The archbishop of Canturburie kept a synod at Herford, the first session whereof began the 24 of September. **1612** DRAYTON *Poly-olb.* v. 81 Each part most highlie pleas'd, then vp the Session brake. **1661** *Bk. Com. Prayer*, A Prayer for the High Court of Parliament, to be read during their Session. **1667** MILTON *P.L.* II. 514 Then of thir Session ended they bid cry With Trumpets regal sound the great result. **1725** POPE *Odyss.* III. 171 Nor herald sworn the session to proclaim. **1827** HALLAM *Const. Hist.* (1876) III. xiii. 1 The frequent session of parliament .. furnished a security against illegal taxation. **1837** CARLYLE *Fr. Rev.* I. III. iii, Already his Majesty .. had held session of Notables. **1841** CATLIN *N. Amer. Ind.* lviii. II. 240 For the sessions of these dignitaries each tribe has .. a Government or council-house. **1869** HUXLEY in *Sci. Opin.* 21 Apr. 464/1 The British geologists .. here in solemn annual session assembled. **1890** P. H. HUNTER *After Exile* II. ii. 33 They proposed further that this court should not confine its sessions to Jerusalem, but should go on circuit. **1928** *Daily Mail* 25 July 19/3 At second session Tin cash £217 15*s.* to £217 17*s.* 6*d.* **1981** *Times* 1 May 20/2 Leading industrials enjoyed one of the best sessions for some time.

**b.** *transf.* and *fig.*

**1594** J. DICKENSON *Arisbas* (1878) 59 Being in these dumpes he held a session in his thoughtes. **1855** TENNYSON *Brook* 127 His pigeons, who in session on their roofs Approved him.

**c.** *pl.* with sing. sense and construction. *rare* (cf. 3 c).

**1613** HEYWOOD *Silver Age* K 4 b, Let's breake this Sessions vp, I am dull. **1847** HELPS *Friends in C.* I. vi. 86 Is it not comfortable to have our sessions here for once, and to be looking out on a good solid English wet day?

†**d.** A number of persons sitting in conference.

**1615** CHAPMAN *Odyss.* II. 40 The old man .. weeping, thus bespake the Session. *a* **1656** USSHER *Ann.* VI. (1658) 468 Both parties appeared to Ptolemei Philometor, and a Session of his friends, for the hearing and decision of the Cause.

**e.** = SÉANCE. *rare.*

**1858** HAWTHORNE *Fr. & It. Note-bks.* (1871) II. 14 Browning and his wife had both been present at a spiritual session held by Mr. Hume.

**3. a.** A continuous series of sittings or meetings of a court, a legislative, administrative, or deliberative body, held daily or at short intervals; the period or term during which the sittings continue to be held; opposed to *recess* or *vacation*.

**1553** in Burnet *Hist. Ref., Rec.* II. I. lvi. (1681) 225 The said Lord President and Council shall keep four general Sittings or Sessions in the Year, every of them to continue by the space of one whole Month. **1871** FREEMAN *Norm. Conq.* (1876) IV. xviii. 130 It was in this Christmas session of the Witan that the vacancy would regularly be filled. **1885** *Act 48 & 49 Vict.* c. 60 §4 A session of the Council shall be held once at least in every two years.

**b.** *spec.* In English parliamentary use, applied to the period between the opening of Parliament and its prorogation.

The term ***autumn session*** (instead of 'autumn sitting') is sometimes used to designate the exceptional resumption of the sittings of the Houses, after an adjournment, in what is normally the autumn recess; but this use is condemned by parliamentary authorities as incorrect.

*a* **1577** SIR T. SMITH *Commw. Eng.* II. iii. (1589) 54 The last day of that parliament or session the Prince commeth in person in his Parliament robes. **1676** LADY CHAWORTH in *12th Rep. Hist. MSS. Comm.* App. v. 34 Parliament .. some says will be dissolved of course by reason of three sessions past without any bill passing. **1683** *Repr. Advantages Manuf. Woollen-cloath* 1 The 20th Act of the third Sess. of the same Parl. **1711-12** SWIFT *Jrnl. to Stella* 21 Mar., I doubt the session will not be over till the end of April. *a* **1832** MACKINTOSH *Hist. Rev.* Wks. 1846 II. 43 At the opening of the Session, that House had contented themselves with general thanks to the King for his speech. **1878** H. S. LEIGH *Town Garland* 195 Very few Members of Parliament only Will wait for the Session to crawl to its close.

†**c.** *pl.* with sing. sense and construction. *Obs.*

**1642** CHAS. I *Message to Both Ho.* 28 Apr. 5 Other Bills passed this Sessions. **1701** *Maryland Laws* v. (1723) 16 Within Six Months from the End of this Sessions of Assembly. **1732** W. PULTENEY in *G. Colman's Posth. Lett.* (1820) 38 This day is to conclude a very tedious Sessions of Parl$^{t}$. **1780** M. MADAN *Thelyphthora* II. 59, I much doubt, whether every sessions of Parliament, for some years past, has not afforded melancholy proofs [etc.].

**d.** (Formerly only in Scotland and the U.S.) The portion of the academic year during which instruction is given. Also, a portion of the day during which classes are held.

***summer session***, in Sc. use, a period of instruction during the summer, additional to the old winter session.

**1714** J. MORICE *Let.* 2 Aug. in W. C. Dickinson *Two Students at St. Andrews* (1952) 53 Alexander Sharp .. being a Double Bajan with M$^{r}$ Pringle last Session. **1775** JOHNSON *West. Isl.* 12 A [St. Andrews'] student of the highest class may keep his annual session, .. which lasts about seven months, for about fifteen pounds. **1807** GRIERSON *Delin. St. Andrews* 108 The session of this college lasts only about four months, .. and the complete course of a student's attendance is, at the shortest, four sessions. **1851** *Catal. Univ. Virginia* 15 (Hall *College Words*) The session commences on the 1st of October, and continues without interruption until the 29th of June. **1861** *Temple Bar Mag.* III. 515 The medical session [at Edinburgh] began on the 1st November. **1862** G. MEREDITH *Let.* 23 Dec. (1970) I. 180, I presume that if I send to Bankers at Norwich, according to direction, before the next session, it will do. **1880** *(title)* The Mason Science College. Calendar for the Session 1880-81. **1891** *Edin. Univ. Cal.* 30 A Summer Session (1st May to 1st October). **1911** *Rep. Labour & Soc. Cond. Germany* (Tariff Reform League) III. VI. 126 Children go to school at seven o'clock in the morning and stay until eleven; then there is a break, the next session commencing at two and going on till five. **1932** *Leader* 9 July 1 The college is recognised and aided by the Government Board of Indian Medicine. The next session begins from 1st August, 1932. **1976** *Billings* (Montana) *Gaz.* 27 June 2-D/6 Temporary shelter became a problem... Ricks College in Rexburg, a junior college on high ground, has opened its doors until its summer session starts.

**4.** A judicial sitting. †**a.** *gen.* A sitting of a judge or judges to determine causes; a judicial trial or investigation. *sing.* and *collect. pl.* (often const. as *sing.*). *Obs.* (exc. *arch.* as contextual use of sense 1 or 2).

**14..** *Customs of Malton* in *Surtees Misc.* (1890) 60 þe sayd Burgoye schall answere .. in all sessyons and inqwyres. **1548** CRANMER *Catech.* 58 He that sayeth to his brother Racha .. is worthye the sessyons. **1557** in *Select Pleas Admiralty* (Selden Soc.) II. 33 At the Sessyons of the same courte which should be holden the .xiij$^{th}$ daye of Decembre then next folloinge. **1585** FLEETWOOD in Ellis *Orig. Lett.* Ser. I. II. 296 Uppon Thursdaye laste .. we kepte a Sessions of Inquyrie in London in the forenone, and in the afternone we kepte the lyke att Fynsburie for Middlesex, in which two severall Sessionses all such as were to be arrayegned for felonye at the Gaole deliverye were indyted. **1604** DEKKER *Honest Wh.* Wks. 1873 II. 159 *Car.* Araigne the poore whore. *Ast.* Ile not misse that Sessions. **1611** SHAKS. *Wint. T.* II. iii. 202 Summon a Session, that we may arraigne Our most disloyall Lady. **1691** CONSET *Pract. Spir. Crts.* (1700) 3 The first general Sessions held in the Court of the Arches .. was kept .. the next day (if no Holy-day) after the Feast of St. Faith the Virgin.

*transf.* and *fig.* **1591** H. SMITH *Lords Supper* ii. 30 This is the priuate araignement or close Sessions, when Conscience sits in her chaire to examine, and accuse, and iudge and condemne her selfe. *c* **1600** SHAKS. *Sonn.* xxx. 1. **1630** BP. HALL *Occas. Medit.* lxxxix. (1633) 225 To hold a privy Sessions, upon my Soule, and actions. **1645** MILTON *Tetrach.* Wks. 1851 IV. 194 The hard hearts of others unchastisable in those judicial Courts, were so remitted there, as bound over to the higher Session of Conscience. **1659** W. BROUGH *Sacr. Princ.* 190 Those particular sessions on my self, prevent His generall assizes. **1879** CHR. ROSSETTI *Seek & Find* 22 Daniel .. beheld the Session of the Ancient of Days, beheld the Judgment set and the Books opened.

**b. sessions of the peace** (in ordinary language simply **sessions**): the periodical sittings of justices of the peace (or, in some instances, of a stipendiary magistrate or a recorder). Often const. as *sing.*

In England the sessions of the peace are of the following kinds: ***petty sessions*** (now *Hist.*), a court held by two or more justices or a stipendiary magistrate, exercising summary jurisdiction in minor offences within a particular district (a 'petty sessional division'): replaced by the magistrates' court; ***special sessions***, a periodical meeting of the justices of a division prescribed by statute for the transaction of some particular kind of business (under this head are included ***brewster*** or ***licensing sessions***, for the hearing of applications for licences to sell alcoholic drinks); ***general*** or ***quarter sessions***, (both now *Hist.*), a court held four times a year (in a county, riding, etc. by the justices of the peace, and in certain boroughs by the recorder), having a limited criminal and civil jurisdiction and certain administrative functions: replaced in 1971 by the Crown Court system. Cf. QUARTER-SESSIONS 1. (*The sessions*, without qualification, usually denoted the quarter sessions.) Quarter sessions were also held in Scotland and Ireland. In certain British colonies the English system of sessions of the peace formerly existed, and was for a time retained in some of the United States.

*c* **1386** CHAUCER *Prol.* 355 At sessiouns ther was he lord and sire. **1453** *Rolls of Parlt.* V. 267/2 The Justicez of the peax in theire Sessions of peax. **1477** *Ibid.* VI. 173/2 Diverse of the Kyng's Justices of the peas .. syttyng in the Kyng's generall Cessions of pease in the same Counte. **1548** in J. H. Glover *Kingsthorpiana* (1883) 108 One Gregorye Cosbye .. was indyted at a cessyons holden at North$^{n}$ for huntyng of the hare in the feld of Pysford. **1556** *Chron. Grey Friars* (Camden) 34 A prisoner brake from the halle at Newgate whan the cecions was done. **1673** SIR W. TEMPLE *Ess. Adv. Trade Irel.* Misc. I. (1680) 116 Sometimes one share of that Money is paid to a single pretender at the Sizes, or Sessions. **1699** *Plea agst. Extr. Price of Corn* 23 Our Country Alehouse-making Justices at their Petty-Sessions, Quarter, and General Sessions. **1754** *Gentl. Mag.* XXIV. 461 The Brewster-Sessions at Bray in Northungria. **1844** LD. BROUGHAM *Brit. Const.* xix. (1862) 315 The Magistrates, when acting singly or in small numbers at petty sessions. **1859** DICKENS *T. Two Cities* II. v, A favourite at the Old Bailey, and eke at the Sessions.

*rarely* in *sing.* **1442** *Rolls of Parlt.* V. 43/1 Ones a yere a gret Cession holden afore the Kynges Justice, .. and also a petit Cession, holden afore the said Justice. **1588** LAMBARDE *Eiren.* IV. i. (1591) 374 *margin*, The description of a Session of the Peace. **1616** B. JONSON *Devil an Ass* v. vi. 21 *Pvg.* How? longer here a moneth? *Ing.* Yes, boy, till the Session. *c* **1710** CELIA FIENNES *Diary* (1888) 160 Appleby .. is the shire town where the session and assizes are held. **1844** *Act 7 & 8 Vict.* c. 101 §2 Such Justice of the Peace shall thereupon issue his Summons to the Person .. to appear at a Petty Session.

†**c.** ***petty*** or ***statute sessions***: see quots. (cf. *petty sessions* in b). *Obs.*

**1562-3** *Act 5 Eliz.* c. 4 §40 That it shalbe laufull to the Highe Constables of Hundredes in every Shire, to holde kepe and contynue Petie Sessions, otherwise called Statute Sessions. **1641** *Termes de la Ley* 247 Petit Sessions or statute Sessions are held by the high Constables of every Hundred for the placing of servants. **1787** W. H. MARSHALL *Rur. Econ. Norfolk* (1795) I. 40 The High Constable of the Hundred in which a statute is held, holds what is called a 'petty sessions'; at which the hiring [of servants] and its attendant circumstances are, or may be, registered.

**d.** ***great*** or ***grand session(s***: a court of justice formerly held half-yearly in each of the counties of Wales, presided over by itinerant judges forming a distinct body from the judges of assize in England. ***court of session***: a court formerly exercising for the County Palatine of Chester a jurisdiction more or less corresponding to that of the courts of assize in the rest of England. *Obs.* exc. *Hist.*

Both these courts were abolished in 1830 by the Act 11 Geo. IV & 1 Will. IV, c. 70 §14.

**1542-3** *Act 34 & 35 Hen. VIII*, c. 26 §4 There shalbe holden .. Sessions twyse in everye yere in everye of the saide Shyres in .. Wales: .. the whiche Sessions shall be called the Kinges Greate Sessions in Wales. **1707** *Lond. Gaz.* No. 4330/4 The Grand Jury, Justices of the Peace, and others .., met together at the Great Sessions holden for the said County [Pembroke]. **1730** *Act 3 Geo. II*, c. 25 *Preamb.*, Judges of the Great Sessions in Wales. *Ibid.* §9 Causes in the Grand Sessions in any County of Wales. *Ibid.*, At least eight Days before every Grand Sessions. §14 The Grand Session in Wales. **1899** W. R. WILLIAMS *(title)*, The history of the Great Sessions in Wales 1542-1830.

**5.** *Scots Law.* **a.** *Hist.* The name given to a court of justice (often called 'the Session of James I'), established in 1425, consisting of the Chancellor and other persons chosen by the king, which sat three times in the year to determine such causes as had previously been brought before the king and his council. The judges of this court were called the ***Lords of Session***. **b.** ***Court of Session***: the supreme civil tribunal of Scotland (otherwise called the ***College of Justice***: see COLLEGE 1 c), established by Act of Parliament in 1532, and uniting in itself the powers and jurisdiction which had belonged to the Session of James I, to the Daily Council of James IV, and to the Lords Auditors of Parliament. The judges of this court are officially styled ***Lords of Council and Session***, but in ordinary language ***Lords of Session***. (Formerly the court was often spoken of as † ***the Session(s)***.)

**1495** *Acc. Ld. High Treas. Scot.* I. 242 Item, gevin to the Freris of Edinburgh at the Kingis commande xviij s. at the sessyon. **1496** *Ibid.* 269 Quhen the King raid to Sanct Jhonistoun to the cessioun. **1500-20** DUNBAR *Poems* ix. 134 At Counsale, Sessioun, and at Parliament. **1503** Lords of Session [see COUNCIL 7]. **1569** *Reg. Privy Council Scot.* I. 665 Gevin and pronunceit be the Lordis of Counsale and Sessioun. **1577-87** HOLINSHED *Hist. Scot.* 317/2 This yeere [1530] the college court of iustice called the sessions was instituted. **1610** HOLLAND *Camden's Brit.* II. 8 The Colledge of Iustice, or as they call it The Session. **1652** LAMONT *Diary* (Bannatyne Club) 37 Lords of Session and Counsell. **1708** J. CHAMBERLAYNE *St. Gt. Brit.* II. II. vi. (1710) 426 None shall be named .. to be ordinary Lords of Session, but such who have been Advocates or principal Clerks of Session for the Space of Five Years. **1711** *Act 10 Anne* c. 13 §2 The Christmas Vacation of the Session or College of Justice.

**6.** *Sc.* = KIRK-SESSION.

*a* **1572** KNOX *Hist. Ref.* III. Wks. 1848 II. 152 That the auld Sessioun befor thair departure, nominat twenty-four in Electioun for Elders, .. and thirty-two for Deacounes. **1672** SIR G. MACKENZIE *Pleadings* Pref. A iij, Our Session having been at first constitute of an equal number of Churchmen and Laicks. **1725** in J. J. Vernon *Hawick* (1900) 187 The Minister did read to ye members of ye Session a petition. **1786** BURNS *Answ. to Trimming Epist. by Tailor* vii, Wi' pinch I put a Sunday's face on, An' snoov'd awa' before the Session. **1846** J. MACFARLANE *Late Secess. Ch. Scot.* 124 The list of parishes vacant, and of sessions dismembered, and of churches thinned, is not to be overlooked.

**7.** *transf.* [Senses not necessarily dependent upon the notion of 'sitting'.] A period of time given to or set aside for the pursuit of a particular activity. **a.** *gen.*

**1920**, etc. [see BULL *sb.*$^{4}$ 3 b]. **1970** [see *rap session* s.v. RAP *sb.*$^{1}$ 7]. **1976** *Cumberland News* 3 Dec. 24/5 A short session of dominoes followed.

**b.** in which musicians perform music, esp. for recording. Also, the music so recorded. Cf. *jam session* s.v. JAM *sb.*$^{1}$ 3; *recording session* s.v. RECORDING *vbl. sb.* 5.

**1927** [see *recording session* s.v. RECORDING *vbl. sb.* 5]. **1929** *Melody Maker* Apr. 381/1 The trouble is due to inferior musicians being engaged for this session. **1947** G. BEALL in R. de Toledano *Frontiers of Jazz* vii. 87 He is present on most of the records, however, taking part in the recording session although the men know his part would not be directly apparent. **1962** *Radio Times* 17 May 43 The jazz musician..is merely inviting himself back to his friend's place for a beer after their session. **1969** R. A. NOBLETT *Stavin' Chain* 7 This version has not been released on record... The session is, however, interesting.

**c.** A disturbance or argument. *colloq.* (chiefly *Austral.* and *N.Z.*).

**1919** H. L. WILSON *Ma Pettengill* iv. 130 Then Ben came down and had a wholehearted session with me. He said I ought to have a talk with Ed and reason him out of his folly. **1930** L. W. LOWER *Here's Luck* i. 5 We had a bit of a session—a 'go in' as they call it. I tried to reason with him. **1949** J. R. COLE *It was so Late* 10 'Don't shoot the barman, he's half shot already.'..'Bit of a session, eh?'

**8.** *attrib.* and *Comb.*, as (sense 2) ***session-bell***; (sense 3) ***session-time***; (sense 4) ***sessions-chamber***, ***session(s day***; (sense 6) ***session-clerk***, ***-clerkship***; (sense 7) ***session fee***, ***man***, ***work***; **session(s-book** *Sc.*, a book kept in each parish to record the proceedings of the kirk-session; **session(s-house**, (*a*) a building in which sessions are held; (*b*) *Sc.*, a room attached to a church in which the session meets; **session musician**, one who is engaged to play music, usu. accompaniments, at a recording session; †**sessions-paper**, a list of cases put down for trial at the sessions.

**1701** *Acts of Sederunt* (1790) 221 After the ringing of the *Session-bell. **1829** TRAIN in Scott *Old Mort.* Introd., His death is not registered in the *session-book of any of the neighbouring parishes. **1778** *Eng. Gazetteer* (ed. 2) s.v. *Weldon-Great*, A handsome market-house, and a *sessions-chamber over it. **1821** GALT *Ann. Parish* xii. (1895) 86 The schoolmaster was likewise *session-clerk and precentor. **1876** Session clerk [see PAROCHIAL *a.* (*sb.*) 1 a]. **1795** *Statist. Acc. Scot.* XVI. 511 This and the *session-clerkship do not belong to him as schoolmaster. **1537** LONDON in Ellis *Orig. Lett.* Ser. I. II. 81 In the *cession dayes and other cowrt dayes. **1602** HEYWOOD *Wom. killed w. Kindn.* (1617) C 1 b, This is the Sessions day. **1977** *Times* 1 Nov. 14/5 The orchestra had a choice: either to take a share of the royalties or settle for what the trade calls a *session fee—a once-and-for-all payment. **1599** LEWKENOR *Contarini's Commw. Venice* I. 22 Euery holliday..this great councell is assembled into a great and spacious hall, which we will call the *Session house. **1600** in *Cath. Rec. Soc. Publ.* (1908) V. 389 They were..bidd to putt on their bootes and to goe to the sessions house. **1647** *Acts of Sederunt* (1790) 55 All the advocates sall come to the Session-hous. **1836** DICKENS *Sk. Boz, Scenes* xxv, The right wing of the prison [Newgate] nearest the Sessions-house. **1958** J. ASMAN in P. Gammond *Decca Bk. Jazz* xiv. 170 Men who worked in a number of musical fields, providing the recording studios with a reliable nucleus of *session-men for every kind of date. **1980** *Oxford Times* 20 June 18 She is expertly backed by..fine sessionmen. **1968** *Guardian* 23 Feb. 10/6 The vast majority of pop records made rely to some extent on *session musicians. **1980** P. GOSLING *Loser's Blues* ii. 12 Separately as session musicians on other pop discs they were occasionally..in the charts. *a* **1704** T. BROWN *Pleas. Lett. to Gent.* Wks. 1709 III. II. 16 The greasy Fragments of a *Sessions-Paper. **1728** GAY *Polly* I. (1777) 18 Every monthly sessions-paper..was a record of his [a thief-taker's] services. **1817** SCOTT *Let.* in *Lockhart* (1837) IV. ii. 59 In the vacation I never sit down; in the *session-time I seldom rise up. **1976** J. WAINWRIGHT *Walther P. 38* 82, I moved around from band to band..and sat in on my share of *session work at the recording studios.

**session** ('sɛʃən), *v.* *Sc.* (see also E.D.D.). [f. prec.] *trans.* To bring before the kirk-session.

**1895** CROCKETT *Men of Mosshags* 125 Was there one of us ..that had not been sessioned time and again?

**sessional** ('sɛʃənəl), *a.* [f. SESSION *sb.* + -AL[1].] Pertaining to a session or sessions. **a.** Belonging or relating to, supplied by, a kirk-session.

**1715** in J. F. S. Gordon *Bk. Chron. Keith* (1880) 89 The Session..thought fit to give them a sessional admonition to make conscience of ordering their affairs [etc.]. **1811** T. CHALMERS in Hanna *Mem.* (1849) I. 218, I gave her sessional assistance. **1849** HANNA *Mem. Chalmers* II. 307 The number of sessional poor (that is, of poor who had been on the session's roll of one or other of the three parishes..) was ninety-eight. **1885** EDGAR *Old Ch. Life Scot.* 240 The Lord's table was not to be approached without a sessional pass.

**b.** Pertaining to the session of a law-court. So ***petty sessional***, ***quarter sessional***, pertaining to petty sessions, quarter sessions.

**1832** *Act 2 & 3 Will. IV*, c. 64 §9 Such other places..as are locally situated within..the said sessional divisions. **1837** LOCKHART *Scott* (1839) VI. 326 Scott being then on one of his short Sessional visits to Abbotsford. **1846** S. G. OSBORNE *Let.* 28 May (1891) I. 6 The sitting on the quarter sessional bench. **1883** *Fortn. Rev.* May 693 To establish petty sessional districts.

**c.** Belonging, relating, or restricted to a session of a House of Parliament; recurring every session. Also Canad., ***sessional indemnity***, the remuneration received by a member of a legislative assembly.

**1834** A. W. FONBLANQUE *Eng. under 7 Administr.* (1837) III. 104 The sessional stages. **1839** *Times* 7 Sept. 4/1 He will make a sessional motion in the House of Commons. **1844** MAY *Parlt.* 132 Sessional orders. At the commencement of each session both houses agree to certain orders and resolutions, which, from being constantly renewed from year to year, are evidently not intended to endure beyond the existing session. **1886** C. E. PASCOE *Lond. of To-day* vii. (ed. 3) 81 The Sessional dinners of each House. **1900** E. B. OSBORN *Greater Canada* 105 The average partisan gets to Ottawa for the sake of his sessional indemnity and what he can make by means of his position. **1963** *Globe & Mail* (Toronto) 12 July 8/2 Increases in sessional indemnities and expenses that the Quebec Legislature has just approved put it in a class by itself.

**d.** Pertaining to, or lasting a session (sense 3 d) in an educational institution.

**1965** *Listener* 28 Jan. 137/2 Each student has to pursue two sessional courses, which last the whole year, designed to give an introduction to some subject not studied at sixth-form level. **1978** *Sci. Amer.* Jan. 12/2 Geesey is a sessional lecturer in the department of biochemistry and microbiology at the University of Victoria in British Columbia.

**e.** Pertaining to any period of activity of limited duration. Cf. SESSION *sb.* 7.

**1973** *Scotsman* 12 Jan. 17/4 (Advt.), Part-time medical officers for sessional work. **1977** *Times* 29 Aug. 6/2 Members of mixed card clubs paid a sessional fee according to the stake at their table.

**sessionally** ('sɛʃənəlɪ), *adv.* [f. SESSIONAL + -LY[2].]

**1.** *Sc.* By the kirk-session.

**1715** in J. F. S. Gordon *Bk. Chron. Keith* (1880) 88 They were sessionally rebucked, till further guilt, if any be, appear. *a* **1732** T. BOSTON *Acc. My Life* (1908) 96 The precentor professing his sorrow for his offence, was re-admitted sessionally. **1887** W. ROSS *Pastoral Work Covenant. Times* viii. 168 Some faults dealt with sessionally would not be looked upon nowadays as sufficiently grave.

**2.** Every session.

**1863** COX *Inst. Eng. Govt.* I. ix. 158 No standing committees of the whole House appointed sessionally now sit.

**sessionary** ('sɛʃənərɪ), *a. rare.* [f. SESSION *sb.* + -ARY.] Of or pertaining to a session or sessions.

**1702** *Case of Schedule Stated* 86 The *Dies Statutus*..is ever the Next Sessionary Day. **1884** *Law Times* LXXVII. 401/2 If the sessionary courts were invested with more discretionary power.

**b.** *transf.* During which business is carried on.

**1837** C. LOFFT *Self-formation* II. 188 The sessionary hours of the shopkeepers.

**sessioneer** (sɛʃə'nɪə(r)). [f. SESSION *sb.* + -EER.] = *session musician* s.v. SESSION *sb.* 8.

**1958** T. HALL in P. Gammond *Decca Bk. Jazz* xix. 235 Joe Muddel is one of the busiest 'sessioneers' in Britain's radio, film and TV studios. **1977** *Sounds* 9 July 34/3 He's marshalled such star sessioneers as Richie Albright..and the Memphis Horns into fine order.

†'**sessioner.** *Sc. Obs.* Also 7 -air. [f. SESSION *sb.* + -ER[1].]

**1.** A member of the Court of Session.

**1597** R. BRUCE *Apol.* in Wodrow *Life* (1843) 169 We take us not to his Majesty, neither to the nobility of Scotland..; we take us only to the Sessioners. **1610** JAS. VI in *Reg. Privy Council Scot.* VIII. 613 The saidis President and Sessionaris sall weir these habitis upoun the streitis of Edinburgh induring the tyme of sessioun. **1641** *Sc. Acts Chas. I* (1814) V. 403/1 And in Lyke maner the sessioners with the advise and approbation of the most part of that hous, w[ch] electiones made in the intervall shalbe allowed or disallowed. *a* **1657** SIR J. BALFOUR *Ann. Scot.* Hist. Wks. 1825 II. 129 That from hencefurth [1626] no judge or sessioner should be a priuey counseller.

**2.** A member of a kirk-session.

**1643** in Boyd *Zion's Flowers* (1855) App. 41/2 That none win to the Sessions loft till the Sessioners be placed. *a* **1670** SPALDING *Troub. Chas. I* (Bannatyne Club) I. 173 Ilk minister haveing ane ruleing elder chosen out of the worthiest of the sessioners of his presbiterie. **1682** J. FINLAY in *Cloud of Witnesses* (1778) 193 They..now are sessioners to this Curate. **1683** in Wodrow *Hist. Suff. Ch. Scot.* (1722) II. 317 That the Ministers give in upon Oath a List of their Sessioners.

**sessions** ('sɛʃənz), *v. slang.* [f. *sessions*, pl. of SESSION *sb.*] *trans.* To commit (a person) to the sessions for trial.

**1857** A. MAYHEW *Paved with Gold* III. vi, I am the only chap they could prove against... They could sessions me, but Ned and Phil are safe enough.

**sessle**, *v. dial.* Also sissle. *intr.* To move uneasily, fidget.

**1695** KENNETT *Par. Antiq.* Gloss. s.v. *Cart-Sadel*, In Kent to *sessle* about is to change seats very often. **1865** GARLAND *Words W. Cornw.* in *Jrnl. Roy. Inst. Cornw.* Apr. 52 *Sissling*, moving uneasily in sleep.

†'**sessment.** *Obs.* Also 6 seas(s)-, 6–7 ses-, sesse-, seaz(e)-, 7 seasse-, seize-. [Aphetic f. ASSESSMENT; cf. CESSMENT. For the variation of quantity in the root-vowel cf. SESS *v.*] = ASSESSMENT in various senses. Also *attrib.*

[**1538** in *Norwich Pageants* (1856) 18 Assembly at Black Fryers, 19 May, 1538, elected Officers; a Sesmant 14[s]. Charges, 19[s] 2[d]. Assembly at Guyldhalle, 9 May, 1539, elected Officers; Assmt. 16[s] 6[d].] *c* **1540** *Plumpton Corr.* (Camden) 239, I marvill greatly that your said manor shold be so highley charged... I could never se no writing of the sesment therof. **1548** in *Vicary's Anat.* (1888) App. III. i. 135 A precept directyd to the Craftes..of London, for payment of their Sessment vnto the poore. **1576** *Act 18 Eliz.* c. 10 §5 By Taxacion and Sessement at one Courte or Lawe-daye. **1598** BARRET *Theor. Warres* II. i. 26, I would wish a generall seazement to be made vpon euery parish. **1620–21** *Shuttleworths' Acc.* (Chetham Soc.) 247 P'd by him for sessement to kinge and churche there, vj[s] viij[d]. **1636** FEATLY *Clavis Myst.* xiii. 179 In other seizements you give as you are in the King's books. **1647** in *Polit. Ball. Commw.* (Percy Soc.) 34 The seazement for the lots and subsydyes, The weekly seazements for the trained bands. **1666–7** MARVELL *Corr.* Wks. (Grosart) II. 208 Our House yesterday perfected the proviso of 380,000 l. of the Sesment Bill. [*Ibid.* 209 Bill of Assessment.]

**sessone, -oun**, obs. Sc. forms of SEASON *sb.*

†**sessor.** *Obs.* [Aphetic f. ASSESSOR. Cf. CESSOR[1].] = ASSESSOR in various senses.

**1481** *Coventry Leet Bk.* 481 The names of þe sessours [of a war-levy]. **1496** *Rolls of Parlt.* VI. 516/1 The Sessours and Ordrers in every of the said Citees and Boroughs. **1527–8** *Rec. St. Mary at Hill* 343 Paid for the drinking of the Sessours of the clerkes wages..vj d. **1579–80** NORTH *Plutarch, P. Æmil.* (1595) 282 They [*sc.* the Censors] be the sessours of the people, and the muster masters. **1642** *Ordin. & Decl. Lds. & Comm.* 29 Nov. 5 To nominate Sessors for the same City and Borough. **1712–13** SWIFT *Jrnl. to Stella* 29 Jan., We also raised sixty guineas upon our own Society; but I made them do it by sessors,..and we fitted our tax to the several estates.

**sess-pool, sestain**, var. ff. CESS-POOL, SEXTAIN.

**sest(e**, obs. ff. pa. t. and pa. pple. of CEASE.

*c* **1380** *Sir Ferumb.* 1017 Þe Sarsyns fleȝe & noȝt ne sest. **14..** *Polit. Rel. & Love Poems* (1903) 137 Of þi seruyse oft hafe I seste.

**seste**, obs. form of SIXTH.

**sester** ('sɛstə(r)). Now only *Hist.* Also 4 cestre, sesster, 6 cester, sestur. [OE. *sester* (also *seoxter*) and AF. *sester* = OF. *sestier*:—L. *sextārium* SEXTAR, SEXTARY.

Cf. OS. *soster*, *suster*, Du. *sester*, *sister*, MLG. *sestere*, OHG. *sehtari* and *sextari* (MHG. *sehtere* and *sehstere*, G. *sechter*, *sester*). See also SEPTIER.]

†**1.** A vessel for holding liquid; in OE. a jar, pitcher; in ME. ? a brewing-vat. *Obs.*

*c* **1000** ÆLFRIC *Gloss.* in Wr.-Wülcker 122/30 *Amfora*, sester. *c* **1000** —— *Judges* vii. 16 Gedeon..het heora ælcne ȝeniman anne æmtiȝne sester oððe ænne wæterbuc to þam ȝewinne forð. *c* **1341** *Durham Acc. Rolls* (Surtees) 542 In 2 novis Sestres factis de novo pro bracina, 20*d.* **1347–8** *Ibid.* 546 In 2 Cestris novis fact. et ferro ligand. pro bracina, 2*s.* 10*d.*

**2.** A liquid measure for beer, wine, etc.

In OE. rendering L. *modius*, *cadus*, *metreta*, and *sextarius*.

**909** in Thorpe *Charters* (1865) 158 Twelf seoxtres beoras. *c* **950** *Lindisf. Gosp.* John ii. 6 Stænino fatto..niomende syndriȝe sestras tuoeȝe *uel* ðrea [*Ags. Gosp.* ælc wæs on twegra sestra ȝemete oððe on þreora]. *c* **1000** *Sax. Leechd.* III. 92 Tweȝen sestres sapan, & tweȝe hunies & þre sestres ecedes, & se sester sceal weȝan twa pund. *c* **1440** *Pallad. on Husb.* II. 410 In half a sester [L. *heminam*] aged wyn do shake. **1494** in *Househ. Ord.* (1790) 113 Then yee must goe to the servant of the seller, and warne him to make readie.. as many sesteres of wine as yee thinke will serve the people. **1528** *Coventry Leet Bk.* 696 No bruer..frome-hensfurth shall sell eny ale within this Citie by the Cester aboue ij s. **1580** HOLLYBAND *Treas. Fr. Tong*, *Demy Sétier*,..halfe sester.

**b.** † **sester-penny**, ? a charge made upon every sester of beer brewed.

**1328** in *Essex Rev.* XIII. 203 Every copieholder that doeth brewe bere or ale to sell, shall paye yerely in the moneth of harvest one penye called Cestre-penye.

**3.** A dry measure for wheat, etc.

In mod. use only *Hist.* with reference to *O.E. Chron.* an. 1043, On þisum wæs..corn swa dyre..swa þæt se sester hwætes eode to .lx. peneȝa & eac furðor.

*c* **1050** *Voc.* in Wr.-Wülcker 444/4 *Mine*, healfsester. *c* **1440** *Pallad. on Husb.* VIII. 148 A sester and a semycicle take Of senuey seed. **1707** BP. FLEETWOOD *Chron. Prec.* 65 A Sester or Sextarius was what we now call a Quarter, or a Seam, containing 8 Bushels. [**1848** PETRIE tr. *Ags. Chron.* 433.]

**sesterce** ('sɛstɜːs). Pl. sesterces ('sɛstəsɪz, -ɜːsɪz). Also *pl.* 6–7 sestercies, 7 -ties; *sing.* 7 sestercie. [ad. L. *sestertius* properly adj. (sc. *nummus* coin) = that is two and a half, f. *sēmis* half + *tertius* third; cf. SESQUI-.] A Roman coin, originally equivalent to $2\frac{1}{2}$ asses, later to 4 asses; the fourth part of a DENARIUS.

*pl.* **1598** GRENEWEY *Tacitus, Ann.* VI. iv. (1622) 127 Putting a hundred million sesterces in bancke. **1601** B. JONSON *Poetaster* III. iv. 64 What does this gentleman owe thee, little Minos? *Mino.* Fourescore *sesterties*, sir. **1611** —— *Catiline* II. i, He, tame Crow,.. would haue kept Both eyes, and beake seal'd vp, for sixe sesterces. **1624** BURTON *Anat. Mel.* II. iii. III. (ed. 2) 267 Rings on his fingers worth 20000 sestercies. **1702** ADDISON *Dial. Medals* I. Wks. 1766 III. 10 That..would rather choose to count out a Sum in Sesterces, than in pounds sterling. **1834** LYTTON *Pompeii* I. i, An additional reason for supping with him while the sesterces last. **1882** FARRAR *Early Chr.* 5 A robe covered with pearls and emeralds, which had cost forty million sesterces. **1885** R. BRIDGES *Nero* III. ii, See, here I give you Two hundred sesterces.

*sing.* **1601** B. JONSON *Poetaster* IV. vii. 9 I'll sell 'hem my share for a sesterce. **1656** BLOUNT *Glossogr.*, *Sesterce*, *Sestercie.* **1771** RAPER in *Phil. Trans.* LXI. 489 The *As* was reduced to one ounce, and the silver denarius made to pass for 16 *Asses*; the quinarius, for eight; and the sesterce, for four. **1850** MERIVALE *Rom. Emp.* lxi. (1865) VII. 338 Costly wars..had drained perhaps to the last sesterce the coffers of the empire. **1861** SHEPPARD *Fall of Rome* ii. 98 Destitute and degraded, without a sesterce and without a friend.

¶ Misused for SESTERTIUM.

**1693** *Dryden's Juvenal* IV. (1697) 76 The lavish Slave Six thousand Pieces for a Barbel gave; A Sesterce for each Pound it weigh'd. **1819** *Pantologia* s.v., Some authors make two kinds of sesterces: the less, called sestertius..and the great one, called sestertium.

†'**sestern.** *Obs.* Also 5 cestron, 6 sestorne, seystarne, 7 sestron. [var. SESTER; cf. *testern*, var. TESTER[1]. See also SEXTERN.] = SESTER.

**1421** *Coventry Leet Bk.* 25 That no breuster sell no derre a Cestron ale to noo hukster but for xviij d. **1502** ARNOLDE *Chron.* 72 b/2 The tonne of burdeux..holdith in sesternes lxiij. sesternes. The..sesterne iiij. galons. **1534** in Sharp *Cov. Myst.* (1825) 183 A Seystarne & a halfe of ale ijs iijd. **1682** *Art & Myst. Vintners* 15 Every Sestron is 4 gallons.

**sestern(e,** obs. forms of CISTERN.

‖**sestertium** (sɛ'stɜːʃɪəm). Pl. sestertia (-ʃɪə); also 6 sex-, -cia, -tiaes, 7 -tias. [L., usually explained as the gen. pl. *sestertium* of *sestertius* SESTERCE (with ellipsis of *mille* a thousand), taken as neut. sing.

The use of the sing. in the sense '1000 sesterces', which must on this view have existed, does not appear to be found in the classics; the pl. for 'thousands of sesterces' was common. On the other hand, the gen. pl. *sestertium*, after *decies* ten times, *centies* a hundred times, was used with ellipsis of *centena millia* (= 100,000), and when so used was sometimes treated as a neut. sing.]

A sum of a thousand sesterces.

**1540–1** ELYOT *Image Gov.* xxx. (1544) 71 b, Euery *Sestertium* (which in englysh money of olde grotes.. amounteth to .iiii. li .xvi. s. viii. d.). **1549** W. THOMAS *Hist. Ital.* 27 b, Plinie saieth, that The conueighaunce of this water [Aqua Claudia] did coste .555. thousande sextertia.. the summe amounteth to .vii. millions and .viii. hundred thousand poundes of our money. **1598** MERES *Palladis Tamia* II. 284 b, Octauia..gaue him [*sc.* Virgil] for making 26 verses, 1137 pounds, to wit, tenne Sestertiaes for euerie verse. **1603** B. JONSON *Sejanus* I. i, There is a Gentleman of Rome would buy... *Sat.* A Tribunes place, my Lord. *Sei.* What will he giue? *Sat.* Fiftie Sestertia. **1770** LANGHORNE *Plutarch* (1851) II. 832/1 They thought it better to deposit five hundred sestertia each. **1834** LYTTON *Pompeii* I. iii, 'I will play no more,' said Glaucus, 'I have lost thirty sestertia.' **1842** *W. Smith's Dict. Class. Antiq.* 875 Up to the time of Augustus..the sestertium = £8. 17. 1; after the reign of Augustus the sestertium = £7. 16. 3.

‖**sestertius** (sɛ'stɜːʃɪəs). Also 7 *erron.* sex-, -ties. Pl. sestertii (-ʃɪaɪ). [L.: see SESTERCE.] = SESTERCE.

In the first two quots. the form app. represents the Lat. acc. pl.

**1567** PAINTER *Pal. Pleas.* II. xiii, She sent one to demaunde .xii. C. Sestercios of siluer. **1584** COGAN *Haven Health* clxxviii. 143 Asinius Celer..paid..8000 Sestertios, which after Tonstals account is fourty pound sterling. **1600** HOLLAND *Livy* XLV. 1231 Twentie millions of Sestertij. *a* **1630** J. TAYLOR (Water-P.) Wks. I. 66/2 An As, a Drachma, a Sesterties. *a* **1700** EVELYN *Diary* 6 May 1645, The Sestertius was a small silver coyne marked H. S. or rather LL[s], valu'd 2 pound and half of silver. **1884** *Encycl. Brit.* XVII. 653/1 Under Severus Alexander there was the latest large issue of denarii and sestertii.

**sestet(t, sestette** (sɛs'tɛt). [ad. It. *sestetto*: see next and -ET[1], -ETTE, and cf. SEXTET.]

**1.** *Mus.* A composition for six voices or instruments.

**1801** BUSBY *Dict. Mus.*, *Sestetto*, or *Sestett*. **1874** OUSELEY *Mus. Form* 52 Thus are constructed..sestetts, septetts, and ottetts. **1883** *Grove's Dict. Mus.* III. 475/2 Instrumental sestets are of two kinds; those for strings only..and those for various combinations of strings, wind and pianoforte.

**2.** *Pros.* The last six lines of a sonnet. Cf. OCTAVE, OCTET.

*a* **1859** L. HUNT *Bk. Sonnet* (1867) I. 10 The Minor division [of the Italian sonnet consists] of six lines, called the Sestette. **1881** *Athenæum* 8 Oct. 459/3 The regular sonnet of octave and sestet. **1882** *Macm. Mag.* Feb. 325 This rhythmic variation of the order in the sestet rhymes. **1896** E. GOSSE *Crit. Kit-Kats* 7 No fault can be found with the structure of her [Mrs. Browning's] octetts and sestetts.

‖**sestetto** (ses'tɛtto). *Mus.* [It., f. *sesto* sixth (:—L. *sextus*) + dim. suffix *-etto*.] = SESTET 1.

**1801** [see SESTET 1]. **1824** MEDWIN *Convers. Byron* II. 261 At the moment he was listening to a sestetto in Mayer's opera of 'Elena'. **1879** LONGF. *Life* (1891) III. 294 The sestetto at the end of the second act was splendid.

†'**sestiad.** *Obs.* In 6–7 sestyad. [ad. Gr. Σηστιάς, -άδος (Musæus) adj., f. Σηστός Sestus, a town on the Hellespont.

Used by Chapman (after *Iliad*) as the title of each of the six divisions of *Hero & Leander* (Linley's ed. 1598); hence in transf. sense below.]

Any one of six cantos or main divisions of a poem.

**1646** S. SHEPPARD (*title*) The Times Displayed in six Sestyads.

‖**sestiere** (sesti'ere). Pl. -ieri. [It., f. L. *sextārius* the sixth part of a measure.] In Italy: one of six districts or areas of a city. Cf. QUARTIERE.

**1599** L. LEWKENOR tr. *Contarini's Commonwealth & Govt. Venice* 185 The Citie of Venice is divided into sixe parts, which they call Sestieri. **1673** J. RAY *Observations Journey Low-Countries* 151 This City [*sc.* Venice] is..divided into six parts or regions, called thence *Sestieri*. **1832** S. DE SISMONDI *Hist. Ital. Republics* iv. 84 The town [of Florence] was divided into six parts, each *sestier*, as it was called, named two *anziani*. **1893** J. A. SYMONDS tr. A. Condivi in *Life of Michelangelo* I. i. 2 He was appointed captain of a Sestiere; for Florence in those days was divided into Sestieri, instead of Quartieri. **1934** *Burlington Mag.* Sept. 100/1 St. Peter, the patron of the *sestiere* of the town which he represented. **1980** *Times* 8 Dec. (Winter Holidays Suppl.) p. v/4 The most satisfactory way of tackling the surface of [Venetian] sights is to concentrate on one of the city's six *sestieri* (districts) at a time.

‖**sestina** (sɛ'stiːnə). *Pros.* Also *erron.* sestino. [It., f. *sesto* sixth.] A poem of six six-line stanzas (with an envoy) in which the line-endings of the first stanza are repeated, but in different order, in the other five.

**1838** GUEST *Engl. Rhythms* IV. v. II. 372 The Sestino-stave, invented by Arnaud Daniel, the Troubadour eulogised by Dante and Petrarch. [**1845** *Encycl. Metrop.* XXV. 818/1 It was from the Provençal *chanzo* that the Italians derived their *Sestina* and *Distichi*.] **1878** SWINBURNE *Poems & Ball.* Ser. II. 60 The Complaint of Lisa. (Double Sestina.) **1880** HUEFFER in *Macm. Mag.* Nov. 49 The sestina is a dangerous experiment, on which only poets of the first rank should venture. **1896** KIPLING *Seven Seas* 158 (*title*) Sestina of the tramp-royal.

**sestine** (sɛ'stiːn). *Pros. rare.* [a. obs. F. *sestine*, ad. It. *sestina* (see prec.). Cf. SEXTAIN.] = prec.

*a* **1586** SIDNEY *Arcadia* II. (1598) 219 To present Basilius with some other of their complaints Eclogue-wise, and first with this double Sestine. *Ibid.* IV. 426 One Agelastus.. framing an vniuersall complaint in that vniuersall mischiefe, vttered it in this Sestine. **1611** COTGR., *Sestine*, a Sestine, or stanzo of six verses. **1879** E. GOSSE *New Poems* 157 Arnaut, great master of the lore of love, First wrought sestines to win his lady's heart.

**sestole, sestolet,** occas. var. ff. SEXTOLE, -ET.

**seston** ('sɛstən). *Biol.* and *Oceanogr.* [a. G. *seston* (R. Kolkwitz 1912, in *Ber. Deut. Bot. Ges.* XXX. 341), ad. Gr. σηστόν, neut. of σηστός that which is filtered, f. σήθειν to strain, filter; cf. PLANKTON.] Fine particulate matter suspended in water, esp. that which is organic or living.

**1916** B. D. JACKSON *Gloss. Bot. Terms* (ed. 3) 344/2 *Seston*, plankton material retained by very fine meshed sieves. **1941** *Ecol. Monogr.* XI. 58/1 The varieties in sestonic phosphorus are correlated with both the mass of organic seston and the quantity of phytoplankton, as measured by its chlorophyll content. **1957** G. E. HUTCHINSON *Treat. Limnol.* I. vi. 417 Seston color of this sort is often observed in highly productive lakes. **1967** *Ibid.* II. xix. 235 The seston consists of bioseston, or plankton and nekton, which latter is ordinarily quantitatively negligible, and of abioseston or tripton. *Ibid.* 243 The entire mass of suspended matter in a volume of free water is called seston, the nonliving part, tripton. **1971** *New Scientist* 15 July 145/2 The evidence suggests that the amount of chlorophyll from phytoplankton ..is diminishing.., while the amount of seston (oxygen consumers) is increasing.

Hence **se'stonic** *a.*, of, pertaining to, or being seston.

**1941** [see above]. **1967** *Oceanogr. & Marine Biol.* V. 221 At a glance these ribbons appeared to be sestonic debris from coastal algae of phanerogams.

**sesto(u)rne,** obs. forms of CISTERN.

**1577** B. GOOGE *Heresbach's Husb.* I. (1586) 28 b, My Barley is fyrst steeped in a Sestorne of water a day or two. **1603** *Inv.* in Gage *Hengrave* (1822) 27 One greate copp[r] sestourne to stand at the coobard.

**sestre,** obscure variant of THESTER *v.*

*a* **1300** *E.E. Psalter* lxxiii. 20 Ful-filled er þai þa þat sestrede [*v.r.* cestered] er in mirkenes.

**sestrone,** obs. form of CISTERN.

**1536** *Cockersand Chartul.* (Chetham Soc.) III. II. 1179 Item oone grete Sestrone of ledd at xx *s*.

**sestuor** ('sɛstjuːɔː(r)). *Mus.* Also SEXTUOR. [f. It. *sesto* sixth, after SEPTUOR.] A sestet.

**1862** T. A. TROLLOPE *Marietta* I. vi. 112 Quartettes, sestuors, quintettes.

**sesun(e, -yn(e,** obs. forms of SEASON.

**Sesuto, Sesutu,** varr. SESOTHO.

**set** (sɛt), *sb.*[1] Also 4–5 sete, 3–6 sette, (6 seat), 5– (now prevalent in many technical senses) sett. [f. SET *v.*[1], partly directly from the vb.-stem, and partly a subst. use of SET *ppl. a.*; the two formations cannot always be distinguished.

OE. had *set* neut., seat (in sing. place of setting of the sun; in pl. *setu, seotu* collect. in the senses camp, stable or cowhouse), corresp. to OHG. *sez* neut., seat (MHG. *sez* neut., masc., seat, siege, mod.G. *sess* masc., seat), ON. *set* neut., abode:—OTeut. **seto-m*, f. **set-*: see SIT *v.* It is doubtful whether this survived beyond OE.; the rare early ME. *sette* seat appears to be (as the rhyme shows in one instance) an irregular spelling for *sete* SEAT *sb.*[1] Sense 1 below can hardly have been influenced by the OE. word, as this occurs (in sing.) only in phr. e.g. *to sete gán* (= to set), and the dat. sb. would have become *sēte* in early ME. On the other hand, sense 1 may be partly due to an adoption of ON. *-setr* neut., *-seta* fem. (in *dagsetr, sólarsetr, -seta*: see SUNSET), which are cogn. with OE. *set*.]

**I.** The action of setting or condition of being set.

**1. a.** The act of setting (of a luminary); the apparent descent of the heavenly bodies towards the horizon at the close of their diurnal period. Now only *poet.* except in SUNSET.

*c* **1386** [see *day set*, DAY *sb.* 24]. **1390** GOWER *Conf.* III. 257 Riht evene upon the Sonne set. *a* **1400–50** *Wars Alex.* 2045 And so to settt of þe son sesid þai neuire. **1592** DANIEL *Compl. Rosamond* Wks. (1717) 39 This fair Morning had a shameful Set. **1594** DRAYTON *Idea* liii [lx], Tell me, if euer since the world begunne, So faire a morning had so foule a set? **1599** SHAKS. *Hen. V*, IV. i. 292 But [the King] like a Lacquey, from the Rise to Set, Sweates in the eye of Phebus. **1605** —— *Macb.* I. i. 5 That will be ere the set of Sunne. **1618** CHAPMAN *Hesiod's Georg.* II. 366 The Seuen-stars, and the Fiue, That twixt the Bulls hornes, at their set arriue. **1654–66** EARL ORRERY *Parthen.* (1676) 569 The Sun was fiue hours from his set. **1724** RAMSAY *Vision* xvii, Frae the sun's rysing to his sett. **1812** CARY *Dante, Purg.* XVIII. 80 When they of Rome behold him [the sun] at his set Betwixt Sardinia and the Corsic isle. **1834** MRS. BRAY *Warleigh* xxxi, The sun had already made a fiery set. **1845** SUMNER *True Grandeur Nations* (1846) 13 Between the rise and set of a single sun.

**b.** *set of day*: (*a*) the time at which the sun sets; (*b*) the west.

**1623** LISLE *Ælfric on O. & N. Test.* Ded. xv, Thou..shalt ..Extend thy fame fro Set to Spring of day. **1830** TENNYSON *Adeline* ii, Looking at the set of day. **1868** NETTLESHIP *Ess. Browning* v. 127 At set of day. **1885–94** R. BRIDGES *Eros & Psyche* Mar. xxiii, Lookt left and right to rise and set of day.

**c.** *fig.* of the close of life.

**1625** in Rushw. *Hist. Coll.* (1659) I. 158 Yet can they never deny but that admired Serenity had its set in a Cloud. **1635** A. STAFFORD *Fem. Glory* 13 Anna..being then in the occident, or set of life.

†**2.** ? A setting oneself to fight, encounter, attack. *Obs.*

*c* **1330** R. BRUNNE *Chron. Wace* (Rolls) 15658 Wyþ Cadwaly so harde he met, & Cadwalyn fley atte ferste set.

†**3. a.** Letting, lease. *Sc. Obs.*

**1439** *Charters*, etc. *Edin.* (1871) 64 Sindry alde charteris, takis, and settis of feefedorme made to thaim. **1471** *Acts Lds. Auditors* (1839) 14/2 þat he sall haue na dale nor entrometing þarwith..without þt he optene tak & set þarof. **1476** *Ibid.* 41/1 Dauid allegiand at þe said landis of logycarroch belangit him be Resone of Sete. **1583** *Exch. Rolls Scot.* XXI. 564 Thair was ane set maid of the kingis majesties landis. **1600** J. MELVILL *Autobiog.*, etc. (1842) 11 Be whome they might gett a new sett and possessioun of thay teind fisches. *a* **1637** SPOTTISWOOD *Hist. Ch. Scot.* (1655) 452 He should not delapidate his Benefice..nor make any set, or disposition thereof. [**1886** *Act 49 & 50 Vict.* c. 50 §3 'Lease' [in this Act] shall include tack and set.]

**b.** (Usually *sett.*) A mining lease. Chiefly *Cornwall.* (Cf. 21.)

**1713** *Lond. Gaz.* No. 5141/4 The Setts heretofore made of the Copper-works..will determine at Michaelmas next. **1778** PRYCE *Min. Cornub.* 326 A Set..sometimes..implies the deed or lease by which they enjoy the premises. **1855** LEIFCHILD *Cornwall* 241 The sett, or lease, frequently extends to twenty-one years.

*attrib.* **1891** *Labour Commission* Gloss., *Sett quarries*, a number of mines or quarries taken on lease.

**4.** *Scots Law.* The action of setting to sale (see quots.).

**1693** STAIR *Inst. Law Scot.* I. xvi. (ed. 2) 135 A Roup at the half or major part of the Owners against the rest, or a Set at any of the Owners instance against the whole, either to take his part at such a rate, or [etc.]. **1838** W. BELL *Dict. Law Scot.* s.v. *Sett*, Where the owners of a ship disagree as to the manner in which a vessel is to be employed, or where one of the owners is desirous to sell his share, he usually offers it, at a certain price, to the other owners; and failing an extrajudicial arrangement, an action of sett is competent.

†**5. a.** The condition of being stopped or checked; a check. Phr. *at a set*, at a standstill, in difficulties, nonplussed (cf. 10 e); ***hard*** or ***sore set*** (Sc.), a serious check or set-back (cf. phr. s.v. SET *v.*[1]).

**1613** PURCHAS *Pilgrimage* III. iv. 211 Our Gull-gallants.. who would sometimes be at a sette in their braue and brauing phrases, if they should not haue varietie of oathes and curses. **1642** D. ROGERS *Naaman* 87 He is at a set, and knows not what to make of it. *c* **1680** *Mem. Mrs. Veitch*, etc. (1846) 26 (E.D.D.) They were both against it, which gave my faith a sore set. **1751** [R. PALTOCK] *Life P. Wilkins* xii, It rose so steep..that I was at a Set upon the first Entrance. **1768** ROSS *Helenore* (1789) 45 Great may the hardships be, that she has met, Gotten for my sake so hard a set. *Ibid.* 70, I shanna tell you..How sad the set was, that my heart did get.

**b.** *Bowls.* (See quot. and RUB *sb.*[1] 2 a.)

**1876** *Encycl. Brit.* IV. 180/2 A 'rub' or 'set' is when a jack or bowl, *in transitu*, comes in contact with any object on the green.

†**c.** *Mech.* (See quot.)

**1763** FITZGERALD in *Phil. Trans.* LIII. 156 The stop, or sett, generally in large engines, when the ends of the leaver come to the springs, is a defect that has been endeavoured to be remedied.

**6.** The act of a dog in setting game. (Cf. 10 f.)

**1727** BOYER *Dict. Royal* I. s.v. *Arrest*, A Dog that makes a fine set. **1737** BRACKEN *Farriery Impr.* (1749) I. 309 Their little Dogs make a Set at them in the Manner of Setting-Dogs. **1897** *Badminton Mag.* Apr. 448 All your senses tingle as you go to the set, and encourage the statue-like animal to go on. **1897** *Outing* XXIX. 479/2 Only twenty years ago the term 'set' was in general use. A sportsman, especially an old-timer, when a setter paused on game, would then say 'There's a set!'

**7. a.** = *dead set*, 10 c, d.

**1829** *Examiner* 609/1 'A set' is made upon him of the most inveterate and splenetic character. **1850** CHUBB *Locks & Keys* 17 When 'a set' is made at a bank, every information is ..sought for, by the burglars. **1857** MRS. MATHEWS *Tea-Table T.* I. 136 On one occasion, at a noble table, a great set was made at him. **1857** A. MAYHEW *Paved with Gold* II. x, A direct set upon Phil was made by the satirical young rogues. **1887** W. E. NORRIS *Major & Minor* xxiii, No one could say that Miss N. was making a set at him.

**b.** A grudge. Chiefly in phr. ***to have*** (or ***take***) ***a set on*** (a person), to have a grudge against. *Austral.* and *N.Z. colloq.* Cf. SET *v.* 125 b.

**1903** 'T. COLLINS' *Such is Life* (1937) i. 36 'Hasn't Warrigal Alf got a set on you, too?' asked Thompson coldly. **1941** BAKER *Dict. Austral. Slang* 64 *Set*, a grudge against (someone), e.g., 'have a set on someone'. **1946** K. TENNANT *Lost Haven* (1947) xiv. 228 If the Old Man hadn't tried to give Mark Thorne such particular hell when he was starting his shop, perhaps Thorne wouldn't have taken a set on all the Sudermans.. If he hadn't the set on the Sudermans.. he wouldn't have wanted to cut off his nose to spite his face. **1948** D. BALLANTYNE *Cunninghams* (1963) II. vi. 155 He had a bit of a set on Frank and Sydney and was always pinching their cheeks and telling them they were young roughnecks.

**8.** (Usually *sett.*) A form of power used by shipwrights: see quots.

**1794** *Rigging & Seamanship* I. 10 The sett is made by driving wedges between the head or heel of the shore. *Ibid.* 19 Both must be set close together with cross-setts. **1815** *Falconer's Dict. Marine* (ed. Burney), *Setts*, in mast-making denotes powers made use of, where force is required to bring or unite two or more pieces together, and is performed by screws, shores, cross-setts, or cleats. **1874** THEARLE *Naval Archit.* 83 A 'set' or pressure is obtained by means of other pins driven and wedged into holes on the opposite side of the angle-iron.

**9. a.** The action of setting or hardening, or the condition of being set. ***to take a set***: to set.

**1837** J. T. SMITH tr. *Vicat's Mortars* 53 The 'time of set' may sometimes transgress the prescribed limits. **1839** *Civ. Engin. & Arch. Jrnl.* II. 69/1 Before the cement was perfectly hardened and had taken a set. **1923** *Rep. Progr. Appl. Chem.* VIII. 231 The time of set has been found to depend upon the proportion of combined water.. in the hydrated calcium aluminate. *Ibid.*, Removal of water.. results in the time of set being reduced. **1957** V. J. KEHOE *Technique Film & Telev. Make-Up* xii. 149 Warm weather hastens the set of the material, so chilling the bowl is advisable to slow down the set. **1963** D. SETON *Essent. Mod. Cookery* 156 The use of lemon juice or citric or tartaric acid is essential to ensure a good set [in marmalade].

**b.** ***initial set*** (*Building*), a condition attained by cement when it begins to stiffen, but before hardening commences.

**1891** T. POTTER *Concrete* (ed. 2) I. iii. 104 If a plasterer finds his mortar for stucco is becoming too stiff.. the initial set has commenced. **1927** *Engineer* 5 Aug. 143/2 At the completion of the operation the concrete has taken an initial set. **1953** VAN DEN BRANDEN & KNOWLES *Plastering* iv. 98 The initial set of Portland cement mortar occurs about two to three hours after the dry materials have been wetted.

**10. dead set**: often in phr. ***to make a dead set at***. †**a.** *slang*. (See quots.)

**1725** *New Cant. Dict.*, *Set*, as *Dead Set*, a Term used by Thief-catchers when they have a Certainty of seizing some of their Clients. **1785** GROSE *Dict. Vulgar T.*, *Set*, a dead set, a concerted scheme to defraud a person by gaming.

†**b.** A fixed look. *Obs.*

**1781** G. PARKER *View Soc.* I. 196 The Doctor.. gave me what I term the dead set with his eye.

**c.** A pointed attack; a determined onslaught; const. *at*, *against*. Also, an attitude or position of hostility.

**1835** FONBLANQUE *Eng. under 7 Administr.* (1837) III. 274 The abhorrence of every thing like a 'dead set', or an attempt to run down a man by abuse and clamour. **1836** GEN. P. THOMPSON *Exerc.* (1842) IV. 91 A dead set is to be made from various quarters, against the abominable innovation of publishing Divisions by authority. **1841** KEBLE *Let. to Newman* 19 July, It was plain from the moment Young went into the room that a dead set was to be made at him. **1859** *Hotten's Slang Dict.* s.v., 'A dead set', a determined stand, in argument or in movement. **1885** *Manch. Evening News* 16 July 2/1 The disaffected sections of the Irish population made a dead set against him from the first.

**d.** Of a woman: A determined attempt to gain a man's affections. Also *occas.* conversely of a man.

**1823** BYRON *Juan* XIV. xlii, Her late performance had been a dead set At Lord Augustus. **1825** T. HOOK *Sayings* Ser. II. *Sutherl.* (Colburn) 3 James had.. made a 'dead set' at a 'fortune'. **1848** THACKERAY *Van. Fair* iii, There was a girl at Dumdum.. who made a dead set at me in the year '4. **1883** F. M. CRAWFORD *Dr. Claudius* xvii, I made a dead set at a new beauty just arrived from the South. **1894** MRS. F. ELLIOT *Roman Gossip* v. 148 Women all through his life made a dead set at Garibaldi.

**e.** An absolute stop; a complete check; phr. ***at a dead set***. Also *Univ. slang* = DEAD *sb.*[1] 5.

**1806** SURR *Winter in Lond.* III. 211 Hollo—what's this! —the duchess of Drinkwater at a dead set! **1848** WEBSTER s.v. *Set*, *To be at a dead set*, is to be in a fixed state or condition which precludes further progress. *a* **1851** in B. H. Hall *College Words* 92 See the front of Logic lower; Screws, dead-sets, and fines. **1854** THOREAU *Walden* i. (1863) 72 The man is at a dead set who has got through a knot hole or gateway where his sledge load of furniture cannot follow him.

**f.** *Sporting*. An abrupt stop made by an animal with its muzzle in the direction of the prey; *esp.* the position taken up by a dog in pointing game. (Cf. 6.)

**1819** T. B. JOHNSON *Shooter's Comp.* 23 Happening to pass a small bush, with the whelp close to me.. when the bitch was at a distance, he made a dead set. **1863** W. C. BALDWIN *Afr. Hunting* v. 122 He made a dead set, getting my wind; and immediately made a desperate charge.

**II.** The manner or position in which a thing is set.

†**11.** The way in which something is set down in writing. *Obs. rare.*

**1535** STEWART *Cron. Scot.* II. 27 Ane herald.. Quhilk schew to him ilk word fra end to end,.. In forme and sett as I haif said ȝow heir.

**12.** Tendency, inclination; determination (of the mind, character, action, etc.) in a certain direction; often = settled direction, fixed habit. Also *spec.* in *Psychol.*, a predisposition or expectation that influences the response of a person or animal: used variously of conscious or unconscious, or of mental or physical, states. Cf. SET *v.* 93 c.

**1567** MAPLET *Gr. Forest* 14 There is another kind of Lodestone.. that is of contrarie set and disposition, which will haue none of Iron. **1603** DANIEL *Def. Rhime* Wks. (1717) 7 Which Frame of Words.. are disposed into divers Fashions, according to the Humour of the Composer, and the Set of the Time. *c* **1620** FLETCHER *False One* II. ii, Here's a strange alteration in the Court; Mens Faces are of other setts and motions. **1692** BURNET *Past. Care* vii. 80 Tully's Offices will give the Mind a noble sett. **1730** T. BOSTON *Mem.* viii. (1899) 168 The Lord was pleased to give my heart a set toward the preaching of Christ. **1847** H. MILLER *First Impr. Eng.* xvi. (1857) 268 The poetical mind of England had taken an inveterate set. **1852** BLACKIE *On Studying Lang.* 10 In the.. process by which the mother tongue is acquired, the mind acquires a habit and a set. **1890** W. JAMES *Princ. Psychol.* I. iv. 124 It is not in the moment of their forming, but in the moment of their producing *motor effects*, that resolves and aspirations communicate the new 'set' to the brain. **1898** *Allbutt's Syst. Med.* V. 843 Strain of the heart,—that is, of a permanent 'after-strain' or 'set' towards other than the normal lines of its action. **1911** E. L. THORNDIKE *Animal Intell.* vi. 249 If a cat pushes a button around with its nose, while.. the act to which its general 'set' impels it.. is that of clawing at an opening, it will be less aided in the formation of the habit than if it had been chiefly concerned in what its nose was doing. **1918** R. S. WOODWORTH *Dynamic Psychol.* iii. 56 Danger arouses a 'set' of the nervous system towards escape. **1931** *Brit. Jrnl. Psychol.* Apr. 379 The theory.. that ability in proof-reading is largely a matter of attitude or mental 'set'. **1953** J. B. CARROLL *Study of Lang.* iii. 77 There are actually prelinguistic organismic events (sets, attitudes, etc.) which can be identified with what expression theorists regard as 'thoughts' and 'ideas'. **1968** *Science* 13 Dec. 1236/1 'Set' refers to the subject's psychological expectations of what a drug will do to him in relation to his general personality structure. **1979** FORGUS & SHULMAN *Personality* i. 9 We can measure the dominant perceptual sets.. and.. these sets, in fact, direct perceptual selectivity.

**13.** The direction in which a current flows or a wind blows; also, the action of the water, etc. in taking a particular direction.

Locally applied to particular currents.

**1719** DE FOE *Crusoe* I. (Globe) 193 How the Sets of the Tide, or Currents lay, when the Flood came in. **1755** J. SHEBBEARE *Lydia* (1769) I. 125 By a sudden sett of the sea.. Jack tumbled forward. **1793** *Phil. Trans.* LXXXIII. 189 Although the northern set was trifling..; yet the wind, being both scant and light, we could never overcome the tendency of the current. **1823** W. SCORESBY *Jrnl.* 350 The set of the ice. **1827** FONBLANQUE *Eng. under 7 Administr.* (1837) I. 13 As straws show the set of the wind. **1876** FARRAR *Marlb. Serm.* ii. 19 A feather will show you the direction of the wind; a straw will prove the set of a current. **1879** *Scribner's Monthly* XIX. 327/1 Often in storms a strong swift current runs along the coast between the outer bar and the shore, called by the surf-men the 'set' or 'cut'.

**14. a.** The build or make of a person. *Obs.* exc. *dial.*

**1611** SPEED *Hist. Gt. Brit.* IX. xxiv. (1623) 1186 Of a bigge and broad set. *c* **1620** FLETCHER *Custom of Country* I. v, A goodly gentleman, Of a more manly set I never look'd on. **1708** *Brit. Apollo* No. 32. 4/2 He is of a Squat Set. **1825** JAMIESON, *Set*.. 8. Shape, figure, cast, make, Aberd[een]. **1888** *Harper's Mag.* Jan. 291/2 Something effective and picturesque in the set of his strongly built frame.

†**b.** *gen.* ? Shape. *Obs.*

**1567** MAPLET *Gr. Forest* 46 Houselike.. for his endurance is resembled to Ambrosia.. for his roundset [? *read* round set] or figure to the Bullocks eie.

**15.** *Weaving*. (Usually *sett.*) The adjustment of the reeds (of a loom) necessary for the making of a fabric of a particular texture; hence, the make of a fabric as determined by this.

**1780** A. YOUNG *Tour. Irel.* I. 324 The grist or fineness of the yarn, determines the set or fineness of the reed through which it is to be wrought. **1833** J. HOLLAND *Manuf. Metal* II. 350 When the set of the web is from three fourths of an inch to forty meshes in the inch. **1879** ASHENHURST *Weaving*, etc. 272 The systems of calculating the sett of reeds. *Ibid.*, If a cloth contains sixty threads per inch, it would be said to be a sixty sett cloth. **1893** *Times* 10 July 4/6 Medium and heavy setts of powerlooms are having most attention, fine descriptions being almost neglected.

**b.** (Usually *sett.*) Each or any of the squares in the pattern of a tartan; the pattern itself.

**1721** RAMSAY *Tartana* 197 The Plaid itself gives pleasure to the sight, To see how all its sets imbibe the light. **1725** —— *Gentle Sheph.* I. i, Scarlet and green the sets, the borders blue. **1811** MRS. A. GRANT *Superst. Highl.* II. 207 Every clan wore a different *set*.. of tartan. **1819** SCOTT *Leg. Montrose* viii, How many checks in the sett of his plaid and trews. **1897** *Standard* 21 Sept. 7/1 The Murray 'sett'.

**16.** The form which a body assumes as the result of strain or pressure or in the process of solidification, etc.; *esp.* the permanent deflexion of a bar or plate of metal or wood.

**1812** P. NICHOLSON *Mech. Exerc.* 85 When the timbers are sagged, either by casting or by a set. **1824** TREDGOLD *Ess. Cast iron* (ed. 2) 81 That iron is to be esteemed the best which will bear the greatest degree of flexure without set. **1847** H. MILLER *First Impr. Eng.* xii. (1857) 204 Like a piece of old elastic parchment that had been acquiring for ages the set of the roll. **1869** MRS. SOMERVILLE *Molec. Sci.* I. ii. 77 The.. phenomena of crystals depends upon unequal conductibility.. and their set is determined by the difference between the forces of attraction and repulsion. **1883** *Science* I. 174/1 The 'set' of a zinc bar when heated. **1886** *Cheshire Gloss.* s.v., When the crystals of bay-salt begin to form upon the strings and thorns, the pan is said to have a good or a bad set according as the crystals are large or small. **1888** *Lockwood's Dict. Terms Mech. Engin.*, *Permanent set*, that amount of deflection from which a beam or structure is unable to return to its original form, but which remains constant. **1903** KIPLING *5 Nations* 24 Turning the shingle, returning the shingle, changing the set of the sand.

**17.** The way in which an article of dress is arranged or 'hangs'; also similarly of a ship's sails.

**1822** *Examiner* 68/2 Studying the set of her bonnet. **1827** FONBLANQUE *Eng. under 7 Administr.* (1837) I. 107 She who shapes the mistress's caps, and gives the set to her head-dress—the lady's maid! **1828** H. LE BLANC *Art of Tying the Cravat* (ed. 2) 65 Scrutinizing examination will be made on the *set* of his Cravat. **1845** MRS. M. J. HOWELL *Hand-bk. Dress-making* 40 In order to give the skirt a pretty 'set'. **1881** *Daily Tel.* 28 Jan., Considering the squareness of her bows and the set of her canvas. **1896** KIPLING *Seven Seas* 166 The set o' the tunic's 'orrid.

**18. a.** The position or attitude (either occasional or habitual) given to a limb or a part of the body.

**1855** BAIN *Senses & Int.* III. i. §3 (1864) 335 A peculiar set of the limb, for example, the turning out of the toes. **1863** B. TAYLOR *Han. Thurston* iv, His yellow hair.. grew back from the temples with a sturdy set. **1876** GEO. ELIOT *Dan. Der.* vii, The set of her head and neck. **1896** KIPLING *Seven Seas* 165 'E saw the set o' my shoulders.

**b.** The action or result of fixing the hair when damp so that it dries in the required style. Also with reference to fixing the hair by other means (with heat, a setting lotion, etc.), and as ***hair-set***. Cf. SET *v.*[1] 81 b.

**1933** G. A. FOAN *Art & Craft Hairdressing Spec. Suppl.* iv. 23/2 The procedure here outlined in reference to the final touch must be followed exactly as indicated in order to prevent entirely spoiling the set. **1938** H. GOODMAN *Princ. Professional Beauty Culture* v. 90 After permanent set the intramolecular breakdown and rebuilding processes have effectively evolved a new.. conformation. **1940** W. PECK *Bewildering Cares* iv. 110, I met her once at the hairdresser's bewailing that she couldn't afford a nice steak for Herbert on their income, and she had obviously spent the price of it on a 'set'. **1946** K. TENNANT *Lost Haven* (1947) xiii. 204 You can't get a hairset here and I have to do my own. **1975** *Country Life* 27 Mar. 806/1 Many women disliked wearing a hat because it squashed their 'set'.

**19. a.** The inclination or dip of the arm of an axle-tree; the elevation of a gun.

**1844** H. STEPHENS *Bk. Farm* III. 1163 Were all wheels made with one uniform degree of dish, we should then have one simple standard for the *set* of the axle-arms. **1852** BURN *Nav. & Milit. Dict.* s.v., To give the proper set or dip. **1876** VOYLE & STEVENSON *Milit. Dict.* **1898** *Encycl. Sport* II. 168/2 (Punt shooting), *'Set' of the gun*, the elevation given to the gun as it lies on the gun-rest.

**b.** The slight lateral deflexion in opposite directions of the alternate teeth of a saw; the amount of this deflexion.

**1837** HEBERT *Engin. & Mech. Encycl.* II. 630 Each successive tooth is placed in opposite directions, at the desired *set*, to allow the blade of the saw to pass through the wood without resistance. **1853** URE *Dict. Arts* II. 584 The 'set' of the saw consists in inclining the teeth at the particular angle known to be the best to facilitate the exit of the sawdust. **1875** KNIGHT *Dict. Mech.* 1047/1 *Hack-saw*, a frame saw of moderate set.

**c.** *Typogr.* (See quots.)

**1892** *Southward's Pract. Printing* (ed. 4) 29 *note*, The set of the types signifies the proper position of the letters, with reference to the precise amount of space between them. **1908** LEGROS in *Proc. Instit. Mech. Engin.* Dec. 1043 As the letters are not only unequal in set, and since the widths of set generally bear no particular relation to the em (or body). *Ibid.* 1075 The mould thus made is of definite size for body but variable for the width of set.

**d.** *Bell-ringing*. The inverted position of a bell when it is set. Cf. SET *v.* 66.

**1677** F. STEDMAN *Campanalogia* 23 A prospect of true ringing at any certain compass under the Sett, may thus be taken. *Ibid.* 39 The reason why one of them is said to move up, is, because he that rings that bell, in the making of the change must hold it up at the Sett a little longer than ordinary, to delay its striking, whereby 'tis made to follow the other note which before it preceded. **1901** H. E. BULWER *Gloss. Techn. Terms Bells* (1904) 33 *Set*, the position of a bell after being 'raised', when it rests mouth upward a little beyond the balancing point [etc.].

**e.** *Carpentry*. The amount that the blade of a plane projects below the sole.

**1898** F. & H. P. FLETCHER *Carpentry & Joinery* xxvi. 281 The set of the plane may be adjusted during use by tapping the iron of the nose. **1950** M. T. TELLING *Carpentry & Joinery* II. 116 All [planes] will do specially true work if properly set and sharpened and many of them have mechanical means of adjusting the cutting iron to a fine set.

**III.** Something which is set.

†**20.** An area marked out for a hunt. *Obs.*

*c* **1410** *Master of Game* (MS. Digby 182) xxxv, The maister of þe game shulde be accorded with þe maister forster or parker whedyr þat it be where þe kynge shall hunte suche a daye. And if þe sette be wyde [etc.]. *Ibid.*, þe maister of þe game shulde be enformed by þe forster or þe parker, what game þe kyng shall fynde withinne his sette.

**21.** (Usually *sett.*) The area of ground worked by a particular mining company. Chiefly *Cornwall*. (Cf. 3 b.)

**1778** PRYCE *Min. Cornub.* 326 A Set is the ground granted to a company of Adventurers. **1835** *English's Mining Rev.* July 113 The setts comprise a circumference of several miles, and abound in lodes producing argentiferous ores. **1839** DE LA BECHE *Rep. Geol. Cornwall*, etc. xv. 537 The bounder had the right of granting the sett. **1855** LEIFCHILD *Cornwall* 136 The lord of the soil grants a *sett*.., or portion of mining soil, for a lease of years. **1893** *Daily News* 11 Jan. 2/1 There are many old workings in Wheal Owles, and several setts have of late years been discontinued.

†**22.** ? An ornament of jewellery set on a garment. *Obs.*

**1502** *Priv. Purse Exp. Eliz. York* (1830) 21 Spangelles settes..sterrys dropes and pointes..for garnisshing of jakettes. **1542** *Inv. Royal Wardrobe* (1815) 67 Upon the samyne bonet tene settis, in every set four dyomonttis,.. with xxiiii settis of perle in every set four perle. *Ibid.* 67–68 Tene plain dyamonttis in settis of gold, xviii settis of perle, & thrie in every set, and nyne set lang, and four in every sett.

**23. a.** 'Any thing not sown, but put in a state of some growth into the ground' (J.); a twig, slip, or sucker, used for planting or grafting; also, a young plant, *esp.* a bedding-out plant.

**1513** DOUGLAS *Æneis* XII. Prol. 133 The plane pulderyt with semely settis sovnd. **1523** FITZHERB. *Husb.* §127 Take a sharpe hatchet..and cutte the settes in a playne place, nyghe vnto the erthe. *Ibid.*, At euery two fote, or iii fote, to leaue one set growyng not plasshed. **1553** T. WILSON *Rhet.* 26b, To ympe or graffe yong settes. **1577** B. GOOGE *Heresbach's Husb.* II. (1586) 67 Do they growe of the seede, or of the sette? **1615** W. LAWSON *Country Housew. Gard.* (1626) 12 It shall grieue you much to see your yong sets rubd loose at the roots. **1618** *Shuttleworths' Acc.* (Chetham Soc.) 233, ij hundrethe setts of lycorise for my M[ris], iiij[s]. **1669** WORLIDGE *Syst. Agric.* (1681) 147 Chuse the largest Sets that you can get; which are to be had best out of a Garden well kept. **1760** BROWN *Compl. Farmer* II. 107 One runner will make many setts. **1848** *Jrnl. R. Agric. Soc.* IX. II. 563 The hop-set is no sooner put in the ground than its enemies find it out. **1877** *N.W. Linc. Gloss.*, *Set*..(2) Young plants of any kind used for bedding out. **1894** *Daily News* 15 Jan. 6/6 Find a swampy place, and get good setts (that is, two or three year old withy).

*fig.* **1605** *1st Pt. Ieronimo* III. ii. 123 This arme neare met So strong a courage of so greene a set. **1662** MARVELL *Corr.* Wks. (Grosart) II. 80 We may..graft an Set of our own upon their motion.

**b.** A potato, or a portion of a potato, used as seed. *local.*

**1767** A. YOUNG *Farmer's Lett. to People* 12 Dropping potatoe setts. **1844** H. STEPHENS *Bk. Farm* II. 655 The tubers are either planted whole, or cut into parts called *sets.* **1896** P. A. GRAHAM *Red Scaur* vi. 83, I found her and Mark and Elsie planting potatoes... She carried a basket of 'sets', ..and Mark was doing the hard work of digging. **1901** *Dundee Adv.* 23 Apr. 4 The common potato growing practice is to allow..six inches from sett to sett of the seed.

†**c.** A shoot. *Obs.*

**1675** EVELYN *Fr. Gard.* 182 When you have cut off the heads of your Cabbages..they will produce small sets, which the Italians call Broccoly.

**d.** An undeveloped or rudimentary fruit; *collect.*, flowers that have been fertilized and should develop into fruit. Also, the development of fruit following fertilization. Cf. SET *v.* 98.

**1888** C. M. DOUGHTY *Trav. in Arabia Deserta* II. xv. 436 Every cluster, which had inclosed in it a spray of the male blossom, was lapped about with a wisp of dry forage; and this defended the sets from early flights of locusts. **1928** *Daily Tel.* 12 June 5/2 Of culinary apples the set appears good on the whole... Dessert cherries have had a fair set. **1929** AUCTER & KNAPP *Orchard & Small Fruit Culture* viii. 369 In such orchards, if the blossoms are properly pollinated, much better sets occur. **1964** H. B. TUKEY *Dwarfed Fruit Trees* xxiii. 422 Bee flight is noticeably reduced at 60 degrees F. or below, and pollination, fertilization, and fruit set are accordingly reduced. **1973** H. G. KINGHAM *U.K. Tomato Man.* xvi. 126 For all crops overhead damping with a course spray helps to improve set.

†**24.** The stake put down at dice, etc. Also *fig.*

**1537** in *Privy Purse Exp. Hen. VIII* (1827) 143 Paied to the iij Cotons for iij settes the whiche the kinges grace loste to them in Grenewiche parke. **1586** A. DAY *Eng. Secretary* II. (1595) 39 The plaie that I vsed was with them, the sette by agreement not great, concluded vppon more to passe time, then wherof to make gaine. **1602** HEYWOOD *Wom. killed w. Kindn.* (1617) E 2, Let them that are taken playing false forfet the Set. **1611** COTGR., *Mommon*..a set, by a Mummer, at dice.

†**25. a.** A game at dice or cards; hence, the number of points to be made in order to be 'up'.

**1594** HENSLOWE *Diary* (1845) 47 [Title of play] The seat at mawe. **1611** FLORIO, *Partita*,..a set or match at any game. **1633** FORD *Love's Sacr.* III. G 2b, You were best to try a set at Maw. **1667** DRYDEN & DK. NEWCASTLE *Sir M. Mar-all* I, I lose all my sets, when I want but one of up. **1680** COTTON *Compl. Gamester* (ed. 2) 58 Picket... The usual Set is an hundred. *Ibid.* 75 At Cribbidge..the number of the Set is sixty one. *Ibid.* 79 This Game I conceive is called All-Fours from Highest, Lowest, Jack, and Game, which is the Set as some play it. **1687** SEDLEY *Bellamira* IV. i. Wks. 1778 II. 161, I lost three sets at back-gammon.

†**b.** *fig.* Match, contest. *Obs.*

*c* **1605** ROWLEY *Birth of Merlin* I. i, Your Sister and Lord Edwin are in game, And all their wits at stake to win the Set. **1649** G. DANIEL *Trinarch., Rich. II*, cclxxxvi, If the sword must try it, Hee had an Equall sett, and choos'd to play it. **1687** DRYDEN *Hind & P.* II. 161 That was but civil war, an equal set, Where Piles with piles, and Eagles Eagles met.

**26.** *Real Tennis* (sometimes spelt *sett*): A group of six games which counts as a unit to the side that wins more than half of them; see also quot. *a* 1769. *Lawn Tennis* (always spelt *set*): A group of games counting as a unit towards a match for the person or pair of persons who win the greater number of games in it.

**1578** FLORIO *1st Fruites* 8, I will goe see some play at Tenise, and perhaps play also: will you play two or three settes with me? **1591** —— *2nd Fruites* 25 *P.* How manie are you my masters? *H.* We are but two that will plaie. *P.* Will you plaie in set? **1630** *R. Johnson's Kingd. & Commw.* 185 Ye shall see them play Sets at Tennis in the heat of Summer. *a* **1769** HOYLE *Games* (1778) 203 Six Games make a Set of Tennis, but if what is called an Advantage Set is played, two successive Games above five Games must be won to decide; or, in Case it should be six Games all, two successive Games must still be won on one Side to conclude the Set. **1822** SCOTT *Nigel* xxiii, Perhaps you would like a set at tennis, or a game at balloon. **1886** *Field* 31 July 182/2 Mr. Joy only beat Mr. Thorpe after all three sets had been exhausted. **1891** 'J. S. WINTER' *Lumley the Painter* 36 I shouldn't have liked to lose my first sett with you. **1949** *Lawn Tennis* ('Know the Game' Ser.) 15 The first player or pair to win six games wins the set, except that should the score become five games each—'Five All'—one player or pair must become two games ahead to win the set. **1980** *Guardian* 14 July 18/5 Miss Jevans..had a bad patch in the second set before winning 6–1, 7–5.

**b.** *Comb.*, as **set point**, the state of a set when one side or player needs only one point to win the set; also, the point itself (cf. *match-point (a)* s.v. MATCH *sb.*[1]).

**1928** *Observer* 1 July 29/3 When that cunning player.. would, at set-point, send one as hard as he could hit it straight down the centre line. **1946** *Times* 26 June 2/3 The Dutch pair, after missing a set point when leading by six games to five, finally secured the first set at 9–7. **1972** D. DELMAN *Sudden Death* vi. 152 Set point. I crouch, racket twirling.

†**27.** One of the pleats of a ruff; also, the arrangement of a ruff in pleats. *Obs.*

**1594** NASHE *Unfort. Trav.* Wks. 1904 II. 255, I warrant you should not see one set of her neckercher peruerted or turned awrie. **1601** DENT *Pathw. Heaven* (1617) 47 Some are as proud of their falling bands and little sets, as others are of their great ruffes. **1608** MACHIN *Dumb Knt.* I. i. B 2b, You haue a pretty set too, how big is the steele you set with? **1610** B. JONSON *Alch.* IV. iii, He speakes out of a fortification 'Pray god, he ha' no squibs in those deep sets. **1651** *Randolph's Hey for Honestie* III. iii. 27 The sets of my old Ruffe lookt like so many Organ-Pipes.

**28.** = *set scene*: see SET *ppl. a.* 8. Also, more widely, the setting, stage furniture, etc., used on stage in a theatre. In *Film-making* and *Television*, the scenery (usu. built up rather than painted) and other properties used in the filming of an individual scene; the place or area in which filming takes place. Freq. in phr. *on* or *off (the) set.* Also *attrib.* and *Comb.* Cf. *film set* s.v. FILM *sb.* 7c.

**1859** E. FITZBALL *Thirty-Five Years of Dramatic Author's Life* I. vi. 91 The vast scenes were pushed into sets, imperfectly painted. **1861** *Cornh. Mag.* IV. 169 In the *Frogs*, we have..a grand full stage 'set' of the Acherusian lake. **1868** MISS BRADDON *Dead-sea Fruit* xxvi. II. 296 If such a set were only manageable at the Bonbonnière! But we have not enough depth for this kind of thing. **1880** *Theatre* Apr. 223 The set was excellent, representing the interior of an Elizabethan house. **1894** MRS. H. WARD *Marcella* I. I. i. 5 The complete disappearance of this earliest 'set', to use a theatrical phrase, from the scenery of her childhood. **1912** F. A. TALBOT *Moving Pictures: How they are made & Worked* x. (caption facing p. 109), Building a solid set for 'The Two Orphans'. **1918** H. CROY *How Motion Pictures are Made* 107 With the sets determined upon, preparation for the taking of the picture is begun. **1936** WODEHOUSE *Laughing Gas* iv. 51 She was supposed to be on the set, made up, at six on the following a.m. for some retakes. **1947** A. HUXLEY *Let.* 27 July (1969) 573 The ticklish situation on the set made it impossible to come to New York for Claire's wedding. **1953** K. REISZ *Technique Film Editing* i. 60 Dialogue-writing, set-design and acting all become subjugated to this central purpose. **1956** C. MCCULLERS in *Mademoiselle* Sept. 174/2 Mabel Goodley, the painter and set-designer. **1961** G. MILLERSON *Telev. Production* i. 15 The set designer, responsible for the scenic treatment. **1973** *Listener* 22 Nov. 727/3 The same people are very much less agreeable in *Meet Pamela* than they are 'off-set' in *Day for Night.* **1977** M. BABSON *Murder, Murder, Little Star* xviii. 154 Had there been a further scene..in the dressing-room? Twinkle was being too good on set.

**29.** (Usually *sett.*) A squared stone (chiefly granite) used for paving.

**1871** WILLIAMSON *Science Lect.* Ser. II. 98 Those square stones which I think are technically called 'sets'. **1880** *Daily News* 7 Dec. 6/3 One of the small steamers which trade with setts from the quarries. *Ibid.* 9 Dec. 1/3 A sett stone quarry. **1905** *Academy* 9 Sept. 935/1 The streets used to be paved with setts taken from the black marble quarry.

**30.** Miscellaneous technical senses.

**a.** *Plastering.* The finishing coat on walls prepared for painting. **b.** In pile-driving, etc., a body placed between the hammer and the object to be struck. **c.** *Fishing.* (*a*) = 'set net' (see SET *ppl. a.*); chiefly *eel-set.* (*b*) See quot. 1867. (Cf. MDu. *set, sete.*) **d.** *Mining.* (See quots.) **e.** *Saddlery.* 'The filling of deer's hair or other stuffing beneath the ground seat of a saddle, to bring the top seat to its shape' (Knight *Dict. Mech.* 1875). **f.** (*a*) A young oyster when first attached; (*b*) the crop of young oysters in a locality. **g.** *N. Amer. Trapping.* A trap or snare; a series of traps.

**a. 1823** P. NICHOLSON *Pract. Builder* 373 As the plasterer lays on the set, he draws the brush backwards and forwards over it, till the surface is smooth. **1825** [see RENDERING *vbl. sb.* 3 a].

**b. 1837** in *Civil Eng. & Arch. Jrnl.* (1838) I. 242/2 A set is then applied to the end of the wedge, and the workman strikes it with a hammer. **1842** GWILT *Archit.* 1031 *Sett*, in piling, a piece placed temporarily on the head of a pile.

**c.** *a* **1808** *State, Leslie v. Fraser* 56 (Jam.) The practice of hauling their fishing-nets and feith-sets to the shore. **1867** F. FRANCIS *Angling* iv. (1880) 106 The angler..hooks the fish on to his line by a certain arrangement of hooks called a flight or set. **1882** *Blackw. Mag.* Jan. 102 The silver-bellied eel..is only caught in the eel-sets. **1892** *Longman's Mag.* Nov. 88 Along the Norfolk rivers a very important eel fishery is carried on by means of fixed nets known as 'eel-sets'.

**d. 1858** R. HUNT *Catal. Mus. Pract. Geol.* 223 The pillars are taken away, commencing at the extreme end of the sett. **1862** *Chamb. Jrnl.* Apr. 216 The strait sets are excavations four or five feet wide..made..in the side of a seam of coal at a distance of about six yards from each other. **1883** GRESLEY *Gloss. Coal-mining*, *Sett*, a measure of length along the face of a stall, usually from say 6 to 10 feet, by which holers and drivers are paid. A certain number of setts comprise a day's work.

**f. 1881** INGERSOLL *Oyster-Industry* 248 'The Set is good in Somerset this year'; *i.e.*, there is an abundance of infant oysters. **1887** GOODE, etc. *Fish. Industr. U.S.* v. II. 515 At only a few places does a breed of oysters, or a 'set', as it is termed, occur with any regularity. *Ibid.* 540 *note*, There is no word in the Northern States for infant oysters, except the terms 'set', 'spat', 'spawn', &c.

**g. 1912** V. E. ROE *Maid of Whispering Hills* 74 What is all this beside that which waits the runner of the trail at every 'set' in those many miles? **1942** *Sun* (Baltimore) 2 Feb. 4/3 Each morning the trapper makes the rounds of his 'set'. He strips the skin from the animals..and takes the pelts to market. **1977** *Globe & Mail* (Toronto) 30 Mar. 33/3 We were still within 20 yards of the trap's position, when a 55-pound beaver, swimming unseen under the ice, hit the set.

**IV.** A place where something is set.

**31.** A place where stationary fishing nets are fixed.

**1745** BLOMEFIELD *Topogr. Hist. Norfolk* II. 866 There were 19 appropriated Fishing-Places, which they called Setts, which were yearly allotted by the Mayor, to certain Fresh-Water Fishermen. **1867** SMYTH *Sailor's Word-bk.*, *Sett*, the particular spot in a river or frith, where stationary nets are fixed.

**32.** The earth or burrow of a badger.

**1898** A. E. PEASE *Badger* 40, I knew of nine badger 'sets' in the vicinity. *Ibid.* 44 A badger's earth or warren is properly and generally called a 'set' or 'cete'. **1908** *Nation* 6 June 340/2 For a year or two past the brocks had held their sett in the brake.

**V. 33.** (Often *sett.*) A tool or device used for 'setting' (in various technical senses); *esp.* a heavy punch or chisel for use on metal or stone. Cf. SATE *sb.*: see quots.

**1750** BLANCKLEY *Nav. Expositor*, *Setts* for Saws, are for setting the Teeth when out of Order, so as they may cut with the greater Exactness. **1812** P. NICHOLSON *Mech. Exerc.*, *Smithing* 353 *Side Set*, a hammer used to set shoulders of rivets to a true square or bevel, as required. **1843** HOLTZAPFFEL *Turning* I. 387 The work..is bent over with the blows of a flat-ended punch or set. **1846** [see *saw-set*, SAW *sb.*[1] 5 d]. **1881** *Design & Work* 24 Dec. 451/2 The operation of 'driving' rivets consists in placing a set on the end of the rivet, and sledging it down to form the head. **1888** *Lockwood's Dict. Terms Mech. Engin.*, *Set*, or *Sett*, (1) a narrow square nosed or round nosed chisel-like tool used by fitters and boiler makers for chipping grooves in metal. (2) Broad chisel-like tools used for cutting off hot or cold bars on the anvil. *Ibid.*, *Hook Wrench*, or *Set*, or *Hand Hook*, a smith's tool used for taking work out of winding or out of twist. **1892** *Labour Commission* Gloss., *Sett*, a piece of bar-iron bent to the same curvature or shape that an iron pipe is required to take. **1905** P. N. HASLUCK *Handyman's Bk.* 134/1 For punching the nail head below the surface of the work, the steel set is used. **1920** A. H. FAY *Gloss. Mining & Mineral Industry* 605/1 *Sett*, a quarryman's term for a square-faced steel tool which is held in position and struck with a sledge to cause a fracture in a rock mass. **1924** [see BOLSTER *sb.*[1]]. **1942** W. H. ATHERTON *Workshop Pract.* (ed. 2) V. 176 The Hot Sate or Sett..is in constant use for cutting away extraneous metal while hot. **1962** J. G. ROBERTSON *Metalwork* viii. 95 The Hot Set (Sett or Sate)..is used for cutting off on the cutting face of the anvil. A smith holds the work and hot set whilst a striker wields the sledge hammer. The hot set is designed to cut hot metal. **1964** H. HODGES *Artifacts* iv. 77 The heads were either cast, or formed as the rivets were closed using sets (setts) or snaps.

**set** (set), *sb.*[2] Also 4–6 sette, 5– sett. [orig. (in sense 1) a. OF. *sette*:—L. *secta* SECT *sb.*[1], but in subsequent developments of meaning influenced by SET *v.*[1] and apprehended as equivalent to 'number set together'. The application to things (branch II) may be partly due to MLG. *gesette* set or suite (of pieces), whence app. G. *gesetz* set of knitting-needles, etc., Da. *sæt* set of china, suit of clothes.]

**I.** A number or group of persons.

†**1.** A religious body, sect. *Obs.*

**1387** TREVISA *Higden* (Rolls) VI. 41 After þe deþ of Machometus þat cursede secte encresede so faste þat it drouȝ myȝti men of Pers to þe corsed lawe of þe Arabes. Al þat sette haþ infecte..al Affrica. *c* **1500** *Melusine* xxxvi. 272 Many other of our sette and lawe. *c* **1520** NISBET *N.T.* Acts xxiv. 14 Eftir the sett [*Wycl.* secte] quhilk thai say herresie, sa I serue to God the fadir. *Ibid.* 2 Pet. ii. 1 Maistris learis, that sal bring in settis [*Wycl.* sectes] of perditioun. **1538** in Archbold *Somerset Relig. Houses* (1892) 80 What ys my lord Audley, a man off ye new sett or arfter ye olde sorte?

*transf.* *c* **1450** *Mankind* 372 ȝe wolde haue me of yowur sett?

**2. a.** A number, company, or group (*of* persons) associated by community of status, habits, occupations, or interests. Often with depreciatory implication (cf. LOT *sb.* 8). In the 17th–18th c. freq. spelt *sett.* [Prob. *transf.* from uses in branch II.]

**1682** TATE *Abs. & Achit.* II. 533 The rest..Who ne'er had wit nor will for mischief yet. But pleased to be reputed of a set. **1693** LOCKE *Educ.* §122. 151 A Sett of Children thus ordered, and kept from the ill example of others, would.. learn to read, write, and what else one would have them, as others do their ordinary Plays. **1701** [W. PATERSON] *Counc. Trade* 72 The Fisheries were become a tempting Morsel for a Sett of avaricious Hucksters, and Monopolists. **1705** ADDISON *Italy, Venice* 105 A Set of Artisans, that by the help of several Poles..build themselves up into a kind of Pyramid. **1712** —— *Spect.* No. 440 ¶1 A Sett of merry Fellows. **1733** J. BARBER *Let. to Swift* 6 Feb., I have been, for many years, plagued with a set of ungrateful monsters, called Cousins, that I tremble at the name. **1774** J. BRYANT *Mythol.* I. 258 This kind of divination is still carried on by a set of priests. **1779** JOHNSON *L.P., Yalden* Wks. III. 229 A very numerous and splendid set of acquaintance. **1815** SCOTT *Guy M.* xlvii, A set of smugglers, gipsies, and other desperadoes. **1837** HT. MARTINEAU *Soc. Amer.* II. 164, I think the abolitionists of the United States the most reasonable set of people that I ever knew to be united together for one object. **1866** ROGERS *Agric. & Prices* I. xxiii. 601 In the hope that a new set of customers might be developed. **1894** E. T. AYERS *Bowls* 26 The six [players] divide or 'cut' into two sets of three.

**b.** *absol.* (cf. sense 3).

**1683** KENNETT tr. *Erasm. on Folly* 34 There will come a new hungry Sett. **1691** DRYDEN *Prol. to K. Arthur* 38 Among the rest there are a sharping Sett. *a* **1704** T. BROWN *Praise Poverty* Wks. 1730 I. 92 If this sett were thrown aside and men of poverty and honesty put in their stead. **1758** JOHNSON *Idler* No. 78 ⁋3 There was a select sett, supposed to be distinguished by superiority of intellects. **1826** DISRAELI *Viv. Grey* II. xiv, 'Who are we among,..?' asked Vivian. 'Oh! an odd set,' said the lady, looking dignified. **1845** FORD *Handbk. Spain* I. 16 A highly trustworthy laborious and hardworking set. **1869** TOZER *Highl. Turkey* I. 292 The shepherds were an uncouth-looking set. **1885** *L'pool Daily Post* 23 Oct. 4/7 He did not speak or preach in the dialect of any party or set.

†**c.** A political group or party. *Obs.*

**1748** THOMSON *Cast. Indol.* I. liv, In comes another sett, and kicketh them downstairs. **1750** in *Priv. Lett. Ld. Malmesbury* (1870) I. 78 That the Bedford set will be honourably kicked up or down stairs. **1790** BURKE *Corr.* (1844) III. 140, I intend no controversy with Dr. Price, or Lord Shelburne, or any other of their set.

**d.** A subdivision of pupils or students (esp. in a single year) for instruction on a particular subject: usu. one of a number of such groupings and often constituted according to ability.

**1882** in R. S. Churchill *Winston S. Churchill* (1967) I. Compan. I. iii. 90 Place in 3rd Set of 14 boys for ½ Term —14th. **1889** *Boy's Own Paper* 7 Sept. 781 Those dry definitions [of Euclid] seem twaddle to me (I admit I am low in my set). **1914** 'I. HAY' *Lighter Side School Life* i. 15 He must know whether Mr. A. in the Senior Science Set is expounding theories of inorganic chemistry which have been obsolete for ten years. **1963** M. BEADLE *These Ruins are Inhabited* vi. 86 Sets are ability groups. In each subject the boys had been divided into fast, average and slower-moving sections; each of these sets met as a class. **1971** P. D. JAMES *Shroud for Nightingale* ii. 41 We haven't used the demonstration room since Nurse Pearce's death but otherwise the set is continuing to work according to plan.

**e.** A gang of pickers assigned to a hop-bin.

**1805** R. W. DICKSON *Pract. Agric.* II. 752 Three, four, or more pickers being employed in clearing the binds of the hops..: these, with the person engaged in sorting the poles, are denominated a set.

**3. a.** A group of persons in society having its own peculiar interests, fashions, and conventions; a social group of a select or exclusive character. Freq. with qualifying adj. or sb. indicating the location, affiliation, or characteristic activities of the group, as ***the Bloomsbury*** (***Chelsea, Cliveden***, etc.) ***set. smart set***: see SMART *a.* 13. Cf. *jet set* s.v. JET *sb.*[3] 11.

**1777** SHERIDAN *Sch. Scandal* I. ii, The set she meets at her house, encourage the perverseness of her disposition. **1798** S. & HT. LEE *Cant. T., Young Lady's T.* II. 91 Sir Edward, not deigning to mingle with the set, leaned on his daughter's chair. *c* **1815** JANE AUSTEN *Persuasion* II. iv. (1833) 346 They will move in the first set in Bath. **1837** HT. MARTINEAU *Soc. Amer.* III. 33 What a delightful 'set' she belonged to at her school: how comfortable they all were once, without any sets, till several grocers' daughters began to come in. **1847** TENNYSON *Princess* Prol. 8, I was there From college, visiting the son..with others of our set. **1855** THACKERAY *Newcomes* xlvi, Your intimacy was with Emma. It has cooled. Your sets are different. The Tomkins's are not *quite* &c. &c. **1890** BESANT *Demoniac* i, These men constituted the best set in the College... All were reading men, and all good men. **1906** BERNARD VAUGHAN *Sins of Society* (1908) 16 What a treacherous world was the Smart Set in which the Prodigal rioted. **1914** [see BLOOMSBURY]. **1922** M. COWLEY in *Dial* LXXIII. 231 She [*sc.* K. Mansfield] has three backgrounds only: continental hotels, New Zealand upper-class society, and a certain artistic set in London. **1938** H. NICOLSON *Diary* 19 Sept. (1966) 361 We talk of..how terrible has been the influence of the Cliveden set. **1944** N. COWARD *Middle East Diary* 49 This place is the last refuge of the soi-disant 'International Set'. **1960** J. BETJEMAN *Summoned by Bells* ix. 107, I climbed,..Until I reached what seemed to me the peak—The leisured set in Canterbury Quad. **1977** *News of World* 17 Apr. 5/5 The Prince of the Beatniks abdicated... He said goodbye to the Chelsea Set.

**b.** A meeting of a street gang or group of 'street people', esp. a party; the place where such a group meets. Also, the group itself. *U.S. colloq.* Freq. in Black English.

**1959** *Esquire* Nov. 70 *Set*, a party. **1967** *Trans-Action* Apr. 5/2 The more or less organized center of street life is the 'set' —meaning both the peer group and the places where it hangs out. **1969** R. L. KEISER *Vice Lords* iv. 40 A set had been planned... Throughout the prior week, the set was a constant topic of conversation. The clothes that were going to be worn and the girls that were going to be present were repeatedly discussed. **1970** E. BULLINS *Theme is Blackness* (1973) 178 What's happenin'? What'cha doin' tonight, baby? Why don't we make the set? **1972** J. MILLS *Report to Commissioner* 100 When junkies and pushers on a particular set learn or suspect an agent's identity, he has 'taken a burn'. **1975** *Amer. Speech 1972* XLVII. 152 Blue eyes, you are not in my set.

**4.** The number of couples required to perform a country dance or square dance.

**1766** GOLDSM. *Vic. W.* ix, We were in want of ladies to make up a set at country-dances. **1809** MALKIN *Gil Blas* x. ix. (Rtldg.) 362 The household of the governor and his lady formed a set. **1815** JANE AUSTEN *Emma* xxxviii, Emma was ..delighted to see the respectable length of the set as it was forming. *Ibid.*, Mr. Knightley leading Harriet to the set! **1837** DICKENS *Pickw.* ii, Quadrilles were being systematically got through by two or three sets of dancers. **1890** GUNTER *Miss Nobody* xviii. (1891) 209 She is at the side of the set, he at the head.

**II.** A number or collection of things.

**5. a.** A collection of instruments, tools, or machines customarily used together in a particular operation; a complete apparatus employed for some specific purpose.

For various specific applications, see quots.

[**1561**: see 6]. **1611** COTGR. s.v. *Ieu, Vn ieu de violles*, a set, or chest of violls. **1669** STURMY *Mariner's Mag.* II. ii. 53 You must have two or three Sorts and Sets of Steel Letters and Figures. **1683** MOXON *Mech. Exerc., Printing* 98 A whole Set of Punches of the same Body of Roman and Italica. **1687** MIEGE *Gt. Fr. Dict.* I. s.v. *Jeu, Un Jeu de Quilles* [Boyer: *neuf quilles pour jouer*], a Set of Pins. **1691** T. H[ALE] *Acc. New Invent.* 70 They will..provide two setts of Rudder-Irons to each Ship. **1711** ADDISON *Spect.* No. 108 ⁋4 A Set of Shuttlecocks. **1773** *Life N. Frowde* 39 A complete Sett of Mathematical Instruments. **1825** *Gentl. Mag.* XCV. I. 215 Five or six of these barbacues form a set close to the pulping-mill. **1842** *Civil Eng. & Arch. Jrnl.* V. 387/1 The 'hanging sets' or columns of pumps, with their 'ground spears' used in sinking the shafts. **1848** *Jrnl. R. Agric. Soc.* IX. II. 567 The bin-man, with his pickers, is placed to a certain number of hills, which is called a set. **1864** A. JEFFREY *Hist. Roxburghsh.* IV. 117 A sett of machines, at this time [*c* 1818], consisted of a double scribbler,..a double carder,..a 36-spindled billy,..and four 48-spindled jennies. **1879** *Man. Artill. Exerc.* 117 A set of scales, consisting of a front and rear scale. **1881** FORGAN *Golfer's Handbk.* 35 *Set*, a pack of clubs. **1884** *Mil. Engin.* I. II. 23 In laying out tools in rows the sets should be one pace apart. **1897** R. F. FOSTER *Compl. Hoyle* 563 Matadore Game... Four dominoes in the set are trumps or Matadores.

**b.** = ***pump-set, pumpset*** s.v. PUMP *sb.*[1] 6 b.

*c* **1889** W. TATE *Princ. Mining* xxi. 157 The lifting set delivers into a cistern from which the forcing set pumps the water to bank. **1950** *Water Power* II. 219 The installation comprises two vertical sets consisting of motor and pump only. **1977** *Pump Costs* (5th Techn. Conf. of Brit. Pump Manuf. Assoc.) 231 The circuits were modified to give a signal 'pump unprimed' but not to shut down the set.

**c.** A piece of electrical or electronic apparatus, as a telephone, a telegraph receiver or transmitter, a radio or television receiver, etc. Also, a radar transmitter and receiver. Cf. HANDSET.

**1891** *Man. Instruct. Army Telegr. Field Telegraphs* Plate II (*caption*) Two single current sets. **1898** *Electrician* 4 Mar. 625/2 A diminutive telephone set..is now being put on the market. **1903** *Science Siftings* XXV. 49/1 The instruments of the portable military out-fits are similar to those of the permanent station sets. **1915** A. FAGE *Aeroplane* iv. 42 A wireless set driven by a motor-cycle engine is mounted in front of the passenger's seat. **1923** *Radio Broadcast* Jan. 181/2 Drug stores, music stores, cigar stores, even men's furnishing stores have radio sets for sale. **1931** B. BROWNE *Talking Pictures* vi. 146 Wherever one looked there seemed space and wide, flat walls. One of the larger-sized sets should have been required to fill such an amount of enclosing surfaces. **1936** W. H. S. SMITH *Let.* 13 Dec. in *Young Man's Country* (1977) ii 46, I dropped in on Stansbury..to hear his wireless which is a very good set. **1948** J. L. HORNUNG *Radar Primer* v. 123 The electrical features of radar sets for use in airplanes are similar to those of sets used on ships. **1955** *Radio Times* 22 Apr. 30/1 (Advt.), Here is a..table radiogram... Fine sets these Ferguson's. **1961** L. MUMFORD *City in Hist.* xvi. 496 Reality has been progressively reduced to what filters through the screen of the television set. **1972** *Works Engineer* June 12 (*heading*) Standby electric generator sets. **1974** P. N. WILSON *Water Turbines* 17 (*caption*) Model of 83,000 HP Francis turbine hydro-electric set at Eildon Power Station, Australia. **1976** M. GILBERT *Night of Twelfth* ix. 88 He used to have that old set going all day. You'll be just in time for the six o'clock news.

**6.** †**a.** A number *of* musical instruments arranged to play together; a band; also ***set of music.*** **b.** A suite *of* bells to be rung together. **c.** A 'pair' of organs, of bagpipes: see PAIR *sb.*[1] 6.

**1561** T. HOBY tr. *Castiglione's Courtyer* II. Miv b, The musike of a sette of Violes. **1660** *Englands Joy* in Somers *Tracts* Ser. IV. II. 142 In many Places Sets of loud Musick. **1670** BAXTER *Cure Church Div.* 75 As a musical instrument in tune or a set of musick, delight the hearer by the pleasing harmony. **1679** LOVELL *Pomey's Indic. Univ.* 165 A set of Violins. **1771** SMOLLETT *Humph. Cl.* 18 July (1815) 263 A variety of tunes played upon a set of bells. **1795** *Diary* in *Antiquary* (1896) Oct. 303 Doncaster... Fine set of organs. **1893** STEVENSON *Catriona* Concl. 368 We were guided up to the garret where he lay by the sound of Highland piping. It seemed he had just borrowed a set of them from Bohaldie to amuse his sickness. **1906** RAVEN *Bells* 11 A treble in a village set of four or five.

†**7.** A 'pair' of beads. *Obs.*

**1593** SHAKS. *Rich. II*, III. iii. 147 Ile giue my Iewels for a sett of Beades. **1634** SIR T. HERBERT *Trav.* 55 Vpon the Coffin lie a set of great Beades.

**8. a.** A collection of volumes by one author, dealing with one subject, belonging to one department of literature, or issued in a series.

**1596** SHAKS. *Tam. Shr.* II. i. 107 And this small packet of Greeke and Latine bookes.. Take you the Lute, and you the set of bookes. *c* **1615** in Walcott *William of Wykeham* (1852) 166 Item, a sett of Ovids 0 5 4. **1712** HEARNE *Collect.* (O.H.S.) III. 461, I want Setts also for several others. **1726** *Advt.* in J. Ker *Mem.*, Price 10 Guineas the small, 15 Guineas the large Paper in Sheets for the whole Set. **1778** MME. D'ARBLAY *Diary* 25 July, My father told me it was a shame that I, the author, should not have even one set of my own work. **1815** SCOTT *Guy M.* xx, Commentaries,..sets of the fathers, and sermons. **1873** ALDRICH *Marj. Daw* i. 10 A complete set of Balzac's works, twenty-seven volumes. **1911** *Publisher's List*, Dickens' Works, 18 vols. Sold in Sets only, excepting the single vols. listed above.

**b.** A number of musical compositions forming a whole, as a church 'service'.

**1590** T. WATSON (*title*) The first sett, of Italian Madrigalls Englished. **1603** *Inv.* in Gage *Hengrave* (1822) 24, vj bookes covered with pchement. contg vj setts in a book, with songs of iiij, v, vj, vij and viij partes. **1788** in *Grove's Dict. Mus.* (1883) III. 476/2 A set of Quartetts. **1829** SCOTT *Anne of G.* xxx, His Highness..composed an entire set of grotesque music for the Festival of Asses. **1883** STAINER in *Grove's Dict. Mus.* III. 472 The *Gloria* has once more been included in the set... The Offertory sentences may perhaps be looked upon as a legitimate addition to the set.

**c.** A complete series of the parts of a periodical publication.

**1701** in *Lett. Lit. Men* (Camden) 302, I wish you would try ..the Philosophical Transactions, our sett reaching not far, and being imperfect in the first Volumes. **1709** STEELE *Tatler* No. 31 ⁋8 They had never heard of the Tatler 'till I brought down a Set. **1830** CARLYLE *Misc., Richter again* (1840) II. 313 He perused the antiquated sets of Newspapers. **1834** MACAULAY in Trevelyan *Life* (1876) I. 354 All the Edinburgh Reviews are being bound, so that we shall have a complete set up to the forthcoming number.

**d.** A series of prints by the same engraver.

**1768** *Boyer's Dict. Royal* II. s.v., A whole set of Prints ingraved by John Audran. **1841** BROWNING *Bells & Pomegr., Pippa Passes* 5/1 You brought those foreign prints. .. Nothing but saying His own set wants the proof-mark, roused him up. **1854** THACKERAY *Newcomes* xi, He could talk the Art-cant..and had a set of Morghens and Madonnas.

**e.** A definite number of copies of a bill of exchange or of lading: see quot. 1818.

**1818** CHITTY *Bills of Exchange* (ed. 5) 81 The several parts of a foreign bill are called a set; each part contains a condition, that it shall be paid, provided the others remain unpaid. **1865** H. PHILLIPS *Amer. Paper Curr.* II. 91 Bills of exchange were directed to be prepared in sets of four. **1883** *Law Rep. 11 Q.B. Div.* 333 The bill of lading had been drawn in a set of three copies.

**f.** A number of pieces of Jazz or popular music performed in sequence by a musician or group. Cf. sense 8 b.

**1946** B. TREADWELL *Big Bk. Swing* 125/2 *Set*, group of musical selections. **1955** S. WHITMORE *Solo* II. v. 159 Between sets at Fack's Jaeger found himself alone. **1967** *New Yorker* 21 Jan. 52, I played two sets and Marsala asked me to join the band. **1977** *Sounds* 1 Jan., We all write lyrics but they're too disgusting to be included in the set.

**9. a.** A number of things connected in temporal or spatial succession or by natural production or formation.

**1604** SHAKS. *Oth.* II. iii. 135 He'le watch the Horologe a double Set, If Drinke rocke not his Cradle. **1674** N. FAIRFAX *Bulk & Selv.* 74 The least bitling of it will so far club and fall in with the laws that bind the whole Set. **1681** H. MORE *Expos. Dan.* App. II. 278 The seven last plagues of the Vials supposing a Sett or Number of plagues antecedent. **1692** BENTLEY *Boyle Lect.* v. 32 You do not cast any given Sett of Faces with four Cubical Dice. **1759** R. SMITH *Harmonics* ix. (ed. 2) 212 The Proper Set of Beats, which the said vths ought to make in the given organ. **1815** SCOTT *Guy M.* xxxviii, A new set of words to the old tune of 'Over the Water to Charlie'. **1841** T. R. JONES *Anim. Kingd.* 574 An elaborate temporary set of muscles provided for the purpose. **1893** SIR H. HOWORTH *Glacial Nightmare* I. 31 A set of low hills also intervene.

**b.** The complement *of* teeth (natural or artificial) with which a person (or animal) is furnished.

**1678** J. BROWN *Disc. Wounds* 236 The Tongue being thus guarded with a Sett of Teeth. **1700** T. BROWN tr. *Fresny's Amusem.* 97 Other knaves..take as much for Drawing out an Old Tooth, as would buy a Sett of New ones. **1705** VANBRUGH *Confederacy* I. i, I have worn out four pair of pattens with following my old lady Youthful, for one set of false teeth, and but three pots of paint. **1854** THACKERAY *Newcomes* xxiv, Her ladyship's teeth (a new and exceedingly handsome set). **1878** L. P. MEREDITH *Teeth* 250 With mouths so unfavourable that it is impossible to adapt a set of teeth to them. **1886** C. SCOTT *Sheep-farming* 15 Each set when complete consists of incisor, canine, and molar teeth.

†**c.** ***set of features***: the lineaments of a person's face. *Obs.*

**1713** ADDISON *Cato* I. iv, 'Tis not a sett of features, or complexion..that I admire. **1779** G. KEATE *Sketches fr. Nat.* (ed. 2) I. 59 That air of sensibility..accompanied with a pleasing set of features. **1815** SCOTT *Guy M.* ii, He had a tall, handsome figure, a good set of features.

**d.** A spell (of weather); = SERIES 3 b. *Obs.* exc. *dial.* (but cf. *set in*, SET *v.*[1] 146 e.)

**1633** T. JAMES *Voy.* 104 Wee must haue a set of faire weather, to passe the Straight. *a* **1700** EVELYN *Diary* 3 Sept. 1666, With a long set of faire and warme weather. **1880** *Antrim & Down Gloss.* s.v., A long set of saft weather.

**10. a.** A number of things grouped together according to a system of classification or conceived as forming a whole.

**1690** LOCKE *Hum. Und.* II. i. §4 Which Operations..do furnish the Understanding with another sett of Ideas. **1701** SWIFT *Contests Nobles & Comm.* Wks. 1755 II. I. 50 He assumes..an entire sett of very different airs. **1730** MALCOLM *New Syst. Arith.* 509 Conceive two or more different Setts (or Systems) of Things, containing each the same, or a different number of Things. **1738** SWIFT *Pol. Conversat.* Introd. 23 My old Friend did..invent a Set of Words and Phrases. **1742** YOUNG *Nt. Th.* VIII. 387 Virtue has her peculiar set of pains. **1774** GOLDSM. *Nat. Hist.* (1776) VII. 240 An exact plan..of Nature's operations in this minute set of creatures. **1802** MAR. EDGEWORTH *Moral T.* (1816) I. xiv. 110 The set of notions which he had acquired from his education. **1837** CARLYLE *Fr. Rev.* I. vi.

i, The Constitution, the set of Laws,..that men will live under. 1857 CAYLEY *Math. Papers* (1890) III. 35 Let *L* denote a set of any four elements, *a, b, c, d*. 1897 W. P. KER *Epic & Rom.* II. vi. 201 The poet is at this point free to make use of a new set of motives.

†**b.** *Math.* Used variously, as defined by the individual author. *Obs.*

1837 W. R. HAMILTON in *Trans. R. Irish Acad.* (Sci.) XVII. 422 The author hopes to publish hereafter..a Theory of Triplets and Sets of Moments. 1848 —— in *Ibid.* XXI. 201 When we have in any manner been led to form successively the separate conceptions of any number of moments of time, we may afterwards form the *new* conception of a system, or momental set, to which all these separate moments belong. 1886 *Phil. Trans. R. Soc.* CLXXVII. 23 If the collection be such that whatever undistinguished components *abcd*..., *pqrs*... we select, and whatever other component *lmno*... we select, *w, x, y, z*... can always be selected from the collection, then the collection will be termed a set.

**c.** *Math.* and *Logic.* An assemblage of distinct entities, either individually specified or which satisfy certain specified conditions. Cf. ELEMENT *sb.* 5 d.

1857 *Phil. Trans. R. Soc.* CXLVII. 717 Any values ($x_1, y_1, z_1, \ldots$) satisfying the equations, are said to constitute a set of roots of the system. 1897 W. BURNSIDE *Theory of Groups* i. 1 Let $a_1, a_2, \ldots, a_n$ be a set of *n* distinct letters. 1903 *Trans. Amer. Math. Soc.* IV. 27 A set of elements in which a rule of combination O is so defined as to satisfy the following three postulates shall be called an Abelian group with respect to O. 1937 *Jrnl. Symbolic Logic* II. 66 According to the leading idea of the von Neumann set theory we have to deal with two kinds of individuals, which we may distinguish as sets and classes. The distinction may be thought of in this way, that a set is a multitude forming a proper thing, whereas a class is a predicate regarded only with respect to its extension. 1965 PATTERSON & RUTHERFORD *Elem. Abstr. Algebra* i. 3 If *x* is an element of a set *S*, we write $x \in S$. 1972 A. G. HOWSON *Handbk. Terms Algebra & Anal.* ii. 8 A set is a totality of certain definite, distinguishable objects of our intuition or thought—called the elements of the set. This classic definition of a set was given by Georg Cantor in 1874. Such attempts to give elementary definitions of a set are, however, doomed to failure, their being in the main based on the use of undefined synonyms, such as 'collection', and leading to logical inconsistencies (see *Russell paradox*..). For this reason, mathematicians now regard the notion of a set as an undefined, primitive concept. 1975 I. STEWART *Concepts Mod. Math.* iv. 47 There is only one empty set. All empty sets are equal.

**d.** *transf.* Used variously in *Linguistics* (see quots.).

1935 W. F. TWADDELL *On Defining Phoneme* 60 A modification occurs only in phonetic fractions corresponding to forms, the relations of which constitute relations of sets of micro-phonemes. 1942 BLOCH & TRAGER *Outl. Linguistic Anal.* iii. 45 A structural set is a group of all the phonemes which occur in a given phonetic environment and hence, in that position, directly contrast with each other. 1964 M. A. K. HALLIDAY et al. *Linguistic Sci.* ii. 22 The range of possibilities in a closed choice is called technically a system, that in an open choice a set... We often talk of 'closed system' and 'open set'.

**11.** The complete collection of the 'pieces' composing a suite of furniture, a service of china, a clothing outfit, or the like.

1687 A. LOVELL tr. *Thevenot's Trav.* I. 160 All these Pavillions are..lined within with sets of lovely Tapistry. 1687 MIEGE *Gt. Fr. Dict.* II. s.v., A fine Set of Silver Plate. 1696 *Lond. Gaz.* No. 3158/4 Fine Sets for Dressing Tables. 1697 tr. *C'tess D'Aunoy's Trav.* (1706) 140 Neither is it enough to have one Sett of Jewels, as our Ladies in France have. 1727 BOYER *Dict. Royal* II, A Set of Diamonds... A Set of Buttons. 1779 *Mirror* No. 40 The fall of a set of Dresden. 1798 in Nicolas *Disp.* (1846) VII. p. clx, I had every man..at work to alter some of her own sails, and some we got from the Serieuse to make up a set for her. 1848 THACKERAY *Van. Fair* xxix, A set of Irish diamonds and cairngorms. 1859 *Habits of Gd. Society* iv. 163 Her set of winter sables. 1867 LATHAM *Black & White* 74 The door-keeper wears a set of shooting dittos.

**12. a.** A series of buildings or apartments associated in use; *esp.* a suite of apartments let as lodgings.

1722 DE FOE *Col. Jack* (1840) 136 He led me into a..set of warehouses. 1820 *Gentl. Mag.* Jan. 79/1 A single room out of the sixteen sets composing that part of the Hall [i.e. Magdalen Hall]. 1833 HT. MARTINEAU *Brooke Farm* iv. 53 His one set of farm buildings. 1840 J. T. J. HEWLETT *P. Priggins* xiv, The Dean's scout was summoned to..show me the rooms..that I might select any set I chose. 1841 THACKERAY *Gt. Hoggarty Diam.* ix, First we went into lodgings,—into three sets in three weeks. a1890 LIDDON *Life Pusey* (1893) I. iv. 89 At Lent term, 1826, Pusey went into rooms in Oriel College. The set he occupied [etc.].

**b.** *Mining.* In full *set of timber(s*: A frame for supporting the side of a level or shaft, or the roof of a gallery.

1830 *Eng. & For. Mining Gloss., Cornw.* (1860) 22 *Set of timber*, a frame complete to support each side of the vein, level, or shaft. 1877 RAYMOND *Statist. Mines & Mining* 263 *note*, The 'set of timbers' may perhaps be fairly assumed to represent 50 cubic yards of material removed. *Ibid.* 276 Replacing the old timbers with new square sets.

**13. a.** A team of (usually six) horses.

1687 MIEGE *Gt. Fr. Dict.* I, *Attelage*, a Set of Horses for a Coach or Cart, or of Oxen for a Cart or plough, four of each. 1701 W. WOTTON *Hist. Rome* 402 He would give Sets of Chariot-Horses. 1748 RICHARDSON *Clarissa* (1768) V. 275 To wait upon my Beloved with a coach-and-four, or a Sett. c1789 GIBBON *Autob.* (1896) 162 The favourite team, an handsome set of bays or greys. 1825 T. HOOK *Sayings* Ser. II. *Man of many Fr.* I. 153 A set of horses for town.

**b.** A train of coal-trucks.

1863 R. SCOTT *Ventil. Mines* 10 [The doors] are at a sufficient distance from each other, so as to admit the set to pass through the one before the other is required to be opened. 1871 *Daily News* 17 Aug., When the sets had arrived at 'meetings', instead of passing each other, they ran on to the same line.

**14.** The series of movements or figures that make up a square dance or country dance, *esp.* the quadrille; the music adapted to this. ***first set***: see quots. 1894, 1898. (Cf. *set dance*, s.v. SET *ppl. a.* 8.) ***running set***: see RUNNING *ppl. a.* 17 f.

1834 DICKENS *Sk. Boz, Tales* vii, He attached himself solely to Miss Julia Briggs, with whom he danced no less than three sets consecutively. 1849 CUPPLES *Green Hand* iii. (1856) 29 They were soon swimming away in the first set. 1865 DICKENS *Mut. Fr.* I. xi, The discreet automaton [at the piano]..played a..tuneless set. 1894 E. SCOTT *Dancing* 119 The Quadrille. (Generally known as the First Set.) 1898 tr. *Vuillier's Hist. Dancing* 431 The 'First Set' came over from Paris,..and was introduced..as the 'Parisian Quadrille'.

**III. 15.** Special Comb.: **set theory**, the branch of mathematics which deals with sets without regard to the nature of their individual constituents; an axiomatization which allows of the discussion of sets; **set-theoretic, -theoretical** *adjs.*, of or pertaining to set theory; hence **set-theoretically** *adv.*

1964 E. MENDELSON *Introd. Math. Logic* p. vii, In the belief that beginners should be exposed to the most natural and easiest proofs, free-swinging set-theoretic methods have been used. 1957 P. SUPPES *Introd. Logic* xi. 232 A function is a set-theoretical, not a linguistic, entity. 1952 S. C. KLEENE *Introd. Metamath.* xiv. 424 B is a 'theorem' set-theoretically. 1936 W. V. QUINE in *Jrnl. Symbolic Logic* June 45 Set-theoretic Foundations for Logic... In his set theory Zermelo uses the variables 'x', 'y', etc. for the representation of 'things' generally. 1937 *Jrnl. Symbolic Logic* II. 65 The system of axioms for set theory to be exhibited in this paper is a modification of the axiom system due to von Neumann. 1971 *Where* Nov. 332/1 Many would probably 'solve' it by using set theory and drawing a Venn diagram. 1975 N. CHOMSKY *Logical Struct. Linguistic Theory* iii. 107 We will assume..that each level includes a full set theory, so that we can also form sets of strings, sequences of strings, etc.

**set** (sɛt), *v.*[1] Forms: see below. Pa. t. and pa. pple. set. [Com. Teut.: OE. *settan* = OFris. *setta* (mod.Fris. *sette*), OS. *settian* (MDu., MLG. *setten*, Du. *zetten*), OHG. *sezzan* beside *sazzan* (MHG. *sezzen*, G. *setzen*), ON. *setja* (Sw. *satta*, Da. *sætte*), Goth. *satjan*; causal of **setjan* (*sitjan*) to SIT.

Confusion between *set* and *sit* arose as early as the beginning of the 14th c., owing partly to the identity or close similarity of the forms of their past tenses and pa. pples., and partly to the identity of meaning in some uses, as between *to be set* (= seated) and *to sit*; cf. SIT *v.* (etym. note and A. 5 *a* note). For cases of mere substitution of forms of *sit* for forms of *set*, see A. 1 γ, 2 ζ below. The spelling *sett* is still sometimes found in technical senses; cf. SET *sb.*[1]]

A. Inflexional Forms.

**1. a.** *Infinitive* and *Present stem.* α1 settan (*Northumb.* setta), 2–5 (6 *arch.*) setten, 3–6 sette (2 setton, seotte, 3 *Orm.* settenn, *Lay.* sætten, 4 *Kent.* zetten, 5 settyn, cettyn, satte, 6 seatt-), 4–9 sett, 7–9 *s.w. dial.* zet, 4– set.

c725 *Corpus Gloss.* (Hessels) P 13 *Pastinare*, settan. a900 *Laws Ælfred* II. v. (Liebermann) 50 We settað æghwelcere cirican..ðis frið. c950 *Lindisf. Gosp.* Matt. xviii. 23 Seðe wil reht setta mið ðegnum his. c1000 *Ags. Ps.* (Th.) c. 3 Ne sette ic me fore eagum yfele wisan. a1122 *O.E. Chron.* (Laud MS.) an. 656, þæt hi scoldon..seotte þa dæi hwonne [etc.]. c1200 ORMIN 3941 Soþ sahhtnesse settenn. c1205 LAY. 17569 Heo wolden al þis lond sætten on hæore tweire hond. a1300 *Cursor M.* 12416 To sett iesu to werld lar. a1340 HAMPOLE *Psalter* ii. 10 Settand vndire ȝoure fote ȝoure enmys. 1362 LANGL. *P. Pl.* A. VI. 32 Boþe to sowen and to setten. c1380 *Sir Ferumb.* 1872 Y set noȝt by þy sawes. c1400 *Pilgr. Sowle* (Caxton) II. xlv. (1859) 51 Prowde men ..that settyn att nought al other men. c1420 *Chron. Vilod.* 1761 How lytull his martrus setton by worldelyche gode. 1499 *Promp. Parv.* 67/2 Cettyn or putten. a1533 LD. BERNERS *Huon* iii. 5 Huon and gerarde who by theyr pryde settyth no thynge by me. 1538 in *Lett. Suppress. Monasteries* (Camden) 199 Setteynge many on worke. 1552 *Bk. Com. Prayer* Exhort. Morn. Pr., To sette foorth his moste worthye prayse. 1584 *Eltham Churchw. Acc.* in *Archæologia* XXXIV. 63 For seatting fourthe of a soldger into Frawnce. 1590 SPENSER *F.Q.* I. iv. 14 Themselues to setten forth to straungers sight. 1605 *Lond. Prodigall* v. i. 470 Che zet not a vig by a wife if a wife zet not a vig by me. 1613 E. WRIGHT *Descr. & Use Sphære* 61 Such starres as sett when the sunne riseth, are said to set cosmically. 1711 in *10th Rep. Hist. MSS. Comm.* App. v. 176, I sett again the quære, how can the Irish..be..deemed rebels? 1801 NELSON *Let.* 28 Jan. in *Quaritch's Catal.* Oct. (1909) 28 To sett in a dark room. 1904 *Blackw. Mag.* Feb. 193/2 Unless you have..seen him ..'sett' the game he fetches.

β. *north.* 3–4 seit(t, 4–5 sete. (Cf. 2 δ, 3 η.)

a1300 *Cursor M.* 1177, I sal seit on þi mi merk. *Ibid.* 6060 To seitt him soru at his hert. c1375 *Sc. Leg. Saints* l. (*Katerine*) 27 Quhar all þe folk..he mycht seit opynly and see. 1455 *Test. Ebor.* (Surtees) II. 215, I sete vij marcs to a preste to syng a yere for me.

γ. 4 sitt, syte, 5 sitte, 6–7 sit. (Cf. 2 ζ.)

13.. *Cursor M.* 1580 (Gött.) þe schame, þe sin,.. To tell war lang to sitt aboute [*Fairf.* syte]. c1420 *Sir Amadace* (Camden) xxxiv, Men sittus ryȝte noȝte him bye. 14.. *Sailing Directions* (Hakl. Soc. 1889) 18 Be ware of your stremes of flode for they sitten north est on the Iron groundes. 1567 *Gude & Godlie B.* (S.T.S.) 57 Sittand thair strenth thy word againe. 1601 SHAKS. *Twel. N.* I. iii. 145 Shall we sit about some Reuels? 1683 *Col. Rec. Pennsylv.* I. 82 For sitting up of Bouyes in the River and Bay.

**b.** *Pres. Ind. 2nd person sing.* 1– settest, 4–5 settist, 5 -yst, 6–7 setst, settst; *north.* 1 settes, 1, 5–6 settis.

c825 *Vesp. Ps.* xx. 4 Ðu settes heafde his beȝ of stane deorwyrðum. c950 *Lindisf. Gosp.* John xiii. 38 Saul ðin fore mec ðu settis [*Rushw.* setes]. c1000 *Ags. Ps.* (Th.) lxxiii. 16 þu dæȝ settest. c1400 *Melayne* 988 Thou settis more by a littill golde,..þan to fighte one goddes foo. 1411 in *26 Pol. Poems* 43 þou settest at nouȝt, y bouȝt so dere. c1460 *Wisdom* 927 in *Macro Plays* 66 Why werkyst þou hys consell? by myn settis lyght? c1460 RUSSELL *Bk. Nurture* 69 in *Babees Bk.*, When þow settyst a pipe abroche. 1535 COVERDALE *Job* vii. 17 What is man that thou..settest so moch by him? 1558 PHAER *Æneid* I. C j b, My son, that of the thonderblastes of hye Ioue settst but light. 1562 J. HEYWOOD *Prov. & Epigr.* (1867) 134 Shall I set at my hart, that thou settst at thy heele. 1611 BIBLE *Deut.* xxiii. 20 In all that thou settest thine hand to. 1682 DRYDEN *Mac-Fl.* 199 With whate'er gall thou settst thy self to write.

**c.** *Pres. Ind. 3rd person sing.* α1–4 setteþ, (*Anglian* seteþ), 3 -eþþ, 4 zetteþ, 5–6 settyth, -ith, 5 -eth.

c825 *Vesp. Psalter* ciii. 3 Se seteð wolcen upstiȝe his. c975 *Rushw. Gosp.* Matt. xxiv. 51 Dæl his [he] seteþ mið liceterum. c1000 *Ags. Ps.* (Th.) lxxxiv. 12 And on weȝ setteð wise gangas. c1200 ORMIN 7821 Drihhtin setteþþ i þin þohht God dede to biginnenn. 1340 *Ayenb.* 6 Huo þet ine þise þinges ageltep zetteþ zuo moche hire herte..[etc.]. c1450 *Mirk's Festial* 283 Ȝe settyth noght by no worldely worschyp. 1551 ROBINSON tr. *More's Utopia* II. (1895) 149 He settethe nothynge by yt. 1637 RUTHERFORD *Lett.* (1664) 169 Let Christ (as it setteth him well) have all the glory.

β. 1–5 set(t, (2 sæt, 4 *Kent.* zet).

c888 ÆLFRED *Boeth.* xxxv. §4 þæt hehste god, ðæt..hit eall set. a1122 *O.E. Chron.* (Laud MS.) an. 963, Nan man buton se abbot ane, & þam þe he þærto sæt. c1200 *Trin. Coll. Hom.* 179 Gief he him set a speche. 1340 *Ayenb.* 7 Ine þe stede of þe sabat..zet holi cherche þane sonday to loky. c1400 *Rom. Rose* 4925 Youthe sett man in all folye. 1422 YONGE tr. *Secreta Secret.* xxxvi. 191 Man be-hettith woman loue when he Set the Ring on hir fyngar.

γ. 1 (*Northumb.*), 5 settes, 4 settus, 4–6 *north.* settis, -ys, (5 setis, sattys), 6– sets (setts).

c950 *Lindisf. Gosp.* Matt. xxiv. 51 Dal his [he] settes mið leȝerum. 1340–70 *Alex. & Dind.* 182 þe..king..þere-on settus his sel. a1400–50 *Wars Alex.* 1221 Sampson on anothire side setis out belyue. 14.. *Erthe upon Erthe* (1911) 32/4 How erthe vpon erthe sattys all at noght. c1450 *St. Cuthbert* (Surtees) 579 He saies he settes here þat he fande. a1586 SIDNEY *Ps.* CIII. ii, He setts thee free. 1601 SHAKS. *Twel. N.* III. iv. 79 And consequently setts downe the manner how. 1607 —— *Cor.* III. i. 270 Which he so sets at naught. 1807 A. YOUNG *Agric. Essex* II. 334 At this Michælmas (1805) he *setts* 2000.

**d.** *Imperative.* 1–5 sete (1 *Northumb.* sett), 3–6 sette, 4 zete, 4–6 sett, 4– set; *pl.* 1 settaþ, 3–4 setteþ, 4–5 settith, *north.* settis.

c950 *Lindisf. Gosp.* Matt. ix. 18 On sett hond ofer hia [*Rushw.* ȝesette]. 971 *Blickl. Hom.* 87 Sete nu þin wuldres tacn in helle. c1000 ÆLFRIC *Hom.* II. 542 Settað eornostlice on eowerum heortum þæt [etc.]. c1205 LAY. 27216 Setteð heom after. *Ibid.* 3699 þu..irum al þat lond and sete hit Cordoille an hond. 1340 *Ayenb.* 254 Zete ane brydel to þine couaytises. 1374 CHAUCER *Troilus* IV. 622 But manly set þe world on sixe and seuene. 1375 BARBOUR *Bruce* XI. 563 Beis nocht abasit..Bot settis speris ȝow befor. 1410 in *26 Pol. Poems* 37 Among seyntes þy soule sete. c1449 PECOCK *Repr.* II. xviii. 257 Sette thou me bisidis thee. c1450 *Mirk's Festial* 139 Castys don þes mawmetys..and settyþe þer a cros. 1482 *Monk of Evesham* (Arb.) 27 Settith before vs the bred. 1535 COVERDALE *Col.* iii. 2 Set youre mynde on the thinges which are aboue.

**2.** *Past Tense.* α1–6 sette (1–3 sætte, 3 seate), 3–5 sete, (4 zette), 4–7 sett, 4– set.

*Beowulf* 325 Setton sæmeþe side scyldas..wið þæs recedes wæl. c975 *Rushw. Gosp.* John xx. 15 Sæȝe hræðe me hwer ðu settes hine. c1000 *Guthlac* 405 (Gr.) Guðlac sette hyht in heofonas. a1122 *O.E. Chron.* (Laud MS.) an. 1066, He sætte mycel deorfrið. c1160 *Hatton Gosp.* Luke xix. 21 þu nymst þæt þu ne settst. a1175 *Cott. Hom.* 221 God him sette nama adam. a1300 *Cursor M.* 4175 Siþen þai settam [= sett þam] dun and ete. c1330 R. BRUNNE *Chron.* (Rolls) 2086 Gwyndolene a child had þan,..When tyme was, [she] set hit to boke. c1380 WYCLIF *Sel. Wks.* III. 208 Wher-to, my modir, settist þou me on þi knees,..and rokkid me, and fed me? c1386 CHAUCER *Prol.* 507 He sette nat his benefice to hyre. 1558 G. CAVENDISH *Poems* (1825) II. 14 Thou didest me avaunce, And settest me uppe in thys great pompe and pryde. 1579 GOSSON *Sch. Abuse* (Arb.) 65 The same proposition..which I sette downe before. c1610 *Women Saints* 35 Some she sett out of prison. a1700 EVELYN *Diary* 21 May 1685, The jeweller and goldsmith who sett them.

β. 5–9 sat, sate.

Frequent in inferior writers of the second half of the 18th c., esp. in intr. senses.

c1420 *Master of Oxf. Catech.* in *Rel. Ant.* I. 231 C[*lerk*] Who sat first vines? *M*[*aister*] Noe set the first vines. 1430–40 LYDG. *Bochas* VIII. xv. (1558) 10 Theodose..Smote of his heed, and sate [*edd.* 1494, 1554 set] it on the gate. a1547 in Fosbrooke *Econ. Mon. Life* (1796) 84 She sate forward aft[er] masse. 1561 NUCE tr. *Seneca's Octavia* (1581) III. iii, That..rage..Sate them agog. 1677 W. HUBBARD *Narrative* II. 66 We sate Sayle. 1716 B. CHURCH *Hist. Philip's War* (1865) I. 119 The fore-most sat down his load and halted. 1742–3 *Observ. Methodists* 19 The Lord sat his Banner over us. 1755 J. SHEBBEARE *Lydia* (1769) II. 74 Like Yorick, he often sat the table on a roar. 1756 TOLDERVY *Hist. 2 Orphans* I. 109 The coach being ready, the ladies.. sate out for the hall. 1790 CATH. GRAHAM *Lett. Educ.* 318 The example which the king and his courtiers sat. 1808 HELEN ST. VICTOR *Ruins of Rigonda* I. 186 He then sat before them some dried fruits. 1824 ELLIS *Orig. Lett.* Ser. I. III. 137 *note*, The Prince and Marquis..sate out with the names of Thomas and John Smith.

γ. *dial.* 8–9 sot, *s.w.* zot.

1776 T. HUTCHINSON *Diary* 5 June (1886) II. 67, I sot out from Falmouth this morning. 1803 MARY CHARLTON *Wife & Mistress* II. 51 Dolly informed her that she was to depart the next day..because, as the caravan *sot off* by five in the morning, they should not catch her travelling before day-light. **1840** SPURDENS *Voc. E. Angl.* s.v. *Sot*, I sot it down. **1857** KINGSLEY *Two Y. Ago* III. 161 If ever he sot a foot here! **1886** *W. Somerset Word-bk.* s.v., Zot his back up purty well.

δ. *north.* [1 *pl.* seton], 4 seit, sete, 5, 8–9 seet(e.

[*c* **950** *Lindisf. Gosp.* Mark xv. 19 Seton cnewa.] *a* **1300** *Cursor M.* 2442 Þar he seit first his auter stan. **1375** BARBOUR *Bruce* III. 394 And certane tyme till him he sete [*rime* meite]. *a* **1400–50** *Wars Alex.* 4654 For many seerties we seet þat sysed all þe werde. *c* **1746** J. COLLIER (Tim Bobbin) *View Lanc. Dial.* vi. (1828) 68 Then they aw seete ogen meh.

ε. 4 settede, 4–5 -ide, 5 -id, -yd, 5–6 -ed, 6 *Sc.* -it, 9 *s.w. dial.* zetted.

Frequent in Caxton.

**1382** WYCLIF *Isa.* liii. 3 Wherfore ne wee setteden by hym. *c* **1449** PECOCK *Repr.* v. ix. 530 Crist..settid the lawe of hise sacramentis to the seid lawe of kinde. *c* **1489** CAXTON *Sonnes of Aymon* ix. 245 Reynawde setted noughte by his lyffe. *c* **1520** NISBET *N.T.* Matt. iv. 5 The feend..settit him on the pynacile of the tempile. **1582** BENTLEY *Mon. Matrones* iii. 330 O heauenlie King, who..settedst me in the regall throne. **1888** *Berks. Gloss.* 12, I zetted.

ζ. 4 sitt. (Cf. 1 γ)

*a* **1300** *Cursor M.* 5058 And þan on bink he sitt him bi [*other MSS.* set, sete, sett].

**3.** *Past Participle.* α 1 ᵹeset(t, -sæt, 2–4 iset, (2–3 *infl.* isette, 3 *Lay.* isæt, hi(i)-sette, 4 ysett, *Kent.* y-, izet), 3–4 (6–7 *arch.*) yset, 4–5 ysett(e, isett(e, 5 i-sete.

*c* **888** ÆLFRED *Boeth.* xi. §2 Þa ᵹesælða þe ᵹe oninnan iow habbað..ᵹeset. *c* **1050** *Ags. Hom.* (Assmann) 183 Hys flæsc wearð eall ᵹesett. *c* **1175** *Lamb. Hom.* 11 Þas daᵹes beoð iset us to muchele helpe. *a* **1225** *Ancr. R.* 416 Þeos riche ancren þet..habbeð rentes i-sette. *c* **1330** *Arth. & Merl.* 9 Childer, þat ben to boke ysett. **1340** *Ayenb.* 167 Erþan hi by yzet ope þet bord. *a* **1440** *Sir Degrev.* 1373 Swythe chayres was i-sete And quyschonis of vyolete. *c* **1450** *Godstow Reg.* 491/11 In tymys I-sette. **1483** CAXTON *G. de la Tour* Prol. 1 My seruice well ysette and quitte. **1596** SPENSER *F.Q.* IV. iii. 24 The stone therein yset. **1610** HOLLAND *Camden's Brit.* I. 387 With words in forme yset.

β. 1–9 sett, 2–3 (*infl.*), 4–6 sette, (5 cette), 3– set, (9 *s.w. dial.* zet).

*c* **1000** *Ags. Ps.* (Th.) cxliii. 14 Settum beamum. **1128** *O.E. Chron.* (Laud MS.), Fulle feoht was sett betwenen ða Cristene & þa heðene. *c* **1200** ORMIN Ded. 101 Wiþþ all swillc rime alls her iss sett. *a* **1300** *Havelok* 2612 Þe helmes heye on heued sette. **1303** R. BRUNNE *Handl. Synne* 189 She shal noght to any be sette Withoutyn leue of my maumette. *c* **1340** *Nominale* (Skeat) 850 Henne is set. *a* **1400–50** *Wars Alex.* 179 Sen it is sett to be soo. *c* **1440** *Promp. Parv.* 67/2 Cette, or putt. **1477** EARL RIVERS (Caxton) *Dictes* 67, I haue not sette by golde ne siluer. **1607** *Stat.* in *Hist. Wakefield Gram. Sch.* (1892) 59 All partialitie sett apart. **1719** in Picton *L'pool Munic. Rec.* (1886) II. 62 To be sett out so as not to p'judice the highway. **1746** *Exmoor Scolding* (E.D.S.) l. 228 When tha art zet agog. **1757** R. ROBERTSON *Let.* in J. Russell *Haigs* (1881) 359 All your neighbours are sett to be upon you. *c* **1850** *Rudim. Navig.* (Weale) 140 To make a sett near to another that cannot be sett on any more.

γ. 1 *Anglian* ᵹeset(t)ed, -et, 5 settyt, 6 -it, 9 *dial.* zetted.

*c* **825** *Vesp. Ps.* ii. 6 Ic soðlice ᵹeseted ic eam cyning. *c* **900** *Bæda's Hist.* III. xviii. §1 Þa wilnade he liif onhyrᵹan, þe he wel ᵹeseted ᵹeseah in Gallia rice. *c* **950** *Lindisf. Gosp.* Mark iv. 21 Ðesetted bið, *ponatur*. *c* **1520** NISBET *N.T.* Luke xix. 21 Thou takis away that that thou has nocht settit. *a* **1532** DU WES *Introd. Fr.* in *Palsgr.* 1055 The soule vegetable..is setted within the myght elemented. **1888** *Berks. Gloss.* 12 Zetted.

δ. 1 *Northumb.* ᵹesatted, 3 isat, 5 sat(t)e, 6–7 sat.

*c* **950** *Lindisf. Gosp.* John xx. 6 Ða linne hræᵹlo ᵹesattedo *vel* asetedo, *linteamina posita*. *c* **1205** LAY. 30229 Þe dæi wes isat. **14..** *Three Chron.* (Camden) 77 Sir Baudwyns hede caryed to Excester and sate upon the castell yate. **14..** *Tundale's Vis.* (Wagner) 2031 A crowne..satte aboute.. Wyth precious stones. **1594** R. ASHLEY tr. *Loys le Roy* 47 b, To be sat at their ease. *a* **1695** WOOD *Life* an. 1683 (1772) II. 324 In the Pump below the Star Inn was a Tub sat.

ε. *dial.* 9 a-sot, sot, zot (see *Eng. Dial. Dict.*).

**1836** HALIBURTON *Clockm.* xxi. (1839) 76 To get it sot to rights. **1888** *W. Somerset Word-bk.* s.v. *Set up*, He's a quiet sort of a man like till he's a zot up.

ζ. Chiefly *north.* 1 ᵹeseten, 5 settyn, 6 settin, 5, 9 setten.

*c* **950** *Lindisf. Gosp.* Luke Pref. 9 Ðeseteno mið bisene, *positaque similitudine*. **1484** CAXTON *Fables of Æsop* I. xvi, Of euery one I am setten aback. ? **1567** *Decl. Lordis just quarrell* 91 in *Satir. Poems Reform.* l. 60 Quhen faceles fuillis sall not be settin by. **1887** *Jamieson's Sc. Dict. Suppl.*, *Setten*... This old part. form is still used by the common people. **1889** *N.W. Linc. Gloss.*, *Setten up*.

η. *north.* 4 seeit, 4–5 seit, 5 seete, seyt, 5, 9 seet, 4–6 sete.

*a* **1300** *Cursor M.* 1166 Mi sin me has seit in vnsell. *Ibid.* 20179 Has he sete me ani dai? *c* **1380** WYCLIF *Wks.* (1880) 74 Goddis curs is seit at nouȝt. *Ibid.* 174 Here herte is seeit to loue his muk. *c* **1380** —— *Sel. Wks.* III. 451 Holy Chirche is seet in virtues and good lif. *c* **1420** *Sir Amadas* (Weber) 370 Full mykyll seyt by. *c* **1449** PECOCK *Repr.* Prol. 3 Thei hem silf..ben despisid and ben not seet bi. **1488** *Registr. Aberdon.* (Maitl. Club) I. 320 The said reuerend fadir..has seit and to male lattin..þe saidis landis. **1584** *Shuttleworth's Acc.* (Chetham Soc.) 21 Payed for a horce showe wᶜʰ was sete on in Chorlaye iijˢ.

**B.** Signification.

*General arrangement of senses.* I. To cause to sit, seat; to be seated, sit. II. To sink, descend. III. To put in a definite place (the manner of the action being implied either in the verb itself or in the context). IV. To place or cause to be in a position, condition, relation, or connexion. (This group embraces a large number of uses in which the precise implication of sense depends mainly on the kind of construction employed.) V. To appoint, prescribe, ordain, establish. VI. To arrange, fix, adjust. VII. To place mentally, suppose, estimate. VIII. To put or come into a settled position or condition. IX. To put in the way of following a course, cause to take a certain direction. X. Senses perhaps arising from reversal of construction or from ellipsis (their origin being often obscure). XI. With prepositions in specialized senses. XII. With adverbs in specialized senses. (Combinations formed on the verb-stem are given in a separate article, SET-.) ☛ A phrase key is given at the end of the article.

**I.** To cause to sit, seat; to be seated, sit.

The intransitive sense 'to sit' (5) was apparently developed out of the reflexive and passive uses of the original transitive sense of 'to seat'. *Set*, being thus used synonymously with *sit*, became capable of taking its other senses and constructions (see 5 d, e, 6, 7).

**1. a.** *trans.* To place in a sitting posture; to cause to occupy a seat; to seat.

This sense is barely exemplified outside certain phraseological expressions, e.g. *to set on a seat, a throne, on horseback*, etc., in which the sense 'cause to sit' is now lost sight of. (Prov. *to set a beggar on horseback*: to give an undeserving person an advantage which he will misuse.)

*c* **888** K. ÆLFRED *Boeth.* viii. §5 Þu settest us on þæt setl ðines sceoppendes. **1130** *O.E. Chron.* (Laud MS.), Þa munecas..setten him on þes abbotes settle. *c* **1205** LAY. 14074 Þe king..sætte hine bi him seoluen. **1300–1400** *R. Gloucester's Chron.* (Rolls) App. xx. 446 To king he was iblessed..& iset in trone. **1377** LANGL. *P. Pl.* B. XII. 198 Riȝt as sum man ȝeue me mete and sette me amydde þe flore. **1470–85** MALORY *Arthur* III. ii. 101 The Bisshop of Caunterbury..sette the viij and xx knyghtes in her syeges. *c* **1485** in *Rutland Papers* (Camden) 19 The King..shalbe sett a gayn in his chair befor the high aulter. **1530** PALSGR. 712/1 Come hyther, Kate, and I wyll set the on my lappe, and daunce the. *Ibid.* 713/1 In the stede of a good man we set a shrewe upon the benche. **1607** TOURNEUR *Rev. Trag.* I. (1608) B 2, *Dut.* Nay set you a horse back once, Youle nere light off. *Spu.* Indeed I am a beggar. **1621** BURTON *Anat. Mel.* II. iii. II. 395 Set a beggar on horseback, and he will ride a gallop. **1660** INGELO *Bentiv. & Ur.* I. (1682) 158 Having set the two Ladies..upon two green Seats. **1692** R. L'ESTRANGE *Fables* lxx. 69 They..Set Boys upon the Back on't [a camel]. **1735** JOHNSON *Lobo's Abyssinia*, Descr. xiv. 132 Who setting us upon Camels, conducted us to Mazna.

†**b.** To cause (a body of persons) to sit in deliberation. *Obs.* (Cf. 4 c.)

*a* **1122** *O.E. Chron.* (Laud MS.) an. 675, Ða heot seo kining þone ærcebiscop Theodorus þæt he scolde setton ealle ᵹewitenemot æt þone stede þæt man cleopeð Heatfelde. **1375** BARBOUR *Bruce* I. 591 The king a parlyament Gert set thareftir hastely. **1560** *Inchaffray Charters* (S.H.S.) 167 With power to gar set and affirme courte or courtis.

**c.** To put (a hen) to sit on eggs.

*c* **1440** *Pallad. on Husb.* I. 575 What wommon connot sette an hen obrood And bringe her briddis forth? **1523** FITZHERB. *Husb.* §146 Whan they waxe brodye, to sette them there as noo beastes..hurte them. **1530** PALSGR. 710/2, I will set sixe hennes a brodyng agaynst this Marche. **1707** MORTIMER *Husb.* 191 The best Age to set a Hen for Chickens, is from two years old to five. **1844** H. STEPHENS *Bk. Farm* II. 709 It is not an unusual practice to set a hen at any time of the day. **1867** *Jrnl. R. Agric. Soc.* Ser. II. III. 522, I never set less than three hens at one time.

**d.** To cause (a bird) to perch.

**1530** PALSGR. 710/2, I set a hauke on her perche, *je perche*. .. Go set my hauke on her perche. **1864** BROWNING *J. Lee's Wife* III. i, The swallow has set her six young on the rail.

†**2.** *refl.* To go down *upon one's knees* (*aknee, a-knewling, on knee(s,* etc.); = SIT *v.* 19. *Obs.*

*c* **1250** *Meid Maregrete* lxvii, Malchus herde thes wordes, he sette him acne. *a* **1300** *K. Horn* 781 He sette him a knewelyng. *c* **1300** *Havelok* 1211 On knes ful fayre he hem setten. *c* **1385** CHAUCER *L.G.W.* 455 Doun I sette me on myn kne.

**3.** *refl.* To seat oneself, take a seat, sit down. (Most freq. *to set oneself down*: see 143 i, *a.*)

*a* **1300** *K. Horn* 1475 He sette him on þe benche His harpe for to clenche. *c* **1374** CHAUCER *Troilus* III. 608 After to þe souper alle and some..þey hym sette. *c* **1400** *Destr. Troy* 5092 Þerfore set you full sone. *Ibid.* 12214 He..set hym to ground. *c* **1500** *Melusine* 154 My doughter, sette you here by me. *a* **1586** SIDNEY *Ps.* IX. ii, Setting thy self, in throne which shined bright, Of judging right.

**4.** *pass.* To be seated. (See also *set down* i, *b.*)

*c* **1330** *Arth. & Merl.* 6516 Afterward her compeinie Was yset,..& next hem..Sat þe kniȝtes of þe rounde table. *c* **1380** WYCLIF *Serm.* Sel. Wks. I. 62 Þe men weren sette as it were fyve þousand. *c* **1400** *Destr. Troy* 1711 When þe souerayne was set in a sete rioll. *c* **1410** *Sir Cleges* 469 The kynge was sett in his parlor, Wyth myrth solas and onor. **1503** in *Lett. Rich. III & Hen. VII* (Rolls) I. 192 Next the ..Saxon, the marques of Brandeburgh..bisshop of Laufenburgh were sett. **1553** T. WILSON *Rhet.* (1580) 156 It so fortuned that as thei were set, the Italian knockt at the Gate. **1697** DRYDEN *Æneid* VI. 821 The Queen of Furies by their sides is set. **1793** SMEATON *Edystone L.* §305 Most of the workmen were set round the fire. **1852** THACKERAY *Esmond* II. xv, Most of the party were set to cards. **1875** FREEMAN in W. R. W. Stephens *Life* (1882) II. 254 Soft chairs, in which, when one is once set, it is hard to get up again.

**b.** To be seated to partake of a meal (*to meat, at* or *to dinner*, etc.). *Obs.* or *arch.*

Partly a spec. use of prec., partly a true passive of sense 1.

**13..** *K. Alis.* 538 To the mete they weoren y-set. *c* **1440** *Generydes* 387 The Kyng was sette and serued in the hall. *c* **1475** *Rauf Coilȝear* 183 Quhen thay war seruit and set to the Suppar. **1523** LD. BERNERS *Froiss.* (1812) I. 396 He.. was set at the table to eate some meate. **1596** DANETT tr. *Comines* (1614) 118 After the K[ing] was set to dinner. **1625** MASSINGER *New Way* III. ii, I play the foole To stand here prating, and forget my dinner. Are they set Marrall? **1760–72** H. BROOKE *Fool of Qual.* (1809) IV. 132 When they were again set to dinner, the page entered.

†**c.** To be seated for deliberation or judgement; (of a court) to be in session. *Obs.*

**1390** GOWER *Conf.* I. 249 Whan the Court is set. *c* **1400** *Pety Job* 422 in *26 Pol. Poems* 134 Thou shalt me call at domesday, When thow art set on iugement. *a* **1548** HALL *Chron., Hen. VIII* (1550) 181 b, After that thei [the Legates] wer set..their Commission was redde. **1592** KYD *Sp. Trag.* III. vi, Bring forth the Prisoner, for the Court is set. **1626** B. JONSON *Staple of N.* III. i. 41 Is the examiner set? *a* **1700** EVELYN *Diary* 26 May 1671, Being all set, our Patent was read.

**d.** Of a rabbit: To be resting.

**1801** [see FORM *v.*²]. **1817** J. MAYER *Sportsman's Direct.* (ed. 2) 195 The stag is said to be harboured,..the hare formed, the rabbit set, the marten-cat treed.

**5. a.** *intr.* To sit, be seated. (Sometimes, as in 4 b, c, with spec. reference to partaking of a meal or sitting in judgement, etc.). Now *U.S., dial.* or *vulgar.* (See also *set down*, 143 i, *c.*)

*c* **1205** LAY. 22913 A bord swiðe hende þat þer maᵹen setten [*c* 1275 sitte] to sixtene hundred & ma. *c* **1275** *Ibid.* 19704 Here vte setteþ [*c* 1205 sitteð] six men. *c* **1375** *Sc. Leg. Saints* Prol. 132 Quhene at he Suld sit in sege of maieste, þai twelf sud set with hym-self. *c* **1400** *Destr. Troy* 5095 Þen set þai sone, as said hom the kyng. **1470–85** MALORY *Arthur* XIII. vii. 620 And soo after vpon that to souper, and euery knyȝt sette in his owne place. *c* **1489** CAXTON *Sonnes of Aymon* xvi. 377 He made theim to set vpon a benche. **1530** PALSGR. 713/2, I set hyest, or upper moste in a companye, *je preside*. **1596** NASHE *Saffron Walden* K 1, Such men as..set on the pillory for..periurie. **1658** SIR T. BROWNE *Hydriot.* iv. 23 They may set in the Orchestra, and noblest Seats of Heaven. **1662** GERBIER *Principles* 30 The King and Queen only remaining..setting under the Cloath of State. **1680** OTWAY *Orphan* III. ii, As with his Guests he set in Mirth rais'd high. **1788** JEFFERSON *Writ.* (1859) II. 385 It is very possible that the President and the new Congress may be setting at New York. **1825** R. P. WARD *Tremaine* I. xxiii. 173 He had set upon tenter-hooks during the whole conversation. **1844** DICKENS *Chimes* I. 30 You must always go and be a settin on our steps must you! **1848** THACKERAY *Van. Fair* lv, I'm thinkin' if I set here until I'm paid my wages, I shall set a precious long time, Mrs. Raggles: and set I will, too. **1884** C. H. SMITH *Bill Arp's Scrap Bk.* vi. 74 Lawyers and doctors have to set about town. **1897** WATTS-DUNTON *Aylwin* VII. ii, When you two was a-settin' by the pool, a-eatin' the breakfiss. **1913** H. KEPHART *Our Southern Highlanders* xiii. 298 'Come in and set.' 'Cain't stop long.' **1938** M. K. RAWLINGS *Yearling* i. 12 'If a feller'd light me a candle,' she said, 'I'd git shut o' the dishwashin' and mebbe have time to set and enjoy myself.' **1974** P. DE VRIES *Glory of Hummingbird* (1975) iii. 37 Lolly came almost every evening to set a spell.

**b.** Of a hen: To sit *upon* eggs.

**1586** [see ABROOD]. **1611** COTGR., *Oeuvé*, layed, or set on, as an egge. **1721** R. BRADLEY *Philos. Acc. Wks. Nat.* 85 Stopping when they have laid as many as they can set upon. **1726** —— *Country Gentl. Monthly Director* 31 Chuse the old Hens to set upon the Eggs, for they will set close. **1840** F. D. BENNETT *Whaling Voy.* I. 371 The boobies..that were 'setting hard', as the schoolboys say,..screamed..on our approach.

**c.** To become lodged *upon.*

**1869** E. J. REED *Shipbuild.* i. 16 Sand is the worst description of ground for a ship to set on as it forms a curved base. **1887** GOODE, etc. *Fish. Industr. U.S.* v. II. 540 The first thing found out was that the floating spawn would not attach itself to, or 'set' (in the vernacular of the shore) upon, anything which had not a clean surface.

**d.** *transf.* and *fig.* = SIT *v.* B. 7, 8, 14. Now *dial.* or *vulgar.*

*c* **1400** *Rule St. Benet* (Verse) 317 Þam..þat for godes sake here sett Vnder þe band of Sant Benett. **1482** *Cely Papers* (Camden) 121 They off Gaunte hath sent to the Inglysch naschon and to Dutch naschon..commaundyng them to sett styll..and entermete wᵗ noo parties. **1536** in *Lett. Suppress. Monast.* (Camden) 113 The emperor him selfe was glad to sett still. **1586** T. B. *La Primaud. Fr. Acad.* I. 484 That which setteth neerest hir husbands hart. **1592** KYD *Sp. Trag.* III. vi, O monstrous times, where murders set so light. **1651** HOWELL *Venice* 2 The Eastern Emperors have divers times set upon her skirts [see SKIRT *sb.* 3]. **1674** N. FAIRFAX *Bulk & Selv.* 34 Setting full as close to the very stamp or innostness of a thinking Being, as [etc.]. **1803** *Forest of Hohenelbe* III. 103 A disappointment that ought not to set very heavily on her mind. **1892** *Harper's Mag.* Dec. 22/1 The cat ate a rat, and it did not set well on her stomach.

**e.** To have a certain set or hang; to sit (well or ill, tightly or loosely, etc.). Cf. SIT *v.* 16 b.

**1804** tr. *La Marteliere's Three Gil Blas* II. 95 Your new clothes, which do not by any means set so well upon you. **1861** *Temple Bar* III. 250 To make the artificial hair curl and set naturally to the head. **1878** NAPHEYS *Phys. Life Wom.* 205 A body-case of strong linen..setting snugly to the form. **1883** J. P. QUINCY *Figures of Past* 129 His brown wig, which set low upon his forehead. **1887** *Lady* V. 46 Sleeves lined with stiff or harsh linings never set well. **1892** *Field* 2 July 30/1 Her sail did not set at all well.

**6. a.** *trans.* To become, befit, suit. Chiefly *Sc.* (in mod. use often ironical).

*c* **1480** HENRYSON *Poems* (S.T.S.) III. 103 Scho woir nevir grene nor gray That set hir half so weill. **1508** DUNBAR *Tua Mariit Wemen* 196 How it settis him so syde to sege of sic materis. *c* **1560** A. SCOTT *Poems* (S.T.S.) iv. 41 It settis not madynis als To latt men lowis thair lace. **1606** ROLLOCK *1 Thess.* 190 (Jam.) It is ouer sore to a Gentleman to doe that, it settes him not. **1637** RUTHERFORD *Lett.* (1664) 55 It sets him well howbeit he be young, to make Christ his garland. **1725** RAMSAY *Gentle Sheph.* IV. i, It sets him weel To yoke a plough where Patrick thought to till! **1814** SCOTT *Wav.* xxx, It wad better set you to be nursing the gudeman's bairns than to be deaving us here. **1827** Carlyle *Germ. Rom.* II. 241 How prettily the lace cap sets her. **1860** Whyte-Melville *Holmby House* II. xxi. 301 It set him well now, a worn and broken man, to be taking thought of his looks like a girl. **1891** Barrie *Little Minister* ii, Gavin,..do you think this bonnet sets me?

**b.** Also said of the person with regard to clothing, etc.

**1892** *Longman's Mag.* Nov. 59 Mysie..was a pretty creature, 'setting', in Scottish phrase, everything she wore.

**7.** To sit (a horse); = sit *v.* 22. *rare.*

**1648** *Petit. Eastern Assoc.* 11 It will try how the new Riders will set the saddle. **1710** Steele *Tatler* No. 248 ¶ 1 She set her horse with a very graceful air.

**II.** To sink, descend.

†**8.** *intr.* To subside, abate. *Obs.*

*c* **1000** *Sax. Leechd.* III. 86 Nim fyrs..& leȝe uppa þat ȝeswollene & hyt sceal sona settan. *a* **1225** *Ancr. R.* 274 þe swell schal setten.

**9. a.** Of the sun or other luminary: To go down; to make an apparent descent towards and below the horizon. (Conjugated, like other intr. verbs of motion, with either *be* or *have.*)

Not in OE.: cf. ON. *setjask.*

*c* **1300** *Havelok* 2671 So þat þei nouth ne blinne, Til þat to sette bigan þe sunne. *a* **1400–50** *Wars Alex.* 3050 Als sone as þe son hup soght þe slaghter begynnys, And to sett was þe same sesytt þai neuer. *c* **1440** *Alphabet of Tales* 74 þou sall dye or þe son sett. *a* **1586** Sidney *Arcadia* II. (Sommer) 172 The Sun was readie to set. **1613** Chapman *Maske Inns Crt.*, The ruddy Sunne was seen ready to be set. **1625** N. Carpenter *Geog. Del.* I. x. 220 With them all the stars equally set & rise. **1792** A. Young *Trav. France* I. 18 The sun, on the point of being set. **1816** Scott *Bl. Dwarf* vi, The sun setting red. **1822** Mrs. Hemans *Siege of Valencia* i. (1823) 121 Till the last pale star had set. **1847** C. Bronte *J. Eyre* v, The moon was set, and it was very dark. **1877** Miss Yonge *Cameos* Ser. III. xxxiv. 360 The sun had long been set.

*transf.* **1665** Dryden *Ind. Emp.* I. ii. (1668) 6 Distant skies that in the Ocean set.

**b.** Of the day: To come to its close. *poet.*

**1604** Drayton *Moyses* II. 48 Euery minute is a day and night That breakes and sets in twinkling of an eie. **1610** B. Jonson *Alch.* II. ii, The euening will set red, vpon you, sir. **1838** S. Bellamy *Betrayal* 67 The third day Had set upon the sepulchre.

**c.** *fig.* To decline, wane.

**1607** Tourneur *Rev. Trag.* IV. I4b, May not we set as well as the Dukes sonne. **1611** *Second Maiden's Trag.* 1302 And rise againe in health, to set in shame? *a* **1627** Middleton *Chaste Maid* v. ii, Your malice sets in death, does it not, sir? **1654** Z. Coke *Logick* Pref., Having absolved your courses through Zodiac of praise worthy actions, you wil set laden with Lustre. **1812** Scott *Let.* in *Lockhart* (1837) II. xii. 396 She should have no twilight, but set in the full possession of her powers. **1890** Tout *Hist. Eng. fr. 1689*, 282 The British Empire in India seemed setting in fire and blood. **1892** *Argosy* June 496 The glory of Egypt seemed to have set.

†**10.** Naut. *to heave and set*: to rise and fall with a heavy sea. *Obs.*

**1509** Hawes *Past. Pleas.* XXI. (1555) 99 Quadrant it was, and did heve and sette At every storme whan the wind was great. **1574** W. Bourne *Regiment for Sea* vi. (1577) 26 The Sea..causeth the shippe to heaue, and sette little or much. **1630** Winthrop *New Eng.* (1825) I. 9 This day the ship heaved and set more than before. **1674** Petty *Disc. bef. R. Soc.* 60 If the said water be so rough, as that the Vessel heavs and sets.

**III.** To put (more or less permanently) in a definite place.

* *Where the manner of the action is implied in the verb itself.*

†**11. a.** *trans.* To place on or as on a foundation; to build, erect; = *set up*, 154 n. *Obs.*

*a* **900** Cynewulf *Crist* 356 þa þu ærest wære mid þone ecan frean sylf settende þas sidan ȝesceaft. *a* **1000** *Cædmon's Gen.* 1881 Ongunnon..heora burh ræran & sele settan. *c* **1250** *Gen. & Ex.* 562 Ðat arche..set and limed a-ȝen ðe flood. *a* **1300** *K. Horn* 1395 Strong castel he let sette. *a* **1300** *Cursor M.* 20902 Quen he of antioche had fund þe kirk, and graytli set on grund. *c* **1330** *Arth. & Merl.* 1238 For mi blod no worþ it þe bet, Neuer more þe bet yset. *a* **1400–50** *Wars Alex.* 1649 Godis awen temple, þat of sir Salamon þe sage sett was & foundid. *Ibid.* 4305 And þat sullepe sire at sett all þe werde, In him we lely beleue & in na laȝe ellis. *c* **1400** *Destr. Troy* 1689 Qwhen this Citie was set & full sure made. **1470** *Little Red Bk. Bristol* (1900) II. 133 A litill newe howse ..is bild and sett vpon the Comyn grond in the hye strete iij fote.

*fig.* **1474** Caxton *Chesse* II. v. (1883) 61 That oure lawe is sette alle vpon loue and charyte.

†**b.** *pass.* Of a figure: To rest (*on* a base). *Obs.*

**1570** Billingsley *Euclid* VI. Prop. xxvi. 173 b, If from a parallelogramme be taken away a parallelograme like vnto the whole and in like sorte set. **1660** Barrow *Euclid* I. xxxviii, Triangles set upon equal bases.

**12. a.** To put (a shoot or young plant) into the ground to grow; to plant (a tree, also by extension, a vineyard, flowers, a crop). Also, less usually, to plant (seed) by hand, as opposed to *sowing*; sometimes said of the plant; formerly also, †to cause to grow from seed (*of a kernel*).

*c* **725** *Corpus Gloss.* P 13, *Pastinare*, settan. *a* **1000** *Cædmon's Gen.* 1558 Ða Noe..winȝeard sette, seow sæda fela. *a* **1225** *Ancr. R.* 378 Ȝe beoð ȝunge impen iset in Godes orcharde. *c* **1250** *Gen. & Ex.* 1278 Abraham..tillede corn and sette treen. *a* **1300** *Cursor M.* 1015 Treis o frut þan es þarsett þat serekin vertu has at ette. *c* **1440** *Pallad. on Husb.* I. 14 His appultreen, what hour Best is to sette. **1523** Fitzherb. *Husb.* §127 If the hedge be of .x. or .xii. yeres growing sythe it was first set. **1530** Palsgr. 713/2, I have set rosemarye and sage ynough in my gardayne. **1538** Elyot *Dict.*, *Sertor*, he that soweth seedes or settethe herbes. **1572** Mascall *Planting & Graff.* (1592) 36 Ye ought to transplant or set your trees from Alhallow-tide vnto March. **1602** Kyd *Sp. Trag.* Add. 1999 This was the tree; I set it of a kiernnell. **1611** Shaks. *Wint. T.* IV. iv. 100 Ile not put The Dible in earth, to set one slip of them. **1612** Hopton *Concord. Yeares* (1615) 112 The time [December] is good.. to set beanes, pease, &c. **1662** Stillingfl. *Orig. Sacræ* III. iii. §2 To order his trees, and set his flowers. **1767** A. Young *Farmer's Lett. to People* 154 Those trees which are propagated by..setting shoots. **1820** Keats *Isabella* lii, She ..cover'd it with mould, and o'er it set Sweet Basil. **1830** *Examiner* 796/1 The seed is to be set by hand. **1890** *Blackw. Mag.* CXLVIII. 717/1 If a man sets potatoes in wet bog.

†**b.** *absol.* or *intr.*

*c* **950** *Lindisf. Gosp.* Matt. vi. 26 Ne settas *vel* sauues *non serunt.* **1340–70** *Alex. & Dind.* 912 For to sowe & to sette in þe sad erthe. **1377** Langl. *P. Pl.* B. VII. 6 Alle þat halpe hym to erie to sette or to sowe. ?*a* **1586** Montgomerie *Misc. Poems* xxxi. 17, I sau, I sett—no flour nor fruit I find. **1690** R. Lucas *Hum. Life* 245 Idleness..never ploughs nor sows ..it never plants nor sets.

**c.** *transf.* and *fig.*

*a* **900** Cynewulf *Crist* 663 And eac moniȝfealde modes snyttru seow and sette ȝeond sefan monna. *a* **1310** in Wright *Lyric P.* xviii. 57 Suete Jhesu,..In myn huerte thou sete a rote Of thi love. *a* **1325** *Prose Psalter* xliii. 3 þyn honde desparplist þe folk, and þou settest hem. *c* **1374** Chaucer *Boethius* II. pr. v. (1868) 48 It is þan so þat ye men ne han no propre goode I-set in ȝow. *c* **1425** *Cast. Persev.* 1011 in *Macro Plays*, And þorwe Mankynde we settyn & sowe þe dedly synnys seuene. *c* **1532** Du Wes *Introd. Fr.* in *Palsgr.* 1055 The soule vegetable..is setted within the myght elemented. **1580** Lyly *Euphues* (Arb.) 367 Faire women are set thicke, but they come vp thinne.

†**d.** As a literalism or contextually: To graft.

**1388** Wyclif *Rom.* xi. 24 For if thou art kit doun of the kyndeli wielde olyue tre, and aȝens kynd art set in to a good olyue tre, hou myche more thei that ben bi kynde, schulen be set in her olyue tre. **1645** Ussher *Div.* 165 We see one tree may be set into another, and it groweth in the stock thereof, and becommeth one and the same tree.

†**13.** To put down, deposit (a pledge, security).

Cf. wedset *v.*

*c* **1000** *Laws Æthelred* I. i. (Liebermann) 218 Ȝif he þonne ful wurðe, æt þam forman cyrre..sette ȝetreowe borȝas, þæt he ælces yfeles ȝeswice eft. **16..** in Turreff *Gleanings* (1859) 29 The said day John Michel is ordaint to be put in kirk wolt, thairin to remain quhile he sett caution to adhear to Margratt Quhytt, his spous. *a* **1670** Spalding *Troub. Chas. I* (Bannatyne Club) I. 38 They with the marquess should sett caution, for keeping of the king's peace.

**14. a.** To put (a sum) down as a stake; to stake, wager. Also *fig.* *Obs.* or *arch.*

*c* **1460** Sir R. Ros *La Belle Dame* 524 He leseth his after game, That surely cannot sette his poyntes double. **1500–20** Dunbar *Poems* xxxvi. 27 Ȝung airis, That his auld thrift settis on ane ess. **1599** Minsheu *Sp. Dict.* Dial. 67, I set him two shillings, he cast and drew them. **1605** Shaks. *Lear* I. iv. 136 Set lesse then thou throwest. **1668** Dryden *Even. Love* IV. i, He is nettled, and sets me twenty: I win them too. **1726** *Art & Myst. Gaming* 23 Whatever Sum you set me, I will do the same to you. **1817** Shelley *Rev. Islam* X. xli. 4 His great Empire's worth Is set on Laon and Laone's head. **1853** Whyte-Melville *Digby Grand* ix, The stakes were 'set', the dice rattled [etc.].

**b.** *absol.* or *intr.* To put down a stake, lay money *on* (or *at*). Also *fig.* to give a challenge *to.* *Obs.* or *arch.*

Freq. with dat. of the person against whom the stake is laid. The dat. being interpreted as a direct obj., a personal pass. const. was evolved (see quot. 1823).

*a* **1553** *Nice Wanton* 212 Heer six come on seuen. *They set them*... Come on fiue. *She casteth and they set.* **1560** *Misogonus* II. iv. 171 Sett lustilye, my boykins... That was knavishlye throwne. **1575** *Gammer Gurton* II. ii. 23 Thou shalt set on the king. **1605** Chapman *All Fools* v. i, Come, Dariotto, set me. **1609** B. Jonson *Sil. Wom.* IV. iv, A very sharke, he set me i' the nicke t'other night at *primero.* **1610** —— *Alch.* I. ii, If I doe giue him a familiar, Giue you him all you play for; neuer set him: For he will haue it. **1667** Dryden *Maiden Q.* Prol. ii. 54 Throw boldly, for he sets to all that write. **1716** E. Parker *Fielding's Acc. Comet* 6 Happy the Man who Punts upon a Knave during the Month of January, or Sets on 6 upon Twelfth Night. **1739** *Act 12 Geo. II*, c. 28 §3 Every Person..who shall..set at, stake or punt at..Ace of Hearts [etc.]. **1807** E. S. Barrett *Rising Sun* I. 132 Come, seven's the main—who'll set me? **1823** *Mirror* I. 176/1 Observing that he was completely set, he stopped short,..saying, 'I believe I am set, gentlemen!' **1825** *Examiner* 631/2 The King would at one time set higher than usual.

**c.** *Dominoes.* To play first.

**1844** W. J. Pell *Treat. Game of Dominoes* 22 The largest count that can be made..is 129. To effect this, the winning hand must set. **1897** R. F. Foster *Compl. Hoyle* 561 The one whose turn it is to set lays down any domino he pleases.

**15. a.** To put (a thing, such as an ornament, fitting, piece of furniture, etc.) in a place allotted or adapted to receive it; (contextually) to fit, fix.

*c* **1205** Lay. 7832 þa Bruttes..nomen longen ræftres..& setten heom i Temese flod. *a* **1483** *Liber Niger* in *Househ. Ord.* (1790) 29 A tortayes to sett his lyverey in the wynter nyghtes. **1531** *Test. Ebor.* (Surtees) VI. 26 The side borde in the haull with the tristillis sett in the ground. **1556** in *Shropsh. Par. Doc.* (1903) 58 For ii Wode Candyllstyckes to set apon tapurs. **1575** *Gammer Gurton* I. iv, Set me a candle, let me seeke. **1590** Barwick *Disc. Weapons* 10 b, There be other peeces [*viz.* guns], to be set vpon Blockes. **1610** *Shuttleworth's Acc.* (Chetham Soc.) 192 For Coventrie blue to sett lettres in the chaffe beddes. **1629** Milton *Hymn Nativ.* xii, While the Creator Great His constellations set. **1632** —— *L'Allegro* 106 How the drudging Goblin swet, To ern his Cream-bowle duly set. **1673** Dryden *Assign.* II. iii. 20 Set the Ladder, and mount first. *a* **1700** Evelyn *Diary* 11 Apr. 1645, Setting the candles in little paper lanterns. **1729** Desaguliers in *Phil. Trans.* XXXVI. 202 If the Pulley be set backwarder still. **1807** Crabbe *Par. Reg.* III. 622 The fire-side chair, still set, but vacant still. **1808** *Lady's Econ. Assist.* 4 The sleeves must be set into the shirt rather full. **1875** Jowett *Plato* (ed. 2) I. 86 When he considers if he shall set a bridle on a horse. **1891** M. Muriel Dowie *Girl in Karp.* vii. 83 No chair is wiped and set for the visitor.

†**b.** To fit or attach (one thing) *to* another.

*c* **1375** *Sc. Leg. Saints* ii. (*Paulus*) 372 þe hed to set þe body till. *c* **1489** Caxton *Sonnes of Aymon* ix. 233, I shall set to your necke an halter. **1497** *Naval Acc. Hen. VII* (1896) 237 Workmanship in..settyng the Newe ledders vnto the seid Bellowes. **1595** Shaks. *John* IV. ii. 174 Be Mercurie, set feathers to thy heels.

†**c.** To place in a certain sequence in a literary work, in writing or print. *Obs.*

**1535** Joye *Apol. Tindale* 19 Tindals vncharitable pistle set before hys newe Testament. **1560** Daus tr. *Sleidane's Comm.* Pref. 3, I have set before the beginnyng of every boke, the some or argument. **1679** Dryden *Pref. to Troilus & Cr.* Ess. 1900 I. 204, I made..an order and connexion of all the scenes; removing them from the places where they were inartificially set.

**d.** To put (eggs) *under* a hen to be hatched.

**1726** R. Bradley *Country Gentl. Monthly Director* 31 You may now likewise set Duck-Eggs under Hens. **1815** *Sporting Mag.* XLVI. 27 The saving of eggs..which you intend to set. **1826** J. Wilson *Noctes Ambr.* (1855) I. 170 James, you shall have a dozen eggs to set.

**16.** *pass.* To have a certain position or arrangement by nature.

*a* **1310** in Wright *Lyric P.* ix. 35 Swannes swyre swythe wel y-sette. **1390** Gower *Conf.* I. 98 Her yhen smale and depe set. **1657** W. Coles *Adam in Eden* vii. 15 At the tops of the stalks come forth the flowers set at certain spaces one above another. **1719** De Foe *Crusoe* I. (Globe) 209 His fine Teeth, well set. **1883** Mrs. F. Mann *Parish of Hilby* iii, Their heads were set on long and graceful necks.

** *Where the manner of the action is implied in the adverbial extension.*

(Many of the divisions under this heading do not indicate a difference of sense, but serve mainly to exhibit the great variety of usage.

The development of phraseological expressions has brought into existence many uses in which the original physical reference is obscured. Cf. IV.)

**17. a.** To put or place, cause to be, lie, rest, or stand, in a locality specified by an advb. expression. (See also branch XII with advs.)

*Beowulf* 1242 Setton him to heafdon hilderandas. *a* **1000** *Cædmon's Gen.* 312 [God] heo..under eorðan neoðan..sette siȝelease, on þa sweartan helle. *a* **1000** Ælfric *Gen.* ix. 13 Ic sette minne renboȝan on wolcnum. *c* **1200** Ormin 11351 þe deofell..brohhte himm o þe temmple, & sette himm heȝhe uppo þe rhof. *a* **1225** *Leg. Kath.* 1972 Her, amid heapes, wes þis meiden iset. *a* **1300** *Cursor M.* 21624 A wessel..Sett vnder þat licure to hint. *c* **1300** *K. Horn* 738 (Laud) He sette sadel on stede. **1387** Trevisa *Higden* (Rolls) V. 179 Basilius awook and fonde..his armour i-sette þere as it was raþer. *c* **1400** Maundev. (Roxb.) xix. 87 þai sett þis mawmet with grete wirschepe in a chariot. *c* **1440** *Jacob's Well* xlii. 260 As an erthyn pott..sett on þe fyir brestyth on-sundir. **1535** Coverdale *Jer.* xlix. 38, I wil set my stole [1611 throne] in Elam. *a* **1548** Hall *Chron., Hen. IV* (1550) 32 b, He caused his crowne to be set on the pillowe at his beddes heade. **1548–9** (Mar.) *Bk. Com. Prayer*, *Communion* Rubr., Settyng both the breade and wyne vpon the Alter. **1588** Shaks. *Tit. A.* v. iii. 179 Set him brest deepe in earth, and famish him. **1617** Moryson *Itin.* III. 82 They set this iuyce vpon the fier, continually stirring it. **1764** Eliza Moxon *Eng. Housew.* (ed. 9) 155 Set it over the fire to melt. **1856** Mrs. Browning *Aur. Leigh* I. 1057 They saw a light at a window now and then, They had not set there. **1867** Augusta Wilson *Vashti* xxv, Two drops of blood had fallen on the tablecloth, and the girl instantly set her cup and saucer over them.

**b.** *pass.* To be situated, lie (in a certain locality); to be placed (at a certain height, interval, etc.).

*c* **950** *Lindisf. Gosp.* Matt. v. 14 Ofer mor ȝeseted, *supra monte posita.* **1297** R. Glouc. (Rolls) 2 Engelond his a wel god lond..Ich wene best Iset in þe on ende of þe worlde as al in þe west. *a* **1300** *Cursor M.* 527 Seuen maister sterns er sette in heuen. *Ibid.* 10005 þe four torels on hei er sett. **1387** Trevisa *Higden* (Rolls) VI. 5 þe citee Oxenford, i-sette bytwene þe tweie riveres of Tame and of Temse. *c* **1440** *Pallad. on Husb.* III. 381 The graffes..With gemmes fele aboute on hem ysette. **1530** Palsgr. 711/2 Rychemonte is very well set. **1585** T. Washington tr. *Nicholay's Voy.* I. vi. 4 b, A small fountaine beeing no higher set then the pauement. **1594** West *1st Pt. Symbol.* §60 d, The said W.M. set, lying, or being in W. **1650** Baxter *Saint's R.* III. i. §6. 275 Betwixt them and you will be a great gulf set. **1756** Mrs. F. Brooke *Old Maid* No. 28. 234 They are gone to their country seat set in Berkshire. **1868** Morris *Earthly Par.*, *Man born to be King* 118 Nor struggle in the net Wherein thine helpless feet are set.

**18. a.** To place (a thing) *upon* or in some kind of contact with some part of a person's body, *esp.* as a part of insignia. *Obs.* or *arch.*

**971** *Blickl. Hom.* 23 [Hi] wundan beaȝ of þornum & him setton on heafod. *a* **1225** *Leg. Kath.* 1571, & te an toc ane guldene crune, & sette on hire heauet. ?*a* **1366** Chaucer *Rom. Rose* 846 His leefe a rosen chapelet Had made, and on his heed it set. **1390** Gower *Conf.* I. 15 Upon the hond to were a Schoo And sette uppon the fot a Glove. *c* **1450** *Mirk's Festial* 17 Then anon com oure lady..and set a garlond on his hedde. **1525** Sir J. Russell in Ellis *Orig. Lett.* Ser. II. I. 298 If your Highnes woll, he woll sett the crowne of Fraunce on your hed. *a* **1533** Ld. Berners *Huon* xlvi. 152 He sette his horne to his mouthe and blewe it. **1575** *Gammer Gurton* II. iv. 44 Chil in, Diccon, a cleene aperne to take and set before me. **1720** Mrs. Manley *Secret Mem.* (1736) IV. 213 It is they that occasioned the Crown having been set upon your Head.

†**b.** To put (a thing) *in a person's hand.* (Cf. 27.)

*c* **1000** *Oaths* iii. (Liebermann) 396 Swa hit me se sealde, ðe ic hit nu on hand sette. *c* **1200** ORMIN 8181 Himm wass sett inn hiss rihht hannd An dere kineȝerrde. *a* **1300** *Cursor M.* 4472 Me-thought..i þis cupe in hand him sette. *Ibid.* 17629 Son in his hand he þe letter sett.

**c.** To put (something) *in one's sight* (or *view*), *before one* or *one's eyes* (or *view*), †*to* SHOW, †*to the sight*, †*to* VIEW.

*to set before*, orig. = to place so as to be seen by, acquired the meanings of to put before one for use, consideration, imitation, etc.

*a* **1000** ÆLFRIC *Deut.* xi. 26 Nu to dæȝ ic sette beforan eow bletsunga and wiriȝnissa [*En propono in conspectu vestro*]. *c* **1000** *Ags. Ps.* (Th.) lv. 7 Ic..sette on ðinre ȝesyhðe sariȝe tearas. **1382** WYCLIF *Gen.* xviii. 8 He toke butter, and mylk ..and sette bifore hem. *c* **1400** *Destr. Troy* 436 With pelur and pall..set to þe sight. **1422** YONGE tr. *Secreta Secret.* lxiv. 241 Whan a man syttyth atte mette, and dyuers maner mettis afor hym Is sette. **1535** COVERDALE *Rev.* iii. 8, I haue set before the an open doore. **1576** GASCOIGNE *Delicate Diet* Wks. 1910 II. 464 They dyd Clarkly in figures, set before us sundry tales. **1671** MILTON *Samson* 1624 What was set before him Which without help of eye, might be assay'd,.. he still perform'd All. **1697** DRYDEN *Æneid* VI. 971 To set before your sight your glorious race. **1725** BROOME *Notes Pope's Odyss.* x. 295 The description sets the figure [of Terror] full before our eyes. **1848** PUSEY *Par. Serm.* I. xix. (1873) 371 He cannot set them before him; he cannot see, believe, grasp them. **1888** BURGON *Lives 12 Gd. Men* II. v. 2 His birth..and his parentage have been fully set before the public.

†**d.** To put (a person) *in prison*. Similarly *to set in (on) the pillory* (see PILLORY *sb.*). *Obs.*

*c* **1100** *O.E. Chron.* (MS. D) an. 1036, Ða let he hine on hæft settan. *a* **1300** *Cursor M.* 23315 Þai sal be sett in þair prisun. *a* **1533** LD. BERNERS *Huon* cxxviii. 468 My wyfe set in pryson. **1535** LAYTON in Ellis *Orig. Lett.* Ser. II. II. 61 We have sett Dunce [*sc.* Duns Scotus] in Bocardo. *a* **1547** in J. R. Boyle *Hedon* (1875) App. 74 Then the maiore to sett theym in presone.

†**e.** With complementary advb. phr. expressing removal or issue *from* or *out of* a place. *Obs.*

*c* **1450** *Brut* 336/20 Þei sette out of þe Tour þe Archebishop of Caunturbury. **1596** DALRYMPLE tr. *Leslie's Hist. Scot.* I. Prol. 25 All this tyme settis na man his heid out of the hous. *a* **1610** HEALEY *Epictetus* (1636) 25 Is the dish set from thee? stay it not. **1667** *Churchw. Acc. Pittington*, etc. (Surtees) 335 For setting the watter away from the church style, 2d. **1684** BUNYAN *Pilgr.* II. 180 Now they..befooled themselves for setting a Foot out of doors in that Path.

**f.** *to set on the sea, water, afloat*, etc.: to launch.

**1559** [see *set afloat*, 137 a]. **1568** C. W[ATSON] *Polybius* 48 They were vndockte, and sette on the water. **1587** [see AFLOAT 1]. *a* **1800** *Fair Janet* i. in Child *Ballads* II. 105 Ye'll build to me a bonnie ship, And set her on the sea.

†**g.** To lay (siege) *before* a place. *Obs.*

**1474** CAXTON *Chesse* III. vi. 130 A prynce that setteth a siege to fore a castell. **1530** PALSGR. 711/2 Whan the kynges good grace dyd set his siege byfore Tournaye.

**h.** To put (pen) *to paper* (†*book*).

**1526** *Pilgr. Perf.* (W. de W. 1531) 1 As I had set the penne to the boke. *c* **1530** [see PEN *sb.*[2] 4]. **1579** HAKE *Newes out of Powles* Ep. Ded. (1872) A ij b, And so shall I..set my Pen to Booke againe. **1581** MELBANCKE *Philotimus* Z j, Setting pen to paper. **1621** T. WILLIAMSON tr. *Goulart's Wise Vieillard* A 4 b, My fingers did euen itch to set pen to paper. **1711** ADDISON *Spect.* No. 62 ¶7, I am apt to think that Euclid was the greatest Wit that ever set Pen to Paper. **1895** KERNAHAN *God & Ant* Apol., The worst of all reasons which inexperienced writers put forward for setting pen to paper.

**19. a.** To place (a part of the body) upon a surface or an object.

*c* **900** tr. *Bæda's Hist.* II. xii. §5 [He] sette his þa swiðran hond him on þæt heafod. **971** *Blickl. Hom.* 239 He sette his hand ofer hiora heortan. *a* **1000** ÆLFRIC *Gen.* xxiv. 2 Sete þine hand under min þeoh. *a* **1300** *K. Horn* 758 To lond he him sette & fot on stirop sette. *c* **1520** *Everyman* 778 Now set eche of you on this rodde your honde. **1607** BEAUM. & FL. *Woman Hater* I. iii, When her husband sets first foot in the bedde. **1692** R. L'ESTRANGE *Fables* xxx. 29 A Child of the Family happen'd to set his Foot upon't [*sc.* a snake]. **1749** SMOLLETT *Gil Blas* II. iii. (1782) I. 136 Fabricius..set his hands in his sides. **1870** ROSSETTI *Dante at Verona* xxxii, At such times, Dante, thou hast set Thy forehead to the painted pane Full oft. *a* **1908** F. THOMPSON *Poppy* i, Summer set lip to earth's bosom bare.

†**b.** *to set* (*one's*) *hand*(*s on*: to lay hands upon, seize; *esp.* to lay violent hands upon, attack. Also *to set one's hand against*, to oppose. *Obs.*

*c* **1290** *Beket* 931 in *S. Eng. Leg.* I. 133 ȝif ani man hond on ov set. *c* **1330** *Arth. & Merl.* 5815 Hir hondes sche sett on hir here & hir fair tresses al totere. *c* **1400** *Beryn* 2290 Macaigne arose..And set hond fast on Beryns othir scleve. *c* **1489** CAXTON *Sonnes of Aymon* iii. 79 Aymon..began to sette sore hande vpon theym. **1635** PAGITT *Christianogr.* (1636) III. 37 Our Princes and Bishops set their hand against Image-worship. *c* **1641** F. HAWKINS *Youth's Behav.* (1663) 36 Without setting hand on any thing before him.

**c.** *to set* (*one's*) *hand to*: to lay hold of, take into one's hand; *fig.* to set about, engage upon (†formerly const. inf.). *to set one's hand to the door*: see DOOR *sb.* 6.

*c* **1477** CAXTON *Jason* 60 b, Argos sette hande unto the werk. **1542** in *Lett. Lit. Men* (Camden) 2 Of your aboundaunt pitie to sette your helpyng hand to the bestowyng of me to suche condition. **156.** *Thersites* (Roxb.) 47 They wyll not ones set hande to fight with me. **1638** W. TIRWHYT tr. *Balzac's Lett.* II. 144 If you appoint him to set hand to his Penne. **1639** FULLER *Holy War* I. ix. 13 God set his hand to this warre. **1662** EVELYN *Sculptura* Table, Painters encouraged to set their hands to the graver. **1788** *Trifler* No. 4. 47, I..resolved to set hand to work. **1865** SWINBURNE *Atalanta* 1972 She set her hand to the wood, She took the fire in her hand. **1889** F. BARRETT *Under Str. Mask* I. iii. 46 He set his hand to this good work.

†**d.** To take (a step). *Obs.*

**1593–1642** [see FOOTING *vbl. sb.* 1]. **1622** MABBE tr. *Aleman's Guzman d'Alf.* I. 219 The first step that I set within those holy gates. **1767** GOOCH *Treat. Wounds* I. 212 He was not able to set a step. **1780** A. YOUNG *Tour Irel.* I. 241 Every step the horse set.

†**20. a.** To plant or deal (a blow); with dat. of the person or *upon*. *Obs.*

*c* **1300** *Havelok* 2405 He robert sette Biforn þe teth a dint ful strong. **13..** *Guy Warw.* (A.) 1382 So wele his strok he sett þat his heued fram þe bodi flei. *c* **1400** *Arth. & Merl.* 2422 And when they were together mett, There were strokes sadlye set. *c* **1430** *Syr Tryam.* 1498 They settyd strokes of mode. *c* **1500** *Lancelot* 3175 Nor he so hard his strok apone hyme set.

†**b.** *transf.* To strike (a person). *Obs.*

**13..** *K. Horn* (Harl.) 714 Wel sone bote þou flette myd suert yshal þe sette. *c* **1400** *Beryn* 577 He..set hym with þe ladill on the grustill on þe nose.

†**c.** To direct, aim (*trans.* and *intr.*). *Obs.*

*a* **1300** *K. Horn* 1201 To herte knif heo sette. **1471** CAXTON *Recuyell* (Sommer) 292 Theseus was the firste.. that sette and cowched his speer ayenst hym. **16..** *Sir Andrew Barton* xxxi, A noble gunner..That can sett well with his eye.

**d.** To apply (a weapon, etc.) *to*.

*to set spurs to*: see SPUR *sb.*

**1388** WYCLIF *Luke* iii. 9 An axe is sett to the roote of the tree. **1593** SHAKS. *3 Hen. VI*, II. ii. 165 We set the Axe to thy vsurping Roote.

**21. a.** (orig. †*to set on write*.) To put down in writing; to put on paper; †*occas.* to depict. Now *set down* (see 143 e).

*a* **900** *Laws Ælfred* I. xlix. (Liebermann) 46 Ic ne dorste ȝeðristlæcan þara minra awuht fela on ȝewrit settan. *a* **900** CYNEWULF *Elene* 654 (Gr.), & þa wintergerim on ȝewritu setton. *c* **1175** *Lamb. Hom.* 75 Þet rihte ileue setten þe twelue apostles on write.

*c* **1450** *Myrr. our Ladye* I. vi. 20 That he shulde se that they were sett in trew and conuenyente termes. **1486** *Bk. St. Albans, Her.* b iv, Y[e] token of a beest..set with in the cootarmure. **1540** PALSGR. *Acolastus* I. i. Metres E ij b, I.. haue soo often as any greke word was to be englished, set ouer him..*græca uox*. **1613** TAPP *Pathw. Knowl.* 38 Therefore I take but 8, which I set in the quotient. **1621** in Kempe *Losely MSS.* (1836) 460 Theyr armes in y[e] window, genealogically sett. **1686** W. HOPKINS *Ratramnus* Dissert. iii. 38, I conceive it will not be unacceptable to the Reader to see them set in parallel. **1810** P. BARLOW in *Nicholson's Jrnl.* XXV. 187 Set the inches, parts, &c. as decimals.

**b.** *Geom.*, etc. To lay or mark off (a line of a definite length). (Cf. *set off*, 147 d.)

**1617** SPEIDELL *Geom. Extract.* 21 From the end A, drawe the line AE,..then set the line C, from A, to F. **1660** BARROW *Euclid* VI. iv, Set the side BC in a direct line to the side CE. **1725** W. HALFPENNY *Sound Building* 42 Take *lm* in your Compasses and set it from D to the Dot in the Line DE. **1805** *Shipwright's Vade-M.* 171 Next proceed to set aft the distance of dead-flat from the foremost perpendicular. **1830** HEDDERWICK *Mar. Archit.* 247 On this line set the half-thickness of the stem from the centre-line.

**22.** To put down in a record, catalogue, etc.; to mention or treat of in a writing or composition; to put down or enter in an account. Now *set down*.

*c* **1200** ORMIN 3282 He badd settenn upp o writt All mannkinn. *a* **1310** in Wright *Lyric P.* viii. 31 Of levedis love that y ha let,..Ofte in song y have hem set. *c* **1386** CHAUCER *Wife of Bath's Prol.* 709 Why sholde men elles in hir bookes sette That a man shal yelde to his wyf hir dette? **1390** GOWER *Conf.* I. 12 Whan Crist him self hath bode pes And set it in his testament. **1474** CAXTON *Chesse* IV. vii. 182 Wherfore he setted not the versis of homere in his book. **1540** PALSGR. *Acolastus* I. i. D iij, Sette in a byll, what thy chyldes parte commeth to. **1601** SHAKS. *Jul. C.* IV. iii. 98 All his faults obseru'd, Set in a Note-booke. **1745** P. THOMAS *Jrnl. Anson's Voy.* 105, I know it was set in the Ship's Log Book by Order.

**23.** To put (one's signature), affix (a seal) *to* (†*on*) a document. (Cf. *set to*, 152 b.)

**13..** *Cursor M.* 6889 (Gött.), He..wrat þe name and set [*v.rr.* sett to, sette on] þe sele. **1405** *Rolls of Parlt.* III. 605/2 In Witnessing of whilk thyng, to thys presentes we have sette our forsaide Seal. **1524** in J. H. Glover *Kingsthorpiana* (1883) 66 We have hereunto set the comon seal of Kyngesthorp. **1567** HARMAN *Caveat* xv. (1869) 60 One should make writinges and set seales for lycences and pasporte. **1600** *Weakest goeth to Wall* I 3 b, Here is your hand set to confirme the deed. **1616** R. C. *Times' Whistle* v. 2029 Hee'l make the landlord set both hand & seale To this new lease. **1626** MASSINGER *Rom. Actor* IV. i, Have you set your hands To the accusation? *a* **1700** EVELYN *Diary* 3 Dec. 1699, For setting the Greate Seale to the pardon of an arch pirate. **1736** *Gentl. Mag.* VI. 473/1 In witness whereof I have hereunto set my Hand and Seal. **1892** *Temple Bar* Nov. 358 He set his hand to the death-warrant.

*fig.* **1611** *Second Maiden's Trag.* 310 Force grace into that cheeke wher impudence setts her seale. **1637** RUTHERFORD *Lett.* (1664) 342 Lend Christ your heart: Set him as a seal there.

**IV.** To place or cause to be in a certain position (other than merely local), condition, relation, or connexion.

* *Where a person or thing is placed in or brought into a condition.*

**24. a.** To place in a state or sphere specified by an adverbial expression.

Now less freq. than *place* or *put*.

*c* **1200** ORMIN 10728 Ȝho doþ þe to settenn þe Bineþenn þine lahȝhre. *a* **1225** *Leg. Kath.* 1758 Ȝef ȝe beoð mine, as under me isette. *a* **1300** *Cursor M.* 11408 Quen ani deid o þat dozein, His sun for him was sett again. *Ibid.* 23552 If it sett þam into will to mak anoiþer erth or heuen. **1377** LANGL. *P. Pl.* B. VI. 48 Þat he worth worthier sette and with more blisse. *c* **1400** *Destr. Troy* 223 Hit wold sothely me set as soueraýne in Joye. *Ibid.* 1728 Þat ben set vnder seruage. *c* **1400** *Rom. Rose* 4957 Celde gan..sette men by her ordinaunce In good Reule and in gouernaunce. **1530** PALSGR. 714/2 And I be set ones in auctorite. **1566** DRANT *Hor., Jer.* K viij b, Preists haue set God, in this chafinge moode. **1567** *Gude & Godlie B.* (S.T.S.) 159 Quhen Sathan was lousit out of hell, And had set man in my place. **1632** BP. HALL *Hard Texts* Matt. v. 13 This holy calling, wherein yee are set. **1662** STILLINGFL. *Orig. Sacræ* II. ix. §1. 253 Everything remains in the course and order wherein it was set at the Creation. **1711** ADDISON *Spect.* No. 255 ¶4 Providence for the most part sets us upon a Level. **1831** SCOTT *Cast. Dang.* ix, My age sets me beyond your cruelty. **1846** TRENCH *Huls. Lect.* Ser. II. viii. (1880) 245 He must be set in those conditions, where to abide by this good shall bring upon him every outward calamity. **1847** H. MILLER *First Impr. Eng.* vi. (1857) 92 It had to be set under a keeper, to insure better behaviour.

†**b.** With complementary advb. phr. expressing removal from a condition or position. *Obs.*

(Now commonly expressed by *put*.)

*c* **1050** *O.E. Chron.* (MS. C) an. 1043, & raðe þæs man sette Stigant of his bisceoprice. **13..** *Cursor M.* 8639 (Gött.) Þe dede childe..es þin, þat þi-selue of lijf has sett [*Fairf.* atte þou fra life to dede has sette]. **1390** GOWER *Conf.* III. 1 This vice, which so out of rule Hath sette ous alle. **1523** LD. BERNERS *Froiss.* I. ccccv. 285 b, His mynde was so sore therof, that no man coude set hym therfro. **1530** PALSGR. 715/1, I feare me he hath set my fote out of joynte. *Ibid.* 715/2 Who hath set my bookes out of order on this facyon? **1548** [see BESIDE *prep.* 4 c]. **1559** in Strype *Ann. Ref.* I. App. x. 31 Note th' end of these men's doctryns, that is to sett us withowt God. **1596** [see BY *prep.* 16 c]. **1596** SHAKS. *1 Hen. IV*, v. i. 88 This present enterprize set off his head. **1606** G. W[OODCOCKE] *Hist. Ivstine* XXXI. 105 It was a far easier labor to depose them of Rome then to set them beside their Empire. **1693** LOCKE *Educ.* §55 Wks. 1714 III. 18 This.. spoils his Mind, and sets that farther out of order. **1756** in *Coltness Collect.* (Maitl. Club) 209 They wanted to have a haggas, but John said we must set our hearts bye that.

**25. a.** In a large number of phraseological expressions (often equivalent to a single verb), in which *set* acquires the sense of: To cause to be or become (so-and-so). Cf. PUT *v.* 25, 26.

***to set at ease, at rest, to rest,*** † ***in*** **or** ***at peace; to set*** † ***at debate,*** † ***at difference,*** † ***at a jar,*** † ***at jars, at odds, at one, at variance,*** † ***at square, at war, by the ears,*** † ***in sunder; to set agog,*** † ***at gaze, astray; to set aglow, afire, on fire, aflame, in flame(s***, etc.; ***to set in array, in order, in readiness, to rights; to set*** † ***in effray,*** † ***on fear; to set at large, at leisure, at liberty; to set on edge; to set in or on a roar; to set in action, motion, operation; to set at bay, at fault,*** † ***in press,*** † ***in stay; to set at contempt, at defiance***; etc.: see also the sbs. and advs. Also, *to set afoot* or *on foot* (see AFOOT 3, FOOT *sb.* 32 c).

*a* **1000** *Cædmon's Gen.* 2728 Ne þearf ðe on edwit Abraham settan. *a* **1000** *Sal. & Sat.* 344 (Gr.), Hine god seteð ðurh ȝeearnunga endȝum to ræste. **1297** [see AFIRE 1]. **1375** BARBOUR *Bruce* X. 257 Settand in pes all the cuntre. *Ibid.* XVI. 427 The Ynglis rout in gret effray War set. *c* **1407** LYDG. *Reson & Sens.* 2188 Sette thyn herte best at ese. **1473** *Paston Lett.* III. 102, I trust to God thatt the ij Dukes of Clarans and Glowcester shall be sette att one. **1509** HAWES *Past. Pleas.* XXV. iii, Whan that God set them [the planettes] in operacyon. **1513** DOUGLAS *Æneis* VIII. iv. 142 That on this wise had Cacus set in pres [L. *telis premit*]. **1530** PALSGR. 715/2 Set your herte at rest. *c* **1530** *Crt. of Love* (MS.) 418 And lovers true to setten at debate. **1568** GRAFTON *Chron.* II. 35 He set that Countrie in good rest and peace. **1575** GASCOIGNE *Glasse of Govt.* IV. i, I have..set al thinges in redynesse for my Sonnes departure. **1578** *Paradise Dainty Devises, Sturdy Rock* 8 The stately stagge..By yalping hounds at bay is set. **1595** SHAKS. *John* III. iii. 9 Imprisoned angells Set at libertie. **1615** R. COCKS *Jrnl.* 30 July (1883) I. 28 An other matter is now set on foote, which I never did heare of till this instant. **1632** LITHGOW *Trav.* II. 48 An vnresolued man..is distracted here, set on feare there. **1638** [see AFOOT 3]. **1668** PEPYS *Diary* 8 Nov., At my chamber all the morning, setting my papers to rights. **1736** T. LEDIARD *Life Marlborough* III. 364 A Treaty of Peace was again set on foot. *a* **1774** GOLDSM. *Hist. Greece* I. 111 The Athenians.. sat many of their ships on fire. **1805–6** CARY *Dante, Inf.* XXVIII. 132 Father and son I set at mutual war. **1809** MALKIN *Gil Blas* X. x. (Rtldg.) 371 Which set my lungs as well as appetite in motion. **1829** SCOTT *Anne of Geierstein* III. ix. 263 He..has in a right godly manner tried to set afoot a treaty of peace with my own father. **1837** CARLYLE *Fr. Rev.* II. VI. ii, They have quite another feat to do: a paralytic National Executive to set in action. **1854** H. MILLER *Sch. & Schm.* (1858) 284 A peculiarity which had set at fault..the modern ship-carpenter. **1867** AUGUSTA WILSON *Vashti* xxiii, At last she was set once more adrift in the world. **1879** GUEST *Lect. Hist. Eng.* xxxi. 316 His followers set themselves in battle array. **1890** *Sunday Mag.* Aug. 531/2 Enquiries were at once set on foot. **1895** *Cornh. Mag.* Mar. 298 That day's incident set the whole neighbourhood agog.

**b.** With complementary adj.; chiefly *to set free, loose, right*: see also the adjs.

**1530** PALSGR. 713/2 As for your costes, take no thought for, I wyll set you fre. *c* **1570** W. WAGER *The Longer thou livest* 1558 (Brandl), Let me helpe you to set your gowne right. **1607** SHAKS. *Timon* III. iii. 31, I cannot thinke, but in the end, the Villanies of man will set him cleere. *a* **1639** W. WHATELEY *Prototypes* II. xxiv. (1640) 8 She is a bad and unloving wife,..who sets him short, and cares not to fit him with pleasing food. **1693** LOCKE *Educ.* §89 Wks. 1714 III. 35 His Practice must by no means cross his Precepts, unless he intend to set him wrong. **1780** *Mirror* No. 92 Who make people laugh, or set them asleep. **1799** KIRWAN *Geol. Ess.* 19 An immense quantity of inflammable air set loose. **1854** THACKERAY *Newcomes* iii, Orme's Hindostan, the book.. which set dear Tom wild to go to India. **1855** BROWNING *Fra Lippo* 45 Let's sit and set things straight now. **1890** TOUT *Hist. Eng. from 1689*, 155 The death of the old king set them free from their last scruple.

†**26. a.** To place (a person) in a certain sphere of activity or occupation; esp. *to set to lore, to*

***book*, *to school***; also, to place *with* an instructor or employer. *Obs.* (Cf. 114.)

*a* **1225** *Leg. Kath.* 115 Hire feder hefde iset hire earliche to lare. *c* **1290** *Beket* 210 in *S. Eng. Leg.* 112 þis child was ȝong to schole i-set. *c* **1330** *Arth. & Merl.* 9 Childer, þat ben to boke ysett. **1340–70** *Alex. & Dind.* 454 We ben lered.. lore of no scole, Ne to no sience i-set vs silue to wisse. **1486–93** *Early Chanc. Proc.* 94/14 (P.R.O.), Your said oratour (when newly set to Courte in Davys Inne). **1513** Bradshaw *St. Werburge* I. 491 He set her for doctryne to the abbesse Saynt Hylde. **1538** Starkey *England* I. ii. 43 Settyng themselfe in relygyouse housys, ther quyetly to serue God. *a* **1548** Hall *Chron., Hen. VII* (1550) 49 b, The sayde Barlo set me with a merchaunt of Middelboroughe too seruice. **1697** Dryden *Virg. Georg.* III. 261 Set him betimes to school.

†**b.** ***to set above*, *aloft*, *high***, or ***on high***: to exalt. ***to set nether***: to bring low. *Obs.*

*c* **1205** Lay. 4049 Feowere here weren riche þe haueden ferden muchele þeo nedden al þæ oðere & heom neðder sætten. **1390** Gower *Conf.* I. 7 Tho was the vertu sett above And vice was put under fote. *c* **1430** *Hymns Virgin* 37 Wrong is an hiȝ seete þere riȝt schulde be. *c* **1470** Henry *Wallace* VI. 58 Feyll sys or than he had beyne set abuff. **1509** Hawes *Past. Pleas.* XXXIII. xxv, Verite on the first fane Did sette aloft of falshoed the hede. **1530** Palsgr. 711/1, I set a lofte, as a man is whan one dothe promote him. **1596** Norden *Progr. Pietie* (Parker Soc.) 28 That God that can give and take away, set aloft and pull down. **1610** Holland *Camden's Brit.* 244 Fortune.. hath set no man so high, but she threatneth to take from him as much. *c* **1675** Waller *Epitaph Col. Cavendish* 25 Equal success had set these champions high.

†**c.** To put (singers) at the proper pitch. *Obs.*

**1506** in Legg *Clerk's bk.* (1903) 76 The said clarkis.. whanne ony seruyce shalbe don by note shall sett the quyer not after his owne brest. **1530** Palsgr. 714/1 Can you nat set these syngyng men in tune yet?

**d.** orig. ***to set upon the muzzle***: To muzzle (a horse) so as to prevent him feeding improperly.

**1834** Medwin *Angler in Wales* II. 115 My training groom had his orders and yet I was afraid Idris would not be set upon muzzle, and so get improperly filled. **1856** 'Stonehenge' *Brit. Rural Sports* II. I. vi. §7 Some [horses] requiring to be set over night after having eaten their hay. **1856** H. H. Dixon *Post & Paddock* (1862) 143 They set them [the horses] very sharp.

**27.** To place (a person or thing) in one's possession or control, or in a condition to be used, dealt with, or occupied.

***to set in hand***: † (*a*) to place in (a person's) possession or control; † (*b*) to take in hand, undertake; also *intr.* with *with*, in the same sense; (*c*) to put out to be done. ***to set to* (*for*, *on*) *sale*, *a-sale***: see sale *sb.*[2] 2 a, c. † ***to set at pawn*, *to pledge*, *to wed***: to pledge, pawn.

*c* **1205** Lay. 12348 Cheorles.. hefden al þis kine-lond iset a cheorlene hond. *Ibid.* 25171 Mi lond ich wulle sette to wedde for seoluere. **1388** Wyclif *Ecclus.* x. 10 For whi this man hath also his soule set to sale. *c* **1420** *Sir Amadace* (Camden) xxxiii, That he had sette, and layd to wedde. *c* **1500** *Robin Hood* liv, My londes beth sette to wedde.. To a ryche abbot. **1535** Coverdale *2 Esdras* v. 3 Let vs set our londes.. to pledge. **1548** Udall, etc. *Erasm. Par. John* vii. 6–10 He left them and set in hand to preache. *Ibid.* x. 19–24 New matter to set in hand and dispute wt him again. **1553**, **1577** [see a-sale]. **1600** W. Watson *Decacordon* (1602) 349 Neither done, nor set in hand withall. **1601** Hakluyt tr. *Galvano's Discov.* 77 He set in hand sending foorth two ships. **1750** Johnson *Rambler* No. 28 §7 A man who has.. set his country to sale. **1812** Crabbe *Tales* XIX. 256 Concerns it you what books I set for sale? **1864** *Builder* 16 Apr. 281/3 The proposed restoration of St. Bartholomew's, Smithfield, is to be set in hand forthwith.

**28. a.** To cause (a thing) to assume a certain physical position expressed by a complementary adj. or advb. phr.; chiefly ***to set open* (†*wide*)**, ***set on end*, *set upright*** (see also these words).

*a* **1300** *Cursor M.* 3804 He it sett vp right. *a* **1300** [see end *sb.* 17 d]. *a* **1400–50** *Wars Alex.* 2142 Werpis þam vp.. & wyde open settis. **1549–62** [see ope *a.*]. **1615** Murrell *New Bk. Cookerie* 32 To make Pancakes so crispe that you may set them vpright. **1678** Phillips (ed. 4), *To set taught the Shrouds*, in the Navigators Dialect, is to make them stiffer when they are too slack. **1715** Leoni *Palladio's Archit.* (1742) I. 101 Seeing that the.. legions were so close and crouded, he commanded them to set themselves more at large. **1724** Calamy *Life Howe* 11 Setting the Top on the piqued end downwards. **1775** Johnson *Jrnl.* 23 Oct. in *Boswell*, The plate.. is.. then set sloping to drop the superfluous mercury. **1837** Carlyle *Fr. Rev.* II. IV. viii, With door set ajar. **1896** *Pall Mall Mag.* May 7 An ill-tempered frown, that set her beauty askew.

**b.** To cause to take a certain shape (defined by an adj. or advb. phr.).

**1677** Moxon *Mech. Exerc.* i. 12 Turn the other side of your work, and with your Hammer set it flat and straight. **1842** *Penny Cycl.* XXIII. 432/2 The sword is then set to the required shape by placing it on a sort of fork upon the anvil, and wrenching it by means of tongs.

**29.** To place (a person, his body or limbs) in a certain posture. Also *refl.*

***to set on one's feet*, *legs***: see foot *sb.* 27, leg *sb.* 2 c.

*c* **1400** *Beryn* 1838 The hoost.. set his hond in kenebowe. **1565** J. Phillip *Patient Grissell* 53, I was set on my legges and reyzed vpright. **1662** Hopkins *Funeral Serm. A. Grevil* (1663) 27 What are they.. but.. Nothings set a strutt? **1665** Hooke *Microgr.* 200 Standing still, and setting itself on its hinder leggs. **1750** Johnson *Rambler* No. 116 ¶10 When a man can set his hands to his sides, and say he is worth forty thousand pounds every day of the year. **1835** Harewood *Dict. Sports* s.v. *Cock-fighting*, When brought beak to beak, and set on their legs. **1837** Lockhart *Scott* I. ii. 82 Unless the old man would set him astride on his shoulder. **1859** *Habits of Gd. Society* vii. 250 In standing, the legs ought to be straight, or one of them bent a little, but not set wide apart.

** *Where something is assigned, applied, allotted, apportioned, etc.*

†**30.** To give, bestow, assign (a name). Const. dat. or equivalent with *to*, *upon*. *Obs.*

*c* **1000** Ælfric *Hom.* I. 12 God him sette naman Adam. *c* **1200** Ormin 722 Whatt name he shollde settenn Uppo þatt illke child. *a* **1635** Sibbes *Confer. Christ & Mary* (1656) 79 God setteth a stile upon us suitable to the excellency of our spirituall being.

†**31.** To apply or allot (money) *to*, spend (a sum) *on* a certain object; to expend, invest. *Obs.*

**1154** *O.E. Chron.* (Laud MS.) an. 1137, [He] wrohte on þe circe & sette þar to landes & rentes. *c* **1400** *Beryn* 2244 Wele settith he his peny, þat þe pound.. savith. **1455** [see A. 1 β]. **1475** *Bk. Noblesse* (Roxb.) 81 Late it be set in money to the remedie and socoure of this gret importunyte and necessite. **1485** *Naval Acc. Hen. VII* (1896) 7 All somes of money sett upon hym for the same [office]. **1507** *Acc. Ld. High Treas. Scot.* III. 334 To the King himself, quhilk was set on the syment riall,.. xx Franch crounis.

†**32.** To apply (a remedy) *to*; to bestow (pains).

*a* **1300** *Cursor M.* 89 To sette traueil On thyng þat may not auail. **1375** Barbour *Bruce* x. 100 And he mycht set no help thar-till. *c* **1375** *Cursor M.* 4722 (Fairf.) Bot ȝe sette bote our life ys gane. *c* **1440** *York Myst.* v. 19 My trauayle were wele sette Myght y hym so betraye. *c* **1450** *Merlin* vii. 114 That alle shull be distroied but god sette remedye. **1481** Caxton *Godfrey* 277 To thende that they myght sette remedye for theyr affayres. *a* **1578** Lindesay (Pitscottie) *Chron. Scot.* (S.T.S.) I. 394 To sett ane remedy thairto.

†**33.** To add (one thing) *to* another. *Obs.*

*c* **1055** *Byrhtferth's Handboc* in *Anglia* VIII. 303 Nim þæt an, & sete onforeweardum þam concurrentium. *c* **1175** *Lamb. Hom.* 19 We wrecche sunfulle.. setteð deihwamliche sunne uppon sunne. *c* **1375** *Lay Folks Mass Bk.* (MS. B) 23 Grett saumpel he settis þer-to, whi hit is ful ille to do. *c* **1449** Pecock *Repr.* I. xi. 55 That to Holi Writt men schulde not sett eny exposiciouns, declaracions, or glosis. **1532** More *Confut. Tindale* Wks. 505/2 If any manne any thing set to these thynges. **1540** Palsgr. *Acolastus* I. i. Metres E iij b, They.. sette a syllable or mo to the nexte verse folowynge.

**34.** ***to set* (†*a*) *fire* †*in*, † *on*, † *upon*, † *of***, now only ***to***: to kindle, ignite. (Cf. 25.) Also *U.S.* ***to set a fire*** (without prepositional complement): to kindle or start a fire.

*c* **1400** *Laud Troy Book* 5879 Thei sette ffir In schip. **1535** Coverdale *Matt.* xxii. 7 The kynge.. destroyed those murtherers & set fyre vpon their Citie. **1568–1700** [see fire *sb.* 1 f]. **1582** N. Lichefield tr. *Castanheda's Discov. E. Ind.* 120 Our men.. did set fire to all the Townes yt were in the Ilande. **1641** T. Jordan *Walks of Islington* IV. ii. (1657) F 4, I will even make bold to set fire of your Bush [tavern], then throw your water and spare not. **1726** Swift *Gulliver* I. vii, By setting fire on your house. **1885** *Manch. Exam.* 8 July 5/2 These set fire by rockets to the straw barracks. **1906** *N.Y. Even. Post* 15 Nov. 3 Two fires in tenement house letter boxes were set to-day at an early hour. **1907** Elinor Glyn *Three Weeks* vi, As a child.. who sets a light to a whole box of matches in play. **1976** *Washington Post* 19 Apr. B1/7 The school had been broken into and the fire had been set.

**35.** To stake the welfare or existence of (something) *upon*; also *pass.* to be dependent for its destiny *upon*.

Phr. ***to set on* (*at*) *cinque and sice*, *on six and seven***: see cinque 3, six.

**1594** Shaks. *Rich. III*, v. iv. 9, I haue set my life vpon a cast, And I will stand the hazard of the Dye. **1601** —— *Jul. C.* v. i. 75 To set Vpon one Battell all our Liberties. **1670** Dryden *Tyr. Love* v. i. 49 Yet all my Fortune on his death is set. **1832** [see die *sb.*[1] 2 b (*d*)]. **1894** W. J. Dawson *Making of Manhood* 74 Their life is set upon a rushing whirling star.

**36.** To put (one thing) in the balance *against* another; to compare (one thing) *by* or *to* another.

[*a* **1000** *Boeth. Metr.* vi. 7 Hiora birhtu ne bið auht to ȝesettane wið þære sunnan leoht.] **1589** Puttenham *Eng. Poesie* III. xix. (Arb.) 241 When a man wil seeme to make things appeare good or bad,.. he sets the lesse by the greater, or the greater to the lesse. **1687** Burnet *Reply to Varillas* 30 Improbabilities ought never to be set against Positive Proofs. **1692** R. L'Estrange *Fables* lxviii. 68 This method of Setting what we Have against What we have Not. **1729** *Act 2 Geo. II*, c. 22 §13 Where there are mutual Debts between the Testator or Intestate, and either Party, one Debt may be set against the other. **1873** Spencer *Study Sociol.* ii. 40 Against his professed theory may be set his actual practice. **1890** *Illustr. Lond. News* 13 Sept. 331/1 Has she no human faults to set against so much sterile virtue?

*** *Where something is made to dwell in or rest upon a person or thing.*

**37. a.** To place (one's hope or trust) *in* (†*on*); to cause (one's thoughts or affections) to dwell *upon* or to be centred *in* something. Phr. ***to set one's heart on* (†*in*)**.

*c* **825** *Vesp. Ps.* lxxvii. 7 Ðæt hie setten in gode hyht. **971** *Blickl. Hom.* 227 Up to heofenum.. þyder his modȝeþanc a ȝeseted wæs. *a* **1300** *E.E. Psalter* lxi. 11 Nil þou set on þam þi hert. **1340** Hampole *Pr. Consc.* 7226 Þai.. on þe world þair hertes sett hard. **1377** Langl. *P. Pl.* B. x. 392 Many men.. more sette here hertis In good þan in god. *c* **1386** Chaucer *Monk's T.* 854 In vengeance he al his herte sette. *c* **1400** *Rule St. Benet* (Verse) 607 In god we set al our thoght. **1470–85** Malory *Arthur* I. xvii. 62 Kyng Arthur sette his loue gretely vpon her. *a* **1548** Hall *Chron., Hen. VII* (1550) 3 b, Whose mindes and studyes he.. knewe to be.. set in the polytique regiment.. of the publique wealth. **1576** Gascoigne *Droomme of Doomes Day* Wks. 1910 II. 307 To set mynde, upon vice and wickednesse. **1617** Moryson *Itin.* II. 195 His heart is very much set upon the enterprize of Ireland. **1714** Addison *Lover* No. 10 ¶3 The fragility of china is such as a reasonable being ought by no means to set its heart upon. **1802** Mar. Edgeworth *Moral T.* (1816) I. xi. 90 He had set his fancy upon his friend's horses. **1848** Thackeray *Van. Fair* xliii, She had set her mind on the Major. **1862** Tyndall *Mountaineer* i. 3 We set our thoughts on the sublime and beautiful. **1870** Rogers *Hist. Glean.* Ser. II. 203 He had set his heart on seeing his son a clergyman. **1891** E. & D. Gerard *Sensit. Pl.* III. III. xii. 91 Jeannette had set her fancy there.

†**b.** *pass.* and *intr.* (said of the affections). *Obs.*

**1607** Tourneur *Rev. Trag.* IV. i. G 3 Where the hearts set, there goes the tongues consent. **1831** Scott *Ct. Robt.* x, Whether, she had.. felt a partiality towards one whose heart was not particularly set upon gaining hers.

†**38.** To cause (a feeling or state of mind) to arise *in* a person; to fix *in* one's mind. *Obs.*

**971** *Blickl. Hom.* 125 Uton we symle þæs dæȝes fyrhto & eȝsan on ure mod settan. *c* **1200** Ormin 2337 Þe laffdiȝ Sannte Marȝe.. haffde sett inn hire þohht To libbenn i clænnesse. *Ibid.* 7187 Iss ned tatt he Dredinng & aȝhe sette On alle þa [etc.]. *a* **1225** *Leg. Kath.* 646 Sete, Iesu, swucche sahen i my muð to marhen. *a* **1225** *Ancr. R.* 32 Alle monne sores setteð in ower þouhte. *a* **1300** *Cursor M.* 6060 To seitt him soru at his hert. *c* **1400** *Apol. Loll.* 24 If ȝe wil not sett to þe hert to ȝef glory to my name. **1540** Palsgr. *Acolastus* I. iii. G ij b, What care goest thou about to set at thy fathers hart.

**39. a.** To rest (one's eye, one's look) *upon*.

*c* **1330** R. Brunne *Chron. Wace* (Rolls) 13821 Ilk on oþer auisement sett. *c* **1386** Chaucer *Clerk's T.* 233 Vp on Grisilde.. this Markys sette his eye. *c* **1386** —— *Man of Law's T.* 1053 At the firste look he on hire sette. *c* **1450** *St. Cuthbert* (Surtees) 4423 His syght on þe lyght he settys. **1575** Gascoigne *Hemetes the heremyte* Wks. 1910 II. 482, I cold nevr more sett eye on her. *a* **1645** Waller *To Amoret* 5 Joy salutes me when I set My blest Eyes on Amoret. **1765** Foote *Commissary* II. (1782) 32 The first time I set eyes on captain Wilkins.. I accost him. **1852** Dickens *Bleak Ho.* xlvi, He.. never has been seen or heard of since, till I set eyes on him just now.

†**b.** ***to set sight of* (*in*)** = to set eyes on, to sight. *Obs.*

*c* **1595** Capt. Wyatt *R. Dudley's Voy. W. Ind.* (Hakl. Soc.) 11 On which daie it pleased God that wee sett sight of a carvell. **1746** *Exmoor Scolding* (E.D.S.) l. 37 Nif zo be tha dest bet zet Zeert [= sight] in Harry Vursdon.

**40.** To put (a mark, impression) *upon*; to place as a distinguishing mark, token, or imprint. Now *rhetorical*.

*a* **1000** *Cædmon's Gen.* 2369 Abraham.. sette friðotacen [*viz.* circumcision].. on his selfes sunu. **1382** Wyclif *Gen.* iv. 15 The Lord sette a signe in Caym [**1611** set a marke vpon]. **1412–20** Lydg. *Chron. Troy* IV. 2156 Al paie is good, be so þe prente be set. **1601** Shaks. *Twel. N.* II. ii. 31 In womens waxen hearts to set their formes. **1653** Manlove *Lead-mines* 21 The Barghmaster.. on the Spindel ought to set a nick, If that the grove unworked be three week. **1653** Marvell *Corr.* Wks. (Grosart) II. 4, I shall hope to set nothing upon his spirit but what may be of a good sculpture.

**41.** To lay or spread (a surface of a certain kind) *on* an object; hence, to put (a favourable or specious appearance) *upon* a thing.

***to set a good face upon***: see face *sb.* 10. ***to set a gloss upon***: see gloss *sb.*

**1540** Palsgr. *Acolastus* II. i. I iij, Seinge thou settest as good a face vpon beanes, as if they were blanched almondes. **1566** Gascoigne *Supposes* IV. v, What a brazen face he setteth on it! **1593** Shaks. *2 Hen. VI*, IV. ii. 7 Iacke Cade the Cloathier, meanes to dresse the Common-wealth and turne it, and set a new nap vpon it. **1602** —— *Ham.* IV. vii. 133 Wee'l.. set a double varnish on the fame The Frenchman gaue you. **1607** —— *Timon* I. ii. 152 You haue.. Set a faire fashion on our entertainment. **1649** Milton *Eikon.* Pref. B 4 b, They took him to set a face upon thir own malignant designes. **1697** Dryden *Virg. Past.* IX. 8 Kick'd out, we set the best face on't we cou'd. **1716** Lady M. W. Montagu *Let. to Pope* 14 Sept., I find that I have.., whatever face I set on't, a strong disposition to believe in miracles.

**42.** To put (an edge or point) *on*, *to*. (Cf. 75.)

**1600** Nashe *Summer's Last Will* F 1, What sets an edge on a knife? the grindstone alone? no, the moyst element powr'd vpon it, which grinds out all gaps, sets a poynt vpon it. **1620** *Westward for Smelts* (Percy Soc.) 11 This did but set an edge to her wanton appetite. **1647** C. Harvey *Schola Cordis* xxxix. 3 What I get Serves but to set An edge upon mine appetite. **1891** *Cornh. Mag.* Dec. 638, I am now setting a very keen edge to my blade.

**43. a.** To fix (a certain price) *upon* a thing; now chiefly in ***to set a price upon one's head*** and the like; otherwise expressed by *put*. (Cf. 89.)

**1530** Palsgr. 715/2 And you set nat a price upon your marchaundyse, howe can it be bought? **1652** Needham tr. *Selden's Mare Cl.* 492 Setting great ransom upon their Fisher-men. **1666–7** Marvell *Corr.* Wks. (Grosart) II. 203 A Bill has bin read for setting the prices of wine as well upon the merchant as retaylor. **1687** Burnet *Contin. Reply to Varillas* 35 There is not a word of any sum set on his Head. **1720** Ozell *Vertot's Rom. Rep.* II. XI. 184 Sylla set a Price upon the Heads of all that were proscribed. **1765** [see premium 1]. **1861** *Temple Bar* I. 521 A price was set upon the head of the Prince. **1880** D. C. Davies *Metallif. Min.* 420 s.v., To set a price upon a share in a mine.

**b.** *fig.* To put (a certain value) *upon*, have (a certain estimate) *of*.

**1611** Shaks. *Cymb.* IV. iv. 48 Since of your liues you set So slight a valewation. **1671** Milton *P.R.* IV. 160 That I On what I offer set as high esteem. **1756** Mrs. Calderwood in *Coltness Collect.* (Maitland Club) 238 After setting a just value upon others, I must next set it on myself.

†**44.** To lay (something burdensome) *upon*; to impose or inflict (a penalty, tax, etc.) *upon*. *Obs.*

*c* **888** Ælfred *Boeth.* xxxix. §10 Þæt God nylle.. nan unaberendlice broc him an settan. *a* **1000** *Cædmon's Gen.* 1266 Hwonne frea wolde on wærloȝan wite settan. *c* **1200** *Trin. Coll. Hom.* 61 Listeð nu wich þreat dauid setteð uppen us. **1338** R. Brunne *Chron.* (1810) 55 Forto reise þe treuage, þat on þe lond was sette. **13..** *Cursor M.* 23666 (Gött) [Pine] þat godd has sett vs for vr sin. *c* **1450** *St. Cuthbert* (Surtees) 6246 þe tax on þaim to sett. **1537** in Leadam *Sel. Cases Crt. Requests* (Selden Soc.) 47 The seid felaweship.. sett vpon euery of the seyd compleynauntes for his contribucion xij d. by the yere. **1552–3** *Act 7 Edw. VI*, c. 12 §10 The somme or sommes upon hym sett to be due. **1617** Moryson *Itin.* I. 115 There being a great penalty set upon any that carry their Armes. **1639** Du Verger tr. *Camus' Admir. Events* 220 This man sets a seisure on Nilamon's lands. *a* **1715** Burnet *Own*

*Time* (1724) I. 399 He was to have a proportion of all the fines that should be set upon this evidence. **1761** *Chron.* in *Ann. Reg.* June, Of which offence he being convicted, the Court set a fine on him.

V. To appoint, institute (a person); to prescribe, ordain, establish (a thing).

**45.** To post or station (a person) in a certain place *to* perform certain duties.

With infin. this sense passes into 112b.

**971** *Blickl. Hom.* 177 Þa he bebyrȝed wæs, settan him hyrdas to. *a* **1225** *Ancr. R.* 270 Isboset lei & slepte & sette ane wummon uorte beon ȝeteward. **1297** R. GLOUC. (Rolls) 8113 Hii..at ech of þe vour ȝates sette an compaynie. *Ibid.* 10685 He astorede þe castel..& sette þer uolk inou to holde him aȝe þe kinge. **1362** LANGL. *P. Pl.* A. x. 22 Þeose sixe ben I-set to saue þe Castel. *c* **1400** *Master of Game* (MS. Digby 182) xxxv. fol. 55 b, Þe stable þat oweth to be sette or þe kyng comme. *c* **1450** *Mirk's Festial* 16 Þen wer þer þefes set for hym yn a wod þat he most nede goo þrogh. *a* **1533** LD. BERNERS *Huon* lxxxiii. 259 Loke that ye set good watche at euery gate. **1598** BARRET *Theor. Warres* II. i. 22 He shall.. assist him..in setting the watch. **1630** WINTHROP *Hist. New Eng.* (1825) I. 10 Our captain, so soon as he had set the watch, at eight in the evening, called his men. **1697** DRYDEN *Virg. Georg.* IV. 607 Like Centries set. **1769** FALCONER *Dict. Marine* (1780) Rr4b, To set the Watch, is to appoint one division of the crew to enter upon the duty of the watch. **1821** SCOTT *Kenilw.* xxxviii, How came he to leave the Castle after the watch was set? **1873** SPENCER *Stud. Sociol.* x. 251 Spies have to be set to check them. **1877** MISS YONGE *Cameos* Ser. III. xxiii. 214 A watch was set all round the castle.

†**46.** To place (a person) in an office, appoint *to* a certain function or *to perform* a certain duty; to appoint (an official). *Obs.*

*c* **1000** *Ags. Ps.* (Th.) civ. 17 He sette hine on his huse to hlafwearde. *c* **1200** ORMIN 13438, I sette ȝuw to ben Amang hæþene lede Lihhtfattess muþ. *a* **1300** *Cursor M.* 11753 Preistes..To do þe folk, als þai war sete, Ma sacrifies to þair maumet. *Ibid.* 23877 Hirdes þat þe lauerd has sett. *c* **1400** *Rule St. Benet* (Prose) 20 Þabbes ah at set nan þar-to bot þat scho is sikir offe. *c* **1450** *Brut* 429 He..made his testament full, and sette his executoris. *c* **1460** *Oseney Reg.* 5 The which sett in the seyde church seculer chanons. *c* **1460** SIR R. ROS *La Belle Dame* 613 There is no iuge yset on such trespace. **1486** *Rec. St. Mary at Hill* (1904) 7 Than I woll.. admytte..an honest preest to the said Chauntry, & hym set & inducte in the same. **1498** *Cov. Leet Bk.* 597 Auditours therupon to be sett.

**47. a.** To place in a position of superiority or control *over* another (e.g. as a ruler, protector, guard).

*c* **1000** *Ags. Ps.* (Th.) xvii. 48 Þa hælo þæs cynges ðe ðu ȝesettest ofer folcum. **1123** *O.E. Chron.* (Laud MS.), Hit wæs toȝeanes riht þæt man scolde setten clerc ofer muneces. *c* **1200** ORMIN 3910 To..setten enngless oferr hemm To ȝemenn hemm. *a* **1225** *Ancr. R.* 72 Þet beoð ouer oðre iset, & habbeð ham to witene. *a* **1300** *Cursor M.* 6222 Ouer al þat ost he sett leders. *c* **1400** *Rule St. Benet* (Verse) 965 Lord, o-bouen set hase þou Souerayns to wham vs bus bew. **1585** T. WASHINGTON tr. *Nicholay's Voy.* III. iv. 76 b, The Ambassadors, vnto whom they are set ouer as theyr gard. **1667** MILTON *P.L.* IX. 941 Us his prime Creatures,..Set over all his Works. *a* **1700** EVELYN *Diary* Sept. 1646, They ..set a guard upon us. **1754** RICHARDSON *Grandison* IV. xiii. 80 The seventh man was set over the post-boy. **1844** H. H. WILSON *Brit. India* I. 235 In the estimation of those whom he was set over. **1879** GUEST *Lect. Hist. Eng.* xiv. 127 He promoted the French clergy, and set them over the English.

**b.** To cause (a person) to act in a grievous way *upon*.

Phr. *to set* (one) *in* another's **neck**: see NECK *sb.* 3c. Similarly *to set on* another's *back*.

**1551** ROBINSON tr. *More's Utopia* II. viii. (1895) 251 They reyse vp the people..and them they sette in theyre neckes vnder the coloure of some olde tytle of ryghte. **1692** DRYDEN *Cleomenes* IV. i, Your Friend was set upon you for a Spy. **1695** WOOD *Life* (O.H.S.) IV. 49 He endeavoured to set Sir William Glynn on his back.

**c.** *to set* (a person) *on* (another): to get him to use influence with. *rare.*

*a* **1715** BURNET *Own Time* (1724) I. 241 He took care to set the English Bishops on the King.

**48.** To appoint (a boundary, limit). Const. dat. of person or equivalent with *to*.

*c* **888** ÆLFRED *Boeth.* xxi, He hæfð heora mearce swa ȝesette þæt hie ne mot heore mearce ȝebrædan. *a* **1000** ÆLFRIC *Exod.* xix. 23 Þu hete settan ȝemæro. **1535** COVERDALE *Ps.* ciii. 9 Thou hast set them their boundes, which they maie not passe. **1576** GASCOIGNE *Grief of Joy* Wks. 1910 II. 521 Asthough yᵉ bounds were sett, How longe mans lyfe, might heere on earthe endure. *a* **1586** SIDNEY *Arcadia* III. (Sommer) 265 Since she found she could set no limits to his passions. **1667** MILTON *P.L.* III. 538 Where bounds were set To darkness. **1678** CUDWORTH *Intell. Syst.* 882 Those narrow Limits, which Vulgar Opinion and Imagination sets them. **1749** SMOLLETT *Gil Blas* IX. i. (1782) III. 226 Ambitious fellows, who set no bounds to their desires. **1827** SCOTT *Highl. Widow* v, My sufferings will soon be over; but yours—Oh, who but Heaven shall set a boundary to them! **1885** 'LUCAS MALET' *Col. Enderby's Wife* II. IV. i. 130 The limits of our nature are set, and we can never cross them.

†**49.** To appoint (a season, festival, etc.) to be observed. *Obs.*

*c* **1000** *Ags. Ps.* (Th.) lxxv. 7 Þæt ic þe symble daȝ sette and ȝyrwe. *c* **1000** ÆLFRIC *Hom.* I. 310 Þes dæȝ [Pentecostes] wæs on ðære ealdan æ ȝesett and ȝehalȝod. *c* **1175** *Lamb. Hom.* 11 Þas daȝes beoð iset us to muchele helpe. *a* **1300** *Cursor M.* 28260 Þe festes þat in kyrk ar sette. **1340** *Ayenb.* 171 Þe festes principals þet byeþ yzet ine holy Cherche vor God to bidde.

**50.** To ordain or establish (a regulation); to lay down (a law); to prescribe (a form or order). †Also, in OE. and ME., to ordain or lay it down (*that* something should be done). *Obs.* or *arch.* Cf. *set law* s.v. SET *ppl. a.* 1 b.

*c* **893** ÆLFRED *Oros.* I. ii. §3 Hio ȝesette ofer eall hyre rice þæt nan forbyrd nære [etc.]. *a* **900** CYNEWULF *Crist* 236 [God] sylfa sette þæt þu sunu wære efeneardiȝende mid þinne engan frean. *a* **1122** *O.E. Chron.* (Laud MS.) an. 1102, Hi þær maneȝa beboda setton þe to Cristendome belimpað. *c* **1200** ORMIN 491 Drihhtin haffde þanne sett, þatt nan ne shollde wurrþenn þa sett to wurrþenn prest, butt iff He prestess sune wære. *a* **1225** *Leg. Kath.* 359 Alle ich iseo þine sahen sotliche isette. *c* **1449** PECOCK *Repr.* IV. vii. 461 Seint Poul..which made this now rehercid lawe and settide it to be had in vce. **1477** NORTON *Ord. Alch.* iv. in Ashm. (1652) 46 Rasis set the Dietary. **15..** BODENHAM in Hakluyt *Voy.* (1599) II. I. 100 The chiefe of the Turkes set order yᵗ none shal do any harme to the people or to their goods. **1666–7** PEPYS *Diary* 14 Feb., When our rules are once set,..no Governor should offer to alter them. **1865** GROTE *Plato* I. xii. 422 Actual positive laws: which..have..been set by some ill-qualified historical ruler, or have grown up insensibly.

*absol.* *c* **1200** ORMIN Ded. 10 An reȝhellboc to follȝhenn Unnderr kanunnkess had & lif, Swa summ Sannt Awwstin sette. *c* **1400** *Destr. Troy* 379 After custome to kepe as the Kyng set.

**51. a.** To fix or appoint (a time) for the transaction of an affair, or as the term of a period. Also, to fix a time for. Cf. SET *ppl. a.* 2 a.

*a* **1056** *Diplom. Angl.* (Th.) 376 [Hi] settan dæȝ to þæt man to ðam lande scolde faran. *a* **1122** [see A. 1 a]. *c* **1205** LAY. 2554 A þon daie þet wes iset þa comen heo to sumne. *c* **1290** *Beket* 782 in *S. Eng. Leg.* 129 Ich þe lende þo fif hondred pound..Sete me þar-of ane schorte day for þov schalt heom ȝelde ech-on. *a* **1300** *Cursor M.* 5939 Sett vs term wen we sal for þe prai. **1387** TREVISA *Higden* (Rolls) VIII. 103 Þere was i-sette a day to answere. **1470–85** MALORY *Arthur* X. lxxxvii. 568 Sette ye a day said sir Tristram that we shalle doo bataille. **1548–77** VICARY *Anat.* i. (1888) 16 They shal.. neuer set any certaine day of the sicke-mans health, for it lyeth not in their power. **1633** BP. HALL *Hard Texts* Isa. xvi. 14 Within three yeares (which shall be as precisely set and observed, as the hireling uses to keep account of the time agreed upon for his service). **1693** LOCKE *Educ.* §127 Wks. 1714 III. 58 Upon his dispatching his Study within the Time set him. **1753** RICHARDSON *Grandison* IV. xxi. 163, I thank my grandmamma and aunt for their kind summons. I will soon set my day. *a* **1810** TANNAHILL *Poems* (1846) 21 Let's set the bridal night afore ye gang. **1890** MARY E. WILKINS *Far-away Melody*, etc. 305 Two o'clock had been the hour set for the wedding. **1893** *Field* 18 Feb. 225/3 The club's opening day..is set for April 22.

**b.** Said of God, destiny, etc.; also in impers. pass.

*a* **1300** *Cursor M.* 15163 Þe tide, þat in his suete wil was sett. **1390** GOWER *Conf.* I. 191 The time set of kinde is come. **1460–70** *Bk. Quintessence* I Þe teerme þat is sett of god, þat noman may a-schape. **1590** LODGE *Rosalynde* (Hunter. Club) I b, You see that Fate hath set a period of my yeares. **1594** KYD *Cornelia* IV. ii. 147 Heauen sets our time. **1611** *Second Maiden's Trag.* 364 Yet sir ther is a date set to all sorrowes. **1667** MILTON *P.L.* x. 499 His Seed, when is not set, shall bruise my head. **1681** H. MORE *Expos. Dan.* 199 God had set his time wherein these afflictions..should end.

†**c.** *intr.* To fix *upon* a time. *Obs.*

**1648** GAGE *West Ind.* 84 We set upon the time that we should take our flight.

†**52.** *trans.* To appoint as one's lot or destiny. Also *absol.* *Obs.*

*c* **1000** ÆLFRIC *Hom.* I. 64 Ac he sette ȝecamp ȝeleaffullum sawlum. *c* **1200** ORMIN 775, & forrþi sette himm Drihhtin Godd To ben Johan ȝehatenn. *Ibid.* 4836 All þatt he setteþþ uppo þe Off sellþe & off unnsellþe. *a* **1300** *Cursor M.* 15548 Als prophetis has sett..I sal rise on þe thrid dai. *a* **1400–50** *Wars Alex.* 522 He..Said it was sett to be so he saȝe by his artis. *c* **1470** HENRY *Wallace* VIII. 691 For Inglismen he settis no doym bot ded.

†**53.** To appoint or provide to be used or observed by a person. *Obs.*

*c* **1000** ÆLFRIC *Hom.* I. 312 On ðam ealdan Pentecosten sette God æ ðam Israhela folce. **1129** *O.E. Chron.* (Laud MS.), Crist sette red for his wrecce folc. *c* **1200** ORMIN 11690 Þe lare off haliȝ boc þatt ȝuw iss sett to follȝhenn. **1340** *Ayenb.* 11 Þe tuelf apostles þet hise zette to hyealde and to loky to alle þon þet wyleþ by yborȝe. *c* **1430** *Life St. Kath.* (Roxb.) 28 After þe offices þat he hath sett vn to hem. *c* **1450** CAPGRAVE *Life St. Aug.* xi, Sche took councell of Seyn Ambrose, and he sette hir þis reule. **1690** LOCKE *Hum. Und.* II. xxvii. §6. 158 It would be in vain for one intelligent Being, to set a Rule to the Actions of another.

**54. a.** To present (an example or pattern) for others to follow; to introduce (a fashion).

*c* **1175** *Lamb. Hom.* 5 Godalmihti..sette us bisne. *a* **1340** HAMPOLE *Psalter* xxvii. 1 Crist..settand him ensaumpile til rightwismen. **1642** MILTON *Apol. Smect.* §12. 57 Their Maister Christ gave them this precept, and set them this example. **1710** ATTERBURY *Serm.* (Matt. xi. 6) (1734) I. 81 To trace all the Steps of that Example which he set us in the Flesh. **1786** *Microcosm* No. II. 130 Homer having prescribed the form, or, to use a more modern term, set the fashion of Epic Poems. **1867** FREEMAN *Norm. Conq.* I. v. 378 A Thegn of Danish descent, Thurcytel.., set the example of flight. **1883** *Ch. Times* 9 Nov. 813/3 He set a pattern of controversial violence at a time when tolerance was the lesson most needed by all parties. **1890** S. LANE-POOLE *Barbary Corsairs* II. xvi. 213 The Genoese and Venetians set the models of these vessels. **1895** A. J. BALFOUR *Found. Belief* I. ii. 54 A fashion, as the phrase goes, has to be 'set'.

**b.** To put before a person (a specimen of work) to be followed, mark out (the lines) on which he is to work or proceed.

**1593** SHAKS. *2 Hen. VI*, IV. ii. 95 We tooke him setting of boyes Copies. **1638** JUNIUS *Paint. Ancients* 8 Children follow the copies which are set them. *c* **1680** BEVERIDGE *Serm.* (1729) I. 586 To walk..in the ways which he hath set them. **1714** POPE *Let. to Caryll* 16 Aug., I could turn writing-master at last and set copies to children. **1862** MACLAREN *Milit. Syst. Gymnastic Exerc.* 9 The instructor will set (*i.e.*, perform in its perfect manner) each exercise. **1912** *Scott. Hist. Rev.* Jan. 193 Successful in a brief military campaign on lines set for him by his circumstances.

†**c.** To start (a hymn, etc.) for others to take up.

*c* **1450** in Aungier *Syon* (1840) 360 The chefe chauntresse. To whos charge..it belongeth for..to sette the songe euen and mensurably. **1712** STEELE *Spect.* No 284 ⁋5, I had one Day set the Hundredth Psalm, and was singing the first Line in order to put the Congregation into the Tune. **1726** *Adv. Capt. R. Boyle* (1768) 148 One Sunday as the Clerk had set the Psalm. **1742** FIELDING *Jos. Andrews* I. vi, I should be very willing to be his Clerk: for which you know I am qualified, being able to read, and to set a Psalm.

**d.** In a chase or race, ***to set the pace***, to proceed at a rate of speed to be followed by another. So ***to set the stroke*** (in rowing).

**1891** *Murray's Mag.* Mar. 367 Walking the pace set by her pupil. **1892** *Field* 2 Apr. 480/1 Elin, in the Cambridge boat, is setting a longer stroke. **1898** NEWBOLT *Isl. Race* 84 He's leading them straight for Blackmoor Gate, And he's setting a pounding pace!

**e.** *Bowls*, etc. (See quots.)

**1886** *W. Somerset Word-bk.* s.v., At each round [of skittles] the loser has to set—i.e. to fix the spot where the bowl shall be delivered in the next. **1897** *Encycl. Sport* I. 129/2 (Bowls), A 'mark' is *set*, *thrown*, or *led*, by the winners of an end after the score has been settled.

**55. a.** To allot or enjoin (a task). Const. dative of person or *upon*.

In mod. use often *pass.* said of what is required to be done.

*a* **1300** *Cursor M.* 29000 Crist..has he sett vs certain task quilk ar þai bones for to ask. **1693** LOCKE *Educ.* §127 (1699) 235 Set him such a Task, to be done in such a time, as may allow him no opportunity to be idle. **1821** SCOTT *Kenilw.* xxxvii, Repeating the words like a task which was set him. **1821** B'NESS BUNSEN in Hare *Life* (1879) I. 187 While I sit working or setting work. **1845** [PYCROFT] *Collegian's Guide* 107, I shall close my door another morning after the first five minutes, and then set impositions. **1847** MARRYAT *Childr. New Forest* xiv, I shall not set him anything to do. **1884** *Manch. Exam.* 17 June 5/1 The master..was in the habit of setting lessons for the children to work upon at home after school hours. **1892** *Standard* 27 July 7/5 The Club were set 94 runs to win. **1892** *Field* 6 Feb. 188/1 We had our work set to keep up with hounds.

**b.** *Mining*, etc. To appoint the amount of (work to be done).

**1742** *De Foe's Tour Gt. Brit.* (ed. 3) I. 141 They appoint ..the Quantity each Dredgerman shall take in a Day, which is usually called Setting the Stint. **1868** BALLANTYNE *Deep Down* xxviii, The manager..read out the names, positions, etc., of the various 'pitches' that were to be 'sett' for the following month. **1880** D. C. DAVIES *Metallif. Min.* 420 To set bargains or work to miners. **1900** *Daily News* 3 Dec. 10/3 Those other bargains which it was impracticable to 'set' on the 19th and 20th November will be 'set' as usual on the same day (December 5th).

**c.** To propound (a question or set of questions) to be solved or answered; to prescribe (a book) for an examination or a course of study.

**1711** [see A. 1 a]. **1845** [PYCROFT] *Collegian's Guide* 317 [It] enabled Williamson.. to answer two of the ethical questions with the *ipsissima verba* of two of the examiners who set them. **1889** MRS. LYNN LINTON *Thro' Long Night* I. I. vii. 101 No mind-reader..could have solved the problem had it been set him. **1890** *Jrnl. Educ.* 1 June 297/2 He will henceforward set no papers either in Greek or in Latin verse. **1891** *Murray's Mag.* X. 743 Milton's 'Areopagitica' is set for examinations. **1895** *Law Times* XCIX. 547/1 The intermediate examination is in special books set from time to time.

†**56. a.** To appoint (a meeting), make (an appointment). Also *absol.* *Obs.*

*c* **1330** *Arth. & Merl.* 4702 Galathin & Gawainet To gider com, þer þai hadde set. *c* **1375** *Sc. Leg. Saints* xviii. (*Egipciane*) 1160 To þe kirk he come but let, quhare scho to hyme triste set. **1596** SHAKS. *1 Hen. IV*, I. ii. 119 (Qo.), Nowe shall we knowe if Gadshill haue set a match. *a* **1810** TANNAHILL *Poems* (1846) 19 They set their tryst where neist again to meet.

†**b.** To appoint (a council, etc.) *to be held*. *Obs.*

**1523** LD. BERNERS *Froiss.* I. l. 30 Ther was a counsell set to be at Uyllenort. *a* **1578** LINDESAY (Pitscottie) *Chron. Scot.* (S.T.S.) I. 394 He sett ane parliament at Edinburgh to be haldin the tent day of Juin.

**57. a.** To let on lease, lease, let. Also ***to set in feu, in feu ferm, in lease, in tack***. Now *local*.

**1422** in Raine *North Durham* (1852) App. 104 For til haue Set & to ferme latty[n] to my der frende all my landis of Eddirham. **1426** in C. Rogers *Chartul. Priory Coldstream* (1879) 43 Be it kend..ws Wilȝame Drax..till haue set and to ferme lattyn al ye landis of Litill Swynton. *c* **1480** *Oseney Reg.* (Exch. MS.) 60 b, Howses..the which, to whoome soo ever they will, they maye sett or lette. **1495** *Rolls of Parlt.* VI. 465/1 Moche lesse Rent..then the said Lordshippes.. myght resonably be sette for. **1523** FITZHERB. *Surv.* 2 b, How moche euery acre is worthe to set by the yere. **1564** *Reg. Privy Council Scot.* I. 304 He..hes..set and disponit the few of the saidis landis owir his heid. **1600** HOLLAND *Livy* XXVII. 635 That these Censors should set and to ferme let the territorie of Capua. **1618** in *Rec. Convent. Roy. Burghs Scot.* (1878) III. 61 Thai..sall nather sell, dispone or sett in few or in tak anie of the saids lands. **1682** G. VERNON *Life Heylin* 120 He removed his Study to Alresford, setting his House for no more than 3 l. a year. **1693** STAIR *Instit.* II. xi. (ed. 2) 347 All Tacks set by the Vassal without the Superiors Consent. **1710** SWIFT *Jrnl. to Stella* 26 Oct., I have had also a letter from Parvisol, with an account how my livings are set; and that they are fallen, since last year, sixty pounds. **1788** BURKE *Sp. agst. W. Hastings* Wks. XIII. 233 By setting the rest to farmers at rents and under hopes, which could never be realized. **1790** WOLCOT (P. Pindar) *Ep. to Jas. Bruce* Wks. 1816 II. 163 A comely spot..; A lease-hold though..; Set..at a moderate rent. **1806** MORISON *Decis.* XXXIII. 14259 The magistrates and council did set in lease to certain persons a stell fishing. **1884** R. HUNT *Brit. Mining* 107 The custom of setting or leasing a mine on tribute. **1910** P. W. JOYCE *Engl. in Irel.* 319 A struggling housekeeper failed to let her lodging, which a neighbour explained by: 'Ah, she's no good at setting'.

†**b.** *intr.* To take a (mining) lease. Cf. SET *sb.*[1] 3 b. *Obs.*

**1653** MANLOVE *Lead-mines* 3 May set In any ground, and there Lead-oar may get. *Ibid.* 37 The Vulgar term, is setting for a Mine, For the grace of God, and what I there can find. *Ibid.* 41 Another Miner for a Crosse-vein sets.

†**58. a.** *trans.* To establish by agreement or authority (a settled condition, an alliance, a peace). *Obs.*

*c* **900** tr. *Bæda's Hist.* III. xviii. §1 Þa wilnode he þæt lif onhyrigan, þe he well ȝesæt ȝeseah in Gallia rice. *c* **1205** LAY. 30031 Heo setten grið, heo sette frið. *a* **1300** *Cursor M.* 25870 Þer has þi schrift sett end o pyne, þat elles war wit-vten fine. *a* **1450** *Le Morte Arth.* 2331 A trews they sette and sekeryd thare. **1523** LD. BERNERS *Froiss.* I. lii. 30 b, The thyrde shulde set agrement bytwene them. **1535** CROMWELL in Merriman *Life & Lett.* (1902) I. 411 As ye can.. sett a fynall ende therin. **1545** in Leadam *Sel. Cases Crt. Requests* (Selden Soc.) 175 To sett suche fynall ordre and determinacion therin as maye stand with our Lawes. **1576** GASCOIGNE *Droomme of Doomes day* Wks. 1910 II. 352 Thynke not.. that I came to set peace in the world. **1581** PETTIE tr. *Guazzo's Civ. Conv.* I. (1586) 31 It is now high time to set an end to this discourse. **1585** T. WASHINGTON tr. *Nicholay's Voy.* I. ii. 2 Hauing sette an order in his householde affaires. **1632** BP. HALL *Hard Texts* Matt. xv. 2 Why do thy disciples violate and neglect this good order, set by our wise Elders in their repast? **1633** *Ibid.* 2 Sam. xix. 29, I have in my first sentence set an order in these affaires. **1652** NEEDHAM tr. *Selden's Mare Cl.* Ep. Ded. 14 You were readie to set an end to the present differences.

†**b.** To settle (an affair). *Obs.*

**1605** STOW *Ann.* 1426 [Jas. I] called a councell to him, and taking order for setting all things in his Realme of Scotland, began his voyage towards England. **1619** CUSHMAN in Bradford *Plymouth Plant.* (1856) 36, I.. could not effecte yt which I aimed at, neither can yet sett things as I wished.

**VI.** To put in position, arrange, fix, adjust.

* *To fix or arrange in a required position or manner.*

**59.** To spread out (a net) to catch animals; to lay (a trap). †Also *absol.*

For *set a gin, snare, trap* used phraseologically in a fig. sense, see the sbs.

*c* **825** *Vesp. Ps.* cxviii. 110 Setten synfulle ȝerene me. *a* **1000** *Colloq. Ælfric* in Wr.-Wülcker 92 Ic brede me max and sette hiȝ on stowe ȝehæpprre. *a* **1250** *Owl & Night.* 1057 Þe louerd.., Lym & grune & wel ihwat Sette & leyde þe for to lacche. ? *a* **1366**, etc. [see GIN *sb.*[1] 4]. **1388** WYCLIF *Jer.* v. 26 Fouleres settynge snaris and trappis. **1530** PALSGR. 711/2 Go set for some connyes. *a* **1578** LINDESAY (Pitscottie) *Chron. Scot.* (S.T.S.) I. 56 As they had ben settand tinchellis for the murther of wyld beistes. **1697** DRYDEN *Virg. Georg.* I. 413 For stalking Cranes to set the guileful Snare. **1815** [see GIN *sb.*[1] 4]. **1817** J. MAYER *Sportsman's Direct.* (ed. 2) 176 To have traps constantly set and baited. **1827** *Act 7–8 Geo. IV*, c. 18 §1 If any Person shall set or place.. any Spring Gun, Man Trap, or other Engine calculated to destroy human Life. **1842** *Act 5 & 6 Vict.* c. 106 §7 Every Person offending by setting or leaving set any such Net. **1889** DOYLE *Micah Clarke* iv, We.. proceeded to set our lines [for fishing]. **1890** *Good Words* Aug. 549/1 The snare was set.. outside the field.

**60. a.** To put (a thing) in place; to fix up in the proper or required manner; †to erect (a tent, a mast); in early use often = *set up*, 154 m.

**1399** LANGL. *Rich. Redeles* III. 166 Kerving þe cloþe all to pecis, þat seuene goode sowers.. Moun not sett þe seemes ne sewe hem aȝeyn. *a* **1400–50** *Wars Alex.* 1143 And þen trussis him to Tyre & þare his tentis settis. **1429–30** *Rec. St. Mary at Hill* (1904) 73 For ijc latthes set.. xvj d. *a* **1530** HEYWOOD *Play of Wether* 742 (Brandl) Except ye be perfyt in settynge your [mill]stones. **1603** *Shuttleworths' Acc.* (Chetham Soc.) 151 A mason, iiij days and halfe settinge the chimly pyppes. *a* **1647** in *Archæologia* XII. 283 We reared our sheers to set our masts. **1669** BOYLE *Contn. New Exp.* II. (1682) 187 Whilst I set the screw all things in the Receiver suffered a compression. **1720** DE FOE *Capt. Singleton* xvii. (1840) 296 She lay to set her mast. **1735** DYCHE & PARDON *Dict.*, *Set*,.. a Term used for turning a Crane round, so as to raise the Weight that is to be shipped from the Shore. **1765** FRANKLIN *Let.* Wks. 1887 III. 390 You mention nothing of the furnace. If that iron one is not set, let it alone till my return. **1830** HEDDERWICK *Mar. Archit.* 280 Having the sheer adjusted and set fair on one side. **1863** G. A. LAWRENCE *Border & Bastille* iv, The fore and hind wheels are nearly the same height, and set very close together. **1870** *Inquiry, Yorksh. Deaf & Dumb* 18 She has been occupied in setting cards to card wool with. **1883** *Law Times Rep.* XLIX. 139/1 He [a slater] was to have 4*s.* a square, 2*d.* a foot for setting the ridge. **1890** BILLINGS *Nat. Med. Dict.* II. 498 The lancets are set and released simultaneously. **1891** *Labour Commission* Gloss., *Setting trees*, the placing of timber props to support the roof in a coal mine.

**b.** = *set going* (114 c).

*c* **1500** MORE *Wks.* ¶ iij, A toppe can I set, and dryue it in his kynde. **1781** COWPER *Let. to Rev. W. Unwin* 28 May, When the press is once set.. [the printers] are rather impatient of any delay. **1819** HAYMAN *Art of Brewing* 16 When the tap is set, the liquor passes perpendicularly through the goods. **1833** BREWSTER *Nat. Magic* xi. 294 He can, by setting an engine, produce [etc.].

**61.** To insert (a stitch). Phr. *to set a stitch*, to use needle and thread, to sew. Formerly † *to set seams.*

**1683** KENNETT tr. *Erasm. on Folly* 94 For a poor Cobbler to set a stitch on the Sabbath day. **1771** FOOTE *Maid of B.* III. Wks. 1799 II. 239, I am almost resolved never to set another stitch for him as long as I live. **1856** MISS YONGE *Daisy Chain* xxvii. 654 Bellairs.. shed a tear for every stitch she set in the trousseau. **1862** —— *C'tess Kate* xiv, She has never let Lily wear a stitch but of her setting.

**62.** *Baking, Glass-making*, etc. To put into the oven or furnace.

**1483** *Cath. Angl.* 263/1 To set in Owen.. *jn fornacem ponere.* **1530** PALSGR. 714/1 At the settyng in to the oven folkes make syde loves. **1735** DYCHE & PARDON *Dict.*, *Set*,.. in particular used by Bakers, as putting their Bread, &c. into the Oven. **1834–6** BARLOW in *Encycl. Metrop.* (1845) VIII. 459/1 The seggars, in *setting-in* the oven, are first placed in the spaces between the bags opposite the entrance. **1839** URE *Dict. Arts* 577 (*Glass-making*) Before *setting the pots* in the furnace. **1845** G. DODD *Brit. Manuf.* IV. 45 The withdrawal of an old pot and replacing it with a new one is called 'setting a pot'. **1854** G. READ *Biscuit Baker's Assist.* (ed. 2) 15 An old practice of setting a suit of biscuits, called 'chuck and shove'. **1885** LOCK in *Workshop Rec.* Ser. IV. 171/1 Before commencing to 'set' the retorts.

**63. a.** To fix (a stone or gem) in a surface of metal as an ornament; †formerly also on a garment (cf. SET *sb.*[1] 22). Also, to fashion (a design or pattern) *in* precious stones.

*a* **1500** *Flower & Leaf* 146 Many a riche stone Was set on the purfiles. **1501** *Bury Wills* (Camden) 91 A ryng of gold wt a toorkes set in. **1530** PALSGR. 710/2, I wyll set my rubye in fyne golde. **1604** E. G[RIMSTONE] *D'Acosta's Hist. Indies* VI. xiv. 459 To cut, and set the stones in worke. **1607–12** BACON *Ess., Beauty* (Arb.) 208 Vertue is like a rich stone, best plaine sett. **1611** BIBLE *1 Chron.* xxix. 2 Onix stones, and stones to be set. **1710** STEELE *Tatler* No. 245 ¶2 A Crochet of 122 Diamonds, set strong and deep in Silver. **1737** [S. BERINGTON] *G. di Lucca's Mem.* (1738) 15 We found several Precious Stones, some Set, some Unset, of a very great Value. **1828** *Mirror* V. 15/2 Fine brilliants are always set open. **1890** W. C. RUSSELL *Ocean Trag.* xxvii, On the back .. were his initials set in brilliants.

*transf.* and *fig.* **1596** SHAKS. *Merch. V.* II. vii. 55 O sinfull thought, neuer so rich a Iem Was set in worse then gold. **1681** DRYDEN *Span. Friar* IV. ii, And him too rich a Jewel to be set In vulgar metal, or for vulgar use. **1827** KEBLE *Chr. Y., 2nd Sunday Adv.* iv, Each tender gem, Set in the figtree's polish'd stem. **1890** *Blackw. Mag.* CXLVIII. 23/2 No vice could be odious when set in so much gold.

**b.** *transf.* and *fig.* To place (a thing) *in* a certain setting; †to frame (a picture).

**1530** PALSGR. 711/1 Now that my picture of the crucifix is set in bordes. **1712** ADDISON *Spect.* No. 328 She.. draws all her Relations Pictures in Miniature; [which].. must be.. set by no body but Charles Mather. **1822** COLERIDGE *Table-t.* 29 Dec., A scrubby boy, with a shining face set in dirt. **1825** *New Monthly Mag.* XVI. 534 It is a dark and terrible picture richly set in a massive framework of old English manners. **1865** TROLLOPE *Belton Est.* iii. 33 Large square windows set in stone.

**c.** To fix (artificial teeth) on the plate.

**1844** P. B. GODDARD (*title*) The anatomy.. of the human teeth; with methods of treatment; including operations, and making and setting teeth. **1878** C. HUNTER *Mech. Dentistry* viii. 100 The models.. must now have wax plates made for them, and upon these the teeth are set.

**64. a.** To put (a sail) up in position to catch the wind. Also said of a ship carrying (so much canvas).

[*a* **1300**: see *set up*, 154 b.] **1627** CAPT. SMITH *Seaman's Gram.* ix. 41 Set your foresaile. **1669** STURMY *Mariner's Mag.* I. ii. 16 Loose the Main-sail, and set him. **1799** *Naval Chron.* I. 377 Their.. ships.. set all their plain sails. **1805** in Nicolas *Disp.* (1846) VII. 166 *note*, All our masts badly wounded and no sail fit to set. **1890** *Chamb. Jrnl.* 26 July 469/2 There was no more canvas on her to set. **1892** *Engl. Illustr. Mag.* X. 42 When under full sail this vessel sets 45,000 square feet of canvas.

*fig.* **1819** CRABBE *T. of Hall* XI. 869 A daily guest the man appear'd, Set all his sail, and for his purpose steer'd. **1843** BETHUNE *Scott. Peasant's Fireside* 15 Setting all the sail they could to catch the gale of admiration.

**b.** phr. *to set sail*: to start on a sea voyage. Also † *to set one's sails*: to sail.

**1513** DOUGLAS *Æneis* V. xiii. 69 That salfie throw the se It may be lefull thai thare salis set. **1599** BODENHAM in *Hakluyt's Voy.* II. I. 100 After the sayde dayes expired, I wayed & set saile for the Iland of Chio. **1615** G. SANDYS *Trav.* 227 On the sixt of June they were licensed to set sail. **1712** ADDISON *Spect.* No. 507 ¶6 When Pompey was desired not to set sail in a tempest that would hazard his life. **1760–72** H. BROOKE *Fool of Qual.* (1809) III. 90 He reimbarked in the frigate, and directly set sail. **1890** TOUT *Hist. Eng. from 1689*, 118 Buonaparte set sail from Toulon.

**65. a.** To put (a movable part of an instrument or piece of mechanism) in a certain position.

*c* **1391** CHAUCER *Astrol.* II. §3 Tho sette I the centre of this Alhabor vpon 18 degrees among myn Almykantaras. **1592** HUES *Treat. Globes* IV. xii, The Globe being set to the latitude of the place. **1675** J. S. *Horol. Dial.* II. 39 What hour soever you would have your Larrums to ring at, to that figure.. set your Larrum hand. **1833** *Encycl. Brit.* (ed. 7) VI. 800 A larger knob or button.. sets the hand of the watch backward or forward as may be necessary. **1857** C. HOARE *Wine & Spirit Merchant's Guide* 49 Set the length on the slide to 18.79 on D. **1879** *Man. Artill. Exerc.* 116, No. 1 having set his scale replaces it in the gun. *Ibid.* 117 He first sets the tangent scale to the required deflection. **1883** R. H. SCOTT *Elem. Meteorol.* 68 Just before setting the vernier.

**b.** *Computers.* To cause (a binary storage unit) to enter a prescribed state, *spec.* that representing 1. Also *intr.*, to enter a prescribed state.

**1948** *Electronics* Apr. 127/1 The initial values can be set into the computer without too much time lag. **1957** R. K. RICHARDS *Digital Computer Components & Circuits* vi. 263 The real problem in devising a large-capacity storage system is not so much in the storage elements themselves as in providing means to gain access to any specified individual storage element for the purpose of sensing.. or setting its status. **1968** MALEY & HEILWEIL *Introd. Digital Computers* vi. 82 The latch is simply a circuit whose output can be set to 1, or reset to 0, and it will remain at either one of these two values until another set or reset operation changes its value. **1971** J. H. SMITH *Digital Logic* i. 12 A binary divider is a modified toggle which has only one input. If electrical pulses are applied to this input the unit will 'set'. The second pulse will 'reset' the circuit.

**66.** *Bell-ringing.* To ring (a bell) up till it stands still in an inverted position, either balanced or held by the stay and the slider. Also *intr.* of the bell.

**1671** *Tintinnalogia* 3 He is able to Set a Bell Fore-stroke and Back-stroke. **1688** [see *set change*, SET *ppl. a.* 8]. **1733** *Campanologia* in *Encycl. Metrop.* XV. 410 The first step he (the learner) makes in this art, is to learn perfectly to set a Bell, both back stroke and fore. [**1788** W. JONES, etc. *Key to Art of Ringing* (repr.) 9 *note*, As the first half-pull sets the bell up at back-stroke..; so the next half-pull brings her at hand or fore-stroke, which is the position we suppose her to have set off from.] **1860** E. BECKETT DENISON *Clocks & Watches* (ed. 4) 420 A bell of about 52 cwt... which he and some other boys used to raise and set. **1871** WIGRAM *Change-ringing Disentangled* 41 The learner should begin his practice on a bell when 'set'. **1875** HAWEIS in *Encycl. Brit.* III. 539/1 The first half-pull 'drops' the bell, the second 'sets' it.

**67. a.** To put (a liquid) in a vessel, at a certain temperature, strength, etc., ready to undergo a process; *spec.* in *Cheese-making* (see quot. 1861 and cf. *set together*, 153 c).

**1736** BAILEY *Dict. Domest.* s.v. *Cheese*, The milk must be set to turn in two different vessels. **1789** W. H. MARSHALL *Glo'stersh.* I. 275 The evening's meal is set for cream; and, being skimmed in the morning, is added to the morning's meal. *Ibid.* 297 The heat of the milk when set 83½°. **1852** *Jrnl. R. Agric. Soc.* XIII. I. 37 The churn should be set at 58° or 60°. **1861** *Ibid.* XXII. I. 50 The temperature of the milk when it is 'set' (that is, when the rennet is added). **1875** F. J. BIRD *Dyer's Hand-bk.* 39 Run your cloth through a jigger, set with cutch at 4° Twaddle, temperature about 180° Fahr.

*transf. a* **1861** T. WOOLNER *My Beautiful Lady, Wild Rose* ii, And sets a crimson rose to bleach.

**b.** *Baking* and *Brewing.* To add barm or yeast to. *to set the sponge*: to leaven a mass of flour.

**1743** *London & Countrey Brewer* IV. (ed. 2) 329 This Servant.. being obliged to set his Drink that Night. **1841** *Guide to Trade, Baker* 41 The.. journeyman.. is occupied in carrying out bread till about half-past four, when he sets the sponge. **1844** T. WEBSTER *Encycl. Dom. Econ.* §4317 The sponge being thus set, cover the whole over with a cloth.

** *To put in a certain order or arrange according to a plan.*

†**68. a.** To compose, write (a treatise, book). *Obs.*

*c* **888** ÆLFRED *Boeth.* ii, Ða lioð.. ic sceal nu.. mid swiþe unȝeradum wordum ȝesettan. *a* **950** *Guthlac* (prose) Prol., For ðisum þingum ic ðas boc sette. *c* **1000** ÆLFRIC *Hom.* II. 576 Dauid ðurh ðone Halȝan Gast ða sealmas sette. **1340** *Ayenb.* 12 Þe uerste article ys þellich. 'Ich beleue ine god þe uader almiȝti..'. Þis article zette saynte peter. *a* **1400** *Launfal* 4 Of a ley that was ysette, That hyght Launval. **1471** CAXTON *Recuyell* (Sommer) 4 Whyche was in prose so well and compendiously sette and wreton.

†**b.** Contextually: To translate. *Obs.* (Cf. *set out*, 149 s, *b.*)

*c* **888** ÆLFRED *Boeth.* Proem, Hwilum he sette word be worde, hwilum andȝit of andȝite. *c* **1425** *Eng. Conq. Irel.* 90 The forme of thay preuyleges.. ne myght I nat comly setten yn Englyshe. **1601** W. T. tr. *Ld. Remy's Civ. Consid.* 1st Ep. Ded., I attempted to set it out of French into our vulgar tongue.

†**c.** To arrange (words) in speech; to phrase, give a particular turn to. *Obs.*

*c* **1400** *Beryn* 3781 Geffrey set his wordis in such manere wise. **1484** CAXTON *Fables of Æsop* II. xii, Of a fewe wordes euyll sette cometh a grete noyse and daunger. **1530** PALSGR. 714/2 Beware of hym, he can sette his wordes, I tell you.

†**d.** *Astrol.* = CAST *v.* 39. *Obs.*

**1570** in *Archæologia* XL. 391 Bedo.. desyred this examynate to cast a fygure for certen monny that was hydden.. and upon his importunat sute this examynate sett a fygure.

†**69.** To settle or dispose of (land). *Obs.*

[**971** *Blickl. Hom.* 79, & þæt land ȝesetton swa hie sylfe woldon.] *c* **1205** LAY. 24088 Arður hafde France and freoliche heo sette. **1297** R. GLOUC. (Rolls) 7780 Þo he adde iset is londes. *c* **1320** *Sir Tristr.* 903 Tvo ȝere he sett þat land, His lawes made he cri.

†**70.** To settle the arrangement of (an army) for battle. *to set the field*: see FIELD *sb.* 8 b. *Obs.*

*c* **1205** LAY. 27430 Ælc king of his folke ȝarkede ferde. Þa hit al was iset & ferden isemed. **1297** R. GLOUC. (Rolls) 432 Brut ordeinede is ost, and sette hom wisliche. *c* **1420** ? LYDG. *Assembly of Gods* 634 The capyteyns.. B[e]st to set hys felde and folow on the chase. **1502** [see FIELD *sb.* 8 b]. **1573** WHITEHORNE (*title*) Certaine Waies for the ordering of Souldiours in battelray, and setting of battailes. **1608** CHAPMAN *Byron's Conspir.* v. H 4, I am not hee that can set my Squadrons ouer-night [etc.].

**71. a.** To make (a table) ready for a meal, spread (a table) *with* food, etc. **b.** To lay (a meal).

*c* **1386** CHAUCER *Clerk's T.* 975 She gan the hous to dighte, And tables for to sette. *a* **1547** in Fosbrooke *Econ. Mon. Life* (1796) 84 The bordes was divers times set. **1575** *Gamm. Gurton* II. i. 23 Was there none at home thy dinner for to set? **1700** DRYDEN *Ovid's Met.* VIII. *Baucis* 83 The good old Huse-wife, tucking up her Gown, The Table sets. **1794** MRS. A. M. BENNETT *Ellen* I. 21 He.. declined partaking of the supper, which was setting on the table. **1861** *Temple Bar* I. 343 Go and set the tea. **1884** J. T. TROWBRIDGE *Farnell's Folly* II. xxxvi. 101 You may as well set the table for two. **1890** *Universal Rev.* Aug. 580 A table is set with refreshments.

**c.** To arrange the colours in the desired order on (a palette).

**1847** *Man. Oil Painting* 126 To set a palette is to arrange the tints and colours in their due order for service. **1866** E. YATES *Land at Last* I. vii. 122 By the easel were a big palette already 'set', a colour-box, and a sheaf of brushes.

**72.** *Printing.* To place (type) in the order in which it is to be printed from; to compose, set up (type); hence, to put (manuscript) into type. Also *absol.*

**1530** Palsgr. 711/2 Your worke must nedes go forwarde, for I have foure that do nothyng else but set upon it. **1535** Joye *Apol. Tindale* (Arb.) 20, I correked but the false copye wherby and aftir whyche the printer dyd sette his boke. **1609** Tourneur *Funeral Poem* 428 As practis'd printers sette and distribute Their letters. **1637** [see compose *v.* 7]. **1708** in Hearne *Collect.* (O.H.S.) II. 126 The third sheet.. is set. **1830** Miss Mitford *Village* Ser. iv. 241 The proprietor of the county newspaper, who keeps the advertisement of this matchless villa constantly set. **1864** *Daily Tel.* 28 June, Next, to the composing-room, where I find about seventy men at work 'setting' small scraps of copy before them. **1892** *Leisure Hour* Feb. 232/2 The type from which the journal is set. **1899** *Tit-Bits* 8 Apr. 36/2 A good compositor can set 12,000 letters a day. **1964** F. Bowers *Bibliogr. & Textual Criticism* vi. i. 161 The sole purpose of saving the printer the labour of setting from a difficult manuscript.

**73. a.** To put (words) *to* (†*in*) music; to write (a musical composition) *for* certain voices or instruments. Also (less freq.) to put (music) *to* words, adapt (a melody) *to*, compose (a tune).

**1502** *Privy Purse Exp. Eliz. York* (1830) 2 For setting an Anthem of oure lady and Saint Elizabeth. *Ibid.* 83 Item to Cornishe for setting of a carralle upon Cristmas day. *a* **1548** Hall *Chron., Hen. VIII*, 8 Exercisyng hym selfe daily.. in settyng of songes, makyng of ballettes, & did set .ii. goodly masses, euery of them fyue partes. **1560** Daus tr. *Sleidane's Comm.* 233 This Psalme.. he made it also in metre, and set a note to it. **1600** Nashe *Summers Last Will* D 2, He.. setteth wanton songs vnto the Lute. **1607** Chapman *Bussy d'Ambois* v. iii. 67 Consorts fit to sound forth harmony Set to the falls of kingdoms! **1645** (*title*) Poems of Mr. John Milton... The songs were set in Musick by Mr. Henry Lawes. **1693** Luttrell *Brief Rel.* (1857) III. 134 A fine consort of musick, wherein the word Maria was soe sett it took up halfe an hour in singing. *a* **1700** Evelyn *Diary* 9 Aug. 1661, [He] plaied 9 or 10 tunes on the bells very finely, some of them set in parts. **1762** Colman *Mus. Lady* ii. 19 *Sophy.* And you really think it is set prettily... *Mask.* Delightfully!.. and sung — O heavens! **1774** Storer in Jesse *Selwyn & Contemp.* (1844) III. 77 An air set to the words of one of his own ballads. **1821** Shelley *Song* iv, Let me set my mournful ditty To a merry measure. **1870** Tennyson *Window* Pref., Sullivan.. had been very successful in setting such old songs as 'Orpheus with his lute'. **1891** *Sat. Rev.* 14 Nov. 558/2 The poem is set for chorus and orchestra. **1965** *Listener* 3 June 836/2 One does not make music 'colloquial' by using it to set colloquial words. **1966** Bennett & Smithers *Early M.E. Verse & Prose* 108 The music to which it [*sc.* a lyric] is set clearly shows that the words were composed to fit the tune. **1970** *Oxf. Compan. Music* (ed. 10) 498/1 The tunes set to these hymns were partly adaptations of the ancient plainsong, partly arrangements of folk song and partly original. **1979** *N.Y. Rev. Bks.* 17 May 32/4 Byrd set this notorious poem to music, and the setting certainly did not escape notice.

**b.** *fig.*

**1789** Mrs. Piozzi *Journ. France* I. 8 He sets his talk to a sounding tune. **1809** Malkin *Gil Blas* x. x. (Rtldg.) 371 Get out of my sight, or I shall set your *solfeggio* in a crying key. **1862** Tyndall *Mountaineer.* xi. 92 Clothing the crags with splendour, and setting the wind to melody. **1879** Morley *Burke* x. 209 Burke's mind was not easily set to these tunes.

**c.** *intr.* To be capable of being put *to* music; to go (*well*) *to* music.

**1697** J. Lewis *Mem. Dk. Glocester* (1789) 82 He thought that they [the verses] would set very well to music.

**74.** trans. *Theatr.* To make up (a scene) on the stage; to arrange (an item of the scenery) in a particular way. Also *to set the stage* (also *fig.*, to prepare the way or conditions *for* (an event, etc.)).

**1779** Sheridan *Critic* ii. i, Sir, the scene is set, and everything is ready to begin. **1889** Mrs. Lynn Linton *Thro' Long Night* II. ii. ii. 4 He wanted to see how he should be received when the stage was not set nor were the lamps trimmed for his reception. **1890** *Harper's Mag.* June 68/2 The palace of the Borgias was 'set' as a modern apothecary's shop. **1892** *Illustr. Lond. News* 23 July 110/2 The time necessary for setting and changing scenes. **1937** *Discovery* June 175/1 Given suitable conditions, the stage is always set for the transformation. **1972** *Review & Herald* 7 Dec. 12/2 However, it is first necessary to 'set the stage'. **1980** *Sci. Amer.* Jan. 122/1, I can best set the stage for describing Morelli's instrument by reviewing the two basic types of spectroscope and spectrophotometer.

*** *To give a required shape or form to.*

**75. a.** To put an edge on (a cutting instrument, *esp.* a razor). Also *to set the edge of.* (Cf. 42.)

In first quot. app. fig. phr. *to set upon the hone*, to sharpen (a person) up.

**1461** Marg. Paston in *P. Lett.* II. 62 As for Wylliam Wyrcestyr, he hathe be set so up on the hone, what by the parson and by othyr,.. that they hope he wole do well i now. **1562** Withals *Dict.* 39 A stone to whette or sette the rasure with. **1667** Wood *Life* (O.H.S.) II. 122 Setting a razor, 2*d.* **1680** Moxon *Mech. Exerc.* x. 192 It is afterwards Set upon a round Whet-stone. **1687** Dryden *Hind & P.* iii. 19 You have ground the persecuting knife, And set it to a razor edge on life. **1749** Smollett *Gil Blas* ii. vii. (1782) I. 165 A case and two razors.. with a thong of leather to set them. **1816** Byron *Parisina* xv, The headsman.. Feels if the axe be sharp and true Since he set its edge anew. **1868** Bemrose *Fret-Cutting* 10 In 'setting' the tools, apply a few drops of sweet oil to the Arkansas stone. **1892** *Leisure Hour* Apr. 387/1 Are my razors set yet?

**b.** fig. phr. *to be sharp* or *keen set*: to be hungry or keen. (See also sharp-set.)

**1540** Palsgr. *Acolastus* ii. iii. M ij, My mynd is al redy in the platters or dishes .i. I am sharpe set. **1606** Bryskett *Civ. Life* 94 Being fed temperatly, our mindes may be the sharper set to fall to those other dainties. **1728** Young *Love of Fame* ii. 120 As in smooth oil the razor best is whet, So wit is by politeness sharpest set. **1891** 'L. Keith' *Halletts* III. iv. 80 Her own appetite was keener set than usual. **1893** Selous *Trav. S.E. Africa* 22, I knew she [a lioness] must be pretty keen set.

**76. a.** To adjust (the teeth of a saw) by deflecting them alternately in opposite directions so as to produce a kerf of the required width. Also *to set a saw.*

**1678** Moxon *Mech. Exerc.* v. 94 Then with the Saw wrest .. they set the Teeth of the Saw. **1806** J. Beresford *Miseries Hum. Life* (ed. 3) iv. 77 Having your impatience soothed by the setting of a saw, close at your ear. **1834–6** Barlow in *Encycl. Metrop.* (1845) VIII. 382 In sawing valuable timber the teeth are not turned out so much (or as the workmen term it, set so rank) as for coarse cheap stuff.

**b.** To adjust (the blade of a plane in relation to the sole) in order to vary the depth of cut.

**1677** J. Moxon *Mech. Exerc.* iv. 63 When you set the Iron of the Fore-Plain, consider the Stuff you are to work upon. **1857–9** E. L. Tarbuck *Encycl. Pract. Carpentry & Joinery* i. iii. 26 The projection of the plane iron may be very nicely regulated, or set, rank, or fine, that is projecting from the face in a greater or less degree. **1938** C. H. Hayward *Carpentry Bk.* i. 27 When a piece of wood with a difficult grain has to be planed, the back-iron is advanced and the plane set as fine as possible.

†**77.** To tune (an instrument). *Obs.*

**1471** Caxton *Recuyell* (Sommer) 324 Orpheus setted & entuned his harpe. **1530** Palsgr. 714/1, I set in tune, as mynstrelles do their instrumentes of musyke. **1590** Barwick *Disc. Weapons* B 3, I doubt not.. we shall haue a Cornelius to set these instruments in better tune.

**78.** †To tenter (cloth); to stretch (leather).

**1473** in *Arnolde's Chron.* (1811) 78 The fullyng teynteryng or settyng and sheryng of wullen cloth.. teyntered sett and drawen out in length and brede. **1884** Knight *Dict. Mech.* Suppl. 797/1 To set a side of leather, it is spread upon the table when wet, and is smoothed out on it. **1897** C. T. Davis *Manuf. Leather* (ed. 2) 217 It is well to have a tub of water by the side of the stuffing table, and dip in each side to soften it before proceeding to set the same.

**79.** To put (a broken or dislocated bone) in a position adapted to the restoration of the normal condition. Also *intr.* said of the bone.

**1572** in Gage *Hengrave* (1882) 192 To Adkyns of Bury, surgon for setting of ij dogges legs. *a* **1586** Sidney *Arcadia* ii. (Sommer) 114 b, Gynecia.. had her shoulder put out of ioinct; which though.. it was set well againe [etc.]. **1672** Wiseman *Wounds* ii. 71 It was doubted, whether the Bone was Set or not. A Bone Setter was sent for. **1709** Steele *Tatler* No. 41 ¶7 The new Man has broke his Leg, which is so ill set, that he can never dance more. **1821** Jefferson *Autobiog.* Writ. 1892 I. 100 A dislocated wrist, unsuccessfully set. **1887** *Encycl. Brit.* XXII. 682/1 Accurate apposition is termed 'setting the fracture'; this is best done by the extension of the limb and coaptation of the broken surfaces. **1891** *Field* 14 Nov. 761/2 Dogs' bones soon set.

*fig.* *a* **1591** H. Smith *Serm.* (1592) 430 Pride doth breake the peace, humilitie doth set it againe. **1647** Ward *Simple Cobler* 65 When a kingdome is broken just in the neck joynt, .. ropes and hatchets are not the kindliest instruments to set it.

†**80.** To pleat (a ruff); to arrange the pleats of (a gown). *Obs.*

**1530** Palsgr. 710/2, I set a gowne, I put the playtes of it in order... I can nat sette a gowne, I was never no taylour. **1576** Gascoigne *Grief of Joy* Wks. 1910 II. 534 They set their ruffes, thei ruffle up theire heare. **1597** Bp. Hall *Sat.* iii. vii, His linnen collar Labyrinthian-set. **1611** Cotgr., *Godronner vne fraise*, to set a ruffe.

**81.** † **a.** To adjust (one's attire, the hair). *Obs.*

**1303** R. Brunne *Handl. Synne* 3206 Be nat proud of þy croket Yn þe cherche to tyfe and set. **1694** Dryden *Love Triumph.* Ded., Combing his Peruke and setting his Cravat. **1695** Congreve *Love for L.* v. i, He's at the great Glass in the Dining-Room,.. setting his Cravat and Wig. **1712** Pope *Rape Lock* i. 146 These set the head, and those divide the hair. [**1722** Steele *Consc. Lovers* i. ii, Such an Author consulted in a Morning, sets the Spirits for the Vicissitudes of the Day, better than the Glass does a Mans Person.]

**b.** To arrange and fix (the hair) when damp so that it dries in the desired style; *occas.*, to fix a hair-style by other means.

**1926** *Hairdressing* 10 Sept. 241/1 This can only be done by superior work; namely, excellent setting of the finished permanent. **1932** *Mod. Woman* Feb. 72/1 A perfectly easy method of keeping your hair perfectly waved, set and curled at home. **1957** V. J. Kehoe *Technique Film & Telev. Make-Up* xv. 214 Hair lacquer or spray.. is used for setting the hair in place after it has been dressed. **1967** N. Freeling *Strike out where not Applicable* 10 Ash-blonde hair cut fairly short and set every week in Leiden. **1976** C. Bermant *Coming Home* i. vii. 105 Her hair was always smartly set.

**82.** *Weaving.* To fix the texture of (a fabric). In first quot. *pass.*, of a tartan: To have a pattern of a certain kind (cf. set *sb.*[1] 15 b).

**1685** *Depred. Clan Campbell* (1816) 114 Item, ane new colored womans wearing plaid, most sett to boday red. Item, ane gray broken plaid, sett most to the green. **1839** Ure *Dict. Arts* 1056 A thorough knowledge of the adaptation of yarn of a proper degree of fineness to any given measure of reed... The art of performing this properly is known by the names of *examining*, *setting*, or *sleying.* **1891** *Yorksh. Coll. Textile Soc. Jrnl.* I. 129 By the sett of a fabric is meant the number of threads it contains in a given space. There are a great many things to be considered in setting any fabric.

**83.** To arrange (a butterfly, etc.) as an entomological specimen. (Cf. *set up*, 154 o.)

**1868** *Rep. U.S. Commissioner Agric.* (1869) 317 In setting long-legged specimens, a square piece of stiff paper or card should be pushed upon the pins under the insect. **1892** *Field* 18 June 904/1 'Setting' the insects, which means the spreading of specimens on blocks of cork or wood to dry.

**84.** To give the requisite adjustment, alignment, or shape to (a mechanical contrivance, an instrument, etc.). (Cf. set *sb.*[1] 33.)

**1879** *Cassell's Techn. Educ.* IV. 413/2 The rough-maker.. smoothes off all the sharp edges and 'sets' them, i.e., bends them into graceful and uniform shape over a block. **1881** Burgess *Coach-building* 78 Setting axles is giving them the bend and slope required. **1886** Walsingham & Payne-Gallwey *Shooting* (Badm. Libr.) I. 70 The next process is to 'set' or straighten the barrel inside. **1898** Rider Haggard *Farmer's Year* (1899) 222 Being able to 'set' a wheel better than anyone about here.

**** *To adjust according to a standard.*

**85. a.** To regulate, adjust *by* a standard; *esp.* to put (a clock, etc.) right.

*c* **1391** Chaucer *Astrolabe* ii. §3 To haue sette Iustly a clokke. **1640** Suckling *Let. to German* Fragm. Aur. (1648) 92 In Court they.. determine his [the king's] good by his desires: which is a kind of setting the Sun by the Diall. **1665** Boyle *Occas. Refl.* iv. xv. (1675) 254 A little Sun-Dyal, furnished with an excited Needle to direct how to set it. *a* **1721** Prior *Ess., Opinion* Wks. (1907) 196 Quare [a clock maker] does not set his Watch more actually than Mathar does his understanding. **1762** *Phil. Trans.* LII. 579 The 16th, at noon, I sat a pendulum-clock.. to solar time. **1772** Foote *Nabob* i. (1778) 21 To set his watch by Tompion's clock in the Hall. **1844** Hood *Workhouse Clock* 8 The Overseer of the Poor Is setting the Workhouse Clock. **1850** *Jrnl. R. Agric. Soc.* XI. ii. 397 We watch vainly every cloud and in vain set our weather-glass. **1857** Hughes *Tom Brown* i. iv, The Tally-ho [coach] was a tiptop goer.. and so punctual that all the road set their clocks by her.

**b.** with immaterial obj.

**1693** Locke *Educ.* §14 (1699) 19 The Seasoning and Cookery which by Custom they [*sc.* our palates] are set to. **1693** Prior *To Montague* iii, Pleas'd, when his Reason He deceives; And sets his Judgment by his Passion. **1717** —— *Alma* i. 88 He.. sets men's faith by his opinions.

**86.** To fix the amount of (a fine or other payment), put down *at* a certain amount.

*c* **1420** in *26 Pol. Poems* 76 And þou nylt 3eue it [*sc.* love] me..; Sette pris to selle it. **1521** *Maldon* (Essex) *Liber B.* 57 Truly affur and sett al maner of mercyaments made. **1525** in Ellis *Orig. Lett.* Ser. iii. II. 24 To set his raunsom at a somme of money reasonable. **1531–2** *Act 23 Hen. VIII*, c. 7 To set the prices of all kinde of wynes. **1653** H. Cogan tr. *Pinto's Trav.* xx. 71 He payd for all that he bought at the price the sellers would set. **1691** Locke *Consid. Lower. Interest* Wks. 1714 II. 5 That Law cannot keep Men from taking more Use than you set. *Ibid.*, The Rate you set, profits not the Lenders, and very few of the Borrowers. **1770** Langhorne *Plutarch, Cicero* ¶13 Verres being thus condemned, Cicero set his fine at 750,000 drachmæ. **1980** M. Boddy *Building Societies* iv. 46 The composite rate [of tax paid by building societies] was set at 79·3 per cent of the basic rate (then 35 per cent), i.e. 27·75 per cent.

**VII.** To place mentally; to suppose, estimate.

†**87.** To posit, assume, suppose. Phr. *set the case* (see case *sb.*[1] 12), chiefly in imper. or pres. pple. as equivalent to a conj. = suppose, supposing.

*a* **1340** Hampole *Psalter* xxii. 4 Gret vertu is in man when he dredis na ill þat may fall for he settis þe werst. *c* **1374** Chaucer *Troilus* ii. 367, I sette þe worste þat ye dredden þis Men wolden wondren to se hym come or gon. *c* **1386** —— *Melib.* ¶525 Yet sette I caas, ye have bothe might and licence for to venge yow. **1387–8** T. Usk *Test. Love* i. ix. (Skeat) 64, I sette now the hardest. *c* **1440** [see case *sb.*[1] 12] **1561** T. Hoby tr. *Castiglione's Courtyer* iv. (1577) X ij, Setting case therefore this be so. **1632** Holland *Cyrupædia* 129 Set case.. that a man should make so much of those dogs which you keepe. **1659** Bunyan *Law & Grace Unfolded* (1685) 286 Set the case that there be two men who make a covenant. **1726** Shelvocke *Voy. round World* Pref. 10 Setting the case I had not their interest at heart, yet it was for my interest to support theirs.

**88. a.** To place mentally or conceptually in a certain category; †to regard as being (so-and-so); to consider (a thing) to reside *in* or to depend *on* (another); †to attribute *to.*

**13..** *E.E. Allit. P.* A. 8 Quere-so-euer I Iugged gemmez gaye, I sette hyr sengely in synglure. **1375** Barbour *Bruce* xvii. 826 That wes mar To myrakill of god almychty; And to nocht ellis it set can I. **1387** Trevisa *Higden* (Rolls) IV. 81 Hircanus, for he was 3ong, was i-sette laste of þe wise men. *c* **1400** *Beryn* 1278 Allas! þat ever a man shuld.. Setten al his wisdom on his wyvis tayll! **1423** Jas. I *Kingis Q.* v, This noble man, That in him-self the full recouer wan Off his Infortune, pouert, and distresse, And in tham set his verray sekernesse. **1549** *Compl. Scot.* xvi. 141 Euerye man settis his felicite to distroy his nychtbour. **1576** Gascoigne *Droomme of Doomes day* Wks. 1910 II. 240 He alwayes setteth his end in thinges which he must have. **1604** E. G[rimstone] *D'Acosta's Hist. Indies* i. xiv. 46 They set Tharsis in Affrike, saying, it was the same Citie which was anciently called Carthage. **1685** Stillingfl. *Orig. Brit.* iv. 209 The want of skill may make Caradoc set his Gildas elder than he ought to have done. **1870** Rogers *Hist. Glean.* Ser. ii. 21 Tradition sets Wiklif's birth in the year 1324.

**b.** To place (a person or thing) *before* or *after* another in estimation. Now *poet.*

*c* **1383** in *Eng. Hist. Rev.* Oct. (1911) 747 Religiouse possessioneris.. shulden sette before [*preferrent*] þe comaundementis of god. **1387** Trevisa *Higden* (Rolls) V. 99 þat þe manere and þe usage of al holy chirche of Grees, of Italy, of Rome, of Gallia, and of Fraunce, schulde be i-sette to-fore þe manere and custom.. of a corner of þe worlde. *c* **1400** *Rule St. Benet* (Verse) 2475 So þat þai set non erthly þing Be-for þe luf of crist. **1592** Hues *Treat. Globes* Pref. (Hakl.) 16 These Globes.. may justly bee preferred before all other that have been set before them. **1648** Milton *Sonn.* xiii. 12 Dante shall give Fame leave to set thee higher Then his Casella. **1671** —— *Samson* 1375 Venturing to displease God for the fear of Man, and Man prefer, Set God behind.

**1732** POPE *Ep. Cobham* 148 And justly set the Gem above the Flow'r.

**89. a.** To fix the value of (a thing) *at* so much. *Obs.* or *arch.*

Cf. the reverse construction in sense 43.

*c* **1460** FORTESCUE *Abs. & Lim. Mon.* x. (1885) 131 That [*sc.* salt] is now sett to so grete prise, þat the bushell, wich the kyng bieth ffor iijd or iiijd, is solde to his peple ffor ijs and a jd. **1530** PALSGR. 712/1, I sette my horse at foure pounde.. How moche set you his plate at? **1585** T. WASHINGTON tr. *Nicholay's Voy.* IV. xxvi. 145 [The women] beyng once set at a price none could marry them, except they first payde the pryce. **1616** R. COCKS *Diary* (Hakl. Soc.) I. 104 Yf the Hollanders set pepper at that rate, they sell other comodetis at a hier. **1617** MORYSON *Itin.* I. 34 At the times of the faires, Coaches are set dearer then any time els. **1692** R. L'ESTRANGE *Fables* clxx. 142 Well.. and what's the Price of that Juno there? The Carver set That a little Higher. **1713** POPE *Let. to Swift* 8 Dec., I cannot set his delivery from purgatory at less than fifty pounds sterling.

*fig.* **1592** SHAKS. *Rom. & Jul.* V. iii. 301 There shall no figure at that Rate be set, As that of true and faithful Juliet. **1602** —— *Ham.* I. iii. 122 Set your entreatments at a higher rate, Then a command to parley. **1648–9** *Eikon Bas.* xvii. 170 Setting Peace at as high a rate, as the worst effects of War.

**b.** Hence in idiomatic phr. connoting disesteem or depreciation: ***to set at naught*** or ***nought*** (see NOUGHT A. 6), ***at little, at the least, at nothing***; ***to set at a pease, at a pie's heel, at a pin's fee***; ***to set at no price, store***, or ***value***.

**1303** R. BRUNNE *Handl. Synne* 3013 And he þat ys vnbuxum al Aȝens hys fadyr spiritual, And setteþ hym ryȝt at þe leste. *Ibid.* 7774 þe mayster fend.. sette at noȝt þat he hadde tolde. **1377** LANGL. *P. Pl.* B VI. 171 Lete liȝte of þe lawe.. And sette Pieres at a pees. *Ibid.* VII. 194, I sette ȝoure patentes.. at one pies hele! *c* **1385** CHAUCER *L.G.W.* 602 Al the worlde he sette at noo value. **1413** in *26 Pol. Poems* 51 Þouȝ all here gold were hider brouȝt, I wolde set hit at lytel store. *c* **1450** tr. *De Imitatione* III. xi, To sette all þinges at no price for þe. **1488** *Rolls of Parlt.* VI. 413/2 Unreverently sette theym at litill or nought. **1596** SPENSER *F.Q.* VII. vi. 44 Shee had.. Long loved the Fanchin, who by nought did set her. **1602** SHAKS. *Ham.* I. iv. 67, I doe not set my life at a pins fee. **1649** EARL MONM. tr. *Senault's Use Passions* (1671) 203 He then sets at nothing what he so much esteemed. **1874** STUBBS *Const. Hist.* I. viii. 238 Canonical custom is set at naught.

†**c.** ***to set light, at light*** (see LIGHT *a.*[1] 13 d), ***lightly, coldly***. (Cf. 91 e, f.)

**1602** SHAKS. *Ham.* IV. iii. 65 Thou maist not coldly set Our Soueraigne Processe. **1652** NEEDHAM tr. *Selden's Mare Cl.* 149 Wee'll not disgrace your Realm, nor lightly set Your Fame. **1718** BP. HUTCHINSON *Witchcraft* vii. 104 He set them light [*ed.* 1720 set them at light].

**d.** To estimate the amount of *at* so much.

**1863** *Jrnl. R. Agric. Soc.* XXIV. I. 21 The yearly increase .. is set at about 8*s.* per acre. **1866** ROGERS *Agric. & Prices* I. xxiii. 599 We cannot set the increase at less than 100 per cent.

**90.** To assess (a person) *at* so much. *Obs.* or *arch.*

**1521** *Maldon* (Essex) *Liber B.* 57 Set every man after the quantyte of the trespace. *c* **1537** in Leadam *Sel. Cases Crt. Requests* (Selden Soc.) 47 Like as all other brethern of the seid felaweship were and be set at. **1538** ELYOT *Dict.* Add., *Duicensus*, he that is sette with an other to pay money for a taxe. **1557** in Marwick *Edinb. Guilds* (1909) 89 Prouyding always thai pay the sowmes to the quhilk thai were sett. **1607** in W. H. Hale *Prec. in Causes of Office* (1841) 9 And so shall sett every parishoner proportionably. **1611** BIBLE *2 Kings* xii. 4 The money that every man is set at. **1831** MACAULAY *Ess., Hampden* (1843) I. 453 The sheriff was blamed for setting so wealthy a man at so low a rate.

**91.** To have (a certain estimate) of a person or thing: in idiomatic phrases expressing high or low regard, great or little esteem, for a person or thing.

Here the construction is the reverse of that of 93 b.

**a.** ***to set*** (***so***) ***little*** (or †***lite***), (***so***) ***much*** (or ***mickle, a great deal***), ***less, least, more, most by***. *Obs.* exc. *arch.* or *dial.*

Originally substantival or pronominal, *little, much*, etc. were capable of being taken as adverbial; whence the substitution of adverbs of equivalent meaning (see f).

*a* **1300** [see LITTLE B. 3]. *c* **1374** CHAUCER *Troilus* II. 432, I se ful wel þat ye sette lite of vs Or of oure deth. *c* **1380** WYCLIF *Sel. Wks.* III. 109 Þey sette more by here lawes ..þan þey dude by þe lawe þat God ȝaf to hem. *c* **1380** *Antecrist* in Todd *Three Treat. Wyclif* (1851) 151 And more þei shal be sett by and wurshiped. **14..** *Why I can't be a Nun* 220 in *E.E.P.* (1862) 144 But alle.. set not by her nether most ne lest. **1456** SIR G. HAYE *Law Arms* (S.T.S.) 33 Tynsale of the body.. that is lytill to sett by. **1545** ASCHAM *Toxoph.* I. (Arb.) 74 Howe moche the Persians.. set by shotinge. **1627** DRAYTON *Agincourt* 4 What set that Conqueror, by their Salique Lawes. **1664–5** PEPYS *Diary* 9 Mar., He did.. give me one of Lilly's grammars.. which I shall much set by. **1690** C. NESSE *Hist. & Myst. O. & N. Test.* I. 23 A pretious soul was no more set-by by them. **1741** RICHARDSON *Pamela* II. 173 He was sure I should set more by it, than the richest Diamond in the World. **1785** B. TUPPER in Sparks *Corr. Amer. Rev.* (1853) IV. 118 A visit, which I shall set more by than the interest I possess in Massachusetts. **1845** S. JUDD *Margaret* II. i. (1874) 190 God knows how hard it is to help setting a good deal by one's children. **1894** *Advance* (Chicago) 5 Apr., A man much set-by.

†**b.** ***to set naught*** or ***nought*** (***nothing, not anything***) ***by***: to have no esteem or regard for. *Obs.*

*c* **1375** *Cursor M.* 23860 (Fairf.) In hert to halde hit as a horde & noȝt to sette be goddis worde [*Cott.* Quen noght es mad o crists word]. **1390** GOWER *Conf.* III. 348 Bot noght forthi Mi will hath nothing set therby. **1470–85** MALORY *Arthur* VIII. xxxviii. 331 By the myghty lord of this yle he setteth nought by. **1483** CAXTON *G. de la Tour* e j b, Mocked & scorned & nought set by. **1535** COVERDALE *John* IV. 44 A prophet is nothinge set by at home. **1549** ——, etc. *Erasm. Par. Heb.* xii. 1–6 By despisyng and settyng naught by worldly reproche. **1598** GRENEWEY *Tacitus, Ann.* I. v. 8 The souldyers.. set nought by all military discipline. **1601** SHAKS. *Twel. N.* V. i. 194, I thinke you set nothing by a bloody Coxecombe.

*absol.* **1456** SIR G. HAYE *Law Arms* (S.T.S.) 14 And suppos it be sum part subtile to understand, settis nocht by.

**c.** By substitution of *not* for *nought*, and by extension of the idiom to negative expressions generally, *set by* came to be equivalent to 'esteem, regard', and, by elimination of the negative, to 'esteem or value highly, think or make much of'. *Obs.* exc. *arch.* or *dial.*

Formerly *to set not by* sometimes = to have no scruples about.

**1393** LANGL. *P. Pl.* C. x. 302 Men setten nat by songewarie. *a* **1400** *Minor Poems fr. Vernon MS.* 692/10 Now is þe selue I-set not by. *c* **1400** *Rule St. Benet* (Verse) 459 Þai wil set bi no man saw. **1426** AUDELAY *Poems* 3 Avoutré ne lechory men set not by. *c* **1435** *Torr. Portugal* 1152 The kyng of Aragon sett her bye. **1467** MARG. PASTON in *P. Lett.* II. 308 Thei set not be a woman as thei shuld set be a man. *c* **1480** HENRYSON *Mor. Fab., Fox, Wolf & Cadger* 1998 (Charteris MS.) To beir ȝour office than wald I not set by. **1508** DUNBAR *Flyting* 238 Quhat man settis by the! **1513** DOUGLAS *Æneis* XI. iv. 98 Onlesum war syk plesour I set by. **1561** T. HOBY tr. *Castiglione's Courtyer* I. H ij b, They do not onelye not sett by letters, but they rather abhorre them. *a* **1659** BP. BROWNRIG *Serm.* (1674) I. iv. 57 Men set by good servants. *a* **1661** FULLER *Worthies, N'hants* (1662) II. 291 Set by and extolled. **1663–4** PEPYS *Diary* 20 Jan., Mr Pierce tells me that my Lady Castlemaine is not at all set by by the King. **1848** LOWELL *Biglow P.* Ser. I. ix, Wite folks aint sot by half ez much.

**d.** ***to set*** (***no, more***, etc.) ***store*** or † ***price by***: see PRICE *sb.* A. a, B. 8, STORE *sb.*

†**e.** ***to set light by*** see LIGHT *a.* 13 d. Also ***to set short by***. *Obs.*

**1377** LANGL. *P. Pl.* B. XI. 2 Scripture scorned me.. and liȝte by me she sette. *Ibid.* XII. 124 No clergie to dispise, Ne sette schort be here science. *c* **1460** *Wisdom* 927 in *Macro Plays* 66 Why werkyst þou hys consell? by myn settis lyght? **1565** T. STAPLETON *Fortr. Faith* 129 Such smal matters were not of good Christians light sett by. **1594–1771** [see LIGHT *a.* 13 d]. **1633** MARMION *Fine Comp.* III. v. F 3, She set as light by me, as by the least feather in her Fanne. **1816** SCOTT *Old Mort.* xxxix, I am a fool.. to set light by that which Heaven has so often preserved.

†**f.** ***to set*** †***greatly***, † ***littly, lightly***, † ***so***, etc. ***by***. *Obs.*

**1530** PALSGR. 713/1 The man is hyghely sette by in our countraye. **1537** *Orig. & Sprynge of Sectes* 28 Hitherto haue they ben in estimacion & greatly set by. **1577** T. KENDALL *Flowers of Epigr.* 30 No man that setts so by hym self, can please the Lorde a right. **1612** T. TAYLOR *Comm. Titus* To Rdr., Things lightly come by are lightly set by. **1729** BP. BUTLER *Serm.* xv. (1862) 209 That in all lowliness of mind we set lightly by ourselves. **1809–10** COLERIDGE *Friend* (1818) I. 104 To set lightly by the emancipation of the human reason.

**g.** In negative context, with a sb. as obj. connoting a negligible or contemptible quantity.

***to set not a cherry, curse, a fly, a haw, a mite, an onion*** (etc.) ***at, by, of***: see also the sbs.

*c* **1374** CHAUCER *Troilus* III. 900, I nolde setten at his sorwe a myte. *c* **1386** —— *Miller's T.* 648 Of paramours he sette nat a kers. **1406** HOCCLEVE *La Male Regle* 380 For by hem two, he settith nat an hawe. *c* **1489** CAXTON *Sonnes of Aymon* xix. 442, I shall not sette a rotyn appull for all the power of Charlemagne. **1500–20** DUNBAR *Poems* xxxi. 22 Lat ws.. sett nocht by this warld a chirry. *a* **1525** *Vergilius* in Thoms *Prose Rom.* (Rtldg.) 223 The roffyans set nat a poynt. *c* **1570** W. WAGER *The Longer thou livest* 1691 (Brandl), By honest men he settest not an Oynion.

**h.** In various constructions, with preps. other than *by*.

† ***to set little, more, nought, not, of; to set a*** (***great, little***) ***price***, † ***rate, store upon; to set no price, littly at***; † ***to set light of, before***; † ***to set little, nought to***; etc.

**1387–8** T. USK *Test. Love* I. i. (Skeat) 67 How shulde ye, lady, sette prise on so foule fylthe. **1390** GOWER *Conf.* II. 211, I sette noght of his beyete. *c* **1400** *Beryn* 1386 Sith he of my wordis so litil prise set. *Ibid.* 2838 To save hir lyvis, & set nat of hir los. *c* **1400** *Sowdone Bab.* 1717 Set not of youre Barons so light. **1422** YONGE tr. *Secreta Secret.* ix. 139 Men that lytill bethe sette of. *Ibid.* xix. 146 Men sholde sette lytillie at this goodis. **1470–85** MALORY *Arthur* V. ii. 162 Of his demaunde and commaundement I sette nothyng. **1481** CAXTON *Myrr.* I. v. 18 They setted not of mete and drynke. **1589** PUTTENHAM *Eng. Poesie* III. xix. (Arb.) 239 We set but light of the matter. **1601** HOLLAND *Pliny* XXXIII. xii. II. 483 Disdaining and setting light by any other bathing-vessels. **1607–12** BACON *Ess., Riches* (Arb.) 232 Doe you not see what fayned prices are sett vpponn litle stones, and rarityes. **1632** LITHGOW *Trav.* Ep. Ded. A 3 b, What a high Value was set upon the Widdowes Mite. **1638** [see RATE *sb.*[1] 2]. **1642** [see LIGHT *a.* 13 d]. **1651** HOBBES *Leviath.* I. x. 42 By comparison to the rate that each man setteth on himselfe. **1662** [see PRICE *sb.* 8]. **1688** *Lett. conc. Pres. St. Italy* 79 Nor would it have been set on so much by their Holy Patriarchs. **1819** SCOTT *Ivanhoe* xxx, Where be these dog-priests now,.. who set such price on their ghostly mummery. **1861** LD. BROUGHAM *Brit. Const.* xx. 396 The grounds upon which so great store has ever been set upon colonial possessions. **1875** MANNING *Mission Holy Ghost* iv. 105 They are continually showing that they set small price on the Eternal God. **1891** F. W. ROBINSON *Her Love & His Life* III. VII. iv. 262 He did not set any value on his own life.

†**i.** To care (so much) for. Also *intr.* (Not) to care *for*. *Obs.*

*c* **1374** CHAUCER *Troilus* III. 832 Yf to lose his Ioye he set a myte Than semeth it þat Ioye is worth but lyte. *c* **1400** *Destr. Troy* 5002 Yf þou set noght our saghe. **1456** SIR G. HAYE *Law Arms* (S.T.S.) 233 Ane unworthy lymmare, that settis nocht for honour bot for pillery.

**VIII.** To put or come into a settled or rigid position or state.

**92. a.** *pass.* To be resolved or determined; to have a settled purpose. Chiefly const. inf. Now usu. in sense 'likely, about (to)'. Also, in *Journalese*, const. *for* followed by *sb.*

*a* **1300** *Cursor M.* 17332 Mi-self es sett to wrek þe wrang. *c* **1375** *Sc. Leg. Saints* xxxvii. (*Vincencius*) 403 [S. Vincent] til ples god wes mar sete, þane ocht þat wes in þe markete. *c* **1420** *Liber Cocorum* (1862) 42 Þerfore to telle you I am set, .. what herbz.. Ben gode to potage. *c* **1470** HENRY *Wallace* III. 324 Thai are set till wndo all thi kyn. **1525** ABP. WARHAM in Ellis *Orig. Lett.* Ser. III. II. 10 Seeing almoste al the people obstinatly sett not to graunte to the request. **1540** PALSGR. *Acolastus* I. iii. F iv b, I am at a poynte, or my mynde is fully sette. *a* **1586** SIDNEY *Arcadia* III. (Sommer) 261 b, But my hart is already set.. to lead a virgins life to my death. *a* **1641** BP. MOUNTAGU *Acts & Mon.* (1642) 256 She was wayward, disdainful, and set to contradict. **1757** in J. Russell *Haigs* (1881) xii. 359 All your neighbours are sett to be upon you. **1827** KEBLE *Chr. Yr., Morning* 30 If on our daily course our mind Be set to hallow all we find. **1890** *Harper's Mag.* Aug. 407/2 Mamma was completely set in her own mind that we must go to the south. **1976** *Daily Tel.* 30 Nov. 1/6 Electricity prices are set to go up again on New Year's Day. **1978** *Sunday Tel.* 10 Dec. 1 (*heading*) Callaghan set for showdown with Benn. **1979** *Daily Tel.* 28 Feb. 2/6 The Inner City partnerships outside London seem set for increases above the average. **1982** *Times* 16 Oct. 9/6 The armchair moralists of Academe.. are now set to carp about the sinking of the Belgrano.

†**b.** *intr.* To resolve. *Obs.*

**1638** EARL MANCH. in *Buccleuch MSS.* (Hist. MSS. Comm.) I. 280 The King hath set to be at Hinchenbrook to bed the 27th of March. **1674** N. FAIRFAX *Bulk & Selv.* 161 Could not God then make the world, when he set with himself that he would do it?

**c.** *trans.* To make (a resolution). *rare.*

**1771** WESLEY *Wks.* (1872) V. 100 If he does but once set a resolution.

**93. a.** *pass.* To have one's mind or will fixed *upon* something.

**1390** GOWER *Conf.* I. 301 He was upon pacience So sett. *c* **1400** *Balade of Pite* 100, I am sette on yowe in suche manere þat.. I moste you loue. *c* **1400** *Rom. Rose* 4829 They are so sette Vpon delite to pley in feere. **1611** SPEED *Hist. Gt. Brit.* IX. xviii. 25 If she be.. so obstinate, and so precisely set vpon her owne will. **1671** MILTON *Samson* 1201 When I perceiv'd all set on enmity. **1740** RICHARDSON *Pamela* (1824) I. xxxi. 50, I am so set upon it, that I am not to be persuaded. **1890** *Universal Rev.* Mar. 457 Cap'n Prust's as set as never was on little Dot. **1893** *Chamb. Jrnl.* 28 Jan. 58/2 Isabell is always set on the news.

†**b.** To have a specified disposition or inclination to be (so) disposed. *Obs.*

**1470–85** MALORY *Arthur* X. lxxxviii. 570 Whanne syre launcelot wyste how his kynnesmen were sette. *c* **1500** *Cocke Lorelles Bote* 1 She is as softe as a lamme yf one do her meue, And lyke to ye deuyll wan a man dothe her greue, So well is she sette. **1513** DOUGLAS *Æneis* II. ix. 58 Bot he.. was nocht to Priame sa hard set. *a* **1670** SPALDING *Troub. Chas. I* (Bannatyne Club) I. 103 The commissioners told how the marquess and burgh of Aberdeen were peaceably sett. *a* **1715** BURNET *Own Time* (1724) I. 598 Were he ever so wickedly set.

**c.** *Psychol.* To predispose (a person or other organism) to a given response; usu. *pass.* Also *intr.* for *pass.* Cf. SET *sb.*[1] 12.

**1909** *Amer. Jrnl. Psychol.* XX. 569 The psychophysical organism 'sets' to meet an imminent situation; and on the conscious side, this 'set' is expectation. **1938** *Mind* XLVII. 88 An observer in an experiment is said to be set towards an aspect of a situation if he is directed to it by the instructions. **1961** LINDGREN & BYRNE *Psychol.* vi. 143/2 Alterations in our familiar surroundings are often missed because we are 'set' to perceive certain stimuli.

**94. a.** ***to set one's*** or ***the face*** (***countenance***): to give a fixed or settled expression to the countenance.

† ***to set a face***: to make it appear (*as though*..). ***to set one's face as a flint***, after Isaiah l. 7.

**1560** BIBLE (Genev.) *Isa.* l. 7 Therefore haue I set my face like a flint. **1564–5** *Buggbears* I. ii. 154 Formosus set a face as thoughe he knew wher to find a cunnyng mane. *a* **1586** SIDNEY *Arcadia* II. (Sommer) 212 When she set her countenaunce to tell the matter. *c* **1610** B. JONSON, etc. *Widow* V. i, Set your countenance then; for here he comes. **1635** CRANLEY *Amanda* 9 She would.. sometimes set her countenance as if shee had bin angry. **1719** D'URFEY *Pills* I. 353 Set thy Face, and thy best Curchy make. **1855** TENNYSON *Maud* I. i. 31, I.. May make my heart as a millstone, set my face as a flint.

**b.** *pass.* and *intr.* (and *refl.*) Of the eyes, the features, the countenance: To have or assume a fixed look or expression.

**1601** SHAKS. *Twel. N.* V. i. 205 O he's drunke.. an houre agone: his eyes were set at eight i' the morning. **1611** BIBLE *1 Kings* xiv. 4 But Ahiiah could not see, for his eyes were set by reason of his age. **1717** GARTH tr. *Ovid's Met.* XIV. *Iphis* 45 Set are her eyes and motionless her limbs. **1861** GEO. ELIOT *Silas M.* i, He saw that Marner's eyes were set like a dead man's. **1865** SWINBURNE *Chastelard* V. iii. 214 His face set, The eyes not curious to the right or left And reading in a book. **1880** MRS. RIDDELL *Palace Gardens* ix, The lines in his face set and hardened. **1881** P. GREG *Ivy* III. iii. 68 Her face sets as it used against your mother. **1884** 'RITA' *My Lord Conceit* I. I. v. 72 A face set in stern, rigid lines. **1888** G. GISSING *Life's Morning* III. xxii. 210 Her features had set themselves in sorrow. **1898** G. B. SHAW *You never can tell* IV. *Stage dir.*, His face set and sulky.

**95. a.** To press (the teeth, lips) together into a rigid position; to clench (the teeth), compress (the lips, mouth).

Phr. *to set one's teeth*: see TOOTH.

1602 MARSTON *Antonio's Rev.* v. iii, Another frets, and sets his grinding teeth. 1702 C. MATHER *Magn. Chr.* VI. vii. 73 They were sometimes hindred from eating their Meals, by having their Teeth set. 1853 KINGSLEY *Hypatia* xxiv, The old woman set her lips firmly, and drew her dagger. 1860 WHYTE-MELVILLE *Mkt. Harb.* xxii, 'I think not!' replied Mr. Sawyer, setting his teeth for a catastrophe. 1867 'OUIDA' *Cecil Castlemaine*, etc. 263 His mouth sternly set, and his forehead paler and more severe than ever. 1886 STEVENSON *Kidnapped* xxii, Each set his mouth and kept his eyes in front of him.

**b.** *refl.* and *intr.* Of the mouth, or the teeth.

1626 BACON *Sylva* §714 [This] maketh the teeth to set hard one against another. 1719 DE FOE *Crusoe* I. (Globe) 191 My Teeth.. would.. set against one another so strong, that for some Time I could not part them again. 1883 MRS. F. MANN *Parish of Hilby* xix, Helen's mouth set itself firmly as she thought of it.

**c.** *pass.* and *intr.* Of muscles, or the like: To have or assume a rigid attitude or state. Also *spec.* of an athlete poised to start a race. In wider use: to be prepared for action; to be ready (*to* do something). Freq. in phr. (*to be*) *all set*. Cf. *on your mark(s)*, (*get set, go*) s.v. MARK *sb.*[1] 12e.

1844 J. GREGG *Commerce of Prairies* I. 51 Each teamster vies with his fellow.. and it is a matter of boastful pride to be the first to cry out—'All's set!' 1851 H. STEPHENS *Bk. Farm* (ed. 2) II. 174/2 The hams should not be too full of flesh, *lyary*, which in a young animal indicates that the carcass will soon set from growing. 1862 TYNDALL *Mountaineer.* vi. 53 The muscles have become set, and some minutes are necessary to render them again elastic. 1868 *Rep. U.S. Commissioner Agric.* (1869) 313 Butterflies generally *set* in one or two weeks. 1882 W. A. BAILLIE-GROHMAN *Camps in Rockies* i. 3 'All set!' echoes from each of the horsemen in front. 1893 *Outing* XXII. 154/1 At the words 'Get set!' the arms are raised, the knees slightly bent, and.. the starter braces his legs apart. 1913 [see CROUCH *sb.*[2] b]. 1930 *Amer. Speech* VI. 120 Set for big bout. 1935 *Encycl. Sports* 580/1 At the words 'Get set' you should let the weight come forward on to the finger tips and the leading foot, raising the left knee but lowering the back and head. 1949 N. MARSH *Swing, Brother, Swing* v. 84 All set, boys? Let's go. 1956 A. H. COMPTON *Atomic Quest* iii. 162 The du Pont Company was getting set to build the plutonium production plant. 1957 DUNCAN & BONE *Oxf. Pocket Bk. Athletic Training* (ed. 2) v. 62 On the command 'set' the body rises up smoothly with the body-weight on the hands and front foot. 1962 J. HELLER *Catch-22* vi. 51 Just when I was all set to really start stashing it away, they had to manufacture fascism and start a war. 1979 *Daily Tel.* 26 Feb. 21/4 National Westminster is set to produce full year figures tomorrow.

**d.** *intr.* To become bent or twisted as a result of strain. (Cf. SET *sb.*[1] 16.)

1798 *Phil. Trans.* LXXXVIII. 485 If a wire is twisted only a little more than its elasticity admits of, then, instead of setting, as it is called, or acquiring a permanent twist all at once, it sets gradually. *c* 1865 *J. Wylde's Circ. Sci.* I. 404/1 The scales will have a tendency to 'set' when over-loaded.

†**e.** *trans.* To stick up, cock. *Obs. rare.*

1708 *Lond. Gaz.* No. 4428/16 Stollen.., a Bay Nag.. sets his Head and Tail.

**96.** *Dyeing.* **a.** To prepare (woad) for dyeing.

1529 *Cov. Leet Bk.* 697 To occupie the Craft of dying and settyng of wadd. 1590 WEST *Symbol.* §82 Euery set of the same woad shall make, when it is set and prooued, fower pound sterling. 1811 *Self Instructor* 535 Wood-wax.. is set with pot ashes.

**b.** To make (a colour) fast or permanent.

1601 HOLLAND *Pliny* XXII. ii. II. 115 To set all other colours that can bee devised, with the juice onely of certaine hearbs. 1882 CROOKES *Dyeing* 15 The brown colouring matter of the flax instead of being removed is fastened, or as it is technically called, 'set'.

**97. a.** To cause to become firm, hard, or rigid in consistency; to curdle, coagulate (milk, etc.).

1736 BAILEY *Dict. Domest.* s.v. *Cheese*, While this rennet is fresh, one spoonful of the liquor will turn or set about 16, 18 or 20 gallons of milk. *Ibid.*, When you would turn or set milk for cheese. 1784 TWAMLEY *Dairying Exempl.* 102 Boiling Water.. will set the Curd in some degree, and fix it hard. 1855 *Jrnl. R. Agric. Soc.* XVI. I. 135 If you clay heavily.. you must muck heavily, or you will set the land. 1875 KNIGHT *Dict. Mech.* 2286/1 [He] uses golden sulphuret of antimony and sets the rubber by vulcanizing it. 1974 M. LINDLAW *Super Sweets & Puddings* 9 *To set jelly quickly.* Dissolve the jelly tablet in ½ pint (1½ dl) hot water, then make up to 1 pint (6 dl) with cold water or ice cubes. Stir until on the point of setting.

**b.** *pass.*

1791 SMEATON *Edystone L.* §168 Dutch Tarras,.. which, after being once set, would afterwards become hard, without ever being compleatly dry. *Ibid. note*, [*Set*], the term used in the application of calcareous mortar, which denotes its first step, or degree of hardening. 1839 CHATTO & JACKSON *Wood Engraving* 723 Recent impressions of a wood-cut, before the ink is set. 1846 *Jrnl. R. Agric. Soc.* VII. II. 493 The skin was set, that is, it would not easily rub off. 1879 *Cassell's Techn. Educ.* III. 99 When the film is just set enough to bear a light touch, without receiving any impression of the finger.

**c.** *intr.* To become firm or solid in consistency; (of milk) to curdle or turn; (of mortar, etc.) to solidify.

1736 BAILEY *Dict. Domest.* s.v. *Cheese*, When it [milk] sets or turns to curd very quick. 1776 SEMPLE *Building in Water* 79 The out-side Mortar.. set, that is, grew hard immediately. 1837 J. T. SMITH tr. *Vicat's Mortars* 9 We say that a lime has set, when it bears without depression a knitting-needle of 0.12 cent... diameter, filed square at its extremity, and loaded with a weight of 0.30 kil. 1839 HANSARD *Print. & Type-founding* (1841) 151 When the varnish has had time to set. 1842 *Jrnl. R. Agric. Soc.* III. I. 16 The soil.. is rather sticky when wet, and sets hard when dry. 1860 PIESSE *Lab. Chem. Wonders* 168 Silver 'sets' before the lead. 1883 *Standard* 17 May 2/2 Nor shall we permit the meat to hang, to 'set' over the reeking fumes of the killing chamber. 1886 J. BLANDY *Baker's Guide* 51 A certain sort of loaf, put into the oven without touching, 'set crusty', as the baker would say. 1963 D. SETON *Essent. Mod. Cookery* 151 The sugar is very important in jam-making. If too much or too little is used, the jam will not set. 1973 *Cooking for Today* (Good Housekeeping) 264/4 Pour one third of this jelly into a picnic jelly mould and put in a cool place to set.

**d.** Of cream: To collect and settle on the top of the milk.

1859 *Jrnl. R. Agric. Soc.* XX. I. 53 The milk.. is.. left until the cream has set.

**98. a.** To cause (fruit) to form on a tree by the process of fertilization; to cause (a flower) to develop into fruit: said of bees, etc. and (also *absol.*) of the tree bearing the fruit.

1693 EVELYN *De La Quint. Compl. Gard.* Dict. s.v. *Bud*, Well Budded or well set Trees; is said of those Fruit-Trees, that have abundance of Fruit Buds. 1721 BRADLEY *Philos. Acc. Wks. Nat.* 25 Concerning the Generation of Plants, and the manner of setting their Fruits. 1729 LANGLEY *Pomona* 77 Our Fruits being plentifully set. *a* 1793 G. WHITE *Selborne, Obs. on Veget.* (1836) 301 When they [bees] are once induced to haunt the frames, they set all the fruit. 1877 DARWIN *Forms of Flowers* i. 28 Flowers legitimately fertilised set seeds under conditions which cause the almost complete failure of illegitimately fertilised flowers. 1892 *E. P. Dixon's* (Hull) *Seed Catal.* 18 It is a robust grower and sets very freely. 1893 *Field* 8 Apr. 530/1 The plant.. 'sets' a larger proportion of the flowers.

**b.** *intr.* Of blossom or fruit: To develop as the result of fertilization. Also said of hemp fibre.

1718 J. LAWRENCE *Fruit-Gard. Cal.* 53 This Blossom Set, and produced me a Peach. 1779 *Phil. Trans.* LXX. 475 February was so mild and fine that the wall-fruit flowered.. and set much fuller, than the apples, which were two months later. 1849 *Jrnl. R. Agric. Soc.* X. I. 177 The fibre has not set, nor has the male stem shed its pollen. 1854 H. MILLER *Sch. & Schm.* (1858) 561 To mark how very few of the blossoms have set. 1891 *Field* 24 Oct. 634/1 About a dozen fruit set, of which six ripened.

**c.** Of a plant: *to set to seed* = SEED *v.* 1.

1897 WILLIS *Man. Flowering Pl.* II. 234 Moneywort.. is said never to set seed in Brit[ain].

**99.** *Plastering.* To put a finishing coat on. (See SET *sb.*[1] 30a.)

1693 MOXON *Mech. Exerc.* (1703) 249 They finish the Plastering when it is almost dry,.. setting it, that is to say, Trowelling and brishing it. 1812 P. NICHOLSON *Mech. Exerc.* 309 (Plastering) *Lath Floated and Set Fair.* These words bear the same meaning as lath pricked-up and floated and set. 1847 SMEATON *Builder's Man.* 128 Render, float, and set, is three-coat work. 1874 J. BIRCH *Country Archit.* 44 Lath, plaster, float, set and twice whiten all ceilings throughout.

**100. a.** *Sheep-breeding.* To settle or establish (a particular stock).

1782 MARSHALL *Norfolk* (1795) II. 321 Bought by those who are increasing, or 'setting' a ewe stock. 1807 A. YOUNG *Agric. Essex* II. 334 His flock has been 1140 breeding ewes; and at this Michælmas (1805) he setts 2000. *a* 1819 REES *Cycl.* XXXII, *Setting*, a term used in sheep-management, which signifies the picking, choosing, and selecting those which are the best formed.. for the purpose of breeding, forming the flock, and keeping as stock. *Ibid.*, *Setting Lamb-Stock.* 1847 *Jrnl. R. Agric. Soc.* VIII. I. 17 In setting the flocks particular attention is paid to size, wool, strength of constitution.

**b.** *intr.* Of a period of time or weather: To become settled; = *set in*, 146e. (Cf. SET *ppl. a.* 6c.)

*a* 1800 *Gil Brenton* vi. in Child *Ballads* I. 74 Till the evening set and birds they sang. 1880 *Antrim & Down Gloss.* s.v., 'The night is set'.. night has come on. 1892 ZANGWILL *Bow Myst.* 98 It's set wet, it'll rain right into the new year. 1894 *Harper's Mag.* Feb. 359/1 The night set very cold.

**c.** *Cricket.* (*pass.*) To have become accustomed to the bowling.

1865 *Lillywhite's Cricketers' Comp.* 127 As a bat he is deficient in defence, though a punishing hitter when once set. 1882 *Daily Tel.* 19 May, The Colonials were firmly set, and the runs came fast.

**101.** To settle the growth of (a plant) in the right way.

1845 *Jrnl. R. Agric. Soc.* V. II. 339 Where the clover is not well set. 1864 *Ibid.* XXV. II. 275 Wheat is rolled.. in spring, to set the young plant.

**102.** To check; to puzzle, nonplus, 'stump'; to tax the resources of. Now *north. dial.*

1586 HOOKER *Irish Hist.* 87/2 in *Holinshed*, At this answer Meth was set. 1601 HOLLAND *Pliny* II. xii. I. 9 The silie mind of men was before sett and to seeke. 1633 G. HERBERT *Temple, Ch. Mil.* 51 Learning was pos'd, Philosophie was set. 1737 BRACKEN *Farriery Impr.* (1757) II. 164 Standing.. will make them [feet] grow so hard,.. that it will set the Smith to drive a Nail in shoeing. *c* 1746 J. COLLIER (Tim Bobbin) *View Lanc. Dial.* Misc. Wks. (1775) 62, I wur warr set to get eawt (if possible) in e wur when Nip an me feel off the Bridge. 1819 *Pantalogia* s.v. *Cart-horse*, Four thorough-shaped horses will draw, with facility, a weight which would set five ordinary ones.

**103.** *Dancing.* (*intr.*) To take up a position and perform a number of steps with one's face *to* one's partner or *to* the dancer on one's right or left. Chiefly in ***set to partners, to corners*** (also ***set corners***).

1652 *Dancing Master* Expl. Charac., Set and turn single, is a single to one hand, and a single to the other, and turn single. *Ibid.* 1 Sides all, set and turn S. *Ibid.* 72 Meet all, back again, set to your own, and to the next. 1711 BUDGELL *Spect.* No. 67 ¶9 A.. Step called Setting, which I know not how to describe to you, but by telling you that it is the very reverse of Back to Back. 1791 BURNS *Tam o' Shanter* 147 The dancers.. reel'd, they set, they cross'd, they cleekit. 1801 R. ANDERSON *Cumbld. Ball.* 18 Tou kens we danc'd a threesome reel, And Betty set to me. 1806 J. BERESFORD *Miseries Hum. Life* iii. (ed. 3) 51 Set corners, ladies. 1811 T. WILSON *Country Dancing* (ed. 2) 6 Foot and set are the same; it is merely dancing in your place to fill up the time of the music. 1894 E. SCOTT *Dancing* 113 The gentleman sets to and turns with the lady on his left hand. *Ibid.* 119 Set to partners and turn. *Ibid.* 120 All set to corners and turn... They set and turn to places.

*transf.* 1835 DICKENS *Sk. Boz, Mr. Watkins Tottle* ii, Two green sauce tureens, with ladles of the same, were setting to each other in a green dish.

**104. a.** *pass.* and *intr.* To get stuck. †Also *trans.* to allow to get stuck.

(There is perhaps a punning reference to this sense in Shaks. *Lear* II. ii. 3 *Stew.* Where may we set our horses? *Kent.* I' th' myre.)

1756 J. CLUBBE *Misc. Tracts, Hist. Wheatfield* (1770) I. 83 Carters.. when their waggons were set in bad roads. 1778 [MARSHALL] *Minutes Agric.* 2 Sept. 1776 If he spill or overturn his load, or if he break his waggon, or set his horses. 1854 THOREAU *Walden* xvi. (1863) 316 A plough got set in the furrow and had to be cut out. 1888 *Sci. Amer.* 4 Feb. 74/1 To prevent the 'setting' and sliding of the wheels.

**b.** *Bowls.* (*intr.*) = RUB *v.*[1] 14b.

1875 'STONEHENGE' *Brit. Rural Sports* III. I. iii. §3 If a bowl be struck and if it do rub or set on the striker's partner.

**IX.** To put in the way of following a certain course, cause to take a particular direction.

** Where physical direction or motion in a certain path is the prevailing notion.*

†**105. a.** To take (a journey), direct (one's course).

*a* 900 CYNEWULF *Elene* 1004 (Gr.) ðif hie.. ȝesundne sið settan mosten. *a* 1000 *Sat.* 189 (Gr.) Ic.. sceal nu wreclastas settan sorhȝeariȝ, siðas wide. *a* 1330 *Sire Degarre* 425 Mani a jorne thai ride and sette. *c* 1375 *Cursor M.* 13668 (Fairf.) To ihesus þe way he sette.

†**b.** To lay (a ship's course). Also *absol. Obs.*

*c* 1485 *Digby Myst.* (1882) iii. 1723 Sett þer-with, yf we mown, for I wott itt is a havyn town. 1513 DOUGLAS *Æneis* VII. v. 10 It is also cummyn to our eris, ȝe set ȝour cours ouer see thir mony ȝeiris. 1585 T. WASHINGTON tr. *Nicholay's Voy.* II. viii. 42 Setting our course east Northeast.

**106.** *intr.* (less freq. *refl.*) To proceed in a specified direction; to begin to move, start off, put out, set out. Now surviving (exc. *Sc.*) only in ***set forth, forward, off, on***, etc. (see XII).

*a* 1000 *Boeth. Metr.* i. 4 Setton suðweardes siȝeþeoda twa. 1052 *O.E. Chron.* (MS. C), Ða ȝeaxedon þæt lið þæt on Sandwic læȝ embe Godwines fare, setton þa æfter. *c* 1205 LAY. 27216 Setteð heom after. *c* 1400 *Beryn* 1999 He set hym in ful purpose to his Shippis ward. *c* 1400 *Destr. Troy* 1828 At Salame full sound þai set into hauyn. *Ibid.* 11109 Sadly ho sete, sewit hym agayne. 1568 C. W[ATSON] *Polybius* 62b, Immediately to set towardes his ennimies. 1599 SHAKS. *Hen. V*, II. Prol. 34 The King is set from London. 1632 LITHGOW *Trav.* x. 440 From thence I set East-ward to Syragusa. 1637 RUTHERFORD *Lett.* (1664) 342 To set up the brae to the King's city. 1697 DRYDEN *Æneid* VII. 508 The faithless Pirate soon will set to Sea. 1786 BURNS *Halloween* xxi, While for the Barn she sets. 1808 JAMIESON s.v., *I set*, or *set out, after him*; I pursued him.

**107. a.** *intr.* Of a current, wind: To take or have a (certain) direction or course.

14.. *Sailing Directions* (Hakl. Soc.) 11 At the Hedelonde the streme settith North West and Southest. 1595 MAYNARDE *Drake's Voy.* (Hakl. Soc.) 19 From hence.. a great currante setts towards the estward. 1685 W. HEDGES *Diary* (Hakl. Soc.) I. 181 The Current (which usually setts to the Northward at this time of the Year). *a* 1700 EVELYN *Diary* 15 Oct. 1644, Blowing very hard from land.. it set so violently as rais'd.. so great a sea. 1748 *Anson's Voy.* I. iv. 51 We found the tide to set S.S.E. and N.N.W. 1835 SYD. SMITH in *Mem.* (1855) II. 362 When the wind sets that way. 1877 HUXLEY *Physiogr.* 174 The current which sets into the Gulf of Mexico. 1890 *Longman's Mag.* July 336 The prevalent winds set from the west.

**b.** Of the tide (cf. *set in*, 146f).

1777–83 LESCALLIER *Voc. Termes Mar.* 64 The tide sets to the South. 1825 *Examiner* 30/1 There was a strong tide setting. 1853 M. ARNOLD *Sohrab & Rustum* 627 As the vast tide Of the bright rocking Ocean sets to shore At the full moon.

**c.** *fig.* and in fig. context: To have a direction, tendency, or bent.

1778 EARL CARLISLE in Jesse *Selwyn & Contemp.* (1844) III. 340, I think I have strength of mind enough to stem the torrent, let it set against me with all its fury. 1842 TENNYSON *Locksley Hall* 24 All the current of my being sets to thee. 1885 *Manch. Exam.* 16 Feb. 5/3 The current of popular fiction in this country has lately set strongly towards pure sensationalism. *Ibid.* 28 Sept. 5/3 The public opinion of the young men is setting against the practice. 1891 *Temple Bar* Nov. 309 Her ambition did not set in the direction indicated. 1893 *National Observer* 1 Apr. 490/1 The sleeve puffings reveal an artful under-garment, setting towards pink.

**108. a.** *trans.* To cause to pass into a certain place or from one place to another; to convey, transport (? orig. by water, cf. *set over*, 150a). Now *rare*, the usual verb being *put*.

1375 BARBOUR *Bruce* XIV. 382 With four schippes that he had tane, He set thame our the Ban ilkane. *c* 1500 in Peacock *Stat. Cambr.* (1841) App. A. 37 The Bedyll shall sett the Masters of Gramer to the Fathers place. 1530 PALSGR. 715/1 Ferye man, what shal I gyve the to set me over the water? 1556 *Chron. Gr. Friars* (Camden) 36 The curet with all the parich and solempnite sette the osttes home with soleme procession. 1575 *Gamm. Gurton* IV. iii. 21, I set him soone inward. *a* 1578 LINDESAY (Pitscottie) *Chron. Scot.* (S.T.S.) I. 394 To.. sett certane bandis of men of weir to the bordouris. 1601 *Acc. Bk. W. Wray* in *Antiquary* XXXII. 80 A laye layde.. for settynge soldyars into Ireland. 1615 W. LAWSON *Country Housew. Garden* (1626) 2 Drifts of snow will set Deere, Hares, and Conies.. ouer your wals. 1819 J. HODGSON in Raine *Mem.* (1857) I. 227 The price my pinch me for cash to set me home. 1856 HAWTHORNE *Engl. Note-bks.* (1870) II. 53 We went back to the ferry, and, after being set across.., we drove back to Melrose.

†**b.** To put *a land, on land, ashore*. *Obs.*

**1375** Barbour *Bruce* III. 425 Ane That rowyt thaim our deliuerly, And set thaim on the land all dry. *c***1482** J. Kay tr. *Caoursin's Siege of Rhodes* (1870) ¶11 Many of the Turkes that were sette a land by the brygge from the shippes. **1617** Moryson *Itin.* I. 47 The barke..set us on land neere the Towne. **1700** S. Parker *Homer in Nutshell* 6 You'll ferry o'r, And at the Pallace-stairs be set a'shoar.

*intr.* for *refl.* **1523** Ld. Berners *Froiss.* I. cxxi. 59 b, He counselled the kyng..to set a lande in Normandy.

**c.** To accompany or escort (a person) for part or all of the way he has to go. Chiefly *north. dial.*

**1737** Bracken *Farriery Impr.* (1757) II. 99, I was setting my Patient a little on the Road. **1802** R. Anderson *Cumbld. Ball.* 34 And monie a time he's set me heame. **1889** M. E. Carter *Mrs. Severn* III. II. ix. 17 I've had a very happy day, and they set me to the stile. **1890** Hall Caine *Bondman* I. vii, I'll set you as far as Ballasalla.

†**d.** *to set home*: to bring to bear closely *upon*; to enforce, emphasize. *Obs.*

*a***1656** Vines *Lord's Supper* (1677) 178 Setting home the sin and danger of it. **1678** Cudworth *Intell. Syst.* I. iv. 422 Which Argumentation is further set home by such Similitudes as these. **1757** Jon. Edwards *Orig. Sin* I. Wks. 1807 II. 97 To set home this awful truth upon their consciences.

**109.** Of a current, wind, etc.: To cause to move, carry along in a (certain) direction.

*c***1450** *St. Cuthbert* (Surtees) 6792 Bot þai were lett, And fra þe se to land sett. *c***1620** Z. Boyd *Zion's Flowers* (1855) 9 She plies that course her compasse sets her on. **1748** *Anson's Voy.* II. v. 180 There was a current which set us to the northward. **1819** Byron *Juan* II. ci, The current..Still set them onwards to the welcome shore. **1823** W. Scoresby *Jrnl.* 74 A breeze sprung up from the south-east, and set the ice so rapidly upon us. **1892** *Field* 6 Feb. 198/3 The current in a rapid usually 'sets' the canoe clear of rocks.

**110.** To propel (a boat or other craft) with a pole; to punt. Also *absol.*, to use a punt pole or setting pole; now *esp.* in punt-shooting, to move up *to* the fowl, to get within shooting distance (cf. *set up*, 154 pp).

*c***1566** Southam in *Hakluyt's Voy.* (1599) I. 366 We departed from Ostroue in the morning before Sunne rising, rowing and setting vp the riuer 5. miles. **1705** tr. *Bosman's Guinea* 338 Those in the Boats are obliged to set 'em along by sticking their Pole in the Ground. **1725** De Foe *Voy. round World* (1840) 325 By the help of towing and setting as well as they could, they came to a flatter shore. **1765** J. Bartram *Jrnl.* 31 Dec., We rowed or set the battoe as far as she could swim. **1823** *Examiner* 719/1 At Shields, as a young keelman..was in the act of setting the keel to which he belonged, the pole slipped. **1859** Folkard *Wild-fowler* xxiv. 145 When 'setting' to birds side by side with other punters. **1882** Payne-Gallwey *Fowler Irel.* 468 When setting to fowl in this style of craft the shooter lies partly on his left side.

**111. a.** To direct or point (one's face, foot, etc.) *to, towards, for* a place.

**1611**, **1632** [see face *sb.* 2 g]. *a***1700** Evelyn *Diary* 30 Aug. 1654, I, with my wife, &c. set our faces towards home. *a***1701** Maundrell *Journ. Jerus.* (1732) 14 That way the Musselmans are obliged to set their faces when they Pray. **1732** Law *Serious C.* iv. 65 With hearts always set towards Heaven. **1850** Tennyson *In Mem.* cii, I turn to go: my feet are set To leave the pleasant fields and farms. **1861** *Temple Bar* I. 394 It was time for him to set his face homewards. **1862** Collins *No Name* II. i. I. 279 The lonely figure of a woman..with her face set towards the westward view. **1885** *Field* 4 Apr. 426/2 As usual he [*sc.* the fox] set his head for Nosely. **1890** Miss I. D. Hardy *New Othello* i, They have set their faces for home.

**b.** To put (a person) *on the way* leading to a destination.

**1678** Bunyan *Pilgr.* I. (1900) 24 By turning thee from the way in which I had set thee. *Ibid.* 46 He directed me to the Wicket-Gate..and so set me into the way that hath led me directly to this house. **1883** J. Gilmour *Mongols* xviii. 212 Your host comes out with you to set you on your way. **1891** Muriel M. Dowie *Girl in Karp.* xviii. 239 He knew the path and could set us on it.

** *Where a person (or thing) is put to perform a task or to act in a certain way.*

(☞ For phr. *set a work, at, in, on,* or *to work*, see awork and work.)

**112. a.** To put (a person) *to* a piece of work or a task.

*c***1200** Ormin 4166 Þe sexe daȝhess sette God Hiss follc to þeȝȝre werrkess. **1522** *World & Child* 848 Folye met me..And vnto all synnes he set me. **1530** Palsgr. 715/1 To set every man to his taske. **1576** Gascoigne *Droomme of Doomes day* Wks. 1910 II. 349 To doe any yᵉ most vyle or paynefull dewty they are set unto. **1695** J. Edwards *Author. O. & N. Test.* III. 487 The 70 seniors disagreed in their translation..and so were set to it again. **1836** B. Hall *Schloss Hainfeld* vi. 77 We set the children to their regular lessons. **1861** *Macm. Mag.* IV. 331/1 He was set to a work for which he had no stomach.

**b.** Const. inf. (occas. †gerund): To put (a person or agent) to the task of doing a certain thing, cause (him) to be so occupied.

Prov. *set a thief to catch a thief.*

*a***1250** *Gen. & Ex.* 3634 Aaron bissop, oðere of ðat kin, Sette he hem for to seruen ðor-in. *a***1300** *Cursor M.* 18563 And o mi knightes sum þai sett For to do his graf be gett. **1387** Trevisa *Higden* (Rolls) V. 311 Paschasius,..in þe peyne of purgatorie, was i-sette for to serve bathes. *c***1450** in Aungier *Syon* (1840) 255 They schal be sette to say..fyftene pater nostres. **1474** Caxton *Chesse* II. iv. 56 That men shold sette poure children to laboure in the felde. **1526** *Pilgr. Perf.* (W. de W. 1531) 142 The free mason setteth his prentyse first longe tyme to lerne to hewe stones. **1599** B. Jonson *Ev. Man out of Hum.* I. i. (1600) D 2, Ile instantly set all my Hinds to thrashing Of a whole Reeke of corne. **1612** Brinsley *Lud. Lit.* 8 To set your children to begin to learne. **1712** Addison *Spect.* No. 435 ¶1 As one set to watch the Manners and Behaviour of my Countrymen. **1833** Ht. Martineau *Loom & Lugger* II. ii. 22 Nurse set us to ask my brother Robert. **1852** Thackeray *Esmond* II. vii, Baubles..for which men have been set to kill and quarrel ever since mankind began. **1886** *Encycl. Brit.* XX. 42/2 The twilight that sends the hens to roost sets the fox to prowl. **1890** *Sat. Rev.* 12 July 37/2 The naval operations our squadrons are set to perform.

**c.** *transf.* with a thing as obj.

**1841** Helps *Ess., Pract. Wisd.* (1842) 6 By setting one evil thing to counteract another. **1871** R. Ellis *Catullus* lxiii. 18 Let a gong clash glad emotion, set a giddy fury to roam.

**113. a.** To direct (one's mind, intention, or will) *to* the consideration or performance of something. Now *rare*.

**1340** Hampole *Pr. Consc.* 97 He þat til ille settes his wille. **1375** Barbour *Bruce* I. 11, I wald fayne set my will,..To put in wryt a suthfast story. *c***1386** Chaucer *Pars. T.* 314 He that wolde sette his entente to thise thynges. **1423** Jas. I *Kingis Q.* xxxviii, Sen him to serue he myght set my corage? *c***1450** Capgrave *Life St. Aug.* xiii, þe loue of his hert is now only sette to serue God. **1513** Douglas *Æneis* v. xiii. 105 My desire was sett..all Troy for to doun bett. **1590** Spenser *F.Q.* II. x. 60 To which whiles absent he his mind did set. *a***1668** Denham *Of Prudence* 133 Our hearts are only set..to be Rich or Great. **1671** Milton *P.R.* I. 202 All my mind was set Serious to learn and know. **1681** H. More *Expos. Dan.* 183 He..will set his mind to the taking of the more strongly fortified places. **1879** Guest *Lect. Hist. Eng.* xxiv. 236 He set his mind to govern his people well.

**b.** *refl.* To apply oneself *to* a piece of work, a task, or employment. Most often (and now always) const. inf.; also †to lay oneself out *for*.

*a***1352** Minot *Poems* (ed. Hall) x. 20, I rede þat þou..sone set þe to schriue. *c***1375** *Cursor M.* 17845 (Fairf.) A-twynne they sette hem to þat note. *c***1450** *Mirk's Festial* 81 Þay maden to take Mathy eftsones, and set hom to throw stonys at hym. **1456** Sir G. Haye *Law Arms* (S.T.S.) 37 That King sett him to have senȝeoury of all the Orient. **1500–20** Dunbar *Poems* xxix. 13 Quhen I sett me to sing or dance. **1611** Speed *Hist. Gt. Brit.* vi. li. §5 178 He set himselfe for their deliuerance. **1624** in *Lett. Lit. Men* (Camden) 131, I had set myselfe close to my worke. **1701** W. Wotton *Hist. Rome* 259 He set himself to redress the Abuses. **1845** Trench *Huls. Lect.* Ser. I. i. 9 They..will yet set themselves ..to look for petty discrepancies. **1880** Meredith *Trag. Com.* v, She set herself to study it.

**c.** *intr.* in the same sense: const. *to* with sb. (pron.) or inf., or *to* or *a-* with gerund. (Cf. *set about*, 127 a.)

**1456** Sir G. Haye *Law Arms* (S.T.S.) 90 Quhether I aw to defend my nychtbour in armys, and men wald sett to sla him. **1611** Cotgr. s.v. *Mettre*, If I vndertake it, if I set to it. **1641** Milton *Animadv.* ii. 18 Your Bishops have set as fair to doe it as they durst. **1668** H. More *Div. Dial.* III. xxix. I. 492 Two Asses..that set a-braying. **1705** tr. *Bosman's Guinea* 395 Most of them set to running before the Enemy appears. **1737** [S. Berington] *G. di Lucca's Mem.* (1738) 14 The Chief of the Inquisition..set to the Scrutiny of his Papers. **1803** Beddoes *Hygëia* IX. 99 A young man..reached a book from a shelf..and set to read. **1837** Carlyle *Fr. Rev.* I. III. iii, He sets to denouncing Stockbrokerage. **1890** *Cornh. Mag.* June 643 The mother and daughters set to the making of beds. **1893** *Black & White* 29 July 124/2 Let us ..set a-hunting once more for the philosopher's stone.

**114. a.** trans. *to set* (a person) *upon*: to put in the way of doing or performing, cause to be occupied with (something): often with implication of urging or impelling (cf. put *v.*[1] 27). Also *refl.*

**1435** *Contract Fotheringhay Ch.* (1841) 29 During all the sayd werke the seid Will. Horwode shall nether set mo nor fewer Free-Masons..thereupon. *c***1475** *Rauf Coilȝear* 394 Ane man..That neuer wald set him on assay withoutin his assent. **1657** W. Rand tr. *Gassendi's Life Peiresc* I. 184 A..Historiographer, who was at that time set upon the same undertaking. **1690** Locke *Hum. Und.* II. xxi. §29 Nothing setting us upon the change of state, or upon any new action, but some uneasiness. **1693** —— *Educ.* §94 Wks. 1714 III. 40 The Studies which he sets him upon. **1711** Addison *Spect.* No. 255 ¶8 This often sets him on empty Boasts and Ostentations of himself. **1825** *New Monthly Mag.* XVI. 406 [It] has set us upon an inquiry into the present state of religion. **1879** M. Pattison *Milton* vi. 75 This rude shock..set Usher upon a more careful examination.

**b.** Const. *on* (occas. †*in, to*) with gerund.

*Obs.* with reference to physical movement, e.g. *set on going, packing*: cf. d.

*c***1440** *Pallad. on Husb.* I. 366 Lond grauel anoon sette in worchinge. **1624** Bacon *Consid. War Spain* (1629) 5 This wheele set on going, did power a Warre vpon the Venetians. **1639** Fuller *Holy War* II. xli. (1640) 100 Suspicion giveth a passe-port to faith to set it on packing. **1690** Locke *Hum. Und.* III. vi. §31 [It] sets them also upon making of one name, that may comprehend both Gold, and Silver. **1695** Dryden tr. *Dufresnoy's Art Paint.* 72 You will do well to..set yourself on designing after the Ancient Greeks. **1745** *Col. Rec. Pennsylv.* V. 27 The pernicious conduct of the French at Canada in setting their Indians on destroying the Inhabitants. **1763** Mills *Pract. Husb.* III. 156 If the ground be..not wet enough to set it on growing. **1832** *Examiner* 91/2 This address set him to dancing again. **1851** Keble *Occas. Papers* (1877) 242 Is not this a thought to set us on praying? **1859** Geo. Eliot *Adam Bede* xxvii, That he might ..set him on persuading the Squire to consent. **1889** F. Pigot *Strangest Journ.* 188 It was perhaps this that set..Jem on stealing my own silver goblet.

**c.** Const. gerund with *a-* prefixed: in this const. and next, often, to put (a thing) in motion or progress, to start; esp. *to set (a-)going*.

**1530** Palsgr. 712/1 Go set these glasses of rose water a sonnyng. **1600** J. Pory tr. *Leo's Africa* IX. 334 Whosoeuer listeth to drinke of it, must set it a cooling for the space of an hower. **1660** Boyle *New Exper. Phys. Mech.* xvii. 129 Which perhaps will set..You..a thinking. **1705** Cheyne *Philos. Princ.* I. v. (1715) 186 The Impulse of an Almighty Hand to set them first a-going. **1794** Gouv. Morris in Sparks *Life & Writ.* (1832) II. 440 Those who set the plan agoing. **1852** Thackeray *Esmond* I. xiv, Those cards set people sadly a-quarrelling. **1855** Bain *Senses & Int.* II. iv. §27. 292 A morsel of food on the tongue sets a-going the movements of mastication. **1861** Thackeray *Four Georges* ii, The abbey bells are set a-ringing.

**d.** Const. simple gerund.

In early use † *to set packing*, etc., where in modern idiom *send* is used.

**1577** Hanmer *Anc. Eccl. Hist.* 43 The..Gadarits set packing the stoutest of them. **1611** *Second Maiden's Trag.* 1653 One touch will set him flyinge. **1662** R. Mathew *Unl. Alch.* 26 Neither let him think that it [ague] will be set going with one violent potion. **1809** Malkin *Gil Blas* x. ix. (Rtldg.) 361 The good wines..were set running at a furious rate. **1832** Fr. A. Kemble *Rec. Girlhood* III. 176 Victor Hugo has set my mother raving. **1843** Dickens *Mart. Chuz.* xxxix, With reference to your duties, I can set you going. **1872** Calverley *Fly Leaves* (1884) 24 Half-a-bar sets several couple Waltzing in convenient spots.

¶ **e.** *to set gone*: to set going, send or let off.

*c***1611** Chapman *Iliad* xv. 429 He..well might haue set gone A hundred arrowes. **1615** —— *Odyss.* XIII. 121 The Rowers..set gone The Ship.

**115.** To cause to be busy *about*. Also *refl.* and *pass.* (For the corresponding *intr.* see 127.)

**1622** Mabbe tr. *Aleman's Guzman d'Alf.* II. 131 Taking little sleepe when I had any thing to set my selfe about. **1693** Locke *Educ.* §202 Wks. 1714 III. 93 The advantages propos'd from what they are set about. **1693** Dryden *Disc. Satire* Ess. 1900 II. 32 The archangel..sets her [Discord].. about her business. **1849** Helps *Friends in C.* II. i. (1854) I. 277 It set me..about thinking of Cicero's *De Senectute*. **1864** Miss Yonge *Trial* I. xiv. 289 Mr. Axworthy had exclaimed that if ever he wanted a thing to be done, he must set Ward about it.

*** *Where attack or opposition is the motive.*

**116. a.** To incite (a dog or other animal, also a person) to make an attack or pursuit: chiefly with preps. *at, on.* (Cf. *set on*, 148 c.)

*c***1440** *Alphabet of Tales* 229 Hondis that & þai be set at any maner of beste, þai wil kill it. **1560** Pilkington *Aggeus* C c vj, If a sheepe runne from hys felowes, the Shepeherde settes hys Dogge after it. **1695** A. Telfair *New Confut. Sadd.* (1696) 6 When any one whistled for him [a dog] to set him on the Cattel. **1776** Earl Carlisle in Jesse *Selwyn & Contemp.* (1844) III. 137, I shall prevent this man from setting ruin like a bull-dog at her. **1840** Thackeray *Barber Cox* Oct., While young Tug set the dog at their heels. **1848** —— *Van. Fair* xlvii, In setting the boys' tutor..on her Ladyship's director, Father Mole. *Ibid.* li, Once or twice they set people at her, but they failed. **1889** Doyle *Micah Clarke* x, They set dogs on us as though we were rats.

**b.** To encourage (an animal) to perform some evolution or feat; to pit (fighting cocks).

*a***1586** Sidney *Arcadia* III. (Sommer) 288 They,..making their horses answer their hands, with a gentle galop, set the one toward the other. **1688** Holme *Armoury* II. 253/1 In Setting of a Cock, none are to be up on the clod but the 2 Seeters [*sic*]... When the Cocks are set Beak to Beak in the middle of the clod,..if the set Cock do not strike in counting of 20, and six times 10, and 20 after all; then the Battle is lost. *Ibid.*, The Cock is to be set, and they are to fight it out. **1884** *Western Daily Press* 16 Apr. 7/2 A well-known Kentish amateur..decided to 'set' his own birds. **1890** F. Barrett *Betw. Life & Death* II. xix. 38 She would set her horse at anything.

**117. a.** To place in a position of hostility or opposition; to cause to be hostile or antagonistic; to pit (one) *against* (another). Phr. *to set* (a person) *against*, to cause him to have an antipathy for.

*to set one's face against*: see face *sb.* 2 g.

**1297** R. Glouc. (Rolls) 9375 Vor setteþ him one hardeliche aȝen an hondred to wende. *a***1340** Hampole *Psalter* xxvi. 5 If castels be set agaynes me my hert shal not drede. *c***1420** in *26 Pol. Poems* 108 Why settyst þou þy herte aȝen resoun? **1576** Gascoigne *Droomme of Doomes day* Wks. 1910 II. 308 To set our owne wicked wills directly against his most holy will. **1680** H. More *Apocal. Apoc.* 261 He wonders that any man should set his wit against it. **1727** Boyer *Dict. Royal* II. s.v., Why would ye set such a man against ye? **1827** Scott *Surg. Dau.* ix, Set a brave spirit, then, against your fortune. **1837** Carlyle *Fr. Rev.* II. II. iv, Man has been set against man. **1879** Miss Yonge *Cameos* Ser. IV. v. 62 Henry VIII tried to set François against it. **1884** *Manch. Exam.* 25 June 5/2 The story..set people against a useful article of fish food. **1891** Fenn *Mahmie Nousie* II. iii. 54 You have been setting her against me.

**b.** Const. *to, at.*

*a***1400–50** *Wars Alex.* 1316 (Dubl.) A sege by hym-self sett to a hundreth. **1595** Shaks. *John* III. i. 264 So mak'st thou faith an enemy to faith, And like a ciuill warr setst oath to oath. **1596** Nashe *Saffron Walden* Wks. 1910 III. 75 Were there a thousand more of them and they should set their wit to his. **1606** Shaks. *Tr. & Cr.* II. i. 94 Will you set your wit to a Fooles? **1822** Lamb *Elia* I. *On some of the old Actors*, I have seen some Olivias..who..have seemed to set their wits at the jester. **1871** R. Ellis *Catullus* lxvi. 20 Whiles her bridegroom bold set to the battle a face.

**c.** *refl.* and *pass.* To be hostile or antagonistic.

*c***1482** in *Cal. Proc. Chanc. Q. Eliz.* II. (1830) Pref. 70 Whoos lordship and ladyship..is so hevely sette ayene the said suppliant. **1535** Coverdale *Ezek.* xxiv. 2 When the kynge of Babilon set himself agaynst Ierusalem. *c***1640** H. Bell *Luther's Colloq. Mens.* (1652) 303 The Cardinals would yield to no Reformation, but set themselvs against it. **1676** Hobbes *Iliad* I. 107 With a mind against me set. **1727** Gay *Begg. Op.* I. xiii, My Papa and Mama are set against thy life. **1889** Jessopp *Coming of Friars* iii. 158 The Cistercians ..at first set themselves against the wholesale pillage of the parochial clergy. **1889** Gissing *Nether World* iii, She only gets more and more set against me.

**d.** *intr.* To make an attack: see *set against* 128 a, *set at* 129, *set on, upon*, 131, 132 a.

**X.** Senses which appear to have arisen by reversal of construction or by an ellipsis.

†**118. a.** To people or garrison (a place) *with.*
971 *Blickl. Hom.* 121 Hie wiston þæt heora eþel þær on heofenum sceolde eft ȝebuen & ȝeseted weorþan mid halȝum sawlum. *a* 1122 *O.E. Chron.* (Laud MS.) an. 964, Her drǣfde Eadgar cyng þa preostas on Ceastre of Ealdanmynstre,..& of Middeltune & sette hy mid munecan. *c* 1205 LAY. 13337 And setten þine castles mid kene monnen.

**b.** To beset (a place) for the purpose of intercepting or capturing a person.
*a* 1425 *Cursor M.* 19717 (Trin.) Ofte þe toun for him þei set And saul wist þat he was þret. *c* 1470 HENRY *Wallace* IV. 56 And tauld how thai the way for his man sett. 1525 *Sc. Acts Jas. V* (1814) II. 298 Setting þe gait Laying wachis. 1535 STEWART *Cron. Scot.* I. 123 With mony spy [he] Gart sett the wod. *a* 1593 MARLOWE *Mass. Paris* 332 That they which haue already set the street May know their watchword.

**119.** To plant (ground) *with* 'sets' or (young) trees; formerly often with *about.* (Cf. 12.)
*to be set with* = to have growing upon it, to be overgrown with.
*c* 1290 *S. Eng. Leg.* 239/695 þicke it was i-set with treon. 1340 *Ayenb.* 95 God zette paradys erþlich uol of guode trawes. 1398 TREVISA *Barth. De P.R.* XIII. iv. (1495) 443 Ampnis is a ryuer arayed and sett wyth woodes. *c* 1450 *St. Cuthbert* (Surtees) 3862 þat fosse whare þe water was ȝett It is aboute with trees sett. *a* 1500 *Flower & Leaf* 56 The hegge ..With sicamour was set and eglatere. *c* 1590 MARLOWE *Faustus* (1631) D, The Riuer Maine..Whose bankes are set with groues of fruitfull Uines. *a* 1700 EVELYN *Diary* 27 Sept. 1644 The Pall Mall is sett with faire trees. *Ibid.* Apr. 1646, Several..walks all set about with orange..trees. 1757 MRS. GRIFFITH *Lett. Henry & Frances* (1767) I. 196, I have set the last acre of Belmont since I came down. 1852 *Jrnl. R. Agric. Soc.* XIII. II. 417 The whole 3 acres were ploughed and set with beans. 1855 TENNYSON *Brook* v, Many a fairy foreland set With willow-weed and mallow. 1891 M. MURIEL DOWIE *Girl in Karp.* xiii. 163 A grassy clearing, set with whortleberries.

**120. a.** To ornament (metal or other surface) by inlaying or encrusting it with stones or gems.
*c* 1370 *Robt. Cicyle* 57 (Camb. MS.) Alle was set with perrye. *a* 1375 *Joseph Arim.* 290 Sencers..set wiþ riche stones. 1431 *Rec. St. Mary at Hill* (1904) 27 A myter of cloth of gold set with stones. 1572–3 in Nichols *Progr. Eliz.* (1823) I. 324 One ring of golde sett with diamondes lozengye. 1681 FLAVEL *Meth. Grace* xxxiv. 575 A sword that hath an hilt of gold, set thick with diamonds. *a* 1700 EVELYN *Diary* 7 Sept. 1651 Whose belt was set with pearle. 1795 *Gentl. Mag.* 607/1 A superb watch, set with brilliants.

**b.** To surround (a large stone) *with* a mount of small stones; to mount (an object) *in* a particular metal. ? *Obs.*
1506 *Acc. Ld. High Treas. Scot.* III. 246 Ane mergreit set with stanes. 1705 EVELYN *Diary* 5 Feb., He had a most rich George in a Sardonyx set with diamonds. 1726 SWIFT *Gulliver* II. viii, I got it [a maid of honour's corn] hollowed into a cup and set in silver. 1727 GAY *Begg. Op.* I. vi, And this snuff-box... Set in gold!

**121. a.** *pass.* To be studded, dotted, lined, etc. *with* a number of objects; *occas.* †to be adorned or trimmed *with. to be set about* (*arch.*) or ***round with***, to be surrounded or encircled with, to have a circle of.
1382 WYCLIF *Song Sol.* vii. 2 As an hep of whete, set aboute with lilies. *a* 1400 *Parlt. 3 Ages* 31 And he assommet and sett of vi and of fyve. *c* 1400 *Anturs of Arth.* (Camden) x, In clething vn-clere Was sette aure [*Thornton MS.* Cerkelytt] with serpentes, that sate to the sidus. 1474 CAXTON *Chesse* III. ii. 90 Enuyrouned and set aboute wyth gardes & wacche-men. 1486 *Bk. St. Albans, Her.* biv, Quadrat is calde in armys whan the felde is set with sum tokyn of armys. 1585 T. WASHINGTON tr. *Nicholay's Voy.* II. xviii. 51 b, A very fayre fountaine, set about with diuers faire cypres trees. *Ibid.* xxii. 60 b, A rich pauillion of..satten set with gold and siluer. 1597 GERARDE *Herbal* I. v. 6 A brownish stalke..set with long sharpe leaues. 1667 MILTON *P.L.* VI. 755 As with Starrs thir bodies all And Wings were set with Eyes. *a* 1700 EVELYN *Diary* 15 Feb. 1645, An admirable picture..set about with columns of alabaster. *Ibid.* 29 May 1660, The windowes and balconies well set with ladies. 1712 ADDISON *Spect.* No. 383 ¶4 How thick the City was set with Churches. 1810 SCOTT *Lady of L.* I. xi, Fantastically set With cupola or minaret. 1889 M. E. CARTER *Mrs. Severn* III. III. viii. 205 The serene sky was set with stars. 1889 DOYLE *Micah Clarke* xxiv, A small ante-chamber, set round with velvet settees.

**b.** *rare* in the corresponding active use.
*c* 1386 CHAUCER *Clerk's T.* 382 A corone on hire heed they han ydressed And sette hire ful of Nowches. 1882 *Century Mag.* XXIV. 398/1 Winter had set them [the summits of the mountain] with snowy castles.

**122.** †**a.** To beset or besiege (a place or a person): esp. with *about. Obs.*
*c* 1400 *Rom. Rose* 7342 They..set the castel al aboute. *c* 1425 WYNTOUN *Cron.* VIII. xxxi. 5408 He was set harde. *c* 1430 *Syr Tryam.* 1307 We here be sett alle abowte. 1530 PALSGR. 715/1, I set rounde aboute, as a man is with his enemyes, or a beest with hunters.

**b.** *fig.* esp. in pass. phr. ***to be hard set***, † ***ill set***, to be in great straits or hard put to it.
1387 TREVISA *Higden* (Rolls) VII. 473 þe kyng..was hard i-sette wiþ tempest in þe see. *c* 1475 *Rauf Coilȝear* 449, I sall hald that I haue hecht, bot I be hard set. *c* 1560 A. SCOTT *Poems* xx. 20 Lufe, Quhilk now setts the so sair. 1653 H. MORE *Antid. Ath.* III. ix *heading*, How hard set the Atheist will be for a subterfuge against this story. 1673 O. HEYWOOD *Diaries* (1883) III. 204 They were ill set to liue. 1737 BRACKEN *Farriery Impr.* (1756) I. 254 The poor Creature is very hard set to drive his Water from him. 1891 *Temple Bar* Dec. 514 He..was hard set to restrain himself in his desire.

**123. a.** Of a hunting dog: To mark the position of (game) by stopping dead and pointing the muzzle towards it. (Cf. SETTER *sb.*[1] 11.)
1621 MARKHAM *Hungers Prevention* 255 If..you chaunce to see your dogge to make a sudden stop..you shall then presently make into him (for he hath set the Partridge). *a* 1674 CLARENDON *Hist. Reb.* XIV. §76 To see a dog set partridge. 1727 BOYER *Dict. Royal* I. s.v. *Arrester*, To set Quails, or Partridges, as a setting Dog does. 1892 *Field* 7 May 666/3, I remember once having a young setter dog out with me, when he set a partridge on her nest.

**b.** *transf.* and *fig.*
1675 J. SMITH *Chr. Relig.* App. I. 23 Yet for all this Tully sets this Royal Game [Varro]. 1781 JOHNSON in *Boswell*, Have I said any thing against Mr.****? You have set him, that I might shoot him: but I have not shot him. 1825 T. HOOK *Sayings* Ser. II. *Sutherl.* I. 5 My reader may perchance have seen a cat *set* a mouse. 1888 *Times* 16 Oct. 10/5 The puppy was..encouraged forward on my trail.. and 'set' me without a fault.

**c.** *intr.* To set game. †Also formerly (of persons), ***to go setting***, to hunt with a setter.
*to set dead*, to make a dead set: see SET *sb.*[1] 10 f.
1775 JOHNSON *Tax. no Tyr.* 12 His dog may refuse to set. 1841 H. MILLER *Old Red Sandst.* iii. (1887) 66 The puppy of the setting-dog squats down and sets untaught. 1892 *Field* 23 July 124/1 He..steals along a few paces, and then sets rigidly, just as an old grey hen flushes. 1897 *Badm. Mag.* Apr. 456 The mother, twenty yards off, backs her point and sets dead.

†**d.** Of persons, ***to go a-setting***: see SETTING *vbl. sb.*[1] 1 c (*b*).

**124.** *Naut.* To take the bearings of (an object).
1626 CAPT. SMITH *Accid. Yng. Seamen* 18 Set him by the Compasse. 1627 —— *Seaman's Gram.* ix. 38 Set the land, how it beares by the Compasse. 1694 MOTTEUX *Rabelais* V. x, We weigh'd Anchor, hois'd up Sail, stow'd the Boats, set the Land, and stood for the Offing. 1769 FALCONER *Dict. Marine* (1780) *Setting*, We set the Tower of Arabia near the port of Alexandria. 1808 ASHE *Trav.* I. 25 Having set the house with a pocket-compass. 1863 HARBORD *Gloss. Navig.* s.v. 1867 SMYTH *Sailor's Word-bk.*, *Set the chase*, to mark well the position of the vessel chased by bearing.

†**b.** To sight or 'make' (land, a vessel). *Obs.*
1632 LITHGOW *Trav.* VII. 328 When they set land, Some this, some that, doe gesse, this Hill, that Cape.

**125. a.** To mark down as prey, fix on as a victim, make a set at; to watch for the purpose of apprehending or robbing. *slang.* (Cf. SETTER *sb.*[1] 7 a.)
1670 *Mem. Du Vall* 8 He, with his Squadron, overtakes a Coach which they had set over night. 1692 SPRAT *Relat. Contriv. Blackhead & Young* I. 50 He might come to Rob, or to Set the House. 1727 GAY *Begg. Op.* III. ii. (1776) 43 There will be deep play to-night at Marybone,..I'll give you the hint who is worth setting. 1732 *Tricks of Town* 11 The Dogs that belong to private Families and Shopkeepers, the proper time for setting them is generally soon after Seven in the Morning. 1800 in *Cornwallis Corr.* (1859) III. 320 The person who procured for me all the intelligence respecting Lord Edward Fitzgerald, and got —— to set him. 1890 *Melbourne Argus* 2 July 8/3 Two of the fraternity 'setting' a young man..and endeavouring to win the gold for which he had laboured.

**b.** Phr. ***to have*** or ***get*** (a person) ***set***: to have a score to settle with, 'have it in for' (that person). *Austral.* and *N.Z. slang.* Cf. SET *sb.*[1] 7 b.
1916 C. J. DENNIS *Songs Sentimental Bloke* 40 This Romeo 'e's lurkin' wiv a crew—A dead tough crowd o' crooks—called Montague. 'Is cliner's push—wot's nick-named Capulet—They 'as 'em set. *c* 1926 'MIXER' *Transport Workers' Song Bk.*, 17 You growl and swear you can't get work Or the boss has got you set. 1945 BAKER *Austral. Lang.* vi. 121 A man who has acquired a strong dislike of another person... He *gets someone set* and *words him*, rebukes him. 1959 —— *Drum* 112 *Get someone set*, to have a grudge against a person; to prepare to pay someone out.

†**126.** *Sc. Law.* To reject, set aside. *Obs.*
1678 SIR G. MACKENZIE *Crim. Laws Scot.* II. xxiii. §6 (1699) 250 Thus an assizer was set..because he was not twenty-five Years of age. *Ibid.* xxvi. §2. 265 To object against a witness in our Law, is called to cast a witness, or to set him.

**XI.** With prepositions in specialized senses (intransitive).

**127. set about ——.**

**a.** (*a*) To begin working at, take in hand, begin upon.
1601 [see A. 1 γ]. 1611 *Second Maiden's Trag.* (Malone Soc.) 1182 He will weigh the work he vndertakes, and sett about it een in the best sobrietie of his Iudgem[en]t. 1637 RUTHERFORD *Lett.* (1664) 189, I purpose God willing to set about Hosea & to try if I can get it to the presse here. 1707 SHAFTESB. *Let. Enthusiasm* (1708) 8 Men..are wonderfully happy in a Faculty of deceiving themselves, whenever they set heartily about it. 1784 *New Spect.* No. 1. 6 My friend sat about it with great diligence. 1818 SCOTT *Br. Lamm.* xxvi, Let every man and woman here set about their ain business. 1865 RUSKIN *Sesame* i. §2 This essential education might be more easily got..if they set about it in the right way. 1889 DOYLE *Micah Clarke* xxx, We had best set about our part of the contract.

(*b*) *const. inf.*
*a* 1300 *Cursor M.* 1580 þe scham, þe sin þat þan was vte At tell war lang to sett aboute [*Gött.* sitt aboute, *Fairf.* syte a-bout]. 1736 LEDIARD *Life of Marlborough* I. 147 The Queen set about to form Her Ministry. 1840 *Jrnl. R. Agric. Soc.* I. IV. 404 He sets about to clean his land in good earnest. 1889 'M. GRAY' *Repr. Annesley* I. I. iv. 94 He scrambled to his feet, and set about to console himself.

(*c*) *const. gerund.*
1749 CHESTERF. *Let. to Son* 24 Nov., I..will set about doing the orders contained therein. *a* 1774 GOLDSM. tr. *Scarron's Com. Romance* (1775) II. 172 Don Sancho's servant..immediately sat about enquiring into Dorothea's conduct. 1865 GLADSTONE *Glean.* vii. (1879) 34, I will set about explaining what I mean. 1890 TOUT *Hist. Eng. from 1689*, 173 Peel..set about forming a new party.

**b.** To set upon, attack. *colloq.*
1879 HORSLEY *Jottings from Jail* (1887) 5 This got to my father's ears; when I went home he set about me with a strap until he was tired. 1906 *Daily Chron.* 22 May 3/3 It is always well to name the antagonist whom you are setting about.

**128. set against ——.**

†**a.** To make an attack upon, be hostile to. *Obs.*
*c* 1330 *Arth. & Merl.* 4874 þis paiens..oȝains þis children set. *a* 1400–50 *Wars Alex.* 2082, I my-selfe with a sowme set þaim agayns. 1542 UDALL *Erasm. Apoph.* 333 He spared not to sette against Philippus w[t] moste vehemente oracions. 1590 SHAKS. *Mids. N.* III. ii. 146. 1611 BIBLE *Ezek.* xix. 8 The nations set against him on euery side. 1685 BAXTER *Paraphr. N.T.* Mark vii. 9 You think it very well done, to set against Godliness and God's own Laws.

**b.** To compensate, balance.
1832 HT. MARTINEAU *Homes Abroad* vii. 104 Such a fright as we have had will set against a great deal of the good.

**c.** To move in a direction opposed to.
1859 TH. PARKER *Exper. as Minister* Wks. 1865 XII. 318 Public opinion, now setting against this beastly vice. 1889 C. LARKING *With Everything agst. her* III. xi. 245 On the last day luck set dead against her.

**129. set at ——.** To assail, attack. (Cf. 127 b, 128 a, 131, 132 a.)
*c* 1430 *Pilgr. Lyf Manhode* I. xliii. (1869) 26 Ne were ye so gret a ladi, ye shulde right soone haue þe werre, and at yow j wolde sette. *a* 1548 HALL *Chron., Hen. VIII*, 49 b, They were prively sett at and in many jeopardies. 1849 *Tait's Mag.* XVI. 262/1 He sets at the church..and he deals it.. strong advice and comment. 1877 MISS YONGE *Cameos* Ser. III. xxxvi. 391, I would go, although as many devils should set at me as there are tiles on the housetops.

**set by ——:** see 91 c.

**130. set into ——.** †**a.** To enter or embark upon.
1591 SAVILE *Tacitus, Agricola* (1622) 188 Boldnesse to challenge and set into dangers. 1605 BACON *Adv. Learn.* II. To the King §12 When Schollars come to the practises of professions, or other actions of ciuill life, which when they set into [etc.].

**b.** To get into (a certain condition).
1825 HONE *Every-day Bk.* I. 292, I begin..setting into wind to follow the foxhounds in November.

**131. set on ——.** = 132.
*c* 1290 *S. Eng. Leg.* 16/530 A cristine man sone he mette, ..and on him faste he sette. *c* 1450 *Brut* II. 434 He set sore on the Frensshe men. 1470–85 MALORY *Arthur* II. x. 87 Syr said a knyght set on arthur for they are wery and forfoughten. *a* 1548 HALL *Chron., Hen. VI*, 136 The Frenchemen, beyng sodainly surprised and set on. 1628 EARLE *Microcosm.* xl. (Arb.) 61 He..sets boldly on good natures, as the most vanquishable. *a* 1700 EVELYN *Diary* 20 Apr. 1644, The company behind us were set on by rogues. 1820 SCORESBY *Acc. Arctic Reg.* II. 447 With despair pictured in every face, the crew set on the pumps. 1892 *Sat. Rev.* 13 Aug. 185/2 If you see a man set on by robbers.

**set to ——:** see 14 b, 103, 113 c.

**132. set upon ——.**

**a.** (*a*) To attack, assail, fall violently upon.
1390 GOWER *Conf.* III. 247 The lordes alle upon him sette With drawe swerdes. 1525 in Ellis *Orig. Lett.* Ser. II. I. 300 Wheere the Emperors thought to have set upon them being encamped, they founde them in array and goode ordre. 1530 PALSGR. 716/1 They dyd sette upon me foure to one. 1562 in *Archæologia* XLVII. 230 His maister..meteth whithe theves..And ys sett vpon by them. 1631 GOUGE *God's Arrows* I. §60. 100 David..set upon a Beare at one time, and on a Lion at another, and slew them both. 1663 PEPYS *Diary* 11 May, I was set upon by a great dogg, who got hold of my garters. 1722 *St. James's Even. Post* 14–16 June 2/1 A young Man was set upon by three Rogues..and robb'd of Bills and Money. 1848 DICKENS *Dombey* xliii, Wounded, hunted, set upon by dogs. 1879 GUEST *Lect. Hist. Eng.* xii. 109 The Danes came against them and set upon them again and again.

(*b*) *in immaterial sense.*
1639 DU VERGER tr. *Camus' Admir. Events* 205 Of all brags the foolishest is, that which sets upon the reputation of a weake sex. 1690 LOCKE *Govt.* I. xi. §118 However sin might set upon him. 1711 ADDISON *Spect.* No. 16 ¶3 If I attack the Vicious, I shall only set upon them in a Body. 1875 JOWETT *Plato* (ed. 2) I. 356 This is the reason why my three accusers ..have set upon me.

**b.** To urge strongly, importune. *rare.*
1652 EARL MONM. tr. *Bentivoglio's Hist. Relat.* 158 The Princesse was secretly set upon in private to suffer herself to bee conveyed away. *a* 1715 BURNET *Own Time* (1724) I. 236 The best of the Episcopal Clergy set upon the Bishops, to lay hold on this opportunity. 1883 [G. N. BANKES] *Cambr. Staircase* vi. 95 Milstead again set upon Oxden for his story.

†**c.** = *set about*, 127 a. *Obs.*
1555 WATREMAN *Fardle of Facions* II. xii. 300 It behoued them to sende for the Bishoppe, to hallowe the firste corner stone... And then might the Masons sette vpon the reste, but not afore. 1648 GAGE *West Ind.* 146 It was my fortune to set upon a hard and difficult building in a Church of Mixco. 1681 R. L'ESTRANGE *Tully's Offices* 69 Him that sets upon Building. 1709 STRYPE *Ann. Ref.* I. xxiii. 234 The Dean..exciting them with all his Rhetorick, to set upon the Reparation of it. 1793 SMEATON *Edystone L.* §103 To level the Sugar-Loaf..would..be a serious work; as it never could be set upon except when the sea was remarkably still.

**d.** *Naut.* To haul or pull upon.
1793 SMEATON *Edystone L.* 196 This tackle being a little slacked,..and then set upon. *Ibid.* 197 The rope..being then set upon by the main tackle.

**XII.** With adverbs in specialized senses.

**133. set about.** To circulate, spread about (a statement, report). Now chiefly *north. dial.*
*a* 1715 BURNET *Own Time* (1724) I. 168 Many discourses were set about upon this occasion. 1890 *Sat. Rev.* 4 Oct. 385/1 Alarming reports have been set about as to the imminence of serious trouble.

**134. set abroach.** *arch.*

**a.** To broach (a cask, liquor).

**1390** GOWER *Conf.* II. 183 Riht as who sette a tonne abroche. *c* **1460** [see A. 1 b]. **1697, 1855** [see ABROACH 1]. *fig.* **14..** LYDG. *Chron. Troy* II. 2464 (Digby MS.) He..gan approche & wiþ his swerd to sette a broche..þe Grekys hatful blood. **1605** CHAPMAN *All Fools* II. i, My Purse set a broch By euerie cheating come you seauen? **1763** C. JOHNSTON *Reverie* I. p. iv, He had drunk of his wine, which now began to warm his heart, and set all his secrets abroach.

**b.** To set on foot, set going, give currency or publicity to.

*c* **1475** *Mankind* 572 in *Macro Plays* 21 Ther xall be sett a-broche a clerycall mater. **1545** ASCHAM *Toxoph.* I. Wks. (1904) 26 Than euery one of them setteth his shiftes abroche. **1579** GOSSON *Sch. Abuse* (Arb.) 32 There set they abroche straunge consortes of melody. **1638, 1835** [see ABROACH 2]. **1702** *Engl. Theophrastus* 324 A studied and a laborious forecast toward the setting of a humour abroach.

**†135. set abroad.** *Obs.*

**a.** To spread abroad, spread wide.

**1526** TINDALE *Matt.* xxiii. 5 They set abroade there philateries, and make large borders on there garmenttes.

**b.** To publish (a treatise); to circulate (a report); to disseminate (a disease); to set (a matter) on foot.

**1555** BRADFORD in Strype *Eccl. Mem.* (1721) III. App. 127 Thoughe yt be never so daungerous to me to sett this lyttell Treatys abroad. **1584** COGAN *Haven Health* ccxliii. 265 The plague..was set abroade in the towne through buying..bedding..infected. **1588** SHAKS. *Tit. A.* I. i. 192 And set abroad new businesse for you all. **1687** MIEGE *Gt. Fr. Dict.* II, To set a Story abroad. **1759** SARAH FIELDING *C'tess of Dellwyn* I. 257 Ingeniously set it abroad that a Fire had happened.

**†136. set adown.** = *set down. Obs.*

*c* **1205** LAY. 19686 We weoren..for gode men iholden a þat Sæxisce men setten us a-dune. **13..** *Coer de Lion* 2142 The steward on knees him set adown. *c* **1350** *Will. Palerne* 2459 þanne as bliue þat barn þe best a-doun sette. *c* **1385** CHAUCER *L.G.W.* 226 Vp-on the..gras They settyn hem ful softely adoun. **1387** TREVISA *Higden* (Rolls) V. 107 And I..deme þat I be disposed and i-sette adoun.

**137. set afloat** (**†on float**). *arch.*

**a.** To launch, float (*lit.* and *fig.*).

**1559** *Mirr. Mag., Cade* xi. 1 See here how fortune setting vs a flote, Brought to our nets a portion of our pray. **1575** GASCOIGNE *Glasse of Govt.* Wks. 1910 II. 62, I trust maister Philosarchus fees will be sufficient to set both thee and me a floate. **1785** BOSWELL *Tour Hebrides* (1897) 537, I got our common friends there to assist in setting him afloat. **1837** CARLYLE *Fr. Rev.* I. II. v, Wondrous leather-roofed Floating-batteries, set afloat by French-Spanish *Pacte de Famille.*

**b.** To bring to the surface (as the dregs of a liquid); hence *fig.* to set (*esp.* something bad) in motion, set agog, stir up, make active.

**1586** [see AFLOAT 8]. **1662** CHARLETON *Myst. Vintners* (1675) 191 Seeing all Unsavouriness of Wines whatever seems to proceed from their impurities set afloat. **1724** WARBURTON *Tracts* (1789) 4 Ill Qualities,..when indiscreetly set on Float become fatal on the Constitution. **1749** [see FLOAT *sb.* 4]. **1809** MALKIN *Gil Blas* IX. x. (Rtldg.) 332 Hold your hand..exclaimed I... You must not set my avarice afloat again.

**†c.** To flood (land). *Obs.*

**1692** RAY *Disc.* II. ii. (1693) 74 So much Water..as..caused a considerable Flood.., setting all the Meadows on flote.

**†d.** To cause to become unsettled, 'carry away'.

*a* **1713** ELLWOOD *Hist. Life* (1714) 320 [Their] Applause setting his Head afloat, he came up to London.

**138. set apart.**

**†a.** To lay aside, put on one side. *Obs.*

**1530** PALSGR. 711/1 You may sette this a parte for a whyle, for we shall nat occupye it.

**†b.** To get rid of, do away with. *Obs.*

**1455** *Rolls of Parlt.* V. 279/2 To..purvey for restfull..reule in Wales, and to sette aparte such riottes and disobeisaunces as have be there. **1475** *Ibid.* VI. 143/2 That the said blessed intent,..and last Will..be not..fordoon and sett a parte.

**†c.** (*a*) To dismiss from one's consideration; to put out of one's mind; to cease to entertain, put aside, discontinue. *Obs.*

**1471** CAXTON *Recuyell* (Sommer) 676 They..sette aparte all dangers and paryllis. **1515** *Sel. Cases Star Chamb.* (Selden) II. 103 To set aparte all suche neue besynes as that thenne they hadde begonne. **1565** J. PHILLIP *Patient Grissell* (Malone Soc.) 1581 Be frollicke and ioyfull, set sorowes aparte. **1609** HOLLAND *Amm. Marcell.* XX. vii. 152 Sequestring and setting apart his anger for that time. *a* **1641** SPELMAN *Hist. Sacrilege* (1698) 144 They all set all other Business a-part.

(*b*) *in absolute ppl. phr.*

**1471** CAXTON *Recuyell* (Sommer) 146 That thou retorne in to the mercy of thy fader..alle excusacions set a part. **1508** FISHER 7 *Penit. Ps.* vi. Wks. (1876) 5 Set aparte the goodnes and gentylnes of almyghty god. **1560** DAUS tr. *Sleidane's Comm.* 14 b, He would..all delaye sette a parte, repaire into Germany. **1595** SHAKS. *John* III. i. 159 All reuerence set apart To him and his vsurp'd authoritie. **1636** HEYWOOD *Challenge Beautie* I. Wks. 1874 V. 11 To parallel the Queene in beauty and vertue?.. Which he may easily doe, her Prerogative of birth set apart.

**d.** To separate for a special purpose; to devote to some use.

**1604–1853** [see APART 6].

**139. set aside** (**†on side**). **a.** See simple physical senses and ASIDE *adv.* 1, 2, 3; to put on one side.

**1412–20** LYDG. *Chron. Troy* II. 2696 Make þi choyse..Whan euery drogge & pot is set a-syde. *c* **1430** *Art of Nombryng* (E.E.T.S.) 10 Write a cifre in the place of the figure sette a-side. **1530** PALSGR. 711/2 Set this asyde, tyll I call for it. **1598** DELONEY *Iacke of Newberie* Wks. (1912) 16 Set your link aside, and giue mee your hand. **1611** COTGR., *Remouvoir*, to remoue, retire, withdraw, set aside, put away. **1614** GORGES *Lucan* VIII. 343 His Roman pile was set aside. **1697** [see ASIDE A. 3].

**†b.** To discontinue the performance or practice of; also, to discard the intention of doing (something). *Obs.*

**1426** LYDG. *De Guil. Pilgr.* 22458 Late lordes..Sette asyde alle fflaterye! *c* **1440** —— *Hors, Shepe & G.* 90 Lett alle werr and stryffe be sett A-syde. **1528** ROY *Rede me* I. (Arb.) 65 Sett thy busynes a whyle a side, And lett vs have fyrst a songe. **1530** PALSGR. 711/2 The kynge wyll, all other thynges set asyde, that you examyne this mannes mater. **1590** SHAKS. *Mids. N.* IV. i. 188 Our purpos'd hunting shall be set aside. **1697** DRYDEN *Æneid* VIII. 584 Set your Tasks aside.

**†c.** ? To repulse. *Obs.*

*c* **1500** *World & Child* 294 To set our enemy sharpely on-syde.

**d.** (*a*) To dismiss from one's mind, abandon the consideration of.

*c* **1407** LYDG. *Reason & Sens.* 3189 And al they mente in honest wyse, Vnleful lust was set a-syde. **1540** PALSGR. *Acolastus* II. ii. K ij, Settynge care and thought a syde. **1562** *Aberd. Kirk Sess. Rec.* (Spalding Club) 4 All vder excusatioun set asyde. **1567** HARMAN *Caveat* Epist. (1869) 21 Settinge asyde all feare. **1593** SHAKS. *3 Hen. VI*, III. iii. 119 All dissembling set aside, Tell me for truth, the measure of his Loue. **1710** WYCHERLEY *Let. to Pope* 1 Apr., Yet..set raillery or compliment aside, I can bear your absence..better than I can your company when you are in pain. **1821** SCOTT *Kenilw.* xxiii, To make her lady's safety the principal object of her care, setting all other considerations aside.

*const. inf.* *c* **1572** GASCOIGNE *Posies, Fruites of Warre* xl, I set aside to tell the restlesse toyle The mangled corps.

(*b*) In imper. or ppl. const.: Excluding, excepting, except for, apart from.

**1610** HOLLAND *Camden's Brit.* I. 567, I saw Solyhill: but in it, setting a side the Church, there is nothing worth sight. **1652** EARL MONM. tr. *Bentivoglio's Hist. Relat.* 55 And set wine aside..they abound in all things necessary for human life. **1657** —— tr. *Paruta's Pol. Disc.* 107 But set this respect aside, to live out of a mans Countrie, hath no resemblance of evil. **1760** *Impostors Detected* III. xi. II. 123 He was a very good kind of a man, setting aside his figure. **1883** EMILY LAWLESS *Millionaire's Cousin* iv. 95 Setting aside this, all inequality so far as I can see ceases.

**†**(*c*) In ppl. const.: Not taking account of, let alone. *Obs.*

**1753** L. M. *Accomplished Woman* I. 61, I think, that setting aside scandal, it were enough to escape their [men's] censure. **1785** *Liberal Amer.* I. 63, I flattered myself that the sight of a country..which is certainly beautiful, setting aside the charm of novelty, would have amused her.

**e.** To reject or throw over as being of no value, cogency, or pertinence; to overrule.

**1594** WEST *2nd Pt. Symbol., Chancerie* §22 Equitie..setting on side the common rules of the law. *a* **1700** EVELYN *Diary* 18 May 1688, Such a dispensing power as might..set aside all Laws. **1762–71** H. WALPOLE *Vertue's Anecd. Paint.* (1786) III. 57 [He] was brought to set aside his evidence. **1870–2** LIDDON *Elem. Relig.* iv. §i. (1904) 133 The existence of moral evil is too patent..a subject, to be permanently set aside by human beings. **1874** STUBBS *Const. Hist.* I. vi. 135 The rule of hereditary succession was..set aside. **1885** R. BRIDGES *Nero* III. i. 12/2 To set our honoured oaths and firm allegiance To you aside, as being unjustly sworn.

**f.** To discard or reject from use or service, in favour of another.

**1576** GASCOIGNE *Droomme of Doomes day* K iij b, Settinge a side such thinges as are requisite for the soules health: And omitting the obseruance of gods holy commaundementes. **1691** *Trials Sir R. Graham*, etc. 24 *Mr. Cradock.* My Lord, I know not how I came to be summoned upon this Jury; for I am no Freeholder. *L. C. J. Holt.* Then set him aside. **1779** *Mirror* No. 39 When a man of acknowledged honour..sees himself set aside, and obliged to give way to the worthless and contemptible. **1849** MACAULAY *Hist. Eng.* vi. II. 5 If that national force [the militia] were set aside, the gentry of England must lose much of their dignity and influence. **1861** LD. BROUGHAM *Brit. Const.* xv. 220 To set aside the elder or Stuart branch, and to substitute..the younger. **1879** M. J. GUEST *Lect. Hist. Eng.* xliii. 440 The English prayer-book was set aside, and the Latin mass said again.

**g.** To annul, quash, render void or nugatory. Chiefly *Law.*

**1760** C. JOHNSTON *Chrysal* (1822) III. 179, I have it in my power to set aside the whole unnatural, nonsensical will. **1790** DURNFORD & EAST *K.B. Rep.* III. 5 A rule to shew cause..why the verdict should not be set aside and a new trial granted. **1877** SPURGEON *Serm.* XXIII. 61 Nor does it set aside the necessity that those men should cheerfully accept the gospel of Christ. **1883** *Law Rep. 11 Q.B. Div.* 591 A rule was subsequently obtained by Mr. Woollett to set that nonsuit aside.

**h.** To separate out for a particular purpose.

**1720** GORDON & TRENCHARD *Indep. Whig* (1728) 66 Particular Persons who are set aside and paid for that Purpose. **1890** TOUT *Hist. Eng. from 1689*, 91 To set aside a part of the national revenue every year. **1891** *Law Times* XCII. 130/2 To set aside a portion of his wages in order to meet Lloyd's debt.

**140. set away. †a.** To remove, do away with.

*c* **1430** *Art of Nombryng* (E.E.T.S.) 16 Settyng away alle that is ouer hym in respect of the doublede. **1549** LATIMER *7th Serm. bef. Edw. VI* (Arb.) 200 Knoweledge..causeth vs to forget all, and set a waye discipline. **1687** MIEGE *Gt. Fr. Dict.* II, To set (or put) away, *oter.*

**b.** = *set by*, 142 b.

**1747** MRS. GLASSE *Cookery* ii. 52 Strain it and set it away for Use.

**c.** *intr.* To set off. *north. dial.*

**1818** SCOTT *Rob Roy* xxvii, Mattie had ill-will to see me set awa on this ride.

**141. set back.**

**a.** To hinder the progress of, give a check to. Hence, with a sum of money as compl.: to cost (a person so much). Also *fig.*, to take aback, to disconcert.

[**1530** PALSGR. 712/2 I set backewarde, or hynder a mater that it gothe nat forwarde... I have set hym backwarde this mornynge more than he shall come forwarde these seven yeres]. **1600** HOLLAND *Livy* III. 118 Thou hadst more need to set me backe with force of arms. **1647** MAY *Hist. Parlt.* I. ii. 20 The endammaging and setting backe of that newly established Kingdome. *a* **1677** BARROW *Serm.* Wks. 1716 I. 62 By so eagerly persuing he effectually setteth back his designs. *a* **1700** EVELYN *Diary* 11 Aug. 1693, This succeeded much wet, and set harvest extremely back. **1748** RICHARDSON *Clarissa* VI. 56 This had like to have set all back again. **1847** *Spirit of Times* 31 May 159/1 The captain used to boast that he could pack a gallon without its setting him back any. **1884** 'MARK TWAIN' *Huck. Finn* viii. 66 The nigger was set back considerable, because he reckoned it was all done with witchcraft. **1900** ADE *Fables in Slang* 131 Daughter was..seated under a Canopy that had set Father back thirty-two Dollars. **1922** S. LEWIS *Babbitt* x. 142 How much'll it set me back? **1937** J. STEINBECK *Of Mice and Men* 79 'What's it set you back?' George asked. 'Two and a half [dollars].' **1940** H. L. ICKES *Secret Diary* (1954) III. 183 This set him back on his heels. **1966** 'J. HACKSTON' *Father clears Out* 53 'Goin' t' leave it?' the prince asked, a bit set back. **1974** *Country Life* 14 Nov. 1445/1 Even a moderately-sized piece of cheesecake sets you back 20p.

**b.** To put (a clock, its hands) to an earlier time.

**1635** QUARLES *Embl.* v. vii. 2 Or has some frolick heart set back the hand Of Fates perpetuall Clock? **1892** *Illustr. Lond. News* 9 Jan. 45/1 They reconcile people to monarchy and set back the clock of progress.

**c.** *intr.* To flow in the reverse direction.

**1803** SYD. SMITH *Wks.* (1859) I. 24/1 Is not the tide of opinions..setting back with a strength equal to its flow?

**142. set by. †a.** To put on one side, lay aside. (*lit.* and *fig.*). *Obs.*

**1602** SHAKS. *Ham.* v. ii. 295 Ile play this bout first, set by a-while. **1626** B. JONSON *Staple of N.* III. ii. (1905) 66 To be separated and set by For Vshers, to old Countesses. *a* **1642** SUCKLING *Goblins* I. Wks. 1874 II. 16 Set him by, till he's sober. **1654** tr. *Scudery's Curia Pol.* 12 You have forced him not onely to set by his Mil[i]tia, and to depose his Crown.

**b.** To lay up or lay by for future use.

**1595** MAYNARDE *Drake's Voy.* (Hakl. Soc.) 8 To trimme his shippes..set by some new pinnaces. **1726** LEONI *Alberti's Archit.* I. 100/2 The Pantry for setting by what is left after meals. **1818** SCOTT *Br. Lamm.* xxvi, Let the house be redd up, the broken meat set by. **1850** MISS WARNER *Wide Wide World* xxxvii, After that many a basket of apples..was set by for her.

**†c.** (*a*) To reject, dismiss; to disregard, scorn.

**1592** NASHE *Strange Newes* Wks. 1910 I. 294 No more set by, but set by, thrust aside. **1636** HEYWOOD *Challenge Beautie* I. Wks. 1874 V. 9 Birth wee set by. **1660** FULLER *Mixt Contempl.* II. xiv. 23 Being now set by, layd aside as uselesse, and not sett by. **1704** NORRIS *Ideal World* II. i. 36 To set by this conclusion for a while. **1758** S. HAYWARD *Serm.* xvi. 481 'Tis indisputable... Devils cannot set it by, and the judge will not.

**†**(*b*) *setting by*: setting aside, not counting.

*a* **1592** GREENE *Alphonsus* I. i, Setting by Alphonsus' power divine, What man alive..Could countervail his courage? **1657** HEYLIN *Undeceiv. People* 7 Setting by all children which live under their parents [etc.]..the number of the residue will be found so small.

**†d.** To give up (doing something). *Obs.*

*a* **1674** CLARENDON *Surv. Leviath.* (1676) 282 To set by disputing with him, as one that is to be convinced only by himself.

**143. set down.** (Cf. *set adown*, 136.)

**a.** See simple trans. senses and DOWN *adv.*

(*a*) To cause to sit down. *rare.*

*a* **1470** GREGORY *Chron.* in *Hist. Coll. Cit. Lond.* (Camden) 222 The Erle of Worseter was take before the mayre and sette downe in the myddys of the hy tabylle. **1525** LD. BERNERS *Froiss.* II. ccxxvii. 295 b, The duke of Orlyaunce set euery man downe. **1835** WILLIS *Pencillings* III. 135 We were set down..at nine, to cold grouse, salmon [etc.]. **1861** S. BROOKS *Silver Cord* v. (1865) 27 The little girl having..been..set down, in a half-darkened apartment, to amuse herself with the pictures in Fox's Book of Martyrs.

**†**(*b*) To encamp (an army or host). *Obs.*

**1607** SHAKS. *Cor.* v. iii. 2 We will before the walls of Rome to morrow Set downe our Hoast. **1621** BP. MOUNTAGU *Diatribæ* 34 Because he did not..spend so many bookes..as Antimachus did, before he sate downe the seuen Princes at Thebes.

(*c*) To place, situate, locate.

**1827** *Edin. Weekly Jrnl.* 28 Feb., in Scott *Chron. Canongate* Introd. App., Wherever the belligerent powers might be pleased to set down this new theatre. **1882** W. MORRIS in Mackail *Life* (1899) II. 67 Lewes is set down better than any town I have seen in England. *a* **1887** JEFFERIES *Field & Hedgerow* (1889) 316 He was the exact counterpart of the London Jew dealer, set down in the midst of the country.

(*d*) *Falconry.* (See quots.)

**1614** LATHAM *Falconry* I. xi. 40 You doe at her first setting downe, giue her as much as she list to take into her gorge. **1891** HARTING *Bibl. Accipitr.* 229 *Set down to moult*, put into the mew.

**b. †**(*a*) To bring low, debase; to depose from office; to put down, quell. *Obs.*

*c* **1369** CHAUCER *Dethe Blaunche* 635 That is broght up she set al doun. **1387** TREVISA *Higden* (Rolls) VII. 261 In þat counsaille were y-sett doun meny bisshops and abbotes. *Ibid.* VIII. 179 He was i-sette doun of the fourþe pope Innocentius. *a* **1578** LINDESAY (Pitscottie) *Chron. Scot.* (S.T.S.) II. 141 Quhat was best to be done aganis..thair new reliegioeun and to sie quhat way thay might sett done the samin.

(*b*) To lower (a person's pride, etc.); to take down, snub.

**1753** RICHARDSON *Grandison* (1754) III. xviii. 251 Sir Harry own'd himself to blame: and thus the Lady's pride was set down softly. **1846** D. JERROLD *Mrs. Caudle* xxxi, Like her impudence!—I set her down for the rest of the evening. **1889** MRS. COMYNS CARR *Margaret Maliphant* I. i. 11, I was such a headstrong girl that it took a deal to set me down.

**c.** †(*a*) To slacken (the strings or pegs of a musical instrument). *Obs.*

**1565** COOPER *Thesaurus* s.v. *Chelys, Intendere chelyn*, to wreste vp the stringes of the lute. *Laxare chelyn*, to sette downe. **1604** SHAKS. *Oth.* II. i. 202 Oh you are well tun'd now: But Ile set downe the peggs that make this Musicke.

(*b*) To beat down to a shape.

**1703** T. N. *City & C. Purchaser* 193 So much of the Sheet as lies over the Cavity is set down into it with the Seaming-mallet. **1843** HOLTZAPFFEL *Turning* I. 213 When the iron is to be set down.. it is first nicked with a round fuller.

**d.** (*a*) To place so as to rest upon a surface; to put down, as upon the ground. Also *absol.*

*a* **1425** *Cursor M.* 12958 (Trin.) On an heȝe pinacle he set him doun Of þe temple. *c* **1530** H. RHODES *Bk. Nurture* in *Babees Bk.* 67 In some places the Caruer doth vse to shew and set down,.. and in some place he beareth the first dish, and.. setteth it downe couered before the degree of a Knight. **1573** G. HARVEY *Letter-bk.* (Camden) 4 He hath set down his staf. *c* **1600** SHAKS. *Sonn.* cxliii, As a.. huswife.. Sets downe her babe. **1796** MRS. M. ROBINSON *Angelina* III. 180 Sir Edward sat down the candlestick. **1825** SCOTT *Betrothed* x, The body was here set down before the door of the chapel. **1878** FR. A. KEMBLE *Rec. Girlhood* II. i. 28 If you attempt to lift or carry me down the stage, I will kick and scream till you set me down.

(*b*) To cause or allow to alight from a vehicle; to 'drop' (a person at a place). Also *absol.*

(Said of the person or persons in charge of or occupying the vehicle, or of the vehicle itself.)

**1668–9** PEPYS *Diary* 18 Mar., My wife and I going by coach, she went with us to Holborne, where we set her down. **1694** CONGREVE *Double-Dealer* V. v, My coach shall set you down. **1715** GAY *Let. to Pope* 8 July, I have just set down Sir Samuel Garth at the Opera. **1782** MISS BURNEY *Cecilia* VII. vi, I knew the postilion very well... And then he told me where he had set you down. **1841** THACKERAY *Gt. Hoggarty Diamond* ii, A number of carriages full of ladies were drawing up and setting down. **1844** *Act 7 & 8 Vict.* c. 85 §6 Such Train shall.. take up and set down Passengers at every Passenger Station. **1889** MRS. ALEXANDER *Crooked Path* I. iv. 110 The carriage is to come back for us after setting you down at the theatre.

**e.** (*a*) To put down in writing or in print; to put on paper; to enter in a catalogue or account; to write out, compose; to put on record; to record, relate, give an account of.

**1574** H. BAKER *Well-spring Sci.* (1617) 9, I set downe 7 vnder the line against the place of penies. **1576** GASCOIGNE *Droomme of Doomes day* II. E viij, [In the Scriptures] there are set down two.. entyer parts of rightuousnesse. **1579** GOSSON *Sch. Abuse* (Arb.) 16 The harshest penne may sette downe somewhat woorth the reading. **1590** SHAKS. *Mids. N.* I. ii. 22 You Nicke Bottome are set downe for Pyramus. **1605** BACON *Adv. Learn.* I. vi. §6. 28 After the Creation was finished, it is sette downe vnto vs that man was placed in the Garden to worke therein. **1610** HOLLAND *Camden's Brit.* I. 288 And here I am willing to set down their names. **1615** R. COCKS *Diary* (Hakl. Soc.) I. 70, I forgot to set downe how I receaved a letter from Martin de Guinia. **1663** S. PATRICK *Parab. Pilgrim* xi. (1687) 59 You will expect.. that I should set down at large the particulars of every days conference. **1687** A. LOVELL tr. *Thevenot's Trav.* II. 182 A great many good Ports that are not set down in the Maps. **1712** STEELE *Spect.* No. 266 ⁋2 Her Women.. are alphabetically set down in her Book. **1779** J. MOORE *View Soc. Fr.* (1789) I. ix. 62, I set down the whole scene as soon as F—— left me. **1806** J. BERESFORD *Miseries Hum. Life* (ed. 3) III. v, My youngest boy.. bethought himself of setting down a few 'School-miseries'. **1863** COWDEN CLARKE *Shaks. Char.* xvi. 393, I have always regretted that Hazlitt set down that passage. **1886** BESANT *Childr. Gibeon* II. v, It would not be fair to set down in cold blood the things he habitually said.

†(*b*) ***to set down the*** or ***one's period***: to come to a final decision. *Obs.*

**1590** GREENE *Never too Late* Wks. (Grosart) VIII. 23 They set downe the period with a deepe sigh. **1590** —— *Mourn. Garm.* ibid. IX. 150 At last she set downe her period on the face of Alexis, thinking he was the fairest.

†(*c*) To fix at a certain amount. *Obs.*

*c* **1593** ? GREENE *George a Greene* (1599) G 1 b, George a Greene, set downe the king of Scots His ransome. **1621** R. COCKS *Diary* (Hakl. Soc.) II. 141 It being the price sett downe. **1654** BRAMHALL *Just Vind.* iv. (1661) 85 Prescribed the indowments of Vicars, set down the wages of Priests.

(*d*) To put down, as in a schedule or table, *to be* performed at a certain time; †to appoint a time for the performance of (something).

**1593** SHAKS. *Rich. II*, IV. i. 319 On Wednesday next, we solemnly set downe Our Coronation. **1594** —— *Rich. III*, III. iv. 44 We haue not yet set downe this day of Triumph. **1795** [C. ABBOT] *Jurisdiction Crt. Gt. Sessions Wales* 120 The plaintiff must.. set down his cause to be heard. **1819** TAUNTON *Rep. Cases Comm. Pleas* VII. 85 Cases out of Chancery.. cannot be set down nor heard, unless they are signed by a Serjeant. **1889** ACWORTH *Railways Eng.* 203 The Great Western express.. was set down to leave Didcot.. 3 minutes earlier. **1893** *Weekly Notes* 68/1 After the cause had been set down for trial.

†**f.** To lay down (a principle), prescribe (a regulation, mode of procedure). *Obs.*

**1576** FLEMING *Panopl. Epist.* 257 Whiles I set doune directions and precepts. **1579** LYLY *Euphues* (Arb.) 193 She endeauoreth to set down good lawes. **1625** BACON *Ess., Simul. & Dissim.* (Arb.) 508 Therfore set it downe; That an Habit of Secrecy, is both Politick, and Morall. **1641** MILTON *Reform.* II. 47 If.. the Constitution of the Church be already set down by divine prescript. **1688** *Lett. conc. Pres. St. Italy* 30 All of that Cabale had set down this for a Rule.

†**g.** (*a*) To determine or resolve upon. Also ***set down one's rest*** (see REST *sb.*[2] 8 b). *Obs.*

**1582** N. LICHEFIELD tr. *Castanheda's Discov. E. Ind.* xxx. 73 b, Of the meeting of the King.. and the Captaine generall, at which time there was set downe a Trade and Factorie. **1611** SHAKS. *Cymb.* I. iv. 178 Wee will haue these things set downe by lawfull Counsell. **1632** BP. HALL *Hard Texts*, Luke xiv. 29–31 [He] must.. set it downe with his owne heart to undergoe resolutely all the difficulties that [etc.].

(*b*) *pass.* and *intr.* To be resolved, resolve. *Obs.* exc. *north. dial.* const. inf.

*a* **1586** SIDNEY *Arcadia* I. (Sommer) 20 One, that to praise well, one must first set downe with himselfe, what it is to be excellent. **1603** KNOLLES *Hist. Turks* (1638) 295 A man set downe to mischiefe. **1684** N. LEE *Constantine* III. ii. 36 If you set down t'enjoy me, Sir.

**h.** (*a*) To estimate, reckon; †in early use with obj. and compl., or with clause; now only, to regard (a person) *as*, take (him) *for*, consider (him) *to be* (so-and-so).

**1798** *Geraldina* I. 183, I never see a library of books with highly gilt bindings, but I set down that the owner seldom opens them. **1799** S. & HT. LEE *Cant. T., Frenchman's T.* (ed. 2) I. 198 The playful unconscious character she had first been set down. **1809** MALKIN *Gil Blas* I. xii. (Rtldg.) 25 The corregidor.. set me down for the culprit. **1815** *Zeluca* III. 9 He sat himself down as invulnerable. **1828** SCOTT *Aunt Marg. Mirror* ii, You had best set him down a Jesuit. **1840** DICKENS *Barn. Rudge* xlviii, Those who cling to the truth and support the right cause, are set down as mad. **1872** J. HARTLEY *Yorksh. Ditties* Ser. II. 118 They used to be sat daan to be young ens 'at hadn't le'nt wit. **1889** F. BARRETT *Under Str. Mask* I. iv. 68 He would set her down at once for an impertinent.. busy-body.

(*b*) To attribute, or put down *to*.

**1822** LAMB *Elia* I. *Mod. Gallantry*, He could not set it down to caprice. **1879** MISS YONGE *Cameos* Ser. IV. xii. 137 This, as usual, was set down to malice prepense on his side.

**i.** Now *dial.* (*a*) *refl.* To seat oneself. (Cf. 3.) †Also, to go down *on one's knees*: cf. sense 2.

*a* **1300** *Cursor M.* 14092 For-wit his fete sco sett hir dun. **1470–85** MALORY *Arthur* I. xix. 65 He sette hym doune by a fontayne. **1548** UDALL *Erasm. Par. John* vi. 1–4 Iesus, beyng sumwhat separate from the people, setteth hym down on the hyll. **1694** *Acc. Sev. Late Voy.* (1711) i. 64 They set themselves down on the Grass. **1719** DE FOE *Crusoe* I. (Globe) 15 We.. set us down to fish.

(*b*) *pass.* To be seated. (Cf. 4.) Also *transf.* to be settled in a place.

*a* **1300** *Cursor M.* 13495 All right þar war þai sett dun. **1575** PAINTER *Pal. Pleas.* II. iv. (1890) II. 178 The king and Ariobarzanes being sette downe at a table. **1622** MABBE tr. *Aleman's Guzman d'Alf.* II. 229 When I was set downe to my meat. **1741** C'TESS HARTFORD *Corr.* (1805) III. 189 When I am set peacefully down at my farm, I shall often read over your letters. **1776** S. J. PRATT *Pupil of Pleas.* II. 74, I was just set down to the card-table at the Delmores. **1815** SCOTT *Guy M.* xvi, When all should be gone to bed, or set down to cards, which is the same thing.

⁋ *With mixed construction.*

**1582** T. WATSON *Centurie of Love* (Arb.) 38 My harte is sett him downe twixt hope and feares Vpon the stonie banke of high desire. **1593** SHAKS. *3 Hen. VI*, IV. iii. 2 The King by this, is set him downe to sleepe.

(*c*) *intr.* To sit down. (Cf. 5.)

*c* **1400** *Rule St. Benet* (Verse) 1741 þai sal set down And mak a schort colacioun. **1442** *Aberdeen Reg.* (1844) I. 7 That.. [he] sal cum.. and set downe on his kneis. **1530** PALSGR. 713/1, I set downe, I rest me on a seate, *je massis.* **1635** HEYLIN *Sabbath* (1636) I. 124 That we should.. set down with modesty,.. to heare the Law. *a* **1700** EVELYN *Diary* 17 Sept. 1685, All the gentlemen in his traine setting down at table with him. **1720** *Humourist* 212 Till he set down to Dinner. **1794** MRS. A. M. BENNETT *Ellen* I. 28 He had just.. set down to his coffee. **1809** SYD. SMITH *Serm.* I. 43 He is ever ready.. to say a grace to God, before he sets down to feast with Mammon.

†(*d*) ***to set down by*** = to put up with. Cf. SIT *v.* 23 d (*a*).

*c* **1618** MORYSON *Itin.* IV. (1903) 64 The Venetians.. having a very rich Shipp robbed by Turkish Pyratts.. were forced to sett down by the losse.

**j.** *refl.* To begin to devote oneself *to*.

**1864** J. H. NEWMAN *Apol.* 243, I set myself down to my translation of St. Athanasius. **1891** *Blackw. Mag.* CL. 173/1 In his green old age, he set himself down to write this great dictionary.

†**k.** *intr.* To be encamped; to 'sit down' *before* (a town) to besiege it. *Obs.* Cf. a (*b*).

**1601** SHAKS. *All's Well* I. i. 129 Man setting downe before you, will vndermine you, and blow you vp. **1606** —— *Ant. & Cl.* III. xiii. 168 Cæsar sets downe in Alexandria. **1621** LADY M. WROTH *Urania* 130 Then did the braue Generall set down before Thessalonica. **1631** HEYLIN *St. George* 248 Nothing to stop our march, till we set downe With all our troopes, before the Holy Towne.

**l.** *intr.* To have a direction downwards.

**1747** HOOSON *Miner's Dict.* S 2 b, If a fair leading sets down under the second Sett, it may in all probability lead down to a third, and so on.

**144. set forth.** See simple senses and FORTH *adv.* †**a.** (*a*) To thrust forth. *Obs.*

*a* **1225** *Leg. Kath.* 827 Ah nu we beoð of se feor for þe iflut hidere, þu schalt setten sikel forð. **1553** T. WILSON *Rhet.* 118 Some settes forth their lippes two ynches good beyonde their teeth.

†(*b*) To direct or send forward, set on the way.

**1525** LEE in Ellis *Orig. Lett.* Ser. III. II. 75 To sett forthe the standard against thies Philistees. **1549** LATIMER *Ploughers* (Arb.) 17, I have assaied to sette furth my plough to proue what I coulde do. **1590** BARWICK *Disc. Weapons* 7 My commaunder commaunds me to set foorth of my band of 200, one hundred, to keepe a straight or passage.

†(*c*) To arrange or dispose in a certain manner; to lay out. *Obs.*

*c* **1450** in Aungier *Syon* (1840) 373 The butler schal sett forthe the pottys.. up on eche table. **1595** SHAKS. *John* II. i. 295 W'el set forth In best appointment all our Regiments. **1651** T. BARKER *Art of Angling* (1653) 1 A man that goeth to the River.. must understand.. to set forth his Tackles. **1667** MILTON *P.L.* VII. 429 There the Eagle and the Stork.. set forth Thir Aierie Caravan high over Sea's Flying.

†**b.** (*a*) To send out (soldiers, etc.) for service; hence, to equip, fit out (men, a fleet, a voyage). *Obs.*

**1451** [implied in SETTER-FORTH]. *a* **1533** LD. BERNERS *Huon* lxi. 213 They sette forth a galay & .xxx. paynyms therin. **1584** [see A 1]. **1603** OWEN *Pembr.* (1891) 41 They are forced to sett furthe manye to theire owne dislike, althoughe the best that cold be founde. **1626** B. JONSON *Staple of N.* II. v, Setting forth some Lady, Will cost as much as furnishing a Fleete. **1635** R. N. tr. *Camden's Hist. Eliz.* I. 54 He intended to set forth a voyage into West India. *a* **1700** EVELYN *Diary* 29 July 1667, The charge of setting forth a fleete. **1702** —— *Diary* 3 May, Every Missioner, besides the 20 *l.* to set him forth, should have 50 *l. per. ann.* **1805** *Act 45 Geo. III*, c. 72 §7 If such Ship or Vessel so retaken shall appear to have been, after the taking by His Majesty's Enemies, by them set forth as a Ship or Vessel of War.

†(*b*) To furnish with what is necessary. *Obs.*

*c* **1610** *Women Saints* 207 Haue you nothing.. lying in store, wherewith her exequies may be sett forth?

†(*c*) To furnish, provide (entertainment). *Obs.*

**1526** TINDALE *John* ii. 10 All men att the begynnynge sett forth goode wyne. **1613** PURCHAS *Pilgrimage* (1614) 330 Certain Priests, whose office it was to set forth publike playes and games in honor of their Gods. **1693** CONGREVE *Dryden's Juvenal* XI. 6 When Poor Rutilus spends all his Worth, Jn hopes of setting one good Dinner forth.

†**c.** (*a*) To provide, allot, or set apart for a purpose.

**1596** DALRYMPLE tr. *Leslie's Hist. Scot.* II. 358 Jn this ordour.. ar mony sett furth to hald sitizenis in peice and in thair office. **1632** BP. HALL *Hard Texts* Matt. xxiv. 29 When as my Church shall have endured that full proportion of affliction, which I have set forth for it. **1684** in Picton *L'pool Munic. Rec.* (1883) I. 318 The wast ground.. formerly set forth for that purpose.

†(*b*) To put aside as tithe; = ***set out***, 149 r (*b*).

**1548** *Act 2 & 3 Edw. VI*, c. 13 §2 Yf any person carrye awaye his corne or haye or his other prediall tythes before the tythe thereof be sett forthe. **1670** W. SHEPPARD *Parson's Guide* 9 The Parson or Vicar is to take away his Tythes in a convenient time after they are set forth.

(*c*) To lay out (money); = ***lay forth***, LAY 52 c; = ***put forth***, PUT 42 j.

**1622** BACON *Hen. VII*, 208 This [sum of money] to bee set forth in Lands, of the best and most certaine Reuenue.

**d.** To promulgate, publish, issue (a regulation, proclamation, etc.).

**1567** HARMAN *Caveat* Epist. (1869) 19 Many good.. lawes and actes made and setforthe in this.. realme. **1583** STUBBES *Anat. Abus.* II. 17 If the prince than doe set foorth a lawe contrarie to the lawe of God. *a* **1700** EVELYN *Diary* 1 Oct. 1651, Our religion, that had neither appointed nor set forth any houres of prayer or breviaries. **1711** STEELE *Spect.* No. 17 ⁋2 The Rules of the Club, as set forth, in a Table, intituled, *The Act of Deformity.* **1837** CARLYLE *Fr. Rev.* I. III. iii, Lafayette.. took upon him to set forth more than one deprecatory oration. **1877** MISS YONGE *Cameos* Ser. III. vii. 64 A proclamation was set forth placing a price.. on his head.

**e.** To publish (a literary work).

**1535** COVERDALE Prol. to Rdr., I toke the more upon me to set forth this speciall translacyon. **1590** GREENE *Mourn. Garment* Concl., Wks. (Grosart) IX. 221, I haue.. set forth many Pamphlets, full of much loue and little Scholarisme. **1628** S. WARD in *Ussher's Lett.* 394 Dr. Jackson hath lately set forth a Book of the Attributes of God. *a* **1700** EVELYN *Diary* July 1645, Father Kirchner, who was then setting forth his great work *Obeliscus Pamphilius.* **1779** *Mirror* No. 21 (1787) I. 154 The latter has set forth his in print.

**f.** (*a*) To express in words, give an account of, present a statement of, *esp.* in order, distinctly, or in detail; to declare, expound, relate, narrate, state, describe; †to describe the features or characters of.

**1530** PALSGR. 713/1 Now have I shewed you in a generaltie the contentes of the chapiter, but to set forthe the partyculers requyreth a further layser. **1548–9** (Mar.) *Bk. Com. Prayer, Commun., Pr. Whole St. Ch.*, That thei maie.. set furthe thy true and liuely worde. **1549** LATIMER *Ploughers* (Arb.) 38 One that wyl set furth papistrie aswel as him selfe wyl do. **1586** A. DAY *Eng. Secretary* II. (1595) 100 As if in setting foorth our most gracious Soueraigne, wee should say: That Goddesse like adorned with high aspectes,.. she issued foorth. **1589** PUTTENHAM *Eng. Poesie* (Arb.) 41 They set forth the dolefull falles of infortunate and afflicted Princes. *a* **1660** N. ROGERS (*title*) The Rich Fool, set forth in an exposition on that parable. Luke 12, 16–22. **1688** *Lett. conc. Pres. St. Italy* 31 A Sect of men that were set forth as Monsters. **1692** R. L'ESTRANGE *Fables* lxxx. 78 In These Three Fables, is set forth the Vanity of Unnatural Wishes, and Foolish Prayers. **1711** STEELE *Spect.* No. 54 ⁋3 A Treatise, wherein I shall set forth the Rise and Progress of this famous Sect. **1746** HERVEY *Medit.* (1818) 151 Even fancy has her merit when she sets forth in such pleasing imagery, the crucified Jesus. **1780** COXE *Russ. Disc.* 254 The instructions given to the Captain set forth that a private ship had in 1762 found there a commodious haven. **1801** *Farmer's Mag.* Jan. 80 An advertisement.. inserted in some of the public papers, setting forth the miseries of the poor. **1865** KINGSLEY *Herew.* i, Hereward, whose history this tale sets forth. **1872** C. E. MAURICE *Stephen Langton* i. 21 One after another he set forth the hideous corruptions which were growing up. **1893** *National Observer* 14 Jan. 201/1 He invites the fault-finders to set forth their grievances.

(*b*) To represent in art. ? *Obs.*

**1585** T. WASHINGTON tr. *Nicholay's Voy.* I. viii. 8 b, I haue thought good..too sette foorth vnto you, a woman as shee goeth in the streete. **1662** EVELYN *Sculptura* 38 But to proceed, Albert [Durer] being very young set forth our Lady, some designes of Horses after the life, [etc.].

**g.** To adorn, decorate. Now *rare.*

**1530** PALSGR. 713/1 This blacke velvet gowne setteth fort this lady verye well. **1585** T. WASHINGTON tr. *Nicholay's Voy.* II. xviii. 51 b, [The gate] is..well set forth, with letters of gold, and leaues of diuers colours. **1633** BP. HALL *Hard Texts* Ezek. xxiii. 6 The Assyrians..which were rich and proudly set forth. **1889** HERRING & ROSS *Irish Cousin* I. I. v. 62 Heavy mahogany tables, each duly set forth with books and daguerrotypes.

†**h.** To further the progress or advancement of; to promote, advance. *Obs.*

**1528** MORE *Dyaloge* IV. Wks. 262/2 To confesse..what he had done for the settinge forth of that secte. **1542** [implied in SETTER-FORTH]. **1551** T. WILSON *Logic* L j, The very cause of thynges, is such a one that if it be practised in very diede, and set forth with other naturall causes, the effect must nedes folowe.

†**i.** To praise, commend. *Obs.*

**1565** COOPER *Thesaurus, Commendare*, to prayse: to sette forth. **1596** SHAKS. *Merch. V.* III. v. 95 *Ies.* Nay, let me praise you while I haue a stomacke? *Lor.* No pray thee, let it serue for table talke... *Iessi.* Well, Ile set you forth. **1662** STILLINGFL. *Orig. Sacræ* II. ii. §2 To set forth a person by that which in its self is no matter of commendation.

†**j.** To exhibit, display, show forth. *Obs.*

**1551** ROBINSON tr. *More's Utopia* I. B j b, Onles I wolde.. set furth the brightnes of the sonne wyth a candell. *Ibid.* II. S ij b, Wretches..whose pouerty she [Pride] might.. encrease by gorgiously setting furthe her riches. **1593** NASHE *Christ's T.* 69 b, Thys woman disdaines..that any should sette forth the porte and maiestie, in gate and behauiour like vnto her. **1611** *Second Maiden's Trag.* 190 Fortunes are but the outsides of true worth, it is the mynde that sets his master forth. **1667** MILTON *P.L.* VI. 310 To set forth Great things by small.

**k.** *intr.* To set out *on* a journey, *against* an enemy, *in* pursuit, etc.

*c* **1400** *Destr. Troy* 4604 Hast you to saile; Sette furthe to þe se. **1530** PALSGR. 713/1 Whan sette you forthe on your journay, and God wyll. **1568** GRAFTON *Chron.* II. 294 They set forth that were appoynted to breake the array of the Archers. **1592** KYD *Sp. Trag.* I. iv. 28, I with my hand set foorth against the Prince. **1601** SHAKS. *Twel. N.* III. iii. 13 My willing loue, The rather by these arguments of feare Set forth in your pursuite. **1675–6** *City Mercury* 10–17 Feb. 2/1 Exeter Coach... Sets forth every Monday morning from the Sarazens head Inn. **1718** ATTERBURY *Serm.* (Acts xxvi. 26) (1734) I. 4 Just as if it [Christianity] were now in its Infant State, and newly setting forth in the World. **1798** CHARLOTTE SMITH *Yng. Philos.* IV. 76 Your fair Columbian,..the moon being at full..sat forth alone. **1845** FORD *Handbk. Spain* I. 55 Before they set forth on their day's journey. **1890** W. E. NORRIS *Misadventure* I. vi. 88 The two young people set forth for the village. **1894** E. SCOTT *Dancing* 110 If the partners join right and left hands in setting forth.

**145. set forward** (†**forwards**).

**a.** (*a*) To carry, send, or thrust forward. *to set one's (best) foot forward*: see FOOT *sb.* 29, 29 b.

*c* **1430** *Art of Nombryng* (E.E.T.S.) 10 Sette forwarde the figures of the nombre multiplying by oo difference. *a* **1547** in Fosbrooke *Econ. Mon. Life* (1796) 83 When hir hors letyr was app[ar]eled..she was set forwards aft[er] this manner. **1555** EDEN *Decades* (Arb.) 70 Settinge forewarde with their ores the brigantine. *a* **1617** BAYNE *Lect.* (1634) 202 That man neuer yet set right foote forward in the way to the Kingdome of God.

(*b*) To put (a clock) on.

**16..** MIDDLETON, etc. *Old Law* III. i, I would have you set forward the Clock. **1848** H. MILLER *First Impr. Eng.* vii. (1857) 115 One of his companions..set forward the house-clock.

†(*c*) To increase, aggravate. *Obs.*

**1611** BIBLE *Job* xxx. 13 They set forward my calamitie. **1684** BURNET tr. *More's Utopia* 24 Luxury likewise breaks in apace upon you, to set forward your Poverty and Misery.

**b.** To assist (a person) in the way of progress; to help on (a matter, plan, etc.); to advance, promote.

**1530** PALSGR. 713/2, I set forwarde a person, or avaunce him to promocyon. *Jaduance.* **1540** CRANMER *Let.* in *Misc. Writ.* (Parker Soc.) 401 To set forwards whatsoever was your Majesty's will. **1561** *Reg. Privy Council Scot.* I. 193 For ..setting fordwart of the commone effaris of the cuntre. *a* **1617** BAYNE *Lect.* (1634) 204 Walking after a potion taken ..setteth forward the working of physicke taken. **1662** *Bk. Com. Prayer, Pr. Ember Weeks*, That..they may..set forward the salvation of all men. **1793** SMEATON *Edystone L.* §7 *note*, To set the workmen forward..I have been obliged to continue on board our store vessel..frequently a week. **1811** SIMEON *Let.* in Carus *Life* (1847) 308 Some of the young men..were endeavouring to set forward a Bible Society.

**c.** To put forward, promulgate; to advance (an opinion).

**1560** *1st Bk. Discipl. Ch. Scot.* (1621) 47 We leave it..to be weighed by your honours wisdome, and set forwards by your authority. **1651** HOBBES *Leviath.* III. xl. 252 To set forward..such doctrine as was agreeable to Moses his doctrine. **1890** *Universal Rev.* Sept. 64 The theory now set forward.

**d.** *intr.* To go forward, set out, start.

**1530** PALSGR. 713/2, I set forward, as an armye..dothe. *Je me auance.* *a* **1548** HALL *Chron., Rich. III*, 12 The erle.. aventured..to set forwarde hym selfe by lande. **1603** KNOLLES *Hist. Turks* (1638) 670 With which fleet..[he] set forward against the Portingals. **1632** LITHGOW *Trav.* IX. 411, I set forward through the vaile of Ombria. **1749** FIELDING *Tom Jones* XVII. v. (1840) 248 Mrs. Miller set forwards to her son-in-law's lodgings. **1815** JANE AUSTEN *Emma* xiii, He..set forward at last in his own carriage. **1889** 'M. GRAY' *Repr. Annesley* III. VI. i. 129 He..set forward again after supper.

**146. set in. a.** (*a*) See simple trans. senses and IN *adv.*; to enter (a name); to insert, put in; to engraft, implant; †to put in office or power, etc.

**1388** WYCLIF *Rom.* xi. 23 3he, and thei schulen be set yn [Vulg. *inserentur*], if thei dwellen not in vnbileue. *c* **1450** in Aungier *Syon* (1840) 361 To sette in the names of sustres and brethren professed in the register of the chapter. **1487** *Cely Papers* (Camden) 169 They hawe dischargyd all the old wytt [= magistrates] of Bruges the whych was sett yn be the Kyng. **1562** *Child-Marriages* 13 The said James Smith toke a Lease of his part of the Tenement, and set-in the said Ellin to have hit after his decesse. **1563–4** in Swayne *Churchw. Acc. Sarum* (1896) 109 John Atkyns to blo y^e organs when he set in y^e pypes vj d. **1587** GOLDING *De Mornay* i. (1592) 6 When a member that was out of ioynt is set in again. **1598** GRENEWEY *Tacitus, Ann.* XII. xi. (1622) 172 [They] set in Companies to robbe and spoile [*immittere latronum globos*]. **1662** PEPYS *Diary* 5 Aug., At Greenwich set in Captain Cocke. **1669** STURMY *Mariner's Mag.* I. ii. 17 Set in your Lee-braces. **1709** *Tatler* No. 37 ¶2 Beau Slimber a Londoner, undertook to keep up with Trips, a whelp just set in. **1808** *Lady's Econ. Assist.* 1 The worked part of the frock body must be set in quite plain. **1859** *Jrnl. R. Agric. Soc.* XX. II. 364 To prevent any escape of the manure while turning [the plough] and setting in again. **1888** *Co-op. News* 16 June 619 If the clothes are placed in cold water out of the boil the fabric will contract, and so set in the dirt. **1888** 'J. S. WINTER' *Bootle's Childr.* xii, I want the ring to be quite plain and heavy, with three stones set in level with the gold. **1889** 'M. GRAY' *Repr. Annesley* I. II. ii. 158 Having now finished setting in a row of young plants.

(*b*) *absol.* (See quot.)

**1530** PALSGR. 714/1, I set in to the oven, as bakers do their breed... We shal nat set in tyll to morowe thre of the clocke.

(*c*) To put (a vessel) in towards the shore. Also *absol.*

**1887** *Pall Mall Gaz.* 22 Feb. 10/2 The ship was set in towards the land by a current. **1891** F. W. ROBINSON *Her Love & His Life* III. VII. i. 236 'Set in to shore,' cried Kerts, roughly.

(*d*) To draw or gather in.

**1858** *Ladies' Cabinet* Jan. 54/1 The skirt..is set in at the waist, in large fluted or hollow plaits.

**b.** †(*a*) To direct into the fight. *Obs.*

**1375** BARBOUR *Bruce* IX. 610 Schir Eduardis cumpany, Quhen thai had thrillit thame hastely, Set stoutly in the hedis agane.

†(*b*) *to set in foot*: to enter upon an undertaking.

**1542** UDALL *Erasm. Apoph.* 78 b, Whoso hath ones stepped foorth, and sette in foote to take charge of a commen weale. **1560** DAUS tr. *Sleidane's Comm.* 122 b, It belongeth.. to the Emperour..to set in foote in counselles. **1562** HEYWOOD *Prov. & Epigr.* (1867) 169 He hath set in foote, thyngs by wyt to be sped.

†(*c*) 'To put in a way to begin' (J.). *Obs.*

**1697** COLLIER *Ess. Mor. Subj.* II. 48, I think I had better decline the Task, than injure the Argument. However, if you please to assist, and set me In, I will endeavour to recollect my self for a short Conference.

†**c.** *intr.* To make one's way into the fight, among the enemy; hence, to offer fight, to intervene in behalf of a person or in support of a cause.

**1450** *Merlin* xxix. 588 Whan thei saugh the hoste comynge thei merveiled fro whens so moche peple myght come. Neuertheles thei sette in a-monge hem. **1630** SANDERSON *Serm. ad Magistr.* i. (1674) II. 258 A rich opportunity..to set in for Gods cause. **1656** BAXTER *Reformed Pastor* 73 It is our duty to set in for the assistance of these,..to help them to a conquest of their corruptions. **1665** SANDERSON *Eight Cases Consc.* (1674) 85 Princes may see cause to set in for their own safety and interest. **1692** RAY *Disc.* II. iv. (1693) 145 May not the Stoicks here set in and help us out at a dead lift?

**d.** To set to work, begin (upon something); *esp.* followed by *to*, *for*. Also *pass.* *Obs.* exc. *dial.*

**1608** WILLET *Hexapla Exod.* 495 Where the fire setteth in, the whole is spoiled. **1650** TRAPP *Comm. Lev.* xiii. 6 God also will set in and wash such with the blood of his son. **1693** TATE *Dryden's Juvenal* II. (1697) 30 To behold your unnerv'd Sex set in To Needle-Work. **1700** CONGREVE *Way of World* IV. i, Sir Wilfull is set in to drinking, madam, in the parlour. **1711** STEELE *Spect.* No. 24 ¶1 A worthy old Batchelor, who sets in for his Dose of Claret every Night. **1764** *Museum Rusticum* II. xxix. 93 To let the first mower and his attendants set-in well before the second follow. **1794** MRS. RADCLIFFE *Myst. Udolpho* xxv, They are all set in to feasting yet. **1835** MOORE *Mem.* (1856) VII. 82, [I] set in hard at work at the remainder of my volume. **1837** DICKENS *Let.* ? Dec. (1965) I. 346, I was in the humour for writing last night—..was regularly set in—when there came a double knock. **1842** DICKENS *Amer. Notes* ix, I go upon the hurricane-deck, and set in for two hours of hard walking up and down. **1893** *Field* 11 Feb. 191/2 It set in to freeze.

**e.** To begin, become prevalent: chiefly of the weather entering upon a particular state.

*a* **1700** EVELYN *Diary* 8 Feb. 1684, The weather was set in to an absolute thaw and raine. **1765** FOOTE *Commissary* III. (1782) 61 The latter end of the year, when the winter sets in. **1769** FALCONER *Dict. Marine* (1780) N 2 b, When the western monsoons set in. **1848** THACKERAY *Van. Fair* lx, Politics set in a short time after dessert. **1856** HAWTHORNE *Engl. Note-bks.* (1870) II. 167 The evening set in misty and obscure. **1857** MILLER *Elem. Chem., Org.* (1862) 137 Though no fermentation had set in. **1890** *Blackw. Mag.* CXLVIII. 32/1 Sooner or later a reaction must set in.

**f.** Of a current or wind: To flow or blow towards the shore.

**1719** DE FOE *Crusoe* I. (Globe) 193 The Current of the Flood set in close by the Shore. **1815** J. SMITH *Panorama Sci. & Art* II. 46 The westerly winds setting in on this coast. **1821** SCOTT *Pirate* i, The current of a strong and furious tide,..setting in betwixt the Orkney and Zetland Islands. **1831** *Mirror* XVII. 102/1 The tide sets in on this part of the coast with extraordinary velocity.

**147. set off. a.** See simple trans. senses and OFF *adv.*: †(*a*) To take away, remove. *Obs.*

**1597** SHAKS. *2 Hen. IV*, IV. i. 145 Euery thing set off, That might so much as thinke you Enemies.

†(*b*) To alienate. *Obs.*

**1632** BP. HALL *Hard Texts* 1 John iii. 15 If any mans heart bee set upon the world, it is set off from God. **1651** —— *Soliloquies* vi, Do Thou set off my heart from all these earthly vanities.

†(*c*) ? To discharge, cancel. *Obs.*

**1642** C. VERNON *Consid. Exch.* 27 Such [sums] as shall appeare to be discharged or set off by such matter of Record. *Ibid.* 30 The Clerk of the Pipe is not to discharge or set off any part of the Sheriffes charge, but by Tallies to be leavied in his Majesties Receipt of Exchequer.

(*d*) To put (a person) off. *Sc.*

**1768** ROSS *Helenore* 75 But think na, man, that I'll be set off sae, For I'll hae satisfaction ere I gae.

(*e*) To stop the working of. *Sc.*

**1728** RAMSAY *Monk & Miller's Wife* 51 Gae warm ye, and crack with our dame, Till I set aff the mill. **1823** SCOTT *Peveril* xxi, The goodman has set off the mill, to come to wait on you himself.

(*f*) To set up in type separately. ? *nonce-use.*

**1770** LUCKOMBE *Hist. Printing* 375 A very close line in the Copy, which we set off, to see how it comes into the measure made to m's.

(*g*) To let. *Sc.*

**1799** J. ROBERTSON *Agric. Perth* 516 He..set off five new farms, formerly waste land.

(*h*) To cause to go off or explode, let off.

**1881** *I. of Wight Gloss.*, *Zet off*,..to explode gunpowder. **1882** *Jamieson's Sc. Dict.* s.v., He set off the cannon. **1898** *Engineering Mag.* XVI. 69 A spark..that might set off the explosives.

**b.** To start off, give (a person or thing) a start; to send off *into* a fit of laughter, etc.

*a* **1625** FLETCHER *Hum. Lieut.* III. vi, I seek a brave hand To set me off in death. **1828** SIR H. STEUART *Planter's Guide* (ed. 2) 478 It is extremely important for the success of Trees, to possess a certain degree of vigour in the outset, or to be what is technically called, 'well set off.' **1830** FR. A. KEMBLE *Rec. Girlhood* (1878) II. 163 The carriage..was set off at its utmost speed. **1863** MRS. GASKELL *Sylvia's Lovers* iii, To divert her attention from the subject which had set her off into hysterics. **1865** LEVER *Luttrell* xix. 132 One of those practised laughs, which, by setting others off, frequently cut short an unpleasant discussion. **1886** *Tip Cat* xxii. 301 Her questions set Dick off thinking. **1889** 'M. GRAY' *Repr. Annesley* III. v. ii. 44 He..set Mr. Rickman off upon one of his interminable monologues.

**c.** To apportion or assign to a particular purpose; to portion off.

**1687** BURNET *Contin. Reply to Varillas* 60 The appointments that were set off for her. **1828–32** WEBSTER s.v., To set off a portion of an estate. **1842** *Penny Mag.* 8 Oct. 395/2 A portion of the stabling is set off as a 'sick-box' for the invalids.

**d.** (*a*) To mark or measure off (a certain distance) on a surface; to lay off (the lines of a ship).

*a* **1647** in *Archæologia* XII. 250 They found by due trial all lines [of the ship] to be truly set off. **1683** MOXON *Mech. Exerc., Printing* xi. ¶1 The varied Measure must be set off from the top of the Cilinder. **1712** J. JAMES tr. *Le Blond's Gardening* 95 Set off 30 Fathom on the Side BD. **1774** M. MACKENZIE *Marit. Surv.* I. iii. 11 Taking the Length of XY from a Scale of equal Parts, set it off from X to Y. **1830** HEDDERWICK *Mar. Archit.* 201 The square measurements of the cant-timbers are set off on the body-plan of the schooner foreward and abaft. **1876** VOYLE & STEVENSON *Milit. Dict.* 335/1 This space is formed by setting off demi-gorges of 30 yards. **1891** *Chamb. Jrnl.* 20 June 400/1 If three hundred and sixty separate degrees be set-off from the centre of a perfect circle.

(*b*) To place along a surface at definite intervals.

**1850** INKERSLEY *Inq. Styles Archit. France* 311 All these windows being set off on the outer face of the wall.

(*c*) To mark off, separate from the context.

**1824** L. MURRAY *Eng. Gram.* (ed. 5) I. 399 When adjuncts or circumstances are of importance,..they may be set off by commas.

**e.** (*a*) To set in relief, make prominent or conspicuous by contrast.

**1596** SHAKS. *1 Hen. IV*, I. ii. 239 My reformation glittering o're my fault, Shall shew more goodly,..Then that which hath no foyle to set it off. **1633** G. HERBERT *Temple, Foil* ii, God hath made starres the foil To set off vertues; griefs to set off sinning. **1634** MILTON *Comus* 801 She fables not, I feel that I do fear Her words set off by som superior power. **1656** EARL MONM. tr. *Boccalini's Advts. fr. Parnass.* I. xix. (1674) 20 Picture-drawers do the better set off the Figures they draw, by dark shadows. **1693** LOCKE *Educ.* §93 (1699) 148 Good qualities are the Substantial Riches of the Mind, but 'tis good Breeding sets them off. **1778** SIR J. REYNOLDS *Disc.* viii. (1876) 454 That the blue, the grey, or the green colours..be used only to support and set off these warm colours. **1825** *New Monthly Mag.* XVI. 121 His raiment served to set his destitution off. **1859** GEO. ELIOT *Adam Bede* ix, The primrose is set off by its nest of green. **1890** *Lippincott's Mag.* Jan. 23 Thick brown hair.. fell down on her shoulders and set off the margins of her smooth pure cheeks.

*absol.* **1611** SHAKS. *Cymb.* III. iii. 13 It is Place, which lessen's, and sets off.

(*b*) *intr.* To form a contrast (*with*).

**1652** *Bk. Drawing*, etc. 34 What Colours set off best together. **1735** *Dict. Polygraph.* II. H h 4, Blues set off with yellows, reds, whites, browns, and blacks. Greens set off well with purples and reds.

**f.** To show to advantage, enhance, embellish.

**1611** SHAKS. *Cymb.* I. vi. 170 He hath a kinde of Honor sets him off, More then a mortall seeming. **1628** EARLE

*Microcosm.* lv. (Arb.) 79 No quality sets a man off like this. **1705** ADDISON *Italy* 439 Claudian has set off his Description of the Eridanus, with all the Poetical Stories that have been made of it. **1747** MRS. GLASSE *Cookery* xvi. 142 Fairy Butter. .. This is a pretty Thing to set off a Table at Supper. **1749** SMOLLETT *Gil Blas* III. v. (1782) I. 255, I adorned myself to the best of my power, the barber lending a helping hand, in order to set me off. **1821** SCOTT *Kenilw.* xix, Thou seest how well the French hose set off the leg and knee. **1849** RUSKIN *Seven Lamps* iv. §42. 133 The sculpture is approved and set off by the colour. **1891** *Temple Bar* July 445 Dress helped to set off her many charms.

**g.** To give a flattering description of, commend, praise.

*a* **1625** FLETCHER *Hum. Lieut.* III. i, Set 'em off Lady I mean sell 'em. **1706** POPE *Let. to Wycherley* 10 Apr., The great Dealers in Wit, like those in Trade, take least pains to set off their Goods. **1785** [R. GRAVES] *Eugenius* II. xviii. 118 Young Scrip, whom Mrs. Banks was going to set off as a young man of great expectations. **1828–32** WEBSTER, *To set off*... To give a pompous or flattering description of; to eulogize; to recommend; as to set off a character.

**h.** (*a*) To take into account by way of compensation or equivalent; to put in the balance (*against* something); *spec.* in *Law*, to allow or recognize as a counter-claim. Also *absol.*

**1735** *Act 8 Geo. II*, c. 24 §5 The Debt intended to be set off, shall be pleaded in Bar, in which Plea shall be shewn how much is truly and justly due on either side. **1775** F. BULLER *Introd. Law Nisi Prius* (ed. 2) 179 A Debt by simple Contract might by the former Act have been set off against a Specialty Debt. **1809** MALKIN *Gil Blas* II. v. (Rtldg.) 56 We may set off their drugs against our specifics. **1818** J. CAMPBELL *Nisi Prius Cases* II. 586 The defendant had therefore a right to set off this loss against the premiums. **1819** TAUNTON *Rep. Cases Comm. Pleas* VII. 481 The Defendants' guaranty does not so make the Defendants parties to the contract, that they can set off. **1880** MUIRHEAD *Gaius* iv. 64 He is required to set off his customer's counter-claim. **1891** *Sat. Rev.* 15 Aug. 192/1 The produce is set off against the advance, the balance is fairly struck.

(*b*) To counterbalance, compensate.

**1749** FIELDING *Tom Jones* v. i, Thus the beauty of day, and that of summer, are set off by the horrors of night and winter. **1819** SCOTT *Ivanhoe* xl, The merry-men of the forest set off the building of a cottage with the burning of a castle. **1893** *Times* 8 May 7/6 The loss feared in one branch of trade would be set off by a gain in another branch.

(*c*) *intr.* To be a set-off *against*.

**1824** *Examiner* 152/2 Prices neither have risen, nor is there the least prospect of their rising, to a rate that will set off against the taxes..that burden the land.

**i.** (*a*) *intr.* To start on a journey or course; *transf.* to start (doing something).

**1774** *Trinket* 91, I sat off in immediate pursuit of them. **1816** SCOTT *Bl. Dwarf* xi, They mounted..and..set off at a round gallop. **1823** SOUTHEY *Hist. Penins. War* I. 473 Messengers set off to solicit succour from Badajoz. **1848** THACKERAY *Van. Fair* iii, They both set off in a fit of laughter. **1888** 'J. S. WINTER' *Bootle's Childr.* viii, He..set off to go home alone.

(*b*) To take off for a leap. *rare.*

**1760–72** H. BROOKE *Fool of Qual.* (1809) III. 95 A mark from whence the rivals were to set off on their leap.

†**j.** To have a certain appearance. *Obs.*

**1601** B. JONSON *Poet.* Epil. 20, I, now, but thinke, how poore their spight sets off, Who,.. Haue nothing left, but the vnsau'ry smoake Of their blacke vomit, to vpbrayd themselues.

**k.** *Printing.* To soil the next leaf or sheet: said of the ink or of the printed page.

**1683** MOXON *Mech. Exerc., Printing* xi. ¶23 Trane-Oyl.. hinders the Inck from drying; so that when the Work comes to the Binders, it Sets off. **1777** in *N. & Q.* Ser. IX. V. (1900) 189/1 [The binder] is particularly desired to beat the work before he places the cuts, in order to prevent the letterpress from setting off on the engravings. **1823** J. BADCOCK *Dom. Amusem.* 27 Some printers' works 'set off', as they term it, when the ink of one page leaves its impression upon the opposite page. **1883** R. HALDANE *Workshop Rec.* Ser. II. 343/2 An undue proportion of lampblack in the ink will cause it to smear,..and to 'set-off' during book-binding operations.

**l.** In the pianoforte, (of the hoppers) to make the proper set-off.

**1853** W. SANDILANDS in *Abridgm. Specif. Patents, Music* (1871) 187, I..claim an improvement through the same means in the setting off of the hopper. **1885** LOCK *Workshop Rec.* Ser. IV. 281/1 Blocking is caused by the hoppers not 'setting off'.

**148. set on. a.** *lit.* To place on or upon something: see simple senses and ON *adv.*: with special implication, e.g. to set (a vessel) on the fire; †to put on (an article of clothing); †to hang (a door).

*c* **975** *Rushw. Gosp.* Mark v. 23 Sete on honda ofer hiæ. *c* **1200** *Trin. Coll. Hom.* 197 He ne mihte finden on al his licame hwar he his finger on sette bute uppen wunden. *c* **1205** LAY. 311 Brutus sette on his flo. *c* **1420** *Avow. Arth.* xxxi, Downe thay take that birde bryȝte, Sette hur one, behinde the knyȝte. *c* **1460** J. RUSSELL *Bk. Nurture* 987 in *Babees Bk.* 183 But furst sett on his sokkis. **1522** in *Archæologia* XXV. 450 Item p$^{d}$..for settyng on of a horne & trymmyng of y$^{or}$ long bowe..iiij d. **1535** COVERDALE *2 Esdras* iii. 6 They..set on the dores, lockes & barres of it. **1582** STANYHURST *Æneis* I. 213 Soom doe set on caldrons, oothers doe kendel a bauen. **1657** R. LIGON *Barbadoes* (1673) 38 Another course [of a meal] is set on. *a* **1700** EVELYN *Diary* 7 Mar. 1690, To protect, set on, and bring off, those who should manage the fire-ships. **17..** in *Ritson's Gammer Gurton's Garl.* (1783) 52 Is John smith within?.. Can he set on a shoe? **1808** *Lady's Econ. Assist.* 22 A welt should be set on to the waist at the back. *c* **1850** *Rudim. Navig.* (Weale) 140 To *relieve*, to make a sett near to another that cannot be sett on any more till it is taken in on each side. **1859** *Jrnl. R. Agric. Soc.* XX. II. 330 The tail is not neatly set on. **1880** *Plain Knitting* 11 Knitting can hardly be set on too loosely. **1884** *Live Stock Jrnl.* 1 Aug. 107/1 A..Setter Dog, good all round, with the exception of his ears, which are set on too high.

†**b.** To set on foot, instigate, promote. *Obs.*

**1639** ROUSE *Heav. Univ.* vii. (1702) 94 They behold the shape of Folly of their own setting on. *c* **1640** H. BELL *Luther's Colloq. Mens.* (1652) 334 The Emperor sent his Embassador to John Frederick, Prince Elector of Saxon, to set on and to further a Council. **1688** *Lett. conc. Pres. St. Italy* 158 The Son of him that set on the Massacres of the Protestants. *a* **1715** BURNET *Own Time* (1724) I. 262 The King was as earnest in the setting it on, as the Duke was in opposing it.

**c.** (*a*) To urge (an animal, *esp.* a dog) to attack.

**1592** NASHE *P. Penilesse* B4 What Cur wil not bawle.. when he is set on by his maister? **1610** SHAKS. *Temp.* IV. i. Stage Dir., Enter diuers Spirits in shape of Dogs and Hounds, hunting them about: Prospero and Ariel setting them on. **1890** MRS. A. MACLEOD *Austral. Girl* I. xxii. 259, I found him setting a puppy on to some sheep.

(*b*) To instigate, incite, urge on (a person) *to do* something.

**1523** BERNERS *Froiss.* I. lviii. 32 b, By the settyng on of Sir Willyam Bayllule. **1540** PALSGR. *Acolastus* I. i. D iij b, The vndewe loue he hath to hym selfe..setteth him on to take this way. *Ibid.* D iij b, He hath priuyly or by secrete menes stered the, or set y$^{e}$ on (to do this thynge). **1560** DAUS tr. *Sleidane's Comm.* 137 Beinge ayded by the Byshop of the same Citie, or set on rather. **1616** R. COCKS *Diary* (Hakl. Soc.) I. 115 The chirurgion is a prating fello, and I think sett on per others. **1622** MABBE tr. *Aleman's Guzman d'Alf.* I. 150 My Master was now bent against me, his Wife had set him on. **1743** T. MORRIS *Serm.* vii. 184 Whether they went out of their..choice, or were set on by others. **1781** D. WILLIAMS tr. *Voltaire's Dram. Wks.* II. 286 The devil set me on to marry you. **1821** SCOTT *Kenilw.* xxxiv, Woman, thou art set on to this. **1892** *Gd. Words* May 300/2 It was..the boys—they set us on to ask.

†(*c*) To carry through to a conclusion; to drive *home*. *Obs.*

**1596** NASHE *Saffron Walden* Wks. 1910 III. 123 Speaking to him, that he shuld not go about to answere me, except he set it soundly on. **1653** H. MORE *Antid. Ath.* App. iii. (1712) 186, I confess the Objection is very ingenious, and set on home.

**d.** †(*a*) To advance, send forward. *Obs.*

**1601** SHAKS. *Jul. C.* II. i. 331 Set on your foote, And..I follow you. *Ibid.* v. iii. 108 Let vs to the Field, Labio and Flauio set our Battailes on.

(*b*) To set in motion, set going. Also *absol.*

**1855** BAIN *Senses & Int.* I. i. §3 By what influence do we draw our first breath, or set on the first stroke of the heart? **1867** SMYTH *Sailor's Word-bk.*, *Set on*, the order to set the engine going on board a steamer.

**e.** To start (a person) doing something. Cf. *set off*, 147 b.

**1854** J. S. C. ABBOTT *Napoleon* (1855) II. xxxi. 58 It is well known to be no easy matter to check the people when they are once set on. **1866** MRS. H. WOOD *St. Martin's Eve* xxi. II. 86, I have coughed a great deal lately..and the coming in from the cold air to the atmosphere of your stifling stove, has set me on now.

**f.** To set or appoint (a person) to do something; = *put on*, PUT *v.* 46 l.

**1852** THACKERAY *Esmond* I. x, He was set on to read Latin. **1856** *Househ. Words* 21 June 546/2 Frazer..set on two or three extra gangs of navvies.

**g.** (*a*) *intr.* To advance, go forward.

*c* **1400** *Sowdone Bab.* 2555 On thay set with herte stronge. *c* **1450** *Merlin* xxii. 383 Loke ye sette on alle to-geder ther as ye shull here an horne blowe right high and lowde. **1605** *1st Pt. Ieronimo* III. iv. 6 Set on to Spaine in most triumphant measure. **1611** SHAKS. *Wint. T.* IV. iv. 682 We set on..to th' Sea-side. **1808** SCOTT *Marm.* IV. iii, Marmion Gave..the signal to set on.

†(*b*) To make a move *for*. *Obs.*

**1616** SIR T. ROE *Jrnl. Embassy* (1899) 342 When I deliuer the Next guiftes to the Mogoll..I will sett on anew for a formall contract.

(*c*) To begin working.

**1889** W. WESTALL *Birch Dene* II. iii. 34 All of you to your places; the engine is setting on again. *Ibid.* xi. 173 Nearly an hour after the engine had 'set on'.

**h.** To make an attack. Now *dial.* in ***set on at*** or ***to*** = attack, assail.

**1670** EACHARD *Cont. Clergy* 120 Countrey People..read not so many Gazetts, as a Citizen, nor concern themselves where the Turk, or King of France sets on next. **1862** MRS. H. WOOD *Mrs. Hallib.* III. vi, His sister..set on at the wife, saying it was her fault.

**149. set out. * a.** See simple senses and OUT *adv.*; to lay out, spread out; to cause to project or extend; to display (a flag); etc.

**1573** in Feuillerat *Revels Q. Eliz.* (1908) 193 Setting owte & Taking in againe..sundry kyndes of Apparell. **1576** PETTIE *Petite Pallace* 54 Setting out flag of defyance. **1592** TIMME *Ten Engl. Lepers* vii. H 2 b, Olde age draweth in the eyes, setteth out the teeth. **1614** GORGES *Lucan* VIII. 331 The light That Pharus tower sets out at night. **1641** J. JACKSON *True Evang. T.* III. 190 Let us a little set out the bounder-stones of this disquisition upon which we are fallen. **1698** FARQUHAR *Love & Bottle* I. i, The Enemy approaches, we must set out our false Colours. **1719** DE FOE *Crusoe* I. (Globe) 121 How many [*sc.* pots] crack'd by the..Heat of the Sun, being set out too hastily. **1888** 'J. S. WINTER' *Bootle's Childr.* xii, The jeweller..set out some trays of pretty inexpensive brooches. **1897** C. T. DAVIS *Manuf. Leather* (ed. 2) 250 The side having been stuffed, and next 'set out'..the next step in the process of manufacturing upper leather is that of whitening.

**b.** To spread (leather) on a flat surface while wet, in order that it may dry free from wrinkles.

**1885** C. T. DAVIS *Manuf. Leather* xxiii. 423 The side having been stuffed, and next 'set out'..the next step in the process of manufacturing upper leather is that of whitening. **1909** H. G. BENNETT *Manuf. Leather* xxi. 261 The butts are now struck out, 'set out' or 'pinned'. **1946** J. W. WATERER *Leather in Life, Art & Industry* II. ii. 147 The butts are piled up to drain... They are 'set out' to remove wrinkles and smooth the grain. **1969** T. C. THORSTENSEN *Pract. Leather Technol.* v. 70 After bleaching, the bends are wrung and sent to an oil wheel... This process usually takes about one hour. The leather is 'set out' to smooth and dry.

†**c.** To set in relief, set off. *Obs.*

**1577** WHETSTONE *Remembr. Life Gascoigne* vii, Euil sets out good, as far as black dooth white. **1611** *Second Maiden's Trag.* 2225 The Body..drest vp in black veluet which setts out the pailenes of the handes and face. **1658** SANDERSON *Graphice* 48 Light and Shadows forward, set out any Painting outwards.

†**d.** To expose. *Obs.*

**1579** TOMSON *Calvin's Serm. Tim.* xxiii. 404/2 That our life seemeth to be set out to Sathan [orig. *exposee à Satan*]. **1611** COTGR. *Exposé*..set out, put or layed open to.

**e.** To accompany or escort on the way. *dial.*

**1725** WALKDEN *Diary* (1866) 7, I rose and set son John out towards the coalpit. **1803** R. ANDERSON *Cumbld. Ball.* 57 Young Susy half consenting To set me out a mile o' geate.

** †**f.** (*a*) To fit out (a ship, fleet) for a voyage; to equip for an expedition; to send out (forces), fit out (an expedition). *Obs.*

*a* **1122** *O.E. Chron.* (Laud MS.) an. 1047, Man sette ut .ix. litsmanna scipa. **1557** in *Sel. Pleas Crt. Admiralty* (1897) II. 31 Another shippe of warre..furnished manned and victualyd and sett out to the seas by Walter Rawleighe. **1601** HAKLUYT tr. *Galvano's Discov.* 20, I know not whether the charge of that voiage was theirs or the kings. But by whom soeuer it was set out [etc.]. **1603** KNOLLES *Hist. Turks* (1638) 783 *marg.*, The Christian Princes set out a fleet for the recouery of Tripolis. **1605** STOW *Ann.* 1402 The Citizens of London set out 500 souldiers into Ireland, with their furniture. *a* **1642** SUCKLING *Goblins* I. i. Wks. 1874 II. 11 Why does not then the state Set out some forces, and suppress them? **1707** SLOANE *Jamaica* I. 1 Christopher Columbus first solicited the king of Portugal to set him out. *a* **1715** BURNET *Own Time* (1724) I. 313 The fleet could not be set out that year.

(*b*) To equip or furnish *with*.

**1585** T. WASHINGTON tr. *Nicholay's Voy.* IV. i. 114 Set out and furnished with bowes and arrowes. **1725** *Fam. Dict.* s.v. *Goose*, They set out Arrows with its Feathers.

†(*c*) To dress for going out. *Obs.*

**1687** MIEGE *Gt. Fr. Dict.* II. s.v., To set out a Child in order to go abroad, *habiller un Enfant pour sortir.*

†(*d*) To put out (a boat). *Obs.*

**1694** tr. *Martens' Voy Spitzbergen* in *Acc. Sev. Late Voy.* II. 128 They set out their Long-boats after the Whale.

†**g.** With immaterial obj.: To cause to go forth, send forth; to give currency or vogue to; to issue, promulgate. *Obs.*

*c* **1100** *O.E. Chron.* (MS. D) an. 1052, & setton stefna ut to Lundene & man bead þa folce þider ut ofer ealne þisne norðende. **1542** UDALL *Erasm. Apoph.* 197 For epitaphies are..not set out till the parties bee deceassed. **1548** in *Wodrow Soc. Misc.* (1844) 9 This confescion was fyrste wrytten and set out by the ministers of the churche and congregacion of Sweuerland. **1560** *Maitl. Club Misc.* III. 216 Traditiones of men sett owt to thirle the consciences of Goddis people. **1687** BURNET *Contin. Reply to Varillas* 83 The Articles of our Religion were agreed on, and set out by Authority. *a* **1700** EVELYN *Diary* 23 Dec. 1695, The Parliament..setting out a proclamation prohibiting the currency of half crowns. *a* **1715** BURNET *Own Time* (1724) I. 500 The King set out a declaration for satisfying his people.

†**h.** ***to set out one's (a, the) throat***: to cry aloud, shout. *Obs.* (Cf. *set up*, 154 c.)

**1574** tr. *Marlorat* in *Marbeck's Bk. Notes* (1581) 1108 Set out thy throte & cry. **1602** MIDDLETON *Blurt* II. i. C, I should cut your throate..but that I know you would set out a throate. **1610** B. JONSON *Alch.* v. iii, His gag is melted, And now he sets out the throte. **1622** MABBE tr. *Aleman's Guzman d'Alf.* II. 263 She thereupon began to set out so loud a throat, as if (like a pig) I had offered to sticke her.

†**i.** To exhibit (a play) on the stage; to exhibit (public games). *Obs.*

**1540** PALSGR. *Acolastus* Prol. B ij b, That same wyll we nowe sette out before you (with personages) in our play. **1565** COOPER *Thesaurus* s.v. *Comparo*, To sette out playes with great charges. **1579** GOSSON *Sch. Abuse* (Arb.) 29 Romulus..set out playes to gather the fayre women togither. **1600** HOLLAND *Livy* XXVII. 635 A decree was graunted, that C. Hostilius the Pretour should vow, and set out the games and playes of Apollo.

†**j.** To put into print, publish (a literary work).

**1559** MORWYNG *Evonym.* Pref. A j, This Arte was.. wryten in our Dutch tung and first set out by him. *a* **1568** ASCHAM *Scholem.* II. Wks. (1904) 285 Which booke I haue in writyng, and is not yet set out in print. **1612** J. CHAMBERLAIN in *Crt. & Times Jas. I* (1848) I 214, I hear of some verses are set out or given to some few, but not publicly sold.

†**k.** To declare, proclaim, show forth, reveal. *Obs.*

*a* **1540** BARNES *Wks.* (1573) 293/2 That..the declaration and setting out of his worde. **1547** HARPSFIELD in *Homilies, Mis. Mankind* ***j b, He is the God, which..setteth out his charitie and exceadyng loue toward vs. **1565** COOPER *Thesaurus* s.v. *Dico*, To employe his studie to set out ones prayse. **1583** *Leg. Bp. St. Androis* 646 Robert Melwene of Carnebie, That with that bischop went about, To sett his feinyeit falsett out. **1648** GAGE *West Ind.* 77 If I should not set out to the publick view the worth of her people. **1665** MANLEY *Grotius' Low C. Wars* 545 If any more eminent matter of Valour or Policy happen, there is given a fair occasion..to set out the Authors or Inventors thereof. **1681** H. MORE *Expos. Dan.* 233 Then will this Antichrist by a publick writing be exhibited or set out to the world in his colours.

†**l.** To express, denote. *Obs.*

**1628** T. SPENCER *Logick* 4 The word *art*, doth set out the generall nature of Logick. **1631** GOUGE *God's Arrows* III. §53. 284 The word whereby the Evangelist setteth out consent in prayer. **1684** H. MORE *Answ.* 41 The Kings of the Earth..calling to the Rocks and Mountains..sets out the fear of those great Men.

*** **m.** To display (wares) for sale.

**13..** *K. Alis.* 7077 Ac theygh the marchaunt sette out his ware, In the stret. **1530** PALSGR. 715/1 This felowe hath set out his marchandyse to the shewe. **1611** COTGR., *Mangonner*, to..set out vnto the eye sale things. **1617** MORYSON *Itin.* I. 198 All vertues become lesse prized in them, who set them out to sale. **1829** *Examiner* 370/1 Shopkeepers set out their goods for the purpose of attracting the gaze.

†**n.** (*a*) To display to advantage, put forward to attract attention, make attractive. *Obs.*

**1586** T. B. *La Primaud. Fr. Acad.* I. Ep. Ded., Seeing they are sent to edifie others, and not to set out themselves. **1605** CHAPMAN *All Fools* v. ii. 195 As for your mother, shee.. could set out her taile with as good grace as any shee in Florence. **1619** W. WHATELY *God's Husb.* I. (1622) 102 Hee that is apt to set out himselfe, and cannot brooke another that goeth not so farre as himselfe: that man doe thou suspect, and from him be thou reserued. **1646** SIR T. BROWNE *Pseud. Ep.* I. iii. 9 Mahomet..when hee set out the felicitie of his heaven, by..the delights of sense.

†(*b*) To extol, 'crack up'. *Obs.*

**1687** MIEGE *Gt. Fr. Dict.* II. s.v., To set one out, or speak much to his Praise. **1693** DRYDEN *Juvenal* Ded. in *Ess.* (1900) II. 68 The colours [of rival charioteers] themselves were but a fancy; but when once a man had taken pains to set out those of his party, and had been at the trouble of procuring voices for them, the case was altered. **1754** RICHARDSON *Grandison* I. viii. 39 How have you over-rated my merits!..should you not..have known something of my mind before you had set me out thus.

†**o.** To embellish, adorn, deck out, trick out. Also *refl.* *Obs.*

**1523** SKELTON *Garl. Laurel* 422 O noble Chaucer, whos pullisshyd eloquence Oure Englysshe rude so fresshely hath set out. **1526** *Pilgr. Perf.* (W. de W. 1531) 84 Not set out with fayre & fyne clothes. **1589** COOPER *Admon.* 56 The Libeller to set out his Pasquill, raketh all things. **1621** BURTON *Anat. Mel.* III. ii. II. iii. 572 Gold and pretious stones doe condescend to set out their shooes. **1662** J. DAVIES tr. *Olearius' Voy. Amb.* 205 They set out their Discourse with all sorts of Fables. *a* **1704** T. BROWN *Ess. on Women* Wks. 1711 IV. 157 They bestow..as much Times and Pains in the Art of Dissimulation, as they do in setting out their Faces. **1714** C'TESS COWPER *Diary* (1865) 36 There she was, set out in all her Airs. **1747** MRS. GLASSE *Cookery* ix. 89 It is good with Vinegar, and a fine Dish to set out a cold Table.

**** †**p.** To put out at interest. *Obs.*

**1533** in *Test. Ebor.* (Surtees) VI. 8 All such goodes..shall ..be sett owte to the use and profett of John Mering, Robert Mering and Nicholes Mering. **1614** RICH *Honestie Age* (1615) 36 Euery man can call him an Vsurer that setteth out his money. **1677** YARRANTON *Eng. Improv.* 22 All such as.. dare not set out their Moneys at interest.

†**q.** To put (a child) out to nurse; to place out with a master or at school. *Obs.*

**1575** GASCOIGNE *Glasse Govt.* IV. iv. Wks. 1910 II. 64, I thinke no mens children are thus set out. **1643** TRAPP *Comm. Gen.* xxi. 7 If the childe must be set out, let a fit nurse be looked after. *c* **1670** WOOD *Life* (O.H.S.) I. 130 Somtimes she would tell him that she would set him out to an attorney or sollicitor. **1729** WALKDEN *Diary* (1866) 61 To-day we set son Henry out to school to Mr. Nabb.

†**r.** (*a*) To set apart *for* certain treatment. *Obs.*

**1607** SHAKS. *Timon* V. iv. 57 Whom you your selues shall set out for reproofe. **1633** BP. HALL *Hard Texts*, Zech. xi. 4 Thus saith the Lord, my God, yet amongst these Jewes, which I have justly set out for this slaughter, there is a flocke of mine, whom I have due care of.

(*b*) To put aside (a tenth part); to reserve as tithe. *Obs.* (Cf. *set forth*, 144 c, *b*.)

**1548** *Act 2 & 3 Edw. VI*, c. 13 §1 Everye of the Kinges subjectes shall..devide sett out yelde and paye all manner of their prediall tythes in their proper kynde. **1670** W. SHEPPARD *Parson's Guide* 41 The common course of setting out and delivering Corn by the Common Law, is by the tenth Shock, Cock, or Sheaf. **1710** PRIDEAUX *Orig. Tithes* iii. 160 Men were forced to set the Tithes duly out, and pay them fully. **1736** *Gentl. Mag.* VI. 697/1 And no Quaker shall after such Notice, and before the setting out, or after such Tythe shall be so set out, withdraw or take away, or cause to be withdrawn or taken away the said Tythes. **1768** *Case of Jeffry Ruffle* 3 He gave him notice every time of the setting out of his tythes.

†**s.** To let or lease out. *Obs.*

**1614** RICH *Honestie Age* (1615) 37 The Land-Lords that doe set out their liuings at those high rates. **1617** MORYSON *Itin.* I. 6 Some boyle not the Salt in their owne name but set it out to others. **1693** STAIR *Instit.* I. xvi. (ed. 2) 135 Letting out of Lands, or setting out of Houses.

***** **t.** (*a*) †To exhibit graphically (*obs.*); to put down on paper in express or detailed form; to describe or enumerate expressly; to detail.

**1560** DAUS tr. *Sleidane's Comm.* 158 Before Luthers booke was sette out a picture. **1568** GRAFTON *Chron.* II. 13 There ye shall see it [pallium] set out in white with a great many of blacke crosses vpon it.

**1545** ASCHAM *Toxoph.* (Arb.) 43 The other [Cicero] setteth oute no poynte of rhetorike, so fullie in all his bookes, as [etc.]. **1585** T. WASHINGTON tr. *Nicholay's Voy.* III. ix. 84 The very same partie by whom the liuely figure before set out was made. *Ibid.* IV. xxix. 150b, The places..most notable, and that doe merite to be set out. **1621** ELSING *Debates Ho. Lords* (Camden) 109 Yt shoulde sett out the matter orderly. **1658** GURNALL *Chr. in Arm.* II. verse 14. xvi. 314 The Christians getting to heaven, is set out as a businesse of so much difficulty. **1693** DRYDEN *Juvenal* x. (1697) 244 The Poets Design in this Divine Satyr, is to represent the various Wishes and Desires of Mankind; and to set out the Folly of 'em. **1775** F. BULLER *Introd. Law Nisi Prius* (ed. 2) 176 In such Case the Jury are not to set out the Value of the Land descended. **1842** *Act 5 & 6 Vict.* c. 45 Sched. 4 Set out the Title of the Book. **1879** M. PATTISON *Milton* 101 This moving situation Gauden, no mean stylist, set out in the best academical language of the period. **1896** *Athenæum* 14 Mar. 339/1 A list of authorities set out in the appendix.

†(*b*) To furnish a translation of. *Obs.*

**1597** MORLEY *Introd. Mus.* To Rdr., I do not doubt, but many..will wonder that..I haue taken vpon mee to set out that in our vulgar tongue. *a* **1668** LASSELS *Voy. Italy* (1670) II. 232 It was he that set us out the life of Sir Thomas More in English. *a* **1700** EVELYN *Diary* 12 Sept. 1649, Dr. Crighton,..a learned Grecian who set out the Council of Florence.

**u.** (*a*) To delimit, define, mark out.

**1653** MANLOVE *Lead-mines* 48 The finder,..May have two meers met, and set out by stake. **1660** STANLEY *Hist. Philos.* XI. *Parmenides* (1687) 747 He..first set out and limited the habitable parts of the Earth. **1690** LOCKE *Hum. Und.* IV. iv. §13 A false Supposition, that these two Names, Man and Beast, stand for distinct Species so set out by real Essences, that there can come no other Species between them. **1727** BOYER *Dict. Royal* II. s.v., Every Man has his Share of Provisions and Business set out. **1847** MARRYAT *Childr. New Forest* xiv, If he is to work..it must not be by having work set out for him. **1870** HUGHES *Alfred the Grt.* xv, The shires and their sub-divisions..were carefully set out.

(*b*) To portion out (land) into lots.

*a* **1700** EVELYN *Diary* 22 Mar. 1675, When the rebells were dividing their conquests in Ireland, he was employ'd by them to measure and set out the land. **1818** CRUISE *Digest* (ed. 2) V. 17 The commissioners should set out, allot, and assign unto the lady of the manor, twenty statute acres of the common and waste grounds. **1893** *Field* 1 Apr. 486/1 My predecessor had set out a large field in allotments.

(*c*) To plan, lay out (a town, road, garden, etc.); to lay out (ground) *with* plants.

**1673** RAY *Journ. Low C.* 3 The present Town having been contrived and set out all at once. **1689** *Col. Rec. Pennsylv.* I. 298 To set out a Cart road according to Statute. *a* **1700** EVELYN *Diary* 17 Jan. 1653, I began to set out the ovall garden at Sayes Court. **1712** J. JAMES tr. *Le Blond's Gardening* 138 A Gardener who has a Parterre or a Grove to set out. **1845** *Jrnl. R. Agric. Soc.* VI. II. 335 A ditch is then to be set out 4 feet wide. **1854** *Ibid.* XV. II. 426 He..himself sets out his drains and his water-meads. **1893** *Cornh. Mag.* May 485 Every year sees another acre or two set out with narcissus bulbs.

(*d*) To mark out, lay out in a pattern or design.

**1838** *Civ. Engin. & Arch. Jrnl.* I. 322/1 Professor Phillips described an Odontograph, or instrument for setting out the teeth of wheels. **1861** *Temple Bar* I. 234 The lines of a floating battery in setting out the lines of a..fast frigate. **1891** DENNING *Art Cabinet-Making* 213 The sketch from which the working drawing is set out. **1892** ELEANOR ROWE *Chip Carving* 45 To set out the borders on Figs. 35 and 36.

**v.** (*a*) To arrange (a table, a room, etc.) for a meal or other purpose; to spread (a table, etc.) *with* ornaments, etc.; to dress (a window). (*b*) To put out or arrange (things necessary for a meal, game, etc.), esp. on a table; to lay (a meal).

**1809** MALKIN *Gil Blas* I. v. (Rtldg.) 10 The next step was to regale after their labours. A large table was set out in the hall. **1850** *Tait's Mag.* XVII. 764/2 The room was set out for dinner. **1856** *Leisure Hour* V. 604/1 Is it beneath his dignity to take down the shutters and 'set out' the window of his establishment? **1859** GEO. ELIOT *Adam Bede* x, Seth.. began to..clear the small round deal table that he might set out his mother's tea upon it. **1872** CALVERLEY *Fly Leaves* (1884) 34, I see her..setting out the tea-things, For a howling herd of hungry boys. **1885** J. PAYN *Luck of Darrells* xliii, The table was brilliantly set out with glass and silver.

(*c*) To arrange (objects) at proper intervals or with a due amount of display; *spec.* to plant out; to leave (plants) at a distance apart, by thinning (cf. SINGLE *v.* 7).

**1812** *New Bot. Gard.* I. 15 Removing the plants..and setting them out in beds. **1831** LOUDON *Encycl. Agric.* (1857) §6009 The planters differ in the number of hills to be made..some choosing to set them out..in rows of equal distances. **1847** *Jrnl. R. Agric. Soc.* VIII. I. 215 The plants are set out with the hoe, the distance varying from 14 to 18 inches. **1860** TYNDALL *Glac.* II. x. 285 This line [of stakes] was set out and numbered from the Trélaporte side of the valley. **1888** B. W. RICHARDSON *Son of Star* II. v. 79 A commander-in-chief who cannot set out troops. *Ibid.* III. xii. 218 The tents..are set out in the order of a city. **1890** *Jrnl. Educ.* 1 Aug. 429/2 The examples are nowhere 'set out', but buried in the body of the page.

****** †**w.** To put (people) at variance. *Obs.*

*a* **1610** HEALEY *Theophrastus* (1636) 51 If he be chosen Arbitrator betwixt two at difference..hee sets them out further then euer they were before. **1649** *Nicholas Papers* (1886) 156 To breed differences with and set him out with the Queene his mother.

******* *intr.* **x.** (*a*) To begin or start on a journey; to start on one's way.

*Set out* is felt as more appropriate than *set off* in this sense when the journey is undertaken with some deliberation or is of an important or arduous character.

**1583** STOCKER *Civ. Warres Lowe C.* IV. 24 b, Thei franckly and freely sette out of the Towne. **1667** MILTON *P.L.* VIII. 111 Mee thou thinkst not slow, Who since the Morning hour set out from Heav'n..and ere mid-day arriv'd in Eden. *a* **1700** EVELYN *Diary* 27 June 1650, The next morning by 4 we sat out for Canterbury. **1748** RICHARDSON *Clarissa* VII. 215, I write this after all are gone to bed; and the fellow is to set out with it by day-break. **1837** LOCKHART *Scott* IV. xi. 366 The Baronet..set out on his return to the North. **1886** MISS SERGEANT *No Saint* ix, He set out resolutely to walk across country. **1887** RUSKIN *Præterita* II. 164 We set out together for the base of the Buet,—I on muleback, he walking.

(*b*) const. *inf.* To begin one's career or start off with the object of doing something; to lay oneself out (*to do*).

**1888** BRYCE *Amer. Commw.* lxxxix. III. 211 It.. accomplished much of what it set out to do. **1893** *Harper's Mag.* Jan. 313/2 Did he..deliberately set out to be a tyrant? **1897** *Bookman* Jan. 126/1 The..stories..don't set out to prove anything.

(*c*) *ellipt.*

**1744** LADY M. W. MONTAGU *Let. to Montagu* 12 June, A new vice-legate,..young, rich, and handsome, and sets out in a greater figure than ever has been known here. **1798** *Geraldina* I. 191 Nor would I set out a Reformer.

**y.** To start on a certain course; to begin or start off (*with* or *by doing* something).

**1693** LOCKE *Educ.* §93 (1699) 151 A young Gentleman, who gets this one Qualification from his Governour, sets out with great Advantage. **1694** ATTERBURY *Serm.* (Isa. lx. 22) (1726) I. 100 But Christianity, when it set out, took none of these methods of recommending it self. **1753** HOGARTH *Anal. Beauty* xi. 89 The two general ideas we sat out with at the beginning of this chapter. **1770** LUCKOMBE *Hist. Printing* 247 Every Printer ought to consult with himself about the scope and nature of the business which he sets out for. **1829** LAMB *Let. to Gillman* 30 Nov., Life opened upon him with comparative brilliancy. He set out as a rider or traveller for a wholesale house. **1853** J. NAPIER *Man. Dyeing* 261 If we start with a protosalt of iron..and if we set out with a persalt. **1884** G. ALLEN *Philistia* III. 22 He set out by admiring his niece's fat arms.

**z.** To project.

**1892** *Black & White* 11 June 758/1, I have observed..that several of the new skirts..show a tendency towards setting out round the feet. **1892** *Pictorial World* 25 June 98/1 It is only cut and stiffly lined to set out round the feet.

†**aa.** = *sit out* (trans. and intr.): see SIT *v.* 37 a, b.

**1714** MRS. MANLEY *Adv. Rivella* 40, I..saw the Person for whom she was accus'd, set the Play out. **1815** *Zeluca* III. 82 Not but I'd rather set out; for it's quite unfair to sing a foolish thing that nobody likes, when I could do better.

**150. set over.** †**a.** To convey to the other side of a piece of water. Also *absol.* or *intr.* (Cf. *put over*, PUT *v.* 49 d.) *Obs.*

*c* **1400** *Destr. Troy* 2998 There light þai full lyfely, lept into bote, And were set ouer soundly into the same yle. **1548** HALL *Chron., Edw. IV* (1809) 292 He was a frayde to set ouer or to geue battayl, knowynge not to what parte his souldiers would enclyne. **1567** HARMAN *Caveat* xi. (1869) 54 By that tyme the boye was sette ouer, his Maister..hadde taken a Bote and followed hym. *a* **1627** HAYWARD *Edw. VI* (1630) 61 Finding the riuer to be fordeable.., he there set ouer his horse.

†**b.** To give up, surrender *to*. *Obs.*

**1575–85** ABP. SANDYS *Serm.* vii. 109 The vineyard of the Lorde is set ouer to the spoile. *a* **1641** BP. MOUNTAGU *Acts & Mon.* (1642) 460 Sorry Ascetæ they were..who could not find in their hearts to set over to Gods service any more then two times or hours in the day.

**c.** To make over, transfer.

**1594** WEST *2nd Pt. Symbol., Chancerie* §141 The said sherife..did..bargaine, sell, assigne, & set ouer the said lease..vnto one G. H. **1613** R. WITT *Arithm. Quest.* 148 This Merchant hauing occasion to imploy money at 3. moneths end after he deliuer the said 300*l.* is desirous to sell or set ouer the said debt. **1818** CRUISE *Digest* (ed. 2) II. 10 A covenant from the lessee, that he would not 'assign, transfer, or set over..the said indenture of demise'. **1820** GIFFORD *Compl. Engl. Lawyer* (ed. 5) 660 The said A. B. hath..assigned, transferred, and set over..unto the said N. O...all that messuage.

†**d.** To brush aside, dismiss. *Obs.*

**1701** *Col. Rec. Pennsylv.* II. 80 Objections..which they could by no means Sett over.

†**e.** *intr.* Of a vessel: To run over. *Obs.*

**1608** BP. ANDREWES *Serm. Holy Ghost* ii. (1641) 609 Filled: not to hold, but to set over.

**f.** *pass.* and *intr.* *Salt-manuf.* Of the pan: To collect a crust in the process of evaporation.

**1808** H. HOLLAND *Agric. Cheshire* 59 When a crust of this kind forms [on the surface of the brine] the salt boilers say that 'the pan is set-over'. **1875** *Ure's Dict. Arts* III. 744 The introduction of a very few grains being amply sufficient to clear the largest pan, and to prevent any recurrence of the 'setting over'.

**g.** To kill or murder. *U.S. Criminals' slang.*

**1931** G. IRWIN *Amer. Tramp & Underworld Slang* 166 *Set over*, to kill, probably since the victim is set over or apart. **1944** W. R. BURNETT *Nobody lives Forever* xxii. 159 I've been trying to find you ever since you set Doc over. **1949** —— *Asphalt Jungle* xxxiii. 211 They have to set a guy over.

**151. set through.** †To carry through, bring to a conclusion. *Obs.*

**1600** J. PORY tr. *Leo's Africa* II. 53 A kind of tribunall.. wherein all contentions..are presently decided and set through [orig. *deciditur ac sedatur*].

**152. set to.** †**a.** *trans.* To add. *Obs.*

*c* **1200** ORMIN Ded. 339, & tale wile icc settenn to, To don ȝuw tunnderrstanndenn Hu fele [etc.]. **1551** TURNER *Herbal* I. H ij, Seynge the place..is proued to be but bastarde, and set to by some other to Dioscorides.

†**b.** To affix (one's seal or signature). *Obs.*

Often written *setto* or *set-to.*

*a* **1300** *Cursor M.* 6889 He..wrat þe nam, and sett to sele [*c* **1375** *Fairf.* sette on sel]. **1418** *E.E. Wills* (1882) 29 In the wytnesse of the wyche thynge, I haue set to my sele. *c* **1450** *Godstow Reg.* 44 He made hyt stronge by settynge to of hys seele. **1464** in *Archæologia* XLVII. 192 In witnesse of the quhilk thing I haf set to my signet. **1534** TINDALE *John* iii. 33 He that hath receaved hys testimonye hath set to his seale that God is true. **1552–3** *Inv. Ch. Goods, Stafford* 43 To thes presents interchaungeabli have setto our handes. **1624** HERIOT *Codicil to Will* in *Mem.* App. III. (1822) 102 In witness whereof to this..I have..set to my seal. **1829** GEN. P. THOMPSON *Exerc.* (1842) I. 38 Men must set-to their hands to being the born thralls of a proprietor of human cattle.

†**c.** To set (a broken limb). *Obs.*

**1596** SHAKS. *1 Hen. IV*, v. i. 133 Can Honour set too a legge?

†**d.** ***to set to one's hands***: to get to work. *Obs.*

**1611** *Second Maiden's Trag.* 1787 Remoue the stone that I maie see my mistres, setto yor handes you villaines, and that nymblie.

**e.** *Cock-fighting.* To put (cocks) beak to beak. (Cf. SETTER-TO 1.)

*c* **1800** in *Hoyle's Games Improv.* (1814) 443 No persons to set-to, but those who are appointed by the masters of the match.

**f.** (*a*) *intr.* To make a beginning; to get to work; *esp.* to begin seriously or energetically.

*c* **1425** *Eng. Conq. Ireland* 130 He sette to, & asked of the out-comen men that ynto the lond wer comen, howe hyt shold be of ham. **1637** RUTHERFORD *Lett.* (1664) 189, I beseech you set to, to goe through scripture. *c* **1830** MRS. SHERWOOD *Houlston Tracts* III. 9 The lass was at the washing-tub till it was quite late in the day, without getting anything forward, so that my wife was obliged to set to. **1847** MARRYAT *Childr. New Forest* viii, Edward then set to with a good appetite. **1858** R. S. SURTEES *Ask Mamma* l. 222 He again set-to on his own account, munching and crunching. **1890** H. M. STANLEY *Darkest Africa* I. v. 100 The engineer set to to repair the rudder.

(*b*) *Pugilism.* To begin fighting (*with*).

**1743** *Broughton's Rules* iii. in Egan *Boxiana* (1830) I. 52 Every body is to quit the stage as soon as the champions are stripped, before they set-to. **1792** *Ann. Reg.* 17 These famous pugilists set-to exactly at a quarter before 3 o'clock. **1823** SYD. SMITH *Wks.* (1859) II. 27/1 They [*sc.* poachers] take a delight in setting-to with the gamekeepers. **1863** 'OUIDA' *Held in Bondage* vi, Du Loo and his pet of the Fancy retired to the far end of the room, and there set-to, delivering from the left shoulder.

(*c*) *Racing.* To make the final effort to get in front. (Cf. SET-TO 3.)

**1856** H. H. DIXON *Post & Paddock* xii. 204 Buckle's great forte was to wait and then set-to on an idle horse.

†**g.** *pass.* or *intr.* Of food: To 'catch' on the bottom or side of a vessel in cooking. *Obs.*

*a* **1610** HEALEY *Theophrastus* (1636) 72 Then he tels you that his Sieges were blacker then broth, that's set to.

**153. set together.** †**a.** (*a*) To put (things) together; to set (a bone); to construct (a framework). *Obs.*

*c* **1205** LAY. 51 Feþeren he nom mid fingren & fiede on boc-felle & þa soþere word sette to-gadere. **1530** PALSGR. 715/2 And you wyll set your horses nere togyther, you have romme ynough in this stabell for two mo. **1553** T. WILSON *Rhet.* (1585) 6 Though a man can finde out good matter and good wordes, though hee can handsomely set them together. **1579** LYLY *Euphues* (Arb.) 58 Doth not he remember that the broken bone once set together, is stronger than ever it was? **1598** CHAPMAN *7 Bks. Iliads* To Rdr., I haue good authoritie that the bookes were not set together by Homer himselfe. **1603** KNOLLES *Hist. Turks* (1638) 670 After it [timber for building a fleet] was framed, and ready to be set together. **1613** SHAKS. *Hen. VIII*, I. i. 46 Who set the Body, and the Limbes Of this great Sport together?

†(*b*) ***to set together by the ears***: see EAR *sb.*[1] 1 e.

**1663** [see EAR *sb.*[1] 1 e]. **1692** R. L'ESTRANGE *Fables* lxvii. 65 So Mean a Rascal, as to set other People together by the Ears, without Fighting your self.

†(*c*) ***to set horses together***, to agree. *Obs.*

**1685** in *Verney Family Mem.* (1899) IV. 344, I wonder how Sir Rich. who is boyling water & the Mayor doe, to set their horses together.

†**b.** To couple together in comparison. *Obs.*

**1628** T. SPENCER *Logick* 117 The Oxe, and Israell are set together, in the quantitie of ignorance.

**c.** *Cheese-manuf.* To prepare (the milk) for the process of coagulation by adding the rennet.

**1837** *Brit. Husb.* II. 426 (Libr. Usef. Knowl.) The firmness of the curd, if the milk be set hot together, will be much greater than that from milk which has been set cold together. **1845** *Jrnl. R. Agric. Soc.* VI. I. 107 They make their cheese 'cold'—that is, set the milk together at a low temperature.

†**d.** *intr.* To curdle. *Obs.*

**1608** WILLET *Hexapla Exod* 215 The word is *kapha*, which properly signifieth the running or setting together of cheese.

**154. set up.** * **a.** (*a*) To place in a high or lofty position; to raise to an elevated situation.

[*c* **1200** ORMIN 3430 He sette a steorrne upp o þe lift.] *c* **1290** *S. Eng. Leg.* 238/680 þis monekes he [a whale] ladde ech-on, And sette heom up hole and sounde. *c* **1300** *Arth. & Merl.* 5911 [They] sett him vp as a king, þat er lay as a breþeling. **1470–85** MALORY *Arthur* VIII. xli. 336 Sir Gawayne..toke the knyghtes lady, and sette her vp behynde his squyer. **1565** COOPER *Thesaurus* s.v. *Pono*, He sette vp a marke on the toppe of an elme for archers to shoote at. **1582** ALLEN *Martyrdom Campion* (1908) 57 M. Forde being set up in the carte. **1631** GOUGE *God's Arrows* v. Ded. 406 You have brought me forth into the open field, and set me up to be gazed on. **1861** C. BEARD *Port Royal* I. 308 They..set up an inscription in the same church. **1879** M. J. GUEST *Lect. Hist. Eng.* xxxvi. 364 [She] caused his head to be set up on the gates of York.

†(*b*) To drive up. *Obs.*

**1496** *Acc. Ld. High Treas. Scot.* I. 305 To ij childer that chasit dukis in the dubbis, and set thaim vp to the halkis, ij s.

†**b.** To hoist (sail, a flag). *Obs.* (Cf. ON. *setja upp segl.*)

*a* **1300** *Cursor M.* 24829 þair sail þai sett up o þair scipp. *c* **1330** *Arth. & Merl.* 115 Vp þai sett sail & mast. **1538** STARKEY *England* I. i. 22 Them wych..wythout wynd wyl set vp the sayle. **1585** T. WASHINGTON tr. *Nicholay's Voy.* II. i. 31 b, [They] set vp a redde flagge. *a* **1674** CLARENDON *Hist. Reb.* XVI. §237 The wind coming fair, he set up his Sails. **1790** *Lond. Comp.* 144 Any waterman who sets up a sail between Lambeth and London Bridge, forfeits for each offence 5*s*.

**c.** To raise (a cry); to utter (vocal sound).

† *to set up one's throat*: see THROAT *sb.* 3 b.

*c* **1250** *Gen. & Ex.* 3717 Ðis folc ðo sette up grot and gred. **1540** PALSGR. *Acolastus* IV. ii. S iij b, Let vs begynne or set vppe a prety songe or balade. **1664** BUTLER *Hud.* II. ii. 657 The whole Rout Set up their throats with clam'rous shout. **1682** BUNYAN *Holy War* (1905) 285 With one voice they set up a cry that reached up to the Heavens. **1720** DE FOE *Capt. Singleton* xii. (1840) 211 They set up a huzza. **1749** SMOLLETT *Gil Blas* I. v. (1782) I. 28 Setting up my pipes, as if he had flayed me. **1809** MALKIN *Gil Blas* X. x. (Rtldg.) 365 The good old man set up a roar of laughter. **1821** SCOTT *Kenilw.* xi, Dame Crane set up her throat, and began a horrible exclamation against Jack Hostler. **1853** HAWTHORNE *Tanglewood T.* (1883) 238 Setting up her childish voice, she called him back. **1887** MISS BETHAM-EDWARDS *Next of Kin Wanted* II. vii. 78 Baby..set up a yell.

†**d.** To open. *Obs.*

**1387** TREVISA *Higden* (Rolls) V. 129 Whan Constantyn was i-cristened he made prisouns i-oponed,..and chirche dores i-sette up [*aperiri*].

†**e.** To put up for sale or auction. *Obs.*

*c* **1395** *Plowman's Tale* III. 1198 They that..sette hem up to any sale. **1707** *Lond. Gaz.* No. 4343/7 On the 4th of July ..will be exposed to Sale.., 10 Bags of..Spanish Wool,.. set up at 20d. per lb. **1812** CARY *Dante, Purg.* XIV. 64 Their flesh, yet living, sets he up for sale. **1819** HAZLITT *Pol. Ess.* 260 Let them set them up at auction, and see what they will fetch.

**f.** To post up (a paper or notice); to give notice of, advertise.

*c* **1540** in *Lett. Lit. Men* (Camden) 24 And in the night season sett upp certeyn refutacions in wrytyng on the churche dore. **1562** in *Vicary's Anat.* (1888) App. III. 163 Peter van Duran..was licensed by the same Courte to set vp bylles vpon postes, in suche partes of this Cytye as to him shall seame good. **1601** SHAKS. *Jul. C.* I. iii. 145 Good Cinna, take this Paper..set this vp with Waxe Vpon old Brutus Statue. **1616** R. COCKS *Diary* (Hakl. Soc.) I. 122 And soe we sett up a bill in writing, that I would geve a bar of plate to him which brought the keyes. **1708** *Constit. Watermen's Co.* liii, A Summons, to be set up at the most noted Plying-places between Gravesend and Windsor. **1727** BOYER *Dict. Royal* II, To set up a Play on the Posts. **1779** STILES *Diary* 1 June (1901) II. 343, I attended eveng prayers in the Chapel and set up College Orders. **1876** J. FERGUSSON *Hist. Ind. Archit.* I. vi. 139 It appears unlikely that Asoka would have been allowed to set up two copies of his edicts in the dominions of such powerful kings as Aira and his father seem to have been.

†**g.** To throw into relief, make brilliant, heighten the lustre of. *Obs.*

**1588** KYD *Househ. Phil.* Wks. (1910) 275 The Pewter so set vppe, the Brasse and yron works so bright [etc.]. **1603** HOLLAND *Plutarch's Mor.* 94 Painters to set up their colours, and to give them more beautifull light and lustre. **1615** S. WARD *Coal from Altar* 24, I haue heard our Marchants complain, that the set vp blewes haue made strangers loath the rich oaded blewes.

**h.** †(*a*) To tighten (strings) so as to raise their pitch. *Obs.*

**1642** M. NEWCOMEN *Serm. bef. Ho. Comm.* 5 Nov. (1643) 25 To proceed as Musicians doe in tuning their instruments: Who straine their strings with a gentle hand, and set them up by little and little.

(*b*) *Naut.* To take in the 'slack' of (shrouds, stays), make taut.

**1748** *Anson's Voy.* I. viii. 80 One mizen-shroud broke,.. which we knotted, and set up immediately. **1750** BLANCKLEY *Nav. Expositor* s.v. *Salvagees*, Salvagees..are used when a Shroud or Back Stay wants setting up. **1840** R. H. DANA *Bef. Mast* xxv, Setting up the weather breast-back-stays. **1875** BEDFORD *Sailor's Pocket Bk.* viii. (ed. 2) 282 The hawser is to be set up by means of the double block tackle purchase.

**i.** (*a*) To stake: only in phr. ***set up one's rest*** (see REST *sb.*[2] 6 b).

†(*b*) To score (so much) at cards. *Obs.*

**1680** COTTON *Compl. Gamester* (ed. 2) 76 Cribbidge... And when they have play'd out their three Cards and set up with Counters their Games in their hands. *Ibid.* 82 He that hath three Honours in his own hand, his partner not having the fourth sets up Eight by Cards, that is two tricks.

**j.** (*a*) To place in an exalted, eminent, or superior position; to raise to power or authority; sometimes *spec.* to put on the throne. Also *absol.*

*c* **1375** *Sc. Leg. Saints* vii. (*Jacobus Minor*) 612 þane Iosaphus þe met gert dycht, & set vpe tytus..to þe bowrde as þare oure-mane. **1387** TREVISA *Higden* (Rolls) VIII. 41 Foure false popes þat Frederik þe emperour had i-sette up. *a* **1586** SIDNEY *Arcadia* I. (Sommer) 21 All the things she did to ouerthrow him did set him vp vpon the height of honor. **1596** SPENSER *F.Q.* v. ii. 41 He maketh Kings to sit in souerainty; He maketh subiects to their powre obay; He pulleth downe, he setteth vp on hy. **1603** LD. CECIL in *Crt. & Times Jas. I* (1848) I. 16 To dispossess his majesty and his royal issue of this crown, and to have set up the Lady Arabella Stuart. **1654** Z. COKE *Logick* Pref., God hath set you up the Oracles of War. **1713** ADDISON *Cato* I. iv, Where's the worth that sets this people up Above your own Numidia's tawny sons! **1818** SCOTT *Rob Roy* xxvi She'll be keen for a that can set up King James, and ding down King George. **1879** M. J. GUEST *Lect. Hist. Eng.* xlvii. 477 Judges ..were almost tools of the king, who could set them up and put them down at his pleasure.

(*b*) To appoint (an officer or functionary).

**1642** VICARS *God in Mount* 45 Lecturers, chosen and set up with the peoples consent. **1678** BUTLER *Hud.* III. ii. 267 Some were for setting up a King. **1879** M. J. GUEST *Lect. Hist. Eng.* xxxi. 308 Two rival popes were set up.

(*c*) To appoint to or nominate for a position.

**1689** T. R. *View Gov. Eur.* 40 A Mountebank was set up for Lord Chancellor. *a* **1700** EVELYN *Diary* 8 Apr. 1685, For this Parliament, very meane and slight persons..were set up. *a* **1715** BURNET *Own Time* (1724) I. 480 When a person was set up to be Sheriff that would not serve. **1754** RICHARDSON *Grandison* I. xvi. 99 Supposing that he would set up his nephew when at age..as a representative for the county.

**k.** To make (a person) elated, proud, or vain; *esp.* in *pass.* to be elated, gratified; to be proud, or 'stuck-up'.

**1526** SKELTON *Magnyf.* 2025 Nowe she wyll laughe; forth-with she wyll frowne; Sodenly set vp and sodenly pluckyd downe. **1601** B. JONSON *Poetaster* IV. iii. 67 Come hither, cockatrice: here's one, will set thee vp, my sweet punke: set thee vp. **1789** CHARLOTTE SMITH *Ethelinde* (1814) II. 168 He's not so set up with it. **1866** MRS. GASKELL *Wives & Daughters* xiv, Sister thought such a message would set you up too much. **1886** RUSKIN *Præterita* I. 392 We were very much set up at making his acqaintance. **1893** KIPLING *Many Invent., Badalia Herodsfoot* 297 She's that set up you wouldn't know her.

**l.** (*a*) †To speak highly of, extol, praise (*obs.*); to put forward *as* a model, 'put on a pedestal'.

**1535** COVERDALE *Song 3 Childr.* 63 O ye spretes and soules of the righteous, speake good of ye Lorde: prayse him, and set him vp for euer.

**1809** MALKIN *Gil Blas* IV. viii. ¶1 This exterior did not prevent her from being set up as the cleverest woman in all Madrid. **1891** 'H. S. MERRIMAN' *Prisoners & Captives* x, I do not set him up as a hero.

(*b*) *dial.* (esp. *Sc.*) in ironical or contemptuous use.

**1824** SCOTT *St. Ronan's* ii, Set him up for confectioner! **1829** BROCKETT *N.C. Gloss.* (ed. 2) s.v., She rides in a coach —set her up, indeed! **1893** STEVENSON *Catriona* xi, Which makes me the keener for your company, Mr. David Balfour of the Shaws, and set ye up!

** **m.** (*a*) To place in an erect position; to set or stand upright; to erect (an image, statue); to raise (a standard).

*c* **1205** LAY. 27244 þa lette he sette up þene drake heremærken unimake. *a* **1225** *Leg. Kath.* 1468 Me schal..setten hit [an ymage] on heh up. *c* **1400** *Beryn* 1746 A Chese [= chessboard] þere was I-brouȝt forth..The meyne were I-set vp. **1530** PALSGR. 716/1 Set up this ladder agaynst the wall. *a* **1533** BERNERS *Huon* lxii. 215 She fell downe in a transe... Than Huon..set her vp, and comfortyd her. **1603** SHAKS. *Meas. for M.* II. i. 2 We must not make a scar-crow of the Law, Setting it vp to feare the Birds of prey. **1626** BACON *Sylva* §435 It hath beene knowne, that a Fruit-Tree hath beene blowne vp (almost) by the Roots, and set vp againe, and the next yeare bare exceedingly. *a* **1700** EVELYN *Diary* 14 June 1685, Certaine intelligence of the Duke of Monmouth..having set up his standard as King of England. **1707** S. SEWALL *Diary* 7 Aug., Peter Weare set up the stone post to shew a mile from the Town-House ends. **1821** SCOTT *Kenilw.* xii, In less than a minute, by setting up his mustaches and his hair, he seemed a different person. **1849** MACAULAY *Hist. Eng.* iii. I. 359 Palisades were set up, and a pleasant garden laid out. **1857** HUGHES *Tom Brown* II. viii, Old Bailey gravely sets up the middle stump again and puts the bails on. **1879** M. J. GUEST *Lect. Hist. Eng.* xxiii. 234 A beautiful monument was set up.

†(*b*) ? To trim or curl up. *Obs.*

*a* **1625** FLETCHER *Wild-Goose Chase* II. iii, Let me set my Beard up. —— *Hum. Lieut.* IV. i, She hates curl'd heads too, And setting up of beards she swears is Idolatry.

(*c*) To 'erect' (lines) in a plan.

**1731** W. HALFPENNY *Perspective* 24 To draw the Steps, first draw their Plan.., then set up their intended Heights.. from G, on the Line G*g*. **1830** HEDDERWICK *Mar. Archit.* 247 Set up the tangent-lines at the exact half-breadth of the midship-frame, on each side of the centre-line.

†(*d*) To set (a top) spinning. *Obs.*

**1607** SHAKS. *Cor.* IV. v. 161 He turn'd me about with his finger and his thumbe, as one would set vp a Top. **1649** LOVELACE *Lucasta* 8 Then, as a Top, he sets it up, And pitifully whips it! **1679** DRYDEN *Troil. & Cress.* III. i, He's an old wooden Top, set up by Father Time three hundred Years ago.

(*e*) ***to set up one's bristles***: to be irate. ***to set up one's comb*** or ***hair***: to be proud. ***to set one's back up***, etc.: see BACK *sb.*[1] 24 f.

**1528** TINDALE *Obed. Chr. Man.* 47 b, Then fume we and rage and sett vp the bristels. *a* **1536** [see COMB *sb.*[1] 5]. **1576** GASCOIGNE *Droomme of Doomes day* Wks. 1910 II. 251 Men thus advaunced..hould up theyr heads, set up their heare, shew theyr pryde. **1845** [see BACK *sb.*[1] 24 f]. **1886** BESANT *Childr. Gibeon* I. ix, I hear you've been to see my mother and you've set her back up.

(*f*) *U.S.* To put (drink, etc.) before customers for their consumption; hence, to 'treat' to (drinks, cigars). Also in phr. ***to set them up***, to provide free drinks.

**1880** A. A. HAYES in *Harper's New Monthly Mag.* Jan. 209/1 You bet he lived high; always set up the drinks. **1883** SWEET & KNOX *On Mexican Mustang* iii. 47 Then he swore, and cussed the 'demmed country, you know', but finally got into good humor, and set 'em up all round. **1884** *Lincoln* (Nebraska) *Jrnl.* Aug., A counter where the beer could be set up. **1888** *Lisbon* (Dakota) *Star* 9 Nov. 2/6 Well, we must make him set up the cigars on that happy event. **1906** C. DE L. CANFIELD *Forty-Niner* ix. 83 Of course, it was drinks all around; you can't do anything in this country without setting 'em up first. **1949** [see *rock candy* s.v. ROCK *sb.*[1] 9 a]. **1965** G. MELLY *Owning Up* vi. 64 In exchange for a song or two from me, he was prepared to set them up all night.

**n.** (*a*) To erect and make ready for use; to pitch (a tent); †to erect (a building). Cf. 60.

*c* **1205** LAY. 8716 þa þet work wes up iset. *a* **1300** *Cursor M.* 10378 Sir Ioachim was fain and blith, And vp he sett an auter suith. *a* **1400–50** *Wars Alex.* 2296 þe powere him grauntis To sett his cite vp agayn. **1471–3** in *Cal. Proc. Chanc. Q. Eliz.* (1830) II. Pref. 55 The seid hous shuld have be..fully sett upp, garnysshed, and doon by the fest of the nativite of our lady Seint Mary. **1485** CAXTON *Chas. Gt.* 241 He made hys tentys to be sette vp there. **1523–4** *Rec. St. Mary at Hill* 323 Paid..for Settyng vpp of a pewe in Seint Annys chappell iiij d. **1585** T. WASHINGTON tr. *Nicholay's*

*Voy.* II. xiii. 49 Constantinople being reedified and new sette vp. **1603** *Shuttleworths' Acc.* (Chetham Soc.) 152 When they were settinge upp the chimle pyppes and the batlement. **1667** MILTON *P.L.* XII. 247 He voutsafes Among them to set up his Tabernacle. **1719** DE FOE *Crusoe* I. (Globe) 212, I made a..fram'd Door-case, and a Door.., and..set it up in the Passage. **1880** LADY F. DIXIE *Across Patagonia* 206 Several vain attempts were made to set up the tents, but the wind was too strong.

†(*b*) To build (a ship). *Obs.*

**1595** MAYNARDE *Drake's Voy.* (Hakl. Soc.) 11 Settinge up more newe pinnaces. **1719** DE FOE *Crusoe* II. (Globe) 481, I oblig'd him to set up the Sloop which I had brought [in frame].

**o.** To set (a trap), lay (a snare). Now *dial.*

**1579** GOSSON *Sch. Abuse* (Arb.) 72 Cupide sets vpp a Springe for Woodcockes. **1687** MIEGE *Gt. Fr. Dict.* II. s.v. *Mouse,* To set up a Mouse-trap. **1887** *Kentish Gloss.* s.v. *Set up* A man 'sets up a trap for vermin'.

**p.** (*a*) To put together the parts of (a machine) and erect it in position.

(Merges in the sense of 'establish, set on foot', see **aa.**)

**1683** *Repr. Advantages Manuf. Woollen-cloath* 18 We have 25 Loomes constantly imployed, and have ordered the setting up 10 more. **1751** LABELYE *Westm. Bridge* 84 Three ..Months were employed..by the Carpenters in new framing and setting up the Centers. **1770** LUCKOMBE *Hist. Printing* 323 [He] ought to know as much of setting-up a Press as the Press-man himself. **1872** POPE *Telegraph* i. 13 In setting up the battery pure water may be used in the porous cell. **1879** M. J. GUEST *Lect. Hist. Eng.* xxviii. 284 Flemish weavers set up their looms and taught the English to weave cloth.

(*b*) To start (a piece of work) on a loom, etc.

**1857** MISS CUMMINS *Mabel Vaughan* xxxiii, Drawing a huge ball of yarn from her pocket, [she] commenced setting up a stocking. **1861** GEO. ELIOT *Silas M.* v, A piece of very fine twine was indispensable to his 'setting up' a new piece of work in his loom.

(*c*) To make the necessary interconnections and initial settings in (a computer) for the performance of a particular calculation; to do this so that the computer will solve (an equation), perform (a calculation), etc.

**1931** *Jrnl. Franklin Inst.* CCXII. 459 A bus shaft is assigned to each significant quantity appearing in the equation. The several relations existing between these are then set up by means of connections to the operating units. **1948** *Electronics* Apr. 124/1 When combining circuit elements to form an analog computer, the first step is to set up the differential equations to be solved. *Ibid.* 126/3 Consider setting up the computer for solving the differential equation $p^2y - 0{\cdot}2py - y = 0$. **1962** MACKAY & FISHER *Analogue Computing at Ultra-High Speed* xiii. 171 The procedure for setting up a given equation on an analyser is not difficult. **1964** G. A. & T. M. KORN *Electronic Analog & Hybrid Computers* ii. 37 The computer is 'set up' for the given problem when a suitable arrangement of computing elements establishes the correct relationships between computer voltages.

**q.** *Typogr.* To put (types) into the composing-stick; to arrange (type) in words or blocks of words; to put (a book, etc.) into type; occas. said of the type (quot. 1770). Also *absol.*

**1668–9** J. LEIGH *Let. to S. Clarke* (MS. Rawl. D. 398 fol. 141), I Request y[u] giue halfe Crown a man to each Composito[r] when hee begins to sett it vp. **1683** MOXON *Mech. Exerc., Printing* xix. ¶6 When the Boy Sets up Letters ..[he] takes the Composing-stick..in his left-Hand. **1770** LUCKOMBE *Hist. Printing* 247 A Fount of English, which sat up about twelve sheets in 4to of the Surgeons Case, in Paris. **1818** BYRON *Ep. to Murray* i, My dear Mr. Murray, Your're in a damn'd hurry, To set up this ultimate Canto. **1832** HALLAM in *Life Tennyson* (1897) I. 89 The (printer's) devils are full of promise to set up immediately. **1891** *Chamb. Jrnl.* 16 May 319/2 The speech..was set up in an incredibly short time.

**r.** To place (the dead body of an animal stuffed or otherwise treated for preservation) in an erect or lifelike position.

**1781** *Nat. Hist.* in *Ann. Reg.* 64/2 These Bats were kept for some time..before they were set up. **1861** *Temple Bar* III. 500 A nearly perfect skeleton has been obtained and is being set up. **1884** G. ALLEN *Philistia* I. 2 Where they stuffed birds or set up exotic butterflies in little cabinets. **1892** *Field* 30 Jan. 133/3, I am sending the skin..to be set up.

**s.** *to be well* (*straight*) *set up*: to have a stalwart, well-knit frame.

**1825** LD. COCKBURN *Mem.* (1856) 159 Charles Hope was tall and well set up. **1861** *Temple Bar* III. 53 Leotard is not straight set up, after the standard so cherished by soldier martinets. **1904** SIR P. BURNE-JONES *Dollars & Democr.* 53 In New York..the women..are so well 'set up', so excellently 'turned out'.

**t.** (*a*) To make erect and soldierly by drill.

**1865** MEREDITH *Rhoda Fleming* i, No master of callisthenics could have set them up better. **1893** *Chamb. Jrnl.* 10 June 364/1 When I joined the [Police] Force I was a big awkward-looking, country Johnny... Drill soon set me up.

(*b*) (See quot.)

**1842** in R. Oastler *Fleet Papers* II. 134 The assault consisted in 'setting her up', that is, making her hold a brush above her head for an hour and forty minutes; and when her arms began to be tired, and dropped a little, he put them up again.

**u.** *Agric.* To earth up (root-crops).

**1801** *Farmer's Mag.* Jan. 52 The turnips thrive better when not set up.

†**v.** To fix (a price or standard); also, to put up the price of. *Obs.*

**1530** *Proper Dyaloge* in Roy *Rede me,* etc. (Arb.) 138 Oure fearmes set vp dayly more and more. *Ibid.* 139 And yet no hygher price was ther vp set Than good conscience did require. **1592** NASHE *P. Penilesse* Wks. 1910 I. 197 In setting vp a sise of Bread.

†**w.** To compose (verses). *Obs.*

**1607** *Stat.* in *Hist. Wakefield Gram. Sch.* (1892) 72 Those which are able shall upon that daye sett upp verses.

†**x.** *Cards.* To make up (a side). *Obs.*

**1609** B. JONSON *Sil. Wom.* III. vi, *Cen.*.. Mavis and shee will set vp a side. *Trv.*..And mistris Mavis, shee will sustaine her part.

*** **y.** (*a*) To put into operation; to bring into use or vogue; to establish a course or series of. Now *rare.*

*a* **1400–50** *Wars Alex.* 2135 And settes vp a sawte to þe towne sydes. **1570** [see PLEA *sb.* 1 γ]. **1612** CHAPMAN *Rev. Bussy d'Ambois* V. iv. 3, I have had lotteries set up for my death. **1622** JAS. I *Let. to Earl Southampton* 9 July (*title-p.*), The present setting up of Silke works..in Virginia. **1685** DRYDEN *Pref. to Alb. & Alb.* Ess. 1900 I. 279 When operas were first set up in France. *a* **1700** EVELYN *Diary* 19 July 1664, The lottery which his Majesty had permitted Sir Arthur Slingsby to set up for one day in the Banqueting House at White-hall. **1700** *Ibid.* 24 Mar., Some Lectures were set up. **1722** DE FOE *Plague* (1754) 35 All the Plays and Interludes, which..had been set up. **1847** L. HUNT *Men, Women, & Bks.* II. iii. 44 The numerous smaller periodical works which were set up by Steele. **1849** *N. & Q.* Ser. I. I. 33 A new post-coach had been set up which performed the journey to Bath in a single day.

(*b*) To cause (a certain condition, *esp.* of disease) to arise. Often *pass.*

**1851** *Jrnl. R. Agric. Soc.* XII. II. 528 Inflammation is set up in the soft tissue. **1853** *Ibid.* XIV. I. 199 Fermentation was more readily set up. **1889** MRS. COMYNS CARR *Marg. Maliphant* II. xxi. 122 Want of proper nourishment..had caused the accident to set up a disease. **1891** *Cornh. Mag.* Dec. 601 This sets up fructification.

**z.** To establish (a state of things, a custom, a form of government, a society, etc.).

**1431** *Acts Privy Council* IV. 95 It alwey pourveide and seene þat..justice be set uppe and stabylysshede þere. **1535** COVERDALE *1 Chron.* xviii. [xix.] 3 Whan he wente to set vp his power by the water Euphrates. **1549** LATIMER *Ploughers* (Arb.) 30 His office is to hinder religion,..to set vp Idolatrie. **1597** SHAKS. *2 Hen. IV,* I. iii. 50 To plucke a Kingdome downe, And set another vp. **1640** *Articles agst. Laud* 3 He went about to subvert Religion, and to set up Papists and superstition. *c* **1710** CELIA FIENNES *Diary* (1888) 200 They have their Coales and 3 shillings p[r] weeke allowed to Each to maintain them,..its set up and allowed to by M[r] Coleson a merch[t] in London. **1765** BLACKSTONE *Comm.* I. 52 The legislature..which was originally set up by the general consent of the society. **1820** W. IRVING *Sketch Bk.* (1859) 184 In consequence of two rival 'Burial Societies' being set up in the place. **1855** MACAULAY *Hist. Eng.* xii. III. 225 Though he had not taken part in setting up the new government. **1861** *Macm. Mag.* IV. 371/1 He succeeded in setting up Episcopacy..in Scotland. **1890** TOUT *Hist. Eng. from 1689,* 151 The house of Savoy now set up a united Italy.

**aa.** (*a*) To set on foot, establish (a business, profession); to begin (housekeeping, life).

*to set up shop*: see SHOP *sb.*

**1525** *Coventry Leet Bk.* 691 Euery persone that haith bene full prentise..doithe sett vp his occupacion or Craft within the same [city]. **1567** HARMAN *Caveat* Epist. (1869) 21 To set vp houses and kepe hospitalytie. **1585** T. WASHINGTON tr. *Nicholay's Voy.* IV. xvi. 130b, They haue also there set vp printing, not before seene in those countries. **1615** G. SANDYS *Trav.* 136 Buying pewter, brasse, and such like implements as if to set up house keeping. **1663** MARVELL *Corr.* Wks. (Grosart) II. 91 The Earl of Carlisle is going upon an extraordinary embassage to Muscovy, in order to setting up the English trade again there. **1738** SWIFT *Pol. Conversat.* Introd. 17, I have often wished, that certain..Instructors..would set up Schools. **1777** *Ann. Reg.* II. 42 He returned to London and set up the small-coal trade. **1852** THACKERAY *Esmond* I. x, He taught the science of the small-sword, and set up a saloon-of-arms. **1869** 'WAT. BRADWOOD' *The O.V.H.* vi, The next thing we shall hear will be that you have set up house and got married. **1894** H. DRUMMOND *Ascent of Man* 299 As new cells budded from the parent they moved away and set up life for themselves.

(*b*) To begin the use or practice of; to adopt as part of one's establishment, etc.

*a* **1704** T. BROWN *Dial. Dead* Wks. 1711 IV. 36 She set up a Basset-Table. **1709** STEELE *Tatler* No. 176 ¶8, [I] have set up a Pack of little Beagles. **1749** SMOLLETT *Gil Blas* VIII. ix. (1782) III. 188, I..bought the coach of a notary, who had set it up through ostentation, and now wanted to get rid of it. **1815** SCOTT *Guy M.* xli, He had lately set up a carriage. **1853** 'C. BEDE' *Verdant Green* II. xi, He conceived the idea of setting up a drum! **1860** MRS. CARLYLE *Lett.* III. 63 You will have heard of my setting up a second servant. **1890** *Cornh. Mag.* July 45 Improved..by the short beard he had set up.

(*c*) To prepare, set in readiness (apparatus, machinery, etc.). (A more generalized application of sense 154 p (*c*).)

**1922** H. D. BURGHARDT *Machine Tool Operations* II. viii. 157 Sometimes an unskilled man or boy can operate several machines after they have been 'set up' by a skilled mechanic. **1962** A. NISBETT *Technique Sound Studio* viii. 142 To be able to put the disc on the turntable, locate the right groove,.. and set the record up ready for playing in. **1977** P. DICKINSON *Walking Dead* I. iii. 39 Foxe felt most fully alive ..when he was setting up a new experiment.

(*d*) *gen.* To make preparations or arrangements for; to contrive, plot (a move, trick, etc.); to arrange (a social engagement).

**1965** P. O'DONNELL *Modesty Blaise* vii. 83 If Gabriel or anyone else has been setting up a job from here, Paco will know about it. **1968** [see NIM *sb.*[2]]. **1971** *Daily Tel.* 28 Oct. 3 (*heading*) Boy, 12, set up cripple's death jury is told. **1973** R. BUSBY *Pattern of Violence* vi. 104 Let's set this thing up. I'll get onto the divisional commander. **1973** *Houston* (Texas) *Chron.* (Suppl.) 14 Oct. 8/4 We set up a date and a couple of weeks later Agnew and I sat down in his suite in a Chicago hotel. **1978** R. THOMAS *Chinaman's Chance* xxii. 228 'Could you set it up?' 'No problem.'

**bb.** To provide (a person) with means; to place in a position of prosperity or in the way of retrieving one's fortune; to set 'on one's legs' *again.*

**1530** PALSGR. 716/1, I shall than be set up agayne. **1584** LODGE *Alarum* 10 Thou maist haue money in thy pursse, and other necessaries to set thee vp againe. **1605** SHAKS. *Macb.* III. i. 10 May they not be my Oracles as well, And set me vp in hope. **1658** *Wit Restor'd* 25 But when a Fammily is sunck, And Titles are a fading, Some Merchant's daughter setts you up. **1728** LAW *Serious C.* viii, She has set up near twenty poor tradesmen that had failed in their business. **1811** MARY TITHERINGTON *Diary* in *Mem.* (1819) 103 Job was set up again by the bounty of his friends. **1840** R. H. DANA *Bef. Mast* xxv, We had a light, fair wind, which set us up again. **1892** *Illustr. Sporting & Dram. News* 10 Dec. 446/3 He soon set us all up in funds.

**cc.** (*a*) To establish or start (a person) in a business or profession; *transf.* said of the money, stock, or outfit sufficient to equip a person.

*to be set up for* (colloq.): to be well provided with.

**1556** *North Country Wills* (Surtees) 238 The same company [of mercers in London] shall deliver yerlie the said rent to one poore yong man to sett hym up that hathe nother father nor mother. **1628** EARLE *Microcosm.* (Arb.) 65 Two Deskes, and a quire of Paper set him vp. **1679–88** *Moneys Secr. Serv. Chas. II & Jas. II* (Camden Soc.) 88 To W[m] Lloyd,..bounty, to sett him up to his trade of a shoemaker. **1722** DE FOE *Col. Jack* (1840) 184, I was..set up in the world, made a master. **1745** *Life Bampfylde-Moore Carew* 52 He expended a small Sum of Money to set her up for a retail Trader in Buckles. **1825** *New Monthly Mag.* XVI. 366 Mistress of as many branches of knowledge as would set up half-a-dozen literary hacks. **1848** THACKERAY *Van. Fair* xxii, He had brilliant under-waistcoats, any one of which would have set up a moderate buck. **1863** MRS. H. WOOD *Verner's Pride* v, I'm set up for cotton gownds. **1865** DICKENS *Mut. Fr.* IV. xiii, Now, John, if you don't fix a time for setting her up in her own house and home, and letting us walk out of it, I'll turn Informer. **1886** MRS. C. PRAED *Miss Jacobsen* II. iii. 48 His father will set him up in business.

(*b*) *refl.* To constitute or establish oneself (*as*).

**1883** FENN *Middy & Ensign* xxiv. 142 Dick had no intention of setting himself up as a prophet. **1891** *Murray's Mag.* X. 728 The Wincauntons set themselves up as judges of their neighbours.

(*c*) To bring (someone) to a position from which he may be knocked down, to make vulnerable (*lit.*, as in *Pugilism*); *fig.* (*colloq.* and *slang*), to lead on in order to fool, cheat, or incriminate (a person); to 'frame'. orig. *U.S.*

**1950** J. DEMPSEY *Championship Fighting* x. 49 If you can land solidly with a straight left or with a left hook, you'll generally knock your opponent off balance, at least, and 'set him up' for a pot-shot with your right. **1956** B. HOLIDAY *Lady sings Blues* xxi. 168 When I saw them running across the rooftops with my money, I knew I'd been had. Somebody had set me up. **1963** L. DEIGHTON *Horse under Water* xxxi. 127 Either Mr. Ivor Batcher was double-crossing his boss or I was being set up. **1964** S. BELLOW *Herzog* 109 Of course he understood that Tennie was setting him up, and that he was a sucker for just the sort of appeal she made. **1979** A. PRICE *Tomorrow's Ghost* ii. 23 'You're deliberately using them for bait, for God's sake.' 'Oh no we're not... We didn't set them up.' **1981** 'E. V. CUNNINGHAM' *Case of Sliding Pool* ix. 101 He had a partner, whom he set up from the very beginning for the kill.

†**dd.** To restore, repair, make good. *Obs.*

**1609** BIBLE (Douay) *1 Macc.* iii. 43 Let us set up [Vulg. *erigamus*] the abasing of our people, and let us fight for our people. *a* **1670** SPALDING *Troub. Chas. I* (Bannatyne Club) II. 286 Whill his loissis wes set wp.

**ee.** To bring to a proper state of health and strength; to restore to health.

**1727** BOYER *Dict. Royal* II, To set one up again..(to recover his Health). **1804** NELSON *Lett.* (1814) II. 63 A little of your good nursing, with ass's milk, will set me up for another campaign. **1863** MRS. CARLYLE *Lett.* III. 170, I returned from that visit quite set up. **1889** MRS. LYNN LINTON *Thro' Long Night* II. II. xiii. 200 Change is just what Estelle wants to set her up again.

**** **ff.** To put away for future use, lay up in store, store away. *Obs.* or *dial.*

**1421** *Coventry Leet Bk.* 33 þat hur hoost haue in charge that they bryng all hur fysche in-to the markett, without they sett up any fysche in any othur fyschers houses. **1530** PALSGR. 716/1 Go, set up this bagge of monaye, tyll I call for it. **1588** KYD *Househ. Phil.* Wks. (1901) 242 Mellons, Cytrons, and such like,..were..reserued and set vp. **1617** MORYSON *Itin.* III. 82 They beginne them in the midst of the broade side, making a round hole there, into which hole, when the cheese is to be set vp, they put some few drops of wine. **1729** SWIFT *Direct. Serv.* ii. ¶7 If your lady orders you to set up a piece of meat for supper. **1730** T. BOSTON in Morrison *Mem.* ix. (1899) 221, I refused to eat;..and the meat was set up again untasted. **1844** H. STEPHENS *Bk. Farm* II. 393 The corn is then set up, that is, set down in the sacks on the floor, and remains there unemptied.

†**gg.** To put (a horse, etc.) up in a stable; *occas.* to keep (cattle) up to fatten them. *Obs.*

*c* **1440** *Alphabet of Tales* 124 He went privalie into þe stabyll þer þe knightis man had sett vp her hors. **1523** FITZHERB. *Husb.* §68 Yf she be rydden vppon, and sette vp hotte. **1540** PALSGR. *Acolastus* V. v. B b j b, The caulfe that is well fatted. *i.* that is set vp to be made fatte. **1622** MABBE tr. *Aleman's Guzman d'Alf.* I. 46 My Companion..sets vp his Asses in the Stable. *a* **1713** ELLWOOD *Autobiogr.* (1714) 21 When I..had set up my Horse at an Inn. **1768** *Boyer's Dict. Royal* II. s.v., To set up a coach..*Dételer les chevaux d'un carrosse.*

***** **hh.** (*a*) To put into an attitude of hostility or opposition; to incite, instigate.

*a* **1586** SIDNEY *Ps.* VII. vi, Arise, O Lord, in wrath thy self up sett Against such rage of foes. **1601** SHAKS. *All's Well* I. i. 35 Hee was skilfull enough to haue liu'd stil, if knowledge could be set vp against mortallitie. **1606** —— *Tr. & Cr.* V.

iv. 13 They set me vp in pollicy, that mungrill curre Aiax, against that dogge of as bad a kinde, Achilles. **1803** *Pic Nic* No. 4 (1806) I. 144 They set up argument against matter of fact. **1804-6** SYD. SMITH *Mor. Philos.* (1850) 218 Sudden variation,..in a great scale, is most commonly either grand or sublime; it sets all the faculties up in arms. **1818** SCOTT *Rob Roy* xxxii, As for them that have abused your Grace's ear, and set you up against a man that [etc.]. **1884** G. ALLEN *Philistia* III. xxvi. 27 The environment is too strong for you; and if you set yourself up against it, it'll crush you. **1894** J. T. FOWLER *Adamnan* Introd. 33 This one has perhaps been set up as a rival to an earlier St. Patrick's Purgatory.

(*b*) *Hunting*. To bring to bay. Also *fig.*

**1608** CHAPMAN *Trag. Byron* v. Q4, As a Sauadge Bore that (hunted longe, Assayld and set vp) with his onely eyes, Swimming in fire keepes of the baying hounds. **1747** *Tricks of Town laid open* (ed. 3) 31 You see, Sir, how naturally all these Beasts of Prey hunt a Country Squire, and..they seldom lose the Scent till they have set him up (as you phrase it) *brought him to a Bay*. **1889** *Field* 12 Jan. 41/3 The hounds ..came up with their stag there, and set him up to bay at this well-known landmark.

****** **ii.** To put forward (a claim, defence, a case in law).

**1697** *Mem. Trans. Savoy* 123 Several Reasons engage the French King to set up anew his Title to Savoy. **1813** SHELLEY *Q. Mab* IV. 77 That apology Which kings who rule, and cowards who crouch, set up For their unnumbered crimes. **1821** SCOTT *Kenilw.* xvii, After setting up a vain and unjust pretence to the throne of England. **1855** [see ALIBI *sb.*]. **1856** *N. Brit. Rev.* XXVI. 201 The best defence is that which..has been set up by M. de Remusat. **1858** [see CLAIM *sb.*[1]]. **1885** BOWEN in *Law Rep. 10 Prob. Div.* 194 The husband sets up in bar a deed of separation.

**jj.** To advance, propose, put forward (a theory, idea, plan).

**1803** *Pic Nic* No. 3 (1806) I. 87 They seem to have set up for themselves a peculiar test of their merit. **1843** RUSKIN *Mod. Paint.* (1851) I. Pref. p. xiv, They are rejoiced to set up a standard of imaginary excellence. **1883** FENN *Middy & Ensign* xii. 70 You set up a theory of your own. **1890** MISS I. D. HARDY *New Othello* III. x. 211 You set up those false and morbid scruples between yourself and me.

******* *intr.* **kk.** To sit up (late at night). Now *U.S.*, *dial.* or *vulgar*.

**1697** *C'tess D'Aunoy's Trav.* (1706) 201 In this Season they set up till four or five a Clock in the Morning because of the heats. **1776** S. J. PRATT *Pupil of Pleas.* II. 208, I find the whole family..is to set up. **1822** MRS. NATHAN *Langreath* I. 176 You forget, my child, how late you set up at night. **1935** R. BASS in *Scribner's Mag.* Feb. 122/1 The body must never be left alone for an instant until it is left in the grave. It must be 'set up' with. **1968** E. R. BUCKLER *Ox Bells & Fireflies* ix. 127 Neighbors took turns 'setting up' with the patient night after night.

**ll.** (orig. *absol.* of aa.) To start in business, begin the exercise of a trade or profession.

Formerly const. *for*, now *as* (with the sb. connoting the occupation); in recent use also with simple sb. as compl.

**1593** NASHE *Christ's T.* 46b, My young Merchant returnes, and settes vppe fresher then euer he did. **1647** N. BACON *Disc. Govt. Eng.* I. iii. (1739) 7 They had but new set up, and had not yet found out the right way of Trade. **1691** WOOD *Ath. Oxon.* I. 377 He set up for a writing-master. *a* **1704** T. BROWN *Laconics* Wks. 1711 IV. 11 A Wit and a Beau set up with little or no Expense. **1779** *Mirror* No. 67 Your predecessor, *The Spectator*, used to be consulted in cases of difficulty. I know not if you, Mr. Mirror, set up on the same footing. **1809** SCOTT *Let.* in *Lockhart* (1837) II. vi. 237 Ballantyne's brother is setting up here as a bookseller. **1882** *Sat. Rev.* 19 Aug. 247/1 When people had set up in business. **1891** *Ibid.* 26 Dec. 728/1 He even set up smuggler on his own account.

**mm. to set up for.** (*a*) ***to set up for oneself***, to start on a career on one's own account.

**1622** MABBE tr. *Aleman's Guzman d'Alf.* I. 55 He got him a Stocke, to set vp for himselfe in the world. **1701** W. WOTTON *Hist. Rome* 268 Three of them set up for themselves, Pescennius Niger in the East, Septimius Severus in Illyricum, and Clodius Albinus in Britain. **1727** BOYER *Dict. Royal* II. s.v., After this Victory over Mark Anthony, Augustus had a mind to set up for himself. **1852** C. W. HOSKYNS *Talpa* xviii. (1854) 153 No sooner is a new thought imparted, than it sets up for itself, and denies its pedigree.

(*b*) To put oneself forward as (a person of a certain kind or class), to lay claim to being (so-and-so). Also, to ***set up for being*** (so-and-so).

**1687** MIEGE *Gt. Fr. Dict.* II, To set up for a Reformer. **1692** R. L'ESTRANGE *Fables* lxvii. 66 Shall any Man..that Willfully..procures the Cutting of whole Armies to Pieces, set up for an Innocent? **1709** E. WARD tr. *Cervantes* 206 Covetous Men commonly set up for being very long sighted. **1716** J. CRAGGS *Let. to Pope* 2 Sept., I fancy I am..setting up for a wit. **1765** FOOTE *Commissary* I. (1782) 17 *Sim*... Why he must be upwards of — *Mrs. Mech.* Fifty, I warrant. *Sim.* Rather late in life to set up for a gentleman. **1849** *Tait's Mag.* XVI. 237/1, I do not set myself up for a purist. **1889** *Harper's Mag.* Mar. 557/1, I don't set up for a beauty.

†(*c*) To have as one's object or goal. *Obs.*

**1685** STILLINGFL. *Orig. Brit.* ii. 50 Clodius Albinus having set up for the Empire in Britain, and being beaten by Severus. **1705** ADDISON *Italy* 504 Whether or no they have done well, to set up for making another kind of Figure, Time will witness. **1707** *Diverting Muse* I. 6 An Old Lady, who has bury'd Six Husbands and sets up for the Seventh.

†(*d*) To support the claims of. *Obs.*

**1689** T. R. *View Gov. Eur.* 4 Ahaz's Dial is no President for our time or measures; nor may the Theocracy of the Jews authorize us to set up for King Jesus. **1691** W. NICHOLLS *Answ. Naked Gospel* 97 The first then that stood up for this Heterodoxy was Michael Servetus..who..set up for the Unitarian Doctrine in Europe.

(*e*) To lay claim to (a quality, virtue, etc.). Also, †to lay claim to having (a concrete possession).

**1698** COLLIER *Immor. Stage* 226 This Spark sets up for Sense. **1698** FARQUHAR *Love & Bottle* II. i, Had the Land-lady but a Highland Piper to joyn with 'em, she might set up for a Collection of Monsters. **1741** RICHARDSON *Pamela* III. 127 If People will set up for Virtue, and all that, let 'em be uniformly virtuous. **1766** GOLDSM. *Vic. W.* xv, No doubt.. you have known ladies set up for wit that had none. **1865** MISS BRADDON *Sir Jasper's T.* xxii, I suppose Pauncefort sets up for originality.

**nn.** (*absol.* of ii.) To lay claim or pretend *to be*.

*a* **1849** MAR. EDGEWORTH *Pop. Tales, Rosanna* v, What more could we have, if we were to set up to be gentry? **1889** MISS SERGEANT *Luck of House* I. xxi. 286 You need not set up to be virtuous.

†**oo.** (orig. *absol.* of gg.) To put up *at* an inn or other lodging. *Obs.*

**1684** MRS. BEHN *Novels* (1722) II. 325 Bellamora..was obliged to lodge..at the same Inn where the Stage-Coach set up. **1745** *Life Bampfylde-Moore Carew* 92 He..then rode away Post-Haste to Exeter; where being arrived he sets up at the Oxford Inn. **1760-72** H. BROOKE *Fool of Qual.* (1809) IV. 105 On setting up for the night, I rejoiced to find ..Louisa was..alive. **1780** S. J. PRATT *Emma Corbett* civ. 209 Every house where the stages set up. **1819** LADY MORGAN in *Mem.* (1862) II. 116 We set up at the Nova-Yorka [Hotel], kept by an Englishwoman.

**pp.** To punt, esp. so as to get close *to* water-fowl to shoot them. (Cf. sense 110.)

**1776** C. CARROLL *Jrnl. Miss. Canada* in B. Mayer *Mem.* (1845) 47 In many places the current was so strong that the batteau men were obliged to set up with poles, and drag the boat by the painter. **1824** HAWKER *Instr. Yng. Sportsmen* (ed. 3) 343 If we can neither find a creek nor a 'latch', with sufficient water to set up to birds. **1882** PAYNE-GALLWEY *Fowler Irel.* 26 Illustr., Wexford floatmen setting up to fowl together.

**qq.** Of a cart: To tip up. *local.*

**1841** *Jrnl. R. Agric. Soc.* II. II. 178 The carts..are.. larger, and with moveable bodies, so as to set up for the purpose of turning out their load at once.

**rr.** Of a soft-nosed bullet: To expand on impact.

**1896** *Times* 16 Dec. 5/2 The metal covering at the point being made thin and the lead core slightly exposed, the result being that the bullet 'set up' on striking any object. **1898** *Engineer* 4 Mar. 216/2 A bullet should do more than make a man rub his leg some hours afterwards. Consequently efforts have been directed to causing bullets to set up on impact.

☛ *Key to phrases and idiomatic uses.*

Uses of the passive: (= be seated) 4, (= be arranged) 16, (= be situated) 176, (= be resolved, determined, fixed, settled, rigid) 92, 93, 94b, 95c, 97b, (= be hostile) 117c; to be *s* with 119; to be *s* round or about (with) 121; to be keen *s*, sharp *s* 75b; to be hard *s*, ill *s* 122b.

Uses of the intransitive: (= sit) 5, (= sit on eggs) 5b, (= subside) 8, heave and *s* 10, (= stake) 14b, (= become fixed, rigid, solid, coagulated) 94b, 95b, c, d, 97c, (of fruit or blossom) 98b, (= set in) 100b, (in dancing) 103, (in bowls) 104b, (= proceed, start off) 106, (of a current) 107, (= punt) 110, (of a setter) 123c; see also branches XI and XII.

Set about (prep.) 127, (adv.) 133; *s* above 26b; *s* abroach 134; *s* abroad 135; *s* adown 136; *s* afloat 137; *s* against (= attack) 128; *s* one person against another 117; *s* aland 108b; *s* aloft 26b; *s* apart 138; *s* ashore 108b; *s* aside 139; *s* at (= attack) 129; *s* away 140; *s* the axe to 20d; *s* back 141; *s* one on another's back 47b; *s* a bargain 55b; *s* before one or one's eyes 18c; *s* a bell 66; *s* a bone 79; *s* to book 26; *s* bounds to 48; *s* a butterfly 83; *s* by 91c, 142; *s* case 87; *s* caution 13; *s* the chase 124; *s* a clock 85; *s* a colour 96b; *s* a copy 54b; *s* (to) corners 103; *s* one's countenance 94; *s* dead 123c; *s* a dog on 116; *s* down 143; *s* an edge on 42; *s* the edge of 75; *s* eggs 15d; *s* an end to 58; *s* on end 28; *s* an example 54; *s* (one's) eyes on 39; *s* a fabric 82; *s* a or one's face 94; *s* a (good) face upon 41; *s* one's fancy on 37; *s* a fashion 54; *s* in feu 57; *s* the field 70; *s* a fine 86; *s* fire to 34; *s* on fire 25b; *s* a flock 100; *s* (one's) foot 19; *s* footing 19d; *s* forth 144; *s* forward(s 145; *s* to fowl 110; *s* free 25b; *s* the fruit 98; *s* game 123; *s* a gin 59; *s* a gloss on 41; *s* (on, a-) going 114b, c, d; *s* gone 114e; *s* in hand 27; *s* in one's hand 18b; *s* one's hand against, on, to 19b, c; *s* one's hand (= signature) to 23; *s* one's heart on 37; *s* a hen 1c; *s* (on) high 62b; *s* home 108d; *s* on horseback 1; *s* in 146; *s* (= tune) an instrument 77; *s* into 107, 130; *s* the keel 110; *s* land 69; *s* on land 108b; *s* the land 124; *s* in lease 57; *s* (at) light 89c; *s* light by 91e; *s* lightly (littly) by 91f; *s* a limit 48; *s* lines 59; *s* little by (of, to) 91, etc.; *s* at little 89b; *s* loose 25b; *s* to lore 26; *s* a mark on 40; *s* a mast 60; *s* a match 56; *s* a meal 71; *s* milk for cream 67a; *s* one's mind on 37; *s* one's mouth 95; *s* much by 91; *s* to music 73; *s* upon the muzzle 26d; *s* at naught 89b; *s* naught by (of, to) 91b, h; *s* a net 59; *s* nether 26b; *s* not by 91c; *s* off 147; *s* on 131, 148; *s* a person on another 47c; *s* open 28; *s* order in 58; *s* in order 25b; *s* out 149; *s* over 150; *s* a person over another 47; *s* the pace 54d; *s* (on, a-) packing 114b, c, d; *s* a palette 71c; *s* to partners 103; *s* a pattern 54; *s* at pawn 27; *s* pen to paper 18h; *s* (= frame) a picture 63b; *s* in (on) the pillory 18d; *s* to places 103; *s* a plant 12, 101; *s* to pledge 27; *s* a pot 62; *s* a price on 91h; *s* a price on one's head 43; *s* in prison 18d; *s* the psalm 54c; *s* a question 55c; *s* a rate 86; *s* at a rate 89; *s* a razor 75; *s* remedy 32; *s* right 25b; *s* a ruff 80; *s* the saddle 7; *s* sail 65b; *s* to sale 27; *s* a saw 76; *s* to school 26; *s* on the sea 18f; *s* one's seal 23; *s* on a seat 1; *s* the scene 74; *s* to seed 98c; *s* a siege before 18g; *s* in one's sight 18c; *s* sight of 39b; *s* a snare 59; *s* a song 73; *s* the sponge 67b; *s* a squadron 70; *s* the stage 74; *s* a stake 14; *s* a step 19d; *s* a stitch 60b; *s* a stock 100; *s* a stone 63, 120b; *s* a stroke 20; *s* the stroke 54d; *s* a table 71; *s* in tack 57; *s* a task 55; *s* teeth on a plate 63c; *s* one's teeth 95; *s* on a throne 1; *s* through 151; *s* a time for 51; *s* to (prep.) 113c, (adv.) 152; *s* (= add) one thing to another 33; *s* together 153; *s* a trap 59; *s* tryst 56; *s* type 72; *s* up 154; *s* upon 132; *s* upright 28; *s* a varnish on 41; *s* a watch 45; *s* on the water 18f; *s* a person on his (or the) way 111b; *s* to wed 27; *s* one's wit at 117b; *s* woad 96a; *s* one's words 68c; *s* on write 21.

See also the lists of phrases under senses 25, 89b, 91.

**set,** *v.*[2] [f. SET *sb.*[2]] *trans.* To group (pupils) into sets (see SET *sb.*[2] 2d); also *absol.* Hence ˈ**setting** *vbl. sb.*[2]

**1953** *Organ. Comprehensive Secondary Schools* (London County Council) 14 A practicable arrangement would be to re-set only across three adjacent forms. 'Setting' in this way would not determine the rate at which each set would work. **1957** B. SIMON *New Trends in Eng. Educ.* II. 46, I will not ask the reader to follow me in the intricacies of fifth-year setting. **1962** J. VAIZEY *Britain in Sixties* v. 56 Some..feel that.. children should be 'setted' for each subject. **1965** *Observer* 7 Nov. 4/8 Mathematics teachers consider it necessary to set after two terms. **1973** MORRISON & MCINTYRE *Teachers & Teaching* (ed. 2) iii. 126 There is reason to believe that the practise of 'setting'— different streaming for each of several subjects—reduces these effects. **1975** *Language for Life* (Dept. Educ. & Sci.) xv. 224 Speaking purely for English, most of us have reservations about arrangements by which pupils are streamed or setted according to ability.

**set** (sɛt), *ppl. a.* Forms: see SET *v.*[1] A. 3. [pa. pple. of SET *v.*[1]]

When in concord with a following sb., it was formerly often hyphened.

**I. 1.** In various strictly participial uses, with reference to corresponding senses of the vb.

**a.** Of a task, a subject of study or discourse: Imposed or prescribed. Now *rare* exc. in ***set book***: a book 'set' or prescribed as one of the subjects; also ***set text***.

*a* **1300** *Cursor M.* 26270 Quen nede es for to slak þe sett penance þat es for plight. **1709** STEELE & SWIFT *Tatler* No. 66 ¶1 When you are to talk on a Set Subject. **1863** W. C. BALDWIN *Afr. Hunting* i. 2 My natural aversion to any set task. **1888** *Daily News* 5 Nov. 5/2 Set books are for a Tripos the exception rather than the rule. **1966** N. NICOLSON in H. Nicolson *Diaries & Lett.* (1966) 28 He read..the whole of Aeschylus' *Seven Against Thebes* because it was my set-book at school. **1968** *Listener* 22 Aug. 244/3 By the end of 1967, however, it had sold more than 15,000 copies, mainly because a few enterprising examining bodies had chosen it as a set book for A-level GCE. **1982** *Times* 12 Aug. 8/3 Mrs. Thatcher's Family Policy Committee has been given a set text in the form of a paper by the recently appointed head of the Downing Street Policy Unit.

†**b.** Of law: Imposed by definite enactment; = POSITIVE 1. *Obs.*

*c* **1200** *Trin. Coll. Hom.* 17 Hit is iset lage..þat me sal children fuluhtnie. *c* **1320** *Cast. Love* 170 Two lawen Adam scholde..holden In Paradis: þat on him was þorw kynde i-let, þat oþer was clept lawe I-set. *Ibid.* 193 þe kuyndeliche and þe set ek, Boþe his lawen he to-brek.

†**c.** Of plants or trees: Planted, not self-sown or growing wild. Also, that has been 'set' or dibbled, not 'sown' broadcast. *Obs.*

**1562** TURNER *Herbal* II. 60, ii. sortes of sowen or set myrtel trees. *Ibid.* 60b, The set or gardin Myrt tre. **1644** SYMONDS *Diary* (Camden) 44 Round about the howse many rowes of sett tall oakes. **1780** *Lett. & Pap. Bath Soc.* I. 15 A whole field was sown, and set, in alternate stetches... The produce of the set part was eight bushels per acre more than the sown.

†**d.** Provided with a musical setting. *Obs.*

**1598** YONG *Diana* 237 The sweetenes of a Set-song. **1600** BODENHAM *Eng. Helicon* 4 M. Birds set Song. **1706** A. BEDFORD *Temple Mus.* xi. 226 Our Psalm Tunes were composed before any of our Set Services.

**e.** Placed in a setting, mounted.

**1535** COVERDALE *1 Chron.* xxx [xxix.]. 2 Onix stones, set Rubyes [1611 stones to be set], and stones of dyuerse coloures. *a* **1732** [see NEW-SET *ppl. a.*].

**f.** Inserted in a fixed framework, built in.

***set bowl*** (U.S.), a lavatory basin. ***set tub*** (U.S.), a tub for washing, fixed in masonry. Also ***set-pot*** (see 8).

**1884** HOWELLS *Silas Lapham* (1891) I. 66 I'll do the wash .., said Mrs. Lapham. I presume you'll let me have set tubs. **1899** —— *Ragged Lady* 185 He sympathized with her in her wish that there was a set-bowl in her room.

**g.** Of the teeth: Clenched.

**1810** SCOTT *Lady of L.* III. xi, With set teeth and clenched hand. **1876** A. J. EVANS *Through Bosnia* viii. 368 The sailors ..with set teeth laboured at the oars as for grim life.

**h.** Of types: That have been 'set up'.

**1837** CARLYLE *Fr. Rev.* II. II. iv, Your military ranked Arrangement going all (as the Typographers say of set types, in a similar case) rapidly to pie!

**i.** Of jelly: that has become firm. Cf. SET *v.*[1] 97a, c.

**1973** *Cooking for Today* (Good Housekeeping) 264/4 Pour half this vanilla jelly on to the set coffee jelly. **1974** M. LINDLAW *Super Sweets & Puddings* 58 Make up the Angel Delight..and pipe or swirl on to the set jelly.

**2.** Appointed or prescribed beforehand; †appointed for observance by the Church. Hence (with sense less distinctly ppl.), Fixed, definite, not subject to uncertainty or alteration.

**a.** Of a point of time.

*c* **1050** *Laws Northumb. Priests* §36 (Liebermann) 382 Ȝif preost on ȝesetne timan tida ne ringe oððe tida ne singe. *c* **1205** LAY. 25459 Arður þa hehte aðelest kinge to ane isette time þat folc isomnien. *a* **1225** *Ancr. R.* 412 Ȝif out limpeð misliche þet ȝe beon nout i-huseled i þeos i-sette termes. **1375** BARBOUR *Bruce* VIII. 213 Quhen the set day cumin was He sped him fast toward the place. *c* **1477** CAXTON *Jason* 14b, The triews faylled at time sette and exspired. **1597** HOOKER *Eccl. Pol.* V. (1617) 377 Festiuall Solemnities and set-dayes. **1628** EARLE *Microcosm.* (Arb.) 37 An old Colledge Butler..keepes the set houres at his booke more duly then any. *a* **1659** BP. BROWNRIG *Serm.* (1674) I. i. 12 God..sets much by them, that put him not off with some set-dayes service. **1701** SWIFT *Contests Nobles & Commons* Wks. 1755 II. I. 28 The set time for payment. **1769** E. BANCROFT *Guiana* 325 The Indians have no set time of eating. **1837** CARLYLE *Fr. Rev.* II. VI. i, There will not have arrived, at the set day, Three-thousand of them in all.

**b.** Of wages, income, rent, quantity. Now *rare*.

*a* **1225** *Ancr. R.* 428 Non ancre seruant ne ouhte..uorto asken i-sette huire, bute mete & cloð. **1504** *Acc. Ld. High*

*Treas. Scot.* II. 262 Item, to the said Maister Andro, that he gaif in almous be the Kingis command, by the set almous.. xxxjs. **1587** R. HOVENDEN in *Collect.* (O.H.S.) I. 217 Which a sett rent can no wise afford. **1593** NASHE *Christ's T.* Wks. 1910 II. 149 Half a Crowne..is the sette pryce of a strumpets soule. **1633** MASSINGER *Guardian* I. i, Some.. make a set living on't. **1651** HOBBES *Leviath.* II. xxii. 123 It is not a set number that makes the Assembly Unlawfull. **1705** ADDISON *Italy, Switzerl.* 480 Handsom Fountains planted at set Distances from one End of the Streets to the other. **1851** HELPS *Comp. Solit.* ix. (1854) 157 There always will be a set amount of wrongdoing. **1891** *Labour Commission* Gloss., *Set wages*, a fixed weekly wage, apart altogether from piece-work.

**c.** Of rules, order, a form of words, etc.

**1570–6** LAMBARDE *Peramb. Kent* (1826) 239 The..Princelike Palaices..which the Archbishops..kept..to perfourme their set solemnities of housekeeping. **1597** HOOKER *Eccl. Pol.* v. xxvi. §1 A strange conceipt, that to serue God with any set forme of common prayer is superstitious. *a* **1619** FOTHERBY *Atheom.* II. i. §7 (1622) 182 As strictly tied vnto his set-motion, as a Mill-horse to his Mill. **1630** BP. HALL *Occas. Medit.* lxxx. (1633) 200 The Monarchical government requires a constant and regular course of the set degrees of rule and inferiority. **1705** STANHOPE *Paraphr.* II. 215 A long preparation of set Diet. **1710** BERKELEY *Princ. Hum. Knowl.* §30 The set rules or established methods. **1871** EARLE *Philol. Eng. Tongue* §292 The set words of a proverb. **1883** JAS. GILMOUR *Mongols* xvii. 201 Our religious system has no set form of liturgy to be got off by heart and repeated.

†**d.** Of persons, things, places: Fixed, specified, definite. *Obs.*

**1594** ? GREENE *Selimus* 327 Things that were as common as the day, Did then to set possessors first obey. **1709** SHAFTESB. *Moralists* I. i. 5 There are formal Set-Places, where..there is enough said and taught of this kind.

**e.** Of a meal in a hotel, etc.: consisting of a predetermined collection of dishes or items of food at a fixed price.

**1914** 'SAKI' *Beasts & Super-Beasts* 308 The one-and-sixpenny set dinner receded..to a Sunday extravagance. **1923** C. STONE *Let.* 30 June in C. Mackenzie *My Life & Times* (1966) V. 250, I fancy F. will get herself set teas, and other meals out. **1938** D. DU MAURIER *Rebecca* xxvi. 423 Colonel Julyan waded through the whole set lunch. **1957** W. CAMP *Prospects of Love* III. i. 148 She promptly chose the five shilling set meal. **1973** J. PATTINSON *Search Warrant* vii. 105 If you have the set lunch, it comes cheaper. **1978** *Times* 3 June 11/4 There was an advertised set lunch at £5.50 plus VAT.

**3.** Deliberate, intentional. **a.** Of a purpose or design: Deliberately conceived. Chiefly in phrases, *of* (or †*on*, †*a*) *set purpose* (see PURPOSE *sb.* 10, 11).

**1456** SIR G. HAYE *Law Arms* (S.T.S.) 84 To byde in felde fermly of sett purpos..cummys of a calde sett mynde confermyt in hardyness with deliberacioun. **1530** PALSGR. 835/1 Evyn a set purpose. **1581** PETTIE tr. *Guazzo's Civ. Conv.* I. (1586) 24 b, How much more hainous those faults are which are committed of set mallice, then those which are done of blinde ignorance. **1600** in R. M. Fergusson *Logie* (1905) II. 22 *note*, Cruellie slaine be yame..vpon sait purpois and foirthocht fellonie. **1695** WOODWARD *Nat. Hist. Earth* VI. (1723) 303 Should a Man go about with never so set Study and Design. **1872** MORLEY *Voltaire* 57 This fatal predominance was first founded, though assuredly not of set design, by Voltaire.

**b.** Of phrases, forms of expression: Deliberately composed, not spontaneously arising. Also, customary, 'stereotyped.' Cf. 5 d.

*in good set terms*: often used (after the context of the Shaks. example) for 'roundly', 'with outspoken severity'.

**1600** SHAKS. *A.Y.L.* II. vii. 17, I met a foole i'th Forrest.. Who..rail'd on Lady Fortune in good termes, In good set termes, and yet a motley foole. **1695** J. EDWARDS *Author. O. & N. Test.* III. 382 The set sayings of the Stoicks. *a* **1700** EVELYN *Diary* 27 Jan. 1689, He did this without any set or formal repetitions, as one who had learn'd things without book. **1827** SCOTT *Surg. Dau.* ix He drew it up in good set terms, like one who had his senses much at his command. **1832** LEWIS *Use & Ab. Pol. Terms* Introd. 1 The set phrase of Scientific inquirers. **1860** MOTLEY *Netherl.* x. (1865) II. 85 The governor-general..often denounced him in good set terms. **1861** DICKENS *Gt. Expect.* xxxii, It had no set beginning, as Dear Mr. Pip, or Dear Pip.

†**c.** Contrived in order to deceive. *Obs.*

**1603** FLORIO *Montaigne* I. v. 10 Nor by surprises, or stratagems by night, nor by set-flights [*par fuittes apostees*].

**4.** (In *set battle, field*) = PITCHED *ppl. a.*[1] 2. Now *rare* (cf. sense 5).

**1375** BARBOUR *Bruce* VIII. 367 The king, in set battalʒe.. Vencust him with a gret menʒe. *c* **1470** HENRY *Wallace* XI. 9 Off set battaillis fyve he dyscumfyt haill. **1551** ROBINSON tr. *More's Utopia* II. (1895) 257 In set fylde the wyues doo stande euerye one by here owne husbandes syde. **1572** J. SADLER tr. *Vegetius* Pref. ¶*. ii. b, Whether they should fight in skirmishe, or set battel. **1664–5** PEPYS *Diary* 17 Feb., He hath fought more set fields than any man in England hath done. **1773** HAMPTON *Polybius* IV. Contents XIV, The Carthaginians..are defeated in a set engagement.

*transf.* **1883** F. M. CRAWFORD *Dr. Claudius* xvii, I challenged her to a set flirtation.

**5.** Formal, ceremonious, regular. **a.** As the designation of a particular style of handwriting: see quots. Now only *Hist.*

**1513** [see HAND *sb.* 16]. **1594** SHAKS. *Rich. III*, III. vi. 2 Here is the Indictment..Which in a set Hand fairely is engross'd. **1685** MATLOCK *Fax Nova Artis Scribendi* 6 The Set-Hand is thought fittest..for Ingrossing all Evidences of Lands. *Ibid.* 11 The English-Ingrossing-Hand, commonly called Set-Secretary. **1784** ASTLE *Orig. Writ.* v. 98 The writing which prevailed in England from..596 to the middle of the eleventh century, is generally termed Saxon, and may be divided into five kinds, namely, the Roman Saxon, the Set Saxon, the Running hand Saxon, the Mixed Saxon, and the Elegant Saxon. *Ibid.* 143 The specimens of the charters..are composed partly of characters called Set Chancery and Common Chancery. **1885** E. M. THOMPSON in *Encycl. Brit.* XVIII. 156/2 In the 8th century appears the set book-hand in an even..character.

**b.** Of a meal, a meeting for business or pleasure: Carefully pre-arranged; attended with some degree of ceremony or formality; stated, regular, formal. So †*set table*.

**1606** HOLLAND *Sueton.* 71 He feasted daily: and never otherwise than at a set table [L. *cena recta*]. **1653** H. COGAN tr. *Pinto's Trav.* ii. 3 Keeping a set table for above seven hundred persons. **1680** COTTON *Compl. Gamester* (ed. 2) 95 They have one most egregious piece of Roguery more, and that is playing the High-Game at Putt; and this is to be done but once at a Sett-meeting. **1693** LOCKE *Educ.* §14 (1699) 21 The Romans usually fasted till Supper; the only set Meal, even of those who eat more than once a Day. **1718** *Free-thinker* No. 19. 133 His Physicians advised him to leave off Set-Suppers. **1818** in Lady Morgan *Autobiog.* (1859) 166 It is not a set party, but one without full dress or ceremony. **1862** *Chamb. Encycl.* s.v. *Curling*, These *bon-spiels* or set matches, are contested with immense spirit. **1868** E. EDWARDS *Ralegh* I. xxii. 495 The ambassador would fain have discussed such grave matters only at a set audience.

†**c.** Of costume: Suited to ceremonial occasions.

**1698** FRYER *Acc. E. India & P.* 390 The set dress of the Persian. **1676** ETHEREGE *Sir Fopling Flutter* IV. ii, We should not always be in a Set Dress.

**d.** Of a discourse, treatise, etc.: Elaborate, composed in due form; expressly or systematically dealing with a subject.

*set speech*: public speech more or less elaborate; an oration, as distinguished from extemporaneous or informal utterances.

**1573** G. HARVEY *Letter-bk.* (1884) 12, I am inforcid rather to bungle up a pelting histori then to write a set epistle. **1608** CHAPMAN *Trag. Byron* v. i. Q 1, The most lawierly deliuery Of his set speeches. **1655** STANLEY *Hist. Philos.* (1701) 4 He did not confine himself to set Lectures in the Chair. **1662** STILLINGFL. *Orig. Sacræ* II. ii. §2 A learned man hath in a set discourse endeavoured to shew the great defects that were in it. **1760–2** GOLDSM. *Cit. W.* xxx, I had prepared a set introductory speech for the occasion. **1817** MOORE *Lalla Rookh* (1824) 126 The young lady dies, in a set speech. **1834** MACAULAY *Ess., Pitt* ¶29 He was no speaker of set speeches. His few prepared discourses were complete failures. **1886** C. E. PASCOE *London of To-day* viii. (ed. 3) 89 It is not easy to learn beforehand when the great popular leaders may be expected to make set orations.

†**e.** Regularly established. *Obs.*

**1702** C. MATHER *Magn. Chr.* IV. Introd. (1852) 9 They soon determined..that set-schools are so necessary there is no doing without them.

**6.** That has assumed a permanent form or condition; immovable, persistent. **a.** Of facial expression, looks, or countenance, tones of voice: Fixed, rigid, unvarying.

**1605** CHAPMAN *All Fools* IV. i, A set countenance Of rage and choller. *a* **1625** FLETCHER *Nice Valour* 1, Look, who comes here, sir! his love fit's upon him: I know it, by that set smile, and those congies. **1760** FRANKLIN *Ess.* Wks. 1840 II. 127 Those even, set tones, so common among readers. **1865** SWINBURNE *Poems & Ball., Two Dreams* 28 The heavy sun's Set face of heat stopped all the songs. **1892** BIERCE *In Midst of Life* 96 In that set immobile face was no sign; it was as hard as bronze.

**b.** Of a feeling, attitude of mind: Fixed, settled, immovable. †Of action: Resolute. Also (*dial.* and *U.S.*) of persons: Obstinate. (Cf. HARD-SET 3.)

*a* **1625** FLETCHER *False One* IV. ii, Why do you frowne? good gods, what a set-anger Have you forc'd into your face! **1650** BAXTER *Saint's R.* IV. vi. (1654) 146 The set and solemn acting of all the powers of the soul. **1748** RICHARDSON *Clarissa* (1811) III. 38, I can not, at present, write to every particular unless I would be in set defiance. **1848** BARTLETT *Dict. Amer.* s.v., He is very set in his ways. **1848** LOWELL *Biglow P.* Ser. I. ix (end), Wen I hev once made up my mind, a meet'nhus aint sotter. **1896** *Harper's Mag.* Apr. 680/1 'You are a terribly set person,' she said,..after she had consented to let him have his own way.

**c.** Of a kind of weather: Persistent, likely to continue some time. So quasi-*adv.* in *set fair* (also *fig.* and in extended use).

*set fair* is usually marked on English barometers at the point indicating that the height of the mercury is 30½ inches.

**1699** DAMPIER *Voy.* II. ii. 55 Then you have set Rains till the latter end of August. **1823–4** *Encycl. Metrop.* (1845) XV. 281 To the next half-inch below this highest point are written *set fair* on the one side, and *set frost* on the other. **1842** DICKENS *Amer. Notes* xiv. (1893) 167 The road..was certainly enough to have shaken tempers that were not resolutely at Set Fair, down to some inches below Stormy. **1873** BROWNING *Red Cotton Night-Cap Country* ii. 108 Like some kindly weathercock..stuck fast at Set Fair. **1921** W. DE LA MARE *Mem. Midget* xxix. 197 Her mood, like our weather that April, was almost always 'set fair'. **1978** J. PEARSON *Façades* xxiii. 399 Everything appeared set fair for the happiest of stays.

†**d.** Of demeanour: Composed, grave. *Obs.*

*a* **1660** in Morris *Troubles Cath. Foref.* (1872) I. vi. 286 She was always of a set and womanly carriage, not wild or given much to play.

**e.** Chiefly predicative: Of settled form or habit of body.

**1861** HUGHES *Tom Brown at Oxf.* ii, The other man was evidently a year or two older than himself, his figure was more set. **1861** *Temple Bar* IV. 53 Their limbs are not sufficiently 'set' to prevent serious accidental injury. **1894** ASTLEY *50 Yrs. Life* I. 144 Orme was, as we should say of a racehorse, 'too set.'

**7.** With prefixed adv.: Having a specified position, location, arrangement, conformation, build, adjustment, disposition, pitch, etc.

See *broad-set* (BROAD *a.* D. 2), DEEP-SET, *fine-set* (FINE *a.* D. 2 b), *firm-set* (FIRM *a.* C. 2), HARD-SET, HIGH SET, ILL-SET, *low-set* (LOW *a.* 5), STRONG-SET, THICK-SET, *thin-set* (THIN *a.* D. II), WELL-SET.

**13..** *K. Alis.* 7112 Cadace was a ferly best, Thries set [*Laud MS.* shet] teth was in his teste.

**II.** Combinations.

**8.** In special collocations (most of which are hyphened as compounds, and often stressed on the first syllable): †**set board** *Sc.*, (*a*) ? a washboard in a ship [cf. Du. *zetboord*, G. *setzbord*]; (*b*) some kind of table; **set changes** *Bell-ringing*, = *set peal*; †**set cloth**, a kind of worsted fabric; **set copper**, a form of metallic copper containing about 6 per cent of cuprous oxide, produced by oxidation during refining; **set dance**, a quadrille, country-dance, or the like; **set iron** [cf. Du. *zetijzer*, G. *setzeisen*] *Ship-building*, a bar of soft iron, admitting of being bent so as to be used for transferring curves from the scrive-board to the bending plate; **set joint** *U.S. slang* (see quots. and *flat joint* (*b*) s.v. FLAT *a.* 15); **set line** [cf. Du. *zetlijn*], a fishing-line with baited hooks, pegged or anchored; also *attrib.*; †**set match**, an agreement, conspiracy, an appointment made for a highway robbery (cf. *to set a match*, SET *v.*[1] 56); **set net**, a fishing net fastened across a stream or channel, into which the fish are driven; †**set peal** *Bellringing*, a ringing of a peal of bells in one position for a considerable length of time before a change is given; **set point**, the value of a physical quantity that an automatic controller or regulator is set to maintain; also *transf.*; **set-pot, 'setpot**, (*a*) *dial.* a fixed cauldron or boiler used for heating water for domestic purposes; (*b*) a copper pan, heated by a special flue, used in making varnish, and for heating oil, size, etc.; †**set-pull** *Bell-ringing*, the position of a bell when raised so that it stands mouth upwards; **set scene**, an apparatus built up and placed in position upon a theatrical stage before the rise of the curtain; a collection of side scenes, 'skies', etc. depending upon one another for a particular effect; so *set scenery*; **set scrum(mage)**, *Rugby Football*, an organized scrummage ordered by the referee during the course of play; opp. *loose scrum(mage)* s.v. LOOSE *a.* 9; **set shot** *Basketball*, a shot at the basket made from a still position; **set sod**, a turf used in building up a bank of a ditch in the operation of water-tabling; **set square**, (*a*) a plate of wood, metal, etc. in the form of a right-angled triangle, the acute angles being either 60° and 30° or both 45°, used by draughtsmen as a guide for drawing lines at one of these angles; (*b*) a form of T-square with an additional arm turning on a pivot, for drawing lines at fixed angles to the head; (*c*) a joiner's square; †**set-stitched** *a.*, ? of 'set-work' embroidery; **set stocking** *Agric.* (orig. *N.Z.*), the grazing of animals, esp. sheep, in the same pasture for a considerable period; so **set-stock** *v. trans.* See also SET-WORK.

**1512** *Acc. Ld. High Treas. Scot.* IV. 456 Item..for xv^c seym and ruf for the *set burdis of the greit schip. **1529** *Reg. Mag. Sig. Scot.* (1883) 178 A comptar burd price 2 markis, a set burd with formis and trestis price 13s. 4d. **1677** [STEDMAN] *Campanalogia* 169 For such as have not yet attain'd the skill to ring these compleat peals, *Sett-changes are very proper for them, being easie. **1688** HOLME *Armoury* III. 462/2 Ringing in Set Changes, that is, the Bells being Set, they order which Bell shall lead away & what to follow. **1872** ELLACOMBE *Bells of Ch.* iii. in *Ch. Bells Devon* 231 Its members rang nothing but rounds and set changes, till about the year 1642, when single changes were first attempted. **1467–8** *Rolls of Parlt.* V. 629 Divers Wollen Clothes, some called brode *sette Clothes, and that other called streite sette Clothes. **1523** *Act 14 & 15 Hen. VIII*, c. 11 Vesses, otherwise called Sette clothes of diuers colours. **1904** *Trans. Amer. Inst. Mining Engineers* XXXIV. 671 Some of the copper is oxidized to cuprous oxide and dissolved by the metal bath. When the quantity of dissolved cuprous oxide has reached about 6 per cent, the metal is said to have been brought to '*set-copper'. **1959** J. NEWTON *Extractive Metallurgy* vi. 376 Usually it is not possible to take any short-cuts in refining copper—the metal must be carried to the set-copper stage and then poled. **1712** ADDISON *Spect.* No. 434 §5 Several Regular Tunes and *Sett Dances. **1800** WEEMS *Washington* ii. (1877) 11 He has carried down many a sett dance with her. **1874** THEARLE *Naval Archit.* 83 When the scrive board is used, a flat rod of soft iron termed the '*set iron' is bent to the curvature. **1926** MAINES & GRANT *Wise-Crack Dict.* 14/1 **Set joint*, unbeatable game. **1931** *Amer. Speech* VI. 335 *Set-joint*,..a gambling device operated with a numbered wheel and arrow-spindle. These are always fitted with a *gimmick* which prevents the customer from winning too often, or which may be used by the operator to lead the customer on until he will place a large bet, when the operator applies the gimmick and the customer loses. **1865** BERTRAM *Harvest of Sea* 160 *Set-line-fishing..can only be practised in places where the tide recedes to a considerable distance. **1586** J. HOOKER *Hist. Irel.* 37/2 in *Holinshed*, These things came not thus to passe, as it were by a *set match. **1592** GREENE *Discov. Coosenage* C 3, When their other trades fail, as..y^e high lawier, when he hath no set match to ride about. **1614** BP.

HALL *Contempl.* VII. *Aaron's Censer* 269 A set match betwixt the brethren. **1481–90** *Howard Househ. Bks.* (Roxb.) 192 A *sett net of ij. fadom. **1745** BLOMEFIELD *Norfolk* II. 866 Two Wardens of the Fishermen-Company..to inspect the Sett Netts belonging to them. **1863** *Rep. Sea Fisheries Comm.* (1865) II. 1190/1 Small quantities of herrings were taken with set-nets close in-shore. **16..** in *Eng. Gilds* 290 If the Master..shall neglect to warn the Company..for to ring a bisett *sett peale, he shall pay..one shilling. **1941** T. J. RHODES *Industr. Instruments for Measurem. & Control* ix. 419 Where it is not permissible for the process temperature to deviate for any appreciable period from the original *set point, it is necessary to use a mode of control previously described as proportional and floating. **1972** *Science* 9 June 1125/1 One of the principal homeo-static 'set points', that for body temperature, seems to depend on the constant ratio of $Na^+$ to $Ca^{2+}$ in the caudal hypothalamus. **1975** D. G. FINK *Electronics Engineers' Handbk.* XXIV. 14 Display of the measurement, set point, and output levels is normally provided. **1839** URE *Dict. Arts* s.v. *Varnish*, Black japan is made by putting into the *set-pot 48 lbs. of Naples or any other of the foreign asphaltums. **1862** ROBINSON *Dial. Leeds*, *Set pot*, a stone boiler or 'copper', with a fire-grate under, for the purpose of boiling and 'stewing' dirty linen. **1873** E. SPON *Workshop Rec.* Ser. I. 65/2 Take the gum pot from the fire; let it cool for a few minutes, then pour it into the oil in the set pot. **1677** [STEDMAN] *Campanalogia* 26 The falling of the bells from a *Set-pull. *Ibid.* 46 Supposing that a peal of 5 bells were raised, and rung at a Sett-pull. **1866** 'OLD STAGER' *Stage Reminisc.* ix. 122 The sizes and sets of yarns occupied his thoughts much less than theatrical 'lengths' and '*set scenes'. **1887** *Spectator* 25 June 857/2 Theatrical speculators now spend such vast sums on the upholstery of their set scenes. **1854** FAIRHOLT *Dict. Terms Art* 382 The scenery..was entirely of the nature of what is now termed *set-scenery, regularly built up by carpenters before the curtain rises, to be taken to pieces again when it falls. **1938** MACDONALD & REES *Rugger Practice & Tactics* ii. 34 Few tries are scored in good football by movements that start from a *set scrum. **1960** E. S. & W. J. HIGHAM *High Speed Rugby* xiv. 185 We deal with the set scrum first, because it forms the basis of loose scrums and loose rucks. **1977** *S. Wales Guardian* 27 Oct. 16/3 By this stage Llandovery's forwards were dominating the set scrums. **1925** R. M. RAYNER *Man. Rugby Football for Public Schools* viii. 47 (*heading*) On getting possession in '*set' scrummages. **1971** *Times* 15 Feb. 9/4 Bryce, Miller and Moroney are an experienced front row and rubbed in the fact..at the set scrummages. **1940** *N.Y. Times* 21 Jan. v-1/3 The cadets, their *set shots hitting the mark with a remarkable degree of accuracy, gained the upper hand at the outset. **1976** *Milton Keynes Express* 9 July 42/3 Wickham, Wynn and Waller were all desperately unlucky with set shots. **1844** H. STEPHENS *Bk. Farm* II. 574 After a few of these smaller sods have been made ready, the hedger lays them, with the grass side downwards, upon the edges of the *set-sods. **1854** in *Specif. Patents, Artists' Instr.* (1872) 73 An improved artizans' tool, which may be used as a measuring rule, straight edge, *set square, T square, bevel, and plumb rule. **1857** BINNS *Orthogr. Projection* 1 One 8-inch set square. **1884** HOLTZAPFFEL *Turning* V. 64 The sliderest is adjusted to it by means of the set square, an instrument with a straight shaft and a steel blade fixed to it at right angles. **1892** ELEANOR ROWE *Chip-Carving* (1895) 15 The set-square of 45°. *Ibid.* 7 The 60° set-square. **1760** STERNE *Tr. Shandy* III. xxix, An old *set-stitch'd chair. **1956** *N.Z. Jrnl. Sci. & Technol.* A. XXXVII. 555 Most New Zealand farmers producing fat lambs..generally prefer to *set-stock the ewes and lambs from lambing time onwards. **1964** *Weekly News* (Auckland) 21 Oct. 54/4 Under New Zealand conditions, ewes and lambs are usually set-stocked from lambing until weaning, although rotational grazing is practised on some farms. **1981–2** *Deer Farmer* (N.Z.) Summer 8/3 Hinds are set-stocked or mob-stocked over winter at about 10 to the acre. **1950** *N.Z. Jrnl. Agric.* Feb. 100/2 Make sure that the calves are rotated through the paddocks at intervals of a few days. *Set stocking at this time of the year is bound to result in..some deaths. **1975** *Country Life* 26 June 1702/1 In the last 35 years we would seem to have gone full circle—from set-stocking, strip-grazing, paddock-grazing..and now the so called 'intensive' set-stocking.

**9.** In parasynthetic derivatives. *rare.*

**1614** CHAPMAN *Androm. Lib.* Ep. Ded. ¶3 b, The one-ear'd Race Of set-eyed vulgars. **1615** —— *Odyss.* XVII. 602 You are a sawcy set-fac't Vagabond. **1633** T. STAFFORD *Pac. Hib.* I. xi. 74 The treacherous Guid, who did upon a set purposed malice draw this Draught, was..hanged.

**10.** With adverbs (see the corresponding combinations of the vb.), as *set-apart* (rare), *set-down*, *-on*, *-out*, etc. With specific meaning: **set-down** *nonce-use*, described in books, recognized; **set-in**, (*a*) inserted, inset; (*b*) of rain, etc. that has set in or become continuous; **set-off** *Sc.*, of part of a tenement, let off to a sub-tenant; **set-on** *Sc.* (see quot. 1825); **set-up**, (*a*) established; (*b*) in phr. *well set-up* (see quot. 1867; also in wider use); (*c*) *dial.* and *colloq.* conceited, 'stuck up'; (*d*) of type, composed.

**1830** GEN. P. THOMPSON *Exerc.* (1842) I. 292 This act of disinterested baseness and *set-apart iniquity. **1858** —— *Audi Alt.* lxxvi. II. 28 All have sunk into a state of lamentable indifference, there is no burning zeal left except among the set-apart. *a* **1850** ROSSETTI *Dante & Circle* II. (1874) 281 'Tis no *set-down sickness that I have, Nor are my pains set down. **1884** RUSKIN *Bible of Amiens* I. 9 *note*, The first fixed and set-down footsteps. **1534** *Acc. Ld. High Treas. Scot.* VI. 185 To be ane *set in nek to ane veluet slop. **1866** LIVINGSTONE *Last Jrnls.* (1873) I. vi. 158 A set-in rain came on. **1875** KNIGHT *Dict. Mech.* 1534/2 *Side-notes*, marginal or set-in notes. **1895** *Montgomery Ward Catal.* Spring & Summer 280/2 Men's overshirts... Set in bosom, yoke back, [etc.]. **1969** *Sears Catal.* Spring/Summer 37/3 Wing collar, set-in sleeves. *a* **1722** FOUNTAINHALL *Decis.* I. 454 One may set *set-off chambers and parts of a house. **1825** JAMIESON, **Set-on*, a term applied to what is singed or slightly burned in the pot or pan. **1864** *Q. Jrnl. Sci.* I. 467 Well set-on tails and very sloping shoulders. **1710** PALMER *Proverbs* 359 If the pomp..be carry'd out of proportion,.. it is an ill *set-out ambition. **1809** MALKIN *Gil Blas* III. iii. (Rtldg.) 87 There was no want of magnificence, good taste, or a well-designed set out table! **1607** New-*set-up [see NEW-SET *ppl. a.*]. **1856** JULIA KAVANAGH *Rachel Gray* iv. 66 Serve her right—the set up thing! **1867** SMYTH *Sailor's Word-bk.* s.v., Soldiers, mariners, and small-arm men, well drilled, and instructed to be upright and soldierlike in their carriage, are 'well set up'. **1878** *Encycl. Brit.* VIII. 116/1 Set-up type is also sometimes copied thus.

† **set**, *conj. Sc. Obs.* [Prob. evolved from the imperative or the pa. pple. (in absolute construction) of SET *v.*[1] in the sense 'to put the case,' 'to suppose (that)'. Cf. G. *gesetzt* = 'on the assumption that'.] Though, although. Also with *at* (= that).

Very frequent in the *Sc. Leg. Saints.*

*c* **1375** *Sc. Leg. Saints* xxvii. (*Machor*) 26 God mad hym to rest syn in fraunce,..til honouryt be, set þare a strangere was he. **1390** GOWER *Conf.* III. 345 And sett thou myhtest lust atteigne, Of every lust thende is a peine. *c* **1425** WYNTOUN *Cron.* I. Prol. 33 And set to þis I gif my will My wit I ken sa skant þartill That I drede saire þame till offend. *c* **1470** HENRY *Wallace* XI. 1432 Blaym nocht the buk, set I be wnperfyt. *c* **1500** *Lancelot* 99 And set yhoue clep one erbis and one treis, Sche heris not thi wo. **1513** DOUGLAS *Æneis* VI. Prol. 31 Set thow think this bot sport.

**set-**, the stem of SET *v.*[1] in comb., chiefly in sbs. derived from phr. with advs. (see SET *v.*[1] XII.): **set-forth**, a setting forth, departure; **set-in**, the beginning of a period of time, a spell of weather, or the like; **set-on**, the way in which a thing is set on. See also SET-BACK, SET-DOWN, SET-TO, SET-UP, etc. Also **set-fair**, the second coat in plastering; **set-hands**, applied to devices connected with setting the hands of a watch or clock; **set-ope** *dial.* [OPE *a.* and *sb.*], a device for holding open a gate, window, etc. (? *obs.*); **set-screw**, a screw that enables two contiguous parts to be brought into and held in their correct relative position, and is usually threaded the full length of the shank; in names of devices for adjusting or shaping, **set-bolt**, **-hammer**, **-stud** (see quots.). See also SETFAST.

**1627** CAPT. SMITH *Seaman's Gram.* ii. 5 *Set bolts for forcing the workes and plankes together. **1770–4** A. HUNTER *Georg. Ess.* (1803) I. 115 Backing out a Bolt, or Trenail, is driving it out by means of a tool called a Set-bolt. **1875** KNIGHT *Dict. Mech.*, *Set bolt*..*a.* One used as a drift, to force another bolt out of its hole. *b.* A bolt used to bring a plank to its bearings. **1812** P. NICHOLSON *Mech. Exerc.* 312 (*Plastering*), *Set Fair, is used after roughing-in and floated or pricked up and floated: it should be well troweled. **1829** SOUTHEY in *Corr. Car. Bowles* (1881) 177 Whether the next *set-forth from the house be for a marriage, or a funeral. **1855** FRANKE *Beil's Technol. Dict.* II. 456 **Set-hammer* (a hammer used in forging a set-off). **1883** CRANE *Smithy & Forge* 29 The 'set-hammer' is employed by being held against a certain portion of the heated iron and its top struck with the hammer. **1884** F. J. BRITTEN *Watch & Clockm.* 240 *Set-hands Arbor..the arbor in a three-quarter plate key-winding watch by which the hands are set. *Ibid.*, Set-hands Dial. *Ibid.*, Set hands Square. **1885** C. G. W. LOCK *Workshop Rec.* Ser. IV. 337/1 The set-hands stud. **1825** *New Monthly Mag.* XVI. 270 A regular *set in of Arabian wind is hardly to be expected. **1830** W. PHILLIPS *Mt. Sinai* IV. 331 At set-in of day. **1852** in Col. Hawker *Diary* (1893) II. 344 A regular set in of wet weather at last. **1847** W. C. L. MARTIN *Ox* 48/2 The *set-on of the tail is prominent, and detracts from their appearance. **1884** *Live Stock Jrnl.* 15 Aug. 154/2 In Puppies the winner..falls away too much from loin to set-on of tail. **1823** E. MOOR *Suffolk Words* 336 The gate oont keep back; the **set-ope* is gone. **1912** *Civ. Serv. Supply Assoc. Catal.* 1351 Melon frames..glazed with 21 oz. sheet glass, and fitted with improved set-opes. **1850** T. TREDGOLD *Steam Engine* (ed. 3) I. IV. 19 When the piston is taken to pieces.., the two *set-screws *h* are taken out of the holes into which they are screwed in the piston cover, and two handles screwed into them. **1855** FRANKE *Beil's Technol. Dict.* II. 456 Set-screw, Adjusting screw, Regulating screw. **1861** FAIRBAIRN *Iron* 129 Set screws,.. and all kinds of small work, are produced at the same rate. **1947** J. C. RICH *Materials & Methods of Sculpture* ix. 277 A setscrew is used [in proportional dividers] to hold the two arms together and to adjust the dividers. **1970** K. BALL *Fiat 600, 600D Autobook* vi. 69/1 Undo the setscrew securing the angled extension piece to the gear-rod. **1855** FRANKE *Beil's Technol. Dict.* II. 456 *Set-bolt*, **Set-stud* (a bolt screwed into the two pieces to be joined, and fastened so as to prevent the play of the pieces).

‖ **seta** ('siːtə). Pl. **setæ** ('siːtiː). [L. *sēta*, *saeta* bristle.]

**1.** *Bot.* A stiff hair or bristle-like body. Also the stalk which supports the theca or capsule of mosses.

**1793** T. MARTYN *Lang. Bot.*, *Seta*, a Bristle. A strong, stiff, roundish hair. A sort of pubescence.—Linneus also puts it for the scape of the capsule in Mosses. **1830** LINDLEY *Nat. Syst. Bot.* 320 *Thecæ* [of mosses], hollow urn-like cases seated upon a seta or stalk. **1832** —— *Introd. Bot.* I. ii. 104 When the *arista* proceeds from the very apex of the bracteæ, and not from below it, it is denominated in the writings of Palisot a *seta*. **1870** HOOKER *Stud. Flora* 219 Leaves covered ..with long flexuous scattered..hairs or setæ with bulbous bases.

**2.** *Zool.* A bristle; a bristle-like appendage.

*c* **1820** *Edin. Encycl.* (1830) VII. 432 *Ampithöe.* Superior antennæ, without a seta at the base of the last joint. **1826** KIRBY & SP. *Entomol.* IV. xliv. 225 A number of small hexapods distinguished by two pairs of anal setæ and a proleg. **1858** W. CLARK tr. *Van der Hoeven's Zool.* II. 553 *Gypaëtus.* Head closely plumed, bearded with rigid setæ under the bill. **1881–82** SAVILLE KENT *Man. Infusoria* II. 779 Two oblique rows of ventral setæ, three caudal, but no anal setæ.

† **setace.** *Obs. rare.* Also **settace.** [ad. mod.L. *sētāce-um* seton, neut. of *sētāceus*: see SETACEOUS *a.*] = SETON.

**1656** RIDGLEY *Pract. Physick* 114 Setaces are principle good, applyed to the Neck. *Ibid.* 155 He set a settace between the first and third Spondil.

**se'taceo-.** Used as combining form of next.

**1829** LOUDON *Encycl. Plants* 1104 *Setaceo-rostrate*, having a beak with the figure of a bristle. **1833** HOOKER in *Smith's Eng. Flora* V. I. 32 Leaves from a broad base setaceo-capillary spreading on all sides flexuose.

**setaceous** (sɪ'teɪʃəs), *a.* Also 9 *erron.* **setateous.** [f. mod.L. *sētāce-us*, f. L. *sēta* bristle: see -ACEOUS.]

**1.** Having the form or character of a bristle. Chiefly in scientific use (*Anat.*, *Zool.*, *Bot.*), of the nature of a seta or setæ.

**1664** H. MORE *Myst. Iniq.* 273 These setaceous prickles. **1713** DERHAM *Phys.-Theol.* VIII. vi. 427 The Parent-Insect with its stiff setaceous Tail, terebrates the Rib of the Leaf. **1769** PENNANT *Brit. Zool.* III. 168 The Gattorugine... The teeth slender, almost setaceous. **1769** BANCROFT *Ess. Nat. Hist. Guiana* 391 The setaceous hairy substance growing on the outside of the pod. **1829** LOUDON *Encycl. Plants* 19 *Justicia nigricans*... Bractes setaceous. **1835** T. BELL in *Todd's Cycl. Anat.* I. 474/1 The cats and..the seals, in which animals the long elastic setaceous whiskers are so useful as feelers. **1882–4** COOKE *Brit. Fresh-w. Algæ* I. 120 Thallus very thick, setaceous.

**2.** Furnished or covered with setæ or bristles, bristly.

*setaceous Hebrew-character*: a book-name for the moth *Noctua C-nigrum* (**1803** HAWORTH *Lepidoptera Brit.* 226. **1869** NEWMAN *Brit. Moths* 346).

**b.** *jocularly.* Bristly, unshaven.

**1787** *Minor* II. i. 66 My father's broad, setaceous visage alternately displayed specimens of all the various colours.

Hence **se'taceously** *adv.*

**1821** W. P. C. BARTON *Flora N. Amer.* I. 14 The serratures or little teeth being sometimes only setaceously armed.

**setaceous**, obs. (erron.) f. CETACEOUS.

**setal** ('siːtəl), *a.* [f. L. *sēta* bristle + -AL[1].] 'Of or pertaining to setæ; as the setal bands of a brachiopod which may run along the pallial margin and denote the site of the setæ.'

**1891** *Century Dict.* (citing *T. Davidson*).

**setar**, var. SITAR.

**setarious** (sɪ'tɛərɪəs), *a. Ent.* [f. L. *sēta* bristle + -ARIOUS.] Of antennæ: Ending in a naked arista or bristle.

**1806** TURTON tr. *Linn. Syst. Nat.* VII. Expl. Terms, *Setarious*, applied to the antennæ of insects, it means, terminating in a simple naked bristle. **1826** KIRBY & SP. *Entomol.* IV. xlvi. 324 Setarious... When the awn or bristle is naked.

**set-aside**, *sb.* and *adj. phr. U.S.* [f. vbl. phr. *set aside*: cf. SET *v.* 139 a, ASIDE *adv.*]

**A.** *sb. phr.* Something set aside; *spec.* a quantity of commodities, agricultural produce, etc., reserved by governmental order for a special purpose (*orig.* for supplying the military forces.) Also, the action of securing thus.

**1943** *Sun* (Baltimore) 16 June 28/8 'Set asides' for the armed forces have increased measurably. **1954** *Ibid.* 21 July B-12/3 One of the foggier sections of the pending overall farm bills would provide for 'set-asides' of surplus commodities now held by the Government. The purpose of the set-aside is clear enough, if the method of effecting it is not. **1966** *Wall St. Jrnl.* (Eastern ed.) 5 Dec. 12/2 The Government ordered drastic increases in defense set-asides on copper during the first half of 1967. **1975** *New Yorker* 26 May 66/2 A visitor asked Butz, who had become Secretary of Agriculture late in 1971, if as Secretary he would have preferred to limit the 'set-aside' of cropland withheld from production in 1972. **1980** *Outdoor Life* (U.S.) (Northeast ed.) Oct. 47/1 Another may be squeaky clean on wilderness set-aside, for example, but falter badly when it comes down to a sensible attitude on gun control.

**B.** *adj. phr.*

**1943** *Daily Progress* (Charlottesville, Va.) 6 Oct. 3/5 A protest..to the War Food Administration against inclusion of smaller sizes of certain varieties of fruit in the government's 'set-aside' order to protect needs for the armed services. **1979** *Financial Times* 19 Jan. 37/7 There is in addition a 'set-aside' programme in the U.S. for both wheat and maize to restrict plantings.

**'set-back.** [f. vbl. phr. *set back*: see SET *v.*[1] 141.]

**1.** *fig.* A check to progress, a retardation or retrograde movement, a relapse, reverse.

**1674** FLAVEL *Husb. Spirit.* i. 20 Even when he is about his work, how many set-backs doth he meet with! **1883** *Century Mag.* July 431 Yet, in the face of all set-backs, the city [New Orleans] that once was almost annually scourged, has, in the twenty-seven years since the great epidemic,..suffered but one mild and three severe epidemics. **1895** *Daily News* 25 Sept. 2/5 Operators are..sore at this sudden set-back, when the boom appeared to be resuming its course on a sounder basis. **1899** *Ibid.* 1 Mar. 5/4 It is now feared that a set-back in the patient's present weakened condition may result in collapse.

**2. a.** *Arch.* A plain, flat set-off in a wall.

**1864** WEBSTER (citing *Weale*). **1887** *Arch. Publ. Soc. Dict.*, *Set-off*; or set-back, or offset.

**b.** *N. Amer.* The setting back or recessing of a building from the edge of a roadway (as an element of environmental planning); the limit of this withdrawal or the open area created.

**1916** *Ann. Rep. Planning Board of Brookline, Mass., 1915* 5 Disregard of the customary setback which has hitherto maintained a margin of cheerful green. **1923** *Stud. Building Height Limitations* (Zoning Comm. Chicago Real Estate Board) 163, I would like to ask in the case of a narrow street whether it would be automatically widened by the establishment of a fixed set-back. **1937** *Sun* (Baltimore) 30 Sept. 24/2 Claiming the building of a stone wall along a lot boundary on Wendover road 'is in total disregard of the theory of setbacks and open spaces in Guildford'. **1947** *Daily Progress* (Charlottesville, Va.) 13 Sept. 2/1 (*heading*) Staples approves rural setbacks. **1961** L. MUMFORD *City in Hist.* Note to plate 51, The architect is freed from arbitrarily uniform prescriptions as to garden allotments, setbacks from roads and obsolete street patterns. **1975** *Canadian Antiques Collector* Mar.–Apr. 27/1 One fence encloses a typical store and defines a deep setback for a distinctive house.

**c.** *N. Amer.* A feature of the design of a skyscraper by which higher storeys are successively set back a certain distance behind the line of lower storeys, leaving a horizontal area in front; the horizontal area so formed.

**1923** *Stud. Building Height Limitations* (Zoning Comm. Chicago Real Estate Board) 23 Additional Heights of Buildings should be allowed, provided proper set-backs are required for such additional stories. **1926** *Daily Colonist* (Victoria, B.C.) 12 Jan. 3/6 It [*sc.* a proposed skyscraper] is to be of the type recently developed..with a reduction of area, or a 'set back' from the street line above the tenth floor and similar reductions taking place at intervals thereafter. **1934** *Sun* (Baltimore) 16 May 2/1 Former Governor Alfred E. Smith..announced that on June 1 the club would open a new terrace cafe on one of the setbacks of the Empire State Building. **1945** *Washington Post* 17 Aug. 1/8 His body cleared more than 100 feet of building setbacks in the seven tiers of parapets designed as obstacles to suicide plunges. **1964** 'J. H. ROBERTS' *Q Document* i. 12 The façade of the building was deceptive, with sculpted indentations and setbacks. **1977** *Guardian Weekly* 6 Nov. 18/4 One of the victims is hurled through a closed window, his body coming to rest on a setback seven floors below.

**3.** A setting back or backward; a thrown-back set (of the shoulders), a backward set (of a golf-club).

**1900** MARY E. WILKINS *Parson Lord*, etc. 188 The old Beau..had a military set-back to his shoulders. **1900** *Westm. Gaz.* 10 Nov. 2/1 The angle..which gives the club the necessary set-back and resulting loft.

**4.** *U.S.* = BACK-SET *sb.* 2.

In recent Dicts.

**5.** *attrib.*, as (sense 2 b) ***setback line, space***; **set-back hinges**, hinges for setting back window-shutters.

**1833** LOUDON *Encycl. Archit.* 269 The hinges used should be what are called set-back hinges, when it is wished to make the shutters fit close to the windows when shut, and to throw them back close to the wall when open. **1917** *Establishment of Setbacks* (City of N.Y. Comm. on City Plan) 4 The set-back line secures on certain streets a uniform set-back of buildings from the street line. **1948** *Daily Progress* (Charlottesville, Va.) 4 Nov. 1/4 An agreement..to permit the super market..to stay four feet inside the prescribed ten-foot setback line. *Ibid.*, If and when the city needs the full ten-foot setback space to widen Preston Avenue, [etc.].

**setchal, setchel(l**, obs. forms of SATCHEL *sb.*

**set-down.** (Stress variable.) [f. vbl. phr. *set down*: see SET *v.*[1] 143.]

**1. a.** A single drive (ending where the passenger first alights) in a vehicle plying for hire; the distance covered by such a drive. (= F. *course.*) **b.** An opportunity of being conveyed some distance on one's way by a passing vehicle; a 'lift'.

**a. 1761** *Ann. Reg.* 220 A guinea for a set-down from any of the squares..to Westminster abbey. **1767** BUSH *Hibernia Cur.* (1769) 23 The rates of hackney-coaches, and sedans, are established here as in London, for the different distances, or set-downs, as they are called. **1891** *Daily News* 27 May, Cabbies..bargain not to be taken by the hour, or for set downs at long distances.

**b. 1727** SWIFT *Let.* 29 Feb. in *Corr.* (1963) III. 268 Mr. Schutz's coach that usd to give you so many a Set-down, is wheeled off to St. James's. **1792** W. ROBERTS *Looker-On* No. 30 (1794) I. 437, I have seen a very able disputant very much humbled..by a cold offer, on the part of his wealthy opponent, to give him a set down in his carriage. **1799** MAR. EDGEWORTH *Pop. Tales, Lame Jervas* ii, Part of the journey I performed on foot; but wherever I could, I got a set down. **1832** G. DOWNES *Lett. Cont. Countries* I. 142, I secured a set-down to Zug in our late vehicle.

**2.** An unexpected and humiliating rebuff. Also, a severe scolding.

**1780** T. PASLEY *Jrnl.* 1 Aug. in *Private Sea Jrnls.* (1931) 105 Gave John a set-down for impertinence. **1786** MRS. A. M. BENNETT *Juvenile Indiscr.* V. 12 Miss Franklin's..ideas of the..felicity of the marriage state received a most mortifying set down. **1809** MALKIN *Gil Blas* v. i. (Rtldg.) 199 The lady then, offended at my words..gave a complete set down to my assurance. **1861** GEN. P. THOMPSON *Audi Alt. Part.* III. 143 The home monopolists..have had a notable though not complete set-down. **1867** J. MACGREGOR *Rob Roy on Baltic* xviii. 216, I gave him such a hearty set-down in good sound English that he was ashamed of himself.

**3.** *U.S. slang.* A sit-down meal.

**1824** J. R. ANTHONY *Diary* 3 Feb. in Z. Pease *Life in New Bedford 100 Yrs. Ago* (1922) 76 After we had got our fill, returned back to our house with a bowl full [of fried oysters] for the girls. Had a good set down and parted at 12 o'clock. **1858** *Harvard Mag.* Sept. 281 We Americans think that we cannot live unless we have our three 'set-downs'..each day, which is absurd. **1900** FLYNT *Tramps* 105 (Farmer) He will almost always give a beggar a set-down. **1907** J. LONDON *Road* 28 At the very next house I was given a 'set-down'. Now a 'set-down' is the height of bliss. **1914** *Sat. Even. Post* 4 Apr. 10/2 That kid don't want no handouts. He gets setdowns. Yes, siree, bo; every time. Setdowns in the kitchen. **1941** J. SMILEY *Hash House Lingo* 48 *Set down*, good meal.

**4.** The action or an instance of landing in or from an aircraft.

**1951** *Sun* (Baltimore) (B ed.) 28 May 28/4 The pilot had called in to report his 'set down'. **1968** O. WYND *Sumatra Seven Zero* xii. 183 Would it surprise him to know..that he had been under observation from the moment of set down?

†**sete**, *sb. Sc. Obs.* (Only *pl.* setis.) [Of obscure origin; perhaps from OE. (Northumb.) pl. *ȝiseto* 'insidias'; OE. *sǣt* 'ambush' would also correspond in form and sense.] A number of men posted to intercept or shoot game.

**1375** BARBOUR *Bruce* III. 479 Thai..soucht schawys, and setis set; Bot thai gat litill for till ete. *c* **1425** WYNTOUN *Cron.* VII. i. 46 Þe kynge þan warnyt his menȝhe Withe hym at huntynge for to be;..þan on þe morn..þe setis [*Wemyss MS.* settis] and þe stabile set [etc.]. **1513** DOUGLAS *Æneis* IV. iii. 58 Quhen that the rangis..Dynnis throw the gravis,..And setis sett the glen on euery side.

†**sete**, *a. Obs.* Also 4 **seete**, 5 **sety** (?). [Related to SIT *v.*; the precise formation is uncertain.]

**1.** Settled or easy in mind, content.

*a* **1310** in Wright *Lyric P.* xxx. 89 Withoute gold other eny tresor, he mai be sound ant sete. *Ibid.* xlii. 114 Whose loveth untrewe, his herte is selde seete.

**2.** Fitting, suitable; (of food or drink) wholesome.

**13..** *Propr. Sanct.* (Vernon MS.) in *Archiv Stud. neu. Spr.* LXXXI. 108/109 Þis is þe ȝok,..þat crist on his meyne wol ley, To Monnes soule hit is ful seete; þerfore he seide, hit was ful sweete. **13..** *Gaw. & Gr. Knt.* 889 Serued..Wyth sere sewes & sete, sesounde of þe best. *c* **1440** *Pallad. on Husb.* II. 420 To this x pounde of hony swete And best: this wol be plesaunt drynke & sete. *Ibid.* IV. 457. **1467** *Ordin. Worc.* in *Eng. Gilds* (1870) 382 Ale conners..to se that the ale be good and sete. *Ibid.* 397 To se that all suche vytelle be able and sete for mannys body. *Ibid.* 425 That the ale be gode, able, and sety.

**sete**, obs. form of CITY, SEAT, SET, SIT.

**setel, setelle**, obs. forms of SETTLE *sb.* and *v.*

‖**setem** ('sɛtɛm). *Egyptology.* Also **Setem**. [ad. Egyptian *sm*, *stm*.] = SEM.

**1963** C. M. FORDE tr. *Desroches-Noblecourt's Tutankhamen* vi. 181 He officiated as the last scion of the royal family in the role of the *Setem* priest at the funeral of his predecessor. **1972** I. E. S. EDWARDS *Treasures of Tutankhamun* 43 (*caption*) King Ay, wearing the leopard skin of a *setem*-priest performs the Opening of the Mouth ceremony.

‖**se-tenant** (sətənɑ̃), *a. Philately.* [Fr., 'holding together'.] Of postage stamps: joined together as when printed; usu. applied to two or more stamps of different denominations or designs. Also as quasi-*adv.*

**1911** F. J. MELVILLE *Chats on Postage Stamps* 49 Se tenant.—A French expression signifying that the stamps referred to have not been separated: usually employed in reference to an error, or variety, when still forming a pair with a normal stamp. **1938** D. B. ARMSTRONG *Key to Stamp Collecting* s.v., *Se Tenant.*—French phrase meaning 'joined together', and applied to a pair of stamps, one of which differs from the other. **1957** *Encycl. Brit.* XVII. 715A/1 *Se-tenant* stamps are two or more unsevered from each other. The term is usually applied to unusual pairs or larger pieces in which one or more of the stamps differs from the other. Sometimes two denominations of stamps will be printed in one sheet and a pair of stamps of the different denominations would be described as 'a *se-tenant* pair'. **1971** [see FUNNY *a.* I b]. **1980** *Jrnl. R. Soc. Arts* July 535/2 The stamps have been printed as four se-tenant designs of one value, that is four different designs joined together on one sheet.

**setenes**, variant of SETNESS[1] *Obs.*

**seter**, var. SAETER, SETTER.

**Seterdai, -day, Seters-dai**, obs. ff. SATURDAY.

**setewale**, obs. form of SETWALL.

**setfast** ('sɛtfɑːst, -æ-). [f. SET *v.*[1] (? vb.-stem or pa. pple.) + FAST *adv.*] A hard tumour on a horse's back; = SITFAST 1. Also *dial.* 'a gathering, tumour; the central part of a wound or boil' (*Eng. Dial. Dict.*).

**1709** *Lond. Gaz.* No. 4591/4 A..Gelding,..with..a Set fast under the Saddle. **1826** COBBETT *Rur. Rides* (1885) II. 192 This man..is a sore to Westminster; a set-fast on its back. **1866** *Morn. Star* 10 July, On examination he perceived it had a bad back, a set-fast [etc.].

**setfoyle**, obs. form of SEPTFOIL.

‖**Seth** (seɪt). *India.* Also 8 **seat, set.** [Hindī *seṭh*, Skr. *śrēṣṭha*, said to be a corruption of *çrēṣṭha* best, chief; in meaning the mod. word corresponds to the Skr. derivative *çrēṣṭhin*.] A leading Hindu merchant or banker.

**1740** in J. Long *Select. Unpubl. Rec. Govt.* (*Ft. William*) (1869) 9 (Y.) The Sets being all present at the Board inform us that [etc.]. **1772** DOW *Hist. Hindostan* III. Diss. I. 109 The well-known bankers, the Jaggat Seats of Murshedabâd. **1880** GROWSE *Mathura* (ed. 2) 15 The Seths..also advanced large sums of money for Government purposes on different occasions. **1884** M. THORNHILL *Pers. Adv. Ind. Mutiny* 79 The Seths held rank next to the sovereign princes. **1895** *Rep. Opium Commiss.* VII. 319 *Seth*, or *Sheth*, or *Sah*, the honorific title of a Hindu merchant.

**seth**, variant of SAITHE, SEATH *Obs.*

**seth, seþ**, obs. forms of SITH.

†**seth(e.** *Obs.* Also 5 **seeth(e, seyth, syth.** [Aphetic f. ASSETH(E, due to apprehending the phr. *make asethe* as *make a sethe*. See also the later (Scottish) SYTH *sb.* and *v.*] Satisfaction, amends, atonement. **a.** ***to make a seth(e***: see ASSETH(E.

**1387** TREVISA *Higden* (Rolls) VII. 91 þat þey schulde make a sethe to þe bisshop [orig. *ut præsuli satisfacerent*]. **1430–40** LYDG. *Bochas* III. v. (1554) 77 To make a seeth for his transgression. *c* **1450** *Cov. Myst., Salut.* 103 He may nevyr make a seyth be resone. *a* **1513** FABYAN *Chron.* VI. cxciv. (1533) I. 119 That he made a seth and amendes to goddes pleasure.

**b.** ***to make (a) full sethe, make amends and sethe.***

*c* **1420** ? LYDG. *Assembly of Gods* 97 Tyll he haue made full seethe and recompence For hurt of my name. *c* **1460** *Wisdom* 122 in *Macro Plays* 39 Wysdam, þat was Gode & man ryght, Made a full sethe to þe fadyr of hewyn. **1461** J. PASTON in *P. Lett.* II. 36 To make amendes and sethe to the pore peple.

**sethe**, variant of SAITHE; obs. form of SITH.

**sethen(ne, -in**, etc., var. ff. SITHEN *Obs.*

**sethence, -ens**, obs. forms of SITHENCE.

**Sethian** ('sɛθɪən). [ad. eccl. L. *Sēthiān-ī* (Gr. *Σηθιανοί*) pl., f. *Sēth* (LXX. *Σήθ*, Heb. *shēth*), the name of the son of Adam who according to the Book of Genesis was the ancestor of Noah and hence of the existing human race.] A member of a Gnostic sect of the second century, holding Seth in great veneration, and believing that Christ was Seth revived.

**1721** BAILEY. **1780** N. LARDNER *Hist. Heretics* II. xiii. Wks. 1788 IX. 449 Irenæus, at the conclusion of his first book, has two chapters, the first of Ophites and Sethians, whom he joins together. **1874** *Blunt's Dict. Sects*, etc.

**Sethic** ('sɛθɪk), *a.* [f. *Seth* (see prec.) + -IC.] Of or pertaining to Seth.

**1882–3** *Schaff's Encycl. Relig. Knowl.* II. 1662/2 Noah..was the tenth and last in the list of the Sethic line.

**sethim, sethin**, obs. forms of SHITTIM.

†**Sethinian.** *Obs.* [f. mod.L. *Sēthīn-us* (f. *Seth*) + -IAN.] = SETHIAN.

**1723** *Dict. Relig.* (ed. 2). **1728** CHAMBERS *Cycl.*

**Sethite** ('sɛθaɪt), *sb.* and *a.* Also **Shethite**. [f. *Seth* (see SETHIAN) + -ITE.]

**A.** *sb.*

**1.** A descendant of Seth (occas. *transf.* a spiritual descendant of Seth).

**1659** GELL *Ess. Amend. Transl. Bible* 102 The Shethites and Shemites were and are taken up wholly or principally with matters of the life to come. **1863** J. G. MURPHY *Comm. Gen.* iv. 23, 4 The Cainites were..an older race than the Shethites. **1896** DAWSON in *Expositor* Sept. 206 The Sethites were thus sons and daughters of Adam by special right.

**2.** = SETHIAN.

**1765** MACLAINE tr. *Mosheim's Eccl. Hist.* Cent. II. II. v. §18 The Sethites..honoured Seth in a particular manner, and looked upon him as the same person with Christ. **1862** *Chamb. Encycl.* IV. 804/1 To the Syrians may also be reckoned the Ophites, Cainites, and Sethites.

**B.** *adj.* Of or pertaining to Seth, descended from Seth.

**1795** T. MAURICE *Hindostan* (1820) I. xii. 382 The virtuous Sethite progeny. **1877** DAWSON *Orig. World* xii. 255 This intermixture of the Sethite and Cainite races.

**seþþe(n, seththe(n**, obs. forms of SITH(EN.

**setiferous** (sɪ'tɪfərəs), *a.* [f. L. *sēta* bristle: see -FEROUS.] Having setæ or bristles.

**1828** STARK *Elem. Nat. Hist.* II. 128 Rows of setiferous papillæ. **1835–6** *Todd's Cycl. Anat.* I. 165/1 The setiferous annelidans. **1856** W. CLARK *Van der Hoeven's Zool.* I. 628 *Bomolochus*... Feet bifid, setiferous in four pairs.

**setiform** ('siːtɪfɔːm), *a.* [f. L. *sēt-a* bristle + -(I)FORM.] Having the form of a seta or bristle; bristle-shaped.

**1816** KIRBY & SP. *Entomol.* xvii. (1818) II. 89 Two setiform tubes. **1826** LINDLEY in *Bot. Register* XII. 992/2 The setiform processes. **1849** OWEN in *Todd's Cycl. Anat.* IV. 874/1 When the teeth are..rather stronger than these, they are called 'setiform'. **1882–4** COOKE *Brit. Fresh-w. Algæ* I. 163 Terminal cell setiform.

**setiger** ('siːtɪdʒə(r)). [a. L. *sētiger*, *sætiger* bristle-bearing, f. *sēta*, *sæta* bristle + *-ger* bearing.] A setigerous worm.

**1842** BRANDE *Dict. Sci.* etc., *Setigers*,..the name of a tribe of Anellidans, including those which like the earthworm, are provided with bristles for progressive motion.

**setigerous** (sɪˈtɪdʒərəs), *a.* [f. L. *sētiger*, *sætiger* bristle-bearing (f. *sēta* bristle + *-ger* bearing) + -OUS.] Furnished with or having setæ or bristles.

**1656** BLOUNT *Glossogr.*, *Setigerous*, that bears or hath bristles on his back. **1721** BAILEY. **1819** SAMOUELLE *Entomol. Compend.* 299 Antennæ inserted near the front, setigerous. **1826** KIRBY & SP. *Entomol.* xlvii. IV. 377 The antennæ..in the other [*sc.* Homoptera]..are very short and setigerous. **1852** DANA *Crust.* I. 14 The feet are usually setigerous. **1882-4** COOKE *Brit. Fresh-w. Algæ* I. 170 Terminal cell often setigerous.

**setil**, obs. form of SETTLE *sb.*

† **Setin.** *Obs.* Also 7 **Setine.** [ad. L. *Sētīn-um*, f. *Sētia*, a city of Latium.] Wine of Setia.

**1693** W. BOWLES *Dryden's Juvenal* v. (1697) 97 Perhaps to morrow he may..drink old sparkling Alban, or Setine. **1764** *Oxf. Sausage* 50 Nectareous Wines, that well may vie With Massic, Setin, or renown'd Falern.

**setiparous** (sɪˈtɪpərəs), *a.* [f. L. *sēt-a* bristle + -PAROUS.] Producing setæ or bristles.

**1870** ROLLESTON *Anim. Life* 125 Due to the development in these segments of the setiparous glands of the inner row of setæ.

**Setirday**, obs. form of SATURDAY.

**setireme** (ˈsiːtɪriːm). [f. L. *sēta* bristle + *rēm-us* an oar.] A name given by Kirby to the setose leg of an aquatic insect, serving as an oar.

**1835** KIRBY *Hab. & Inst. Anim.* II. xvii. 133 These might be named *Setiremes*.

**setirostral** (siːtɪˈrɒstrəl), *a.* *Ornith. rare.* [f. L. *sēta* bristle + *rostr-um* beak + *-al*: see ROSTRAL.] 'Having the bill furnished with conspicuous bristles along the gape; having long rictal vibrissæ.'

**1891** *Century Dict.* (citing *P. L. Sclater*).

**setl(e**, obs. forms of SETTLE *sb.* and *v.*

**setling** (ˈsɛtlɪŋ). Also 6-8 **settling.** [f. SET *sb.*[1] + -LING. Cf. LG. *settling*, G. *setzling*.] A slip taken from a tree and planted.

**1387-8** T. USK *Test. Love* III. v. (Skeat) l. 23 Every yonge setling lightly with smale stormes is apeyred. **1502** ARNOLDE *Chron.* lxiiij, A setlyng yᵗ spryngeth out of a nother trees Roete. **1564** BECON *Wks.* I. Pref. B vj, Such as be..newly planted in the religion of Christ, and haue taken no sure roote in the same, are easily moued, as young setlings & caryed away. **1664** EVELYN *Sylva* xix. 41 For setlings, those are to be preferr'd which grow neerest to the stock. **1725** *Bradley's Fam. Dict.* s.v. *Sallow*, Some there are who plant them [*sc.* Sallows] at full Height,..but then they are less useful for Staves and Settlings, nor do they grow so speedily.

† **ˈsetly**, *adv. Obs. rare.* [f. SET *ppl. a.* + -LY[2].] In a set manner; resolutely, of set purpose.

**1678** E. COLES *God's Sov.* Pref. 6 This put him upon searching the Scriptures more Setly touching the Doctrine. *Ibid.* i. 11 That Honour..which they setly intended to prevent.

† **ˈsetness**[1]. *Obs.* Also 3 **sett-**, **sæt-**, **sætt-**, **sete-**, 4 **zet-**. [OE. *setnes* (also *ȝeseines*), f. (*ȝe*)*set*, pa. pple. of *settan* SET *v.*[1] + -NESS.]

**1.** Constitution; establishment; imposition (of a law).

*law of setness*: positive law as opposed to law of nature ('kind'). Cf. SET *ppl. a.* 1 b.

*c* **950** *Lindisf. Gosp.* Matt. xiii. 35 Ic loccete deiglo from setnesse middanȝeardes [*a constitutione mundi*]. *a* **1300** *Cursor M.* 29517 Þat cursing tald vn-laghful es þat ordir wantes and right settnes o lagh. **13..** *Ibid.* 1571 (Gött.) Þai left þe lede of oþer laue, þat es of setnes and of kind.

**2.** What is decreed or determined; a statute, ordinance.

*c* **950** *Lindisf. Gosp.* Matt. xv. 2 Ðeȝnas ðinne hia oferȝæs *vel* oferhoȝas selenise *vel* setnesa [*traditionem*] ðara ældra. *c* **1200** ORMIN 16837 Godess laȝhe & Godess rihht & hiss hallȝhe settnesse. *c* **1205** LAY. 4258 Heo makeden ane sætnesse, and mid aȝe heo semde. *a* **1300** *Cursor M.* 11292 Þai bar þe child..vn-to þe temple, For to do fore him þat dai, þe settenes of þe ald lai. *Ibid.* 24958 Þis ilk abbot... A settnes set in his abbai. **1340** *Ayenb.* 223 Huanne þe lost ne paseþ naȝt þe markes ne þe zetnesses of spoushod.

**3.** ? Fixed abode.

*c* **1200** *Trin. Coll. Hom.* 23 Chireche is cleped..kiriaca .i. dominicalis,..and is þerto nemned for þe heuenliche kinges lichame is to setnesse þarinne.

**4.** Appointed time.

*a* **1400-50** *Wars Alex.* 5553 Sone so þe setnes was gane þat him-selfe made [*Tempus..quod militibus suis predixit Alexander completum erat*].

**setness**[2] (ˈsɛtnɪs). [f. SET *ppl. a.* + -NESS.] The quality, state, or character of being set, in various senses; also an instance of this.

**1642** D. ROGERS *Naaman* 187 Looking sometime more..at the setnesse of our sentences..then at Gods awfull presence. **1741** RICHARDSON *Pamela* II. 67 Don't you see by the Setness of some of these Letters..that it is the Hand of a Person bred in the Law-way. **1818** HAZLITT *Eng. Poets* viii. (1869) 195 There is in the chief character..a setness of purpose which John Kemble alone was capable of giving. **1852** MRS. STOWE *Uncle Tom's C.* xxvi, Her little peculiarities and setnesses, so unlike the careless freedom of southern manners. **1899** R. H. CHARLES *Eschatol.* xi. 380 There is a setness and rigidity in the teaching of the Apostle.

**Seto** (ˈsɛtɔː). The name of a city 12 miles north-east of Nagoya in Japan used *attrib.* and *absol.* to designate the pottery and porcelain produced from the kilns established there in the 13th century.

**1881** AUDSLEY & BOWES *Keramic Art of Japan* 125 The specimens..cost about four times as much as corresponding articles of Arita or Seto make. *Ibid.* 226 Other descriptions are called..Seto-Suke, Seko-Kuro, and..Ki-Seto, or yellow Seto after the colour of the glaze used. **1925** W. WESTON *Wayfarer in Unfamiliar Japan* xii. 127 The region whose chief and oldest settlement, Seto, gives its name to the Japanese term *Seto-mono* (lit. 'Seto ware'), porcelain, just as we ourselves employ the word 'china' to connote articles of a similar nature. **1945** W. B. HONEY *Ceramic Art of China & Other Countries of Far East* v. 181 The 'yellow Seto' (*ki-seto*) was possibly suggested by a variety of the *temmoku*, but more probably by late Corean ware. **1959** R. KIRKBRIDE *Tamiko* ix. 67 The tea arrived in small porcelain cups which Ivan recognized as Seto, very old and rare, from the kiln at Nagoya. **1972** P. MURRAY tr. *Shoya Yoshida's Folk-Art* (ed. 2) 52 (*caption*) Seto water dropper with peony relief.

**ˈset-off.** Pl. **set-offs** (*incorrectly* **sets-off**). [f. vbl. phr. *set off*: see SET *v.*[1] 147.]

**1.** Something used to set off or adorn; an adornment, decoration, or ornament.

**1621** FLETCHER *Wild Goose Chase* III. i, This course creature, That has no more set off, but his jugglings, His travell'd tricks. **1662** STILLINGFL. *Orig. Sacræ* Ep. Ded. a 4 b, The plain dress of the Scriptures, without the paint and set-offs which are added to it by the severall contending parties of the Christian World. **1702** *Eng. Theophrastus* 347 A fine woman charms us without any other set-off than that of her beauty and youth. **1856** J. H. NEWMAN *Serm. Var. Occas.* i. (1881) 13 Nor is science..an ornament and set-off to devotion.

**2.** The act of setting off on a journey, etc.; a start.

**1759** FRANKLIN *Hist. Rev. Pennsylv.* Wks. 1840 III. 425 What the governor's set-off could not effect, was to be re-attempted by this put-off. **1798** *Geraldina* II. 189 This is but a dull set-off. **1806** SOUTHEY *Lett.* (1856) I. 376, I suppose the new Magazine will start with the new year, in which case I must lend a helping hand for awhile, and give a hearty shove at the set-off. **1893** 'Q' [Quiller-Couch] *Delect. Duchy* 52 Never do I mind such a gay set-off for the journey.

**3.** *Comm.* and *Law.* An act of 'setting off' one item of account against another, i.e. of reckoning the former as a counterbalance to or a deduction from the latter; an item or amount which is or should be set off against another in the settlement of accounts; a counter-claim, or a counterbalancing debt, pleaded by the defendant in an action to recover money due; also, this mode of defence. Cf. OFFSET *sb.* 5.

**1766** BURROW *Cases K.B.* II. 820 There was a Plea of a Set-off. **1768** BLACKSTONE *Comm.* III. xx. 304 The practice of what is called a set-off: whereby the defendant acknowleges the justice of the plaintiff's demand on the one hand; but, on the other, sets up a demand of his own, to counter-ballance that of the plaintiff, either in the whole or in part. **1775** F. BULLER *Introd. Law Nisi Prius* (ed. 2) 181 Defendant..gave a Notice of Set-off. **1838** W. BELL *Dict. Law Scot.* 195 This plea, however, is not properly a bar to the action, but of the nature of a set-off or counter-claim, which extinguishes or modifies the pursuer's claim. **1844** MILL *Pol. Econ.* III. xii. 6 If the cheque is paid into a different bank, it will not be presented for payment, but liquidated by set-off against other cheques. **1854** *Act 17 & 18 Vict.* c. 104 §191 If in any Proceeding..touching the Claim of a Master to Wages any Right of Set-off or Counter-claim is set up. **1861** GOSCHEN *For. Exch.* 16 Otherwise, involving no immediate claim, they [American securities] cannot be regarded as a set-off to the debts which we incur to the Americans for cotton and corn. **1868** ROGERS *Pol. Econ.* iv. (1876) 39 The debts may be made to act as a set-off against each other.

**b.** In wider sense: A taking into account of something as a counterbalance to a partial compensation for something else; a counter-balancing or compensating circumstance or consideration.

**1773** *Hist. Eur.* in *Ann. Reg.* 106*/2 The idea of a set-off of services against offences was trivial. **1799** JEFFERSON *Writ.* (1859) IV. 263 Something is required from you as a set off against the sin of your retirement. **1809** MALKIN *Gil Blas* IV. vii. (Rtldg.) 151 As a set-off against his hen-pecked cowardice..he gave me fifty ducats. **1848** DICKENS *Dombey* xxiv, Her own delight was no set-off to this. **1864** *Reader* 5 Nov. 567/3 We must take her evidence with great allowances and sets-off.

**4. a.** *Arch.* (Also *sett-off*.) A reduction in the thickness of a wall, buttress, etc.; the sloping or flat projection or ledge formed when the portion above is reduced in thickness; = OFFSET *sb.* 7.

**1717** TABOR in *Phil. Trans.* XXX. 554 There was a Set-off (as our Masons term it) in the inside of the Wall, eight Inches broad. **1721** PERRY *Daggenh. Breach* 81 My Dam had hitherto from the Foundation been carry'd up by Set-offs on each Side, of about seven foot in breadth. **1823** P. NICHOLSON *Pract. Builder* 427 The sets-off thus made..will also afford a secure support to the floors. **1842** GWILT *Archit.* Gloss., *Sett-off.* **1850** PARKER *Gloss. Archit.* (ed. 5) s.v. *Buttress*, The set-offs dividing the stages [of Early English buttresses] are generally sloped at a very acute angle. **1867** A. BARRY *Sir C. Barry* vii. 254 Set-offs would have caused dislocation in the panelling.

**b.** A similar reduction or shoulder in a metal bar, etc.

**1830** *Eng. & For. Mining Gloss.*, *Cornw.* (1860) 22 *Set-off*, the part of a connecting rod to which the bucket rod is attached. **1846** HOLTZAPFFEL *Turning* II. 821 The safe-edge file is principally required in making a set-off, or shoulder at any precise spot in the work. **1883** CRANE *Smithy & Forge* 42 A set-off is a reduction from the original size of the bar with a square shoulder or two square shoulders.

**5.** *Printing*, etc. The transference of ink from one page to another.

**1842** *Penny Mag.* 24 Sept. 379 The rolling-press is found to be more efficacious than the hammer in producing less 'set-off', or transference of ink from one page to another. **1882** SOUTHWARD *Pract. Printing* 436 In this way only can 'set off' be prevented.

**b.** An impression transferred.

**1839** HANSARD *Print. & Type-founding* (1841) 138 Impressions in reverse, which, whilst the ink was yet fresh, were to be pressed strongly between clean paper, the set-off upon which would be fit for use. **1854** *Ev. Man Own Printer* 26 This will leave upon the stone what is termed a 'set off', or light transfer of the drawing.

**6.** In a pianoforte, the space left between the hammer at its full rise and the strings.

**1896** HIPKINS *Pianoforte* 33 A prolongation, forming the escapement lever *k*, controls the escapement or set-off from the strings by the screw and button *h*.

**7.** *attrib.*: **set-off button**, a button to control the 'set-off' (sense 6) in a pianoforte; **set-off paper**, **sheet** *Printing* (see quots.).

**1822** SAVAGE *Hints Decorative Printing* 45 These Set off Sheets..prevent the ink setting off from one sheet to another while it is newly printed. **1839** HANSARD *Print. & Type-founding* (1841) 111 The master should not grudge ample supplies of set-off paper. **1896** HIPKINS *Pianoforte* 36 The set-off button.

**setoler**, var. CITOLER *Obs.*, citole-player.

*c* **1420** *Anturs of Arth.* 343 (Thornton MS.).

**seton** (ˈsiːtən), *sb. Surg.* Forms: 5-6 **ceton**, 7 **setton**, 8 **seaton** (9 *illiterate* **seething**), 5- **seton**. [ad. med.L. *sētōn-em*, app. f. L. *sēta* bristle, in med.L. also silk. Cf. OF. *seton*, *ceto* (mod.F. *séton*), It. *setone*.]

**1.** A thread, piece of tape, or the like, drawn through a fold of skin so as to maintain an issue or opening for discharges, or drawn through a sinus or cavity to keep this from healing up (*Syd. Soc. Lex.*).

*c* **1400** *Lanfranc's Cirurg.* 308 The .x. cauterie is clepid ceton. *Ibid.* 310 Alle þese cauterijs wolen be maad best wiþ seton. **1541** COPLAND *Guydon's Quest. Chirurg.* P ij b, Rounde cauteres, or cauteres with cetons, that kepeth it better open. **1597** A. M. tr. *Guillemeau's Fr. Chirurg.* 22/1 Applyinge of the corrosive in place of a Seton. **1651** BIGGS *New Disp.* ¶255 A Seton or coard of twisted thred or silk is runne through on both sides the skin of the neck. **1714** [see ROWEL *sb.* 6]. **1813** *Sporting Mag.* XLII. 75 The defendant attempted to pass a seething up the wound. **1844** H. STEPHENS *Bk. Farm* III. 841 Some farmers introduce a seton into the dewlap of all their calves... The seton consists of a piece of tape or soft cord passed under a portion of the skin by a seton-needle. **1895** *Brit. Med. Jrnl.* 14 Dec. 1492/1 It was replaced by a tight seton of quadrupled cord.

**b.** *seton-needle*, a needle used for passing a seton through the skin.

**1672** WISEMAN *Wounds* I. vii. 61, I passed a Seton-needle through, and that way discharged the Matter. **1831** LOUDON *Encycl. Agric.* (1857) §6537 When the seton needle is removed, the ends of the tape should be joined together.

**2.** The issue so formed.

**1597** A. M. tr. *Guillemeau's Fr. Chirurg.* 43/1 The Seton, properlye, the threde which we drawe through the skinne with the needle... Improperly, a longe stretchinge vlceration which is cleane thrust throughe the dubble skinne with a glowinge Cauterye. **1688** HOLME *Armoury* III. 430/1 This Needle being..heated red hot..makes a Seton, or perforates the flesh almost paineless. **1725** *Bradley's Fam. Dict.* s.v. *Glanders*, First to make a Seaton under the Tail and in the Withers. **1846** BRITTAN tr. *Malgaigne's Man. Oper. Surg.* 59 The seton is a kind of issue made by piercing the skin in two corresponding points, and passing through them a *mèche* of cotton, or a bit of linen unravelled at the edges. **1860** JESSIE WILSON *Mem. G. Wilson* 323 Lecturing ten, eleven, or more hours weekly..frequently with torturing setons and open blister wounds.

*fig.* **1849** CLOUGH *Dipsychus* II. i. 32 A sort of seton, I suppose, A moral bleeding at the nose.

Hence **ˈseton** *v.*, to apply a seton. **ˈsetoned** *ppl. a.*, **ˈsetoning** *vbl. sb.*

**1541** COPLAND *Guydon's Quest. Chirurg.* P ij, The fyfth place is the necke where as cetons are applied with tonges cetoned or with a nedle cetonned. **1845** YOUATT *Dog* vi. 118, I have bled, and physicked and setoned, and blistered, and used the moxa. **1897** *Yearbk. U.S. Dept. Agric.* 254 Many plans of prevention [of blackleg] have been adopted, such as bleeding, setoning [etc.].

**setose** (ˈsiːtəʊs), *a.* [ad. L. *sētōs-us*, *sætōs-us* bristly, f. *sēta*, *sæta* bristle: see -OSE.]

**1.** *Anat.* and *Zool.* Set or covered with bristles or stiff hairs, bristly. Also, of a bristly nature.

**1661** LOVELL *Hist. Anim. & Min.* Isagoge b 1 b, The taile ..setose in those that are longish, as horses. **1819** MACLEAY *Horæ Entomol.* I. 35 Porrect mandibles, and setose maxillæ. **1881-2** SAVILLE KENT *Man. Infusoria* II. 779 Three or four distinctly differentiated setose cilia.

**2.** *Bot.* Having setæ or bristles.

**1760** J. LEE *Introd. Bot.* I. xvii. (1765) 43 *Setose*, bristly. **1832** LINDLEY *Introd. Bot.* I. ii. 114 If those hairs..are very unusually stiff, it [*sc.* the *pappus*] is setose. **1881** BABINGTON *Brit. Bot.* (ed. 8) Gloss., *Setose*, having bristles or setæ usually ending in glands.

Hence **seˈtosity.**

**1731** BAILEY vol. II, *Setosity*, fulness of bristles.

**setous** ('siːtəs), *a. rare.* [ad. L. *sētōs-us, sætōs-ūs*: see prec. and -OUS.] = SETOSE.

**1822** J. PARKINSON *Outl. Oryctol.* 120 Their spines are various, never uniformly setous. **1828–32** WEBSTER, *Setous*, bristly; having the surface set with bristles; as, a setous leaf or receptacle [citing MARTYN who in *Lang. Bot.* (1793) has *Setosus*].

**set-out.** (Stress variable.) Chiefly *colloq.* and *dial.* Pl. **set-outs** (*incorrectly* **sets-out**). [f. vbl. phr. *set out*: see SET *v.*[1] 149.]

**1.** A display.

**a.** A display or set of plate, china, etc.

**1806–7** J. BERESFORD *Miseries Hum. Life* (1826) x. xxi, Every dish..being served up on the kitchen table, with a set-out of crockery from the same apartment. **1823** 'JON BEE' *Dict. Turf*, etc., *Set out*,..'tis also applied to a sideboard, decked out, or a dinner table, set out. **1830** COL. HAWKER *Diary* (1893) II. 14 He and his punt came home looking like a set-out of glass, and himself half-frozen. **1851** MAYHEW *Lond. Labour* I. 368/1 The lady..wanted me to go and buy expressly for her a green and white chamber service all complete,..and all this here grand set-out she wanted for a couple of old washed-out light waistcoats.

**b.** A 'spread' of food.

**1809** MALKIN *Gil Blas* III. viii. (Rtldg.) 101 There was a grand set-out, and mirth, the best relish, was not wanting to the banquet. **1815** JANE AUSTEN *Emma* xlii, 'There shall be cold meat in the house.' 'Well, as you please; only don't have a great set-out.' **1850** L. HUNT *Autobiog.* I. iv. 161 A becoming set-out of coffee and buttered toast. **1898** MRS. H. WARD *Helbeck* I. v. 98 It wor a varra poor set-oot, wor Jenny's buryin. Nowt but tay, an sic-like.

**c.** A 'turn-out'; i.e. a carriage with its horses, harness, etc.

**1810** *Sporting Mag.* XXXVI. 82 The set out of these gentlemen excited admiration. **1819** *Ibid.* V. 123 The Corinthians, in their bang-up sets-out of blood and bone. **1827** *Ibid.* XX. 47 The fame of the Western sets-out is recorded in Nimrod's best style. **1833** T. HAMILTON *Men & Mann. Amer.* vi. (1843) 86, I thought of the impression the whole set-out would be likely to produce on an English road. *a* **1837** [APPERLEY] *Road* (1852) 62 The vis-à-vis,.. with all its *set-out*, has cost at least a thousand pounds. **1837** J. F. COOPER *England* (ed. 2) III. 119 A procession of mail-coaches, which however neat and seemly the set-outs, had too much the air of a cockney show. **1851–61** MAYHEW *Lond. Labour* II. 46/2 The 'whole set out'..poney included, cost 50*l.* when new. **1856** WHYTE MELVILLE *Kate Coventry* iv. 38 As we pulled up in front of the Castle Hotel..''Ere's a spicy set-out, Bill!' said one.

*transf.* **1819** LADY MORGAN in *Mem.* (1862) II. 114 He said he had orders to bring the Captain's boat and ten men for me as often as I pleased. He came with this set-out twice.

**d.** A person's costume or 'get-up'; the way in which a person is dressed.

**1834** L. RITCHIE *Wand. Seine* 192 Her cap is..a plain set-out, round which is thrown loosely a piece of white muslin bordered with lace. **1834** *Tait's Mag.* I. 605/2 Both at a glance seemed to make a rapid inventory and appraisement of Mrs. Mark Luke, and her entire set-out. **1837** DICKENS *Pickw.* ii, He called his companion's attention to the large gilt button, which displayed a bust of Mr. Pickwick in the centre, and the letters 'P.C.' on either side. 'P.C.', said the stranger,—'queer set out—old fellow's likeness, and "P.C."'. **1892** *Daily News* 7 Sept. 6/5 In a blue and green dress, with bows flying, and every one turning round to look and laugh at her set-out.

**e.** A show or public performance; an entertainment for a number of people, a party of pleasure.

**1818** LADY MORGAN *Autobiog.* (1859) 290 He excited some sensation here last Wednesday, when I had a most brilliant set-out. **1823** W. ROBINSON in J. A. Heraud *Voy. & Mem. Midshipm.* (1837) 140 We went to the play here; but it was a horrid set out. **1834** DICKENS *Sk. Boz, Tales* i. ch. ii, Never saw anything like that Captain Ross's set-out—eh? *Ibid. Tales* vii, The best way will be, to have a committee of ten, to..manage the whole set-out. **1887** *Kent. Gloss.*, *Set out*,.. a grand display; an event causing excitement and talk. 'There was a grand set-out at the wedding.'

**f.** A party, set (of people), company.

**1854** DICKENS *Hard T.* I. viii, She must just hate and detest the whole set-out of us.

**g.** A commotion, disturbance, 'to-do'.

**1833** DICKENS *Let.* ? Jan. (1965) I. 14, I am consequently unable to tell the story and to deliver a plain unvarnish'd tale of the set out. **1875** PARISH *Sussex Gloss.* 101 There's been a pretty set-out up at the forge. **1887** *Kent Gloss.*, *Set-out*, a great fuss and disturbance. **1903** SOMERVILLE & 'ROSS' *All on Irish Shore* i. 15 'I'm sure Fennessy wishes to hear no more of it,' said Barnet acridly to Mrs. Griffen, when Mrs. Alexander had passed swiftly out of hearing, 'after the way those girls have been worryin' on at him about it all the morning. Such a set out!' **1933** D. L. SAYERS *Murder must Advertise* x. 166 'Coo! that was a set-out, that was.'

**2.** A beginning or start.

**1821** BYRON *Diary* 18 Feb. in Moore *Lett.* etc. (1830) II. 429 The commotions left every body a side to take; and the parties were pretty equal at the set out. **1863** W. BARNES *Dorset Dial.*, *Set out*, an outset; a starting, or a proceeding. **1893** *Nat. Observer* 4 Mar. 392/1 The children..might have had such a good set-out in the world.

**3.** Outfit, equipment.

**1831** *Lincoln Herald* 7 Oct. 4/4 Gambling set-outs of every description. **1832** COL. HAWKER *Diary* (1893) II. 45 But my grand object was to try all the tackle, having (except the gun, newly done up) an entirely new set-out, on a somewhat different, and I hope, improved plan. **1864** *Gd. Words* 788/1 The teacher..is supposed to have on his shelf a full set-out of the most approved elementary volumes.

**4.** *Coal mining.* (See quot.) Also *set-out tub.*

**1849** GREENWELL *Gloss. Terms Coal Trade* (1851) 46 *Set-out*, a tub or corf of coals filled insufficiently, and consequently forfeited. **1891** *Labour Commission* Gloss., *Set-out Tub*, a tub of coal insufficiently filled by a miner.

**set piece.** Also set-piece, setpiece. [SET *ppl. a.*]

**1. a.** A painting, or a sculptured group of people.

**1846** DICKENS *Pictures Italy, Rome* 190 The hollow-cheeked monk..went down on his knees, in a corner before this set-piece. **1901** *Westm. Gaz.* 22 May 6/3 A group [of flowers] of the set-piece kind in the form of a grotto.

**b.** A picture or design composed of fireworks.

**1874** W. H. BROWNE *Art Pyrotechny* 118 'Set pieces' (as they are called).

**c.** A (passage of) formal composition in prose or verse; a discourse, narrative, etc., composed according to a set pattern.

**1932** C. BROWN *Eng. Lyrics of 13th Cent.* p. xiv, In the English romance *Arthour and Merlin* a series of lyrics on the various months—May, June, February, &c.—are introduced as set pieces to divide the romance into Fitts. **1954** *Essays in Criticism* IV. 1 Little reason to suppose that Menenius is as impartial or as wise as his famous set-piece, the fable of the belly and the members, might at first sight suggest. **1959** I. & P. OPIE *Lore & Lang. Schoolch.* ix. 156 And there is the recurrent set-piece: 'What's your name?' 'Sarah Jane.' 'Where do you live?' 'Down the lane' [etc.]. **1968** *Listener* 10 Oct. 475/3 Amis's prose is very good, and some of his little set-pieces are brilliant, as well as modish. Thus, the American road-scene. **1977** *Broadcast* 7 Nov. 13/3 'Hard Times'..as a novel..has a few splendid set pieces and many incidental pleasures. **1980** *Times Lit. Suppl.* 19 Sept. 1012/1 The ceremony of the Holy Fire in the Holy Sepulchre in Jerusalem—the major set-piece of the novel.

**2.** *Theatr.* A piece of scenery, either flat or three-dimensional and usu. free-standing, that represents a single feature such as a tree, a gate, or the like.

**1859** E. FITZBALL *Thirty-Five Years of Dramatic Author's Life* I. vi. 140 His long costly robes, becoming entangled with a set piece, pulled down with it, the orange tree excepted, every morsel of scenery on the stage. **1884** [see CLOTH *sb.* 7]. **1930** SELDEN & SELLMAN *Stage Scenery & Lighting* I. vi. 163 The character of an outdoor setting is better suggested by a few plastic 'set' and 'built' pieces, such as ground rows, silhouette hills, rocks, trees, and fences placed in front of the sky than by anything placed on the drop. **1970** H. NELMS *Scene Design* ii. 19/1 Except for the cyc and the ground row needed to mask its lower edge, the whole setting..consists of a single set piece. This is a flat piece of scenery placed by itself somewhere in the playing space.

**3.** An organized movement, action, or manœuvre; *spec.* in *Sport*, a prescribed (and usu. rehearsed) movement or feature of the game by which the ball is returned to play, as at a scrummage in Rugby or a free kick in Football.

**1938** D. S. MILFORD *Hockey* vi. 122 We have now finished our survey of the full-back positions for what may be called 'set pieces'. **1947** *Jrnl. R. Aeronaut. Soc.* LI. 840/1 The fourth and last type of operation is the raid against an enemy shore base, usually referred to as a 'set-piece'. This is really rather similar to a Bomber Command operation at shorter range and with smaller aircraft. **1960** E. S. & W. J. HIGHAM *High Speed Rugby* xx. 314 Set-piece Rugby. This is not a game in the strict sense, but a series of set pieces, following rapidly, one on another, at a word from the coach or referee. **1977** *Western Mail* (Cardiff) 5 Mar. 18/5 Modern rugby is a game of pressure and most of this is upon the halves, from set pieces and loose play.

**4.** (with hyphen) *attrib.* passing into *adj.* Having the attributes of a set-piece; formally or elaborately planned or composed; set (cf. SET *ppl. a.*).

**1947** *Jrnl. R. Aeronaut. Soc.* LI. 840/1 (*heading*) The 'set-piece' attack. **1962** E. GODFREY *Retail Selling & Organization* ii. 11 The windows themselves may be enclosed, providing a background for set-piece displays. **1968** *Economist* 17 Feb. 43/1 The not quite universal tendency of reporters to compare the setpiece battle situation that has been building up at Khe Sanh, close to the boundary between South and North Vietnam, to Dienbienphu. **1976** H. WILSON *Governance of Britain* 9 The prime minister is not only required to make a set-piece ministerial or other broadcast on major occasions; he is constantly in the news.

**setrack**, obs. form of CETERACH.

**1570** LEVINS *Manip.* 5/36 Setrack, herbe, *lepidium.*

**Setre(t)-day, Setry(s)day**, obs. ff. SATURDAY.

**setryne**, obs. form of CITRINE.

**set sames**: see SEPT PSAUMES.

**setsayne**, rare obs. form of CITIZEN.

**setsman** ('sɛtsmən). [f. *sets* pl. or genit. of SET *sb.*[1] + MAN *sb.*] A workman who makes 'sets' or paving-stones.

**1881** *Instr. Census Clerks* (1885) 86 Stone quarrier... Sett Miner, Maker, Setsman, Setsman Finisher.

**Setswana** (sɛt'swɑːnə). Also **Sechuana, Sechoana, Sechwana, Secuana,** †**Sichuana.** [a. Tswana *se-*, prefix meaning 'language' + TSWANA.] = TSWANA *sb.* b. Also *attrib.* or as *adj.*

**1811** [see KORI[1]]. **1815** A. PLUMPTRE tr. *H. Lichtenstein's Trav. S. Afr.* II. li. 407 Under the name of *Beetjuana, Sihtjuana*, or *Muhtjuana* are to be included all the tribes that inhabit the country which extends from the river Kurahman. **1824** W. J. BURCHELL *Trav. S. Afr.* II. xi. 295 The Bachapins call this language the Sichuána. **1839** W. C. HARRIS *Wild Sports S. Afr.* ii. 11 This..individual.. possessed a fair smattering of the English and Sichuana languages. **1850** [see BECHUANA]. **1905** G. W STOW *Native Races S. Afr.* xxi. 407 The Bachoana proper, including the Batlapin, Barolong, etc., speaking the Sechoana and Serolong. **1916** S. T. PLAATJE *Sechuana Proverbs* 15/1 The present confusion..is apt to hamper missionary enterprise among Sechuana-speaking Natives. **1919** H. H. JOHNSTON *Bantu & Semi-Bantu Langs.* iii. 317 *Secuana* dialects are spoken in Bechuanaland, north of the 28th degree of South latitude. **1935** A. L. JAMES *Broadcast Word* i. 10 There is a story told of the Bechuana that..the early missionaries taught them the Lord's Prayer in the native language, Sechuana. **1961** L. VAN DER POST *Heart of Hunter* I. vii. 110 A language they had evolved in the course of the journey out of a little Swahili, some Sechuana and a lot of onomatopœia. **1964** D. VARADAY *Gara-Yaka* xii. 108 When at a loss for a word he helped himself in Afrikaans, Chivenda, Sechwana, Zulu, and Shangaan. **1977** 'J. MCVEAN' *Bloodspoor* iii. 22 *Morena*. 'Chief.' The Setswana term for any white man of authority.

**sett** (sɛt). *Sc.* Also 9 **set.** [Possibly a use of SET *sb.*[1] (though its relation to the other senses is difficult to assign); it may, however, be a. MLG. *set, sette* (also *gesette* = G. *gesetz*) ordinance, law, f. *setten* to SET.] The constitution or form of government of a burgh, fixed by charter.

**1683** (*title*) The Sett, and Decreet Arbitral of King James the 6th..containing the Fundamentall Principles of the Government of the City of Edinburgh. **1739** in *Edin. Antiq. Mag.* (1849) 133 The Council of Dingwall, by the act of sett, consists of a Provest, two Bailies [etc.]. **1806** FORSYTH *Beauties Scot.* IV. 109 The set or constitution [of Kirkcaldy]. **1818** SCOTT *Hrt. Midl.* i, An anxious.. discussion, concerning provosts, bailies, deacons, sets of boroughs [etc.]. **1838** W. BELL *Dict. Law Scot.* s.v., The setts are either established by immemorial usage, or were at some time or other modelled by the convention of Burghs.

**sett**: see SET *sb.*; also obs. f. SET *a.* and *v.*

**settable** ('sɛtəb(ə)l), *a.* [f. SET *v.*[1] + -ABLE.] That may be set. (In quot. *a* 1657 perh. that may be planted with trees.)

*a* **1657** BRADFORD *Plymouth Plant.* (1856) 216 They should only lay out settable or tillable land. **1967** *Electronics* 6 Mar. 6/2 The synthesized center-frequency marker and side markers are accurate, stable, and precisely settable. **1981** *Times Lit. Suppl.* 22 May 573/2 So much of modern poetry has no sense of rhythm or rhyme, and therefore is neither memorable nor settable to music.

‖**settaine.** *Obs. rare*$^{-1}$. [a. F. *septain*, pronounced (sɛtɛ̃), f. *sept* seven: cf. QUATRAIN.] A stanza of seven lines.

**1589** PUTTENHAM *Eng. Poesie* II. x[i]. (Arb.) 101 The huitain or staffe of eight verses, hath eight proportions such as the former staffe, and because he is longer he hath one more then the settaine.

**sette**, obs. form of SEAT *sb.*, SET, SETTEE[1].

‖**settecento** (sette'tʃɛnto). [It.: short for *mil settecento* one thousand seven hundred.] The eighteenth century considered as a period of Italian art, architecture, music, etc.

**1926** E. HUTTON tr. *A. Venturi's Short Hist. Ital. Art* vi. 286 The secret of the fascination Corregio exercised on the art of the *Seicento* and *Settecento*..must be sought in the extraordinary sensibility of his nature. **1936** A. HUXLEY *Olive Tree* 151 It is a scene from a *settecento* Earthly Paradise —before the Fall of 1789. **1941** *Burlington Mag.* Aug. 38/2 With our last selection, we pass from the Cinquecento to the Settecento. **1966** T. PYNCHON *Crying of Lot 49* i. 10 The Fort Wayne Settecento Ensemble's variorum recording of the Vivaldi Kazoo Concerto.

**settee**[1] (sə'tiː). Now only *Hist.* Forms: 6 **settea,** 7 **sattie, -y, satia, sett(y)e,** 7–8 **sattee,** 8 **cettee, saetia, setye,** 7– **settee.** [a. It. *saettia* (pronounced (-'tia)), 'a very speedie pinnace' (Florio 1598), of obscure origin, commonly viewed as f. *saetta* arrow. Cf. F. *scétie, setie, scitie.*] A decked vessel, with a long sharp prow, carrying two or three masts with a kind of lateen sails, in use in the Mediterranean. Also *attrib.* **settee-sail** (see quot. 1794).

In some of the early quots. the vessel appears to have been a fairly large merchant ship.

**1587** T. SANDERS *Voy. Tripoli* C iv, M. Barton with all the residue of his companie departed from Tripolie to Oezant in a vessell called a Settea of one Marcus Segoorus. **1628** DIGBY *Voy. Mediterr.* (Camden) 13 To take that opportunitie to cleanse my shippes and to furnish myselfe with a sattie and other necessaries, and to change my ballast. **1653** H. APPLETON *Fight Legorn-Road* 1 The Warwick.. takes a French Sattee coming in to the Road. **1665** *Oxf. Gaz.* No. 17/4 A Sette came also from Malaga, a Vessel rarely seen in these parts; she is about fifty Tuns, and her Masts like a pair of Taylors Sheers opened. **1667** *Lond. Gaz.* No. 133/1 An English Satia from Tangier. **1686** W. HEDGES *Diary* (Hakl. Soc.) I. 237 We came up and spoke with a French Settee of Marseles. **1712** BLINSTON in *Lond. Gaz.* No. 5026/6 Three Marineco Ships, a Cettee and Gavilan. **1755** *Acts Gen. Assembly Georgia* (1881) 53 For every Snow Brig Polacre or Saetia [*printed* Sactia] Twenty Two Shillings and Six pence for every Sloop or Schooner [etc.]. **1786** in *Amer. St. Papers* (1833) I. 107, 1 Setye of 34 guns. **1794** *Rigging & Seamanship* I. 136 Boat's Settee Sail. This sail is quadrilateral. The head is bent to a latteen-yard. *Ibid.* 236 *Polacre-settee* is a vessel with three masts, usually navigated in the levant or mediterranean,..generally rigged with square-sails upon the main and mizen mast, and a latteen-sail upon the foremast, like a xebec. *Ibid.* 238 *Settee*, a vessel used in the mediterranean, rigged and navigated similar to xebecs or galleys, with settee-sails instead of latteen-sails. **1860** DUNDONALD *Autobiog. Seaman* (1862) 181 On the 11th [Nov. 1808] we captured a settee.

†**settee**². *Obs. rare.* [Of unknown origin.] A double pinner for the head.

**1688** HOLME *Armoury* II. 482/1 A Coronet settee..covers the Head, and by doubling it makes it stand at a great height both above and besides the Face. **1692** *Scarronides* II. 63 With top-knots fine, to make 'em pretty, With tippet, pallateen and settee. **1694** N. H. *Ladies Dict.* 11/1 A Settee is only a double Pinner.

**settee**³ (sɛ'tiː). [perh. a fanciful variation of SETTLE *sb.*: see -EE².] A seat (for indoors) holding two or more persons, with a back and (usually) arms; occasionally also with divisions (see quot. 1784). In America sometimes furnished with rockers.

**1716** *Lond. Gaz.* No. 5494/4 All Sorts of Hangings for Rooms and Stair-cases, Chairs, Settees and Screens. **1718** *Free-thinker* No. 44. 317 The Damask Settee was placed in the Center. **1756** AMORY *Buncle* (1825) I. 321 An oak settee, on which his bones lay. **1784** COWPER *Task* I. 75 Ingenious Fancy..devis'd The soft settee; one elbow at each end, And in the midst an elbow it receiv'd, United yet divided, twain at once. **1823** E. MOOR *Suffolk Words* 336 *Settee*, a sopha or moveable window-seat; in more modern language called, I believe, conversation stool. I have not heard the word of many years, and believe it is going out. **1839** BARHAM *Ingol. Leg.* Ser. I. *Gengulphus*, The aforesaid *barbe gris*..Had been stuff'd in the seat of a kind of settee Or double-arm'd chair. **1888** EGGLESTON *Graysons* i. 6 There was a green settee with three rockers beneath and an arm at each end. **1893** LELAND *Mem.* II. 141 An abundance of velvet 'settees', or divan sofas. **1895** *Stores' Price List* 192 Cane Settee.

**b.** *U.S.* (See quot.)

**1891** *Century Dict.*, *Settee*,..(*b*) A small part taken off from a long and large sofa by a kind of arm: thus, a long sofa may have a settee at each end partly cut off from the body of the piece.

**c. settee-bed**, a bed that can be folded up so as to form a settee.

**1769** FALCONER *Dict. Marine* (1780) II, *Banc à coucher*, a sort of folding bedstead, or settee-bed. **1786** in W. Macgill *Old Ross-sh.* (1909) 141 Settee bed with blue and white cheque covers.

**settel(l**, obs. forms of SETTLE.

**setter** ('sɛtə(r)), *sb.*¹ Also 5-6 *Sc.* settar, 6 *Sc.* -are, 7 seter. [f. SET *v.*¹ + -ER¹. Cf. Du. *zetter*, OHG. *sezzari* (Ger. *setzer*), Sw. *sättare*, Dan. *sætter*.]

**I.** One who or something which sets, in various senses of the vb.

**1. a.** *gen.* One who sets something specified or contextually implied. Often as the second element of a compound, in which the first element denotes the thing 'set,' as in BONE-SETTER, EEL-*setter*, TYPE-*setter*.

**14..** *Voc.* in Wr.-Wülcker 604/34 *Prepositor*, a setter of mes. **1538** ELYOT *Dict.*, *Finitor*, a setter of boundes. **1557** in Marwick *Edin. Guilds* (1909) 89 Thai wer ordanit be the settaris of the said taxt to pay ane pairt thairof. **1648** HEXHAM II, *Een Zetter*, a Setter, or a Compositor of letters. **1652** URQUHART *Jewel* Wks. (1834) 181, I usually afforded the setter copy at the rate of above a whole printed sheet in the day. **1859** *Lancet* 24 Dec. 649/2 Having the special repute of being a first-class..setter of stoves, grates, &c. **1889** RIDER HAGGARD *Cleopatra* II. iv, Who..would believe that she was the setter of that snare in which the Queen..should miserably perish? **1964** *New Statesman* 20 Mar. 455/1 Mr Holloway is severe on other people's abuses of English—particularly the setters of examination questions. **1976** *Listener* 23 & 30 Dec. 820/3 The *Listener* setter [of crossword puzzles] caters..for the cognoscente.

**b.** With adverbial extension or complement. See also SETTER-FORTH, -ON, -OUT, -TO, -UP.

**1548** UDALL, etc. *Erasm. Par. John* xix. 16-22 He was and is..a setter of all them at libertie whiche professeth his name. **1560** DAUS tr. *Sleidane's Comm.* 228b, Neyther wanted the matter setters foreward. **1591** SAVILE *Tacitus, Hist.* II. xx. 89 Maricus..pretending to be the setter of France at freedome. **1623** LISLE *Ælfric on O. & N. Test.* Pref. to Serm. Easterday M 4, An earnest louer and a great setter forward of monkery. **1654** WHITLOCK *Zootomia* 30 They come as Refiners of thy Drosse, or gilders (setters off) of thy Graces. **1656** BLOUNT *Glossogr.*, *Spretor*, a contemner,..a setter-light by. **1846** TRENCH *Mirac.* xxiv. (1862) 352 *note*, He was come now a Redeemer, that is a setter free of man..from alien powers which held him in bondage. **1866** W. COLLINS *Armadale* III. xii, 'Gin-and-bitters will put you on your legs again,' whispered this Samaritan setter-right of the alcoholic disasters of mankind.

**2.** A workman employed to 'set' something.

†**a.** One who 'sets' or lays stone or brick in building. *Obs.* Also ***rough-setter***: see ROUGH *a.* 21.

?**1403** *Fabric Rolls York Minster* (Surtees) 21 In remuneracione data cementariis vocatis setters ad parietes. **1435** *Contract Fotheringhay Ch.* (1841) 30 The Setters shall be chosyn and takyn by such as shall haf the governance and oversight of the sayd Werke by my seid Lord. **1526** *Pilgr. Perf.* (W. de W. 1531) 142 Choseth hym as a connynge man, ..& maketh hym a setter or orderer of yᵉ same stones. **1601-2** *Accts. Trin. Coll.* in Willis & Clark *Cambridge* (1886) II. 486 To laborers diging foundacions..and seruing the setters at the fountaine.

**b.** *Woollen Manuf.* (See quot. 1757.)

*c* **1515** *Cocke Lorelles B.* (Percy Soc.) 9 Lyne webbers, setters, with lyne drapers. **1713** ADDISON *Trial Count Tariff* 3 He was Huzza'd into the Court by several Thousands of Weavers, Clothiers,..Packers, Calenders, Setters, Silk-men, Spinners [etc.]. **1757** R. CAMPBELL *Lond. Tradesman* (ed. 3) 201 Setters..are called so only because they rent Tenter-grounds and stretch Cloths after they are milled, upon Frames called Tenters.

**c.** A workman who sets jewels.

**1819** *P.O. Lond. Direct.* 382 Woolcott & Co.,..Cutters and Glaziers' Diamond Setters, 127 High Holborn. **1874** *Dieulafait's Diamonds*, etc. 275 The setter has at his command a furnace filled with burning charcoal. His work is to solder the diamond into a quantity of alloy [etc.]. **1884** *B'ham Daily Post* 23 Feb. 3/4 Jeweller's Setter.—Wanted a good Hand, used to flush work.

**d.** *Agric.* (See quot.)

**1707** MORTIMER *Husb.* (1721) I. 90 To each Cart [of marl] must be a Driver and a Setter, whose Office is to shew where 'tis to be laid, and to assist in the unlading of it.

**e.** A workman who sets or puts into working condition saws, razors, gun-barrels, etc.

**1833** J. HOLLAND *Manuf. Metal* II. 29 A celebrated setter or whetter of razors. **1837** HEBERT *Engin. & Mech. Encycl.* II. 630 They [saws] are next handed to the setter, who places each alternate tooth over the edge of a little anvil [etc.]. **1881** GREENER *Gun* 234 To determine if a barrel is straight, the setter holds it a few inches from his eye with one end pointing towards the top of a high shop-window.

†**3.** 'A officer on the Border, who, with a searcher, was responsible for setting the appointed watch' (*Northumbld. Gloss.* 1893-4). *Obs.*

**1552** in Nicolson *Leges Marchiarum* (1705) 235 The Ford of Bellester..to be watched nightly, with two Men at either Watch..; Setters and Searchers, Thomas Blenkensop and John Orsby. *Ibid.*, Setters and Searchers of the same Watch, Christopher Bowman, Nichol Blaykloke.

**4.** In *Dice-play.* The player who stakes on the throw of the 'caster'.

**1726** J. KER *Mem.* II. 93 And when the Cullies that are not in the Secret, throw at All, they commonly throw out, and lose the Box, which the Bites take, and the Setters go round, laying Guineas, and most extravagant Odds upon the Success. **1726** *Art & Myst. Gaming* title-p., Tables calculated betwixt the Caster and Setter, throughout the whole Course or Changes of the Dice. **1814** *Hoyle's Games Impr.* 367 If the main be seven, and each person stakes a guinea, the gain of the setter is about 3½d. per guinea. **1856** CARLETON in Bohn's *Hand-bk. Games* (1867) 359 (Hazard), If the Caster throw 2, 3, 11 or 12, next after the main is declared, the Setter wins the stake.

**5.** †**a.** *gen.* One who places a combatant in position. *Obs.*

**1648** BP. HALL *Select Th.* xv. 60 This duel [between the flesh and the spirit] may well beseem God for the Author, and the Son of God for the setter of it.

**b.** *spec.* In cock-fighting: = SETTER-TO 1.

**1688** HOLME *Armoury* II. 253/1 When the Cocks are set Beak to Beak in the middle of the Clod, and there left by the Setters. **1835** H. HAREWOOD *Dict. Sports* s.v. *Cock-fighting*, The battle is conducted by two setters, as they are called, who place the cocks beak to beak. **1884** *West. Daily Press* 16 Apr. 7/2 The whole number at the pit side, including the 'setters' was only 37 persons.

**6.** †**a.** *Sc.* One who grants or makes a lease. *Obs.*

**1484** in *Exch. Rolls Scot.* IX. 603 Our commissioneris and settaris of all and sindri our landis. **1586** in *Extracts Edin. Burgh Rec.* (1882) IV. 478 The said setters of thair land to sic persouns sall be poynded or wairdet for ane vnlaw of fyve pund swa aft as thai failyie. **1638** R. BAILLIE *Lett. & Jrnls.* (1841) I. 163 He was a setter of tacks to his sones and goodsones, for the prejudice of the church. **1754** ERSKINE *Princ. Sc. Law* (1809) 186 Tacks necessarily imply a *delectus personæ*, a choice by the setter of a proper person for his tenant.

**b.** 'One who lets anything to another for hire' (Jam.). *north. dial.*

**1806** *Sporting Mag.* XXVII. 42 A person in the city of Chester, who is noted for a high setter of shops, as they express it in the north. **1825-82** JAMIESON s.v., A *horse-setter*, a horse-hirer.

**c.** In quarrying and mining work: The foreman by whom the contracts are made with the workmen. See also SETTING *vbl. sb.*¹ 1 e.

**1884** *West. Morn. News* 5 Sept. 2/4 The setter will engage that the bridge shall ply..daily... The setter also will appoint engineers and pay their wages. **1892** *Labour Commission* Gloss., *Setter*, a *bargain-setter* (or *letter*) is the official who *sets* or *lets* the contract to the quarrymen. **1901** *Daily News* 29 Jan. 6/5 At the beginning of each month, upon what is called bargain day, one, two, or three skilled quarrymen agree with a foreman, or 'setter', upon the tonnage rate at which they will work out a given portion of the quarry for the following month.

**7. a.** A confederate of sharpers or swindlers, employed as a decoy; also (? with transferred notion of sense 11), one who is employed by robbers or murderers to spy upon their intended victims.

**1592** GREENE *Discov. Coosenage* A 4, There be requisite effectually to act the art of Conny-catching, three seuerall parties, the Setter, the Verser, and the barnacle. The nature of the Setter, is to drawe anie person familiarly to drinke with him [etc.]. **1596** SHAKS. *1 Hen. IV*, II. ii. 53 *Poin.* O 'tis our Setter, I know his voyce: Bardolfe, what newes? **1647** DIGGS *Unlawfuln. Taking Arms* iv. 137 It is beyond my skill to..determine, whether the slye and cunning setter, or the stout thief can claim greatest share in the spoyle. **1722** SWIFT *Dying Words Elliston* Wks. 1761 III. 357 We have setters watching in corners, and by dead walls, to give us notice when a gentleman goes by. **1755** *Connoisseur* No. 86 ¶4, I became Setter to a Fleet-Parson.

**b.** 'A person employed by the vendor at an auction to run the biddings up' (*Hotten's Slang Dict.* 1860).

**1698** DUNTON *Life & Errors* 547, I had not one Setter (to advance the price, and draw on unwary Bidders) in any of my five Sales. **1732** *Tricks of Town* 36 Away to the place of Auction; the Orator,..surrounded by his Puffs and Setters, shows away.

**c.** A police spy or informer.

**1630** J. LANE *Contn. Squire's T.* 2nd vers. (1887) 134 So maie wee doe and live, woold Algarsive and his state setters, all vs thus reprive. *a* **1661** FULLER *Worthies*, *Lond.* (1662) II. 222 It was not long before he [Campian] was caught by the Setters of the Secretary Walsingham, and brought to the Tower. **1778** WARNER in Jesse *Selwyn & Contemp.* (1844) III. 314, I shall have the satisfaction at last of finding something that I am fit for,—a setter, a dun, a catchpole, or a bum-bailiff, to recover bad debts. **1866** FITZPATRICK *Sham Squire* 125 All the information regarding the movements of Lord Edward Fitzgerald came through Francis Higgins, who employed a gentleman..'to set' the unfortunate nobleman. The 'setter' we believe to have been Mr. Francis Magan, barrister-at-law. **1890** BARRÈRE & LELAND *Dict. Slang*, *Setter*,.. a policeman in disguise or a man in the employ of the police (the French 'indicateur') who points out the thief for others to arrest.

†**d.** (See quot.) *Obs.*

*a* **1700** B. E. *Dict. Cant. Crew*, *Setters*..also..an Excize-Officer to prevent the Brewers defrauding the King.

**e.** *transf.* and *fig.*

**1600** SIR W. CORNWALLIS *Ess.* I. iii. C 8, They are the effect of need, or wantonnesse, venial faults. Age commonly reclaimeth the one, and the other is punished by the setter Pouertie. **1667** *Decay Chr. Piety* v. (1668) 82 Self-love, which is, as it were, the common Setter to all those cheats which circumvent and fool us. **1683** CAVE *Eccles.*, *Basil* 218 Their first care was to lodge him in the House of some Friend, or Country-man, or at least one of those Setters, that plied up and down in the behalf of that Sophist.

**8.** One who sets to music.

**1605** J. DAVIES (Heref.) *Wit's Pilgr.* (Grosart) 8/1 Thy Soule vpon so sweet an Organ plaies As makes the Parts, she plaies, as sound as sweete; Which sounds the heau'nly Setters, and thy praise. **1635** WALLER *To Mr. H. Lawes* 23 The Writers and the Setters skill At once the ravisht Ears do fill.

†**9.** One who devises or instigates. *Obs.*

**1600** HOLLAND *Livy* XXVI. 605 As well the misters that were the setters thereof, as the servants that were privie and accessarie thereto, had their deserts, and suffered for it.

**10. a.** That which fertilizes a flower, so that the plant is able to 'set' or develop fruit (see SET *v.*¹ 98).

*a* **1793** G. WHITE *Selborne*, *Obs. on Veget.* (1836) 301 If bees, who are much the best setters of cucumbers, do not happen to take kindly to the frames, the best way is to tempt them by a little honey put on the..bloom.

**b.** A plant which 'sets' or develops fruit; only with adj. as ***good, bad setter***.

**1888** M. T. MASTERS in *Encycl. Brit.* XXIV. 237/2 Some ..varieties [of the vine] are, as gardeners say, 'bad setters', —i.e. do not ripen their fruit owing to imperfect fertilization.

**11.** A dog trained to 'set' game.

**a.** As the name of a special breed. ***Irish setter*** = *red setter* s.v. RED *a.* 17 a. ***English, Gordon setter***: see under first element.

Of the breed now so called, there are three varieties, the *English*, the *Irish*, and the *Gordon setters*. The name was formerly applied to a kind of spaniel.

**1576** FLEMING tr. *Caius' Dogs* (1880) 16 When he approcheth neere to the place where the birde is, he layes him downe, and with a marcke of his pawes, betrayeth the place of the byrdes last abode, whereby it is supposed that this kinde of dogge is called *Index*, Setter. **1616** SURFL. & MARKH. *Country Farm* VII. xxii. 680 There is also another sort of land spannyels which are called Setters. **1774** GOLDSM. *Nat. Hist.* II. 167 The setter that crouches down when it scents the birds, till the net be drawn over them. **1859** DARWIN *Orig. Spec.* i. (1873) 25 Some..authorities are convinced that the setter is directly derived from the spaniel. **1866** J. WALKER in *Field* 6 Jan. 3/2, I should feel obliged by your allowing me to say a word or two..on the colour and general characteristics of the Irish setter. **1912** A. HUXLEY *Let.* 13 May (1969) 42 He, the dog, is a beautiful Irish setter, the only one of his kind within a radius of miles, as the beast has only just been introduced into Germany. **1975** J. M. BREARLEY (*title*) This is the Irish Setter.

*attrib.* **1885** *Field* 17 Jan. Advt., For Sale, handsome highly bred Setter Bitch. *Ibid.*, A gentleman is desirous of placing Two Red Setter Pups..with a first-class breaker.

†**b.** *gen. Obs.*

**1678** *Lond. Gaz.* No. 1317/4 A little Land Spaniel, red and white, no Setter. **1741** *Compl. Fam.-Piece* II. i. 314 But Water Spaniels may be brought to be Setters, if they have a perfectly good Scent.

†**c.** One who practises 'setting': see SETTING *vbl. sb.*¹ 1 c (*b*). *Obs.*

**1780** T. DAVIES *Garrick* I. 3 Mr. Hunter was..a great setter of game. Happy was the boy who could inform his offended master where a covey of partridges was to be found.

**II. 12.** An instrument or tool used in setting, in various senses.

†**a.** A net or trap for catching or killing birds.

**1526** *Househ. Exp. Sir T. Le Strange* (MS.), Item. a wood-cocke and ij partriches kylled with the setter. **1540** *Acts Privy Counc.* (1837) VII. 56 Taking or killing..any partriches and fesantes with any nettes setters horses trameles or other gynnes.

**b.** *Gunnery.* A wooden instrument used, with the aid of a mallet, to set the fuse into a shell.

**1802** C. JAMES *Milit. Dict.*, *Setter*, in *gunnery*, a round stick to drive fuzes, or any other compositions, into cases made of paper. **1828** J. M. SPEARMAN *Brit. Gunner* (ed. 2) 79 Wood Setters. **1854** F. A. GRIFFITHS *Artil. Man.* (ed. 6) 82 They are carefully driven into the Shell with a mallet and setter. **1876** VOYLE & STEVENSON *Milit. Dict.* 377/2.

**c.** ? = SETTING-POLE.

**1853** SIR H. DOUGLAS *Milit. Bridges* 31 The appurtenances were as follows:—6 balks,..2 oars; 1 anchor; 1 grapnel; 1 pole or setter.

**d.** *Porcelain Manuf.*

**1853** URE *Dict. Arts* II. 454 A plate sagger will hold twenty plates placed one on the other of earthenware, but china plates are fired separately in 'setters' made of their respective forms. **1873** SPON *Workshop Rec.* Ser. I. 43/2 Setters also should be used at the bottom of each piece, and ground flint applied, but not sand, for the placing or seating.

**e.** A kind of lifting-jack.

**1895** *Stores' Price List* 15 Sept. 490 Carriage Setter. Best Wood Setter—each 15/0.

**13.** *dial.* (See quot.)

**1849** GREENWELL *Gloss. Terms Coal Trade* (1851) 46 *Setters*, large pieces of coal; so called by the landsale cartmen, from their use in piling or setting round the sides of their carts, to enable them to hold a larger quantity of coals than could otherwise be placed upon them.

**'setter,** *sb.*[2] *dial.* [f. SETTER *v.*] A seton or issue produced by 'settering': see the vb.

**1766** *Complete Farmer, Setter*, a kind of setom [*sic*] or issue, made by cutting a hole in the dewlap of an ox or cow, and putting into the wound a sort of tent formed out of the root of helleboraster. **1788** [see SETTERGRASS].

**setter** ('sɛtə(r)), *v. dial.* Also 6 **syter.** [f. SETTER- in SETTERWORT.] *trans.* To insert a piece of setterwort under the skin of (an animal) in order to produce an issue.

[**1523**: cf. SEVER *v.* 5c.] **1551** TURNER *Herbal* I. Lvj, Dyuerse husband men..vsed to put the roote of berefoot into beastes eares, and called the puttynge in of it, syterynge of beastes. **1577** B. GOOGE *Heresbach's Husb.* III. (1586) 133 The order of Settring a Bullocke is this, take setterwoort [etc.]. *Ibid.* 151 Some again cure them with settering. **1691** RAY *N.C. Words*, To *Setter*; to cut the Dewlap of an Ox or Cow, into which they put Helleboraster, which we call Setterwort. **1741** *Compl. Fam.-Piece* III. 506 It is necessary at the same Time to setter the Hog in the Ear with the common Hellebore. **1863** ATKINSON *Danby Gloss.* s.v. *Seton*, We took care that she [a cow] was weel setter'd.

**setter:** see SAETER, SETTER.

**Setterday,** obs. form of SATURDAY.

**setter-forth.** [See SET *v.*[1] 144.] One who sets forth (in various senses); one who promulgates an opinion, who equips an expedition, etc.

**1451** *Rolls of Parlt.* V. 225/1 Noon owner, Vitailler, nor setter-forth of eny Shippe or Vessell. **1542** UDALL *Erasm. Apoph.* 5 *marg.*, Mecænas was..so great a fauourer, promouter, and setter fourthe of Virgil, Horace, & suche other learned menne, that [etc.]. **1611** BIBLE *Acts* xvii. 18 He seemeth to be a setter foorth of strange gods. **1616** CAPT. SMITH *Descr. New Eng.* 48, I was beholden to the setters forth of the foure ships that went with Cooper. *a* **1700** EVELYN *Diary* Aug. 1641 (1879) I. 22 Mr. Bleaw, the setter forth of the Atlas's and other workes of that kind. **1721** STRYPE *Eccl. Mem.* III. xl. 319 Sebastian Cabota..was the chief Setterforth of the first Voyage into those Parts. **1840** BROWNING *Sordello* I. 26 Your setters-forth of unexampled themes.

**'settergrass.** *Obs.* exc. *dial. rare.* In 4 **saturgresse,** 5 **setyr grysse.** [f. *setter- in SETTERWORT + GRASS.] = SETTERWORT.

*a* **1387** *Sinon. Barthol.* (Anecd. Oxon.) 18 *Elleborus*, i. saturgresse. **1483** *Cath. Angl.* 331/2 Setyr grysse, *eleborus niger, herba est.* **1597** GERARDE *Herbal* II. ccclxi. 827 *Consiligo* is called in English Bearfoote, Setterwoort, and Setter-grasse. **1788** W. H. MARSHALL *Yorksh.* II. 350 Setter-grass, *helleborus fœtidus*; a species of bear's-foot; used in making 'setters' or issues in cattle. **1868** ATKINSON *Cleveland Gloss.* 439 The plant setter-wort, or setter-grass.

†**setter-on.** *Obs.* [See SET *v.*[1] 148.]

**1.** One who sets on; an instigator or inciter.

*c* **1550** BALE *K. Johan* 2482 (Manly) Tyll my setters-on were of their purpose wyde. **1560** DAUS tr. *Sleidane's Comm.* Pref. 4b, I sent unto them that were my setters on, at Woormes. **1616** R. COCKS *Diary* (Hakl. Soc.) I. 163 The Jesuistes and other padres are the fyre brands and setters on of all this, in provoking children against parents and subjects against their naturall princes. **1749** FIELDING *Tom Jones* VI. ix, The great Dowdy who acts the part of a madman as well as some of his setters-on do that of a fool.

**2.** One who 'sets on' or makes an onset. *rare.*

**1568** GRAFTON *Chron.* II. 294, I made once a vowe that the first battaile that eyther the king your father or any of his children should be at, how that I would be one of the first setters on, or else to die in the trauaile.

**setter-out.** *rare.* [See SET *v.*[1] 149.]

**1.** One who sets out; one who publishes, proclaims, etc.

*c* **1553** ASCHAM *Disc. Germ.* (1570) 21 A noble setter out, and as true a follower of Christ and his Gospell. **1582** in Row *Hist. Kirk* (Wodrow Soc.) 101 That the autors, dyters, setters out of that infamous lybell be punished accordinglie. **1824** [W. CARR] *Craven Gloss.* Introd. 5 T'Setter-out o't book.

**2.** *spec.* (See quot.)

**1892** *Labour Commission* Gloss., *Setter out*, an under or assistant foreman of joiners or leading joiner, whose work is to accurately set or line out every detail of each piece of joinery.

**setter-to.** ? *Obs.* [See SET *v.*[1] 152.]

**1.** A professional handler of game-cocks in a cock-fight; = SETTER *sb.*[1] 5.

**1794** *Sporting Mag.* III. 169 To these another class become annexed, called 'handers' or 'setters to'. **1835** H. HAREWOOD *Dict. Sports* s.v. *Cock-fighting*, When once the cocks are pitted, neither of the setters-to can touch his cock ..unless [etc.].

**2.** *Pugilism.* With epithet: One who has a particular style of 'setting to' or beginning the fight.

**1810** *Sporting Mag.* XXXVI. 125 A shewy setter-to, but a slight hitter. **1824** EGAN *Boxiana* II. 493 The most accomplished setter-to of the day, Tom Belcher.

**setter-up.** [See SET *v.*[1] 154.] One who sets up (in any sense).

**1563** *Homilies* II. *Agst. Peril Idol.* III. 59b, The erecter, setter vp, and mainteyner of Images in Churches and Temples. **1593** SHAKS. *3 Hen. VI*, II. iii. 37 Thou setter vp, and plucker downe of Kings. **1607** MIDDLETON *Michaelm. Term* II. iii, I am but a yong setter vp; the vttermost I dare venture vppon't is three-score pound. **1613** BEAUM. & FL. *Honest Man's Fort.* II. i, Old occupations have too many setters up to prosper. **1713** BERKELEY *Hylas & Phil.* iii. Wks. 1871 I. 359, I do not pretend to be a setter-up of new notions. **1853** R. S. HAWKER in *Life & Lett.* (1905) 251 Neither can I congratulate your Setter-up [i.e. compositor] on his accuracy. **1876** MORRIS *Æneids* VIII. 134 Dardanus first setter-up and sire of Ilian wall. **1881** *Instr. Census Clerks* (1885) 43 Spinning and weaving machine maker... Setter-up.

**setterwort** ('sɛtəwɜːt). Also 6 **syter wurt.** [Perh. adopted from MLG.; Diefenbach s.v. *Elleborum* gives a great variety of synonymous forms in MHG. and MLG. such as *sitro, sutir-, sittir-, sitti-, siter-, sutten-, -sutwurz, -wort* (f. HG. *wurz*, LG. *wort* WORT[1]). The first element is of unknown origin; cf. ME. (14th *c.*) *satur(gresse)* SETTERGRASS.] The plant Bear's-foot or Fetid Hellebore, *Helleborus fœtidus*; also the Green Hellebore, *H. viridis*.

**1551** TURNER *Herbal* I. Lvj, The herbe syter wurte. **1577** B. GOOGE *Heresbach's Husb.* III. (1586) 124b, The hearbe called blacke Ellebor, of some Bearfoot, and others Setterwort. **1597** [see SETTERGRASS]. *c* **1710** PETIVER *Cat. Ray's Eng. Herbal* Tab. 42 Setterwort. Greenish. **1778** G. WHITE *Selborne, Let. to Barrington* 3 July, *Helleborus fœtidus*, stinking hellebore, bear's-foot, or setterwort. **1907** *Daily News* 25 Feb. 3 The tender green of the setterwort does not own the power of the frost by a single black spot.

**settewale,** obs. form of SETWALL.

**setthe(n,** obs. variant forms of SITH, SITHEN.

**Settherday,** dial. form of SATURDAY.

**settil,** obs. form of SETTLE.

**setting,** *sb. Orkney & Shetl.* Also 6 **settein,** 7–9 **setten,** 9 **settin, -een.** [a. ON. *séttung-r* sixth part, f. *sétte* sixth.] A unit of weight in the Orkney and Shetland Isles; the sixth part of a 'meal' (MEAL *sb.*[4]); identical with the LISPOUND.

**1576** in *Oppress. Orkney & Zetl.* (1859) 72 Ane barrell of malt of nyne setteins wecht. **1588** *Rot. Scacc. Reg. Scot.* XXI. 390 Selling..63 lastis 23,003 settingis 4 marks coist, 125 lasts 1002 settingis beir, 95 lastis 1004 settingis flesche. **1703** M. MARTIN *Descr. West. Isles* 370 A Young Boy..stole a setten of Barley, which is about twenty eight Pound Weight. **1814** SHIRREFF *Agric. Shetl.* 159 Twenty-four marks make a settin or lispund... Six settins or lispunds make a meil.

**setting** ('sɛtɪŋ), *vbl. sb.*[1] [f. SET *v.*[1] + -ING[1].]

**I. 1. a.** The action of the verb SET in various transitive senses; putting, placing, planting, etc. Also, the fact of being set.

**1398** TREVISA *Barth. De P.R.* XVII. cxxxvi. (1495) 692 The rose tree spryngith somtyme by settynge and plantynge and somtyme by graffynge. **1427–8** *Rec. St. Mary at Hill* 68 Also for settyng of þe same ston iij dayes. **1561** T. HOBY tr. *Castiglione's Courtyer* III. (1577) Pj, M. Thomas..writte to his wife, and did hir to weete hys setting at libertie. **1626** BACON *Sylva* §423 A Tree, at the first Setting, should not be Shaken, vntill it hath taken Root fully. **1769** FALCONER *Dict. Marine* (1780), *Setting*, when applied to the sails, is the loosening and expanding them. **1796** W. JONES, etc. *Key to Art of Ringing* Pref. 1 Instructions for the attainment of the practical part of the art, from the setting of a Bell itself to the perfect knowledge of the most difficult peals. **1841** *Guide to Trade, Baker* 38 This is called the quarter sponge, and the operation is denominated setting. **1881** GREENER *Gun* 235 At that time setting or straightening was so little known that many of the barrels were far from being straight. **1892** *Labour Commission* Gloss., *Setting of the Brick*, the fixing of the bricks in a kiln. **1921** H. G. CROCKETT *Pract. Leather Manuf.* II. x. 141 When the goods have become sufficiently dry for setting, and in a fairly stiff condition, they are taken down and brushed over with water. **1953** D. WOODROFFE *Leather Dressing* xiv. 144 Sometimes the setting is done by striking out a second time on the same machine. **1965** M. MCINTYRE *Place of Quiet Waters* ii. 23 There was a.. bucksaw, badly in need of setting.

†**b.** An ambush or trap. *Obs.*

*c* **1430** *Pilgr. Lyf Manhode* IV. viii. (1869) 180 Keepe þee.. from hise settinges and from hise nettes.

**c.** *Sport.* (*a*) The action of a dog in indicating game.

**1621** MARKHAM *Hungers Prev.* 265 To make a true election of your dogge, which you intend to apply to this purpose of Setting. **1725** *Bradley's Fam. Dict., Setting-dog*, a Dog train'd up to the Setting of Partridges. **1819** T. B. JOHNSON *Shooter's Comp.* 22 Dogs, called setters, are now to be met with of all forms, miserably deficient in the most prominent quality, setting.

(*b*) The sport of 'putting up' game with a setter.

**1661** BOYLE *Certain Physiol. Ess.* (1669) 36 When I go a Hawking or Setting. *a* **1700** EVELYN *Diary* 20 Aug. 1654, I went a setting and hawking. **1770** G. WHITE *Selborne, Let. to Pennant* 12 May, I knew a lover of setting, an old sportsman. **1818** *Gentl. Mag.* LXXXVIII. II. 113 His great skill in all the sports of the field, especially that of Setting, of which diversion his Lordship was passionately fond.

**d.** *Sc.* and *dial.* The action of letting or leasing (land, etc.); the right to do this; a lease.

**1397** in *Spalding Club Miscell.* V. 252 All giftys, taliees, settyngys, and condysyoungs mad or to be mad be dame Isabell, Contas of Mar, to the sayd George hir brothir. **1546** *Yorks. Chantry Surv.* (Surtees) 246 The saide founder.. shall have the lettinge, settinge, boynes, services and customes of all the landes. **1634–46** ROW *Hist. Kirk* (1842) 173 Cruell oppression of the poore tenants; evidenced, 1°. By deare setting of rowms. **1760** *Patrington Haven Act* 16 The intention of such letting or setting. **1898** *Longman's Mag.* Apr. 546 The lettings, here called 'settings' or 'takings', are at Candlemas.

**e.** *Mining.* The act of contracting with miners for work to be done.

**1839** DE LA BECHE *Rep. Geol. Cornwall*, etc. xv. 569 Of the remainder he paid the adventurers one-half, or one-quarter, as may have been agreed upon according to the supposed prospects of the mine at the time of setting. **1892** *Labour Commission* Gloss., *Setting*, sometimes termed 'letting',..in the slate industry,..means agreeing upon a contract for a month.

**2. a.** The manner or position in which anything is set, fixed, or placed. In *Croquet*, any one of the different arrangements of the hoops and pegs on the ground.

**14..** *Wycliffite Bible, 2 Kings* ii. 19 *marg.*, That is, the setting of the citee was best for profetis. *c* **1450** *Mirk's Festial* 279 How ȝe schull pray to God, þe settyng of þe chyrch hyt tellyþe you: Hit ys sette yn þe est, techyng [etc.]. **1523–34** FITZHERB. *Husb.* §4 The temperynge to go brode and narrowe is in the settyng of the culture [= coulter]. **1625** MIDDLETON *Game at Chess* Induct. 40, I saw the bravest setting for a game now That ever mine eye fix'd on. **1868** W. J. WHITMORE *Croquet Tactics* ii. 19 There are as many as eight different settings. **1897** *Encycl. Sport* I. 254/1 (Croquet) The original setting had ten hoops... Finally came the six-hoop or championship setting. **1948** 'DUPLEX' *Sharpening Small Tools* iv. 71 To adjust the setting of the plane..the tension screw is slightly slackened and the set adjustment lever is moved upwards or downwards. **1979** *Homes & Gardens* June 154/1 Some recent models also have a thermometer and control dial so you are able to alter the setting.

**b.** The inclination or dip of an axle: = SET *sb.*[1] 18a.

**1844** H. STEPHENS *Bk. Farm* III. 1162 The setting or form of the axle.

**c.** *Gas-works.* The manner of placing retorts in a furnace; *concr.* a group or set of retorts placed together.

**1872** W. C. HOLMES & CO. *Manag. Gas Works* 15 The setting of the retorts is a matter of the utmost importance. **1877** W. RICHARDS *Manuf. Coal Gas* 354 Of all the apparatus of a gasworks, unquestionably the most important are the settings of retorts. **1879** *Encycl. Brit.* X. 91/2 A furnace or bed of retorts is composed of a group or setting, heated by a separate fire.

**d.** *Type-founding.* The position of the face of a letter on the body or shank. Cf. SET *sb.*[1] 19c.

**1887** J. SOUTHWARD in *Encycl. Brit.* XXIII. 710/1 All founders now supply imitations of the old types. Comparing the old face and the modern characters, the latter are more regular in size, lining, setting, and colour,—using these words in the technical sense of the founder.

**e.** A set of cutlery or crockery, or of both, sufficient for one place at table. Cf. *place-setting* s.v. PLACE *sb.*[1] 29.

**1952** A. VANDERBILT *Compl. Bk. Etiquette* ix. 98 A young bride can do very well with four- or six-place settings consisting of dinner knife, dinner fork, salad fork, butter knife, teaspoon, and dessert spoon. **1961** *Times* 30 May 15/6 Veneered oak canteen containing settings for 8 people, including fish knives and forks, in Mappin Plate. **1975** M. ORR *Rich Girl, Poor Girl* xxi. 278 Maggie..was given..a twelve-piece setting of Danish flatware.

†**3.** Putting into words, redaction. *Obs.*

*c* **1450** LOVELICH *Grail* lvi. 519 For þ[e] ton storie the tothir Medlyth withal, After the settyng Of the forseid Robert That somtym it translated. **1450–1530** *Myrr. our Ladye* I. vi. 21 Therefore thus after the settynge of mayster Alphonse is youre legende red in all places of this order.

†**4.** A stake at play; a bet or stake. *Obs.*

**1540** PALSGR. *Acolastus* IV. iii. Tj, All the stakes and settynges that be sette within the dyce borde, whiche lye on lyttell heapes.

†**5.** A set (of stones) with which a surface is 'set' or studded. *Obs. rare*[−1].

**1611** BIBLE *Exod.* xxviii. 17 And thou shalt set in it settings of stones [*margin*, Hebr. fill in it fillings of stone].

**6. a.** The manner in which a jewel is 'set' or mounted; *concr.* the frame or bed (of precious metal or the like) in which a jewel is set.

**1815** W. H. IRELAND *Scribbleomania* 192 *note*, A very valuable antique ring, the setting of which did not meet his approbation. **1822** HAZLITT *Table-t.* Ser. II. ii. *Aristocr. Lett.* (1869) 48 The setting is more valuable than the jewel. **1879** *Cassell's Techn. Educ.* IV. 350/2 There are two systems of setting practised—viz., Roman setting, and what is called colletting.

**b.** *transf.* and *fig.* The environment or surroundings in which a person or thing is 'set'; the literary framework of a narrative or other composition; the mounting of a play.

**1841** MYERS *Cath. Th.* III. §8. 30 The connecting links —the framing and setting—of these Revelations. **1874** SAYCE *Compar. Philol.* viii. 315 Mythology has a setting in geography and history. **1885** *Manch. Exam.* 27 Jan. 5/4 The setting of the piece is charming, and it is quite wonderful how much has been made of a little stage.

**c.** *Psychol.* and *Sociol.* A person's disposition or cast of mind formed by experience and colouring his behaviour. Also, the immediate environment considered as an influence upon behaviour; *spec.* an environment designed to create a particular atmosphere, esp. for experiments with mind-affecting drugs.

**1914** M. PRINCE *Unconscious* x. 311 Antecedent experiences of life..conserved in the unconscious formed a setting that gave the point of view and attitude of mind. **1954** BARKER & WRIGHT *Midwest & its Children* iii. 45 A behavior setting has been defined as a standing pattern of behavior and as part of the milieu which are syno-morphic and in which the milieu is circumjacent to the behavior. *Ibid.* vi. 223 A day from the life of a child in the settings of a community gives a sample of behavior and habitat that is ..limited. **1963** E. GOFFMAN *Behav. in Public Places* ii. 21 The same physical space can come to be used as a setting for more than one social occasion, and hence as a locus for more than one set of expectations. **1968** *Science* 13 Dec. 1236/1 It is necessary to control set and setting... The total environment in which the drug is taken is the setting. **1974** M. C. GERALD *Pharmacol.* xviii. 341 Among the variables that modify the marijuana response are dosage, route of administration, set, and setting.

**7.** The manner in which a poem or form of words is set to music; a piece of music composed for a particular poem or form of words.

**1871** D. G. ROSSETTI *Lett.* (1967) III. 923 Dr. Bennett.. can publish his setting if he makes no alteration in the words. **1879** HUSK in *Grove's Dict. Music* I. 84/2 Arne gave to the world those beautiful settings of the songs 'Under the greenwood tree' [etc.]. **1881** CROWEST *Phases Mus. Eng.* 93 Settings for the Canticles by modern Church writers.

**8. a.** *Plastering.* The finishing coat of plaster, the *setting-coat* (see 14, SET *sb.*[1] 30 a, SET *v.*[1] 101).

**1823** P. NICHOLSON *Pract. Builder* 390 The term setting is commonly used, when the third coat is made of fine stuff for papering. **1825** J. NICHOLSON *Oper. Mech.* 606 With this tool all the first coats of plaster is laid on, as are also the last, or, as it is technically termed, the setting. **1873** SPON *Workshop Rec.* Ser. I. 121/2 Setting may be either a second coat upon laying or rendering, or a third coat upon floating.

**b.** A wash of gum or other suitable material applied to the surface of a pencil, charcoal or crayon drawing to prevent it being rubbed; a fixative.

**1895** in *Funk's Stand. Dict.*

**9. a.** A crop of fruit developed by fertilizing (see SET *v.*[1] 98). ? *Obs.*

**1731** MILLER *Gard. Dict.* s.v. *Cucumis*, For Want of which kindly Heat, the first Setting or Crop of Fruit..drops off.

**b.** A clutch (of eggs).

**1902** E. NESBIT *Five Children & It* iii. 85 A setting of Buff Orpington eggs that had not turned out well. **1938** M. K. RAWLINGS *Yearling* xiv. 140 The setting was hatched. The young quail, each no bigger than the end of his thumb, scattered like small windblown leaves.

**II.** Senses related to intransitive uses of SET *v.*[1]

**10. a.** The sinking of a heavenly body towards and below the horizon; the quarter or direction in which a heavenly body sets. Also, the fall of night or darkness.

*a* **1400–50** *Wars Alex.* 5508 Þan sewis furth þat souerayn ay by þa salt strandis Toward þe settynge of þe son. **1592** HUES *Treat. Globes* xii, You shall in like manner have the houre of the setting. **1607, 1728** [see HELIACAL 1]. **1699** *Relat. Sir T. Morgan's Progr. France* 13 The Major-General reply'd he would fall on just at the setting of the Night, and when the dusk of the Evening came on. **1823** CLISSOLD *Ascent Mt. Blanc* 22 The sun being now near his setting. **1877** BROWNING *Agamemnon* 67 The shield-bearing people That made a leap, at setting of the Pleiads.

**b.** *fig.*

**1613** SHAKS. *Hen. VIII*, III. ii. 225, I haue touch'd the highest point of all my Greatnesse, And from that full Meridian of my Glory, I haste now to my Setting. **1702** C. MATHER *Magn. Chr.* II. x. (1852) 156 Upon the setting of Mr. Francis Newman, there arose Mr. William Leet. **1807** WORDSW. *Ode Intim. Immortality* v, The Soul that rises with us, our life's Star, Hath had elsewhere its setting, And cometh from afar. **1839** LONGF. *Hyperion* I. i, The setting of a great hope is like the setting of the sun.

**11.** The process or fact of becoming set, hard, or stiff; coagulation.

**1791** E. DARWIN *Bot. Gard.* I. Addit. Notes xii. 24 The clay becomes as hard as before, being pressed together..by its self-attraction, called setting by the potters. **1805** R. W. DICKSON *Pract. Agric.* I. 456 An almost impenetrable crust may be produced by the quick exhalation of the moisture, and what is termed by farmers the setting of the clay. **1812** P. NICHOLSON *Mech. Exerc.* 312 (Plastering) *Setting* is also the quality that any kind of stuff has to harden in a short time. **1883** *Hardwich's Photogr. Chem.* (ed. 9) 166 If too much Alcohol be employed, the setting of the Pyroxyline will be..greatly retarded. **1969** *Jams, Preserves & Homemade Sweets* (Good Housekeeping Libr. Cooking) i. 10 Lemon juice..aids the setting. *Ibid.* 11 After the sugar has been added, the jam should be watched carefully and tested for setting without undue delay.

*attrib.* **1825** J. NICHOLSON *Oper. Mech.* 610 The coagulating or setting power of burnt alabaster. **1878** ABNEY *Treat. Photogr.* vii. 52 The alkali decomposes the pyroxyline, rendering it..defective in setting qualities. **1963** D. SETON *Essent. Mod. Cookery* 150 The setting property of jam is due to the presence of pectin in the fruit. *Ibid.* 151 Setting-point is reached when the jam forms a flake and drops off the spoon cleanly or sharply when shaken.

**12.** The flowing of a current in a particular direction; the direction of flow. Also *fig.*

*c* **1595** CAPT. WYATT *R. Dudley's Voy. W. Ind.* (Hakl. Soc.) 52 The settinge of head seas in soe darke a night within soe straight and daingerous a passage. **1670** NARBOROUGH *Jrnl.* in *Acc. Sev. Late Voy.* I. (1694) 10 You are to..observe all..Courses of Tides, flowings and settings of Currents. **1769** FALCONER *Dict. Marine* (1780) N 2 b, The setting, or progressive motion of the current. **1835** SIR J. ROSS *N.-W. Passage* xl. 533 It was attempted to explain this appearance, by supposing the setting of a current here from west to east. **1875** GLADSTONE *Glean.* (1879) VI. 199 That powerful setting of the current of human motive and inclination.

**III.** Combinations.

**13. a.** With various advs., as ***setting-down, -forth, -in, -off, -out, to***: see the corresponding combinations of SET *v.*[1]

*c* **1375** *Sc. Leg. Saints* Prol. 6 As sais 'þe romance of þe rose', but settyng to of ony glose. **1439** *Little Red Bk. Bristol* (1900) II. 157 Atte the settyng vp of his Crafte he schal pay ijs. **1551** ROBINSON tr. *More's Utopia* II. H iv, The gallaunt garnishing, and the bewtiful setting furth of it. **1606** BACON *Consid. Plant. Irel.* Resuscit. (1657) 259 So that, this must rather be an Adventure, for such as are full; Then a setting up, of those, that are of low Means. **1614** MARKHAM *Pleas. Princes* 52 From his [the Cock's] head to the setting on of his shoulders. **1711** STEELE *Spect.* No. 132 ¶1 The first preparation for our Setting out was, that the Captain's Half-Pike was placed near the Coachman. **1778** HALHED *Bengal Gram.* Advt., Till the setting in of the dry season. *c* **1800** in *Hoyle's Games Improv.* (1814) 444 The person appointed.. is to tell ten between each setting-to, till one of the two cocks has refused fighting ten times successively. **1845** YOUATT *Dog* iii. 82 Their teeth and the setting-up of their backs will confirm this. **1859** H. H. DIXON *Silk & Scarlet* 216 We do not just like the setting on of his [a horse's] neck. **1894** J. E. DAVIS *Elem. Mod. Dressmaking* (1895) 46 The setting-in of the second sleeve [is] proceeded with. **1942** P. I. SMITH *Princ. & Processes Light-Leather Manuf.* v. 161 After dyeing and fat-liquoring the next process is setting-out or striking out, which today is usually done by hand. **1942** W. S. CHURCHILL *End of Beginning* (1943) 27 It was agreed that I should propose to those concerned the setting-up of a Pacific Council in London. **1953** D. WOODROFFE *Leather Dressing* xiv. 144 Striking out forms an excellent treatment prior to the setting out process. **1959** *20th Cent.* Nov. 345 The setting-up of an alternative..television service. **1962** A. NISBETT *Technique Sound Studio* viii. 146 If wear is noticeably accelerated,..rather complicated ways of setting up have to be devised. **1975** BRAM & DOWNS *Manuf. Technol.* vi. 168 To assist 'setting up', tenon blocks are provided to engage in table slots. **1979** A. B. EMARY *Woodworking* viii. 37 The steps..are setting out, which means making certain full-size drawings—in the trade this is called making a workshop rod, compiling a list of timber required for the job, and placing the necessary marks on the timber from the information on the rod.

**b.** Specific uses: **setting-down**, †a siege; **setting-forth**, †a means of advancement or bringing into celebrity; **setting-off**, †something that enhances the charm of a thing; **setting-out**, (*a*) a working drawing; (*b*) *U.S.* = SET-OUT 3; **setting-up** *U.S. dial.*, an all-night vigil, esp. one kept by relatives beside the body of a dead person (cf. SET *v.*[1] 154 kk).

**1601** B. JONSON *Poetaster* II. ii. 217 O Ioue, what a setting forth it is to a man, to haue many courtiers come to his house! **1605** SHAKS. *Macb.* v. iv. 10 The confident Tyrant Keepes still in Dunsinane, and will indure Our setting downe befor't. **1633** MASSINGER *Guardian* II. v, A Bed-fellow, To whose rare entertainment all these are But foils and settings off. *a* **1635** NAUNTON *Fragm. Reg.* (Arb.) 48 They were rather excursions than sieges or settings down, for he staid not long in a place. **1835** C. GILMAN *Recoll. Southern Matron* in *Southern Rose* 14 Nov. 41/2 This solemnity is usually styled by the negroes 'a setting up'. **1848** *Ladies' Repository* VIII. 337, I think you can afford to give that to Hen and Kate as part of their 'setting-out'. **1891** DENNING *Art Cabinet-Making* 220 The setting out or working drawing may be made on paper. **1900** J. DE F. SHELTON *Salt-Box House* xxi. 169 Despite the high prices caused by the war, her [bridal] setting-out was not inferior, having its full complement of silver, china..Irish-stitch (damask), [etc.]. **1905** 'P. PENNINGTON' *Jrnl.* 25 Dec. in *Woman Rice Planter* (1913) viii. 272 All the grown servants have gone to the 'setting up', which is one of the strongest articles of their creed..the feeling that they must not be found in their beds on this mysterious night when the King of the world was born. **1949** 'J. NELSON' *Backwoods Teacher* xv. 160 Most of them stayed a few minutes and departed, perhaps leaving one member of the family for the 'settin'-up'.

†**c.** Phr. *to cost one the setting on*, ? to cost one dear. Also, *to cost one* (*dear*) *in the setting on*.

**1594** LYLY *Mother Bombie* II. v, This good fellowshippe shall cost mee the setting on at our next meeting. **1615** JACKSON *Creed* IV. II. viii. 255 Carthages often prouocation of Rome cost it dearer in the setting on, then other Citties vanquished by the Romanes.

**d.** Phr. *setting-to-rights*, the action of putting things in their correct places (on a shelf, etc.). Cf. SET *v.*[1] 25 a.

**1847** C. M. YONGE *Scenes & Characters* xxiii. 284 That wearisome operation, a complete setting-to-rights; Eleanor ..extended her cares from the stores to every other household matter. **1911** K. D. WIGGIN *Mother Carey's Chickens* xiv. 124 Dozens of shelves in odd spaces helped much in the tidy stowing away of household articles... In the midst of all this delightful and cheery setting-to-rights a letter arrived.

**14.** Attributive, in many names of technical instruments and appliances, as *setting-chisel, -dibble, -hammer, -iron, -knife, -pin, -screw, -trowel*, etc.; **setting-board**, (*a*) a board used by glaziers in lead-work (see quot. 1825), (*b*) a board of wood or cork, usually grooved, for setting insect specimens; **setting-circle**, a graduated circle attached to a telescope for ascertaining the position of a star (1891 in *Cent. Dict.*); **setting coat**, a finishing coat of fine plastering (cf. 8 a); **setting lotion**, lotion that is applied to the hair in order to assist the process of setting; **setting muzzle**, a muzzle used for preventing a horse from feeding (cf. SET *v.*[1] 26 d); **setting-net**, ? a SET-NET; **setting-room** *N. Amer. dial.* = SITTING-ROOM 1; **setting-rule**, a composing-rule; **setting stuff**, the fine plaster from which a setting coat is made; **setting-up drill**, a course of gymnastic exercises used to give an erect carriage, etc.; also **setting-up exercise**. Also SETTING-POLE, SETTING-STICK.

**1825** J. NICHOLSON *Oper. Mech.* 638 The *setting-board is that in which the ridge of the light is marked and divided into squares, struck out with a chalk line, or drawn with a lath, which serves to guide the workmen. **1826** KIRBY & SP. *Entomol.* I. IV. 534 The English plan, except in the case of some large-bodied moths or hawk-moths, requires no groove in the setting-board. **1894** W. FURNEAUX *Butterflies & Moths* ix. 122 The most important requirement is the setting boards, of which several are necessary. **1976** V. NABOKOV *Details of Sunset* 158 He would first pin the carefully killed insect in the cork-bottomed groove of the setting board. **1399** in *Fabric Rolls York Minster* (Surtees) 18 Magnæ *settyng chisiles. **1812** P. NICHOLSON *Mech. Exerc.* 312 **Setting Coat*. **1916** E. A. DONCASTER *Limes & Cements* xiii. 144 The setting coat..is made of the pure lime as it runs from the basin. **1927** A. H. TELLING *ABC of Plastering* 206 The setting coat should be about one-eighth of an inch thick. **1626** T. H. tr. *Caussin's Holy Court* 28 To handle the scepter, with the same humility of heart..that one would do a *setting-dibble. **1688** HOLME *Armoury* III. ix. 382/1 Tools used by Jewellers... A *Setting Hammer. **1611** COTGR., *Fiche*, a gardeners dible, or *setting yron. **1854** H. MILLER *Sch. & Schm.* (1858) 186 With what are known as masons' setting-irons stuck into the stone-work behind. **1825** J. NICHOLSON *Oper. Mech.* 638 The *setting-knife [used by glaziers in lead-work] consists of a blade with a round point, loaded with lead at the bottom and terminating in a long square handle. **1926** *Hairdressing* 27 Aug. 181/1 No *setting lotion nor dressing of any kind was used. **1941** N. MARSH *Death & Dancing Footman* (1942) ii. 42 She was met by the..familiar smells of hot hair, setting lotion, and the sachets used in permanent waving. **1977** J. WILSON *Making Hate* xiii. 157 That thick sweetish smell you always get in ladies' hair-dressers..setting lotion or hairspray. **1835** H. HAREWOOD *Dict. Sports* s.v. *Muzzle*, There are two descriptions of muzzles: 1. the dressing muzzle..2. the *setting muzzle. **1840** BLAINE *Encycl. Rural Sports* §1127. 319 A setting muzzle prevents it [*sc.* wind-sucking in horses] usually. ? *c* **1690** *Bagford Ball.* (1877) 757 This Honourable Covey met, Hodge draws the Members *Setting-Net, And gets from all, without regret, Subscriptions. **1789** W. H. MARSHALL *Glocester* I. 144 The *setting pin resembles the gardener's dibble. **1741** *Probate Rec. New Hampshire* (1915) III. 30, I give to my Beloved Wife..ye furniture of ye Chamber over our *Setting room. **1832** W. D. WILLIAMSON *Hist. Maine* II. xxviii. 703 Our indigenous cherry, black-birch, and curl maple,..were shoved from the parlour and setting-room, to admit articles of foreign mahogany. **1908** J. C. LINCOLN *Cy Whittaker's Place* iii. 38 It's your dad's house come back alive, it is so! Look at this settin' room. **1770** LUCKOMBE *Hist. Printing* 376 Having made and secured our measure, we look for a *setting Rule. **1867** *Chamb. Encycl.* IX. 608/2 A thin slip of brass called a setting-rule, which he places in the composing-stick when he begins. **1733** TULL *Horse-Hoeing Husb.* xxii. 329 The Use of this *Setting-Screw is, to increase or diminish the Proportion of seed to be turned out by the Notches. **1911** *Encycl. Brit.* XXI. 785/1 *Setting stuff should not be applied until the floating is quite firm and nearly dry, but it must not be too dry or the moisture will be drawn from the setting stuff. **1927** A. H. TELLING *ABC of Plastering* 187 Setting or fine stuff consists of one part of plasterer's putty to two or three parts of sand. **1939** W. VERRALL *Solid & Fibrous Plastering* v. 64 Setting or skimming stuff can be applied in its raw state or an addition of 10 to 15 per cent. of plaster of Paris added. **1693** MOXON *Mech. Exerc.* (1703) 249 A *Setting Trowell, being less than the Laying Trowell, with which they finish the Plastering when it is almost dry. **1862** MACLAREN *Milit. Syst. Gymnastic Exerc.* 26 The *setting up and position drill of recruits. **1935** O. NASH *Primrose Path* 37 A few *setting-up exercises. **1970** *Soviet Weekly* 25 Apr. 2 He gets up at half past five, does a few setting-up exercises, takes a bath, has breakfast, goes for a walk before starting work.

**setting**, *vbl. sb.*[2]: see SET *v.*[2]

**setting** (ˈsɛtɪŋ), *ppl. a.* [f. SET *v.*[1] + -ING[2].] That sets, in various senses of the verb.

**1.** Becoming, suitable, graceful. *Obs.* exc. *Sc.* Cf. SITTING *ppl. a.* 2.

**1535** *Goodly Primer* Admon. to Rdr. (1537), It is not mete, comely, nor settynge, that [etc.]. **1768** ROSS *Helenore* (1789) 50 Says she, that lad was a' her care, That was so setting with his yellow hair. *Ibid.* 94 The ither too was a right setting lass, Though forthersome.

**2.** Of a dog: That sets or indicates game. See also SETTING-DOG.

**1551** *Richmond Wills* (Surtees) 71 To my brother Rayff Thompsone my setting spanyell doge, with all netts and geyr pertenyng to it. **1687** *Lond. Gaz.* No. 2275/4 Lost.., a large Setting-Bitch about 4 years old.

**3.** Of a hen: Sitting. Now *dial.*

**1829** MRS. S. C. HALL *Sk. Ir. Char.* II. 29 Mr. Billy..sent her a setting hen and seven eggs. **1879** HOWELLS *L. Aroostook* (1883) II. 14 A ship's time is worth no more than a setting hen's.

**4.** Sinking below or nearing the horizon; said of the sun or other heavenly body, its light, etc.

**1593** SHAKS. *Rich. II*, II. i. 12 The setting Sun. **1697** DRYDEN *Æneid* VIII. 79 When the setting Stars are lost in Day. **1704** POPE *Windsor For.* 194 His shadow lengthen'd by the setting sun. **1798** WORDSW. *Tintern Abbey* 97 Whose dwelling is the light of setting suns. **1814** SCOTT *Ld. of Isles* II. xix, A flush like evening's setting flame Glow'd on his cheek. **1882** SIR W. W. HUNTER in Skrine *Life* (1901) 314 By the light of a setting half-moon.

**b.** *fig.*

**1595** DANIEL *Civ. Wars* II. i, All turn'd their faces to the rising sunne And leaues his setting-fortune night begun. *a* **1639** WOTTON *Parall. Essex & Buckhm.* Reliq. W. (1651) 11 First, he was to wrastle with a Queens declyning, or rather with her very setting Age (as we may term it). **1658** SIR T. BROWNE *Hydriot.* v. 26 We whose generations are ordained in this setting part of time. **1829** SCOTT *Anne of G.* i, That important period, when chivalry still shone with a setting ray, soon about to be totally obscured.

†**c.** *transf.* Western. *Obs.*

**1612** DRAYTON *Poly-olb.* v. 248 The Flemings were inforc't to take them to their Ores, To try the Setting Maine to find out firmer shores. **1622** *Ibid.* xxix. 22 Yorkshire which doth lye vpon my Setting side. **1646** SIR T. BROWNE *Pseud. Ep.* VI. vii. 305 Magnifying the condition of..the Easterne Countries, above the setting and occidentall Climates.

**d.** ***setting-sun***: an edible bivalve mollusc, *Psammobia vespertina.*

**1867** LOVELL *Edible Mollusks* 150.

**5. a.** Of fruit: Beginning to develop from the flower. **b.** Of jam, etc.: coagulating; in the process of becoming hard or stiff.

**1891** *Macm. Mag.* Apr. 438 The setting plums or apples. **1969** *Jams, Preserves & Homemade Sweets* (Good Housekeeping Libr. Cooking) ii. 38 Poor setting fruits can be combined with the better ones to give added colour or flavour. **1974** M. LINDLAW *Super Sweets & Puddings* 53 Make up the Dream Topping..or whisk the cream until it begins to thicken. Whisk into the setting jelly.

**6.** With adverbs, *down, in, up*, etc. (see the vb.).

**1805** FORSYTH *Beauties Scot.* II. 413 Here the sea has formed caverns, which are rendered dreadful by a setting-in tide. **1874** *Hislop's Bk. Scot. Anecd.* 514 'Did ye ever hear a cuddie bray, Hawkie', said a youth to him one day... 'Never till the noo,' was the setting-down and quick answer. **1881** *Instr. Census Clerks* (1885) 51 Type Founding... Setting-up Boy.

†**setting dog.** *Obs.* A dog trained to 'set' game; = SETTER *sb.*[1] 11.

**1611** COTGR., *Braque*, a kind of short-tayled setting dog. **1621** MARKHAM *Hungers Prev.* 253 A Setting Dogge is a certaine lusty land Spaniell, taught by nature to hunt the Partridge before, and more then any other chase whatsoeuer. **1697** *Post Boy* 12–14 Aug. b/2 An old Brown and white Setting-dog. **1751** JOHNSON *Rambler* No. 116 ¶1 He was eminent for a breed of pointers and setting-dogs. **1780** H. WALPOLE *Let. to W. Cole* 5 Feb., Dr. Birch was.. running about like a young setting-dog in quest of anything. **1835** H. HAREWOOD *Dict. Sports* s.v. *Setter*, It is said that Dudley, Duke of Northumberland, was the first person that broke a setting-dog to the net, doubtless the spaniel.

**b.** *transf.* and *fig.*

**1643** *True Chr. Subj. under Heathen Prince* 5 Looke to the twentieth part, which is but a setting dogge to shew where the covey of nineteen are. *a* **1700** B. E. *Dict. Cant. Crew*, *Setters*, or *Setting-dogs*, they that draw in Bubbles, for old Gamesters to Rook; also a Sergeant's Yeoman, or Bailiff's Follower, or Second, and an Excize-Officer to prevent the Brewers defrauding the King. *c* **1730** RAMSAY *Address of Thanks* xii, Even sell K. T. that gart us ban, And eke that setting-dog his man.

**setting-pole.** Chiefly *N. Amer.* A pole, esp. one used by wild-fowlers for propelling a boat or punt on mud-banks, securing wounded birds, etc.

**1763** J. BELL *Trav. from St. Petersburg* II. xiii. 140 The barques..run often a-ground..and the people were obliged to..heave them off..with levers and setting poles. **1765** *Universal Mag.* XXXVII. 370/1 When they go against a current, they use setting-poles. **1797** F. BAILY *Tour* (1856) 270 The longest setting poles we had would not reach the bottom. **1824** HAWKER *Instr. Yng. Sportsman* (ed. 3) 345 Let one go out for the birds, taking with him the setting pole. **1875** 'STONEHENGE' *Brit. Rural Sports* I. I. ix. §2. 121 The shooter proceeds, generally by night, with an assistant in the punt, using the oars, paddle or setting-pole. **1931** G. L. NUTE *Voyageur* 40 Up to this point they had used 'setting poles' as well as paddles whenever the current was too swift for the ordinary method of propelling the canoe. **1959** *Moosehead Gaz.* (Dexter, Maine) Feb. 18/3 Junior eased the canoe down through the rocky rips with a setting pole.

**setting-stick.**

**1.** A stick used for making holes for 'setting' or planting. Now *dial.*

**1556** WITHALS *Dict.* (1562) 19b, A dibell or settynge sticke, *pastinum.* **1658** EVELYN *Fr. Gard.* (1675) 233 Plant them with the setting-stick, or dibber. **1669** WORLIDGE *Syst. Agric.* vii. §4 (1681) 121 Make the holes with an ordinary Setting-stick. **1793** *Trans. Soc. Arts* (ed. 2) V. 54 The plant is then to be planted with a setting-stick so that the upper part of the root shall appear about half an inch out of the ground. **1817–8** COBBETT *Resid. U.S.* (1822) 66 A setting-stick which should be the top of a spade-handle cut off, about ten inches below the eye. **1886** *Cheshire Gloss.*, *Setting-stick*, a short pointed stick, used for planting cabbages.

†**2.** A rod used for stiffening the plaits or 'sets' of ruffs, a poking-stick. *Obs.*

**1575** LANEHAM *Let.* (1871) 37 Marshalld in good order: wyth a stetting [*sic*] stick, and stoout, that euery ruff stood vp like a wafer. **1583** STUBBES *Anat. Abus.* II. 36 They haue also another instrument called a setting sticke,..and with this they set their ruffes. **1615** HOWES *Stow's Chron.* 948/2 About the sixteenth yeere of the Queene, began the making of steele poking-stickes, and vntill that time all Lawndresses vsed setting stickes, made of wood, or bone. **1621** BURTON *Anat. Mel.* III. ii. II. (III.) iii. 568 Pots, glasses, oyntments, irons, combes, bodkins, setting stickes.

**3.** A composing-stick.

**1875** SOUTHWARD *Dict. Typogr.* (ed. 2) 123.

**Settirday**, obs. form of SATURDAY.

**settle** ('sɛt(ə)l), *sb.*[1] Forms: α. 1 **setl, setel, setol, seotl, sotl, seatl, sitl (-el, -ol, -ul)**; 3 **sættel, seotel, seotle**, 3, 6, **setle**, 3–4 **settel**, 4 **setill(e, setil(e**, 5 **setyl**, 4– **settle**. β. 1 *Northumb.* **seð(e)l, sedl**, 5 *north.* **sedylle**; see also LANGSETTLE. [OE. *setl* neut., pl. *setlu* (also, in Northumb., pl. *setlas, seatlas*, etc., as if masc.) corresponds to OHG. *sezzal* (MHG. *sezzel*, mod.G. *sessel*) masc., Goth. *sitl-s* masc.:—OTeut. **setlo-*:—pre-Teut. **sedlo-*, cogn. w. L. *sella* (:—**sedlā*), f. Indogermanic root **sed-*, OTeut. **set-*: see SIT *v.* The β forms, OE. (Anglian) *seð(e)l, sedl*, ME. *-sedil, sedylle*, mod. north. dial. *-seddle, -saddle* see LANGSETTLE), represent a WGer. variant **seþl* (with the irregular variation in the articulation of the dentals sometimes found before *l* and *m*: see BOTTLE *sb.*[1], BOTTOM *sb.*), which is found also in OFris. *sedel*, OS. *sethal, sedal, sedel* masc., OHG. *sethal, sedal* (MHG. *sedel*) neut., masc., whence MHG. *sidelen* (mod.G. *siedeln*) to settle in a place. Cf. the metathetic form SELD *sb.*

In Eng. the β type appears only in Anglian dialects (after the OE. period almost exclusively in the forms of LANGSETTLE), and does not show (as it does in OHG.) any differentiation in application from the α type.]

†**1.** A sitting place. Also *transf.* and *fig.*, a 'seat', position, abode. *Obs.*

*Beowulf* 1782 (Gr.) Ga nu to setle. *a* **900** tr. *Bæda's Hist.* III. xiv. [xvi.] (1890) 202 Ond mon mæȝ ȝen to dæȝe þa stowe his seðles [orig. *locum sedis ejus solitariæ*] on þæm ilcan ealonde sceawian. *c* **1000** ÆLFRIC *Ags. Bible* (Gr.) 2/45 Þa næfde he nan setl, hwær he sittan mihte, for þan þe nan heofon nolde hine aberan. **13..** *Cursor M.* 17872 (Gött.) Adam..wid patriark and wid prophete, In mirk settlis þar þai sete. *a* **1340** HAMPOLE *Psalter* iv. 9, I sall rest in þe bed of endles blis & in þe setil of heuen. *Ibid.* Cant. 504 Þou did down ill gastis & vicys of þaire alde setile, þat þai hafe na powere in my saule.

†**2.** Something to sit upon; a chair, bench, stool, or the like. *Obs.*

*c* **897** K. ÆLFRED *Gregory's Past. C.* lvi. 435 Hit is swiðe ȝewunelic ðætte domeras & rice menn on setelum sitten. *c* **1000** *Ags. Gosp.* Matt. xxi. 12 Hyra setlu [*c* 975 *Rushw.* settlas] þara þe culfran sealdon he tobræc. *a* **1250** *Owl & Night.* 594 Among þe wede, among þe netle, þu syttest & singst bihinde seotle. *a* **1300** *Cursor M.* 14734 Þair setles þat þai in can sete, He kest þam dun. **13..** *Gaw. & Gr. Knt.* 882 A cheyer by-fore þe chemné..Was grayþed for sir Gawan ..& he sete in þat settel semlych ryche. **1483** CAXTON *Golden Leg.* 226/2 He dyd do make a siege or a stole of yron..and after to sette fyre under it..but the siege or setyl malte like waxe. **1483** *Cath. Angl.* 327/2 A Sedylle, *sedile.*

**b.** ***high settle*** (OE. *héahsetl* = OHG. *hôhsedal*): an elevated seat, a chair of dignity or state; a seat of honour at table; a throne, seat of judgement. *Obs.* exc. *arch.* after OE. use.

*c* **950** *Lindisf. Gosp.* John xix. 13 Fore þæm hehsedle [Vulg. *pro tribunali*]. *c* **1000** ÆLFRIC *Hom.* (Th.) I. 272 Se rica man ðe sitt on his heahsetle hraðe ȝeswicþ he his ȝebeorscipes ȝif ðu þeowan ȝeswicaþ ðæra teolunga. *c* **1205** LAY. 16646 Þa sat Agag þe king inne his hæh sættele. *a* **1225** *Juliana* 20 He lette bringen hire biuoren him to his heh seotel as he set in dome as reue. **1877** GREEN *Hist. Eng. People* I. i. 16 The high settle of King or Ealdorman.

**3.** *spec.* A long wooden bench, usually with arms and a high back (often extending to the ground), and having a locker or box under the seat. Cf. LANGSETTLE.

**1553** *Rec. St. Mary-at-Hill* 53 Item, In yᵉ qvire ij settelles with lockars apece. **1590** in *Archæologia* (1866) XL. 327 Itm. an olde standing bedsted wᵗʰ a settle unto it. **1596** NASHE *Saffron Walden* To Rdr., D, His Booke..I hauing kept idle by me in a by settle out of sight amongst old shooes and bootes almost this two yere. **1658** tr. *Ussher's Ann.* 114 They rap and make a noise with their hands or mallets, upon the deskes or settles in their Synagogues. **1678** BUNYAN *Pilgr.* I. 47 Looking down under the Settle there he espied his Roll. **1700** DRYDEN *Ovid's Met.* VIII. *Baucis & Phil.* 44 The Man ..A common Settle drew for either Guest, Inviting each his weary Limbs to rest. **1859** TENNYSON *Geraint & Enid* 579 And cast him..Down on an oaken settle in the hall. **1868** EASTLAKE *Hints Househ. Taste* 145 The common wooden settle which forms so comfortable and snug-looking a seat by rustic hearths.

**b.** A bench or seat in a boat (see quot.).

**1867** SMYTH *Sailor's Word-bk.*, *Settle*, now termed the stern-sheets.

**4.** A ledge, raised platform. †**a.** In the Bible, used to render Heb. *ʿăzārāʰ* (Vulg. *crepido*), app. either of two platforms or stages, surrounding the great altar, the one on a level with its base, and the other between this and the ground. *Obs.*

**1611** BIBLE *Ezek.* xliii. 14 And from the bottom vpon the ground, euen to the lower settle [*R.V.* or ledge], shalbe two cubits,..and from the lesser settle euen to the greater settle shalbe foure cubites. *Ibid.* 17. *Ibid.* xlv. 19.

**b.** (*a*) = *settle-gang* (*b*): see 6. (*b*) See quot. 1833.

**1799** J. ROBERTSON *Agric. Perth* 183 For this purpose, I have seen the settles of the byre (cow-house) sometimes floored. **1833** LOUDON *Encycl. Archit.* §1206 The settles (gutters) for carrying off the urine.

**c.** (See quots.)

**1695** KENNETT *Par. Antiq.* s.v. *Cart-Sadel*, The frame of wood to support the barrels in a buttery or cellar, is call'd the Seddle and Settle. **1881** *Isle of Wight Gloss.*, *Settle*,..a foundation, usually raised, for a rick. **1886** *Chesh. Gloss.*, *Settle*, any bench or frame for supporting heavy weights. Thus a barrel of beer might be said to be stillaged 'on a stone settle'.

**5.** *Firework Manuf.* A projection on the upper surface of the block used in filling tourbillon cases; it fits into the end of the case and forms a base for the composition during the process of filling.

**1873** SPON *Workshop Rec.* Ser. I. 135/2 Tourbillon cases are filled by means of an apparatus which consists of a block of wood, provided with a settle, on which one end of the tourbillon case is placed... The settle projects into the case about ⅛ of an inch. **1888** W. H. BROWNE *Firework Making* xx. 144 To fill the piece..fit the end on to the settle, and see that it stands perfectly upright.

**6.** *attrib.* and *Comb.*, as ***settle-back***; **settle bed**, a settle adapted for alternative use as a seat or bed; †**settle-bench, -chair** = sense 3 above; **settle-gang**, †(*a*) the setting (of the sun); (*b*) *dial.*, 'the raised part of a cow-house on which the animals lie' (*Eng. Dial. Dict.*).

**1900** H. SUTCLIFFE *Shameless Wayne* vii. (1905) 97 Reaching across the *settle-back. **1641** in *Burlington Mag.* Mar. (1912) 342/2 A *settle bed of wanscote in Fashion of a Fourme, wherein is a Fetherbed. **1781** C. JOHNSTON *Hist. J. Juniper* I. 8 A settle-bed, which served the double purpose of being sat upon, and slept in. **1818** SCOTT *Hrt. Midl.* xix, His eyes involuntarily rested upon the little settle-bed. **1741** RICHARDSON *Pamela* (1824) I. 67 Sitting down upon a *settle-bench. **1688** HOLME *Armoury* III. xiv. (Roxb.) 14/2 Some terme it a *settle chaire, being so weighty that it cannot be moued from place to place.., haueing a kind of box or cubbert in the seate of it. *c* **1000** *Ags. Ps.* (Th.) xlix. 2 Fram sunnan up-gange, oð hire *setl-gang. *a* **1300** *E.E. Psalter* xlix. 1 Fra sonne springe to setelgange.

**settle** ('sɛt(ə)l), *sb.*[2] *Obs.* exc. *Sc. rare.* [f. SETTLE *v.*] The action of the verb SETTLE; settling, settlement. ***to take settle***: to be settled, to be at ease.

*a* **1660** *Contemp. Hist. Irel.* (Ir. Archæol. Soc.) II. 24 Castlhaven did continue in Mariborough 9 or 10 daies givinge orders for the settle therof. *Ibid.* 166 For the settle of his freinds. **1822** AINSLIE *Pilgr. Land of Burns* 39 Frae the settle o' the night To the income o' the light. **1889** BARRIE *Window in Thrums* 153 I'll tak no settle till ye're awa.

**settle** ('sɛt(ə)l), *v.* Forms: α. 1 **setlan**, 3–7 **setle**, 4, 6–7 **settell, seatle, settill**, (4 **sedle, setel**, 5 **setelle, setyll**), 3– **settle**. β. 4–6 **satle**, (4 **satille**), 5–6 **sattyl, -yll**, (5 **sattil**), 6 **satell, sat(t)ill**, 4–7 **sattell**, 5–7, 9 *dial.* **sattle**. [OE. *setlan* (only once), f. *setl* seat, place of rest: see SETTLE *sb.*[1] Cf. mod.Du. *zetelen*, to place, settle. The β forms seem to represent another formation from the same Teut. root; ? OE. **sætlan*:—prehistoric **satuljan* f. **sat-*, ablaut variant of *set-*: see SIT *v.*

In some uses the vb. became synonymous with the like-sounding ME. *saȝtle* to appease, reconcile (SAUGHTEL *v.*), association with which may perhaps have influenced the development of these uses.

In many of the senses explained below, the verb frequently appears with a colouring derived from senses of different origin, so that the position of many of the examples is open to dispute.]

**I.** To seat, place.

The examples here treated as passive uses of senses in this branch mostly admit of being interpreted as intransitive uses (branch II) conjugated with *be*.

†**1. a.** *trans.* To seat; to put in a seat or place of rest; also, to cause to sit down. *Obs.*

*c* **1000** *Whale* 15 (Gr.) Wæȝliþende..setlaþ sæmearas [= 'stable their sea-horses'] sundes æt ende. *c* **1200** ORMIN 14049 Þatt hæfedd mann þatt heȝhest wass Att tatt bridale settledd. *a* **1300** *Cursor M.* 23340 Bot suld þai [*sc.* the righteous] haf a gret delite, To se þam [*sc.* the wicked] setlid [*MS.* seclid] in þair site. **1561** T. HOBY tr. *Castiglione's Courtyer* I. Kij b, And assone as he had saluted the Dutchesse, and setled the reste that were risen vp at his comminge, he satte hym downe. **1632** J. HAYWARD tr. *Biondi's Eromena* 129, I kept my selfe setled on the plancke till the morning. **1663** WOOD *Life* 24 Sept. (O.H.S.) I. 495 After they were setled in their chaires under the canopy. **1691–2** *Ibid.* 26 Jan. III. 381 A meeting in the Apoditerium before the vice-chancellor, Doctors, and Masters setled in the house.

†**b.** *fig.* in *passive*: To be 'seated', situated.

*a* **1400–50** *Wars Alex.* 4429 For all ȝoure wisdom, I-wis, is wroken to ȝour tongis, And all þe sauour of ȝoure sauls is sattild in ȝour mouthis.

**2. a.** To place (material things) in order, or in a convenient or desired position; to adjust (e.g. one's clothing).

**1515** BARCLAY *Eclogues* III. (1570) B vj/2 Or els must he rise and walke him selfe a space, Till time his ioyntes be setled in their place. **1582** STANYHURST *Æneis* II. (Arb.) 66, I twisted a wallet On my broad shoulders, my nape did I settle eke vnder. **15..** *Sir Andrew Barton* xliv. in Child *Ballads* (1889) III. 341/1 With that hee lett his gun-shott goe; Soe well hee settled itt with his eye, The ffirst sight that Sir Andrew sawe, Hee see his pinnace sunke in the sea. *c* **1650** in Gutch *Hist. & Antiq. Univ. Oxford* (1796) II. 943 *note*, That they [*sc.* Selden's books] bee placed..in the new built west end of the publique Library,..with such inscription upon the place where they shall bee soe settled as the said Executors..shall directe. **1709** STEELE *Tatler* No.

48 ¶4 He adjusted the cock of his hat a-new, settled his sword-knot. **1719** De Foe *Crusoe* I. (Globe) 69 Having settled my houshold Stuff and Habitation. **1784** Cowper *Task* III. 486 Th' uplifted frame.. He settles next upon the sloping mount. **1796** C. Marshall *Garden.* xiv. (1813) 196 Thus having settled the plants, shut the lights close. **1815** Scott *Guy M.* xxxvi, He washed his face and hands, settled his wig in the glass. **1818** —— *Hrt. Midl.* i, They immediately began to settle their clothes, which were a little deranged. **1861** Trollope *Orley Farm* I. xxxiii. 264 I'll come for the answer when you're settling the room after breakfast tomorrow. **1866** G. Macdonald *Ann. Q. Neighb.* I. vii. 192 As I was settling her pillow for her. **1894** Crockett *Raiders* xi, May Maxwell settled her shawl closer about her.

†**b.** To dispose in order (an argument, the parts of a discourse). *Obs.*

**1551** T. Wilson *Logic* G vj, Now.. I will declare howe to seatle & place an argumente, that any bodie may geue a reason, why euery worde is set in an argument, in this, or that place. **1553** —— *Rhet.* (1580) 159, I thinke meete to speake of framyng, and placyng an Oration in order, that the matter beeyng aptly seteld and couched together: might better please the hearers.

**3. a.** To place (a person) in an attitude of repose, so as to be undisturbed for a time. Chiefly *refl.* to dispose oneself comfortably, adjust one's position on a chair, etc. with the intention of remaining seated.

**1515** Barclay *Eclogues* III. (1570) B vj b/1 Neuer shalt thou knowe thy lodging or thy nest, Till all thy betters be setled and at rest. **1546** J. Heywood *Prov.* I. x. (1562) L j b, In no place could she sit hir selfe to settle. **1627** Drayton *Nimphidia* 516 Yet scarce he on his back could get, So oft and high he did coruet, Ere he himselfe could settle. **1712** Hearne *Collect.* (O.H.S.) III. 381 They soon came away and settled themselves at the East part of the Library. **1781** Cowper *Ep. Lady Austen* 39 Thus we were settled when you found us, Peasants and children all around us. **1848** Thackeray *Van. Fair* lxi, When her patient above was settled for the night. **1893** 'Q' *Delect. Duchy* 16 The man.. settled her comfortably in the stern-sheets. **1901** W. S. Walker *In the Blood* vi. 71 You were asleep like a child almost as soon as you were settled. **1905** R. Bagot *Passport* ii. 12 Settling himself in his saddle, Sor Beppe started off at an easy canter.

**b.** In *passive.* To be installed in a residence, to have completed one's arrangements for residing. Also, *rarely*, in *active*: to install (someone) in a residence.

*c* **1643** Ld. Herbert *Autobiog.* (1824) 185, I was but newly settled in my Lodging. **1722** De Foe *Plague* (1840) 130 Why should we make you remove now you are settled in your lodging? **1782** Miss Burney *Cecilia* VI. i, Such was the house in which Cecilia was now settled. **1813** W. Bingley in *Lady Morgan's Mem.* (1862) II. 31 You, I presume, are by this time comfortably settled in your new residence. **1837** Lever *H. Lorrequer* i, We were soon settled in barracks. **1853** Geo. Eliot *Lett.* (1954) II. 97 What do you think of my going to Australia with Chrissey and all her family?—to settle them, and then come back. **1901** W. S. Walker *In the Blood* viii. 97 Billy's sisters.. were at length settled in a small cottage out Redfern way.

**4. a.** To cause to take up one's residence in a place; *esp.* to establish (a body of persons) as residents in a town or country; to plant (a colony, †a town).

**1573–80** Tusser *Husb.* (1878) 198 So God I trust for Christes sake, Shall settle me in blis. **1582** Stanyhurst *Æneis* I. (Arb.) 17 Ere towne could statelye be builded, Or Gods theare setled. **1599** Shaks. *Hen. V*, I. ii. 47 Charles the Great.. There left behind and settled certaine French. **1667** Milton *P.L.* IV. 940 My afflicted Powers To settle here on Earth. **1670** Denton *Brief Descr. N. York* (1845) 1 Part of the Main Land belonging to New York Colony, where several Towns and Villages are setled. *a* **1700** Evelyn *Diary* 4 Jan. 1665, I went.. to settle physitians, chirurgeons, agents, marshals and other officers in all the Sea Ports. **1797** *Encycl. Brit.* (ed. 3) V. 149/1 The practice of settling commercial colonies in distant countries hath been adopted by the wisest nations of antiquity. **1830** M. T. Sadler *Law Popul.* I. 483 Maryland.. was first settled by Roman Catholics. **1831** Scott *Ct. Robt.* xxxiii, What interest I have .. shall be strained to the uttermost to settle thee in thine own beloved native country. **1845** *Encycl. Metrop.* XIV. 392/1 The first town that was settled by the English in North America.

**b.** *refl.* Also in *passive*, to have taken up one's abode.

**1550** Bale *Eng. Votaries* II. C j b, The Romysh clergy satled them selues all the worlde ouer. **1572** *Act 14 Eliz.* c. 5 §16 That the said aged ympotent and poore People should have convenient Habitacions and Abydinge Places throughout this Realme to settle themselves uppon. *c* **1610** *Women Saints* 22 She went to Bethleem,.. where she settled her self. **1686** tr. *Chardin's Trav. Persia* 30 That the Grand Signior should not entertain.. any European Nation, except what were already setl'd there, but under the French Banners. **1711** Addison *Spect.* No. 12 ¶1 It was some time before I could settle my self in a House to my likeing. **1738** *Whitehall Even. Post* 12–15 Aug. 3/2 This is to give Notice, That Mr. Isaac De Vic, Jun., Wine-Merchant, of Southampton, is settled in this City. **1780** Harris *Philol. Enq.* (1841) 470 He induced.. many of the first families in Italy.. to leave their country, and there settle themselves. **1827** O. W. Roberts *Voy. Centr. Amer.* 45 One of the rivers on which they are settled has its source in a kind of lake. **1853** J. H. Newman *Hist. Sk.* (1876) I. I. ii. 52 A tribe of them.. settled themselves between the high Tartar land and the sea of Aral.

**c.** To fix or establish permanently (one's abode, residence, etc.). † *to settle one's rest*: to take up one's residence. (Cf. *to set up one's rest*, REST *sb.*$^{2}$ 7 f; and see REST *sb.*$^{1}$ 5.)

**1562** J. Hopkins *Ps.* lxxxiv, Much rather would I keepe a dore within the house of God: Then in the tentes of wickednes, to settle myne abode. **1633** Bp. Hall *Hard Texts, Isa.* XI. 10 And he shall settle his rest among them, which shall be glorious for himselfe, and happy for them. **1678** J. Godolphin *Repert. Canon.* (1680) 17 St. Augustine .. took on him the Title of Archbishop of England, settling his See at Canterbury. **1727** Boyer *Fr. Dict.*, To settle one's Abode somewhere. **1823** Scott *Quentin D.* Introd., The town at which I had settled my temporary establishment.

**d.** To assign to (a person) a legal domicile in a particular parish. Chiefly in *passive.* Cf. SETTLEMENT 3.

**1572** *Act 14 Eliz.* c. 5. §16 Then the said Justices.. shall.. settle the same poore People for their Habitacions and Abydynges, yf the parishe within the whiche they shalbee founde shall not.. provide for them. **1662** *Act 14 Chas. II*, c. 12 §1 To such Parish where he or they were last legally setled either as a native Householder Sojourner Apprentice or Servant for the space of forty dayes. **1773** *Observ. State Poor* 77 Children whose parents settlements cannot be discovered and illegitimate children, are all settled wherever they are born. **1814** Maule & Selwyn *K.B. Rep.* I. 380 If the pauper lived 40 days under that assignment we should hold him settled in the parish.

**e.** To furnish (a place) with inhabitants or settlers.

**1702** *Propos. Effectual War in Amer.* 18 The.. setling and fortifying that large Island of Newfoundland. **1768** J. Byron *Narr. Patagonia* (ed. 2) 112 The country hereabouts .. is so circumstanced as to discourage the most sanguine adventurers from attempts to settle it. **1823** Cobbett *Rur. Rides* (1885) I. 321 Margate.. is so thickly settled with stock-jobbing cuckolds at this time of year, that [etc.]. **1855** Kingsley *Westw. Ho!* xiii, Your.. brother, sir, is better bestowed than in settling Newfoundland.

†**f.** To establish, set up (an institution, a business, etc.) in a particular town or country. *Obs.*

**1582** N. Lichefield tr. *Castanheda's Conq. E. Ind.* I. xxx. 75 He was come thether.. to settle a trade in y$^{e}$ citie. **1624** in Foster *Eng. Factories India* (1909) III. 16 Hee should have a howse and there to settell a factorye in his towne of Pullasera. **1645** Durye *Israel's Call* (1646) 48 Next unto the Schooles of the Prophets (whereof besides the Universities, it were to be wisht that some lesser ones might be setled in every Province). **1687** A. Lovell tr. *Thevenot's Trav.* II. 157 This might be made one of the richest Cities in the World, because of the commerce that might be settled there. **1705** De Foe *Consolidator* Wks. 1840 IX. 354 They.. settled a sub-cash, depending upon the grand bank, in every province of the kingdom. **1773** *Life N. Frowde* 6 Having by his frequent Voyages settled a good Correspondence on the Continent.

**g.** *U.S. slang.* To sentence (a person) to imprisonment, put in prison.

**1899** 'J. Flynt' *Tramping with Tramps* 396 *Settled*, in prison. **1914** Jackson & Hellyer *Vocab. Criminal Slang* 75 *Settled*,.. convicted of misdemeanor or statutory offence. Example: 'He's settled for a two spot.' **1916** *Literary Digest* 19 Aug. 425/1 Foley was 'pinched' and 'settled' in San Quentin. **1930** *Amer. Mercury* Dec. 457/2 He goes to the counter and gets settled for a nickel. **1955** D. W. Maurer in *Publ. Amer. Dial. Soc.* XXIV. 151 Maybe he will get *settled*, or sent to prison; among pick-pockets this term does not carry the implication of a long sentence or a life-term..; it usually means two years.

†**5.** To fix, implant (something) *in* (a person's heart, mind, etc.). *Obs.*

**1560** Ingelend *Disob. Child* G ij, All such sayinges as in my mynde At the fyrst tyme ye studied to sattell. **1579** Lodge *Def. Poetry* 6 Witt hath wrought that in you, that yeares and studie neuer setled in the heads of our sagest doctors. **1607** Shaks. *Timon* v. i. 54 What a Gods Gold..? 'Tis thou that Setlest admired reuerence in a Slaue. **1646** Sir T. Browne *Pseud. Ep.* I. ix. 37 [Poets' inventions] setling impressions in our tender memories, which our advanced judgements, doe generally neglect to expunge. **1690** Locke *Hum. Und.* IV. vii. §11 Before Custom has setled Methods of Thinking and Reasoning in our Minds.

†**6.** To set firmly on a foundation; to fix (a foundation) securely. *lit.* and *fig. Obs.*

**1560** Bible (Geneva) *Prov.* viii. 25 Before the mountaines were setled.. was I begotten. **1583** H. Howard *Def. Pois. Supposed Prophesies* A j b, The higher any man will rayse his toppe, the lower must he settell hys foundation. **1590** Spenser *F.Q.* II. xii. 1 That goodly frame of Temperaunce .. Formerly grounded and fast setteled On firme foundation of true bountyhed. **1604** E. G[rimstone] *D'Acosta's Hist. Indies* VI. xiv. 461 The water is so deep as they can not settle any foundation. **1666** Stillingfl. *Serm.* (1673) 21 That the glory of the City may not be laid upon the tears of the Orphans and Widows, but that its foundations may be setled upon Justice and Piety.

**II.** To come to rest after flight or wandering.

†**7.** *intr.* To take a seat, sit down (? OE.). Of the sun: To set. *Obs.*

[*c* **1000** ? Implied in *setlung*, sitting down, setting (of the sun), *Lambeth Ps.* cxxxviii. 2, *Sax. Leechd.* III. 266.] *c* **1350** *Will. Palerne* 2452 Till þe semli sunne was setled to reste.

**8. a.** Of a bird, flying insect: To take up a position of rest from flight; to alight *on* something.

**13..** *K. Alis.* 484 Him thoughte a goshauk with gret flyght Setlith on his beryng [*MS. Bodl.* settleþ on his herbergeynge]. *Ibid.* 488 A dragon out of his den flygth.. And setled [*MS. Bodl.* settleþ].. On the stude there the quene was. **1728** *Congress of Bees* in *Arbuthnot's Misc. Wks.* (1751) II. 135 The Bees.. all settled. **1791** Cowper *Yardley Oak* 91 Time was, when, settling on thy leaf, a fly Could shake thee to the root. **1845** J. Coulter *Adv. in Pacific* iii. 29, I have often seen flocks of snipe.. settling to the left of the town. **1859** Tennyson *Merlin & V.* 221 The gnat That settles, beaten back, and beaten back Settles. **1875** *Encycl. Brit.* I. 260/1 The common blue fly which settles on meat.

*fig.* **1601** Shaks. *All's Well* III. i. 21 All the honors that can flye from vs, Shall on them settle. **1611** —— *Wint. T.* IV. iii. 106 This man.. (hauing flowne ouer many knauish professions) he setled onely in Rogue. **1781** Cowper *Retirem.* 672 A mind.. after poising her advent'rous wings, Settling at last upon eternal things. **1842** Tennyson *Gard. Dau.* 220 We coursed about The subject most at heart, more near and near, Like doves about a dovecote, wheeling round The central wish, until we settled there.

**b.** Of things, esp. flying or floating objects, also *transf.* and *fig.* of darkness, silence, etc.: To come down and remain.

**13..** *E.E. Allit. P.* C. 409 Muche sorȝe þenne satteled vpon segge Ionas. *c* **1380** *Sir Ferumb.* 3281 Þat fyr þat setlede so on þe walle ȝerne hit gan to brenne. **1715** Pope *Iliad* IV. 527 Shades eternal settle o'er his eyes. **1779** *Mirror* No. 50 ¶4 A deep gloom settled on his spirits. **1802** Mar. Edgeworth *Moral T.* (1816) I. 232 The dust which had settled on the white figures. **1810** Scott *Lady of L.* I. iii, And silence settled, wide and still, On the lone wood. **1829** *Chapters Phys. Sci.* 239 The dog had inhaled the noxious air which, sinking to the bottom, had settled there. **1864** E. Yates *Broken to Harness* I. xv. 271 You find.. a yellow fog settling down. **1866** G. MacDonald *Ann. Q. Neighb.* III. ix. 208 Suddenly from out of the dark a hand settled on my arm. **1890** R. Bridges *Shorter Poems* III. ii. 3 The snow came flying.. Stealthily and perpetually settling and loosely lying.

**9.** To come together from dispersion or wandering. †**a.** Of a body of persons: To direct their course to a common point. *Obs.*

? *a* **1400** *Morte Arth.* 2465 Thane the price mene prekes, and proues þeire horsez, Satilles to þe cete, appone sere halfes.

**b.** *Hunting.* Of hounds: To keep steadily to the scent.

**1781** Beckford *Th. Hunting* xiv. 185 By this time his hounds get together, and settle to the scent. **1827** [Apperley] *Chace* (1852) 44 The scent being good, every hound settles to his fox. **1885** *Field* 7 Feb. 148/2 The music of the pack as they settled to the line. **1897** *Encycl. Sport* I. 551/2 Hounds settle like bees upon the line.

**10. a.** Of things: To lodge, come to rest, in a definite place after wandering.

**1622** Venner *Via Recta* (ed. 2) 190 Those crude and superfluous humors.. fluctuating from part to part, doe at length settle and produce morbificall affects. *a* **1634** Chapman *Revenge for Hon.* v. i, Where like a fixt Star 't [*sc.* love's flame] settles, never to be removed thence. **1660** Stanley *Hist. Philos.* XI. ix. §6 (1687) 764/2 The Earth at first wandred up and down..; but in time growing thick and heavy, it setled down immoveable. **1682** Creech *Lucretius* VI. 202 The Earth.. Inclining only from its usual Plain, Then turns, and settles in its seat again. **1829** Scott *Anne of G.* ii, Down went the huge fragment,.. settling at length in the channel of the torrent.

**b.** Of pain or disease: To establish itself *in* or *on* a definite part of the body.

**1594** Kyd *Cornelia* III. i. 99 And suddainly.. A chyl-cold shyuering (setled in my vaines) Brake vp my slumber. **1768** Earl Carlisle in Jesse *Selwyn & Contemp.* (1843) II. 301 A cold which chose to settle in my eyes. **1856** Julia Kavanagh *Rachel Gray* xvii, A cough settled on her chest. **1877** *Five Yrs. Penal Serv.* i. 26 Poor A. caught a cold he never recovered from; it settled on his lungs.

**c.** Of the wind: To become 'set' *in* (*at*, *into*) a specified quarter.

**1626** Bacon *New Atl.* 1 But then the Winde came about, and setled in the West for many dayes. **1628** Digby *Voy. Mediterr.* (1868) 75 It continued all day verie foule weather ..: in the end it settled a stiffe gale at N.W. **1719** De Foe *Crusoe* I. (Globe) 40 [The hurricane] came about to the North-West, and then settled into the North-East. **1773** *Life N. Frowde* 140 A.. Storm.. which in the space of forty-eight Hours varied to every Point of the Compass, and at length, settled in the East by North.

**d.** Of affections, etc.: To come after wandering *to*, become fixed *on* an object.

**1628** Feltham *Resolves* I. xxx. 95 Finding my affections settle to them [*sc.* the world's choicest solaces] without resistance, I cannot but distrust my selfe. **1639** S. Du Verger tr. *Camus' Admir. Events* 16 Friendship is not idle where it settles, it presently falls to worke. **1714** *Spect.* No. 605 ¶6 When Time hath worn out their natural Vanity, and taught them Discretion, their Fondness settles on its proper Object. **1884** *Manch. Exam.* 17 May 4/7 The interest.. which led to the inquiry too often evaporates or settles on some new object before it is finished.

**11. a.** Of persons: To cease from migration and adopt a fixed abode; to establish a permanent residence, take up one's abode, become domiciled; also with *down.* With *in*, to become established in a new home; hence, to become accustomed to a new abode or to new surroundings.

**1627** Earl Manch. in *Buccleuch MSS.* (Hist. MSS. Comm.) I. 267, I hope to be settling at Kimolton for a while. **1685** Wood *Life* 1 Sept. (O.H.S.) III. 158 He setled for a time in Shropshire. **1719** De Foe *Crusoe* I. (Globe) 1 My Father being a Foreigner of Bremen, who settled first at Hull. **1779** Lady A. Howard in Jesse *Selwyn & Contemp.* (1844) IV. 235, I.. go into Hertfordshire on Sunday. When I come to settle, I hope, Mr. Selwyn, you will do me the favour to call upon me. **1874** Green *Short Hist.* i. §3. 25 If trouble befell the Christian preachers who came settling among them. **1891** *Law Times* XCII. 127/2 Riley had left his father's house.. for America, where he intended to settle down. **1904** Dor. P. Hughes *Life H. P. Hughes* i. 6 When he finished his wanderings as a Methodist preacher.. and settled in Carmarthen as a supernumerary. **1929** *Star* 21 Aug. 15/1 The Jellicoes.. are 'settling in' at their new London home this autumn. **1951** M. McLuhan *Mech. Bride* (1967) 67/2 It will want to 'settle in' and enjoy the sense of belonging in America. **1960** J. Stroud *Shorn Lamb* xiii. 151 He'll settle in, I feel sure. It'll be a long job though. **1977** 'A. York' *Tallant for Trouble* iii. 48 We met the Brices after we came. We threw a party, to settle in, and the Brices were top of the list.

**b.** Of a people: To take up its abode in a foreign country. Also, to establish a colony.

*a* **1682** Sir T. Browne *Tracts* (1683) 138 The Saxons settling over all England, maintained an uniform Language. **1700** Evelyn *Diary* 4 Feb., The Parliament voted against the Scots settling in Darien. **1726** Shelvocke *Voy. round World* 358 They are secure from the attempt of any European nation to settle on them. **1872** Freeman *Europ. Hist.* xiii. §28 (1874) 277 So men tried to get more freedom by settling in distant lands. Thus the French Huguenots tried to settle in America.

*indirect passive.* **1845** J. Coulter *Adv. in Pacific* xi. 147 The greatest surprise I experienced was, that they [these islands] were not colonized and settled upon long before this.

**12.** = *to settle oneself* (sense 3). Sometimes of birds, etc. with mixture of sense 8. ***to settle in***: to dispose oneself for remaining indoors.

**1818** Scott *Rob Roy* xvii, The little irritable citizens [*sc.* bees], were settling in their straw-thatched mansion for the evening. **1827–35** Willis *Idleness* 55 When..the birds settle to their nests. **1833** Lady Morgan *Mem.* (1862) II. 377 On my return, settled in to write. **1859** Tennyson *Geraint* 250 Like a clamour of the rooks At distance, ere they settle for the night. **1864** E. Yates *Broken to Harness* I. xv. 272 The inhabitants of the neighbouring houses had pulled their blinds down and settled in for the night. **1865** Kingsley *Herew.* xlii, The clang of the wild-fowl settling down to rest. **1902** 'M. Fairless' *Roadmender* 24 The child ..extracted from the basket a small black cat, and settled in for the afternoon.

**III.** To descend, sink down; to lower. [From sense 8.]

**13. a.** To sink down gradually by or as by its own weight. Of the ground: To subside. Of a structure or part of a structure: To sink downwards from its proper level.

*c* **1315** Shoreham *Poems* I. 758 Ase oþer mete In to þy wombe hyȝt sedlyþ. *c* **1330** R. Brunne *Chron. Wace* (Rolls) 8186 þen schok þe ground [*v.r.* þe grounde satled]. *c* **1440** *York Myst.* xxxiii. 248 Whan it [*sc.* a standard] settles or sadly discendis. *c* **1440** *Promp. Parv.* 440/2 Saggyn, or sallyn [? *read* satlyn] (*P.* satelyn), *basso.* **1545** Ascham *Toxoph.* (Arb.) 131 For with shoting it [*sc.* the feather] wyll sattle and faule very moche. **1576** Lambarde *Peramb. Kent* 287 Ye very earth..did continually, for euer after, setle and sinke downeward. *a* **1597** Peele *David & Bethsabe* II. iii. (1599) E j b, As doth the daylight settle in the west. **1601** [see sag *v.* 1]. **1693** Moxon *Mech. Exerc.* (1703) 256 These Arches.. must be made of Bricks and Morter that are very good,.. that they do neither settle nor give way. **1751** Labelye *Westm. Bridge* 76 The..Pier..was observed to settle. **1791** W. Hutchinson *Treat. Pract. Seamanship* 15 Which caused their..floors to sag downwards, so much as to make their hold stanchions amidships..settle from the beams. **1868** *Rep. U.S. Commissioner Agric.* (1869) 251 The single-row fence..must sag and settle toward the ground, if pleached without staking. **1898** Watts-Dunton *Aylwin* I. i, The *débris*..again falling and settling into new and permanent shapes. *Ibid.*, A great mass of loose earth settled, carrying me with it in its fall.

† **b.** *fig.* Of feeling, conviction: To sink deeply *into* (the mind, heart). *Obs.*

*a* **1300** *Cursor M.* 24225 And al þe baret þat he bar, It setteld [*Gött.* satlid] in þi hert ful sare. **1513** More in Grafton *Chron.* (1568) II. 814 This olde adage so sanke, and setled in my heade, that [etc.]. **1525** *St. Papers Hen. VIII*, IV. 361 And nowe the said newes doe satell and synke into the Scottes myndes. **1574** Dee in *Lett. Lit. Men* (Camden) 35 Onely God can make the perswasion of the truth hereof to settel into the bottom of your Lordships hart.

† **c.** ? *transf.* Of troops: To fall back, yield ground, retire. Also *trans.* (*causatively*). *Sc. Obs.*

**1513** Douglas *Æneis* IX. xiii. 28 Turnus a lityl..Begouth frawart the bargane to withdraw, And sattyl towartis the ryveris syde alaw. **1535** Stewart *Cron. Scot.* (Rolls) III. 429 So cruell counter..Quhilk satlit hes the Sutheroun far abak Beȝond the place quhair that tha first began. *a* **1578** Lindesay (Pitscottie) *Chron. Scot.* (S.T.S.) I. 97 Ane companie of fresche men..come so fercelie wpoun the Earle of Huntlieis wangaird quhill they war compellit to satill a littill abak. *Ibid.* 275 Thay causit the inglismen to sattill frome thame.

† **14.** *trans.* (*causatively*). **a.** To lower in condition; to reduce in degree. *Obs. rare.*

**1338** R. Brunne *Chron.* (1810) 225 þis legate Ottobone mad a cursyng hard..& som of þer heyres..it peyres, & som has satled sore. *c* **1350** *Will. Palerne* 4562 þe comli quen of palerne oft crist þonked, þat..hade setteled hire sorwe so sone, þat was huge.

**b.** To lower (a commodity, rent) in price or value. Also *intr.*, to go down in price. *dial.*

**1812** in W. Cudworth *Round abt. Bradford* (1876) 412 Mr. Joseph Dawson settled his coals at Wrose Pit from sevenpence to sixpence a load. **1868** Atkinson *Cleveland Gloss.* s.v., Corn's sattled a vast sen last market. Ah's quit at May-day gin he weeant sattle me [*i.e.* reduce my rent] a bit. **1886** *W. Somerset Word-bk.* s.v., Arter all this dry weather, an no keep, stock's bound to settle.

† **c.** To put *down* to the original place. (Cf. 2.)

**1731** Miller *Gard. Dict.*, s.v. *Cucumis*, If you find your bed too hot, it is but raising up the Baskets..and when the violent Heat is over, they may be settled down again.

**15.** *Naut.* **a.** *intr.* Of a ship: To sink gradually; also with *down*.

**1819** Byron *Juan* II. xliv, The ship was evidently settling now Fast by the head. **1836** *Uncle Philip's Convers. Whale Fishery* 289 The ship began to settle down in the water. *transf.* **1818** Scott *Hrt. Midl.* i, The ancient vehicle used to settle quietly down, like a ship scuttled and left to sink. **1840** F. D. Bennett *Narr. Whaling Voy.* II. App. 174 The whale will occasionally sink in the horizontal position, or, as it is technically expressed, 'settle down'. **1873–5** Henley *In Hospital* xiii. *Bk. Verses* (1888) 22 Raised, he settled stiffly sideways: You could see the hurts were spinal.

**b.** *trans.* To diminish the height of, to reduce to a lower level (a deck, topsail). †Also, to cause (the land) to appear lower in the water by receding from it (cf. lay *v.*[1] 5).

*a* **1625** *Nomenclator Navalis* (Harl. MS. 2301) To Setle a Deck. **1626** Capt. Smith *Accid. Yng. Seamen* 28 We shall haue wind, sattle your top sailes. **1669** Sturmy *Mariner's Mag.* I. ii. 17 Settle our fore and main Top-sails two thirds of the Mast down. **1704** J. Harris *Lex. Techn.* I, *Settle a Deck*, is the Word at Sea for taking a Deck lower than it was at first. **1769** Falconer *Dict. Marine* (1780), *Settled*, lowered in the water; as, we have settled the land, or sunk it lower, by sailing further out to seaward. This phrase is usually opposed to raising. **1867** Smyth *Sailor's Word-bk.*, *To settle*, to lower;..as..'we settled the land'. 'Settle the main topsail halliards', *i.e.* ease them off a little, so as to lower the yard.

**16. a.** *intr.* Of soil, loosely compacted materials: To subside into a solid mass. Of new masonry or brickwork: To become consolidated by its own weight and drying of the mortar.

**1560** Ingelend *Disob. Child* F j, I wyll make thy skyn to rattell, And the braynes in thy Scull more depely to sattell. **1618** W. Lawson *New Orch. & Garden* vii. (1623) 20, I shake the Set easily to and fro, to make the earth settle the better to his roots. **1664** Gerbier *Counsel* II. 27 See the Morter well tempered, since if unequall in thicknesse; that which is thin, will cause the work to settle more in one place then in the other. **1791** Mawe & Abercrombie *Every Man his own Gardener* 157 Shaking the plant gently as the earth is filled in, to cause it to settle close between all the roots and fibres. **1800** Wellington in Gurw. *Desp.* (1837) I. 60 The people cannot build more than about a foot and a half in a day which must be allowed to dry and settle for three or four days. **1828–32** Webster, *Settle*, to sink after being heaved, and to dry; as, roads settle in spring after frost and rain. **1886** *W. Somerset Word-bk.* s.v., 'Tis a maain gurt heap, but he on't look so big arter he've a settled a bit.

**b.** To shrink in size. *dial.* (? *obs.*) and *techn.*

**1641** Best *Farm. Bks.* (Surtees) 12 When sheepe are first putte out of the closes into the field, they will sattle and goe backe extreamely for the space of a weeke. **1889** C. T. Davis *Bricks* v. 139 The bricks are now ready to shrink, or as it is termed in burning, to 'settle'.

**c.** *trans.* To cause to subside into a solid mass; to consolidate, compact. Also with *down*, *home*.

**1611** Bible *Ps.* lxv. 10 Thou waterest the ridges thereof abundantly: thou settlest the furrowes thereof. **1669** Sturmy *Mariner's Mag.* v. xii. 68 With the Rammer give two or three strokes more to settle it home. **1673** Ray *Journ. Low C.* 123 Mud or Clay..which in tract of Time hath been setled together and hardned. **1706** E. Ward *Wooden World Diss.* (1708) 75 A short Breakfast upon the Crumbs of Comfort well settl'd down with a humming Stroke at the Brandy-Bottle. **1712** J. James tr. *Le Blond's Gardening* 106 The Earth should be trod upon to settle it. **1751** Labelye *Westm. Bridge* 91 They are all built..and both the Abutments of the Bridge compleated and settled. **1791** Mawe & Abercrombie *Ev. Man his own Gardener* 157 If they are watered as soon as planted, it will settle the earth about all the roots. **1828–32** Webster, *Settle*, to cause to subside after being heaved and loosened by frost; or to dry and harden after rain. Thus clear weather settles the roads. **1845** *Florist's Jrnl.* 33 Then give the whole a good watering to settle the soil.

**IV.** To come or bring to rest after agitation.

**17. a.** *intr.* Of a liquid: To become still after agitation or fermentation, so that the suspended particles or impurities are separated as scum or sediment. Also in figurative context.

*c* **1467** *Noble Bk. Cookry* (1882) 101 Sye it throughe a clothe and let yt stond and setelle. **1471** Ripley *Comp. Alch.* v. x. in Ashm. (1652) 150 For they together lyke lyquyd Pyche that tyde, Shall swell and burbyll, setyll, and Putrefye. **1530** Palsgr. 698/1 And so for wyne, or ale, or any thynge that fyrst swelleth and afterwarde sattylleth. **1560** Bible (Geneva) *Jer.* xlviii. 11 Moab..hathe setled on his lees, & hathe not bene powred from vessel to vessel. *a* **1634** Chapman *Trag. Chabot* I. i. 197 And not be like a dull and standing lake, That settles, putrefies, and chokes with mud. **1758** Reid tr. *Macquer's Chym.* I. 298 If you let the turbid water settle, and distill the sediment. **1799** G. Smith *Laboratory* I. 290 Pour the ingredients of the three glasses into one, stop them up, and let them settle. **1857** Miller *Elem. Chem.*, *Org.* 361 The mixture is left to settle. **1866** Lowell *Study Wind.*, *Swinburne's Trag.*, Goethe, in whose capacious nature..the spiritual fermentation of the eighteenth century settled and clarified.

**b.** *trans.* To cause (liquor) to deposit dregs or work off impurities; to clarify.

**1599** Sir J. Davies *Nosce Teipsum* Introd. xl, So working seas settle and purge the wine. **1883** *Harper's Mag.* Mar. 578/1 Should the coffee be settled with an egg or with fish-skin?

**c.** *Soap-making.* To refine or purify (soap) by fusing in water or weak lye.

**1906** L. L. Lamborn *Manuf. Soap* ix. 343 Soap to be filled with soda-ash solution..may be settled finer or thinner; i.e., more heavily hydrated than the various kinds of soaps just mentioned.

**18. a.** *intr.* Of suspended particles or impurities in a liquid: To come to rest after agitation or disturbance; to collect as scum or sediment by gravitation; now chiefly (with mixture of sense 13), to sink to the bottom as sediment. Also ***to settle out***. Also *fig.*

*c* **1420** *Pallad. on Husb.* XII. 480 Whanne her dregges sattled doun beth go. *c* **1425** tr. *Arderne's Fistula* etc. 59 Poudry resolucions which..ar..putte out with þe vryne. And for þai ar heuy and erþi þai satle in þe grounde. **1626** Bacon *Sylva* §14 The Wine setling in the top..and the Water descending & setling in the bottome. **1630** R. Johnson *Kingd. & Commw.* 14 The melancholike [humours]..remaine, and as dregges settle at the base of all their actions. **1634** Milton *Comus* 595 But evil..shall..mix no more with goodness, when at last Gather'd like scum, and setl'd to it self It shall [etc.]. **1678** Moxon *Mech. Exerc.* vi. 102 Especially if the Small Beer chance to be new, and its Yest not well settled from it. **1695** Woodward *Nat. Hist. Earth* II. 75 That which had the least Gravity sinking not down till last of all, settling at the Surface of the Sediment. **1860** Maury *Phys. Geog. Sea* (Low) xiv. §587. 326 When they die their shells settle to the bottom. **1883** Haldane *Workshop Rec.* Ser. II. 302/2 The liquor is kept..in a fluid condition, to allow mechanical impurities to settle out.

**b.** Of food or a meal: to be digested.

**1944** L. P. Hartley *Shrimp & Anemone* iv. 44 What about these toboggans? We've given our tea time to settle.

**19. a.** Of passion: To subside, calm down. Of the brain, mind, etc.: To become calm or composed.

**1591** Savile *Tacitus, Hist.* II. xv. 61 The feare, which at first is most terrible, settling by litle and litle. **1611** Shaks. *Wint. T.* IV. iv. 482 Then till the fury of his Highnesse settle Come not before him. **1680** Dryden *Span. Friar* II. i, Your fury then boil'd upward to a foam; But since this message came, you sink and settle, As if cold water had been pour'd on you. **1693** Prior *'While blooming Youth'* 28 The Heat, with which thy Lover glows, Will settle into cold Respect. **1779** Johnson *Let. Mrs. Thrale* 28 Oct., I dined on Tuesday with *** and hope her little head begins to settle. **1818** Scott *Hrt. Midl.* xvi, Better let her mind settle a little. **1823** —— *Quentin D.* xxviii, Risks which raise a man's blood so, that, by Saint Andrew, it will not settle for an hour or two.

**b.** Of persons: To become composed; to compose oneself *to* sleep; to come to a quiet or orderly state after excitement or restless activity. Also with *down*, and *spec.* of an infant or a child.

*a* **1578** Lindesay (Pitscottie) *Chron. Scot.* (S.T.S.) I. 111 He waxit irefull aganis all consperatouris bot zeit wald settill of his ire sa sune as they became penitent of thair offences and cryme. **1784** Cowper *Task* VI. 69, I again perceive The soothing influence of the wafted strains, And settle in soft musings as I tread The walk. **1848** Dickens *Dombey* xxxi, It is impossible to settle down after this, and why not go, in a party, to the play? **1896** Bodkin *Ld. Edw. Fitzgerald* xiii, Maurice Blake was too excited..to settle at once to sleep. **1972** P. D. James *Unsuitable Job* iii. 88 The Webbers couldn't bear the boy to go to hospital; they'd tried it once and he didn't settle. **1976** 'D. Halliday' *Dolly & Nanny Bird* viii. 106 You can let go now, he won't settle.

**c.** ***to settle down***: To subside into indolence or contentment.

**1853** F. W. Faber *All for Jesus* (1854) 328 It is incredible how soon people can make themselves comfortable in low things... If it were not for this fatal facility of *settling down* [etc.]. **1862** *Lady Morgan's Mem.* II. 22 Lady Morgan was always anxious that Sir Charles should exert himself and not settle down into indolent comfort.

**20. a.** *trans.* To quiet, tranquillize, compose (a person, his mind, brain, nerves, etc.); to allay (passion). Also *refl.*

**1530** Palsgr. 698/1, I sattyll, or sober, or appayse my selfe from myne anger, or any passyon, *je me rassis.* **1550** Bale *Apol.* 30 If all thys wyll not sattle his wyld wytlesse head. *a* **1619** Fletcher *Mad Lover* IV. i, How still he sitts: I hope this Song has setled him. **1684** Bunyan *Pilgr.* I. (1900) 12 Hoping that sleep might settle his brains, with all haste they got him to bed. **1694** Congreve *Double Dealer* I. i, We'll.. drink a dish of tea to settle our heads. **1833** Ht. Martineau *Manch. Strike* i. 8 A glass of gin..to settle him to his sleep. **1848** Leigh Hunt *Town* (1906) 581 [Charles II] was a rapid and constant walker, to settle his nerves. **1865** Trollope *Belton Est.* xiii, Cold pudding is good to settle a man's love.

**b.** ***to settle the stomach***: to check vomiting or nausea.

**1622** J. Davies *tr. Mandelslo's Trav.* 195 There is not any thing that..settles the stomack better than this herb doth. **1756** Mrs. Calderwood in *Coltness Collect.* (Maitland Club) 129 The minister..made a large pot of coffee,.. declaring it to be the finest thing to settle the stomachs of the whole company. **1898** P. Manson *Trop. Dis.* vi. 122 Effervescing mixture often helps to clean the tongue and settle the stomach.

**c.** To recover from the effects of (drink).

**1639** S. Du Verger tr. *Camus' Admir. Events* 62 They let him sleepe..and whilest he settles his drinke, the Duke prepares [etc.].

**21. a.** To quiet with a blow; to knock down dead or stunned; to finish, 'do for'.

*c* **1611** Chapman *Iliad* XIII. 587 It settled him, and set his spirit gone Amongst the hands of his best friends. **1660** Fuller *Mixt Contempl.* I. xxvii. 44 They [of Northamptonshire] used to say when at Cudgel playes..one gave his Adversary such a sound blow, as that he knew not whether to stand or to fall that he Settled him at a blow. *a* **1661** —— *Worthies, Lancash.* (1662) I. 124 He [Lambert] at Preston gave the Scotch Army such a Blow, as setled or stun'd it. **1709** *Brit. Apollo* II. No. 44. 3/1 Clowns..Call it Settling a Man when they knock him down dead. **1738** Swift *Pol. Conversat.* 103 There's nothing will settle me but a Bullet. **1834** Dickens *Sk. Boz, Boarding Ho.*, 'She says she'll settle her missis's life,' replied Mrs. Tibbs. 'The wretch! they're plotting murder.' **1888** Kipling *Soldiers Three, In Matter of a Private*, 'Come to——' laughed Simmons, sending a cartridge home with his thumb. 'Not before I've settled you an' Jerry Blazes.'

**b.** *to settle* (a person's) *hash*: see hash *sb.*[1] 3 b.

**1822** A. Thornton *Don Juan* II. xii, Which..settled his hash, or, to speak in the language of real science, floored him.

**c.** To compel to cease from opposition or annoyance; to silence, nonplus.

**1850** Dickens *Dav. Copp.* xi, [He] rebelled against my being so distinguished [as to be called by my Christian name], but Mick Walker settled him in no time. **1900** H. A. Jones *Mrs. Dane's Defence* II. 39 We will very soon settle Mrs. Bulsom-Porter.

† **22.** In occasional physical uses: **a.** *trans.* To steady, keep from quivering. **b.** In *passive*, of the blood: To cease to move or pulsate. **c.** *intr.* of the eyes: To become set. *Obs.*

**1592** SHAKS. *Rom. & Jul.* IV. v. 26 Alas shee's cold, Her blood is settled and her ioynts are stiffe. **1615** G. SANDYS *Trav.* 267 His tongue hung out and his eyes setled in his head. **1631** GOUGE *God's Arrows* III. §48. 273 To settle his hand, and to make it the more steddy..Aaron and Hur staid up his hands. **1824** MISS FERRIER *Inher.* viii, 'Miss Pratt!' cried the Earl, in a tone enough to have settled quicksilver itself.

**23. a.** *intr.* To come to an end of a series of changes or fluctuations and assume a definite form or condition. Const. *in, into.* Also *to settle down* (*to*).

**1684** BURNET *Th. Earth* I. v. 53 The Chaos..was wrought by degrees from one form into another, till it setled at length into an habitable Earth. **1731** ARBUTHNOT *Aliments* vi. (1735) 191 Our Aliment in the Form of Chyle..is whitish; by..Circulation it runs through all the intermediate Colours, till it settles in an intense Red. **1828** D'ISRAELI *Chas. I,* II. ii. 32 The elements of war are often gradually accumulating before they settle into an open rupture. **1851–4** *Tomlinson's Cycl. Useful Arts* (1866) I. 775/2 [The ball of glass] settles by cooling into a form similar to that of Fig. 1078. **1858** CARLYLE *Fredk. Gt.* VII. vi. II. 236 The Duke..blushed blue, then red, and various colours; at length settling into steady pale. **1859** *Habits of Gd. Society* vii. 250 This smile should not settle into a simper. **1900** 'Q' *Old Fires* viii, Young men who have run through all beliefs by the age of twenty and settled down to a polite but weary atheism.

**b.** Of the weather: To become steadily fine. Also *to settle* (*in*) *for*: to come gradually to a steady condition of (rain, frost, etc.); *to settle down* or *in*, of the weather, a season, etc.: to set in.

**1719** DE FOE *Crusoe* I. (Globe) 106 As soon as the Rains were over, and the Weather began to settle. **1818** SCOTT *Rob Roy* xiv, Howsomever, I'm no denying that it may settle.. till Monday morning. **1825** HONE *Every-day Bk.* I. 879 His cautious neighbour..waited for the weather to 'settle'. **1863** MRS. GASKELL *Sylvia's L.* (ed. 2) I. xiv. 294 The air was very still, settling in for a frost. **1889** J. K. JEROME *Three Men in Boat* v. 70 'Going to clear up, d'ye think?'.. 'Well, no, sir; I'm afraid it's settled down for the day.' *a* **1912** *Mod.* It seems to be settling for a storm. **1939** K. PINKERTON *Wilderness Wife* x. 110 By the first week in December the winter began to 'settle in', as they say in the North.

**c.** *to settle down*: to drop into a regular or uniform rate of movement.

**1899** *Daily News* 5 June 3/7 Sweet Mart colt settled down with a clear lead.

**V.** To render or become stable or permanent; to fix or become fixed in a certain condition.

**24. a.** *trans.* To ensure the stability or permanence of (a condition of things, a quality, power, etc.).

*c* **1386** CHAUCER *Merch. T.* 2405 Til that youre sighte ysatled [*v.r.* ystabled] be a whyle Ther may ful many a sighte yow bigile. **1526** *St. Papers Hen. VIII,* IV. 441 Till the peax were some deall moore firmely satilled. **1569** *Reg. Privy Council Scot.* I. 667 To settill and estableis universall peace. **1610** B. JONSON *Masques, Sp. Pr. Henry's Barriers* Wks. (1616) 969 Th' increase Of trades and tillage,..Begun by him [Edw. I.], but settled and promou'd By the third Heroe of his name. **1648–9** *Eikon Bas.* xiii. 106 Other violent motions..shall never either shake or settle my Religion. **1693** LOCKE *Educ.* §41. 43 Thus much for the Setling your Authority over your Children in general. **1710** PRIDEAUX *Orig. Tithes* iv. 172 After they had settled peace between the Father and the Son. **1748** *Anson's Voy.* III. vi. 345 The eastern monsoon was now, we reckoned, fairly settled. **1833** TENNYSON *Lotos-eaters* 127 'Tis hard to settle order once again.

†**b.** To adopt firmly (an opinion, mental attitude). *Obs.*

*a* **1586** SIDNEY *Arcadia* I. (Sommer) 38 They rather increased new doubts, then gaue him ground to settle any iudgement. **1697** CIBBER *Woman's Wit* III. 34 When he does that, I shall know how to settle my Opinion. **1756** TOLDERVY *Hist. 2 Orphans* IV. 210 Mr. Richmond had settled so great a respect for that accomplished gentleman, that he could not suffer him to depart [etc.].

**25.** To fix, make steadfast or constant (a wavering, irresolute or doubting person, heart, mind, etc.). Const. *in, to.*

**1435** MISYN *Fire of Love* 99 þerfore my mynde to þi power take & make itt stabyll, þat..my mynde so in þe sattyld so in þi lufe byrne þat, with no chauns..it be kelyd. **1535** COVERDALE *Ecclus.* ii. 2 My sonne,..sattle thine hert, and be pacient. **1581** in Allen *Martyrdom Campion* (1908) 49 If a man were not setled in his religion there was inough to convert him. **1606** SHAKS. *Ant. & Cl.* II. ii. 246 If Beauty, Wisedome, Modesty, can settle The heart of Anthony. **1611** BIBLE *Col.* i. 23 If ye continue in the faith grounded and setled. **1639** S. DU VERGER tr. *Camus' Admir. Events* 52 He kept back his anger, and setled his minde to sufferance. **1643** BAKER *Chron.* (1653) 475 All these being..Papists yesterday, and to day Protestants, who being scarce setled in their Religion, how should they be setled in their Loyalty? *c* **1665** MRS. HUTCHINSON *Mem. Col. Hutchinson* (1846) 26 There was no opinion which he was most settled in,..but he would patiently and impartially hear it debated. **1714** SWIFT *Public Spirit of Whigs* 5 It is a Pamphlet..against the Ministry..; it will settle the Wavering, confirm the Doubtful. **1720** DE FOE *Capt. Singleton* xix. (1840) 331 However, William settled my mind to more prudent steps than these. **1882** MOZLEY *Remin.* (ed. 2) I. 61 A sermon designed to recall and settle the troubled spirits of Oxford, ..in what to him was the faith and practice of his forefathers.

**26. a.** *refl.* To fix one's attention *upon* an object; to make up one's mind *to do* something; to dispose or set oneself steadily *to* some employment. Now usually with mixture of sense 20, to compose oneself after excitement or restlessness and apply oneself quietly to work. (Often with *down.*) **b.** *intr.* In the same senses, with or without prepositional compl. †Also, to become fixed or steadfast *in* (affection, etc.).

**a. 1530** PALSGR. 698/1 The mans mynde is so wandringe that he can sattell hym upon nothyng. **1548** ELYOT *Dict., Comparare se ad respondendum,* to prepare or settle hym selfe to make an answere. **1576** FLEMING *Panopl. Epist.* 356 Let vs take the axe,..and settle our selues to cleauing and riueing. **1579** HAKE *Newes out of Powles* i. (1872) Bj b, Then Paule began..To settle forth him selfe to speake. *c* **1582** M. PHILLIPS in *Hakluyt's Voy.* (1600) III. 432, I could neuer throughly settle my selfe to marry in that countrey. **1675** DUPPA *Rules Devotion* 70 When thou art therefore setling thy self to thy devotions. **1833** HT. MARTINEAU *Briery Creek* iv. 78 When I settle myself down to my pursuits. **1881** SHORTHOUSE *J. Inglesant* II. 378 After some talk of this nature we settled ourselves to our music and to tune our instruments.

**b. 1576** PETTIE *Petite Pallace* 65 She began to settle so surely in good wyl towardes him. **1667** PEPYS *Diary* 1 June, It troubles me to see how hard it is for me to settle to it [*sc.* business] sometimes when my mind is upon pleasure. **1699** DAMPIER *Voy.* II. II. vi. 128 When the violent Storm..took us, I was but just settling to Work. **1756** WALPOLE *Let. Conway* 22 Jan., The Opposition, like schoolboys, don't know how to settle to their books again after the holidays. **1848** THACKERAY *Van. Fair* lix, His daughter could not induce him to settle down to his customary occupations. **1865** MRS. GASKELL *Wives & Dau.* I. xix. 215 She went down into the drawing-room, and could not settle to anything. **1883** *Law Times* LXXVI. 118/2 The horse.. when checked..broke into a canter, and would not trot and settle down to its work afterwards. **1976** *Cambridge Independent Press* 16 Dec. 1. 10/5 But Felixstowe settled and after 25 minutes they took the lead when Bailey touched home Goffin's cross.

**27. a.** To secure or confirm (a person) *in* a position of authority, an office; to install permanently, establish *in* an office, an employment.

*a* **1548** HALL *Chron., Hen. VI,* 187 b, When Kynge Henry was somewhat setteled in the realme of Scotlande. **1553** BALE *Vocacyon* 42, I thought my selfe..wele satteled in the bishoprycke of Ossorye. *a* **1586** SIDNEY *Arcadia* II. (Sommer) 180 After the death of Tiridates, and setling Erona in her gouernement. **1634** SIR T. HERBERT *Trav.* 35 He beheaded and strangled most of them..to settle himselfe in a more quiet tyranny. **1660** WOOD *Life* Dec. (O.H.S.) I. 360 Many..being absent from the University either to get, or settle themselves in their preferments. **1694** E. CHAMBERLAYNE *Pres. St. Eng.* III. i. (ed. 18) 356 How a Clergyman becomes settled in a Living. **1705** DE FOE *Consolidator* Wks. 1840 IX. 354 They went on to settle themselves in all sorts of trade in open companies. **1857** KINGSLEY *Two Y. Ago* I. i, He had made to himself a practice large enough to enable him to settle two sons well in his own profession.

**b.** (Chiefly *Sc.* and *U.S.*) To appoint (a minister) to the charge of a parish; also, to appoint a minister to (a parish). In U.S. also *intr.*: see quot. 1828–32.

**1719** WODROW *Corr.* (1843) II. 448 The Presbytery of Ayr are appointed..to go on and settle the parish. **1726** *Ibid.* III. 253 That Mr. Chambers being now settled, the Magistrates ..and Communicants in Aberdeen..could not be deprived of him. **1756** in [N. Morren] *Ann. Gen. Assembly Ch. Scot.* (1840) II. 77 That the blood of the parish of Nigg would be required of them if they should settle a man to the walls of the kirk. **1773** BOSWELL *Johnson* 1 May, In some cases the Prebytery having refused to induct or settle, as they call it, the person presented by the patron. **1828–32** WEBSTER, *Settle,* to be ordained or installed over a parish, church or congregation. A. B. was invited to *settle* in the first society in New Haven. **1890** MARY E. WILKINS *Faraway Melody,* etc. 32 He was settled over a neighbouring parish [New England].

**28. a.** To establish (a person) in the matrimonial state. Phr. *to settle in the world* or *in life.* Now chiefly *refl.* and *pass.*

**1566** KINWELMARSHE *Jocasta* I. in *Gascoigne's Wks.* (1907) I. 247 Thou knowst what care my carefull father tooke, In wedlockes sacred state to settle me With Laius. **1693** DRYDEN *Ovid's Met.* IX. *Iphis & Ianthe* 70 The fond Father thought the time drew on Of settling in the World his only Son. Ianthe was his choice. **1704** STEELE *Lying Lover* II. i. 27, I therefore have resolv'd to settle thee, and chosen a young Lady, witty, prudent, rich and fair. **1772** FOOTE *Nabob* III. (1778) 71 And as to my young cousins within, I hope we shall be able to settle them without Sir Matthew's assistance. **1825** T. HOOK *Sayings* Ser. II. *Doubts & F.* iii, The prudent gentlewoman..wishes to settle her daughter. **1831** T. L. PEACOCK *Crotchet Castle* v, I have been very much in love; but now I am come to years of discretion, and must think..of settling myself advantageously. **1864** TROLLOPE *Can you forgive her?* vii, How are you to settle yourself in life if you don't care for them [*sc.* amusements]?

**b.** *intr.* 'To establish a domestic state' (J); chiefly in phr. *to marry and settle, to settle in life.* Also *to settle down.*

**1718** PRIOR *Alma* II. 49 As people marry now, and settle, Fierce love abates his usual mettle. **1738** SWIFT *Pol. Conversat.* 102 Why don't you marry, and settle? **1822** DE QUINCEY *Conf.* 29 My landlady..had but lately married away and 'settled' (as such people express it) for life. **1830** M. T. SADLER *Law Popul.* I. 564 Their very object in leaving their native countries is to settle in life, a phrase that needs no explanation. **1869** J. GREENWOOD *Seven Curses London* ii. 19 At sixteen..the pair embark in housekeeping and 'settle down'. **1891** G. CHAMIER *Philosopher Dick* v. 120 'Didn't I tell you he was a looking hout for some crib to settle down.' 'Settle down, indeed! What do you mean?' 'Why, he's about to get spliced.' **1911** G. B. SHAW *Getting Married* 118 They had all, as they called it, settled down, like balloons that had lost their lifting margin of gas. **1928** E. O'NEILL *Strange Interlude* VI. 230 He looks pretty dissipated..too many women..ought to get married and settle down.

†**29.** To establish (a person) in legal possession of property. *to be settled of*: to be seised of.

**1617** MORYSON *Itin.* II. 10 This man dying without heires males, his said brother came up to the State, that he might be setled in his inheritance. **1647** N. BACON *Disc. Govt. Eng.* I. xli. (1689) 64 If the man was settled of such estate..and died, his Wife surviving,..she had her Dower, or third part of such estate of inheritance.

**30. a.** To secure (payment, property, title) *to, on,* or *upon* (a person) by decree, ordinance, or enactment.

**1625** BURGES *Pers. Tithes* 32 By yeelding that to be a Due, which the Law hath setled vpon the Minister. **1651** HOBBES *Leviath.* III. xl. 250 The succession to that Office was setled upon Aaron, and his heirs after him. **1659** MILTON *Consid. Means to remove Hirelings* title-p., Wherein is also discourc'd..whether any maintenance of ministers can be settl'd by law. **1697** DRYDEN *Æneid* I. 8 He..setl'd sure Succession in his Line. **1708** *Constit. Watermen's Co.* lv, So much Money as shall from time to time be settled to and for each of them in the Poor's List. **1765** BLACKSTONE *Comm.* I. I. iii. 207 They therefore settled the crown, first on king William and queen Mary..for their joint lives. **1859** MISS PIDDINGTON *Last of Cav.* xxxiv, The conditions on which the crown was to be settled. **1863** H. COX *Inst.* III. iii. 620 The statute settling the present title to the Crown.

**b.** Of a private individual: To secure (property, succession) *to, on* or *upon* (a person) by means of a deed of settlement.

*a* **1661** FULLER *Worthies, Somerset.* (1662) II. 37 She would have setled on that House Lands to the value of five hundred pounds *per annum.* *a* **1700** EVELYN *Diary* 6 Jan. 1692, Boyle ..had settled a fund for preachers who should preach expressly against Atheists [etc.]. **1711** ADDISON *Spect.* No. 106 ¶6, I..have settled upon him a good Annuity for Life. **1766** BLACKSTONE *Comm.* II. 137 It became usual, on marriage, to settle by express deed some special estate to the use of the husband and his wife, for their lives, in joint-tenancy or jointure. **1818** CRUISE *Digest* (ed. 2) IV. 285 A tenant for life, with power to settle a jointure. **1844** J. WILLIAMS *Real Prop.* (1877) 103 The modern English custom of settling the family estates on the eldest son. **1884** FLOR. MARRYAT *Under Lilies* xiii, The day that Miss Rayne becomes Lady Coombe, I will settle a thousand a year on her for her private use.

**c.** *absol.* To make a jointure (see JOINTURE *sb.* 4).

**1713** GARTH *Epil. to Cato,* He sighs with most Success that settles well.

†**d.** *intr.* Of an estate: To pass legally. *Obs.*

*a* **1626** BACON *Use of Law* (1629) 65 Vpon Feofments and Recoveries, the estate doth settle as the vse and intent of the parties is declared..before the Acts was done.

**31. a.** *trans.* To subject to permanent regulations, to set permanently in order, place on a permanent footing (institutions, government); to bring (a language) into a permanent form.

**1597** HOOKER *Eccl. Pol.* V. lxxvi. §4. 223 The greatest felicitie they wish to the common wealth..is that..no faulte may be capitall besides dislike of things settled in so good termes. **1629** SELDEN in *Lett. Lit. Men.* (Camden) 143 For the Library is not yet so setled as that books may not be lent if the founder will. **1642** J. M[ARSH] *Argt. conc. Militia* 1 The King refusing to settle the Militia for the defence and securitie of his people. **1643** BAKER *Chron.* (1653) 93 King Richard at his going out of England, had so well setled the Government of the kingdome, that [etc.]. **1659** MILTON *Treat. Civ. Power Eccl. Causes* 44 [They] who think the gospel..cannot stand or continue..unless it be enacted and settled, as they call it, by the state. **1662** *Bk. Com. Prayer, For the High Court of Parlt.,* That all things may be so ordered and setled by their endeavours, upon the best and surest foundations. **1712** SWIFT *Propos. Corr. Eng. Tongue* 45 If You will not take some Care to settle our Language, and put it into a state of Continuance. **1849** MACAULAY *Hist. Eng.* V. I. 575 The government should be settled on principles favourable to liberty. **1874** GREEN *Short Hist.* viii. §10 They proceeded at once to settle the Government on a Parliamentary basis. **1886** T. L. K. OLIPHANT *New Engl.* II. 1 Tyndale, Coverdale, and Cranmer had done so much to settle our language.

*absol.* *a* **1700** EVELYN *Diary* 19 Aug. 1660, The National Assemblies beginning to settle, and wanting instruction. **1718** PRIOR *Solomon* II. 704 Her Will alone could settle or revoke; And Law was fix'd by what She latest spoke.

†**b.** To vest the control of (something) *in* a person. *Obs.*

**1671** E. CHAMBERLAYNE *Pres. St. Eng.* II. 279 Besides, the fore-mentioned forces there is the standing Militia..setled in the King.

**c.** *to settle one's estate, one's affairs*: to arrange for the disposal of one's property, the payment of one's debts, etc., esp. with a view to one's death, removal to a distance, or retirement from business. Occas. with *up.*

In the first quot. perh. rather: to render one's worldly position secure (sense 24).

**1652** BP. HALL *Rem. Wks.* (1660) 144 Oh the poor and base thoughts of men! How may I raise my house? how may I settle my estate? *a* **1700** EVELYN *Diary* 10 Sept. 1647, Being call'd into England to settle my affaires after an absence of about 4 yeares. **1710** STEELE *Tatler* No. 164 ¶6, I several months since made my Will, settled my estate, and took leave of my friends. **1719** DE FOE *Crusoe* II. (Globe) 555 He had settled all his affairs so well at Bengal, and left his Effects in such good Hands, that [etc.]. **1884** J. GILMOUR *Mongols* xxxi. 363 They..are expected to settle up their affairs and return to their remote abodes. **1894** A. ROBERTSON *Nuggets* 84 Besides, hasn't he settled his affairs —made his will, in fact, most sensibly.

**VI.** To fix (what is uncertain), to decide (a question).

**32. a.** To appoint or fix definitely beforehand, to decide upon (a time, place, plan of action, price, conditions, etc.); †to adjust (one's action) *to* something.

**1596** DALRYMPLE tr. *Leslie's Hist. Scot.* IX. II. 158 The Wardanis setlis a day. **1608** CHAPMAN *Byron's Trag.* III. i. 50 My lord, I stand not on these deep discourses To settle my course to your fortunes. **1754** COWPER *Ep. R. Lloyd* 31 Thus, the preliminaries settled. **1782** MISS BURNEY *Cecilia* VI. v, His journey to Bristol was settled to take place in three days. **1798** SOPHIA LEE *Canterb. T., Young Lady's T.* II. 164 Having settled his route..[he] set out. **1825** COBBETT *Rur. Rides* (1885) II. 14 The allowance settled by the magistrates for a young, hearty, labouring man! **1837** CARLYLE *Fr. Rev.* I. IV. iv, The Hall is ready: the very costume [of the Deputies], as we said, has been settled. **1867** MRS. OLIPHANT *Madonna Mary* III. xiv. 236, I came that it might be all settled out of hand. **1891** 'J. S. WINTER' *Lumley* iii, 'Then it's as good as settled,' he remarked, smiling broadly.

†**b.** To appoint or arrange (something to be done or to take place). *Obs.*

**1694** PENN *Trav. Holland* 162 Being the first monthly meeting that was setled for Frieslandt. **1705** *New Jersey Archives* XI. 13 These are to give notice, That Her Majesty ..Hath settled Packet-Boats for the West-Indies. **1709** STEELE *Tatler* 143 ¶3 There is a Stage-Coach settled from the One-Bell in the Strand to Dorchester.

**c.** To fix by mutual agreement.

**1620** R. COCKS *Diary* (Hakl. Soc.) II. 122 Capt. Speck came..to talke about going to Nangasaque to Gonrok Dono, to settell the price of the lead. **1687** MIEGE *Gt. Fr. Dict.* s.v., We have at last settled that Business. **1716** ADDISON *Freeholder* No. 23 ¶3, I think it is very convenient there should be a cartel settled between them. **1786** MME. D'ARBLAY *Diary* 8 Aug., The conversation concluded with nothing being settled. **1824** MISS FERRIER *Inher.* viii, All these matters being settled, Miss Pratt then accepted the arm of her companion. **1848** THACKERAY *Van. Fair* iv, If a dear girl has no dear Mamma to settle matters with the young man. **1896** BODKIN *Ld. Edw. Fitzgerald* xi, Meanwhile the two seconds were settling the fatal formalities in the library.

**d.** *intr.* To come to a decision; to decide *to do* something; to decide *upon* (a plan of action, an object of choice).

**1782** MISS BURNEY *Cecilia* IV. vii, Two other young ladies, who were..settling to dance in the same cotillon. **1814** MME. D'ARBLAY (Miss Burney) *Wanderer* (1817) I. 122 A comedy that we have been settling to massacre. **1833** HT. MARTINEAU *Manch. Strike* xii. 127 The masters met and settled that they would give no more than the medium wages. **1867** MRS. OLIPHANT *Madonna Mary* III. xiii. 222 This was what Will had always intended and settled upon. **1885** H. FINCH-HATTON *Advance Australia!* 196, I settled to shift my camp up the creek. **1886** HARDY *Mayor Casterbr.* xxiv, But settling upon new clothes is so trying.

**e.** *to settle for*, to decide or agree on, to content oneself with.

**1959** P. BULL *I know Face* i. 11 My father wanted me to be a chartered accountant, a profession which seemed to me to lack glamour. However, in order to show willing, I did settle for 'journalism'. **1963** H. GARNER in R. Weaver *Canad. Short Stories* (1968) 2nd Ser. 27 There were plates of doughnuts..but I settled for a mug of coffee. **1972** C. FREMLIN *Appointment with Yesterday* xi. 82 'You couldn't start straight away, could you?.. Or would you rather have some coffee?'.. Milly found the courage to settle for the coffee.

**33. a.** *trans.* To decide, come to a fixed conclusion on (a question, a matter of doubt or discussion); to bring to an end (a dispute) by agreement or intervention.

**1651** HOBBES *Leviath.* I. iv. 15 In Geometry..men begin at settling the significations of their words; which settling of significations, they call Definitions. **1666** BOYLE *Orig. Formes & Qual.* 111 This being thus setled in the First place, we may in the Next consider, that [etc.]. **1716** ADDISON *Freeholder* No. 53 ¶3 Casuists..that will settle you the right of Princes. **1793** *Blackstone's Comm.* (ed. 12) I. 114 *note*, At the great council assembled in 1072, to settle the claim of precedence between the two archbishops. **1883** *Law Rep. 11 Q.B. Div.* 575 In settling the value of a copyhold fine. **1886** *Manch. Exam.* 16 Jan. 5/4 The dispute at Llandulas quarries has been settled. **1895** ROWLANDS in *Law Times* XCIX. 564/2 Now that this point has been definitely settled, it seems too clear for argument.

**b.** With indirect question as obj.

**1796** MME. D'ARBLAY *Camilla* I. 282 Mr. Tyrold intreated him to stay till they had settled how to get rid of the business. **1874** SYMONDS *Sk. Italy & Greece* (1898) I. xii. 237, I have to settle with myself what I mean by art in general.

**c.** Of a fact or argument: To be decisive of (a question).

**1825** COBBETT *Hist. Prot. Reform.* (1899) xvi. §468 There! that settles the matter. **1857** KINGSLEY *Two Y. Ago* Introd., You shall see enough to-day to settle for you the question whether we old-country folk are in a state of decadence.

**d.** *Law.* To decide (a case) by arrangement between the contesting parties. More fully, *to settle out of court.*

**1900** *Daily News* 14 Feb. 6/4 After one of the plaintiffs.. had been in the box, it was agreed to settle the case.

**e.** To put beyond dispute, establish (a principle, fact) by authority or argument.

**1733** ARBUTHNOT *Ess. Effects Air* v. 97 Another Fact, settled by a fair Experiment of the ingenious Mr. Hales, is, that [etc.]. **1883** KAY in *Law Rep. 24 Chanc. Div.* 107 It is well settled that the transmissibility of contingent interest is a doctrine applying equally to real and personal estate.

**34. a.** *intr.* To arrange matters in dispute, to come to terms or agreement *with* a person.

**1527** *St. Papers Hen. VIII*, I. 272, I have first depeched Mons[r] Gregory, who, after he hathe satelled with Mons[r] de Lotrik..shall [etc.]. **1647** *Caldwell Papers* (Maitland Club) I. 110 For my awin chargis..in settling w[t] y[e] ladie, and resaving of y[e] rents. **1682** *Rec. Scott. Cloth. Manuf. New Mills* (S.H.S.) 33 Ordered thatt upon settleing with Smith in the teerms thatt the rest of the silk stocken men are upon thatt he have a gratuity of 3 legg dollars. **1800** PAGET in *P. Papers* (1896) I. 191 It was not till yesterday that I was enabled to settle with the Master of an English Merchantman for my conveyance.

**b.** To make an arrangement, compound *with* a creditor.

**1838** W. BELL *Dict. Law Scot.* 197 In extra-judicial arrangements for settling by composition, no creditor can be required to accept the composition offered, unless he pleases. **1855** THACKERAY *Newcomes* II. xxxii. 294 The reverend Baptist Bellman..had helped himself to 73,000l. more, for which he settled in the Bankruptcy Court. **1885** *Law Rep. 15 Q.B. Div.* 11 The underwriters of the ship ultimately settled with her owners at 88 per cent.

**35. a.** *trans.* To close (an account) by a money payment; to pay (an account, bill, score); also *dial.* to write 'settled' to a bill, to receipt (it).

**1687** MIEGE *Gt. Fr. Dict.* s.v., To settle an Account, *regler un Conte.* **1765** FOOTE *Commissary* I. (1782) 26 Let us settle accounts, Mr. Paduasoy; you'll see no more of my money. **1840** THACKERAY *Shabby-genteel Story* ii, [At the foot of a bill.] Settled, Juliana Gann. **1848** —— *Van. Fair* xxxiv, I'd best go and settle the score. **1868** ATKINSON *Cleveland Gloss.* s.v., Gan an' pay John Lewis' bill, an' mahnd an' git him to sattle 't.

*fig.* **1794** MRS. RADCLIFFE *Myst. Udolpho* xxxiii, If I was they, I would settle accounts with myself, for all my hard fighting, the same way. **1852** MRS. STOWE *Uncle Tom's C.* xvi. 148 What an awful account these wicked creatures will have to settle, at last, especially for being lazy! **1887** W. E. NORRIS *Major & Minor* III. xi. 199, I am here to settle accounts with you, my fine fellow. I suppose you thought it was a very safe thing to insult and desert a girl who had nobody at hand to protect her except an old man.

**b.** *absol.* or *intr.* To settle accounts by payment. Chiefly const. *with.*

**1788** CLARA REEVE *Exiles* III. 105, I was obliged to go to the inn to settle with the landlord. **1796** *Hist. Ned Evans* II. 192 He had still upwards of £300 in his hands, for which he would be ready to account whenever he chose to settle. **1827** SCOTT *Chron. Canongate* i, Some change that was due to me on settling with my landlady. **1844** MACAULAY in Trevelyan *Life* (1876) II. 155, I then called to the steward, and pretended to be very anxious to settle with him about some coffee that I had taken. **1873** *Money Market* ix. (ed. 3) 113 The 'settling' days occur twice in each month, when the transactions of the preceding fortnight are settled for in cash. **1886** ELWORTHY *W. Somerset Word-bk.* s.v., I went and begged o' un vor to settle; he've a got a plenty o' money.

*fig.* *c***1820** S. ROGERS *Italy, Arqua* 40 When he had done and settled with the world.

**VII. 36.** Comb.: †**settle-brain**, something that calms the brain; **settle-down**, *nonce-wd.*, a flock settling down.

**1629** FORD *Lovers Mel.* II. ii, Sir, is your stomacke vp yet? get some warme porredge in your belly, 'tis a very good settle-braine. **1640** BROME *Antipodes* V. vii, I have yet an entertainment for him, Of better Settle-braine, then Drunkards porridge. **1692** TRYON *Good Housew.* xxvi. 213 Coffee is the Drunkards Settle-brain. **1855** BROWNING *Cleon* 15 Like the chequer-work Pavement..Now covered with this settle-down of doves.

**'settleable**, *a.* [-ABLE.] **1.** Capable of being settled. *nonce-wd.*

**1837** MOORE *Mem.* (1856) VII. 202 He seemed to consider the whole thing as settled, or, at least, settle-able without any difficulty.

**2.** Having the property of settling or sinking to the bottom of a liquid.

**1940** IMHOFF & FAIR *Sewage Treatment* ii. 30 It is important to know how much of the solid matter is in suspension, how much is settleable, and how much is in solution. **1947** [see FLOC]. **1969** *Sci. Jrnl.* Mar. 81/2 In the activated sludge process the ability of the organisms to flocculate into settleable clumps is automatically inbred.

**settled** ('sɛt(ə)ld), *ppl. a.* [f. SETTLE *v.* + -ED[1].]

**1.** Of mental states, purposes, habits, etc.: Fixed, firmly embraced or implanted; become regular or customary; unchanging, undeviating.

**1556** HEYWOOD *Spider & F.* ii. 8 Oh sodayne sorowe, from setled solas. **1568** *Gismond of Salerne* IV. iii. 17 There stayed in me so settled trust, that thy chast life..wold not haue yelded to vnlawfull lust. **1599** THYNNE *Animadv.* (1875) 12 But I judge the beste, for in dobtes I will not resolue with a settled iudgemente. *a***1617** HIERON *Penance for Sin* xv. Wks. 1628 I. 235 A settled bent of the soule, in nothing to sinne against God. **1693** NORRIS *Pract. Disc. Div. Subj.* (1722) IV. 17 For alas what is a Mode or Fashion, but only a continued and settled Practice of a great Many? **1712** ADDISON *Spect.* No. 349 ¶7 He died under a fixed and settled Hope of Immortality. **1784** COWPER *Tiroc.* 778 Where..His virtuous toil may terminate at last In settled habit and decided taste. **1796** SOUTHEY *Mary, Maid of the Inn* i, Her silence implies The composure of settled distress. **1856** *N. Brit. Rev.* XXVI. 41 To remain to the end of life destitute of any settled religious opinions. **1874** GREEN *Short Hist.* iv. §5 It was his settled purpose to fling off the yoke of the Baronage.

**b.** Of the mind, character, etc.: Rendered staid, steadfast, or sober.

**1557** *Tottel's Misc.* (Arb.) 203 Pacience thy setled minde dothe guide and stere. **1604** SHAKS. *Ham.* (Qo. 2) IV. vii. 81 For youth no lesse becomes The light and carelesse liuing that it weares Then setled age, his sables, and his weedes. **1611** —— *Wint. T.* V. iii. 72 No setled Sences of the World can match The pleasure of that madnesse. **1650** H. MORE *Observ.* in *Enthus. Tri.* (1656) 96 What you have delivered.. concerning the Soul of man..might become a man of a more settled brain than Anthroposophus. **1670** DRYDEN *Tyr. Love* II. i. 16 Nor pride nor frenzy, but a setled mind. **1821** SCOTT *Kenilw.* xli, Wayland, now a man of settled character.

**c.** Of the countenance or bearing: Indicating a settled purpose, mind, character, etc.

*a***1586** SIDNEY *Arcadia* II. (Sommer) 111 With a setled countenance, not accusing any kind of inwarde motion. **1603** SHAKS. *Meas. for M.* III. i. 90 This outward sainted Deputie, Whose settled visage, and deliberate word Nips youth i'th head. **1622** MABBE tr. *Aleman's Guzman d'Alf.* I. 225 With..a graue countenance, a settled gate, and words well plaste. **1680** OTWAY *Orphan* II. iv, In your settled Face And clouded Brow methinks I see my Fate. **1825** SCOTT *Betrothed* xv, Rose saw her cheek assume a paler but more settled hue, instead of the angry hectic which had coloured it. **1839** G. DARLEY *Nepenthe* II. 31 Antiquity, thou Titan-born! That..look'st with dim but settled eye O'er thy deep lap.

**2.** Of a matter in dispute, an arrangement, regulation, etc.: Determined, decided, enacted or agreed upon. Of a truth, a principle: Established, placed beyond dispute.

**1579** LYLY *Euphues* (Arb.) 82, I finde it now for a setled truth, which earst I accompted for a vaine talke, that the purple dye will neuer staine [etc.]. **1638** JUNIUS *Paint. Ancients* 11 It is then expedient that we should not wander, but rather follow a settled short way. **1662** J. DAVIES tr. *Olearius' Voy. Ambass.* 325 Those who are entertain'd into his Service have a setled pay at all times. **1666** STILLINGFL. *Serm.* (1673) 21 That there be no complaining..in the Churches for want of a settled maintenance. **1749-50** JOHNSON *Rambler* No. 1 ¶1 The settled and regular forms of salutation which necessity has introduced into all languages. **1803** *Vesey's Chanc. Cases* (1827) XI. 537, I cannot upon any doubt of mine..shake what is the settled law upon the subject. **1860** RUSKIN *Unto this Last* iv. §60, I wish this were a settled question in London markets. **1870** MORRIS *Earthly Par.* III. 386 We look to have from him a settled day When we must change our faith or bide the worst.

**b.** Phr. *a settled thing* (or *matter*), used predicatively (often = something about which there is considered to be no room for doubt or question).

**1818** SCOTT *Br. Lamm.* xxi, 'I thought', said he,..'that was a settled matter—they are continually together'. **1839** THACKERAY *Stubb's Cal.* Apr. (1841) 305 She was told to call me her little husband; and she did; and it was considered a settled thing from that day. **1845** DISRAELI *Sybil* V. vii, 'Is it a settled thing between Lady Joan and Mr. Mountchesney?' 'Not the slightest foundation... She is not in a hurry to marry'. **1853** MRS. GASKELL *Cranford* vii, Still, it was not at all a settled thing that Mrs. Fitz-Adam was to be visited. **1864** E. YATES *Broken to Harness* I. xv. 272, The twilight had been a settled thing for at least an hour. **1868** H. BLACKBURN *Artists & Arabs* i. 7 At Marseilles, where..it is an understood and settled thing that every Englishman is on his way, to or from Italy or India.

**3.** Of affairs, an institution, or the like: Established on a permanent footing and under fixed conditions or regulations.

**1648-9** *Eikon Bas.* xvii. 149 Since the first Age,..not one Example can bee produced of anie settled Church, wherein were manie Ministers and Congregations, which had not som Bishop above them. **1650** HUBBART *Pill Formality* 152 Man..in his most settled estate is altogether vanity. **1672-5** COMBER *Comp. Temple* (1702) 7 Such a liberty therefore cannot be granted in a setled Church. **1724** DE FOE *Mem. Cavalier* (1840) 259 The parliament had no settled army. **1765** JOHNSON *Shaks.* Wks. (1773) I. Pref. D 8, Grammatical and settled languages. **1794** BURKE *Corr.* (1844) IV. 254 Settled governments have not the bold resources of new experimental systems. **1842** TENNYSON '*You ask me, why*' iii, A land of settled government. **1858** FROUDE *Hist. Eng.* xix. IV. 119 A settled age can imperfectly comprehend an age of revolution. **1883** P. H. HUNTER *Story Daniel* i. 8 At such time as this..when the settled order of things was breaking up.

**4.** Fixed in place or position; having a fixed abode.

**1591** SHAKS. *1 Hen. VI*, II. v. 106 But now thy Vnckle is remouing hence, As Princes doe their Courts, when they are cloy'd With long continuance in a settled place. **1611** BIBLE *1 Kings* viii. 13, I haue surely built thee an house to dwel in, a settled place for thee to abide in for euer. **1633** P. FLETCHER *Pisc. Ecl.* I. xvii, The setled rock seem'd from his seat remove. **1645** *Direct. Lords & Comm. for Elect. Ruling-Elders* 2 In the place where his most settled dwelling and imployment doth lie. *a***1700** EVELYN *Diary* 9 Mar. 1652, No more intending to go out of England, but endeavour a settl'd life, either in this or some other place. **1735** JOHNSON *Lobo's Abyssinia* Descr. i. 47 They..live like the Arabs, without any settled Habitation. **1830** M. T. SADLER *Law Popul.* I. ix. 146 Since mankind have become more settled and numerous. **1862** STANLEY *Jew. Ch.* (1877) I. x. 191 Becoming a settled..instead of a nomadic people.

**b.** Of an ailment: Fixed in the system.

**1811** LADY MORGAN *Mem.* (1862) I. 479 A bad cold and a settled cough.

**5.** Of weather of a specified character: Established and maintaining itself without change or break (cf. SET *a.* 6c). Of wind: Blowing continuously in one direction.

**1628** DIGBY *Voy. Mediterr.* (1868) 8 The current did then sett strongly out of the straightes, which I vnderstand is vsuall after settled Leuant windes. **1710** *Loyal Mourner* 9 The smiling Aspect of Earth, Sea, and Air, All for a lasting Calm, and Settled Fair. **1719** DE FOE *Crusoe* I. (Globe) 72 Now it began to be settled fair Weather. **1737** [S. BERINGTON] *G. de Lucca's Mem.* (1738) 143 It was the most settled and downright Rain (as the Saying is) that ever I saw. **1798** S. ROGERS *To Friend on Marr.* Poems (1812) 162 And settled sunshine on her soul descend! **1818** BYRON *Juan* I. cxcvi, As roll the waves before the settled wind. **1837** SOUTHEY *Poems* IV. Pref., Raising my spirits to the degree of settled fair. **1870** L'ESTRANGE *Life Miss Mitford* I. v. 136 What is a thunder shower..to settled, set-in, bad weather?

**b.** Of weather (without other specification): Calm and fine.

**1717** in J. O. Payne *Rec. Eng. Catholics 1715* (1889) 156 Such brave settled weather as't has been ever since you left us. **1731** MILLER *Gard. Dict.* s.v. *Cucumis*, Towards the latter End of May, when the Weather appears settled and warm. **1830** T. MOORE in *Lady Morgan's Mem.* (1862) II. 312, I am preparing to take advantage of the very first appearance of more settled weather.

†**6.** Of a liquid: Not flowing, stagnant, coagulated. Also of wine: That has 'settled on the lees'.

**1597** SHAKS. *2 Hen. IV*, IV. iii. 112 The warming of the Blood: which before (cold, and setled) left the Liuer white, and pale. **1604** DRAYTON *Moyses* II. 36 The fleet hurrying flood..As a black lake or setled marish stood At th'extensure of the Hebrewes wand. **1659** HOWELL *Vocab. Arts & Sci.* xviii, Settled wine; *vin riposato*; *vin rassis*. **1681** CROWNE *Hen. VI*, IV. 58 His Face is black and swell'd with settled Blood.

**7.** That has sunk down or subsided. Of earth: Compacted, consolidated.

**1642** HEXHAM *Princ. Art Milit.* II. (ed. 2) 48 The stopping which is made newly is not so firme as the old setled Earth, which hath lain a long time in it. **1751** LABELYE *Westm. Bridge* 80 The further Loading of the settled Pier would be dangerous.

**8.** Of a person: Established in life, esp. by marriage; brought into a regular way of life.

*a* **1706** EVELYN *Mrs. Godolphin* (1888) 128 Wee will looke vpon this Lady now, as a setled Woman, and in the Armes of that excellent Person the most worthy to possess her. **1777** SHERIDAN *Sch. Scandal* II. iii. Plays (1902) 169 Mercy on me—He's greatly altered—and seems to have a settled married look. **1884** 'C. E. CRADDOCK' (Miss Murfree) *In Tennessee Mts.* 83 A settled married man, a-behavin' no better 'n them fool boys.

**b.** Established in an office or living; *spec.* of Presbyterian ministers (cf. SETTLE *v.* 27 b).

**1773** *Ann. Reg.* 148 Mrs. Greeve was to have procured the place of a settled-tidesman for Mr. John Smith. **1785** *Gentl. Mag.* LXIV. II. 391 The settled Relief minister at Irvine. *a* **1817** T. DWIGHT *Trav. New-Eng.* (1823) IV. 397 In the year 1798 there were..two hundred and forty-two ministers; of whom thirty-three were without any charge; or, in the language of New-England, were not settled ministers.

**9.** Of an estate or property: Secured to a person by a legal act or agreement; held by a tenant for life under conditions defined by the deed.

**1856** *Act 19 & 20 Vict.* c. 120 (*title*), An Act to facilitate Leases and Sales of Settled Estates. *Ibid.* §1 The Term 'Settled Estates'..shall signify all Hereditaments..and all Estates..which are the Subject of a Settlement. **1882** *Act 45 & 46 Vict.* c. 38 (*title*), An Act for facilitating Sales, Leases, and other dispositions of Settled Land. **1889** *Wharton's Law Lex.* (ed. 8), *Settled land*, land limited by way of succession, to a person other than the person for the time being entitled to the beneficial enjoyment thereof.

**10.** Of a country: Peopled with new-comers; colonized. Also ***settled-up***.

**1831** SIR J. SINCLAIR *Corr.* II. 12 In the settled part of it, the land is divided into smaller farms. **1839–40** W. IRVING *Wolfert's Roost*, etc. *R. Ringwood* (1855) 196, I had relatives in Lexington, and other settled places. **1897** BEATRICE HARRADEN *Hilda Strafford* 146 She had seen some of those settled-up parts.

**11.** Of soap: Refined by fusing in water or weak lye.

**1898** G. H. HURST *Soaps* vii. 228 Three chief varieties of hard soap..known as 'curd', 'fitted', or, in America, 'settled', and 'run' soaps. **1906** L. L. LAMBORN *Manuf. Soap* ix. 328 Settled Rosined Soap.

†**'settledly,** *adv. Obs.* [-LY².] In a settled manner.

**1602** WARNER *Albion's Eng.* XIII. Epit. 360 The first Kingdome..was Kent... It settledly began about the yeere ..475. *a* **1617** HIERON *Penance for Sin* xviii. Wks. 1628 I. 263 When hee doth aduisedly, and setledly, and with deliberation and purpose doe that which is naught. **1635** STRAFFORD *Lett.* (1739) I. 412 To shew you how chearfully and settledly I remain Your Lordship's..most humble Servant, Wentworth. **1668** H. MORE *Div. Dial.* IV. ii. (1713) 291 Those that either slight or misbelieve Christianity..do not seriously or settledly believe there is a God. **1692** T. BEVERLEY *Concil. Disc.* 5 Men, among whom Scripture is setledly receiv'd.

**settledness** ('sɛt(ə)ldnɪs). [-NESS.] The state or quality of being settled (in various senses).

Frequent in 17th c.

**1571** GOLDING *Calvin on Ps.* i. 1 The 'seate' by which word he betokeneth..the settlednesse that is concieued of the continuall custome of liuing. **1607** BEAUMONT *Woman Hater* v. iii, *Coun.* You are your self my Lord, I like your setel'dnes. **1622** MABBE tr. *Aleman's Guzman d'Alf.* I. 151 Their eyes [turn] to a swolne settlednesse & dulnesse of look. **1642** FULLER *Holy & Prof. St.* III. xxiv. 221 §1 The Scythian wandring Nomades,..wanting both civility and settlednesse. **1648** BP. HALL *Breath. Devout Soul* xxxiv. 53 Lord, work my heart to so firme a setlednesse upon thee, that it may never be shaken. **1663** BP. PATRICK *Parab. Pilgr.* xxiii. (1665) 248 Setledness and stediness of mind. *a* **1676** HALE *Prim. Orig. Man.* II. vii. (1677) 196 The Antiquity and Setledness of this Monarchy. *a* **1866** GROTE *Exam. Utilit. Philos.* xii. (1870) 195 The discriminateness or settledness, with which moral notions present themselves to the mind. **1875** J. H. RIGG *Living Wesley* II. ii. 43 The pleasant and old-fashioned settledness of the town of Epworth. **1877** BRYCE *Transcaucasia & Ararat* i. 25 The general want of settledness [in Russia] is seen in the ease with which the population move from place to place.

**settlement** ('sɛt(ə)lmənt). [f. SETTLE *v.* + -MENT.]

**I.** The placing of persons or things in a fixed or permanent position.

**1.** The act of fixing (a thing, material or immaterial) in a secure or steady position; the state of being so fixed; a fixed or steady position.

**1648** BP. HALL *Breath. Devout Soul* §3. 3 Can ye hope to finde rest in any of these sublunary contentments. Alas? how can they yeeld any stay to you, that have no settlement in themselves? **1677** YARRANTON *Engl. Improv.* 5 The Winds and Tide trouls them [*sc.* the Sands], and give them a settlement along the Shores. **1825** SCOTT *Talism.* xii, Bring, if thou canst, thy wavering understanding to a right settlement for a minute or two. **1837** DISRAELI *Venetia* I. xii, A vast trunk uprooted from its ancient settlement. **1902** ALLBUTT in *Encycl. Brit.* (ed. 10) XXX. 611/2 Even more set diseases began to lose their settlements, and were recognized as terms of series, as transitory or culminating phases.

**2.** Establishment of a person in life, in marriage, in an office or employment.

**1651** WALTON *Life Wotton* in *Reliq. Wotton.* c 4 b, This [*sc.* the Provostship of Eton Coll.] was a faire setlement for his minde. **1660** R. COKE *Justice Vind.* 21 A magistrate of an hour's settlement is as much a magistrate as if he had been one never so long. **1692** R. L'ESTRANGE *Fables* ccxci. 254 Every Man..Applies himself..toward the Attaining of his End; whether it be Honour, Wealth, Power, or any other sort of Advantage, or Settlement in the World. **1749** SMOLLETT *Gil Blas* III. i. (1782) I. 212, I shall find no difficulty in procuring for you a good settlement. **1788** GIBBON *Decl. & F.* lii. V. 445 Thirty thousand Persians, who had obtained service and settlement in the Byzantine empire. **1861** MRS. H. WOOD *E. Lynne* xii, That Mr. Carlyle was not of rank equal to her own she scarcely remembered: East Lynne seemed a very fair settlement in life,..superior to the home she was now in. **1861** *Two Cosmos* I. 294 Contrary to all that Mr. Caird had ever dreamed or planned for a settlement of his daughter in the married state.

**3.** Legal residence or establishment in a particular parish, entitling a person to relief from the poor rates; the right to relief acquired by such residence.

**1662** *Act 14 Chas. II*, c 12 §3 If the person..shall not returne to the place aforesaid when his..worke is finished.. it shall not bee accounted a Setlement in the cases abovesaid. **1689** in G. T. Lawley *Hist. Bilston* (1893) 59 Forasmuch as some persons by sculking w^tin this Constablewick, have surreptitiously gain'd a settlement here. **1704** J. CHAMBERLAYNE *St. Gt. Brit.* I. III. x. (ed. 21) 425 There is a Workhouse in Bishopsgate-Street, for employing..all such as have no Settlement. **1722** DE FOE *Plague* (1754) 113 Many of them were without what we call legal Settlements, and so could not claim of the Parishes. **1791** 'G. GAMBADO' *Ann. Horsem.* (1809) xvii. 138 But I soon convinced 'em he had not staid long enough in the parish to gain a settlement. **1857** A. MAYHEW *Paved with Gold* Introd. iii, At one Union..they had told her that she must go back to where she had been born, for her settlement was there. **1898** *Daily News* 20 July 8/4 The appeal involved a question as to the settlement of a pauper..who was born at Plymouth, but had done no act to gain a settlement.

**4.** The act of settling oneself, or state of being settled, in a fixed place or position, in a permanent abode, etc.

*a* **1700** EVELYN *Diary* 9 Mar. 1652, I went to Deptford, where I made preparation for my settlement, no more intending to go out of England. **1719** DE FOE *Crusoe* I. (Globe) 112 This little wandring Journey, without settled Place of Abode, had been so unpleasant to me, that my own House, as I call'd it to my self, was a perfect Settlement to me, compar'd to that. **1791** LD. AUCKLAND *Corr.* 12 Dec. *Jrnl. & Corr.* (1861) II. 396 Nothing can be known till the settlement in the new house and in society is completed. **1882** BESANT *Revolt of Man* iv. 85 She began..with a comfortable settlement in the chair, which meant a good long talk.

**5.** In Presbyterian churches: The placing or installing of a minister in a pastoral charge.

**1723** WODROW *Corr.* (1843) III. 14 Our settlements are turning extremely vexatious. **1825** JAMIESON Suppl. s.v. *Settle* v., A congregation is said to get a settlement, when the Pastor is introduced to the discharge of the pastoral office among them, S. **1842** W. M. HETHERINGTON *Hist. Ch. Scot.* 666 Great opposition was made to the settlement by the pious parishioners. **1854** H. MILLER *Sch. & Schm.* ii. 31 Gillespie had been deposed..for refusing to assist in the disputed settlement of Inverkeithing.

**6.** The act of settling as colonists or new-comers; the act of peopling or colonizing a new country, or of planting a colony. (Cf. sense 14.)

Phrase, ***to effect a settlement.***

**1827** P CUNNINGHAM *N.S. Wales* II. 83 It would be well, also, to attempt the cultivation of tea in some part of our colony, by a settlement of Chinese. **1850** W. MURE *Lit. Greece* I. v. §1. 89 The settlement of Oriental colonies in Greece produced no sensible effect on the character either of the language or the nation. **1851** D. WILSON *Preh. Ann.* (1863) II. IV. i. 170 A band of pioneers effected a settlement on the southern part of Argyleshire. **1874** GREEN *Short Hist.* iv. §2 We have traced the rudiments of our Constitution to the first moment of the English settlement in Britain. **1884** *Pall Mall Gaz.* 8 Sept. 5/1 That region is now divided into four distinct provinces—Assiniboia, Saskatchewan, Alberta, and Athabasca—in all of which, except the last, settlement is rapidly progressing.

*transf.* **1896** NEWTON *Dict. Birds* 897 Being a great wanderer, it [*sc.* the Tree-Sparrow] has effected settlements even in such remote islands as the Færoes.

**II.** Arrangement or regulation (of affairs, etc.).

**7. a.** The act or process of regulating or putting on a permanent footing; the act of establishing (public affairs, etc.) in security or tranquillity; the state of being settled and established; a settled arrangement, an established order of things.

**1645** DURYE *Israel's Call* (1646) 47 Then look to the further settlement of the civill state. *Ibid.* 48 With the settlement of the Church, as a body compact together. **1661** COWLEY *College* Ess. etc. (1906) 254 That every third year (after the full settlement of the Foundation) the Colledge shall give an account..of the fruits of their triennial Industry. **1681** H. NEVILE *Plato Rediv.* 23 People..who think that the growth of Popery is our only Evil, and that if we were secure against that, our Peace and Settlement were obtain'd. **1696** EVELYN *Let. Wotton* 30 Mar. *Diary* (1879) III. 484 In religious matters..I could not but discover in him the same free thoughts which he had of philosophy... For the rest always conformable to the present settlement. **1716** ADDISON *Freeholder* No. 50 ¶6 A sufficient force for the reformation of such disorders, and the settlement of the publick peace. **1796** MORSE *Amer. Geog.* II. 197 These [*sc.* manufactures and commerce] are the offspring of peace and settlement. **1849** MACAULAY *Hist. Eng.* v. I. 555 A settlement such as Argyle would have made..seemed to them not worth a struggle. **1900** *Sat. Rev.* 24 Mar. 350 The settlement that should be made after the war.

**b.** Determination or decision of a question, dispute, etc.; the establishing of an opinion, the text of a document, etc.

**1777** PRIESTLEY *Matt. & Spir.* (1782) I. xx. 249 The opinion..does not seem to have tended to a settlement before the fifth century. **1855** PALEY *Æschylus* (1861) Pref. p. xi, The settlement of the text of Aeschylus..has been a gradual process of restoration and recovery. **1856** FROUDE *Hist. Eng.* (1858) I. ii. 159 The settlement of the question.. could not long be delayed. **1866** LOWELL *Study Wind.*, *Swinburne's Trag.*, That is an affair of taste, which does not admit of any authoritative settlement.

**8.** *Law.* The act of settling property upon a person or persons; the particular terms of such an arrangement; the deed or instrument by which it is effected. Often spec. = ***marriage settlement***: see MARRIAGE 8.

**1677** YARRANTON *Engl. Improv.* 9, I have been a Commissioner in the Third part of the greatest Estates in the County, wherein I have seen the Settlements two ways. **1685** DRYDEN tr. *Idylls of Theocritus* xxvii. Misc. Wks. 1727 II. 68 My Flocks, my Fields, my Wood, my Pastures take, With Settlement as good as Law can make. *a* **1700** EVELYN *Diary* 30 Dec. 1679, I went to meete Sir John Stonehouse, and give him a particular of the settlement on my sonn, who now made his addresses to..his daughter-in-law. **1731** SWIFT *Strephon & Chloe* 40 But, Strephon sigh'd so loud and strong, He blew a Settlement along. **1782** MISS BURNEY *Cecilia* II. vii, All the world..would approve the connection, and the settlement made upon her should be dictated by herself. **1848** DICKENS *Dombey* xxx, The deed of settlement, the professional gentlemen inform me, is now ready. **1858** LD. ST. LEONARDS *Handy Bk. Prop. Law* xi. 69 Your wife.. may..claim a settlement out of it for herself and her children. **1861** M. PATTISON *Ess.* (1869) I. 36 The splendid settlement which Rudolf was ready to make upon his son.

*attrib.* **1879** CHAMPNESS *Insur. Dict.* (1883) 302 *Settlement policies*, life policies in which are introduced clauses giving them all the effect of marriage settlements so far as the moneys assured are concerned.

**b.** The settling the succession to the Crown. ***Act of Settlement***, the Act passed in 1701 (12 & 13 Will. III, c. 2) by which the succession to the British crown was settled upon Princess Sophia of Hanover and her descendants.

**1714** R. STEELE (*title*) The Crisis, or, a Discourse Representing..The several Settlements of the Crowns of England and Scotland on Her Majesty. **1765** BLACKSTONE *Comm.* I. I. i. 124 These liberties were again asserted..in the act of settlement, whereby the crown is limited to his present majesty's illustrious house. **1827** HALLAM *Const. Hist.* (1876) III. xv. 179 The immediate settlement of the crown at the Revolution extended only to the descendants of Anne and William.

**c.** *Scots Law.* The disposition of property or heritage by will; also, the document by which this is effected. ***disposition and settlement***, a deed by which a person provides for the disposal of his property, heritable and movable, after his death.

**1815** SCOTT *Guy M.* xxxv, This lady..made a general settlement of her affairs in Miss Lucy Bertram's favour. *Ibid.* xxxviii, Mr. Protocol..began to read the settlement aloud in a slow, steady, business-like tone. **1838** W. BELL *Dict. Law Scot.* s.v. *Testament*, Testament or Will disposing of Moveables only... Disposition and Settlement or Will disposing of Heritage as well as Moveables.

**d.** The amount settled upon a person.

**1811** T. C. MORGAN in *Lady Morgan's Mem.* (1862) I. 525 My wife's settlement is vested in the Three per Cents.

**e.** *U.S.* A sum of money or other property formerly granted to a minister on his ordination, in addition to his salary.

**1828–32** in WEBSTER. *a* **1840** NATH. EMMONS *Autobiog.* in Bartlett *Dict. Amer.* (Cent.), Before the war began, my people punctually paid my salary, and advanced one hundred pounds of my settlement a year before it was due by contract.

**9. a.** The settling or payment of an account; the act of satisfying a claim or demand, of coming to terms (*with* a person).

**1729** *Act 2 Geo. II*, c. 23 §23 Upon the Taxation and Settlement of such Bill and Demand. **1818** SCOTT *Br. Lamm.* ix, Ye might say..that the carline awed ye rent, and that ye wad allow it in the settlement. **1837** CARLYLE *Fr. Rev.* II. II. v, From the Townhall he..emits..fresh plans of settlement with Château-Vieux. **1873** MRS. H. WOOD *Master Greylands* I. x. 172 In an incredibly short..time.. the affairs of the bank were in a way of settlement. **1878** MRS. J. H. RIDDELL *Mother's Darling* I. vii. 197 No heavy bills were sent to Dilfield for settlement.

**b.** *spec.* The fortnightly (or, for government securities, monthly) settling of accounts on the Stock Exchange.

**1772** FOOTE *Nabob* II. (1778) 41 For de next settlement, would your honour be de bull or de bear? **1897** *Westm. Gaz.* 23 Dec. 8/2 With regard to Mining markets preparations are now in full progress for the settlement.

**10.** In India: The process of assessing the government land-tax over a specific area.

**1789** EARL CORNWALLIS *Let.* 2 Nov. *Corr.* (1859) I. 443 The Board continued..to form and issue the necessary instructions for making a settlement of the land revenues of the province of Bahar. **1849** *Direct. Revenue Off. N.W. Prov. Bengal* (1850) 7 There are evidently two distinct operations in the formation of a Settlement. The one is fiscal—the determination of the Government Demand—the other is judicial, the formation of the record of rights.

*attrib.* **1849** *Direct. Revenue Off. N.W. Prov. Bengal* (1850) 27 Directions for Settlement Officers.

**III.** The act of becoming set or still, sinking, subsiding, etc.

**11. a.** The act of settling and clarifying after agitation or fermentation.

**1626** BACON *Sylva* §302 First for Separation; It is wrought by Weight; As in the ordinary Residence or Settlement of Liquors. **1662** CHARLETON *Myst. Vintners* (1675) 156 The too frequent or violent motion of Wines after their settlement in their vessels. *Ibid.* 179 They counsel to rack it from the Milky bottom, after a weeks settlement.

*fig.* **1881** JOWETT *Thucyd.* I. 9 In the age which followed the Trojan War, Hellas was still in process of ferment and settlement.

**b.** The deposition of grosser particles or solid matter. Also *concr.*, a deposit or sediment. *Obs.* exc. *dial.*

**1687** MIEGE *Gt. Fr. Dict.* s.v., This Liquour is not right, there is a Settlement. **1692** J. HOUGHTON *Coll. Improv. Husb.* No. 9 ⁋ 3, I dry'd both the Settlements asunder. **1739** W. MONTAGU *Let.* 16 Aug. in *Lady M. W. Montagu's Lett.* (1893) II. 43 They are occasioned by a settlement of humours, which are removed by exercise. **1739** LABELYE *Westm. Bridge* 64 The Tide of Ebb having so long a Time to deposit its Settlement. **1890** *Glouc. Gloss.*, *Settlements*, sediment.

**c.** The sinking of floc and other solid particles in liquid sewage. Also *attrib.*, as ***settlement tank***.

**1912** H. LEMMOIN-CANNON *Textbk. Sewage Disposal in U.K.* xviii. 62 Tanks of the same kind..are used for the purpose of attaining the settlement of the suspended organic solids by sedimentation. **1927** T. H. P. VEAL *Disposal of Sewage* v. 54 Quiescent settlement tanks are operated on what is known as the fill-and-draw principle. *Ibid.* 55 The amount of clarification effected in a given time by quiescent settlement is greater than that effected by the continuous flow method. **1977** C. B. CAPPER in A. G. Callely et al. *Treatment Industrial Effluents* vi. 90 Probably the oldest method of removing suspended solids was by the use of horizontal-flow settlement tanks.

**12.** A sinking down or subsidence (of a structure, loose earth, etc.).

**1793** SMEATON *Edystone L.* §283 Twelve pieces..of near a ton each,..laid upon the first vaulted floor, without..the least degree of settlement. **1799** KIRWAN *Geol. Ess.* 410 After a certain degree of desiccation their masses were capable of a much closer approach to each other, or of what builders commonly call settlement. **1820** TREDGOLD *Carpentry* §298 By shrinkage, or settlement, the joints will bear only upon the angular points of the joint. **1833** DE LA BECHE *Geol. Man.* (ed. 2) 135 The whole may be explained by the settlement of loose sand..during the violent shocks of an earthquake. **1842** GWILT *Archit.* Gloss., *Settlements*, those parts in which failures by sinking in a building have occurred. **1898** WATTS-DUNTON *Aylwin* I. i, These landslips are sometimes followed, at the return of the tide, by a further fall, called a 'settlement'.

**13.** The process of becoming calm or tranquil.

**1837** CARLYLE *Fr. Rev.* III. VII. v, It is like the settlement of winds and waters, of seas long tornado-beaten.

**IV.** An assemblage of persons settled in a locality.

**14. a.** (Cf. sense 6.) A community of the subjects of a state settled in a new country; a tract of country so settled, a colony, esp. one in its earlier stages.

***back settlement***: see BACK *a.* 1 a. ***Straits Settlements*** (now *Hist.*), the collective name given to the British possessions in the Malay Peninsula.

**1697** DAMPIER *Voy.* I. vii. 163 In some River where the Spaniards have neither Settlement nor Trade with the native Indians. **1725** DE FOE *Voy. round World* (1840) 280 Have the Spaniards no..ports or towns, settlements or colonies in it? **1753** *Scots Mag.* Feb. 65/2 British subjects in the back settlements. **1776** A. SMITH *W.N.* I. viii. I. 89 The present state of Bengal, and of some other of the English settlements in the East Indies. **1844** BROUGHAM *Brit. Const.* xvii. (1862) 280 The endless variety of our settlements in all the most remote quarters of the globe! **1874** GREEN *Short Hist.* i. §4 Offa resolved to create a military border by planting a settlement of Englishmen between the Severn and the huge 'Offa's Dyke'. **1877** *Encycl. Brit.* VI. 159/1 The English settlements in Virginia, New England, Maryland, and Pennsylvania had..developed into a new nation.

**b.** Of a religious community.

**1708** J. CHAMBERLAYNE *St. Gt. Brit.* I. III. i. (ed. 22) 201 According as their [*sc.* the Quakers'] Settlements are more Numerous and Thick. **1884** R. PATON *Scott. Ch.* viii. 75 St. Finnian had twelve chief disciples, who filled the land with religious settlements. *Ibid.* 81 There was the earthen rampart enclosing the settlement.

**15.** In the outlying districts of America and the (former) Colonial territories: A small village or collection of houses. Also, the huts forming the living quarters of the slaves on a plantation.

**1827** O. W. ROBERTS *Voy. Centr. Amer.* 31 The terms settlement and plantation mean the residences of the natives. **1839** FR. A. KEMBLE *Resid. in Georgia* (1863) 18 There are four settlements or villages (or, as the negroes call them, camps) on the island, consisting of from ten to twenty houses. **1856** OLMSTED *Slave States* 417 At another plantation..I found the 'settlement' arranged in the same way, the cabins only being of a slightly different form. **1884** 'C. E. CRADDOCK' (Miss Murfree) *In Tennessee Mts.* 81 And certainly the instinct of the eagle built that eyrie called the Settlement..far above the towering pine forest. **1896** *Trans. Roy. Soc. Canada* II. ii. 210 Topographical terms actually used by the people of New Brunswick... *Settlement*, rarely village.

**16.** An establishment in the poorer quarters of a large city where educated men or women live in daily personal contact with the working class for co-operation in social reform.

**1884** *Oxf. Mag.* 23 Apr. II. 171/2 Oxford and East London. The Executive Committee of the University Settlement have issued a prospectus and appeal for donations towards the initial expenses of the Settlement. *Ibid.* 172/1 Nine men have undertaken to commence residence in the Settlement. **1892** *Ch. Times* 4 Nov. 1094/1 Those 'settlements', or missions, which have become of late such a striking feature in the religious life of London. **1904** D. PRICE HUGHES *Life H. P. Hughes* ix. 207 A site in the City Road, where it was proposed to erect premises containing full accommodation for a Settlement.

**V. 17.** *attrib.* and *Comb.*, as (senses 6, 14) ***settlement area***, ***pattern***; (sense 9 b) ***settlement price***, ***terms***; **settlement day** = *settling day* s.v. SETTLING *vbl. sb.* 3 b; **settlement house** *U.S.*, an institution in an inner city area, usu. sponsored by a church or college, that gives educational, recreational, and other social services to the community (cf. sense 16).

**1963** H. N. SAVORY in Foster & Alcock *Culture & Environment* iii. 31 The south Wales seaboard was a primary settlement-area of the continental colonists. **1977** *Word 1972* XXVIII. 72 Brittany is a dispersed settlement area, and farms are either isolated or in small clusters. **1896** W. H. S. AUBREY *Stock Exch. Investm.* 314/2 (Index), Settlement days. **1901** C. DUGUID *How to read Money Article* xvii. 75 Directly one account is ended by the fortnightly settlement, another account begins. It commences at noon on the first settlement day. **1907** J. STRONG *Challenge of City* 307 Your letter..was duly received and reply thereto delayed awaiting report from the inspection districts wherein are located the Settlement houses you mentioned. **1959** *New Statesman* 24 Oct. 534/2 In relation to the street gangs, most of these disquisitions regard the conventional 'agencies'—boys' clubs, mixed clubs, settlement houses, community centres—as ineffectual. **1978** G. VIDAL *Kalki* v. 114 Of course, Amelia did work in settlement houses, helping the poor. **1958** G. LIENHARDT *Tribes without Rulers* 98 Dinka settlement-patterns differ from each other according to the two broadly different kinds of country. **1928** *Daily Mail* 25 July 19/3 Tin: Standard cash quoted £217 10*s.* to £217 12*s.* 6*d.*; three months, £214 10*s.* to £214 12*s.* 6*d.*; settlement price, £217 10*s.* **1931** C. MAUGHAN *Markets of London* 122 Rubber is also sold on 'settlement terms', which means that a buyer receives a profit or pays a loss every fortnight, in a similar way to settlements on the Stock Exchange.

**settler** ('sɛtlə(r)). [f. SETTLE *v.* + -ER[1].]

**1. a.** One who or a thing which, settles, fixes, decides, etc.

**1598** FLORIO, *Acconciatore*,..a mender, a setler, an order. **1611** COTGR., *Ficheur*, a fixer, fastener, setler, or setter in. **1659** *England's Universal Distraction 1643–5* 16 True Religion is rather a Setler then Stickler in Policy, and rather confirmes men in obedience to the Government. **1687** WOOD *Life* 9 Dec. (O.H.S.) III. 245 Mr. A[rthur] Ch[arlet] of Trin. Coll., the chief setler of unsetled minds in Oxford. **1825** *New Monthly Mag.* XVI. 113 He fancied himself a settler of destinies. **1846** GREENER *Sci. Gunnery* Introd. 6 This powerful settler of disputes [*sc.* artillery]. **1898** *Daily News* 6 July 4/6 That sum was..paid by him over to Mr. Goodson, who acted as Sir John's settler.

**b.** *colloq.* Something that settles or 'does for' a person, a finisher; something that settles an antagonist in an encounter or argument; a crushing or finishing blow, shot, speech, etc.

**1744** M. BISHOP *Life & Advent.* ix. 124, I endeavoured to revive them by saying I intended to have a Bowl of Punch, by way of a Settler and then to go to Bed upon it. *c* **1817** HOGG *Tales & Sk.* V. 221 This was a settler; I could make no answer to that. **1819** MOORE *Tom Crib's Memorial* (ed. 3) 15 So he tipp'd him a settler..Full plump in the whisker. **1833** FONBLANQUE *Eng. under 7 Administr.* (1837) II. 338 Cook knocked him on the head instantly; this is what the English call a settler, that is, in this way they settle their accounts. **1837** HALIBURTON *Clockm.* Ser. I. xx, That shot was a settler, it struck poor Sall right atwixt wind and water. **1888** *Sportsman* 22 Dec. (Farmer), A mistake at the last hurdles proved a complete settler, and he succumbed by six lengths. **1894** BLACKMORE *Perlycross* 239 After this settler [a crushing speech], the man sat down, and turned his back on the Parson.

**c.** A clerk in a betting shop who calculates the winnings.

**1963** L. MEYNELL *Virgin Luck* vii. 172 'But what do you do..?' 'Settle. I'm a settler. I work out a bet. It goes down on a slip and after the race the settlers go through the slips and work them out.' **1966** P. WILLMOTT *Adolescent Boys of East London* vi. 102 Non-manual jobs of a more 'routine' kind, mainly clerks and shop assistants, draughtsmen and betting-shop 'settlers'. **1977** *Evening Post* (Nottingham) 27 Jan. 14/1 (Advt.), Saturday settler required by independent licensed Betting Office.

**2. a.** One who settles in a new country; a colonist. ***old settler***: see OLD *a.* D 4. orig. *Amer.*

**1696** *Rec. Early Hist. Boston* (1881) VI. 51 The first goers or first setlers of Woodstock. **1739** W. STEPHENS *Jrnl.* 15 Dec. in *Colonial Records State of Georgia* (1906) IV. 469 One Bunyon, a Builder of Boats and a Settler there. **1786** T. DUNDAS *Let.* 28 Dec. in Cornwallis *Corr.* (1859) I. 279 The half-pay provincial officers are valuable settlers. **1788** GIBBON *Decl. & F.* lii. V. 442 The fields and vineyards were divided among the new settlers. **1802** G. BARRINGTON *New South Wales* iv. 98 The natives taking advantage of the distance settlers lived from each other. **1867** EMERSON *Lett. & Soc. Aims, Progr. Culture* Wks. (Bohn) III. 225 Land without price is offered to the settler. **1874** GREEN *Short Hist.* i. §1 Each dweller within the settlement was jealous of his own isolation and independence among his fellow-settlers. **1904** W. M. RAMSAY *Lett. 7 Churches* xi. 133 Hence the Jewish settlers formed a counterpoise against the Greek colonists in the Seleucid cities.

**b.** *gen.* One who settles in a place as a resident.

**1815** SCOTT *Guy M.* vii, Nor was Mr. Bertram in a hurry to exert his newly-acquired authority at the expense of these old settlers. *Ibid.* xii, If..he should become a settler in that part of Scotland. **1834** DICKENS *Sk. Boz, Boarding Ho.*, He resides among the original settlers at Walworth.

**c.** A worker at a social settlement (see SETTLEMENT 16).

**1884** *Durham Univ. Jrnl.* 5 July VI. 44 What then are Settlements, and their Settlers, to do in the East End of London? **1887** *Charity Organiz. Rev.* III. 408 The university settlers [at Toynbee Hall]. **1899** *Daily News* 26 June 4/7 The 'settlers' at Mansfield House look forward to having one of the best-equipped boys' clubs in London.

**3.** *Law.* One who settles property: = SETTLOR.

**1800** *Act 39 & 40 Geo. III*, c. 98 §1 The Term of Twenty-one Years from the Death of any such Grantor, Settler, Devisor, or Testator.

**4.** A pan or vat into which a liquor is run off to 'settle' or deposit a sediment. In *Metallurgy* (see quot. 1881).

**1674** RAY *Collect. Words, Allom Works Whitby* 140 Which [kelp] being put in so soon as the Liquor boils or flows up.., they draw it off into a settler. **1731** MILLER *Gard. Dict.* s.v. *Anil*, There are three of these [indigo] Vats commonly built one above another... This last Vat is also call'd at St. Domingo, a Settler. *a* **1864** GESNER *Coal, Petrol.*, etc. (1865) 161 The pump..draws the petroleum from the settler. **1874** RAYMOND *6th Rep. Mines* 193 The roasted ore is amalgamated in 8 pans, with as many settlers. **1881** —— *Mining Gloss.*, *Settler*, a tub or vat, in which pulp from the amalgamating pan or battery-pulp is allowed to settle, being stirred in water, to remove the lighter portions.

**5.** *attrib.* and *Comb.*, as ***settler-folk***, †***slam*** (SLAM *sb.*[3]); **settler's** or **settlers' clock**, *Austral.* (see quots.); **settler's effects** *Canad.*, goods brought into the country by an immigrant for his personal use that are exempt from import duty; also *transf.*; **settler's matches, twine** *Austral.* (see quots.).

**1896** *Harper's Mag.* Apr. 716/2 The westward march of the *settler-folk. **1743** in *6th Rep. Dep. Kpr.* App. II. 121 A Method of making Alum out of Dross (commonly called *Settler Slam). **1827** P. CUNNINGHAM *Two Years in N.S.W.* I. 232 The loud and discordant noise of the laughing jackass (or *settler's clock, as he is called)..acquaints us that the sun has just dipped behind the hills. **1847** L. LEICHHARDT *Jrnl. Australia* viii. 234 The laughing Jackass (*Dacelo gigantea*) which, from its regularity, has not been unaptly named the settlers' clock. **1911** *Daily Colonist* (Victoria, B.C.) 2 Apr. 14/3 She landed 150 tons of cargo here, including three boilers..*settler's effects, and general freight. **1939** K. PINKERTON *Wilderness Wife* i. 13 Beside us on the station platform that morning were our canoe, camp outfit and a few 'settler's effects'. **1965** I. REEKIE *Along Old Melita Trail* ii. 12 Coming to Manitoba with two cars of settlers' effects. **1891** H. LAWSON in *Bulletin* (Sydney) 19 Dec. 21/2 And we walked so very silent—being lost in reverie—that we heard the '*settlers'-matches' gently rustle on the tree. **1898** MORRIS *Austral Eng.*, *Settlers' Matches*,..the long pendulous strips of bark which hang from the Eucalypts and other trees, during decortication and which..are used as kindling wood. **Settler's Twine*, a fibre plant, *Gymnostachys anceps*, R. Br[own]..used by farmers as cord or string.

**'settlerdom.** *nonce-wd.* [f. SETTLER + -DOM.] Settlers collectively.

**1863** DICEY *Federal St.* II. 123 *Veni, vidi, aedificavi*, should be the motto of Western settlerdom, so rapid is the growth of cities in the West.

**settling** ('sɛtlɪŋ), *vbl. sb.* [-ING[1].] The action of the verb SETTLE.

OE. *setlung* = a sitting down, also the setting of the sun. The latter sense is recorded by Ash (1775) and Todd (1818) for *settling*, but this is prob. an error for *setting*.

**1. a.** The action of fixing, establishing, arranging permanently, adjusting, deciding, etc.

**1553** T. WILSON *Rhet.* (1560) 3 The setling or ordering of things inuented for this purpose, called in Latin *Dispositio*. *a* **1569** KYNGESMILL *Confl. with Satan* (1577) Pref. A v b, This I say must be a setlinge vnto thee, if thou hast tasted how good and gracious God is. **1619** W. SCLATER *Expos. 1 Thess.* 173 To Gods children let it be a settling of their Faith, that it neuer wauer. **1629** *Reg. Privy Council Scot.* Ser. II. III. 21 To gif thair advise anent the satling of the disordouris of the Middle shyris. *a* **1642** SUCKLING *Let.* in *Fragm. Aurea* (1648) 62 Since the setling of your Family would certainly much conduce to the setling of your mind. **1662** STILLINGFL. *Orig. Sacræ* II. ix. §2. 261 The miracles done at the setling of their Law. **1669** R. MONTAGU in *Buccleuch MSS.* (Hist. MSS. Comm.) I. 465 This thing will be an absolute settling of my fortune, which..is in no good condition. **1747** *Col. Rec. Pennsylv.* V. 141 Has desir'd me to take upon myself the settling of the Terms for paying the Men off. **1817** SELWYN *Law Nisi Prius* II. 917 The adjustment of a loss is the settling and ascertaining the amount of the indemnity. **1909** GWATKIN *Early Ch. Hist.* I. vi. 112 We get a general impression of apostolic superintendence..and of settling of churches.

†**b.** The state of being settled, a settlement; a station. *Obs.*

**1582** N. LICHEFIELD tr. *Castanheda's Conq. E. Ind.* I. lxvii. 137 Those that went in the vangard, as soone as they came to their setling [orig. *chegando à estancia*], did giue fire to theyr ordinance. **1641** MILTON *Ch. Govt.* I. vi. 26 Those Epistles of Peter and John, which are likely to be latest written, when the Church grew to a setling.

**2.** The action of planting a country with colonists, or of establishing a colony. †Also the result of this, a settlement.

**1609** SALISBURY in *Buccleuch MSS.* (Hist. MSS. Comm.) I. 83 An enterprise of plantation in the Indies, where..the King of England..might have a settling as well as the King of Spain. *a* **1680** BUTLER *Rem.* (1759) I. 2 To search the Moon by her own Light;..And make the proper'st Observations, For settling of new Plantations. **1707** J. ARCHDALE (*title*) A New Description of..Carolina: with a brief account of its Discovery, Settling, and the Government Thereof to this Time. **1797** *Encycl. Brit.* (ed. 3) V. 149/1 That the settling of colonies would have been a cheaper and better method of bridling modern countries, than building fortresses in them. **1877** *Ibid.* (ed. 9) VI. 159/2 The ultimate constitution of a colony depends but little on the manner in which the territory for settling was originally acquired.

**3. a.** The adjusting or liquidating of accounts; also ***settling up***.

**1761** T. MORTIMER *Ev. Man his own Broker* ii. (1762) 28 The four principal times, for which contracts or bargains are made,..are called in 'Change Alley, the Rescounter settlings. *Ibid.* 82 Against the day of settling he has made out, what he calls his list. **1852** R. S. SURTEES *Sponge's Sp. Tour* (1893) 377 After a great event—a Derby, Oaks, or Leger..the newspapers generally devote a neat paragraph or two to what is called 'the settling'. **1893** *Baily's Mag.* Oct. 275/2 A backer, who..refused to face an adverse settling, and quietly skedaddled.

*fig.* **1910** *Blackw. Mag.* Feb. 183/1 After dinner there would be a settling up with the two rebels.

**b. settling day**, a day appointed for settling accounts; *spec.* the fortnightly pay-day on the Stock Exchange. **settling room**, a room (esp. at the Stock Exchange) in which accounts are settled.

**1806–7** J. BERESFORD *Miseries Hum. Life* (1826) XII. xviii, Attending at the Stock-exchange on settling-day. **1822** SCOTT *Nigel* xxi, The score of pieces that must be made up at settling-day. **1859** H. H. DIXON *Silk & Scarlet* 97 In the yard of Tattersall's, on Priam's settling day. **1902** *Westm. Gaz.* 20 Mar. 9/1 The Settling-room underneath the House [Stock Exchange].

**4.** (Cf. SETTLE *v.* 21 c.) ***to get a settling*** (*Sc.*): 'to be frightened into quietness' (Burns *Gloss.* 1785).

**1785** BURNS *Halloween* xxiv, But Och! that night, amang the shaws, She gat a fearfu' settlin!

**5. a.** The action of coming to rest, taking up a fixed or permanent position, becoming quiet or composed, etc. Also ***settling down***.

**1605** SHAKS. *Lear* IV. vii. 82 The great rage You see is kill'd in him:..Trouble him no more till further setling. **1711** ADDISON *Spect.* No. 106 ¶6 At his first settling with me. **1744** M. BISHOP *Life & Advent.* viii. 111, I hope you have no Thoughts of going again to Sea, as I have waited so many Years in Expectation of your settling, when you came home. **1796** MME. D'ARBLAY *Camilla* I. 344 Dr. Marchmont..had been introduced to Sir Hugh upon the baronet's settling in the large mansion-house of that village. **1911** G. B. SHAW *Getting Married* 118 The process of settling down would go on until they settled into their graves.

**b. *settling in***, the action of establishing one's residence in a new place or of becoming accustomed to new surroundings. Chiefly *attrib.*, as ***settling-in allowance, grant***.

**1955** *Times* 16 July 2/4 Generous settling-in allowance during first month, and housing assistance can be afforded to selected applicants. **1965** *Wireless World* Aug. 120 (Advt.), Free air travel will be provided for a successful applicant..and a 'settling in' allowance will also be paid on arrival in Salisbury. **1973** *Soviet Weekly* 17 Feb. 11/3 Some redundant teachers were willing to be sent to localities where there was a shortage of teachers. They were given settling in grants totalling two or three months average earnings, plus a quarter of that sum for each member of their family. **1974** *Economist* 31 Aug. 83/1 (Advt.), A settling-in allowance of up to £400 is payable in approved circumstances and assistance with housing for a short time is a possibility.

**c.** Special Comb.: **settling time**, the time taken for a measuring or control instrument to get within a certain distance of a new equilibrium value without subsequently deviating from it by that amount.

**1951** CHESTNUT & MAYER *Servomechanisms & Regulating System Design* I. xiv. 410 (*heading*) Settling time $t_s$ to reach 5 per cent of final value. **1974** J. W. BREWER *Control Systems* x. 285 Rise time is a measure of the speed of response, and the ratio of settling time to rise time is a measure of damping.

**6. a.** The action of sinking down, subsiding, forming a deposit or sediment, etc.; also, the result of this.

*c* **1440** *Promp. Parv.* 440/2 Saggynge, or satlynge, *bassacio.* **1540** JONAS tr. *Roesslin's Byrth Mankynde* I. vii. 32 After the delyueraunce happeneth to women other the feuer or ague, ..or els commotion or settelynge out of order of the.. matrice. **1601** HOLLAND *Pliny* XXXI. iii. II. 408 [These plants] come up..in some low grounds where there is a settling or stay of raine water fallen from higher places. **1650** FULLER *Pisgah* IV. iv. 70 Purple being severall sanguine colours, differing onely in degrees, and the severall setlings thereof. **1655** MOUFET & BENNET *Health's Improv.* 294 For as too long sitting..hindereth the full descent of meat to the depth of our stomachs; so too speedy rising causeth an overhasty setling. **1663** GERBIER *Counsel* 26 The unequall setling of the Work. **1693** MOXON *Mech. Exerc.* (1703) 260 Which occasions Cracks and Setlings in the Walls. **1742** *De Foe's Tour Gt. Brit.* (ed. 3) I. 174 The Shifting of the Beach without, and Settling of the Sullage within. **1880** *Standard* 10 Dec., The ground..immediately over a disused rock salt-mine, began to show signs of 'settling'. **1881** *19th Cent.* 247, I have known a settling down of strata crumple up 14 feet of solid masonry, as though it were paper.

*attrib.* **1782** WEDGWOOD in *Phil. Trans.* LXXII. 320 After complete vitrification, the heat is abated for some hours to 28 or 29°, which is called the settling heat. **1834–6** *Encycl. Metrop.* VIII. 422/2 The strong liquor is drawn off into settling cisterns. **1857** MILLER *Elem. Chem., Org.* 667 The solution is allowed to run into a deep vessel or settling back. **1867** J. A. PHILLIPS *Mining & Metallurgy of Gold & Silver* ix. 183 When settling pits are used for the purpose of collecting the tailings for subsequent treatment, it is necessary that at least two of them should be provided, so that whilst one is being filled the other may be cleaned up. **1868** *Times* 4 Aug. 4/3 A complete churning and intimate union are effected by the sewage passing through a number of small apertures into cells, in each of which revolves a stirrer, and thence out of the cells into two very spacious settling tanks. **1884** *Encycl. Brit.* XVII. 506/1 As these.. naturally act as settling-ponds they get rapidly silted up. **1894** G. E. WARING *Mod. Meth. Sewage Disposal* xvii. 234 The flocculent matter passing the screen clogged the 4-inch absorption-tiles after a time. This was obviated by constructing a settling-chamber. **1899** *Rep. Dept. Mines on Goldfields N.Z. 1898–99* 45 The crushed ore passes over amalgamated copper-plates, 12 ft. long, into four sets of spitzlutten or settling-boxes. **1915** G. B. KERSHAW *Sewage Purification & Disposal* iv. 117 In most settling towers the bottom of the tank is formed in the shape of a cone, the sludge drain being placed at the apex. **1928** W. A. MITCHELL *Civil Engineering* v. 572 The term settling basin is ordinarily applied to a reservoir which contains from one to four days' supply of water. **1940** IMHOFF & FAIR *Sewage Treatment* iv. 72 In these tanks, the lower story serves as a sludge chamber and the upper one as a settling chamber. **1941** C. A. WARD *Those Raw Materials* vi. 272 The separation of sludge [from oil] may take place in settling tanks or may be brought about by centrifugal means. **1955** LINSLEY & FRANZINI *Elements Hydraulic Engin.* x. 249 Settling basins..just below the point of diversion so that sediment can be collected and sluiced back into the river. **1964** *Grouts & Drilling Muds in Engin. Pract.* 29/2 Retention [of the mud] in settling pits should be not less than 12 min. **1978** *Sci. Amer.* July 99/1 Conventional sewage treatment employs a combination of large settling tanks, bacterial cultures and sludge-thickening devices to decontaminate waste water and to concentrate the solid residue.

**b.** *concr.* Sediment, lees, dregs. Chiefly *pl.*

**1594** PLAT *Jewell-ho.* III. 23 The residence or setling, which you find in the bottom therof. **1634** MILTON *Comus* 810 Yet 'tis but the lees And setlings of a melancholy blood. **1646** P. BULKELEY *Gospel Covt.* I. 180 The Lord formed man ..out of the earth, the dregs and setlings of all creatures. **1747** MRS. GLASSE *Cookery* v. 65 Fill these Cups with the Jelly, which you must take clear from the Settling at the Bottom. *Ibid.*, Take the fine Jelly clear from the Settlings at Bottom. **1832** G. R. PORTER *Porcelain & Glass* ix. 240 A layer of the finer settlings of the enamel is to be spread..over the convex side. **1895** *Daily News* 11 May 7/7 The stuff [illicit spirit] was made..from sugar and wine settlings.

**settling** (ˈsɛtlɪŋ), *ppl. a.* [f. SETTLE *v.* + -ING².] That settles (in the senses of the verb).

*c* **1611** CHAPMAN *Iliad* II. 82 [As bees] So from the ships, ..The rabble..Hurried together;..earth did grone Beneath the setling multitude. **1681** DRYDEN *Span. Friar* III. 36 You call it Settling of a man; just as when a fellow has got a sound Knock upon the head, they say he's settled: Marriage is a Settling blow indeed. **1762–3** MACPHERSON *Ossian's Poems, Coulath & Cuthona* (1806) II. 287 Go; view the settling sea; the stormy wind is laid. **1844** MRS. BROWNING *Drama of Exile* 1701 The settling hush A bird makes in her nest with feet and wings. **1850** J. H. NEWMAN *Let.* 11 Oct. in 'J. Oldcastle' (W. Meynell) *Newman* (1885) 27, I have just received Maskell's able and settling pamphlet. **1902** MABEL BARNES-GRUNDY *Thames Camp* xii. 256 'Of course you refused him', I said, in my most settling manner. **1908** *Westm. Gaz.* 1 Aug. 7/1 The wild little black [horse]..stood trembling and snorting in the settling dust.

**settlor** (ˈsɛtlə(r)). *Law.* [Altered form of SETTLER (sense 3): see -OR 2 d.] One who makes a settlement of property.

**1818** CRUISE *Digest* (ed. 2) II. 317 Where an estate was limited to the use of the settlor for 99 years. **1848** MILL *Pol. Econ.* II. x. §2 (1876) 207 Every settlor and testator has an almost unbounded licence to multiply interests in land. **1875** POSTE *Gaius* IV. (ed. 2) §151 A settlor of dower. **1876** K. E. DIGBY *Real Property* vii. §2. 329 The great object of settlements of lands, the preserving them in the settlor's family.

**set-to.** Pl. set-tos (-to's); *incorrectly* sets-to. [f. vbl. phr. *set to*: see SET *v.*¹ 152.]

†**1.** A talking-to, dressing-down. *Obs. rare*⁻¹.

**1774** MME. D'ARBLAY *Early Diary* (1889) I. 313, I gave her a good *set-too* just now.

**2. a.** orig. *Pugilism.* The action of 'setting to' (SET *v.*¹ 152 f. (*b*)); hence, a bout or round; a pugilistic encounter or boxing match. Also, a bout, engagement, or match at some other sport.

**1743** *Broughton's Rules* in Egan *Boxiana* (1830) I. 51 Every fresh set-to after a fall, or being parted from the rails. **1789** *Chron.* in *Ann. Reg.* 199/2 The set-to was prodigiously fine, and after a few feints on each side, Ryan put in the first blow. **1818** *Sporting Mag.* (N.S.) III. 31 They will exhibit two grand set-to's in boxing. **1821** EGAN *Boxiana* (1830) I. 67 Taylor died in three months after this set-to. **1824** SCOTT *St. Ronan's* xxxi, Gentlemen of the fancy hastening to a set-to. **1882** DE WINDT *Equator* 41 A rattling set-to at lawn tennis. **1899** A. DOBSON *Paladin Philanthr.* xii, [He] proposed a preliminary set-to with the gloves.

**b.** *gen.* and *fig.* A fight, contest. Also, in weakened sense: an argument, a heated debate.

**1794** MRS. RADCLIFFE *Myst. Udolpho* xxxiii, Signor Verezzi is always losing..and Signor Orsino wins from him, ..and they have had several hard set-to's about it. **1816** J. SCOTT *Vis. Paris* App. (ed. 5) 333 There were many set-to's of dogs, chiefly mastiffs. **1819** SCOTT *Let.* in *Lockhart* (1837) IV. viii. 253 My stomach is now getting confirmed, and I have great hopes the bout is over; it has been a dreadful set-to. **1829** BROCKETT *N.C. Words* (ed. 2), *Set-to*, an argument, a strong contest, a warm debate. **1833** MARRYAT *P. Simple* lv, Every gun was ready,..and every soul..was anxious for the set-to. **1881** JEFFERIES *Wood Magic* I. ii. 42 The starlings on the chimney began to quarrel, and had a terrible set-to. **1894** FENN *Real Gold* xii, Didn't you ever have a set to at school? **1898** LLOYD GEORGE *Let.* 25 Dec. (1973) 116 We have had several sets to over church matters & female suffrage & we hit without sparing. **1912** LD. FISHER *Let.* 2 Aug. in R. H. Bacon *Life Ld. Fisher* (1929) II. xvi. 155 At the Defence Committee yesterday..we had a regular set-to with Lloyd George. **1976** NICHOLS & ARMSTRONG *Workers Divided* II. 135, I like nothing better than a good set-to with a good shop steward.

**c.** An attack or 'go' (*at*); *dial.* a drinking-bout.

**1801** SOUTHEY *Lett.* (1856) II. 191 There are materials before me for another set-to at the Evangelicals. **1813** W. DUNLAP *Mem. G. F. Cooke* I. iv. 63, I doubt not that his dinner with the Irish manager was a roaring set-to, a full and convincing proof of what is called Irish hospitality. **1818** *Blackw. Mag.* III. 407 The dinner much invited a set-to. **1828** *Life Planter Jamaica* 358 His noise soon procured him materials for a set-to at sangaree.

**3.** *Racing.* (See quot. 1842 and SET *v.*¹ 152 f (*c*).)

**1840** *Spirit of Times* 9 May 115 For two miles he trailed, keeping his horse in position for a set-to in the last mile. **1842** APPERLEY *Life Sportsman* xvi. 329 The struggle of the last few yards between two horses very nearly equal—which we call the set-to. **1894** *Field* 9 June 829/1 After a tremendous set-to, Haut Brion beat her by three-quarters of a length.

**Settres-, Setturday**, obs. ff. of SATURDAY.

**setule** (ˈsiːtjuːl, ˈsɛtjuːl). (Also in Latin form.) [ad. mod.L. *sētula*, dim. of *sēta*; see SETA.] A small seta or bristle.

**1826** KIRBY & SP. *Entomol.* xlvi. IV. 302 *Setule*, a little bristle. **1852** DANA *Crust.* II. 702 The most prominent setules are at the outer apex of the penult joint at base.

Hence **ˈsetuliform** *a.*, having the form of a setule; **ˈsetulose, ˈsetulous** *adjs.*, covered with setules.

**1826** KIRBY & SP. *Entomol.* xlvi. IV. 276 Setulose (*Setulosa*). Setose with the bristles truncated. **1852** DANA *Crust.* II. 882 Having two very low prominences near base of finger, the first rounded and minutely setulous. **1857** M. J. BERKELEY *Cryptog. Bot.* §386 Substance various;.. sometimes setulose. **1879** W. A. LEIGHTON *Lichen-flora* (ed. 3) 522 *Setuliform*, thread-like.

**ˈset-up**, *sb.* [f. vbl. phr. *to set up*: cf. SET *v.* 154.]

**1.** An object set up or upright, an upright. Also *spec.* a stand or display at a carnival, etc.

**1841** *Civ. Engin. & Arch. Jrnl.* IV. 264/1 The set-ups on the rail with the line fixed. **1841** *Guide to Trade, Baker* 30 Set-ups..are four-sided oblong pieces of beech of proper dimensions. They are placed on both sides, the back, and in the front of the oven, to keep the loaves in their places. **1875** KNIGHT *Dict. Mech.*, *Set up*,..the steam-ram used in the squeezer which operates on the loup or ball of iron from the puddling-furnace. The action is to up-set or condense longitudinally the bloom. **1925** C. R. COOPER *Lions 'n' Tigers* v. 135 Mike..responded almost immediately,.. returning to his various 'stands' and 'set-ups' as though he had never been away. Mike is still on the job with the circus. **1938** E. CALDWELL *Southways* 53 'You win the set-up!' Bess cried, ducking under the railing. 'It's all yours! Go on in there and take it!'

**2. a.** The way in which something is organized, arranged, or constituted; an organization, arrangement, system, or situation; *U.S.*, personal bearing or carriage; *Billiards*, etc., a position of the balls (e.g. as left by the last player) from which it is easy to score.

*Set-up* occurs in a vague and indefinite sense in a large number of contexts, but several reasonably distinct areas of use can be isolated: (*a*) a business or administrative structure or organization; also, an economic, social, or political system (both with reference to the system or the persons involved); (*b*) a domestic situation, as determined either by lifestyle or personal relationships; (*c*) a team (esp. in *Sport*); (*d*) the layout of some mechanical apparatus or equipment.

**1890** T. C. CRAWFORD *Eng. Life* 147 (Cent.), They [English soldiers] have a set-up not to be found in any of the soldiers of the Continental armies. **1895** *Outing* (N.Y.) XXVI. 66/1, I found an easy set-up and pocketed fifteen straight. **1922** *Proc. IRE* X. 249 Oscillograms of the essential current and voltage relations existing in the systems of the type illustrated by Figures 1 and 2 were obtained with the set up of apparatus illustrated in Figures 5 and 6, respectively. **1928** *Daily Express* 12 Mar. 13/2 The national set-up of motion picture chairmen. **1932** *Sun* (Baltimore) 31 Oct. 8/2 It develops that this Princeton 'set-up' actually outrushed Michigan, to produce what..ought to be classed..as at least a Class B 'upset'. **1932** D. FROME *By-Pass Murder* v. 39 Servants..belong to that..class of people whose public and private lives have no connection with each other... Publicly and privately their set-ups are as different as Fulham Road and Grosvenor Square. **1933** *Sun* (Baltimore) 29 July 1/1 They provided the set-up for the conspiracy. They helped organize the groups responsible for bombings, sluggings and strikes. **1939** [see AMPUTEE]. **1942** *Archit. Rev.* XCII. 52/2 The reason for this must be found in the general economic set-up of these countries. **1943** F. L. WRIGHT *Autobiogr.* (rev. ed.) v. 403 Other workmen.., learning of our set-up, asked us to take them on. **1946** E. G. WEBBER *Johnny Enzed in Italy* 9 Nice set up you've got here, Dig. **1949** E. L. MASCALL *Existence & Analogy* iii. 48 Before we know where we are we shall have the best possible world and the whole Leibnitian set-up. **1951** *Sport* 27 Jan.–2 Feb. 7/1 The transfer had had full notice in the Press and yet he was shown included in the home set-up. **1952** H. READ *Philos. Mod. Art.* xiii. 233 What the work of art 'expresses', in an emotional sense, depends very largely on what the spectator brings, in the way of an emotional set-up, to the work of art. **1953** W. BURROUGHS *Junkie* 7 But these people were jerks for the most part and, after an initial period of fascination, I cooled off on the setup. **1958** *Times* 19 May 11/2 At the time of the battle of Marathon the Athenians had.. a rather inefficient command set-up. **1962** A. NISBETT *Technique Sound Studio* xi. 191 In a full-scale studio 'telephone conversation' set-up it is usual to have two microphones, one normal and the other with a filter in the circuit. **1962** J. LUDWIG in R. Weaver *Canad. Short Stories* (1968) 2nd Ser. 254 What a set-up for those two kids! Jimmy would spend a fortune on Shirley, but Maxie would spend the night. **1971** *Physics Bull.* Sept. 513/1 Multinational Data, a joint setup linking ICL with the French Compagnie International pour l'Informatique and the American Control Data Corporation. **1973** B. BROADFOOT *Ten Lost Years* xi. 122 A fellow.. offered us a job. This was the set-up and.. we jumped at it. *a* **1974** R. CROSSMAN *Diaries* (1976) II. 295 Burke is now far the most powerful of the Prime Minister's confidants, and has got Harold tightly integrated into the Whitehall set-up. **1977** *Western Morning News* 30 Aug. 3/5 The family atmosphere certainly grips those who come from abroad, many of whom can find nothing to compare with the set-up in their own countries.

**b.** *Computing.* The arrangement of inter-connections and setting of parameters in a computer, esp. an analogue one, necessary for the performance of a particular calculation.

**1935** *Mem. & Proc. Manchester Lit. & Philos. Soc.* LXXIX. 67 A second diagram is then drawn up showing the various gear ratios, positive directions of rotation of the various shafts, [etc.].., and from this second diagram the actual set-up of the machine is made. **1945** *Jrnl. Franklin Inst.* CCXL. 277 After a few days of operation the 'set-up' time per solution became tolerably small. **1952** G. A. & T. M. KORN *Electronic Analog Computers* ii. 32 A number of computer laboratories have successfully used so-called setup sheets as an intermediate step between the preparation of the block diagram and the actual computer setup. **1970** D. E. HYNDMAN *Analog & Hybrid Computing* iv. 82 A considerable amount of time is generally required to patch and check out a problem set-up.

**c.** The arrangement of guns, decoys, etc., for shooting wildfowl.

**1939** *Sun* (Baltimore) 6 Nov. 7/4 Mr. Leichhardt has directed them to.. examine the shooting 'set-ups' at the various lodges. **1957** R. SCHARFF *Compl. Duck Shooter's Handbk.* iv. 105 You'll get more ducks if you have some goose decoys in your setup. **1973** G. GRESHAM *Compl. Wildfowler* x. 150 Some days the birds just won't decoy properly. They.. pitch in before they reach your setup.

**d.** *Cinematogr.* (See quot. 1959.)

**1941** B. SCHULBERG *What makes Sammy Run?* xi. 284 A director.. worrying.. about the camera set-ups. **1957** V. J. KEHOE *Technique Film & Telev. Make-Up* i. 17 In motion pictures, where the scene is shot from each angle separately in different lighting set-ups and schemes, the lighting effect can be designed to be complementary to the make-up. **1959** W. S. SHARPS *Dict. Cinematogr. & Sound Recording* 128/1 *Set-up*, the arrangement of the scenery, props, performers, lights, microphones and cameras for a particular shot. **1963** *Movie* Feb. 31/1 The open court scenes are presented within a framework of two medium close camera set-ups. **1976** C. LARSON *Muir's Blood* xviii. 101 He got here at a quarter after nine. We won't get our first setup before noon.

**e.** The difference between the maximum and minimum heights of a water surface tilted by wind action.

**1951** *Jrnl. Res. Nat. Bureau of Standards* (U.S.) XLVI. 373/1 An attempt was made to establish the relationship between set-up and the depth of water for the case where waves were present. **1968** R. W. FAIRBRIDGE *Encycl. Geomorphol.* 235/1 The intertidal zone is not a simple transition but rather a zone of maximum energy, whose peak level ranges through the tide cycle (plus storm-wave 'setup').

**3.** *colloq.* (orig. and chiefly *U.S.*). In *Boxing*, a fighter who can be easily defeated by his opponent (with the implication that he has been deliberately chosen on these grounds); *gen.*, an opponent who is easy to defeat; a thing that is easily overcome or accomplished, a 'push-over'. *spec.* in *Lawn Tennis*, a ball that is easy to hit or smash.

**1926** R. HUGHES in *Hearst's Internat.* Feb. 44/2 A guy was tellin' me that set-ups are has-beens or never-wases who get paid to stand up just long enough to be knocked out. **1926** *Clues* Nov. 162/2 *Set-up*, something easy; soft. **1932** *Sun* (Baltimore) 23 Sept. 1/2 Blaine himself did not take him [*sc.* Chapple] seriously, considered his opposition a 'set-up'. **1946** *College Topics* (Univ. of Va.) 7 Dec. 3/1 It must not be forgotten that Georgia had pretty much of a set-up as far as the schedule was concerned and it would have been a real surprise if Georgia had been beaten. **1950** *Sun* (Baltimore) 24 Mar. B 22/4 Marciano has fought a string of set-ups, and there are few known boxers on La Starza's list. **1957** M. MILLAR *Soft Talkers* vi. 63, I went after him anyway, tooth and nail. It was easy. Ron was a perfect set-up. **1961** *Times* 18 May 5/2 He is well aware that the best players never miss a 'set-up'. **1969** *New Yorker* 14 June 44/3 Graebner could now probably explode one. He has what is almost a set up on his power side.

**4.** *U.S. colloq.* The glass, ice, soda, etc., required for mixing a drink, which is served to customers, who supply their own spirits, in unlicensed premises.

**1930** *Sun* (Baltimore) 24 Dec. 11/1 If the club did not ban liquor drinking on the premises and cease serving 'set-ups' its lease would be in danger. **1944** C. HIMES *Cotton gonna kill me Yet* in *Black on Black* (1973) 197 You pays two bucks to get in this joint, fo' bucks for a half-pint grog, two bucks for a coke setup. **1954** F. P. KEYES *Royal Box* xiii. 186 But Herb asked did I want to turn him into a lone drinker, and where was the icebox, he could make his own setups, and the first thing I knew we were sitting at the table drinking ice-cold highballs. **1964** *Listener* 19 Nov. 803/3 The head waiter will probably relieve him of the bottle, place it on his table, and then serve him unlimited quantities of what are called 'set-ups' to make it palatable. These are the tonic-water, the ice, the soda, or whatever it is. **1973** W. MCCARTHY *Detail* i. 65 He looked over to the sideboard and saw a complete assortment of liquors, rums and set-ups.

**5.** *U.S. colloq.* A place- or table setting at a restaurant; the dishes, cutlery, etc., which make up this.

**1934** in WEBSTER. **1941** J. SMILEY *Hash House Lingo* 48 *Set up*, table eating utensils. **1978** J. D. MACDONALD *Empty Copper Sea* iii. 34 He led us to a corner booth set up for four, whipped away the extra setups.

**6.** *colloq.* (orig. *U.S.*) A scheme or trick whereby an innocent person is caused to incriminate himself or a criminal is caught red-handed; a 'frame-up'.

**1968** *Sun Mag.* (Baltimore) 13 Oct. 28/3 That's how the narcs get most guys on possession of narcotics—through set-ups. **1970** W. BURROUGHS JR. *Speed* iv. 78 A set-up crossed my mind, but Jesus, who cared if it was a set-up or not, we were still busted. **1973** *Black Panther* 7 Apr. 8/2 As he was bringing the food inside he noticed the driver of the truck had turned and was running away. Grady immediately realized it was all a set-up. **1978** J. GARDNER *Dancing Dodo* xxix. 236 Arthur's clean... It was a set-up... I had him checked like you'd check a dodgy engine.

**7.** Special Comb.: **set-up man**, (*a*) *U.S.* (see quot. 1953); (*b*) *N. Amer.* a man who sets up machinery or equipment.

**1953** W. BURROUGHS *Junkie* i. 18 They are always looking for a 'setup man', someone to plan jobs and tell them exactly what to do. **1954** [see *job enlargement* s.v. JOB *sb.*[2] 7]. **1968** *Globe & Mail* (Toronto) 13 Jan. 48/2 (Advt.), Foreman and set-up man, polyethylene film extrusion, for afternoon shift. **1978** *Detroit Free Press* 16 Apr. F1/3 (Advt.), Willing to train experienced set-up man who has leadership potential.

**set-up**: see SET *ppl. a.* 10.

**setwall** ('sɛtwəl). Forms: α. 3 **zedewal**, 3, 5 **zeduale**, 5 **zedewal(l)e**, 6 **zedual**; 4 **sed(e)wale**, 5 **seduale**, 6 **-wale**. β. 4 **ceteuall**, **setewale**, 4–5 **sette-**, 4–7 **cetewale**, 6 **cety-**, 7 **setywall**. γ. 4–6 **setuale**, 4–8 **setwell**, 5 **cetuall**, 5 **set(t)well**, **setwaly** (?), 5–6 **setwale**, 6 **setual(l**, **-waule**, **settwelle**, 7 **set(t)wal(l**, 6– **setwall**. [a. AF. *zedewale* = OF. *citoual*, *citual*, *sotoval* (Palsgr.), also *citouar(t*, etc., ad. med.L. **zedoāle*, var. *zedoārium*, ad. Arab. *zedwār*: see ZEDOARY.]

†**1.** The root of the East Indian plant *Curcuma Zedoaria*, used as a drug; also the plant itself; = ZEDOARY. *Obs.*

α. *a* **1225** *Ancr. R.* 370 Ne makeden heo neuer strencðe of gingiuere ne of gedewal [*MS. T.* ȝedewal, *MS. C.* zeduale], ne of clou de gilofre. *c* **1305** *Land Cokayne* 74 In þe praer is a tre... þe rote is gingeuir and galingale, þe siouns beþ al sedwale. *a* **1310** in Wright *Lyric P.* v. 27 With gyngyvre ant sedewale ant the gylofre. *c* **1400** MAUNDEV. (1839) xviii. 187 Canelle, Zedewalle, Notemuges and Maces. **14..** *Voc.* in Wr.-Wülcker 621/16 *Zeduarium*.. zeduale. **1547** BOORDE *Brev. Health* iii. 8 Take of Anys sedes, of Fenell sedes, of Zedual, of eche the weyght of xii d.

β. **1310–11** *Durham Acc. Rolls* (Surtees) 507 In 3 *li.* di. de Ceteuall. *c* **1386** CHAUCER *Miller's T.* 21 As sweete as is the root Of lycorys or any Cetewale [*v.r.* Settewale]. *a* **1400** in *Sc. Acts Parl.* (1844) I. 669 Gynger setwell almondis. *c* **1440** *Promp. Parv.* 454/1 Setuale, or seduale, herbe (*K.* setwale, *P.* setwaly), *Zedoarium*. **1496** *Halyburton's Ledger* (1867) 57 Item a li. settwell. **1530** PALSGR. 269/2 Setwall. **1567** MAPLET *Gr. Forest* 37 Cetewale, is an Herbe whose roote the Phisitions vse to gather in Sommer. **1610** MARKHAM *Masterp.* II. clxxiii. 495 *Nardi radix*, which wee call setwal. **1640** PARKINSON *Theat. Bot.* 1612 Zedoaria.. the Setwall that we have usually in our shops.

*attrib.* **1639** O. WOOD *Alph. Bk. Phys. Secrets* 211 Take the powder of Setwell Roots.

**2.** The plant valerian, *Valeriana pyrenaica*.

**1548** TURNER *Names Herbes* (E.D.S.) 62 Phu is called in englishe setwal, of other some Capones tayle. **1590** SPENSER *Muiop.* 196 Dull Poppie, and drink-quickning Setuale. **1593** DRAYTON *Ballad of Dowsabell* 33 This mayden.. Went forth.. to get sweete Cetywall [? **1605**, **1619**, Setywall].. to deck her summer hall. **1658** PHILLIPS, *Settwall*, a kind of herb growing near walls. **1741** *Complete Fam.-Piece* I. iv. 254 Take red Sage, Betony,.. Setwell. **1865** 'C. BEDE' *Rook's Gard.* 9 Clusters of the red valerian or setwall.

**set work**, **'setwork**. [SET *ppl. a.*]

†**1.** A kind of embroidery used in working tapestry; also *attrib. Obs.*

**1503** *Acc. Ld. High Treas. Scot.* II. 214 Ane gret liar of set werk of worsait. **1624** *Inv.* in *Archæologia* XLVIII. 136 A set work chare. **1649** in *Bury Wills* (Camden) 220 My posted settworke bedstead.

†**2.** Regular or fixed employment. *Obs.*

*a* **1661** FULLER *Worthies, Leic.* (1662) II. 132 Especially making it his Set-work (what was Pits his by-work) to observe the Natives of this Shire.

†**3.** Piece-work. In quot. *attrib. Obs.*

**1720** S. SEWALL *Diary* 12 Nov., His Trade of Set-Work Coopering.

**4.** Two-coat plastering on lath.

**1812** P. NICHOLSON *Mech. Exerc.* 312 The plasterers denominate set work by the compound term of layed and set.

**5. a.** A method of boat-building in which the strakes are placed edge to edge and battened inside. **b.** Mechanism for feeding transversely material that is being sawed. (In recent U.S. dicts.)

**setye**, obs. form of CITY.

**1536** *Cal. Anc. Rec. Dublin* (1889) 497.

**setyn**, obs. f. and pa. t. SIT *v.*

**Setyrday**, obs. f. SATURDAY.

**seu**, obs. f. SEW, SUE; obs. pa. t. SOW *v.*

**seuer**, **seuerance**, **seuerte**, obs. ff. SURE, SURANCE, SURETY.

**seuge**, **seuggen**, obs. ff. SAY *v.*

**seugh**, var. SHEUGH.

**seuȝ**, obs. pa. t. SOW *v.*

**seuir**, obs. Sc. f. SURE.

†**seul**, *a. Obs. rare.* Also 5 **seulle**, 6 **seile** (?). [a. F. *seul* alone, SOLE *a.*] Sole, unique.

*c* **1477** CAXTON *Jason* 32 Jason.. thought.. onely, upon the seulle and oultrepassed beaute of the uertuouse myrro. **1512** *Helyas* in Thoms *Prose Rom.* (1858) III. 26 If I thought to haue endomaged you of one seile farthyng [*sic*; Fr. *d'un seul espy*]. [*Ibid.* 106 Seul heritier of his brother.]

†**seur**. *Obs.*[−1]. [? a. F. *seur* 'a kind of Net, or Engine to catch fish with' (Cotgr.).] A kind of fishing-net.

**1558** [see LAMMET].

**seur(e**, **seur(e)ly**, **seur(e)te**, etc., obs. ff. SURE, SURELY, SURETY, etc.

**seute**, obs. f. SUIT.

**sevagerous**, var. SAVAGEROUS *a.*

[**sevant** *a.*, **sevantly**, *adv.* See note s.v. SUANTLY *adv.*]

‖**sève** (sɛv). [Fr. = sap.] The fineness and strength of flavour proper to any particular wine.

**1742** POPE *Dunc.* IV. 556 The *Sève* and *Verdeur* of the Vine. **1851** REDDING *Mod. Wines* (ed. 3) vi. 175 When carefully kept until old, it approaches Barsac in *sève*. **1888** *Encycl. Brit.* XXIV. 605/2 Sauterne.. possessing a special *sève*, or, in other words, having that special taste which, while it remains in the mouth, leaves the palate perfectly fresh.

**seve**, obs. form of SIEVE; see also SÈVRES.

**seveare**, **seveirlie**, obs. ff. SEVERE, SEVERELY.

**seven** ('sɛv(ə)n), *a.* and *sb.* Forms: α. 1–2 **seofon**, **-en**, (1 **seofan**, **-un**, **siofun**, **sibun**, **sifun**, **sufon**, **syfan**, **-on**, 2 **soven**), 2–3 **seoven**, (*Ormin* **se(o)ffne**, **se(o)fenn**), 2, 5 **sefen**, 3 **seovene**, **seofne**, 3–5 **sevene**, 4 **sefne**, **seyven**, 4–5 **seyvyn**, **sevon**, **sevyan**, 4–6 **sevin**, **-enne**, **ceven(e**, **-yn**, 5–6 **sevyne**, 5–7 **seaven**, 6 **sevn**, 7 **seavne**, **seivine**, 3– **seven**. β. Chiefly *Sc.* 4 **sewine**, 5 **sewne**, 5–7 **sewin**, 6 **seweyne**, **sewn**, **sawin**. γ. 4 **sen**, **sene** (?); see also SENNIGHT. δ. 1 **seofo**, **-a**, **siofo**, **sefo**, 1–2 **seofe**, 2 **sefe**, 2–4 **sove**, 2–5 **seve**, 3 **seove**, 4 *Kent.* **zeve**, 5 **sef(f**. [Com. Teut.: OE. *seofon* (infl. *seofone*, *-u*, etc.) = OFris. *sowen*, *sawen* (later *sân*, *saan*, mod. *saun*), *sigun*, *siugun* (mod. *sjûggen*), etc., OS. *sibun*, *sivon* (MLG. *seven*, *soven*, MDu. *seven*, Du. *zeven*), OHG. *sibun* (MHG. *siben*, G. *sieben*), ON. *sjau* (Icel. *sjö*, Norw. dial. *sjau*, *sju*, etc.; Sw. *sju*, Da. *syv*), Goth. *sibun*:—OTeut. **sebun*. The Indo-germanic **septḿ* is more closely represented by Skr. *saptá*, Gr. ἑπτά, L. *septem*, OSl. *sedmĭ*, Lith. *septynì*, OIr. *secht n-*.] The cardinal number next after six, represented by the symbols 7, VII, vii.

**A.** *adj.* **1. a.** In concord with a sb. expressed.

α. *Beowulf* 3122 þeᵹnas syfone. **971** *Blickl. Hom.* 193 An ᵹear & seofan monaþ. *c* **1000** ÆLFRIC *Gen.* xli. 53 þa þa seofon godan ᵹear agane wæron. *c* **1175** *Lamb. Hom.* 13 þa oðre souen laȝe. *c* **1200** ORMIN Ded. 252 Godnessess seffne. *Ibid.* 8399 Forr sefenn winnterr haffde he been Tosamenn inn Egippte. *c* **1330** *Arth. & Merl.* 3845 þo seiȝe þai seuen baners. **1390** GOWER *Conf.* I. 140 So that.. he be bereined Be times sefne and sore peined. *c* **1440** *Promp. Parv.* 67/2 Ceventymes, *septies*. **1591** DIGGES *Pantam.* 8 The line AB which I would diuide into seauen equall portions. **1596** DALRYMPLE tr. *Leslie's Hist. Scot.* I. 35 Sax, sevin, or viii. cubites hich. **1683** EVELYN *Diary* 18 June, For the last seaven yeares. **1813** SOUTHEY *Nelson* I. 198 The capture of seven sail of the line. **1865** BARING-GOULD *Werewolves* viii, When seven girls succeed each other in one family.

β. *c* **1375** *Sc. Leg. Saints* viii. (*Philepus*) 79 Sewyne dais.. before his ded. **1422** tr. *Secreta Secret., Priv. Priv.* 153/10 He makyd the Cite of Rome afyre to sette, and Sewyn dayes and Sewyn nyghtes to brente. **1500–20** DUNBAR *Poems* lx. 5 All thing wrocht in dayis seweyne. **1559** in J. Campbell *Ch. & Par. Kirkcaldy* vi. (1904) 59 Sewn pundes and twelf shillinges. **1612** in *Scott. Hist. Rev.* (1905) 394 Of erras wark tâpestrie sewin stand ewerie stand contenying fywe pieces.

γ. *a* **1340** HAMPOLE *Psalter* xi. 7 þe sen [*v.r.* seuen] giftis of þe halygast. *c* **1380** WYCLIF *Sel. Wks.* III. 500 In hevene it [God's body] is sene fote in fourme. *a* **1400** *Octouian* 1386 Sene yere and more.

δ. *c* **950** *Lindisf. Gosp.* Luke ii. 36, & lifde mið wer hire wintrum seofo. *c* **1175** *Lamb. Hom.* 41 He him sceaude an ouen on berninde fure; he warp ut of him seofe leies. *a* **1200**

*Moral Ode* 140 Wa wurð sorȝe seueȝer for souenihte blisse. *c* **1275** LAY. 3970 þo soue ȝer were a-gon. **1297** R. GLOUC. (Rolls) 88 þe saxons.. Seve kynges made in engelond. **1340** *Ayenb.* 4 þe zeue stapes of chastetė. *c* **1475** *Partenay* 4181 A lytell body of sixe or sef yere age.

**b.** Used predicatively.

**1622** FLETCHER *Beggar's Bush* II. i, We are seven of us. **1655** F. W. *Observ. on Fulke's Meteors* 162 Metalls are seven in number, as the Planets are. **1798** WORDSWORTH (*title*) We are seven. *a* **1847** ROSSETTI *Blessed Damozel* i, The stars in her hair were seven.

**c.** With *day*, *night*, *month* in more or less specific uses.

*seven days*: a week; often referred to as the period of the Creation; in England, formerly a common term of imprisonment. Also ***seven days and seven nights***. ***seven months' child***: one born at the seventh month; a type of weakliness. Cf. SEVEN-DAY(S, SEVEN-YEAR(S, and SENNIGHT.

*c* **1200** ORMIN 4356 Forr seffne daȝhess brinngenn aȝȝ þe wuke till hiss ende. *c* **1250** *Gen. & Ex.* 2952 Ðis wreche.. Lestede fulle seuene niȝt. *a* **1300** *Leg. Rood* (1871) 42 þer wiþþoute mete and drinke seue dawes he lay. *c* **1375–1500–20** [see I β above]. **1470–85** MALORY *Arthur* IV. xix. 144 And rode daye by day wel a seuen dayes or they fond ony auenture. *a* **1513** DUNBAR *Compl. to King* 5 God, that.. all thing wrocht in dayis seweyne. **1611** BIBLE *Job* ii. 13 They sate downe with him vpon the ground seuen dayes, and seuen nights. **1798** COLERIDGE *Anc. Mar.* IV. ix, Seven days seven nights I saw that curse. **1817** *2nd Rep. Committee Police Metrop., Min. Evid.* 352 He is sent for seven days to the House of Correction. **1847** *Act 10 & 11 Vict.* c. 89 §29 Liable.. to Imprisonment for a Period not exceeding Seven Days. **1850** [I. WILLIAMS] (*title*) The Seven Days, or the Old and New Creation. **1859** TENNYSON *Merlin & V.* 561 A seven-months' babe had been a truer gift. **1892** *Oxf. Chron.* 19 Mar. 6/7 Fined 1*s.* and costs 3*s.* 6*d.*, or seven days. **1898** J. HUTCHINSON in *Archives Surg.* IX. 364 In December of the same year his wife was delivered of a seven months' child. **1903** *Ladies' Field* 7 Nov. 346/1 The Crystal Palace Cat Show.. Neila Billi, a grand seven-month son of Orange Blossom of Thorpe.

**d.** Used (*a*) symbolically, often denoting completion or perfection (esp. in echoes of biblical phraseology), or (*b*) typically in expressions of time, etc. for a large number or quantity, esp. †(*this*) ***seven year***(*s*, etc. (= a long period). See also SEVENSITHE(S.

† ***seven times fold*** = SEVENFOLD *adv.*; ***seven-times-folded*** = SEVENFOLD *a.*

*c* **1000** ÆLFRIC *Judges* xvi. 7 Ʒif ic beo ʒebunden mid seofon rapum of sinum ʒeworhte, sona ic beo ʒewyld. **1362** LANGL. *P. Pl.* A. IX. 66, I haue suwed þe þis seuen ȝer. *c* **1386** CHAUCER *Nun's-Pr. Epil.* 7 The were nede of hennes, as I wene, Ʒa, moo than seuene tymes seuentene. **1470–85** MALORY *Arthur* VII. xiii. 232 Men sayen that he hath seuen mens strength. *c* **1475** *Rauf Coilȝear* 664 Thocht he had socht sic ane sicht all this seuin ȝeir. *c* **1475** *Partenay* 4182 Better.. seff tymes fold. **1549** *Compl. Scot.* ii. 24, I sal strik ȝou vitht ane plag, seuyn tymes mair vehement. **1611** SHAKS. *Wint. T.* IV. iv. 591 There shall not, at your Fathers House, these seuen yeeres Be borne another such. **1657** AUSTEN *Fruit Trees* I. 32 The Lord recompenceth and will give thee seauen-times as much. **1671** MILTON *Samson* 1122 Add thy Spear, A Weavers beam, and seven-times-folded shield. **1855** KINGSLEY *Westw. Ho!* xiii, And gold seven times tried he was, when God.. took him home at last.

**e.** In *Naut.* slang phrs. ***to knock seven bells out of*** (someone): to beat (someone) severely; similarly, ***to scare seven bells out of***: to terrify. Cf. BELL *sb.*[1] 3 b.

**1929** F. C. BOWEN *Sea Slang* 121 *To knock seven bells out of a man*, to give him a hiding or knock him out. **1932** J. W. HARRIS *Days of Endeavour* ix. 158 Three angry Norwegians ..knocked seven bells out of him. **1933** M. LOWRY *Ultramarine* iv. 206 Yis. He's knocked seven bells out of harder cases than you in his time. **1943** F. C. HENDRY *True Tales of Sail & Steam* i. 11 She [*sc.* a ship] scared seven bells out of us and gave us the worst month I have ever known at sea.

**2. a.** With ellipsis of sb., which may usually be supplied from the context.

*c* **900** tr. *Bæda's Hist.* IV. iii. (1890) 262 Mid feaum broðrum, þæt is seofonum oððe eahtum. *a* **1000** *Cædmon's Gen.* 1335 (Gr.) Ond þu seofone ʒenim on þæt sundreced tudra ʒehwilces ʒeteled rimes. *c* **1175** *Lamb. Hom.* 27 Erðon he nefde bute enne deofel, nu he haued sefene. *c* **1205** LAY. 15878 Joram þe witie & seofne of his iueren. *a* **1300** *Cursor M.* 1455 Nine hundret yeir and seuen a[nd] fiue, Sua lang it lasted seth liue. **1382** WYCLIF *Gen.* vii. 2 Of alle hauynge sowles clene, thow shalt take seuene and seuene, maal and femaal. **1411** in *26 Pol. Poems* x. 34 Wiþ water, for synne þe world y slow, Saue seuene, and noe þat was my gest. **1500–20** DUNBAR *Poems* lxvi. 47 Bot beneficis ar nocht leill devydit; Sum men hes sewin, and I nocht ane. **1603** SHAKS. *Meas. for M.* III. i. 111 Sure it is no sinne, Or of the deadly seuen it is the least. **1656** STANLEY *Hist. Philos.* III. 89 He first divided an oration into four parts, some say into seaven. **1667** MILTON *P.L.* III. 648 Th' Arch-Angel Uriel, one of the seav'n Who in God's presence.. Stand. **1849** MACAULAY *Hist. Eng.* viii. II. 357 It was known all over London that the Bishops were before the Council... When the Seven came forth under a guard [etc.].

**b.** With ellipsis of *parts*.

**1297** R. GLOUC. (Rolls) 8372 Her ost hii delde a seuene [*MS.* β departed in seuene].

**c.** *esp.* With ellipsis of *hours* (of the day) or *minutes*, as ***seven o'*** (†***of the***, †***a***) ***clock***; also simply ***seven***; ***half-past seven***, ***seven fifteen***, etc.

*c* **1412** HOCCLEVE *De Reg. Princ.* 2008 O-boute þe hour of seuene. **1470–85** MALORY *Arthur* XX. v. 804 Or it be seuen of the clok. **1596** SHAKS. *Tam. Shr.* IV. iii. 193 It shall be seuen ere I go to horse. **1664** BUTLER *Hud.* II. iii. 512, I meant what time o'th' day 'tis? Quoth Ralpho, between seven and eight 'tis. **1779** *Mirror* No. 43 ¶6 A clock was heard to strike seven. **1859** GEO. ELIOT *Adam Bede* iv, It's gone seven by th' clock. **1872** CALVERLEY *Fly Leaves* (1903) 93 Ere yet the minster clock chimed seven.

**1580** G. HARVEY *Letter-Bk.* (Camden) 72 Afternoone seavenaclocke dinnars. **1898** WATTS-DUNTON *Aylwin* V. ii, To dress for her ridiculous seven o'clock dinner.

**d.** With ellipsis of *years* (of age). ***to be more than seven***: to 'know one's way about'.

**1608** SHAKS. *Per.* IV. vi. 81 Did you goe too't so young, were you a gamester at fiue or at seuen? **1693** LOCKE *Educ.* §199. 254 The first Season to get Foreign Languages,.. I should think, should be from Seven to Fourteen or Sixteen. **1872** CALVERLEY *Fly Leaves* (1884) 65 A dull little varmint Of seven or eight. **1898** GISSING *Town Trav.* viii. 81 Oh, we all know that Mr. Gammon's more than seven.

**e.** With ellipsis of *shillings* or *pence*, as in ***seven and seven*** (***pence***). ***seven-and-sixer***: an article (in quot., a hat) costing seven shillings and sixpence.

**1839** THACKERAY *Stubb's Cal.* Dec., I had charged a gentleman in the coffee-rooms seven-and-sixpence for a glass of ale and bread and cheese. **1857** HUGHES *Tom Brown* I. v, We are allowed two seven-and-sixers a half.

**f.** Specific uses.

***the Seven***: (*a*) the seven deacons of Acts vi. 5; †(*b*) the Seven Sages of Greece (see SAGE *sb.*[2] 1); (*c*) the seven Argive heroes that made war against Thebes; (*d*) in soldier's slang (see quot. 1898). †***the erring seven***: the planets.

**1382** WYCLIF *Acts* xxi. 8 Philip euangelist, that was oon of the seuene. **1605** BACON *Adv. Learn.* II. iv. §3 Which later kind of Parabolical wisedome was much more in vse in the ancient times, as by the Fables of Aesope, and the briefe sentences of the seuen.. may appeare. **1612** SELDEN *Illustr. Drayton's Poly-olb.* x. 220 As the old verses of the Seven tells us. **1642** H. MORE *Song of Soul* II. iii. III. xv, So doth the earth one of the erring seven Wheel round the fixed sunne. **1842** W. C. TAYLOR *Anc. Hist.* viii. §6 (ed. 3) 216 The memorable war of 'the Seven against Thebes'. **1888** *Encycl. Brit.* XXIII. 230 War of the 'Seven' (under Adrastus of Argos). **1898** *United Service Mag.* Mar. 649 In their way soldiers are very philosophical. If anything in their work annoys them they say, 'It's all in the seven', *i.e.*, the seven years for which they join the army. **1902** T. M. LINDSAY *Ch. Early Cent.* iv. 117 They are never called deacons; the Seven is the technical name they were known by.

**g.** ***seven-a-side***(*s*, a form of Rugby Union football played with only seven men on each side; hence, a rugby match or tournament played with teams of this size. Cf. sense 2 e of the sb.

**1900** *Scottish Sport* 13 Apr. 6/1 Melrose.. will tomorrow resound with a Babel of tongues.. eager and excited over the first of the Border seven-a-side tournaments. *a* **1917** E. C. SMITH *Braid Haaick* (1927) 24 The 'Greens' hev wun the seevin-a-sides at their ain spoarts. **1935** *Encycl. Sports* 529/1 *Seven-a-Side*. This variant of the Rugby Union game is much played by the better clubs towards the end of the season... There are, usually, three forwards and four backs on either side. **1961** *Times* 5 May 11/1 We would much rather have seen the seven-a-sides at Twickenham.

†**3.** = seven times. *Obs.*

**1303** R. BRUNNE *Handl. Synne* 6834 More þank þou getest for swych ȝyuyng þan seuene so moche with chydyng. *a* **1425** *Cursor M.* 9382 (Trin.) Sonne & mone þat is so briȝt Had seuen so michel more liȝt.

**4. a.** Multiplying another numeral.

*c* **893** ÆLFRED *Oros.* II. v. §2 His heres wæs seofon hund þusenda. *c* **1205** LAY. 364 We habbeð seoue þusund of gode cnihten. *a* **1300** *Cursor M.* 1488 Lameth his sun his eild to neuen, Seuen hundret yeir seuenti and seuen. **1362** LANGL. *P. Pl.* A. III. 141 Seuen score dayes. *a* **1400** *Morte Arth.* 3788 One seuenschore knyghtes. *c* **1400** *Laud Troy Bk.* 8669 Douȝti knyȝtes thousandes seuene. **1596** DALRYMPLE tr. *Leslie's Hist. Scot.* I. 4 Seuin hundir thousand pace lang. **1626** BACON *Sylva* §755 Who lived till she was seuen-score yeares old. **1650** in *Fasti Aberd.* (1854) 587 Seivine dusson egges 0 14 0. **1774** GOLDSM. *Nat. Hist.* (1776) I. 216 The river Mississippi is of more than seven hundred leagues in length. **1837** CARLYLE *Fr. Rev.* III. II. i, Then do but touch some spring dexterously, the whole machine, clattering and jerking seven-hundredfold, will whirl with huge crash. **1859** FITZGERALD tr. *Omar* xx, To-morrow I may be Myself with Yesterday's Sev'n Thousand Years.

**b.** Coupled with a higher (cardinal or ordinal) numeral, so as to form a compound (cardinal or ordinal) numeral.

*c* **1000** *Ags. Ps.* (Th.) xxvii. *heading*, Dauid sang þisne seofen and twentiʒoþan sealm. *c* **1250** *Gen. & Ex.* 594 Seuene and .xx.ti dais. *c* **1470** HENRY *Wallace* VI. 107 Tuelff hundred ȝer, tharto nynte and sewyn. **1579** FULKE *Heskins' Parl.* 302 The seuen and sixtieth Chapter. *a* **1586** SIDNEY *Arcadia* II. (Sommer) 163 b, A young girle of a seuen and twenty yeare old. **1601** HOLLAND *Pliny* II. 270 The seven and twentieth Booke of Plinies Naturall Historie. **1837** CARLYLE *Fr. Rev.* I. IV. iv, Slashed by seven-and-twenty wounds.

**c.** Forming fractional numerals.

**1726** *Act 13 Geo. I*, c. 26 §11 In Breadth full Three quarters of a Yard, or full Seven eighths. **1832** J. RENNIE *Consp. Butterfl. & M.* 64 Wings one inch one-half to seven-twelfths. **1900** *Jrnl. Sch. Geog.* (U.S.) Jan. 16 We must divide the number of days between the time of the observation and the nearest equinox by three and seven-eighths.

†**5.** = SEVENTH *a. Obs.*

The ME. *sevenday* may be either an instance of this or a contraction of *sevende day* (see SEVENTH); cf. SEVENDELE.

*c* **1250** *Gen. & Ex.* 247 Ðe seuendai morʒen sprong. *c* **1305** *Pop. Treat. Sci.* 137 Ther nis bote the sove del that men wonyeth on i-wis. *c* **1320** *Sir Tristr.* 800 To his castel.. He sailed þe seuenday. *c* **1375** *Sc. Leg. Saints* vi. (*Thomas*) 422 þat in lele pennance we suld dwel, as fore þe sewine gre ve ma tell. *a* **1400** *Relig. Pieces fr. Thornton MS.* 23 The seuen braunche of pryde es elacion. *c* **1475** *Partenay* 1261 The seffe child Ffromont that tyme callyd was. **1491** *Cal. Anc. Rec. Dublin* (1889) 375 The yer of the regn of Kyng Harry the Seventh the sewne yer. **1513** DOUGLAS *Æneis* I. xi. 755 For now the sevin symmir hidder careis the Wilsum, and errant, in euery land and see. **1588** A. KING tr. *Canisius' Catech.* 39 Ye sawin commandiment.

**6.** In special collocations.

**seven bishops** *Eng. Hist.*, Archbishop Sancroft, and Bishops Ken, Lake, Lloyd, Trelawney, Turner, White, who in 1688 protested against the Declaration of Indulgence of James II. **seven brethren**, the seven sons of St. Felicitas, whose festival is assigned to July 10th. **seven champions**, the national saints of England, Scotland, Wales, Ireland, France, Spain, and Italy, viz. George, Andrew, David, Patrick, Denys, James, and Anthony. Hence sing. † ***seven-champion*** allusively (see quot. 1676). **seven islands**, the Ionian Islands (cf. SEPTINSULAR). **seven jargons** (see quots.). **seven names of God**, cf. quot. 1905; a partial coincidence with this Jewish list appears in the incantatory formula (in Heinrich *ME. Medizinbuch* 149) *El, Elye, Sabaoth, Adonay, Alpha, Omega, Messias, Pastor, Agnus, Fons*. The 14th c. quots. below point to a use of *Seven* as a name of God. **seven seas**, the Arctic, Antarctic, North and South Pacific, North and South Atlantic, and Indian Oceans. Also SEVEN SISTERS, SEVEN SLEEPERS, SEVEN STARS. For others see AGE *sb.* 5, ART *sb.* 7, BELL *sb.* 3 b, COMMAND *sb.* 2, DEADLY *a.* 5 (*s. deadly sins*), HEAD *sb.*[1] 71 b (*s. head-sins*), HEAVEN *sb.* 4, MERCY *sb.* 7 (*s. works of mercy*), PLANET *sb.*[1] 1, PSALM *sb.* 2, SACRAMENT *sb.* 1, SAGE *sb.*[2], SCIENCE *sb.* 3, SENSE *sb.* 10, STAR, VIAL, VICE, VIRTUE, WHISTLER, WISE (*s. wise masters* and *men*), WONDER, WORD.

**1731** TINDAL *Rapin's Hist. Eng.* XV. 142 *marg.*, Tryal of the *Seven Bishops [1688]. *c* **1450** *Godstow Reg.* 19, I pray ȝou þen *Brethren seuyn, That I may be one of Benet ys heyre. **1588** A. KING tr. *Canisius' Catech.* in *Cath. Tract.* (S.T.S.) 189 The 7 brether sones of S. Foelicite martt. at Rome vnder Antoninus 136. **1596** R. JOHNSON (*title*) The Famous History of the *Seauen Champions of Christendome. **1676** *Poor Robin's Intell.* 28 Mar. 1/1 He is a Seaven-Champion in Quackery, that delights in nothing but dangerous adventures. **1735** BOLINGBROKE *Study Hist.* i. (1752) 5 Some.. read the life of Aristides or Phocion,.. just as.. they would read the story of the seven champions. **1803** G. ROSE *Diaries* (1860) II. 20 The republic of the *Seven Islands. **1880** *Encycl. Brit.* XIII. 206/2 In 1800, the emperor Paul erected the Republic of the Seven United Islands. **1843** BORROW *Bible in Spain* xxxix, I heard one of them [the alguazils] say 'he understands the *seven Gypsy jargons'. **1896** *Gentl. Mag.* CCLXXX. 129 It was very galling for one who had just been discussing the Seven Jargons with a past master to be now floored in a missing word competition. *a* **1325** *Adam & Eve* 125 in Horstm. *Altengl. Leg.* (1878) 140 Yblisced be his *nam seuen. **13..** *Guy Warw.* 2841 God, for his name seuene He bring ȝou to gode heuene! *c* **1460** *Towneley Myst.* xiii. 191 Now lord, for thy naymes sevyn, that made both moyn and starnes, Well mo then I can neuen thi will, lorde, of me tharnys. [**1905** *Jewish Encycl.* IX. 163/2 The number of divine names that require the scribe's special care is seven: El, Elohim, Adonai, YHWH, Ehyeh-Asher-Ehyeh, Shaddai, and Zeba'ot.] **1872** FITZGERALD tr. *Omar* xlvii, Which of our Coming and Departure heeds As the *Sev'n Seas should heed a pebble-cast. **1896** KIPLING (*title*) The Seven Seas.

**B.** *sb.* **1. a.** The abstract number seven.

*at* or *on six and seven*, *at sixes and sevens*: see SIX *sb.* 5. † ***be sic seven***: see SIC *a.* 1 b.

*c* **1055** tr. *Byrhtferth's Handboc* in Anglia VIII. 303 Twia seofon beoð feowertyne. *c* **1200** ORMIN 5351 Forr tale off seoffne tacneþþ uss þatt seofennkinne bene. **1398** TREVISA *Barth. De P.R.* XIX. cxx. (1495) 922 Seuen hyghte Septenarius and is the thyrde amonge odde nombres. *c* **1425** *Crafte Nombrynge* (E.E.T.S.) 10 Cast 3 to foure, þat wole be seuen. ? **1593** DRAYTON *Man in Moon* Poems (1619) 484 The which foure Seuens the Eight and Twenty make. **1621** T. WILLIAMSON tr. *Goulart's Wise Vieillard* 42 The number of seuen, is otherwise iudged of in the holy Scriptures.

†**b.** ***to set on seven***: said of the work of God in creation. *Obs.*

*a* **1400** *Pistill of Susan* 264 þou maker of myddelert,.. Boþe þe sonne and þe see þou sette vpon seuene. *c* **1460** *Towneley Myst.* xiii. 738 The fader of heuen god omnypotent, That sett all on seuen. *c* **1470** *Gol. & Gaw.* 1045, I swere be suthfast God, that settis all on sevin.

**c.** Short for the date of the seventh year of a particular century, e.g. 1707. Also, ***two sevens***: 77th year.

**1818** SCOTT *Hrt. Midl.* xxiv, At the last riding of the Scots Parliament, and that was in the gracious year seven. **1889** GRETTON *Memory's Harkback* 63 When he was in his 'two sevens', I followed him from church on Christmas Day in his Doctor's red gown, big wig, and silk stockings.

**2. a.** A set of seven persons or things.

*sevens*: a ball game (see quot. 1868).

**1590** H. BROUGHTON *Let. to Friend* A 2 Seauen seauens (of yeeres) and sixtie and two seauens. **1599** PONT *Right Reckoning of Years* 76 The wicked spirites also are numbred by seavens. **1611** BIBLE *Gen.* vii. 2 Of euery cleane beast thou shalt take to thee by seuens. **1667** MILTON *P.L.* XI. 731 Of everie Beast, and Bird, and Insect small Came seavens, and pairs. **1853** *N. Brit. Rev.* Feb. 397 Till the end of the forty-ninth annual revolution, a period of seven sevens. **1868** *Routledge's Ev. Boy's Bk.* 48 Sevens. This game is very like Catch-ball. The object is to catch a ball seven times in a particular fashion.

**b.** A playing card marked with seven pips.

**1656** EARL MONM. tr. *Boccalini's Pol. Touchstone* (1674) 288 The fair advantage which he had of three Sevens in hand. **1680** COTTON *Compl. Gamester* (ed. 2) 90 You then play your seven of Clubs. *Ibid.* 102 They may lay out the threes, fours, fives, sixes and sevens. **1783** W. HOOPER *Rat. Recr.* (ed. 2) I. 120 With the seven and eight of diamonds. **1873** *Routledge's Young Gentl. Mag.* Jan. 121 Gather up the four sevens, and place them on the top of the pack.

**c.** *Cricket.* A score of seven runs from one hit.

**1765** in Waghorn *Cricket Scores* (1899) 59 Harding fetched 24 notches off his own bat at four strokes: that was one 5, two 6's, and one 7. **1886** PYCROFT *Oxford Mem.* II. 101 He hit Mr. Lowth for a fair seven.

**d.** *pl.* Verses of seven syllables.

**1825** *Collect. Psalms & Hymns* 197 Hymn 170. (Sevens.) Gracious Spirit, Love Divine. **1891** J. C. PARSONS *Eng. Versif.* 35 Sevens. Trochaic trimeter, with added syllable.

**e.** Short for *seven-a-side(s* (see sense 2 g of the adj.).

**1926** *Times* 26 Apr. 5/5 Cussen showed in the semi-final what pace means in the game of Sevens. **1977** *Daily Mirror* 15 Mar. 30/1 Rosslyn Park are angry that they cannot call their famous schools sevens tournament by the names of their sponsors.

**3.** † **a.** In the game of hazard, with reference to the throwing of a main. *Obs.*

***seven's the main***: see MAIN *sb.*[3] ***seven is (my) chance***: see CHANCE *sb.* 3 b. ***seven and eleven***: the two casts upon which the highest expectation can be wagered when seven is the main. ***come on seven***: ? = 'seven's the main'; ? so ***come you seven***, in quot. used as sb., a hardened gamester.

*c* **1386** CHAUCER *Pard. T.* 653 Seuene is my chaunce, and thyn is cynk and treye. *a* **1553** *Nice Wanton* 212 Heer six come on seuen. **1596** SIR J. DAVIES *Epigr.* xxi, Hee still doth swear By come on seauen that al is lost and gone. **1605** CHAPMAN *All Fools* II. i. 42 Shall I be made A foolish novice ..By everie cheating come you seaven? **1680** COTTON *Compl. Gamester* (ed. 2) 121 (Hazzard) If again Seven be the Main, and the Caster throws eleven, that is a Nick. **1684** OTWAY *Atheist* v. i, Farewel for ever Old Hock..Seven and Eleven, Sink-Tray, and the Doublets. **1693** *Humours Town* 25 But at Seven and Eleven to shake away an Estate to known Rooks that live by the Dice, is an unaccountable piece of folly. **1726** *Art & Myst. Mod. Gaming* 13 Whereas of the 36 Changes 24 only are Mains, viz. 8 Fives and Nines, 10 Sixes and Eights, and 6 Sevens. **1814** *Hoyle's Games Impr.* 362 If seven is thrown for a main, and four the chance, it is 2 to 1 against the person who throws. **1839** THACKERAY *Lect. Fine Arts* ii. Wks. 1900 XIII. 273 A gambling-house, where many a bout of seven's-the-main..has been had.

† **b.** ***to set (all) on seven***: to make a desperate venture; hence, to make an attack. Cf. *to set (all) on six and seven*: see SIX *sb.* 5. *Obs.*

? *a* **1400** *Morte Arth.* 2131 Thus he settez on seuene with his sekyre knyghttez. *a* **1440** *Sir Degrev.* 1279 Ȝet wold I sett all one seven ffor Myldor the swet. *c* **1470** *Gol. & Gaw.* 668 With seymely scheildis to schew, thai set vpone seuin.

**c.** Phr. ***to throw a*** (or ***the***) ***seven*** and varr., to die; also, to faint or vomit. *Austral. slang.*

**1894** H. LAWSON *Martin Farrell* in *Coll. Verse* (1967) I. 269, I am pretty cronk and shaky—too far gone for hell or heaven, An' the chances are I'm goin'—that I'm goin' to 'do the seven'. **1899** W. T. GOODGE *Hits! Skits! & Jingles!* 17 You could bet on me chuckin' the seven If she slung me for some other bloke! **1908** [see MARBLE *sb.* 4 b]. **1932** A. UPFIELD *Royal Abduction* xxvi. 201 If she sees the thing she won't scream and throw a seven. She'll shoot. **1966** T. RONAN *Once there was Bagman* x. 217 The partially digested fruit must have swollen inside me, for before long I was chucking sevens around the flat as I had done a few years before when I had that touch of ptomaine poisoning.

**d.** ***seven-and-a-half***, a round game of cards in which the object is to make the number seven-and-a-half without exceeding it, by counting the pips on the cards.

Court cards (except for the King of Diamonds) are counted as worth half a point.

**1937** *Sun* (Baltimore) 26 Jan. 5/5 All other games and machines—..twenty-one, blackjack, seven-and-a-half, big Injun, Klondyke and craps are mentioned specifically—require a $50-per-month license. **1964** A. WYKES *Gambling* vii. 178 Blackjack and seven-and-a-half are found more rarely in the casinos of Europe than those of America.

**4.** A person or thing to which the number seven is attached in a set or series, e.g. in an eight-oared boat, the rower occupying the seat behind stroke. Also ***number seven***.

**1830** MARRYAT *King's Own* xli, 'Had not I better get a piece of duck for that?' 'No, no—number seven [*sc.* canvas] will do as well.' **1872** H. KINGSLEY *Hornby Mills*, etc. II. 59 You spoilt the boat by carrying away young Dickson,..and instead of rowing a good seven in the boat, he was bowled out with five runs at Kennington. **1891** *Cambr. Rev.* 12 Mar. 267/1 On Saturday with a new seven they rowed so well [etc.].

† **5.** A seventh in music. *Obs. rare.*

**1561** T. HOBY tr. *Castiglione's Courtyer* I. (1577) Ej, The verie sense of our hearing..oftentymes delyteth in a second or in a seauen. **1598** MARSTON *Sco. Villanie* III. xi. (1599) 228 When they sute Some harsher seauens for varietie My natiue skill discernes it presently.

**C.** Combinations.

**1. a.** In parasynthetic adjs. with suffix -ED[2], as ***seven-branched, -caped, -channelled, -chorded, -cornered, -eyed, -formed*** [after eccl. L. *septiformis*], ***-gated, -headed, -horned, -maned, -mouthed, -piled, -quired, -sealed, -sided, -stringed, -syllabled, -thorned, -tined, -toned, -tongued, -towered, -twined, -twisted***; **seven-footed**, seven feet high; † **seven-mountain-seated** = SEVEN-HILLED; † **seven-ported**, seven-gated. See also SEVEN-HILLED, SEVEN-LEAGUED.

**1863** STANLEY *Jew. Ch.* xvii. 377 On the left of the Entrance, stood the *seven-branched candlestick. **1859** *All Year Round* No. 34. 176 She calls the *seven-caped cabman. **1621** G. SANDYS *Ovid's Met.* I. (1626) 11 *Seuen-chanel'd Nile. **1647** H. MORE *Triumph* 27 But Æther..Tunes his *seven-corded Harp. **1841-6** LONGF. *To a Child* xii, Pythagoras..formed the seven-chorded lyre. **1611** FLORIO, *Settangolare*, *seuen-cornered. **1649** ROBERTS *Clavis Bibl.* 615 The vigilant *seven-eyed Providence of the Lord. [See Zech. iv. 10.] **1787** COLMAN *Inkle & Yarico* I. iii, Some grim, *seven-footed fellow ready to scalp us. **1561** DAUS tr. *Bullinger on Apoc.* (1573) 47 b, He is sayd..to haue the *seuen formed spirite, whom he also powreth out vpon the faithfull. **1581** A. HALL *Iliad* IV. 71 The *seauen gated Thebes towne. **1729** G. ADAMS tr. *Sophocles' Antig.* I. ii. II. 14 Round the seven gated City. **1849** M. ARNOLD *Strayed Rev.* 247 Seven-gated Thebes. **1561** DAUS *Bullinger on Apoc.* (1573) 5 b, The old *seuenheaded, and the new twohorned beast. **1646** [S. GORTON] (*title*) Simplicities Defence against Seven-headed Policy. Or Innocency vindicated, being unjustly accused by that Seven-headed Church-Government united in New England. **1810** SOUTHEY *Kehama* XIV. i, Joy in the seven-headed Idol's shrine! **1847** TENNYSON *Princess* Prol. 200 Seven-headed monsters only made to kill Time by the fire in winter. **1835** I. WILLIAMS in *Lyra Apost.* cxi[ii]. (1836) 139 And old imperial Rome Looks up, and lifts again half-dead Her *seven-horned head. **1849** ROSSETTI *Mary's Girlhood* ii, The seven-thorn'd briar and the palm *seven-leaved. **1949** S. SPENDER *Edge of Being* 29 The *seven-maned Golden lions. **1624** *Nero* II. (1633) C 3 b, Empire-crown'd *seven mountaine-seated Rome. **1590** SPENSER *F.Q.* I. v. 18 As when a wearie traueller that strayes By muddy-shore of broad *seven-mouthed Nile. **1850** MARG. FULLER *Wom. in 19th C.* (1862) 187 Their ever weeping skies and *seven-piled velvet of verdure. **1603** MURRAY in *Stirling's Darius* In praise Author, *Seauen-ported Thebes wals. **1897** F. THOMPSON *New Poems* 20 Where *seven-quired psalterings meet. **1826** E. IRVING *Babylon* II. 339 The 14th chapter, which is no portion of the *seven-sealed book. **1766** B. MARTIN *New Art Survey* 27 A Heptagon, or *seven-sided Figure. **1853** LYNCH *Self-Improvem.* iv. 96 Seven-sided subjects. **1965** J. A. MICHENER *Source* (1966) 251 He carried a small *seven-stringed lyre made of fir wood trimmed with antique bronze and strung with twisted sheep's gut. **1869** HOOD *Rules of Rhyme* 30 Tetrameter (*seven-syllabled). **1849** *Seven-thorned [see *seven-leaved*]. **1844** H. STEPHENS *Bk. Farm* II. 682 The implement..is now very frequently used with five tines, in place of the original *seven-tined implement. **1853** *N. Brit. Rev.* Feb. 399 The *seven-toned rhythm of the universe. **1913** E. STOCK *Heroic Bishop* ii. 12 In later days he became known in India as 'the *seven-tongued man'. **1959** E. POUND *Thrones* xcvi. 19 From the Palace, half-circle that street is, ending near the *seven-towered castello. **1853** *N. Brit. Rev.* Feb. 399 A pencil of light..*seven-twined and beautiful. *Ibid.*, A web of *seven-twisted thread.

**b.** *Nat. Hist.*

**1812** SHAW *Gen. Zool.* I. I. 190 *Seven-banded Armadillo. **1881** *Cassell's Nat. Hist.* V. 32 The third *seven-gilled Shark, called *Notidanus indicus*. **1591** PERCIVALL *Sp. Dict.*, *Siete en rama*, *seauen leaued grasse. **1822** *Hortus Anglicus* II. 175 Seven-leaved Tooth Wort. **1927** E. SITWELL *Rustic Elegies* 81 The seven-leaved man-plant. **1821** W. P. C. BARTON *Flora N. Amer.* I. 14 Leaves..*seven-nerved. **1812** SHAW *Gen. Zool.* VI. I. 55 The common or *seven-spotted Lady-Bird.

**2.** Combined with sbs. forming adjs., as ***seven-carbon, -course, -cubit, -eighths, -feet, -figure, -foot, -inch, -line, -octave, -ounce, -part, -point, -sacrament, -shilling, †-shot, -wire***; **seven-water**, containing seven parts of water to one of spirit. See also SEVEN-LEAGUE.

**1852** *Jrnl. Chem. Soc.* IV. 233 *Seven-carbon ether, Amylate of ethyle, or Ethylate of amyle. **1933** C. DAY LEWIS *Magnetic Mountain* 12 The penny-a-liner, the *seven-course diner. **1858** M. ARNOLD *Merope* 28 Agamemnon's unhappy,..world-fam'd, *Seven-cubit-statur'd son. **1881** O. WILDE *Poems* 117 The seven-cubit spear. **1939** M. B. PICKEN *Lang. Fashion* 123/1 **Seven-eighths length*, length of coat that is shorter than dress or skirt by a little less than one-eighth of the length from shoulder to hem. **1963** BIRD & HUTTON-STOTT *Veteran Motor Car* 186 A patent plate clutch, a new form of universal joint and seven-eighths-elliptic back springs of which the upper portions were cantilevered. **1979** *Tucson* (Arizona) *Citizen* 20 Sept. 2B/1, I was told that nothing will make my fall wardrobe look more up-to-date than a seven-eighths-length coat. **1782** 'J. H. ST. JOHN DE CRÈVECŒUR' *Lett. from Amer. Farmer* vi. 169 The right whale, or *seven feet bone..about sixty feet long. **1829** W. PEARSON *Pract. Astron.* II. 367 Mr. South's seven-feet instrument. **1842** *Penny Cycl.* XXIII. 498/1 *Seven-figure numbers to 100 thousand. **1865** DE MORGAN & SCHROEN (*title*) Seven-figure Logarithms. **1933** *Brit. Jrnl. Psychol.* XXIII. 358 Seven-figure logarithms were used in all calculational work. **1972** *Daily Tel.* 10 Apr. 3/8 Lord Salisbury..died before the Budget so his family cannot benefit from the top duty scale reduction..for seven-figure fortunes. **1935** *Discovery* Feb. 62/1 We read on p. 42 that Watt's 'Old Bess' had a single cylinder of 33 inches diameter—usually termed bore—and a *7 foot stroke. **1950** *Amer. Speech* XXV. 237/2 *Seven-foot line*, a line of sight seven feet off the property line from one seven-foot point to another. **1805** R. W. DICKSON *Pract. Agric.* I. Plate xx, A small *seven-inch drain. **1869** HOOD *Rules of Rhyme* 38 The *Seven-line Stanza. **1869** 'MARK TWAIN' *Innoc. Abr.* lix. 580 Any one can see a part of the unquestioned and undisputed Temple of Solomon, the same consisting of three or four stones lying one upon the other, each of which is about twice as long as a *seven-octave piano. **1885** *Encycl. Brit.* XIX. 77/2 Broadwood's seven-octave concert grands. **1896** KIPLING *Seven Seas* 97 (Lost Legion) We've shouted on *seven-ounce nuggets. **1883** *Grove's Dict. Mus.* III. 464/1 Several short pieces for female voices in *seven-part harmony. **1889** *Cent. Dict.*, **Seven-point*.., *a.*, related to seven points, as the seven-point circle. **1939** A. RODGER in F. C. Bartlett et al. *Study of Society* II. xi. 259 Causes of occupational failure..are..classifiable under seven headings. [*Note*] This seven-point plan, has, of course, other uses. **1977** *Word* 1972 XXVIII. 310 A seven-point scale. **1935** *Burlington Mag.* Feb. 81/1 The well-known series of *Seven Sacrament fonts, nearly all confined to.. Norfolk and Suffolk. **1955** M. D. ANDERSON *Imagery Brit. Churches* III. i. 54 There are about forty Seven Sacrament fonts... The bowls are carved with panels of figure sculpture, each representing one of the Sacraments. **1780** H. WALPOLE in Jesse *Selwyn & Contemp.* (1844) IV. 317 Last night I saw a proof-piece of *seven-shilling pieces struck in 1776. **1821** BYRON *Juan* III. lx, A lady with her daughters or her nieces Shine like a guinea and seven-shilling pieces. **1870** HENFREY *Engl. Coins* I. 87 One-third guinea or Seven-shilling piece. **1681** GREW *Musæum* IV. §ii. 366 A *Seven-Shot Gun, or a Gun which carries Powder and Bullets, for seven Charges and Discharges. **1688** HOLME *Armoury* III. ix. 382/1 A Wax Box, with a *seven Stone Ring set in it. **1836** MARRYAT *Three Cutters* ii, *Seven-water grog. **1876** PREECE & SIVEWRIGHT *Telegraphy* 242 To the old *seven-wire cable ..four new wires are added.

**3.** With sbs. FOOTER, POUNDER, SHOOTER (q.v.).

**1860** *Charleston* (S. Carolina) *Mercury* 6 Nov. 3/5 (Advt.), Allen & Wheelock's seven shooters. **1872** 'MARK TWAIN' *Roughing It* ii. 23, I was armed to the teeth with a pitiful little Smith & Wesson's seven-shooter..and it took the whole seven to make a dose for an adult. **1890** 'R. BOLDREWOOD' *Col. Reformer* (1891) 205 A very effective seven-shooter. **1896** *Daily News* 22 Apr. 7/7 A Hotchkiss seven-pounder. **1899** *Westm. Gaz.* 13 Sept. 3/3 That giant seven-footer.

**4. seven-bark**, (*a*) = 'nine-bark' (*Spiræa opulifolia* and other species); (*b*) *Hydrangea arborescens* (Syd. Soc. Lex. 1891); **seven-bore**, a shotgun with calibre seven; **seven-eye(s** [cf. G. *siebenauge*], the lamprey, in allusion to its seven gill-openings; **seven-gills**, a shark of the genus *Heptanchus* or *Notidanus* (Cent. Dict. 1891; cf. *seven-gilled* in 1 b); **seven-holes** = *seven-eyes*; † **seven-leaf, -leaves** = SEPTFOIL.

**1814** LEWIS & CLARKE *Trav. Missouri* (1815) III. 18 The *seven bark, or as it is usually denominated, the nine bark of the United States. **1863** W. C. BALDWIN *Afr. Hunting* ix. 375, I have shot for ten years constantly with a *seven-bore of his make. **1740** R. BROOKES *Art of Angling* I. xxxviii. 81 The Lamprey..is called by Dr. Plot, the Pride of the Isis, and by others, *Seven-Eyes. **1839** T. C. HOFLAND *Brit. Angler's Man.* xv. (1841) 186 The lamprey,..or seven eyes. **1883** DAY *Fishes Gt. Brit.* II. 360 Names—Lampern, lampron, and lamper-eel; nine-eyes, nine-holes, the eye and nasal orifice appear to be here counted; *seven-holes, when only the gill-openings are enumerated. *c* **1000** *Sax. Leechd.* I. 232 Ðeos wyrt þe man eptafilon & oðrum naman septifolium nemneð & eac sume men *seofenleafe hatað. **1657** COLES *Adam in Eden* 76 Tormentil, Setfoil or Seven-leaves.

**seven-day(s, -days'**, *attrib. phr.*

**1.** Consisting of or extending over seven days or a week. Also Comb. ***seven-days-long*** adj.

**1823** BENTHAM *Not Paul* 354 The seven-days-long false oath. **1862-3** (*title*) The Seven Days' Journal of Literature, Science, Art, and General Information. **1879** *Law Rep.* (*Ireland*) II. 386 It is competent to him..to exchange such six-day license for a general or seven-day license. **1885** 'H. CONWAY' *Family Affair* vii, The seven days wonder about the boy had almost died away.

**2.** ***seven-day(s disease***, a form of tetanus. ***seven-day fever***, a kind of relapsing fever; septan fever.

**1797** UNDERWOOD *Dis. Childhood* I. 377 Having escaped the seven-days-disease, they thrive well until the third or fourth month. **1888** FAGGE *Princ. Med.* (ed. 2) I. 153 *note*, Synonyms [of Relapsing Fever]..bilious remittent, seven-day fever, famine fever. **1891** *Syd. Soc. Lex.*, *Seven-day disease*, a term for *Trismus*.

† **'sevendele.** *Obs.* [f. *sevende* (see SEVENTH) + *dele* (see DEAL *sb.*[1] 1 b). Cf. OFris. *sawendel*, MHG. *sibenteil*.] Seventh part.

[*c* **1305**: see SEVEN A. 5.] **1387** TREVISA *Higden* (Rolls) I. 45 þe roundenesse of a cercle aboute conteyneþ þre so moche as þe brede [MS. *a adds* and the seuendele of the brede]. [*a* **1400-50** *Wars Alex.* 2342 A-losed mare of strenth þan I my-selfe or my seggis be þe seuent dele.]

† **seven-double**, *a. Obs.* [Cf. THREE-DOUBLE, etc.] Sevenfold.

*a* **1586** SIDNEY *Arcadia* I. Ecl. (1598) 86 Her hands which pierc'd the soules seau'n-double shield. **1611** FLORIO, *Setteplico*, seauen-fold, seauen-double.

**sevener** ('sɛv(ə)nə(r)). [-ER[1].] **a.** A criminal who is sentenced to seven years' imprisonment. **b.** A hit for seven runs.

**1897** P. WARING *Old Regime* 219 Pedder was a 'sevener', Blake was a 'niner'. **1898** in Bettesworth *Chats Cricket Field* (1910) 417 Stephens again hit me to leg, but this time he only made a sevener!

**sevenfold** ('sɛv(ə)nfəʊld), *a.*, *adv.*, *sb.* [OE. *seofonfeald* = OFris. *sivonvald, saunfald*, OHG. *sibunfalt* (MHG. *sibenvalt*, G. *siebenfalt*), ON. *sjaufalde*: see SEVEN and -FOLD.] **A.** *adj.*

**1.** Consisting of seven together or seven in one; having seven parts, divisions, elements, or units.

Formerly a frequent epithet of the river Nile.

*c* **960** ÆTHELWOLD *Rule St. Benet* (Schröer) xvi. 40 Ðæt seofonfealde ȝetæl bið þus þurh us ȝefylled, ȝif [etc.]. *c* **1055** tr. *Byrhtferth's Handboc* in *Anglia* VIII. 302 Witodlice hine ofer stigað þæt seofonfealde ȝetæl þære sunnan ȝeares daȝas. **1340** *Ayenb.* 268 þe dede of alle ine mennesse ys zeueuald: Hy lybbeþ, hy smackeþ, hy louyeþ, hy byeþ glede, hy heryeþ, hy byeþ zuyfte, hy byeþ zikere. **1590** GREENE *Orl. Fur.* 3 From seuenfold Nilus to Taprobany. **1606** SHAKS. *Ant. & Cl.* IV. xiv. 38 The seuen-fold shield of Aiax. **1634** SIR T. HERBERT *Trav.* 156 The Alcoran bids a seuen-fold daily worship. **1728** POPE *Dunc.* I. 244 The Master of the sev'nfold Face. **1807** CRABBE *Par. Reg.* III. 816 He fill'd the sevenfold surplice fairly out. **1864** PUSEY *Lect. Daniel* (1876) 168 A sevenfold period of years. **1882** *Encycl. Brit.* XIV. 696/1 A 'litania septiformis', that is to say a sevenfold procession of clergy, laity, monks, virgins, matrons, widows, poor, and children.

**b.** *Theol.* [tr. eccl.L. *septiformis.*] Applied to seven gifts of the Holy Ghost enumerated in Isaiah xi. 2 (Vulg. and LXX.); see also Rev. i. 4.

*a* **1000** ÆLFRIC *Hom.* (Thorpe) I. 326 We wurðiað þæs Halȝan Gastes to-cyme mid lofsangum seofon daȝas, forðan ðe he onbryrt ure mod mid seofonfealdre ȝife. *c* **1200** ORMIN Ded. 301 Þiss sefennfald godleȝȝc þatt Crist Uss dide þurrh hiss are. *a* **1400** *Minor Poems Vernon MS.* xx. 9 Þou art in ȝifte seuenfold, Godus riht hond ffinger art þou. *c* **1450** *Mirour Saluacioun* (Roxb.) 21 The sevenfold haly gast. **1526** *Pilgr. Perf.* (W. de W. 1531) 1 The vij folde graces of the holy goost. **1563** WINȜET tr. *Vincent. Lirin.* vii. Wks. (S.T.S.) 27 The seuinfald licht of the Haly Gaist. **1627** COSIN *'Veni Creator'*, Thou the anointing Spirit art, Who dost thy sevenfold gifts impart. **1738** WESLEY *Hymns, Creator Spirit, by whose Aid* iii, Plenteous of Grace, descend from high, Rich in thy sevenfold Energy. **1827** KEBLE *Chr. Y., Confirmation*, Draw, Holy Ghost, Thy sevenfold veil, Between us and the fires of youth.

**2.** Seven times as great or numerous; seven times increased or repeated. Hence, typically = very great, strong, etc.

*c* **1000** ÆLFRIC *Saints' Lives* (1881) I. 66 Iulianus wycode wið þa ea eufraten and him ofer-wacedon syfan-fealde weardes. **1382** WYCLIF *Isa.* xxx. 26 The liȝt of the sunne shal be seuene fold, as the liȝt of seuene daȝes. **1557** RECORDE *Whetst.* B ij, Septupla 7 to 1: 14 to 2..Seuenfolde. **1694** SALMON *Bate's Dispens.* (1713) 359/2 Chymists advise a sevenfold Rectification. **1736** *Gentl. Mag.* VI. 601/2 A seventy times seven-fold Vengeance from above. **1742** YOUNG *Nt. Th.* IV. 204 And foul transgression dips in sev'nfold guilt. **1852** BAILEY *Festus* 298 With A sevenfold blessing and inviolate rest, Yea, with His sabbath. **1872** SPURGEON *Treas. Dav.* Ps. lxxiv. 20 In some places a sevenfold night of superstition and unbelief has settled down. **1908** *Grove's Dict. Mus.* IV. 670/2 Among his [*sc.* Stainer's] most successful..pieces of church music must be named the well-known 'Sevenfold Amen'.

**3.** Seven in number. *poet.*

**1614** GORGES *Lucan* VI. 232 Here stood..Echions Thebes with seauenfolde gates. **16..** MIDDLETON, etc. *Old Law* I. i, Never did Greece, Not when she flourished in her sevenfold sages,..Produce a law more grave and necessary. **1812** CARY *Dante, Purg.* XXXII. 17, I mark'd that glorious army..turn, Against the sun and sevenfold lights, their front. **1887** MORRIS *Odyssey* XI. 263 Thebes of the gates sevenfold.

**B.** *adv.* (OE. had *seofonfealdlice*.)

**1.** In a sevenfold manner or degree; seven times. Hence, exceedingly, greatly.

*c* **1200** *Trin. Coll. Hom.* 171 Ðe rihtwise shulle ben seuefeald brihtere þane þe sunne. *a* **1225** *Juliana* 18 So mare ȝe me helpeð seoueuald to heouene. *a* **1340** HAMPOLE *Psalter* xi. 7 Syluyre examynd in fire proued of þe erth, purged seuenfald. **1382** WYCLIF *Dan.* iii. 19 He bad, that the fourneyse shulde be sette on fijre seuen fold hatter than it was wont for to be tendid. *c* **1460** *Towneley Myst.* ii. 373 For he that sloys yong or old It shall be punyshid sevenfold. **1567** *Gude & Godlie B.* 119 Seuinfald, their sin, gude Lord, mot punist be. **1607** SHAKS. *Timon* I. i. 289 Plutus the God of Gold Is but his Steward: no meede but he repayes Seuenfold aboue it selfe. **1632** W. FORSTER tr. *Oughtred's Circles of Proportion* 16 Let the ratio given be septuplicated, that is multiplied sevenfold into it selfe. **1849** MACAULAY *Hist. Eng.* I. iii. 340 The population of some [country towns] has multiplied sevenfold.

**2.** In seven folds or coils. *nonce-use.*

**1830** TENNYSON *Mermaid* ii, That great sea-snake..From his coiled sleeps in the central deeps Would slowly trail himself sevenfold Round the hall where I sate.

**C.** *sb.* (*nonce-uses.*) **a.** *the sevenfold*, a sevenfold amount. **b.** A group of seven.

**1382** WYCLIF *Prov.* vi. 31 Caȝt therewith forsothe he shal ȝelde the seuene fold [Vulg. *septuplum*]. **1864** PUSEY *Lect. Daniel* iv. 165 *note*, Some of the poets have said, who measure age ταῖς ἑβδομάσι, by the sevenfolds.

Hence †**sevenfold** *v.*, to make sevenfold; **'sevenfolded**, †**-folden** = SEVENFOLD *a.*; **'sevenfoldness**, the quality of being sevenfold.

**1611** FLORIO, *Settiplicare*, to *seauen-fold or double. **1590** SPENSER *F.Q.* II. v. 6 His *seuenfolded shield. **1876** MORRIS *Æneids* XII. 925 The..outer rim of that seven-folded shield. **1561** DAUS tr. *Bullinger on Apoc.* (1573) 66 b, I tolde you..how the seuen spirites of God are put for the *seuen folden, full, and perfect spirite of God. **1856** P. FAIRBAIRN *Prophecy* II. iii. 306 The *sevenfoldness ascribed to it must be..seven different states or forms of dominion.

**seven-hilled**, *a.* [Cf. L. *septicollis* (Prudentius).] Standing on seven hills: epithet of the city of Rome.

**1608** H. CLAPHAM *Errour Right Hand* 73 The Seauen hilled Citie (Rome). **1681** H. MORE *Expos. Dan.* Pref. 24 The seven-hilled City of Rome. *c* **1743** FRANCIS tr. *Hor., Sec. Poem* 117 Mayst thou, in all thy radiant course, Nothing more great than seven-hill'd Rome behold! **1818** BYRON *Ch. Har.* IV. lxxx, The Goth, the Christian, Time, War, Flood, and Fire, Have dealt upon the seven-hill'd city's pride. **1835** LYTTON *Rienzi* I. xii, Rome..with her seven-hilled diadem.

So **seven-hilly** *a. rare.*

**1561** DAUS tr. *Bullinger on Apoc.* (1573) 281 The seuen hilly Rome. **1824** BYRON *Def. Transf.* I. ii. 149 In old Rome, the seven-hilly, We'll revel at ease.

**sevenight(e**, etc., obs. forms of SENNIGHT.

**seven-league(d**, *a.* ***seven-league(d) boots*** [F. *bottes de sept lieues*], the boots in the fairy story of Hop o' my Thumb, which enabled the wearer to cover seven leagues at each step. Hence allusively = of enormous size or speed.

**1793** W. B. STEVENS *Jrnl.* 27 Feb. (1966) I. 70 Wrote to Dewe that I would put on my seven league boots next weekend and stretch my course to Appleby. **1799** SOUTHEY in Robberds *Mem. W. Taylor* (1843) I. 254 He has advanced with such seven-leagued strides as to overtake everybody. **1813** L. HUNT in *Examiner* 26 Apr. 262/2 Heaven grant he may not have put on his seven-league boots in vain! **1818** SCOTT *Rob Roy* iv, Giants with seven-leagued boots. **1826** —— *Woodst.* xxviii, Leave swelling phrase and seven-leagued words at home. **1849** HAWTHORNE *Twice-told T., Mr. Higginbotham's Catastr.*, The stranger on foot must have worn seven-league boots, to travel at such a rate. **1855** DICKENS *Dorrit* II. xii, With a..rapid step, as if he wanted to get his seven-league dress-shoes on and go round the world. **1890** 'R. BOLDREWOOD' *Miner's Right* (1899) 141/2 The sergeant strode forward with one of his characteristic seven-leagued movements.

*Comb.* **1864** A. J. WARDEN *Linen Trade* 240 The rapid progress in this seven-league-booted century.

**sevenpence** ('sɛv(ə)npəns). [f. SEVEN + PENCE.] A sum of money equal to seven pennies. Hence ˌ**sevenpence-'halfpenny**; ˌ**seven-'pennyworth**; (**-penn'orth**). Also *transf.*, †transportation for seven years.

**1671** E. LEIGH *Three Diatribes* 73 In Venice a Liver is about seven pence half peny. **1756** MRS. CALDERWOOD in *Coltness Collect.* (Maitland Club) 229 Peices..of sevenpence (called a skillen). **1821** P. EGAN *Life in London* II. iii. 230 My Lord, if I am to stand *seven-pence*, my Lord, I hope you'll take it into your consideration. **1824** URE tr. *Berthollet's Dyeing* I. 8 A measure of corn, which would at present cost sevenpence-halfpenny English. **1859** *Hotten's Slang Dict.*, *Seven pennorth*, transportation for seven years. **1865** RUSKIN *Sesame* i. §33 Now £700 is to £50,000 roughly, as sevenpence is to two thousand pounds. **1885** *Pall Mall Gaz.* 11 Mar. 4/1 Mary L. warmly asserted that 'she had been married at the sevenpence-halfpenny-church'... The sevenpence-halfpenny demanded pays only for the legal stamp.

**sevenpenny** ('sɛv(ə)npənɪ), *a.* [See PENNY *sb.* 10.] Costing or valued at sevenpence; hence, †trifling, contemptible. Also as *sb.*, a volume that costs sevenpence.

*c* **1380** *Antecrist* in Todd *Three Treat. Wyclif* (1851) 147 Antecrist makiþ hise [priests] knowen..bi her sevenpeny wedding & haliwater spryngynge. **1664** J. WEBB *Stone-Heng* (1725) 122 Readers would never be induced to swallow such a Gudgeon, as that seven-penny Men should be fed with Venison. **1711–12** SWIFT *Jrnl. to Stella* 8 Jan., I forgot Catherine's sevenpenny dinner. **1908** *Daily Chron.* 17 Aug. 5/4 The neatly-bound, well-printed sevenpenny or shilling volume of fiction. **1908** *Westm. Gaz.* 7 Sept. 4/3 The 'sevenpenny' has come to stay as a form for the circulation of English literature.

**seven sisters.** Also Seven Sisters. [See also SISTER *sb.*]

†**1.** The Pleiades. *Obs.*

**1412–20** *Lydg. Chron. Troy* II. 3334 Sche allone among þe susters seuene Schroudeth to vs schamfastly hir chere. [**1667** MILTON *P.L.* x. 673 To Taurus with the Seav'n Atlantick Sisters, and the Spartan Twins Up to the Tropic Crab.] **1742** GRAY *Propertius* II. 35 Whence the seven Sisters' congregated fires.

**2.** *Hist.* Seven cannon, resembling each other in size and make, cast by Robert Borthwick and used at the battle of Flodden.

? **1513** SKELTON *Agst. Scottes* 162 Your Seuen Systers, that gun so gay. *a* **1578** LINDESAY (Pitscottie) *Chron. Scot.* (S.T.S.) I. 259 Sewin cannonis that he tuik fourtht of the castill of Edinburgh, quhilk was callit the sewin sisteris. **1808** SCOTT *Marmion* IV. xxvii, Borthwick's Sisters Seven.

**3. a.** A name of two common spurges. *dial.*

**1886** BRITTEN & HOLLAND *Plant-n.*, Seven Sisters. *Euphorbia Helioscopia* and *E. Peplus*, in allusion to the seven branches of the stem. Co. Donegal, Ireland.

**b.** ***seven sister(s') rose***: a climbing rose producing densely clustered heads of white, cream, or pinkish flowers.

**1864** HIBBERD *Rose Bk.* 27 One of the finest is *Grevillei*, or the Seven Sisters' rose, a climber which grows with tremendous vigour. **1906** *Westm. Gaz.* 3 Aug. 10/1 The seven-sister rose Blossoms about the gabled close.

**4.** A popular name for *Malacocercus terricolor*, an Indian bird of gregarious habits.

**1878** P. ROBINSON *In Ind. Garden* 31 The Seven Sisters pretend to feed on insects, but that is only when they cannot get peas. **1901** KIPLING *Kim* 90 The chattering, gray-backed Seven Sisters.

**5.** The seven international oil companies noted for their dominant influence on the production and marketing of petroleum (see quot. 1976).

**1962** *Times* 29 Oct. 11/2 Mattei..liked to take the view that the 'Seven sisters'—as he called the majors—were making excessive profits out of both Governments and consumers. **1966** J. ALDRIDGE *Statesman's Game* xviii. 137 Was this..a challenge to the Seven Sisters of the oil world? **1976** *N.Y. Rev. Bks.* 15 Apr. 20/1 The group of international oil companies often referred to as 'the Seven Sisters'—Exxon, Mobil, Gulf, Standard Oil of California, Texaco, British Petroleum, and Royal Dutch Shell.

**6.** The group of long-established colleges (originally for women only) which were formerly regarded as the most prestigious women's colleges in the U.S. Cf. IVY LEAGUE.

**1962** *Changing Times* Apr. 37/2 The most difficult women's colleges to get into are the so-called 'Seven Sisters'—Barnard, Bryn Mawr, Mount Holyoke, Radcliffe, Smith, Vassar and Wellesley. **1979** *N.Y. Rev. Bks.* 17 May 43/2 (Advt.), Yale grad..would like to meet a 'seven sisters' graduate. **1980** L. BIRNBACH et al. *Official Preppy Handbk.* 86/2 The feminine equivalent of the Ivy League is the group of colleges known as 'The Seven Sisters'.

†**sevensithe(s**, *adv. Obs.* Forms: see SEVEN and SITHE *sb.*[1] [OE. *seofon síþa, síþum*: cf. ON. *sjausinnum*.] Seven times.

*c* **825** *Vesp. Psalter* cxviii. 164 Seofen siðum in deȝe lof ic seȝde ðe. *c* **950** *Lindisf. Gosp.* Matt. xviii. 21 Huu oft synngiȝa mæȝe in mec broðer min & ic forgefo him, wið sefo siða? *c* **1055** tr. *Byrhtferth's Handboc* in *Anglia* VIII. 303 Seofon siðon seofon beoð niȝon & feowertiȝ. *c* **1175** *Lamb. Hom.* 39 Seofesiðe brihtre þene þa sunne. *a* **1225** *Leg. Kath.* 1680, & alle þe burhmen seouen siðes brihtre þen beo þe sunne. *c* **1250** *Gen. & Ex.* 1825 Seue siðes he fell him biforen. *a* **1300** *Cursor M.* 1851 Til seuensith tuenti dais war gan. *a* **1300** *Floriz & B.* 650 Hu ihc hire boȝte apliȝt For seuesiþe of gold hire wiȝt. **1410** *26 Pol. Poems* ix. 89 Seuene syþes on þe day, Men seyn, the riȝtwis man doþ falle. **1483** *Cath. Angl.* 331/2 Seven sithe, *sepcies*. *c* **1530** *Crt. Love* 436 Seven sith at night thy lady for to please.

**seven sleepers.** [tr. L. *septem dormientes.*] Seven youths of Ephesus said to have hidden in a cave during the Decian persecution and to have slept there for several hundred years.

*c* **1000** ÆLFRIC *Saints' Lives* (1881) I. 488 Her efne ongin̄ð þæra eadiȝra seofon slæpera ðrowung. *c* **1310** *Leg. Saints* (MS. Ashm. 43) lf. 122 b, Seue sleparis. **1387** TREVISA *Higden* (Rolls) VII. 221 þe array of þe sevene slepers. *c* **1450** *Godstow Reg.* 19 Make us to study þe seuen slepars. **1599** NASHE *Lenten Stuffe* Wks. 1905 III. 163 The forty yeares vndermeale of the seauen sleepers. **1641** MILTON *Prel. Episc.* Wks. 1851 III. 77 The seven Sleepers, that slept..three hundred seaventy, and two years. **1781** GIBBON *Decl. & F.* xxxiii. (1787) III. 350 The memorable fable of the Seven Sleepers. **1831** CARLYLE *Sartor Res.* I. iv, A peal of laughter, enough to have awakened the Seven Sleepers!

**b.** Hence *sing.* **seven-sleeper**: *allusively*, one who has been asleep for years; *dial.* a dormouse or other hibernating (or migrating) animal. [So G. *siebenschläfer*.]

**1671** GLANVILL *Further Discov. M. Stubbe* 30, I thought there was something in 't, that you now publish him for a Seven Sleeper, that knows not the Transactions of the Learned World. **1837** CARLYLE *Fr. Rev.* II. III. i, But in seasons of Revolution..your miraculous Seven-sleeper might, with miracle enough, awake sooner. **1873** W. P. WILLIAMS & JONES *Somerset Gloss.*, *Seven-sleeper*, dormouse. **1899** H. C. HART in *Phil. Soc. Trans.* 13 *Seven sleepers.* The summer migrants supposed to sleep through the Winter.

**sevensome** ('sɛv(ə)nsəm), *sb.* and *a.* [f. SEVEN *a.* + -SOME. Cf. Fris. *saunesom.*]

**A.** *sb.* Seven together. *Sc.*

**17..** RAMSAY *Wyfe of Auchtermuchty* viii, He draif the gaislings forth to feid, Thair was but sevensum of them aw.

**B.** *adj.* Consisting of seven. *rare*$^{-0}$.

**1864** in WEBSTER.

Hence '**sevensomeness**, the quality of being 'sevensome'. *rare*$^{-1}$.

**1853** *N. Brit. Rev.* Feb. 398 The Sevensomeness of the microcosm. *Ibid.* 407 The sevensomeness of the luminous, or of the musical octave.

†**seven stars.** *Obs.* (Also ME. *sterres seven.*) [OE. *seofon steorran*: see SEVEN and STAR *sb.*, but OE. had also collect. neut. *sifun-, sibunsterri* = WFris. *saunstjerre*, WFlem. *zeven(ge)sterre*, MLG. *sevensterne*, Du. *zevengesternte*, OHG. *sibunstirni, -stirri* (MHG. *sibensterne*, G. *siebenstern* and *siebengestirn*), ON. *sjaustirni*. Cf. med.L. *septistellium*.] **a.** The Pleiades. **b.** ? The planets. **c.** The Great Bear.

*c* **725** *Corpus Gloss.* (Hessels) P 451 *Pliadas*, sibunsterri. *a* **900** *O.E. Martyrol.* 7 Nov. 202 Ond þonne gongað þa seofon steorran up on æfen. **1340–70** *Alex. & Dind.* 477 þe sonne set in his cours & þe seue sterres. *a* **1400–50** *Wars Alex.* 1961 (Dublin MS.) One of þe souerenest syres vndir þe seuen sternes. **1412–20** LYDG. *Chron. Troy* II. 3323 Pliades, þe seuene sterris briȝt, Of whiche sixe apperen to oure siȝt. **1483** *Cath. Angl.* 331/2 þe Seven sterns, *plias, septemtriolis, septemtrio.* **1513** DOUGLAS *Æneis* VIII. Prol. 151 The pleuch, and the polys, the planettis begane, The son, the sevin sternis, and the Charll wane. **1535** COVERDALE *Amos* v. 8 [so **1611**; *Revised* 1884 Pleiades]. **1577** B. GOOGE *Heresbach's Husb.* IV. (1586) 182 b, The best time for the first haruest, the rising of the seuen starres, or the beginning of May. **1605** SHAKS. *Lear* I. v. 38 The reason why the seuen Starres are no mo then seuen, is a pretty reason. **1630** *R. Johnson's Kingd. & Commw.* 85 Where so many kingdomes are united, making a more perspicuous shew over the universe, than the seven starres doe in the Firmament, over the single planets. **1754** J. HILL *Urania*, *Seven Stars*, a common denomination of the constellation, called, by astronomers, the Pleiades. [**1818** SCOTT *Hrt. Midl.* xxviii, Mrs. Bickerton, lady of the ascendant of the Seven Stars, in the Castle-gate, York.]

**1430–40** LYDG. *Bochas* I. ii. (1544) 5 b, He would haue raught vp to y^e^ sterres seuen. *c* **1450** METHAM *Wks.* (E.E.T.S.) 10 Hys bryght plowgh of sterrys, and eke the systyrrys at ther stent, The qwyche be namyd the sterrys seuyn. **1500–20** DUNBAR *Poems* xxv. 66 We pray to all the Sanctis of hevin, That ar aboif the sterris sevin.

**sevent**, obs. form of SEVENTH.

**seventeen** (ˌsɛv(ə)n'tiːn, 'sɛv(ə)ntiːn; see -TEEN), *a.* and *sb.* Forms: see SEVEN and -TEEN; also 3 sceoven-, 5 cevyn-; 3–5 -ten; 6 *Sc.* sewinteine, sewinttein. [OE. *seofontíene, -téne, -týne* = OFris. *sogen-, soven-, savntene* (WFris. *sauntsien*), OS. *sivontein*, MDu. *seventien* (Du. *zeven-*), OHG. **sibunzehan* (MHG. *sibenzehen*, G. *siebzehn*), ON. *sjautján* (Sw. *sjutton*, Da. *sytten*): see SEVEN and -TEEN.] The cardinal number next after sixteen, composed of ten and seven, represented by the symbols 17, XVII, xvii. **A.** *adj.*

**1.** In concord with a sb. expressed. Also, qualifying a higher numeral.

*c* **900** tr. *Bæda's Hist.* III. xxiv. (1899) 315 Wæs he Wulfhere Mercna cyning seafontyne winter. *c* **1205** LAY. 27200 Seouentene þusend selere cnihten. **1297** R. GLOUC. (Rolls) 6487 þe ȝer of grace a þousend & seuentene. *a* **1300** *Cursor M.* 9124 þis roboam þat i of mene, Regned winters seuentene. *c* **1330** *Arth. & Merl.* 8895 A kniȝt of dede vertuous þat on hur gat kniȝtes seuentene. *a* **1400–50** *Wars Alex.* 2105 Saudiours him to sewe seuyntene thousand. **1592** NASHE *P. Penilesse* Wks. 1904 I. 225 Scotland, Denmarke, and some more pure partes of the seauenteene Prouinces. *a* **1627** HAYWARD *Edw. VI* (1630) 94 A proclamation vnder the hands of seuenteen persons. **17..** in

*Ritson's Gammer Gurton's Garl.* (1783) 23 There was an old woman toss'd in a blanket, Seventeen times as high as the moon. **1777** (*title*) Seventeen Hundred and Seventy-Seven; or, a picture of the manners and characters of the age. **1814** SCOTT in *Lockhart* (1837) III. iii. 132 A..dissenting clergyman, who has..brought up..sixteen or seventeen children..upon L.150 a-year. **1879** MORLEY *Burke* 161 A Lyons silk weaver, working..for over seventeen hours a day. *a* **1890** LIDDON *Life Pusey* (1893) I. iv. 76 In all Germany the number of professors who then contended for the truth of the Gospel..was thought to be seventeen.

**2.** With various ellipses, esp. of *years*.

***sweet seventeen*** is used typically for the most attractive period of a girl's life. ***the seventeen-eighties***: the decade extending from 1780 to 1789.

*c* **1290** *S. Eng. Leg.* 264/107 3eot heo leouede twenti 3er after þe seuentene bi-fore þat heo ne et no mannische mete bote weodes and wilde more. **1375** BARBOUR *Bruce* XIII. 645 Scho set hym in so hard assay, That he with sevintene in a bat Wes fayne for to hald hame his gat! *c* **1386** [see SEVEN A. 1 d]. *a* **1568** ASCHAM *Scholem.* (1904) 205 From seuentene to seuen and twentie (the most dangerous tyme of all a mans life). **1662** STILLINGFL. *Orig. Sacræ* III. iv. §9 That the posterity of Noah might beget children at seventeen. **1712** STEELE *Spect.* No. 266 ¶2 A slim young girl about Seventeen. **1767** H. WALPOLE in Jesse *Selwyn & Contemp.* (1843) II. 190 The lottery tickets which I have bought for you at twelve pounds seventeen and sixpence apiece. **1855** TENNYSON *Brook* 113 Claspt hands and that petitionary grace Of sweet seventeen subdued me ere she spoke. **1878** H. S. LEIGH *Town Garland* 29 The gushing heart of seventeen. **1896** E. V. LUCAS *Willow & Leather* (1898) 32 The Hambledon Club's ground was changed..somewhere in the seventeen-eighties.

†**3.** = SEVENTEENTH. *Obs.*

*c* **1400** *Destr. Troy* 6369 Polidarius, the porknell, and his pere Machaon, Suet with the xvij, sad men & noble. **1551** RECORDE *Pathw. Knowl.* I. xxviii, As the seuentene conclusion doth teache. **1580** in *Cath. Tractates* (S.T.S.) 68 As hie declaris in the sewintein buik of the Citie of God.

**4.** *Comb.* (chiefly parasynthetic), as ***seventeen-branched*** adj.; ***seventeen-day, -foot, -mark, -mile***, attrib. phr.; **seventeen-hander**, a horse of 17 hands; **seventeen-hunder linen** (*Sc.*), linen in the weaving of which 1700 threads go to the warp; **seventeen-year cicada** = *seventeen year(s') locust*; **seventeen-year(s') locust**, *Cicada septemdecim* (see quot. 1882).

**1861** HAGEN *Synopsis Neuroptera N. Amer.* 207 Sector 1 *seventeen-branched. **1890** BILLINGS *Nat. Med. Dict.*, **Seventeen-day fever*, relapsing fever. **1900** KIPLING in *Daily Express* 29 June 4/5 The *seventeen-foot Union Jack. **1886** MISS BRADDON *One Thing Needful* xxii, The horses were her own particular *Seventeenhanders, grand, upstanding bays. **1790** BURNS *Tam o' Shanter* 154 Snaw-white *seventeen hunder linnen! **1861** *Two Cosmos* I. 228 Sheets o' seventeen hunder linen. **1824** G. CHALMERS *Caledonia* III. iv. 438 Gilbert Macdoual..who held the *seventeen-mark lands. **1897** *Outing* XXX. 357/1 Regular watches were once more set upon the boats as they entered the upper or *seventeen-mile level. **1870** *Amer. Naturalist* III. 106 The eggs and young of the *seventeen-year Cicada. **1950** *Chicago Daily News* 13 Jan. 42 The periodic or 17-year cicada lives the longest of any known insect. **1817** *Columbian Centinel* (Boston) 14 May 1/4 The southern papers have announced that the present is the year for the appearance of what is called..the *Seventeen Years Locust. .. The insect lives above ground about two months, and 17 years in it. **1843** H. D. THOREAU *Let.* 7 July (1958) 121 Have you seen the Seventeen year locust in Concord? **1882** *Cassell's Nat. Hist.* VI. 112 One North American species is called the Seventeen-years' Locust (*Cicada septendecim*) because it is said to appear only at intervals of seventeen years in any given locality. **1975** *Islander* (Victoria, B.C.) 3 Aug. 3/1 The juice-sucking 17-year locusts—which are really cicadas—were also around.

**B.** *sb.* The abstract number seventeen; the symbol representing this.

**1594** NASHE *Unfort. Trav.* Wks. 1905 II. 211, I vp with a long circumstance, alias, a cunning shift of the seuenteenes. **1596** HARINGTON *Apol. Ajax* Aa2, Lyke a trycke of seuenteene in a sinkapace.

**seventeenth** (ˈsɛv(ə)ntiːnθ, sɛv(ə)nˈtiːnθ), *a.* and *sb.* Forms: α. 1 **seofonteȝeða, -teoȝeða, -tiȝeþa, -teoða**, 4–5 **seventeþe**; β. 3–4 **seventenþe**, 5 **-tenyth**, 6 **-tenth**, 6– **teenth**; γ. 4–5 **sevintende**. [OE. *seofontéoþa*, f. *seofontíene* SEVENTEEN: see -TEENTH. The later developments (β and γ forms) are parallel with those of FIFTEENTH (q.v.); with the γ-form cf. ON. *sjautjánde*. See also TENTH.]

**A.** *adj.* The ordinal number corresponding to the cardinal seventeen; qualifying a sb. expressed or implied.

*c* **900** tr. *Bæda's Hist.* I. v, Severus casere..se wæs seofonteoȝeða [*v.r.* seofonteoða] fram Agusto. *Ibid.* III. xxiv, þi seofanteoþan [*v.r.* -tiȝeþan] dæȝe Kalendarum Decembrium. *c* **1300** *Havelok* 2559 Of marz þe seuentenþe day. *c* **1400** *St. Alexius* (Laud 108) 325 At þe seuenteþe 3eres ende. *c* **1400** *Rule St. Benet* (Prose) xii. 17 þe hundred seuintende [psalm]. *c* **1450** *Godstow Reg.* 147/27 The 3ere of þe reyne of kyng Edwarde þe seventenyth. **1530** PALSGR. 372 *Dixseptiesme*, sevynteenth. **16..** MIDDLETON, etc. *Old Law* v. i, September the seventeenth. **1805** WORDSW. *Prelude* II. 386 My seventeenth year was come. **1839** DE LA BECHE *Rep. Geol. Cornwall*, etc. xv. 590 About the end of the seventeenth century. **1862** MISS BRADDON *Lady Audley* xxxv, He..married me three months after my seventeenth birthday.

**B.** *sb.* **1.** A seventeenth part.

**1728** CHAMBERS *Cycl.* s.v. *Measure*, One Paris Ell, and fifteen Seventeenths.

**2.** *Mus.* A note seventeen degrees above or below a given note (both notes being counted); the interval between, or consonance of, two notes seventeen degrees apart; a chord containing this interval. Also, an organ stop (see quot. 1855.)

**1597** MORLEY *Introd. Mus.* 126 Though I do in it talke of fifteenth and seuententhes, yet are these cordes seldome to be taken in three parts. **1609** DOWLAND *Ornith. Microl.* 79 A seuenteenth, which is equall to a third, and a tenth. **1694** W. HOLDER *Princ. Harmony* 102 A Seventeenth Major. **1797** *Encycl. Brit.* (ed. 3) XII. 509/2 The double octave of the third is called a seventeenth. **1855** HOPKINS *Organ* 120 *Tierce-Seventeenth*. A Stop formed of open metal cylindrical pipes, the pitch of which is a major third above the Fifteenth, or a seventeenth above the Diapasons. **1897** tr. *Riemann's Dict. Mus.* 372/1 The (major) Seventeenth (second octave extension of the major third..),..the Minor Seventeenth (second octave extension of the minor third). *Ibid.* 730/1 *Seventeenth*, the seventeenth degree of the scale; also called the 10th or 3rd.

Hence **seven'teenthly** *adv.*, in the seventeenth place (in an enumeration).

**1623** in *Fasti Aberd.* (1854) 283 Seventintlie, that [etc.]. *c* **1643** CLEVELAND *Let.* Poems, etc. (1677) 127 Cheverel-Lungs that will stretch as far as Seventeenthly. **1725** tr. *Dupin's Eccl. Hist. 17th C.* VI. II. iv. 250 Seventeenthly, That baptiz'd Infants..ought to be instructed in the Faith of Jesus Christ. **1819** SCOTT *Leg. Montrose* xiv, The Captain heard sixteenthly—seventeenthly—eighteenthly, and to conclude, with a sort of feeling like distracted despair.

**seventh** (ˈsɛv(ə)nθ), *a.* and *sb.* Forms: α. *north.* (and *Kentish*). 1 **seofunda, -onda, siofunda**, 2 **seofende**, 3 (*Ormin*) **se(o)ffnde, sefennde**, 3–4 **sevende**, 3–5 **sevend**, 4 **zevende, seyvend(e**, 4–5 **sevind, -ynd**. β. 1 **seofoþa, -eða, sufoþa**, 1–2 **-oþe**, 2 **seofeþe**, 3 **seoveþe**, 3–4 **sovethe, seveþe**; 3 **sefþe**, 5 **sefth**. γ. 3 **seouenþe**, 3–5 **seventhe**, 4 **sevenethe, sefnthe**, 4–5 **seveneth**, 5 **sevynthe, (senthe)**, 6 **sevoenthe, sevinth**, 6–7 **seaventh**, 4– **seventh**. δ. *north.* 4 **seyvent, sevente, sewinte, sevynte**, 4–6 **sevent, sevint**, 4, 6 **sewint**, 5 **sevenete, sente, (senfte)**, 6 **sewent**. [Formations of different types are here represented: α. OE. (Anglian) *seo-, siofunda*, ME. (Northern and Kentish) *sevende*, corresp. to OFris. *siugunda, sogunda, savnda* (mod. *saunde*), OS. *sivondo*, OHG. *sibunto* (MHG. *sibente, sibende*, G. *siebente*), ON. *sjaunde* (Norw. *sjaunde*, Sw. *sjunde*, Da. *syvende*):—OTeut. **sebundo-*; cf. late OE. *niȝende* ninth, ME. *tende* tenth. β. OE. *seofoþa, -eþa* = OS. *sivoðo*:—OTeut. **sebunþo-*, f. **sebun* SEVEN; cf. OE. *niȝoþa* ninth, *téoþa* tenth. γ. ME. *seventhe*, a new formation on SEVEN and -TH[2]; cf. NINTH, TENTH. The δ-forms exhibit the by-form (*-t*) of the suffix characteristic of Sc.] The ordinal number corresponding to the cardinal number SEVEN. **A.** *adj.*

**1. a.** In concord with a sb. expressed or understood.

α. *c* **950** *Lindisf. Gosp.* Matt. xxii. 26 ðelic ðe æftera & ðe ðirda wið to ðæm seofunda [*c* **975** *Rushw. Gosp.* siofund; *c* **1000** *Ags. Gosp.* seofoþan, *v.rr.* seofeðan, sufoþon; *c* **1160** *Hatton Gosp.* seofende, *v.r.* seofeðen]. *c* **1200** ORMIN 4168 þe sefennde, þe lattste da33. *Ibid.* 5598 þe seoffnde 3ife Godess Gast Her 3ifeþþ. *c* **1250** *Gen. & Ex.* 445 Lamech is at ðe sexte kne, ðe seuende man after adam. **1340** *Ayenb* 3 þe zeuende bene of þe holy pater noster. *c* **1350** *Leg Rood* (1871) 93 For hunger he cried on þe seuynd day. *c* **1400** *Rule St. Benet* (Prose) vii. 14 þe seuind degrece o mekeness. *c* **1400** MAUNDEV. (Roxb.) xvi. 73 þis faire lady sall com to him at þe seuend day, or þe thridd day, end.

β. **971** *Blickl. Hom.* 47 Ærest on ærne morȝen..seofoþan siþe on uhtan. *c* **1175** *Lamb. Hom.* 43 Innan þan sea weren vii bittere uþe..þe seofeþe [wes] ful stunch. *a* **1225** *St. Marher.* 8 þe seoueðe time of þe dei. **1297** R. GLOUC. (Rolls) 2577 þe seueþe 3er it was after þat hii to londe come. *Ibid.* 9068 In þe seueþe & tuenti 3er of þe kinges crouninge. *a* **1300** *Signs bef. Judgm.* 97 in *E.E.P.* (1862) 10 þe sefþe dai hit sal grow a3e. **1393** LANGL. *P. Pl.* C. XVII. 144 The syxte, hit is a paþ of pees... The seueþe, hit is a welle of wysedome. *c* **1475** *Partenay* 4427 Thys Grymold is the fifte Geant found, The sixte, or the sefth of thaim hath be last. *a* **1550** *Six Town Chron.* (1911) 186 Kyng henry the sevethe.

γ. *c* **1290** *Beket* 1815 in *S. Eng. Leg.* 158 þe seuenþe 3er þat he wende furst out of engelonde. *c* **1374** CHAUCER *Troilus* II. 681 Blisful Venus wel arayed Sat in here seuenethe hows of heuene þo. **1390** GOWER *Conf.* III. 130 The sefnthe sterre in special Of this science is Arial. *c* **1425** *Eng. Conq. Irel.* xxiv. 58 He arryued, the yer of hys kyngedome, senthe [*v.r.* the Senfte]. *c* **1430** *Chev. Assigne* 42 Sex semelye sonnes & a dow3ter þe seueneth. **1493** *Dives & Pauper* III. xiii. 1j b, God bad reste in the seuynthe day. **1596** DALRYMPLE tr. *Leslie's Hist. Scot.* I. 84 Henrie the seuinth. **1605** SHAKS. *Macb.* IV. i. 118 Another yet? A seaventh? **1667** MILTON *P.L.* VIII. 128 Thir wandring course..In six thou seest, and what if sev'nth to these The Planet Earth..Insensibly three different motions move? *Ibid.* XI. 696 Hee the seventh from thee, whom thou beheldst The onely righteous in a World perverse. **1710** SWIFT *Jrnl. to Stella* 31 Oct., I have sent my seventh [letter] to your fourth, young women. **1899** *Allbutt's Syst. Med.* VII. 353 In both cases the focus [of disease] seems to have affected the issuing seventh [cerebral nerve].

δ. *c* **1375** *Cursor M.* 6844 (Fairf.), vj. dayes sal 3e wirke..and 3e sal rest þe seyuent day. *c* **1375** *Sc. Leg. Saints* vii. (*Jacobus Minor*) 95 The sewynt 3ere of his bischophad. *c* **1380** WYCLIF *Sel. Wks.* III. 169 þe sevent werke of mercy. **1456** SIR G. HAYE *Law Arms* (S.T.S.) 23 Pape Gregore the sevynt. *a* **1500** *Signs of Doomsday* 95 in *Brome Bk.* 74 The sente day schall fall down Chyrch, and castyll. **1576** in *Oppress. Orkney & Zetld.* (1859) 47 This Sewint Article. **1588** A. KING tr. *Canisius' Catech.* 183 The sext is bontie... The Sewent is gentilnes.

**b.** *ellipt.* for *seventh day, chapter, regiment*, etc. ***to commit the seventh*** (slang), to transgress the seventh commandment, to commit adultery.

**1598** J. CHAMBERLAIN *Lett.* (Camden) 29 The seventh of this moneth. **1674** BREVINT *Saul at Endor* 298 The seventh of St. John's Revelation. **1841** LEVER *O'Malley* cxvii, He ordered me to picket two squadrons of the seventh. **1874** HARDY *Far fr. Madding Crowd* viii, As soon as he could..fancy he was doing wrong and committing the seventh.

**2. a.** ***seventh part***, or †***deal*** (see also SEVENDELE), one of the seven equal parts into which a thing may be divided.

*c* **1290** *S. Eng. Leg.* 318/657 þare nis bote þat seouenþe del þat men woniez on, i-wis. *Ibid.* 318/665 þe seuenþe part. **1387** TREVISA *Higden* (Rolls) I. 45 þe seuenþe parte of þe þridde. *a* **1400–50** *Wars Alex.* 2157 þai pleyne more þe pouirte & þe pite of þar horsis þan þe soro3e of þam-selfe by þe seuynt parte [*Dubl. MS.* seuent dele].

**b.** ***seventh heaven***, see HEAVEN *sb.* 5 c, 7 c.

Hence ***seventh-heaven-arian*** (nonce-wd.), one who is always in the seventh heaven of ecstasy.

**1818** SCOTT *Hrt. Midl.* xxxiii, You will find that, when you have heard my counsel, you may go to the seventh heaven with it in your pocket, if you have a mind, and not feel yourself an ounce heavier in the ascent. **1857** KINGSLEY *Two Y. Ago* II. 104 What a blue stocking, pre-Raphaelite seventh-heaven-arian she would have been. **1892** MRS. CLIFFORD *Aunt Anne* xiv, Florence was in a seventh heaven of happiness.

**c.** ***seventh wave***, the wave traditionally thought to be the biggest in an increasing swell of the sea; also *fig.*, a culminating act or experience.

**1891** KIPLING *City of Dreadful Night* i. 3 Six moderately pure mouthfuls of [Calcutta] air may be drawn without offence. Then comes the seventh wave and the queaziness of an uncultured stomach. **1908** G. MEREDITH *Let.* 24 Jan. (1970) III. 1623 You know the seventh wave. There must be a gathering of the waters before a big surge is thrown on shore. **1940** L. MACNEICE *Poems 1925–1940* 251 The Northern Lights and the Seventh Wave. **1976** E. WARD *Hanged Man* i. 3 A seventh wave pulled him backwards into undertow.

**3.** = SEVENTHLY. *rare.*

**1576** GASCOIGNE *Droome of Doomes day* Wks. 1910 II. 330 Seventh, he ought in all things to [etc.]. **1840** *Dom. Brewing* 8 The following articles only are requisite... Seventh, a stirring stick.

**B.** *sb.* **1.** = Seventh part.

**1557** RECORDE *Whetst.* B ij b, *Sesquiseptima*. 8 to 7 : 16 to 14..(1⅐) a seuenth more. **1623** J. JOHNSON *Arith.* 229 Because your fractions are seuenths, cut off 7 figures. **1762** RAMSBOTTOM *Fractions Anatomized* 33 For if to 4 Sevenths We add 4 Eighths..it is neither 8 Sevenths nor 8 Eighths. **1844** R. ROUSE *Turf Betting* 8 Different denominators, as fifths, sevenths, elevenths. **1897** GÜNTHER in Mary Kingsley *W. Africa* 711 Eye two-sevenths of the length of the head.

**2.** *Mus.* **a.** A note seven degrees (see DEGREE *sb.* 11 a) above or below a given note (both notes being counted); the note immediately below the octave in a scale, = *leading note*. **b.** The interval between two notes seven degrees apart; it is either *major, minor*, or *diminished*: see these words. **c.** (In full, ***chord of the seventh***.) A chord consisting of a note together with its third, fifth, and seventh: denominated from that note of the scale which forms the root, as ***dominant seventh, tonic seventh***; also ***minor, diminished seventh*** (see quots. 1880, 1883), ***leading seventh*** (see LEADING *ppl. a.* 1 b).

**1591** J. FARMER *Plainsong* B vj, 2 parts in one in the seuenth, the Basse before, the Meane follow a sembreefe, the plainsong in the midst. **1597** MORLEY *Introd. Mus.* 71 *Phi.* Which distances make discord..? *Ma.*..a second, a fourth, a seuenth. **1694** W. HOLDER *Princ. Harmony* 169 These Discords, the Tritone, and Semidiapente; as also, the Seconds, and Sevenths, are of very great use in Music. **1730** *Treat. Harmony* 15 The Seventh of the key. **1752** tr. *Rameau's Treat. Mus.* 28 The perfect Chord, and that of the Seventh. **1797** *Encycl. Brit.* (ed. 3) XII. 508/2 An interval consisting of four tones and two semitones, as from *re* to *ut*, is called a *seventh minor*. **1818** T. BUSBY *Gram. Mus.* 326 The chord of the Seventh is susceptible of three changes. **1839** *Penny Cycl.* XV. 297/1 The dominant 7th and the diminished 7th, or their inversions. **1855** BROWNING *Toccata of Galuppi's* vii, Those lesser thirds so plaintive.. Those commiserating sevenths. **1880** *Grove's Dict. Mus.* I. 673 The use of the minor seventh, which we call the Dominant seventh, without preparation. **1883** *Ibid.* III. 477/2 The chord of the Diminished seventh..is in its complete form composed of a set of minor thirds.

**seventh-day.** (Also 5–6 *north.* sevent, -ynt.) †**1.** = WEEK'S-MIND. *Obs.*

**1462** *Test. Ebor.* II. 256, I wille that I be brought forthe at the day of beriall as my degre askis withouten any sevent-day. **1527** *Ibid.* V. 238, I witt a quarter wheate and ij barils bere to be delt in the kirke of Hornese opon my sevynt daye.

**2. a.** The seventh day of the week, Saturday; the (Jewish) Sabbath; *transf.* Sunday. Also *attrib.*

**1692** T. WATSON *Body Divinity* 332 The old Seventh-day Sabbath (which was the Jewish Sabbath) is abrogated. **1710** O. SANSOM *Acc. Life* 226 On the Seventh Day we went to Youghall, and on the First Day had two Meetings there. **1870** CONWAY *Earthward Pilgr.* xxviii. 345 The sanctity of the Seventh Day is the survival of the old worship of Ashtaroth. **1872** O. W. HOLMES *Organ-Blower* 27 When the seventh day's sunshine falls Through rainbowed windows on the walls. **1885** R. BUCHANAN *Matt* iii, I thought her ordinary costume far more becoming than her seventh-day finery.

**b.** In the designations of bodies of Christians who observe the seventh day of the week

(Saturday) as the principal day of rest and religious observance.

*Seventh-day Adventists*: a millenarian sect holding sabbatarian principles. *Seventh-day Baptist*: see SABBATARIAN *sb.* 3. † *Seventh-day man*: see TRASKITE.

**1684** LUTTRELL *Brief Rel.* (1857) I. 302 The seventh day minister, in Newgate. **1694** E. CHAMBERLAYNE *Pres. St. Eng.* (ed. 18) III. i. 378 Traskitts, now called Seventh-day-men, who keep the Jewish Sabboth. **1784** BACKUS *Ch. Hist. New Eng.* II. Index 15 Seventh-day Baptists. **1860** *Advent Rev. & Sabbath Herald* (Washington) 23 Oct. 179/2 *Resolved*, that we take the name of Seventh-day Adventists. **1876** *Direct. Amer. Publ.* 19 in *Amer. Catal.* (1880), Seventh Day Adventists. **1880** *Libr. Univ. Knowl.* (U.S.) s.v., Traces of seventh-day keepers are found in the days of Gregory I. **1931** *Times Lit. Suppl.* 19 Feb. 139/2 Seventh Day Adventist missions. **1956** R. MACAULAY *Towers of Trebizond* v. 49 The local Anglican priest .. would give him news of the Seventh-Day Adventist Mission. **1977** *Hongkong Standard* 12 Apr. 5/1 Seventh Day Adventist Church Conference.

**seventhly** ('sɛv(ə)nθlɪ), *adv.* [f. SEVENTH *a.* + -LY².] In the seventh place (in an enumeration).

*c* **1532** DU WES *Introd. Fr.* in *Palsgr.* 929 Seventhly, *septiesmement.* **1574** WHITGIFT *Def. Answ.* XVII. 631 Master Gualter .. sayth: He comprehendeth seuenthly in this order, gouernours vnder whom [etc.]. **1648** D. JENKINS *Wks.* 38 Seventhly, we maintaine that the King is the onely supreme Governour in all causes. **1725** *Fam. Dict.* s.v. *Rules*, Seventhly, Galloping is the last, and must be join'd to all the other Paces. *a* **1887** JEFFERIES *Field & Hedgerow* (1889) 328 Seventhly, no one can find these footpaths, which probably led nowhere.

**b.** As *sb.* with ref. to the heads of a sermon.

**1815** SCOTT *Paul's Lett.* i. (1816) 4 The Parson has spared his flock one Seventhly of his text. **1860** DICKENS *Uncomm. Trav.* ix, I have been .. catechised respecting Boanerges Boiler, his fifthly, sixthly, and his seventhly.

**'seventh-night.** *Obs.* [f. SEVENTH *a.* + NIGHT.] = SENNIGHT.

**1625** B. JONSON *Staple of N.* I. v. 86 His Father dy'd on this day seuenth-night. **1672** LOCKE *Let. to Mapletoft* 19 Oct., That day seventhnight I parted from you.

**seventieth** ('sɛv(ə)ntɪɪθ), *a.* Forms: 3-4 seventiþe, 4 seveteþe, (*north.* seven-, seyvintiand), 4-6 seventeþe, 6 seventyth, 7 seaventieth, 7- seventieth. [f. next + *-eth*, -TH². The forms in Cursor Mundi are after the ON. ordinal ending *-tugonde.*] The ordinal numeral corresponding to the cardinal SEVENTY.

**1297** R. GLOUC. (Rolls) 5730 Yssryned he was nyn hondred & on & seuentiþe ȝere. **13..** *Cursor M.* 21209 (Gött.) þe seuentiand and feird ȝere [*Fairf.* seyuintiand]. **1382** WYCLIF *Zech.* i. 12 This is now the seuentithe ȝeer. **1530** PALSGR. 372 *Septantiesme*, seventyth. **1570** LEVINS *Manip.* 88/41 Yᵉ Seuenteth, *septuagesimus.* **1611** FLORIO, *Settuagesimo*, the seauentieth. **1635** A. STAFFORD *Fem. Glory* 206 She liv'd to her seaventieth yeare. **1900** (*title*) Report of the Seventieth Meeting of the British Association for the Advancement of Science.

**seventy** ('sɛv(ə)ntɪ), *a.* and *sb.* Forms: [1 hundseofontiȝ, -sifontiȝ, etc.: cf. SEVEN], 3 seoventi, (*Ormin*) seof(f)enntiȝ, 4 seyventi, sewinty, zeventy, 4, 6 sevinty, -te, 5 ceventye, senty, 7 seaventy, 3- seventy. [OE. (*hund*)*seofontiȝ* = OFris. *siugun-*, *sogen-*, *soventich* (mod. *sauntich*), OS. *sivuntig* (MLG. *seven-*, *soventich*, MDu. *seventich*, Du. *zeventig*), OHG. *sibunzug* (MHG. *sibenzec*, etc., G. *sieb(en)zig*), ON. *sjau tiger* (Norw. *sjautti*, *sytti*, Sw. *sjuttio*): see SEVEN and -TY.] **A.** *adj.*

**1.** The cardinal number equal to seven tens, represented by 70 or lxx: **a.** with sb. expressed or implied in the context.

*c* **1200** ORMIN 4319 þe feorþe staff iss nemmnedd O & seofenntiȝ bitacneþþ. *a* **1300** *Cursor M.* 1486 Til þat nine hundret yeir war gan And seuenti. **1340** *Ayenb.* 1 Blind, and dyaf, and alsuo domb. Of zeuenty yer al uol rond. *a* **1400-50** *Wars Alex.* 634 In foure or in fyfe ȝere he ferre was in lare þan othire at had bene þare seuynte wynter. *c* **1440** *Promp. Parv.* 67/2 Cevyntye, *Septuaginta.* **1530** PALSGR. 367 *Septante*, seventy. *a* **1674** CLARENDON *Hist. Reb.* XI. §151 A ship .. that carried seventy guns. **1814** WORDSW. *Excurs.* II. 600 The still contentedness of seventy years. **1848** THACKERAY *Van. Fair* li, 'Lend me a hundred, Wenham, for God's sake,' poor Rawdon said—'I've got seventy at home.'

**b.** With ellipsis of *years* (*of age*).

*c* **1645** HOWELL *Lett.* (1650) II. 114 He .. who at seventy odd forsakes this light. **1729** POPE *Let. to Swift* 28 Nov., My first friendship at sixteen, was contracted with a man of seventy. **1831** SCOTT *Ct. Rob.* vi, His age was some seventy and upwards. **1884** RYLE *Princ. Churchmen* (ed. 2) 424 By the time we are seventy, our memories and intellects begin to fail.

**c.** Specific elliptical uses.

*the Seventy*: (*a*) the seventy disciples of our Lord whose mission is recorded in Luke x. 1; (*b*) the Seventy Interpreters = SEPTUAGINT 1; (*c*) in the organization of Mormonism, a body of seventy elders acting as missionaries.

**1520** NISBET *N.T.* (S.T.S.) I. 10 He sendithe the sevinte befoire him to preche. **1614** RALEIGH *Hist. World* I. vii. §8. 110 The Geneua Translation calls it [Gopher] Pinetree, the Rabbine Cedar, the Seuentie square timber. **1662** STILLINGFL. *Orig. Sacræ* I. ii. §11. 37 The Seventy render it .. τὰ γλυπτά, by which they understand graven Images. [**1669** BARROW *Expos. Creed* (1697) 143 Fitly rendered κύριος by the Seventy interpreters.] **1681-6** J. SCOTT *Chr. Life* II. vii. Wks. 1718 I. 485 Matthias, who .. was one of the Seventy that was Chosen and Ordained by the other Apostles to succeed Judas in the Apostolate. **1858** *Trans. Phil. Soc.* 72 The Greek rendering of the Seventy. **1861** R. F. BURTON *City of Saints* ix. 484 The fourth body in rank is the Seventies. The 'Seventy' act in the name of the Lord, under direction of the 'Twelve', in building up the church, and like them are travelling ministers.

**2. a.** In comb. with numbers below ten (ordinal and cardinal), as ***seventy-one***, ***one and seventy***, ***seventy and one***, ***seventy-first***; often with ellipsis (e.g. of *years*).

*a* **1225** *Ancr. R.* 62 Seouene & seouenti lefdies. **1297** R. GLOUC. (Rolls) 7672 In þe ȝer of grace a þousend & seuenti & þre. *c* **1375** *Sc. Leg. Saints* Prol. 139 And disciplis ȝet had he may, forowtin þir, sewinty and twa. *c* **1420** *Chron. Vilod.* 414 After þe Incarnacyon ayȝte hundreth ȝere senty and fyue hit was. **1562** WINȜET *Cert. Tractates* Wks. (S.T.S.) I. 17 His Apostolis and seuinty-twa Discipulis. **1615** W. BEDWELL *Moham. Impost.* III. §109 You shal be separated farre off from me vnto the seuenty three generation. **1788** GIBBON *Decl. & F.* l. V. 218 Seventy-two Houris .. of resplendent beauty. **1791** J. TOWNSEND *Journ. Spain* (1792) III. 266 On the seventy-first day. **1862** LOWELL *Biglow P.* Ser. II. ii, Wal, by heaven, Thet's the wust news I've heerd sence Seventy-seven! **1873** *All Year Round* 3 May 13/2, In 1791, the Seventy-third, now the Seventy-first, that had won a name in Indian warfare, again took a foremost part against .. Tippoo. **1885** TENNYSON *To E. FitzGerald* 43, 44 And I am nearing seventy-four, While you have touch'd at seventy-five.

**b.** Specific uses.

*seventy-twos*, *seventy-twomo* [reading of the symbol 72mo; cf. *sixteenmo*, etc.], the size of the page of a book in which each leaf is one seventy-second part of a whole sheet. *seventy-three(s* (U.S. slang), best wishes, good-bye; also written *73*. *seventy-four*: (*a*) a ship carrying seventy-four guns (now *Hist.*); (*b*) see quot. 1853. *seventy-five*: (*a*) a bow requiring a power of 75 lbs; (*b*) a gun of 75 mm. calibre formerly used in the armies of the French Republic and the U.S.A.; also written *75*. *seventy-eight*, a gramophone record designed to be played at a speed of seventy-eight revolutions per minute (a speed that was standard until the introduction of the long-playing record); also written *78*.

**1797** NELSON in Duncan *Life* (1806) 44 Two first-rates and a seventy-four are with him. **1840** G. A. HANSARD *Bk. Archery* 368 A seventy-five, which commands all lengths within four hundred yards. **1841** SAVAGE *Dict. Printing*, *Seventy-twomo*, a sheet of paper folded into seventy-two leaves or one hundred and forty-four pages is termed seventy-twos or seventy-twomo. **1853** PAPPE *Edible Fishes C. Good Hope* 21 *Dentex Rupestris* .. (Bastard Silverfish; Seventy-four). **1860** DICKENS *Uncomm. Trav.* xv, The dark hold of an old Seventy-four. **1882** SOUTHWARD *Pract. Printing* (1884) 110 A variety of formes from folio to seventy-twomo. **1894** C. N. ROBINSON *Brit. Fleet* 238 For fifteen years the seventy-four was the ideal fighting ship for the line of battle. **1915** E. WHARTON *Fighting France* 56 We begin to come more and more frequently on big colonies of 'Seventy-fives'. **1941** *Traffic World* LXVIII. 198/1 Morse code operators .. used many arbitrary numbers to shorten their work .. 4 meaning 'where', .. 73 'best regards' and 22 'kisses'. **1951** SACKVILLE-WEST & SHAWE-TAYLOR *Record Guide* 720 The wise collector will retain his 78 gramophone and the pick of his 78 recordings, continuing to buy good new 78s (especially single discs). **1967** R. PETRIE *Foreign Bodies* xi. 156 Stina looked out her two old seventy-eight records and the four tunes on them sounded through the villa all day. **1969** A. HORNE *To lose a Battle* xxi. 510 Amongst the guns taken were some 7,000 French '75s' of First War vintage. **1971** G. STEINER *In Bluebeard's Castle* iv. 92 There is a science and market .. in worn 'seventy-eights'. **1976** *S9* (N.Y.) May/June 31/2 Seventy-threes, and 'bye. **1977** *Gramophone* Apr. 1527/1 The LP, at 33⅓ revolutions per minute, and the single, at 45 rpm, have retained their popularity with record-buyers, at the same time sounding the death-knell of the 78, which was finally abandoned in 1958.

**3.** *Comb.* (chiefly parasynthetic), as ***seventy-horse*** (= horse-power), ***-mile***; ***seventy-footer*** (see FOOTER *sb.*¹ 5); ***seventy-times-seventh***, ***seventy-year-old*** adjs.; also ***seventy-fold*** adv. and vb. (see -FOLD).

**1387** TREVISA *Higden* (Rolls) II. 231 Lamech his synne was i-punsched seuene and seuenty folde. **1611** FLORIO, *Settantiplicare*, to seauentie-fold. **1834-6** *Encycl. Metrop.* (1845) VIII. 705/1 The propelling powers are two seventy-horse steam-engines. **1877** BESANT & RICE *Son of Vulcan* II. iv. 198 His seventy-times-seventh flogging. **1893** KATE F. SANBORN *Truthful Woman* 50 From San Diego to Los Angeles, a seventy-mile run along the coast. **1896** *Harper's Mag.* XCII. 761/2 The seventy-year-old Blücher. **1900** *Daily News* 9 July 8/5 The new seventy-footers .. now being sailed in American waters.

**B.** *sb.* **1.** A set of seventy persons or things; †a period of seventy years.

**1590** H. BROUGHTON (*title*) A Letter to a Friende, tovching Mardochai his Age, which helpeth much to holde the trueth, for that chiefe prophecie of our saluation, in Gabriels seuenties. **1741** in *Buccleuch MSS.* (Hist. MSS. Comm.) I. 398 Many companies that were seventy's when we embarked, have not six men left in them. **1883** *Encycl. Brit.* XVI. 828/2 There are eighty seventies in Utah. [Cf. A. 1 c, 1861.] **1892** GUNTER *Miss Dividends* 106 A Mormon empire .. ruled over by the Priesthood of the faith of Joseph Smith and the Council of Seventies.

**2.** *the seventies*: the decade 70 to 79 in a particular century or in a person's life.

**1865** 'C. BEDE' *Rook's Gard.*, etc. 96, I have heard the word sparrowgrass from the lips of a real Lady—but then she was in her seventies. **1887** W. E. S. FALES *Brooklyn's Guardians* iv. 57 Before the 'Seventies', Brooklyn was essentially a city of homes. **1895** SAINTSBURY *Corr. Impr.* 173 It was not easy to reconcile these two laws in the late seventies and early eighties with regard to Mr. Anthony Trollope. **1922** JOYCE *Ulysses* 630 The tattoo .. was all the go in the seventies or thereabouts, even in the House of Lords. **1977** *Rolling Stone* 21 Apr. 66/1, I was fascinated with the notion that Mike was what I might have become had I been a man, the lastborn instead of the first—, a child of the Seventies rather than the Sixties.

**seven-up.** *U.S.* **1.** The game of all-fours when played for seven 'chalks'.

**1830** *N.Y. Constellation* 11 Sept. 2/5 Some tugged at the bottle, .. and some played seven-up. **1845** J. J. HOOPER *Simon Suggs* (Bartlett), Simon and Bill were .. very earnestly engaged at seven-up. **1847** RUXTON *Adv. Mexico* xxvii. 245 'Euker', 'poker', and 'seven-up', the regular mountain-games. **1890** L. C. D'OYLE *Notches* 47 There sat four 'cow-punchers', .. playing 'seven-up'.

**2. Seven up.** Also **Seven-Up**, etc., and as **7-Up.** The proprietary name of a popular carbonated soft drink.

**1928** *Official Gaz.* (U.S. Patent Office) 13 Nov. 304/2 'Seven Up.' For carbonated, nonalcoholic, noncereal, maltless beverages sold as soft drinks and syrups, extracts, and flavors used in making the same. **1953** *Trade Marks Jrnl.* 24 June 555/2 Seven-up... Non-alcoholic drinks and preparations for making such drinks, all included in Class 32. **1968** N. FLEMING *Counter Paradise* v. 78 Crystal ordered a coffee for herself and a Seven-Up for Jake. **1978** *Washington Post* 5 Sept. 10A/1 Bottles of 7-Up, suddenly the hottest commodity in Egypt.

**seven year(s, -years',** *attrib. phr.* Consisting of or lasting for seven years; having a period of seven years. † ***these*** (***this***) ***seven years day***, this long time: cf. SEVEN A 1 c, d.

*seven-year(s apple*, a fruit of tropical America, *Genipa clusiæfolia*, supposed to require seven years to ripen. † *seven-years bean, pea*: see quot. 1666. *Seven Years' War*, the third Silesian war (1756-1763), in which Austria, France, Russia, Saxony, and Sweden were allied against Frederick II of Prussia. *seven-year-vine*, the West Indian *Ipomœa tuberosa*. *seven year(s' itch* (orig. *U.S.*), used to designate conditions supposed to last for, appear, or recur after, seven years; freq. applied *joc.* to an urge towards infidelity after seven years of marriage.

**1593** SHAKS. *2 Hen. VI*, II. i. 2, I saw not better sport these seuen yeeres day. **1647** SYMMONS *Vind.* To Rdr. b 3 b, It hath been mine endeavour this seaven years day, and my usuall Prayer, that I may be able to conclude as M. Bradford the Martyr did. **1666** J. DAVIES *Hist. Caribbee Isles* 64 Those called the Seven-years Beans, because the same stalk bears seven years one after another. **1672** W. HUGHES *Amer. Physit.* 20 Of the seven years Pease. **1730** *Phil. Trans.* XXXVI. 434 The Seven Years Apple. **1788** TOWERS *Mem. Fredk. III of Prussia* II. 325 Thus ended [1763], what is called in Germany, The Seven Years War. **1837** CARLYLE *Fr. Rev.* II. III. i, In that seven-years sleep of his, so much has changed! **1854** H. D. THOREAU *Walden* 355 These may be but the spring months in the life of the race. If we have had the seven-years' itch, we have not seen the seventeen-year locust yet in Concord. **1856** H. H. DIXON *Post & Paddock* i. 17 We lately met with a seven-year-old. **1864** GRISEBACH *Flora W. Ind. Islands* 787 Seven-year-vine. **1880** J. C. HARRIS *Uncle Remus* i. (1881) 17 'Miss Sally' missed her little seven-year-old. **1899** C. W. CHESNUTT *Conjure Woman* 154 Lawsuits wuz slow ez de seben-yeah eetch. **1900** *Jrnl. Sch. Geog.* (U.S.) Apr. 141 The seven-year periods. **1936** C. SANDBURG *People, Yes* 112 'May you have the sevenyear itch,' was answered, 'I hope your wife eats crackers in bed.' **1955** *Sun* (Baltimore) 16 May 12/7 When I was a boy we called the skin rash from poison ivy .. 'the seven-year-itch' and firmly believed that it would reappear every year for seven years. **1959** 'O. MILLS' *Stairway to Murder* xiv. 149 Lapse understood and sympathised with. It's so common they've even got a name for it. It's the seven-year itch. **1980** P. MOYES *Angel Death* x. 132 There's something called the seven-year itch .. middle-aged men quite suddenly cutting loose.

**sever** ('sɛvə(r)), *v.* Also 5 sevyr, severe, *Sc.* sevir, 6 sevour, seaver, *Sc.* siver, -ir, syver, sewer. [a. AF. *severer*, *ceverer*, OF. *sevrer*, *severer*, mod.F. *sevrer* to wean:—pop.L. **sēperāre*, L. *sēparāre* to SEPARATE. Cf. It. *sceverare*, *scevrare*.]

**I.** Transitive senses.

**1.** To put apart, set asunder (two or more persons or things, or one *from* another); to part or separate by putting in different places.

**1382** WYCLIF *Gen.* xxv. 6 He seueryde [Vulg. *separavit*] hem fro Ysaac .. to the est plage. **1387** TREVISA *Higden* (Rolls) VII. 307 Eueriche in his owne celle .. i-served [*v.r.* ysevered] by hem self [orig. *ab aliis separatus*]. *c* **1440** *Pallad. on Husb.* III. 147 And seuered by hem self sette euery kynd. *c* **1450** *Merlin* xxii. 402 Than he seuered a part of his peple. **1535** COVERDALE *Ezek.* xxxiv. 20, I will seuer the fat shepe from the leane. **1591** SPENSER *Virg. Gnat* 623 By which iust Minos righteous soules doth seuer From wicked ones. **1605** BACON *Adv. Learn.* II. xxv. §9. 112 The chaffe may and ought to be seuered from the corne in the Eare. **1623** MASSINGER *Dk. Milan* II. E 1 b, *Franc.* What winde hath rais'd this tempest? Seuer 'em, I command you. **1667** MILTON *P.L.* IX. 252 Least harm Befall thee sever'd from me. **1788** COWPER *Negro's Compl.* 11 What are England's rights, .. Me from my delights to sever? **1908** S. A. COOK *Relig. Anc. Palestine* v. 56 Cremation .. may have been intended to sever the soul from the body.

**b.** To part or open (the lips, eyelids).

**1398** TREVISA *Barth. De P.R.* v. xvii. (1495) h iij b, Mannes lippes .. maye be seueryd & departed. *a* **1586** SIDNEY *Arcadia* III. (1598) 372 Pyrocles, then first seuering his eye liddes, and quickly apprehending her danger. **1842** TENNYSON *Day-Dream*, *Sleeping Pal.* iv, Her lips are sever'd as to speak.

**c.** To disjoin, dissociate, disunite (persons or things normally united by some immaterial tie).

**1382** WYCLIF *Prov.* xvi. 28 The man ful of woordis seuereth princis. **1412-20** LYDG. *Chron. Troy* v. 24 Amonge hem silf to bring in variaunce, And her hertis .. Contagiously to seueryn & deuyde. **1495** *Act 11 Hen. VII*, c. 34 §1 That all the same .. Hereditamentes shuld be .. seperat severed and disanexed from the Duchie of Cornwall. **1593** SHAKS. *3 Hen. VI*, IV. i. 21 God forbid, that I should wish them sever'd, Whom God hath ioyn'd together. **1601** —— *All's Well* I. iii. 57 How somere their hearts are seuer'd in Religion. **1605** CAMDEN *Rem.* 3 In whose person the two mightie Kingdomes of England and Scotland hitherto severed, are now conioyned. **1831** SCOTT *Cast. Dang.* v, I will..take an opportunity of severing these two young men. **1856** FROUDE *Hist. Eng.* (1858) I. iii. 188 A revolution which severed England from the papacy. **1875** JOWETT *Plato* (ed. 2) IV. 529 Plato sees that the ideal of the state in his own day is more and more severed from the actual. **1898** WATTS-DUNTON *Aylwin* II. xi, I would trample it [a coronet] in the mud, if it were to sever me from Winifred.

**d.** in legal phraseology (cf. 7).

**1532** *Dial. Laws Eng.* II. vii. 19b, The fealtie can nat be seuered fro the reuercion. **1579** *Termes de la Ley* 44b/2 Such common [*viz.* common appurtenant]..may bee seuered from the land to which it is appurtenaunte. *a***1625** FINCH *Law* I. iii, Things incident cannot be seuered. **1884** *Law Times Rep.* 12 Apr. 201/1 Where a fund is directed to be at once set apart and severed from the rest of the testator's estate, it carries income from the testator's death.

†**e.** To part or remove by some technical process (a substance) *from* another with which it is combined or mixed; = SEPARATE *v.* 5. *Obs.*

**1626** BACON *Sylva* §311 It is vsuall in Clarifying Ippocrasse to put in Milke; Which after seuereth and carrieth with it the Grosser Parts of the Ippocrasse. **1661** BOYLE *Certain Physiol. Ess.* (1669) 251 The thinner and more serous Liquor..being thus sever'd from the grosser parts of the milk. **1667** MILTON *P.L.* I. 704 A second multitude With wondrous Art founded the massie Ore, Severing each kinde, and scum'd the Bullion dross. **1796** KIRWAN *Elem. Min.* (ed. 2) I. 485 A general method of discriminating and severing them [*sc.* earths].

*fig.* **1626** BACON *Sylva* §490 This Axiome is of large extent; And therefore would be seuered, and refined by Triall.

†**f.** (In Biblical language.) To set apart or segregate for a special purpose. Also with *out*.

**1382** WYCLIF *Deut.* iv. 41 Thanne Moyses seuerde thre citees, biȝonde Jordan. [Also **1611**.] **1609** BIBLE (Douay) *2 Esdras* iii. 16 Iacob thou didst sever to thy selfe, but Esau thou didst separate. **1611** —— *Ezek.* xxxix. 14 And they shall seuer out men of continual emploiment. **1718** PRIOR *Callimachus' Hymn to Jupiter* 93 The Soldier..rich with hostile Spoil, Severs the Bull to Mars.

†**g.** In occasional uses: To deprive *of*; to hinder *from*; to free *from*. *Obs.*

**1508** DUNBAR *Tua Mariit Wemen* 337 Quhen I seuerit had that syre of substance in erd. **1533** BELLENDEN *Livy* II. xx. (S.T.S.) I. 208 The Inemyis..mycht skairslie be severit fra oppugnatioun of þare tentis [orig. *aegre abstinent quin castra oppugnent*]. **1577** B. GOOGE *Heresbach's Husb.* I. (1586) 29b, Weeding when it is knotted, seuereth the Corne from all anoyances. **1601** *2nd Pt. Return fr. Parnassus* I. vi. 484 What slimie bold presumtious groome is he, Dares with his rude audacious hardye chatt Thus seuer me from skybredd contemplation?

**h.** *refl.*

**1568** GRAFTON *Chron.* II. 61 The most part of them that came with the Archebishop and accompanied him before, for feare of the kinges displeasure seuered themselues from him. **1589** NASHE *Pref. to Greene's Menaphon* (Arb.) 10 Amongst others in that Age, Sir Thomas Eliots elegance did seuer it selfe from all equalls. **1611** BIBLE *Judges* iv. 11 Now Heber the Kenite..had seuered himselfe from the Kenites. **1617** MORYSON *Itin.* II. 14 Their Lordships advised the Lord Deputy to offer Odonnel pardon, so as he would sever himselfe from Tyrone. **1845** SARAH AUSTIN *Ranke's Hist. Ref.* II. IV. v. 537 Switzerland, which had now severed itself from the empire. **1863** GEO. ELIOT *Romola* II. iv. (1880) II. 44 To sever herself from the man she loved no longer. **1872** RAE tr. *Taine's Notes Eng.* xvi. 206 The Englishman does not sever himself from public affairs.

**2.** To separate in thought or idea; to distinguish, treat as distinct; to mark off *from*.

**1426** LYDG. *De Guil. Pilgr.* 2032, I [Reason] am she By whom that ye yknowe be ffrom other bestys..And seueryd in especyal. *c***1510** MORE *Picus* (W. de W.) A iv, Suche vnknowen and straunge tokens..severynge the cradyls of suche specyall chyldren fro yᵉ company of other of the comune sorte. **1594** HOOKER *Eccl. Pol.* I. iii. §2 Expedient it will be that we seuer the law of nature obserued by the one from that which the other is tied vnto. **1605** B. JONSON *Volpone* V. v, *Volp.* Am I then like him? *Mos.* O, Sir, you are hee: No man can seuer you. *c***1652** MILTON *Sonn. to Sir H. Vane* 11 To know Both spirituall powre & civill, what each meanes, What severs each. *a***1654** SELDEN *Table-T., Books* (Arb.) 31 He is a poor Divine that cannot sever the good from the bad. **1909** *Expositor* Sept. 222 In another letter he severs his own position most definitely from that of Sabbatier. **1910** *Ibid.* Aug. 127 We cannot sever religious cult from social custom.

**3.** To keep distinct or apart by an intervening space or barrier. Of the intervening medium: To occupy the space or interval between. Also *fig.*

**1422** YONGE tr. *Secreta Secret.* lviii. 223 That the rybbis Bene wel departid or Seueret. **1533** BELLENDEN *Livy* II. xi. (S.T.S.) I. 171 Belive all municiouns, quhilkis war laid be Industrye to sivir þe armyis, war removit. **1584** COGAN *Haven Health* ccxli. 240 Let your lodging be in an vpper chamber, yet seuered from the roufe with some false flower. **1600** NASHE *Summer's Last Will* H 4, Ile beate downe the partition with my heeles Which as a mud-vault seuers hell and thee. **1611** BIBLE *Exod.* viii. 22, I will seuer in that day the lande of Goshen..that no swarmes of flies shall be there. **1665** HAVERS *P. della Valle's Trav. E. India* 102 A large cover'd room in the poop, sever'd from the banks of rowers. **1805** WORDSW. *Prelude* XI. 94 With such general insight into evil, And of the bounds which sever it from good. **1814** —— *Excurs.* III. 661 Immense The space that severed us! **1850** MRS. BROWNING *Prometh.* (near end) *Poems* I. 183 The gulf which severs rule from servitude. **1874** GREEN *Short Hist.* ii. §1 Fens nearly one hundred miles long severed East Anglia from the midland counties.

**4.** To divide into (two or more) parts. Also *refl.* Now *rare* or *Obs.* exc. as in 5.

**1435** *Cov. Leet Bk.* 182 For & the Craft were severed in the maner as hit [is] seide aboue, Then the Cardwirdrawers and the myddelmen most nedes bye the wire that they shull wirche of the smythiers. **1533** GAU *Richt Vay* (1888) 83 Part of psalmis ar sewert be this vord sela that singnifeis rest and pece. **1566** *Act 8 Eliz.* c. 16 §3 The Tayle of Rewarde of everie of the foresayd Counties..shalbe severed and devyded. **1577** HANMER *Anc. Eccl. Hist., Euseb.* v. xii. (1619) 85 He sheweth this heresie in his time to have been severed into sundry sects. **1584** B. R. tr. *Herodotus* II. 73b, Running in one streame til it come to the city of the Cercasians, and afterwards seuering it selfe into three sundry chanels. **1617** MORYSON *Itin.* II. 95 The rest were severed into small companies, and unlike to draw to any dangerous head. **1654** [ELLISTONE & SPARROW] tr. *Behmen's Myst. Magn.* iv. 11 Now the will Severs it selfe..into two Kingdomes, where each dwelleth in it selfe.

†**b.** To divide according to kind or quality, to sort. *Obs.*

**1523–34** FITZHERB. *Husb.* §36 To seuer pees, beanes, and fytches... Let theym be well reed with syues, and seuered in thre partes, the great from the small. *Ibid.* §53 Whan thou haste all shorne thy shepe, it is than best tyme to drawe them, and soo seuer theym in dyuers sortes. **1573–80** TUSSER *Husb.* (1878) 33 Now friend, as ye wish, goe seuer thy fish: When friend shall come, to be sure of some.

†**c.** To divide and distribute. *Obs. rare*$^{-1}$.

**1548** GESTE *Agst. Pr. Masse* I ij, He bad vs seuer the consecrate breade charitablye emong vs & not eche of vs to reserue it to hym selue.

**5.** To part or divide suddenly or forcibly; to cut in two, cleave or rend asunder. With a material or immaterial thing as object.

**1412–20** LYDG. *Chron. Troy* III. 2056 Eueryche on oþer lik tigers or lyons Be-gan to falle, and proudly to assaille, And furiously seuere plate and maille. *Ibid.* v. 648 þe þondre, þat seuerede seil & mast. *a***1450** *Knt. de la Tour* 49 No man shulde putte betwene hem no thinge that might seuere the loue that God and the churche hathe ioyned in hem. **1560** DAUS tr. *Sleidane's Comm.* IV. 52b, Many they were yᵗ sought to seaver and break that societie. **1595** DANIEL *Civ. Wars* VI. xciv, There the closest ranks hee seuereth. **1667** MILTON *P.L.* IX. 958 Our State cannot be severd, we are one, One Flesh. **1791** MACKINTOSH *Vind. Gallicæ* Wks. 1846 III. 163 Let the Court of Madrid..sever every tie that unites her to Europe. **1837** WHEWELL *Hist. Induct. Sci.* (1857) I. 190 Under their hands, the pediment was severed at its vertex, and divided into separate halves. **1852** ROBERTSON *Serm.* Ser. III. (1857) xii. 171 Not many years ago the Church of Scotland was severed into two great divisions. **1861** BUCKLE *Civiliz.* (1873) III. iii. 166 Thus it was that this great tie was severed. **1867** BAKER *Nile Tribut.* xiv. (1886) 246 Another galloped up behind, and severed the hamstring. **1870** BRYANT *Homer* I. VIII. 240 The aged man Hastened to sever with his sword the thongs That bound him to the car. **1875** *Encycl. Brit.* III. 377/1 Having discovered that this company was merely a swindling concern, he severed his connection with it.

**b.** To break up, scatter, disperse (an assemblage or company of individuals). Also *refl.* Now *rare.*

**1412–20** LYDG. *Chron. Troy* IV. 2301 But Troylus ay hem chaseth her & ȝonder, And seuered hem maugre al her myȝt. *a***1513** FABYAN *Chron.* V. xcii. (1516) 36b/1 Yᵉ Brytons.. that were disparkled and seueryd in many countres. **1568** GRAFTON *Chron.* II. 976 On Friday at night blewe such a storme that seuered all the nauie. **1590** SHAKS. *Mids. N.* III. ii. 23 As..russed-pated choughes, many in sort (Rising and cawing at the guns report) Seuer themselues, and madly sweepe the skye. **1591** SPENSER *Virg. Gnat* 638 Let the flitting aire my vaine words sever. **1853** KANE *Grinnell Exp.* xxi. (1856) 168 A gale of wind has severed the pack, and the drift begins.

¶**c.** To cut the dewlap of (cattle). (? Misprint for *setter*: see SETTER *v.*)

**1523** FITZHERB. *Husb.* §59 (1525?) 26b, There be many men that can seuer theym, & that is to cutte the dewlappe before.

**6.** 'To part by violence from the rest' (J.); to separate suddenly and forcibly; to cut, tear, or pull off.

**1626** BACON *Sylva* §400 It is reported..that a Sacrificed Beast hath lowed, after the Heart hath been seuered. *a***1700** EVELYN *Diary* 12 May 1641, The fatal stroke which sever'd the wisest head in England from the shoulders of the Earle of Strafford. **1712** ADDISON *Spect.* No. 519 ¶6 That Species of Shell-fish..that grow to the Surface of several Rocks, and immediately die upon their being sever'd from the Place where they grow. **1784** COWPER *Task* v. 38 He from the stack carves out th' accustom'd load,..With such undeviating and even force He severs it away. **1798** WORDSW. *Simon Lee* 86, I struck, and with a single blow The tangled root I severed. **1815** J. SMITH *Panorama Sci. & Art* II. 27 By which any length desired will instantly be severed from the rest of the tube. **1839** LANE *Arab. Nts.* I. 108 The blow, which I gave with the view of severing his head, only cut the gullet and skin and flesh. **1908** S. A. COOK *Relig. Anc. Palestine* ii. 16 The heads had evidently been severed before burial, and there was no trace of the bodies.

**7.** *Law.* **a.** To divide (a joint estate) into independent parts.

**1544** tr. *Littleton's Tenures* 69 Whan the Ioyntenauntes were ioyntly seased in fee symple..thoughe that one of them made estate of that, that vnto him belongeth for terme of lyfe ..yet he hath nat seuered the fee symple. **1628** COKE *On Litt.* 182b, If a man maketh a lease to two for their liues, and after granteth the reuersion to one of them in fee, the ioynture is seuered. **1766** BLACKSTONE *Comm.* II. 185 How an estate in joint-tenancy may be severed and destroyed. **1818** CRUISE *Digest* (ed. 2) II. 499 The question was, whether the jointure was severed or not. **1895** STRAHAN *Law of Property* (1908) 89 On the reversion being severed the conditions of all kinds are to be apportioned between the persons among whom the reversion is divided. *Ibid.* 132 A joint tenancy, where the joint tenants are beneficial owners, may be severed either (a) by a partition of the joint estate, or (b) by alienation by one of the joint tenants of his undivided share.

**b.** To detach (growing fruit or trees, minerals, fixtures, etc.) from the soil or realty.

**1602** FULBECKE *1st Pt. Parall.* 37 If a man..deuiseth the corne growing vpon the lande, and dyeth before it bee seuered, the deuisee shall haue it. **1628** COKE *On Litt.* 55b, If a Disseisor sowe the ground and seuer the corne. **1911** ODGERS *Common Law* I. 329 All these become personal property as soon as they are severed from the soil, and until they are severed they cannot, of course, be carried away. *Ibid.* II. 700 The produce of the trees, when they should be cut down and severed from the freehold.

**c.** To separate and remove (one of the plaintiffs in a joint action, when he is nonsuited). (See also SUMMON *v.*).

**1602** FULBECKE *1st Pt. Parall.* 29 By our law if two bring a writ of warde of the body of the heire beeing within age, and the one of them is summoned and seuered, and the other recouereth, hee which was seuered may haue a writte of accompt against the other for the profites. **1628** COKE *On Litt.* 139 In reall or mixt actions the Nonsuite of one Demandant is not the Nonsuite of both, but he that makes default shall be summoned and seuered. **1652** tr. *Fitzherbert's Nat. Brev.* 36 If one of those who is named by his proper name, will not sue..he shall be severed. **1741** T. ROBINSON *Gavelkind* I. vi. 109 If two Coparceners join against the Alienee in a Writ of Partition at Common Law, and one of them does not proceed, yet he may be summoned and severed, as his Part shall be parted and severed, as well as the other Parts.

**d.** To part (two or more defendants) in their trial. (Cf. 10a.)

**1660** *Trial Regicides* 57 Are you all agreed as to your Challenges?.. No, my Lord... Then we must do as before, sever you, and go to tryal severally. **1691** *Arraignmt. Sir R. Graham*, etc. 22 Since they are pleased to declare they will sever in their Challenges, we must desire to sever them in their Tryal, and to begin with the Tryal of my Lord Preston.

**8.** *absol.* To make a separation or division (*between*). *rare.*

**1611** BIBLE *Exod.* ix. 4 The Lord shall seuer betweene the cattel of Israel, and the cattell of Egypt. **1622** J. TAYLOR (Water-P.) *Water-cormorant* A 4, The Pope sends stormes forth, seuers or combines, According to his mood it raines or shines. **1648–9** *Eikon Bas.* xi. 82 There remain's in far the Major part of both Houses..so much Learning, Reason, Religion, and just Moderation, as to know how to sever between the use and abuse of things. **1882** PUSEY *Paroch. & Cathedr. Serm.* xvii. 243 He stands between the dead and the living. He severs between her past and her future life.

**II.** *intr.* (Cf. the reflexive uses in branch I.)

**9.** Of a person: To go away, part, be sundered *from*. Of two or more: To be separated, quit each other, go asunder, part.

**13..** *Gaw. & Gr. Knt.* 1797 Ho..semly hym kyssed, & siþen ho seueres hym fro. *Ibid.* 1987, & vche segge as sore, to seuer with hym þere, As þay hade wonde worþyly with þat wlonk euer. *c***1375** *Lay Folks Mass Bk.* (MS. B.) 396 In oure last day..when þis worlde & we shal seuer. *c***1470** HENRY *Wallace* III. 86 Gude lycht harnes, fra that tyme, wyst he euir; For sodeyn stryff, fra it he wald nocht seuir. **1533** BELLENDEN *Livy* I. x. (S.T.S.) I. 60 Sone eftir baith þe armyis siverit and returnit hame. **1618** FLETCHER *Isl. Princess* II. i, Come, all sever, But keep still within sight. **1667** MILTON *P.L.* IX. 366 Seek not temptation then, which to avoide Were better, and most likelie if from mee Thou sever not. **1715** POPE *2nd Epist. to Miss Blount* 5 From the dear man unwilling she must sever, Yet takes one kiss before she parts for ever. **1791** BURNS *Ae Fond Kiss* i, Ae fond kiss, and then we sever. **1825** JEFFERSON *Autobiog.* Wks. 1859 I. 31 Should we sever from each other,..no foreign power will ally with us. **1842** W. A. BUTLER *Serm.* Ser. I. x. (1849) 166 The more the parties sever, the closer the knot is bound.

**b.** of things.

**1545** RAYNALD *Byrth Mankynde* I. xiv. (1552) 39 Manye tymes the one [vein] seuereth from the other before conuenient season and so causeth aborcement. **1598** DRAYTON *Heroic. Ep., C'tess Salisb. to Black Prince* 47 If modesty and women once doe seuer, Farewell our fame, farewell our name for euer. **1605** BACON *Adv. Learn.* II. xxii. §17. 86b, Theis three as in the bodye, so in the minde seeldome meete, and Commonly seuer. *a***1626** —— *Physiol. Rem.* Baconiana (1679) 140 Spirit of Wine mingled with common Water, although it be much lighter than Oyl,.. severeth not again, as Oyl doth. **1859** LD. LYTTON *Wanderer, Once* xxiii, These lips from thine, I know, must sever.

**c.** Of the lips, doors, or the like: To go apart, open.

**1797** MRS. A. M. BENNETT *Beggar Girl* (1813) III. 267 Her lips severed, but no voice was heard. **1811** MISS MITFORD *Blanch of Castile* in L'Estrange *Life* (1870) I. 130 The deaf man..Felt her hands' pressure soft and warm, Saw her lips sever. **1871** B. TAYLOR *2nd Pt. Faust* I. i, 'T is thus,..The portals of fulfilment widely sever.

**d.** Of a whole or aggregate: To part, become divided, be separated into parts.

*c***1407** LYDG. *Reson & Sens.* 2527 Her companye Ne seuereth nat, but y-fere Eche ys to other so entere. **1412–20** —— *Chron. Troy* IV. 4084 She..slowe of hem vp-on euery syde, Makynge her rengis for to seuere wyde. *a***1548** HALL *Chron., Hen. VI*, 102b, This fortresse stode in such a place, that what with waters and what with marishes, the army must sever in thre partes. **1608** CHAPMAN *Byron's Conspir.* III. i, As, the soul departed from the body, The body wants coherence in his parts Can not consist but seuer and dissolue. **1805–6** CARY *Dante, Inf.* xxv. 124 His tongue, continuous before and apt For utterance, severs [*si fende*]; and the other's fork Closing unites.

**10.** *Law.* **a.** Of two or more defendants: To plead independently. More fully ***to sever in their challenges, in their defence***, etc.

*a***1625** HOBART *Rep.* (1650) 245 Now though the Defendants shall not sever in Dilatories, yet in Bars they may. **1660** *Trial Regicides* 57 If one challenge one [of the Jury-panel], and another challenge another, we must sever, and go to Tryal one by one. **1691** *Arraignmt. Sir R. Graham*, etc. 23 If you had joyned in your Challenges, then you had been tryed all together... That Advantage you lose by severing in your Challenges. **1824** STEPHEN *Princ. Pleading*

270 If the defendants have once united in the plea, they cannot afterwards sever at the rejoinder. **1855** MACAULAY *Hist. Eng.* xx. IV. 523 The prisoners who were first arraigned did not sever in their challenges, and were consequently tried together. **1884** *Law Times Rep.* 10 May 321/1 The defendants had severed in their defence to the action. **1884** *Law Rep. 26 Chanc. Div.* 701 Motion made by counsel for the Defendants..for leave to sever in their defences.

**b.** Of joint tenants: To divide their jointure.

**1895** STRAHAN *Law of Property* (1908) 131 When joint tenants for life sever, each takes a tenancy in severalty or in common for his own life in his share.

**severable** (ˈsɛvərəb(ə)l), *a.* [f. SEVER *v.* + -ABLE.] Capable of being severed or separated; †distinct, separate. ***severable contract***: see quot. 1848.

**1548** GESTE *Agst. Pr. Masse* G v b, By Paules doctryne to serue the aultare & to preache be soundrye and seuerable offices and ministeryes. **1641** *Termes de la Ley* s.v. *Apportionment*, Common appendant is of common right and severable. **1651** tr. *Kitchin's Courts Leet* (1653) 292 Suit by two is not severable. **1818** CRUISE *Digest* (ed. 2) V. 470 A joint estate given to the husband and wife before marriage.. is severable. **1847** C. G. ADDISON *Contracts* II. i. §1 (1883) 250 The ornamental fixtures now held severable and removable by the tenant are..stoves, tapestry,..and ornamental cornices capable of being detached without injury to the building. **1848** WHARTON *Law Lex.* s.v. *Contract*, A severable contract is one, the consideration of which is, by its terms, susceptible of apportionment on either side, so as to correspond to the unascertained consideration on the other side. **1852** C. WORDSWORTH *Occas. Serm.* Ser. III. 42 Whether secular knowledge can rightly be regarded as severable from religion. **1878** A. MITCHELL *Past in Present*, etc. (1880) 231 A state could not give up its gods, nor could the gods give up a state. The connection was not severable. **1884** *Law Times Rep.* LI. 532/1 Two causes of action which are severable and distinct.

**several** (ˈsɛvərəl), *a.*, *adv.*, and *sb.* Also 4–8 -all, (5 -ell, -ele, *pl.* -alx), 5–6 el(le, alle, (7 -ale); *poet.* 7–8 sev'ral (7 -all). [a. AF. *several* adj. and sb. (whence med.L. *severālis*), ad. med.L. *sēparālis* (neut. sb. *-āle*), f. L. *sēpar* separate, distinct.

*Seuerel* in Trevisa's translation (1387) of Higden's *Polychronicon* (Rolls) VIII. 49 (MS. St. John's, Camb. H 1) 'seuerel werkes', is an error for *servile*.]

**A.** *adj.*

**I.** Existing apart, separate.

†**1.** Having a position, existence, or status apart; separate, distinct: (*a*) in predicative use. *Obs.*

**1422** YONGE tr. *Secreta Secret.* xlvi. 209 So oweste thow, Alexander, to haue v messagers and v consaillours, and euery of tham shall be seuerall [orig. *per se separatus*]. *c* **1430** *Freemasonry* (ed. Halliw. 1844) 22 The thrydde poynt most be severele, With the prentes knowe hyt wele, Hys mayster cownsel he kepe and close, And hys felows by hys goode purpose. **1539** BIBLE (Great) *2 Chron.* xxvi. 21 Uzia.. dwelt seuerall in an house [**1611** in a seuerall house] beynge a leper. **1577** B. GOOGE *Heresbach's Husb.* III. (1586) 145 Varro doth commend sundry little flocks kept seuerall, rather then greate flockes together. **1612** BREREWOOD *Lang. & Relig.* 109 Many Mahumetans be also found..both several in sundry provinces, and otherwise mingled with idolaters. **1642** FULLER *Holy & Prof. St.* IV. i. 243 Severall are the causes of Favourites falls,..different the degrees and manner of their ruine. **1652** SPARKE *Prim. Devot.* (1660) 553 Mistaking the Son of Alphæus, and St. James the Brother of our Lord, for several; which were but one and the same person. **1654** WHITLOCK *Zootomia* 330 Keeping the Delivery of others Opinions and my own severall. **1707** MORTIMER *Husb.* (1721) II. 334 Then grind or beat them, keeping the Fruit several, in case you have enough to fill a Vessel of one kind.

(*b*) in attributive use, with *a* and *pl.*

**1511** GUYLFORDE *Pilgr.* (Camden) 79 They haue.. seuerall cloysters and seuerall lodgynges, but they kepe all theyr dyuine seruyce in one quere all togyther. *a* **1533** FRITH *Disput. Purgat.* I. (end) F vij, What soeuer is not answered in this parte, shalbe..fully conuynced in the thyrde, which shall be a seuerall boke agaynst my lorde of Rochestre. **1594** PLAT *Jewell-ho.* III. 5 Receaue the oile into a seuerall glasse by it selfe. **1597** MORLEY *Introd. Mus.* 3 If you shoulde aske them, why two men of one name should not both giue one Armes? they will straight answere you, that they be of seuerall houses. **1603** OWEN *Pembrokeshire* ii. (1891) 33 In seuerall and lone houses. **1620** E. BLOUNT *Horæ Subs.* 518 The commixture of seuerall sexes, which we call Marriage. **1635** SWAN *Spec. M.* iv. §2 (1643) 60 Every scale of an onyon is a severall and differing scale. **1690** MILTON *Hist. Eng.* II. (end), But so different a state of things requires a several relation. *a* **1700** EVELYN *Diary* June 1645, From hence we visited St. Spirito and St. Lawrence, faire Churches in severall islands. **1700** DRYDEN *Fables* Pref. *C 1 b, The Reeve, the Miller, and the Cook, are several Men. **1768** TUCKER *Lt. Nat.* (1834) II. 311 It is the custom of Providence to perfect mighty works by a multitude of.. instruments, each performing a small and several part of the whole.

†**b.** Separate, distinct, or different *from*. *Obs.*

**1533** TINDALE *Supper of Lord* Wks. (1573) 467/2 So be we now by Baptisme rekened to bee consigned vnto Christes Church seuerall from Iewes, paynyms, &c. **1551** RECORDE *Pathw. Knowl.* II. xxvi, The thirde likeiamme..hathe his grounde line.., seuerall from the other, but yet equall vnto it. **1560** DAUS tr. *Sleidane's Comm.* 373 b, It [penance] is also a severall Sacrament from Baptisme. **1566** T. STAPLETON *Ret. Untr. Jewel* iii. 58 Saint Luke.., if that crye of the Lycaonians hade bene in greke, woulde not haue termed it a seuerall language from the greke, as he doth, calling it Lycaonicall. **1599** *Broughton's Lett.* xii. 40 Christianity hath vsed many words in seuerall sence from the common phrase. **1612** T. TAYLOR *Comm. Titus* iii. 1 But the precept is entire of it selfe, and seuerall from the other before. **1636** *Recorde's Gr. Artes* 302 Either the whole number is seuerall from the Fraction..or else the whole number is ioyned with one, or both of the Fractions.

†**c.** With reference to function or use: Distinctive, particular. *Obs.*

**1564–5** *Form Prayers Genev. & Scot.* (1584) H 8, That the Minister..also vse some forme of prayer..to the which he may appoint..some seuerall daye after the Sermon, weekely to be obserued. **1582** BENTLEY *Mon. Matrones* To Rdr. B 3, Vnder the pretense of seuerall deuotion to commit manifold vngodlinesse. **1584** B. R. tr. *Herodotus* II. 79 b, Euery one.. doth seruice to all the gods indifferently, no man being clarked or chosen to be the seuerall minister of any one god alone. **1596** SPENSER *State Irel.* Wks. (Globe) 681/2 All men should marke theyr cattell with an open severall marke upon theyr flanckes. **1614** CAMDEN *Rem.*, *Armories* 178 The ancient Picts and Britans..adorned their bodies with figures and blazons of diuers colours, which they coniecture to haue bene seuerall for particular families. **1648** GAGE *West Ind.* 214 There are no severall terminations for cases, as in Latine.

†**d.** Acting separately or individually; having separate responsibility. *Obs.*

**1466** *Cal. Anc. Rec. Dublin* (1889) I. 322 That every person..have his accion of trespas agaynes all manner person or persones of Chester..juncte or severell at his plesyre. **1475** in *10th Rep. Hist. MSS. Comm.* App. v. 312 The payne..to be levid by thofficers and by every of them, juncte and severall.

**2.** Qualifying a pl. sb.: Individually separate; different.

**a.** Preceded by an adj. of number or plurality.

**1448** in *Wars Eng. in France* (Rolls) I. 483 There is due unto him the somme of vij. c. xlij. li...as by iij. severalx accomptes. **1562** TURNER *Herbal* II. 127 Although diuerse.. learned men haue made one herbe of Thymbra and satureya, yet it is playne..that they are two seuerall herbes. **1588** *Marprel. Epist.* (Arb.) 42 Two seuerall Iohns, the father and the sonne, that had beene both recusants. **1602** SHAKS. *Ham.* v. ii. 20 An exact command, Larded with many seuerall sorts of reason. **1617** ABP. ABBOT *Descr. World* (1634) 91 China..containeth in it very many severall Kingdomes. **1641** R. BROOKE *Disc. Nat. Episc.* II. iv. 75 The word *Elder*, is used twenty severall times in the New Testament. **1719** DE FOE *Crusoe* I. (Globe) 70 All these Days entirely spent in many several Voyages. **1800** WORDSW. *Hart-Leap Well* 67 Three several pillars, each a rough-hewn stone. **1879** GEO. ELIOT *Theo. Such* i. 3 Three several times astonished.

**b.** Preceded by the def. article, a possessive, etc.: Each and all of *the*, *these*, †*one's* (etc.) various or different.

**1445** tr. *Claudian* in *Anglia* XXVIII. 279 So that yf thou woldist nat enclyne to her severel preyers At Romys request thou sholdist not lette her wille soon to perfourme. **1594** SHAKS. *Rich. III*, III. ii. 78, I doe not like these seuerall Councels. **1596** —— *Merch. V.* II. vii. 2 Draw aside the curtaines, and discouer The seuerall Caskets to this noble Prince. **1634** SIR T. HERBERT *Trav.* 33 Hee had well viewed her seuerall forces. **1681** POPPLE tr. *Locke's 1st Let. Toleration* L.s' Wks. 1727 II. 253 All the several separate Congregations,..will watch one another. **1711** ADDISON *Spect.* No. 205 ¶2 Besides a great many little Blemishes which you have touched upon in your several other Papers. **1731–8** SWIFT *Pol. Conversat.* Introd. 39 In the Compass of my own several Acquaintance. **1794** LD. GRENVILLE in *Paget Papers* (1896) I. 64 Your several Dispatches have been duly received and laid before the King. **1844** LINGARD *Anglo-Saxon Ch.* (1858) II. x. 107 During the several weeks which they spent on the coast of Natolia. **1866** J. MARTINEAU *Ess.* I. 198 Now combine these several propositions. **1893** SIR R. BALL *Story of Sun* 1 It is to the control of the Sun that the several planets are indebted for the regulation of their movements.

**c.** Without limiting word: A number of different; various, divers, sundry. (Now merged in 4.)

**1509** HAWES *Past. Pleas.* XLIII. (1555) 212 Whose goodly stories in tongues severall About were sent for to be perpetuall. **1563** *Homilies* II. *Almsdeeds* I. 168 b, When seuerall matters are seuerally handeled. **1601** SHAKS. *Jul. C.* I. ii. 320, I will this Night, In seuerall Hands, in at his Windowes throw, As if they came from seuerall Citizens, Writings. **1628** T. SPENCER *Logick* 12 Seuerall respects of things, considered alone, and by themselues. **1650** FULLER *Pisgah* I. iv. 11 Dates, Almonds, Nuts,..and other severall fruits. **1690** LOCKE *Hum. Und.* III. vi. §25 Were they Nature's Workmanship, they could not be so various..in several Men. **1710** J. CHAMBERLAYNE *St. Gt. Brit.* II. I. ii. (1743) 329 It seems to have been built at several times, and by different Persons. **1823** J. BADCOCK *Dom. Amusem.* 51 Two or three lenses may be kept, of several focal lengths. **1855** J. PHILLIPS *Man. Geol.* 206 Upper limestone, cavernous, with coral bands in several stages.

**d.** In legal use: More than one.

**1531** *Dial. Laws Eng.* I. viii. 15 b, They be set in this writyng for seuerall groundes and he that lysteth may so accompt them, or if he wyll he may take them for one grounde after his pleasure. **1628** COKE *On Litt.* III. i. §241. 164 They be but one heire, and yet seuerall persons. **1824** STEPHEN *Princ. Pleading* 279 The use of several counts, and the allowance of several pleas. **1853** in W. Williams *Introd. Pleading* (1857) 307 Several pleas, replications or subsequent pleadings, or several avowries or cognizances founded on the same ground of answer or defence. *Ibid.*, Several counts on the same cause of action shall not be allowed.

**3.** Being one of a number of individuals of the same class. **a.** ***every*** or ***each several***: every or each individual or single.

*a* **1562** G. CAVENDISH *Wolsey* (1893) 112 Under the sealls of every severall unyversitie. **1568** GRAFTON *Chron.* II. 2 That euery seuerall person, aswell horsemen as footemen should carye a greene bough in his hand. **1591** SHAKS. *Two Gent.* I. ii. 108 Ile kisse each seuerall paper, for amends. **1622** MABBE tr. *Aleman's Guzman d'Alf.* I. 237 The tearing of euery seuerall hayre seemed vnto him the plucking out of so many eyes out of his head. **1665** MANLEY *Grotius' Low C. Wars* 193 Without the consent of every severall Province. **1823** B'NESS BUNSEN in Hare *Life* (1879) I. vi. 214 Each several person wishes each several cardinal a happy conclave. **1847** MRS. GORE *Castles in Air* xviii. (1857) 154 Unless the families said to inhabit Bark's Buildings were hoisted up by the crane attached to each several house. **1861** MANNING in *Ess. Relig. & Lit.* Ser. I. (1865) 39 Every several Greek is bound to submit to the Catholic Church, one by one. **1883** PARRY in *Grove's Dict. Mus.* III. 477/2 Any of its elements can be treated as the discordant note, with the result of leading to a different key in each several case.

†**b.** ***a*** or ***one several***: a single, one and only one. Also ***many a several*** = many a. *Obs.*

**1543** *Necessary Doctr.* F iij, The church of Rome being but a seuerall church, chalenginge that name of Catholyke aboue all other. **1563** *Homilies* II. *Prayer* I. 122 b, Why dyd the Apostles immediatly after his ascention, gather them selues together into one seuerall place? **1582** *N.T.* (Rhem.) Rev. xxi. 21 Every gate was of one several pearle. **1597** SHAKS. *Lover's Compl.* 206 These tallents of their heir,..I haue receau'd from many a seueral faire.

**4.** As a vague numeral: Of an indefinite (but not large) number exceeding two or three; more than two or three but not very many. (The chief current sense.)

In earlier instances that may be brought under this definition, it is difficult to determine how far the sense of 'different, various' remains; cf. the remarks s.v. DIVERS *a.* 3.

?**1661** in *12th Rep. Hist. MSS. Comm.* App. v. 6 During which times he received severall sums of money to the value of 300*l.* **1662** J. DAVIES tr. *Olearius' Voy. Ambass.* 154 The current having forc'd the Ship upon the shore, where we were constrained to stay for several hours. **1671** MILTON *P.R.* III. 276 Ninevee, of length within her wall Several days journey. **1711** ADDISON *Spect.* No. 159 ¶1 When I was at Grand Cairo, I picked up several Oriental Manuscripts. **1748** *Anson's Voy.* I. vi. 65 A thong of several fathoms in length,..with a running noose at one end of it. **1860** TYNDALL *Glac.* I. v. 37 Which may be seen by several hundred persons at once. **1883** STEVENSON *Treas. Isl.* iv, Some of the men..remembered..to have seen several strangers on the road.

†**b.** A good many. *Obs.*

**1712** SWIFT *Let. Eng. Tongue* 24 Several young Men at the Universities, terribly possessed with the fear of Pedantry, run into a worse Extreme. **1733** BUDGELL *Bee* IV. 341 A French-Celtick, or French-British Dictionary..useful and curious..for finding the Etymology of several French and British Words. **1753** L. M. *Accomplished Woman* II. 26 We must not be surpris'd that this passion hath so great influence on the mind of several women.

**c.** *ellipt.* and *absol.*, esp. followed by *of*. ***a good several*** (nonce-use): a good many.

**1685** LUTTRELL *Brief Rel.* (1857) I. 340 His majestie hath turn'd off severall of his servants, as is said, near 200. **1686** tr. *Chardin's Trav. Persia* 7 The French are very numerous ..over all the Levant, there not being a Port of Turkie upon the Mediterranean sea, wherein there are not several. **1705** ADDISON *Italy* Pref., There are still several of these Topicks that are far from being exhausted. **1748** *Anson's Voy.* II. x. 232 Commerce was the reigning passion of several of the European Princes. **1774** *Chesterfield's Lett. to Son* I. xi. 30 Cicero, the greatest Orator that Rome ever produced; although it produced several [orig. Fr. *plusieurs*]. **1839** URE *Dict. Arts* etc. 605 France contains no workable gold mines; but it presents in several of its rivers auriferous sands. **1865** CARLYLE *Fredk. Gt.* XIX. v. V. 525 A good several of them cut and wounded. **1883** STEVENSON *Treas. Isl.* iv, While we could get several who were willing enough to ride to Dr. Livesey's.

†**5.** Consisting of different elements or parts; of diverse origin or composition. Chiefly *poet.*

**1590** SPENSER *F.Q.* I. iii. 16 A heavy load he bare Of nightly stelths, and pillage severall. **1649** G. DANIEL *Trinarch., Hen. IV*, cxxvi, How Richard fell, the various Reports Of many writing, make it seuerall; Some say that he was starv'd. *a* **1674** MILTON *Hist. Moscovia* v. Wks. 1851 VIII. 515 Seventy Messes with three Carts of several Meath [*i.e.* mead = drink] sent after him.

**6.** *Comb.* (parasynthetic).

**1633** SHIRLEY *Triumph Peace* I. i. Stage Direct., Fancy in a suit of several-coloured feathers, hooded, a pair of bat's wings on his shoulders. **1677** MOXON *Mech. Exerc.* xi. 201 There are several fashion'd Collers: As the Joynt-Coller marked G, the Round Coller marked H, and the Coller marked I, in Plate 13. **1830** LINDLEY *Nat. Syst. Bot.* 181 Seeds nut-like, sometimes cohering into a several-celled putamen. **1866** *Treas. Bot.* s.v. *Poa*, The spikelets..are for the most part several-flowered and without awns. **1882** SYMONDS in *Macm. Mag.* XLV. 325 It is a several-chorded lute on which they play. **1882–4** COOKE *Brit. Fresh-w. Algæ* I. 270 Or even forming transverse, several-celled bands.

**II.** Pertaining to an individual person or thing.

**7.** Chiefly *Law.* (Opposed to *common.*) Private; privately owned or occupied.

**a.** of land, *esp.* of enclosed pasture.

**1421** *Cov. Leet Bk.* 33 That þe Trinite gilde haue hur close feldis severell. *c* **1440** *Jacob's Well* 37 þe tythe awȝte to be payed..of pasture, comoun & seuerall. **1483** *Rolls of Parlt.* VI. 257/1 All the seid XL Acres of Lande..as their proper and severall grounde and soil. **1580** TUSSER *Husb.* (1878) 50 Good land that is seuerall, crops may haue three, in champion countrie it may not so bee. **1583** STUBBES *Anat. Abus.* II. (1882) 27 The commons..are inclosed, made seueral. **1614** MARKHAM *Cheap Husb.* I. iii. (1623) 42 This ground is best if it be seuerall and inclosed, yet may be bred vpon though it bee open and in common. *a* **1656** VINES *Lord's Supper* (1657) 183 A severall not a common field.

**b.** Of a house, water, or any possession or commodity. *Obs.* exc. in ***several fishery***, a right to fish derived through or on account of ownership of the soil.

**1426** LYDG. *De Guil. Pilgr.* 2352 Sestow nat how a comoun welle Mor avaylleth..Than doth A-nother seuerel? *a* **1450** *Fysshynge w. angle* (1883) 35 That ye fysshe not in noo poore mannes seuerall water. *c* **1450** *Godstow Reg.* 401 The abbesse of Godestowe..yaf..to henry kyngeston and to william more, Fysshers, ther seuerell fysshwere in the subarbis of Oxenford that is I-called Charwelle. *a* **1547** T. Key *Erasm. Par. Mark* v. 35-43 This thyng dyd Iesus then in a nother mannes seuerall house. **1618** Dalton *Countrey Justice* ciii. (1630) 263 To take fishes that be kept in a trunke or severall pond. **1766** Blackstone *Comm.* II. 39 He that has a several fishery must also be the owner of the soil. **1842** *Act 5 & 6 Vict.* c. 106 §114 The Words 'several Fishery' shall, for the Purposes of this Act, be construed to mean an exclusive Fishery, possessed and enjoyed as such by virtue of Grant, Patent [etc.]. **1885** *Act 48 & 49 Vict.*, c. 79 §3 A right of several fishery or of regulating a fishery shall not exceed sixty years.

†**c.** Const. *to*, also *by*, *for* (the possessor); esp. *to himself* (etc.). *Obs.*

**1423** *Cov. Leet Bk.* 47 The tenement..schal-be seuerall to þe priour of Couentre. **1450-1530** *Myrr. our Ladye* 284 The olyue that growyth in gardyns is seueral to the owners. **1523** Fitzherb. *Husb.* §18 He that hath a falowe felde, seueral to hym-selfe. **1551** Robinson tr. *More's Utopia* I. (1895) 101 Here..euerye man hath hys possessyons seuerall to hymselfe, and there all thinges be common. **1593** *Rites of Durham* (Surtees 1903) 83 Euery one of the old monkes had his Carrell seuerall by him selfe. **1612** Brerewood *Lang. & Relig.* 112 The Jews have not for their mansion any peculiar countrey;..neither have they..any other region in the world, several to themselves.

**d.** *fig.* and *allusively.*

*c* **1430** Lydg. *Min. Poems* (Percy Soc.) 207 The bastyle. longith of verray dewe ryght, To fals bakerys it is trewe herytage, Severelle to them. **1526** Tindale *Expos. Matt.* v. (*c* 1550) 24b, The lyght of Christes gospell may not bee hidden nor made a seuerall thinge, as though it parteyned to some certayne holy parsons onelye. **1569** in Strype *Ann. Ref.* (1709) I. lv. 558 Many of your Disordered.. Wives are much agrieved that Priests, which were wont to be Common, be now made Several. **1588** Shaks. *L.L.L.* II. i. 223 *La.* My lips are no Common, though seuerall they be. *Bo.* Belonging to whom? *La.* To my fortunes and me. *c* **1600** —— *Sonn.* cxxxvii, Why should my heart thinke that a seuerall plot, Which my heart knows the wide worlds common place? **1611** W. Sclater *Key* (1629) 303 So enuious is our nature, and so gladly would we make seuerall Gods common fauours.

**8.** Belonging, attributed, or assigned distributively to certain individuals referred to; different for each respectively. **a.** Preceded by a possessive (or its equivalent) referring usually to a collective or distributive adj. or pron.; (*a*) qualifying a pl. sb.

**1457** in *Rep. Hist. MSS. Comm.* Var. Coll. IV. 85 Bothe my lord and we haue now late writen vnto you diuers times our seueralx lettres of especial Recommendation. **1579** Gosson *Sch. Abuse* (Arb.) 51 As to the body, there are many members, seruing to seuerall vses. **1617** Moryson *Itin.* I. 285 Now I will set downe the divers moneys of Germany, with the severall values of them. **1633** P. Fletcher *Purple Isl.* I. xxxix, Bid each kinde their severall places fill. **1667** Milton *P.L.* III. 714 Swift to thir several Quarters hasted then The cumbrous Elements, Earth, Flood, Aire, Fire. *a* **1716** South *Serm.* (1744) X. 118 Moses and our Saviour Christ himself; both of them in their several times, the meekest persons upon the earth. **1819** Scott *Ivanhoe* xxxviii, They embraced accordingly, and departed on their several roads. *a* **1842** Arnold *Hist. Rome* III. xliv. 175 The officers for the year being thus appointed, it remained to determine their several provinces. **1881** Jowett *Thucyd.* I. 149 The Acharnians..did not attempt any united action, but guarded their several districts.

(*b*) qualifying a sing. sb.

**1577** B. Googe *Heresbach's Husb.* I. (1586) 33 They are to be sowed in tyme and place as I haue tolde before, in my seuerall entreatyng of them. **1599** Shaks. *Much Ado* v. iii. 29 Good morrow masters, each his seuerall way. **1629** Milton *Hymn Nativ.* xxvi, Each fetter'd Ghost slips to his severall grave. **1633** G. Herbert *Temple, Ch. Porch* viii, All in a shipwrack shift their severall way. *c* **1750** Shenstone *Ruin'd Abbey* 18 Ambitious to display Their several merit. **1807** Wordsw. *White Doe* I. 161 While each pursues his several road. **1866** Lowell *Study Wind., Swinburne* (1870) 214 Each was natural in his several way. **1894** K. Grahame *Pagan P.* 4 But most of them, avoiding classification, keep each his several tender significance.

**b.** Preceded by the indef. article. *Obs.* or *arch.*

**1526** Tindale *1 Cor.* xv. 38 To every seed a severall body. **1583** Stubbes *Anat. Abus.* I. (1879) 102 To euery dish a seuerall sawce appropriat to his kinde. **1634** Ford *Perkin Warbeck* Epil., Here ha's appear'd, though in a severall fashion, The Threats of Majestie; the strength of passion; Hopes of an Empire; change of fortunes. **1635** Pagitt *Christianogr.* III. (1636) 83, I finde added to the end of every Psalme a severall Prayer. **1672** Villiers (Dk. Buckhm.) *Rehearsal* III. ii. (Arb.) 77, I see, Sir, you have a several design for every Scene. **1707** Cibber *Com. Lovers* IV. Stage Direct., Florimel and Celadon walk carelessly by one another, humming a several Tune. **1732** Pope *Ess. Man* II. 237 Each individual seeks a sev'ral goal. **1879** J. Earle *Philol. Eng. Tongue* (ed. 3) 193 To observe the distinction.. by a several [*ed.* 1871 distinct] orthography, writing the interjection *wo*, and the substantive *woe*.

†(*b*) *ellipt. Obs.*

**1628** Feltham *Resolves* I. xliii. 127 Opinions are as various, as false. Iudgement is from every tongue, a severall. **1651** Hobbes *Gov. & Soc.* vi. §1. 86 In neither sense can a multitude be understood to have one will given to it by nature, but to either a severall. **1670** J. Smith *Eng. Improv. Reviv'd* 182 Within these Ovals do grow Saffron, Anniseed, Carroway, and Coriander-seed in each Plot a several.

†**c.** Preceded by other limiting words. *Obs.*

**1614** Tailor *Hog hath lost Pearl* III. E 1 b, Search through the guts of greatnes, and behold What seueral sin best pleas'd them. **1647** Clarendon *Hist. Reb.* IV. §131 He repeated the Several, and Distinct discourse every man had made.

**d.** Not preceded by a limiting word, and qualifying a sing. or pl. sb. *Obs.* or *arch.*

**1571** Digges *Pantom.* III. xi. R iv, To teach seuerall rules for euery sorte it were ouer tediouse. **1587** Fleming *Contn. Holinshed* III. 1428/1 My lord gaue to them seuerall thanks, and they seuerallie did giue to him the like. **1594** Drayton *Idea* xxxvii, How happy are all other liuing Things, Which though the Day dis-ioyne by seu'rall flight, The quiet Eu'ning yet together brings. **1615** T. Adams *White Devil* 2 Every one shewed him severall kindness. **1667** Milton *P.L.* x. 610 This said, they betook them several wayes. *Ibid.* 650 The Creator calling forth by name His mightie Angels gave them several charge. **1732** Pope *Ess. Man* II. 166 A mightier Pow'r the strong direction sends, And sev'ral Men impels to sev'ral ends. **1838** Wordsw. '*Serving no haughty Muse*' 4 My hands have here Disposed some cultured Flowerets..Each kind in several beds of one parterre.

**9.** *Law.* (Opposed to *joint*.) Pertaining separately to each of the tenants of an estate, parties to a bond or suit, etc. Of inheritance, tail: By which land is conveyed or entailed to two persons separately by moieties. Of an obligation to which several are parties: Enforceable against each of the parties independently of the others. *several tenancy*: see quot. 1607.

**1532** *Dial. Laws Eng.* II. xxx. 64 That writte lyeth where two presente by seuerall tytles. **1544** tr. *Littleton's Tenures* 67 Tenauntes in comon be they that haue landes and tenementes..by seueral tytle, and nat ioynt tytle, and none of them knowe that, that is seuerall to him. [**1581** Kitchin *Court Leet* 198 Cestuy que plede seueral tenancy.] **1607** Cowel *Interpr.*, *Several tenancie* (*tenura separalis*) is a plee, or exception taken to a writ, that is laide against two as ioynt, which are seuerall. **1628** Coke *On Litt.* 189 Joyntenants haue the Lands by one ioynt Title, and in one Right, & Tenants in common by seuerall Titles, or by one Title, and by seuerall Rights. **1684** Manley *Cowel's Interpr.*, *Several tayle*, is that whereby Land is given or entayled severally to Two: For example Land is given to two Men and their Wives, and to the Heirs of their Bodies begotten; the Donees have joynt Estate for their two Lives, and yet they have several Inheritance. **1821** Archbold *Digest* 307 If several tenancy be pleaded to parcel, the tenant must also plead over to the action or vouch. **1826** G. J. Bell *Comm. Laws Scot.* (ed. 5) I. 346 *note*, A bill drawn abroad, without the words jointly and severally, settled to be joint and several on a report of mercantile usage. **1847** C. G. Addison *Law of Contracts* I. i. §2 (1883) 38 Wherever several persons agree to perform a particular act, they are bound jointly and not severally in the absence of express words creating a several liability. **1863** *Chamb. Encycl.* V. 732/2 The general rule of law is, that a contract of several persons is joint and not several.

†**10.** *Logic.* Used as designation of the minor proposition: see minor *a.* 4. *Obs.*

**1551** T. Wilson *Logic* F viij, The seconde is called *Minor*, that is to saie, the seuerall proposicion. *Ibid.*, The second terme is called the seuerall, whiche is in the second proposicion. *Ibid.* G j, The terme at large, is in the first proposicion, and the terme seuerall, is in the second proposicion.

†**B.** *adv.* = severally *adv.*; separately, apart; distinctly, differently; each in his own place, way, turn, etc. *Obs.*

**1551** Robinson tr. *More's Utopia* II. v. (1895) 157 Euerye kynde of thynge is layde vp seuerall in barnes. **1560** Daus tr. *Sleidane's Comm.* VI. 78 They al pourged them selves every man several [orig. L. *separatim*]. **1576** G. Baker *Gesner's Jewell of Health* 228 b, These beaten severall and apart, and compounded after altogether,..keepe to your use. **1596** Spenser *F.Q.* VI. i. 10 Both tooke goodly leaue, and parted seuerall. *c* **1615** W. Gordon in Purchas *Pilgrims* III. III. xii. 555 Foure or fiue Wiues, with whom he lyeth by turn euery night seueral. **1667** Milton *P.L.* v. 697 Hee together calls, Or several one by one, the Regent Powers. *a* **1777** *Robin Hood & Golden Arrow* xiii. in Child *Ballads* III. 224/1 We'll dress us all so several They shall not us perceive. One shall wear white, another red [etc.].

**C.** *sb.*

**1.** in several [AF. *en several*]: †**a.** Of land, pasture: As private property; in private hands, under separate ownership, not common. *Obs.*

**1473** *Acta Audit.* (1839) 27/1 þe landis of Wistoune pertening to him in seuerale & propirte. **1573-80** Tusser *Husb.* (1878) 145 More profit is quieter found (where pastures in seuerall bee:) Of one seelie aker of ground, than champion maketh of three. [**1602** Carew *Cornwall* 13 Their workes, both Streame and Load, lie either in seuerall, or in wastrell, that is, in enclosed grounds, or in commons.] **1652-62** Heylin *Cosmogr.* III. (1673) 24/1 Where the Lands lie in several, and are duly cultivated, it answereth to the former character. **1707** Mortimer *Husb.* (1721) I. 204 Good store of Pasture, either in several or common.

**b.** Separately, individually; apart from others or the rest; as a separate member, unit, etc. Now *rare.*

*to know one's part in several* (Law): see 2 c.

**1586** A. Day *Eng. Secretary* I. (1595) 47 As touching these particularities which we have tearmed Motions and affects let vs consider if you wil in seuerall, and see [etc.]. **1601** Holland *Pliny* VI. xxxiii. I. 149 Now are we to compare respectively the greatnes of ech part of the world in severall. **1607** Topsell *Four-f. Beasts* 11 Concerning their members or parts in seueral, they are black and hairy,..a long Dogges face, and teeth stronger and longer then Dogges. *c* **1611** Chapman *Iliad* II. 320 They all, will fight in seuerall then, (Easie for note). **1652-62** Heylin *Cosmogr.* III. (1673) 3/1 So it retained that name [Asia] to it self in several, distinct both from the Greater and the Lesser Asia. **1862** F. Hall *Hindu Philos. Syst.* 160 *note*, Nescience and ignorance, when referred to souls in several, are only fractional portions of illusion.

†**c.** Divided into separate portions. *Obs.*

**1652** W. Brough *Sacred Princ.* (ed. 2) 28 If thou wouldest have a reason, why these Prayers are so short, and in severall, which use to make a long one, all put together.

**2.** Land in private ownership or over which a person has a particular right; chiefly in particularized use, a plot of such land; *esp.* enclosed pasture land, as opposed to common. *Obs.* exc. *dial.* (see quots. 1787, 1895).

*c* **1460** *Oseney Reg.* 139 Thabbot and Couent.. purposenne..to close all þe forsayde ffelde of le heth and lynlonde as here seuerell. **1473** *Acta Audit.* (1839) 27/1 Quhethir þe said land..has been broukit..be þe saide Johne of carmichell..as propirte & seuerale til him. **1523** Fitzherb. *Surv.* 7 The lorde may haue an actyon of Trespace agaynst any man that chaceth or kylleth any of theym in his commen as well as in his seuerall. **1587** Mascall *Govt. Cattle, Sheep* (1627) 229 They haue no seuerals to put their lambs in when they should bee weaned. **1642** Fuller *Holy & Prof. St.* v. xiii. 409 He counts to enter common with others as good as his own severall. **1669** Worlidge *Syst. Agric.* (1681) 15 A Farm divided into many Severals. **1787** Marshall *Norfolk* (1795) II. 378 *Dole*, or *Several*, a piece of land upon a heath or common, off which only one particular person hath a right to cut fuel. **1895** *E. Angl. Gloss.*, *Several*, a portion of common land allotted to a certain person.

†**b.** *gen.* Private property or possession. *Obs.*

**1555** Watreman *Fardle Facions* Pref. A ij, When no man claimed aught for his seueralle, but lande and water ware as commune to al, as Ayer and Skie. **1616** Chapman *Homer's Hymn Apollo* 734 No more Yee must be made, your owne Reciprocalls To your lou'd Cittie, and faire seueralls Of wiues, and houses. **1636** B. Jonson *Discov.* (1640) 89 Truth lyes open to all; it is no mans severall. **1642** Fuller *Holy & Prof. St.* IV. i. 242 Some are so boysterous, no severals will hold them, but lay all Offices common to their power.

†**c.** *to know one's several* [AF. *savoir son several*]: see quots. *Obs.*

[**1539** *Act 31 Hen. VIII*, c. 1 None of them [joynt tenauntes] by the lawe..maye knowe their severall partes or porcions in the same. **1544** tr. *Littleton's Tenures* 67 Which haue suche landes & tenementes by seueral tytle, and nat ioynt tytle, and none of them knowe that, that is seuerall to him. **1628** Coke *On Litt.* §292 Their occupation is indeuided, and neyther of them knoweth his part in seuerall.]

**1598** *Termes de la Ley* §267 Though two tenants in common be seised throughly & of the whole and none knoweth hys seueral, yet if one die the other shall not haue the whole by yᵉ suruiuor. **1628** Coke *On Litt.* §292 None of them [tenants in common] know of this his seuerall.

*transf.* **1639** Fuller *Holy War* II. viii. (1640) 54 The deluge of the Saracens tyranny had washed away the bounds of the Churches jurisdictions, that now they knew not their own severals, where Mahometanisme so long had made all common and waste.

**3.** *pl.* †**a.** Particular or individual points, parts, or qualities; particulars, details. *Obs.*

**1599** Shaks. *Hen. V*, I. i. 86 There was not time enough to heare..The seueralls and vnhidden passages Of his true Titles to some certaine Dukedomes. **1606** —— *Tr. & Cr.* I. iii. 180 All our abilities, gifts, natures, shapes, Seuerals and generals of grace. **1628** Feltham *Resolves* I. xii. 32 No man can leaue his Successor rules for seuerals. **1673** *Ladies Call.* I. i. §7 This will be found true in all the severals we are to pass thro. *a* **1703** Burkitt *On N.T.* Matt. vi. 13 In this comprehensive and compendious prayer, the following severals are remarkable.

(*b*) *rarely* in *sing.*

**1606** Hieron *Truths Purchase* 65 This is the first thing which I will..commend as a direction, for the meaner sort, (who cannot enter into the examination of every seuerall). **1706** Phillips (ed. Kersey), A *Several*, a Particular.

†**b.** Different parts, branches, or heads. *Obs.*

**1639** Fuller *Holy War* v. xix. (1640) 260 Herein we branch our opinion into these severals. **1654** Whitlock *Zootomia* 26 Make Infallibility minced (as I may terme it) into severalls, and private Interpretation the Canon of our owne and other mens beleife. **1659** Bp. Walton *Consid. considered* iii. 39 This [general charge] will appear to be most untrue in the severalls, by him mentioned, when we shall come to them.

†**c.** Individual persons or things. *Obs.*

**1611** Shaks. *Wint. T.* I. ii. 226 Not noted, is't, But of the finer Natures? by some Seueralls Of Head-peece extraordinarie? **1650** Jer. Taylor *Holy Living* ii. §3 (1686) 73 Besides these general acts of Chastity which are common to all states of men and women, there are some few things proper to the severals.

**d.** Several persons or things; = A. b. (Cf. *others*.) *Sc.*, *Irish*, and *U.S.*

**1654** *Nicholas Papers* (Camden) II. 106 He spoak with severalls that were com in. **1693** Stair *Inst. Law Scot.* I. iii. §5 (ed. 2) 21 They remain only as bonds upon the good-will and honesty of these who are thereby bound, of which there are severals. *a* **1699** Lady Halkett *Autobiog.* (Camden) 58 Itt was knowne to severalls about the Court what my concerne in him was. **1711** *Countrey-Man's Lett. to Curate* 70 In all the Impressions of the Genevan Liturgie that ever I saw, and I have seen severals, there is a Table for the Moveable Feasts. **1756** Mrs. Calderwood in *Coltness Collect.* (Maitland Club) 155 They..were acquented with severalls of the great folks. **1860** Bartlett *Dict. Amer.* (ed. 3), *Severals*, for *several*, is used in Pennsylvania. 'How many hats have you?' 'I used to have severals, but now have got only one.' **1875** W. Alexander *Sk. Ain Folk* (1882) 121 Severals o' them wud lickly be cautioners or hae len't sooms till 'im. **1880** *Antrim & Down Gloss.* s.v., Severals told me about it.

†**4.** ? A partition or boundary. *Obs.*

[Possibly another word, f. sever *v.* + -al.]

**1597** Hooker *Eccl. Pol.* v. xiv, [The Jews] had..their seuerall for the Priests, and for the high Priest alone their seuerall. Their being in ours for locall distinction betwene the Clergie and the rest..but one partition. *a* **1661** Fuller *Worthies, Suffolk* (1662) III. 55 High stiles troublesome to be clambred over. But the owners grudge not the pains in climbing them sensible that such severals redound much to their own advantage.

†ˈ**several**, *v. Obs. rare.* [f. several *a.*]

**1.** *trans.* To make (a field) 'several' or enclosed and private property.

1482 *Cov. Leet Bk.* 510 My lorde Priour severels the Brodwok wast. *Ibid.* 511 The Maister of þe Trinite Gilde severels a feld in Stychall-hiron calde Miry-felde. 1577–87 Harrison *England* I. x. 36 in *Holinshed*, The people of this Ile vsed not to seuerall their grounds. 1794 W. Pearce *Agric. Berks.* 49 The advantage resulting from inclosing, or at least severalling common fields, is so very obvious.

2. To divide or break up into separate parts or branches.

1570 Dee *Math. Pref.* *j b, Our Seuerallyng, distinctyng, and Numbryng, createth nothyng: but of Multitude considered, maketh..distinct determination. 1642 D. Rogers *Naaman* 55 Wee will severall the story into her branches.

**'several-fold**, *a.*, *adv.*, and *sb.* [f. several *a.* + -fold.] Used like manifold, but with the implication of not very many.

1738 Medley tr. *Kolben's Cape Gd. Hope* (ed. 2) I. 194 Some of the grown Women have above a Hundred of those Rings upon each Leg, lying several-fold one upon another. 1833 Carlyle *Misc. Ess., Cagliostro* I. (1872) V. 79 As for the other question, of his resources, these we perceive were several-fold, and continually extending. 1884 Bower & Scott *De Bary's Phaner.* 33 In P[eperomia] magnoliifolia and rubella, it [the epidermis] exceeds several-fold the rest of the substance of the leaf, and in P. pereskiifolia it exceeds it seven-fold. 1892 *Advance* (Chicago) 13 Oct., There is a growing interest in the cause, and..we may look for an increase of severalfold. 1945 *Times* 7 Aug. 4/2 The Secretary of War..said later that an improved bomb would be forthcoming soon. It would increase by 'severalfold' the present effectiveness of the new weapon. 1979 *Nature* 29 Mar. 468/1 The rate of protein synthesis increases severalfold during the early cleavage stages. 1981 *Spectator* 7 Nov. 29 The reasons were severalfold.

**severality** (sɛvəˈrælɪtɪ). *rare.* [f. several *a.* + -ity. Cf. the earlier severalty.]

1. *pl.* Individual or particular points, matters, or objects.

1562 [see severalty 4]. 1649 Bp. Hall *Cases Consc.* iv. v. (1654) 332 All the severalities of the degrees prohibited run still upon the male. 1830 W. Taylor *Hist. Surv. Germ. Poetry* II. 359 He..Packs up his severalities. 1843 Emerson *Misc. Papers, Carlyle* Wks. (Bohn) III. 315 And no such glaring contrasts or severalities in that or this.

†2. Separateness, distinctness. *Obs.*

1664 Power *Exp. Philos.* Pref. 9 Multiplicity of parts, diversity of figures, severality of functions.

3. *in severality*: separately, singly, each by itself.

1665 J. Webb *Stone-Heng* (1725) 31 Reckoning up the Parts of Structures in Severality. 1836 J. Abbott *Way to do Good* ix. 284 The objects, though..trifling when regarded in severality and detail rise to..importance when we consider their fast aggregation.

**'severalize**, *v. rare.* [See -ize.] *trans.* To separate or distinguish (*from*). Cf. severize *v.*

1645 Bp. Hall *Peace-maker* i. §3. 14 There is one and the same Church of Christ, however farre disterminate in places, however segregated and infinitely severallized in persons. 1649 J. E[llistone] tr. *Behmen's Epist.* vi. §17. 85 The properties of the Severalized distinguishing or separating will [orig. *die Eigenschafften des schiedlichen Willens*]. 1862 F. Hall *Hindu Philos. Syst.* 284 Its epithet visuddha, 'pure', is intended to severalize it from 'modificational cognition'.

**severall**: see several and severon.

**severally** (ˈsɛvərəlɪ), *adv.* [f. several *a.* + -ly².]

1. Separately, individually; each of a number of persons or things by himself or itself; each successively or in turn.

(*a*) with distributive adj. or pron.

1399 *Rolls of Parlt.* III. 451/1 The Answeres of certeins Lordes..ware herd, iche man severallyche by hymself. *a* 1533 Frith *Disput. Purgat.* Wks. (1573) 13/2 Let us see how he aunswereth the argument, and seuerally examine euery part. 1549 *Form Consecr. Archbishops*, etc. rubric, The Bisshop with the Priestes presente shall laye their handes seuerally vpon the heade of euery one that receaueth orders. 1560 Daus tr. *Sleidane's Comm.* xvi. 228 b, He had spoken with eyther of them severally. 1597 Hooker *Eccl. Pol.* v. lxviii. §2 In speaking vnto euery communicant seuerally. 1700 Dryden *Fables* Pref. *C, All his Pilgrims are severally distinguish'd from each other. 1760–2 Goldsm. *Cit. W.* xxx, He turned severally to each for their opinion. 1812 H. & J. Smith *Rej. Addr.* v. (1873) 39, I take it for granted that every intelligent man, woman, and child..has stood severally and respectively in Little Russell Street.

(*b*) referring to plural subject or object.

*c* 1400 tr. *Secreta Secret., Gov. Lordsh.* 101 It nedys noght þat a kyng aske conseyll of vs, of any of his pryue doynges, But þat he aske seuerally of some his conseill. 1456 *Cov. Leet Bk.* 286 Endentures seuerally made be-twix the seyde Meyre & the Collectours. 1528 More *Dial. Heresies* iii. iii. Wks. 209/2 Whan thei be wisely & seuerally examined, thei can seldome so well make their tale before, but that their vntrouth shall in some parte appere. 1603 Drayton *Bar. Wars* vi. xxxiii. 133 Yet heere and there they seu'rally withdrew. 1660 *Trial Regic.* 33 We must needs try them severally. 1828 Scott *F.M. Perth* xiii, Receiving the mute salutations of the members of the council whom he had severally addressed. 1890 Gladstone in *Daily News* 31 Dec. 5/7 My own inability to acknowledge severally the gifts ..which have reached..me. 1892 Westcott *Gospel of Life* 33 We severally think with a mind which is more or less in harmony with a universal mind.

b. In legal language, opposed to *jointly*.

1447 *Rolls of Parlt.* V. 140/1 An action of trespasse ayenst such takers and ayenst all thaym, to whom the possession.. comes..joyntly or severally. 1474 *Ibid.* VI. 115/2 That the same Shires..stond and be severally chargeable and charged of the same men Archers. 1528 Gardiner in Pocock *Rec. Ref.* (1870) I. 1. 104 To proceed jointly or severally with your grace. 1628 Coke *On Litt.* §296 In this case of the two Abbots in respect of their seuerall capacities, albeit the words be ioynt, yet the Law doth adiudge them to be seuerally seised. 1652 tr. *Fitzherbert's Nat. Brevium* 38 Whether they shall recover severally damages upon that joynt count, it is a doubt. 1875 Poste *Gaius* iii. 396 In Correality each creditor is *severally* entitled to receive, and each debtor is *severally* bound to discharge, the whole Object of the obligation. *a* 1887 J. Grant *Royal Highlanders* 19 Holcroft would in some way or other bring trouble upon them conjunctly or severally.

(*b*) *jointly* (Sc. *conjunctly*) *and severally.*

1454 *Registr. Aberdon.* (Maitland Club) I. 261 Be it kende til al men me Edwarde of þe Vesthale til haf maide [the several persons named] coniunctly and seuerly my ful procuratoris. 1467 *Godstow Reg.* 347 They made..Iohn Baywell and Symond Turnere..there trew and lawfull attorneyes, ioyntly and severally, to entre and delyver in ther name. 1554 *Acts of Sederunt* (1790) 1 That thay, and ilk ane of thaim, conjunctlie and severalie, suld lelelie and trewlie minister in the said office of curatry. 1597 in *Spalding Club Misc.* (1841) I. 117 The quhilk to do we commit to you, coniunctlie and severallie, our full power, be this our precept. 1766 Blackstone *Comm.* ii. xii. II. 193 A devise to two persons, to hold jointly and severally, is a joint-tenancy. 1826 G. J. Bell *Comm. Laws Scot.* (ed. 5) I. 346 If the co-obligants be bound jointly and severally, any one may be taken for the whole debt. 1838 W. Bell *Dict. Law Scot.* s.v. *Conjunctly*, When two or more persons are bound conjunctly and severally to perform an obligation, they are liable *singuli in solidum*, and it is in the option of the creditor to exact performance, either from each of them proportionally, or to enforce the obligation to the full extent against any one of them, leaving him to seek his relief from the rest.

†c. Preceded by numeral adv.: On two (etc.) separate occasions. *Obs.*

1576 Gascoigne *Kenelworth Castle* Wks. 1910 II. 121 Twise severally summoned to appeare before the great Gods.

2. Apart from others or from the rest; not together or in a company; independently. *arch.*

1530 Elyot *Image Gov.* (1541) 104 The thyrde state was of the base people or communers to whom seuerally should not be committed any authoritee. 1548 Geste *Agst. Priv. Masse* L j, In the pryuate masse where the priest seuerally all alone hath hys loofe & eateth it alone. 1577 Hanmer *Anc. Eccles. Hist., Euseb.* ii. xvii. (1663) 29 They assembled together, severally men, and severally women. 1615 Markham *Eng. Housew.* i. 25 Take knot grasse and shepheards purse, and plantaine, and stampe them seuerally. 1630 Pagitt *Christianogr.* i. ii. (1636) 55 These Christians live severally by themselves without any mixture of Mahometans or Pagans. 1660 Barrow *Euclid* i. xxxii, Two angles (taken severally, or together). 1709 Atterbury *Serm.* (Rom. xi. 6) (1726) II. 256 Abraham, Isaac, and Jacob ..to whom the Promise of the Blessed Seed was severally made. 1883 Stevenson *Silverado Sq.* 9 A great variety of oaks stood, now severally, now in a becoming grove, among the fields.

const. *from.* 1649 Milton *Eikon.* xi. 102 [The King is] not to be consider'd severally from them [the Parliament]. 1862 F. Hall *Hindu Philos. Syst.* 99 It is the same as concerns the experience of cognition, or the like, considered severally from its experience.

†b. Specially, particularly. *Obs. rare.*

*c* 1610 *Women Saints* 70 The place cutt for the head seuerallie was made so iust for her head as could be deuised.

3. Respectively.

1585 T. Washington tr. *Nicholay's Voy.* ii. vii. 37 b, Grecians and Geneuoises, and..Iewes..seuerally haue one streete to dwell in. 1756 Burke *Subl. & B.* i. x, They stick severally to their own species in preference to all others. 1827 C. Wordsworth *Chas. I* (1828) 2 The parts which I and they have severally taken are openly justified. 1875 Jowett *Plato* (ed. 2) I. 33 The great benefits which mankind would obtain from their severally doing the things which they knew. 1909 *Athenæum* 20 Mar. 345/1 'The Constitution is saved.' 'A Commission is needed at once.' So say severally the very old and the very young amongst our legislators.

†4. Differently, variously. *Obs.*

1605 Bacon *Adv. Learn.* i. i. §3 To deliuer it [*sc.* learning] from the discredites and disgraces which it hath receiued; all from ignorance; but ignorance seuerally disguised. 1625 —— *Ess., Of Building* (Arb.) 549, I vnderstand both these Sides..to be vniforme without, though seuerally Partitioned within. 1628 Feltham *Resolves* i. xciii. 271 There are, and that seuerally, that be much troubled with the disease of speaking. *a* 1644 Chillingworth *Serm.* ii. §42 How severally Satan plants his Engines for the subversion of the Church.

**severalth**, *a. U.S. dial.* Also severaleth. [f. several *a.* + -th².] The ordinal form of several *a.* 4 as an indefinite number.

1902 A. H. Lewis *Wolfville Days* xvi. 238 Re-fillin' his glass for the severaleth time. 1949 'J. Nelson' *Backwoods Teacher* ii. 23 But presently, apologizing for the 'severalth' time—to use a good word we learned at Big Piney—..Mrs Helms did sit down.

**severalty** (ˈsɛvərəltɪ). [a. AF. *severalte*, *-aute*: see several *a.* and -ty.]

1. The condition of being separate or distinct; separateness, distinctness, independence.

1449 Pecock *Repr.* i. x. 50 ȝit herfore tho craftis in thilk man ben not the lasse dyuerse, ne neuer the lasse kepen her seueralte in boundis and markis as in hem silf. 1571 Golding *Calvin on Ps.* lxxiv. 16 Insatiable covetousnes and ambition breaketh whatsoever severaltie [*quicquid distinctionis*] is made in the world. 1648 Bp. Hall *Select Th.* 269 He singles them out in a familiar kinde of severalty both of knowledg and respect. 1650 B. *Discolliminium* 37 A respective severalty, that each Nation should operate separately..in cases peculiar to their severall interests. 1679 Puller *Moder. Ch. Eng.* (1843) 21 The several societies of Christian men, unto every of which the name of a Church is given, with addition betokening severalty, as the Church of Rome, Corinth, Ephesus, England. 1847 Grote *Greece* ii. x. III. 92 The original severalty and subsequent consolidation of the different portions of Attica. 1849 *Ibid.* ii. xxxviii. V. 8 The discordant severalty of agents conspicuous in the Homeric theology. *a* 1882 T. H. Green *Proleg. Ethics* (1883) 31 Something other than the manifold things themselves which combines them without effacing their severalty.

2. **in severalty** [AF. *en severalte*]. a. *Law.* Of land: (Held) in a person's own right without being joined in interest with another (opposed to joint-tenancy, coparcenary, and tenancy-in-common); (held) as private enclosed property (opposed to common).

*to know in severalty*: = 'to know one's several': see several C. 2 c.

*c* 1475 *Partenay* 3640 Thi land shal be..Parted in partes.. Neuer to-geders hold in seueralte. 1480 *Cov. Leet Bk.* 447 He kepeth diuerse pastures in seueralte, which owen to be comen. 1523 Fitzherb. *Surv.* 2 And than is nat an acre so moche worthe as & it were in seueralty inclosed or in seuerall pasture. 1540 *Act 32 Hen. VIII*, c. 1 §3 The same in three partes to be divided in certainety and by speciall divisions as it may be knowen in severaltie. 1581 W. S. *Compend. Exam.* 18 b, Tenaunts in common be not so good husbandes as when euery man hath his parte in seueralty. 1653 tr. *Kitchin's Courts Leet* (ed. 2) 476 They are Tenants in severalty. 1766 Blackstone *Comm.* II. 185 If two joint-tenants agree to part their lands, and hold them in severalty, they are no longer joint-tenants. 1807 Vancouver *Agric. Devon* (1813) 102 Coarse moor-land, lying in severalty. 1818 Cruise *Digest* (ed. 2) I. 329 Not in the nature of dower, that is, in severalty, but in common with the heir. 1875 Maine *Hist. Instit.* iv. 101 The arable lands are held in severalty, while pasture and bog are in common. 1895 Strahan *Law of Property* (1908) 132 By partition is meant the dividing up of the joint estate among the joint tenants, who henceforth hold their individual shares in severalty.

(*b*) Const. *to* or *for* (the possessor).

1523 *Act 14 & 15 Hen. VIII*, c. 6 §1 Yt shalbe leafull to your said besecher [etc.]..to enclose the said olde Waye.. and that frohensforthe to holde in Severaltie to them and to their Heires and Assignes to their owne use and profitt for ever..without any comon Waye or passage ther. 1652 Heylin *Cosmogr.* iii. 44 Every one..should..take as much ground in severalty for his own inheritance, as he could overcome.

b. Separately, apart from others, particularly.

1588 Fraunce *Lawiers Logike* ii. iii. 89 b, If the same Logicall Doctor..should affirme the same of all the other kindes of causes specially and in seueralty. 1624 Wotton *Archit.* i. 64 Hauing considered the precedent Appertions or Ouertures, in seueraltie according to their particular Requisites. 1768 Tucker *Lt. Nat.* (1834) I. 240 That all should enjoy the produce of their skill and industry in severalty, without interruption from others. 1893 Traill *Soc. Eng.* Introd. 17 It has seemed best to treat of each great department of our social life in severalty.

c. In or into several divisions or parts.

1824 J. Davison *Disc. Prophecy* vi. iii. 388 Polytheism divided the world, and its own creed, in severalty; it set up its deities over particular regions. 1868 Gladstone *Juv. Mundi* viii. §12. 304 One group of these traditions..which when associated compose a nebula, appears before us in severalty, divided between the three individualities of Artemis, Persephonè, and Aphroditè.

3. Land held by an individual not joined with other owners. Also, the condition of land so held; a state of being owned by individuals.

1570 Dee *Math. Pref.* a ij, Which was when..ground sold were to be layd out: or (when disorder preuailed) that Commons were distributed into seueralties. 1766 Blackstone *Comm.* ii. xii. II. 194 Estates in common can only be dissolved two ways: 1. By uniting all the titles and interests in one tenant..which brings the whole to one severalty: 2. By making partition between the several tenants in common, which gives them all respective severalties. 1801 *Farmer's Mag.* Nov. 400 Reducing all common and intermixed possessions into severalty. 1814 Shirreff *Agric. Shetld.* 179 Till land is placed in a state of severalty,..inclosures are seldom erected in any country. 1844 *Min. Evid. Sel. Comm. Commons' Inclosure* 27 It often happens that in these shifting severalties the occupier of lot one this year goes round the whole of the several lots in rotation. 1862 Merivale in *Macm. Mag.* July 265 Not inclosed from the waste, but merely converted from 'common field' into severalty.

b. *attrib.*

1844 *Min. Evid. Sel. Comm. Commons' Inclosure* 27 After the crop has been removed, these lands become commonable to all the parties having a severalty right, and to no others. *Ibid.*, The severalty crop. *Ibid.*, Circumstances under which the severalty ownership of these lands shifts from time to time. 1892 *Pall Mall Gaz.* 30 May 6/2 A private arrangement between the lord, the severalty owners, and the owners of lammas rights.

†4. A separate, distinct, or particular thing, point, feature, etc. *Obs.*

1561 T. Norton *Calvin's Inst.* i. xiii. 37 Lette it not come in our myndes ones to imagine suche a Trinitie of Persons as may hold our thought withdrawen into seueralties [ed. 1562 seueralities]. 1610 Healey *St. Aug. Citie of God* viii. vii. tr. *Vives* 309 The first apprehensions..nature hath giuen man, whence the knowledge of many great seueralties arise [*vnde rerum multarum magnarumque oritur cognitio*]. 1637 Heylin *Answ. Burton* 163 These are the severalties contained in that generall head; and they relate either to preaching or to praying. 1640 Bp. Hall *Episc.* ii. vii. 124 Here is a manifest distinction betwixt the Pastor or Bishop, and those of his charge; and they are described by the severalties of their estates. 1667 Waterhouse *Narr. Fire in London* 17 Many other Authors have given us severalties which summed up together, makes out such secret policies.

5. (See quot.)

1867 Smyth *Sailor's Word-bk.*, *Severalty*, the denomination under which disagreements respecting accounts amongst the part owners of a ship are referred, either to equity courts, or the common law.

**severance** ('sɛvərəns). [a. AF. *severance*, OF. *sevrance*, f. *sevr-er*: see SEVER *v.* and -ANCE.]

**1. a.** The act or fact of severing; the state of being severed; separation.

**1467–8** *Rolls of Parlt.* V. 574/1 Severaunces from Shires, and makyng of Shires by theymself. **1491** *Act 7 Hen. VII*, c. 12 §1 To preserve the possessions of the Crown hoolly and entierly without any severaunce or decreasing therof. **1565** *Act 8 Eliz.* c. 16 §2 The wch sayd severance and Devision of the sayd proffers shalbe entred of Recorde. **1602** CAREW *Cornw.* II. 152 These 2. riuers..doe enclose betweene them ..a neck of land..in regard of his fruitfulnesse, not vnworthy of a seuerance. **1786** JEFFERSON *Writ.* (1859) II. 66 This measure..gives me serious apprehensions of the severance of the eastern and western parts of our confederacy. **1787** J. BARLOW *Oration 4 July* 8 Our severance from the British empire. **1864** PUSEY *Lect. Daniel* (1876) 501 A meeting..after this first severance. **1873** J. GEIKIE *Gt. Ice Age* xxxiii. 474 The sea again stole in between our islands and the Continent, until a final severance was effected. **1875** M. ARNOLD *God & Bible* Pref. 34 Their religion involved severance from Rome. **1876** MISS BRADDON *J. Haggard's Dau.* II. 81 He..kissed her with more warmth of feeling than he had ever shown after so short a severance. **1879** CALDERWOOD *Mind & Br.* iv. 91 There is no real severance of the lobes.

**b.** const. *between* (two or more objects). †Formerly, a distinction or difference *between*.

**1422** YONGE tr. *Secreta Secret.* 180 Mekenesse is the Seuerance and the difference betwene a kynge and a tyraunt. **1508** DUNBAR *Tua Mariit Wemen* 311 For, thocht I say it my self, the seuerance wes mekle, Betuix his bastard blude, and my birth noble. *c* **1642** *Contra-Replicant's Compl.* 28 The Law itself makes ever a distinction betwixt the King and his agents: though our Replicant will not allow any such severance. **1845** MAURICE *Mor. Philos.* in *Encycl. Metrop.* II. 665/1 Now more than at any former time there was a severance between religion and philosophy. **1851** GLADSTONE *Glean.* VI. xlviii. 32 To draw in practice those lines of severance between truth and falsehood. **1865** PUSEY *Truth Eng. Ch.* 59 The temporary severance between Rome and both Asiatic and African Churches. **1883** CHALMERS & HOUGH *Bankruptcy Act* Introd. 9 A severance is made between judicial and administrative functions. **1912** *Blackw. Mag.* Jan. 148/2 The severance between the Parliament and the country is complete.

**2.** *Law.* **a.** The division of a joint estate into independent parts; the destruction of the unity of interest in a joint estate.

**1539** *Act 31 Hen. VIII*, c. 1 §1 Forasmuche as..diverse of the Kinges Subjectes being seised of Mannors landes [etc.] as joynt tenauntes..cannot..make any severans division or particion thereof, without either of their mutuall consentes and assentes. **1628** COKE *On Litt.* 192 If two Joyntenaunts be, and one maketh a Lease, this is a seuerance of the joynture. **1766** BLACKSTONE *Comm.* II. 185 Joint-tenants being seised *per my et per tout*, every thing that tends to narrow that interest..is a severance or destruction of the jointure. **1818** CRUISE *Digest* (ed. 2) II. 501 A mortgage by a joint tenant, for a term of years, will operate as a severance of the joint tenancy. **1895** STRAHAN *Law of Property* (1908) 89 The severance of the reversion..that is, the dividing between two or more of the estate in reversion. *Ibid.* 134 Severance of joint tenancies in land may also be brought about by merger.

**b.** The detaching of fruit, minerals, fixtures, etc. from the soil or realty.

**1602** FULBECKE *1st Pt. Parall.* 38 After the sowing and before the seuerance [of the corn]. **1628** COKE *On Litt.* 55 b, Seuerance or remouing of the corne. **1684** MANLEY *Cowel's Interpr.* s.v., Severance of Corn is the cutting and carrying it off from the ground, and sometimes the setting out the Tythe from the rest of the Corn is called Severance. **1769** BLACKSTONE *Comm.* IV. 232 Of things..that adhere to the freehold, as corn, grass, trees, and the like, or lead upon a house, no larciny could be committed by the rules of the common law; but the severance of them was, and in many things is still, merely a trespass. **1817** W. SELWYN *Law Nisi Prius* (ed. 4) II. 1208 The right to tithes accrues immediately on the severance. **1911** ODGERS *Common Law* II. 700 When things annexed to the freehold are sold in contemplation of an immediate severance.

**c.** The separation of two or more parties that are joined in a writ, as when one is nonsuited and the other is allowed to proceed in the action. Also, 'the putting in several or separate pleas or answers by two or more disjointly' (Bouvier).

**1607** COWEL *Interpr.*, *Severance* is the singling of two or more, that ioyne in one writ, or are ioyned in one writ. **1628** COKE *On Litt.* 139 If two be Plaintifes in a *Natiuo habendo*, if one be nonsuit this is the Nonsuite of both, and no sommons and seuerance doth lie in that case. *Ibid.* 139 b, *Note*, Seuerance is twofold, *viz.* by Sommons *ad sequendum simul*, and that is when one of the Demandants or Plaintifes neuer appeared; and by award of the Court of Nonsuit without any sommons, and that is after appearance. **1684** MANLEY *Cowel's Interpr.* s.v., Severance in Debt [is] where two, or more, Executors are named Plaintiffs, and the one refuses to prosecute. **1741** T. ROBINSON *Gavelkind* I. vi. 110 It is the less unreasonable that the Part of him not proceeding should be divided with the rest in this Case, because he does not by the Severance absolutely cease to be Party to the Record. **1824** STEPHEN *Princ. Pleading* 270 Where in respect of several subjects or several defendants, a severance has thus taken place in the pleading, this may.. lead to a corresponding severance in the whole subsequent series.

**d.** Discharge from contractual employment. Also *ellipt.* = *severance pay* below.

**1941** *North Western Reporter* CCXCVII. 652/1 There was a complete 'severance of employment' and compensation would be calculated on basis of $2.50 per day. **1945** *Monthly Labor Rev.* Jan. 48 The American Newspaper Guild.. regards dismissal pay as an equity which the individual builds up on his job and for which he should be compensated regardless of the reason of severance. **1965** *Bull. U.S. Dept. Labor* No. 1425-2. ii. 9 Some agreements gave no details of the plan's characteristics—i.e., when severance would be paid, [etc.]. **1977** *Time* 5 Dec. 72/2 When CBS decided that Schorr must go, its lawyers in February 1976 agreed to pay Schorr more than two years' salary, and severance besides.

**3.** *attrib.* and *Comb.*, as (sense 2 d) ***severance arrangement, money, payment***; **severance cutting** (see quot. 1928); **severance felling** = *severance-cutting*; **severance pay**, money paid in compensation to one whose contractual employment is terminated; cf. *redundancy pay* s.v. REDUNDANCY 3.

**1971** *Guardian* 14 Jan. 13/3 Some kind of compulsory *severance arrangement..will have to be negotiated. **1905** *Terms Forestry & Logging* (U.S. Dept. Agric.) 20 *Severance cuttings are made to strengthen the trees on the edge of a stand. **1928** R. S. TROUP *Silvicultural Systems* ii. 8 'Severance cuttings'..are cleared lines of varying breadth, usually 30–50 feet, cut through the wood while it is still comparatively young in order to induce low branching by the border trees. **1895** W. R. FISHER tr. *Schlich's Man. Forestry* 469 *Severance-fellings should be forty to fifty feet broad. **1951** W. L. TAYLOR *Estate Forestry* xiv. 131 Gale and flood are countered by..correct orientation of forest rides and severance fellings. **1975** *N.Y. Times* 5 Nov. 23/3 The parent company closed down the edition [*sc.* the Scottish Daily Express] 18 months ago.., and the employees decided to keep it going as a cooperative. They put *severance money of $1.3 million into the venture. **1953** P. C. BERG *Dict. New Words* 143/1 *Severance pay. **1956** *Economist* 7 July 12/2 The unions now appear to be ready to lay rather more emphasis on bargaining for higher severance pay. **1979** *Now!* 21–27 Sept. 95/1 The £1,750 tax-free severance pay provides a cushion for defeated MPs. **1962** *Listener* 19 July 86/1, I believe a compensation scheme—*severance payment—is important.

**severane**, obs. form of SOVEREIGN.

**severans, -ant**: see SEVERON.

†**severat(e**, *a. Obs.* Altered form of SEPARATE *a.*, after *sever*. Hence †**severatly** *adv.*

**1470–85** MALORY *Arthur* IV. vii. 127 He tooke vs seuerately as we rode on oure auentures. **1563** *Homilies* II. *Right Use Ch.* II. Ddj, When euery man and woman in seuerate [*edd.* 1567–71 seuerat, *later edd.* seuerall] pretence of deuotyon prayeth priuately.

**severation** (sɛvə'reɪʃən). *rare.* [f. SEVER *v.* + -ATION.] Separation, severance.

**1649** J. E[LLISTONE] tr. *Behmen's Epist.* vi. §60 The humane Science..may in that same light see, not onely it selfe, but likewise all other naturall things according to the severation of the Word. **1654** [ELLISTONE & SPARROW] tr. *Behmen's Myst. Magn.* iv. 12 Now we are to consider of the Severation in the fire. **1821** W. P. C. BARTON *Flora N. Amer.* I. 27 Michaux deemed it sufficiently at variance with that genus in its fruit, to justify a severation. **1852** W. JERDAN *Autobiog.* II. 282 The last severation of all human ties.

**severe** (sɪ'vɪə(r)), *a.* Also 6 sever, *Sc.* seveir(e, (7 seveere, seveare). [a. F. *sévère* or ad. L. *sevērus*. Cf. It., Sp., Pg. *severo*.]

**I.** Rigorous in condemnation or punishment.

**1. a.** Of persons, their temper, disposition, etc.: Rigorous in one's treatment of, or attitude towards, offenders; unsparing in the exaction of penalty; not inclined to indulgence or leniency.

**1548** ELYOT *Dict.*, *Asper*,..rude, seuere, rigorous. *Ibid.*, *Austerus*,..cruelle, austere, seuere. **1560** DAUS tr. *Sleidane's Comm.* xv. 197 b, In a steade of a gentle and mercifull Prince, you shall haue a seuere executour of iustice. *a* **1568** ASCHAM *Scholem.* I. (Arb.) 47 One of the greatest benefites, that euer God gaue me, is, that he sent me so sharpe and seuere Parentes, and so ientle a scholemaster. **1603** SHAKS. *Meas. for M.* III. ii. 276 He who the sword of Heauen will beare, Should be as holy, as seueare. **1611** BIBLE *Wisd.* v. 20 His seuere wrath shall he sharpen for a sword. **1611** HEYWOOD *Golden Age* I. i, Why should not I proue as seuere a mother As he a cruell father. **1667** MILTON *P.L.* IX. 1169 And am I now upbraided, as the cause Of thy transgressing? not enough severe, It seems, in thy restraint. *a* **1715** BURNET *Own Time* (1823) I. 290 They were men of severe tempers, and kept good discipline. **1780** HARRIS *Philol. Enq.* Wks. (1841) 463 [Athens] found the cruel Sylla her severest enemy. **1829** SCOTT *Anne of G.* xiv, Charles of Burgundy deserved the character of a just though severe prince. **1849** MACAULAY *Hist. Eng.* viii. II. 342 The King's temper was arbitrary and severe. **1878** DALE *Lect. Preach.* iii. 74 Nature is sometimes kindly if she is often severe.

*absol.* **1817** SHELLEY *Rev. Islam* II. xxxiv, Nor are the strong and the severe to keep The empire of the world.

**b.** Const. *to, with, against.*

[**1561**: cf. 3.] **1648** *Hamilton Papers* (Camden) 216 The Houses haue been of late very seuere against the poore Caualiers. *a* **1699** STILLINGFL. (J.), What made the church of Alexandria be so severe with Origen for, but holding the incence in his hands..? yet for this he was cast out of the church. *a* **1700** EVELYN *Diary* 22 July 1674, A severe master to his servants. **1725** POPE *Odyss.* IX. 132 Each rules his race, his neighbour not his care, Heedless of others, to his own severe. **1742** GRAY *Adversity* 31 Justice, to herself severe.

**c.** Of a person's looks, demeanour, etc.: Betokening a severe mood or disposition.

**1565** COOPER *Thesaurus* s.v. *Seuerus*, Seuere grauitie of countenance. **1600** SHAKS. *A.Y.L.* II. vii. 155 The Iustice,.. With eyes seuere, and beard of formall cut. **1603** KNOLLES *Hist. Turks* (1621) 709 Saying with a severe countenance, that they were worthie of such death. **1675** COVEL in *Early Voy. Levant* (Hakl. Soc.) 206 A full, roundish high forehead, a severe brow. **1819** SCOTT *Ivanhoe* xxxvi, 'There is in this mansion..,' said the Grand Master, in a severe tone, 'a Jewish woman.' **1848** THACKERAY *Van. Fair* xlix, The Lady Bareacres..to whom the Colonel's lady made also a most respectful obeisance: it was returned with severe dignity by the exalted person in question.

**2. a.** Of law, judgement, punishment, discipline, restraint, and the like: Involving strict and rigorous treatment; executed or carried out with rigour; not leaning to tenderness or laxity; unsparing.

**1562** WINȜET *Cert. Tractates* ii. Wks. (S.T.S.) I. 21 The seueir punisment of Core, Dathan, and Abiron. *c* **1570** W. WAGER *The Longer thou livest* 1752 (Brandl), I represent Gods seuere iudgement, Which dallieth not where to strike he doth purpose. **1592** SHAKS. *Rom. & Jul.* v. iii. 269 Let my old life be sacrific'd..Vnto the rigour of seuerest Law. **1661** *Act 13 Chas. II*, c. 9 §21 None shall presume to quarrell with his Superior Officer, upon pain of severe punishment. **1662** STILLINGFL. *Orig. Sacræ* III. i. §12 It is not evident that the Laws of all the antient Common-wealths were so severe against Atheism. **1669–70** MARVELL *Corr.* Wks. (Grosart) II. 306 The House..voted..that severe provision be made against all frauds upon the importation [of wine]. **1797** MRS. RADCLIFFE *Italian* x, Schedoni hinted that the obedience of youth was hopeless unless severer measures were adopted. **1819** SHELLEY *Cenci* v. ii. 73 To pursue this monstrous crime By the severest forms of law. **1838** F. A. P[ALEY] tr. *Schömann's Assemb. Athen.* Introd. 19 The people.. disliking the severe controll of the four hundred. **1861** M. PATTISON *Ess.* (1889) I. 47 Severer penalties awaited drunkenness, dissipation, or dicing.

**b.** Of a compact: Imposing rigorous conditions, stringent. Of an account: Unsparingly exacted.

**1591** SHAKS. *1 Hen. VI*, v. iv. 114 If we conclude a Peace, It shall be with such strict and seuere Couenants, As little shall the Frenchmen gaine thereby. **1684** *Contempl. St. Man* I. ix. (1699) 106 Let us not misspend the time of this Life, since so severe an account will be demanded of all the benefits which we have received. **1751** JORTIN *Serm.* (1771) I. vii. 135 Power wantonly exercised is the undesirable opportunity of doing mischief, for which a severe account is to be given in the next state.

**c.** Of a prisoner: Rigorously confined. *nonce-use.*

**1740** RICHARDSON *Pamela* (1824) I. 138 You told me once she was in London waiting on a bishop's lady, when all the time she was a severe prisoner here.

**3. a.** Unsparing in censure, criticism, or reproof.

**1561** B. GOOGE *Palingenius' Zodiac of Life* Ep. Ded., As the deuine Plato (although a Iudge somethynge to seuer agaynste them)..doth confesse. **1581** J. HAMILTON *Cath. Traict.* 21 S. Hierom, the seueir impugner of all hæritiks in his age. **1638** BAKER tr. *Balzac's Lett.* (vol. II.) 83 Your friend therefore, is certainly more severe than he neede to be. *c* **1673** WALLER *To the Duchess, when he presented this Book* 8 While we your wit and early knowledge fear, To our productions we become severe. **1680** DRYDEN *Pref. Ovid's Ep.* (1716) 9 The most severe Censor cannot but be pleas'd with the Prodigality of his [Ovid's] Wit. **1683** SIR J. TURNER *Pallas Armata* 39 *marg.*, Lipsius severe to Vegetius. **1711** ADDISON *Spect.* No. 124 ¶1 As the most severe Reader makes Allowances for many Rests and Nodding-places in a Voluminous Writer. **1760–2** GOLDSM. *Cit. W.* xcix, Her very appearance was sufficient to silence the severest satirist of the sex. **1780** *Mirror* No. 70 His good-nature..prevented him from viewing, with too severe an eye, the occasional excesses of some of his companions. **1825** MACAULAY *Ess.*, *Milton* ¶7 Nor..will the severest of our readers blame us. **1837** WHEWELL *Hist. Induct. Sci.* (1857) I. 138 The exact but severe historian of astronomy, Delambre,..loses all his bitterness when he comes to Hipparchus. **1858** MRS. PAUL *Maiden Sisters* xii. 119 'There is no depth in the talk of general society, but plenty of lightness and flippancy.' 'I think you are severe,' said Ellen, courageously.

*absol.* *c* **1614** SYLVESTER *Micro-cosm.* 374 Wks. (Grosart) II. 100 If I be merry, I am mad (say the Severe).

**b.** *to be severe on* (or *upon*): to pass harsh or sarcastic judgement on, 'to be hard upon'.

**1672** WYCHERLEY *Love in Wood* II. i. 26 His wit properly lies in..being severe as they call it, upon other peoples cloaths. **1713** ADDISON *Guardian* No. 162 ¶1 The good Lady Lizard..desired her Cosin Thomas..not to be so severe on his Relations. **1731–8** SWIFT *Pol. Conversat.* 103, I suppose the Colonel was cross'd in his first Love, which makes him so severe on all the Sex. **1858** MRS. PAUL *Maiden Sisters* xiv. 138 'One must not be severe on a little inequality of temper,' said Norah, laughing.

**c.** Of an utterance, opinion, etc.: Unsparing in censure; strongly condemnatory.

**1561** B. GOOGE *Palingenius' Zodiac of Life* Ep. Ded., Humbly requesting that..the simple frutes of a yong head, may strongly be defended from the seuer reprehensions of Momus. **1668** MARVELL *Corr.* Wks. (Grosart) II. 253 We on Munday send to the Lords severe votes against their proceedings. **1692** NORRIS *Two Treat. Div. Light* I. 15 He.. very gravely applies to me two of the most severe Texts of Scripture that he could pick out in all the Bible. **1709** SWIFT *T. Tub* Apol. (1710) a 3, The severest Stroaks of Satyr in his Book. **1781** COWPER *Table-t.* 103, I grant the sarcasm is too severe. **1873** B. HARTE *Fiddletown* 27 He was arrested..and discharged with a severe reprimand. **1879** LUBBOCK *Addr. Pol. & Educ.* ix. 151 English travellers in Oriental countries frequently make severe remarks on the manner in which the ..remains of antiquity are allowed to go to ruin.

**II.** Conforming to a rigorous standard.

**4. a.** Extremely strict in matters of conduct or behaviour; rigorous in self-discipline and self-restraint; austere with oneself; shunning laxity or self-pleasing.

**1565** COOPER *Thesaurus* s.v. *Seuerus*, A seuere man eschewynge all sensuall pleasures. **1604** SHAKS. *Oth.* II. iii. 301 Come, you are too seuere a Moraller. **1643** SIR T. BROWNE *Relig. Med.* II. §7 To doe no injury, nor take none, was a principle, which to my former yeers..seemed to contain enough of Morality, but my more setled yeares, and Christian constitution have fallen upon severer resolutions. **1671** MILTON *P.R.* IV. 280 The Stoic severe. **1709** STEELE *Tatler* No. 4 ¶8 He is held in the highest Veneration imaginable for a severe Honesty, and Love of his Country.

*a* **1715** BURNET *Own Time* (1766) I. 459 He was a man of severe morals. **1798** SOPHIA LEE *Canterb. T., Young Lady's T.* II. 411 Emily affected severe economy in her travelling expences. **1818** SCOTT *Rob Roy* xiii, A man of severe temperance. **1822** MRS. HEMANS *Siege of Valencia* i, We must fall As men that in severe devotedness Have chosen their part, and bound themselves to death. **1869** TOZER *Highl. Turkey* II. 306 [His] severe impartiality adds weight to his authority. **1879** FROUDE *Cæsar* xxviii. 481 A Roman matron of the strictest and severest type.

**b.** Of habits, etc.: Dictated by strict and austere principles of living.

**1828** SEWELL in *Oxf. Prize Ess.* 36 The Spartan manners were rough, simple, and severe. **1879** FROUDE *Cæsar* vi. 49 The habits of the household were simple and severe.

**c.** Of a secret: Strictly kept (? *obs.*). Of a resolution: Unyielding, rigid.

**1734** FIELDING *Univ. Gall.* IV. i, I beg this thing may be kept a severe secret. **1849** DE QUINCEY *Engl. Mail Coach* Wks. 1890 XIII. 276 The Emperor..descended in great pomp from his throne, with the severest resolution never to remount it.

**5. a.** Of intellectual operations, thought, etc.: Conforming to an exacting standard of mental effort; rigidly exact or accurate; grave, serious, not light or recreative; not shrinking from what is toilsome or difficult. (Cf. 9.)

**1605** BACON *Adv. Learn.* II. i. §3. 8 A substantiall and seuere Collection of the Heteroclites, or Irregulars of Nature, well examined & described. *c* **1645** HOWELL *Lett.* (1655) II. xli. 50, I find you have a genius for the most solid and severest sort of studies. **1662** STILLINGFL. *Orig. Sacræ* II. viii. §6. 235 And upon severe enquiry we shall find the grand principle which [etc.]. **1682** DRYDEN *Relig. Laici* 233 Those hours hast thou to Nobler use employ'd, And the severe Delights of Truth enjoy'd. **1757** GRAY *Bard* 127 Truth severe, by Fairy Fiction drest. **1812** CRESSWELL *Maxima & Min.* I. 10 In haste to quit the province of severe reasoning. **1821** HAZLITT *Table-t., Milton's Sonn.*, A day spent in social retirement and elegant relaxation from severer studies. **1839** DE QUINCEY *Recoll. Lakes* Wks. 1862 II. 203 Under the continual restraint of severe good sense. **1863** GEO. ELIOT *Romola* I. xii, [He] is held in high honour for his severe scholarship.

*absol.* **1683** SOAME & DRYDEN tr. *Boileau's Art Poet.* I. 76 Happy who in his verse can gently steer From grave to light, from pleasant to severe [orig. *du plaisant au sévère*]. **1734** POPE *Ess. Man* iv. 380 Form'd by thy converse, happily to steer From grave to gay, from lively to severe.

**b.** said of a student, thinker, etc.

**1603** DANIEL *Def. Rhyme* H 5 b, Peraduenture there will be found in the now contemned recordes of Ryme matter not vnfitting the grauest Diuine and seuerest Lawyer in this kingdome. **1706** HEARNE *Collect.* 8 Mar. (O.H.S.) I. 201 Mr. Smith..has been..a severe Student.

**6. a.** In reference to style or taste, literary or artistic: Shunning redundance or unessential ornament; not florid or exuberant; sober, restrained, austerely simple or plain.

**1665** BOYLE *Occas. Refl.* VI. i. (1848) 341 To expect that Piety and Vertue were able, by their native charms, so much to endear my dress, as to win themselves adorers in a plain, or even a severe one. **1676** DRYDEN *State Innoc.* Pref. (1677) b 3 Virgil and Horace, the severest Writers of the severest Age. **1693** —— *Disc. Satire* Ess. 1900 II. 65 Lucilius, who was more severe, and more correct. **1820** KEATS *Hyperion* I. 211 That inlet to severe magnificence Stood full blown, for the God to enter in. **1849** RUSKIN *Sev. Lamps* ii. §24. 56 The forms of the tracery were still severe and pure. **1856** EMERSON *Eng. Traits, Manners* Wks. (Bohn) II. 50 Even Brummel their fop was marked by the severest simplicity in dress. **1860** RUSKIN *Mod. Paint.* V. IX. xi. 319 He would have been remembered as one of the severest of painters. **1872** BLACK *Adv. Phaeton* x, Queen Titania's more severe but no less graceful costume.

†**b.** Of a language: Concise, terse, not redundant. *Obs. rare.*

**1680** DRYDEN *Pref. Ovid's Ep.* (1716) 15 The Latin (a most Severe and Compendious Language).

**III.** Of impersonal agencies or conditions: Pressing hardly, rigorous.

**7. a.** Of the weather, etc.: Causing great discomfort or injury to living beings; hard, rigorous; very cold, wet or stormy.

**1676** in *12th Rep. Hist. MSS. Comm.* App. v. 32 God bless your two deare sweet babies and keep them from the sharp colds of this seveare weather. *a* **1700** EVELYN *Diary* 7 Mar. 1658, This had been the severest winter that any man alive had known in England. **1768** H. WALPOLE *Let. to Earl Strafford* 25 June, We have had some severe rain; but the season is now beautiful. **1774** PENNANT *Tour Scotl. in 1772* 175 The climate is very severe. **1788** M. CUTLER in *Life*, etc. (1888) I. 420 Very severe shower in the night. **1812** *New Bot. Gard.* I. 59 In case the frost is not so severe as to destroy the flowers. **1866** G. MACDONALD *Ann. Q. Neighb.* xxviii. (1878) 477 Very severe weather came. **1884** *Harper's Mag.* Jan. 283/2 They would require slightly severer cold to affect them.

**b.** Of fire or light: Painfully or searchingly intense. *rare.*

**1652** CRASHAW *Carmen Deo Nostro* Wks. (1904) 252 O that Book! whose leaves so bright Will sett the world in severe light. **1667** MILTON *P.L.* II. 276 Our torments also may in length of time Become our Elements, these piercing Fires As soft as now severe. **1822** SHELLEY *Tri. Life* 424 In that light's severe excess.

**c.** Of an attack of illness or disease: Attended with a maximum of pain or distress, violent.

**1725** N. ROBINSON *Th. Physick* 265 It is the way Nature her self often takes, in solving the severer Fevers. **1756** MRS. CALDERWOOD in *Coltness Collect.* (Maitland Club) 224 The coldness of the inn had given Mr. Calderwood a severe cold. **1803** *Med. Jrnl.* X. 522 The complaint was in many cases very severe, but fatal to very few. **1823** WHEWELL in *Life* (1881) 83, I finally caught a severe cold. **1899** *Allbutt's Syst. Med.* VIII. 507 In severe cases [of eczema] there may be some prodromal symptoms.

**8. a.** Of pain, suffering, loss, or the like: Grievous, extreme.

**1742** GRAY *Eton* 80 Moody Madness laughing wild Amid severest woe. **1781** COWPER *Truth* 101 His voluntary pains, severe and long. **1794** MRS. RADCLIFFE *Myst. Udolpho* xxxviii, The silence of Valancourt..oppressed Emily with severe anxiety. **1808** *Med. Jrnl.* XIX. 173 Severe shooting pains in the head were felt. **1838** PRESCOTT *Ferd. & Isab.* I. xi. (1854) I. 272 The loss inflicted on the infantry was also severe. **1844** H. H. WILSON *Brit. India* III. 200 Their exposure beyond the trenches to the fire of the garrison would have been attended with still severer loss of life. **1848** THACKERAY *Van. Fair* xxxii, She..watched incessantly by the wounded lad, whose pains were very severe. **1888** *Spectator* 30 June 874/2 There has been a severe fall in the value of the shares.

*absol.* **1802** BEDDOES *Hygeïa* VIII. 141 The gouty, besides having to struggle with every thing that pain has of severe, are [etc.].

**b.** Qualifying an agent-n., as ***a severe loser***.

**1748** FOOTE *Knights* II. Wks. 1799 I. 80 'Tis odd, that the same cause that increases the passion in one sex should destroy it in the other; the reason is above my reach, but the fact I am a severe witness of. **1863** FAWCETT *Pol. Econ.* II. v. 185 Individuals engaged in the trade might be severe losers.

**9. a.** Of events or circumstances, labour or exercise, a struggle or contest, a test, trial, etc.: Hard to sustain or endure; making great demands on one's powers or resources; arduous.

**1774** BRYANT *Mythol.* II. 58 Osiris..then entered Thrace, with the King of which he had a severe encounter. **1784** COWPER *Task* IV. 389 The man feels least, as more inur'd than she To winter, and the current in his veins More briskly mov'd by his severer toils. **1798** FORESTER in *Paget Papers* (1896) I. 114 This day..met near Oakham, have had a very severe day. **1826** DISRAELI *V. Grey* IV. xiii. 244 De Bœffleurs once more assisted me, though his terms were most severe. **1827** SCOTT *Two Drovers* Introd., The master of the pack takes as severe exercise as his whipper-in. **1838** PRESCOTT *Ferd. & Isab.* II. xiv. (1854) II. 220 This action was one of the severest which occurred in these wars. **1860** TYNDALL *Glac.* II. xxii. 347 In the following experiment the ice was subjected to a still severer test. **1867** BAKER *Nile Tribut.* xiv. (1886) 244 The pace was too severe, and, although running wonderfully, he was obliged to give way to the horses. **1880** C. T. NEWTON *Art & Archæol.* viii. 323 Universities where this elaborate training was tested by competitive examinations of the severest kind.

**b.** *transf.* Of geographical terrain, etc.: causing exertion or making great demands of endurance or skill; taxing, hard to 'negotiate'. Also *spec.* of a rock or mountain or the route by which it may be climbed. Hence as *sb.* (usu. with capital initial).

**1881** *Sportsman's Year-bk.* 49 Twenty miles a day is often the work of a crack greyhound intended to run in a severe country. **1897** *Daily News* 1 Sept. 3/1 This is again a very difficult piece of running. There are severe curves at Smethwick and at Worcester Foregate. **1897** O. G. JONES *Rock-Climbing in Engl. Lake District* p. xxiii, Exceptionally Severe Courses: Screes Great Gully. **1935** D. PILLEY *Climbing Days* iv. 66 It was bizarre that a *severe* should sometimes seem simple, when a *moderate* caused nerve storms of impotent despair. **1951** C. COXHEAD *One Green Bottle* iii. 86 'Ah yes, the Amphitheatre Buttress... An easy Difficult, isn't it?' She..herself led Very Difficults, and occasionally..an easy Severe. **1958** E. NEWBY *Short Walk in Hindu Kush* iii. 34 Easy, moderate, difficult, very difficult, severe, very severe, exceptionally severe, and excessively severe. **1970** *Guardian* 28 Aug. 18/6 The Wen Slab, a broad expanse of smooth, sheer rock classed as 'very severe'. **1975** G. MOFFAT *Miss Pink* iii. 43 It's the big stack off the north headland: a hundred and fifty feet high... A good Severe, we thought. **1976** H. MACINNES *Death Reel* iii. 23 'Is there any climbing on Bidean?' 'I reckon Lilly's route is the best line on this side. About 600 feet, Severe.'

**10.** *Naut.* (See quot. 1867.)

**1830** MARRYAT *King's Own* xiii, Belay all that; take a *severe* turn, and don't come up an inch. **1867** SMYTH *Sailor's Word-bk.*, *Severe*, effectual; as, a severe turn in belaying a rope.

**11.** *colloq.* (chiefly *U.S.*) A vague epithet denoting superlative quality; very big or powerful; hard to beat.

**1805** T. E. WHITE *Jrnl.* (1904) 32, I got up this morning with the determination to have a severe nap before night. **1834** J. HALL *Kentucky* II. 9 Your whiskey is as good as your fire, and that is saying a great deal, for you are the severest old beaver to tote wood that I've seen for many a long day. **1847** DE QUINCEY *Sp. Milit. Nun* Wks. 1890 XIII. 209 *note*, These Andes, in Jonathan's phrase, are a 'severe' range of hills. **1864** ATKINSON *Stanton Grange* 75 The whole party arrived, quite ready for a 'severe tea'. **1889** C. D. WARNER in *Harper's Mag.* Jan. 270/1 A well-known character in the mountains, who has killed twenty-one men... He is called, in the language of the country [Kentucky], a 'severe' man.

**12.** Epithet of a small snake, *Coluber severus*.

**1802** SHAW *Gen. Zool.* III. 421 Severe snake. *Coluber Severus.*

**13.** quasi-*adv.* = SEVERELY.

**1599** NASHE *Lenten Stuffe* 20 Not any where is the word seuerer practised, the preacher reuerentlier obserued and honoured. **1653** MILTON *Ps.* ii. 9 The Lord shall scoff them, then severe Speak to them in his wrath. **1725** POPE *Odyss.* I. 446 No blame severe his choice. **1802** J. WOODFORDE *Diary* 13 July (1931) V. 401 It was like to be a severe contested Election.

**IV.** *Comb.*, as ***severe-faced***, ***-looking*** adjs.

**1939** W. FORTESCUE *There's Rosemary* xxxv. 220 Together we hurried down the garden path—to meet Queen Alexandra, Princess Victoria, and a severe-faced lady coming out of the garden door. *a* **1957** J. CARY *Captive & Free* (1959) xliii. 186 A very severe-looking young woman.

**severe**, obs. form of SEVER *v.*

**severed** ('sɛvəd), *ppl. a.* [f. SEVER *v.* + -ED[1].] In senses of the verb.

**1581** HOWELL *Devises* L iiij, Then eche a seuerde peece doth spoyle, Which late conioynde, no force could foyle. **1588** T. HUGHES *Misfort. Arthur* III. i. 107 How close the seuered skinne vnites againe. **1606** SHAKS. *Ant. & Cl.* III. xiii. 170 Our seuer'd Nauie too Haue knit againe. **1621** G. SANDYS *Ovid's Met.* I. (1626) 6 Part of his seuer'd scarce-dead lims he boyles. **1634** MILTON *Comus* 274 How to regain my sever'd company. *a* **1635** SIBBES *Confer. Christ & Mary* (1656) 49 We must not think of the ascension of Christ as a severed thing from us. **1814** WORDSW. *Excurs.* IV. 746 Take, running river, take these locks of mine..This severed hair. **1837** CARLYLE *Fr. Rev.* III. IV. i, The executioner lifted the severed head. **1860** TYNDALL *Glac.* II. xxiii. 352 We have, in the case of ice, the actual regelation of the severed surfaces.

Hence **'severedly** *adv. rare*[−1].

**1605** BACON *Adv. Learn.* II. viii. §5. 35 But heere I must giue warning, that it bee done distinctly and seueredly.

**severee**: see SEVERY.

**severely** (sɪ'vɪəlɪ), *adv.* [f. SEVERE *a.* + -LY[2].]

**1.** With rigour or extreme strictness in the treatment of offenders; with severity in judgement, punishment, censure or rebuke.

**1548** ELYOT *Dict.*, *Asperè*,..rigorously, seuerely. *Ibid.*, *Duriter*,.. cruelly, seuerely. **1573** T. CARTWRIGHT *Reply Whitgift's Answ.* 27 The transgressyons of the lawe in the tyme of the gospell oughte rather to be seuerelyer punyshed then they were vnder the lawe. **1591** SHAKS. *Two Gent.* III. i. 108 She..is..kept seuerely from resort of men. **1647** CLARENDON *Hist. Reb.* I. §74 Olivarez had been heard to censure very severely the duke's..want of respect towards the Prince. **1695** BLACKMORE *Pr. Arth.* v. 564 Be mercifully Just, severely Kind. **1712** STEELE *Spect.* No. 431 ¶2 My Master received Orders every Post to use me very severely. **1759** HUME *Hist. Eng. Tudors* I. Mary i. 356 Taylor..was very severely handled, and was violently thrust out of the house. **1855** MACAULAY *Hist. Eng.* xii. III. 209 Of legislation such as this it is impossible to speak too severely. **1878** LECKY *Eng. in 18th C.* I. i. 121 The treaty of 1709..was severely censured as too favourable to the Dutch.

**b.** With severe looks or demeanour.

**1565** COOPER *Thesaurus*, *Exuere vultus seueros*, to look no more seuerely. **1697** DRYDEN *Æneid* VI. 779 Whose Jaws with Iron Teeth severely grin. **1757** W. WILKIE *Epigoniad* VII. 225 Severely smiling, thus the hero spoke. **1898** W. W. JACOBS *Sea Urchins, Money-changers* (1906) 223 The fare, who had been leaning back in the stern with a severely important air.

**c.** With rigour or strictness in examining, revising, or the like.

**1600** JER. TAYLOR *Worthy Commun.* ii. §3. 141 Here therefore it concerns us to examine our selves strictly and severely. *a* **1700** EVELYN *Diary* 6 July 1679, Dr. Lloyd.. with Dr. Burnet, who had severely examin'd him, came away astonish'd. **1821** LAMB *Elia* Ser. I. *Old Benchers*, His housekeeping was severely looked after, but he kept the table of a gentleman. **1897** *Daily News* 6 May 6/2 He wrote best, as most Frenchmen do, in the morning, and corrected much less severely than Victor Hugo.

**d.** ***to leave*** or ***let severely alone***: to avoid of set purpose; to pursue a deliberate policy of ignoring or isolating.

**1880** PARNELL *Sp.* 19 Sept. in R. B. O'Brien *Life* (1898) I. 237 You must show him..by leaving him severely alone, by putting him into a moral Coventry..your detestation of the crime he has committed. **1886** *Referee* 20 June 5 (Cass.), England and her wants..are to be severely let alone. **1898** *Dubl. Rev.* Oct. 276 The question was regarded as quite insoluble, and severely left alone.

**2.** With rigour or strictness in one's own practice or conduct; rigidly, inflexibly.

**1649** J. H. *Motion to Parl.* 38 Halfe a life need to be severely spent in learning them. **1703** ROWE *Fair Penitent* I. i. 207 With deadly Imprecations on her Self, She vow'd severely ne'er to see me more. **1726** POPE *Odyss.* XVI. 36 Severely chaste Penelope remains. **1821** SCOTT *Kenilw.* xxii, My father is stern and strict in his temper, and severely true to his trust. **1873** M. ARNOLD *Lit. & Dogma* iii. 79 Bishop Butler, in general the most severely exact of writers. **1889** *Sat. Rev.* 6 Apr. 415/1 Though they were severely orthodox.

**3.** With austere plainness or simplicity of style or taste.

**1635–56** COWLEY *Davideis* III. Wks. 1905 I. 337 On's head an helm of well-wrought brass is place'd, The top with warlike Plume severely grace'd. **1849** RUSKIN *Sev. Lamps* iii. §xv. 79 Severely rectilinear forms were associated with the curved ones in the cornice. **1878** MISS BRADDON *Open Verdict* I. 335 Dog-cart, severely painted darkest olive. **1885** *Harper's Mag.* Mar. 524/2 The fire-places..are severely plain.

**4.** Painfully, grievously; in a manner, or to a degree, that is distressing or hard to bear.

**1682** SIR T. BROWNE *Chr. Mor.* II. x. (1716) 64 This the fallen Angels severely understand,..and more afflictively feel the contrary state of Hell. **1687** A. LOVELL tr. *Thevenot's Trav.* I. 74 He..received the great and small Shot of one half of the Turkish Fleet, which he mawled severely. **1711** SWIFT *Cond. Allies* Wks. 1841 I. 414/2 We have shamefully misapplied [our strength]..to effect [ends], which after a peace we may severely repent. **1778** MISS BURNEY *Evelina* xxi, I now most severely felt the folly of my plan. **1807** WILKINSON in Pike *Sources Mississ.* (1810) II. App. 25 The night was severely cold. **1861** GEO. ELIOT *Silas M.* vi. 38 After this feeble delusive thaw, the silence set in as severely as before. **1867** BAKER *Nile Tribut.* viii. (1886) 107 The plague of boils broke out, and every one was attacked more or less severely. **1885** *Manch. Exam.* 16 May 6/1 The extremely cold nights..tell very severely on the elderly members of the House. **1897** MARY KINGSLEY *W. Africa* 121 The mangrove-swamp..stank severely.

**5.** *colloq.* To a great or excessive degree, 'not wisely but too well'. (Cf. SEVERE *a.* 11.)

1854 WHYTE MELVILLE *General Bounce* xii, That officer has dined 'severely', as he calls it, and is slightly inebriated.

**se'vereness.** Now *rare.* [-NESS.] Severity.

1579–80 NORTH *Plutarch, Phocion* (1595) 792 This fault of seuerenes was in Cato the younger. 1597 I. T. *Serm. Paules Crosse* 37 We doubt he will execute it with seuerenesse. 1610 DONNE *Pseudo-Martyr* 118 The certainety, seuereness, and length of Purgatory. 1667 H. MORE *Div. Dial.* v. xxi. (1713) 476 That Severeness and Austerity observable in the Baptist. 1673 TEMPLE *United Prov.* i. 20 The Severeness and Gravity of the [Spanish] Nation.

**severer** ('sɛvərə(r)). *rare.* [f. SEVER *v.* + -ER[1].] One who severs or separates.

1662 *Comenius' Janua Ling. Triling.* 102 The severer separateth (severeth) the stony filth, the washer washeth the things thus separated. 1887 in *Cassell's Encycl. Dict.*

**severey:** see SEVERY.

**Severian** (sɪ'vɪərɪən). [ad. L. *Sevēriān-ī* (pl.), f. the name *Sevērus* (see below) + -IAN.]

**1.** A member of an Encratite or Gnostic sect of the 2nd century which condemned marriage, etc.

'It may reasonably be doubted whether there really was an Encratite teacher named Severus, or whether sects did not merely get the Latin name of Severians from the austerity of their rule of life' (*Smith's Dict. Chr. Biog.*).

1607 T. ROGERS *39 Art.* vi. (1633) 30 Of the former sort [*i.e.* those who rejected the books of the O.T.] were the Seuerians, .. and the Manichies. 1656 BLOUNT *Glossogr.*, *Severians* .. a sort of Hereticks that condemned marriage, abstained from eating flesh and drinking wine, &c. 1702 ECHARD *Eccl. Hist.* (1710) 500 The Severians .. who rejected the Epistles of St. Paul and the Acts of the Apostles. 1887 SALMON in Smith & Wace *Dict. Chr. Biog.* IV. 633/1 A sect of Severians is described by Epiphanius (*Haer.* 45) which except the feature of Encratism has little in common with the sect described by Eusebius.

**2.** A follower of Severus, the Monophysite patriarch of Antioch (early 5th c.).

1698 FRYER *Acc. E. India & P.* 272 Severus Bishop of Antioch .., from whom they were denominated Severians. 1765 MACLAINE tr. *Mosheim's Eccl. Hist.* Cent. VI. II. v. §5. 1878 P. SMITH *Hist. Chr. Ch.* xvi. §6. 368 *note*, The Severians .. held that the body of Christ before the resurrection was mortal and corruptible. 1882–3 SCHAFF *Encycl. Rel. Knowl.* II. 1137 The Egyptian Monophysites called themselves .. Theodosians, or Severians.

**b.** *attrib.* or *adj.*

1718 J. SHARPE *Hist. Acc. Heresie* II. 51 The Severian Sect (in the Year 521) .. took its Name from Severus.

**severiga,** obs. variant of SEVRUGA.

**severing** ('sɛvərɪŋ), *vbl. sb.* [-ING[1].] The action of the verb SEVER; an instance of this.

1382 WYCLIF *Isa.* vii. 17 Fro the daȝes of the seueryng of Effraym fro Juda. 1533 BELLENDEN *Livy* I. x. (S.T.S.) I. 59 Afore þe seuering [*v.r.* syvering] of þare armyis. 1712 ADDISON *Spect.* No. 349 ⁋7 The severing of his Head from his Body. 1805 WORDSW. *Prelude* IX. 271 In memory of the farewells of that time, Domestic severings. 1807 —— *Ode Intim. Immortality* 192 And O, ye Fountains, Meadows, Hills, and Groves, Forebode not any severing of our loves!

†**b.** *concr.* A division, partition, separated part.

*c* 1400 LOVE *Bonavent. Mirr.* xiii. (1907) 83 Thei had no grete hous but a litel in the whiche thei hadde thre seuerynges as it were thre smale chambres there specially to praye and to slepe.

**'severing,** *ppl. a.* [-ING[2].] That severs.

1592 SHAKS. *Rom. & Jul.* III. v. 8 Looke Loue what enuious streakes Do lace the seuering Cloudes in yonder East. *a* 1635 SIBBES *Confer. Christ & Mary* (1656) 92 That spirit of God .. is a severing spirit. 1793 WORDSW. *Descr. Sk.* 310 Th' insuperable rocks and severing tide. 1836 J. H. NEWMAN in *Lyra Apostol.* (1891) 217 Thou shrinkest now From urgent rule, and severing vow. 1888 MEREDITH *Night frost in May* Poems 1898 II. 238 In this shrill hush of quietude, The ear conceived a severing cry.

Hence **'severingly** *adv.*

*a* 1390 WYCLIF *Isa.* Jerome's Prol., And off euer either rewme, now togidere, now seuerendely [Vulg. *nunc commistim, nunc separatim*], he ordeynede the profecie.

**se'verish,** *a. rare.* [-ISH.] Somewhat severe.

1819 *Blackw. Mag.* IV. 566 One don't sift Such trifling doggrel strains with eye severish. 1863 J. BROWN *Lett.* (1907) 158 Russel was severish, but justish.

†**Severite**[1]. *Obs.* [f. the name *Sevērus* (see SEVERIAN) + -ITE[1].] = SEVERIAN 1 and 2.

1607 T. ROGERS *39 Art.* ii. (1633) 13 The Seuerites .. who affirmed the diuinitie and humanity of Christ, to be of one and the same nature. *Ibid.* vi. 32 Others, of all other bookes reiected the said Acts, as the Manichies, and the Seuerites. 1716 M. DAVIES *Athen. Brit.* II. 284 The Eutychians, Nestorians, Apollinarists, and the Severits or Acephalians.

**severite**[2] ('sɛvəraɪt). *Min.* [Named from Saint-*Sever* (Landes, France) + -ITE[1]. Cf. F. *sévérite.*] A synonym of LENZINITE.

1823 W. PHILLIPS *Introd. Min.* (ed. 3) 87 Severite .. occurs in small masses [etc.]. 1854 DANA *Syst. Min.* (ed. 4) II. 504 Severite, a variety of halloysite.

**severity** (sɪ'vɛrɪtɪ). [a. F. *sévérité*, ad. L. *sevēritās*, f. *sevērus*: see SEVERE *a.* and -ITY. Cf. It. *severità*, Sp. *severidad*, Pg. *severidade.*]

**1.** Strictness or sternness in dealing with others; stern or rigorous disposition or behaviour; rigour in treatment, discipline, punishment, or the like.

1530 WOLSEY in Ellis *Orig. Lett.* Ser. II. II. 33 Your most excellent nature wych hath ever be moved and propensyd to clemency and mercy then to rygor and severyte. 1538 *St. Papers Hen. VIII*, VIII. 50 Wher as severitie is to be used ayenst the anabaptistes. 1582 *N.T.* (Rheims) *Rom.* xi. 22 See then the goodnes and the seueritie of God. 1591 SHAKS. *1 Hen. VI*, II. iii. 47, I laugh to see your Ladyship so fond, To thinke, that you haue ought but Talbots shadow, Whereon to practise your seueritie. 1622 BACON *Hen. VII*, 235 As for the Seueritie vsed vpon those which were taken in Kent, it was but vpon a Scumme of People. 1680 DRYDEN *Pref. Ovid's Ep.* Ess. 1900 I. 231 The Emperor who condemned him had as little reason as another man to punish that fault with so much severity. 1752 HUME *Polit. Disc.* x. (ed. 2) 203 Excessive severity in the laws is apt to beget great relaxation in their execution. 1838 THIRLWALL *Greece* xli. V. 178 His regulations were .. enforced with inflexible severity. 1856 KANE *Arctic Explor.* I. xxxii. 443, I have to guard its ventilation with all the severity that would befit a surgical ward. 1868 E. EDWARDS *Ralegh* I. iii. 41 An illustrious poet .. apologises for it [the massacre] as an act of unavoidable severity.

**b.** An act or instance of severity.

1538 STARKEY *England* 120 A lyke seueryte I fynd in the punnyschment of treson. 1689 LUTTRELL *Brief Rel.* (1857) I. 613 The severityes towards the protestants were continued. *a* 1715 BURNET *Own Time* (1766) I. 201 That so a colour might be put on their severities against such as should refuse it. 1726 AYLIFFE *Parergon* 157 There is a Difference between an Ecclesiastical Censure, and an Ecclesiastical Severity: For under the Appellation of a Censure we only include Excommunication, Suspension, and an Interdict; but under the Denomination of an Ecclesiastical Severity, every other Punishment of the Church is intended... But according to some, a Censure and a Severity is the same Thing. 1871 FRASER *Berkeley* ii. 19 The severities of Tyrconnel obliged Molyneux to fly to England.

**c.** Harshness of judgement, criticism, or rebuke. Also *pl.*, severe rebukes or criticisms.

1660 F. BROOKE tr. *Le Blanc's Trav.* 2 Though I received some severities from my mother on this occasion. 1665 BOYLE *Occas. Refl.* Ep. Ded., The Devout .. will be scrupulous to be more Severe to these Papers, than a Person in whom, upon the score of her own Style, Severity were more justifiable than in most Readers. 1713 STEELE *Englishm.* No. 50. 326, I should be very loth to see you fall with too particular a severity upon the Error. 1784 COWPER *Task* v. 170 'Twas but a mortifying stroke Of undesign'd severity, that glanc'd .. On human grandeur and the courts of kings. 1859 BAGEHOT *Lit. Stud.* (1879) I. 176 We should think it unseemly to criticise the .. work .. with extreme severity. 1871 R. ELLIS *Catullus* v. 2 Sour severity, tongue of eld maligning. 1884 R. W. CHURCH *Bacon* i. 2 Bacon has been judged with merciless severity.

**d.** Sternness of aspect or countenance; a severe look or expression.

1711 ADDISON *Spect.* No. 160 ⁋11, I think, says the Author, I never saw a greater Severity than in this Man's Face. 1770 LANGHORNE *Plutarch, Cleomenes* V. 177 In the court, where, with a silent severity of aspect, he observed all that passed. 1782 MISS BURNEY *Cecilia* VII. vi, How will his noble mother disdain me! how cruelly shall I sink before the severity of her eye! 1828 J. W. CROKER *Diary* 21 Apr., [Sir J.] Moore's countenance assumed a great severity.

**e.** *transf.* in reference to handling or dealing with inanimate objects.

1878 J. MARSHALL *Ann. Tennis* 112 Though not playing with so much severity as some others, he yet can cut the ball so as to make and win short chases on the floor with some certainty. 1898 W. W. JACOBS *Sea Urchins, Grey Parrot* (1906) 219 Mr. Gannett .. with a small knife dug with much severity and determination a hardened plug from the bowl [of his pipe].

**2.** Strictness or austerity of life, morals, etc.

1481 BOTONER *Tulle on Old Age* (Caxton) g ij (R.), Seuerity is continuance and perseuerance of oon maner of lyuyng as wele in the thyngys within as in theym withoute. 1565 COOPER *Thesaurus* s.v. *Seuere*, Life passed in great seueritie and grauitie. 1579 LYLY *Euphues* (Arb.) 178 We would .. with more seueritie direct the sequele of our life, for the feare of present death. 1592 SHAKS. *Rom. & Jul.* I. i. 225 Beauty steru'd with her seuerity, Cuts beauty off from all posteritie. 1680 DRYDEN *Pref. Ovid's Ep.* Ess. 1900 I. 230 'Tis true, they [Ovid's Elegies, etc.] are not to be excused in the severity of manners. 1728 LAW *Serious C.* xviii. (1732) 329 Such severity of behaviour, such abstinence [etc.]. 1741 MIDDLETON *Cicero* II. viii. 256 He affected the severity of the Stoic. 1903 in Westcott *Life Bp. Westcott* I. 23, I had ever before me what I may call the severity of his example.

**b.** *pl.*

1673 *Ladies Calling* I. i. ⁋10. 8 Tho these first severities were soon lost in the successes of that Empire. 1797 MRS. RADCLIFFE *Italian* vi, O, Ellena! let the severities of custom yield to the security of my happiness. 1826 LAMB *Elia* Ser. II. *Wedding*, The tristful severities of a funeral. 1890 'R. BOLDREWOOD' *Col. Reformer* (1891) 291 The ordinary prudences and severities of conscience.

**3.** Strictness in matters of thought or intellect; rigid accuracy or exactness; undeviating conformity to truth or fact. Also *pl.* instances of this.

1638 JUNIUS *Paint. Ancients* 73 Then the Artists themselves, the severitie and integritie of whose judgements is often weakened by the love of their owne and the dislike of other mens workes. *a* 1676 HALE *Prim. Orig. Man.* I. i. 27 A sort of Men that pretend to much severity of Wit, and would be thought too wise to be imposed upon by Credulity. 1693 DRYDEN *Disc. Satire* Ess. 1900 II. 24, I may say it, with all the severity of truth, that every line of yours is precious. 1791 BURKE *Let. Memb. Nat. Assembly* Wks. 1834 I. 477 The process of reasoning called *deductio ad absurdum*, which even the severity of geometry does not reject. 1834 *Burke's Wks.* I. Introd. 75 A vagueness and looseness of language quite incompatible with precision of thought, and utterly inconsistent with the severity of philosophy. *a* 1859 DE QUINCEY *Syst. Heavens* Wks. 1889 III. 194 A wish for the naked severities of science, with a total absence from all display of enthusiasm. 1864 HAMERTON *Doré* in *Fine Arts Q. Rev.* III. 2, I have but one law of conduct in criticism which is to judge .. neither with indulgence nor prejudiced harshness, but with severity (in its true sense) stating qualities and defects with equal force.

**4.** Austere purity or simplicity of style, taste, etc.

1709 FELTON *Diss. Classics* (1718) 18 Considering the Disadvantage of the Language, and the Severity of the Roman Muse, the Poem is still more Wonderful. 1768 GOLDSM. *Goodn. Man* III. i, The severity of French taste. 1858 KINGSLEY *Misc.* (1860) I. 153 Look at that old hound. .. Look at the severity, delicacy, lightness of every curve. 1859 JEPHSON *Brittany* iii. 36 The modest severity of the Breton dress. 1883 *Eng. Illustr. Mag.* Nov. 90/2 That severity of treatment on which the success of iron-work greatly depends.

**5.** Rigour or inclemency (of weather or climate); esp. extremity of cold.

*a* 1676 HALE *Prim. Orig. Man.* II. ix. 210 The severity of the Winter finds them [*sc.* Insects] out and destroys them. 1794 MORSE *Amer. Geog.* 112 Winter continues with such severity from December to April, as that the largest rivers are frozen over. 1826 LAMB *Let. to V. Novello* 9 May, Summer, as my friend Coleridge waggishly writes, has set in with its usual severity [also alleged to be a phrase of H. Walpole's]. 1863 GEO. ELIOT *Romola* II. v, The bare wintry morning, the chill air, were welcome in their severity. 1880 HAUGHTON *Phys. Geog.* iv. 175 The severity of the climate in this part of Asia may be estimated by a comparison of this January and July temperatures of Astrachan. 1912 *Cowley Evangelist* 181 We have had on three successive evenings thunderstorms of increasing severity.

**6.** Violence or acuteness (of illness).

1808 *Med. Jrnl.* XIX. 362 Nor does this disease at all seem to increase either in severity or in frequency. 1879 *St. George's Hosp. Rep.* IX. 126 The eruption .. increased in severity till death. 1893 ECCLES *Sciatica* 68 After a period of rest .. varying in duration .. according to the severity of the case.

**7.** Grievousness (of pain, affliction, penalties, etc.).

1849–50 ALISON *Hist. Eur.* xxix. (1854) IV. 309 They now felt the severity of the confiscation they had inflicted on others. 1890 NICOLAY & HAY *Lincoln* X. 314 The news [of Lincoln's assassination] fell with peculiar severity upon the hearts which were glowing with the joy of a great victory. 1893 *Law Times* XCIV. 600/2 The [income] tax falls with excessive and undue severity upon one class, and with unreasonable lightness upon others.

†**severi'zation.** *Obs. rare* [Formed as next + -ATION.] The action of severing or cutting in two.

1849 *Theatrical Programme* 20 Aug. 84 Brilliant Feats of Swordsmanship, including the Severisation of a Leg of Mutton. 1861 *Temple Bar* I. 248 A Scottish *fête* in Holland Park, where .. sergeants of the Life Guards effected the 'severisation of the leg of mutton', and performed the 'Saladin feat'.

†**'severize,** *v. Obs. rare.* [f. SEVER *v.* + -IZE.] *trans.* To sever or separate. (Cf. SEVERALIZE *v.*) Hence †**'severized** *ppl. a.*

1649 J. E[LLISTONE] tr. *Behmen's Epist.* vi. §65. 91 All Beings are but one onely Being, which hath breathed forth it selfe out of it selfe, and hath severized, and formized it selfe. *Ibid.* §66 The severized, parted, and divided will. 1691 TAYLOR *Behmen's Theos. Phil.* 381 Mutually unfolded and severized.

**severly,** obs. Sc. form of SEVERALLY *adv.*

†**severon.** *Arch. Obs.* Forms: 5 **severonne, -yn, -ant,** *pl.* **-ans,** 6 **severall,** *pl.* **se(y)verns.** [a. OF. *sev(e)ronde, souv(e)ronde, souverante, severonne,* etc. (Godefroy):—L. *suggrunda, subgrunda* eaves, ? f. *sub* under + *grunda* (only in a gloss) roof, projecting part of roof: cf. It. *gronda* eaves, gutter of a roof.] 'Some kind of water-table or cornice' (Parker *Gloss. Archit.* 1850). Also ***severon table.***

1412 *Contract Catterick Ch.* (1834) 10 And also forsaide Richarde sall make tablyng of the endes of the forsaide Kirke of a Katrik with seueronne tabill. 1422–3 *Fabric Rolls York Minster* (Surtees) 48 Et in ix. m waltiell emptis .. pro j severyn facto ex parte Archiepiscopi. 1443 in Willis & Clark *Cambridge* (1886) I. 386, iiij[c]xvj fote of Seuerant table scapled with poynts aftur a molde. 1450 in *Hist. Dunelm. Script. Tres* (Surtees) p. cccxxvi, Pro factura xxiiij ulnarum de severans. 1517 in *Hearne's Hist. Glastonbury* (1722) 287, vii[c]. and iii[xx]. footes off cresse table, and severall table att iii. d. the foote. 1527–8 *Fabric Rolls York Minster* (Surtees) 101 In les fre stone, in evis bordes, severns et j soletre. 1532–3 *Durham Househ. Bk.* (Surtees) 173 Pro sarracione ½ rod [cf. ROOD 8 c] pro molendinis, in seyverns.

**severy** ('sɛvərɪ). *Arch.* Forms: 5 **severy, -ee,** 6 **-ey;** *pl.* 4 **sewerwus,** 5 **severyse, civerys, (civers, cyfres),** 6 **severey(e)s.** [ad. OF. **civorie, civoire* ciborium:—L. *cibōri-um* (see CIBORIUM), used by Gervase of Canterbury (12th c.) in the following sense.] A bay or compartment of a vaulted roof. Also, a compartment or section of scaffolding.

1399 *Mem. Ripon* (Surtees) III. 131 In j porcione meremii empta de Willelmo Kyrkby pro sewerwus pro præd. tenemento, 6*d.* 1422–3 *Fabric Rolls York Minster* (Surtees) 47 Pro vj magnis saplyngs emptis pro scaffaldyng in le severy Archiepiscopi. *Ibid.* 48 Pro bruscis porcinis pro bruscis faciendis ad dealbacionem le severyse in le yle ecclesiæ, 15d. *a* 1490 BOTONER *Itin.* (1778) 244 Memorandum de le severee duarum fenestrarum. *Ibid.* 302 Ab illo hostio usque ad illas

les civerys in quibus mariatagia dependent. **1506** in *Rel. Ant.* II. 115 Which roof conteyneth vii. seuereys [*printed* senereys]. **1512** in Willis & Clark *Cambridge* (1886) I. 608 The tymber of ij seuereys of the said grete scaffold. *Ibid.*, For euery seuerey in the seid churche.
**1859** GWILT *Archit.* (ed. 4) 838 App., The vault of the chapel in question [*i.e.* King's Coll. Chapel at Cambr.] is divided into oblong severies. **1866** R. WILLIS *Archit. Hist. Glastonbury* 35 The nave contained ten severies, the eastern arm of the cross four severies. **1883** *Archæol. Cantiana* XV. 64 It projects a severy eastward of the rest of the range.

†**se'vidical**, *a.* *Obs.*$^{-0}$ [f. L. *sævidic-us* (f. *sævus* fierce, furious + *dic-* stem of *dīcĕre* to say, speak) + -AL[1].] 'That speaks cruel and rigorous words, that threateneth' (Blount *Glossogr.* 1656).

**sevier**, var. SIEVIER *Obs.*, sieve-maker.
**1630** in Mayo *Munic. Rec. Dorchester* (1908) 403.

‖**sévigné, sevigné.** [Prob. named after Mme. de *Sévigné* 1627–96.] A kind of bandeau, *esp.* one for the hair; a jewel or ornament of the kind used to decorate a head-dress. Also *attrib.* Now *Hist.*
[**1817** LADY MORGAN *France* III. (1818) I. 364 The *chignon à la Sevigné*, or *coëffure de Ninon*, now triumph over *la tête à l' Agrippina*.] **1826** M. WILMOT *Let.* 29 Feb. (1935) 239 Black velvet stomacher..fastened to the top with a sevigné, garnett and pearl..and another garnett sevigné on her forehead. **1835** *Court Mag.* VI. p. vi/2 Some are ornamented with Sevignés of *tulle*, disposed in regular plaits. **1837** [MISS MAITLAND] *Lett. fr. Madras* (1843) 55 They were covered with gold and jewels,..bands round their heads, sévignés, and rings on all their fingers and all their toes. **1840** M. EDGEWORTH *Let.* 30 Dec. (1971) 574 Sevigné headdress of black velvet with Sevigné jewels in front. **1843** *Commissioner* 221 A..damsel with long black ringlets..and a sevigné on her forehead.

**sevile, sevilioun**, obs. ff. CIVIL, CIVILIAN.
*c* **1400** *Beryn* 2069 For they were grete Sevilliouns & vsid probate law. *Ibid.* 2665 Sevile law.

**Sevillan** (sɛ'vɪlən), *a.*, (*sb.*) [f. *Seville* (see SEVILLE *a.*) + -AN.] = SEVILLIAN *a.* ***Sevillan ware***, an earthenware made in Seville in imitation of Italian majolica. Also as *sb.*
**1883** G. MEREDITH *Let.* 16 Mar. (1970) II. 690 We have just produced pots [of marmalade], which are Sevillan. **1891** in *Century Dict.* **1930** H. BAERLEIN *Spain* x. 138 Three hundred Murillos of the best period used to be the quota of a Sevillan gentleman when Théophile Gautier travelled in these parts, and the Sevillan was willing to sell one or two of his treasures. **1971** D. CORY *Sunburst* iv. 50 The Sevillan summer was getting into its blazing stride.

**Sevillano** (sɛvɪ'ljɑːnəʊ, ‖sevi'ʎano), *sb.* and *a.* Also fem. **-a** and erron. **Sevilliana.** [Sp.] = SEVILLIAN *a.* and *sb.*
**1884** O. PATCH *Sunny Spain* i. 14 The Sevillanas, as the ladies of Seville are called, are remarkable for their beauty. **1897** H. C. CHATFIELD-TAYLOR *Land of Castanet* iv. 93 The fair Sevilliana sits in her darkened chamber. **1904** B. KENNEDY *Tramp in Spain* iv. 25, I like the Sevillanos. They are a fine, free and easy people. **1932** E. HEMINGWAY *Death in Afternoon* 324 Now Ronda means sober and tragic in the Plaza with a limited repertoire and sevillano means light-hearted..with flowery style and a lengthy repertoire. **1970** R. A. H. ROBINSON *Origins of Franco's Spain* 325 Protest of 2,000 Sevillano farmers to Alcalá-Zamora. **1976** E. P. BENSON *Bulls of Ronda* iii. 14, I see..that you are a Sevillano.

**Seville** ('sɛvɪl), *a.* Forms: 5 Syvyle, Cyvylle, 6 Cyvyl, 6–7 Cyvill, Civil(l, 7 Civile, Sivil, 7–8 Sevil(l, 8– Seville. [The name (Sp. *Sevilla*) of a city and province of Andalusia, used attributively.]
†**1.** ***Seville oil***: olive oil brought from Seville.
**1436** *Libel Eng. Policy* 54 in *Pol. Poems* (Rolls) II. 160 Lycorys, Syvyle [*marg. note* Cyvylle] oyle, and grayne. **1541** in *Sel. Pleas Crt. Admiralty* (1894) I. 112 On hogs hede of Cyvill oyle. **1610** MARKHAM *Masterp.* II. lxxx 358 Other Farriers take of Ciuill oyle and brimstone, of each like quantity. *a* **1618** *Rates Marchandizes* I 4 b, Seuill oile, Maiorca oile [etc.].
**2.** ***Seville orange***: the bitter orange, *Citrus Bigaradia*, used for making marmalade.
**1593** NASHE *Strange Newes* Wks. (Grosart) II. 282 For the order of my life, it is as ciuil as a ciuil orenge. [**1599** SHAKS. *Much Ado* II. i. 304 The Count is neither sad, nor sicke,..: but ciuill Count, ciuill as an Orange.] **1657** W. COLES *Adam in Eden* clxvii. 256 In Spaine about Sivil, where the best Orenges grow, and are called by us Civil-Orenges. **1710–11** SWIFT *Jrnl. to Stella* 11 Feb., I wish you had some of our Seville oranges. **1796** *Campaigns 1793–4* II. xi. 81 The whole tribe of Oranges, seville and sweet. **1877** *Cassell's Dict. Cookery* 482/2 Take some Seville oranges.
*ellipt.* **1892** *Garrett's Encycl. Cookery* II. 31 Oranges are capable of being adapted to many culinary purposes..; the Seville being preferred..as having the stronger flavour.

**Sevillian** (sɛ'vɪlɪən), *a.* and *sb.* Also Sevilian. [f. prec. + -IAN.] **a.** *adj.* Of or pertaining to Seville. Cf. SEVILLAN. **b.** *sb.* An inhabitant of Seville.
**1830** DISRAELI *Let.* 26 July (1885) 30 The Sevillians say that *Cadiz es toda facada*. *Ibid.* 32 You see what a Sevillian écritoire is by this despatch. **1842** BORROW *Bible in Spain* xlviii, This grove is the favourite promenade of the Sevillians. **1849** *Athenæum* 3 Mar. 233/2 [Murillo] the prince of Sevillian painters. **1886** *Encycl. Brit.* XXI. 709/2 The Casa de los Abades is in the Sevillian plateresque style. **1926** E. A. PEERS *Royal Seville* i. 18 The ceramic art which is so noted a Sevilian industry. *Ibid.* ii. 29 The Sevilians like to say that the Guadalquivir salts the sea. **1957** A. MACNAB *Bulls of Iberia* xv. 170 A Sevilian from the classic San Bernardo quarter. **1967** A. ROSIN tr. *G. Pillement's Unknown Spain* 55 The charm of the Sevillians, who are known for their laughter.

**sevocation** (sɛvə'keɪʃən). *rare*$^{-0}$. [n. of action f. L. *sēvocāre*: see SEVOKE *v.* and -ATION.] The action of calling apart or aside.
**1623** COCKERAM II, A Calling aside, *Seuocation.* **1656** BLOUNT *Glossogr.* Hence in PHILLIPS, BAILEY, and later Dicts.

†**se'voke**, *v.* *Obs.*$^{-0}$ [ad. L. *sēvocāre*, f. *sē-* apart, aside + *vocāre* to call.] *trans.* To call apart or aside.
**1623** COCKERAM II, To Call aside, *Seuoke.*

†'**sevous**, *a.* *Obs.* *rare*$^{-1}$. [ad. L. *sēvōs-us*, *sēbōsus*, f. *sēv-um*: see SEVUM and -OUS.] Of the nature of suet or tallow.
**1725** *Phil. Trans.* XXXIII. 223 A thick Layer of sevous Fat.

‖**Sèvres** (sɛːvr), *a.* Forms: 8 Sève, Seve, 8–9 Sèvre, Sevre, 9– Sèvres. [The name of a town in France, near Paris.] The designation of a costly porcelain made at Sèvres.
**1764** LD. HOLLAND in Jesse *Selwyn & Contemp.* (1843) I. 287 We saw the china you speak of at Poiriers,..; it is Sevre china. **1782** H. WALPOLE *Let. to T. Walpole* 6 Sept., A cup and saucer of the Sève china. **1789** A. YOUNG *Trav. France* (1892) 101 A table formed of Seve porcelain. **1825** T. HOOK *Sayings* Ser. II. *Sutherl.* I. 81 A salver of Sèvre coffee-cups. *Ibid.*, *Man of Many Fr.* I. 294 Etruscan vases, and Sèvres tables. **1862** MISS BRADDON *Lady Audley* xxxii, The Benvenuto Cellini carvings and the Sèvres porcelain. **1908** R. BAGOT *A. Cuthbert* xxi. 254 A basket of beautiful old Sèvres china.
*absol.* **1862** MISS BRADDON *Lady Audley* xxxii, The Sèvres and bronze, the buhl and ormolu. **1870** 'OUIDA' *Held in Bondage* 40 The breakfast, in dainty Sèvres and silver.

‖**sevruga** (siv'rjuga, sɛv'ruːgə). Forms: 6 severiga, 9 sewruga, 8–9 sevruga. [Russ. *sevriúga*.] **1.** A species of sturgeon, *Acipenser stellatus*.
**1591** G. FLETCHER *Russe Commw.* (1857) 12 The fish called bellougina, the sturgeon, the seueriga, and the sterledey. **1799** W. TOOKE *View Russian Emp.* III. 143 The several kinds of sturgeon, namely beluga, sturgeon, and sevruga. **1802–3** tr. *Pallas's Trav.* (1812) I. 218 One thousand sevrugas produce one pood and a quarter of isinglass. **1814** tr. *Klaproth's Trav. Cauc.* 308 The most common fishes in the Terek are carp, barbel, sturgeon and sewruga. **1940** A. SIMON *Conc. Encycl. Gastron* II. 14/2 The Ship caviar is light in colour and small; that from the Sevruga is smaller still. **1964** A. LAUNAY *Caviare & After* i. 18 There are three varieties of acipenser used in the production of caviare, the Beluga, the Ocietrova or sturgeon and the Sevruga.
**2.** Caviare made from the roe of this fish.
**1959** W. HEPTINSTALL *Hors d' Œuvre & Cold Table* 29 Beluga Malossol caviar..has..the largest grain and..the highest price. Next comes Sevruga Malossol at about two-thirds of the price of the Beluga caviar. **1977** *Times* 16 Nov. 18/5, I have never been able to say 'when', whether it be a second helping of Sevruga or just another wee drop of the hard stuff.

‖**sevum** ('siːvəm). [L. *sēvum*, *sēbum*. Cf. SEBUM.] Suet, as used in pharmacy.
*c* **1440** *Pallad. on Husb.* I. 1141 Or siftid askis clene And seuum molton, held in euery chene. **1693** tr. *Blancard's Phys. Dict.* (ed. 2), *Sevum*, Suet. **1853** ROYLE *Mat. Med.* (ed. 2) 733 *Sevum*... Fat of Ovis Aries, the Sheep. Suet... Useful in giving consistence to ointments and plasters.

**sevyan, sevyne**, obs. forms of SEVEN.

†**sew**, *sb.*[1] *Obs.* Forms: 1 séaw, séa, (3 -sæw), 4–5 seew, seue, 4–6 sewe, 5 cewe, seau, 5–7 sew, 6 seu. [OE. *séaw* neut. = NFris. *sâie*, *sei*, *sii*, OHG. *sou*, MHG. (genit. *sowes*) juice, poison, food:—OTeut. *sawwo-. Cf. ON. *sǫgg-r* wet, dank. The root may be identical with that of Gr. ὕει (:—*su-) it rains.]
**1.** Juice, moisture, humour. (OE. only; but cf. ME. ELESÆW oil, in Ormin.)
Cf. the combs. *lipséaw* synovia, *plúmséaw* plum-juice.
*c* **900** *Bede Glosses* in Sweet *O.E. Texts* 182 *Sucum*, sea. *a* **1000** *Sax. Leechd.* I. 268 Wiþ ðæra earena sare, ʒenim þisse sylfan wyrte [*sc.* of foxglove] seaw, mid rosan seawe. *Ibid.* II. 176 Cumaþ þa adla..on [? *read* of] yflum seawum.
**2.** Pottage, broth; a mess of pottage. (Cf. *fig-sue*, FIG *sb.* 10.)
In the 15th c. sometimes used as the equivalent of OF. *civé* onion broth, minced meat stewed with onions. (Cf. quot. *c* 1440.) There may have been a disyllabic *seve* (a. OF. *civé*) which may have been confused with the native word because of the ambiguity of the spelling.
**13..** *E.E. Allit. P.* B. 108 þyse ilk renkez..Schul neuer..suppe on sope of my seve. *Ibid.* 825 þenne ho sauerez with salt her seuez vchone. *c* **1386** CHAUCER *Squire's T.* 59, I wol nat letten of hir strange sewes. **1388** WYCLIF *Gen.* xxvii. 4 Whanne thou hast take ony thing bi huntyng, make to me a seew therof. **1422** YONGE tr. *Secreta Secret.* lxix. 246 Flesh y-rostid, wych is more hottyr than in seau, or sode in watyr. *c* **1440** *Promp. Parv.* 67/2 Cewe, *sepulatum*. *Ibid.* 454/2 Sew, *cepulatum*. **14..** *Voc.* in Wr.-Wülcker 572/7 *Cepiarium*, sewe. *c* **1500** LACY *Wyl Bucke's Test.* a iij, The potage stued tripes and Noumbles in sewe. **1547** BOORDE *Brev. Health* §309 Beware of eatyng of frutes, potages, and sewes. **1586** WARNER *Alb. Eng.* v. xxv, To have gud spiced Sewe and Roste, and plum-pies for a King. **1601** HOLLAND *Pliny* xx. xvi. II. 63 If a thicke grewell or sew be made thereof. **1633** J. FISHER *Fuimus Troes* III. ix, Hidder, eke and shidder, With spiced sew ycramd.
*fig.* **1645** *Answ. Pref.* 89 You..durst not upon the peril of quenching your kitchin-fire; put forth your single sew of translation, without the Coloquintida of your Annotations.
*attrib.* **1459** *Durham Acc. Rolls* (Surtees) 89 Item ij sewpottez.

**sew**, *sb.*[2] *Obs.* exc. *dial.* [a. OF. **sewe*, *saiwe*, aphetic f. **esseve*, *escheve*, f. *essever* SEW *v.*[4]
But cf. the synonymous SOUGH (north. dial. *seugh*), which may conceivably have undergone alteration through association with SEW *v.*[4] and SEWER *sb.*[1]]
A sewer, drain.
**1475** *Engl. Misc.* (Surtees) 27 The hows of Robert Raynald next by stoppes the watyr sew, that the water may not hawe it reght corsse. *Ibid.*, The new sewes in Gouththorp..is defectyve. **1585** HIGINS *Nomenclator* 391/2 *Cloaca*, the towne sinke: the common sew. **1610** HOLLAND *Camden's Brit.* I. 237 Common Sewes or Sinks. **1710** FULLER *Pharm. Extemp.* 244 Julep..scoms out feculent Rubbish..of the Body [and] sweeps it into the Common-Sew of the Circulating Blood. **1875** PARISH *Sussex Gloss.*, *Sew*, an underground drain. **1898** B. KIRKBY *Lakeland Words* 127 *Sew*—Mig hole, sewer, muck midden.

**sew** (sjuː), *a.* *dial.* Also sue, zoo, etc. [? Shortened form of *a-sew* (s.w. dial.): see *Eng. Dial. Dict.*
This word may possibly represent OE. *ásiwen*, pa. pple. of *áséon* to strain, drain.]
Of a cow: Dry of milk. Chiefly in phr. ***to go sew***, also ***to go to sew***.
**1674** RAY *S. & E.C. Words* 76 To go Sew: i.e. to go dry, Suss[ex] spoken of a cow. **1746** *Exmoor Scolding* (E.D.S.) 36 Thee hast a let the Kee go zoo vor Want o' strocking. **1875** PARISH *Sussex Gloss.* s.v., A cow is said to be gone to sew when her milk is dried off. **1886** *W. Somerset Word-bk.* s.v. *Zoo*, We milks twenty cows, but you know they never baint all in milk to once, some be always zoo.
¶**b.** The alleged subst. use = 'a cow which gives no milk' is perh. based on an erroneous analysis of *a-sew* (see above).
**1681** WORLIDGE *Syst. Agric.* 331 A Cow is a Sew when her Milk is gone. **1706** PHILLIPS (ed. Kersey), *Sew* (Country-word), a Cow, when her Milk is gone. **1885** SWEETMAN *Wincanton Gloss.* (E.D.D.).

**sew** (səʊ), *v.*[1] Pa. t. **sewed** (səʊd). Pa. pple. **sewed, sewn** (səʊn). Forms: 1 seowan, siwan, seowian, siowian, siwian, 2 sewen, 3 seouwen, 4 seu, souwe, sowen, 4–6 sewe, 4–8 sowe, (5 sawe), 6 *Sc.* schew, 6–7 sow, 7–9 *Sc.* shew, 5– sew. *Pa. pple.* 1 seowed, 3 ise(o)uwed, 4 isued, y-sewed, 4–8 sowed, (5 saude, sawede), 6 soude, sowd, *Sc.* sowit, 7 sewit, 4– sewed; 4–6 sowen, 7 sewen, 9– sewn. [Com. Teut. and Indogermanic: OE. *siwan*, *siowan* (usually, with change of conjugation, *siwian*, *siowian*, *seowian*) = OFris. *sîa* (mod.Fris. dial. *siije*), OHG. *siuwen*, ON. *sýja* (Sw. *sy*, Da. *sye*), Goth. *siujan*:—OTeut. **siwjan*, cogn. w. the synonymous L. *su-ĕre*, Gr. (κασ-)σύειν, Lett. *schuju*, OSl. *šiti* (Russ. *shit'*, *shivat'*), Skr. *siv* (3 sing. pres. *sīvyati*, pa. pple. *syūtá*; derivatives are *syū* fem., needle or thread, *syūman* suture).
The root (for which Hirt suggests a primary form **seyewa-*) appears in the words above quoted as **syū-*: **sīw*. Another ablaut-grade, **syou-*, is found in OTeut. **saumo-* SEAM *sb.* The pronunciation (səʊ) is abnormal (cf. *strow*, var. of *strew*, repr. OE. *streowian*); the written forms show that it goes back at least to the 14th c. In the 17th c. *sew* sometimes rhymes with *clue*, *new*; the mod.Sc. pronunciation is (ʃu).]
**1. a.** *trans.* To fasten, attach, or join (pieces of textile material, leather, etc.) by passing a thread in alternate directions through a series of punctures made either with a needle carrying the thread, or with an awl; to make the seams of (a garment, etc.).
*c* **725** *Corpus Gloss.* 1773 *Sarcio*, siouu. *c* **1000** ÆLFRIC *Gen.* iii. 7 Hiʒ..siwodon ficleaf and worhton him wædbrec. *c* **1000** —— *Saints' Lives* xv. 23 Sum sutere siwode [*v.r.* seowode] þæs halʒan weres sceos. *a* **1225** *Ancr. R.* 420 Schepieð, and seouweð, and amendeð chirche cloðes. *a* **1300** *Cursor M.* 19766 To seu þe pouer þair clething. *c* **1386** CHAUCER *Parson's T.* ⁋256 They sowed of fige-leves a manere of breches. *c* **1420** *Liber Cocorum* (1862) 36 Fylle thy bagge..And sew hit fast. **1566** in Hay Fleming *Mary Q. of Scots* (1897) 506 Item of lyncum tuyne to schew the Quens curges tua unce. **1576** G. BAKER *Gesner's Jewell of Health* 21 A Bagge..shaped and sowen after this manner. **1576** GASCOIGNE *Steele Gl.* Wks. 1910 II. 171 When shoemakers make shoes, That are wel sowed. **1666** *Third Adv. to Painter* 29 Bring home the old ones, I again will sew And dearn them up to be as good as new. **1756** MRS. CALDERWOOD in *Coltness Collect.* (Maitland Club) 243 A boy who sowes point in the forenoon. **1843** HOOD *Song Shirt* 31 Sewing at once, with a double thread, A Shroud as well as a Shirt. **1880** 'OUIDA' *Moths* I. 40 She can get a girl to sew them for her.
**b.** To fasten, attach, or fix (something) by this process *on*, *upon*, *in*, *to*, *round* (etc.) something else.
*a* **1000** *Ags. Gosp.* Mark ii. 21 Nan man ne siwaþ niwne scyp to ealdum reafe. *c* **1290** *Beket* 1804 in *S. Eng. Leg.* 158 In þe schipes seile an heiʒ þis holi man let do Ane Croiz, þat Man fer isaiʒ Iseuwed faste þer-to. **1382** WYCLIF *Job* xvi. 16, I souwide a sac vpon my skin. *c* **1386** CHAUCER *Prol.* 685 A vernicle hadde he sowed on his cappe. **1464** *Nottingham Rec.* II. 376 As it appiers in a cedule to þis sewed. **1483** *Act 1 Rich. III*, c. 8 Preamble, The seid Diers..uppon the lystes of the same Clothes festen and sowe greate Risshes. **1588** SHAKS. *Tit. A.* II. iv. 39 Faire Philomela she but lost her

tongue, And in a tedious Sampler sowed her minde. **1635** R. N. *Camden's Hist. Eliz.* III. 261 His head was soone after sewed to his body by his friends, and committed to buriall. **1681** DINELEY *Jrnl. Visit Irel.* in *Trans. Kilkenny Arch. Soc.* Ser. II. II. 28 [They] adorn it with flowers, sewen to the shroud. **1815** SCOTT *Guy M.* vi, Two slips of parchment, which she sewed round it, to prevent its being chafed. **1908** [MISS E. FOWLER] *Betw. Trent & Ancholme* 362 She had a black ribbon sewn round her lame finger.

*fig.* **1598** Q. ELIZ. *Hor. de Arte Poet.* 20 Oft to beginnings graue and shewes of great is sowed A purple pace. **1831** SCOTT *Cast. Dang.* i, My own good breeding is not so firmly sewed to me but that I can doff it, and resume it again without its losing a stitch.

**c.** with adv., esp. *on, together.*

*c* **1290** *St. Edmund Conf.* 54 in *S. Eng. Leg.* 433 And euere ȝwane heo sende heom cloþes..þare-with heo wolde herene sende faste i-seuwede with-inne. **1382** WYCLIF *Gen.* iii. 7 Thei soweden to gidre leeues of a fige tree. **1560** DAUS tr. *Sleidane's Comm.* 424 The other two and Paule also, had as it were sowed together certen fragmentes and patches. **1634** SIR T. HERBERT *Trav.* 105 Prams, sowed together with hempe and cord. **1709** FELTON *Diss. Classics* (1718) 32, I can compare such Productions to nothing but rich Pieces of Patchwork, sewed together with Pack-thread. **1836** W. IRVING *Astoria* I. 269 Mere tents of dressed buffalo skins, sewed together and stretched on long poles. **1855** LADY E. FINCH *Sampler* (ed. 2) 83 To Sew on a Button. **1901** L. F. DAY & M. BUCKLE *Art in Needlework* (ed. 2) xii. 116 A thread may be laid across and sewn down—couched, as it is called.

**d.** *Surgery.* = *sew up*: see 4 a.

*c* **1502** *Joseph Arim.* 269 The wounde to sewe fast he began to spede. **1795** J. BELL *Disc. Wounds* 17 *note*, The older Surgeons..called it a Continued Suture when they sewed the wound all along like a seam. **1801** —— *Princ. Surg.* II. 52 Except in those cuts which are so slight as only to require a cloth to be wrapped about the part, every wound ought to be sewed.

**e.** *Bookbinding.* To fasten together the sheets of (a book) by passing a thread or wire backwards and forwards through the back fold of each sheet, so as to attach it to the bands: distinguished from *stitch*.

**1637** *Star Chamber Decree* in *Milton's Areop.* (Arb.) 9 Nor cause any such [books] to be bound, stitched, or sowed. **1809** C'TESS CHARLEVILLE in *Lady Morgan's Mem.* (1862) I. 366, I read *Ida* before it was all issued from the press, a volume being sent me as soon as sewed. **1880** J. W. ZAEHNSDORF *Art of Bookbinding* v. 21 A third sheet having been sewn.., the needle brought out at the kettle-stitch, must be thrust between the two sheets first sewn. **1929** A. J. VAUGHAN *Mod. Bookbinding* I. 24 Before a book is sewn by hand the back is required to be marked..as a guide for the needle. **1968** I. ROBINSON *Introd. Bookbinding* 27 When the second section has been sewn the long and short ends of thread are drawn taut.

**f.** With cogn. obj.: To make (a seam).

**1399** LANGL. *Rich. Redeles* III. 166 Kerving þe cloþe all to pecis, þat seuene goode sowers sixe wekes after Moun not sett þe seemes ne sewe hem aȝeyn. *c* **1400**, **1630** [see SEAM *sb.*[1] 1].

**2.** *absol.* and *intr.* To work with a needle and thread.

*c* **1450** *Mirk's Festial* 136 þis man..toke hys schone to hym, and began forto sawe on hit. And as he sewet full helt [etc.]. **1526** *Pilgr. Perf.* (W. de W. 1531) 67 Whan a virgyn begynneth fyrst to lerne to sewe in the samplar. **1602** SHAKS. *Ham.* II. i. 77 As I was sowing in my Chamber. *a* **1700** DRYDEN *Ovid's Art Love* I. 780 What means Eacides to spin and sow? **1846** J. E. TAYLOR *Fairy Ring* 65 She sat steadily at her work, sewing away at the shirts. **1855** BROWNING *In a Year* iii, When I sewed or drew. **1891** MORRIS *Poems by the Way* (1896) 162 Hellelil sitteth in bower there, And seweth at the seam so fair.

**3.** *trans.* To enclose *in*, put *into* a cover or receptacle secured by sewing; = *sew up*, 4 b.

*c* **1350** *Will. Palerne* 3060 þan þa komeli quen kast in hire hert, Sche wold wirche in þis wise wel to be sewed In an huge hindes hide as þe oþer were. **1387** TREVISA *Higden* (Rolls) VII. 195 Peraventure ȝe schal kepe my body if it be sewed [**1432–50** sawede] in a hertes skyn. **1555** EDEN *Decades* (Arb.) 124 Her picture sowd in his apparell nere vnto his breste. **1596** SHAKS. *Tam. Shr.* IV. iii. 137 Master, if euer I said loose-bodied gowne, sow me in the skirts of it. *a* **1648** DIGBY *Closet Opened* (1677) 27 Sow these spices in a little bag. **1663** BUTLER *Hud.* I. i. 797 They sow'd them in the Skins of Bears And then set Dogs about their Ears. **1840** DICKENS *Old C. Shop* xxx, Nell had still the piece of gold sewn in her dress. **1848** THACKERAY *Van. Fair* xxxii, The diamonds were sewed into her habit.

**4. sew up.**

**a.** To close (an orifice, a wound, also anything that envelops) by stitching the edges together.

**1490** CAXTON *Eneydos* li. (1890) 143 Merencyus..made his wounde to be shwed [? *read* sewed; orig. *faisoit couldre sa playe*] vppe, that was yet full sore. *a* **1548** HALL *Chron., Hen. VI*, 181 The lordes sat still..neither whisperyng nor spekyng, as though their mouthes had been sowed up. **1596** SHAKS. *Tam. Shr.* IV. iii. 148, I commanded the sleeues should be cut out, and sow'd vp againe. **1712** STEELE *Spect.* No. 436 ⁋9 The Wound was exposed to the View of all who could delight in it, and sowed up on the Stage. **1776** *Trial Nundocomar* 31/1, I sewed up the bag with my own hand. **1812** *Ann. Reg., Chron.* 37 A surgeon sewed up the wound. **1885** *Riverside Nat. Hist.* (1888) III. 224 The fisher-men.. generally sew up the mouth before placing it with others.

¶ *transf.* To keep (one's mouth) resolutely closed. ? *nonce-use.*

**1785** H. WALPOLE *Let. to C'tess Upper Ossory* 20 June, I sewed up my mouth, and though he addressed me two or three times, I answered nothing but yes or no.

**b.** To enclose *in* a cover or receptacle and secure it by sewing.

**1611** BIBLE *Job* xiv. 17 My transgression is sealed vp in a bagge, and thou sowest vp mine iniquitie. **1633** FORD *Love's Sacrif.* II. ii, A Creature Sow'd vp in painted cloth, might so be styl'd. **1648** HERRICK *Hesper.*, *Nuptial Song* xv, But since It must be done, dispatch, and sowe Up in a sheet your Bride. **1848** THACKERAY *Van. Fair* li, He has sewn up ever so many odalisques in sacks and tilted them into the Nile. **1855** MACAULAY *Hist. Eng.* xii. III. 234 A piece of paper sewed up in a cloth button.

**c.** *slang.* (*a*) To tire out (a horse). (*b*) To tire out, exhaust (a person); to nonplus, bring to a standstill; to put *hors de combat*; to outwit, cheat, swindle; also, to bring about the conviction of (a person). (*c*) To make hopelessly drunk. (*d*) *to sew up one's stocking*: to put to silence, confute.

(*a*) **1826** *Sporting Mag.* XIX. 17 He preserves his cattle in such rare condition, that with great difficulty are they to be 'sewn up'. **1862** WHYTE MELVILLE *Inside Bar* x, I like you young fellows to enjoy yourselves..and sew up your horses and come home.

(*b*) **1837** DICKENS *Pickw.* xxxix, Here's Mr. Vinkle reg'larly sewed up vith desperation, miss. *Ibid.* lv, 'Busy!' replied Pell; 'I'm completely sewn up'. **1838** HALIBURTON *Clockm.* Ser. II. x. 154 You might have traded with him, and got it for half nothin'; or bought it and failed, as some of our importin' marchants sew up the soft-horned British. **1849** ALB. SMITH *Pottleton Legacy* xiii. 113, I have introduced him to you as soon as I could, and you must sew him up as quickly as you can. **1855** SMEDLEY *H. Coverdale* ii. 12, I did not think there was a man living who could have sewn me up in ten minutes like that; but you are..quick with your fists. **1857** A. MAYHEW *Paved with Gold* II. xvii, He told Fred Tattenham in confidence that if the men who were in his debt did not come up to the scratch on settling day he should be regularly 'sewed up'. **1927** *Dialect Notes* V. 462 *Sew up*, v., to convict on overwhelming evidence. **1929** D. HAMMETT *Red Harvest* vii. 80, I expected something like that. That's why I sewed you up. And you are sewed up. **1945** E. S. GARDNER *Case of Gold-Digger's Purse* xv. 159 The police have sewed him up on a written statement.

(*c*) **1829** BUCKSTONE *Billy Taylor, Kitty.* (*Aside, and taking out a vial.*) This liquid, sent me by Monsieur Chabert, The fire-king, will sew him up. **1840** J. T. J. HEWLETT *P. Priggins* xx, We must ply him with liquor, for I don't think a little will sew him up. **1842** LOVER *Handy Andy* v, To use Jack Horan's own phrase, the apothecary was sewed up before he had any suspicion of the fact.

(*d*) **1859** READE *Love me Little* xxvi, At this home thrust Mrs. Wilson was staggered... 'Eh! Miss Lucy', cried she, 'but ye've got a tongue in your head. Ye've sewed up my stocking'.

**d.** *colloq.* To bring (something) to a desired conclusion or condition; to complete satisfactorily; to organize or gain control of (a person or thing); *spec.* to ensure the favourable outcome of a game or match. Freq. in phr. ***all sewn*** (or ***sewed***) ***up***.

**1904** ADE *True Bills* 136 The Man with the Megaphone Voice cut no Ice whatsoever, for they had him sewed up. **1915** *Dialect Notes* IV. 235 *Sew up, v. phr.*, to make certain of (a place on a team, in a club, etc.). **1933** E. E. CUMMINGS *eimi* 245 We glide to marriage 'they've got that all sewed up' blonde's mari affirms. **1936** 'P. QUENTIN' *Puzzle for Fools* xxi. 198 He said that..he had Broadway sewed up—him and a few other fellows. **1942** E. S. GARDNER *Case of Careless Kitten* (1944) xii. 100 By the time you get there, Lieutenant Tragg will have things sewed up so tight you'll have to pay admission to get within a block of the place. **1945** —— *Case of Gold-Digger's Purse* xv. 165 The police have all the witnesses sewed up tight. **1953** A. UPFIELD *Murder must Wait* xxi. 191 A Chinese I..played draughts with..let me win a man..and I'd think I had him well sewn up..and then he'd clean the board. **1960** T. MCLEAN *Kings of Rugby* xi. 163 It was Henderson who sewed up the match a moment later. **1977** *News of World* 17 Apr. 23/3 Charlton appeared to have the game sewn up. **1979** *Quarto* Oct. 3/1 During this period the novelists had it all sewn up.

**e.** To enclose or seal off. *colloq.*

**1962** *New Statesman* 21 Dec. 899/1 Knowing that it's only a matter of minutes before the Law would sew up the district with a cordon, we drop one of the team at the local railway station.

**5.** *Comb.*: **sew-and-fell** *attrib.*, made by sewing and felling; **sew-on** *a.*, attached by sewing; **sew-round**, used *attrib.* to designate a method of sewing the upper of a shoe directly to the sole; also *sb.*, a shoe so made.

**1880** *Plain Hints* 27 The edge of the patch should be turned down as for a sew-and-fell seam. **1885** LENO *Boot & Shoemaking* xi. 94 In the best sewrounds, the sole is reduced to the thickness of the upper. **1889** *Pall Mall Gaz.* 20 Nov. 4/3 Men engaged in the sewround branch of the boot trade. **1900** C. RUSSELL & H. S. LEWIS *Jew in London* 78 In the 'sew-round' or slipper-making trade. **1905–6** *T. Eaton & Co. Catal.* Fall & Winter 158/4 Sew-on Hose Supporters, which are stitched on to corset. **1977** *Evening Post* (Nottingham) 24 Jan. 8/1 (Advt.), Sew on Patches By Leomotif. Fantastic range of over 300 designs.

†**sew**, *v.*[2] *Obs.* Also 5 cew, 5–6 shew, 6 sewe. [Back-formation from SEWER *sb.*[2]] *trans.* To place (food) on the table as a sewer does; *intr.* to act as a sewer.

The gloss *cepulo* in *Promp. Parv.* is due to association with SEW *sb.*[1]

*c* **1440** *Promp. Parv.* 67/2 Cewyn, *cepulo*. *Ibid.* 454/2 Sewyn, at mete.., *ferculo, sepulo*. *c* **1440** LYDG. *Hors, Shepe, & G.* 208 A fatt goos..is sewid [*v.r.* served] vp atte kingis table. *a* **1483** *Liber Niger* in *Househ. Ord.* (1790) 36 He [the sewer] seweth at one mele, and dyneth and soupeth at another mele. *c* **1500** *For to serve a Lord* in *Babees Bk.* (1868) 366 First, mustard and brawne, swete wyne shewed therto. **1530** PALSGR. 716/2, I sewe at meate, *je taste*. *a* **1548** HALL *Chron., Hen. IV*, 14 b, The esquier whiche was acustomed to sewe and take the assaye before kyng Rychard. **1560** RHODES *Bk. Nurture* in *Babees Bk.* (1868) 67 In some places the Caruer doth vse to shew and set down. **1609** B. JONSON *Silent Wom.* III. vii. *marg.*, La-Foole passes ouer sewing the meate.

†**sew**, *v.*[3] *Falconry. Obs.* [aphetic a. OF. *essuer*, *essuier* (mod.F. *essuyer*) to wipe, cleanse:—L. *exsūcāre* to deprive of juice, f. *ex-* out + *sūcus* juice.] *trans.* Of a hawk: To wipe (the beak) after feeding.

*c* **1450** *Bk. Hawking* in *Rel. Ant.* I. 296 An hawke suyth is beke and not wypith. **1486** *Bk. St. Albans* a vj, An hawke snytith or sewith hir beke and not wipith hir beke. **1575** TURBERV. *Faulconrie* 289 Let hir tire against the Sunne, snyting and sewing hir beake a little at your discretion.

**sew** (sjuː), *v.*[4] Also 6 seaw, sewe, 7 siew, 7–9 sue. [a. OF. (north-eastern) **sewer* (latinized *sewāre*), aphetic a. OF. *essewer*, *essever* :—popular L. **exaquāre*, f. L. *ex-* out + *aqua* water.

The OE. *séon* (pa. pple. *ȝesiwen*) had precisely the sense 2 below. It is possible that in this sense the vb. may be a distinct word, from the OE. pple. The F. *suer* to sweat may also be a partial source.]

**1.** *trans.* To drain, draw off the water from. Now *dial.* Also, †to draw off (water).

*a* **1513** FABYAN *Chron.* VII. (1811) 487 [They] slewe and hurte many of the abbottes tenauntes, and spoyled and brake his closures and warynes, and sewyd their pondes and waters. **1573** TUSSER *Husb.* (1878) 32 Sewe ponds, amend dams. **1579–80** NORTH *Plutarch, J. Cæsar* (1595) 785 He determined to draine and seaw all the water of the marishes. **1610** FOLKINGHAM *Art of Survey* I. xiii. 45 Mills, for Siewing of surrounded grounds. **1669** WORLIDGE *Syst. Agric.* (1681) 268 A good time to sew Fish-ponds, and take Fish. **1853** W. D. COOPER *Sussex Gloss.* (ed. 2), *Sue*, to make furrows to draw off water from land. **1887** *Kent Gloss.*, *Sew*, to dry; to drain; as, 'To sew a pond.'

**2.** *intr.* Of a liquid: To ooze out, exude. (Said also of the containing vessel.) Now *dial.*

**1565** GOLDING *Ovid's Met.* IV. (1567) 53 The droppes of bloud that from the head did sew Of Gorgon being new cut off. **1575** TURBERV. *Faulconrie* 292 Whensoever the humor makes a shew to sew out at the hawkes eares. **1626** BACON *Sylva* §79 The Percolation or Suing of the Veriuyce through the wood. *Ibid.* §410 Some Wheat lay vnder the Pan, which was somewhat moistned by the Suing of the Pan. **1648** J. BEAUMONT *Psyche* II. clxvii, The deadly juice that from his brain doth sue. **1807** W. TAYLOR in *Monthly Mag.* XXIV. 549 The water sues through the brick work. **1823** E. MOOR *Suffolk Words* 337 *Sew*, to ooze out. Water, from wet land—blood, from a bound-up wound. *a* **1825** FORBY *Voc. E. Anglia*, *Sue*, to issue in small quantities; to exude as a fluid from a vessel not sufficiently tight to confine it.

**3.** *Naut.* **a.** Of a ship: To be grounded, to be high and dry; also (with specifying addition), to have its water-line (so much) above the water.

*c* **1588** in *Defeat Sp. Armada* (Navy Rec. Soc.) I. 16 For that she was aground and sewed two foot, and could not be gotten off. **1627** CAPT. SMITH *Seaman's Gram.* ix. 45 When the water is gone and the ships lie dry, we say she is Sewed; if her head but lie dry, she is Sewed a head; but if she cannot all lie dry, she cannot Sew there. **1676** WOOD *Jrnl.* in *Acc. Sev. Late Voy.* (1694) I. 166 The Water did Ebb, and the ship Sued above 3 Foot. **1745** P. THOMAS *Voy. S. Seas* 178 At Low-Water she Sued about one Foot and a half. **1750** BLANCKLEY *Nav. Expositor* s.v., When a Ship at low Water comes to be on the Ground to lie dry, they say, she is Sewed; and if she be not quite left dry, then they say, she Sews to such a Part. **1769** FALCONER *Dict. Marine* (1780) s.v. *Sewed*, If a ship runs aground on the tide of ebb, and it be required to know if she has sewed, the water line..is examined, and this mark being found above the water, she is said to be sewed by as much as is the difference. **1882** NARES *Seamanship* (ed. 6) 109 If the water has left her two feet, she has sued two feet.

†**b.** Of the water: To subside or diminish in depth. *Obs.*

**1748** *Anson's Voy.* III. vii. 355 The tide of ebb making, the water sewed to sixteen feet.

†**sew**, *v.*[5] *Obs.*[−0] *intr.* Of a cow: To go dry. (Perh. only a compiler's error; cf. SEW *a.*)

**1766** *Complete Farmer* s.v., To Sew, or go Sew, to go dry; spoken of a cow.

**sew**, obs. f. SAW *v.*, SHOW *v.*, SOW *sb.*, *v.*, SUE *v.*

**sewable** (ˈsjuːəb(ə)l), *a.* [f. SEW *v.*[4] + -ABLE.] Capable of being drained.

**1848**, **1894** [see DIKE-REEVE].

**sewage** (ˈs(j)uːɪdʒ), *sb.* [Formed after SEWER *sb.*[1] (apprehended as a derivative with -ER[1]) by substitution of suffix: see -AGE.

The assumed verb-stem implicit in this formation coincides in form and sense with SEW *v.*[4], but, unless the sb. is much older than the evidence shows, it was prob. framed without any knowledge of the verb as having been actually used.]

**1.** Refuse matter conveyed in sewers.

**1834** *Rep. Sel. Comm. Metrop. Sewers* 169 A grating.. through which the lighter and thinner parts of the sewage would rise. **1849** in *Mech. Mag.* Aug. (1850) 177/1 The separation of the sewage from the surface waters. **1869** E. A. PARKES *Pract. Hygiene* (ed. 3) 25 Shallow wells are very apt to be contaminated..by sewage soaking from cesspits.

*fig.* **1868** *Sat. Rev.* 5 Dec. 749/1 (art.) Newspaper Sewage. **1884** *Bookseller* 6 Nov. 1190/1 The literary sewage which is pouring forth from the Paris press.

**2.** = SEWERAGE 1, 2. *rare.*

**1834** *Rep. Sel. Comm. Metrop. Sewers* 136 The public have..built more sewage within the same level and the same term of years. *Ibid.* 182 Have you any communication to make..respecting the want of sewage in Holloway? **1850** OGILVIE, *Sewerage, Sewage*, The system of sewers or subterranean conduits for receiving and carrying off the superfluous water and filth of a city; as, the *sewage* of the city of London.

**3.** *attrib.* and *Comb.*, as *sewage disposal, -outfall, -question, -water, -works*; **sewage farm**, a farm on which sewage irrigation is practised; so **sewage farming; sewage grass**, grass grown on land fertilized by sewage; **sewage irrigation**, the system of disposing of liquid sewage by turning it on to land; so **sewage-irrigated** *a.*; **sewage lagoon** *N. Amer.* = LAGOON[1] 4.

**1873** *Practitioner* XI. 381 The health-aspect of *sewage disposal. **1939** *Country Life* 11 Feb. p. xxi/1 (Advt.), Sewage disposal for country houses, factories, farms, etc. **1978** J. WAINWRIGHT *Thief of Time* 29 The septic tank.. forms part of the sewage-disposal system of the bungalow. **1870** CORFIELD *Treatm. Sewage* 234 Examples of *Sewage Farms. *Ibid.* 271 Influence of *Sewage-Farming on the public health. **1888** *Science* 30 Mar. 156/1 *Sewage-grass is very inferior to normal herbage. **1867** B. LATHAM *Purif. Sewage* 10 The *sewage-irrigated farm of Beddington. **1870** CORFIELD *Treatm. Sewage* 237 Near Edinburgh, *sewage irrigation has been going on for the last 200 years. **1930** S. H. ADAMS *Mod. Sewage Disposal & Hygienics* 472/2 (Index), *Sewage lagoon. **1958** *Progress* (Preeceville, Sask.) 28 May 1/6 Northwest of town the earthwork for the sewage lagoon has been completed. **1976** *Billings* (Montana) *Gaz.* 30 June 4-D/3 Froid's water, sewer and sewage-lagoon systems. **1858** *Prel. Rep. Comm. Sewage Towns* 11 The present state of *sewage outfalls. **1850** *Mech. Mag.* Aug. 177/1 The Metropolitan *Sewage question. **1854** BAZALGETTE & HAYWOOD *Rep. to Metrop. Sewers Comm.* 5 The commercial value of *sewage water, and the cost of its conversion into dry manure. **1884** *Punch* 16 Feb. 82/1 The Vestry strongly object to *sewage-works being there erected.

**sewage** ('s(j)uːɪdʒ), *v.* [f. prec. sb.]

**1.** *trans.* To irrigate or fertilize with sewage.

**1861** *2nd Rep. Comm. Sewage Towns* 24 Plot 2. To be irrigated with sewage at the rate of 3,000 tons per acre per annum. Plot 3. To be sewaged at the rate of 6,000 tons per acre per annum. **1880** [cf. SEWAGED 1].

**2.** To furnish with sewers, drain with sewers.

**1884** *Pall Mall Gaz.* 9 Dec. 11/2 The streets.. are badly paved, abominably sewaged [etc.]. **1887** *Cassell's Encycl. Dict.*

**sewaged** ('s(j)uːɪdʒd), *ppl. a.* [f. SEWAGE *v.* or *sb.* + -ED.]

**1.** Fertilized by the application of sewage.

**1861** *2nd Rep. Comm. Sewage Towns* 28 Ten Hereford oxen were tied up in a shed; two to be fed on unsewaged grass, and the remaining eight to receive sewaged grass. **1880** H. ROBINSON *Sewage Disposal* 25 Weeds which are a source of trouble and expense on sewaged land.

**2.** Contaminated with sewage.

**1865** *Pall Mall Gaz.* 18 Aug. 9/2 'Sewaged water never can get pure' says another.

**'sewaging**, *vbl. sb.* [f. SEWAGE *v.* + -ING[1].

In quot. 1610 app. an independent word, f. SEW *v.*[4]]

**1.** The action of draining by means of sewers.

**1610** FOLKINGHAM *Art of Survey* II. ii. 50 Banckíng, balking, dyking, drayning, sewing, sewaging, rilling.

**2.** The action of irrigating with sewage.

**1894** *Jrnl. R. Agric. Soc.* June 348 Berlin adopted very stringent regulations for the management of the [sewage] farms and for the sewaging of each field in particular. *Ibid.*, A careful systematic sewaging of the land.

†**sewane.** *Obs. rare*[−1].

**1513** DOUGLAS *Æneis* XII. Prol. 145 Seroppis, sewane, sugour, and synamome.

**sewant, sewantly:** see SUANT *sb.* and *a.*, SUANTLY.

**sewar**, obs. form of SEWER, SOWAR.

**sewarry**, variant of SOWARRY.

**sewch, sewdarie**, obs. ff. SHEUGH, SUDARY.

**sewe**, obs. form of SEW, SIEVE, SOW *v.*, SUE *v.*

**sewed** (səʊd), *ppl. a.* [pa. pple. of SEW *v.*[1] Cf. SEWN.] Joined, fastened, etc. by stitching.

**1585** HIGINS *Nomenclator* 113/2 *Corona sutilis.* A sowed garland, or a garland the flowers wherof are tied together with thread. **1601** in *T. Pont's Topogr. Acc. Cunningham* (Maitl. Club) 179 Twa pair curtingis with sewit rebbenis. **1652** in Beck *Gloves* (1883) 152 Twenty four shillings for the Doz. of twice shewed sheep leather. **1763** in Macgill *Old Ross-sh.* (1909) 148 A Black gauze sewed hood. **1861** *Ladies' Gaz. Fashion* Oct. 79/2 Bonnet of sewed rice straw. **1861** *Times* 4 Oct. 7/4 The trade in sewed muslins. **1885** *Harper's Mag.* Jan. 279/1 Whether 'sewed' or 'open-tanned' goat-skins are preferable.

**b.** Of books: Having the sheets stitched together, but not bound.

**1766** *Catal. Mod. Bks.* 87 Young's (Dr. Edward).. Conjectures on Composition 8vo, sewed, 0 1 0. **1834** *J. R. Smith's Catal. Bks.* May 5/2 Historie of Friar Rush, 4to, sewed 2s 6d.

**sewed**, obs. form of SUET.

†**sewee.** ? Variant of SOY. (Cf. F. *soui.*)

**1737** WESLEY *Jrnl.* 2 Dec., Sewee Beans, about the Size of our Scarlet, but to be shelled and eaten like Windsor Beans.

**sewel**, variant of SHEWEL *Obs.*, scarecrow.

**sewellel** (sɪ'wɛləl). [See quot. 1893.] A small rodent of the Western coast of the United States, *Haplodon rufus.* Called also *mountain-beaver* (see MOUNTAIN 9 c).

**1814** LEWIS & CLARKE *Trav. Missouri* (1815) III. 39 Sewellel is a name given by the natives to a small animal found in the timbered country on this coast. **1859** S. F. BAIRD *Mammals N. Amer.* 353 *Aplodontia leporina*, Rich. Sewellel; Showt'l. **187.** *Cassell's Nat. Hist.* (1896) III. 97 The sewellel is torpid during the winter. **1893** COUES in *Lewis & Clark's Exped.* III. 861 *note*, It seems by the later researches of George Gibbs into the unspellable jargon of the Columbia River Indians, that 'sewellel' is their name for the robes, mistaken by Captain Lewis for the name of the animal.

**sewelling**, var. SHEWELLING *sb.*

**sewen**, obs. f. SEWIN, SUE *v.*; obs. pa. pple. of SEE *v.*, SEW *v.*[1]

**sewer** ('s(j)uːə(r)), *sb.*[1] Also 5 suer(e, 6 sewar, souer, 7 sewre, sure, 7 seward. See also SYRE, SYVER (*Sc.*; prob. unconnected), and SHORE *sb.*[4] [a. OF. (north-eastern) *se(u)wiere* channel to carry off overflow from a fishpond (latinized *seweria*, 1264 in Du Cange):—L. type **exaquāria* (cf. med.L. *exaquātōrium*), f. **exaquāre* (L. *ex-* out + *aqua* water), whence OF. *essever* to drain off, with which are connected OF. *essevour, -eur, esseouer, essouere* drain, ditch. (For the phonology cf. EWER.)

Until the 16th c. chiefly in legal formulæ as representing the earlier Anglo-Latin *sewera* or Anglo-Fr. *sewer(e.*]

**1.** An artificial watercourse for draining marshy land and carrying off surface water into a river or the sea. Also *water-sewer.*

[**1299** *Memoranda LTR* 26 & 27 Edw. I, m. 51 (Public Rec. Office), Per defectum reparacionis Walliarum Watergangarum et Sewerarum contra impetum fluctuum aque Humbrie.] **1402-3** [see *sewer-gate* in 5]. **1461** *Rolls of Parlt.* V. 493/1 For Sewers, Walles of Mersshes, Dyches, Gutters. **1482** *Ibid.* VI. 210 Makyng of Sewers for avoidyng of lake waters. **1543** in *Lett. & Pap. Hen. VIII*, XVIII. II. 118 For skoryn of a water souer. **1610** *N. Riding Rec.* I. 200 Tho. Skarth of Carlton in Cleveland, theldest, [presented] for stopping of the water-sewer upon the West Shortflatt. **1622** DRAYTON *Poly-olb.* xxv. 5 One general sewer which seemeth to divide Low Holland from the high. **1833** *Act 3 & 4 Will. IV*, c. 22 §22 It shall.. be lawful for the Occupier.. of Land .. adjoining to any.. Sewer.. to take.. such Gravel, Soil,.. and Weeds.

*transf.* *a* **1548** HALL *Chron., Hen. VI*, 187 The great ryuer of Wharfe, which is the great sewer of yᵉ broke, and of all the water comyng from Towton.

**2. a.** An artificial channel or conduit, now usually covered and underground, for carrying off and discharging waste water and the refuse from houses and towns. ***common sewer***: a drain through which all or a large part of the sewage of a town passes, a main drain collecting and discharging the contents of auxiliary drains. Cf. SHORE *sb.*[2]

The development of this sense (*c* 1600) is prob. due to the fact that the drainage of towns near tidal rivers had come under the control of the commissioners of sewers. See Act 3 Jas. I, c. 14 (1606).

Technically, 'sewer' is distinguished from 'drain', the latter being restricted to channels used 'for the Drainage of one Building only or Premises within the same Curtilage' (Act. 11 & 12 Vict. c. 112 §147).

**1606** SHAKS. *Tr. & Cr.* v. i. 83 *Ther.* Sweet draught: sweet quoth-a? sweet sinke, sweet sure. **1610** HOLLAND *Camden's Brit.* I. 423 A sewer within the ground to ridde away filth. **1611** COTGR., *Gesse*, a common sinke or sewer. **1619** DRAYTON *Bar. Wars* v. xli, Vnder whose Floore, the common Sewer past Vp to the same, a loathsome stench that cast. **1628** WITHER *Brit. Rememb.* II. 387 It was no noysome Ayre, no Sewre or Stinke. **1667** MILTON *P.L.* IX. 446 As one who long in populous City pent, Where Houses thick and Sewers annoy the Aire. **1684** I. PETER *Siege of Vienna* 42 Some Men were discovered in the Common-Sewer. **1739** LABELYE *Westm. Bridge* 72 Drains or Sewers discharging themselves into a small Arch. **1834** *Rep. Sel. Comm. Metrop. Sewers* 136 Open and Covered Sewers built within the Ranelagh Level. **1851** MAYHEW *Lond. Labour* II. 389 Fleet Ditch, which was perhaps the first main sewer of London. **1886** *Encycl. Brit.* XXI. 713/1 For small sewers, circular pipes of glazed earthenware.. are used, from 6 inches to 18 inches in diameter... Where the capacity of an 18-inch circular pipe would be insufficient, built sewers are used in place of earthenware pipes.

**b.** *transf.* and *fig.*

**1647** N. BACON *Disc. Govt. Eng.* I. iv. 16 This Island hath from time to time been no other than as a sewer to empty the superfluity of the German Nations. **1738** JOHNSON *London* 94 London! the needy villain's general home, The common sewer of Paris, and of Rome. **1765** FALCONER *Demag.* 240 His black entrails, faction's common sewer. **1859** TENNYSON *Enid* 39 A territory Wherein were bandit earls,.. Assassins .. this common sewer of all his realm. **1884** MRS. C. PRAED *Zero* ix, The moral sewer of Europe. **1945** N. MITFORD *Pursuit of Love* vii. 56 Who is that sewer with Linda?

**3.** *Law.* **a.** ***Commission of Sewers***: (*a*) a royal commission issued to a number of persons (hence called ***Commissioners of Sewers***) constituting them a temporary court with authority for the repair and maintenance of 'walls, ditches, banks, gutters, sewers, gotes, causeys, bridges, streams and other defences by the coasts of the sea and marsh ground lying and being within the limits of' a specified district liable to inundation from the sea or rivers; also, the body of commissioners of sewers for a district; (*b*) a body of municipal officers (abolished by Act 60 & 61 Vict. c. 133, 1897) who were responsible for the control of the 'sewers' (sense 2) in the City of London; these officers were first appointed in pursuance of the Act 19 Chas. II, c. 8 (1667), and were invested with the title and jurisdiction of commissioners of sewers by the Act 7 Anne, c. 32 (1708).

The term 'Commission of Sewers' (AF. *Commission de Sewerez, de Sewers*) occurs first in 1427 (Rolls of Parlt. IV. 333/1 and Act 6 Hen. V, c. 5), but the issue of similar commissions is recorded in 1314 (Rolls of Parlt. I. 319/1) and in 1322 (Placit. Abbrev. 339/1).

**1444** *Rolls of Parlt.* V. 109/1 Hit was ordeyned.. that by x yere then next folwyng, severals Commissions of Sewers shuld be made unto divers persones. **1504** in Leadam *Sel. Cases Crt. Requests* (Selden Soc.) 9 The kynges Commyssioners of Sewers. *c* **1530** in Ellis *Orig. Lett.* Ser. III. II. 227 One of the Kyngs Commysioners of Sewers. **1531-2** *Act 23 Hen. VIII*, c. 5 §2 The authoritie to you yoven by the Commission of Sewers. **1622** CALLIS *Stat. Sewers* (1647) 135 If a Collector or Officer of Sewers do distrain a man, or do any other act contrary to an Inhibition of Sewers to him directed by the Commissioners of Sewers. **1623** BACON *Ordin. Chancery* §94 (1642) 20 The Commission of Sewards. **1708** *Lond. Gaz.* No. 4442/4 The Commissioners of Sewers for the Levels of Havering and Dagenham. **1833** *Act 3 & 4 Will. IV*, c. 22 §60 The Words 'Court' and 'Court of Sewers'.. shall.. be deemed to mean every Court.. of any Six or more Commissioners of Sewers .. named in any Commission of Sewers. **1848** *Act 11 & 12 Vict.* c. 112 §3 The Metropolitan Commissioners of Sewers. **1881** *Ann. Local Taxation Returns* 112 Monies Raised and Expended by Commissioners of Sewers during the Year last ended.

**b.** ***law of sewers***: a local law relating to embankment and draining. ***Statute of Sewers***: the Act 23 Hen. VIII, c. 5, relating to the issuing of Commissions of Sewers. †***work of sewers***: any of the works of defence against floods (e.g. a sea-wall, ditch, bank, gutter, sewer, etc.) to which commissions of sewers relate.

**1571** *Act 13 Eliz.* c. 9 §3 Concerning the execution of any suche Lawes Ordynaunces and Constitutions of Sewers. **1605-6** *Act 3 Jas. I*, c. 14 The saide Statute of Sewers [23 Hen. VIII, c. 5]. **1622** CALLIS *Stat. Sewers* (1647) 133 If one oppose against a Law of Sewers. *Ibid.* 138 If one do suffer a Wall, Bank, or other work of Sewers to fall into decay for want of repairing. **1661** N. N. *Narrative Drain. Fens* in Arb. *Garner* I. 317 A Law of Sewers made at Saint Ives. **1835** *Tomlins' Law Dict., Romney-marsh.* A large tract of land in the county of Kent.. which is governed by certain.. laws of sewers.

**4.** Ellipt. for: Commissioner of Sewers. *Obs.*

**1616** BULLOKAR *Eng. Expos.*, *Sewer*.. one that hath authoritie to ouerlooke water courses. **1641** *Termes de la Ley* 247 The Sewers are Commissioners that sit by vertue of their Commission and authority grounded upon divers statutes, to enquire of all nusances and offences committed by the stopping of rivers [etc.]. **1675** ASHMOLE *Mem.* (1717) 53 This Morning a Jury of Sewers set out my Brick Wall made towards the High-way. **1706** PHILLIPS (ed. Kersey), *Clerk of the Sewers*, an Officer belonging to the Commissioners of Sewers, who writes down all Things they do, by virtue of their Commission. **1901** *N. & Q.* Ser. IX. VII. 436 Some of the family were 'sewers' of Wisbech.

**5.** *attrib.* and *Comb.*, *as sewer-assessment, authority, -ditch, grating,* † *law* (see 3 b), *-man, -rate, -scent, -stench, -water*; **sewer-air, -gas**, atmospheric air mixed with gas formed by the decomposition of sewage; **sewer-block**, a stoneware brick used for building the walls of sewers; †**sewer-gate**, a floodgate at the mouth of a drain or water-course; **sewer-heading** (see HEADING *vbl. sb.* 11); **sewer-hunter**, one who searches sewers; **sewer lagoon** *U.S.* = *sewage lagoon* s.v. SEWAGE *sb.* 3; **sewer line** *U.S.*, a pipeline that is a sewer; **sewer-rat**, the brown rat (*Mus decumanus*) common in sewers and drains.

**1861** FLOR. NIGHTINGALE *Nursing* ii. (ed. 2) 23 A stream of *sewer air coming up the back staircase of a grand London house from the sink. **1899** *Allbutt's Syst. Med.* VIII. 313 Similar symptoms may follow poisoning by sewer air, if this be concentrated. **1814** *Regent's Park* 72 He misunderstood the nature of the *sewer assessments. **1893** *Daily News* 25 Nov. 5/1 The Corporation.. are at once the *sewer authority and the road authority. **1884** *Health Exhib. Catal.* 50/1 Sanitary stoneware.. including drain-pipes.. *sewer-blocks [etc.]. **1851** MAYHEW *Lond. Labour* II. 390 Open *sewer-ditches, into which drains were emptied. **1849** in E. R. Pike *Human Docs. Victorian Golden Age* (1967) 276 These gases, which so many people are daily inhaling.. are identically the same in nature with.. *sewer-gas. **1870** CORFIELD *Treatm. Sewage* 174 It would be difficult to imagine a more ingenious method for delivering sewer gases at high pressure into houses than the one above described. **1886** *Encycl. Brit.* XXI. 716/1 The corrosive action of sewer gas. **1402-3** *Doc. New Romney*, [An entry about new gates to the sluice of the] *suergate. **1897** W. RYE *Norfolk Songs* 42 He cut his wife up into small pieces and dropped her down *sewer gratings. **1890** *Hardwicke's Sci. Gossip* XXVI. 236/2 Note on a Boulder met with in driving a *Sewer-Heading in Liverpool. **1851** MAYHEW *Lond. Labour* II. 151 The *sewer-hunters usually go in gangs of three or four for the sake of company. **1959** *Washington Post* 31 Oct. B1/5 To construct the outfall line to the location of the *sewer lagoons would require trenches in excess of 25 feet. **1785** J. PHILLIPS *Treat. Inland Navig.* 40 The works done in pursuance of this Act, not to be subject to the *sewer-laws. **1977** *It* May 6/3 (*caption*) Rosselli and his back-up man went down a manhole behind the fence.. and followed the *sewer-line away from Dealey Plaza. **1851** MAYHEW *Lond. Labour* II. 383 Of the *Sewermen and Nightmen of London. *Ibid.*

(1861) II. 431/1 The *sewer-rat is..said by the Jacobites to have come in with the first George. **1888** WOOD *Farmer's Friends* 23 Sewer-rats, of course, are to some extent beneficial. **1823** *Rep. Sel. Comm. Sewers Metrop.* 15 Laying a *sewer rate over the whole district. **1848** *Act 11 & 12 Vict.* c. 112 §77 Every District Sewers Rate to be made under this Act. **1929** D. H. LAWRENCE *Pansies* 54 And it's funny my dear young men, that you in your twenties should love the *sewer scent Of obscenity. *Ibid.*, A vapour of rottenness out of their mouths, like *sewer-stench wreathing. **1851** MAYHEW *Lond. Labour* (1864) II. 463, I..regard the Thames in the neighbourhood of the metropolis as nothing less than diluted *sewer-water.

[*Note.*—In the collocations 'Commission of sewers', 'works of sewers', etc., the word had virtually a much wider meaning than sense 1 above; it practically denotes any means of defence against inundation from the sea. The formula enumerating the things placed under the control of the commissioners begins with 'walls' (1322 more fully 'sea-walls', *murorum maritimorum*) and mentions 'sewers' only in the fifth or sixth place. This had already attracted the attention of lawyers early in the 17th c.; in 1622 Callis (*Stat. Sewers*, ed. 1647, p. 57) states that 'some compound the word of *sea* and *were*' (= WEIR, defence). Although sense 1 is certainly genuine, and the etymology stated at the head of this article is well established, it seems not impossible that there may have been some early confusion with a native compound of the formation suggested by the writers referred to by Callis. No instance of OE. *sǽ-wer, however, is known; a (? plural) *sǽ-wǽre*, of obscure meaning, occurs A.D. 1045 (Kemble *Cod. Dipl.* No. 776): 'Se ịȝȝað æt portes bricge & healfe sæ-wære & se mylnstede æt Mannæs bricge.' The Anglo-Latin derived verb *sewerare* (1314 in *Rolls of Parlt.* I. 319/1) appears to mean 'to protect from flood'.

The pseudo-etymological spelling *seward* (quot. 1623 in 3) is noteworthy. Skinner (Etymol. 1671, s.v.) erroneously attributes to Minsheu the statement that the word 'was formerly written *seward*, perhaps from *seaward*, either because they [*sc.* sewers] are made towards the sea, or because they ward off the sea'.]

**sewer** ('sju:ə(r)), *sb.*[2] Now only *Hist.* Forms: α. 4–6 sewere, 4–7 sewar, 5 seware, ceware, 5–6 sever, 6 sawere, 7 sewre, 4– sewer; β. 6 shewere, shower, 6–7 shewer. [aphetic a. AF. *asseour*, f. OF. *asseoir* to cause to sit, seat:—L. *assidēre*, f. *ad-* + *sedēre* to sit. ASSEWER (q.v.) is not recorded so early as the aphetic form. The β-forms are assimilated to *shew*, *show*.] An attendant at a meal who superintended the arrangement of the table, the seating of the guests, and the tasting and serving of the dishes.

Down to the 15th c. it was the designation of an officer of the Royal Household; it survived somewhat later as the title of a ceremonial office at coronations.

α. **13..** *E.E. Allit. P.* B. 639 As sewer in a god assyse he serued hem fayre, Wyth sadde semblaunt & swete of such as he hade. **1387** TREVISA *Higden* (Rolls) VI. 251 Olyver, cheef sewere of þe kynges bord. *c* **1440** *Promp. Parv.* 67/2 Ceware at mete. **1447–50** Q. MARG. *Lett.* (Camden) 97 Oure trusty and welbeloved Squier Thomas Burneby, sewer of our mouth. **1464** *Rolls of Parlt.* V. 535/2 Oure Servaunt William Wade, Squier, Sewer of oure Chambre. **15..** in W. Jones *Crowns & Coronat.* (1883) 119 [At the coronation of Elizabeth, queen of Henry VII, 1487] the lorde Fitz-water, sewer, or dapifer, attended.. and served the messes. **15..** *Bk. Precedence* in *Q. Eliz. Acad.* 17 A viscount..may haue Caruer and Sewer, with there Towells, when they sett there seruisse on the table. **1605** SHAKS. *Macb.* I. vii. Stage Direct., Enter a Sewer, and diuers Seruants with Dishes and Seruice ouer the Stage. **1637** N. WHITING *Albino & Bellama* 129 The dropsied Host, like to a Sewre did strut To marshall every dish. **1669** E. CHAMBERLAYNE *Pres. St. Eng.* (ed. 2) 257 The Sewers of the Chamber are 8. *a* **1700** EVELYN *Diary* 23 Apr. 1661, Gent. Ushers, Daily Waiters, Sewers, Carvers. **1791** COWPER *Odyss.* I. 178 The sewer with savoury meats Dish after dish, served them. **1821** SCOTT *Kenilw.* xvii, Let the master of my lord's household see that both clerk and sewer taste the dishes which the one dresses and the other serves. **1864** BURTON *Scot Abr.* I. iv. 168 *note*, Atholl performed the part of sewer, and Morton of carver.

β. **1525** BERNERS *Froiss.* II. xxxi. 36 b/1 Sir yuan of Leschell was shewer and sir Gracyen bare his cuppe. **1533** MORE *Answ. poysoned Bk.* Wks. 1036/2, I beshrew such a shewer as so serueth in the supper, that he conueieth away the best dysh. **1553** *Rutland Papers* (Camden) 119 Therle of Sussex claymethe to be shewer at dyner the daye of the coronacion. **1565** in Ellis *Orig. Lett.* Ser. I. II. 204 Athall shower, Morton carvar, Crayforde cupbearer. **1602** W. S. *Life Cromwell* IV. iv. Stage Direct., Enter the Vsher and the Shewer, the meate goes ouer the Stage.

**b.** *fig.* and in fig. context.

**1501** DOUGLAS *Pal. Hon.* III. lviii, His maister sewar hecht verteous discipline. **1641** MILTON *Animadv.* 7 It shew'd but green practise..to blurt upon the eares of a judicious Parliament with such a presumptuous and over-weening Proem: but you doe well to be the Sewer of your owne messe. **1649** —— *Eikon.* xxiv. 192 Som such place, as may stile them the Sewers, or the Yeomen Ushers of Devotion.

**sewer** ('səʊə(r)), *sb.*[3] Forms: 4–5 sower, 5 sawer, 7 shewer, 5, 8– sewer. [f. SEW *v.*[1] + -ER[1].] One who sews.

**1399** LANGL. *Rich. Redeles* III. 165 Seuene goode sowers sixe wekes after Moun not sett þe seemes ne sewe hem aȝeyn. *c* **1475** *Pict. Voc.* in Wr.-Wülcker 795/21 *Hec sutrix*, a sewer. **1481** in *Eng. Gilds* 314 That no man of the forsayde crafte [of tailors] set no new sawer a-warcke a-bofe the spasse of xv. days. **1483** *Cath. Angl.* 331/2 A Sewer, *filator, sutor, sutrix*. **1652** in Beck *Gloves* (1883) 152 [The Craft] ordains every boy and fial to take such work from his Master as his shewers cast. **1755** JOHNSON, *Sewer*..He that uses a needle. **1870** *Echo* 30 Dec. The sewer has it placed on a long table round which she travels, stitching as she goes. **1880** ZAEHNSDORF *Bookbinding* 21 It will be better if the cords are a little to the right of the press, so that the sewer may get her or his left arm to rest better on the press. **1891** E. PEACOCK *N. Brendon* II. 108 She was not only a neat sewer, but could cut out men's shirts.

**sewer** ('s(j)u:ə(r)), *v.*[1] Also 6 sewar. [f. SEWER *sb.*[1]]

†**1.** *trans.* To drain. *Obs.*

**1565** in *Arch. Cantiana* XIII. 269 A cricke, or water-wey, sewared or dryed upp.

**2.** To furnish (a town, road, etc.) with a system of sewers. Hence '**sewering** *vbl. sb.*

**1854** *Jrnl. R. Agric. Soc.* XV. I. 155 These towns have been sewered under the improved system. **1865** *3rd Rep. Comm. Sewage of Towns* 210 The sewering of towns on correct principles ought to be promoted, so as to ensure cleanliness, comfort, and health. **1884** *Pall Mall Gaz.* 9 July 2/1 In some of the southern cities of America..sewering, draining, and scavenging have brought about great improvement. **1888** BRYCE *Amer. Commw.* II. li. II. 287 To grade, pave, and sewer streets.

†'**sewer**, *v.*[2] *Obs. rare.* [f. SEWER *sb.*[2]] *intr.* To act as sewer at a meal.

*c* **1553** in Grose *Antiq. Rep.* (1809) IV. 652 A Gent. to sewerer yf they were not otherwise occupyed in the Q. busynesse. **1623** MINSHEU *Sp. Dict.*, To Sewer or taste before, *vide Hazer salva.* *a* **1641** FINETT *Observ.* (1656) 156 His assertion was not followed for the better convenience of the said Officers carving and sewering. **1647** HEXHAM II, To Sewer, *Voor-smaecken, voor-tasten.*

**sewer**, obs. form of SURE.

**sewerage** ('s(j)u:ərɪdʒ). [f. SEWER *sb.*[1] + -AGE.]

**1.** Drainage by means of sewers; a method or system of draining by sewers.

**1834** *Rep. Sel. Comm. Metrop. Sewers* 149 The tenantry are paying sewer-rates; they never have enjoyed sewerage. *Ibid.* 150 To prepare a sewerage and manage it themselves. **1841** *Penny Cycl.* XXI. 317/2 How imperfectly the advantages of good sewerage are appreciated. **1892** EMINSON *Epid. Pneumonia* 12 Good sewerage will, I trust, banish this disease as effectually.

*attrib.* **1848** *Act 11 & 12 Vict.* c. 112 §34 The Limits of such Sewerage Districts. **1862** *Catal. Internat. Exhib.* II. x. 57 Glazed sewerage-pipes. **1865** *Times* 5 Apr. 3/1 The opening..of the great sewerage works.

**b.** The carrying away *of* refuse.

**1856** STANLEY *Sinai & Pal.* v. 246 The hole [in the altar rock] is an aperture for the sewerage of the blood of victims.

**2.** *concr.* Sewers collectively; the system of sewers belonging to a particular locality.

**1834** *Rep. Sel. Comm. Metrop. Sewers* 150, I have seen a programme of the street; I think that is the position in which the sewerage is. **1851** MAYHEW *Lond. Labour* II. 389 Our arched and subterraneous sewerage. **1889** GUNTER *That Frenchman* v. 46 Whose foul-smelling gutters have been replaced by under-ground sewerage.

**3.** Sewage.

**1851** MAYHEW *Lond. Labour* II. 383 Which forms a part of the street mud..of the scavenger's cart, rather than of the sewerage. **1858** HAWTHORNE *Fr. & It. Jrnls.* II. 182 The Tiber..enriched with city sewerage. **1900** *Jrnl. Sch. Geog.* (U.S.) June 207 To carry sewerage of Chicago toward the Mississippi river.

**b.** *fig.* Moral filth or garbage.

**1859** MEREDITH *R. Feverel* xl, [She] poured a little social sewerage into his ears. **1868** SWINBURNE *Blake* 131 The weltering sewerage of Aphra's unreadable and unutterable plays. **1874** L. STEPHEN *Hours in Library* (1892) I. vi. 230 The foulest depths of literary sewerage.

**sewering**, *vbl. sb.*: see SEWER *v.*[1]

'**sewerless**, *a.* [f. SEWER *sb.*[1] + -LESS.] Having no sewers.

**1854** *Chamb. Jrnl.* I. 209 The saturated and sewerless ground. **1885** *Truth* 28 May 850/1 Sewerless cities.

'**sewery**, *sb. rare.* [f. SEWER *sb.*[2] + -Y.] The office or apartment used by a sewer.

**1851** TURNER *Dom. Archit.* I. 68 In household rolls of the thirteenth century the daily expenditure is almost always classed under the following heads; 1. The amount of bread, wine and beer supplied from the sewery and butlery.

'**sewery**, *a.* [f. SEWER *sb.*[1] + -Y[1].] Characteristic of sewers.

**1851** MAYHEW *Lond. Labour* II. 390 The Fleet Ditch seems always to have had a sewery character. **1896** *Punch* 1 Dec. 257/1 Some thought them [the smells] like Eau-de-Cologne, whilst their foes Denounced them as sickly and sewery.

**sewet**, obs. form of SUET, SUIT.

**seweyne**, obs. Sc. form of SEVEN.

**sewin**[1] ('sju:ɪn). Forms: 6 suwynge, sewing, 8 shewin, 9 sewen, suin, 8– sewin. [Of obscure origin: app. not Welsh. Cf. SUANT *sb.*] A fish of the Salmon tribe (*Salmo cambricus* or *eriox*), the bull-trout, found in Welsh rivers.

**1532** in G. T. Clarke *Cartæ Glamorgan* IV. 454 Yeldyng and paynge yerely to the sayd abbotte..x. samones v. gyllynges and xliiij[te] suwynges..or elles..for euery cuple sewinges I. d. **1769** PENNANT *Brit. Zool.* III. 248 Taken in the river Wye, where it is known by the name of Sewin, or Shewin. **1805** DUNCUMB *Agric. Heref.* 17 The botcher resembles the suin taken in the Welsh rivers. **1834** *Proc. Berw. Nat. Club* I. ii. 52 The sewin will most likely prove our Scotch hirling or whiting. **1861** *Act 24 & 25 Vict.* c. 109 §4. **1900** *Field* 28 July 153/1 There is not a better sea trout or sewin river in North Wales.

**sewin**[2] ('sju:ɪn). Corrupt form of *sewel*, SHEWEL.

**1886** WALSINGHAM *Shooting* (Badm. Libr.) I. 201 A substitute for nets in covert shooting, where it is desirable to stop the winged game rather than the ground game, is commonly known as 'sewin'. **1898** *Encycl. Sport* II. 85/2 (Pheasant) The number of stops may be materially reduced by the use of the sewin.

**sewin(e**, obs. Sc. forms of SEVEN.

**sewing** ('səʊɪŋ), *vbl. sb.*[1] Forms: 3 seuwingue, 4–5 sewinge, 4–6 sowinge, 5 sawyng, sowenge, soyng, 5–6 sewin, 5, 7, sowing, 6 *Sc.* schiuine, 7 soweing, soeing, 4– sewing. [f. SEW *v.*[1] + -ING[1].]

**1. a.** The action of SEW *v.*[1]; the use of a needle and thread; the uniting of pieces of material (etc.) by this means. In *Bookbinding*: see SEW *v.*[1] 1 e.

*c* **1290** *S. Eng. Leg.* 261/18 With spinningue and with seuwingue hire liflode heo wan. **1428–9** *Rec. St. Mary at Hill* 71 The lauendere for a hole ȝere wasshynge & sowenge ..ij s. **1484** CAXTON *Fables of Alfonce* xiii, [A tayller] whiche surmounted alle the other in shapynge or sewynge. **1566** in Fleming *Mary Q. of Scots* (1897) 506 Item for schiuine and the fassoune and pontis. **1597** A. M. tr. *Guillemeau's Fr. Chirurg.* 13/3 Sowinge of a wounde is a vnitinge and coupling together of the dissevered partes with a threded needle. **1691** RAY *Creation* III. (1704) 322 To manage the Needle in Sowing and the Pen in Writing. **1835** J. A. ARNETT *Bibliopegia* 20 There are various ways of sewing, according to the size and thickness of the sheets of a book. **1872** YEATS *Techn. Hist. Comm.* 155 The rise of the tailor's art did not take the constant occupation of sewing out of the hands of women. **1874** KNIGHT *Dict. Mech.* s.v. *Bookbinding*, A machine for folding sheets for gathering, sewing and binding. **1880** J. W. ZAEHNSDORF *Art of Bookbinding* v. 22 This is the strongest sewing executed at the present day. **1951** L. TOWN *Bookbinding by Hand* v. 99 If the sewing is done too tightly the book will be 'nipped in' at the kettle-stitches.

**b.** with prefixed word denoting the kind.

**1878** JEVONS *Primer Pol. Econ.* 72 Those who were not.. wise enough to learn machine-sewing, receive better wages for hand-sewing than they would formerly have done.

**2.** *concr.* Work sewn; materials to be sewn; the stitches or seams of anything.

*c* **1400** *Lanfranc's Cirurg.* 143, & þanne bynde þe nose wiþ two bandis..þe toþir schal be leid aboue þat he mowe kepe þe plumaciols, poudre, & þe sowynge. **1565** in Fleming *Reform. Scot.* (1910) 610 Four coffarris with hir clayis and sewingis. **1706** HEARNE *Collect.* (O.H.S.) I. 177 (Near to the Sewing), not at ye Top of ye Page. **1845** MRS. M. J. HOWELL *Hand.-bk. Dress-making* 47 No opportunity should be lost in making the sewing look well. **1865** HATTON *Bitter Sweets* iii, Mrs. Grey looked up from her sewing.

**3.** *pl.* Sewing thread or silk: see 4.

**1844** G. DODD *Textile Manuf.* vi. 184 Sewings are compound threads of silk, wound, cleaned, doubled and thrown, with especial reference to their ultimate use as sewing-silk. **1853** PERKINS *Haberdashery* (ed. 8) 24 Cloth Sewings—coarse large skeins for tailors' use. **1862** *Catal. Internat. Exhib.*, Brit. II. No. 3656, Dyed and polished yarns and sewings.

**4.** *attrib.* and *Comb.*, as ***sewing card, chair, -room, -work***; = employed in sewing or in teaching sewing, as ***sewing-class, girl, -maid, -mistress, -society, -woman***; of materials used for sewing, as ***sewing cotton*** (COTTON *sb.*[1] 3), †***gold*** (GOLD *sb.* 4), ***silk, silver*** (SILVER *sb.* 4), ***thread, worsted***; of contrivances, etc. for holding materials to be sewn, as ***sewing bird, -frame*** (FRAME *sb.* 13 b), ***-horse, -press*** (PRESS *sb.*[1] 10), ***table***; of a gathering for the purpose of sewing, as ***sewing bee, circle***; **sewing-brod** *Sc.*, a tailor's board; **sewing-clerk**, in the glove trade, a district collector of sewing done by home-workers; †**sewing-rope**, ? some kind of rope used for scaffolding.

**1862** M. COLT *Went to Kansas* 23 Have had two *sewing bees; one for the old ladies, and one for the young. **1936** F. CLUNE *Roaming round Darling* xxi. 209 Funds are raised in various ways, such as dances, sewing-bees, jam and wood days. **1976** R. BARNARD *Little Local Murder* iii. 35 Mrs. Smith, a woman of no importance who had had a forlorn hope of starting a sewing-bee. **1857** *Spirit of Times* (N.Y.) 21 Nov. 192/3 (Advt.), Gold bracelets, gold pencils, *sewing-birds. **1875** KNIGHT *Dict. Mech.*, *Sewing-bird*,..a device for holding the work while sewing... It has assumed many forms, the bird being ornamental and holding the work in its beak. **1949** R. J. SIM *Pages from Past* 10 Who can say when the ancestor of the sewing bird made its appearance on the edge of the table? **1790** A. WILSON *Callamphitre's Elegy*, He at the *sewing-brod was bred, And wrought gude serge and tyken. **1887** A. M. SULLIVAN *Let.* 20 Mar. in H. Keller *Story of my Life* (1903) III. iii. 312 Her father..sees her contentedly stringing her beads or making horizontal lines on her *sewing-card. **1961** M. K. ASHBY *Joseph Ashby* vii. 87 Tripping round in action songs..and the sewing cards.. certainly made them [*sc.* the children] happier. **1868** *Ann. Rep. Secretary Michigan State Board Agric.* VII. 354 A. Dondero, Detroit..[exhibited] 1 willow ladies' *sewing chair. **1978** D. CLARK *Liberties* v. 99 He looked at Mrs. Middleton on the sewing chair. **1846** *Knickerbocker* XXVII. 373 As if I too belonged to a *sewing-circle, and read charity sermons. **1912** L. M. MONTGOMERY *Chron. Avonlea* ii. 50 The minister's wife..asked her if she wouldn't come to their Sewing Circle. **1979** B. PARVIN *Deadly Dyke* ix. 47 Find out if there's a local sewing circle..in the village. **1864** LAYCOCK *Lanc. Rhymes* 62 We couldn't have an easier job nor goin' to th' *sewin' class. **1884** *Pall Mall Gaz.* 16 May 4/1 The glove-making counties are mapped out into circuits, each of which has its *sewing clerk or commercial traveller. **1826** *Haberdasher's Guide* 13 Coloured *Sewing Cottons. **1818** *Art Book-binding* 1 *Sewing-frame, with brass or iron keys, to fasten the cords or bands. **1876** *Encycl. Brit.* IV. 43/1

When taken out of the sewing-frame the fly-leaves are pasted on. **1848** 'N. Buntline' *Mysteries & Miseries N.Y.* 11 What, a little *sewing girl, eh? **1870** O. Logan *Before Footlights* 576 Among the same number of sewing-girls of our great cities. **1534** *Acc. Ld. High Treas. Scot.* VI. 191 Twa gret hankis.. *sewing gold. **1566** in Fleming *Mary Q. of Scots* (1897) 505 Item of schiuine gold iiij doubil hankis. **1875** Knight *Dict. Mech.*, **Sewing-horse*, a harness-maker's clamp for holding leather while being sewed. **1886** *York Herald* 23 Aug. 1/5 Useful *Sewing-maid. **1870** *Act 33 & 34 Vict.* c. 75 §3 The term 'teacher' includes assistant teacher, pupil teacher, *sewing mistress. **1613** M. Ridley *Magn. Bodies* 6 Smaller wiers, *sowing-needles and such like small waights. **1779** *Phil. Trans.* LXIX. 540, I stuck the point of this sewing needle to the lower extremity of a steel magnet. **1860** Tyndall *Glac.* I. xx. 144 If a common steel sewing needle be substituted for the iron [etc.]. **1728** Chambers *Cycl.* s.v. *Bookbinding*, They are then sew'd in the *Sewing-Press. **1842** *Penny Mag.* 24 Sept. 380/2 When the book is taken from the sewing-press, an inch or two of each string is left hanging to it. **1852** E. E. Hale *If, Yes & Perhaps* (1868) 56, I always offered my services in the Sunday-schools and *sewing-rooms. **1978** R. Hill *Pinch of Snuff* v. 50 We use this as a sewing-room... Alice.. makes all our clothes in here. **1336** *Acc. Exch. K. R.* 19/3 m. 4 *Sewenge rope [made of skin (*pelle*)]. *a* **1515** *Build. Louth Steeple* in *Archæologia* X. 74 Paid to Robert Beverley for 6 bunch sewing rope, 0 0 5. **1809** *Sporting Mag.* XXXIII. 281 The *sewing-school, the pastry-school, were then essential branches of female education. **1480** *Wardr. Acc. Edw. IV* (1830) 136 *Sowing sylk, j lb. ij unces and a quarter. **1621** in Kempe *Losely MSS.* (1836) 426 Stitching and soeing silke, 4*s.* 6*d.* **1826** Miss Mitford *Village* II. 190 Trimmings, ribands, sewing-silk, and lining. **1546** in *Extracts Edin. Burgh Rec.* (1871) II. 126 *Sewing sylver, to be sawld in punds. **1842** Dickens *Amer. Notes* (1850) 32 They have among themselves a *sewing Society to make clothes for the poor. **1863** A. D. Whitney *Faith Gartney's Girlhood* xxi. 199 In her low chair by her *sewing-table, sat the young sister. **1875** Knight *Dict. Mech.*, *Sewing-table*, a table or bench at which signatures of books are sewed to the cords or bands by which they are fastened together, and also secured in the cover. **1924** H. T. Lowe-Porter tr. *T. Mann's Buddenbrooks* I. i. 6 There was a sewing-table by the window. **1979** *Country Life* 27 Sept. Suppl. 59/3 Faded mahogany sewing table. **1566** in Fleming *Mary Q. of Scots* (1897) 499 Four pound of fyne *suyng threide. **1850** Miss Pratt *Comm. Things Sea-side* iv. 247 Scarcely larger than a sewing thread. **1847** Mrs. Carlyle *Lett.* II. 15 All the *sewing women I knew of being unable to come. **1722** De Foe *Col. Jack* (1840) 343 She.. took up her *sewing-work. **1612** *Sc. Bk. Rates* in *Halyburton's Ledger* (1867) 296 *Sewing worsett the dozen pound weght thairof.

† **'sewing**, *vbl. sb.*[2] *Obs.* [f. SEW *v.*[2] + -ING[1].] The action of a sewer; the arrangement of the guests and serving up of dishes or courses.

*a* **1483** *Liber Niger* in *Househ. Ord.* (1790) 37 The manner of sewing of dishes at the dressour. **1513** *Bk. Keruynge* in *Babees Bk.* 270 Here foloweth sewynge of flesshe. *Ibid.*, The borde of sewynge. *Ibid.* 286 Here endeth the boke of seruyce, & keruynge, and sewynge. **1627** Hakewill *Apol.* (1630) 430 Dinner and supper was served in with all accustomed ceremonies, as sewing, water, grace, carving, say taking, &c. **1660** R. May *Accompl. Cook* (1665) B 4 b, The Sewing of Fish... To go to the sewing of fish, muscalade, minews in sew [etc.]. [**1812** Southey *Omniana* II. 71 The terms of carving and sewing.]

**'sewing**, *ppl. a.* [f. SEW *v.*[1] + -ING[2].] That sews.

**1837** Carlyle *Fr. Rev.* I. VII. iii, The fair sewing fingers.

**sewing, -ly**, var. ff. SUING, SUINGLY.

**'sewing-maˌchine.** [SEWING *vbl. sb.*[1]]

**1.** A machine designed to perform the operation of sewing. Freq. *attrib.* as ***sewing-machine oil***.

**1847** *Artizan* Mar. 65/1 Sewing Machine. A new machine for sewing has recently been invented [etc.]. **1858** Hogg *Shelley* II. 457, I thought very little of it [*sc.* Cleopatra's Needle],.. after having seen the sewing-machine in London. **1869** E. A. Parkes *Pract. Hygiene* (ed. 3) 411 Two pieces of waterproof cloth, sewn together by the sewing-machine.

*attrib.* **1863** in *Rebellion Rec.* V. I. 70 Elias Howe, Jr., the inventor of the sewing-machine needle, was a private in this regiment. **1873** 'Susan Coolidge' *What Katy Did at Sch.* ii. 37 The nice half-dozens of pretty underclothes came home from the sewing-machine woman's. **1875** Knight *Dict. Mech.* s.v. *Bobbin*, A bobbin for sewing-machine shuttles. **1895** *Montgomery Ward Catal.* 262/3 See Index for Sewing Machine Oil. **1977** A. Scholefield *Venom* v. 205 He found a can of.. sewing-machine oil and squirted it into the lock.

**2.** *Bookbinding.* (See quot.)

**1880** Zaehnsdorf *Bookbinding* 176 *Sewing-machine*, a recent invention for the sewing of books with wire instead of thread.

**3.** *attrib.* **a.** Designating a musical instrument whose operation resembles the action of a sewing-machine. **b.** *fig.* Of rhythm: precise, regular, inexpressive.

**1874** J. Codman *Mormon Country* viii. 80, I found the solitary musician seated at one of those sewing-machine 'melodeons', and grinding out the Missionary hymn. **1934** C. Lambert *Music Ho!* IV. 247 Bach's sewing-machine counterpoint. **1974** *Early Music* Apr. 119/2 His purpose is to counter the 'sewing-machine' style of playing Bach by the 'purists'.

Hence **'sewing-maˌchinist.**

**1881** *Instr. Census Clerks* (1885) 75 Sewing Machinist.

**sewinti**, obs. form of SEVENTY.

**sewirer**, obs. comparative of SURE.

**sewit**, obs. f. SUIT.

**sewl**, var. f. SULL *sb. dial.*

**sewn** (səʊn), *ppl. a.* [pa. pple. of SEW *v.*[1]]

**a.** Stitched, fastened by means of sewing. Chiefly with prefix, as ***hand-sewn***, ***machine-sewn***.

**1866** *Chamb. Encycl.* VIII. 645 The operator, who keeps drawing the sewn cloth off at the eye-end of the needle. **1881** *Instr. Census Clerks* (1885) 73 Sewn Ornament Maker. **1895** *Hasluck's Boot Making* iii. 57 Shoemakers call all work sewn that is treated with a round awl; while stitching is only technically applied where the square awl is used.

**b.** With advbs. forming adjs., as ***sewn-in***, ***-on***.

**1961** *Guardian* 15 Sept. 10/1 Garments.. will have sewn-in labels giving simple washing instructions. **1965** E. C. Hiscock *Cruising under Sail* (ed. 2) I. vii. 136 In way of the grommet the boltrope is usually protected against chafe by sewn-on leather or plastic. **1977** *Guardian* 10 Jan. 8/1 The pallid youth in the tie-die shirt with a sewn-on picture of Marx.

**sewn(e**, obs. forms of SEVEN.

**sewr(e, sewrance**, obs. ff. SURE, SURANCE.

**sewre**, obs. form of SEWER *sb.*[1], *sb.*[2]

**'sewster.** *Obs.* exc. *Sc.* Forms: 4–5 **sewestre, -stare, sou-, sowe-, sywester(e**, 4–9 **sewster**, 5 **sew-, sowstare**, 5–9 **sowster**, 6 **seu-, sewe-, sewstar**. [f. SEW *v.*[1] + -STER. Cf. Fris. dial. (Hinderloopen) *syster*.] A sempstress.

**1391** *Earl Derby's Exped.* (Camden) 86/26 Edwyne Moreyn sewster pro filo ab ipsa empto. **1393** Langl. *P. Pl.* C. VII. 362 Sesse þe sywestere [*v.rr.* sowester, sewestare, sewestre, soustere; A. v. 158 souters, *v.r.* soustere; B. v. 315 souteresse, *v.r.* sowestere]. *c* **1440** *Promp. Parv.* 454/2 Sewstare, or sowstare (sowares) *sutrix*. *c* **1440** *Jacob's Well* 40 Tayllourys, sowsterys. **1519** Horman *Vulg.* 238 Brotherers, sylkewomen, and all seusters craftis occupye redyls. **1550** Bale *Engl. Votaries* II. 29 A yonge wenche.. whych was a very connynge sowster. **1567–9** Jewel *Def. Apol.* (1611) 450 Labouring Women, and Sewsters, and Seruants, and Handmaids. **1590** *Maldon* (Essex) *Liber C.* 121 Le sewester sive silkewoman. *a* **1637** B. Jonson *Sad Shepherd* II. iii, At every twisted thrid my rock let flie Unto the sew'ster, who did sit me nigh. **1657** C. Beck *Universal Char.* K 7 b, A sewster. **1824** MacTaggart in Trotter *East Galloway Sk.* (1901) 370/1 When plowman Tam meets sewster Bess His dogg'rel rhymes he'll chime till her. **1825** Jamieson, *Sewster*, a sempstress. [ed. **1882** also *Sowster*.]

**sewte**, obs. f. SUIT *sb.*

**sewy**, obs. f. SUE.

**sewyn**, obs. pa. pple. of SEE *v.*

**sewyr**, obs. form of SURE *v.*

**sex** (sɛks), *sb.* Also 6–7 **sexe**, (6 **seex**, 7 pl. **sexe**, 8 *poss.* **sexe's**). [ad. L. *sexus* (*u*-stem), whence also F. *sexe* (12th c.), Sp., Pg. *sexo*, It. *sesso*.
Latin had also a form *secus* neut. (indeclinable).]

**1. a.** Either of the two divisions of organic beings distinguished as male and female respectively; the males or the females (of a species, etc., esp. of the human race) viewed collectively.

**1382** Wyclif *Gen.* vi. 19 Of alle thingis hauynge sowle of ony flehs, two thow shalt brynge into the ark, that maal sex and femaal lyuen with thee. **1532** More *Confut. Tindale* II. 152, I had as leue he bare them both a bare cheryte, as wyth the frayle feminyne sexe fall to far in loue. **1559** Aylmer *Harborowe* E 4 b, Neither of them debarred the heires female .. as though it had ben.. vnnatural for that sexe to gouern. **1576** Gascoigne *Philomene* xcviii, I speake against my sex. *a* **1586** Sidney *Arcadia* II. (1912) 158 The sexe of womankind of all other is most bound to have regardfull eie to mens judgements. **1600** Nashe *Summer's Last Will* F 3 b, A woman they imagine her to be, Because that sexe keepes nothing close they heare. **1615** Crooke *Body of Man* 274 If wee respect the.. conformation of both the Sexes, the Male is sooner perfected.. in the wombe. **1634** Sir T. Herbert *Trav.* 19 Both sexe goe naked. **1667** Milton *P.L.* IX. 822 To add what wants In Femal Sex. **1671** —— *Samson* 774 It was a weakness In me, but incident to all our sex. **1679** Dryden *Troilus & Cr.* I. ii, A strange dissembling sex we women are. **1711** Addison *Spect.* No. 10 ¶6 Their Amusements.. are more adapted to the Sex than to the Species. **1730** Swift *Let. to Mrs. Whiteway* 28 Dec., You have neither the scrawl nor the spelling of your sex. **1742** Gray *Propertius* II. 73 She .. Condemns her fickle Sexe's fond Mistake. **1763** G. Williams in Jesse *Selwyn & Contemp.* (1843) I. 265 It would astonish you to see the mixture of sexes at this place. **1780** Bentham *Princ. Legisl.* VI. §35 The sensibility of the female sex appears.. to be greater than that of the male. **1814** Scott *Ld. of Isles* VI. iii, Her sex's dress regain'd. **1836** Thirlwall *Greece* xi. II. 51 Solon also made regulations for the government of the other sex. **1846** *Ecclesiologist* Feb. 41 The propriety and necessity of dividing the sexes during the publick offices of the Church. **1848** Thackeray *Van. Fair* xxv, She was by no means so far superior to her sex as to be above jealousy. **1865** Dickens *Mut. Fr.* II. i, It was a school for both sexes. **1886** Mabel Collins *Prettiest Woman* ii, Zadwiga had not yet given any serious attention to the other sex.

**b.** *collect.* followed by plural verb. *rare.*

**1768** Goldsm. *Good-n. Man* IV. (Globe) 632/2 Our sex are like poor tradesmen. **1839** Malcom *Trav.* (1840) 40/1 Neither sex tattoo any part of their bodies.

**c.** ***the fair(er), gentle(r), soft(er), weak(er) sex***; ***the devout sex***; ***the second sex***; † ***the woman sex***: the female sex, women. ***the †better, sterner sex***: the male sex, men.

[**1583** Stubbes *Anat. Abus.* E vij b, Y[e] magnificency & liberalitie of that gentle sex. **1613** Purchas *Pilgrimage* (1614) 38 Strong Sampson and wise Solomon are witnesses, that the strong men are slaine by this weaker sexe.]

**1641** Brome *Jovial Crew* III. (1652) H 4, I am bound by a strong vow to kisse all of the woman sex I meet this morning. **1648** J. Beaumont *Psyche* XIV. l, The softer sex, attending Him And his still-growing woes. **1665** Sir T. Herbert *Trav.* (1677) 22 Whiles the better sex seek prey abroad, the women (therein like themselves) keep home and spin. **1665** Boyle *Occas. Refl.* v. ix. 176 Persons of the fairer Sex. *a* **1700** Evelyn *Diary* 12 Nov. an. 1644, The Pillar.. at which the devout sex are always rubbing their chaplets. **1701** Stanhope *St. Aug. Medit.* I. xxxv. (1704) 82, I may.. not suffer my self to be outdone by the weaker Sex. **1732** [see FAIR *a.* 1 b]. **1753** Hogarth *Anal. Beauty* x. 65 An elegant degree of plumpness peculiar to the skin of the softer sex. **1820** Byron *Juan* IV. cviii, Benign Ceruleans of the second sex! Who advertise new poems by your looks. **1838** *Murray's Hand-bk. N. Germ.* 430 It is much frequented by the fair sex. **1849** C. Brontë *Shirley* III. xiv. 312 'Mama' is rather a misanthropist, is she not? Not the best opinion of the sterner sex? **1894** C. D. Tyler in *Geog. Jrnl.* III. 479 They are beardless, and usually wear a shock of unkempt hair, which is somewhat finer in the gentler sex. **1928** D. K. Parker tr. *Schopenhauer: Selections* 443 Women.. form the *sexus sequior*—the second sex. **1953** H. M. Parshley tr. S. de Beauvoir (*title*) The second sex. **1961** 'F. O'Brien' *Hard Life* v. 42 Decent people should look after women—isn't that right? The weaker sex. **1974** J. Mitchell *Psychoanalysis & Feminism* II. ii. 306 Woman is the archetype of the oppressed consciousness: the second sex.

**d.** Used *occas.* with extended notion. ***the third sex***, (*a*) eunuchs (in quot. 1820); (*b*) *sarcastically* (see quot. 1873); (*c*) homosexuals regarded as a separate sexual group.

**1820** Byron *Juan* IV. lxxxvi, From all the Pope makes yearly, 'twould perplex To find three perfect pipes of the third sex. *Ibid.* v. xxvi, A black old neutral personage Of the third sex stept up. **1873** Ld. Houghton *Monogr.* 280 Sydney Smith.. often spoke with much bitterness of the growing belief in three Sexes of Humanity—Men, Women, and Clergymen. **1896** J. A. Symonds *Probl. Mod. Ethics* vi. 78 Burton.. was led to surmise a crasis of the two sexes in persons subject to sexual inversion. Thus he came to speak of 'the third sex'. **1924** J. Riviere et al. tr. *Freud's Coll. Papers* II. xviii. 230 A very considerable measure of latent or unconscious homosexuality can be detected in all normal people. If these findings are taken into account, then, to be sure, the supposition that nature in a freakish mood created a 'third sex' falls to the ground. **1977** C. Isherwood *Christopher & his Kind* ii. 20 Hirschfield.. was.. notorious all over western Europe as a leading expert on homosexuality. Thousands of members of The Third Sex, as he called it, looked up to him as their champion.

**e.** ***the sex***: the female sex. [F. *le sexe*.]

**1589** Puttenham *Eng. Poesie* III. xix. (Arb.) 235 As he that had tolde a long tale before certaine noble women, of a matter somewhat in honour touching the Sex. **1608** D. T[uvill] *Ess. Pol. & Mor.* 101 b, Not yet weighing with himselfe, the weaknesse and imbecillitie of the sex. **1631** Massinger *Emperor East* I. ii, I am called The Squire of Dames, or Servant of the Sex. **1697** Vanbrugh *Prov. Wife* II. ii, He has a strange penchant to grow fond of me, in spite of his aversion to the sex. **1760–2** Goldsm. *Cit. W.* xcix, The men of Asia behave with more deference to the sex than you seem to imagine. **1792** A. Young *Trav. France* I. 220 The sex of Venice are undoubtedly of a distinguished beauty. **1823** Byron *Juan* XIII. lxxix, We give the sex the *pas*. **1863** R. F. Burton *W. Africa* I. 22 Going 'up stairs', as the sex says, at 5 a.m. on the day after arrival, I cast the first glance at Funchal. **1892** 'Mark Twain' *Amer. Claim.* xvii. 160 The customers applauded, the sex began to flock in. **1920** D. Lindsay *Voyage to Arcturus* i. 2 He was used to such receptions at the hands of the sex.

**f.** Without *the*, in predicative quasi-adj. use = feminine. *rare.*

*a* **1700** Dryden *Cymon & Iph.* 368 She hugg'd th' Offender, and forgave th' Offence, Sex to the last!

**2.** Quality in respect of being male or female.

**a.** With regard to persons or animals.

**1526** *Pilgr. Perf.* (W. de W. 1531) 282 b, Y[e] bee, whiche neuer gendreth with ony make of his kynde, nor yet hath ony distinct sex. **1577** T. Kendall *Flowers of Epigr.* 71 b, If by corps supposed may be her seex, then sure a virgin she. **1616** T. Scot *Philomythie* I. (ed. 2) A 3 Euen as Hares change shape and sex, some say Once euery yeare. **1658** Sir T. Browne *Hydriot.* iii. 18 A critical view of bones makes a good distinction of sexes. *a* **1665** Digby *Chym. Secrets* (1682) II. 225 Persons of all Ages and Sexes. **1667** Milton *P.L.* I. 424 For Spirits when they please can either Sex assume, or both. **1710–11** Swift *Jrnl. to Stella* 7 Mar., I find I was mistaken in the sex, 'tis a boy. **1757** Smollett *Reprisal* IV. v, As for me, my sex protects me. **1825** Scott *Betrothed* xiii, I am but a poor and neglected woman, feeble both from sex and age. **1841** Elphinstone *Hist. India* I. 349 When persons of different sexes walk together, the woman always follows the man. **1882** Tenison-Woods *Fish N. S. Wales* 116 Oysters are of distinct sexes.

**b.** with regard to plants (see FEMALE *a.* 2, MALE *a.* 2).

**1567** Maplet *Gr. Forest* 28 Some seeme to haue both sexes and kindes: as the Oke, the Lawrell and such others. **1631** Widdowes *Nat. Philos.* (ed. 2) 49 There be sexes of hearbes.. namely, the Male or Female. **1720** P. Blair *Bot. Ess.* iv. 237 These being very evident Proofs of a necessity of two Sexes in Plants as well as in Animals. **1790** Smellie *Philos. Nat. Hist.* I. 245 There is not a notion more generally adopted, than that vegetables have the distinction of sexes. **1848** Lindley *Introd. Bot.* (ed. 4) II. 80 Change of Sex under the influence of external causes.

**3. a.** The distinction between male and female in general. In recent use often with more explicit notion: The sum of those differences in the structure and function of the reproductive organs on the ground of which beings are distinguished as male and female, and of the other physiological differences consequent on these; the class of phenomena with which these differences are concerned.

*organs of sex*: the reproductive organs in sexed animals or plants.

*a* **1631** DONNE *Songs & Sonn., The Primrose* Poems 1912 I. 61 Should she Be more then woman, she would get above All thought of sexe, and think to move My heart to study her, and not to love. *a* **1643** CARTWRIGHT *Siedge* III. vi, My Soul's As Male as yours; there's no Sex in the mind. **1748** MELMOTH *Fitzosborne Lett.* lxii. (1749) II. 119 There may be a kind of sex in the very soul. **1751** HARRIS *Hermes* Wks. (1841) 129 Besides number, another characteristic, visible in substances, is that of sex. **1878** GLADSTONE *Prim. Homer* 68 Athenè..has nothing of sex except the gender, nothing of the woman except the form. **1887** K. PEARSON *Eth. Freethought* xv. (1888) 429 What is the true type of social (moral) action in matters of sex? **1895** CRACKANTHORPE in *19th Cent.* Apr. 607 (art.) Sex in modern literature. *Ibid.* 614 The writers and readers who have strenuously refused to allow to sex its place in creative art. **1912** H. G. WELLS *Marriage* ii. §6. 72 The young need..to be told..all we know of three fundamental things; the first of which is God, ..and the third Sex.

**b.** Sexual intercourse. Freq. in phr. ***to have sex (with)***.

**1929** D. H. LAWRENCE *Pansies* 57 If you want to have sex, you've got to trust At the core of your heart, the other creature. **1952** S. KAUFFMANN *Philanderer* (1953) x. 174 Her arms went around his neck and his hand rested on her waist, and they had a brief moment of friendship before the sex began. **1960** R. EAST *Kingston Black* viii. 82 She refused to have sex with him. **1962** *Listener* 7 June 1006/2 Why wasn't Bond 'more tender' in his love-making? Why did he just 'have sex' and disappear? **1962** *Woman's Own* 18 Aug. 29/3 Those trends in our society that make sex before marriage so easy. **1971** *Petticoat* 17 July 6/2 The most conspicuous consequence of sex before marriage is the possibility of pregnancy. **1980** *Times* 6 Sept. 2/2 Michael was alongside me, and in due course, on top of me. We had not had sex, but we were contemplating it.

**c.** Genitalia; a penis. *slang.*

**1938** D. GASCOYNE *Hölderlin's Madness* 18 And the black cypresses strained upwards like the sex of a hanged man. **1956** H. GOLD *Man who was not with It* (1965) xviii. 162 His eyes turned to his pants, gaping open, and his sex sick as an overhandled rattler gaping through. **1977** T. ALLBEURY *Man with President's Mind* i. 9 The narrow white briefs that barely captured her sex.

¶**4.** Used, by confusion, in senses of SECT (q.v. 1, 4b, 7, and cf. 1d *note*).

**1575–85** ABP. SANDYS *Serm.* xx. 358 So are all sexes and sorts of people called vpon. **1583** MELBANCKE *Philotimus* L iij b, Whether thinkest thou better sporte & more absurd, to see an Asse play on an harpe contrary to his sex, or heare [etc.]. **1586** J. HOOKER *Hist. Irel.* 180/2 in *Holinshed*, The whole sex of the Oconhours. **1586** T. B. *La Primaud. Fr. Acad.* I. 359 O detestable furie, not to be found in most cruell beasts, which spare the blood of their sexe. *a* **1704** T. BROWN *Dial. Dead, Friendship* Wks. 1711 IV. 56 We have had enough of these Christians, and sure there can be no worse among the other Sex of Mankind [i.e. Jews and Turks]? **1707** ATTERBURY *Large Vind. Doctr.* 47 Much less can I imagine, why a Jewish Sex (whether of Pharisees or Saducees) should be represented, as [etc.].

**5.** *attrib.* and *Comb.*, as ***sex activity, affair*** [AFFAIR 3], ***aid, -anger, antagonism, awareness, behaviour, circuit*** [CIRCUIT 7], ***clinic, complex*** [COMPLEX *sb.* 3], ***-compulsion, -consciousness, -contrast, -craving, difference, -distinction, distribution, education, emotion, equality, -excitement, -experience, -exploitation, -feeling, fiend*** [FIEND 4a], ***film, -flow, function, game, -hate, -hatred, hygiene, -inertia, -instruction, joke, life, -longing, -love, -machine*** [MACHINE *sb.* 4d], ***magazine, mania, maniac, manifestation, manual*** [MANUAL *sb.* 1b], ***-morality, novel, obsession, organ*** [ORGAN *sb.*[1] 5], ***orgy, partner, -party*** [PARTY *sb.* 9], ***-power, problem, question, repression, show, -specificity, starvation, stereotype, -stereotyping, story, -talk, -thrill, -union, war, warfare***, etc.; ***sex-abusing, -alive, -angry, -conscious*** [CONSCIOUS *a.* 12], ***-crazed, -emancipated, -influenced, -mad*** [MAD *a.* 4c], ***-obsessed, -segregated, -smelling, -specific, -starved, transforming*** adjs.; **sex act**, the (or an) act of sexual intercourse; **sex-appeal**, sexual attractiveness; qualities which attract members of the opposite sex; also *fig.*; hence **sex-appeal** *v. trans.* and *intr.*, to attract sexually; **sex-appealing** *ppl. a.*, having or exerting sex appeal; **sex attractant**, a substance produced by one sex of a species that attracts members of the opposite sex, or a synthetic substance with the same property; also *attrib.* or as *adj.*; **sex-blind** *a.*, not discriminating between the sexes; **sexboat** *U.S. slang*, **sex-bomb** *slang* = *sexpot* below; **sex-cell**, a reproductive cell, with either male or female function; a sperm-cell or an egg-cell; **sex change**, a change of sex; *spec.* an apparent change of sex brought about by surgical means, treatment with hormones, etc.; also *attrib.*; **sex chromatin**, the material of a small heterochromatic body (believed to be an inactivated X chromosome) of which there is one in a normal (XX) female cell and in general one less than the number of X (or Z) chromosomes in a cell; also *attrib.*; **sex chromosome**, each of the chromosomes (normally two in number) in a cell's chromosomal complement the particular combination of which (as XX or XY) determines an individual's sex; opp. AUTOSOME; hence ***sex-chromosomal*** adj.; **sex crime**, a crime involving sexual assault or with a sexual motive; a sexual act regarded as a crime; hence ***sex criminal***; **sex-determinant**, that which determines an individual's sex; **sex determination**, the biological process that settles the sex of an individual; **sex determiner**, a gene which determines the sex of the individual bearing it; **sex-determining** *ppl. a.*, determining an individual's sex; **sex discrimination** orig. *U.S.*, unfavourable treatment motivated by prejudice against members of a particular sex; hence ***sex-discriminating*** ppl. adj., ***sex-discriminatory*** adj.; **sex drive**, the principle which motivates satisfaction of sexual needs; **sex factor**, (*a*) a sex-determining chromosome or gene; (*b*) [tr. F. *facteur sexuel* (Jacob & Wollman 1957, in *Compt. Rend.* CCXLV. 1840)], a bacterial plasmid which can promote the transfer of genetic material from its ('male') host to another ('female') bacterium in which recombination then takes place; **sex-free** *a.*, (*a*) having a liberated attitude towards sex; (*b*) not involving sex; **sex hormone**, any of the (natural or synthetic) hormones that affect sexual development or behaviour, esp. those produced by the gonads; **sex impulse**, the impulse towards satisfaction of sexual needs; **sex instinct**, the behaviour and feelings associated with sexual reproduction considered as an instinct for the survival of the species; **sex-interest**, concern with a sexual relationship, esp. as a theme or episode in a story, film, etc.; **sex-intergrade**, an intersex; **sex-killer**, a murderer who sexually assaults his victim; hence ***sex-killing*** vbl. sb.; **sex kitten** *colloq.*, a young woman who exploits her sex appeal; hence ***sex-kittenish*** adj.; **sex-mosaic** *Biol.*, an individual some of whose cells are of one sex and the rest of the other; **sex object**, a person towards whom or thing towards which the sexual impulse is directed; a person regarded only as the object of sexual desire; **sex offence**, (*U.S.*) **offense**, a breach of law or etiquette involving sex; **sex-offender**, a person guilty of a sex offence; **sex play**, (*a*) a play about sex or with sexual content; (*b*) sexual activity stopping short of intercourse; **sexpot, sex-pot** *colloq.*, a sexually exciting person, esp. a woman; also, a sexually very active or sex-obsessed person; also *attrib.* or as *adj.*; **sex ratio**, the ratio of the numbers of individuals of each sex; **sex relation**, (*a*) sexual relationship; (*b*) *pl.* sexual intercourse; also ***sex relationship***; ***sex-related*** adj.; **sex-reversal**, adoption of a form or role characteristic of the opposite sex; hence **sex-reversed, -reversing** *ppl. adjs.*; **sex role** *Social Psychol.*, the culturally determined role or behaviour which a person learns as appropriate to his or her sex; **sex shop**, a shop selling sex magazines, aids, etc.; **sex surrogate**, a person employed as a sexual partner for a person undergoing therapy for sexual problems; **sex symbol**, (*a*) a person who is for many the epitome of sexual attraction and glamour; (*b*) a symbol with a sexual signification; **sex therapy**, therapy that deals with a person's psychological impediments to sexual intercourse or with other sexual problems; so ***sex therapist***; **sex-typed** *ppl. a. Sociol.* and *Psychol.*, typified as being characteristic of either the male or the female sex; so ***sex-typing*** ppl. adj. and vbl. sb.; **sex urge** = *sex drive* above. (Many combs. are paralleled by a collocation with SEXUAL *a.* 3.)

**1887** *Jrnl. Educ.* No. 210. 29 If this examination craze is to prevail, and the *sex-abolitionists are to have their way. **1781** COWPER *Expost.* 415 Sin, that in old time Brought fire from heav'n, the *sex-abusing crime. **1918** M. STOPES *Married Love* vi. 62 What must be taking place in the female system as a result of the completed *sex act? **1958** *Listener* 21 Aug. 263/1 A consciousness of guilt in the sex act. **1972** J. SYMONS *Bloody Murder* xii. 160 Detailed accounts of sex acts is [*sic*] still less frequent in the crime story than in ordinary novels. **1898** C. P. STETSON *Women & Econ.* iii. 44 Woman..has developed in the lines of action to which she was confined; and those were always lines of *sex-activity. **1949** M. MEAD *Male & Female* x. 208 The burden of choosing between sex activity and other activities has been taken off the individual. **1933** DYLAN THOMAS *Let.* Nov. (1966) 51 She who lives serene..And drags her tea-time *sex affair all fresh To the dinner table. **1949** M. MEAD *Male & Female* v. 118 Two inexperienced adolescents had a first sex-affair. **1977** *Gay News* 7–20 Apr. 14/3, I should like to dismiss this neat little toy as a *sex-aid for sadomasochists. **1923** *Sex-alive [see *ranch dog* s.v. RANCH *sb.*[2] 3a]. **1923** D. H. LAWRENCE *Kangaroo* xiii. 294 And if for a time you *do* overcome her with reason, the *sex-anger only arises more hideously. *Ibid.*, You can reason with a *sex-angry woman till you are black in the face. **1909** E. ROBINS *Votes for Women* I. 44 This ferment of feminism..[is] likely to bring a very terrible thing in its train... *Sex antagonism. **1952** A. CHRISTIE *Mrs McGinty's Dead* xii. 93 We really get a feeling of sex antagonism between the chap and the girl. **1924** *Amer. Mercury* II. 318/1 An actress with *sex appeal is four times out of five a more effective actress. **1924** G. R. CHESTER *On Lot & Off* 25 She'd sex appeal me all right! **1953** *Encounter* Nov. 32/2 For the frustrated and starved, it [*sc.* Communism] has all the sex-appeal of a strong, monolithic creed. **1979** *Guardian* 30 Mar. 9/6 Two conflicting general [education] policies have been put forwards by the Conservatives... Both have political sex appeal. **1980** N. FREELING *Castang's City* xi. 68 A very feminine charm, next door to sex appeal. **1928** *Daily Express* 24 Nov. 4/1 *Sex-appealing women should cut out the hurt feelings, the dewy eyes, trembling lips, the 'Please, I'm just a woman' stuff. **1932** *News Chron.* 20 June 4/1 Both [stories] are glittering, glamorous, sex-appealing. **1937** G. FRANKAU *More of Us* v. 61 'Ergo et propter hoc festina lente', Remarked Athene from that smoke-blue ceiling. But Innocent continued sex-appealing. **1964** *Listener* 27 Aug. 291/2 The study of *sex-attractant odours in insects has shown that these may be so highly specific that a very slight change in their chemical structure may make them less effective or even quite ineffective. **1976** *Globe & Mail* (Toronto) 13 Sept. 5/1 Many species manufacture and use chemicals as sex attractants. **1925** *John o' London's Weekly* 5 Dec. 360/1 In many fishes..there seems little hint of *sex-awareness. **1949** M. MEAD *Male & Female* xiv. 284 The period between childhood sexuality focussed on the parent and the stirring of adolescent sex awareness. **1923** J. S. HUXLEY *Ess. of Biologist* IV. 144 Castrated animals fail to realize either possibility of normal *sex-behaviour. **1949** M. MEAD *Male & Female* xvii. 354 The exaggerated over-concern with the other..puts an extraordinary strain on sex behaviour. **1975** *New Yorker* 29 Sept. 29/1 Even in an ideal *sex-blind situation you are going to encounter different kinds of blocksmanship between you and your goals. **1977** *N.Y. Post* 30 Mar. 3 Spokesmen for several liberal groups..declared yesterday that totally sex-blind job assignments are a violation of prisoners' rights. **1962** E. LACY *Freeloaders* ii. 22, I don't buy the bit that every mademoiselle is automatically a *sexboat because she's French. **1963** L. DEIGHTON *Horse under Water* xxii. 98 I've got the photo of your secretarial *sex-bomb. **1976** P. CAVE *High Flying Birds* iii. 42 Sex-bomb, Sonya Stelling might be. Oscar contender she was not. **1889** GEDDES & THOMSON *Evol. Sex* 91 Very commonly the *sex-cells originate in the ectoderm and ripen there. **1946** *Nature* 3 Aug. 173/2 These results.., while providing virtual proof of *sex-change from male to female in a section of the male population, point also to the probable occurrence of two types of males in *P*[*atella*] *vulgata*. **1960** *Twentieth Century* Mar. 258 Sex-change may well seem, as *The Times* said, 'unprepossessing' as a subject for comedy. **1970** *Daily Tel.* 21 Dec. 2/6 More people with transsexual problems are seeking National Health sex-change operations. **1952** GRAHAM & BARR in *Anat. Rec.* CXII. 709 The term 'sex influenced chromatin', or simply '*sex chromatin', will be used in the description to follow for the nuclear structure characterized by a size relation to sex. **1962** *Lancet* 27 Jan. 216/2 In all cases the sex-chromatin pattern was shown to be consistent with the morphological sex. **1913** *Jrnl. Exper. Zool.* XV. 593 The two white females ..came from the union of the two-X egg with the no-X sperm of the vermillion pink male, and should be entirely maternal and entirely non-paternal in *sex chromosomal composition, i.e., they should be exact counterparts..of their mother. **1906** E. B. WILSON in *Jrnl. Exper. Zool.* III. 28 These chromosomes are the bearers of the male and female qualities (or the factors essential to the production of these qualities) respectively. They may also be designated (whenever it is desirable to avoid circumlocution) as *sex-chromosomes. **1926** J. S. HUXLEY *Ess. Pop. Sci.* 46 From all the facts, we can, I think, be sure that all the higher animals possess special X or sex-chromosomes, two in one sex, one in the other, by whose agency sex is determined. **1974** GOODENOUGH & LEVINE *Genetics* x. 466 The sex of a fly is determined, in part, by the number of euchromatic sex chromosomes, called X chromosomes, possessed by an individual. **1920** D. H. LAWRENCE *Women in Love* xvi. 221 Each acknowledges the perfection of the polarised *sex-circuit. **1951** R. CAMPBELL *Light on Dark Horse* 319 These Germans had money from the Komintern and they set up *sex-clinics and communist-cells. **1972** *Newsweek* 27 Nov. 65 The sex clinic is fast becoming as vital a part of the modern hospital as the emergency room. **1921** R. MACAULAY *Dangerous Ages* vi. 111 You prefer to avoid discussing certain aspects of your life. You obviously have a *sex complex. **1928** D. H. LAWRENCE *Lady Chatterley's Lover* vi. 64 Be damned to the artificial *sex-compulsion! refuse it! **1912** T. DREISER *Financier* xx. 222 From the first she was somewhat *sex-conscious. **1952** S. KAUFFMANN *Philanderer* (1953) ii. 30 But she's certainly a sex-conscious girl. It's in her voice, in the way she sits, the way she drinks. **1911** *Freewoman* 7 Dec. 56/1 The impression given..is that the editors and most of the contributors picture the average woman as an individual wallowing in *sex-consciousness. **1953** D. A. BANNERMAN *Birds Brit. Isles* II. 193 'Sex consciousness'..remains for a long time, the male continuing to feed the female..even after the young are hatched. **1911** J. A. THOMSON *Biol. Seasons* iii. 263 The male 'ends' are salmon red or dull pink; the female 'ends' are greenish-grey or drab—the *sex-contrast eking itself out in colour. **1949** M. MEAD *Male & Female* v. 110 The little boys will feel..the potential sex-contrast with the mother. **1921** D. H. LAWRENCE *Psychoanal. & Unconscious* i. 20 The incest-craving is not the result of inhibition of normal *sex-craving. **1954** R. BISSELL *High Water* xx. 218 Well I'm reading this here story about a *sex-crazed maniac. **1925** *Amer. Mercury* Feb. 196 *Sex crimes, which are commonly regarded as a natural result of drug taking, actually never occur among addicts. **1965** G. MCINNES *Road to Gundagai* vi. 99 The murder of Alma Tirtschke by Colin Ross..was a sex crime which gripped Melbourne for weeks. **1977** *Gay News* 7–20 Apr. 10/1 Three gay people locked away in a private house constitutes a public meeting, and sexual acts that take place between any or all of them are sex crimes.

1972 J. Symons Players & Game xv. 100 Inadequacy. That's the mark of *sex criminals. 1902 Biol. Bull. III. 73 If we accept the theory that chromatin is the bearer of hereditary qualities, there could be little doubt regarding the necessary chromosomic character of a *sex determinant. 1889 Geddes & Thomson Evolution of Sex iii. 49 The temperature of the time, not of birth but of *sex determination, must of course be noted. 1977 Dædalus CVI. iv. 137 Primitive wasps..evolved the sex determination mechanism of haplodiploidy, whereby unfertilized eggs yield males and fertilized eggs yield females. 1912 Jrnl. Exper. Zool. XII. 509 Bateson and Punnett ('11) describe certain exceptions occurring in their sex-linkage experiment with fowls, which they suggest may be due to a failure of the usual association between the sex-linked factor and the *sex-determiner, i.e., to 'crossing over' in the female. 1960 E. J. Gardner Princ. Genetics vii. 123/2 When the parallelism was discovered between the chromosome cycle and gene behaviour it was generally assumed that genes other than sex determiners were also located in the sex chromosomes. 1901 Geddes & Thomson Evol. Sex (ed. 2) 51 In regard to rotifers (Hydatina), Maupas maintains that temperature is the *sex-determining factor. 1966 Lancet 24 Dec. 1397/1 This discrepancy between mammals and birds..might reflect different evolutionary origins of chromosomal sex-determining mechanisms in the two classes. 1918 M. Stopes Married Love iii. 19 Vaguely, perhaps, men have realised that much of the charm of life lies in the *sex-differences between men and women. 1979 Bull. Amer. Acad. Arts & Sci. Feb. 25 Clear sex differences in the probability of labor force participation and in the kinds of jobs held. 1964 C. Barber Ling. Change in Present-Day Eng. iv. 105 The *sex-discriminating word used to indicate that the member of some profession or the holder of some office is a woman. 1976 Listener 4 Mar. 264/3, I do not care if it is unfair, or sex-discriminating, for a woman to get an old age pension five years before a man. 1916 Campaign Text-Bk. (National Woman's Party) 62 Enfranchised women in the United States regard the removal of *sex discrimination from our national constitution as a political need of primary importance. 1965 Financial Times 24 Nov. 3/3 New guide-line interpretations on sex discrimination have just been issued by the Commission... So far the Commission has received over 400 complaints of sex discrimination. 1976 Times 6 Jan. 2/3 Employers who have cheated women of equal pay by job-grading schemes..may be taken to court for sex discrimination. 1976 A. Oakley in Mitchell & Oakley Rights & Wrongs of Women i. 27 This practical equality challenged the law which was *sex-discriminatory. 1894 H. Drummond Ascent of Man 317 The *sex-distinction slowly gathers definition. 1949 M. Mead Male & Female xiii. 266 The very simple accidents of *sex distribution inside any family give a structure within which a child can feel unwanted. 1918 R. S. Woodworth Dynamic Psychol. vii. 173 The association is not entirely a spreading of the *sex drive into the esthetic sphere. 1963 A. Heron Towards Quaker View of Sex 54 There may be a period.. when the sex-drive is latent. 1979 J. Sherwood Hour of Hyenas ii. 23 You are very striking-looking, but..my power drive is far stronger nowadays than my sex drive. 1920 Jrnl. Amer. Med. Assoc. 25 Sept. 884/2 The conference will.. consider the topic of venereal disease from these..aspects: (1) medical measures; (2) enforcement of repression and protection laws; and (3) *sex education. 1969 Guardian 7 Aug. 7/6 A series of sex-education talks I'd been giving at a North-east London youth club. 1936 D. H. Lawrence Pornography & So On 46 The most high-flown *sex-emancipated young people. 1911 O. Schreiner Women & Labour 232 The ignorant savage,..who violates and then clubs a female into submission, may be dominated, and is, by *sex emotions of a certain class. 1967 A. Marshall in Coast to Coast 1965–6 108 He was sure the men he knew were incapable of any sex emotion other than an animal lust. 1907 E. Densmore (title) *Sex equality. 1921 Daily Mail Year Bk. 42/1 The organization of the League of Nations has from the outset been founded on the principle of sex equality. 1977 'J. Gash' Judas Pair i. 14 She settled weeping while I found a coat. I'm all for sex equality. 1922 Ld. Dawson of Penn Love-Marriage-Birth Control 23 If this harmful restraint succeeds in preventing conception there eventuates the inevitable prevalence of *sex excitement. 1936 D. H. Lawrence Pornography & So On 30 Sex-excitement of a secretive, furtive sort. 1919 M. Stopes Married Love (ed. 7) ix. 141 Women so harried by the undue drains of unregulated *sex-experience. 1953 Sex experience [see sex play below]. 1914 J. London Let. 26 Mar. (1966) 419 The recent *sex-exploitation in our magazines and books. 1911 R. C. Punnett Mendelism (ed. 3) xi. 107 The factor which repels the red-eye factor is in this case to be found in the male, and here consequently it is the male which must be regarded as heterozygous for a *sex factor that is lacking in the female. 1931 E. B. Ford Mendelism & Evolution i. 14 Two doses of the sex factors carried by the X-chromosomes evoking the development of one of the sexes. 1955 Science 25 Feb. 305/1 The sex alleles of monosporoidal lines from a cross can be determined by matings in corn seedlings with lines representing each of the four haploid combinations of the parental sex factors. 1959 Genetics XLIV. 497 (heading) A variant sex factor in Escherichia coli. Ibid., The wild type sex factor (F′) of strain K-12 is characterized by its low affinity for the chromosome and its lack of any preferential site of attachment. 1968 W. Hayes Genetics of Bacteria & their Viruses (ed. 2) xiv. 799 If the sex factor happens to be inserted into the chromosome.., the replication initiated in the sex factor proceeds around the complete, integrated structure so that the chromosome is transferred as well. 1973 R. G. Krueger et al. Introd. Microbiol. xv. 423/2 The spread of a sex factor like Δ through successive populations of cells carrying different resistance genes on nontransmissible plasmids could result at each step in a strain carrying more and more genes for antibiotic resistance. 1918 M. Stopes Married Love v. 50 Even after a woman's dormant *sex-feeling is aroused..it may even take as much as from ten to twenty minutes of actual physical union to consummate her feeling. 1937 Discovery May 162/2 Conjugal affection, as distinct from sex-feeling. 1970 Women Speaking Apr. 4/2 The nearest man ever comes to this reduction to a word is when he offends society sexually: he is a *sex fiend. 1976 T. Heald Let Sleeping Dogs Die vi. 111 She was picked up by a sex fiend..and raped. 1970 *Sex film [see sex-instruction below]. 1936 D. H. Lawrence Pornography & So On 44 The *sex-flow is dying out of the young. 1929 —— Pornography & Obscenity 24 But the bohemian is '*sex free'. 1960 Encounter Sept. 72/1 Gerda is one of those sex-free affairs between tormented men and life-accepting women. 1897 J. Hutchinson in Arch. Surg. VIII. 230 Loss of *Sex Function. a1911 D. G. Phillips Susan Lenox (1917) II. x. 244 The favorite children's games, often played in the open street..were *sex games. 1976 J. Crosby Nightfall xxvi. 148 'Don't you like sex games?' she said. a1930 D. H. Lawrence Last Poems (1932) 140 All this talk of equality between the sexes is merely an expression of *sex-hate. 1913 J. London Let. 11 Oct. (1966) 408 She cherishes a *sex hatred for a woman who was bigger than she. 1917 Jrnl. Exper. Zool. XXIII. 371 (heading) The free-martin; a study of the action of *sex hormones in the foetal life of cattle. 1965 New Scientist 22 Apr. 218/3 The materials contained in the various forms of The Pill are synthetic sex hormones. 1951 M. McLuhan Mech. Bride (1967) 23/2 The reader is treated as the sluggish male is treated by the *sex-hungry cave woman in the shirt ads. 1912 G. F. Lydston (title) *Sex hygiene for the male and what to say to the boy. 1949 M. Mead Male & Female i. 17 Proper diet, rest, and sex hygiene have taken care of that. a1911 D. G. Phillips Susan Lenox (1917) II. xi. 281 In the streets the *sex impulse shows stripped of all disguise. 1957 J. S. Huxley Relig. without Revelation ix. 223 The powerful emergence of the sex-impulse in adolescence. 1936 D. H. Lawrence Pornography & So On 45 You may even bring about a state of utter indifference and *sex-inertia. 1951 H. A. Lindsay et al. in Jrnl. Nat. Cancer Inst. XII. 244 During accelerated synthesis of Nissl material the *sex-influenced chromatin moves from its usual position, next to the nucleolus, toward the nuclear membrane. 1898 C. P. Stetson Women & Econ. iii. 56 What business has a little girl with the instincts of maternity?.. They are *sex-instincts, and should not appear till the period of adolescence. 1976 A. Montagu Nature of Human Aggression (1978) iv. 64 Everyone 'knows' from his or her own experience that there is such a thing as a sex instinct. 1935 E. Bowen House in Paris i. iii. 42 We do not consider him ripe for direct *sex-instruction yet, though my husband is working towards this through botany. 1970 Guardian 10 Dec. 10/4 From time to time we have to see, not sex films, but sex-instruction films. 1911 Maclean's Mag. Apr. 139/2 There is scarcely any '*sex interest' in it at all. 1940 'G. Orwell' in Horizon Mar. 189 Both of these papers admit a certain amount of sex-interest into their stories. 1917 *Sex-intergrade [see intersex]. 1962 Lancet 27 Jan. 216/2 The hypothesis, advanced by Lang, that some male homosexuals are sex intergrades—i.e., morphologically male but genotypically female. 1941 'G. Orwell' in Horizon IV. 155 More than half, perhaps three-quarters, of the jokes are *sex jokes. 1959 M. Gilbert Blood & Judgement ii. 26 You'd be surprised..how many *sex-killers turn out to be their mothers' favourite sons. 1972 J. McClure Caterpillar Cop ii. 15 Murders..kept things going... But wanton *sex killings involving the young were quite another matter. 1958 Daily Sketch 2 June 11/4 Clever film men have moulded her *sex-kitten type. 1966 Guardian 7 Jan. 9/2 Brigitte Bardot..the original sex kitten with the French charm. 1977 D. Morris Manwatching 256 This is why we like 'sex kittens' more than females who are 'catty'. 1963 J. Fowles Collector ii. 166 Antoinette was almost parodying herself, she was so *sex-kittenish. 1898 C. P. Stetson Women & Econ. vii. 143 It should be..understood ..that the higher development of social life following the economic independence of women makes possible a higher *sex-life than has ever yet been known. 1922 S. Paton Signs of Sanity vi. 205 Some phases of our instinctive activities.. we discuss frankly..; others, notably the sex-life, we treat in a..furtive manner. 1936 'P. Quentin' Puzzle for Fools xx. 181, I get no kick out of the sex-life of the white-tailed baboon. 1976 Vogue 15 Mar. 13/2 He is being reviled for apparently having absolutely no sex life, none at all. 1979 R. Jaffe Class Reunion i. v. 47 Richard was the only boy..who had a regular sex life with a girl, and so he was a celebrity. 1925 T. Dreiser Amer. Tragedy (1926) II. iii. xiv. 183 All those..*sex-longings..had long since been covered with an easy manner. 1898 C. P. Stetson Women & Econ. xii. 260 The generous giving impulse of *sex-love. 1976 R. Delmar in Mitchell & Oakley Rights & Wrongs of Women ix. 281 There are several conditions which, in Engels..make sex love the rule within the proletariat. 1935 H. Edib Clown & his Daughter viii. 43 Now she wants to burden me with another *sex-machine. 1970 Times 9 Dec. 16/4 Lulu herself, from her first days as an insatiably successful sex-machine to her last days as an amateur prostitute, has no existence outside her appetite. 1943, 1974 *Sex-mad [see mad a. 4 c]. 1931 *Sex magazine [see confession magazine]. 1980 P. Kinsley Vatchman Switch vii. 66 The customs officer..sold any sex magazines he could confiscate from foreign tourists. 1895 Fortn. Rev. 1 Apr. 592 *Sex mania in art and literature can be but a passing phase. 1895 H. Garland Rose of Dutcher's Coolly viii. 90 The brakeman came through and eyed her with the glare of a *sex-maniac. 1971 Daily Tel. 14 Dec. 3 The Jersey sex maniac..was jailed for 30 years yesterday for 13 indecent and sexual offences against young girls and boys. 1975 'D. Rutherford' Mystery Tour i. 8 Wasn't that [sc. the murder] the work of some sadistic sex maniac? 1911 O. Schreiner Women & Labour v. 187 It is among certain orders of birds that *sex manifestations appear to assume their most harmonious and poetical forms on earth. 1949 M. Mead Male & Female viii. 167 These [sc. seizures] are extremely violent, but without specific sex manifestations. 1975 H. McCloy Minotaur Country iii. 21 He would be a sober, industrious lover. He would read all the *sex manuals. 1926 W. R. Inge Lay Thoughts iii. 254 The pleasantest side of our civilization—the ease with which innocent friendships are made between men and women—stands or falls with that Christian *sex-morality which is now being openly flouted. 1958 Listener 4 Dec. 933/2 Queen Victoria..instituted a new reign of sex-morality. 1903 Bull. Museum Compar. Zool. Harvard Coll. XL. 197 Unilateral and mixed hermaphrodites are an exceptional form of *sex-mosaic. 1926 J. S. Huxley Ess. Pop. Sci. 296 It is possible in the case of abnormal distribution of the sex-chromosomes during development to obtain some parts of the body with the male-determining, others with the female-determining complement of chromosomes, with the result that a sex-mosaic or gynandromorph is the result [sic]. 1955 Japanese Jrnl. Zool. XI. 350 The 1st gynandromorph is a simple bilateral sex mosaic showing yellow Ww gene in the left male wings and white Ww gene in the right female wings. 1923 in C. D. Stelling Yea & Nay 33 (heading) Is there any alternative to the *sex novel? 1951 M. McLuhan Mech. Bride (1967) 23/2 Amid the unmitigated torrent of sadistic sex novels works of reflection are tolerated only if they are..'warmly human'. 1911 Amer. Jrnl. Psychol. XXII. 423 Instead of sublimating the sex impulse, he [sc. Leonardo da Vinci] directed it towards the physical Jesus in toto. It was simply the substitution of one *sex object for another. 1963 B. Friedan Feminine Mystique (1965) xi. 266 For the woman who lives according to the feminine mystique, there is no road to achievement, or status, or identity, except the sexual one: the achievement of sexual conquest, status as a desirable sex object, identity as a sexually successful wife and mother. 1980 G. Greene Doctor Fischer of Geneva ix. 59 Deane is not an actor: he is a sex object. Teenage girls worship him. 1914 New Republic 26 Dec. 27/1 An almost lyrical open-airness.. saved 'The Garden Without Walls,'..from being *sex-obsessed. 1979 London Rev. Bks. 25 Oct. 13/1 Civilised human beings are remarkable among animal species for being sex-obsessed. 1920 F. M. Ford Let. 19 Sept. (1965) 127 The end would be the most horribly costive neurastheniac you can imagine, with incredible *sex obsessions sedulously concealed. 1911 J. London Let. 8 Jan. (1966) 330 You are suffering from what you deem a *sex-offence. 1977 J. Thomson Case Closed vii. 85 The offences..included fraud, burglary,..assault, sex offences of various sorts. 1939 Columbia Law Rev. Mar. 535 Prior to the enactment of this statute in Illinois, a criminal *sex offender received no special treatment. 1976 K. Bonfiglioli Something Nasty iii. 33 We 'ave only two known sex-offenders worth the name in this Parish. 1902 W. James Var. Relig. Exper. i. 12 That without the chemical contributions which the *sex-organs make to the blood, the brain would not be nourished so as to carry on religious activities..may be true or not true. 1978 Times 15 Mar. 6/3 Old symbols like mutilation of sex organs..are passé. 1962 J. Heller Catch-22 xxi. 208 Officers' clubs everywhere pulsated with blurred but knowing accounts of lavish, hushed-up drinking and *sex orgies there. 1949 M. Mead Male & Female ix. 195 But patterns that regulate competition in the choice of *sex partners are learned patterns. 1970 Sex partner [see sex therapy below]. 1958 J. Kerouac On Road i. i. 8 He told him of..his innumerable girls and *sex-parties and pornographic pictures. 1916 G. B. Shaw Overruled 63 Plays occupied wholly with the conventional results are..unsatisfying as *sex plays. 1932 Wodehouse Louder & Funnier 270 When I write my daring sex-play, I have to submit it to Lord Cromer, who starts licking his blue pencil the moment he has opened the envelope. 1953 H. M. Parshley tr. De Beauvoir's Second Sex II. vii. 682 The excessive sentimentality,..and platonic crushes of adolescent girls,..are much more injurious than a little childish sex play and a few definite sex experiences. 1961 W. Brown Bedeviled 17 Gradually, however, the fondling developed into open sex play which frightened her. 1957 F. Morton Art of Courtship 156 How pitiful the American who cannot command the smile of a *sexpot. 1961 Harper's Bazaar May 57/2 Ovid..the dirty old sexpot. 1963 J. T. Story Something for Nothing i. 17 'I like the hockey type,' Albert said. 'I can't stand these sex-pots.' 1975 New Yorker 5 May 115/1 Graham Chapman, John Cleese..with Connie Booth and Carol Cleveland as their sexpot aides. 1981 London Mag. July 89/2 Tough Games Mistress. Rebellious sexpot pupil (pregnant again). 1918 M. Stopes Married Love viii. 76 The periods of complete abstinence should be opportunities for transmuting the healthy *sex-power into work of every sort. 1977 London's Outrage i. 7 The bully-boy sex-power of Nazism/fascism is very attractive and an easy solution to our complex moral and social dilemmas. 1876 Hardy Ethelberta xxxvii, You cannot have celebrity and *sex-privilege both. 1900 J. X. Merriman Let. 1 July (1966) 222 The shrieking sisterhood who write on *sex problems and scream out for votes. 1979 Guardian 10 July 9/1 Professional partners used in the treatment of sex problems. 1902 G. B. Shaw Mrs. Warren's Profession p. xx, Plays which treat *sex questions as problems for thought instead of as aphrodisiacs will be freely performed. 1917 F. W. S. Browne in Proc. Brit. Soc. for Study Sex Psychol. 7 General early marriage, even if possible under present conditions, does not solve the sex question. 1906 Biometrika V. 79 The *sex-ratio for the family of each individual is directly calculated and tabled. 1974 J. Burnett Useful Toil i. 48 Because of the unequal sex ratio one in three [Victorian] women were 'doomed' to spinsterhood. 1977 Detroit Free Press 11 Dec. 9-c/1 A high-ranking official of Planned Parenthood says television's standards on *sex-related programming should be as much a public issue as its standards on televised violence. 1898 C. P. Stetson Women & Econ. i. 5 The economic status of the human female is relative to the *sex-relation. 1911 O. Schreiner Let. in First & Scott Olive Schreiner (1980) vii. 291 [She] thinks it's wrong for people, even if married, to have sex relations with each other except just when they want to make a child. 1949 M. Mead Male & Female i. 14 The infant..before he can toddle has absorbed a particular style of sex relations. 1980 First & Scott Olive Schreiner viii. 307 A cutting about sex relations between Indians and white women. 1898 C. P. Stetson Women & Econ. iv. 74 Let us bear in mind that all the tender ties of family are ties of blood, of *sex-relationship. 1963 A. Heron Towards Quaker View of Sex i. 8 There are certain historical characteristics of the Society of Friends that ought specially to lead to..understanding of the significance of the sex relationship. 1926 M. Leinster Dew on Leaf v. 29 He talked ..about health, climate, and *sex-repression. 1958 J. Cannan And be Villain i. 27 Richard used to treat me as a case of sex repression. 1916 Amer. Naturalist L. 388 In the generic crosses which give all, or nearly all, males at the beginning of the season and all, or nearly all, females in the autumn what is happening?—true *sex reversal? or is it selective fertilization, differential maturation or a selective elimination of ova in the ovary? 1926 J. S. Huxley Ess. Pop. Sci. iv. 53 Hens which had undergone sex-reversal to cocks. 1949 M. Mead Male & Female vi. 129 Peoples may provide sex-reversal rôles for both sexes. 1926 J. S. Huxley Ess. Pop. Sci. iv. 53 Similar results have now been obtained..by breeding from *sex-reversed moths. 1959 Sex-reversed [see feminization 2]. 1926 J. S. Huxley Ess. Pop. Sci. iv. 52 Some sexually abnormal human beings are the victims of this *sex-reversing power. 1927 W. B. Wolfe tr. Adler's Understanding Human Nature i. vii. 135 There are only two *sex rôles possible. One must orient oneself according to one of two models, either that of an ideal woman, or according to that of an ideal man. 1969 W. H. Sewell in E. F. Borgatta Social Psychol. 218/1 The sex-role concepts of children and..sex-role pressure in the socialization of the male child. **1977** *China Now* July/Aug. 3/3 The sex-roles are traditionally presented and the girl who helps Mummy to hang out the washing is rewarded. **1955** T. H. Pear *English Social Differences* 200 This class-segregated, *sex-segregated regime. **1970** *Guardian* 26 Nov. 4/2 '*Sex-shops'..are now established in many West German cities. **1974** K. Millett *Flying* (1975) III. 307 Sarah stops by and gives us an account of the new sex shop in Tottenham Court Road. **1981** *Observer* 4 Jan. 3/2 How do you designate a sex shop anyway? Does selling contraceptives make Boots a sex shop? **1959** P. Bull *I know Face* x. 187 A city almost entirely devoted to *sex-shows. **1922** Joyce *Ulysses* 535 The dark *sexsmelling theatre unbridles vice. **1961** *Giornale di Microbiologia* IX. 149 Two phages have been isolated which are *sex-specific on *E[scherichia] coli* K 12. **1976** P. Marks in Mitchell & Oakley *Rights & Wrongs of Women* v. 179 They may differ among themselves about how far vocations, and thus education, should be sex-specific. **1961** *Giornale di Microbiologia* IX. 147 The same strains used to test the '*sex-specificity of phages $\mu_2$ and $\phi_1$ were challenged with phages $T_1$,.., $T_7$. **1912** M. Hastings *New Sin* II. 57 *Sex-starvation, they call it. It's awful, but it can be done because it must be done. **1977** 'D. Rutherford' *Return Load* i. 12 He wondered whether sex starvation had..started to provoke hallucinations... He had seen..a gorgeous red-head. **1927** A. Huxley *Proper Studies* 292 St. Anthony and the unwashed, underfed, *sex-starved monks of the Thebaid. **1978** M. Birmingham *Sleep in Ditch* 164 Their first guess is that I'm a sex-starved grass-widow, glimpsing seducers behind every door. **1949** M. Mead *Male & Female* vi. 137 A *sex stereotype that decries the interests..of each sex is usually not completely without a basis. **1977** *N.Z. Herald* 8 Jan. 2-2/7 The society has new projects planned for its second decade, including a survey into *sex-stereotyping. **1936** *Sex-story [see *crime-story*]. **1979** *Guardian* 10 July 9/1 Dr. Martin Cole's Institute for Sex Education and Research..has been supplying *sex surrogate therapy for ten years. *a* **1911** D. G. Phillips *Susan Lenox* (1917) II. xx. 442 Men..might regard her as nothing but *sex symbol; she regarded herself as an intelligence. **1951** M. McLuhan *Mech. Bride* (1967) 94/2 The 'line' [of chorus girls] itself..is even more basic than the sex symbol of the flower. **1976** Botham & Donnelly *Valentino* i. 12 The olive skin of the man who would..become the world's first and most enduring sex symbol. **1931** G. T. Renier *English: Are they Human?* iv. 85 The wide-spread ignorance of the technique of love among average Englishmen..results from the taboo on direct *sex-talk. **1977** C. Fremlin *Spider-Orchid* xiii. 94 They have these sex talks..at school from the age of nine. **1978** J. Pudney *Thank Goodness for Cake* 80 At the football club sex talk proliferated, constantly spiced with dirty stories. **1976** *National Observer* (U.S.) 13 Mar. 6/3 American life-styles: a TV anchorman,..a rock star,..a groupie, a *sex therapist. **1977** DeLora & Warren *Understanding Sexual Interaction* iv. 90 Sex therapists, who direct their creative energy toward the specifically sexual difficulties of individuals or couples. **1961** R. A. & F. R. Harper in *Encycl. Sexual Behaviour* I. 348/2 Individuals and groups vary..in the quality and quantity of *sex therapy they need. **1970** Belliveau & Richter *Understanding Human Sexual Inadequacy* (1971) III. vii. 77 Success in sex therapy is dependent upon communication between the sex-partners. **1928** D. H. Lawrence *Lady Chatterley's Lover* i. 6 In the actual *sex-thrill within the body, the sisters nearly succumbed to the strange male power. **1642** H. More *Song of Soul* I. III. lxxi, Mad-making waters, *sex trans-forming springs. **1941** Miller & Dollard *Social Learning & Imitation* xii. 198 The punishments meted out to adults who actually exhibit such tendencies tend to maintain and strengthen the *sex-typed habits acquired. **1979** *Bull. Amer. Acad. Arts & Sci.* Feb. 31 The modal pattern for each sex is, nonetheless, conventionally sex-typed. **1941** Miller & Dollard *Social Learning & Imitation* xii. 198 By the time a child reaches his second year *sex-typing has already begun. **1976** *New Society* 4 Mar. 509/1 The 'blue/gun for a boy: pink/dolly for a girl', sex-typing syndrome. **1898** C. P. Stetson *Women & Econ.* x. 213 We confuse the natural result of marriage in children, common to all forms of *sex-union, with the family,—a purely social phenomenon. **1923** M. Stopes *Contraception* iii. 39 The type of woman who..has acquired the view that all sex union after the procreation of the desired number of children has been accomplished, is wrong. **1920** M. Sanger *Woman & New Race* ix. 111 This man is not concerned with his wife's *sex urge, save as it responds to his own at times of his choosing. **1966** D. Francis *Flying Finish* vi. 74 Bravery is built in... You can't stamp it out any more than the sex urge. **1912** L. Housman (*title*) *Sex-war and woman's suffrage. **1978** J. Irving *World according to Garp* xvii. 362 'Fucking *women*,' the cabby said. 'Fucking *men*,' said Garp, feeling..that he had done his duty to ensure that the sex war went on. **1911** 'I. Hay' *Safety Match* I. i. 4 The sides of the house are equally balanced both for purposes of companionship and in the event of *sex-warfare.

**sex** (sɛks), *v.* [f. sex *sb.*] **1.** *trans.* To determine the sex of, by anatomical examination; to label as male or female.

**1884** Gurney *Diurnal Birds Prey* 173 The specimen is not sexed, neither is the sex noted on the drawing. **1888** A. Newton in *Zoologist* Ser. III. XII. 101 The..barbarous phrase of 'collecting a specimen' and then of 'sexing' it.

**2.** *to sex up* (slang), to give a sexual flavour to, to increase the sexual content of.

Examples of the adj. or quasi-adj. *sexed-up* 'sexually aroused' are included here for convenience.

**1942** Berrey & Van den Bark *Amer. Thes. Slang* §361/5 *Make sexy, sex it up*, to introduce sex into, as a story. *Ibid.* §361/9 Passionate; amative; lustful..(*all*) *sexed up*. **1958** *Observer* 24 Aug. 5/7 The business of 'sexing up' the titles of foreign films is..a trick well known in both France and Britain. **1959** *Ibid.* 11 Oct. 21/4 Reads rather like an old-time boy's book sexed up and sadistified for the 1950s. **1969** J. Gardner *Compl. State of Death* vi. 97 What do you do when you get sexed up? Mortify the flesh? **1976** *Nature* 15 July 177/3 Erickson and Zenone tested the reaction of 35 males to two groups of females... The males..showed more aggression and less courtship towards the 'sexed up' females.

**3.** *intr.* To have sexual intercourse. *slang.*

**1966** 'G. Black' *You want to die, Johnny?* ix. 172 The surprising thing isn't the number of teenagers who sex and dope, but rather..that there are so many that don't. **1980** J. Barnett *Palmprint* i. 6 Maybe we sex together at yo' place.

**sex**, obs. form of six.

**sex-** (sɛks), repr. L. *sex* six in combination (as in *sexangulus* sexangular, *sexennis* sexennial), occurs in many mod. formations, chiefly scientific or technical. (In some of these sexi- is also used.)

**1.** Forming parasynthetic compounds, as ***sexannulate*** (= six-ringed), ***sexarticulate***, ***sexcuspidate***, ***sexlocular***, ***sexradiate***, ***sex-tubercular***, ***-tuberculate*** adjs. (see annulate, etc.); **sex'digital**, **-'digitate**, **-'digitated** (also **sedigital**, etc. after L.) *adjs.*, having six digits (fingers or toes); **sex'digitism**, the condition of having six digits; **sex'digitist**, one who has six digits; **sex'farious** *a. Bot.* [mod.L. *sexfarius*], see quot.; **'sexfid** *a.* [mod.L. *sexfidus*], divided into six segments; **sex'tactic** *a. Math.*, pertaining to or involving six coincident points of contact.

**1856** W. Clark *Van der Hoeven's Zool.* I. 317 *Loxocera*,..Abdomen elongate, *sexannulate. *Ibid.* 345 *Chironomus*,..Antennæ filiform,..in females *sexarticulate. **1899** *Proc. Zool. Soc.* 560 In the molars..the derivation from the *sexcuspidate type is equally recognizable. **1898** *Syd. Soc. Lex.*, *Sexdigital, having six digits. **1868** Darwin *Anim. & Pl.* II. xii. 13 The child of the fifth generation would have only 1-32nd part of the blood of his *sedigitated ancestor. **1775** Ash *Suppl.*, *Sexdigitism. **1825** A. Clarke *Bible Comm.* II. 2 Sam. xxi. 20 Maupertius..says, that he met with two families near Berlin, where sexdigitism was equally transmitted on both sides of father and mother. **1880** Proctor *Rough Ways* 211 In a branch of a well-known Scotch family sex-digitism—after continuing for three or four generations—has apparently disappeared. **1775** Ash *Suppl.*, *Sexdigitist. **1900** B. D. Jackson *Gloss. Bot. Terms*, *Sexfarious, presenting six rows, extending longitudinally round an axis. **1760** J. Lee *Introd. Bot.* I. xi. (1776) 26 In respect to its Segments..it [a calyx] is..*Sexfid, in six. **1785** Martyn *Rousseau's Bot.* xxiv. (1794) 341 The exterior calyx..in Alcea is sexfid. **1777** Robson *Brit. Flora* 34 *Sexlocular, divided into six cells, as in Asarum. **1853** Macdonald & Allan *Bot. Word-bk.* 29 *Sexlocular*, applied to a pericarpium which has six internal divisions or cells. **1874** J. E. Gray in *Ann. Nat. Hist.* Ser. IV. XIII. 288 Sponges with spicules of the *sexradiate type. **1859** Cayley *Math. Papers* (1890) IV. 228 The twenty-seven *sextactic points form nine groups of three each. **1893** *Ibid.* (1897) XIII. 387 Halphen assumes that $a^2d - 3\ abc + 2\ b^3$ is the sextactic reciprocant. **1890** *Nature* 20 Mar. 467/1 The addition of a postero-internal cusp in the bunodont series gives us the *sextubercular molar. **1899** *Proc. Zool. Soc.* 558 The unworn molars..are..*sextuberculate.

**b.** *Chem.* In the names of classes of compounds, denoting the presence of six atoms, molecules, or combining proportions of the substance indicated by the second part of the compound, as ***sexa'luminate***, ***sex'borate***, ***sex'decyl***. Also in other kinds of words: †**sex'basic** *a.*, having six combining proportions of the base; **sex'valent** *a.*, having an equivalence of six, combining with or replacing six hydrogen atoms.

**1836** T. Thomson *Min., Geol.*, etc. I. 219 The mineral might be considered as composed of 2 atoms sexaluminate of magnesia 1 atom tersilicate of magnesia. **1841** Brande *Chem.* (ed. 5) 839 A hydrated sexbasic nitrate of lead is formed. **1849** Watts tr. *Gmelin's Handbk. Chem.* III. 89 Sexborate of soda. **1868** *Fownes' Chem.* (ed. 10) 632 Sex-decyl, or Cetyl Alcohol,..also called Ethal, is obtained from spermaceti. **1872** Watts *Dict. Chem.* VI. 243 Sulphur, regarded as sexvalent, may take with it into combination the quinquivalent group. **1877** —— *Fownes' Chem.* I. 256 Sexvalent elements, or Hexads.

**2.** Combined with a numerical element: **sex'decimal**, **,sexduo'decimal**, **se'xoctonal** *adjs.* (see quots. 1816, 1822); **sex'decimo** = sextodecimo; **sexmille'narian** *a.*, holding the doctrine of the 'sexmillenary duration' of the world: **sexmi'llenary**, **-mi'llennial** *adjs.*, of 6000 years.

**1816** R. Jameson *Char. Min.* (ed. 2) 201 **Sex-decimal*, when the planes that belong to the prism..and those which belong to the two summits, are the one six, and the other ten in number, or *vice versa*. In the same manner, we say, *octo-decimal*, **sex-duodecimal* [etc.]. **1870** J. Power *Handy-bk.* 112 *Sex-decimo,—sixteenmo; contraction, 16mo, now called foolscap 8vo. **1851** A. P. Stanley in *Life & Lett.* (1893) I. 429 A conversation..going on between the Dean, Dr. Spry, and the *sexmillenarian C——. **1728** Earbery tr. *Burnet's St. Dead* II. 16 The Prophecy of the Jews..of the *Sex-millenary Duration thereof [*sc.* of the World]. **1684** T. Burnet *Th. Earth* II. 34 The prophecy..concerning the *sexmillennial duration of the world. **1822** P. Cleaveland *Min.* (ed. 2) I. 36 Quadridecimal, octodecimal,..octosexdecimal, *sexoctonal, &c. when..a prism or the middle part of a crystal, and the two summits have the number of faces, indicated by the several names respectively. Thus..plomb carbonaté (carbonate of lead) sexoctonal.

**sexa-**, irreg. for sex-, sexi-.

**1891** *Century Dict.*, *Sexadecimal*. **1905** Kamensky *Mendeléeff's Princ. Chem.* (ed. 3) I. 441 *note*, Sulphur is bivalent towards hydrogen, and sexavalent as regards oxygen.

**sexagecuple**, *a. rare.* [f. L. *sexāgintā* sixty, after *decuple*.] Proceeding by sixties.

**1728** Chambers *Cycl.* s.v. *Minute*, The Divisions of Degrees are Fractions, whose Denominators increase in a Sexagecuple Ratio.

**se'xagenal**, *a.* [f. L. *sexāgēnī* 60 each + -al[1].] = sexagenary *a.*

In recent Dicts.

**sexagenarian** (ˌsɛksədʒɪˈnɛərɪən), *a.* and *sb.* [f. L. *sexāgēnāri-us*: see sexagenary and -ian.]

**A.** *adj.* Of the age of sixty years. Also, characteristic of one sixty years old.

**1862** T. A. Trollope *Marietta* I. ii. 27 A sexagenarian sire. **1889** Gunter *That Frenchman* iii. 28 He gives a sexagenarian nudge to his companion.

**B.** *sb.* A person sixty years old.

**1738** Chambers *Cycl.* (ed. 2) s.v. *Sexagenary*, Some casuists dispense with sexagenarians for not fasting. **1826** Syd. Smith *Wks.* (1859) II. 88 The rouged cheek of the sexagenarian. **1870** Disraeli *Lothair* xxxv, Your enamoured sexagenarians.

Hence **,sexage'narianism**, the state of being sixty years old.

**1876** Hardy *Ethelberta* xlii, The sort of sexagenarianism beside which a young woman's happiness can sometimes contrive to keep itself alive in a quiet sleepy way.

**sexagenary** (sɛkˈsædʒɪnərɪ), *a.* and *sb.* [ad. L. *sexāgēnāri-us*, f. *sexāgēnī* sixty each, distributive of *sexāgintā* sixty.

In some dicts. of the 18th and 19th c. the word is accented '*sexagenary*, in some of the 18th *sexa'genary*.]

**A.** *adj.*

**1.** *Math.* Of or belonging to the number 60; composed of or proceeding by sixties; pertaining to a scale of numbers of which the modulus is 60.

***sexagenary arithmetic*** = sexagesimal *arithmetic*. ***sexagenary table***, a table of proportional parts which shows at sight the product or quotient of any two sexagenary numbers to be multiplied or divided.

**1594** Blundevil *Exerc.* I. (1597) 34 (*bis*), The Sexagenary progression is alwaies to be vsed, as well in Diuision as in Multiplycation. *Ibid.* 37 b, The description and vse of the Sexagenarie Table. **1669–70** Flamsteed in Rigaud *Corr. Sci. Men.* (1841) II. 93 In the study of..Mr. Halton I once saw one [*sc.* a mathematical canon] of Vlaccus to every ten sexagenary seconds. **1721** Bailey, Sexagenary Arithmetick. **1785** Hutton *Math. Tables* I Ptolemy, who used the sexagenary arithmetic for this division of chords and arcs, and for astronomical purposes. **1795** T. Maurice *Hindostan* (1820) I. I. viii. 274 The emperor Yu,..who flourished..about the middle of the third great sexagenary cycle. **1819** Jas. Wilson *Dict. Astrol.* 398 Leaving the left hand column for the seconds, but they may be made to answer to any sexagenary proportion.

**2.** = sexagenarian *a.*

**1638** Mayne *Lucian* (1664) 141 Though he was a Sexagenary Bridegroome. **1755** Chesterf. in *World* IV. 132 The sexagenary widow remembers that she was handsome, but forgets that it was thirty years ago. **1819** Byron *Wks.* (1846) 799/1 Having a sexagenary aunt of my own. **1821** *Blackw. Mag.* X. 88 Some will have this to be the due consequences of sexagenary decay. **1856** Mrs. Browning *Aur. Leigh* I. 1038, I count it strange..That nearly all young poets should write old, That Pope was sexagenary at sixteen.

**B.** *sb.*

†**1.** *Math.* and *Astr.* = sexagesimal B. *sb.*

**1668** Glanvill *Plus Ultra* 23 The Decimal Arithmetick, which avoids the tedious way of computing by Vulgar Fractions in..Sexagenaries in Astronomy. **1704** J. Harris *Lex. Techn.* I. s.v., Sexagesimal Fractions, or Sexagenaries, are such as have always 60 for their Denominator. **1728** Chambers *Cycl.*, *Sexagenary Tables*, are Tables of proportional Parts, shewing the Product of Two Sexagenaries, or Sexagena's that are to be multiplied; or the Quotient of Two, to be divided.

**2.** = sexagenarian *sb.* Now *rare* or *Obs.*

**1814** Scott *Wav.* xliii, The lad can sometimes be as dowff as a sexagenary like myself. **1841** Moore *Mem.* (1856) VII. 290, I..went down an English country dance of fifty couples on the stone floor, no trifling achievement for a sexagenary.

**'sexagene.** *Math.* Also in L. form. [ad. mod.L. *sexāgēna* fem. sing. f. L. pl. *sexāgēnī*, *-æ*, *-a*: see prec.] A quantity or number multiplied by sixty or a power of sixty; an arc of sixty degrees. ***first***, ***second***, etc. ***sexagene***: the first, second, etc. stage in ascending order of a sexagesimal scale of numeration or measurement.

**1570** Dee *Math. Pref.* *ij, The Astronomers, for spede..haue deuised a peculier maner of orderyng numbers, about theyr circular motions, by Sexagenes, and Sexagesmes. **1597** Blundevil *Exerc.* I. (ed. 2) 37 In those Tables are often vsed two kinds of denominations,..Sexagenæ and..Sexagesimæ,..the denomination Sexagenæ being set ouer any number doth signifie that the vnite of the Integrum is multiplyed by 60. But the denomination Sexagesimæ doth signifie that the vnite of the Integrum is diuided by 60. **1674** Jeake *Arith.* (1696) 233 Bring all the Circles and Signs, or Sexagenae thereof, into Degrees. **1694** tr. *Oughtred's Key Math.* 32, 53″·09′ 34°· *i.e.* 53 second Sexagenes; 9 first Sexagenes; and 34 Unites. **1709** Mandey *Syst. Math., Arith.* (1729) 77 Days also are accounted in Sexagenes, so that 60 Days make one Prime Sexagene: and sixty Prime Sexagenes, or 3600 Days makes one Second Sexagene, etc. **1728** [see sexagenary B].

**Sexagesima** (sɛksəˈdʒɛsɪmə). *Eccl.* Also 4 **sexagesime**, 5 **-ym(e**, **-in**, **sexagesme**, 7 **sexagesm.** [Eccl. L., fem. (sc. *diēs*) of L. *sexāgēsimus* sixtieth, f. *sexāgintā* sixty. For the etymological meaning see SEPTUAGESIMA.] In full *Sexagesima Sunday*: the second Sunday before Lent. (Also † *Sunday in S.*: cf. SEPTUAGESIMA 2.) Hence *Sexagesima week.*

*c* **1380** WYCLIF *Sel. Wks.* I. 102 Sexagesime Sonday Gospel. *c* **1400** *Table of Lessons*, etc. in *Wycl. Bible* IV. 685 The Sonday in Sexages. *c* **1450** *Godstow Reg.* 193 At the fest of Sexagesyme fyfty shillyngis. *c* **1450** *Mirk's Festial* 69 þys day ys called yn holy chirch Sonday in Sexagesin. **1483** CAXTON *Golden Leg.* (1892) I. 30 The sexagesme sygnefyeth the tyme of reuocacion. **1549** *Bk. Com. Prayer*, The Sunday called Sexagesima. **1658** in Morris *Troubles Cath. Foref.* (1872) I. vi. 314 Upon Sexagesima Sunday before Prime. **1710** WHEATLEY *Bk. Com. Prayer* v. §9 The Gospel for Sexagesima-Sunday..admonishes us to be careful in the performance of our duty. **1883** *Cath. Dict.* (1897) 559/2 To fast three days in Sexagesima and three in Quinquagesima week. **1886** E. MILLER *Text. Guide* 111 The Tuesday after Sexagesima.

**sexagesimal** (sɛksəˈdʒɛsɪməl), *a.* and *sb.* [ad. med.L. *sexāgēsimālis*, f. L. *sexāgēsimus* (see next).]

**A.** *adj.* Proceeding by sixties; *esp.* pertaining to, involving, or based upon division into sixty equal parts (as seconds and minutes).

*sexagesimal arithmetic*, a method of computation based on the number 60. *sexagesimal table* = SEXAGENARY *table*.

**1685** WALLIS *Alg.* vii. 20 Concerning this Process, by Sexagesimal Multiplication. *Ibid.*, The Sexagesimal Tables of Multiplication. *Ibid.* 21 The Arabs..have introduced..their Table of Sines.., expressed in like manner by Sexagesimal Parts. **1694** tr. *Oughtred's Key Math.* 29 If there be several Sexagesimal Species joined to Integers, suppose 127. 32′·00″·09‴·45⁗. **1728** CHAMBERS *Cycl.*, *Sexagesimal*, or *Sexagenary Arithmetic*, a Method of Computation, proceeding by Sixties. **1780** M. TAYLOR (*title*) A Sexagesimal Table, exhibiting, at sight, the result of any proportion, where the terms do not exceed sixty minutes. **1785** HUTTON *Math. Tables* 1 The sexagesimal division both of the radius and of the parts [of every circle]. **1826** *Encycl. Metrop.* (1845) I. 439/2 Stifelius ventured to simplify the sexagesimal notation. **1876** tr. *J. Verne's Adv. Engl. & Russ.* iv. 36 The length of the pendulum that beats the sexagesimal second. **1887** *Academy* 3 Sept. 144/2 The sexagesimal numeration which we employ for the division of the hour.

**b.** *sexagesimal fraction*: a fraction whose denominator is 60 or a power of 60.

**1685** WALLIS *Alg.* vii. 19 Writers of Astronomical or Sexagesimal Fractions. **1749** S. LOWE *Arithm.* 72 Thus it is ..that Sexagesimal fractions..are reduc'd to decimal. **1858** *Catal. MSS. Univ. Libr. Camb.* III. 61 A table of the square roots of numbers from 1 to 102, calculated to three places of sexagesimal fractions.

**B.** *sb. pl.* Sexagesimal fractions; also, the system of sexagesimal fractions.

**1685** WALLIS *Alg.* vii. 20 By this way of Multiplication and Division in Sexagesimals. **1694** tr. *Oughtred's Key Math.* 29 The Conversion of Sexagesimals into Decimals. **1706** W. JONES *Syn. Palmar. Matheseos* 93 By this Proposition, Fractions are reduced..into Decimals, Sexagessimals &c. **1794** CUNN *Doctr. Fractions* 62 Sexagesimals are such places of Figures below Unity, that decrease in a 60th rate. **1873** *Rep. Brit. Assoc.* I. 25 The table is prepared as if for three places of sexagesimals. **1907** *Athenæum* 9 Nov. 589/1 The Elamites appear also to have used a decimal system of notation instead of the Babylonian sexagesimals.

Hence **sexaˈgesimally** *adv.*, into sixtieths.

**1888** *Encycl. Brit.* XXIV. 489/1 The talent of the 80 grain system was sexagesimally divided. **1900** *N. & Q.* Ser. IX. V. 290/1 There is no utility, only needless complexity, in dividing 1° of arc sexagesimally.

† **sexaˈgesime**, *a.* and *sb. Obs. rare.* [As next.] Sixtieth (part).

**1632** W. FORSTER tr. *Oughtred's Circles of Proportion* 66 To reduce sexagesime parts into Decimals. Diuide the sexagesimes giuen by 60.

† **ˈsexagesm.** *Math. Obs.* [ad. mod.L. *sexāgēsima* (sc. *pars*), fem. of L. *sexāgēsimus*, ordinal of *sexāgintā* sixty.] A sexagesimal fraction. Also, the sixtieth part of a degree, a minute.

**1570** [see SEXAGENE]. **1635** GELLIBRAND *Variation Magn. Needle* 13 The differ. is 11⁰⁰⁰⁸ MZB..which converted into sexagesmes is 11 gr. 0 min., 0 Sec. [**1674** JEAKE *Arith.* (1696) 233 To turn *Sexagenae* into Integers, or Decimals into *Sexagesimae*, multiply continually by 6, every time removing the *Separatrix* one place.] **1685** WALLIS *Alg.* vii. 18 For ⅐, (because this cannot be exactly expressed in Sexagesms) they would put 8′. **1734** *Phil. Trans.* XXXVIII. 470 The Declination of all needles (especially if touched by different Magnets) is different a few Sexagesms.

**sexagon** (ˈsɛksəgən). [mod.L. *sexagōnum*, alteration of *hexagonum* HEXAGON by substitution of L. *sex* 'six' for the first syllable.] = HEXAGON.

**1616** RATHBORNE *Surveyor* IV. 114 To inscribe a Sexagon within a circle giuen. **1688** HOLME *Armoury* III. ix. 377/2 A Sexagone, Hexagone, or Exagon. **1873** 'OUIDA' *Pascarèl* III. vi, The white sexagons of the stars of Bethlehem grew amongst the grasses. **1908** *Daily Chron.* 19 Feb. 9/6 Show-case,..sexagon shape.

**sexagonal** (sɛkˈsægənəl), *a.* [f. mod.L. *sexagōn-us* (see prec.).] = HEXAGONAL.

**1750** tr. *Leonardus' Mirr. Stones* 76 The beryl has a clear sexagonal form [orig. L. *sexagonam formam*]. **1802–3** tr. *Pallas's Trav.* (1812) I. 409 Sepulchral buildings of a sexagonal, heptagonal, or octagonal form. **1882** *Harper's Mag.* July 192 *note*, A reticulated sexagonal pattern, which gives the surface the appearance of being honey-combed.

† **sexangle.** *Obs. rare.* [ad. L. *sexangulus*, f. *sex* six + *angulus* ANGLE *sb.*[2] Cf. SISEANGLE (1551).] A hexagon.

**1651** J. F[REAKE] *Agrippa's Occ. Philos.* II. xxiii. 253 Triangle, quadrangle, sexangle [orig. L. *hexagonum*], septangle, octangle, and the rest. **1788** T. TAYLOR *Proclus* I. Pref., As Barocius observes, why..should not πεντάγωνος and ἑξάγωνος be rendered quinquangle and sexangle. **1795** HUTTON *Math. Dict.*, *Sexangle*, in Geometry, a figure having 6 angles, and consequently 6 sides also.

So † **sexangled** *a. rare*⁻¹ [after late L. *sexangulātus*], = next.

**1509** HAWES *Past. Pleas.* III. iv, The fayre tower..Was all about sexangled. **1730** BAILEY (folio), *Sex-Angled* [with Geometricians] having six Angles, as in the Figure.

**sexangular** (sɛkˈsæŋgjʊlə(r)), *a.* [ad. late L. *sexangulār-is*, f. *sexangulus*: see SEXANGLE.] Having six angles; hexagonal.

**1608** TOPSELL *Serpents* 94 If you eye well their [*sc.* hornets'] nestes, you shall finde them all for the most part exactly sexangular or sixe cornered. **1637** WOTTON *Will* in Walton *Life* (1670) 71 Item, A piece of Christal Sexangular, (as they grow all). **1701** GREW *Cosm. Sacra* I. iii. §27. 15 The known Figure of Nitre, is a Sexangular Prisme. **1860** *Merc. Marine Mag.* VII. 25 The Beacon is sexangular. **1880** GÜNTHER *Fishes* 344 Teeth sexangular.

So † **seˈxangularly** *adv.*, in a sexangular form; † **seˈxangulary** *a.* = SEXANGULAR *a.*

**1658** R. WHITE tr. *Digby's Disc. Cure Wounds* (ed. 2) 72 Armoniac salt [doth form it self] in Hexagons of six points, as the snow doth, which is sexangulary. **1681** GREW *Musæum* I. iii. 35 Cancellated with little squares..on the top of the back, sexangularly. **1701** —— *Cosm. Sacra* I. iii. §21. 14 Diamonds are often sexangularly pointed.

**sexational** (sɛkˈseɪʃənəl), *a. slang* (orig. *U.S.*). Also **sexsational**. [Blend of SEX *sb.* and SENSATIONAL *a.*] Sexually sensational. So **seˈxationalism**.

**1927** *Time* 16 May 39 Newspaper sensationalism has developed into sex-ationalism. **1928** *Daily Express* 30 July 3/3 You send us films of sexational novels and pornographic plays, which our censors cut to pieces. **1937** *Time* 27 Dec. 30/2 Sexational, robustious Cinemactress Mae West appeared on a commercial broadcast for the first time in four years. **1957** R. HOGGART *Uses of Literacy* viii. 213 Their authors' favourite descriptive epithet for them is 'sexational'. **1968** *Punch* 29 May 789/3 These are the qualities that save the film from being what *Variety* often calls 'sexsational'. **1976** *West Lancs. Evening Gaz.* 8 Dec. 3/2 (Advt.), 1st Blackpool showing of the Sexsational *Highway through the Bedroom* (X).

**sexcapade** (ˈsɛkskəpeɪd). *colloq.* [Blend of SEX *sb.* and ESCAPADE.] A sexual escapade.

**1965** F. RAPHAEL *Darling* xxvii. 134 We are not complicating our holiday with disgusting sexcapades. **1976** *Honolulu Star-Bull.* 21 Dec. A-11/1 A generally less swinging group than the lone men off on sexcapades who helped give tourism a bad name.

**sexcentenary** (sɛksˈsɛntɪnərɪ, -sɛnˈtiːnərɪ), *a.* and *sb.* [In A. 1, f. L. *sexcentēnī*, distributive of *sexcentī* 600; in A. 2 and B, f. SEX- + CENTENARY.]

**A.** *adj.*

**1.** Pertaining to the number 600: see quot.

**1779** J. BERNOULLI (*title*) A Sexcentenary Table; exhibiting, at sight, The Result of any Proportion, Where the Terms do not exceed 600 Seconds or 10 Minutes. **1841** *Penny Cycl.* XXI. 320/1. **1888** *Encycl. Brit.* XXIII. 9/1.

**2.** Relating to a period of 600 years.

**1864** *Times* 15 June 11/3 The sexcentenary Festival of Merton College, Oxford.

**B.** *sb.* The six-hundredth anniversary (of an event).

**1885** *Encycl. Brit.* XVIII. 98/1 Worcester College..has recently celebrated the sexcentenary of its first building in 1283 as Gloucester Hall. **1909** *Q. Rev.* Jan. 158 The sexcentenary of the birth of Dante.

† **sexcuple**, *v. Obs. rare.* [irreg. f. L. *sex* six, after DECUPLE.] *trans.* To multiply by six.

**1674** JEAKE *Arith.* (1696) 200 The Square of 16, sexcupled and multiplyed by the square of 8, makes 98, 304.

**sexduction** (sɛksˈdʌkʃən). *Microbiology.* Also **sex-duction.** [Blend of SEX *sb.* and TRANSDUCTION.] The transfer of part of a bacterial genome from one bacterium to another by a sex factor.

**1960** [see F III. 1 l]. **1964** G. H. HAGGIS et al. *Introd. Molecular Biol.* x. 277 It is possible by exploiting a special phenomenon, known as sex-duction, to bring about a stable state of diploidy for a short length of the chromosome containing all the genes involved in the lactose system. **1974** *Molecular & Gen. Genetics* CXXX. 99 The number of sexductants in a λ-immune recipient is not significantly affected while sexduction into a non-immune recipient is increased by a factor 10–20.

**sexe**, obs. form of SIX.

**sexed** (sɛkst), *a.* [f. SEX *sb.* + -ED².]

**1.** As the second element of a parasynthetic compound: Pertaining to one or both of the sexes (specified by the prefixed word).

**1598, 1873** Double-sexed [see DOUBLE C. 1]. *a* **1616** BEAUM. & FL. *Four Plays in one* Wks. (1647) 27/2 Tie up my sight, let not soft nature so transformed be (and lose her gentler sex'd humanitie) to make me see my lord bleed. **1621** J. TAYLOR (Water P.) *Superbiæ Flagellum* C 6, Shamelesse double sex'd Hermophradites, Virago Roaring Girles. **1883** MEREDITH *Poems & Lyrics* 140 Alas, that I should have to say it! bad Is two-sexed upon earth.

**2.** Of an animal or plant: Having sex; not neuter or asexual.

**1891** *Century Dict.*

**3. a.** With prefixed adv.: having the sexual desires, emotions, or functions developed in a specified way.

**1898**, etc. [see OVER-SEXED *a.*]. **1921** *Outward Bound* Mar. 13/2 Had Elizabeth been as strongly sexed as she. **1949** M. MEAD *Male & Female* vi. 139 The tall, fiery, infinitely proud, specifically nervously sexed man and woman. **1974** M. TAYLOR tr. *Metz's Film Lang.* i. 9 Each one is disguised by a whole rigorously sexed body.

**b.** *sexed-up*: see SEX *v.* 2.

**4.** Of poultry: divided into the two sexes.

**1960** *Farmer & Stockbreeder* 1 Mar. 148/3 (Advt.), Day old sexed pullets. **1971** *Farmers Weekly* 19 Mar. 92/2 (Advt.), Sexed poults.

† **sexenary**, *a. Obs. rare.* [irreg. f. L. *sex* six, after SEPTENARY.] = SENARY *a.*

**1815** HUTTON *Math. Dict.*, *Sexenary* or *Sextuple Scale* of Notation. **1864** WEBSTER.

**sexeˈnnarian.** *rare*⁻¹. [f. L. *sexenn-is* (f. *sex* six + *annus* year) + -ARIAN.] A six-year-old child. So **seˈxennary** *a.*, sexennial; **seˈxennate** [after SEPTENNATE], a period of six years.

**1753** W. MAITLAND *Hist. Edin.* II. 223 A Sexenary [*sic, for* sexennary] Account of Burials in the City of Exeter. **1821** *Blackw. Mag.* X. 118 Scholars..mostly quinquennarians, or at most sexennarians. **1890** *Times* 7 Feb. 5/2 The Government contemplated the consolidation of the sexennary bonds. **1898** *Ibid.* 16 Dec. 5/1 A further increase in the navy beyond the limits of Admiral Tirpitz's sexennate.

**sexennial** (sɛkˈsɛnɪəl), *a.* [f. L. *sexennis* or *sexennium* (see prec.) + -AL¹.] Continuing for a period of six years; occurring every six years.

**1646** J. TEMPLE *Irish Reb.* 81 That as in England there past an Act for a Trienniall Parliament, there may passe in Ireland another for a Sexenniall Parliament. **1676** in *Fasti Aberd.* (1854) 347 The sexennial residence of the regents and masters of philosophie in the colledges. **1790** BURKE *Fr. Rev.* 300 Your new contrivance of sexennial elective judicatories. **1818** COLEBROOKE *Import Colonial Corn* 230 The recent sexennial period (1812–1817). **1890** *Daily News* 21 Feb. 4/6 The sexennial bonds will be consolidated in Perpetual Three per Cent. Rentes.

Hence **seˈxennially** *adv.* (1854 in Webster.)

**sexennium** (sɛkˈsɛnɪəm). [L.: see SEXENNARIAN.] A period of six years.

**1959** *Amer. Jrnl. Phys. Anthropol.* XVII. 132/1 Over the sexennium from age 5 years to age 11 years, some children augment their skeletal face depth more than twice as much as other children. **1970** D. M. WALKER *Princ. Scottish Private Law* I. li. 882 When the sexennium has run the constitution and resting—owing of the debt must be proved by the writ or oath of the debtor.

**sexern**, var. SIXERN.

**sexfoil** (ˈsɛksfɔɪl), *a.* and *sb.* [f. SEX-, after *trefoil*, *cinquefoil*.] **A.** *adj.* Having six foliations.

**1848** *Rickman's Styles Archit.* Introd. 26 A small sexfoil gable window. **1906** *Proc. Soc. Antiq.* 6 Dec. 261 The chalice is 5⅝ inches high, with a sexfoil foot. **1907** E. A. JONES *Ch. Plate I. Man* Introd. 16 The sexfoil depression is superseded..by a single circular depression.

**B.** *sb. Arch.* and *Her.* = SIXFOIL.

**1688** HOLME *Armoury* II. iv. 60 He beareth Argent, a Sexfoile, or a Sisefoile, Sable. **1828–40** BERRY *Encycl. Her.* I, *Sexfoil*, or *Sisefoil*, is a grass, or flower, with six leaves, formed like the cinquefoil which has five. **1851** PUGIN *Chancel Screens* 85 With images of angels in sexfoils.

**sexfoiled** (ˈsɛksfɔɪld), *a.* [f. prec.] = prec. A.

**1846** *Ecclesiologist* VI. 69 The clerestory is Middle-Pointed, of sexfoiled circles. **1851** TURNER *Dom. Archit.* II. iv. 167 The highest part of which [window] is sex-foiled.

**sexful** (ˈsɛksfʊl), *a. rare.* Also **sexfull.** [f. SEX *sb.* + -FUL.] Conveying sexual emotions; sexy.

**1898** G. MOORE *Evelyn Innes* xvii. 232 Soprano voices of a rarer and more radiant timbre than any woman's sexful voice. **1959** D. BARTON *Loving Cup* 144 A sexless voice..was singing a sexfull dance lyric.

**sexhindman.** *Hist.* [Altered form of OE. *siexhynde mon* (in Instituta Cnuti, *c*1110, *sexhende-*, *-hændeman*, also *sexhindus*) lit. six-hundred man.] A thane of the middle class, assessed at 600 shillings.

**1729** JACOB *Law-Dict.* s.v. *Hindeni*, The middle Class [were] valued at Six hundred Shillings, and called Sexhindmen.

**sexhood** (ˈsɛkshʊd). [f. SEX *sb.* + -HOOD.] The quality or condition of belonging to one or other sex; status with reference to sex.

**1866** J. B. ROSE *Ovid's Met.* 79 For seven long years to a changed sexhood bound. **1891** *Advance* (Chicago) 5 Mar., To lift women from mere sexhood up toward glorious womanhood.

*attrib.* **1869** BUSHNELL *Woman Suffrage* vii. 62 Their sexhood qualities of variation.

**sexi-**, occas. used as combining form of L. *sex* six: ˈ**sexifid** = *sexfid* (see SEX- 1). ˈ**sexiped(e** [L. *ped-*, *pēs* foot] = HEXAPOD. **sexiˈpolar** *a.*, having or involving six magnetic poles. **sexisyˈllabic** *a.*, of six syllables; so **sexi'syllable**. **sexitu'bercular**, **sexi'valent** *adjs.* = *sextubercular*, *sexvalent* (see SEX- 1, 1 b).

**1860** WORCESTER **Sexifid.* **1847** *Blackw. Mag.* LXI. 756 The delicate monsters, the savoury *sexipedes, with whom Typee and his comrades had to wage incessant war. **1889** MACCOLL *Mr. Stranger's Sealed Packet* v, All the creatures ..were quadrupeds; there were no quintipeds, sexipeds, or anything of that sort among them. **1854** EMERSON *Lett. & Soc. Aims* (1883) 35 The decasyllabic quatrain, or the octosyllabic with alternate *sexisyllabic, or other rhythms. **1855** OGILVIE Suppl., **Sexisyllable.* **1872** *Phil. Mag.* XLIII. 260 Carbon is quadrivalent; two carbon atoms may unite by mutually saturating 1, 2, or 3 pairs of affinities, thus giving rise to a radical $C^2$, which may be *sexi-, quadri-, or bivalent accordingly: thus, $C^2H^6$, $C^2H^4$, $C^2H^2$. **1874** J. P. COOKE *New Chem.* 244 The four sexivalent atoms of sulphur are the centres of subordinate groups connected with this nucleus.

**sexiferous** (sɛk'sɪfərəs), *a. Bot.* [f. L. *sex-us* SEX *sb.* + -FEROUS.] Bearing sexual organs.

**1819** LINDLEY tr. *Richard's Obs. Fruits & Seeds* 15 There is then no such thing as a naked seed..proceeding from an ovulum with a covering that is simple, and consequently immediately sexiferous.

**se'xillion.** [f. L. *sex* six, after *million, billion.*] = SEXTILLION.

**1850** in OGILVIE.

**'sexing,** *vbl. sb.* [f. SEX *v.* + -ING[1].]

**1.** Attribution of sex.

**1834** GEN. P. THOMPSON *Exerc.* III. 6 'That blind and unconscious matter cannot, by any of her combinations,' (Why *her*? This sexing is a stock receipt for mystification). **1970** *Nature* 11 July 190/1 None of these specimens was sufficiently mature to allow accurate sexing. **1973** *Ibid.* 14 Dec. 423/2 Final proof of an increase in frequency of Y sperm must await sexing of offspring conceived of spermatozoa exposed to the isolation process.

**2.** With *up*: see SEX *v.* 2.

**1954** KOESTLER *Invisible Writing* xxxi. 330 [Otto] thought that a little sexing-up of the war could do no harm.

†**sexious,** *a. nonce-wd.* [? for **sectious*, f. SECT *sb.* + -IOUS.] ? Sectarian.

**1592** MARLOWE *Massacre Paris* 857 (Brooke), To ouerthrow those sexious Puritans.

†**sexism**[1]. *Obs. rare*$^{-1}$. [ad. OF. *sixiesme* (mod. *sixième*) sixth.] = SIXIEME.

**1688** HOLME *Armoury* III. xvi. (Roxb.) 73/2 A Sexism, is a sequence of 6 cards.

**sexism**[2] ('sɛksɪz(ə)m). [f. SEX *sb.* + -ISM after RACISM.] The assumption that one sex is superior to the other and the resultant discrimination practised against members of the supposed inferior sex, esp. by men against women; also conformity with the traditional stereotyping of social roles on the basis of sex.

**1968** C. BIRD in *Vital Speeches* (U.S.) 15 Nov. 90 Sexism is judging people by their sex where sex doesn't matter. **1968** S. VANAUKEN *Freedom for Movement Girls—Now* 7 The parallels between *sexism* and *racism* are sharp and clear. Each embodies false assumption in a myth. **1971** *Guardian* 15 Jan. 11/4 The concept of a 'woman's page'..perpetuates sexism by stressing the 'special' domestic interests supposedly adhering to women. **1971** *Publishers' Weekly* 22 Mar. 14 The Women's National Book Association panel during NBA Week on 'sexism' in children's books. **1973** *Ms.* Nov. 39/2 An insidious form of sexism pervades most biographies of famous women, a tendency to treat women's work as peripheral to their lives. **1981** *Amer. Speech* LVI. 84 Although they recognize the inherent sexism of the generic masculine, the Fowlers see no real alternative.

**sexist** ('sɛksɪst), *sb.* and *a.* [f. SEX *sb.* + -IST after RACIST *sb.* and *a.*] **A.** *sb.* One who advocates, practises, or conforms to sexism. **B.** *adj.* Of, pertaining to, or characteristic of sexism or sexists.

**1965** P. M. LEET *Speech* 18 Nov. (mimeographed), When you argue..that since fewer women write good poetry this justifies their total exclusion, you are taking a position analogous to that of the racist—I might call you in this case a 'sexist'—who says that since so few Negroes have held positions of importance..their exclusion from history books is a matter of good judgment rather than discrimination. **1968** C. BIRD in *Vital Speeches* (U.S.) 15 Nov. 90 There is recognition abroad that we are in many ways a sexist country. *Ibid.*, Women are sexists as often as men. **1968** S. VANAUKEN *Freedom for Movement Girls—Now* 2 The sexist myth is the greatest and most pervasive myth the world has ever told itself. *Ibid.* 7 A *sexist* is one who proclaims or justifies or assumes the supremacy of one sex (guess which) over the other. **1971** *Publishers' Weekly* 22 Mar. 20/2 We live in a sexist society. By sexist we mean predetermining social roles on the basis of sex alone. **1976** *New Yorker* 5 Apr. 57/1 He was very stern and disagreeable and a gross sexist. **1977** MILLER & SWIFT *Words & Women* ix. 143 The language of American school books mirrors the sexist assumptions of society. **1978** J. IRVING *World according to Garp* xvi. 344 The sexist notion that women are..the acceptable prey of predatory males.

**sexit,** obs. Sc. form of SIXTH.

**sexless** ('sɛkslɪs), *a.* [f. SEX *sb.* + -LESS.] Without sex; lacking the characteristics of sex; asexual.

**1598** [see SIRELESS]. **1714** MANDEVILLE *Fab. Bees* (1733) II. 99, I perfectly lothe the sight of those sexless animals [*sc.* eunuchs.] **1853** KINGSLEY *Hypatia* II. ii. 40 Which..I must leave to be uttered only by the pure lips of sexless priests. **1865** LECKY *Ration.* I. 374 Sometimes the soul was pourtrayed as a sexless child, rising out of the mouth of a corpse. **1903** F. W. MAITLAND in *Camb. Mod. Hist.* II. xvi. 583 One reading of her character, and perhaps the best, makes her heartless and nearly sexless.

**b.** *Nat. Hist.* = NEUTER *a.* 4.

**1827** *Blackw. Mag.* XXII. 363 Like two sexless bees, from flower to flower, They wander'd unreproved. **1858** LEWES *Sea-Side Studies* 283 The insect which issues from the egg [of the aphis] is a wingless sexless insect. **1877** DARWIN *Forms of Fl.* Introd. 6 Between the sexless, female and hermaphrodite states of these latter flowers, the finest gradations may be traced.

Hence **'sexlessly** *adv.*, in a sexless manner; without reference to sex; **'sexlessness**, absence of sexual power or characteristics.

**1864** JAS. MANNING *Possessive Argument* 56 In Wicliff's translation, 'And Mary..turnid again to *his* own house' Luke i. 56, the masculine possessive pronoun appears to be applied sexlessly. **1873** PATER *Renaissance* viii. 194 Here, there is a moral sexlessness, a kind of impotence. **1891** ELIZ. R. PENNELL in *Mary Wollstonecraft's Rights Wom.* Pref. 23 The new sham sexlessness of emancipation. **1965** F. RAPHAEL *Darling* ix. 38 The West End was sexlessly bent on commerce. **1978** *Daily Tel.* 6 July 13/1 He is frequently bidden to the neat little house..where Leonora flirts with him, mothers him, indeed sexlessly gobbles him up.

**sex-limited** (stress variable), *a.* [f. SEX *sb.* + LIMITED *ppl. a.*] †**1.** = SEX-LINKED *a.* 1. *Obs.*

**1909** W. BATESON in A. C. Seward *Darwin & Mod. Science* v. 94 A study of the sex-limited descent of certain features in other animals. **1919** R. C. PUNNETT *Mendelism* (ed. 5) 95 Sex-limited inheritance..has been demonstrated in other birds besides poultry.

**2.** Of a genetic character or a phenotype: capable of occurring only in individuals of one sex. Of an individual: having such a character or phenotype.

[**1871** C. R. DARWIN *Descent of Man* viii. 282 (*heading*) Inheritance as limited by sex. *Ibid.* 285 If any variation appeared in a female pigeon, which was from the first sexually limited in its development to the females, it would be easy to make a breed with the females alone thus characterized. **1905** *Brit. Med. Jrnl.* 28 Oct. 1094/1 The abnormality, though affecting both boys and girls, is mainly limited to one sex in each family.] **1923** *Jrnl. Genetics* XIII. 215 As a contribution towards the adoption..of uniform terminology for the various modes of inheritance (at present, such terms as 'sex-limited' and 'sex-linked' are often used at random), I would point out that the denomination '*sex-linked*' (geschlechtsgebunden) ought to be applied only to conditions of inheritance explainable by the presence of the factor in question in those sex-chromosomes which are normally found in individuals of both sexes. *Ibid.* 216 The expression 'sex-limited inheritance' is not very judicious... 'Sex-limited manifestation' would be better. **1944** *Genetics* XXIX. 520 The mutant is strongly sex-limited in phenotypic expression. **1975** *Jrnl. Zool.* CLXXVII. 330 In butterflies, most sex-limited morphs are controlled by autosomal genes, their expression being dependent on the sex of the developing individual.

**3.** *transf.* Occurring only in one sex.

**1949** M. MEAD *Male & Female* xi. 237 To the phrasing of any piece of human behaviour, however sex-limited it may seem to be, both sexes contribute their imaginations.

Hence **sex-limi'tation**.

**1911** *Jrnl. Genetics* I. 189 The operation of the system of sex-limitation is similar in all these examples, the only difference being that in the one group the repulsion is from the factor *F*, in the other from the factor *M*. **1922** *Encycl. Brit.* XXXII. 419/2 (*heading*) Sex-limitation and sex-linkage. **1975** *Jrnl. Zool.* CLXXVII. 329 Polymorphism in butterflies is complicated by various factors, notably sexual dimorphism and sex-limitation.

**sex-linked** (stress variable), *a.* [f. as prec. + LINKED *ppl. a.*] **1.** Being or determined by a gene that is carried on a sex chromosome.

[**1905** *Brit. Med. Jrnl.* 28 Oct. 1095/1 Thus, in haemophilia, the abnormality is habitually linked with one sex.] **1912** *Jrnl. Exper. Zool.* XIII. 80 In the male-producing sperm, where no X is present, the sex-linked characters are always absent. **1923** [see SEX-LIMITED *a.* 2]. **1974** *Encycl. Brit. Micropædia* III. 23/2 Colour blindness, which affects about 20 times as many males as females, is a sex-linked recessive character.

**2.** Occurring only or characteristically in one sex.

**1932** AUDEN *Orators* II. 42 Self-regard, in origin a mere accident of overcrowding, like haemophilia is a sex-linked disease. **1956** H. W. PAPASHVILY *All Happy Endings* v. 75 In the writing of *Uncle Tom's Cabin*, Mrs. Stowe had exhibited many of those qualities considered by her contemporaries to be sex-linked to females—sympathy, tact, sensitivity, sensibility.

So **sex-linkage**, the state or condition of being sex-linked.

**1912** *Jrnl. Exper. Zool.* XII. 512 In this case it would seem that complete sex-linkage, such as that found..in barred fowls, would not occur at all. **1975** *Zool. Jrnl.* CLXXVII. 330 Such sex-linkage..may give rise to a situation where a morph is common in one sex, and very rare in the other.

**'sexly,** *a. arch. rare.* [f. SEX *sb.* + -LY[1].] Characteristic of one's sex.

**1601** Q. ELIZ. *Sp. to last Parlt.* 30 Nov. A 3 b, Should I ascribe any of these things vnto my selfe or my sexly weakenesse, I were not worthy to liue. *a* **1945** E. R. EDDISON *Mezentian Gate* (1958) xxxviii. 203 You [*sc.* a woman] are hampered by no sexly weakness: as fit as any man living to undertake it.

**sexology** (sɛk'sɒlədʒɪ). orig. *U.S.* [f. SEX *sb.* + -OLOGY.] The scientific study of sex and of the relations between the sexes.

**1902** W. H. WALLING (*title*) Sexology. **1912** *Amer. Jrnl. Urology* VIII. 441 The author believes that..there is practically no individual who can claim to have entirely avoided sexual activities of any kind, an opinion in which Lowenfeld, whose experience in sexology is so extensive, concurs. **1936** C. S. LEWIS *Allegory of Love* I. 13 The second factor is the medieval theory of marriage—what may be called, by a convenient modern barbarism, the 'sexology' of the medieval church. **1977** E. J. TRIMMER et al. *Visual Dict. Sex* (1978) i. 18 Reich is..in all the history of sexology, perhaps the most single-minded believer in the centrality of sex to human lives.

Hence **sexo'logical**, *a.*, of or pertaining to sexology; **se'xologist**, one who studies sexology.

**1914** *Amer. Jrnl. Clinical Med.* Aug. 687/1 There may be some homosexuals who are reconciled to or even proud of their abnormality, as some sexologists claim, but I must confess that I have not met such types. **1920** *Contemp. Rev.* July 93 A point of some sexological interest. **1949** KOESTLER *Insight & Outlook* xiv. 196 The distinction made by some sexologists between the detumescent and contractile components of the sexual drive. **1973** I. ROBINSON *Survival of English* v. 178 The only happy aspect of the sexological misapplication of the jargon of science is that the common language is strong enough to make it appear at times what it is, howlingly funny. **1980** *Times Lit. Suppl.* 28 Nov. 1355/1 The sexual inclinations of a sexologist presumably have to be investigated in some detail, even if the whole truth is not intrinsically interesting.

**sexophone** ('sɛksəfəʊn). *rare.* [Blend of SEX *sb.* + SAXOPHONE.] An imaginary musical instrument resembling a saxophone and producing sexual sensations. Also *attrib.* So **se'xophonist**.

**1932** A. HUXLEY *Brave New World* v. 88 The Sixteen Sexophonists were playing an old favourite. *Ibid.* 89 The sexophones wailed like melodious cats under the moon. **1945** V. NABOKOV *Real Life Sebastian Knight* xi. 93 Physical love is but another way of saying the same thing and not a special sexophone note, which once heard is echoed in every other region of the soul.

**sexpartite** (sɛk'spɑːtaɪt), *a.* [ad. mod.L. *sexpartīt-us*: see SEX- and PARTITE *a.*] Divided into or consisting of six parts.

**1760** J. LEE *Introd. Bot.* I. xiv. (1776) 39 In respect to their Number the Stigma may be Sexpartite, divided into six Parts. **1775** J. JENKINSON *Brit. Plants* 234 The cup is monophyllous, sex-partite, campanulated. **1830** WHEWELL *Archit. Notes* 25 A roof consisting of six cells, which may be called, therefore, sexpartite. **1849** FREEMAN *Archit.* 367 The vaulting is usually quadripartite, but sometimes sex-partite.

**sexpert** ('sɛkspɜːt). *slang* (orig. *U.S.*). [Blend of SEX *sb.* and EXPERT *sb.*] An expert on sexual matters.

**1924** [see DIM *a.* 4 b]. **1979** *Radio Times* 9–15 June 78/1 Every other interviewed sexpert seemed to come from California where..you can graduate in any old spurious subject.

**sexploitation** (sɛksplɔɪ'teɪʃən). [Blend of SEX *sb.* and EXPLOITATION.] The exploitation of sex, esp. in films. Also *attrib.*

**1942** in Berrey & Van den Bark *Amer. Thes. Slang* §361/1. **1948** G. V. DESANI *All about Mr. Hatterr* ii. 73 Damme, make the eternal triangle pay out a dividend! First that Portuguese feller victimised, then self! Damme, sexploitation! **1967** *Time* 17 Feb. 99 Jack Smith's four-year-old *Flaming Creatures*, an incredible tedious parody of a sexploitation picture, demonstrates how easy it is to fall asleep in the steamy midst of an hour-long transvestite orgy. **1977** E. J. TRIMMER et al. *Visual Dict. Sex* (1978) xxiv. 272 Sexploitation in advertisements seeks to tell the public that the problems of human sexuality are easily solved by the purchase of manufactured goods. **1981** *Times* 29 Jan. 4/4 It will become the 164th 'sexploitation' establishment in an area of less than one square mile.

So **sex'ploit** *v. trans.* to exploit sexually; **sex'ploitative** *a.*

**1970** M. PEI *Words in Sheep's Clothing* App. A 218 Lastly, there is the entrancing possibility of a vast extension of *sex*-portmanteau forms, for which a precedent already exists in 'sexploit' and 'sexploitation'. **1977** *Gay News* 24 Mar. 29/2 *Inserts* advertises itself as..simultaneously serious and sexploitative. **1977** M. SOKOLINSKY tr. *Merle's Virility Factor* ix. 180 That sociologist broad..she never stopped telling me: 'Bess, you've been sexploited by men.'

**sexsational,** var. SEXATIONAL *a.*

**sexst,** obs. 2nd sing. ind. pres. of SEE *v.*

**sex sum,** obs. form of SIXSOME.

**sext** (sɛkst). Also 5 **sexte, syxt.** [In sense 1, ad. L. *sexta* (sc. *hōra* hour), fem. of *sextus*, ordinal of *sex* SIX. In sense 2, ad. L. *sextus* (sc. *liber* book). In sense 3, ad. L. *sexta* (sc. *pars* part). Cf. F. *sexte*, G. *sexta, sexte.*]

**1.** *Eccl.* The third of the lesser canonical hours; so called because belonging orig. to the sixth hour of the day (midday). Also *pl.* (cf. NONES).

An early name was 'midday': see MIDDAY 1 b.

*c* **1425** *St. Eliz. of Spalbeck* in *Anglia* VIII. 118/7 Atte a dewe oure, and, as me meniþ, bytwix sexte & noon. **1446** LYDG. *Nightingale Poems* I. 342 Sygnyfinge all the tydes,.. Whech that haue be fro tierce vnto syxt. **1481** CAXTON *Reynard* v. (Arb.) 10, I will now go forth, for I haue yete to saye my sexte, none, and myn euensonge. **1526** *Pilgr. Perf.* (W. de W. 1531) 164 b, All the seruyce of god & houres canonicall.., matyns, pryme, tierce, sext, none, euensonge & complyn. **1753** CHALLONER *Cath. Chr. Instr.* 212 Terce, Sext, and None, begin with *Pater, Ave* &c. **1805** SOUTHEY *Ballads & Metr. T.* Poet. Wks. VI. 118 'Tis the hour of noon ..And the Sexts are begun. **1877** J. D. CHAMBERS *Div. Worship* 195 On Ash Wednesday, after Sext there might be a Sermon. **1898** Chr. Wordsw. *Med. Services* 28 On Sundays and semi-doubles at Lincoln Terce was followed by High Mass; and Sext and None then were sung after the Mass.

**2.** *Eccl.* The sixth book added to the Decretals by Pope Boniface VIII.

**1656** in Blount *Glossogr.* **1883** *Cath. Dict.* (1897) 115/1 Of these five collections—namely, the Decretals, the Sext, the Clementines, the Extravagants of John XXII., and the Extravagants Common—the 'Corpus Juris Ecclesiastici' is made up.

**3.** *Mus.* **a.** An interval of a sixth. **b.** An organ stop of two ranks of pipes having an interval of a sixth between them.

**1876** Stainer & Barrett *Dict. Mus. Terms, Sext*, the name of an organ stop of two ranks, having the interval of a sixth between them, namely, a twelfth and tierce.

**sext**, obs. form of sixth.

**sextain** (ˈsɛksteɪn). *rare.* Also 7 **sestain.** [? Alteration of obs. F. *sestine*, after *quatrain*, *sixain*.] = sestina.

**1639** Drumm. of Hawth. *Conv. w. B. Jonson* Wks. (1711) 226 Sextains, madrigals, and songs, echoes and equivoques. **1658** Phillips, *Sestain*, a stanza consisting of six verses. **1880** *Macm. Mag.* XLIII. 49/1 Dante..has paid him the practical compliment of imitating one of his favourite metres, viz. the sestina, or sextain.

**sextal** (ˈsɛkstəl), *a.* [f. L. *sext-us* sixth + -al.] Pertaining to a system of numerical notation with 6 as base.

**1943** *Trans. Philol. Soc. 1941* 10 A purely native six-system; that is what we have in Finno-Ugrian... The sextal system, though not common among the languages of the world, is quite well-attested. **1962** *Punch* 4 Apr. 554/3 Age-grouping would be standardised (on the sextal scale, of course). **1971** *Nature* 12 Mar. 133/3 Like the SI prefixes, it perpetuates the sextal (and ternary) system for counting indices, while the rest of our number system is decimal.

**sextan** (ˈsɛkstən), *a.* [ad. mod.L. *sextāna* (sc. *febris* fever), f. L. *sext-us* sixth: see -an.] Designating a fever of which the paroxysms recur every fifth (according to old reckoning, every sixth) day.

**1657** *Expert Physician* 123 The Quintan, Sextan, Septan, and Nonan Feavers. **1897** *Allbutt's Syst. Med.* II. 318 Further modifications have been recognised by nosologists as quintan, sextan, octan.

**sextant** (ˈsɛkstənt). Also formerly in Latin form 6–7 **sextans** (7 **-ance**?). [ad. L. *sextant-*, *sextans*, sixth part (of an as, acre, etc.), f. *sextus* sixth: see -ant.]

†**1.** The sixth part of the Roman as. *Obs.*

**1601** Holland *Pliny* xxxiii. x. II. 480 That purse.. wherein every man put his sextant, *i.* the sixt part of an As. **1656** Blount *Glossogr., Sextant*, a coin less then that called Quadrant, by the third part.

†**2.** The sixth part of a circle. *Obs.*

**1596** Blagrave *Uran. Astrolabe* H 2, The Sextans of a circle. **1609** —— *Dyalling* 141 Describe the Sextans, A.B.C. **1656** J. B. *Descr. Carpenters Rule*, etc. 137 The Dyal it self is in form of a Quadrant, Sextance, or Circle, according as you please. *Ibid.* 139. **1730** Bailey (folio), *Sextant*, with Mathematicians is the 6th Part of a Circle, or an Arch comprehending 60 Degrees.

**3.** An astronomical instrument resembling a quadrant, furnished with a graduated arc equal to a sixth part of a circle, used for measuring angular distances between objects, esp. for observing altitudes of celestial objects in ascertaining latitude at sea.

Tycho Brahe, *Astron. Instaur. Mech.* (1602) A 5, states that he gave the name *sextans* to this instrument.

**1628** Burton *Anat. Mel.* ii. ii. iv. (ed. 3) 264 To examine and calculate the motions of the Planets..by those curious helps of glasses, astrolabes, sextantes [**1632**, sextants], quadrants. **1726** Swift *Gulliver* iii. iii, Stored with great variety of sextants, quadrants, telescopes [etc.]. **1774** M. Mackenzie *Marit. Surv.* 32 Hold the Sextant vertically, and direct the Sight to some Object in the Horizon, or between you and the Sky, under the Sun. **1828** Moore *Pract. Navig.* 156 Hadley's Sextant is constructed on the same principles as the Quadrant; but..the Arch is extended to 120°..; it is also provided with some appendages not generally annexed to a Quadrant. **1860** Dickens *Lett.* (1880) II. 125 His sextant (which is about the size and shape of a cocked hat), on being applied to his eye, entirely concealed him. **1868** Lockyer *Elem. Astron.* §520 If we require to measure simply the angular distance of one celestial body from another, we employ a sextant.

**4.** *Bot.* Each of a group of six segment-cells; also *attrib.*

**1875** Bennett & Dyer tr. *Sach's Bot.* 122, 123 The section of the stem now appears as if composed of six cells or sextants, whose walls are placed nearly radially, forming a six-rayed star... Hence the walls..are called sextant-walls. .. The sextant-cells are still further broken up. **1884** Bower & Scott *De Bary's Phaner.* 19 Then follows in each of these the division into alternately dissimilar sextants.

**5.** *Astr.* The constellation *Sextans.*

**1795** Hutton *Math. Dict., Sextans*, the Sextant, in Astronomy, a new constellation, placed across the equator, but on the south side of the ecliptic. **1875** *Encycl. Brit.* II. 817/1 The constellations added by Hevelius are the following..:——..10. Sextans, The Sextant.

**sextantal** (sɛkˈstæntəl), *a.* [f. L. *sextans* (see prec.) + -al[1].] Pertaining to or based on the ancient Roman *sextans* (see prec. 1).

**1887** B. V. Head *Hist. Num.* 37 Bronze coins of the Roman sextantal and uncial systems.

†**sextantary**, *a. Obs.*$^{-0}$ [ad. L. *sextantāri-us*.] (See quot.)

**1656** Blount *Glossogr., Sextantary*, of or belonging to the measure, quantity or weight of Sextant.

**sextar** (ˈsɛkstɑː(r)). *rare.* [ad. L. *sextār-ius*: see next. Cf. sester.] = sextary.

**1559** Morwyng *Evonym.* Pref., Sieth ij sextars of the juice of Roses. **1601** Holland *Pliny* xiv. xiii. I. 418 Among donatives..certaine sextars or quarts of milke have been many times given. **1656** Dugdale *Warwicksh.* 340/1 In the time of the said King Edward [the Confessor] the Shirivalty of this County..answered lxv *li.* in money and xxxvi. Sextars of honey. **1707** Fleetwood *Chron. Prec.* 68 In 1125, a Sextar or Quarter of Wheat, at 01*l* 00*s* 00*d*. *Ibid.* 73 Sir H. Spelman says, that at Paris, a *Modius Vini* holds 36 *Sextarios*, and that a *Sextar* is 8 Pints. **1774** T. West *Antiq. Furness* ii. 33 [transl.], I also grant that they shall sell each sextar of ale dearer by one penny than is done at Appleby.

**sextary** (ˈsɛkstərɪ). Also in Latin form. [ad. L. *sextāri-us*, f. *sextus* sixth: see -ary. Cf. sester, septier.]

**1.** An ancient Roman liquid measure containing the sixth part of a congius. Also used loosely = sester 2, septier.

**1382** Wyclif *Lev.* xiv. 10 He shal take..bisides a sextarie of oyle. **1398** [see congius 1]. *a* **1483** *Liber Niger* in *Househ. Ord.* (1790) 24 One sextarie of wyne; viii gallons of ale. **1559** Morwyng *Evonym.* Pref., It consisteth of v sextaries of water, ii sextaries of hony. **1607** Topsell *Four-f. Beasts* 256 Let the fasting patient..take three sextaries Warme of that milke. **1633** N. Hunt *Handmaid Arith.* 387 The Spanish Sextarius. **1679** Blount *Anc. Tenures* 76 A Sextary of July-Flower Wine. **1737** Whiston *Josephus, Antiq.* viii. ii. §9 The bath is able to contain seventy-two sextaries. **1809** Bawdwen *Domesday Bk. York*, etc. 291 Value in King Edward's time forty shillings and two sextaries of honey. **1833** *Penny Cycl.* I. 472 The Attic amphora contained.. seventy-two sextaries, equal to about two gallons, five pints and a half of English wine-measure.

**2.** A dry measure containing the sixteenth part of a modius. (Cf. sester 3.)

**1382** Wyclif *Exod.* xxix. 40 The fourthe part of hyn, that is a sextarye, that is a mesure of two pownd. **1398** Trevisa *Barth. De P.R.* xix. cxxviii. (1495) 932 Sextarius is the mesure of two pounde..and is Cenix in grewe. **1646** Sir T. Browne *Pseud. Ep.* vii. xviii. 380 If every man of the Army had had a chenix of Corne a day, that is a sextary and halfe, or about two pints and a quarter. **1674** Jeake *Arith.* (1696) 89 Whether by confounding the Attick and Roman Sextaries..I know not. **1707** [see sester 3]. **1737** Whiston *Josephus, Antiq.* ix. iv. §4 The Hebrews bought a sextary of dove's dung, instead of salt. **1837** Wheelwright tr. *Aristoph. Clouds* ii. i, I ask..what thou thinkest the most perfect measure, The trimeter or the tetrameter? *Str.* I think that nought beats the half sextary.

†**3.** Any of the six divisions of the city of Venice.

**1617** Moryson *Itin.* i. 78 The City [of Venice]..is of old divided into six sextaries, or six parts vulgarly *sestieri*. **1651** Howell *Venice* 13 Six Councellors, whose peculiar priviledg is to be chosen out of the six Precincts or Sextaries of the Citty.

**sexte, sexten**, obs. forms of sixth, sixteen.

**sextend**, obs. Sc. form of sixteenth.

**sextene** (sɛkˈstiːn). *Chem.* [f. L. *sext-us* sixth + -ene.] = hexene.

**1873** Watts *Fownes' Chem.* (ed. 11) 554.

**sextene**, obs. form of sixteen.

**sextennial** (sɛkˈstɛnɪəl), *a. rare*$^{-1}$. [irreg. f. L. *sext-us* sixth, after *sexennial*.] = sexennial.

**1814** J. Adams *Lett. J. Taylor* x. Wks. 1851 VI. 468 The legislatures of the several states are balanced against the senate by sextennial elections.

†**sextern**[1]. *Sc. Obs.* Variant of sestern.

**1425** *Sc. Acts Jas. I* (1814) II. 12/1 The ald boll first maid be king Dauid contenit a sexterne [orig. *sextarium*] þe sexterne contenit xij galonnis. **14..** *Assize of Measures* in *Sc. Acts* (1844) I. 310 Item þe boll sall contene a sexterne viz. xij gallonis of aile.

**sextern**[2] (ˈsɛkstɜːn). [ad. med.L. *sexternum*, *-us*, f. L. *sex* six, after *quaternum*, *-us* (see quire *sb.*[1]), variants of *quaternio*, quaternion.] A quire consisting of six sheets.

**1885** E. Maunde Thompson in *Encycl. Brit.* XVIII. 144 Sexterns, or quires of six sheets (twelve leaves).

**sexters**, rare obs. pl. of sesterce.

**1541** Paynell tr. *Felicius' Conspir. Catiline* xiv. 20 b, Who so euer wolde detect the conspiracie,..shoulde haue his freedome, and an hundred sexters.

**sextes**, obs. pl. form of sect *sb.*[1]

**sextet** (sɛksˈtɛt). Also **-ett.** [Alteration of sestet after L. *sex* six. (In sense 1, a. G. *sextett*.)]

**1.** = sestet 1.

**1841** tr. *Schindler's Beethoven* II. 380 Sextett in E flat, for two Violins, Alto, two Horns, and Violoncello. **1880** *Academy* 28 Feb. 168/1 A sextett in A major, op. 48, for two violins, two violas, and two violoncellos, by Anton Dvorák.

**2.** A stanza of six lines.

*a* **1850** Rossetti *Dante & Circle* i. (1874) 36 Two sextetts followed by two quattrains. **1877** Dowden *Shaks. Primer* vi. 86 Paris scatters his blossoms with one of those graceful love-speeches in the form of a rhymed sextet.

**3.** A group or set of six persons or things.

**1873** W. Boyd (*title*) Sextet of Morse Alphabets. **1896** (*title*) A Sextet of Singers, or Songs of Six.

**4.** 'A bicycle for six riders' (*Cent. Dict.* Suppl. 1909). Cf. sextuplet.

**sextetto.** Alteration of sestetto: cf. prec.

**1876** Stainer & Barrett *Dict. Mus. Terms.*

†**sexti-**, occas. combining form of L. *sextus* sixth, used in the sense of 'six': **sextipartite** *a.*, drawn up in six copies; **sextipartition**, division by six; **sexti'section**, division into six parts. *Obs.*

*a* **1548** Hall *Chron., Hen. IV*, 12 The sedicious congregacion..made an indenture sextipartite..in the whiche eche bounde him selfe to other..for the destruccion of Kynge Henry. **1674** Jeake *Arith.* (1696) 34 Sextipartition, or to divide by 6. **1697** G. K. *Discov. Geom. Problems* 9, I shall begin with the Sextisection, and then proceed to the Quinquisection.

**sextic** (ˈsɛkstɪk), *a.* and *sb. Math.* [f. L. *sext-us* sixth + -ic.] **A.** *adj.* Of the sixth degree or order.

**1853** [see quintic *a.*]. **1867** Cayley *Math. Papers* (1893) VI. 249 The discriminant of this sextic function contains the factor *c*. **1872** —— in *Proc. Lond. Math. Soc.* IV. 105 On the Mechanical Description of Certain Sextic Curves.

**B.** *sb.* A quantic, or equation, of the sixth degree; a curve of the sixth order.

**1872** Cayley in *Proc. Lond. Math. Soc.* IV. 110 The curve is consequently a unicursal sextic, or sextic with 10 dps. **1885** J. Hammond in *Amer. Jrnl. Math.* VII. 327 On the Syzygies of the Binary Sextic and their Relations.

**sextiene**, obs. form of sixteen.

†**sextier**, variant of sester.

*c* **1483** Caxton *Dialogues* 7/19 *Cannes dun sestier* Cannes of a sextier. *Ibid.* 21/8 By quarters or by sextiers, By poundes or by half poundes.

**sextile** (ˈsɛkstaɪl, -ɪl), *a.* and *sb.* Also 7 **-il**(l. [ad. L. *sextīlis* (in class. L. only with *mēnsis* or ellipt., as the earlier name of August), f. *sextus* sixth: see -ile.] **A.** *adj.*

**1.** Astrol. ***sextile aspect***, the aspect of two heavenly bodies which are 60° or one sixth part of the zodiac distant from each other.

**1557** H. Baker *Rules Use Almanacs* B vij b, ✱ Signifieth sextile aspecte: whiche is caused, by the distaunce of two sygnes betwene two planettes. **1614** Chapman *Androm. Lib.* C 4 b, Venus in aspect Sextile or Trine. **1638** Wilkins *New World* v. (1707) 40 When she [the Moon] is about a Sextile Aspect distant from the Sun. **1715** tr. *Gregory's Astron.* (1726) I. 204 If a Sixth Part of the Zodiac lies between them, they are said to have a Sextile Aspect. **1815** Scott *Guy M.* iii, Signs and planets, in aspects sextile, quartile, trine, conjoined or opposite. **1856** [see quartile *a.*].

†**2.** (See quot.) *Obs. rare*$^{-0}$.

**1656** Blount *Glossogr., Sextile* or Sextilian moneth,..the month of August.

**B.** *sb.*

**1.** *Astrol.* A sextile aspect. Phr. *in* (*a*) *sextile.*

**1592** *Greene's Vision* Wks. (Grosart) XII. 278 Canst thou ..tell the course of the Starres, setting downe their aspects, oppositiues, times, and sextiles? *c* **1610** Sir C. Heydon *Astrol. Disc.* (1650) 74 Six Sextiles equal to six aequilater Triangles, fill the whole space about a point, which is equal to four right Angles. *a* **1625** Fletcher *Bloody Brother* iv. ii, Mars being Lord of the Geniture in Capricorne, Is..now a Sextile here, With Venus Lady of the Horoscope. **1638** Wilkins *New World* i. (1684) 114 If you behold the Moon ..when she is in a Sextile with the Sun. **1667** Milton *P.L.* x. 659 Thir planetarie motions and aspects In Sextile, Square, and Trine, and Opposite. **1837** Whewell *Hist. Induct. Sci.* (1857) I. 176 By observation of the moon, when she was nearly in trine and in sextile with the sun. **1880** Shorthouse *J. Inglesant* xvi, Venus also casting a sextile to the cusp of the ascendant.

**2.** A sixth form boy at Eton.

**1825** C. M. Westmacott *Eng. Spy* (1907) I. 33 He is our captain, a Sextile, a Roue. **1838** W. Cory *Lett. & Jrnls.* (1897) 3 Westmacott, Bullock, and Tarver, all sextiles.

†**sex'tilian**, *a. Obs. rare*$^{-0}$. [f. L. *sextīlis* sextile: see -ian.] (See quot.)

**1623** Cockeram i, *Sextilian moneth*, the moneth of August. **1656** [see sextile 2].

**sextillion** (sɛksˈtɪljən). *Arith.* [ad. F. *sextillion*, f. L. *sex* six, after *septillion*, *octillion*.] The sixth power of a million, denoted by 1 followed by 36 cyphers. In American (following the later Fr.) use, the seventh power of a thousand, denoted by 1 followed by 21 cyphers. Hence **sex'tillionth** *a.* and *sb.* (in recent Dicts.).

**1690** Locke *Hum. Und.* ii. xvi. §6 Sextilions. **1730** Malcolm *New Syst. Arith.* 8 Quintillions, (or a Million of Quadrillions;) Sextillions, (or a Million of Quintillions). **1861** T. L. Peacock *Gryll G.* xxi, He..adorned the surface of the ice with successions of 898, till they amounted to as many sextillions, with their homogeneous sequences. **1870** Phipson *Guillemin's Sun* 39 This sum of work is represented by 510 sextillions of kilogrammetres. **1881** Walt Whitman *Leaves of Grass, Song of Myself* xxxi, I believe..a mouse is miracle enough to stagger sextillions of infidels.

**sextine** ('sɛkstiːn). [ad. F. *sextine*, ad. Pg. *sextina* = It. SESTINA.] = SESTINE.

**1598** YONG *Diana* 31 After she had plaied a while on it, she began to sing this Sextine following. **1884** R. F. BURTON *(title)* Camoens. The Lyricks. Part I. (Sonnets, Canzons, Odes, and Sextines) Englished by Richard F. Burton.

*attrib.* **1823** ROSCOE tr. *Sismondi's Lit. Eur.* IV. 438 Camoens also wrote some sextine pieces [orig. F. *sextines*].

**sextine**, obs. form of SIXTEEN (*a.* 3).

**1599** NASHE *Lenten Stuffe* 7 This sextine centurie.

**sextin'variant.** *Math.* [f. L. *sext-us* sixth + INVARIANT.] An invariant of the sixth degree.

**1878** SYLVESTER in *Amer. Jrnl. Math.* I. 112 On the principal forms of the general sextinvariant to a quartic and quartinvariant to a sextic.

†**'sextiply**, *v.* *Obs. rare.* [ad. med.L. *sextiplicāre*, inferior form of *sextuplicāre* SEXTUPLY *v.*] *trans.* To multiply by six.

**1602** J. DAVIES (of Heref.) *Microcosmos* 86 So, some Affections our soules browes vnbend, And other some doe sextiply each dent. **1602** —— *Mirum in Modum* xv. Wks. (Grosart) I. 6/2 And thus executes Their pow'res as one, though sextiplied in sutes.

**sexto** ('sɛkstəʊ). [a. L. *sextō*, ablative case of *sextus* sixth: cf. QUARTO, etc.] The designation of the size of a book, or of the page of a book, in which each leaf is one-sixth of a sheet.

**1847** DE MORGAN *Arithm. Bks.* Introd. 11 When he folds a sheet of paper into six leaves, making what ought to be a sexto book, he calls it a duodecimo printed in half sheets.

**sexto-decimo** (ˌsɛkstəʊ'dɛsɪməʊ). = DECIMO-SEXTO, q.v. (Cf. SIXTEENMO.)

[**1626** S. WARD *Let.* in R. Parr *Life of Usher* (1686) 344 A Book of large 16°.] **1688** HOLME *Armoury* III. xv. (Roxb.) 23/1 A sextodecimo booke, is of 16 leaues in a sheete. **1819** DIBDIN *Typogr. Antiq.* IV. 282 Justification of Man, &c. 1548. Sextodecimo.

**sextole** ('sɛkstəʊl). *Mus.* Also (Dicts.) sestole. [a. G. *sextole*, arbitrarily f. L. *sext-us* sixth: cf. QUINTOLE.] A group of six notes to be played in the time of four. So **'sextolet**.

**1854** J. SCHUBERTH *Mus. Hand-bk.* (ed. 4) 233 *Sextole*, a group of 6 notes, having the value of 4 equal notes. **1876** STAINER & BARRETT *Dict. Mus. Terms*, *Sextolet*, or *Sextuplet*. **1883** *Grove's Dict. Mus.* III. 478/1 Sextolet.

**sexton** ('sɛkstən). Forms: α. 4-5 segerstone, 4-6 -ane, 6 -en, (sequestern, segerson), 6-7 segerston, 7 seggerston; 6 sagar-, sacarston, 6-7 sagerston. β. 5 secristeyn, -ane, -oun, sekyrsteyn, 6 secri-, secra-, secrestan. γ. 4 sekesteyn, 4-6 sexteyn(e, -eine, (4 -eyene, -ein, 5 -een, cexteyne, 6 cyxten, seixten), 5-6 sextayn(e, -ene, 5-7 sexten, (5 sex(e)sten, 6 sextine, 7 -aine, -an, -in, sixeteene), 6- sexton; 6 saxten, 7 saxton. [a. AF. *segerstaine*, = OF. *segrestein*, *secrestein*, *-in*, etc. (whence med.L. *segrestanus*), semi-popular ad. med.L. *sacristānus* SACRISTAN (of which this word is a doublet). The trisyllabic (α and β) forms are almost entirely confined to northern texts; cf. the early quots. s.v. SACRISTAN.]

**1.** A church officer having the care of the fabric of a church and its contents, and the duties of ringing the bells and digging graves.

In early use often = the sacristan in a religious house, cathedral, etc., having charge of the vestments, sacred vessels, relics, and the like. In popular use from the 16th c. usually = bell-ringer and grave-digger.

α. [**1330** *Rolls of Parlt.* II. 47/2 Benefices appurtenantz al Segerstaine d'Everwik.] **1391** *Mem. Ripon* (Surtees) III. 110 In salario Johannis Segerstane mundantis ecclesiam in le flore ejusdem, item parietes et fenestras vitreas ejusdem. **1537** *Whalley Abbey Inv.* (P.R.O.), The sequestern that had the keping of al the seid copes. **1546** *Yorksh. Chantry Surv.* (Surtees) II. 353 Yerlie to the segezstane [*read* seger-] and belman, iiij^s. vj^d. *Ibid.* 530 In the saide collegiate churche bee..fower segersons. **1637** *Churchw. Acc. Pittington*, etc. (Surtees) 100 For the seggerston, 3s.

**1575-6** *Durham Depos.* (Surtees) 280 Being..sagarston of the same church 20 yeres togither. **1597** *Churchw. Acc. Pittington*, etc. (Surtees) 127 Item the sacarston for his fourth quarter's wages, xij d. **1687** *Ibid.* 255 That John Riddam shall make and assist the sagerston to make graves.

β. **14..** *Nom.* in Wr.-Wülcker 680/36 *Hic sacrista*, a secristoun. **1463** *Bury Wills* (Camden) 26 To the Secristeyn and to the Priour of Dusgylde. **1483** *Cath. Angl.* 327/2 A Secristane; vbi Sacristane. **1513** BRADSHAW *St. Werburge* II. 1588 Werburge appered to the secristan alone. **1537** *Aberdeen Reg.* (1844) I. 151 Quhen thai ar warnit be the secrestanis seruand, or him self. *Ibid.*, Gyf the secrastan preevis nocht his warning.

γ. **1303** R. BRUNNE *Handl. Synne* 11093 A nyȝt, whan þe sekesteyn yn bede was leyd, Hym þoȝt [etc.]. **13..** *St. Alexius* (Cott. MS.) 192 That Images spake, þat was so bryght, to the sexteyene vppon a nyght. *c* **1386** CHAUCER *Monk's Prol.* 48 Thou art som Officer Som worthy sexteyn or som Celerer. *c* **1440** *Promp. Parv.* 67/2 Cexteyne (*edd.* **1508, 1516** cyxten), *sacrista.* **1463** *Bury Wills* (Camden) 17 Y^e Sexteyn of y^e chirche to haue..xij d. for his rynggyng and his mete. **1498** in *Somerset Med. Wills* (1901) 363 The said cruetts and paxebrede to be in the kepyng of the Sexten of the said priorie. *a* **1539** in *Archæologia* XLVII. 56 That the president of your religion or sextene kepe them [*sc.* church keys]. **1581** PETTIE tr. *Guazzo's Civ. Conv.* III. (1586) 168 b, As a sextine said, a man cannot carie the crosse, and ring the bells altogether. **1596** NASHE *Saffron Walden* O, [The] continuall crashing of sextens spades against dead mens bones. **1602** SHAKS. *Ham.* v. i. 177, I haue bin sixeteene heere, man and Boy thirty yeares. **1624** BEDELL *Lett.* xi. 140 As if all that are made Priests among you were Psalmists, Sextens, Readers, Exorcists, Torch-bearers, Subdeacons, and Deacons before. **1638** in Legg *Clerk's Bk.* (1903) 99 Whether your Parish Clark or Sexton hath had due regard to the Ornaments of your Church. **1708** J. CHAMBERLAYNE *St. Gt. Brit.* I. II. vii. (1755) 71 Where the Office of the Clerk and Sexton are distinct, the Minister chooses the former, the people the latter. **1766** BLACKSTONE *Comm.* I. 395 Parish clerks and sextons are also regarded by the common law, as persons who have freeholds in their offices. **1826** HOOD *Faithless Sally Brown* 67 They went and told the sexton, and The sexton toll'd the bell. **1866** GEO. ELIOT *F. Holt* I. i. 18 The sexton waited in the belfry ready to set the one bell in joyful agitation just at the right moment.

**1593** in Legg *Clerk's Bk.* (1903) 81 And also that the same Saxten shall..rynge the fowerthe Bell for a daye Bell. **1696** *Churchw. Acc. Pittington*, etc. (Surtees) 260 If the said saxton be negligent therein, he shal hereby incurr the forfeiture of his place.

†**b.** Applied to the pope's sacristan. *Obs.*

**1667** P. A. *Acc. Pope Alex. VII*, etc. 25 The Sandals were taken up by the hand of the Lord Sexton. **1728** CHAMBERS *Cycl.* s.v., The Office of Sexton of the Pope's Chapel is particularly affixed to the Order of the Hermits of Saint Augustin: He is generally a Bishop... He takes the Title of Prefect of the Pope's Sacristy.

†**c.** *transf.* Applied to custodians of heathen temples, etc.; a keeper, warden. *Obs.*

**1582** STANYHURST *Æneis* IV. 78 Seixten of Hesperides Sinagog. **1603** FLORIO *Montaigne* II. xii. (1632) 298 Varro..writeth, that Hercules his Sextaine [etc.]. **1606** HOLLAND *Sueton.* 39 The warden and Sextaine of that ground or soyle, which Augustus of happy memory touched first.

**d.** *fig.*

**1502** ARNOLDE *Chron.* 61/1 O tho most noble bishop..thou art y^e clere lyght of thy feyth & y^e sexten of y^e crysten relygion. **1595** SHAKS. *John* III. i. 324 Old Time the clocke setter, y^t bald sexton Time. **1603** HOLLAND *Plutarch's Mor.* 1150 A Sextaine [*orig.* μυσταγωγός], who leadeth by the hand those that are professed in some religion, shewing unto them all the holy reliques and sacred ceremonies. **1867** BAKER *Nile Trib.* i. (1872) 7 The usual sextons were the crows.

**2.** = SEXTONESS, SACRISTAN 2.

*c* **1400** *Rule St. Benet* (Verse) 1472 The Priores, & oþer nane, Aw for to ches a segerstane To ring þe bels in right aray. *c* **1440** *Jacob's Well* 271 A nunne þat hyȝte Beatrix, sexteyn of here hows. *c* **1450** in Aungier *Syon* (1840) 284 Sche that is sexteyne moste ordeyn that the awter in the sustres quyer be honestly arayed. *c* **1475** *Pict. Voc.* in Wr.-Wülcker 780/16 *Hic et hec secrista*, a sekyrsteyn.

**3.** A sexton beetle.

**1885** *Riverside Nat. Hist.* (1888) II. 385 *Necrophorus*... These beetles are often called sextons or grave-diggers.

**4.** *attrib.* and *Comb.*: **sexton beetle**, a beetle of the genus *Necrophorus*; a burying beetle.

**1839** G. DARLEY *Nepenthe* II. 31 Floods of dust..Heaped o'er thee by the sexton winds! **1840** *Cuvier's Anim. Kingd.* 516 *Necrophorus*, Fabr... The instinctive habits which these insects possess of burying small quadrupeds, has caused them to be named Sexton, or Burying Beetles. **1854** A. ADAMS, etc. *Man. Nat. Hist.* 195 Sexton-Beetles (Blapsidæ). **1891** MEREDITH *One of Our Conq.* xli, That worm-like thread of voice [of a dying woman] came up to him still from sexton-depths.

**sextoncy** ('sɛkstənsɪ). *nonce-wd.* [f. SEXTON + -CY.] Sextonship.

**1831** CARLYLE *Misc.* (1857) II. 288 While Eulenspiegel held this Sextoncy.

**sextoness** ('sɛkstənɪs). Also 5 **sexteynes, sextenesse.** [f. SEXTON + -ESS.] A female sexton (or sacristan).

*c* **1420** *Chron. Vilod.* 2843 Þe sexstenes rong þe belles þo alle abouȝte. *c* **1450** in Aungier *Syon* (1840) 306 The sexteynes schal ordeyne be fore the profession the bere with fayre newe erthe,..and thys bere sche schal sette forthe at the dore. *c* **1450** CAPGRAVE *Life St. Gilbert* xl. 121 Þe nunne, þe sextenesse, rang to mateyns. **1826** MISS MITFORD *Village* Ser. II. 117 He..even dug a grave for the sextoness, an old woman of eighty. **1842** BARHAM *Ingol. Leg.* Ser. II. *Sir Rupert*, It reach'd such a pass That the sextoness hasten'd to turn on the gas. **1888** BURGON *Lives Twelve Gd. Men* I. iv. 397 Rebecca (the dear old sextoness of S. Mary's).

†**'sextonry.** *Obs. rare*^{-1}. In 6 **sextenry.** [f. SEXTON + -RY.] = SEXTONSHIP.

**1525** LD. BERNERS *Froiss.* II. cxcvii. 250/2 He..retayned to hymselfe but a small lyueng, and that was the sextenry of our lady churche in Renes.

**sextonship** ('sɛkstənʃɪp). [f. SEXTON + -SHIP.] The office or position of a sexton.

**1511-2** *Rec. St. Mary at Hill* (1905) 279 Paid to William Wylde for his wages this yere for the sextenship. **1597** *Return fr. Parnass.* II. i. 671, I am double benefisde with my sextonshipp and my clearkeshippe! **1731-2** SWIFT *Consid. 2 Bills* Wks. 1737 VI. 152 They may get a Dispensation to hold the Clerkship and Sextonship of their own Parish *in Commendam.* **1816** BYRON *Churchill's Grave* 13 And thus he answer'd—..'He died before my day of Sextonship, And I had not the digging of this grave.' **1833** SIR F. PALGRAVE *Corporate Reform* 7 The Candidate for the sextonship grounds his pretensions on being an 'Old inhabitant'. **1903** *Macm. Mag.* Feb. 269/1 [He] cherished open aspirations towards the sextonship, presently vacant.

†**'sextress, -trice.** *Obs. rare.* [f. SEXTON by substitution of the suffixes -TRESS, -TRICE. Cf. next.] = SEXTONESS.

*a* **1400** *Minor Poems fr. Vernon MS.* 138 *note*, Hou vre lady dude þe offys of a sextresse fyftene ȝeer for a nonne. **1476** *Crabhouse Reg.* (1889) 11 The mony..remaynyd..to the profiht of the sextrice.

**sextry** ('sɛkstrɪ). Also 4 **sextriȝe**, 5 **cextrye**, 5-6 **sextrye**, 6 **sextre**, 6-7 **sextery(e**, **sextrie**, 7 **sextary.** [Of obscure formation; perh. f. SEXTON after *vestry*, or an alteration of OF. *sacrestie* (mod.F. *sacristie*), med.L. *sacristia*, by metathesis of *r*.]

†**1.** = SACRISTY. *Obs.*

*a* **1400** *Minor Poems fr. Vernon MS.* xxix. § I. 51 Seþen him-self goþ to be Sextriȝe, þat was þe Munstres treserye. *c* **1440** *Promp. Parv.* 67/2 Cextrye, *sacristia.* *c* **1450** in Aungier *Syon* (1840) 350 The tapers schal be lyghte abowte the sepulcre be the minister of the sextry. **1483** CAXTON *Gold. Leg.* 358/2 Whan he sawe he taryed ouer long to clothe hym he entryd in to the Sextrye. **1519** HORMAN *Vulg.* 10 Bere these iewelles into the sextrye. *c* **1530** in Strype *Cranmer* (1694) App. 25 There are in the Sextre five Crosses of gold. **1594** O. B. *Quest. Profit. Concern.* L 3 b, His sextrie or vestry, wherin he was wont to bestow his holy relicks. **1611** COTGR., *Secretainerie*, a Sextrie, or Vestrie. **1691** *d'Emiliane's Frauds Rom. Monks* 222 The Abbot and his Officers, having put off their Ornaments, went into the Sextry.

**2.** The residence of a sacrist or sacristan.

**1585** in *Acc. Obedientiars Abingdon* (Camden) App. 167 The soil of divers houses pulled down..called the Abbottes lodging..the Sexterye [etc.]. **1829** J. BRITTON *Hist. Abbey & Cath. Glouc.* Ess. 13 The Under-Steward of the Abbey...His dwelling was in a chamber, with a garden annexed to it, called 'the sextry'.

**3.** *attrib.*: **sextry barn, land** (see quots.).

**1675** DUGDALE *Baronage* I. 324/1 All the Lands called Sextery-Lands, lying in the Towns of Hellingley..and Hailesham, in that County of Sussex. **1691** BLOUNT *Law Dict.* (ed. 2) Sextery lands..are Lands given to a Church or Religious House, for maintenance of the Sexton or Sacristan. **1843** R. WILLIS *Descr. Sextry Barn* 5 The Tithe-Barn at Ely... This was commonly known by the name of the Sextry Barn (or Sacrist's Barn), because..the Tithes, for the reception of which this building was erected, belonged to the Sacrist of the monastery.

‖**sextula** ('sɛkstjʊlə). *Antiq.* Also (in Dicts.) anglicized **sextule.** [L., dim. of *sexta* (sc. *pars*), fem. of *sextus* sixth.] The sixth part of a Roman ounce (*uncia*). Also a Roman land measure, the sixth of an *uncia*. Hence †**'sextulary** *a.* [after mod.L. *sextulāris*], of a 'sextula'.

**1656** BLOUNT *Glossogr.*, *Sextule.* **1657** W. RAND tr. *Gassendi's Life Peiresc* II. v. 114 Both being added, make five Sextulæ (for half an ounce contains three of them) so that by this means all the parts of an ounce might be computed, both the duellary and sextulary parts. **1658** J. ROWLAND tr. *Moufet's Theat. Ins.* 1056 Rabby Moyses prescribes one Sextula of Frankincense with Wine sufficient. **1888** PETRIE in *Encycl. Brit.* XXIV. 488/2 The sextula after Constantine had the name of solidus as a coin weight.

**sex'tumvirate.** *rare.* [Badly f. L. *sex* six, with reminiscence of TRIUMVIRATE, SEPTEMVIRATE. Cf. *quartumvirate*.] A group of six persons.

**1726** SWIFT *Gulliver* III. vii, A sextumvirate, to which all the ages of the world cannot add a seventh. **1906** *Westm. Gaz.* 26 Feb. 2/2 It is curious to read the reasons alleged for their action by this Lordly Sextumvirate.

**sextuor** ('sɛkstjuːɔː(r)). *Mus.* [a. F. *sextuor*, f. L. *sex* six, after QUATUOR. Cf. *septuor*.] = SEXTET I.

**1824** *Dict. Musicians* II. 184 Grand Sextuor, for Piano-forte. **1829** J. JOUSSE *Dict. Terms Mus.*, *Sestetto* or *Sextuor*...Mozart's sextuor in Don Juan. **1876** STAINER & BARRETT *Dict. Mus. Terms*, *Sextuor*, a composition in six parts.

‖**sextupla.** *Mus. Obs.* [mod.L., neut. pl. of *sextuplus*: see next.] See quot. (cf. SEXTUPLE A. 2).

**1597** MORLEY *Introd. Mus.* 32 Wee call that sextupla, where wee make sixe black minymes to the semibriefe.

**sextuple** ('sɛkstjuːp(ə)l), *a.* and *sb.* [ad. med.L. type **sextuplus*, f. *sex* six, after late L. *quintuplus*, *septuplus*: see QUINTUPLE, SEPTUPLE. Cf. F. *sextuple*, Sp., Pg. *sextuplo*, It. *sestuplo*.] **A.** *adj.*

**1.** Sixfold; six times as great or numerous; consisting of six parts or things.

**1626** BACON *Sylva* § 186 Cause some halfe dozen Pipes to be made..with a single, double, and so on to a Sextuple Bore. **1646** SIR T. BROWNE *Pseud. Ep.* IV. v. 192 The proportion of man, whose length..is sextuple unto his breadth. *a* **1687** PETTY *Pol. Arith.* i. (1691) 6 But what is exported out of Holland into England is worth three Millions; and what is exported thence into all the World besides, is Sextuple to the same. **1784** HERSCHEL *Catal. Double Stars* in *Phil. Trans.* LXXV. 90 In the quadruple or n. preceding set, the two nearest very unequal... In the sextuple or s. following set, the two largest pretty unequal. **1805** T. WEAVER tr. *Werner's Ext. Charac. Fossils* 170 A sextuple-passage [occurs] when the folia of a fossil intersect each other in six different directions. **1841** ELPHINSTONE *Hist. India* I. 459 The fourfold division of the army (horse, foot, chariots, and elephants) was the same as that of Menu; but Strabo makes a sextuple division. **1868** LOCKYER *Guillemin's Heavens* (ed. 3) 393 *note*, The great nebula which surrounds the sextuple star θ Orionis. **1884** *Fortn. Rev.* June 835 Our nearest continental neighbour..may have much to lose, by a quadruple or sextuple control.

†**2.** *Mus.* (See quots.) *Obs.*

**1738** CHAMBERS *Cycl.* (ed. 2), *Sextuple*, *Sestuplo*, in music, denotes a mixed sort of triple time, which is beaten in double time. **1746** TANSUR *New Mus. Gram.* 32 The next Species [of Time] is Sextuple (or Binary-Tripla-Time..) and call'd Six to Four; each Bar containing six Crotches.

†**3.** = SENARY *a.*

**1815** [see SEXENARY].

**B.** *sb.* The number which is six times a specified number.

**1657** HOBBES *Absurd Geom.* 5 The excesse shall be that proportion which unity hath to the sextuple of the number of termes after o. **1692** J. SMITH *Seaman's Gram.* II. xv. 123 The Sextuple thereof is 1.817.

**sextuple** ('sɛkstju:p(ə)l), *v.* [f. SEXTUPLE *sb.*]

**1.** *trans.* To multiply by six; to make six times as large, numerous, powerful, etc.

**1632** W. FORSTER tr. *Oughtred's Circ. Proportion* 14 Bring the Anticedent arme unto the quadrupled space and the consequent arme, keeping that duplicated opening, will cut the space sextupled. **1656** HOBBES *Six Lessons* iii. 22 Your instance therefore of six, three, one, is here impertinent, there being in them no doubling, no tripling, no sextupling of Proportions, but of numbers. **1864** MAINE *Village-Commun.* (1876) 248 We have sextupled our students. **1884** *Edin. Rev.* Oct. 358 The range of vision was more than sextupled.

**2.** *intr.* To increase sixfold.

**1861** M. ARNOLD *Pop. Educ. France* 157 *note*, The number of schools has more than doubled in the last twenty years..; the number of girl-scholars has sextupled. **1870** *Daily News* 18 June, In Ulster during 90 years the value of land was trebled, and in Scotland..it had sextupled.

**sextuplet** ('sɛkstju:plɛt, -'tju:plət). [f. SEXTUPLE *a.* after *triplet*.] A group, set, combination, etc. of six things. **a.** *Mus.* = SEXTOLET. **b.** Any of six children born at one birth. **c.** A cycle for six riders.

**1852** [see OCTUPLET]. **1876** STAINER & BARRETT *Dict. Mus. Terms*, *Sextolet*, or *Sextuplet*, a double triplet, six notes to be performed in the time of four. **1894** GOULD *Illustr. Dict. Med.*, *Sextuplet*, one of six offspring from a single gestation. **1896** *Daily News* 17 July 7/1 A proposal was recently made ..to match a sextuplet [*sc.* cycle] against a railway train. **1905** *Daily Chron.* 19 Oct. 5/3 Professor Hamy..reported that a negress living in the Gold Coast Colony gave birth recently to sextuplets.

**sextuplex** ('sɛkstju:plɛks), *a.* [a. med.L. *sextuplex*, f. *sex* six, after *triplex*, *quadruplex*, etc. Cf. SEXTUPLE *a.*] Sixfold.

**1668** WALLIS in Rigaud *Corr. Sci. Men* (1841) II. 495 Sextuplex is as much the double of triplex as 6 is the double of 3.

**b.** *Electric Telegr.* Applied to a system by which six messages may be transmitted simultaneously by the same wire. Hence **'sextuplex** *v.*

**1889** [see OCTUPLEX]. **1891** PREECE & SIVEWRIGHT *Telegraphy* x. (ed. 9) 202 The application of the same terms, duplex, quadruplex and sextuplex..to the corresponding arrangements in multiplex working would tend to confusion. **1895** *Times* 29 Jan. 6/6 The wires were all worked on the simplex plan 25 years ago; now the processes are simplex, duplex, quadruplex, and sextuplex.

**sex'tuplicate,** *a.* and *sb.* [ad. med.L. *sextuplicāt-um*, pa. pple. of *sextuplicāre*: see SEXTUPLY *v.*] †**A.** *adj.* Sixfold. *Obs. rare*⁻¹.

**1657** HOBBES *Absurd Geom.* 10 An infinite row of Arithmetically proportionalls in proportion quadruplicate, quintuplicate, sextuplicate &c.

**B.** *sb.* (See quot. 1934.) Also in phr. ***in sextuplicate***, in sixfold quantity, in six copies.

**1934** WEBSTER, *Sextuplicate*, *n.*, a sixth thing corresponding to five others of the same kind; an exact copy of something of which five other exact copies exist. **1975** *Daily Tel.* 1 Aug. 12 Contestants..have been asked to submit their entries in sextuplicate. **1978** *Nature* 31 Aug. 897/2 (*caption*) Each column represents the result for one patient, averaging 4 to 10 separate assays (in sextuplicate) per tissue. **1979** *Ibid.* 29 Mar. 465/1 After pre-incubation, the tubes were returned to ice and ³H-5-HT was added in sextuplicate.

**sextupli'cation.** *rare.* [n. of action f. med.L. *sextuplicāre*: see next.] Multiplication by six.

**1674** JEAKE *Arith.* (1696) 24 Sextuplication, or to multiply by 6. **1935** *Antiquity* IX. 298 The sextuplication of the King's Chamber roof.

†**'sextuply,** *v.* *Scots Law. Obs. rare.* Cf. SEXTIPLY *v.* [ad. med.L. *sextuplicāre*, f. *sextuplic-*, *-plex*: see SEXTUPLEX *a.*] *intr.* To make a rejoinder to a quintuplication.

**1673** *Rec. Justic. Crt. Edinb.* (S.H.S.) II. 167 Quintuplyes his Majesties Advocate, that..Sextuplyes Sir Geo. McKenzie, that [etc.].

**sextuply** ('sɛkstju:plɪ), *adv.* [f. SEXTUPLE *a.* + -LY².] In a sixfold manner.

**1873** MAXWELL *Electr. & Magn.* I. 175 In the sextuply connected part of the spherical surface.

**sextupole** ('sɛkstju:pəʊl), *a.* and *sb. Physics.* [f. *sextu-*, in SEXTUPLE *a.* and *sb.* and related words + POLE *sb.*²] **A.** *adj.* Having six magnetic (or electric) poles, three of each polarity. **B.** *sb.* A sextupole device.

**1961** in *Progr. Nucl. Physics* (1964) IX. 114 A Sextupole Magnet Design. **1969** [see QUADRUPOLE *sb.* b]. **1976** *Physics Bull.* Nov. 499/2 Extra dipoles, sextupoles and octupoles act as correcting magnets in case of defects in the magnet lattice and for superfine control. **1979** *Sci. Amer.* May 64/1 The atoms emerge from a nozzle as a low-energy beam, then pass into the strongly nonuniform field of a sextupole, or six-pole, magnet... It discriminates strongly between spin-up and spin-down electrons.

**sexual** ('sɛksju:əl), *a.* Also 7 -all. [a. late L. *sexuāl-is* (5th c.), f. L. *sexu-s* SEX. Cf. F. *sexuel* (18th c.), Sp., Pg. *sexual*, It. *sessuale*.]

Many collocations are paralleled by and equivalent to combs. with *sex* (see SEX *sb.* 5). These are not individually listed or defined below.

**1.** Of or pertaining to sex or the attribute of being either male or female; existing or predicated with regard to sex.

**1651** BIGGS *New Disp.* ¶69 The same simple rotteth, and is changed into little animals, these are..of both sexes, which truly would not come to passe if those simples had already a sex or sexuall powers within them. **1760** J. LEE *Introd. Bot.* (1776) Pref. 9 The Honour of having first suggested the true sexual Distinctions in Plants appears to be due to..Sir Thomas Millington. **1794** SULIVAN *View Nat.* II. 222 One only single sexual pair of every species of living things. **1803** SYD. SMITH *Wks.* (1859) I. 46/1 Delphine is said to be intended for the authoress, and Madame de Vernon (by a slight sexual metamorphosis) for Talleyrand. **1874** SAYCE *Compar. Philol.* vii. 249 We may take, by way of illustration, the question of gender. What.. was the source..of the sexual relation of nouns? **1877** HUXLEY *Anat. Inv. Anim.* ii. 81 These extremely simple organisms have not yet reached the stage of sexual differentiation. **1968** S. HYNES *Edwardian Turn of Mind* vi. 201 It was an easy grammatical step..to shift the blame from sexual discrimination to sex itself. **1981** N. TUCKER *Child & Book* vii. 212 Children's perceptions of their sexual roles are built up from many different sources.

(*b*) *spec.* in ***sexual politics***, the principles determining the relationship of the sexes; so ***sexual-political*** adj., ***sexual politician***.

**1970** K. MILLETT *Sexual Politics* p. xii, The prospect of radical change in sexual politics. *Ibid.* II. iii. 110 The sexual-political predilections of each faction. *Ibid.* iv. 233 So we proceed to the counter-revolutionary sexual politicians themselves—Lawrence, Miller and Mailer.

**2. a.** Pertaining to sex as concerned in generation or in the processes connected with this. ***sexual dimorphism***, the condition in which there exist marked differences in form or appearance between the sexes of a species in addition to differences in the sexual organs themselves; ***sexual intercourse***, copulation; ***sexual interference*** (euphem.), sexual assault or molestation; ***sexual selection***: see SELECTION 3 b.

**1799** *Med. Jrnl.* II. 323 The act of sexual intercourse. **1800** WORDSWORTH *Lyrical Ballads* I. p. xxxii, From this principle the direction of the sexual appetite, and all the passions connected with it take their origin. **1803** *Med. Jrnl.* X. 509 Sexual function is impaired. **1821** *Blackw. Mag.* IX. 282/1 Some one has said that Sir George Etherege was the first who founded a comedy barefacedly upon the sexual passion. **1826** KIRBY & SP. *Entomol.* III. 334 It is most probably for sexual purposes. **1836–9** *Todd's Cycl. Anat.* II. 695/1 We are inclined to attribute very little weight to the nature of the sexual desires of the malformed individual. **1849** W. M. THACKERAY *Pendennis* I. xxv. 239 That anxiety with which brooding women watch over their sons' affections... I have no doubt there is a sexual jealousy on the mother's part, and a secret pang. **1861** EMERSON *Soc. & Solit.* Wks. (Bohn) III. 133 To insure the existence of the race, she [Nature] reinforces the sexual instinct. **1863** E. V. NEALE *Anal. Thought & Nat.* 183 The sexual impulse. **1868** H. MAUDSLEY *Physiol. & Pathol. of Mind* (ed. 2) II. iii. 405 Acute dementia..connected, he believes, with the effect produced on the nervous system by sexual intercourse. **1876** BRISTOWE *Theory & Pract. Med.* (1878) 329 It [acne] has a special connection with the period of development and maturation of the sexual functions. **1880** BESSEY *Bot.* 206 No sexual organs are known [in Protophytes], and whether the sexual act occurs or not is somewhat doubtful. **1888** Sexual dimorphism [see DIMORPHISM b]. **1898** *Alienist & Neurologist* Oct. 613 From whatever side and from whatever symptoms we start, we always unfailingly reach the region of the sexual life. **1898** 'S. GRAND' *Beth Bk.* xliv. 417 The sex question..is the stock-in-trade of every author, as if there were nothing..in the lives of men and women but their sexual relations. **1902** *Encycl. Brit.* XXVII. 625/2 *Bonellia* and *Hamingia* are very interesting examples of sexual dimorphism... The male is reduced to a minute.. organism, which passes its life..in a special recess of the nephridia of the female. **1903** G. B. SHAW *Man & Superman* p. xvi, The Don Juan play..is to deal with sexual attraction. **1928** W. S. MAUGHAM *Sacred Flame* III. 142 You can't go without food... But you can go without the satisfaction of your sexual appetites. **1929** D. H. LAWRENCE *Pornography & Obscenity* 18 The young man and the young woman went and had sexual intercourse together. **1932** S. ZUCKERMAN *Soc. Life Monkeys & Apes* xiii. 212 It is possible that sexual dimorphism plays some part in determining the monogamy or polygyny of a species. **1934** BLUNDEN *Choice or Chance* 58 You saw the mystical idea of course—..roughly, my Tristram is the Sexual Force. **1951** N. MITFORD *Blessing* xi. 118 If you don't empty your mind and heart of sexual jealousy..you will never be happy with me. **1957** R. CHANDLER *Let.* 28 Apr. (1981) 441, I had not filled myself with sexual fantasies. **1960** C. DAY LEWIS *Buried Day* vi. 107 The conflict and guilt set up by masturbation..and the sexual fantasies attached to it. **1968** S. HYNES *Edwardian Turn of Mind* vi. 195 The biological facts of sexual attraction and the urge to reproduce. **1968** 'A. GILBERT' *Night Encounter* iv. 45 Quite a young girl... No attempt at sexual interference, no signs of pregnancy. **1970** *Cambr. Anc. Hist.* (ed. 3) I. I. v. 156 Even allowing for marked sexual dimorphism it is still obvious that more than one species [of Australopithecine] demands recognition. **1971** P. D. JAMES *Shroud for Nightingale* vii. 246 The late Mr. Dettinger hadn't understood [many things], his wife's sexual needs among them. **1973** B. A. TONKIN tr. *Lorenz & Leyhausen's Motivation Human & Animal Behaviour* iii. 53 The sexual drives bring forces of a new kind pulling in a new direction. **1974** H. R. F. KEATING *Underside* xi. 108 She must know.. that men had sexual urges, that they could not live without any sexual experience of any sort. **1978** P. G. WINSLOW *Coppergold* 163 Post-mortem had shown that the girl had had sexual relations with a man just before her death. **1979** *Times Lit. Suppl.* 23 Nov. 20/1 Edel..suggests..that after it was clear that a sexual relationship with Virginia was impossible he [*sc.* Leonard Woolf] sublimated his sexual drives in work. **1980** D. NEWSOME *On Edge of Paradise* 382 He had no sexual life; all his sexual instincts had to be sublimated. **1981** A. EDWARDS *Sonya* xix. 321 Her diary.. is filled with musings on her sexual needs, frustrations, and fantasies. **1981** G. MARKSTEIN *Ultimate Issue* 261 'And at these places sexual intimacy took place—' Christ almighty.. how many more times is he going to say it. Sexual misconduct. Sexual intercourse.

**b.** ***sexual organs***, the organs of sexual generation in animals or plants.

**1828** STARK *Elem. Nat. Hist.* II. 407 Worms..with..the sexual organs separate. **1861** J. R. GREENE *Man. Anim. Kingd.*, *Cœlent.* 74 If the producing zoöid possess sexual organs. **1882** VINES *Sachs' Bot.* 224 The morphological characters of the sexual organs.

**c.** Of or pertaining to the organs of sex.

**1836–9** *Todd's Cycl. Anat.* II. 695/1 In attempting to determine the true sex in such doubtful instances of sexual formation. **1898** *Syd. Soc. Lex.*, *Sexual diseases*, diseases of the sexual organs.

**d.** ***sexual system*** (or ***method***): the Linnæan classification of plants, based on the differences in their sexual organization.

In 1735 Linnæus (*Bibl. Bot.*, ed. 1747, p. 64) has *systema sexuale*, referred to 1731.

**1760** J. LEE *Introd. Bot.* (1776) Pref. 6 Dr. Linnæus; whose Labours..and whose Invention of the Sexual System in particular, are well known. **1825** T. K. CROMWELL *Colchester* 352 The herbaceous collection will be arranged according to the sexual system of Linnæus.

**3.** Relative to the physical intercourse between the sexes or the gratification of sexual appetites, as ***sexual morality, vice, excess***, etc. ***sexual athlete***, a sexually vigorous person, a skilled performer in sexual intercourse; so ***sexual athleticism, athletics***; ***sexual inversion***: see INVERSION 11; ***sexual psychopathy***: see PSYCHOPATHY 1; hence ***sexual psychopath, psychopathic*** adj.; ***sexual revolution***, the liberalization of established social and moral attitudes to sex.

**1792** M. WOLLSTONECRAFT *Rights of Woman* vii. 273 (*heading*) Modesty.—comprehensively considered, and not as a sexual virtue. **1878** GLADSTONE *Prim. Homer* 112 Sexual frailty exists among Achaians, only in narrow measure. **1888** K. PEARSON *Ethics of Freethought* v. 120 Another good example is that of sexual morality; here the most difficult questions arise. **1897** C. LOMBROSO in T. L. Stedman *Twentieth Century Practice* XII. 402 We have seen that in the most extraordinary tendencies of sexual psychopathy.. the somatic and hereditary signs are epileptoid in character. **1908** G. B. SHAW *Getting Married* 182 Whilst the subject is considered shameful..we shall have no systematic instruction in sexual hygiene. **1910** tr. *Freud's Lectures* in *Amer. Jrnl. Psychol.* XXI. 218 The claims of our civilization make life too hard for the greater part of humanity..without producing an excess of cultural gain by this excess of sexual repression. **1911** *Contemp. Rev.* Sept. 383 Berlin is outbidding Paris in its sexual immorality. **1924** *Internat. Jrnl. Psycho-analysis* V. 95 (*heading*) The sexual offender. **1934** A. HUXLEY *Beyond Mexique Bay* 44 Places where people..every other sexual taboos. **1936** 'R. WEST' *Thinking Reed* viii. 265 It sounded insincere, as if she were merely obeying a sexual convention. **1938** *John Marshall Law Q.* III. 407 The proposed law is as follows: An Act to Provide for the Commitment and Detention of Criminal Sexual Psychopathic Persons. **1939** R. PEARL *Nat. Hist. Population* 293 Some present-day examples of sexual athletes who make Casanova, the traditional star, seem a somewhat puny performer. *Ibid.*, I thought you might be interested in some cases of—as it seems to me—prodigious sexual athleticism. **1941** *Horizon* Sept. 161 All societies, as the price of survival, have to insist on a fairly high standard of sexual morality. **1945** T. P. WOLFE tr. *Reich's Sexual Revolution* ix. 64 Soviet sexual legislation was the clearest expression of the first attack of the sexual revolution on the reactionary sexual order. **1950** *Amer. Jrnl. Sociol.* LVI. 142/1 Since 1937 twelve states and the District of Columbia have enacted sexual psychopath laws. *Ibid.* 142/2 The concept of the 'sexual psychopath' is so vague that it cannot be used for judicial and administrative purposes. **1954** B. KARPMAN *Sexual Offender* xii. 224 Determination of the question of sexual psychopathy is by a superior court and commitment is for an indefinite period. **1957** H. M. HACKER in *Marriage & Family Living* XIX. 232/1 In societies which differentiate strongly between masculine and feminine social roles, individuals who manifest personality traits ascribed to the opposite sex or who feel inadequate in fulfilling their part of the sexual division of labor may become confused in their sexual identification, and feel that they must also change their sexual object. **1958** J. BYROM *Or be He Dead* iii. 37 Essays about sexual perverts. **1961** R. F. C. HULL tr. *Jung's Freud & Psychoanal.* in *Coll. Works* IV. IV. 321 As soon as we enter the field of neurosis, this antithesis is stretched to the limit. God becomes the symbol of the most complete sexual repression. **1963** B. FRIEDAN *Feminine Mystique* (1965) xi. 266 A woman who is herself only a sexual object, lives finally in a world of objects, unable to touch in others the individual identity she lacks herself. **1967** B. W. TUCHMAN in *Sat. Rev.* (U.S.) 25 Feb. 28/3 Sexual perversion and hallucinatory drugs..'are not what human history is about.' **1968** S. HYNES *Edwardian Turn of Mind* vi. 201 The [suffrage] movement never made sexual freedom a goal. **1968** A. DIMENT *Bang Bang Birds* II. vi. 81 You'd think his life work was spreading American sexual mores around the world. **1969** *Daily Tel.* (Colour Suppl.) 24 Oct. 35/2 The family is not composed of sexual athletes and cannot make love 20 times a day and so cannot try everything. **1970** *Guardian* 12 Nov. 10/3 Would he have to do anything awful in the way of sexual athleticism? **1970** K. MILLETT *Sexual Politics* iii. 62 A sexual revolution would require..an end of traditional sexual inhibitions and taboos. **1971** G. STEINER *In Bluebeard's Castle* I. 15 Bourgeois sexual ethics were a veneer, masking a great area of turbulent hypocrisy. **1971** H. LEE *Surrogate Wife* (1972) 27 Nice girls..were less likely to be able to copulate with strangers, even if those strangers were sexual therapists. **1972** P. D. JAMES *Unsuitable Job* iv. 144 One of the more innocuous of sexual deviations. **1972** P. COUSINS (*title*) Christianity and sexual liberation. **1975** G. HOWELL *In Vogue* 62 Sexual deviation was becoming respectable. *Ibid.*, The sexual education of the jazz age.

**1975** L. FARLEY in *N.Y. Times* 19 Aug. 38/1 Sexual harassment of women in their place of employment is extremely widespread. **1976** *Globe & Mail* (Toronto) 16 Feb. 1/6 Police said the report of a pathologist who examined the bodies makes no mention of a sexual assault. **1976** *Jrnl. R. Soc. Arts* June 351/2 The 4,500 magazines dealing in specialized trades or tastes from ironmongery to sexual athletics. **1977** *Evening Gaz.* (Middlesbrough) 11 Jan. 3/4 Sexual offences, mainly indecent assault on females, increased by 17. **1977** R. GREEN in W. H. Masters et al. *Ethical Issues in Sex Therapy & Research* vii. 198 There are clinicians of considerable sophistication utilizing sexual surrogates. **1977** C. FREMLIN *Spider-Orchid* viii. 61 In spite of Permissiveness and the Sexual Revolution.. nothing had changed! **1978** *Times* 7 Aug. 2/4 Contraception.. is producing.. a profound alteration in sexual behaviour. **1979** J. CROSBY *Party of Year* xvi. 99 Decadent bourgeois sexual perversions. **1981** J. B. HILTON *Surrender Value* xiv. 104 He was a mild man... There was no record.. of sexual aberration. **1982** R. GRAYSON *Montmartre Murders* xi. 91, I have been told that Suji's sexual appetite is formidable.

**4. a.** Of animals and plants: Having sex; sexed; separated into two sexes; having sexual organs; producing offspring by means of sexual congress. (Opposed to *asexual*.)

**1830** LINDLEY *Nat. Syst. Bot.* Introd. 18 Plants are naturally and primarily divided into two great divisions, called Sexual and Asexual. **1861** HULME tr. *Moquin-Tandon* II. vii. 329 The Linguatulæ are at first asexual... They pass.. into the bodies of the carnivora.., where they complete their development, and become sexual. **1880** BESSEY *Bot.* 361 They [*sc.* Vascular Cryptogams] present an alternation of sexual and asexual generations. **1882** VINES *Sachs' Bot.* 273 It is only towards the close of the period of growth that sexual individuals make their appearance.

**b.** ***sexual cell***, a reproductive cell which is either male or female; a sperm-cell or an egg-cell.

**1868** DARWIN *Anim. & Pl.* II. xii. 2 Some trifling peculiarity.. transmitted through the male or female sexual cells. **1883** AVELING tr. *Haeckel's Pedigree Man*, etc. 242 That blending of the two kinds of sexual cells that is the sole essential in sexual reproduction.

**c.** Of reproduction in animals or plants: Taking place by means of the congress of the two sexes. Opposed to *asexual* or *agamic*.

**1872** H. C. WOOD *Fresh-w. Algæ U.S.* 100 The propagation is both sexual and non-sexual. **1882** VINES *Sachs' Bot.* 251 Conjugation is the simplest form of sexual reproduction.

**5.** Characteristic of or peculiar to the one sex or the other.

***secondary sexual characters***: those marks of sex (e.g. the beard in man, the distinctive plumage in birds) which are not immediately connected with the reproductive structure.

**1815** *Sporting Mag.* XLVI. 74 Her looks, her turns, her whole manner of speaking and acting is sexual. **1826** KIRBY & SP. *Entomol.* III. 316 Of all the organs of the head, none seem so little subject to sexual variation as the under-jaws. **1839** DE QUINCEY *Recoll. Lakes* Wks. 1862 II. 204 To ingraft, by her sexual sense of beauty, upon his masculine austerity those graces, which [etc.].

**6.** Having reference to the sexes.

**1879** *St. George's Hosp. Rep.* IX. 719 The sexual distribution of this disease.

**sexualism** (ˈsɛksjuːəlɪz(ə)m). [f. SEXUAL *a.* + -ISM.] Sexuality as a principle of action or thought.

**1857** *Blackw. Mag.* LXXXII. 751 Siva.. is most useful and popular as the god of reproduction and sexualism. **1867** *Contemp. Rev.* V. 187 Cecco Angiolieri.. drives his master, Dante, into the strangest development, refusing to see anything in him save merely a sort of artistic sexualism.

**sexualist** (ˈsɛksjuːəlɪst). *rare.* [ad. mod.L. *sexuālista* (Linnæus 1735), f. *sexuāl-is*: see SEXUAL *a.* + -IST.] **a.** One who attributes sexuality to certain organisms. **b.** An adherent of the 'sexual system' of botanical classification.

**1790** W. SMELLIE *Philos. Nat. Hist.* I. 246 Here, then, the analogy stops; and, instead of bringing aid to the sexualist, operates powerfully against his favourite hypothesis. **1839** LINDLEY *Introd. Bot.* I. iii. 261 It was difficult for sexualists to believe that plants of so large a size were destitute of such organs [of fecundation].

**sexuality** (sɛksjuːˈælɪtɪ). [ad. mod.L. **sexuālitās*: see SEXUAL *a.* and -ITY. Cf. F. *sexualité*.]

**1.** The quality of being sexual or having sex.

*a* **1800** COWPER *Wks.* (1836) VII. 320 It is on their sexuality that he has built his poem [Loves of the Plants]. **1826** KIRBY & SP. *Entomol.* III. 325 The wonderful diversity of forms.. to which mere sexuality gives rise amongst insects. **1882–4** COOKE *Brit. Fresh-w. Algæ* I. 63 Larger cœnobia,.. with daughter-cœnobia enclosed within the mother, evolved without sexuality.

**b.** (See quot.)

**1888** *Buck's Handbk. Med. Sci.* VI. 436/2 According to a strict biological definition sexuality is the characteristic of the male and female reproductive elements (genoblasts), and sex of the individuals in which the reproductive elements arise. A man has sex, a spermatozoon sexuality.

**2.** Possession of sexual powers, or capability of sexual feelings.

**1879** J. M. DUNCAN *Dis. Wom.* xxvii. (1889) 223 In removing the ovaries, you do not necessarily destroy sexuality in a woman. **1899** *Allbutt's Syst. Med.* VIII. 191 Precocious sexuality.. interferes with normal mental growth.

**3.** Recognition of or preoccupation with what is sexual; *pl.* (*nonce-use*), allusions to sexual matters.

**1848** KINGSLEY *Yeast* viii, Paradise and hell.. as grossly material as Mahomet's, without the honest thorough-going sexuality, which you thought made his notion logical and consistent. **1893** C. A. CLARKE *Knobstick* xiii. 137 Under the unsteady inspiration of.. alcohol, there was rude and uproarious bawling of music hall ditties.. and chuckling sexualities were tossed to and fro.

**4.** Appearance distinctive of sex.

**1908** S. A. COOK *Relig. Anc. Palestine* iii. 29 [The Astarte-plaques] offer a large variety of types from the coarsest exaggeration of sexuality to highly conventionalised forms.

**sexualization** (ˌsɛksjuːəlaɪˈzeɪʃən). [f. SEXUALIZE *v.* + -ATION.] The act or process of sexualizing; the state of being sexualized; adaptation to a sexual role.

**1889** *Classical Rev.* III. 391 We are inclined to doubt Pott's confident assumption that sexualization is a necessary consequence of personification. **1977** A. H. WILLIAMS in A. W. Franklin *Challenge of Child Abuse* xii. 168 In sadism, it is important to recognize the sexualization of the pleasure in the cruel transaction. **1979** *Country Life* 29 Mar. 947/4 The lives available to a woman.. education, sexualisation, part-time prostitution, suburbanisation.

**sexualize** (ˈsɛksjuːəlaɪz), *v.* [f. SEXUAL *a.* + -IZE.] *trans.* To make sexual, endow with sex, attribute sex to.

**1839** *Blackw. Mag.* XLV. 462/2 The French [language].. has no resources for elevating its diction... The single misfortune of having no neuter gender,.. by sexualising in all cases, neutralises the effect. **1876** FAIRBAIRN *Stud. Philos. Relig.* 31 The bright divinity of Heaven may have been sexualized and married to a goddess of Heaven before [etc.]. **1900** POSTGATE *Pref. to Mrs. H. Cust's Transl. Bréal's Semantics* 12 Even in the case of animals the sexualizing, if I may so call it, of the endings *-us* and *-a* was by no means complete.

**sexually** (ˈsɛksjuːəlɪ), *adv.* [f. SEXUAL *a.* + -LY[2].] **a.** In a sexual manner; by means of sexual congress. **b.** With respect to sex.

**1655** in Hartlib *Ref. Commonw. Bees* 21 These Wormes.. engender sexually. **1862** HUXLEY *Lect. Working Men* 86 Whether we consider the reproduction.. of organic beings as they take place asexually or as they may take place sexually. **1878** BELL tr. *Gegenbaur's Comp. Anat.* 131 These are developed into the sexually mature form.

**sexualogy** (sɛksjuːˈælədʒɪ). *rare*[−1]. [f. SEXUAL *a.* + -LOGY.] The science of sexual relations. Hence **sexuaˈlogical** *a.*, of or belonging to sexualogy.

**1885** K. PEARSON *Ethic of Freeth.* xiii. (1888) 371 Not until we have ample statistics.. will it be possible to lay the foundations of a real science of sexualogy. *Ibid.* 387 The whole question of Neo-Malthusianism is fraught with immense social and sexualogical difficulties.

**sexuate** (ˈsɛksjuːeɪt), *a. Ent.* [f. L. *sexu-s* SEX + -ATE[2].] Having sex, separated into sexes = SEXUAL *a.* So **ˈsexuated** *a.*

**1882** *Entomol. Mag.* Mar. 225 This last genus is sexuate; it has males and females which copulate. *Ibid.* 226 A single egg.. will produce.. males and females; and before these sexuated insects appear, would be seen winged insects [etc.].

**sexupare** (ˈsɛksjuːpɛə(r)). *Ent.* [ad. mod.L. *sexupar-um*, neut. of *sexuparus*: see next.] 'In the plant lice, one of the parents of the sexed generation, usually developed late in the season' (*Cent. Dict.* 1909).

**18..** *U.S. Dept. Agr.*, Div. Entom., Bulletin 44 p. 8 (Cent.) The sexupares or return migrants.

**sexuparous** (sɛkˈsjuːpərəs), *a. Biol.* [f. mod.L. *sexupar-us*, L. *sexu-s* SEX: see -PAROUS.] Producing offspring sexually.

**1899** D. SHARP *Insects* II. 586 One [series of Chermes] is wingless, and exclusively parthenogenetic,.. while the other part becomes winged; these latter are called sexuparous.

†**sexvirate.** *Obs. rare*[−1]. [ad. late L. *sexvirātus* (*sēvirātus*), f. *sexvir* (*sēvir*) one of six colleagues (back-formation from *sex virī* six men): see -ATE[1].] A body of six colleagues.

**1762** tr. *Busching's Syst. Geog.* II. 374 The eldest of the six professors which constitute the sexvirate of the college is styled primicerius.

**sexy** (ˈsɛksɪ), *a.* [f. SEX *sb.* + -Y[1].] **a.** Concerned with or engrossed in sex. **b.** Sexually attractive or provocative, sexually exciting; also *fig.* Also *Comb.*, as ***sexy-looking*** adj.

[**1925** *La Nouvelle Revue Française* Jan. 313 Depuis que Joyce a publié un livre qu'ils croient 'sexy'—cet état d'esprit n'a pas d'équivalent français—on s'en empare.. que sa méthode sert de modèle à des gens qui.. se disent surréalistes.] **1928** *Sunday Dispatch* 2 Dec. 19/2 Australian audiences.. like sex plays, but they mustn't be to sexy. **1934** DYLAN THOMAS *Let.* 9 May (1966) 120, I shall now attempt to.. look all sexy at the mantel-piece. **1935** J. T. FARRELL *Judgment Day* ii. 22 He watched the dark sexy-looking waitress scurry with a large tray of food. **1940** N. MITFORD *Pigeon Pie* ii. 29 He had been most famous as a singer of those sexy ballads which were adored by our grandparents. **1942** [see GLAMORIZE *v.*]. **1947** J. STEINBECK *Wayward Bus* 84 Her voice was throaty and sexy. **1959** *Housewife* Oct. 131/2 Did she keep her figure beautiful and wear sexy nightgowns? **1963** A. ROSS *Australia 63* 23 A sexy-looking torch singer breathed huskily into her microphone. **1970** *Wall St. Jrnl.* (Eastern ed.) 22 Sept. 1/6 Corn and soybeans may not sound as sexy as electronics or aerospace. **1975** R. PLAYER *Let's talk of Graves* iii. 80 The seminarists were.. casting perplexed eyes to Heaven, the Immaculate Conception being far too sexy to explain to adolescents. **1977** *New Scientist* 17 Mar. 638/1 Expensive, high-technology, politically sexy.. small wonder the big dam is popular all round. **1978** *Rolling Stone* 12 Jan. 44 A 'sexy' (TV for a good story) news idea. **1981** V. GLENDINNING *Edith Sitwell* iv. 57 Nancy Cunard—sexy, vital, unpredictable.

Hence **ˈsexily** *adv.*, **ˈsexiness.**

**1925** *Glasgow Herald* 28 May 4/2 The stallion seems to vanish altogether near the end of the story, and the Welsh groom is put into prominence, with mere 'sexiness' thus supplanting magnificent vitality. **1947** J. STEINBECK *Wayward Bus* 83 Wide-set eyes meant sexiness. **1953** R. LEHMANN *Echoing Grove* 240 Late party, the latest place, place of lugubrious eroticism, sexily spot-lit. **1971** *Ink* 12 June 6/3 So-called permissiveness, sexiness, moral relaxation have gone as far as they can without beginning to alter *radically* our civilization. **1978** P. BRYERS *Cat Trapper* ix. 61 She curled sexily on a cushion.

**sey**[1] (seɪ). Also 7 sye, 9 sei. [var. of SAITHE. Cf. Norw. *sei.*] = SAITHE. Also ***sey-fish, -pollack.***

**1698** M. MARTIN *Voy. St. Kilda* (1749) 27 Their food is Herring, Mackarels, and Syes. **1842** BONNYCASTLE *Newfoundld.* I. 264 The gadus carbonarius, the sey-fish of Norway, or coal-fish. **1863** KINGSLEY in *Reader* 29 Aug. 213/1 A two-pound 'sei' (*Pollachius viridis*), the most beautiful in form and colour of all British fish. **1864** COUCH *Brit. Fishes* III. 84 Sey Pollack.

**sey**[2] (seɪ). *Sc.* Also 8 **say.** [Of obscure origin.] (See quot. 1844.)

**1719** RAMSAY *Ep. J. Arbuckle* 89 A healthfu' Stomach sharply set Prefers a Back-sey pipin het. **1724** —— *Health* 259 His squeamish Stomach loaths the savory Sey. *Ibid.* Gloss., *Back-sey*, a Surloin. **1737** *Ochtertyre House Bk. Acc.* (S.H.S.) 65 Sent a hinde quarter of the cow to Gray and a fore say to Fentry. **1816** SCOTT *Antiq.* xv, He'll make as muckle about buying a forequarter o' lamb in August as about a back sey o' beef. **1819** —— *Bride Lamm.* xxxiv, This bit morsel o' beef.. is out o' the back sey. **1844** H. STEPHENS *Bk. Farm* II. 168 The sirloin, or back sey. The spare rib, or fore sey. [In the Scotch mode of cutting up a carcass of beef.]

**sey**[3] (sɛɪ). *Sc.* and *Ulster.* Also **sie, sye,** etc. (see E.D.D.). Cf. SCYE. [Of obscure origin.]

**1825–80** JAMIESON *s.v.*, The sey of a gown or shift is the opening in which the sleeve is inserted. S.

**sey:** see SAY, SEA, SEE, SYE (sieve).

‖**seyal** (seɪˈjɑːl). Also **sayall.** [Arab. *sayāl.*] The acacia.

**1844** KITTO *Phys. Hist. Palestine* vii. 251 The Arabs of the desert now use the epidermis of the *seyal*.. for tanning. **1873** TRISTRAM *Moab* ii. 36 Some fine acacia or 'seyal' trees. **1907** *Daily Chron.* 18 Nov. 8/6 The sayall bushes began to grow more densely.

**seyalle,** obs. form of SEAL *sb.*[2]

**seybertite** (ˈseɪbətaɪt). *Min.* [Named after H. *Seybert*: see -ITE.] A synonym of clintonite.

**1833** *Amer. Jrnl. Sci.* XXIV. 171 Mr. Clemson.. proposes for it [Bronzite] the trivial name of Seybertite, after the distinguished American analyst, Mr. Henry Seybert. **1854** DANA *Syst. Min.* (ed. 4) II. 297.

**seybie,** Sc. variant of SYBOW, young onion.

**seych,** obs. Sc. form of SIGH *v.*

**Seychellois** (seɪʃɛlˈwɑː), *sb.* and *a.* Fem. Seychelloise (-ˈwɑːz). Pl. **Seychellois,** fem. **-oises** (-ˈwɑːz). [Fr.] **A.** *sb.* A native or inhabitant of the Seychelles, a group of islands in the Indian Ocean. **B.** *adj.* Of or pertaining to the Seychelles or their inhabitants.

**1898** F. A. BARKLY *From Tropics to North Sea* viii. 34 The Seychellois have a method of walling houses with the bark of the lathe palm. **1936** J. A. F. OZANNE *Coconuts & Créoles* xii. 184 The young Seychellois is quite safe from European competition. *Ibid.* 186 Most of these young Seychellois boys are very keen sportsmen. **1960** I. FLEMING *For Your Eyes Only* 207 The only conceivable security hazard in the Seychelles lay in the beauty and ready availability of the Seychelloises. **1971** *Vogue* Dec. 73, I took passage on the launch with a crew of Seychellois police. **1978** T. ALLBEURY *Lantern Network* iii. 34 She was a Seychelloise from Mahé. **1980** *Illustr. London News* Mar. 67/2 As a tourist you will find both English and French spoken and understood; the Seychellois speak their own patois.

**Seyd,** var. SAYYID.

**seyde,** obs. f. SAID, SEED *sb.*

**seye,** obs. f. SAY *sb.*[1], *sb.*[2], SAY *v.*, SEE *v.*

**Seyed,** var. SAYYID.

**seyen,** obs. f. SAY *v.*[1]

**seyer,** variant of SYRE *Sc.* (gutter, drain).

**seyetyka,** obs. form of SCIATICA.

**seyf(e,** obs. form of SIEVE, SIEGE.

**Seyfert** (ˈseɪfɜːt). *Astr.* The name of Carl K. *Seyfert* (1911–60), U.S. astronomer, who first described such galaxies in 1943 (*Astrophysical Jrnl.* XCVII. 28), used *attrib.* with reference to a class of galaxies characterized by bright compact cores that show strong infra-red emission.

**1959** *Astrophysical Jrnl.* CXXX. 26 Another characteristic feature of many of the Seyfert galaxies is the apparently small size of their nuclei in which the broad emission features arise. **1963** *Ibid.* CXXXVII. 1032 It is possible that an event of the Seyfert type is experienced by all spiral galaxies and not only by the Sa and Sb systems. We believe this to be a reasonable assumption, but it has the effect only of reducing the frequency of Seyfert objects among spirals by a factor of 2 or less. **1969** *Ibid.* CLVIII. 859 The detection of such [nonstellar] absorption features in Seyfert spectra is rather difficult. **1970** *Nature* 31 Jan. 410/2 Seyfert galaxies with their extraordinarily bright and unusual nuclei could easily be intermediaries between quasars and normal galaxies. **1970** *Sci. Jrnl.* Feb. 57/1 Many of the phenomena observed in Seyfert galaxies are similar to those seen in quasi-stellar objects. **1971** *New Scientist* 17 June 695/1 A compact infrared source with a spectrum similar to that of the Seyfert nuclei, but with a smaller energy output.., appears to be located at the centre of our Galaxy.

**b.** *absol.* A Seyfert galaxy.

**1968** *Physical Rev. Lett.* XXI. 1540/1 NGC1275 and 3C120..are a hundred times more luminous in the radio than most of the Seyferts. **1977** *Dædalus* Fall 56 The association of X-ray emitters with active compact galaxies.. has been confirmed by the discovery of an X-ray emission by the Seyfert galaxy 3C120..and of a dozen more Seyferts by Pounds and his associates working with Ariel-5.

**seyge**, obs. form of SIEGE.

**seygnery, -o(u)rye**, etc., obs. ff. SEIGNIORY.

**seyin**, variant of SYNE *adv.*, since.

**seyk, -nes**, obs. forms of SICK, -NESS.

**seyl(l(e:** see SAIL, SEAL, SELE.

**seym**, obs. form of SEAM *sb.*[1], *sb.*[2], SEEM *v.*[2]

**Seym**, var. SEJM.

**seymar**, variant of SIMAR.

**seyme**, obs. f. SEAM *sb.*[1], *sb.*[2]; Sc. var. SEAM *sb.*[3]

**seymland**, var. SEMBLAND *sb. Obs.*

**seymme**, obs. form of SEEM *v.*[2]

**seymouriamorph** (siːˈmɔərɪəmɔːf). [a. mod.L. name of suborder *Seymouriamorpha*, f. generic name *Seymouria* (F. Broili 1904, in *Palæontographica* LI. 81), f. *Seymour* name of a town in Baylor County, Texas + -IA[1].] A fossil tetrapod belonging to the suborder Seymouriamorpha, considered to include transitional forms between amphibians and reptiles.

**1945** A. S. ROMER *Vertebr. Paleontol.* (ed. 2) xxvii. 527 The degenerate genus *Kotlassia* represented the seymouriamorphs in the late Permian. **1977** A. HALLAM *Planet Earth* 269 The terrestrial anthracosaurs, known as seymouriamorphs, include the only large terrestrial amphibians known.

**seyn:** see SAY, SEE, SEEN, SENE, SYNE.

**seynct**, obs. form of SAINT.

**seynd**, obs. form of SIND *v.*, to rinse.

**1597** in *Spalding Club Misc.* (1841) I. 180 The said Isobel ..gatherit ane number of deid folkis baines, and seyndit thame in water.

**seynd, seyndil(l:** see SINGED *ppl. a.*[1], SENDLE.

†**ˈseyne.** *Obs. rare*[−1]. [a. OF. *seigné*, pa. pple. of *seigner* in the sense to assign, designate.] = ASSIGN *sb.*[2]

*a* **1500** *Brome Bk.* 140 [To] J. B. [and] T. P., to þe eyrys and seyneys of them.

**seyne:** see SAY, SEE, SENE, SENYE, SYNE.

**seyng(e:** see SAY *v.*[1], SEE *v.*, SING *v.*

**seynorye, -ourye**, obs. forms of SEIGNIORY.

†**seynt.** *Obs.* Also 4 saynt, (sayn), ceint, 4–5 seinte, ceynt(e, 4–6 seint, 5 saint, (sent). [a. OF. *ceint* masc., *ceinte* fem.:—popular L. *cinctum* neut., *cincta* fem. (whence Sp., Pg., It. *cinto, cinta*) = older L. *cinctu-s* (*u*-stem), f. *cingĕre* to gird.] A girdle.

*a* **1350** *Assumpt. Mary* 473 in Horstm. *Altengl. Leg.* (1881) 118 A saynt of silk..þat was obut hir medel done. **13..** *Gaw. & Gr. Knt.* 589 With silk sayn vmbe his syde. *Ibid.* 2431. *c* **1386** CHAUCER *Prol.* 329 A Sergeant of the Lawe.. Ther was..He rood but hoomly in a medlee cote Girt with a ceint [*v. rr.* ceynt, seynt, seint, sent] of silk with barres smale. **1399** LANGL. *Rich. Redeles* III. 140 For they..settith all her siluer in seintis and hornes. *c* **1400** *Ywaine & Gaw.* 1772 A riche robe als gan sho ta, And a saint of silk alswa. **1413** *Pilgr. Sowle* v. v. (1859) 76 Aungels..clothed..of reed bloody purpure, gyrd with ceyntes of gold. *c* **1440** *Promp. Parv.* 451/2 Seynt, or cors of a gyrdylle, *textum*. *c* **1530** *Crt. of Love* 817 With aureat seint about her sydes clene. **1530** PALSGR. 268/1 Seynt of a gyrdell, *tissu*.

**seynt**, obs. form of SAINT, SINGED *ppl. a.*[1]

**seyntery, -tuarie**, etc.: see SANCTUARY *sb.*[1]

**seynt graal**, obs. form of SANGRAIL.

†**seynture.** *Obs. rare*[−1]. [a. F. *ceinture*. Cf. CENTURE.] A waist-belt.

*c* **1400** *Beryn* 3925 The second brouȝt a swerd I-shethid, with seynture I-fretid all with perelis orient & pure.

**seyntwar(e**, variant forms of SAINTUAIRE *Obs.*

**seyntwary(e**, obs. forms of SANCTUARY *sb.*[1]

**seynur(r)ye, seyon:** see SEIGNIORY, SCION.

†**ˈseyny.** *Obs.* [a. OF. *seigné* bled, or *seignée* bleeding.] Used *attrib.* in ***seyny book*** (= *liber sanguinatorum* in *Consuet. Mon. S. Petri Westmon.* §317), a choir book provided for the use of monks who had lately been bled.

*c* **1492** in J. A. Robinson & M. R. James *MSS. Westm. Abbey* 9 Payments for the newe repairyng of the Seyny bookes. *Ibid.* 10.

**seyper**, var. SIPER.

**seyrch**, obs. f. SEARCH *v.*

**seys(e, seysere**, etc., obs. ff. CEASE *v.*, SEIZER.

**seyson(e, -oun, -yne**, obs. forms of SEASON *sb.*

**Seyssel** (ˈseɪsɛl). The name of two villages on the upper Rhône, used *attrib.* or *absol.* to designate various white wines made there.

**1926** P. M. SHAND *Book of Wine* v. 171 The best-known Savoy wine is Seyssel... Much of the wine sold as Seyssel only enjoys the type-name by courtesy. **1968** V. & M. PETTITT *Len Deighton's Travel Dossier* 46 *Savoy*... Seyssel wines (much is made into 'vin mousseux'). **1968** [see ROUSSETTE 3].

**seyt, -tte**, obs. forms of SEAT *sb.*

**seyth**, obs. form of SAITHE *Sc.*; var. SYTHE.

**Seyud, Seyyad, -id**, variant forms of SAYYID.

**seyverns**, pl. form of SEVERON *Obs.*

**seywinge**, obs. form of SHOWING *vbl. sb.*

**sez** (sɛz). ¶. Jocular spelling of *says*, 3rd person sing. pres. of SAY *v.*[1], esp. in representations of uneducated speech, and in phrase ***sez you*** (see SAY *v.*[1] 3 b).

**1844** 'J. SLICK' *High Life in N.Y.* I. i. 8 Cousin John took out his watch..and, sez he,—'Come, Mr. Slick.' **1886** F. H. BURNETT *Little Lord Fauntleroy* i. 9 Sez he to me: 'Mary,' sez he, 'I'm very much int'rusted in the 'lection,' sez he. **1904** WODEHOUSE *William Tell* vii. 45 'What I sez,' said Friesshardt, 'is, wot's the use of us wasting our time here?' **1930** *Outlook* (N.Y.) 12 Nov. 417/3, I am so tired of hearing sap, oh boy, and how, sez you, guts and dirty bum, that I could almost leave for the Fiji Islands to escape them. **1931** *Week-end Rev.* 24 Oct. 513/1 Mr. Lowe is well known for his invention of the famous catch-phrase 'Sez you!' **1933** DYLAN THOMAS *Let.* Nov. (1966) 53 May I borrow that foul expression of yours—it isn't yours, really—and whisper Sez You into his ear. **1940** H. G. WELLS *Babes in Darkling Wood* II. i. 125 They must not attempt either to monopolise or possess. (Sez we.) **1960** J. STROUD *Shorn Lamb* xi. 128 If I make a movement, he sez: 'Oh, don't be disgusting!' he sez. **1973** B. GRAEME *Two & Two make Five* xiii. 123 'He's..not nearly so useful in a rough house.' 'Sez you!' Sanders growled. **1977** [see SAY *v.*[1] 3 b].

‖**Sezession** (zetsɛsiˈoːn). *Art.* Pl. Sezessionen. [G.] = SECESSION 3 d.

**1905** *Burlington Mag.* VI. 422/2 The Austrian Government..did not look with a favourable eye upon this 'Sezession', and withheld all support which the 'Sezession' claimed as well as other societies of artists. **1959** P. & L. MURRAY *Dict. Art & Artists* 296 The *Sezessionen* were groups of artists in Germany and Austria who resigned from established academic bodies and exhibiting societies in order to forward the aims of various modern (usually Impressionist) movements. **1962** *Listener* 1 Mar. 384/3, I said nothing about..the artists of the *Sezession*. **1970** *Oxf. Compan. Art* 106/1 When in 1910 a number of young painters were rejected by the Sezession—among them members of Die Brücke—they started the *Neue Sezession*.

Also **Sezessioˈnist**, an artist belonging to the *Sezession*; **Sezessionstil** (-ˈʃtiːl) [G. *stil* style], the style of the *Sezession*.

**1958** M. L. WOLF *Dict. Painting* 264 *Sezessionists*, an art group in Vienna associated with the *art nouveau* movement, popular between 1890 and 1905. **1967** J. N. BARRON *Lang. of Painting* 19 In Belgium, it [sc. *Art Nouveau*] was associated with *Les Vingt* (The XX); in Vienna, with the Sezessionists. **1970** *Oxf. Compan. Art* 80/1 In Germany the style was called *Jugendstil*..; in Austria it was called *Sezessionstil*. **1978** *Country Life* 10 Aug. 394/1 (*caption*) The Bull Inn, Paisley. Built in 1900–1901..it combines Scottish Baronial features with a curved gable akin to the contemporary Viennese *Sezessionstil*.

**sferics** (ˈsfɛrɪks), *sb. pl.* orig. *U.S.* Also with capital initial; (*rarely*) **spherics**. [Contraction and respelling of ATMOSPHERICS *sb. pl.*] Atmospherics; sometimes used to denote a radio direction-finding system used to locate storms by means of the atmospherics they produce. Hence **ˈsferic** *a.*, of or pertaining to sferics.

**1945** in *U.S. Army Signal Res. & Development Lab., Techn. Rep.* 2199 (AD 266–795) (1961) 97 (*heading*) Military characteristics for automatic atmospherics (sferics) equipment. **1949** *Marine Observer* XIX. 199 'Sferic' is the code word which has been used for some years now to designate reports of positions of areas in which thunderstorms are taking place. **1951** R. C. WANTA in T. F. Malone *Compendium Meteorol.* 1297/1 Sferics (less commonly spherics) is a contraction of the word atmospherics meaning natural electrical phenomena detected by radio methods. **1963** T. PYNCHON *V.* ix. 230 As it turned out, the whistler was only the first of a family of sferics whose taxonomy was to include clicks, hooks, risers, nose-whistlers and one like a warbling of birds called the dawn chorus. **1968** B. W. ATKINSON *Weather Business* ii. 41 Sferic fixes depend on the radiation of electromagnetic waves caused by lightning flashes in the clouds. **1974** *Nature* 10 May 134/2 Observers under the balloon reported no thunder or lightning; thus we attribute the spherics to an intense thunderstorm system that was over the eastern United States at the time. *Ibid.*, Our local v.l.f. monitor recorded strong spheric activity.

†**S'fire,** *int. Obs. rare*[−1]. [See 'S.] Used as a minced oath.

**1791** O'KEEFFE *Wild Oats* I. i, *Sir Geo.* S'fire, my Lady.

†**'Sflesh,** *int. Obs.* [See 'S.] = FLESH *sb.* 9 d.

**1705** [T. WALKER] *Wit of a Woman* III. 29 'Sflesh I'm a Gentleman Soldier now. *Ibid.* 30.

†**'Sfoot,** *int. Obs.* Also 'sfut, sfut, sfoot(e, s'fut, s'foote. Shortened form of *God's foot*: see GOD 14 a.

**1602** MARSTON *Antonio's Rev.* IV. iii, Gods neakes he has wrong, that he has: and S'fut, an I were he, I would beare no coles. **1602** —— *Ant. & Mel.* v. H3, Sfoote, a sits like Lucifer himselfe. **1606** SHAKS. *Tr. & Cr.* II. iii. 6. **1616** B. JONSON *Ev. Man in Hum.* II. iv, 'Sfoot [**1598** *reads* Gods foot], I haue lost my purse, I thinke. **1662** [see FOOT *sb.* 1 b].

‖**sforzando** (sforˈtsando). *Mus.* [It., gerund of *sforzare* to force.] **a.** A musical direction indicating that the note so marked is to be specially emphasized or rendered louder than the rest. Abbreviated *sf.*, *sfz. Sfz. p.*, abbreviated form of ***sforzando piano***, suddenly loud followed by diminuendo or piano.

**1801** BUSBY *Dict. Mus.* (1811), *Sforzando*, or *Sforzato*, or SF. (Ital.). **1876** STAINER & BARRETT *Dict. Mus.* **1883** GROVE *Dict. Mus.*

**b.** As *sb.* Pl. sforzandi, sforzandos. A note or group of notes specially emphasized or rendered louder than the rest; an increase in loudness and emphasis; also *transf.* Also *attrib.* or as *adj.*

**1849** *Belfast News-Letter* 6 Feb. 4/4 Prima donna instrumentalists of the sforzando order. **1890** G. B. SHAW in *Scots Observer* 28 June 143/2 The smoothing-out of all the old jerks and jigs and *sforzandos* from the surface of the stream of melody. **1902** R. HICHENS *Londoners* 34 'Instant destruction', he repeated, with a slight sforzando. **1947** AUDEN in *Amer. Scholar* Autumn 405 Fill a Dwarf's ears with sforzandos and the dwarf will Believe he's a giant. **1956** T. BEECHAM 26 Apr. in H. Procter Gregg *Beecham Remembered* (1976) II. 180 Well, you know what dramatic effects are in my experience? It's making loud thumps on a percussion instrument, *sforzandi* in the strings—constant *sforzandi*—a few pathetic whinings on the wind, and sudden blasts on trumpets..and trombones. **1965** *New Statesman* 7 May 736/3 The woodwind skirls and *sforzando* brass exclamations still evoke the native dance-song. **1976** *Gramophone* Mar. 1463/1 He is meticulous in observing the jab of sudden sforzandos.

**c.** *Comb.* **sforzando coupler, pedal**: see quots.

**1876** HILES *Catech. Organ* iii. (1878) 20 The Sforzando coupler is a movement for increasing the power of the Swell instantaneously. **1881** C. A. EDWARDS *Organs* 114 The sforzando pedal is a coupler of great value.

‖**sforzato** (sforˈtsato). *Mus.* Pl. sforzati, sforzatos. [It., pa. pple. of *sforzare*: see prec.] = SFORZANDO.

**1801** [see SFORZANDO]. **1876** STAINER & BARRETT *Dict. Mus. Terms.* **1969** *Listener* 17 July 89/2 The hard sound of the first 'g' in the word is reflected in *sforzato* harp notes. **1976** *Daily Tel.* 8 Mar. 8/3 Presumably, if the lost autograph of the 32 in C minor had meanwhile surfaced,..with all *sforzatos* abolished, this fact would have been mentioned. **1977** 'E. CRISPIN' *Glimpses of Moon* iii. 41 '*Dernghl*' he exclaimed in his nose, imitating sforzato stopped horns. **1977** *Gramophone* Dec. 1098/2 No. 2 in E minor has as its first movement a funeral march that alternates between minor and major and is full of suspensions and *sforzati*. **1978** *Jrnl. R. Soc. Arts* CXXVI. 354/1 It is impossible for us to say definitely how soft is soft, or how loud is loud or how much emphasis to put on a sforzato.

‖**'sforzato.** *Obs. rare*[−1]. [Error for It. *forzato*.] A galley-slave. = FORSADO.

**1605** B. JONSON *Volpone* II. ii, I was condemn'd a 'Sforzato to the Galleys, for poysoning the Cardinall Bemboo's Cooke.

‖**sfumato** (sfuˈmato), *a.* (*sb.*) *Painting.* [It., lit. 'smoked'.] (See quot. 1869.) Also as *sb.*, the technique of softening outlines and allowing tones and colours to shade gradually into one another; a softened outline or hazy form produced in this way.

**1847** *Manual of Oil-Painting* 126 *Sfumato.* Painted with a light, vapoury touch. **1869** EASTLAKE *Mater. Hist. Oil Painting* II. 206 Another quality which was adopted from Leonardo..was the 'sfumato' system—the imperceptible softening of the transitions in half-tints and shadows. **1909** R. FRY *Let.* 16 Feb. (1972) I. 312 The black is a wonderful *sfumato* with scarcely any modelling. **1935** *Burlington Mag.* Feb. 72/2 The fine 'sfumato' and the delicacy of the surface. **1936** *Ibid.* Oct. 192/1 The influence of Venice is said to have succeeded the abandonment of Leonardo's *sfumato*. **1965** *New Statesman* 7 May 732/2 In all encounters with Leonardo there is never a definite answer to any of the artistic, aesthetic, historical or psychological questions which he raises. The *sfumato*—the suggestive smoke-like contour—is as much a characteristic of his personality as it is a feature of his drawing.

†**s'gad**, *int. Obs. rare*⁻¹. = EGAD.

**173.** FIELDING *Eurydice* Wks. 1771 III. 212 *Auth.* Ay! s'gad, I should as soon have suspected half the Dutchmen to be dancing-masters.

**sge**, early ME. form of SHE.

‖**sgraffiato** (sgraffi'ato). *Pottery.* Pl. **sgraffiati** (-ti). [It., pa. pple. of *sgraffiare* to scratch, to produce sgraffito: see SGRAFFITO.] = SGRAFFITO b.

**1862** J. C. ROBINSON in *Catal. Special Exhibition Wks. of Art S. Kensington Mus.* (1863, rev. ed.) Section xxi. 400 (*heading*) Sgraffiato or Incised Wares. **1900** F. LITCHFIELD *Pott. & Porc.* ii. 13 This ware has been termed *sgraffiati, sgraffiato*, or incised ware. **1957** MANKOWITZ & HAGGAR *Conc. Encycl. Eng. Pott. & Porc.* 71/2 Several important slipware potteries existed in North Devon... Jugs and other presentation wares decorated in *sgraffiato* style with mariner's compasses, Royal arms, country scenes, or birds and foliage are typical. **1973** *Times Lit. Suppl.* 28 Dec. 1590/3 The medieval sgraffiato pottery of north and north-west Iran was based on Sasanian metal-work. **1980** *Catal. Fine Chinese Ceramics* (Sotheby, Hong Kong) 24 A large sgraffiato jar with shouldered ovoid body.

‖**sgraffito** (sgraf'fito). Also 7 **sgrafit**. Pl. **sgraffiti** (sgraf'fiti). [It.: see GRAFFITO; the prefix *s-* represents L. *ex-* (see EX-).] **a.** (See quots. Cf. GRAFFITO.)

**1730** BAILEY (fol.), *Sgrafit*, a method of Painting in black and white only, not in *fresco*. **1847** *Manual of Oil-Painting* 126 *Sgraffito.* A kind of bold design, in black and white, done by scratching a wall where it was purposely painted of the former hue. **1847** EASTLAKE *Mater. Hist. Oil Painting* I. 150 Works so produced must have resembled the *nielli*, or, on a small scale, the *sgraffiti* of the Italians. **1902** BALDRY *Mod. Mural Decoration* 101 The term sgraffito is now limited to a particular method of scratching lines upon a plaster surface... The plaster is so laid that the incisions in an upper coat reveal a lower stratum of a contrasting colour.

*attrib.* **1883** *L'pool Daily Post*, Panels in Sgraffito work. **1886** *Offic. Catal. Col. & Ind. Exhib.* 53 Layer upon layer of coloured lac are laid. Then, with a stylus, these coats are scratched through in a manner analogous to Italian *sgraffito* decoration.

**b.** *Pottery.*

**1878** [see DOULTON]. **1889** C. T. DAVIS *Pract. Treat. Bricks*, etc. xv. 463 Each clay is to be separately compressed, unless sgraffito effects are desired. **1897** SPARKES & GANDY *Potters* 237 The introduction, in 1867–1870, of the 'Doulton-ware Sgraffito' pottery. These were vases and jugs made in the common pipe-clay, with simple incised or stamped patterns, coloured equally simply.

**Sgt.**, abbrev. of SERGEANT *sb.*

**1899** *Morning Post* 6 Dec. 5/2 No. 3732 Squad.-Sgt.-Maj. should be Shoeing-Smith John Hobbs. **1909** *Army & Navy Gaz.* 10 Apr. 342/2 Sgt. Huntley beat Sgt. Kilvert. **1948** *R.A.F. Rev.* June 22/3 Sgt. A. Roff, R.A.F., Selitar, Singapore. **1977** *Belfast Tel.* 28 Feb. 1/7 'Sgt. Joe', as he was affectionately known, was considered to be the model village policeman.

**sh**, a consonantal digraph representing the simple sound (ʃ). In late OE. this sound was represented by the combination *sc*, which retained its original phonetic value (sk) only in words of foreign origin. The sound (ʃ) did not exist in early OF., and hence the early ME. texts, written by French-educated scribes, show great diversity of attempts to find expression for it. The OE. notation by *sc* became rare after the 12th c. Some scribes of the 12–13th c. used the single *s* initially and finally. More frequent was *ss* (used in all positions), which is found as late as 1340 (*Ayenbite*). In medial and final positions *ssh* was common from the 13th to the 16th c.; Coverdale (1535) has frequently *szsh*, sometimes *szh* (but also often *sh*). The prevailing form from the end of the 12th c. to the end of the 14th c. was *sch* (initially; in other positions it was less frequent); in the north it was common down to the end of the 16th c. In the 13th c. we occasionally find *sge*, *sȝe*, *sze* for *she* (rarely *sȝ* or *sz* in other words), and in the 14–15th c. some East Anglian scribes wrote *xal*, *xulde* for *shall*, *should*. In ME. texts the suffix *-ship* is often written *-chipe*, and sometimes *ch* occurs as the symbol of (ʃ) in other positions.

The combination *sh* (probably to be regarded as a simplification of *sch*) is regularly used in the *Ormulum c* 1200 and frequently in the *Trinity College Homilies* of about the same date. It is the usual symbol in the London documents of the 14th c. and in the MSS. of Chaucer, and from the time of Caxton onwards it has been the established notation for (ʃ) in all words except those which (as *machine*, *schedule*, *Asia*, the derivatives in *-tion*, etc.) are spelt unphonetically on etymological grounds.

In some compounds as *dishonest*, *mishap*, *Gateshead*, *s* and *h* come together without forming a digraph. The pronunciation of some proper names in which this sequence occurs has been affected by misinterpretation of the spelling; e.g. Evesham is often called ('iːvʃəm), Petersham ('piːtəʃəm).

**sh** (ʃ), *int.* Also written **'sh** (as if an abbrev. of *hush*). An exclamation used to enjoin silence or noiselessness; = HUSH *int.* The reduplication or prolongation of the sound is indicated by *sh-sh*, *s-s-sh*, and the like (see quots.).

**1847** *Man in the Moon* II. 114 He..imposed silence by a long-drawn S-s-s-s-s-s-sh! **1848** THACKERAY *Van. Fair* xix, When anybody entered the room, she uttered a *shshshsh* so sibilant and ominous, that it frightened the poor old lady in her bed. **1867** MISS BROUGHTON *Cometh Up* xxvi, Sh! Sh! don't make a scene! **1883** HOWELLS *Register* ii. in *Harper's Mag.* Dec. 79/2 'Sh! Listen. **1893** ASHBY-STERRY *Naughty Girl* vii. 66 S-s-sh! Don't make a noise!

**b.** Used (in reduplicated form) to express a low faint rustling or swishing sound. Cf. SHISH.

**1878** BESANT & RICE *Monks of Thelema* xli, The gardener's boy sharpened his scythe musically, and then began again his low and gentle sh-sh-sh over the lawn.

**sh** (ʃ), *v.* Also **sh-sh-sh**. [f. SH *int.*; cf. SHSHSH, SHUSH *v.*] **a.** *trans.* To reduce to silence or tranquillity with the sound of 'sh!', or attempt to do so.

**1887** A. J. EVANS *At Mercy of Tiberius* vii. 125, I patted and, 'she-e-d' her [*sc.* a baby], but she got her head above cover..and..set up a squall. **1916** 'B. CABLE' *Action Front* 62 Ainsley 'sh-sh-sh-ed' him to silence.

**b.** *intr.* To become quiet in response to an order 'sh!'.

**1925** 'R. CROMPTON' *Still—William* iii. 53 'Sh!' William said fiercely. Violet Elizabeth 'Sh'd' obediently. **1972** WODEHOUSE *Pearls, Girls, & Monty Bodkin* ix. 136 She uttered a 'Sh!' of such significance that Grayce instinctively lowered her voice. 'Mrs. Molloy!' 'Sh!' Grayce might have retorted that she *had* sh-ed and that if she sh-ed any further she could become inaudible.

**sh.**, abbreviation of *shilling.*

**1607–8** *Aberd. Acc.* in *Spalding Club Miscell.* V. 135 Item, for four buistis, at ten sh. the buist, is 2 lib. **1730** A. MALCOLM *Syst. Arith.* 79 The Sum is 68*d.* which I divide by 12 (because 12*d.* = 1 *sh.*).

**sh-, sh'**, formerly used for *she* in certain elisions, as *sh'as* for 'she has'.

**1575** *Gammer Gurton's Needle* III. iv. 8 Shase as much wyt in her head almost as chaue in mine! *Ibid.* IV. ii. 23 Chad thought shad stopt hir throte. **1611** MIDDLETON & DEKKER *Roaring Girl* II. i. D 1 b, Life, sh'as the Spirit of foure great parishes. **1620** *Westward for Smelts* (Percy Soc.) 20 Twice thirtie yeeres, Sha'd past with cares. **1631** KNEVET *Rhodon & Iris* III. i. E 3, Sometimes sh'applauds a pavement-sweeping traine.

‖**sha** (ʃɑː). [? Shortened f. SHAPOO.] The oorial (*Ovis cycloceros*). Also applied to *O. vignei*.

**1842** VIGNE *Trav. Kashmir* II. 280 The Shâ is a tragelaphus, or goat-deer. **1893** LYDEKKER *Horns & Hoofs* 77 The so-called sha (Ovis-vignei) of the upper Indus valley. **1894** *Lydekker's Roy. Nat. Hist.* II. 223 The Asiatic wild sheep known in the Punjab as the urial, but in Ladak as the sha.

**sha**, obs. form of SHAH.

**shaake, shaar(e, shaarpe**, obs. ff. SHAKE, SHARE, SHARP.

**shab** (ʃæb), *sb.* Forms: 1 **sceabb, scæb, sceb**, 3 **schabbe**, 4 **shabbe**, 4– **shab**. [OE. *sceabb* masc. corresponding to ON. **skabbr* SCAB *sb.*, f. Teut. root **skab-* to scratch, SHAVE:—Indogermanic **skăbh-*, whence L. *scabiēs* itch, *scabĕre* (perf. *scābī*) to scratch. From the same root are Flem. dial. *schab* (Kilian *schabbe*), mod.G. *schäbe* (*schabe*, dial. *schabbe*) itch.]

**1.** = SCAB *sb.* 1–3. Now only *dial.*, a cutaneous disease in sheep (= SCAB *sb.* 2).

*c* **897** K. ÆLFRED *Gregory's Past. Care* xi. 70 Se hæfð singalne sceabb þe næfre ne blinð unȝestæððiȝnesse. *c* **1000** *Sax. Leechd.* I. 322 Eac hyt afeormaþ ðone leahtor ..þe hy achoras nemnað þæt ys sceb [*v.r.* scæb]. *c* **1290** *St. Francis* 309 in *S. Eng. Leg.* 62 Þo bi-gan þe souwe a-non.. To beo ful of schabbe and of buyles. **13..** *Pol. Songs* (1839) 239 He shrapeth on is shabbes. **1382** WYCLIF *Lev.* xxii. 22 Litil bleynes, or with shab, or drye round shab. **1806** *Med. Jrnl.* XV. 518 They were afflicted, not with the sheep-pox, but with the scab, or shab. **1810** *Sporting Mag.* XXXV. 30 Our poor kiddy..which died yesterday of the shab. **1825** LOUDON *Encycl. Agric.* §6522 (Sheep) The scab, shab, ray, or rubbers. **1886** *W. Somerset Word-bk.*, *Shab*, scab in sheep.

**2.** *slang.* A low fellow (= SCAB *sb.* 4). ? *Obs.*

**1637** BASTWICK *Litany* I. 19 Neither are those Shabs for any merit in themselues..worthy to giue guts vnto a beare. **1735** DYCHE & PARDON *Dict.*, *Shab*, a mean, sorry, pitiful Fellow, one that is guilty of low Tricks &c. **1837** BAYLY *Songs & Ball.* (1844) II. 40, I belong to the Club, which is very genteel—We ne'er let a Scamp or a Shab in. **1851** BORROW *Lavengro* xcviii, 'Any name but that, you shab,' said Black Jack.

**shab** (ʃæb), *v. Obs.* exc. *dial.* [Of obscure origin; sense 2 suggests connexion with SHAB *sb.* 2.]

**1.** *trans.* with *off*: **a.** To get rid of; get (a person) out of the way.

**1677** W. HUBBARD *Narrative* Postscr. T 3 b, Certain Nipnets intended to have sheltred themselves under Vncas; but he perceiving it would be distastful to the English, soon shab'd them off. **1698** FARQUHAR *Love & Bottle* IV. iii, I have shabb'd him off purely. *a* **1824** in Mactaggart *Gallovid. Encycl.* 347 They shab'd puir Thomas aff to hell Wi nimble feet. **1828** CROKER *Fairy Leg. S. Irel.* II. 212 But when that [money] was gone..they soon shabbed him off.

**b.** To put (a person) off *with* (something inferior or unsatisfactory). Cf. FOB *v.* 3.

**1840** J. P. KENNEDY *Quodlibet* iii. (1860) 61, I hold the people in too much esteem to shab them off with anything of a secondary quality.

**2.** *intr.* with *off* or *away*: To slink away, sneak off. Also, to fall away from one's engagement.

*a* **1700** B. E. *Dict. Cant. Crew*, *Shab'd off*, sneakt, or slid away. **1720** *Humourist* 185 And so the fat Parson shabb'd off. **1829** BROCKETT *N.C. Words*, *Shab-off*, *Shab-away*, to sneak away. **1880** *W. Cornw. Gloss.* s.v., He wanted to shab-off without paying.

**b.** (See quot.)

**1755** JOHNSON, To *Shab* v.n., to play mean tricks; a low barbarous cant word.

†**3.** *trans.* ? To rob. *Obs.*

**1787** W. HUTTON *Courts of Requests* xxxvii. 187 He bore it like a philosopher; to be shabbed was nothing new, he had often lost everything he had, but himself.

†**shabaroon, shabroon.** *slang. Obs.* Also 7 **shabberoon**, 9 **shabbaroon**. [? f. SHAB *sb.*, after *picaroon*.] A disreputable person, ragamuffin.

*a* **1700** B. E. *Dict. Cant. Crew*, *Shabberoon*, a Ragamuffin. **1703** E. WARD *London Spy* xv. (1706) 366 Poor loose Shabroons in Bawdy-Houses Bred. **1762–7** T. BRIDGES *Hom. Trav.* (1797) II. 11 That no more rogues to-day may drop, Go you and all your shabroons stop. **1797** MRS. A. M. BENNETT *Beggar Girl* (1813) I. 21 Letting a tribe of shabroons and painted Jezebels into their honest house. **1838** *New Monthly Mag.* LIV. 214 If..a recognition from a coroneted carriage stamps you a lord,..the notice of a shabaroon can be nothing less than a hint to your tailor to send in his bill. **1847** HALLIWELL, *Shabbaroon*, a mean shabby fellow.

*attrib.* **1786** MRS. A. M. BENNETT *Juvenile Indiscr.* V. 56 Trap answered, he believed he had nobody belonging to him worth seeking after, for that he was but a shabroon sort of a gem'man.

**Shabas**, var. SHABBOS.

‖**shabash** (ʃa'baʃ), *int.* [Hindi or Urdu.] Well done! Also as *sb.*, an exclamation of *Shabash!*

**1843** C. I. C. DAVIDSON *Travels in Upper India* I. 209, I was awakened at night from a sound sleep by the repeated *savâshes! wâh! wâhs!* from the residence of the thannadar. **1886** YULE & BURNELL *Hobson-Jobson* 618/1 *Shabash!* interj. 'Well done!' 'Bravo!' Pers. *Shāh-bāsh*. 'Rex fias!' **1901** KIPLING *Kim* iv. 105 'Oh, *shabash*!' murmured Kim..'Well done, indeed?' **1907** P. S. ALLEN *Let.* 8 Mar. (1939) 58 However in 10 days I shall be clear for Erasmus for the rest of the year. Shabash! **1974** H. R. F. KEATING *Bats fly up for Inspector Ghote* iii. 24 Cries of 'Jolly good show' and 'Shabash, Inspector, shabash.'

**shabbaron**, obs. form of CHAPERON.

**shabbaroon**, variant of SHABAROON.

‖**Shabbat** (ʃa'bat). Also **Shabat, Shabbath**. [Heb. *šabbāṯ* SABBATH. Cf. SHABBOS.] Among Sephardic Jews and in the State of Israel: the Sabbath. Also in phr. ***Shabbat shalom*** [SHALOM *int.* and *sb.*], 'peaceful Sabbath', a form of salutation used on the Sabbath.

**1934** WEBSTER, Shabbath. **1965** J. A. MICHENER *Source* 42 After we see it, why don't we go on to Zefat? It'll be Shabbat and we can attend the Vodzher Rebbe's synagogue. **1966** L. DAVIDSON *Long Way to Shiloh* viii. 116 'All right. Thanks. Shalom.' 'Shabat Shalom.' **1971** D. MEIRING *Wall of Glass* ii. 21 What would Arabs be doing on Tel Aviv beach?.. Above all on a Shabat? *Ibid.* v. 40 I'd been waiting for the sound of the ram's horn, to light my Shabat candles. **1976** C. BERMANT *Coming Home* I. iii. 47 There is a traditional Jewish dish called *cholent*..normally eaten for Shabbat lunch. **1980** *Encounter* Oct. 56/2 We bade each other *shabbat shalom.*

**b.** *Comb.*, as **Shabbat-goy** = *Sabbath goy* s.v. SABBATH 4.

**1859** [see REMNANT *sb.* 2 b].

**shabbed**, *a. Obs.* exc. *dial.* Forms: 1 **sceabbede, scæbbede**, 4–5 **schabbed, shabbid, -yd**, 7– **shabbed**. [f. SHAB *sb.* + -ED². Cf. SCABBED.]

**1.** Afflicted with scab or scabs; = SCABBED *a.* 1.

*a* **1100** in Napier *O.E. Glosses* 126/4929 *Purulentus*, scæbbede [*v.r.* sceabbede], ættræn. **1362** LANGL. *P. Pl.* A. VIII. 17 Hou heore schabbede schep schal heore wolle saue. *a* **1400–50** *Stockh. Med. MS.* 101 For schabbed hands.

**2.** = SHABBY.

**1674** R. GODFREY *Inj. & Abus. Physick* 63 The Chymical Doctor..offered him his help contrary to his custome, (for I believe he hateth that shabbed trick of asking people to buy health). *a* **1687** COTTON *Poems* (1689) 94 We..Had happy been had we chang'd features, Garments at least, though theirs be shabbed, With those who that cold place inhabit. **1716** HEARNE *Collect.* (O.H.S.) V. 210 He died in a shabbed Condition, as he lived. **1891** 'M. GRAY' *In Heart of Storm* Prol. i. I. 28 My best bonnet was that shabbed I didn't like to go to church of a fine Sunday.

**shabberoon**, variant of SHABAROON.

**shabbify** ('ʃæbɪfaɪ), *v.* [f. SHABBY *a.* + -FY.] *trans.* To make shabby. Also *fig.*

**1866** *All Year Round* 9 June 518 Walking over Mont Cenis..has somewhat shabbified my travelling attire. **1961** E. WILLIAMS *George* xi. 149 Thomas became, for life, Tom, ..and Biblical Job..was overnight shabbified into Joe.

**shabbily** ('ʃæbɪlɪ), *adv.* [-LY².] In a shabby manner (see the adj.).

**1755** JOHNSON, *Shabbily*, meanly; reproachfully; despicably; paltrily. A cant word. **1756** MRS. DELANY *Autobiog.* (1861) III. 417 Madame de Sevigné goes on but shabbily: this cold weather numbs my faculties. **1781** J. Ripley *Sel. Orig. Lett.* 47 The caparisons upon his horse, shabbily splendid. **1821** J. W. Croker *Diary* 12 June, Burdett.. comes shabbily off, for he denies a meaning which his words have. **1829** Lytton *Devereux* III. vi, A little dark man, shabbily dressed. **1870** Miss Bridgman *R. Lynne* II. ii. 23 The rooms were furnished shabbily. **1879** F. W. Robinson *Coward Consc.* IV. i, Fanny behaved so shabbily to your brother.

**shabbiness** ('ʃæbɪnɪs). [-ness.] The quality or state of being shabby (in various senses).

**1711** Addison *Spect.* No. 31 ¶1 The Shabbiness of his Dress. **1712** Steele *Ibid.* No. 264 ¶2 His gay Shabbyness of Clothes. **1827** Syd. Smith *Cath. Quest.* Wks. 1859 II. 120/1 Explaining away this sale of your soul by every species of falsehood, shabbiness, and equivocation. **1863** Miss Braddon *Eleanor's Vict.* I. i. 3 In spite of.. the shabbiness of her straw bonnet. **1899** Doyle *Duet* (1909) 69/1 His occasional shabbiness in money matters.

**shabble**: see shable.

‖**Shabbos** ('ʃabəs). Also Shabas, Shabbes, Shabbuss, Shabes, Shabus. Pl. -im. [Yiddish *shabes* ad. Heb. *šabbāṯ* Sabbath. See also Shabbat.] Among Ashkenazi Jews: the Sabbath. Also *attrib.* Phr. ***to make Shabbos***, to prepare for the Sabbath.

**1876** Geo. Eliot *Dan. Der.* II. iv. xxxiii. 348 'Shlav'm Shabbes fyock on,' said Adelaide Rebekah. 'Her Sabbath frock... She'll have her Sabbath frock on this evening.' **1892** I. Zangwill *Childr. Ghetto* I. 151, I shall have no fish for Shabbos. **1959** H. Pinter *Birthday Party* I. 14 After lunch on Shabbus we'd go and sit in a couple of deck-chairs. **1960** F. Raphael *Limits of Love* III. iv. 317 The chauffeur always carried a box of good things.. which the inmates came to enjoy on the following *shabas* eve. **1968** M. Richler in R. Weaver *Canad. Short Stories* 2nd Ser. 150 We're orthodox here. Today is *shabus*. **1968** L. Rosten *Joys of Yiddish* 318 *Shabbes* begins just before sunset on Friday. The wife and mother, dressed in her very best, lights the *Shabbes* candles and offers a benediction. **1975** C. Potok *In Beginning* ii. 126 Yesterday was such a nice day. It was a pleasure to make Shabbos yesterday. *Ibid.* iii. 185 I'll read it [*sc.* the Torah].. in the synagogue, for Shabbosim and holidays. **1979** H. Howard *Sealed Envelope* xiv. 181 Every week she expects you for shabbos dinner but always you have excuses.

**b.** *Comb.*, as **Shabbos-goy** [goy] = *Sabbath goy* s.v. Sabbath 4; also fem. **Shabbos-goya(h**; also *fig.*

**1892** I. Zangwill *Childr. Ghetto* I. 158 Poor women, frequently Irish, known as *Shabbos-goyahs* or *fire-goyahs*, acted as stokers to the Ghetto at twopence a hearth. **1959** M. Wilson *They came as Strangers* III. iii. 194 Victor Gollancz's parents were strictly orthodox,.. never took a bus on the Sabbath and had a *Shabbes goy* to light the fires on that day. **1962** B. Abrahams tr. *Life of Glückel of Hameln* IV. 102 Send the *shabbos-goya* to me. I want to send her somewhere. **1969** A. Laski *Dominant Fifth* v. 187 Perhaps.. we.. have deliberately assimilated him, made him a tame cat, or *Shabbos-goy*. **1978** *Maledicta* 1977 I. 323 Reinhold Aman, president, director, chief-lucubrator and *shabes-goy* of Maledicta, edits, typesets and publishes this journal considered by the repressed as a Gross Encounter of the Worst Kind.

**shabby** ('ʃæbɪ), *a.* [f. shab *sb.* + -y. Cf. scabby; also LG. *schabbig, schäbbig*, MHG. *schebic* (mod.G. *schäbig* = sense 1 below).

'A word that has crept into conversation and low writing; but ought not to be admitted into the language' (J.).]

**1. a.** That has lost its newness or freshness of appearance; dingy and faded from wear or exposure. Said of clothes, furniture, houses, etc.

**1685** *Lond. Gaz.* No. 2070/4 Having a Gray Coloured Coat and a shabby Perriwig. **1716** Lady M. W. Montagu *Let. to C'tess of Bristol* 22 Aug., In the other, you see a sort of shabby finery. **1763** R. Lloyd *New-River Head* 11 With the drap'ry she had got Within her little shabby cot. **1765** Goldsm. *Ess.* xxi. [vi.] ¶1 A man in very shabby cloaths. **1838** Dickens *Nich. Nick.* xvi, There was a stream of people pouring into a shabby house. **1866** G. Macdonald *Ann. Q. Neighb.* vi. (1878) 82 It was an old book in very shabby binding. **1884** W. C. Smith *Kildrostan* 65, I should have been a poacher In shabby velveteen. **1889** Jessopp *Coming of Friars* iii. 123 The surest token that a monastery was in a bad way was that its church was in a shabby condition.

**b.** Of persons, their appearance, etc.: Poorly-dressed, 'seedy'.

**1669** Ogilby *Odyss.* xxiii. 334 Shabby my looks, so mean my garments be, That for her lord she'll not acknowledge me. **1688** Clarendon *Diary* 7 Dec., They were very shabby fellows, pitifully mounted, and worse armed. *a* **1700** B. E. *Dict. Cant. Crew*, *Shabby*, in poor, sorry Rigging. **1782** Miss Burney *Cecilia* II. i, [She] was shewn, by a little shabby footboy, into a parlour. **1882** Miss Braddon *Mt. Royal* II. ix. 179 He lived with a shabby old half-pay father.

**c.** *transf.* Discreditably inferior in quality, making a poor appearance.

**1805** T. F. Fremantle *Let.* 1 Aug. in P. Fremantle *Wynne Diaries* (1940) III. vii. 195, I shall not apologise.. for the very shabby letters I have been.. writing to you. **1820** Lady Granville *Lett.* (1894) I. 191 Excuse this shabby letter. **1824** Syd. Smith *Wks.* (1859) II. 46/2 We Scotch, who live in a little shabby scraggy corner of a remote island. **1852** Thackeray *Esmond* II. xiv, My Lord Duke's entertainments were both seldom and shabby. **1865** Mill *Exam. Hamilton* 448 Who, then, would expect such shabby, not arguments, but mists of arguments, as the author presents us with. **1880** E. A. Freeman in W. R. W. Stephens *Life & Lett.* (1895) II. 198 Unless they have mended their ways at Laon since 1869, you will hear the shabbiest of masses there.

**2. a.** Of persons, their actions, etc.: Contemptibly mean, ungenerous, or dishonourable. Often applied, in a lighter tone, to conduct which is less friendly or generous than one had hoped for.

**1679** J. Sheffield (Dk. Buckhm.) *Charac. Tory* Wks. 1729 II. 66 These shabby fellows who pretend to be robbed. *a* **1720** Sewel *Hist. Quakers* VII. (1722) 374 Among these was a shabby Fellow, who to get Victuals without working, had thrust himself among the Quakers. **1763** Ld. Holland in Jesse *Selwyn & Contemp.* (1843) I. 270 Stephen gives his compliments, but says you left Paris in a shabby manner. **1840** Thackeray *Bedford-Row Consp.* i, It was voted a shabby excuse. **1850** Smedley *Frank Fairlegh* xv, It would be horribly shabby of you to desert us now. **1892** W. S. Gilbert *Mountebanks* I, What shabby things a man will do when he's eaten up with jealousy.

**b.** Mean or ungenerous in giving or paying.

**1766** [Anstey] *Bath Guide* v. 7 So I took out my Purse, as I hate to be shabby. **1863** P. Barry *Dockyard Econ.* 154 The Admiralty, always generous to profusion to unworthy people,.. is shabby to the sailor.

**c.** Of a gift or the like: Small or poor as estimated by the giver's means.

**1753** Miss Collier *Art Torment.* II. iii. (1811) 139 Make him some shabby allowance, hardly enough to keep him from starving. **1857** Livingstone *Trav. S. Africa* iii. 68, I, being.. familiar with their customs, knew that this shabby present was an insult to us.

**3.** †**a.** ? Dirty, muddy. *Obs. rare*$^{-1}$.

**1705** Berkeley *Cave of Dunmore* Wks. 1871 IV. 504 A spacious vault, the bottom whereof is always shabby by reason of the continual distillation of rock-water.

**b.** *dial.* and *colloq.* Of weather: Wet and unpleasant.

**1853** D. G. Rossetti *Let.* 12 July (1965) I. 148 The weather had been generally very shabby. **1855** *Whitby Gloss.* s.v., A wet shabby day. **1950** W. Stevens *Let.* 1 Feb. (1967) 663 While we have had an occasional day of proper winter, mostly it has been pretty shabby.

**4.** Of the pulse: Weak.

**1843** R. J. Graves *Syst. Clin. Med.* xiv. 175 His pulse was 140 in a minute and remarkably shabby. **1906** *Brit. Med. Jrnl.* 13 Jan. 70 A rapid shabby pulse.

**5.** *dial.* Diseased with 'shab' or scab; = scabby 1.

App. the original meaning, though not recorded early.

**1825** Jennings *Obs. Dial. W. Eng.* 66 *Shabby*, affected with the shab. **1886** *W. Somerset Word-bk.* s.v., They sheep be shabby.

**6.** *Comb.*, as †***shabby-looked, -looking*** adjs.

**1705** Mrs. Centlivre *Gamester* I. i, But, Sir, here was a kind of a—kind of a shabby-look'd fellow. **1853** Kane *Grinnell Exp.* xl. (1856) 365 We are an uncouth, snobby, and withal, shabby-looking set of varlets.

**shabby** ('ʃæbɪ), *v.* [f. the adj.] **1.** *intr.* To act shabbily. *rare.*

**1898** M. Deland *Old Chester Tales* 213 'They'll be shabbying on me,' said Katy.

**2.** *trans.* and *intr.* To make or become shabby.

**1912** *Daily Chron.* 5 Mar. 9/2 She will probably find that a good deal of the.. 'shabbying' of her clothes is caused by .. throwing her dresses carelessly down on chairs. **1920** H. Begbie *Life of W. Booth* I. iii. 56 The shadow of poverty deepening every day upon the shabbying walls of his unhappy home. **1962** D. Lessing *Golden Notebk.* IV. 536 You'll be one of those tough, square, solid middle-aged men, like a shabbying brown bear, your golden crew-cut greying judiciously at the temples.

'**shabby-gen'teel**, *a.* Attempting to look genteel and keep up appearances in spite of shabbiness. Also *absol.*

**1754** in *Connoisseur* No. 25. 146 The numerous fraternity of the shabby-genteel, who are the chief support of the clothiers in Monmouth-street. **1800** Helena Wells *Const. Neville* (ed. 2) II. 342 A tall meagre female,.. whose habiliments might come under the description of shabby genteel. **1821** W. Cobbett *Rur. Rides* (1885) I. 50 Shabby-genteel houses, surrounded with dead fences, and things called gardens. **1868** Alex. Smith *Last Leaves* 76 He has.. a feeling of respect for shabby-genteel virtues. **1874** Micklethwaite *Mod. Par. Churches* 341 A shabby-genteel imitation of an expensive building.

Hence **shabby-gentility**.

**1829** Carlyle *German Playwrights* in *Foreign Rev.* III. 115 Old threadbare material, scoured up into a state of shabby-gentility. **1836** Dickens *Sk. Boz, Charac.* x, This compound of the two—this shabby-gentility. **1898** G. B. Shaw *Plays Pleasant & Unpleasant* II. 156 The shifts of impecunious shabby-gentility.

'**shabbyish**, *a.* [-ish.] Somewhat shabby.

**1830** Carlyle *Let.* 21 Aug. in Froude *Life* (1882) II. 120 A cold-hearted, shabbyish, dandy parson. **1864** Burton *Scot Abr.* I. i. 25 The advancement of one of his brothers from the shabbyish bishopric of Poitiers to the brilliant see of Paris.

**Shabes**, var. Shabbos.

**shable, shabble** ('ʃæb(ə)l). *Sc.* Also 7 shabel, schable. [ad. It. *sciabla, sciabola*, or Hungarian *szábl̲ya*, Polish *szabla*, parallel forms to Du. *sabel*, G. *sabel* (now *säbel*): see sable *sb.*³, sabre.]

**1.** A sabre or curved sword.

'Now generally used to denote an old rusty sword' (Jam.).

**1632** Lithgow *Trav.* v. 208 Shables, or short crooked swords. **1683** Sir J. Turner *Pallas Arm.* 171 The Persians, Turks, Russians, Polonians, and Hungarians, for most part wear Scimiters and Shables. **1689** *Lond. Gaz.* No. 414/2 One of them had his left Arm cut off with one blow of a Schable or Polish sword. **1749** Crookshank *Hist. Ch. Scot.* II. 22 At last, the Commander struck him with a shabble on the face. **1818** Scott *Rob Roy* xxviii, He tugged for a second or two at the hilt of his *shabble*, as he called it. **1895** Crockett *Men of Mosshags* 75 He would strike them on the face with the basket hilt of his shable.

**2.** 'Any little person or thing' (Jam.).

**1842** Carlyle *Let.* 19 Apr. in Froude *Life Lond.* (1884) I. ix. 251 Fly away with your shabble of a Duke.

‖**shabracque, shabrack** ('ʃæbræk). Also 9 shubrach, (chabrague, shabrag), schabraque, shabraque. [a. G. *schabracke*, F. *schabraque* (also *chabraque*), from some lang. of Eastern Europe: cf. Russ. *chaprak*, Czech *čabrak(a, čapraka, šabraka*, Magyar *csabrág*, Turkish *čāprāq*.] A saddle-cloth used in European armies.

*c* **1808** Porter *Russ. & Swed.* (1813) II. xxxi. 59 The leopard-skin shubrach (or saddle covering). **1821** *Sporting Mag.* VII. 151 A saddle-cloth vying in size with the shabrack of a heavy dragoon. **1838** *Hist. Rec. Life Guards* 190 Sheepskin Shabraques, black for the Officers, and white for the Men. **1865** Miller *Equipm. Artillery* 74 Shabraque. .. Worn by officers of horse brigades only. **1904** *Dress Regulat. Officers* 17, 18 Shabracque. **1908** Bain *Slav. Europe* 213 Their.. shabracks ablaze with precious stones.

'**shab-rag**, *a.* and *sb. dial.* and *slang.*

**A.** *adj.* Shabby, damaged, the worse for wear.

**1762–7** T. Bridges *Hom. Trav.* (1797) II. 254 None of your Bromingham affairs, Nor any such like shabrag wares, But good new halfpence from the mint, With honest George's face in print. **1880** *W. Cornw. Gloss.* s.v. *Horny-wink*, An old tumble-down house has been revilingly described as an old shabrag horny-wink place.

**B.** *sb.* A mean beggarly person, a ragamuffin.

**1828** [Carr] *Craven Gloss.* **1829** Brockett *N.C. Words.* **1869** R. B. Peacock *Lonsdale Gloss.* **1879** Miss Jackson *Shropsh. Word-bk.*, *Shab-rag*, a term of contempt applied to persons of dirty, depraved appearance.

**shabroon**: see shabaroon.

‖**shabti** ('ʃæbtiː). *Egyptology.* [a. Egyptian *šbty*.] = ushabti. Cf. shawabti.

**1864** *Zeitschrift für Ägyptische Sprache und Alterhumskunde* Oct./Nov. 90 The principal variants of the names of these figures have been given by M. Chabas as ..*šuabti*,..*šabt*,..*šabti* and..*šebti*; to these.. may be added many additional forms. **1935** W. M. F. Petrie (*title*) Shabtis. **1936** *Times Lit. Suppl.* 18 July 601/1 Next to the scarab the *shabti* is perhaps the object most readily acquired by visitors to Egypt... This book is of first importance for the study of *shabti*-figures. **1953** *Flinders Petrie Centenary Exhib.* 21 The *shabti* is a figure placed in tombs to answer by magic for the deceased when called to labour in the Fields of the Blessed. **1964** I. E. S. Edwards et al. *Introd. Guide Egyptian Collections in Brit. Mus.* vi. 155 *Shabti*-figures are exhibited in the Third Egyptian Room. The name *shabti* is of uncertain meaning. The same figures were called *shawabtis* in the New Kingdom and *ushabtis* in the Late Period.

†**shabub, shawbubbe.** *Obs.* [app. repr. G. †*schabab*, explained as black coriander; f. *schab ab* imper. of *abschaben* to get away, be off.] Alleged name for the plant Honesty (*Lunaria biennis*).

**1548** Turner *Names Herbes* (E.D.S.) 85 It maye be called in englishe great Lunari. Some cal it Shabub. **1568** —— *Herbal* III. 52 Some call this herbe Shawbubbe.

**Shabus**, var. Shabbos.

‖**shabu-shabu** ('ʃabu'ʃabu). [Jap.] A Japanese dish of thinly sliced beef or pork cooked with vegetables in boiling soup.

**1970** T. Egami *Oriental Cookery* 130 Shabu-Shabu. The word *shabu-shabu* derives from the sound of thin slices of succulent beef being gently swirled with chopsticks.. in hot broth. **1973** *Times* 9 June 11/2 The speciality dish shabu-shabu (£1.80); raw beef and geometrically cut vegetables, briefly cooked by the waitress in a pagoda-shaped pot of broth, and served with rice and savoury dip. **1979** *United States 1980/81* (Penguin Travel Guides) 179 You can sample delicious shabu-shabu, Japan's answer to Swiss fondue.

**Shabzieger**, var. Schabzieger.

**shach**, obs. form of shah.

**shachle**, variant of shauchle *v. Sc.*

**shack** (ʃæk), *sb.*¹ Now *dial.* [f. *shack*, dial. variant of shake *v.* Cf. shake *sb.*¹ 2 e.]

**1.** Grain fallen from the ear, and available for the feeding of pigs, poultry, etc., after the harvest; a supply of fallen grain for this purpose. Also, fallen beech-mast or acorns.

**1536** *Rolls House MS.* in Froude *Hist. Eng.* (1185–6) III. 93 *note*, Able and sufficient with the help of the shakke in the stubbe to succour and feed as many great beasts.. as the land would keep. **1563** *Homilies* II. *Rogat. Week* IV. 251 b, The common balkes and walkes, whiche good men before tyme, made the greater and broder,.. partlye for the better shacke in haruest tyme, to the more comfort of his poore neyghbours cattell. **1764** *Museum Rust.* III. lxxiv. 322 [Produce of farm (Suffolk)] One hundred coomb of wheat ..£75 0 0. Shack for cattle, £1 10 0. **1802** *Sport. Mag.* XX. 64 Lonely watch'd he the grunters all day, As they rooted the stubbles for shack. **1823** E. Moor *Suffolk Words* 337 *Shack*, the corn left in a barley or pea field, after the crop has been carried. Pigs and poultry are then turned in to 'to shack'. 'Tha's good shack in that there filld'. *a* **1825** Forby *Voc. E. Anglia, Shack*... The shaken grain remaining on the ground when harvest and gleaning are over; or, in woodland countries, the acorns, or mast under the trees. **1858** *U.S. Newspaper* in J. F. Morgan *Eng. Norm. Occup.* iii. 57 *note*, The woods in the vicinity of Sandusky.. were frequented by vast numbers of wild hogs, which.. grew fat upon the shack which every where abounded.

**2. a.** In phrase ***to be, go*** or ***run at shack, to go to shack***, said of pigs, poultry, etc., when turned into the stubble to feed on the 'shack' (sense 1) after the harvest. Hence **b.** The right of sending pigs or poultry to 'run at shack' on another's land after the harvest; also, in extended sense, the right of pasturing cattle in winter on another's land.

**1629** COKE *Rep.* VII. II. 5 Ceux parolx, daler Shack, sont tant adire comme daler a libertie ou daler alarge. *Ibid.*, Le dit common appel Shacke. **1641** *Termes de la Ley* 247 *Shack* is a peculiar name of Common, used in the Countrey of Norfolke. **1706** PHILLIPS (ed. Kersey), *Shack*, (in Norfolk and Suffolk) the liberty of Winter-Pasturage;.. Also a Custom in Norfolk to have Common for Hogs, from the end of Harvest till Seed-time in all Mens Grounds: Whence *to go at Shack* in that County, signifies as much as to go at large. **1787** W. H. MARSHALL *Norfolk* (1795) II. 387 *Shack.* Stock turned into the stubbles after harvest are said to be at shack. Grounds lying open to common fields are said to 'lie quite shack'.

**c.** *attrib.*, as ***shack-land, -time*** (cf. SHAKE-*time*).

**1821** *Monthly Repos.* Feb. 97/1 A great part.. of our lands were formerly *shack lands, of which the occupant had the use only whilst his crop was on, the land then reverting to the community for pasturage. **1573-80** TUSSER *Husb.* (1878) 42 Yoke seldom thy swine while the *shacktime doth last. *Ibid.*, Where loue among neighbors do beare any stroke, While shacktime indureth men use not to yoke. *a* **1825** FORBY *Voc. E. Anglia*, *Shack-time*, the time when pigs are at shack.

**3.** An animal or animals 'at shack'.

**1842** C. W. JOHNSON *Farmer's Encycl.* 1087/1 *Shack*,.. the stock turned upon the stubble after harvest. **1859** *All Year Round* No. 33. 160 The pig is an admirable gleaner, 'a shack' they call him in Norfolk.

**shack**, *sb.*[2] *dial.* and *U.S.* [? Short for SHACK-RAG. Cf. SHAKE *sb.*[2]]

**1.** An idle disreputable fellow, a vagabond.

**1682** HICKERINGILL *Black Non-Conf.* Concl. 64 Such vile Shacks as will swear an hundred Oaths for Nothing, or a Whisker for Something. *a* **1734** NORTH *Exam.* II. iv. §120 (1740) 293 Great Ladies are more apt to take Sides with talking flattering Gossips than such a Shack as Fitzharris. *c* **1800** *Derbysh. Rhyme* in W. Andrews *Bk. Oddities* (1882) 84 Ripley ruffians, Butterley blacks, Swanwick bull-dogs, Alfreton shacks. **1862** BORROW *Wales* lxxviii, A fellow.. having much the appearance of a town shack. **1892** HOLE *Mem.* xvi. 192 The shack is a man [in Notts] who objects to regular employment, but can and will do anything except ordinary work.

**2.** 'A worthless horse; a plug' (Webster 1911).

**shack**, *sb.*[3] [Of obscure origin.

The late J. Platt, Jun., suggested (*N. & Q.* Ser. x. XII. 306/2) that the source might be the Mexican *jacal*, Aztec *xacalli*, wooden hut. Cf. SHACKLE *sb.*[3]]

**1. a.** A roughly built cabin or shanty of logs, mud, etc. Also applied to other similar structures.

**1878** *Rep. Indian Affairs* (U.S.) 42 Too much praise cannot be given to these homesteaders for.. the erection of this building, while they, themselves, were living in shacks. **1881** *N.Y. Times* 18 Dec. in *N. & Q.* Ser. VI. V. 65/2 The average 'shack' comprises but one room, and is customarily roofed with earth, supported by poles. **1882** *Century Mag.* Sept. 774/1 He [a stockman in the north-west] lives, as a rule, in a wretched dirt-roof 'shack'. **1932** A. CHRISTIE *Peril at End House* v. 70 We saw a lot of messy-looking shacks, and then by good luck we found this. **1936** D. GLOVER *Home Thoughts* 18 A mountain shack Where blankets, candles, frying-pan Bespeak the only needs of man. **1939** *Denver Post* 2 Jan. 16-B/6 Other work will include the building of a ski shack. **1950** J. BAXTER in *Landfall* (N.Z.) XIII. 10 There in a corrugated iron shack Behind a brushwood fence, he lives alone. **1960** *Daily Mail* 11 Apr. 4/4 In Durban.. Bren guns and heavy machine-guns covered the hillsides spotted with native shacks.

**b.** *attrib.* and *Comb.*

**1885** *Home Missionary* (N.Y.) Mar. 426 The rude shack-like store has changed to an imposing structure of stone. **1909** *N.Y. Even. Post* 4 Feb. in Thornton *Amer. Gloss.* s.v., An Italian was murdered in his bunk by his shack-mate. **1923** H. STEELE *Spirit-of-Iron* 105 Where little shack-towns rose, it knew there should be cities. **1962** G. MACEWAN *Blazing Old Cattle Trail* i. 4 The residents of what had been an unprepossessing shack-town found their community overrun with rip-roaring cowboys, gamblers, gunmen, even women.

**2.** *U.S. slang.* A house.

**1910** C. E. MULFORD *Hopalong Cassidy* xiii. 128 You stay in that shack. Don't leave it for a second, understand? **1930** *Living Age* 1 Apr. 188 I've gotta tote this outfit of waffles and candy to grandmomma's shack.

**3.** *U.S. slang.* = *radio shack* s.v. RADIO *sb.* 7.

**1929** *Amer. Speech* V. 49 *Shack*, wireless room or office. **1947** *Christian Science Monitor* 15 Jan. 9/1 Al's [ham radio] station, like most of the other 75,000 American amateurs, is a bedroom converted into what they call a 'shack'. **1960** [see RIG *sb.*[6] 3 d].

**shack**, *sb.*[4] *U.S.* Also (in comb.) shag-. [Of obscure origin.

There is some affinity of meaning with SHACK *sb.*[1] 1.]

**1.** Bait picked up at sea, refuse fish, flesh of porpoises or of sea-birds, etc., as distinguished from regular bait carried on the vessel. More fully ***shack-bait.*** Also *attrib.*, ***shack-fisherman, -fishing.***

**1891** in *Century Dict.*; and in later Dicts. **1897** KIPLING *Capt. Cour.* 75, 'I mistrust shag-fishin' will pay better, ez things go.' That meant the boys would bait with selected offal of the cod as the fish were cleaned.

**2.** A catch of sea-fish, made up of cheap varieties, esp. of the cod species. Also *attrib.* or *adj.*

**1904** *Rep. Mass. Comm. Fisheries & Game* 78 (Cent. Suppl.) Such fish, tumbled in together, without effort at classification, are known as shack. *Ibid.*, At first a shack trip referred particularly to a voyage on which cheap species of fishes constituted the bulk of the catch.

**shack** (ʃæk), *sb.*[5] *U.S.* [prob. f. SHACK *sb.*[2] or SHACK *v.*[2]] A slow trot. Also *attrib.*

**1881** *Harper's Mag.* Feb. 375/2 [He] walked with a peculiar shack gait. **1900** H. GARLAND *Eagle's Heart* 144 He continued his steady onward 'shack' toward the West. **1938** G. BUTLER *Running & Runners* iii. 85 Probably the best exercise of the whole lot is the 'shack' a word derived from the ponderous movement of a cart-horse. This is a movement mid-way between running and walking.

**shack** (ʃæk), *sb.*[6] *N. Amer. slang.* Also **shacks.** [Origin obscure.] The brakeman or guard on a train.

**1899** 'J. FLYNT' *Tramping with Tramps* 397 *Shack*, a brakeman. **1907** J. LONDON *Road* 213 As the freight got out of Philadelphia she began to hit up speed. Then I understood what the shack had meant by suicide. **1926** *Amer. Speech* I. 652/2 *Shacks*, brakeman on train. **1931** 'D. STIFF' *Milk & Honey Route* ii. 27 A great many hobo writers .. are full ready to tell the novice how to outwit the brakemen, or shacks. **1947** L. M. BEEBE *Mixed Train Daily* 313 The stock was valuable and a roundup was imperative, but, as the shacks and hoggers of the S.V. were unaccustomed to the saddle, a score of professional cowpokes were engaged for the task. **1976** LIEBERMAN & RHODES *Compl. CB Handbk.* vi. 136 *Shack*, railroad conductor.

†**shack**, *a.*[1] *Obs. rare.* [? Evolved from SHACK-HAIRED *a.*] Shaggy.

**1577** HARRISON *Descr. Scot.* vii. 9/1 in *Holinshed*, White Bulles with shack [1587, p. 13/2 shackt] hears and curled manes like fierce Lions.

**shack**, *a.*[2] *dial.* [f. SHACK *sb.*[1]] Used predicatively in phrase ***to lie shack***, said of land so situated as to be liable to 'shack'.

**1787** [see SHACK *sb.*[1] 2].

**shack** (ʃæk), *v.*[1] *dial.* [f. SHACK *sb.*[1]]

†**1.** *intr.* ? To 'run at shack' (in quot. *transf.*).

**1674** N. FAIRFAX *Bulk & Selv.* 196 Those rayes of other atoms that are shacking all over the worlds wasts.

**2.** *trans.* To turn (pigs or poultry, etc.) into stubble-fields; also, of animals, to feed on (stubble). Also *intr.* to feed *upon* stubble.

[**1658-** cf. *shaking-time*: SHAKING *vbl. sb.* 4.] *a* **1825** FORBY *Voc. E. Anglia*, *Shack*..To turn pigs or poultry into the stubble-fields, to feed on the scattered grain. **1867** *Jrnl. R. Agric. Soc.* Ser. II. III. II. 533 They [turkeys] are then sold ..to the larger farmers to 'shack' upon the barley or oat stubbles. **1887** SUFFLING *Land of Broads* 253 *Shack*, to turn cattle out to graze after the corn has been carted. *a* **1904** in *Eng. Dial. Dict.* s.v. *Shake* 9 The pigs shack the barley.

**shack**, *v.*[2] *dial.* [f. SHACK *sb.*[2], or of cognate formation. Cf. SHACKLE *v.*[2] (sense 2).]

**1. a.** *intr.* To idle away one's time; to loaf *about.*

**1787** [implied in *shacking* ppl. a., see below]. *a* **1825** FORBY *Voc. E. Anglia*, *Shack*..To rove about; as a stroller or mendicant. **1865** *Good Words* Feb. 125/2 What makes the work come so heavy at the end of the week, is, that the men are 'shacking' at the beginning. **1896** E. PHILLIPS OPPENHEIM *False Evid.* xxvi, What would you have me do? Shack about with my hands in my pocket all day?

**b.** To move with a slow ambling gait, to go at a slow trot. *U.S.*

**1833** in B. F. Hallett *Full Rep. Trial E. K. Avery* 61, I *shacked* down some of the hills, (partly run). **1916** H. TITUS *I Conquered* ii. 31 Yonder [was] a man shacking along on a rough little horse, head down, listless. **1947** *Sat. Even. Post* 8 Mar. 53/1 Each winter Steve shacked in to Barry's camp a couple of times, sat in the log office a day and shacked out.

**2.** *Western U.S.* 'To hibernate, as an animal, especially the bear: also said of men who "lay up" or "hole up" for the winter, or go into winter quarters' (*Cent. Dict.* 1891).

Hence **'shacking** *ppl. a.* (in sense 1).

**1787** W. H. MARSHALL *Norfolk* (1795) II. 387 *Shacking*, a shabby rambling fellow (living at shack). **1881** *Dr. Gheist* 227 I'm tired enough of this shacking night-work. **1891** *Rutland Words* Add., *Shacking*, idle good-for-nothing. He's a shacking chap.

**shack**, *v.*[3] *U.S.* [Of obscure origin.] *trans.* 'To go after, as a ball batted to a distance' (*Cent. Dict.* 1891); 'to chase and fetch, as a batted ball' (*Funk's Stand. Dict.* 1895).

**shack** (ʃæk), *v.*[4] *slang* (orig. *N. Amer.*). [f. SHACK *sb.*[3]; cf. SHACK *v.*[2] 2.] **1.** *intr.* To live in a shack.

**1895** *Dialect Notes* I. 393 *Shack*..(v.) to live in a *shack* or keep a bachelor's hall in general. 'They sent away their wives and *shacked* for a time.' **1935** Z. N. HURSTON *Mules & Men* I. vi. 127 You ain't de Everglades Cypress Lumber Comp'ny sho nuff. Youse just shacking in one of their shanties. **1954** C. BRUCE *Channel Shore* 16 Men had sailed east from here to the Cape Breton coast, to shack on the beaches and fish the waters off Petit de Grat. **1975** *Maclean's Mag.* (Toronto) May 43/3 We used to shack there, camp ourselves where the mine was.

**2. a.** *intr.* Usu. with *up.* To obtain temporary accommodation, to shelter for the night; to lodge *with* (esp. as a sexual partner), to set up house *with*, to cohabit (*with*); hence, to have sexual intercourse *with.*

**1935** Z. N. HURSTON *Mules & Men* I. vii. 161 Ah..was doin' fine till Ah shacked up with a woman dat had a great big ole black cat. **1942** BERREY & VAN DEN BARK *Amer. Thes. Slang* §62/9 *Shack up*, to stay in a camp for the night. **1945** *Sun* (Baltimore) 1 Mar. 6/6 More wanderlust grips the sow and she shacks up with half a dozen families before the original owner gets wind of her again. **1946** *Time* 14 Oct. 40/3 The medicine man..had shacked up with a halfbreed cook. **1947** L. WALLER *Show me Way* III. xxii. 191 She wanted me to shack with her tonight. **1949** R. CHANDLER *Little Sister* xviii. 120 I'm not talking about her love life... She doesn't have to shack up with a red-hot. **1951** J. D. SALINGER *Catcher in Rye* ix. 73, I was going to shack up in a hotel for a couple of days and not go home till vacation started. **1959** H. HOBSON *Mission House Murder* iii. 22 Besides appearing at performances she has to shack up with Johnny. **1965** S. T. OLLIVIER *Petticoat Farm* ix. 128 A man's got to have something to offer a girl before he asks her to shack up with him. **1968** *Listener* 15 Feb. 210/1 Some [trusted prisoners] even had their own cars to go up town and shack in some motel with a woman. **1972** P. LIVELY *Driftway* x. 136 We'll shack up for the night. There's a field farther on where the farmer's not one of those choosy fellows as'll turn me off after half an hour. **1976** W. GREATOREX *Crossover* 193 Galina's not my wife... We shack up, that's all. **1981** A. MORICE *Men in her Death* viii. 80 This must have been.. before they become friendly enough to shack up together.

**b.** *trans.* Usu. with *up.* To provide with accommodation or lodging, esp. as a sexual partner. Chiefly in pass. ***to be shacked (up)***, to be staying or lodging, to be cohabiting (*with*).

**1927** *Dialect Notes* V. 462 *Shack up*, v., to put up for the night. **1946** *Amer. Speech* XXI. 252 'I'm shacked up around here' means that the speaker has found a friendly *fräulein* who in substance maintains a home for him. The *fräulein* herself is a 'shack job'. **1953** P. FRANKAU *Winged Horse* IV. 242 He's shacked up with Celia. **1957** *Economist* 30 Nov. 787/1 Private Girard's marriage to the Japanese girl with whom he had been 'shacked up'. **1958** 'E. MCBAIN' *Killer's Payoff* (1960) ii. 19 'Where is this Newton?' 'He's shacked in a hotel..downtown.' **1967** [see GIRL *sb.* 2 g]. **1973** *Globe & Mail* (Toronto) 29 Sept. 1/2 Even the mayor was shacked up and everybody knew. **1975** D. LODGE *Changing Places* iii. 125 Philip Swallow is shacked up with Melanie at that address.

So **'shacking** *vbl. sb.*

**1884** *Prince Albert* (Saskatchewan) *Times* 13 June 3/2 Of all the enjoyments Prince Albert can number, there's none equals shacking on a *pre-emption* claim. **1945** *Yank* 8 June 14 Must be. I'm sure not crackin' up from shackin' up. **1980** M. UNDERWOOD *Clear Case of Suicide* xiii. 96 Casual shacking up was quite different from holy matrimony.

**shack**, dial. variant of SHAKE *sb.* and *v.*

**shackage** ('ʃækɪdʒ). [f. SHACK *sb.*[1]] The turning (of pigs, etc.) into the stubble or 'shack'. Also *attrib.*

**1885** W. RYE *Hist. Norfolk* 59 *note*, Open fields over which the manor tenants had grazing and shackage rights during certain times of year. **1903** *Westm. Gaz.* 14 Sept. 3/1 To this day in Bygrave.. the different occupiers of lands in the open fields enjoy the right of 'shackage'—that is, of pasturing beasts on one another's lands after harvest.

**shackal(l**, obs. forms of JACKAL *sb.*

†**shackatory.** *Obs. rare.* Also shockatory. [Of obscure origin: possibly a blundered reproduction of It. *cacciatore* hunter.] ?A huntsman's underling, a beater.

In Dicts. erroneously explained 'an Irish hound'.

**1630** DEKKER *2nd Pt. Honest Wh.* III. i. E 1 b, The Irish Footman can tell you all his hunting houres..that Irish Shackatory beates the bush for him, and knowes all. **1640** W. M. *Wand. Jew telling Fortunes* 34 For Time..is an excellent footman; no Shockatory comes neere him if hee once get the start, hee's gone, and you gone too.

**shack-bag.** Also **shack-back.** [variant of SHAKE-BAG.]

**1.** *dial.* = SHACK *sb.*[2] 1.

**1855** *Whitby Gloss.*, A *Shackbag*, a loose trustless fellow. **1886** FENN *This Man's Wife* I. xiv, I was a fool to come down as I did before, such a shackbag as I was.

**2.** The name of a large breed of fowls.

**1816** 'B. MOUBRAY' *Treat. Poultry*, etc. (ed. 2) 25 Shack-bags. Formerly the largest variety, but in probability it has been entirely worn out for some years. It was called the duke of Leeds' breed, [etc.]. **1849** D. J. BROWNE *Amer. Poultry Yd.* (1855) 75 The famous 'shack-backs', 'shack-bags', or 'Duke of Leeds' fowl',.. were supposed to have been a cross between the jago and Dorking fowls.

**shackbolt** ('ʃækbəʊlt). *Her.* [? Shortened from *shackle-bolt*: see SHACKLE *sb.*] A shackle or fetter used as a charge.

**1610** GUILLIM *Heraldry* IV. xvii. (1660) 349 He beareth, Argent, a Shackbolt sable. **1656** BLOUNT *Glossogr.*, *Shack-bolt* or *Shackle*, a prisoners Bolt, a Fetter or Give. **1688** [see SHACKLE-BOLT]. **1712** *Lond. Gaz.* No. 4973/4 A Lion's Head erased in a S[h]ackbolt on a Wreath. **1868** CUSSANS *Handbk. Her.* vii. (1893) 115 Fetter-lock, or Shack-bolt: a somewhat rare Charge.

†**shacked**, *a. Obs. rare.* Also 6 shackt. [f. SHACK *a.*[1] + -ED[2]. Cf. SHAGGED *a.*[1]] Shaggy.

**1587** [see SHACK *a.*[1]]. **1587** HARRISON *England* I. x. 41/1 in *Holinshed*, Their haire is betweene the wooll of a sheepe and the haire of a goat, resembling both, shacked, and yet absolutelie like vnto neither of both.

**shacker** ('ʃækə(r)). *U.S.* [f. SHACK *sb.*$^{4}$ (sense 2) + -ER$^{1}$.] See quot.

**1902** *Boston* (Mass.) *Transcript* 20 Aug. 13/6 A shacker, as the vessels, which bring fresh cod and haddock to the wharf are called.

† **shackerell.** *Obs.* Also 5 **shaker(e)l.** [? f. SHAKE *v.*] A vagabond.

*c* **1420** ? LYDG. *Assembly of Gods* 675 Shamefull shakerles, soleyn shaueldores. **1610** B. RICH *Descr. Irel.* 9 The meanest Shackerell, that hath scarce a mantle to wrap himselfe in, hath as proud a mind as Oneal himselfe.

**shackfork,** dial. variant of SHAKEFORK.

† **shack-haired,** *a.* Also **shak-, shake-.** [? Altered form of SHAG-HAIRED; cf. *shock-haired.*] Shaggy or shock-haired.

**1555** WATREMAN *Fardle Facions* II. viii. 187 Certeine saluages with dogges heades, and shacke heared on their bodies. **1567** GOLDING *Ovid's Met.* XIII. 1084 Herbes which neuer calf . . nor shakheard Goate did feede. **1587** HARRISON *England* III. vii. 230/1 in *Holinshed,* Of which sort [of dogs] also some be smooth, . . and some shake haired.

**shack-job** ('ʃækdʒɒb). *U.S. slang.* Also **shack job.** [f. SHACK *v.*$^{4}$ + JOB *sb.*$^{2}$ 4 f.] = SHACK-UP 2.

**1946** [see SHACK *v.*$^{4}$ 2 b]. **1951** *New Yorker* 10 Mar. 112/2 Allowing him to sleep with their daughter (this was an early shack-job, not the girl mentioned above). **1955** W. GADDIS *Recognitions* I. iv. 158 Look, rabbit, I'm looking for a shack-job, see? **1966** *Sunday Times* (Colour Suppl.) 4 Dec. 73/3 *Shack job,* easy-woman.

**shackle** ('ʃæk(ə)l), *sb.*$^{1}$ Forms: α. 1 sceacul, scacul, 3 scheakel, 4 schackle, schakel, 4–5 schakle, 5 shakill, schakyl(l, -ylle, schakkyl, 5–6 shakyl, 5–7 shakel, 6 schakill, schaccle, shakyll, shackil, -yll, 6–7 shackel(l, 6–9 *now dial.* shakle, (7 schackell), 9 *dial.* sheakle, 6– shackle. β. *north.* and *Sc.* 5 shekyl, 6 scheckill, 7 schaikill, 8 shekle, shekel, 9 sheckle, shaikle. [OE. *sceacul* masc., fetter, corresp. to LG. *schakel* link of a chain, hobble for a horse, Du. *schakel,* HG. dial. *schakel* link of a chain, ON. *skǫkull* masc., pole of a wagon (Sw. *skakel,* Da. *skagle*):—OTeut. type **skakulo-*. A cognate word is LG. *schake* link of a chain.

The notion common to these words appears to be that of 'something to fasten or attach'. On this ground it seems difficult to refer them to the Teut. root **skak-* SHAKE *v.* Falk and Torp suggest a Teut. root **skǣk-*:—pre-Teut. **skēg-*, a doublet of **kēg-*, whence Teut. **hǣk-* (:*hak-* :*hōk-*) found in G. *haken,* OE. *hóc* HOOK *sb.*$^{1}$; but this is very doubtful.]

**I.** A kind of fetter.

**1.** A fetter for the ankle or wrist of a prisoner, usually one of a pair connected together by a chain, which is fastened to a ring-bolt in the floor or wall of the cell. In the OE. examples, a ring or collar for the neck of a prisoner. **a.** *sing.*

*a* **1000** ÆLFRIC *Gloss.* in Wr.-Wülcker 107/10 *Columbar,* sceacul, *uel* bend. [*Ibid.* 116/10 *Nerui boia* fotcopsa, *uel* sweorscacul.] *c* **1425** *Cast. Persev.* 2655 in *Macro Plays* 156 Þou schalt be schakyn in myn schakle. *c* **1440** *Promp. Parv.* 443/2 Schakkyl, or schakle, *murella, numella.* *a* **1591** H. SMITH *Serm.* (1594) 262 At last his shackell falleth from him, . . the prison openeth and [etc.]. **1688** HOLME *Armoury* III. 336/1, I should rather take it [a Cop-sole and Pin] for a Shackle and Bolt. *a* **1779** COOK *Voy. Pacific* III. vi. (1784) II. 102 He carried with him the shackle of the bilboo-bolt that was about his leg. **1851** ROBERTSON *Serm.* Ser. I. xviii. (1855) 303 It is not the shackle on the wrist that constitutes the slave—but the loss of self-respect.

**b.** *pl.*

**1540** *Star Chamber Cases* (Selden Soc.) II. 220 There was put vpon your sayd poore subiecte . . a great payer of Shackels. *a* **1548** HALL *Chron., Hen. VIII,* 91 b, A prison and a man loking out at a grate . . and all his apparel was garded with shakelles of syluer. **1555** EDEN *Decades* (Arb.) 252 Then caused two payre of shackels of iron to bee put on theyr legges. **1597** *Aberd. Acc.* in *Spalding Club Miscell.* V. 69 Tua pair of scheckills to the witches in the stepill. **1641** EARL MONM. tr. *Biondi's Civil Wars* v. 167 They resolved rather to dye fighting then to live in schackells. **1652** COTTERELL tr. *Calprenede's Cassandra* III. (1676) 51 You go to offer your hands to the shackles that are already prepared for you. **1784** COWPER *Task* II. 42 Slaves cannot breathe in England; . . They touch our country, and their shackles fall. **1852** MRS. STOWE *Uncle Tom's C.* x, Haley, drawing out from under the waggon-seat a heavy pair of shackles, made them fast around each ankle. **1864** SEATON *Cadet to Colonel* xiii. 272 Shackles were put on their legs. **1867** SMYTH *Sailor's Word-bk., Shackles,* semicircular clumps of iron sliding upon a round bar, in which the legs of prisoners are occasionally confined on deck. *Manacles* when applied to the wrists.

**c.** *Her.* A shackle used as a bearing.

**1780** EDMONDSON *Her.* II. Gloss. In mod. Dicts.

**2.** *fig.* and in figurative context. Applied to restraint on freedom of action. Chiefly in *pl.*

*a* **1225** *Ancr. R.* 94 Auh ancren . . schulen beon þer [i.e. in heaven] . . lihture & swifture & ine so wide scheakeles pleien ine heouene, ase me seið ine heouene is large leswe, þet tet bodi schal beon hwar so euer þe gost wule, in one hondhwule. *a* **1400** *Minor Poems Vernon MS.* 145/13 For synne is cald þe deueles schakel, His net, his tool, his takyng takel. *a* **1592** GREENE *Mamillia* II. Ded., Wks. (Grosart) II. 142 Staying thus in suspence, I shaked off the shakles with calling to remembraunce the saying of a poore Painter in Sienna, who [etc.]. **1681** TEMPLE *Mem.* III. Wks. 1731 I. 337 They would leave the Crown after him in Shackles, which . . would not be easily knock'd off by any Successor. **1690** C. NESSE *Hist. & Myst. O. & N. Test.* I. 13 This body is become a prison, a shackle, a sepulchre to the soul. **1738** *Gentl. Mag.* VIII. 4/1 To knock off the Shackles of Ignorance and Prejudice. **1752** YOUNG *Brothers* II. i, Virtue's a shackle, under fair disguise, To fetter fools, while we bear off the prize. **1776** MICKLE tr. *Camoens' Lusiad* Introd. 152 That rhyme makes the poet walk in shackles is denied. **1872** YEATS *Growth Comm.* 281 Elizabeth . . removed the chief shackle upon British trade.

**b.** ***the shackles***: the bonds of matrimony.

[*c* **1460** *Towneley Myst.* xiii. 72 Bot begyn she to crok, To groyne or to clok, Wo is hym is of oure cok, ffor he is in the shekyls.] **1780** *Mirror* No. 89 Were I to enter the shackles, I have too much regard to my own ease to chuse a lady of reflection.

† **3.** A fetter-like bond, esp. one used as an ornament, an armlet or anklet. *Obs. rare.*

**1571–2** in Nichols *Progr. Eliz.* (1823) I. 294 An armlet or skakell [*sic*] of golde. **1634** SIR T. HERBERT *Trav.* 10 They bury his Armolets, Bracelets, Shackles and such Treasure. **1697** DAMPIER *Voy.* I. 514 Most of the Men and Women on the Island . . had all Ear-rings made of Gold, and Gold Shackles about their Legs and Arms.

**4.** [Short for SHACKLE-BONE.] The wrist; also *rarely* the ankle. *dial.*

**1788** W. H. MARSHALL *Yorksh.* II. 350 *Shackle of the arm,* the wrist. **1861** C. C. ROBINSON *Dial. Leeds, Shackle,* the wrist. 'Spreined one o' my shackles'. **1902** HYNE *Thompson's Progr.* 195 'T' sheckle willn't mend . . .' . . The fool of a woman ought to have had her shackle set at the infirmary.

**5. a.** A hobble for a horse. ? *Obs.*

**1529** *Acc. Ld. High Treas. Scot.* V. 366 Ane pair of schakillis to the grete hors. **1562** WITHALS *Dict.* (1568) 38 b/2 Shakels or spannes vpon the horse legges, *numelli.* **1573** TUSSER *Husb.* (1878) 38 Soles, fetters, and shackles, with horselock and pad. **1594** CAREW *Huarte's Exam. Wits* (1616) 171 Those shackles which we clap on the legs of an vntrained Mule, which going with them many dayes, taketh a steddie and seemly pace. **1610** MARKHAM *Masterp.* II. lxxxiv. 364 If a horse be galled in the pastorne, on the heele, or vpon the cronet, either with shackell or locke, as it many times happens in the Champion countries, where the Farmers vse much to teather their horses: then for such a soare you shall [etc.]. **1814** SOUTHEY *Roderick* xxv. 91 Some sleek and sober mule Long trained in shackles to procession pace.

**b.** A chain, rope, twisted band of straw or the like, used for securing cows. Now *dial.*

*c* **1400** *Beryn* 1064 A plant, whils it is grene . . A man may with his fyngirs ply it wher hym list, And make ther-of a shakill, a withey, or a twist. **1858** M. A. DENHAM in *D. Tracts* (1891) I. 275 The custom of twisting birch twigs in a peculiar manner, to serve instead of hempen bands for the purpose of tying up cattle. These are called 'sheakles'. **1869** PEACOCK *Lonsdale Gloss., Shackle,* . . a cow chain.

**II.** In various technical senses.

**6.** A ring, clevis, or similar device, used for attaching or coupling, so as to leave some degree of freedom of movement; often a **U**-shaped piece of iron, closed by a movable bar passing through holes in the ends. **a.** A coupling for a plough, harrow, wagon, carriage, etc.

**1343** *Durham Acc. Rolls* (Surtees) 205, 1 clitta pro moldebredd; 2 schackles de ferro pro carucis; 2 coupewaynes. *Ibid.* 543, 3 Reyns, 3 paribus de pastrons, 3 Schakles et 1 croper pro longa carecta, 26*s.* 9*d.* **1422–3** *Ibid.* 619 Pro 5 novis Reynes de corr. pro stabulo d'ni Prioris, 3 Shakelys de correo, 2 heltres de corr. **1523–34** FITZHERB. *Husb.* § 15. C 4 b, The fote teame shall be fastened to the same [*i.e.* 'the formest slote' of the harrow] with a shakyll, or a withe to drawe by. **1530** *Knaresb. Wills* (Surtees) I. 27 A wayne and yoke with bolte and shakyll. **1832** *Scoreby Farm Rep.* 3 in *Libr. Usef. Knowl., Husb.* III, The price charged . . is for the plough fit for use, but not including the shackle, by which it is drawn and regulated. **1881** J. W. BURGESS *Coach-Building* x. 98 Shackles are iron staples, which serve to receive the leather suspension braces of C spring carriages on the springs; they are also used for coupling springs together. **1894** *Northumbld. Gloss., Sheckle, sheakle, shaikle,* . . the sling that fastens the double-tree to a plough-head or bridle.

**b.** *Naut.* A fastening for a port-hole; a coupling for lengths of chain cable, an anchor, etc.

**1627** CAPT. SMITH *Seaman's Gram.* xiv. 68 Shackels are a kinde of Rings but not round, . . fixed to the middest of the ports within boord, through which wee put a billet to keepe fast the port for flying open in foule weather. **1793** SMEATON *Edystone L.* § 142 A large swivel, with shackles and bolts, . . the western chain . . joined to the eastern . . by a bolt and shackle. **1805** *Shipwright's Vade-M.* 130 *Shackles,* the small ring-bolts driven into the ports, or scuttles, and through which the lashing passes when the ports are barred in. **1831** J. HOLLAND *Manuf. Metal* I. 190 A large shackle is also fixed at one end to be joined to the anchor. **1875** BEDFORD *Sailor's Pocket Bk.* x. (ed. 2) 363 Each length is to be provided with a shackle and shackle bolt, to be tested as part of the chain. **1891** WINN *Boating Man's Vade-M.* 78 *Shackle* is a small half hoop shaped iron, fitted with a screw pin connecting the two open ends. Anchor shackles have the lug or pin countersunk [etc.].

**c.** A ring, hook, or the like for lifting, holding, carrying, etc. a weight or something heavy.

**1552** in R. H. Hore *Wexford* (1901) II. 243, 2 Iron Shackells for bucketts. **1896** *Westm. Gaz.* 2 Nov. 10/1 The immense wooden beams on which it [the bell] formerly hung have long since been broken down at the shackle.

**d.** The hinged and curved bar of a padlock which passes through the staple.

**1850** CHUBB *Locks & Keys* 7.

**7.** *Telegr.* A form of insulator used in overhead lines for supporting the wire where a sharp angle occurs.

**1855** *Lardner's Mus. Sci. & Art* III. 143 The conducting wire of the main line in passing the station is cut and the ends jointed by a shackle. **1859** *Abridgm. Specif. Patents, Electr. & Magn.* 288 Non-conducting shackles (used at stations to break the continuity of the wire) consist of a solid piece of gutta percha inserted into metal hooks [etc.]. **1876** PREECE & SIVEWRIGHT *Telegraphy* 213 A special form of insulator known as a shackle is employed, which confines the strain of the wire to one spot. *Ibid.* 214 The shackle is formed of porcelain, with a hole through the centre, into which a $4\frac{1}{2}$in. bolt is inserted.

**8.** A device for gripping anything; *spec.* 'either of the pivoted gripping devices for holding a test piece in a testing machine' (Webster 1911).

**1838** *Civ. Engin. & Arch. Jrnl.* I. 380/1 A shackle was placed round the centre of the block [of concrete], and two others at the extremities.

**9.** A length of cable $12\frac{1}{2}$ fathoms (orig. the distance between two 'shackles', in sense 6 b).

**1886** J. M. CAULFEILD *Seamanship Notes* 4 The length of the bower cable is generally 12 shackles, a shackle is $12\frac{1}{2}$ fathoms.

† **10.** Some implement used by chimney-sweepers; ? a link for fastening poles together. *Obs.*

**1719** D'URFEY *Pills* IV. 198 A Chimny-sweeper, with his Brooms, his Poles and Shackles.

**III. 11.** *attrib.* and *Comb.*, **shackle-bar,** (*a*) the swingle-tree of a coach, etc.; (*b*) *U.S.* 'the coupling between a locomotive and its tender' (Webster 1864); **shackle-breeching** (see quot.); **shackle-crow,** 'a bar of iron slightly bent at one end like the common crow, but with a shackle instead of a claw at the end . . . used for drawing bolts or deck-nails' (Smyth *Sailor's Word-bk.* 1867); † **shackle-dancer,** a performer who dances in shackles; † **shackle-gall,** a sore under the fetlock of a horse, caused by the galling of the shackle (cf. 5 a), hence ***shackle-galled*** adj.; † **shackle-hammed** *a.*, knock-kneed, so also † **shackle-hams,** knock-knees; **shackle-head** *dial.*, a seine-net; **shackle-irons** *dial.*, hand-cuffs; **shackle-jack** (see quot.); **shackle-joint,** (*a*) a joint in the form of a shackle (sense 6), esp. one for adjusting the tension of rods, wires, etc.; (*b*) a peculiar kind of articulation in the vertebræ of some fishes (see quot. 1872); **shackle-net** *dial.* (see quots.); **shackle-pin,** † (*a*) the pin or bolt of a shackle; (*b*) 'the small pin of wood or iron that confines a shackle-bolt in place' (*Cent. Dict.* 1891); **shackle-plate** (see quot.); † **shackle-vein,** 'a vein of the horse, apparently the median ante-brachial, from which blood used to be let' (*Cent. Dict.*); † **shackle-wise** *adv.*, in the form of a shackle. See also SHACKLE-BOLT, SHACKLE-BONE.

**1834** *D. Walker's Manly Exerc.* 201 *Shackle- or swing-bars. **1867** SMYTH *Sailor's Word-bk.*, **Shackle-breeching,* two shackles are turned into [*i.e.* fastened to] the breeching, by which it is instantly disconnected from the port-ringbolts. **1709** E. SMITH *Poem Death J. Philips* 102 So the stretch'd Cord the *Shackle-Dancer tries. **1596** MASCALL *Bk. Cattle* II. *Horses* 164 *Shakell-gall, is on the pastornes. **1627** J. TAYLOR (Water-P.) *Armado* C 6, The Chinegall, the Nauellgall, Windgall, Spurgall, Lightgall, and Shacklegall. **1684** *Lond. Gaz.* 1958/4 Her two fore Feet *Shackel-gald. **1592** GREENE *Upst. Courtier* D 1 b, His legges *shackle hamd, as if his knees had beene laced to his thighes with points. **1674** *Lond. Gaz.* No. 907/4 A Red Roan Nag about 13 hands high, shakle hammed. **1750** W. ELLIS *Mod. Husbandm.* III. I. 180 (E.D.D.) Colts broken too young are often shackle-hammed. **1603** H. CROSSE *Vertues Commw.* (1878) 132 The Grashopper . . with his *shackle hammes weakely skips too and fro. **1762** *Gentl. Mag.* June 287/2 If I lies than Bessy, than I wishes The *Shackleheads may never close the fishes. **1876** *Whitby Gloss.*, **Shackle-irons,* prison hand-cuffs. **1896** J. K. SNOWDEN *Web of Old Weaver* xv. (1897) 176, I looked to be taen any day, and I did not want all to see me wear the shackle-irons. **1875** KNIGHT *Dict. Mech.*, **Shackle-jack,* an implement for attaching the thills to the shackle on the axle where an anti-rattling box of india-rubber is used. **1837** *Civ. Engin. & Arch. Jrnl.* I. 48 A round wrought-iron tie-bar . . with a *shackle joint in the centre. **1872** MIVART *Anat.* ii. 25 Some spiny bones of Siluroid fishes have a perforation at their base, through which passes a bony ring . . a shackle-joint. **1824** [CARR] *Craven Gloss.*, **Shackle-net,* a net, called a flue. **1446** *Wills & Inv. N.C.* (Surtees 1835) 95, vij shakels ferri, unde ij sine *shakelpynnez et v cum shakylpynnez ferri. **1874** THEARLE *Naval Archit.* 67 At *K* is shown a *shackle plate to receive rudder pendants, which secure the rudder to the vessel in the event of the former becoming accidentally unshipped. **1607** MARKHAM *Caval.* VII. ix. 22 The cuer is to let them blood very much in the *shackle veins to draw the humors from the vpper parts. **1610** —— *Masterp.* II. cxv. 414 A slender string, which commeth from the shackell veine to the gristell in the nose and betweene the lippe. **1639** T. DE GRAY *Compl. Horsem.* 347 Take up the shackle veynes. **1596** MASCALL *Bk. Cattle* I. 73 Yee shall fasten them vnto the postes, with a bowe-withe made *shacle wise.

'**shackle,** *sb.*$^{2}$ *dial.* [f. SHAKE *v.*: see -LE.]

**1.** Stubble.

*a* **1800** PEGGE *Suppl. Grose, Shackle,* stubble. Herefordsh.

**2. a.** Sc. ***silver shackle***: the quaking-grass, *Briza media.* (Cf. *silver shaker,* SHAKER 7.) **b.** *pl.* The yellow rattle, *Rhinanthus Crista-galli* (E.D.D.).

*a* **1824** in *Mactaggart's Gallovid. Encycl.* 427 The sillar shakle wags its pow, Upon the brae.

3. A game of dice; a raffle. Cf. SHAKE *sb.* 2g. **1881** *Chequered Career* 350 The shanty-keeper now produces the dice-box and proposes a 'shackle'. **1885** *Western Gaz.* 30 Jan. in *N. & Q.* Ser. VI. XI. 245/2 He..was asked by a young man to join in a 'shackle' for live tame rabbits. He consented, and a box was brought containing three threepenny pieces, and those who threw the highest gained the rabbits.

**shackle** ('ʃæk(ə)l), *sb.*[3] [See SHACK *sb.*[3]] = SHACK *sb.*[3]

**1835** D. WEBSTER *Original Scottish Rhymes* 194 There'll be gude tents an' shachels For drinkers to roar an' to rift. **1890** *Advance* (Chicago) 18 Sept., I found lots of families living in the most miserable shackles.

**shackle** ('ʃæk(ə)l), *v.*[1] Forms: 5 **schaklyn, -ylle**, 6 **shakel, shakle, shakkle**, 6-7 **shackel**, 6- **shackle**. [f. SHACKLE *sb.*[1]]

**1.** *trans.* To confine with shackles; to put a shackle or shackles on.

*c* **1440** *Promp. Parv.* 443/2 Schaklyn, *numello.* *c* **1530** *Hickscorner* 237 (Manly) In Newgate we dwelled togyder, For he and I were bothe shakeled in a fetter. *a* **1548** HALL *Chron., Hen. IV*, 20 Edmond Mortimer..whome..Owen Glendor kepte in filthy prison shakeled with yrons. **1577** B. GOOGE *Heresbach's Husb.* IV. (1586) 158 This mischiefe you may easily preuent, with shackling him with a shooe sole. **1635** SWAN *Spec. M.* vi. §4 (1643) 252 To find their horses unfettered in the morning, although they were fast shackled over night. **1760-72** H. BROOKE *Fool of Qual.* (1809) III. 90 Sore and shackled as I was, I got..on deck. **1874** GREEN *Short Hist.* iii. §5 (1882) 139 A smith was ordered to shackle him. **1886** STEVENSON *Kidnapped* xviii, It's harder yet to lie shackled in a red-coat prison.

**b.** of a chain.

**1646** H. LAWRENCE *Comm. Angels* 58 These chaines shall shackle and binde them for ever.

**2.** *transf.* and *fig.*

*a* **1568** ASCHAM *Scholem.* II. (Arb.) 121 They will say, it were a plaine slauerie, and iniurie to, to shakkle and tye a good witte. **1594** CAREW *Huarte's Exam. Wits* i. (1596) 7 Our vnderstanding shackled with the rules and precepts of Logicke. **1655** *Nicholas Papers* (Camden) II. 245 The last post day I was shackled in my bed with an humour fallen into my right foot. **1692** R. L'ESTRANGE *Fables* lxxv. 74 His Claws were so Shackled in the Fleece..that the Shepherd..caught him. **1763** MILLS *Pract. Husb.* IV. 345 Moss likewise, which shackles the vine, as with a fetter,..must be carefully scraped off. **1779** J. MOORE *View Soc. Fr.* I. xv. 123 Had she been shackled to a morose,..jealous fellow..the case would have been different. **1879** FARRAR *St. Paul* (1883) 326 The views of Paul were..less shackled by associations. **1901** EARL SPENCER in *Parl. Deb.* 5 July 948 The work which they did hindered and shackled me in my endeavours to do what I considered right..for the Navy.

†**3.** *Chem.* To fix in combination. *Obs.*

**1675** GREW *Anat. Pl.* Lect. VI. iv. (1682) 288 A Sulphur well impregnated, either with an Alkaline, or an Acid Salt, but also shackled with Earth. **1681** —— *Musæum* II. §ii. ii. 224 A little of that Fixed Salt, serves, it seems, to Shackle or Crystallize..a very great quantity of the Essential Salt of this Plant. **1694** WESTMACOTT *Script. Herb.* 227 Sulphur, well impregnated with an Alkaline Salt, shackled with Earth.

**4.** To join, couple, or fix by means of a shackle.

**1834-5** M. SCOTT *Cruise Midge* i. I. 18 Its [the yard's] heavy iron-shod heel was shackelled by a chain of a fathom long, to a strong iron-bar. **1845** *Ann. Reg.* 131/2 A goods truck was placed across the up line at the 'points'..ready to be shackled to a down train. **1882** NARES *Seamanship* (ed. 6) 171 Shackle the cable.

**b.** *intr.* for *refl.*

**1865** *Times* 19 Aug. 9/3 Up came the cable and wire rope shackling together on the V-wheel in the bow. **1882** NARES *Seamanship* (ed. 6) 50 The foremost ends shackle on to dolphin striker.

**5.** *Telegr.* To attach to or furnish with a shackle (SHACKLE *sb.*[1] 7). *to shackle off*: to terminate (involving the use of a shackle).

**1852** in *Abridgm. Specif. Patents, Electr. & Magn.* (1859) 257 Shackling the wires. **1876** PREECE & SIVEWRIGHT *Telegraphy* 224 When the wire has to be terminated, or 'shackled off', as it is termed, at intermediate points. **1910** *N. Hawkins' Electr. Dict., Shackling*, connecting a line wire to a shackle insulator.

Hence '**shackling** *vbl. sb.* and *ppl. a.*

**1556** J. HEYWOOD *Sp. & Flie* lxxii. 20 Rather then bide their perpetuall shakling, To stand agaynst them, and stick to our takling. **1674** N. FAIRFAX *Bulk & Selv.* 3 A medly made to the everlasting shackling of that head or question. **1753** HOGARTH *Anal. Beauty* xvii. 229 They then have recourse to steel collars and other iron machines [to prevent children from stooping]; all which shacklings are repugnant to nature, and may make the body grow crooked. **1861** PALEY *Æschylus* (ed. 2) *Choeph.* 484 *note*, The entangling and shackling garment called ποδιστὴρ πέπλος. **1862** CARLYLE *Fredk. Gt.* XI. i. (1865) IV. 13 Censorship, or the shackling of men's poor tongues and pens. **1894** BLACKMORE *Perlycross* 307 For the miserable floods, and the long snowtime, and the shackling of the stream is over.

'**shackle**, *v.*[2] *dial.* (See *Eng. Dial. Dict.* for other senses, and forms.) [Frequentative f. SHAKE *v.*]

**1.** *trans.* To lay (standing corn); also, to litter, disorder (see *Eng. Dial. Dict.*). Also *to send hogs a shackling*, to send them to feed in the stubble (cf. SHACK *sb.*[1] and *v.*[1]).

**1670** EACHARD *Cont. Clergy* 83 Every neighbour's horse or cow, that breaks their hedges, or shackles their corn. **1790** GROSE *Prov. Gloss.* (ed. 2) s.v. *Shacking*, To send hogs a shackling, to send hogs to feed in the stubble. Essex. **1891** *Rutland Gloss.* s.v., After some heavy rain the corn is 'so shackled that you cannot reap it'.

**2.** *intr.* To idle or loaf *about*, to shirk work. (Cf. SHACK *v.*[2])

**1809** BATCHELOR *Anal. Eng. Lang.* 143 *Shakling*, idling. **1845** F. E. PAGET *Tales Village Childr.* Ser. II. 120 That good-for-nothing fellow, rat-catcher Falkener, who is always shackling about. **1859** —— *Curate Cumberworth* 266 There's a lot of lads that are always shackling about, ready for any mischief on Sundays.

**shackle**, variant of SHAUCHLE *v. Sc.*

**shackle-bolt.** [f. SHACKLE *sb.*[1] + BOLT *sb.*[1]]

**a.** The bolt which passes through the eyes of a shackle. **b.** *Her.* This used as a bearing. **c.** 'A bolt having a shackle or clevis on the end' (Knight *Dict. Mech.* 1875). **d.** *dial.* A handcuff.

**1688** HOLME *Armoury* III. 311/1 He beareth sable, a double shake-bolt or shackle-bolt, Argent. **1706** PHILLIPS (ed. Kersey), *Shackle-bolts* or *Shackles*, a sort of Fetters put upon Malefactors in Prison. **1819** SCOTT *Ivanhoe* xxix, A fetter-lock and shacklebolt azure. **1852-63** BURN *Nav. & Mil. Techn. Dict.* (ed. 4), Shackle bolt of a triangle gin. **1876** PREECE & SIVEWRIGHT *Telegraphy* 214 Through the hole in the arm or bracket a 4½ in. bolt is placed; connecting this with the shackle-bolt are two galvanized iron straps..which [etc.]. **1897** *Leeds Merc. Suppl.* 1 May (E.D.D.), Shackle-bolts [= handcuffs].

**shackle-bone.** *Sc.* and *dial.* [SHACKLE *sb.*[1]]

**1.** The wrist.

**1571** in *Reg. Privy Counc. Scot.* XIV. 93 The tormentaris ..band baythe my handis at the schakilbanes withe a coird. **1622** in Pitcairn *Crim. Trials* III. 509 Scho..tuik him be þe schaikill-bane with the ane hand. *c* **1730** RAMSAY *Boy & Pig* 13 [He] drugs till he has maist disjointed His shekelbane. **1824** SCOTT *Redgauntlet* ch. xi, The shackle-bones are of the largest, and so they were obliged to keep the handcuff wide. **1868** G. MACDONALD *R. Falconer* I. 65 His shackle-bane was as thick as baith mine.

**2.** The knuckle-bone; also 'the hind leg of a pig's carcase, between the foot and the joint at which it is cut off' (Miss Jackson *Shropsh. Word-bk.*).

**1822** GALT *Sir A. Wylie* lxxxviii, Gin ye hae the shachle bane o' a mutton ham.

**shackled** ('ʃæk(ə)ld), *ppl. a.* [f. SHACKLE *sb.*[1] + -ED[1].] Wearing or bound in shackles.

*c* **1440** *Promp. Parv.* 443/2 Schakklyd, *numellatus.* **1562** J. HEYWOOD *Prov. & Epigr.* (1867) 185 We wrestle alone: And shall, tyll tyme our shakled breeches be gone. **1600** *Maids Metam.* v. i, Hee's as good a footeman as a shackled sow. **1671** WOODHEAD *St. Teresa* I. xxxv. 259 To make them, who fly like eagles..to walk no faster than a shackled Hen. **1842** LONGF. *Witnesses* i, With shackled feet and hands. **1861** DICKENS *Gt. Expect.* liv, The hunted wounded shackled creature.

**b.** *transf.* and *fig.*

**1837** WHITTIER *Lines Celebr. 3rd Anniv. Brit. Emancip.* 14 The shackled soul and hand are free. **1894** E. LEE-HAMILTON *Sonn. Wingless Hours* 22 Let not this shackled body drag thee down Into that stagnant sea.

†**c.** *shackled-ham'd* = *shackle-hammed* s.v. SHACKLE *sb.*[1] 11. *Obs.*

**1733** W. ELLIS *Chiltern & Vale Farm.* 112 A Colt, who is check'd by being work'd too soon, will be shackled-ham'd, stunted, and complain ever after.

'**shackledom.** *nonce-wd.* [f. SHACKLE *sb.*[1] + -DOM.] The condition of being bound with shackles. (In quot. = marriage.)

**1771** T. HULL *Sir W. Harrington* (1797) IV. 121 Why does the sage Julia S. so soon after the commencement of her own shackledom, ask such a question?

**shackles** ('ʃæk(ə)lz). *dial.* and *slang.* [Prob. f. SHACKLE-BONE.] Broth, soup, or stew.

**1886** F. T. ELWORTHY *West Somerset Word-Bk.* 658 *Shackles*.., broth. Every mornin' my old 'ummun makth me a basin o' *shackles*, and her knowth how to make 'em too, mind, way a plenty o' liks (leeks) in 'em. **1909** W. H. DAVIES *Beggars* xiii. 104 The following are a few slang words used by beggars...soup—shackles. **1931** 'G. ORWELL' *Coll. Essays* (1968) I. 70 New words (i.e. words new to me)... *Shackles*, broth or gravy. **1969** *Tel.* (Brisbane) 29 July 2/4 Mr. Coppard records how one night he stumbled on a field kitchen and enjoyed a wonderful meal of schackels, a soup made up from leftovers.

**shackle-up** ('ʃæk(ə)lʌp). *slang.* Also **shackle up.** [Origin uncertain: cf. prec.] An act of preparing food in a pot.

**1935** H. NEVILLE *Sneak Thief on Road* 347 Shackle-up —a great cooking of food in a pot. **1936** J. CURTIS *Gilt Kid* xx. 202 A spare shirt and a couple o' tins in case they want to have a shackle up.

**shackling** ('ʃæklɪŋ), *ppl. a.* [f. SHACKLE *v.*[2] + -ING[2]. In sense 2 perh. influenced by RAMSHACKLE.]

**1.** Loafing, dissipated.

**1788** PARR *Let. Burney* 16 Feb., Wks. (1828) VII. 407 And upon this account I call him a shuffling, shilly-shally, shackling fellow. **1889** DOR. E. HURST *Horsham* (ed. 2) 267, I can't employ him, he is such a shackling fellow.

**2.** *U.S.* Rickety, ramshackle.

**1790** W. MACLAY *Jrnl.* 24 May (1890) vii. 272 His whole figure has a loose, shackling air. **1793** J. LINDLEY in *Friends' Misc.* (1836) (ed. 2) II. 63 And the wagon very shackling, made the tour very disagreeable. **1846** J. K. POLK *Diary* 9 June (1929) iii. 114 Mr. Bancroft reminded Mr. Buchanan of a remark which he had made in the Cabinet some months ago, that the title of the United States north of 49° was a shackling one. **1872** J. T. TROWBRIDGE *Coupon Bonds* 387 (Farmer) The gate itself was such a shackling concern, a child couldn't have leaned on it without breaking it down. **1884** *Harper's Mag.* Oct. 738/2 A poor old black horse, harnessed to a shackling buggy.

†'**shacklock.** *Obs.* [? Contr. of **shackle-lock*, f. SHACKLE *sb.*[1] + LOCK *sb.*] A fetterlock.

The surname *Shacklock* is known in Derbyshire.

**1613-16** W. BROWNE *Brit. Past.* I. v. 98 The swarty Smith ..bids his Man bring out..His shackles, shacklockes, hampers, giues and chaines.

**shackly** ('ʃæklɪ), *a. U.S.* and *dial.* Also **shackley.** [f. SHACKLE *sb.*[2] or *v.*[2] + -Y.] Shaky, rickety; ramshackle.

**1843** *Indiana Q. Mag. Hist.* III. 121, I stopped at a small poverty-stricken little town called Mt Meridian; shackly houses, huts and hovels..gave no great expectation of refinements. **1843** *New Mirror* 18 Nov. 116/2 Hitched with oakum before a shackley go-cart, the rocking evolution of whose wheels showed that it was long since they had firmly revolved in their own proper axis. **1848** BARTLETT *Dict. Amer.* s.v., What a shackly old carriage! *c* **1850** Dow *Serm.* III. (Bartlett 1860), The general fly-offs and moral unhitches incident to poor shackly mortality. **1884** 'MARK TWAIN' *Huck. Finn* xxi. 208 All kinds of old shackly wagons. **1897** —— *More Tramps Abroad* lxxi, A gaunt, shackly country lout six feet high. **1896** DE VINNE *Moxon's Mech. Exerc., Printing* Pref. p. xvii, The poverty of the old printing-house... Its scant supply of types, its shackly hand-presses [etc.]. *Ibid.* 426 The needless wearing of elastic or shackly-fitted parts of the press.

†'**shack-rag.** *Obs.* = SHAKE-RAG, SHAG-RAG.

**1611** CHAPMAN *Widow's T.* v. i. K4, To send a man abroad vnder guard of one of your silliest shack-rags; that he may beate the knaue, and run's way.

**shack-shack, shac-shac** ('ʃækʃæk), vars. CHAC-CHAC. Cf. SHAK-SHAK.

**1848** in *Caribbean Q.* (1956) IV. III & IV. 184 Bands of music (soi-disant) including those inelegant instruments, the tin kettle and salt box, the bangee and shack shack. **1953** P. L. FERMOR *Violins of Saint-Jacques* 58 The leaders wielded shackshacks: cylinders of bamboo filled with rattling seeds. **1955** *Caribbean Q.* IV. II. 101 The band includes..a cuatro..a set of home-made drums with cymbal and triangle, and shac-shacs. **1959** P. CAPON *Amongst Those Missing* 243 The music..was strongly rhythmic and the rhythm was marked by the rattling of shack-shacks and maracas.

**shack-up** ('ʃækʌp). *slang* (chiefly *U.S.*). Also **shack up, shackup.** [f. SHACK *v.*[4] 2.]

**1.** Cohabitation. Also *attrib.*

**1935** Z. N. HURSTON *Mules & Men* I. ii. 54 'Oh, you kin be had,' Gold retorted... 'Yeah? But not wid de trace chains. Never no shack up. Ah want dis tip-in love and tip yo' hat and walk out.' **1974** *Times Lit. Suppl.* 18 Oct. 1155/2 An affair with David,..a shack-up with Colin. **1977** *Toronto Star* 21 May B5 One down-to-earth mother referred to 'my child's shack-up partner'.

**2.** A partner in cohabitation or sexual intercourse.

**1969** E. R. JOHNSON *Mongo's back in Town* ii. 20 That's not like Angel. She was still Mike's shackup. **1972** J. GORES *Dead Skip* (1973) xxiii. 163 He didn't even know if the guy was married or single. He might have a shack-up there for the night.

†'**shacky**, *a. Obs. rare*[−1]. = SHAGGY *a.*

**1567** GOLDING *Ovid's Met.* I. 275 His garments turnde to shackie heare.

**shaco**, variant of SHAKO.

**shac-shac**: see SHACK-SHACK.

**shad** (ʃæd), *sb.* Forms: 1 **sceadd**, 6-7 **shadde**, (7 **shed**), 7, 9 **chad**, 6- **shad.** *Pl.* **shad**, also **shads** (? 7 **shades**). [OE. *sceadd*, of unknown origin; cf. Welsh *ysgadan* pl. (sing. *ysgadanyn*), Irish and Gaelic *sgadan*, herring.

The LG. *schade* shad, herring, may be from Eng.; in Dicts. it has been confused with *scheide* sheat-fish, catfish.]

**1.** Any clupeoid of the genus *Alosa*; the British species are the allice, *A. communis* or *vulgaris*, and the twaite (or herring-shad), *A. finta*; the common or white shad of America is *A. sapidissima*, and the Chinese shad is *A. reevesi.*

**1002** *Will* in Kemble *Cod. Dipl.* VI. 147 On ðæt ȝerad, ðonne sceaddgenge sy, ðæt heora æȝðer sylle. III. þusend sceadda into ðære stowe æt Byrtune. **1538** ELYOT *Dict.* Addit., *Acon, aconis*, a fyshe, whiche after the description of Paulus Iouius, I suppose to be that, whiche at London is callid a shad [**1545** a shadde]. **1584** COGAN *Haven Health* clxxviii. 143 Shad & Mackerel are both sweete in tast & soft in substance. **1602** CAREW *Cornwall* 30 Of round fish there are..Chad, &c. *a* **1623** FLETCHER *Love's Cure* II. ii, Whilst I [had]..seen poor rogues retire all gore and gash'd Like bleeding shads. **1629** CAPT. SMITH *Virginia* II. 28 (Arb.) I. 356 Of fish we were best acquainted with Sturgeon, Grampus, Popus..Catfish, Shades, Pearch of three sorts,.. and Muscles. **1634** WOOD *New Eng. Prosp.* (1865) 38 The Shaddes be bigger than the English Shaddes and fatter. **1792** WASHINGTON *Let.* Writ. 1792 XII. 245 To furnish me with a certain quantity of shad and herreing. **1819-20** W. IRVING *Sketch Bk., Sleepy Hollow* (1865) 440 There was.. broiled shad and roasted chickens. **1833** J. RENNIE *Alph. Angling* 24 Ælian again tells us, that the chad is allured by the sound of castanets. **1848** JOHNS *Week at Lizard* 238 Bream, chads, or young bream, gurnards. **1886** R. C. LESLIE *Sea-painter's Log* viii. 164 A herring-shad—a large bony flat-fish like a magnified fresh-water bream.

**2.** *U.S.* Applied, usually with defining word, to other fishes, as **gizzard shad**, the genus *Dorosoma*, esp. *D. cepedianum* (called also *mud, white-eyed, winter shad*); **green-tailed, hard-head(ed, yellow-tailed shad**, the menhaden; **hickory** or **tailor shad**, see TAILOR *sb.* 6; **long-**

**boned shad** = MOHARRA a; **Ohio shad**, *Pomolobus chrysochloris*; **trout shad**, the squeteague.

1884 GOODE, etc. *Nat. Hist. Aquatic Anim.* 569 The Menhaden... 'Hard-head Shad'... 'Yellow-tailed Shad.' *Ibid.* 607 The Hickory Shad. *Ibid.* 608 The 'Tailor Shad.' *Ibid.* 610 The..'Mud-Shad', 'Winter Shad', or 'Stink Shad',.. the 'Gizzard Shad',..or 'White-eyed Shad'.

**3.** As a term of abuse. *rare.*

1610 B. JONSON *Alch.* IV. vii, Then you are an Otter and a Shad, a Whit, A very Tim. 1894 'MARK TWAIN' in *St. Nicholas* Jan. 252/2 Spiders in a desert, you shad?.. You don't ever reflect, Huck Finn, and I reckon you really haven't got anything to reflect with.

**4.** *attrib.* and *Comb.* **a.** Simple attrib., as *shadbone, -box, -fish, -fisher, -fry, genus, -hatcher, roe, -seine.*

1962 AUDEN *Dyer's Hand* (1963) 303 Thus, she describes a tomcat's face: the *shadbones regularly set about the mouth. 1884 GOODE, etc. *Nat. Hist. Aquatic Anim.* 409 These eggs were placed in *shad boxes. 1679 A. LOVELL *Indic. Univ.* 35 A *Shed fish, *Alosa.* 1908 LD. CROMER *Mod. Egypt* II. 326 Six live electric shad-fish from the Nile. 1860 *Harper's Mag.* Nov. 795/1 A party of *shad-fishers, pulling in their seine. 1904 GALLICHAN *Fishing & Shooting in Spain* 195 The shad-fishers of Seville. 1857 PERLEY *Hand-bk. N. Brunswick* 25 Upwards of two hundred boats and five hundred men are employed in the *shad fishery, every season, in Cumberland Basin. 1879 MISS JACKSON *Shropsh. Word-bk.* s.v. *Shad-bird,* It is probable that the Severn fishermen, connecting the appearance of the bird with the advent of the *shad-fishing season, gave to it the local appellation of Shad-bird. 1904 GALLICHAN *Fishing & Shooting in Spain* 164 Shad-fishing is still a flourishing industry in the Valley of the Minho. 1884 GOODE, etc. *Nat. Hist. Aquatic Anim.* 606 The *shad fry..spend the first six months in our rivers. 1891 *Century Dict.*, *Shad-hatcher, one who engages in the artificial propagation of shad. 1888 *All about Alaska* (Pacific Coast Steamship Co.) 54 Herring roe is to the native Sitkans what the *shad roe is to the dwellers on the Susquehanna and the Potomac. 1976 *National Observer* (U.S.) 23 Oct. 19/4 And, this is the place for exotic fish eating, with surprises like..shad roe, wolf fish. 1891 *Century Dict.*, s.v. *Seine*, *Shad-seine, a seine especially adapted or used for taking shad, and generally of great size. 1884 GOODE, etc. *Nat. Hist. Aquatic Anim.* 604 In the Albemarle the important Shad seine-fisheries begin early in March.

**b.** Special comb. [Chiefly U.S. names of plants which are in flower or fruit when the shad are found in the rivers, and of birds, insects, etc. that appear about that time.] **shad-berry**, the shad-bush or its fruit; **shad-bird**, (*a*) *dial.* the common sandpiper, *Tringoides hypoleucus*, ?*Obs.*; (*b*) 'the common American snipe, *Gallinago wilsoni* or *G. delicata*' (*Cent. Dict.* 1891); **shad-blossom**, the shad-bush or its blossom; **shad-blow** = *shad-bush*; †**shad-brid** (see quot.); **shad-bush**, the genus *Amelanchier*, esp. *A. canadensis*, also called *June-berry* or *service-berry*; **shad-flower**, (*a*) = *shad-bush* (Miller *Plant-n.* 1884); (*b*) the whitlow-grass, *Draba verna* (*Cent. Dict.*); **shad-fly**, a fly which appears when shad are running; **shad-frog**, *Rana halecina* or *virescens*; **shad-herring**, a gizzard shad; **shad-salmon**, the whitefish or freshwater herring, *Coregonus clupeiformis* of Lakes Erie and Ontario; **shad-splash** = *shad-wash* (1891 in *Cent. Dict.*); **shad-tree** = *shad-bush* (1895 in *Funk's Stand. Dict.*); **shad-trout**, the squeteague; **shad-waiter**, the Menomonee whitefish, *Coregonus quadrilateralis*; **shad-wallow**, the spawning ground of shad; **shad-wash**, 'the wash, swish, or splash of the water by shad in the act of spawning; hence a place where shad spawn' (*Cent. Dict.*); **shad-worm**, a 'worm' which is the food of shad. See also SHAD-BELLY.

1861 BENTLEY *Man. Bot.* 537 *Amelanchier canadensis.*— The fruit is known in Rupert's Land, &c., under the name of '*Shad-berry or Service-berry. 1879 MISS JACKSON *Shropsh. Word-bk.*, *Shad-bird. 1883 KRIGER in Trumbull *Names & Portraits Birds* 157 (Cass. Suppl.) [In Delaware] snipe are called shad-birds by many of the fishermen. 1821 T. DWIGHT *Trav.* I. 42 *Shad blossom. This tree grows about fifteen feet in height. 1860 MISS WARNER *Say & Seal* li, Under the trees were various low shrubs in flower: shad-blossom, with its fleecy stems, and azalia, in rosy pink. 1846 D. J. BROWNE *Trees Amer.* 282 The Canadian Amelanchier ..[also called] June Berry, *Shad-blow, Shad-flower. 1890 *Harper's Mag.* Apr. 710/2 Shadblow, with leaves of bluish green, white flowers or green berries waiting for the sun to make them red. 1960 *Washington Post* 25 Jan. B1/4 Trees considered to be worth only 60 per cent..are..common horse-chestnut, shadblow serviceberry, [etc.]. 1688 HOLME *Armoury* II. 325/2 A Minnow [is] first a *Shad-brid, then a Sprat, then a Minnow. 1818 A. EATON *Man. Bot. N. & Middle States* 145 *Aronia..botryapium* (*shad-bush). 1856 BRYANT *Old Man's Counsel* 28 Within the woods..the shadbush, white with flowers, Brightened the glens. 1892 *Nation* (N.Y.) 11 Aug. 114/2 The Eastern shadbush, with its two varieties, and the northwestern (species of *Amelanchier*) come next. 1817 A. EATON *Man. Bot. Northern States* 55 *Aronia..botryapium*, (*shad-flower). 1825 *Canad. Mag.* IV. 474 The ephemeral Spring Fly, called..by the English the *Shad Fly, as they are supposed to indicate the approach of the fish. 1857 THOREAU *Maine Woods* (1894) 316 We met with ephemerae (shad-fly) midway, about a mile from the shore. 1791 W. BARTRAM *Trav.* 278 The *shad frog, so called in Pennsylvania from their appearing and croaking in the spring season, at the time the people fish for shad. 1852 THOREAU *Autumn* (1894) 79 Painted tortoises and shad frogs. 1845 STORER in *Mem. Amer. Acad.* (1846) II. 462 *Chatoëssus signifer* Dekay...Called '*Shad-Herring', 'Thread-Herring', and 'Thread-fish' in New York. 1842 *Ibid.* 452 *Coregonus clupeiformis*, Common *Shad-Salmon. 1884 GOODE, etc. *Nat. Hist. Aquatic Anim.* 362 In the Southern Atlantic States it [the Squeteague] is called 'Grey Trout', 'Sun Trout', and '*Shad Trout'. 1879 GOODE *Catal. Anim. Res. U.S.* 57 Prosopium quadrilaterale, (Rich.) Milner.—*Shad-waiter. 1884 GOODE, etc. *Nat. Hist. Aquatic Anim.* 606 The favorite spawning grounds of the Shad, or '*Shad Wallows', as they are termed by the fishermen. 1851 M. H. PERLEY *Rep. Fisheries Bay of Fundy* 88 At Windsor, the '*Shad-worm' is found upon the mud flats. 1857 PERLEY *Hand-bk. N. Brunswick* 25 Their [shad's] favourite food, the shad-worm and the shrimp.

**shad**, *v. rare.* [f. SHAD *sb.*] *intr.* To fish for shad. Cf. SHADDER *sb.*

1863 T. W. HIGGINSON *Out-Door Papers* ix. 240 (Funk) Along our maritime rivers the people associate April, not with 'sugaring' but with 'shadding'. 1884 *Pall Mall Gaz.* 2 Aug. 4/2 Fishing mainly consists, it is true, of pnollocking (whiffing), and chadding.

**shad**, obs. form of SHADE, SHED.

**'shad-belly.** *U.S.* [f. SHAD *sb.* + BELLY *sb.*] A Quaker coat, so called from its shape (see quot. 1860), hence a Quaker. More fully *shad-belly coat.*

1842 *Philad. Spirit of Times* 18 Mar. (Thornton *Amer. Gloss.*), A gentleman in a shad-belly coat. 1854 J. C. BALDWIN *Flush Times* 67 (*Ibid.*) He had doffed the cassock, or rather the shadbelly, for the gown. 1860 BARTLETT *Dict. Amer.* (ed. 3), *Shad-belly coat*, one which slopes gradually from the front to the tails, and has no angle. Drab coats of this shape are worn by Quakers, who are hence sometimes called shad-bellies.

Hence **shad-bellied** *a.*, (*a*) Of a coat (*rarely* of a waistcoat) = SHAD; (*b*) Of a person, having an abnormally thin or flat belly.

1832 J. P. KENNEDY *Swallow Barn* III. i. 3 A shad-bellied blue bobtail coat. 1845 S. JUDD *Margaret* I. xiii. (1874) 83 Many wore three-cornered hats, shad-bellied coats, shoe and knee buckles. 1847 [see NIGHT-OWL 2]. 1851 H. MELVILLE *Whale* xvi, A harpooner in a broad shad-bellied waistcoat. 1871 MRS. STOWE *Oldtown Fireside Stor.* 12 He was kind o' mournful and thin and shad-bellied. 1874 EGGLESTON *Circuit Rider* xx. (1895) 146 His coat is straight-breasted,—shad-bellied, as the profane call it.

‖**shadchan** ('ʃadxən). Also **schadchen, schatchen, shadchen, shadkhan, shadkin, shatchen.** [Yiddish *shadkhn*, ad. Heb. *šaddǝḵān*, f. *šiddēḵ* to arrange a marriage; cf. SHIDDUCH.] A Jewish professional matchmaker or marriage-broker. Also *fig.*

a1890 in Barrère & Leland *Dict. Slang* (1890) II. 219/2 Ten per cent of the dowry goes to the shadkin when the others become kin. 1892 I. ZANGWILL *Childr. Ghetto* I. 60 He sent a *Shadchan* to propose to her, and they were affianced, Chayah's father undertaking to give a dowry of two hundred gulden. 1897 F. MOSS *Amer. Metropolis* iii. 216 A man named J—— H——..acted as schatchen (match-maker). 1950 D. RIESMAN in *Psychiatry* May 177/1 The lies and sales talk of the schadchen, the Jewish marriage brokers. 1957 L. STERN *Midas Touch* I. viii. 68 'Shatchen,' Israel muttered into his beard, 'Matchmaker.' 1959 'W. HAGGARD' *Venetian Blind* vii. 98, I married her..because my parents, on the advice of a reliable *shadchan*..considered the match suitable. 1968 [see *marriage broker* s.v. MARRIAGE 8]. 1976 *Publishers Weekly* 11 Oct. 94/2 Taking the role of *shadkhan*, the authors bring together seeker and supplier.

**shadd**, doubtful var. SHOAD.

‖**shadda** ('ʃadda). *Gram.* Also **šedda, shaddah.** [a. Arab. *šadda*, lit. strengthening.] In Arabic, a sign, also called *tašdīd*, written or printed above a consonant to indicate that it is doubled.

1896 W. WRIGHT tr. *Caspari's Gram. Arabic Lang.* (ed. 3) I. I. iii. 14 In African Mss. the vowel is not always written with the šedda. 1925 W. H. T. GAIRDNER *Phonetics of Arabic* ix. 58 The sign written over the consonant-letter in Arabic writing is called aʃ ʃadda ('force'). 1958 D. COWAN *Introd. Mod. Literary Arabic* 5 If two identical consonants come together and are not separated by a vowel only one is written with the mark ـّ above it. This mark is called..*s͟hadda* or 'strengthening'. 1962 HAYWOOD & NAHMAD *New Arabic Gram.* i. 10 A doubled letter is not written twice, unless separated by an intermediate vowel. Instead, the sign ـّ (called..tas͟hdīd or..s͟hadda) is written over the letter. 1969 A. G. CHESNE *Arabic Lang.* ii. 28 Other diacritical marks were..introduced. Among these are..the *shaddah* for doubling a consonant. 1971 R. A. WISBEY *Computer in Lit. & Ling. Research* 228 Though the vowels are not to be included, as they are usually omitted in the script, shadda, the sign which denotes the doubling of a letter, and the various combinations with hamza are to be plotted.

‖**Shaddai** ('ʃadai). *Judaism.* Also **Shadai.** [Heb., of uncertain meaning; in the English versions of the Bible usu. translated 'Almighty'.] One of the names of God in the Bible and cabbala, inscribed on certain ritual objects and on talismans.

1620 J. DONNE *Sermon* (1957) III. 191 Shaddai is the name of God, and yet Shaddai is spoyle, violence and depredation. 1881 *Encycl. Brit.* XIII. 812/1 The angel Metatron inhabits this world. He alone constitutes the world of pure spirit, and is the garment of Shaddai, *i.e.*, the visible manifestation of the Deity. 1892 I. ZANGWILL *Childr. Ghetto* I. 133 The doorposts twinkled with *Mezuzahs*—cases or cylinders containing sacred script, with the word *Shaddai* (Almighty) peering out of a little glass eye at the centre. 1926 W. & E. MUIR tr. *Feuchtwanger's Jew Süss* I. 37 Three furrows, sharp, deep, short and almost vertical above his nose cleft his forehead; and they formed the sacred letter Shin, the first letter of God's name, Shaddai. 1962 I. B. SINGER *Slave* ii. 219 The incantation a scribe had written out for her:..*Yuhah* will guard me! *Shaddai* will save me! *Taftifiah* will be a wall for me. 1969 E. STEWART *Heads* 91 There was an amulet..the little golden heart with the letters that spelled *Shadai*..*Shadai*, he thought: *eternal.*

**shadde**, obs. f. SHED and *shod* pa. pple. of SHOE *v.*

**shadden**, bad spelling of SCHADON.

1750 W. ELLIS *Mod. Husbandm.* v. i. 107 (E.D.S.) Else the honey will be corrupted by the shaddens in the comb.

†'**shadder**, *sb. Obs.* $rare^{-1}$. [f. SHAD *sb.* + -ER[1].] A fisher for shad.

1630 in Binnell *Descr. Thames* (1758) 78 None of the said Shadders shall go forth to fish until they have received Leave and Licence.

**shadder** ('ʃædə(r)), *v.* [Cf. SHALDER *v.*] *trans.* To break up (the larger pieces of crude lead ore).

1622 MALYNES *Anc. Law-Merch.* 264 [He delivered] 20 pound weight of the said Ore, grinded, shaddered and washed. 1890 WALLACE *Alston Moor* 145 (E.D.D.) The larger pieces were shaddered.

**shaddo**, obs. form of SHADOW *v.*

**shaddock** ('ʃædək). Also 8 **shattuck, shaddoc, shadock, chad(d)ock.** [Named after a Captain *Shaddock*: see quot. 1707.] The fruit of *Citrus decumana* (also called POMPELMOOSE) resembling an orange, but very much larger. In stricter use, applied to the large pear-shaped varieties of the species, the smaller and rounder varieties being called *grape-fruit.*

1696 [see *shaddock tree*]. 1707 SLOANE *Jamaica* I. 41 In Barbados the Shaddocks surpass those of Jamaica in goodness. The seed of this was first brought to Barbados by one Captain Shaddock, Commander of an East-India Ship, who touch'd at that Island in his Passage to England, and left the Seed there. 1720 S. SEWALL *Diary* 1 Jan., Mr. Cooper sends my wife a present of oranges and a shattuck. 1764 GRAINGER *Sugar Cane* I. 44 The golden shaddoc, the forbidden fruit. 1773 Chaddock [see POMPELMOOSE]. 1823 BYRON *Island* I. viii, A seaman..Held the moist shaddock to his parched mouth. 1884 *De Candolle's Orig. Cultivated Pl.* 181 Oranges are distinguished from shaddocks by the complete absence of down on the young shoots and leaves.

**b.** The tree bearing this fruit.

1785 MARTYN *Rousseau's Bot.* xxv. (1794) 371 Shaddock, which has them [the leaves] obtuse, and emarginate or notched at the end. 1885 LADY BRASSEY *The Trades* 139 The orange, lemon, shaddock, pomelo,..were weighed down by their own golden fruit.

**c.** *attrib.*, as *shaddock-bower*, etc.

a1818 M. G. LEWIS *Jrnl. W. Ind.* (1834) 23 My coffee walks and *shaddock bowers. 1892 KIPLING *Barrack-r. Ballads* 130 He has stripped my rails of the *shaddock-frails. 1731 BRADLEY *Gardening* 592 The *Chadock Orange. 1797 *Encycl. Brit.* V. 29/1 s.v. *Citrus*, The great Shaddock orange, or pumplemoes. 1825 *Greenhouse Comp.* I. 81 The orange is best propagated by grafting or budding on lemon or *shaddock stocks. 1696 *Shaddock-tree [see POMPELMOOSE]. 1884 *Leisure Hour* Feb. 78/2 The fragrant blossoms of large shaddock-trees.

**shaddow**, obs. form of SHADOW.

†**shaddrew**, var. CHEDREUX *Obs.*, a kind of wig.

1678 D'URFEY *Fool turn'd Critick* I. ii. 5 And let me see you strut it in the Streets, Display thy Garniture, Hat, Curl'd Shaddrew.

**shaddup** (ʃʌ'dʌp), repr. a colloq. or vulg. pronunc. of imper. *shut up!* (see SHUT *v.* 19 m).

1959 R. CONDON *Manchurian Candidate* iv. 78 Shaddup! You hear? Shaddup! 1977 *Daily News* (Perth, Austral.) 19 Jan. 3 (*caption*) 'Forget it, mother it doesn't bother me.' 'It bothers me! People'll think I'm gettin' old!' 'Shaddup.' 1977 *Daily Mirror* 6 Apr. 24 (*caption*) 'Snooker isn't a trifle!' 'Aw, Shaddup!!'

**shaddy**, obs. form of SHADY.

**shade** (ʃeɪd), *sb.* Forms: 1 sceadu, scead, scad, sced, scæd, 3 ssade, 3–4 schade, 4 ssed(e, 5, 7, 9 *dial.* shad(de, 6 shaad, 6–7 *Sc.* schad, 4, 6– shade. [ME. *schade*, repr. OE. *sceadu* str. fem. (oblique cases *sceadwe*, also irreg. *sceade*) and the by-form *scead* neut. (dat. sing. *sceade*, pl. *sceadu*). The flexional form *sceadwe* is represented by SHADOW *sb.*, q.v. for the further etymology.

The ME. *schade*, mod.Eng. *shade*, descend regularly from the nom. *sceadu* of the fem. sb., and from the dat. *sceade*, which is common to the fem. and the neut. sb. The neut. nom. *scead* is represented by ME. *schad(de*, mod. dial. *shad.*

The OE. *sceade* for *sceadwe* genit. and dat. is due to the analogy of other sbs. with nom. sing. in *-u*. The neuter *scead* prob. arose from taking the sing. *sceadu* as a plural.]

I. Comparative darkness.

**1. a.** Partial or comparative darkness; absence of complete illumination; esp. the comparative darkness caused by a more or less opaque object intercepting the direct rays of the sun or other luminary.

a1000 *Sal. & Sat.* 116 (Gr.) Hydeð hine æghwylc æfter sceades sciman. c1374 CHAUCER *Anel. & Arc.* 18 Thou Polymya..that..Singest with vois memorial in the shade Vnder the laurer. ?c1400 LYDG. *Æsop's Fab.* i. 84 (Trin.) [Cock-crow] Causeþ merchauntys and pylgryms to be glad, The theuys swerde hyd vndyr þe shad. 1596 SHAKS. *1 Hen.*

*IV*, I. ii. 29 Let vs be Dianaes Forresters, Gentlemen of the Shade. **1629** MILTON *Hymn Nativ.* xx, In twilight shade of tangled thickets. **1730–46** THOMSON *Autumn* 1139 The night begins to fall, A shade immense. **1791–2** WORDSW. *Descr. Sk.* 98 Aloft, here, half a village shines arrayed In golden light; half hides itself in shade. **1794** MRS. RADCLIFFE *Myst. Udolpho* xlviii, The pensive shade of twilight was pleasing to her. **1797** —— *Italian* Prol., The shade of the long aisles. **1827** SCOTT *Surg. Dau.* viii, The lady stood in the shade. **1850** TENNYSON *In Mem.* Concl. xxx, And touch with shade the bridal doors, With tender gloom the roof, the wall. **1870** ROSSETTI *Last Conf.* 253 As when a bird flies low Between the water and the willow leaves, And the shade quivers till he wins the light.

†**b.** ***shade of death*** = SHADOW of death.

*a* **900** [see SHADOW 1 b]. **1591** SHAKS. *1 Hen. VI*, v. iv. 89 But darkness, and the gloomy shade of death Inuiron you. **1593** —— *2 Hen. VI*, III. ii. 54.

**c.** *fig.* Comparative obscurity. Chiefly in phrases, ***to be in the shade***, to be in retirement, to be little known; ***to cast, throw into the shade, put into the shade***, to obscure by contrast of superior brilliancy, to surpass so as to render insignificant.

**1650** R. STAPYLTON *Strada's Low C. Wars* I. 3 Though I am a stranger to the Court and Camp, a man.. of the shade, yet [etc.]. **1796** BURKE *Regic. Peace* i. (1892) 55 They throw the light on one side only of their case; though.. the other side which is kept in the shade has it's importance too. **1806** *Med. Jrnl.* XV. 556, I have chosen to remain in the shade. **1819** SCOTT *Ivanhoe* xxvii, Hast thou.. sought refuge from oppression in the shade of the convent? **1824** BYRON *Juan* XVI. xliv, Adeline would throw into the shade.. Their sort of half profession. **1852** *Beck's Florist* 229 Young's Crimson King.. puts all other bedding varieties into the shade. **1854** THACKERAY *Newcomes* v, How can we see a man's brilliant qualities if he is what we call in the shade? **1884** *Manch. Exam.* 2 May 4/7 Internal taxation.. is so excessive in other Portuguese colonies as to cast even an illiberal tariff into the shade. **1884** R. W. CHURCH *Bacon* iii. 68 Bacon still remained in the shade.

**d.** *transf.* A fleeting look of displeasure, a 'cloud' on a person's brow or countenance.

**1818** SCOTT *Rob Roy* xii, The whole countenance loses its sterner shades, and becomes serene and placid. **1838** LYTTON *Alice* I. iv, A shade came over her forehead. **1879** E. K. BATES *Egypt. Bonds* I. viii. 183 A shade of annoyance crosses his face.

**2.** In plural. **a.** ***the shades*** (***of night, of evening***, etc.): the darkness of night; the growing darkness after sunset. Also *fig.*

**1582** STANYHURST *Æneis* IV. 8 Watrye shaads Aurora remooued. **1593** SHAKS. *Rich. II*, I. iii. 177 To dwell in solemne shades of endlesse night. **1634** MILTON *Comus* 580 O night and shades, How are ye joyn'd with hell in triple knot. **1667** —— *P.L.* IV. 1015 The Fiend.. fled Murmuring, and with him fled the shades of night. **1682** DRYDEN *Religio Laici* 182 Sin spread once again the Shades of Night. **1717** POPE *Let. to Mrs. M. Blount*, The shades of the evening overtook me. **1744** AKENSIDE *Pleas. Imag.* II. 6 How faint, How slow, the dawn of Beauty and of Truth, Breaks the reluctant shades of gothic night. **1814** SCOTT *Ld. of Isles* III. xx, The shades come down—the day is shut. **1837** CARLYLE *Fr. Rev.* II. IV. vii, The thick shades of night are falling. **1840** THACKERAY *Shabby-genteel Story* vii, The shades of evening had by this time fallen upon the quiet city. **1841** LONGF. *Excelsior* I.

**b.** ***the shades***: the darkness of the nether world; the abode of the dead, Hades. (Often indistinguishable from the collective plural of sense 6).

**1594** KYD *Cornelia* III. i. 107 When shall this soule of mine Come visite thee in the Elisian shades? **1601** CAMPION *Bk. Ayres* I. xx, When thou must home to shades of vnder ground. **1638** G. SANDYS *Paraphr. Job* xxxiv. (1648) 50 No mufling Clouds, nor Shades Infernall, can From his inquiry hide offending Man. **1718** POPE *Iliad* XVII. 349 Sent by great Ajax to the Shades of Hell. **1749** SMOLLETT *Regic.* v. ii, Then let our swords.. Dismiss him to the shades. **1812** BYRON *Ch. Har.* I. vi, And e'en for change of scene would seek the shades below. **1907** QUILLER-COUCH *Introd. to Coleridge's Poems* 1 After a third attempt to embrace his mother in the Shades.

**c.** Applied to the condition of the present life in contrast to that of heaven. *nonce-use.*

**1816** J. WILSON *City of Plague* II. i. 53 Us poor dwellers in the woeful shades Of mortal being.

**3. a.** *Drawing* and *Painting.* Absence of complete illumination as represented pictorially; the parts, or a particular part, of a picture which represent this; the darker colour expressing absence of illumination. Often in ***light and shade***.

**1662** EVELYN *Sculptura* I. (1906) 89 Perel has discovered a particular talent for Landskips, if not a little exceeded in the darknesse of his shades. **1710** WHITWORTH *Acc. Russia* (1758) 40 Miserable paintings without shade or perspective. **1756–7** *Keysler's Trav.* (1760) II. 167 Streaks of *verde antico* inlaid by way of shades. **1768** W. GILPIN *Ess. Prints* (1781) 158 The whole is in dark shade, except three figures on the fore-ground. **1779** *Mirror* No. 48 ¶ 10 By the distribution of light and shade, to make every figure stand out from the canvas. **1799** [G. SMITH] *Laboratory* I. 179 Delineate the outlines or capital strokes and where the shades appear soft. **1812** CARY *Dante, Purg.* XII. 29 What master of the pencil or the style Had traced the shades and lines. **1840** *C. O. Müller's Hist. Lit. Greece* xi. §2 He contemplates it as the shade in a picture. **1907** J. A. HODGES *Elem. Photogr.* (ed. 6) 112 A good contrast of light and shade.

**b.** *transf.* and *fig.* In various applications: those portions of a story, a literary work, or the like, which are designedly less brilliant in effect than others; the less praiseworthy features of a character, the sadder portions of a person's history, etc. ***light and shade***: in a literary work, a musical performance, or the like, the contrast necessary to artistic effect, of passages of lighter and graver tone, or of greater and less brilliancy.

**1732** [see LIGHT *sb.* 12]. **1768** BOSWELL *Corsica* ii. (ed. 2) 80 The shades which were in his private conduct, are to be forgotten. **1818** T. BUSBY *Gram. Mus.* 480 The Voluntary, like the Organ Concerto, should have its lights and shades. *Mod.* (*Conductor loq.*) You must be careful of your light and shade in this passage.

**c.** *Ent.* An ill-defined patch of darker colour on the wing of a moth.

**1869** E. NEWMAN *Brit. Moths* 415 The hind margin is chiefly occupied by a darker band-like shade. *Ibid.* 417 The discoidal spots are green,.. the reniform having.. a gray-brown shade on the median area. In recent Dicts.

**4. a.** Degree of darkness or depth of colour; hence, any of the many minutely differing varieties of quality that may exist in what is broadly considered as one and the same colour; a tint.

By chromatologists (after Clerk Maxwell, *Sci. Papers* 1890 I. 131) the word is used in a more restricted sense, distinguished from *hue* and *tint*. Two varieties of a mixed colour (e.g. lilac) differ in *shade* when one is lighter or darker than the other; in *hue* when the one is more red more blue, etc., than the other; and in *tint* when the one is more or less decided in colour than the other. For a different distinction see quot. 1879.

**1690** LOCKE *Hum. Und.* II. iii. §1 Colours, as white, red, yellow, blue; with their several Degrees or Shades, and Mixtures. **1783** WEDGWOOD in *Phil. Trans.* LXXIII. 285 Darker or lighter shades of black and brown. **1857** MILLER *Elem. Chem., Org.* 274 Various shades of rose, violet, and dark red. **1879** POLE in *Nature* 6 Nov. 15/2 *note*, In technical language mixtures of a colour with white are called *tints*, with black, *shades*. **1885** RIDER HAGGARD *K. Solomon's Mines* xix, My stubbly hair came out of the treasure cave about three shades greyer than it went in.

**b.** *transf.* and *fig.* A minutely-differentiated degree or variety (of a quality, a condition, meaning, etc.). Often advb. with comparatives, ***a shade better, less***, etc.

**1749** SMOLLETT *Gil Blas* IX. ii. (1782) III. 229 He put (to use the expression) different shades of consideration in the civilities he shewed. **1781** GIBBON *Decl. & F.* xviii. II. 89 Among the different branches of the human race, the Sarmatians form a very remarkable shade. **1820** J. W. CROKER *Diary* 2 Feb., The King is a shade better. **1858** O. W. HOLMES *Aut. Breakf.-t.* ix. (1891) 211, I drew my chair a shade nearer to her. **1888** BURGON *Lives 12 Gd. Men* II. v. 13 Men of all shades of opinion.. combined against him.

**c.** A tinge, a minute qualifying infusion (of some quality); colloquially, a minute quantity or portion added or removed.

**1791** BURKE *App. Whigs* 6 Without any shade of sorrow. **1816** SCOTT *Old Mort.* xliii, There was now in his conduct a shade of lunacy. **1860** TYNDALL *Glac.* II. xi. 290, I.. was unwilling to accept an observation of such importance with a shade of doubt attached to it. **1888** PAYN *Myst. Mirbridge* III. l. 257 A touch of pity, just the merest shade, but still a touch, crept into those threatening eyes. **1890** W. J. GORDON *Foundry* 194 Up came Whitworth's highly scientific foreman to tell the American that in their shop they did not work to 'shades', but to measurement.

**II. 5. a.** A dark figure 'cast' upon a surface by a body intercepting light, a shadow. Now *dial.* and *poet.*

*a* **1000** *Cædmon's Exod.* 113 (Gr.) Blace stodon ofer sceotendum scire leoman, scinon scyldhreoðan, sceado swiðredon. *a* **1300** *Cursor M.* 20883 Peter.. a ded he quickend wit his schade. **1340** *Ayenb.* 179 Zuich uolk is ylich þe horse þet heþ drede of his ssede. *c* **1400** *Pety Job* 308 in *26 Pol. Poems* 131 And thus I chaunge in euery shoure, And fle away ryght as a shade. **1561** W. KETHE in *Sc. Psalter* XC. v, They are.. euen lyke a slepe or shade. **1662** EVELYN *Sculptura* v. 122 You see likewise in this very Figure, that the oblique, and direct shades *o u x y* are caused by the cathetus *m t n*. **1750** JOHNSON *Rambler* No. 80 ¶ 2 After a few hours, we see the shades lengthen. **1868** MORRIS *Earthly Par., Cupid & Psyche* 641 And when she woke the shades were lengthening. **1891** HARDY *Tess* xxi, I zid you kissing his shade.

**b.** *fig.* An unsubstantial image of something real; an unreal appearance; something that has only a fleeting existence, or that has become reduced almost to nothing; = SHADOW *sb.* 6. Now only *poet.* or *rhetorical.* Also, with strengthened hyperbole, ***the shadow of a shade***.

**1297** R. GLOUC. (Rolls) 2330 þe king nas him sulf bote as a ssade & let im worþe al out. *a* **1300** *Sarmun* xxxviii. in *E.E.P.* (1862) 5 Man-is lif nis bot a schade nov he is and nov he nis. **1340** *Ayenb.* 77 Holy wryt þet hise clepeþ leazinges and ssed and metinges and uanites. *c* **1580** SIDNEY *Ps.* XXXIX. iv, They are but shades, not true things where we live. **1664** S. CROSSMAN in Palmer *Bk. Praise* (1865) 166 My life's a shade, my days Apace to death decline. **1741–2** GRAY *Agrippina* 43 The consulate, that empty shade Of long-forgotten liberty. **1814** COLERIDGE *To Lady with Falconer's 'Shipwreck'* vi, Remembrances of Friend, Or absent or no more! Shades of the Past, Which Love makes substance! **1815** SCOTT *Guy M.* xxxvii, I am a member of the suffering and Episcopal Church of Scotland—the shadow of a shade now, and fortunately so. **1874** O'SHAUGHNESSY *Music & Moonlight* 185 We die.. And shades, we hunt some shade of our desire.

**c.** *transf.* An inseparable follower or companion. *poet. nonce-use.* Cf. SHADOW *sb.* 8.

**1667** MILTON *P.L.* x. 249 Thou my Shade Inseparable must with mee along.

**6. a.** The visible but impalpable form of a dead person, a ghost. Also, a disembodied spirit, an inhabitant of Hades (= L. *umbra*); chiefly with allusion to pagan mythology. Often collective plural, ***the shades***: the world of disembodied spirits, Hades (cf. sense 2 b).

**1616** SIR W. MURE *Misc. Poems* xvii. 26 Glorefied amidst the schads dewyne. **1697** DRYDEN *Virg. Georg.* IV. 726 The youth essay'd To stop her flight, and strain the flying shade. **1742** GRAY *Eton* 4 Where grateful Science still adores Her Henry's holy Shade. **1798** FERRIAR *Illustr. Sterne* iii. 85 Lucian.. allows only a foot to each of the shades. *a* **1839** PRAED *Poems* (1864) II. 299 Peace to his hallowed shade! **1879** C. F. KEARY *Dawn Hist.* x. 149 A journey after death to reach the home of shades.

**b.** A spectre, phantom. *rare.*

**1598** SHAKS. *Merry W.* v. v. 42 Fairies blacke, gray, greene, and white, You Moone-shine reuellers, and shades of night.

**c.** Orig., in humorous invocation of the spirit of a deceased person, as likely to be horrified or amazed by some action or occurrence. Now usu. in *pl.* and no longer exclusively in humorous use. Also *loosely*, with reference to some person or thing in the past of which a present event is reminiscent.

**1818** MOORE *Fudge Fam. Paris* (ed. 4) 167 Oh, shade of the Cheesemonger! [*Note.* One of the Fancy, who.. was killed .. at Waterloo.] **1863** W. PHILLIPS *Sp.* i. 8 Shades of Hugh Peters and John Cotton, save us from such pulpits! **1866** WYNTER *Our Social Bees* Ser. II. 96 Shade of my aunt! why, her Dresden china poodle dog cost more money. **1899** R. WHITEING *No. 5 John Street* xviii. 183 Shade of Tilda! not a bud but would outvalue your entire stock. **1928** H. CRANE *Let.* 22 Feb. (1965) 317 A paean from Venusberg! Oy-oy-oy! I have just had my ninth snifter of Scotch. O shades of Bert Savoy! **1968** *Listener* 25 July 98/2 The persistent.. demand .. for a major change in the relationship between a free people and the state, for an end to arbitrary, secretive and alien government and for the restoration and maintenance of free institutions. Shades of Disraeli, maybe. **1977** *Times* 26 Nov. 4/3 Colleges.. were.. conducting campaigns to ban Jewish societies... Shades of Nazi Germany (he said). **1978** H. WOUK *War & Remembrance* xxiv. 238 There's a fridge, but it doesn't work. Shades of Singapore.

**7.** = SILHOUETTE *sb.* 1. Now chiefly *Hist.*

**1781** *Advt.* in *N. & Q.* (1900) Ser. IX. VI. 356/2 Old Shades reduced with Care and Expedition. **1793** HOLCROFT *Lavater's Physiogn.* xlii. 219 No art can attain to the truth of the shade taken with precision. **1809** 'J. A. ANDERSEN' *Dane's Excurs.* I. 22 Lord Nelson pointed out to me a profile, and then observed 'You see it is but a shade: yet I had great difficulty in obtaining it'. **1842** *Penny Cycl.* XXII. 8/1. **1960** H. HAYWARD *Antique Coll.* 255/1 Edward Foster of Derby often painted faces in brown, blue or some other colour, and unless details are shown in the faces, such may also be termed shades. **1970** *Oxf. Compan. Art* 1065/1 The great vogue of silhouette portraits (more often known in England as 'shades') came between 1750 and 1850. **1979** *Jrnl. R. Soc. Arts* July 513/1 Anything but an average shade, it is, none-the-less, a competent head-and-shoulders in strict profile.

**III.** Protection from glare and heat.

**8. a.** Cover afforded by the interposition of some opaque or semi-opaque body between an object and light, heat, etc.; esp. the shelter from the sun afforded by trees; quasi-*concr.* (*sing.* and *pl.*) overshadowing foliage.

*c* **1000** *Ags. Ps.* (Th.) xxxv. 8 Manna bearn soðlice symle hopiað to þæm sceade þinra fiðera. **1340** *Ayenb.* 95 þis trau is to alowe and to louie uor manye þinges. Vor þe rote... And uor his uayre ssed. *c* **1350** *Will. Palerne* 22 þe buschys þat.. lent grete schade. **1574** HELLOWES *Gueuara's Fam. Ep.* (1577) 42 When his souldiers saide, the enimies did shoote arrowes so thicke that the sunne was couered, He aunswered: Then let vs fighte in the shade. **1584** B. R. tr. *Herodotus* II. 108 Fayre braunched trees, ouershadowing y[e] waters with a coole & pleasant shade. **1600** SHAKS. *A.Y.L.* II. vii. 111 Vnder the shade of melancholly boughes. **1667** MILTON *P.L.* I. 303 In Vallombrosa, where th' Etrurian shades High overarch't imbowr. **1765** *Museum Rust.* IV. 458 The canal ought not to be under shade. **1841** JAMES *Brigand* i, The high swelling of the mountains round, still gave a pleasant shade to one side of the valley. **1855** BAIN *Senses & Int.* III. iii. §19 Too much light impels us to seek the shade. **1892** *Photogr. Ann.* II. 431 Printing.. should be done in shade by preference.

*fig.* **1599** SHAKS. *Hen. V*, II. ii. 28 There's not I thinke a subiect That sits in heart-greefe and uneasinesse Vnder the sweet shade of your gouernment. **1789** W. BLAKE *Songs Innoc., Cradle Song* 1 Sweet dreams, form a shade O'er my lovely infant's head! **1832** LONGF. *Coplas de Manrique* liii, And he, the good man's shield and shade.

**b.** ***in the shade***: in a position screened from the direct action of the sun's rays; opposed to *in the sun*. Also *fig.*

**1621** T. WILLIAMSON tr. *Goulart's Wise Vieillard* 130 If from his youth he.. hath not bin brought vp in the shade, but hath endured stormes, cold, and extreame parching heate [etc.]. *a* **1700** EVELYN *Diary* June 1645, One may walk all round it, dry, and in the shade. **1826** S. COOPER *First Lines Surg.* (ed. 5) 371 The patient distinctly perceives the light, and can even plainly discern in the shade,.. large objects, or bright colours. **1883** E. A. PARKES *Pract. Hygiene* I. xv. (ed. 6) 435 Two maximum thermometers are issued —one to observe the greatest heat in the sun, the other in the shade.

**9. a.** A place sheltered from the sun; chiefly, a piece of ground overshadowed by trees. Now rare exc. in *collective plural*, with poetical colouring.

*c* **1000** *Sax. Leechd.* I. 284 þone man sceal mid linenan claþe befealdan & on sceade ahon oððet he ȝedriȝed beon mæȝe. *a* **1400–50** *Wars Alex.* 3800 A kniȝt þat zephall was callid fand in a cole schade A litill drysnyng of dewe. **1577** B. GOOGE *Heresbach's Husb.* III. (1586) 140 b, In the noone time.. you must driue them to the valleies and shades. **1646** CRASHAW *Delights* Wks. (1904) 126 No lone shade, but rings With chatting Birds delicious murmurings. **1705** ADDISON

*Italy, Brescia* 61 Corn, that in these warm countries ripens much better among the Mulberry Shades, than if it were expos'd to the open Sun. **1830** J. G. STRUTT *Sylva Brit.* 59 The respectability which leafy shades, of apparently long standing, always confer on a habitation. **1845** KITTO *Cycl. Bibl. Lit.* s.v. *Egypt* (1849) I. 599/2 The climate is.. exceedingly hot..; a shade is not easily found.

**b.** *transf.* A retired spot. Hence, an abode sheltered from the world, a quiet habitation. Chiefly *pl.* Now only *poet.* or rhetorical.

**1605** SHAKS. *Macb.* IV. iii. 1 Let vs seeke out some desolate shade, & there Weepe our sad bosomes empty. **1630** *R. Johnson's Kingd. & Commw.* 536 Delighting in nothing but in ease, in shades, in dancing and drinking. *c* **1710** LADY M. W. MONTAGU *Let. to Mrs. Hewet* (1887) I. 30 People mistake very much in placing peace in woods and shades. **1729** T. COOKE *Tales, Proposals*, etc. 48 Hail to those Shades where, in our golden Age, The godlike Sidney pen'd the deathless Page. **1751** JOHNSON *Rambler* No. 180 ¶9 Men bred in shades and silence.. may be allowed to feel terror at personal danger. **1823** LAMB *Elia* Ser. II. *Poor Relations*, In the depth of college shades..or in his lonely chamber, the poor student shrunk from observation. **1837** DISRAELI *Venetia* I. i, Sought the retired shades of Cherbury.

**c.** In dial. use: A meadow open to the breeze, into which cattle are turned in hot weather.

**1806** [see SINGLE *sb.* 2]. *a* **1847** in F. Sheldon *Minstrelsy Eng. Border* 421 He raced thro' reise and shad. **1893** *Cornhill Mag.* June 591 When they say the cattle come 'to shade' they mean they seek a spot where they are open to the cooling influences of water and breeze.

**10.** *the Shades*: originally, a name for wine and beer vaults with a drinking-bar, either underground or sheltered from the sun by an arcade. Hence subsequently used, both in England and in the U.S., as a name for a retail liquor shop, or a drinking-bar attached to a hotel.

**1823** 'J. BEE' *Dict. Turf, Shades* (the) at London-bridge are under Fishmongers' hall. **1872** SCHELE DE VERE *Americanisms* 315 In the cities Shades are perhaps the most numerous. **1882** E. EDWARDS *Words, Facts & Phrases* 507 *Shades*... The name originated at Brighton... Numbers of other publicans, in London and elsewhere, adopted the name 'Shades', which is now fully established in the language as a synonym for wine vaults.

**11.** Something which affords protection from light, heat, etc. **a.** A shelter from wind and weather, a screen from excessive heat or cold. Also, *U.S.* a window-blind.

**1624** *Capt. Smith's Virginia* III. vii. 73 To keepe vs from the winde we made a shade of another Mat. **1730** A. GORDON *Maffei's Amphith.* 349 The first who invented a Shade in the Theatre. **1814** T. HAYNES *Treat. Strawberry*, etc. (ed. 2) 70 Such shade or skreen will admit of being removed and taken away. **1867** AUGUSTA WILSON *Vashti* xviii, A window opened from the hall, and to-day, though a rose-coloured shade was lowered, the sash had been raised. **1894** HOWELLS *Trav. fr. Altruria* 126 The windows had paper shades.

**b.** A lace scarf for the head worn by women. *Obs.* exc. *dial.*

**1706** PHILLIPS (ed. Kersey), *Shade*,..an Ornament for a Woman's Head. **1738** *Boston News Let.* in Alice M. Earle *Costume Col. Times* (1894) 213 Worsted Shades. **1753** *Ibid.*, White Paris net shades. **1755** *Ibid.* 214 Gauze for Shades. **1766** [ANSTEY] *Bath Guide* iii. 76 All that Fancy's self has feign'd In a Band-Box is contain'd: Painted Lawns and chequer'd Shades. **1800** ELIZA S. BOWNE *Girl's Life* (1888) 42 Why can't you go and see McLellan's lace shades? Perhaps he may let you have one reasonably. **1868** LADY VERNEY *Stone Edge* vii. 81 Lydia appeared in her black 'shade' (a sort of mantle) and hood.

**c.** A dome-shaped cover of glass to protect ornaments from dust or accidental injury.

**1705** HAUKSBEE in *Phil. Trans.* XXV. 2130 A Shade (as they generally call such as are put o're Images to keep them from Dust). **1863** KINGLAKE *Crimea* (ed. 3) I. xiv. §8. 267 One shot broke the mirror over the chimney-piece, another the shade of the clock. **1894** MORRISON *Mean Streets* 115 A 'shade of fruit'—a cone of waxen grapes and apples under a glass cover.

**d.** A globe or cylinder of some semi-transparent substance placed over the flame of a candle, lamp or gas-jet to soften or diffuse the light or to protect the flame from draughts; also, a screen of silk, paper, metal, etc., supported upon a light framework and placed above an illuminant to reflect, concentrate, or soften the light. Also (Westminster School) a lamp with a fixed shade. ***wall shade*** = SCONCE *sb.*[1]

**1780** *Hickey's Bengal Gaz.* 8 Apr. (Y.) Borrowed last Month by a Person or Persons unknown..a very elegant Pair of Candle Shades...—N.B. The Shades have private marks. **1789** I. MUNRO *Narr. Milit. Operat.* 186 His tent is furnished with..a folding-table, a pair of shades for his candles [etc.]. **1825-9** MRS. SHERWOOD *Lady of Manor* III. xxi. 251 It was well lighted up, with many wall-shades and standing-shades. **1884** FORSHALL *Westminster Sch.* 64 The Juniors had then..to clean the 'shades' of the Seniors and third Election. **1891** HARDY *Tess* liii, The two customary candles were burning under their green shades in the Vicar's study.

**e.** A covering worn to protect the eye from light (see quot. 1857). Also *pl.*, sunglasses, tinted glasses (*colloq.*, chiefly *U.S.*).

**1801** NELSON *Let. to Lady Hamilton* 28 Jan., He has directed me..to have green shades for my eyes. **1818** LADY MORGAN *Autobiog.* (1859) 71 The dear Comte de Ségur, with a green shade over his eyes, and almost blind. **1857** BARWELL *Care of Sick* 80 The proper method is to use what is called a shade, made of a piece of cardboard, large enough to hang over the eye. **1958** *Amer. Speech* XXXIII. 225 Less frequently used among nonmusicians (primarily for lack of an occasion) are *shades* (dark glasses). **1965** *N.Y. Times* 11 Apr. E14/6 Your teen-age daughter asks what you think of her 'shades', which you are canny enough to know are her sunglasses. **1976** *National Observer* (U.S.) 10 Apr. 1/4 'Hiya, Rog,' says somebody else, popping up clip-on shades. **1980** G. V. HIGGINS *Kennedy for Defense* vi. 68, I looked at Emerson, hiding behind his shades and his imported-cigarette smoke.

**f.** The part of a head-dress that projects in front so as to shade the eyes; the peak of a cap.

**1818** SCOTT *Hrt. Midl.* xiii, The projecting shade of a curch, or coif.

**g.** In scientific apparatus: a shutter or other mechanical means of intercepting light falling upon or through an object.

**1837** GORING & PRITCHARD *Microgr.* 74, I likewise drew a shade over the objective end of the microscope. **1848** *Knapp's Chem. Technol.* I. 156 Reflectors, shades, &c.

**h.** (See quot. 1894.)

**1894** T. ELLISTON *Organs & Tuning* 127 *Shade*, a flap of metal at the top of a reed pipe to regulate the power, at the top of a flue pipe to tune by—also applied when the tone, pitch, or power of a pipe is affected through being shaded or shadowed by an obstruction. **1925** H. F. MILNE *How to build Small Two-Manual Chamber Pipe Organ* 127 The pipes in many reed stops are of an inverted conical shape, and the regulating device may take the form of either a cap or shade. **1951** R. WHITWORTH *Organ Stops & their Uses* i. 13 The pipe represented at letter L is the much over-used swell oboe for 4 ft C. The bell and its shade on the top should be noticed.

**IV.** *attrib.* and *Comb.*

**12. a.** Simple attrib., as (sense 8) ***shade-mantle, -side***; (sense 8 b) ***shade-heat***; (sense 9) ***shade-plot***; (sense 11) ***shade-frame, -stone***; **b.** objective, as ***shade-giving, -loving, -seeking*** adjs.

**1909** *Cent. Dict. Suppl.*, **Shade-frame*. A frame for the partial shading of a seed-bed. **1859** LANG *Wand. India* 282 A clump of *shade-giving mango trees. **1896** *Allbutt's Syst. Med.* I. 249 We distinguish between radiant or sun heat, and *shade or air heat. **1830** LINDLEY *Nat. Syst. Bot.* 264 Ferns and other *shade-loving plants. **1880** O. CRAWFURD *Portugal* 318 Detached clouds..shall throw their *shade-mantles on the land. **1586** W. WEBBE *Eng. Poetrie* (Arb.) 73 Thou Tityr, at ease in a *shade plott. **1826** MISS MITFORD *Village* II. 173 That..cold-braving, *shade-seeking plant. **1856** MRS. BROWNING *Aur. Leigh* VI. 429 The artist's eye, That keeps the *shade-side of the thing it loves. **1904** H. C. BUTLER *Archit. & other Arts* 126 Another interesting detail of the domestic architecture of Northern Syria is the shed or *shade-stone frequently found over the doorways.

**c.** Instrumental, as ***shade-softened*** adj.

**1866** G. M. HOPKINS *Jrnls. & Papers* (1959) 138 Very level clouds, long pelletted sticks of shade-softened grey in the West.

**13.** Special comb.: **shade-bearer**, a plant which is shade-tolerant; **shade-bearing** *a.*, = *shade-tolerant* adj. below; **shade-card**, a card illustrating the range of colours in which goods are supplied; also *fig.*; **shade-cord**, *U.S.* a blind-cord; **shade-deck**, an upper deck of a passenger vessel, covered at the top but open at the side, forming a sheltered promenade in hot weather; hence **shade-decked** *a.*; **shade-fish**, = MAIGRE *sb.*; **shade-lover, plant**, a plant which thrives in shady conditions; **shade maximum**, the highest temperature recorded in a single day by a thermometer placed in the shade; **shadepull** *U.S.*, a cord for pulling down a window-shade; **shade-reading**, the indication of a thermometer protected from direct influence of the sun's rays; **shade-tolerant** *a.*, able to grow normally in the shade of taller plants; **shade-tree**, a tree planted for the purpose of affording shade.

**1891** *Shade-bearer [see *light-demander* s.v. LIGHT *sb.* 16]. **1959** *Times* 7 Dec. (Agric. Suppl.) p. viii/4 Beech can be the underplant used for amenity work, because it is a shade-bearer. **1889** W. SCHLICH *Man. Forestry* I. ii. 117 Certain species cannot thrive unless they enjoy a large measure of light throughout life, while others will bear a certain amount of shade. Accordingly, the former are called 'light demanding', and the latter *shade bearing species. **1975** T. C. WHITMORE *Tropical Rain Forests of Far East* vi. 71/2 The population structure of light-demanding and shade-bearing species in a stand of high forest is markedly different. **1895** *British Warehouseman* Feb. 38/2 A new and very attractive *shade-card, comprising all the newest tints. **1955** *Radio Times* 22 Apr. 22/2 A free illustrated colour booklet about Snowcem and a shade card. **1961** P. MASON *Common Sense about Race* IV. i. 120 There are words conveying..subtle nuances of skin-colour..a kind of verbal shade-card. **1904** RIIS *Roosevelt* xii. 298 When he passed each window [he] would seize the *shade-cord and give a little abstracted pull. **1894** *Times* 22 Oct. 7/5 The boats are carried on a *shade deck, which forms a covered promenade. **1894** W. H. WHITE *Man. Naval Archit.* (ed. 3) 382 A tank steamer of the 'shade-deck' type. **1902** *Encycl. Brit.* (ed. 10) XXXII. 550/1 Most of the latter have a continuous upper deck above the main deck: if this be of light construction..the vessel is called a *Shade-decked Vessel. **1722** DIAPER tr. *Oppian's Halieut.* I. 214 Here..tim'rous *Shade-Fish the blind Haunts pursue. **1863** COUCH *Brit. Fishes* II. 54 Sciæna. Shade Fish. Maigre. **1960** *Farmer & Stockbreeder* 9 Feb. (Suppl.) 4/2 Other worthwhile *shade-lovers—the climbing fig..and the sweetheart plant. **1896** *Daily News* 20 July 7/3 In London the *shade maximum on Friday was only 67 degrees. **1926** H. A. SPOEHR *Photosynthesis* ii. 103 It would be interesting to determine whether *shade plants such as the *Oxalis*..do not utilize a greater proportion of the light absorbed than plants growing in the direct sunlight. **1974** Shade plant [see SOLARIZATION 1 c]. **1955** W. GADDIS *Recognitions* I. vi. 202 The housefly..drawn to a new destination the instant it halted, from the *shade-pull to the floor, from there to the lampshade. **1973** *Philadelphia Inquirer* (Today Suppl.) 7 Oct. 41/3 Meg is replacing such geegaws with tasteful black shadepulls. **1897** *Ibid.* 21 Sept. 5/2 There was no *shade reading below 40 deg. reported. **1952** J. D. U. WARD *Woodman's Diary* 310 Some other species, mostly in the *shade-tolerant category..allow a wide latitude for neglect and error. **1964** V. J. CHAPMAN *Coastal Veg.* ix. 214 On Fair Isle, Red campion (*Melandrium rubrum*) grows well in the fescue swards, probably because being a woodland species it is shade-tolerant. **1806** *Balance* 22 July 228 (Thornton *Amer. Gloss.*) It is to be regretted that a *shade tree, useful and ornamental as the poplar, should be in danger. **1885** LADY BRASSEY *The Trades* 179 Through plantations of fine coffee, protected by the usual 'shade-trees'.

**shade** (ʃeɪd), *v.*[1] Also 4 **schade**, 8-9 *dial.* **shad.** [f. SHADE *sb.*]

†**1.** *intr.* To cast a shadow. *Obs. rare*$^{-1}$.

**1393** LANGL. *P. Pl.* C. XXI. 479 May no grysliche gost glyde þer hit [the cross] shadeweþ [MS. M. schadeþ].

**2. a.** *trans.* To screen from light or heat, to protect from the glare or heat of the sun's rays.

*c* **1400** in *26 Pol. Poems* (1904) 143 A place I fonde shadyd with bowes I-bent. *c* **1420** ? LYDG. *Assembly of Gods* 65 The grettest trees that any man may fynde In forest to shade the deere for her comfort. **1615** G. SANDYS *Trav.* 120 Barges, shaded with damasks, and stuffes of India. **1697** DRYDEN *Virg. Past.* VII. 16 Here wanton Mincius..shades his happy Banks with bending Reeds. **1707** MORTIMER *Husb.* (1721) II. 58 They cannot well stand too dry, if they are but shaded in dry Weather. **1820** SHELLEY *Orpheus* 12 The overhanging rock That shades the pool. **1874** O'SHAUGHNESSY *Music & Moonlight* 20 Aloe, I made thee A garden to shade thee.

†**b.** To place in the shade; *refl.* To take shelter from light or heat. *Obs.*

*a* **1586** SIDNEY *Arcadia* II. (Sommer) 120b, How to feede his beastes before noone, where to shade them in the extreame heate. **1733** W. ELLIS *Chiltern & Vale Farm.* 140 The Cattle..lie and shade themselves under their Boughs. *fig.* **1639** FULLER *Holy War* II. xxvi. 77 Many retired themselves to solitary places..chiefly to shade themselves from the heat of persecution.

**c.** To protect (one's eyes or face) from the glare of the sun, with the hand or with something used as a screen.

**1782** MISS BURNEY *Cecilia* VI. ix, You have indeed a bad cold my love; but shade your eyes with your hat, and after dinner [etc.]. **1831** SCOTT *Ct. Robt.* xiii, His hand interposed between his eyes and their faces, like a man that would shade his eyesight from the level sun. **1902** 'MICHAEL FAIRLESS' *Roadmender* 74 He shaded his keen old blue eyes, and looked away across the water.

†**d.** *transf.* To overshadow protectingly; to protect. ? *Obs.*

**1613** SHAKS. *Hen. VIII*, v. i. 160 Now good Angels.. shade thy person Vnder their blessed wings. **1667** MILTON *P.L.* IX. 266 Leave not the faithful side That gave thee being, stil shades thee and protects. **1701** DE FOE *Trueborn Eng.* 18 Whose Female Glories shade them from my Song.

¶ **e.** Misused for: To shelter (from wind). *rare.*

**1845** J. COULTER *Adv. in Pacific* viii. 102 They [the hills] shaded it from the trade winds.

**f.** To cover with a screen, to protect (a light) from draughts.

**1827** SCOTT *Surg. Dau.* viii, A large chandelier, which, shaded opposite to his face, threw all the light to the other side of the table. *c* **1885** CHR. G. ROSSETTI *Sick Child's Medit.* 4 Fresh air blows in, and mother shades the light.

**3.** To conceal from view; to hide partially, as by a shadow; to veil, obscure; to disguise.

*c* **1530** *Crt. of Love* 1272 'How is', (quod I) 'that he [Prevy Thought] is shaded thus With yonder cloth, I not of what colour?' **1596** SPENSER *F.Q.* VI. x. 42 Through hollow caues, that no man mote discouer For the thicke shrubs, which did them alwaies shade From view of liuing wight. **1667** MILTON *P.L.* v. 277 A Seraph wing'd; six wings he wore, to shade His lineaments Divine. **1704** SWIFT *T. Tub* Introd. §3 All this he cunningly shades under the following allegory. **1813** SHELLEY *Q. Mab* i. 41 Her golden tresses shade The bosom's stainless pride. **1837** CARLYLE *Fr. Rev.* II. IV. iii, A Lady shaded in broad gipsy-hat. **1908** [MISS E. FOWLER] *Betw. Trent & Ancholme* 72 Shaded from view on the South side.

**4. a.** To cover with shadow, to darken. Also *transf.* and *fig.*

**1599** SHAKS., etc. *Pass. Pilgr.* x, Bright orient pearl, alack, too timely shaded! **1634** SIR T. HERBERT *Trav.* (1638) 253 From this accursed root branching out so many sects as in short time infected and shaded all the orient, in an eclipse of fearfull darknesse. **1794** MRS. RADCLIFFE *Myst. Udolpho* xxxiv, Never..had she watched with so much pleasure.. twilight shade and darkness veil the scene. **1700** PRIOR *Carm. Sec.* xii, The Piece by Virtue's equal Hand is wrought, Mix'd with no Crime, and shaded with no Fault. **1827** SCOTT *Highl. Widow* v, A melancholy smile shaded his cheek.

**b.** To appear like a shadow upon.

*a* **1704** T. BROWN *On Duke Ormond's Recov.* Wks. 1730 I. 49 Ee'r rising down to shade his cheeks began. **1750** tr. *Leonardus's Mirr. Stones* 132 Nassonites is a stone of a sanguin colour, marked or shaded with black veins.

**c.** To cast one's shadow upon, to be close to. *nonce-use.*

**1717** POPE *Iliad* x. 183 But sleep'st thou now? when from yon' Hills the Foe Hangs o'er the Fleet, and shades our Walls below.

**5.** In occasional figurative uses. **a.** To cast into the shade; to surpass, eclipse. **b.** To obscure, dim the lustre of (good qualities). **c.** To throw a veil over (faults).

*c* **1746** J. COLLIER (Tim Bobbin) *View Lanc. Dial.* Wks. (1862) 49 This had like't o shad awth' tother! **1785** ADAMS

*Let.* 17 Nov. in Boswell *Johnson* Advt. ¶4, I wish..a few of our hero's foibles had been a little more shaded. **1813** *Sk. Character* (ed. 2) I. 14 His good qualities were not a little shaded by an inherent pride of ancestry, and an austerity of manners. **1865** Brierley *Irkdale* xiii. I. 210 Queer! It shads Guilliver ut thy feyther ust read abeawt. **1928** S. Lewis *Man who knew Coolidge* I. 45 And I got to admit that Walt's radio shades mine just the least little bit. **1972** *Sydney Morning Herald* 26 Aug. 31/7 University slightly shade Gordon in points scored for and against. **1973** *Observer* 3 June 28/7 Denness, whose 534 runs in first-class matches this season have him shading even Boycott. **1975** *Cork Examiner* 30 May 15/1 Womble survived a bad last hurdle mistake to shade strongly challenging Glenicmurrin by a short head.

**6.** To represent as by a shadow, to shadow forth, symbolize. ***to shade out***: to sketch faintly.

**1591** Sidney *Astrophel* lxxxi, How faine would I paint thee to all mens eyes, Or of thy gifts at least shade out some part! **1596** Spenser *F.Q.* v. vii. 2 Calling him [Iustice] great Osyris..With fayned colours shading a true case.

**7.** *Painting* and *Drawing.* To represent the shade or shadow on (an object); to furnish (a picture) with the indications of shade. In black-and-white or monochrome work: To furnish (a drawing) with the gradated dark markings (produced by lines more or less close together, rubbing of crayon or pencil, a wash of tint, or the like) indicating shade and colour of the object. Hence *occas.* to darken (parts of a diagram, etc.) in a similar manner. ***to shade up***: to fill in (an outline sketch) with markings indicative of contour.

**1797** *Encycl. Brit.* (ed. 3) VI. 116/1 After the learner has made himself..perfect in drawing outlines, his next endeavour must be to shade them properly. **1815** J. Smith *Panorama Sci. & Art* II. 718 The perspective drawing thus produced, may then be completed, by shading it according to the manner in which the light appears to fall on the original. **1848** Thackeray *Van. Fair* l, She buys a couple of begilt Bristol boards..and paints..a shepherd with a red waistcoat on one, and a pink face smiling in the midst of a pencil landscape—a shepherdess on the other..with a little dog, nicely shaded. **1875** Seaton *Fret Cutting* 64, I have not shaded the leaf to show any depth of the carving. **1886** W. N. Brown *Wood Engraving* 33 Filling in or 'shading up' with a softer and darker pencil and washes of Indian ink.

**b.** ***to shade in***: to insert by shading. *fig.*

**1878** *Irish Monthly* VI. 506 And then the eloquent Member for Louth proceeds to shade in the darker tints of this companion picture.

**8.** To colour (a textile fabric) with shades gradually passing one into another.

**1841** *Penny Cycl.* XIX. 495 Shading [of ribbons] 6d. per gross extra. **1845** Mrs. M. J. Howell *Hand-bk. Dress-making* 27 Observe, in silks and satins that are shaded, there is an up and a down.

**9. a.** *intr.* Of a colour, hence *gen.*: To pass by imperceptible degrees *to* or *into* something else; also with *away*, *off*. Also ***to shade away***: to disappear gradually.

**1819** Scott *Let.* in *Lockhart* (1837) IV. viii. 272 It will perhaps shade off into a mild chronic complaint. **1845** Budd *Dis. Liver* 162 The colour of the skin is a golden yellow shading into green. **1855** Brewster *Newton* I. v. 123 Three primary spectra..having their intensity of illumination and maximum at different points, and shading to nothing at their extremities. **1880** E. White *Certainty Relig.* 80 Their own teaching was at once definite and vague, carrying a central lustre and a dimmer enfolding radiance, shading away into the Infinite. **1901** *N. Amer. Rev.* 15 Feb. 235 No other nation has company officers of the average ability and education of our own; but the superiority shades away as their service progresses.

**b.** *trans.* To change or make to pass by imperceptible degrees *into* something else; also with *away*, *off*. Also ***to shade away, down***, to soften the abruptness of (a statement) by qualifying words.

**1818** Scott *Rob Roy* iii, A touch of coarseness and hardness about the manners of the times, which has since, in a great degree, been softened and shaded away. **1864** Bowen *Logic* x. 336 Their various sorts and degrees are shaded into each other imperceptibly. **1873** Symonds *Grk. Poets* viii. 235 The thoughts of Aristophanes are not shaded down, concealed or wrapped up in symbols.

**c.** *trans.* To make a slight or gradual reduction in (a price, value, etc.). Also *intr.* of shares, prices, etc.: to decline slightly in value, cost, etc.

**1875** *Chicago Tribune* 27 Oct. 6/4 Prices are not strong, the quotations being shaded on fair orders. **1899** *Pitman's Commercial Correspondence & Commercial English* xii. 119 Please, therefore, do your best to deliver the finest quality you possibly can at the figure named, or, if you can shade the price a little, it would be advisable to do so. **1903** *Boston Transcript* 24 Oct. 22 To spur his freight traffic manager to get business without shading rates. **1928** *New Statesman* 28 July (Finance Suppl.) p. x, The newsprint and pulp industry..has..been developed rather faster than the demand, with the result that prices have been shaded. **1966** *Times* 17 June 16/4 If a favourite or near-favourite was being quoted at two-to-one as its price in the ring and on the rails, and if a certain bookie had not got it in his book, far from 'shading the odds', he had to increase them to attract money on that horse for his book. **1973** 'R. MacLeod' *Burial in Portugal* iv. 90 When he'd bought, Consolidated had already been shading at 130 and Maltsters had been on the upswing at 146. **1978** *Daily Tel.* 29 Mar. 21 Banks may be invited..to shade the margin over base rate which they charge private customers and small businesses. **1981** *Times* 7 May 24 General Accident..shaded 10p to 334p.

**d.** *trans.* To modify the pitch of (an open organ stop) by placing something near the top of the pipe. *rare.*

**1876** Stainer & Barrett *Dict. Mus. Terms* 395/1 *Shading of pipes*, the placing of anything so near the top of an organ pipe as to affect the vibrating column of air which it contains. **1894** [see shade *sb.* 11 h].

**shade**, *v.*[2] Forms: 3–5 schade, 9 shade. [Northern repr. OE. *scādan*, *sceādan*: see shed *v.*]

†**1.** *intr.* To distinguish *between*. *Obs. rare*$^{-1}$.

*c* **1300** *Cursor M.* 22930 Wel bituix þam can he schade.

†**2.** *trans.* To shed, scatter abroad. *Obs. rare*$^{-1}$.

*c* **1425** *Cast. Persev.* 2329 in *Macro Plays* 146 Gostly grace I spylle & schade.

**3.** *Sc.* To part (the hair). Also *transf.*

**1818** Scott *Hrt. Midl.* xvii, Hastily shading her dishevelled hair back from her wasted, but still beautiful countenance. **1824** Mactaggart *Gallovid. Encycl.* 116 He'd shade the binwud door aside. **1869** [McLennan] *Peasant Life* Ser. I. 265 To have her hair combed and shaded.

**shade**, doubtful form of shoad.

**shaded** ('ʃeɪdɪd), *ppl. a.* [f. shade *v.*[1] + -ed[1].]

**1. a.** Protected from light or heat.

**1634** Habington *Castara* I. (Arb.) 49 I'de rather like the violet grow Vnmarkt i'th shaded vale. *a* **1691** Boyle *Hist. Air* (1692) 153, I placed a piece of amber in a shaded part of a window. **1756** Mrs. Calderwood in *Coltness Collect.* (Maitl. Club) 186 There are shaded walks for study and contemplation. **1827** Keble *Burial of Dead* 45 in *Lyra Apost.* (1849) 59 If human anguish o'er the shaded brow Pass shuddering, when the handful of pure earth Touches the coffin lid. **1897** Mary Kingsley *W. Africa* 276 These narrow shaded swamps gave us a world of trouble.

**b.** Of a lamp, candle: Covered with a shade. Also as second element with a specifying colour.

**1836** Dickens *Sk. Boz* (1837) 2nd Ser. 352 A shaded lamp by the bed-side. **1865** Dickens *Mut. Fr.* III. v, He was standing with some papers in his hand by a table with shaded candles on it. **1866** Mrs. H. Wood *St. Martin's Eve* xxxviii, A small shaded reading lamp. **1881** Lady D. Hardy *Through Cities & Prairie Lands* 96 The shaded lamps were lighted. **1903** H. James *Ambassadors* xvi. 222 His dinner with Maria Gostrey, between the pink-shaded candles. **1956** E. Grierson *Second Man* i. 32 The secluded corner table with the shaded lights. **1973** I. Drummond *Jaws of Watchdog* xii. 157 A red-shaded lamp.

**2.** Covered with shadow.

**1670** Dryden *1st Pt. Conq. Granada* III. i. Song (1673) 27 From her white Temples fell her shaded Hair, Like Cloudy Sunshine, not too brown nor fair. **1725** Pope *Odyss.* XI. 12 O'er the shaded billows rush'd the night. **1829** *Chapters Phys. Sci.* 402 If the moon indeed be attentively viewed, some days after her conjunction, the boundary of the shaded part will be seen as it were indented.

†**3.** Obscurely hinted, shadowed forth. *Obs.*

**1583** Melbancke *Philotimus* K iv, His highnes perceiuing the shaded drift, called a counsell of diuers noble men [etc.].

**4. a.** Having colours gradually passing into one another, marked with gradations of colour.

**1710** Steele *Tatler* No. 151 ¶1, The artificial nosegay, and shaded furbelow. **1799** *Hull Advertiser* 25 May 3/1 A complete stock of shaded worsted. **1891** 'J. S. Winter' *Lumley* v, These shaded pink geraniums are exquisite.

**b.** In collectors' names of moths: see quots.

**1832** J. Rennie *Butterfl. & Moths* Index 277 Shaded Broad Bar. **1869** E. Newman *Brit. Moths* 151 The Shaded Broad Bar (*Thera obeliscata*). *Ibid.* 122 The Shaded Pug (*Eupithecia subumbrata*).

**5.** Of a drawing, etc.: see shade *v.*[1] 7. Also, of a colour or coloured object: Edged or variegated *with* some darker colour.

**1796** Withering *Brit. Plants* (ed. 3) IV. 188 Gills extremely white: pileus mouse-colour, shaded with brown. **1813** Shelley *Q. Mab* ii. 17 Those far clouds of feathery gold, Shaded with deepest purple. **1839** R. S. Robinson *Naut. Steam Eng.* 107 The shaded spaces *b b*, representing the position of the valve when shut. **1869** *Athenæum* 20 Feb. 279/1 An outline woodcut copy, and also a shaded one, of Occleve's beautiful miniature of Chaucer. **1871** *Amer. Encycl. Printing* (ed. Ringwalt) 405 *Shaded*, a general name for many varieties of job-letter, in which the main character is shaded.

**6.** Of prices, values, etc.: see shade *v.*[1] 9 c.

**1960** *Farmer & Stockbreeder* 26 Jan. 4/1 Oilcakes in limited demand at shaded rates. **1976** *Birmingham Post* 16 Dec. 9/11 R. and A. G. Crossland at 16½p and Moss Engineering 44p shaded, brighter contrasts being provided by Willmot Breeden at 49p.

**shadeful** ('ʃeɪdfʊl), *a. rare.* [f. shade *sb.* + -ful.] Abounding in shade; umbrageous.

**1563** B. Googe *Eclogs* i. (Arb.) 34 Then shadefull places oute he lookes, and all alone he lyues. **1596** R. L[inche] *Diella* (1877) 78 O'regrowne it was with mighty shadefull Trees. **1613** Drayton *Poly-olb.* iii. 78 The Easterne Avon vaunts..To be the onelie child of shadefull Sauernake.

**shadeless** ('ʃeɪdlɪs), *a.* [f. shade *sb.* + -less.]

**1.** Lacking shade, without shelter (from heat, etc.).

**1814** Wordsw. *Excurs.* VII. 143 An opening Shadeless, and shelterless. **1882** Arnold in *Macm. Mag.* XLVI. 145 The shadeless streets of a hot and dusty town.

**2.** Affording no shade.

**1890** H. H. Johnston in *Nature* 13 Nov. 46 The shadeless acacias with their cruel thorns.

**3.** Not marked by shadows; unrelieved by shade, monotonously faultless.

**1835** Mrs. Browning *Felicia Hemans* 2 Thou bay-crowned living One, that o'er the bay-crowned Dead art bowing, And, o'er the shadeless moveless brow, the vital shadow throwing. **1894** H. Nisbet *Bush Girl's Rom.* 13 Walter Scott was a little heavy for her with his introductions, while his heroines were just a trifle shadeless and uninteresting.

**4.** Not furnished with a shade.

**1852** Maitland *Eight Ess.* 237 Though for reasons of his own he might incessantly wear a shadeless cap.

Hence '**shadelessness.**

**1894** H. Nisbet *Bush Girl's Rom.* 153 Its sunny shadelessness filled him with a strange tremor of dread. **1909** *Eng. Rev.* Apr. 70 In the wonderful light and shadelessness of that noon..I looked at you.

**shader** ('ʃeɪdə(r)). *rare.* [f. shade *v.*[1] + -er[1].] One who or something which shades (in various senses of the verb).

**1728** *Capt. G. Carleton's Mem.* 151 In every Age Virtue has its Shaders or Maligners. **1765** J. Brown *Chr. Jrnl.* 221 Black and deep the night begins to fall; a shader immense. **1881** *Instr. Census Clerks* (1885) 55 Flower Making.. Shader. *Ibid.* 64 Woollen Cloth Manufacture..Shader.

**shadew(e**, obs. forms of shadow.

**shadewy**, obs. form of shadowy.

‖**shadi** ('ʃɑːdiː). [Hind. *shādī.*] In the Indian subcontinent: a wedding, marriage.

**1893** Kipling *Many Inventions* 223 Make the *shadi* swiftly, and the girl will make him a Mussalman. **1897** F. A. Steel *Potter's Thumb* 299 There's going to be a big shâdi (wedding)..to-morrow morning. **1978** 'M. M. Kaye' *Far Pavilions* xxx. 443 A canopy..beneath which the sacred fire would be lighted and the officiating priests perform the *shadi*, the marriage ceremony.

**shadine** (ʃæ'diːn). [f. shad *sb.*, after sardine.] A trade name for the menhaden, preserved in oil like a sardine.

**1782** Crevecoeur *Lett.* 132 It is on the shores of this part of the island..where they catch their best fish, such as sea-bass, tew-tag or black fish,..shadine, pike, &c. **1842** in *Mem. Amer. Acad.* (1846) II. 260 *Alosa sadina*, Spotted Shadine. **1888** Goode *Amer. Fishes* 386 'American Sardine', 'American Club-fish', 'Shadine' and 'Ocean Trout'.

**shadiness** ('ʃeɪdɪnɪs). [f. shady *a.* + -ness.] The quality or condition of being shady.

**1611** Cotgr., *Opacité*, opacitie, shadinesse, vmbrage. **1652** J. Wright tr. *Camus' Nat. Paradox* xii. 361 The.. Shadiness of the Chamber. **1863** Bates *Nat. Amazons* I. 82 It is difficult to see the bird in the woods, on account of..the shadiness of its dwelling-places. *Mod.* I agree with you as to the shadiness of their transactions.

**shading** ('ʃeɪdɪŋ), *vbl. sb.* [f. shade *v.*[1] + -ing[1].] The action of shade *v.*[1] in various senses.

**1.** Protection from light or heat.

**1611** Cotgr., *Ombragement*, a shading or shadowing. **1821** Scott *Kenilw.* ii, I thought I might take the privilege of an old comrade to ride across through the trees, both for shading..and for avoiding of dust. **1858** Glenny *Everyday Bk.* 210/1 Attention to the watering and shading is all that is required for the established plants.

**2.** A foreshadowing, adumbration.

**1850** Wordsw. *Prel.* iv. 248 Whatever shadings of mortality,..Had come among these objects heretofore.

**3. a.** Delineation of shade; a marking or colouring resembling this.

**1663** Gerbier *Counsel* 85 Painting..upon flat moulding, and set off with shading. **1766** Fordyce *Serm. Young Women* (1767) I. vi. 253 The business of shading with the needle is now..seldom thought of but at school. **1839** Dickens *Nich. Nick.* iv, Gilt letters and dark shading. **1882** Morris *Hopes & Fears for Art* iv. (1903) 148 Gradation, which in more naturalistic work is got by shading.

*fig.* **1896** Mrs. Caffyn *Quaker Grandmother* 254, I fear the finer shading was entirely omitted in the making of me.

**b.** *Mus.* The imparting of 'light and shade'.

**1881** Broadhouse *Mus. Acoustics* 331 That expression.. was obtained..by the much more delicate shading of various transpositions of consonant chords.

**4. a.** A minute variation or difference (of a colour, hence of a quality, species, etc.).

**1775** Ash, *Shading*, the different gradation of colours. **1858** Sears *Athan.* xix. 168 The seven colors and their shadings. **1863** Dana *Man. Geol.* 602 Appearances suggesting the idea of such shadings among species are.. rare.

**b.** ***shading-off***: decrease in the intensity of a colour, or its passage *into* some other, by imperceptible gradations; also *fig.* of a quality, species, or the like.

**1858** Mallet in *Rep. Brit. Assoc.* I. 60 The shading-off or evanescence of tint. **1885** *Manch. Exam.* 6 Mar. 5/4 In Egypt..there is no gradual shading off from fertile into waste ground. **1892** *Spectator* 16 Jan. 77/2 The University ..lends its influence even to the shading-off of one political class into another.

**c.** A spurious variation in brightness over parts of a televised image. Freq. *attrib.*

**1940** D. G. Fink *Princ. Television Engin.* ix. 414 The remaining item of equipment necessary to produce a composite video signal of adequate quality is the shading correction generator required with cameras of the iconoscope (storage-mosaic) type. **1961** G. Millerson *Technique Television Production* iii. 50 Shading is reduced manually, by adjusting electronic correction circuits. **1969** G. L. Hansen *Introd. Solid-State Television Systems* xi. 269 If the red, green, and blue channels were called upon to reproduce a white scene, the unbalance caused by the corner shading in the red channel would produce a red hue in the corner. *Ibid.*, Shading generators..supply waveforms to the cathodes of the camera tubes to offset the variations that are present because of shading irregularities.

**5.** A toning-down, qualifying (of a statement).

**1818** Scott *Rob Roy* xiii, The circumlocutions, shadings, softenings, and periphrasis, which usually accompany explanations betwixt persons of different sexes in the higher orders of society.

**shading** ('ʃeɪdɪŋ), *ppl. a.* [f. SHADE *v.*[1] + -ING[2].] That shades, in various senses of the vb.

**1.** Affording protection from heat or light.

*a* **1586** SIDNEY *Arcadia* I. x. ¶7 (1912) 63 Grasse (which plentifully grewe, brought up under the care of those wel shading trees). **1671** MILTON *P.R.* III. 221 A shelter and a kind of shading cool Interposition, as a summers cloud. *c* **1709** PRIOR *First Hymn of Callim.* 15 Wild Lycæus, black with shading Pines. **1910** *Westm. Gaz.* 19 Feb. 14/2 If such a shading hood were applied at all times.. the clearness of the photograph taken would be very much clearer.

†**2.** Delineating shade. *Obs. rare*⁻¹.

**1667** MILTON *P.L.* III. 509 Thick with sparkling orient Gemmes The Portal shon, inimitable on Earth By Model, or by shading Pencil drawn.

**shadkhan, shadkin,** vars. SHADCHAN.

**shadock,** obs. form of SHADDOCK.

**shadoing,** obs. form of SHADOWING *sb.*

**shadoof** (ʃə'du:f). Also schaduf, shadouf, shaduf, shayduf; chadous. [Egyptian Arabic *shādūf.*] A contrivance used in the East for raising water for irrigation purposes, consisting of a rod or pole working upon a pivot, at one end of which is fastened a bucket and at the other a weight to serve as a counterpoise.

**1836** LANE *Mod. Egypt.* xiv. (1890) 300 The most common of these machines is the 'shadoof'. **1837** WILKINSON *Mann. & Cust. Anc. Egypt.* ii. (1841) I. 53 The mode of irrigation was by the *shadoof.* **1858** HOMANS *Cycl. Comm.* 440/1 The cotton plants [in Egypt] are watered periodically by means of Sakyiehs, Shadoufs, or water-wheels. **1885** LOCK *Workshop Rec.* Ser. IV. 90/2 The shadoof or chadous of Egypt. **1904** H. SPENCER *Autobiog.* II. 338 The fellahs.. work all day with their shadoofs, raising water to irrigate their lands. **1937** *Times Lit. Suppl.* 10 Apr. 268/2 The sounds which run as an undercurrent beneath the activities of Egyptian life.. are the creak of the water-wheel and of the *shaduf.* **1961** G. CLARK *World Prehist.* v. 109 For any great extension of the fertile zone it was necessary to cut channels and lift the Nile waters into them by some such device as the *schaduf.* **1974** *Encycl. Brit. Micropaedia* IX. 100/3 (*caption*) Villagers in the state of Tamil Nadu, India, using a shaduf to raise water from a stream into irrigation channels.

**shadow** ('ʃædəʊ), *sb.* Forms: 1 *dat.* sceadwe, sceaduwe, 2 sceadewe, 2–3 scadewe, 2–5 shadewe, 3 scheadewe, scaudu, sadue, 3–4 schadw(e, 3–5 schadew(e, 3–7 schadow, 4 schadu(e, shaldw, shadw, shadu, shodow, sadwe, szadewe, *Sc.* schedow, -aw, 4–5 shadue, shadwe, 4–6 schadowe, 4, 6 *Sc.* schaudow, 4, 6–7 shaddowe, 4–7 shadowe, 4, 7 schadou, 5 schado, shadew, shedow, 5–7 shaddow, 6 shadoe, shadoo, shadou, shoddowe, *Sc.* schaudou, schaddou, 6–7 *Sc.* schaddow, 7 shaddou, 8 shadoue, 4– shadow. [repr. OE. *scead(u)we*, oblique case of *sceadu* str. fem.; the nom. sing., with the variant form *sceade* of the oblique case, and the by-form *scead* neut., are represented by SHADE *sb.*, q.v. The Teut. cognates show some variation in declension and gender: OS. *scado* masc. or fem. (MLG. *schade, schadewe*, mod. LG. *schadde, scharde, scharre, scharr*); cf. mod. WFris. *skaed*, EFris. *schād*, NFris. *skaar*); MDu. *schade, schaduwe* (mod.Du. *schaduw* fem.); OHG. *scato* masc., genit. *scatewes* (MHG. *schate, schatte* str. and wk. masc., also *schatewe*, early mod.G. *schatte* wk. masc., mod.G. *schatten* masc.); wanting in ON. (the mod.Norw. *skadda, skodda* fog, is of doubtful origin); Goth. *skadus* masc. The OTeut. form was prob. **skadwo-z* masc. or **skadwā* fem. (the traces of *u* declension in Goth. and OE. being due to analogical alteration):—pre-Teut. **skotwó-s, -wā́* or **skatwó-s, -wā́*; cf. Gr. σκότος masc. and neut., darkness, OCeltic **skāto-s* masc. (Irish *scáth*, Cornish *scod*, Breton *squeut*, Welsh *cy-sgod*, shadow).]

**I.** Comparative darkness.

**1. a.** Comparative darkness, esp. that caused by interception of light; a tract of partial darkness produced by a body intercepting the direct rays of the sun or other luminary. Cf. sense 11.

*a* **1220** *Bestiary* 648 Ðanne cumeð ðis elp unride, and.. slepeð bi ðe tre in ðe sadue. *c* **1325** *Gloss. W. de Bibbesw.* in Wright *Voc.* 159 E pus au boys en umbrail [*glossed* in the sadwe (szadewe)] Passerom desouz l'overayl. *a* **1366** CHAUCER *Rom. Rose* 1411 And fayre in shadowe was euery wel. *c* **1421** *26 Pol. Poems* 104 So soþfast sunne, by hys pouste, Dryueþ awey shadewe. **1555** EDEN *Decades* II. i. (Arb.) 106 The shadowe of the tree is contagious. **1603** SHAKS. *Meas. for M.* III. i. 257 That the time may haue all shadow, and silence in it. **1820** BELZONI *Egypt & Nubia* III. 400 Where there is no index to direct the stranger on his way,.. nor even a stone or a shadow to shelter him from the sun. **1860** TYNDALL *Glac.* I. vi. 42 The fronts of the ridges ..remain in shadow all the day. **1902** R. BAGOT *Donna Diana* xxi. 258 She quietly withdrew from the bedside, and stood in the shadow of the curtains at its head.

**b.** *shadow of death*: a Biblical expression (= LXX and N.T. σκιὰ θανάτου, Vulg. *umbra mortis*) embodying an ancient interpretation of Heb. צלמות, traditionally vocalized *çal'māveth*, as if f. *çēl* shadow + *'māveth* death.

Ewald and many other scholars, however, think the word should be pronounced *çalmūth* (or as pl. *çᵉlāmōth* = Arab. *ḍalamāt*), and that it comes from the Semitic root found in Arab. as *ḍalima* to be dark. However this may be, it is in the Old Testament merely a poetic word for intense darkness (so the margin of the Revised Version, 'deep darkness'). But the phrase 'shadow of death' has (in Eng. as in Christian Latin and other langs.) often been used with various meanings naturally suggested by the words; the commonest use is to denote the gloom and horror of approaching dissolution.

*the valley of the shadow of death* (Ps. xxiii. 4 in Eng. versions from Coverdale 1535; the earlier versions follow the Vulg. and LXX, which read 'midst' instead of 'valley'): often applied to the experience of being brought by illness apparently near to the grave.

*The Land of the Shadow of Death*: a rhetorical name for a tract of Western Africa in which the mortality among the white inhabitants is very great.

[*a* **900** CYNEWULF *Christ* 118 þa þe longe ær.. deorc deaþes sceadu dreogan sceoldan.] *c* **1050** *Lambeth Ps.* cvi. 10 Ða sittendan on þeostrum & on sceaduwe deaþes. *a* **1340** HAMPOLE *Psalter* cvi. 10 In shadow of ded, þat is in vicious life, þat is, ymage of endles ded. *c* **1386** CHAUCER *Pars. T.* 177 The lond of mysese and of derknesse, where as is the shadwe of deeth [= *Job* x. 22, Vulgate]. **1535** COVERDALE *Ps.* xxii[i]. 4 Though I shulde walke now in the valley of the shadowe of death [so **1611**]. **1678** BUNYAN *Pilgr.* I. (1900) 58 Now at the end of this Valley, was another, called the Valley of the Shadow of Death. **1889** 'MARK TWAIN' *Yankee at Crt. K. Arthur* xli. 480 If you've watched your child through the valley of the Shadow and seen it come back to life. **1897** MARY KINGSLEY *W. Africa* 441 The.. depressing scenery of the Land of the Shadow of Death—a land that stretches from Goree to Loanda. **1910** *Lond. Mag.* Dec. 478/2 That Valley of the Shadow of Death which lies between Wolverhampton and Birmingham.

**c.** *fig.* with various notions: Gloom, unhappiness; a temporary interruption of friendship; something that obscures the lustre of a reputation.

**1855** LONGF. *Hiawatha* x, Love is sunshine, hate is shadow. **1894** DOYLE *Sherlock Holmes* 38 There never was a shadow between us until this accursed affair began. **1905** *Century Mag.* Aug. 484/1 The episode left an unfortunate shadow on the sportsmanship of the visitors.

**d.** *Psychol.* In the theory of C. G. Jung (1875–1961), the dark aspect of personality formed by those fears and unpleasant emotions which, being rejected by the self or persona of which an individual is conscious, exist in the personal unconscious; an archetype in which this aspect is concentrated.

**1923** H. G. BAYNES tr. *Jung's Psychological Types* iv. 203 For the sake of understanding, it is, I think, a good thing to detach the man from his shadow, the unconscious... One sees much in another man which does not belong to his conscious psychology, but which gleams out from his unconscious. **1940** S. DELL tr. *Jung's Integration of Personality* (1941) iii. 70 To take his [*sc.* the devil's] place there are human beings to whom we gratefully resign our shadows. With what pleasure.. we read newspaper reports of crime. *Ibid.* 88 The three archetypes so far mentioned —the shadow, the anima, and the wise old man—are of the kind immediately experienced in personified form. **1959** *Listener* 29 Oct. 723/2 Jung defined an archetypal image which he called the shadow... The shadow actually became, in his designation, a term which covered a wide variety of impulses and wishes, most of which were felt to be evil or at least inadmissible. **1973** *Jrnl. Genetic Psychol.* Mar. 165 The shadow is described as the dark side of the personality or representing the original conception of evil in the world. The latter conception places the shadow in the collective unconscious.

**2.** *pl.* **a.** The darkness of night; the growing darkness after sunset.

**1382** WYCLIF *Song Sol.* ii. 17 To the time that the dai springe, and shadewes be bowid in. *a* **1611** BEAUM. & FL. *Four Plays in One, Tri. Death* Wks. 1912 X. 349 Give me such kisses as the Queen of shadows Gave to the sleeping boy she stole on Latmus. **1728** YOUNG *Ocean* xix, The stars are bright To chear the night, And shed, thro' shadows, temper'd fire. **1865** BARING-GOULD *Hymn*, '*Now the day is over*' i, Shadows of the evening Steal across the sky.

†**b.** *the shadows*: the shades, Hades. *Obs. rare.*

**1490** CAXTON *Eneydos* xx. 73 Wherof I shalle make my reporte vnto the pryue goddis, beyng in the lowe shadowes.

**3. a.** *Painting* and *Drawing.* The darker part of a picture, etc. representing the less illuminated portions of the original. Also the colour used in the tincture of such a part. = SHADE *sb.* 3 (which is now more usual).

**1486** *Bk. St. Albans, Her.* c viij, A dowte theer is yit of a certayn shadow of a mylnerys cros as it shewith here folowyng [etc.]. **1565** COOPER *Thesaurus, Vmbræ pictorum..* Shadows cast in peynctyng. **1675** A. BROWNE *App. Art Limning* 9 An Excellent Shadow for Old Mens Bodies, temper Pink, Lake, and Red Lead. **1778** SIR J. REYNOLDS *Disc.* viii. (1779) 19 One of the first rules.. respecting his conduct and management of light and shadow, would be what Leonardo Da Vinci has actually given. **1885** LOCK *Workshop Rec.* Ser. IV. 365/1 The result is a negative harmonious from high light to clear shadow. **1907** J. A. HODGES *Elem. Photogr.* (ed. 6) 116 The lights being hard and the shadows dense.

**b.** = *eye-shadow* s.v. EYE *sb.*[1] 28.

**1936** *Time* 26 Oct. 39/2 Make-up Man Senz 'deepened' Miss Phillips' bulgy eyes with dark brown 'shadow'. **1966** *Vogue* Dec. 84/3 Soft liquid shadows in browns, greys and seaweed greens to put near the curve. **1976** 'E. MCBAIN' *Guns* vii. 198 She wears orange lipstick... There is green shadow on her eyelids.

**II.** Image cast by a body intercepting light.

**4. a.** The dark figure which a body 'casts' or 'throws' upon a surface by intercepting the direct rays of the sun or other luminary; the image (approximately exact or more or less distorted) which this figure presents of the form of the intercepting body. Phr. ***under*** or ***in the shadow of***: within the purlieus of, close up against, in proximity to.

*a* **1300** *Cursor M.* 19277 Þe seke war born þam for to mete, þat petre scaudu on þaim suld rine þar-of had mani seke medicine. *c* **1386** CHAUCER *Pars. T.* 212 Certes a shadwe hath the liknesse of the thyng of which it is shadwe. *c* **1450** *Mirk's Festial* 188 Wher þat euer he ȝeode, and his schadow glod on a seke body, he was hole anon. **1553** T. WILSON *Rhet.* II. 56, I solde you not the shadowe of the Asse. **1635** N. CARPENTER *Geog. Del.* I. x. 226 The shaddow is alwayes found to be opposite in place to the Sunne-beams. **1785** MISS FIELDING *Ophelia* I. xxiii, Lord Larborough.. followed me about like a shadow. **1822** IMISON *Sci. & Art* I. 467 Eclipses of the moon are owing to the shadow of the earth falling upon the moon. **1874** tr. *Lommel's Light* 14 An opaque body is illuminated on that side of its surface only which is turned towards the light, its opposite surface, as well as a space covered by it, the shadow, remains dark. *fig.* **1801** CAMPBELL *Lochiel's Warn.* 56 Coming events cast their shadows before. **1853** C. BRONTË *Villette* I. v. 85, I lie in the shadow of St. Paul's. **1931** *Times Lit. Suppl.* 20 Aug. 625/4 The gradual rise of Innsbruck from a little village lying under the shadow of the great castle of the Dukes of Andechs to the.. capital city of Tyrol.

**b.** Phrases, ***to be afraid of one's own shadow***: to be unreasonably timorous. ***may your shadow never grow (be) less!*** may you keep on increasing (in prosperity)! [A Persian phrase.]

**1568** GRAFTON *Chron.* II. 659 Whether shee were afrayed of her awne shadowe.. the truth is, that the whole army returned to their Shippes. **1824** [MORIER] *Hajji Baba* xxviii. II. 64 'May his shadow never be less', said another. **1863** R. F. BURTON *Wand. W. Africa* I. 9 *note*, The little fleet—may its shadow never be less!—began with chartered ships. **1887** *Referee* 2 Jan. (Cass.), The recipients hope.. that Sara's shadow may never grow less.

**c.** As a type of what is fleeting or ephemeral.

*a* **1272** *Luue Ron* 32 in *O.E. Misc.* 94 Þus is þes world as þu mayht seo al so þe schadewe þat glyt away. **1340** HAMPOLE *Pr. Consc.* 715 Man.. passes away Als a shadu on the somers day. ? *c* **1415** HOCCLEVE *Min. Poems* 67 Lyf passith as a shadwe in euery age. **1830** SCOTT *Jrnl.* II. 160 In this phantasmagorial place [London] the objects of the day come and depart like shadows. **1871** CASWALL *Hymn*, '*Days and Moments*' II. i, As a shadow life is fleeting.

**d.** *Optics*, etc. †***right shadow***: the figure thrown by an opaque body upon a horizontal plane to which it is perpendicular. †***contrary***, †***versed shadow***: the figure thrown by an opaque body upon a vertical plane to which it is perpendicular. ***geometric shadow***: the figure produced upon a vertical screen by extending the lines from a luminous point which envelop an opaque body placed between the screen and the point. †***line of shadows***: a scale engraved upon some mathematical instruments used in taking altitudes; = QUADRAT.

**1571** DIGGES *Pantom.* I. xii. D iij b, Marke well the diuisions of pointes touched in your scale, if they be of right shadow... But and if they bee of contrarie shadow, worke contrarely. **1644** NYE *Gunnery* II. (1670) 37 But if of contrary or vers'd shadow, multiply the distance from the middle of your foot by the parts cut. **1727–52** CHAMBERS *Cycl., Quadrat, Quadratum*, called also *geometrical square*, and *line of shadows*, is an additional member on the face of the common Gunter's and Sutton's quadrants. **1882** *Encycl. Brit.* XIV. 581/1 How to place a plane quadrilateral of given form so that its geometric shadow may be a square.

**e.** *transf.* (See quots.)

**1873** *Proc. London Math. Soc.* IV. 271 Immediately in the rear of a sufficiently large sphere there will be a sound shadow. **1875** TYNDALL *Sound* vii. (ed. 3) 317 The possible influence of a sound-shadow. **1883** *Ibid.* (ed. 4) 299 *heading*, Acoustic Shadows. **1895** *Funk's Stand. Dict.*, *Shadow*, A region protected or screened off from radiation of any kind: used with qualification or in composition; as, a sound-shadow; an electric shadow.

**f.** A dark area in a (positive) radiograph (appearing as a light area in a negative).

**1903** PUSEY & CALDWELL *Practical Application Röntgen Rays* I. v. 120 (*caption*) Apparatus for orthographic projection of *x*-ray shadows on fluorescent screen. **1928** A. TURNBULL tr. *Köhler's Röntgenol.* 187 Dense bean-like shadows lateral to the upper opening of the hip-joint.. have been observed. **1964** LE ROUX & DODDS *Portfolio Chest Radiographs* i. 17 (*caption*) A normal P.A. chest radiograph of a young adult female with dense mammary shadows.

**5.** In loose or extended use.

**a.** A reflected image.

A similar use of the corresponding sb. is found in many other langs.

*c* **1175** *Lamb. Hom.* 29 Hu maht þu iseon þine sceadewe in worie watere? *c* **1200** *Trin. Coll. Hom.* 29 Hie [*sc.* þe wimman] bihalt hire sheawere, and cumeð hire shadewe þaronne, þe shadewe hire tacheð [etc.]. *a* **1366** CHAUCER *Rom. Rose* 1529 He [*sc.* Narcissus] louede his owne shadowe soo That atte laste he starf for woo. *c* **1470** HENRYSON *Mor. Fab.* x. (*Fox & Wolf*) xxiv, The schadow of the mone schone in the well. **1601** SHAKS. *Jul. C.* I. ii. 58 Such Mirrors.. That you might see your shadow. **1692** R. L'ESTRANGE *Fables* vi. 5 But out of a Greediness to get Both, he [*sc.* the dog] Chops at the Shadow, and Loses the Substance. **1797–8** COLERIDGE *Anc. Mar.* VI. xvi, And on the bay the moonlight lay, And the shadow of the Moon. **1803**

WORDSW. *Yarrow Unvisited* 44 Let..The swan on still St. Mary's Lake Float double, swan and shadow! **1823** SCOTT *Quentin D.* xxix, The planets which shine above us as little influential of our destiny, as their shadows, when reflected in the river, are capable of altering its course.

†**b.** The faint appearance of something seen through an obscuring medium. *Obs.*

**1594** PLAT *Jewell-ho.* I. 42 Let the scholler write vpon the shadowe of the text lines.

**c.** Applied to the appearance of degenerate corpuscles, bacilli, etc. faintly visible under the microscope; also known as ***shell-shadows***.

**1885** *Buck's Med. Handbk.* I. 204 (Cent. Suppl.), The occurrence of..'shell shadows' in the blood after release from the bell jar. **1896** *Allbutt's Syst. Med.* I. 83 In tuberculosis..it is not unusual to find in the giant-cells some bacilli..but faintly traceable as unstained, translucent shadows.

**6.** *fig.* **a.** An unreal appearance; a delusive semblance or image; a vain and unsubstantial object of pursuit. Often contrasted with *substance*.

*a* **1225** *Ancr. R.* 366 He þet neuede nout of sunne, bute scheadewe one. **1526** ABP. WARHAM in Ellis *Orig. Lett.* Ser. III. II. 42, I..shulde bee as a shadoo and ymaige of an Archebisshop and Legate, voide of auctoritie and jurisdiction. **1602** SHAKS. *Ham.* II. ii. 265 The very substance of the Ambitious is meerely the shadow of a Dreame. **1611** MURE *Misc. Poems* i. 52 Thy pleasour is bot paine, A dreame, a toy, a schadou. **1701** DE FOE *Trueborn Eng.* 41 Titles are Shadows, Crowns are empty things. **1780** BURKE *Sp. Bristol declining Poll* ¶5 The worthy gentleman ..has feelingly told us, what shadows we are, and what shadows we pursue. **1809** MALKIN *Gil Blas* XI. vi. (Rtldg.) 405 The minister..was now determined to seize the substance as well as catch at the shadow. **1840** J. H. NEWMAN *Par. Serm.* V. i. 4 At present we are in a world of shadows.

†**b.** Applied rhetorically to a portrait as contrasted with the original; also to an actor or a play in contrast with the reality represented. *Obs.*

**1580** LYLY *Euphues* (Arb.) 259 For Appelles shadowes are to be seene of Alexander, but not Alexanders of Appelles. **1590** SHAKS. *Mids. N.* V. i. 213, 430. **1591** —— *Two Gent.* IV. ii. 126 To your shadow, will I make true loue. **1609** *Ev. Woman in Hum.* III. i. in Bullen *O. Pl.* IV. 347, I have a dumbe-shewe of all their pictures, each has sent in his several shadow. **1679** in *Spalding Club Miscell.* V. 186 He was wont to gaze away whole days on her picture,.. practising upon the shadow to fit himself for the substance.

**c.** An obscure indication; a symbol, type; a prefiguration, foreshadowing.

**1382** WYCLIF *Col.* ii. 17 The whiche ben schadowe of thingis to come; forsoth the body is of Crist. **1526** *Pilgr. Perf.* (W. de W. 1531) 3 b, But all these were but fygures and shadowes of thynges to come. **1667** MILTON *P.L.* XII. 233 Religious Rites Of sacrifice; informing them, by types And shadowes, of that destind Seed to bruise The Serpent. **1704** SWIFT *Mech. Operat. Spir.* Misc. (1711) 305 Certain curious Figures,..which were so many Shadows and Emblems of the whole Mystery. **1855** KINGSLEY *Westw. Ho!* xix, That eternal world, whereof all here is but a shadow and a dream.

**d.** Something of opposite character that necessarily accompanies or follows something else, as shadow does light.

**1830** TENNYSON *Love & Death* 10 Thou [Death] art the shadow of life. **1872** MORLEY *Voltaire* (1886) 1 A new type of belief, and of its shadow, disbelief.

**e.** An imitation, copy; a counterpart. *spec.* The Opposition counterpart of a cabinet minister; a member of the shadow cabinet (see sense 16 b below).

**1693** *Humours Town* 31, I desire you to parallel the Follies and Vices of the Town with the shadows of such in the Country. **1825** T. HOOK *Sayings* Ser. II. *Passion & Princ.* xv. III. 362 Everything [on a voyage] goes on with the precision of clockwork, and one day is only the shadow and echo of another. **1864** BRYCE *Holy Rom. Emp.* xviii. (1875) 330 The Roman Empire was the shadow of the Popedom. **1912** LD. LANSDOWNE *Let.* 23 Feb. in R. Blake *Unknown Prime Minister* (1955) v. 103 But if the House of Commons 'shadows' are to number 11, I don't see how I can leave out Londonderry. **1961** *Daily Tel.* 1 Dec. 14 The five members of the Labour front bench who have exchanged 'shadows'. **1975** R. LEWIS *Margaret Thatcher* i. 4 When he resigned from the leadership, out of all the Shadows, only Lord Carrington, one of nature's gentlemen, went round to his old chief to express his consolation and regrets. **1980** *Times* 8 Dec. 2/4 Mr Denis Healey..has continued as shadow on Treasury affairs.

**f.** Used *hyperbolically* to designate a person extremely emaciated or feeble. Freq. in phr. ***to wear*** (oneself or another) ***to a shadow***.

**1588** GREENE *Pandosto* Wks. (Grosart) IV. 262 This tragicall discourse of fortune so daunted them, as they went like shadowes, not men. **1590** SIR J. SMYTHE *Disc. Weapons* Ded. 11 Great numbers of miserable and pitiful ghosts or rather shadowes of men. **1590** SPENSER *F.Q.* III. i. 45 All were faire knights, and goodly well beseene, But to faire Britomart they all but shadowes beene. **1773** *Life N. Frowde* 8, I hardly eat or drank, and became a perfect Shadow. **1815** SCOTT *Guy M.* xli, He appeared to wither into the shadow of himself. **1840** DICKENS *Lett.* (1969) II. 51 Commend me to him though he *does* wear me to a shadow. **1847** C. M. YONGE *Scenes & Characters* xviii. 236 And poor Lily wearing herself to a shadow, in vain attempts to mend matters. **1887** BOWEN *Virg. Æneid* III. 590 A stranger, by want to a shadow worn. **1977** *Grimsby Even. Tel.* 14 May 1/6 He was wearing himself to a shadow touring the country and Holland and Sweden trying to get new contracts.

**g.** An attenuated remnant; a form from which the substance has departed. Also, ***the shadow of a name*** (L. *nominis umbra*), a shadowy or faintly surviving renown.

*a* **1569** KYNGESMILL *Godly Adv.* (1580) 13 Least instead of a man, ye finde but the shadowe of a man. *a* **1674** CLARENDON *Hist. Reb.* xv. §152 But his greatness at home was but a shadow of the glory he had abroad. **1781** GIBBON *Decl. & Fall* xvii. II. 29 The emperors themselves, who disdained the faint shadow of the republic. **1837** CARLYLE *Fr. Rev.* I. IV. iv, Who shall become the eloquent orator of Royalism, and earn the shadow of a name. **1862** BROUGHAM *Brit. Const.* iii. 52 The prerogative of the Crown was reduced to a shadow.

**h.** A slight or faint appearance, a small insignificant portion, a trace.

**1586** A. DAY *Eng. Secretary* I. (1625) 8 Simple, plaine, and of the lowest and meanest stile, utterly devoide of any shadow of high and loftie speeches. **1678** CUDWORTH *Intell. Syst.* I. iv. §18 (1743) 321 There was no shadow of reason, why [etc.]. **1736** BUTLER *Anal.* I. i. Wks. 1874 I. 28 There is not so much as this shadow of probability, to lead us to any such conclusion. **1831** KEBLE *Serm.* v. (1848) 113 For the shadow of anything like proof of it, we may search far and wide in vain. **1867** FREEMAN *Norm. Conq.* (1876) I. App. 774 There is not a shadow of evidence that Harold ever reigned as Under-king in England.

**7.** A spectral form, phantom; = SHADE *sb.* 6.

*c* **1375** *Sc. Leg. Saints* ii. (*Paulus*) 1151 þan come a schadow full hugly, blak and blay, & stud hyme by. **1460** CAPGRAVE *Chron.* (1858) 266 Eke he [Rich. II] thoute evyr that a schadow of a man walkid before him. **1588** SHAKS. *Tit. A.* I. i. 100 That so the shadowes be not vnappeased. —— *Mids. N.* III. ii. 347 Beleeue me, King of shadowes, I mistooke. *c* **1590** MARLOWE *Faust.* 146 And I..Will be as cunning as Agrippa was, Whose shadowes made all Europe honor him. **1667** MILTON *P.L.* x. 264 Whom thus the meager Shadow answerd soon. **1790** COWPER *Iliad* II. 71 At mine head The shadow took his stand. **1812** CARY *Dante, Purg.* VIII. 45 To the valley now..let us descend; and hold Converse with those great shadows. **1871** R. ELLIS *Catullus* lxiv. 153 No handful of earth shall bury me, pass'd to the shadows. **1888** HONNOR MORTEN *Sk. Hosp. Life* 48 Every second the silent shadow feared of man drew nearer.

**8.** One that constantly accompanies or follows another like a shadow.

**a.** A parasite, toady; also (= L. *umbra*) a companion whom a guest brings without invitation.

**1579** GOSSON *Sch. Abuse* (Arb.) 40 Though the pryde of their shadowes (I meane those hangebyes whome they succour with stipend) cause them to be somewhat il talked of abroade. **1609** B. JONSON *Sil. Wom.* II. ii, Laught at by the Lady of the Colledge, and her shadowes. **1639** MASSINGER *Unnat. Combat* III. i, I must not haue my boord pester'd with shadowes, That under other mens protection breake in Without invitement.

**b.** A spy or detective who follows a person in order to keep watch upon his movements. Cf. SHADOW *v.* 12.

**1859** MATSELL *Rogue's Lex.* 78 *Shadow*, a first-class police officer, one who possesses naturally the power..to follow his quarry. **1890** *Daily News* 4 Oct. 4/6 The refusal of the magistrates to allow a policeman to be asked whether he was a 'shadow'. **1908** *Westm. Gaz.* 8 Aug. 10/2 His duties as official police 'shadow' to the Prince of Wales.

**c.** *Westminster School.* (See quot.)

**1884** FORSHALL *Westminster Sch.* 4 The master..called me to him, and along with me another boy, whom he assigned to me as my 'Substance'. I was the 'Shadow'. The 'Substance' was, for the space of a week, responsible for the proper conduct of his 'Shadow'. **1903** F. MARKHAM *Recoll. Town Boy Westminster* 231.

**d.** *Football.* A player who marks (MARK *v.* 15 c) another player in the opposing team.

**1976** *Southern Even. Echo* (Southampton) 15 Nov. 13/7 The rare occasions he outwitted his experienced close-marking shadow, Billy Tucker. **1976** *Times* 2 Dec. 12/2 The ability of Everton's forwards to escape from their marking shadows had been apparent throughout.

†**9.** An outline for a picture. *Obs.*

**1656** JEANES *Fuln. Christ* 14 Painters, whose first rude or imperfect draught is termed a shadow, or adumbration.

**10.** *Algebra.* A symbol having no meaning apart from a symbol of another kind to which it is attached.

**1898** A. N. WHITEHEAD *Univ. Algebra* I. 87 The Greek letters have no meaning apart from the Roman letters to which they assign properties, and therefore should not be written alone. Let these Greek letters be called shadows or umbral letters; and let the Roman letters denoting regions be called regional letters.

**III.** Shelter from light and heat.

**11. a.** Protection from the sun; shade. Now *rare.* † ***in the shadow*** = 'in the shade' (SHADE *sb.* 8 b).

'Dry it in the shadow' is a constant direction in pharmaceutical recipes in the 17th c.

*c* **1350** *Will. Palerne* 754, & vnder a tri appeltre tok him tid a sete, þat was braunched ful brode & bar gret schadue. *c* **1425** *Cursor M.* 8451 (Trin.) Vndir þe shadow of þat tre þe kynde of þingis lerned he. **1525** BERNERS *Froiss.* II. ciii. [xcix.] 299 They shall be in the sonne and in great heate, and we shall be in the shadowe and in the fresshe ayre. **1601** HOLLAND *Pliny* XXVIII. ix. II. 320 Prepared they ought to bee and dressed, before Autumne, when they be new and fresh washed, & dried in the shaddow.

†**b.** *concr.* That which affords shade. Cf. 13.

**1667** MARVELL *Corr.* Wks. (Grosart) II. 402 Though an only son be inestimable, yet it is like Jonah's sin, to be angry at God for the withering of his shadow.

†**c.** A shady place. *Obs.*

**1526** *Grete Herball* lxii. (1529) D iv, Betony..groweth on hylles, woodes, & shadowes, and about trees. **1688** HOLME *Armoury* II. 176/1 A Shepheards Bower..[is] called Shades, or shaddows, by the Poets.

†**d.** Retirement, seclusion. *Obs. rare*$^{-1}$.

**1612** BACON *Ess., Of Gt. Place* (Arb.) 280 They..are impatient of priuatenesse, euen in age and sicknesse, which require the shadow.

**12. a.** Overshadowing (of wings, etc.), as affording security; protection or shelter from danger or observation.

*c* **1200** *Vices & Virtues* 101 Vnder ðare scadewe of ðine fiðeres. *a* **1300** *E.E. Psalter* xvi. 10 Hile me vnder schadou of þi wenges twa. **1474** CAXTON *Chesse* IV. viii. (1883) 187 Praynge your good grace to resseyue this litylI and symple book made vnder the shadowe of your noble protection. **1607** SHAKS. *Timon* v. iv. 6 Such As slept within the shadow of your power. **1719** WATTS *Hymn, 'O God our Help'* ii, Beneath the shadow of Thy throne Thy Saints have dwelt secure. **1821** SCOTT *Kenilw.* i, There is no treason, sure, in a man's enjoying his own thoughts, under the shadow of his own bonnet? **1827** —— *Surg. Dau.* xii, She is under the shadow of the British flag, and she shall experience its protection. **1871** FREEMAN *Norm. Conq.* (1876) IV. xviii. 106 Deeds were done under the shadow of his name which we may be sure that in his own heart he abhorred.

†**b.** ***under the shadow of*** [= Fr. †*en l'ombre de, sous (l')ombre de*, It. *sotto ombra di*]: = under colour of, on pretence of. *Obs.*

**1523** BERNERS *Froiss.* I. cccxxvi. 206 b, He was nat worthy to holde any herytage in the realme of Fraunce, vnder the shadowe of his children. **1632** LITHGOW *Trav.* IV. 146 He stroue (vnder the shaddow of inuented lies) to mitigate the fury of her..disdaine.

†**13.** Denoting various appliances for affording shade. **a.** A handscreen; also a parasol, sunshade. **b.** A woman's headdress, or a portion of a headdress, projecting forward so as to shade the face. **c.** A tester or canopy for a bed. *Obs.*

**a. 1604** E. G[RIMSTONE] *D'Acosta's Hist. Indies* v. xxix. 418 They put vpon him certaine ensignes of feathers, with fannes, shadowes and other things. **1611** COTGR., *Ombraire*, an Vmbrello, or shadow. *Ibid.*, *Ombrelle*.

*fig.* **1623** FLETCHER *Rule Wife* III. (*init.*), Now you have got a shadow, an *umbrella* To keep the scorching worlds opinion From your fair credit.

**b. 1579** LYLY *Euphues* (Arb.) 116 Besides all this their shadows, their spottes, their lawnes, their leefekyes, their ruffes, their rings, shew them rather Cardinals curtisans, then modest Matrones. **1598** FLORIO, *Velaregli*, bone-graces, shadowes, vailes or launes that women vse to weare on their foreheads for the sunne. **1631** KNEVET *Rhodon & Iris* III. i. E 3, Shadowes, rebatos, ribbands, ruffes, cuffes and fals. **1641** BEST *Farm. Bks.* (Surtees) 106 Lawne..is much used for fine necke-kerchers, and fine shadowes, and dressinges.

**c. 1604** T. M. *Black Bk.* in *Middleton's Wks.* (Bullen) VIII. 25 The testern, or the shadow over the bed.

**14.** *Theatr.* A penthouse or roof over the stage. *Obs.* exc. *Hist.*

**1600** in Greg *Henslowe Papers* (1907) 5 W[th] a shadowe or cover over the saide Stadge. **1831** J. P. COLLIER *Dram. Poetry* III. 305 The projecting tiled roof over the stage [at the 'Fortune'] is called in this agreement 'the shadow', but it is also technically termed 'the heavens'.

**IV.** *Comb.*

**15. a.** Simple attrib., as ***shadow-side***, ***-streak***; (sense 4) ***shadow-leaf***, ***-pattern***, ***-show***, ***-tackle***, ***-tracery***, ***-train***; (sense 4 c) ***shadow-wave***; (sense 7) ***shadow-crown***, ***-king***, ***-patriarch***, ***-shape***, ***-wife***, ***-word***, ***-world***; (sense 13) ***shadow-plant***; ***shadow-like*** adj. (and adv.); also quasi-adj. = SHADY, as †***shadow ditch***, †***hedge***, †***hilet***, †***place***, †***tree***.

**1844** MRS. BROWNING *Vis. Poets* cccxiv, The figure of a palm-branch brown Traced on its brightness up and down In fine fair lines,—a *shadow-crown. **1568** TURNER *Herbal* III. 54 *Nummularia*..groweth by hedge sydes, and in *shaddowe ditches. **1602** tr. *Pastor Fido* I 1, Where a *shadow hedge [*vna siepe ombrosa*] doth close it in. **1382** WYCLIF *Isa.* iv. 6 And a tabernacle shal ben in to a *shadewe hilet of the dai, fro brennyng. **1896** LINA ECKENSTEIN *Wom. Monasticism* 75 Ebruin..again became house-mayor to one of the *shadow kings, *rois fainéants*, the unworthy successors of the great Merovech. **1957** C. DAY LEWIS *Pegasus* 55 Frecklings of sunlight and flickerings of *shadowleaf. **1601** HOLLAND *Pliny* XXXII. ix. II. 444 The garbage and skales of the *shadow-like Sciæna. **1623** DRUMM. OF HAWTH. *Flowres of Sion* (1630) 31 Glories breath, which Shadow-like on wings of Time doth glide. **1863** I. WILLIAMS *Baptistery* I. Imag. xiii. (1874) 170 A something deep, And shadowlike, yet shadowless. **1639** FULLER *Holy War* III. ii. (1640) 111 Let those who are delighted with Sciographie, paint out.. these *shadow-Patriarchs. **1943** KOESTLER *Arrival & Departure* III. 86 He stared at the ceiling of the dim room on which the shutters projected a streaky *shadow-pattern of grey and white ribs. **1967** E. SHORT *Embroidery & Fabric Collage* i. 32 *Shadow patterns.* If any three-dimensional object is suspended between a bright light and a sheet of white card or paper, and the object revolved, a series of patterns will be made by the shadow of the object on the card. **1551** TURNER *Herbal* I. E v b, Astragalus..groweth in places open to the wynde in *shadowe places. **1885** LADY BRASSEY *The Trades* 140 '*Shadow-plants' which have to be grown in order to protect the young cacao-plants. **1872** FITZGERALD *Omar* (ed. 3) lxviii, We are no other than a moving row Of Magic *Shadow-shapes. **1859** *Ibid.* xlvi, 'Tis nothing but a Magic *Shadow-show. **1570** T. WILSON *Demosth. Orat., Life* 117 When the sunne was verie hote about noonetide, they both would go on the *shadow side of the Asse. **1890** *Anthony's Photogr. Bull.* III. 147 If the light is too strong on the nose it must be lowered by bringing up the shade on the cheek, especially on the shadow side. **1833** TENNYSON *Pal. Art* 76 The ragged rims of thunder brooding low, With *shadow-streaks of rain. **1888** G. M. HOPKINS *Poems* (1967) 72 Shivelights and *shadowtackle in long lashes lace, lance, and pair. **1885** WARREN & CLEVERLY *Wand. Beetle* 72 Lying on the sunny sward, dappled with the restless *shadow-tracery of the trees. **1932** AUDEN in *Rev. Eng. Stud.* (1978) Aug. 282 A *shadow-train flitted foreshortened through fields. **1602** tr. *Pastor Fido* F 3 b,

Among these *shadow trees. **1871** G. MACDONALD *Wks. Fancy & Imag.* II. 11 Scaring *shadow-waves o'er fields of corn. **1939** AUDEN & ISHERWOOD *Journey to War* 279 Loss is their *shadow-wife. **1932** D. H. LAWRENCE *Etruscan Places* ii. 42 Pelasgian is but a *shadow-word. **1957** E. PARTRIDGE *English gone Wrong* II. 38 In the U.S.S.R., *right* is a shadow-word; and rights, something one possesses only theoretically. **1853** *Shadow-world [see LIVE *v.*[1] 5]. **1891** F. THOMPSON *Sister Songs* (1895) 50 A shadow-world, wherethrough the shadows wind Of all the loved and lovely of my kind. **1953** S. SPENDER *Creative Element* 93 What Lawrence protested against was not intellect but the kind of intellectualization whereby men create a shadow-world for themselves.

**b.** Instrumental, as ***shadow-chequered***, ***-coloured***, ***-dappled***, ***-haunted***, ***-hung***, ***-peopled***, ***-stroked-vested***, ***-winged*** adjs.; also similative, as ***shadow-white*** adj.

**1830** TENNYSON *Arab. Nts.* 102 Many a *shadow-chequer'd lawn. **1947** K. TENNANT *Lost Haven* x. 147 In these sweeps of land were *shadow-coloured birds and the beautiful midnight blue of the wild pigeons. **1952** R. CAMPBELL tr. *Baudelaire's Poems* 43 When you're asleep, dear shadow-coloured wench. **1857** KINGSLEY *Two Y. Ago* xxv, Gazing out over the *shadow-dappled lawn. **1887** MORRIS *Odyss.* XII. 285 To wander o'er the *shadow-haunted sea. **1913** 'SAKI' *When William Came* (1914) xviii. 288 A grey *shadow-hung land which seemed to have been emptied of all things that belonged to the daytime. **1820** SHELLEY *Hymn Merc.* xxix, But we will leave this *shadow-peopled cave And live among the Gods. **1866** G. M. HOPKINS *Jrnls. & Papers* (1959) 144 Prettily *shadow-stroked spikes of pale green grain. **1832** SHELLEY *Invoc. Misery* i, *Shadow-vested Misery. **1918** D. H. LAWRENCE *New Poems* 54 Into the shadow-white chamber silts the white Flux of another dawn. **1871** PALGRAVE *Lyr. Poems* 131 *Shadow-winged night hovers nearer above.

**c.** Objective, as ***shadow-bringer***, ***-fighter***, ***-hunting***, ***-maker***, ***-painting***, ***-pursuer***; ***shadow-bringing***, ***-fighting***, ***-grasping*** adjs.

**1902** W. S. CROCKETT *Scott Country* xix. 479 The great *Shadow-bringer was fast approaching. **1730** BAILEY (fol.), *Umbriferous*,..*Shadow-bringing. **1845** MAURICE *Mor. Philos.* in *Encycl. Met.* II. 582/1 He becomes a mere *shadow-pursuer and *shadow-fighter. **1768–74** TUCKER *Lt. Nat.* (1834) I. 473 Locke..then addressed the *shadow-fighting champion in these words. *a* **1644** QUARLES *Sol. Recant.* VI. 81 Thou, whose *shadow-grasping hand even tires Vpon the vanity of thy vast desires. **1856** RUSKIN *Mod. Paint.* IV. v. v. §11 The strange shapes it [a cast shadow] gets into..cannot be imagined until one is actually engaged in *shadow-hunting. *a* **1887** JEFFERIES *Field & Hedgerow* (1889) 226 That singular *shadow-painting seen on the wings of moths.

**16. a.** Special comb., as †**shadow-adder** (tr. L. *coluber*, pseudo-etymologically 'qui colit umbram'), a serpent lurking in shady places; **shadow-band**[1], a company of or resembling phantoms; **shadow-band**[2], one of a series of parallel bands, alternately light and dark, seen passing over any light-coloured surface immediately before and after totality in a solar eclipse; **shadow-bird**, a popular name for *Scopus umbretta*, a bird of nocturnal habits native in Africa and Madagascar; **shadow box**, a case with a protective transparent front in which is displayed a painting, jewel, etc.; also *attrib.*; **shadow-box** *v. intr.* and *trans.*, to box (against) an imaginary opponent, as a form of training; also *fig.*; so **shadow-boxing** *vbl. sb.*; **shadow-building** (see quot.); **shadow canoe** (cf. *shadow-building*); **shadow catcher**, (*a*) one who grasps at and retains trifles; (*b*) a photographer; **shadow-check** (see quot. 1957); chiefly *attrib.*; **shadow cretonne**, **-print**, **-tissue**, a reversible material having a woven-in pattern which gives a shadowy, blurred effect; †**shadow dial**, ? a sundial; **shadow embroidery** = *shadow work* below; **shadow-fight**, a fighting with shadows (i.e. imaginary foes), or a fight between shadows, a sciamachy; **shadow figure**, a silhouette; = *shadow puppet* below; **shadow-fish** = SCIÆNA; †**shadow grass**, ? *Luzula sylvatica*; **shadow-grey** *a.* and *sb.*, (a) dark grey; **shadow-half**, **-part**, 'that portion of land which lies towards the north, or is not exposed to the sun' (Jam.); †**shadow-house**, a summer-house; **shadow lace**, a lace with an indistinct pattern; **shadow-light**, a reflected light; **shadow-line**, (*a*) = *line of shadows* (sense 4 d); (*b*) a line cast by the shadow of an upright post or by the gnomon of a sun-dial; **shadow mask** *Television*, a perforated metal screen situated directly behind the phosphor screen in certain types of colour television tube, and having a pattern of precisely located holes through which the electron beams pass so as to strike the correct dots on the phosphor screen; freq. *attrib.*, as ***shadow-mask tube***; **shadow-photograph**, a picture taken by means of the Röntgen rays; hence **shadow-photography**; **shadow-picture**, (*a*) a shadow-photograph; (*b*) a picture formed by a shadow (usu. of a person's hand or hands) thrown upon a screen or other surface (cf. SHADOWGRAPH 1); **shadow-pin** (see quot.); **shadow-play**, a play in which the actors appear as shadows cast upon a screen placed between the stage and the auditorium; also, a puppet play of the shadow theatre; also *attrib.* and *fig.*; †**shadow-plough**, ? a PLOUGH (sense 3 a) on the shady part of an estate; **shadow-price** (see quot. 1965); also *transf.*; hence **shadow-pricing** *vbl. sb.*; **shadow print**: see *shadow cretonne* above; **shadow puppet**, a puppet used in a shadow play; **shadow-script** (? *nonce-use*), markings in shadow; **shadow-site**, an archaeological site revealed by shadowing on the ground; **shadow-stick**, an upright post used for casting a shadow line; **shadow-stitch**, (*a*) 'in *lace-making*, a mode of using the bobbins so as to produce delicate openwork borderings and the like' (*Cent. Dict.* 1891); (*b*) a criss-cross embroidery stitch used on sheer materials for filling in spaces, and which, being worked on the wrong side, shows through on the right side in a shadowy way with an outline resembling a back-stitch; **shadow stripe** (see quots. 1940, 1947); so **shadow-striped** *a.*; **shadow tag** *N. Amer.* (see quot. 1977); **shadow test**, (*a*) a method of finding out by refraction whether an eye is myopic or hypermetropic; (*b*) a method of examining the outer side of an eye affected with cataract in its second stage (*Syd. Soc. Lex.* 1898); **shadow theatre**, a form of puppetry in which flat figures are passed between a strong light and a translucent screen, the audience watching on the other side of the screen; also, a place where such puppet shows are performed; **shadow tissue**: see *shadow cretonne* above; **shadow work**, embroidery done in shadow-stitch; also *attrib.* and *fig.*

**1382** WYCLIF *Prov.* xxiii. 32 It shal bite as a *shadewe eddere. **1891** C. DAWSON *Avonmore* 156 In dear memory's hallowed land They move a silent *shadow band. **1900** S. P. LANGLEY in *Science* 22 June 977 (Cent. Suppl.) Shadow bands were seen. **1905** *Westm. Gaz.* 1 Sept. 6/3 The shadow-bands were splendidly exhibited before and after totality. **1869–73** T. R. JONES *Cassell's Bk. Birds* IV. 62 The Hammer-head, or *Shadow-bird. **1909** *Cent. Dict.* Suppl., *Shadow-box..*n.* **1969** [see OPTICAL *a.* 2 c]. **1973** *Houston Chron.* 21 Oct. 18 (Advt.), Giant hutch mirror with shadow-box frame and shelves. **1976** *National Observer* (U.S.) 17 Jan. 14/1 (Advt.), This stunning golden shadow box pendant. **1924** S. LEWIS *Free Air* i. 8 She fought the steering-wheel as though she were *shadow-boxing. **1927** [see *punch-bag* s.v. PUNCH *sb.*[2] 3]. **1932** H. S. DRAGO *Champ* i. 15 Andy protested that it wasn't necessary as he shadow-boxed an imaginary opponent. **1951** *Scott. Jrnl. Theol.* IV. 321 Unlike many Fundamentalists he is aware that the battle has passed into new phases and he is not satisfied to shadow box on deserted fields. **1971** *Nature* 22 Oct. 510/1 These representatives of European governments are still shadow-boxing with each other. **1977** *Time* 19 Dec. 68/2 It was O.K. to shadowbox at a professional gym. **1919** E. CORRI *Refereeing 1,000 Fights* 69 The mascot stripped to the waist to do some *shadow boxing. **1939** *Sun* (Baltimore) 17 Feb. 10/1 Shadow boxing over the selection of a site for the Leakin Memorial Park will continue next week. **1966** *Illustr. London News* 10 Sept. 10/3 But in any case, the gnomes know that a good deal of what is going on is 'shadow-boxing'. **1978** A. GARVE *Counterstroke* I. 60 He did a little shadow boxing and some skipping. **1891** WINN *Boating Man's Vade-M.* 9 The construction of small boats without regard to particular lines and without special intermediate dimensions is termed '*Shadow building'. **1883** *Fisheries Exhib. Catal.* 197 Full-size whale boat, dories, *shadow canoe,..Indian birch canoe, &c. **1774** MITFORD *Ess. Harmony Lang.* 53 *note*, Such a *shadow-catcher as I. Vossius..seems to have been. **1907** *N. & Q.* Ser. x. VII. 67 A firm of photographers in Bishopsgate Street are now describing themselves as 'Shadow-catchers'. **1908** *Sears, Roebuck Catal.* 1058/2 The background is a fairly dark *shadow check effect. **1957** *Terms & Definitions* (Textile Inst.) (ed. 3) 89 *Shadow stripe*.., an effect, due to different reflections of light, produced in woven fabrics by employing yarns of different physical properties, usually of 'S' and 'Z' twist, in warp or weft (or in both, when it becomes a shadow check). **1960** *Woman* 23 Apr. 9/1 Dainty shadow-check shirt-waisters. **1932** *Sale Catal.*, Made of good quality *Shadow Cretonne. **1943** E. BOWEN *Seven Winters* 48 Pink-and-cream 'shadow' cretonne. **1973** 'D. HALLIDAY' *Dolly & Starry Bird* xviii. 284 His bruises stood out like shadow cretonne on a chesterfield. **1669** STURMY *Mariner's Mag.* VII. Aaaa 2, A Globe with two Pole-Dials, and one *Shadow-Dial. **1920** J. HERGESHEIMER *Linda Condon* ii. 11 *Shadow embroidery and fine shell edges. **1768–74** TUCKER *Lt. Nat.* (1834) I. 471 Who is that antagonist whom he bumps and pummels so furiously in his *shadow-fight? **1816** COLERIDGE *Statesm. Man.* 34 While the latter present a shadow-fight of Things and Quantities, the former gives us the history of Men. **1851** MAYHEW *Lond. Labour* I. 311 The *shadow-figures sold this winter by one of my informants were of Mr. and Mrs. Manning, the Queen, Prince Albert [etc.]. **1935** H. EDIB *Clown & his Daughter* xliii. 240 It meant that she could easily buy a leather set of shadow figures for Tewfik. **1976** *Jrnl. R. Soc. Arts* Apr. 254/2 Flat Figures and Shadow Figures are a distinct type of puppet... In the Shadow Theatre the figures are placed between a light and a translucent screen. **1598** *Epulario* F iiij b, To dresse a Latus or *shadow fish. **1705** DALE *Pharmacol.* Suppl. 348 Umbra... The Grunter or Shadow-Fish. **1597** GERARDE *Herbal* I. vi. 8 Wood grasse or *Shadow grasse. **1918** W. BEEBE *Jungle Peace* (1919) ii. 26 The *shadow-grey sea. **1932** *Sale Catal.*, A beautiful quality plain silk... Shades:..shadow grey and gunmetal. **1505** *Reg. Mag. Sig. Scot.* 600/2, 6 mercatas terrarum bine partis de Smythtoun de Noth, viz., le *Schaddow-half earundem. **1574** *Ibid.* 1585, 263/1 The *schaddow or myd thrid part and how schaddow thrid part. **1586–[87]** *Reg. Privy Council Scot.* IV. 149 With the barnis, byris, biggingis and uthiris abonespecifeit standing upoun the shaddow halff thairof. **1869** C. LESLIE *Family Leslie* III. 45 George Leslie of Tocher granted a charter of the shadow half of the town and lands of Drumdurno. **1649** in *Archæologia* X. 419 One garden summer or *shadowe house. **1914–15** *T. Eaton Catal.* Fall & Winter 32 All White Evening Dress of Paillette Silk and Allover *Shadow Lace. **1977** C. MCCULLOUGH *Thorn Birds* iii. 61 His mother clad in a long bustled gown of palest pink shadow lace. **1623** DRUMM. OF HAWTH. *Flowres of Sion* (1630) 6 Of which that golden Eye, which cleares the Skies, Is but..a *Shadow light. **1764** J. FERGUSON *Lect.* 207 So as the uppermost edge of the shadow of the gnomon may just cover the *shadow-line. **1900** *Jrnl. Sch. Geog.* (U.S.) Jan. 2 The shadow-line is marked at each hour during the school day. **1902** *Westm. Gaz.* 17 Oct. 4/2 They watched the slowly moving shadow-line and cast sorrowful glances towards the erratic clocks in the neighbourhood. **1951** *Proc. IRE* XXXIX. 1187/1 The first public demonstration of..*shadow-mask color tubes..was made in March, 1950. *Ibid.* 1188/2 The triangular pattern [of holes] was chosen for the shadow mask in experimental tubes primarily because of its mechanical properties. **1965** *Wireless World* July 354/2 The Mullard colour-selection shadow mask with graded holes. **1975** K. WICKS *Television* 54 The most common type of picture tube in use today is the shadow-mask tube. **1896** *Daily News* 13 Feb. 2/1 At least two years ago a German scientist took what are now called *shadow photographs in a small way. *Ibid.*, '*Shadow photography', nevertheless, is the term that has 'caught on'. **1889** J. POLLARD *Plays & Games for Little Folks* 32 **Shadow Pictures.* In order to make these pictures show well on the wall, there must be but one lamp in the room, and that must stand back of the performer. **1896** *McClure's Mag.* VI. 415/2 A Crookes tube..with which he has taken all his shadow pictures. **1977** O. SCHELL *China* (1978) III. 244 At break we sit on the freshly turned earth and make shadow pictures with our hands. **1891** *Naut. Mag.* Sept. 809 The *shadow-pin..attached to a compass card, to indicate the bearing of the sun at noon. **1890** CHAMPLIN & BOSTICK *Young Folks' Cycl. Games & Sports* 625/2 **Shadow plays*, plays in which not the actors, but their shadows, are seen by the audience. **1895** MRS. GRINDROD *Siam* 49 Burlesques, comedies introducing current events, and shadow-plays, are productive of much mirth at fair-times. **1900** W. W. SKEAT *Malay Magic* vi. 514 Another very characteristic performance is the Shadow-Play. **1910** *Handbk. Ethnogr. Coll. Brit. Mus.* 102 The first two forms of Wayang are shadow-plays, the puppets being cut from leather. **1932** E. WAUGH *Black Mischief* iii. 92 He liked..to appear in society ..to survey the shadow-play of fashion. **1938** *Burlington Mag.* Aug. 87/2 Shadow-play puppets. **1964** *Catal. National Mus. Kuala Lumpur* 3/1 The shadow play exhibit is arranged so that the visitor can see backstage and learn how the figures are manipulated during the drama. **1971** *Country Life* 17 June 1544/1 A shadow play, the Wayang Kulit of parchment puppet figures manipulated from behind a lamplit screen. **1544** in *Reg. Mag. Sig. Scot.* 1587, 402/1 Octo bovatas terre..vocatas the *Schaddow-pleuch of Sonny-syde. **1965** A. WATERSTON *Development Planning* ix. 322 If the true economic cost of a project is to be determined in situations where market prices are out of line..it may be necessary to 'adjust' the prevailing prices by estimating the extent to which they deviate from 'equilibrium' prices. The adjusted prices, variously known as '*shadow' or 'accounting' prices, are then substituted for prevailing prices and used to determine real costs and benefits to an economy and to compare the project under consideration with other projects on a comparable basis. **1970** S. L. BARRACLOUGH in I. L. Horowitz *Masses in Lat. Amer.* iv. 157 Should labor be counted as a cost valued at current wage rates when there are no alternative job opportunities? If not, what 'shadow prices' should be used? **1981** *Sci. Amer.* June 116/3 Marginal values are sometimes called shadow prices or imputed prices. **1965** A. WATERSTON *Development Planning* ix. 323 *Shadow-pricing can also permit valid comparisons to be made of a public sector project with a private sector project. **1976** *Nature* 8 July 84/1 Does this justify the attachment of a money-tag to all values, even though this means what economists call 'shadow pricing' (for example, the 'value' of a view of the South Downs is the extra cost of not defacing the view if a road or a line of electric pylons has to be built in the neighbourhood)? **1926** G. G. DENNY *Fabrics* (ed. 2) I. 111 *Warp print or *shadow print.* Silks, ribbons and cretonnes woven with plain filling on a printed warp which gives a faint and shadowy design. **1968** J. IRONSIDE *Fashion Alphabet* 246 *Shadow print*, the warp yarns are printed with the design before weaving, giving a shadowy print effect. **1923** H. W. WHANSLOW *Everybody's Theatre, & How to make It* iv. 42 A fine collection of these Javanese *shadow puppets. **1971** H. TREVELYAN *Worlds Apart* iii. 43 There were the ingenious hand-made toys, the shadow-puppets manipulated on sticks. **1898** *Edin. Rev.* Apr. 312 The Fraunhofer spectrum, being a *shadow-script on a bright ground. **1929** O. G. S. CRAWFORD *Air-Photography for Archaeologists* 3/1 Inequalities in the surface of the ground produce shadows. All sites where remains are visible on the ground fall into this class. They may be called **shadow-sites.* **1946** R. J. C. ATKINSON *Field Archaeol.* I. 47 Shadow-sites are those whose surface is irregular, consisting of banks, mounds, ditches and terraces whose presence is revealed by the shadows they cast when seen in the low light of the rising or setting sun. **1900** *Jrnl. Sch. Geog.* (U.S.) Jan. 2 The *shadow-stick aids in teaching latitude. **1882** CAULFEILD & SAWARD *Dict. Needlework* 248 *Shadow Stitch..is used in Pillow Lace making to form the shadow of a pattern, to fill in the inside of curves [etc.]. **1932** *Mod. Woman* Feb. 56/1 This shadow stitch is just like herring-boning worked rather closely together... It gives you the shape of the leaf outlined in back-stitch on the right side and padded with long, crossed stitches on the wrong. **1932** *Pontings Whitsun Sales Catal.* 11 Morning Washing Frock for the larger than stock size in *shadow stripe art. silk. **1940** *Chambers's Techn. Dict.* 762/2 *Shadow stripes*,..cotton cloths, of plain or satin weave, in which stripes are produced by using warp yarns of different directions of twist. The shadow effect is due to light being reflected in different directions by the different twists. **1947** J. STEVENSON-HAMILTON *Wild Life S. Afr.* vi. 52 Burchell's zebra..'Shadow stripes', that is to say light brown bands impinged upon the white ground which separates the black markings. **1930** *Economist* 18 Oct. 713/1 As a result a substantial amount of business was booked, principally in *shadow striped poplins. **1969** I. & P. OPIE *Children's Games* ii. 86 The game [*sc.* Shadow Touch] is also played in Canada and the United States ('*Shadow Tag'). **1977** *Hartford* (Conn.) *Courant* 6 June 15/3 There was 'Shadow Tag' on sunny days—the 'It' player ran after the others, trying to jump on a shadow with a foot. **1884** H. E. JULER *Ophthalmic Sci. & Pract.* xiv. 363 The two following [methods] are very useful in estimating refraction; in both the ophthalmoscopic mirror alone is employed, and is held at a considerable distance from the eye. The first of these may be called the 'Fundus-Image' test; the other has been called 'Retinoscopy', but would be more appropriately designated by some such term as '*Shadow Test'. **1889** G. A. BERRY *Dis. of Eye* xiv. 462 It has been called the shadow test because attention is directed perhaps more to the dark shadow which borders the illuminated area than to the area itself. **1964** S. DUKE-ELDER *Parsons' Dis. of Eye* (ed. 14) vii. 69 Retinoscopy, or, more correctly, skiascopy or the shadow test, is the most practicable method of estimating the conditions of the refraction objectively. **1923** H. W. WHANSLOW *Everybody's Theatre, & How to make It* iv. 41 China..has had its *shadow-theatres for many centuries. **1932** J. NICOLL tr. *Van Boehn's Dolls & Puppets* viii. 35 The Chinese shadow theatre..has no public, and the educated classes pay no attention to it now. **1970** *Guardian* 22 July 20 Mr P. L. Amin Sweeney, who has just gained a Ph.D. for a thesis on the Malay shadow theatre, yesterday demonstrated the art with a lamp, a screen, and 40 flat hide puppets. **1920** *Queen* 3 Apr. 17 (Advt.), *Shadow Tissue. **1939–40** *Army & Navy Stores Catal.* 1073/2 Shadow tissues at 1/3 per yard. **1919** 'C. DANE' *Legend* 94, I possess that underlying *shadow-work (I admit it's no more) of fact to guide me in deciphering her method in the first book. **1932** D. C. MINTER *Mod. Needlecraft* 25/1 If the material is very transparent, a white thread on a white ground is..effective. This 'shadow work', as it is called.., can be prettily used on collars and cuffs and small articles. **1932** *Mod. Woman* Feb. 56 The shadow work tea cloth and cosy. **1967** Shadow work [see *pattern darning* s.v. PATTERN *sb.* 13 b].

**b.** Designating members of an opposition party nominated as counterparts of members of the government in power holding cabinet or other offices, or the offices held, as ***shadow cabinet***, ***minister***, ***ministry***, etc.

**1906** A. J. BALFOUR *Let.* in Ld. Newton *Ld. Lansdowne* (1929) 354 If we are to have, as you suggest, a Committee consisting of members selected from the Front Bench in both Houses,..what we should really have would be a shadow Cabinet once a week. **1925** J. O'CONNOR *Hist. Ireland 1798–1924* II. xxiii. 302 The Dail might go on to the crack of doom passing secret resolutions, appointing shadow ministers, [etc.]. **1953** EARL WINTERTON *Orders of Day* p. xi, I was in Mr. Churchill's 'Shadow Cabinet' from 1945 to 1950. **1958** *Spectator* 20 June 799/2 The Chancellors and Shadow-Chancellors. **1965** *New Statesman* 19 Mar. 436/2 Mr Ernest Marples, 'Shadow' Minister of Technology, will start work today at the English Electric Leo-Marconi works at Kidsgrove, Staffs. **1970** C. HAMPTON *Philanthropist* ii. 18 The Shadow Minister of Health..was hit in the ankle by a ricochet. **1973** *Ottawa Jrnl.* 21 Feb. 29/2 Opposition Leader Stanfield and his shadow cabinet have been using it to try and discredit Liberal economic policies in advance of the budget. **1976** H. WILSON *Governance of Britain* vii. 150 As shadow chancellor, I had..made some strong comments on some of the projects. *Ibid.* viii. 158 The Conservative leader ..also nominates the members of the so-called Shadow Cabinet and allocates the shadow 'portfolios'. **1977** M. WALKER *National Front* iii. 57 The Shadow Home Secretary ..supported the motion. **1980** *Austral. Financial Rev.* 11 Apr. 15/2 Labor's energy policy for the next Federal election, which was unveiled..by the Leader of the Opposition.. and the Shadow Minister for Minerals and Energy.

**c.** Designating organizations, structures, etc., built or instituted to substitute for or duplicate those existing in an emergency or to fulfil special needs, esp. before and during the war of 1939–45. Also as *adj.*

**1936** *Economist* 31 Oct. 195/2 There was the scheme for the 'shadow' industry... This..was to consist of a set of new factories built at the expense of the Government, but supplied with skilled labour and management by the private companies. **1937** *Sunday Express* 24 Jan. 14/2 Experts other than Lord Nuffield have doubts whether the Government's shadow factory system for air-craft production is wise or workable in war time. **1938** *Times* 16 Mar. 7/2 Both in the regular industry..and in the shadow scheme, which was designed as a reinforcement and an insurance, engines were somewhat ahead of air-frames. **1939** *Sun* (Baltimore) 6 July 1/5 The factories themselves, conventional and 'shadow', are turning out a certain number of aircraft and engines each month—the actual number could not be learned. **1939** *Air Ann. Brit. Empire* 3 The Standard Motor Company is also concerned in shadow manufacture of new engine components. **1940** *Ann. Reg. 1939* 20 The whole 'shadow' organisation should be in a position to function as soon as an emergency arose. **1944** *Jrnl. R. Aeronaut. Soc.* XLVIII. 370 Considerable experience had been gained by the Bristol Co., in their licence manufacture all over the world, which had already taught them the method of laying out drawings and preparing data remote from the parent factory, and this was of the utmost help in getting going on the 'shadow' production. **1946** *R.A.F. Jrnl.* May 160 He may have spent his last few years before donning a uniform on a war job in a shadow factory—a shadow factory which, with the coming of peace, has now closed. **1980** J. DITTON *Copley's Hunch* II. iv. 178 The war came..then they put up one of those shadow factories at—well, I'd best not say where.

**shadow** ('ʃædəʊ), *v.* Forms: 3–4 shadu, 3–5 schadow, 4 sseduy, 4–5 shadew, -dwe, schadew(e, 4, 6 schadou, 4–7 shadowe, 4, 6–7 schadow, 5 schado, schad(o)we, 6 schaddow, shad(d)o, 6–8 shaddowe, 4– shadow. [OE. *sceadwian* f. *sceado* SHADOW *sb.* (cf. OS. *skadowan*, *skadoian*, OHG. *scatewen*, also OE. *ofer-sceadwian* OVERSHADOW *v.*, and its Teut. equivalents).]

**1. a.** *trans.* To protect or shelter (a person or thing) from the sun; to shade. Now *rare* or *Obs.*

*a* **1366** CHAUCER *Rom. Rose* 1511 Whan he was to that welle comen, That shadowid was with braunches grene. **1530** PALSGR. 699/2 The sonne can nat come hyther, yonder house shadoweth me. **1577** B. GOOGE *Heresbach's Husb.* II. (1586) 98 Against the heat of the sun..shadow them as wel as you may. **1630** *R. Johnson's Kingd. & Commw.* 69 The Land is..shadowed with huge woods. **1675** COVEL in *Early Voy. Levant* (Hakl. Soc.) 202 Two more in like manner went fanning him all the way and shadowing him (for it was about ten o'clock, and a most excessive hot day). **1726** LEONI *Alberti's Archit.* I. 48 These..Stones..make a kind of pavement at top to shadow and protect the Substructure.

†**b.** *refl.* To obtain shade, take shelter from the sun. *Obs.*

**1340** *Ayenb.* 97 Ine þe ssede of þise trawe him ssel guod herte sseduy. **1530** PALSGR. 700/1, I wyll go shadowe my selfe under yonder fayre oke. **1648** GAGE *West Ind.* 69 A rock, under which they shadowed themselves. **1682** LISTER *Gœdart Of Insects* 138 These Spiders delight to be about the herbe Balm; and in Summer time they shaddow them-selves under it.

†**c.** *intr.* for *refl. Obs.*

*a* **1533** BERNERS *Gold. Bk. M. Aurel.* (1546) Z j, Agaynste enuye is no..thycke wodde to shadowe in. **1607** NORDEN *Surv. Dial.* v. 205, I find that under these trees the grasse is most rancke and fruitefull,..by reason of..the cattle sheltring and shadowing under them.

**2. a.** *trans.* To shelter or protect as with covering wings; to enfold with a protecting and beneficent influence; = OVERSHADOW *v.* Chiefly in Biblical use. *Obs.* exc. *poet.* with *over.*

*c* **1000** *Lambeth Ps.* xc. 4 His sculdrum he scaduaþ þe [*obumbrabit tibi*]. *a* **1325** *Prose Ps.* xc. 4 And he shal shadow þe wyþ hys shulderis. *c* **1420** HOCCLEVE *Lam. Green Tree* 18 in *Reg. Princes* App. p. xxxvii, O holy gost,..That of heye vertue shadowist me. *c* **1450** CAPGRAVE *Life St. Gilbert* xxxv. 112 þe commemoraciones of holy seyntis used in þe cherch, be whech we be schadowyd fro wyndes of temptaciones. **1526** *Pilgr. Perf.* (W. de W. 1531) 202 The holy goost shall comme ouer the, and the vertue or myght of the moost hye god shall shadowe the. **1595** SHAKS. *John* II. i. 14 You giue his offspring life, Shadowing their right vnder your wings of warre. **1830** TENNYSON *Supposed Conf.* 181 Let Thy dove Shadow me over, and my sins Be unremember'd.

¶**b.** *intr.* with prep. *on*, *over*, *up* (= L. *obumbrare* with *super*), in the same senses. *Obs. rare.*

*a* **1300** *E.E. Psalter* cxxxix. 8 [cxl. 7] Lauerd..þou schadowed ouer mi heued in dai ofe fighte. *a* **1325** *Prose Psalter*, þou shadued, Lord, vp min heuede. **1382** WYCLIF, Thou al aboute shadewedest on myn hed.

†**3. a.** *trans.* To screen, protect from attack. *Obs.*

**1489** CAXTON *Faytes of A.* I. xix. 56 A rowte of folke on horsbake that ouer ranne about the felde here and there for to shadowe theyre fote men. **1558** LD. WENTWORTH *Let. to Q. Mary* 2 Jan. *Cal. State Pap., For. 1553–8*, 355 The enemy, shadowing themselves under the turnpike wall.. kept themselves so secure that the pieces from the bridge could not touch them. **1598** BARRET *Theor. Warres* V. iii. 154 The Cauallerie, in their quarters.., would be defended and shadowed by the Infanterie.

†**b.** In immaterial sense: To be a security or protection to; to take under one's protection or patronage; to screen from blame or punishment, or from wrong. Also, to put (oneself, one's rights, etc.) under the protection of another. *Obs.*

*a* **1548** HALL *Chron., Hen. VI*, 127 b, And so, shadowed with this counsaill..he tooke a determinate peace. **1565** J. PHILLIP *Patient Grissell* 2116 (Malone Soc.), Shadow and defend them, with thy glorious spright. **1577–87** HOLINSHED *Chron.* I. 161/1 Though she were no nun, yet the offense seemed verie heinous, for that he should not once touch anie woman shadowed vnder that habit. **1588** GREENE *Pandosto* Ep. Ded. (1607) A 2 b, But I hope my willing minde shall excuse my slender skill, and your Honours courtesie shadowe my rashnesse. **1621** FLETCHER *Isl. Princess* III. i, Was't not enough I saw thou wert a Coward, And shadowed thee? **1630** *R. Johnson's Kingd. & Commw.* 420 He invaded Livonia.., which had shadowed it selfe under the protection of the said Sigismund. **1704** TRAPP *Abra-Mulé* I. II. 286 Those Laurels which his conqu'ring Sword has won Should shadow this Miscarriage.

**4. a.** To cast a shadow upon, to cover or obscure with a shadow.

**1382** WYCLIF *Acts* v. 15 That..the schadowe of him schulde schadowe [Vulg. *obumbraret*] ech of hem. [Similarly TINDALE **1526**.] **1414** BRAMPTON *Penit. Ps.* (Percy Soc.) 64 (Harl. MS.), My dayes..ben shadowed and waxen drye and derke. **1563** SHUTE *Archit.* D iiij b, The Proiecture, shalbe as before..sauing onely that Mutili shall hange ouer so farre as ye maye conueniently not hyddinge or shadowing his Cymatium. **1590** SPENSER *F.Q.* II. vii. 56 The warlike Elfe much wondred at this tree, So faire and great, that shadowed all the ground. **1613** CHAPMAN *Maske Inns Court*, Her tresses in tucks braided with siluer: The hinder part shadowing in waues her shoulders. **1683** MOXON *Mech. Exerc., Printing* ii. ¶ 1 When the Compositer is at work the Light may come in on his Left-hand; for else his Right-hand ..might shadow the Letter he would pick up. **1795** SOUTHEY *Joan of Arc* x. 168 The dark battalions of the foe Shadowing the distant plain. **1825** SCOTT *Talism.* xxiii, The features..no longer shadowed by the mass of hair. **1850** TENNYSON *In Mem.* xlv[i], The path we came by, thorn and flower, Is shadow'd by the growing hour.

†**b.** In *passive* of a shadow: To be 'cast' by an object. (If the reading be genuine: other MSS. read 'shadwe'.)

*c* **1386** CHAUCER *Pars. T.* 212 (Camb. MS.) Certis a schadewe hat the liknesse of the thyng of whiche it is schadewid.

**c.** *intr.* To cast a shadow. Now *rare.*

**13..** *E.E. Allit. P.* A. 42 On huyle þer perle hit trendeled doun, Schadowed þis wortez ful schyre & schene. **1377** LANGL. *P. Pl.* B. XVIII. 431 May no grysly gost glyde þere it [the cross] shadweth. **1513** DOUGLAS *Æneis* IV. Prol. 2 Thow bricht Cytheria, Quhilk only schaddowist amang sterris lite. **1821** CLARE *Vill. Minstr.* II. 100 To seek the brook that down the meadows glides, Where the grey willow shadows by its sides. **1847** TENNYSON *Princess* v. 515 As comes a pillar of electric cloud,..shadowing down the champaign till it strikes On a wood.

**d.** To grow dark or gloomy. Also *transf.*

**1888** *Harper's Mag.* Apr. 753 Evening shadowed; the violet deepened. **1891** MEREDITH *One of Conq.* III. 12 'There's the mother too', said he; and Nesta saw that the ladies shadowed.

†**5.** *trans.* To intercept or dim the light of (the sun or other luminary). *Obs.*

*c* **1430** *Pilgr. Lyf Manhode* II. xl. (1869) 91 Whan the sunne is shadewed, and at time of miday is shoven vnder a cloude. *a* **1548** HALL *Chron., Hen. IV*, 1 The bright glory of the triumphant Rome was eclipsed and shadowed. **1561** B. GOOGE *Palingenius' Zodiac Life* I. B j, As the sonne behinde the cloude, or shadowde of the moone. **1608** WILLET *Hexapla Exod.* 117 They are in such multitudes that they shadow the sun. *a* **1633** AUSTIN *Medit.* (1635) 42 He [Christ] was borne in the Night, to shew that the dignity and glory of his Godhead was shaddowed and darkened with the Night, and vaile of our flesh.

†**6. a.** To screen from view or knowledge; to keep dark, conceal. *Obs.*

**1432–50** tr. *Higden* (Rolls) VII. 369 Thenkynge to schado his rape by the simplicite of seynte Wulstan. **1436** *Rolls of Parlt.* IV. 501/1 Under ye umbre of such vidimus, all an hole Navye of Adversaries myght been and been shadewed. *c* **1560** *Trag. Rich. II* (1870) 51 You and I will heere shadowe ourselues, and writ downe the speches. **1581** PETTIE tr. *Guazzo's Civ. Conv.* II. (1586) 71 Manie, to the ende they may be taken for others then they are, vse to shadow the trueth. **1588** KYD *Househ. Philos.* Wks. (1901) 257 Neyther are their [women's] faces shadowed with beards. **1605** SHAKS. *Macb.* v. iv. 5 Let euery Souldier hew him downe a Bough, And bear't before him, thereby shall we shadow The numbers of our Hoast. **1608** MIDDLETON *Mad World* III. i. 29 Though I shadow it, that sweet virgin's sickness grieves me not lightly!

**b.** ? To clothe (a person) *with* a garment, to wrap, enfold.

**1605** B. JONSON *Masque of Blackness*, Oceanus.. shaddowed with a robe of sea-greene. *Ibid.*, Niger.. shaddowed with a blue, and bright mantle.

**7. a.** To represent by a shadow or imperfect image; to indicate obscurely or in slight outline; to symbolize, typify, prefigure. Now chiefly with adv. *forth*, *out*.

**1575** tr. *Marlorat's Apocalips* 47 The mysterie of the election and sealyng vp of Gods children by the holie Ghoste, seemeth too be ryghte trimly shadowed vnder this figure of speeche. **1606** BACON *Consid. Plant. Irel.* Resuscit. (1657) 257 That Glorious Embleme or Allegory, wherein the wisdome of Antiquity, did figure, and shadowe out, works of this Nature. **1625** T. GODWIN *Moses & Aaron* VI. viii. 312 By the same foure [creatures], in the opinion of many of the Fathers, are shadowed forth the foure Euangelists. **1697** DRYDEN *Æneid* Ded. (b) 2, Augustus is still shadow'd in the Person of Æneas. **1712** ADDISON *Spect.* No. 327 ¶ 5 Tho' the Catastrophe of the Poem is finely presag'd on this Occasion, the Particulars of it are so artfully shadow'd, that they do not anticipate the Story which follows in the ninth Book. **1715** CHAPPELOW *Right way Rich* (1717) 18 As the times grew nearer that dispensation which they shadowed out. **1820** SHELLEY *Prometheus* I. 247 Tremendous Image, as thou art must be He whom thou shadowest forth. **1843** GRAVES *Syst. Clin. Med.* xxix. 370 Some of them [i.e. symptoms] will be faintly shadowed out, or altogether absent. **1894** *Knowledge* 1 May 99/2, I have ventured..to shadow forth what I believe will be the most hopeful principle on which to mount a monster reflecting telescope.

†**b.** *intr.* To hint *at* something. *Obs.*

**1621** BRATHWAIT *Nat. Embassie* (1877) 150 My purpose is rather to shadow at some, then amply to dilate on all.

†**8.** *trans.* To portray, paint the likeness of; to draw or paint (a picture). *Obs.*

Very common in Lyly and some of his contemporaries.

**1576** FLEMING *Panopl. Epist.* 58 It surpasseth all the pictures shadowed with the painters pencill. **1580** LYLY *Euphues* (Arb.) 213 The first picture that Phydias the first Paynter shadowed, was the portraiture of his owne person. **1584** B. R. tr. *Herodotus* II. 89 A Phœnix..I neuer saw but portrayed and shadowed in colours. **1589** LODGE *Scillaes Met.* D 3, The pencile man that with a careles hand Hath shaddowed Venus, hates his slack regard. **1603** H. CROSSE *Vertues Commw.* (1878) 130 Apelles would not loose a day without shadowing a phisnomie. **1615** W. LAWSON *Country Housew. Gard.* (1626) 36 This is the best forme of a fruit-tree, which I haue here only shadowed out for the better capacity of them that are led more with the eye, than the mind. **1635** H. GELLIBRAND in J. W[ells] *Sciographia* ¶ 3 b, Others voice it on that witty Samian Aristarchus,..as first shadowing out the houre lines on a Plane. **1669** STURMY *Mariner's Mag.* VII. iv. 8 The Stile..you may make with Copper.., in form as you see shadowed.

†**9.** To depict the shadows in (an object, a scene); to place the shadows in (a picture or a part of it); to shade. *Obs.*

**1612** PEACHAM *Gentl. Exerc.* I. ix. 29 The shinbone from the knee to the instep, is made by shadowing one halfe of the leg with a single shadow. **1674** LEYBOURN *Surv.* 311 Vmber is good to shadow upon Gold. **1682** T. A. *Carolina* 23 A deep Green, shadow'd with a Murry. **1714** JERVAS *Let. to Pope* 20 Aug., I have done Homer's head, shadow'd and heighten'd carefully. **1735** *Dict. Polygraph.* II. Hh 4, Umber is shadowed with umber burnt... Masticote is shadowed with red orpiment. *c* **1790** IMISON *Sch. Art* II. 2 With the pencil and gold size touch the places you would have shadowed. **1821** CRAIG *Lect. Drawing*, etc. vii. 367 He cannot by means of his art singly, delineate and shadow the face and person of his friend.

**10.** *intr.* †**a.** To be tinged *with* a darker colour. *Obs.* †**b.** To agree in shade of colour *with* (in quot. *fig.*); to border or verge *upon* a certain colour. *Obs.* **c.** (Also *passive.*) To pass by degrees, shade off *to* or *into* a certain hue; also *fig.*

**1648** J. GOODWIN *Right & Might* 32 Nor doth the Act of the Army in that dissociation of the Parliament..colour, or shadow (in the least) with the act of the King, breaking into their House. **1656** EARL MONM. tr. *Boccalini's Pol. Touch-stone* (1674) 256 [She] is of so sallow a complexion, that she shadows upon the Moor. **1666** BOGHURST *Loimogr.* (1894) 39 A urine shadowing with a greenish black. **1839** *Standard* 25 Feb., This sphere [of falsehood] is so wide, and its several degrees so shadowed into one another. **1868** LOWELL *Pict. Appledore* ii, Now pink it blooms, now glimmers gray, Now shadows to a filmy blue.

†**11.** *trans.* To reflect, to imitate. *Obs. rare*$^{-1}$.

**1553** BRENDE *Q. Curtius* Ffvij, I have not thought it unsemely for the Percians to shadow y[e] customes of the Macedons.

**12. a.** To follow (a person) like a shadow; in mod. journalistic language said of a detective who dogs the steps of a person under surveillance.

**1602** ROWLANDS *Greenes Ghost* 17 Then did Gibson sweare that he shuld not buy one peniworth of ware that day ..and thereupon he shadowed him vp and downe, and mard his market quite. **1876** BESANT & RICE *Gold. Butterfly* i, A bear who was 'shadowing' the man and meant claws. **1899** *Yorksh. Post* 20 Dec. 3 A Spanish Steamer shadowed by a British Cruiser.

**b.** *Speech Therapy. trans.* and *intr.* To repeat (another's words) with the minimum of delay, as a treatment for stuttering.

**1955** *Nature* 5 Nov. 874/2 The subject 'shadows' an unseen message read by the operator steadily and continuously. *Ibid.*, It now seems that stammerers..find little difficulty and can be induced to 'shadow' fluently. **1973** C. VAN RIPER *Treatment of Stuttering* iii. 80/2 When stutterers 'shadowed' the speech of a model speaker almost complete 'suppression' of stuttering occurred. **1977** D. FRY *Homo Loquens* x. 149 A stammerer who is shadowing will hear the appropriate sequence of sounds in advance and this should cancel out any built-in delay in his system.

**c.** *trans.* To act as a shadow (see SHADOW *sb.* 6e) in respect to (a parliamentary minister, ministry, etc.). Also *absol.*

**1969** *Daily Tel.* 28 Oct. 16 An unusual trio of Tory political partners is associated with the..gallery... One is Geoffrey Rippon, who 'shadows' Defence. **1971** F. R. LEAVIS in *Human World* Aug. 8 The politician..was at that time 'shadowing' Education. **1974** *Times* 12 Mar. 1/1 Mr Carr shadows Mr Healey at the Treasury. Sir Alec Douglas Home maintains..foreign affairs and Mr Rippon will shadow on Europe. **1977** *Times* 5 Nov. 1/5 The new spokesman on Treasury and economic affairs..will be Mr Peter Tapsell, who formerly helped to 'shadow' the Foreign Office.

**13.** *Microscopy.* To subject (a specimen) to the process of SHADOW-CASTING *vbl. sb.* I.

**1945** *Proc. Soc. Exper. Biol. & Med.* LVIII. 267 (*caption*) A micrograph of a similar preparation after it has been shadowed by the oblique deposition upon it of a thin layer of chromium. **1966** D. G. BRANDON *Mod. Techniques Metallogr.* 48 By shadowing the surface of the replica with a heavy metal from a carefully collimated source at a known angle, the intensity differences from point to point on the surface can be related directly to the surface topography of the specimen. **1978** *Nature* 19 Jan. 231/2 Increased ammoniation is indicated principally by the change in morphology of particles collected (during ascent) on a carbon surface and 'shadowed' with silicon oxide later in the laboratory.

**shadow-casting,** *ppl. a.* and *vbl. sb.*

**A.** *ppl. a.* That casts a shadow or shadows.

**1859** TENNYSON *Merlin & V.* 479 To him the wall That sunders ghosts and shadow-casting men Became a crystal. **1882** *Encycl. Brit.* XIV. 584/1 The shadow-casting object should be near the screen. **1904** W. DE LA MARE *Henry Brocken* 145 Laid embraced in the shadow-casting moonlight. **1953** *Jrnl. Exper. Psychol.* XLV. 206/1 The shadow-casting object is placed as close to the screen as possible, whereas the distance between the light source and the object is made large.

**B.** *vbl. sb.* **1.** *Microscopy.* A technique for enhancing an electron-microscope image by projecting a beam of small particles or atoms (usu. of a heavy metal) on to the sample at a small angle to the horizontal, so as to form a deposit giving the appearance of shadows cast by sideways illumination.

**1944** WILLIAMS & WYCKOFF in *Jrnl. Appl. Physics* XV. 712/2 Information was needed in our work other than that provided by stereoscopic photography. A procedure for measuring heights based on shadow-casting was accordingly developed to meet this need. **1947** *Ann. Rev. Microbiol.* I. 11 With the addition of the shadow casting technique, about eleven fibrils were clearly seen to compose the cilium of *Paramecium*. **1971** V. A. PHILLIPS *Mod. Metallogr. Techniques & Applications* v. 183 It is customary to enhance the contrast of replicas by shadow casting, that is, by evaporating a heavy metal from an angle to give shadow effects in the final electron micrograph, equivalent to oblique light illumination.

**2.** *lit.* The casting of shadows, esp. in *Psychol.* as a technique of perceptual research. Also *attrib.*

**1957** *Psychol. Rev.* LXIV. 291/2 Previous shadow-casting devices..have not been constructed for this systematic purpose. **1971** *Nature* 3 Sept. 55/2 The geometric principles of shadow casting and the use of chromatic filters for dichoptic stimulation are established techniques.

Hence (as a back-formation) **'shadow-cast** *v. trans.*, to enhance (a microscopic image) by shadow-casting; to subject (a microscopic specimen) to shadow-casting; also as *ppl. a.*; **shadow caster,** a device employed in perceptual research in order to cast shadows, esp. one for producing seemingly three-dimensional shadows.

**1944** *Jrnl. Appl. Physics* XV. 715/2 (*caption*) Example of a shadow-cast electron micrograph for the determination of the heights of objects. **1957** *Psychol. Rev.* LXIV. 291/2 Considering the mount and the screen as two geometrical planes, changes in the position of the mount will yield all possible perspective transformations of the shadow relative to the shadow caster. **1969** *Vision Res.* IX. 154 The principal advantage of the stereoscopic shadow-caster over other stereoscopic projection methods lies in its versatility in the study of binocular kinetic space perception. **1971** V. A. PHILLIPS *Mod. Metallogr. Techniques & Applications* v. 187 After being allowed to harden, it is dry-stripped and shadow cast. **1971** *Nature* 3 Sept. 55/2 To produce this effect, a stereoscopic shadow caster was used, in which two point sources slightly separated horizontally cast the shadows of three vertical rods on a rear-projection screen. **1979** *Ibid.* 27 Sept. 287/2 Film samples were transferred to..electron microscope grids... Transferred films were shadowcast in the direction of compression with platinum-palladium at an angle of 10° before examination in a Siemens Elmiskop.

**shadowed** ('ʃædəʊd), *ppl. a.* [f. SHADOW *v.* + -ED[1].]

**1.** Protected from light and heat; furnished with shade.

**1400** tr. *Secreta Secret., Gov. Lordsh.* lviii. 79 Wyn..þat growys in playn and moyst valeyes, and stedys shadwyd. **1526** *Grete Herball* cxxxiv. (1529) Hvb, Candelacia.. groweth in shadowed and humourous places. **1600** SURFLET *Country Farm* II. xlii. 277 Pimpernell..craueth a moist and shadowed ground. **1713** C'TESS WINCHILSEA *Misc. Poems* 27 A Shepherd seeking with his Lass, To shun the Heat of Day; Was seated on the shadow'd Grass. **1857** KINGSLEY *Two Y. Ago* xx, That peak is four miles from us now; and yet the shadowed cliffs at its foot seem double that distance.

†**2.** *Her.* = UMBRATED. *Obs.*$^{-1}$

**1486** *Bk. St. Albans, Her.* cviij, He berith of golde with a mylneris cros umbratid or shadowyd. **1611** COTGR., *Ombré*, vmbred, or shadowed; (a tearme of Blason).

**3.** Obscured or darkened by shadow or shadows. Also *transf.* and *fig.*

**1596** SHAKS. *Merch. V.* II. i. 2 Mislike me not for my complexion, The shadowed liuerie of the burnisht sunne. **1729** SAVAGE *Wanderer* III. 290 Winter more nitrous chills the shadow'd sky. **1825** LONGF. *Burial of Minnisink* i, On sunny slope and beechen swell, The shadowed light of evening fell. **1867** AUGUSTA WILSON *Vashti* xxv, He scrutinized the sadly sharpened and shadowed features. **1908** ALICE SHIELD *Henry Stuart* Pref., The quiet shadowed story of the last Stuart prince.

**4.** Of a portion of a visible object or scene: Lying in shadow or shade. (Chiefly with implied reference to artistic representation.)

**1657** G. THORNLEY *Daphnis & Chloe* 171 The shadowed beauty of the ripened grapes. **1778** SIR J. REYNOLDS *Disc.* viii. (1779) 19 You must oppose a light ground to the shadowed side of your Figure. **1830** in *Builder* 9 Jan. (1864) 22/3 [Fuseli:] 'Don't say shadowed, it is incorrect'. 'Shaded, then, sir?' 'Yes. I know Sir Joshua uses "shadowed"; but it is not right.' **1879** LINTON *Hints Wood Engraving* 28 The shadowed face of the boy,..and it may be the level sky, are engraved in regular lines.

†**5.** Of textile fabrics: Having colours or tints gradually passing one into another. *Obs.*

**1639** in *Verney Mem.* (1907) I. 154 Some shadoede sattine ribbinge.

†**6.** ?Faintly written; ?showing faintly through a semi-opaque medium. (Cf. SHADOW *sb.* 5b.) *Obs.*

**1588** W. KEMPE *Educ. Children* F3b, The Maister shall teach his Schollar to write by practise of drawing the Pen upon the figures of shadowed letters.

**7. a.** Indicated obscurely, or by symbol or type; disguised, veiled.

**1635** R. N. tr. *Camden's Hist. Eliz.* I. 32 Whether this proceeded from any virtue of his, whereof he gave some shadowed tokens. **1726** POPE *Odyss.* XIX. 627 A visionary thought I'll now relate, Illustrate, if you know, the shadow'd fate. **1850** TENNYSON *In Mem.* xxxiii, Leave thou thy sister when she prays, Her early Heaven, her happy views; Nor thou with shadow'd hint confuse A life that leads melodious days.

†**b.** Adopted as a disguise. *Obs. rare*$^{-1}$.

**1615** BRATHWAIT *Strappado* 173, I know your place and haue an ayme, To shewe your merits in a shadow'd name.

†**8.** Reduced to a shadow; shadowy, unreal.

**1597** MIDDLETON *Wisd. Solomon* ix. 7 What were it to be shadow of a king? A vanity; to wear a shadow'd crown?

**9.** Followed by a 'shadow' or spy, kept under observation.

**1889** *Daily News* 12 Oct. 2/1 At last the shadowed man seized his opportunity, and slipped into the Irish mail unobserved.

**10.** *Microscopy.* Subjected to the process of SHADOW-CASTING *vbl. sb.* I.

**1944** *Jrnl. Appl. Physics* XV. 714/2 Photographing and measuring the lengths of the shadowed areas thus formed on the preparation. **1949** *Proc. Soc. Exper. Biol. & Med.* LXXI. 80/1 (*caption*) Chromium shadowed preparation of the same slide. **1973** P. J. GOODHEW *Specimen Preparation in Materials Sci.* v. 151 If a high resolution is required then the grain size of the shadowed replica is important.

**shadower** ('ʃædəʊə(r)). [f. SHADOW *v.* + -ER[1].]

**1.** One who or something which shadows, adumbrates, or portrays.

**1600** SURFLET *Country Farm* Ep. Ded. A4, Those..liuely shadowers and setters forth of natures workes. [**1618** *Owles Alman.* 56 *Painters*, You Beauty-shadowers, that robbe the raine-bow of her colours.] **1822** BEDDOES *Brides' Trag.* II. ii, His words are feeble shadowers Of such pure beauty!

**b.** One who portrays shadow: tr. Gr. σκιαγράφος.

**1842** WORNUM in Smith *Dict. Grk. & Rom. Antiq.* 691/1 s.v. *Painting*, Apollodorus..was surnamed the shadower.

†**2.** Something affording protection. *Obs. rare*$^{-1}$.

**1691** E. TAYLOR *Behmen's Theos. Philos.* 162 (Tho' not in the holy Book, yet) in the adjunct, shadower or cover.

**3.** One who follows another in order to keep watch upon his actions, a spy.

**1889** *Daily News* 12 Oct. 2/1 This seems to have taken the shadowers a little aback. There was a delay in getting out the police cars. **1893** F. F. MOORE *I Forbid Banns* (1899) 186 Lupus has several shadowers.

**'shadowgram.** [f. SHADOW *sb.* + -GRAM.] = SKIAGRAM.

**1896** *Brit. Med. Jrnl.* 29 Feb. 558, I sent her to Dr. Mackenzie Davidson that a shadowgram of the foot might be obtained. **1896** *Q. Rev.* Apr. 496 Actual shadowgrams, realizing all that had been reported of them, passed into circulation.

**shadowgraph** ('ʃædəʊgrɑːf, -æ-), *sb.* [f. SHADOW *sb.* + -GRAPH.]

**1. a.** A picture formed by a shadow (usually, of the operator's hand or hands) thrown upon a screen or other lighted surface; an exhibition of a series of such pictures as a form of entertainment. Also *fig.*, and = SHADOW-GRAPHIST.

**1886** *St. Stephen's Rev.* 27 Mar. 5/2 At the New Club..on Saturday next..Mason and Titus, the American shadowgraphs, who nightly provoke so much laughter at the Oxford, will appear at 11.30 p.m. **1888** *Glasgow Even. Times* 10 Sept. 4/3 Prof. Wynne brings his shadow-graph to the Gaiety and Star this week. **1893** *Westm. Gaz.* 14 Dec. 4/3 An account of Trewey's famous shadowgraphs. **1928** A. S. EDDINGTON *Nature of Physical World* p. xvi, In the world of physics we watch a shadowgraph performance of the drama of familiar life. **1965** J. VON STERNBERG *Fun in Chinese Laundry* i. 2 To disembody human beings into shadowgraphs of my concepts of them is no labor of love.

**b.** An image formed by light which has passed through a fluid and been refracted differently by regions of different density (used esp. in the study of fluid flow).

**1926** *Proc. R. Soc.* A. CXI. 336 Shadowgraphs of the jets emerging into the atmosphere from nozzles of different forms and at different initial pressures were obtained by the method described above. **1945** *Jrnl. Optical Soc. Amer.* XXXV. 505/2 If one places a viewing screen between the jet ..and the second mirror, the image of the jet as seen on the screen will show what is commonly referred to as a shadowgraph. **1955** F. J. WEYL in *High Speed Aerodynamics & Jet Propulsion* IX. 21 By far the most extensive use of shadowgraph techniques..concerns the recording of shock waves and slip discontinuities. **1974** W. MERZKIRCH *Flow Visualization* iii. 85 Shadowgraphs made with short-duration light pulses display a scale of details much finer than that which the hot-wire technique can resolve. **1978** *Nature* 5 Jan. 47/1 (*caption*) Shadowgraph photograph showing the tilted layers and interfaces produced by inserting a block of ice into salt-stratified water at room temperature.

**2.** A picture or photograph taken by means of X-rays, a radiograph.

**1896** *Dubl. Rev.* Apr. 422 A shadowgraph is produced on the plate, revealing the skeleton stripped of flesh and muscle. **1975** *Nature* 25 Sept. 276/2 The X-ray shadowgraph image is converted into a charge image on a dielectric by the ionisation of a gas or liquid in a chamber. **1978** *Sci. Amer.* Nov. 62/1 The simplest and most successful way to produce an image with X rays is with contact X-ray microscopy. This technique, which achieves a resolution substantially better than that of the light microscope, creates a shadowgraph of the specimen.

Hence **'shadowgraph** *v.*, *intr.* to produce shadowgraphs; *trans.* to depict by shadowgraphs, take shadowgraphs of. **shadow'graphic** *a.*, pertaining to shadowgraphs. **'shadowgraphist,** one who produces shadowgraphs. **'shadowgraphy,** the production of shadowgraphs.

**1888** *Weekly Scotsm.* 29 Sept. 4/8 Mons. F. Trewey, famed as a shadowgraphist. **1896** *Daily News* 29 Feb. 5/4 Mr. Stanley Kent photographed, shadowgraphed, electrographed, or radiographed..a fractured finger bone at St. Thomas's Hospital. **1896** *Brit. Med. Jrnl.* 14 Mar. 678 Shadowgraphy is an impossible monster. **1897** *Strand Mag.* Dec. 625/2 Mr. Devant..actually gave his shadowgraphic entertainment in the dazzling glare of a mid-day sun. **1902** *Music Hall & Showman* 28 Mar., His *répertoire* consists of shadowgraphy, conjuring [etc.].

**shadowily** ('ʃædəʊɪlɪ), *adv.* [f. SHADOWY *a.* + -LY[2].] In a shadowy manner, like a shadow.

**1845** E. WARBURTON *Crescent & Cross* I. 336 Numerous torches here gleamed upon walls, shadowily giving out pictured battles, and kneeling priests, and stern deities. **1890** *Chamb. Jrnl.* 1 Mar. 133/1 The sailors..went staggering shadowily under their burden along the poop.

**shadowiness** ('ʃædəʊɪnɪs). [-NESS.] The quality or condition of being shadowy.

*a* **1672** STERRY *Freed. Will* (1675) 213 [Christ] takes away ..the shadowyness of the shadowy Image in its dissolution and restauration. **1682** H. MORE *Annot. Glanvill's Lux O.* 116 And the shadowyness of the Night may help them in the more composing Introversions of their contemplative mind. **1881** *Contemp. Rev.* Mar. 479 The shadowiness and want of concreteness in the portraiture.

**shadowing** ('ʃædəʊɪŋ), *vbl. sb.* [-ING$^{1}$.] The action of the verb SHADOW in various senses.

**1. a.** The action of affording shadow or protection from the sun; the state of being protected from the sun; protective overshadowing or sheltering.

*a* **1340** HAMPOLE *Psalter* ciii. 4 Thoro shadoyng of þi grace we are taken in contemplatyf life. *a* **1366** CHAUCER *Rom. Rose* 1503 For Narcisus,..By auenture come to that welle To resten hym in that shadowing. **1450–1530** *Myrr. Our Ladye* 329 Whiche hathe conceyued thyne only gotten sonne by shadowyng of the holy goste. *a* **1850** ROSSETTI *Dante & Circle* I. (1874) 252 And there my lady 'mid the shadowings Of myrtle-trees..Singing I saw.

†**b.** *concr.* Something affording shade, a canopy, curtain. *Obs. rare.*

**1598** FLORIO, *Vela*,..a vaile or shadowing, a couering, a curteine. *c* **1710** CELIA FIENNES *Diary* (1888) 256 Then she [the Queen] was anoynted in this manner; there was a Cloth of silver twilight Embroyder'd, held a Little shaddowing over her head.

**2.** The act of casting a shadow upon something; obscuration of light; quasi-*concr.* shadows cast upon something. Also *transf.* and *fig.* (cf. SHADOW *sb.* 4 f).

*c* **1000** *Sax. Leechd.* III. 258 On sumum earde hi [*sc.* days] beoð længran, on sumon scyrtran, for þære eorðan sceadewunge [*v.r.* sceadwunge]. **1382** WYCLIF *Jas.* i. 17 Anentis whom is not ouerchaunginge, nether schadewing of whileness [Vulg. *obumbratio vicissitudinis*]. *a* **1619** FOTHERBY *Atheom.* II. i. §9 (1622) 197 Peter [healed], by his onely shadowing. **1868** LOCKYER *Guillemin's Heavens* (ed. 3) 169 It is by projecting these total and partial shadowings one on the other that they produce the phenomena of eclipses. **1878** NEWCOMB *Pop. Astron.* 556 *Penumbra*, a partial shadowing. **1977** *Lancet* 3 Sept. 512/1 A chest radiograph showed slight inflammatory shadowing in the right upper zone.

**3.** The position or distribution of shadow, in a visible object or scene; the placing of the shadows in a picture. †Also, in *Drawing* and *Painting*, = SHADING.

**1603** DEKKER *Wonderf. Yeare* C 3, Lend me Art (without any counterfeit shadowing) to paint..the whole story. **1622** PEACHAM *Compl. Gent.* xii. 115 You must obserue the shaddowing of Taffata's. **1705** ADDISON *Italy* 371 An infinite Variety of Inequalities and Shadowings, that naturally arise from an agreeable Mixture of Hills, Groves and Vallies. **1732** BERKELEY *Minute Philos.* iv. §23 A little soft shadowing of evil sets off the bright and luminous parts of the creation. **1799** G. SMITH *Laboratory* II. 35 This way of drawing and shadowing is generally performed with black chalk.

**4.** A variation of colour, a shade, tint. *rare.*

**1580** LYLY *Euphues* (Arb.) 352 When Phydias first paynted, they vsed no colours, but blacke, white, redde, and yeolow: Zeuxis added greene, and euery one inuented a new shadowing. **1827** J. F. COOPER *Prairie* I. 17 The martin's fur ..was of a fineness and shadowing that a queen might covet.

**5.** An imperfect or obscure representation; a prefiguring or adumbration. Also with *forth*.

**1642** R. C. *Union Christ & Ch. Shadowed* 4 God.. delighted to draw some Shadowings and Adumbrations of it here below. **1805** A. KNOX *Rem.* (1834) I. 15 If every species of the sublime be..a shadowing of Deity [etc.]. **1872** A. P. FORBES *Kalendars Sc. Saints* p. xlvii, The first shadowings forth of the minsters and cathedrals of the best days of pointed architecture.

**6. a.** The action of dogging a person's steps to spy on his proceedings.

**1890** *Guardian* 9 July 1085/1 The real author of shadowing is..the National League.

*attrib.* **1904** SWEENEY *At Scotl. Yard* iii. 35 Nominally, you are not on shadowing duty for more than a certain time.

**b.** *Speech Therapy.* Repetition of another's words with the minimum of delay, as a treatment for stuttering.

**1955** *Nature* 5 Nov. 874/2 'Shadowing' means repeating concurrently. **1975** in J. Eisenson *Stuttering: 2nd Symposium* 347 It would appear that speech behavior during shadowing shares something in common with singing.

**7.** *Microscopy.* = SHADOW-CASTING *vbl. sb.* I.

**1945** *Science* 8 June 596/1 Their orientation with respect to the direction of shadowing. **1973** P. J. GOODHEW *Specimen Preparation in Materials Sci.* v. 148 Much shadowing is performed with heavy elements, a wide variety of which have been used.

**8.** *Comb.*: †**shadowing place**, a place of shade, a shelter, an arbour. *Obs.*

**1382** WYCLIF *Ecclus.* xxxiv. 19 The hilet, or the schadowyng place [Vulg. *umbraculum*], of the myd-day. **1426** LYDG. *De Guil. Pilgr.* 16750, I se that ffolkys..ffynden a Shadwyng place and an holsomme Refuge whan they ffen to the ffor socour and helpe. **1509** FISHER 7 *Penit. Ps.* cxxx. Wks. (1876) 231 After this Ionas..made hym a shadowynge place. **1580** HOLLYBAND *Treas. Fr. Tong*, *Auvent*, an arbour, a shadowyng place.

**shadowing** ('ʃædəʊɪŋ), *ppl. a.* [-ING$^{2}$.] That shadows, in various senses of the verb.

**1.** Affording shade, shelter, or protection.

**1552** HULOET, Shadowynge or makynge shadowe as wood doth, *umbrifer*. **1562** TURNER *Herbal* II. 81 Peplis..hath a brode shaddowyng bushe which is full of whyte iuice. **1634** SIR T. HERBERT *Trav.* 214 Shadowing trees. **1797** MRS. RADCLIFFE *Italian* i, Shadowing pines and thickets of oak. **1816** SCOTT *Old Mort.* xxix, The horseman..pulled the shadowing hat still deeper on his forehead.

**2.** Indicating obscurely or by symbol; prefiguring, boding.

**1579** FULKE *Heskin's Parl.* 58 [The pascal lamb is] a shadowing figure, like the first draught of a painter. **1604** SHAKS. *Oth.* IV. i. 41 Nature would not inuest her selfe in such shadowing passion, without some Instruction. **1795** SOUTHEY *Joan of Arc* III. 350 The dark and shadowing visions of the night. **1877** TENNYSON *Harold* III. i, The king Is holy, and hath talk'd with God, and seen A shadowing horror.

**3.** Spying, following for purposes of information.

**1889** GUNTER *That Frenchman* v. 46 Of Hermann and his shadowing Jolly [a detective] he sees nothing.

Hence †'**shadowingly** *adv. Obs.*$^{-1}$

**1635** BRATHWAIT *Arcad. Princ.* 24 Hee shadowingly deliuers unto her, in what manner they are handled.

†'**shadowish,** *a. Obs.* Also 6 **shadowysshe, shaddoish, shadowishe.** [f. SHADOW *sb.* + -ISH.]

**1.** Characterized by shadow, shady.

**1530** PALSGR. 323/1 Shadowysshe, *vmbrageux*. **1568** TURNER *Herbal* III. 66 Sanicle..groweth commonlye in colde and shadoish woddes and hedges.

**2.** Of the nature of or resembling shadow.

**1642** J. EATON *Honey-c. Free Justif.* 278 As the walls of the house cannot of their own nature but cast forth all day long a shadowish darkness.

**b.** *transf.* and *fig.* Unsubstantial, fleeting; figurative, mystical.

Very common in the 16th and 17th c.

**1561** T. NORTON *Calvin's Inst.* I. 8 Euen thys is it, to make a shadowishe God, to driue farre away the true God whome we ought to feare and worshyp. **1621** *Three Quest. Answ. Fourth Commandment* 30 Take heed this doctrine bee not rather shadowish then substantiall. **1685** BUNYAN *Seventh-day Sabb.* iv, The nature of that law is moral, but the.. circumstances thereunto belonging are shadowish and figurative.

Hence †'**shadowishly** *adv.*, indistinctly. *rare*$^{-1}$.

**1681** GLANVILL *Sadducismus* I. (1682) 155 A certain faculty in the soul, which, in some manner, though very shadowishly, answers to that power in God of creating Matter.

**shadowist** ('ʃædəʊɪst). [f. SHADOW *sb.* + -IST.]

†**1.** A constructor of dials. *Obs. rare.*

**1635** H. GELLIBRAND in J. W[ells] *Sciographia* ¶4 The Surveyour may search out Altitudes..by the only helpe of three right lines; But the compleat Shadowist cannot here rest without further helpe from above. **1650** T. RUDD *Pract. Geom.* Bj, The compleat Shadowist can teach the Sun to trace out his way upon the Earth.

**2.** One who gives an entertainment consisting of shadow pictures.

**1902** *Music Hall & Showman* 28 Mar., Another well-known conjurer and shadowist.

**shadow-land. 1.** A place conceived as the abode of phantoms and ghosts, an imaginary land of spirits.

**1821** LAMB *Elia* Ser. I. *Witches*, A peep..into the shadow-land of pre-existence. **1862** LYTTON *Str. Story* II. 16 Trials and visitations from the shadowland of ghosts and sorcerers. **1877** *Outl. Hist. Relig.* 181 [The soul] then sets off on its journey to the shadow-land. *a* **1887** JEFFERIES *Field & Hedgerow* (1889) 243, I shall start forth from my burial-mound upon the chase in the shadow-land just as now I start forth from my cave. **1908** *Contemp. Rev.* Oct. 425 The country suddenly felt itself face to face with reality when it heard M. Clemenceau, and M. Jaurès faded away into shadowland.

**2.** A place in shadow; a gloomy, unhappy place; an indeterminate border-land between other places, states, etc.

**1923** *Daily Mail* 13 July 13 To lead Ireland out of the shadow-land of much unnecessary suffering and turmoil into a brighter and happier state. **1949** BROOKS & WARREN *Fundamentals of Good Writing* vi. 241 If we understand the extremes..we can use common sense to discriminate among the examples of the shadowland in between. **1960** AUDEN *Homage to Clio* 18 Within a shadowland of trees. **1966** *New Statesman* 27 May 775/3 Malcolm X the Harlem hustler had gloried in the sexual power-game of the race war's shadowlands.

**shadowless** ('ʃædəʊlɪs), *a.* [f. SHADOW *sb.* + -LESS.]

**1.** Casting no shadow.

**1638** SIR T. HERBERT *Trav.* (ed. 2) 6 They cast their shadowes both wayes according as the Sunne is in declination, and Ascij or shadowlesse, when Sol is Zenith. **1804** MAR. EDGEWORTH *Ennui* i. (1809) 38 She had a large assortment of fairies and shadowless witches, and banshees. **1862** MISS BRADDON *Lady Audley* xxviii. 186 Under the bare and shadowless trees in the grey February atmosphere.

**b.** Of a lamp or its furniture: So constructed as to cast no shadow.

**1859** F. S. COOPER *Ironmongers' Catal.* 77 Gas chimneys, per dozen. Shadowless ditto. *c* **1865** LETHEBY in *J. Wylde's Circ. Sci.* I. 111/1 Parker's Sinumbra Lamp..was called the shadowless lamp. **1884** *Health Exhib. Catal.* p. liv, Gasaliers and brackets with improved shadowless burners.

**2.** Having no shadows on its surface; unsheltered from the sun. Of light, the sky, etc.: Unclouded.

**1827** POLLOK *Course T.* v. 145 Black Ethiopia, that, shadowless, Beneath the Torrid burned. *c* **1810** T. MOORE *Song of Hyperborean* iii, That shadowless orb [the moon]. **1845** E. WARBURTON *Crescent & Cross* II. 144 There was something startlingly new and strange in that wild, shadowless landscape. **1870** MORRIS *Earthly Par.*, *Ring given to Venus* 1275 And in the shadowless still morn A sense of rest to him was born.

*fig.* **1830** PRAED *Poems, My Little Cousins* 42, I used to have as glad a face, As shadowless a brow. **1854** GREENWOOD *Haps & Mishaps* 94 A day of shadowless pleasure.

Hence '**shadowlessness.**

**1881** HARDY *Laodicean* I. I. iii. 51 He saw the dinted nose of the De Stancys distinctly outlined with Holbein shadowlessness against the blue-green of the distant wood.

†'**shadowly,** *a. Obs. rare*$^{-1}$. [f. SHADOW *sb.* + -LY$^{1}$.] Of the nature of a shadow.

**1434** MISYN *Mending of Life* 128 Myendly sight truly is takyn vp heuenly to behald be schadoly syght ȝit & meroly, not clere and opyn.

**shadowly** ('ʃædəʊlɪ), *adv.* [f. SHADOW *sb.* + -LY$^{2}$.] In the manner of a shadow, obscurely.

**1866** BLACKMORE *Cradock Nowell* xxx, He could see her shadowly. **1892** DOYLE *Round Red Lamp* (1894) 221 Terrible possibilities loom ever shadowly upwards.

†'**shadowous,** *a. Obs. rare.* [f. SHADOW *sb.* + -OUS.] Shadowy, shady; also *fig.* (see quot. 1483).

**1483** CAXTON *Gold. Leg.* (1892) I. 313 He was vmbrouse or shadewous. That is to saye he was cold & refrigerat fro all concupyscence of the flesshe. **1585** T. WASHINGTON tr. *Nicholay's Voy.* I. xvi. 17 b, They study to seek places coole & shadowous, to eschew the heat of the Sun.

**shadowy** ('ʃædəʊɪ), *a.* Forms: 4 **shadewy, schadewy, shadwye,** 5 **shadwy, schadowye,** 6 **shaddowy,** 7 **shadowey,** 4– **shadowy.** [f. SHADOW *sb.* + -Y.]

**1.** Resembling or of the nature of a shadow.

**a.** Unsubstantial, impalpable; transitory, fleeting; unreal, imaginary.

**1374** CHAUCER *Boeth.* II. pr. iv. (Skeat) II. 60 Thise shadewy transitorie dignitees [L. *has umbratiles dignitates*]. **1632** MILTON *L'Allegro* 108 When in one night..His shadowy Flale hath thresh'd the Corn That ten day-labourers could not end. **1712** ADDISON *Spect.* No. 419 ¶8 We find a whole Creation of the like shadowy Persons in Spencer. **1814** BYRON *Lara* I. vii, He did not follow what they all pursued..; Nor shadowy honour, nor substantial gain. **1855** LONGF. *Hiawatha* v. 58 Gazing with half-open eyelids Full of shadowy dreams and visions. **1884** LINDLEY in *Law Times Rep.* LI. 277/1 The plaintiff's case is of such a shadowy, frivolous, and vexatious character.

**b.** Spectral, ghostly.

**1681** J. SCOTT *Chr. Life* I. iii. (1684) 72 Their Monuments and Sepulchres, where the shadowy Phantasms of such Souls have sometimes appeared. **1727** DE FOE *Hist. Appar.* v. (1840) 45, I come now to the main and most disputed part of shadowy appearance, viz, the apparition of unembodied soul. **1804** MOORE *Passing Deadman's Isl.* iv, Yon shadowy bark hath been to that wreck. **1887** BOWEN *Virg. Æneid* IV. 243 From the river of Death he recalls Shadowy ghosts.

**c.** Faintly perceptible, indistinct, vague.

**1797** MRS. RADCLIFFE *Italian* i, He perceived a shadowy figure station itself at the entrance of the arch. **1819** BYRON *Juan* II. cxlvii, Where the blue veins look'd shadowy, shrunk and weak. **1862** SPENCER *First Princ.* I. v. §32 (1875) 113 A belief seeming to them so shadowy and indefinite. **1888** HENLEY *Bk. Verses* 160 A shadowy sail, silent and gray, Stole like a ghost across the bay.

†**d.** Of the nature of a faint or reflected image; symbolic, typical. *Obs.*

**1641** MILTON *Ch. Gov.* ii. Wks. 1851 III. 103 Indeed the description is as sorted best to the apprehension of those times, typicall and shadowie. **1676** GALE *Crt. Gentiles* II. III. 90 Philosophers had some kind of..dark adumbration or shadowy description of the first principles of Nature. **1726** PENN *Tracts* Wks. I. 578 That it might the better end the Jews shadowy services.

**e.** quasi-*adv.*

**1797** COLERIDGE *Christabel* I. 60 A silken robe of white, That shadowy in the moonlight shone. *c* **1804** MOORE *Odes to Nea* vii, The broad banana's green embrace Hung shadowy round each tranquil grace. **1897** OLIVE CUSTANCE *Opals, A Pause*, In silver mail all shadowy pale, The moon shines white.

**2. a.** Abounding in shade; protected from the sun.

**1398** TREVISA *Barth. De. P.R.* XVIII. lviii. (Bodl. MS.), His modre huydeþ hym..in schadewi places. *c* **1450** BURGH *Secrees* 1918 In placys pleyn moyst and shadwy. **1526** *Grete Herball* xcii. (1529) F ij, It ought to be gadred when it bereth floures & than be hanged to dry in a shadowy place. **1657** W. COLES *Adam in Eden* xi. 23 Primroses and Cow-slips joy most in shadowy places. **1794** MRS. RADCLIFFE *Myst. Udolpho* 35 The bluish tints that pervaded their shadowy recesses. **1824** MRS. SHERWOOD *Waste Not* III. 3 The various shadowy lanes branching off from the high road. **1871** R. ELLIS *Catullus* lxiii. 41 When he smote the shadowy twilight with his healthy team sublime.

**b.** Enveloped in shadow; obscured by shadows.

**1840** SUSAN E. MILES in Palmer *Bk. Praise* (1865) 70 Our spirits shall not dread The shadowy way to tread. **1855** TENNYSON *Maud* II. I. ii, A shadow there at my feet, High over the shadowy land. **1876** HARDY *Ethelberta* xlvi, From the shadowy archway came a shining lantern which was seen to be dangling from the hand of..the hostler, John.

†**c.** Screened from observation, retired; hence, remote, inaccessible. *Obs.*

**1555** WATREMAN *Fardle Facions* II. viii. 177 These [Gymnosophistæ] haunte the outemoste borders, and shadowie partes of that countrie. **1591** SHAKS. *Two Gent.* V. iv. 2 This shadowy desart, vnfrequented woods I better brooke then flourishing peopled Townes. **1613** PURCHAS *Pilgrimage* (1614) 369 Then they wash it with the bloud of a slaine Wolfe, and carry it into a shadowie place.

**3.** Casting a shadow, affording shade.

**1607** TOPSELL *Four-f. Beasts* 605 About noon when the season groweth hot, they lead them [sheep] to shaddowey trees and rocks. **1796** W. TAYLOR in *Monthly Rev.* XX. 515 The shadowy palm. **1871** L. STEPHEN *Playgr. Eur.* x. (1894) 250 To climb the rocks when the sun is hot and creep into cool shadowy ledges.

†**4.** Of an inflorescence: Shaped like a 'shadow' or umbrella. *Obs.*

**1562** TURNER *Herbal* II. 107 b, A shaddowy or spokye top with a round circle as dyll. **1578** LYTE *Dodoens* v. xlii. 606 The stalkes..be full of branches, vppon the which grow spoky tufts or litle shadowy toppes with white flowers. *Ibid.* VI. lxxx. 760 The flowers [of the *Viburnum Opulus*] be white, and grow in brode round shadowy tuffetes.

**5.** *Comb.*

**1855** TENNYSON *Daisy* xviii, A thousand shadowy-pencill'd valleys And snowy dells.

**Shadrach** (ˈʃeɪdræk). [Allusive use of the name of one of the 'Three Children' delivered unharmed from the fiery furnace (Dan. iii. 26, 27).] **1.** See quot. 1847. Cf. SALAMANDER *sb.* 3.

**1847** WEBSTER, *Shadrach*, in the smelting of iron, a mass of iron on which the operation of smelting has failed of its intended effect.

**2.** (See quots.) *local.*

**1827** in S. Holland *Mem. Sydney Smith* (1855) I. 259 His fires are blown into brightness by *Shadrachs*, tubes furnished with air from without, opening into the centre of the fire. **1954** D. HARTLEY *Food in England* iv. 46 In some places, a draught is obtained by shadrack, an underground arrangement like a small blast furnace through which the blast of a rotary fan is carried under the [peat] fire.

**shaduf**, var. SHADOOF.

**shady** (ˈʃeɪdɪ), *a.* Also 7–8 **shaddy.** [f. SHADE *sb.* + -Y.]

**1.** Affording shade.

**1579** SPENSER *Sheph. Cal.* Jan. 31 You naked trees, whose shady leaues are lost. **1611** BIBLE *Job* xl. 22 The shady trees couer him with their shaddow. **1697** DRYDEN *Virg. Georg.* IV. 74 The winged Nation..o'er the Plains and shady Forrest flies. **1825** WORDSW. *To Skylark* 7 Leave to the nightingale her shady wood. **1879** 'EDNA LYALL' *Won by Waiting* xxvi, There was a shady hat to be chosen.

**2.** Shaded, protected by shade.

**1589** GREENE *Menaphon* (Arb.) 36 The shadie valleies [shall be] thy euenings arbour. **1590** SPENSER *F.Q.* I. iii. 4 Her angels face..made a sunshine in the shady place. **1661** BOYLE *Certain Physiol. Ess.* (1669) 191 Those little moats that from a shady place we see swimming up and down in the Sun-beams. **1717** LADY M. W. MONTAGU *Let. to Pope* 17 June, I am in the middle of a wood..divided into many shady walks. *a* **1821** KEATS *Hyperion* I. 1 Deep in the shady sadness of a vale. **1875** JOWETT *Plato* (ed. 2) V. 29 There are shady places under the trees, at which..we may often rest and talk.

**b.** fig. phr. ***on the shady side of***: older than (a specified age).

**1807–8** W. IRVING *Salmag.* (1824) 87 The younger being somewhat on the shady side of thirty. **1872** CALVERLEY *Fly Leaves* (1884) 74 Thou art on the shady Side of sixty too.

**c.** Inhabiting or loving the shade; choosing retirement and security. *nonce-use.*

*a* **1586** SIDNEY *Apol. Poetry* (Arb.) 51 We were full of courage, giuen to martiall exercises;..and not lulled a sleepe in shady idlenes with Poets pastimes.

†**3.** Opaque; also, not luminous, dark. *Obs.*

**1605** BACON *Adv. Learn.* II. xxiii. §48. 118 This Globe which seemeth to vs a dark and shady body is in the view of God as Christall. **1709–29** V. MANDEY *Syst. Math., Astron.* 343 And that 'tis not Pellucid or Shining, but is the same shady Body, is evident from this [etc.].

**b.** said of night. *poet.*

**1746** FRANCIS tr. *Horace, Epist.* II. ii. 281 From dawning Day till shady Night [L. *ad umbram lucis ab ortu*]. **1896** A. E. HOUSMAN *Shropshire Lad* xix, Eyes the shady night has shut.

†**c.** Of qualities: Of the nature of shade or defect. *Obs.*

**1719** OLDISWORTH *E. Smith's Wks.* Charac. Author A 8, If the World had half his good Nature, all the shady Parts would be entirely struck out of his Character.

†**4.** Shadowy, indefinite in outline, faintly perceptible. *Obs.*

**1626** BACON *Sylva* §249 You shall see..diuers such Super-Reflexions, till the *species speciei* at last die. For it is euery Returne weaker, and more shady. **1710** NORRIS *Chr. Prud.* iv. 332 The light of Conscience..may be..made shine very dim, so as to give but a very faint and shady direction.

**5.** *colloq.* **a.** Of questionable merit or prospects of success; uncertain, unreliable. [? Orig. university slang.]

**1848** CLOUGH *Bothie* i. 24 The Tutor..Shady in Latin, said Lindsay, but topping in plays and Aldrich. **1858** BP. FRASER in Hughes *Life* (1887) 97 We have twenty-one candidates for the Ireland—a shady lot. **1858** R. S. SURTEES *Ask Mamma* xxv. 95 What looks very well one way may look very shady the other. ? *c* **1880** JOWETT in Tollemache *Mem.* (1895) 21 [Commenting on the remark that England had one living poet of the first order, but hardly another even of the second class.] I think that Browning deserves a shady first. **1884** *Pall Mall Gaz.* 16 Oct. 5/2 The chances of the Underground Railway against the omnibuses will be very shady.

**b.** Not bearing investigation, of a nature or character unable to bear the light; disreputable.

**1862** *Sat. Rev.* 8 Feb. 156 Balls and bazaars continue to be the refuge of institutions, whether charitable or religious, whose balance-sheets are 'shady'. **1873** *Punch* 25 Oct. 167/2 Have always heard that 'shady people' went to Boulogne. **1882** SERJ. BALLANTINE *Exper.* iv. 42, I was entrusted with a brief by a rather shady attorney. **1894** SIR E. SULLIVAN *Woman* 52 A Roman lady of extraordinary beauty and somewhat shady character.

**shae, shaeling,** obs. ff. SHE, SHIELING.

**SHAEF** (ʃeɪf). Also **S.H.A.E.F., Shaef.** [Acronym f. the initials of *S*upreme *H*eadquarters *A*llied *E*xpeditionary *F*orce.] The operational headquarters of the allied expeditionary force that invaded occupied Europe in 1944–5.

**1944** *N.Y. Times* 21 May IV. 8/2 'SHAEF' stands for Supreme Headquarters Allied Expeditionary Force. **1944** C. MILBURN *Diary* 6 June (1979) 215 The great assault is known as S.H.A.E.F., pronounced 'shafe'—Supreme Headquarters Allied Expeditionary Force. **1945** *Times* 28 May 3/3 Shaef announced yesterday that it is expected that the port of Hamburg will be open on June 1 to allied shipping and supplies for our armies in the liberated countries. **1958** *Listener* 21 Aug. 272/3 The Cossac spirit carried on into Shaef and through to triumph. **1977** P. USTINOV *Dear Me* xi. 145 SHAEF, the Allied Supreme Headquarters, wished an official film to be made about the war in the West.

**shaell, shaet,** obs. ff. SHELL, SHAHI.

**shafe, shaff,** obs. ff. SHEAF *sb.*

**shaferne, shafferoon:** see SHAFFRON.

**shaff(e-hoke,** obsolete forms of SHAVE-HOOK.

**shaffle** (ˈʃæf(ə)l), *v. dial.* [In sense 1 (northern), app. a variant of SHAUCHLE *v.*; sense 2 may be developed from this, or belong to a distinct word, perh. of imitative or symbolic formation: cf. *shiffle-shaffle*, *shiffle* vbs. (E.D.D.) and SHUFFLE *v.*]

**1.** *intr.* To shuffle in walking.

[**1552**: implied in SHAFFLER.] **1781** HUTTON *Tour to Caves* (ed. 2) 95 *Shaffle* and *Shiffle* v. to hobble in walking. **1818** TODD, *To Shaffle*, to move with an awkward or irregular gait; to hobble. Used in the north of England. **1894** *Northumbld. Gloss.*, *Shaffle, Shaughle*, to shuffle in walking.

**2. a.** To work or move in a lazy fashion; to be undecided in plan or action; to vacillate, delay.

[**1703** implied in SHAFFLES.] **1828** [CARR] *Craven Gloss.*, *Shaffle*..to do things ineffectually. **1873** R. FERGUSON *Dial. Cumbld.* 121 *Shaffle*, to be undecided, to vacillate. **1890** *Sheffield Gloss.*, *Shaffle*, to move in a lazy way; to delay, to put off.

**b.** 'To retreat from a bargain or engagement, make excuses, prevaricate' (*Eng. Dial. Dict.*).

**1781** HUTTON *Tour to Caves* (ed. 2) 95 *Shaffle*,..also to act unfairly. **1866** BROGDEN *Provinc. Words Lincolnsh.* 178 Don't shaffle with me.

Hence **'shaffler**, one who 'shaffles'; **'shaffles**, a bungler, shiftless person.

**1552** HULOET, Shaffler with his fete whych fayleth in going, *atta*. **1703** THORESBY in Ray *Philos. Lett.* (1718) 336 A *Shaffles*, a Bungler. **1828** [CARR] *Craven Gloss.*, *Shaffler*, one who walks lame. 2. A bungler in business. **1885** HALL CAINE *Shadow of Crime* xxiv, Or mayhap ye'll ask yon shaffles, yer father.

†**'shafflin.** *Obs. rare.* Also 6 **shafflynge** (in Continental authors **schafoling, schafling, -lyng**). [Perh. the same word with SHAFTLING, though applied to a different fish. Cf. SHAFT-EEL.] A kind of eel.

**1553** BELON *De Aquatil.* 273 Anglorum autem pisces.. hisce nominibus agnoscuntur,..Eils, Lampres, Schafolings, Fausen, Griggs. **1555** —— *La Nat. des Poissons* 267 Eils, Lampres, Schaflings, Fauson, Griggs. **1558** *Gesner's Hist. Anim.* IV. 54 Minima Anguilla iisdem [Anglis] *Grigge* uocatur. *Schaflyng* uero media inter *Grigge* & *Fausen ele*. **1572** HULOET (ed. Higins), Shafflinge, or eele of a middle bignesse, *anguilla media*. **1747** MRS. GLASSE *Cookery* xxi. 163 Fish in Season..Midsummer Quarter Grigs, Shafflins and Glout [etc.].

**shaffolde,** obs. form of SCAFFOLD *sb.*

†**shaffron.** *Obs.* Forms: 5 **shawfron,** 6–7 **shaf(f)ron,** 7 **shafrone, shaferne,** 8 **shafferoon;** 6 (*Sc.* in sense 2) **schaifron, saferon, schaffroun, chaffrone, cheffroun, chaiffer, schaiffer.** [Variant of CHAFFRON, CHAMFRAIN.]

**1.** The frontlet of a barbed horse: = CHAFFRON, CHAMFRAIN.

**1465** Shawfron [see CHAMFRAIN]. **1547–8, 1610, 1617** [see CHAFFRON]. **1590** SIR J. SMYTHE *Disc. Weapons* 31 b, Their shafrons, cranets, or steele pectorells. **1660** in *Archæologia* XI. 100 Shaffroones.

**2.** *Sc.* 'A piece of ornamental head-dress anciently worn by ladies' (Jam.).

**1511** *Acc. Ld. High Treas. Scot.* IV. 210 Item, to be schaiffronis to the sam hudis, half ane elne crammesy. *Ibid.* 230 Item, for half quartar crammesy satin, to be ane schaiffer to hir hud, viij s. ix d. *Ibid.*, Item, for making of the hud and chaiffer, viij s. **1512** *Ibid.* 213 For ane chaffrone of gold. **1516** *Inv. R. Wardrobe* (1815) 24 Ane saferon with ane chenye of gold of blak veluous. *Ibid.* 27 Item, ane schaffroun with ane burd of gold with lxxxi perle... Item, ane cheffroun sett with goldsmyth werk with xxxv perle.

†**b.** = CHAPERON 2. *Obs.*

[Possibly *shafferoon* may be the correct form, and the form *chaperon*, *-oon* may be due to pseudo-etymology.]

**1725** J. COATS *Dict. Her.* (1739) 73 Those little Shields, containing Death's Heads, and other Funeral Devices, plac'd upon the Foreheads of the Horses, that draw Hearses at Pompous Funerals vulgarly now call'd, by Corruption *Chaperoons*, or *Shafferoons*.

**Shafiite** (ˈʃæfiaɪt). Also **Shafeite, Shafæite.** [f. Arab. *shāfiʿī* + -ITE[1].] A member of one of the four sects or schools of the Sunnites or orthodox Muslims, named from the cognomen (*ash-Shāfiʿī*) of their founder, Abu Abdallah Muhammad ibn Idris, 767–819. Also *attrib.* or *adj.*

[**1704** PITTS *Acc. Mahometans* vii. 93 The Malachees and Shaffees lift up their Hands in a sort of careless manner, and then let them fall down and hang by their sides.] **1838** G. C. RENOUARD in *Encycl. Metrop.* (1845) XXIV. 440/2 The Sect of the Shâfi'is or Shafeïtes, is named from Mohammed ibn Idrîs Al Shâfi'î. **1886** Shafeite [see HANBALITE]. **1887** *Encycl. Brit.* XXII. 661/1 The Hanafite praxis is the least rigorous, then the Shâfi'ite. *Ibid.*, In Egypt and North Africa Shâfi'ites are more numerous than Mâlikites, while the opposite is the case in Arabia.

**shaflie,** obs. (non-literary) form of SAFELY *adv.*

**1639** *Hamilton Papers* (Camden) 94.

**shafman, -ment,** obs. forms of SHAFTMENT.

**shafnet,** corrupt form of SHAFTMENT.

†**shaft,** *sb.*[1] *Obs.* Forms: 1 **sceaft** (also with **ȝe-**), **scæft,** 2–3 **sceft-e, saft-e,** 2–3 *Ormin.* **shafft,** 2–4 **scaft,** 3 **seft,** 3–4 **schafte,** (**scaf** *Cursor M.*), 3–5 **shafte, schaft,** 4 **chaft,** *pl.* **schefte,** *Ayenb.* **ssepþe,** (**ssefþe**), 2–5 **shaft.** [OE. *sceaft*, *ȝesceaft* fem.:—OTeut. **(ga)skapti-z* f. **skap-* to make, create: see SHAPE *v.* Cf. OS. *giscaft*, OHG. *gascaft*, *giscaft* fem.]

**1.** Creation, origin (*OE.* only); make, constitution, nature or species.

**888** K. ÆLFRED tr. *Boeth.* xxx. §2 Ealle sint emnæþele, ȝif ȝe willað þonne fruman sceaft ȝeþencan, & þone scippend. [*c* **1175** *Lamb. Hom.* 81 He is..þe king of heuene þe com in to herþe and auenede him in to his iscefte.] *c* **1250** *Gen. & Ex.* 349 Flesses frenðe and safte same boðen he felten on here lichame. *a* **1300** *Cursor M.* 739 A littel best þe quilk es noght vnwiliest, þe nedder þat es of a scaft þat mast kan bath on crok and craft. *a* **1300** *E.E. Psalter* cii[i]. 13 [14] Fore our schaft wele knawes he. **13..** *Guy W.* 7168 Gret wenges he haþ wiþ to fle, His schaft to telle alle ne mow we. *c* **1320** *Cast. Love* 661 He moste be boren of a wommon, þulke schaft to vnderfonge wiþ-alle þat ouȝte to monnes kynde bi-falle. *c* **1330** R. BRUNNE *Chron. Wace* (Rolls) 9386 He [Merlin] can ynow of swylke craftes, Of alle vigures he turnes þe schaftes. **1340** *Ayenb.* 62 þe dyeuel him ssseweþ ine uele ssefþes. *Ibid.* 158 Me be-houeþ to zyenne..ine þe perle of þe eȝe þe sseppe of the þinge þet is him be-uore. **1377** LANGL. *P. Pl.* B. XIII. 297 Feyrest of feytures of fourme and of schafte. *c* **1400** *Arth. & Merlin* (Linc. Inn MS.) 1579 His schaft may nomon telle, He loked as a feond of helle.

**2.** That which is created; a creature.

*c* **888** K. ÆLFRED tr. *Boeth.* xli. §2 Ȝif God næfde on eallum his rice nane friȝe ȝesceaft [**11..** *Bodl. MS.* sceaft] under his anwalde. *c* **1175** *Lamb. Hom.* 59 Lauerd he is of alle scafte. *a* **1200** *Moral Ode* 84 He wit and waldeð alle þing and scop alle scefte [*c* **1200** safte]. *c* **1200** ORMIN 19444 Acc hallȝhe weress sæȝhenn Godd I shafftess onnlicnesse. *c* **1220** *Bestiary* 456 Seftes sop ure seppande. *a* **1225** *Leg. Kath.* 239 þæt schafte of mon þæt he schop. *c* **1250** *Gen. & Ex.* 127 God saȝ his safte fair and good. *a* **1300** *Cursor M.* 23640 Wit alkin scaf [*Gött.* schaft] þai sal discord. **1340** *Ayenb.* 84 He [man] wes lhord of alle sseppes þet were onder heuene.

**shaft** (ʃɑːft, -æ-), *sb.*[2] Forms: 1 **sceft,** 1–3 **sceaft, scæft,** 3 **scaft, saft,** 3–4 **ssafte, scheft,** 4 **shafth,** 4–5 **schafft, schafte,** 4–7 **schaft, shafte,** 5 **chaft(e,** 4– **shaft;** *rare* 4 **schaf,** 4–5 **shaffe,** 4, 7 **shaff,** 7 **shafe.** [Com. Teut. (wanting in Gothic): OE. *sceaft* masc. = OFris. *skeft* (Hettema), OS. *skaft* masc. (MLG., MDu., Du. *schaft*, *schacht* fem.), OHG. *scaft* masc., pl. *scefti* (MHG., mod.G. *schaft* masc.), ON. *skapt* neut. (Sw., Da. *skaft*):—OTeut. **skafto-*, **skafti-z*:—preTeut. **skapto-*, *-ti-s*.

App. cogn. w. L. *scāpus* shaft, stem, shank; somewhat more doubtfully with Gr. (Dor.) σκᾶπτον staff (Ion., Att. σκηπτο- in σκηπτοῦχος staff-bearer, σκῆπτρον staff, SCEPTRE, σκήπτειν to prop.). The Teut. word might, with regard both to form and meaning, be plausibly explained as a passive ppl. derivative from the root of SHAVE *v.*; but it is doubtful whether the supposed cognates can be similarly accounted for.]

**1. a.** The long slender rod forming the body of a lance or spear, or of an arrow. Also of a staff, harpoon, etc.

*c* **1000** ÆLFRIC *Gloss.* in Wr.-Wülcker 143/7 *Contus*, spereleas sceaft. **1297** R. GLOUC. (Rolls) 8658 He sset þe kyng [William Rufus] in atte breste þat neuereft he ne speke Bote þe ssafte þat was wyþoute grisliche he to brek. **1382** WYCLIF *1 Sam.* xx. 5 The brother of Goliath Jethee, whos spere schaft was as the beme of websters. *c* **1386** CHAUCER *Knt.'s T.* 504 (Morris), His sleep, his mete, his drynk is him byraft, That lene he wexe, and drye as eny schaft. **1506** *Acc. Ld. High Treas. Scot.* III. 358 Item, for xij staf schaftis.. xxiiij s. **1533** *Ibid.* VI. 188 For v dosane shaftis to Jedburcht stavis coft to his grace. **1688** HOLME *Armoury* III. xvii. (Roxb.) 113/1 Parts of a Pike. The shaft, for military service is reputed 16 or 18 foot long or there about. **1801** T. ROBERTS *Engl. Bowman* 293 *Shaft*, an arrow: properly so called when it wants only the head. **1814** SCOTT *Ld. of Isles* VI. xvi, His broken weapon's shaft survey'd The King, and careless answer made. **1836** LANDOR *Pericles & Aspasia* Wks. 1846 II. 419, I can compare the Lacedemonians to nothing more fitly than to the heads of spears without the shafts. **1907** C. HILL-TOUT *Brit. N. Amer., Far West* vii. 132 Points being held to the haft of the harpoon by long plaited lines. When the fish is struck these points detach themselves from the shaft.

**b.** A spear or lance. Now *arch.*

*c* **1000** ÆLFRIC *Lives Saints* xii. 53 His sceaft ætstod ætforan him..swa þæt þæt spere him eode þurh ut. *c* **1205** LAY. 23907 Þe an an his ænde..and þæ oðer an his ænde.. heo quehten heore scaftes [*c* 1275 saftes]. **13..** *Guy Warw.* 1404 So miȝti strokes þer wer ȝiuen, þat strong schaftes al to-driuen. *c* **1380** *Sir Ferumb.* 1594 So harde þay acoupede on hur scheldes þat broke buþ boþe hure schafte, & þe peces fulle on þe feldes þe hedes on þe tre by-lafte. *c* **1430** *Chev. Assigne* 301 And whenne þat shafte is schyuered take scharpelye another. **1483** *Cath. Angl.* 57/2 A Chafte; *vbi* spere, &c. **1697** DRYDEN *Virg. Georg.* II. 627 War from stubborn Myrtle Shafts receives: From Cornels Jav'lins; and the tougher Yeugh Receives the bending Figure of a Bow. **1754** GRAY *Poesy* 53 Hyperion's march they spy, and glitt'ring shafts of war. **1847** TENNYSON *Princess* v. 492 All the plain,—brand, mace, and shaft, and shield—Shock'd.

**2. a.** An arrow. ***cloth-yard shaft***, see CLOTH-YARD.

*c* **1400** *Rom. Rose* 1747 So at the last the shaft of tree I drough out, with the fethers three. *c* **1480** *Test. Ebor.* (Surtees) III. 253 Item xiiij shaffe of bolts and shoytyng shaftes, price xiiij s. Item v shaffe of rowyng shaftes iiij s. Item xlvij shaffe of childre shaftes. **1483** *Cath. Angl.* 57/2 A Chafte; *vb*[*i*] Arowe. **1541** *Act 33 Hen. VIII*, c. 9 §3 Euerie man, hauynge..men children..shall prouide..a bowe and two shaftes. **1596** SHAKS. *Merch. V.* I. i. 140 In my schoole dayes, when I had lost one shaft, I shot his fellow in the selfesame flight The selfesame way. **1599** B. JONSON *Ev. Man out of H.* v. iv, Draw me the biggest shaft you haue out of the butt you wot of. **1624** BP. HALL *True Peace-maker* Wks. (1625) 539 Thou wounded heart [*sic*]..; alas, the shaft sticks still in thee, or if that bee shaken out, the head. *a* **1711** KEN *Edmund* Poet. Wks. 1721 II. 236 Shafts aim'd at Trees can never mount so high, As those we shoot directly tow'rds the sky. *a* **1854** H. REED *Lect. Eng. Lit.* iv. (1878) 129 The air was darkened by the shafts from the hosts of English archers.

**b.** *Proverbial phr.* See BOLT *sb.*$^{1}$ 1 b.

**1594** NASHE *Terrors of Nt.* Wks. 1904 I. 368 To make a shaft or a bolt of this drumbling subiect of dreames, from whence I haue bin tost off and on I know not how.

†**c.** In various occasional scientific uses, as transl. of L. *sagitta*: (*a*) *Astr.* The Pole-star and its companion; (*b*) *Anat.* (see quot. 1552); (*c*) *Geom.* A versed-sine: cf. ARROW *sb.* 6. *Obs.*

**1551** RECORDE *Cast. Knowl.* (1556) 263 The lesser Beare.. is the chiefe marke whereby mariners gouerne their course in saylinge by nyghte, and namely by 2 starres in it, which many do call the shafte. **1552** UDALL tr. *Geminus' Anat.* B vij b, In the bone of the temple is a bone lyke a smal pyller, or a nedle, and therefore called the nedlelyke bone,..the quyll bone, the shafte, and the staffe bone. **1594** BLUNDEVIL *Exerc.* II. (1597) 49 b, A.H. is the Shaft, called in Latine *Sinus versus.* [See also ARROW *sb.* 6.]

†**d.** An 'arrow' on a plan or diagram showing the direction. *Obs. rare.*

**1730** A. GORDON *Maffei's Amphith.* 293 The Bending of the Stairs; the Knowledge of which..will be much facilitated by the Shafts which shew their Extension.

**e.** *loosely.* A missile. *rhetorical.*

**1786** tr. *Beckford's Vathek* (1836) 80 By my formidable art, the clouds shall pour grape-shot in the faces of the assailants, and shafts of red-hot iron on their heads. **1817** SHELLEY *Rev. Islam* VI. xi, Then the shaft Of the artillery from the sea was thrown More fast and fiery. **1835** W. IRVING *Tour Prairies* 196 The trees and thickets with which it was bordered would be sufficient to turn aside any shaft of the enemy. **1838** PRESCOTT *Ferd. & Isab.* I. x. (1846) I. 427 Some threw away their arms; hoping by this means to facilitate their escape, while in fact it only left them more defenceless against the shafts of their enemies.

**f.** *fig.* and in figurative context.

**1576** GASCOIGNE *Droome Doomes Day* Wks. 1910 II. 409 To wound and wearye theyr soules, with..the shaftes of sundrye shamefull concupyscences. **1600** FAIRFAX *Tasso* II. xxxiv, Death hath exchang'd againe his shafts with loue, And Cupid thus lets borrow'd arrowes flie. **1608** HIERON *Help Devot.* Wks. 1632 II. 760 Let his children be as chosen shafts in thy quiuer. **1667** MILTON *P.L.* IV. 763 Here Love his golden shafts imploies, he lights His constant Lamp. **1779** J. MOORE *View Soc. Fr.* I. xxx. 281 It is..to be regretted, that he allowed the shafts of his ridicule to glance upon the Christian religion. **1847** TENNYSON *Princess* II. 444 And often came Melissa hitting all we saw with shafts Of gentle satire, kin to charity, That harm'd not. **1873** DIXON *Two Queens* XIX. vii. IV. 41 Having suffered for a whole year past from the shaft of love.

**g.** *transf.* A beam or ray (of light, etc.), a streak of lightning, etc. Chiefly *poet.*

**13..** *E.E. Allit. P.* A. 982 By-ȝonde þe brok fro me warde keued, þat schyrrer þen sunne with schaftez schon. *Ibid.* C. 455. *a* **1400–50** *Wars Alex.* 1544 A Mitre,..Stiȝt staffull of stanes þat straȝt out bemes, As it ware shemerand shaftis of þe shire son. **1798** BLOOMFIELD *Farmer's Boy, Summer* 264 When midnight and the frightful Tempest come, The Farmer wakes, and sees..The angry shafts of Heaven gleam round his bed. ? **1799** COLERIDGE *On a Cataract* 13 It embosoms the roses of dawn, It entangles the shafts of the noon. **1864** TENNYSON *En. Arden* 588 The sunrise broken into scarlet shafts Among the palms and ferns and precipices. *a* **1878** W. C. BRYANT *Leg. Delawares* 4 A thousand shafts of lightning pass. **1898** WATTS-DUNTON *Aylwin* XIV. iv, Masses of vapour..blazing..whenever the bright shafts of morning struck them.

**3. a.** A pole, flagstaff; *spec.* †a may-pole; also †the pole on which the candle lighted at the 'new fire' was carried in the ceremonies of Easter Eve. Also, †a gate-post. *rare.*

*a* **1000** *Boeth. Metr.* i. 11 Fana hwearfode scir on sceafte. *c* **1250** *Gen. & Ex.* 3899 Moyses ðor made a wirme of bras, And heng et hege up on a saft. **1419** *26 Pol. Poems* 71 Of here banere of grace, god broken haþ þe shaft. **1428** in Peacock *Eng. Ch. Furniture* (1866) 179 Et Thomas harpmaker pro emendacione de la schafte xj d. *c* **1450** in Aungier *Syon* (1840) 351 The holy water schal go before, the schafte after with ij tapers unlyght... Aftyr the sensyng of the fyre the schafte schal be lyght only. **1522** *Churchw. Acc. St. Giles, Reading* 17 Paid for a whope of Iron to the Shafts of the churche gate iij d. **1598** STOW *Surv.* 107 On May day..a high or long shaft (or May pole) was set vppe there,..which shaft when it was set on end..was higher then the Church steeple. *a* **1819** REES *Cycl.* XXXII, *Set*, a term used for a pole or shaft, used to shove boats along a canal, &c. **1852–63** BURN *Techn. Dict.* I. (ed. 4), *Trabe*,..pole or shaft of an ensign or colour.

†**b.** A guild in the parish of St. Dunstan's, Canterbury; ? named from a pole carried by the warden in procession. Also, ? the pole itself. *Obs.*

**1486** *Churchw. Acc. St. Dunstan's, Canterb.* in *Archæol. Cant.* XVI. 294 The acompte of the Schafte made be..[the two] then beyng wardeyns. **1511** *Ibid.* 321 We haue receyud of Wyllyam Carpenter of his gyfte a gyrdyll for to bere the Schaft contynuyng for euer from Warden to Wardeyn. **1535** *Ibid.* 98 For the expensis of the dyner, Seynt Dunstones lyght, mendyng of the Shaft, and other charges xxiij s. xj d. **1539** *Ibid.* 102 Wardens of a Brotheryd caulyd the Shafte in the parysch of Seynt Dunstone.

**4.** A stem, columnar or straight portion of something. **a.** The stem or trunk of a tree. Now *rare.*

**1398** TREVISA *Barth. De P.R.* XVII. i. (Bodl. MS.), þe schafte of a tree þat streccheþ fro the rote vp to þe toppe is propreliche cleped lignum. **1449** PECOCK *Repr.* I. vi. 28 Tho bowis grewen out of stockis or tronchons, and the tronchons or schaftis grewen out of the roote. **1605** BACON *Adv. Learn.* II. xvii. §4. 62 If you will haue sciences growe, it is lesse matter for the shafte or bodie of the Tree, so you looke well to the takinge vp of the Rootes. **1825** COBBETT *Rur. Rides* 98 By far the finest tree that I ever saw in my life. The stem or shaft is short. **1842** MRS. KIRKLAND *Forest Life* I. 203 They were the shafts of bee-trees, found in the forest. **1889** B. HARTE *Cressy* x. II. 113 The dim colonnade of straight pine shafts.

**b.** In various Natural History uses. (*a*) The main stem or scape of a feather. [So G. *schaft.*] (*b*) The part of a hair between the root and the point. (*c*) *Anat.* The middle portion of a long bone. (*d*) *Ent.* The SCAPE of an antenna or of a halter. †(*e*) *Bot.* = STYLE (1787 Withering *Brit. Pl.* ed. 2, *passim*).

(*a*) **1748** *Phil. Trans.* XLV. 161 The Shafts of the Tail Feathers are very stiff. **1826** STEPHENS in Shaw *Gen. Zool.* XIV. I. 177 The white on the shafts of the feathers is broader. **1886** P. L. SCLATER *Catal. Birds Brit. Mus.* XI. 345 Feathers of head and neck lanceolate and with shining shafts.

(*b*) **1851** CARPENTER *Man. Phys.* (ed. 2) 200 The constituent fibres of the shaft are marked out by delicate longitudinal striæ, which may be traced in vertical sections of the hair. **1876** DUHRING *Dis. Skin* 33 In considering the hair we distinguish two portions,—the shaft, and the root.

(*c*) **1835–6** *Todd's Cycl. Anat.* I. 431/1 The long bones.. are never exactly cylindrical, being always contracted in the middle or shaft, and enlarged at each end. **1858** HOLDEN *Hum. Osteol.* (1878) 165 The 'shafts' are slightly concave towards the palm, to form the hollow of the hand.

**c.** The part of a candlestick which supports the branches.

**1388** WYCLIF *Exod.* xxv. 31 Thou schalt make a candilstike..and thou schalt make the schaft [**1382** staf, **1535** Coverdale, **1611** shaft] therof, and ȝerdis, cuppis, and litle rundelis, and lilies comynge forth therof. *Ibid.* 33 Sixe ȝerdis, that schulen be brouȝt forth of the schaft. *a* **1586** CARTWRIGHT in *Answ. to Cartwright* 88 The shaft..of the candlesticke.

†**d.** 'The Spire of a Church-Steeple' (Phillips 1706). [Cf. F. *flèche.*] *Obs.*

*c* **1450** *Chron. London* (Kingsford 1905) 156 The Steple of Seynt Pawlis chirche was sette on fire aboute the medyll of the Shafte in the tymbir. **1581** *Churchw. Acc. Dunmow* (MS.) fol. 49 In repayringe the steple in stone worke xxxix$^{li.}$ iii$^{s.}$ i$^{d.}$ Item, repayringe the shafte and tymber therof, v$^{li.}$ xvi$^{s.}$ ix$^{d}$. **1612** PEACHAM *Gentl. Exerc.* I. vi. 19 Practise to draw small and easie things,..as a cherry with the leafe, the shaft of a steeple [etc.]. *a* **1700** EVELYN *Diary* 20 Aug. 1654, Famous is the Steeple [at Grantham] for the exceeding height of the shaft, which is of stone.

**e.** Of a chimney, a blast-furnace: (see quots. and *chimney-shaft* s.v. CHIMNEY 11).

*c* **1450** *Nominale* (Harl. MS. 1002) 146 b, *Caminus*, a chymney. *Epicaustorium*, þe chaft þer-of. *a* **1548** in J. Bayley *Tower Lond.* (1821) I. App. p. xxv, To fynyshe x. shaftes upon x. chymneys. **1662** GERBIER *Brief Disc.* (1665) 10 Neither are those high Shafts of Chimnies real Ornaments to a Building. **1706** PHILLIPS (ed. Kersey), *Shaft*,..the Tunnel of a Chimney. **1836–50** PARKER *Gloss. Archit.* (ed. 5) s.v., The part of a chimney-stack between the base and cornice is called the shaft. **1855** FRANKE *Beil's Technol. Dict.* II. 457/2 *Shaft* of a blast-furnace (the internal cavity of the furnace), *der Schacht*; *Cuve, cheminée.*

**f.** *Arch.* The body of a column or pillar between the base and the capital. Also the 'die' of a parapet. See also quot. 1842.

**1483** *Cath. Angl.* 332/1 A schafte of a pylar, *stilus.* **1598** HAYDOCKE tr. *Lomazzo* I. xxiv. 86 The shaft or trunke of the columne is to be diminished a fourth parte at the toppe. **1624** WOTTON *Archit.* 31 They [the Columns] are all Diminished or Contracted..from one third part of the whole Shaft vpwards. **1756–7** *Keysler's Trav.* (1760) II. 461 The pedestal [of this pillar] consists of one stone, the base of eight, the torus of one, the shaft of twenty-three, and the capital of one. **1823** P. NICHOLSON *Pract. Build.* 310 The shaft or die, which is the part immediately above the plinth. **1842** GWILT *Archit.* Gloss., *Shaft of a King Post*, the part between the joggles. **1849** FREEMAN *Archit.* 16 Then gradually bringing within its power the details of shaft and capital.

**g.** The upright part of a cross; *esp.* the part between the arms and the base.

**1781** LEDWICH in Vallancey *Collect. de Rebus Hibern.* II. 446 The arms were broken, but the shaft [of the market cross of Kilkenny] remained adorned with beautiful figures. **1810** SCOTT *Lady of L.* III. viii, A slender crosslet form'd with care,..The shaft and limbs were rods of yew. **1836–50** PARKER *Gloss. Archit.* (ed. 5) s.v. *Cross*, In some instances they had small niches..round the top of the shaft below the cross. **1870** F. R. WILSON *Ch. Lindisf.* 90 The limbs and a portion of the shaft of a Saxon cross were found. *a* **1887** JEFFERIES *Field & Hedgerow* (1889) 279 One of them has retained its top perfect, and really is a cross, not a shaft only.

**h.** The stem or long straight handle of a tool, etc.; the shank of an anchor; the stem of a pipe; †the stalk or foot of a goblet or wine-glass.

**1530** PALSGR. 266/1 Shafte of any edged tole, *manche.* **1769** FALCONER *Dict. Marine* (1780), *Shank*, the beam or shaft of an anchor. *a* **1837** J. HOGG *Tales & Sk.* I. 297, I then took out my brandy bottle, and a small crystal glass without the shaft, that I carried in my pocket. **1841** CATLIN *N. Amer. Ind.* xxix. (1844) I. 235 The shafts or stems of these pipes. **1851** GREENWELL *Coal-trade Terms, Northumb. & Durh.* 46 *Shaft*,..the handle of a pick, hack, shovel, or maul. **1855** FRANKE *Beil's Technol. Dict.* II. 457/2 Shaft of a forge hammer (the helve or handle of the hammer), *der Helm, Stiel*; *Manche.* **1897** *Encycl. Sport* I. 473/1 (Golf), *Shaft*, the handle of the club.

**i.** †(*a*) Of a cannon: = CHASE *sb.*$^{3}$ 2. (*b*) 'The forward, straight part of a gun-stock' (Knight *Dict. Mech.* 1875).

**1626** CAPT. SMITH *Accid. Yng. Seamen* 32 Her shaft or chase, her trunnions.

**5. a.** *Arch.* A slender column, *esp.* one of 'the small columns which are clustered round pillars, or used in the jambs of doors or windows, in arcades and various other situations' (Parker *Gloss. Archit.*).

**1835** R. WILLIS *Archit. Mid. Ages* ii. 27 But the compound archway did not long remain in this simple form, its component archways were early decorated in various ways with shafts and mouldings. **1838** LYTTON *Leila* I. ii, The ceiling of cedar-wood..was supported by slender shafts, of the whitest alabaster. **1873** DIXON *Two Queens* I. i. I. 8 Images of the goddess on her jasper shaft. **1878** M$^{c}$VITTIE *Christ Ch. Cathedral* 67 The inside moulded jambs are decorated with six short limestone shafts.

**b.** *U.S.* An obelisk or column erected as a memorial.

**1847** EMERSON *Poems, Hymn* Wks. (Bohn) I. 494 Spirit, that made those heroes dare To die, and leave their children free, Bid Time and Nature gently spare The shaft we raise to them and thee. **1873** B. HARTE *Washington in N. Jersey* in *Fiddletown*, etc. 93 The gray shaft that commemorated the Morristown dead of the last civil war. **1878** JOAQUIN MILLER *Songs of Italy* 49 The whole country round vaunts our deed and the town Raised that shaft on the spot.

†**6.** A kind of balance: = AUNCEL, POUNDER (app. orig. ***auncel's shaft***).

**1429**, **1439** [see POUNDER *sb.*$^{1}$]. **1502** [see AUNCEL].

**7. a.** One of the long bars, between a pair of which a horse is harnessed to a vehicle; a thill. Also (? *U.S.*) 'the pole of a carriage, also called *tongue* or *neap*' (Webster 1828–32).

**1613** PURCHAS *Pilgrimage* (1614) 325 The shafts or beam of Gordius his cart. **1725** POPE *Odyss.* xv. 208 The bounding shafts upon the harness play. *a* **1764** LLOYD *Cobbler of Cripplegate's Let.* 124 The racer stumbles in the shaft, And shews he was not meant for draft. **1794** W. FELTON *Carriages* (1801) I. 61 The Shafts of a Carriage are the side framings, by which it is supported by the horse. **1894** K. GRAHAME *Pagan P.* 77, I found him smoking his vesper pipe on the shaft of his cart.

**b.** Either of the two side-pieces of a ladder which support the rungs or steps.

**1888** STEVENSON *Across the Plains* (1892) 197 The weedy spokes and shafts of the ladder.

**c.** (See quot.)

**1825** J. NICHOLSON *Oper. Mech.* 630 The sides of this table [for casting sheet lead]..are guarded by a frame or edging of wood, 3 inches thick, and 4 or 5 inches higher than the interior surface, called the shafts. *Ibid.* 631 So that its ends, which are notched.., may ride upon the shafts.

**8.** *Mech.* A long cylindrical rotating rod upon which are fixed the parts for the transmission of motive power in a machine; also, a separable portion of a line of shafting.

Also with qualifying word indicating a specific kind of shaft, as *crank, paddle, propeller, screw shaft*, COUNTERSHAFT, etc.: see those words.

**1688** HOLME *Armoury* III. 340/2 The Shaft [of a Wind-Mill], that on which the Sail Rods are set. **1764** CROKER, etc. *Dict. Arts* s.v. *Mill*, The undershot-wheel, upon whose shaft is fixed a spur or cog-wheel. **1814**, etc. [see JOURNAL *sb.* 10]. **1825** J. NICHOLSON *Operat. Mechanic* 43 In forming couplings, great care should be taken to make them fit, so that the coupled shaft may move as though of the same piece with the driving shaft. **1841** R. WILLIS *Princ. Mechanism* 44 *note*, Axis is the general and scientific word, shaft the millwright's general term, and spindle his term for smaller shafts. **1873** J. RICHARDS *Wood-working Factories* 4 The last shaft, or the one farthest from the engine, can be driven at a higher speed than the other shafts to suit joiners' machines on an upper floor. **1887** D. A. LOW *Machine Draw.* (1892) 30, Fig. 25, which represents a brake shaft carrier of a locomotive tender.

**9.** *Weaving.* Each of a pair of long laths between which the heddles are stretched; also applied to the pair taken together. Also in parasynthetic compounds with prefixed numeral, as ***four-shaft, ten-shaft*** adjs., designating makes of cloth.

Although no early examples have been found, the sense is certainly old; the G. *schaft* and Du. *schacht* are similarly used. Cf. '*thre-schaptyd cloth*, triplex' (*Promp. Parv.*, c 1440): see THREE III. 2.

[**1801** see LAM *sb.*[2]] **1839** URE *Dict. Arts*, etc. 1230 The heddles being stretched between two shafts of wood, all the heddles connected by the same shafts are called a leaf. **1878** BARLOW *Weaving* 173 With four shafts and twenty pairs of leashes.. the effect that may be produced will be noticed at ABCDE and F. *Ibid.*, At D the leashes are raised, and the shafts also. *a* **1904** W. THORNTON in *Eng. Dial. Dict.* s.v., [*Obs.* in W. Yorksh.] Long thin flat rods of wood, upon which the 'gems' or 'healds' were stretched. The stretching was effected by a 'top' and 'bodom' shaft, and the whole was also termed a 'shaft', when describing the pattern or make of cloth to be produced, as 'four shaft', 'ten shaft', &c.

†**b.** *Sc.* A kind of woollen cloth. *Obs.*

[Prob. generalized from designations like *four-shaft*, *ten-shaft*, etc.: see above.]

**1797** *Statist. Acc. Scot.*, *Aberd.* XIX. 208 Cloths manufactured from the above wool,.. three quarters to yard broad seys, sarges, shafts, plaidings, baizes, linseywoolseys, jemmies, and stripped apron stuffs.

**10.** In various slang uses. **a.** The penis. Also † ***shaft of delight.***

[**1719** T. D'URFEY *Wit & Mirth* IV. 72 It is a Shaft of Cupid's cut, 'Twill serve to Rove, to Prick, to Butt.] **1772** G. A. STEVENS *Songs, Comic, & Satyrical* 11 For Cupid's Pantheon, the Shaft of Delight Must spring from the Masculine Base. **1971** B. W. ALDISS *Soldier Erect* 45 It was never enough merely to lower your trousers—they had to come off,.. so that you could crouch there naked but for your shirt, frantically rubbing your shaft.

**b.** A human leg. *U.S.*

**1935** A. J. POLLOCK *Underworld Speaks* 103/2 *Shaft*, a woman's leg. **1939** C. MORLEY *Kitty Foyle* 95 If anyone showed a good shaft Pop would wink at me.

**c.** *U.S.* An act or instance of unfair or harsh treatment; slighting, rejection, 'the push'; esp. in ***to give*** or ***get the shaft.***

**1959** *Amer. Speech* XXXIV. 155 A girl or boy who makes a play for another's date is *snaking*... If he succeeds, the loser gets the *shaft* (sometimes *with barbs*), *the purple shaft*, or *the maroon harpoon*, depending upon the degree of injury to his pride. **1960** WENTWORTH & FLEXNER *Dict. Amer. Slang* 461/1 *Shaft*.., an act or an instance of being taken advantage of, unfairly treated, deceived, tricked, cheated, or victimized; a raw deal. Usu. in 'to get the (*or* a) shaft'. Fig., the image is the taboo one of the final insult, having someone insert something, as a barbed shaft, up one's rectum. **1964** *Mad Mag.* July 14 Looks like somebody gave him the shaft! **1977** *Amer. Speech* *1975* L. 65 She gave him the shaft after he broke their date last weekend. **1979** *Mod. Photography* Dec. 86/2, I would give more of my business to Minolta but for the company's uncooperative, anti-consumer thinking. Doubtless there are many such as myself who have gotten the shaft.

**11.** *attrib.* and *Comb.* **a.** In sense 2 (arrow, etc.), as ***shaft-arm***, †***-end***, ***-hand***, ***-head***, ***-maker***; ***shaft-armed***, ***-like***, ***-straight***, ***-strong*** adjs.; †**shaft-wise** *adv.*, ? in cylindrical form.

**1801** T. ROBERTS *Engl. Bowman* 293 **Shaft-arm, Shaft-hand*, the arm, the hand, employed in drawing the arrow. **1790** COWPER *Iliad* I. 18 His hands charged with the wreath And golden sceptre or the God *shaft-arm'd. **1545** ASCHAM *Toxoph.* II. Wks. (1904) 116 Yf I should shoote at a line and not at the marke, I woulde alwayes loke at my *shaft ende. **1801** *Shaft-hand [see *shaft-arm* supra]. **1545** ASCHAM *Toxoph.* II. Wks. (1904) 115 To looke at your *shafte hede at the lowse, is the greatest helpe to kepe a lengthe that can be. **1821** BYRON *Sardanap.* IV. i. 90 A huge quiver rose With shaft-heads feather'd from the eagle's wing. **15..** J. BRYAN *Ps.* cxxvii. 7 in Farr *S.P. Eliz.* II. 335 Straight, *shaft-like sprowts in shape and mind. **1899** R. B. SHARPE in *Daily News* 21 Feb. 6/2 A long shaft-like plume. **1904** WINDLE *Preh. Age Eng.* iv. 80 Here the object was.. to shape off the roughnesses of a stick, so as to convert it into an arrow-shaft—for which reason this kind of scraper is sometimes called a '*shaft-maker'. **1849** CHARL. BRONTË *Shirley* II. v. 127 Her *shaft-straight carriage and lightsome step. **1519** HORMAN *Vulg.* 105 b, All preciouse stonys may be made *shaft wyse, saue pearlys. *Omnes gemmæ teretes fieri possunt, extra vnum vnionem.*

**b.** In sense 5 a (*Arch.*), as ***shaft-architecture***, ***-cap***, ***-ring***.

**1851** RUSKIN *Stones Venice* I. viii. §xxiii, The earliest and grandest shaft architecture which we know, that of Egypt. **1882** *Archæol. Cant.* XIV. 364 The segmental arch of its head springs not from shaft-caps but from vertical stilts. **1909** *Century Dict.* Suppl., *Shaft-ring*, an annular band.. which seems to surround a shaft of a column. It is often the wrought edge of a stone plate which separates two stones that make up a shaft, the inclosing ring being an appearance only.

**c.** In sense 4 h (handle), as **shaft-hole**, *Archæol.* the hole in an axe-head or similar implement for the insertion of the haft or handle.

**1852–63** BURN *Techn. Dict.* II. (ed. 4), Shaft prop, *servante. Ibid.*, Shaft stay, *cravate.* **1865** LUBBOCK *Preh. Times* iii. (1878) 62 The British lance-heads frequently have loops at the side of the shaft-hole,.. which is never the case with Danish specimens. **1894** J. MACINTOSH *Ayrsh. Nt.'s Entert.* 201 A stone axe.. having a shaft-hole one inch in width. **1928** [see *core-casting* s.v. CORE *sb.*[1] 16]. **1958** W. WILLETTS *Chinese Art* I. ii. 75 (*heading*) Objects derived from the shaft-hole adze. **1971** *Listener* 7 Jan. 14/1 (*caption*) Copper shaft-hole tools of the Balkan late neolithic.

**d.** In sense 7 a (thill of a carriage, etc.): as ***shaft-bar***, ***-bender***, ***-bolt***, ***-jack***, ***-loop***, ***-man***, ***-ring***, ***tug***; **shaft-horse**, the horse which goes in the shafts.

**1802** C. JAMES *Milit. Dict.*, **Shaft-bars*, are two pieces of wood to fasten the hind ends of the shafts together, into which they are pinned with wooden pins. **1881** *Instr. Census Clerks* (1885) 56 Coach making.. *Shaft Bender. **1852–63** BURN *Techn. Dict.* II. (ed. 4), *Shaft-bolt, *boulon de limonière.* **1769** WESLEY *Jrnl.* 28 July, The *shaft-horse.. boggled and turned short. **1886** RUSKIN *Præterita* I. vi. 182 The four horses were driven by one postillion riding the shaft horse. **1875** KNIGHT *Dict. Mech.*, **Shaft-jack*, (Vehicle) an iron attaching the shafts to the axle. *Ibid.*, **Shaft-loop*, (Harness) the ring of leather suspended from the gig-saddle to hold the thill or shaft. **1881** *Instr. Census Clerks* (1885) 56 Coach making.. *Shaftman. **1802** C. JAMES *Milit. Dict.*, *Rings*, in artillery, are of various uses such as, the *shaft-rings to fasten the harness of the shaft-horse by means of a pin. **1856** 'STONEHENGE' *Brit. Rural Sports* III. III. iv. 543 A buckle and strong loop on each side, called the *Shaft Tug, by which the shaft is supported.

**e.** *Ornith.* (sense 4 b), as ***shaft-mark***, ***-spot***, ***-streak***, ***-stripe***; **shaft-tailed bunting**, Latham's name for one of the buntings of the genus *Emberiza*; **shaft-tailed whidah, widow bird**, a dark-coloured African weaver-bird, *Vidua regia*, having long tail-feathers with bare shafts.

**1884** J. H. GURNEY *Diurnal Birds Prey* 157 The dark *shaft-marks much narrower than in the female [Kestrel]. **1888** P. L. SCLATER *Argentine Ornith.* I. 164 Above plumbeous, with slight darker *shaft-spots. **1874** R. B. SHARPE *Catal. Accipitres B. Mus.* 438 Crown rufous, with blackish *shaft-streaks. **1867** P. L. SCLATER & SALVIN *Exotic Ornith.* 71 There are linear elongated *shaft-stripes on the head and on portions of the under plumage. **1783** LATHAM *Gen. Synopsis Birds* II. I. 183 *Shaft-tailed Bunting. **1881** F. & C. G. OATES *Matabele Land & Victoria Falls* facing p. 220 (*caption*) *Shaft-tailed Whydah Bird. **1900** A. C. STARK *Birds S. Afr.* I. 148 Shaft-tailed Widow Bird... The four central, elongated tail-feathers are webbed at their ends.., the rest of them consists of bare shaft. **1948** C. D. PRIEST *Eggs of Birds breeding S. Afr.* 135 Shaft-tailed Whydah.. undoubtedly parasitic. **1974** *Sci. Amer.* Oct. 96/2 The shaft-tailed widow bird of South Africa.. mimics the repertory of its host, the violet-eared waxbill.

**f.** In sense 8 (axle or revolving bar), as ***shaft-bearing***, ***-boss***, ***-bracket***, ***-coupling***, ***-drive*** (so ***-driven***), ***-eye***, ***-gearing***, ***-governor***, ***-head***, ***-passage***, etc. **shaft-alley** *Naut.* (see quot. 1884); also used *attrib.* to designate unofficial or unreliable information or its source, attributed to gossip in shaft-alley; **shaft horsepower**, brake horsepower, *spec.* power delivered to a propeller shaft or the shaft of a turbine; **shaft turbine** (see quot. 1958).

**1884** *Naval Encycl.* 732/1 **Shaft-alley*, a passage extending from the engine-room to the stern.. in which is contained the propeller-shaft and its bearings. **1922** L. HISEY *Sea Grist* 155 It was rumored by shaft alley wireless that we would reach Antwerp, Belgium, in two days. **1941** R. G. M. EHLERS *Diary of Ship's Surgeon* (1944) 67 A 'shaft alley' rumor brought word that all ships had been ordered out of Hong Kong. **1945** *Sun* (Baltimore) 30 Aug. 7-0/5 It's the job of these six men to go down to the nethermost portion of this ship in 'Shaft Alley', where the big propeller shafts whirl. **1875** KNIGHT *Dict. Mech.*, *Shaft-bearing. **1863** BARRY *Dockyard Econ.* 236 This is 42 feet in length, and, with its sole and *shaft-boss, weighs 40 tons. **1894** W. H. WHITE *Man. Naval Archit.* (ed. 3) 415 (Cent. Suppl.), Stems, sternposts, *shaft-brackets, rudders, etc., are now commonly made of cast steel instead of forged iron or steel. **1906** *Westm. Gaz.* 26 June 4/1 As regards transmission, fourteen of the cars are employing chains, as against twenty relying on *shaft drive. **1906** *Daily Chron.* 14 Nov. 9/3 These cars are *shaft-driven. **1835** URE *Philos. Manuf.* 34 The recent innovations in.. adjusting the movements of the system of *shaft-geering. **1898** *Engineering Mag.* XVI. 146/2 The Design and Setting of *Shaft Governors. **1825** J. NICHOLSON *Operat. Mechanic* 130 A gudgeon from the end of each cylinder runs into an iron fastened to the *shaft-head. **1908** A. E. TOMPKINS *Marine Engin.* (ed. 3) v. 61 The torsion-meter is used to measure this angular twist between two points of a shaft, and from this angle the *shaft horse-power is calculated. **1974** *Petroleum Rev.* XXVIII. 490/1 The high shaft horsepower was the conditioning factor for this proportion of pilot fuel. **1874** THEARLE *Naval Archit.* 115 The bulkheads of the *shaft passages are sometimes made watertight. **1958** *Chambers's Techn. Dict.* Add. 1013/1 **Shaft turbine*, any gas turbine aero-engine wherein the major part of the energy in the combustion gases is extracted by a turbine and delivered, through appropriate gearing, to a shaft. **1970** LAMBERMONT & PIRIE *Helicopters & Autogyros of World* (ed. 2) 147 It had two shaft-turbine engines mounted on the cabin top instead of two Pratt and Whitney piston engines.

**g.** *Weaving* (sense 9), as ***shaft harness***, ***monture.***

**1878** BARLOW *Weaving* 168 The second [contrivance] is generally used in weaving the richest silks now made, and is termed the split harness, or 'shaft monture'. *Ibid.* 170 The above contrivance entirely dispenses with a separate set of treadles to work the shaft harness.

**h. shaft-furnace**, 'a high furnace, charged at the top and tapped at the bottom' (Raymond *Mining Gloss.* 1881).

**1874** RAYMOND *Statist. Mines & Mining* 393 Those shaft-furnaces which use charcoal as fuel.

**shaft** (ʃɑːft, -æ-), *sb.*[3] Also 5 shafte. [Corresponds in sense to MHG. *schaht*, mod.G. *schacht* masc., which is prob. a. LG. *schacht* (also Du.) of the same meaning, usually regarded as a specific application of *schacht* = SHAFT *sb.*[2], the primitive notion being that of something cylindrical. It is possible, however, that the type **skafto-* represented by LG. *schacht*, Eng. *shaft* 'pit-hole', may be a separate formation on the Teut. root **skab-* of SHAVE *v.*, in its original sense to dig (cf. Gr. σκάπτειν). On either of these views, it is doubtful whether *shaft* 'pit-hole' goes back to OE. (though not recorded before the 15th c.), or was introduced into England by foreign miners.

Some scholars still adhere to the view of Grimm, that the HG. *schacht* (and LG. *schacht* in this sense) represent a Teut. type **skaχto-z.* On this supposition the Eng. word would necessarily be a loan word from the continent. Grimm's hypothesis is formally possible, but leaves the ultimate etymology obscure, as the suggested connexion with the root **skak-* SHAKE *v.* is semasiologically improbable.]

**1.** A vertical or slightly inclined well-like excavation made in mining, tunnelling, etc., as a means of access to underground workings, for hoisting out materials, testing the subsoil, ventilation, etc.

For *air-shaft*, *engine-shaft*, *pumping-shaft*, etc. see those words.

**1433–4** *Durham Acc. Rolls* (Surtees) 711 Pro factura unius shaft infra campum de Heworth pro carbonibus ibidem lucrandis, 20s. **1443** *Ibid.* 713 Cum thirlyng unius shafte. **1602** CAREW *Surv. Cornw.* 8 b, There they sincke a Shaft, or pit of fiue or sixe foote in length [etc.]. **1665** *Phil. Trans.* I. 80 By letting down shafts from the day (as Miners speak). **1733** ARBUTHNOT *Ess. Effects Air* ii. 34 Suppose a Tube, or, as the Miners call it, a Shaft were sunk from the Surface of the Earth to the Centre. **1815** CLANNY in *Thomson's Ann. Philos.* (1816) VII. 369 In this district there are several coal-mines that have only one shaft, which serves the double purpose of ventilation and working. **1843** *Penny Cycl.* XXV. 369/2 Shafts of at least four feet diameter should be sunk along the line of the tunnel. **1868** MORRIS *Earthly Par.*, *Rhodope* 14 Nor as yet had any one Sunk shaft in hill-side there, or dried the stream To see if 'neath its sand gold specks might gleam. **1888** F. HUME *Mme. Midas* I. i, She.. sank a shaft in the place indicated.

**2.** *Mil. Mining.* (See quot. 1876.)

**1834** J. S. MACAULAY *Field Fortif.* (1847) 183 The top frame of the shaft is then let into the ground. *Ibid.* 184 In unfavourable soil the whole shaft must be lined with sheeting. **1876** VOYLE & STEVENSON *Milit. Dict.* (ed. 3), *Shaft*, in military mining is the perpendicular passage sunk from the surface of the ground to the required depth, from which the branches of the mine diverge, termed 'galleries'. .. Shafts and galleries are lined with timber to prevent the soil from breaking in.

**3.** *transf.* Applied to other well-like excavations, or passages.

**1820** BELZONI *Egypt & Nubia* II. 270 Where the granite work finishes at the end of this passage [in the 2nd Pyramid], there is a perpendicular shaft of fifteen feet. **1860** TYNDALL *Glac.* I. ii. 18 Numerous shafts, the forsaken passages of ancient 'moulins'. **1861** FLOR. NIGHTINGALE *Nursing* (ed. 2) 28 It often happens that the sick room is made a ventilating shaft for the rest of the house. **1912** *World* 25 June 1005/2 The second floor [of the burning house] seemed a furnace, and the shaft of the lift acted as a chimney.

**4.** *attrib.* and *Comb.* **a.** simple attrib., as ***shaft ladder***, ***mouth***, ***work***, etc.; ***shaft sinking*** vbl. sb. Also objective, as ***shaft-sinker.***

**1844** F. W. SIMMS (*title*) Practical tunnelling, explaining in detail.. shaft sinking, and heading driving. **1862** *Times* 21 Jan., Mr. Coulson.. has had vast experience in shaft work. c **1868** C. WARREN *Recov. Jerus.* (1871) 128 The shaft mouth is on the south side of the Sanctuary wall. **1909** *Chamb. Jrnl.* Apr. 239 They started to descend the shaft-ladders. **1922** D. H. LAWRENCE *Aaron's Rod* vii. 70 His father had been a shaft-sinker.

**b.** *Comb.*: **shaft-drill**, 'a rotary drilling-machine, armed with diamond points, for boring vertical shafts' (Knight *Dict. Mech.* 1875); **shaft-grave** *Archæol.*, applied to ancient interments in a 'shaft'; **shaft-house**, 'the heavy framework for the pulleys and landing-place at the top of a mining shaft, some-times enclosed for protection from the weather' (*Funk's Stand. Dict.* 1895); **shaftman**, a man employed to keep the shaft in repair (*Northumbld. Gloss.*); also, a workman employed to sink shafts (cf. SHAFTSMAN); **shaft pillar** *Mining*, a body of coal or rock unworked in order to provide support for an adjacent shaft; **shaft-rent** (see quot.); **shaft-riding**, ascending by means of a lift or cage in a shaft; **shaft-tackle** = POPPET-HEAD 2; **shaft tomb** = *shaft-grave.*

**1910** D. G. HOGARTH in *Encycl. Brit.* I. 248/1 The *shaft graves in the Mycenae circle are also a late type. **1872** *Statistics of Mines & Mining 1870* (U.S. Treasury Dept.) 344 The quartz is brought from the mine, unless the mill is in or near the *shaft-house, in wagons. **1874** RAYMOND *Statist. Mines & Mining* 332, I cannot see the need or use of a shaft-house of such a shape and only 10 feet in diameter. **1881** *Instr. Census Clerks* (1885) 84 Tin miner.. *Shaftman. *Ibid.* 85 Lead miner.. shaftman. **1893** W. C. BORLASE *Age Saints* Introd. 21 Many a first-rate Cornish miner—a 'shaftman', that is to say—belongs to it [the German type]. **1855** G. C. GREENWELL *Pract. Treat. Mine Engin.* vi. 155 The situation of coal pits varies so much, together with the position of the seams of coal, dykes and slips, that no rule can be laid down for the form of the pillars of coal, left near the shaft, which are called the *shaft pillars. **1929** I. C. F. STATHAM *Winning & Working* xxx. 499 This subsidence was not.. wholly due to the removal of the shaft pillar, but was partly accounted for by crushing of the shaft pillar in an upper seam. **1977** *Irish Press* 29 Sept. 8/4 A third semipermanent pillar, known as the shaft pillar, cuts across the orebody from north to south. **1849** GREENWELL *Coal-trade Terms, Northumb. & Durham* (1851) 42 **Shaft rent*, for the privilege of drawing up the shaft the coal worked from another royalty by outstroke. **1887** P. McNEILL *Blawearie* 57 In those days the miners who worked the coalfields on the estate of Blawearie were but rarely allowed to indulge in the luxury of '*shaft riding'. **1874** J. H.

COLLINS *Metal Mining* 81 The cost of preparing and fixing this *shaft-tackle should not exceed 25s. or 30s. for timber, ironwork, and labour. **1895** W. LEAF *Iliad* I. Introd. 15 The '*shaft tombs' discovered by Dr. Schliemann in the Acropolis of Mykenai.

†**shaft**, *v.*$^{1}$ *Obs. rare*$^{-1}$. [Of obscure origin.] *intr.* Of the sun: ? To set.

13.. *Gaw. & Gr. Knt.* 1467 He rechated, & r[ode] þurȝ ronez ful þyk, Suande þis wy[ld]e swyn til þe sunne schafted.

**shaft** (ʃɑːft, -æ-), *v.*$^{2}$ [f. SHAFT *sb.*$^{2}$]

**1.** *trans.* To fit (an arrow-head, a weapon or tool) with a shaft.

**1611** FLORIO, *Alberáre*,..Also to shaft or stave any weapon as a holbard. *a* **1775** *Hobie Noble* xvi. in Child *Ballads* IV. 3/1 Gar warn the bows o' Hartlie-burn See they shaft their arrows on the wa! **1853** G. J. CAYLEY *Las Alforjas* II. 256 Many of our modern authors live by..new shafting and feathering old arrow heads.

**2.** *to shaft out*: to shoot as an arrow or shaft.

**1862** THORNBURY *Turner* II. 88 There was the storm rolling..and shafting out its lightning over the Yorkshire hills.

**3.** To propel (a barge, etc.) with a pole.

**1869** A. DAVIS *Velocipede* 5 Like unto the method of punting or shafting vessels. **1906** *Daily Chron.* 19 Feb. 10/5 Sometimes a boat is 'shafted' through [a tunnel] with a pole.

**4.** To treat unfairly or harshly; to cheat, deceive; to take advantage of; to slight, reject. *slang* (orig. and chiefly *N. Amer.*).

**1959** *Amer. Speech* XXXIV. 155 A raw deal from any other source may also be referred to in this way; for example, one may be *shafted* or *jabbed* by the opposite sex, a professor, a policeman, parents, or anyone else for any real or imagined injury. **1966** 'E. LATHEN' *Murder makes Wheels go Round* xiii. 108 He was a menace to Wahl... He'd railroaded Orin Dunn into jail... He was shafting Buck Holsinger! **1970** *Deb. Senate Canada* 1 June 755l/2 As I have told my constituents in Hamilton, Ontario, which seems to have been continually shafted by this government. **1971** B. MALAMUD *Tenants* 19 Rent control..is an immoral situation. The innocent landlord gets shafted. **1976** M. MACHLIN *Pipeline* xxxv. 397, I think how they're shafting us with this whole deal.

**5.** = FUCK *v.* 1 *trans. coarse slang.*

**1970** G. LORD *Marshmallow Pie* xxi. 185 There was this young girl among them, not even sixteen yet..like as not being shafted by every dirty long-haired crud in town. **1971** B. W. ALDISS *Soldier Erect* 82 How sinful he looked, squatting there by the water while his wife was being shafted by some dirty big Mendip only a few feet away! **1971** J. WAINWRIGHT *Last Buccaneer* II. 228 He was Jimmy Needler —that's all...and the rest of the world could go shaft itself.

Hence ˈ**shafting** *vbl. sb.*

**1971** B. W. ALDISS *Soldier Erect* 124 Hello there, gran! What do you do? Gobble? Where are the birds? We want three as are fit enough to stand a gude shafting. **1972** J. WAINWRIGHT *Requiem for Loser* iii. 50 What a monumental shafting he'd deliver to some lucky bint. **1973** *Farm & Country* 20 Nov. 23/3 Hugh Blaine charged that farmers 'suffered a shafting at the hands of feed dealers last year'. **1975** R. H. RIMMER *Premar Experiments* i. 94 After double-dealing with his own people and selling them to the slavers, some slaver gave the king and his family a shafting and enslaved them too.

**shafted** (ˈʃɑːftɪd, ˈʃæft-), *a.* [f. SHAFT *sb.*$^{2}$ + -ED$^{2}$.] Having or furnished with a shaft or shafts. **a.** *Her.* Of a spear, arrow, or similar weapon: Having the shaft of a specified tincture.

**1586** FERNE *Blaz. Gentrie* 221 Tomyris, Queene of Scythia: did beare Iupiters thunder-bolt Or: shafted and winged Argent. **1661** MORGAN *Sph. Gentry* I. iv. 50 Jupiters Thunderbolt in pale or,..shafted saltirewayes argent.

**b.** Furnished with a shaft or handle. Chiefly in parasynthetic derivatives, as *long-shafted*.

**1641** *D. Fergusson's Sc. Prov.* (1785) 14 He should hae a long shafted spoon that sups kail wi' the devil. **1869** BOUTELL *Arms & Armour* App. (1905) 273 Fourteen Examples of Shafted Weapons. **1870** MORRIS *Earthly Par.* III. IV. 46 He crept along, Poising a spear, thick shafted, strong, In his right hand. **1879** *Echo* 21 Mar. 2/5 Those [assegais]..are thrown by the hand..and are less strongly shafted than the charging weapon.

**c.** *Arch.* Ornamented with or resting upon shafts.

**1801** A. RANKEN *Hist. France* I. I. v. 452 Hence proceeded the pointed arches, the shafted columns [etc.]. **1805** SCOTT *Last Minstr.* II. i, When the broken arches are black in night, And each shafted oriel glimmers white. **1835** R. WILLIS *Archit. Mid. Ages* iii. 29 These imposts are divided into two classes, which may be called Shafted and Banded. In shafted archways the horizontal section of the upright is different from that of the arch taken immediately above the impost, and generally much plainer. **1878** SIR G. G. SCOTT *Lect. Archit.* (1879) 279 Even when the exterior is shafted the inner splay often comes close to the face of the recessed order. **1812** *Archæol. Cant.* XIV. 364 Seven-foiled lights, with shafted mullions of Decorated character.

**d.** *Ornith.* In comb. with prefixed word: Having the shafts (of feathers) of a specified character or number.

**1809** SHAW *Gen. Zool.* VII. 496 Six-shafted Paradise-bird. **1831** Red-shafted [see RED *a.* 14b].

†**shaft-eel.** *Obs.* [? SHAFT *sb.*$^{2}$, referring to the shape.] A kind of eel. Cf. SHAFFLIN.

**1411** *Cal. Let. Bks. Hen. IV*, I. 102 [*printed* shastele]. **15..** in Dugdale *Monasticon* (1655) I. 81/2 Schafte eles to bake for the covent on shere thursday. **1545** *Rates Custom Ho.* bjb, Elis called shaft kyue or dele elis. **1583** *Ibid.* Bvijb, Shaft, kine or dole Eeles. [So in later schedules.]

**shafter** (ˈʃɑːftə(r), -æ-). [f. SHAFT *sb.*$^{2}$ + -ER$^{1}$.] A shaft-horse.

**1840** HALIBURTON *Clockm.* Ser. III. x. 137 A London brewer's shafter wouldn't make the smallest part of a circumstance to him. **1877** *Holderness Gloss.*, *Shafther*, the horse, where there are more than one, which is placed between the shafts of a cart. **1904** *Blackw. Mag.* June 824/2 The cook alternately crooned and swore at the old shafter.

**Shaftesburian** (ʃɑːftsˈbjʊərɪən, -æ-), *a.* Also **Shaftsburean, -ian.** [f. *Shaftesbury* (see below) + -IAN.] Of or pertaining to the moral philosophy or literary style of Anthony Ashley Cooper, third Earl of Shaftesbury (1671–1713), author of 'Characteristicks of Men' (1711).

**1752** *Gray's Inn Jrnl.* No. 10 (1756) I. 68 Mr. Plastic is a compleat Shaftesburian Philosopher. *Ibid.* 69 This with him is the Test of Truth which he opposes..to the Shaftesburian Rule. **1755** MISS TALBOT in Pennington *Life Mrs. Carter* (1808) I. 196 Shaftsburian Heathens [will read this book] because Epictetus was an honour to Heathenism. **1828** D. IRVING *Elem. Composition* (ed. 8) 243 That parade of language which distinguishes the Shaftesburean manner.

†ˈ**Shaftesbury.** *slang. Obs. rare*$^{-0}$. [The name of a town in Dorset.] (See quot.)

*a* **1700** B. E. *Dict. Cant. Crew*, *Shaftsbury*, a Gallon-pot full of Wine, with a Cock.

**shafting**$^{1}$ (ˈʃɑːftɪŋ, -æ-). [f. SHAFT *sb.*$^{2}$ + -ING$^{1}$.]

**1.** A system of connected shafts for communicating motion from the prime mover to the machinery. Also, material from which to cut lengths of shafts.

**1825** J. NICHOLSON *Oper. Mech.* Descr. Frontisp. 16 The rotary motion which the crank has received from the engine is imparted to the shafting. **1845** I. FARRELL *Archimedean Railway* 5, I have therefore made several experiments on different lengths of shafting. **1862** *Catal. Internat. Exhib.* II. XII. 2 The motion of the handle on deck is transmitted..by means of a series of shaftings and tooth-wheels. **1889** F. COLYER *Public Instit.* 192 The Shafting must be 2½ inches diameter, and the pulleys of suitable sizes to the machines they have to drive. **1895** *Daily News* 3 June 7/3 The demand for marine shafting in the city has been fairly good for nine months. **1912** *Times* 19 Dec. 19/3 Bolts, shaftings, and miscellaneous products.

*attrib.* **1881** *Instr. Census Clerks* (1885) 99 Factory Labourer... Shafting Oiler. **1898** *Engineering Mag.* XVI. 148/1 A Shafting Lathe. Describes a lathe..intended both for general lathe work and for turning shafting.

**2.** Shafts or ornamental columns.

**1868** *Morn. Star* 25 June, A large quantity of shafting belonging to the north piers of the chancel..had been smashed with a hammer.

**3.** *U.S.* 'A darkening of the shaft, or quill of a feather, as in some breeds of poultry' (*Cent. Suppl.*).

**1896** *Yearbk. U.S. Departm. Agric.* 462 (Cent. Suppl.), Shafting on the back will also help the black stripe in the saddles.

ˈ**shafting**$^{2}$. [f. SHAFT *sb.*$^{3}$ + -ING$^{1}$.] The sinking of a shaft; also, the shafts of a mine collectively.

**1872** RAYMOND *Statist. Mines & Mining* 297 Aggregate of shafting over 5,000 feet. **1877** *Ibid.* 273 About 1,000 feet of shafting and drifting well represent the amount of work done.

**shaftless** (ˈʃɑːftlɪs, -æ-), *a.* [f. SHAFT *sb.*$^{2}$ + -LESS.] Without or lacking a shaft (in any sense of the sb.).

**1811** BYRON *Curse of Min.* vii, The broken lance Seem'd weak and shaftless. **1812** —— *Ch. Har.* II. xc, The flying Mede, his shaftless broken bow. **1881** PALGRAVE *Vis. Eng.* 116 One high gracious curve Of shaftless windows frames the limpid blue. **1881** MAYNE REID *Free Lances* I. xvii. 189 His irony was shaftless, being understood. **1895** *Daily News* 21 Sept. 5/5 The doctors went to look for the Lefebvre light carts but found them shaftless.

ˈ**shaftlet.** *nonce-wd.* [f. SHAFT *sb.*$^{2}$ + -LET.] A small shaft or column.

**1890** *Murray's Handbk. Lincolnsh.* 148 The font is E.E., with two crosses on each face, and shaftlets round the stem.

†ˈ**shaftling.** *Obs.* [Perh. f. SHAFT *sb.*$^{2}$ + -LING, with allusion to the shape. Cf. SHAFFLIN.] The stickleback.

**1558** *Gesner's Hist. Anim.* IV. 896 De Pungitio... Angli Scharplyng uel Shaftlyng nominant. **1572** HULOET (ed. Higins), Shaftling, sharplinge, stickling, sticklebanke, or banstickle, *aculeatus pisciculus, Pungitius, Centriscus.* **1598** FLORIO, *Spinaruólo*, a sharpling, or shaftlin fish [**1611** shaftin-fish].

ˈ**shaftment**$^{1}$. *Obs.* exc. *dial.* Forms: 1 **sceaftmund,** 4 **schaftmonde,** 5 **schafftmon, schaftemonde, schaft-mun, shaftmone, -mon(d, -mount, chaftmonde,** 5–6 **shafmond,** 6 **shaft-man, shaftemente,** (**shafts-man** *Florio*), 7 **shaftmont, -men, -met, shafman,** (*corruptly* **shafnet**), 7, 9 **shafment,** 9 **shaffment,** 6–9 **shaftment** (see also *Eng. Dial. Dict.*); 8–9 *Sc.* **shathmont.** [OE. *sceaftmund* (only once), f. *sceaft* SHAFT *sb.*$^{2}$ + *mund* hand, handbreadth. (Probably *sceaft* was intended to denote the extended thumb.)] The distance from the end of the extended thumb to the opposite side of the hand, used as a measure = about 6 inches.

*c* **910**–*c* **1060** *Pax* in Liebermann *Gesetze Ags.* 390 Ðus feor sceal beon ðæs cinges grið fram his burhȝeate,..III. mila & .III. furlang, and .III. æcera bræde, and .IX. fota, and .IX. scæftamunda [? *read* sceaftmunda], and .IX. berecorna. ? *a* **1400** *Morte Arth.* 3843 He schare hyme one the schorte rybbys a schaftmonde large! *c* **1400** *Laud Troy Bk.* 6658 He hadde a strok a schafftmon long. *c* **1400** *Anturs of Arth.* xli, Thro his shild and his shildur a schaft-mun [*Douce MS.* shaftmone] he share. **1474** *Coventry Leet Bk.* 399, iij schafmond and a half a-bout and a yerde of lenthe. *a* **1483** in W. G. Benham *Red Paper Bk. Colchester* (1902) 19 His fagot of wode shall be a yard of length and iij shaftmonds and an half abowte. *a* **1483** *Liber Niger* in *Househ. Ord.* (1790) 49 The Deane of the Chapell hathe all the offerings of wax.. when the tapers be consumed into a shaftmount. **1483** *Cath. Angl.* 57/2 Chaftmonde. **1545** ASCHAM *Toxoph.* II. (Arb.) 112 Therfore lette youre bowe haue good byg bend, a shaftemente and .ii. fyngers at the least. **1558** *Cranmer's Confut. Verities* Oivb, A lytle young prety babe, about a shaftmond long. **1598** FLORIO, *Quattraggio*, a certaine rate of cloth that is giuen aboue measure, as we say a shaft man or a handfull. **1620** J. TAYLOR (Water-P.) *Praise Hemp-seed* (1623) 13 Once heaue the Lead againe and sound abaff, A shafnet lesse, seauen all. **1626** CAPT. SMITH *Accid. Yng. Seamen* 18 Fadome by the marke, 3 od and a shaftment left. **1640** PARKINSON *Theat. Bot.* 486 This Scabious hath a thicke whitish stemme next the ground for a shaftmont high. **1647** HEXHAM I, A Shaftmen, *Een mate van een halven voet.* **1656** BLOUNT *Glossogr.*, *Shafment*, is a kinde of measure used in some parts of England, and is the breadth of a mans hand, and the length of the thumb. **1674** *Ibid.* (ed. 4), *Shaftmet*, or *Shaftment.* **1762** [W. YOUNG] *Treat. Weights & Meas.* 19 A shaftment, which is the length from the bottom of the wrist to the end of the thumb when the hand is extended, is reckoned 6 inches. *a* **1769** *Wee wee man* ii. in Child *Ballads* I. 330/1 His legs were scarce a shathmont's length. **1816** SCOTT *Antiq.* viii, Not a step, not a pace, not an inch, not a shathmont, as I may say; the meaning of which word has puzzled many that think themselves antiquaries.

**shaftment**$^{2}$ (ˈʃɑːftmənt, -æ-). *rare.* [f. SHAFT *sb.*$^{2}$ + -MENT. (Perh. suggested by misunderstanding of prec.)] †**a.** An arrow. *Obs.* **b.** The feathered part of an arrow.

**1634** WOOD *New Eng. Prosp.* II. xiii, Let fly their winged shaftments without eyther feare or wit. **1801** T. ROBERTS *Engl. Bowman* 293 *Shaftment*, that part of the arrow occupied by the feathers. **1903** *Amer. Anthropologist* Jan.–Mar. 60 (Cent. Suppl.) The dice were originally made of canes, being the shaftments of arrows, painted or burned with marks corresponding with those used to designate the arrows of the four world-quarters.

**shaftsman** (ˈʃɑːftsmən, -æ-). *Mining.* [f. SHAFT *sb.*$^{3}$ + MAN *sb.*$^{1}$ after CRAFTSMAN, etc. Cf. *shaftman*, SHAFT *sb.*$^{3}$ 4b.] A man employed in sinking shafts.

**1881** *Instr. Census Clerks* (1885) 84 Coal Miner.. Shaftsman. **1892** *Pall Mall Gaz.* 21 Mar. 7/3 Walking from eight to ten miles a day before and after his underground work (much of it as a shaftsman).

**shafty** (ˈʃɑːftɪ, -æ-), *a.* [f. SHAFT *sb.*$^{2}$ (sense 9) + -Y.] Of wool: 'having a close, compact, free, long, and strong staple' (Webster 1911).

**1891** *Times* 3 Oct. 13/1 Good shafty wools, both merinos and cross-breds. **1895** *Argus* (Melbourne) 4 Oct., At the London wool sales yesterday..deep shafty and scoured merinoes sold at 20 per cent. [above previous prices]. **1911** A. F. BARKER in *Encycl. Brit.* XXVIII. 806/2 A long but fine wool technically termed a long and shafty 60's to 64's quality.

**shag** (ʃæg), *sb.*$^{1}$ Forms: 1 **sceacga,** 6–7 **shage,** 7 **shagge,** 7–9 **shagg,** 7– **shag.** [OE. *sceacga* wk. masc.:—prehistoric **skaggon-*, cogn. w. ON. *skegg* neut., beard (:—**skagjo-m*), OE. *sceaȝa* wk. masc., coppice, SHAW (formally = ON. *skage* wk. masc., promontory:—**skagon-*), ON. *skaga* to project; the ON. *skóg-r*, a wood, shows a different ablaut-grade of the root. Cf. OHG. *scahho* wk. masc., promontory (:—**skakon-*), which may be more distantly related.

The OE. word occurs once (in a gloss), and the derivative *sceacgede* SHAGGED *a.*$^{1}$ twice. Otherwise neither the sb. nor any of its derivatives has been found before the latter part of the 16th c.]

**1. a.** Rough matted hair, wool, etc. *rare* or *arch.*

*c* **1050** *Voc.* in Wr.-Wülcker 379/41 *Coma*, feax, sceacga. **1601** HOLLAND *Pliny* VIII. xxxiii. I. 214 Of the same kind is the Goat hart, and differing onely in the beard and long shag about the shoulders. **1697** *Phil. Trans* XIX. 410 Many Prickles interspersed among the Hairy Shag that covered the sides. *a* **1732** GAY *Fables* II. v. 69 A Bear of shagg and manners rough, At climbing trees expert enough. **1771** tr. *Pernety's Voy. Malouine Isl.* (1773) 289 They have a sort of buskins or half-boots, made of the same skins, with the shag on the inside. **1809** W. IRVING *Knickerb.* v. vii. (1820) 343 A rugged mop of hair, not a little resembling the shag of a Newfoundland dog. **1869** BUSHNELL *Woman Suffrage* iii. 50 The base in his voice and the shag on his face. **1898** C. F. LUMMIS *Awak. Nation* 104 It is a purely leonine type—not by bulk or shag, but by look and port.

**b.** A mass of matted hair; also shreds (of bark).

**1607** TOPSELL *Four-f. Beasts* 626 For what [wool] which was rough and thicke in ancient time, was vsed for this purpose, and also to make garments, hauing the shags thereof hanging by it like rugs. **1610** GUILLIM *Her.* III. xv. (1660) 180 The King of Judah was then like a Sleeping Lyon, which did not shew his rage with his erected shag. **1882** *Harper's Mag.* May 870/1 Nuts which have been packed away and wedged beneath the loose shags of bark.

**c.** The nap (esp. long and coarse) of cloth.

*a* **1661** HOLYDAY *Juvenal* II. Notes (1673) 25 Then their *Galbana rasa*, white smooth sarcenet without hair or shag;.. of this our Women now wear hoods. **1716** GAY *Trivia* I. 47 Fine Witney Broad-Cloath with it's Shag unshorn. **1844** G.

DODD *Textile Manuf.* vi. 201 The face [of velvet] has a short shag, or 'pile', occasioned by the insertion of short pieces of silk thread doubled under the shoot. **1851-3** *Tomlinson's Cycl. Usef. Arts* (1867) II. 329/1 *Plush*, a textile fabric, with a sort of velvet nap or shag on one side.

**d.** *transf.* Applied to thick down on plants.

**1773** *Phil. Trans.* LXIII. 365 The shag [Fr. *la pluche*], or inner part of these flowers. **1854** PAPPE *Silva Capensis* (1862) 18 Twigs, petioles, calyces and underside of leaves densely coated with brown shag. *Ibid.* 19 Petioles and veins clothed with a dense rusty shag.

**e.** A (tangled) mass of shrubs, trees, foliage, etc.

**1836** STRUTHERS *Dychmont* i. Poet. Wks. (1850) II. 50 Were thy broomy shag but shorn, Thou might'st be made to wave with corn. **1855** BROWNING *Up at Villa* iii, Stuck like the horn of a bull Just on a mountain's edge as bare as the creature's skull, Save a mere shag of a bush with hardly a leaf to pull! **1877** BLACKMORE *Erema* lii. III. 190 Dark shags of ling, and podded spurs of broom. **1905** MARY E. WILKINS *Debtor* 60 He could see the gleam of the current through the shag of young trees which found root in the unpromising soil. *Ibid.* 396 Only the oak-leaves, a brownish-red shag mostly on the lower branches, were left on the trees.

**f.** *fig.* Roughness, brutality of manner.

**1784** COWPER *Task* v. 693 As if, like him of fabulous renown [*i.e.* Orpheus], They had indeed ability to smooth The shag of savage nature. **1809** MALKIN *Gil Blas* VIII. xiii. (Rtldg.) 308 This metamorphose into the shag of a savage is not perceptible to myself.

**2.** A cloth having a velvet nap on one side, usually of worsted, but sometimes of silk. Also, a kind or variety of this.

**1592** *Wills & Inv. N.C.* (Surtees 1860) II. 211 Three quarters of blacke shage, 12s. **1598** SYLVESTER *Du Bartas* II. ii. III. *Colonies* 71 Chiorze, where Buls as big As Elephants are clad in silken shag. **1612** [F. BEAUMONT] *Masque Inner Temple* D 1 b, The high Priest a cap of white silke shagge close to his head, with two labels at the eares [etc.]. **1623** SIR R. BOYLE in *Lismore Papers* (1886) II. 86, I..gaue him ordre to bring for me..crymson shagg and Spangled Lace for winter Clothes for my Children. **1769** DE FOE, etc. *Tour Gt. Brit.* (ed. 7) III. 280 The Woollen Manufacture called Half-thicks, Frizes, and Shags. ? **1725** *Sadberge* (*Durham*) *Par. Reg.*, A..cushion of red shagg. **1781** *Phil. Trans.* LXXI. 72 The Indians make a most elegant cloathing..as fine as a silk shag. **1805** LUCCOCK *Nat. Wool* 277 The blanket manufacture at Witney, and that of worsted shaggs at Banbury. **1825** SCOTT *Talism.* xvii, A cap of rough shag. **1855** LEIFCHILD *Cornwall* 179 Engine Shag and Poldavey 1,119 yards. **1887** *Fortn. Rev.* Aug. 294 The King, says Petion, wore a coat of dark shag, and his linen was not clean.

**3.** †**a.** A garment, rug, or mat of shaggy material.

**1634** SIR T. HERBERT *Trav.* 97 At the end sate the Pot-shaugh or great King..his seat hauing two or three white silke shags vpon the Carpets. **1664** POWER *Exp. Philos.* I. 50 A [magnified] Sage Leaf looks like a white Rugge, or Shagge, full of Knots, tassel'd all with white silver Thrums. **1681** T. JORDAN *London's Joy* 9 St. Patric..a gray Mantle with a thick shag about his Neck of large green Silk and Gold fringes. **1738** [G. SMITH] *Cur. Relat.* II. 361 Twelve Royal travelling Coaches..; one Set of Shags. **1827** CARLYLE *Germ. Rom.* III. 229 The Regiments-Quartermaster..embaled in a long woollen shag. **1854** R. S. SURTEES *Handley Cross* xiv, His hunting clothes, consisting of a roomy scarlet coat,..drab shags, and mahogany-coloured tops.

**b.** *Westminster School slang.* (See quot. 1902.)

**1902** R. AIRY *Westminster* 108 Any coat other than an 'Eton' or 'tails' is a 'shag'.

**c.** *ellipt.* A shag carpet or rug; shag pile. See sense 6 c below.

**1951** K. R. GILLESPIE *Home Furnishings* v. 164 A few cotton floor coverings woven on standard carpet backs have come into the market, in addition to the bouclé weaves, shags, [etc.]. **1974** *Anderson* (S. Carolina) *Independent* 18 Apr. (Sears Advts. Suppl.) 5 Nylon pile shag. Long shag that's slow to show soil! **1976** H. NIELSEN *Brink of Murder* xii. 108 The floor was carpeted with soft yellow shag.

**4.** (In full *shag tobacco*.) A strong tobacco cut into fine shreds.

**1789** *Act 29 Geo. III*, c. 68 §127 Upon the exportation of any short cut tobacco, shag tobacco, roll tobacco, and carrot tobacco. **1823** in *Spirit Publ. Jrnls.* 527 Porter and pop, mirth-moving max, and fragrant shag. **1840** THACKERAY *Shabby-genteel Story* i, A constant and agreeable odour of shag tobacco. **1862** *Cornh. Mag.* VI. 607 One pipe..of Virginian tobacco in the shape of bird's-eye or shag. **1876** J. DUNNING *Tobacco* 17 'Shag' is the generic name of all those varieties of leaf which have passed through the cutting machine.

¶**5.** ? Used for *snag*. [Cf. SHAGGED *a.*$^{1}$ 2 c; but perh. a misprint.]

**1649** J. TAYLOR (Water-P.) *Wand. West* 6 At a stile I had a great disaster, for a shagge or splinter of the stile tooke hold of my one and onely breeches.

**6.** *attrib.* and *Comb.* **a.** simple attrib., as ***shag edging***, ***manufactory***, ***manufacture***; **shag boy**, *dial.* = *shag foal* (b); **shag end** *N. Amer. colloq.* = FAG-END 2; **shag foal**, *dial.*, (*a*) 'a foal with its first year's coat on' (*N.W. Linc. Gloss.* 1877), (*b*) a hobgoblin (see quots. 1847, 1856); †**shag sponge**, a 'muricate' sponge.

**1882** M. G. WATKINS *In Country* (1883) 210 Fairies and *shag-boys! lasses are often skeart at them, but I never saw none. **1884** G. S. STREATFEILD *Linc. & Danes* 357 *Shag-boy* also *Shag-foal*, a ghost. **1808** *Trans. Soc. Arts* XXVI. p. x, The ingenious Implement..for cutting *Shag Edgings. **1972** J. MOSHER *Adultery* IV. xxi. 176 It was the *shag end of winter and there were several things to be had. **1977** G. V. HIGGINS *Dreamland* i. 13 The years that came between that night..and the shag end of 1971. **1847** HALLIWELL, **Shag-foal*, a sort of ghost or spectre, which under this appearance is thought by the common people to haunt different parts of the county. *Linc.* **1856** P. THOMPSON *Hist. Boston* 722 *Shag-foal*, a hobgoblin in the shape of a small rough horse. *Ibid.* 736. **1780** A. YOUNG *Tour Irel.* I. 278 Bandon was once the seat of the stuff, camblet, and *shag manufacture. **1794** R. DAVIS *Agric. Oxford* 26 The *shag manufactory at Banbury. *a* **1776** J. ELLIS *Zoophytes* (1786) 185 *Spongia muricata.* *Shagg Sponge.

**b.** passing into *adj.*, composed or made of 'shag' (sense 2).

**1611** MIDDLETON & DEKKER *Roaring Girl* II. i. D 1 b, I am going to buy a shag ruffe. **1621** in Kempe *Losely MSS.* (1836) 426 For 17 yards of fyne doble shagg bayes, for Gilbert's murning cloake [etc.]. **1706** in C. N. Robinson *Brit. Fleet* (1894) 493 Striped shag breeches, lined with linen. **1836** MARRYAT *Japhet* xxxix, He was dressed in highlow boots,..a shag waistcoat, and a blue frock overall. **1911** B. CAPES *Loaves & Fishes* 181 Wandering unsociable in a shag coat.

**c.** Of carpets, rugs, etc.: having a long, rough, pile. Also ***shag pile***. Cf. SHAGGY *a.* 1 c.

**1946** *House Beautiful* Oct. 199 (Advt.), Charm Tred Shag Cotton Rugs. **1947** *Sun* (Baltimore) 1 Dec. 13/4 (Advt.), Heavy Loop Pile Shag Rugs. **1969** D. E. WESTLAKE *Up your Banners* (1970) xlii. 309 The silence had the texture of a shag rug. **1974** *Times* 3 May 11/4 Kosset Panorama, the cheapest shag carpet I have seen. *Ibid.* 12 Aug. 22/8 (Advt.), *Carpets*..Shag Piles and Berber Weaves.

**shag** (ʃæg), *sb.*$^{2}$ Forms: 6 schagge, 7 shagge, 7-9 shagg, 7- shag. [Perh. a use of SHAG *sb.*$^{1}$ or SHAG *a.*, with reference to the 'shaggy' crest.]

**a.** A cormorant, esp. the crested cormorant, *Phalacrocorax graculus*, which in the breeding season has a crest of long curly plumes.

Also with defining name, applied to several varieties of the cormorant, and sometimes erroneously to the common shag at different periods of its age, under the idea that it is a different variety.

**1566** *Act 8 Eliz.* c. 15 §2 For euery head of..Busarde, Schagge, Carmeraunt, or Ryngtayle, two pence. **1602** CAREW *Cornwall* I. 35 Curlewes, Teale, Widgeon, Burranets, Shags, Duck and Mallard. *a* **1672** WILLUGHBY *Ornith.* (1676) 249 *Corvus aquaticus minor sive Graculus palmipes.* The Shag. **1729** J. WOOD *Voy.* 85 An island which is much frequented by a sort of Fowl which are called Shaggs, that live mostly upon fish. **1769** COOK *1st Voy.* in Hawkesworth *Voy.* (1773) II. 339 Plenty of wild fowl, principally shags, ducks, curlieus, and the sea-pie. **1785** LATHAM *Gen. Synopsis Birds* III. II. 600 Crested Shag. *Pelecanus cristatus. Ibid.*, Violet Shag. *Ibid.* 601 Red-faced Shag. *Ibid.* 602 Spotted Shag. *Ibid.* 603 Caruncculated Shag. *Ibid.* 604 Magellanic Shag. *Ibid.* 605 Pied Shag. *Ibid.* 606 Tufted Shag. *Ibid.*, African Shag. *Ibid.* 607 Dwarf Shag. **1824** —— *Gen. Hist. Birds* X. 423 Chinese Shag. *Ibid.* 425 Brown-necked Shag. *Ibid.* 431 New Holland shag. **1841** J. T. HEWLETT *Parish Clerk* I. 288 Cormorants, or shaggs, as they are more commonly termed. **1841** SELBY in *Proc. Berw. Nat. Club* I. No. ix. 255 The common cormorant (*Phalacrocorax carbo*), and the crested shag (*P. cristatus*), are permanent residents. **1861** COUES in *Proc. Philad. Acad.* 241 Both this [*Graculus dilophus*] and the *G. carbo* are universally known as 'Shags'. **1879** BEERBOHM *Patagonia* ii. 12 We startled a large covey of shag, which, to judge by the accumulation of guano, appeared to roost there habitually. **1885** *Riverside Nat. Hist.* (1888) IV. 191 New Zealand is especially rich in shags,..having not less than thirteen species, amongst these the curiously colored spotted shag (*Phalacrocorax punctatus*). *Ibid.*, Flock after flock of violet-green shags (*P. pelagicus*) came up to the steamer.

*Phrase.* **1835** MARRYAT *Jac. Faithf.* xx, I'm as wet as a shag, and as cold as charity. **1841** in Col. Hawker *Diary* (1893) II. 197 Came home in the middle of the day 'as wet as a shag', it having come on to pour.

**b.** *transf.* ***a shag on a rock***: used in various Austral. colloq. phrases as a type of the isolated or exposed.

**1845** R. HOWITT *Impressions of Australia Felix* 233 'Poor as a bandicoot', 'miserable as a shag on a rock', &c.; these and others I very frequently heard them make. **1929** J. RAESIDE *Golden Days* 16 The flood waters did not subside, and we were there like three shags on a rock. **1971** D. IRELAND *Unknown Industrial Prisoner* 275 It's easy enough to curse England. Leaving us out here like a shag on a rock.

**c.** *attrib.* **shag cormorant**, †**pelican**, the shag; **shag-like** *adv.*, in the manner of a shag.

**1826** STEPHENS in Shaw *Gen. Zool.* XIII. I. 82 *Shag cormorant (*Phalacrocorax Graculus*). **1896** T. E. BROWN *Lett.* (1900) II. 165 Indications (stage-directions, hints like yours) send one skimming *shag-like over the water. **1785** PENNANT *Arctic Zool.* II. 581 *Shag Pelecan.

**shag**, *sb.*$^{3}$ In 6 shagge. [f. SHAG *v.*$^{1}$] †**a.** A shake. *Obs.* **b.** *dial.* The refuse of barley, corn, oats, etc. Cf. SHACK *sb.*$^{1}$ 2.

**1581** RICH *Farew.* (1846) 166 When she sawe she waked not, she laied her hand upon her, and givyng her a shagge, she said withall, Mistres, awake! my maister calleth for you. **1822** *Edin. Caled. Mercury* 9 Dec. (Jam.), Mr. Robert Meiklejohn, brewer, Alloa, sowed a quantity of shag, from English barley,..being the skimmings of his malt cisterns. **1823** *Ibid.* 13 Nov. (Jam.), Oats have about ten times the quantity of shag they had last year. **1856** MORTON *Cycl. Agric.* II. 725 (Provincialisms.) *Shagg*, (Stirlings.), tail corn.

**shag**, *sb.*$^{4}$ In 7 shagge. [? var. of SHACK *sb.*$^{2}$ Cf. SHAG-RAG.] A low, rascally fellow.

**1620** T. GRANGER *Div. Logike* 170 Shagge, a terme of reproach semes to come of *Shog, Shagag*, or *Shag heb.* to do vnadvisedlie [etc.]. **1790** GROSE *Prov. Gloss.* (ed. 2), *Shag*, or *Shack*, a blackguard. Suffolk. **1801** CHARLOTTE SMITH *Lett. Solit. Wand.* I. 352 Was now under the hard necessity of becoming shag, fag, skip, or whatever the boys in the higher forms chose to insist upon.

**shag**, *sb.*$^{5}$, variant of SHACK *sb.*$^{4}$

**shag**, *sb.*$^{6}$ *coarse slang.* [f. SHAG *v.*$^{3}$] **a.** An act of copulation.

**1937** PARTRIDGE *Dict. Slang* 748/2 *Shag*, a copulation; also, copulation generically. **1971** B. W. ALDISS *Soldier Erect* 114 It was not just a good shag I needed. It was romance.

**b.** One who copulates. *rare.*

**1971** K. AMIS *Girl, 20* ii. 76 Ageing shag tries to stimulate jaded appetite by re-creating situation of days of first discovery of sex. **1978** —— *Jake's Thing* ix. 94 The moustached shag and the flat-chested bint..had moved away from the bar with their drinks.

**shag**, *sb.*$^{7}$ [Perh. f. SHAG *v.*$^{2}$ or *v.*$^{3}$] A dance popular esp. in the U.S. in the 1930s and 1940s, and characterized by vigorous hopping from one foot to the other. Hence as *v. intr.*, to dance the shag; **'shagger**$^{1}$, one who dances the shag.

**1932** (*title of jazz tune*) Shag. **1937** [see *Big Apple* s.v. BIG *a.* B. 2]. **1938** *Sun* (Baltimore) 24 June 4/3 The Virginia reel, the shag, the sugarfoot and trucking predominate on the dance program. **1939** RAMSEY & SMITH *Jazzmen* xiii. 271 The Crescent Billiard Hall..frequented by the best shaggers in town. *Ibid.*, Usually when Brunions reaches the third chorus..the kids have stopped shagging. **1940** *Time* 29 Jan. 17/1 A citizenry shagging to the tune of *Oh Johnny!* refused to take the 1940 Campaign seriously. **1954** DANNETT & RACHEL *Down Memory Lane* 131 The shag is a fast, nervous, hopping dance, performed in time to a strongly accentuated rhythm. **1963** *N.Y. Times Mag.* 27 Oct. 104/2 [The Negroes'] body rhythm and frank sensuality turned the formal European waltz into..the shag, the Susie Q. and the big Apple.

**shag** (ʃæg), *a.* Now *rare* or *arch.* Also 6 shagg, 7 shagge. [From attrib. use of SHAG *sb.*$^{1}$]

**1.** Having shaggy hair.

Formerly sometimes hyphened, as ***shag-dog***.

**1592** SHAKS. *Ven. & Ad.* 295 Round hooft, short ioynted, fetlocks shag, and long. **1634** SIR T. HERBERT *Trav.* 201 Black—long—shag—curld heads. **1638** FORD *Lady's Trial* III. i, A' has chang'd Haire with a shagge dogge. **1642** (*title*) An exact Description of a Roundhead and a long-headed Shag-Poll. *c* **1645** HOWELL *Lett.* IV. xxxiii. (1892) II. 612 The Shag-dog was so well bred, that his Master us'd to send him by himself to Smithfield Shambles. *c* **1670** WOOD *Life* (O.H.S.) I. 199 He..had a curl'd shag-pate, was squint-ey'd and purblind. **1760** *Impostors Detected* III. viii. II. 77 Two hundred of these creatures [monkeys], mounted on shag dogs came first. **1883** A. DOBSON *Old World Ballads* 181 Huddling they came, with shag sides caked of mire, With hoofs fresh sullied from the troughs o'erturned. **1892** KIPLING *Barrack-r. Ballads* 97 The picketed ponies, shag and wild, Strained at their ropes.

**2.** Of hair, a mane, etc.: Long and rough, shaggy.

*c* **1596** *Sir T. More* III. ii. 111 How long Hath this shagg fleece hung dangling on thy head? *Ibid.* 118 When were you last at barbars? how longe time Have you vppon your head woorne this shagg haire? **1601** HOLLAND *Pliny* XVII. xxii. I. 532 Sheepe..with their shag-coats. **1611** TOURNEUR *Ath. Trag.* II. F 2, The Gentleman took the dog in shagge-haire to be some Watch-man in a rugge gowne. **1639** T. DE GRAY *Compl. Horsem.* 314 Clip away the long shag haire from about the pasternes. **1647** HEXHAM I, Shagge haire, *Ruygh hayr.* **1975** R. L. DUNCAN *Dragons at Gate* (1976) i. 12 Jenkins feigned the appearance of his early thirties..sandy-colored shag hair.

**3.** Comb., as ***shag-bearded***, ***-eared***, ***-faced***, ***-footed***, ***-woolled***, etc.

**1907** H. TRENCH *New Poems* 10 *Shag-bearded pines, All gnarled, loom down. **1907** *Black Cat* June 26 Dogged at every step by the sinister, velvet-footed march of *shag-coated wolves. **1605** SHAKS. *Macb.* IV. ii. 83 Thou ly'st thou *shagge-ear'd [*mod. edd.* shag-haired] Villaine. *Mur.* What you Egge? **1884** *N. & Q.* Ser. VI. IX. 133/2, I have frequently heard a Shetland pony called 'shag-ear'd just like a moke'. **1716** R. ARBUTHNOT in *Stuart Papers* (Hist. MSS. Comm. 1904) II. 218 Macdonald..is a *shag-faced, thin fellow. **1901** JANE BARLOW *Land of Shamrock* 222 Gulls..swooping about among the *shag-footed, tramping plough-horses. **1821** SCOTT *Kenilw.* xv, Half a score of *shag-headed Irish kernes. **1612** DRAYTON *Poly-olb.* xiii. 139 Flocks of *shag-wooll'd Sheepe.

†**shag**, *v.*$^{1}$ *Obs. rare.* Also 4-5 schagge. [Of obscure origin: cf. SHAKE *v.*, SHOG *v.*] **a.** *trans.* To toss about. **b.** *intr.* To shake, waggle. Hence †**'shagging** *vbl. sb.*

*c* **1380** WYCLIF *Sel. Wks.* I. 374 And þe boot, amydde þe water, was shaggid [*v.r.* schoggyd; **1388** —— *Bible* Matt. xiv. 24 schoggid; Vulg. *jactabatur*] wiþ wawis. *a* **1400** *Pistil of Susan* 106 þe chouwet, þe cheuerol, þat schaggen on niht. *c* **1440** *Promp. Parv.* 443/1 Schaggynge, schoggynge, or waverynge, *vacillacio.* **1572** MASCALL *Plant. & Graff.* v. (1592) 28 But alwayes take good heede to the binding of your heds that they waxe slack, or shagge, neyther on the one side or other, but remaine fast vpon the clay.

**shag** (ʃæg), *v.*$^{2}$ [f. SHAG *sb.*$^{1}$]

†**1.** *intr.* To be shaggy; to hang down in a shaggy manner. *Obs. rare.*

**1596** SPENSER *F.Q.* v. ix. 10 Long curld locks, that downe his shoulders shagged. **1801** CHARLOTTE SMITH *Lett. Solit. Wand.* II. 90 But here are vines planted on hills, and shagging like copse-wood in England.

**2.** *trans.* To render rough or shaggy, *esp.* the surface of the earth, a hill-side, a rock, etc. (*with* a growth of trees or the like). Chiefly in pa. pple.

**1612** PEACHAM *Gentl. Exerc.* II. vi. (1634) 121 His neather parts of a Goate declare the inequality of the earth being rough and shagged as it were with trees, plants, hils, &c. **1634** MILTON *Comus* 429 Caverns shagg'd with horrid shades. **1726-46** THOMSON *Winter* 281 The Swain..sees other hills ascend, Of unknown joyless brow; and other scenes, Of horrid prospect, shag the trackless plain. **1806** R. MANT *Poems* I. 32 Where seas extend of everlasting ice, And horror shaggs the unsunn'd precipice. **1873** HOWELLS *Chance Acquaintance* iii. 74 The woods that hitherto have shagged the hills with a stunted and meager growth,..now assume a stately size. **1894** BLACKMORE *Perlycross* 196 The fringe of the dominant black weed, like heavy brows, shagging the outlook. **1897** F. THOMPSON *New Poems, Ode Setting Sun* 113 Who lit the furnace of the mammoth's heart? Who shagged him like Pilatus' ribbèd flanks?

†**b.** To make a long or rough nap or pile on (a cloth or other material). *Obs. rare.*

**1671** E. BLOOD in *Abridgm. Specif. Patents, Weaving* (1861) 1 A rich silk shagg..made of a silke wast..and shagged by tezell or rowing cardes, like as English bayes, rowed fustians, or dimatyes.

**shag** (ʃæg), *v.*³ *coarse slang.* [Origin unknown, perh. f. SHAG *v.*¹] **1.** *trans.* and *intr.* To copulate (with).

**1788** GROSE *Dict. Vulgar Tongue* (ed. 2), *Shag*, to copulate. **1879–80** *Pearl* (1970) 258 A fellow who's had the mishap, To forget, when he shagged her, to button his flap. **1958** N. LEVINE *Canada made Me* iv. 102 You know what they're talking about? If they got shagged last night. **1969** J. WOOD *Three Blind Mice* iii. 32 We..go and shag ourselves half-stupid all night..and *pay* them for it in the morning! **1973** *Nation Rev.* (Melbourne) 24–30 Aug. 1417/4 The credo of the new fashioned mammy is if you shag, I shag. **1977** C. MCCULLOUGH *Thorn Birds* xvii. 413 There are plenty of men who will shag anything if it's a virgin. **1980** R. ADAMS *Girl in Swing* xxi. 279 'He's never absent.' And the corporal next to Jack muttered, 'Well, I 'ope 'e ain't 'angin' around when I'm shaggin' my missus.'

**2.** Used profanely in imprecations and exclamations. Cf. FUCK *v.* 2 and sense 1 of next.

**1933** M. LOWRY *Ultramarine* ii. 88 'Paddy—give us Paddy McGulligan's daughter, Mary Ann.' 'Oh shag off!' **1971** R. LUDLUM *Scarlatti Inheritance* iv. 43 'Get four men and get out there.' 'Go *shag*, Captain.' 'Are you disobeying your superior officer?' **1973** G. PINSENT *Rowdyman* 135 'Then shag you!' I shouted, as he swaggered away.

Hence '**shagger**²; '**shagging** *vbl. sb.*² and *ppl. a.*

**1970** G. GREER *Female Eunuch* 41 All the vulgar linguistic emphasis is placed upon the *poking* element;..*rooting, shagging* are..acts performed upon the passive female. **1971** B. W. ALDISS *Soldier Erect* 9 God, what sodding, shagging, scab-devouring misery it all was! *Ibid.* 12, I could watch my reflection in the mirror of the wardrobe... Now *there* was a born shagger, if ever I saw one, given the chance. **1977** *Zigzag* Aug. 4/3 Plus the fact it gets hotter than shagging in the back of a car during the summer of '76.

**shag** (ʃæg), *v.*⁴ [Origin unknown. Possibly connected with SHAG *v.*¹ or (esp. in sense 1) *v.*³; but it is not even certain that senses 1 and 2 belong to the same verb.] **1.** *intr.* To make off; to wander aimlessly; to traipse. Freq. with advbs. *slang.*

When followed by *off* there is some overlap with sense 2 of SHAG *v.*³

**1851** *Gloss. Provinc. Words Gloucs.* 11 *Shag*, to steal away. **1932** J. T. FARRELL *Young Lonigan* iv. 192 He watched a familiar looking airedale dog shag about. **1938** D. RUNYON *Furthermore* xiv. 278 The Princess is getting too grown-up to be shagging around Broadway, and..she is now going to public school. **1968** 'B. MATHER' *Springers* xv. 162 I'll take you into Russia with me—or you can shag off on your own. **1976** W. H. CANAWAY *Willow-Pattern War* xiv. 140 We'd been shagging around over these mountains for four days now, and we hadn't seen one single musk deer.

**2.** *trans.* To chase. Also const. *up. spec.* in *Baseball*, to go for or catch (fly balls). *U.S. colloq.*

**1913** C. H. CLAUDY *Battle of Baseball* 318, I was allowed to 'shag' foul balls. **1932** J. T. FARRELL *Young Lonigan* ii. 66 Demons..would come and lean over his bed..until his old man came and shagged them away. **1955** *Sun* (Baltimore) 3 Mar. 19/8 Coan..shagged flies under the tutelage of Coach Tom Oliver. **1979** *Navajo Times* (Window Rock, Arizona) 24 May 15/1, I was originally picked as an outfielder, so I played two years shagging balls in the outfield. **1981** G. V. HIGGINS *Rat on Fire* v. 37 Every so often..I got to shag up a couple of guys who haven't told a clean joke in years and give the guy free entertainment.

†'**shagamuffin.** *Obs. rare*⁻¹. [Alteration of RAGAMUFFIN, after SHAG *sb.*⁴] A term of abuse.

**1642** *Compl. to Ho. Commons* B2b, Debauched Shaggamuffins whose words no wise man will regard.

**shaganappi** (ʃægəˈnæpɪ), *sb.* and *a. N. Amer.* Also **shaganappy, shagginappi, -eppi,** etc. [Name in one of the western dialects of Ojibwa.] **A.** *sb.* Thread, cord, or thong made from raw hide, raw hide cut into strips. Also a rough pony. **B.** *adj.* 'Tough, rough' (*Cent. Dict.* 1891). Also, cheap, inferior, makeshift.

**1743** J. ISHAM *Obs. Hudsons Bay* (1949) 46 Shag, a nap, pee or a string of Leather tauk' a miss. **1820** G. SIMPSON *Jrnl.* 10 Sept. (1938) 58 Any dressed skins, sinews, and Shaganapy lines that can be spared, you will send here for New Caledonia. **1873** G. M. GRANT *Ocean to Ocean* v. 122 When any part broke before, a thong of Shaganappi had united the pieces. Shaganappi, in this part of the world does all that leather, cloth, rope, nails, glue, straps, cord, tape ..[etc.] are used for elsewhere. **1892** J. ROBERTSON in C. W. Gordon *Life* (1908) 338 In the old days..every one had his pocket full of shaganappi. **1895** W. ELKINGTON *Five Years in Canada* xi. 101 A few years ago the only horses in the country were bronchos and Indian 'shaganappies' as they are called. **1900** W. A. FRASER *Mooswa* 35 Have patience, little shaganappi (cheap) Bird. **1908** *Outlook* 5 Sept. 302/2 The women..hanging on their shaganappies (native ponies). **1961** W. O. MITCHELL *Jake & Kid* i. 2 At the Rabbit Hill school concert last night, folks heard a shaganappy speech. *Ibid.* viii. 106 Thinka anybuddy havin' a shaganappy thing like that in their house!

'**shag-bag,** *sb.* and *a. colloq.* [A jingling alteration of SHAKE-BAG; cf. SHAKE-BAG, SHAG-RAG, SHAG *sb.*⁴] **a.** *sb.* A shabby or worthless fellow. **b.** *adj.* Shabby and worthless; poor in quality.

**a.** *a* **1700** B. E. *Dict. Cant. Crew*, *Shag-bag*, a poor, shabby Fellow. **1865** W. S. BANKS *Prov. Words Wakefield* 62 *Shegbeg*,..a loosely (baggily) and raggedly drest, or worthless man.

**b.** **1888** *Star* 17 Apr. 4/5 A particularly shag-bag field started for this event. **1892** LD. BRAMWELL in *Times* 10 May 10/1, I was sitting in my chambers when there came a shagbag attorney with a brief.

**shagbark** (ˈʃægbɑːk). *West Indian* and *U.S.* [f. SHAG *a.* + BARK *sb.*¹

So called on account of the rough and shaggy appearance of the bark when the tree is old.]

**1.** *West Indian.* = SAVONETTE b.

**1691–6** PLUKENET *Almagestum* Wks. 1769 III. 373 *Shagbarke* Barbadensibus dicta, eo quod in hac Arbore cortex scabritie valde asperatus est. **1864** GRISEBACH *Flora W. Ind. Islands* 787 Shag-bark: *Pithecolobium micradenium.*

**2.** *U.S.* A variety of HICKORY; also the wood or the nut of this tree. Also *attrib.* or *adj.* as a designation of this tree.

**1751** J. BARTRAM *Observ.* 67 A great hill, cloathed with large Magnolia,..shagbark-hickery, chesnut and chesnut oak. **1788** J. MAY *Jrnl.* 20 June, My men employed in planting shagbarks, which out here [at Marietta, Ohio] are the largest one can conceive of. **1827** J. Q. ADAMS *Mem.* 12 Aug., Two more of my shagbark walnut-trees have come up. **1856** LOWELL *Lett.* (1894) I. 304 There were the same high-heaped shagbark trees. **1860** WORCESTER, *Shag-bark*,..the nut of the tree *Carya alba.* **1866** WHITTIER *Snow-bound* 348 From the shagbark overhead The grizzled squirrel dropped his shell. **1878** MRS. STOWE *Poganuc P.* xx. 179 For the frost ripened the shag-bark walnuts. **1902** GREENOUGH & KITTREDGE *Words* 340 In some parts of America the name walnut is given to the 'shagbark', a kind of hickory nut, and the true walnut is known as the 'English walnut'.

So †**shag-barked** *a.*

**1786** ABERCROMBIE *Gard. Assist., Arrangemt.* 35 Walnut tree,..Black American, or hickory,..Shag barked.

**shagbot(e, -bush, -but,** obs. ff. SACKBUT¹.

**shaggamitie,** obs. form of SAGAMITÉ.

**shaggareen, -in:** see SHAGREEN, CHAGRIN *a.*

**shagged** (ʃægd, ˈʃægɪd), *a.*¹ Now *rare.* Forms: 1 sceacgede (sceagode), 6 shagd, 7 shag'd, 7, 9 shagg'd, 6– shagged. [OE. *sceacgede*, f. *sceacga* SHAG *sb.*¹: see -ED².]

**1. a.** Having or covered with shaggy hair; rough with hair. Chiefly said of animals.

*shagged foal* = *shag-foal* s.v. SHAG *sb.*¹ 5.

*a* **1000** *Voc.* in Wr.-Wülcker 206/9 *Comosus*, sceagode. *c* **1050** *Ibid.* 380/14 *Comosus*, sceacgede. *c* **1611** CHAPMAN *Iliad* VI. 184 A Gotes shagg'd forme she bore. **1612** DRAYTON *Poly-olb.* xi. 109 Of whose shagg'd Siluans shee Hath in the Rockes been woo'd, their Paramour to bee. **1653** H. MORE *Antid. Ath.* III. vii. §4 (1712) 104 A shagged Dog with great eyes. *a* **1720** W. GIBSON *Diet Horses* vii. (ed. 3) 95 Otherwise in cold Weather the finest Horses will look shagged, if they are not kept cloathed. **1821** CLARE *Vill. Minstr.* I. 23 A shagged foal would fright the early-rising swain. **1822** T. TAYLOR *Apuleius* 114 The shagged god [*sc.* Pan]..called her gently to him. **1825** SCOTT *Talism.* iii, I will strike thy shagged head from thy meagre shoulders. **1848** LYTTON *Harold* VI. i, Round them grazed the rough shagged ponies which they had used for their journey.

†**b.** *transf.* (Said, e.g., of a comet.) *Obs.*

**1648** HERRICK *Hesper., Farewell to Sack*, And like to those Comets we see by night; whose shagg'd portents Fore-tell the comming of some dire events. **1679** ECCLESTONE *Noah's Fl.* II. 18 I'le shake off all these shagged shades of Night, And will adorn my self with Robes of Light.

†**c.** ? Unkempt; ? ill-clad, ragged. *Obs.*

**1622** J. TAYLOR (Water-P.) *Water-Cormorant* C2, Attended fitly..With two shag'd Ruffians, and a pyde coat Page. **1711** E. WARD *Don Quix.* I. 7 Yet look'd so shagged and forlorn.

**2.** †**a.** Of textile fabrics, garments: Having a rough or long nap. *Obs.*

**1649** J. TAYLOR (Water-P.) *Wandering* 8 My chamber-pot seemed to be lined within the crimson plush, or shag'd scarlet bayes. **1665** HOOKE *Microgr.* 3 A very course piece of shag'd cloth. **1679** T. JORDAN *Lond. in Luster* 7 An old Woman clad all in white Flannel, with a white shag'd Irish Mantle. **1679** A. LOVELL *Indic. Univ.* 65 Shagged or high-napped cloth. **1691** *Bragadocio* v. ii. 63 *Stage-direct.*, Enter the Quack in a Fur Cap, and shag'd Gown.

**b.** *transf.* Of a hill-side, etc.: Covered with scrub, trees, or some rough or shaggy growth.

**1784** J. BYNG *Jrnl.* 11 July in *Torrington Diaries* (1934) I. 161 A most fearful mountain, call'd Drwsycood, of awful, and shagged front. **1820** W. IRVING *Sketch Bk., Rip* I. 69 He looked down into a deep mountain glen, wild, lonely, and shagged. **1831** LYTTON *Godolphin* xv, Constance..pointed admiringly to the blue course of the waters as they wound through their shagged banks. **1927** F. B. YOUNG *Portrait of Clare* III. viii. 350 The twisted apple-trees stood shagged with a silvery blight.

**c.** Jagged; having a rough, uneven surface.

**1589** PUTTENHAM *Eng. Poesie* III. iv. (Arb.) 156 Teeth euen and not shagged. **1750** G. HUGHES *Barbados* 116 The bark..is rough and shagged. **1764** *Museum Rust.* II. xxv. 80 His crop [of 'coleseed'] will receive great damage by the stumps being left very shagged and torn. **1858** G. P. SCROPE *Geol. Central France* (ed. 2) 64 Replacing the rivulet that flowed there with a black and shagged current of lava.

**3. a.** Of hair, etc.: Long and rough; shaggy.

**1587** HUGHES *Misfort. Arthur* II. Argt., A man..with blacke long shagged haire downe to his shoulders. **1609** HOLLAND *Amm. Marcell.* XXV. iii. 270 His beard, which was shagged and rough. *c* **1620** Z. BOYD *Zion's Flowers* (1855) 120 His long black lockes hang shagg'd adowne his shoulder. **1719** D'URFEY *Pills* (1872) III. 318 And like him made a noble Shield of She-goat's shagged Coat. **1775** ADAIR *Amer. Ind.* 7 Skins of buffalo calves, with the wintery shagged wool inward. *c* **1800** R. CUMBERLAND *John De Lancaster* (1809) I. 71 Monstrous white bulls with shagged manes and hairy foreheads. **1814** SCOTT *Ld. of Isles* III. xxv, Eyebrows shagg'd and grey.

**b.** *transf.* Of plants, etc.: Having a rough or shaggy appearance.

**1798** BLOOMFIELD *Farmer's Boy, Autumn* 45 Some warm slope with shagged moss o'erspread. **1830** SCOTT *Auchindrane* II. i, Rough with..shagged sea-weed.

†**4.** *Comb.* **shagged-ragged** *a.* (cf. SHAG-RAG), shaggy and ragged. *Obs.*

**1612** ROWLANDS *Knaue of Harts* 13 Rose Hat-bands, with the shagged-ragged-Ruffe.

Hence '**shaggedness.**

**1660** H. MORE *Myst. Godl.* IV. ix. 121 The colour, shaggedness and other qualities of the Dog.

**shagged** (ʃægd), *a.*² *slang.* [Origin uncertain: perh. rel. to SHAGGED *a.* or SHAG *v.*³ Cf. also FAGGED *ppl. a.*] Weary, exhausted. Also with *out.*

**1932** AUDEN *Orators* III. 99 Wakeful at night, in the morning fagged; They feel like angels, but they look just shagged. **1947** D. M. DAVIN *Gorse blooms Pale* 178 They're all in pretty good nick, considering. Shagged, of course. **1950** DYLAN THOMAS in *Circus* Apr. 8/2 He is..thin, not to say of a shagged-out appearance. **1960** *Observer* 20 Mar. 10/3 Oh cut it out, Sarge—let up! I'm shagged. **1971** *Peace News* 10 Sept. 8/2 The haggard and shagged-out end products of a lifetime spent in the pursuit of materialism. **1975** G. W. TARGET *Strike Strikers* iii. 51 The two other-rankers were now sitting in the back of the jeep, with all of 'em looking shagged out.

**shaggery** (ˈʃægərɪ). *N.Z.* [f. SHAG *sb.*² + -ERY.] A breeding colony of shags.

**1882** W. D. HAY *Brighter Britain!* II. vi. 222 They [*sc.* Kawau] build in trees, in large 'shaggeries'. **1921** H. GUTHRIE-SMITH *Tutira* xxii. 207 Fish are attracted to the vicinity of shaggeries.

**shaggily** (ˈʃægɪlɪ), *adv.* [-LY².] In a shaggy manner; so as to be shaggy.

**1859** GEO. ELIOT *Adam Bede* I. x. 196 His hair was tossed shaggily about his forehead. **1891** *Century Dict.* s.v., Shaggily pilose. **1921** D. H. LAWRENCE *Birds, Beasts & Flowers* (1923) 82 It was a fiery fortress frowning shaggily on the world. **1977** T. HEALD *Just Deserts* i. 11 A dark, shaggily suave person.

**shagginess** (ˈʃægɪnɪs). [f. SHAGGY *a.* + -NESS.] The quality of being shaggy.

**1778** COOK *3rd Voy.* IV. v. (1784) II. 377 From the colour and shagginess of the hair..we judged it might probably be that of the large male ursine seal, or sea-bear. **1881** V. SHAW *Bk. Dog* ix. 82 General appearance, tail, strength, and shagginess without too much length of coat, should be taken into consideration.

**shaggreen, shaggrin:** see SHAGREEN, CHAGRIN.

**shaggy** (ˈʃægɪ), *a.* Also 6–7 shaggie, 8 shagy. [f. SHAG *sb.*¹ + -Y.

The altered form *shackie*, SHACKY *a.*, appears in our quots. somewhat earlier.]

**1. a.** Covered with or having long coarse or bushy hair. Of persons: Unkempt.

*c* **1590** MARLOWE *Jew of Malta* IV. 1858 He sent a shaggy totter'd staring slaue. **1607** N. FIELD *Woman a Weathercock* II. i. (1612) D3, Wilde Virginia, Blacke Affricke, or the shaggy Scithia, Must send it ouer as a Merchandize Ere thou shew any heere. *a* **1612** B. JONSON *Masque Oberon* Wks. (1616) 978 Trap our shaggie thighs with bels. **1690** C. NESSE *Hist. & Myst. O. & N. Test.* I. 42 Some black shaggy dog. **1754** GRAY *Poesy* 55 Shaggy forms o'er ice-built mountains roam. **1755** in Macgill *Old Ross-sh.* (1909) 169, 2 two-year-old she cattle and a shagy bull. **1822** SCOTT *Nigel* xvii, Shaggy, uncombed ruffians, whose enormous mustaches were turned back over their ears. **1848** DICKENS *Dombey* ii, He was a strong, loose, round-shouldered, shuffling shaggy fellow. **1882** 'OUIDA' *In Maremma* I. 151 A mounted shepherd on his wild and shaggy horse.

**b.** Of a skin, or garment, etc.: Covered with coarse bushy hair.

*c* **1611** CHAPMAN *Iliad* XV. 282 Ioues huge and each-where shaggie shield. **1705** J. PHILIPS *Blenheim* 408 While Volga's Stream Sends Opposite, in shaggy Armor clad, Her Borderers. **1790** COWPER *Odyss.* XVII. 107 Tunic and shaggy mantle. **1816** GALT *Life B. West* 94 A peasant dressed in shaggy skins.

**c.** Of a textile material: Having a long, rough nap; rough or coarse in texture.

**1664** PEPYS *Diary* 11 Nov., Put on my new shaggy purple gown with gold buttons and loop lace. **1728** POPE *Dunc.* II. 135 A shaggy tap'stry, worthy to be spread On Codrus' old, or Dunton's modern bed. **1831** SCOTT *Ct. Robt.* ii, A surcoat composed of strong shaggy silk, so woven as to exhibit, at a little distance, no inaccurate representation of a bear's hide. **1837** WHITTOCK *Bk. Trades* (1842) 113 (*Carpet-Weaver*), But in Wilton, or other carpets that are required to be 'shaggy', the wires are made thin, and sharp at one end.

**d.** *Bot.* and *Zool.* Having or covered with rough or stiff hairs (hirsute) or long soft hairs (villous). Also in renderings of specific names, as *shaggy maple, spunk.*

**1796** WITHERING *Brit. Plants* (ed. 3) I. 81 Shaggy (*hirsutus*), rough with stiff hairs. *Ibid.* II. 218 Blossom shaggy. **1802** WILLICH *Dom. Encycl.* IV. 455 The Shaggy

Spunk, or *Boletus hirsutus*, a species of Mushroom. **1833** *Penny Cycl.* I. 78/2 *Acer villosum*, the shaggy maple. **1840** LOUDON tr. *Köllar's Treat. Insects* 363 This beetle is somewhat shaggy and black. **1854** PAPPE *Silva Capensis* (1862) 6 Flowers terminal on short, shaggy peduncles. *Ibid.* 14 Drupe shaggy.

**e.** *Phys.*, *Path.*, etc. Bristling with hair-like processes.

***shaggy chorion***, that part of the chorion which develops long villous processes, and thus enters into the formation of the placenta, the rest of the chorion remaining smooth.

**1799** *Med. Jrnl.* II. 2 Upon maceration in water for a certain time, it put on the usual shaggy appearance formed by the tubuli seminiferi. **1835–6** *Todd's Cycl. Anat.* I. 780/1 An epidermic layer..covering a thick and shaggy membrane. **1855** RAMSBOTHAM *Obstet. Med.* 62 And imbed themselves in the semi-fluid deciduous secretion, like roots in the soil, these have been called the shaggy chorion. **1888** W. H. DICKINSON in *Lancet* 24 Mar. 565/1 The Furred or Shaggy Tongue. *Ibid.*, When there is great projection of the papillæ, so that these stand out distinctly, the term furred or shaggy represents this condition. **1898** *Allbutt's Syst. Med.* V. 739 It's [i.e. the inflamed pericardium's] surface is covered with floating shaggy processes.

**f.** *transf.* Of the earth, a hillside, etc.: Covered with a rough, tangled growth. Also of a comet: 'Hairy'.

**1591** SYLVESTER tr. *Du Bartas* I. ii. 407 And liberally the shaggy Earth [He will] adorn With Woods, and Buds of fruits, of flowers and corn. **1612** DRAYTON *Poly-olb.* xii. 524 Those fallow Deere, and huge-hancht Stags that graz'd Vpon her shaggy Heaths. **1653** RAMESEY *Astrol. Rest.* IV. vi. 319 [Other comets] become shaggy and compassed as it were with hair or frindge round about. **1667** MILTON *P.L.* IV. 224 A River Through the shaggie hill Pass'd underneath ingulft. **1780** G. CUMBERLAND *Landscapes* (1793) 8 Nor less I joy, at parting day, to trace The sun-gilt forms of Enfield's shaggy chace. **1898** WATTS-DUNTON *Aylwin* II. xiii, The little flower-beds looked shaggy, grass-grown, and uncared for.

**g.** Having a rough surface. ***shaggy metal***: in the Cheshire salt mines, 'porous clay in the side of the shaft, which admits the ingress of fresh water' (*Cheshire Gloss.* 1886).

**1693** EVELYN *De La Quint. Compl. Gard.* II. 83 Some by growing Soft first, as many Pears do,..others by growing Dry and Shaggy, as most Musc-Pears do; all which are different ways Conducing to Rotteness and Destruction. **1811** H. HOLLAND in *Trans. Geol. Soc.* I. 50 Where this [porous] structure of the clay occurs it goes by the name of the shaggy metal. **1813** SCOTT *Rokeby* IV. viii, A mantle long and loose he wore, Shaggy with ice, and stain'd with gore. **1849** MURCHISON *Siluria* xiii. 332 Chocolate-coloured porphyres..highly shaggy and amygdaloidal. **1856** A. GRAY *Man. Bot.* 402 Fruit globular, its husk very thick: bark of old trunk shaggy, exfoliating in strips or plates.

**2. a.** Of hair, etc.: Rough, coarse, tangled.

**1638** BP. MOUNTAGUE *Art. Enq. Norwich* B 1 b, Doth he [your Minister] weare long shaggy haire? **1721** MORTIMER *Husb.* (ed. 2) II. 78 Moss growing on Trees is of several sorts, cold and moist Ground produces a long shaggy, moist and dry Ground a short thick Moss. **1735** SOMERVILLE *Chase* III. 256 Thy shaggy Mane. **1828** SCOTT *F.M. Perth* xiv, The bushy red hair and shaggy beard. **1829** LYTTON *Disowned* iv, Eyebrows sage and shaggy. **1868** C. GIBBON *R. Gray* xxii, His short shaggy hair was shaggier than usual. **1901** ALLDRIDGE *Sherbro* xiv. 141 Her dress is of long shaggy fibre.

**b.** *Bot.* ***shaggy hairs***: see quots. Cf. SHAG *sb.*[1]

**1884** BOWER & SCOTT *De Bary's Phaner.* 55 Shaggy hairs are thread-like bodies, consisting of two or many layers or rows of cells. *Ibid.* 56 The multiseriate shaggy hairs of the Melastomeæ.

**c.** *transf.* Of a wood, trees, etc.: Resembling a rough growth of hair.

**1789** GILPIN *Wye* 38 A woody hill..rudely hung with shaggy furniture. **1791** NEWTE *Tour Eng. & Scot.* 303 The rocks and shaggy wood that fringe that river. **1805** SCOTT *Last Minstr.* VI. ii, Land of brown heath and shaggy wood, Land of the mountain and the flood. **1890** A. J. C. HARE *Story Life* xxvi. (1900) VI. 193 A poor town hanging shaggy on the hillside.

**3.** Comb., as ***shaggy-bearded***, ***-bodied***, ***-chested***, ***-fleeced***, ***-footed***, ***-haired***, ***-legged***, ***-throated*** adjs.; **shaggy dog story**, a lengthy tediously detailed story of an inconsequential series of events, more amusing to the teller than to his audience, or amusing only by its pointlessness; also ***shaggy dog yarn***, etc.; **shaggy (ink-)cap** = next; **shaggy mane**, an edible fungus, *Copinius comatus* (Cent. Dict. Suppl.).

**1861** L. L. NOBLE *Icebergs* 68 They were a..shaggy-bearded set. **1593** NASHE *Christ's T.* Wks. (Grosart) IV. 173 A grizly shaggy-bodied deuill. **1894** M. C. COOKE *Edible & Poisonous Mushrooms* 57 Shaggy Caps... This is one of the best of edibles, and common enough everywhere. **1979** *Guardian* 31 Oct. 14/1 The delightful pleasures of Shaggy Cap soup or Lawyer's Wig stew. **1922** JOYCE *Ulysses* 510 Ben Jumbo Dollard, rubicund,..shaggychested, shockmaned,..stands forth. [**1945** D. LOW in *N.Y. Times Mag.* 4 Feb. 40/1 The logical lunacy of 'Shaggy Dog'.] **1946** *Coll. Shaggy Dog Stories* facing p. 1 Stories of the Shaggy Dog variety are essentially tales to be told rather than read. **1947** *Beat* Apr. 6/3 Here's one of my favourite 'shaggy dog' stories. **1952** A. R. K. BARNARD in A. Redman *Somewhat 'Shaggy'* 4 The comparatively recent type of story—the 'Shaggy Dog' yarn. **1952** KOESTLER *Arrow in Blue* I. viii. 68 The people of Budapest have a peculiar shaggy-dog kind of humour. **1958** *Listener* 16 Oct. 623/1 It was a shaggy-dog story about a small-town worthy who shams madness to avoid paying bills. **1972** P. RUELL *Red Christmas* xi. 102 He seemed to be in the middle of an autobiographical shaggy-dog story. **1879** SALA in *Daily Tel.* 15 May, The black-faced shaggy-fleeced sheep. *a* **1593** MARLOWE *Hero & L.* i. 114 Wretched Ixions shaggie footed race. **1610** G. FLETCHER *Christ's Tri.* II. xlvi, Foolish Sheapheards, that wear woont esteem, Your God all rough, and shaggy-hair'd to bee. **1866** GEO. ELIOT *Felix Holt* II. xvi. 15 The shaggy-haired, cravatless image of Felix Holt. **1974** L. DEIGHTON *Spy Story* i. 14 A shaggy-haired giant, complete with kilt. **1840** CARLYLE in Froude *Life in Lond.* (1884) I. 190 A fine..shaggy-headed man is Alfred [Tennyson]. **1953** J. RAMSBOTTOM *Mushrooms & Toadstools* Pl. 22 (*caption*) Shaggy Ink-Cap..often in enormous numbers on made-up ground. **1970** J. WEBSTER *Introd. Fungi* II. iv. 311 *Coprinus comatus* is a large terrestrial species (the shaggy ink-cap or lawyer's wig) which is edible. **1822** *Hortus Anglicus* II. 128 Shaggy-leaved Toad Flax. **1927** D. H. LAWRENCE *Etruscan Places* (1932) i. 16 He grins and drinks wine, and immediately one sees again the shaggy-legged faun. [**1885** J. A. PALMER *Mushrooms Amer.* Pl. II (*caption*) Shaggy-Maned Mushroom.] **1895** W. H. GIBSON *Our Edible Toadstools & Mushrooms* 28 The Shaggy-mane..is conspicuously even-gilled, and is a decided delicacy. **1976** *National Observer* (U.S.) 13 Mar. 19/2 Now is the time of the shaggy manes and field mushrooms. **1946** R. S. THOMAS *Stones of Field* 17 Thunder-browed and shaggy-throated All the men were there.

**shagh**, obs. form of SHAH.

†**shag-hair**, *a.* and *sb.* *Obs.* [f. SHAG *a.* + HAIR *sb.*] **a.** *adj.* = next. **b.** *sb.* A 'shag-haired' dog.

**1584** LYLY *Sapho* IV. iv. 33 *Vulcan.* My shag-haire Cyclops, come, lets ply Our Lemnion hammers lustily. **1598** FLORIO, *Lacno*, a dogs name, as we say a shag-haire or ruffian. **1612** PEACHAM *Gentl. Exerc.* I. xvi. 54 Shag hair dogs.

**shag-haired**, *a. arch.* [f. SHAG *a.* + HAIRED *a.* Cf. SHACK-HAIRED *a.*] Having shaggy hair.

**1577** B. GOOGE *Heresbach's Husb.* III. (1586) 154 The Mastie..his breast great, and shaghaird. *Ibid.* IV. 182 Some of them be shaghearde, and ill coloured. **1577** tr. *Bullinger's Decades* III. vi. 381 They were called Nazarites, as who should say, longe locked, or shagge haired people. **1593** SHAKS. *2 Hen. VI*, III. i. 367 Like a shag-hayr'd craftie Kerne. **1604** *Meeting of Gallants at Ordinarie* B 3, Infection ..was saide to skip into wollen cloathes, and lie smothring in a shag-hayrde Rugge. *a* **1693** *Urquhart's Rabelais* III. xxiv, The Shaghaired Argives..vowed to carry never any hair on their Heads, till [etc.]. **1901** H. TRENCH *Deirdre Wed* 18 And the shag-hair'd guard, with a mock, laid spears in their passage house Athwart. **1904** M. HEWLETT *Queen's Quair* III. i. 358 Every horse in the country was saddled and manned by some shag-haired Hepburn.

**'shaglet.** *nonce-wd.* [f. SHAG *sb.*[2] + -LET.] A young shag or cormorant.

**1898** E. STEP in *Good Words* Sept. 622, I..put the uncomplaining shaglet into my empty lunch-bag.

†**'shagling**, *a. Obs. rare.* [Of obscure origin. ?Cf. SHACKLING *ppl. a.* and SHAG *sb.*[1]] **a.** A designation at Oxford for persons permitted to lecture, but having no official status; also for the lectures given by them. **b.** Used (? through misapprehension) by Davies for: Feeble, ineffective.

**1691** WOOD *Ath. Oxon.* I. 18 Lynacre..was incorporated Doctor of Physick in this University read a shagling Lecture in that faculty [etc.]. *Ibid.* 90 Robert Warde..became a shagling Lecturer in Philosophy before the University in the publick Schools. **1716** M. DAVIES *Athen. Brit.* II. 245 Yet 'tis from the same confus'd and confounding Magazine of artful Sandius, that our Modern Arians borrow all their Shagling Weapons and Sophistical Quivers. *Ibid.* III. *Diss. Author Lat. Drama* 27 That University..permitted him to read a shagling Lecture in that Faculty.

**'shag-rag**, *a.* and *sb.* Now *rare* or *Obs.* exc. *dial.* [A jingling alteration of SHAKE-RAG. Cf. SHAG *sb.*[4], SHACK-RAG, SHAB-RAG, SHAG-BAG.]

**A.** *adj.* Of a person: Ragged, rascally.

*c* **1590** MARLOWE *Jew of Malta* IV. 1913 To haue a shag-rag knaue to come [etc.]. **1615** *Band, Ruffe & Cuffe* (Halliw.) 9 A scurvie shag-ragge gentleman new come out of the North, a punie, a freshman come up hither to learn fashions, and seeke to expell me?

*transf.* **1693** *Bacchanalian Sessions* 6 Upon which, in clean Vessel, not tatter'd and shagrag, Appears Rhenish, Hock, Old and Young, Moselle, and Backrag.

**b.** Shaggy, unkempt.

**1868** BROWNING *Ring & Bk.* v. 389 An old bruised and battered year-by-year..With shag-rag beard and doleful doublet.

**B.** *sb.* A ragged, disreputable person; a low rascally fellow.

**1611** CHAPMAN *May Day* Plays 1873 II. 340 I'de hire some shag-ragge or other for half a chickeene to cut's throat. **1611** COTGR., *Guerluset*, (Somewhat like our Shagrag;) a by-word for a beggerlie souldior. **1622** MABBE tr. *Aleman's Guzman d'Alf.* I. 69 Your poore Shag-rags, and silly snakes, that steale from the Armie to returne home. **1719** D'URFEY *Pills* II. 327 Sharks, Shagrags, Shatter-brains, Panders. **1829** BROCKETT *N.C. Gloss.* (ed. 2). **1881** *Cumberld. Gloss.* etc.

**b.** *shag rag and bobtail* = tag rag and bobtail.

**1708** MOTTEUX *Rabelais* IV. xxxiii, It will swallow us all, Ships and Men, Shag, Rag, and Bobtail, like a dose of Pills. **1762** STERNE *Tr. Shandy* V. i. 5 There was a good farcical house, large enough to hold..them, *shag rag and bob-tail*, male and female, all together. **1828** [CARR] *Craven Gloss.* II. 113 Shag-rag and bobtail.

**shagreen** (ʃə'griːn). Also 7–8 **shagrin**, **shaggreen**, 8 **shaggareen**, 7–9 CHAGRIN. [Var. CHAGRIN *sb.*]

**1.** A species of untanned leather with a rough granular surface, prepared from the skin of the horse, ass, etc., or of the shark, seal, etc., and frequently dyed green. Also, an imitation of this.

**1677** [see 3]. **1698** FRYER *Acc. E. Ind. & P.* 264 Hides and Leather from Bulgaria, Turky, and of their own dressing, which excels that we call..Shagreen for Durableness. **1710** STEELE *Tatler* No. 245 ¶2 A Bible bound in Shagreen. **1774** GOLDSM. *Nat. Hist.* (1776) VI. 239 His [the shark's] skin.. being that substance which covers instrument cases, called shagreen. **1777** COOK *3rd Voy.* III. ix. (1784) II. 174 The men of Mataia..cover..their bodies with a sort of shagreen, being skin of fishes. **1852** MORFIT *Tanning & Currying* (1853) 443 The genuine oriental shagreen is not a true leather, but a skin prepared by drying. **1891** E. PEACOCK *N. Brendon* II. 327 A thin oval case covered with dark shagreen. **1907** GALSWORTHY *Country House* I. i. 2 A tall man..whose tall wife carried a small bag of silver and shagreen.

**b.** The skin of various sharks, rays, etc., which is covered with close-set calcified papillæ, forming a hard rough surface: used for polishing, etc.

**1870** NICHOLSON *Man. Zool.* lviii. (1875) 434 The so-called 'shagreen' of the Dog-fishes and sharks is composed of very small and close-set tooth-like processes. **1871** HUXLEY *Anat. Vert.* iii. 126 Very commonly it [the integument of sharks, etc.] is developed into papillæ, which become calcified, and give rise to toothlike structures; these, when they are very small and close-set, constitute what is called shagreen. **1873** MIVART *Elem. Anat.* vii. 277 These [calcifications] may be quite small and thickly distributed all over the body. A skin so furnished is called shagreen.

**c.** *transf.* in *Ironfounding*. (See quot.)

**1884** KNIGHT *Dict. Mech.* Suppl., *Shagreen*, hard, colored, metallic spots found on the surface of iron castings.

†**2.** A silk fabric. *Obs. rare.*

**1702** LADY G. BAILLIE *Househ. Bk.* (1911) 197 For 5½ ells black shagrin..18 9 0. **1728** MRS. DELANY in *Life & Corr.* (1861) I. 177, I..bought eighteen yards of very pretty white silk for Trott, something in the nature of shagreen, but a better colour than they ever are. **1741** *Anti-Pamela*; *Mem. Mr. J. Parry* 129 Nicholas advised him..to have the suit lined with white Shagreen.

**3.** *attrib.* and *Comb.* **a.** *attrib.* passing into adj., made of shagreen, as ***shagreen case***, ***cover***, ***skin***.

**1706** PHILLIPS (ed. Kersey), *Shagreen*,..a sort of rough, green Leather; as *A *Shagreen Case.* **1730** *Inventory D. Bond's Goods* (1732) 34 A Shaggareen Case for Bottles. **1852** THACKERAY *Esmond* III. vii, She held out the black shagreen-case. *c* **1696** PRIOR *Cupid & Gan.* 19 Two Table-Books in *Shagreen Covers. **1677** J. P. tr. *Tavernier's Trav.* I. iv. 21 [They] wear Boots or Shooes of *Shagrin-Leather. *Ibid.*, *Shagrin-Skins. **1782–3** W. F. MARTYN *Geog. Mag.* I. 42 In this country are also manufactures of..shagreen skins and other leather.

**b.** (Sense 1 b.) ***shagreen-granule***, ***point***, ***scale***; **shagreen-ray**, **-skate**, *Raiia fullonica*.

**1896** H. WOODWARD *Guide Fossil Reptiles Brit. Mus.* 82 In the majority of instances, the fossils [of sharks] consist merely of detached spines, *shagreen-granules, teeth, or pieces of cartilage. **1857** H. MILLER *Test. Rocks* ii. 58 An external armature, consisting of plates, spines, and *shagreen points of solid bone. **1776** PENNANT *Brit. Zool.* III. 77 *Shagreen Ray. I met with this species at Scarborough, where it is called the French Ray. **1849** MURCHISON *Siluria* vii. 138 The fish-remains are chiefly those of the minute *Shagreen scales. **1882** TENISON-WOODS *Fish New South Wales* 191 *Shagreen-skate. *Raiia fullonica.* Britain.

**c.** *Comb.*: ***shagreen-covered***, ***-like*** adjs.

**1857** H. MILLER *Test. Rocks* i. 62 The dorsal spines and *shagreen covered skin of the common dog fish. **1864** SALA *Quite Alone* I. viii. 131 Limp, green, shagreen-covered registers to keep the accounts in. **1840** tr. *Cuvier's Anim. Kingd.* 317 Others [of the subgenus *Pimelodes*] have the head oval, and a kind of helmet of *shagreen-like bones.

**shagreened** (ʃə'griːnd), *a.* [f. prec. + -ED[2].]

**1.** Having a roughened consistence or appearance like 'shagreen' or shark-skin.

**1721** BRADLEY *Philos. Acc. Wks. Nat.* 74 Its Skin is Shagreen'd, like that of the Dog-Fish. **1801** PENNANT *Journ. Lond. to I. Wight* II. 73 The back and tail shagreened. **1822** J. PARKINSON *Outl. Oryctol.* 301 With a rough and shagreened surface in the soft tortoises. **1841** E. NEWMAN *Hist. Insects* 28 The microscope shews the case of the egg to be shagreened in squares. **1866** E. C. RYE *Brit. Beetles* 47 Their elytra are shagreened in texture. **1899** *Allbutt's Syst. Med.* VIII. 595 These patches [of neurotic lichen], which have a shagreened aspect, spread quickly.

**2.** Covered with shagreen.

**1847** WEBSTER; and in later Dicts.

**shagroon** (ʃə'gruːn). *N.Z. slang* (now *Hist.*). [Perh. ad. Ir. *seachrán* wandering.] An early settler in Canterbury, New Zealand, from anywhere except Britain, esp. one from Australia.

**1851** W. LYON (*title*) Dream of a shagroon. **1851** E. WARD *Jrnl.* 20 Feb. (1951) 132 Started with Henry and a 'shagroon' cattle-driver. **1898** E. E. MORRIS *Austral English* 410/2 The men who came from England were called *Pilgrims*, all others *Shagroons*; probably a modification of the Irish word *Shaughraun*. **1930** L. G. D. ACLAND *Early Canterbury Runs* 1st Ser. i. 3 The Australians were known as 'Prophets' or 'Shagroons'. **1966** G. W. TURNER *Eng. Lang. Austral. & N.Z.* i. 16 In Canterbury, immigrants from Victoria, locally called *shagroons*, set up sheep stations on the plains and were contemptuous of the wealthier agricultural enterprises of the *pilgrims* as the Canterbury Association's settlers were called.

**shah** (ʃɑː). Forms: 6 **shawgh**, 6–7 **shaugh**, **xa**, 6–9 **shaw**, 7 **sa(a**, **saha**, **scha**, **shawe**, **shagh**, 7–8 **s(c)hach**, **schah**, **sha**, 9 **shauh**, 7– **shah**. [a. Pers. *shāh*, shortened from OPers. *χšāyaþiya* king, prob. orig. an adj. = 'mighty', allied to Skr.

kšatra dominion, Gr. κτᾶσθαι to acquire, get, κεκτῆσθαι to possess.] A Persian title equivalent to 'king'; in Europe the usual designation of the monarch of Persia (Iran), the PADISHAH.

**1566** A. EDWARDS in Hakluyt *Voy.* (1589) 378 A noble man..in great fauour with the Shaugh. *c* **1575** DUCKET *Ibid.* 422 The king of Persia..is called the Shawgh. **1625** PURCHAS *Pilgrims* I. II. i. 32 Ismael the Persian Xa, or Sophi. **1662** J. DAVIES tr. *Olearius' Voy. Ambass.* 250 The Kings of Persia were not called Schachs, as they are now. **1664** MARVELL *Corr.* Wks. (Grosart) II. 146 The Shagh of Persia? **1747** *Gentl. Mag.* XVII. 449/1 Advices from Ispahan confirm the death of the late Schah. **1825** T. HOOK *Sayings* Ser. II. *Passion & Princ.* xv. III. 396 Punkah'd by Ranees and salamed by Shaws. **1828** [MORIER] *Hajji Baba in Eng.* I. xiv. 158 The shah's throne, on which he sits to administer justice. **1897** L. J. TROTTER *Life J. Nicholson* ii. (1908) 30 Calcutta had heard of the Shah's triumphant return to the Bala Hissar.

**b.** followed or preceded by a proper name.

**1564** A. JENKINSON in Hakluyt *Voy.* (1589) 370, I was sent for to come before the sayd Sophie, otherwise called Shaw Thamas. **1566** A. EDWARDS *Ibid.* 378 Thomas the Shaugh. **1601** HAKLUYT *Galvano's Discov. World* 49 Shaugh Ismael king of Persia. **1614** SELDEN *Titles Hon.* 110 Ismael is vsually calld Ismael Schah, Shah, or Shach. **1683** W. HEDGES *Diary* (Hakl. Soc.) I. 87 Buglagotte, a place where Shaw Susa [*i.e.* Shujā'] fought a great battle with his brother, y[e] present Emperour Aureng Zeeb. **1685** *Ibid.* 211, I went to see y[e] King of Persia, Sha Soliman, ride abroad to take y[e] aire. **1698** FRYER *Acc. E. Ind. & P.* 171 His Grandfather was a Man in Esteem under Nisham Shaw. **1738** [G. SMITH] *Cur. Relat.* II. 570 Shach Sefi caused not many Years ago one Side of the Wall to be lined with Marble Slabs. **1815** ELPHINSTONE *Acc. Caubul* (1842) I. 104 His voice and manner strongly resembled Shauh Shujah's. **1841** —— *Hist. Ind.* XII. i. II. 567 The death of Bahádur Sháh [at Lahor] was followed by the usual struggle among his sons.

**Shah Abbas** (ʃɑː 'æbəs). The name of a Shah of Persia (1558–1628) used *attrib.* and *absol.* to designate Persian rugs and carpets like those made for him or their characteristic design.

**1901** J. K. MUMFORD *Oriental Rugs* vi. 74, I have known a Persian who paid thirty dollars..for a fragment of one of these old Shah Abbas rugs. *Ibid.*, The Shah Abbas pattern is still made in rug factories. **1913** W. A. HAWLEY *Oriental Rugs* ix. 105 Only a few Persian rugs have the formal repetitive patterns, such as the Herati, Guli Hinnai, Mina Khani, and Shah Abbas. **1973** P. O'DONNELL *Silver Mistress* i. 16 The sumptuous silken glow of the Shah Abbas carpet.

‖**shahāda** (ʃa'haːda). Also **shahādah**. [Arab. *šahāda* testimony, evidence.] The Muslim profession of faith, 'Lā ilāha illā Allāh, Muḥammad rasūl Allāh' ('there is only one God, and Muḥammad is his prophet').

**1885** T. P. HUGHES *Dict. Islam* 571/1 *Shahādah*.., 'evidence'. **1929** E. D. ROSS tr. *Lammens's Islam* iii. 56 The customary offering of prayer, of which the *shahāda* forms an integral part, takes the place of this obligation. **1970** *New Yorker* 29 Aug. 45/1 A European who repented the error of his faith and proclaimed the *shahada*—'There is but one God and Mohammed is His Prophet'—before dying would always go directly to Heaven. **1981** *Daily Tel.* 19 June 15/8 Everything in Islamic art and thought should be seen in the light of the *shahada*, or profession of faith.

‖**Shahanshah** ('ʃɑːən'ʃɑː). Also **Shahenshah, Shahinshah, Shah-in-Shah,** etc. [Pers. *šāhanšāh* king of kings: see SHAH.] 'King of kings': a title given to the Shah of Iran (Persia).

**1815** J. MALCOLM *Hist. Persia* I. vi. 92 The son of Babek was hailed..with the proud title of Shahan Shah, or King of Kings. **1824** J. MORIER *Hajji Baba* II. iii. 63 The *Shah-in-Shah* speaks like an angel. **1877** E. S. DALLAS *Kettner's Bk. of Table* 478 It is to be hoped that the land of vegetable marrows sometimes makes a dish of them for the Shah en Shah—king of kings. **1892** LD. CURZON *Persia & Persian Question* I. xiv. 434 He remains the Shahinshah, or King of Kings. **1938** 'M. ESSAD-BEY' et al. *Reza Shah* iii. 44 The trim appearance of the Cossacks..impressed the Shahanshah tremendously. **1953** J. H. ILIFFE in A. J. Arberry *Legacy of Persia* i. 31 The Shāhanshāh (King of kings) is..always aloof from his subjects. **1972** N. GORDIMER *Livingstone's Companions* 5 He had been sent to Iran for the coronation of the Shahanshah. **1980** *Listener* 14 Feb. 199/3 The set book was the historic speeches of the Shahenshah published in English translation.

**Shahaptan**, var. SAHAPTIN.

‖**shahbandar** (ʃɑː'bʌndə(r)). Forms: 7 sabandar(e, -er, sabendor, savendar; shabandar, xabandar, shawbander, chabandar, -er, 7–8 shabander, -bender, shah-, shawbunder, 8 shebandar, 9 shahbendar, Also shabunder, shahbender. [a. Pers. *shāh-bandar*, lit. 'king of the port'. Cf. Pg. *xabandar*.] 'The title of an officer at native ports all over the Indian seas, who was the chief authority with whom foreign traders and ship-masters had to transact. He was often also head of the Customs' (Yule). Also, the title of an officer with wider responsibilities; *spec.* one of three chief local officials who administered Sarawak under the Sultan of Brunei.

**1599** J. DAVIS in Purchas *Pilgrims* (1625) I. III. 120 The Sabandar tooke off my Hat, and put a Roll of white linnen about my head. *c* **1603** *Ibid.* 161 The Sauendar, or Gouernour of the Citie. **1606** *Sir H. Middleton's Last East-Ind. Voy.* E 4, Then came the Sabendor with light, and brought the Generall to his house. **1613** in Purchas *Pilgrims* (1625) I. IV. 462 The Xabandar. **1619** in Foster *Eng. Factories Ind.* (1906) I. 150 Choja Hasanaly, Shabandar. **1628** *Ibid.* III. 212 Cojah Tellaldine, Shawbander or admirall of this port. **1678** J. PHILLIPS tr. *Tavernier's Trav.* II. 18 The Chabander and Mint-master are very observant to the Company. **1698** FRYER *Acc. E. India & P.* 98 The Shawbunder..who is King of the Port, or Chief Customer. *aa* **1711** in C. Lockyer *Acc. Trade India* 223 The *Shabander* or Custom-Master. **1795** M. SYMES *Embassy Ava* (1800) 160 The important office of Shawbunder, or intendant of the port, and receiver of the port customs. **1797** *Encycl. Brit.* (ed. 3) XVIII. 62/2 At Batavia..the Shabander exacts a dollar *per* pecul on all sugar exported. [**1833–5** LANE *Mod. Egyptians* (1836) I. 137 The Shah-bendar (chief of the Merchants of Cairo).] **1922** O. RUTTER *Brit. North Borneo* v. 135 The Padas Damit district..was taken over..as a result of the operations against Pengiran Shabandar Hassan. **1960** S. RUNCIMAN *White Rajahs* III. ii. 93 It [*sc.* the land] belonged to a Brunei Princess, whose brother, the Pangiran Shabandar, administered it. **1964** D. K. BASSETT in Wang Gungwu *Malaysia* II. vii. 122 The chief *shahbandar* of Kedah. **1969** J. M. GULLICK *Malaysia* ii. 40 Control of the port, supervision of the merchants and collection of customs duties were divided among four harbour-masters, called *shahbandars*, who looked after the traders in one region. **1971** N. TARLING *Britain, Brookes & Brunei* I. i. 4 The system of offices, of a mixed Hindu-Muslim character, included..men of noble blood or *pengirans*, the most important being the *shahbandar*. **1974** S. E. MORISON *European Discovery of America: Southern Voyages* xviii. 443 The Shahbender (title of the ruler of Brunei) sent out..a beautiful prao with gilt work on bow and stern.

‖**Shahbanu** ('ʃɑːbɑːnuː). Also **Shahbanou, Shahr-banu.** [Pers., f. *šāh* SHAH + *bānū* lady.] The title of the wife of the Shah of Iran (Persia).

**1915** P. M. SYKES *Hist. Persia* II. xlvii. 44 It is universally believed by Persians, that Husayn married the daughter of Yezdigird, who is known throughout Persia as 'Shahr-bánu' or the 'Queen'. **1975** *Vogue* Dec. 149 The Shahanshah and Shahbanou and the Imperial Family. **1976** *Times* 6 Apr. 9/1 (*caption*) H. I. M. Farah Pahlavi, Shahbanu of Iran. **1980** J. CARTWRIGHT *Horse of Darius* xi. 155 A stiff family group.. with the Shah.., the Shahbanu and the younger children.

**shahdom** ('ʃɑːdəm). *rare.* [f. SHAH + -DOM.] The position, dignity, or territory of the Shah.

**1884** MARVIN *Region Eternal Fire* xix. 334 Desert or mountain-severed provinces, susceptible of being easily broken off the Shahdom in detail. **1895** *Athenæum* 9 Mar. 314/1 The difficult task of tutoring Shahdom.

**shahee**, variant or obs. form of SHAHI.

**shaheed**, var. SHAHID.

‖**shaheen** (ʃɑː'hiːn). Also **shahin.** [Urdū, a. Pers. *shāhīn*, lit. royal (bird), f. *shāh* SHAH.] An Indian falcon, *Falco peregrinator* and other species.

**1839** JERDON in *Madras Jrnl. Lit. & Sci.* X. 81 The shaheen is a native of India, and breeds pretty generally among rocky mountains. **1851** J. GOULD *Birds Asia* III. Pl. 2, *Falco peregrinator*. Shaheen Falcon. **1852** R. F. BURTON *Falconry Valley Indus* ii. 13 The Bahri..and her tiercel, here vulgarly called the Shahin, are found in some parts of the province [Scinde]. **1897** *Encycl. Sport* I. 366/1 (Falconry), In India there are used..the black shaheen, *Falco peregrinator*; the red-naped shaheen, *Falco babylonicus* [etc.].

**Shahenshah**, var. SHAHANSHAH.

**shahgoest**, variant of SYAGUSH.

‖**shahi** ('ʃɑːɪ). Forms: *α.* 6 shaugh, 7 scahy, -i, shawhee, schai, 8 s(h)ahie, chaye, 7–9 shahee, 9– shahi; *β. erron.* 7 shehide, shaet, schaied. [Pers. *shāhī* royal, f. *shāh*: see SHAH.

It has been suggested that the erroneous *β* forms are due to confusion (by Europeans) with the word *shāhid* martyr.]

*Hist.* Orig., a small silver coin of Persia varying between 4*d.* and 10*d.*; subsequently, a copper coin of Persia worth about $\frac{3}{8}$*d.*

*α.* **1566** A. EDWARDS in Hakluyt *Voy.* (1589) 378, 200 shaughes is a tumen, reckoning euery shaugh for 6. pence Russe. **1617** MORYSON *Itin.* I. 293 Eight aspers at Cyprus made one scahy (a Turkish money which the Italians call Seya) being esteemed at little more then sixe pence English, and fifteene scahy made a zechine. **1619** in Foster *Eng. Factories India* (1906) 140 Two shahees maketh a ma[hmudi]. **1634** SIR T. HERBERT *Trav.* 151 Their [Persian] Coines..Larrees.. are worth ten pence, Shawhees four pence. **1687** A. LOVELL tr. *Thevenot's Trav.* II. 89 The Piastres are commonly worth there thirteen Schais. **1753** HANWAY *Trav.* (1762) I. v. lxiv. 292 Shahie, or sahie. **1882** E. O'DONOVAN *Merv Oasis* I. xxiv. 400 Small copper coins called pools and shahis.

*β.* *c* **1583** NEWBERY in Purchas *Pilgrims* II. IX. iii. 1418 The cariage of a Mule from Arzerum to Arsingam, costeth twelue Shehides. **1677** J. P. tr. *Tavernier's Trav.* I. I. xii. 51 There are four several pieces of Silver Coyn [in Persia]; Abassi's, Mamoudi's, Shaet's, and Bisti's. *Ibid.*, Two Shayet's make a Mamoudi. **1687** A. LOVELL tr. *Thevenot's Trav.* II. 32 At Aleppo..the Schaied is worth five Aspres, sixteen Schaieds go for a Piastre.

‖**shahid** ('ʃɑːiːd). Also **shaheed.** [Arab. *šahīd* witness, martyr.] A Muslim martyr.

**1881** *Calcutta Rev.* LXXVII. 74 The martyrs of the new Indian religion, known by the Musalman name *shahid*, were to have their exceeding great reward in a future state. **1934** *Encycl. Islam* IV. 259/1 The Muslim who falls on the battlefield is called *Shahid*..'witness, martyr'. **1967** P. M. HUBBARD *Custom of Country* (1969) vii. 87 All Pakistanis killed fighting the Indians were *shaheeds*, martyrs of Islam. **1977** *Bangladesh Times* 20 Jan. 8/3 Shaheed Asaduzzaman, a student of Dacca University, was one of the many shaheeds who laid down their lives during the mass movement of 1969.

**Shahinshah, Shah-in-Shah,** vars. SHAHANSHAH.

**shahmanism**, variant of SHAMANISM.

‖**shahnai** ('ʃɑːnaɪ). Also **shannai, shehnai.** Pl. same. [ad. Hindi and Urdu *śahnāī*, f. Pers. *šāhnāy*.] An Indian wind instrument of the oboe class.

**1914** A. H. FOX STRANGWAYS *Music of Hindostan* i. 46 In the temple at Madura I heard the *nāgasāram* (N. India *shahnai*), a kind of oboe with a very loud tone. **1957** *New Oxf. Hist. Music* I. iv. 223 Among the imported wind-instruments we may count the different varieties of the oboe class, such as *shannai* (*surnahi*) which spread from the Near East across continents and to the far islands of the Indonesian archipelago. **1967** *Evening Standard* 20 Sept. 10/2 There has also been this extraordinary blossoming of Indian music... You are now expected to know about Bismillah Khan and his shehnai. **1969** R. SHANKAR *My Music* i. 40/2 The oboelike *shahnai*..is thought to be an auspicious instrument and is often played..to celebrate.. marriage. **1971** *Illustr. Weekly India* 18 Apr. 27 No Mendelssohn's Wedding March for her. She must have *shehnai* and Gujarati songs! **1981** LD. HAREWOOD *Tongs & Bones* xii. 195 The two greatest woodwind players I ever heard—Heinz Holliger, the Swiss oboist, and Bismillah Khan, the Indian *shahnai* player.

**Shahr-banu**, var. SHAHBANU.

**shahstah**, obs. form of SHASTRA.

‖**shahzadah** (ʃɑː'zɑːdə). Forms: 7 shawh-zawdeh, 9 shahzadeh, shazada, shah zadeh, shahzada, 8– shahzadah. [Pers. *shāhzādah*, f. SHAH + *zādah* son.] The son of the SHAH; a king's son.

**1662** PHILLIPS (ed. 2), *Shawh-zawdeh*, the Grand-Signior's son; the word signifieth in Persian tongue, a King's son. **1800** WELLINGTON in *Suppl. Desp.* (1858) I. 461 You have heard of the conspiracy here [Seringapatam] to..carry off the Shah-zadahs. **1817** JAS. MILL *Brit. India* II. IV. v. 172 The Shazada (such was the title by which the eldest son of the Mogul was then distinguished in Bengal). **1840** J. B. FRASER *Trav. Koordistan*, etc. I. iii. 56 Thus, however, the Beglerbeggee becomes regarded nearly in the light and rank of a Shah Zadeh, and maintains the state of one. **1859** *Hodson's Twelve Yrs. India* 310 *note*, The three Princes [*footn.* called Shahzadahs]..were in a tomb six miles off.

**shaik(h**, variant of SHEIKH.

**shaikha(h**, var. SHEIKHA.

**shaikhdom**, var. SHEIKHDOM.

†**shail**, *sb.*[1] *Obs. rare.* Also **shayle.** [Cf. SHEWEL.] A scarecrow.

**1531** ELYOT *Gov.* I. xxiii, The good husbande..setteth up cloughtes or thredes, whiche some call shailes [**1557** shayles],..to feare away birdes.

**shail**, *sb.*[2] *dial. rare.* In 6 shayle. [f. SHAIL *v.*[2]] A crooked gait; a shuffling, awkward manner of walking. First in **a-shayle** *adv.*, moving or walking in a shuffling, awkward manner.

**1530** PALSGR. 831/1 A shayle with the knees togyther, and the fete outwarde, *a eschays*. **1887** HARDY *Woodlanders* I. xi. 202 Fancy..her bounding walk becoming the regular Hintock shail-and-wamble.

†**shail**, *v.*[1] *Obs. rare*[−1]. [An alteration of SKAIL *v.* (perh. a scribal error; the MS. elsewhere has *skail*.)] *intr.* = SKAIL *v.* 9.

*c* **1375** *Cursor M.* 18836 (Fairf.), His hare..bi his eres shailande sumdele [*a* **1300** *Cott.* skailand].

**shail** (ʃeɪl), *v.*[2] *Obs.* exc. *dial.* Forms: 4–5 schayle, 5 scheyle, (6 shoyle, scayle), 6, 9 shayl, 6–7, 9 shale, (7 ? shael), 7– shail. [Possibly a metathetic derivative of OE. *sceolh* oblique.]

**1.** *intr.* To stumble, to walk or move in a shuffling, shambling manner.

? *a* **1400** *Morte Arth.* 1098 Schovelle-fotede was þat schalke, and schaylande hyme semyde, With schankez unschaply, schowande to-gedyrs. *c* **1440** *Promp. Parv.* 443/1 Schaylyn, or scheylyn. (*Disgredior.*) **1483** *Cath. Angl.* 332/1 To Schayle (*v.r.* Schaylle), *degradi & degredi.* *a* **1529** SKELTON *Sp. Parrot* 85 Our Thomasen she doth trip, our Ienet she doth shayle. **1530** PALSGR. 700/1, I shayle with the fete, *jentretaille des piedz.* I never sawe man have a worse pace, se how he shaylleth. **1565** GOLDING *Ovid's Met.* II. (1567) 17 The Waine for want of weight..Did hoyse aloft and scayle and reele, as though it empty were. **1575** TURBERV. *Venerie* lv. 155 They [wild swine] set not their hinderfoote within their forefoote, and their gards fall straight vpon the ground and neuer shoyle or leane outwards. **1593** *Passionate Morrice* (1876) 82 Other, which were well legde, shaled with their feete, or were splafooted. **1692** R. L'ESTRANGE *Fables* ccxxi. 193 Child [a young crab], (says the Mother) You must Use your self to Walk Streight, without Skewing, and Shailing so Every step you set. **1887** HARDY *Woodlanders* I. xi. 202 She may shail; but she'll never wamble.

**b.** *fig.* To blunder, be wrong.

*a* **1529** SKELTON '*Womanhood, wanton*' 19 Good mastres Anne, there ye do shayle. —— *Col. Cloute* 401 What, Colyne, there thou shales! —— *Replyc.* 172 Ye shayle *inter enigmata* And *inter paradigmata*.

**2.** ? To blink. *rare*[−1]. (See SHAILING *vbl. sb.*)

**3.** *dial.* **a.** *intr.* To glide or move in a slanting direction. **b.** *trans.* To throw (a flat missile) with a gliding motion. [Possibly a distinct word.]

**a. 1895** A. PATTERSON *Man & Nat. on Broads* 78 High over-head some great grey gulls are 'shayling' in erratic flight, making seaward.

**b. 1832** tr. *Tour Germ. Prince* III. v. 127 It is also no rarity for some one to throw the fragments of his 'gouté'..on the heads of the people in the pit, or to shail them with singular dexterity into the boxes. **1840** SPURDENS *Suppl. Forby*, *Shail*, to throw a flat missile, as a tile or an oyster shell.

Hence **'shailing** *vbl. sb.* and *ppl. a.* Also **'shailer**, one who shambles in his gait.

**1398** TREVISA *Barth. De P.R.* VIII. xii. (Tollemache MS.), þe scrabbe is schaylynge beste [**1495** a sheylynge, **1535** shelynge, **1582** shelling beest] and gooþ bakwarde. *c* **1440** *Promp. Parv.* 443/1 Schaylare. *Ibid.*, Schaylynge (or scheylynge, *loripedacio*). *c* **1460** *Ibid.* (Winch. MS.) 395 Schey, or skey, or horsys or schyttyl scheylere, idem quod schaylare, supra. **1530** PALSGR. 266/1 Schayler that gothe a wrie with his fete, *boytevx*. **1611** COTGR., *Fauquet*,..a shaling wry-legd fellow. **1653** BULWER *Anthropomet.* VI. 106 The word..was *Hippos*, which signifies a perpetuall shaeling of the Eyes. **1658** GURNALL *Chr. in Arm.* verse 14. vi. II. 237 This is too narrow a path, for many shaleing professours to walk in now adays.

**shair(d**, obs. Sc. forms of SHARE *v.*, SHERD.

[**shairl**, spurious word: see SHAWL (*-goat*).]

**shairman, shairn**, Sc. ff. SHEARMAN, SHARN.

‖**Shaitan** (ʃeɪ'tɑːn). Forms: 7 shitan, sceithan, 7, 9 sheitan, 9- shaitan. [Arab. *shaiṭān*, corruptly a. Heb. *sāṭān* SATAN.]

**1.** The Devil, Satan; an evil spirit.

**1638** SIR T. HERBERT *Trav.* (ed. 2) 241 Ozman in his parody assures them, The Devil (Shitan they call him) ever diets so. **1662** J. DAVIES tr. *Olearius' Voy. Ambass.* 233 But as soon as they were gone, Sceithan, that is to say, the Devil, presented himself to Hagar. **1698** A. BRAND *Emb. Muscovy into China* 41, I could not meet with any thing worth taking notice of all over the Hall but their Sheitan, or (as they themselves call'd it) their God. **1863** YULE *Friar Jordanus' Mirabilia* (Hakl. Soc.) 37 *note*, Certain mysterious footsteps, more than thirty or forty paces asunder, which the natives alleged to be Shaitan's.

**2.** *transf.* An evil-disposed or vicious person or animal.

**1834** MORIER *Ayesha* I. i. 18 Cara Bey! oof! he is a Sheitan, he is Satan, he is a black Yezidi, a worshipper of the devil! **1849** LAYARD *Nineveh* I. ix. 287 *note*, The term Sheitan (equivalent to Satan) is usually applied in the East to a clever, cunning, or daring fellow. **1884** F. BOYLE *On Borderland* 377 Ranjit Singh, that Shaitan, turned it into a magazine. **1895** MRS. B. M. CROKER *Village Tales* (1896) 21 The shaitan [*i.e.* a tiger] has slain my man and my son. *Ibid.* 230 But Zālim Sing had no such excuse—he is a shaitan, the son of a she ass.

**3.** A dust-storm.

**1900** *Daily News* 17 Apr. 5/5 In India and the East a dust storm rejoices in the name Shaïtan, otherwise Satan... To-day thousands of sightseers were the playthings of a Shaïtan in the Champ-de-Mars. **1911** in WEBSTER.

**shaitel**, var. SHEITEL.

**Shaivism, Shaivite**, vars. SAIVISM, SAIVITE.

**shakal**, obs. variant of JACKAL *sb.*

**shakbott, -but(t**, obs. forms of SACKBUT.

**1519** *Lett. & Pap. Hen. VIII*, III. II. 1533 To the shakbutts, 50*s*. **1593** G. PEELE *Hon. Garter* B 1 b, Therewith I heard the Clarions and the Shalmes, The Shakbuts.

**shake** (ʃeɪk), *sb.*[1] Also 4 schak, 5 schakke, 8–9 shack. [f. SHAKE *v.*]

†**I. 1. a.** With prefixed adj., as advb. cognate obj. to *shake* vb., or other vbs. of motion, *a good, great*, etc. *shake*: quickly, with headlong speed.

**13..** *K. Alis.* 232 Away he rod from heom god schak. **13..** *Propr. Sanct.* (Vernon MS.) in *Archiv Stud. neu. Spr.* LXXXI. 84/72 And aftur þei schoken a ful gret schak. ?*c* **1475** *Hunt. Hare* 96 Thei wente a nobull schakke.

†**b.** A charge (of men in battle), onrush. (Cf. SHOCK *sb.*). *Obs.*

*c* **1380** *Sir Ferumb.* 2663 So þat þe furste schak was ouercome of hure enymys. ?*a* **1400** *Morte Arth.* 1759 The Bretons..Schokkes in with a schakke, and schontez no langere.

**II.** The action or an act of shaking.

**2. a.** An act of shaking a person or thing.

**1581** A. HALL *Iliad* IV. 72 And as down leaped he, His gay and gorgeous armor rich so sounded in the shake. **1632** J. HAYWARD tr. *Biondi's Eromena* 2 The dogge..pinch'd him in the eye, with so terrible a shake, that the Lion..was constrained to forsake himselfe. **1683** MOXON *Mech. Exerc.*, *Printing* 172 Sometimes it happens that by a Shake..the Metal may spill. **1715** ADDISON *Freeholder* No. 1 ¶5 Blossoms, that would fall away with every shake of wind. **1764** ELIZA MOXON *Eng. Housew.* (ed. 9) 138 Give them a shake together before you lie in your eggs. **1823** LAMB *Elia* Ser. II. *Amicus Rediv.*, It seemed to have given a shake to memory, calling up notice after notice of [etc.]. **1845** POE *Purloined Let.* Tales 206 We turned over every leaf in each volume, not contenting ourselves with a mere shake.

**b.** (Usually in full *a shake of the hand.*) An act of shaking hands or a person's hand, a handshake. (See SHAKE *v.*)

**1712** ADDISON *Spect.* No. 269 ¶5 Our Salutations..consisting of many kind Shakes of the Hand. **1820** L. HUNT *Indicator* No. 40 I. 315 The shake [was] as close, as long, and as rejoicing, as if the semi-unknown was a friend come home from the Desarts. **1908** R. BAGOT *A. Cuthbert* vii. 75 Jim Sinclair gave her hand a very British shake.

**c.** ***shake of the head***: see SHAKE *v.* 6 b.

**1713** J. HUGHES in J. Duncombe *Lett.* (1772) I. 74, I may have called a man a knave by a shake of the head and a shrug of the shoulders. **1779** SHERIDAN *Critic* III. i, *Puff.* Why, by that shake of the head, he [Ld. Burleigh] gave you to understand that [etc.]. **1848** DICKENS *Dombey* l, Captain Cuttle observed with a shake of his head, that Jack Bunsby himself hadn't made it out. **1889** PARNELL in R. B. O'Brien *Life* (1898) II. 228 Is there any one of them who..sitting in his place, by a shake of the head, or a nod, or a word, will venture to say that [etc.]?

**d.** An act of shaking oneself. Also *fig.*

**1712–14** POPE *Rape Lock* i. 15 Now lap-dogs give themselves the rousing shake. **1726** W. PENN *Tracts* Wks. I. 490 Having given my self a loose shake of the Calumnies of his first Section. **1830** *Blackw. Mag.* XXVIII. 596 That long shake [of a dog] that bedrizzled the sunshine. **1857** HUGHES *Tom Brown* I. viii, The speaker got up from a bench on which he had been lying unobserved, and gave himself a shake.

**e.** *dial.* The shaking out of corn from the ear. Also in Comb. ***shake-time***. Cf. SHACK *sb.*[1]

**1668** WORLIDGE *Dict. Rust.*, *Shake-time*, the season of the year that Mast and such Fruits fall from Trees. **1786** *Har'st Rig* vi, And aye they tell, that 'a green shear Is an ill shake.' **1899** *Cumbld. Gloss.* s.v. *Shear*, A green shear's as bad as a shak.

**f.** *Paper-making.*

**1885** *Encycl. Brit.* XVIII. 225/1 He..then gives the mould the 'shake', a gentle shake both along and across the mould. **1890** A. WATT *Paper-making* xii. 131 He gives the mould a gentle shake from his chest forward and back again, which is called the fore-right shake; this shake takes place across the wires... He next gives a shake from right to left, and back again.

**g.** *dial.* A raffle.

**1877** E. LEIGH *Chesh. Gloss.*, *Shake*, a raffle. 'My mon won the picture in a shake.'

**h.** *colloq.* or *slang.* Used as the type of instantaneous action, esp. in the phrases ***in a shake, in a brace*** or ***couple of shakes***. Also, ***in three*** (or ***two***) ***shakes of a sheep's*** (or ***lamb's***) ***tail, (in) half a shake***.

**1816** G. MUIR *Clydesdale Minstrelsy* 98 (E.D.D.) In the shake of a hand I received my sight. **1840** BARHAM *Ingol. Leg.* Ser. I. *St. Aloys*, He'll be up at the church in a couple of shakes. **1841** J. T. HEWLETT *Parish Clerk* I. xvi. 283 I'll just..run whome wi' un, and be back agin in a brace of shakes. **1858** S. A. HAMMETT *Piney Woods Tavern* xxiv. 260 Out come my mare, and in a couple of shakes of a sheep's tail we was a doin' our three minits jest as fine as silk. *Ibid.* xxvi. 283 In hafe a shake Bingham broke through 'em. **1867** G. W. HARRIS *Sut Lovingood* 113 Pat tuck me at my word, an' wer outen site in the shake ove a lamb's tail. **1883** STEVENSON *Treasure Isl.* xiii, 'Well, if I speak back, pikes will be going in two shakes. **1884** 'MARK TWAIN' *Huck. Finn* xli. 414, I says to myself spos'n he can't fix that leg just in three shakes of a sheep's tail, as the saying is? spos'n it takes him three or four days? **1902** E. NESBIT *Five Children & It* ii. 51 He'll be ready in a brace of shakes, he says. **1904** E. NESBIT *Phœnix & Carpet* vii. 145 Wait a shake, and I'll undo the side gate. **1934** N. SCANLAN *Tides of Youth* 117 Half a shake—any more beer? **1936** W. GREENE *Death in Deep South* II. 93 If you boys will just hold your horses, I'll have a statement for you. Harmon's typing it now. It'll be ready in a shake. **1958** J. WAIN *Contenders* xii. 265 In two shakes he's solved the problem. Or shaken it anyway. **1966** *Guardian* 29 July 8/7 Then they are off again... I nearly wrote 'in two shakes of a lamb's tail'. **1973** E. LEMARCHAND *Let or Hindrance* xii. 140 I'll knock you up bacon and eggs in a brace of shakes.

**i.** ***a fair shake***: a fair deal. Also, ***an even shake, a good shake***, and opp., ***an unfair shake***. *U.S. slang.*

**1830** *Central Watchtower & Farmer's Jrnl.* (Harrodsburg, Kentucky) 22 May 1/3 Says I, any way that will be a fair shake. **1902** S. E. WHITE *Blazed Trail* xxxi. 218 'That ain't a fair shake,' cried the man excitedly. **1949** E. B. WHITE *Let.* 20 Nov. (1976) 315 *The New Yorker* disagrees with practically everything Boyer believes in... Nevertheless, it has given Boyer a fair shake. **1969** L. G. ARTHUR in A. E. Wilkerson *Rights of Children* (1973) x. 124 What does the child receive in return:..just psychiatric screen, shiny tiled walls, and electronic listening. It doesn't seem an even shake! **1972** *Time* 17 Apr. 33/1 The Administration took office..expecting an unfair shake. **1976** M. MACHLIN *Pipeline* xix. 243 What about the natives? They're not getting such a good shake. **1980** in S. Terkel *Amer. Dreams* 341 I'd like to see an America where so much power was not in the hands of the few. Where everybody'd get a fair shake.

**j.** orig. *Naut.* An act of shaking a sleeper to rouse him. Also *fig.*, a morning call.

**1933** P. A. EADDY *Hull Down* 49 If I'm asleep give me a shake at eight bells. **1945** 'TACKLINE' *Holiday Sailor* iv. 47 A shake. Another shake. I peer muzzily down at Gordon's upturned face. 'Quarter to four, Smiler, if you want any tea.' 'Uh? Oh, righto—thanks. I'll be up.' **1979** D. GURR *Troika* vii. 43 The knocking intruded slowly into consciousness. The room was dark, although my shake was for six-thirty.

**k.** A party, *esp.* a rent party. *U.S. slang.*

**1946** [see PERCOLATOR c]. **1956** S. LONGSTREET *Real Jazz Old & New* xvi. 126 Depression came... You could always wrassel up a piano and get together to listen and charge a few coins and have a skiffle. Or, as some said, a rent party, or a shake. **1977** *Amer. Speech 1975* L. 65 *Shake*.., party. 'There's a shake at Jim's house.'

**3. a.** Irregular vibratory or tremulous movement, esp. as the result of impact or disturbance of equilibrium; irregular lateral movement (of something revolving or moving in a line). *Naut.*, a fluttering or shivering (of a sail).

**1665** HOOKE *Microgr.* 12 The cause of fluidness..I conceive to be nothing else but a certain pulse or shake of heat. **1690** BOYLE *Effects of Motion* iii. 18 The Shake is first communicated by the Cannon to the earth or floor on which they play. **1764** J. FERGUSON *Lect.* 48 The bush must embrace the spindle quite close, to prevent any shake in the motion. **1797** *Encycl. Brit.* (ed. 3) XV. 663/2 A square box made to slide along this wooden trunk without shake. **1825** J. NICHOLSON *Oper. Mech.* 529 The earth must be struck with a rammer, and if found to shake, must be bored, to ascertain whether the shake be local or general. **1844** H. STEPHENS *Bk. Farm* II. 320 Diagonal braces..to resist the shake from the action of the wheel upon the pinion. **1882** NARES *Seamanship* (ed. 6) 223 The sail will come in without a shake. **1883** *Science* I. 101/1 Care should be taken..that there is no 'shake' or lateral motion in the adjustments for focus. **1885** LOCK *Workshop Rec.* Ser. IV. 328/2 See that the cannon pinion does not confine the shake of the centre wheel.

**b.** The shock of an earthquake. Now *U.S.* and *N.Z.*

**1622** W. BURTON *Leicestersh.* 270 The bell in the Townehall at Denbigh knowled with the violence of the shake [of an earthquake]. **1731** *Gentl. Mag.* I. 224 In that and some following Days they had no less than 50 Shakes. **1793** SMEATON *Edystone L.* Introd. 3 It has been destroyed by the shake of an earthquake. **1845** E. J. WAKEFIELD *Adventure in N.Z.* II. xv. 368 The most severe earthquake occurred that I have yet felt... The natives..acknowledged that they had never experienced so bad a *ru*, or 'shake'. **1907** *Westm. Gaz.* 13 Apr. 3/2 That earthquake at San Francisco—the 'shake', as the local papers lightheartedly called it within a fortnight. **1929** 'E. MILTON' *Love & Chiffon* 219 In good old New Zealand, you'd realize these shakes are mere nothings. **1948** J. COURAGE in *Landfall* II. 298 The earthquake happened late..but the shake woke Mr Blakiston immediately. **1949** *Los Angeles Times* 14 May 1/4 Newspaper and police switch-boards were flooded immediately with requests for information on the shake.

**4. a.** A shivering or trembling of the body or limbs; also, a state of tremor. ***the shakes***, nervous agitation caused by fear or horror.

**1624** FLETCHER *Rule a Wife* IV. i, I must stand to it stoutly, And show no shake of fear. **1837** LYTTON *E. Maltrav.* I. x, She was pale and agitated, or, as she expressed it, 'had a terrible fit of the shakes'. **1851** HAWTHORNE *Ho. Sev. Gables* xvi, Her nerves were in a shake. **1966** M. WOODHOUSE *Tree Frog* xii. 93 It was like getting the shakes on an exposed pitch of rock. **1976** B. BOVA *Multiple Man* xiii. 135 The sliding glass doors..were locked... So I sat around and waited, trying not to get the shakes.

**b.** An attack of a shaking disease. ***the shakes***, a name popularly applied to any disease characterized by a trembling of the muscles and limbs, esp. delirium tremens.

***dumb shakes***, (*U.S.*) ?masked intermittent fever. ***hatters' shakes***, a disease incident to some workers in hat-making.

**1782** MME. D'ARBLAY *Diary* 28 Dec., A man who has had two shakes of the palsy! **1838** *Penny Cycl.* XI. 220/2 When 'the shakes' have taken possession of their unhappy victim [of mercury-poisoning]. **1856** OLMSTED *Slave States* 355 Even in the midst of a severe 'shake', they would generally insist that they were 'well enough to dive'. **1867** H. LATHAM *Black & White* 109 The Dismal Swamp is a first-rate place for concealment, if you are not afraid of shakes and agues. **1871** NAPHEYS *Prev. & Cure Dis.* III. ii. 640 The 'dumb shakes' of the Wabash Valley. **1884** *Cornhill Mag.* June 616 An attack of delirium tremens, or, as she and her neighbours style it, a 'fit of the shakes'. **1902** *Brit. Med. Jrnl.* 15 Feb. 378 Muscular tremors ('hatters' shakes') are most often observed in those engaged in dusty post-carotting processes. **1927** *New Republic* 9 Mar. 72/1 The following is a partial list of words denoting drunkenness now in common use in the United States..to have the shakes. **1947** A. MARSHALL in *Coast to Coast 1946* 177 The longest bender I ever had was eight months. It took me three years to get over the shakes it gave me. **1977** *New Yorker* 3 Oct. 40/1 Have you ever had the D.T.s? The shakes?

**c.** A tremor (in the voice).

**1859** LEVER *Dav. Dunn* liv, If I'd have detected one line in your face, or one shake in your voice, like treachery.

**d.** A shaking movement in a dance; ***the Shake***, a dance characterized by such movements.

**1946** [see BUMP *sb.*[1] 1 f]. **1956** B. HOLIDAY *Lady sings Blues* (1973) iv. 41 The Cotton Club—a place Negroes never saw inside unless they played music or did the shakes or shimmies. **1962** *Guardian* 31 Dec. 5/1 The Madison threatens to become compulsory dancing; creeping up behind it come the Slop, the Shake, the Waddle,..the Bossa Nova. **1966** [see JERK *sb.*[1] 2 f].

**5.** *Mus.* (See quot. 1881.)

†*close, open shake* (see quot. 1674). *Obs.*

**1659** [see *shaking stop*, SHAKING *vbl. sb.*]. **1674** PLAYFORD *Skill Mus.* I. xi. 47 Trill, or plain shake. *Ibid.* 53 The Trill, or Shake of the Voice, being the most usual Grace. *Ibid.* II. 104 The close Shake is when you stop with your first Finger on the first Fret, and shake with your second Finger as close to it as you can; the open Shake is when you stop with your first Finger on the first Fret, and shake with your third Finger on the third Fret. **1711** [see QUAVER *sb.* 2]. **1775** MME. D'ARBLAY *Early Diary* Nov. (1889) II. 98 She has a very pretty shake, and sings very chastly, not with vile graces and trills. **1825** SOUTHEY *Paraguay* III. xl, And sometimes high the note was raised, and long Produced, with shake and effort sensible. **1881** F. TAYLOR in *Grove's Dict. Mus.* III. 479 *Shake* or *Trill*..consists of the regular and rapid alternation of a given note with the note above,..continuing for the full duration of the written note... Immediately before the final note of a shake a new subsidiary note is introduced, one degree *below* the principal note. This and the concluding principal note together form what is called the *turn* of the shake.

**6. a.** A concussion or blow which impairs the stability of something; often *fig.* a damaging blow (e.g. to an institution, a state of things, a person's health); a shock (to the mind or nerves).

**1565** W. ALLEN *Def. Purgatory* xvii. 283 One of these ouer-throwers frameth..his negatiue argument, to the more sure shake of oure faithe herein after this sorte. **1673** TEMPLE *Observ. United Prov.* Wks. 1731 I. 35 The States-General..consisted of about Eight Hundred Persons, whose meeting..gave too great a Shake to the whole Body of the Union. **1685** BAXTER *Paraphr. N.T.* Acts xxiv. 8-9 This is a great shake to the credit of most History. **1704** SWIFT *Tale Tub* ix. 168 His Brain hath undergone an unlucky Shake. *a* **1722** FOUNTAINHALL *Decis.* (1759) I. 13 Being thought..a great shake to the security of men's lives and fortunes. **1862** SPENCER *First Princ.* I. i. §5 (1875) 18 The rude shakes which Science has given to many of their cherished convictions. **1894** H. NISBET *Bush Girl's Rom.* 44 He was the life of us before he had that shake, but it's only nerves.

**b.** *to give* (someone) *a* or *the shake* or *the cold shake*: to cold-shoulder, rebuff; evade, escape. *U.S.*

**1875** E. EDDY *Let.* 29 Oct. in J. F. Daly *Life A. Daly* (1917) xxv. 215, I desire to give the 'Two Orphans' a shake. **1883** 'MARK TWAIN' *Life on Miss.* iii. 33 None of them herded with Dick Allbright. They all give him the cold shake. **1930** D. RUNYON in *Collier's* 1 Feb. 13/3 Although I give her..all my affection, she will probably give me the shake. **1970** N. FLEMING *Czech Point* (1971) viii. 106 If these jokers want to tail us, they've damn well got to do it properly from behind. Overtake and give them the shake.

**7.** *to be no great* (*some great, considerable*, etc.) *shakes*: to be nothing (something, etc.) extraordinary in ability or importance.

[Perh. alluding to shaking of dice.]

[**1816** LD. BROUGHTON *Recoll.* (1865) II. 2 W. said that a piece of sculpture there was '*nullae magnae quassationes*', and the others laughed heartily.] **1819** MOORE *Tom Crib's Memor.* (ed. 3) 41 Though no great shakes at learned chat. **1820** *Blackw. Mag.* VIII. 89 Ten years ago, the young Whig was 'non sordidus auctor', considerable shakes; but now they are all asses. **1820** BYRON *Let. to Murray* 28 Sept. (1875) 733, I had my hands full, and my head too, just then [when he wrote 'Marino Faliero']; so it can be no great shakes. **1845** CARLYLE *Cromwell* (1850) II. 222 No great shakes at metre. **1876** BROWNING *Pacchiarotto, Shop* xi, This article, no such great shakes, Fizzes like wild fire? **1894** *Cornhill Mag.* June 564 Bannock can't hit a haystack at fifty yards, and I'm no great shakes. **1913** D. H. LAWRENCE *Sons & Lovers* x. 266 You think you're terrific great shakes, and that you live under the eternal insult of working in a factory. **1939** *Sun* (Baltimore) 8 Nov. 6/8 Women feel..that, no matter what poor shakes of wives they are, their husbands are blessed beyond their deserts in getting them. **1948** G. H. JOHNSTON *Death takes small Bites* vii. 159 He couldn't have been any great shakes as a driver because he didn't beat you by much. **1970** H. MCLEAVE *Question of Negligence* xxiii. 191 I'm no great shakes at this modern dancing. **1976** *Daily Mirror* 18 Mar. 2/3 Sir Richard may not have been particularly great shakes. But he was never given much chance to show his paces.

**8.** In combination with adv. (subst. use of phrases: of SHAKE *v.*: see also SHAKE-DOWN, -OUT). ***shake-up***: an act of shaking up or being shaken up, or the result of this; a thorough or drastic change or rearrangement; a disturbing or unsettling experience.

**1847** J. S. MILL *Lett.* (1910) I. 131 To give that general shake-up to the torpid mind of the nation which the French Revolution gave to Continental Europe. **1857** HUGHES *Tom Brown* II. ii, Tom gave the prisoner a shake-up, took away his list, and stood him up on the floor. **1880** 'MARK TWAIN' *Tramp Abr.* xxxviii. 438 My nerves had hardly grown quiet after this affair when they got another shake-up,—one which utterly unmanned me for a moment. **1882** *National Police Gaz.* 18 Nov. 7/2 (*heading*) The Union Square Company has a matrimonial shake-up all around. **1899** R. H. BARBOUR *Half-back* vi. 59 There'll be a shake-up to-morrow... He's going to put Greer on the scrub to-morrow. **1903** *Westm. Gaz.* 21 Feb. 7/1 The Board has had a healthy 'shake-up'. **1912** *Contemp. Rev.* Nov. 654 Indictments and bills in equity became the order of the day, and 'probings' and 'shake-ups' the common talk of business men. **1916** 'TAFFRAIL' *Pincher Martin* xvi. 312 But, orl the same, Tubby boy, I reckons it's done us orl good ter 'ave a bit of a shake up like this 'ere [*sc.* a naval engagement]. **1938** E. BOWEN *Death of Heart* III. i. 325, I can't see that this change has done you harm. Nor the shake-up either; you were getting too quiet. **1962** E. SNOW *Red China Today* (1963) xxii. 165 'Rectification', self-criticism, retraining and restudy among party and nonparty cadres are followed by shake-ups which affect millions. **1967** D. PINNER *Ritual* viii. 85 You didn't half give me a shake-up. **1969** *Listener* 27 Mar. 410/2, I read that BBC radio is due for a programme shake-up. **1970** 'D. HALLIDAY' *Dolly & Cookie Bird* iii. 35 It was sporting of your father to ask me. I can imagine what a shake-up it must have been, without taking me on as well. **1980** *Christian Sci. Monitor* (Midwestern ed.) 4 Dec. 4/1 As a result of the latest shake-up, which occurred at the party meeting, the political balance has shifted away from the conservatives.

**III.** Something produced by shaking.

**9.** A natural cleft or fissure produced during growth or formation. **a.** in timber.

For *cup, heart, star, wind shake*: see those words.

**1651** J. WHITE *Rich Cabinet* (1677) 29 Get a streight piece of wood.., let it be free from knots, or shakes, then plain it. **1769** FALCONER *Dict. Marine* (1780), *Shakes*,..the cracks or rents in a plank, occasioned by the sun or weather. **1851** *Rural Cycl.* IV. 178 *Shake*, a disease in trees, consisting of long splits up the stem. **1894** *Times* 31 Aug. 3/5 Yellow pine, without a single knot, shake, or other blemish in its whole surface.

**b.** in rock, mineral strata, etc.

***water shake***, one in which a stream empties itself.

**1747** HOOSON *Miner's Dict.* L 2, The Shaft was Sunk in a great and loose Shack of Chirts. **1771** MRS. GRIFFITH *Hist. Lady Barton* I. 41 That same want of stability..like a shake in marble, runs thro' the whole block. **1802** J. MAWE *Mineral. Derbysh.* iii. 38 In this limestone stratum are frequently found openings or caverns, which are commonly called shakes, or swallows. **1846** J. BAXTER *Libr. Pract. Agric.* II. 305 They..were as compact as when first moved by the plough, without even the appearance of a water shake or fissure. **1856** *Jrnl. R. Agric. Soc.* XVII. II. 373 The more feeble springs that empty themselves..through some loose or porous soil, shakes in the rocks, or otherwise. **1893-4** *Northumberld. Gloss.*, *Shake*, a thickening or 'belly' in a vein of lead ore..or the cavity sometimes found in such places.

**10.** *pl.* **a.** A set of barrel staves = SHOOK *sb. U.S.*

**1820** SCORESBY *Arct. Regions* I. 207 *note*, Empty casks are ..taken to pieces, and the staves closely packed up in a cylindrical form, constituting what are called shakes or packs. **1841** DANA *Seaman's Man.* 122 *Shakes*, the staves of hogs-heads taken apart.

**b.** Pieces of split timber, a kind of shingles. Also *sing.* when *attrib.* or *comb.* (see sense 13 below). Chiefly *U.S.*

**1772** TILLINGHAST & HOLROYD *Let.* 23 Nov. in *Commerce of Rhode Island* (1914) I. 420 We herewith send you all the Shakes we can yet get in. **1845** C. MATHEWS *Writ.* I. 164 in R. H. Thornton *Amer. Gloss.* s.v., A..house, shingled with what they call 'shakes' all over the West and Southwest. **1893** *Advance* (Chicago) 16 Mar., By and by..shakes can be split for a roof, and fastened on. **1939** I. BAIRD *Waste Heritage* xviii. 240 Weathered barns with the lichen growing on the shakes. **1964** L. LINTON *Of Days & Driftwood* ix. 51 The first place of worship was a very small building of shakes. **1977** *Tel.* (Brisbane) 20 Dec. 36/5 Shakes are hand split and have a rustic appearance. **1982** *Times* 26 Jan. 11/3 The design of these shakes was identical to that of the traditional oak shakes used in England for many centuries.

**11.** *Printing.* (See quot.)

**1888** JACOBI *Printers' Voc.*, *Shake*, a slur on a printed sheet through some defect in the impression.

**12.** (See quot. 1911.)

**1911** *Webster's Dict.*, *Shake*... Short for *milk shake* or *egg shake*, etc., beverages of milk, or milk and egg, flavored and shaken thoroughly. *Colloq.*, *U.S.* **1948** D. BALLANTYNE *Cunninghams* I. xxix. 146 You sat..sucking raspberry shakes through straws. **1953** [see PARFAIT]. **1966** B. H. DEAL *Fancy's Knell* iii. 44 'I'll have a burger too,' the redhaired boy said. 'And a shake.' **1981** J. D. MACDONALD *Free Fall in Crimson* x. 114 She sucked up the shake.

**IV. 13.** *attrib.* and *Comb.* as (sense 10 b) ***shake cabin, house, roof, shanty***; ***shake-maker***; ***shake-sided*** adj.; **shake-bog**, a bog which shakes or quakes when trodden upon; **shake culture**, a CULTURE (3 c) in which the organisms are distributed through the medium by a gentle shake; **shake dancer** *slang* (see quot. 1968); so (as a back-formation) **shake dance**; **shake-hole** (see quots.); **shake music** (see quot. 1942); **shake wave** = *S wave* s.v. S 6; **shake willey, willow**, a machine used in the preparation of cotton and wool (see quot.).

**1815** J. SMITH *Panorama Sci. & Art* II. 599 That kind of bog called the *shake-bog. **1885** L. W. SPRING *Kansas* v. 64 Big Springs in the autumn of 1855 was a place of four or five *shake-cabins and log-huts. **1967** M. CRAVEN *I heard Owl* (1968) v. 36 Old Marta was there and the girl called Keetah, and the two small children.., come from the shake cabins to pick blueberries. **1894** E. KLEIN in *Brit. Med. Jrnl.* 13 Oct. 799/1 It does not form gas bubbles in gelatine *shake cultures. **1968** J. LOCK *Lady Policeman* xi. 102, Her daughter..did bare-breasted *shake dances. **1956** B. HOLIDAY *Lady sings Blues* (1973) x. 98 A *shake dancer with her pimp. **1968** J. LOCK *Lady Policeman* xi. 102, I was.. assigned..to the women entertainers. They were known as 'shake dancers'... The art consisted of shaking bare or almost bare breasts to music. **1976** *National Observer* (U.S.) 2 Oct. 21/5 She becomes a shake-dancer and B-girl. **1823** BUCKLAND *Reliq. Diluv.* 6 *note*, Open fissures, locally called *shake-holes, or swallow-holes, from their swallowing up the streams that cross the limestone districts. **1828** [CARR] *Craven Gloss.*, *Shack-hole*, a hollow in the ground, resembling a funnel, which receives the surface water. **1857** *Lawrence* (Kansas) *Republican* 9 July 3 You are always welcome to his log or *shake house. **1901** J. MUIR *Our National Parks* ix. 298, I found many *shake-makers at work in it, access to these magnificent woods having been made easy by the old mill wagon road. **1935** *Shake music [see JUNGLE *sb.* 3 c]. **1942** BERREY & VAN DEN BARK *Amer. Thes. Slang* §579/1 *Syncopated music; jazz*... Shake music, a savage style similar to 'jungle music'. **1947** *Michigan Hist.* June 178 It was a small log cabin with a *shake roof. **1978** J. HYAMS *Pool* vi. 68 It had..a steep moss-covered shake roof that turned green in the rain. **1879** *Atlantic Monthly* Aug. 154/1 Every one of the frail *shake shanties is a centre of destruction. **1970** J. HANSEN *Fadeout* i. 8 The overhang of a *shake-sided cabana. [**1929** H. JEFFREYS *Earth* (ed. 2) vi. 86 The type (9) are called the longitudinal, irrotational, condensational, primary, or *P* waves; (10) and (11) the transverse, distortional, equivoluminal, secondary, or *S* waves. Prof. H. H. Turner has very appropriately called them the 'push' and the 'shake'.] **1944** A. HOLMES *Princ. Physical Geol.* xvii. 369 The S or '*shake' waves are distortional waves, in which each particle vibrates at right angles to the direction of propagation. **1969** *Daily Tel.* 2 Sept. 12 Seismic records obtained so far from the landing site show the absence of the so-called 'shake-waves'. **1875** KNIGHT *Dict. Mech.*, **Shake-willy* (Cotton-manufacture), a willy or willowing machine for cleaning cotton, preparatory to carding. **1884** W. S. B. MCLAREN *Spinning* 181 In order ..to shake loose any matted pieces, the wool is usually passed through a shake willey or willow.

**shake** (ʃeɪk), *sb.*[2] *slang* and *dial.* [Short for SHAKE-RAG. (Cf. SHACK *sb.*[2])] A disreputable person.

**1846** *Swell's Night Guide* 36 Many of the Haymarket shakes frequent this lumber. **1859** *Hotten's Slang Dict.*, *Shake*, a disreputable man or woman. *North.*

**shake** (ʃeɪk), *v.* Pa. t. shook (ʃʊk); pa. pple. shaken (ˈʃeɪk(ə)n). Forms: *Inf.* 1 sceacan, scacan, 3 sceki, sceky, sake, scheken, schek(e, 3-4 scake, ssake, schak(e, sshake, (4 schac, scha(a)k, s(c)haken, 5 schakyn), 4-6 schake, 6 *Sc.* scha(i)k, 8-9 *Sc.* and *dial.* shack, 4- shake. *Pa. t.* α. 1 sceóc, scóc, 3 scoc, scok(e, ssoc, ssok, 3-4 schok, choke, 4-5 schook, 4-6 schoke, *Sc.* schuk(e, 4-7 (9 *dial.*) shoke, (4 shok, shuke), 6-7 shooke, (6 showke, *Sc.* schuik, 6, 9 sheuk), 9 *dial.* shu(c)k, *north.* shuik, 5- shook. β. 4 shakid, 5 shakyd, 6 schaked, shakte, 6-7 shakt, shak't, 9 *dial.* shacked, sha(c)kt, shakked, *Sc.* and *north.* shaket, -it, 5-9 shaked, 6-9 shak'd. γ. 3 scæken (*pl.*). *Pa. pple.* α. 1 sceacen, scacen, scæcen, 4 schaken, (yshaken), s(c)hakun, schake, 4-6 shake, 5 i-sake, 5-6 *Sc.* schakyn, 6-7 *Sc.* scha(i)kin, 6 *Sc.* shaikne, shacken, shakken, 5- shaken. β. 5 schacked, 6-7 shak'd, shakt, 6 shakte, 7 shak't, 9 *dial.* shacked, shakked, shak't, 6- shaked. γ. (6 shooken), 7 shooke, 9 *dial.* shock, shooken, shookt, shu(c)k, -en, *Sc.* sheuken, shooken, 7- shook. [OE. *scacan* str. vb. (*scóc, scacen*) corresponds to OS. *skakan* to depart (once only, in pa. t. *skôk*), mod.Fris. dialects (Sylt) *skaake*, (Föhr) *skaaki* to push, displace, LG. *schacken* to shake, ON. *skaka* (*skók, skekinn*) to shake (Sw. *skaka*):—OTeut. **skakan*. (Not found in Goth. or in HG.; the OHG. gloss '*untschachondes*, fluctivagi' seems to prove the existence of a derivative vb. **scachôn* to wander.) Outside Teut. the only probable cognate is Skr. *khaj* to agitate, churn (*khaja, khajā* a churn).]

†**I. 1.** *intr.* A poetical word for: To go, pass, move, journey; to flee, depart. Said of persons and things, and both in physical and non-physical senses. Also with *away, forth, down. Obs.*

It is not clear that the notion of rapidity of movement, which may be found in some of the examples, is other than merely contextual.

*Beowulf* 1803 (Gr.) þa com beorht leoma scacan ofer scadu. *Ibid.* 3118 þonne stræla storm..scoc ofer scildweall. *a* **1000** *Andreas* 1594 (Gr.) [Hi] ȝewiton mid þy wæȝe in forwyrd sceacan under eorþan grund. *a* **1122** *O.E. Chron.* (Laud MS.) an. 992, Ða sceoc he on niht fram þære fyrde him sylfum to mycclum bismore. *a* **1220** *Bestiary* 264 Ðe mire..suneð it and sakeð forð, so it same were. *Ibid.* 660. *a* **1300** *Childhood Jesus* 1387 in Horstm. *Altengl. Leg.* (1875) 46 þo Josep was fram him i-schake. *a* **1300** *Cursor M.* 21228 Quider-ward sum-euer he scok. *c* **1330** R. BRUNNE *Chron. Wace* (Rolls) 7084 Out of his abite he hym schok. **1338** —— *Chron.* (1810) 217 Symoun did doun schake [to the king's side]. *Ibid.* 323 With þam away þei schoke. *c* **1380** *Sir Ferumb.* 928 Duke Rolant saw hymen awayward schake. *c* **1400** *Sege Jerus.* 18/315 (E.E.T.S.) Clerkes & comens of contrees aboute, Wer schacked to þat cite. *c* **1450** LOVELICH *Merlin* 2744 Grete diches we scholen here make, wherthorwgh this water schal forth Schake. *c* **1450** —— *Holy Grail* xiv. 282 And whanne Of his Swowneng tho he Awook, Anon there Into A Sadel he Schook. ? *c* **1475** *Hunt. Hare* 66 To the town the husbond wentt, As fast as he myght schake. **15..** *Wedding of Syr Gawene* 741 in *Syr Gawayne* (Bannatyne Club) 298 Syr Gawen rose, and in his hand he toke His fayr lady, and to the dore he shoke.

**II.** To vibrate irregularly, tremble.

**2. a.** Of things having more or less freedom of movement: To move irregularly and quickly to and fro, up and down, or from side to side; to quiver, quake, vibrate, waver.

*c* **950** *Lindisf. Gosp.* Matt. xi. 7 Huæt eada ȝe in uoestern ȝesea ȝerd from uinde sceæcende. *c* **1386** CHAUCER *Merch. T.* 605 The slakke skyn aboute his nekke shaketh. *c* **1440** *Promp. Parv.* 443/2 Schakyn or qwakyn.., *tremo*. Schakyn or waveryn, *vacillo*. **1575** GASCOIGNE *Kenelworth* II. v. Wks. 1910 II. 127 Her Majestie came by a close Arbor,..and whiles Silvanus pointed to the same, the principall bush shaked. **1684** R. WALLER *Ess. Nat. Exper.* 62 Her Wings.. upon the Ingress of the air shoke very much. **1780** COWPER *Progr. Err.* 129 The full concerto swells upon your ear; All elbows shake. **1800** WORDSW. *Pet Lamb* 10 His tail with pleasure shook. **1847** TENNYSON *Princess* IV. 3 The long light shakes across the lakes. **1860** LONGF. *Wayside Inn, K. Olaf* II. xiv, While the rifted Streamers o'er him shook and shifted. **1872** CALVERLEY *Fly Leaves* (1884) 65 The mighty pine-forests which shake In the wind.

**b.** *Naut.* Of a sail: To shiver, vibrate, flutter.

**1769** FALCONER *Dict. Marine* (1780), *Shivering*, the state of a sail when it shakes or flutters in the wind. **1846** CODRINGTON in Nicolas *Disp. Nelson* VII. 154 *note*, She kept her starboard and lee studding-sails set and shaking. **1867** SMYTH *Sailor's Word-bk.* s.v., To shake in the wind.

†**c.** Of a person or animal: To throw oneself or one's limbs about. *Obs.*

**1538** ELYOT *Dict.*, *Succusso*, to shake as a horse doth whan he trotteth. **1611** COTGR., *Iacter*,..to swing, tosse, tumble, or shake vp and downe.

**3. a.** Of things normally stable or still: To vibrate irregularly, tremble, either as a whole or in its parts, as the result of impact or disturbance of equilibrium. Hence, to totter, lose stability, become weakened.

**1297** R. GLOUC. (Rolls) 4241 Al þe hul mid þe vallinge ssoc. *a* **1300** *Cursor M.* 19211 And in þat erth-din þar scok, þe haligast eft-sith þai tok. *c* **1489** CAXTON *Sonnes of Aymon* ix. 217 The trompettes..sowned soo sore that the chambre where as he laye shoke of it. **1523** SKELTON *Garl. Laurel* 1508 The starry heuyn, me thought, shoke with the showte.

a 1530 J. HEYWOOD *Play of Love* (1534) Biv, And therwithall I fet a sygh such one As made the forme shake which we both sat on. 1605 *1st Pt. Jeronimo* III. i. 24 Now, Spaine, sit firme; ile make thy towers shake. 1634 MILTON *Comus* 797. 1785 BURNS *Jolly Beggars*, He ended; and the kebars sheuk Aboon the chorus roar. 1819 SCOTT *Ivanhoe* xxix, The postern gate shakes,..it crashes—it is splintered by his blows. 1842 BARHAM *Ingol. Leg.* Ser. II. *Sir Rupert*, From base to turret the castle shook. 1859 TENNYSON *Elaine* 459 So..that a man far-off might well perceive..The hard earth shake. 1864 —— *Voyage* ii, We felt the good ship shake and reel.

**b.** *fig.* Of a person: To lose firmness. ? *Obs.*

1340 *Ayenb.* 116 Make oure herten ueste and stedeuest þet hi ne ssake uor none uondynge þet to hare comþ.

**c.** Of a band of persons: To become unsteady, to reel, give way.

1375 BARBOUR *Bruce* II. 380 And in the stour sa hardyly He ruschyt, that all the semble schuk. a 1586 SIDNEY *Arcadia* I. (Sommer) 26b, The great bodie of them beginning to shake, and stagger. 1849 MACAULAY *Hist. Eng.* v. I. 611 The pikes of the rebel battalions began to shake; the ranks broke.

**4. a.** Of a person, his body, limbs, etc.: To quake or tremble with physical infirmity or disease; to quiver with emotion; to shiver with cold, to quake with fear.

***to shake in one's shoes***: to tremble with fear.

[a 1100 *Aldh. Gl.* in Napier *O.E. Glosses* i. 4160 *Exhorruit*, ofscoc.] a 1300 *Cursor M.* 3565 Quen þat sua bicums ald ..þe heued biginnes for to scak. 1398 TREVISA *Barth. De P.R.* XVII. clxxxv. (1495) 726 The dronklew mannys honde tremblyth and shakyth. c 1489 CAXTON *Sonnes of Aymon* vii. 161 He shoke all for angre. *Ibid.* xxiv. 528 He shoke all for fere. 1581 A. HALL *Iliad* x. 183 He stoode so tremblingly, That one full wel might heare his teeth togither so to shake. 1611 SHAKS. *Wint. T.* IV. iv. 641 Why shak'st thou so? Feare not (man). 1615 R. COCKS *Diary* (Hakl. Soc.) I. 31 And about midnight..my frend came home againe, shaking every joint of hym. 1735 POPE *Donne Sat.* iv. 279, I sweat, I fly, And shake all o'er, like a discover'd spy. 1781 COWPER *Conversat.* 333 He shakes with cold. 1818 COBBETT *Polit. Reg.* XXXIII. 497 This is quite enough to make Corruption and all her tribe shake in their shoes. 1848 THACKERAY *Van. Fair* lviii, Was that she? He began to shake at the mere possibility. 1873 *Punch* 15 Mar. 107/2 It had set the whole Liberal party 'shaking in its shoes'. 1909 MRS. H. WARD *Daphne* iv. 90 Her small frame shook with weeping.

**b.** To be convulsed with laughter. Cf. 11 c.

1728 POPE *Dunc.* I. 22 Whether thou choose Cervantes' serious air, Or laugh and shake in Rab'lais' easy chair. 1748 JOHNSON *Van. Hum. Wishes* 61 How wouldst thou [Democritus] shake at Britain's modish tribe. 1905 F. YOUNG *Sands of Pleasure* II. ii, If the whole of France is shaking with the antics of Venus, the whole heavens are shaking with laughter.

**III.** To cause to vibrate, agitate.

**5. a.** *trans.* To brandish or flourish threateningly (a weapon or something used as a weapon); †to wield. Also, to flourish, wave (something) in ostentation or triumph.

c 1000 *MS. Bodl.* 577 lf. 63b, Macheram stricto mucrone uibrabat, *gloss* sceoc. c 1205 LAY. 26481 Heo scæken on heore honden speren swiðe stronge. c 1320 *Sir Tristr.* 885 Schaftes þai gun schake. 1470–85 MALORY *Arthur* VIII. xxxi. 321 He shoke the swerd to the kynge. 1570–6 LAMBARDE *Peramb. Kent* (1576) 185 A picture of woode, that wulde shake a speare, and rolle the eyes. 1601 SHAKS. *All's Well* II. v. 96 Go thou toward home, where I wil neuer come, Whilst I can shake my sword. 1667 MILTON *P.L.* XI. 489 And over them triumphant Death his Dart Shook, but delaid to strike. 1712 STEELE *Spect.* No. 382 ¶1 The Prince.. shaked a Cane at the Officer. 1813 SCOTT *Rokeby* I. ii, Conscience..calls her furies forth, to shake The sounding scourge and hissing snake. 1838 DICKENS *O. Twist* xx, 'Take heed, Oliver! take heed!' said the old man, shaking his right hand before him in a warning manner. 1862 W. COLLINS *Basil* III. vi, He has no marriage-certificate to shake over our heads, at any rate. 1896 A. E. HOUSMAN *Shropshire Lad* xlvii, And the people passing by Stop to shake their fists and curse.

**b.** *fig.* Chiefly in phrases. †***to shake boast***: to boast, swagger. †***to shake the feather***: see FEATHER *sb.* 8b. ***more than you can shake a stick at*** (and vars.): more than one can count, a considerable amount or number (*colloq.*, orig. and chiefly *U.S.*).

c 1380 *Sir Ferumb.* 3645 After hym folwede & schoke bost xxx[ti] þowsant on an host. 1509 BARCLAY *Shyp of Folys* (1570) 45 Thou shakest boast [*jactas*] oft of her foly in vayne. 1818 *Lancaster* (Pa.) *Jrnl.* 5 Aug. 3/1 We have in Lancaster as many Taverns as you can shake a stick at. 1843 R. CARLTON *New Purchase* I. xii. 86 Our queen snake was.. retiring, attended by more of her subjects than we even dared to shake a stick at. 1883 R. W. DIXON *Mano* I. viii. 21 A reckless star Seemed shaking over him malific powers. 1904 J. C. LINCOLN *Cap'n Eri* iv. 56 There's more Snows in Nantucket than you can shake a stick at. 1939 L. M. MONTGOMERY *Anne of Ingleside* xxi. 137, I had more beaus than you could shake a stick at. 1960 'E. MCBAIN' *Give Boys* (1962) iv. 32 We get more damn cancellations than you can shake a stick at. 1982 *Folio* Spring 4 More consuls and dictators hanging from her family tree than a prudent man would shake a bundle of twigs at.

**6. a.** To move to and fro irregularly or tremulously, agitate (some part of the body); (of an animal) to 'wag' (its tail) (? *obs.*); (of a bird) to flap, flutter (its wings) esp. as preparing to fly. Also said of a thing personified. Also with *down*, *wide*.

[a 1000 *Phœnix* 144 þonne..he..þriwa ascæceþ feþre flyht-hwate.] 1388 WYCLIF *Jer.* li. 38 Thei schulen schake lockis, as the whelpis of liouns. a 1400–50 *Wars Alex.* 5018 þan schogs hire þe son-tree & schoke hire schire leues. 1486 *Bk. St. Albans* c viij b, She..drawith booth her wyngys ouer the myddys of her boeke..and softely shakyth them. 1590 SPENSER *F.Q.* II. iv. 15 [Furor] Shakt his long lockes..And bit his tawny beard to shew his raging ire. 1600 FAIRFAX *Tasso* I. xiv, On Libanon at first his foote he set, And shooke his wings with roarie maydewes wet. 1667 MILTON *P.L.* VII. 66 The Tawnie Lion..Rampant shakes his Brinded main. a 1700 EVELYN *Diary* 19 Sept. 1658, Rattle-snakes..swiftly vibrating and shaking their tailes. 1797 HT. LEE *Canterb. T.*, *Frenchm. T.* (1799) I. 192 Dorsain shook his grey locks— 'That's as much as to say our dancing days are past!' added Antoine, observing it. 1818 SCOTT *Rob Roy* v, Shaking down a profusion of sable ringlets. 1819 SHELLEY *Cyclops* 66 Shaking wide thy yellow hair. 1837 CARLYLE *Fr. Rev.* I. IV. iv, He steps proudly along,..and shakes his black *chevelure*, or lion's-mane. 1852 THACKERAY *Esmond* II. i, His cruel goddess had shaken her wings and fled. 1909 J. G. FRAZER *Psyche's Task* iv. 38 The sun-scorched stocks of the fruitless Indian corn shook their rustling leaves in the wind.

**b.** ***to shake one's head***: to turn the head slightly to one side and the other in sorrow or scorn, or to express disapproval, dissent or doubt.

a 1300 *Cursor M.* 24503 On him mi hefd i scock, and said, 'Vngretli, leif sun, er þou graid!' c 1320 *Seuyn Sag.* (W.) 1069 '*Par fai*, dame', he saide, 'no!' And schok his heved vpon the quen. c 1385 CHAUCER *L.G.W.* 2344 And pitously he wep & shok his hed. c 1400 *Rom. Rose* 3164 So cherlishly his heed he shook. 1551 ROBINSON tr. *More's Utopia* I. (1895) 71 And as he was thus saying, he shaked his heade, and made a wrie mouth. 1607 SHAKS. *Timon* IV. ii. 25 Let's shake our heads, and say..We haue seene better dayes. 1697 DRYDEN *Virg. Georg.* III. 819 The Learned Leaches in Despair depart: And shake their Heads, desponding of their Art. 1743 BULKELEY & CUMMINS *Voy. S. Seas* 10 The Captain shook his Head, and said, Carpenter! that is not the Reason. 1808 COBBETT *Pol. Reg.* XIII. 161 It is he who now nods *yes*, or shakes *no*, while the ministers are speaking. 1865 MRS. GASKELL *Wives & Dau.* I. xi. 134 'No, I shan't!' said Molly, shaking her head. 1897 MAX PEMBERTON *Queen of Jesters* iv. 176 The Corsican shook his head, implying that he doubted.

**c.** ***to shake one's ears***: lit. of an animal, hence *fig.* of a person likened to an animal, (*a*) to wake up, bestir oneself; (*b*) to show indifference or dislike, pleasure in freedom, mirth, etc.

1580 LYLY *Euphues* Wks. 1902 II. 35 Euphues..began to shake his eares, and was soone apparailed. 1583 GOLDING *Calvin on Deut.* i. 34–40 When Gods threatenings are vttered vnto vs, a great many of vs do but shake our eares at them. *Ibid.* viii. 1–4. 1592 SHAKS. *Ven. & Ad.* 924 [Hounds] Shaking their scratch'd ears, bleeding as they go. 1601 —— *Jul. C.* IV. i. 26 Then take we downe his Load, And turne him off (Like to the empty Asse) to shake his eares, And graze in Commons. 1601 —— *Twel. N.* II. iii. 134. 1645 G. DANIEL *Poems* Wks. 1878 II. 42 Thriftie villagers Have long since shak'd their Ears. 1654 GAYTON *Pleas. Notes* IV. viii. 220 The Mountebanck shak'd his ears, (as if he drank base wine). 1747 H. WALPOLE *Let. to H. S. Conway* 8 June, How merry my ghost will be, and shake its ears to hear itself quoted as a person of consummate prudence!

**d.** To wave (the hand) in farewell.

1569 W. HUBBARD *Ceyx & Alcyone* Av, She sawe him becking with his hand: And she likewise her hands did shake [Ovid: *concussaque manu dantem sibi signa maritum prima videt, redditque notas*]. a 1700 DRYDEN *Ceyx & Alcyone* 77 [She] first her Husband on the Poop espies Shaking his Hand..; She took the Sign; and shook her Hand again. 1848 THACKERAY *Van. Fair* xxix, Amelia..acknowledged her presence..by kissing and shaking her fingers playfully in the direction of the vehicle.

**e.** ***to shake one's elbow***: to gamble with dice.

1623 WEBSTER *Devil's Law Case* II. i, This comes of your ..Shaking your elbow at the Taule-boord. 1705, 1826 [see ELBOW 4e]. 1721 AMHERST *Terræ Fil.* No. 10. 47 A famous gamester..was elected Margaret-professor of divinity: so great, it seems, is the analogy between dusting of cushions, and shaking of elbows.

**f.** ***to shake a foot***, ***hoof*** (*U.S.*), ***leg*** (see LEG *sb.* 2b; also, to hurry), ***toe***, ***one's bones***, ***feet***, ***heels***, ***hough*** (Sc.), ***shanks***; also ***to shake it*** = to dance (*obs.* exc. *U.S. Blacks'*); also, ***to shake that thing***.

1661 *Thrac. Wonder* II. C4, Son, set down thy Hook, and shake it lustily. 1667 DRYDEN *Tempest* IV. iii, Now wou'd I lay greatness aside, and shake my heels, if I had but Musick. 1828 J. RUDDIMAN *Tales & Sk.* 62 When he shakes his bowed houghs to the sound o' Rab Murray's creaking catgut. 1830 BUCKSTONE *Wreck Ashore* II. i, Dance with? with me, to be sure; though I hav'n't shaken a toe these twenty years. 1842 LOVER *Handy Andy* xvii, They hav'nt a lilt to shake their bones to. 1848 *Buffalo Gals* (song) 3, I ax'd her would she hab a dance... I taught dat I might get a chance, To shake a foot wid her. 1850 THACKERAY *Mr. Malony's Acc. Ball* x, in *Punch* Aug. XIX. 53 And I'd like to hear the pipers blow, And shake a fut with Fanny there! 1884 D. GRANT *Lays & Leg. North* 99 Resolved to shak' their heels,..In jigs and Highland reels. 1904 *N.Y. World Mag.* 1 May 6/3 Shake a leg..meaning to 'hurry up'. 1927 *Jrnl. Abnormal & Social Psychol.* XXII. 16 'Shake it', 'shake that thing', etc. Such expressions are very frequent in the blues. Ostensibly they refer to dancing, but they are really Negro vulgar expressions relating to coitus. 1927 S. LEWIS *Elmer Gantry* xxv. 333 Come on, Reverend. I bet you can shake a hoof as good as anybody! The wife says she's gotta dance with you! 1935 F. M. DAVIS *Black Man's Verse* 34 Strut it in Harlem, let Fifth Avenue shake it slow Plink plank plink a plink. 1952 WODEHOUSE *Barmy in Wonderland* viii. 82 'Clean this place up.'.. 'Yes, sir.' 'And shake a leg.' 1967 M. C. MELNICK in A. Dundes *Mother Wit* (1973) 273/1 If you shake it, I'll buy you a diamond ring.

†*transf.* 1595 A. B. *Noblen. Asse* D3, Whereupon, he caused him with the rest, to be hanged by the neckes, and (as the common prouerbe is) sent them to shake their heeles against the winde. 1611 CHAPMAN *May-Day* I. 10 Let her shake her heeles..I would make her shake her heeles too, afore I would shake mine thus.

**g.** *refl.* Of a person or animal: To give a shake to his or its body (e.g. in order to throw off wet, snow, dust, etc., or to remove the stiffness caused by repose); *fig.* to bestir oneself, arouse oneself to activity. Also with complement, ***to shake oneself free***, ***loose***, ***awake***, ***sober***, and with const. *from*.

1390 GOWER *Conf.* III. 75 Into an Egle he gan transforme after that himself he schok. c 1489 CAXTON *Sonnes of Aymon* xxiv. 497 He [Bayard] shaked hymselfe for to make falle the water from hym. 1535 COVERDALE *Isa.* lii. 2 Shake the [1611 shake thy selfe] from the dust, arise & stonde vp, o Ierusalem. 1759 ROBERTSON *Hist. Scot.* v. Wks. 1851 II. 55 The regent saw the danger of allowing the duke to shake himself loose, in this manner, from his engagements. 1845 D. JERROLD *St. Giles* i, 'What's the matter?' asked the watchman..surlily shaking himself. 1859 FARRAR *Jul. Home* xvii. 222 A large and fierce mastiff also shook himself from sleep. 1861 GEO. ELIOT *Silas M.* iii, Just shake yourself sober and listen, will you? 1888 STOKES *Celtic Ch.* 153 The Roman Church determined at last to shake itself free from this thraldom. 1899 B. MARIE DIX *Hugh Gwyeth* xvi. 261 "Twill be sunrise soon', Hugh said, and shook himself awake.

**h.** *intr.* for *refl.*

1893 SIR R. BALL *Story of Sun* 255 They shake clear from one surrounding group merely to ally themselves with another.

**7. a.** *trans.* To cause to move irregularly to and fro by external force; to make to flutter or quiver; to agitate. *Naut.* To cause (a sail) to flutter in the wind. Also with adv., as *about*, *abroad*.

a 1000 *Cædmon's Exod.* 176 (Gr.) Guðweard gumena.. wælhlencan sceoc. c 1386 CHAUCER *Prol.* 406 With many a tempest hadde his berd been shake. 14.. *Beryn* 1762 Who so shoke a rynge, Ther no man is within, þe rynging to answere. 1523–34 FITZHERB. *Husb.* §25 Whan thy medowes be mowed,..if the grasse be very thycke, it wolde be shaken with handes, or with a shorte pykforke. 1534 TINDALE *Matt.* xi. 7 Went ye out to se a rede shaken with the wynde? c 1570 *Buggbears* I. ii. 134 Ther they shaked Iron chaynes. 1648 T. HILL *Strength Saints* 5 It is clean water indeed, that when the glasse is shaked, there is no filth appeares. 1770 LANGHORNE *Plutarch*, *Demetrius* (Rtldg.) 615/2 Bocchoris.. ordered the man to tell the gold that she demanded into a bason, and shake it about before her, that she might enjoy the sight of it. 1797 COLMAN *Br. Grins*, *Night-gown & Slippers* (1804) 30 When taken, To be well shaken. 1813 SHELLEY *Q. Mab* I. 205 The Queen Shaking the beamy reins Bade them [the coursers of the air] pursue their way. 1825 SCOTT *Betrothed* xxvii, Genvil slowly unrolled the pennon —then shook it abroad. 1842 TENNYSON *Locksley Hall* 32 The glass of Time..Every moment, lightly shaken, ran itself in golden sands. 1851 MRS. BROWNING *Casa Guidi Wind.* II. 175 At which we shook the sword within the sheath Like heroes. c 1860 H. STUART *Seaman's Catech.* 41 Keeping the ship close to the wind without shaking the sails.

*slang.* 1788 GROSE *Dict. Vulgar T.* (ed. 2), To shake a cloth in the wind; to be hanged in chains.

**b.** With additional notion of a purpose of dislodging or discharging something adhering or contained.

c 1386 CHAUCER *Clerk's T.* 922 She gan the hous to dighte, ..Preyynge the chambreres..To hasten hem, and faste swepe and shake. 1388 WYCLIF *2 Esdras* [*Neh.*] v. 13 Y schook [1382 shakide out] my bosum, and Y seide, So God schake awei [1382 shake out] ech man, that fillith not this word. 1530 PALSGR. 700/1 Shake the table clothe or you laye it on agayne. 1595 SHAKS. *John* III. iii. 7 And ere our comming see thou shake the bags Of hoording Abbots. 1697 DRYDEN *Virg. Georg.* I. 238 You may..shake for Food the long-abandon'd Oak. 1784 COWPER *Task* IV. 499 Society, grown weary of the load, Shakes her encumber'd lap. 1847 *Act 10 & 11 Vict.* c. 89 §28 Every Person who beats or shakes any Carpet, Rug, or Mat.

**8. a.** To grasp or seize and move (a person) roughly to and fro; esp. (*a*) as a punishment or in a struggle; also in phr. ***to shake by the beard*** or ***ears***.

***to shake a fall*** (Wrestling): see FALL *sb.*[1] 13.

a 1300 *Cursor M.* 7509 And i..scok þam [*sc.* a bear and a lion] by þe berdes sua. c 1330 R. BRUNNE *Chron. Wace* (Rolls) 1823 [The wrestlers'] brestes to-gyder met;..Ilk oþer pulled, ilk oþer schok. 1471 CAXTON *Recuyell* (Sommer) 253 And so they shoke and lugged eche other, but finably hercules cast theseus. 1565 J. PHILLIPS *Patient Grissell* 541 (Malone Soc.), Jacke sauce I shake you by the eares. 1611 BIBLE *Job* xvi. 12 He hath also taken me by my necke, and shaken me to pieces. 1665 in *Extr. St. Papers rel. Friends* Ser. III. (1912) 237 P. J...gript him and shakt him and tould him tythes should quickly be putt downe. 1795 BURNS *To Collector Mitchell* Postscr., Grim loon! he [Death] got me by the fecket, And sair me sheuk. 1838 DICKENS *O. Twist* vi, Oliver..shook him, in the violence of his rage, till his teeth chattered in his head. 1856 MISS YONGE *Daisy Chain* II. vi. 390 Dr. May stepped towards her, almost as if he could have shaken her.

(*b*) for the purpose of arousing him. Also *transf.* of an inanimate agency: To rouse or startle (a person *from* sleep).

1530 PALSGR. 706/1, I shake one that is aslepe tho [*sic*] wake him, *je sace*. 1610 SHAKS. *Temp.* II. i. 319, I heard a humming,..which did awake me: I shak'd you Sir, and cride. 1728–46 THOMSON *Spring* 1024 Sudden he starts, Shook from his tender trance. 1823 SCOTT *Quentin D.* xxiv, Though he shake thee something roughly by the shoulders to awake thee. 1872 J. G. HOLLAND *Marble Prophecy* 84 Silence thy strong pulse repeating Wakes me—shakes me —from my rest.

**b.** Of an animal: To worry (its antagonist or prey).

1565 COOPER *Thesaurus* s.v. *Excutio*, A lamme shaken in pieces. 1589 L. WRIGHT *Hunt. Antichrist* 11 John Wicklif an eger bloudhound..so hunted and shaked that venemous Dragon in his time, as the woundes he gave him, coulde neuer yet be cured. 1611 COTGR., *Goussepiller*, to shake, or tug, as a Dog doth a Cat, &c. 1807 *Med. Jrnl.* XVII. 272 A mad dog..met two men, both of whom he shook and bit. 1824 Mactaggart *Gallovid. Encycl.*, *Shack*, a word used in encouraging a curr-dog to worry a fox; 'shack him!' is the cry.

**c.** To rouse up (an animal) to activity; to 'shake up' a horse (see 21 c), also *absol.*

1853 Whyte Melville *Digby Grand* xi, This is the time to shake to the front, and cut down three of the best riders England can produce. 1904 *Eng. Dial. Dict.* s.v. *Shake* 5 A farmer buying a horse said, 'Shack him over the stones, let's see if he's got a thistle in 'is toe.'

**9.** To clasp and move to and fro (another person's hand) as a customary salutation or an expression of friendly feeling. **a.** ***to shake hands*** (said of two persons mutually saluting thus); also (of one person) ***to shake hands with*** (another):

(*a*) as a greeting, sign of friendship or goodwill, confirmation of a promise, bargain, etc.; (of combatants) as a sign of the absence of ill-feeling. Also *fig.*, *spec.* in phr. ***to shake hands with an old friend, the wife's best friend*** (colloq.), of men: to urinate.

1535 Coverdale *2 Macc.* xii. 12 Whervpon they shoke hondes [Gr. λαβόντες δεξιάς], and so they departed to their tentes. 1540 Palsgr. *Acolastus* ii. iii. L ij b, That they maye shake handes with me. 1579 Gosson *Sch. Abuse* (Arb.) 46 But bothe [combatants] be contented and shake handes. 1657 R. Ligon *Barbadoes* (1673) 52 And coming near together, they [*sc.* wrestlers] shake hands, and embrace one another with a cheerful look. 1719 De Foe *Crusoe* ii. (Globe) 357 They shook Hands, and swore to one another that they would be reveng'd. 1826 Coleridge *Six Months W. Ind.* 287, I would rather shake hands with a highwayman than with a gentleman who [etc.]. 1827 Scott *Surg. Dau.* iv, Let me see you shake hands, and let us have no more of this nonsense. 1865 Dickens *Mut. Fr.* i. xv, 'Sit down, sir', said Mr. Boffin, shaking hands with him. 1908 R. Bagot *A. Cuthbert* v. 48 Now we have shaken hands on the bargain. *fig.* 1565 W. Allen *Def. Cath. Ch. Doctr.* Pref. 20, I feare me they haue indented with deathe, and shaked handes withe helle. 1593 Shaks. *3 Hen. VI*, i. iv. 102. 1659 D. Pell *Impr. Sea* 588 *note*, Resolve, that the Orient shall sooner shake hands with the West. 1797 T. Holcroft tr. *Stolberg's Trav.* II. lx. (ed. 2) 367 Thus do..harvest and the..spring shake hands together. 1809 Malkin *Gil Blas* x. x. (Rtldg.) 372 Here it was..that I first shook hands with sensuality. 1829 Lytton *Devereux* i. iii. 12 Application and I, having once shaken hands, became very good acquaintance. 1874 Blackie *Self-Culture* 21 That famous son of Philip of Macedon, who with his conquering hosts caused the language of Socrates and Plato to shake hands with the sacred dialect [etc.]. 1952 M. Tripp *Faith is Windsock* iii. 44 'I'm going out for a crafty smoke; anyone coming?' 'Sure, I'll come... I want to shake hands with an old friend, anyway.' 1965 *Times Lit. Suppl.* 16 Sept. 812/2 Expressive Australianisms to describe this prosaic function;..pointing Percy at the porcelain, shaking hands with the wife's best friend, [etc.].

(*b*) as a farewell.

1546 J. Heywood *Prov.* (1867) 37 We shoke handes, and parted. 1602 Shaks. *Ham.* i. v. 128. 1826 Coleridge *Six Months W. Ind.* 74 Having shaken hands with kind Antonio ..we mounted our horses. 1850 Tennyson *In Mem.* xl. 29 But thou and I have shaken hands, Till growing winters lay me low.

*fig.* 1577–87 Harrison *England* ii. xi. 186/2 in *Holinshed*, It is the custome of the more idle sort hauing once serued, ..to shake hand with labour, for euer. 1674 S. Vincent *Yng. Gallants Acad.* 99 His word and his meaning are quadrate, and never shake hands and part. 1742 Wesley *Wks.* (1872) I. 386, I have long since shook hands with the world. 1867 Augusta Wilson *Vashti* xxxii, A lonely woman, who has shaken hands with every earthly hope.

**b.** ***to shake*** (a person's) ***hand, to shake*** (a person) ***by the hand*** = to shake hands with.

1540 Palsgr. *Acolastus* ii. iii. L ij b, That they maye.. shake me by the fyste. *a*1566 R. Edwards *Damon & Pithias* (1908) F j, Let vs agree like friends, and shake eche other by the fist. 1567 *Satir. Poems Reform.* iii. 231 With that he.. shuik our handis twa. 1606 Shaks. *Ant. & Cl.* ii. vi. 75 Let me shake thy hand, I neuer hated thee. 1712 Addison *Spect.* No. 329 ¶ 15 He shook him by the Hand at parting. 1865 Dickens *Mut. Fr.* i. v, He shook Silas earnestly by the hand. 1886 Ruskin *Præterita* I. 357 The Dean gave me his first and second fingers to shake at our parting.

**c.** *absol.* ***to shake*** = to shake hands. Now chiefly *U.S.*

[1601 Shaks. *Jul. C.* iii. i. 185 Let each man render me his bloody hand. First Marcus Brutus will I shake with you.] 1891 J. Newman *Scamping Tricks* vii. 59 Shake. That's right. 1903 F. Norris *Deal in Wheat* iv, 'Sold! Sold!' shouted Hornung... Billy, shake on it. 1911 M. Beerbohm *Zuleika Dobson* xv. 228 'Are you going to die to-day, or not?' 'As a matter of fact, I am, but—' 'Shake!'.. Oover wrung the Duke's hand. 1927 *Punch* 20 Apr. 444/3 'Long may it flourish!' said Roger, shaking vigorously. 1938 M. K. Rawlings *Yearling* vii. 61 'You got to promise..not to beat the very puddin' outen me after you've hunted him.' 'Shake.' A hairy paw closed over Penny's hand. 1966 'J. Hackston' *Father clears Out* 199 Tom..said, almost benignly, 'Now shake!' and they shook,..in the true spirit of eternal friendship. 1972 J. Gores *Dead Skip* viii. 55 He stood up, stuck out his hand... They shook.

**10. a.** To put into a quaking, quivering, or vibrating motion (a thing normally firm or fixed); to cause (a structure) to totter; hence, to impair the stability of, to weaken; occas. †to loosen (something rooted). ***to shake down***: to cause to totter and fall.

*c*1050 *Byrhtferth's Handboc* in *Anglia* VIII. 320 Þe þænne swyðlice þa heannyssa þæs roderes sceceð mid his þodenum. *a*1300 *Cursor M.* 7259 Þe post þat al þat huse vpbare Wit bath his handes he it scok. *c*1400 Maundev. (Roxb.) v. 17 He tuke þe post in his armes and schoke doune all þe hous apon þam. 1569 Stocker tr. *Diod. Sic.* iii. xi. 123 And with his great artillary [he] sore battered and shaked the Walles. 1582 N. Lichefield tr. *Castanheda's Conq. E. Ind.* i. lxxi. 146 With yᵉ other shot past, they had somwhat shaken their yron works. 1610 *Gaultier's Rodomont.* E 2, A Bullet..fel into my mouth, shook two of my formost teeth, without iniury or offence vnto mee. 1643 Baker *Chron., Hen. VI*, 64 The Regent..by secret mining and violent Batteries so shook the Walls, that they agreed to yeild it up. 1690 Boyle *Ess. Effects of Motion* iii. 17 The tremulous motion of the Air ..has been able sensibly to shake..the glass-windows of houses. 1715 Pope *Iliad* xv. 119 Jove..Shakes all the thrones of heaven. 1812 Byron *Ch. Har.* ii. lxxxviii, Age shakes Athena's tower, but spares gray Marathon. 1850 Tennyson *In Mem.* xc. 19 Not less the yet-loved sire would ..shake The pillars of domestic peace. 1860 Tyndall *Glac.* i. ix. 63 A peal like that of thunder shook the air. 1869 Tozer *Highl. Turkey* I. 58 Parts of two monasteries had been shaken down by earthquakes.

**b.** *fig.* (*a*) with object a person (in faith, resolution, etc.) or his faith, purpose, testimony, etc.

*c*1375 *Sc. Leg. Saints* xxxi. (*Eugenia*) 159 He..fel in disputacion with ane erretike, þat richt wise wes in clergy at dewyse, þat sa wele schoke þe abbot, til [etc.]. 1605 Shaks. *Macb.* i. v. 47 That no compunctious visitings of Nature Shake my fell purpose. 1625 Donne *Serm.* 3 Apr. 6 The righteous is bolde as a Lyon, not easily shaked. 1646 in *12th Rep. Hist. MSS. Comm.* App. ix. 18 The confidence her Majesty had formerly in mee was ever after much shaken. *a*1729 J. Rogers *Twelve Serm.* viii. (1730) 241 Our Religion, which no Arguments can shake. 1825 Scott *Talism.* xxiii, These attentions were intended to shake him in his religious profession. 1838 T. Mitchell *Clouds of Aristoph.* 798 *note*, It may almost be thought impertinent to endeavour to shake their testimony. 1859 Geo. Eliot *Adam Bede* xl, Adam had not been shaken in his belief that Hetty was innocent. 1884 W. C. Smith *Kildrostan* 48 Let nothing shake your trust in her.

(*b*) with object (the health or strength of) a person, his body or mind.

1588 Shaks. *Tit. A.* iv. iii. 17 It comes from old Andronicus, Shaken with sorrowes in vngratefull Rome. 1651 R. Wittie tr. *J. Primrose's Pop. Err. Physic* ii. ix. 109 The body is shaked, and weakened by the violence of diseases. 1783 Anna Seward *Lett.* (1811) II. 75 Shook as his frame has been, his mind has lost, as yet, none of its energy. 1818 Scott *Br. Lamm.* xxx, Her health also began to be shaken. 1846 *Edin. Rev.* LXXXIV. 176 If your nerves are apt to be shaken by the click of a knife in the dark passage of a hostelry. 1848 Thackeray *Van. Fair* xxxiv, Too much shaken in mind and body to compose a letter.

(*c*) with object a person, institution, etc., with regard to his or its stability of position.

1545 *Primer of Hen. VIII* (1546) D diij b, We haue now suffered much punishment, being..shaken with so many fluddes. 1560 Daus tr. *Sleidane's Comm.* 48 It is onely the preaching of Gods word, that shaketh theyr [*sc.* the Papists'] power and dignitie. 1587 Golding *De Mornay* Pref. 10 Now God vouchsafe..to confute them which go about to shake downe his doctrine. 1625 Donne *Serm.* 3 Apr. 17 That great Storme, that shaked the State, and the Church. 1660 Dryden *Astræa Redux* 104 Her blows not shook but riveted his Throne. *a*1715 Burnet *Own Time* iii. (1724) I. 457 A great part of the property of the Nation..was shaken by the prospect. 1764 Goldsm. *Hist. Eng.* (1772) II. 17 Such a conduct would have shook him on the throne. 1821 Scott *Kenilw.* xvii, Such reflections on government..as tend to..shake the solid foundations of civil society. 1871 Freeman *Norm. Conq.* (1876) IV. xviii. 224 An attempt was made to shake the dominion which he had established over Wessex. 1879 B. Taylor *Germ. Lit.* 145 The Thirty Years' War..hardly shook a single society out of existence. 1883 R. W. Dixon *Mano* i. v. 14 With wrongs would they redub the wrongs they felt, Shake down the state, and furiously be freed.

**11. a.** Of physical infirmity, emotion, etc.: To cause (a person, his frame, etc.) to quiver or tremble; to agitate, convulse.

1382 Wyclif *Matt.* viii. 14 He say his wyues moder liggynge, and shakun with feueris. 1390 Gower *Conf.* II. 146 Bot if this Fievere a womman take, Sche schal be wel mor harde schake. 1599 Shaks. *Hen. V*, ii. i. 124 Hee is so shak'd of a burning quotidian Tertian, that it is most lamentable to behold. 1750 Gray *Long Story* 119 A sudden fit of ague shook him. 1797 Ht. Lee *Canterb. T.*, *Frenchm. T.* (1799) I. 287 Extreme emotion..seemed to shake his whole frame. 1842 Tennyson *Locksley Hall* 27 And she turn'd—her bosom shaken with a sudden storm of sighs. 1895 P. Hemingway *Out of Egypt* i. xi. 112 The memory of his loss shook him with sobs.

**b.** To move or stir the feelings of; to disturb, upset. Also, to upset the composure or complacency of (someone) (*colloq.*).

1567 Drant *Horace Ep.* i. x. D viij, Who so was to much rauished..In flow of wealth, his chaunge of flow yea to much shall yshake. 1610 Donne *Pseudo-martyr* 217 Vpon a mistaking, that the euennesse of his Maiesties disposition might be shaked by this insinuation. 1715 Rowe *Lady Jane Grey* i. i, The genius of our isle is shook with sorrow. 1842 Tennyson *Locksley Hall* 166 Enjoyment..in the thoughts that shake mankind. 1848 Thackeray *Van. Fair* xv, She will be shaken when she first hears the news. 1891 Hardy *Tess* xxxvi, The unexpected quality of this confession.. shook him indescribably. 1943 C. H. Ward-Jackson *It's a Piece of Cake* 54 'That'll shake him,' as the transport officer said when he refused to provide a vehicle for the Group Captain without written authority. 1966 *New Yorker* 25 June 52 It shook me some when I looked at the label.

**c.** To cause (a person, his sides) to quiver with laughter or mirth. Also of a person, ***to shake one's sides***, to be convulsed with laughter.

?1593 Drayton *Eglog* vi. Poems (1619) 454 The Man alone, Which once with laughter shook'st the Shepheards Boord. 1736 Ainsworth *Eng.-Lat. Dict.* s.v., She shaked her sides with laughter. 1781 Cowper *Expost.* 548 It shakes the sides of splenetic disdain. 1847 Tennyson *Princess* i. 197 A sight to shake The midriff of despair with laughter. 1859 H. Kingsley *G. Hamlyn* xiv, [To] shake his honest sides with many an old half-forgotten tale of fun.

**d.** *Austral.* and *N.Z. slang.* ***to be shook on***: have an infatuation for. Also, less strongly, to be keen on, to be impressed by, to admire, and const. *after*.

1888 'R. Boldrewood' *Robbery under Arms* II. 46 He was awful shook on Mad; but she wouldn't look at him. *Ibid.* II. 291, I must have a dance; blest if I don't!.. I'm regular shook on the polka. 1907 H. Lawson in *Austral. Short Stories* (1951) 84 The trouble is that I'm so long, and I always seem to get shook after little girls. 1926 K. S. Prichard *Working Bullocks* 301 Didn't know she was so shook on Mark Smith. 1934 L. G. D. Acland in *Press* (Christchurch) 27 Jan. 15/7 *Shook on, to be*, to admire; to be keen on; e.g., 'I'm not s.o. his horse.' 1940 F. Sargeson *Man & his Wife* (1944) 22 Mother wasn't too shook on our doing it at first, but afterwards she didn't mind. 1947 D. M. Davin *Gorse blooms Pale* 78, I wasn't as shook on Phyllis as all that. 1965 M. Shadbolt *Among Cinders* xxii. 209 The bush. Still not too bloody shook on it, are you? 1975 *Sunday Tel.* (Sydney) 29 June 49 I'm not all that shook on cocktail parties myself.

**12. a.** With adv. or phrase: To reduce by shaking (sense 7) to a specified condition. ***to shake down***: to cause to settle or subside by shaking. ***to shake together***: to shake so as to ensure intimate mixture or subsidence into smaller compass.

1382 Wyclif *Luke* vi. 38 A good measure, and wel fillid, and shakun to gidere. 1601 Shaks. *All's Well* iv. iii. 191 [They] dare not shake the snow from off their Cassockes, least they shake themselues to peeces. 1611 Cotgr. s.v. *Voiturer*, Throughly to digest, (or, as we say, to shake downe) his meat by..exercise. 1656 Heylin *Surv. France* 127 Some [of the dancers] there were so ragged, that a swift Galliard would almost have shaked them into nakedness. 1735 Pope *Ep. Lady* 280 Heav'n..Shakes all together, and produces—You. 1747 Lady M. W. Montagu *Let. to C'tess Bute* 24 July (1893) II. 153 The land so stony, I was almost shook to pieces. 1815 J. Smith *Panorama Sci. & Art* II. 792 Shake the mixture well together. 1883 *Century Mag.* XXVI. 117/2 She was shaking her match out, as women do [after lighting the gas]. 1898 G. B. Shaw *You never can tell* Plays II. 209 She shakes her dress into order..and goes to the window.

**b.** *intr.* for *refl.* (*a*) ***to shake down***: to find temporary accommodation, esp. with reference to sleeping, to occupy a 'shake-down'.

1858–9 W. H. Russell *Diary India* (1860) I. iii. 40 An eligible apartment in which some five or six of us 'shook down' for the night. 1869 *Punch* 24 July 31/1, I have often professed myself able to shake down anywhere and rough it. 1888 Rider Haggard *Mr. Meeson's Will* xi, She was led off to the cabin occupied by the captain and his wife.., the captain shaking down where he could.

(*b*) ***to shake down into***: to settle *into*, to accommodate oneself to (circumstances, a condition, position, etc.). ***to shake together***: (of a company of persons) to mix, get on friendly terms with each other.

1861 Hughes *Tom Brown at Oxf.* i. i, I spent a day or two ..before I got shaken down into my place here. *Ibid.* i. xi, The rest of the men had shaken together well, and seemed to enjoy themselves. 1865 Mrs. Gaskell *Wives & Dau.* I. x. 107 'We shall shake down into uniformity before long..,' said he [referring to his second marriage]. 1889 *Cornhill Mag.* June 561 We have scarcely had time to shake down into the usual routine of a well-ordered household.

**c.** ***to shake down*** *intr.* and *refl.*, to settle down, to accommodate oneself to circumstances, a condition, position, etc.

1864 C. M. Yonge *Trial* II. x. 178 Mr. Cheviot, as the family shook down together, became less afraid of Ethel. 1875 Trollope *Prime Minister* (1876) I. vii. 109 You'll find they'll shake down after the usual amount of resistance and compliance. 1916 'Taffrail' *Pincher Martin* i. 4 You needn't look so scared. You'll soon shake down. Is this your first ship? 1959 *Times* 31 May 11/2 By the time a new American President has..shaken himself down in the White House, the West German federal elections..will be approaching. 1973 *Times* 26 Apr. 17/1 Agricultural prices.. produced..several sharp clashes of interest. This is an integral part of the process of shaking down. 1980 R. Adams *Girl in Swing* (1981) xxii. 307 And how is the beautiful Karin? Is she shaking down nicely in England?

**13. a.** *trans.* To dislodge or get rid of (something, a person's hold, etc.) by shaking one's body, limbs, clothes, etc. Const. *from*, *off*; also with adv., *away*, *aside*, *down*. (For *shake off* see 19.)

*a*1300 *Cursor M.* 20962 (Gött.), Bot of his hand..He schok and in þe fire it kest. 1388 Wyclif *Gen.* xxvii. 40 And tyme schal come whanne thou schalt shake awei..his ȝok fro thi nollis. *c*1440 *Alphabet of Tales* 473 Sho..bear hym.. vnto þe galous, & evyn vndernethe þe galows sho shuke hym down. 1590 Shaks. *Mids. N.* iii. ii. 261 Vile thing let loose, Or I will shake thee from me like a serpent. 1622 Mabbe tr. *Aleman's Guzman d' Alf.* i. 112, I haue shak't that Vermine from off my fingers ends. 1774 Goldsm. *Nat. Hist.* (1776) I. 365 He was obliged..to shake the sand from his cloaths. 1791 Cowper *Judgem. Poets* 11 [She would] shake with fury, to the ground, The garland that she wore. 1847 Tennyson *Princess* Prol. 137 She shook aside The hand that play'd the patron with her curls. 1848 James *Beauchamp* II. ix. 195 If the gentleman..seizes us, we can often shake him away.

*fig.* 1340 *Ayenb.* 4 Vor to ssake a-way heuinesse an drede. *c*1380 Wyclif *Wks.* (1880) 291 Vnderstond, ȝe kyngis; and schaak of ȝou rudenesse. 1581 N. Burne *Disput.* in *Cath. Tract.* (S.T.S.) 155 Iohne Kmnox..schuke louse all the actis of Paipis..maid be continual success of tyme. 1605 Shaks. *Lear* i. i. 40 And 'tis our fast intent, To shake all Cares and Businesse from our Age. 1821 Lamb *Elia* Ser. i. *My First Play*, I never pass it without shaking some forty years from off my shoulders. **1850** Mrs. Jameson *Leg. Monast. Ord.* (1863) 3 He could not wholly shake from his mind the influences of the age in which he lived.

**b.** *to shake the dust from* or *off one's feet*: lit. in the Gospel passages (see also *shake off*, 19 a); hence *allusively*, to take one's departure from an uncongenial place.

*c* **950** *Lindisf. Gosp.* Mark vi. 11 Sceacas.. þæt asca of.. fotum iurum, *excutite puluerem de pedibus uestris.* **1382** Wyclif *ibid.*, Shake awey the powdre fro ȝoure feet. **1672** tr. *J. de Luna's Pursuit Lazarillo* vii. O 7, I shaked upon them the dust off [1622 of] my shoes. **1782** Miss Burney *Cecilia* viii. i, I then paid off my lodgings, and 'shaking the dust from my feet', bid a long adieu to London. **1826** Disraeli *Viv. Grey* iv. vi, At length the pilgrim shook the dust off his feet at Heidelberg. **1921** Galsworthy *To Let* vii. 181 Impressions of the United States, whose dust he had just shaken from off his feet—a country.. so barbarous in every way.

**c.** orig. *U.S.* To get rid of, cast off (a person); to give up (a habit). Also, to give (a person) the slip; to jilt; occas. to abandon (a place); to shake off (an illness, feeling, etc.).

**1872** 'Mark Twain' *Roughing It* xlvii. 336 He never shook his mother... No indeedy.. he looked after her and took care of her. **1873** B. Harte *Fiddletown* 24 But she should shake you, Kernel, thet she should just shake you—is what gits me. **1874** (song) *I'll Never Get Drunk Any More*, Chorus: The pledge I will take, the whisky I'll shake, Oh I'll never get drunk any more. **1884** 'Mark Twain' *Huck. Finn* xxxi. 323 That little rascal has stole our raft and shook us, and run off. **1893** Kipling *Seven Seas* 96 We've shaken the Clubs and the Messes To go and find out and be damned. **1896** *Harper's Mag.* Apr. 779/1 Then Ruth shook me. **1903** *Smart Set* IX. 13/2 You'll have to shake the drink; that goes without saying. **1907** R. W. Service *Songs of Sourdough* 13, I was all caked in on a dance-hall jade, but she shook me in the end. **1934** in J. A. & A. Lomax *Amer. Ballads & Folk Songs* xx. 459 She shook me for the driver. **1935** M. de la Roche *Young Renny* iv. 28 'He was paying us a visit and the time went on and—he just came with us.' 'You mean you couldn't shake him?' **1949** R. Chandler *Let.* 21 Mar. (1981) 157 I'm going down to Palm Springs for a week to try to shake this cough. **1953** 'S. Ransome' *Drag Dark* (1954) xiii. 131 We deliberately shook you that night, then tailed you back here. **1958** J. Kerouac *On Road* v. 34 'I have a date with my boy friend.' 'Can't you shake him?' **1965** V. Canning *Whip Hand* v. 51 If anyone was following you must have shaken them. **1972** 'T. Coe' *Don't lie to Me* (1974) vii. 75 The picture of the murderer stayed in my head... Trying to shake it, trying to shake the mood it was giving me, I searched for other things to think about. **1974** 'J. Ross' *Burning of Billy Toober* x. 97 If you don't shake it [*sc.* heroin], it'll kill you in the end. **1977** *Rolling Stone* 16 June 34/4 Blauer had admitted himself to a New York state hospital hoping to shake a debilitating depression. **1979** 'S. Woods' *This Fatal Writ* 129 If you know you're being followed, it isn't too difficult to shake a tail.

**14.** To dislodge or eject by shaking the receptacle or support: **a.** const. *from*, etc., or with adv. *down*, *off*, etc. (For *shake out* see 20.)

**1500–20** Dunbar *Poems* vii. 3 The levys are doun schakyn with the schouris. *a* **1529** Skelton *E. Rummyng* 198 Than Elynour taketh The mashe bolle, and shaketh The hennes donge away. **1545** in Leadam *Court Requests* (Selden Soc.) 187 He.. lyked theym nott whervpon he showke theym forthe of hys bagg. **1607** Shaks. *Cor.* iii. i. 179 Hence rotten thing, or I shall shake thy bones Out of thy garments. *Ibid.* iv. vi. 99 As Hercules did shake downe Mellow Fruite. **1726** Swift *Gulliver* ii. viii, The first jolt had like to have shaken me out of my hammock. **1842** Loudon *Suburban Hort.* 31 Shake this earth away from the roots. **1889** *N.W. Linc. Gloss.* s.v. *Shack*, I'll goä shack sum cherries doon.

†**b.** *simply*. To cast down, scatter (fruit, blossom, corn, etc.) by shaking; = *shake down* above. Also, to turn out (a fox) from a bag (cf. 20 a, quot. 1856).

**1576** Gascoigne *Grief of Joye* Wks. 1910 II. 535 The weakest wynde, can shake their bravest bloomes. **1583** Melbancke *Philotimus* T ij, The wallnut tree wel bet when his nuts are shaken, beareth more fruit the yeare ensuing. **1596** Shaks. *Tam. Shr.* v. ii. 140 It.. Confounds thy fame, as whirlewinds shake faire budds. **1605** —— *Macb.* iv. iii. 238 Macbeth Is ripe for shaking. **1611** Tourneur *Ath. Trag.* iii. i, A sweet young blossome shak'd before the time. **1812** *Sporting Mag.* XXXIX. 185 On Thursday the 2d instant, a fox was shook near Mr. Markey's.

*Proverbial phr.* **1557** Edgeworth *Serm.* ccxxx. C 1, All this wynde shoke no corne, all this moued him not. **1589** R. Harvey *Pl. Perc.* 1 All this wind shakes none of my Corne, quoth Perceuall. **1629** J. Taylor (Water-P.) *Wit & Mirth* Wks. 1630 ii. 200/2 Wel quoth Sara, all this winde shakes no corne.

**c.** *intr.* Of fruit, blossom, corn: To fall, scatter. Now *dial.*

**1725** P. Blair *Pharmaco-Bot.* iii. 130 Being again timely ripe, it mixes and shakes before any other Grain. **1788** W. H. Marshall *Yorksh.* II. 350 To *Shack* (that is, to shake); to shed, as corn at harvest. **1799** J. Robertson *Agric. Perth* 155 These [kinds of oats] are apt to shed the grain or shake, if allowed to be fully ripe before they are cut down. **1813** T. Busby *Lucretius* II. iv. *Comm.* 6 The fine seeds of southernwood.. slightly shook. *a* **1904** in *Eng. Dial. Dict.* s.v. *Shake*, This corn shacks out wi' t' wind.

**15. a.** To distribute with a shake, to scatter, sprinkle. Also with *forth*, *down*.

*c* **1400** *Destr. Troy.* 2206, I graunt thee þe gouernaunse of þis gret mode, And shake it on þi shulders. **1508** Dunbar *Gold. Targe* 14 The perly droppis schake [*pa. pple.*] in silvir schouris. **1523** Skelton *Garl. Laurel* 595 Wheron stode a lybbard,.. And with his forme foote he shoke forthe this wrytyng. **1620** *Hist. Frier Rush* (1810) 32 With his forke he shaked the straw abroad. **1667** Milton *P.L.* ii. 711 Satan.. like a Comet burn'd, That.. from his horrid hair Shakes Pestilence and Warr. **1728–46** Thomson *Spring* 318 The Winter keen Shook forth his waste of snows. **1747** Mrs. Glasse *Cookery* ii. 25 Shake a little Flour over it. **1819** Scott *Leg. Montrose* vi, 'Shake down plenty of straw in the great barn,' said the Laird. **1857** T. Moore *Handbk. Brit. Ferns* (ed. 3) 11 When shaken over a sheet of paper they [the spores] are scarcely visible to the naked eye.

**b.** To cast (dice) usually with a preliminary shake; hence to gamble *away* (an estate); also with personal object, to 'throw' against (a person) *for* whatever is staked.

**1570** B. Googe *Pop. Kingd.* 47 Dice are shakte. **1693** *Humours Town* 25 To shake away an Estate to known Rooks that live by the Dice. **1875** Wood & Lapham *Waiting for Mail* 79 I'll shake you for drinks.

**16.** † **a.** *to shake* (a person) *out of* (property): to rob, plunder. *Obs.* **b.** *slang.* To steal (goods); to rob (a person). Now *Austral.*

*c* **1412** Hoccleve *De Reg. Princ.* 4514 He þat schakith Men out of hire good. **1538** Elyot *Dict.* Add., *Excutere aliquem*, to robbe one, to shake oone out of his clothes. **1567** Harman *Caveat* xix. (1869) 67 When these [walking morts] get ought .. as money or apparell, they are quickly shaken out of all by the vpright men. **1811** *Lex. Balatron.*, *Shake*, to draw any thing from the pocket. He shook the swell of his fogle; he robbed the gentleman of his silk handkerchief. **1812** J. H. Vaux *Flash Dict.*, *Shake*, to steal or rob; as I *shook* a chest of *slop*, I stole a chest of tea; I've been *shook* of my *skin*, I have been robbed of my purse. **1859** H. Kingsley *G. Hamlyn* xix. II. 22, I shook a nag, and got bowled out and lagged. **1903** W. Craig *Adv. Austral. Goldf.* 191 The man.. wondered if 'he' was worth 'shaking'.

**c.** *to shake down*, to extort money from, to blackmail or otherwise pressurize (a person) *for* (occas. *of*) money, etc. *slang* (orig. and chiefly *U.S.*).

**1872** G. P. Burnham *Mem. U.S. Secret Service* p. viii, *Shake, out* to 'shake down'; to extort money from individuals. **1916** J. London *Let.* 12 Oct. (1966) 473 'Uncle Charley'.. then proceeded to shake you down in proper money-lender.. fashion. **1927** J. Barbican *Confess. Rum-Runner* xiv. 148 For only last week they were shook down for five hundred by a stray fellow from the Department. **1949** *Los Angeles Times* 5 May 1/3 Ferguson.. accused them of trying to 'shakedown' Mickey Cohen of $5000. **1956** H. Kurnitz *Invasion of Privacy* vii. 54 'You weren't by any chance trying to shake him down?'.. 'No, sir. Not a penny.' **1966** T. Pynchon *Crying of Lot 49* ii. 28 He left after shaking her down for four bits for carrying the bags. **1976** 'J. Ross' *'I know what it's like to Die'* xxii. 144 Sickert had been shaken down for protection money.

**d.** *to shake down*, (esp. of police, etc.) to search (a person or place). *slang* (orig. and chiefly *U.S.*).

**1915** *N.Y. World* 9 May (Suppl.) 14/1 *Frisk*, to shake down or search. **1955** D. W. Maurer in *Publ. Amer. Dialect Soc.* xxiv. 46 They.. shook down my hotel. **1968** *Listener* 15 Feb. 210/1 Inmate guards have been in complete control of the prison. They.. shook down incoming prisoners to take radios and watches and so on. **1977** D. Bagley *Enemy* xvii. 141 Once Mayberry had been shaken down the guards were taken from Penny and Gillian. **1979** D. Anthony *Long Hard Cure* xxv. 198 The Sony had been in plain sight.. Billy Combs was shaking down the rest of the house.

**17. a.** *refl.* and *intr.* Of timber: To split or crack. Also *refl.*

**1679** Moxon *Mech. Exerc.* (1703) 149 The Boards will Tear or Shake, which is in vulgar English, Split or Crack. **1703** T. N. *City & C. Purch.* 136 The.. Boards are set.. under some cover'd Shed... For if.. the Sun shine fiercely upon 'em.. they will tear or shake 'em,.. that is, in plain English, split or crack. **1844** W. Barnes *Poems Rur. Life* Gloss., *Shook*, split, as wood by shrinking.

**b.** *trans.* To separate the staves of (a cask). Cf. shake *sb.* 10 a.

**1867** Smyth *Sailor's Word-bk.* s.v., *To shake a cask*, to take it to pieces, and pack up the parts. **1882** Nares *Seamanship* (ed. 6) 95.

**18.** *Mus.* To accompany or execute with a shake; also *absol.* or *intr.* to execute a shake (see shake *sb.* 5).

**1611** Cotgr., *Gringoter*, to warble quauer, shake with the voice. **1632** Sherwood *s.v.*, To shake the voice (in singing), *gringoter*. **1659** C. Simpson *Division-Violist* i. 9 Open [-shake] is, when a Finger is shaked in that distance from when it was removed, or is to be set down. *Ibid.*, Wider then that [*sc.* an interval of a tone] we never shake. **1676** T. Mace *Musick's Monum.* 104 The Back-fall may be either Plain, or Shaked. **1746** Tansur *New Mus. Gram.* 23 A Shake, or Trilloe.. is, to shake, tremble, or warble your Voice, or Instrument. **1828** *Examiner* 664/1 She.. absolutely introduced two consecutive fifths by shaking on F instead of descending to D.

**19. shake off. a.** To cast off or get rid of with a shake or an effort. *lit.* and *fig.*

**1393** Langl. *P. Pl.* C. vii. 13 Repente þe,.. And shryf þe sharpliche and shak of alle pruyde. **1535** Coverdale *Mark* vi. 11 Shake of the duste from your feet. **1611** Bible *ibid.* **1567** Maplet *Gr. Forest* 42 b, Through the onely.. eating hereof, they shake off many sicknesses. **1588** Shaks. *L.L.L.* iv. iii. 243 A withered Hermite fiuescore winters worne, Might shake off fiftie, looking in her eye. **1642** J. Eaton *Honey-c. Free Justif.* 366 Having shaken off our sinne (as Sampson had shaked off his new ropes). **1671** Milton *Samson* 409, I Might easily have shook off all her snares. **1711–12** Swift *Jrnl. to Stella* 11 Jan., I walked lustily in the Park by moonshine till eight, to shake off my dinner and wine. **1719** Ozell tr. *Misson's Mem. Trav. Eng.* 26 Then the Bull bellows and bounds, and kicks about to shake off the Dog. **1774** Goldsm. *Nat. Hist.* (1776) VII. 365 The most industrious shake off their old garments about eight o'clock. **1827** N. P. Willis *Widow of Nain* 18 The sentinel Shook off his slumber. **1864** Bryce *Holy Rom. Emp.* xvii. (1875) 305 Poland, once tributary, had shaken off the yoke. **1888** Payn *Myst. Mirbridge* III. xlvii. 223, I know from experience how difficult it is to shake off old associations.

**b.** To get rid of (a person); to draw away from (a competitor in a race).

**1530** Palsgr. 700/2, I shake of, as one shaketh of or awaye from hym a person or matter that he wolde be rydde of. **1571** *Satir. Poems Reform.* xxix. 34 Quhen he listis, he schaks hir of be diuorce or hir wirreis. **1608** Tarlton *Cobler Canterb.* (1844) 117, I shakt him off as well as I could, but he would haue no nay at all. **1710** Swift *Jrnl. to Stella* 9 Sept., I am glad I have wholly shaken off that family. **1823** Scott *Quentin D.* vi, Exerting his strength, he suddenly shook off both the finishers of the law. **1856** H. H. Dixon *Post & Paddock* xiii. 324 'You thought to shake me off, did you?' roared Mr. T. as they landed together in a large grass field. **1878** Tennyson *The Revenge* viii, And a dozen times we shook 'em off as a dog that shakes his ears.

†**c.** To let off (a shot). *Obs. rare*$^{-1}$.

**1583** Stocker *Civ. Warres Lowe C.* iv. 32 a, Either parte shooke of their shotte, and coupled them selues together in a braue Skirmishe.

**d.** Of a plant: To shed (leaves, fruit).

**1388** Wyclif *Isa.* xxiv. 13 If a fewe fruitis of olyue trees that ben left ben schakun of fro the olyue tre. **1575** Gascoigne *Kenelworth* ii. v. Wks. 1910 II. 123 The Trees shooke off their leaves.

**e.** *Naut.* To unfasten (a sail).

**1627** Capt. Smith *Seaman's Gram.* v. 22 When we shake off a Bonnet. **1867** Smyth *Sailor's Word-bk.* s.v., To *shake*, to cast off fastenings, as.. To shake off a bonnet of a fore-and-aft sail.

**20. shake out. a.** To cast out or remove with a shake. *lit.* and *fig.*

*a* **1225** *Ancr. R.* 206 Þe scorpiunes cundel þet heo bret in hire boseme, schek hit ut mid schrifte. *c* **1330** R. Brunne *Chron. Wace* (Rolls) 14682 Luytel notes þey toke, & holede þem, þe kerneles out schoke. *c* **1450** in Aungier *Syon* (1840) 368 Mynyster of the sextry schal.. haue oute the tapettes.. and the duste schake oute. **1576** Gascoigne *Droomme of Doomes day* i. Wks. 1910 II. 238 You shall never shake a brybe out of your hand, unlesse you shut covetousnesse out of your brest. *a* **1700** Evelyn *Diary* 24 Aug. 1678, This they dextrously turning, shake out like a pancake. **1842** Loudon *Suburban Hort.* 449 We shook the plants out, and shortened their roots.. and repotted them. **1856** 'Stonehenge' *Brit. Rural Sports* i. ii. v. 135 A bag-fox being shaken out before hounds by the keeper.

**b.** *nonce-uses.* To bring about by 'wagging'; to produce by shaking.

**1601** Shaks. *All's Well* ii. iv. 24 Many a mans tongue shakes out his masters vndoing. **1608** Middleton *Trick to catch Old One* v. ii, Chiefly dice, those true outlanders, That shake out beggars, thieves, and panders.

†**c.** To cast out the contents of; to empty. *Obs.*

**1382** Wyclif *2 Esdras* [*Neh.*] v. 13, I shakide out my bosum. **1639** R. Baillie *Lett. & Jrnls.* (1841) I. 213 Harie Rollock, by his sermons, moved them to shake out their purses.

**d.** To unfasten or unfurl and let out with a shake (a flag, sail); to straighten out by shaking (something crumpled or folded).

**1549** *Compl. Scot.* vi. 41 Schaik out the flag on the top mast. **1800** *Naval Chron.* IV. 394, I dare not shake the reefs out of the sail. **1849** Lever *Confess. Con Cregan* I. xiv, Old Ben Crosseley, of the 'Lively Biddy', that wouldn't stand being ordered to shake out his canvas. **1853** Kane *Grinnell Exp.* xx. (1856) 153 We had shaken out our reefs, and were driving before the wind. **1902** Snaith *Wayfarers* xvii, He.. produced a fresh wig.. and having shook it out, discarded the modest wig he was wearing.

**e.** *intr.* To show visible signs of trembling.

**1843** Sir T. Watson *Lect. Physic* I. xl. 709 [In] the dumb ague, or the dead ague; the patient is said not to shake out.

**21. shake up.** † **a.** To rattle (a chain). *Obs.*

*c* **1430** *Chev. Assigne* 356 Þey.. shoken vp þe cheynes þer sterten vp þe swannes; Eche on chese to his.

**b.** To shake together for the purpose of combining or mixing; to shake (a liquid) so as to stir up the sediment.

**1753** *Chambers' Cycl.* Suppl. s.v. *Eye*, [The mixture is to be] thoroughly shook up every time it is to be used. **1837** Dickens *Pickw.* xxiii, Mr. Weller, shaking up the ale, by describing small circles with the pot, preparatory to drinking. **1878** Huxley *Physiogr.* 84 If we shake up a mixture of liquids of different densities.

**c.** To rouse up with or as with a shake.

**1850** Allingham *Poems, Morning* i, The wind shakes up the sleepy clouds. **1857** Hughes *Tom Brown* i. iv, Bob.. hollers to his 'osses, and shakes 'em up, and away we goes. **1896** *Daily News* 30 Apr. 3/4 The favourite always had his race well won,.. although.. Loates had to shake him up.

**d.** To loosen (bedding, etc.) by shaking.

**1833** W. H. Maxwell *Field Bk.* s.v. *Training*, After he [the horse] has had his food, the litter is to be shook up. **1857** Anne Marsh *Rose of Ashurst* vi, [He] had.. shook up and arranged my pillows, in a way most comfortable to me.

**e.** *Naut.* (See quot.)

**1769** Falconer *Dict. Marine* (1780) ii. E e e 2, Shake her up in the wind, let the sails touch! the order to the helmsman to steer the ship so as to let the sails shake with their edges to the wind.

†**f.** To rate soundly, abuse violently. (Very common in 16–17th c.) Also, to harass, afflict.

*a* **1553** Udall *Roister D.* ii. ii. (Arb.) 33, I was nere so shoke vp afore since I was borne. **1576** Pettie *Petite Pallace* 53 b, The king.. sent for my youth Iphis, shooke him vp with sharpe threatninges, and charged him.. neuer after to be seene at the Court. **1600** Shaks. *A.Y.L.* i. i. 30. **1620** Sanderson *Serm.* I. 145 What was Eliah to Ahab?.. that he durst.. shake him up roundly for.. his bloody abominable oppressions? **1637** Heylin *Antid. Lincoln* iii. 9 Your next vagarie is upon the Doctor... The Doctor thus shaked up, you goe on againe unto the point of Iurisdiction.

**g.** To upset the nerves of, agitate, confuse.

**1884** 'Mark Twain' *Huck. Finn* vi. 40 People allowed there'd be another trial to.. give me to the widow for my guardian... This shook me up considerable, because I didn't want to go back to the widow's. **1897** Kipling *Capt. Cour.* ii. 31 'Well, you was shook up and silly', said Dan.

**IV. 22.** The verb-stem in combination: †**shake-brained** *a.*, of unsound mind, crazy, crack-brained; †**shake breast** = WAVE-*breast* (cf. *Geneva Bible* 1560, *Lev.* x. 15 shakẽ breast, *Num.* vi. 20 shaken breast); †**shake-day-sheaf** = WAVE-*sheaf*; **shake-hands**, an act of shaking hands with another person; hence ***shake-hand*** attrib.; **shake-lurk** *slang*, a sham official document falsely declaring that the bearer has suffered shipwreck; †**shake offering**, a WAVE *offering*; †**shake rotten** *a.*, a term of abuse; †**shake-sheaf** = *shake-day-sheaf*; **shake-tail** *a.*, of a woman, loose.

**1793** *Gentl. Mag.* Feb. 126 A..*shake-brained fellow. **1647** *Husbandm. Plea agst. Tithes* 38 Then the custome is (in some Parishes) for the Parson to have a tenth joynt, a heave shoulder, or a *shake breast. *c***1659** BP. BROWNRIG *Serm.* (1674) I. xxi. 278 God, saith Gregory, requires not only *pectus fidei*..the shake-breast of faith, but [etc.]. **1650** TRAPP *Comm. Levit.* xxiii. 11 This *shake-daie-sheaf was a pregnant type of Christ's rising again. **1856** LEVER *Martins of Cro' M.* l. 491 Not a little provoked at the *shake-hand salutation her son had accorded him. **1800** F. BURNEY *Let.* 18 July (1973) IV. 436 William will be much pleased by a private congratulatory **shake hands* from you in his own Apartment. **1811** *Ora & Juliet* I. 235 After..a hearty shake-hands with Brewster. **1889** D. C. MURRAY *Dangerous Catspaw* 33 He..executed a hearty shake-hands. **1851** MAYHEW *Lond. Labour* I. 219 Armed with these [sham official documents], the patterer becomes a 'lurker'... Shipwreck is called a '*shake lurk'. **1608** WILLET *Hexapla Exod.* 574 The *shake offering was shaken to and fro. **1595** PEELE *Old Wives T.* D, This *shake rotten parish that will not burie Iack. **1650** TRAPP *Comm. Levit.* xxiii. 17 The *shake-sheaf..of their barlie-harvest. **1782** ELIZ. BLOWER *Geo. Bateman* II. 120 A couple of *shake-tail jabbering wenches.

**shakeable** (ˈʃeɪkəb(ə)l), *a.* [f. SHAKE *v.* + -ABLE.] That may be shaken.

**1869** RUSKIN *Q. of Air* §54 Anything you can find in the universe that is shakeable.

**ˈshake-bag.** *Obs.* exc. *dial.* [f. SHAKE *v.*]

**1.** *Cock-fighting.* (See quots. 1688, 1709). Cf. SHACKBAG 2.

**1663** *State-Scuffle* 3 And when two shake-bags are thrown out, To try the Battel yet in doubt, When weary still they wheele about More eager. **1688** HOLME *Armoury* II. 252/1 A Shake-bag, is a Cock turned out of the Bag to fight another Cock, unsight, unseen, or unmatched; a Battle at a venture. **1688** *Lond. Gaz.* No. 2328/4, 40 Cocks on each side will be shewn... And every Battel 5 l. each side, and 50 l. the odd Battel, and four Shake Bags for 10 l. each Cock. **1709** R. H. *Roy. Pastime Cock-fighting* iv. 19 Yet are these Birds commonly reduced into two sorts only,..the great Game Cock, or Shake-bag, and the little Match, or Battle-Cock. **1777** [T. SWIFT] *Gamblers* I. 829 The Pit shall roar, fierce Shake-bag flap the wing. **1881** *Isle of Wight Gloss.*, *Shakebag*, a game-cock of the largest size.

*transf.* **1700** CONGREVE *Way of World* I. 65 *Wit*... Will you go to a Cock-match? *Sir Wil.* With a Wench, Tony? Is she a shake-bag Sirrah? **1771** SMOLLETT *Humph. Cl.* 30 Apr., I would pit her..against the best shake-bag of the whole main.

**2.** A rogue, scoundrel. Also (see quots. 1796 and 1823 in 3). Cf. SHACKBAG I.

[Cf. the following: **1592** *Arden of Feversham* (title-p.), His ..wife, who..hyred two desperate ruffins Blackwill and Shakbag, to kill him. (See also quot. **1595** SHAKE *v.* 7 b.)] **1794** *Sporting Mag.* III. 104 Being estimated..by the blacklegs, rooks and shakebags as a complete knowing one. **1796** GROSE *Dict. Vulgar T.* (ed. 3), *Shag-bag*, or *Shake-bag*, a poor sneaking fellow, a man of no spirit: a term borrowed from the cock-pit.

**3.** *attrib.*

**1688** HOLME *Armoury* II. xi. 252 *Shake-back* [sic] *Battle*, is a fight between two Cocks unmatched, unsight, unseen. **1823** 'JON BEE' *Dict. Turf*, *Shake-bag match*—in cocking; the fighting adventitiously, or guessing at weights and pairing, while the fowls are still in their respective bags. 'A Shake-bag fellow', if he be no pick-pocket, is at least a seedy cove.

†**ˈshakebuckler.** *Obs. rare.* [f. SHAKE *v.* + BUCKLER *sb.* Cf. *swashbuckler*.] Only in ***Sim Shakebuckler***, a nickname for a serving man.

**1550** BECON *Gov. Virtue* Wks. 1564 I. 257 That a poore mayde and a simple Sym Shakebuckelare, made him [Peter] both to denye [etc.]. **1560** —— *Catech.* VI. ibid. 523 Nor [suffer their children] to be of the nomber of suche simme shakebucklers, as in theyr yong yeares fal vnto seruing.

**shakebut(t**, obs. forms of SACKBUT.

**1593** G. PEELE *Hon. Garter* D 1, Then Shalmes and Shake-butts sounded in the ayre. **1628** P. SMART *Serm.* (*Ps.* xxxi. 7) 22 With Shakebuts, and..all kinde of Musicke.

†**shaked**, *ppl. a. Obs. rare.* [f. SHAKE *v.* + -ED[1].]
**a.** Shaken. **b.** *Mus.* Trilled.

**1625** MILTON *Ode Death Fair Infant* 44 Wert thou some Starr which from the ruin'd roofe Of shak't Olympus by mischance didst fall. **1659** C. SIMPSON *Division-Violist* I. 9 Graces done with the Fingers are of two sorts: viz. smooth and shaked. *Ibid.*, Shaked Graces.

**ˈshake-down.** [f. vbl. phrase *to shake down*: see SHAKE *v.* 12.]

**1.** A bed made upon straw loosely disposed upon the floor or ground; hence, any makeshift bed, esp. one made up on the floor.

*c***1730** BURT *Lett. N. Scot.* (1754) I. 107 The same Blanket ..is made a Part of their Bedding at Night, which is generally spread upon the Floor; this I think they call a Shake-down. *a***1820** A. YOUNG *Autobiog.* iv. (1898) 72 A 'shake-down' when I was in Ireland [1776–8] meant some clean straw spread upon the floor, with blankets and sheets. **1838** DICKENS *Nich. Nick.* vii, You can give him a shake-down here to-night, can't you? **1883** S. C. HALL *Retrospect* I. 77 When the party broke up there was no leaving at so late an hour, and shake-downs were improvised for at least forty ..guests.

*attrib.* **1891** *Catholic News* 29 Aug. 8/4 Shake-down straw beds with a rug or two for covering.

**2. a.** An act of shaking down: see SHAKE *v.* 12.

**1878** HARDY *Ret. Native* VI. iv, Now gie the bed a shake down. We've put in seventy pound of best feathers.

**b.** A forced contribution; an instance of extortion. Cf. SHAKE *v.* 16 c. orig. and chiefly *U.S.*

**1902** in *Dict. Americanisms* (1951) s.v. *shake*, To the historic phrase 'blackmail'..have been added, as words of similar evil omen, the new and expressive terms shake-down and rake-off. **1903** A. H. HODDER *Fight for City* 219 He [*sc.* a New York policeman] was fined 30 days' pay because he would not stand for a 'shake-down', which means that he had refused to give from time to time upon demand 5 or 10 dollars..to his superiors to be used for purposes unknown. **1916** J. LONDON *Let.* 12 Oct. (1966) 473 A usurer..slunk out because..he saw the shake-down of me would not go through. **1941** *Sun* (Baltimore) 31 Mar. 1/7 Jack Pollack.. was named..as the man behind a demand for a $2,500 'shakedown' to kill a liquor license bill in the Legislature. **1978** S. BRILL *Teamsters* ix. 329 While the shakedown was proved, it was never shown that the money went to Presser personally.

**c.** A search of a person or a place. Cf. SHAKE *v.* 16 d. orig. and chiefly *U.S.*

**1914** JACKSON & HELLYER *Vocab. Criminal Slang* 75 *Shake down*, noun. General currency. A personal search; a deprivation of one's personal belongings... Example: 'If this dick nails you you'll have to stand a shake down.' **1936** *Sun* (Baltimore) 31 Jan. 3/5 A sudden 'shakedown' of the Stateville Penitentiary resulted in the seizure of several knives. **1958** *Landfall* (N.Z.) XII. II. 123 But about nine o'clock, without any warning, there was a shake-down [of prisoners]. **1977** D. BAGLEY *Enemy* viii. 53, I really wanted ..to give Ashton's study a good shake-down. But..it's bad form..to be found searching through your host's private papers.

**3.** *attrib.* (sense 2 a) ***shakedown test***; (sense 2 b), as ***shake-down dodge***, ***scheme***; (sense 2 c), as ***shake-down party***; **shake-down cruise** *Naut.* (orig. *U.S.*), a cruise designed to test a newly-launched ship and its equipment and to train its crew; also *fig.*; similarly **shake-down flight** *Aeronaut.*

**1927** G. BRADFORD *Gloss. Sea Terms* 156/1 *Shakedown cruise*, one for the purpose of adjusting machinery and instruments, and familiarizing a crew with a new vessel. **1933** *Sun* (Baltimore) 21 Jan. 16/7 The newest addition to the navy..is on its 'shake-down' cruise. **1968** *Wall St. Jrnl.* (Eastern ed.) 12 Sept. 1/1 The first week on the road..has been a shakedown cruise for the Senator and his staff—enabling the candidate to test stump themes,..giving aides experience at writing speeches and organizing motorcades, [etc.]. **1978** P. O'DONNELL *Dragon's Claw* ii. 27 The boat's 'ad a shakedown cruise and..it 'andles beautifully. **1934** D. RUNYON in *Collier's* 24 Nov. 52/2 He is only going back to his old shake-down dodge, so all you have to do is to buy him off. **1939** *Sun* (Baltimore) 25 Mar. 20/3 The 10,000-mile shakedown flight will require about two weeks. **1952** *Here & Now* (N.Z.) II. IV. 32 The shake-down parties have been through the cells pretty often. **1976** *Honolulu Star-Bull.* 21 Dec. A-2/4 The mayor's own press secretary was convicted in a shake-down scheme. **1942** *R.A.F. Jrnl.* 2 May (recto rear cover), To send them into actual service..without modification or further shakedown test.

**ˈshakefork.** Also shackfork. [f. SHAKE *v.*] A wooden fork with two tines or prongs used by threshers to shake and remove the straw from the grain; also, a pitchfork. Now *dial.*

**1338** *Durh. Acc. Rolls* (Surtees) 200 It. 8 rastra cum schakforkes, pr. 12*d*. **1483** *Cath. Angl.* 332/2 A Schake forke, *pastinatum*. **1597** BP. HALL *Sat.* III. vii. 66 So slender wast with such an Abbots loyne,..Like a broad shak-forke with a slender steale. **1607** MARKHAM *Cavel.* v. 15 You shall take a shakeforke..and with it you shall shake vp..all the horses dung, and wet litter. **1788** W. H. MARSHALL *Yorksh.* II. 350 Shack-fork (that is, shake-fork); a wooden fork,.. generally made of a forked ozier; the tines or branches about two feet long, and one foot wide at the points. **1847** *Jrnl. R. Agric. Soc.* VIII. II. 297 The swaths are gathered into shocks with a shack-fork. **1876** *Whitby Gloss.*, *Shackfork*, a wooden fork for lifting the thrashed straw... 'His clothes look as if they were flung on to his back with a shackfork.'

**b.** *Sc. Her.* (See quots.)

**1680** G. MACKENZIE *Sci. Her.* xi. 33 This is called a Shakfork with us, and should not touch the corners of the Escutcheon. **1780** J. EDMONDSON *Her.* II. Gloss., *Shake-fork*, is in form like the Pall, but doth not touch the top of the shield, and is pointed at each end. **1894** J. MACINTOSH *Ayrsh. Nights' Entert.* xv. 286 [Stewarton Ch.] Over the.. doorway..is a rather long window-like compartment, in which the shake-fork forms, as it were, the mullion.

**shaken** (ˈʃeɪk(ə)n), *ppl. a.* [pa. pple. of SHAKE *v.*]

**1.** Put into a quick or violent alternating motion; agitated; (of seed, etc.) sprinkled.

**1725** P. BLAIR *Pharmaco-Bot.* III. 130 If..no Care has been taken to Till the Ground over the shaken Seed. **1849** M. ARNOLD *Strayed Reveller* 189 A Chief, With shout and shaken spear, Stands at the prow. **1876** GEO. ELIOT *Dan. Der.* xxxvi, For the moment she felt like a shaken child.

**2.** Moved abruptly or violently with a blow or shock; hence, weakened in structure.

**1614** GORGES *Lucan* II. 68 And bands of foot come follow on, This shaken bridge goe set vpon. **1822** SHELLEY *Scenes fr. Faust* II. 136 And through the ruins of the shaken mountain The airs hiss and howl. **1858** MALLET in *Rep. Brit. Assoc.* I. 58 The shaken area [of an earthquake].

**b.** *transf.* and *fig.*

**1641** MILTON *Reform.* II. 87 This our shaken Monarchy, that now lies labouring under her throwes. **1890** GALL *Mod. Tactics* (ed. 2) 131 Against shaken troops the opportunities will possibly be as great..in the future. **1896** F. MATHEW *Wood of Brambles* ix. 176 He is a shaken irritable kindly lean little man.

**3.** Of a cask: Taken to pieces and bound up in a compact form for transport. (Cf. SHAKE *sb.* 10 a, SHOOK *sb.*)

**1557** in Hakluyt *Voy.* (1599) I. 300 We haue laden in these ships..94. tunnes shaken Caske and 46. tunnes whole. **1575** *Ibid.* 414 There must be..800 empty shaken hogsheds. **1792** *Descr. Kentucky* 41 In 1787 were exported Shaken hogsheads 4,775.

**4.** Of timber: Cracked or split defectively.

**1523–34** FITZHERB. *Husb.* §132 (1882) 84 If it be noo tymbre tree but a shaken tree or a hedge-rote full of knottes. **1679** MOXON *Mech. Exerc.* ix. 172 Such Stuff as is crackt either with the heat of the Sun or the drought of the wind, is called Shaken Stuff. **1680** *Ibid.* xii. 206 If your Stuff prove shaken, or otherwise unsound. **1852** FINCHAM *Ship Building* II. (ed. 3) 32 The refuse of the other planking through its being shaken, or otherwise defective.

**5.** *Mining.* (See quots.)

**1747** HOOSON *Miners Dict.* U 4, *Swallow*, a loose and shaken place in a Vein. **1839** URE *Dict. Arts* 965 Troubles in coal-fields are..3. Shaken coal. It resembles the rubbish of an old waste.

**ˈshakenly**, *adv. rare.* [-LY[2].] In a shaken manner.

**1890** *Blackw. Mag.* CXLVIII. 545/1 'You do not trust me,' he said, low and shakenly.

**ˈshake-out.** [f. vbl. phr. *to shake out*: see SHAKE *v.* 20.] **1.** *Stock Exch.* A crisis in which the weaker speculators are driven out of the market. Also, a sudden fall in prices, a sudden general disposal of particular stocks, etc.

**1895** *Daily News* 23 Jan. 2/2 The 'shake-out' in speculative accounts..has strengthened the Stock markets. .. The recent 'shake out' of weak holders, referred to above. **1910** *Westm. Gaz.* 13 Apr. 10/1 All traces of last week's Rubber 'shake out' have vanished. **1928** *Sun* (Baltimore) 7 Dec. 1/3 Measured by the Associated Press averages of twenty leading industrials and twenty leading rails, which dropped $9.45 and $4.38, respectively, it was one of the quickest and most drastic shakeouts in recent market history. **1981** *Times* 14 Aug. 18/3 Properties came in for a small shake out with Stock Conversion a weak market 10p lower at 370p.

**2.** An upheaval or reorganization, esp. one involving contraction, streamlining, shedding of personnel, closure of some businesses, etc.

**1939** *Times* 9 Mar. 8/1 There had been what was sometimes called a 'shake-out' in the film industry during the past year. A number of those elements which did not raise the repute of the film industry had been removed. **1956** *Sun* (Baltimore) 20 Jan. 13/1 New claims for jobless pay increased about 20 per cent in Maryland last week under the impetus of the usual year-end economic 'shake out'. **1957** *Time* 2 Sept. 59/1 In downtown Washington, D.C., eight, or about half, of the city's big discount houses went out of business in the past year. The shake-out is almost as severe in Los Angeles, Boston and Dallas. **1963** *Listener* 21 Feb. 319/2 Public-house gossip is perhaps most busy about the need for a shake-out of the party system. **1964** *Financial Times* 3 Mar. 12/7 A shake-out in the business world, with pressure on profits and profit margins forcing the inefficient producer, or..retailer, out of business or into efficiency. **1967** *Listener* 19 Jan. 80/3 A nation-wide witch-hunt and counterbalancing resistance movement which could well make the upheaval of the past year [in China] seem like the mildest of shake-outs. **1974** *Howard Jrnl.* XIV. 39 Successive recessions and mechanization have meant a 'shake-out' of labour in traditionally labour-intensive industries. **1981** *Economist* 28 Nov. 26/1 Workers left in droves, because they were laid off. The worst of that shake-out is over.

**shaker** (ˈʃeɪkə(r)). Also 5 schakare, -ere, 6 *Sc.* schakar, (-car), schekkar. [f. SHAKE *v.* + -ER[1].]

**1. a.** One who or something which shakes (in the transitive senses of the verb). Also in phr. ***mover and shaker***, ***shaker and mover*** (U.S.), a person who influences events, a person who gets things done.

*c***1440** *Promp. Parv.* 443/1 Schakare, *excussor*. **1500–20**, *a***1605**, **1785**, **1816** [see HALLAN-SHAKER]. **1581** A. HALL *Iliad* II. 35 Who were..cunning shakers of the staffe to hit their foe a farre. *c***1611** CHAPMAN *Iliad* VII. 104 Thou mightie shaker of the earth, thou Lord of all the seas. **1613** PURCHAS *Pilgrimage* (1614) 711 Strangers..scarsely in twentie daies, with great care, can shake off this Shaker [*sc.* ague]. **1823** SCOTT *Quentin D.* Introd., The Marquis was no shaker of hands. **1852** TENNYSON *Death Wellington*, O shaker of the Baltic and the Nile. **1874** A. O'SHAUGHNESSY *Music & Moonlight* 1 Yet we are the movers and shakers Of the world for ever, it seems. **1901** F. H. SKRINE *Life Sir W. W. Hunter* xxi. 452 The fortune made in India by the Thackerays and other shakers of the pagoda-tree. **1972** F. KNEBEL *Dark Horse* (1973) ix. 124 The rich movers and shakers..always manage to manipulate the Congress for their own benefit and screw the rest of us. **1975** J. F. BURKE *Death Trick* iv. 61 Beniamino Tucci was..known as the Little Godfather of the Upper West Side. A mover and shaker with many interests. **1977** *Time* 10 Oct. 1/2 Perish the thought that a shaker and mover should work for the Government.

**b.** ***shaker off***: cf. SHAKE *v.* 19.

**1638** HEYWOOD *Wise Wom. Hogsdon* IV. G 4 b, *Harring.* Hee what art thou; *Sencer.* A hanger on, if it please you. *Harring.* And I a shaker off,..You shall not hang on mee. **1764** *Museum Rust.* II. xxv. 82 There are two men, called shakers off, that immediately follow the threshers; the first of them throws the coleseed straw up; the other strikes it as it rises, which helps to knock out what seed may be left.

**2. a.** One who or something which shakes, trembles, vibrates, etc. †Also, a boaster, swaggerer.

c 1440 *Promp. Parv.* 443/1 Schakare, or craker, or booste maker, *jactator*. 1573 Baret *Alv.* Sh. 265 Such a shaker or trotter. 1823 *Blackw. Mag.* XIV. 701 The pluckless shakers at his authority.

**b.** A simple percussion instrument that is shaken; *spec.* = chac-chac. Cf. shack-shack, etc.

[1837 I. M. Belisario *Sk. Negro Pop. in Jamaica* (caption to Plate 7), Shaka, a rattle used by the French Set Dancers.] 1943 *Penguin New Writing* XVIII. 96 He finished with a flourish of the shakers and threw his drumstick into the air. 1958 E. Borneman in P. Gammond *Decca Bk. Jazz* xxi. 275 A male leader and a small group..who accompanied themselves on..shakers and gong-gong. 1965 E. M. Matterson *Play with Purpose for Under-Sevens* ix. 145 Shakers can be made from a wide variety of empty containers to make a number of sounds. 1972 S. Dickinson *Mother's Help* iii. 45 Shakers or rattles, are probably the easiest instrument of all to make.

**†3.** ? A person of loose life. *Obs.*

?a 1500 *Nominale MS.* in Halliwell s.v. *Shake* (5), *Lascivus*, Anglice a schakere. 1694 Motteux *Rabelais* V. Pantagr. Prognost. v, Those whom Venus is said to Rule, as ..Wenchers, Leachers, Shakers [etc.].

**4.** With capital initial. **†a.** In the 17th c. applied to various sectaries whose devotional exercises were accompanied by 'shaking' or convulsions; often used as equivalent to quaker. *Obs.*

1648 *Scottish Mist Dispel'd* 17 If the Lord in mercy doe not afford us more liberty..in things Civill and Religious,.. we may be quickly reckoned amongst the new Sect of Shakers: you would make us tremble under your hands. 1654 Pagitt *Heresiogr.* (ed. 5) 136 The Shaker or Quaker. 1694 E. Chamberlayne *Pres. St. Eng.* III. i. 378 The other sort of Anabaptists are called Quakers or Shakers, from the Trembling and Quaking, caused in them by Vapours in their Ecstatick Fits.

**b.** One of an American religious sect (calling itself 'The Society of Believers in Christ's Second Appearing'), which exists in the form of mixed communities of men and women living in celibacy. Also *attrib.*, esp. of artefacts produced by or of a type produced by Shakers.

The first of these communities was founded by Ann Lee or Stanley, who emigrated from England in 1774.

1784 J. Belknap *Tour to White Mts.* (1876) 21 A man from Saco whose wife had run away with the Shakers. 1821 Coleridge *Lett.* (1836) II. 18 The Essenians for several ages subsisted by adoption: we shall see if the Shakers continue so long. 1842 Dickens *Amer. Notes* xv, These people are called Shakers from their peculiar form of adoration, which consists of a dance, performed by the men and women of all ages, who arrange themselves for that purpose in opposite parties.

*attrib.* 1817 *Niles' Reg.* XII. 371/1 At Enfield, Vermont, he visited the '*Habitation of the Shaken* [sic] *community*', to use their own phraseology, or in more familiar language the Shaking Quakers. 1837 Ht. Martineau *Soc. Amer.* II. 55, I visited two Shaker communities in Massachusetts. 1856 in C. C. Richards *Village Life in Amer.* (1912) 77 We went down town this morning and bought us some shaker bonnets to wear to school. 1863 *Trans. Illinois Agric. Soc.* (1865) V. 256 Your committee would..suggest that they put on their..shaker bonnet, [etc.]. 1864 T. Norris *Amer. Angler's Bk.* xiii. 371 Two or three pairs of stout yarn socks ('Shaker' socks are best). 1866 A. D. Whitney *Summer in Leslie Goldthwaite's Life* vi. 92 On this little green stood her Shaker rocking-chair. 1883 *Century Mag.* XXV. 525/1 A bonnet, hey?.. It looks like a Shaker cap. *Ibid.*, The Shaker sisters don't wear crimps. 1895 *Montgomery Ward Catal.* 561/3 Baby Carriage Robes..Shaker flannel, pinked edge and embroidered center. 1928 *Antiques* XIV. 134 A study of the characteristic forms of Shaker furniture suggests the hypothesis that the early craftsmen adapted to their own designs existing Colonial models. 1967 D. Skirrow *I was following this Girl* iii. 20 Early American Engraving up this way. Early Shaker Woodwork in the Brook Street Foyer. 1975 J. Gores *Hammett* i. 11 He wore a maroon worsted Shaker coat over a wool shirt. 1978 *Jrnl. R. Soc. Arts* CXXVI. 305/2 The Fraktur and Shaker artists, many of whose works..seem to have anticipated Paul Klee.

**c.** A member of a community in the New Forest, formed in 1864 by Mrs. Mary Ann Girling, who claimed to be an incarnation of God. (The name was popularly given to the sect from some resemblance to the Shaker communities of the U.S.)

1878 *Irish Monthly* Oct. 556 Hordle, where what are usually called the New Forest Shakers reside. *Ibid.* 559 The first Shaker I met.

**5.** The fan-tail pigeon. More fully ***shaker pigeon***.

1668 Charleton *Onomast.* 77 *Tremulæ*... Quakers or Shakers. a 1672 Willughby *Ornithol.* II. xv. §2 (1676) 131 Columbæ tremulæ laticaudæ; Anglicè Broad-taild Shakers. *Ibid.* 132 Columbæ tremulæ angusticaudæ..Narrow-tail'd Shakers. 1678 Ray *Willughby's Ornithol.* II. xv. § 2. 181 Broad-tail'd Shakers, called Shakers because they do almost constantly shake or wag their Heads and Necks up and down... Narrow-tail'd Shakers... This kind we have not as yet seen. 1735 J. Moore *Columbarium* 54. 1854 Meall *Moubray's Poultry* 252–3, II. Fantail, or Shaker... 12. Narrow-tailed Shaker.

**†6.** *pl. Sc.* An ornamentation or trimming for the dress composed of thin plates of metal which vibrate with the movements of the wearer; also *transf.*, vibrating drops of dew. *Obs.*

1506 *Acc. Ld. High Treas. Scot.* III. 313 Item, for xv goldin skinnis to stomois for thaim, and schakaris and bordouris to the tailes. 1513 Douglas *Æneis* v. vii. 18 And all his heid Of goldin schacaris and rois garlandis reid Buskit full weill. *Ibid.* XII. Prol., And syluer schakaris gan fra levis hyng. a 1568 *Tayis Bank* 21 (Bannatyne MS.) With schakeris of the schene dew schour, Schynnyng my courtenis schew. c 1600 Montgomerie *Cherrie & Slae* (Ever-green) 49 Floras fragrant flouris, Quhairon Apollos paramouris Had trinklit mony a teir; The quhilk lyke silvir schaikers shynd, Embroydering Bewties bed.

**7.** *pl. dial.* The quaking-grass, *Briza media*; also ***hayshakers*** and Sc. ***silver shakers***.

1597 Gerarde *Herbal* I. lvii. 80 Shakers, or quaking grasse. 1845 *New Statist. Acc. Scot.* IV. Kirkcudbr. 68 Shaking grass (the 'silver shaker'). 1889 *N.W. Linc. Gloss.* 1893 *Wiltshire Gloss.*, *Shakers*.

**8.** An implement, machine, etc. used for shaking.

**a.** A contrivance for shaking straw or hay.

1812 Sir J. Sinclair *Syst. Husb. Scot.* I. 90 An ingeniously-devised shaker..for clearing all the loose grain from among the straw. 1856 Morton *Cycl. Agric.* II. 966 (*Thrashing machine*) The straw, being taken off by the shakers..drops on the slide.

**b.** *Dyeing.* (See quot.)

1791 Hamilton *Berthollet's Dyeing* I. I. ii. 159 The silk is stretched out on a moveable pole, called a Shaker—kept continually in motion. 1837 Whittock *Bk. Trades, Dyer* (1842) 191.

**c.** A riddle or sieve (see quot.).

1906 J. Paterson *Wamphray* ii. 61 *note*, [A riddle] exactly like shakers used by masons at the present day to riddle lime.

**d.** A container in which cocktails or other mixed drinks are blended by shaking. Freq. as the second element of a comb.

1868 [see *cocktail shaker*]. 1889 J. G. Woolley *Seed Number One hard* (1893) 96 The bartender..makes the bits of ice, the spoon, the shaker, the strainer, the glasses, fairly play a tune. 1895 *Montgomery Ward Catal.* 435/1 Liquor Mixers or Lemonade Shakers of tin. 1922 S. Lewis *Babbitt* viii. 110 He did not possess a cocktail-shaker. A shaker was proof of dissipation. 1929 E. Linklater *Poet's Pub* II. 39 Holly poured his chosen liquors into a long silver shaker, added broken fragments of ice, screwed down the top, and, like a man with the palsy, shook. 1946 'P. Quentin' *Puzzle for Fiends* v. 35 She carried a small shaker of Manhattans. 1959 A. W. Sherring *Tip Off* xiii. 135 Big Boy Gale watched them in the bar mirror as he poured drinks from a shaker. 1971 *Scope* (S.Afr.) 19 Mar. 77/2 Many people consider the shaker and mixer as being the same thing, but there is a considerable difference: cocktails with clear ingredients are prepared by stirring in a mixer, cloudy liquids are agitated in a shaker.

**e.** A machine for mechanically agitating fluids.

1897 *Brit. Med. Jrnl.* 27 Mar. 776/2 The residue [was] extracted with water. This was accomplished in twenty-four hours and was assisted by an electrically-driven 'shaker'.

**f.** *U.S.* = castor[2] I.

1910 J. W. Tompkins *Mothers & Fathers* 29 Miss Elsie would be terribly shocked at this shaker. 1969 J. A. McPherson in A. Chapman *New Black Voices* (1972) 153 Shouldn't you polish the shakers or clean out the Pantry or squeeze oranges? 1978 S. Brill *Teamsters* vii. 284 The small formica booth table with the mini-juke box built into the wall just above the salt and pepper shakers.

**9.** Short for *Shaker bonnet*: see sense 4 b above. *U.S. local.*

1858 M. D. Colt *Let.* in *Went to Kansas* (1862) xiii. 238, I did not wear the green silk calash, but a shaker, made of brown muslin smoothed over a pasteboard frame; it was very fashionable; besides it kept the sun out of my face, and was very genteel for a school-ma'am. 1881 *Harper's Mag.* May 854/2 The bonnet is far too fine. I will buy me a shaker at the store. 1905 K. D. Wiggin *Rose o' River* 9 Rose had tried on..children's gingham 'Shakers', mourning bonnets for aged dames, [etc.]. 1909 *Dialect Notes* III. 415 *Shaker*, a palm leaf sunbonnet.

Hence **'Shakerdom**, the Shakers as a class. **'Shakeress**, a female Shaker. **'Shakerism**, the principles and practice of the Shakers.

1818 *Catholic Vindicator* 5 Dec. 41 Anabaptism or independentism, quakerism or shakerism. 1822 Mary M. Dyer (*title*) A Portraiture of Shakerism. 1861 J. G. Holland *Lessons in Life* vi. 87, I object to their style of life and piety, and to everything outside of Shakerdom. 1860 *Reynolds's Misc.* 15 Sept. XXV. 180/2 Two comely Shakeresses wait upon you. 1868 *Morn. Star* 8 June, The Owenite experiments in England and America have failed, but Shakerism is a living and triumphant fact. 1870 D. Macrae *Amer. at Home* II. xxx. 358 We followed the Shakeress..within doors.

**'shake-rag.** [f. shake *v.* + rag *sb.*] A ragged disreputable person; also *attrib.* or *adj.*, beggarly. Cf. shack-rag, shag-rag.

1571 Golding *Calvin on Ps.* lxix. 13. 259 It is no maruell that shakerags [orig. *sordidos homines*] (which haue no regarde of honestie) did..raile with out shame. 1610 Healey *St. Aug. Citie of God* VII. xi. 269 Pecunia,..one of the shake-rag goddesses in our forth booke. 1641 Brome *Jovial Crew* III. (1652) H 4 b, Do you talk Shake-rag: Heart yond's more of 'em. I shall be Beggar-mawl'd if I stay. 1815 Scott *Guy M.* xxvi, 'He was a shake-rag like fellow', he said, 'and..had gipsy blood in his veins'.

Hence **† shake-ragged** *a.*

1560 Becon *Fortress of Faithful* Wks. II. 129 Who wyll be troubled..with suche a sorte of shake ragged slaues in a towne, whyche do nothynge but..fyll the towne full of beggers braules?

**shakerful** (ˈʃeɪkəfʊl). [f. shaker 8 d + -ful.] The contents of a (cocktail) shaker; the amount that a shaker will hold.

1946 E. Hodgins *Mr Blandings builds his Dream House* vii. 95 A second shakerful of still paler Martinis. 1966 T. Pynchon *Crying of Lot 49* i. 15 Gliding like a large bird in an updraft toward the sweating shakerful of booze. 1977 [see screwdriver 3].

**Shakescene** (ˈʃeɪksiːn). *arch. rare.* [f. shake *v.* + scene *sb.*; in allusion to the name *Shakspere*.

Cf. B. Jonson *To Memory of Author* in *Shaks. Wks.* (1623), I would..call forth..Æschilus..To life againe, to heare thy Buskin tread, And shake a Stage.]

(Of uncertain or vague meaning: used by Greene in his attack on Shakspere.)

a 1592 Greene *Groatsw. Wit* (1874) 30 He..is in his owne conceit the onely Shake-scene in a countrie.

**'shake-spear,** *a. nonce-wd.* [f. shake *v.*] That brandishes a spear (tr. Gr. δορυσσόος).

1853 M. J. Chapman tr. *Theocritus* Idyll XXII. xvii, Castor ..The brass-mailed, shake-spear knight.

**Shakespeare** (ˈʃeɪkspiːə(r)). [The name of William *Shakespeare*: see Shakespearian *a.* (and *sb.*).] **1.** A person (occas. a thing) comparable to Shakespeare, esp. as being preeminent in a particular sphere.

1821 M. Edgeworth *Let.* 23 Oct. (1971) 243 Humboldt is the Shakespear of travellers—as much superior in genius to other travellers as Shakespear to other poets. 1859 A. J. Munby *Diary* 17 Mar. (1972) 28 When..the poetic soul.. has learnt..to see the poetic side of all such things, *then* we may have a Homer of the railway and a Shakespeare of the Ballot. 1905 'Mark Twain' in *N. Amer. Rev.* Jan. 3 The telegraph, the telephone..the Pullman car..the Shakespeares of the inventor-tribe, so to speak. 1931 R. Campbell *Georgiad* ii. 36 A Fabian Shakespeare of the Summer Schools To other poets laying down my rules.

**2.** *attrib.*, as **Shakespeare collar**, (*a*) = *polo collar* s.v. polo[1] 4; (*b*) (see quot. 1960); **Shakespeare country**, the part of Warwickshire around Stratford-on-Avon, birthplace of Shakespeare; **Shakespeare industry**, the large-scale production of writings about Shakespeare, items commemorating Shakespeare, etc.; the commercial exploitation of objects, places, etc., associated with Shakespeare.

1907 *Yesterday's Shopping* (1969) 873/1 Cotton Football Shirts..Shakespeare collar, and three buttons. 1913 [see *polo collar* s.v. polo *sb.*[1] 4]. 1960 C. W. Cunnington et al. *Dict. Eng. Costume* 192/1 *Shakespeare collar.* 1860's on. A shallow turn-over collar, the points projecting downwards onto the shirt-front. 1900 J. Leyland *Shakespeare Country* 92 This survey of Shakespeare Country has traversed a rich district of middle England that was familiar to the great poet in his boyhood. 1966 J. Wainwright *Crystallised Carbon Pig* iv. 20 The plan worked..as smoothly..as an American tourist's trip through the Shakespeare country. 1972 *Times* 4 Aug. 4/2 The 'Shakespeare country' around Stratford-upon-Avon, Oxford and Cambridge are the main non-metropolitan attractions. 1939 Brown & Fearon (*title*) Amazing monument: a short history of the Shakespeare industry. 1958 *Listener* 2 Oct. 523/1 Is not much of this book-making on the Bard another branch of the Shakespeare industry? 1962 *Observer* 4 Mar. 13/6 The 1864 affair..marked the dawn of the Shakespeare industry. At Stratford..'streets were adorned with flags and banners; the townsfolk and visitors wore the..Shakespeare badge', [etc.].

Hence **'Shakespeare** *v. intr.* (*nonce-wd.*), to act in a Shakespeare play.

1896 G. B. Shaw *Our Theatres in Nineties* (1932) II. 90 Madame de Navarro has declaimed, spouted, statuesqued, Shakespeared, and all the rest of it.

**Shakespearian** (ʃeɪkˈspɪərɪən), *a.* (and *sb.*) Also **Shakespearean, Shakspe(a)rian, -ean.** [f. *Shakespeare* + -ian.

The forms in *-ian* are alone correct according to the relevant analogies. The other variations follow the diversities of spelling of the poet's name. The spelling *Shakspere*, adopted in the first edition of this Dictionary, was advocated by Sir F. Madden on the ground of the signature in the poet's copy of Florio's *Montaigne*, and accepted by Dr. Furnivall and the New Shakspere Society; the standard form is now *Shakespeare*.]

**A.** *adj.* Of or pertaining to, or having the characteristics of William Shakespeare (1564–1616) or his dramatic and poetical productions.

1755 H. Fielding *Voy. to Lisbon* 100 A poetic, if not a Shakespearian genius. 1805 C. Wilmot *Let.* 4 Aug. in *Russ. Jrnls.* (1934) II. 164, I rooted out Hamlet's Garden..& got into a *Shakespearian tantrum* at finding myself in the place. 1817 Keats *Wks.* (1889) III. 10 The acting of Kean is Shakespearian. 1820 Coleridge *Lett.* (1836) I. 49 The almost Shakespearian old witch-wives at the funeral [in Scott's *Bride of Lammermoor*]. 1886 C. E. Pascoe *Lond. of To-day* xxxiv. (ed. 3) 304 The Princess's Theatre, in the days of Charles Kean famous for its Shakespearian revivals.

**B.** *sb.* An authority on or student of the writings of Shakespeare; a Shakespearian scholar. Also, one who believes that Shakespeare wrote the plays usually attributed to him; an imitator of Shakespeare's style, one of his school; an admirer of Shakespeare's works.

1837 Lockhart *Scott* II. viii. 294 She was, however, about as devout a Shakspearian as her nephew. 1874 [see Baconian *a.* and *sb.* 2]. 1912 E. Nesbit *Let.* in D. L. Moore *E. Nesbit* (1933) xv. 268 Are you a Baconian or a Shakespearean? 1930 N. Streatfeild *Ballet Shoes* iii. 38 We'll read some more one day. I'll make a Shakespearean of you. 1964 *English Studies* XLV. 353 It also establishes the negative method of praising Heywood, as a minor Shakespearian. 1971 *Daily Tel.* 8 Mar. 10/4 One of those devoted Shakespeareans who knows his author backwards. 1979 F. Kermode *Genesis of Secrecy* iv. 79 Shakespearians may find explanations of the mysteriousness .. of *Hamlet*, by considering instead the *ur-Hamlet*.

Hence **Shake'spearianism**, (*a*) a form of expression peculiar to or imitated from Shakespeare (*Cent. Dict.* 1891, and in later Dicts.); (*b*) the imitation of Shakespeare, or the effects of his influence generally. Similarly **Shakespeari'ana** (see -ANA). **Shake'spearianizing** *vbl. sb.*, the action or instances of imitating passages from the works of Shakespeare. **Shake'spearianly** *adv.*, in a Shakespearian manner. **'Shakespearism** = *Shakespearianism* (*a*). **'Shakespearite**, one who believes that Shakespeare wrote the plays traditionally attributed to him. **'Shakespearize** *v.*, *trans.* to imbue with the spirit or ideas of Shakespeare; *intr.* to imitate Shakespeare. **Shakespea'rolater**, a worshipper of Shakespeare. **Shakespea'rolatry**, worship of Shakespeare. **Shakespea'rology**, the branch of study concerned with the works and life of Shakespeare.

**1718** C. GILDON *Compl. Art Poetry* I. 305 Shakespeariana: or Select Moral Reflections, Topicks, Similies, and Descriptions from Shakespear. **1823** LAMB *Lett.* (1888) II. 79 In the same collection I find several Shakspearisms. **1836** EMERSON *Nature, Amer. Schol.* Wks. (Bohn) II. 178 The English dramatic poets have Shakespearized now for two hundred years. **1847** —— *Repr. Men, Shakespeare* Wks. (Bohn) I. 359 Now, literature, philosophy, and thought are Shakespearized. **1861** *Sat. Rev.* 30 Nov. 557/2 'The national pulse beats Shaksperianly.' So at least says Mr. James Orchard Halliwell in one of two circulars .. which have lately reached us about 'the National Shaksperian Fund'. **1862** *Daily Tel.* 20 Jan., The most commendable act performed of late years in Shakespeareology. **1864** *Realm* 9 Mar. 6 In these days of Shakspearolatry. **1865** F. THIMM (*title*) Shakespeariana from 1564 to 1864. **1875** L. TOLLEMACHE in *Fortn. Rev.* Mar. 335 The strained efforts of the Shakespearolaters to find dramatic propriety in the most inappropriate passages. **1886** *Contemp. Rev.* Aug. 250, I think that the spirit of modern Shakespearianism, among readers, critics, and actors, is quite false to Shakspeare himself. **1890** *Merry England* July 242 A fine, Shakespearianly virile bit of poetry. **1903** G. B. SHAW *Let.* 12 Jan. (1972) II. 303 Ben Jonson never could quite get over the absurdity of the Shakespearisms which he knew so well at the Mermaid passing off in cold ink as literature. **1908** *Daily Chron.* 21 Mar. 5/1 But Shakespeareanism is not dead yet a while. **1909** 'MARK TWAIN' *Is Shakespeare Dead?* v. 50 Two of these cults are known as the Shakespearites and the Baconians... The Shakespearite knows that Shakespeare wrote Shakespeare's Works. **1921** G. B. SHAW in *John Keats Memorial Volume* 176 The lines beginning (Shakespearianly) with How fever'd is the man who cannot look Upon his mortal days with temperate blood! **1936** F. R. LEAVIS *Revaluation* vi. 223 *The Cenci* .. is full of particular echoes of Shakespeare... This Shakespearianizing .. is .. quite damning. **1953** *John o' London's* 12 June 520/4 A musical piece, with Arthur Askey .. Shakespeareanly disguised. It was called *The Kid from Stratford.* **1955** *Times* 3 Aug. 9/5 One such foundation has for many years placed a standing order for the purchase of Shakespeariana offered at our leading sale rooms. **1964** *Economist* 11 Apr. 144/3 The appetite for Shakespeareana.

**shake-up:** see SHAKE *sb.*[1] 8.

**shakily** ('ʃeɪkɪlɪ), *adv.* [f. SHAKY *a.* + -LY[2].] In a shaky manner, unsteadily.

**1863** HUXLEY *Man's Place Nat.* I. 36 On the ground, the Orang always goes laboriously and shakily, on all fours. **1877** BOX *Eng. Game of Cricket* 337 The 'glorious Tennent' next appeared [as batsman], and began very shakily indeed. **1912** *Engl. Review* Feb. 461 Frances laughed shakily.

**shakiness** ('ʃeɪkɪnɪs). [f. SHAKY *a.* + -NESS.] The condition of being shaky.

**1862** *Cornhill Mag.* VI. 613 Shakiness of the hand [is] a sign of poisoning. **1884** CHURCH *Bacon* i. The shakiness of current doctrines .. on religion and policy.

**shaking** ('ʃeɪkɪŋ), *vbl. sb.* [-ING[1].]

**1. a.** The action of the verb SHAKE, in any sense.

*c* **1380** WYCLIF *Sel. Eng. Wks.* III. 313 Bi here newe dampnacion þat þei maden at London in þe erþe schakyng. *c* **1450** CAPGRAVE *Life St. Gilbert* xxiv. 98 All þe toknes [of the fever] wer come, as schakyng, akyng of þe hed and swech oþir. **1575** GASCOIGNE *Kenelworth* II. ii. Wks. 1910 II. 113 It was the shaking of some leafe. **1586** T. B. *La Primaud. Fr. Acad.* I. 326 Few there are, who, in great overthwarts and shakings of fortune, have harts sufficiently staied to practise .. that which they commend. **1685** tr. *St. Evremond's Mixt Ess.* 24 With their warblings and shakings, they [the Spaniards] seem to mind nothing in their singing, but to contend with Nightingales. **1782** J. ADAMS *Fam. Lett.* (1876) 404 But shaking on horseback guards pretty well against it. **1891** EARL LYTTON *Lett.* (1906) II. 430 The shaking I got on my way from London to Paris made last Sunday a terribly painful one to me. **1899** R. WHITEING *No. 5 John St.* 157 The great need of the age is a good sound shaking, to get the nonsense out.

†**b.** The gathering, harvesting, falling or shedding (of fruit or grain). *lit.* and *fig.* *Obs.*

**1623** in Foster *Eng. Factories Ind.* (1908) II. 237 These fellowes are growne ripe; I hope wee shall have the shakinge of them. **1637** *MS. Acc. St. John's Hosp., Canterb.*, Payd for shakinge of our frute o 2 o. **1658** [see *shaking-time* in 4]. *c* **1750** *MS. relating to Suffolk Manors*, No person shall in the time of Shaking .. keep any drove cattle in the fields.

**c.** With advs.

*c* **1440** *Promp. Parv.* 443/2 Schakynge a-wey, *excussio.* **1613** HIERON *Back-parts Jehovah* Serm. (1614) 180 A shaking off of that due obedience we owe vnto him. **1683** MOXON *Mech. Exerc., Printing* XII. xix. 172 The Break made by the Shaking out of the Mettal. **1866** W. COLLINS *Armadale* II. vii, A good shaking-up is just the thing for you, after being so long indoors. **1897** H. A. JONES *Case Rebell. Susan* I. 19, I allow every married couple twelve months for what I call the shaking-down process. **1926** J. S. HUXLEY *Ess. in Pop. Sci.* ix. 118 Taking them [*sc.* Infusoria] on a railway journey to give them a good shaking-up. **1928** *Daily Mail* 9 Aug. 12/4 The best opinion is that a thorough shaking-out will do much good, but there is no need for alarm. **1958** L. DURRELL *Mountolive* vi. 134 Only Pursewarden had not put in an appearance... Mountolive planned to give him a shaking-up at the first opportunity.

†**d.** ***the shaking of the sheets***: the name of a dance (in the 16–17th c. very often used jocularly for sexual intercourse). *Obs.*

? *c* **1570** *Misogonus* II. iv. 272 To that daunce of all other I see he is bent. *Sr.* Faythe no I had rather haue shakinge oth shetes. **1589** *Pappe w. Hatchet* Lyly's Wks. 1902 III. 411 O tis his best daunce next shaking of the sheetes. **1633** ROWLEY *Match at Midn.* III. i, Thee and I shall dance the shaking of the sheetes together. **1654** GAYTON *Pleas. Notes* I. vii. 25 He knew not what a dance the Don would lead him, before he return'd to the shaking of the sheets, with his Joan Gutierez.

*transf.* **16..** *Ballad, Doleful Dance & Song of Death* i, Can you dance the shaking of the Sheets, a Dance that every one must do?.. Make ready then your winding sheet. **1604** *Meeting of Gallants at Ordinarie* C 3, But this youngster daunced the shaking of one sheet [*i.e.* died] within fewe dayes after.

**2.** A disease in sheep and swine (see quot. *a* 1722). Also the ague. Chiefly in plural.

**1642** FULLER *Holy & Prof. St.* v. xi. 401 Being good Physick for the sheep to keep them from the Shakings. *a* **1722** LISLE *Husb.* (1757) 339 Some years the sheep will be apt to be taken with a disease they call the shaking .. : it is a weakness which seizes their hinder quarters, so that they cannot rise up when they are down. **1736** BAILEY *Househ. Dict.* s.v. *Tremour*, The tremour or shaking in Swine. **1877** *Holderness Gloss.*, *Shakkins*, the ague. 'Thoo dodhers as if thoo'd getten shakkins.'

**3.** *concr.* That which is shaken off, out, down, etc. *Naut.* (see quots. 1867–86). Also with advs. *down*, *off*, *out*. Chiefly in plural.

**1382** WYCLIF *Isa.* xvii. 6 As the shaking out of the oile berie. **1388** *Ibid.*, As the schakyng doun of the fruyt of olyue tre. **1682** *J. Houghton's Coll. Lett. Husb.* etc. No. 7 I. 70 The Shakings of the Cloth. **1754** P. H. *Hiberniad* iv. 29 Luxuriant Congreve (the .. Shakings-off of whose Pen, would invigorate twenty of our late spiritless miscall'd Comedies). **1839** *Nautical Mag.* 726 [Heading of miscellaneous items of news.] Shakings. **1867** SMYTH *Sailor's Word-bk.*, *Shakings*, refuse of cordage, canvas, &c., used for making oakum, paper, &c. **1886** *Tinsley's Mag.* Sept. 287 Shakings are the sweepings of the deck gathered together after the day's work is done. *Ibid.*, 'Mere shakings' is a term used by seamen to express worthless men.

**4.** *attrib.* and *Comb.*, as ***shaking time***; also in the names of machines used for agitating materials, as ***shaking barrel***, also ***shaking frame***, ***table*** (Knight *Dict. Mech.* 1875); **shaking cure, machine** (see quots.); **shaking stop**, the tremolo organ stop.

**1884** *B'ham Daily Post* 23 Feb. 2/4 Boot-rivet Machines, Spring Punches, *Shaking Barrel. **1898** *Syd. Soc. Lex.*, **Shaking cure*, the treatment of certain nervous diseases, such as paralysis agitans, by means of a vibrating arm-chair. **1850** HOLTZAPFFEL *Turning* III. 1090 Rumble or *Shaking Machine. This is a contrivance sometimes used for polishing small articles principally by their attrition against each other. **1659** C. SIMPSON *Division-Violist* I. 9 Some also affect a kind of Shake or Tremble with the Bow, like the *shaking Stop of an Organ. **1665** in Hopkins *Organ* (1845) *Hist.* 52 One Shaking Stopp. **1658** GURNALL *Chr. in Arm.* verse 14 xii. II. 284 Away they runne with their enjoyments, .. like hogges in *shaking time. **1706** PHILLIPS (ed. Kersey), *Shacking-time*, the Season when Mast is ripe.

**shaking** ('ʃeɪkɪŋ), *ppl. a.* [f. SHAKE *v.* + -ING[2].]

**a.** In the senses of the verb. Of a bog, morass, etc.: Quaking. ***shaking stone***, a rocking stone.

*a* **1225** *Ancr. R.* 60 [Lechery] mid schekinde word ȝiueð speres wunden. *c* **1380** WYCLIF *Wks.* (1880) 210 þei .. suffre pore men haue nakid sidis & schakynge lippis & hondis for cold. **1578** J. DERRICKE *Image Irel.* (1581) D iij b, And brought from Boggs to champion ground, .. Yet doe thei loke to shaking boggs. **1660** R. MAY *Accompl. Cook* (1665) 180 To make a Shaking Pudding. **1662** RAY *Itin.* iii. Sel. Rem. (1760) 240 Here lies a Stone, called the shaking Stone. **1763** MILLS *Pract. Husb.* I. 137 Mr. Eliot's contrivance to drain a piece of shaking meadow, as he calls it. **1773** GOLDSM. *She stoops to conq.* II, Item .. a Florentine, a shaking pudding. **1842** LOVER *Handy Andy* xxiii, The cat made for a shaking bog—the loneliest place in the whole country. **1889** P. H. EMERSON *Eng. Idyls* 133 Holding their shaking sides.

**b.** Of a disease: Characterized by a tremulous agitation of the head or limbs.

**1528** PAYNELL *Salerne's Regim.* Y ij, White pepper is holsome for a shakynge feuer. **1615** CROOKE *Body of Man* 401 The disease called Tremor, or the shaking palsie. **1888** [see PARKINSON[1]]. **1905** *Brit. Med. Jrnl.* 25 Feb. 406/1 He had a shaking chill followed by a sweat. **1955** [see PARKINSON[1]].

*transf.* **1595** SHAKS. *John* II. i. 228 Bulletts wrapt in fire To make a shaking feuer in your walles.

**c.** ***Shaking Quaker*** = SHAKER 4 b.

**1784** *Mass. Spy* 1 Jan., in R. H. Thornton *Amer. Gloss.* (1912), The people in the Western part of this State, who stile themselves Shaking Quakers. **1839** MARRYAT *Diary Amer.* Ser. I. I. 114, I had intended to .. proceed from thence to New Lebanon to visit the Shaking Quakers.

**d.** quasi-*adv.*

**1890** 'R. BOLDREWOOD' *Col. Reformer* (1891) 240 What a lot of rattling bullocks, shaking fat too.

Hence **'shakingly** *adv.*

**1889** *Cornhill Mag.* Oct. 438 'Tell her, please, Bryan', I say, shakingly.

**shako** ('ʃækəʊ). Also **schakos, schako;** and see CHACO. [a. Magyar *csákó*, short for *csákó süveg*, more correctly *csákos süveg* peaked cap (*csákos* being an adj. f. *csák* peak, believed by native scholars to be a. G. *zacken* point, spike).

The word has been adopted into several European langs.; the F. *schako* may be the proximate source. While the shako was still worn in the British army, the pronunciation was ('ʃækəʊ) among officers, but (ʃə'kuː) in the ranks.]

A military cap in the shape of a truncated cone, with a peak and either a plume or a ball or 'pompom'. (Not now worn by British soldiers.)

**1815** SCOTT *Paul's Lett.* xiii. (1816) 317 [The French guide] puts on the *schakos*, which he has hitherto held in his hand. **1852** LIEUT.-COL. J. LUARD *Dress Brit. Soldier* 158 We have introduced the large-topped, overweighted shako from the French. **1868** *Queen's Regul. Army* ¶67 Officers in uniform are not to take off their shakos or forage Caps in Saluting. **1903** J. CONRAD & F. M. HUEFFER *Romance* II. ii. 60 The little worsted balls on the infantry shakos.

**shak-shak**, variant of CHAC-CHAC.

**1905** *Contemp. Rev.* Oct. 510 An African revivalist .. who should attempt to arouse the ecstasies of a West Indian meeting with no more elaborate orchestra than a bull-roarer and a shak-shak.

**Shaksper-:** see SHAKESPEARIAN, etc.

**Shakti**, var. SAKTI.

‖**shaku** ('ʃaku). Also 8 **sackf, sak, saku.** Pl. same. [Jap., ad. Chinese *chǐ* a foot.] **1.** A Japanese measure of length, equal to 11·9 inches (30·3 cm.); (see also quot. 1974).

**1727** J. G. SCHEUCHZER tr. *Kæmpfer's Hist. Japan* I. xi. 136 One *Sackf* and a half long. *Ibid.* II. iv. 180 Snow .. to the height of four *Sak* and five Suns, that is about four foot and a half. *Ibid.* III. vi. 246 His Stature .. of nine *Saku*, and nine *Suns*, proportionable to the greatness of his Genius. **1878** *Trans. Asiatic Soc. Japan* VI. II. 249 The seismograph consisted of a copper vessel, whose diameter was 8 *shaku* or feet. **1884** tr. *J. J. Rein's Japan* ii. 415 The interval of three shaku (1 metre). **1893** E. ARNOLD *Adzuma* I. i. 2 He could .. run so fleetly that a cord of thirty *shaku*, tied to his waist, would stream in a straight line behind him. **1974** *Encycl. Brit. Micropædia* IX. 106/3 *Shaku*, a unit of length, area, and volume in Japan, equivalent to 10/33 metre, 3·306 square decimetres, and 18·039 cubic centimetres.

**2.** A flat baton made of wood or horn, a little over a foot in length, upon which a Japanese court noble formerly would note memoranda, but later carried as a mark of honour in the presence of the emperor, or by the emperor himself.

**1875** F. V. DICKINS tr. *Chiushingura* (1876) 208 'Twas the Emperor's whim That the tree should from him Have a *shaku* with Ta-iu writ on. **1880** *Trans. Asiatic Soc. Japan* VIII. 351 A short staff called the *Shaku*, which was generally held vertical in the right hand. **1894** C. M. SALWEY *Fans of Japan* 6 The *shaku* .. was a stick in the shape of the outside frame of a folding fan, about two feet in length, about an inch and a half to two inches at the top, decreasing at the base to about one inch. **1928** *Daily Express* 12 Nov. 3/7 The Emperor, after seating himself on the throne, was presented with the small wooden baton (shaku) which is a traditional symbol of authority found in many Shinto rites.

‖**shakudo** ('ʃakudo). [a. Japanese *shakŭ dō*, ad. an older form of Chinese *ch'ih t'ung* red copper.] A Japanese alloy of copper and gold. Also *attrib.*

It is often subjected to a chemical process, which produces a blue patina.

**1860** S. B. KEMISH *Jap. Empire* 114 The beautiful work called *syakfdo*, in which various metals are partly blended, partly combined, producing an effect much resembling fine enamel. **1878** *Jrnl. Applied Sci.* Apr. IX. 61/2 The dark blue colour .. is that of the Shakudo, composed of copper, and three or four per cent. of gold. **1911** *Encycl. Brit.* XV. 179/2 To apply a lining of silver to a shakudo box. **1981** G. MACBETH *Kind of Treason* ix. 91 The little black cups of the *nanako* on the *shakudo* grounds.

‖**shakuhachi** (ʃaku'hatʃi). [Jap., f. SHAKU + *hachi* eight (tenths).] An end-blown Japanese flute, made of bamboo.

**1893** F. T. PIGGOTT *Music & Musical Instruments of Japan* I. 43 The Shakuhachi, introduced into Japan from China by Prince Tsuneyoshi as far back as .. 1335, seems to have been treated from the first as a solo instrument. **1949** *Western Folklore* July 202 Their melodies are found to be very pleasing, especially if the *shakuhachi*, or bamboo flute, is used as accompaniment. **1965** W. SWAAN *Jap. Lantern* ii. 22 Two itinerant beggar-priests playing the shakuhachi, an archaic type of bamboo flute. **1981** *Daily Tel.* 17 Mar. 11/7 The first half was devoted to traditional pieces, performed on the shakuhachi, a simple bamboo flute.

**shaky** ('ʃeɪkɪ), *a.* Also **shakey.** [f. SHAKE *v.* or *sb.*[1] + -Y.]

**1.** Of timber: Fissured = SHAKEN 4.

**1703** T. N. *City & C. Purch.* 241 Such Stuff as is crack'd, either with the Heat of the Sun, or the Drought of the Wind, is call'd shaky, or shaken Stuff. **1851** *Palace of Industry* 18 If found to be shaky, they [*sc.* sash-bars] are rejected as unfit to be used. **1868** *Harper's Mag.* XXXVI. 418 Some of the pines were short and scraggy, some were shaky.

**2. a.** Of a structure: Given to shaking by the looseness of its parts; liable to break down or give way; unsound. Of ground: Not firm or solid.

**1850** OGILVIE, *Shaky*, 2. loosely put together; ready to come to pieces. *Familiar*. **1860** TYNDALL *Glac.* I. xxv. 182 The bridge was so frail and shaky at the place of junction. **1871** *Punch* 2 Dec. 228/2 The chair.. so shaky in the legs. **1894** *Bookseller's Catal.*, Binding shaky.

**b.** *the Shaky Isles* (colloq.), New Zealand (from the frequency of earthquakes).

**1933** *Bulletin* (Sydney) 2 Aug. 20/2 The widespread notion that they're peculiar to the Shaky Isles. **1941** S. J. BAKER *N.Z. Slang* vi. 49 New Zealand was no longer merely a colony; it became *the Dominion, the Shakey Isles*,.. and so on. **1971** *Sunday Tel.* (Sydney) 16 May 37/2 He came over from the Shaky Isles in his early 30s.

**3. a.** Of a person or his limbs: Trembling with age, infirmity, apprehension or fear.

**1850** THACKERAY *Pendennis* lxx, The old fellow's hand was very cold and shaky. **1871** O. W. HOLMES *Smiling Listener* 46 Well, Time with.. his shaky old fingers will soon snuff us out.

**b.** Of writing: Tremulous.

**1848** THACKERAY *Van. Fair* xxxviii, All he did was to sign the circulars.. and direct them in a shaky, clerk-like hand. **1891** C. JAMES *Rom. Rigmarole* 92 At this point the writing began to grow very shaky and weak.

**4.** Characterized by or causing shaking or jolting.

**1860** *Merc. Mar. Mag.* VII. 290 It is rather a shaky business.. riding over those roads in a cart. **1883** C. HOWARD *Roads Eng. & Wales* (ed. 3) 138 The surface is rather shaky for quick riding.

**5.** In immaterial sense.

**a.** Of a person's position, credit, securities, etc.: Insecure, liable to fail or be upset, unreliable.

**1841** THACKERAY *Gt. Hoggarty Diam.* x, Our director was —what is not to be found in Johnson's *Dictionary*—rather shaky. Three of his companies had broken, four more were in a notoriously insolvent state. **1853** WILBERFORCE 3 Nov., *Life* (1881) II. 225 Lord Aberdeen now growing to look upon Gladstone as his successor... Cabinet shaky. **1865** MISS BRADDON *Sir Jasper's Tenant* I. xiv. 302 With a view to raising money on very shaky security. **1884** *Law Times* 1 Nov. LXXVIII. 10/2 The manufacturer, whose credit is so shaky. **1908** *Blackw. Mag.* July 130/2 His seat in Parliament was shaky.

**b.** Unsettled in allegiance or belief.

**1853** LYTTON *My Novel* XI. xvii, Well,.. I must be off presently to see those three shaky voters in Fish Lane. **1857** LADY CANNING in A. J. C. Hare *Two Noble Lives* (1893) II. 202 The shaky regiment, the 37th, had tried to tamper with the Seiks. **1884** *Contemp. Rev.* Jan. 141 A work.. calculated to render persons who are shaky in their belief in religion.. more shaky still.

**c.** Not completely sound in health.

**1844** DICKENS *Let.* 26 Feb. *Lett.* (1880) I. 100, I am rather shaky just now, but shall pull up. **1856** H. H. DIXON *Post & Paddock* 26 If his legs are shaky, he [the racehorse] is trained 'through the muzzle', as a forlorn hope.

**d.** Of knowledge, or persons with reference to this: Uncertain, doubtfully adequate, not to be depended on.

**1860** *Hotten's Slang Dict.*, *Shaky*, said.. at the University, of one not likely to pass his examination. **1881** *Century Mag.* XXIII. 934/2 In shaky but intelligible Spanish he asked.. to see her father. **1889** W. S. GILBERT *Gondoliers* II, He is shaky in his spelling, so we help him if we can.

**e.** *shaky do* [DO *sb.*[1] 2 b], a difficult or risky situation, a close shave. *slang* (orig. *R.A.F.*).

**1942** T. RATTIGAN *Flare Path* III. 150 They had rather a shaky do last night. **1943** C. H. WARD-JACKSON *It's a Piece of Cake* 54 *A shaky-do*, any occurrence that has serious consequences or just escapes them. This may vary from a pilot temporarily losing control of his Whitley as a result of being hit by flak, to an erk who is out of station bounds without a pass and only just avoids a Service policeman. **1944** T. H. WISDOM *Triumph over Tunisia* ix. 79 No. 18 Squadron, which had been involved in many similar 'Shaky do's', was asked to lay on the raid. **1949** F. MACLEAN *Eastern Approaches* II. vi. 244 The earth all round was kicked up by a burst from the plane's tail-gunner... 'This,' said the Australian, 'is going to be a shaky do.'

**shalche**: see SHALL *v.* A. 6 a.

†'**shalder**, *sb.*[1] ? *Obs.* *rare*⁻¹. [related to SHALDER *v.*] ? A flake, split-off piece of stone.

**1577** HARRISON *England* III. xv. [ix.] 114 b, Yᵉ flint and chalke, the shalder and the peble.

**shalder** ('ʃɔːldə(r)), *sb.*[2] Also 9 chalder, shelder, schalder, shaalder. [Of obscure origin. Cf. SCOLDER[2], SCALEDRAKE, SHELDEN, SHELDRAKE.] The oyster-catcher, *Hæmatopus ostralegus*.

**1828** FLEMING *Brit. Anim.* 115 *Hæmotopus Ostralegus*. Common Oyster-catcher... *N.*, Chalder, Skeldrake. **1866** T. EDMONSTON *Shetl. & Orkney Gloss.*, Schalder. S. **1877** G. STEWART *Shetl. Fireside T.* ix. 68 The scream of the frighted shelder.

**shalder** ('ʃɔːldə(r)), *sb.*[3] *dial.* Also shelder. [Of unknown origin.] A rush or sedge growing in ditches, esp. the yellow iris, *Iris Pseudacorus*.

**1825** JENNINGS *Observ. Dial. W. Eng.* 66 *Shalder*, a kind of broad flat rush, growing in ditches. **1873** W. P. WILLIAMS & W. A. JONES *Somerset. Gloss.* 32 *Shalder*.

†'**shalder**, *v.* *Obs. rare*. Also 8 shelder. [? Cogn. w. SHALE *sb.* Cf. SHALDER *sb.*[1], SHADDER *v.*] *intr.* To crumble.

**1577** HARRISON *England* II. iii. [I. xv.] 69 b, Till such time as two hils betwixt which it ran, did shalder & so choke vp his [the river's] course. **1707** MORTIMER *Husb.* (1721) I. 75 Rising in gross Clods at the first breaking up of the Plough, and sheldring with the Frost. *Ibid.* II. 200 If you dig them often, the Sun, Rain, and Frosts will mellow them, so as to cause them to shelder into Dust.

**shale** (ʃeɪl), *sb.*[1] *Obs.* exc. *dial.* (in various senses see *Eng. Dial. Dict.*). Forms: 1 scealu, scalu, 3–5, 7, 9 *dial.* schale, 4 schal, 5 *pl.* shalus, 6 shaell, (7 *erron.* shalt), 4 shale. [OE. *sc(e)alu* str. fem.:—OTeut. **skalō*, ablaut-variant of **skǣlō*, represented by ON. *skál* SCALE *sb.*[1], q.v. for the Teut. cognates.]

†**1.** A dish; a cup or goblet: = SCALE *sb.*[1] 1. *Obs.*

*c* **1075** in Kemble *Cod. Dipl.* IV. 275, .VI. mæsene sceala. *a* **1225** [see SCALE *sb.*[1] 1 β]. *c* **1325** *Metr. Hom.* 120 Seruanz war at this bridale, That birled win in cupp and schal.

†**2.** A shell, husk, esp. the shell or outer covering of a nut, which encloses the kernel; also the pod of peas or beans, etc. *Obs.*

[Also in †*nutshale*, examples of which (*c* 1205–1577) are given under NUTSHELL *sb.*, where see the equivalent forms in continental Teut.]

*c* **825** *Epinal Gloss.* 462 *Glumula*, scalu. [*c* **1050** *Voc.* in Wr.-Wülcker 371/1 *Cittis*, uilmenum, æpelscealum ymb ða cyrnlu. *a* **1100** in Napier *OE. Glosses* i. 608 *Quisquiliarum*, æswæpe, beanscalu.] *c* **1384** CHAUCER *H. Fame* 1281, I saugh him carien a wind-melle Under a walsh-note shale. *c* **1430** LYDG. *Letabundus* 227 in *Minor P.* (1911) 56 The husk is falle, brokyn is the shale, The noote kernel, Closyd in scripturys.. Al openly shewith his swetnesse. **1532** MORE *Confut. Tindale* Wks. 644/2 From the tone [sacrament] take they the swete carnel within, the blessed body of Christ, and leaue the people the shales. **1540** PALSGR. *Acolastus* Argt. C j, He releued his hunger with peskod shales, or the huskes of other graynes. **1584** HANMER *Anc. Eccl. Hist.* (1585) Ep. Ded. *ij b, There is found wheate among tares,.. a kearnell within the shale [**1663** shaell], marrow within the bone. **1659** ROBOTHAM *Gate Lang. Unlocked* xi. §121 He that hath a minde to get out the kernel.. must put away the husk [*marg.* Peel, coat, shalt]. **1668** WILKINS *Real Char.* II. vi. §1. 171 Cod, Husk, Pod, Shell, shale, siliquous.

*fig.* **1599** SHAKS. *Hen. V*, IV. ii. 18 Doe but behold yond poore and starued Band, And your faire shew shall suck away their Soules, Leauing them but the shales and huskes of men. **1617** tr. *A. de Dominis' Serm.* (*Rom.* xiii. 12) 52 They stuffe them vp with swines meat, the huskes, and shales of these superfluous, and superstitious deuotions.

†**b.** As an example of something without value.

*c* **1400** *Laud Troy Bk.* 7234 So wonderly the wynd it blewe, That alle here tentis ouerthrewe; Al ȝede to grounde bothe tent and hale, Here ropes vayled not of a schale.

†**c.** The shell of an egg or a shell-fish. *rare.*

**1561** HOLLYBUSH *Hom. Apoth.* 11 b, Beat egges shales to pouder. **1567** MAPLET *Gr. Forest* 99 Periwinckles.. are alwaies clothed with one and the same shale.

†**d.** The refuse of hemp: = SHEAVE *sb.*[2]

**1577** B. GOOGE *Heresbach's Husb.* I. 39 b, Of Hempe.. the Shales or Stalkes serue for the heating of Ouens.

**3.** A scale (of a fish, of metal, of a scaly disease, etc.). *Obs.* exc. *dial.*

**1398** TREVISA *Barth. De P.R.* XIII. xxix. (Tollemache MS.), Fische þat ben bred in þe see haue harde shales and þikke,.. and ryuer fische haueþ sotel schales. *c* **1420** *Chron. Vilod.* 4601, & dame Alfyne woke of hurre slepe þo after anone: And mony shalus he syȝe falle from hurre heyȝe þo, —þen myȝt he syȝe welle, & alle hurre sekenesse was agone. **1611** COTGR., *Finfreluches*, shales, or scales, or scalie excrements; as dandriffe, &c. **1655** W. F. *Observ. Fulke's Bk. Meteors* 170 Iron.. purged in the fire,.. in such sort as that which is earthy, doth at last turn to schales and dross. **1880** *W. Cornw. Gloss.*, *Shale*, a scale of a fish; a flake.

†**b.** Comb., *shale-fish* = shell-fish. *Obs.*

**1596** DALRYMPLE tr. *Leslie's Hist. Scot.* I. 41 Ostiris, Buckies, and vthiris schal fishe.

**4.** A mesh of a net. *Obs.* exc. *dial.*

**1606** S. GARDINER *Bk. Angling* 37 Some.. breake the shales of the net. **1855** ANNA GURNEY *Norf. Words* in *Trans. Phil. Soc.* 36 *Shale*, the mesh of a net.

**5.** *dial.* 'Loose substance from a mine or quarry; loose ore' (*Eng. Dial. Dict.*); see also quots.

[Cf. OE. *stánscalu*, ? a rocky stratum denuded of soil, whence *stánscyliȝ* stony (ground).]

**1793** A. YOUNG *Agric. Sussex* 16 The various sorts of limestone.. with the thickness and shale of each different sort. **1860** *Eng. & Foreign Mining Gloss.* (ed. 2) Cornw. 21 *Scal*, a shale or portion of earth, rock &c., which separates and falls from the main body. **1882** JAGO *Cornw. Gloss.* 256 *Schale*, a scale, as a 'schale of earth', or earth slide in an excavation.

**shale** (ʃeɪl), *sb.*[2] [Perh. a use of SHALE *sb.*[1], or a derivative of SHALE *v.* (sense 5).

There is no sufficient reason for the common view that it is a. G. *schale* (= SHALE *sb.*[1]), which is not used in this sense (the G. equivalent being *schieferthon* 'slate clay'); *schale* however occurs for a thin layer of ore or stone, and the *Deutsches Wbuch.* has *schalstein* a laminated limestone, *schalgebirge*, explained as 'a layer of stone in a stratified range of mountains'.]

**1. a.** An argillaceous fissile rock, the laminæ of which are usually fragile and uneven, and mostly parallel to the bedding; often overlying a coal formation. Also with qualifying word as *bituminous shale*, etc.

**1747** HOOSON *Miner's Dict.* L iv b, Strong Beds, Shale, or Chists. **1796** KIRWAN *Elem. Min.* (ed. 2) I. 182 Slate Clay, Shale. **1811** J. FAREY *Derbyshire* I. 443 It is not uncommon with colliers to call any Argillaceous Stratum in very thin lamina by the name of Shale. **1833** LYELL *Princ. Geol.* III. 334 The conversion of clay into shale, and of sand into sandstone, may, in many cases, be attributed to simple pressure. **1884** *Times* (weekly ed.) 19 Sept. 3/2 A ring of shale, part of a large ribbed bead of delf.

**b.** A variety or specimen of this rock.

**1830** [see BITUMINOUS *a.* b]. **1832** DE LA BECHE *Geol. Man.* (ed. 2) 315 Shales, grits, &c. **1873** C. ROBINSON *N.S. Wales* 52 Deposits of brown cannel oil coals and oil shales. **1878** A. H. GREEN etc., *Coal* i. 25 Tasmanite is a shale containing from 26 to 30 per cent. of combustible matter. **1890** *Hardwicke's Sci. Gossip* XXVI. 245/2 Next in order above the sandstones.. occur the black shales.

**c.** *spec.* = ALUM-*shale*. *dial.*

**1825–80** JAMIESON, *Shale*, a name given to alum ore. **1847** HALLIWELL, *Shale*,.. alum ore. **1876** *Whitby Gloss.*, *Shale*, the gray alum rock of this quarter.

**2.** *attrib.* and *Comb.* **a.** simple attrib., as ***shale distillation, limestone, mine, miner***; instrumental, as ***shale-sprinkled*** adj.

**1842** SEDGWICK in *Hudson's Guide Lakes* (1843) 209 *Third Group, or Shale Limestone.*—This group forms the upper part of the calcareous zone on the north side of the Cumbrian mountains. **1884** *Times* (weekly ed.) 19 Sept. 3/2 Beyond.. turning up a large, ornamental shale ring, nothing could be done. **1887** *Pall Mall Gaz.* 21 Sept. 11/2 The shale miners of Scotland. **1894** *Westm. Gaz.* 30 May 5/3 Mr. Robert Bell.. was the first to manufacture oil from shale distillation in Scotland. **1901** KIPLING *Kim* xiv. 358 They held the shale-sprinkled grass for an hour.

**b.** Special comb.: **shale-naphtha, -oil**, naphtha and oil obtained by the destructive distillation of bituminous shale; **shale shaker**, a vibrating screen used in oil and gas drilling to remove drill cuttings from the circulating drilling mud that is passed through it; †**shale-shiver**, laminated shale; **shale-stone** *dial.*, slate; **shale-tar**, tar derived from bituminous shale.

**1855** *Q. Jrnl. Chem. Soc.* VII. 106 The existence in *shale naphtha of the isomer of cumidine. **1857** MILLER *Elem. Chem.*, *Org.* ix. 580 (heading) *Shale oils. **1886** *Pall Mall Gaz.* 14 Dec. 4/1 The Midland has begun to burn shale oil in the lamps hung in its suburban trains. **1945** HEALD & AYRES in L. M. Fanning *Our Oil Resources* vi. 185 Crude shale oil is produced from oil shale by retorting. **1976** *Time* 20 Dec. 41/1 Prices for getting shale oil or using wet-steam deposits in the earth to generate electricity are also far from commercially acceptable. **1959** *Petroleum Handbk.* (Shell) (ed. 4) 85 On reaching the well head it is diverted via a horizontal flow line to a vibrating screen or '*shale shaker'. **1974** G. S. ORMSBY in P. L. Moore et al. *Drilling Practices Manual* vi. 152 The term 'shale shaker' is used in drilling mud work to cover all the devices that in another industry might be differentiated as 'shaking' screen, 'vibrating screens', and 'oscillating screens'. **1794** T. HUTCHINSON *Hist. Cumbld.* I. *Catal. Anim.*, etc. 46 *Shale Shiver. **1880** *W. Cornw. Gloss.*, **Shale-stone*, *Shilstone*, slate. **1857** MILLER *Elem. Chem.*, *Org.* ix. 580 *Shale tar is particularly rich in basic substances.

**shale** (ʃeɪl), *v.*[1] *Obs.* exc. *dial.* Also 5 schale, 6 shaell, (7 shalle, 9 shail). [f. SHALE *sb.*[1]]

**1.** *trans.* To free from the shell or husk; to remove, take *off* (the shell or husk) from a nut, bean, fruit, etc.; to decorticate (hemp). ? *Obs.*

**1398** TREVISA *Barth. De P.R.* XVIII. liii. (1495) 812 Amptes shale the greynes that they done togyders for they sholde not growe ayen and wexe grene corn. *c* **1420** *Liber Cocorum* (1862) 25 Take smalle notes, schale not [? out] harde, As þou dose of almondes, fayre and wele. *c* **1430** *Two Cookery-bks.* xl. 13 Take grete Oystrys, an schale hem. *c* **1518** *Kal. Sheph.* i. A v, Yet may they syt and shalell peson. **1577** B. GOOGE *Heresbach's Husb.* I. 41 Hempe haruest.. The Male ..is made vp in bundels to be knockt and shaled [orig. *confringenda, decorticataque repurganda*] in Winter euenynges. **1607** TOPSELL *Four-f. Beasts* 643 Parched barley which hath bene well shaled. **1613–16** W. BROWNE *Brit. Past.* II. iv. 97 A little Lad set on a bancke to shale The ripen'd Nuts pluck'd in a woody Vale. **1622** SIR R. HAWKINS *Voy. S. Sea* xxiv. 55 They haue hudds, as our Beanes, which shaled off, the kernell parteth it selfe in two. **1693** *Urquhart's Rabelais* III. xviii. 145 The Bean is not seen till.. its swad.. be shaled.

*fig.* *a* **1680** T. GOODWIN *Blessed State* x. Wks. 1703 V. III. 64 This Abundancy of Life, that is in God, instantly shales off, Works out all that Filth, Frailty, Misery.

†**b.** *intr.* To allow of being shelled. *rare.*

**1600** SURFLET *Country Farm* III. lxv. 581 The vttermost pilling of common walnuts, whether it shale willingly or no may be distilled in the moneth of September.

**2.** Of grain, seed, etc.: To drop out.

[**1578** ? Implied in SHALING *ppl. a.*] **1642** D. ROGERS *Naaman* 616 Suffer it to shale and fall to the ground for lack of reaping. **1764** *Museum Rust.* II. xxv. 80 Coleseed is a seed that will shed or shale very greatly, if it is not reaped in proper time. **1895** *E. Angl. Gloss.*, *Shail*.. to drop out.

†**3.** *trans.* To shed (a tooth). *Obs. rare.*

**1686–7** AUBREY *Rem. Gentilisme* (1881) 11 When Children shaled their Teeth. *Ibid.* 27 When children did shalle a tooth they rubbed salt upon it, and then threw it into the fire.

**4.** *intr.* Of water: To form an incrustation. *rare*⁻¹.

**1844** H. HUTCHINSON *Treat. Pract. Drainage Land* 160 In some drains water will shale or form an incrustation upon the flat tile.

**5.** To cleave, as stones in being raised.

**1712** J. MORTON *Nat. Hist. Northampt.* 129 Rammel, a Stone unfit for Building, because in the raising it cleaves or shales into many small uneaven Pieces. **1851** STERNBERG *Northampt. Gloss.* 93.

†**6.** *to shale out*: ? to strip (a tree). *Obs.*

**1618** W. LAWSON *New Orch. & Garden* xiii. (1623) 45 The Bul-finch is a deuourer of your Fruit in the bud, I haue had whole trees shald out with them in Winter-time.

**shale** (ʃeɪl), *v.*² *rare.* [app. echoic: see quot. 1834.] *intr.* Of water: To make the sound characteristic of tidal movement near the shore.

**1834** M. SCOTT *Cruise Midge* xvi. (1842) 299 The water in the bay.. again rushed in with a loud *shaling* noise,—I coin the word for the sound—in *bores* nearly ten feet high. **1890** CLARK RUSSELL *Marriage at Sea* ix, A gentle *shaling* noise of waters broken by the passage of the vessel. **1897** —— *Last Entry* 57 The stream of tide softly shaled along the bends of the schooner.

**shale**, variant of SHAIL *v.*²

† **shaled**, *ppl. a. Obs.* [f. SHALE *sb.*¹ and *v.*¹]

**1. a.** Encased as in a shell.

?*a* **1400** *Morte Arth.* 766 His [*sc.* a dragon's] scoulders ware schalyde alle in clene syluere, Schreede ouer alle the schrympe with schrinkande poyntez.

**b.** Consisting of a shell.

**1567** MAPLET *Gr. Forest* 77 Plinie vsed this Latine worde *Cancer*, for a generall or common name for all such as haue, & weare shaled garments.

**c.** Having a 'shale', shell, or pod.

*c* **1575** DUCKET in Hakluyt *Voy.* (1599) I. 397 Hasell nuts, ..as good and thin shaled as are our Filberds. **1622** *Comenius' Janua Ling. Triling.* 19 The fruits of the earth bring grains; those which are eared in ears,..those which are shal'd in shales [*siliquatæ in siliquis*].

**2.** *schalyd hed*: app. = SCALD HEAD 2.

**1400–50** *Stockh. Med. MS.* 100 To holen a schalyd hed.

**3.** Peeled or stript of shell, shelled.

**1598** FLORIO, *Snocciolato*, crackt nuts, shaled nuts. **1661** LOVELL *Hist. Anim. & Min.* 110 Tosted and shaled Barly.

**shalemuse**, obs. form of SHAWM.

† **'shaler.** *Obs. rare*⁻⁰. [f. SHALE *v.* + -ER¹.] One who 'shales' or shells.

**1611** COTGR., *Escailleur*, a..piller, shaler of. **1648** HEXHAM II, *Een scheller*, A Peeler, a Rinder, or a Shaler.

**shaler**, var. SHEILA.

† **shaleur.** *Obs. rare*⁻¹. [a. F. *chaleur* heat.] = HEAT *sb.* 13.

**1509** WATSON *Ship of Fools* ix. (1517) C ij b, Some hath recours vnto vyces lyke as an olde dogge hath after a bytche that is in shaleur.

‖ **shalgram** ('ʃælgrɑːm). Also **salgram.** [Hindī *çālgrām*, repr. Skr. *çālagrāma* the name of a village where this stone was found.] An ammonite or other fossil, sacred to Vishnu.

**1784** F. GLADWIN tr. *Ayeen Akbery* II. 29 Salgram, is a black stone which the hindoos hold sacred. **1905** MACPHAIL *Kenneth S. Macdonald* x. 133 The Shalgram, from the geological point of view, is an ammonite fossil. *Ibid.*, The Shalgram, he explained, was one of the three things essential to daily worship in an orthodox Hindu house.

**'shaling**, *vbl. sb.* ? *Obs.* [f. SHALE *v.*¹ + -ING¹.] The action of removing the outer shell or husk; also pl. the shell or husks removed.

**1611** COTGR., *Chaloppes*, the huskes, parings, or shalings, of a nut, or nut-kernell. *Ibid.*, *Escaillement*, a..pilling, shaling of. *Ibid.* s.v. *Fabal*, *Le fa: de febues*, the chaffe, hulls, or shalings of beanes. **1686** PLOT *Staffordsh.* 170 These are ..used..chiefly for Rye, Barley, and Mault, or for shaling of Oates.

† **'shaling**, *ppl. a. Obs. rare*⁻¹. [f. SHALE *v.*¹ + -ING².] ? Falling from the husk as ripe.

**1578** *Procter's Gorg. Gallery Gallant Invent.* G ij b, The shaling nuts and mast, that falleth from the tree, Should serue for my repast.

**shalk.** *poet. Obs.* Forms: 1–3 **scealc**, 3 **scalk, scalc, scælk**, 4–5 **skalke, schalke**, 4–6 **schalk**, 5 **shalk(e.** [Com. Teut.: OE. *sc(e)alc* masc. = OFris., OS. *skalk*, OHG. *scalc, scalh* servant (MHG. *schalk* servant, mod.G. *schalk* rogue, wag), ON. *skalk-r* (Icel. *skálk-r* rogue, Sw., Da. *skalk*), Goth. *skalk-s* servant:—OTeut. **skalko-z*. No cognates outside Teut. have been found; the word forms the second element in **marho-skalko-z* 'horse-servant', MARSHAL *sb.*]

Originally, a servant; in alliterative poetry one of the common synonyms for 'man'. (In the last example used contemptuously.)

*Beowulf* 939 Nu scealc [Beowulf] hafað..dæd ȝefremede, ðe we ealle ær ne meahton snyttrum besyrwan. *c* **1000** *Ags. Ps.* (Th.) lxxxv. 2 Hæl þinne scealc [*salvum fac servum tuum*]. *c* **1205** LAY. 4219 Heo wenden bi þen scelden þat hit heore scalkes weoren. *Ibid.* 19126 þer wes moni bald scalc. **13..** *E.E. Allit. P.* C. 476 þe schyre sunne hade hem schent, er euer þe schalk wyst. *a* **1400–50** *Wars Alex.* 1391 Archars with arows of atter envemonde Schotis vp scharply at shalkis [*Dubl. MS.* salkez] on þe wallis. *c* **1440** *York Myst.* xxxiii. 2 ȝe schappely schalkes and schene for to schawe, I charge ȝou as ȝour chiftan þat [etc.]. *c* **1450** *Golagros & Gaw.* 891 Sexty schalkis full schene, Cled in armour sa clene. **1508** DUNBAR *Tua Mariit Wemen* 105 Quhen schaiffyn is that ald schalk with a sharp rasiour, He schowis on me his schewill mouth.

**shalke**, obs. form of CHALK *sb.*

**shall** (ʃæl), *sb.* [f. SHALL *v.*]

**1.** An utterance of the word 'shall'; a command, promise, or determination (such as is expressed by means of 'shall').

It is doubtful whether quots. 1553 and 1608 belong to this word or to SHALE *sb.*¹ Quots. 1566 and 1593 imply the existence of a punning phrase *to feed* or *serve with shalls* (*shales*).

**1553** *Respublica* (Brandl) III. iii. 90 *Adul.* Ye shall prove att length by theffecte yᵗ shall ensue. *Peop.* Nai, and we shall alwaie bee served but with shales, than chil beleve een still yᵗ vaire woordes beeth but tales. **1566** ASCHAM *Let.* in Harington *Nugæ Antiq.* (1804) I. 101 As now another man shall enjoye the sweet kirnell of this hard and chardgeable nutt, which I have bene so long in cracking; and nothing left unto me but shells and shalls to feed me with all. **1593** CHURCHYARD *Challenge* 153 Y 2, You shall haue Nuts, they say when ploms are ripe. Thus all with shalles or shalles ye shal be fed, And gape for gold, and want both Gold and lead. **1607** SHAKS. *Cor.* III. i. 90 Marke you His absolute Shall? **1608** *Merry Devil Edmonton* II. ii. 2 What? hast thou fed me all this while with shalles. And com'st to tell me now, thou lik'st it not? **1677** GILPIN *Dæmonol.* I. xiii. 103 These *wills* and *shalls* of wicked Men, are for the most part God's interpretation of their Acts and Carriage. **1870** M. ARNOLD *St. Paul & Protestantism* (1875) 85 The external *shalls* and *shall nots* of the law.

**2.** The word 'shall' as idiomatically used in contradistinction to 'will'.

**1837** MACAULAY *Ess.*, *Bacon* (1843) II. 408 Not one Londoner in a million ever misplaces his *will* and *shall*. **1861** JOS. ANGUS *Handbk. Engl. Tongue* 219 These 'Shalls' are sometimes wrongly emphasized. **1882** A. J. ELLIS *Presid. Addr.* in *Trans. Philol. Soc.* 23 These *shalls* and *wills* are still shibboleths. **1891** *Daily News* 26 June 5/2 Perhaps no Scot ever yet mastered his 'shalls' and 'wills'.

**shall** (ʃæl, *unstressed* ʃ(ə)l), *v.* Pa. t. **should** (ʃʊd, ʃəd). Forms: see below. [A Com. Teut. preterite-present strong verb: OE. *sceal, sculon, sc(e)olde* = OFris. *skil* (*skel, scol*), *skilun* (*skalun*, etc.), *skolde* (*sculde*, etc.), OS. *skal, skulun, skolda*, OLow Frankish *sal, sulum, solde* (MDu. *sal, sullen, solde*, mod.Du. *zal, zullen, zou*), OHG. *scal, sculun, scolta*, also *sal* (*sol*), *sulun, solta* (MHG. *schal* and *schol, schulen, scholte*, also *sal* and *sol, sulen, solte*; mod.G. *soll, sollen, sollte*), ON. *skal, skulu, skylda* (Sw. *skall*, pa. t. *skulle*; Da. *skal*, pa. t. *skulde*), Goth. *skal, skulum, skulda*. The Teut. root (**skel-*:) **skal-*: **skul-* to owe (:—pre-Teut. **skel-*: **skol-*: **sk'l*) is represented by Goth. *skula*, OHG., OS. *scolo*, OE. *ȝescola* wk. masc., debtor, OHG. *sculd, sculda* (mod.G. *schuld*), OS. *sculd*, OE. *scyld* fem., debt, guilt. Outside Teut. the only certain cognates are Lith. *skelěti* to be guilty, *skilti* to get into debt, *skolà* debt, guilt, OPrussian *skallisnan* (acc.) duty, *skellânts* guilty, *po-skulit* to admonish.

The northern English dialects (including Sc.) have a form *sal*, pa. t. *suld*, with initial *s* instead of *sh*. This does not occur in the remains of ONorthumbrian, but first appears in the 13th c. It is remarkable that a similar form, with *s* irregularly representing OTeut. *sk*, existed as a dialectal variant in OHG. (*sal, sol, sulun*) and OFris. (*sal, sel*), and has ousted the regular form in Ger. (*soll, sollen*) and Du. (*zal, zou*). Some scholars regard the *s* form as representing an OTeut. variant, originating from the euphonic dropping of *k* in inflexional forms like the subjunctive **skli-*. It seems more probable that it was independently developed in the different dialects at an early period, while the *sk-* retained its original pronunciation; in stressless position the *k* might naturally be dropped, and the simplified initial afterwards extended by analogy to the stressed use.

In Eng. the vb. has no inf. or pples. (the evidence of an OE. inf. *sculan, sceolan*, is doubtful). Some of the other Teut. langs. have an infinitive: OHG. *scolan, solan* (MHG., mod.G. *sollen*), MDu. *sullen* (Du. *zullen*), ON. *skulu* (pa. t. inf. *skyldu*); Goth. has the pres. pple. *skuland-s* and the pa. pple. *skuld-s*; OHG. has the pres. pple. *scolanti* (mod.G. *sollend*), and early mod.G. the pa. pple. *gesollt*; ON. has a ppl. adj. *skyld-r* bound by duty.]

**A.** Inflexional Forms.

**I.** Present tense.

**1.** *1st and 3rd pers. sing.* α. 1 **sceall, scell, scyl**, 1–3 **sc(e)al, scel, scæl**, 3 **scall**, *erron.* **swal**, 3–4 **ssal**, 3–6 **schal**, 3–7 **shal**, 4 **schel, ssel**, 4–5 **schalle, xal**, 4–6 **schall**, 5 **shalle, schawl(l, schaul, chall, schel(e, schill**, 5–6 **xalle**, 5–7 **shale**, 3– **shall.**

*Beowulf* 438 (Gr.) Ic mid grape sceal fon wið feonde. *c* **831** *Charter* in *O.E. Texts* 445 Hwet man elce ȝere..aȝiaban scel. *c* **888** ÆLFRED *Boeth.* xxxix. §5 Hu hit ȝeweorðan sceall ær ær hit ȝeweorðe. *c* **950** *Lindisf. Gosp.* Matt. x. 8 *marg.*, Biscop scæl cunneȝe..ðone preost. *a* **1000** *Andreas* 1483 (Gr.) þæt scell æglæwra mann..findan on ferðe. *c* **1000** *Ags. Gosp.* Luke xxii. 37 ðyt scyl beon ȝefylled þæt be me awriten is. *a* **1175** *Cott. Hom.* 219 For wan hi beoð þuss icweðe me scel sigge, an oðre stowe. *c* **1200** ORMIN 17684 All þatt follc þatt æfre wass & all þatt ȝet shall wurrþenn. *c* **1205** LAY. 5435 Eow swal beon þe betere. *Ibid.* 32149 No scal hit eou reouwe nauere. *c* **1250** *Owl & Night.* 1195 Ich wot hwo schal [*v.r.* sal] beon anhonge. **1297** R. GLOUC. (Rolls) 138 Her after.. me ssal ihere al þis. *a* **1300** *K. Horn* 1312 Ischal þe to hewe [*v.r.* ich schal]. **1340** *Ayenb.* 2 (*heading*), Hou me ssel knawe guod and kuead. **13..** *Sir Beues* (A.) 155 Me self schel dobbe þe to kniȝt. *c* **1375** *Lay Folks Mass Bk.* (MS. B) 357 Be my helpe whils I shal lyue. **1382** Shall [see B. 7 c]. **1389** in *Eng. Gilds* (1870) 54 He xal paye ye rytes of ye hows at his entre, viij.d. **1426** AUDELAY *Poems* 10, I schal say ȝou the soth, that wel schul ȝe wyt. *c* **1450** *Mankind* 586 in *Macro Plays* 22, I xall goo ronde in hys ere. **1463** MARG. PASTON in *P. Lett.* II. 143, I trowe it shall apeyer. **1525** SAMPSON in Ellis *Orig. Lett.* Ser. I. I. 261 A synnar..nevyr..schall.. deserve such a singulier goodnesse. **1535** COVERDALE *Amos* ix. 11, I shal repayre it. **1536** in *Lett. Suppress. Monasteries* (Camden) 126, I thynke longe to know wherto I xall hold me. **1660** *Act 12 Chas. II*, c. 24 §15 Who doth or shall tap out such Beere. **1663** *Extr. St. Papers rel. Friends* Ser. II. (1911) 164 This Shal be your warrant.

β. 3 **sel, sæl**, 3–4 **sale**, 4–5 **salle**, (5 **sill**, 6 **sell**), 3– **sal**, 4– **sall.**

From 14th c. onwards only *north.* In the early southern and midland examples (Layamon, etc.) the initial *s* represents (ʃ).

*c* **1205** LAY. 8904 þi mon he sæl bi-cumen. *c* **1220** *Bestiary* 25 Sal he neure luken ðe lides of hise eȝen. *c* **1275** LAY. 701 þe bet ȝou sel worþe. *a* **1300** *Sarmun* xxx. in *E.E.P.* (1862) 4 þe erþe þe watir þan sal sprede. *a* **1325** *MS. Rawl. B* 520 lf. 28 b, Ase ofte as þe tressepas multipliez so sal þe torment wexen of þe peine.

*a* **1300** *Cursor M.* 119, I sal yow schew..Brefli of aiþere testament. **1338** R. BRUNNE *Chron.* (1725) 5 Dede him toke .. als it salle do vs. *a* **1400–50** *Wars Alex.* 3194 Quat sall I dreȝe. *c* **1461** in *Jarrow & Wearmouth* (Surtees) 246 He sall knawe hyme by yir takynis. **1473** *Acc. Ld. High Treas. Scot.* I. 14 For the quhilk he sal ansuer to the compt. **1508** DUNBAR *Tua mariit wemen* 372 Ane othir sall the worschip haif. **1646** *Hamilton Papers* (Camden) 112, I sall represent the necessitie of it the best way I can. **1784** BURNS *Addr. Illegit. Child* v, If thou..tak' the counsel I sall gie thee. **1887** *S. Chesh. Gloss.* 89 Unemphatic Form *Sall* (sŭl, sl).

γ. 3 **sol, shol**, 3–4 **schul(l**, 4 **sul**, 5 **scholl, shul**, 6 **schol**, 9 *dial.* **sholl, shull**, etc.

*c* **1250** *Owl & Night.* 1025 (Cott.) Wat sol ich þar mid mine songe? *c* **1330** *King of Tars* 32, I schul hire winnen in pleyn batayle. **1455** *Cal. Anc. Rec. Dublin* (1889) 287 No maner of man ne woman scholl lad no corne. **1526** J. TAYLOR in Ellis *Orig. Lett.* Ser. II. I. 333 At whos commyng I schol wryte more at large.

**2.** *2nd pers.* α. 1–2 **scealt**, 2–3 **scalt**, 3 **scælt, scelt, sælt, sschalt, shallt, schald, sald, scald**, 3–5 **schalt**, (also 9 *dial.*) **salt**, 4 **schelt, sselt, shelt, shult**, 5 **schild, xalt**, 5–6, *dial.* 8–9 **shat**, 4– **shalt.**

*c* **888** ÆLFRED *Boeth.* xlii, An þing ðu scealt nede þæran witan. *c* **950** *Lindisf. Gosp.* Mark x. 21 Ðu scealt habba ȝestrion in heofne. *c* **1175** *Lamb. Hom.* 39 þu scalt bi-wepen þine sunne. *c* **1200** ORMIN Ded. 38 Tekenn mare inoh þu shallt tæronne findenn. *c* **1205** LAY. 11492 þu scælt habben wurhscipe muchele. *a* **1225** *Leg. Kath.* 1613 þu schalt stihen biforen me to drihtin in heouene. *c* **1250** *Hymn* 31 in *Trin. Coll. Hom.* App. 256 þu sschalt us in to heouene lede. *c* **1250** *O.E. Misc.* 156/22 þenne þu schald wel do. *a* **1300** *Cursor M.* 26406 þar-of salt þou þe vmlok. **1303** R. BRUNNE *Handl. Synne* 3737 þou shalt haue charge of þo boþe. **1340** *Ayenb.* 100 þis zuete word vader..þe sseaweþ þet þou sselt yleue. **1393** LANGL. *P. Pl.* C. XII. 113 To clergie shult þow neuere come. **1435** MISYN *Fire of Love* II. iv. 77 þow salt chawnge. *c* **1440** *Stac. Rome* 281 in *Polit. Rel. & L. Poems* 152 þou shat haue gret mede. *c* **1450** LOVELICH *Grail* xxi. 277 In pes ne Reste Schat thow neuer be. *c* **1450** *Cov. Myst.* (Shaks. Soc.) 37 Thou xalt be ded. *c* **1475** *Partenay* 2166 What shalt thou now don? *c* **1560** *Trag. Rich. II* (1870) 55, I com ouer them for ther blancke charters, shat heere else. **1667** MILTON *P.L.* VIII. 330 Inevitably thou shalt dye. **1749** FIELDING *Tom Jones* XV. v, Shat ha un, d——n me, shat ha un. **1879** *Shropsh. Word-bk.* p. lxxi, Thou sha't, or sha'st be.

β. 3–4 **salle**, 3–5 **sale, schal**, 4–5 **shal**, 5 **schall(e, shal(l)e**, 7–8 *dial.* **shall**, 3– (now *dial.*) **sal(l.** (Cf. note on 1 β.)

*c* **1250** *Gen. & Ex.* 1815 Ðu sal ben hoten israel. *a* **1300** *Cursor M.* 1252 Toward þe est end of þis dale Find a grene gate þou sale. **1375** BARBOUR *Bruce* IV. 659 Feill anoyis thoill ȝhe sall. *a* **1400** HYLTON *Scala Perf.* (W. de W. 1494) I. lxxv, Kyndely hunger whiche thou shal nedelynges fele. *a* **1400–50** *Wars Alex.* 688 þou sall..se þe same with þine eȝen. *c* **1485** *Mary Magd.* 1176 in *Digby Myst.* 100 Stryppys on þi ars þou xall have. **1513** DOUGLAS *Æneis* I. viii. 97 Nor thou sall nevir repent the sickirlie. *a* **1592** GREENE *Jas. IV*, I. iii, *Eust.*.. I'll see her whom the world admires so much... *Sir Bar.* Be gad, and sall both see and talk with her. **1869** *Lonsdale Gloss.* s.v. *Sal*, Thou sal du it.

**3.** *pl.* α. 1 **sculon, sceolon, sciolon, -un, scilon, sceulon, scolan, scylun**, 2 **sceolen**, 2–3 **sculen, sul(l)en**, 3 **scullen, sceollen, shulenn, scholen, sollen, sulin, sullen**, 3–5 **schullen, schulen**, 4 **ssollen, sshullen, schollen, shullon, ssulin, sullen, solen**, 4–5 **shul(l)en, schulyn**, 5 **shullan, -yn, -on, schulun.**

*c* **888** ÆLFRED *Boeth.* xxxiii. §4 Hwæt sculon we nu don? *c* **950** *Lindisf. Gosp.* Matt. v. 46 ðie sciolun habba, *habebitis*. *Ibid.* xx. 18 We stiȝes *vel* we scilon stiȝe, *ascendimus*. *a* **1000** *Cædmon's Gen.* 1902 (Gr.) Ne sceolon unc betweonan teonan weaxan. *c* **1100** *O.E. Chron.* an. 870 (MS. F) Oððe þas preostas scolan munecas beon, oððe [etc.]. *c* **1175** *Lamb. Hom.* 5 þet we sulen habben ure heorte..to ure drihten. *c* **1200** *Vices & Virtues* 7 For hire we sculen alle deað þolien. *c* **1200** [see B. 10 b]. *c* **1205** LAY. 8780 To-gaderen wit scullen [*c* **1275** sollen] libben. *Ibid.* 9518 Faren wit swullen to-somne. *a* **1275** *Prov. Ælfred* 16 in *O.E. Misc.* 103 Whu we ȝure lif lede sulin. *c* **1300** *Havelok* 621 We sholen þe wel fede. **1435** *Cov. Leet Bk.* 181 Poor chapmen..shullon be gretely hyndered. *c* **1449** PECOCK *Repr.* II. xiii. 223 Thei schulen no longer so erre.

β. *contracted.* 4 **schulne, shuln**, 4–5 **schun, schin, schyn**, 5 **schyn(n)e, shyn, schone**, 9 *dial.* **shan, sun**, etc.

**13..** *E.E. Allit. P.* C. 1810 þose þat seme arn & swete schyn se his face. **1362** LANGL. *P. Pl.* A. XI. 237 Godis word witnessiþ we shuln ȝiue & dele oure enemys. **1389** in *Eng. Gilds* (1870) 67 They schun holdyn..foure dayes of spekyngges tokedere. *c* **1420** *Liber Cocorum* (1862) 34 þer bene bestes þat schyne be rost. **1447** BOKENHAM *Seyntys, Cecilia* 408 Fynd we shuln a ful cruel fal. *c* **1450** *Bk. Curtasye* 590 in *Babees Bk.*, Baylys, and parker, Schone come to acountes euery ȝere. **1887** *S. Chesh. Gloss.* 89 Emphatic Form..Wey shaan... Unemphatic Form..Wey sŭn, sn.

γ. 1 (*Northumb.*) **scilo**, 2–3 **scule**, 2–4 **sculle**, 3 **shul(l)e, solle, schule, sul(l)e, ssulle, sul**, 3–4 **ssolle, schole**, 4 **schoulle, ssolle, schol, sschulle, scolle, chul, sul**, 4–5 **scholle, shulle, schul(e, schulle, shul**, 5 **shule, shole, chull, schil(l, xul.**

*c*950 *Lindisf. Gosp.* Matt. x. 19 Huæt ȝespreca scilo, *quid loquamini.* *c*1175 *Lamb. Hom.* 41 Ne scule ȝe neure god don unforgolden. *c*1200 ORMIN 8655 Siþþenn shule witt anan Off hunngerr deȝenn baþe. *c*1250 *Gen. & Ex.* 303 For adam sul ðus and his wif In blisse ðus leden lesteful lif. *c*1300 *K. Horn* 1262 (Laud MS.), To day we schole hem keche. 1340 *Ayenb.* 186 Wel ssolle we habbe reuþe. *c*1350 *Will. Palerne* 3339 Redli chul ȝe spede. 1390 GOWER *Conf.* I. 38 Pes and acord awey schol wende. *c*1410 *Sir Cleges* 227 Ye schill to Cardyffe to the kynge. 1426 AUDELAY *Poems* 5 ȝe schul have grace. 14.. *Pol. Rel. & L. Poems* (1903) 277 In tyme quan we xul dey. *c*1450 *Mirk's Festial* 203 ȝe chull come þat day to holy chyrch. 1471 CAXTON *Recuyell* (Sommer) 44 What shulle we now doo thynke ye. *c*1500 *Melusine* i. 16 Al thoo that shal demande the without cesse,.. shul be putt from theire prosperytees.

δ. 3 **scul(l)eð, sulleð, ssuleþ, s(s)olleþ,** 3–4 **schul(l)eþ,** 4 **shulleþ, scholleþ.**

*c*1205 LAY. 27376 Heo sculleð beon islaȝene. 1297 R. GLOUC. (Rolls) 724 þine sostren ssolleþ abbe al. 1387 TREVISA *Higden* (Rolls) III. 451 þey schulleþ [MS. γ scholleþ] goo out at þe worldes ende. 1393 LANGL. *P. Pl.* C. IV. 53 For mede we shulleþ synge. 1395 *E.E. Wills* (1882) 10 To do and to preye as othere Reclus.. Shulleth don and preye.

ε. 2 **scale,** 3–4 **sal(e,** 3–6 **sall,** 4 **sschal, salle, shal(le,** 4–5 **schal(l,** 5 **shalle, shal, xal(l,** (etc. as in 1) 4– **shall.**

*c*1175 *Lamb. Hom.* 83 Hwan we scale festen. *c*1250 *Owl & Night.* 1206 Ic wot if smithes sale vuele clenche. *a*1300 *Cursor M.* 11450 To hend and fete we sal him fall. 13.. *Gaw. & Gr. Knt.* 2405 We schal yow wel acorde. *c*1380 WYCLIF *Serm.* Sel. Wks. I. 141 þei shal not see him. 1390 GOWER *Conf.* I. 44 Remembrance Of that thei schall hierafter rede. *c*1400 *26 Pol. Poems* 149/232 All that lyuen.. Shall dye. *c*1450 *Mankind* 358 in *Macro Plays* 14 We xall bargen with yow. 1552 LYNDESAY *Monarche* 6242 Quhen the Childryng of God.. Sall do appeir. 1660 CHAS. II, in *Cath. Rec. Soc. Publ.* VI. 39 Yᵘ shale find yᵗ hearafter I will do all I can. 1664 *Extr. St. Papers rel. Friends* Ser. III. (1912) 220 We shal easily provide els-where.

4. *Subjunctive.* 1 **scule, sceole, sciele, scile, scyle,** (*pl.* 1 **scylen, -un, sceulen),** 3 **sculle, shul(l)e, sule, schulle, schille,** 3–5 **schule.**

*c*888 ÆLFRED *Boeth.* xxxviii. §7 Ne scyle [*v.r.* sceal] nan mon siocne monnan.. swencan. *c*897 —— *Gregory's Past. C.* v. 40 Hu hie selfe scylen fulfremedeste weorðan. *c*1000 ÆLFRIC *Exod.* v. 2 Hwæt ys se drihten, þæt ic hym hiran scile? *c*1200 ORMIN 3546 þatt illc mann shule cumenn ham. *a*1225 *Ancr. R.* 178 þet heo muwe & schule þuruh ham þe betere beon iboruwen. *c*1250 *Owl & Night.* 1683 (Cott.) Schille [*Jesus* schulle] ich an utest uppen ow grede, ich shal swo stronge ferde lede [etc.]. *c*1275 *Passion our Lord* 144 in *O.E. Misc.* 41 þeyh ich to þe deþe schulle myd þe go. *c*1450 MYRC 587 ȝef hyt schule in greyþe fare.

5. Reduced enclitic forms (all persons and numbers). *a.* 6 **-sh, -s,** 7 **-ce,** 6– **-se,** 7– **s';** *miswritten* 7–9 **'s,** 8–9 **'se.**

Very frequent in the north, in the expressions *Ise uphaud, Ise warrant*: see Uphold, Warrant in Eng. Dial. Dict.

1560 ROLLAND *Seven Sages* Prol. ii, For Dialogs (quod I) weis get anew. *c*1566 *Merie Tales of Skelton* Wks. 1843 I. p. lviii, In gewd faith, saith the Kendallman, do see, and Ise bay for your skott to London. 1575 *Gammer Gurton* I. v. 39 Yoush beare the blame for mee. 1575 *Ibid.* III. iii. 44 Thouse pay for al. 1578 WHETSTONE *Promos & Cass.* II. IV. ii, Yuse haue a blew one soone. 1585 JAS. I *Ess. Poesie* (Arb.) 63 *Iis neir cair*, for *I sall neuer cair*. *a*1592 GREENE *Jas. IV* Ind., Ays gar thee recon me nene of thay friend. 1605 SHAKS. *Lear* IV. vi. 246 Ice try whither your Costard, or my Ballow be the harder. 1647 CHAS. I *Let. to Dk. York* 15 July, Where I s'have the contentment of seeing you. *c*1780 in Child *Ballads* III. 489/1 Thy dinner's be dressd in Annan Holme. 1825 JAMIESON s.v. *Ise*, In Lanarks. and other counties, *ye'se, he'se, she'se, we'se, they'se, that'se*, are also used... *Thou'se* also for *thou shalt.* *a*1864 in R. A. Arnold *Cotton Famine* 303 Aw feel better neaw. We's be reet enough tomorn, lass.

*β.* 6–9 **-st;** *miswritten* **'st.** *dial.*

*a*1590 *Marr. Wit & Wisd.* (Shaks. Soc.) 8, I promise the, before these folke, Thoust neuer cost me grote. 1728 VANBRUGH & CIBBER *Provok'd Husb.* I. 27 We'st ta' the best care we can of 'um.

6. a. With pronouns affixed: *sing. 1st pers.* 6 **shalche.** *2nd pers.* 1 **scealtu,** 3 **s(c)haltu, saltu,** 3–4 **shaltou,** 3–5 **shaltow,** 4 **schal(s)tow, saltou, -ow(e, schaltou, scheltou.** *3rd pers.* 6 **shalla.** *pl. 1st pers.* 7 **shalles, shals, shal's** (= *shall us*). *2nd pers.* 3 **sollie** (= *soll ye*).

1553 *Respublica* v. vii. 1609 And what shalche zai to om? *a*1000 *Andreas* 220 (Gr.) Scealtu.. mid ærdæȝe.. ceol ȝestiȝan. *a*1225 *Leg. Kath.* 2094 Ne schaltu nower neh se lihtliche esterten. *c*1300 *Havelok* 1322 Alle þe castles þat aren þer-inne Shal-tow.. winne. *c*1350 *Will. Palerne* 325 þat alle þi frendes fordedes faire schalstow quite. *a*1352 MINOT *Poems* (ed. Hall) xi. 25 Say now,.. how saltou fare? *c*1380 *Sir Ferumb.* 1436 To Egremoygne-ward scheltou fare. *c*1400 *Rom. Rose* 7467 But shaltow never of apparence Seene conclude good consequence In none argument.

1556 PHAER *Æneid* IV. Lij, And shalla go? Indeede? and shalla flowte me thus?

1605 *1st Pt. Ieronimo* (1901) II. i. 50 Prince Balthezer, shalles meete? 1613 HEYWOOD *Brazen Age* II. ii, Shals to the field. 1626 B. JONSON *Staple of N.* IV. i. 3 What shal's doe with our selues?

*c*1250 *Kent. Serm.* in *O.E. Misc.* 32 Comeþ to srifte .. þanne sollie habbe þo helþe of heuene.

b. With *not* (*na*) affixed: 7–9 (now *dial.*) **shannot, shan'not, sha'not;** *Sc.* and *north.* 8 **sha'na,** 8–9 **shanna (shinna,** etc.); 7 **shann't, sha'nt,** 7– **sha'n't, shan't** (9 *dial.* **sant,** etc.).

1664 S. CROSSMAN in Palmer *Bk. Praise* (1865) 167 My Life and I sha'nt part. 1668 DRYDEN *Secret Love* I. ii, By this leg but you shan'not. 1675 COTTON *Burlesque upon B.* 48 Nay but I wonnot, so I wonnot, Nor you shan't keep me, no you shannot. 1677 RAVENSCROFT *Scaramouch* I. 10 It cannot be, it must not, it sha'not. 1682 N. O. *Boileau's Lutrin* III. 29 Doctors, Proctors, Paritors together Shann't leave upon thy Naked back one Feather. 1741 RICHARDSON *Pamela* (ed. 3) I. 121, I shan't stir from this House. 17.. RAMSAY *O'er Bogie* ii, We shanna part For siller or for land. 1792 BURNS *Bonie Lesley* v, Misfortune sha'na steer thee. 1819 R. ANDERSON *Cumbld. Ball.* 55 Tou sant git a kiss! 1825 JENNINGS *Observ. Dial. W. Eng.* 67 *Shatt'n*, shalt not. 1826 J. WILSON *Noctes Ambr.* Wks. 1855 I. 148 The same shinna befa' the year. 1862 MRS. H. WOOD *Channings* iii, Shan't I have a fine time of it! 1876 BLACK *Madcap Violet* xii, He sha'n't marry Violet. 1878 *Cumbld. Gloss., Sallant, Sal n't, Säan't, Sannat, Sanna*, shall not.

c. Written continuously with an infin. (esp. *be*).

*c*1400 *Pety Job* 7 in *26 Pol. Poems* 121, I shalbe wormes ware. 1456 SIR G. HAYE *Law Arms* (S.T.S.) 189 The tyme salcum that thare salbe bot a pastour and a schepe faulde. 1458–9 *Cal. Anc. Rec. Dublin* (1889) 300 Ther selbe no ladyng of corn. 1502 *Bury Wills* (Camden) 92 Ther where it xalbe moste nedefull. 1523 LD. BERNERS *Froiss.* I. cccxxxviii. 214 b, Let vs assemble togyder, and so we shalbe the stronger. 1555 *Act 2 & 3 Phil. & Mary* c. vi. §4 Every person or persons.. wᶜʰ shalbee.. auctorised. 1597 *Reg. Mag. Sig. Scot.* 1599, (1890) 304/1 The.. personis quha salhappin to be querrellit. 1632 SANDERSON *Serm.* 560 He shalbe able to avoyd any sinne.

II. Past tense.

7. *a.* 1–2 **sceolde,** 1–3 **scolde, sculde,** (1 **sc(e)alde,** 3 **shollde, scholte, seolde,** *erron.* **swulde),** 3–4 **ssolde,** 3–5 **schulde, scholde,** 3–6 **shulde,** (4 **sschulde, shullde, chold),** 4–6 **sholde, schold, shuld,** 4–7 **shold,** 5–6 **shoulde, xuld(e,** (5 **schulld, shoolde, xwld, sculd, schud(e,** 6 **shalld,** 7 **shoo'd, sho'd, shu'd,** 8 **shou'd)** 6– **should.**

*c*888 ÆLFRED *Boeth.* xxxviii. §1 Se Job.. licette þæt he sceolde bion se hehsta god. *a*900 *Martyrol.* in *O.E. Texts* 178 Ðæt ða wildan hors scealden iornan on hearde weȝas. *c*975 *Rushw. Gosp.* Matt. xviii. 24 An seþe scalde ten þusende. *Ibid.* xx. 10 þa ærestu wendon þæt hie mare sculdon onfoon. 1154 *O.E. Chron.* (Laud MS.) an. 1140, Xpist ne wolde ðæt he sculde lange rixan. *c*1205 LAY. 4267 þenne and auere mare heo swulden habben are. *a*1300 *K. Horn* 906 Wiþ wronge Scholte [*Laud MS.* Scholde] ihc hit vnderfonge. 13.. *Seuyn Sages* 1057 (W.) Who sschulde him biyete but the king? 13.. in Ritson *Anc. Songs & Ball.* (1877) 62 That such a knight ssold falle. *c*1350 *Will. Palerne* 2014 Sche chold sone be bi-schet here-selue al-one. 1382 WYCLIF *Matt.* ii. 15 That is shuld be fulfillid. 1393 LANGL. *P. Pl.* C. xx. 154 þe fyngeres þat folde sholden. 1399 —— *Rich. Redeles* Prol. 14 For he shullde hem serue of þe same after. 1411 *Rolls of Parlt.* III. 650/1 That the said William Gascoigne shoolde treete bitwen the forsayd Lord.. and hym. *c*1449 PECOCK *Repr.* II. vii. 176 Which pilgrimage.. he wolde that no Cristen man schude do. 1461 C. PASTON in *P. Lett.* 26 June, The mony that I xwld have. 1471 CAXTON *Recuyell* (Sommer) 14 þᵗ he shold not suffre hyt. *Ibid.* 37 That.. they shuld go to þe ryuage of the see. 1471 *Paston Lett.* III. 19 That I chuld goo and comon with the woman. 1515 BARCLAY *Egloges* v. (1570) Dij, A man on his cloke should not espye a heare. *c*1550 BALE *K. Johan* 1387 (Pollard), What ye mene.. I wold ye shuld opynly tell. 1608 D. T[UVILL] *Ess. Pol. & Mor.* 39 As that I shold erect a Tabernacle. 1648 HERRICK *Hesp., To Dean-bourn*, I never sho'd behold. 1662 in *Extr. St. Papers rel. Friends* Ser. II. (1911) 154 All are troubled that they shoulde make an Order and I should not obey it. 1697 CIBBER *Woman's Wit* I. 2 D'ee believe it impossible you shu'd ever Love? 1767 GOOCH *Treat. Wounds* I. 387 These considerations shou'd make us the more attentive. 1785 BURNS *To Rev. J. M'Math* viii, I'm no' the thing I shou'd be.

*β.* 3 **sol(l)de, sulde, soolde;** *Sc.* and *north.* 4–9 **sulde, soulde,** 4–8 **sould,** (4 **salde, suuld, sold,** 4, 8 **sud,** 5 **sald,** 6 **sowld,** 8 **soud),** 3– **suld.**

*c*1200 ORMIN 7239 þær Messyass.. To manne cumenn sollde. *c*1220 *Bestiary* 149 He fleð fro him als he fro fir sulde. *c*1275 LAY. 3485 So man his fader solde. *a*1325 *MS. Rawl. B* 520 lf. 62 Ilke lond.. wuche soolde retournen to þilke R. *a*1300 *Cursor M.* 146 þe law.. þe quilk the Iuus in suld life. 13.. *Ibid.* 6106 (Gött.), [Moyses] for-bed þat þai Sould vte of hous cum. *Ibid.* 16464, þar was na soygne, bot his lauerd sud dei. *a*1375 *Ibid.* 1197 (Fairf.), Our lorde.. bad he salde wiþ his wyf dele hit sulde him turne to myche wele. 1497 *Acc. Ld. High Treas. Scot.* I. 357 The gallory quhilk he suld mak. 1500–20 DUNBAR *Poems* xiv. 8 That sowld haif ay thair God afoir thair ene. 1567 *Satir. Poems Reform.* iii. 5 That euer I sould byde to se that day! *c*1620 A. HUME *Brit. Tongue* (1870) 18 Quhither quho, quhen, quhat, etc. sould be symbolized with q or w. 1725 RAMSAY *Cock Laird* v, We maun hae braw things, Abeit they soud break. 1785 BURNS *To W. S*****n* ii, I sud be laith to think ye hinted Ironic satire. 1822 SCOTT *Nigel* iii, That I suld have held up my hand to my brow. *a*1862 in C. C. Robinson *Dial. Leeds* 213 Ah wur sorely flääd 'at ah sud säay my text wreng.

8. *2nd pers. sing.* *a.* 1 **sceoldes,** 3–4 **suldes,** 5 **shuldes, xulddes;** 1 **sceoldest,** 2–3 **scoldest, sculdest,** 3–5 **schuldest,** 5–6 **shuldest,** (3 **ssholdest,** 4 **ssoldest, scholdest,** 5 **sholdest,** 6 **souldest),** **shouldest, shouldst.**

*c*888 ÆLFRED *Boeth.* v. §3 Eac þæt wæs swiðe micel pleoh þæt ðu swa wenan sceoldes. *c*1250 *Gen. & Ex.* 3984 Her suldes ðu nu wurðen slaȝen. *c*1300 *K. Horn* 106 (Laud MS.) þat micte so bi falle þou suldes slen us alle. *a*1425 *Cursor M.* 2986 (Trin.) þat þou shuldes not synne in me. *c*1485 *Mary Magd.* 1163 in *Digby Myst.* 99 And þou xulddes ryde.

*Beowulf* 2056 (Gr.) þone þe ðu mid rihte rædan sceoldest. 1154 *O.E. Chron.* (Laud MS.) an. 1137, All a dæis fare sculdest thu neure finden man in tune sittende. *c*1175 *Lamb. Hom.* 15 þat ilke uuel þe ic dude þe þu scoldest don me. 1399 LANGL. *Rich. Redeles* III. 170 As þou shuldist mete of a myst. *c*1400 *Pilg. Sowle* (Caxton 1483) IV. xxiv. 70 Yf thou haddest ..entended to this scole duely as thou sholdest. 1445 tr. *Claudian* in *Anglia* XXVIII. 259 That to trespassours thou sholdist pardon.. graunte. 1573 J. SANFORD *Hours Recr.* (1576) 109 That thou shuldest buye that which thou must occupie. 1582 BENTLEY *Mon. Matrones* ii. 198 Speciallie that thou shouldest not despaire. 1667 in *Extr. St. Papers rel. Friends* Ser. III. (1912) 263 Thou shouldest take parte with the opressed. 1820 SCOTT *Monast.* xx, Shouldst thou point out to me.. an enemy more worthy of my resentment. 1862 CALVERLEY *Verses & Transl.* (1894) 97 He shall teach thee that thou shouldest not dream.

*β. contracted.* 3 **s(s)ost,** 4 **s(c)host, schust,** 4–5 **shust.**

1297 R. GLOUC. (Rolls) 8974 Ich clupede þe ek up þat þou it ssost ise [*v. rr.* (*14th* c.) shost, schost, scholdest, schuldest]. *c*1300 *Harrow. Hell* (A.) 195 Lord crist,.. þou schust com to helle pine. 13.. *Medit.* 714 þou shust pray for hem þat þy foos be. 1426 LYDG. *De Guil. Pilgr.* 6824 Rather than thow shust forsake Thy skryppe.

*γ.* 4–5 **shuld(e,** 4–6 **suld(e,** 6 **should.**

*a*1300 *Cursor M.* 12088 Til oþer thues þou suld him won. *c*1375 *Lay Folks Mass Bk.* (MS. B) 244 How þou shulde praye, I wold þou wyst. 1411 *26 Pol. Poems* 46/207 For þou shuld ȝeue, god dede þe sende. 1500–20 DUNBAR *Poems* xc. 28 Thow sulde it tell with all the circumstance.

9. a. With pronouns affixed: *1st pers. sing.* 3 **schuldich.** *2nd pers. sing.* 4 **shuldestou,** 5 **schuldestow.**

*a*1300 *Vox & Wolf* 163 in Hazl. *E.P.P.* I. 63 What shuldich ine the worlde go? 1377 LANGL. *P. Pl.* B. XI. 97 þinge that al þe worlde wote wherfore shuldestow spare To reden it? *c*1450 *Cursor M.* 9611 (Trin.) þenne shuldestou be douted nouȝt.

b. With *not* (Sc. and dial. *na*) affixed.

*c*1420 *Chron. Vilod.* 2147 How.. Sathanas Dude hurre þere lette wᵗ alle his myȝt, þat he shulnot haue come to þat ioyfulle place. *a*1796 BURNS *'Dear——, I'll gie ye some advice'*, You shouldna paint at angels mair. 1848 THACKERAY *Van. Fair* xxv, Perhaps I was a fool, Becky, but you shouldn't say so. 1859 GEO. ELIOT *Adam Bede* xxxii, I shouldna wonder if he's come about that man [etc.].

B. Signification and uses.

†I. 1. *trans.* a. To owe (money). *Obs.*

*c*975 *Rushw. Gosp.* Matt. xviii. 28 Seþe sculde him undred denera. *c*1000 *Ags. Gosp.* Luke xvi. 5 Hu mycel scealt þu minum hlaforde? *c*1290 *Beket* 820 in *S. Eng. Leg.* 130 þar-of þritti þousent pound þov me schalt. 1340 *Ayenb.* 115 Ich ne habbe huer-of maki þe yeldinge: uoryef me þet ich þe ssel. *Ibid.* 145 þise dette ssel ech to oþren and huo mest his yelt mest he ssel. *a*1400 *New Test.* (Paues) Rom. xiii. 7 ȝelde ȝe to alle men ȝoure dettes: to hym þat ȝe schuleþ trybut, trybut. *c*1425 HOCCLEVE *Min. Poems* xxiii. 695 The leeste ferthyng þat y men shal.

†b. To owe (allegiance). *Obs.*

*c*1325 *Poem temp. Edw. II* (Percy Soc.) xxxiv, Be the fayth ic schal to God. *c*1374 CHAUCER *Troilus* III. 1649 And by that feyth I shal to god and yow. [*c*1530 *Crt. of Love* 131 By the feith I shall to god.]

II. Followed by an infinitive (without *to*).

Except for a few instances of *shall will, shall may* (*mowe*), *shall conne* in the 15th c., the infinitive after *shall* is always either that of a principal verb or of *have* or *be*.

* The present tense *shall*.

†2. In general statements of what is right or becoming: = 'ought'. *Obs.* (Superseded by the pa. subjunctive *should*: see sense 18.)

In OE. the subjunctive present sometimes occurs in this use (e.g. *c* 888 in A. 4).

*Beowulf* 20 (Gr.) Swa sceal ȝeong guma gode ȝewyrcean .. þæt [etc.]. *c*700 CÆDMON *Hymn* 1 Nu scylun herȝan hefænricæs uard. *c*888 ÆLFRED *Boeth.* xli. §3 Hwy sceall þonne æniȝ mon bion idel, þæt he ne wyrce? *a*1100 *Gerefa* in *Anglia* IX. 259 Se scadwis ȝerefa sceal æȝðer witan ȝe hlafordes landriht ȝe folces ȝerihtu. *c*1175 *Lamb. Hom.* 19 Al þet þe licome luueð þet þa saule heteð.. Nu sculle we forlete þes licome lust for-þon. *a*1225 *Ancr. R.* 96 Ancren schulen brihtluker, uor hore blindfallunge her, iseon ant understonden þer Godes derne runes. *c*1300 *Havelok* 2419 Mine knihtes, hwat do ye? Shule ye þus-gate fro me fle? 1340 *Ayenb.* 5 þe hestes ten þet loki ssolle alle men. *Ibid.* 136 Ase moche ase he ssel and may do wyþ-oute misdo. 13.. *Cursor M.* 20538 (Gött.) Inogh þai did me vilete, þat wid right min aune sul be. *c*1420 *Pol. Rel. & L. Poems* (1903) 242 Alle cristen pepill glad xal bene þat crist is boþe king and prest. *c*1420 *Liber Cocorum* (1862) 29 Pekokys, and pertrikys perboylyd schyn be. *c*1460 FORTESCUE *Abs. & Lim. Mon.* vii. (1885) 125 The kynge shall often tymes sende ..his juges, to.. punysh riatours and risers. 1562 LEGH *Armory* 149 Whether are Roundells of all suche coloures, as ye haue spoken of here before? or shall they be named Roundelles of those colours?

†3. a. In OE. and occas. in ME. used to express necessity of various kinds (for the many shades of meaning in OE. see Bosworth-Toller): = 'must', 'must needs', 'have to', 'am compelled to', etc.

*c*888 ÆLFRED *Boeth.* xxxiv. §3 þonne scealt þu nede ȝelefan þæt sum anwald sie mara þonne his. *c*897 —— *Gregory's Past. C.* iii. 34 On ðæm ȝeswincum he sceal hine selfne ȝeðencean, ðeah he nylle. *c*1250 *Gen. & Ex.* 308 We ðe ben fro heuene driuen, sulen ðusse one in sorwe liuen. *c*1275 *Passion our Lord* 159 in *O.E. Misc.* 41 If ich hine schal drynke iworþe þine wille. *c*1350 *Will. Palerne* 5422, I wold it were þi wille wiþ vs forto lenge, hit forþinkes me sore þat we schul de-parte. 1387 TREVISA *Higden* (Rolls) I. 369 Tweyne þat beeþ i-wedded a man and a wom̄an schal nedes be outlawed out of þat contray. *c*1440 *York Myst.* XVI. 18, I am fairer of face.. (þe soth yf I saie sall).. þan glorius gulles.

†b. In stating a necessary condition: = 'will have to', 'must' (if something else is to happen).

*a*1000 *Boeth. Metr.* v. 26 ȝif þu nu wilnast.. þæt soðe leoht sweotole oncnawan.. þu forlætan scealt idle ofersælða. 1596 SHAKS. *Merch. V.* I. i. 116 You shall seeke all day ere you finde them, & when you haue them they are not worth the search. 1605 —— *Lear* v. iii. 22 He that parts vs, shall bring a Brand from Heauen. 1818 SCOTT *Hrt. Midl.* xviii, He shall hide himself in a bean-hole, if he remains on Scottish ground without my finding him.

†c. In hypothetical clause, accompanying the statement of a necessary condition: = 'is to'.

*c* **1440** *Alphabet of Tales* lxv. 48 Right so muste hym chastes his flessh with fastyng if he sal be savid. **1612** Bacon *Ess., Greatn. Kingd.* (Arb.) 482 Neither must they be too much broken of it, if they shall be preserued in vigor.

†**4.** Indicating what is appointed or settled to take place = the mod. 'is to', 'am to', etc. *Obs.*

*c* **1000** Ælfric *Gram.* xxiv. (Z.) 136 *Lecturus sum cras*, ic sceal rædan to meriȝen, *lecturus es*, þu scealt rædan, *lecturus est*, he sceal rædan. *Ibid.* xli. 248 *Osculandus*, se ðe sceal beon ȝecyssed. *a* **1122** *O.E. Chron.* (Laud MS.) an. 565, Nu sceal beon æfre on Ii abbod næs bisceop, & þam sculon beon under þædde ealle Scotta biscopes. *c* **1205** Lay. 5964 Belin ..hit [*sc.* Rome] bi-tæcheð Brenne þe scæl bi-læuen here. **1297** R. Glouc. (Rolls) 56 We ssulleþ her after in þise boc telle of al þis wo. **1526** Tindale *Luke* vii. 19 Arte thou he that shall come..? **1600** Shaks. *A.Y.L.* II. iv. 89 What is he that shall buy his flocke and pasture? **1625** in Ellis *Orig. Lett.* Ser. I. III. 199 Tomorrow His Majesty will be present..to begin the Parliament which is thought shall be removed to Oxford.

**5.** In commands or instructions. **a.** (*a*) In the second person, equivalent to an imperative.

Chiefly in Biblical language, of Divine commandments, rendering the jussive future of the Heb. and Vulgate. (In OE. the imperative is used in the ten commandments.)

*a* **1000** *Andreas* 950 (Gr.) Nu ðu, Andreas, scealt edre ȝeneðan in gramra gripe. *c* **1000** *Ags. Ps.* (Th.) civ. 13 Ne sceolon ȝe mine þa halȝan hrinan. **1340** *Ayenb.* 5 Þe uerste heste þet god made..is þis: þou ne sselt habbe uele godes. **1382** Wyclif *Exod.* xx. 7 Thow shalt not tak the name of the Lord thi God in veyn. [So Coverdale, etc.] **1405** *Lay-Folks Mass Bk.* 64 Ȝe sal mak your prayers specially..for the state and the stabilnes of al halykirk. **1533** Gau *Richt Vay* 8 Thou sal haif na oder strenge godis. **1567** *Gude & Godlie Ball.* 8 Thou sall not slay, in na kin wyse. **1604** *Bidding Prayer* (still in use), Ye shall pray for Christ's Holy Catholic Church.

†(*b*) In expositions: ***you shall understand***, etc. (that). *Obs.*

*c* **1175** *Lamb. Hom.* 5 Nu ic eou habbe þet godspel iseid anfaldeliche, nu scule ȝe understonden twafaldeliche þet hit bi-tacnet. **1303** R. Brunne *Handl. Synne* 10663 A Frysoun ȝe shul vndyrstande To a marchaunde of Fryslande. *c* **1400** Maundev. (1839) vii. 73 Ȝee schulle undirstonde, that it stont fulle faire betwene Hilles. **1423** Jas. I *Kingis Q.* cxxviii, Thou sall wele knawe and witt, Thou may thy hert[e] ground on suich a wise [etc.]. **1523** Cromwell in Merriman *Life & Lett.* (1902) I. 313 Ye shall also understond the Duke of Suthffolke..goyth ouer in all goodlye hast [whit]her I know not.

†(*c*) In the formula ***you shall excuse*** (***pardon***) ***me***. *Obs.* (now *must*).

**1595** Shaks. *John* v. ii. 78 Your Grace shall pardon me, I will not backe. **1630** *R. Johnson's Kingd. & Commw.* 191 You shall excuse me, for I eat no flesh on Fridayes.

**b.** In the third person.

*a* **900** *Durham Admon.* in *O.E. Texts* 176 [Ðis mon] scal reda ofer ða feta ða ful infalleð. *a* **1225** *Ancr. R.* 24 Þenne schal siggen, hwo se con, 'Domine labia mea aperies'. *a* **1325** *MS. Rawl. B* 520 lf. 32 b, Ȝif þe lord ne mai noȝt suffisen to uellen þe vnder wode, þe contreie him sal helpe. *c* **1386** Chaucer *Prol.* 794 Ech of yow, to shorte with your weye, In this viage, shal telle tales tweye. *c* **1450** *Godstow Reg.* 206 The said Abbesse and her successours whan they ben resonably somoned shul send thedir their certayn steward. **1560** Daus tr. *Sleidane's Comm.* 246 b, It shall be free for every man to joyne hym selfe unto thys league. **1623–4** *Act 21 Jas. I*, c. 28 §7 No Sanctuarie..shalbe hereafter admitted. **1645** *Ordin. Lords & Comm.* 5 Scandalous persons shal be kept from the Sacrament. **1744** in Atkyns *Chanc. Cases* (1782) III. 166 The words *shall and may* in general acts of parliament, or in private constitutions, are to be construed imperatively, they *must* remove them.

**6.** In the second and third persons, expressing the speaker's determination to bring about (or, with negative, to prevent) some action, event, or state of things in the future, or (occasionally) to refrain from hindering what is otherwise certain to take place, or is intended by another person.

**a.** In the second person.

*a* **1000** *Cædmon's Gen.* 909 (Gr.) Þu scealt greot etan þine lifdaȝas. *a* **1175** *Cott. Hom.* 221 Ȝif þu þanne þis litle bebod to brecst, þu scealt deaðe sweltan. *c* **1205** Lay. 26587 Abuggen ȝe scullen þa dede. *c* **1275** *Sinners Beware* 316 in *O.E. Misc.* 82 To day ye schuleþ..vnder-fo luþre mede. *c* **1350** *Will. Palerne* 2257 Þe soþe, felawes, ful sone ȝe schol it wite. **1447** Bokenham *Seyntys, Cecilia* 591 Ye shul hens pace, Or ellys, certeynly, ye shule deye. **1470–85** Malory *Arthur* VII. xviii. 240 And syker assuraunce and borowes ye shal haue. *a* **1596** *Sir T. More* I. i, Followe me no further; I say thou shalt not haue them. **1633** P. Fletcher *Purple Isl.* VI. lxxvii, To morrow shall ye feast in pastures new. **1777** Sheridan *Trip Scarb.* v. ii. ad fin., Well, 'fore George, you shan't say I do things by halves. **1777** —— *Sch. Scandal* II. ii, Positively you shall not be so severe. **1833** Tennyson *Death of Old Year*, Old year, you must not go;..Old year, you shall not go. **1891** 'J. S. Winter' *Lumley* xi, If you would rather not stay then, you shall go down to South Kensington Square then.

**b.** In third person.

*c* **1000** Ælfric *Gen.* xviii. 10 Þin wif Sarra sceal habban sunu. **1310** *St. Brendan* (Bälz) 603 We wolleþ ous wel awreke, up him sulve it schal go. *c* **1386** Chaucer *Reeve's T.* 167 By goddes herte he sal nat scape us bathe. *c* **1422** Hoccleve *Jereslaus's Wife* 37 With goddes grace my comynge ageyn Shal nat be longe. **1591** Shaks. *Two Gent.* v. iv. 129 Verona shall not hold thee. **1604** —— *Oth.* v. ii. 334 If there be any cunning Crueltie, That can torment him much,..It shall be his. **1777** Sheridan *Sch. Scandal* I. ii, Though your ill-conduct may disturb my peace of mind, it shall never break my heart, I promise you. **1840** Thackeray *Barber Cox* Feb., Others, whose names may be found in the Blue Book, but shan't, out of modesty, be mentioned here. **1849** Noad *Electricity* (ed. 3) 174 The occasion of mentioning this gentleman's name shall be taken as an opportunity of describing his..form of the constant battery. **1891** 'J. S. Winter' *Lumley* xiv, 'Oh, yes, sir, she shall come back,' said the nurse. 'I'll take care of that.' 'I will come back,' said Vere.

**7.** In special interrogative uses related to senses 5 and 6.

**a.** In the first person, used in questions to which the expected answer is a command, direction, or counsel, or a resolve on the speaker's own part.

(*a*) in questions introduced by an interrogative pronoun (in oblique case), adverb, or adverbial phrase.

*c* **900** tr. *Bæda's Hist.* IV. xxv, Cwæð he: Hwæt sceal ic singan? Cwæð he: Sing me frumsceaft. **971** *Blickl. Hom.* 169 Hwæt sceal ic ðonne ma secgean fram Sancte Iohanne.. buton þæt [etc.]. *c* **1200** Ormin 9289 Whatt shule we nu forrþwarrd don? *c* **1250** *Gen. & Ex.* 3358 'Louered', quad he, 'quat sal ic don? He sulen me werpen stones on'. *a* **1300** *Cursor M.* 11205 Quat schal [*Trin.*, *Laud*, shulde] i tell yow, less or mare, Bot ihesu crist hir barn sco bar? *c* **1449** Pecock *Repr.* III. xi. 342 Frowhens schule we trowe this came, that so manye..false Apostlis..weren in the chirche. *c* **1450** Holland *Howlat* 69 Quhom sall I blame in this breth, a bysyn that I be? **1513** Douglas *Æneis* I. vi. 38 Bot, O thou virgine, quham sall I call the? **1600** Fairfax *Tasso* VIII. lxix, What shall we doe? shall we be gouern'd still, By this false hand? **1611** Beaum. & Fl. *Philaster* I. i, How shall we devise To hold intelligence? **1848** Thackeray *Van. Fair* xxii, 'It's rather slow work', said he, 'down here; what *shall* we do?' **1865** Kingsley *Herew.* xxxiii, Where shall we stow the mare?

(*b*) in categorical questions.

Often expressing indignant reprobation of a suggested course of action, the implication being that only a negative (or, with negative question an affirmative) answer is conceivable.

**1600** [see (*a*)]. **1611** Shaks. *Wint. T.* v. iii. 83 Shall I draw the Curtaine? **1622** Wither *Philarete* (1633) I 7 Shall I wasting in Dispaire, Dye because a Womans faire? ? *a* **1700** D'Urfey *Pills* (1719) V. 113 Shall you and I Lady, Among the Grass lye down a. **1777** Sheridan *Sch. Scandal* II. iii, What! shall I forget..when I was at his years myself? **1802** Wordsw. *To the Cuckoo* i, O Cuckoo! shall I call thee Bird, Or but a wandering Voice? **1865** Swinburne *Chastelard* I. i. 22, I am bound to France; Shall I take word from you to any one? **1891** 'J. S. Winter' *Lumley* xiii, 'Are you driving, or shall I call you a cab?' 'Oh, no; I'm driving, thanks'.

¶(*c*) In ironical affirmative in exclamatory sentence, equivalent to the above interrogative use. (Cf. Ger. *soll.*) *rare.*

**1741** Richardson *Pamela* (1742) III. 89 A pretty thing truly! Here I, a poor helpless Girl, raised from Poverty and Distress,..shall put on Lady-airs to a Gentlewoman born.

†(*d*) ***to stand shall I, shall I*** (later ***shill I, shall I***: see shilly-shally), ***to be at shall I, shall I*** (***not***): to be vacillating, to shilly-shally. *Obs.*

**1674** R. Godfrey *Inj. & Ab. Physic* 85 Such Medicines.. that will not stand shall I? shall I? but will fall to work on the Disease presently. *c* **1689** *Popish Pol. Unmaskt* 34 in *Third Coll. Poems* (1689) 23 Who follows him that standeth, shall I, shall I? **1727** Boyer *Dict. Royal* II. s.v., To be at shall-I shall-I, (to be at a stand, or in suspence).

**b.** Similarly in the third person, where the subject represents or includes the speaker, or when the speaker is placing himself at another's point of view.

**1610** Shaks. *Temp.* v. i. 22 Hast thou (which art but aire) a touch, a feeling Of their afflictions, and shall not my selfe, One of their kinde,..be kindlier mou'd then thou art? **1871** R. Ellis *Catullus* xxx. 6 O where now shall a man trust?

**c.** In the second and third person, where the expected answer is a decision on the part of the speaker or of some person other than the subject.

As in sense a, the question often serves as an impassioned repudiation of a suggestion that something shall be permitted.

*c* **1205** Lay. 13531 Wha scal an hirede beon ure lauerd Nu Vortiger is iuaren? **13..** in *Ayenb.* (1866) Descr. MS., Þe kyng Alesandre acsede hwan ssal þat be. **1382** Wyclif *Ps.* xii. 3 Hou longe shall ben enhauncid myn enemy vp on me? *c* **1450** *Merlin* i. 14 'What shalbe his name?' 'I will', quod she, 'that it haue name after my fader.' *c* **1590** Montgomerie *Sonn.* liv. 2 Vhase praise, Apollo, sal my pen proclame? **1600** Shaks. *A.Y.L.* IV. ii. 11 What shall he haue that kild the Deare? **1737** Pope *Hor. Epist.* I. i. 97 And say, to which shall our applause belong, This new Court jargon, or the good old song? **1812** Crabbe *Tales* xviii, Shall a wife complain? **1850** Tennyson *In Mem.* lvi. 8 And he, shall he, Man,..Be blown about the desert dust, Or seal'd within the iron hills?

**d.** In indirect question.

In quot. 1470–85 irregularly in pres. tense when the principal clause is in pa. t.

*c* **888** Ælfred *Boeth.* v. §3 Þæt ic þonan onȝietan mæȝe hwonon ic þin tiliȝe scyle & hu. *c* **950** *Lindisf. Gosp.* Matt. x. 19 Nallað ȝe ȝeðence huu vel huæt ȝe spreca scilo [*quomodo aut quid loquamini*]. *a* **1225** *Leg. Kath.* 638 Ne þenche ȝe neauer hwet ne hu ȝe schulen seggen. *c* **1380** Wyclif *Wks.* (1880) 147 Þei stryuen not who schal be most meke. *c* **1400** Love *Bonavent. Mirr.* xiii. (Gibbs MS.) lf. 32 He taught.. vs in what manere þis vertue of mekenesse schal be goten. **1450** W. Lomner in *Paston Lett.* 5 May, The shreve of Kent ..sent his under shreve to the juges to wete what to doo, and also to the Kenge whatte shalbe doo. **1470–85** Malory *Arthur* II. xiii. 91 On the morne they fond letters of gold wryten how syr Gaweyn shalle reuenge his faders deth. *c* **1489** Caxton *Sonnes of Aymon* viii. 181 That ye counseille me how I shall maye avenge me. *a* **1500** *Tretyce of Husb.* in *W. Henley*, etc. (R. Hist. Soc. 1890) 41 The vj chapitur tellithe nowe howe you shall lay youre lande at seede tyme. **1610** Shaks. *Temp.* I. ii. 495 Harke what thou else shalt do mee. **1756** Mrs. Calderwood in *Coltness Collect.* (Maitland Club) 185, I beg to know..who I shall inform him inquired so kindly after him. **1777** Sheridan *Sch. Scandal* III. i, Let our future Contest be, who shall be most obliging. **1865** Kingsley *Herew.* x, Let her say what shall be done with it.

**8.** As a mere auxiliary, forming (with present infinitive) the future, and (with perfect infinitive) the future perfect tense.

In OE. the notion of the future tense was ordinarily expressed by the present tense. To prevent ambiguity, *wile* (will) was not unfrequently used as a future auxiliary, sometimes retaining no trace of its original sense. On the other hand, *sceal* (shall) even when rendering a Latin future, can hardly be said to have been ever a mere tense-sign in OE.; it always expressed something of its original notion of obligation or necessity. In ME. the present early ceased to be commonly employed in futural sense, and the future was expressed by either *shall* or *will*, the former being much more common. The usage as to the choice between the two auxiliaries has varied from time to time; since the middle of the 17th c. the general rule (subject to various exceptions) has been that mere futurity is expressed in the first person by *shall*, in the second and third by *will*. In indirectly reported speech, usage permits either the retention of the auxiliary used by the original speaker or the substitution of that which is appropriate to the point of view of the person reporting.

**a.** In OE. *sceal*, while retaining its primary sense, served as a tense-sign in announcing a future event as fated or divinely decreed. Hence *shall* has always been the auxiliary used, in all persons, for prophetic or oracular announcements of the future, and for solemn assertions of the certainty of a future event.

*a* **900** Cynewulf *Crist* 1030 Sceal þonne anra ȝehwylc fore Cristes cyme cwic arisan. *c* **950** *Lindisf. Gosp.* Luke xiii. 5 Alle ȝelic ȝie sciolon losiȝa, *omnes similiter peribitis*. *c* **1200** Ormin 211 Fra þiss daȝȝ þu shallt ben dumb. *c* **1250** *Gen. & Ex.* 4039 Of ðe sal risen sterre briȝt. **1297** R. Glouc. (Rolls) 5133 Hii ssolleþ ȝut keuery moche lond þat hii abbeþ y lore. *c* **1400** *Brut* lxix. 64 Ȝe shul bigete a douȝter þat shal be quene of Irland. *c* **1475** *Partenay* 2168 Thy contre shalt se put in exile all, Distroed, robbed. **1546** Heywood *Prov.* (1867) 43 That shalbe, shalbe. **1577** in Allen *Martyrdom Campion* (1908) 110 The queene neither ever was, nor is, nor ever shall be the head of the Church of England. **1601** Shaks. *Jul. C.* III. i. 262 Now do I Prophesie..A Curse shall light vpon the limbes of men. **1653** W. Ramesey *Astrol. Rest.* 273 It signifies men shall be scoffers and jeerers one of another. **1746** Francis tr. *Hor. Epist.* II. i. 26 No Prince so great, so wise, Hath ever risen, or shall ever rise. **1852** Tennyson *Ode Death Wellington* 191 Whatever record leap to light He never shall be shamed. **1864** J. H. Newman *Apol.* 181 A General Council, truly such, never did, never shall err in a matter of faith. **1891** F. Thompson *Sister-Songs* (1895) 46 So it may be, so it shall be,—Oh, take the prophecy from me!

**b.** In the first person, *shall* has, from the early ME. period, been the normal auxiliary for expressing mere futurity, without any adventitious notion. (*a*) Of events conceived as independent of the speaker's volition. (To use *will* in these cases is now a mark of Scottish, Irish, provincial, or extra-British idiom.)

*c* **1200** Ormin Ded. 143, I shall hafenn forr min swinnc God læn..Ȝiff þatt I..Hemm hafe itt inntill Ennglissh wennd. *c* **1205** Lay. 8371 Nu we sulleð for heore beone bliðe iwurðen. *c* **1300** *K. Horn* 1406 (Laud MS.) Þis lond we schollen winne And sle al þat þere ben inne. **1470–85** Malory *Arthur* I. xx. 67, I shalle dye a shameful deth. **1595** in *Cath. Rec. Soc. Publ.* V. 357 My frend, yow and I shall play no more at Tables now. **1605** Shaks. *Macb.* I. i. 1 When shall we three meet againe? **1613** —— *Hen. VIII*, I. iv. 44 Then wee shall haue 'em, Talke vs to silence. **1667** Milton *P.L.* VI. 737, I..shall soon..rid heav'n of these rebell'd. **1777** Sheridan *Trip Scarb.* II. i, So—carry him off!.. We shall have him into a fever by-and-by. **1781** Johnson in *Boswell* (1904) II. 402 You cannot suppose that we shall rise with a diseased body. **1806** Wordsw. *Addr. to a Child* 39 He may work his own will, and what shall we care? **1822** Shelley *Chas. I*, i. 40 My travel's done,—Before the whirlwind wakes I shall have found My inn of lasting rest. **1852** Mrs. Stowe *Uncle Tom's C.* xvii, 'But what if you don't hit?' 'I *shall* hit', said George coolly. **1863** Geo. Eliot *Romola* vi, Our personal characters will be attacked, we shall be impeached with foul actions.

(*b*) Of voluntary action or its intended result. Here *I* (*we*) *shall* is always admissible exc. where the notion of a present (as distinguished from a previous) decision or consent is to be expressed (in which case *will* must be used). Further, *I shall* often expresses a determination insisted on in spite of opposition, and *I shall not* (colloq. *I shan't*) a peremptory refusal.

In the 16th c. and earlier, *I shall* often occurs where *I will* would now be used.

*c* **1200** Ormin 11557 Icc shall beon aȝȝ occ aȝȝ wiþþ ȝuw Whil þatt tiss weorelld lassteþþ. *a* **1225** *Leg. Kath.* 396 We schulen bringen to ende þat we bigunnen habbeð. *a* **1300** *K. Horn* 833 Ischal..Wiþ mi swerd wel eþe Bringe hem þre to deþe. *c* **1320** *Sir Tristr.* 621 Cherl! go oway, Oþer y schal þe smite. **1382** Wyclif *Exod.* xx. 19 Spek thow to vs, and we shulen here. *a* **1400** *Sir Perc.* 1466 A schafte salle I one hym sett, And I salle fonde firste to hitt. **1559** W. Cunningham *Cosmogr. Glasse* 91 This now shall I alway kepe surely in memorye. **1601** Shaks. *All's Well* v. iii. 27 Informe him So 'tis our will he should.—I shall my liege. **1693** Evelyn *De la Quint. Compl. Gard.* I. 91, I shall begin my Discourse of this Russelet-pear by telling you [etc.]. **1779** *Mirror* No. 25, I.. shall let my wife and daughters know, that I will be master of my own house. **1819** Shelley *Cenci* v. iii. 86 Say what ye will. I shall deny no more. **1833** [see sham *v.* 5]. **1885** Ruskin *On Old Road* II. 57 *note*, Henceforward..I shall continue to spell 'Ryme' without our wrongly added *h*.

**c.** In the second person, *shall* as a mere future auxiliary appears never to have been usual in affirmative or negative senses (exc. in the uses treated under 9 b and 11); but in categorical questions it is normal: e.g. '*Shall* you miss your train? I am afraid you will.'

**d.** In the third person. *Obs.* (superseded by *will*) exc. when another's statement or expectation respecting himself is reported in the third person, e.g. 'He says he shall not have time to write.' (Even in this case *will* is still not uncommon, but in some contexts leads to ambiguity; it is therefore preferable to use *he shall* as the indirect rendering of *I shall*.)

*c* **1200** ORMIN Ded. 79 Þeʒʒ shulenn lætenn hæþeliʒ Off unnkerr swinnc. *a* **1300** *Thrush & Night.* 128 in Hazl. *E.P.P.* I. 55 Come thou heuere in here londe, Hy shulen don the in prisoun stronge. *c* **1475** *Rauf Coilʒear* 56 Traist quhen thow will, For I trow and it be nocht swa, sum part salbe thyne. **1477** EARL RIVERS (Caxton) *Dictes* 19 Parauenture in aduersite my power shal lak. *c* **1489** CAXTON *Sonnes of Aymon* ii. 64 Yf your fader come agayn from the courte, he shall wyll yelde you to the kynge Charlemayne. **1581** E. CAMPION in *Conf.* II. (1584) L iv, It shalbe he reported that I sayd this and that, and my wordes shalbe depraued. *c* **1656** *Roxb. Ball.* (1891) VII. 492 'Tis very like they shall be sent, soon after, to relieve you. **17..** RAMSAY *Some of the Contents* ix, Montgomery's quatorsimes sall evir pleis. **1799** J. ROBERTSON *Agric. Perth* 361 The effect of the statute labour ..has always been, now is, and probably shall continue to be, less productive than it might. **1837** MACAULAY *Ess., Bacon* (1843) II. 406 That method leads the clown to the conclusion that if he sows barley he shall not reap wheat. **1850-8** MILL 3 *Ess., Util. Relig.* (1874) 92 People do not really believe that..they shall be punished by God, any more than by man.

¶**e.** Down to the 18th c., *shall*, the auxiliary appropriate to the first person, was sometimes used when a person wrote of himself in the third person.

Cf. the formula: 'And your petitioner shall ever pray.'

**1531** in *Sel. Cases Crt. Requests* (1898) 33 And your seid Orator shall dayly pray to Ihesu for the preseruacion of your most ryall grace. **1642** *Chas. I's Wks.* (1662) I. 203 (Though His Majesty shall be deeply..sensible of their sufferings) He shall wash His hands..from the least imputation of slackness. **1798** KEMBLE *Let.* in *Pearson's Catal.* (1900) 45 Mr. Kemble presents his respectful compliments to the Proprietors of the 'Monthly Mirror', and shall have great pleasure at being at all able to aid them.

†**f.** In negative (or virtually negative) and interrogative use, *shall* often = 'will be able to'. *Obs.*

*a* **1000** *Guthlac* 337 (Gr.) Hu sceal min cuman gæst to ʒeoce, nemne ic gode sylle hyrsumne hiʒe? *a* **1375** *Joseph Arim.* 104 Let breken hem a-two and bren hem al to pouder, Schaltou neuer gete grace þorwʒ none suche goddes. *c* **1386** CHAUCER *Merch. T.* 318 Ye shul nat plese hir fully yeres three, This is to seyn, to doon hir ful plesaunce. **1565-6** ABP. PARKER *Corr.* (Parker Soc.) 263 If I draw forward, and others draw backwards, what shall it avail? *c* **1600** SHAKS. *Sonn.* lxv, How with this rage shall beautie hold a plea. **1652** BLITH *Eng. Improver Impr.* II. xxviii. (1653) 192 He shall never make a Plough to go with ease by his rules. **1773** [T. DAY] *Dying Negro* 2 How shall I soothe thy grief, my destin'd bride!

**g.** Used (after a hypothetical clause or an imperative sentence) in statements of a result to be expected from some action or occurrence. Now (exc. in the first person) usually replaced by *will*; but *shall* survives in literary use.

*c* **1205** LAY. 8018 ʒif þu ileuest ælcne mon selde þu sælt wel don. *a* **1225** *Ancr. R.* 406 Weop for his sunnen. þus þu schalt, seið Salomon, rukelen on his heaued bearninde gleden. **1398** TREVISA *Barth. De P.R.* XVIII. xcii. (1495) 840 Yf that matter towchyth a mannys body the heere shal fall. *c* **1400** MAUNDEV. (1839) xviii. 189 ʒif ony thing falle in to that Lake, it schalle nevere comen up aʒen. *c* **1400** LOVE *Bonavent. Mirr.* xiii. (Gibbs MS.) lf. 31 ʒyfe we woleth hier take good entent we schull mowe see þat [etc.]. **1534** TINDALE *1 Cor.* xiv. 9 When ye speake with tonges..how shall it be vnderstonde what is spoken? For ye shall but speake in the ayer. **1594** BARNFIELD *Affect. Sheph.* (Arb.) 22 Who tutcheth pitch, with pitch shalbe defiled. **1605** SHAKS. *Lear* II. ii. 144 You shall..show too bold malice Against the .. Person of my Master, Stocking his Messenger. **1709** STEELE *Tatler* No. 118 ¶1, I shall disoblige Multitudes of my Correspondents, if I do not take Notice of them. **1851** DASENT *Jest & Earnest* (1873) II. 140 Visit Rome and you shall find him [the Pope] mere carrion. **1865** RUSKIN *Sesame* i. §12 Make yourself noble, and you shall be. **1882** *Harper's Mag.* Dec. 24/2 Examine the book-shelves, and you shall find the novelist's favorite authors.

**h.** In clause expressing the object of a promise, or of an expectation accompanied by hope or fear. Now only where *shall* is the ordinary future auxiliary; but down to the 19th c. *shall* was often preferred to *will* in the second and third persons. Cf. sense 11.

**1475** J. PASTON 22 Feb. in *P. Lett.*, Iff the markett be nott goode yit, I hope it shall be better. *c* **1475** in *Eng. Gilds* (1870) 318 Ye schall swere that ye schall well and truelly byhaue you. **1508** DUNBAR *Flyting* 111, I tak on me ane pair of Lowthiane hippis Sall fairar Inglis mak,..Than thow can blabbar with thy Carrik lippis. **1538** STARKEY *England* I. i. 20 We are sure they schal bryng vs to our saluatyon. **1628** in Ellis *Orig. Lett.* Ser. I. III. 266 He is confident that the blood of Christ shall wash away..his..sins. **1643** in Mrs. A. Hope *Franciscan Martyrs* xiv. (ed. 3) 195, I hope nobody shall have any harme by anything I have saide, and for myself the worst they can doe to mee is the best and most desired. **1654** E. NICHOLAS in *N. Papers* (Camden) II. 142, I hope neither your Cosen Wat. Montagu nor..Walsingham shall be permitted to discourse..with..the D. of Glocester. **1749** FIELDING *Tom Jones* xv. iii, I hope his visits shall not be intruded upon me. **1820** SOUTHEY *Wesley* (ed. 2) I. 70, I trust in God your labour shall not be in vain.

†**i.** In impersonal phrases, ***it shall be well, needful***, etc. (to do so and so). *Obs.* (now *will*).

**1571** DIGGES *Pantom.* I. xviii. F b, It shalbe needfull at the time of your measuring to haue ground at libertie on the one side. **1585** T. WASHINGTON tr. *Nicholay's Voy.* III. x. 90 It shall not be impertinent nor out of my purpose, if I do speak ..of the kitchin of the great Turke. **1602** DEKKER *Satirom.* Ad Lect. A 4 b, It shall not be amisse (for him that will read) first to beholde this short Comedy of Errors.

†**j.** ***shall be***, added to a future date in clauses measuring time. Cf. *was* in BE *v.* 20. *Obs.*

**1617** SIR T. WENTWORTH in *Fortescue Papers* 25 To which purpose my late Lord Chancelour gave his direction about the 3. of Decembre shallbe-two-yeares.

**9.** In the idiomatic use of the future to denote what ordinarily or occasionally occurs under specified conditions, *shall* was formerly the usual auxiliary. In the second and third persons, this is now somewhat formal or rhetorical; ordinary language substitutes *will* or *may*. Often in antithetic statements coupled by an adversative conjunction or by *and* with adversative force.

**a.** in the first person.

**1712** STEELE *Spect.* No. 326 ¶2 In spite of all my Care, I shall every now and then have a saucy Rascal ride by reconnoitring..under my Windows.

**b.** in the second person.

*c* **1200** ORMIN 423 Full cweme wærenn baþe..& tu shallt findenn swillke nu Bitwenenn uss well fæwe. *c* **1449** PECOCK *Repr.* I. xx. 119 Thou schalt not fynde expresseli in Holi Scripture that the Newe Testament schulde be write in Englisch tunge to lay men. **1596** DALRYMPLE tr. *Leslie's Hist. Scot.* I. 5 Sa plentifull is the ground, that mekle esier ʒe sall expone quhat it nocht beiris, than quhat it beiris. **1597** MORLEY *Introd. Mus.* Annot., You shall not finde one side in all the booke without some grosse errour or other. **1625** BACON *Ess., Atheism* (Arb.) 333 You shall haue Atheists striue to get Disciples, as it fareth with other Sects. **1760** *Impostors Detected* I. iv. I. 26 He was as handsome a man, as you shall see on a summer's day. **1810** CRABBE *Borough* iii, A man so learn'd you shall but seldom see, Nor one so honour'd. **1852-4** SPENCER *Ess.* (1858) 414 After knowing him for years, you shall suddenly discover that your friend's nose is slightly awry. **1909** *Sat. Rev.* 29 May 692/1 You shall meet ten thousand men every day in the year between the Bank and the Mansion House..who are as poor as Church mice.

**c.** in the third person.

*c* **1000** *Sax. Leechd.* II. 236 Be þære frecnan coþe þe se mon his utgang þurh ðone muð..sceal aspiwan. He sceal oft bealcettan. **14..** *Pol. Rel. & L. Poems* (1903) 271 Quan a chyld to scole xal set be, A bok hym is browt. *a* **1568** ASCHAM *Scholem.* I. (Arb.) 39 If a father haue foure sonnes, three.. well formed..the fourth..deformed, his choice shalbe, to put the worst to learning. **1598** SYLVESTER *Du Bartas* II. ii. IV. *Columnes* 234 Here-by the Printer, in one day shall rid More Books, then yerst a thousand Writers did. **1652** FELTHAM *Low Countries* 18 Your man shall be..saucy, and you must not strike him. **1711** ADDISON *Spect.* No. 23 ¶5 There is indeed something very..inhuman in the ordinary Scriblers of Lampoons. An Innocent young Lady shall be exposed, for an unhappy Feature. **1773** W. ROBERTS *Looker-On* (1794) III. 179 One man shall approve..the same thing that another man shall condemn. **1821** LAMB *Elia* I. *My Relations*, He has some speculative notions against laughter, ..when peradventure the next moment his lungs shall crow like Chanticleer. **1870** M. ARNOLD *St. Paul & Prot.* 2 It may well happen that a man who lives and thrives under a monarchy shall yet theoretically disapprove the principle of monarchy. **1870** LOWELL *Study Wind.* 175 That which one shall hide away..another shall make an offensive challenge to the self-satisfaction of all his hearers.

**10.** In hypothetical, relative, and temporal clauses denoting a future contingency, the future auxiliary is *shall* for all persons alike. (Where no ambiguity results, however, the present tense is commonly used for the future, and the perfect for the future-perfect; the use of *shall*, when not required for clearness, is apt to sound pedantic.)

†Formerly sometimes used to express the sense of a present subjunctive.

**a.** In hypothetical clauses.

(†*shall I* = 'if I shall'. *rare.*)

*c* **1250** *Owl & Night.* 1683 Schille [*v.r.* schulle] ich an utest uppen ow grede, ich shal swo stronge ferde lede, þat ower proude shal auall̄e. *c* **1300** *Havelok* 1782 Shol ich casten þe dore open, Summe of you shal ich drepen! **1382** WYCLIF *Ecclus.* xxiii. 13 If he shul bigile the brother, the gilte of hym vpon hym shal be. *c* **1400** *Gamelyn* 115 If I schal algate be beten anon, Cristes curs mot thou have but thou be that oon! **1588** [see c]. **1590** in C. S. *Right Relig.* A ij b, If your Worship shall read with patience and with great aduise see into the work. **1680** *New Hampsh. Prov. Papers* (1867) I. 388 If any Christian..shall speak contemptuously of the Holy Scriptures,..such person..shall be punished. **1885** TENNYSON *The Fleet* I If you shall fail to understand, What England is..On you will come the curse of all the land.

**b.** In relative clauses (where the antecedent denotes an as yet undetermined person or thing).

*c* **1200** ORMIN 1205 Forrþi sinndenn alle þa þatt shulenn inntill helle Effnedd wiþþ gæt. *c* **1250** *Gen. & Ex.* 305 Alle ðo, ðe of hem sule cumen, sulen ermor in blisse wunen. **1382** WYCLIF *Luke* x. 8 In to what euere citee ʒe schulen entre, and thei schulen receyue ʒou, ete ʒe tho thingis that ben put to ʒou. **1417-18** *E.E. Wills* (1882) 38 Eny goude þat schele be solde, yt ys my wyll þat Wyllyam Aluowe haue it. *c* **1450** *Merlin* 33, I go thider as thei shullen lede me. **1502** *Bury Wills* (Camden) 92, I will..vj s. viij d. to be delte in bedred men..ther where it xalbe moste nedefull. **1576** *Aberdeen Reg.* (1848) II. 26 To consent to sic uther thingis as salbe thocht expedient. **1665** in *Rep. Hist. MSS. Comm.* Var. Coll. IV. 244 Mr. Mayor is desired to..pay the fees that shalbe due to the officers. **1718** ROWE *Lucan* III. 171 With humble Votes obedient they agree, To what their mighty Subject shall Decree. **1794** MRS. RADCLIFFE *Myst. Udolpho* xliii, I will lay all the spirits that shall attack me in the Red Sea. **1811** SOUTHEY *Let. to G. C. Bedford* 16 Feb. The minister who shall first become a believer in that book..will obtain a higher reputation than ever statesman did before him. **1874** R. CONGREVE *Ess.* 417 We extend our sympathies ..to the unborn generations which..shall follow us on this earth.

**c.** In temporal clauses.

**1382** WYCLIF *1 Cor.* xi. 26 How ofte euere ʒe schulen ete this breed,..ʒe schulen schewe the deeth of the Lord, til he come. *c* **1394** *P. Pl. Crede* 9 Whan y schal schewen myn schrift schent mote y worþen. *c* **1421** *26 Pol. Poems* 111/117 Whenne þou al þe world shal deme, Dampne me noʒt after my dede. **1480** *Bury Wills* (Camden) 67 And this to be doon as ofte as such case xall require. **1588** J. UDALL *Diotrephes* (Arb.) 33 If this way shall be thought good, when there shalbe some aduice taken vpon it. **1655** *Nicholas Papers* (Camden) II. 313 When you shall licence mee, I shall bee free. *a* **1763** W. KING *Pol. & Lit. Anecd.* (1819) 159 The seat of happy souls; who, after they shall have continued in it the space of 10,000 years, will be removed to a more glorious orb. **1830** *Laws of Cricket* in Nyren *Yng. Cricketer's Tutor* (1902) 20 If in striking, or at any other time, while the ball shall be in play, both his feet be over the popping-crease. **1865** KINGSLEY *Herew.* xxxi, Pray St. Etheldreda to be with us when the day shall come. **1896** A. AUSTIN *England's Darling* II. iv, When War's loud shuttle shall have woven peace.

**11.** In clauses expressing the purposed result of some action, or the object of a desire, intention, command, or request. (Often admitting of being replaced by *may*; in OE., and occas. as late as the 17th c., the pres. subj. was used as in Latin.)

**a.** in final clause usually introduced by *that*.

In this use mod. idiom prefers *should* (22 a): see quot. 1611 below, and the appended remarks.

*c* **1200** ORMIN 7640, I þiss child iss borenn her to þann þatt fele shulenn fallenn, & fele shulenn risenn upp. *c* **1250** *Owl & Night.* 445 Bit me þat ich shulle singe vor hire luue one skentinge. **1375** BARBOUR *Bruce* I. 156, I sall do swa thow sall be king. **1390** GOWER *Conf.* II. 213 Thei gon under proteccioun, That love and his affeccioun Ne schal noght take hem be the slieve. *c* **1450** *Mirk's Festial* 289, I wil.. schew ʒow what þis sacrament is, þat ʒe schullon in tyme comyng drede God þe more. **1470-85** MALORY *Arthur* XIII. xv. 633 What wille ye that I shalle doo sayd Galahad. **1558** in J. M. Stone *Hist. Mary I*, App. 518 My mynd and will ys, that the said Codicell shall be accepted. **1611** BIBLE *Luke* xviii. 41 What wilt thou that I shall doe vnto thee? [So in *Matt.* xx. 32; 'should' in *Mark* x. 51; 1881 (Revised) has 'should' in all three passages. Coverdale (1535) has 'shal' in *Matt.*, in the other gospels 'that I do'.] *c* **1643** LD. HERBERT *Autobiog.* (1824) 139 Were it not better you shall cast away a few words, than I lose my life? **1698** in J. O. Payne *Rec. Engl. Cath.* 1715 (1889) 111 To the intent they shall see my will executed. **1829** MACAULAY *Mill on Govt.* in *Edin. Rev.* Mar. 177 Mr. Mill recommends that all males of mature age ..shall have votes. **1848** THACKERAY *Van. Fair* xxiv, We shall have the first of the fight, sir; and depend on it Boney will take care that it shall be a hard one. **1879** M. PATTISON *Milton* xiii. 167 At the age of nine and twenty, Milton has already determined that this lifework shall be..an epic poem.

**b.** in relative clause.

**1545** RAYNALD *Byrth Mankynde* Prol. (1552) B iij, The foundation & grounde, by the perceauerance wherof, your ..vnderstanding shal be illuminat. **1599** SHAKS. *Hen. V*, II. iv. 40 As Gardeners doe with Ordure hide those Roots That shall first spring. *a* **1631** DONNE *Paradoxes* (1652) 35 To know those vertues require some Judgement in him which shall discerne. **1769** JOHNSON in *Boswell* (1904) I. 399 I'll take you five children from London, who shall cuff five Highland children. **1874** L. STEPHEN *Hours in Libr.* Ser. I. 287 To hit off that delicate mean between the fanciful and the prosaic which shall satisfy his taste.

** The past tense *should* with temporal function.

†**12.** Expressing a former obligation or necessity: = 'was bound to', 'had to'. *Obs.*

*Beowulf* 10 (Gr.) He..weox under wolcnum..oð þæt him æʒhwylc þara ymbsittendra ofer hronrade hyran scolde. *Ibid.* 704 Sceotend swæfon, þa þæt hornreced healdan scoldon. *c* **893** ÆLFRED *Oros.* I. i. §14 þa sceolde he ðær bidan ryhtnorþanwindes, for ðæm þæt land beaʒ þær suþryhte. *c* **1205** LAY. 4301 þer fore his mon he bicom & hærdsumnesse him solde don. *c* **1250** *Gen. & Ex.* 1326 Ysaac was leid ðat auter on, So men sulden holocaust don. *c* **1380** WYCLIF *Serm.* Sel. Wks. I. 77 In þe olde lawe weren þei wont to offre a lombe wiþouten wem, þe whiche shulde be of o ʒere. ? *a* **1400** *Arthur* 481 Arthour, as he scholde done, Sende lucyes body to Rome.

†**13.** In statements of what was formerly intended or settled to take place; = 'was to', or (contextually) 'was about to'. *Obs.*

*Beowulf* 1443 (Gr.) ðyrede hine Beowulf eorlʒewædum.. scolde herebyrne hondum ʒebroden..sund cunnian. *a* **1000** *Andreas* 1132 (Gr.) Hæfdon æglæcan sæcce ʒesohte, sceolde sweordes ecg..feorh acsiʒan. *a* **1122** *O.E. Chron.* (Laud MS.) an. 1000, His scipu wendon ut abuton Leʒceastre and sceoldan cumon onʒean hine, ac hi ne mihton. *c* **1205** LAY. 10322 Heo makeden enne hehne cniht heore here-toʒe..he heom scolde læden. *c* **1275** *Passion our Lord* 532 in *O.E. Misc.* 52 Seþþe hi dude heore sel vpe þene ston Lutel hi wiste wrecches hw hit sculde gon. *a* **1300** *K. Horn* 1412 þe schup bigan to blenche, His lemman scholde adrenche. *c* **1380** WYCLIF *Sel. Wks.* III. 58 Whanne Abraham schulde have offrid Isaac..he hadde a greet ooþ to God. *c* **1420** *Sir Amadace* (Camden) lix, Quo schuld his stede to stabulle haue? Knyʒte, squier, ʒoman, ne knaue, Nauthir with him he broʒte. **14..** in *Pol. Rel. & L. Poems* (1903) 273 Mary hys moder went þe weye To caluery þer he xuld deye. **14..** *Three 15th Cent. Chron.* (Camden) 78 The Egill on Poulis stepell was take downe.., but whan hit shulde be set up a yene he that shulde have set it up fell downe and was dede. **1523** BERNERS *Froiss.* I. xlii. 24 The same friday that the batell shulde haue ben the french kynge..was sore dyspleased, bycause he departed without batayle. **1537** *Matthew's Bible, Luke* vii. 19 Arte thou he yᵗ shulde come: or shall we loke for another? **1560** DAUS tr. *Sleidane's Comm.* 57 b, When he shoulde die [orig. *moriturus*]. *Ibid.* 433 The common assemble of thempire yᵗ shuld be holden at Auspurge. **1622** S. WARD *Life of Faith* (1627) 12 When hee should haue been tyed to the stake, he required to stand vntyed.

**14.** Used in indirect reported utterances, or other statements relating to past time, where *shall* would be used if the time referred to were present.

**a.** corresponding to *shall* in sense 5, 6, or 7.

*Beowulf* 691 (Gr.) Næniȝ heora þohte, þæt he þanon scolde eft eardlufan æfre ȝesecean. *c* **897** ÆLFRED *Gregory's Past. C.* xxxix. 284 We cwædon ær ðæt se sceolde lytel sawan, se þe him ðone wind ondrede. *c* **950** *Lindisf. Gosp.* Mark xiv. 40 *Ignorabant quid responderent ei*, ne wiston huæd scealdon onduearda him. *a* **1122** *O.E. Chron.* (Laud MS.) an. 1070, þæt land folc comen him ongean & griðedon wið hine, wændon þæt he sceolde þet land ofer gan. *c* **1175** *Lamb. Hom.* 13 Vre drihten cweð to moyses þet he scolde wissien his folc. *c* **1205** LAY. 2079 He hehte þat luue scolde liðen heom bi-tweonen. *c* **1330** *Arth. & Merl.* 1937 A begger þer com in..; þai seyd, he schuld nouȝt haue, Bot strokes & bismare. **1340–70** *Alex. & Dind.* 781 ȝe ben soþli þe same of wham þei so tolde, þat scholde lenge aftur lif in lastinge paine. *c* **1450** *Mirk's Festial* 57 The lawe of the Iewes was þen suche þat a woman þat was delyuerde of a man-chyld sculd be holden vnclene. **1470–85** MALORY *Arthur* x. lvii. 511 Yet wold not sire Launcelot telle me certeynte of you where I shold fynde yow. **1535** COVERDALE *Dan.* iii. 19 He charched and commaunded, that the ouen shulde be made seuen tymes hoter. **1579** GOSSON *Sch. Abuse* (Arb.) 74 His Pypers were ready too rounde him in the eare, what he should speake. **1611** SHAKS. *Cymb.* III. iv. 129 'Tis commanded I should do so. **1697** DRYDEN *Virg. Georg.* IV. 732 What shou'd He do, who twice had lost his Love? **1719** DE FOE *Crusoe* I. (Globe) 249 He answer'd.. That he would make Conditions with them.. That they should be absolutely under my Leading. **1818** CRUISE *Digest* (ed. 2) V. 497 The husband and wife covenanted to levy a fine, which was thereby declared should be to the use of the cognizees and their heirs. **1848** THACKERAY *Van. Fair* vi, So long as his friend was enjoying himself, how should he be discontented? *Ibid.* xxi, Old Osborne thought she would be a great match, too, for his son. He should leave the army; he should go into Parliament. **1849** MACAULAY *Hist. Eng.* v. I. 575 James was declared a mortal..enemy... No treaty should be made with him. **1859** GEO. ELIOT *Adam Bede* xxiv, After all, what had he done? Gone a little too far, perhaps,..but..no harm could come—no harm *should* come. **1865** KINGSLEY *Herew.* xxv, Where were Sweyn and his Danes? Whither should they go till he came?

**b.** corresponding to *shall* in sense 8.

Here *should* is the auxiliary of the 'anterior future' or 'future in the past' tense. With perf. inf. it forms the 'anterior future perfect' or 'future perfect in the past'.

*c* **1175** *Lamb. Hom.* 19 Heo wisten..þet he sculde cumen to þisse middeleard for ure neode. **1297** R. GLOUC. (Rolls) 225 Wane he wolde iwite ȝwat man þe child ssolde be þat he adde bi ȝete. *c* **1375** *Sc. Leg. Saints* xliv. (*Lucy*) 109 Venand þat he suld at his weding þare-thru hafe doublyt al his thing. *c* **1450** *Merlin* i. 1 We ne trowed not that eny man myght be bore of woman, but that he sholde ben oures. **1470–85** MALORY *Arthur* VII. xxxiii. 266, I made promyse vnto your lady that I shold yelde me vnto yow. **1568** GRAFTON *Chron.* II. 694 He was sure that with the Erle of Warwike, he should haue no peace. *a* **1586** SIDNEY *Arcadia* III. (Sommer) 255 b, She tolde him, that he should doo well to do so. **1620** *Westward for Smelts* (Percy Soc.) 11 He feared he was, or should be a cuckold. **1700** DRYDEN *Ovid's Met., Acis*, etc. 39 The Prophet Telemus.. Foretold the Cyclops, that Ulysses hand In his broad eye shou'd thrust a flaming Brand. *a* **1715** BURNET *Own Time* (1724) I. 199 The French did thus set on the war between the English and the Dutch, hoping that our Fleets should mutually weaken one another so much, that [etc.]. **1760–72** H. BROOKE *Fool of Qual.* (1809) IV. 114 Sectarians..would make a monopoly of the Saviour; they should shut him up into a conventicle. **1809** SYD. SMITH *Serm.* II. 240 Joseph in the dungeon knew not that he should be the lord of Egypt. **1846** MRS. KIRKLAND *West. Clearings* 129, I thought I never should have got out. **1855** MACAULAY *Hist. Eng.* xix. IV. 279 He had expected that he should be able to push forward without a moment's pause. **1893** 'SARAH GRAND' *Heav. Twins* (1894) 134 They never doubted but that they should discover him hard at work.

**c.** in hypothetical, temporal, and final clauses, and relative clauses with hypothetical or final implication. (Cf. 10.)

*Beowulf* 965 (Gr.) Ic hine..heardan clammum..wriþan þohte, þæt he..scolde licgean lifbysiȝ. *c* **1250** *Gen. & Ex.* 175 He made on werlde al erue tame, ðe sulde him her..to fode, and srud. *a* **1300** *Cursor M.* 410 Hymself þan gaf us sample þare, þat we suld hald it euer mare. **1340–70** *Alex. & Dind.* 108 For þat enchesoun god ches oþur chef kinguus, þat scholde maistrus be maad ouur mene peple. **1390** GOWER *Conf.* I. 14 The tresor of the benefice, Wherof the povere schulden clothe And ete and drinke. *c* **1400** LOVE *Bonavent. Mirr.* xiv. (Gibbs MS.) 34 Shewynge vs þe trewe wey wher by we schuld mowe come þer to. **1510** *Sel. Cases Star Chamb.* (Selden Soc.) II. 73 They wer bound..to reentre the seid prison when the seid Priour shulde commaunde them. *a* **1578** LINDESAY (Pitscottie) *Chron. Scot.* (S.T.S.) I. 47 Wtheris thocht that..he sould haue had sic men about him at his command as suld haue suppressed all oppressioun. **1794** MRS. RADCLIFFE *Udolpho* xxv, Emily ..determined to attempt the outer door of the turret as soon as Barnardine should withdraw. **1821** SCOTT *Kenilw.* xxvii, He..resolved..to retire..until the tolling of the great castle-bell should announce the arrival of Elizabeth. *a* **1859** MACAULAY *Hist. Eng.* xxiii. V. 31 Clancarty was pardoned on condition that he should leave the kingdom. **1902** J. K. MANN *Hist. Popes* I. I. 35 They offered to submit their case to the emperor himself as soon as the Lombards should be overcome.

**d.** In noun-clause dependent on expressions of willing, desiring, commanding, requesting, etc. (in the pa. t.). Similarly (esp. with the verb *want*) in the pres. tense (*colloq.*, orig. and chiefly *U.S.* and in representations of Jewish speech). (Cf. 11 and 22 a.)

*a* **1000** *Guthlac* 636 (Gr.) Wendun ȝe & woldun..þæt ȝe scyppende sceoldan ȝelice wesan in wuldre. *c* **1000** ÆLFRIC *Hom.* I. 310 God bebead Moyse,..þæt he and eall Israhela folc sceoldon offrian..an lamb anes ȝeares. *a* **1122** *O.E. Chron.* (Laud MS.) an. 1101, On þa ȝerad..þet se eorl Rotbert..sceolde..þreo þusend marc seolfres habban. *a* **1225** *Leg. Kath.* 1439 Het eft þe keiser þat me schulde Katerine bringen biforen him. *a* **1300** *Cursor M.* 381 þe thrid day þat drightin..bad a dri sted suld be. *a* **1352** MINOT *Poems* (ed. Hall) iii. 53 He cumand þan þat men suld fare Till Ingland. *c* **1400** *Gamelyn* 19 He sente hem word by lettres they schulden hye blyve. **1471** CAXTON *Recuyell* (Sommer) 71 He comandyd that thou sholdest be put to deth. **1594** ASHLEY tr. *Loys Le Roy* 42 Aristotle did write vnto Calisthenes..that..he should diligently inquire of the antiquitie of the Chaldees. **1665** *Extr. St. Papers rel. Friends* Ser. III. (1912) 245 His sweet highnes would not haue giuen it to your honour but that he intended you should doe good in it. **1780** *Mirror* No. 96 My parents..were determined I should have a good education. **1861** T. L. PEACOCK *Gryll Grange* xxxii, He had wished that the doctor should inquire into the cause of his trouble. **1891** 'J. S. WINTER' *Lumley* xii, Blackwood had a not unreasonable desire that such an event should not come about.

**1852**, **1903** [see WANT *v.* 5 b]. **1920** W. D. HOWELLS *Vacation of Kelwyns* 188 Want I should drive ye home? **1960** F. RAPHAEL *Limits of Love* 3 You want we should go bankrupt? **1970** R. MILLAR *Abelard & Heloise* I. iii. 11 He asks you should go to him. **1978** J. ROSENTHAL *Evacuees* iv. 89 They want they should take you away.

**e.** In statements of a former likelihood, unlikelihood, expectation, hope, fear, etc.

In present usage the rules for the choice of the auxiliary are the same as apply to the future tense (see 8). Until the middle of the 19th c., however, *should* was common in this use in the second and third persons, where *would* is now normal.

**1340** *Ayenb.* 12 Alle þon þet..storue..ine hope þet hi ssolden by y-borȝe be him uor þe zenne of the uerste manne. *c* **1489** [see FEAR *v.* 4 b]. **1653** DOROTHY OSBORNE *Lett.* (1888) 94 We could not reasonably hope he should outlive this day. **1671** tr. *Palafox's Conq. China* xvi. 312 [They] expected it should have defended it self better. **1749** FIELDING *Tom Jones* XIII. ix, He thought it most likely that some of his servants should be acquainted with the same secret. **1788** MRS. HUGHES *Henry & Isab.* III. 94 From his age and infirmities it was not likely Lord Belford should live long. **1820** SHELLEY *Ess.* (1852) II. 232 There was no danger that it should become a model to the age of that false taste. **1855** MACAULAY *Hist. Eng.* xiv. III. 428 It was not to be expected that men who would not help themselves should help each other. **1867** THIRLWALL *Lett.* (1881) II. 118 You had reason to expect that I should have returned the enclosed papers before now.

**f.** In statements of what habitually occurred. (Cf. sense 9.) Now *rare* (? *dial.*).

**1722** DE FOE *Col. Jack* 23 Every now and then dropping asleep, I should dream that my money was lost. **1745** P. THOMAS *Jrnl. Anson's Voy.* 314 Sometimes we should have seven Fathom on one Side.

**15. a.** Forming with the inf. a substitute for the pa. t. indic. (or, with perf. inf., for the pluperf.) in the oblique report of another's statement in order to imply that the speaker does not commit himself to the truth of the alleged fact. (The perf. inf. was often substituted for the pres. inf. merely in order to express the notion of past time more unambiguously. *Obs.* exc. *dial.*

The corresponding use of *shall* (= G. *soll*, 'is said to') is not evidenced in Eng., the OE. instances alleged by Bosw.-Toller having apparently a different meaning.

*c* **888** ÆLFRED *Boeth.* xxxv. §4 Ic wat þæt ðu ȝeherdest oft reccan on ealdum leasum spellum þætte Iob Saturnes sunu ..sceolde ricsian on heofenum. *c* **1000** ÆLFRIC *Saints' Lives* xviii. 197 Fundon ða lease ȝewitan þe forluȝon naboð þæt he sceolde wyriȝan wælhreowlice god. *a* **1122** *OE. Chron.* (Laud MS.) an. 1098, Ðises ȝeares..æt Finchamstæde an mere blod weoll, swa swa maniȝe trywe men sædan þe hit ȝeseon sceoldan. **13..** *Guy Warw.* (A.) 6918 In edwite it worþ þe adrawe, Swiche a man þou schust haue slawe. **1460** CAPGRAVE *Chron.* (Rolls) 7 In othir bokes..is told that Adam schuld a sent Seth onto the gates of Paradyse for the oyle of mercy. **1472** SIR J. PASTON 4 Nov. in *P. Lett.*, Thys daye rennyth a tale that the Duke of Bretayne sholde be ded. I beleeff it not. **1506** *Engl. Misc.* (Surtees) 52 Oon Bartrame Dawson of the citie of York..is senysterly defamed that he shulde be a Scottysshman borne. **1518** *Sel. Cases Star Chamb.* (Selden Soc.) II. 137 They harde one Thomas Wynwyck say that he shuld here John Sucklyng say that [etc.]. **1561** in Froude *Engl. Seamen* (1895) 26 When I was arraigned I was charged that I should say our mass was as good as theirs. *a* **1578** LINDESAY (Pitscottie) *Chron. Scot.* (S.T.S.) II. 174 It was alledgit that my lord of Arrane in his mirienes sould oppin this consperacie. *a* **1586** SIDNEY *Apol. Poetry* (Arb.) 51 To the second [*sc.* imputation]..that they should be the principall lyars; I aunswere..that of all Writers vnder the sunne, the Poet is the least lier. **1600** SHAKS. *A.Y.L.* III. ii. 182 But didst thou heare without wondering, how thy name should be..carued vpon these trees? **1663** MARVELL *Corr.* Wks. (Grosart) II. 92 There are some rumors that the conspirators should have taken some other places. **1764** *Museum Rust.* II. 134 My neighbour,.. being told that I should say I would do for them, charged me with destroying them. **18..** *Let.* in Sir J. T. Coleridge *Mem. Keble* (1869) 64 Some one raised a report that he should say that herring and potatoes were good enough for anyone. **1822** SCOTT *Nigel* xv, They had a braw sport in the presence last Friday, how ye suld have routed a young shopkeeper. **1886** *W. Somerset Word-bk.* s.v. *Should*, I zeed Mr. Jones, and he zaid how you should zay I told ee that there zeed come vrom he.

¶ **b.** with omission of the *have* of the perf. inf.

*c* **1465** *Eng. Chron.* (Camden) 63 The peple..demed that it sholde betokened sum harm sone aftirward. *a* **1566** *Hist. Estate Scot.* (Wodrow Soc. Misc.) 71 It appeared that they should matched.

**16.** In indirect question relating to a past matter of fact. *Obs.* exc. *arch.*

Present usage prefers the pa. t. or perf.; when the notion of uncertainty is emphasized, *might* or *could* is used instead of the earlier *should*.

*a* **1300** *Cursor M.* 4931 þe folk asked quat þai suld be, 'Theues,' coth ioseph. *Ibid.* 21579 And quatkin tre it suld ha bene His eldres tald him all be-dene. *c* **1440** *Gesta Rom.* xxiii. 84 (Harl. MS.), þere was no man cowde discryve wheþer of hem shuld be Emperour. **1530** TINDALE *Prol. Hebr.* Wks. (1573) 56/1 About this epistle hath euer ben much doubting..who should be the authour thereof. **1534** —— *Mark* ix. 10 They..demaunded one of a nother, what the rysinge from deeth agayne shuld meane. **1640** YORKE *Union Hon.* 122 Who should be the mother I find not mentioned by M. Vincent. **1704** N. N. tr. *Boccalini's Advts. fr. Parnass.* II. 19 The Assembly were wondring what should be the meaning of it. **1851** KEBLE *Occas. Papers* (1877) 238 Some..may have wondered what this 'present distress' should mean.

**17.** In questions introduced by *who*, *whom*, *what*, and followed by *but*, serving to express the unexpectedness of some past occurrence.

**1626** BP. HALL *Contempl., O.T.* XXI. v, Whiles his hart is taken vp with these thoughts, who should come ruffling by him, but..Haman. **1833** TENNYSON *May Queen* iv, As I came up the valley whom think ye should I see, But Robin? **1842** BROWNING *Pied Piper* iv, Just as he said this, what should hap At the chamber door but a gentle tap? **1945** R. GIBBINGS *Lovely is Lee* xxvii. 133 On the 23rd of March 1889 who should be born in Cork but myself?

*** The past tense *should* with modal function.

As with other auxiliaries, the pa. t. (orig. subjunctive) of *shall* is often used to express, not a reference to past time, but a modal qualification of the notion expressed by the present tense. Where in addition the notion of past time is to be expressed, this can often be effected by the use of the perf. instead of the pres. inf. (though sometimes this produces ambiguity); the temporal notion may however be merely contextually implied, and in that case the pa. t. has the appearance of having both functions (temporal and modal) at once.

**18. a.** In statements of duty, obligation, or propriety (originally, as applicable to hypothetical conditions not regarded as real). Also, in statements of expectation, likelihood, prediction, etc.

This conditional form of expression was from an early period substituted for the unconditional *shall* in sense 2, and in mod.Eng. the pres. tense in this use is obs., and *should* = ought to.

*Beowulf* 2708 (Gr.) Swylc sceolde secg wesan, þeȝn æt ðearfe. *c* **897** ÆLFRED *Gregory's Past. C.* iv. 36 Ðonne mon forlet ðone eȝe..þe he mid ryhte on him innan habban sceolde. *c* **1175** *Lamb. Hom.* 21 We scolden halden his heste us bitwenan. *c* **1275** *Passion our Lord* 472 in *O.E. Misc.* 50 þu ne schuldest nouht þi wryt habben iwryte so. *c* **1315** SHOREHAM I. 749 He despyseþ ihesu cryst, Wanne he hym scholde herye. *c* **1350** *Will. Palerne* 3685 Whi make ȝe þis sorwe? ȝe schuld now make ȝow merie. **1411** *Rolls of Parlt.* III. 650/2 He knoweth wel that..he ne hath noght born hym as he sholde hav doon. ? *c* **1570** *Misogonus* III. i. 189 (Brandl) Thoughe I sait and shoulde not sait. **1607–12** BACON *Ess., Counsel* (Arb.) 318 Neither is it necessarye, that he that consulteth what he should doe, should declare what he will doe. **1756** MRS. CALDERWOOD in *Coltness Collect.* (Maitland Club) 214 Some men should have been women, and he, I think, is one. **1819** SCOTT *Ivanhoe* xxxii, Conquest, lady, should soften the heart. **1845** POE *Tales, Gold Bug*, I draw tolerably—*should* do it at least—have had good masters. **1896** *Law Times Rep.* LXXIII. 616/2 He should have looked up and down the line before he ventured to cross it.

**1922** GALSWORTHY *Loyalties* III. i. 82 'Mr. Twisden's not in, then?'..'No. He's at the Courts. They're just up; he should be in directly.' **1954** WODEHOUSE & BOLTON *Bring on Girls* viii. 101 'It will run a bit short, I suppose, but it should have a wide appeal.' 'Very wide,' said Guy. 'You've got a winner.' **1961** E. F. SCHUMACHER in *Small is Beautiful* (1973) II. iii. 117 Proved oil reserves should be enough for forty years. **1963** 'J. LE CARRÉ' *Spy who came in from Cold* x. 94 A couple of weeks should see you through. **1966** T. FRISBY *There's a Girl in my Soup* I. 2 That blanket should be warm by now. **1970** R. MILLAR *Abelard & Heloise* I. ii. 27 A makeshift effort, but it should serve. *Ibid.* xiv. 35 Master Simon says he should be up in a week.

*Phrases.* **1764** MRS. SHERIDAN *Journ. to Bath* I. i, That same Lord Stewkly is no better than he should be, (between ourselves). **1780** *Mirror* No. 104 Every woman who passed much of her time in town, he made no scruple to say, was no better than she should be. **1829** CARLYLE in *Edin. Rev.* June 458 This is as it should be; for not in turning back,..but only in resolutely struggling forward, does our life consist. **1860** J. W. PALMER tr. *M. J. Michelet's Love* IV. i. 184 The mother lives entirely in that cradle; the world is as nothing to her. This is as it should be, for it is the saving of the babe.

¶ with omission of *have* in perf. inf.

*a* **1529** SKELTON *Agst. Scottes* 106 Regarded ye should your lord. **1561** *Godly Q. Hester* (1873) 23 And they that should assisted, I wote not how they were brysted. *c* **1730** RAMSAY *Wyfe of Auchtermuchty* xv, Scho fand all wrang that sould been richt.

**b.** ***should be***: ought according to appearances to be, presumably is. Also, ought according to expectation to be, presumably will be (cf. sense 18 a).

**1605** SHAKS. *Macb.* I. iii. 45 You should be Women, And yet your Beards forbid me to interprete That you are so. **1631** HEYWOOD *2nd Pt. Fair Maide West* IV. i, Pursue the Ruffin,.. He should be Captain of those bloody theevs, That haunts our mountains. **1661** COSIN *Corr.* (Surtees) II. 36, I saw a letter to-day which tells us that the great Presbyterian preacher in London is silenced; but the letter names him not. I guesse it should be Mr. Baxter. **1821** BYRON *Cain* I. i. 365, I have heard it said, That seraphs *love most*—cherubim *know most*—And this should be a cherub

—since he loves not. 1855 KINGSLEY *Westw. Ho!* II. ix. 249 That should be Barbados.. unless my reckoning is far out.

**c.** ***you should hear, see*** = I wish you could hear, if only you could hear, etc.

1811 LADY GRANVILLE *Let.* 6 Oct. (1894) I. 21 You should have heard the shout when he said by mistake, [etc.]. 1842 TENNYSON *Walking to Mail* 63 You should have seen him wince As from a venomous thing. 1857 HUGHES *Tom Brown* II. v, Ah! but you should just have seen the fight between Slogger Williams and Tom Brown! 1908 BELLOC *Cautionary Tales for Children* 26 That Night a Fire *did* break out—You should have heard Matilda Shout! 1971 S. GRAY *Butley* II. 58 But you should see our flat. Even Joey's room is like a pigsty.

**d.** Used ironically, expressing the inappropriateness or unlikeliness of the action advocated or state envisaged, as ***I should worry***, there is no reason for me to worry, I am not worried. *colloq.* (orig. a Yiddishism).

1892 KIPLING *Naulakha* xiii. 154 [Amer. loq.] I should murmur!.. It makes me feel good all over. 1906 F. H. BURNETT *Shuttle* (1907) xxxviii. 381 'Hope you had a fine time, Mr. Selden?' 'Fine! I should smile! Fine wasn't in it.' 1914 'HIGH JINKS JR.' *Choice Slang* 13 *I should worry*, I do not care. 1929 'E. QUEEN' *Roman Hat Myst.* vi. 80 'Well,' grinned the District Attorney, 'I carry a lot of insurance, so I should worry.' 1937 D. L. SAYERS *Busman's Honeymoon* x. 224 'You watch your step, Polly. Maybe 'e's married three times a'ready.' 'I *should* worry,' said the girl, with a toss of the head. 1945 A. KOBER *Parm Me* 155 'The cilling you think he's going to fix?' 'You should live so long!' he'll say. 1957 *N.Y. World-Telegram* 13 Sept. 22/5 All I ask of these scientists is that they put in writing their guarantee that insects will get us yet. We should be so lucky. 1967 V. C. WELBURN *Johnny So Long* II. iii. 76 Don't try to digest everything at once. Hell, I should talk. 1970 M. O'BRINE *Crambo* lxiii. 170 If that's the best their gunners can do, we should worry. *Ibid.* lvii. 230 'It's your life,' said Waterhouse. 'I should live that long,' said Gesing. 1975 R. RENDELL *Shake Hands for Ever* iii. 29 They both came in at about ten—my God, I should be so lucky!

**19.** In the apodosis of a hypothetical proposition (expressed or implied), indicating that the supposition, and therefore its consequence, is unreal.

**a.** Where *shall* (in sense 5, 6, 7, 8, or 9) would be used if the hypothesis were accepted.

1154 *O.E. Chron.* an. 1137, Wel þu myhtes faren all a dæis fare sculdest thu neure finden man in tune sittende. *a* 1225 *Ancr. R.* 332 ȝif ure Louerd demde him al efter rihtwisnesse ..wo scholde him iwurðen. *c* 1250 *Gen. & Ex.* 194 Hadde he wel loked him wið skil, Ilc beste sulde don his wil. *a* 1300 *K. Horn* 347 þanne scholde wiþuten oþe þe kyng maken vs wroþe. *c* 1386 CHAUCER *Frankl. T.* 47 Pacience.. venquysseth.. Thynges þat rigour sholde neuere atteyne. 1408–9 *26 Pol. Poems* (1904) 32 And it were soþ þat clerkis telle, ffewe folkes shulde come in heuene. 1535 FISHER *Wks.* (1876) 384 If one deadly sin were found in their soules, they should incontinent be throwen into the darke dungeon of hell. 1581 in Allen *Martyrd. Campion* (1908) 35, I will not belie myself, for so should I condemne my owne soule. 1601 B. JONSON *Poet.* III. i. 183 You shoo'd see mee [*sc.* dance], were it not i' the street. 1604 SHAKS. *Oth.* III. iv. 62 If she lost it,.. my Fathers eye Should hold her loathed. 1718 EARL COWPER in J. Duncombe *Lett.* (1773) I. 198 You and your horse should have been very welcome. 1779 JOHNSON in *Boswell* (1904) II. 308 We should have robbed the Scotch, if they had had any thing of which we could have robbed them. 1790 COWPER *Let. to Lady Hesketh* 8 Mar., I should be unreasonable indeed not to be highly gratified by it. 1802–12 BENTHAM *Judic. Evid.* (1827) II. 404 Cross-examination.. a term for which.. one should have expected to have found an equivalent in every language. 1848 THACKERAY *Van. Fair* xli, I often think we should all be better without it. 1878 O. W. HOLMES *Motley* 37 He knew that he should not have been satisfied with himself, if he had not made it. 1878 MISS BRADDON *Open Verd.* vi, After this, I shouldn't be at all surprised at his going over to Rome. 1887 BROWNING *Parleyings, B. de Mandeville* iv, So should wrong merely peep abroad to meet Wrong's due quietus.

*interrogatively.* 1834 K. H. DIGBY *Mores Cath.* v. iii. 84 But where should one finish if one were to speak of the 'lauda Sion' [etc.].

**b.** When the pres. tense of the principal vb. would be used if the hypothesis were accepted. (Where the pa. t. or the perf. would be used, *should* is followed by the perf. inf.)

In this use the combination of *should* with inf. forms a periphrastic past subjunctive: thus 'I should be' = the archaic 'I were'. Similarly with perf. inf.: 'Then I should have been' = 'then had I been'.

The choice between *should* and *would* follows the same rules as that between *shall* and *will* as future auxiliaries, except that *should* must sometimes be avoided on account of liability to be misinterpreted as = 'ought to' (sense 18). In present Eng. *should* occurs mainly in the first person; in the other persons it follows the rule for *shall* in 8 c, d.

*c* 1430 *Two Cookery Bks.* 45 Bete alle to-gederys as þikke as þou schuldyst make oþer bature in fleyssche tyme. 1432–50 tr. *Higden* (Rolls) I. 337 Thei scholde haue writen more circumspectely, if they hade seide [etc.]. *c* 1435 *Torr. Portugal* 1534 Nyne oxen of that lond Shold not drawe the tre. 1467 MARG. PASTON 11 July in *P. Lett.*, Thei set not be a woman as thei shuld set be a man. 1481 CAXTON *Reynard* (Arb.) 35, I haue so grette scatte and good of syluer.. that seuen waynes shold not conne carye it away. *c* 1489 — *Sonnes of Aymon* xvi. 377 Yf it had be at our wyll ye sholde have had goode peas wyth the kyng charlemagn. 1753 CHALLONER *Cath. Chr. Instr.* 91 At the Confiteor.. I should advise the Assistants to an humble Confession of their Sins to God. 1882 'L. KEITH' *Alasnam's Lady* III. 284, I shouldn't know how to begin. 1908 BAGOT *A. Cuthbert* v. 42, I should say that Aunt Jane.. is perfectly right in regarding me.. as an intruder.

¶ with omission of *have* in perf. inf.

1585 NORDEN *Sinful Mans Solace* 25 b, Then should not thus my silly soule Bene wrapt in irkesome woe.

**c.** With verbs of liking, preference, etc., *should* in the first person (and interrogatively in the second) is regarded as more correct than *would*, though this is often used.

In the third person *should* is used only in indirect speech (when *he* represents *I*); uses like quot. 1862 are abnormal.

The forms *I should have liked to (see)* and *I should like to have (seen)* are alternative ways of adding the temporal notion to the modal sense of *should*. Another form, sometimes met with, but certainly faulty, is *I should have liked to have (seen)*.

1779 BOSWELL *Johnson* (1904) II. 308 Should you not like to see Dublin, Sir? 1785 TRUSLER *Mod. Times* III. 81 Should you like any thing up stairs, or would you prefer it in the kitchen? 1838 MACAULAY *Ess., Sir W. Temple* (1843) III. 98 Corneille was said to unite the merits of Æschylus, Sophocles, and Euripides. We should like to see a Prometheus after Corneille's fashion. 1860 RUSKIN *Unto this Last* i. §21, I should like the reader to be very clear about this. 1862 G. C. LEWIS *Lett.* (1870) 418 One should like to know what it was that they numbered. 1869 FREEMAN in W. R. W. Stephens *Life* (1895) I. 427, I should like to have stayed longer at Noyon.

*erroneous use.* 1883 L. OLIPHANT *Altiora Peto* I. 8, I should much preferred to have seen you there.

**d.** The original conditional notion is obscured in the phrases ***it should seem*** (see SEEM *v.* 7 f); ***one should think*** (now somewhat *arch.* and perh. sometimes interpreted in the sense of 18). Similarly ***I should think*** (***suppose***, etc.) = 'I am inclined to think (suppose, etc.)'; also *colloq.* as a strong affirmation in reply to a tentative suggestion, e.g. 'I should (rather) think he *did* object'.

In the last phrase (as used idiomatically), *would* is never substituted; in the second person the phrase is used only in questions, and in the third person only in oblique narration.

1432–50 tr. *Higden* (Rolls) II. 79 Hit scholde seme to a man beholdenge the fundacion of hit that werke to be rather of the labor of.. Romanes, then of Britones. 1508 FISHER 7 *Penit. Ps.* i. Wks. (1876) 15 It sholde seme that he was create of god but in vayne. 1577 AYLMER in H. N. Birt *Eliz. Relig. Settlem.* (1908) x. 465 *note*, He hath divers *Agnus Dei* [etc.]. .. It should appear that he hath bestowed many, and these be the refuses. 1617 MORYSON *Itin.* I. 195, I should thinke, that these old ornaments are taken away. 1630 *R. Johnson's Kingd. & Commw.* 249 It should seeme that nature herselfe hath armed this people, in giving them the Iron Mines of Biskay, Guipuscoa, and Medina. 1741 C'TESS HARTFORD *Corr.* (1805) III. 324 So vast a stock of vivacity.. one should think, could only proceed from a head and heart entirely at ease. 1775 C. JOHNSTON *Pilgrim* 105, I should rather think he has a mind to finger its finances. 1835 MACAULAY *Ess., Sir Jas. Mackintosh* (1843) II. 261 It might, one should think, have crossed the mind of a man of fifty, who had seen a great deal of the world. 1856 —— *Johnson* Misc. Writ. (1882) 321/2 It should seem that a full half of Johnson's life, during about sixteen years, was passed under the roof of the Thrales. 1861 GEO. ELIOT *Silas M.* vi, 'You remember when first Mr. Lammeter's father came into these parts, don't you, Mr. Macey?'.. 'I should think I did.' 1889 SWINBURNE *Study B. Jonson* 4 That singing power.. was not, it should seem, a natural gift of this great writer's.

†**e.** ***should have been*** = 'would have had to be': see 3 b. (In quot. with omission of *have*.)

15.. *Christ's Kirk* xvii, He suld bene swift that gat him Throw speid.

**f.** *I should* (*do* so and so): orig. with expressed or understood protasis 'if I were you', but in mod. colloquial language often used loosely = 'I would advise you to (do, etc.)'.

1908 R. BAGOT *A. Cuthbert* iii. 19, I should get her back as soon as you can, otherwise perhaps the painter will marry her!

**20.** In a hypothetical clause expressing a rejected supposition. †**a.** Where *should* has notional force = 'were obliged to', 'must', 'were about to'. Often with ellipsis of *if* after *as*. *Obs.*

With the use as in quot. 1530 cf. the modern 'as if his heart *would* break'.

1340 HAMPOLE *Pr. Consc.* 4306 Devels aftir sal bere hym .. In-til þe ayre als he suld stey to heven. 1362 LANGL. *P. Pl.* A. I. 132 No dedly sunne to do dyȝe þauȝ þou scholdest. *c* 1400 *Destr. Troy* 10795 þai drepit in dole, as þai degh shuld. 1526 TINDALE *Matt.* xxvi. 35 Yff I shulde dye with the [Gr. κἂν δέῃ με σὺν σοὶ ἀποθανεῖν] yet wyll I not denye the. 1529 MORE in Scoones *Four Cent. Eng. Lett.* (1893) 12 If I shold not leave myself a spone, there shall no poore neighbour of mine bere no losse by any chance happened in my house. 1530 PALSGR. 724/1 The poore boye sobbed, as his herte shulde brust. 1568 *Satir. Poems Reform.* xlvi. 34 Na pedderis pak scho will ressaif, Althocht hir travell scho sowld tyne.

**b.** Where the future tense (or the present with future import) would be used if the supposition were entertained. (With pa. t. subjunctive, usually *should* or *would*, also *could*, *might*, arch. *were*, etc., in the apodosis. Cf. 21.) Now somewhat *rare*, mod. usage preferring *were to*.

*c* 1520 *Everyman* 146 (Pollard) Yf I sholde this pylgrymage take,.. Shewe me,.. Sholde I not come agayne shortly? 1598 SHAKS. *Merry W.* IV. ii. 237 Me thinkes there would be no period to the iest, should he not be publikely sham'd. 1664 BUTLER *Hud.* II. iii. 53 If he should forbear to go She might conclude h'had broke his Vow. 1743 BULKELEY & CUMMINS *Voy. S. Seas* 176 If any Misfortune should attend the Vessel,.. we should be put very hard to it for a Subsistence. 1782 MISS BURNEY *Cecilia* IX. i. (1882) II. 298 Should I think, sir, to eternity,.. I could never conjecture what you mean! 1884 TENNYSON *Becket* III. i, And no flower, not The sun himself, should he be changed to one, Could shine away the darkness of that gap.

†**c.** With reference to the past (e.g. 'if he should have done' = if he had done). *Obs.*

1576 KNEWSTUB *Confut.* etc. (1579) R 7 The gift had beene exceeding great, if wee should haue had no more at his hands, then [etc.]. 1611 SHAKS. *Cymb.* v. i. 8 If you Should haue tane vengeance on my faults, I neuer Had liu'd to put on this.

**d.** In relative clause with hypothetical import.

1800 C. BUTLER *Life Alban Butler* xvi, A person would deserve well of the English Catholics who should translate it into English. 1843 MACAULAY *Ess., Addison* (1853) III. 420 Pope writing dialogue resembled.. a wolf, which, instead of biting, should take to kicking. 1886 MRS. LYNN LINTON *Paston Carew* xxxii, The bank was perfectly solvent. He who should have said otherwise.. would have been made to eat his libellous talk [etc.].

**e.** ***as who should say*** [cf. F. *comme qui dirait*] = as much as to say. *arch.* Also † ***as if he should say*** (***should have said***).

1551 T. WILSON *Logic* (1580) 70 It is asmuche as who should saie: He that made thee, without thee, can not saue thee without thee. 1568 GRAFTON *Chron.* II. 251 Then one of them behelde another, as who should say, who is he that dare go foorth to cary this message. 1600 C. SUTTON *Disce Mori* (1607) x. 168 He declared as thus, his integrity of life: Behold here I am, beare record of mee... As if hee should haue sayd, Giue me my Quietus est at parting. 1641 J. SHUTE *Sarah & Hagar* (1649) 112 Some conceive the Apostle to use that phrase by way of excellency, (as if he should haue said), though I were of the most excellent elocution. 1687 R. L'ESTRANGE *Brief Hist. Times* I. 150 As who should say; 'tis e'en a Mercy that we have not had All our Throats Cut. 1883 SHERER *At Home & in India* 110 Rameshur bowed his head, following the action by two or three affirmative nods, as who should say, 'Yes, yes' [etc.].

**21. a.** In a hypothetical clause relating to the future, *should* takes the place of *shall* (indicative or subjunctive), or of the equivalent use of the present tense, when the supposition, though entertained as possible, is viewed as less likely or less welcome than some alternative. (With future, future perf., or imperative in the apodosis.)

1675 HANNAH WOOLLEY *Gentlew. Comp.* 247, I shall swell this Volume into too great a bulk, should I give you patterns of Letters for all occasions. 1791 COWPER *Let.* 13 June, Should I thunder ever so loud, no efforts of that sort will avail me now. 1842 TENNYSON *Lady Clare* xii, 'And he shall have it', the lady replied, 'Tho' I should die to-night.' 1846 J. BAXTER *Libr. Pract. Agric.* (ed. 4) I. 50 Should any soluble salt remain it will be soda. 1896 A. AUSTIN *England's Darling* I. iii, And, should the looked for shock be on us soon, I must be there!

**b.** Similarly, with perf. inf., in a hypothetical clause relating to what may have happened in the past.

1794 WINDHAM in *Eng. Hist. Rev.* Oct. (1912) 714 Let me recall to your recollection the business of Mr. Burke, in case it should not have been mentioned to you by Mr. Dundas.

**22.** In a noun-clause (normally introduced by *that*).

**a.** In dependence on expressions of will, desire, command, advice, request.

Where the verb of the governing clause is in the pa. t., this use is indistinguishable from that treated in 14 d.

The substitution of *should* for the earlier *shall* (itself a periphrastic substitute for the more primitive use of the pres. subjunctive: see 11 a) may have arisen from instances in which the governing vb. was in the modal pa. t. (as in quots. *c* 1200, 1340).

*c* 1200 ORMIN Ded. 133, I wollde bliþeliȝ þatt all Ennglisshe lede Wiþþ ære shollde lisstenn itt. *c* 1290 *S. Eng. Leg.* 420 Manie gon nakede and bidde þat sum man heom scholde biweue. 1340 HAMPOLE *Pr. Consc.* 1625 þai luf swa þis worldes vanytе þat þai wald never other lyfe suld be. 1482 *Cely Papers* (Camden) 94 My emer & I be agreed that I schold have xi li. 1594 HOOKER *Eccl. Pol.* III. ix. §3 Their iudgment is.. that the Church of Christ should admit no Law-makers but the Euangelists. 1611 [see 11 a]. 1746 FRANCIS tr. *Hor., Sat.* I. ix. 12 'What's your will with me?' —'That one of your profound discerning Should know me'. 1819 in Moore *Mem.* (1853) III. 77 Chantrey.. wishes I should sit to Bartolini. 1833 T. HOOK *Parson's Dau.* I. ix, 'I would much rather she did not come', said Fanny... '*I* would rather she *should* come', said the squire. 1883 *St. James's Gaz.* 25 Aug., It is suggested that the black bass.. should be acclimatized in these waters. 1887 L. OLIPHANT *Episodes* 41, I found it to contain a request.. that I should repair.. to the Horse Guards.

**b.** In statements relating to the necessity, justice, propriety, etc. of something contemplated as future, or as an abstract supposition.

1527 WOLSEY in *St. Papers Hen. VIII* (1830) I. 195, I think convenient.. Your Grace shuld handle her both gently and doulcely. *a* 1578 LINDESAY (Pitscottie) *Chron. Scot.* (S.T.S.) II. 133 It is aganes the lawis of haly kirk that thow souldest be ane preist and marie ane wyff. 1641 MILTON *Animadv.* 65 It is most just, that all their faults should be imputed to yee. 1724 RAMSAY *Vision* xx, Quhats proper we suld know. 1780 *Mirror* No. 75, It is of high national importance that the very earliest notice should be given of the near appearance of a figure-dancer. 1818 CRUISE *Digest* (ed. 2) II. 326 We are now to consider the time at which it is requisite a contingent remainder should vest in interest. 1855 TENNYSON *Maud* III. iii, It is time.. That old hysterical mock-disease should die.

**c.** In expressions of surprise or its absence, approval or disapproval, of some present or past fact.

*c* 1330 *Arth. & Merl.* 6803 Woleway.. þat ich euer schuld sen þus miche rewþe on erþe ben! *c* 1440 *Generydes* 35 Gret pite that she.. Shuld sette hyr wurchippe atte so litill prise. 1508 DUNBAR *Poems* iv. 91 Gud Maister Walter Kennedy,..

lyis veraly, Gret reuth it wer that so suld be. **1580** R. PARSONS *Brief Disc.* 1 b, So was it no meane comforte..to consider..that their should be fownde in Ingland so many gentlemen..so precyse [etc.]. **1650** ELIZ. CROMWELL 27 Dec. in Carlyle *Cromwell*, I wonder you should blame me for writing no oftener, when I have sent three for one. **1780** *Mirror* No. 92 That folly and ugliness should thrust themselves forward to public notice, might be matter of surprise. **1817** KEATS *I stood tip-toe* 44 It may haply mourn That such fair clusters should be rudely torn From their fresh beds. **1820** SOUTHEY *Wesley* I. 199 It is somewhat remarkable, that Wesley should have said nothing of their customs respecting matrimony. **1848** THACKERAY *Van. Fair* lxi, The coachman, who grumbled that his 'osses should be brought out.

¶ with omission of *have* in the perf. inf.

**1537** *Wriothesley's Chron.* I. 119 Which was great pitie that so good a ladie as she is should so sone lost her great joy.

**d.** In clause dependent on sentence (negative, interrogative, or hypothetical) expressing possibility, probability, or expectation.

Cf. 'Is it possible that he should do this?' with 'It is possible that he may do this'. Similarly, 'It is unlikely that he should have been there', but 'It is likely that he was (or may have been) there'.

**1600** FAIRFAX *Tasso* VIII. lxxix, Perchance you look I should entreaties bring. **1749** FIELDING *Tom Jones* VII. xv, The Reader may, perhaps, expect..that..she should immediately have interposed in his Behalf. **1780** *Mirror* No. 104 It is..vain to expect, that persons in that rank of life should be able to withstand the attractions of a court. **1824** LANDOR *Imag. Conv.* Wks. 1846 I. 187 The popes..were under no apprehension that the new religion should itself be subverted. **1850** THIRLWALL *Lett.* (1881) I. 198, I think it is quite impossible that I should not at least have looked into it enough to remember having seen it.

**e.** In clause (now almost always with *lest*) expressing the object of fear or precaution.

**1402** HOCCLEVE *Let. of Cupid* vii, They [*sc.* women] graunte hem grace..for that men shulde nat for her sake dey. *c* **1440** *Jacob's Well* 107 þou leuyst almesse-dede fro þe poore for dreed þat þou schuldyst after fallyn in pouert. **1594** LYLY *Mother Bombie* I. i, She is mewed vp..least she should by some roisting courtier be stollen away. **1686** PARR *Life Usher* 81 Which he..was much concerned at, for fear he should have neglected his duty. **1753** CHALLONER *Cath. Chr. Instr.* 117 In such Cases 'tis much to be feared, lest their Self-love should biass their Judgment. **1777** MISS BURNEY *Early Diary* (1889) II. 202 The subject is melancholy, and I am afraid it should give you the vapours. **1857** BORROW *Rom. Rye* xl, However, lest conversation should lag, I'll give it you. **1893** F. THOMPSON *Poems* 5 Others shall fear lest, heavened thus long, Thou should'st forget thy native song.

**23.** In special interrogative uses. **a.** In questions introduced by *why* (or equivalent word), implying the speaker's inability to conceive any reason or justification for something actual or contemplated, or any ground for believing something to be fact.

**971** *Blickl. Hom.* 69 To hwon sceolde þeos, smyrenes þus beon to lore ʒedon? *a* **1300** *Cursor M.* 461 Qui suld I him seruis yeild? *c* **1420** *Avow. Arth.* xxxiii, I conne notte say the ther-tille, Hit is atte the quene wille, Qwi schuld I layne? **1528** MORE *Dyaloge* I. xxvii. (1529) G vj b/2 Yf we fell at dyuers oppynions, why shuld thae tone parte more beleue the tother, than be beleuyd of the tother. **1583** MELBANCKE *Philotimus* H ij, Why then shouldest not thou aswell deceyue me as others? *c* **1600** SHAKS. *Sonn.* li, From where thou art, why should I hast me thence. **1779** *Mirror* No. 21 They tell us, 'that men have one common original, and why should relations quarrel?' **1791** COWPER *Let. to W. Bagot* 5 Dec., Why should you suppose that I did not admire the poem you showed me? I did admire it. **1831** SCOTT *Ct. Rob.* Introd. Addr. ¶38 Why should not the same triumph be repeated now? **1890** 'L. FALCONER' *Mlle. Ixe* i, 'I do hope she will not be dull', said Evelyn... 'Why should she be dull?'

**b.** In questions introduced by *how*, implying that the speaker regards something as impossible or inadmissible.

*c* **1200** *Vices & Virtues* 65 Hu scolde godd, oðer ani of his halȝen,..hauen rewðe..of ðe, seððen ðu ðe seluen ne hafst nu hier none of ðe seluen? **1303** R. BRUNNE *Handl. Synne* 732 How shulde y þan be meke to ȝow? *a* **1375** *Joseph Arim.* 83 Hou scholde I gon with childe with-oute felau-schupe of mon? *a* **1400** *Pistill of Susan* 46 (MS. P.), þei wold enchaunte þat child; how shold she eschewe? **1500–20** DUNBAR *Poems* lxxiv. 34 How sould ony gentill hart indure To se this sycht on ony creature! *a* **1585** MONTGOMERIE *Cherrie & Slae* 570 How suld it be said? **1782** MISS BURNEY *Cecilia* II. x, How *should* you understand what is so little intelligible? **1819** SCOTT *Ivanhoe* xliv, If a tinge of the world's pride..may mix with an expression so lovely, how should we chide that which is of earth for bearing some colour of its original?

†**c.** In questions relating to meaning, cause, or reason, the form with *should* was formerly often substituted for an indicative tense. *Obs.*

**1532** HERVET *Xenoph. Househ.* 9 What shulde be the cause of it, gentil Socrates, but that [etc.]. *a* **1548** HALL *Chron., Edw. IV*, 237 b, What should signifie, that dumpishenes of mynde, and inward sighyng? **1592** A. DAY *Eng. Secretary* II. (1625) 128 What should be the cause hereof? **1662** STILLINGFL. *Orig. Sacræ* I. v. §5 What should be the reason of this diversity?

**III.** Elliptical and quasi-elliptical uses.

**24.** With ellipsis of verb of motion: = 'shall go'. Now *arch.*

[The use is common in OHG. and OS., and in later HG., LG., and Du. In the mod. Scandinavian langs. it is also common, and instances occur in MSw.]

*Present tense.* *Beowulf* 1179 (Gr.), þonne ðu forð scyle metodsceaft seon! *c* **1000** ÆLFRIC *Saints' Lives* xxxiii. 86 Loca nu þin fæder sceal mid me to mynstre. *a* **1225** *Leg. Kath.* 811 Schome ow is to..schunien þat ȝe schulen to. **1297** R. GLOUC. (Rolls) 7213 þe ssephurdes & þe ssep al so ssolleþ to þe pine of helle. **1387** TREVISA *Higden* (Rolls) VIII. 75 Of þe devel þey come, and to þe devel þey schulleþ. *c* **1450** CAPGRAVE *Life St. Aug.* xi, þe same man stand in study wheithir he schal to þe good wey or nowt. **1506** *Kal. Sheph.* (Sommer) 91 If thy boke be nat sure of rekenynge Thou shalt to hell. *a* **1596** *Sir T. More* IV. iii. 48 He shall straite to courte. **161.** GIBBES *Expos. 3rd Chap. Philipp.* (1619) 237 The decree of God is, that to dust wee must, as all the rest of our fellow Saints and servants shall. *a* **1628** PRESTON *New Cov.* (1629) 324, I will plant my Law in thy heart, it shall neuer out againe. **1756** MRS. CALDERWOOD in *Coltness Collect.* (Maitland Club) 117 They..say, with a sort of flutter that they shall to Vauxhall and Ranelagh, but do not seem to enjoy it when there. **1828** SCOTT *F.M. Perth* xxix, Thou shalt with me to Iona.

*Past tense.* *c* **893** ÆLFRED *Oros.* III. v. §4 þonne andydan hie þa duru þe on þa healfe open wæs, þæt hie be þæm wiston hwider hie sceoldon. **971** *Blickl. Hom.* 225 þæt hit ða rihte wære þæt he of ðisse worlde sceolde. **1297** R. GLOUC. (Rolls) 7375 Willam & alle his þat into þis bataile mid him ssolde. **1303** R. BRUNNE *Handl. Synne* 2484 Wheþer he wulde, or he ne wulde, he toke hym vp, and furþe he shulde. **1377** LANGL. *P. Pl.* B. XV. 13 One with-outen tonge and teeth tolde me whyder I shulde. **1462** MARG. PASTON 18 May in *P. Lett.*, Sche seithe her brother and other of her frendes thynke that she schulde up to London. **1596** SHAKS. *1 Hen. IV*, IV. i. 37 That with our small coniunction we should on. **1598** —— *Merry W.* III. v. 14 If the bottome were as deepe as hell, I shold down.

†**25.** In questions, ***what shall*** = 'what shall (it) profit', 'what good shall (I) do'. *Obs.* (*rare* after OE.).

*Present tense.* *a* **1000** *Cædmon's Gen.* 663 (Gr.), Hwæt scal þe swa laðlic strið wið þines hearran bodan? *c* **1250** *Owl & Night.* 1025 (Cott.), Wat sol ich [*Jesus MS.* schold ich] þar mid mine songe, Ne sunge ich hom neuer so longe?

*Past tense.* *c* **893** ÆLFRED *Oros.* II. v. §4 He ascade, hwæt sceolde æt swa lytlum weorode mara fultum. *c* **1250** [see above].

†**26.** With the sense 'is due', 'is proper', 'is to be given or applied'. *Obs.* [Cf. G. *soll.*]

*c* **1000** *Ags. Gosp.* Matt. ii. 1 *Rubric*, þys [*sc.* godspel] sceal on twelftan dæʒ. *c* **1325** *Poem temp. Edw. II* (Percy) xli, He wol aske half a pownd To bygge with spiserye: The eyȝt shillyngs schul up To wyn and to ale. *c* **1375** *Cursor M.* 1724 (Faif.), Sir noe..hew þe timbre þat sulde þerto.

**27. a.** With ellipsis of active infinitive to be supplied from the context.

*Present tense.* *a* **1225** *Leg. Kath.* 2390 Leste ȝe eft wepen echeliche in helle,..as ȝe schullen alle, buten ȝef [etc.]. **1297** R. GLOUC. (Rolls) 4092 Vorto anhansy vre king as we ssolle on alle wyse. *a* **1300** *Cursor M.* 19071 'þat i mai giue', he [*sc.* St. Peter, *Acts* iii. 6] said, 'i sale'. **1377** LANGL. *P. Pl.* B. XI. 203 Loue we as leue bretheren shal. *c* **1400** LOVE *Bonavent. Mirr.* xxxix. (Gibbs MS.) lf. 86, I haue ouercome þe world Alse who seyth And so schulle ȝe. **1526** TINDALE *Rom.* viii. 25 Who shall seperate vs from goddes love? shall tribulacion? *a* **1592** GREENE *Jas. IV*, Ind., *Ober.* That would I fain see. *Boh.* Why, thou shalt. **1610** SHAKS. *Temp.* V. i. 20 *Ar...* If you now beheld them, your affections Would become tender. *Pro.* Dost thou thinke so, Spirit? *Ar.* Mine would, Sir, were I humane. *Pro.* And mine shall. **1633** FORD *'Tis Pity* V. vi, *Soran...* Bring the strumpet forth. *Vas.* I shall Sir. **1710** SWIFT *Jrnl. to Stella* 22 Oct., This would vex me, but it shall not. **1777** SHERIDAN *Trip Scarb.* IV. i, You shall have your choice... *Miss Hoyd.* Shall I? **1878** SWINBURNE *Poems* Ser. II. *Compl. Lisa* 49 Ah, but, forgetting all things, shall I thee? **1892** MRS. H. WARD *David Grieve* IV. ii, 'No, indeed, I havn't got all I want', said Lucy. .. 'I never shall, neither'.

*Past tense.* *Beowulf* 2585 (Gr.) Guðbill ʒeswac nacod æt niðe, swa hyt no sceolde. *a* **1023** WULFSTAN *Hom.* ii. (1883) 13 þæt hi næfdon to gode naðer ne lufe ne eʒe, swa swa hy scoldan. *c* **1120** *Ranks* in *Gesetze der Angels.* (Liebermann) 456 Se moste..his onspæce ʒeræcan mid rihte, swa hwær swa he sceolde. *a* **1200** *Moral Ode* 60 in *O.E. Hom.* I. 163 Vfel we doð al to muchel and god lesse þenne we sculden. *c* **1350** *Will. Palerne* 3810 þat þei hent swiche herte as hardi men schuld. **1377** LANGL. *P. Pl.* B. VI. 49 Bot þou do bette And lyue as þow shulde. **1458** in Parker *Dom. Archit.* (1859) III. 42 For his fadir soule and his frendes he dyd as he scholde. **1509** BARCLAY *Shyp of Folys* 71 Blame it blynde dryuyll: by the lawe so thou sholde And nat therat to gyggyll. **1583** in W. Kelly *Notices illustr. Drama* (1865) 213 The..playours..crawed lycense ageyne to play at there Inn, & he told them they shold not. **1601** SIR W. CORNWALLIS *Disc. Seneca* (1631) 9 It is not pleasure to doe what we list, but never to stray from what we should. **1735** PEGGE *Kenticisms* Introd. Let. (E.D.S.) 11, I wou'd remind you, and indeed it is altogether a necessary I shou'd, that [etc.]. **1848** THACKERAY *Van. Fair* xxxi, I knew he would come. I prayed so that he should. **1872** CALVERLEY *Fly Leaves* (1884) 81, I knew..That she was uttering what she shouldn't.

**b.** Phrase, ***if I shall*** (see quots.). Now *dial.*

**1390** GOWER *Conf.* II. 96 Doun knelende on mi kne I take leve, and if I schal, I kisse hire. *Ibid.*, I wolde kisse hire eftsones if I scholde. **1871** EARLE *Philol. Engl. Tongue* 203 The familiar proposal to carry a basket,..*I will if I shall*, that is, I am willing if you will command me; I will if so required. **1886** *W. Somerset Word-bk.* s.v., I'll warn our Tom'll do it vor ee, nif he shall—i.e. if you wish.

†**c.** With generalized ellipsis in proverbial phrase: ***needs must that needs shall*** = 'he must whom fate compels'. *Obs.*

**1390** GOWER *Conf.* I. 99 Bot nede he mot that nede schal. *a* **1592** GREENE *Jas. IV*, Ind., Then needs must, needs sall.

†**28. a.** With ellipsis of *do* (not occurring in the context). *Obs. rare.*

*c* **1000** ÆLFRIC *Saints' Lives* v. 370 He axode þone casere hu he embe hi sceolde. **1477** NORTON *Ord. Alch.* in Ashm. (1652) 5 O King that shall These Workes!

**b.** The place of the inf. is sometimes supplied by *that* or *so* placed at the beginning of the sentence.

The construction may be regarded as an ellipsis of *do*. It is distinct from the use (belonging to 27) in which *so* has the sense of 'thus', 'likewise', or 'also'; in the latter there is usually inversion, as *so shall I*.

**13..** *Seuyn Sag.* (W.) 2735 'Rightfulliche thou him awreke'. Th' Emperour saide, 'So ich schal'. **1470–85** MALORY *Arthur* X. lvii. 510 That shall I not said sir Dynadan. **1818** SCOTT *Br. Lamm.* xxi, 'His Mastership will do well to look to himself'. 'That he should', re-echoed Craigengelt. **1888** 'J. S. WINTER' *Bootle's Childr.* iv, 'I should like to see her now she's grown up'. 'So you shall'.

†**29.** With ellipsis of *be* or passive inf., or with *so* in place of this (where the preceding context has *is*, *was*, etc.). *Obs.*

*Present tense.* *a* **900** CYNEWULF *Elene* 895 (Gr.) Ða wæs þam folce on ferhðsefan inʒemynde, swa him a scyle. *c* **1320** *Cast. Love* 719 þe castel lihteþ al abouten, And is raddore þen euere eny rose schal. *c* **1386** CHAUCER *Nun's Pr. T.* 4284 Then dreme of thing that never was ne shal. *c* **1412** HOCCLEVE *De Reg. Princ.* 1631 þus haþ it ben, & ay schal, I bileue. *c* **1560** *Misogonus* III. iii. 153 Yf thou best askt as I know thou shalt. **1566** STERNHOLD & H. *Ps.* cxliii. 12 For I thy seruant am and shal. **1615** J. CHAMBERLAIN in *Crt. & Times Jas. I* (1848) I. 362 He is not yet executed, nor I hear not when he shall.

*Past tense.* *c* **1300** *K. Horn* 326 (Harl.) þah horn were vnder molde & oþer elle[s] wher he sholde. *c* **1380** WYCLIF *Serm.* Sel. Wks. II. 269 ȝif þis epistle of Poule were fulli executid as it shulde. **1426** LYDG. *De Guil. Pilgr.* 2155 That ye be shorn as ye sholde As chose shepe of Crystys folde. ? **15..** *K. Estmere* vii. in Child *Ballads* II. 52/1 Many a man throughe fals messengers is deceived, And I feare lest soe shold wee. **1654** DOROTHY OSBORNE *Lett.* (1888) 285 When I was not satisfied with it myself, I had no reason to hope that anybody else should. **1749** FIELDING *Tom Jones* XVI. i, The Sentiments in all these are very little varied, nor is it possible they should.

**shallal** ('ʃæl'læl). *dial.* [Echoic.] 'A serenade of kettles and pans given to a notorious wedding couple' (Eng. Dial. Dict.); 'rough music'.

**1864** *West. Morn. News* 17 June 4 It has been the custom in this town (S. Ives, Cornwall) for some years, on the occasion of a marriage, for a number of young men in disguise to go to the house of the newly-married pair on the night of the wedding and make a 'shallall', that is [etc.]. **1892** 'Q.' (Quiller-Couch) *Three Ships* vii. 120 'Twill be time enough to talk of shal-lals when the weddin'-day's fixed.

†**shalle.** *Obs.* [App. shortened from *shallemuse* or some other form of SHAWM.] = SHAWM.

*c* **1407** LYDG. *Reas. & Sens.* 5590 Ther wer trumpes and trumpetes, Lowde shallys and doucetes. **1420–2** —— *Thebes* 4298 And in Thebes loud as any shalle The Cry aroos. **1426** —— *De Guil. Pilgr.* 14305 Thys ffloutys ek, with sotyl musys, And thys shallys loude crye.

†**shallen.** *Obs.* *rare*$^{-1}$. [Perh. a variant of CHALON; but the quot. is obscure.]

**1588** *Wills & Inv. N.C.* (Surtees) II. 178 Shallen wever couerletts.

**shallon, shallun** ('ʃælən). [Prob. related in some way to SALAL, the native form of which is given by Lewis & Clark (II. 731) as *shelwel, shellwell.*] = SALAL.

**1806** LEWIS & CLARK *Exped.* (1893) II. 791 An evergreen called shallun, resembling the laurel. **1866** [see SALAL].

**shalloon**[1] (ʃə'lu:n). Forms: 7–9 **shaloon**, 8 **saloon**, 7– **shalloon**. [a. F. *chalon*, which had been earlier adopted as CHALON, q.v. Cf. MHG. *schalûne*, mod.G. *schalaune*.]

**1.** A closely woven woollen material chiefly used for linings.

[**1270–1** *Pipe Roll* 55 Hen. III m. 1 *d*, Pro..xxxvij chalonibus de Reyns.] **1678** *Ancient Trades Decayed* 16 (Stant.), And instead of a Perpetuana or a Shalloon to Lyne Mens Coats with, is used sometimes a Glazened Calico. **1701** *Lond. Gaz.* No. 3701/4 All sorts of Mercery Goods, viz...Shaloons,..Silk Shags, Chenies,..will be sold by Auction. **1706** E. WARD *Hud. Rediv.* (1707) II. I. 18 Her Honour's Petticoat and Gown, Were nicely made of blew Saloon. **1721** SWIFT *Epil. Benefit-play* 21 In blue shalloon shall Hannibal be clad. **1753** SMOLLETT *Cnt. Fathom* xxix, The mummy of an Egyptian king, most curiously rolled up in bandages of rich figured gold shalloon. **1837** BARHAM *Ingol. Leg.* Ser. I. *Monstre Balloon* 6 The netting had burst —the silk—the shalloon. **1877** J. W. HAYES *Draper & Haberdasher* (ed. 4) 104 Shalloons, a very loosely made stuff, used by tailors for lining coats, &c. A similar article is also made and used for dresses.

**b.** A wig-tie made of shalloon.

*a* **1845** BARHAM *Cousin Nicholas* xxiv, The end of his pigtail..contrasts well with the sable shalloon that unites it to his occiput. *a* **1845** —— *Ingol. Leg.* Ser. III. *Wedding-day*, And bright the shalloon of his little quill'd *queue*.

†**c.** *transf.*

**1775** S. J. PRATT *Liberal Opin.* lxxviii. (1783) III. 84, I was so disgusted..at the baseness of this shred of shalloon, that ..the only business I had..was to mortify, disgrace, and punish the scoundrel who had injured you.

**2.** *attrib.* passing into *adj.* Made of shalloon.

**1665** WOOD *Life* 24 Apr. (O.H.S.) II. 35, I bought a black shaloone suit. **1841** *Blackw. Mag.* XLIX. 298 The red shalloon lining of his coat.

**3.** *Comb.*, as ***shalloon-maker***, ***-manufacturer***.

**1723** *Lond. Gaz.* No. 6221/2 Joseph Alford and John Alford,..Shalloon-makers. **1857** *P.O. Directory Yorksh.* 1052 Shalloon Manufacturers.

†**sha'lloon**[2]. *Obs.* *rare*$^{-1}$. In 7 **shaloon(e, shallown.** (See quot.)

**1688** HOLME *Armoury* III. 345/2 A Shaloone..is a kind of Diminutive Coach, which runneth upon two Wheels, and holdeth two people; it is drawn with one Horse. *Ibid.* III. 449/2 A Shallown.

**shallop** ('ʃæləp), *sb.*, †**shalloop.** Forms: α. 6 **schalop,** (6–7 *erron.* **scallop, skallop**), 7 **sallop, shallupp, shawlopp,** 7–9 **shalop;** β. 7 **shalupe, shaloup,** 8 **shalloup, shalloop.** See also CHALOUPE. [a. F. *chaloupe*, prob. either a. Du. *sloep* (see SLOOP) or the source of that word. Cf. Sp. *chalupa*, It. *scialuppa*, G. *schaluppe*. The β forms may be viewed either as a re-adoption of the Fr. word, or as an assimilation of the Eng. word to its original; the spellings suggest final stress, but the only verse quot. has '*shaloup*.

The form *scallop, skallop*, in Florio 1598–1611 s.v. *Schiffetto, Schiffo*, and Minsheu 1617, is due to erroneous identification with SCALLOP *sb.*]

**1.** A large, heavy boat, fitted with one or more masts and carrying fore-and-aft or lug sails and sometimes furnished with guns; a sloop.

*a* **1578** LINDESAY (Pitscottie) *Chron. Scot.* (S.T.S.) II. 278 Ane schip with ane schalop to keip the narrow vatteris fra thame of blaknes. *c* **1595** CAPT. WYATT *R. Dudley's Voy. W. Ind.* (Hakl. Soc.) 18 Shee was in some harde fight with two pinnesses and a shallop of the Frenchmen. **1626** in Foster *Eng. Factories India* (1909) III. 143 The comanders sent their shallupps to chase fisher boats. **1666** *Lond. Gaz.* No. 29/1 A double Shallop, well mann'd, with two guns. **1740** JOHNSON *Life Drake* Wks. 1787 IV. 408 Were surprized with the sight of seven Spanish shallops. **1783** in Nicolas *Disp. Nelson* (1846) IV. p. iv, The Albemarle and Pandora recaptured a Shallop, and on the 12th they recaptured a Sloop laden with wine. **1876** BANCROFT *Hist. U.S.* I. ii. 31 One shallop was commanded by Alonso de Castillo and Andres Dorantes, another by Cabeza de Vaca.

**2.** A boat, propelled by oars or by a sail, for use in shallow waters or as a means of effecting communication between, or landings from, vessels of a large size, a dinghy.

α. **1590** SPENSER *F.Q.* III. vii. 27 Into the same she leapt, and with the ore Did thrust the shallop from the floting strand. **1619** W. PHILLIP tr. *Schouten's Wonderf. Voy.* 60 We sent out our Shalop to sound the depth. *a* **1645** WALLER *On Danger His Majesty escaped* 93 Our Hero, set In a small shallop. **1832** TENNYSON *Lady of Shalott* I. iii, The shallop flitteth silken-sail'd Skimming down to Camelot. **1889** P. H. EMERSON *Eng. Idyls* 37 Fain would I have slumbered in my frail shallop.

β. **1646** SIR P. OSBORNE in Tupper *Hist. Guernsey* (1876) 281 It is a shore full of rocks..insomuch that all must be done with shalupes. **1691** TATE *Poem H.M. Voy. to Holland* 6 A distant Fleet, and open Shaloup nigh. **1692** LUTTRELL *Brief Rel.* (1857) II. 394, 25 shalloops are ordered to be built with oares, and wells for fresh water. **1700** S. L. tr. *Fryke's Voy. E. Ind.* 31 Upon this we fell to tricking up our selves, painting our Long-Boat and Shalloop, and making our Ship very fine. **1719** DE FOE *Crusoe* II. (Globe) 344 Coasting from one Island to another, sometimes with the Ship, sometimes with the French Man's Shalloup. **1772** *Ann. Reg. 1771*, 99/2 The Gaillard..sent her shalloop with 40 men to carry provisions and refreshments on board.

**3.** *Comb.*

*a* **1660** *Contemp. Hist. Irel.* (Ir. Archæol. Soc.) I. 104 The shawlopp men were kept within. **1905** HOLMAN HUNT *Pre-Raph.* II. 64 Over this floated shallop-shaped clouds.

'**shallop,** *v. nonce-wd.* [f. SHALLOP *sb.*] *intr.* To sail or row in a shallop.

**1736–7** *Pennsylv. Gaz.* 13–20 Jan., Shalloping up and down the bay to Egg Harbour.

**shallot, shalot** (ʃə'lɒt). Also 7 **shelot,** 9 **shalott, 'schalot.** [aphetic f. ESCHALOT. Cf. LG. *schalotten, scharlotten* (Brem. Wb.).

The spelling *shallot*, though inferior to *shalot* because it suggests a wrong pronunciation, is now the more common.]

**1.** A small onion, *Allium Ascalonicum*, native in Syria and cultivated for use as a flavouring ingredient for salads, sauces, etc.

**1664** S. BLAKE *Compl. Gard. Pract.* 121 Shalot. Or Spanish Garlick. **1670** L. MEAGER *Eng. Gardener* 188 Shelot. *Ibid.* 189, 213. **1687** MIEGE *Gt. Fr. Dict.* II, Shalot, ..*echalote.* **1693** EVELYN *De La Quint. Compl. Gard.* II. VI. 146 Shalots or Eschalots. *Ibid.* 201 *Shallots*, otherwise Rocamboles, or Spanish Garlick. **1741** *Compl. Fam.-Piece* II. iii. 358 Plant Garlick, Shallots, Rocambole. **1747** MRS. GLASSE *Cookery* ii. 35 Take five or six Shalots peel'd. **1822** LAMB *Elia* I. *Diss. upon Roast Pig*, Steep your whole hogs in shalots, if you wish. **1838** BARHAM *Ingol. Leg.* Ser. I. *Witches' Frolic* xliv, And they wound up the meal with rumpsteaks and 'schalots. **1882** *Garden* 11 Feb. 106/2 Shallots often become mildewed.

*attrib.* **1747** MRS. GLASSE *Cookery* ii. 35 Shalot-Sauce for roasted Fowls. **1842** MERLE *Domestic Dict.* 255 *Shalot Vinegar.* Same as garlic vinegar.

**2.** [After F. *échalote.*] A name for the metal 'reed' in some kinds of organ-pipes.

**1727** CHAMBERS *Cycl.* s.v. *Organ*, A Reed-pipe consists of a Foot..which carries the Wind into the Shalot, or Reed.., which is a hollow Demi-cylinder, fitted [etc.]. **1746** TANSUR *New Mus. Gram.* 65 The Shallot or Reed. **1938** *Oxf. Compan. Mus.* 658/1 A certain number [*sc.* of organ pipes] have a tongue of metal like that of a toy trumpet, vibrating against the open (or partially open) side of a little brass tube (called *eschallot* or *shallot*) at the bottom of the pipe.., and these are called *Reed Stops.* **1969** J. CURNUTT tr. *Andersen's Organ Building & Design* iii. 51 The *shallot*..consists of a tube which is closed at the lower end and planed flat on one side so that a throat-shaped opening is produced.

†'**shallow,** *sb.*[1] *Sc. Obs.* In 6 **schallaw, schallow.** [a. Gael. *sealbh.*] A drove, a flock.

**1550** *Rec. Elgin* (New Spald. Club 1903) I. 102 Ilk schallow of scheip xii d. to be pait to the pundoris..and it salbe lesum to the takaris to pund the haill guiddis or ane best of the schallaw.

**shallow** ('ʃæləʊ), *sb.*[2] *dial.* [OE. *scealȝa, scylȝa* wk. masc., perh. f. **scealiȝ* scaly, f. *scealu* SHALE *sb.*[1], scale.] A freshwater fish, the RUDD[1].

*c* **1050** *Suppl. Ælfric's Gloss.* in Wr.-Wülcker 180 *Rocea*, scylȝa. *a* **1100** *Ags. Voc.* ibid. 319 *Rocea*, scealȝa. **1712** J. MORTON *Nat. Hist. Northampt.* 419 The Fish here called a Shallow, found in..our Rivers,..a Scaly Fish, in shape betwixt a Roache and a Breame. **1880–4** F. DAY *Brit. Fishes* II. 184 *Leuciscus erythrophthalmus*..Rudd,..Shallow (East).

**shallow** ('ʃæləʊ), *a.*[1] and *sb.*[3] Forms: 4–5 **schalowe,** 5–7 **shalow,** 6 *Sc.* **schallow,** 6–7 **shallowe,** 6– **shallow.** [Early 15th c. *schalowe*, prob. related in some way to the synonymous *schald* (OE. *sceald*): see SHOAL *a.*

There may have been an OE. **scealu* (:—**skalwo-*) or **scealȝ* (:—**skalgo-*), f. the root of *sceald* (**skaldo-*) with a different suffix; but no such formation is known in Eng., and the cognate langs. afford no light. It is unlikely that *schalowe* is a compound f. *schald* SHOAL *a.* + LOW *a.*]

**A.** *adj.*

**1. a.** Not deep, having little extension in a downward direction: said e.g. of water, of a dish or tray, of a depression or excavation in the ground.

**14..** *Trevisa's Higden* (Rolls) III. 131 [Camb. MS.] þanne þe kyng..made his auowe þat he wolde make þat greet ryuer so schalowe [*Cotton MS. a* **1400** schoolt] þat þe water schulde nouȝt reche to women kneen þat wolde wade ouer. *c* **1440** *Partonope* 739 The Shippe was grete he myght not passe For the water so shalow was. *c* **1440** *Promp. Parv.* 447/2 Schold, or schalowe, noȝte depe, as water or oþer lyke. **1577** B. GOOGE tr. *Heresbach's Husb.* I. 22 If it [*sc.* the furrow] be shallowe in one place, and deepe in another, it declares the grounde to be euill handled in the plowing. **1610** HOLLAND *Camden's Brit.* (1637) 739 When the River in Summer time is very ebbe and shallow. **1717** BERKELEY *Tour in Italy* Wks. 1871 IV. 543 Port shallow, not admitting ships of any burden. **1865** METEYARD *Wedgwood* I. iii. 98 Their [*sc.* pot-works] vicinity marked by shallow excavations for clay. **1907** J. A. HODGES *Elem. Photogr.* (ed. 6) 27 The various manipulations..are usually carried out in shallow dishes, or trays.

**b.** Of the soil of agricultural land: Forming only a thin stratum over rock.

**1733** TULL *Horse-hoeing Husb.* xx. (Dublin ed.) 290 If the Soil be shallow, it may be broke up with a narrow Furrow. **1760** BROWN *Compl. Farmer* II. 63 On poor light shallow land some sow a small white pea. **1849** ROBERTSON *Serm.* Ser. I. ii. 22 Shallow soil is like superficial character.

**c.** *absol.* in superlative = shallowest part.

**1587** FLEMING *Contn. Holinshed* III. 271/2 The same snow was found in London to lie two foot deepe in the shallowest.

**d.** *transf.* Of actions, etc.

**1815** J. SMITH *Panorama Sci. & Art* II. 626 Experienced agriculturists..upon the whole advise shallow ploughings. **1860** MAURY *Phys. Geog.* (Low) ix. 234 Now compare the shallow soundings in these lakes with the great depths of the arctic ocean.

**e.** In collocations, as ***shallow end***, *spec.* of a swimming-pool; also *fig.*; ***shallow well***, a well that is not deep; *spec.* (see quot. 1972).

**1924** 'I. HAY' (*title*) The *shallow end. **1929** R. HUGHES *High Wind in Jamaica* i. 9 The little ones, of course, only splashed about the shallow end: but John and Emily dived. **1972** J. ROSSITER *Rope for General Dietz* vi. 78 She broke away, swimming to the shallow end and climbing out. **1877** J. T. FANNING *Practical Treat. Water Supply Engin.* I. vii. 104 *Shallow well and spring supplies are, usually, yields of water from the drift formation alone. **1943** *Bull. Amer. Assoc. Petroleum Geologists* XXVII. 838 Of the shallow wells drilled for gas, 80 per cent were producers and 20 per cent were dry. **1959** ACKERMAN & LÖF *Technol. in Amer. Water Development* x. 281 The first irrigation was from shallow wells within the suction lift of centrifugal and piston pumps. **1972** *Gloss. Geol.* (Amer. Geol. Inst.) 650/2 *Shallow well.* (a) A water well..that taps the shallowest aquifer in the vicinity. The water is generally unconfined ground water. (b) A well whose water level is shallow enough to permit use of a shallow-well (suction) pump, the practical lift of which is taken as 22 ft.

**2.** Extending only a short distance inward from the surface or from the front towards the back. Of a lens: Having slight convexity or concavity.

**1545** ASCHAM *Toxoph.* II. (Arb.) 127 The nocke of the shafte is dyuersly made, for some be greate and full..some depe, some shalowe. *Ibid.*, The shalow, and rownde nocke is best for our purpose in prickyng for cleane delyuerance of a shoote. **1679** MOXON *Mech. Exerc.* vii. 130 Or you may make the Rooms next the Front deeper, or shallower, and leave the remainder for the Back Room. **1764** G. WILLIAMS in Jesse *Selwyn & Contemp.* (1843) I. 320, I wish you would let me trouble you to buy two pair of point-ruffles,..and pray let them be shallow. **1837** GORING & PRITCHARD *Microgr.* 60 If you use the focus of a very deep lens to measure that of a shallow one, then [etc.]. **1849** PARKER *Introd. Gothic Archit.* ii. 49 If the sculpture is early it is very rude, and the work is shallow. **1886** WILLIS & CLARK *Cambridge* II. 619 A shallow bow-window. **1899** *Allbutt's Syst. Med.* VIII. 842 The ulcer is shallow.

†**3.** Placed not far below the surface. *Obs. rare.*

**1697** DRYDEN *Virg. Georg.* III. 798 The lab'ring Swain Scratch'd with a Rake, a Furrow for his Grain; And cover'd, with his Hand, the shallow Seed again.

†**4.** Of sound: Lacking resonance, 'thin'. *Obs.*

**1626** BACON *Sylva* §223 If a Virginall were made with a double Concaue..as the Harpe hath; It must needs make the Sound perfecter, and not so Shallow and Iarring.

**5.** Of respiration: Slight, 'diaphragmatic'.

**1875** H. C. WOOD *Therap.* (1879) 435 The respiration progressively rendered slower and shallower by a direct action upon the centre.

**6.** *fig.* **a.** Of thought, reasoning, observation, knowledge, or feeling: Lacking depth, superficial.

*c* **1586** C'TESS PEMBROKE *Ps.* XCII. ii, What witt can.. deeply sound thy shallow'st thought? **1591** SHAKS. *Two Gent.* I. i. 21 That's on some shallow Storie of deepe loue, How yong Leander crost the Hellespont. **1771** SMOLLETT *Humph. Cl.* 13 July (1815) 237 That were but shallow policy; it would only serve to make the satire more cutting and severe. **1812** BYRON *Ch. Har.* I. xxv, He..turn'd a nation's shallow joy to gloom. **1875** JOWETT *Plato* (ed. 2) IV. 269 The term 'sensational' is rightly used to express what is shallow in thought and feeling.

**b.** Qualifying an agent-noun, or said of a person with reference to knowledge, exposition, etc. Also †not deeply versed *in*.

**1601** SHAKS. *All's Well* I. iii. 45 *Clo.*.. I hope to haue friends for my wiues sake. *Cou.* Such friends are thine enemies knaue. *Clo.* Y'are shallow Madam in great friends, for the knaues come to doe that for me which I am a wearie of. **1667** MILTON *P.L.* IX. 544 Beholders rude, and shallow to descerne Half what in thee is fair. **1771** WESLEY *Jrnl.* 25 Aug. (1827) III. 428 O how hard it is to be shallow enough for a polite audience! **1818** COBBETT *Pol. Reg.* XXXIII. 58 Shallow, indeed, must be those observers, who regard the predictions of Paine as having been falsified. **1899** *Allbutt's Syst. Med.* VII. 484 Thus a shallow observer may be led to give the assurance that there is no cause for further anxiety.

**c.** Of persons and their attributes: Wanting in depth of mind, feeling, or character.

**1593** SHAKS. *Lucr.* 1016 Out, idle words, servants to shallow fools! **1628** DIGBY *Voy. Mediterr.* (1868) Pref. 7 Not merely kept the shallow and impetuous Sir Everard steady, but [etc.]. **1712** STEELE *Spect.* No. 504 ¶4 Shallow fops, who are governed by the eye, and admire every thing that struts in vogue. **1870** NEWMAN *Gram. Assent* I. iii. 32 To apprehend notionally is to have breadth of mind but to be shallow.

**d.** Indicative of shallowness.

**1822** HAZLITT *Table-t.* Ser. II. ii. (1869) 36 To be deceived by shallow boasting. **1829** SOUTHEY *Ep. to Allan Cunningham* 185 The..shallow laugh Of one who would [etc.].

**7.** quasi-*adv.* To or at a slight depth.

**1662** EVELYN *Sculptura* II. v. (1906) 27 Grave your vernished plate with a very fine poynt..and eate it but shallow with your Aqua Fortis. **1707** MORTIMER *Husb.* xvi. 334 They should be sow'd but shallow, an Inch or an Inch and a half being deep enough. **1799** A. YOUNG *Agric. Lincolnsh.* 71 It includes a scarificator, with a bush of thorns, and cuts deeper or shallower at pleasure. **1867** F. FRANCIS *Angling* iv. (1880) 107 It is sometimes necessary to..fish shallow. **1892** *Photogr. Ann.* II. 269 The notches..had better be filed very shallow at first.

**8.** *Comb.* **a.** Parasynthetic derivatives, as ***shallow-conceited, -footed, -forded, -headed, -hearted, -hulled, -minded,* †*-mored, -rooted, -sighted, -soiled, -thoughted, -toothed, witted*** adjs.

*a* **1674** TRAHERNE *Chr. Ethics* (1675) 339 These self, but *shallow-conceited ranters. **1592** NASHE *Strange Newes* H 4, Some superficial slime of poison hast thou driueld from thy pen in thy *shallow footed sliding through my Supplication. **1678** DRYDEN *All for Love* IV. i, But I am made a *shallow-forded Stream, Seen to the bottom. **1647** TRAPP *1 Cor.* iv. 10 These Corinthians undervalued and depressed Paul under their silly *shallow-headed verbalists. **1588** SHAKS. *Tit. A.* IV. ii. 97 What, what, ye sanguine *shallow harted Boyes. **1842** TENNYSON *Locksley Hall* 39 O my cousin, shallow-hearted! O my Amy, mine no more! **1901** *Munsey's Mag.* XXIV. 454/1 *Shallow-hulled vessels are particularly liable to this defect. **1817** LADY MORGAN *France* III. (1818) I. 272 *note*, Mad. de Pompadour has left behind her, in France, the character of an ignorant, *shallow-minded, and vindictive woman. **1757** LISLE *Husb.* 452 In treading on such barley as was *shallow-mored it would stick to their shoes. **1593** SHAKS. *2 Hen. VI*, III. i. 31 Now 'tis the Spring, and Weeds are *shallow-rooted. **1705** CIBBER *Perolla* III. 35 Poor *shallow-sighted Man! **1827** POLLOK *Course T.* IV. (1860) 95 These, like ephemera, sprang in a day From lean and *shallow soiled brains of sand. **1858** SPENCER *Ess.* I. 145 Men who..prove themselves *shallow-thoughted and cold-hearted. **1857** T. MOORE *Handbk. Brit. Ferns* (ed. 3) 43 [Pinnules] *shallow-toothed. **1656** EARL MONM. tr. *Boccalini's Advts. fr. Parnass.* I. lxxiv. (1674) 92 They were ..held for..*shallow-witted people.

**b.** Attributive use of phrases, as †***shallow-bay, -draught, -level, -sea, -water.***

**1795** PHILLIPS *Hist. Inland Navig.* 319 No vessel drawing above six feet and a half can navigate it, unless the practice of shipping in *shallow-bay harbours be adopted. **1894** *Daily News* 28 Nov. 2/5 A contract..for the immediate construction of two *shallow-draft stern-wheel gunboats. **1902** *Daily Chron.* 2 Dec. 6/5 The report of the.. Commission, which pronounced strongly in favour of the *shallow-level 'tube'. **1855** KINGSLEY *Glaucus* (1878) 82 Deep-sea or *shallow-sea deposits. **1880** A. R. WALLACE *Isl. Life* 90 They are all comparatively *shallow-water forms.

**c.** Adverbial with pres. and pa. pples., as ***shallow-read, -rooting, -searching*** adjs.; complementary, as † ***shallow-ebbed*** adj.

**1600** S. NICHOLSON *Acolastus* (1876) 17 Perchance thou seest my *shallow-ebd estate. **1704** SWIFT *T. Tub* v, The Art of being deep-learned and *shallow-read. **1887** *Daily News* 16 July 3/8 The *shallow-rooting turnip plants were going through a struggle for life in the parched surface soil. *a* **1645** MILTON *Arcades* 41 And lead ye where ye may more neer behold What *shallow-searching Fame hath left untold.

**B.** *sb.*

**1. a.** A shallow part of a piece of water, of the sea, of a lake or river; shallow water; a shallow place.

**1571** *Act 13 Eliz.* c. 18 §5 The Shyriffes..shall..cause.. the saide newe Cut..to be suffyciently clensed of all the Shelfes and Shallowes. **1596** *Edw. III*, III. iii. 2 By whose cunning guide We found the shalow of this Riuer Some.

**1630** *R. Johnson's Kingd. & Commw.* 121 Jarsey..is environed with Rocks and dangerous Shallowes. **1670** Milton *Hist. Eng.* II. 37 Ours who well knew thir own advantages, and expertly us'd them, now in the shallows, now on the Sand. **1777** Robertson *Hist. Amer.* IV. (1778) I. 376 Two men can carry them, wherever shallows or cataracts obstruct the navigation. **1810** Scott *Lady of L.* I. xxxi, And the bittern sound his drum, Booming from the sedgy shallow. **1849** Macaulay *Hist. Eng.* v. I. 556 A place where it was protected by rocks and shallows. **1874** O'Shaughnessy *Music & Moonlight* 21, I have gleaned them from tide And cavern and shallow.

**b.** *fig.*

**1601** Shaks. *Jul. C.* IV. iii. 221 There is a Tide in the affayres of men, Which taken at the Flood, leades on to Fortune; Omitted, all the voyage of their life, Is bound in Shallowes, and in Miseries. **1818** Scott *Br. Lamm.* xxx, She sounded every deep and shallow of her daughter's soul. **1890** Chr. G. Rossetti *Poet. Wks.* (1904) 280/2 Thy will Chose love not in the shallows but the deep.

†**2.** A kind of hat. *Obs.*

***Shaking in the Shallow***: ? some game in which a hat of this kind was used as a dice-box or the like.

**1795** *Sporting Mag.* VI. 139 They went into a back parlour to play at Shaking in the Shallow. **1812** Vaux *Flash Dict.*, *Shallow*, a hat. **1823** in *Spirit Publ. Jrnls.* 421 A great flaming bunch of blood-red ribbons pinned upon his battered whitey-brown shallow. **1830** N. S. Wheaton *Jrnl.* 190 The tightly-laced dandy, with his fan-tailed shallow smartly stuck on one side of his bison-head.

**3. a.** A flat basket used by costermongers and street-hawkers.

**1851** Mayhew *Lond. Labour* I. 29 Baskets of various kinds; as..the square and oval 'shallow', fastened in front of the fruit-woman with a strap round the waist. **1889** *Standard* 20 Sept., The common flowers they hawk in their hand-barrows and 'shallows'.

**b.** A costermonger's cart.

**1859** Sala *Tw. round Clock* (1861) 33 There is a cobweb of wheeled vehicles of all sorts, from a cab to a hybrid construction something between a wheel-barrow and a costermonger's shallow. **1896** Morison *Child Jago* 33 A donkey employed to drag a cranky shallow, stored with glass bottles.

**4.** *Astr.* (See quot.)

**1801** Herschel in *Phil. Trans.* XCI. 267 Shallows are extensive and level depressions of the luminous solar clouds, generally surrounding the openings to a considerable distance. *Ibid.* 270, Jan. 4, 1801. There is a large opening much past the centre of the sun, with a shallow about it.

Hence **'shallowist** *nonce-wd.*, †**'shallowling**, a shallow, superficial person; **'shallowish** *a.*, somewhat shallow.

**1616** Sylvester *Tobacco Battered* 346 Can wee suppose, that any Shallowling Can find much Good in oft Tobacconing? **1799** Coleridge *Lett.* 16 Sept. (1895) 306 Kendall, a poet, who really looks like a man of genius pale and gnostic, has the merit of being a Jacobin or so, but is a shallowist. **1853** G. J. Cayley *Las Alforjas* II. 69 A slight dip, which gradually deepened into a shallowish valley.

**'shallow**, *a.*[2] *slang.* [Perh. suggested by *shall-I-go-naked*, used *dial.* as adj. applied to scanty clothing.] Used in ***shallow cove, dodge, mort, screever***: see quots.

**1839** H. Brandon in W. A. Miles *Poverty, Mendicity & Crime* 165/1 *Shallow Coves*, or *Shallow Fellows*,—fellows who go about the country, half-naked, with a Guernsey jacket, but no hat, shoes, nor stockings. **1842** *Edin. Rev.* July 484 'Shallow Coves' are impostors begging through the country as shipwrecked sailors. They generally choose winter, and always go nearly naked. *Ibid.*, 'Shallow Motts' are females who, like the Shallow Coves, go nearly naked. **1859** *Hotten's Slang Dict.*, *Shallow screever*, a man who sketches and draws on the pavement. **1869** Greenwood *Seven Curses of Lond.* 245 The 'shaller' or more properly 'shallow' dodge, is for a beggar to make capital of his rags and a disgusting condition of semi-nudity.

**shallow** ('ʃæləʊ), *v.* [f. shallow *a.*[1]]

**1.** *trans.* To make shallow.

**1510** *Sel. Cases Star Chamb.* (Selden Soc.) I. 74 The seid Priour..by subtill and crafty meanes by his Fisshe-garthes so ebbeth and shalloweth the same porte. *a* **1682** Sir. T. Browne *Misc. Tracts* (1684) 190 The Silt and Sands shall so choak and shallow the Sea in and about it. **1870** Orton *Andes & Amazon* II. xli. (1876) 563 The great equatorial lake, already shallowed by sediment, was drained. **1879** Boddam-Whetham *Roraima* 141 The long drought had shallowed the river.

**b.** *fig.*

**1742** Young *Nt. Th.* IX. 785 That thought alone thy state impairs, Thy *lofty* sinks, and shallows thy *profound.* **1821** R. Pollok in D. Pollok *Life* 117 This, instead of shallowing or enfeebling the current of language, deepens and invigorates it. **1872** Bushnell *Serm. Liv. Subj.* 16 These sayings..are not vaporized and shallowed by much talk.

**c.** *transf.* To pass from a greater to a less depth of.

**1793** Rennell in *Phil. Trans.* LXXXIII. 189 In effect, in running 120 miles, we shallowed the water only nine fathoms.

**2.** *intr.* To become shallow, to diminish in depth.

**1770** Cook *1st Voy.* III. iv. in Hawkesw. *Voy.* (1773) III. 504 The deepest water on that side is seven fathom, shallowing to five a good way up. **1823** W. Scoresby *Jrnl. Whale Fishery* 342 The sea shallows considerably on approaching the West Land. **1883** Fenn *Middy & Ensign* xli. 247 The water,..as the river shallowed, came only to his waist.

**shalloway** ('ʃæləʊweɪ). *Canad. Obs.* exc. *Hist.* [Origin unknown.] A small coastal sailing craft.

**1676** in D. W. Prowse *Hist. Newfoundland from Eng., Colonial, & Foreign Rec.* (1895) viii. 206 No Indians come [to Placentia] but some Canida Indians from forts of Canida in french shallowayes. **1774** G. Cartwright *Jrnl. Residence Coast of Labrador* (1792) II. 14 Hooper's shalloway having sprung her foremast,..I sent the boat-builder to make her a new one. **1971** E. R. Seary *Place Names* v. 86 The fishing boats in the cod and seal fishery were formerly called shallops and shalloways... The shalloways were open boats, what are now called punts.

†**'shallow-brained.** *Obs.* [f. shallow *a.*[1]] Having shallow brains; having no depth of intellect.

**1592** Nashe *P. Penilesse* Wks. (Grosart) II. 88 To this effect, the pollicie of Playes is verie necessary, howsoeuer some shallow-braind censurers..mightily oppugne them. *a* **1634** ? Chapman *Alphonsus* I. i. 7 No, Englishman, thou art ..Too shallow-brain'd to undermine my throne. **1667** South *Serm.* (*Prov.* x. 9) (1697) II. 43 Lewd Shallow-brain'd Huffs making Atheism and Contempt of Religion the sole Badge and Character of Wit. **1810** Loveden *2 Reports Thames Navig.* (1811) 5 He must be very shallow-brained indeed, who cannot perceive [etc.].

†**'shallow-brains.** *Obs. rare*[−1]. [Formed after prec.] A shallow-brained person.

**1707** tr. *Wks. C'tess D'Anois* I. (1715) 102, I am no more a Visionary, said he, nor a jealous Shallow-brains than another.

**shallowed** ('ʃæləʊd), *ppl. a.* [f. shallow *v.* + -ed[1].] Lessened in depth.

**1832** S. Ferguson *Forging of Anchor* 57 Where 'mid Norwegian isles He lies, a lubber anchorage for sudden shallow'd miles. **1879** *St. George's Hosp. Rep.* IX. 488 The primary incision for each iridectomy was by transfixion with a Graefe's knife, which, in crossing the shallowed anterior chamber of the left eye, became entangled in the iris.

**shallowing** ('ʃæləʊɪŋ), *vbl. sb.* [-ing[1].] The action of shallow *v.*; a making or becoming shallow.

**1727** A. Hamilton *New Acc. E. Ind.* I. xxxii. 392 Within 50 Paces of the Bank are sixteen Fathoms Water, which sudden Shallowings make it the more dangerous. **1854** H. Miller *Sch. & Schm.* (1858) 555 *note*, The increasing roll of the sea showed the gradual shallowing of the water. **1891** Stalker *Preacher & Models* i. 27 Such a shallowing of the general mind as will render it [etc.].

**shallowing** ('ʃæləʊɪŋ), *ppl. a.* [f. shallow *v.* + -ing[2].] That shallows; that becomes shallow.

**1858** Chr. G. Rossetti *Poet. Wks.* (1904) 205/2 They.. count the creep Of time, and sound the shallowing deep, Till we in port shall also sleep. **1886** Froude *Oceana* 323 We were running quietly through smooth and shallowing water.

**shallowly** ('ʃæləʊlɪ), *adv.* [f. shallow *a.*[1] + -ly[2].] In a shallow manner.

**1593** Nashe *Christ's T.* 89 What dullards and block-heads are wee, that hearing these tearmes of hell and eternall, so often souned in our eares, sound them so shallowly..? **1694** Motteux *Rabelais* IV. lxvii, Shallow of Judgment, and judging shallowly. **1871** W. A. Leighton *Lichen-Flora* 112 Margins broadly and shallowly crenate.

**shallowness** ('ʃæləʊnɪs). [f. shallow *a.*[1] + -ness.] The quality of being shallow:

**a.** in physical senses.

**1552** Huloet, Shallownes or sholenes in water, *uadum.* **1555** Eden *Decades* I. III. (Arb.) 77 The keeles of the shippes often tymes rased the sandes for shalownes of the water. **1613** Purchas *Pilgrimage* (1614) 512 The cause of greater tides he thinketh to be the shallownesse, and narrower shoares. **1707** Mortimer *Husb.* xiii. 284 It may prove very commodious to place the Bed of the Cart under the Axle-tree at such a distance as the depth or shallowness of the Ways or Waters you are to go thro' requires. **1849** Parker *Introd. Gothic Archit.* (1874) I. iii. 45 The wide-jointing of the masonry and the shallowness of the carving distinguish the old work from the new. **1878** Huxley *Physiogr.* 17 The extreme shallowness of the Thames basin. **1898** *Allbutt's Syst. Med.* V. 891 An increasing shallowness of breathing down to absolute cessation.

**b.** Want of depth of character, thought, knowledge, etc.; superficiality.

**1590** Greenwood *Answ. to Gifford* 25 This bewrayeth your shallownes. **1623** Bingham *Xenophon* 8 What a shallownesse it would be, to require that of a Generall, which if he granted, his enterprise should be quite ouerthrowne. **1736** Butler *Anal.* II. vi. 317 There are other persons without this shallowness of temper, persons of deeper sense as to what is invisible and future. **1827** Hare *Guesses* Ser. II. (1873) 445 Some persons give one the notion of an abyss of shallowness. **1871** B. Taylor *Faust* II. i. (1875) II. 91, I was a fool: My shallowness I now must ridicule.

**'shallow-pate.** Now *arch.* [f. shallow *a.*[1] + pate *sb.*] A person of shallow intellect.

**1600** *Garzoni's Hosp. Incur. Fooles* A 3 b, Shallow-pates and ninnie-hammers. *a* **1700** B. E. *Dict. Cant. Crew*, *Shallow-pate*, a foolish, silly, empty Fellow. [*c* **1730** Young *Ep. to Pope* 65 Each shallow pate, that cannot read your name, Can read your life, and will be proud to blame.] **1930** [see dowd *sb.*[1]]. **1964** *Listener* 24 Dec. 1002/1 That complicated shallow-pate, Jean-Paul Sartre,..makes of his subjective and personal passions a sort of objective truth.

So **'shallow-pated,** *a.*

**1616** R. C. *Times' Whistle* (1871) 37 This age such shallow pated men affords. **1870** Disraeli *Lothair* lxxv, The Prince was a shallow-pated coxcomb.

**shallowy** ('ʃæləʊɪ), *a.* [f. shallow *sb.*[3] + -y[1].] Characterized by shallows.

**1890** *Murray's Mag.* June 738 Nyanza's shallowy silver flood.

†**'shally.** Anglicized var. of challis. *Obs.*

**1840** T. Hook *Fitzherbert* I. vii. 72 An elegant shally wrapper trimmed with Mechlin lace.

**shalm(e, -ewe, eye, -ie, -oyse:** see shawm.

‖**shalom** (ʃa'lɔm), *int.* and *sb.* [Heb., lit. 'peace'.] In Jewish society, a word used as a salutation at meeting or parting. See also *Shabbat shalom* s.v. Shabbat. So **shalom aleichem** (a'lexɛm) *int.* [Heb. *'alêḵem*], peace be with you.

**1881** E. B. Tylor *Anthropology* i. 11 The Arab still salutes the stranger with *salâm alaikum*, 'peace upon you', nearly as the ancient Hebrew would have said shâlôm lâchem, that is, 'peace to you'. **1898** I. Zangwill *Dreamers of Ghetto* p. vi, I saw two Jews that met by chance... *Shalom Aleichem*, mournfully each said. **1959** I. Jefferies *Thirteen Days* iv. 49 Shalom. Cigarette, Sarge? **1962** L. R. Banks *End to Running* II. xiii. 265 There would be cries of 'Shalom, Shalom! Come in! Have a drink!' **1972** O. Sela *Bearer Plot* xxxix. 219 With a whispered '*Shalom*' she was gone. **1977** *Rolling Stone* 19 May 6/4, I was ready to say goodbye America, shalom Israel.

**shalop,** obs. form of shallop.

**shalot,** variant of shallot.

**shalt** (ʃalt, ʃolt), *sb. Sc. dial.* Also 9 shault, shawlt. [See Sheltie.] A small horse, a pony.

**1813** W. Beattie *Tales* 29 (Jam.), He made a halt, And lighted there, and left the shalt. **1858–61** Ramsay *Remin.* (1874) 31 The minister's shault's got lowse frae his tether.

†**'shaltree.** *Obs.* In 4 **schaltrow, skaltre, skaltrow,** *pl.* **scaltreen,** 5 **scaltre, scalter, shaltre.** [Partial translation of MHG. *schaltbaum* (or MLG. *schaldbôm*) pole used as an oar or a rudder, f. *schalten* (MLG. *schalden*) to push, shove + *baum* (see beam *sb.*); the Ger. word was also adopted in the 14th c. as *scheltbeme* sheltbeam. (Some of the spellings in the examples below may however represent G. *schalter*, used in the same sense.)] A pole (? used for propelling vessels).

**1307–8** *Acc. Exch. K.R.* Bd. 14 No. 14 (P.R.O.), In .viij. paribus de schaltrowes emptis..pro dicta bargia. **1336** in Nicolas *Hist. Navy* (1847) II. 472 [For 24 spars ('spres') bought to make 24] 'skaltres' [with]. **13..** *Domesday de Sippewyz* in *Black Bk. Admiralty* (Rolls) II. 195 De chescune nefe ovesqes scaltreen qe vyent a la vyle [*transl.* (15th c.) Of eche ship with scaltreen that comyn to the toun]. **1419** *Liber Albus* III. III. (Rolls) 344 Item, de navi cum shaltre, quantum dabit.

‖**shalwar** ('ʃʌlvɑː(r)). Also **salvar, salwar, shalvar, shulwar, shulwaur**[Urdu *šalwār*, Hindi *salvār*, ad. Pers. *šalwār*; Cf. sherryvallies, sherwal] **a.** Loose trousers worn by both sexes in some South Asian countries, esp. those worn by women together with a ***kameez***.

**1824** J. Morier *Adventures Hajji Baba* II. ix. 144 Can I offer him five tomâuns, and a pair of crimson *shalwars*? **1828** J. B. Fraser *Kussilbash* I. xv. 200 His huge shulwars, or riding trowsers..fell in folds over the large red leather boots. **1840** —— *Koordistan* II. v. 118 The Sheikh's cloaks and shulwârs. **1951** P. Miles *They came to Mountain* ix. 91 Over her *salvar* she wore stockings tied up with bootlaces. **1955** R. Prawer Jhabvala *To whom she Will* xv. 102 She was very fine now in a pink silk kamiz with blue roses on it and a pink salwar. *Ibid.* 295 The salwar is 104 inches wide at the waist and tied with a cord: when the cord is pulled the material falls in a bunch of folds over the stomach. The legs taper towards the ankles. **1957** *Geogr. Mag.* Aug. 198/1 A sophisticated taste will prefer the fashions of Paris and Bombay to the unbecoming *qamis* and *shalwar* of the North. **1967** *Times* 28 Sept. 2 (*caption*) Muslim children wearing their traditional baggy trousers outside Moat Girls' School, Leicester, yesterday. The shalwars will be allowed by the education authority on religious grounds. **1972** H. R. F. Keating *Inspector Ghote trusts Heart* iii. 34 She was wearing not a sari but a bright, cherry-red kameez and salwar. **1973** *Observer* (Colour Suppl.) 28 Oct. 72/1 Semi-transparent trousers (shalvar) approx £30.

**b.** *Comb.*, as **shalwar-, salwar-kameez(e** [see kameez(e], a woman's outfit consisting of *shalwar* and *kameez* or loose tunic.

**1955** R. Prawer Jhabvala *To whom she Will* xxx. 222 A lively sturdy girl in coloured salwar-kamiz. **1966** J. & R. Godden *Two under Indian Sun* iv. 104 She in salwar-kameeze, the loose tunic and trousers..worn by Muslim and up-country girls. **1977** A. Desai *Fire on Mountain* III. xi. 136 A bunch of schoolgirls in bright indigo *salwar-kameez.*

**shaly** ('ʃeɪlɪ), *a.* [f. shale *sb.*[2] + -y[1].] Composed of, or having a resemblance to shale.

**1681** Cotton *Wond. Peak* 41 A shaly Earth,..from the crown With a continual motion mouldring down. **1781** *Phil. Trans.* LXXI. 345 The soil was..in parts rather inclining to a shaly structure. **1863** Baring-Gould *Iceland* 354 The Saxifraga hirculus, like a golden star, sprinkled the shaley slopes. **1886** Fenn *Patience Wins* 51 Along the short rough turf and over the shaly paths.

**sham** (ʃæm), *sb.*[1] and *a.* Also 7 shamm(e. [Of obscure origin; the word first appears as slang, together with the related verb, about 1677, and immediately came into very frequent use.

Commonly explained as in some way connected with *sham*, north. dial. form of shame *sb.* and *v.* This is not impossible, on the supposition that the slang word arose from some once well-known anecdote or incident in a play. The following quot. may possibly contain a genuine tradition, but the alleged origin does not seem to account satisfactorily for the sense in the early examples. (North says that the word was introduced into general use, in the phrase 'sham plot', by Dangerfield; but it was already common some years before 1680, the date to which this statement refers.)

*a* **1734** NORTH *Exam.* II. iv. §1 (1740) 231 The word *Sham* is true Cant of the Newmarket Breed. It is contracted of *ashamed*. The native Signification is a Town Lady of Diversion, in Country Maid's Cloaths, who to make good her Disguise, pretends to be so *sham'd*! Thence it became proverbial, when a maimed Lover was laid up, or looked meager, to say he had met with a *Sham*.]

**A.** *sb.*

†**1. a.** A trick, hoax, fraud, imposture; something devised to impose upon, delude, or disappoint expectation; a 'sell'. ***to put a sham upon***: to hoax, defraud. ***to cut a sham***: 'to play a Rogue's trick' (B.E. *Dict. Cant. Crew*, *a* 1700). *Obs.*

**1677** [see SHAM *v.*[1]]. **1678** LADY CHAWORTH in *12th Rep. Hist. MSS. Comm.* App. v. 53 A letter to the Secretary.. some feare..that tis rather a sham to prevent stricter scherch. **1678** OTWAY *Friendship in F.* I. i, The Sham won't pass upon me, Sir, it won't look you. **1680** *Refl. Late Libel on Curse-ye-Meroz* 19 'Tis but a Tale, and a Story of his own making, like all the rest of the Sham's he would gladly put upon the Author. **1681** LUTTRELL *Brief Rel.* (1857) I. 66 Some scruple not to think this a shamm, and only an accusation to draw in others. **1688** *Eng. Prot. Mem. to Pr. & P'cess Orange* 19 They thought it an easie sham to say women misreckoned very often. *a* **1696** AUBREY *Lives, Chaloner* (1898) I. 160 He [Chaloner] wrote..an anonymous pamphlett, 8vo, scil. An account of the Discovery of Moyses's Tombe... 'Twas a pretty while before the shamme was detected. **1727** DE FOE *Hist. Appar.* viii. 141 He..seem'd to laugh that she should first put such a Sham upon him, and then to tell such a formal Story to make it good. **1751** *Affect. Narr. of Wager* 31, I own, I ever look'd upon the whole Affair as a Sham. **1821** PRAED *Gog* i. 191 You think I'm playing off a sham.

†**b.** In generalized sense: Trickery, hoaxing.

**1682** OLDHAM *Sat. Imit. Juv.* III. Wks. (1703) 429 Let the Plot-mongers stay behind, whose Art Can Truth to Sham, and Sham to Truth convert. **1713** M. HENRY *Folly of Despising our own Souls* Wks. 1855 I. 160 A man justly reckons himself affronted and resents it accordingly, who is imposed upon by sham and banter.

†**c.** ***upon the sham***: fraudulently, with deceitful purpose. *Obs.*

**1689** T. R. *View Govt. Europe* 87 They negotiate upon the square, frankly, and without artifice, or double dealing, not disguised, or upon the sham. *c* **1691** *Virgin's Compl.* 25 in *Bagford Ballads* (1878) 931 Robin came upon the Sham, Told me many [a] Lye and Flam.

†**d.** One who tries to delude, a humbug. *Obs.*

**1677** OLDHAM *Dithyr.* Wks. (1703) 451 Hence holy Sham! .. To some raw ent'ring Sinner cant and whine, Who never knew the worth of Drunkenness and Wine.

**2. a.** [Prob. developed from the adjectival or attributive uses.] Something that is intended to be mistaken for something else, or that is not really what it purports to be; a spurious imitation, a counterfeit.

**1728** MORGAN *Algiers* I. List of Subscribers, By retaining such a number of Names tho' Shams I might have showed away pompously. **1822** W. FOWLER in *Corr.* 437 One window wanted in west front as sham. **1835** CAMPBELL *Epist. Algiers* ix, For the pain of my thirst is no sham. *a* **1850** ROSSETTI *Dante & Circle* I. (1874) 237 That direst wolf shall seem like sweetest lamb Beneath the constant sham. **1861** *Sat. Rev.* 23 Nov. 524 To see whether the promised reduction of the naval and military forces of France is to be a reality or a sham. **1874** MICKLETHWAITE *Mod. Par. Churches* 215 As dishonest a sham as the stucco stone 'orders' of modern Regent Street. **1877** MRS. FORRESTER *Mignon* I. 244 She will have no shams, no imitations if she knows it. **1902** BUCHAN *Watcher by Threshold* 312 The hollow shams of life with their mincing conventions had departed.

**b.** Applied to a person. Cf. 1 d.

**1850** CARLYLE *Latter-d. Pamph.* i. 15 The greatest sham, I have always thought, is he that would destroy shams. **1867** TROLLOPE *Chron. Barset* I. xxiv. 214 Who can undertake to say that he is not a sham in anything?

**c.** in generalized sense.

**1843** CARLYLE *Past & Pr.* I. v. 36 The laws of Sham and Semblance, which are called the Devil's Laws. **1857** HUGHES *Tom Brown* I. ix, It's all sham—he's only afraid to fight it out.

**3.** *spec.* †**a.** A false shirt-front or 'dicky'; also see quot. 1785. **b.** (See quot.) **c.** A pillow-sham, see PILLOW *sb.* 6. **d.** (? *U.S.*) A strip of fine linen put under the upper edge of the bedclothes and turned over, as if forming the upper end of the sheet (*Cent. Dict.*, 1891).

**a.** **1721** STEELE *Conscious Lover* I. i, Wearing shams to make linen last clean a fortnight. **1772** NUGENT *Hist. Fr. Gerund* II. 67 A silk handkerchief round their necks,..half shirts or shams of coarse linen. **1785** GROSE *Dict. Vulgar T.* s.v. *Sham*, Shams, false sleeves to put on over a dirty shirt, or false sleeves with ruffles to put over a plain one.

**b.** **1863** R. B. GIRDLESTONE *Anat. Scepticism* 68 He fills up the rest of his shop with shams (i.e. boxes supposed to be filled with everything that can be required).

**c.** **1884** *Cottage Hearth* (Boston) Aug. 254/1 Large shams made of four very small handkerchiefs..are elegant in appearance over blue or pink under covers. **1893** *Scott. Leader* 12 June 1 Beautifully embroidered..tray cloths, tea cloths, pillow cases, shams and sheets.

**d.** **1891** *Century Dict.* **1906** WILLIAMSON *Lady Betty Across the Water* 280 There are stiff square 'shams' to hide the pillows and turn down over the top of the sheet.

**B.** *attrib.* and *adj.* (Sometimes with hyphen.)

**1. a.** Of immaterial things: Pretended, feigned, false, counterfeit; not genuine or true. ***sham fight***: a mimic battle between two divisions of a military or naval force, either for exercise or display.

**1681** *Relig. Clerici* To Rdr., Let Sham-truths be drawn as severally as mens fancies and humours please (yet) she [*sc.* Truth] her self hath nevertheless one regular, uniform, eternal Face. **1682** OTWAY *Prol. to Mrs. Behn's City Heiress*, Who..Wou'd lay sweet Money out in Sham-Thanksgivings? Sham-Plots you may have paid for o'er and o'er: But who ere paid for a Sham-Treat before? **1697** J. LEWIS *Mem. Dk. Glocester* (1789) 91 Thus these sham fights began and ended, to the no small entertainment of the little Duke and his boys. **1699** E. S——CY *Country Gentl. Vade M.* 98 After a little Sham-squabble between the two Cheats, says the first, If [etc.]. **1708** *Deplor. St. New Eng.* 22 in *Sewall's Diary* (1879) II. 118* As soon as the Sham-Vote.. was Gained, the Governour draws the Council in. **1714** *Lond. Gaz.* No. 5238/4 Known by the Sham Title of the Lady Rich. **1724** WELTON *18 Disc.* 70 We find our Blessed Saviour upbraiding those puritanick Jews..with a conscious hypocrisy and sham zeal. **1741** RICHARDSON *Pamela* (1824) I. 90 Perchance, some sham-marriage may be designed, on purpose to ruin me. **1770** FOOTE *Lame Lover* II. Wks. 1799 II. 71 Demurrers, sham-pleas, writs of error.., and imparlance. **1770** *Junius Lett.* xxxvi. (1788) 195, I do not refer to the sham prosecution which you affected to carry on against him. **1839** LEVER *H. Lorrequer* i. 11 A sham-battle in the Fifteen Acres. **1846** O. W. HOLMES *Urania* 24 And these ..Are all impatience till the opening pun Proclaims the witty shamfight is begun.

**b.** ***sham operation*** (*Biol.*), an operation in which an incision is made but nothing is removed, performed on animals of an experimental control group so that they suffer the same incidental effects of the operation as the animals on which a true operation is performed. Hence ***sham-'operate*** vb. trans., to perform a sham operation on; ***sham-'operated*** ppl. adj.

**1963** *Life Sci.* II. 475 Rats..were thymectomized within the first eighteen hours after birth. Approximately half of the litters were sham-operated. The polyoma virus was injected subcutaneously either immediately after thymectomy or sham-operation or two to three weeks afterwards. *Ibid.* 477 Rats thymectomized at birth seem to be much more sensitive to the oncogenic action of the polyoma virus than are normal or sham-operated rats. **1970** *Physiol. Zool.* XLIII. 91/1 Matched animals in an approximately 1:1 ratio were 'parietalectomized'..or sham-operated according to standard procedures. **1975** *Nature* 27 Mar. 349/1 Pinealectomy and sham operation were performed as described previously, and 10 d later a 2-mm semicircular wound was made in the right ear of each animal, including the controls. *Ibid.* 349/2 The result indicated that control, sham-operated, and melatonin-treated animals form one group.

**2.** Of a person: That pretends or is falsely represented to be (what is denoted by the sb.).

Now only as a transferred use of sense 3; hence several of the examples below are not quite in accord with present usage.

**1683** *Roxb. Ballads* (1884) V. 251 When zealous Sham-Sheriffs the City oppose. **1690** WOOD *Life* 4 Oct. (O.H.S.) III. 341 The discovery of the sham Prince of Wales is said to be very manifest. **1697** [J. DRAKE] (*title*) The Sham Lawyer: or the Lucky Extravagant. **1722** DE FOE *Moll Flanders* 123 Not venturing to go myself, I sent several sham Messengers. **1727** —— *Syst. Magic* II. ii. 278 The witch of Endor raised a sham Samuel in the room of the true prophet Samuel. **1756** C. SMART tr. *Horace, Art P.* [433] (1826) II. 351 So the sham-admirer is always more affected, than he that praises with sincerity. **1820** KEATS *Hyperion* II. 319 Dost thou forget, sham Monarch of the Waves, Thy scalding in the seas? **1841** DICKENS *Barn. Rudge* lxxi, He had his foot upon the breast of their sham deliverer. **1841** THACKERAY *Shrove Tuesday in Paris* Wks. 1900 XIII. 567 As the sham-fiends do in Don Juan. **1850** CARLYLE *Latter-d. Pamph.* i. 13 The Kings were Sham-Kings, playacting as at Drury-Lane;—and what were the people withal that took them for real?

**3.** Of material things or substances: Made in imitation of something else; made to appear to be something which it is not; made of inferior or base materials.

Now always implying reprobation; but in the earlier part of the 19th c. often used in tradesmen's price-lists, etc. as equivalent to 'imitation'.

**1699** E. S——CY *Country Gentl. Vade M.* 99 One of the other two conveys a Sham-bill under the Table, which [etc.]. *a* **1700** B. E. *Dict. Cant. Crew*, *Masons-mason'd*, a Sham-sore above the Elbow, to counterfeit a broken Arm, by a fall from a Scaffold. **1708** SWIFT *Hist. Vanbrugh's Ho.* 26 And so [he] resolved a house to build: A real house... Not a sham thing of clay or cards. **1722** DE FOE *Moll Flanders* 239 She kept a sham Gold Watch..in her Pocket. **1762** *Gentl. Mag.* May 212 Behind the doors..is discovered a beautiful sham front of an organ. **1780** MME. D'ARBLAY *Lett.* 9 June, Send me a line by the diligence... Charlotte.. will make it into a sham parcel. **1798** *Hull Advertiser* 24 Mar. 2/3 A very handsome..light airy chariot, with sham joints. **1848** THACKERAY *Van. Fair* xxxv, The sham coat of arms which Osborne had assumed from the Peerage. **1876** BLACK *Madcap Violet* xvii. 149 Not one of the girls dared to wear a bit of sham jewellery. **1898** J. T. FOWLER *Durham Cath.* 28 Decorated and Perpendicular windows have..been replaced by sham Norman ones.

†**4.** False, deceptive. *Obs. rare.*

*a* **1721** PRIOR *Ess. Opinion* Wks. (1907) II. 194 Another.. likes to see the Butcher of the West really wounded at the Bear-Garden, not content with the sham red that glows upon the Skirt of Banco's Ghost. **1727** DE FOE *Syst. Magic* I. ii. (1840) 49 If they could have amused the king with any sham answer,..they would certainly have done it.

**5.** *Comb.* Prefixed to other adjs. as ***sham-ancient***, ***-dead***, ***-serious***, ***-Tudor***; also with sbs. forming compounds used attributively, as ***sham-twist***. Also †***sham-legged*** *a.*, ? wooden-legged (but perh. error for ***shamble-legged***).

**1688** *Lond. Gaz.* No. 2339/4 One James Caulket,..a Dyer ..sham leg'd, goes somewhat foundered. **1840** CARLYLE *Heroes* v. (1841) 303 He who has once seen into this, has seen the difference of the True from the Sham-True. **1843** —— *Past & Pr.* I. v. 42 It is not governed by the wisest it has.. but by the sham-wisest. **1850** —— *Latter-d. Pamph.* i. 26 My Christian friends, and indeed my Sham-Christian and Anti-Christian, and all manner of men, are invited to reflect on this. **1847** MRS. GORE *Castles* ix. (1857) 69 A suite of sham-ancient steam-carved furniture. **1880** E. MAITLAND in *Encycl. Brit.* XI. 279/2 A sham-twist [gun-] barrel..[which] has all the appearance of a genuine twisted barrel. **1889** 'F. ANSTEY' *Pariah* III. viii, The shabby little sham-marble mantle-piece was draped with embroidered cloth. **1909** *Nation* May 153/2 To this agitation we apply the term sham-serious. **1934** *Discovery* Oct. 304/1 It cannot be long before the incongruity of the sham-Tudor house with the 1934 interior is generally recognised. **1945** [see JACOBETHAN *a.*]. **1970** T. HUGHES *Crow* 53 So in one hand he held a sham-dead spider.

**sham**, *sb.*[2] *slang.* Short for CHAMPAGNE *sb.*

**1849** THACKERAY *Pendennis* iv, A bottle of sherry, a bottle of sham, a bottle of port and a shass caffy, it ain't so bad hay, Pen? **1870** M. COLLINS *Vivian* III. xii. 240 Late hours and lots of hiced sham makes a man nervous.

**sham** (ʃæm), *v.* [See SHAM *b.*[1]]

†**1.** *trans.* To cheat, trick, deceive, delude with false pretences; to impose upon, take in, hoax. *Obs.*

**1677** WYCHERLEY *Pl. Dealer* III. i. 44 *Law.* Why, I'm sure you jok'd upon me, and shamm'd me all night long. *Man.*.. Shamming! What does he mean by't Freeman? *Free.* Shamming, is telling you an insipid, dull Lye, with a dull Face, which the slie Wag the Author only laughs at himself; and making himself believe 'tis a good Jest, puts the Sham only upon himself. **1688** SHADWELL *Sq. Alsatia* II. Wks. 1720 IV. 42 Sirrah! most audacious rogue! do you sham me? do you think you have your uncle to deal with? **1693** *Humours Town* 69 Their highest Excellence is, to banter the Vintner, to bilk their Lodgings, to sham their Bookseller. **1821** BYRON *To Mr. Murray* iv, So, if *you will*, I shan't be shamm'd.

†**b.** To bring *into*, *out of* a condition, etc., or to deprive *of* something by 'shamming' or deception. *Obs.*

**1681** T. FLATMAN *Heraclitus Ridens* No. 31 (1713) I. 201 These true Protestant Juries have the best luck at Shamming their Friends into Halters, that ever I knew in my Life. **1682** *New News fr. Bedlam* 9 Those Youths, who lately came..To sham us of our Lives and Liberty. **1692** R. L'ESTRANGE *Fables* ccliii. 220 When they find themselves Fool'd and Shamm'd (as we say) into a Conviction. *a* **1733** J. DUNTON *Life & Err.* (1818) I. iii. 44, I fell into my first amour like a Knight Errant, being purely shammed into it.

†**c.** To put off, 'fob off' with something deceptive or worthless; to get rid of (a person) by some paltry excuse. Also with *off*. *Obs.*

**1682** *Tory Plot, or Discov. Design carried on by Addressers* 9 William..was advanced to the Crown, and his Eldest Brother Robert shamm'd off with a Dukedom. **1683** KENNETT tr. *Erasm. on Folly* 53 Princes..miss the advantage of being told the truth, and are shamm'd off by a parcel of insinuating Courtiers. **1712** BETTERTON in *Misc. Poems* 248 For Priests with empty thanks are never shamm'd. **1726** M. HENRY *Wks.* (Fullarton) I. 142 Men may be shammed with a frivolous excuse. **1749** LAVINGTON *Enthus. Meth. & Papists* II. (1754) Pref. 21 Seeing then you have thus shammed us off with Counterfeit Coin.

**d.** ? To make to appear a sham; to rid oneself of (an accusation) by deceit. Also with *off*.

**1681** *Trial of S. Colledge* 57 If they can make me a Traytor, they will try it upon others, and so hope to sham off their own Treasons. *Ibid.* 76 They talk up and down the Town as if I did intend to sham the Popish Plot, and to make a Protestant Plot. *Ibid.* 131 When he was told of this, he began to put it off, and to use his own words, had a great mind to sham off the business. **1691** *Providences of God* 124 Edward Ivy had often Conference with Mrs. Collier, and the Popish Priests in Newgate, and had received Money to Sham the Popish Plot and to swear to a Protestant one.

**e.** To make *up* deceitfully, to 'fake' *up*.

**1679** 'TOM TICKLEFOOT' *Obs. Trials of Wakeman*, etc. 8 But by all that's good, it was my Old Master Clodpate's disease,..alwayes to Sham up an Evidence when any body had bin with him the Morning before.

†**2.** To impose or attempt to pass off (something) *upon* (a person) by deceit; to palm *off*. *Obs.*

**1682** T. FLATMAN *Heraclitus Ridens* No. 68 (1713) II. 174 Then he Shams upon us, that the great Poets could not give Johnson his due Praise. *a* **1683** OLDHAM *Sat. Jesuits* Prol. 15 Are Texts, and such exploded Trifles fit T'impose, and sham upon a Jesuit? **1687** R. L'ESTRANGE *Answ. to Dissenter* 48 To say nothing how Artificially the Writer of that Letter has Shamm'd upon the People his Majesties Act of Grace in favour of the Dissenters, for a Matter Concerted betwixt Them, and the Papists. **1692** —— *Fables* clxii. 136 Not..to Sham Fallacyes upon the World for Current Reason. **1722** DE FOE *Moll Flanders* 44 Don't go to sham your Stories off upon me. **1751** LAVINGTON *Enthus. Meth. & Papists* III. (1754) 90 Franciscan Fryars, who never fail to sham them [Hysteric Fits] upon the World for Divine Ecstasies.

†**3.** *intr.* To practise deception or deceit. *Obs.*

**1678** OTWAY *Friendship in F.* III. i. 26 *Malag.* Oh, hang money Sir, your Father was an Alderman. *Sir Nob.* Well, get thee gone for an Arch-wagg—I do but sham all this while. **1682** OLDHAM *Sat. Imit. Juv.* III. Wks. (1703) 434 Tho we say the same, He is believ'd, and we are thought to sham. **1689** PRIOR *Ep. F. Shephard* 171 All your Wits, that flear and sham.

**4.** *trans.* **a.** To be or to produce a deceptive imitation of; † to pretend falsely to be (a person of a certain rank or character). †*to sham one's glass*: to make a pretence of drinking.

**1698** FARQUHAR *Love & Bottle* IV. ii, A compound of practical rake and speculative gentleman, who..shams the beau and squire with a whore or chambermaid. *a* **1704** T. BROWN tr. *Æneas Sylvius' Lett.* xlv. Wks. 1709 III. II. 74 Paint and fine Washes sham a complexion, which is none of their own. **1754** CHESTERF. *World* No. 90 ¶7 He keeps up his spirits bravely, and never shams his glass. **1775** SHERIDAN *Rivals* I. i, Why does your master pass only for an ensign?—Now if he had shammed general indeed—. **1874** SYMONDS *Sk. Italy & Greece* (1898) I. x. 190 Tawdry frescoes shamming stonework.

**b.** To assume the appearance of, counterfeit (a specified condition, action, etc.).

**1775** MISS BURNEY *Early Diary* (1889) II. 44 Shamming a little confusion, I confessed I knew not where it was. **1812** W. TAYLOR in *Monthly Mag.* XXXIV. 235 Read all thy spells, and I will hear, And fold my claws, and sham a tear. **1837** CARLYLE *Fr. Rev.* II. v. v, Shamming death, '*faisant le mort!*' **1843** F. E. PAGET *Warden of Berkingholt* 246 She held the candle to my face while I was shamming sleep till I began to suspect she was up to me. **1869** 'W. M. COOPER' *Flagellation* xxii. 205 Persons shamming an epileptic fit.

**c.** To 'scamp' (work). *rare.*

**1848** *Jrnl. R. Agric. Soc.* IX. II. 538 There is great room for the workmen to sham their work, without its being observable in appearance.

**5.** *intr.* To make false pretences; to pretend to be, do, etc. what one is not, does not, does not mean, etc.; to feign.

**a.** Followed by an adj. complement.

**1787** *Generous Attachment* IV. 155, I preferred this scheme to that of shamming sick, as I looked so well. **1833** T. HOOK *Parson's Dau.* II. ii, If I had shammed sorry when I heard of old Alexander Marc Antony Anderson's death, I should have been as great a hypocrite as—I shan't say who. **1834** MARRYAT *P. Simple* xviii, What did you sham dead for? **1879** MEREDITH *Egoist* xxxv. (1889) 351 If you want me for a friend you must not sham stupid.

**b.** *simply.*

**1855** MACAULAY *Hist. Eng.* xii. III. 169 Wondering within himself whether those who lectured him were such fools as they professed to be, or were only shamming. **1878** BAYNE *Purit. Rev.* x. 407 He was canting and shamming.

**6.** Phrase *to sham Abra(ha)m* (orig. *Naut. slang*), to feign sickness: see ABRAHAM-MAN.

**1752** *Gentl. Mag.* Mar. 140/2 As he [capt. Lowry] went along some sailors cry'd out..that He must not sham Abram (a cant sea phrase when a sailor is unwilling to work on pretence of sickness, and used by the captain when Hossack was almost expiring under his blows). **1760** GOLDSM. *Cit. World* cxix, The boatswain..swore..that I shammed Abraham merely to be idle. **1827** SCOTT *Surg. Dau.* vi, It's good enough, and too good, for a set of lubbers, that lie shamming Abraham. **1860** [see ABRAHAM-MAN]. **1863** READE *Hard C.* xxxi. (1868) 265 He's shamming Abraham.

**b.** Hence *sham-Abra(ha)m* quasi-*sb.*, malingering, deception. Also quasi-*adj.*, hypocritical.

**1828** [J. P. COLLIER] *Punch & Judy* 87 None of your sham-Abram. **1840** T. HOOK in *New Monthly Mag.* LVIII. 442 She is all shamabram and humbug before me.

**1837** HOOD *Ode to Rae Wilson* 62, I..treat sham Abr'am saints with wicked banters.

Hence †**shammed** *ppl. a.*, **'shamming** *vbl. sb.* and *ppl. a.*

? *c* **1677** *Obscure Prince* in *Roxb. Ballads* (1883) IV. 625 Call't the shamm'd Story of the blackened Box. **1677** WYCHERLEY *Pl. Dealer* IV. ii. 66 You noble Wits are so full of shamming, and droling, one knows not where to have you, seriously. **1682** MRS. BEHN *City Heiress* v. i. 50 A Shamming Rogue; the right Sneer and Grin of a dissembling Whig. **1682** *London's Joy & Loyalty* in *Roxb. Ballads* (1883) IV. 632 Now the loud threat'ning Tempest is dispers'd, And all their shamming Plots are quite revers'd. **1692** *Scarronides* II. 11 What glavering shamming toads the rest are.

‖**shama**[1] ('ʃɑːmə). [Hindī *çāmā*.] A cereal cultivated in India, *Panicum frumentaceum* (*colonum*), yielding a millet-like grain used as food. Also *shama millet*.

[*a* **1815** ROXBURGH *Flora Ind.* (1820) I. 307 *Panicum frumentaceum.* R... *Beng.* Shama. *Teling.* Bonta-shama; shamaloo, the grain.] **1874** *Treas. Bot.* Suppl., *Shama*, a species of *Mesembryanthemum*, the seeds of which are used as food by the desert Arabs. **1886** A. H. CHURCH *Food-Grains India* 50 Shama Millet... This millet, sometimes called 'Wild Rice' or 'Jungle Rice', is a poor food.

‖**shama**[2] ('ʃɑːmə). Also **shamah.** [Hindī *çāmā*.] An Indian song-bird, *Cittocincla tricolor*.

**1839** JERDON in *Madras Jrnl. Lit. & Sci.* X. 252 *Petrocincla Pandoo*..Indian Rock Thrush—*Shamah*, H. *Ibid.*, The *Shamah* is a rare bird in the southern part of the Peninsula. **1894** *Times* 5 Feb. 4/6 One or two mynahs and shamahs, and a piping crow. **1895** *Daily News* 30 Dec. 5/3 Indian 'shamas' are also in great demand in Germany.

**shama**, var. SHAMMA.

**shamade**, obs. form of CHAMADE.

**1706** PHILLIPS (ed. Kersey), *Shamade*, a beat of Drum for a Parley. See *Chamade*.

‖**shamal** (ʃə'mɑːl). Also 7 **shemaul**; **shamaal, shemmal.** [Arab. *shamāl* left (hand), north, north wind. (Sometimes confused with SAMIEL.) (See quots.)]

**1698** FRYER *Acc. E. Ind. & P.* 226 The Periodical and stated Winds of the Gulph are the North-west, by the Inhabitants termed Shemauls, which begin when the Cowshees or South-East leave off. **1900** S. M. ZWEMER *Arabia* x. 107 The prevailing wind at Bahrein..is the *shemmāl* or Northwester. **1901** *Scotsman* 13 Sept. 5/2 The bay suffers only from a swell when the nor'wester known as the Shamal blows. **1980** D. CREED *Scarab* xiii. 129 The Shamaal blows strong from the north.

‖**shamalo** ('ʃæmələʊ). Also **shamaloo, shamoola.** [Telinga.] = SHAMA[1]. Also *shamalo-grass*.

[*a* **1815**: see SHAMA[1].] **1846** LINDLEY *Veg. Kingd.* 113 Panicum frumentaceum, called Shamoola, in the Deccan. **1891** *Century Dict.*, *Shamalo-grass*.

**shaman** ('ʃɑːmən, 'ʃæmən), *sb.* (and *a.*). Also 8 **schamane**, 8–9 **schaman**, 9 **shuman.** Formerly usu. with capital initial. [a. G. *schamane*, Russian *sha'man*, a. Tungusian *samân* (Castren *Tung. Sprachl.*). Cf. F. *chaman*.

The Persian *shemen*, idol, idol temple, sometimes cited as the source, is unconnected. Evidence seems to be wanting for the plausible suggestion that the Mongolian word is an adoption of Chinese *sha mên*, an ordained member of a Buddhist fraternity, a. Skr. *çramaṇa*, Pali *samana* Buddhist monk or mendicant.]

**A.** *sb.* A priest or priest-doctor among various northern peoples of Asia. Hence applied by extension to similar personages in other parts, esp. a medicine-man of some of the north-western American Indians. Occas. in wider sense: an adherent of shamanism. Also more recently, with recognition of the widespread similarity of primitive beliefs, the term denotes esp. a man or woman who is regarded as having direct access to, and influence in, the spirit world which is usu. manifested during a trance and empowers them to guide souls, cure illnesses, etc. Also *fig.*

**1698** A. BRAND *Emb. Muscovy into China* 50 If five or six of these Tonguese Families happen to live near one another ..they maintain betwixt them a Shaman, which signifies as much as Sorcerer or Priest. **1706** tr. *Evert Ides' Trav.* vii. 29 Several Tunguzians, amongst which is also their famed Schaman or diabolical artist. **1780** TOOKE *Russia* III. 245 Among all the Schamanes, women are looked upon as beings vastly inferior to men. **1848** S. W. WILLIAMS *Middle Kingdom* II. xviii. 258 The ritual of the Shamans..has been translated by Neumann, a German sinologue. **1868** F. WHYMPER *Trav. Alaska* 255 The Schaman, pronounced exactly like our word showman. **1900** T. ADNEY in *Harper's Mag.* Mar. 495 A former chief and medicine-doctor, or shuman. **1907** C. HILL-TOUT *Brit. N. Amer.*, *Far West* x. 199 If the corpse was that of a woman it was prepared for interment by a female shaman. **1910** HADDON *Races of Man* 62 After a death they [the Veddas of Ceylon] perform certain dances and rites through a shaman to the recently departed spirit. **1921** R. H. LOWIE *Primitive Society* xii. 328 It was indeed through the shaman, who revealed the will of the spirits, that the chief was chosen. **1925** G. RÓHEIM *Austral. Totemism* vii. 350 This rite..is based on the scheme of death and rebirth and..the vocation of a shaman is often chosen at puberty. **1938** in F. Boas *Gen. Anthropol.* ix. 469 Because the North Californian woman happens to be a shaman does not mean that she treats her family and friends differently. **1952** KOESTLER *Arrow in Blue* xiii. 106 Vladimir Jabotinsky ..became the first political shaman in my life. **1964** W. R. TRASK tr. *Eliade's Shamanism* i. 4 The shaman is also a magician and medicine man... But beyond this, he is a psycho-pomp, and he may also be priest, mystic, and poet. *Ibid.*, Through this whole region in which the ecstatic experience is considered the religious experience par excellence, the shaman, and he alone, is the great master of ecstasy. **1971** I. M. LEWIS *Ecstatic Relig.* ii. 56 We are perfectly justified in applying the term shaman to mean..a 'master of spirits'. **1971** *Times Lit. Suppl.* 19 Nov. 1453/3 The Maori shaman clasps in his arms the tree on which his people rely for food, clothing, shelter and transport. **1972** P. M. BARTZ *South Korea* 42/1 Primitive spirit worship (shamanism) was followed by Buddhism... Today, there are said to be 27,000 shamans, 10,000 of them women. **1979** *London Rev. Bks.* 25 Oct. 1/1 America lacks this type of magician—the shamans there are grander, more worldly, more pretentious.

**B.** *adj.* (or *attrib.*) Of or pertaining to a shaman or to shamanism.

**1780** TOOKE *Russia* III. 243 The Schamane religion is undoubtedly one of the most antient that exists. **1882** LANSDELL *Through Siberia* xxx. (1883) 374 The Russian missionaries..find the conversion of the Shaman Buriats tolerably easy. **1901** *Contemp. Rev.* Jan. 95 The necessary spiritual gifts entitling to the Shaman-office often are bestowed.

Hence †**sha'manian** *sb.*, a shamanist; **sha'manic** *a.*, akin to shamanism; also, of or connected with a shaman. Also **'shamanka, 'shamaness, 'shamanin,** terms sometimes applied to a female shaman.

**1802** PINKERTON *Mod. Geog.*, *Russ. Emp. in Asia* ii. II. 47 The Schamanians even believe that the Burchans, or gods themselves, arose from the general mass of matter and spirit. **1899** *Athenæum* 11 Mar. 303/2 The mental attitude of the composers is shamanic and archaic. **1936** *Jrnl. R. Anthropol. Inst.* LXVI. 80 The term *shamanka* is used by travellers and anthropologists for all female shamans. This usage is unscientific and misleading... For the sake of convenience, however, I shall follow current usage. **1955** H. V. ELWIN *Relig. Indian Tribe* v. 146 A shamanin who has done the wrong things is regarded rather as a nun who has broken her vows. **1964** W. R. TRASK tr. *Eliade's Shamanism* vii. 241 A shamaness..resolves to bring back his soul and goes down to the 'world of the dead'. **1964** *Listener* 29 Oct. 677/2 The initiation dreams, the general schema of shamanic flight.. are not a shaman monopoly. **1968** N. K. SANDARS *Prehist. Art of Europe* i. 26 In Siberia there were also women who were shamankas. **1977** D. R. MCCANN *Black Crane* p. i, These oracles to *Chesŏk*..were recited by a *mudang*, or shamaness.

**shamanism** ('ʃɑːmənɪz(ə)m, 'ʃæmənɪz(ə)m). Also 8 **schamanism**, 9 **shahmanism.** Formerly usu. with capital initial. [f. SHAMAN + -ISM.] The primitive religion of the Ural-Altaic peoples of Siberia, in which all the good and evil of life are thought to be brought about by spirits who can be influenced only by shamans (see SHAMAN *sb.*); hence applied to similar religions, esp. of North-West American Indians. Also the beliefs, rituals, techniques, etc., associated with a shaman, the general pattern of which is found almost universally in primitive cultures at the food-gathering stage of social development.

**1780** TOOKE *Russia* III. 243 Of Schamanism. **1841** *Penny Cycl.* XX. 382/2 They [Samoyedes] are heathens, and profess the religion called Shamanism. **1848** S. W. WILLIAMS *Middle Kingd.* II. xviii. 258 The form of Budhism prevailing among the Mongols and Tibetans differs more in its state and power than in its doctrines; it is called Shamanism, or *Hwang kiau*, the Yellow doctrine, from the color of the priestly robes. **1870** DALL *Alaska & Resources* 88 The belief in shamánism is universal among the natives of Alaska, Eskimo as well as Indians. **1875** SAYCE in *Encycl. Brit.* III. 192/2 The earliest religion of Accad was a Shamanism resembling that of the Siberian or Samoyed tribes of to-day. **1906** PETRIE *Relig. Anc. Egypt* i. 3 Others, as the Turanians,..do not adopt the worship of great gods, but deal with a host of animistic spirits, ghosts, devils, or whatever we may call them; and Shamanism or witchcraft is their system for conciliating such adversaries. **1930** G. RÓHEIM *Animism, Magic, & Divine King* III. iv. 166 The sexual organs play a large part in Chukchee shamanism. **1947** H. C. E. ZACHARIAS *Protohistory* iv. 109 Shamanism.. by which term I mean not merely the forms of hysteria and of falling into a trance. **1963** in H. N. Michael *Stud. in Siberian Shamanism* 120 Evenk shamanism was characterized by such phenomena as..a special shamanistic language, numerous and extremely effective pieces of equipment, [etc.]. **1964** W. R. TRASK tr. *Eliade's Shamanism* i. 4 A first definition of this complex phenomenon, and perhaps the least hazardous, will be: shamanism = *technique of ecstasy*. **1972** G. JONES *Kings, Beasts, & Heroes* III. i. 129 They nourished him with foaming hornfuls drawn from the deep casks of wonder, myth, shamanism, make-believe, wish-fulfilment, unreason.

So **'shamanist**, a believer in shamanism; also *attrib.* or *adj.* **shama'nistic** *a.*, pertaining to shamanism. **'shamanite** = SHAMANIST. **'shamanize** *v.*, *intr.* [= G. *schamanieren*] to perform the incantations proper to a shaman; *trans.* to imbue with shamanistic beliefs; hence **'shamanizing** *vbl. sb.* and *ppl. a.*

**1842** PRICHARD *Nat. Hist. Man* xxi. (1845) 223 The Kamtschatkans..are Shamanists. **1854** LATHAM *Native Races Russ. Emp.* 103 A name which we expect amongst Jews and Mahometans rather than amongst shamanistic Voguls. **1871** MATEER *Travancore* 191 The Shamanites acknowledge the existence of a supreme God but offer him no worship. **1882** LANSDELL *Through Siberia* xxxii. (1883) 405 The people worship the spirits of the mountains, a superstition of the Shamanist Buriats. **1901** *Contemp. Rev.* Jan. 87 Old Russian settlers in those far-off regions have to a high degree become 'Shamanized'. **1908** *Q. Rev.* Oct. 522 A Lama disguised as a Shamanist dancer. **1912** *Man* XII. 171 The shamanistic ceremonies of the races occupying the northern parts of the Eurasian continent. **1949** W. HOWELLS *Heathens* viii. 126 Evans-Pritchard has the same thing to say about Zande witch doctors, who do shamanizing of a less distinct type. **1963** in H. N. Michael *Stud. in Siberian Shamanism* 8 The people were beating the drum ('shamanizing'). **1964** *Listener* 29 Oct. 677/2 The vital function shamanizing can take on..may be seen in the *Bardo Thodol*, the Tibetan 'Book of the Dead'. *Ibid.*, In a shamanizing society, 'Venus and Adonis'.., 'The Wanderings of Oisin', 'Ash Wednesday', would all qualify their authors for the magic drum.

**shamas(h** (‖'ʃaməs). Also **shammas(h, shammes, shammos,** etc. Pl. **-im.** [Yiddish *shames*, Heb. *šammāš* attendant, f. *šimmēš* to serve.] **1.** A beadle or sexton in a Jewish synagogue.

**1650** [see CHAZZAN]. **1675** L. ADDISON *Present State of Jews* xi. 90 First the Summas, or Sacristan. **1862** *Once a Week* VII. 191/2 The shamas, a kind of curate and clerk combined, brings a glass of wine. **1892** I. ZANGWILL *Childr. Ghetto* I. 6 Many of the worshippers were tempted to give beyond their means for fear of losing the esteem of the *Shammos*, or beadle, a potent personage only next in influence to the President. **1896** I. ABRAHAMS *Jewish Life Mid. Ages* 8 It was an ancient custom in several places for the Shamash or verger to announce every Saturday the result of law-suits, and to inform the congregation that certain properties were on the market. **1903** *Standard* 27 Apr., There is a 'shammas' acting as beadle, door-keeper, collector, cook, and utility-man in emergencies. **1909** *Cent. Dict.* Suppl., Shammash. **1946** KOESTLER *Thieves in Night* 288 It was opened by the *shamash* or door-keeper. **1960** L. P. GARTNER *Jewish Immigrant in England 1870–1914* vii. 189 The observant immigrant in the East End..could not look to..the rabbi nor to the more commonplace *shammash* (sexton) for edification. **1967** C. POTOK *Chosen* i. 27 You should see his father. He's one of Reb Saunders' shamashim. **1968** L. ROSTEN *Joys of Yiddish* 329 The visiting rabbi stopped in the middle of his sermon and signaled to the *shammes*. **1973** *Jewish Chron.* 2 Feb. 26/2 The death of Mr Harry Goldman in his 74th year has cast a shadow over the members of the Singers Hill Synagogue, where he served as shammas for 40 years. **1976** *New Yorker* 29 Mar. 64/2 The divinely inspired shammes, or custodian, of the synagogue.

**2.** An extra candle used for lighting the Chanukah candles.

**1961** in WEBSTER. **1976** Y. L. BIALER *Jewish Life* 161 The Hanukkah lights are..not to be used for ordinary purposes.

.. Alongside each Hanukkah lamp the sages instituted the use of a special candle for normal household purposes, calling it the 'caretaker' (*shamash*).

**shamateur** ('ʃæmətɜː(r), ʃæmə'tɜː(r)). [f. SHAM *a.* + AM)ATEUR.] A sportsman who is classed as an amateur but behaves like a professional, esp. one who makes money out of his performances.
**1896** *Badminton Mag.* II. 533 For frank and open professionalism there may be a good deal to be said, but nothing can make the 'promateur' and the 'shamateur' attractive. **1928** *Sunday Dispatch* 8 July 22/3 The Football Association do not regard their clean-up of non-professional Soccer as completed by the sensational exposure and punishment of four hundred 'shamateurs' and their accomplices in the North. **1955** T. H. PEAR *Eng. Social Differences* 247 An Oxbridge college which trained its 'eight' so rigidly that they did not take a reasonable part in university life, was criticised as exposing the University to the suspicion of encouraging 'shamateurs'. **1962** *Punch* 18 Apr. 627/2 The bitchery of high shamateur tennis. **1973** RIESSEN & EVANS *Match Point* I. x. facing p. 92 (*caption*) It was hard work being a 'shamateur'—lugging all that booty around.
Hence '**shamateurism**.
**1928** *Sat. Rev.* 4 Feb. 126 Where the interests of amphitheatre and arena come first, 'shamateurism' must pass eventually into an honest professionalism. **1964** *Punch* 6 May 668/1 Shamateurism has grown steadily in lawn tennis. **1979** *Financial Rev.* (Sydney) 27 Aug. 25/2 Shamateurism is common enough and their activities probably do not inflict any real damage.

‖**shamba** ('ʃæmbə). *East African.* [Swahili.] A cultivated plot of ground. Also, a farm or plantation.
**1878** H. M. STANLEY *Dark Cont.* ii. 51 But the highest ambition of a Mgwana [freeman of Zanzibar] is to have a house and shamba or garden of his own. **1901** *Geog. Jrnl.* Nov. 551 The greater number of whom [manumitted slaves in East Africa] have settled on 'shambas' upon conditions entered into with the Arab cultivators. **1942** *E. Afr. Ann. 1941–2* 17/2 They are to be found in every kind of work.. from shamba labourer to school teacher. **1952** *Chambers's Jrnl.* Apr. 247/1 There would be rain soon and the ground must be ready for planting before it came. There were two shambas to be cultivated, one for millet and one for beans. **1973** *Reader's Digest* Feb. 200/1 Most Kenyans, for example, have *shambas* (small farms) back in their tribal homelands. **1980** *Times* 23 Feb. 6/2 Jos had pegged out several acres to turn into a coffee shamba.

**shambe**, obs. form of SHAWM *sb.*

**shamble** ('ʃæmb(ə)l), *sb.*[1] Forms: α. 1 **scomul, -el, scoemel, sceamel, -ol, -ul, scæmol, scamul, -ol, 1–2 scamel, 2 scæmel, 3 scheomel, schamel, 4 schamil, shamyll, 4–5 shamel, 5 schamel, -ylle, sh(e)amle, schamylle, shaumelle, 5–6 shamell, 6 (9 *dial.*) shammel, shamil, shamwelle, shammoulle.** β. 5 **sheamble, 5–6 schambylle, 6** *pl.* **sh-, chambulles, shambylles, 7 shambel, 6– shamble.** [OE. *sc(e)amel* masc., = OS. (*fôt*) *skamel* (MLG. *schemel*, MDu. *schamel, schemel*, mod.Fris. *skammel*), OHG. (*fuoz*) *scamel, -il* (MHG. *schamel, schemel*, mod.G. *schemel*); a Com. WGer. adoption of L. *scamellum* dim. of *scamnum* bench. From LG. is prob. ON. *skemill* (Da. *skammel*), whence SCAMBLE *sb.*]
†**1.** A stool, footstool. Chiefly in fig. context.
*c* **825** *Vesp. Ps.* cix. 1 Oð ðæt ic sette feond ðine scomul [*scabellum*] fota ðinra. *a* **1225** *Ancr. R.* 166 Vor þi alle þe halewen makeden of al þe worlde ase ane stol [*MS. Cleopatra* scheomel; *MS. Titus* schamel] to hore uet, uorto arechen þe heouene. *a* **1340** HAMPOLE *Psalter* xcviii. 5 Heghis þe lord oure god, and loutis þe shamyll of his fete: for it is haly. **1483** *Cath. Angl.* 333/1 A Schamylle (*MS. Addit.* Schambylle), vbi A stule (*MS. Addit.* Macellum).
**2.** † **a.** In OE., a table or counter for exposing goods for sale, counting money, etc. *Obs.*
**971** *Blickl. Hom.* 71 He þa ineode on þæt haliȝe Salemannes templ, & þa ut aweарp þa sceomolas þara cypemanna. **1289** in *Wood's MS.* C. 1. lf. 36 Shopa cum sponda quae dicitur schamel [in the Bucherow].
**b.** *spec.* A table or stall for the sale of meat.
α. *c* **1305** *Of Men Lif*, etc. xv, in *E.E.P.* (1862) 155 Hail be ȝe potters [? bochers] wiþ ȝur bole ax..ȝe stondiþ at þe schamil [*printed* sthamil in *Rel. Ant.* II. 176], brod ferlich bernes. **1548** in E. Green *Somerset Chantries* (1888) 191 [John Spiringe and Peter Leighe hold a] shamell [there, and render per ann. xxiiij s.]. *Ibid.* 201 [John Kape holds a meat] shamell [in Fore strete].
β. **1577** V. LEIGH *Surv.* D iij b, And in like maner of profites of Bothes, standinges, shambles and tolles or other profits of a wekely market..kept within. **1844** W. BARNES *Poems Rural Life* 346 *Shambles*, Butchers' benches or stalls. **1850** S. DOBELL *Roman* i. 11 The form that served The world for signs of beauty, parcell'd out A carcase on the shambles. **1886** *W. Somerset Word-bk.*, *Shambles*, portable covered stalls, set up in a market-place for the sale of meat. Not applied to the market itself. Precisely the same erection for the sale of any other article would be a 'standing'.
*fig.* **1830** J. MILNE *Widow & Son* ii. (1851) 155, I mean to give a short preamble Because it tallies with the common run Of tales laid on the literary shamble.
**3. a.** *pl.* A place where meat (or occas. fish) is sold, a flesh- or meat-market. ? Now *local.*
*a* **1410–** [see FLESH-SHAMBLES]. **1484** *Nottingham Rec.* III. 229 The twychell betwix þe Shaumelles and þe Draperie. *a* **1490** BOTONER *Itin.* (1778) 170 In vico de Worshyp-strete alias shamellys sive bocherye. *Ibid.*, In vico vocato le shamelys. **1554** *Roll of Totnes Guild Merchants*, Received ffor the fishe shamells at the hands of James Pelliton, beeyng lett unto hym at ferme, liij[s] viij[d]. **1574** in *10th Rep. Hist. MSS. Comm.* App. v. 424 To send ther fleash..to the fleash shammoulles ther to be sold.
β. **1477** in *10th Rep. Hist. MSS. Comm.* App. v. 312 If ony man..sill fleshe within the citie..till it come to the Kyngs sheambles. **1556** *Chron. Grey Friars* (Camden) 55 Sent Martyns at the chambulles end, sent Nicolas in the chambulles, and sent Ewyns. *Ibid.* 58 The viij. day of March [1549] a bucher of sent Nicolas shambulles was put on the pyllery. *Ibid.* 77 Item the xvij. day of May [1553] the market in Newgate market was removyd unto..the shambylles where sent Nicolas church sometyme was. **1565** COOPER *Thesaurus*, *Carnarium*, a lardar: the shambles: flesh meate. *c* **1570** W. WAGER *The longer thou livest* 251 (Brandl), In S. Nicholas shambles, ther is inough. **1634** SIR T. HERBERT *Trav.* 10 They haue Shambles of men and womens flesh, ioynted and cut in seuerall Morsels. **1653** H. COGAN tr. *Pinto's Trav.* xxxiv. 137 This City hath an hundred and three score Butchers shambles, and in each of them an hundred stalls. **1688** HOLME *Armoury* III. 292/2 At the Shambles, where they [*sc.* Butchers] sell their meat. **1699** DAMPIER *Voy.* II. I. 31 Dogs and Cats are killed purposely for the Shambles. **1725** WATTS *Logic* (1736) 319 Raw Meat is bought in the Shambles. **1835** *Munic. Corp. Rep.* IV. 2627 (Chester), The Shambles are let weekly upon the market day, in standings.
**b.** Construed as a singular; also in sing. form.
**1570** LEVINS *Manip.* 18/31 Y[e] shamble, *macellum.* **1617** MORYSON *Itin.* I. 87 There is the Pallace of a Gentleman, who proving a Traytor, the State..turned the same into a shambles, and some upper chambers to places of judgement. The fish market lies by this shambles. **1623** FLETCHER *Rule a Wife* III. i, I stink like a stal-fish shambles. **1636** BRATHWAIT *Rom. Emp.* 64 He was called of many Macellinus, of the Latine word *Macellum* a shambles, or butchery.
**c.** *transf.* and *fig.*
**1608** [see FLESH-SHAMBLES b]. **1610** DONNE *Pseudo-martyr* Pref. C 2, As..he would make in this Kingdome a spirituall shambles of your soules, by corrupt doctrines: so..he labours to make a Temporall shambles and market of your bodies, by selling you for nothing, and thrusting you vpon the Ciuill sword. **1843** WHITTIER *Massach. to Virginia* 50 Watching round the shambles where human flesh is sold.
**4. a.** *pl.* The place where animals are killed for meat; a slaughter-house.
**1548** UDALL, etc. *Erasm. Par. John* x. 1–5 They bee called to their foode, and not to the fleshe shambles to be killed. **1605** B. JONSON *Volpone* I. i, I..fat no beasts, To feede the shambles. **1726** SWIFT *It cannot rain but it pours*, A Flock of Sheep, that were driving to the Shambles. **1841** DICKENS *Barn. Rudge* lxxi, He was felled like an ox in the butcher's shambles. *a* **1873** LYTTON *Pausanias* I. ii. (1876) 65 Savage though the custom, it smells not so foully of the shambles.
**b.** Construed as a singular; also in sing. form.
**1696** BP. PATRICK *Comm. Exod.* xxx. (1697) 598 The vast number of Beasts that were slain..at the Sanctuary..would have made it smell like a Shambles. **1828** SCOTT *F.M. Perth* xv, Like the disgusting refuse of a shambles. **1885** M. BRIDGES *Pop. Mod. Hist.* 433 Nobles, priests and women were slaughtered like sheep in a shamble.
**5.** *transf.* and *fig.* **a.** A place of carnage or wholesale slaughter; a scene of blood. Chiefly *pl.* construed as *sing.*; rarely in sing. form.
**1593** NASHE *Christ's T.* 12 b, The Infidell-Romaines.. shall inuade thee, and make thy Citty..a shambles of dead bodies. **1607** CHAPMAN *Bussy d'Ambois* V. iv. 34 If I scape Monsieur's 'pothecary shops, Foutre for Guise's shambles! **1638** DRUMM. OF HAWTH. *Irene* Wks. (1711) 170 The Bodies of Common-wealths are already turned into Skeletons, the Cities into Sepulchres, the Fields into Schambles. **1641** J. JACKSON *True Evang. T.* I. 48 That it may appeare indeed, what bloud-hounds the Papists are, what a Shambles their Church is, consult a grand Witnesse of their own. *a* **1649** DRUMM. OF HAWTH. *Poems* (1711) 33/2 Earth turns an hideous Shamble, a Lake of Blood. **1741** WATTS *Improv. Mind* xviii. Wks. (1813) 139 When a person or his opinion is made the jest of the mob or his back the shambles of the executioner. **1794** COLERIDGE *Robespierre* I. i. 79 I've fear'd him, since his iron heart endured To make of Lyons one vast human shambles. **1868** FARRAR *Seekers* I. iii. 51 A brutal.. barbarity..often turned a house into the shambles of an executioner. **1901** 'LINESMAN' *Words by Eyewitness* ix. (1902) 177 What a shambles the deep valley between Inkweloane and Spitz Kop would have been!
**b.** *pl.* In more general use, a scene of disorder or devastation; a ruin; a mess. orig. *U.S.*
**1926** P. H. DE KRUIF *Microbe Hunters* III. iv. 83 Once more his laboratory became a shambles of cluttered flasks and hurrying assistants. **1942** E. WAUGH *Put out More Flags* ii. 150 Alastair learned, too, that all schemes ended in a 'shambles' which did not mean, as he feared, a slaughter, but a brief restoration of individual freedom of movement. **1966** M. R. D. FOOT *SOE in France* viii. 184 Helped the commandos to make a thorough shambles of the main dockyard. **1979** *Daily Tel.* 5 Sept. 6/6 Haiti remains a dictatorship, its economy in a shambles.
**6.** *Mining.* See quot. 1819. Also SHAMMEL *sb.*
**1671** *Phil. Trans.* VI. 2102 A Tin-shaft..which we sink down about a fathom, and then leave a little long square place, termed a Shamble, and so continue sinking from cast to cast. **1819** *T. Mortimer's Commerc. Dict.*, *Shambles*, among miners, a sort of niches or landing-places, left at such distances in the adits of mines, that the shovel-men may conveniently throw up the ore from shamble to shamble, till it comes to the top of the mine. **1881** RAYMOND *Mining Gloss.*, *Shambles*, shelves or benches, from one to the other of which successively ore is thrown in raising it to the level above, or to the surface.
**7.** *dial. pl.* 'The frame of wood that hangs over a shaft-horse in a cart' (Halliwell 1847).
[**1596**: see *shamble-stave* in 9]. **1677** PLOT *Oxfordsh.* 257 Having also a head of boards, and shambles over the thills. **1854** MISS A. E. BAKER *Northampt. Gloss.* II. 219.
**8.** ? A shoal. Perh. only *pl.* the name of a shoal off Portland Bill (hence Cook's use in quot. 1769).
**1769** COOK *Jrnl. 1st Voy.* (1771) 70 About three miles N.E. from Portland [in the Pacific] are several shoals, which we called the Shambles. **1774** J. HUTCHINS *Dorset* I. 587 The Shambles, called by Hollingshed the *Shingles*, is a bank of sand, lying about four miles E. by S. from the Bill [Portland]. **1800** C. STURT in *Naval Chron.* (1801) IV. 394 Carrying me dead upon the Shambles [off Portland], where the sea was running tremendously high.
**9.** *attrib.* and *Comb.*, as ***shamble door, -fly, -house, -oozing, warden***, also ***shambles-blood, shambles keeping***; ***shamble-seeking, -smelling*** adjs.; † **shamble-hook**, a hook for hanging meat upon; **shamble(s)-meat**, butcher's meat; **shamble-stave**, one of the bars forming 'shambles' (sense 7).
**1803** A. HUNTER *Georg. Ess.* I. 325 A compost made of *shambles-blood and saw-dust. **1889** RIDER HAGGARD *Cleopatra* II. vii, No lamb skipping at the *shamble doors can be more innocent of its doom than is Queen Cleopatra. **16..** MIDDLETON, etc. *Old Law* III. ii, Those *Shamble flies Which Butchers boyes snap betweene sleepe and waking. **1688** HOLME *Armoury* III. 313/2 A *Shamble Hook. **1847** LYTTON *Lucretia* II. xviii, [These] left the murderer leisure ..to render the insurances on the life of the latter less open to suspicion than if effected immediately on her entrance into that *shamble-house. **1559** FECKNAM in Strype *Ann. Ref.* (1709) I. II. App. ix. 26 There was no open Flesh eatinge, nor *Shambles kepeinge, in the Lent and Daies prohibitid. **1618** *Licence to eat Flesh* in *Penny Mag.* (1836) V. 259 Forbidding them all manner of *shamble-meates whatsoever. **1736** DRAKE *Ebor.* I. vi. 219 This city is as well supplied with all sorts of shambles-meat as most markets in England. **1891** *Reports Provinc.* (E.D.D.), I mind the time when old people [in Devonshire] said, 'It's more'n a month since we had any shammel-mate'. **1894** LEE-HAMILTON *Sonn. Wingless Hours* 102 A Paris gutter of the good old times, Black and putrescent in its stagnant bed, Save where the *shamble oozings fringe it red. **1638** G. DANIEL *Eclog.* i. 122 You..might..Scorne These *Shamble-seeking birds. **1603** DEKKER *Wonderf. Yeare* B 4, In *shamble-smelling roomes. **1596** MASCALL *Bk. Cattle* II. 120 Preparing the cart. ..Al the *shamble staues to be made of good dry and tough ash, which are to beare a burthen from the thyller. **1835** *App. Munic. Corpor. Rep.* II. 1095 (Axbridge), The *Shamble Wardens have the inspection of meat, fish and butter. *Ibid.* 1370 (Wells), Two officers, named Shamble Wardens are appointed..to inspect the meat.

**shamble** ('ʃæmb(ə)l), *sb.*[2] [f. SHAMBLE *v.*[2]]
**1.** A shambling gait.
**1828** DISRAELI *Viv. Grey* III. iii, His coronation pace degenerated into a strut, and then into a shamble. **1855** BAIN *Senses & Int.* II. iv. §9 The shamble of the elephant. **1881** J. GRANT *Cameronians* I. iii. 34 His once firm and stately stride had given place to what he called 'a species of half-pay shamble'. **1887** MARY E. WILKINS *Humble Rom.*, *Old Lady Pingree* 53 She..went across the room with a long shamble.
†**2.** *slang.* (See quot.) *Obs.*
*a* **1700** B. E. *Dict. Cant. Crew* s.v. *Shamble-legg'd*, *Shake your Shambles*, haste, begon.

'**shamble**, *a. rare.* [Prob. an attributive use of SHAMBLE *sb.*[1]; the expression *shamble legs* prob. meant originally 'legs straddling like those of the trestles of a shamble' (SHAMBLE *sb.*[1] 2 b). Cf. WFris. *skammels* (pl. of *skammel* shamble, board on trestles) used in the sense 'legs, esp. when badly formed' (Dijkstra *Fries. Woordenboek*).] Shambling, ungainly, awkward; ill-shaped, wry, distorted; also *Comb.*
**1607** G. WILKINS *Mis. Inforced Marr.* II. B 4 b, A leane fellowe, with sunke eyes, and shamble legges. **1639** [J. TAYLOR (Water-P.)] *Divers Crabtree Lect.* 100 He had a cleane Legge and a handsome Foote; but thou hast neither, a very shamble-shinne, and hast a foote of the slovings Last. *a* **1700** B. E. *Dict. Cant. Crew*, *Shamble-Legg'd*, one that goes wide, and shuffles his Feet about. **1709** MRS. CENTLIVRE *Man's Bewitched* III, Death, you shamble-ham'd Dog! I'll beat your head off. **1785** R. FORBES *Ulysses Answ.* 24 Thersites, Wha for's ill-scrappit tongue, An' shamble chafts, got on his back Puss wi' the nine tails hung. **1869** 'WAT. BRADWOOD' *The O.V.H.* xii, Butchers' ponies, and rough-coated, shamble-kneed cobs, just up from grass. **1897** LD. E. HAMILTON *Outlaws* xxvii. 303 'Hand up, ye shammel-shankit brute,' he continued, as his horse stumbled forward.

**shamble** ('ʃæmb(ə)l), *v.*[1] *rare.* [f. SHAMBLE *sb.*[1]] *trans.* To cut up or slaughter as in the shambles. † ***to shamble forth***: to cut up and dispose of (a corpse). Also '**shambled** *ppl. a.*
**1601** R. YARINGTON *Two Trag.* II. vi. E 2 b, [*Stage direction*] Merry begins to cut the body... *Enter* Truth. Ye glorious beames [of the moon]..Why doost thou lend assistance to this wretch, To shamble forth with bolde audacitie His lims, that beares thy makers semblance! **17..** *Remonstr. Prot. agst. Papists* in *Somers Tracts.* (1748) II. 248 (*bis*), As if their Intention were to convert the World, and not to Kill the King, Garble the Parliament, Shamble all good and sober Protestants of every Party. **1869** LD. LYTTON *Orval* V. ii. 249 It was a desperate sortie. *The Count.* Desperate? ay, They shambled us like sheep.

**shamble** ('ʃæmb(ə)l), *v.*[2] [Prob. f. SHAMBLE *a.* Cf. Fris. *skammelje*, 'to walk irregularly, esp. with badly-formed legs' (Dijkstra).] *intr.* To go with an awkward ungainly gait, to walk awkwardly or unsteadily, usually with adv. as ***to shamble along***.
**1681** [see SHAMBLING *vbl. sb.*]. **1690–** [see SHAMBLING *ppl. a.*]. **1717** GARTH *Ovid's Met.* XIV. *Vertumnus & Pomona* 36 The heedless lout comes shambling on. **1746** FRANCIS tr. *Horace, Ep.* II. i. 233 Dossennus slip-shod shambles o'er the Scene. **1764** GRAY *Jemmy Twitcher* 9 He shambles and straddles so oddly. **1837** DICKENS *Pickw.* xxiv, Jinks.. shambled to a seat, and proceeded to write it down. **1867** TROLLOPE *Chron. Barset* xlix. II. 54 Every morning he

shambled across from the deanery to the Cathedral. **1902** BUCHAN *Watcher by Threshold* 83 He turned and shambled down the passage.

**b.** of an animal.

**1859** *Blackw. Mag.* LXXXVI. 244/2 The bears of the north have scented their quarry—they come near you and nearer, shambling and rolling their bulk. **1878** BOSW. SMITH *Carthage* xxi. 439 Each [camel] grunting and grumbling as he shambles along.

**c.** quasi-*trans.* To make (one's way) or move (one's feet) shamblingly.

**1847** LYTTON *Lucretia* II. vii, The sweep..let himself out, and shambled his way to his crossing. **1859** *Habits of Gd. Society* vii. 250 Another shambles his feet along the pavement.

**shamble**, obs. form of SHAWM.

**'shambled**, *ppl. a.* [f. SHAMBLE *v.*[1] + -ED [1]]

**1.** Cut up or slaughtered as in the shambles. *rare.*

**1900** *Daily News* 26 May 3/3 To..slaughter the British soldiers like shambled deer.

**2.** *U.S.* Wrecked, ruined. Cf. SHAMBLE *sb.*[1] 5 b.

**1940** *Newsweek* 17 June 21/2 (*caption*) Nazis photographed the shambled Dunkerque's water front. **1952** *Time* 11 Aug. 25/1 (*caption*) Reconstruction of the shambled town..is expected to take at least five years.

**shambling** ('ʃæmblɪŋ), *vbl. sb. rare.* [f. SHAMBLE *v.*[2] + -ING[1].] An awkward motion in walking or progression.

**1681** DRYDEN *Span. Friar* I. ii, By that shambling in his walk, it should be my rich old banker Gomez. **1862** F. W. ROBINSON *Owen* IV. ix, Presently he heard the rustling of her dress, and the shambling of her feet across the narrow landing-place. **1887** JESSOPP *Arcady* iv. 116 Think of the weary shambling through the mud and rain.

**shambling** ('ʃæmblɪŋ), *ppl. a.* [f. SHAMBLE *v.*[2] + -ING[2].]

**1.** That shambles or is characterized by an awkward, irregular gait or motion.

**1690** DRYDEN *Amphitryon* II. i, One pair of shambling legs, with two splay feet. **1697** VANBRUGH *Relapse* V. v. 67 A long, loose, shambling sort of a Horse. **1771** SMOLLETT *Humph. Cl.* 15 July (1815) 249 Mounted on a tall, meagre, raw-boned, shambling grey gelding. **1798** M. PILKINGTON *Dict. Painters* (new ed.) 791 [Francis Heyman is] easily distinguishable by the large noses and shambling legs of his figures. **1837** DICKENS *Pickw.* xx, A shambling pot-boy. **1838** —— *Nich. Nick.* xxxiv, Who..made a great many shambling bows. **1880** A. H. HUTH *Buckle* II. 72 His gait was stooping, and his walk rather shambling.

**b.** *transf.* and *fig.* Often of metre and style, etc.

**1802** MAR. EDGEWORTH *Rosanna* iii, Upon the profits of this place, Simon contrived to live in a shambling sort of way. **1875** SWINBURNE *Ess. & Stud.* 283 The slippery style and shambling license which we pardon in Decker. **1882** STEVENSON in *Longman's Mag.* I. 78 He crams all this matter, tail foremost, into a single shambling sentence. **1887** SAINTSBURY *Elizab. Lit.* iv. 151 A third [characteristic].. makes them..tedious reading, independently of their shambling metre.

**2.** Of jointed tools: Rickety in action.

**1829** HOGG *Sheph. Cal.* I. 45 A pair o' shambling shears. **1833** J. HOLLAND *Manuf. Metal* II. 204 The brass articles [tongs]..are liable to get loose and shambling.

Hence **'shamblingly** *adv.*

**1872** *Daily News* 2 Oct. 5 A grimy miner..slouched shamblingly homeward. **1894** SALA *London up to date* vi. 73 On rare occasions I do contrive to crawl shamblingly through the streets for half an hour or so.

**†'shambo.** *Sc. Obs.* Also 8 shamboe, 9 shambeau. [? Corruption of CHAMOIS *sb.*] *Attrib.* in ***shambo leather***, chamois leather (CHAMOIS *sb.* 2). Also in ***shambo skin.***

**1612** *Sc. Bk. Rates* in *Halyburton's Ledger* (1867) 310 Gloves of shambo lether the dozen pair xlviii s. *a* **1706** in *J. Watson's Collect. Sc. Poems* I. 28 No windy flowrish'd flying Feathers, No sweet permusted shambo Leathers. **1755** in Macgill *Old Ross-sh.* (1909) 154, 5 large Shamboe skins for lyning breeches and pockets 7s 6d. **1807** J. HALL *Trav. Scot.* II. 516 The miniature figure of a man made of stuffed shambeau leather.

**shambo, -ok**, obs. forms of SJAMBOK.

**1810** *Barrington's Voy. N.S. Wales* I. 186 These sort of whips, which they call shambos, are most horrid instruments.

**shambolic** (ʃæm'bɒlɪk), *a. colloq.* [f. SHAMBLE *sb.*[1] 5 b, perh. after SYMBOLIC *a.*] Chaotic, disorderly, undisciplined.

Reported to be 'in common use' in 1958.

**1970** *Times* 18 June 9 His office in Printing House Square is so impeccably tidy that it is..a standing reproach to the standard image of shambolic newspaper offices. **1975** *Times* 14 June 8/5 The average listener is in the position of anybody who encounters an organization at work for the first time. It may appear shambolic but how much is that because he hasn't yet made sense of it. **1978** R. JANSSON *News Caper* xiii. 110 We may have a shambolic landing, Jean. I want you to go right through the aircraft reminding people about the emergency drill. **1980** *Jrnl. R. Soc. Arts* July 509/1 It will continue in a much more shambolic manner than the urbanization that has occurred in the Western World.

**†shambrier.** *Obs.* Also 6 shambriere, 9 shammbrie. [a. F. *chambrière*, etc.] A long lash used by the master of a manège.

**1667** W. CAVENDISH *Meth. Dressing Horses* 182 The Shambriere is too Dull a thing; and so are all Whips, Hand-whips, and all. **1728** CHAMBERS *Cycl.* s.v. *Rope*, When they begin to..teach him to flee from the Shambner [*later edd. corrected* shambrier], and not to gallop fastly or incompactly. **1852–63** BURN *Technol. Dict.* (ed. 4), *Shambrier*, (long leathern thong), *chambrière.* **1891** FLÜGEL *Eng.-Germ. Dict.* (ed. 4), *Shammbrie.*

**shambrogue**, obs. form of SHAMROCK.

**†shambrough.** *Her. Obs.*—[0] (See quots.)

**1780** EDMONDSON *Heraldry* II. Gloss., *Shambroughs*, a kind of shoe. [But the engraving represents a ship.] **1828–40** BERRY *Encycl. Her.* I. Gloss., *Shambroughs*, a kind of ship. **1847** *Gloss. Heraldry.*

**shambuc**, obs. form of SJAMBOK.

**1828** *Life Planter Jamaica* 141 The cow-skin,..of the West Indies, or the shambuc of the Cape.

**shambulle, -ylle**, obs. forms of SHAMBLE *sb.*[1]

**'sham-'damn**, *a.* [f. SHAM *sb.*[1] + DAMN *v.*] The distinctive epithet of an inferior kind of scrap-iron, used for making gun-barrels. Hence of firearms: Of wretched quality, 'shoddy'.

**1846** GREENER *Sci. Gunnery* 197 Sham damn iron is similar in nature to brass, a metal with fibres certainly, but they are like the fibres of willow compared to oak... All slave gun-barrels are made of it. **1851–4** *Tomlinson's Cycl. Usef. Arts* (1866) I. 818/1 These [pieces of scrap-iron] are sorted and used in preparing iron of various qualities, known as wire-twist,..twopenny, or Wednesbury-skelp, sham-damn-skelp. **1895** *Outing* XXVII. 63/2 A cheap, sham-dam arm should not be given to a boy, for it may prove his executioner.

**shame** (ʃeɪm), *sb.* Forms: α. 1 scamu, sceamu, 1–4 scame, 2–3 same, 3 seame, 3–4 scam, ssame, 3–5, 6 *Sc.* scham, 3–5, 6–7 *Sc.* schame, (4 chame), *Sc.* schaym(e, 4, 6 sham, 6 *Sc.* schamme, scheyme, (schaheme), 3– shame. β. 1 scomu, scomo, sceomu, 2–3 scome, 3 sceome, some, 3–4 scheome, schom, 3–5 schome, shome. [Com. Teut.: OE. *sc(e)amu*, *sc(e)ǫmu*, corresponds to OFris. *scome*, OS. *skama*, MDu. *schame* (mod.Du. *schaam-* in compounds), OHG. *scama* (MHG., mod.G. *scham*), ON. *skǫmm* with unexplained gemination (Sw., Da. *skam*), Goth. **skama* (inferred from the derivative *skaman* refl. to be ashamed):—OTeut. **skamō*.

From the Teut. root **skam-* are also OHG. *scant* ashamed (:—**skamdo-*), Goth. *skanda*, OHG. *scanda* (G. *schande*) fem., disgrace, OE. *scand* masc., infamous man, *scand* fem., infamous woman, disgrace, *scendan* (:—**skamdjan*) SHEND *v.*

Outside Teut. no root of corresponding form and sense has been found, but many scholars assume a pre-Teut. **skem-*, variant of **kem-* to cover (Teut. **hem-*: *ham-* as in HAME[1]), 'covering oneself' being the natural expression of shame.]

**I. 1. a.** The painful emotion arising from the consciousness of something dishonouring, ridiculous, or indecorous in one's own conduct or circumstances (or in those of others whose honour or disgrace one regards as one's own), or of being in a situation which offends one's sense of modesty or decency.

*c* **725** *Corpus Gloss.* (Hessels) P. 844 *Pudor*, scomo. *c* **950** *Lindisf. Gosp.* Luke xiv. 9 Ðu inginnas mið sceoma [*cum rubore*] þæt hlætmesto stoue ȝehalda. *a* **1225** *St. Marher.* 7 Ah þe schulde scheomien..ȝef þu scheome cuðest þat þulli mot haldest wið a ȝung meiden. *c* **1250** *Gen. & Ex.* 349 Flesses fremeðe and safte same boðen he felten on here licham. **1471** CAXTON *Recuyell* (Sommer) I. 240 Alle shame and vergoyne redowblith in me. **1595** SHAKS. *John* IV. i. 114 You will but make it blush, And glow with shame of your proceedings, Hubert. **1623** FLETCHER & ROWLEY *Maid in Mill* I. iii, But for my part (in all humility And with no little shame) I ask your pardons. **1711** STEELE *Spect.* No. 114 ¶4 Shame of Poverty makes Laertes lanch into unnecessary Equipage. **1842** TENNYSON *Ld. of Burleigh* 63 As it were with shame she blushes. **1860** PUSEY *Min. Proph.* 240 Shame at the evil which sin is, works repentance.

*Personified.* **1590** SPENSER *F.Q.* II. vii. 22 Lamenting Sorrow did in darknesse lye, And Shame his vgly face did hide from liuing eye. **1742** GRAY *Eton* 64 Pallid Fear, And Shame, that sculks behind.

**b.** *pl.*

**1851** HELPS *Comp. Solit.* viii. 152 Being free from many of the usual small shames, petty ends, trivial vanities.

**c.** ***sense of shame***: the consciousness of this emotion, guilty feeling; also, the right perception of what is improper or disgraceful (cf. 2).

**1647** C. HARVEY *Schola Cordis* xv. 29 Untill the sense of shame Makes me contemne my self-dishonour'd name. **1700** DRYDEN *Cinyras & Myrrha* 307 Another, and another Night she came; For frequent Sin had left no Sense of Shame. **1766** FORDYCE *Serm. Yng. Women* (1767) I. i. 11 All but those who..have..lost their sense of shame. **1847** TENNYSON *Princess* IV. 330 And full of cowardice and guilty shame, I grant in her some sense of shame, she flies. **1872** DARWIN *Emotions* xiii. 321 Under a keen sense of shame, there is a strong desire for concealment.

**d.** ***past shame, dead to shame***, no longer capable of feeling shame, grown callous to shame.

**1509** [see PAST *prep.* 3]. **1647** HEXHAM I. s.v., He is past shame. **1780** WARNER in Jesse *Selwyn & Contemp.* (1844) IV. 325 His wife and her sister are not great enough or little enough to be dead to shame.

**2.** Fear of offence against propriety or decency, operating as a restraint on behaviour; modesty, shamefastness. ***without shame***, shameless(ly.

*c* **1386** CHAUCER *Wife's Prol.* 342 In habit maad with chastitee and shame Ye wommen shul apparaille yow. **1576** GASCOIGNE *Grief of Joye* IV. xxxv. Wks. 1910 II. 555 The dark-some nyght, sharpe enemye to shame, By candles light, betrayethe many a dame. **1590** SHAKS. *Mids. N.* III. ii. 285 Haue you no modesty, no maiden shame, No touch of bashfulnesse? **1622** MABBE tr. *Aleman's Guzman d'Alf.* II. 131 Discouering those parts which shame bids vs hide. **1692** R. L'ESTRANGE *Josephus, Antiq.* IV. viii. (1733) 97 A Debtor that hath neither the Shame nor the Conscience to restore what he borrowed. **1780** BENTHAM *Princ. Legisl.* xii. §10 Where robberies are frequent and unpunished robberies are committed without shame. **1875** JOWETT *Plato* (ed. 2) V. 45 To infuse into them that divine fear, which we call shame. *Mod.* I am not surprised at his request; he is quite without shame.

*Personified.* *c* **1400** *Rom. Rose* 3058 And grauntid hir.. That Shame, bicause she is honest, Shal keper of the roser be. **1754** GRAY *Poesy* 64 Her track, where'er the Goddess roves, Glory pursue, and generous Shame.

**3. a.** Disgrace, ignominy, loss of esteem or reputation.

*a* **990** CYNEWULF *Crist* 1274 Hi þær scoma mæste dreoȝað. *c* **1175** *Lamb. Hom.* 59 To..kepen us from hearm and scome. *a* **1300** *K. Horn* 327 Schame mote þu fonge & on hiȝe rode anhonge. **1362** LANGL. *P. Pl.* A. IV. 28 For to sauen hem-self from schome and from harme. *c* **1385** CHAUCER *L.G.W.* 1028 Thour out the worl oure shame is kid so wyde. **1535** COVERDALE *Ezek.* xvi. 52 Therfore beare thine owne shame. **1590** SHAKS. *Com. Err.* IV. iv. 70 Free from these slanders, and this open shame. **1729** BUTLER *Serm.* Wks. 1874 II. 14 Men, to avoid the shame of one villainy, are sometimes guilty of a greater. **1764** BURN *Poor Laws* 199 By once inflicting shame on a criminal, we for ever remove that fear of it, which is one very strong preservative against doing evil. **1845** SARAH AUSTIN *Ranke's Hist. Ref.* I. 194 After such high-raised expectations, the result was shame and ignominy. **1859** TENNYSON *Enid* 101 Far better were I laid in the dark earth..Than that my lord thro' me should suffer shame.

**b.** An instance or piece of disgrace.

*c* **1230** *Hali Meid.* 8 (Bodley MS.) Teonen þolien, & gromen & scheomen. *c* **1385** CHAUCER *L.G.W.* 589 So fil it as fortune hym aughte a schame. *a* **1470** HARDYNG *Chron.* CXIV. xviii, Thus synnes olde make shames come full newe. *a* **1586** SIDNEY *Arcadia* II. (Sommer) 99 Though..euery death were followed with a thousand shames. **1606** SHAKS. *Ant. & Cl.* I. iv. 72 Let his shames quickely Driue him to Rome. **1633** LD. BROOKE *Poems, Treat. Warres* vii. 71 So be the Shames of Peace, the Pride of Warre. **1880** MCCARTHY *Own Times* IV. 32 The calamities and shames of 1865 might have been avoided. **1891** FARRAR *Darkn. & Dawn* i, The name of her sister Drusilla had been already stained with a thousand shames.

**c.** *spec.* Violation of a woman's honour, loss of chastity. † ***to do (a) shame***, to offer violence (to). ***child, son of shame***, a child born out of wedlock.

*c* **1205** LAY. 12101 Melga nom Oriene..& scome hire bihedde & ladde heo to his bedde. *c* **1385** CHAUCER *L.G.W.* 488 That al here lyf ne don nat but asayen How manye wemen they may don a schame. **1590** SPENSER *F.Q.* III. v. 13 After that foster fowle he fiercely rid, To bene auenged of the shame, he did To that faire Damzell. **1603** SHAKS. *Meas. for M.* III. i. 140 Is't not a kind of Incest, to take life From thine owne sisters shame? **1722** DE FOE *Col. Jack* (1840) 2 My nurse..bred me up very carefully with her own son, and with another son of shame like me. **1813** BYRON *Giaour* 421 And every woe a tear can claim, Except an erring sister's shame. **1827** SCOTT *Surg. Dau.* ii, A child of shame, deserted by its father and mother. **1833** TENNYSON *Sisters* 8 She mix'd her ancient blood with shame. **1864** —— *Aylmer's Field* 687 The poor child of shame.

**†d.** ***shames death*** (***deid, dede***, etc.), a shameful death. *Obs.*

*a* **1300** *Cursor M.* 1619 He suar his ath þat þai suld all thole schammes deid. *c* **1386** CHAUCER *Merch. T.* 1133 God yeve yow bothe on shames deeth to dyen! *c* **1440** *Bone Flor.* 1823 God gyf the schames dedd. *c* **1450** *St. Cuthbert* (Surtees) 7829 Þai had aftir an yuel spede, Shames deed or outelawde. **16..** *Sir John Butler* iv. in Child *Ballads* III. 330/1 A shames death may hee dye!

**†e.** Infliction of disgrace, injurious language or conduct. (Cf. the phrases in 11.) *Obs.*

*c* **975** *Rushw. Gosp.* Mark xii. 4 Mið scomum miclum toȝiworhtun [*contumeliis affecerunt*]. *a* **1225** *Ancr. R.* 108 In his earen he hefde,..al þe schorn, & alle þe scheomen þet earen muhte iheren. **1526** *Pilgr. Perf.* (W. de W. 1531) 300 b, Than began all the multytude with moost shame and abhomynacyon..to spyt in thy blessed face.

**†4.** What is morally disgraceful or dishonourable; baseness in conduct or behaviour. ***to do shame***, to do something disgraceful or wicked.

*a* **1300** *Cursor M.* 25497 Ken us lauerd, for þi nam, Forsak bat sin and scam. *c* **1386** CHAUCER *Wife's T.* 295 Men may wel often fynde A lordes sone do shame and vileynye. *c* **1400** *Destr. Troy* 13704 He cast hym by course..To venge of his vilany & his vile schame. *a* **1520** DUNBAR '*Be ȝe ane luvar*' 6 Be layth alway to do amiss or schame. **1682** SIR T. BROWNE *Chr. Mor.* III. §17 If that degenerous vice possess thee, hide thyself in the shadow of thy shame, and pollute not noble society.

**5. a.** Used predicatively (without article) for: A fact or circumstance which brings disgrace or discredit (*to* a person, etc.); matter for severe reproach or reprobation. Now *poet.*

*a* **1000** *Colloq. Ælfric* in Wr.-Wülcker 100 Micel hynd and sceamu [*uerecundia*] hyt is menn nelle wesan þæt þæt he ys. *c* **1200** ORMIN 11956 Forr þatt wass, alls he wisste itt wel, Hiss aȝhenn shame & shande. *c* **1380** WYCLIF *Wks.* (1880) 72 It is schame to written it but more to done it in dede. *c* **1386** CHAUCER *Prol.* 505 And shame it is, if a preest take keep, A shiten shepherde and a clene sheep. *c* **1475** *Rauf Coilȝear* 87

For first to lofe and syne to lak, Peter! it is schame. **1538** STARKEY *England* I. iv. 125 Thys ys not only grete hurte to the commyn wele, but also grete schame and dyshonowre to our cuntrey. **1593** SHAKS. *Rich. II*, II. i. 238 Now afore heauen, 'tis shame such wrongs are borne In him a royall Prince. **1784** COWPER *Tiroc.* 78 Truths.. That 'tis our shame and mis'ry not to learn. **1819** SCOTT *Ivanhoe* xl, It were shame to our profession were we to suffer it. **1850** TENNYSON *In Mem.* xlviii. 11 She.. holds it sin and shame to draw The deepest measure from the chords. **1896** A. E. HOUSMAN *Shropshire Lad* v, Some lads there are, 'tis shame to say, That only court to thieve.

**b.** Similarly ***a shame, a great shame***. Now common in colloq. use.

**1390** GOWER *Conf.* II. 28 Which were a schame unto his trowthe. *c* **1450** *Mirk's Festial* 27 Hit was a gret schame to all hom þat werne gret clerkes. **1577** B. GOOGE *Heresbach's Husb.* I. (1586) 16 b, If it be a shame for.. a pleadar of causes to be ignorant of the lawe wherein he dealeth, a greater shame is it for a professor of husbandry, to be vnskilful in the ground whereon his whole trade lyeth. **1648** *Hunting of Fox* 36 'Tis a foul shame that you should be last in returning to a sence of your duty. **1662–3** PEPYS *Diary* 19 Jan., They.. pay fifteen or twenty sometimes per cent. for their money which is a most horrid shame. **1799** HT. LEE *Canterb. T.*, *Frenchman's T.* (ed. 2) I. 199 What a shame yon pretty cot should be suffered to go to ruin! **1809** MALKIN *Gil Blas* VII. v, It was a burning shame to see such a waste of provisions. **1815** SCOTT *Guy M.* xxxix, I envy you the concatenation, Colonel—it is a shame to me not to have drawn the same conclusion. **1858** S. BROOKS *Gord. Knot* xvi. 119 'It's a —— shame', jerked out Mr. Spenser. **1866** GEO. ELIOT *F. Holt* xxii, It's a sin and a shame. **1889** J. K. JEROME *Three Men in Boat* 166 George said it was a wicked shame of Mrs. G.

**c.** Occas. in non-predicative use: A disgraceful thing, something to be ashamed of. *poet.*

*c* **1600** SHAKS. *Sonn.* lxi. 7 Into my deeds to prye, To find out shames and idle houres in me. **1850** TENNYSON *In Mem.* li. 7 Shall he for whose applause I strove.. See with clear eye some hidden shame And I be lessen'd in his love? **1855** —— *Maud* III. iv, A peace that was full of wrongs and shames.

**6. a.** A person or thing that is a cause or source of disgrace. Const. *to*, *of*, †*on*.

*a* **1586** SIDNEY *Arcadia* II. (Sommer) 99 That only I.. should become a plague to my selfe and a shame to womankind. **1607** SHAKS. *Cor.* I. iv. 31 You Shames of Rome. **1675** J. OWEN *Indwelling Sin* xiii. (1732) 165 It may be this Day you had been a Terror to your selves, a Shame to your Relations. **1681** COTTON *Wond. Peak* 76 Environ'd round with Natures shames and Ills, Black Heaths, wild Rocks, bleak Craggs, and naked Hills. **1709–11** POPE *Ess. Crit.* 694 Erasmus, that great injur'd name, (The glory of the Priesthood, and the shame!). **1757** GRAY *Bard* 87 Ye towers of Julius, London's lasting shame. **1778** [W. H. MARSHALL] *Minutes Agric., Digest* 113 Colleges of Agriculture, reared in those Wastes which are now a shame on their Country. **1819** SHELLEY *Cenci* III. i. 287 Nature casts him off, who is her shame.

**b.** *colloq.* A thing which is shockingly ugly or indecent, or of disgracefully bad quality.

**1764** GRAY *Jemmy Twitcher* 8 His nose is a shame,—and his eyes are so lewd! **1815** SCOTT *Guy M.* v, Luckie Finniston sent up three [hens] that were a shame to be seen. **1880** TENNYSON *Village Wife* vii, An' 'e bowt little statutes all-naäkt an' which was a shaame to be seen.

**7.** *concr.* The privy members or 'parts of shame'. Now *rare* or *Obs.*

*a* **1000** *Cædmon's Gen.* 942 (Gr.), Het heora sceome þeccan frea frumhrægle. *c* **1050** *Voc.* in Wr.-Wülcker 470/23 *Preputia*, scama, þa wæpenlican limo. *c* **1250** *Gen. & Ex.* 351 Ðo gunen he same sriden, And limes in leues hiden. *a* **1300** *Cursor M.* 2026 His midelst þat right cam, Bihild, and sagh his fader schame. **1584** B. R. tr. *Herodotus* II. 86 Other [women] cast vp their clothes, & openly discouer and bewray their shame. **1599** T. M[OUFET] *Silkwormes* 3 Then fig-tree fannes uppon their shame they wore. **1611** BIBLE *Rev.* xvi. 15 Least hee walke naked, and they see his shame. [**1795** tr. *Thunberg's Trav.* (ed. 2) II. 78 The Hottentots universally wore a bag just before the parts of shame.] **1922** JOYCE *Ulysses* 533 And with loving pencil you shaded my eyes, my bosom and my shame.

**II.** Phrases.

**8.** ***to have shame***: to be ashamed, feel ashamed. Const. *of*, inf., *that*. Now *poet.*

*c* **888** ÆLFRED *Boeth.* xi. §1 Hi habbað sceame þæs welan ȝif hi ne beoð swa æþele on ȝebyrdum swa hi woldon. *c* **1175** *Lamb. Hom.* 137 And þere mide hine aleseð of scome þe he habben sculde ȝif he heo ne ȝef. *c* **1375** *Sc. Leg. Saints* i. (*Petrus*) 535 Sic schent and schame at hart had he. *Ibid.* xxvii. (*Machor*) 1014 Alswa had he schame to tell quhy [etc.]. *c* **1400** MAUNDEV. (1839) xii. 133 Sche had gret schame, that sche hadde a Child. *c* **1400** *Rule St. Benet* (Prose) 30 þat tay haue shame of þair faute. **1842** TENNYSON *Vision of Sin* IV. vi, Sit thee down, and have no shame, Cheek by jowl, and knee by knee.

**9.** ***to think shame***, to be ashamed. (Occas. *to think it shame*.) Const. *of*, *for*, inf., or *that*...

†**a.** The early examples belong to the impersonal THINK *v.*, const. *dative* (*him* etc. *thinketh shame*). *Obs.* **b.** In the 15th c. this construction gave place to that in which the verb is the personal THINK *v.*[2] Now somewhat *arch.*

**a.** *c* **1205** LAY. 28850 For mucchel scome heom þuhte þat wepmen heom ne rohte. *a* **1300** [see THINK *v.*[1] B. 2 a]. *a* **1400** *St. Alexius* 5 (Vernon MS.), To seruen god þhuȝte him no schome.

**b.** *c* **1470** HENRY *Wallace* x. 517 And for hys wrang reyff othir he sall think schame Or de tharfor. **1648** J. BEAUMONT *Psyche* I. cxi, And then eleven great Stars thought it no shame To couch before me who admired them. **1724–7** RAMSAY *Wyfe of Auchtermuchty* xv, I trow the man thocht mekle schame. **1791** [see THINK *v.*[2] B. 1 c]. **1816** SCOTT *Bl. Dwarf* ix, Thinkna ye shame o' yoursells, to come here.. to frighten a lone widow woman? **1871** FREEMAN *Norm. Conq.* (1876) IV. xviii. 187 Men thought it shame to dwell at such a time under the shadow of a house.

**10.** ***to take shame***. †**a.** To be disgraced, incur disgrace (*obs.*). **b.** To conceive shame, feel ashamed; to accept blame or disgrace as merited; to acknowledge that one is in fault. More fully ***to take shame to (unto, upon) oneself***.

**1338** R. BRUNNE *Chron.* (1810) 323 Grete pite it was, þat þe hede of Cristendam Suld for suche trespas take so foule a scham. **1509** HAWES *Past. Pleas.* XXXII. (Percy Soc.) 156, I was not proude, I toke of him no shame. **1603** SHAKS. *Meas. for M.* II. iii. 36, I doe repent me, as it is an euill, And take the shame with ioy. **1607** B. BARNES *Divils Charter* I. iii. B 2, Take to thee Gismond both the skorne and shame. **1712** STEELE *Spect.* No. 448 ¶3, I take shame upon myself for this Crime. **1727** BOYER *Dict. Royal* II. s.v., I take shame to my self, that, *J'avouë à ma honte, que*. **1821** SCOTT *Kenilw.* xv, I take shame to say, that [etc.]. **1869** GOULBOURN *Purs. Holiness* x. 91 So long as they take shame to themselves for the evil which is in them.

†**11.** ***to do*** (a person) ***shame***: to inflict injury or dishonour, offer reproach or obloquy (see also 3 c). Also ***to say*** or ***speak*** (one) ***shame***; ***to say*** or ***speak shame of, on, by***. Also with ***a*** and pl. *Obs.*

*c* **950** *Lindisf. Gosp.* Luke xi. 45 *Nobis contumeliam facis* us sceoma ðu does. *a* **1200** *Vices & Virtues* 51 Alle ðe scames and ðe bismeres ðe hie arrer him hadde idon. *a* **1225** *Leg. Kath.* 349 Ah gað ȝet & seggeð scheome bi ure undeadliche godes. *a* **1250** *Owl & Night.* 363 Yet þu me seyst an oþer schome þat ich an on Myn eye lome. **1297** R. GLOUC. (Rolls) 3239 Hii þoȝte to do þis lond ssame. *c* **1385** CHAUCER *L.G.W.* 467 Ne a trewe louere may me nat blame Thaw that I speke a fals louere sum schame. **1470–85** MALORY *Arthur* x. xxvii. 457 The letter spak shame by her and by sir launcelot. **1535** COVERDALE *Dan.* xi. 18 A prynce shal stoppe him, to do him a shame. **1595** SHAKS. *John* IV. iii. 97 If thou.. teach thy hastie spleene to do me shame. **1603** —— *Meas. for M.* III. i. 81 Why giue you me this shame? **1611** BIBLE *1 Sam.* xx. 34 Hee was grieued for Dauid, because his father had done him shame.

**12.** ***to put to shame***: to bring into disgrace, bring disgrace upon; also *fig.* to outshine, eclipse. Similarly, ***to bring***, †***shape***, †***turn to shame***. Also †***to go to shame***, to be ruined or spoilt.

*a* **1250** *Owl & Night.* 522 Hwenne þu hauest ido þi gome þi stefne goþ anon to schome [*Cotton MS.* shome]. *c* **1290** *Sancta Crux* 318 in *S. Eng. Leg.* 12 Cristine men þat he miȝte i-finde Alle he brouȝte to schame. *c* **1375** *Sc. Leg. Saints* ii. (*Paulus*) 521 He schupe þam all to schame, þat euir trowit in cristis name. *a* **1440** *Sir Degrev.* 127 He sey, 'Alle ȝoode to schome!' And went one hys wey. **1445** tr. *Claudian* in *Anglia* XXVIII. 269 With her also thou puttist to shame her loothsom norice ambicion. *c* **1470** HENRY *Wallace* x. 1004 The Roman [buikis] at than was in Scotland, He gart be brocht to scham, quhar thai thaim fand. **1591** SHAKS. *Two Gent.* IV. iv. 67 A Slaue, that still an end turnes me to shame. **1611** BIBLE *Heb.* vi. 6 They crucifie to themselues the Sonne of God afresh, and put him to an open shame. **1752** 'SIR H. BEAUMONT' tr. *Attiret's Acc. Emp. China's Gard.* 29 If any one of them is caught in the Fact [i.e. Thieving] he is brought to Shame. **1780** COWPER *Progr. Error* 245 Has time worn out, or fashion put to shame, Good sense, good health, good conscience, and good fame? **1855** THACKERAY *Newcomes* xli, No young woman of this year has come near her: those of the past seasons she has distanced, and utterly put to shame. **1865** F. PARKMAN *Huguenots* i. (1875) 5 Every ship from the New World came freighted with marvels which put the fictions of chivalry to shame.

**13. a.** ***for shame***: from a sense of shame, because one feels shame; also, for fear of shame, in order to avoid shame; so †***for shame of***, in order not to bring shame upon. Also ***for shame's sake***.

*c* **900** tr. *Bæda's Hist.* IV. xxiv. (1899) 482 þonne aras he for scome from þæm symble. *c* **1200** ORMIN 16971 Forrþi þatt he ne mihhte nohht O daȝȝ forr shame lernenn. *c* **1386** CHAUCER *Frankl. T.* 24 Save that the name of soveraynetee, That wolde he have for shame of his degree. **1592** SHAKS. *Ven. & Ad.* 36 He red for shame, but frosty in desire. **1592** MORYSON *Let.* 21 Oct. in *Itin.* (1617) I. 38 When I looked my face in a glasse, I could not for shame take this course. **1823** SCOTT *Quentin D.* xxxiii, I will grant you as fair terms as for very shame's sake you ought to ask in my present condition. **1859** TENNYSON *Vivien* 548 The shame that cannot be explain'd for shame.

**b.** esp. in adjuration or remonstrance. Hence often as an int. = 'shame on you!' 'you should be ashamed'; also *fie for shame!* (see FIE *int.* 1).

*a* **1300** *Cursor M.* 2794 For scam ne dos þam na males. *c* **1374** CHAUCER *Anel. & Arc.* 272 Mi swete fo, whi do ye so, for shame. *c* **1412** HOCCLEVE *De Reg. Princ.* 1057 Ffor shame! why makest þou al this wo? **1575** *Gammer Gurton's Needle* IV. ii. 42 Canst thou for shame deny it? **1592** SHAKS. *Ven. & Ad.* 379 'For shame', he cries, 'let go, and let me go'. *a* **1642** SUCKLING *Fragm. Aurea*, '*Why so pale and wan*', Quit, quit for shame. **1775** SHERIDAN *Rivals* II. ii, *Lucy.* For shame now! here is some one coming. **1840** THACKERAY *Shabby Genteel Story* v, At which remark.. Miss Caroline very properly said 'For shame, Becky!' **1850** MISS WARNER *Wide World* xxx, 'Oh, William!—William!—for shame! for shame!' said Ellen again.

†**14.** ***in shame of***: in order to put to shame. *Obs.*

**1596** DALRYMPLE tr. *Leslie's Hist. Scot.* I. 101 To put a gluue vpon the poynte of ane speir in exprobratione and schame of him quha crakit his creddence. **1601** SHAKS. *Jul. C.* II. ii. 41 The Gods do this in shame of Cowardice.

**15.** ***to one's shame***, so as to cause one shame, in a way that brings one discredit. Also parenthetically, with ellipsis of 'be it spoken'. In early use also †***to*** or †***for*** (one) ***to shame***.

*c* **1205** LAY. 21008 Heore ȝelp & heore gome ilomp heom seoluen to scame. **1382** WYCLIF *1 Cor.* vi. 5, I seie to ȝoure schame. **1390** GOWER *Conf.* II. 30 And yit for Demephon to schame Into this dai it berth the name. **1526** *Pilgr. Perf.* (W. de W. 1531) 42 His credytours claymeth dette of hym to his payne & great shame. **1596** SHAKS. *1 Hen. IV*, V. i. 93 For my part, I may speake it to my shame, I haue a Truant beene to Chiualry. **1815** SCOTT *Guy M.* xlvii, It is greatly to the shame of our young lover's apprehension, that [etc.]. **1835** MACAULAY in Trevelyan *Life* (1876) I. 444, I read some of his Dialogues of the Dead when I was thirteen; and to my shame, I never.. read a line of him since.

**16. a.** In ejaculatory formulae of imprecation or indignant disapproval, as (*a*) ***shame*** (or †***a shame***) ***betide*** (***take***, etc.).. *!*; (*b*) ***shame to*** or ***on***..*!*; (*c*) ***(the) more shame for***..; (*d*) ***shame!*** simply. Also ***for shame!*** (see 13 b); (*e*) used simply in S. Afr., as an expression of sympathy or pleasure.

(*a*) *a* **1352** MINOT *Poems* (ed. Hall) ii. 12 Schame bityde þe Skottes for þai er full of gile. *c* **1400** *Rom. Rose* 4267 God yeve him shame! **1568** GRAFTON *Chron.* II. 968 Shame come to him that is the cause thereof. **1593** SHAKS. *2 Hen. VI*, III. i. 307 Nay, then a shame take all.

(*b*) **1595** SHAKS. *John* II. i. 167 Now shame vpon you where she does or no. **1728** POPE *Dunciad* I. 113 Now (shame to Fortune!) an ill Run at Play Blank'd his bold visage. **1819** SHELLEY *Cenci* V. ii. 60 Shame on these tears! **1855** KINGSLEY *Westw. Ho!* xv, It can't be expected, and no shame to them!

(*c*) **1591** SHAKS. *Two Gent.* IV. iv. 138 The more shame for him, that he sends it me. **1662** STILLINGFL. *Orig. Sacræ* II. vi. §16 Did they not? the more shame for them: and if they did, the more shame for this great Rabbi thus to belie them. **1848** DICKENS *Dombey* vi, 'Ah! true! more shame for him,' thought Walter.

(*d*) **1605** SHAKS. *Macb.* III. iv. 66 Shame it selfe, Why do you make such faces? **1709** STEELE *Tatler* No. 21 ¶13 The whole Town cries out, Shame! That one of his Coat should be such an Atheist? **1834–51** MARY HOWITT *Sk. Nat. Hist.*, *Wolf* ii. 82 Oh, shame, that ever it hath been said, That bloody war is a glorious trade! **1848** *Times* 14 Nov. 5/2 A great many voices cried out 'Shame! shame!' **1887** *Pall Mall Gaz.* 29 Jan. 5/1 Sir Michael Hicks-Beach's proposal.. elicited cries of 'Shame!' from the Irish benches.

(*e*) **1932** *Grocott's Mail* (Grahamstown, S. Afr.) 9 Jan. 3 During the address of our local dairy representatives.. I heard several murmurs of Oh! and Shame! and grant the statements were given in a manner that commanded much sympathy. **1952** N. GORDIMER *Soft Voice of Serpent* (1953) i. 6 'Shame, isn't he a funny old man,' she said. **1976** *Sunday Times* (Johannesburg) 14 Nov., Oh, look, look!.. those foals. Oh, shame, aren't they sweet.

**b.** ***to cry shame on, upon***, †***of***: to express vigorous reprobation of.

**1599** SHAKS. *Much Ado* IV. i. 123 Why doth not euery earthly thing Cry shame vpon her? **1617** MORYSON *Itin.* II. 155 Don Jean.. commended highly the valour of our men, and cried shame upon the cowardise of his owne. **1721** DE FOE *Mem. Cavalier* (1840) 255 The people cried shame of them. **1849** MACAULAY *Hist. Eng.* iii. I. 360 The pavement was detestable: all foreigners cried shame upon it.

**III. 17.** *Comb.*, as (sense 7) ***shame-cloth***, ***-rag***; ***shame-burnt***, ***-closing***, ***-eaten***, ***-making***, ***-proof***, ***-shrunk***, ***-sick***, ***-stricken***, ***-swollen***, ***-wounded*** adjs.; **shame culture**, a culture in which conformity of behaviour is maintained through the individual's fear of being shamed; †**shamefish** = *pintle fish* (see PINTLE 3); **shameworthy** *a.*, of which one ought to be ashamed.

**1849** HELPS *Friends in C.* II. ii. (1854) 287 The shrinking, downcast, *shame-burnt woman. **1922** JOYCE *Ulysses* 55 She blinked up out of her avid *shameclosing eyes. **1963** M. LAURENCE *Tomorrow-Tamer* 226 Not yet five years old, she wore only a *shamecloth, a mere flutter of red and beaded rag around her middle and between her legs. **1947** R. BENEDICT *Chrysanthemum & Sword* x. 223 True *shame cultures rely on external sanctions for good behaviour. **1953** M. B. SINGER in Piers & Singer *Shame & Guilt* II. iii. 56, I shall consider whether the test data support the conclusion that American Indian cultures are predominantly shame cultures. **1977** A. GIDDENS *Stud. in Social & Polit. Theory* 393 Some anthropologists have sought to contrast the 'guilt cultures' of Western Europe with 'shame cultures'. **1859** MEREDITH *R. Feverel* viii, His diversion only irritated and confused our *shame-eaten youth. **1655** MOUFET & BENNET *Health's Improv.* xviii. 174 Yards or *shamefishes (*Colybdænæ*). **1672** JOSSELYN *New-Eng. Rarities* 32 Yardfish, Asses Prick or Shame-fish. **1934** R. MACAULAY *Going Abroad* xxxv. 297 He adoring some one else, that was *shame-making and humbling too. **1977** D. RAMSAY *You can't call it Murder* I. 26 Nothing to do with her, thank God. Offering such thanks was shame-making. **1588** SHAKS. *L.L.L.* v. ii. 513 We are *shame-proofe my Lord. **1938** R. GRAVES *Coll. Poems* 166 Those froward hermits.. Wore but a *shame-rag, dusk or dawn, And rolled in thorny places. **1631** QUARLES *Samson* Med. xvi. 97 Wee can trample Vpon our *shame shrunke cloakes, by your example. **15..** G. ELLIS *Lament. Lost Sheepe* in Farr *S. P. Eliz.* (1845) 410 With *shame-sick Adam haue I hid my head. **1848** THACKERAY *Van. Fair* xxix, Heart-stained, and *shame-stricken, he stood at the bed's foot. **1592** NASHE *P. Penilesse* Wks. 1904 I. 197 Would you.. gesse it were possible for any *shame-swolne toad to haue the spet-proofe face to out liue this disgrace? **1382** WYCLIF *Lev.* xvi. 4 And with lynnen breches he shal hile the *shame worthi [**1388** schamefast] membres. **1600** HOLLAND *Livy* xxxiv. 855 If they begin once to shame at that which is not shame-worthy. **1802** LAMB *Let. to Manning* 24 Sept., If I should have formed a diabolical resolution.. of not admitting any spirituous liquors into my house, will you be my guest on such shameworthy terms? **1922** JOYCE *Ulysses* 49 Our souls, *shamewounded by our sins, cling to us yet more.

**shame** (ʃeɪm), *v.* Pa. t. and pa. pple. shamed (ʃeɪmd). Forms: *α.* 1–2 sceamian, scami(ȝ)an, 2–3 scamien, 3 shamien, samie, schamie, ssame, scam, 3–6 schame, 4 ssamie, scham, 5 schamyn, 6

*Sc.* schaam, scheyme, 8 *dial.* sheame, sham, 3– shame; *β.* 1 scomian, sceomian, 3 scomien, sceomien, scheomen, schomye, scomye, scumi, 3–4 schome. [OE. *sc(e)amian, sc(e)ǫmian*, f. *sc(e)amu, sc(e)ǫmu* SHAME *sb.*

The verb corresponds formally to OS. *skamon*, OHG. *scamôn* (MHG. *schamen*), mod.NFris. *skaame, skômi*; an older Teut. formation is represented by Goth. *skaman*, OHG. *scamên*; and a third type by MHG. *schemen* (mod.G. *schämen*), ON. *skemma* (Sw. *skemma*, Da. *skjæmme* to disgrace, injure); ON. had also *skamma* (Da. *skamme* refl. to be ashamed).]

**1.** *intr.* To feel or conceive shame; to become or be ashamed. Const. *of, at, with, for. Obs.* exc. *dial.* (see *Eng. Dial. Dict.*).

(In OE. with genit. of cause, also of refl. pron. = to be ashamed of oneself.)

*Beowulf* 1026 (Gr.) No he þære feohȝyfte for sceotendum scamiȝan ðorfte. *c* **897** ÆLFRED *Gregory's Past. C.* lii. 409 Ðios sæ cwið ðæt ðu ðin scamiȝe, Sidon. *a* **1225** *Ancr. R.* 312 Nolde þe kniht beon sori & scheomen ful sore? *a* **1240** *Ureisun* in *O.E. Hom.* I. 185 þe sunne..leoseþ here liht and scomeþ aȝein þi brihte leor of hir þesturnesse. *a* **1300** *Cursor M.* 17429 Wit þis word scomed þan þe Iuus. **1340** HAMPOLE *Pr. Consc.* 7159 Þai salle swa schame ay of þair syn. *c* **1440** *Alphabet of Tales* 120 Som þat shamyd with þer syn, went & shrafe þaim clene þerof. **1534** in *Lett. Suppress. Monasteries* (Camden) 49 He hath a brasyn forehed, which shameth at nothing. ? *a* **1586** MONTGOMERIE *Misc. Poems* xxxii. (1887) 50, I thank my God I shame not of my shap. **1588** GREENE *Pandosto* (1607) E 3, And yet Dorastus, shame not at thy shepheards weede. **1606** W. CRASHAW *Rom. Forgeries* 52 The brazen face of the whore of Babylon, who shames with no sinne. **1651** JANE *Image Unbr.* 95 They..shame not at such assertions of falshood as common States blush to be detected of.

**b.** With clause expressing the reason. *arch.*

*c* **897** ÆLFRED *Gregory's Past. C.* x. 62 Ȝif we ðonne scomiað þæt we to uncuðum monnum swelc sprecen. *c* **1470** HENRY *Wallace* x. 491 Schamys thow nocht, that thow neuir ȝeit did gud? **1593** SHAKS. *Lucr.* 1143 Thou sing'st not in the day, As shaming any eye should thee behold. **1847** MRS. NORTON *Fisher's Drawing Room Scrap-bk.* 28, I shame that a creature so light, should bid me thus quiver and bleed.

**c.** Const. *to* (or †*for to*) and inf. Now *rare.*

**1375** BARBOUR *Bruce* VII. 436 Ȝhe aucht to shame..For to schut at me on fer! *c* **1400** MAUNDEV. (Roxb.) xx. 89 Men and wymmen..schamez noȝt for to schew þam as Godd made þam. *a* **1513** FABYAN *Chron.* VII. (1811) 328 Elyzabeth ..shamyd not, for Crystis sake, to wesshe yᵉ sorys & bylis of lazars. *a* **1541** WYATT *Compl. upon Love* in *Tottel's Misc.* (Arb.) 48 Now shames he not on me for to complain. **1598** B. JONSON *Ev. Man in Hum.* II. v. (1616) 28 Art thou a man? and sham'st thou not to beg? **1659** MILTON *Hirelings* Pref., Clergie who shame not..to maintain..their Popish and oft refuted positions. **1840** LADY C. BURY *Hist. of Flirt* xv, A folly I shamed to confess. **1862** MISS MULOCK *Dom. Stories* 210, I shame to say that [etc.].

**2.** *trans. impers.*, as in (*it*) *shames me* = I am ashamed. Const. *to* (or *for to*) and inf., a clause, or *for*; in OE. also genit. of cause. In later use only with *it*. Now *rare.*

*c* **897** ÆLFRED *Gregory's Past. C.* xxi. 164 Oððe hwa bið ȝescended, ðæt me forðæm ne scamiȝe? *c* **1000** ÆLFRIC *Gen.* ii. 25 Hi wæron þa butu nacode..and him þæs ne sceamode. *c* **1205** LAY. 4851 Him swiðe scomede þat he swa i-scend wes. *c* **1380** WYCLIF *Serm.* Sel. Wks. I. 22 Delve may Y not, and me shameþ for to begge. *c* **1386** CHAUCER *Man of Law's Prol.* 3 To asken help thee shameth in thyn herte. **1470–85** MALORY *Arthur* VIII. xxxix. 332 Me shamed att that tyme to haue more a doo with you.

**1577** *St. Augustine's Man.* 17 It shameth and irketh me to abide such thyngs as this world doth. **1652** NEEDHAM tr. *Selden's Mare Cl.* 77 It shamed that noble Nation to pay Tribute, who were wont to command it. **1847** LYTTON *Word to Public* 10 Omitting it from the list of those [writings] it does not shame me to acknowledge.

**3.** *trans.* To feel shame in regard to (a person or thing); to hold in awe or reverence; to dread or shun through shame. *Obs.* or *arch.*

**1382** WYCLIF *Mark* xii. 6 For by hap thei schulen schame my sone [*gloss* or drede with reuerence, Vulg. *reverebuntur*]. —— *Heb.* xi. 27 Not schamynge [*gloss* or dredynge, Vulg. *non veritus*], the hardnesse of the kyng. *a* **1592** GREENE *Jas. IV*, v. vi, My maister sad—(for why he shames the Court) Is fled away. **1885–94** R. BRIDGES *Eros & Psyche* May xxviii, And when at night her love flew to his place More than afore she shamed his fond embrace.

**4.** To make ashamed, fill with shame, cause to feel shame.

**1530** PALSGR. 701/1 I shame one,..I make one chaunge colours. **1593** SHAKS. *3 Hen. VI*, I. iv. 120 To tell thee whence thou cam'st, of whom deriu'd, Were shame enough to shame thee, Wert thou not shamelesse. **1639** MAYNE *City Match* IV. v. 43 Then, Sir, she is so modest... The least Obscene word shames her. **1735** POPE *Prol. Sat.* I. 89 Who shames a Scribbler? break one cobweb thro', He spins the slight, self-pleasing thread anew. **1847** TENNYSON *Princess* Prol. 132, I wish I were Some mighty poetess, I would shame you then, That love to keep us children! **1859** —— *Elaine* 207 Nay, father,..shame me not Before this noble knight. **1889** BARRIE *Window in Thrums* xviii. 166 The love Leeby bore for Jamie was such that in their younger days it shamed him.

†**b.** *refl.* To be ashamed. Const. *of, for*, or inf.

*a* **1250** *Owl & Night.* 161 (Jesus MS.) Schomye [*Cott.* Schamie] þe vor þine vnrede. *c* **1375** *Cato* 573 in *Minor Poems fr. Vernon MS.* 603 Þat þou ne const, schome þe not Of oþere to ben I-tauht. **1526** *Pilgr. Perf.* (W. de W. 1531) 64 And so he shameth hymselfe. **1825** SCOTT *Betrothed* xxxi, 'Rise, rise, De Lacy; and shame thee of thy petition,' said the King.

**c.** *pass.* To be ashamed. Const. *of, at, for, with,* †*upon*, inf., or subord. clause. Now *poet.*

**13..** *Cursor M.* 636 (Gött.) Naked war þai bath tway, þai were noght schamed par ma fay. *c* **1374** CHAUCER *Troilus* v. 1727 For sory of his frendes sorwe he is, And shamed, for his nece hath doon a-mis. *c* **1400** *Destr. Troy* 8250 Than shamet was the shalke for the shene ladies. *a* **1400–50** *Wars Alex.* 469 So was scho schamed of þe schont þat hire þe shalk made. **1613–16** W. BROWNE *Brit. Past.* I. ii. 31 The flowers pull'd in their heads as being sham'd Their beauties by the others were defam'd. **1815** SCOTT *Guy M.* xxvi, He's sair shamed o' himsell. **1847** TENNYSON *Princess* III. 35 Pardon, I am shamed That I must needs repeat for my excuse What looks so little graceful. **1877** BROWNING *Agamemnon* 119 The opposite to say I shall not shamed be.

**d.** ***to tell (say, speak) the truth and shame the devil***: to tell the truth boldly in defiance of temptation to the contrary.

**1552** LATIMER *Serm. Lincolnsh.* iii. (1562) 85 b, There is a common saying amongst vs, Say the truthe and shame the diuel. **1562** T. WILSON *Rhet.* 76 b, Saie on beast, and shame the deuil. **1596** SHAKS. *1 Hen. IV*, III. i. 58–9. **1598** —— *Merry W.* IV. ii. 124 Now shall the diuel be sham'd. **1658** BRAMHALL *Consecr. Bps.* i. 7 Compell him..to shame the divell, and eate his owne words. **1731–8** SWIFT *Pol. Conversat.* 93 Come, tell Truth, and shame the Devil. **1893** G. ALLEN *Scallywag* I. 151 'Because he's so much richer', Paul answered, boldly shaming the devil.

**5.** To inflict or bring disgrace upon; to disgrace, dishonour; to be a cause of disgrace to.

*c* **1200** ORMIN 18284 Hefiȝlike he shameþþ þe & shendeþþ & unnwurrþeþþ. *c* **1330** R. BRUNNE *Chron. Wace* (Rolls) 15209 Þey wyþ tailles þe godeman schamed. *c* **1386** CHAUCER *Frankl. T.* 837 Heer may I nat dwelle, And shamen al my kinrede in this place. **1398** TREVISA *Barth. De P.R.* XV. xii. (1495) 492 Yf it happe that thou be ouercome thenne arte thou shamyd for euermore. **1530** PALSGR. 701/1, I was of good name and fame afore he shamed me by this yvell reporte. **1556** OLDE *Antichrist* 64 b, This John..shamed the Church of Rome wonderfully wᵗ his lyuing. **1644** NYE *Gunnery* (1670) 28 When Gunpowder is moist..it shameth the Gunner which useth it. **1667** MILTON *P.L.* I. 461 Where he fell flat, and sham'd his Worshipers. **1784** COWPER *Task* II. 807 Rusting there..What wonder if, discharg'd into the world, They shame their shooters with a random flight. **1820** BYRON *Mar. Fal.* IV. ii, *Doge*... Let us go worthy of our sires and selves. *Ber. F.* I shall not shame you, uncle. **1900** *Daily Tel.* 18 Oct. 11/1 We tortured no prisoners,..we shamed no women.

**b.** with a thing as object.

*a* **1340** HAMPOLE *Ps.* xiii. 10 Þe counsaile of þe helples ȝe shamed. **1581** MARBECK *Bk. of Notes* 1124 S. Paule saith, yᵗ euery man which prayeth or precheth wᵗ couered head, shameth his head. **1784** COWPER *Task* II. 427 He.. prostitutes and shames His noble office. **1812** BYRON *Ch. Har.* II. viii, If..there be A land of souls beyond that sable shore, To shame the doctrine of the Sadducee. **1842** TENNYSON *Lady Clare* 66 O Lady Clare, you shame your worth! **1865** BUSHNELL *Vicar. Sacr.* I. v. (1866) 71 The losses..that shame His saving work.

**6.** To confound or put to shame by superior excellence; to outrival.

*c* **1400** *Rule of St. Benet* (prose) 47 Bot we..þat er..of febil lif, þis gude lif schamis vs, and confundis. **1592** SHAKS. *Ven. & Ad.* 732 Wherein she framed thee in high heaven's despite, To shame the sun by day and her by night. **1611** *Second Maiden's Trag.* 1741 (Malone Soc.) How pittie strikes een throughe inscensible thinges and makes them shame our dullnes. **1741** SHENSTONE *Judgm. Hercules* 82 Her blushing cheeks, that sham'd the purple morn. **1841–44** EMERSON *Ess., Nature* Wks. (Bohn) I. 224 Here [in the forest] is sanctity which shames our religions. **1848** DICKENS *Dombey* lviii, She'll shame 'em with her good looks, yet.

**7.** With complementary adv. or advb. phr.: To drive *away* (etc.) through shame.

**1596** SHAKS. *1 Hen. IV*, III. i. 61 And Ile be sworne, I haue power to shame him hence. *c* **1644** CLEVELAND *Rebel Scot* Poems (1659) 53 Hyperbolus by suffering did traduce The Ostracism, and sham'd it out of use. **1682** D'URFEY *Butler's Ghost* 36 My Head's not such a thing of no worth, 'Tis to be sham'd away, and so forth. **1790** BURKE *Fr. Rev.* 53 You would have shamed despotism from the earth. **1859** *Habits of Gd. Society* 52 The turbulent state of the country.. leaving, when bloodshed was shamed back, the same deadly hatred.

**b.** To drive (one) *out of, into* (a state, course of action, etc.) through shame or fear of shame.

**1679** J. GOODMAN *Penitent Pardoned* III. iv. (1713) 330 Railery may go about to shame him out of his course. *c* **1680** BEVERIDGE *Serm.* (1729) II. 545 When the practice of others ..shames you into a compliance with them. **1775** SHERIDAN *Rivals* Epil., Shamed into sense,..Our beaux from gallantry would soon be wise. **1839** THIRLWALL *Greece* xlvi. VI. 81 Philip..shamed his son out of his suspicions by an indignant expostulation. **1878** BOSW. SMITH *Carthage* 284 The considerable armament, which the news of Hannibal's triumphant progress through Italy had at last shamed the Carthaginians into raising for him.

Hence **shamed** *ppl. a.*

**1508** KENNEDIE *Flying w. Dunbar* 549 Defamyt, blamyt, schamyt, Primas Paganorum. *a* **1586** SIDNEY *Arcadia* III. (Sommer) 319 No, shamed Musidorus, worthie for nothing, but to keepe sheepe. **1874** O'SHAUGHNESSY *Music & Moonlight* 125 In the shamed and the ruined love's stead. **1880** MEREDITH *Tragic Com.* (1881) 275 With..secret aim, which he nursed like a shamed mother of an infant.

**shame**, obs. form of SHAWM.

**shameanah**, variant of SHAMIANA(H.

'**shamedly**, *adv. rare.* [f. SHAMED *a.* + -LY².] In an ashamed manner, with shame.

**1890** *Murray's Mag.* May 692 'No, sir', the young man said, shamedly. **1913** D. H. LAWRENCE *Sons & Lovers* x. 260 Then she herself took her place on the sofa, shamedly.

**shameeana**, variant of SHAMIANA(H.

**shameface** ('ʃeɪmfeɪs). *rare.* [f. SHAME *sb.* + FACE *sb.* (After *shamefaced* adj.)] **a.** A bashful aspect. **b.** *nonce-use.* A shamefaced person.

**1636–41** *Politick Maid* ii. in Child *Ballads* II. 491 But it seemd he had a shame-face, He did not court and play. **1691** MRS. D'ANVERS *Academia* 4 Being told at home that a shame Face too, Was a great sign he had some Grace too. **1892** W. BESANT in *Critic* 12 Sept. 143/2 One could see all the way across the Atlantic her cheeks blush; one could observe the shameface. **1898** M. HEWLETT *Forest Lovers* xvi. (1911) 138 You mean that I may not venture into a lady's chamber, Shameface?

**shamefaced** ('ʃeɪmfeɪst), *a.* [f. SHAME *sb.* + FACE *sb.* + -ED²; originally an etymological misinterpretation of SHAMEFAST *a.*]

**1.** Modest; bashful, shy.

**1555** [implied in SHAMEFACEDNESS]. **1593** R. HARVEY *Philad.* 19 Cordeil being euer modestly and maydenly shamefaced. **1629** MILTON *Hymn Nativ.* xi, A Globe of circular light, That with long beams the shame-fac't night array'd. **1634** W. CARTWRIGHT *Ordinary* IV. v. Song, Her blush doth shed All o'r the bed Clean shamefac'd beames. **1712** ADDISON *Spect.* No. 458 ¶5 Our Excess of Modesty makes us shamefaced in all the Exercises of Piety and Devotion. **1810** SCOTT *Lady of L.* II. xxiv, The flush of shame-faced joy to hide The hounds, the hawk, her cares divide. **1873** MORLEY *Rousseau* I. 218 He felt shamefaced as a schoolboy before the great world.

**b.** *absol.* (See quot.)

**1598** SYLVESTER *Du Bartas* II. i. I. *Eden* 625 There quakes the plant, which in Pudefetan Is call'd The shame-fac'd [orig. *L'arbre en Pudefetan Vergongneux appellé*], for asham'd of man, If toward it one doe approch too much It shrinkes his boughes to shunne our hatefull tuch.

**2.** Ashamed, abashed.

**1873** MORLEY *Rousseau* I. 70 That unwritten chapter of their lives which even the most candid persons keep privately locked up in shamefaced recollection. **1896** 'IAN MACLAREN' *Kate Carnegie* 237 The minister..hears the shamefaced confession of some lassie whom love has led astray.

**shamefacedly** ('ʃeɪmfeɪstlɪ), *adv.* [-LY².] In a shamefaced manner, modestly, bashfully.

**1620** SHELTON *Quix.* II. xlix. 327 She, with her eyes fixt vpon the earth, most shamefac'dly answered [etc.]. **1865** MRS. WHITNEY *Gayworthys* iii. (1879) 31 He had shamefacedly essayed it. **1881** 'RITA' *My Lady Coquette* i, 'Oh yes', says the boy, shamefacedly, 'that's all right'.

**shamefacedness** ('ʃeɪmfeɪstnɪs). [-NESS.] The state or quality of being shamefaced.

**1.** Modesty, bashfulness, shyness.

**1555** WATREMAN *Fardle Facions* II. viii. 181 A couering of honeste shamefacednesse. **1608** *Pennyless Parl.* §3 in *Harl. Misc.* (1744) I. 176 Some Maidens shall blush more for Shame, than for Shame-facedness. **1621** G. SANDYS *Ovid's Met.* IV. (1626) 74 He blusht for shame; Not knowing loue: whom shamefac'tnesse became. **1693** LOCKE *Educ.* §135. 167 There is often in People, especially Children, a clownish shamefac'dness before Strangers. **1741** RICHARDSON *Pamela* (1824) I. 131 My poor grateful heart was like a too full river, which overflows its banks; and it carried away my fear and my shamefacedness. **1803** WORDSW. *To Highland Girl* 31 The embarrassed look of shy distress, And maidenly shamefacedness. **1888** SPURGEON *Serm.* in *Voice* (N.Y.) 31 May, A woman of few words and much shamefacedness.

**2.** The state of being ashamed, ashamedness.

**1641** J. TRAPPE *Theol. Theol.* x. 365 Shee [*sc.* the soule] stands off in a sinful shamefac'dnesse. **1653** A. WILSON *Jas. I*, 20 A certain Shamefacedness to be thought curious or changeable. **1894** WEYMAN *Man in Black* i. 8 The boy.. stood looking round him with a dark shamefacedness.

¶**3.** Misused for: Shamelessness. Cf. SHAMEFASTNESS 3.

**1827** LONGF. *Life* (1891) I. vii. 101 The French ministry is..with the most bold shamefacedness endeavoring to retrench their liberty of thought.

**shamefast** ('ʃeɪmfɑːst, -æ-), *a. arch.* Forms: see SHAME *sb.* [OE. *sc(e)amfæst*, f. *sc(e)amu* SHAME *sb.* + *fæst* FAST *a.*

The etymological sense appears to be 'restrained by shame'; but *-fæst* was a common element in OE. adj. compounds, in some of which it has hardly any definable meaning.]

**1.** Bashful, modest. In a good or neutral sense: Modest or virtuous in behaviour and character. In a depreciatory sense: Shy, awkward in the company of others, 'sheepish'. Also *absol.*

*c* **897** ÆLFRED *Gregory's Past. C.* xxxi. 204 On oðre wisan sint to læronne ða scamleasan, on oðre ða scamfæstan. *c* **1200** ORMIN 2175 Ȝho wass wiss wiþþ alle Shammfasst, & daffte, & sedefull. *c* **1320** *Sir Beues* 3201 Wimmen beþ schamfast in dede And namliche maidenes. *c* **1385** CHAUCER *L.G.W.* 1535 Ther nas no lak, but that he was agast To loue, & for to speke shamefast. **1422** tr. *Secreta Secret., Priv. Priv.* 229 Tho that haue the face sumwhate ruddy bene schamefaste. *c* **1530** *Crt. of Love* 731 Demene you liche a maid with shamefast dred. **1535** COVERDALE *Ecclus.* xxvi. 10 Yf thy daughter be not shamefast, holde her straitly. **1590** SPENSER *F.Q.* I. ii. 27 With chaunge of cheare the seeming simple maid Let fall her eyen, as shamefast to the earth. **1615** BRATHWAIT *Strappado* 119 So humble was the prelate, as to please The shamefast maid, he oft fell on his knees. **1652** GAULE *Magastrom.* 185 A neck leaning to the right hand for shamefast; to the left hand for shamelesse.

*transf.* **1567** MAPLET *Gr. Forest* 15 Kaman the stone may well be called a turncote, for that it is now blacke, now white, now shamefast and blushing.

**b.** Of actions, behaviour, appearance: Characterized by or indicating modesty or bashfulness.

*c* **1386** CHAUCER *Pars. T.* ¶985 The firste is þat confession moste be shamefast. **1505** HEN. VII *Instruct. to Ambass.* vi. (1761) 10 The said quyn ys..not liȝght nor boldehardy in speche but with a demewre womanly shamefast contenance. **1611** MURE *Misc. Poems* ii. 9 Hir schamefast, blusching smyles. *a* **1835** MOTHERWELL *Poet. Wks.* (1847) 124 The rose with its sweet shamefast look. **1868** MORRIS *Earthly Par., Doom of K. Acrisius* 264 The damsel's shamefast blood Made all her face red to the golden hair.

†**2.** Ashamed, abashed, full of shame. *Obs.*

*c* **1275** *Sinners beware!* 80 in *O.E. Misc.* 240 And þeos gedelynges summe. Hwenne heo to schrifte come. Heo beoþ schomeuaste. **1382** WYCLIF *Ps.* xxxiv. 26 Be thei clad with confusioun and shamefast drede. *c* **1450** *Merlin* vii. 111 The quene was shamefaste, and discouerid to hym the very trouthe, how the childe was be-geten the same nyght that the Duke was slain. *c* **1557** ABP. PARKER *Ps* xxxiv. 80 They had an eye: full bent in hym, and so they lightened were: A shamefast face not one of them, from that tyme forth dyd beare. **1634** SIR T. HERBERT *Trav.* 130 With their hands couer their shamefast faces.

†**3.** = SHAMEFUL 4. *Obs.*

**1388** WYCLIF *Lev.* xvi. 4 He schal hide the schamefast membris with pryuy lynnun clothis. **1563** HYLL *Art Garden.* (1593) 165 The ashes made of the rinds of the Gourds, and strawed on the vlcers of shamefast places,.. bringeth them vnto a scarre. **1565** T. STAPLETON *Fortr. Faith* 110b, Hauing a desease in some shamefast parte of their body.

**shamefastly** (ˈʃeɪmfɑːstlɪ, -æ-), *adv.* [f. SHAMEFAST *a.* + -LY[2].] In a 'shamefast' manner.

**1382** WYCLIF *Ps.* xxxix. 15 Be thei confoundid and shamefastli drede thei togidere; that sechen my soule, that they do it awei. **1485** CAXTON *St. Wenefryde* 2 She..a lytyll cast down shamefastly her chere. **1567** GOLDING *Ovid's Met.* IX. 119b, Shee calld a servant shamefastly. **1902** *Encycl. Brit.* XXVI. 482/2 He..confessed, rather shame-fastly, that he had never killed anybody at any time.

**shamefastness** (ˈʃeɪmfɑːstnɪs, -æ-). *arch.* [f. SHAMEFAST *a.* + -NESS.]

**1.** Modesty, sobriety of behaviour, decency, propriety; bashfulness, shyness. Also, †a feeling of shame, ashamedness.

*c* **1200** *Trin. Coll. Hom.* 73 Min shamfestnesse is togenes me. *c* **1380** WYCLIF *Sel. Wks.* III. 193 Wymmen..in convenable abite, wiþ schamefastnesse and sobirnesse ournynge hem. *c* **1386** CHAUCER *Prol.* 840 And ye, sire clerk, lat be your shamefastnesse, Ne studieth noght. *c* **1460** SIR R. ROS *La Belle Dame* 120 in *Pol. Rel. & L. Poems* (1903) 84 To syng also, by force he wasse constrayned, ffor no plesaunce, but verrey schamfastnesse. **1513** *Life Hen. V* (1911) 144 The Kinge..kissed..the Ladye Katherine,..w[ch] was not done w[th]out some shamefastnes of that virgin. **1545** ASCHAM *Toxoph.* II. (Arb.) 141 And in stede of the feruente desyre, which prouoketh a chylde to be better than hys felowe, lette a man be as much stirred vp with shamefastnes to be worse than all other. **1642** D. ROGERS *Naaman* 324 Others out of bashfulnesse and shamefastnesse, loath to be troublesome. **1646** W. PRICE *Mans Delinq.* 11 Even Nature (saith Tertullian) hath cast a shamefastnesse on all sinfull evill. **1697** J. SERGEANT *Solid Philos.* a6, Out of Niaiserie and Shamefastness says at every turn (I think, or perhaps this is true, or may be true). **1856** MISS YONGE *Daisy Chain* II. iii. 360 Blanche..almost cried with indignant 'shamefastness'. **1882** SWINBURNE *Tristram* iii. 69 She looked on him and loved him; but being young Made shamefastness a seal upon her tongue.

†**b.** *personified.*

**1509** HAWES *Past. Pleas.* xxxii. (1845) 159 And first she led me to the upper ward, Where Shamefastnes did us well regarde, For he was gayler. **1596** SPENSER *F.Q.* IV. x. 50 And next to her sate goodly Shamefastnesse, Ne euer durst her eyes from ground vpreare.

†**2.** Misused for: Shamelessness. *Obs.*

**1589** NASHE *Anat. Absurditie* Wks. (Grosart) I. 26 It seemes that law is turned to libertie, and honest ciuilitie into impudent shamefastnes.

**shameferon, shamfron,** var. ff. CHAMFRAIN, CHAMFRON.

**1537** *North Country Wills* (Surtees 1908) 148 One paier of greate pottes pounced with Talbottes and shameferons. *Ibid.*, Shamfron.

**shameful** (ˈʃeɪmfʊl), *a.* Forms: see SHAME *sb.* Also 5 shem(e)ful. [f. SHAME *sb.* + -FUL.]

†**1.** Modest, shamefaced. *Obs.*

*a* **950** *Durh. Ritual* (Surtees) 108 Sceomfull [glosses L. *pudica*]. *a* **1225** *Ancr. R.* 90 Ich am woware scheomeful. *a* **1300** *Cursor M.* 3367 And þof sco scamful was, i-wiss, Sco tint na contenance wit þis. *c* **1425** *St. Eliz. of Spalbeck* in *Anglia* VIII. 109/46 A merueilous onest and schameful gladnesse of cheer, caused of goostly ioye. *a* **1625** FLETCHER *Q. Corinth* IV. i, For certain Sir, his bashfulness undo's him, For from his Cradle h'had a shameful face.

†**b.** *transf.* (See quot.)

**1659** R. LOVELL *Herbal* 542 Shamefull-shrub, *Pinahuihuiztlis, Herba verecunda.*

†**2.** Permeated with a feeling or appearance of shame, full of shame, ashamed. *Obs.*

**1375** BARBOUR *Bruce* VIII. 359 So schamfull that he vencust wes, That..He gaf vp thar his vardanry. *c* **1440** *Alphabet of Tales* 191 When he hard þis he wex ferd & shamefull. **1594** KYD *Cornelia* I. 22 Vnder a Tyrant see our bastard harts Lye idely sighing, while our shamefull soules Endure a million of base controls. **1702** MATHER *Magn. Chr.* III. IV. vii. 231 With what shameful Reflections on all our past Behaviours. **1713** in Keble *Life Bp. Wilson* (1863) 215 She is one of the most penitent and shamefull offenders that hath been for many years. **1760–72** H. BROOKE *Fool of Qual.* (1809) IV. 1 The house-tops began to be cleared with a shameful caution.

**3.** That brings to shame; that causes or ought to cause shame; disgraceful, scandalous, degrading.

*c* **1330** *Arth. & Merl.* 1157 (Kölbing) Sore he worþ adrad, ywis, Of schameful deþ to haue of þe. **1340** *Ayenb.* 117 Vor þet were a fole bezechinge and ssamuol. **1474** CAXTON *Chesse* IV. i. (1883) 161 And shamefull pouerte is the more greuous whan hit cometh by nature of an hyhe and noble burth or hous. **1535** COVERDALE *Wisd.* ii. 20 Let vs condemne him with the most shamefull death. **1605** SHAKS. *Lear* II. ii. 179 Take vantage heauie eyes, not to behold This shamefull lodging. **1635** CRANLEY *Amanda* 41 And as thou shame-lesse of all shame dost live, So death to thee a shamefull end will give. **1781** COWPER *Hope* 715 The shameful close of all his mispent years. **1813** SHELLEY *Q. Mab* II. 140 There once old Salem's haughty fane..in the blushing face of day Exposed its shameful glory. **1837** CARLYLE *Fr. Rev.* VII. vii, Shameful! Three against one! **1871** R. ELLIS *Catullus* lxvii. 41 Many a shameful time I heard her stealthy profession.

†**4.** *shameful parts*: the secret parts, organs of sex. *Obs.*

**1382** WYCLIF *Ezek.* xxii. 10 Fadris vnhilliden in thee more shameful thingis. **1617** MORYSON *Itin.* III. 180 Their said breeches are so close, as they expose to view, not onely the noble but also the shamefull parts. **1693** DRYDEN *Sat. Persius* iv. 94 Not all thy Pincers, nor unmanly Arts, Can smooth the roughness of thy shameful parts.

†**5.** Applied to language: Casting shame, opprobrious, vituperative. *Obs.*

**1500–20** DUNBAR *Poems* lxxii. 12 Judas..Tuke blissit Jesu..And schot him furth, with mony ane schow, With schamefull wourdis of dishonour. **1568** GRAFTON *Chron.* II. 729 Reprouing and reuiling him with such yll wordes, and so shamefull termes, that all the hearers abhorred it. **1570** LEVINS *Manip.* 187/9 Shameful, *contumeliosus*.

†**6.** Shaming, affording shame *to*. *Obs. rare*[−1].

**1572** *Lam. Lady Scot.* 107 in *Satir. P. Reform.* (S.T.S.) I. 230, I grant I had ane Douchter was ane Quene,..Lusty, gude lyke, to all men fauourabill; Schamefull to euill, baith honest, meik and law.

**shamefully** (ˈʃeɪmfʊlɪ), *adv.* [f. SHAMEFUL *a.* + -LY[2].]

**1.** In a manner that causes shame or disgrace; with indignity; disgracefully.

*a* **1300** *Cursor M.* 28735 Qua mar tas þan he bere might oþere he sal leue it wit-alle or schamfulli þar vnder stand. **1340** *Ayenb.* 181 His [*sc.* Samson's] yuo þet him deden grinde ate querne ssamuolliche. *c* **1430** *Pilgr. Lyf Manhode* III. iii. (1869) 138, I shal make thee shamefullich and vileynesliche dye. **1549** *Compl. Scot.* ix. 79 He vas schamefully chaissit furtht of France. **1625** BACON *Ess., Of Boldness* (Arb.) 519 They haue promised great Matters and failed most shamefully. **1712** BUDGELL *Spect.* No. 401 ¶6 The World has seen me shamefully lose that Time to please a fickle Woman. **1855** MACAULAY *Hist. Eng.* xviii. IV. 160 The allies whom he had shamefully abandoned were accused of persecuting him without a cause. **1879** R. MORRIS *Blickl. Hom.* Pref. 8 The leaves have been shamefully clipped, I suppose by the binders. **1884** *Manch. Exam.* 20 Feb. 4/7 Ordinary license of speech has seldom been more shamefully exceeded.

**2.** Shamefacedly, modestly, bashfully, ashamedly. Now *rare*.

*c* **1375** *Sc. Leg. Saints* xvi. (*Magdalena*) 106 Nocht for-þi scho come eftir þame schamfully, & gat in handis cristis fete. *c* **1489** CAXTON *Sonnes of Aymon* i. 33 The whiche trybute your sone asked hym shamfully. *c* **1525** SIR T. MORE in More *Life* (1626) 183 You aske monye, deare Megg, too shamefully & fearefully of your father. ?**1595–6** CAREW *Excell. Eng. Tongue* in *Camden's Rem.* (1614) 40 We borrow (and that not shamefully [*Cott. MS.* shamfully]) from the Dutch, the Britaine, the Romane [etc.]. **1887** HALL CAINE *Deemster* xxxv, Shamefully..they told what he had to do, and then his vacant face became suddenly charged with passion.

**shamefulness** (ˈʃeɪmfʊlnɪs). [f. SHAMEFUL *a.* + -NESS.]

†**1.** Sense of shame or disgrace. Also, bashfulness, modesty. *Obs.*

*a* **1340** HAMPOLE *Ps.* lxxxii. 18 Fulfil þaire faces of schamefulnes. ?*a* **1487** *How Good Wife taught Dau.* 45 Bot euir with dreid and schamfulnes Scho suld draw to the lawast plass. **1552** LYNDESAY *Compl.* 59 Allace! my sleuth and schamefulnes Debarrit fra me all gredynes. **1638** JUNIUS *Paint. Ancients* 103 It is fit we should endue children with shamfulnesse and desire of glorie.

**2.** Disgracefulness, scandalousness. Also, disgraceful conduct.

**1564** RASTELL *Confut. Jewell's Serm.* 101b, No absurditie or shamefulnes shall euer be concluded of them. **1610** HEALEY *St. Aug. Citie of God* II. v. 59 The whole kinred.. would blush, and bee ashamed at her shamefulnesse. **1862** TENNYSON *Coming of Arthur* 238 While the King debated with himself If Arthur were the child of shamefulness, Or born the son of Gorloïs, after death. **1903** *Blackw. Mag.* Aug. 243/1 An enterprise whose shamefulness was obvious now to himself.

†**3.** 'Shame,' secret parts. *Obs.*

**1561** T. NORTON *Calvin's Inst.* (1634) Table Script. Quot., None shall come neere any of the next of his bloude that he should reveale there shamefulnesse [*sa vergongne*].

**shamel(l,** obs. form of SHAMBLE *sb.*[1]

**shameless** (ˈʃeɪmlɪs), *a.* Forms: see SHAME *sb.* Also 7 *superl.* shamelest. [OE. *sc(e)amléas, sc(e)omléas*: see SHAME *sb.* and -LESS.]

**1.** Lacking shame, destitute of feelings of modesty; impudent, audacious, immodest; insensible to disgrace.

*c* **897** ÆLFRED *Gregory's Past. C.* ix. 60 Se læce bið micles to bald & to scomleas þe gæð æfter oðerra monna husum lacniende, & hæfð on his agnum nebbe opene wunde unlacnode. *a* **1225** *Ancr. R.* 170 Schomeleas is þe mon oðer þeo wummon þet deð eni untoweschipe, oðer seið, biuoren ancren. **1340–70** *Alex. & Dind.* 20 To þe schamlese schalk schewden hur lettres. *c* **1412** HOCCLEVE *De Reg. Princ.* 3508 Fy! schamēles vnworthy gouernour! **1591** SHAKS. *1 Hen. VI*, III. ii. 45 Scoffe on vile Fiend, and shamelesse Curtizan. **1598** GRENEWEY *Tacitus, Ann.* XV. viii. (1622) 232 Vatinius was one of the shamelest monsters of his [Nero's] court. **1683** W. HEDGES *Diary* (Hakl. Soc.) I. 63 Though these men are so shameless as to deny it. **1725** POPE *Odyss.* VIII. 358 But there remain, ye guilty, in my pow'r, 'Till Jove refunds his shameless daughter's dow'r. **1859** TENNYSON *Elaine* 100 Lo the shameless ones who take Their pastime now the trustful King is gone! **1891** FARRAR *Darkn. & Dawn* ix. 65 A man of refined culture..but the most cynically shameless liver and talker even in Rome.

*absol.* *c* **897** ÆLFRED *Gregory's Past. C.* xxxi. 204 On oðre wisan sint to læronne ða scamleasan, on oðre ða scamfæstan. **1825** SCOTT *Talism.* xv, 'Peace, shameless!' said the King.

**2.** Indicating or characterized by absence of shame or modesty. Of actions: Indicating absence of shame on the part of the agent, impudent.

*c* **1000** *Ags. Ps.* (Th.) l. 3 Of þysse scamleasan scylde ȝeclænsa me. **1533** FRITH *Answ. More* (1829) 156 Then fall they to a shameless boldness & let not to deny the Scripture & all. **1675** BAXTER *Cath. Theol.* II. ix. 200 This is the same shameless self-contradicting Accusation, and needs no other Answer. **1853** GROTE *Greece* II. lxxxiv. §xi. 145 It was found practicable to convict the delinquent of shameless falshood. **1874** GREEN *Short Hist.* viii. §2. 472 He [James] degraded the nobility by a shameless sale of peerages.

*absol.* *c* **897** ÆLFRED *Gregory's Past. C.* xxxi. 206 Forðæm he spræc ðas word þe he wolde ðara scamleasena scylda tælende ȝeopenian.

†**3.** Suffering no shame, free from disgrace. *Obs.*

**1390** GOWER *Conf.* III. 151 For hou so that the cause wende, The trouthe is schameles ate ende, Bot what thing that is troutheles, It mai noght wel be schameles. *c* **1440** *Alphabet of Tales* 144 Lorde Jesu! delyuer me & safe me shameles of þis Iewis at þis tyme.

†**4.** (See quot.) *Obs. rare.*

**1552** UDALL tr. *Geminus' Anat.* Bvij b, The bone of the foreheade,..of some other it is called the shameles bone [orig. *os inuerecundum*], or the bone of the common senses.

**5.** quasi-*adv.*

*a* **1541** BARNES *Wks.* (1573) 311/2 Open whoredome, & abhominable and detestable vncleannes, that is now vsed shamelesse in the worlde. **1590** SHAKS. *Com. Err.* V. i. 202 Beyond imagination is the wrong That she this day hath shamelesse throwne on me.

**6.** *Comb.*

**1555** RIDLEY in Coverdale *Godly Lett.* (1564) 87 The abhominable desolacion..of proude Senacheryb, of the shameles faced kyng & of the Babilonical beaste.

**shamelessly** (ˈʃeɪmlɪslɪ), *adv.* [f. prec. + -LY[2].] In a shameless manner, without shame.

*c* **897** ÆLFRED *Gregory's Past. C.* xix. 144 Hie..swiðe scamleasliche ȝilpað ðisses hwilendlican onwaldes. **1535–6** *Act 27 Hen. VIII*, c. 28 Ther vycyous lyvyng shamelesly encreasseth and augmentith. **1611** BIBLE *2 Sam.* vi. 20 As one of the vaine fellowes shamelessely vncouereth himselfe! **1736** BUTLER *Anal.* I. iv. Wks. 1874 I. 79 There are men.. who shamelessly avow..their mere will and pleasure, to be their law of life. **1885** *Manch. Exam.* 26 Aug. 3/1 Those bounds of reticence which have been so shamelessly disregarded by some contemporary writers.

**shamelessness** (ˈʃeɪmlɪsnɪs). [f. SHAMELESS *a.* + -NESS.]

**1.** The quality of being destitute of shame or modesty; impudence.

**1540** PALSGR. *Acolastus* Prol. Bijb, But I here whysperynges amongest you, I wote not what, of a new shamelesnesse. **1628** WITHER *Brit. Rememb.* IV. 713 There sate a peece of shamelesnesse, whose flaring Attires and looks, did show a monstrous daring. **1741** RICHARDSON *Pamela* I. 85 Here's Shamelessness for you! **1865** KINGSLEY *Herew.* i, Both were abashed by the lad's utter shamelessness.

**2.** In a good or neutral sense: Freedom from shame, unashamedness.

**1667** H. MORE *Div. Dial.* III. vi. (1713) 191 That is very consequentially done, Euistor, to that simple shamelessness of being stark naked. **1679** OLDHAM *Sat. Jesuits* iii. Wks. (1686) 49 Let Wine..train him to a well-bred Shamelesness. **1901** *Edin. Rev.* July 68 The splendid shamelessness of the early Greeks.

**shameliche,** obs. form of SHAMELY *adv.*

†ˈ**shamely,** *a.* and *adv.* *Obs.* Forms: see SHAME *sb.* [f. SHAME *sb.* + -LY[1] and [2].] **A.** *adj.*

**1.** Shamefaced, modest; abashed. *rare.*

*a* **1100** *Aldhelm Gloss.* 3671 in Napier *O.E. Glosses* 97/2 *Pudibunda*, .i. *pudica*..sceamlic. *Ibid.* 144/2 *Pudibunda*, .i. *erubescens*, scamlic. *c* **1482** J. KAY tr. *Caoursin's Siege of Rhodes* (1870) ¶12 The Turkes wyth loe chiere and halfe shamely contenaunce, departed from theym.

**2.** Shameful, disgraceful.

*c* **1205** LAY. 20462 þenne were his cun iscend mid scomeliche witen. *c* **1350** *Will. Palerne* 556, & þat were a schamly schenchip to schende me euer. *c* **1425** *Cast. Persev.* 2051 in *Macro Plays* 138 Mankynde for to schylde & schete fro dedly synne & schamely schot.

**B.** *adv.* Disgracefully, shamefully.

*c* **1200** *Trin. Coll. Hom.* 69 Shameliche hem oigredeð and fule shendeð. *a* **1225** *Ancr. R.* 310 A mon þet were idemed uor a luðer murðre to beon forbernd al cwic, oðer scheomeliche anhonged. **13..** *E.E. Allit. P.* C. 128 Bot, I trow, ful tyd, ouer-tan þat he were, So þat schomely to schort he schote of his ame. **1471** CAXTON *Recuyell* (Sommer) I. 27 My..husband..will schamely put me to deth yf y accomplyssh not..his comaundement. **1558** G. CAVENDISH *Poems* (1825) II. 66 Who shamely doth, of long will not be raced.

†ˈ**shameness.** *Obs. rare*[−1]. In 4 ssamnesse. [f. SHAME *sb.* + -NESS.] Shamefacedness, modesty.

**1340** *Ayenb.* 142 Þous biginþ þe zaule to louie onhede and stillehede and þanne him wext ine herte ane holy ssamnesse þet is one of þe uariste doþter of mildenesse.

**ˈshamer.** *rare.* [f. SHAME *v.* + -ER[1].] One who or something which shames.

*a* **1625** FLETCHER *Woman's Prize* I. iii, My means and my conditions are no shamers Of him that owes 'em. **1832** S. FERGUSON *Forging of Anchor* 68 But shamer of our little sports! forgive the name I gave.

**shameuse,** obs. form of CHAMOIS *sb.*

†**ˈshamevous,** *a. Obs.* [f. SHAME *sb.* after *bountevous, plentevous.* Cf. SHAMOUSLY *adv.*] Shameful, disgraceful.

*c* **1475** *Partenay* 3407 Aforn all will declare the Auenture, hou Gaffray hym put to shameuous oppressure. *Ibid.* 3444 He wold make hym ende, And shameuous deth dight! *Ibid.* 5135 Which that he hath lost by dedes shameuous.

**shamewe,** variant of SHEMEWE *Obs.*

**shamfering,** obs. variant of CHAMFERING.

**1728** R. MORRIS *Anc. Archit.* 81 Shamfering.

**shamfron,** obs. form of CHAMFRAIN, -FRON.

‖**shamiana(h** (ʃæ-, ʃɑːmɪˈɑːnə). *Indian.* Forms: 7 semijane, semane, semian(e, symmeane, semeano, 9 shamyana, shameanah, shameeana, shimiana, 9- shamiana(h. [Urdu, Pers. *shāmiyāna.*] 'An awning or flat tent-roof without sides' (Yule); a flat awning or canopy. †Also (quots. 1609, 1613), a material used for such awnings, a striped calico.

**1609** in Danvers *Lett. E. Ind. Comp.* (1896) I. 29 A sort of Calico here called Semijanes are also in abundance. *c* **1610** W. FINCH in Purchas *Pilgrims* (1625) I. IV. iv. 432 Another open Chounter of stone to sit in, couered with rich Semianes. **1616** F. FETTIPLACE in Danvers & Foster *Lett. E. Ind. Comp.* (1900) IV. 239 Semanes, whereof they gave us order from Suratt to buy for one-third of our stock. **1616** *Ibid.* 239 Symmeanes. **1616** SIR T. ROE in Purchas *Pilgrims* (1625) I. IV. xvi. 543 There is erected a throne foure foote from the ground, in the Durbar Court, from the backe whereof, to the place where the King comes out a square of fiftie sixe paces long, and fortie three broad was rayled in, and couered with faire Semianes or Canopies of Cloth of Gold, Silke, or Veluet ioyned together, and sustained with Canes so couered. **1622** R. COCKS *Diary* (Hakl. Soc.) II. 287 Fyne Semian chowters and white baftas are good for presentes. **1676** in Forrest *Bombay Lett.* Home Ser. (1887) I. 89 We desire you to furnish him with bridle and sadle, semeanoes, canatts [etc.]. **1814** J. FORBES *Oriental Mem.* II. 455 To pitch my tent or erect my summiniana, or shamyana. **1857** M. THORNHILL *Personal Adv. Ind. Mutiny* (1884) 14 Our beds were arranged under large canopies, open on all sides, and which are termed..'Shameanahs'. **1902** *Times* 13 Aug. 4/1 On the lawn, a shamiana with silver uprights had been erected.

**shamil,** obs. form of SHAMBLE *sb.*[1]

**shaming** (ˈʃeɪmɪŋ), *vbl. sb.* [f. SHAME *v.* + -ING[1].] The action or fact of putting to shame.

**13..** *Minor Poems fr. Vernon MS.* (1901) 534 Þou miȝtest procure wiþ such prouyng To þi-self newe schamyng. *c* **1440** *Jacob's Well* xliii. 272 Beatryx, wyth-oute schamyng of here susterys, was schreuyn priuely. *c* **1510** MORE *Picus* Wks. 5/1 Thei serued of nought but to the shaming of such other folke as wer in very science much better lerned, and in those trifles ignorant. **1680** C. NESSE *Church Hist.* 212 Calling it..Nehustan..for the shameing of such as had so doted upon it. **1844** MRS. BROWNING *Lady Geraldine's Courtship* lxxii, I..trod them down with words of shaming.

**ˈshaming,** *ppl. a.* [f. SHAME *v.* + -ING[2].] That shames or puts to shame. Hence **ˈshamingly** *adv.*

**1741** RICHARDSON *Pamela* III. 407 For convincing me, in so kind, yet so shaming a manner, how wrong I was. **1868** GEO. ELIOT *Span. Gypsy* I. 111 An added Present, sketching still In hope unchecked by shaming memories. **1970** D. NEVILLE-ROLFE *Power without Glory* II. 247 Shorthand and typing... I originally took a shamingly long time to learn both. **1979** *Homes & Gardens* June 169/1 Eventually my bus arrived; a collection of shamingly healthy-looking people in breeches and clumpy boots gathered round.

**shamisen,** var. SAMISEN.

**shamle, shamly:** see SHAMBLE *sb.*[1], SHAMELY.

‖**shamma** (ˈʃæmə). Also **chamma, shama.** [Amharic.] A long loose robe resembling a toga, worn by both men and women in Ethiopia.

**1862** H. A. STERN *Wanderings among Falashas in Abyssinia* xxi. 311 The costume of the Abyssinian is exceedingly simple. Men of all ranks..wear a *shama*, or loose dress of white cotton. **1893** J. T. BENT *Sacred City of Ethiopians* ii. 35 A young stripling in cotton drawers and the red-striped *shamma* of everyday wear. **1930** H. NORDEN *Africa's Last Empire* iii. 62 She was swathed in the usual *chamma*. **1969** *Daily Tel.* 18 Oct. 10/8 The streets are full of the gentle flutter of the white muslin *shammas* worn by the shy, slim Ethiopian women.

†**shammade,** *v. Sc. Obs. rare*$^{-1}$. [app. a blundered adoption of F. *chamarrer.*] *trans.* To ornament with lace.

**1665** J. FRASER *Polichron.* (S.H.S.) 359 Cloathed in a scarlet cloake richly shammaded with golden lace.

**Shammar** (ˈʃæmɑː(r)). [Native name.] (A member of) a Bedouin tribe originating in the Nafud desert of Saudi Arabia. Also *attrib.* or as *adj.*

**1911** G. BELL *Let.* 14 Apr. (1927) I. xii. 300 Now the Shammar are *Beda*; only the Shammar and the Anazeh are real Bedawin, the others are just Arabs. **1916** T. E. LAWRENCE *Home Lett.* (1954) 311 There is a very heady old Shammar, and an Aneyze. **1929** F. STARK *Let.* 24 Nov. (1974) I. 215 He..has now suggested a visit to one of the Shammar chiefs up the Tigris. **1959** W. THESIGER *Arabian Sands* iii. 54 In Syria I had seen the Shammar migrating, a whole people on the move, covering the desert with their herds.

**shammas(h, shammes, -os,** vars. SHAMAS(H.

†**ˈshammatize,** *v. Obs.* Also 7 **samatize, schamatize.** [a. mod.L. *samatizāre* (1583 in Drusius *Quæst.* I. 16), **schamatizāre*, f. Jewish Aramaic *sh'mattā* excommunication, whence the denom. vb. *shammēth* to excommunicate.

According to Levy *sh'mattā* (:—**sh'madtā*) is a derivative of שמד, in causative conjugations to destroy, curse. Modern scholars believe the word to have been a general term for excommunication; the statement of Elias Levita that there were three degrees of excommunication, of which *sh'mattā* was the most severe, appears to be destitute of authority.]

*trans.* In mediæval Judaism: To excommunicate.

**1613** PURCHAS *Pilgrimage* (1614) 113 If they did not amend, they were excommunicated with a greater curse, or Anathema: and if they persisted obstinate, they did Samatize them. **1661** STILLINGFL. *Irenicon* I. viii. §5. 147 A most dreadful sentence of excommunication..whereby they do Schamatize, curse and devote the persons against whom it is pronounced. **1684** tr. *Lightfoot's Horæ Hebr.* Wks. II. 538 [They] anathematiz'd, shammatiz'd, excommunicated the Samaritans.

**shammbrie,** variant of SHAMBRIER.

**shammel** (ˈʃæm(ə)l), *sb. Mining.* See also SHAMBLE *sb.*[1] 6. [Dialect form of SHAMBLE *sb.*[1]] (See quots.)

**1778** PRYCE *Min. Cornub.* 142 The Miners prefer a Shammel, which is a stage of boards, for the more light and easy use of their shovels. **1855** LEIFCHILD *Cornwall* 201 The product was raised by being thrown upon successive platforms (called *shammels*). **1880** D. C. DAVIES *Metallif. Min.* 420 *Shammel*, a stage for shovelling ore upon, or for raising water.

*attrib.* **1803** POLWHELE *Hist. Cornw.* I. 175 The shammel-working indeed, which appears in several places between Bovey and Dartmoor,..may be considered as relics of the Romans. *Ibid.* III. 9 In the mean time the shammel-works must, I think, have been almost superseded by shafts.

Hence **ˈshammel** *v. intr.*, to work a mine by the use of a series of 'shammels'.

**1778** PRYCE *Min. Cornub.* 142 The custom of Shammeling both above and under-ground at this time. **1860** *Eng. & For. Mining Gloss.* (ed. 2) *Cornw.* 22 *Shammel*, when ore or water is lifted part of the required height by one machine or person and part by another.

**shammel,** obs. form of SHAMBLE *sb.*[1]

**shammer** (ˈʃæmə(r)). [f. SHAM *v.* + -ER[1].] One who shams.

†**a.** One who deceives or tricks with false pretences. *Obs.*

**1677** WYCHERLEY *Plain Dealer* III. i. 45, I shou'd make the worst Shammer in England. **1681** R. L'ESTRANGE (*title*), The Shammer Shamm'd. *a* **1696** AUBREY *Lives, Sir H. Blount* (1898) I. 110 He was heretofore a great shammer, i.e. one that tells falsities not to doe any body any injury, but to impose on their understanding.

**b.** One who shams illness, death, etc.

**1861** *All Year Round* 13 July 371 Mutiny shall be punished. Skulkers and shammers shall get their deserts. **1870** *Daily News* 24 Dec., Many of them are genuine invalids, but many are mere shammers. **1875** HOUGHTON *Sk. Brit. Insects* 143 Like the Skip-jacks, these Death-watch-beetles are great shammers.

†**ˈshammish,** *a. Obs.* [f. SHAM *sb.*[1] + -ISH[1].] Of the nature of 'a sham', hoax, or fraud.

*a* **1734** NORTH *Exam.* I. ii. §128 (1740) 100 The Overture was very shammish.

**shammock** (ˈʃæmək), *sb. dial.* Also **shammocks, shommacks, shammick(s** (see *Eng. Dial. Dict.*). [? f. SHAMMOCK *v.* Cf. dial. *slammock(s, slammick(s* of similar meaning.] Used as a term of depreciation, with many varieties of meaning; a lazy, slovenly person; a starved, miserable-looking person or animal.

**1828** [CARR] *Craven Gloss.* II. 113 He's a sad shammocks. **1891** 'Q.' (Quiller-Couch) *Noughts & Crosses* 97 If These-an'-That, there, wasn' but a poor ha'f-baked shammick, he'd ha' killed that wife o' his afore this. **1897** MARY KINGSLEY *W. Africa* 213 So the poor old chief worried himself to a shammock.

**shammock** (ˈʃæmək), *v. dial.* Forms: (see *Eng. Dial. Dict.*). [Cf. SHAMBLE *v.*; also *slammock* vb., widely used dial. in similar senses.] *intr.* To walk with a shambling or unsteady gait; to slouch; to dawdle; to idle about.

**1857** SCHOLES *Tim Gamwattle* 6 (E.D.D.) As aw wur shammokin alung shore.

Hence **ˈshammocking** *ppl. a.*, awkward, clumsy; slovenly, untidy; idle, worthless. **ˈshammocky** *a.* = prec.; also, shaky, infirm.

**1702** T. BROWN, etc. *Lett. Dead to Living* II. (1707) 73 Pox take you both for a couple of shammocking Rascals. **1841** HARTSHORNE *Salop. Ant.* 564 *Shomacky*, slovenly, awkward in gait. **1852** *Tait's Mag.* XIX. 42 An idle, boozing, and shammocking scamp weds an industrious girl. **1891** DOYLE *White Company* xiv, You shammocking yaping over-long good-for-nought! **1900** H. SUTCLIFFE *Shameless Wayne* xix. (1905) 241 But ye poor, shammocky sheep-drivers think there's nowt save ewes an' tups i' th' world.

†**shammoe,** *v. Obs.*$^{-0}$ [Of obscure origin: is it a misprint for *shammoc* SHAMMOCK *v.* ?]

**1688** HOLME *Armoury* II. 427/2 Shammoe, to cast the toes outward in going.

**shammoulle,** obs. form of SHAMBLE *sb.*[1]

**shammoy,** obs. form of CHAMOIS *sb.*

**shammy**[1] (ˈʃæmɪ). Also 7 **shammie,** 8 **shamy, shammey.** [A phonetic spelling of CHAMOIS *sb.*]

**1.** In full *shammy-leather*: a kind of soft, pliable leather. Cf. CHAMOIS *sb.* 2. Also a piece of this, a wash-leather.

**1714** *Fr. Bk. Rates* 142 Goat-Skins and Sheep-Skins drest ..in Imitation of Shammy. **1767** S. PATERSON *Another Trav.* I. 364 They are more capable of labour, than if they wore shammy, or dog-skin. **1823** J. BADCOCK *Dom. Amusem.* 93 Cover it with a piece of buff or shammy leather. **1851** MAYHEW *Lond. Labour* I. 443/2 The wash-leathers, sometimes called 'shammys' (chamois), now sold extensively in the streets, are for the most part the half of a sheep-skin, or a larger lamb-skin. **1883** R. HALDANE *Workshop Rec.* Ser. II. 367/1 The process of manufacturing 'chamois' or 'shammy' leather is thus described.

**2.** *attrib.* passing into *adj.* **a.** Composed or made of 'shammy' or chamois leather.

**1651** T. BARKER *Art of Angling* (1820) 7 Some make them [*sc.* May-flies] with a shammie [eds. 1653, 1659 shammy] body. **1673** SHADWELL *Epsom Wells* I. 17 A couple of Gentlemen in Buff Belts, Red Coats, and Shammey Breeches. **1706** *Sir W. Calverley's Note-bk.* (Surtees) 112 A pair of good shamy gloves. **1766** H. WALPOLE *Let. to H. S. Conway* 12 Jan., I have got my cravat and shammy shoes. **1874** G. WALCH *Head over Heels* 83 Here it is—in this old Shammy bag.

†**b.** Of the colour of this leather; yellowish brown or light fawn. *Obs.*

**1661** *Peacham's Compl. Gent.* xiv. 156 Shammy colour, a smoakie, or rain colour, which is a kind of yellow.

**3.** *Australia.* 'A bag of chamois leather in which miners keep their gold dust' (*Cent. Dict.* 1891).

[**1874**: cf. 2 a.]

**shammy**[2] (ˈʃæmɪ). ? *nonce-wd.* [f. SHAM *a.* + -Y, after *dummy.*] A spurious imitation.

**1822** *Sporting Mag.* IX. 214 This may be the case with horses' tails—real ones may be deliberately cut off, and some celebrated professor's shammies annexed to the beast's back in their stead.

**shamois,** variant of CHAMOIS *sb.*

†**ˈshamously,** *adv. Obs.* Also **shamesly.** [f. **shamous* (f. SHAME *sb.* + -OUS: cf. SHAMEVOUS) + -LY[2].] Shamefully.

*c* **1440** *York Myst.* xxxii. 143 Shamously my selfe þus schente I So sone for to sente to his slayng. **14..** *Wars Alex.* 739* (Dubl. MS.) Þus shamesly of hys awne childe hym chevyd such end.

**shamoy** (ˈʃæmɔɪ), *v.* Also **shammoy, shammy.** [f. *shamoy* sb., var. CHAMOIS *sb.* 2.] *trans.* To prepare (leather) by working oil or grease into the skin. Hence **shamoyed** *ppl. a.*, **shamoying** *vbl. sb.*

**1837** HEBERT *Engin. & Mech. Encycl.* II. 67 Any subsequent operation, of tawing, or dyeing, oil-dressing, or shammoying. **1842** *Penny Cycl.* XXIV. 40/2 The process by which it is made is called shamoying or shammying... When whole skins are shamoyed, the grain surface is removed by scraping or rubbing with pumice-stone. **1857** MILLER *Elem. Chem., Org.* III. 675 Shamoying consists in working into the skin a quantity of oil, which supplies the place of the vegetable astringent..in the processes of tanning and tawing. *Ibid.*, A large portion of shamoyed leather forms what is known as wash-leather. **1858** HOMANS *Cycl. Comm.* s.v. *Leather* 1195/2 Deer and antelope [skins] are usually *shamoyed*, or dressed in oil. **1882** PATON in *Encycl. Brit.* XIV. 380/2 Shamoyed leather, consisting of skins combined with oils or fatty substances.

**shamoy(es,** etc.: see CHAMOIS *sb.*

**shampany,** obs. variant of CHAMPANY.

**shampin(n)ion,** obs. forms of CHAMPIGNON.

**1661** RABISHA *Cookery Dissected* 7 To pickle Shampinnions. **1706** PHILLIPS (ed. Kersey), *Shampinion*, a Mushroom.

**shampoo** (ʃæmˈpuː), *sb.* [f. SHAMPOO *v.*] **1.** The act or operation of shampooing; also a 'wash' used for shampooing. Also *attrib.*

**1838** HALIBURTON *Clockm.* Ser. II. xii, Prince Shleek, will you have one shampoo? said she. A shampoo? said I; to be sure I will. **1866** COOLEY *Toilet* 477 The 'Shampoo Liquid' often used by the hairdressers, after cutting the hair. **1880** WEBSTER *Suppl.* **1888** *Pall Mall Gaz.* 21 May 14/1 The shampoo room and the general swimming tank..are the same size. **1897** *Times* 9 Aug. 10/3 The vessel was labelled 'Antiseptic shampoo'. **1951** *Good Housek. Home Encycl.* 172/1 Soiled silk lampshades can be given a soap-and-water shampoo. **1970** *Which?* Aug. 251/2 Which carpet shampoo you choose depends on how much carpet you have to clean and how often you want to clean it.

**2.** *shampoo and set* (cf. SET *sb.*[1] 18 b).

**1935** A. CHRISTIE *Death in Clouds* xiii. 136 Is it a shampoo and set, or are you having a tint to-day? **1977** *Belfast Tel.* 22 Feb. 1/4 Customers will have to shell out an extra 10–15 pc for a snip of the scissors or a shampoo and set in many cases.

**3.** *slang.* Arbitrary alteration of CHAMPAGNE. Cf. SHAM *sb.*[2]

**1957** R. LONGRIGG *Switchboard* 192 'You'd better have some shampoo, darling.'.. 'Shampoo?' 'Champagne.' **1959** A. SINCLAIR *Breaking of Bumbo* ii. 31 The waiter brings a bottle of champagne... Shampoo, Sheila dear?

**shampoo** (ʃæm'puː), *v.* Also 8–9 **shampo,** 9 **champo(e, champoo, champou, shampoe.** [Prob. a. Hindī *čāmpo*, imper. of *čāmpnā* to press. Cf. CHAMPING *vbl. sb.*[2] (from 1698).]

**1. a.** *trans.* To subject (a person, his limbs) to massage. Now *rare* or *Obs.*, exc. as designating a part of the process of a Turkish bath.

**1762** [? NOBLE] *Voy. E. Indies*, etc. 226 Had I not seen several China merchants shampooed before me, I should have been apprehensive of danger. **1780** J. CAPPER *Let.* in *Observ. Passage India* (1785) 26 Some people have their nails cut and also are Shampoed. **1800** BEATSON *View War with Tippoo* 159 The Sultaun generally rose at break of day: after being champoed, and rubbed, he washed himself. **1813** J. FORBES *Oriental Mem.* II. 52 She [a Mahratta wife] first champoes her husband, and fans him to repose; she then champoes the horse. **1848** DICKENS *Dombey* viii, Miss Pankey was shampooed every morning. **1898** JEAN A. OWEN *Hawaii* iii. 65 In Tahiti, too, a traveller, on entering a house, is always given a mat to lie on, and his weary limbs are shampooed whilst food is prepared for him.

*absol.* **1823** *Mirror* I. 424/1 A man and his wife who profess to Shampoo, according to the Indian manner.

†**b.** *transf.* and *fig. Obs.*

**1837** DICKENS *Pickw.* v, The other shampoo'd Mr. Winkle with a heavy clothes brush. **1838** HALIBURTON *Clockm.* Ser. II. xii, So our diplomatists shampoo the English, and put 'em to sleep. How beautiful they shampoo'd them in the fishery story. **1848** THACKERAY *Van. Fair* xvii, Pinching the bed-curtains, poking into the feathers, shampooing the mattresses.

**2. a.** (The ordinary modern sense.) To subject (the scalp) to washing and rubbing with some cleansing agent, as soap and water, shampoo powder, etc. Also *absol.*

**1860** WORCESTER. **1881** *Times* 6 Jan. 4/3 The patient should have.. the hair cut and shampooed, and the whole body well cleansed with carbolic soap. **1976** *Glasgow Herald* 26 Nov. 17/4 This conditioning treatment is used before you shampoo, and so resembles the sort of reconditioning treatments available at a salon.

**b.** *transf.* To wash (a carpet, upholstery, etc.) with a cleansing agent. Also *absol.*

**1954** A. C. MOORE *How to clean Everything* I. 138/1 Synthetic (soapless) detergents.. are available in liquid, paste and powder form to shampoo hair, rugs and upholstery. **1969** *Sears Catal.* Spring/Summer 1359 Outdoor carpets... They'll take whatever comes in stride.. resist spots, stains.. just vacuum or shampoo clean. **1970** *Which?* Aug. 252/1 If you are going to shampoo your carpet only now and then.. a cheap aerosol would be most economical.

Hence **shampooed** (-'puːd) *ppl. a.*

**1821** SIR R. K. PORTER *Trav.* I. 232 This over, the shampooed body.. is rubbed all over with a preparation of soap confined in a bag, till he is one mass of lather.

**shampooer** (ʃæm'puːə(r)). [-ER[1].] **a.** One who shampoos, in either sense of the verb.

**1829** LYTTON *Disowned* iv, The stranger's horse.. being by no means in a good humour with the clumsy manœuvres of his Shampooer, the ostler. **1859** *Habits of Gd. Society* iii. 144 It [a rough hair shirt] acts the part of a shampooer, and with its perpetual friction soothes the surface of the skin [etc.]. **1884** BRACHET *Aix-les-bains* I. 95 At Aix are found thoroughly trained shampooers. **1885** E. GREEY *Bakin's Captive of Love* iii. (1904) 21 At that moment two blind shampooers came along the road. **1906** BEGBIE *Priest* viii. 156 His reddish hair fresh from the shampooer's hand.

**b.** A device for applying carpet shampoo.

**1960** *Farmer & Stockbreeder* 22 Mar. (Suppl.) 11/2 The new mechanical shampooers simplify the job greatly. **1974** *Spartanburg* (S. Carolina) *Herald* 25 Apr. A5 (Advt.), Rent a twin brush carpet shampooer.

**sham'pooing,** *vbl. sb.* [-ING[1].] The action or operation of SHAMPOO *v.*

**1762** [? NOBLE] *Voy. E. Indies*, etc. 226 Shampooing is an operation not known in Europe and is peculiar to the Chinese. **1823** J. BADCOCK *Dom. Amusem.* 114 We had long ago seen negroes employed in percussion upon their Barbadean masters, by whom it is termed 'Champooing'. **1829** *Good's Study Med.* (ed. 3) IV. 350 To these [remedies] should be added a series of friction, and especially of shampooing or manipulation applied down the whole course of the spine. **1829** *Health & Longevity* 235 In the East Indies, friction with the hand, or what is called champouing, is generally practised. **1869** M. WILKS *Hist. Sk. S. India* (ed. 2) I. xii. 276 *note*, Shampooing may be compared to a gentle kneading of the whole person. **1899** *Allbutt's Syst. Med.* VIII. 778 In all these [remedies] the shampooing necessary for their thorough application plays an important part in the treatment.

*attrib.* **1815** *Sporting Mag.* XLVI. 213, I set up a sort of shampooing scheme for the cure of the lumbago. **1825** C. M. WESTMACOTT *Eng. Spy* I. 313 A shampooing or vapour bath. *a* **1881** R. W. PROCTER *Barber's Shop* xvii. (1883) 160 Brilliant with gas, and redolent of rich perfume, are the modern shampooing saloons.

**shamrock** ('ʃæmrɒk). Forms: α. 6 shamrote, 7 shamroot; β. 6 shamrocke, sham-roke, 7 schamrock, shamrook, 7 shamocke, 8 shammock, shamroque, 6– shamrock; γ. 7 shamrogh, -rogth, shamerag, shamrug, -rogue, (chamroch), 7–8 shamrog(e, 8 shamrogge, (shambrogue, -brogh). [a. Irish *seamróg* (= Gael. *seamrag*), dim. of *seamar* clover.]

**1.** A plant with trifoliate leaves, used (according to a late tradition) by St. Patrick to illustrate the doctrine of the Trinity, and hence adopted as the national emblem of Ireland; a spray or leaf of this plant.

The 'shamrock' of the legend has been conjecturally identified with many different plants, e.g. the white clover *Trifolium repens*, the red clover, *T. pratense*, the black medic, *Medicago lupulina*, the wood-sorrel, *Oxalis Acetosella*, and the water-cress. The name is now most commonly applied to the lesser yellow trefoil, *Trifolium minus*, which is the plant most frequently worn as an emblem on St. Patrick's Day.

α. **1571** CAMPION *Hist. Irel.* I. vi. (1633) 18 Shamrotes, Water-cresses, Rootes, and other hearbes they feede upon. **1610** HOLLAND *Camden's Brit.* II. 147 They feed willingly upon.. Mushromes, Shamroots and rootes. **1613** WITHER *Abuses Stript* I. viii. Juvenilia (1633) 61 In no more cloathing than a mantle goe; And feed on Sham-rootes as the Irish doe.

β. **1577** STANYHURST *Descr. Irel.* viii. 28/1 in *Holinshed*, Water cresses, which they terme shamrocks, rootes and other herbes they feede vpon. **1596** SPENSER *State Irel.* Wks. (Globe) 654/2 Yf they founde a plotte of water-cresses or sham-rokes, there they flocked as to a feast for the time. **1597** GERARDE *Herbal* II. ccccLxxvii. 1018 Medow Trefoile is called.. in Irish Shamrockes. **1617** MORYSON *Itin.* III. 163 They willingly eate the hearb Schamrock. **1627** J. TAYLOR (Water-P.) *Armado* C 1 b, Their fare being many times shamrookes, oaten-bread, beanes and butter-milke. **1630** DEKKER *2nd Pt. Honest Wh.* III. i. E 2 b, Worse then damnation, a wild Kerne,.. Longed you for Shamocke? **1682** PIERS *Descr. West-Meath* (1770) 121 Butter, new cheese, and curds and shamrocks, are the food of the meaner sort all this season. **1775** SHERIDAN *St. Patrick's Day* I. i, I put a great shammock in his hat this morning. **1781** C. JOHNSTON *Hist. J. Juniper* I. 28 He marked our young hero on the left breast with a shamroque. **1813** T. MOORE *Oh the Shamrock!* 16 Chosen leaf Of Bard and Chief, Old Erin's native Shamrock! **1856** O. W. HOLMES *For Meeting Burns Club* 52 We drink a triple health,—the Rose, The Shamrock, and the Thistle! **1901** *Daily Express* 18 Mar. 5/7 Covent Garden sent King Edward a four-leaved shamrock on Saturday.

γ. **1611** SPEED *Theat. Gt. Brit.* IV. i. 138/2 Feeding vpon water-cresses, rootes, mushromes, shamrogh, butter tempered with oate-meale. **1622** J. TAYLOR (Water-P.) *Sir Greg. Nonsence* Wks. 1630 II. 4/2 Whilst all the Hibernian Kernes in multitudes Did feast with Shamerags stew'd in Vsquebagh. **1632** HOLLAND *Cyrupædia* I. i. 4 *margin*, Cresses.. of which the Irish Shamrogth are a kinde. **1643** J. TAYLOR (Water-P.) *Preter-pluperfect* 4 Some Bookes also of Irish Rebellion were devoured as they had been Shamrogs [*misprinted* Shamroys]. **1681** DINELEY in *Jrnl. Kilkenny Archæol. Soc.* (1858) I. 183 The 17[nth] day of March yeerly is S[t] Patricks, an immoveable feast, when.. the vulgar superstitiously wear shamroges, 3 leav'd grass. **1699** E. LHWYD in *Phil. Trans.* (1712) XXVII. 506 Their Shamrug is the common Clover. **1712** STEELE *Spect.* No. 455 ¶2 The Scotch Thistle, the Irish Shambrogue. **1741** *Gentl. Mag.* XI. 438/1 Go little Shamrogge, and adorn My pretty Flavia's breast this morn.

**b.** *to drown the shamrock*: to drink, or go drinking, in honour of the shamrock, on St. Patrick's day.

[**1726** THRELKELD *Syn. Stirpium Hibern.* s.v. *Trifolium*, This Plant is worn by the People.. upon.. St. Patrick's Day. It being a current Tradition, that by this Three Leafed Grass, he emblematically set forth to them the Mystery of the Holy Trinity. However that be, when they wet their *Seamar-oge*, they often commit Excess in Liquor, which is not a right keeping of a Day to the Lord.] **1888** *Daily Tel.* 22 Mar. (Farmer), An Irishman.. on Saturday last resolved to drown the shamrock in the orthodox fashion. **1901** *Ibid.* 18 Mar. 10/6 The oportunities for 'drowning the shamrock' were commendably abbreviated by the law.

**2.** Applied with defining word to some other plants (see quots.).

**1884** W. MILLER *Plant-n.* 124/2 Shamrock, Blue-flowered. *Parochetus communis*... Shamrock, Indian. *Trillium latifolium*. **1889** J. H. MAIDEN *Usef. Native Plants* 143 *Trigonella suavissima*.. is the 'Australian shamrock' of Mitchell. **1898** MORRIS *Austral Eng.*, *Shamrock, Native*, a forage plant, *Lotus australis*.

**3.** *attrib.* and *Comb.*: **shamrock pea,** *Parochetus communis* (Miller, *Plant-n.* 1884); †**shamrockshire,** a jocular name for Ireland.

**1581** DERRICKE *Image of Irelande* (1883) 8 My soule dooeth detest their wilde shamrocke manners. **1689** *Irish Hudibras* 80 Which.. Makes Wit so scarce in Shamrogeshire. **1724** MOFFET *Hesperi-neso-gr.* (1755) 3 Priests in Shambroghshire, they say, Can women kiss, as well as pray. **1900** *Daily News* 9 Apr. 5/6 The same shamrock-embroidered bonnet.

**Shamscrit,** obs. form of SANSKRIT.

‖**shamsheer.** Also 7 **chemchir,** 9 **shumsheer.** [Pers. *shamshīr* (see SCIMITAR). The form *shumsheer* is Anglo-Ind.] = SCIMITAR I.

**1634** SIR T. HERBERT *Trav.* 111 Three Cozel-bashawes standing by, in an instant whipt off all their heads, with their slicing Shamsheers or Semiters. **1686** tr. *Chardin's Coronat. Solyman* 41 The third Piece was a Chemchir, or sword. **1834** *Baboo* I. viii. 128 (Stanf.) With my shumsheer's point I directed the march towards the fort.

**shamshin,** var. SAMISEN.

**shamshue,** obs. variant of SAMSHOO.

**1744** J. PHILIPS *Jrnl. Exped. Anson* 217 They have another strong Liquor besides Shamshue. [*Ibid.* 155 Samshue.]

†**'shamster,** ? *nonce-wd.* [f. SHAM *v.* + -STER.] A shammer, impostor.

**1716** *Coll. State Songs, Poems*, etc. 40 They swore the lov'd Shamster [*i.e.* the Pretender] to Britain they'd bring.

**shamulle(r,** obs. forms of SHAWM, SHAWMER.

**shamus** ('ʃɑːməs, 'ʃeɪməs). *U.S. slang.* Also **sharmus, shommus.** [Orig. uncertain: perh. f. SHAMAS(H or the Irish proper name *Seamus*.] A police officer; a private detective.

**1925** H. LEVERAGE *Dict. Underworld* in *Flynn's Mag.* 28 Mar. 660 *Sharmus*, a detective; a cop. **1928** J. O'CONNOR *Broadway Racketeers* xvii. 186 Every Shommus on the beat knew we were going South with the stuff, but they couldn't prove it. **1930** [see KOSHER *a.* (*sb.*) c]. **1950** 'S. RANSOME' *Deadly Miss Ashley* ii. 19 Men in my profession don't call each other shamuses... We private operatives call ourselves private operatives. **1960** WODEHOUSE *Jeeves in Offing* iv. 49 You mean that I'm to be a sort of private eye or shamus, tailing them up? **1977** *New Yorker* 2 May 38/3, I think my wife is having me tailed by a private shamus.

**Shamvaian** (ʃæm'vaɪən), *a. Geol.* [f. *Shamva* + -IAN.] Of or pertaining to rocks in the vicinity of Shamva, a town in northern Zimbabwe; *spec.* the epithet of a Pre-Cambrian mountain-building episode in southern Africa when these were affected.

**1947** A. M. MACGREGOR in *Bull. S. Rhodesian Geol. Surv.* No. 38. 8 Although the Shamva Grits of the Mazoe Valley were not the first to be described they occupy the largest continuous area... The name 'Shamvaian' is proposed. *Ibid.* 15 The Shamvaian rocks of the Bembesi valley are generally similar to the upper series at Que Que. **1951** *Trans. Geol. Soc. S. Afr.* LIV. p. xxix, The largest area of these rocks.. is that of the Shamva grits in the Mazoe Valley which is selected as the type area of the Shamvaian system. **1964** A. E. PHAUP in S. H. Haughton *Geol. Ore Deposits S. Afr.* II. 2 Some reefs may be pre-Bulawayan and pre-Shamvaian in age, but the majority are post-Shamvaian. **1971** I. G. GASS et al. *Understanding Earth* xxii. 317/1 At least seven major mountain-building events (periods of orogenesis) are recorded in Africa and are.. (ii) 2500–2800 million years ago (Shamvaian orogeny); [etc.].

**shamway,** obs. form of CHAMOIS *sb.*

**shamwelle,** obs. form of SHAMBLE *sb.*[1]

**shamy,** obs. form of SHAMMY *sb.*[1]

**shamyana,** variant of SHAMIANA(H.

**shamyll,** obs. form of SHAMBLE *sb.*[1]

**shan** (ʃæn), *sb.*[1] [Of obscure origin.] The SHANNY.

**1713** JAGO in Ray *Synopsis Pisc.* 164 *Cataphractus lævis, Cornubiensis.* Smooth Shan. **1851** GOSSE *Nat. Hist., Fishes* 168 The most common of our Blennies is the Shanny (*Blennius pholis*, Linn.), sometimes called the Smooth Shan, an epithet probably alluding to the absence of those fringed appendages to the head with which all our other true Blennies are furnished.

**shan,** *sb.*[2] *slang.* ? *Obs.* Also **shand.** [Cf. SHAN *a.*] Counterfeit or base coin. Also *fig.*

**1812** J. H. VAUX *Flash Dict.*, *Shan*, counterfeit money in general. **1815** SCOTT *Guy M.* xxxii, I doubt Glossin will prove but shand after a'..; but this is a gude half-crown ony way. [*Note*, Cant expression for base coin.]

**shan** (ʃæn), *sb.*[3] *Naut.* [Of obscure origin; the Norwegian *skaan* hard crust (ON. *skán* thin membrane, film) has been compared.] (See quot.)

**1867** SMYTH *Sailor's Word-bk.*, *Shan*, a defect in spars, most commonly from bad collared knots; an injurious compression of fibres in timber: the turning out of the cortical layers when the plank has been sawed obliquely to the central axis of the tree.

**Shan** (ʃɑːn), *sb.*[4] and *a.*[2] Also **Sciam, Shaan.** [Burmese.] **A.** *sb.* (A member of) a group of Mongoloid peoples of the Tai family, inhabiting parts of Burma, south China, and Indo-China. Also, the Tai language spoken by these peoples. **B.** *adj.* Of or pertaining to the Shan or their language.

**1800** M. SYMES *Acc. Embassy Ava* xi. 274 An intelligent man.. informed him, that.. the first Shaan town was called Thangdat. *Ibid.*, Shaan, or Shan, is a very comprehensive term given to different nations, some independent, others the subjects of the greater states. **1833** W. TANDY tr. *Sangermano's Descr. Burmese Empire* ix. 57 The zaboà or petty princes of the Sciam, subject to the Burmese. **1898** [see LOLO]. **1920** *Blackw. Mag.* June 839/1 You sell liquor and opium to Burmans and Shans. **1927** *Ibid.* June 819/1 Men armed with.. long Shan knives were patrolling the approaches. **1951** R. FIRTH *Elem. Social Organiz.* iv. 145 The Pai of the Chinese Shans; the *anga* of the Tikopia.. are ..examples of the allocation of large-scale resources in goods and labour with primary reference to status yields. **1968** O. WYND *Sumatra Seven Zero* ii. 25 Your companion knows Shan. She learned it to pass the time. **1977** *Whitaker's Almanack 1978* 828 Burmese is the official language, but minority languages include Shan, Karen, Chin, and the various Kachin dialects.

**shan,** *a.*[1] *Sc.* and *north.* ? *Obs.* [Of obscure origin.] Pitiful, silly; poor, mean, paltry, shabby.

**1714** RAMSAY *Elegy on John Cowper* xiii, Of umquhile John to lie or bann, Shaws but ill will, and looks right shan. **1719** —— *To Hamilton, 1st Answ.* vi, Ye're never rugget, shan, nor kittle. **1776** HERD *Sc. Songs* II. 264 Gloss. **1906** A. M[c]CORMICK *Tinkler-Gypsies Galloway* iii. 128 A flat-fitted or shan-winklered (bad-eyed) body.

**shanachie, -y,** variant forms of SENNACHIE.

**shananacking,** var. SHENANIGAN.

‖**Shanavest** (ˈʃænəvɛst). *Irish.* Also *erron.* Shanavat. [According to Dr. P. W. Joyce, f. Irish *sean* old + VEST *sb.* (The opposing faction were called *caravats* = 'cravats'.)] *pl.* The name of one of the fighting factions into which the peasantry of the South of Ireland were formerly divided.

**1811** J. JEBB in C. Forster *Corr. betw. J. & Knox* (1834) II. 41 The Archbishop..promises to insure you against caravats, shanavests, and all such marauders. **1823** *Blackw. Mag.* XIV. 518 Whiteboys, Shanavats,..and Captain Rock. **1862** BORROW *Wales* c. III. 380 My father..was the best fighting man with a stick that the Shanavests ever had.

**shancre,** obs. form of CHANCRE.

†**shand,** *a. Sc. Obs. rare.* In 5 **schand.** ? Beautiful, handsome.

*c* **1450** HOLLAND *Howlat* 84 The plesant Pacock..schand in his schap. *Ibid.* 112 That ȝe wald cry apon Crist..To schape me [*sc.* an Owl] a schand bird.

**shand,** var. f. SHAN *sb.*[2]

**shandaradan,** obs. form of SHANDRYDAN.

**shande,** variant of SHOND *Obs.*, disgrace.

**Shandean** (ˈʃændɪən, ʃænˈdiːən), *a.* (and *sb.*). Also 8 **Shandeyan,** 9 **Shandyan** (*sb.*), **Shandeian.** [f. (*Tristram*) *Shandy*, the title of a novel (1759–67) by Sterne + -AN.] Pertaining to *Tristram Shandy*, or the Shandy family there portrayed.

**1762** STERNE *Tr. Shandy* VI. xvii, I write a careless kind of a civil, nonsensical, good-humoured Shandean book, which will do all your hearts good. **1767** S. PATERSON *Another Trav.* I. Pref. 8 A couple of Shandean duodecimos. **1769** CHATTERTON *Jrnl. Sixth* Poet. Wks. (1886) 153 But Hudibrastics may be found To tire ye with repeated sound, So changing for a Shandeyan style, I ask your favour and your smile. **1782** T. JEFFERSON *Notes State of Virginia* (1787) 234 His stile is easy and familiar, except when he affects a Shandean fabrication of words. **1887** SAINTSBURY *Ess. Eng. Lit.* (1891) 107 Scott's delightful Shandean jest on him. **1909** SICHEL *Sheridan* I. 3 [Sheridan's] inner texture is Shandeian.

*Comb.* **1762** STERNE *Let.* 9 July, Wks. 1885 IV. 496, I had hired a chaise and horse.., but, Shandeanlike, did not take notice that the horse was almost dead when I took him.

**b.** *sb.* One who has the 'Shandean' spirit.

**1866** P. FITZGERALD *Lamb* (ed. 2) 187 Another point of resemblance between these two great Shandyans [*sc.* Sterne and Lamb] was their both writing little quaint autobiographies.

So also †**Shanˈdaic** *a.* ˈ**Shandeism** (ˈ**Shandyism**), the style or the philosophy of the novel *Tristram Shandy*. ˈ**Shandy** *v.* quasi-trans., *to Shandy it*, to play a Shandean part; *trans.* to bandy in Shandean fashion. †ˈ**Shandyize** *v.* = prec.

*a* **1761** J. GILBERT *Let. to Sterne*, Shandyise. **1761** STERNE *Let.* ? Aug., Wks. 1885 IV. 479 If God..had not poured forth the spirit of Shandeism into me, which will not suffer me to think two moments upon any grave subject. **1762** —— *Let.* 19 Mar., *Ibid.* 485, I Shandy it away fifty times more than I was ever wont, talk more nonsense than ever you heard me talk in your days. **1766** —— *Let.* 25 Nov., *Ibid.* 542, I am going to lie in of another child of the Shandaick procreation, in town. **1831** *Mirror* XVII. 234/2 The book is altogether *Shandean*, and the satire *shandied* to and fro with great vivacity. **1891** *Daily News* 15 Oct. 6/1, I..imbibed Shandyism from him [Sterne] to the dregs. **1903** *Blackw. Mag.* May 712 He invented a Shandeism perfectly consistent with his own age and his own taste.

**shandeller,** obs. variant of CHANDLER[1].

**1547** in *Spalding Club Misc.* V. 313 Twa silver shandellers.

**shanderadan, -erydan,** obs. ff. SHANDRYDAN.

**shandigaff,** variant of SHANDYGAFF.

**shandite** (ˈʃændaɪt). *Min.* [ad. G. *shandit* (P. Ramdohr in *Sitzungsber. d. Deutsch. Akad. d. Wissensch. zu Berlin* (*Math.-naturwissensch. Kl.*) *1949* (1950) VI. 26), f. the name of S. J. Shand (1882–1957), Scottish geologist: see -ITE[1].] A sulphide of nickel and lead, $Ni_3Pb_2S_2$, found as yellow rhombohedral crystals.

**1950** *Amer. Mineralogist* XXXV. 450 On receiving this result Dr. Ramdohr intimated in a private communication (Nov., 1949) that he proposed to name the new mineral shandite, after Professor S. J. Shand,..who had suggested ..the study of the Insizwa nickel ores which led to the discovery of parkerite. *Ibid.*, Two lots of artificial shandite were prepared by fusing charges of 1 gm. and 2 gm. of the powdered elements in the proportions 3Ni:2Bi:2S. **1968** I. KOSTOV *Mineralogy* 117 Shandite has a distorted spinel structure, the nickel atoms being arranged along the pseudocubic diagonals; this explains its ferromagnetic properties.

**shandry** (ˈʃændrɪ). *North-west dial.* Also **shanderee, shandray.** [Perh. shortened from next, which however is later in our quots.] A light cart or trap on springs. Also ***shandry cart.***

**1802** MRS. WHEELER *Westmld. Dial.* iv. 95 Dud the cusen keep a horse an a shanderee? **18..** J. BRIGGS *Rem.* (1825) 93 (E.D.D.), We hired a shandry to carry us to Little Langdale. **1836** SIR G. HEAD *Home Tour* 427, I saw this happy couple drive away from the inn together, in a light shandry cart. **1859** DICKENS *Haunted Ho.* VII. 45 I'll drive yo' in the shandry. *a* **1865** MRS. GASKELL *Sexton's Hero* in *Cousin Phillis*, etc. 280 We borrowed a shandry, and harnessed my old grey mare. **1882** *Lanc. Gloss.*, *Shandray*, a one-horse carriage. **1888** *Bury Times* 1 Sept. 6 Damages to a milk shandry.

**shandrydan** (ˈʃændrɪdæn). Also **shandrydan, shandridan, -redan, -radan, shan-dradam; shandaradan, -ery-dan, -eradan; shatterydan, shattaradan.** [Of obscure origin: in some way related to prec.] A kind of chaise with a hood. In later use, a jocular designation for any rickety old-fashioned vehicle.

**1820** HOGG in *Blackw. Mag.* VI. 391 Dr. Morris wheeling ..yon furious shandrydan. **1823** in *Spirit Publ. Jrnls.* 277 [A parody of Moore's *Loves of the Angels.*] When in Hyde Park we grac'd the ride In the old royal shandaradan. **1829** A. SEDGWICK in Clark & Hughes *Life & Lett.* (1890) I. 353 A machine with two seats, but in every other respects like a Dent's shandery-dan. **1830** MRS. ELIZ. HOLMES *Scenes in our Parish* 276 To be sure Haynes the cobler has a curious shandridan, sometimes open and sometimes covered. **1838** MOORE *Mem.* (1856) VII. 235 One of those cabs (or shanderadans, as they call them). **1849** J. COLQUHOUN *Rocks & Rivers* 15 Now, landlord, out with the shan-dra-dam. **1858** R. S. SURTEES *Ask Mamma* xxxii. 134 Having got the last shandry-dan deposited under the hay-house, he had just time [etc.]. **1860** H. MAYHEW *Upper Rhine* Introd. 3 The only private carriage that appears in the streets is the Princess's shandredan. **1861** MUSGRAVE *By-Roads* 75 When ..gigs and shandradans of every grade would be bespoken by special retainers. **1873** R. A. FITZGERALD *Wickets in West* 70 Shatterydans of various kinds conveyed them to the Russell House [Ottawa]. **1900** ELIN. GLYN *Visits of Eliz.* 158 A few of the really odd kinds of shandrydans that one sees coming to country garden parties in England.

**shandy** (ˈʃændɪ), *sb.* Short for SHANDYGAFF. Also, a mixture of beer and fizzy lemonade.

**1888** *Daily News* 4 June 3/1 Sparkling hop, shandy, and other new-fangled drinks. **1893** *Westm. Gaz.* 10 Oct. 5/2 The witness..supplied him with some bitter-shandy. **1919** *Chambers's Jrnl.* Sept. 593/1 Staff-Sergeant Jack Dorley, R.E., finished off his shandy with a long draught. **1947** K. TENNANT *Lost Haven* xvii. 267 Miss O'Shea was drinking ginger-beer and her escort had a shandy. **1969** A. CHRISTIE *Hallowe'en Party* v. 39 For me, I think a shandy. The ginger beer and the beer? **1976** *Milton Keynes Express* 30 July 2/7 He said Mr Westley had drunk four pints of shandy during the evening but his driving had not appeared to be affected.

**shandy** (ˈʃændɪ), *a. dial.* Also **shanny.** [Of obscure origin; connexion with OE. *sceand* masc., buffoon, charlatan, *sceand* fem., disgrace (see SHOND) is unlikely.] Wild, boisterous; also visionary, empty-headed, half-crazy. See also *Eng. Dial. Dict.*

**1691** RAY *N.C. Words* 62 *Shandy*, wild. **1788** W. H. MARSHALL *Yorksh.* II. 351 *Shandy*, a little crack-brained; somewhat crazy. *a* **1825** FORBY *Voc. E. Anglia*, *Shanny*, shatter-brained. **1855** ROBINSON *Whitby Gloss.*, *Shandy*, crack-brained, shallow, crazy. 'He's quite shandy.' Also, slender in person. 'A spare shandy sort of a figure.' **1884** TROLLOPE *Old Man's Love* I. 107 Could there be anything more moonstruck, more shandy, more wretchedly listless, than for a girl..to indulge in dreams of an impossible lover. **1895** A. PATTERSON *Man & Nat. on Broads* 27 Master'll wonder if I'm clean gone tu sleep or if I'm shanny.

*Comb.* **shandy-pated** *a.*, giddy, thoughtless.

**1806** BLOOMFIELD *Wild Flowers, Horkey* 47 A shanny-pated crew. **1863** TROLLOPE *Rachel Ray* I. 250 Mrs. Ray.. was so inconsequent in her mental workings, so shandy-pated if I may say so, that [etc.]. **1867** —— *Chron. Barset* I. xxxii. 276, I am in such matters so shandy-pated, that I can trust myself to be sure of nothing.

**shandygaff** (ˈʃændɪgæf). Also **shandigaff.** [Of unknown origin.] A drink composed of a mixture of beer and ginger-beer.

**1853** 'C. BEDE' *Verd. Green* I. xii, He taught me..to make shandy-gaff and sherry-cobbler. **1861** HUGHES *Tom Brown at Oxf.* xv, With a large pewter, foaming with shandygaff, in each hand. **1881** J. PAYN *Grape from a Thorn* li, A glass of 'shandigaff'. **1903** F. MARKHAM *Recoll. Town Boy Westminster* 135 What with the charge for the [racquet-] court, our luncheon, and frequent shandy-gaffs, our money only just lasted out.

**shane,** Sc. f. SANE *v.*; obs. pa. t. of SHINE *v.*

**Shang** (ʃæŋ). Also **Chang, Xanga.** [Chinese *shāng*.] The name of a dynasty which ruled China during part of the second millennium B.C., probably from the 16th to the 11th century B.C. Also *attrib.* or as *adj.* Also called **Shang-Yin** [f. the place-name *Yin* in Honan Province, the dynasty's final capital].

**1669** J. OGILBY tr. *Nieuhoff's Embassy Grand Tartar Cham* xviii. 281 [Then] arose the family of Xanga, whereof the Emperor Tangus, in the year before Christ's Birth 1766, was the first who called it Xanga, from a Lordship of the same name he possessed. **1736** R. BROOKES tr. *Du Halde's Gen. Hist. China* I. 298 (*heading*) The Second Dynasty, called *Chang*, which comprehends the Lives of Twenty Eight Emperors in the Space of 644 Years. **1797** *Encycl. Brit.* IV. 653/1 The whole of their [*sc.* of the Chinese] emperors..are comprehended in 22 dynasties, mentioned in the following table... 2. Shang, or Ing. **1877** *Ibid.* VI. 259/2 Confucius's own ancestry is traced up, through the sovereigns of the previous dynasty of Shang, to Hwang-ti. **1933** R. FRY *Let.* 15 Dec. (1972) II. 686 Some..accomplished pre-Cheou bronzes: Shang they say but anyhow earlier than anything I knew. **1939** *Burlington Mag.* Feb. 85/2 Practically everything is problematical... This applies to the use of Shang weapons, though their date seems fairly safe. **1958** W. WILLETTS *Chinese Art* I. 108 Writing in Shang-Yin times may have been more widespread through society than was at first believed. **1972** S. H. HANSFORD *Gloss. Chinese Art & Archaeol.*, *Ku*..is applied especially to objects attributed to the..Hsia, Shang-Yin and Chou, and the Han Dynasty. **1978** *New Archaeol. Finds in China* II. 2 Shang relics have been newly discovered in regions other than the Central Plains.

**Shangaan** (ʃæŋˈgɑːn). [Native name.] (A member of) a Bantu people inhabiting Zimbabwe, Mozambique, and South Africa; the language of the south-east Bantu group spoken by this people. Also *attrib.* or as *adj.*

**1887** J. W. MATTHEWS *Incwadi Yami* 183 The native labour of the diamond fields..includes nearly twenty different tribes such as Zulus, Swazees, Basutos, Shangaans, [etc.]. **1911** *Encycl. Brit.* XXVII. 189/2 The Shangaan are members of a Bantu tribe from the Delagoa Bay region who took refuge in the Transvaal between 1860 and 1862 to escape Zulu raids. **1932** C. FULLER *Louis Trigardt's Trek* 39 Trigardt adopted a version from other than local natives, probably his Shangaan guides. **1948** *Rep. Native Laws Comm. 1946–48* (Dept. Native Affairs, S. Afr.) 38/1, I have had in hand a most valuable document, prepared by a young Shangaan. **1968** C. BURKE *Elephant across Border* iv. 118 An elderly man..got out, speaking quietly in Shangaan to an African. *Ibid.* 128 They suddenly saw Murray and his Shangaan tracker. **1973** *Standard Encycl. S. Afr.* IX. 601/1 The Transvaal Tsonga—called Machangana (Shangaans), ..—have been recognised as one of the eight Bantu peoples living in the Republic of South Africa.

†**shangan.** *Sc. Obs.* Also **shangin, shanjan.** [a. Gael. *seangan*, ? f. *seang* slender, narrow.] 'A stick cleft at one end for putting on a dog's tail' (*Eng. Dial. Dict.*). Cf. SHANGY *sb.*

**1786** BURNS *Ordination* ii, He'll clap a shangan on her tail, An' set the bairns to daud her Wi' dirt this day. **1789** D. DAVIDSON *Thoughts on Seasons* 20 And Gibby skelp'd before the fae, Like Colly wi' a shangin. **1824** MACTAGGART *Gallovid. Encycl.* 425.

**shanghai** (ʃæŋˈhaɪ), *sb.* Also **shanghae, -hay.** [f. *Shanghai* or *Shanghae*, the name of one of the chief seaports of China.]

**1.** With capital initial. A long-legged, large breed of domestic fowls, with feathered shanks, reputed to have been introduced from Shanghai; now developed into the brahmas and cochins.

**1853** TEGETMEIER *Profit. Poultry* 19 Cochins or Shanghaes. **1853** FORTUNE in Wingfield & Johnson *Poultry Bk.* 3 The Shanghae breed. *Ibid.*, Some of the Shanghae fowls' eggs have double yolks. **1857** AGASSIZ *Contrib. Nat. Hist. U.S.* I. 164 Varieties..such as the Shanghae fowl, for instance.

**2.** *Austral.* and *N.Z.* Also as **shangeye.** A catapult.

**1863** *Leader* 24 Oct. 17/1 (Morris), Turn, turn thy shanghay dread aside, Nor touch that little bird. **1875** *Spectator* (Melbourne) 15 May 22/1 The lads had with them a couple of pistols, powder, shot, bullets, and a shanghai. **1901** DYSON *Gold-stealers* viii. 81 The plan brought Dicky, 'shanghai' in hand, under the tree where Hardy sat. **1940** F. SARGESON *Man & Wife* (1944) 7, I was out in the backyard with my shanghai, and..I took a shot at a thrush. **1947** D. M. DAVIN *Gorse blooms Pale* 57 Bits of shangeye as they called their catapults. **1972** M. GEE *In my Father's Den* 44 He made me shanghais and bows and arrows.

**3.** *U.S.* (See quot.).

**1880** *Scribner's Monthly* Jan. 365/1 The 'shanghai' is the glaring daub required by some frame-makers for cheap auctions. They are turned out at so much by the day's labor, or at from $12 to $24 a dozen, by the piece.

**4.** *Shanghai oil*: an oil extracted from the seeds of *Brassica chinensis*.

**1861** BENTLEY *Man. Bot.* 453.

**5.** *Darts.* With capital initial. [f. SHANGHAI *v.* 1.] A popular variation of the game of darts, in which players amass points by throwing three darts at each number in succession, players failing to score during a round being eliminated or 'shanghaied' (but see also quot. 1953); a winning shot or score of a single, double, and treble of a number.

**1930** *Anchor Mag.* (Barclay Perkins, Brewers) 196 'Shanghai' may be played by teams of 8, in pairs, individually, or, in fact, any number. **1936** R. CROFT-COOKE *Darts* vii. 44 Of all the lesser-known games which can be played on a dart-board, there is none which combines such fascinating elements as Shanghai. And it remains exciting till the very last throw. **1953** *Word for Word* (Whitbread & Co.) 31/2 *Shanghai*, a popular variant of the standard game of darts, usually played by four or more people. Each player is given a number which he must first score; he then proceeds to score the numbers of all the other participants. **1968** N. E. WILLIAMSON *Darts* v. 46 *Shanghai.* One of the more popular dart games for a number of players... Usually two or three numbers most often 5, 7 and 9 are nominated as 'Shanghai' numbers, and a player not scoring on any one of these is 'Shanghaied' or out of the game. **1977** *Daily Mirror* 10 May 30/2 The hot twenty—including local favourites George Simmons, Tony Brown, Nick Norris and Lew Walker—have to sweat through nineteen 501s, one 1,001, one 2,001, one round-the-board-on-doubles, one shanghai and one halve-it. **1980** K. TURNER *Darts* ix. 89 There is however a special shot that will automatically win the game on any number: scoring 'Shanghai'—hitting the single, double and treble of that number (in any order).

**shang'hai**, *v.* [Formed as prec.]

**1.** *trans.* **a.** *Naut. slang* (orig. *U.S.*). To drug or otherwise render insensible, and ship on board a vessel wanting hands.

**1871** *N.Y. Tribune* 1 Mar. (Schele de Vere *Americanisms*, p. 347), And before that time they would have been drugged, shanghaied, and taken away from all means of making complaint. **1887** S. SAMUELS *Forecastle to Cabin* 46 To be carried or forced on board of a ship in this manner is what is termed in sailor parlance being shanghaied.

*transf.* **1909** *Chamb. Jrnl.* July 440/2, I have got the Grand Duke pretty well shanghaied.

**b.** *transf.* To transfer forcibly or abduct; to constrain or compel. *colloq.* (orig. *U.S. Mil. slang*).

**1919** in *Amer. Speech* 1972 (1975) XLVII. 97 The second third has been 'shanghaied' for garrison duty. **1934** *Sun* (Baltimore) 21 May 7/5 Arguments will be heard..on Insuli's plea that that court has no jurisdiction over him because he was 'shanghaied' from Istanbul. **1958** *People* 4 May 15/6 We began to wonder if she'd got herself shanghaied. **1974** *Sunday Times* 15 Dec. 3/1 Hunt..thought he was being 'Shanghai-ed'—prison jargon for a transfer to another prison as a punishment. **1976** J. GIBSON *As I saw It* xxviii. 491 Most of my guests get shanghaied into giving a general knowledge talk to the boys.

**c.** *Darts.* To eliminate (a player) from a game of shanghai. See sense 5 of the sb.

**1968** [see SHANGHAI *sb.* 5]. **1980** K. TURNER *Darts* ix. 90 A more common variation is to 'Shanghai' players out of the game.

**2.** *Australian.* [See prec. sb. 2.] 'To shoot with a shanghai' (*Webster's Suppl.* 1902).

Hence **shang'haier**, one who shanghais.

**1917** *Chambers's Jrnl.* Jan. 19/1 Once..a shanghaier had been shanghaied by a rival shanghaier. **1926** J. BLACK *You can't Win* xii. 152 Here I learned to beware the crafty shanghaier with his knockout drops.

**Shanghailander** (ʃæŋ'haɪlændə(r)). [f. *Shanghai* (see SHANGHAI *sb.*), after HIGHLANDER, ISLANDER, etc.] A native or inhabitant of Shanghai.

**1917** *China Press* (Shanghai) 20 June 6/3 The Shanghailanders are still working to get a pipe band together and yesterday there were two leathery-lunged Scots extracting sounds from their machines in the Town Hall. **1937** E. LINKLATER *Juan in China* vii. 123 They were Shanghailanders. **1959** *Time* 8 June 36/3 The impertinent, self-assured Shanghailander of the past has disappeared.

**Shanghainese** (ʃæŋhaɪ'niːz). [f. *Shanghai* (see SHANGHAI *sb.*) + *-n-* + -ESE, after CHINESE, etc.] The Chinese dialect of the Wu group spoken in Shanghai; a native or inhabitant of Shanghai (also *collect.*). Also *attrib.* or as *adj.*

**1964** *Asia Mag.* 12 July 22/3 The Chinese [in Hong Kong]..speak no less than seven tongues—Cantonese, Hoklo,..Shanghainese, Chiuchow and Fukienese. **1965** M. WEST *Ambassador* vi. 116 He looked more like a Shanghainese than a Viet. **1970** T. LILLY *Projects Section* iv. 36 The Shanghainese must surely be among the most handsome people in the world. **1971** K. HOPKINS *Hong Kong* 225 Shanghainese firms were mainly established in Hong Kong, in the late 1940s and early 1950s, by capitalists from Shanghai who fled from Communism. **1977** H. FAST *Immigrants* II. 114 'You see, my mother is Shanghainese—.' 'Not really,' Feng Wo interrupted. 'She comes from a tiny village to the south of the city.' *Ibid.* 115, I was speaking Shanghainese and Mandarin before I ever knew a word of English.

**Shango** ('ʃæŋgəʊ). Also **shango**. [f. the name *Shango* of the god of thunder and lightning in the Yoruba religion of W. Nigeria.] **1.** A syncretistic cult practised in the Caribbean. Freq. *attrib.*

**1953** *Caribbean Q.* III. I. 16 In 1916 I had the first experience of the Shango. **1958** J. CAREW *Wild Coast* xi. 155 The shango gods, Dumbhalla, Legba, Moko. **1963** G. J. MCCALL *Social Problems* x. 364/2 'Hoodoo'..corresponding to..*shango* in Trinidad. **1974** *Trinidad Guardian* 2 Nov. 7/6 Sometimes they used the heady chants heard at 'wakes', shango meetings, and other such ceremonies.

**2.** A dance associated with the Shango cult.

**1948** E. LEAF *Isles of Rhythm* vi. 142 It had a more pronounced sex base than the Afro-Caribbean religious dances such as *Voodoo*, *Shango* and *Obeah*. **1971** *Advocate-News* (Barbados) 17 Sept. (Guyana Suppl.) p. i/1 *Cumfa*, a spirit dance like the Trinidad 'Shango'.

**Shangri-La** (ʃæŋgrɪ'lɑː). Also **Shangrila**, **shangri-la**, etc. The name of *Shangri-La* [f. Tibetan *la* mountain pass], a Tibetan utopia in *Lost Horizon* (1933), a novel by James Hilton, used *transf.* to designate an earthly paradise, a place of retreat from the worries of modern civilization. (In quot. 1945 as quasi-*adj.*)

[**1933** J. HILTON *Lost Horizon* ix. 212 When the High Lama asked him whether Shangri-La was not unique in his experience..he answered..'To be quite frank, it reminds me very slightly of Oxford, where I used to lecture.' **1938** 'E. QUEEN' *Four of Hearts* xv. 197 'It's a simply hideous place.' ..'It's not exactly another Shangri-La.'] **1941** *Time* 23 June 53/1 The Captain operates an insular Shangri-La in the South Pacific. **1945** L. DURRELL *Let.* 15 Dec. in *Spirit of Place* (1969) 81, I was afraid I would sound so heartlessly healthy and the country so Shangri la that you would write me a stinker. **1960** D. LESSING *In Pursuit of English* i. 15 Their Shangri-La would be populated..with nice professional people. **1971** *Sat. Rev.* (U.S.) 11 Dec. 53/1 The Windward Islands..excel any of the shangri-las of the South Pacific. **1977** *China Now* July/Aug. 19/1 The lamasery, for all its association with the Shangrila myth of eternal youth and joy, brought misery.

**shangy** ('ʃæŋɪ), *sb. Sc.* and *north.* Also **shangie**. [? Altered form of SHANGAN.]

**1.** A shackle; *pl.* handcuffs.

**1808** JAMIESON, *Shangie*, a shackle that runs on the stake to which a cow is bound in the byre. **1839** *Dundee Advertiser* 12 Apr., As he remained obstreperous, the policeman put on the shangies. **1864** LATTO *Tammas Bodkin* x. 89 Clappin' the shangies on my wrists.

**2.** = SHANGAN.

**1825** JAMIESON, Shangan, Shanjan, Shanjie... It is pronounced *shangie*, Roxb. **1843** M. A. RICHARDSON *Local Hist. Table Bk.*, Legend. Div. I. 117 Tom..sneaket off like a tyke wi' a shangy on his tail.

**shank** (ʃæŋk), *sb.* Forms: α. 1 sceanca, scanca, scance, 2–3 scanke, 3 (*Ormin*) shankk, 3–7 schank(e, shanke, 4 sschanke, 4–5 schanke, 6 shainke, shankke, sanke, shaunck, 6–7 shanck(e, 5– shank. β. 1 sconca, sconc, 3 sconke, shonke, (soncke), 3–4 schonke. [OE. *sc(e)anca* wk. masc. corresponds to LG. *schanke* leg, thigh, Flem. *schank* bone (Sw., Da. *skank*, Norw. *skonk* thigh, prob. from LG.):—WGer. **skankan-*; also, with difference of declension, to MLG. *schenke*, Du. *schenk* leg-bone (:—**skanki-*); a derivative from the same grade of the root is MLG., MHG., mod.G. *schenkel* thigh (WGer. **skankila-*). From other grades of the root (**skink-*: **skank-*: **skunk-*) are OS. *scinka*, gl. L. 'basis', 'tibia' (MLG. *schinke* thigh, ham), OHG. *scinko* masc., *scinka* fem., leg-bone, thigh (MHG. *schinke* masc., thigh, ham, mod.G. *schinken* masc., ham); OFris. *skunka*, *sconck* (mod.Fris. *skonk*, *schunk*), LG. (Koolman) *schunke* thigh, ham, Du. *schonk* bone. The OE. str. form *sconc* neut. (see 1 e) may belong to either the *a* or the *u* grade.

The root agrees formally, and may be identical, with that of ON. *skakk-r* wry, distorted (:—OTeut. **skanko-*), which is prob. cogn. w. Gr. σκάζειν (:—pre-Hellenic **sq'ngy-*) to limp. Even assuming the identity of the root, however, the etymological meaning of the Teut. sbs. remains obscure.]

**1. a.** That part of the leg which extends from the knee to the ankle; the tibia or shin-bone. Also (now *jocularly*) the leg as a whole; chiefly *pl.* one's legs.

α. *c* **1000** *Ags. Gosp.* John xix. 33 Þa hi to þam hælende comon & ȝesawon þæt he dead wæs ne bræcon hi na his sceancan. *c* **1000** ÆLFRIC *Gloss.* in Wr.-Wülcker 160/15 *Crus*, scance; *crura*, sceanca. *c* **1200** ORMIN 4775 Brest, & wambe, & þes, & cnes, & fet, & shannkess. *a* **1300** *Cursor M.* 14064 And sco hir vnttement me broght And smerd has me fote and schank. *Ibid.* 28002 If þou..has bituix hir scankes gan or tirid or tut or skirt vptan. *c* **1400** MAUNDEV. (Roxb.) xviii. 81 Men ballokes hyngez doune to þaire schankes. *c* **1430** *Chev. Assigne* 326 Thenne thei styrte vp on hy with staloworth shankes. **1538** ELYOT *Dict.*, *Parastata*, also one of the bones in the shanke of the legge. **1596** SPENSER *F.Q.* IV. x. 25 Sundry flowring bankes, To sit and rest the walkers wearie shankes. **1635** [GLAPTHORNE] *Lady Mother* II. i. in Bullen *O. Pl.* II. 131 Come, stir your shanks nimbly or Ile hough you. **1674** SCHEFFER *Lapland* v. 12 Slender wasts, spindle shanks, and swift of foot. **1784** COWPER *Task* v. 16 With eye askance I view the muscular proportion'd limb Transform'd to a lean shank. **1888** STEVENSON *Kidnapped* xiv, My stockings..were quite worn through, so that my shanks went naked. **1890** H. G. DAKYNS tr. *Xenophon's Anab.* III. ii. Wks. I. 156 In fact we, on our stout shanks, are better mounted than those cavalry fellows.

β. *a* **900** *Kent. Glosses* 58 in *O.E. Texts* 173 *Tibiis*, sconcum. *a* **1000** *Sal. & Sat.* 101 (Gr.), Læteð flint brecan scines sconcan. *c* **1200** *Trin. Coll. Hom.* 211 At pleȝe þih and shonkes and fet oppieð, wombe gosshieð, and shuldres wrenchieð. *c* **1205** LAY. 5863 Lihteð of eowre blanken and stondeð on eowre sconken. *a* **1225** *Ancr. R.* 258 Þeo ilke reouðfulle garcen of þe luðere skurgen, nout one in his [Christ's] schonken, auh ȝeond al his leofliche licome. *a* **1225** *Juliana* 48 Ich habbe i-blend men ant ibroken ham þe schonken & te schuldren baðen. *a* **1450** MYRC *Par. Pr.* 780 Wrynge þou not wyth þy schonkes.

**b.** ***Shanks'*** (or ***Shanks's***) ***mare, pony***, etc.: one's own legs as a means of conveyance.

*a* **1774** FERGUSSON *Poems* (1807) 333 And auld shanks-naig wad tire, I dread, To pace to Berwick. *a* **1795** S. BISHOP *Poet. Wks.* (1796) I. 204 I'd rather..ride on Shanks's Mare. **1823** SCOTT *Fam. Lett.* 11 Feb. (1894) II. xix. 167, I found shanksnaigie..the only way of moving by which I could get out to dinner. **1898** WATTS-DUNTON *Aylwin* XII. iii, I'll start for Carnarvon on Shanks's pony.

**c.** The lower part of the foreleg of some animals, *spec.* of a horse, that part between the so-called knee and the fetlock, corresponding to the metacarpus. Also, the tarsus of a bird; the tibia or fourth joint of the leg of an insect.

[*c* **1000** *Sax. Leechd.* I. 362 Nim blæces hundes deades þone swyþran fotsceancan.] *a* **1000** *Phœnix* 310 (Gr.), Sindon þa scancan [of the Phœnix] scyllum biweaxen, fealwe fotas. **1545** T. SCALON *Treat. Astron.* (MS. Ashm. 391) lf. 1 In Tauro..the schank or sperlure. **1584** B. R. tr. *Herodotus* II. 82 b, Making him [Pan] to haue the head and shankes of a goate. **1661** LOVELL *Hist. Anim. & Min.* 147 The marrow of the shanks [of the Crane] is used in ophthalmick unguents. **1669** WORLIDGE *Syst. Agric.* (1681) 194 The Bees by their pale coloured Shanks at their return home, shew whence they have their Store. *a* **1777** GOLDSM. *Epil. Harlequin* 31 'The deuce confound,' he [the stag] cries, 'these drumstick shanks.' **1816** KIRBY & SP. *Entomol.* xxii. (1818) II. 286 These legs..vary in larvæ of the different orders: but they seem in most to have joints answering to the hip (*coxa*); trochanter; shank (*tibia*). *a* **1843** J. F. SOUTH *Zool.* in *Encycl. Metrop.* (1845) VII. 284/1 The legs [of insects] are divided into five parts,—the hip, trochanter, thigh, shank, and foot. **1881** ROMANES in *Fortn. Rev.* Dec. 751 The so-called knee of the horse is really the wrist or ankle, and the so-called shank, the middle toe or finger very much enlarged.

**d.** As part of a joint of meat, e.g. in a ham, a leg of mutton, etc.

**1806** A. HUNTER *Culina* (ed. 3) 180 Good broth, made of shank of beef, or veal and mutton. **1837** M. DONOVAN *Dom. Econ.* II. 279 A ham without its shank. **1877** MRS. FORRESTER *Mignon* I. 60 He brings in triumph a basket out of which sticks the shank of a huge leg of mutton. **1908** C. H. SENN *Pocket Dict. Foods & Culinary Encyclopædia* 132 *Shank Jelly*, a kind of savoury jelly, lightly seasoned, recommended to weak people.

†**2.** *pl.* A kind of fur obtained from the legs of animals, esp. kids, goats or sheep, used for trimming outer garments. *Obs.*

**1480** *Wardrobe Acc. Edw. IV* in *Privy Purse Esp. Eliz. York*, etc. (1830) 116 A furre of blac bogy shanks. **1502** *North Country Wills* (Surtees) 268 My gowne of tawney furred with shankles [*sic*]. **1531** *Rec. St. Mary at Hill* 43 A nolde gowne of blake furryd with blake sankes. **1570** *Wills & Inv. N.C.* (Surtees 1860) 330 One gowne faced with Shanks. **1607** COWELL *Interpr.* s.v. *Furre*, Shankes be the skin of the shanke or legge of a kind of kid which beareth the furre that we call Budge.

**3.** *Sc.* A stocking, or that part of it which covers the leg; esp. a stocking in process of being knitted. Also *U.S. pl.* leggings.

*c* **1546** P. VAUS in Agnew *Hered. Sheriffs Galloway* (1893) I. 362, I pray yow vat ye vaild send me sum mo schankis, for them that I haine vill be schone doine. **1603** *Philotus* xxx, Ȝour schankis of silk ȝour veluot schone. **1611** in W. Macgill *Old Ross-sh.* (1909) 142 Twa pair of schanks wᵗ ane hatt [etc.]. **1644–5** *Aberd. Acc.* in *Spalding Club Misc.* V. 164 Item, two pair wovin whyte shankis to him, at threttie shillings ye pair, 3 lib. *a* **1867** W. ANDERSON in *Mod. Sc. Poets* Ser. II. (1881) 235 Jean scrapit a livin' wi' weavin' at shanks. **1871** W. ALEXANDER *Johnny Gibb* (1873) 213 The lang evenin's 's drawin' on noo, an' it's tiresome nae to hae a bit shank to tak i' yer han' files. **1888** *Harper's Mag.* Oct. 510/1 Four or five pairs of heavy woollen socks cover his feet, and over them is placed a pair of caribou shanks.

**4.** *transf.* †**a.** Each of the 'legs' of a pair of compasses. Also each of the 'legs' of a triangle. *Obs.*

**1587** GOLDING *De Mornay* vii. 87 In the drawing of a Circle, the one shanke of the Compasses is set fast in some place, and the other shanke is caried round about. **1611** SPEED *Hist. Gt. Brit.* VII. xxxix. §5. 344 All men [have]..the shank of their Compasse so set in a center that the Circle of their lines are [etc.]. **1679** A. LOVELL *Indic. Univ.* 159 The Isocele, or Triangle of equal Shanks.

**b.** Each of the two portions of a pair of scissors between the bow and the joint.

**1833** J. HOLLAND *Manuf. Metal* II. 40 Ladies' and fancy scissors, the shanks of which have been composed of rich open work. **1859** F. S. COOPER *Ironmonger's Catal.* 63 Scissors..Bent Blade and Shank.

**c.** *Arch. pl.* The plane spaces between the grooves of the Doric triglyph.

**1823** P. NICHOLSON *Pract. Build.* 593 Shanks; the intersticial spaces between the channels of the trigliph, in the Doric frieze; sometimes called Legs. **1836–50** PARKER *Gloss. Archit.* (ed. 5).

**d.** Each of the two checks or side-pieces of a spur.

**1891** in *Century Dict.*

**5.** The stem or straight part of anything. Cf. SHAFT *sb.*² **a.** The stem of a goblet, glass, etc.

**1553** *Inv. Ch. Goods York*, etc. (Surtees) 168 The foote, shancke, and knoppe of the challaice. **1583–4** *New Yrs. Gifts* in Nichols *Progr. Eliz.* (1823) II. 420 Oone sault, the foote, shainke, and cover of lapis-lazule. **1625** in Rymer *Fœdera* XVIII. 238/1 One Salte of Goulde..haveing uppon the Shanke three great course Saphires. **1826** GALT *Last of Lairds* iii. 28 He had the shank o' the very glass in his hand he had held to his old frien's lips.

**b.** The straight part of a nail or pin, between the head and the taper of the point. Also of a drill or borer.

**1483** *Act 1 Rich. III*, c. 12 §2 No Merchant Stranger..shall bring into this Realm..Latten Nails with Iron Shanks. **1542–3** *Act 34 & 35 Hen. VIII*, c. 6 Pinnes..such as shal..haue the heads souldered fast to the shanke. **1677** MOXON *Mech. Exerc.* i. 7 An hole..to set the blunt end of the shank of the Drill in. **1725** *Bradley's Fam. Dict.* s.v. *Shoeing Horses*, The Shanks of the Nails should be somewhat flat, and the Points sharp. **1815** J. SMITH *Panorama Sci. & Art* I. 20 A shank or small mandrel..with a square hole..at the end of it, into which drill bits of various sizes can be alternately inserted. **1840** *P. Parley's Ann.* I. 174 The coral animal is..not much larger than a pin's shank.

**c.** The stem of a plant (†*Sc.* also the trunk of a tree); the pedicel or footstalk of a flower; the footstalk or connecting part of any organ in a plant.

**1513** DOUGLAS *Æneis* IV. viii. 70 And like as quhen the anciant aik tre, With his byg schank, be north wynd oft we se Is vmbeset. **1565** *Reg. Privy Council Scot.* I. 413 Ane penny..havand on the one syde ane palmetre crownit, ane schell padocke crepand up the schank of the samyn. **1617** MARKHAM *Country Housew. Garden* ix. (1648) 96 Set slips without shankes any time, except [etc.]. [*a* **1693** *Urquhart's Rebelais* III. xiii. 109 One Apple of the shortshank Pepin-kind.] **1710** RUDDIMAN *Gloss. Douglas' Æneis* s.v. *Schank*, And Scot. the stalk of any herb or plant is called the shank. **1750** G. HUGHES *Barbados* 211 Its long tubular shank is finely rayed, the inside with purple-bluish veins. **1751** CHAMBERS *Cycl.* (ed. 7) s.v. *Clove*, Cloves must be chosen dry,..and if possible, with the shank on. **1796** C. MARSHALL *Gardening* xiv. (1813) 197 Earth up the shanks [of cucumber plants] with dry mould. 1820 SHELLEY *Sensit. Pl.* III. 56 And the dock, and henbane, and hemlock dank, Stretched out its long and hollow shank. 1884 BOWER & SCOTT *De Bary's Phaner.* 235 They are connected..by means of shanks or diverging limbs, which are attached to the neighbouring bundles on either side.

†d. The tunnel of a chimney. *Obs.*

c1525 *Contract* in Gage *Hengrave* (1822) 42 The schanck of the chymnies. 1538 ELYOT *Dict.*, *Fumarium*,..also the shanke or tonell of a chymneye. 1706 PHILLIPS (ed. Kersey).

e. The shaft or stem of an anchor, connecting the arms and the stock.

1549 *Compl. Scot.* vi. 40 Than thai maid fast the schank of the ankyr. 1626 CAPT. SMITH *Accid. Yng. Seamen* 16 The Anchor hath a stocke, a ring, a shanke, a flouke. a1779 COOK *3rd Voy. Pacific* III. viii. (1784) II. 129 The ring, with part of the shank, and the two palms [of the anchor] were now wanting. 1882 NARES *Seamanship* (ed. 6) 165 The shank lying athwartships under the boat. 1905 GEIL *Yankee in Pigmy Land* xxv. 375 Had the steering gear of the 'Flandre' broken, we should have gone over the cataracts in spite of the shanks being ready to cast.

†f. The stem of a candlestick. *Obs.*

1577 tr. *Bullinger's Decades* III. v. (1592) 347 So then Christ is the shanke or shaft of the candlesticke. 1611 CORYAT *Crudities* 244 Hard by this Altar are two very rich candlestickes..; the whole shanke betwixt the base and the socket being about eight foot high. 1706 PHILLIPS (ed. Kersey), *Shank*,..the Stem of a Candle-stick.

g. The straight part of a fish-hook, to which the line is attached.

a1613 DENNIS *Secrets Angling* I. xviii, His Shank should neither be to short nor long, His point not ouersharpe, nor yet too dull. 1741 *Compl. Fam.-Piece* II. ii. 331 Lay your Line on the Inside of the Shank. 1910 H. T. SHERINGHAM in *Encycl. Brit.* II. 28/2 (*Angling*), A leaded hook round the shank of which is twisted bright-coloured wool.

†h. The neck of a still or alembic. *Obs.*

1600 SURFLET *Country Farm* III. lxxvi. 608, C Is the shanke, which must be a foote long at the least, and is otherwise called the neck of the stillitorie.

i. The cylindrical portion of a stop-cock.

1660 BOYLE *New Exp. Phys. Mech.* Proem 11 There was soder'd on to the shank of the Cock..a Plate of Tin. 1797 CURR *Coal Viewer* 55 Injection Cocks. To be made of brass with square shanks.

j. *Typog.* The body of a type, as distinguished from the shoulder, face, and foot.

1683 MOXON *Mech. Exerc.*, *Printing* 390 The square Mettle the Face of a Letter stands on, is called the Shank of a Letter. 1885 LOCK *Workshop Rec.* Ser. IV. 219/2 Low spaces and quads must all be raised to the level of the height of the shanks of the letters prior to moulding.

k. The stem of a key, between the bow and the bit.

1677 MOXON *Mech. Exerc.* i. 6 The shank of a Key also, or some such long hole, the Punch cannot strike. 1686 *Lond. Gaz.* No. 2132/4 Lost.., a large Key with a Coronet and fluted Shank filed cross.

l. The stem of a tobacco-pipe.

1688 HOLME *Armoury* III. xxii. (Roxb.) 271/2 Long shanks [of a Tobacco-pipe]... Short shanks or ends. *Ibid.* 272/1 A Shanking toole..to rub and polish and make smooth the shanks of the pipes. 1758 REID tr. *Macquer's Chym.* I. 404 Keep stirring the mixture with the shank of a tobacco-pipe. 1898 MACMANUS *Bend of Road* 46 He ran a straw down the shank of his pipe.

m. The slender part between the flattened handle and the bowl of a spoon; the narrow part of a spoon-handle. Also, the handle of a ladle.

1688 HOLME *Armoury* III. xiv. (Roxb.) 6/1 Spoons are made plaine, but with wrought shanks, and heads with diuerse devises. 1839 URE *Dict. Arts* 585 By lifting it [the glass] out in flat copper ladles with iron shanks.

n. The blank part of a screw, or screw-bolt, between the thread and the head.

1677 MOXON *Mech. Exerc.* ii. 28 You must make wide holes, big enough to receive the shank of the Screw. *Ibid.* 29 The shank of the Screw..must be Forged square near the Head. 1770 LUCKOMBE *Hist. Printing* 300 The shanks of these Screws are made so long as to reach through the Head and through the Cap: at the upper-end of these shanks is made male-screws. 1892 *Photogr. Ann.* II. 217 The narrow part of slot slips down over shank of screw, and the head holds the shelf firmly in its place.

o. *Arch.* The shaft of a column.

1736 *Gentl. Mag.* VI. 652/2 It [Pompey's Column] is made up of three Pieces, of which the Chapiter is one, the Shank and three Feet of the Basis forms the second, and the Basis compose the third.

p. *Sc.* The shaft of a pit or mine.

1790 A. WILSON *Poems* 265 (Jam.) Nine score o' fathoms shanks down lead, To let the hammerin' core in. 1887 SERVICE *Dr. Duguid* xxi. 138 This lowsing the stanes in the shank, so chirted oot the bratticing that at last [etc.].

q. The tang of a knife, chisel, etc. or part which is inserted in the handle; the continuation of the tang of a tool or instrument.

1688 HOLME *Armoury* III. 388/1 The Shank [of a chisel]. 1807 J. BARLOW *Columb.* VII. 346 Strong bayonets, with short firm shanks Protruded from their tubes.

r. (*a*) The part of a harpoon between the 'socket' and the 'mouth'. (*b*) The tapering part of an oar between the handle and the blade. (*c*) *dial.* The handle of a broom, rake, spade, etc.: see *Eng. Dial. Dict.*

(*a*) 1820 W. SCORESBY *Acc. Arctic Reg.* II. 223.
(*b*) 1857 P. COLQUHOUN *Comp. 'Oarsman's Guide'* 30 The oar or scull [consists] of handle, loom, shank, and blade. 1898 *Encycl. Sport* II. 297/2 (Rowing) *Oar*... Its chief parts are—the *blade*, broad and thin, which is dipped in the water, the *loom* or *shank*, and the *handle*, which the oarsman grips.

s. The stylet of a trocar.

1846 BRITTAN tr. *Malgaigne's Man. Oper. Surg.* 393 The surgeon..then plunges in the trocart by a sharp quick blow. .. He instantly withdraws the shank, supporting with his left hand the canula.

t. The fang of a tooth. *rare.*

1851 MANTELL *Petrifactions* iii. §5. 245 The germ of the coronal portion of the tooth was first secreted and the entire crown completed before the formation of the shank or fang commenced.

u. The narrow part of a boot or shoe which connects the sole with the heel; the waist.

1875 KNIGHT *Dict. Mech.*, *Shank-cutter*, a machine or tool for cutting shanks for boots and shoes. 1886 *Encycl. Brit.* XXI. 830.

v. That part of an axe-head which is between the edge and the back, which in some old forms is drawn out long and thin.

1891 in *Century Dict.*

w. A straight piece of metal tubing fitted to a brass instrument to lower its pitch.

1885 G. B. SHAW in *Our Corner* Nov. 313 Brass instruments have resources in shanks and tuning-slides for flattening. 1938 *Oxf. Compan. Mus.* 114/1 By the addition [to a horn or trumpet] of a crook (a curved additional length of tubing) or a shank (a straight additional length), the fundamental note could be altered. 1977 *Early Music* V. 221/2 Every hand horn that we found..had a C alto shank among the set of crooks.

6. A part or appendage by which something is attached. (Cf. 6 c, 'footstalk'.)

a. That part of a ring which encircles the finger.

1688 HOLME *Armoury* III. 91/1 (Jewellers' terms.) Shank, is that part as compasseth the Finger, the Ring part. 1710 *Lond. Gaz.* No. 4691/4 A large enamelled Ring set like a Lozenge, with 18 Diamonds about the Stone and Shank. 1873 *Catal. Loan Exhib. Anc. & Mod. Jewellery* (South Kensington Museum) 72 Gold ring, the shank formed of leaves; in centre a transparent stone. 1928 *Daily Express* 18 June 5/2 The middle stone may be placed into a knife-edged shank with a 'coronet' setting, producing a solitaire ring. 1978 *Morecambe Guardian* 14 Mar. 16/5 Mrs Tyson was fined a further £20 for stating orally..that a ring was solid gold when it had a hollow shank filled with wax.

b. A lug, stud, or ear, projecting from an object, by which it is held, or which affords a bearing or point of attachment.

1677 MOXON *Mech. Exerc.* ii. 28 This spring is..fixed at the bottom of the Main-plate, by two small shanks proceeding from that edge of the spring that lies against the Main-plate..: These shanks are to be rivetted..on the other side of the Main-plate.

c. (See quot.)

1688 HOLME *Armoury* III. 462/1 The Shank [of the Clapper of a Bell], the length of it to the Ball.

d. The wire loop by which some kinds of buttons are attached.

1790 H. CLAY *Patent* in *Repertory of Arts* (1800) XII. 242 If a shank of metal is wanted or preferred,..the shank is to be put into or through a single piece or pieces of slate or slit stone,..leaving a metal stud, or other ornament, on the top of the button. 1837 WHITTOCK *Bk. Trades* (1842) 86 (*Button-maker*), To this plate is soldered the eye or 'shank' made of wire. 1904 QUILLER-COUCH *Fort Amity* xv. 180 She ..began with her embroidery scissors to snip at the shanks of its breast-buttons.

7. In names of various tools and implements.

†a. A bone pin for slating. *Obs.*

1716 *Ford* (Northumbld.) *Ch.-bks.* (MS.), Paid for three pecks of shanks, from Newcastle, 3s. 8d.

b. *Founding.* A clay-lined ladle having long handles, one of them T-shaped, in which to carry molten metal from the furnace to the mould.

1843 HOLTZAPFFEL *Turning* I. 369 A double hand-ladle, or a shank. 1858 SIMMONDS *Dict. Trade*, *Shank*, a double hand-ladle, capable of holding 2 to 4 cwt. of melted metal, carried in foundries by from three to five men.

c. *pl.* (See quot.)

1850 HOLTZAPFFEL *Turning* III. 1265 The lenses..are brought to the circular form with flat pliers called shanks, the jaws of which are made of soft iron that they may more readily..take a firm hold.

d. A short rope or chain (*spec.* = †short for *shank-painter*); 'a tie-strap of a halter; the loose end of a rope or chain' (*Funk's Stand. Dict.* 1895).

1706 PHILLIPS (ed. Kersey), *Shank*, or *shank-Painter*, (in Sea-Affairs) a short Chain [etc.]. 1879 MISS JACKSON *Shropsh. Word-bk.*, *Shank*, a rope by which a horse is tied up in the stall.

e. *Fishing.* (*a*) A line of pots attached to a rope, used to catch crabs, whelks, etc. (*b*) = *shank-net* (see sense 12).

1962 *Listener* 28 June 1105/2 Not far short of 600 fathoms of rope go to one shank of pots (a shank holds thirty-six pots). 1971 *Country Life* 29 Apr. 1000 (*caption*) Fishermen shooting out their shank of pots. Between 24 and 70 pots are attached at intervals along the rope to form the shank. 1973 W. ELMER *Terminol. Fishing* ii. 72 Shanks are designed to be dragged in shallow waters.

8. *Sc.* and *north.* 'The projecting part of a hill, or the narrow ridge, which, like a stem, joins the mass to the level ground' (*Northumbld. Gloss.* 1894).

1602 *Reg. Mag. Sig. Scot.* 485/2 The south schank of ane hill callit the peithill. 1820 *Blackw. Mag.* Nov. 201, I thought I heard a queer unearthly greet coming down the shank, and wizing ay nearer, and nearer to the byre door. 1887 *Scotsman* 19 Mar., The long 'shanks' and the abounding waterfalls.

9. *dial.* and *U.S.* The latter end or part of anything: the remainder or last part of a thing. Esp. in phr. ***shank of the evening***.

1828 [CARR] *Craven Gloss.* II. 113 'The shank of the evening', twilight. 1829 *Virginia Lit. Museum* I. 418/2 'Won't you spend the *balance* of the evening with me?' In some places, shank is quaintly used with the same signification. 1854 MISS A. E. BAKER *Northampt. Gloss.* II. 220 The shank of the day. 1856 P. THOMPSON *Hist. Boston* 722 *Shank of the evening*, the twilight or dusk of the evening, and in some cases the latter part of it. 1903 A. ADAMS *Log of Cowboy* xviii. 280 Miller made him knock off along in the shank of the evening. 1972 WODEHOUSE *Pearls, Girls, & Monty Bodkin* vii. 97 'It's very late.' 'Shank of the evening.' 1973 *Publishers Weekly* 19 Nov. 56/2 The stuff that makes the antennae of music pros and music-lovers twitch during cultural quarrels in the shank of a Lincoln Center evening.

10. a. Some unidentified plant (quot. 1657). b. 'A name applied to plants of the genus *Bryonia*' (Worcester 1860 citing *Johnson*).

1657 BECK *Universal Charac.* K 8, Shanke herb.

11. *Golf.* An act of striking the ball with the heel of the club.

1942 *Sun* (Baltimore) 8 July 12/7 It should be stated here that a slice isn't a shank. 1960 *Times* 31 May 4/1 Miss Price had a shank at the 13th.

12. *attrib.* and *Comb.*, as ***shank-end***; †**shank-hook**, a hook to secure the shank of an anchor when it is being drawn up to the ship's side; **shank-jelly** (see quot.); †**shank-main**, the pastern (of a horse); **shank-net**, a trawl-net used in shrimping; **shank-painter** = PAINTER[2] 1; **shank-piece** (see quot.); †**shank-pillion**, a pommel.

1837 A. BYWATER *Sheffield Dial.* (1839) 170 Nah, mo lads, we'n get'n tot *shank end at year ageean. 1884 LOCK *Workshop Rec.* Ser. III. 197/1 Put one [file] in a vice and knock the shank end off. 1485 *Naval Acc. Hen. VII* (1896) 38 Catte hokes with tree..v, *Shanke hokes..iij. 1824 *New Syst. Cookery* 372 *Shank Jelly. Soak twelve shanks of mutton four hours... Pour three quarts of water to them [etc.]. 1898 SENN *Culin. Encycl.* 86 Shank Jelly. 1580 HOLLYBAND *Treas. Fr. Tong*, *Paturon de cheval*, the *shanke-maine of a horse. 1883 *Fisheries Exhib. Catal.* 14 *Shank Net or Shrimp Net, to be used from a Boat. 1495 *Naval Acc. Hen. VII* (1896) 258 *Shankpayntours feble..ij, Bowpayntours for destrelles feble..j, Shankpayntors for destrelles worne & feble..ij. 1627 CAPT. SMITH *Seaman's Gram.* vii. 31 The Shank-painter is a short chaine fastend vnder the fore masts shrouds with a bolt to the ships sides, and at the other end a rope to make fast the Anchor to the Bow. 1642 H. BOND *Boat Swains Art* 17, 4 Shank Panters of 3½ inches. 1 Shank Panter for the Streame Anchor 3 inches. 1711 W. SUTHERLAND *Shipbuild. Assist.* 37 To have Bolts for the Top-tackles, standing Parts of the Sheets, Shank-painter Chains. c1860 H. STUART *Seaman's Catech.* 57 The shank painter is then passed. 1885 *Harper's Mag.* Jan. 280/1 The sole in a machine-made shoe would mean a sole, an inner sole, *shank piece [etc.]. 1596 SPENSER *State Irel.* Wks. (Globe) 639/2 The furniture of his horse,..his *shaunckpillion without stirrops.

**shank**, variant of CHANK (*-shell*).

1861 P. P. CARPENTER *Mollusca* 33 (Cent.) The shank-shell is carved by the Cingalese; when found reversed it is considered sacred.

**shank** (ʃæŋk), *v.* [f. SHANK *sb.*]

1. *dial.* a. *intr.* To walk, to travel on foot; also with const. *away*. Often *to shank it*.

a1774 FERGUSSON *Poems*, *King's Birthday* 83 If baudrins slip but to the door,.. I fear, She'll no lang shank upon all four This time o'year. 1862 HISLOP *Prov. Scot.* 186 Them that canna ride, maun shank it. 1894 P. H. HUNTER *James Inwick* ii. 29 He was michty weel pleased to..shank awa hame to Lempockshaws. 1901 G. DOUGLAS *Ho. Green Shutters* 198 Let him shank it! We're in no hurry to have him home.

b. *trans.* To cause to walk *off*, to march (a person) *off*; *refl.* to take oneself *away*.

1816 SCOTT *Antiq.* xxvii, Then shank yoursell awa to the double folk, or single folk. *Ibid.* xxxvi, Ye should baith be shankit aff till Edinburgh Castle. 1856 J. BALLANTINE *Poems* 55 He shankit the snab hame to cobble his shoon. 1898 LD. E. HAMILTON *Mawkin* iv. 47 And now shank yourself awa before I put hand till ye.

2. *intr.* Of a plant or fruit: To decay at the stem or footstalk; to be affected with shanking; usually *to shank off*. Also *pass.* Cf. SHANKING 1.

1848 TURNER in *Beck's Florist* I. 24 Entire beds [of pansies] have been known to shank off during a very hot summer. 1863 DARWIN in *Jrnl. Proc. Linnean Soc.*, *Bot.* VII. 70 Only four capsules [of a *Linum*] shanked off. 1892 *Garden* Aug. 193/3 The first season..the Grapes shanked badly.

*fig.* 1871 H. MACMILLAN *True Vine* v. 223 How often alas, is it true of the believer, that his fruit is shanked, remaining sour when it should become sweet and palatable!

3. a. *trans. Sc.* To sink (a shaft) Also *absol.* b. *intr. dial.* To knit stockings. c. *trans.* in lens-making (see SHANKING *vbl. sb.* 2).

1821 GALT *Ann. Parish* vi. 64 Three new coal-heughs were shanked. 1825 JAMIESON s.v., To shank for coals.
1825 JAMIESON, *To Shank*,..to knit stockings. 1900 C. MURRAY *Hamewith* 79 The auld wife's eident wheel gaes birr, The thrifty lasses shank wi' virr.

4. *Golf.* To strike (the ball) with the heel of the club.

1927 *Daily Express* 26 Oct. 3/4 Of all the awful things a man may do to a golf ball the most demoralising and the most mystifying is to 'shank' it. 1942 *Sun* (Baltimore) 8 July 12/7 Try to shank one. That's about the best cure I know after thirty years of golf. 1976 *Par Golf* Aug. 39/2 He had shanked his second and bunkered his third.

**shank-bone.** The tibia of an animal.
*a* **1330** *Otuel* 796 Wiþ þe fal þe steede a noon, To-barst þat o sschanke bon. *a* **1552** LELAND *Itin.* (1768) V. 65 A broken Shank Bone of a Horse. **1659** *Comenius' Gate Lang. Unlocked* Foundation T, They also played on flutes made of the shank bones of Cranes. **1747** MRS. GLASSE *Cookery* 24 Take off the Skin..and the Shank Bone with it at the End [of a shoulder of mutton]. **1867** BAKER *Nile Tribut.* ix. (1872) 150, I took a good drink through my gazelle shank-bone.

**shanked** (ʃæŋkt), *a.* [f. SHANK *sb.* and *v.* + -ED.]
**a.** Furnished with, or having a shank or shanks (in any sense).
**1593** G. HARVEY *Pierce's Super.* 74 His art [was] shanked like a lath. **1600** SURFLET *Country Farm* III. xxviii. 486 The best of all the rest, is the short shanked apple. **1676** *Lond. Gaz.* No. 1057/4 Lost.., one single Rose Diamond set in a Ring close shankt. **1683** MOXON *Mech. Exerc., Printing* xxiv. ℙ7 To large Paper he chuses Short Shanked Points, and to small Paper Long Shanked Points. **1904** H. G. WELLS *Food of Gods* I. ii. 53 Industrious research discovered..three shanked buttons entire.
**b.** [f. SHANK *v.* 2.] Affected with shanking.
**1882** *Garden* 3 June 388/3, I completely got rid of shanked berries. **1901** *Gard. Chron.* 16 Mar. 175/2 We could never get a crop of Black Hamburgh Grapes without some shanked bunches.

**shanker** (ˈʃæŋkə(r)). [f. SHANK *sb.* and *v.* + -ER[1].]
† **1.** *nonce-use.* A shank-bone. *Obs.*
**1622** MABBE tr. *Aleman's Guzman d'Alf.* I. 148 It was my hap to meet with the shanke-bone [orig. Sp. *cañilla*] of a Heyfer..and presently..I had lapt vp my Shanker [orig. Sp. *cancarron*] in the Paste that remained.
**2.** *Sc.* One who 'shanks' or knits stockings.
**1636** *List Inhab. Aberdeen* in *Scot. N. & Q.* July (1893) 21 Elspet Torrie. Shanker. **1802** SIBBALD *Chron. S.P.* IV. Gloss., *Schankers*, the women who knit them [stockings].
**3.** One who makes, forms or finishes the shanks of nails, buttons, etc.
**1881** *Instr. Census Clerks* (1885) 76 Button maker... Shanker. *Ibid.* 91 Nail manufacture... Wrought nail: Maker. Shanker... Header. Pointer.
**4.** *Sc.* One who sinks shafts.
**1882** *Jamieson's Sc. Dict.*, *Shanker*,..a sinker of shafts; as, 'a well-shanker, a pit-shanker,' West of S[cotland]. **1887** P. MCNEILL *Blawearie* 46 Some shankers, who had been engaged sinking the sump at the bottom of the shaft a little deeper.

**shanker**, obs. form of CHANCRE.

**shanking** (ˈʃæŋkɪŋ), *vbl. sb.* [f. SHANK *v.* + -ING[1].]
**1.** (See quot. 1846. Cf. SHANK *v.* 2.)
**1842** LOUDON *Suburban Hort.* 462 That shanking (shrivelling) may not be induced in the berries. **1846** G. W. JOHNSON *Dict. Mod. Gard.* 593 *Shanking* is the technical term for a gangrene which attacks the footstalks of grapes and the stems of cabbages which have vegetated through the winter.
**2.** The action or process of using the pliers called shanks: see SHANK *sb.* 7 c.
**1850** [see NIBBLING *vbl. sb.* 2].
**3.** The process of making tobacco-pipe-shanks. In quots. *attrib.*
**1688** HOLME *Armoury* III. xxii. (Roxb.) 271/2 A Shanking or smoothing board..is that on which their clay is rolled to the length of their shankes. *Ibid.* 272/1 A Shanking Wyer.. is onely a plaine smooth wyer, by which the hole is made through the pipe Shank. *Ibid.*, A Pen knife, or a Shanking knife. *Ibid.*, The third is a Shanking toole.
**4.** *Golf.* The action of striking (the ball) with the heel of the club.
**1924** C. J. H. TOLLEY *Mod. Golfer* 247 Shanking is a fault which is frequently occurring. **1942** *Sun* (Baltimore) 8 July 12/6 Shanking, in golf, is hitting the ball deep in the heel of the club, thereby causing the ball to fly away at a right angle. **1976** *Sunday Mail* (Glasgow) 26 Dec. 34/2 Norman..had a comparatively poor season last year..(mainly due to a bout of shanking which he is convinced has cleared).

**shannachie**, variant of SENNACHIE.

**shannai**, var. SHAHNAI.

**Shannon**[1] (ˈʃænən). An artificial salmon fly used on the river Shannon in Ireland. In full *Shannon fly*.
**1867** F. FRANCIS *Angling* xii. 357 The large heavy-water Shannon flies are very showy affairs. **1872** *Ibid.* xiii. (ed. 3) 393 The Shannon... Tag, gold tinsel and lemon-yellow floss.

**Shannon**[2] (ˈʃænən). *Information Theory.* The name of Claude Elwood *Shannon* (b. 1916), U.S. mathematician, used *attrib.* and in the possessive to designate various concepts arising from his work, esp. ***Shannon's*** (***second*** or ***capacity***) ***theorem***, a theorem regarding the ability of a noisy channel to carry information with no more than an arbitrarily small frequency of errors (see quot. 1970).
**1956** L. BRILLOUIN *Sci. & Information Theory* i. 7 This is exactly Shannon's formula..for a problem with just two signals. **1956** *IRE Trans. Information Theory* II. 102/1 In the discrete case this quantity [of information] is evaluated correctly according to the well-known Shannon formula. **1963** N. ABRAMSON *Information Theory & Coding* vi. 173 Shannon's second theorem can..be characterized as a little more than an existence proof. **1970** H. A. RODGERS *Dict. Data Processing Terms* 98/1 *Shannon's capacity theorem*, in information theory, a theorem stating that it is possible to encode a source of messages having an information rate $H$ bits/sec so that its information can be transmitted through a noisy channel with an arbitrarily small frequency of errors, provided that $H \leqslant C$ bits/sec, where $C$ is called the limiting capacity of the channel. **1972** L. L. GATLIN *Information Theory & Living System* iv. 98 A fundamental condition under which the Shannon theorem is valid is that the rate of emission from the source..must not exceed the channel capacity.

**shanny** (ˈʃænɪ), *sb.* Also (in Dicts.) shaning. [Related to the synonymous SHAN.] The smooth blenny, *Blennius pholis.* Also applied to several fishes of the genus *Chasmodes* of Eastern North America.
**1836** YARRELL *Brit. Fishes* I. 230 The Shanny or Smooth Shan. **1873** T. GILL *Catal. Fishes East N. Amer.* 20 *Chasmodes Boscianus*... Bosc's shanny. *Chasmodes quadrifasciatus*... Four-banded shanny. *Chasmodes novemlineatus*... Nine-lined shanny. **1878** T. CORNISH in *Zoologist* Ser. III. II. 423 Smooth Shanny.

**shanny** (ˈʃænɪ), *a. dial.* Bashful, shy.
**1821** CLARE *Vill. Minstr.* I. 32 Downcast eye, and blush of shanny lass. **1890** *Cassell's Fam. Mag.* Dec. 23 All sweethearts are shanny.

**shanny**, variant of SHANDY *a. dial.*

**Shanscrit(t)a**, obs. forms of SANSKRIT.

**shant** (ʃænt). *slang.* [Cf. SHANTY *sb.*[2]] A quart, a pot; a pot of drink. Hence *loosely*, a drink.
**1851** MAYHEW *Lond. Labour* I. 218 They have a 'shant of gatter' (pot of beer) at the nearest 'boozing ken'. **1864** *Hotten's Slang Dict.* 225 *Shant*, a pot or quart. 'Shant of bivy' a quart of beer. **1893** P. H. EMERSON *Signor Lippo* v. 13 To show you mean it stand a couple of shants of bevarly to square the boys. **1960** *News Chron.* 5 Aug. 7/8 We did not want to roll anybody but we had a few shants and I always get a bit garritty then. *Ibid.*, We all like a fight when we have had a few shants. **1970** A. DRAPER *Swansong for Rare Bird* vii. 52 'So I had a few shants,' I said.

**shan't, sha'n't** (ʃɑːnt). A colloq. contraction of *shall not*: see SHALL *v.* A. 6 b. Also used *subst.*
**1850** SMEDLEY *Frank Fairlegh* vi, A sulky, half-muttered 'shan't' was the only reply. **1887** BARING-GOULD *Gaverocks* xxxiii, 'Hoity toity!' exclaimed Madam. 'No cant's and shan'ts with me. What I have settled shall be.'

**shantrews** (ʃanˈtruz). *Sc.* Also 9 **shawintrewse, shantreus.** [? Gael. *sean-triubhas*, old trousers.] The name of a Highland tune and dance.
**1807** TANNAHILL *Poems, Kebbuckston Wedding* (1846) 139 Sauney M'Nab..Has hecht to..gi'e us three wallops of merry shan trews, With the true Highland fling of Macrimmon the piper. **1881** *Autobiog. J. Younger* viii. 71, I was then allowed..to skip over the old barn floor at shantrews.

**shantung** (ʃænˈtʌŋ). [f. the name of a province of North-east China where it is manufactured.] A soft undressed Chinese silk (formerly undyed, since 1907 dyed to any shade of colour).
**1882** CAULFEILD & SAWARD *Dict. Needlework* 445 *Shantung Pongee Silk*..is a soft undyed, and undressed Chinese washing silk, and much resembles the Indian goods of the same character; but is somewhat duller in colour. **1895** *Stores' Price List* 15 Sept. 1095/1 Coloured silks... Shantung Pongee, in pieces of about 19 yards. **1908** *Daily Graphic* 21 Mar. 13/1 The hat..might be made of Shantung to match the mantelet.

**shanty** (ˈʃæntɪ), *sb.*[1] Also **chanty, shantie, shantee.** [Prob. corruptly a. F. *chantier* (see CHANTIER) used in Canada in the senses: 'an establishment regularly organized in the forests in winter for the felling of trees; the head-quarters at which the woodcutters assemble after their day's work' (Clapin, *Dict. Canad.-Fr.*, 1894).
See 1 c below; it is uncertain whether this is a survival of the original sense, or a late specific application suggested by the Fr. word. It may be further remarked that *shantyman*, a lumberman, is precisely synonymous with *homme de chantier* (Dunn, *Gloss. Franco-Canad.*, 1880, p. 38.]
**1. a.** Chiefly *U.S.* and *Canada.* A small, mean, roughly constructed dwelling; a cabin, a hut.
**1820** Z. HAWLEY *Tour* (1822) 31 (Thornton *Amer. Gloss.*), [These people (in Ohio)] lived in what is here called a shanty. This is a hovel of about 10 feet by 8, made somewhat in the form of an ordinary cow-house. **1827** J. F. COOPER *Prairie* II. xvi. 256, I offer you, as my side of the business, one half of my shanty. **1830** GALT *Lawrie T.* III. ii. I. 191 Our shanty was completed in good time before the evening. [The scene is Canadian.] **1832** [MRS. TRAILL] *Backwoods of Canada* vi. (1836) 93 The shanty is a sort of primitive hut in Canadian architecture, and is nothing more than a shed built of logs. **1836** *Crockett's Exploits in Texas* i. (1837) 4 When we entered the shantee, Job was busy dealing out his rum.., and I called for a quart of the best. **1842** MRS. KIRKLAND *Forest Life* I. 173 Not a few lounged around the wide door of a temporary building or 'shanty', as we say, erected for the refreshment of the guests. **1853** KANE *Grinnell Exp.* xxvii. (1856) 224 And driving, like the shanty on a raft, before a howling gale. **1871** ALABASTER *Wheel of Law* 254 They pass the temples,..and then village after village of poor-looking bamboo shanties. **1891** 'J. S. WINTER' *Lumley* i, It's on the Essex coast just a rambling old farm-house standing rather high..; it's just in fact, a picturesque shanty.
**b.** *transf.* and *fig.*
**1841-44** EMERSON *Ess., Nature* Wks. (Bohn) I. 226 He has delineated estates of romance, compared with which their actual possessions are shanties and paddocks. **1851** H. MELVILLE in J. Hawthorne *N. Hawthorne & Wife* (1885) I. 399, I have been building some shanties of houses..and likewise some shanties of chapters and essays.
*attrib.* **1888** DK. ARGYLL *New Brit. Constit.* 98 One of the group of men who have been building a shanty-constitution for us to replace the spacious palaces of our ancient laws.
**c.** = Canadian Fr. *chantier* (see the etymology).
See the comb. *shanty-gang*, *-team*, *shantyman* (3 below).
**1824** *Canadian Mag.* III. 201 They commence by building a log cabin called a *Chanty* to shelter them from the weather, and hence another appellation they are known by, namely *Chanty Men.* **1829** J. MACTAGGART *Three Years in Canada* I. 242 In these shanties they pass the time pretty well, considering them to be made up of Highlandmen, Irishmen, and Yankees. **1876** D. WILSON in *Encycl. Brit.* IV. 774/1 Lumber shanties are constructed capable of accommodating from 25 to 50 men.
**2.** *Austral.* and *N.Z.* A public-house, esp. unlicensed; a 'sly-grog shop'.
**1862** *Otago Goldfields & Resources* 28 These accommodation houses are not mere 'shanties' and the traveller, with ordinary precautions, is always safe. **1864** J. ROGERS *New Rush* II. 52 The Keepers of the stores and shanties grieve. **1880** H. LAPHAM in D. M. Davin *N.Z. Short Stories* (1953) 57 When I first saw it..nearly every second house was a 'shanty' or a store. **1902** H. LAWSON *Childr. of Bush* 209 They got up a darnse at Peter Anderson's shanty acrost the ridges.
**3.** *attrib.* and *Comb.*, as (sense 1) ***shanty-cook, shanty-dweller, home, hovel, shop, slum***; (sense 1 c) ***shanty-gang, -team***; (sense 2) ***shanty-bar, -keeper, liquor***; **shanty-boat**, a kind of house-boat used by lumbermen; **shanty-cake**, a cake baked on or in hot ashes; **shanty Irish** *a. U.S.*, belonging to the Irish lower-classes; also *ellipt.*; so **shanty Irish** *sb. pl.*, **shanty Irishman; shantyman**, a lumberman; **shanty town**, a suburb consisting of shanties, *spec.* a poor or depressed area of a city or town.
**1902** H. LAWSON *Childr. of Bush* 240 What damned fools we'd been throwing away our money over *shanty bars. **1880** N. H. BISHOP *Four Months in Sneak-Box* iv. 58 *Shanty-boats..are sometimes called, and justly too, family boats. *Ibid.* 59 The *shanty-boatman looks to the river not only for his life, but also for the means of making that life pleasant. **1897** *Outing* XXIX. 368/1 We were joined by a very small boy from a shanty-boat. **1847** *Knickerb. Mag.* XXXI. 223 (Thornton *Amer. Gloss.*), The backwoodsman [must have] his 'chicken-fixins' and '*shanty-cake'. **1876** D. WILSON in *Encycl. Brit.* IV. 774/1 (*Canada*), The *shanty-cook is an important member of the little community. **1970** *E. Afr. Standard* (Nairobi) 23 Jan. 1/3 Rich-quick land racketeers who leased small plots to *shanty-dwellers in return for 'rent'. **1894** *Outing* XXIV. 94/2 We came along just as a *shanty gang had turned a drive of square timber out of the branch [of the river]. **1970** *E. Afr. Standard* (Nairobi) 2 Jan. 15/4 The fire..destroyed some 98 *shanty homes. **1862** DICEY *Federal St.* (1863) II. 46 Miserable wooden *shanty hovels. **1928** J. TULLY *Shanty Irish* xi. 117 I'm just plain *Shanty Irish an' I'll go to hell when I die. **1966** [see RESIDENCY 1 a]. **1975** J. F. BURKE *Death Trick* (1976) v. 79 That shanty Irish bitch!..She hit me..and got away. **1934** J. T. FARRELL *Young Manhood Studs Lonigan* xx. 334 The Irish made a *shanty Irishman out of Christ. **1874** V. PYKE *Adventures G. W. Pratt* I. iii. 6 The *shanty-keeper interposed. **1875** WOOD & LAPHAM *Waiting for Mail* 45 Mrs. Smith was a shanty-keeper's wife. **1886** H. C. KENDALL *Poems* 209 He'll..swig at *shanty liquors. **1824** *Shanty man [see sense 1 c above]. **1858** SIMMONDS *Dict. Trade*, *Shantyman*, a lumberer or wood cutter; one who lives in a shanty. **1893** *Scribner's Mag.* June 702/2 The typical shantyman works only fitfully in summer. **1891** H. MELVILLE *Timoleon* 63 And here and there a *shanty-shop Where Fez-caps, swords, tobacco, shawls Lay orderless. **1969** *Cultural News from India* Nov. 20 Shanty shops on pavements, packed buses and tram cars..mark the biggest annual festival of Bengal. **1969** A. G. FRANK *Latin Amer.* (1970) xix. 300 The wealth and elegance of downtown Mexico City dazzle the visitor..but equally do the miles of Mexico City's *shanty slums depress. **1878** *Lumberman's Gaz.* 6 Apr., The last of the *shanty-teams of the season have about gone through here on their way home. **1876** *Potter's American Monthly* Oct. 400/2 (*caption*) *Shanty town. **1880** *New York Daily Graphic* 4 Mar. 38 (*caption*) A scene in shantytown, New York. **1917** U. SINCLAIR *King Coal* 36 There's lots of people have boarders in shanty-town. **1946** [see HOOVERVILLE]. **1954** H. GIBBS *Background to Bitterness* II. vii. 121 By the end of 1871 over 10,000 diggers occupied the hot, corrugated iron shanty-town of Kimberley. **1980** *Times* 4 Jan. 6/5 The overpopulated [Turkish] cities are girdled with slummy shanty towns.

**shanty** (ˈʃæntɪ), *sb.*[2], **chant(e)y** (ˈtʃɑːntɪ, ˈtʃæntɪ, ʃ-). [Said to be a corruption of F. *chantez* imper. of *chanter* to sing.]
A sailor's song, esp. one sung during heavy work.
α. **1869** *Chamb. Jrnl.* 11 Dec. 794 (*Article*) Sailors' Shanties and Sea-Songs. **1885** RUNCIMAN *Skippers & Sh.* 93 He began to try singing shanties.
*attrib.* **1876** C. D. WARNER *Winter on Nile* xi. 153 The 'shanty man' the English sailors call their leader from the French *chanter*.
β. **1867** G. E. CLARK *7 Years of Sailor's Life* xvi. 165 The anchor came to the bow with the chanty of 'Oh, Riley, Oh'. **1883** CLARK RUSSELL *Sailors' Lang.* Pref. 11 So the same 'chantey', as the windlass or halliard chorus is called, furnishes the music to as many various indignant remonstrances as Jack can find injuries to sing about. **1888** LAURA A. SMITH (*title*) The Music of the Waters: a Collection of the Sailors' Chanties, or Working Songs of the Sea, of all Maritime Nations. **1896** KIPLING *Seven Seas, Last Chantey* 40 May we lift a Deepsea Chantey such as seamen use at sea? **1900** *Daily News* 9 Apr. 5/1 The British chantey, 'For he's a jolly good fellow'. **1925** D. GARNETT *Sailor's Return* 16 The seaman began a loud and rolling

chanty. **1955** *Times* 24 Aug. 7/4 The sea chanty was essentially a working song.

*attrib.* **1856** C. NORDHOFF *Merchant Vessel* in *Nine Years a Sailor* (1857) iv. 40 The foreman is the chantey-man, who sings the song, the gang only joining in the chorus. **1867** G. E. CLARK *7 Years of Sailor's Life* iv. 41 A chanty gang was engaged to hoist out the cargo. *Ibid.* 44 The chanty men wanted biscuit. **1890** HENLEY *Views & Rev., Lit.* 153 The melancholy song of the chanty-men.

**'shanty**, *a.* *Obs.* exc. *dial.* Forms: 7 **shante, shauntee,** 9 **shantee, shaunty, shawnty,** 8- **shanty.** [a. F. *gentil* (ʒɑ̃ti): see GENTEEL, JAUNTY *adjs.*] Showy, smart.

**1685** CROWNE *Sir C. Nice* Epil., Each Shante Spark, that can the Fashion hit. *c* **1730** J. HAYNES *Dorset Voc.* in *N. & Q.* Ser. VI. VIII. 45/1 *Shanty-man*, genteel man. **1737** R. DRURY *Rival Milliners* II. xiii, Where is the gay, engaging, shanty Mien? *a* **1800** J. WARTON *Fashion* 79 'Tis thine for sleeves to teach the shantiest cuts. **1811** WILLAN *Words W. Riding Yorksh.* in *Archæologia* XVII. 157 *Shantee*, or *Shanty*, gay, showy. **1824** [CARR] *Craven Gloss.*, *Shanty*, smart, flanting. **1895** *E. Angl. Gloss.*, *Shaunty*, showy, flashy, affecting to be tasteful in apparel or ornament.

**shanty** ('ʃæntɪ), *v.* [f. SHANTY *sb.*[1]]

**1.** *intr.* To live in a shanty or temporary log hut.

**1840** C. F. HOFFMAN *Greyslaer* I. v. 97 You see..the comfort to a man—who shanties out as much as I do—of having a home all fixed and ready for you. **1857** S. H. HAMMOND *Wild Northern Sc.* 197 (Bartlett 1860), Mark Shuff and a friend of his, who were trapping, shantied on the outlet, just at the foot of Tupper's Lake.

**2.** *Austral.* 'To visit a grog-shanty habitually; drink frequently or habitually at a public-house' (*Cent. Dict. Suppl.* 1909).

**1888** 'R. BOLDREWOOD' *Robbery under Arms* iii, I was put out at his laying it down so about the Dalys and us shantying and gaffing.

Hence **'shantying** *vbl. sb.*

**1824** *Canadian Mag.* III. 202 Such is the usual routine of what is called *Shantying* in Canada. **1857** S. H. HAMMOND *Wild Northern Sc.* 212 (Bartlett 1860), When we got back to our shantying ground we were tuckered out, as you may believe. **1926** F. RICKABY *Ballads & Songs of Shanty-Boy* 47 Shantying I'll give o'er when I'm landed safe on shore, And I'll lead a different life.

**Shaoshing** (ʃaʊ'ʃɪŋ). Also **shao hsing, shaohsing, shao shing.** The name of a town (Pinyin *Shaoxing*) in the Zhejiang province of China, used *attrib.* to designate the rice wine produced there. Also *ellipt.*

**1961** *Sunday Express* 26 Nov. 19/4 Everything I wanted to cook called for 'shao shing' or yellow rice wine. **1965** O. A. MENDELSOHN *Dict. Drink & Drinking* 306 There are three types of shaohsing: Shan Niang is full-bodied [etc.]. **1969** *Times* 9 Dec. (Taiwan Suppl.) p. viii/7 I would praise Shanghai because the best *Shaoshing* wine once came from spring-water on a hill on the outskirts. **1980** E. BEHR *Getting Even* vii. 90 They drank the ritual toast, in hot shao hsing wine.

**shap** (ʃæp). [a. F. *chape* in the same sense (Littré *Suppl.*).] (See quot. 1904.)

**1882** CAULFEILD & SAWARD *Dict. Needlework* 445 *Shap-faced*, a term employed to denote that the plush or velvet cloth is faced with the short ends of waste silk. **1904** *N. & Q.* Ser. x. I. 307/2 Foulard is not made of silk proper, but of a certain refuse-part of the cocoon known as 'shap'.

**shap**, obs. Sc. form of SHOP.

**shapable**, variant of SHAPEABLE.

†**'shapand.** *Obs. rare*[−1]. Also 4 **schaphand.** [pres. pple. of SHAPE *v.*; cf. SHEPPEND.] One who 'shapes' or predetermines: said of the Fates.

**1303** R. BRUNNE *Handl. Synne* 572 Ȝyf þou trowest..þat þre sustren ben shapandys [*v.r.* schaphandys], And comen þere þe chylde ys bore, And shapyn hyt wele or euel before.

**shape** (ʃeɪp), *sb.*[1] Forms: 1 **ȝescap, ȝesceap, sceap,** 2-6 **schap,** 3 **scap(p, scape, scheap,** 3 (*Ormin*), 5 **shapp,** 3-6 **schape,** 3-7, 9 *dial.* **shap,** 4-6 **schapp(e,** 4-7 **shappe,** (5 **chap**), 5-7 **schaip,** 6 **scheaip, scheap,** 3- **shape.** [repr. OE. *ȝesceap* neut., creation, creature; make, structure, natural character; form, figure, configuration; pudendum (in this sense also *sceap* neut.); also decree, destiny; f. Teut. root **skap*-: see SHAPE *v.* Cf. OS. *giskap*, only pl. *giskapu* creatures, also ordinances, decrees (of God), ON. *skap* neut., state, condition; pl. fate, destiny, also, with suffixed article *skǫp-in* the genitals.

The OE. word is normally represented by the dial. form *shap*; the form *shape* (with lengthened vowel due to the influence of SHAPE *v.*) did not become common till the 15th c., though occasional examples, perh. due to inflexion, are found early in the 13th c.]

**I. 1. a.** External form or contour; that quality of a material object (or geometrical figure) which depends on constant relations of position and proportionate distance among all the points composing its outline or its external surface; a particular variety of this quality.

*c* **1050** *Suppl. Ælfric's Gloss.* in Wr.-Wülcker 179/26 *Uolubile scema*, sinewealt ȝesceap. *c* **1200** *Trin. Coll. Hom.* 99 Ac on þe holi fleis bileueð þe shap and hiu, and smul of ouelete. *a* **1300** *Cursor M.* 370 Al scaples was [þe matere] noght for-þi þat it o scap ne had parti. *c* **1386** CHAUCER *Knt.'s T.* 1031 Round was the shap, in manere of compass. *a* **1425** tr. *Arderne's Treat. Fistula*, etc. (1910) 9 'Siringa' is an holow instrument by þe middez, and it ow to be made of the shappe as it is peynted here. **1560** DAUS tr. *Sleidane's Comm.* 25 An Appell of Golde, representynge the shape of the rounde worlde. **1611** SHAKS. *Cymb.* IV. ii. 309, I know the shape of 's Legge. **1710** J. CLARKE tr. *Rohault's Nat. Philos.* (1729) I. 145 A Glass of the common Shape. **1860** TYNDALL *Glac.* II. xxii. 346 By pressure ice can be moulded to any shape. **1896** WELLS *Wheels of Chance* xxxvii. 284 The clerical person on the tricycle assumed the shape of a note of interrogation. *Mod.* All circles have the same shape; ellipses have different shapes.

**b.** ***to keep in shape***: to secure from change of shape. ***out of shape***: changed from its proper shape.

**1696** J. F. *Merch. Wareho. laid open* 6 English Canvas.. will not retch, nor let Stays out of shape. **1834** J. FORBES *Laennec's Dis. Chest* (ed. 4) 5 A cylinder of paper, formed of three quires, compactly rolled together, and kept in shape by paste.

**c.** The contour or outlines of the trunk of the body.

*c* **1393** CHAUCER *Scogan* 31 On alle hem that ben hore and round of schap. *c* **1450** HOLLAND *Howlat* 68, I se be my schadowe my schape has the wyte. **1702** tr. *Le Clerc's Prim. Fathers* 102 It's said that he was a Man of large Shape. **1753** A. MURPHY *Gray's Inn Jrnl.* No. 53 You may meet a Lady To-day with an elegant Shape, fine by Degrees and delicately less. **1805-6** CARY *Dante, Inf.* xx. 114 That other, round the loins So slender of his shape, was Michael Scot. **1855** TENNYSON *Maud* I. x. 29 Maud could be gracious too, no doubt To a lord, a captain, a padded shape.

**d.** Impressed or represented form; a picture, image. *Obs.* exc. *dial.* (see *Eng. Dial. Dict.*).

*c* **1400** MAUNDEV. (1839) viii. 96 There schewethe the schapp of his left Foot, in the Ston. *a* **1578** LINDESAY (Pitscottie) *Chron. Scot.* (S.T.S.) I. 252 Quhair ye sall find the schap of the kingis schipe and hir pictour. **1600** SHAKS. *Sonn.* xxiv, Mine eyes haue drawne thy shape. **1649** MILTON *Eikon.* 218 An ill Painter by writing on the shapeless Picture which he hath drawn, is fain to tell passengers what shape it is.

†**e.** In certain Biblical expressions, used for *form* (= L. *forma*, Gr. μορφή). Also, used for *form* in philosophical sense. *Obs.*

**1362** LANGL. *P. Pl.* A. x. 32 Bote Mon is him Most lyk of Marke and of schap. ? **1380** *Lay Folks Catech.* (L.) 943 His lord þat is his maker and made hym thorwe his kendnesse lyk to hym-self in schap. **1526** TINDALE *Rom.* xii. 2 But be ye chaunged in youre shape [μεταμορφοῦσθε], by the renuynge of youre wittes. **1551** T. WILSON *Logic* II. L vij, Whan the shappe or fourme is made: theffect or thyng doen may folow: take awaie the shape, & the vse also is taken awaye. **1587** GOLDING *De Mornay* viii. 111 In asmuch as the essentiall shape of man [orig. *la forme essentielle de l' homme*] is to acknowledge a certeine Godhead [etc.].

†**2. a.** The make or cut of a garment. [Cf. SHAPE *v.*] *Obs.* as specific sense.

*a* **1225** *Ancr. R.* 424 Hore weaden beon of swuche scheape, & alle hore aturn swuch þet hit beo eðcene hwarto heo beoð i-turnde. **1380** *Lay Folks Catech.* (L.) 1221 Ne worschipe not men for here fayre cloþes, ne for here qweynte schappis, þat sum men usen. *c* **1440** *York Myst.* xxix. 364 Lo, here a shrowde for a shrewe, and of shene shappe!

†**b.** Fashion of dress. *Obs.*

*a* **1425** *Brut.* II. 296 þey ordeyned and chaungyd ham euery ȝere diuers schappis of disgy[se]ngez of cloþing. *c* **1449** PECOCK *Repr.* v. xii. 548 Oon schap of outward habit (name-lich such a schap which is rather foul than gay).

†**3. a.** The manner in which a thing is fashioned (by nature or art); make, structure, arrangement of parts; visible aspect. *Obs.*

*a* **1300** *Cursor M.* 23659 Efter þat þe dome be giuen þe werld..sal haue a scape al neu. **1340** HAMPOLE *Pr. Consc.* 4893 þe shappe of þe world sal for-done be. *c* **1400** MAUNDEV. (1839) xxvi. 269 Sum men seyn, that thei han the Body upward as an Egle, and benethe as a Lyoun: and treuly thei seyn sothe, that thei ben of that schapp. *a* **1500** *Adrian & Epotys* 138 in *Brome-bk.* 29 On the Fryday god made Adam After hys chap he ȝaffe hym name. *a* **1700** EVELYN *Diary* 27 Aug. 1666, The shape of what stood was very meane.

†**b.** Form, order and arrangement (of words, etc.); course, order (of a story). *Obs.*

*c* **1350** *Will. Palerne* 1160 But schortly for to telle þe schap of þis tale, þe duk hade þe douȝtiere men. **1357** *Lay Folks Catech.* (T.) 284 Ane is right saying and shap of wordes That him augh to sai, that gyffes this sacrement.

†**4. a.** The appearance of a human or animal body or its parts, (often, of the general form as distinguished from the face) considered as beautiful or the contrary. *Obs.*

*a* **1000** *Cædmon's Gen.* 503 (Gr.) þin lichoma leohtra micle, þin ȝesceapu scenra. *a* **1225** *Juliana* 20 As he biheold ant iseh..hire leofliche schape He sikede as þing þat sare were iwundet. *c* **1330** R. BRUNNE *Chron. Wace* (Rolls) 7312 þe kyng byheld þyse bachelers Were faire of schap, & face clers. *c* **1381** CHAUCER *Parl. Foules* 373 A formele egle of shap the gentilleste. **1471** CAXTON *Recuyell* (Sommer) II. 542 Palamydes..was of ryght fayr shapp. **1565** J. PHILLIP *Patient Grissell* 1927 (Malone Soc.) Her comly shape Nature hath framd aright. *a* **1605** MONTGOMERIE *Misc. Poems* xxxii. 50, I thank my God I shame not of my shap. **1700** T. BROWN *Amusem. Ser. & Com.* 49 Hither come the Country Gentlemen to shew their Shapes. **1734** tr. *Rollin's Rom. Hist.* (1827) II. 245 His daughter who was of a majestic shape.

†**b.** Excellence of form; beauty: = L. *forma.*

**1382** WYCLIF *Isa.* liii. 3 Ther is not shap to hym, ne fairnesse. *c* **1450** *Mirour Saluacioun* (1888) 144 Beutee and shappe with out deformytee. *a* **1535** MORE *Fortune* 43 in *Songs, Carols*, etc. (1907) 73 Thow þat arte prowde of honour, shape or kyne.

**c.** *colloq.* or *slang.* ***show your shapes***: come into view. See also quots. *a* 1700 and 1785.

*a* **1700** B. E. *Dict. Cant. Crew*, *Show your Shapes*, turn about, march off. **1785** GROSE *Dict. Vulgar T.* s.v., To shew one's shapes; to be stript, or made peel at the whipping post. **1828** SCOTT *F.M. Perth* ii, Step forward, I say, and show us thy shapes, man.

**d.** *slang.* (See quots.) ? *Obs.*

*a* **1700** B. E. *Dict. Cant. Crew*, *Shapes*, said (often) to an ill-made Man. **1735** DYCHE & PARDON *Dict.*, *Shapes*, a Cant Name for a nice finikin Lass that goes extream tightly laced; also of an ill-made, irregular Lump of Flesh, &c.

†**e.** An empty fop, a dandy. *Obs.*

**1688** SHADWELL *Sqr. Alsatia* IV. i, The most silly beau and shape about the town.

**5. a.** The visible form or appearance characteristic of a particular person or thing, or of a particular species of animate or supernatural beings.

*a* **1000** in Cockayne *Narratiunculæ* (1861) 36 Hi beoð oð ðene nafolan on menniscum ȝesceape. **13..** *Cursor M.* 17915 (Gött.), I sau apon his licam light In schap of douue þe haligast. *c* **1375** *Sc. Leg. Saints* xxxii. (*Iustin*) 382 The feynde..þe schape of a ȝung man tuk. *c* **1400** *Rom. Rose* 6320 For Protheus that cowde hym chaunge In euery shap homely and straunge. **1474** CAXTON *Chesse* III. i. (1883) 76 In the forme & shappe of a man holdynge in his ryght hande [etc.]. **1535** COVERDALE *Dan.* iv. 36, I was restored to the honoure of my kingdome, to my dignite, and to myne owne shappe agayne. **1602** SHAKS. *Ham.* I. iv. 43 Thou com'st in such a questionable shape That I will speake to thee. **1727** DE FOE *Hist. Appar.* i. (1840) 9 So even in Paradise the Devil assumed a shape. **1833-42** TENNYSON *To* —— 19 Not for this Was common clay..temper'd with the tears Of angels to the perfect shape of man. **1910** HIRTH in *Encycl. Brit.* VI. 191/2 The heroes of their accounts appear in shapes somewhat resembling human beings rather than as gods and demigods.

*fig.* **1642** FULLER *Holy & Prof. St.* II. xvi. 111 No wonder if his scholars hate the Muses, being presented unto them in the shapes of fiends and furies.

†**b.** Species, kind (of animate beings). *Obs.*

*c* **1400** MAUNDEV. (1839) Prol. 4 Where dwellen many dyverse Folkes..and of dyverse Schappes of Men. *c* **1475** *Hunt. Hare* 38 Jac of the Bregge and Wylle of the Gappe, Thei have dogges of thei olde schappe.

**6.** *concr.* †**a.** A creature. *Obs.*

*a* **1000** *Elene* 789 (Gr.) Swa ic þe, weroda weard..þurȝ þæt beorhte ȝesceap biddan wille þæt [etc.]. *a* **1400** *R. Brunne's Chron. Wace* (Rolls) 8050 Y ne wiste neuere, ne y ne herde, What maner wyght [*Petyt MS.* schap] wyþ me so ferde.

**b.** A person's body considered with regard to its appearance.

**1601** B. JONSON *Poetaster* V. i. 13 You both haue vertues, shining through your shapes. **1617** MURE *Misc. Poems* xviii. 1 Thou, thou, quhose lovelie schaip, of all admyr'de, In robs most rich a richer spreit attyrd. **1812** SHELLEY *Devil's Walk* xxiv, A statesman passed—alone to him, The Devil dare his whole shape uncover. **1837** CARLYLE *Fr. Rev.* I. VI. iii, Shapes rawboned, in high sabots.

**c.** An imaginary, spectral, or ethereal form; a phantom. Now *rare.*

**1591** SHAKS. *Two Gent.* IV. ii. 131 To worship shadowes, and adore false shapes. **1610** BEAUM. & FL. *Philaster* I. i. He ..diues into my fancy, and there giues me shapes that kneele and doe me seruice, crie me king. **1667** MILTON *P.L.* II. 649 Before the Gates there sat On either side a formidable shape. **1798** COLERIDGE *Wand. Cain* 110 And the Shape shrieked, and turned round, and Cain beheld him. **1820** SHELLEY *Prometh. Unb.* III. i. 51 Awful shape, what art thou? Speak! **1859** FITZGERALD *Omar* xlii, And lately by the Tavern Door agape, Came stealing through the Dusk an Angel Shape.

*fig.* **1734** WATTS *Reliq. Juv.* (1789) 150 Minds released from flesh..may smile at some of the fooleries and airy shapes of reason which we hug and embrace. *c* **1806** WORDSW. *Poems Sentim.*, *Charac. Happy Warrior* 72 Whom neither shape of danger can dismay, Nor thought of tender happiness betray.

**d.** A figure dimly or uncertainly perceived.

**1834** WHITTIER *Mogg Megone* 477 He hears quick footsteps—a shape flits by. **1847** C. BRONTE *Jane Eyre* xxxvii, That narrow front-door was unclosing, and some shape was about to issue from the grange.

**7.** Assumed appearance, guise, disguise.

**1594** SHAKS. *Rich. III*, II. ii. 27 Ah! that Deceit should steale such gentle shape. **1616** B. JONSON *Devil an Ass* V. iii. 18 My cossen has knowne These gallants in these shapes. *Eve.* T'haue don strange things, Sir. One as the Lady, the other as the Squire. **1667** MILTON *P.L.* X. 495 The brute Serpent in whose shape Man I deceav'd. **1726** W. PENN in *Life* Wks. I. 138 There are but Goats and Sheep at last, whatever Shapes we wear here. **1839** LANE *Arab. Nts.* I. 117 A devil named Sakhr, came to her in the shape of Solomon.

**8.** *Theatr.* †**a.** A part, a character impersonated; the make-up and costume suited to a particular part. *Obs.* **b.** A stage dress or suit of clothes.

**1603** DEKKER *Magnif. Entert. K. Jas.* (1604) H 4, The foure Elements, in proper shapes, (artificially and aptly expressing their qualities). **1623** MASSINGER *Bondman* V. iii, Consider This Persian shape laid by, and she appearing In a Greekish dresse,..If she resemble not Pisanders sister? **1661** PEPYS *Diary* 7 Jan., Kinaston, the boy, had the good turn to appear in three shapes: first as a poor woman in ordinary clothes..; then [etc.]. **1886** *Pall Mall Gaz.* 19 July 2/1 Some want money to bring them up to town; some borrow to supply the *addenda* to a wardrobe—such as shapes, shoes, and wigs.

**9. a.** One of the forms or diversities of appearance, structure, or properties, in which a thing may exist.

**1667** MILTON *P.L.* XI. 467 Death thou hast seen In his first shape on man. **1727** DE FOE *Syst. Magic* I. iii. (1840) 69 The new magic coming thus in play, let us see..in what shapes it began to appear. **1771-2** COWPER *Olney Hymns* III. xviii, Dangers of ev'ry shape and name Attend the followers of the Lamb. **1800** *Med. Jrnl.* IV. 324 An atony of the uterus, or an irregularity of contraction of the muscular fibres, assuming various shapes. **1842** T. J. ARNOLD *Schiller's Lied von der Glocke* (1846) Pref. 5 The following translation, in its original shape, was published in Germany. **1871** FREEMAN *Norm. Conq.* (1876) IV. xvii. 51 They were familiar with the thing in all manner of shapes.

**b.** The phrase *in any (no) shape (or form)* is often loosely used for: In any (no) manner, (not) at all.

**1751** HOLLIS in *Lett. Lit. Men* (Camden) 381 If you will please to inform me how I may be useful to you in any shape. **1818** SCOTT *Br. Lamm.* xxi, The Lord Keeper resolved that he would do nothing to commit himself, either in one shape or other. **1825** —— *Betrothed* xxviii, I am in no shape worthy of your farther care.

**c.** Phr. *in all shapes and sizes*: in a great variety of forms.

**1958** J. TOWNSEND *Young Devils* xxi. 196 Parents come in all shapes and sizes. **1967** 'A. CORDELL' *Bright Cantonese* xvii. 189 You've got competition.. in all shapes and sizes. **1980** P. MOYES *Angel Death* v. 60 Tourists come in all shapes and sizes.

**10.** *in the shape of*: **a.** Represented by, embodied in (a person or thing).

**1750** GRAY *Long Story* 41 Fame, in the shape of Mr. Purt, ..Had told, that [etc.]. **1837** CARLYLE *Fr. Rev.* II. II. ii, We there saw Military Rule, in the shape of poor Besenval. **1968** *Listener* 28 Mar. 400/3 The BBC in the shape of Harman Grisewood referred him to the government. **1976** *Eastern Even. News* (Norwich) 22 Dec. 14/4 Gothic had mixed luck, falling foul of County Council in the shape of David Simpson.

**b.** Of the nature of.

**1754** H. WALPOLE *Let. to Mann* 23 May, There is nothing else in the shape of news but small-pox and miliary fevers. **1863** W. C. BALDWIN *Afr. Hunting* iii. 90, I had nothing in the shape of food. **1871** L. STEPHEN *Playgr. Eur.* (1894) ii. 67, I love everything in the shape of a mountain.

**c.** In the form of, existing or presenting itself as.

[**1822** LAMB *Elia* Ser. II. *Thoughts on Books*, I can read anything which I call *a book*. There are things in that shape which I cannot allow for such.] **1823** SCOTT *Quentin D.* xii, I pique not myself upon managing steel in any other shape than that of a razor. **1835** T. MITCHELL *Acharn. of Aristoph.* I *note*, To gain admission even into this place, it was necessary for the anapæst to present itself in an unbroken form, or..in the shape of a preposition with its case immediately following. **1880** C. R. MARKHAM *Peruv. Bark* 272, I made an earnest appeal for recognition of his services in the shape of a small pension.

**11.** Definite, regular or proper form; orderly arrangement. Phr. *to take shape*; *to put into shape*.

**1633** FORD *Loves Sacrif.* III. ii, I am so busie with his friuolous proiect, and can bring it to no shape, that it almost confounds my capacity. **1756** EARL OF HOLDERNESSE in Ellis *Orig. Lett.* Ser. II. IV. 390 Things begin to take a shape. **1820** SHELLEY *Witch of Atlas* iv, Since in that cave a dewy splendour hidden Took shape and motion. **1884** CHURCH *Bacon* ix. 220 He was quite as much a talker as a writer, and beat out his thoughts into shape in talking. **1893** *Law Times* XCV. 26/1 It is high time that this branch of the law should be thrown into statutory shape. **1939** *Daily Tel.* 18 Dec. 1/2 The great grey hulk of Germany's pocket-battleship.. began to take shape. **1982** *New Scientist* 2 Sept. 609/1 The idea that nuclear armaments could be used..had taken firm shape in the minds of the technical people.

†**12.** An attitude (in the manege, dancing, etc.).

**1576** GASCOIGNE *Grief of Joy* IV. xxxix. Wks. 1910 II. 555 Nor he that vaults, or gambolds best in shape, Can coome abowt (yet) nymbly lyke an Ape. **1602** SHAKS. *Ham.* IV. vii. 90, I in forgery of shapes and trickes, Come short of what he did.

*punningly*. **1634** FORD *Perk. Warbeck* II. iii, [A tailor says:] For fashioning of shapes, and cutting a crosse-caper turne me off to my trade againe.

**13.** Condition, state of health, repair, or fitness. orig. *U.S.*

**1865** O. W. NORTON *Army Lett.* (1903) 249, I got through it all in good shape. **1901** *Scotsman* 4 Sept. 7/5 She [a yacht] seems in a worse shape than at the beginning of the season. **1924** J. GALSWORTHY *Forest* II. ii. 52 With only nine Soudanese..and less than thirty carriers—all in bad shape; it's precious long odds against our getting through. **1976** *National Observer* (U.S.) 24 July 3/5 Most of the corn-growing areas..were in pretty good shape for moisture.

**14.** *concr.* in technical uses. **a.** *Cookery.* A mould for forming jelly, blanc-mange, etc., into a particular shape; a portion of jelly, blanc-mange, etc. moulded into an ornamental shape.

**1769** MRS. RAFFALD *Engl. Housekpr.* (1778) 201 You must not put the shapes on the jelly till you are going to send it to the table. **1850** SURTEES *Sponge's Sp. Tour* lix. (1853) 340 She had just stolen a shape of blanc-mange. **1889** BARING-GOULD *Arminell* xliv, The puddings were ground rice mould, 'shape' Mrs. Welsh called it, rice milk [etc.].

**b.** *Millinery.* The body of a straw bonnet or woman's hat or cap previous to trimming.

**1880** *Girl's Own Paper* 20 Mar. 191/3 You might also buy a shape, and make a little hat to match. **1881** *Milliner & Dressmaker* Feb. 15/1 First-class milliners prefer to cover their own shapes with plush.

**c.** A portion of material cut or moulded so as to have a particular shape; *spec.* a piece of rolled or hammered iron of cross-section differing from that of merchant bar; also (see quot. 1875).

**1845** MRS. M. J. HOWELL *Hand-bk. Dress-making* 71 Before the velvet is cut out in shapes, a thin paper should be gummed at the back. **1875** KNIGHT *Dict. Mech.*, *Shape*, a piece of metal roughed out as nearly as may be to the shape it will assume when finally forged and finished.

**d.** *Naut.* A cone, ball, or drum of metal or canvas used in signalling.

**1879** in Nares *Seamanship* (ed. 6) 100 Three black balls or shapes, each two feet in diameter.

**e.** pl. *Gambling.* (See quot. 1936.) *U.S. slang.*

**1928** [see MISS-OUT]. **1936** *Flynn's Mag.* 21 Mar. 139/2 'Shapes' are dice which have beveled faces on some sides of the cube. These cause the dice to trip faster when these surfaces strike the playing table.

**f.** *Bridge.* The distribution of suits in a hand of cards.

**1954** G. S. COFFIN *Bridge Play from A-Z* i. 17 There are in bridge three dominant Playing Shapes: I. No-trump Shape. II. Trump/No-trump Shape. III. Ruff Shape. **1958** *Listener* 27 Nov. 901/3 The shape is unsuitable for a double —the bidding might go too high. **1961** A. TRUSCOTT *Bridge* ii. 22 The shape of a hand is the way the cards are divided between the four suits.

†**II. 15.** What is decreed. *Obs.*

*Beowulf* 3084 (Gr.) Wicum wunian oð woruldende, healdon heah ȝesceap. *a* **1000** *Riddles* xl. 24 (Gr.) Long is to secganne, hu hyre ealdorȝesceaft æfter gongeð, woh wyrda ȝesceapu. **1338** R. BRUNNE *Chron.* (1725) 101 Of Godes ordinance he forsoke þe schap. *a* **1400–50** *Wars Alex.* 180 Sen it is sett to be soo & slipe it ne may, Ne schewid to be na noþire schap.

**III. 16.** The sexual organs; the distinctive organ of either sex. Now *dial.* in narrower sense, 'the private parts of a female' (*Eng. Dial. Dict.*).

*a* **1000** in *Anglia* (1888) XI. 2 þær he on his sceape locode & his to bismere hloh. *c* **1175** *Lamb. Hom.* 153 Et þe schape þe douel smuȝeð in derneliche hwenne hit bið ȝaru to galiche deden. *c* **1200** *Trin. Coll. Hom.* 67 þi shape dide þat hit ne sholde. *c* **1386** CHAUCER *Pars. T.* ¶ 423 Allas! somme of hem shewen the boce of hir shap. *c* **1450** *Mirk's Festial* 35 But as sone as þay haden synned, þay seen hor schappe, and wern aschamet þerof, and hydden hit wyth leues of fygge-tre. *a* **1529** SKELTON *E. Rummyng* 507 Couer thy shap Wyth some flyp-flap. **1639** T. DE GRAY *Compl. Horsem.* 8 Let him cast the cold water upon her shape.

**IV. 17.** *Comb.*, as (sense 5) *shape-changer*, *-shifter*; *shape-changing*, *-shifting* (both adj. and sb.); (sense 14 b) *shape-coverer*; **shape elastic** *adj. phr. Physics*, pertaining to or designating a component of the scattering cross-section of an atomic nucleus that is regarded as independent of the formation of a compound nucleus; **shape factor** *Physics*, an algebraic factor in the expression predicting the profile of a spectral line; † **shape-like** *a.*, comely, fitting; **shape memory**, a property exhibited by certain alloys of recovering their initial shape when they are heated after having been plastically deformed; † **shape mistress** (see quot.); **shape-note** (chiefly *U.S.*), one of a series of notes having heads of different shapes, used to represent the degrees of a scale; † **shape-smith**, *jocular*, a corset-maker.

**1906** W. B. YEATS *Poems, 1899–1905* 63 Shadows, illusions, That the *shape-changers..have cast into his mind. **1978** H. R. E. DAVIDSON in Porter & Russell *Animals in Folklore* 141 The tales of shape-changers in the Sagas are not told 'for true'. **1621** G. SANDYS *Ovid's Met.* II. (1626) 21 Blew Gods the billowes crown'd, *Shape-changing Proteus, Triton shrill. **1978** H. R. E. DAVIDSON in Porter & Russell *Animals in Folklore* 127 (*heading*) Shape-changing in the Old Norse Sagas. **1901** *Daily Chron.* 6 May 9/4 *Shape Coverer wanted for net work. **1954** H. FESHBACH et al. in *Physical Rev.* XCVI. 449/2 It will be practical..to subdivide the elastic cross section into two parts... We call the second part ..the 'compound elastic' cross section... The first part we call '*shape elastic' cross section; this is the part of the elastic scattering which occurs without the formation of a compound [nucleus]. **1971** P. E. HODGSON *Nuclear Reactions & Nuclear Structure* vii. 142 The method of analysis described..applies only to the shape elastic part of elastic-scattering cross-sections. **1955** E. KONOPINSKI in K. Siegbahn *Beta- & Gamma-Ray Spectrosc.* x. 301, *Sn* will be called the '*shape factor'... Whenever *Sn* happens to be independent of the energy $W$,..the spectrum has the 'statistical shape' $\sim pW(W_0-W)^2$, modified only by the Coulomb effect. **1970** *Physical Rev.: C* I. 644/1 It is important that the correlation coefficients and the energy dependence of the shape factor be known to an accuracy of a few percent to provide a meaningful test of nuclear models. **1672** WISEMAN *Treat. Wounds* I. 15 Be sure in your stitching, you bring the Artery and Vein to his wounded fellow, so shall you the likelyer secure your self, and make the work more *shape-like. **1968** DE LANGE & ZIJDERVELD in *Jrnl. Appl. Physics* XXXIX. 2195/1 On heating above 90°C the reverse transformation takes place. The sudden change of configuration into the original shape, which occurs then, is called here the *shape-memory effect. **1975** *Nature* 22 May 281/2 The spring has to be made of one of the alloys—a select band—which exhibit shape-memory. **1820** J. CAULFIELD *Portraits* IV. 70 Mrs. Sarah Mapp..was called the bone-setter, or *shape mistress. **1932** V. RANDOLPH *Ozark Mountain Folks* 248 Right hyar is whar I get in some good licks for *shape-notes, too. **1980** P. M. YOUNG *George Grove* vii. 146 The congregational singing in the enthusiastic manner derived from *Sacred Harp*,..and the 'shape-note' books. **1887** A. LANG *Myth, Rit. & Relig.* II. 19 He was also, like Odin, a '*shape-shifter'. **1884** A. LANG in M. Hunt *Grimm's Household Tales* I. p. lxvii, He escapes with her..by her magical gift of *shape-shifting. **1887** A. LANG *Myth, Rit. & Relig.* I. 50 Belief in..Metamorphosis or 'shape shifting'. **1895** A. NUTT in Kuno Meyer *Voy. Bran* I. 211 We obtain a glimpse of the shape-shifting self-concealing powers of Tuatha De Danann. **1715** GARTH *Claremont* 98 Not yet..broad eyebrows were reduc'd by paste: No *shape-smith set up shop, and drove a trade To mend the work wise Providence had made.

**SHAPE** (ʃeɪp), *sb.*² Also S.H.A.P.E., Shape. [Acronym f. the initials of *S*upreme *H*eadquarters *A*llied *P*owers in *E*urope, set up in 1951.] An organization established by the N.A.T.O. Council embodying a structure of command for the defence of western Europe.

**1950** *Sun* (Baltimore) 20 Dec. 4/3 The 60-year-old five-star general..will create another international staff at SHAPE (Supreme Headquarters, Allied Powers in Europe). **1951** *N.Y. Times* 3 Apr. 8/3 General of the Army Dwight D. Eisenhower formally assumed command and activated the Supreme Headquarters of the Allied Powers in Europe (Shape) into an operational headquarters this morning [2 Apr.]. **1955** *Times* 20 July 8/2 He had accepted the leadership of the Supreme Headquarters in Europe (S.H.A.P.E.) as being a true agency for peace. **1958** *Listener* 25 Sept. 453/1 The signatures of the four Shape Supreme Commanders. **1976** H. WILSON *Governance of Britain* vii. 136 On 8 March the list concludes with southern Africa, Staffordshire, the United Nations and SHAPE.

**shape** (ʃeɪp), *v.* Pa. t. shaped (ʃeɪpt); pa. pple. shaped (ʃeɪpt), *arch.* shapen (ˈʃeɪp(ə)n). Forms: *Inf.* and *pres.-stem*: *α.* 1 **sceppan, scyppan,** 4 **schippe;** *3rd pers. sing.* 3 **shuppieð,** (**for-**) **schuppeð,** 4 **scheppeð, ssepþ.** *β.* 3 **ssape** (*3rd pers. sing.* **schepieð**), 4–5 **shappe,** 3– **shape.** *Pa. t. α. strong* 1 **sc(e)óp,** 3 **shop,** 4 **shoop,** 6 **shoope, schope,** 4–6 **shope,** *Sc.* **schupe,** 6 **showpe;** 4 **schep;** *β.* 3 **scupte, scopte, sipte,** 3–4 **schupte;** *γ.* 4 **schapit** (*Sc.*), **shapte, schapide,** 6– **shaped.** *Pa. pple. α.* 1 **sceapen, scepen,** 3 **shapenn** (*Orm.*), **isceapen, yssape,** 4 **shape, ischape, shappen,** 4– **shapen.** *β.* 3 (**for-**) **schupped,** 4– **schept.** *γ.* 3 **ischeaped,** 4 **yschaped,** 4– **shaped.** [A Com. Teut. str. verb, the original conjugation of which is found unaltered only in OE., OFris., OS., and Gothic, while in the other Teut. langs., and in Middle and Modern English, the primitive flexional forms have been more or less completely replaced by analogical new formations. OE. *scieppan, scóp, scapen* corresponds to OFris. **skeppa, skôp, eskepen* (WFris. *skeppe, skoep, skepen*), OS. **gisceppian, -scôp* (*scuop*), **-scapan*, Goth. *gaskapjan, -skôp, -skapan*: the sense in all these langs. is 'to create', occas. 'to fashion'. In early ME. a new pres.-stem *shape* was formed on the analogy of the pa. pple., and after the 14th c. completely took the place of the older *sheppe, shippe*. The str. pa. t. survived into the 14th c. (in Sc. still later), but in ME. two different weak formations are also found: *shupte* (y) from the original present-stem, and *shapide* from the altered form *shape*. In the pa. pple. ME. similarly developed two distinct weak forms, of the types *schept* and *shaped*. From the 16th c. onwards, *shape* has been a 'regular' weak verb (pa. t. and pa. pple. *shaped*), though the pa. pple. *shapen* still survives in archaizing use. The verb has been influenced in sense-development by SHAPE *sb.*¹, of which it is apprehended as a derivative.

In continental Teut. the changes in conjugation were similar to those that took place in ME.; in addition, a cognate verb repr. an OTeut. type **skapōjan* became in some dialects coincident in form with the verb represented by the OE. and Gothic forms above. Further, German and Du. have from their earliest known periods had a verb meaning 'to draw water', identical in form (and perhaps in etymology) with the verb meaning 'to create'; in the older stages of those langs. all the conjugational varieties occur with both meanings, but subsequently the verb meaning 'to create' and that meaning 'to draw water' came to be distinguished throughout by difference of inflexion. The forms are as follows:—OFris. **skeppa, skôp, eskepen* to create, OS. *giscôp*, pa. t., created, *skeppian* wk., to draw water; Du. *scheppen, schiep, geschapen* to create, *scheppen, schepte, geschept* to draw water; OHG. *scephen, scuof, giscaffan*, also *scaffan, scafta, gaskeft* to create, to draw water, also *scaffôn* wk., to form; MHG. *schepfen, schepfte, geschepft*, also *schaffen, schuof, geschaffen*, and occas. *schaffen, schaffte, geschafft* to create, to do, to draw water; mod.G. *schöpfen, schöpfte, geschöpft* to draw water, earlier also to create (cf. *schöpfer* creator); *schaffen, schuf, geschaffen* to create; *schaffen, schaffte, geschafft* to do, procure; ON. *skepja, skóp* and *skapða, skapt-r*, also *skapa, skapaða, skapað-r* to shape, make, ordain; Sw. *skapa*, Da. *skabe* to create, make, shape.

The ultimate etymology is obscure. Some scholars have suggested that the original sense is 'to draw (water) from a source', and that the senses 'to create', 'to ordain' are developed from this. Others regard **skapjan* to draw water (which is related to OTeut. **skapo-*, OS. *scap*, OHG. *scaf*, mod.G. *schaff*, vessel, bucket) as a distinct word from **skapjan* to create, ordain. For other derivatives of the Teut. root **skap-* see SHAFT *sb.*¹, -SHIP; outside Teut. no cognates are known, unless the root **skap-* be an altered form of **skab-* (:—pre-Teut. **skabh-*): see SHAVE *v.*]

**I.** To create, fashion, form.

†**1. a.** *trans.* To create; in later use, to form, fashion (said of God or Nature).

From the beginning of the 14th c. there are indications that the verb in this use was sometimes apprehended as meaning 'to form, fashion, give shape to', and in the 16th c. the verb, though still used of God, would prob. have been regarded as corresponding to *formare*. In the 17th c. it was felt to be an inappropriate word to apply to God: cf. 'God makes, and the Tailor shapes' (Bulwer *Anthropom.* 256).

*a* **1000** *Cædmon's Gen.* 1278 (Gr.) þa he Adam sceop. *c* **1200** ORMIN 11505, & sawle iss shapenn all off nohht, & hafeþþ þrinne mahhtess. *a* **1240** *Ureisun* in *O.E. Hom.* I. 189 His hwas dohter þu art, his þat wrahte and walt þat ischapen [203 ischeapen] is. *c* **1300** *Harrow. Hell* 196 (Harl. MS.)

Habraham..þou seidest..þat mi leue moder wes boren & shaped of þi fleyhs. *c* **1386** Chaucer *Clerk's T.* 847 Hir fader ..Curseth the day and tyme that nature Shoop him to been a lyves creature. *c* **1460** *Towneley Myst.* ii. 174 God that shope both erth and heuen, I pray to the thou here my steven. **1539** Bible (Great) *Ps.* li. 5, I was shapen in wickednesse. **1557** Turner *Bathes* (1562) Pref. A iij b, [These] byrdes..beynge taught of their nature, whiche almighty God grafted in them, when he shope them and made them to do so.

†**b.** In *pa. pple.*: Naturally fitted or likely (to do something). *Obs.*

**1375** Barbour *Bruce* xx. 206 The douchty lord Dowglass Best schapen for that travell was. *c* **1500** *Melusine* 151 That man is able and shappen for to subdue & putte vndre hym all the world. **1525** Berners *Froiss.* II. ccvi. 264 b, Ladyes.. were nat shapen nor made to endure such payne.

**2. a.** To make, fashion out of pre-existing materials. In later use, to make by alteration of shape (as by moulding or carving) *out of* something else; to make in a definite shape.

*c* **1000** Ælfric *Gram.* xxviii. (Z.) 174 *Fingo*, ic hiwiȝe oððe scyppe. *a* **1300** *Cursor M.* 16573 þe rode þai scop þan as þai wald,..O cedre, cipres, and o pine. *c* **1374** Chaucer *Anel. & Arc.* 357 (Tanner MS.) The temple..That shapyn was as ye shall aftyr here. *a* **1400–50** *Wars Alex.* 113 He shapis him of shire wax litill schipis many. **1470–85** Malory *Arthur* xvii. vi. 698 And whan these thre spyndels were shapen, she made hem to be fastned vpon the selar of the bedde. **1598** Shaks. *Merry W.* iv. ii. 240 Come, to the Forge with it, then shape it. **1665** Hooke *Microgr.* 154 She does begin to Geometrize, ..shaping..plane regular figures, as triangles..cubes, &c. **1802** Leyden *Lord Soulis* lxii, The ropes..Shaped of the sifted sand you see. **1893** D. J. Rankin *Zambesi Basin* xiv. 240 A large wooden mortar shaped out of a log.

**b.** Of the organs of speech: To form, frame, produce (sounds).

*c* **1200** *Trin. Coll. Hom.* 211 Tunge and teð and lippe word shuppieð muð sent ut þe stefne. **1398** Trevisa *Barth. De P.R.* v. xxiii. (Bodl. MS.), To schape þe voice aier is ifonge in þe leues of þe lungen.

**c.** To frame, fashion (an immaterial thing); to make conformable *with* (a pattern).

*a* **1300** *Cursor M.* 28073 Laud men mai sumquat lere, to scape þair scrift wit þis samplere. *c* **1400** *Destr. Troy* 72 Cornelius..translated it into latyn..but he shope it so short þat [etc.]. **1874** Sayce *Compar. Philol.* viii. 299 The statue does not represent more truly the artistic imagination of its sculptor than does the word the mind that shaped it.

**d.** ***to shape out***: to form, produce by giving shape to material.

**1600** J. Pory tr. *Leo's Africa* Introd. 29 At the very mouth or out-let, dispersing it selfe into two branches, it shapeth out a great island. **1756** C. Smart tr. *Horace, Epist.* ii. ii. (1826) II. 293 You may shape out any thing with such moist clay. **1830** Lyell *Princ. Geol.* I. 312 Currents..and tides, cannot..shape out or silt up estuaries..without [etc.].

**e.** ***to shape over*** (*U.S.*): to refashion. Cf. *make over*, make *v.* 92 d.

**1875** Whitney *Life Lang.* iv. 53 The same influence helped..to shape over certain pronominal elements into the personal endings *anti*, *masi*, and *ti*.

**3.** *passive.* To have a certain shape.

*c* **1000** Ælfric in Sweet *Sel. Hom.* iii. 7 þa wæs þæs teoþan werodes hafes ealdor swiþe fæȝer and wlitiȝ ȝesceapen. **13..** *K. Alis.* 6465 Folke heo buth ful eovel yschapen. Heore mouth is from that on ere to that othir [etc.]. *c* **1350** *Will. Palerne* 126 How faire & how fetis it was & freliche schapen. **1423** Jas. I *Kingis Q.* xlviii, Lyke to ane hert schapin verily. **1560** Daus tr. *Sleidane's Comm.* 209 b, The cloth was so shapen, that it covered also the other partes. **1610** Holland *Camden's Brit.* 739 Shaped in forme, as one would say, of an egge. **1796** Withering *Brit. Plants* I. 215 Receptacle very long, shaped like a style. **1884** Mrs. Walford *Baby's Grandm.* I. 262 The head was well shapen.

†**4.** To cut out or fashion (clothing). *Obs.* as specific sense.

*a* **1225** *Ancr. R.* 200 Hu se euer hire kurtel beo ischeaped oðer iseouwed, heo [etc.]. **1387** Trevisa *Higden* (Rolls) VII. 269 Sche cam into þe bisshop his chambre, oon caas for to schape þe chamberlay his lynnen cloþes. **1583** Melbancke *Philotimus* M ij, It is not hard for the Tayler to shape a fitte garment for a straight bodie. **1654** Bramhall *Just Vind.* ii. (1661) 24 Therefore it is as hard a task to shape a coat for Schismaticks, as for the Moon, which changeth its shape euery day. **1828** Scott *F.M. Perth* v, I was thinking of her poor mother when I shaped them [gloves].

*absol.* *c* **1412** Hoccleve *De Reg. Princ.* 473 The taillours, trow I, moot heer-after soone Shape in þe feeld. **1568** Charteris *Pref. to Lyndesay's Wks.* (1871) 4* The King.. sayis to him: 'Qhairto wald thow be my tailȝeour? thow can nouther schaip nor sew?' **1728** Ramsay *Widow* 2 The Widow can shape, and the Widow can shew. **1821** Scott *Pirate* xiv, Thimblethwaite let no one but himself shape for glorious John, and he had a slashing hand at a sleeve.

†**5. a.** To fashion an image of, portray. *Obs.*

*c* **1350** *Will. Palerne* 3214 Swete sire, ȝe me saye what signe is þe leuest to have schape in þi scheld. *c* **1400** *Arth. & Merl.* (Kölbing) 1587 Apon his tayles ende þer was schaped a grysly hed. *a* **1650** *Old Robin of Portingale* xxxii. in *Percy Fol. MS.* I. 240 He shope the crosse in his right sholder of the white flesh & the redd.

†**b.** To present, set (an example). *Obs.*

*c* **1610** *Women Saints* 185 You women doe not leaue this example vnimitated, which she hath shaped you.

†**c.** ***to shape out***: to depict, describe. *Obs.*

**1633** Marmion *Fine Comp.* iii. v. F 3, I am sure she shapt me out to bee the ridiculousest old asse in Europe.

**d.** ***to shape forth***: to picture to view; to give an outline of.

**1579** W. Wilkinson *Confut. Fam. Love* 29 b, That course which the sonne of God by his example shaped forth vnto them. **1810** Scott *Lady of L.* iii. vii, The lone Seer.. Shaped forth a disembodied World. **1831** —— *Ct. Robt.* xiii, 'My humble understanding,' said Agelastes, 'had been infinitely inferior to the management of so..sagacious a scheme, had it not been shaped forth and suggested by the inimitable wisdom of your..Imperial Highness.'

†**6.** To produce, cause, bring about. Also with clause as obj. *Obs.*

*c* **1315** Shoreham i. 111 And glorie Hit scheppeþ, ȝef man deyþe, And schilt fram purgatorie. **1377** Langl. *P. Pl.* B. xx. 138 He made lele matrimonye Departen ar deth cam & deuors shupte. ? *a* **1500** *Chester Pl., Temptation* (Shaks. Soc.) 204 For I shall shape honour for thee. **1831** Scott *Ct. Robt.* xxxiii, Nor is there an opportunity of acquiring honour which I can shape for thee, to which, as it occurs, I will not gladly prefer thee.

†**7. a.** To transform or turn *into*, *to*. *Obs.*

**1362** Langl. *P. Pl.* A. Prol. 54 Summe schopen hem to hermytes heore ese to haue. **1470–85** Malory *Arthur* iv. xiv. 138 She shope her self hors and man by enchauntement vnto a grete marbyl stone. **1648** Gage *West Ind.* 12 Yet from a rich covetous Merchant did it shape him to a Courtier in pleasures.

†**b.** To put *into* clothing. Also *intr.* for refl.

**1362** Langl. *P. Pl.* A. Prol. 2, I schop me in-to a schroud. ? **1370** *Robt. Cicyle* 165 in Hazl. *E.P.P.* I. 275 In a clothyng ye schalle be schape. *a* **1400** *Pistill of Susan* vii. (Ingilby MS.), þe schene briddes in þe schawe þei schappyn in schrowde.

†**c.** To cause to assume an alien shape or appearance. *Obs.*

*c* **1400** *Arth. & Merl.* (Kölbing) 723 And þey [*sc.* fiends] han bothe strengthe & myȝt, After man to schapen here body. **1613** Heywood *Silver Age* ii. i, Enter at one dore.. at the other Iupiter shapt like Amphitrio.

†**8.** To prescribe a form to. *Obs.*

**1340** *Ayenb.* 209 þeruore ous tekþ oure guode mayster Iesu crist uor to asci wysliche and ous sseþþ oure ascinge þo he zede.

†**9. a.** *intr.* To attain maturity of form and proportions. **b.** *trans.* Of a tree: To bring (its fruit) to maturity. *Obs.*

**1605** Bacon *Adv. Learn.* i. v. §4. 24 b, Young men, when they knit and shape perfectly, doe seldome grow to a further stature. **1618** Lawson *New Orch. & Garden* vii. (1623) 16, I haue knowne a tree..for want of strength could neuer shape his fruit.

**10.** To trim, cut, or mould to a particular shape; to adapt in shape *to*.

**1457** Hardyng *Chron.* in *Eng. Hist. Rev.* Oct. (1912) 750 The lawe is lyke vnto a Walshmannes hose, To eche mannes legge that shapen is and mete. **1717** Lady M. W. Montagu *Let. to C'tess Mar* 1 Apr. (1887) I. 175 They generally shape their eyebrows. **1861** *Ladies' Gaz. Fashion* Apr. 30/2 Some [sleeves] are shaped to the elbow, and have cuffs. **1891** Kinns *Graven in Rock* viii. 300 The scarcophagus is slightly shaped to the body.

**11. a.** To give definite form to; to put *into* a certain form, to embody in words. †Also with *out*.

**1589** Greene *Menaphon* (Arb.) 22 That oracles were foretold at the Delphian Caue, but were shapte out and finished in the Counsell house. **1796** W. Taylor in *Monthly Rev.* XX. 535 We knew into how complete and fascinating a whole the selecting taste of Wieland had shapen the enterprise of Huen of Bourdeaux. **1842** Tennyson *Godiva* 3 And there I shaped The city's ancient legend into this. **1875** Geo. Eliot in Cross *Life* (1885) III. 258 The trivial questions I want to put could hardly be shapen in a letter.

**b.** *refl.* To assume a definite form or structure; to develop from vagueness or confusion *into* something coherent.

**1837** Carlyle *Fr. Rev.* I. iv. ii, This multitudinous French People..begins heaping and shaping itself into organic groups. **1869** Tozer *Highl. Turkey* I. 37 The valleys ..shape themselves..into a succession of graceful curves.

**c.** *intr.* To assume a shape or form; to develop or progress. Freq. const. *up*.

**1865** O. W. Norton *Army Lett.* (1903) 278 As things are shaping I do not much think I shall try till after Congress meets. **1903** *N.Y. Times* 10 Sept. 6/3 Matters are shaping for an effort on the part of the organized teamsters to reproduce in this city the..conditions which exist in Chicago. **1921** R. D. Paine *Comr. Rolling Ocean* xvii. 293 Here is how it shapes up to me. **1941** B. Schulberg *What makes Sammy Run?* vii. 153 It's shaping up something terrific... It looks like the biggest opening this town ever had. **1951** *Sport* 27 Apr.–3 May 12/1 How will Yorkshire shape up this summer? **1965** *Listener* 25 Nov. 871/1 The autumn output has shaped up most satisfactorily, far better than its schedules might suggest. **1980** N. Marsh *Photo-Finish* vi. 156 He pulled out... He didn't fancy the way things shaped up.

**12.** To give a direction and character to (one's life, conduct, etc.).

**1823** Keble *Serm.* iv. (1848) 85 Every one shapes his conduct, in regard to his worldly interests, upon the notion that sin and wickedness abound. **1863** Geo. Eliot *Romola* (1880) I. Introd. 2 The great river-courses which have shaped the lives of men have hardly changed. **1886** *Athenæum* 30 Oct. 562/2 It would be absurd to say that his life was shaped for him by the force of circumstances.

**II.** To devise, plan, prepare.

**13.** To devise (a plan, a remedy.)

*c* **1381** Chaucer *Parl. Foules* 502, I can shappe herof a remedie. **1423** Jas. I. *Kingis Q.* lxix, Bot venus, of hir grace, Will schape remede. *c* **1530** *Hyckescorner* 355 But at the last God shope a remedy. **1584** Lodge *Alarum agst. Usurers* 10 According as I finde your aunswere, I will shape your deliueraunce. **1819** Scott *Ivanhoe* xxxiv, Can I shape no means for myself when I am deserted by these cravens?

†**14. a.** To take measures for, contrive, endeavour to bring about. *Obs.*

*c* **1330** R. Brunne *Chron. Wace* (Rolls) 4565 þat schopen hym [Caesar] yuel & outrage, þey diden hym fewte & homage. *a* **1400–50** *Wars Alex.* 3267* And had he shapyn Ay to shalkez shendship & illys. *c* **1450** *Mirk's Festial* 257 And soo for he schapput a fowle deth to oþer, hit fell apon hymselfe.

†**b.** With inf. or clause as obj. *Obs.*

**13..** *E.E. Allit. P.* B. 762 I schal schape no more þo schalkkez to helpe. **1387–8** T. Usk *Test. Love* i. vi. (Skt.) 148 Thilke governour..shoop to have letted thilke eleccion, and have made a newe. *c* **1440** *York Myst.* xvii. 318 Herowde the kyng has malise ment, And shappis with shame yow for to shende. **1500–20** Dunbar *Poems* xxxiii. 61 A fedrem on he tuke, And schupe in Turky for to fle. **1567** *Gude & Godlie Ball.* 142 Send vs support and conforting, Aganis our fais that byssie is, That schapis till stroy, baith auld and zung. *a* **1585** Montgomerie *Cherrie & Slae* 261 Bot ay the mair I schape [? *read* schupe] to smorit The baulder it brak out.

†**c.** *absol.*

**1338** R. Brunne *Chron.* (1725) 201 þanked God & him so wele for him had schaped. *c* **1456** Pecock *Bk. Faith* (1909) 255 Therfore God so schope that the feith schulde bi a notable tyme be preched.

†**15.** *refl.* To set oneself, prepare. Const. *to* with inf., or *for*. *Obs.* Very common in Chaucer.

*c* **1374** Chaucer *Boeth.* i. pr. iv. (1868) 21 And I se þat euery lorel shapiþ hym to fynde oute newe fraudes. **1377** Langl. *P. Pl.* B. xi. 429 'Certes', quod he, 'þat is soth' and shope hym for to walken. *c* **1386** Chaucer *Prol.* 774 As ye goon by the weye, Ye shapen yow to talen and to pleye. **1462** in *Extracts Burgh Rec. Edin.* (1869) I. 20 That no nychbour schaip thame to by ony vittuallis or to bid ony price thairfoir befoir the entrie. *a* **1568** *Bannatyne MS.* (Hunter. Club) 78 Schaip the no moir with ws to stryve. **1570** *Satir. Poems Reform.* xix. 95 Gif ȝour fais tryumphis ouer ȝow to stand, Schaip ȝow for deid.

†**b.** Of the sky: To prepare (to rain). *Obs.*

*c* **1374** Chaucer *Troilus* iii. 551 Right sone vpon the chaunging of the mone Whan..that the welken shoop him for to reyne.

†**16. a.** To direct the course of; to equip, send forth. Also, of a motive: To prompt, induce. *Obs.*

*c* **1330** R. Brunne *Chron. Wace* (Rolls) 12050 Arthur.. schop his host to Southaumptone. **1362** Langl. *P. Pl.* A. viii. 69 Bidders and Beggers Beoþ not in þe Bulle, Bote þe suggestion be soþ þat schapeþ hem to Begge. *c* **1386** Chaucer *Man of Law's T.* 155 Bisshopes ben shapen with hir for to wende. *c* **1470** Henry *Wallace* xi. 403 Throuch auld malice he wox ner wod for teyn; Apon the Scottis schup thaim all with gret mayn.

†**b.** *refl.* To direct one's course. Also *intr.*

*c* **1400** *Destr. Troy* 1144 He will..shape hym to our shippes with his shene knightes. *c* **1470** Henry *Wallace* x. 408 Feyll Sotheroun than to Wallace fast can schaip. **1480** Caxton *Chron. Eng.* xiii. bj b, At the last he [Leir] shope hym to the see and passed ouer in to fraunce.

†**c.** ***to shape*** (a person's) ***way***: to assist one in a course of action. *Obs.*

**1362** Langl. *P. Pl.* A. iii. 17 We wolen wysen þe kyng and þi wey schapen. **1622** Bacon *Hen. VII*, 237 Whereas Empson and Dudley..did not giue way onely..but shape him way to those Extremities, for which himselfe was touched with remorse at his Death.

**d.** ***to shape one's course***: *Naut.*, to steer *for*, *to* a place. Also *transf.* and *fig.* (occas. ***to shape one's passage, way***, etc.). Also *absol.* or *intr.* (*rare*).

**1593** Peele *Hon. Garter* C 4 b, And Sheffeilde, shape thy course no otherwise, Then loyaltie..Directs. **1627** Capt. Smith *Seaman's Gram.* xii. 56 Shape your course as he doth to meet him at the neerest angle you can. *a* **1700** Evelyn *Diary* 16 Sept. 1644, Minding now to shape my course so as I might winter in Italy. *c* **1750** Shenstone *Love & Hon.* 325 To the cloister's pensive scene Elvira shap'd her solitary way. **1816** Tuckey *Narr. Exped. R. Zaire* i. (1818) 9 We now shaped a course for the west end of Madeira. **1848** J. F. Cooper *Oak Openings* I. iv. 49 Perhaps it would be best for me to shape at once for Ohio. **1877** 'H. A. Page' *De Quincey* I. iv. 80 Two considerations caused him to shape his course differently.

**17.** †**a.** To direct, address (speech); to aim (a blow). *Obs.*

**13..** *Gaw. & Gr. Knt.* 1626 He schewez hem þe scheldez, & schapes hem þe tale. **1456** Sir G. Haye *Law Arms* (S.T.S.) 270 He wald..prevene the strakis, and geve him the dedely straikis first that he schapis till him. **1596** Spenser *F.Q.* v. v. 39 Which speaches she applying to the scope Of her intent, this further purpose to him shope.

**b.** Phrase, ***to shape an answer***. In early use const. *to* or *dative*. (Now with mixture of sense 11.)

*c* **1420** ? Lydg. *Assembly of Gods* 160 Wherefore thow Eolus, without more delay Shape vs an answer to thyne accusement. **1528** More *Dyaloge* iii. i. (1529) 67 b/2 That shall I gladly here quod I, and shape you such answere as my pore wytte wyll serue me. **1581** A. Hall *Iliad* ix. 171 Achilles thus an answere shapes. **1625** Bacon *Ess., Cunning* (Arb.) 441 It is a good Point of Cunning, for a Man, to shape the Answer he would haue, in his owne Words, and Propositions. **1670** Milton *Hist. Brit.* iv. 151 Well perceaving which way the King enclin'd, every one thereafter shap'd his reply. **1812** Cary *Dante, Parad.* vi. 28 To thy first question thus I shape mine answer.

**18.** *intr.* †**a.** To turn out, take a course. *Obs.*

**1338** R. Brunne *Chron.* (1725) 301 For him & us alle myght it better schape. *c* **1400** *Laud Troy Bk.* 8415 Iff happe so with me schape That thow may no wyse askape Fro me. *c* **1440** *Wars Alex.* (prose) 69 (E.E.T.S.), And when Alexander saw it schope thus..he commanded þat all men schulde wende armed.

†**b.** To arise, come to pass. *Obs.*

**13..** *E.E. Allit. P.* C. 160, & al to lyȝten þat lome, ȝif leþe wolde schape. *c* **1420** Hoccleve *Min. Poems* xxii. 332 And on a nyght vnhappyly shoop it, Left was the Erles Chambre dore vnstoken. *c* **1430** —— *New Cant. Tale* 15/29 (E.E.T.S.) It schoop so þat this man had a yong sone.

†**c.** To be conducive, tend. *Obs.*

**1611** Shaks. *Cymb.* v. v. 346 Their deere losse, The more of you 'twas felt, the more it shap'd Vnto my end of stealing them.

†**d.** Of a coast-line: to trend. *Obs.*

**1769** E. BANCROFT *Guiana* 7 The sea-coast..from thence ..shapes nearly south by east half east.

**19. a.** To appear promising (chiefly *Sc.* and *dial.*: see Eng. Dial. Dict.). Often with reference to physical exercises, as drill, rowing, etc.: To show signs of becoming efficient.

**1865** CARLYLE *Fredk. Gt.* XIV. viii. V. 264 How their Grand Army of the Netherlands shaped to prosper. *Ibid.* XVIII. vii. VII. 211 Your Brother does not the least shape towards giving in. **1899** KIPLING *Stalky* 205 They [the cadet company] shape well—extremely well they shape. **1913** *Daily Chron.* 22 Feb. 7/4 No. 7 rowed light, but the other men in the stern and right down to 4 shaped finely.

**b.** *Cricket.* Of a batsman: To get into the proper attitude and position for dealing with the particular kind of ball delivered by the bowler. Also in *Golf*: to get into the proper attitude or stance for a stroke.

**1884** I. BLIGH in *Lillywhite's Cricket Ann.* 4 Davis and Powell shaping well. **1930** WODEHOUSE *Very Good, Jeeves!* vi. 160 It was while I was shaping for a rather tricky shot that the front-door bell went.

**c.** Of a horse: To exhibit capabilities; to develop *into*.

**1887** *Daily News* 16 May 3/4 Mr. C. Clark's son of Outfit, who gives promise of shaping into a grand weight-carrier. **1891** GOULD *Double Event* xvii. 123, I am very anxious to see how my horse shapes.

**d.** *to shape up*: to pull oneself together or meet a required standard; to show one's capabilities. Also, to get oneself into good physical condition.

**1938** E. BOWEN *Death of Heart* I. v. 98 There seemed no reason why he should not shape up. **1951** *Chambers's Jrnl.* Nov. 645/1 He shaped up awkwardly against a man who was not only champion but twelve years his junior. **1963** *Time* 8 Nov. 10/3 You stated that an icosahedron is a two-sided solid figure... Shape up, sir! It's really a 20-sided solid figure. **1976** *National Observer* (U.S.) 10 July 8/2 After that [*sc.* adolescence] one is expected to shape up, get a job, get married. *Ibid.* 14 Aug. 11/1, I have gained 5 more pounds, and so once again am embarked on a semiserious effort to shape up. **1977** N. MARSH *Last Ditch* vi. 154 He taught her to ride and was uncommon proud of the way she shaped up.

**e.** Phr. *to shape up or ship out*: used as a threat of transference or dismissal if a satisfactory performance is not achieved. *slang* (orig. *U.S. Mil.*).

**1956** *Amer. Speech* XXXI. 108 *Shape up or ship out!*, start soldiering or be sent to a combat zone. **1968** *Review & Herald* 19 Sept. 24/2 We ought to tell them to 'shape up or ship out'. **1977** *Guardian Weekly* 30 Oct. 15/1 If the International Labor Organization didn't shape up within two years, the U.S. government would ship out.

**20.** *Pugilism.* To 'square' for fighting. Also with *out* or *up*.

**1855** R. CARBONI *Eureka Stockade* 9 By this time two covies..had stripped to their middle, and were 'shaping' for a round or two. **1878** *Athletic World* 31 May 99/2 Bassano.. without the least attempt at shaping, hit him sharply on the nose. **1899** S. MACMANUS *In Chimney Corners* 12 'I'll fight you,' says Billy, shaping out and winding the bit of stick three times over his head. **1927** *Daily Express* 31 May 7 He shaped up to Murphy, when he punched the watchman on the jaw with his fist and knocked him insensible. **1977** N. MARSH *Last Ditch* ii. 47 If you feel like a fight you've only to say so and we'll shape up and make fools of ourselves.

**III.** To appoint, decree, determine.

†**21.** *trans.* **a.** Of God, fate, fortune, etc.: To destine, decree. *Obs.*

*Beowulf* 2913 Wæs sio wroht scepen heard wið Hugas. *a* **1000** *Be manna wyrdum* 95 (Gr.) Weoroda god ȝeond middanȝeard monnes cræftas sceop & scyrede. *c* **1200** *Trin. Coll. Hom.* 105 Werpeð þat gilt uppen ure drihten and seið ..ne was me no bet shapen. **1297** R. GLOUC. (Rolls) 4391 Ac euere vouȝte as hom nere deþ issape non. **13..** *E.E. Allit. P.* C. 247 A wylde walterande whal, as wyrde þen schaped, þat was beten fro þe abyme. *c* **1386** CHAUCER *Monk's Prol.* 21 'Allas!' she seith, 'that ever I was shape To wedde a milksop'. **1423** JAS. I *Kingis Q.* xxiv, Fortune It schupe non othir wayis to be. *c* **1440** CAPGRAVE *Life St. Kath.* 1257 (Rawl. MS.) ȝet is þer to ȝow schape a hyer chaunce. *a* **1547** SURREY *Æneid* II. 153 To whom that fate was shapte, whom Phebus wold.

†**b.** *gen.* To decree, determine. *Obs.*

*c* **1330** R. BRUNNE *Chron. Wace* (Rolls) 4364 When alle were set in ylka bataille, & schept ho scholde formest assaille, Toward þe Romayns faste þey nomen. **13..** *E.E. Allit. P.* B. 742, & quat if faurty be fre & fauty þyse oþer Schalt þow schortly al schende & schape non oþer. *c* **1380** WYCLIF *Wks.* (1880) 419 Siþ no cause is of þis almes, þei seyen þat god shoop þis wiþ-oute cause.

†**22.** To give (a name) to a person or thing. *Obs.*

*Beowulf* 78 Scop him Heort naman. *c* **1000** ÆLFRIC *Hom.* (Th.) I. 478 Rice menn sceopon heora bearnum naman be him sylfum. *c* **1205** LAY. 14232 þa þe burh wel [*read* wes] al ȝare þa scop he hire nome. **1387** TREVISA *Higden* (Rolls) I. 277 In þe same manere kynges sones of Engelond hadde names i-schape by hir fadir names. **1555** PHAER *Æneid* III. 22 And of my name their name I shoope, and Eneads them call.

†**23.** To deliver (a judgement), appoint (a penalty); condemn (a person) to punishment.

*a* **1300** *Cursor M.* 9714 Til an behoues al assent And siþen schap þe iugement. **1340-70** *Alex. & Dind.* 809 To bale were ȝe þanne bore for bannede werkus, þat schullen schamly be schent & schapen to paine. **1377** LANGL. *P. Pl.* B. I. 159 Riȝt so is loue a ledere and þe lawe shapeth. *c* **1425** *Cast. Persev.* 1828 in *Macro Plays* 131, I schape þese schrewys to mekyl schame.

**shape**, obs. form of CHAPE *sb.*

**1540** in Gage *Hengrave* (1822) 114 Paid for gylting of the handle of the swarde and for the shape ijs.

**shape**, obs. form of SCAPE *v.*[1]

**shapeable, shapable** (ˈʃeɪpəb(ə)l), *a.* [f. SHAPE *v.* and *sb.* + -ABLE.]

**1.** Capable of being shaped, plastic.

**1647** WARD *Simp. Cobler* 35 My task is to sit and study how shapeable the Independent way will be to the body of England. **1832** CARLYLE in Froude *Remin.* (1881) I. 19 What strange shapeable creatures we are! **1860** RUSKIN *Unto this Last* (1862) 71 Soft, and shapeable into love-syllables.

**2.** Shapely, characterized by shapeliness.

**1719** DE FOE *Crusoe* I. (Globe) 146 With a Wheel..I made Things round and shapable, which before were filthy Things..to look on. **1889** H. B. WHEATLEY *How to Catalogue* iii. 71 As it forms a more shapable and better-looking volume.

**shapeau**, obs. form of CHAPEAU.

**shaped** (ʃeɪpt), *ppl. a.* [f. SHAPE *v.* and *sb.* + -ED. Cf. SHAPEN *ppl. a.*]

**1.** In senses of the verb. Often with prefixed adv.

**1540** PALSGR. *Acolastus* III. iii. Pivb, That hurtful or noysom yll which..did cast away our first formed or shaped fathers. **1720** OZELL *Vertot's Rom. Rep.* II. XIII. 340 Caius Julius Cæsar..was the best shap'd Man of his Time. **1845** MRS. M. J. HOWELL *Hand-bk. Dress-making* 53 For cambrics, or muslins, this shaped body is most eligible. **1857** DICKENS *Dorrit* xv, That fair ship began to steer steadily on a shaped course. **1862** H. B. WHEATLEY *Anagrams* 18 Shaped verses are instances of the most egregious folly. It was the fashion among the minor poets to compose poems formed in the shape of every conceivable thing. **1863** *Q. Rev.* CXIV. 387 Shaped bones and chipped flints lay in the same deposit. **1890** *Hardwicke's Sci. Gossip.* XXVI. 33/2 The curiously shaped rhinoceros beetle.

**2.** In parasynthetic derivatives of adj. + *shape* sb., as ***many-shaped*** adj.

**1593** Q. ELIZ. *Boeth.* II. pr. i. 20, I vnderstand the many shaped [*multiformes*] deceites of her wonder. **1866** *Field* 6 Jan. 10/2 The first-named..being as fine a shaped hound as ever I saw.

**3.** Special collocations: **shaped charge**, an explosive charge having a cavity which causes the blast to be concentrated into a small area; **shaped note** = *shape note* s.v. SHAPE *sb.*[1] 17.

**1889** F. H. GILSON *Hist. Shaped or Character Notes* 4 The great variety of systems embodying the same idea,—that is, a separate shape for each syllable,—came to be so confusing that the majority of the advocates of shaped notes finally agreed to adopt one system. **1945** *Chicago Tribune* 18 Nov. VII. 1/5 We sang from song books printed with old time shaped notes. **1948** *Sun* (Baltimore) 2 Jan. 1/3 A light but potent recoilless gun of the new type, using a 'shaped charge' like that of the bazooka. **1979** A. HAILEY *Overload* I. ii. 14 What the saboteur used, they decided, was a 'shaped charge'—a cone of dynamite which, when detonated, had a forward velocity similar to that of a bullet.

**shapeful** (ˈʃeɪpfʊl), *a.* [f. SHAPE *sb.*[1] + -FUL.]

†**1.** Having or taking (any) shape. *nonce-use.*

**1615** CHAPMAN *Odyss.* XVII. 648 The Gods Haue often visited these rich abods..since their pow'rs (Being alwayes [? = all ways] shapefull) glide through Townes and Tow'rs.

**2.** Shapely.

**1621** G. SANDYS *Ovid's Met.* IV. (1626) 73 But now in her owne Fountayne bathes her faire And shapefull lims. **1842** J. STERLING *Ess.*, etc. (1848) I. 437 The..struggle for power and riches absorbs the energies that would otherwise exert themselves in shapeful melody. **1867** G. MACDONALD *Disciple*, etc., *Somnium Myst.* xi, Their floral speech, Their lovely silences of shapeful lore.

**shapeless** (ˈʃeɪplɪs), *a.* [f. SHAPE *sb.*[1] + -LESS.]

**1.** Without shape or form; having no definite or regular shape.

*a* **1300** *Cursor M.* 350 þat es þe elementes to sai, þat first scapless al samen lay. **1587** GOLDING *De Mornay* vii. 103 The sayd Chaos was as a shapelesse Child [*vn Embryon*].. scarce set together in the moothers wombe. **1592** SHAKS. *Ven. & Ad.* 415 Who weares a garment shapelesse and vnfinisht? **1636** EARL MANCH. *Contempl. Mortis & Immort.* 33 But what is this soule that so delights in futures? Though it be shapelesse and immateriall, yet [etc.]. **1698** FROGER *Voy.* Ded., I cou'd not forbear, how shapeless soever the same [*sc.* this Relation] may be, to present it to Your Honour. **1709** POPE *Ess. Crit.* 158 Some objects please our eyes..The shapeless rock, or hanging precipice. **1770** GOLDSM. *Des. Vill.* 47 Sunk are thy bowers in shapeless ruin all. **1799** SIR J. MACKINTOSH *Disc. Law Nat.* 17 A shapeless compilation, in which reason lies buried under a mass of authorities and quotations. **1821** SHELLEY *Prometh. Unb.* I. 36 And shapeless sights come wandering by, The ghastly people of the realm of dream. **1891** FARRAR *Darkn. & Dawn* xlix. 157 The statue had been fused and disfigured into a mass of shapeless metal.

**2.** Destitute of beauty or elegance of form, unshapely.

**1588** SHAKS. *L.L.L.* v. ii. 303 Let vs complaine to them what fooles were heare, Disguis'd like Muscouites in shapelesse geare. **1590** —— *Com. Err.* IV. ii. 20 He is deformed, crooked, old, and sere, Ill-fac'd, worse bodied, shapelesse euery where. *a* **1661** HOLYDAY tr. *Juvenal* Sat. x. (1673) 191 A shape-less Lad no Tyrant e're did make His dear Court-Eunuch. **1750** GRAY *Elegy* 79 Some frail memorial still erected nigh, With uncouth rhimes and shapeless sculpture deck'd. **1813** SCOTT *Trierm.* III. xv, In shapeless characters of yore, The gate this stern inscription bore. **1868** GEO. ELIOT *F. Holt* i, The old women at Smyrna are like sacks. You've not got clumsy and shapeless.

**3.** Without guidance or direction, aimless. *rare.*

**1591** SHAKS. *Two Gent.* I. i. 8 To..Weare out thy youth with shapelesse idlenesse. **1890** 'R. BOLDREWOOD' *Col. Reformer* (1891) 133 The drunkard's nerveless, hopeless, shapeless life in death.

Hence **ˈshapelessness**.

**1587** GOLDING *De Mornay* vii. 102 A proper imagination surely,..to father his so orderly essence vppon the shapelessenesse of a Chaos. **1872** *Echo* 3 Oct. 3 The incoherence and shapelessness which Sir George Jessel vaunts as the perfection of human contrivance.

**shapeliness** (ˈʃeɪplɪnɪs). [f. SHAPELY *a.* + -NESS.] The condition of being shapely.

**1388** WYCLIF *Song Sol.* v. 15 His schapplinesse [1382 fairnesse] is as of the Liban. —— *Ps.* xliv. 5 Biholde thou in thi schaplynesse. **1755** in JOHNSON. **1762-71** H. WALPOLE *Vertue's Anecd. Paint.* (1786) III. 294 The shapeliness of the lime and horse-chesnut. **1865** SWINBURNE *Chastelard* I. i. 23 True, a goodly man. What shapeliness and state he hath. **1884** J. R. SEELEY in *Contemp. Rev.* Oct. 497 When we speak of Goethe as having created the literature of Germany, do we mean that he brought it back from wildness to Greek shapeliness and decorum?

†**ˈshapeling.** *Obs. rare*[−1]. [f. SHAPE *sb.*[1] + -LING 2.] A small form or embryo.

**1674** N. FAIRFAX *Bulk & Selv.* 35 The shaplings or tiny keeles of the great Malpighiuses eggs.

**shapely** (ˈʃeɪplɪ), *a.* Also 4-5 **shaply**, (4 **schapliche, schap(p)li, schap(p)ely**, *comparative* **schaploker**), 4-6 **schaply**. [f. SHAPE *sb.*[1] + -LY[1]. (OE. had *ȝesceaplíce* adv., fitly.)]

†**1.** Fit, likely, suitable; also like (*to* something).

*c* **1374** CHAUCER *Troylus* IV. 1452 Tho sleyghtes yet þat I haue herd yow stere Ful shaply ben to fayllen alle y-fere. *c* **1386** —— *Prol.* 372 Euerich for the wisdom þat he kan Was shaply for to been an Alderman. **1390** GOWER *Conf.* I. 264 Envie..is noght schaply forto wyve In Erthe among the wommen hiere. *c* **1435** *Chron. London* (ed. Kingsford 1905) 53 For Sorowe and Remoors, that he ys shaply to make with Inne this Rewme. *c* **1440** HYLTON *Scala Perf.* (W. de W. 1494) II. xxviii, Thyse that god knewe before sholde be made shapely to the ymage of his sone.

**2.** Of good or elegant shape, well-formed.

**1382** WYCLIF *Exod.* ii. 2 [She] bar a child, and, seynge hym shaply [Vulg. *elegantem*], hydde hym thre monethis. **1388** —— *Gen.* xxxix. 6 Forsothe Joseph was fair in face, and schapli in siȝt [Vulg. *decorus aspectu*]. *a* **1400** *Pistil of Susan* 118 (Vernon MS.) Als þis schaply þing ȝede in hire ȝarde. *Ibid.* 194 Hire scholdres schaply and schire. *c* **1400** *Lanfranc's Cirurg.* 30 þe þridde [profit is], þat þe makynge of lymes were þe more schaploker. **1406** HOCCLEVE *La Male Regle* 139 Children deere, þat so goodly so shaply were, and feir. **1513** DOUGLAS *Æneis* VI. xv. 38 A sembly springald, a fayr ȝowng galland, Rycht schaply maid. **1687** A. LOVELL tr. *Thevenot's Trav.* I. 237 The Ambassadour..had the end of his Nose, part of the upper and under Lip cut off, but was otherwise a shapely Man. **1785** COWPER *Task* II. 76 Rude fragments now Lie scatter'd where the shapely column stood. **1883** *Contemp. Rev.* Oct. 613 In physique, they are taller, slighter, more lithe, shapelier, than their congeners at home.

*absol.* **1382** WYCLIF *Song Sol.* ii. 11 My culuer, my shapli [Vulg. *Formosa mea*]. —— *Isa.* lxiii. 1 Who is this..? this shapli in his stole. **1709** SHAFTESB. *Moralists* III. ii. 225 An inward Eye distinguishes, and sees the Fair and Shapely. *a* **1834** COLERIDGE in *Academy* 15 Aug. (1885) 104/2 The distinct Perception of a Whole arising out of a distinct simultaneous perception of the Parts, in the relations of all to each, and of each to each and to all, constitutes—the Shapely.

**b.** Having definite form. *rare.*

**1827** HOOD *Hero & Leander* lxxix, She..spies blurr'd images obscurely drawn,..But her true grief grows shapely by degrees, A perish'd creature lying on her knees. **1863** *Edin. Rev.* Apr. 500 The plastic power of the imagination, taking up and using the existing data, forms them into a shapely conception.

†**3.** Pertaining to form. *Obs. rare*[−1].

**1387** TREVISA *Higden* (Rolls) II. 177 þe makere of alle þinges þat haþ wiþ him schapliche resouns, of al manere resouns and þinges [orig. *ideales rerum rationes*].

**shapen** (ˈʃeɪp(ə)n), *ppl. a.* [Strong pa. pple. of SHAPE *v.* (OE. had *earmsceapen* wretched.) Cf. SHAPED *ppl. a.*]

**1.** Having a shape (of the kind specified by the qualifying word). *Obs.* exc. in ***well shapen*** (somewhat *arch.*).

*a* **1300** *Cursor M.* 8076 þat sagh man neuer for-wit þat hore, Sua fraward scapen creature. *a* **1425** tr. *Arderne's Treat. Fistula*, etc. (1910) 6 Haue the leche also clene handes and wele shapen nailez. **1470-85** MALORY *Arthur* IX. ii. 341 The knyȝt with the euylle shapen cote. *c* **1500** *Melusine* xxxiii. 235 His fayre and wel shappen body. **1549** COVERDALE *Erasm. Par. Rom.* Prol. ✠✠ iij, That the righte shapen workes abyde not behynde, but accompanye faythe. **1603** STOW *Surv.* (ed. 3) 197 An vglie shapen sight appeared to them, comming in at the south Window. **1625** BACON *Ess., Innovations*, The Births of Liuing Creatures, at first, are ill shapen. **1703** T. N. *City & C. Purch.* 85 A well shapen Man. **1859** GEO. ELIOT *Adam Bede* vi, She was a good-looking woman.., well shapen.

**2.** Furnished with a definite shape; fashioned, shaped.

**1483** *Cath. Angl.* 333/1 Schapyne, *aptus, aptatus, adplasmatus.* **1558** *Knaresb. Wills* (Surtees) I. 88, I bequith all my shappen apparell as jacketts, dubletts and others unto my children. *Ibid.* 141, 200. **1887** MORRIS *Odyss.* XII. 15 And withal on the topmost tomb we set the shapen oar. **1891** —— *Poems by Way* (1896) 214 Yet on he went until he heard The cry become a shapen word.

**shapen** (ˈʃeɪp(ə)n), *v. rare.* [f. SHAPE *sb.*[1] + -EN[5]; cf. SHAPEN *ppl. a.*] *trans.* To shape, impart a shape to.

**1535** COVERDALE *1 Kings* xxviii. 14 He sayde: How is he shapened? She sayde: There commeth vp an olde man, and is clothed with a longe garment. **1587** GOLDING *De Mornay* vii. 90 Seeing this Chaos could not receiue either shape or order but by the said Soule,..how met they together,..the one to shape, and the other to be shapened? **1603** FLORIO *Montaigne* I. xxiv. 65 Their speciall charge was first to shapen his limmes and bodie, goodly, and healthie. **1618** W. LAWSON *New Orch. & Gard.* vii. (1623) 20 When it [*sc.* the sap]..shapens his buds for next yeeres fruit. **1819** CRABBE *Tales of Hall* I. 235 The minor portions of his creed hung loose, For time to shapen and an whole produce. **1905** *Westm. Gaz.* 10 Aug. 1/3 Wait..until the creature has..shapened itself into the form of a cottage loaf.

Hence **'shapening** *vbl. sb.*

**1647** H. MORE *Song of Soul* II. ii. I. ix, This is the nourishing Of all; but spermall form, the certain shapening. *Ibid.* II. iii. I. xix, The soul doth imitate and bring Thy eye to such a temper in her shapening.

**shaper** ('ʃeɪpə(r)). Forms: 3 **scaper**, 4–5 **shapere**, 5 **schaper**, **schapare**, 4– **shaper**. Also (in sense 1) 4 **shapper(e**, **schappere**. [f. SHAPE *v.* + -ER[1]; the form *s(c)happere* is influenced by the doublet SHEPPER.]

†**1.** The Creator or Maker (of the universe). *Obs.*

*a* **1300** *Cursor M.* 12899 þe scaper þat wroght al thing. **1303** R. BRUNNE *Handl. Synne* 579, 581 þer nys no shapper [*v.rr.* shaper, schappere] but god almyȝt... He ys shapper of al þyng. *Ibid.* 585, 9663, 9668. **1382** WYCLIF *Deut.* xxxii. 18 Thow..hast forȝet the Lord thi shaper. —— *Isa.* xliii. 15, li. 13. *a* **1400** *Prymer* (1891) 88 Schappere of alle þynges god þat fourmedest me. **1496** *Dives & Paup.* (W. de W.) I. xi. 42/2 God..is..shaper & sauer of all creatures.

**2. a.** One who or something which makes (a thing) in the required shape; one who fashions (material).

*c* **1425** *Noah's Ark* 87 in *Non-Cycle Mystery Plays* 22 [*Noah loq.*] Christ be the shaper of this ship, For a ship need make I must. *c* **1440** *Promp. Parv.* 444/1 Schapare, *aptator, formator.* **1569** J. SANFORD tr. *Agrippa's Van. Artes* 182 b, That auncient Serpente the shaper of such Gods. **1589** R. HARVEY *Pl. Perc.* (1590) 14 Another..wil be none otherwise termde then a shaper of garments. **1831** CARLYLE *Surv. German Poetry* in *Misc. Ess.* (1888) III. 250 Mind is the creator and shaper of matter. **1867** O. W. HOLMES *Guardian Angel* II. 10 He was by nature an artist; a shaper with the pencil or the chisel. **1893** F. THOMPSON *Poems* 51, I..made them shapers Of mine own moods.

**b.** *spec.* in various trades as the designation of an operative. Also ***shaper up.***

**1881** *Instr. Census Clerks* (1885) 42, 45, 74, 97. **1890** *North Lindsey Star* 19 July 5/1 A shaper at the Britannia Iron Works. **1902** *Brit. Med. Jrnl.* No. 2146. 380 [Hat-making.] Curlers including 'shapers'. **1902** *Daily Chron.* 28 Oct. 10/7 Carver and Shaper-up..for shaped blocks.

**3.** quasi-*arch.* A poet. *rare.* (Cf. MAKER 5.)

Suggested by OE. SCOP, fancied to be cogn. w. SHAPE *v.* **1816** W. TAYLOR in *Monthly Mag.* LXXXI. 518 In this hall, we are told, a shaper, or poet, sang the lay of the creation. **1892** S. A. BROOKE *Eng. Lit.* I. iv. 103 If we want to feel whether *Beowulf* is good poetry or not, let us place ourselves in the hall..filled with warriors and seamen,..—and then hear the Shaper strike the harp.

**4. a.** A machine or tool for shaping material, spec. a shaping-machine (see SHAPING *vbl. sb.* 4).

**1853** *Pract. Mechanic's Jrnl.* VI. 230/2 The shaper..is capable of working out differentially-curved..figures. **1893** *Sci. Amer.* 25 Nov. 344/1 Among notable exhibits..was an improved shaper.

**b.** *attrib.* and *Comb.*

**1846** HOLTZAPFFEL *Turning* II. 466 By the use of figured guides, cams, or shaper-plates, by which the motion is constrained. **1884** KNIGHT *Dict. Mech.* Suppl., *Shaper Vise*, one adapted to hold work to a planer, at any horizontal angle. **1901** *Feilden's Mag.* IV. 480/1 The form of the shaper tool would have to exactly coincide with the tooth space of the wheel to be cut.

**5.** *Electronics.* A device which modifies an input to produce an output having a specific waveform.

**1967** [see KEYER]. **1971** J. H. SMITH *Digital Logic* vi. 109 When the count of ten is reached..a gate will produce a signal which is shaped by the shaper unit.

**shaperne, -ed:** see CHAPOURN *Her. Obs.*

†**shapet.** *Obs. rare*[−1]. ? variant of SERPET.

*a* **1657** R. LOVEDAY *Lett.* lx. (1659) 116 Mr. R. left a Shapet of Turkey-Carpets and Hangings, which in all probability he designed..at Lighorn.

**'shape-up.** *U.S.* Also **shapeup.** [f. vbl. phr. *to shape up*: see SHAPE *v.*]

**1.** A system of hiring dock workers for the day or half-day by arbitrary selection from a gathering of men on site. Also *transf.*

**1940** *Sun* (Baltimore) 8 Nov. 22/7 Under the shape-up system..longshoremen are forced to gather on the docks..every morning from 5 o'clock on..for the sake of a half day's pay. **1948** *Ibid.* 26 Nov. 2/2 Retention of the traditional twice-a-day 'shapeup' or work call, with the guarantee of four hours work for men called to work only once in a single day. **1954** *Ibid.* 9 Apr. 20/4 There are now from 22 to 24 cities being considered for the major leagues... This is the opinion of Ford Frick, baseball's high commissioner... 'Of course,' Frick said, 'I don't know when their shape-up will take place.' **1967** *Boston Sunday Herald* 30 Apr. I. 7/1 Boston's union long-shoremen have sounded the death knell of their traditional but unwieldy dock shape-up. **1977** *Time* 17 Oct. 57/2 When Marlon Brando starred in *On the Waterfront* (1954), the morning shape-ups of New York Dock workers were pretty much as the movie portrayed them—noisy, brawling scenes of men fighting for the jobs available.

**2.** The action or an instance of shaping up.

**1963** *Washington Post* 2 Oct. D2 The United States Olympic track and field team will have a final 'shapeup' meet in the Los Angeles Coliseum. **1977** *Time* 7 Feb. 20/2 He [*sc.* Lipshutz] presides at the daily 8 a.m. staff meetings... She is the only..outspoken liberal at Lipshutz's daily shape-ups. *Ibid.* 4 Apr. 60/2 Then, as the Central Intelligence Agency became mired in inefficiency, Schlesinger was tapped for the shape-up operation. As CIA director he immediately began to demythologize the agency.

**shaping** ('ʃeɪpɪŋ), *vbl. sb.* Forms: see the verb. [f. SHAPE *v.* + -ING[1].]

**1. a.** The action of SHAPE *v.*: an instance of this.

*a* **1310** in Wright *Lyric P.* x. 38 'Thah y swore by treuthe ant othe, that God hath shaped me y-nou at luppe'. 'Mid shupping ne mey hit me ashunche.' *c* **1440** *Promp. Parv.* 444/1 Schapynge, *aptura, formacio.* **1484** CAXTON *Fables of Alfonce* xiii, [A tayller] whiche surmounted alle the other in shapynge or sewynge. **1568** CHARTERIS *Pref. to Lyndesay's Wks.* (1871) 4* Seing teiching and preiching is na les requisite to thair vocatioun, than schaiping & sewing is to ane tailȝeouris. **1691** T. H[ALE] *Acc. New Invent.* 124 We come to the like shaping of the remaining part of the Logg. **1795** SOUTHEY *Joan of Arc* III. 361 Canst thou remember, Maid, what vision first Seem'd more than fancy's shaping? **1815** SCOTT *Guy M.* xiv, It was the housekeeper who did teach her those unprofitable exercises of hemming and shaping. **1850** TENNYSON *In Mem.* ciii. 36 As one would sing the death of war,..And one the shaping of a star.

**b.** *Electronics.* The process of modifying the waveform of an electrical signal.

[**1902** *Electr. Rev.* 10 Oct. 641/2 On adjusting the inductance and resistance of the shunt, along with the receiving condenser and its shunt, the signals are effectively curbed and shaped at the receiving end without reference to the sending station.] **1924** *Jrnl. Inst. Electr. Engineers* LXII. 192/1 The relation of damping to the reception of wireless signals, viz. its relation to the 'shaping' of the received dots and dashes. **1949** H. E. PENROSE *Princ. & Pract. Radar* x. 152 A diode may..be employed with the primary object of exercising amplitude control, or..with the primary object of shaping. **1971** J. H. SMITH *Digital Logic* iv. 68 The output of the shaping circuit is fed to the $S_r$ trigger pulse input and a 20 $\mu$F capacitor is used to control the pulse length.

**c.** *Radar.* Modification of a radar beam so as to obtain a desired spatial configuration.

**1945** C. S. PAO *Shaping Primary Pattern of Horn Feed* (M.I.T. Radiation Lab. Rep. No. 655) 2 Such beam shaping cannot usually be achieved by merely changing the geometrical dimensions of the horn. **1975** D. G. FINK *Electronics Engineers' Handbk.* xxv. 66 In the horn-fed reflector the shaping can be achieved by either the reflector or the feed.

**2.** Something shaped, fashioned, or created; a creature, form, shape; a creation (of the mind or fancy).

**1340** *Ayenb.* 64 Oþer huanne me zuereþ be þe sseppinges, ase me zayþ; be þe zonne þet ssinþ [etc.]. *Ibid.* 158 þe dyeuel ssewеþ to þe goste zuiche ssеppinges and zuiche figures ase he wyle. **1629** GAULE *Holy Madn.* 136 Oh blot not out the louely Image of God; in faining, and framing so vaine a shaping to your selues! **1794** COLERIDGE *Relig. Musings* 338 Pale Fear Haunted by ghastlier shapings than surround Moon-blasted Madness when he yells at midnight! **1795** —— *Lines at Shurton Bars* 85 How oft, my Love! with shapings sweet I paint the moment, we shall meet! **1892** GREENER *Breech-Loader* 86 This shaping of the stock is a very modified form of pistol grip.

**3.** *Sc.* (See quot. 1825–80.)

**1814** W. NICHOLSON *Tales, Peacock* 91 Decamp [tailor loon], or by my bloody weapons, I'll cut thy buckram soul to shapin's! **1825–80** JAMIESON, *Shapings*, the small bits of cloth that are cut off with the scissors in shaping any piece of dress, S.

**4.** *attrib.* and *Comb.*: **a.** simple attrib. as ***shaping machinery***; ***shaping implement***, ***mould***, ***process*** (1869 C. Knight *Mechanician* 77–8). **b.** Special comb., as †**shaping apparel**, **clothes** *Sc.*, outer garments; †**shaping board**, a board on which a tailor or shoemaker shapes his materials; **shaping engine**, an early name for the *shaping machine* (*b*); †**shaping knife**, a shoemakers' knife; **shaping machine**, (*a*) a machine for shaping metal pieces and parts of machinery; also *attrib.*; (*b*) a machine for shaping ship's blocks; (*c*) a finishing blocking machine for hats (Knight *Dict. Mech.* Suppl. 1884); **shaping-shop**, that building in a shipwright's yard in which the steel framework, plates, etc. are shaped.

**1564** *Richmond Wills* (Surtees) 170 His *shappinge apparell. A yowlowe sattane dublet and a payre of housse. **1442** *Court-Roll Gt. Waltham Manor, Essex* 11 July, [Proceedings against Joan, widow of William 'Taillor', who] asportavit unam tabulam vocat. a *shepping-bord nuper fixam infra tenementum suum. **1483** *Cath. Angl.* 333/1 A Schapynge burde, *sculpatorium, serdecelita.* **1541** *Aberdeen Reg.* (1844) I. 176 Item, ane shaiping knyf, ane schawing irne,..ane schaiping buird. **1894** CROCKETT *Raiders* xxxiii, 'Deed, Jen,' said Lady Grizel,..'I wad hae gien a' my *shapin' claes to sit there.' **1819** REES *Cycl.* XXII. B 2/1 [Brunel's machinery for making ships' blocks.] The outside surfaces of the blocks are next formed to their true figure by the three *shaping engines. *c* **1340** *Nominale* (Skeat) 553 *Trenket et subiloun* *Shappyngknyf and al. *c* **1440** *Promp. Parv.* 444/1 Schapynge knyfe, *scalprum.* Schapynge knyfe of sowtarys, *ansorium.* **1535** LYNDESAY *Satyre* 3139 How cal thay ȝou, sir, with the schaiping knife? Ane sowtar, sir. **1541** [see *shaping board* above]. **1815** *Ann. Reg., Chron.* (1816) 84 The *shaping machine-room [at the Mint]. *a* **1849** BRUNEL in Beamish *Mem.* (1862) iii. 38 The shaping machine I conceived while [etc.]. **1867** *Rep. Paris Univ. Exhib.* (1868) IV. 373 The same firm also show a milling, or, as it is frequently termed in England, a shaping machine, in which circular cutters are employed. **1911** J. G. HORNER in *Encycl. Brit.* XXVI. 29/2 The shaping machine does for comparatively small pieces that which the planer does for long ones. **1872** J. RICHARDS *Wood-working Machines* 263 *Shaping machinery. **1890** W. J. GORDON *Foundry* 63 The *shaping-shop.

**shaping** ('ʃeɪpɪŋ), *ppl. a.* [f. SHAPE *v.* + -ING[2].] That shapes, in the senses of the verb.

**1398** TREVISA *Barth. De P.R.* VI. xii. (1495) 196 In the male ben vertues formale and shapynge and werkynge and in the female materyal suffringe and passyf. **1674** N. FAIRFAX *Bulk & Selv.* 133 In like manner, another man whose plastick, shaping, or enkindling powers, are fraught with more of manhood,..may [etc.]. **1850** ROBERTSON *Serm.* Ser. III. vi. (1857) 88 Our creative shaping intellect projected its own fantasies on him. **1897** DOWDEN *Fr. Lit.* V. iv. 409 He had..the artist's shaping hand.

†**shapio(u)n.** *Sc. Obs.* In 6 sch-. [Of obscure formation; related to F. *chapeau* hat.] Some kind of head-dress.

**1504–6** *Acc. Ld. High Treas. Scot.* III. 90 Item, for vj schapiois [? *read* schapionis] and quhit hattis..iiij *li.* iiij*s.* **1512** *Ibid.* IV. 205 Item..to James Bassindin for ane schapioun and ane bever..v *li.*

‖**shapka** ('ʃapka). [Russ., = hat.] A brimless Russian hat of fur or sheepskin. (See also quot. 1945.)

**1945** *Richmond* (Va.) *News-Leader* 2 Aug. 14/3 Newest thing in casual headgear is called a 'shapka' (meaning a small informal hat in Hungarian)... This headpiece is a cross between a 'babushka' and a snood, and can be worn over any kind of coiffure. **1958** *Philadelphia Sunday Bull.* 30 Mar. V. 1/3 Wearing one of those 'shapka', or tall Russian hats, the wisecracking Hope descended on a Moscow shivering in six-degree-below-zero temperature. **1963** V. NABOKOV *Gift* iv. 271 He never removed either his fur-lined dressing gown or his lambskin shapka. **1977** *Time* 14 Feb. 33/2 Every [Russian] man wears a *shapka*, a fur..hat with ear flaps.

**shapman, -mann,** obs. forms of CHAPMAN.

‖**shapoo** ('ʃɑːpuː). Also **shapu**, **sharpoo**; shortened SHA. [Tibetan *sha-pho* 'wild sheep' (Jaeschke).] A kind of sheep (*Ovis vignei*) found in Ládák (Kashmír) and Tibet.

**1858** A. L. ADAMS in *Proc. Zool. Soc.* 526 *Caprovis vignei* (Blyth)... 3. Shapoo of Ladakh and Tibet. *c* **1880** *Cassell's Nat. Hist.* III. 8 The Oorial and the Shapoo are bearded Sheep... The Shapoo is brownish-grey, white below, with a short brown beard. **1902** RONALDSHAY *Sport under Eastern Sky* v. 88 One of the men..had returned, having seen some sharpoo.

**shapournet,** obs. f. CHAPOURNET *Her. Obs.*

**shapparoon, shapperoon,** obs. f. CHAPERON.

**1622** J. TAYLOR (Water-P.) *Whore* B8, Her Shapperoones, her Perriwigs and tires. **1640** —— *Praise Needle* A 1 b, No shadowes, Shapparoones, Caules, Bands, Ruffs.

**shappeau, shappo,** obs. ff. CHAPEAU.

*a* **1700** B. E. *Dict. Cant. Crew*, *Shappeau*, or *Shappo*, for *Chappeau*, a Hat, the newest Cant, *Nab* being very old, and grown too common. **1725** *New Cant. Dict.*

**shappester, -yster,** variant ff. SHEPSTER.

**shaps** (ʃæps), *sb. pl.* *U.S.* Also CHAPS. [Shortened from Mexican Sp. *chaparejos.*] Leather riding breeches.

**1885** T. ROOSEVELT *Hunting Trips* 8 (Cent.) The spurs, pit, and revolver silver-mounted, the shaps of sealskin, etc. **1904** E. ROBINS *Magnetic North* x. 181 A fellow who went about in 'shaps', as his California cousins called chaparejos.

**shapsister,** variant of SHEPSTER.

**shar,** obs. f. SHARE; obs. pa. t. SHEAR *v.*

**sharable,** var. SHAREABLE *a.*

**sharan,** dial. variant of SHARN.

**Shararat,** var. SHERARAT.

‖**sharav** (ʃa'rav). Also **Sharav.** [ad. Heb. *šārāḇ* parching heat.] A hot desert wind occurring in the Middle East in April and May; = KHAMSIN.

**1968** *Listener* 27 June 827/2 In Crete they really cannot help it if the killingly hot *sharav* has blown across from the Levant. **1969** O. HESKY *Sequin Syndicate* ix. 96 Mornings when the *sharav* would blow. **1973** *New Scientist* 14 June 670 Ill winds such as the Föhn in Germany and the Sharav in the Near East can produce a malaise in humans. **1980** *Times* 4 Sept. 2/6 Seasonal 'ill-winds' such as the Mediterranean föhn and sirocco and the Middle Eastern sharav.

**Sharawaggi.** (ʃærə'wædʒɪ). Also with small initial. Also **sharawadgi.** [Of unknown origin; Chinese scholars agree that it cannot belong to that language. Temple speaks as if he had himself heard it from travellers. For a discussion of etymological hypotheses see 1949 *Archit. Rev.* CVI. 391/2.] Orig. (see quot. 1685). Revived in the twentieth century with particular application to landscape gardening and architecture. Also *attrib.*

**1685** SIR W. TEMPLE *Gard. Epicurus* Misc. II. ii. (1690) 58 The Chineses..have a particular Word to express it [*sc.* the beauty of studied irregularity]; and where they find it hit their Eye at first sight, they say the *Sharawadgi* is fine or is admirable. **1724** POPE *Let. Digby* 12 Aug., For as to the hanging Gardens of Babylon, the Paradise of Cyrus, and the Sharawaggi's of China, I have little or no Idea's of 'em. **1750** H. WALPOLE *Let. to Mann* 25 Feb., I am almost as fond of the Sharawaggi, or Chinese want of symmetry, in buildings, as in grounds or gardens. **1781** —— *Let. to Earl Strafford* 13 June, Though he was the founder of the Sharawadgi taste in England, I preached so effectually that his every pagoda took the veil. **1933** *Times Lit. Suppl.* 28 Dec. 913/4 Gothicism, *Chinoiserie*, all that may be summed up in the magic word *Sharawadgi* that was imposed by ignorance or mystification upon the connoisseurs of the time as a genuine Oriental art term. **1937** A. R. HUMPHREYS *William Shenstone* II. 41 Sharawadgi, as understood in England, has three main ingredients... It has no faith in mathematics and deifies irregularity... It finds beauty in infinite variety... It treats natural material according to that material's own potential organic pattern. **1944** *Archit. Rev.* XCV. 3 (*heading*) Exterior furnishing or sharawaggi: the art of making urban landscape. **1965** NAIRN & PEVSNER *Buildings of England: Sussex* 294 What Petworth shows more than anything else is Sharawaggi..:, good buildings of all dates mixing perfectly at least up to 1920.

**shard, sherd** (ʃɑːd, ʃɜːd), *sb.*[1] Forms: 1 sceard, 4 shord, 4–5 schoord, (5 schorde, schourde), 4–6 scherd(e, 5–6 sherde, (6 shered), 6 sharde, 6–7 sheard(e, 7–8 *Sc.* shaird, 8 *dial.* shoard, 9 shord, sheard, 4– sherd, 5– shard. [OE. *sceard* neut., cogn. w. OFris. *skerd* (? neut.) cut, notch (WFris. *skird*, NFris. *skård*, *schaard*, *scherd*), MDu. *scharde* fem., *schart* (*schard-*) masc., flaw, fragment (mod.Du. *schaard* fem.), MLG. *schart* neut., crack, chink, mod.LG. *schaard* potsherd, also breach, gap (e.g. in an embankment), MHG., mod.G. *scharte* fem., notch, gap, ON. *skarð* neut. (Da. *skaar* chink, potsherd, MSw. *skardh* neut., gap, chink, *skardher* masc., potsherd); subst. uses of the adj. OE. *sceard*, OS. *skard*, OFris. *skerde*, OHG. (*lida-*)*scart* (MHG. *schart*), ON. *skarð-r*:—OTeut. **skardo-* cut, notched, diminished, a ppl. formation on the root **skar-* (:—**sker-*: **skur-*): see SHEAR *v.*]

**I.** A cleft, gap.

**1.** A gap in an enclosure, esp. in a hedge or bank. Now chiefly *dial.*

*a* **1000** in Kemble *Cod. Dipl.* (1848) VI. 220 Swa on ðæt lytle sceard ðæt is on burhhlinceas. [*a* **1100** *Gerefa* xiii. in *Anglia* IX. 262 Dicsceard betan.] *c* **1430** LYDG. *Min. Poems* (Percy Soc.) 114 The other twayen was elle aferd, They sparyd nethe stylle ne sherd. **1471** *Yatton Churchw. Acc.* (Somerset Rec. Soc.) 107 For makyng a schorde at the wyte croste ijd. **1488** *Cal. Anc. Rec. Dublin* (1889) 493 And be cause the dyche of that lane was faste, they brake a shard and put men over the dyche. **1523–34** FITZHERB. *Husb.* §141 If he..fynde a gap, or a sherde in his hedge. **1581** J. BELL *Haddon's Answ. Osor.* 454 But here was one sharde left open which must neede be stopt up with some brambles and Bryars. **1789** W. H. MARSHALL *Glocester* I. 331 *Shard*, a gap in a hedge; the common term. **1863** KINGLAKE *Crimea* (1877) III. i. 111 His practised eye soon showed him a fit 'shard' or break in the scarped face of the bank.

*fig.* **1581** J. BELL *Haddon's Answ. Osor.* 68b, Now for asmuch as you have stopt up a fewe shardes in these your last tedious Commentaries,..I thought good to reply.

†**2.** Used by Spenser for: ? A dividing water.

**1590** SPENSER *F.Q.* II. vi. 38 Vpon that shore he spied Atin stand, There by his maister left, when late he far'd In Phædrias fleet barke ouer that perlous shard.

**3.** A gap or notch in the blade of a tool. *dial.*

**1787** GROSE *Provinc. Gloss.*, *Shard*, a gap or notch. This knife has a great shard. Glouc.

**II. 4. a.** A fragment of broken earthenware. *spec.* in *Archæol.*, a piece of broken pottery. Phrase: *to break*, etc. *into sherds*: to reduce to fragments, break beyond repair.

Cf. POTSHERD and OE. *crocsceard*. *Sherd* is now established as the normal *Archæol.* spelling.

*c* **1000** *Gl. Prud.* in *Germania* (N.S.) XI. 398/257 *Testarum*, scearda. **13..** *Childh. Jesus* 340 in *Archiv Stud. neu. Spr.* LXXIV. 331 His pechere he brake..And Ihesu gadirde þe skarthes [*v.r.* scherdys]. **1382** WYCLIF *Job* ii. 8 Job..with a sherd [1388 schelle] scrapide awei the quyture. —— *Ps.* xxi. 16 My vertue driede as a shord [1388 tiyl stoon]. —— *Ecclus.* xxii. 7 Who techeth a fool, as that glueth togidere a sherd. **1387** TREVISA *Higden* (Rolls) IV. 151 Hayle stones i-medled with scherdes. **1426** LYDG. *De Guil. Pilgr.* 4197 Thogh that a pot be broke smal On sherdys & on pecys ek. *c* **1440** *Promp. Parv.* 445/2 Scherde, or schoord, of a broke vesselle (*P.* schourde of broken vessel), *testula*, *testa*. **1483** CAXTON *Golden Leg.* 208b/2 He put not away the wodenes of his flessh with a sherde or shelle. **1602** SHAKS. *Ham.* v. i. 254 Shardes, Flints, and Peebles. **1610** B. JONSON *Alch.* IV. v. (1612) K2b, There will be, perhaps, Something, about the scraping of the Shardes, Will cure the Itch. **1656** COWLEY *Davideis* II. 715 And scarce ought now of that vast Citie's found But shards and rubbish. **1725** *Bradley's Fam. Dict.*, *Drain*, a small Passage made for Water to run Underground, with dry Shards at Bottom. **1796** STEDMAN *Surinam* II. xx. 114 Several of the poor rebel negroes..had only the shards of Spa-water cans, instead of flints. **1837** CARLYLE *Fr. Rev.* III. II. v, Mirabeau's treason: wherefore his Bust.. is instantly broken to sherds. **1865** TYLOR *Early Hist. Man.* viii. 217 The mutilation of the priests of Cybele was done with a sherd of Samian ware. **1877** MISS A. B. EDWARDS *Up Nile* xix. 531 Fragments of black, red, and yellowish pottery, like the shards of Elephantine and Philæ. **1881** BLACKMORE *Christowell* iv, He took up a shord..and went down to the river, with that for his cup. **1937** *Jrnl. R. Anthrop. Inst.* LXVII. 233, I could find no bronze-age sherds. **1955** *Sci. Amer.* July 46/3 We came upon a few fragmentary sherds of Aegean painted pottery. **1971** *World Archaeol.* III. 203 Many historic Amphlett sherds were recovered.

*Proverbs.* **1641** *D. Ferguson's Sc. Prov.* (1785) 34 Where the pig's broken let the sherds lie. **1678** RAY *Prov.* (ed. 2) 351 When Tom's pitcher's broken I shall have the sheards (*i.e.* kindness after others have done with it).

**b.** *fig.* and in figurative context.

**1579** J. STUBBES *Gaping Gulf* D5b, Which makes hym esteeme himselfe as the iron pot, and vs as the earthen crock, with whom..he weens he can dash vs into shards at hys pleasure. **1647** C. HARVEY *Schola Cordis* xiv. 31 I'll breake it [*sc.* my heart] all In pieces small; Sinne shall not finde a shearde without a flaw Wherein [etc.]. **1847** LONGF. *Evang.* II. i. 67 Thus did that poor soul wander..Bleeding, barefooted, over the shards and thorns of existence. **1883** D. C. MURRAY *Joseph's Coat* xxvii, Love's idol..was long since broken, and the worshipper was still sorely wounded by the shards.

**c.** *transf.* A fragment (of other material).

**1561** HOLLYBUSH *Hom. Apoth.* 39b, If the rubbel or shardes of the stone [*i.e.* calculus] do put the to payn. **1565** COOPER *Thesaurus*, *Assula*..a sharde of marble, or other stone. **1577** HARRISON *England* II. vi. (1877) I. 147 All [glasses] go one waie, that is, to shards at the last. *a* **1611** CHAPMAN *Iliad* v. 297 The hip of Anchisiades..which all in sherds it droue. **1829** BROCKETT *N.C. Words* (ed. 2) s.v., Many of the common people, in the lower parts of Newcastle, used to resort to the Quayside.., where they gathered up coals with the half of a wooden dish, called a shard. **1847** TENNYSON *Princess* v. 132 What were I nigher this altho' we dash'd Your cities to shards with catapults. **1858** CARLYLE *Fredk. Gt.* III. xx. I. 268 Suddenly with huge jingle, the glass-door of his room went to sherds. **1877–8** HENLEY in *Ballades & Rondeaus* (Canterb. Poets) 77 A melon's dripping sherds. **1910** *Spectator* 11 June 968/1 The bark was blown clean off the stem; there were great shards and slices of bark lying twenty and thirty yards away.

**d.** *Sc.* A remnant (of something worn or decayed).

**1785** BURNS *Ep. W. Simpson* Postscr. xii, An' when the auld Moon's gaun to lea'e them, The hindmost shaird, they'll fetch it wi' them, Just i' their pouch. **1866** CARLYLE in Froude *Remin.* (1881) II. 164 Badams..was living..in a big old rambling sherd of a house among waste gardens. **1883** A. LANG in *Fortn. Rev.* Dec. 846 Everything he carried was more or less broken and outworn... His tomahawk was a mere shard of rusted steel.

†**5.** A scale (in quot. of a dragon). *Obs. rare*⁻¹.

[Cf. OHG. *scartifedar*, shell fish or tortoise.]

**1390** GOWER *Conf.* III. 68 Sche sih, hir thoghte, a dragoun tho, Whos scherdes schynen as the Sonne.

**shard** (ʃɑːd), *sb.*[2] *Obs.* exc. *dial.* In 6 sharde. [app. cogn. w. SHARN.] A patch of cow-dung. (Cf. COW-SHARD.)

**1545** ELYOT *Dict.* s.v. *Bonasus*, In his runnynge [he] flyngeth, and shoteth furth his sharde and dunge thre furlonge from hym. **1576** PETTIE *Petite Pallace* 82b, The Humblebee..at nyght taketh no scorne to lodge in a Cowes foule sharde. **1606** SHAKS. *Ant. & Cl.* III. ii. 19 They are his Shards, and he their Beetle. **1687** DRYDEN *Hind & Panther* I. 321 Such souls as Shards produce, such beetle things As only buz to heaven with ev'ning wings. **1828** [CARR] *Craven Gloss.* **1876** *Whitby Gloss.*, *Sharn*, *Shard*, *Sharra*, or *Skarn*, cow's dung.

**b.** Comb.: **shard-beetle**, a beetle of the family *Geotrupidæ*, found under dung, a dor-beetle.

**1854** A. ADAMS, etc. *Man. Nat. Hist.* 188 Shard-Beetles (Geotrupidæ).

**shard** (ʃɑːd), *sb.*[3] Variant of CHARD[2].

**1685** DRYDEN tr. *Hor. Epode* ii. 81 More pleasing morsels ..Than Shards [L. *herba lapathi*] or Mallows for the pot. **1856** KANE *Arct. Expl.* II. i. 25 With furs and woollens layer upon layer inside, like the shards of an artichoke.

**shard** (ʃɑːd), *sb.*[4] [Evolved from a misunderstanding of Shakespeare's use in SHARD-BORN: see also quot. 1606 s.v. SHARD *sb.*[2]] The elytron or wing-case of a coleopterous insect.

[**1755** JOHNSON s.v. *Shardborn*, Perhaps shard in Shakespeare may signify the sheaths of the wings of insects.] **1811** R. WILLAN *List Words W.R. Yorks.* in *Archæologia* XVII. 157 *Shard*, the shell or hard outward covering of the tribe of insects denominated *Coleoptera*. **1842** LONGF. *Hiaw.* XII. 182 The shining shards of beetles. **1884** *Mag. Art* Jan. 116 The glittering shards of insects.

**shard**, obs. form of CHAR *sb.*[3]

**1668** CHARLETON *Onomast.* 155 *Trutta Minor*..a Shard. **1755** JOHNSON, *Shard*..4. A sort of fish.

**shard** (ʃɑːd), *v. rare.* Also sherd. [f. SHARD *sb.*[1]]

**1. a.** *trans.* To break into fragments. Also with *off*. **b.** *intr.* Of a tree: To shed its bark in 'shards'. Hence **'sharding** *ppl. a.*

**1582** [implied in SHARDED *ppl. a.*[1]]. **1891** NISBET *Colonial Tramp* I. 4 Dead, white branches and sharding trunks. **1900** CONAN DOYLE *Gt. Boer War* xvi. 269 The artillery fire..was then turned..upon..the isolated Vaalkranz... The hillside was sharded off in great flakes. **1910** *Contemp. Rev.* Mar. 339 The veils and filaments of queens are torn aside, their bracelets sherded on their wrists.

**2.** *trans.* To notch the edge of (a tool). *dial.*

**1879** *Exmoor Scolding & Courtship* (E.D.S.) Gloss. *s.v.*, Thee's a shorded my knife. **1886** *W. Somerset Word-bk.* s.v. *Shord*, Zee how he've a-bin and a-shorded my plane ire.

**Shardana, Sherden** (ʃɑːˈdɑːnə, ˈʃɜːdən), *collect. pl.* [ad. Egyptian *Šrdn.*] One of the Sea Peoples, tentatively identified with the later Sardinians, who fought against the Egyptians in the 13th century B.C. and afterwards served them as mercenaries. Hence **'Shardan**, a member of this people. Also *attrib.*

**1877** *Encycl. Brit.* VII. 739/2 The king of the Rebu (Libyans), with the warriors of several tribes joined the Shardana (Sardones), the Shakalasha (Sikels), [etc.]. **1910** *Ibid.* IX. 85/2 The Sherden had been in the armies of Rameses II., and are distinguished by their remarkable helmets and apparently body armour of metal. **1928** C. DAWSON *Age of Gods* xiii. 300 The Shardana..were especially important and formed the royal bodyguard. **1952** O. R. GURNEY *Hittites* i. 35 The Sherden..appear frequently in Egyptian inscriptions. **1960** K. M. KENYON *Archæol. in Holy Land* ix. 224 For centuries Shardans..had been in the habit of serving the Egyptians as mercenaries. *Ibid.* 227 It is known on literary evidence that Shardan mercenaries were employed by the Egyptians.

**'shard-born, -borne**, *a.* [f. SHARD *sb.*[2] + BORN *a.*] **a.** Of a beetle: Born in dung; *spec.* applied to the *shard-beetle* (see SHARD *sb.*[2] b). **b.** Used with the meaning (due to misinterpretation of Shaks.): Borne on shards (SHARD *sb.*[4]).

**1605** SHAKS. *Macb.* III. ii. 42 Ere to black Heccats summons The shard-borne Beetle, with his drowsie hums, Hath rung Nights yawning Peale. **1830** SCOTT *Doom of Devorgoil* I. i, This was a shard-born beetle, heavy, drossy. **1843** CARPENTER *Anim. Phys.* xii. 443 The Dung or Shard-borne Beetle. **1859** LD. LYTTON *Wanderer* (ed. 2) 23 The advancing twilight's shard-born trumpeter.

**sharded** (ˈʃɑːdɪd), *ppl. a.*[1] [f. SHARD *sb.*[1] and *v.* + -ED[1].] †**a.** Of a serpent: Scaly (*obs.*). **b.** Reduced to shards or fragments; of the moon, reduced to a crescent.

**1390** GOWER *Conf.* II. 251 That Serpent..was so scherded al aboute, It hield all eggetol withoute, He was so ruide and hard of skin, Ther mihte nothing go therin. **1582** STANYHURST *Conceits* in *Æneis*, etc. (Arb.) 137 With rent rocks chamferye sharded. **1876** MORRIS *Sigurd* II. 120 The sharded moon.

†**'sharded,** *ppl. a.*[2] *Obs. rare*⁻¹. [f. SHARD *sb.*[2] + -ED[2].] Of a beetle: Living in dung.

**1611** SHAKS. *Cymb.* III. iii. 20 And often to our comfort, shall we finde The sharded-Beetle, in a safer hold Then is the full-wing'd Eagle.

**shardy** (ˈʃɑːdɪ), *a. rare*⁻¹. [f. SHARD *sb.*[4] + -Y.] Having shards or wing-cases.

**1819** J. R. DRAKE *Culprit Fay* vii, Tied to the hornet's shardy wings.

**share** (ʃɛə(r)), *sb.*[1] Forms: 1 scær, scear, scer, 3 ssare, 4 schar, shaar, (*pl.* scharres, -is, sharris), 4, 6 shar, 4–6 schare, (7 shere, sheare, 8 sharr), 4– share. [OE. *scear*, *scær* (masc. or neut.) = OFris. *skere*, *schere*, MLG. *schar* neut., *schare* fem. (Da. *skær* from LG.), OHG. *scar*, *scaro* masc., *scara* fem. (MHG. *schar* masc., fem., neut., mod.G. *schar* fem., f. Teut. root **skar-*: **sker-*: see SHEAR *v.*]

**1.** The iron blade in a plough which cuts the ground at the bottom of the furrow; a ploughshare.

*c* **725** *Corpus Gloss.* (Hessels) 8 *Uomer*, scær. *c* **1000** [see COULTER I]. *a* **1050** *Liber Scintill.* xxxii. (1889) 124 Scer tungan ure [L. *vomer linguæ nostræ*]. **1297** R. GLOUC. (Rolls) 6890 Lat nime foure yrene ssares [*v.r.* scharres] vor hire sulue al a fure. **1340–70** *Alex. & Dind.* 294 Hit is no leue in oure lawe þat we land erie Wiþ no scharpede schar to schape þe forwes. **1382** WYCLIF *1 Kings* xiii. 21 Thanne al Yrael descendide to Philistiym, that echon sharpe his shaar [**1388** schar]..for eggys of the sharis [**1388** scharris]..weren blunt. *c* **1386** [see COULTER I]. **1483** CAXTON *Golden Leg.* 130/1 Whan he toke the share to make clene hys cultre hyt cleuyd to hys hond. **1523–34** FITZHERB. *Husb.* § 3 The share is a pece of yren, sharpe before and brode behynde, a fote longe, made with a socket. **1594** *Selimus* in *Greene's Wks.* (Grosart) XIV. 204 The earth knew not the share, nor seas the barke. **1604–5** *Shuttleworths' Acc.* (Chetham Soc.) 160, ij sheres to plow with, iiij^s viij^d. **1686** PLOT *Staffordsh.* 161 If a Workman should forge out a sheare of this for a plough, it is so brittle [that etc.]. **1703** POPE *Thebais* 187 As stubborn steers..Alike disdain with servile necks to bear Th' unwonted weight, or drag the crooked share. **1733** W. ELLIS *Chiltern & Vale Farm.* 21 Great Clots, that will not yield to the Coulter's Cut, nor the Sharr's Break. **1870** MORRIS *Earthly Par.* II. III. 279 As the bright share carved out the furrow clean. **1880** JEFFERIES *Greene Ferne Farm* 111 An upturned plough with rusty share.

*fig.* **1815** BYRON *Parisina* xx. Those furrows which the burning share Of sorrow ploughs untimely there. **1837** HT. MARTINEAU *Soc. Amer.* III. 238 In whom the very foundations of belief have been ploughed up by the share of authority.

**b.** The analogous part of a seed-drill, or similar implement.

**1731** TULL *Horse-hoeing Husb.* xxii. (Dublin 1733) 351 But I soon contrived a Plow with four Iron Shares, to make Channels [for seed] in any Ground. *Ibid.* xxiii. 352 This [Drill-] Plow makes its Channels by three Sheats, and their Shares and Trunks. **1763** *Museum Rust.* I. lxxxi. 346 After sowing, it will be proper to plow the ground, where the lucern grows, with a drill-plow, with a round share. **1861** *Times* 11 July, The same implement frame..serves for ploughing, scarifying, trenching, digging, ridging, &c., according as it is fitted with shares for these various operations.

**2.** *attrib.* and *Comb.*, ***share-fin***, ***-point***; † **share acre**, an acre charged with supply of a ploughshare yearly to the manor; so ***share acre rent***; **share-beam**, in a plough of the ancient type, the beam which carries the share; **share-head**, the share-beam.

**1641** *Surv. Pleshebury Manor, Essex* (MS.) fol. 6b, For 1 acre of land called a *share acre..12*d.* *Ibid.* fol. 4b, For rents that the saide Smyth receiveth of diverse other persons, called Share acre rents, payeth to this manor yearely. *a* **1000** *Voc.* in Wr.-Wülcker 196/28 *Brigacus*, *scearbeam. **1523–34** FITZHERB. *Husb.* §3 The sharbeame is the tre vnderneth, where-vpon the share is set. **1884** *Longman's Mag.* Feb. 403 The 'hardy rustic' [in Tuscany] still goes into the woods and seeks for an elm . . for the share-beams with double backs, called 'dentale a due dorsi'. **1653** *Share-fin (phin) [see FIN *sb.*[1] 3 b]. **1846** KEIGHTLEY *Notes Virg.*, Terms Husb. 355 The share-beam or *share-head: a piece of wood . . to which the share was fitted. **1665** D. DUDLEY *Metallum Martis* (1855) 31 The Ploughman often breaks his *Share point off if it be made of coldshare Iron. **1733** W. ELLIS *Chiltern & Vale Farm.* 40 Just before the Sharr Point. **1852** C. W. H[OSKYNS] *Talpa* i. 3 The plough comes to a standstill, just revealing, at the share-point, the bruised side of a quartz pebble.

†**share** (ʃɛə(r)), *sb.*[2] *Obs.* Forms: α. 1 **scaru**, 4 **shzare**, 4–5 **schar(e, schore, shaar**, 6 **shaare, shayre**, 8–9 **shear (-bone)**, 5– **share**; β. 3 **scher**, 3–4 **sheer**, 3–6 **schere**, 4–5 **shere**, 6 *Sc.* **scheir**. [The same word as next.] The division or fork of the body; the pubic region, groin.

α. *c* **1000** *Sax. Leechd.* II. 232 Leȝe ofer þa scare oþ þone nafolan. *c* **1050** *Voc.* in Wr.-Wülcker 356/22 *Aluus*, mannes scaru. *c* **1325** *Gloss. W. de Bibbesw.* in Wright *Voc.* 148 *Le penul*, the schore [*v.r.* shzare]. **1398** TREVISA *Barth. De P.R.* VII. lv. (1495) 268 The ache is abowte the shaar and the twyste bytwene the genytours. *c* **1400** *Laud Troy Bk.* 6242 But he smot him aȝeyn so sore, That fro his heued doun to his schore He cleue him doun by the chyn. *c* **1440** *Promp. Parv.* 448/1 Schore, privy parte of a mann, *pubes*. **1545** RAYNALD *Byrth Mankynde* I. iv. (1552) 7 From the mydryffe to the flankes or share. **1657** W. COLES *Adam in Eden* xxi. 44 If the Share and parts thereabouts be anointed therewith. **1694** *Phil. Trans.* XVIII. 22 These Bones, viz. the Share or Pubes.

β. *a* **1225** *Ancr. R.* 272 Heo þuruhstihten Isboset adun into [þe] schere. *a* **1290** *Pains of Hell* (MS. Digby 86) 102 He þat wes owre [= whore] oþer kopiner þat stondeþ in to hoere sheer. **1382** WYCLIF *2 Kings* ii. 23 Thanne Abner . . smoot hym in the sheer [**1388** schar]. *c* **1400** *Laud Troy Bk.* 9679 Some is cloven In-to the shere, Some has lorn bothe cheke & ere. *c* **1475** *Pict. Voc.* in Wr.-Wülcker 750/25 *Hec pubes*, schere. **1536** BELLENDEN *Cron. Scot.* XII. viii, This Edrik . . straik hym throw the scheir in his bowellis.

**b.** *Comb.*: **share-artery**, the pubic artery; **share-bone** = PUBIS 1; †**sharewort**, a plant (Gerarde's drawing, according to Britten and Holland, represents *Pallenis spinosa*).

**1545** RAYNALD *Byrth Mankynde* I. xiv. (1552) 38 Thee *shares artyres. **1541** R. COPLAND *Guydon's Quest. Cyrurg.* I iv, These two bones . . ioyneth to $y^e$ share before, and therfore are they called the *share bones. **1615** CROOKE *Body of Man* 935 The bone without a name . . hath three parts; the Hip, the Hanches and the Sharebones. **1732** ARBUTHNOT *Rules of Diet* in *Aliments*, etc. 423 A sensation of Weight in the Lower Belly under the Shear-Bone. **1827** *Lancet* 6 Oct. 7/1 Vernacular terms... The pubis, the shear bone. **1578** LYTE *Dodoens* I. xxiv. 36 *Aster Atticus*... This herbe is called . . in English *Sharewurte or Sterrewurte: . . in high Douch . . Scartenkraut, and Sternkraut. *Ibid.*, Layd to the botches . . about the share or priuie members [it] preuayleth much against the same. **1601** HOLLAND *Pliny* XXVI. ix. II. 256 Inguinaria, which some name Argemony. [*Margin.*] Some call it Sharewort or Codwort.

**share** (ʃɛə(r)), *sb.*[3] Forms: 5 **schar, chare**, 6 **schare, shaire**, 4, 6– **share**. See also SKAIR. [ME. *share, schar*:—OE. *scearu* str. fem., cutting, division (recorded in the senses 'tonsure' and 'division or fork of the body', SHARE *sb.*[1]; also in comb. *landscearu* land, boundary, *folc-, léodscearu* division of people, nation, *hearmscearu* penalty), corresponding formally to OS. *scara* share in a common field, troop (Gallée), also in comb. as *harm-scara* penalty, MLG. *schare* troop, share, OFris. *-skere* (in *hermskere* penance), Du. *schaar* fem., troop, multitude, OHG. *scara* troop, share of forced labour (MHG., mod.G. *schar* troop, multitude), OTeut. **skarō*, f. root **sker-* to cut, divide: see SHEAR *v.*]

**1. a.** The part or portion (*of* something) which is alloted or belongs to an individual, when distribution is made among a number; also, the portion or quota which is contributed by an individual.

In the earliest instances used for: (*a*) a custom paid by fishing-boats; (*b*) the portion of prize-money due to each of the officers and men of a ship.

**1372** *For. Acc.* 6, A (P.R.O.), Custuma navium batellorum piscentium super mare ibidem [Winchelsea] vocat' shares. **1375** in *Black Bk. Admiralty* (Rolls) I. 172 Item, de prendre et saisir pour ladmiral les shares a lui dues doffice de toutes maneres de biens pris ou gaignez sur la mer. *c* **1400** *Ibid.* 400 Ladmiral aura un share del entierte. **1411** *Exch. Acc. Q.R.* Bundle 67 No. 18 (P.R.O.), Et ibidem cepit unum schar de Thos Ise magistro unius ballenger. **1481** *Howard Househ. Bks.* (Roxb.) 80 My Lord paid John Petman ix. li. x. s. For xxxviij. chares; that is the maister ij. chares, and him self ij. chares and xxxiiij persones, that is xxxiiij. chares. **1530** PALSGR. 266/1 Schare of a man of a prise of warre tyme, *butin*. **1544** in *Sel. Pleas Crt. Admiralty* (1894) I. 141 All suche maryners as wyll not sail in the said shippe for their shaires. **1562** *Mirr. Mag., Shore's Wife* lii, When almes was delt I had a hungry share. **1575** GASCOIGNE *Weedes* Wks. 1907 I. 454 Antonius who conquered prowde Egipt . . Chose Cleopatra for his love... He snapt but hir for his owne share. **1617** MORYSON *Itin.* I. 94 Thus hath one Poet, three crownes to his share. **1653** *Descr. & Plat Sea-coasts Eng.* A 3, As to the Shares in Prizes. *a* **1667** COWLEY *Ess., Agric.*, '*Happy the Man*' 21 Of which large shares, on the glad sacred daies He gives to Friends. *a* **1700** EVELYN *Diary* 5 July 1646, Taking our turns to row, of which I reckon my share came to little less than 20 leagues. **1801** *Farmer's Mag.* Jan. 77 Lord Somerville, the late President, comes in for a share of the general thrashing. **1809** BYRON *Let.* 11 Aug. in R. C. Dallas *Corr.* (1825) I. 90 She offered a share of her apartment, which my *virtue* induced me to decline. **1844** H. H. WILSON *Brit. India* I. 307 They insisted upon their shares, and refused to fight unless they obtained a portion of the spoil. **1880** L. STEPHEN *Pope* iii. 79 We could have wished that he had been a little more liberal with his share of the plunder. **1888** F. HUME *Mme. Midas* I. Prol., There is gold here, my friend, and we must get our share of it.

**b.** In pregnant sense = One's due, proper, or fair share; one's full share (of something enjoyed or suffered in common with others).

*c* **1645** HOWELL *Lett.* (1650) II. lxv. 102 One who by this recluse passive condition hath his share of this hideous storm. **1697** DRYDEN *Virg. Georg.* IV. 356 Lazy Drones, without their Share of Pain, In Winter Quarters free, devour the Gain. **1745** SIR C. H. WILLIAMS in Jesse *Selwyn & Contemp.* (1843) I. 65 Lady Lucy indeed was very plentifully abused, and Mr. Hobart had his share. **1856** SIR B. BRODIE *Psychol. Inq.* (1862) II. iv. 141 It cannot be denied that the lower animals have their share of whatever evil exists in the universe. **1871** MORLEY *Voltaire* 10 Whole generations that might have produced their share of skilful and intrepid mariners.

**c.** The measure or degree *of* a quality, condition, etc. which is allotted to an individual by nature or Providence.

**1722** DE FOE *Hist. Plague* (1756) 285 Those Physicians, who had the least Share of Religion in them, were oblig'd to acknowledge that it was all supernatural. **1742** M. WHITEWAY in *Earl Orrery's Rem. Swift* xi. (1752) 90 Mr. Nichols thought it possible he might return to a share of understanding. **1816** J. SMITH *Panorama Sci. & Art* II. 258 When it contains less than its natural share [of electric fluid], it is said to be negative, or electrified minus. **1816** SCOTT *Old Mort.* xliii, Exerting that youthful agility of which he possessed an uncommon share. **1848** THACKERAY *Van. Fair* xxxiii, Her mamma and sister . . regarded her with that amiable pity, of which your really superior woman always has such a share to give away.

**2.** *Comm.* A definite portion of a property owned by a number in common; *spec.* each of the equal parts into which the capital of a joint-stock company or corporation is divided.

***deferred, preference*** (or ***preferred***) ***shares***: see DEFERRED, PREFERENCE 8. ***ordinary shares***, the shares which form the common stock and are without 'preference'.

**1601** B. JONSON *Poetaster* III. iv. 373 Commend me to seuen-shares and a halfe. **1629** SHERLEY & HATHERLEY in Bradford *Plymouth Plant.* (1856) 259, I thinke it conscionable and reasonable $y^t$ you should beare your shares and proporcion of $y^e$ stock. **1660** F. BROOKE tr. *Le Blanc's Trav.* 4 The ship, wherein my Father had halfe share. *a* **1700** EVELYN *Diary* 2 July 1667, He was endeavouring to bring me into the project, and proffered me a share. **1708** *Lond. Gaz.* No. 4484/3 All Persons that have any Demands . . , on account of their Old Additional Stock, commonly called the Shares, are desired . . to repair to Skinner's Hall. **1818** CRUISE *Digest* (ed. 2) I. 58 A share in the New River water is held to be real property, as also a share in the navigation of the river Avon. *Ibid.* II. 515 The last mode by which an estate in joint tenancy may be destroyed, is by the devolving of all the shares on one of the joint tenants, by survivorship. **1863** KINGLAKE *Crimea* I. xiv. 228 He was a buyer and seller of those fractional and volatile interests in trading adventures, which go by the name of 'shares'. **1891** *Law Rep., Weekly Notes* 68/2 The company had been most successful . . paying a very large dividend on the ordinary shares. **1893** *Law Times* XCV. 305/2 If she wished to be sure of her income she should of all things avoid dabbling in the shares of new companies.

**3. a.** A part taken *in* (an action, experience, etc.). Chiefly in phr. ***to have, take, bear a*** (***one's***, etc.) ***share in***, to have or take part in, participate in.

**1592** KYD *Sp. Trag.* I. ii. 125 Hieronimo, it greatly pleaseth vs That in our victorie thou haue a share. **1687** BURNET *Contn. Reply to Varillas* 103 Somerset came again into a Share in the Government. **1687** A. LOVELL tr. *Thevenot's Trav.* I. 267 Our ship had also some share in the danger. **1721** DE FOE *Mem. Cavalier* (1840) 93, I had no share in the business of Donawert. **1779** *Mirror* No. 60 The philosopher . . took little share in the conversation. **1855** MACAULAY *Hist. Eng.* xix. IV. 362 *note*, He is extolled as having borne a principal share in the emancipation of the press. **1871** FREEMAN *Norm. Conq.* (1876) IV. xviii. 105 We may fully acquit William of any personal share in the evil deeds of Odo and his fellow viceroy. **1875** JOWETT *Plato* (ed. 2) V. 89 He who has no share in the administration of justice, appears to himself to have no share in the state.

†**b.** ***to take share of***: to share (something) *with* another. *Obs.*

**1738** SWIFT *Pol. Conversat.* 127, I took Share of a Beefstake and Two Muggs of Ale with my Chapman.

**4.** †**a.** *gen.* A part, piece, or portion (*of* anything).

*c* **1400** *Rule St. Benet* (Verse) 881 Our gude angel Al our warkes to god wil tel, Al be it neuer so litil a schar. **1664** in *Extr. St. Papers rel. Friends* Ser. III. (1912) 214, I intend . . to have them . . out of $y^e$ custody of our Kendall gaoler who is a great share of a Fanatick himselfe. **1751** T. SHARP in *Lett. Lit. Men* (Camden) 377 No small share of their time was taken up with a trust they were engaged in. **1760–72** H. BROOKE *Fool of Qual.* (1809) I. 116 My friends . . have engaged to spend a share of to-morrow in a party of pleasure upon the Thames.

**b.** One of several parts into which anything is divided; a section or division. Now *dial.*

**1598** STOW *Surv.* 156 Where turning south, and breaking it selfe into many small shares, rilles or streames, it left the name of Share borne lane. **1793–1813** *Reports Agric.* 76 (E.D.D.) In a dry [seed time] the barley sown on the sand land frequently comes up in two shares, and ripens unequally. **1893–4** *Northumbld. Gloss.* s.v., The skate fish is usually dressed for sale and cut into slices or *shares*.

†**c.** *spec.* One of the portions into which land or territory is divided; a portion of land assigned to a particular holder, a lot. *Obs.*

[**1570–6** LAMBARDE *Peramb. Kent* 20 Alfred . . diuided the whole Realme into certein parts, or Sections . . , whiche . . he termed shires, or (as we yet speake) shares, and portions.] **1643** BAKER *Chron., Jas I*, 158 So as now they began to divide the Country [Bermuda] into Tribes and the Tribes into Shares. **1682** PIERS *Descr. W. Meath* (1770) 116 Of these they make so many lots or equal shares, as there are ploughs in the town. *Ibid.*, To each plow they reckon a certain number of acres, which by a general name is called a share; each share hath particularly such and such half acres or stangs assigned to it by name to make up the given number.

**d.** In a salmon-weir: see quot.

**1842** *Act 5 & 6 Vict.* c. 106 §41 A free Gap or Queen's Share shall be left or formed in the deepest Part of such River.

†**e.** With etymological reference to *shear*: A piece hewn out, or cut or torn away. (Cf. *potshare* var. POTSHERD.) *Obs.*

**1590** SPENSER *F.Q.* I. ii. 18 Therewith vpon his crest With rigour so outrageous he smitt, That a large share it hewd out of the rest. **1641** MILTON *Ch. Govt.* I. vii, No wonder then in . . the fierce encounter of truth and falshood together, if, as it were, the splinters and shares of so violent a jousting, there fall [etc.]. **17..** *Clerk Colvil* vii. in Herd *Sc. Songs* (1776) I. 161 Frae her sark he cut a share.

**5.** Phrases. (See also 3.) **a.** ***share and share alike*** (earlier † ***share and share like***), with equal shares, having each a like share. Also ***to go share and share alike*** (†***like***).

*a* **1566** R. EDWARDS *Damon & Pithias* (1908) G j b, Let vs into the Courte to parte the spoyle, share and share like. **1651** N. BACON *Disc. Gov. Eng.* vii. 68 Edward the Third . . promiseth them [the Flemings] share and share like with his own People. **1692** R. L'ESTRANGE *Fables* vii. 6 Every one to go share and share-like in what they took. **1702** YALDEN *Æsop at Court* II. 10 The Articles were these: Share and share like whate'er they got. **1719** DE FOE *Crusoe* II. ii. 30 He declar'd he had reserv'd nothing from the Men, and went Share and Share alike with them in every Bit they eat. **1766** BLACKSTONE *Comm.* II. xiv. 218 Their representatives . . shared the inheritance *per capita*, that is, share and share alike. **1840** MARRYAT *Poor Jack* xxxi, I bequeath to my nephews and nieces . . the whole of my . . personal effects, *share and share alike*. **1859** THACKERAY *Virgin.* lviii, She fondly hoped that he might be inclined to go share and share alike with Twin junior. **1886** LAING-MEASON *Sir William's Specul.* 75 All costs, charges, and similar payments should be share and share alike.

**b.** ***to fall to one's share***: to be assigned as one's portion; hence, to fall to one's lot (*to do*, etc.).

**1637** EARL MONM. tr. *Malvezzi's Romulus & Tarquin* 169 Had it fallen to the common people of Romes share to give their vote. *a* **1700** EVELYN *Diary* 25 Dec. 1658, It fell to my share to be confin'd to a roome in the house. **1813** SCOTT *Rokeby* v. xxiii, And oh! when Passion rules, how rare The hours that fall to Virtue's share! **1865** *Nat. Hist. Rev.* July 387 They divided the field of work between them... To Kotschy's share fell the flowering plants.

**c.** ***for my share***, for my part, as regards my part in the matter. Now *rare*.

**1674** N. FAIRFAX *Bulk & Selv.* 24 And verily, for my share, I cannot see why [etc.]. **1794** GODWIN *Caleb Williams* 114 For my share, misfortunes come so thick upon me, that [etc.]. **1799** H. MITCHELL *Scotticisms* 76 For my share I scorn a sycophant; Sc.—For my part. **1837** CARLYLE *Fr. Rev.* III. v. v, Busy sits Carnot, . . busy, for his share, in 'organizing victory'.

**d.** ***on shares***. Applied to a system whereby two or more persons participate in the risks and profits of an undertaking; as ***to go on shares*** (***with***); ***to work***, etc. ***on shares***. Also, ***upon shares, on the shares***.

**1792** BELKNAP *Hist. New Hampsh.* III. 216 Men can always be had to go on shares, which is by far the most profitable method, both to the employers and the fishermen. **1817** *Massachusetts Spy* 29 Jan. 1/2 To be let, upon Shares or *Hire*, a *Farm*. **1830** GALT *Lawrie T.* II. v. (1849) 55 He had proposed to me to send a venture by the same ship or go on shares with him. **1878** J. S. CAMPION *On Frontier* (ed. 2) 6 The Captain resided in a good house on his own farm, . . which was worked for him on shares by a smart Yankee. **1882** [see RENTER *sb.*[1] 4 b]. **1901** *Munsey's Mag.* XXV. 345/2 It all came out of his own pocket, for he was sailing the vessel on shares.

**e.** ***to go shares with*** (another or others) ***in*** (a possession, enterprise, etc.): to enjoy a part in, paticipate in, contribute towards. Also ***to run shares, to club shares. shares!*** an exclamation demanding to be allowed to 'go shares' in something found, stolen, etc. by another person; hence ***to cry shares***.

**1818** SCOTT *Hrt. Midl.* i, Bubbleburgh is only one of a set of five boroughs which club their shares for a member of parliament. **1821** SHELLEY *Let. to L. Hunt* 26 Aug., Go shares with him and me in a periodical work. **1850** *Tait's Mag.* XVII. 182/1 The two scoundrels . . have run shares in this imposition. **1869** BROWNING *Ring & Bk.* XI. 841 Why touch the thing myself When I could see you hunt and then cry 'Shares! Quarter the carcass or we quarrel'. **1879** SALA *Paris Herself Again* II. xi. 153, I went shares with a friend in the purchase of . . a whole ticket. **1888** RIDER HAGGARD *Col. Quaritch* iv, If you find the treasure we will go shares.

**6.** *attrib.* and *Comb.*, as (sense 2) ***share bonus, broker, capital, -certificate, -dealing, index, -list, -market, -mart, -owner(ship), premium, price, -warrant***; †**share-book**, a book brought out by a number of booksellers or publishers with a collective imprint; **share-farmer** chiefly *Austral.*, one who works on a farm for an agreed portion of the profits; so **share-farming** *vbl. sb.*; **share-fisherman** = *shareman*; **share-hand** *N. Amer.*, a farm-worker or tenant who raises crops on shares; **shareman**, a fisherman who shares with the owner of the vessel in the profits in lieu of wages; **share-milker** *N.Z.*, one who works on a dairy farm for an agreed portion of the profits (cf. *share-farmer* above); hence **share-milk** *v. trans.*, **share-milking** *vbl. sb.*; **share-pusher** (see quot. 1914); hence **share-pushing** *vbl. sb.* and *ppl. a.*; **sharesman**, †(*a*) one who has his share *of* something; (*b*) = *shareman*. Also SHAREHOLDER, -HOLDING.

**1928** *Daily Chron.* 9 Aug. 8/4 A *share bonus of 50 per cent. was provided on account of the year 1917–18. **1851** Bohn in *De Lolme's Constit. Eng.* (1853) 4 In 1781 the work was bought of De Lolme by the trade, and was thereafter published under their mutual protection as what is technically called a *share book. **1909** GROWOLL *Three Cent. Eng. Booktrade Bibliogr.* 23 The books that were thus issued under a collective imprint were first known as 'Sharebooks'; later they were called 'Chapter-books'. **1845** (*title*) Railway Maria; or, The Irish *sharebroker. **1851** (*title*) Ralph's Stock & Share Brokers' Directory. **1848** *Bradshaw's Railway Almanack* 57 Guaranteed 5 per cent. in perpetuity upon £3,000,000 (the authorized *Share Capital). **1974** *Terminol. Managem. & Financial Accountancy* (Inst. Cost & Managem. Accountants) 62 *Equity share capital*, the issued share capital of a company which carries an unrestricted right to participate beyond a specified amount in a distribution. **1888** *Act 51 Vict.* c. 8 §12 The holder of any Foreign or Colonial *Share Certificate. **1955** *Times* 17 May 18/4 Not inconsiderable profits have been made from time to time in *sharedealing. **1969** *Times* 2 May (Suppl.) p. viii/4 The finance houses do not distribute as dividend the profits made on the realization of investments, colloquially known as share-dealing profits. **1928** R. G. STAPLEDON *Tour in Austral. & N.Z.* iv. 28 Many successful men have started as *share-farmers. **1966** *Southerly* XXVI. 203 *Sharemilker*..is a New Zealand term, which is certainly not in use in New South Wales, where the popular term is *sharefarmer*. **1927** *Austral. Encycl.* I. 46 The details of '*share-farming' contracts varied with the district: thus in some cases the landowner provided everything but the labour and took two-thirds of the crop in return, in others the farmer provided plant, labour, and half the bags required and took half the crop. **1932** A. JOSE *Australia Human & Economic* 262 Thus there came into favour a system of 'share-farming' (in Europe better known as metayage), which gave the actual cultivators an interest in good tillage while retaining in the owner's hands full control of his property. **1960** *Farmer & Stockbreeder* 12 Jan. 51/1 Several new variations of the old share-farming system were propounded. **1901** *Scotsman* 11 Sept. 8/5 The Grimsby owners and the *share fishermen last night arrived at a final settlement of all outstanding questions between them. **1911** JENKS & LAUCK *Immigration Problem* 83 How much value careful cultivation, kitchen gardens and small store accounts may be to the cotton '*share hand' and tenant. **1930** *Financial News* 13 Aug. 1/5 (*heading*) Industrial *Share Index. **1982** *Financial Times* 1 May 24/2 The FT-Actuaries 500 share index eased only 0.9 per cent from Thursday's record high. **1846** *Daily News* 21 Jan. 5/5 *Leeds Exchange.*—Notice was given on the *share list of Monday that [etc.]. **1687** *Connecticut Colony Public Rec.* (1859) III. 425 Fishermen..shall not presume to break off their voyage..without the consent of the owner, master and *share-men. **1820** in C. R. Fay *Life & Labour in Newfoundland* (1956) viii. 139 Sharemen are frequently indigent planters who have fallen into debt with their merchant and who cannot afford to use their own boats. **1901** *Westm. Gaz.* 31 Aug. 4/3 The sharemen, as the skippers and the mates of the trawlers are called—for the reason that they have never been paid a wage, but shared with the owners the profits of their voyages to the fishing-grounds. **1966** A. R. SCAMMELL *My Newfoundland* 26, I was shareman with his father..three summers on the lower Labrador. **1841** THACKERAY *Gt. Hoggarty Diam.* vii, Our great men in the *share-market. **1870** J. K. MEDBERY *Men & Mysteries Wall St.* 19 In all the great European *share-marts there is a general executive organization. **1937** GORDON & BENNETT *Gentlemen of Jury* ii. 67 Two months later the mother is 'out in the sheds' helping to *share-milk 100 cows. **1935** J. GUTHRIE *Little Country* xii. 203 Advertisements..for a farm-hand or a *share-milker. **1977** *N.Z. Herald* 8 Jan. 4–7/2 (Advt.), A position has become available for a 50-50 sharemilker on a 130-acre dairy farm. The present sharemilker has purchased his own farm property. **1937** H. G. PHILPOTT *Hist. N.Z. Dairy Industry* I. iii. 65 [He] adopted the system of farm labour now commonly known as '*share milking'. **1958** *Times* 16 June 12/7 In New Zealand 'share milking', as it is called, is controlled by a wages board award. **1973** *Massey Ferguson Rev.* (N.Z.) Mar.–Apr. 5/3 Sharemilking is an important cornerstone of the dairy industry in New Zealand. **1968** *Sci. Jrnl.* Nov. 89/1 Competitors, suppliers, customers, *shareowners, bankers and the government. **1978** *Detroit Free Press* 5 Mar. B 13/3 [They] have made lifetime careers of trying to give shareowners a voice in the running of publicly held companies. **1962** *Economist* 24 Mar. 1149/2 (*heading*) Wider *shareownership. **1930** *Daily Express* 6 Oct. 14/2 The discount on this issue has been entirely written off from *share premium and capital reserve accounts. **1930** *Economist* 19 Apr. 896/2 Rayon *share prices were found to have fully discounted in advance the retention of the duties. **1980** W. ASH *Incorporated* xiii. 156 You can imagine what could've happened to share prices if..that got out beforehand. **1914** H. HALFORD *Dict. Stock Market Terms* 79 **Share pusher*, one who endeavours to dispose of Shares to the public by circular or advertisement, instead of selling them on the market. **1938** 'N. SHUTE' *Ruined City* xii. 247 We're a precious pair... Couple of bloody share-pushers, if you ask me. **1965** B. SWEET-ESCOTT *Baker Street Irregular* i. 34 A look which suggested that I must be a cross between a share-pusher and a black marketeer. **1928** *Daily Mail* 3 Aug. 19/3 The day on which the sections penalising *share-pushing shall come into force. **1928** *Evening News* 18 Aug. 11/3 Shares of this sort are among those that figure prominently in the share-pushing circulars of the 'bucket-shop' brigade. **1972** *Times* 28 Dec. 17/4 The City section.. has developed considerable expertise in cases involving prospectuses, sharepushing and market rigging operations. **1977** N. FAULKS *No Mitigating Circumstances* xi. 152 A number of other persons were charged with having taken part in share-pushing transactions. **1640** MURE *Counter-Buff* 245 Yea, though he should undo them, He's *sharesman of the harme. **1867** G. E. CLARK *Seven Years of Sailor's Life* xxvii. 272 The sharesmen were all looking at the steamer that lay just ahead. **1895** *Outing* XXVII. 20/1 'Sharesmen'..are credited with a certain share of what they catch, a third to a half usually going to the planter. **1912** *Oysterman & Fisherman* Mar. 14/1 The crew wage and crew feeding system practiced by the 'sharesmen'-outfitters. **1867** *Act 30 & 31 Vict.* c. 131 §28 A *Share Warrant shall entitle the Bearer of such Warrant to the Shares or Stock specified in it.

†**share**, *v.*[1] *Obs.* Also 7 **shayre**. [A variant of SHEAR *v.* (cf. *bare* var. of BEAR *v.*); in some uses associated with SHARE *sb.*[1] (For other senses see SHEAR *v.*)] *trans.* To cut into parts; to cut off.

**1553** [cf. SHARING *vbl. sb.*[1]]. **1565** J. PHILLIP *Patient Grissell* 1149 (Malone Soc.), I will share with sword, the Infants corpes by force. **1596** SPENSER *F.Q.* IV. ii. 17 Like two mad mastiffes each on other flew, And shields did share, and mailes did rash, and helmes did hew. **1614** GORGES *Lucan* VI. 232 Where now the cultor shares the soyle, And plough-men daily eare and toyle. *Ibid.* 237 That lumpe.. Which on a young colts forhead breeds,..Before the louing damme so share It with her teeth, and make it bare. **1667** MILTON *P.L.* VI. 326 The sword..deep entring shar'd All his right side. **1673** *Essex Papers* (Camden) I. 139, I would rather run yᵉ hazard of shayring a point of my Orders. **1735** SOMERVILLE *Chase* III. 210 When ev'ry Art has fail'd the captive Fox Has shar'd the wounded Joint, and with a Limb Compounded for his Life.

**b.** with adv. or advb. phrase.

**1577** B. GOOGE *Heresbach's Husb.* III. (1586) 120 Some vse to geue them [horses] aples shared in peces. **1596** SPENSER *F.Q.* V. v. 9 For with his trenchant blade at the next blow Halfe of her shield he shared quite away. **1608** TOPSELL *Serpents* 28 While they share them asunder, they are stung or bitten by the serpent. **1691** RAY *Creation* I. (1692) 124 Pieces of Rose or other Leaves which she [the Bee] shares off with her mouth.

Hence †**shared** *ppl. a.*, cut, divided, cloven.

**1598** BP. HALL *Sat.* V. ii. 69 If perchance thou..with thine elbow shad'st thy shared meat. **1614** GORGES *Lucan* VII. 301 We do not seeke that they should burne In parted flames and shared vrne [orig. *Petimus non singula busta, Discretosque rogos*]. **1697** DRYDEN *Æneid* IX. 1019 Scalp, Face, and Shoulders, the keen Steel divides; And the shar'd Visage hangs on equal sides.

**share** (ʃɛə(r)), *v.*[2] Also 6 **shaire**, **shayre**, 7 *Sc.* **shair**. [f. SHARE *sb.*[3]]

**1. a.** *trans.* To divide and apportion in shares between two or more recipients. *Obs.* or *arch.*

**1590** SPENSER *F.Q.* II. x. 28 In his crowne he counted her no haire, But twixt the other twaine his kingdome whole did shaire. **1607** SHAKS. *Timon* IV. ii. 23 Good Fellowes all, The latest of my wealth Ile share among'st you. **1610** HOLLAND *Camden's Brit.* I. 641 He..shared the Country among his companions. **1624** QUARLES *Job Milit.* Med. ix. 43 To Good and Bad, both Fortunes Heauen doth share, That both, an after-change, may hope, and feare. **1708** SWIFT *Let. conc. Sacram. Test* ¶19 Misc. (1711) 340 Suppose I share my Fortune equally between my own Children and a Stranger, whom I take into my Protection; will that be a Method to unite them? **1711** W. SUTHERLAND *Shipbuild. Assist.* 48 The But Ends, which are shared with as much Indifferency as possible, that every Part of the Ship may be of equal Strength. **1743** BULKELEY & CUMMINS *Voy. S. Seas* 160 We shar'd all the Provisions among the Company. **1837–9** HALLAM *Lit. Europe* III. v. §7 Their parental love forbids all preference, and an impartial law of gavel-kind shares their page among all the offspring of their brain. **1863** NEALE *Med. Hymns* (ed. 2) 197 Midst his people thus the Clerk Scripture nurture shareth.

**b.** Now chiefly with *out*.

**1644–52** J. SMITH *Sel. Disc.* VII. iv. (1821) 347 Those immortal inheritances which he shares out amongst his spiritual sons and subjects in heaven. **1723** *Present St. Russia* I. 52 The Senate shares that Service out among the several Governments. **1761** HUME *Hist. Eng.* I. xiii. 314 The landed property was gradually shared out into more hands. *Ibid.* III. liii. 135 Worldly glory had been shared out to them with a sparing hand. **1898** BRABROOK *Provid. Societies* 57 The funds..diminish so rapidly that the old men share out what there is and close the society. **1901** ALLDRIDGE *Sherbro* xxiii. 242 When there is 'flesh kind' for the carriers, it is given to the head-man, who shares it out most carefully.

**c.** To apportion to an individual as his share. Also with *out*. *arch.*

*c* **1586** C'TESS PEMBROKE *Ps.* LVIII. iv, There is a God that shares to each his own. **1596** SPENSER *F.Q.* IV. viii. 5 And euery day, for guerdon of her song, He part of his small feast to her would share. **1602** CAREW *Cornwall* I. 13 In Wastrell, it is lawfull for any man to make triall of his fortune that way, prouided, that hee acknowledge the Lordes right, by sharing out vnto him a certaine part, which they can toll. **1633** P. FLETCHER *Purple Isl.* VI. xxxi, He all in all..Does share to each his due, and equall doie impart. **1893** STEVENSON *Catriona* vi. 62 And here I am with my foot in the stirrup again and some of the responsibility shared into my hand of prosecuting King George's enemies.

**d.** To divide (what one has or receives) into portions, and give shares to others as well as one's self. Const. *with*.

**1592** *Arden of Feversham* II. i. 35 Were it not that I see more company comming down the hill, I would be fellowes with you once more, and share Crownes with you to. **1636** [FREEMAN] tr. *Seneca's Shortn. Life* (1663) 4 To share his money no man can abide; Their lives 'twixt many all men will divide. **1771** GOLDSM. *Hist. Eng.* I. 149 These had a power of sharing their grants to inferior tenants. **1819** SHELLEY *Cyclops* 538 *Cyclops.* Should I not share this liquor with my brothers? *Ulysses.* Keep it yourself, and be more honoured so. **1901** HALL & OSBORNE *Sunshine & Surf* xxiii. 297 The natives had only brought enough [water] for themselves..which, however, they generously shared with us.

**e.** To divide *into* parts or shares. *rare.*

**1591–5** SPENSER *Colin Clout* 138 First into many parts his streame he shar'd. **1719** DE FOE *Crusoe* I. (Globe) 311, I shar'd the Island into Parts with 'em. **1847** C. BRONTË *Jane Eyre* v. I. 74 A thin oaten cake, shared into fragments. *Ibid.* xxi, Take one day; share it into sections; to each section apportion its task.

†**f.** *refl.* To divide one's service, devotion, etc. between (two different objects). *Obs.*

**1680** C. NESSE *Church Hist.* 164 Solomon had been sharing himself betwixt God and idols.

**2.** Of two or more persons: To divide into shares and take each a portion. Also *absol.*

**1594** SHAKS. *Rich. III*, I. iii. 159 You wrangling Pyrates, that fall out, In sharing that which you haue pill'd from me. **1596** —— *1 Hen. IV*, II. ii. 104 Come my Masters, let vs share, and then to horsse. **1660** STANLEY *Hist. Philos.* XIII. *Epicurus* i. (1687) 836/1 The Two thousand Citizens, whom the Athenians sent to Samus to share the Land by Lots.

**3. a.** To grant or give another or others a share in. Also const. *with*.

**1662** DRYDEN *To Ld. Chanc.* 44 Well may he then to you his Cares impart And share his Burden where he shares his Heart. **1717** POPE *Eloisa to Abelard* 49–50 Then share thy pain, allow that sad relief; Ah, more than share it, give me all thy grief. **1818** SHELLEY *Marenghi* xii, There was set A penalty of blood on all who shared So much of water with him as might wet His lips. **1847** TENNYSON *Princess* VI. 235 Now had you got a friend of your own age, Now could you share your thought. **1860** E. WASHBURN *Amer. Law Real Property* I. 364 (Funk) A mode of letting lands..where the tenant is to cultivate them, and share the crops with his landlord. *Mod.* I will share my room with you for to-night if you cannot get a bed anywhere else.

¶**b.** *nonce-use.* To cause (one thing) to share its place *with* another.

**1813** SCOTT *Rokeby* I. viii, A scorching clime, And toil, had done the work of time,..And sable hairs with silver shared.

**4. a.** To receive, possess, or occupy together with others.

**1592** SHAKS. *Rom. & Jul.* I. iii. 93 So shall you share all that he doth possesse. *c* **1600** *Histriomastix* VI. i. (1610) H 1 b, *Cun[stable]*. Soft sirs, I must talke with you for taxe mony, To releeue the poore, not a penny paid yet. *Post.* Sir, at few words we shar'd but xv. pence last weeke. *a* **1640** DAY *Peregr. Schol.* (1881) 75 Lookeing downe I might perceive a white mowse and a blacke mowse shareinge the roote of the tree. **1697** DRYDEN *Virg. Georg.* IV. 698 Longing the common Light again to share. **1762** GOLDSM. *Cit. W.* xv, He was born to share the bounties of heaven, but he has monopolized them. **1804** J. GRAHAME *Sabbath* 35 He shares the frugal meal with those he loves. **1825** T. HOOK *Sayings* Ser. II. *Man of Many Fr.* I. 283 She quitted the sofa she had been unwillingly sharing with the self-pleased beau.

**b.** *fig.* (with a thing as subject.)

*c* **1652** MILTON *Sonn. Fairfax* 14 In vain doth Valour bleed While Avarice, and Rapine share the land. **1742** YOUNG *Nt. Th.* V. 17 We wear the chains of pleasure, and of pride; These share the man; and these distract him too.

†**c.** To receive or possess (a portion allotted to one); to take or receive as one's share. *poet. Obs.*

**1594** SHAKS. *Rich. III*, V. iii. 268 But if I thriue, the gaine of my attempt, The least of you shall share his part thereof. *c* **1600** —— *Sonn.* xlvii, An other time mine eye is my hearts guest, And in his thoughts of loue doth share a part. **1618** ROWLANDS *Sacred Mem. Miracles* (1876) 37 Who seeing now her sorrowes cause to liue, Had such a fulnesse of a ioyfull heart, That neuer woman sharde a greater part.

†**d.** *to share from*: to gain at the expense of.

**1599** SHAKS. *Hen. V*, IV. iii. 32, I would not loose so great an Honor, As one man more me thinkes would share from me, For the best hope I haue. **1606** —— *Tr. & Cr.* I. iii. 367 What glory our Achilles shares from Hector.

¶**e.** *to share alone*: incorrectly, to possess unshared.

**1626** MASSINGER *Rom. Actor* V. ii, You shall not share alone The glorie of a deed that will endure To all posteritie.

**f.** *Chem.* Of an atom, orbital, etc.: to hold (one or more electrons) in common with another atom or orbital, so as to form a covalent bond. (See also SHARED *ppl. a.*)

**1919** *Jrnl. Amer. Chem. Soc.* XLI. 888 An octet may share an even number of its electrons with 1, 2, 3, or 4 other octets. **1923** *Trans. Faraday Soc.* XIX. 461 In chemically stable molecules we have only to consider atoms sharing pairs of electrons. It is well known that such structures do not exhibit any signs of electrical polarity. One must therefore suppose that the net charge on both atoms is zero, *i.e.* that the two shared electrons are in general so distributed that when one is in one atom the other is in the other. **1964** J. W. LINNETT *Electronic Structure of Molecules* ii. 29 The two electrons may be regarded as being shared between the 1*s* orbital of the hydrogen and one of the 2*p* orbitals of the fluorine.

**5.** To participate in (an action, activity, opinion, feeling, or condition); to perform, enjoy, or suffer in common with others; to possess (a quality) which other persons or things also have. Const. *with*.

**1590** SHAKS. *Mids. N.* III. ii. 198 Is all the counsell that we two haue shar'd, The sister vowes,..O, is all forgot? **1604** —— *Oth.* III. iv. 95 A man that all his time Hath..Shar'd dangers with you. **1667** DRYDEN *Ind. Emp.* V. ii. (1668) 62, I am content in Death to share your Fate. **1761** GRAY *Fatal Sisters* 27 Where our Friends the conflict share. **1815** SCOTT *Guy M.* xvi, That love of admiration which all pretty women share less or more. **1848** THACKERAY *Van. Fair* xxix, How could we, with our means, live at all, but for a friend to share expenses? *Ibid.* xlii, His dinner, which he and his daughter took in silence..or which they shared..with a party of dismal friends. **1856** FROUDE *Hist. Eng.* (1858) I. iii. 267 The bribery was equally shared between both parties. **1860** TYNDALL *Glac.* I. xviii. 131 Their willingness to share my fate whatever that might be. **1874** GREEN *Short Hist.* iv. §3. 177 He [Edward I] shared to the full his people's love of hard fighting. **1885** EAGLES *Constr. Geom. Plane Curves* 99 The ellipse shares with the hyperbola the property of satisfying five geometrical conditions. **1895** *Law Times* C. 4/1 Lord Macnaghten's satisfaction with things as they are will not be shared by anyone.

**6. a.** *intr.* To have a share (*in* something); to participate *in*, to take part *in*.

**1598** SHAKS. *Merry W.* II. ii. 14 Didst not thou share? hadst thou not fifteene pence? **1605** —— *Macb.* IV. i. 40, I commend your paines, And euery one shall share i'th' gaines. **1669** N. MORTON *New England's Mem.* (1910) 35 In which sickness the seamen shared also deeply, and many died. **1690** LOCKE *Govt.* §91 (1692) 91 A Right of Inheritance gave every one..a Title to share in the Goods of his Father. **1781** COWPER *Hope* 686 Good-breeding..if in masculine debate he shar'd, Ensur'd him mute attention and regard. **1849** MACAULAY *Hist. Eng.* ii. I. 156 Was it not enough..that he shared, with the rest of the nation, in the blessings of that mild government of which he had long been the foe? **1912** *Eng. Hist. Rev.* Jan. 53 The king would not share in the expense of raising opposition to the candidature of the electoral prince of Saxony.

**b.** To participate *with* (a person) *in* something. (? *Obs.*) *rare*.

**1594** SHAKS. *1 Hen. IV*, V. iv. 64, I am the Prince of Wales, and thinke not Percy, To share with me in glory any more. **1677** MILTON *P.L.* IX. 831 Adam shall share with me in bliss or woe. **1709** ATTERBURY *Serm.* (Luke x. 32) (1726) II. 244 We cannot, surely, think it beneath us, to share with those glorious Beings, in such an Administration! **1771** GOLDSM. *Hist. Eng.* II. 281 They had shared with him in all his former dangers and distresses.

†**c.** To partake *of*. *Obs. rare*.

**1649** EARL MONM. tr. *Senault's Use Passions* (1671) 6 The one and the other shares of servitude. **1720** *Humourist* 71 Those deplorable Wretches, who, as they share of our Likeness and Nature, ought to share of our Compassion. **1736** WELSTED *Wks.* (1787) 472 Any other people..must have shared, more or less, of the same frailty.

†**d.** To be equal with. *Obs. rare*⁻¹.

**1601** SHAKS. *All's Well* I. i. 73 Succeed thy father In manners as in shape: thy blood and vertue Contend for Empire in thee, and thy goodnesse Share with thy birthright.

**e.** Used in reduplicated form ***share and share*** (***alike***, etc.): the phrase in SHARE *sb.*³ being misapprehended grammatically.

**1821** SCOTT *Pirate* xvii, They say, that a' men share and share equals-aquals in the creature's ulzie. **1841** LYTTON *Nt. & Morn.* I. vi, And a pretty boy is always a help in a linen-draper's shop. He shall share and share with my own young folks. **1841** MACAULAY *Lit. Copyright* Sp. (1853) I. 286 In Kent the sons share and share alike. **1906** MARIE CORELLI *Treas. Heaven* x, I've no money—we all share and share alike in camp.

**7.** *intr.* and *trans.* In the language of Moral Rearmament: to confess one's sins openly; to impart to others one's spiritual experiences. Also const. *with*. Also in wider use.

**1932** [implied at SHARING *vbl. sb.*² 2]. **1933** S. A. KING *Challenge to Oxford Groups* v. 48 What does the Bishop think a man feels when he has 'shared' for 'witness' and finds that God has used that 'sharing' to bring a brother out of.. bondage? **1934** R. MACAULAY *Going Abroad* xiv. 111 She would, thought he, be able to share with another girl in a way she could not with him. *Ibid.* xvii. 135, I must say, I did annoy my father a bit by sharing with him a few things I'd thought about him. **1940** GRAVES & HODGE *Long Week-End* xii. 205 One of their practices was to 'share' confessions of their sins. **1949** A. WILSON *Wrong Set* 19, I do believe you're trying to get me to 'share'. And I never even guessed that you were a Grouper. **1981** B. PAUL *Your Eyelids are growing Heavy* (1982) ix. 121 She 'shared' with the group the fact that she'd begun to have severe bouts of depression.

**8.** *Comb.*: **share-out** [subst. use of the vbl. phrase in 1 b], the act of distributing in shares. Occas. *attrib.* in ***share-out club*** or ***society***. Also that which is distributed; a portion or share (of profits, interest, etc.), a 'cut'.

**1902** *Daily Chron.* 7 Jan. 7/1 A share-out club. **1906** *Westm. Gaz.* 24 Dec. 10/1 There was disappointment for a very large number of members of the Church Institute Slate Club..when it was found that the expected 'share-out' would not take place. **1909** *Daily Chron.* 17 Dec. 1/3 'Share-out night' is a very big event..in the Sick and Provident Club. **1941** *Sun* (Baltimore) 27 Jan. 4/1 It could be 'well in at the head of the table for the shareout' when the war ended. **1951** A. L. ROWSE *England of Elizabeth* viii. 325 The new nobility around the young king helped themselves to a vast share-out of Crown and Church lands. **1963** *Times* 7 May 18/2 No, a share-out it may be—and each shareholder may have his own private, affectionate name for it—but in..the businesslike print of The Birmingham Post, 'dividend' is the better term. **1976** *Scottish Daily Express* 23 Dec. 6/2 Kilkerr was forced to accept his share-out from Soho vice bosses on Friday nights.

Hence **shared** *ppl. a.*

**1884** *Lit. World* (Boston U.S.) 19 Apr. 134/2 Hopes and plans for a shared life, a household which should be his own. **1897** *Westm. Gaz.* 30 June 1/3 The boy is a shared property: he has to serve two masters. **1923** [see sense 4 f above]. **1939** L. PAULING *Nature Chem. Bond* i. 6 In methane the carbon atom, with its two inner electrons and its outer shell of eight shared electrons, has assumed the stable ten-electron configuration of neon. **1977** H. S. PICKERING *Covalent Bond* ii. 17 A variant of the covalent bond occurs in which the two shared electrons of the bond come originally from one of the two atoms.

**shareable** ('ʃɛərəb(ə)l), *a.* Also **sharable**. [f. SHARE *v.*² + -ABLE.] That may be shared. Hence **sharea'bility**.

**1920** *Q. Rev.* July 161 It must be shared or at least must be shareable; otherwise it were nothing at all. **1932** W. T. STACE *Theory of Knowl. & Existence* 332 Shareability of perception is what distinguishes the real from the unreal. **1935** W. DE LA MARE *Early One Morning* I. 19 In the telling of these vividly sharable experiences no direct hint is given that the author is actually seeing himself..as a child. **1977** FONTANA & VAN DE WATER in Douglas & Johnson *Existential Sociol.* iii. 102 The potential shareability of human understanding..is so great that complex systems of exchange can be constructed by groups who share no language. **1980** *Dædalus* Spring 20 Scientific understanding is essentially and eminently shareable.

**share-bone**: see SHARE *sb.*² b.

**share-crop** ('ʃɛəkrɒp), *v.* Chiefly *U.S.* Also **sharecrop, share crop**. [f. SHARE *sb.*³ + CROP *v.*] **a.** *intr.* To farm on shares (see SHARE *sb.*³ 5 d). **b.** *trans.* To grow (a crop) on this system; also *transf.* So **'share-crop** *sb.*, a crop raised on shares; also *attrib.*; **'share-cropper**, one who share-crops; also *attrib.*; and hence **'share-cropped** *ppl. a.*; **'share-cropping** *vbl. sb.* and *ppl. a.*

[**1867** in J. H. Easterby *S. Carolina Rice Plantation* (1945) 231 This will be cheaper in the end than the contract or share of the crop system.] **1907** *Springfield* (Mass.) *Weekly Republ.* 25 Apr. 1 The 'share crops' system is what its name implies, the immigrant being housed and fitted with all the necessaries and then sharing the proceeds of the harvest with the landowner. **1925** *Annals Amer. Acad.* Jan. 61/1 Number of farmers operated by tenants of various kinds (cash, share and share-cash 'croppers', standing tenants, etc.) increased about 100,000. **1928** J. PETERKIN *Scarlet Sister Mary* xxi. 235 The..thing would cost as much as his whole share-crop of cotton would make in five years. **1929** L. R. GOTTSCHALK *Era French Revolution* 33 Most of them had become métayers, who, like our share-croppers, farmed a piece of land for a stipulated portion..of the harvest. **1930** *Dialect Notes* VI. II. 83 *Share-crop*, v., to farm 'on shares'... The word, like the practice, is very common. **1936** *Daily Progress* (Charlottesville, Va.) 3 Nov. 1/5 Bridges, who sharecrops for W. G. Gray, Senath attorney, sat in a big chair and poked wood in the fire. **1944** *Chicago Daily News* 2 Dec. 4/6 The Capone gang owned several locals of the hotel and restaurant workers in Chicago, and had Lou Romano share-cropping them. **1945** *Reader's Digest* Nov. 26/1 He found hundreds of blacks who share-cropped cotton. **1945** B. A. BOTKIN *Lay My Burden Down* 225 That was the beginning of the sharecropping system. **1947** *Social Forces* Dec. 202/1 One hundred Negro sharecropper families on the King and Anderson plantation. **1960** H. E. BATES *Aspidistra in Babylon* 215 A toothless Chinaman.. share-cropped vanilla farther up the hill. **1962** E. SNOW *Red China Today* (1963) lvi. 427 The 'well-to-do' peasants (living at a prosperous share-crop level) resented anything that looked like loss of control over their savings, homes and land. **1970** S. L. BARRACLOUGH in I. L. Horowitz *Masses in Lat. Amer.* iv. 104 When legalized slavery and forced labor were abolished..various forms of share-cropping took their place. **1973** W. MCCARTHY *Detail* i. 62 Paul..came from a large, poor, sharecropper family, in the heart of the delta land of Mississippi. **1973** *Advocate-News* (Barbados) 17 Feb. 8/2 A depression time share-cropping family. **1974** *Evening Herald* (Rock Hill, S. Carolina) 18 Apr. 13/2 He was born in Greenville County, S.C., and spent his youth helping his father sharecrop. **1976** *Jrnl. Devel. Econ.* III. 345 In this exercise, we limit ourselves in focus to a single sharecropped plot on the fazenda.

**shareef**, variant of SHEREEF.

**share-grass**, variant of SHEAR-GRASS.

**shareholder** ('ʃɛəˌhəʊldə(r)). [f. SHARE *sb.*³ + HOLDER¹.] One who owns or holds a share or shares in a joint-stock company, or other joint fund or property.

**18..** *Med. Repos.* (Webster 1828–32), One of the proprietors of the mine..was a principal shareholder in the company. **1841** THACKERAY *Gt. Hoggarty Diam.* vi, Are you insured as a shareholder in the West Diddlesex? **1872** R. B. SMYTH *Min. & Min. Statist.* 55 The company consisted of ten working shareholders. **1876** F. S. WILLIAMS *Midl. Railw.* iii. 70 The shareholders of the..Midland Railway Company. **1912** *Times* 19 Dec. 18/5 The preference shareholders would be entitled to half the profits after payment of the preferential dividend.

Hence **'shareholdership**, the fact or condition of being a shareholder. **'shareholding** *ppl. a.*, that possesses shares. **'shareholding** *vbl. sb.*, the possession of shares; also *pl.*, the shares held by a person in various undertakings.

**1859** LEVER *Dav. Dunn* xli. 331 Our scheme is a great shareholding company. **1866** *Standard* 27 Aug. 4/7 Other.. matters..must be brought before the shareholding body. **1902** *Pall Mall Gaz.* 14 Mar. 4/3 A syndicate..has been privately formed for..taking over the whole of Mr. Rhodes's shareholdings. **1904** *Edin. Rev.* Oct. 348 The right to participate in this wealth—shareholdership, in fact, in this joint-stock concern, the commerce of Venice—was strictly defined and limited.

**share-line.** *rare*⁻⁰. [Cf. SHEAR *sb.*² 4, SHEAR *v.* 8 b.] 'The summit line of elevated ground' (Ogilvie 1850).

**shareman, sharen**: see SHEARMAN, SHARN.

†**share-penny.** *Obs. rare*⁻¹. [f. SHARE *v.*¹] One who would shear a penny, a miser.

**1606** *Wily Beguiled* B 1, Ile goe neere to cosen olde father share-penny of his daughter.

**sharer** ('ʃɛərə(r)). [f. SHARE *v.*² + -ER¹.]

**1.** One who shares something (const. *of*) or shares *in* something (see the senses of the verb). Also const. *with* (a person).

† *to go sharers*: = 'to go shares': see SHARE *sb.*³

**1603** DEKKER *Wonderf. Yeare* Wks. (Grosart) I. 114 A fourth sharer likewise (these winding-sheete-weauers) deserues to haue my penne giue his lippes a Iewes letter. **1609** DANIEL *Civ. Wars* IV. iv, Most it seem'd the French King to import, As sharer in his daughters iniurie. **1622** ROWLANDS *Gd. Newes & B.* 13 That had beene sharers long and many a day Of what they got vpon the common way. **1627** MAY *Lucan* I. (1631) 4 Rule brookes no sharers. **1631** *Star Chamber Cases* (Camden) 87 These men..were plotters, they were sharers, they gave the tooles. **1643** FALKLAND in *Chas. I's Wks.* (1662) II. 282 Those dangerous Distractions which the interest of any Sharers with Him would have infallibly produced. **1733** *Oxford Act* II. 19 If we can write an Answer, I fancy we shall get something by it, and so, Sir, we will go Sharers. **1755** WARBURTON *Serm.* (Luke xiii. 1, 2) Wks. 1788 V. 293 The old Manichean impiety,..which makes an evil Principle, a sharer with him [God] in the direction of the Universe. **1782** J. BROWN *View Nat. & Revealed Relig.* IV. ii. (1796) 302 Till Jesus have.. made me an effectual sharer in the virtue of his intercession. **1821** SCOTT *Kenilw.* xxxv, I have made her sharer of my bed and of my fortunes. **1837** DICKENS *Pickw.* xxix, The sharer of all his cares and troubles followed him. **1869** FREEMAN *Norm. Conq.* (1876) III. xi. 7 Already a sharer in some sort in the honours of royalty. **1874** L. STEPHEN *Hours in Library* (1892) I. ix. 301 He excited little attention..except amongst the sharers of his own religious persuasions. **1885** *Manch. Exam.* 30 Dec. 5/3 To make them sharers with ourselves in all the reforms which are necessary to good government.

†**2.** *spec.* A member of a company of players, who paid the expenses, and received the profits, and employed the 'journeymen' members of the company. *Obs.*

(Quot. 1589 is perh. a forgery by Collier.)

**1589** [?] in J. P. Collier *Shaks.* (1844) I. Life p. cviii. *note*, Her Majesty's poore Playeres..being all of them sharers in the blacke Fryers playehouse, have [etc.]. *c* **1600** *Histriomastix* v. (1610) F 2 b, You that are maister-sharers Must prouide you vpon your own purses. *Ibid.* G 1, *Soul[diers]*. Come on Players, now we are the Sharers And you the hired men. **1601** B. JONSON *Poet.* IV. iv. 8 *Hist[rio]*... They directed a letter to me, and my fellow-sharers. *Lvpv.* Speake lower, you are not now i' your theater, Stager. **1604** T. M. *Ant & Nightingale* C 1, Whilst the Ant began to stalke like a three Quarter sharer. *c* **1613** in Greg *Henslowe Papers* (1907) 23 Fower or ffive Sharers of the saide Company. **1699** J. WRIGHT *Hist. Histrion.* 11 For several Years next after the Restauration, every whole Sharer in Mr. Hart's Company, got 1000 *l.* per an. **1704** *Royal Order* 17 Jan. in *Lond. Gaz.* No. 3985/1 The Managers, Sharers and Actors of the said Companies.

†**b.** A shareholder, one who owns a share in a joint concern. (In quot. 1664 *fig.*) *Obs.*

**1664** COWLEY *On Death Kath. Philips* iii, The Trade of Glory mannag'd by the Pen..Does bring in but small profit to us Men; 'Tis by the number of the sharers drown'd. **1715** *Lond. Gaz.* No. 5348/9 They hereby require, That all the Sharers do pay..two Guineas per Share. **1740** W. DOUGLASS *Disc.* 12 They who take up this Loan Money are called Sharers. **1812** H. & J. SMITH *Horace in Lond.* 102 But fire, alas! to smoak will turn, And sharers, though no houses burn, Are sure to burn their fingers.

**sharewort**: see SHARE *sb.*² b.

**sharg.** *Sc.* ? *Obs.* In 7 scharge. [a. Gael. *searg.*] = next.

**1623** in Pitcairn *Crim. Trials* II. 538 Hir bairne that wes ane scharge. **1825** in JAMIESON.

**shargar** ('ʃɑːgə(r)). *Sc.* Also **sharger**. [Altered form of prec.] A lean, thin, stunted person or animal; a weakly child. Also *attrib.*

**1742** R. FORBES *Ajax, Shop Bill* (1755) 39 Far wary-draggle, an' sharger elf. **1820** G. BEATTIE in MᶜCyrus *Life* (1863) 284 We'll put the sharger down—The wee, wee German lairdie O. **1874** G. MACDONALD *Malcolm* xxv, Maist mithers, gien there be a shargar..amo' their bairns, mak mair o' that ane nor o' a' the lave putten thegither. **1912** C. MURRAY in *The Odd Vol.* 20 A wee sharger collie was a' that she had To cuddle at e'en.

**sharge**, obs. form of SERGE.

**shargoss**, variant of SYAGUSH.

**shargras(s)e**, obs. forms of SHEAR-GRASS.

**Sharia** (ʃəˈriːə). Also **Shariah, Shariat,** †**Sharieh,** †**Sheriat**, and with small initial. [Arab. *šarī'a.*] The Islamic religious law, including the teachings of the Koran and the traditional sayings of Muhammad.

**1855** R. F. BURTON *Personal Narr. Pilgrimage to El-Medinah* II. xxi. 281 In fact, justice at El Medinah is administered in perfect conformity with the Shariat or Holy Law. **1877** *Encycl. Brit.* VII. 113/2 Shi'at or Sher'iat, *i.e.* legal religion under the supervision of a murshid. **1920** *19th Cent.* Sept. 500 Questions of divorce and inheritance are decided by the religious or Sharieh judge, from whom there is an appeal to the Sharieh Court of Appeal in Jerusalem. **1921** *Glasgow Herald* 16 July 7 A code based on the Shariat and prepared upon his orders would come into force. **1927** *Ibid.* 21 Oct. 11 The Sheriat (Moslem) canonical law has practically been abolished, a civil code borrowed from Switzerland being substituted for all questions of marriage and inheritance. **1936** F. STARK *Southern Gates Arabia* iii.

39 The law is the Muhammedan shari'a. **1965** *Mod. Law Rev.* XXVIII. v. 543 The marriage was dissolved, according to Mohammedan law by the unilateral declaration of *talak* divorce in the appropriate Sharia Court. **1971** *Illustr. Weekly India* 4 Apr. 47/1 For long *Sharia* has not been administered by a Caliph or Imam. **1979** *Guardian* 28 Mar. 18/4 At the basis of a way of life which was remarkable for its homogeneity, is the Shariah—meaning simply the way or path.

**sharif, Sharifian**, varr. SHEREEF, SHEREEFIAN *a.*

**shariffe, -iff**, variants of SHEREEF, SHERIFI.

†'**sharing**, *vbl. sb.*[1] *Obs. rare.* [f. SHARE *v.*[1] + -ING[1].] The action of SHARE *v.*[1]; *concr.* that which is shorn or cut off.

**1553** *Respublica* I. i. 94 The paringes, The baggage, the trashe, the fragmentes, the sharinges.

**sharing** ('ʃɛərɪŋ), *vbl. sb.*[2] [f. SHARE *v.*[2] + -ING[1].]

**1. a.** The action or an act of SHARE *v.*[2]

**1625** BACON *Ess., Riches* (Arb.) 237 Sharings, doe greatly Enrich, if the Hands be well chosen, that are trusted. **1720** DE FOE *Capt. Singleton* xiii. (1840) 228 Further sharing of profits. **1879** GEO. ELIOT *Theo. Such* 20 Another form of the disloyal attempt to be independent of the common lot, and to live without a sharing of pain. **1903** A. J. BUTLER *Arab Conq. Egypt* 201 Mohammed answered, 'Verily the profession of Islâm and the sharing of the Flight cancel all the past.'

**b.** *attrib.*

**1640** NABBES *Bride* III. ii, As if the enterteinment of constables on a sharing day were not chargeable enough, but you must complement away wine and sweet meats. **1871** *2nd Rep. Comm. Friendly Soc.* II. (1872) 37/2 The sharing out clubs.. mostly exist from year to year. **1885** J. K. JEROME *On the Stage* 156 He was ready to keep on with us for a week or two longer upon sharing terms. **1910** *Stage Year Bk.* 49 Sharing terms, as understood in England, are rarely arranged for in Australia.

**2.** *spec.* The action of SHARE *v.*[2] 7.

**1932** A. J. RUSSELL *For Sinners Only* ii. 25 They [*sc.* The Oxford Group] defined Sharing as meaning two distinct things—further definable as Confession and Witness. **1945** N. L. MCCLUNG *Stream runs Fast* xxx. 298 They have class meetings, too, but they call them 'quiet times', and they tell their spiritual experiences, but they call that 'sharing', and they care nothing about money. **1964** T. DRIBERG *Mystery of Moral Re-Armament* ii. 38 An ill-judged attempt by Buchman to promote, if only vicariously, the practice of Sharing.

†'**sharing**, *ppl. a. Obs.* [f. SHARE *v.*[1] + -ING[2].] That 'shares' or shears.

**1573** TUSSER *Husb.* (1878) 37 A skuttle or skreine,.. and sharing sheares readie for sheepe to be shorne.

**shark** (ʃɑːk), *sb.*[1] Also 6–7 **sharke.** [Of obscure origin.

The word seems to have been introduced by the sailors of Captain (afterwards Sir John) Hawkins's expedition, who brought home a specimen which was exhibited in London in 1569. The source from which they obtained the word has not been ascertained. Cf. Ger. dial. (Austrian) *schirk* sturgeon: see SHIRK *sb.*[2]

The conjecture of Skeat that the name of the fish is derived from SHARK *v.*[1] is untenable; the earliest example of the vb. is *c* 1596, and the passage alludes to the fish.]

**1. a.** A selachian fish of the sub-order *Squali* of the order *Plagiostomi*; in popular language chiefly applied to the large voracious fishes of this suborder, as the genera *Carcharodon*, *Carcharias*, etc.

**1569** in *B.L. Ballads & Broadsides* (1867) 147 Ther is no proper name for it [a 'marueilous straunge Fishe'] that I knowe, but that sertayne men of Captayne Haukinses doth call it a SHARKE. **1589** SPARKE *Sir J. Hawkins' 2nd Voy.* [landed home 1565] in Hakluyt *Voy.* 528 Many sharks or Tuberons.. came about the ships. **1622** R. HAWKINS *Observ. Voy. S. Sea* xix. 43 The Sharke, or Tiberune, is a Fish like vnto those which wee call Dogge-fishes, but that he is farre greater. **1655** TERRY *Voy. E. India* 8 The Shark hath not this name for nothing, for he will make a morsell of any thing he can catch, master, and devour. **1697** DAMPIER *Voy.* I. 79 We caught several great Sharks. **1774** GOLDSM. *Nat. Hist.* (1776) VI. 240 The shark is the dread of sailors in all hot climates. **1814** SCOTT *Ld. of Isles* IV. xi, So darts the dolphin from the shark. **1873** DAWSON *Earth & Man* vi. 158 Sharks, whose mouths are paved with flat teeth for crushing shells. **1879** E. P. WRIGHT *Anim. Life* 460 The True Sharks, or Carchariadæ, form a family most numerous in species, which are to be found in all seas. *Ibid.* 464 This shark [the Australian Saw Fish, *Pristiophorus cirratus*] is said to attain a length of about twelve feet. **1883** *Fisheries Exhib. Catal.* (ed. 4) 381 There is no dearth of shark and scar-fish.

**b.** With defining word, as **angel-shark**, the monk-fish, *Squatina angelus*; **Gangetic shark**, *Carcharias gangeticus*, inhabiting some rivers; **Greenland shark**, the North Atlantic shark *Læmargus borealis*; **grey shark**, the sand-shark *Carcharinus americanus*; **hammer-headed shark**, the *Zygæna malleus*; †**long-tailed shark**, the Fox-shark; **sea-shark**, a shark of the high seas, esp. 'a large shark of the family *Lamnidæ*' (*Cent. Dict.* 1891); **spine shark**, the Picked Dogfish, *Acanthias*; **spinous shark**, a shark of the genus *Echinorhinus*, as *E. spinosus*; **white shark**, a man-eating shark, *Carcharodon rondeleti*.

(See also BASKING *ppl. a.* 2, BLUE *a.* 12, COW *sb.*[1] 8, FOX *sb.* 16 b, HOUND *sb.*[1] 7 b, MACKEREL[1] 4, ROCK *sb.*[1] 9 d, SAND *sb.*[2] 10 b, TIGER *sb.* 14, WHALE, etc.).

**1655** TERRY *Voy. E. India* 8 This Sea-shark is a Fish as bad in eating as he is in quality. *a* **1672** WILLUGHBY *Hist. Pisc.* (1686) Tab. B. 8 The blew Sharke *Galeus glaucus* Rond. **1674** RAY *Coll. Words, Sea Fishes* 98 White Sharks. **1752** [see HAMMER-HEADED]. **1769** PENNANT *Brit. Zool.* III. 78 The Basking Shark... This species has been long known to the inhabitants of the south and west of Ireland. **1776** *Ibid.* III. 86 Angel Shark. *Ibid.* 97 Long-tailed Shark. *Ibid.* 104 Beaumaris Shark. **1804** SHAW *Gen. Zool.* V. 334 Spotted shark. *Ibid.* 339 Dusky shark. *Ibid.* 346 Grey shark. **1823** BYRON *Island* IV. ix, His.. mates.. Or deem'd him mad, or prey to the blue shark. **1828** J. FLEMING *Brit. Anim.* 166 *Scymnus borealis.* Greenland Shark. **1836** BUCKLAND *Geol. & Min.* (1837) I. 290 The common Dog-Fish, or Spine Shark (Spinax Acanthias, Cuv.). **1873** T. GILL *Catal. Fishes East N. Amer.* 35 *Reniceps tiburo*... Shovel-head shark. **1879** E. P. WRIGHT *Anim. Life* 460 The Gangetic Shark (*Carcharias gangeticus*). *Ibid.* 464 The Spinous Shark (*Echinorhinus spinosus*) is a rare British fish. **1881** *Cassell's Nat. Hist.* V. 31 The Grey Shark is sometimes eleven or twelve feet long. **1886** GÜNTHER in *Encycl. Brit.* XXI. 776/2 Hammerheaded Sharks (*Zygæna*) are sharks in which the anterior portion of the head is produced into a lobe on each side, the extremity of which is occupied by the eye.

**c.** *transf.* **fresh-water shark**, a jocular name for the pike, alluding to its voracity.

**1799** G. SMITH *Laboratory* II. 267 The audacity and voraciousness of this fish [the pike] justly entitle him to the name which he has acquired of the fresh-water shark. **1902** *Daily Chron.* 16 Dec. 8/4 Several fine pike have been captured lately, the heaviest.. coming from a lake at Redhill, the 'freshwater shark' scaling 21lb. 2oz.

**d.** *transf. Naut. slang.* A sardine.

**1916** 'TAFFRAIL' *Pincher Martin* viii. 144 There was a peculiar tang in the air... He found out afterwards that it emanated from various sardine-preserving factories, and the discovery put him off canteen 'sharks' for quite a week.

**2.** *fig.* **a.** (Cf. SHARK *sb.*[2]) Applied to persons, with allusion to the predatory habits and voracity of the shark; one who enriches himself by taking advantage of the necessities of others; a rapacious usurer, an extortionate landlord or letter of lodgings, etc., a financial swindler.

**1713** *Guardian* No. 73 The sharks, who prey upon the inadvertency of young heirs. **1804** *Naval Chron.* XII. 249 The slopsellers, and other sharks, at this port. **1832** G. DOWNES *Lett. Cont. Countries* I. 385 Our guide, a genuine shark, did his best to defraud his brethren, and thereby secure the entire fee. **1857** TROLLOPE *Three Clerks* I. iii. 58 He expected to pay £200 a year for his board and lodging, which he thought might as well go to his niece as to some shark, who would probably starve him. **1886** C. E. PASCOE *Lond. To-day* xix. (ed. 3) 187 Brighton is less plagued with 'sharks' than seaside resorts usually are. **1904** SHUDDICK *How to arrange with Creditors* 35 The.. simplest way of checking the rapacity of the money-lending shark. **1907** H. WYNDHAM *Flare of Footlights* xxx, Even to his untrained eye several of them [*i.e.* theatrical advertisements] obviously emanated from sharks.

*attrib.* **1904** SHUDDICK *How to arrange with Creditors* 31 Another gentleman who is to be avoided at creditors' meetings is the shark accountant.

†**b.** *spec.* (See quots.) *Obs.*

**1707** J. STEVENS tr. *Quevedo's Com. Wks.* (1709) 242 A meer Shark or Pick-pocket. **1788** GROSE *Dict. Vulgar T.* (ed. 2) s.v. *Shark*, Sharks; the first order of pick-pockets. Bow-street term, A.D. 1785.

**c.** A customs officer; also *pl.* the press-gang.

**1785** GROSE *Dict. Vulgar T.*, *Shark*... Also a custom house officer, or tide waiter. **1796** ELIZA HAMILTON *Lett. Hindoo Rajah* (1811) II. 52 The loss you had sustained from the sharks of the custom-house. **1828** D. JERROLD *Ambrose Gwinett* I. iii, *Gil.* A word with you—the sharks are out to-night. *Label.* The sharks? *Gil.* Ay, the blue-jackets—the press-gang. **1851** MAYHEW *Lond. Labour* I. 384/1 They.. look mysteriously around to see if there be any of 'them ere Custom-house sharks afloat'. **1866** 'MARK TWAIN' *Lett. from Hawaii* (1967) 81 The professional 'sharks' in New Bedford and New London who furnish crews to ships.

**d.** *Naut.* A lawyer.

**1806** *Port Folio* 17 May 304/1, I got plenty of promises, Latin, and jaw, And who ever got more from a lawyer? Of the sport I got sick, so threw up the game, For my cash by the sharks had got eaten. **1840** MARRYAT *Poor Jack* xxvii, I'm what the sailors call a shark, that is, I'm a lawyer.

**e.** *U.S. College slang.* A highly intelligent or able student. ? *Obs.*

**1895** W. C. GORE in *Inlander* Dec. 111 *Shark*,.. a person who is very bright either in a general way or (more often) in some particular line of work. **1903** *Williams College Class Book* 29 'Dido' is a Math. shark of the first water. **1909** *Springfield* (Mass.) *Weekly Republ.* 8 July 12 The 'shark' does well in his lessons, but recognizes that study is the first thing in college. 'Sharks' play games. **1920** [see ELOCUTE *v.*].

**3.** *Ent.* Any moth of the genus *Cucullia* (formerly *Noctua*); there are several varieties as camomile, tansy, lettuce, mugwort shark.

**1819** SAMOUELLE *Entomol. Compend.* 418 *Noctua umbratica*... The large Pale Shark. *Ibid.* 419 *N. Tanaceti.* The Tansy Shark. *N. Lactucæ.* The Lettuce Shark. *N. Lucifuga.* The large Dark Shark. **1869** E. NEWMAN *Brit. Moths* 436. **1890** POULTON *Colours Anim.* iv. 58 The appearance of splinters of wood is also often suggested by moths such as the 'Sharks' (*Cucullia*).

**4.** *attrib.* and *Comb.* **a.** Obvious comb., as ***shark-bite, -fisher, genus, -hook, kind, (-liver) oil, -steak, trap; shark-fishing; shark-infested, -like, -mouthed, -proof*** adjs.

**1888** *Daily News* 25 Dec. 5/2 Death by *shark-bite. **1897** 'MARK TWAIN' *Following Equator* xiii. 142 He was passing by a nodding *shark-fisher. **1852** MUNDY *Antipodes* (1857) 89 *Shark-fishing is merely the best sport to be had in New South Wales. **1914** *Chambers's Jrnl.* Feb. 89/1 Shark-fishing is regarded as being as much a trade as a sport. **1976** L. DEIGHTON *Twinkle, twinkle, Little Spy* xi. 117 Is she interested in stud farms or shark fishing? **1822–29** *Good's Study Med.* (ed. 3) V. 6 The squalus, or *shark genus. **1849** CUPPLES *Green Hand* viii. (1856) 74, I hauled up the *shark-hook from astern. **1978** *Detroit Free Press* 5 Mar. A 17/1 Rescue crews Saturday searched *shark-infested waters for the bodies of.. crewmen killed in the crash of a.. domestic airliner. **1758** BORLASE *Nat. Hist. Cornw.* 265 Of the *shark kind.. we have the sea-fox, *Vulpecula* or *Simia marina* of authors. **1885** HORNADAY *2 Yrs in Jungle* xxii. 257 A very strange.. *shark-like fish. **1868** ROYLE & HEADLAND *Mat. Med.* (ed. 5) 745 *note*, *Shark-liver Oil has been lately imported into Liverpool. **1806** J. BERESFORD *Miseries Hum. Life* IV. i, Should you chance to have a wish for what is in the baskets or barrows of these *shark-mouthed bawlers. **1615** R. COCKS *Diary* (Hakl. Soc.) I. 11 And we bought 40 gants of *shark oyle for the junk. **1888** BRANNT *Anim. & Veg. Fats* 310 Shark oil, prepared from the livers of various species of the shark. **1923** 'R. DALY' *Enchanted Isl.* x. 92 She had been bathing in the *shark-proof palisade below. **1967** *Coast to Coast 1965–66* 162 Some evenings the Roebourne mob.. would.. swim in.. our shark-proof pool beside the wharf. **1847** H. MELVILLE *Omoo* xiv. 65 A *shark-steak and be hanged to you! **1885** LADY BRASSEY *The Trades* 209 The pilot.. telling me.. what excellent things shark-steaks were. **1896** A. J. BUTLER tr. *Ratzel's Hist. Mankind* I. 254 Fig., *Shark-trap with wooden float, from Fiji.

**b.** Special comb.: **shark-bait**, *Austral. colloq.*, a lone or daring swimmer well out from shore; hence **shark-baiter, -baiting; shark-barrow**, 'the egg-case of a shark; a sea-purse' (*Funk's Stand. Dict.* 1895); **shark-charmer**, one professing to protect the pearl-divers in Sri Lanka from sharks by incantations; **shark-fin**, the fin of a shark, considered a table delicacy by the Chinese; **shark's fin** = *shark-fin*; also in **shark's fin soup; shark's head** *nonce-word*, a jocular name for the elongated prow of a grab; **shark-headed** *a.*, the designation of a kind of screw, so **shark-header**, a screw of this kind; **shark-louse**, a parasitic crustacean infesting sharks; **shark-moth** = sense 3; **shark's mouth** *Naut.* (see quot.); also 'the opening for the breeching in the cascabel of a cannon' (*Funk's Stand. Dict.* 1895); **shark net** *S. Afr. local*, a length of netting positioned off-shore to protect bathers from sharks; also ***shark netting*; shark-ray**, the angel-fish, also a rhinobatid or beaked ray; **sharkskin**, (*a*) the skin of sharks used for making shagreen, and also used for polishing, etc.; also *attrib.*; (*b*) (i) a woven or warp-knitted fabric of wool, silk, or rayon with a smooth, slightly lustrous, finish; freq. *attrib.*; (ii) an outfit made of this fabric; **shark-sucker**, 'any remora that adheres to sharks,' esp. *Echeneis naucrates*; **shark's tooth, shark-tooth**, the tooth of a shark, also † = GLOSSOPETRA; also *attrib.* quasi-*adj.* in similative use; also in ***shark's teeth sword, weapon***, a weapon armed with shark's teeth, in use among some primitive peoples; **shark-toothed** *a.*, applied to a tooth ornament suggesting shark's teeth.

**1920** A. H. ADAMS *Australians* 177 Farther out in the deep water swam the venturous line of experts, technically known as '*shark-bait'. **1937** K. S. PRICHARD *Intimate Stranger* i. 16 'Shark-bait', boys and girls on the beaches called her, she was so daring. Always swimming out there beyond the reef. **1924** A. WRIGHT *Rung In* iii. 31 It might be only some foolhardy '*shark baiter', as he heard the more venturesome of the bathers termed. **1965** *Austral. Encycl.* VIII. 82/2 Solitary bathers are more often attacked than groups, but the 'shark-baiter' farthest off shore is not necessarily the victim. **1951** CUSACK & JAMES *Come in Spinner* 221 I've given up *shark-baiting. Mug's game. **1967** K. S. PRICHARD *Subtle Flame* 99 I'm no good at shark baiting. **1866** *Cornh. Mag.* XIV. 169 The *shark-charmer.. is considered so indispensable to the fishery that he is paid by Government. **1793** J. TRAPP *Rochon's Voy. Madagascar*, etc. 390 The Chinese pay likewise a liberal price for *shark-fins. **1933** *Gourmet's Bk. Food & Drink* iii. 49 In his own country the Chinaman's evening meal is a somewhat variegated affair.. and includes.. shark's fins, cucumber, fish brawn. *c* **1938** *Fortnum & Mason Price List* 58/1 Soups.. Sharks' Fins per bot. 7/6. **1966** *Guardian* 30 July 7/3 In the heart of Chinatown, shark's fin soup with crab sauce. **1978** *Nagel's Encycl.-Guide: China* 379 Sharks' fins need lengthy preparation, because they are bought dried. **1831** TRELAWNY *Adv. Younger Son* I. 178 Knock the *shark's head off her, and ship a bowsprit in its place. **1861** DICKENS *Gt. Expect.* xv, A gross or two of *shark-headed screws for general use. *Ibid.*, And *shark-headers is open to misrepresentations. **1850** A. WHITE *List. Specim. Crustacea Brit. Mus.* 122 *Dinemoura alata.* Winged *Shark-louse. **1819** G. SAMOUELLE *Entomol. Compend.* 250 *Noctua Tanaceti* (*shark moths). **1881** HAMERSLY *Naval Encycl.*, *Awning*, the *shark's mouth is an opening to accommodate the masts and stays abaft. **1970** *Studies in English* (Univ. Cape Town) I. 33 These bracelets were originally made out of shark netting. The surfer would dig his way out to the *shark nets, cut himself a piece and tie it around his wrist. **1977** J. MCCLURE *Sunday Hangman* ix. 95 The shark nets protecting the bathers off its [*sc.* Durban's] beaches. **1836** YARRELL *Brit. Fishes* II. 408 The Angel-fish.. is also called *Shark-Ray, from its partaking of the characters of both Shark and Ray. **1851** GOSSE *Nat. Hist., Fishes* 314 *Rhinobatina.* The Shark-rays. **1873** T. GILL *Catal. Fishes East N. Amer.* 35 *Squatina Dumerili*... Angel-fish; shark-ray. **1851** H. MELVILLE *Whale* xv. I. 107 His account books bound in superior old *shark-skin. *Ibid.* III. xxvii. 174 With matted beard, and swathed in a bristling shark-skin apron.. Perth was standing between his forge and anvil. **1877** G. MACDONALD *Marquis of Lossie* xlv, What the final touches of the shark-skin are to the marble.. that only can [etc.]. **1932** C. BEATON *Diary* Mar. in *Wandering Years* (1961) xiii. 255, I bought vast quantities, at almost negligible cost, of football vests, exotic footgear, the scantiest shorts in all colours and in white sharkskin. **1944** R. Chandler *Lady in Lake* ii. 11 The man wore trunks and the woman what looked like a very daring white sharkskin bathing suit. **1957** L. Durrell *Justine* III. 183 Now in his ice-smooth shark-skin with the scarlet cummerbund he seemed..the richest and most handsome of the city's bankers. **1974** D. Ramsay *No Cause to Kill* II. 110 Ivy Eastbrook..in silk shirt and sharkskin trousers. **1979** E. Koch *Goodnight, Little Spy* ii. 6 During the winter he wore..five serge suits and two sharkskins. **1850** A. White *List Specim. Crustacea Brit. Mus.* 124 *Anthosoma Smithii*, Bud-like *Shark-Sucker. **1692** Ray *Disc.* II. iv. (1693) 162, I might have added *Sharks-teeth or Glossopetræ. **1845** C. H. Smith in Kitto *Cycl. Bibl. Lit.* s.v. *Arms* Fig. 99 Sharks-teeth Sword. **1853** Kingsley *Westw. Ho!* vi, Jagged shark's-tooth rock. **1885** Hornaday *2 Yrs. in Jungle* xxii. 257 They certainly are more like shark-teeth than spines. **1886** *Guide Exhib. Galleries Brit. Mus.* 216 The singular armour made of cocoanut fibre, worn by the natives [of Micronesia] as a protection against the shark's teeth weapons. **1794** T. Dwight *Greenfield Hill* 79 What stretches Avarice's gulphy maw, And opens wide her *shark-tooth'd jaw. **1860** Thackeray *Round. Pap., Lazy Idle Boy* (1876) 3 The sacristan..espies the traveller eyeing ..the old shark-toothed arch of his cathedral. **1935** C. Day Lewis *Time to Dance* 42 Over the shark-toothed Timor sea Lost their bearings.

†**shark**, *sb.*$^2$ *Obs.* Also **sharke**. Cf. shirk *sb.* [Of uncertain etymology.

It is noteworthy that shirk occurs with the same meaning frequently from 1639 down to the beginning of the 18th c., and that the G. *schurke* (now in wider sense, scoundrel, villain) had in the 16th c. precisely the same sense. Words with meanings of this character were *c* 1600 often adopted from Ger., and it is not unlikely that this word represents an adoption of G. *schurke* (earlier *schurk, schorck*), assimilated in form to shark *sb.*$^1$, of which it seems often to have been felt as a figurative use.]

A worthless and impecunious person who gains a precarious living by sponging on others, by executing disreputable commissions, cheating at play, and petty swindling; a parasite; a sharper. In later use influenced by shark *sb.*$^1$ 2.

**1599** B. Jonson *Ev. Man out of H.* Charac., Shift. A Thredbare Sharke. One that neuer was Soldior, yet liues vpon lendings. His profession is skeldring and odling, his Banke Poules, and his Ware-house Pict-hatch. *c* **1600** *Distr. Emperor* I. i. in Bullen *Old Pl.* (1884) III. 166 To give attendance on the full-fedd gueste, Not on the hungry sharke. **1601** B. Jonson *Poetaster* III. iv. 200 Doe not we serue a notable sharke? **1609** —— *Silent Wom.* IV. iv, *La-f.* A very sharke, he set me i' the nicke t'other night at primero. **1628** Earle *Microcosm., Sharke* (Arb.) 35 A Sharke. One whome all other meanes haue fayl'd, and hee now liues of himselfe. **1678** South *Serm.* (*1 Sam.* xxv. 32, 33) (1697) II. 427 And thus David's Messengers are sent back to him, like so many Sharks, and Runnagates. **1684** Wood *Life* 4 Sept. (O.H.S.) III. 108 Wright Croke..was posted up for a shark and coward in Day's coffey house. *a* **1700** Evelyn *Diary* 19 July 1664, The master of it [the lottery],..was, in truth, a meer shark.

**b.** *Comb.* **shark-gull**, ? one who is both knave and dupe.

**1604** T. M. *Black Bk.* C 4, Alas, poore Skark-Gull [*sic*], that put off is idle.

†**shark**, *sb.*$^3$ *Obs.* [f. shark *v.*$^1$] The action or an act of 'sharking'. ***to live upon the shark***: to live by sharking.

*c* **1692** South *Serm.* (1697) II. vi. 253 Wretches who live upon the Shark, and other men's Sins,..getting their very Bread by the Damnation of Souls.

**shark** (ʃɑːk), *v.*$^1$ Also 7 **sharke**; and see shirk *v.* [Of uncertain origin.

It seems likely that two different words have been more or less confused from the time of the earliest examples; the one (which has the variants *sherk(e, shirk(e*: see shirk *v.*) f. shark *sb.*$^2$, and the other f. shark *sb.*$^1$ The senses naturally resulting from these derivations respectively are so nearly allied, and the use with mixed notions is so frequent, that the two verbs cannot be distinguished.

Skeat conjectured that this verb (which he regarded as the source, not the derivative, of the two sbs.) was a north-eastern Fr. *cherquier* = F. *chercher* to seek, orig. to go about to find. He refers to the phrase '*cercher le broust*, to hunt after feasts, to play the parasite or smell-feast' (Cotgr.), and to the similar It. '*cercare del pane*, to shift for how to live' (Torriano). In view of the senses of this verb and those of shark *sb.*$^2$ (parasite, one who lives by shifts), the citation of these phrases gives striking plausibility to Skeat's hypothesis, which would also account for the divergent forms *shark, sherk, shirk*. But the sense in which the Fr. verb is assumed to have been adopted is merely contextual in the phrase quoted; further, the importation of the Fr. word in a dialectal form at the end of the 16th c. would be surprising, and if (which is unlikely) the adoption took place early the initial sound would normally be *ch*, not *sh*.]

**1.** *intr.* †**a.** ***to shark on*** or ***upon***: to prey like a shark upon; to victimize, sponge upon, swindle; to oppress by extortion. *Obs.*

*c* **1596** *Sir T. More* II. iv. 106 For other ruffians, as their fancies wrought,..Woold shark on you, and men lyke rauenous fishes Woold feed on on another. **1628** Wither *Brit. Rememb.* IV. 895 Then citizens were sharkt, and prey'd upon. *a* **1652** Brome *New Acad.* II. i. (1658) 28 This woman ..is vertuous And too discreet for him to shark upon. *a* **1668** Davenant *Plots* Wks. (1673) 304 Who sharkt on the People much more then the Crown.

**b.** To depend on or practise fraud or the arts of a 'shark', parasite, or sharper; to live by shifts and stratagems. Often to ***shark for*** (something).

**1608** Middleton *Mad World* v. i, I name it gently to you; I term it neither pilfer, cheat, nor shark. **1610** B. Jonson *Alch.* I. i, 'Slid, proue to day, who shall sharke best. **1615** J. Taylor (Water-P.) *Revenge* Wks. 1630 II. 144/1 Couldst thou find no other way, To Sharke, or Shift, or Cony-catch for mony, But to make me thy Asse, thy Foole, thy Cony? **1616** Capt. Smith *Descr. New Eng.* 33 Who would..by relating newes of others actions, sharke here or there for a dinner or supper? **1633** Hart *Diet of Diseased* III. xxiv. 326 Hee had not a morsell of bread..but what he begged, or else sharked for. **1635** L. Foxe *N.-W. Fox* 107 He see him doe nothing but sharke up and downe. **1641** Trapp *Theol. Theol.* 365 To shift and sharke in every bie-corner for comfort. *c* **1672** Wood *Life* (O.H.S.) I. 167 Others that..had no money were forced to shark and live as opportunity served. *Ibid.* 179 To row hastily from it [the little devil], and leave it to shark for it self. **1692** R. L'Estrange *Fables* ccxli. 210 It was Nature that taught This Boy to Shark. **1709** Hearne *Collect.* 27 Sept. (O.H.S.) II. 269 He sneaks and sharks about at Bathe. **1765** C. Johnston *Chrysal* (1783) IV. 124 It is only slipping a puffer or two of quality at them, enough of whom come sharking to every sale for that purpose only. **1809** W. Irving *Knickerb.* vi. ii. (1820) 359 Those vagabond cosmopolites who shark about the world, as if they had no right or business in it. **1837** Carlyle *Diam. Neckl.* Misc. Ess. 1888 V. 160 Thou must hawk and shark to and fro, from anteroom to anteroom.

**2.** *trans.* **a.** ***to shark up***: to collect hastily (a body of persons, etc.) without regard to selection. Now *arch.*, as an echo of the Shakspere passage.

**1602** Shaks. *Ham.* I. i. 98 Young Fortinbras,..Hath in the skirts of Norway, heere and there, Shark'd vp a List of Landlesse Resolutes. **1827** Gifford *Ford's Wks.*, *'Tis Pity* II. iii. *note*, What a detestable set of characters has Ford here sharked up for the exercise of his fine talents! **1900** *Edin. Rev.* July 209 The hard fisted ruffian first of all sharks up the crew out of hospitals and gambling-dens.

**b.** To steal, pilfer, or obtain by underhand or cheating means. Usually const. *from, out of*, also with adv. *away, out*. Now *arch.*

**1612** T. Adams *Heav. & Earth reconc.* (1613) 6 If to digge they are too lazie,..to cheate want witte, and to liue, meanes, then thrust in for a roome in the Church; and once crope in at the window, make haste to sharke out a liuing. **1650** Milton *Eikon.* i. (ed. 2) 15 Having sharkd them [*sc.* prayers] from the mouth of a Heathen worshipper. **1653** Holcroft *Procopius, Pers. Wars* I. 30 John was irksome to all the world,..sharking all kind of booty. **1665** Wood *Life* (O.H.S.) II. 49 He..pretended to joke and play the rogue; and at length shark away a cloak, coat, or something else, when mass was done. **1896** A. Dobson *18th Cent. Vignettes* Ser. III. viii. 166 His classical quotations were not..sharked out of Burton's 'Anatomy'.

†**c.** To swindle (a person). *Obs. rare*$^{-1}$.

*a* **1650** May *Old Couple* v. (1658) 42 But think not..that I sharke, Or cheat him in it.

**3.** *dial.* (See quot.). Cf. shirk *v.*

**1828–32** Webster, s.v., *To shark out*, to slip out or escape by low artifices (Vulgar). **1844** W. Barnes *Poems Rur. Life* Gloss., *Shark* or *Shurk off*, to sneak off softly from shame or an apprehension of danger.

†**shark**, *v.*$^2$ *Obs. rare.* [Perh. f. shark *sb.*$^1$; less probably, an extended form of share *v.*$^1$, shear *v.* (cf. *lur-k, tal-k*).] *trans.* To cut or tear.

**1611** Cotgr., *Coigniaux*, a kind of small, and bright-greene vermine, which sharke off, and cut in peeces, the tendrels and grapes, of Vines. **1614** Gorges *Lucan* VII. 303 Neither could they [the birds] so sharke and share The flesh, whereby the bones were bare.

**shark**, *v.*$^3$ [f. shark *sb.*$^1$] *intr.* To fish for sharks (*Cent. Dict.* 1891). Only as **'sharking** *vbl. sb.*$^2$ [formed after *fishing*, etc.], shark-fishing; also *attrib.*

**1860** Bartlett *Dict. Amer.* (ed. 3), *Sharking*, fishing for sharks. A favorite sport in the waters of Narragansett Bay. **1881** A. J. Northrup *'Sconset Cottage Life* xi. 100 No summer experience at 'Sconset is complete without..one 'sharking' expedition. **1882** E. K. Godfrey *Island of Nantucket* 329 A visit can be made to the 'sharking grounds'. **1937** J. W. Day *Sporting Adventure* 219 The Isle of Arran, off the Scottish coast, is the centre from which the new sport is being followed. A fishing-smack has been fitted out specially there for parties who wish to go out 'sharking'. **1960** *Sunday Express* 24 July 13/5 Good sharking!

**sharka** (ˈʃɑːkə). Also (*rare*) **sarka**. [f. Bulg. *sharka na slivite* pox of plums.] = ***plum pox*** s.v. plum *sb.* 6 d.

**1961** *Tidsskrift for Planteavl* LXV. Saernummer 138 The sarka virus disease (plum pox) is the most significant virus of fruit trees in Yugoslavia. **1973** *Plant Virol.* 167 Sharka has become one of the very serious problems for the plum production in Europe. **1974** K. M. Smith *Plant Viruses* (ed. 5) ii. 13 In the parenchyma cells of fruit from plum trees infected with the 'Sharka' virus, 'plum-pox', cytoplasmic and intranuclear inclusion bodies have been observed. **1976** [see *plum pox* s.v. plum *sb.* 6 d].

**sharke**, obs. variant of charqui.

**1791** *Ann. Reg., Charac. Peasantry Norway* 75 As a luxury the peasants eat sharke; or thin slices of meat, sprinkled with salt and dried in the wind like hung-beef.

†**'sharker**$^1$. *Obs.* Also 7 **sharkor**. [f. shark *v.*$^1$ + -er$^1$.

Some early examples suggest the possibility of a confusion with Du. *schaker* robber.]

One who 'sharks' or lives by cheating and dishonesty; a cheat, thief, swindler.

**1594** Nashe *Terrors of Nt.* Wks. 1904 I. 379 Next a companie of lusty sailers (euerie one a sharker or a swaggerer at the least). **1603** Knolles *Hist. Turks* (1621) 1127 His baggage..was assailed and taken by the Haiducks and such other sharkers enured to prey. **1616** T. Scot *Philomythie* I. (ed. 2) A 8, And passing Smithfield..The owle-eyd Sharkers spied him. **1631** R. H. *Arraignm. Whole Creature* xiii. §1. 168 To kicke them, as we use to doe with discovered Cheators, and Sharkors, as meere deluders, and Impostors. **1663** *Recr. for Ingen. Head-pieces* A 5, Epigrams..12. Of Shift the Sharker. **1672** *Reliq. Wotton* Life, etc. f 1, A hungry Renegado, a dirty Sharker about the Romish Court.

**sharker**$^2$ (ˈʃɑːkə(r)). [f. shark *sb.*$^1$ or *v.*$^3$ + -er$^1$.] One who fishes for sharks.

**1885** C. F. Holder *Marvels Anim. Life* 182 The sharkers had not been idle.

†**'sharking**, *vbl. sb.*$^1$ *Obs.* [f. shark *v.*$^1$ + -ing$^1$.] The action of shark *v.*$^1$

**1602** Lyly *Entert. at Harefield* Wks. 1902 I. 499 If euer I be brought to answere my sinnes, God forgiue me my sharking, and lay vsurie to my charge. I am a Mariner. **1628** Earle *Microcosm., Poor Man* (Arb.) 101 His best seruices [are] suspected as handsome sharking, and tricks to get money. **1674** Staveley *Rom. Horseleech* vii. 51 All immaginable shifts, sharking, and tricks were used.

**sharking** (ˈʃɑːkɪŋ), *ppl. a.* [f. shark *v.*$^1$ + -ing$^2$.]

**1.** That 'sharks'; †that oppresses by extortion (*obs.*); that cheats, steals, cadges, or sponges.

**1608** Day *Hum. out of Br.* III. i, Lend me this iewell. *Flo.* Iewell? away you sharking companion. **1615** Brathwait *Strappado* 150 That..Harbours the sharking Lawyer for his pence. **1692** Wood *Ath. Oxon.* II. 157 This Hicks..was a sharking and indigent Fellow. **1760** C. Johnston *Chrysal* I. iv. I. 22 Making my fortune a prey to every sharking projector who flattered my vanity with promises of success. **1851** Borrow *Lavengro* lxvii, Some sharking priest who has come over to proselytise and plunder. **1856** Masson *Ess.* iii. 78 Nothing to be seen under the sun but hypocritical priests, sharking attorneys [etc.].

**b.** Of a condition, quality, or manner, etc.

**1613** Jackson *Creed* I. 160 Præsaging that rude and sharking life, whereunto this wilde slippes progenie was ordained. **1629** Maxwell tr. *Herodian* (1635) 373 The procurator..hath received his reward, being slaine by our hands, for his barbarous sharking Cruelty. **1676** South *Serm.* (*1 Cor.* iii. 19) (1692) 433 We are degenerated into a mean, sharking, fallacious, undermining Way of Converse. *a* **1694** Tillotson *Serm.* xxxi. (1742) II. 364 Those miserable and sharking shifts which the foolish virgins were driven to, of begging or borrowing, or buying oil. **1705** Dunton *Life & Errors* (1818) I. vii. 289 They [Parents] should not put their Children on any sharking tricks to supply their wants. **1809** W. Irving *Knickerb.* vi. ii. (1820) 360 His hair..added not a little to his sharking demeanour.

†**2.** Behaving like a shark (the fish). *nonce-use.*

**1613** Purchas *Pilgrimage* IX. xv. (1614) 917 By their Dogges at Land they worried them: and in their Pearle-fishing exposed them to the rauening Sharkes, themselues more dogged and sharking than the bruite creatures.

Hence †**'sharkingly** *adv.*

**1659** Torriano, *Alla-scrócca*, sharkingly, shiftingly. **1665** Wood *Life* (O.H.S.) II. 49 He..looked sharkingly, having a reddish-blew nose and cheeks of the same colour. **1670** R. Coke *Disc. Trade* 67 From hence it is that the Trade of England is managed..sharkingly by the Traders.

**sharkish** (ˈʃɑːkɪʃ), *a. rare.* [f. shark *sb.*$^1$ and $^2$ + -ish.] **a.** Of the nature of a 'shark' (*sb.*$^2$) or cheat. **b.** Of the nature of, resembling, or characteristic of, a shark (*sb.*$^1$).

**1844** *Blackw. Mag.* LV. 682 Our Father..got the better of Satan..and pitched him head-foremost out of heaven.., and his whole sharkish band of retainers after him. **1880** Senior *Trav. & Trout in Antipodes* 70 A strong objection to showing mercy to anything of a sharkish nature.

**sharklet** (ˈʃɑːklɪt). *rare.* [f. shark *sb.*$^1$ + -let.] A young shark.

**1898** in *Daily News* 2 Nov. 6/4 Some sharks are viviparous, bearing fifteen sharklets at once. **1904** F. T. Bullen *Creatures of Sea* x. 105 Next morning..sees her lying quietly upon the waves..surrounded by sixteen sharklets.

**sharkling** (ˈʃɑːklɪŋ). *rare.* [f. shark *sb.*$^1$ + -ling$^1$.] = prec.

**1900** F. T. Bullen *Idylls of Sea* 14 Fourteen sharklings were now restlessly darting in and out of their cosy cave at the far end of her capacious throat.

**'sharkship.** *rare.* [f. shark *sb.*$^1$ and $^2$ + -ship.] (*his*) ***sharkship***: a mock-title for a shark.

**1791** A. Wilson *Poet. Wks.* (1876) II. 60 And 'Rump the petticoats and spots' His Sharkship roared wi' Vigour. **1894** R. H. Savage *Flying Halcyon* ix. 141 We will bring a couple of rifles and shoot his sharkship.

**sharky** (ˈʃɑːkɪ), *a. rare.* Also **sharkey**. [f. shark *sb.*$^1$ + -y.] Abounding in, infested with, or characterized by the presence of sharks.

**1854** Badham *Prose Halieut.* 425 *note*, When they bathed in sharky localities. **1897** Mary Kingsley *W. Africa* 653 The way those Kruboys..hauled their 'Massa' out from among the sharkey foam every time he went into it, on the lifeboat upsetting.

**sharling**, obs. form of shearling *sb.*

**sharm**, obs. form of charm *sb.*$^2$

**1674** Fairfax *Bulk & Selv.* 64 An harshness in these things not being so harmless as the cutting of Cork, whereby, though you saw and wring the ears with the sharm, yet still 'tis but a light business you have to deal with.

**sharm**, *v. Obs.* exc. *dial.* Also 9 **shalm, shawm**. [Cf. charm *v.*$^2$] *intr.* = chirm. Hence **'sharming** *vbl. sb.*

*c* **1485** *Digby Myst., Killing of Child.* 142 Though thei sharme and crye, I care not a myght. **1823** Moor *Suffolk Words* 339 What a sharmin them there children dew keep. *a* **1825** Forby *Voc. E. Anglia* II. 295 *Shalm, Sharm, Shawm*, to scream shrilly and vociferously.

**sharman**, obs. form of SHEARMAN.

**sharn** (ʃɑːn). *dial.* and *Sc.* Forms: 1 scearn, scern, 4 ssarn, scharne, 4-5 sheren, scherne, 5, 7 shearne, 6-7 shearne, 6-9 shorn, 7 sherne, shurn, 8 shern, 9 shearn, scharn, shurne, shairn, sharen, -an, -on, shairin, 6- sharn. [OE. *scearn* neut. corresp. to OFris. *skern* (mod.WFris. *skern*, NFris. *sjaarn, sjuarn*), MLG. *scharn*, ON. *skarn* (Sw., Da. *skarn*):—OTeut. **skarno-m*, a pass. ppl. formation on the root **sker-*: *skar-* to separate (cf. SHARE *sb.*, SHEAR *v.*).

Northern dialects have the form *scarn* (a. ON. *skarn*).]

Dung, esp. dung of cattle.

*c* **825** *Vesp. Ps.* lxxxii. 11 Forwurdun ȝewordne werun swe swe scearn eorðan. *c* **1000** ÆLFRIC *Gram.* xiii. (Z.) 83 *Fimus* scern. *c* **1000** *Sax. Leechd.* II. 92 Gose scearn. **1398** TREVISA *Barth. De P.R.* XIX. cxiv. (1495) 918 The Lapwynge layeth and syteeth on broode on dyrte sheren and vnclene thynges. *a* **1585** MONTGOMERIE *Flyting w. Polwart* 406 They fand the shit all beshitten in his awne shearne. **1601** HOLLAND *Pliny* XVII. x. I. 509 They should be well soked or infused in soft beast shearne or thin dung. *Ibid.* XVII. xiv. 518 Mixed togither with oxe or cow shearn. **1645** *Shetl. Witch Trial* in Hibbert *Descr. Shetl. Isl.* (1822) 595 Quhilk stinked and tasted of sharn a long tyme. **1688** HOLME *Armoury* II. 173/1 Shorn is the Dung of Oxen and Cows. **1728** RAMSAY *Daft Bargain* 26 Frae this tale, confed'rate states may learn To save their cow, and yet no eat her sharn. *a* **1774** D. GRAHAM *Hist. Reb.* x. Writ. 1883 I. 171 A poor palace without a door, A bed of state, all wet with shern. **1811** SIR A. BOSWELL *Poet. Wks.* (1872) 150 Tho' he's coupit i' the shearn 'Troth I ken nought ill about him. **1824** CARLYLE *Early Lett.* (1886) II. 286 Shouting, jostling, cursing in the midst of rain and shairn and braying discord. **1893** CROCKETT *Stickit Minister* 30 But oor minister.. hae garred anither thrawn stick o' a farmer body lift his een abune the nowt an' the shairn.

**b.** *attrib.* and *Comb.* as *sharn-smeared* adj.; **sharn-fly**, a fly used by anglers as bait.

**1787** BEST *Angling* (ed. 2) 115 The **Shorn-Fly*. Comes on about the same time as the Canon-fly... They are generally found in mowing grass. **1867** F. FRANCIS *Angling* vi. (1880) 230 Shorn Fly, Hazel Fly, Marlow,.. by all of which names this little beetle is known. **1550** BALE *Image Both Ch.* (1560) B j b, The execrable cytezens of Gomorra with their *shorne smered captaines wyll sturre about them.

†ˈ**sharnbud.** *Obs.* Forms: 1 scearnbudda, 4 ssarnbodde, scharnebude, 4-5 scherne-bodde, 5 scharnebodde, 7 shorn-bud, 6-7 sharnbud. [OE. *scearnbudda* masc.; see SHARN and BUDDE beetle.] A dung-beetle.

*c* **1000** ÆLFRIC *Gloss.* (Z.) 308 *Scarabeus* scernwibba [*MS. W* scearnbudda]. **1340** *Ayenb.* 61 þet byeþ þe ssarnboddes þet beuleþ þe floures and louieþ þet dong. **1390** GOWER *Conf.* I. 173 Lich to the Scharnebudes kinde. **1398** TREVISA *Barth. De P.R.* XII. iv. (Tollemache MS.), Scherne-boddes beþ gendrid of careynes of horses. *a* **1440** *Pallad. on Husb.* IX. 60 Now sharnebodde encumberith the bee; Pursue on hym that slayn anoon he be. [*c* **1475** *Pict. Voc.* in Wr.-Wülcker 767/28 *Hic stabo*, a scarbude.] **1596** MASCALL *Bk. Cattle* I. 57 A bettle fly, cald of some a shumbarb [*sic* mispr.], which creepeth commonly on horse dung, or other dung. **1681** CHETHAM *Angler's Vade-m.* iv. §25 (1689) 56 A young Beetle, or Sharn-bud, which is found in a Cow-turd. **1688** HOLME *Armoury* II. 213/1 The Sweet Scented Beetle, or Shorn-Bud.

ˈ**sharn-bug.** *Obs.* exc. *dial.* Also shorn-. [f. SHARN + BUG *sb.*] = prec.

**1608** TOPSELL *Serpents* 180 The meat of Frogges.. are greene Hearbes, and Humble-Bees, or shorne-bugs. **1668** CHARLETON *Onomast.* 46 *Pilularius*.. the Dung-Beetle, or Shurn-bugg. **1887** *Kent Gloss.*, Shorn bug, sharn bug, the stag beetle.

†**sharn-penny.** *Obs.* In 2 sor-peni, schar-, schornpenny. [f. SHARN + PENNY.] A payment of a penny yearly for each cow, which was due from the burgesses of Bury St. Edmunds to the Abbey as lord of the manor, in lieu of the profit which the Abbey would have obtained from the dung by observance of the manorial custom of folding the tenant's cattle on the lord's land.

?*c* **1200** *Deed of Abbot Sampson* (*Cart. S. Edm.*, MS. f. 247) in Kennett *Cowel's Interpr.*, Facta est compositio.. quod Præpositus ejusdem villæ dabit singulis annis.. denarios pro faldagio vaccarum ipsius villæ quos nominabant scharpenny. **12..** *Cart. S. Edm.* MS. f. 31, *ibid.*, Burgensibus villæ S. Edmundi data est quitantia cujusdam consuetudinis quæ dicitur *Schorn-penny*.. Solebat enim Cellerarius accipere unum denarium per annum de qualibet vacca hominum villæ pro exitu. **1200** *Chron. Joc. de Brakelonda* (Camden) 73 Data eis alia quietantia cujusdam consuetudinis que dicitur sor-peni, pro iiij solidis.

**sharny** (ˈʃɑːnɪ), *a. dial.* chiefly *Sc.* [f. SHARN + -Y.] Bedaubed with dung. So *sharny-faced* adj.; **sharny-peat** (see quot. 1808).

*a* **1625** F. SEMPILL *Blythsum Bridal* v. in Herd *Sc. Songs* (1776) II. 25 Flea-lugged sharney-fac'd Lawrie. **1737** RAMSAY *Sc. Prov.* (1750) 125 Ye shine like the sunny side of a sharney weght. **1808** JAMIESON, *Sharny-peat*, a cake consisting of cows' dung mixed with coal-dross, dried in the sun, and used by the poor for fuel in some places. **1821** SCOTT *Pirate* v, Nane of your sharney peats, but good aik timber. **1871** W. ALEXANDER *Johnny Gibb* x. 77 Gyaun in owre's bed wi's sharnie beets on. **1896** CROCKETT *Cleg Kelly* xliv. 291 Ye sufferin', shairny blastie o' the byres.

**b.** as *sb.* (see quot. 1825).

**1825-82** JAMIESON, *Sharnie*, a name given to the person who cleans a cow-house. **1897** LD. E. HAMILTON *Outlaws of Marches* xviii. 207 Hout! you auld sharnie... Gae round to the byre and see till the kye.

**sharon**, dial. variant of SHARN.

**sharoot**, obs. form of CHEROOT.

**sharp** (ʃɑːp), *a.* and *sb.*[1] Forms: 1-2 scearp, 2-3 scærp, 3 sc(h)erp, scarp, ssarp, *Orm.* sharrp, 3-4 sarp, 3-6 scharp, 4, 6 sharppe, 4-7 sharpe, 5 sherpe, sarpe, scarpe, 5-6 scharpe, scharp, 6 sharpp, *Sc.* schairp, scherpe, schirpe, 3- sharp. [Com. Teut. (wanting in Gothic): OE. *scearp* corresponds to OFris. *skarp, skerp*, OS. *skarp*, MLG., MDu. *scharp, scherp* (mod.Du. *scherp*), OHG. *scarpf, scarf* (MHG. *scharpf, scharf, scherpfe, scherf(e*, mod.G. *scharf*), ON. *skarp-r* (Sw., Da. *skarp*):—OTeut. **skarpo-*.

The Teut. root **skerp-*: *skarp-*: *skurp-* appears also in OHG. *scurfan*, MHG. *schürfen* to cut open (mod.G. to poke a fire), OE. *scearpe* scarification, *scearpian* to scarify. The Teut. root **skrep-*: *skrap-* (see SCRAPE *v.*) appears to be related; no cognates outside Teut. are known. The OHG. and MHG. *sarpf* (early mod.Du. *sarp*) sharp is prob. unconnected.]

**A.** *adj.*

**1.** Well adapted for cutting or piercing; having a keen edge or point: opposed to *blunt*.

**a.** Having a keen cutting edge. Also said of the edge.

*c* **825** *Vesp. Ps.* li. 4 Swe swe scersæx scearp. *Sic ut novacula acuta.* *c* **1205** LAY. 2310 Mid scearpe mire eaxe. *a* **1225** *Leg. Kath.* 2266 Streche forð þine swire scharp sweord to underfonne. *a* **1400** *Minor Poems fr. Vernon MS.* 758/38 Deþþ draweth his sarpe knif. *c* **1460** *Urbanitatis* 42 in *Babees-bk.*, Fyrste loke.. þat þy knyf be sharpe & kene. **1508** DUNBAR *Tua Mariit Wemen* 105 Quhen schaiffyn is that ald schalk with a scharp rasiour. **1613** SHAKS. *Hen. VIII*, I. i. 110, I know, his Sword Hath a sharpe edge. **1719** DE FOE *Crusoe* I. (Globe) 207 They make their wooden Swords so sharp.. that they will cut off Heads even with them. **1822** SHELLEY *Faust* ii. 399 A single blood-red line, Not broader than the sharp edge of a knife. **1907** J. A. HODGES *Elem. Photogr.* (ed. 6) 106 A good sharp penknife may be used.

*trans.* and *fig.* *c* **1400** MAUNDEV. (1839) xxiii. 254 My woord from hens forthe, is scharp and bytynge as a Swerd. **1567** *Gude & Godlie B.* (S.T.S.) 99 Fra thame that hes thair tungis scharp & ground. **1781** COWPER *Hope* 597 He laughs, whatever weapon truth may draw, And deems her sharp artillery mere straw. **1807-8** W. IRVING *Salmag.* (1824) 268 The sharp edge.. of public curiosity.

**b.** Having a tapering end brought to a fine point so as to be used for piercing. Said also of the point itself.

*c* **825** *Vesp. Ps.* xliv. 6 Strele ðine scearpe, *Sagittae tuae acutae.* *a* **1122** *O.E. Chron.* (Laud MS.) Introd., Da ȝe namon þa Walas & adrifon sumre ea ford ealne mid scearpum pilum greatum innan þam wetere. *c* **1205** LAY. 30752 Swe scarp wes þe pic. *a* **1225** *Ancr. R.* 212 He.. pleieð mid sweordes, & bereð ham bi þe scherpe orde uppen his tunge. *c* **1386** CHAUCER *Prol.* 114 A gay daggere, Harnessed wel, and sharp as point of spere. **1484** CAXTON *Fables of Æsop* v. xv, A busshe full of sharp thornes. **1513** *Life Henry V* (1911) 55 The Kinge had geuen commaundement.. that euerie man shoulde prouide him a stake sharpe at both endes. **1588** SHAKS. *Tit. A.* IV. ii. 91 He dies vpon my Semitars sharpe point. **1688** HOLME *Armoury* III. 324/2 [An instrument] with a sharp point, called a Lancer. **1774** GOLDSM. *Nat. Hist.* (1776) VII. 307 Three very sharp teeth. **1819** SCOTT *Ivanhoe* xli, Deep and sharp rowels. **1887** MORRIS *Odyss.* I. 104 Then she took the mighty spear, headed and sharp with brass.

*transf.* and *fig.* *c* **1550** COVERDALE *Calvin's Treat. Sacram.* C j, And wyth sharper prickes can we not be pricked, than in that he compelleth vs (as it were) to see with oure eies [etc.]. **1605** SHAKS. *Macb.* I. vi. 23 But he rides well, And his great Loue (sharpe as his Spurre) hath holp him. **1820** SHELLEY *Prometh. Unb.* IV. i. 192 As the sharp stars pierce winter's crystal air. **1866** G. MACDONALD *Ann. Q. Neighb.* viii. (1878) 130 Hope was a sharp goad to my resolution.

**c.** As complement, esp. with pa. pples.

*c* **1350** *Ipomadon* 8413 (Kölbing), Wythe sperys, that were sharpe grovnde. **1412-20** LYDG. *Chron. Troy* IV. 1014, I hadde of Hector swiche a mortal wounde, With a quarel sharpe whet & grounde. **1508** DUNBAR *Goldyn Targe* 111 Dredefull arowis grundyn scharp and square.

**d.** In similative phrases, *sharp as a razor, as a needle*, etc. (often *transf.* and *fig.* in senses 3-10).

*a* **1000** *Soul's Address* 120 Ðifer hatte se wyrm, þe þa eaȝlas beoð nædle scearpran. **1611** SHAKS. *Cymb.* I. iii. 19 To looke vpon him, till the diminution Of space, had pointed him sharpe as my Needle. *a* **1732** GAY *New Song of Similes* 51 Sharp as a needle are her words. **1836** *Col. Crockett's Exploits in Texas* i. 20 A fellow.. who in those parts was considered as sharp as a steel trap. **1848** THACKERAY *Van. Fair* lxiii, Epigrams that were as sharp as razors. **1851** MEREDITH *Love in Valley* xv, Sharp as a sickle is the edge of shade and shine. **1858** [see 4j]. **1866** GEO. ELIOT *F. Holt* i. I. 46 Denner.. had a mind as sharp as a needle. **1912** *Dialect Notes* III. 589 They won't fool him; he's a *sharp as tacks*. **1976** *National Observer* (U.S.) 10 Apr. 13/4 Mrs. Owen.. is not only as sharp as a tack but is perhaps the best-looking school principal in Texas or elsewhere.

†**e.** Prickly. *Obs.*

*c* **1000** *Sax. Leechd.* II. 314 Ðenim þæs scearpan þistles moran. **1154** *O.E. Chron.* (Laud MS.) an. 1137, [Hi] diden an scærp iren abuton þa mannes throte. **1297** R. GLOUC. (Rolls) 6794 þe rose springþ of þe brer þat ssarp & kene is. *a* **1300** *Cursor M.* 16616 A crun apon his heued þai sett o scarpe tre þai wroght. *c* **1400** *Brut* ccix, Men sette vppon her Heuedes chapelettes of sharpe netles. **1610** SHAKS. *Temp.* IV. i. 180 Tooth'd briars, sharpe firzes, pricking gosse, & thorns. **1611** BIBLE *Micah* vii. 4 The most vpright is sharper then a thorne hedge.

**f.** Of sand, gravel, etc.: Composed of materials having sharp points; hard, angular, gritty. Now *technical*.

**1618** W. LAWSON *New Orch. & Gard.* xiii. (1623) 46 Sift the earth with coale ashes an inch or two thicknesse, and that is a plague to them [worms], so is sharpe grauell. **1693** MOXON *Mech. Exerc.* (1703) 244 They make use of the sharpest Sand they can get (that being the best) for Morter. **1806** *Gazetteer Scot.* (ed. 2) 69 The soil of the arable part is thin and sharp, but very fertile. **1857** T. MOORE *Handbk. Brit. Ferns* (ed. 3) 26 Add to it an eighth part of clean but coarse sharp sand. **1868** JOYNSON *Metals* 96 Sharp slag, 8 cwts.

†**2.** Rough, rugged. *Obs.*

Chiefly as a rendering of L. *asper*.

*c* **893** ÆLFRED *Orosius* I. i. §7 Swiþe scearpe weȝas & stanihte. **1382** WYCLIF *Acts* xxvii. 29 Thei dredinge lest we schulden falle into scharp places. *c* **1450** CAPGRAVE *Life St. Gilbert* xvi. (1910) 86 Wrecchid mete, scharp cloth, þis wold he þei schuld haue. **1574** HELLOWES *Guevara's Fam. Epist.* (1577) 173 He commaunded to be made in the moste sharp mounteines of Argos a most solemne Oracle. **1596** DALRYMPLE tr. *Leslie's Hist. Scot.* I. 9 The montane Grampius, and vtheris ruch, scharpe and hard hillis.

*fig.* and *absol.* *a* **1536** *Songs, Carols*, etc. (1907) 54 Thow hade þe sharpe, & we the smothe.

**3.** Acute or penetrating in intellect or perception. **a.** Of persons or their faculties: †(*a*) Intellectually acute, keen witted, discerning, sagacious (*obs.*). (*b*) Now in less dignified use: Quick-witted, clever (said esp. of children).

Cf. the dialectal 'not right sharp' = half-witted, imbecile.

*c* **888** ÆLFRED *Boeth.* xxxix. 4 Buton he hæbbe swa scearp andȝit swaðær fyr. *c* **1000** *Christ's Desc. Hell* 76 Eala Gabrihel! hu þu eart gleaw & scearp. *c* **1200** *Vices & Virtues* 23 þat ðu understande mid scarpe witte hwat hie bien. *c* **1375** *Sc. Leg. Saints* xxvii. (*Machor*) 670 For þu ȝongare is þane I, scharpare of wyt & mare mychtty. **1474** CAXTON *Chesse* III. vi. (1883) 131 Wherof cometh forgetenes of his mynde and destruction of alle quyk and sharp reson. *c* **1500** *Lancelot* 2885 In his consell wonder scharp and wys. **1590** SPENSER *F.Q.* II. ix. 49 He had a sharpe foresight, and working wit. *c* **1610** *Women Saints* 161 What was more ingenious and sharp of witt than she. **1697** DAMPIER *Voy.* I. 337 Raja Laut is a very sharp man. **1705** EVELYN *Diary* 4 Jan., Dr. King, a sharp ready man in politics. **1837** CARLYLE *Fr. Rev.* II. v. vii, Sharp Guadet transfixes you with cross-questions. **1870** E. PEACOCK *Ralf Skirl.* II. 147 A very sharp lad.

**b.** Of reasoning or discourse: acute, sagacious. Also, of remarks: pointed, apt, witty.

**1580** *Three Familiar Lett.* in *Spenser's Poet. Wks.* (Oxf. 1912) 616 Master H[arvey]s short, but sharpe, and learned Iudgement of Earthquakes. **1613** SHAKS. *Hen. VIII*, II. i. 14 He.. alleadged Many sharpe reasons to defeat the Law. **1700** T. BROWN *Amusem. Ser. & Com.* 152 Your Gentlemen that speak sharp and witty Things. **1851** WILLMOTT *Pleas. Lit.* xxi. (1857) 126 It was thus that.. the sharp, quick sentence flashed from the lips of Buonarotti. **1968** *Observer* 14 Apr. 24/7 It was a sharp idea of the BBC's Religious Department, letting Malcolm Muggeridge wander round the Holy Land.

**c.** Of sight, hearing, the eyes or ears: Acute, keen. Often in figurative expressions.

*c* **1000** *Sax. Leechd.* II. 30 Sio syn biþ þy scearpre. *c* **1381** CHAUCER *Parl. Foules* 331 The royal egle.. That with his sharpe look perceth the sonne. **1599** SIR J. DAVIES *Nosce Teipsum* Introd. iii, When their Reason's Eye was sharp and clear. **1630** *R. Johnson's Kingd. & Commw.* 8 The grey eye ..is sharpest of sight. **1821** SCOTT *Kenilw.* xxxi, The Queen's sharp eye soon distinguished Raleigh amongst them. **1894** BLACKMORE *Perlycross* 77 My ears are pretty sharp.. and I heard you muttering.

**d.** Hence of observation, an observer: Vigilant. Phrase, *to keep a sharp look-out*.

**1535** COVERDALE *Lam.* iv. 18 They laye so sharpe waite for vs, that we can not go safe vpon the stretes. **1584** R. SCOT *Discov. Witchcr.* XIII. xxiii. 265 The sharpest lookers on will saie it is in your other hand. **1828** P. CUNNINGHAM *N.S. Wales* (ed. 3) II. 333 As the majority of mankind have a stronger appetite for censure than for praise of those above them, he will naturally keep a sharp look-out with that view. **1889** JESSOPP *Coming of Friars* iii. 158 The bishop kept a sharp look-out upon them.

**e.** Keen-witted and alert in practical matters, businesslike, smart; often with unfavourable implication, quick to take unfair advantage of others. (Cf. SHARP PRACTICE.)

**1697** DAMPIER *Voy.* I. 228 They found that the Don had been too sharp for them. **1722** DE FOE *Col. Jack* (1840) 4 He was.. sharp as a street-bred boy must be. **1818** SCOTT *Rob Roy* vii, They got a sharp Newcastle attorney. **1853** R. S. SURTEES *Sponge's Sp. Tour* xlv. 252 Among youths of his own age he was reckoned rather a sharp hand. **1855** DICKENS *Dorrit* I. xxiii, I have seen so much business done on sharp principles that.. I am tired of them. **1859** LEVER *Davenport Dunn* lii, All of them ready to do a sharp thing. **1880** L. STEPHEN *Pope* iv. 94 He.. was accordingly pretty sharp at making a bargain with a publisher.

**f.** In colloq. phr. *you're so sharp you'll cut yourself* and varr.: variously used as an observation, reproof, or warning implying over-cleverness.

[**1903** 'T. COLLINS' *Such is Life* (1944) 278 Gosh! you've been on the turkey; you'll be cutting yourself some of these times.] **1910** 'H. H. RICHARDSON' *Getting of Wisdom* xiv. 142 If you're so sharp, you'll cut yourself! **1930** W. S. MAUGHAM *Cakes & Ale* x. 116 You're so sharp you'll cut yourself if you don't look out. **1968** J. FLEMING *Kill or Cure* xiv. 189 He was as sharp as a bag of monkeys, that sharp he'd cut himself.

**4.** Eager, impetuous, violent. †**a.** Of warriors: Eager for battle. *Obs.*

*c* **1000** *Ags. Hom.* (Assmann) 61/244 Ac ða þa hi ne dydon nane dædbote, þa sende him god to þone scearpan here Romanisce leode. *a* **1272** *Luue Ron* 69 in *O.E. Misc.* 95

Hwer is..Ector wiþ his scharpe meyne. **1471** Caxton *Recuyell* (Sommer) I. 246 That men of armes shold haue no wyues to thende that they myght be more sharpe & fiers in the warre.

†**b.** Of feelings: Keen, ardent. *Obs.*

*c* **1375** *Sc. Leg. Saints* v. (*Johannes*) 501 Rycht sa manis deuocione þat quhile fra contemplacione Is drawyne, sal þe scharpar be. *c* **1400** *Destr. Troy* 1780 Then he shope hym to ship in a sharp haste. **1599** Sandys *Europæ Spec.* (1605) Z 3, Time-servers, who..follow Christ vpon a sharpe devotion, but to his bread, not to his doctrine.

**c.** Of conflict, warfare, an attack: Carried on with vigour, fierce, keen.

**13..** *Cursor M.* 7753 (Gött.) Ful scharp [*Cott.* snaip] it was, þat stour and snell, All fledd þe folk of israell. *c* **1381** Chaucer *Parl. Foules* 2 Thassay so hard, so sharp the conquering. *c* **1425** Wyntoun *Cron.* vii. viii. (Cott.) 1982 Betweyn þis Rollande of Galoway And Kylkpatrik a batel fel Was don, bath sar, scharpe and snel. **1508** Dunbar *Goldyn Targe* 170 Thair scharp assayes mycht do no dures To me. *a* **1586** Sidney *Arcadia* i. (Sommer) 27 Then began the fight to grow most sharpe. **1610** Holland *Camden's Brit.* (1637) 816 The fight continued sharpe and hot on both parts. **1761** Hume *Hist. Eng.* II. xxvii. 131 Huntley..after a sharp conflict, put to flight the left wing of the English. **1845** M. Pattison *Ess.* (1889) I. 4 The contest between good and evil becomes sharp and deadly. **1890** *Spectator* 3 May, Though the discussion will be sharp, it will be short.

**d.** Of a storm, a shower, †waves, etc.: Heavy, violent.

**13..** *Minor Poems fr. Vernon MS.* 716/33 Scharpe wawes þat Schip has sayled. **1377** Langl. *P. Pl.* B. xviii. 409 'After sharpe shoures', quod pees 'moste shene is þe sonne'. *c* **1422** Hoccleve *Learn to Die* 556 Whan deeth, as tempest sharp & violent, With woful trouble hem shal vexe & trauaill. **1585** T. Washington tr. *Nicholay's Voy.* ii. xii. 46 A sharpe showre of rayne, whiche contynued vntyll the morning.

**e.** Of an attack of disease: Acute, violent. †Also = acute *a.* 2.

**1607** Topsell *Four-f. Beasts* 341 Of diseases, some be called long, and some sharpe and short.

**f.** (*a*) Of a hawk: Eager for prey; hungry. (*b*) †Of persons (sometimes with allusion to the hawking sense): Hungry, 'sharp-set' (*obs.*). (*c*) Of the appetite: Keen. Of the stomach: Craving for food.

**1486** *Bk. St. Albans, Hawking* c viij b, Also she may be calde an aspare hawke of sharpenesse or hir corage..she is moost asper and sharpe in all thyngs that belong vnto hir of any other hawkys. **1575** Turberv. *Faulconrie* 133 Then set hir sharpe against an evening and go out to seeke some game. **1577** *St. Aug. Manual* (Longman) 95, I am come with a sharpe stomacke, let me not goe awaye fastyng. **1596** Shaks. *Tam. Shr.* iv. i. 193 My Faulcon now is sharpe, and passing emptie. **1642** Fuller *Holy St.* iii. xxv. 231 Nowa-dayes, does not wealth make them lazy, and poverty keep them painfull? like Hawks they flie best when sharp. **1678** L'Estrange *Seneca's Morals* ii. xxiv. 317 When we have fasted our selves Sharp, and Hungry. **1707** [E. Ward] *Barbacue Feast* 7 Their Stomacks were a little too sharp to admit of time enough to crave a Blessing on their Food, but all fell to. **1771** Goldsm. *Haunch of Venison* 5 Though my stomach was sharp, I could scarce help regretting, To spoil such a delicate picture by eating.

**g.** (*a*) Quick or active in bodily movement. Of movements, esp. a run, gallop, etc., also of action of any kind: Brisk, energetic.

*c* **1440** *Promp. Parv.* 444/1 Scharp, or delyuer, *asper, velox.* **1766** Goldsm. *Vic. W.* xvi, Setting my two little ones to box, to make them sharp, as he called it. **1817** J. Mayer *Sportsman's Direct.* (ed. 2) 23 But endeavour to pull quick the instant you see the gun cover the object; you cannot be too sharp. **1842** W. C. Taylor *Anc. Hist.* xvii. §9 (ed. 3) 557 A sharp gallop. **1869** Boutell *Arms & Armour* i. 3 A rapid succession of little sharp blows. **1889** Gretton *Memory's Harkback* 192 After a sharp run, several hunting men baited their horses at the Three Crowns.

(*b*) *Proverbial phr.* (Used as an injunction to promptitude; for another use see quot. 1788.)

**1706** Vanbrugh *Mistake* iii. i, Are you thereabouts, i'faith? Then sharp's the word. **1788** Grose *Dict. Vulgar T.* (ed. 2) s.v. *Sharp*, Sharp's the word and quick's the motion with him; said of any one very attentive to his own interest, and apt to take all advantages. **1837** T. Hook *Jack Brag* ii, Be alive, my fine fellow!..sharp's the word and quick's the motion, eh? **1875** 'Pathfinder' *Breaking & Training Dogs* 44 'Come into heel, sir!' and sharp is the word.

**h.** Of a stream: Rapid. Now *rare*.

**1655** Walton *Angler* vi. (1661) 132 All Fish that live in clear or sharp streams. **1787** Best *Angling* (ed. 2) 36 From that time they delight to be in sharp streams, and such as are very swift. **1875** *Encycl. Brit.* II. 32/2 (art. *Angling*) A deep eddy off some sharp stream.

**i.** Of the pulse.

**1843** R. J. Graves *Syst. Clin. Med.* xiv. 161 Pulse 120, sharp; slightly dicrotous. **1897** *Allbutt's Syst. Med.* III. 621 The pulse becomes small, sharp, wiry or thready.

**j.** Of winter, wintry weather, frost, wind, air: Cuttingly cold, keen.

*c* **1435** *Chron. London* (Kingsford 1905) 2 This same yere was a Riht Sharpe Wynter. **1560** Daus tr. *Sleidane's Comm.* 197 In the most sharpe time of winter. **1610** Shaks. *Temp.* i. ii. 254 Thou..thinkst it much..To run vpon the sharpe winde of the North. **1722** De Foe *Plague* (1884) 13 With sharp tho' moderate Winds. **1762** Sterne *Let. to Mrs. Sterne* 15 Mar., There has been no snow here, but the weather has been sharp. **1858** Hawthorne *Fr. & It. Jrnls.* (1872) I. 44 Keen and cutting air, sharp as a razor. **1894** Hall Caine *Manxman* v. viii, Though the air was sharp, he had been carrying his cloak over his arm.

**k.** Of vehicular transport: ahead of schedule, early; hence of a time-table, etc.: tight, demanding. *colloq.*

**1942** Berrey & Van den Bark *Amer. Thes. Slang* §768 *Hot, sharp*, ahead of schedule. **1945** *Transit News* (Capital Transit Co., Washington, D.C.) 15 June, When a car or bus is ahead of schedule, it's 'Hot or Sharp', while when late it's 'Dragging'. **1977** *Modern Railways* Dec. 480/2 Certain of the intermediate schedules are quite sharp.

**5.** Severe, strict, harsh. **a.** †Of persons: Severe or harsh in temper or mood (*obs.*). Of temper, etc.: Irritable, irascible.

*c* **1000** *Sax. Leechd.* III. 162 He bið scarp & biter & swiðe wær on his wordum. *c* **1250** *Gen. & Ex.* 3577 So wurð he wroð, o mode sarp, His tables brokun dun he is warp. *c* **1540** tr. *Pol. Verg. Eng. Hist.* (Camden) 147 He was verie sharpe in manners, sterne of nature, exceading crewell. **1638** R. Baker tr. *Balzac's Lett.* (vol. II.) 84 Whether hee bee of these sharpe and soure ones that would take from heaven its starres, and from the earth its flowers. *a* **1668** Lassels *Italy* ii. (1698) 96 The Eccho in the well, which answers you indeed, but like a sharp scold, too quick and short.

**b.** Of persons and their utterances: Cutting in rebuke, invective, or satire; harsh and peremptory in command. Also of looks, tones, etc.: Indicating anger or rebuke.

*a* **1225** *Ancr. R.* 212 Sweord & knif eiðer beoð scherpe & keoruinde wordes. *c* **1386** Chaucer *Wife's Prol.* 14 Lo! which a sharp word for the nones..Iesus..Spak in repreve of the Samaritan. **1471** Caxton *Recuyell* (Sommer) II. 654 Eneas..answered to the kynge wordes sharpe and poynaunt ynowhe. **1568** Grafton *Chron.* II. 984 King Henry wrote to him an aunswere with verie sharpe and grieuous wordes reprouing his vntruth. **1589** Puttenham *Eng. Poesie* i. xxxi. (Arb.) 76 Skelton a sharpe Satirist. **1620** Brent tr. *Sarpi's Counc. Trent* viii. (1629) 728 The Cardinall of Loraine also wrote a sharpe letter to the Pope. *a* **1704** T. Brown *Prol. 1st Sat. Juv.* Wks. 1730 I. 52 Nor sharp Juvenal's stronger verse Perverted into doggrel farce. *a* **1720** Sewel *Hist. Quakers* (1795) I. ii. 139 Yet they were not for using sharp language against such teachers. **1833** Tennyson *May Queen* i. iv, He thought of that sharp look, mother, I gave him yesterday. **1868** Freeman *Norm. Conq.* (1876) II. App. 677 Tostig has sharp words with his brother.

**c.** Of punishment, persecution, laws, etc., also of a judge, lawgiver, etc.: Severe, merciless.

*a* **1340** Hampole *Psalter* ix. 25 To punysch him in sharp & bittire pyne. *c* **1375** *Cursor M.* 9103 (Fairf.) Sa sare and sharpe martiring was neuer sene on siche a king. **1533** Gau *Richt Vay* (1888) 85 Supposz thow may richtuslie be ane scherp iuge apone wsz. **1576** Gascoigne *Philomene* xcvi. Wks. 1910 II. 192 But in hir minde a sharpe revenge, She fully did reserve. **1663** Bp. Patrick *Parab. Pilgr.* xxx. (1687) 365 This sluggish temper must be banished by a rigorous and sharp penance. **1720** Sewel *Hist. Quakers* (1795) I. Pref. 16 Who will ere long fall under a sharper persecution. **1851** Helps *Comp. Solit.* vi. 96 Those we have lived with are the sharpest judges of our conduct.

**d.** *to be sharp upon*: to be hard or severe upon (now only, by way of censure or criticism).

**1561** in *Exch. Rolls Scot.* XIX. 475 The said Thomas not to be scharp upoun the said Alexander for payment of the said soum. **1596** Dalrymple tr. *Leslie's Hist. Scot.* I. 161 He was so scharpe vpon his abuses. **1678** Rymer *Trag. last Age* 32 Polynices seems ill treated, and his Brother is much too sharp upon him. **1713** Addison *Guardian* No. 109 ¶5 One of those Untucker'd Ladies whom you were so sharp upon. **1833** Lytton *Godolphin* iv, You are sharp on me, young Sir.

**e.** Of pain, suffering, grief, etc.: Keen, acute, intense. Of experiences: Intensely painful.

*c* **1000** *Sax. Leechd.* II. 206 þonne biþ þæt sar scearpre þonne þæs welmes sar þe on þære lifre selfre beoð. *a* **1122** *O.E. Chron.* (Laud MS.) an. 1086, & syððan com se scearpa hungor. *c* **1205** Lay. 21944 Heo weoren swiðe iharmede mid scærpen þan hungre. *c* **1250** *Gen. & Ex.* 2989 Gnattes..smale to sen, and sarp on bite. **1340** Hampole *Pr. Consc.* 6563 þe ferthe [payne of helle] es hunger sharpe and strang. *c* **1386** Chaucer *Pars. T.* ¶130 This sorwe..shal been hevy and grevous, and ful sharpe and poinant in herte. *c* **1477** Caxton *Jason* 115 b, A sorowe moche aygre and sharp. **1548–9** (Mar.) *Bk. Com. Prayer, St. Andrew's Day, Collect*, The sharp and painful death of the crosse. **1565** J. Phillips *Patient Grissell* 331 (Malone Soc.) The bitter pangs of death, Whose gripes most sharp semd to close my breath. **1592** Shaks. *Rom. & Jul.* v. i. 41 Sharpe miserie had worne him to the bones. *a* **1627** Sir J. Beaumont *Bosworth F.* 74 The sharp Conclusion of a sad success. **1697** Dryden *Virg. Georg.* iii. 803 The nightly Wolf..now plots not on the Fold; Tam'd with a sharper Pain. **1722** Wollaston *Relig. Nat.* ix. 216 Such injoyments..are followed many times by sharp reflections and bitter penances in the rear. **1843** R. J. Graves *Syst. Clin. Med.* xxvii. 340 Sharp, lancinating pains were felt most frequently in the knee. **1898** Watts-Dunton *Aylwin* xi. iii, A pang at my heart as sharp as though there had been a reasonable hope till now.

†**f.** *transf.* Said of a scourge: = smart *a.* 1.

*a* **1300** *Cursor M.* 5876 And qua ne dos noght yur bidding, Wit scarp scurges yee þam suing. *c* **1450** *Mirk's Festial* 44 To ȝeue hym dyscyplyn apon his bare backe wyth a scharpe ȝerde.

†**g.** Of a mode of life: Austere. *Obs.*

**1340** *Ayenb.* 165 þe oþer del is zuo þet hi makeþ..þet lyf þet zuo moche ssseweþ ssarp an dreduol to chiese. **1577** tr. *Luther's Comm. Galat.* v. 19 (1580) 270 b, The Carthusians or Charterhouse monkes, whose order..is of all other the straitest & sharpest. **1588** Parke tr. *Mendoza's Hist. China* 254 They were certaine religious men who liued in common, a sharpe and asper life. **1611** Shaks. *Cymb.* iii. iii. 31 Hap'ly this life is best, (If quiet life be best) sweeter to you That haue a sharper knowne.

**6. a.** Pungent in taste; also, having strong acid, alkaline, or caustic properties. †Of wine: Sour.

*c* **1000** *Sax. Leechd.* I. 354 Nim gate tord meng wið scearpum ecede. **1377** Langl. *P. Pl.* B. xx. 304 Shrifte shope sharpe salue and made men do penaunce For her mysdedes. *c* **1386** Chaucer *Prol.* 352 Wo was his cook, but if his sauce were Poynaunt and sharp. **1477** Norton *Ord. Alch.* v. in Ashm. (1652) 73 As Sharpe tast, Unctuous, and Sower. **1546** J. Heywood *Prov.* (1867) 46 This medicine thus ministred is sharpe and colde. **1577** B. Googe *Heresbach's Husb.* iv. (1586) 187 b, The like quantitie of manna kneaded togither, and giuen them in sharpe wine. **1584** Veron *Lat. Eng. Dict.*, *Pallacana*, a sharpe onion causing the eies to water. **1617** Moryson *Itin.* i. 252 Pomegranates, Olives, Bread, and sharpe Wine. **1639** [J. Taylor (Water-P.)] *Divers Crabtree Lect.* 167, I can weepe no more, unlesse I get a good sharpe Onion in my handkerchiefe. **1641** Murrel *Cookerie* (ed. 5) 21 To boyle a Chine of Mutton or Veale, in sharp broth. **1661** Boyle *Scept. Chem.* iv. 254 As soon as I found the Lixivium sufficiently sharp upon the tongue, I reserv'd it for use. **1709** Felton *Diss. Classics* (1718) 106 Every body can tell Sweet from Bitter, what is Sharp, or Sour, or Vapid, or Nauseous. **1732** Arbuthnot *Rules of Diet* in *Aliments*, etc. 262 What renders the Blood acrimonious or sharp. **1815** J. Smith *Panorama Sci. & Art* II. 429 Arsenic acid..has a sharp caustic taste. **1853** Soyer *Pantropheon* 71 If you prefer a sharper sauce, mix well some green mint with rue.

**b.** *fig.*

**1604** in Challoner *Missionary Priests* (1803) II. 21 Although I shall have a sharp dinner, yet I trust in Jesus Christ I shall have a most sweet supper. **1668** R. Steele *Husbandm. Calling* vi. (1672) 152 Drudging at the harrow, that's sharp; but sweeping down the wheat, that's sweet. **1886** Mrs. Lynn Linton *Paston Carew* xxxii, That sharp sauce which carries costs and awards damages.

**c.** Of water: (*a*) ? Charged with carbonic acid. †(*b*) Hot, scalding (*rare*$^{-1}$).

**1660** F. Brooke tr. *Le Blanc's Trav.* 18 The water was sharp and hard. *a* **1700** Evelyn *Diary* 21 Sept. 1644, A fountaine of sharp water which they report wholesome against the stone. **1742** *Lond. & Country Brew.* i. (ed. 4) 28 Water lukewarm put over at first with the Bowl, but soon after sharp or boiling Water.

**d.** In various technical collocations, as ***sharp lime***, ? unslaked lime; ***sharp vat*** (Dyeing), a vat containing a considerable excess of lime (Ure *Dict. Arts* 1839, p. 674); ***sharp gas*** (see quot. 1886).

**1772** T. Simpson *Vermin Killer* 15 If you sow sharp lime with the grain. **1886** *Times* 12 Apr. 9/3 Miners had..discovered that some outbursts of gas are what they call 'sharp', and are capable of forming a dangerous mixture with much less warning than is usually given. The experiments of the Commissioners show that the 'sharp' gas of the miners contains a larger proportion of marsh gas.

**7.** As a general term of approbation. orig. *U.S. slang.* **a.** Excellent, fine.

**1940** J. O'Hara *Pal Joey* 97, I sound like everything was sharp. **1963** in C. Booker *Neophiliacs* (1969) viii. 186 WIP'S opens late february london's sharpest nightclub. **1979** *Arizona Daily Star* 5 Aug. (Advt. Section) 20/4 The home is sharp with four bedrooms. *Ibid.* 20/3 Sharp and roomy 4 bdrm split plan with spacious modern kitchen.

**b.** Of clothes: stylish, fashionable, smart, 'snappy'. Hence of the wearer: well-dressed, attractive.

**1944** C. Calloway *Hepsters Dict.*, *Sharp*.., neat, smart, tricky. Ex., 'That hat is sharp as a tack.' **1956** B. Holiday *Lady sings Blues* i. 20, I was always the sharpest kid in the block when I was dressed up. **1962** *Observer* 18 Feb. 23/2 It's more a desire for things you haven't got but feel you've a right to, because other people have them—a sharp suit, good things, neat things, flashy things. **1969** W. Ash *Take-off* iv. 57 When Jacques turned up, he was looking pretty sharp..in the sort of dark suit which..looks expensive. **1977** N. Marsh *Last Ditch* iii. 55 Louis..looked almost embarrassingly smooth in breeches, boots, sharp hacking-jacket and gloves.

**c.** Of a motor vehicle: smart, well-equipped; in good condition. Cf. sharp *sb.*[1] 13.

**1970** *Globe & Mail* (Toronto) 28 Sept. 27/4 (Advt.), Chevrolet convertible, fully equipped, a real sharp car. **1974** *Anderson* (S. Carolina) *Independent* 19 Apr. 10B/6 (Advt.), V-8, automatic power steering, electric seats..one of the sharpest around. **1977** *Drive* Sept.–Oct. 16/1 The Saab interior, however, is drab—not sharp at all.

**8. a.** Of sound: Penetrating, shrill, high-pitched.

**1390** Gower *Conf.* III. 90 Nou scharpe notes and nou softe. **1420–2** Lydg. *Thebes* i. 205 Be vertue only of the werbles sharpe That he made in Mercuries harpe. **1604** E. G[rimstone] *D'Acosta's Hist. Indies* v. xxix. 418 A flute of earth, having a very sharpe sound. **1687** Dryden *Song St. Cecilia's Day* 37 Sharp Violins proclaim Their jealous Pangs, and Desperation. **1774** Goldsm. *Nat. Hist.* (1776) IV. 9 Their voice is not so sharp as the note of some other animals. **1810** Scott *Lady of L.* iii. x, A sharp and shrieking echo gave, Coir-Uriskin, thy goblin cave! **1866** Whittier *Maids of Attitash* 20 The wood-bird's plaintive cry, The locust's sharp reply. **1871** R. Ellis *Catullus* lxiv. 262 A sharp shrill tinkle.

†**b.** Of an accent: = acute *a.* Also of a syllable: Bearing the acute accent. *Obs. rare.*

**1589** [see accent *sb.* 1, 6]. **1611** Cotgr., *Accent aigu*, a sharpe accent marked thus, ´, & much vsed. **1612** Brinsley *Pos. Parts* (1615) 46 b, Euery Nowne Substantiue common, increasing sharpe or long in the Genitiue case, is the feminine Gender.

**c.** *Phonetics.* (*a*) Used to express the acoustic quality of the high-front vowels; (*b*) a designation for unvoiced consonants. *Obs.* in technical use.

(*a*) *c* **1532** Du Wes *Introd. Fr.* in *Palsgr.* 899 Ye shal pronounce..your *i*, as sharpe as can be. **1871** *Public Sch. Lat. Gram.* 9 §12, I [is] the thin sharp palatal.

(*b*) **1841** Latham *Eng. Lang.* i. 104 Concerning the Mutes we may predicate that one half of them is Flat, and the other half Sharp. **1899** *Allbutt's Syst. Med.* VII. 450 The voiceless group containing the sharp consonants.

**9.** *Mus.* **a.** Of a note: Relatively high in pitch. **b.** Of a note, singing, an instrument: Above the regular or true pitch; too high. **c.** *A, C, D* etc. ***sharp***: the sound which is a semitone higher than A, C, D, etc. Also the key or other contrivance in a musical instrument for producing such a note. **d.** Of an interval, †key, or †scale: = MAJOR. **e.** Of a key: Having sharps in the signature. †**f.** ***B sharp***: the early name for the sign ♮, used to counteract a flat.

**1597** MORLEY *Introd. Mus.* 3 The ♭ cliefe which is common to euery part, is made thus ♭ or thus ♮ the one signifying the halfe note and flatt singing: the other signifying the whole note or sharpe singing. **1662** PLAYFORD *Skill Mus.* I. i. (1674) 5, B duralis or B sharp. **1694** W. HOLDER *Harmony* (1731) 151 The Differences of those we call Flat, or Sharp Keys; the Sharp, which take the Greater Intervals within Diapason, as Thirds, Sixths, and Sevenths Major, are more brisk and airy. **1746** TANSUR *New Mus. Gram.* 73 Observe, to Tune all Sharp-Thirds, as sharp as the Ear will admit. **1752** tr. *Rameau's Treat. Mus.* 36 If that Concord was a Major, or a Sharp, as the Third and the Sixth may be. *Ibid.* 107 Chromatick may be practised in sharp Keys, upon the sharp Third to a Governing-note. **1782** MRS. H. COWLEY *Bold Stroke for Husb.* II. iii, Trying a semibreve in G sharp, has made me as flat as double F. **1818** BUSBY *Gram. Mus.* 318 *note*, The Chord of the extreme Sharp Sixth. **1848** RIMBAULT *Pianoforte* 19 The black key which lies Between C and D, is called C-sharp or D-flat. quasi-*adv.* **1880** *Athenæum* 17 Jan. 96/2 There was on Saturday a tendency to sing sharp, which was at times unpleasantly noticeable.

**10.** With reference to form only (without implication of cutting or piercing).

**a.** Tapering to a (relatively) fine point.

**1340** HAMPOLE *Pr. Consc.* 820 Hys nese, at þe poynt, es sharp and smalle. **1561** HOLLYBUSH *Hom. Apoth.* 23 [Tokens of death.] When..the nose waxeth sharpe. **1599** SHAKS. *Hen. V*, II. iii. 16 His Nose was as sharpe as a Pen. **1613** PURCHAS *Pilgrimage* IV. xiii. (1614) 413 Long and sharpe chins. **1712** J. MORTON *Nat. Hist. Northampt.* 106 Turbinated Shells.., some with a broader, others with a narrower and sharper Spire. **1784** COWPER *Task* III. 157 Travel nature up To the sharp peak of her sublimest height. **1821** SCOTT *Kenilw.* xvii, A perpetual blush, which occupied rather the sharp nose than the thin cheek of this personage.

†**b.** Ending in an angle, pointed, peaked. ***sharp moon***: the crescent moon. ***crooked and sharp*** (*Her.*): angular zigzag. *Obs.*

*c* **1420** *Two Cookery Bks.* 38 Take blaunchid Almaundys, & kerf hem long, smal, & scharpe. **1486** *Bk. St. Albans, Her.* d vii, He berith pale crokyt and sharpe of Sable and Syluer. **1530** PALSGR. 266/1 Scharpe ende of the moone, *corne.* **1617** MORYSON *Itin.* I. 142 With a long visage and a little sharpe beard upon the chin. **1686** WOOD *Life* 6 July (O.H.S.) III. 191 Tuesday, between 11 and 1 a sharp or new moone was seene in the skies. **1687** A. LOVELL tr. *Thevenot's Trav.* II. 85 A heap sharp at the top like a Sugar-Loaf.

**c.** Of an angle: †(*a*) Less than a right angle: = ACUTE *a.* (*Obs.*: common in the 16th c.). (*b*) Relatively small or acute. (*c*) Abrupt, not rounded off or blunted; involving sudden change of direction; so ***sharp turn***.

(*a*) *c* **1537** DE BENESE *Meas. Lande* A iiij, The last is a sharpe angle, lyke to one of the angles of a tryangle. **1594** BLUNDEVIL *Exerc.* I. (1597) 57 b, For the one [angle] is right, and the other sharpe. **1688** HOLME *Armoury* III. 376/2 A sharp angle or corner, being less than a square Angle. (*b*) **1589** IVE *Pract. Fortif.* 2 The angles that do happen in it, may be made the flatter or sharper. (*c*) **1825** J. NICHOLSON *Oper. Mech.* 537 Knocking off the sharp angles with the thick end of a tool called a scabling hammer. **1877** MISS A. B. EDWARDS *Up Nile* xx. 574 A sharp turn to the right. **1910** HIRTH in *Encycl. Brit.* VI. 191/1 Lines drawn through the eyes of one of the oldest Chinese hieroglyphics cross each other at a sharp angle.

**d.** Of an ascent or descent, a rise or fall (*lit.* or *fig.*): Abrupt.

**1725** DE FOE *Voy. round World* (1840) 257 We had gone up upon a sharp ascent. **1785** COWPER *Task* I. 326 Hence the declivity is sharp and short, And such the re-ascent. **1877** HUXLEY *Physiogr.* xviii. 313 A very sharp rise leads from the Pacific to the range of the Andes.

**e.** *Naut.* Of the shape of a vessel: Having a narrow and wedge-shaped bottom.

**1709** DAMPIER *Voy.* III. II. 47, I would have..hal'd my Ship ashore..but my Ship being sharp, I did not dare to do it. **1721** PERRY *Daggenh. Breach* 115 Ships, more especially such as are sharp and built for Sailing. **1815** *Falconer's Dict. Marine* (ed. Burney), *Sharp-Bottom*, is synonymous with a sharp floor, and used in contradistinction to a flat floor. **1886** *Encycl. Brit.* XXI. 821/1 This tendency on the part of a sharp ship..by her wedge-shaped form in the fore and after bodies, is great.

**f.** Of features: Emaciated, peaked, thin.

[**1561**, **1599**: see a.] **1833** TENNYSON *Death Old Year* 46 His face is growing sharp and thin. **1865** WHITTIER *Changeling* 29 My face grows sharp with the torment.

†**11.** *Naut.* Of the wind: ? Almost dead ahead. (Cf. SHARP *adv.* 2.) *Obs. rare*$^{-1}$.

**1669** STURMY *Mariner's Mag.* I. ii. 17 The Wind is sharp, hawl forward the main Bowline.

**12. a.** Having the angles or edges not rounded off or flattened; hence, clear or distinct in outline or contour. Often in immaterial sense, of contrasts, distinctions, etc.: Not shaded off, abrupt, strongly marked. *spec.* of the definition of a photographic image; also *transf.* of a lens producing a sharp image.

**1675** A. BROWNE *App. Art of Limning* 8 The Complexions of Virgins and Fair Young Women are not so much different from the other in the Colouring: as in the Sharpness of the Work, those few and sharp Muscles in the Body [etc.]. **1815** J. SMITH *Panorama Sci. & Art* II. 809 The plaster.. hardens in a few minutes, and takes a very sharp impression. **1855** *Orr's Circ. Sci., Inorg. Nat.* 207 The chiselled margins of the pillars and cornices of the latter, are still as sharp as when first carved. **1856** STANLEY *Sinai & Pal.* ii. (1858) 133 Those who..are brought into the sharpest geographical contrast. **1883** J. H. T. ELLERBECK *Amateur's First Handbk.* iv. 22 Screw out the whole until, having taken the cap off the lens, you find the image, upside down, coming up sharp, then take a magnifier and see that it is perfectly sharp. **1895** SAINTSBURY *Corr. Impr.* 38 The very musical poets are too apt to let the sharp and crisp definition of their picture be washed away in floods of sound. **1899** *Allbutt's Syst. Med.* VIII. 921 With regard to the first three forms [of drug eruption] no sharp lines can be drawn. **1921** *Daily Colonist* (Victoria, B.C.) 6 Apr. 5/1 (Advt.), Negatives which are exceptionally clear and 'sharp' make splendid enlargements. **1961** G. MILLERSON *Technique Television Production* iii. 34 Many simple photographic and motion-picture cameras have no focusing mechanism. And yet, at the push of a button, they produce acceptably sharp pictures. **1979** *SLR Camera* Jan. 42/3 Although we did not shoot our optical test target we can say that this is a very sharp lens.

**b.** *Physical Sci.* Of a phenomenon, condition, or state, esp. resonance: having, or occurring over, a narrow range of values of energy; capable of graphical representation by a curve showing a sharp peak; clearly defined.

**1906** G. EICHHORN *Wireless Telegr.* vi. 40 The slighter the damping, the sharper the resonance. **1936** R. S. GLASGOW *Princ. Radio Engin.* ix. 248 The effect of resistance predominates and the tuning is sharpest at the low-frequency end. **1960** DICKE & WITTKE *Introd. Quantum Mech.* xvi. 308 The longer a particle can stay trapped before escaping, the sharper the energy level is. **1971** P. E. HODGSON *Nuclear Reactions & Nuclear Structure* xiv. 414 If the resonance is sharp..the cross-section due to the resonating partial waves greatly exceeds that due to all the other partial waves.

**B.** *sb.*

**1. a.** A sharp weapon; *spec.* a small sword (in 18th cent. part of a civilian's attire); a rapier used for duelling as opposed to a 'blunt' or buttoned weapon. *Obs.* or *arch.*

**13..** *Gaw. & Gr. Knt.* 424 þe scharp of þe schalk schyndered þe bones. *a* **1375** *Joseph Arim.* 513 Mony swouȝninge lay þorw schindringe of scharpe. **1654** GAYTON *Pleas. Notes* 67 Through blunts to sharpes, through surcingles to the garters and Zones of Amazones. **1723** MRS. CENTLIVRE *Beau's Duel* III. i, I think a Gentleman ought to wear a sharp for a terror to the Vulgar, and because 'tis the fashion. **1775** SHERIDAN *Rivals* IV. i, But for your curst sharps and snaps, I never knew any good come of 'em.

†**b.** Phr. ***to fight, play***, etc. ***at the sharp, at sharp(s***: to fight with unbated swords, to fight in earnest, in contradistinction to fencing. ***to go*** or ***come to the sharp***: to come to bloodshed. *Obs.*

**1579–80** NORTH *Plutarch, Romulus* (1595) 26 A combate of fensers (called *Gladiatores*) fighting at the sharpe. **1600** HOLLAND *Livy* IX. xl. 344 As for that other furniture, it was rather a good bootie than armour of proofe; faire and resplendent, before men come to the sharp, but foule and unseemely amongst bloudie wounds. **1615** G. SANDYS *Trav.* 297 One goodly Amphitheater..where Fencers at sharpe succeeded the actors. **1694** JER. COLLIER *Misc., Of Duelling* 37 If Butchers had but the Manners to go to Sharps, Gentlemen would be contented with a Rubber at Cuffs. **1748** SMOLLETT *Rod. Rand.* xii, He would even fight captain Weazel at sharps; but it should be with such sharps as Strap was best acquainted with, namely razors. **1826** SCOTT *Woodst.* xviii, There is daylight enough now for a game at sharps.

**c.** *fig.*

**1596** NASHE *Saffron Walden* F 4 b, Put a whole million of *Iohannes Mabusiusses* of them together, and they shall not handle their matters at sharpe so handsomly as I [*marg.* Painters sharp handling]. **1643** SIR T. BROWNE *Relig. Med.* II. §vii. 156 The Devill that did but buffet Saint Paul, playes mee thinkes at sharpe with me. **1720** SHADWELL *Epsom W.* I, Since they were so much too hard for us at Blunts, we were fools to go to Sharps with them.

†**2. a.** A sharp edge; *spec.* the edge of a sword. *Obs.*

**13..** *Gaw. & Gr. Knt.* 1593 For þe mon merkkez hym wel as þay mette fyrst, Set sadly þe scharp in þe slot euen. *c* **1430** *Pilgr. Lyf Manhode* I. xxvii. (1869) 19 Bi the flatte of the swerd j vnderstonde good and trewe avisement... With the flatte ye shulden vsen to smite whan ye seen youre subiectes erre... And if ye mown so haue hem it is bettere than to smite with the sharpe. **1625** PURCHAS *Pilgrims* IV. 1596 The Captaine commanded that they should be put to the sharpe of the sword.

**b.** *fig.*

**1602** DANIEL *Musophilus* lxxii, They present, with the sharp of envy, strain To wound them with reproaches and despite. **1679** OLDHAM *Sat. Jesuits* Prol. 26 'Tis pointed Satyr, and the sharps of Wit For such a prize are th' only Weapons fit. *a* **1734** NORTH *Examen* I. ii. §96 (1740) 82 At present I haue to do only with the Matter of a Treaty (which the Rebels expected) and not with the Sharps, which to their great Surprise and Confusion fell upon them.

**c.** ***the sharp of the hand***: the edge of the hand.

**1840** R. H. DANA *Bef. Mast* xxx. 108 An old salt, pointing with the sharp of his hand to leeward. **1896** CLARK RUSSELL *Tale of Ten* III. 272 Six men..standing up, staring under the sharp of their hands.

†**3.** The termination of anything which is pointed or which tapers to a point. *Obs. rare.*

**1633** in *Verney Mem.* (1892) I. 108 The cloath sute, the skirts wrought in Pickendell, with two sharps on the hoase. **1638** MAYNE *Lucian* (1664) 248 The decent slendernesse of her fingers, ending in a beautiful sharpe. **1848** *Jrnl. R. Agric. Soc.* IX. II. 553 Those poles where the sharp has not been broken off are likely to break when put up and loaded with bine.

**4.** *Mus.* **a.** A high-pitched note. (*rare.*) **b.** A note raised half a tone above the natural pitch. **c.** In musical notation, the sign ♯ which indicates this raising of the note; †also the sign ♮ (see quot. 1653 and cf. A. 9 f). ***double sharp***: the sign **x** indicating that a note must be raised two semitones. **d.** ***sharps and flats***: see FLAT *sb.*³ 14.

**1576** GASCOIGNE *Grief of Joy* IV. xix. Wks. 1910 II. 551 Whiles I searcht, the semyquaver toyes, The glauncing sharpes, the halfe notes for the nones. **1592** SHAKS. *Rom. & Jul.* III. v. 28 It is the Larke that sings so out of tune, Straining harsh Discords, and vnpleasing Sharpes. **1612** DRAYTON *Poly-olb.* XIII. 55 The throstle with shrill sharps, as purposely he song T' awake the lustlesse sun. **1653** LD. BROUNCKER tr. *Des Cartes' Compend. Mus.* 37 Finally, the voyce ♮, is called a Quadrate, or Sharp, because it is the most Acute, and the opposite to ♭ Soft or Flat. **1746** FRANCIS tr. *Hor., Art of Poetry* 474 In vain his tuneful Hand the Master tries, He asks a Flat, and hears a Sharp arise. **1806** CALLCOTT *Mus. Gram.* v. 58 The Double Sharp is sometimes marked with a single Cross. **1842** BROWNING *Pied Piper* ii, Shrieking and squeaking In fifty different sharps and flats. **1855** TENNYSON *Brook* 40, I chatter over stony ways, In little sharps and trebles.

**e.** *allusively.*

**1599** in Farr *S.P. Eliz.* (1845) II. 382 Let all your sharps Bee feares of faithfull harts; And all your flats The death of your desarts.

†**5.** A shoal in a river-bed. *Obs. rare.*

**1776** G. SEMPLE *Building in Water* 56 Shoals or Sharps in navigable Rivers.

†**6.** Some kind of fish. Cf. SHARPLING. *Obs.*

*a* **1636** WESTCOTE *View Devonsh.* (1845) 39 Fish... Shott. Seal. Sharpe. Sturgeon.

**7.** Each of the two raised ledges forming the sides of the mould upon which sheet-lead is cast. Usually in plural.

**1703** NEVE *City & C. Purchaser* (1736) s.v. *Lead*, This Mold..consists of..Boards..nail'd down fast, and upon these, at a due Distance..the Sharps are fixed... At each end [of the strike] is cut a Notch..; so that when the Strike is us'd, it rides upon the Sharps with those Notches... [Settle the sand] by lifting up one end of the Strike, letting the other rest upon the other Sharp. **1825** J. NICHOLSON *Oper. Mech.* 360.

**8. a.** = SHARPER.

**1797** MRS. M. ROBINSON *Walsingham* IV. 277 The sharps have queered me. **1812** J. H. VAUX *Flash Dict.*, *Sharp*, a gambler, or person, professed in all the arts of play; a cheat, or swindler. **1894** MASKELYNE *Sharps & Flats* ii. 25 The successful sharp..must have unbounded self-confidence if his wiles are to be of any avail.

**b.** *colloq.* An expert, connoisseur, a wise man or one professing to be so.

**1840** *Spirit of Times* 12 Sept. 330/2 This race completely took in the 'sharps', who brought the bay filly as a 'bite' on purpose to beat the chesnut, who won the race. **1865** *Pall Mall Gaz.* 11 Sept. 10/1 The long list of 'sharps' who advertise their 'tips' in the sporting journals. *a* **1872** B. HARTE *Poems, Cicely* 44, I never saw such a star, And I thought of them sharps in the Bible, and I went for it then and thar. **1880** ASA GRAY *Lett.* II. 702 You know I am no picture sharp. **1885** HORNADAY *2 Yrs. in Jungle* i. 5 Unless he is a scientific sharp, the chances are he cannot name a living species..which cannot be found represented there.

**9.** *pl.* The finer particles of the husk and the coarser particles of the flour of wheat and other cereals (separated from the bran and the fine flour in the process of milling); the 'middlings' between bran and flour.

The *Lutterworth Advertiser* of 3 Feb., 1912, reports a case heard at Petty Sessions in which the plaintiff, supported by the County Analyst, maintained that the term was applied to the 'middlings' of wheat only, while the defendant and trade witnesses asserted that 'sharps might contain rice, oats, tapioca; it was a general name for mill offals'.

**1801** *Farmer's Mag.* Apr. 215 These sharps were ground a second time, and boulted a third time, and the produce was 46 lb. of second flour of barley. **1824** [CARR] *Craven Gloss.*, *Sharps*, coarse ground flour with a portion of bran. **1844** H. STEPHENS *Bk. Farm* II. 352 The sharps, or that portion which consists of the heart of the grain, and which is broken and escapes from between the millstones. **1896** A. AUSTIN *England's Darling* II. i, None o' your sharps nor dog-bran, but real Earl's barley-meal.

**10.** *pl.* One of three grades of needles, including those of greatest length and most acutely pointed.

**1834** *Chambers's Edin. Jrnl.* III. 129/2 The traveller, knowing the fondness of the Africans for needles, had brought..a great quantity of *Whitechapel sharps.* **1849** LONGF. *Kavanagh* v, If I do not like the sizes, he offers to exchange them for others, either sharps or betweens. **1862** MORRALL *Needle-making* 38 The Sharps are those usually called 'Sewing needles'. **1892** 'F. ANSTEY' *Voces Pop.* (1907) 241, I want..two packets of egg-eyed sharps.

**11.** = SHARPIE.

**1891** *Century Dict.*, *Sharp.* A kind of boat used by oystermen. Also *sharpie, sharpy.*

**12.** *Diamond-cutting.* **a.** (See quot.)

**1891** *Century Dict.*, *Sharp.* In *diamond-cutting*, the edge of the quadrant when an octahedral diamond is cleft into four parts.

**b.** A sharp piece of diamond used to mark the point of intended cleavage; a pencil-like tool to which such a diamond is attached.

**1903** W. R. CATTELLE *Precious Stones* 67 To cleave, the crystal is fastened to the end of a stick and a V-shaped incision made in the grain with a sharp piece of diamond, called a 'sharp'. **1973** G. JENKINS *Cleft of Stars* iii. 36 Called technically a 'sharp', my diamond pencil looked like an ordinary pencil made of metal.

**13.** *N. Amer. slang.* A second-hand car in excellent condition (see quot.). Cf. sense 7 c of the adj. above.

**1960** WENTWORTH & FLEXNER *Dict. Amer. Slang* 463/2 *Sharp*,..a used but well-cared-for automobile having extra accessories.

**C.** *Comb.*

**1.** In parasynthetic adjs., as ***sharp-angled, -beaked, -bellied, -bladed, -boned, -bottomed, -bowed, -breasted, -clawed,*** † ***-copped, -cornered, -eared, -faced,*** † ***-haired,*** † ***-headed, -keeled, -leaved,*** † ***-nebbed,*** † ***-piled,*** † ***-quilled, -ribbed, -ridged, -scented, -snouted,*** † ***-staked,*** -† ***tailed, -tasted, -tempered, -textured, -thorned, -toed,*** † ***-visaged, -winged.***

**1832** J. Rennie *Butterfl. & Moths* 143 The *Sharp Angled Peacock. **1611** Cotgr. *Belenne*, a certaine little,..small-mouthed, and *sharp-beaked, fish. *a* **1661** Holyday *Juvenal, Sat.* v. (1673) 77 By sharp-beak'd Ships. **1804** Shaw *Gen. Zool.* V. 76 *Sharp-bellied Salmon. **1913** J. London *Let.* 5 Sept. (1966) 397 You must in your dealings be..as straight as the edge of the *sharpest-bladed sword. **1933** W. de la Mare *Fleeting* 119 A homelier music than this bleaching wind's In these sharp-bladed grasses. **1794** T. Dwight *Greenfield Hill* 44 His *sharp-bon'd horse..Tied, many an hour, in yonder tavern-shed. **1976** W. Trevor *Children of Dynmouth* i. 14 Timothy Gedge was..a boy with a sharp-boned face and wide, thin shoulders. **1792** J. Phillips *Hist. Inland Navig.* (1795) 319 Busses, and other unavoidably *sharp-bottomed vessels. **1865** W. Whitman *Drum-Taps* 41 O the beautiful, *sharp bow'd steam-ships. **1946** I. Irving *Royal Navalese* 155 *Sharp-bowed*, the description of a man who has had a very close-cropped hair-cut. **1698** *Phil. Trans.* XX. 262 Deformities.., as Hunch Back'd, Pot Belly'd, *Sharp Breasted. **1838** Mary Howitt *Birds & Fl., House-sparrow* 8 You find..everywhere the *sharp-clawed and the bigger still pressing on the lesser and forlorn! **1639** Horn & Rob. *Gate Lang. Unl.* xxiii. §281 Such as have *sharp-coppid crowns, are very subject to fall mad. **1773** *Gentl. Mag.* XLIII. 597 They are sprinkled with small projecting pebbles, and *sharp-corner'd flints. **1890** 'R. Boldrewood' *Col. Reformer* (1891) 211 There was..no danger of the *sharp-eared blacks' dogs giving tongue in time to warn them. **1889** J. K. Jerome *Idle Thoughts* 32 A timid maiden, driven by a hard and *sharp-faced matron. **1706** J. Stevens *Span. Dict., Peliagudo*, *sharp-hair'd, so they call the Kid, Calf, and Rabbet. **1755** Smollett *Quix.* (1803) IV. ii. iii. xv. 71, I would not have you touch these ragoo'd rabbits, because they are a sharp-haired food [orig. Sp. *manjar peliagudo*]. **1420-2** Lydg. *Thebes* 4223 On..with a quarel *sharpe heded for his sake, Markede hym with a bowe of brake. **1545** Ascham *Toxoph.* i. (Arb.) 73 A sharpe heeded shafte. **1697** Dryden *Virg. Georg.* iii. 126 The Colt, that for a Stallion is design'd,..Sharp headed, Barrel belly'd, broadly back'd. *c* **1600** Horsey *Trav.* (Hakl. Soc.) 186 [The ships are to be] *sharpe-kielled not flatt-bottomed. **1667** Dryden *Ann. Mirab.* clvii, In shipping such as this, the Irish Kern, And untaught Indian, on the Stream did glide: Ere sharp-keel'd Boats to stem the Floud did learn. **1777** Lightfoot *Flora Scot.* I. 306 Red *sharp-leav'd Mint. **1604** Drayton *Owle* 206 The *sharp-nebd Hecco stabbing at his braine. **1615** Chapman *Odyss.* xx. 201 And then the Prince ..Tooke to his hand his *sharp-pil'd Lance. **1593** Shaks. *2 Hen. VI*, iii. i. 363 A *sharpe-quill'd Porpentine. **1844** J. R. Lowell *Poems* 220 Grim Boaz, who, *sharp-ribbed and gaunt, yet feared A thing more wild and starving than himself. **1910** W. de la Mare *Three Mulla-Mulgars* xvii. 224 Thimble lay in a sleep so quiet..it seemed to Nod the heart beneath the sharp-ribbed chest was scarcely stirring. **1872** Coues *Key N. Amer. Birds* 48 The tarsus of the vast majority of land birds is seen..to be *sharp-ridged behind. **1927** E. Sitwell *Rustic Elegies* 81 The *sharp-scented rose-boughs. **1611** Cotgr., *Raye au long bec*, the..*sharp-snowted Ray. **1804** Shaw *Gen. Zool.* V. 91 Sharp-snouted Salmon. **1815** Milman *Fazio* (1821) 23 The broad and *sharp-staked trenches of the law. **1430-40** Lydg. *Bochas* iii. xvi[i.] (1494) m iv, And vnder that falshede Hony shed oute *sharpe tayled lyke a bee. **1697** Dryden *Virg. Georg.* ii. 175 *Sharp tasted Citrons Median Climes produce. **1829** Scott *Anne of G.* xix, Thin Moselle wine, so light and sharp-tasted, that [etc.]. **1837** Carlyle *Fr. Rev.* I. vi. iii, Our *sharp-tempered Arthur has been 'pestered for some days past', by shot. **1864** G. M. Hopkins *Let.* 20 July (1956) 213 *Roughed it*; I believe it means irritating the skin on *sharp-textured blankets. **1967** *Coast to Coast 1965-66* 195 You lie down in the sharp-textured air of the desert night. **1912** W. de la Mare *Listeners* 92 Wreathed shall with incense be Thy *sharp-thorned may. **1965** J. A. Michener *Source* (1966) 76 Sharp-thorned vines clutched at them and sucking mud tried to grasp their ankles. **1804** *European Mag.* XLV. 20/1 *Sharp-toed shoes. *a* **1676** Hale *Prim. Orig. Man.* ii. vii. (1677) 200 The Welsh that inhabit the Mountains [are] commonly *sharp-visaged. **1687** *Lond. Gaz.* No. 2250/4 A tall lean Man with curl'd short Hair, small Eyes, and sharp visag'd. **1634** Sir T. Herbert *Trav.* 18 A small blacke Bird long and *sharp-winged. **1832** J. Rennie *Butterfl. & Moths* 26 The Sharp Winged Hawk.. appears in July.

**2. a.** Special combinations and collocations, as † **sharp artery** [L. *arteria aspera*: see ARTERY 1 and TRACHEA], the wind-pipe; † **sharp bone**, the breast-bone of a bird; **sharp-cone** *Math.* (see quot.); **sharp end** *Naut. slang*, the bows of a ship; also *transf.*, the front line, the centre of activity; esp. in phr. *at the sharp end*; **sharp-eyed** *a.*, keen of sight; *transf.* observant, penetrating; **sharp eyespot**, a fungal disease of cereals similar to eyespot but caused by *Corticium solani* (*Thanetophorus cucumeris*) and characterized by more clearly defined markings; **sharp-fanged** *a.*, having a sharp tooth; *fig.* biting (in speech), caustic, sarcastic; **sharp featured** *a.*, peaked, thin; **sharp-fin**, 'an acanthopterygian fish' (*Cent. Dict.* 1891); **sharp-heeled** *a.*, (of a cock) spurred, wearing spurs; **sharp-iron** *Naut.*, a caulkers' reeming-iron; **sharp land** *north.*, soil containing a large proportion of gritty matter; **sharp-nail**, 'a nail with a forged point, used in some trades' (Knight *Dict. Mech.* 1875); **sharp-nails** *dial.*, in *Jack Sharpnails*, the stickleback; † **sharp-new** *a.*, a term applied to the appearance of the crescent moon; † **sharp-nose**, a mean person; **sharp-shinned** *a.*, slender shanked; *spec.* as the distinctive epithet of a hawk, *Accipiter fuscus*, common in N. America; **sharpshins** *dial.*, (*a*) a fleet-footed person; (*b*) a sharp-witted person; an intelligent child; **sharp-tailed** *a.*, having a tapering tail or pointed tail-feathers; *spec.* in names of birds and animals having this characteristic; **sharp-tongued** *a.*, bitter of speech; **sharp-toothed** *a.*, keen of tooth; *transf.* rending, tearing; **sharp-Tuesday** *dial.*, Shrove Tuesday; **sharp-ware**, edged tools (in quot. attrib.); **sharp-whites** (see quot.).

**1578** Lyte *Dodoens* iv. lxxx. 544 The..*sharpe Arterie or wind pipe. *a* **1756** Eliza Haywood *New Present* (1771) 29 Cut the goose down both sides of the breast, half an inch from the *sharp bone. **1872** Cayley *Math. Papers* (1895) VIII. 102 The special forms of (quadri-)cones; these are: 1° The *sharp-cone, or plane-pair; that is, a pair of two planes, intersecting in a line called the axis, the vertex being in this case an indeterminate point on the axis. **1948** Partridge *Dict. Forces' Slang* 166 **Sharp end, the*, the bows of the ship. .. (Navy.) (2) Hence, *at the sharp end*..at the front, well forward. **1973** D. Francis *Slay-Ride* i. 9 Arne pointed the sharp end back... The dinghy slapped busily through the little waves. **1976** *New Scientist* 28 Oct. 230/2 Within a few months I was appointed financial controller... But I still wasn't at the sharp end. **1980** A. Price *Hour of Donkey* ii. 36 The distant sound of bombing indicated that he was very close to the sharp end of the war. **1670** Dryden *1st Pt. Conq. Granada* ii. i, To *sharp-eyed reason this would seem untrue. **1820** Scott *Monast.* xxxii, He knew it not, he saw it not—but I was sharper-eyed. **1843** *Chamb. Jrnl.* 46/1 The coarse-coated, sharp-eyed, snarling terrier. **1943** *Nature* 7 Aug. 161/1 In the first wheat crop after grass, eyespot is generally absent or rare, but *sharp eyespot is found just as commonly as on old arable land. **1980** F. Hope in E. Gram et al. *Recognition & Control of Pests & Dis. Farm Crops* (ed. 2) 136/1 Sharp Eyespot (*Rhizoctonia cerealis*/*Corticium solani*) is similar in appearance to Eyespot, the main difference being that the lesions are more defined and angular, whilst the dark borders are easily distinguished from the linear areas. **1598** Marston *Sco. Villanie* i. ii. B 8 b, What power will'th desist? Or dares to stop a *sharpe fangd Satyrist? **1643** Trapp *Comm. Gen.* xlvii. 1 How potent that quick-sighted and sharp-fanged malignity is. **1887** Meredith *Ballads & P.* 39 'Twixt her and sharp-fanged nature Honour first did plant the fence. **1824** Miss Mitford *Village* I. 239 Mr. Beck..was a little, insignificant, perking, *sharp-featured man. ? *c* **1660** R. Wilde *Poems* (1870) 51 The skilful judges of the play Brought forth their *sharp-heeled warriors. **1686** Blome *Gentl. Recr.* ii. 277/2 That Cock is said to be sharp Heel'd. **1887** Röhrig *Technol. Wörterbuch* I, *Scharfeisen*,..(Schiffb.) *Sharp iron. **1895** in *Funk's Standard Dict.* **1808** W. H. Marshall *Rev. Northern Rep. Agric.* I. 6 The soil appears to be pretty uniformly of a sandy or gravelly nature, what in Scotland is termed '*sharp land'. **1497** *Naval Acc. Hen. VII* (1896) 293 CC of *Sharpe nayle price of euery C—ij$^{s}$ iiij$^{d}$..D sharpenayle price the hundred ij. **1734** *Builder's Dict.*, s.v. *Nail*, Sharp Nails..are made with sharp Points and flat Shanks. **1787** Grose *Prov. Gloss.*, **Jack-sharp-nails*, a prickle-back, called also in Middlesex, a strickle-back. Derb. **1635** Person *Varieties* i. iii. 10 [The Moon] hath a glimps of light indeed of her selfe, but that is dimme and obscure; as may be seene in the *sharp-new (as we say). **1611** Cotgr., *Visage de rebec*, a sneake-bill, *sharp-nose, chittiface. **1704** *Lond. Gaz.* No. 4034/4 A short Negro Man,..*sharp Shin'd, long Heel'd. **1826** Stephens in *Shaw's Gen. Zool.* XIII. ii. 31 Sharp-shinned Hawk. **1884** *Harper's Mag.* Mar. 621/1 The sharp-shinned is our most abundant hawk. **1883-6** C. S. Burne *Shropshire Folk-Lore* xxxv. 581 '*Sharpshins' is still applied in Shropshire, 1st, to light heels, 2nd, to sharp wits, *e.g.* 'Be off, sharpshins!' = run away, make haste... 'Now then, sharpshins! taking me up as usual!'..said in rebuke to some smart speech, display of cleverness, or captious criticism. **1915** D. H. Lawrence *Rainbow* iii. 76 'What does she say, that I'm a fawce little thing?' the small girl asked afterwards. 'She means you're a sharp-shins.' **1678** Ray *Willughby's Ornith.* 364 The *sharp-tail'd Island Duck of Wormius. **1785** Pennant *Arct. Zool.* II. 306 Sharp-tailed Grous. **1793** *Buffon's Nat. Hist. Birds* VI. 461 The Sharp-tailed Goat-sucker. **1834** J. J. Audubon *Ornith. Biogr.* II. 281 The Sharp-tailed Finch. **1837** Wheelwright tr. *Aristophanes* I. 172 The *sharp-tongu'd rival's whetted teeth. **1875** McLaren *Serm.* Ser. ii. iv. 75 The questions of a sharp-tongued servant-maid. **1604** Hieron *Preachers Plea* To Rdr. A 3 Let the most professed and *sharpe-toothed carper say what he please. **1605** Shaks. *Lear* ii. iv. 137 She hath tied Sharpe-tooth'd vnkindnesse, like a vulture heere. **1855** W. Whitman *Leaves of Grass* 62 Blind loving wrestling touch! Sheathed hooded sharptoothed touch! **1938** M. K. Rawlings *Yearling* xxi. 270 They had found..the weak and the strong brought together to earth, the sharp-toothed and the dull. **1858** *N. & Q.* Ser. ii. V. 209 The curious custom existing in that town [Crewkerne] 'of throwing stones against people's doors on what the boys called "*Sharp Tuesday"'. **1874** Whitcombe *Bygone Days Devon & Cornw.* 187 Shrove Tuesday is known by the boys as 'Sharp Tuesday'. **1688** Holme *Armoury* iii. xiv. (Roxb.) 3/1 The badge of the company of *Sharp-ware men, such as make all sorts of edge tooles. **1820** Accum *Adulterat. Food* 14 *Sharp whites (a term given to flour contaminated with..alum).

**b.** In names of birds, as **sharp-bill** = OXYRHYNCHUS 2; **sharp-tail** *U.S.*, (*a*) the sharp-tailed grouse, *Pediœcetes phasianellus*; (*b*) any bird of the sub-family *Synallaxinæ*.

**1826** Stephens in *Shaw's Gen. Zool.* XIV. i. 199 *Oxyrhynchus*, Sharpbill. **1867** T. R. Jones *Nat. Hist. Birds* 119 Synallaxinæ. The Sharptails.

**c.** In names of plants. (*a*) With reference to the pointed or prickly nature of their foliage, as † **sharp-bind** = *sharp smilax*; **sharp cedar** [= F. *cèdre piquant*], a tree, *Juniperus oxycedrus*; **sharp club-rush**, *Scirpus pungens* (Miss Pratt, *Brit. Grasses* 1859); **sharp-pry-grass** *dial.*, *Carex glauca*; **sharp rush**, *Juncus acutus*; † **sharp smilax**, *Smilax aspera*; **sharp thistle** (see quot.). (*b*) With reference to the acid properties of the plant, as **sharp dock** (see DOCK *sb.*[1] 1 b); † **sharp-herb**, ? = *sharp dock*.

**1548** Turner *Names of Herbes* (E.D.S.) 75 Smilax aspera. .. It maye be called in englishe Pryckewynde or *Sharp-bynde. **1840** Paxton *Bot. Dict.*, *Sharp Cedar. *c* **1050** *Voc.* in Wr.-Wülcker 464/1 *Oxylapatium*, sio *scearpe docce. **1693** Evelyn *De La Quint. Compl. Gard.* II. vi. 193 Sharp Dock, or Dock-Sorrell. **1659** R. Lovell *Herbal* 544 *Sharp-herb *Cocoxihuitl*, *Herba acris*. **1803** Hunter *Georgical Studies* III. 88 (E.D.D.), I pared and burnt some *sharp-pry-grass ings that had not been ploughed in the memory of man. **1597** Gerarde *Herbal* i. xxiii. 31 The *sharpe Rush. **1562** Turner *Herbal* ii. 141 The *sharpe smilax hath leaues lyke vnto wodbinde. **1878** *Cumberld. Gloss.* p. xix, *Cnicus arvensis*, *Sharp thistle.

**3.** Quasi-advb. as complement with ppl. adjs., as † ***sharp-built, -cut,*** † ***-grinded,*** † ***-ground, -looking, -whetted.***

**1755** Magens *Insurances* II. 256 If it be desired to insure a *sharp-built Ship or Vessel [etc.]. **1865** Tylor *Early Hist. Man.* ix. 240 They then seizing the *sharp-cut stake. **1700** Dryden *Pal. & Arc.* iii. 513 The Turney is allow'd but one Career, Of the tough Ash with the *sharp-grinded Spear. *a* **1300** *Cursor M.* 21437 *Scarp grunden knijf in hand he bar. **1592** Shaks. *Rom. & Jul.* iii. iii. 44 Had'st thou..no sharpe ground knife. **1590** —— *Com. Err.* v. i. 240 A needy-hollow-eyed-*sharpe-looking-wretch. **1887** Morris *Odyss.* x. 535 Thou shalt sit with thy sword *sharp-whetted drawn from thy thigh.

**sharp** (ʃɑːp), *sb.*[2] *dial.* [? Corruption of SHAFT *sb.*[2]] A shaft of a cart. Usually *pl.*

**1733** Tull *Horse-Hoeing Husb.* xxiii. 363 Part of the Limbers, which are also called Shafts, Sharps, and Thills. **1844** W. Barnes *Poems Rur. Life* Gloss., *Sharps*, the shafts of a cart or other carriage.

**sharp** (ʃɑːp), *adv.* Forms: 1 scearpe, 4 charpe, 4–6 sharpe, scharpe, 6 *Sc.* scherp, scharp, 6– sharp. [OE. *scearpe*, f. *scearp* SHARP *a.*]

**1. a.** In a sharp manner, = SHARPLY in various senses; †shrilly; †niggardly, stingily. Also, smartly, nattily (after SHARP *a.* 7 b).

*c* **1000** *Ags. Ps.* (Th.) xciii. 9 And him eaʒena ʒesyhð eallum sealde, and he scearpe ne mæʒe ʒesceawian? *c* **1000** *Hexam. St. Basil* viii, Ða fuʒelas..ðe be flæsce lybbað syndon clyferfete and scearpe ʒebilode. *c* **1330** R. Brunne *Chron. Wace* (Rolls) 1010 [*v.r.*] So scharpe þei com. **1377** Langl. *P. Pl.* B. xviii. 39 Al her courte on hym cryde crucifye sharpe. *c* **1384** Chaucer *H. Fame* 774 For whan a pipe is blowen sharpe The aire ys twist with violence. **1500-20** Dunbar *Poems* xxvi. 42 Knyvis that scherp cowd scheir. *c* **1590** Marlowe *Jew of Malta* iv, *Pil.* Farewell Fidler: One letter more to the Iew. *Curt.* Prethe, sweet loue, one more, and write it sharp. **1607** *Lingua* i. vi. B 3, How princely do I speake, how sharpe I threaten. **1635** Markham *Eng. Husbandm.* i. iii. (ed. 2) 11 If Flies and small Gnats bite sharpe and sore. **1763** Foote *Mayor of G.* ii. Wks. 1799 I. 182, I hunted and hunted as sharp as if it had been for one of my own minikens. **1822** Scott *Peveril* vii, What makes you ride so sharp this morning? **1852** M. Arnold *Tristram & Is.* i. 55 Loud howls the wind, sharp patters the rain. **1951** J. H. Smyth *I, Mobster* xiii. 142 He was dressed sharp, like the wise guys on Broadway. **1981** 'D. Shannon' *Murder most Strange* i. 15 He was..dressed real sharp, a gray suit, not just sports clothes.

**b.** Abruptly, suddenly.

**1836** Dickens *Sk. Boz, Scenes* xxv, He turns sharp round to the left, and pauses before another gate. **1859** Lever *Dav. Dunn* xlvi, The odds are, he'd pull me up pretty sharp for doing so without his authority. **1860** Mrs. Carlyle *Lett.* III. 42 The horse..turns sharp round and stands stock still. **1885** *Spectator* 25 July 961/1 The Government..have this week been pulled up sharp.

**c.** In an invitation or appointment: Punctually, precisely (at the hour specified).

**1840** Thackeray *Shabby-genteel Story* iii, They should dine that day at three o'clock sharp. **1844** W. H. Maxwell *Sports & Adv. Scot.* x. (1855) 101 Dinner had been ordered at 'sharp five'. **1893** G. Allen *Scallywag* I. 35 At ten sharp the first arrivals began to greet one another.

**d.** Phrases. *look sharp*: see LOOK *v.* 5. *look sharp after*: see LOOK *v.* 5 and cf. 12 e and f. *look out sharp*: see LOOK *v.* 40 c.

**2.** *Naut.* As near fore and aft as possible, trimmed as near as possible to the wind.

**1669** Sturmy *Mariner's Mag.* i. ii. 17 Thus have you all the Sails trimm'd sharp. **1769** Falconer *Dict. Marine* ii. (1789), *Bouter le Lof*, to trim all sharp; to spring the luff. **1815** *Falconer's Dict. Marine* (ed. Burney) s.v. *Sharp*, *To Brace up Sharp*, is to turn the yards to the most oblique direction possible, so that the ship may lie well up to the wind. **1849** W. S. Mayo *Kaloolah* ii. (1850) 24 In a moment more the frigate braced sharp up. **1899** F. T. Bullen *Log Sea-waif* 215 Away we went, braced sharp up on the starboard tack to the north-westward.

**3.** *Comb.* Qualifying a ppl. adj. used attrib., and commonly hyphened.

**1562** J. Heywood *Prov. & Epigr.* (1867) 184 Where shooteth this sharpe shootyng archer? **1580** Tusser *Husb.* (1878) 38 Sharp cutting spade, for the deuiding of mow. **1590** Spenser *F.Q.* ii. ix. 52 Bent hollow beetle browes, sharpe staring eyes, That mad or foolish seem'd. **1725** Pope *Odyss.* v. 621 Nor here the sun's meridian rays had pow'r, Nor wind sharp-piercing. **1842** Tennyson *Morte D'Arthur* 190 Juts of slippery crag that rang Sharp-smitten with the dint of armed heels. **1876** Green *Hist. Eng. People* I. i. 4 The forger of mighty shields and sharp-biting swords. **1895** Kipling *2nd Jungle Bk.* iii. 30 The sharp-smelling wood-smoke.

**sharp** (ʃɑːp), *v.* Forms: α. 1 scyrpan, 1–2 scerpan, 5 schyrpe, 6 scherp, 6, 9 *dial.* sherp, 9 *dial.* shirp; β. 3–6 scharp, 4–5 scharpe, 4–7 sharpe, 5 shaarp, 6 *Sc.* schairp, 4– sharp. [OE. *scierpan, scęrpan, scyrpan, = OS. (*gi*)*scerpian* (L.G., Du. *scherpen*), MHG. *scherpfen* (mod.G. *schärfen*), Icel. *skerpa*, Sw. *skärpa*, Da. *skærpe* (perh. from LG.):—OTeut. type **skarpjan-*, f. **skarpo-* SHARP *a.* In later Eng. this formation probably blends with a new formation on the adj.]

**1. a.** *trans.* = SHARPEN *v.* 1. Now *dial.* or *arch.*

α. **14..** *Voc.* in Wr.-Wülcker 565/48 *Ascio*, to thwyte or schyrpe. **1503** DUNBAR *Thistle & Rose* 121 Syne crownit scho the Egle King of Fowlis, And as steill dertis scherpit scho his pennis. **1583** *Shuttleworths' Acc.* (Chetham Soc.) 7 Sherpeinge the harrove pennes ij[d]. **1883** *Berks. Gloss.*, Sherp this knife vor I, 'ooll 'e.

β. *a* **1340** HAMPOLE *Psalter, Song of Moses* 60 If .i. had sharpid as leuynynge my swerd. *c* **1375** *Sc. Leg. Saints* ii. (*Paulus*) 839 [He] fand a tre, and it scha[r]pit [L. *exacuit*] With his tetht. *c* **1412** HOCCLEVE *De Reg. Princ.* 1905 Sharpe thi penne, and write on lustily. **1513** DOUGLAS *Æneis* XIII. ii. 127 The cristit foule.. For to resist hir sa scharpand hir byll [etc.]. **1614** GORGES *Lucan* VI. 255 And therewithall he sharpes the rocks. **1626** BRETON *Fantast.* (Grosart) 6/2 Now Cupid begins to nocke his Arrowes and sharpe their heads. **1684** HAN. WOOLLEY *Queen-like Closet* Suppl. 92 Pieces of Wire sharped at one end. **1815** SCOTT *Lord of Isles* V. xxiv, Let Ettrick's archers sharp their darts. **1858–61** RAMSAY *Remin.* iv. (1870) 82 He's sharping his teeth. *a* **1945** E. R. EDDISON *Mezentian Gate* (1972) xxviii. 137 A ready means lay to hand in converse with brother: a merry war, sharping and training up the claws of her wit.

**b.** *transf.* and *fig.*

α. *c* **825** *Vesp. Ps.* cxxxix. 4 Scerptun tungan heara. *c* **1000** *Ags. Ps.* (Spelman) *Ibid.* [*Trin. MS.*], Scyrptun.

β. *a* **1340** HAMPOLE *Psalter* cxxxix. 3 þai sharpid þaire tunges as neddirs. **1411** *26 Pol. Poems* 45 To sharpe my wreche y wole bygynne, Take vengeance for his trespas. *a* **1542** WYATT *Ps.* vi. 51 See how my soul doth freat it to the bones: Inward remorse so sharp'th it like a knife. **1600** FAIRFAX *Tasso* XX. lxii, Disdaine her ire new sharpt and kindled hath.

†**2.** *intr.* = SHARPEN *v.* 7. *Obs.*

α. *a* **1200** *Fragm. Ælfric's Gram.* (1838) 5 Him scerpeþ pe neose him scrinckeþ þa lippen.

β. *c* **1325** *Old Age* ii. in *E.E.P.* (1862) 149 Eld me awarpeþ, þat mi schuldern scharpiþ, and ȝouþe me haþ let. *a* **1400** in *Pol. Rel. & L. Poems* (1903) 253, & his nese shal sharpen. *a* **1536** *Proverbs* in *Songs, Carols*, etc. (1907) 128 Sone hit sharpith, that thorn will be.

†**3.** *trans.* = SHARPEN *v.* 2. *Obs.*

α. *a* **1100** *Gerefa* in *Anglia* IX. 260 Symle he sceal his hyrmen scyrpan mid manunge to hlafordes neode. **1527** ANDREW *Brunswyke's Distyll. Waters* G j, The same water put in the iyen in the mornyng.. sherpeth the syght.

β. *c* **1380** WYCLIF *Sel. Wks.* I. 52 But Crist sharpide þes mennis bileve. *c* **1400** tr. *Secreta Secret., Gov. Lordsh.* xxxvii. 69 It.. makys þe sight clerer, shaarpys þe wittes. **1590** SPENSER *F.Q., Dedic. Sonn., To Ladies in Crt.* 7 Much more me needs.. To sharpe my sence with sundry beauties vew. **1633** B. JONSON *King's Entert. Welbeck* (1640) 274 Whom the Whetstone sharpes to eat, And cry Milstones are good meat.

†**4.** = SHARPEN *v.* 3. *Obs.*

*a* **1340** HAMPOLE *Psalter* ix. 25 þe synful sharpid [L. *exacerbavit*] god. **1387** TREVISA *Higden* (Rolls) IV. 121 [He] schewed hem þe juse of grapes.. forto scharpe hem to þe bataille [L. *ad acuendum eos in prælium*]. *c* **1440** *Promp. Parv.* 444/1 Scharpyn, or steryn to hastynesse, *exaspero*.

**5.** To make sharp (in various transferred senses of the adj.). †**a.** = SHARPEN *v.* 2 b.

*a* **1425** tr. *Arderne's Treat. Fistula*, etc. 58 When blode is aduste it is scharped. **1564–78** BULLEIN *Dial. agst. Pest.* (1888) 39 Let euery one of them.. vse the regiment of diet to driyng, sharped with vinegar or tart thynges.

†**b.** To roughen (the sea). *Obs. rare*[−1].

**1513** DOUGLAS *Æneis* III. v. 2 Frosty wynter scharpit [L. *asperat*] the watter cleir With cald blastis.

**c.** *Mus.* = SHARPEN *v.* 4. Occas. used *intr.* with personal subject.

**1662** PLAYFORD *Introd. Skill Mus.* I. vi. 21 Mi and Fa do serve for the flatting or sharping the ordinary Notes in the Scale. **1746** TANSUR *New Mus. Gram.* 93 Where E is sharp'd and becomes Mi. **1895** [see FLAT *v.*[2] 7].

†**d.** = ROUGH *v.*[1] 1 d, SHARPEN *v.* 5. *Obs.*

**1841** FR. A. KEMBLE *Rec. Later Life* (1882) II. 145 Finding the roads dangerously slippery for our horses, which were not sharped,.. we dismounted.

†**e.** To brighten (a colour). *Obs.*

**1398** TREVISA *Barth. De P.R.* XIX. xvii. (1495) 874 In olde tyme men vsyd to sharpe [L. *acuere*] this colour Minius wyth the blode of a certayne worme.

**f.** *intr.* for *refl.* To dress *up*, to dress smartly. Cf. SHARP *a.* 7 b. *U.S. colloq.*

**1957** J. KEROUAC *On Road* (1958) I. ix. 53 Tim, Rawlins, and I decided to sharp up for the big night.

†**6.** *to sharp up*: to admonish sharply. *Obs.*

**1647** TRAPP *Comm. Matt.* xxiii. 33.539 See how our Saviour sharps up these Heresiarchs, that, if possible, they might be made sound in the faith.

†**7.** *intr.* To play the sharper. *Obs.*

**1709** MRS. MANLEY *Secret Mem.* (1720) II. 255 To sharp, deceive, and run into Debt. **1785** COWPER *Task* III. 86 Then he that sharp'd, And pocketted a prize by fraud obtain'd, Was mark'd and shunn'd as odious.

**8.** *trans.* **a.** To cheat, swindle, trick (a person).

*a* **1700** B. E. *Dict. Cant. Crew* s.v. *Clear*, The Fellow is.. Drunk, let's Sharp him. **1720** *Lett. Lond. Jrnl.* (1721) 39 Throngs of Setters and Cullies, sharping and cheating one another. **1882** *Daily News* 19 Jan., A gang of men (probably the same as those who would have sharped me) try the same trick.

**b.** To obtain by swindling, to steal.

**1706** E. WARD *Wooden World Diss.* (1708) 13 Should a half starv'd Sailor sharp a Pair of old Shoes from him. **1716** M. DAVIES *Athen. Brit.* III. *Suppl. Diss. Drama* 31 Those must be only Popish Amusements, for to sharp a little Popish Subsistance-Money.

**Sharpa**, obs. var. SHERPA.

**sharpe**, obs. form of SHRAPE.

**sharped** (ʃɑːpt), *ppl. a.* [f. SHARP *v.* + -ED[1].]

**1.** = SHARPENED *ppl. a.* 1. Now *rare* or *Obs.*

**1340–70** *Alex. & Dind.* 294 Wiþ no scharpede schar to schape þe forwes. **1557** in *Tottel's Misc.* (Arb.) 145 He [Cupid] shot his sharped fiery dart. **1591** SPENSER *Ruines of Rome* 16 Her haughtie walls.. And sharped steeples high shot vp in ayre.

**2.** *Mus.* Of a note: Raised in pitch, *spec.* raised a semitone by a sharp.

**1746** TANSUR *New Mus. Gram.* 23 All descending sharp'd Notes.

**sharp-edged**, *a.* Having a sharp edge or sharp edges.

*c* **1000** ÆLFRIC *Hom.* (Th.) I. 92 God.. het þæt he name scearpecgedne flint. **1548** COOPER *Elyot's Dict.*, *Acutus*, sharpe edged or pointed. **1582** STANYHURST *Æneis* II. (Arb.) 54 They brandish weapons sharp edgde. **1647** HEXHAM I, A sharpe edged sword. **1768** BOSWELL *Corsica* (ed. 2) 282 A sharp-edged crook. **1854** RONALDS & RICHARDSON *Chem. Technol.* (ed. 2) I. 55 A conchoidal, sharp-edged fracture. **1896** H. WOODWARD *Guide Fossil Reptiles Brit. Mus.* 4 Jaws, which were a yard in length, sharp-edged and pointed.

*fig.* **1847** HELPS *Friends in C.* I. viii. 151 There are other precise angular persons, and these sharp-edged persons wound each other terribly. **1870** DICKENS *E. Drood* viii, Sharp-edged words have sharp edges to wound me.

**sharpen** (ʃɑːp(ə)n), *v.* Also 5 scharpen. [f. SHARP *a.* + -EN[5].]

**1. a.** *trans.* To put a sharp edge or point upon, to whet; to furnish (a weapon, implement, etc.) with a cutting edge or fine point.

**1530** PALSGR. 701/1, I sharpen a knyfe or an edge toole to cutte the better, *je aguyse*. **1535** COVERDALE *Eccles.* x. 10 When an yron is blont, and y[e] poynt not sharpened, it must be whett againe. **1697** DRYDEN *Virg. Georg.* I. 357 Let him .. sharpen Stakes, or head the Forks. **1719** DE FOE *Crusoe* I. (Globe) 59 The biggest End being.. sharpen'd on the Top. **1880** G. W. CABLE *Grandissimes* liv. (1898) 352 He sat and sharpened a small pen knife. **1890** S. R. GARDINER *Student's Hist. Eng.* (1896) I. 1 Flints sharpened by chipping.

**b.** *transf.* and *fig.*

**1606** SHAKS. *Tr. & Cr.* V. ii. 75 *Cres.* I prythee Diomed visite me no more. *Ther.* Now she sharpens; well said Whetstone. **1709** STEELE *Tatler* No. 44 ¶3 He was only sharpening Darts for his own Destruction. **1817** SHELLEY *Rev. Islam* IV. xxxi. 8 When the cold moon sharpens her silver horn Under the sea. **1876** J. PARKER *Paraclete* I. xi. 169 When life is sharpened into a crisis, and the whole world seems to have become our assailant.

**c.** In fig. phr. ***to sharpen one's pencil***: to prepare to work; to revise or improve one's work.

**1957** *Times Lit. Suppl.* 15 Nov. 689/3 This is where the post-historic Ph.D. men will sharpen their pencils. **1965** *Daily Progress* (Charlottesville, Va.) 17 June 33/5 He suggested that Stahr and Hovde go home and suggest to local power officials that they 'sharpen their pencils' and figure out lower rates. **1969** *Listener* 2 Jan. 10/2 We.. published our findings. Radio telescopes all over the world were trained on the sources, while theoreticians sharpened their pencils.

**2.** To make sharp or sharper (in various transferred and figurative senses of the adj.). Now freq. const. *up*. **a.** To render more acute (a person's wits, sight, appetite, zeal, etc.); to intensify (hostile feeling).

*c* **1450** *Mirk's Festial* 173 þen forto scharpen ȝoure beleue þe better, I telle ȝou þis example. *c* **1570** W. WAGER *The Longer thou livest* 1417 (Brandl) You shall neuer want a witty page, To sharpen your intelligence. **1606** SHAKS. *Ant. & Cl.* II. i. 25 Epicurean Cookes, Sharpen with cloylesse sawce his Appetite. **1779** *Mirror* No. 59 The military genius is sharpened by exercise. **1818** SCOTT *Br. Lamm.* xix, My hearing.. has been sharpened by my blindness. **1835** LYTTON *Rienzi* X. vi, He had never confided but he had been betrayed; he had never forgiven but to sharpen enmity. **1870** EMERSON *Soc. & Solit.*, *Art* Wks. (Bohn) III. 21 A study of admirable works of art sharpens our perceptions of the beauty of Nature. **1947** 'L. STARR' *Corrie* xii. 161 Just a little cocktail.. to sharpen up our appetites for lunch. **1953** S. PLATH *Let.* 15 May (1978) I. 114 Sharpening up writing again, once it's rusty, is very painful.

**b.** To give an acid flavour or quality to, to make (a liquid) sour or bitter.

**1675** E. W[ILSON] *Spadacrene Dunelm.* 55 Spring-water, sharpened with Spirit of Sulphur. **1747** WESLEY *Prim. Physick* (1762) 90 Drink very largely of Water sharpened with Spirit of Vitriol. **1887** *Encycl. Brit.* XXII. 203/1 s.v. *Soap*, Potash lyes are, however, principally sharpened or causticized by the soap boiler himself from potash carbonate.

**c.** To increase the severity of (a law, a punishment, etc.). Cf. G. *schärfen*.

**1709** STRYPE *Ann. Ref.* I. xxvi. 278 A Law was past for sharpening Laws against Papists. **1769** BLACKSTONE *Comm.* IV. viii. 111 It was found necessary to sharpen and strengthen these laws. **1888** *Times* 6 Sept. 3/2 [Referring to Austria.] He will be lucky if he escapes with six months, 'sharpened' by one fast day a month. **1962** *Listener* 2 Aug. 160/1 French anti-cartel policy was sharpened up by the act of 1958.

†**d.** To embitter, exacerbate (persons, their temper). *Obs.*

*a* **1715** BURNET *Own Time* III. (1724) I. 381 He was much sharpened against Popery. **1768** STERNE *Sent. Journ.* (1778) I. 5 (Calais) What is there in this world's goods which should sharpen our spirits. **1792** BURKE *Corr.* (1844) IV. 35 Their enemies will be more and more sharpened against them by frequent conflicts.

**e.** To render more painful, to aggravate (pain or suffering).

**1768** STERNE *Sent. Journ.* (1778) I. 196 (Dwarf) An injury sharpened by an insult. **1862** STANLEY *Jew. Ch.* (1877) I. xvi. 305 Her grief is.. sharpened by the peculiar horror of the Hebrew women at a childless death.

**f.** To make (the features) sharp or thin.

**1835** W. IRVING *Tour on Prairies* iii. 22 His features were .. not unlike those of Napoleon, but sharpened up, with high Indian cheek-bones. **1849** T. WOOLNER *My Beautiful Lady, My Lady in Death* xvi, Her beauty by degrees Sank, sharpened from disease.

**g.** *refl.* To improve one's appearance; to smarten oneself up.

**1952** S. SELVON *Brighter Sun* ii. 24 Since the Americans came the girls sharpened themselves up and wouldn't be had for less than five Yankee dollars.

†**3.** To render eager for attack; to goad *on*. *Obs.*

**1483** *Cath. Angl.* 333/2 To scharpyn, *jnstigare*. **1587** HUGHES, etc. *Misfort. Arthur* III. Chorus 27 The name of peace doth edge our mindes, And sharpeneth on our furie till we fight. **1733** NEAL *Hist. Purit.* II. 555 Whereby.. the spirits of people [were] sharpened for war.

**4.** *Mus.* To raise the pitch of a note sounded upon a musical instrument. In quot. 1824 *absol.*

**1824** *Mirror* III. 105/2 Flattening and sharpening and rosining bows. **1881** *Nature* 18 Aug. 358/2 If two stopped organ-pipes are brought to unison, and then one of them is sharpened by gradually pushing in its stopper [etc.].

**5.** = ROUGH *v.*[1] 1 d, SHARP *v.* 5 d.

**1897** *Leeds Mercury Suppl.* 15 May (E.D.D.), Hes ta getten t'horse sharpened this morning?

**6.** *Naut.* To brace sharp up.

**1841** R. H. DANA *Seaman's Man.* ix. 47 When the tack is well down, sharpen the yard up again by the brace.

†**7.** *intr.* **a.** To become sharp, to taper to a point; to grow thin. *Obs.*

**1611** COTGR., *Cone*, a Cone.. or any figure, that is broad, and round below, and sharpens toward the top. **1693** DRYDEN *Ovid's Met.*, *Acis, Pol. & Gal.* 48 A Promontory, sharp'ning by degrees, Ends in a Wedge. **1804** W. TAYLOR in Robberds *Mem.* I. 504 The features of the dead are said to be clung when they sharpen and lose their roundness of contour. **1851** D. JERROLD *St. Giles* ix. 85 His face.. sharpened like the face of a sick man.

**b.** To light *up* with a gleam of intelligence.

**1828** LYTTON *Pelham* II. xii, The blunt blue eyes of Mr. Gordon sharpened up in an instant.

**c.** Of faculties: To grow more acute.

**1811** tr. *Zimmerman's Solitude* (ed. 8) I. ii. 55 The faculties sharpen; the mind becomes more clear [etc.].

**d.** To grow more shrill.

**1868** GEO. ELIOT *Sp. Gypsy* IV. 327 A shout of promise, sharpening into cries That seemed to plead despairingly with Death.

**sharpened** (ʃɑːp(ə)nd), *ppl. a.* [f. SHARPEN *v.* + -ED[1].] In senses of the verb.

**1594** WILLOBIE *Avisa* xlv. (Grosart) 94 Your wanny face & sharpened nose Shew plaine, your mind some thing mislikes. **1604** DRAYTON *Moyses* II. 36 The sharpned Reed That with the fluxure of the waue is fed. **1707** MORTIMER *Husb.* (1721) I. 195 By driving a sharpened Stick into every such Hill. **1730** *Treat. Harmony* 19 That would have no Sharpned or Flatned Notes. **1805–6** CARY *Dante, Inf.* xxv. 121 He, on the earth who lay, meanwhile extends His sharpen'd visage. **1819** SHELLEY *Mask of Anarchy* lxxiv, Be your strong and simple words Keen to wound as sharpened swords. **1857** BUCKLE *Civiliz.* I. xiii. 733 With.. sharpened intellect, he returned to the great field of history. **1905** H. D. ROLLESTON *Dis. Liver* 229 The face gets sharpened.

**sharpener** ('ʃɑːp(ə)nə(r)). [f. SHARPEN *v.* + -ER[1].] One who or something which sharpens.

**1640** BP. REYNOLDS *Passions* viii. 58 They are the sharpners and.. the Whetstones of Vertue. **1807** W. IRVING *Salmag.* xvi. (1824) 289 That marvellous sharpener of the wits, a salt-water voyage. **1838** T. MITCHELL *Clouds of Aristoph.* 193 The water-bearers throw the guilt upon the sharpener of the axe and knife. **1867** MILL *Inaug. Addr. St. Andrews* 66 There never was any sharpener of the intellectual faculties superior to the Berkeleian controversy. **1876** GOODE *Classif. Collect. Anim. Resources U.S.* 27 Arrow-head sharpeners.

**sharpening** ('ʃɑːp(ə)nɪŋ), *vbl. sb.* [-ING[1].] The action of making sharp.

**1580** HOLLYBAND *Treas. Fr. Tong*, *Aguisement*, sharpening. **1680** MOXON *Mech. Exerc.* xi. 195 The Hooks when they want sharpening cannot be ground as the Gouges and Chissels are. **1842** LOUDON *Suburban Hort.* 235 The asperities produced in the edge of the knife by sharpening. **1893** W. H. HUDSON *Idle Days in Patagonia* xi. 184 The sharpening of its sense of smell has dimmed the armadillo's eyes. **1900** ELINOR GLYN *Visits Elizabeth* 72 It is a continual sharpening of wits.

*Comb.* **1843** *Penny Cycl.* XXV. 426/1 Some of these sharpening tools are rubbed upon the oil-stone. **1896** BADEN-POWELL *Matabele Campaign* xv, Sharpening-stones lying about.

**sharpening** ('ʃɑːp(ə)nɪŋ), *ppl. a.* [-ING[2].] That sharpens; becoming or making sharp.

**1834** WORDSW. *Redbreast* 1 Driven in by Autumn's sharpening air. **1876** MEREDITH *Beauch. Career* xxxv, Two or three hours of the sharpening air would screw his human nature to the pitch.

**sharper**[1] ('ʃɑːpə(r)). [f. SHARP *v.* + -ER[1].]

**1.** One who or something which 'sharps' or sharpens.

**1567** MAPLET *Gr. Forest* 42 The Latine worde [sc. *fæniculum*: cf. It. *finocchio*] signifieth, that it should be sharper of the eiesight. **1611** FLORIO, *Aguzzatore*, a grinder ..of any weapon. Also a sharper. *a* **1891** *Elect. Rev.* (Amer.) XV. vii. 10 (Cent.) Upright drills, milling machines, sharpers, etc.

**2.** A cheat, swindler, rogue; one who lives by his wits and by taking advantage of the simplicity of others; esp. a fraudulent gamester. Cf. SHARK *sb.*[2]

**1681** LUTTRELL *Brief Rel.* (1857) I. 99 Many of them sharpers about town. **1709** PRIOR *Cupid & Ganymede* 45 A Sharper, that with Box and Dice Draws in young Deities to Vice. **1742** LADY M. W. MONTAGU *Let. to Montagu* 22 Mar. (1893) II. 102, I hear he [*sc.* her son] avoided coming near the sharpers, and is grown a good manager of his money. **1819** SCOTT *Let.* in *Lockhart* (1837) IV. ix. 301 The resort of black-legs and sharpers. **1894** MASKELYNE *Sharps & Flats* iv. 72 [He] falls an easy prey to the sharper.

†**3.** (See quot.) *Obs.*

**1768** PENNANT *Brit. Zool.* II. 334 A bird, acquainted with the nets, is by the birdcatchers termed a sharper.

**4.** *attrib.* and *Comb.* (sense 2).

**1822** BYRON *Vis. Judgem.* xciv, With a hook nose and a hawk's eye, which gave A smart and sharper-looking sort of grace. **1842** MRS. GORE *Fascination* 22 Where is your master, pray?—Your sharper marquis.

'**sharper**[2]. *U.S.* [f. SHARP *a.* + -ER[1].] An oyster having the end of the shell unusually sharp.

**1881** INGERSOLL *Oyster-Industr.* (Hist. Fish. Industr. U.S.) 248 *Sharpers*, elongated, protruding, sharp-ended oysters, dangerous to the feet in moving about the reefs (Gulf coast). **1887** GOODE, etc. *Fish. Industr. U.S.* v. II. 548.

**Sharpey's fibre** ('ʃɑːpɪ). *Anat.* [Named after William *Sharpey* (1802–80), Scottish anatomist, who described such fibres in 1856 (J. Quain *Anat.* (ed. 6) I. p. cxx).] A fibre of connective tissue passing from the periosteum through the lamellæ of a bone or tooth.

[**1878** *Q. Jrnl. Microsc. Sci.* XVIII. 132 The lamellæ when stripped off from a bone that has been softened in acid but subsequently freed from all traces of the acid by long steeping in water or spirit exhibit under the microscope the appearance of intercrossing fibres (the reticulating fibres of Sharpey).] **1890** G. M. GOULD *New Med. Dict.* 400/2 *Sharpey's fibers*, calcified fibers of white, fibrous tissue bolting together the peripheric lamellæ of bone. **1896** A. CLARKSON *Text-bk. Histol.* vi. 151 In addition to fibres forming the lamellæ themselves, there are others—perforating, or Sharpey's fibres—to be found in bone. **1946** *Nature* 24 Aug. 269/1 Superficially placed osteocytes with their processes, and Sharpey's fibres, stand out black against the colourless matrix. **1962** BLAKE & TROTT *Periodontology* ii. 12 The parts of the fibres which lie embedded within cementum or bone are known as Sharpey's fibres.

**sharpie** ('ʃɑːpɪ). [app. f. SHARP *a.*] **1.** = SHARP *sb.*[1] 11. (See quots.) *U.S.*

**1860** *Diary* 10 Dec. in *Outing* (1913) Mar. 688/2, I took some of the skiffs and sharpies behind the Emma S...and we went down to Whig inlet. **1864** WEBSTER, *Sharpie*, a long, sharp, flat-bottomed sailboat. (*Local U.S.*) **1876** GOODE *Classif. Collect. Anim. Resources U.S.* 43 Dorys, sharpies, and dingies. **1882** H. HALL *Ref. Ship-build. Industry U.S.* (1884) 22 A large fleet of small flat-bottomed fishing boats are employed, called 'sharpies', which have a family resemblance to the dory.

*attrib.* **1886** *Boston* (Mass.) *Jrnl.* 1 Sept. 1/8 Orders for five sharpie yachts. **1895** *Outing* XXX. 488/1 A balancelug sail, ..subsequently replaced by a sharpie sail and jib.

**2.** *colloq.* (orig. *U.S.*). **a.** = SHARPER[1] 2; **b.** = SHARP *sb.*[1] 8 b.

**1942** BERREY & VAN DEN BARK *Amer. Thes. Slang* §461 *Clever Crook*,..sharper, sharpie, sharpshooter, slicker. *Ibid.* §637 *Sports predictor*,..dopester, sharp, sharpie. **1944** *Chicago Daily News* 4 Nov. 6/1 Central characters of both plays are engaging highbinders and sharpies who are not exactly thieves, but more than slightly overoptimistic in their use of..other people's money. **1949** W. R. BURNETT *Asphalt Jungle* xiv. 92 He..couldn't make up his mind whether he'd been a chump or a sharpie. **1964** S. BELLOW *Herzog* 3 He had chosen to be dreamy..and the sharpies cleaned him out. **1974** *Times Lit. Suppl.* 3 May 465/4 The same wise-cracking, classless sharpie..can make throwaway remarks about Ingrid Haebler in his own tatty old flat. **1979** T. GIFFORD *Hollywood Gothic* vi. 71, I had drunks.. directors, producers, New York sharpies of every kind.

**3.** *Austral. colloq.* A young person who adopts certain extreme or provocative styles of hair, dress, etc. (see quot. 1975); the Australian counterpart of the SKINHEAD.

**1965** W. DICK *Bunch of Ratbags* 202 The more a sharpie protested he was not a bodgie, the more they [*sc.* the police] laughed and belted him. **1972** *Sydney Morning Herald* 20 Jan. 2 It was alleged in evidence that Still died during an incident involving 'sharpies' and 'long-hairs' outside Greystanes Progress Hall. **1975** *Sun-Herald* (Sydney) 13 Apr. 7 A sharpie is usually aged between 14 and 19 years. The boys wear their hair cropped short on the top and sides and longer at the back. The girls often wear 'dolly' makeup and have their ears pierced. Tattoos are often worn by both sexes. The sharpies wear blue jeans or high-waisted slacks supported by old-fashioned braces, matched with a tee shirt and sometimes a woollen cardigan. **1977** *Sunday Mail* (Brisbane) 21 Aug. 37/3 Carmel says her mother accepted her being a sharpie—even a punk—till she shaved her hair off.

**4.** *N. Amer. colloq.* That which is smart or in good condition. Used esp. of cars. Cf. SHARP *a.* 7 a, c; SHARP *sb.*[1] 13.

**1970** *Globe & Mail* (Toronto) 26 Sept. 47/7 (Advt.), Chevrolet Malibu 2-door hardtop, fully equipped, a real sharpie. **1979** *Tucson* (Arizona) *Citizen* (Advt. Suppl.) 28 Apr. 17/1 Starter home..carpeting, drapes and remodeled kitchen. Call..to see this little sharpie.

**5.** *attrib.* or as *adj.* in above senses.

**1961** W. BROWN *Bedeviled* 19 He was a tall, slender youth with the sharpie clothes and the long sideburns of the juvenile delinquent. **1975** *Sunday Mail* (Brisbane) 13 Apr. 30/1 Police will mount an all-out campaign against Sydney's sharpie gangs. **1980** *Times Lit. Suppl.* 7 Nov. 1270/4 Higgins..tells his latest story from the point of view of a hustling Irish-American sharpy lawyer.

**sharping** ('ʃɑːpɪŋ), *vbl. sb.* [f. SHARP *v.* + -ING[1].] The action of the verb SHARP.

**1. a.** = SHARPENING *vbl. sb.* in various senses.

**1398** TREVISA *Barth. De P.R.* XIX. xvii. 874 In olde tyme men vsed to sharpe this colour Minius wyth the blode of a certayne worme:..and for suche sharpyng that red was callyd Vermiculus. *a* **1400** *Minor Poems fr. Vernon MS.* 71/499 þei..þat hedden tonges of scharpynge And [? *read* As] swerd þat keruep Mayle. **1475** *Bk. Noblesse* (Roxb.) 33 Late the case be taken for a new lerning, and to the sharping of goode corages. **1575** *Richmond Wills* (Surtees) 256 For horse showing, sharping of irons, and ale, xj[d]. **1662** PLAYFORD *Introd. Skill Mus.* I. ii. 9 The Flatting and Sharping of Notes. **1747** HOOSON *Miner's Dict.* E 2 b, This sort [chirtt] will wear a new Steel'd Pick off, in three or four times Sharping. **1895, 1956** [see FLATTING *vbl. sb.* 3].

**b.** *Comb.*: †**sharping-corn**, an annual grant of corn formerly made to a blacksmith in return for sharpening farm implements; **sharping-stone** *Sc.*, a whetstone.

**1681** *Rec. Baron Crt. Stitchill* (S.H.S.) 89, 15 sheaves of shairping corne. **1714** LADY G. BAILLIE *Househ. Bk.* (S.H.S.) 254, 2 sharping stones 3s. **1905** 'H. HALIBURTON' *Excurs.* i. 9 The Bruce stood aimlessly with his sharping-stone in one hand.

**2.** The action of a sharper, swindling, roguery.

**1692** R. L'ESTRANGE *Fables* xxxiv. 33 Cheating and Sharping, one Half of the Year, and Starving, the Other. **1748** SMOLLETT *Rod. Rand.* lviii, Sharping and other infamous practises. **1870** W. R. GREG *Polit. Probl.* 275 Shameless jobbery, cruel swindling and sharping.

**sharping** ('ʃɑːpɪŋ), *ppl. a.* [f. SHARP *v.* + -ING[2].] That acts as a sharper, fraudulent, swindling, cheating, knavish.

**1691** DRYDEN *K. Arthur* Prol. 38 A sharping Sett. *a* **1700** B. E. *Dict. Cant. Crew, Hedge-Tavern*,..a Jilting, Sharping Tavern. **1796** PEGGE *Anonym.* (1809) 47 A sharping attorney. **1829** W. IRVING *Granada* I. xxvi. 237 All wandering minstrels, sharping pedlars,..and other camp trumpery..were drummed out of the gates of Alhama. **1880** W. HOOE (*title*) Sharping London,..a book for honest people.

**sharpish** ('ʃɑːpɪʃ), *a.* and (*adv.*) [f. SHARP *a.* + -ISH.] **1.** Somewhat sharp.

**1589** FLEMING *Virg. Georg.* II. 39 Sowre and sharpish iuces. **1651** FRENCH *Distill.* iii. 87 A water somewhat sharpish. **1725** *Bradley's Fam. Dict.* s.v. *Service*, An acid or sharpish Liquor. **1823** J. BADCOCK *Dom. Amusem.* 208 The pontons, should be..sharpish fore and aft. **1880** R. B. WATSON in *Jrnl. Linn. Soc., Zool.* XV. 118 A minute, sharpish spiral thread.

**2.** quasi-*adv.* = SHARPLY *adv.* (esp. sense 4); somewhat sharply. *colloq.*

**1886** BAUMANN *Londinismen* 174/1 He looks sharpish for his rents. **1899** *Longman's Mag.* July 273 When a barge does come, Dorcas 'bustles her about sharpish', and there is a great to-do. **1952** *Chambers's Jrnl.* Feb. 119/1 We're late ourselves. Better be off sharpish if we're going to be home for tea. **1975** T. ALLBEURY *Special Collection* viii. 54 They shuffled him back to Moscow pretty sharpish.

**sharpite** ('ʃɑːpaɪt). *Min.* [a. F. *sharpite* (J. Mélon 1938, in *Bull. Séances Inst. R. Colonial Belge* IX. 333), f. the name of Major R. R. *Sharp*, who discovered the uranium deposit where it was first found: see -ITE[1].] A hydrated carbonate of uranium found as greenish yellow crusts of thin radiating fibres.

**1939** *Mineral. Abstr.* VII. 225 Sharpite forms yellowish-green, radially fibrous crusts on curite and becquerelite from Shinkolobwe, Katanga. **1971** *Ibid.* XXII. 92/1 Secondary uranium mineralization occurs among secondary Fe, Cu, and Pb minerals in Kletno; it is represented by nasturan, uranium black, gummite, fourmarierite, and traces of sharpite.

**sharpling** ('ʃɑːplɪŋ). Also 6 shapling. [f. SHARP *a.* + -LING[1].]

†**1.** ? A kind of nail. *Obs.*

**1415** in Rogers *Agric. & Prices* (1882) III. 447 Sharplings. **1456** in *Fabric Rolls York Minster* (Surtees) 67, cc sharplynges. **1465** *Mann. & Househ. Exp.* (Roxb.) 201 Item, for a quarter of sharpenge [*sic*: ? an error] for the rother, iiijd. **1526** in *Fabric Rolls York Minster* (Surtees) 100 Pro vij c. sharpling, 4s. 8d. **1538** *Ibid.* 109 Pro vj. m. shaplyng 4s.:.. c shaplinges 8d.

**2.** *dial.* The Stickleback. Cf. SHAFTLING.

**1558** *Gesner's Hist. Anim.* IV. 10 De Piscicvlo Acvleato.. Anglicum eius nomen Scharplyng. *a* **1672** WILLUGHBY *Hist. Pisc.* (1686) 341 A Stickleback, Banstickle, or Sharpling. **1740** R. BROOKES *Art of Angling* I. xxx. 67 The Stickleback or Sharpling. **1836** YARRELL *Brit. Fishes* I. 76 The Roughtailed Stickleback. Banstickle. Sharplin. *Scotland.*

**sharply** ('ʃɑːplɪ), *adv.* [f. SHARP *a.* + -LY[2].] In a sharp manner.

**1.** Severely, sternly, harshly. **a.** Of punishment, discipline, etc. Now *rare.*

*c* **900** *Bede Glosses* in *O.E. Texts* 181/47 *Acerbatim*, scearplice. *c* **1380** WYCLIF *Wks.* (1880) 67 In tokene þat he scharpliest schal ponysche hem þat don symonye. **1415** HOCCLEVE *To Sir J. Oldcastle* 278 Yee heretikes..I doute it nat, your wages shal be payed sharply, but yee correct your trespas. **1526** *Pilgr. Perf.* (W. de W. 1531) 82 b, The body must be entreated sharpely, that it waxe not wanton and wylde. **1557** N. T. (Genev.) *Matt.* xxii. 6 And the remnant toke his seruantes, and intreated them sharpely. **1677** J. LEVERETT in *Jrnl. Friends' Hist. Soc.* (1912) July 134 [The Lord] was pleased to lay his hand so sharply upon me by fits of the stone in a time of great business.

**b.** Of speech, rebuke, command: Sternly, severely, harshly, peremptorily; in cutting terms; in stern or angry tones.

**1340** HAMPOLE *Pr. Consc.* 3450 When þou spekes sharppely til þe pure, þat sum gode askes at þi dore. *c* **1386** CHAUCER *Pars. T.* ¶ 583 Whan a man is sharply amonested in his shrift to leve his sinne. *c* **1450** in Aungier *Syon* (1840) 269 Repreve scharply. **1568** GRAFTON *Chron.* II. 971 The king wrote sharpely to him to accomplish y[t] which appertayned to his duety. **1662** STILLINGFL. *Orig. Sacræ* I. iv. §4. 61 Though he be sharply censured by Strabo. **1829** SCOTT *Anne of G.* xxv, 'By Saint George, never!' answered the Duke, sharply and shortly. **1870** MISS BROUGHTON *Red as Rose* I. 169 'He hates the game', replies Miss Blessington, rather sharplier than is her wont.

**2.** With sharp or painful effect; keenly, smartly.

*a* **1023** WULFSTAN *Hom.* xxix. (1883) 141 Se deofol..cwæð ..'stingað hine scearplice on þone muð'. *c* **1400** MAUNDEV. (Roxb.) ii. 6 It was of iunkes of the see, þat ware whyte and prikked scharpely as thornes. *c* **1470** *Gol. & Gaw.* 930 Sa woundir scharply he schair, The berne that the brand bair. **1602** *2nd Pt. Return fr. Parnass.* V. iv. 2162, I wish thee store of gall, Sharpely to wound the guilty world withall. **1724** *Lond. Gaz.* No. 6240/5 It froze..sharply. **1831** SCOTT *Ct. Robt.* xx, Her own well aimed, but feeble shaft, wounded him [the boar] sharply. **1851** GLADSTONE in Lathbury *Corr. Ch. & Relig.* (1910) I. 358 Such griefs..must be sacred to me, even did they not touch me sharply with a reflected sorrow. **1852** THACKERAY *Esmond* II. i, A fever..which attacked him that night pretty sharply. **1865** KINGSLEY *Herew.* ii, An arrow struck him sharply in the back.

**3.** †**a.** With intellectual acuteness; acutely, sagaciously, shrewdly. *Obs.*

*c* **897** ÆLFRED *Gregory's Past. C.* xi. 68 Ða þe meahton smealice & scearplice mid hiera ondʒiete ryht ʒesion. **1382** WYCLIF *Prol.* 58 Men miȝten expoune..the bible in English,..myche sharpliere and groundliere than manie late postillatouris. *c* **1450** HOLLAND *Howlat* 268 Mony allegiance leile, in leid nocht to layne it, Off Arestotill and ald men, scharplie thai schewe. **1621** S. WARD *Happiness of Practice* (1627) 10 His scope sure was not to make trial of the wits of men, who could sharpliest conceiue. **1699** BENTLEY *Phalaris* 497 Who can deny now, but this is sharply observ'd?

**b.** Attentively, with penetration and keen observation; vigilantly, closely.

*c* **1055** *Byrhtferth's Handboc* in *Anglia* VIII. 309, & hawa swyðe scearplice hwær sy .xii. kl' aprelis. *a* **1340** HAMPOLE *Psalter* lxiii. 6 þe sharpliere þat þai thynke, þe mare þai faile fra sothfastnes. *c* **1420** *Wars Alex.* (prose) (E.E.T.S.) 40 Alexander..biheld þe Phisician in þe vesage riȝte scharpely. **1582** STANYHURST *Æneis* I. (Arb.) 32 Æneas..thee towne top sharplye beholding. **1666** PEPYS *Diary* 16 Dec., This Committee of Accounts will enquire sharply into our office. **1869** TOZER *Highl. Turkey* II. 191 A salutary hint as to..the benefit of being tolerably sharply on the look out. **1879** B. TAYLOR *Germ. Lit.* 144 Their business was to listen sharply.

**4. a.** Briskly, swiftly, quickly.

*a* **1000** *Voc.* in Wr.-Wülcker 226/33 *Efficaciter*, i. *uelociter*, caflice, scearplice. **1338** R. BRUNNE *Chron.* (1725) 244 To Wales he went his way fulle scharply, & fulle brim. *c* **1400** *Brut* (1906) 283 þe Scottis..come fast and sharpely aȝeynes evesong tyme. **1568** GRAFTON *Chron.* II. 426 The Englishe men shot so closely and so sharpely together, that the Flemynges and footemen began to flie. **1688** CLAYTON in *Phil. Trans.* XVIII. 121 They Ride pretty sharply. **1741** SHORT *Ibid.* XLI. 628 It went all over this Country from North to South, pretty sharply, but nothing near so quick as a Glade of Lightning. **1829** SCOTT *Anne of G.* xix, [He] drew in his head, and shut the window sharply against the guest. **1859** TENNYSON *Marr. Geraint* 196 Geraint..Made sharply to the dwarf, and ask'd it of him. **1912** *Times* 19 Dec. 19/6 Prices soon recovered and advanced sharply in the afternoon.

**b.** Of conflict or attack: Eagerly, vigorously.

*c* **1380** *Sir Ferumb.* 724 Al so scharply þes men of mayn þan smyte to-gadre aȝy. **1535** COVERDALE *Lam.* iii. 52 Myne enemies hunted me out sharpely like a byrde. **1678** WANLEY *Wond. Lit. World* v. ii. §82. 478/2 Solyman..sharply besieged and assaulted Vienna. **1737** WHISTON *Josephus, Antiq.* XIV. xv. §12 He pursued them sharply, and killed them.

**c.** Abruptly.

**1828** SCOTT *F.M. Perth* viii, Some of them [*sc.* the blows] lighted upon Jezabel, who, turning sharply round, laid her rider upon the moor. **1889** GUNTER *That Frenchman* i. 9 'Which, by the by, isn't his right name', remarks de Verney, sharply closing his speech.

**5.** With a sharp edge or point; at or with an acute angle.

*c* **1400** *Rom. Rose* 1723 He took an arowe ful sharply whet. **1567** MAPLET *Gr. Forest* 47 b, It is like that figure which the Geometricians call Pyramis, we may say sharpely topped. **1796** WITHERING *Brit. Plants* (ed. 3) III. 543 Leaves egg-shaped, streaked, sharply toothed. **1827** FARADAY *Chem. Manip.* xvi. (1842) 424 It is to be bent, not sharply, but obtusely and roundly. **1860** L. REEVE *Elem. Conchol.* I. 149 Shell.., apex rather sharply acuminated.

**6.** With a sharp sound.

**1387** TREVISA *Higden* (Rolls) III. 29 Oon of þe goldene calues..lowede ful scharpliche. **1808** SCOTT *Marm.* VI. xxii, Deep need that day that every string By wet unharmed should sharply ring. **1825** —— *Talism.* v, A shrill whistle.. was heard to ring sharply through the vaulted chapel.

**7.** Definitely, distinctly.

**1817** COLERIDGE *Biog. Lit.* II. 156 In no system is the distinction between the individual and God..more sharply drawn than in that of Spinoza. **1874** H. H. COLE *Catal. Ind. Art S. Kens. Mus.* 127 Sharply and well carved decoration. **1893** LIDDON *Life Pusey* I. x. 198 This election [Peel v. Inglis] divided men sharply throughout Oxford. **1907** J. A. HODGES *Elem. Photogr.* (ed. 6) 123 The image having been sharply focussed.

**8.** Smartly, fashionably.

**1965** V. CANNING *Whip Hand* ii. 15, I was sharply dressed for the part, young man on holiday, well-heeled. **1981** P. INCHBALD *Tondo for Short* vii. 73 He was dressed as sharply as he could manage.

**9.** *Comb.* With pples., forming adjs., as ***sharply-bitted, -chiselled, -defined, -discerning, -focussed***; †**sharply-conceived**, having a keen, ready wit.

**1844** H. G. ROBINSON *Odes of Horace* I. viii, Why now no more..Does he..with the *sharply bitted rein His Gallic courser's mouth restrain? **1854** tr. *Hettner's Athens*, etc. 54 These bold, *sharply-chiselled, expressive faces. **1630** *R. Johnson's Kingd. & Commw.* 56 The Italian is more courteous... *Sharply conceived, of fresh memory. **1865** VISCT. MILTON & W. B. CHEADLE *N.-W. Passage by Land* viii. (1867) 116 The clear, *sharply-defined track of the active mink. **1879** *St. George's Hosp. Rep.* IX. 601 A sharply-defined ulcer. **1837** CARLYLE *Fr. Rev.* I. II. i, A quick, choleric, *sharply discerning, stubbornly endeavouring man. **1892** *Photogr. Ann.* II. 265 A *sharply focussed representation of a distant object.

**sharpness** (ˈʃɑːpnɪs). [f. SHARP *a.* + -NESS.] The quality of being sharp.

**1.** Keenness or fineness of edge or point.

*c* **725** *Corpus Gloss.* (Hessels) A 117 *Acumen ferri*, ecg *uel* scearpnis. *c* **1375** *Sc. Leg. Saints* xxxvii. (*Vincencius*) 317 þe scharpnes of þe schellis. *c* **1440** *Promp. Parv.* 444/1 Scharpnesse, of egge, *acuties*. *a* **1586** SIDNEY *Arcadia* III. (Sommer) 293 b, The vnfaythfull armour yeelding to the swoordes strong-guided sharpenesse. *c* **1611** CHAPMAN *Iliad* xx. 387 My lance as well as thine Hath point and sharpenesse. **1787** *Hist. Jack & Giants* 13 Taking with him the cap of knowledge, sword of sharpness [etc.]. **1837** CARLYLE *Fr. Rev.* III. III. v, Herein has Sansculottism fashioned for itself a Sword of Sharpness. **1888** *Pall Mall Gaz.* 22 Aug. 5/2 A bar of steel..of wonderful temper and sharpness.

**2. a.** Intellectual acuteness, shrewdness.

*c* **897** ÆLFRED *Gregory's Past. C.* xvi. 99 Swæðeah for ðære sceawunge ðara unȝesewenlicra ðinga ðeah he upaðened wære on his modes scearpnesse. **1398** TREVISA *Barth. De P.R.* II. xx. (1495) 47 The euyll angellis haue thre maner of sharpenesse [orig. *Triplici acumine vigent demones*]. **1532** SIR B. TUKE *Chaucer's Wks.* Pref. A ij b, Suche sharpnesse or quycknesse in conclusyon. **1646** H. P. *Medit. Seige* 55 Nor let them want sharpnesse to discerne, nor courage to execute what should be done in such exigencies. **1814** W. WILSON *Hist. Dissent. Churches* IV. 486 Wickliff..possessed a sharpness of wit. **1895** *Law Times* XCIX. 547/1 An articled clerk of average sharpness may rely upon getting through with three months' coaching.

**b.** Acuteness of the senses or organs of sense.

*c* **888** ÆLFRED *Boeth.* xxxiv. §8 Ne heora scearpnesse nauht ȝebetað to þære sceawunga þære soðan ȝesælðe. **1604** JAS. I *Counterbl. to Tobacco* (Arb.) 105 So loath will they be, to be thought inferiour to their fellowes..in..sharpnesse of sight. **1709** BERKELEY *Ess. Vision* §80 Wks. 1871 I. 73 No exquisite formation of the eye, no peculiar sharpness of sight. **1835** JAMES *Gipsy* ii, The hearing of those whose safety often depends upon the sharpness of their ears.

**c.** Keenness (of observation).

**1822** SCOTT *Peveril* xiii, The utmost sharpness of attention which Julian applied, could not discover if Bridgenorth spoke seriously or ironically to the above purpose.

**3.** Pungency to the taste; acidity, sourness, tartness.

*c* **1000** *Sax. Leechd.* II. 224/22 Þæs ecedes afre scearpnes. *a* **1023** WULFSTAN *Hom.* v. (1883) 35 Þæs sealtes scearpnesse. *a* **1425** tr. *Arderne's Treat. Fistula*, etc. 59 Emoroidez ar caused of scharpnes of blode and ouer mych hete brennyng þe blode. **1555** EDEN *Decades* II. (Arb.) 110 These apples..haue a certeyne sweetnes myxt with a gentell sharpnes. **1662** CHARLETON *Myst. Vintners* (1675) 155 The Sulphur..infects the whole mass of liquor with Sharpness or Acidity. **1701** G. STANHOPE *Anselm's Medit.* xvii. (1720) 348 Make me sometimes taste the sharpness of thy Vinegar. **1839** MRS. KIRKLAND in Griswold *Prose Writers Amer.* (1847) 464 Her vinegar is..the *ne plus ultra* of sharpness.

**4. a.** Severity, harshness in punishment; censure, rebuke, etc.; asperity in behaviour.

*a* **1325** *Prose Psalter* ii. 9 Þou schalt gouernen hem in Scharpnes. *c* **1425** *Found. St. Bartholomew's* (E.E.T.S.) 25 A certeyne bocheyr, Goderyke by name, A man of grete sharpnesse more than semyd hym. *a* **1558** ABP. SANDYS *Serm.* xv. (1585) 262 The sharpenesse of his correction. **1606** SHAKS. *Ant. & Cl.* III. iii. 38 Thou must not take my former sharpenesse ill. *a* **1721** SHEFFIELD (Dk. Buckhm.) *Wks.* 1753 I. 75 Some did our follies with just sharpness blame. **1827** SCOTT *Surg. Dau.* i, An eye of much sharpness and severity of expression. **1867** TROLLOPE *Chron. Barset* lxvii. II. 245 In spite of the sharpness of her tongue.

†**b.** Austerity, asceticism. *Obs.*

**1340** *Ayenb.* 187 Vele men makeþ to god sacrefices of uestinges, of peregrinages, of ssarpnesses of bodye. *c* **1440** *Jacob's Well* 10 Þou louedyst no scharpenesse of penaunce. **1450–1530** *Myrr. our Ladye* 83 Penaunce..ys done in sorowe of harte and sharpenesse of body.

†**c.** Acrimony, exasperated condition. *Obs.*

**1673** TEMPLE *United Prov.* v. 181 All the violence and sharpness, which accompanies the differences of Religion in other Countreys, seems to be appeased or softned here. *a* **1715** BURNET *Own Time* (1766) II. 217 He expressed a very Christian temper, without sharpness or resentment. **1733** NEAL *Hist. Purit.* II. 601 Such was the sharpness of men's spirits on both sides.

†**d.** Severity (of weather), keenness, intensity (of heat, cold, etc.). *Obs.*

**1482** *Monk of Evesham* (Arb.) 94 And yette y am constrayned ful sore to sofyr the scarpnes of colde. **1553** EDEN *Treat. Newe Ind.* (Arb.) 33 At whiche tyme ye sharpenes of winter exceadeth with them. **1662** *Gusman's Ephemeris* B, It will not be common this Month [January] to see Women go with naked shoulders by reason of the Sharpnesse of the Air. **1712** *Lond. Gaz.* No. 4971/1 The badness of the Roads, and the sharpness of the Season, have hindered the march. **1778** COOK *3rd Voy.* IV. ix. (1784) II. 455 The sharpness of the air..seemed to indicate some sudden change.

**e.** Severity, acuteness (of pain or sorrow); painfulness, hardship.

*a* **1400** *Prymer, Te Deum* (1895) 7 Whanne þou haddist ouercome þe scharpnesse of deeþ [L. *mortis aculeo*]. *c* **1410** LYDG. *Life Our Lady* lx. (1484) i v, For sharpenes of the sodayn smerte The chylde gan wepe. **1526** *Pilgr. Perf.* (W. de W. 1531) 204 b, He suffred the sharpnes and smart of payne, ye suche as neuer was suffred. **1631** GOUGE *God's Arrows* II. §24. 166 What need is it to shew the sharpnesse of this famine by things that want life? **1709** *Lond. Gaz.* No. 4521/2 Our Loss has been very great, the Action having been so severe, and the sharpness of the whole having lain upon our Ship.

†**5.** Shrillness, high pitch (of voice). *Obs. rare*$^{-1}$.

**1398** TREVISA *Barth. De P.R.* v. xxiii. (Bodl. MS.), It is seide þat cause of scharpenes and of chaunging of voice is by chaungeing of age.

†**6.** Craving (of the stomach) for food. *Obs.*

**1581** W. STAFFORD *Exam. Compl.* i. (1876) 15 When we had eate somewhat to satisfie the sharpenesse of our stomackes. **1675** HANNAH WOOLLEY *Gentlew. Comp.* 67 The sharpness of my Stomach shall never make me feed uncleanly.

†**7.** Steepness. *Obs. rare*$^{-1}$.

**1585** T. WASHINGTON tr. *Nicholay's Voy.* I. i. 1 The height and sharpnesse of the mount Rhodope. *Ibid.* IV. xxiii. 139 A mount of great highnesse and sharpnesse.

†**8.** Prickling sensation, smarting. *Obs.*

**1694** SALMON *Bate's Dispens.* (1713) 82/1 Inflammations, Pains, and Sharpness of the Eyes.

**9. a.** Distinctness of outline or impression.

**1771** RAPER in *Phil. Trans.* LXI. 475 Three gold coins of Philip, which have all the sharpness of new money fresh from the mint. **1837** GORING & PRITCHARD *Microgr.* 82 A picture whose sharpness and clearness is a maximum. **1884** *Macm. Mag* Oct. 444/2 That word which still retains the sharpness of its stamp and milling. **1907** J. A. HODGES *Elem. Photogr.* (ed. 6) 20 This question of definition, or sharpness of image.

**b.** *Physical Sci.* The extent to which a phenomenon, condition, etc., is sharp (sense 12 b).

**1906** G. EICHHORN *Wireless Telegr.* vi. 40 Wien clearly demonstrated the greater sharpness of resonance in loosely-coupled systems than in the simple system. **1921** [see PEAKINESS]. **1966** COTTON & WILKINSON *Adv. Inorg. Chem.* (ed. 2) xxvii. 733 (*caption*) Note the greater sharpness of the solution spectra.

**sharp-nosed**, *a.*

**1.** Having a pointed nose.

**1675** *Lond. Gaz.* No. 1053/4 A Pied Dog,..shap't like a Lurcher, sharp Nosed. **1769** PENNANT *Brit. Zool.* III. 64 The Sharp-nosed Ray. **1829** J. RICHARDSON *Fauna Boreali-Amer.* I. 126 Sharp-nosed Meadow-Mouse. **1837** DICKENS *Pickw.* xxii, An important-looking sharp-nosed, mysterious-spoken personage. **1881** *Cassell's Nat. Hist.* V. 140 The Sharp-nosed Eel. *Anguilla vulgaris.*

†**2.** Having a keen 'scent'; *fig.* quick at fault-finding, captious. *Obs.*

**1561** T. NORTON *Calvin's Inst.* I. 19 Now let come foorth al these sharpnosed fault finders. **1579** TOMSON *Calvin's Serm. Tim.* 891/1 That wee bee not sharpe nosed to striue against the doctrine of God.

**sharp-pointed**, *a.*

**1.** Tapering or tapered to a point.

**1530** PALSGR. 323/1 Sharpe poynted, *pointu*. **1749** FIELDING *Tom Jones* IV. ii, The sharp-pointed nose of bitter-biting Eurus. **1864** BOWEN *Logic* xi. 365 A sharp-pointed rod. **1890** S. L. GWYNNE *Musset's Comedies* 123 Dame Pluche, repulsing them on either side with her sharp-pointed elbows.

**b.** *Bot.* Acuminate, mucronate.

**1565** COOPER *Thesaurus, Mucronata folia*, sharpe poynted leaues. **1653** RAMESEY *Astrol. Restored* 54 All such herbs..as have sharp-pointed leaves. **1828** SIR J. E. SMITH *Engl. Flora* II. 16 Leaves ovate, sharp-pointed. **1857** MISS PRATT *Flower. Pl.* IV. 130 *Linaria Elatine* (Sharp-pointed Fluel-lin or Toad-flax).

**2.** Having a fine point adapted for purposes of piercing or stabbing.

**1594** SHAKS. *Rich. III*, I. ii. 175 Loe heere I lend thee this sharpe-pointed Sword. *c* **1614** DRUMM. OF HAWTH. *Madrigals & Epigr., The Rose*, This sharpe pointed Thorne. **1707** MORTIMER *Husb.* (1721) I. 189 A sharp pointed Stick. **1875** R. WILSON tr. *Figuier's Hum. Race, Brown Race* iii. 441 The oars are sharp-pointed, and can be used, in case of need, as weapons against an unforeseen attack.

*fig.* **1894** *Outing* XXIV. 5/1 Certain sharp-pointed reports had reached her of where her husband's evenings were spent.

**3.** Having irregular sharp projections.

**1748** *Anson's Voy.* III. ii. 315 The bottom..is full of sharp-pointed coral rocks. **1861** NOBLE *Icebergs* 148 Back slid the Candle, followed by a charge of sharp-pointed baggage.

**sharp practice.**

**1.** Work that demands brisk activity. *rare.*

In some debating societies, applied to a debate intended for practice in readiness of speech, the rule being that each member must speak when called upon, on a subject proposed at the moment.

**1847** J. PAGET in *Mem.* (1901) 157, I..see from 180 to 220 patients on each of my days—sharp practice for a beginner.

**2. a.** Hard bargaining; relentless pursuit of advantage. **b.** Now in more unfavourable sense: Dishonourable taking of advantage, trickery. (Cf. SHARP *a.* 3 e.)

**1836** DICKENS *Pickw.* (1837) xx. 209 'Dodson and Fogg—sharp practice their's—capital men of business is Dodson and Fogg, Sir.' Mr. Pickwick admitted the sharp practice of Dodson and Fogg. **1845** C. M. KIRKLAND *Western Clearings* 42 His 'law studies'..were comprised in six months' 'sharp practice', as clerk to a gentleman who had quitted the shoe-maker's bench for the law. **1847** HELPS *Friends in C.* I. viii. 142 The sharp practice of the world drives some logic into the most vague of men: women are not so schooled. **1869** TOZER *Highl. Turkey* II. 306 Their fondness for trickery and sharp practice. **1914** WODEHOUSE *Man Upstairs* 182 He could not say exactly that it was sharp practice on Owen's part. **1944** 'BRAHMS' & 'SIMON' *Titania has Mother* ix. 95 'Sharp practice?' said the Fairy Peaseblossom. 'Oh no, ma'am. Just diplomacy.'

**Sharps** (ʃɑːps). *U.S.* Also with small initial. The name of Christian *Sharps* (1811–74), American gunsmith, applied *absol.* to any of a number of firearms invented and manufactured by him; esp. a celebrated variety of breech-loading, single-shot rifle. Also in the possessive and *attrib.*

**1850** *Sci. Amer.* 9 Mar. 193/2 (*heading*) Sharps' breech-loading patent rifle. **1873** *Forest & Stream* XXIX. 2 As long as the Indian agents send cases of breech-loading Sharps marked 'hardware'..as Government annuity, we must expect these murders, robberies, etc., on the part of the Indians. **1929** B. DAVIS *Truth about Geronimo* 161 His gun, an antiquated Sharps rifle, had gone off accidentally. **1958** 'W. HENRY' *Seven Men at Mimbres Springs* xv. 176 Doc Harnaday and his old Sharps could..'hit a yearling bull..at 900 yards'.

**sharp-set**, *a.* [f. SHARP *a.* (as compl.) + SET *ppl. a.*

See SET *ppl. a.* 75 b. The hawking use (1 b) may be the original: cf. *to set sharp*, SHARP *a.* 4 f (quot. 1575).]

**1. a.** Eager or keen for food, very hungry. Also said of the stomach.

**1540** PALSGR. *Acolastus* II. iii. M ij, My mynd is al redy in the platters or dishes .i. I am sharpe set. **1586** STANYHURST *Descr. Irel.* ii. 19/2 in *Holinshed*, If anie were so sharpe set..as to eat fried flies, butterd bees, stued snailes. **1692** R. L'ESTRANGE *Fables* clxxv. 146 A Fox that was Sharp-set, Surpriz'd a Crab,..and carry'd him away. **1725** LADY HERVEY in *C'tess Suffolk's Lett.* (1824) I. 192 My stomach is so much sharper set than my wit, that I fancy it will be as well for us both to conclude. **1809** MALKIN *Gil Blas* VII. v, I asked..if there was any eating-house in the neighbourhood.., and went thither sharp set. **1886** STEVENSON *Kidnapped* iii. 17 'Are ye sharp-set?' he asked... 'Ye can eat that drop parritch'.

**b.** Of a hawk, hound, etc.

**1575** TURBERV. *Faulconrie* 116 If shee bee very sharpe set and do plume eagerly. **1781** BECKFORD *Hunting* 48 Hounds, I think, should be sharp-set before hunting: they run the better for it. **1852** BURTON *Falconry Valley Indus* iii. 31 Unfortunately..for the hawk..she had not been 'sharp set' that morning. **1883** SALVIN & BRODRICK *Falconry Brit. Isles* Gloss. 152 *Sharp set*, very hungry. **1918** V. WOOLF *Diary* 5 Feb. (1977) I. 119 She [*sc.* a dog]..wags her tail as hard as she can, & snatches at any scrap of talk as if she were sharp set.

**2.** *transf.* Keen, eager; having desire fixed *upon*, craving *after*.

**1580** LYLY *Euphues* (Arb.) 388 Euphues seeing such speedye retourne of an other aunswere, thought Philautus to be very sharp set. *a* **1586** SIDNEY *Arcadia* II. xvi. (Sommer) 175 b, She being sharp-set vpon the fulfilling of a shrewde office, in ouer-looking Philoclea. **1667** MARVELL *Corr.* Wks. (Grosart) II. 222 Although the House be sharpe set upon finding out..things..yet neither are other publick matters neglected. **1711** CROMWELL *Let. to Pope* 7 Dec., The town is sharp-set on new plays. **1860** *Times* 5 Oct., The public comes back from glacier and moor and breezy sea-coast perfectly sharpset for more oratory. **1889** RIDER HAGGARD *Allan's Wife* 54, I did not feel particularly sharp set on elephants at the moment.

†**b.** Having a craving for sexual indulgence.

**1597–1626** DELONEY *Jack of Newbery* Wks. (1912) 14 Sir (said shee) because you are so sharpe set, I would wish you as soon as you can to wed. **1633** FORD *'Tis Pity* v. iv. **1691** *Comedy, Win Her & Take Her* I. iii. 8. **1695** CONGREVE *Love for L.* III. ix. **1794** *Har'st Rig* liv, Some lown as sharp set as a knife Wi' her they fand.

†**c.** Eager to attack. Const. *on*. *Obs. rare*$^{-1}$.

*a* **1633** AUSTIN *Medit.* (1635) 98 The Pharisees..who were too sharpe set on his Disciples, for not Fasting with them, at that present time.

†**3.** Set with sharp thorns. (Cf. *quick-set*.) *Obs.*

**1601** WEEVER *Mirr. Mart.* A 5, Within the sharp-set thickets.

**4.** Of eyes: ? Having a set eager look.

**1865** SWINBURNE *Chastelard* I. ii. 34 Do you know that lord With sharp-set eyes?

Hence **sharp'setness.** *rare.*

**1673** S. PARKER *Reproof Reh. Transp.* 261 Lest this race [*sc.* capons] be totally extinguish'd by the sharpsetness of the Presbyterians.

**sharpshin** (ˈʃɑːpʃɪn). [In sense 2, a back-formation from *sharp-shinned* (*hawk*). Sense 1 is prob. a jocular allusion to the eagle on the coin.]

**1.** App. orig. a name for some coin of very small value; later, used as a type of what has little value. *U.S.*

**1804** *Lancaster* (Pa.) *Jrnl.* 14 July (R. H. Thornton *Amer. Gloss.*), Three Sharpshins Reward [offered for a run-away apprentice]. **1832** J. P. Kennedy *Swallow B.* x. (1872) 93 This inconsiderable claim—for it is not of the value of a sharpshin. **1834** Marryat *P. Simple* xxx, Four sharp shins to a pictareen. **1872** Schele de Vere *Americanisms* 631 *Sharpshin*, a slang term, denoting the smallest quantity.

**2.** Usu. hyphened. The small North American sharp-shinned hawk, *Accipiter striatus*; cf. *sharp-shinned* s.v. sharp *a.* C. 2.

**1912** W. B. Barrows *Michigan Bird Life* 264 There were Sharp-shins everywhere—sweeping about through the woods. **1937** *Nat. Geogr. Mag.* July 132/2 We have watched the sharp-shin dodge through the thickest brush after its quarry. **1960** R. T. Peterson *Field Guide Birds Texas* 58 Sharp-shin's square-tipped tail can look slightly rounded when spread.

† **'sharpship.** *Obs. rare*$^{-1}$. In 3 scharpschipe. [f. sharp *a.* + -ship.] Hardship, rigour.

*a* **1225** *Ancr. R.* 380 þet te best of helle, hwon he snakereð toward ou uorto biten on ou, hurte him oðe herdschipe [*MSS. T.C.* scharpschipe], & schunche aȝeinwardes.

**sharp-shod,** *a.* Chiefly *N. Amer.* [f. sharp *adv.* + shod *ppl. a.*] Of a horse: provided with caulked shoes; rough-shod. Also [as a back-formation] **sharp-shoe** *v. trans. rare.*

**1889** *Cent. Dict.*, Sharp-shod. **1904** in *Eng. Dial. Dict.* **1906** *Daily Colonist* (Victoria, B.C.) 20 Jan. 8/2 It was quite apparent from the horses' tracks in the snow that one saddle horse was sharp shod. **1935** H. Davis *Honey in Horn* xviii. 305 A man run down by a bunch of sharp-shod horses has a tendency to scatter around badly. **1962** J. Onslow *Bowler-Hatted Cowboy* xi. 100 We sharp-shod our horses in front with shoes that had sharp calkins at the heels and one on each toe.

**sharpshooter** (ˈʃɑːpʃuːtə(r)). [f. sharp *a.* + shooter. (So G. *scharfschütz(e, scharfer schütze.*)] **1. a.** A marksman of accurate aim; *spec.* in naval and military use, a member of a division engaged in skirmishing and outpost work.

**1802** C. James *Milit. Dict.*, *Tirolians*, a body of sharp shooters in the Austrian service. **1803** Scott *Let.* 27 Aug. in *Lockhart* (1837) I. xi. 389 Armies of Reserve, and Militia, and Pikemen, and Sharpshooters, who are to descend from Ettrick Forest to the confusion of all invaders. **1805** in Nicolas *Disp. Nelson* (1846) VII. 224 Lord Nelson was wounded by a French Sharpshooter. **1809** Wellington in Gurw. *Desp.* (1835) IV. 331 On the 11th the enemy tried their usual manœuvres with their sharpshooters in the woods. **1897** *Century Mag.* Jan. 352 [He] had been struck by a sharp-shooter and killed.

**b.** *fig.*

**1824** Dibdin *Libr. Comp.* 695 Hundreds of black-letter sharp-shooters spring up. **1885** J. Martineau *Types Eth. Th.* I. p. x, A fusillade of questions from a class of sharp-shooters. **1933** *Sun* (Baltimore) 26 May 1/3 They were set apart as a shining target upon which all political sharpshooters practiced. **1960** *Twentieth Cent.* May 447 Sociology is not at present and is not likely to become in the near future a subject for intellectual sharpshooters.

**c.** *U.S. Mil.* A rifleman of a particular grade; *spec.* one who has attained the level of proficiency between that of marksman and expert.

**1889** *N.Y. Times* 15 Sept. 13/2 Until within a comparatively recent period all officers and members of organizations armed with the Remington rifle scoring 25 points or better at 200 and 500 yards, 6 shots at each distance ..were accounted 'marksmen'... Later on a distinction was made in respect of men making 42 points or better, by classing them as 'sharpshooters'. **1918** E. S. Farrow *Dict. Mil. Terms* 551 *Sharpshooter*,..in small-arms firing, a grade of rifleman just below that of expert rifleman. **1974** M. Allen *Super Tour* i. 6 The entrance was guarded..by the chief gatekeeper or one of his three sons, all armed with rifles and all rating as sharpshooters when they had done their military service. **1977** *Time* 22 Aug. 34/3 He flunked his first rifle-shooting test but eventually qualified as an infantry sharpshooter (the middle ranking between marksman and expert) with the M-16 rifle.

**2.** Transferred senses. † **a.** *Cricket.* = shooter 9. *Obs.*

**1863** *Boy's Own Vol.* Christmas 218 Among the best men with sharpshooters were Wenman, among the old players, Carpenter and Daft, and last, not least, Mr. E. Grace.

**b.** *Sport.* A player whose aim is particularly accurate. *U.S.*

**1912** *N.Y. Tribune* 21 Sept. 12/1 Devore..was the principal sharpshooter of the second encounter, as he answered for all four runs. **1974** *State* (Columbia, S. Carolina) 27 Feb. 3-B/1 Virginia Military..builds its offense around freshman sharpshooter John Krovic.

**c.** *U.S. colloq.* = sharp *sb.*[1] 8 b.

**1942** *Sun* (Baltimore) 7 Mar. 10/5 The sharpshooters have been saying that Market Wise should romp in. **1944** *Ibid.* 21 Sept. 17/5 The real romance of the race track..is the betting crowd. First you get the experts or the sharp-shooters.

**3.** One of several leafhoppers of the family Cicadellidæ, feeding on grasses, grape-vines, and other plants.

**1902** *Yearbk. U.S. Dept. Agric. 1901* 377 Early cotton.. avoids to a great extent damage to the plant by the boll-worm, cotton worm, and sharp-shooter. **1959** *Washington Post* 23 July A20/2 Priesendorfer identified them as leafhoppers, commonly called sharpshooters.

Hence **'sharpshooting** *vbl. sb.* and *ppl. a.*

**1806** A. Duncan *Nelson* 311 The system of sharp-shooting practised by the enemy. **1840** Thackeray *Shabby-genteel Story* vi, Mrs. S. attacked the punch with some sharp-shooting, and fierce charges of vulgarity. **1844** Dickens *Mart. Chuz.* xliv, After some little sharp-shooting on both sides, Mr. Pecksniff became grave. **1863** in *Advance* (Chicago) (1892) 28 Jan., On Tuesday he..kept his men busy sharp-shooting across the river. **1865** Kingsley *Herew.* xxxii, I am too old a campaigner to take much harm by woman's sharpshooting, at fifteen score yards off. **1872** *Routledge's Ev. Boy's Ann.* 215/1 He was out sharp-shooting in the Crimea. **1899** *Westm. Gaz.* 30 Dec. 3/2 Artillery would be put out of action by sharp-shooting riflemen. **1948** *Sporting Mirror* 19 Nov. 5/1 First Division clubs are queuing up to bid for Vic Lambden, Bristol Rovers' sharpshooting centre forward. **1976** *Norwich Mercury* 10 Dec., It was the same Carrow player who had scored the first goal, and he was certainly giving Old Boys a lesson in sharpshooting. **1978** M. Puzo *Fools Die* xvi. 172 The client was a sharpshooting Wasp Wall Street broker named Buddy Stove.

† **sharp-shot.** *Obs.* [f. sharp *a.* + shot *sb.* (in the sense of shooting). (So G. *scharfschuss.*)] Firing with shot (as opposed to blank cartridge).

**1725** *Wodrow's Corr.* (1843) III. 217 Captain Bushel, unprovoked, and without reading the proclamation,..shot sharp-shot, without the least care, to dispel a poor contemptible mob. **1837** Carlyle *Fr. Rev.* I. iii. ix, The Torch Procession is met with sharp shot.

**sharpsighted** (ʃɑːpˈsaɪtɪd), *a.* [f. sharp *a.* + sighted *a.*]

**1.** Having acute or quick sight.

**1571** Golding *Calvin on Ps.* Ep. Ded. 2 Though he were otherwise as sharpsighted as Argus. **1648** Crashaw *Delights of Muses* (1904) 156 Sharp-sighted as the Eagles eye. **1791–1823** D'Israeli *Cur. Lit.* (1859) II. 445 He often trembled lest some future explorer of manuscripts might be found as sharpsighted as himself. **1832** Ht. Martineau *Life in Wilds* v. 62 So sharpsighted and timid are these birds. **1905** A. R. Wallace *My Life* xiv. 209 The Welshman is by no means sharp-sighted when his cattle are enjoying themselves in a neighbour's field.

**2.** *fig.* Having acuteness of mental vision.

**1583** Golding *Calvin on Deut.* ix. 49 Because we be not sharpesighted ynough to spie out the things that God perceiueth. **1745** *De Foe's Eng. Tradesm.* i. (1841) I. 6 For want of this knowledge, he is liable to be imposed upon..by the sharp-sighted World. **1869** Trollope *He knew*, etc. xiv. (1878) 82 [She] was sharpsighted and clear-witted.

Hence **sharp'sightedness.**

**1647** Trapp *Comm. Matt.* xxiv. 28. 553 Eagles the Saints are called,..for their sharp-sightednesse. **1838** Dickens *Nich. Nick.* xxvii, She had never felt so satisfied with her own sharp-sightedness as she did that day.

**sharpster** (ˈʃɑːpstə(r)). *colloq.* (chiefly *U.S.*). [f. sharp *sb.*[1] + -ster.] **1.** = sharper[1] 2.

**1942** Berrey & Van den Bark *Amer. Thes. Slang* §436 *Cheat*,..sharpster, shaver, shyster. **1955** *Archivum Linguisticum* VII. 153 An adjectival derivative..with the pejorative sense of 'sharpster'. **1965** *English Studies* XLVI. 465 A boxer, among scores of other appellations, may be a *fightster*..; a dishonest gambler, a *sharpster*.

**2.** A 'sharp' or stylish dresser. (In quot. *attrib.*)

**1957** J. Kerouac *On Road* (1958) ii. vi. 144 Once I knocked on his door..and he opened it wearing..a vest with nothing underneath, and long striped sharpster pants.

**sharp-witted** (ʃɑːpˈwɪtɪd), *a.* [f. sharp *a.* + wit *sb.* + -ed[2].] Sagacious, intelligent.

*a* **1586** Sidney *Arcadia* i. xii. (1912) 81 O Lord (saide Musidorus) how sharp-witted you are to hurt your selfe? **1623** Cockeram ii, Sharp witted. *Acute, sagax.* **1756** C. Smart tr. *Hor.*, *Sat.* i. iii. (1826) II. 27 To bear the sharp-witted sneers of these men. **1855** Macaulay *Hist. Eng.* xxi. IV. 538 It was beyond the power of the great King to prevent his..sharpwitted courtiers from whispering to each other. **1854** J. H. Newman *Hist. Sk.* Ser. i. (1872) 45 The sharp-witted provincial of Greece or Asia Minor.

Hence **sharp'wittedness.**

**1647** Hexham i, Sharpwittednesse, *Vernuftigheyt, scherpsinnigheyt.* **1858–61** E. B. Ramsay *Remin.* vi. (1870) 194 The sharp-wittedness of the knave.

**sharrag, -ig, -og,** dial. forms of shear-hog.

**sharrer** (ˈʃærə). *colloq.* Also **sharra.** Short for char-à-banc. Cf. chara[2].

**1934** D. L. Sayers *Nine Tailors* 114 There's a regular party comin'..in Jack Brownlow's sharrer. **1966** 'L. Lane' *ABZ of Scouse* 102 She fell outer ther sharrer. **1977** *Listener* 15 Dec. 801/2 And charabanc: it went from bang to bong and back again to bang... 'Meanwhile,' says Mr Ferris, 'the nation went about its business and called it either a coach or a sharra.'

**sharry** (ˈʃærɪ). *colloq.* Also **sharrie.** As prec. Cf. charry.

**1923** *Chambers's Jrnl.* Dec. 7/1 Many who travel by 'sharry' do so because they want the pleasures of the road. **1974** P. Wright *Lang. Brit. Industry* ix. 79 Part of many a market square..was daily reserved as a parking area for motor-coaches (then called *sharries* or *charry-bangs*).

**s'hart** (= God's heart!): see heart *sb.* 53.

**shartfort,** variant of shortford *Obs.*

**sharute,** obs. form of cheroot.

**shas, shash,** obs. ff. sash *sb.*[1] and *sb.*[2]

‖ **shashlik** (ˈʃæʃlɪk). [ad. Russ. *shashlýk*, ult. f. Turk. *şiş* a spit, skewer; cf. shish kebab.] An Eastern European and Asian kebab of mutton and garnishings often served on a skewer. Also *attrib.*

**1925** R. F. Wilson *Paris on Parade* vi. 163 He gives them ..*shashlik*, alternately spitted morsels of mutton and bacon grilled over charcoal. **1951** 'A. Garve' *Murder in Moscow* xv. 144, I was giving Watson luncheon..and he had to dash away with his *shashlik* almost untouched. **1960** *Guardian* 29 Aug. 5/6, I ate..shashlik with retsina. **1977** *N.Y. Times* 9 May L2/2 An outdoor shashlik stand just off Ashkhabad's Marx Prospekt was pulling in passers-by.

**shashoon, -une, shasoon,** obs. ff. sashoon.

**shass(e,** obs. forms of sash *sb.*[1]

**Shasta** (ˈʃæstə, locally ˈʃæstɪ), *a.* and *sb.* Also **Saste, Shaste, Shasty.** [Native name.] **A.** *adj.*

**1.** Designating an American Indian people living in the highlands of northern California or the language of the Hokan group spoken by this people.

**1843** T. J. Farnham *Trav. Gt. Western Prairies* II. 208 The doctor..had his face very much slashed in a contest with the Shasty Indians near the southern border of Oregon. **1851** G. Gibbs *Jrnl.* in H. R. Schoolcraft *Indian Tribes* (1853) III. iv. 161 This man was afterwards dispatched..to make another attempt to assemble the Shasté tribes. **1963** *Language* XXXIX. 40 The Shasta language of northern California and southern Oregon has a long history of relevance for Hokan studies.

**2.** Special collocations in *Nat. Hist.*: **Shasta cypress,** the Macnab cypress, *Cupressus macnabiana*, a small tree native to California; **Shasta daisy,** a perennial herb, *Chrysanthemum × superbum*, of the family Compositæ, a hybrid developed by Luther Burbank (1849–1926) and bearing large white flowers; **Shasta (red) fir,** a large red fir, *Abies magnifica* var. *shastensis*, native to western North America; **Shasta lily,** a yellow-flowered fragrant lily, *Lilium kelleyanum*, native to the mountains of central and northern California.

**1897** G. B. Sudworth *Nomencl. Arborescent Flora U.S.* 76 *Cupressus macnabiana.* Macnab Cypress..[also called] Shasta Cypress. **1908** N. L. Britton *N. Amer. Trees* 101 The tree..is also called Fragrant cypress, Shasta cypress, Macnab's cypress. **1901** L. Burbank *New Creations* (Suppl.) 8 When 'Shasta Daisies' were being bred and educated up to their present state more admiration has been bestowed upon them by visitors than upon any other flowering plant growing on my grounds. **1977** *Monitor* (McAllen, Texas) 26 June 1C/7 The church was decorated with pedestal urns of white Shasta daisies. **1897** G. B. Sudworth *Nomencl. Arborescent Flora U.S.* 58 *Abies magnifica* Shasta Fir..[also called] Shasta Red Fir. **1949** Collingwood & Brush *Knowing your Trees* 106 Red Fir, also known as red-barked fir, Shasta fir and golden fir, is found on high mountain slopes and meadows. **1915** Armstrong & Thornber *Western Wild Flowers* 34 Shasta Lily is a variety with a small bulb. **1937** J. H. McFarland et al. *Garden Bulbs in Color* 155 There are several varieties of this Washington or Shasta Lily.

**B.** *sb.* **1.** (A member of) the Shasta people.

**1843** T. J. Farnham *Trav. Gt. Western Prairies* II. 311 (*population table*) Shastys 500. **1846** H. Hale *Ethnogr. & Philol.* (U.S. Exploring Exped.) 218 The women of the Saste..are tattooed in lines from the mouth to the chin. **1855** *Crescent City* (California) *Herald* 27 Oct., Some of the Shastas..are represented as having been the last to retreat. **1903** G. W. James *Indian Basketry* 79 The fine white grass, used by the Shastas in the manufacture of their baskets is gained from great elevations in the mountains. **1935** R. Benedict *Patterns of Culture* ii. 42 Among the Shasta it was the convention that only women were so blessed. **1973** A. H. Whiteford *N. Amer. Indian Arts* 47 The..Shasta..had ..food baskets.

**2.** Their language. Also *Comb.*, as **Shasta-Achomawi.**

**1851** G. Gibbs *Jrnl.* 12 Oct. in H. R. Schoolcraft *Indian Tribes* (1853) III. iv. 151 Higher on the main river, the prevailing language is the Shasté. **1905** *Amer. Anthropologist* VII. 213 (*heading*) The Shasta-Achomawi: a new linguistic stock, with four new dialects. **1913** [see Hokan]. **1965** *Language* XLI. 175 Dixon's Shasta-Achomawi group..was placed in Dixon and Kroeber's Hokan stock.

Hence **'Shastan** *a.* and *sb.* [-an], (designating) a linguistic grouping of the Shasta and certain other peoples (formerly including the Achomawi-Atsugewi), or the peoples so comprised.

**1910** *Bull. U.S. Bureau Amer. Ethnol.* XXX. ii. 528/2 Shastan Family..a linguistic stock comprising two principal groups, the Sastean and the Palaihnihan of Powell. **1963** *Language* XXXIX. 43 This neatly validates the theory of contraction with the Shastan subfamily. *Ibid.*, There may have been as many as five such families a little over a century ago, viz. *Shastan*..; *Palaihnihan*..; *Pomoan*..; *Chumashan* ..; and *Yuman.* **1974** *Encycl. Brit. Micropædia* IX. 118/2 *Shastan Indians*, a group of Indian peoples speaking related languages of the Shastan family of Hokan stock... The culture of the Shastans was imitative of the Yurok and Karok.

‖ **shastra** (ˈʃɑːstrə). Forms: 7 **shastram, -um,** 7–9 **shaster,** 8 **shahstah,** 8–9 **shastah,** 9 **shastra, shastru;** 9– **sastra** Also with capital initial. [a. Hindī *çāstr*, Skr. *çāstra* (nom. sing. *çāstram*). The scholarly transliteration *śāstra* is now freq. used.] Any one of the sacred writings of the Hindus. Also, a body of teaching, a science; a treatise. Hence **Sha'straic, Sa'straic** *a.*

**1630** Lord *Banians* 40 This Booke by them called the Shaster. **1698** *Phil. Trans.* XX. 275 The *Shastram* being to them what the Bible is to Christians. **1763** Scrafton *Indostan* (1770) 4 A comment thereon [i.e. on the Vedas], called the Shahstah. **1838** [Miss Maitland] *Lett. fr. Madras* (1843) 198 They know that the Bible is our Shaster, and suppose it to be as good for *us*, as their own Shasters are for *them.* **1845** *Encycl. Metrop.* XXI. 673/1 Those who study the Védas..are styled *Waïdik*,..when learned in the six Sástras they are called *Sástrí*. **1872** SHERRING *Hindu Tribes* I. 3 The Brahman..possesses..the holy canon—Vedas, Shástras, and Puránas. **1887** W. J. WILKINS *Mod. Hinduism* 127 The position of the Brāhman as taught by the Sāstras. **1932** S. DASGUPTA *Hist. Indian Philos.* II. xiv. 445 At the first stage a man performs his duties in accordance with the injunctions of the *śāstras*. **1956** V. RAGHAVAN *Indian Heritage* p. lvii, These systems later came to be called *Sastras*, meaning thereby merely that they are authoritative and systematic schools of thought. **1960** KOESTLER *Lotus & Robot* i. 59 It is significant that every science in India is called a Sastra—a system of thought with a spiritual purpose. **1961** WEBSTER, Shastraic. **1967** SINGHA & MASSEY *Indian Dances* i. 33 The shastraic literature which kept it alive. **1968** *Indian Mus. Jrnl.* V. 46 Its gigantic volume, comprehensive subject-matter, *śāstraic* treatment of the subject-matter. **1974** *Encycl. Brit. Macropædia* III. 433/1 From the 2nd century AD onward, Mahāyāna authors wrote 'treatises' (*śāstras*) in their own names.

‖**shastri** ('ʃɑːstriː). Also 7 **shastre**, 9 **shastree**. [Hindī *çāstrī*, Skr. *çāstrin*, nom. sing. *çāstrī*, f. *çāstra* SHASTRA.] One who is learned in, or teaches, the shasters.

*c* **1645** HOWELL *Lett.* Suppl. xiv. (1892) 662 As they who have conversed with Shastres and Turbants doe well know. **1826** J. G. DUFF *Hist. Mahrattas* I. 23 *note*, Bramins learned in the Shasters have the title of Shastree. **1855** H. H. WILSON *Gloss. Judic.* etc. *Terms India* 470 *Sástrí*, vulgarly *Shastree*.

**shastyse**, obs. form of CHASTISE.

†**shat**[1]. *Obs.* [Ir. *séad*, lit. jewel.] Used as a term of endearment in addressing an Irish person.

*a* **1616** BEAUM. & FL. *Coxcomb* II. i, Come hither shat, are you an Irish mon?

†**shat**[2]. *Obs. rare*$^{-1}$. Mentioned as a colloq. or slang term for a tattler.

**1709** STEELE *Tatler* No. 71 ¶7 Bambouzling is exploded; a Shat is a Tatler.

**shat**, *pa. pple.* of SHIT *v.*; also var. SHOTT.

**shatchen**, var. SHADCHAN.

**shate**, obs. pa. t. of SHOOT.

**shathmont**, *Sc.* variant of SHAFTMENT[1].

**shatranji**, var. SITRINGEE.

**shattaradan**: see SHANDRYDAN.

**shatter** ('ʃætə(r)), *sb.* [f. SHATTER *v.*]

**1.** *pl.* Fragments into which a thing is broken, rent, or torn. Chiefly in phrases (*to break*, etc.) *into* or *to shatters*, (*to be*) *in shatters*. *Obs.* exc. *dial.*

*a* **1640** FENNER *Serm.* xvii. Wks. (1657) 225 If ever the heart come to be sensible of its blow, it will break all to shatters. **1691** MRS. D'ANVERS *Academia* 35 His..Gown.. hangs about his Legs in shatters. **1727** [E. DORRINGTON] *Philip Quarll* (1816) 38 A sea which dashed the ship to shatters against the rock. **1750** H. WALPOLE *Let. to Mann* 19 Nov., For the Ministry, it is all in shatters. *a* **1814** *Last Act* II. v. in *New Brit. Theatre* II. 398, I..run my chaise so effectually against theirs, that smash both went all to shatters. **1821** CLARE *Vill. Minstr.* I. 93 The proudest triumph art conceives..Grey-bearded time in shatters leaves. **1872** *Argosy* XIII. 199 It's a sad thing..for men like you to be obliged to work yourselves to shatters to keep them. **1890** *Gloucester Gloss.*, *Shatters*, sherds of pottery, etc.

**2.** A shattered state of nerves. *rare.*

**1777** MISS BURNEY *Early Diary* (1889) II. 166 You can have no idea what a shatter every new comer gave me. **1849** CARLYLE in *Century Mag.* (1882) May 23/2 If the nerves are to be continually in a shatter with want of sleep.

†**3.** 'Shattery' or friable stone. *dial. Obs.*

**1712** J. MORTON *Nat. Hist. Northampt.* 123 [Strata] 2. Stiff Clay almost four Foot. 3. Shatter, as they there call it, that is a shattering Stone, two Foot.

**4.** Something scattered or shed; a crop (of hops); a shower (of rain). *dial.* Cf. SCATTER *sb.* 2.

**1875** PARISH *Sussex Gloss.*, There's a tidy shatter of hops this year. **1887** *Kentish Gloss.*, We've had quite a nice little shatter of rain.

**shatter** ('ʃætə(r)), *v.* Forms: 4–5 **schater, -ir**, 6 **shater, shattar**, 6– **shatter**. [Of obscure origin: see SCATTER *v.*]

**1.** *trans.* To scatter, disperse, throw about in all directions; to cause (seed, leaves, etc.) to fall or be shed. Also with *out*. *Obs.* exc. *dial.*

*c* **1330** *Arth. & Merl.* 553 (Kölbing) Ac þo þai come hider eft, Her werk was al vp aleft & yschatred here & þere. *c* **1400** *Apol. Loll.* (Camden) 81 ȝe schal mak counseil and it schal be schaterid [Vulg. *Isa.* viii. 10 *dissipabitur*]. **1577** B. GOOGE *Heresbach's Husb.* I. (1586) 32 Least the whot weather shatter the seedes. **1637** MILTON *Lycidas* 5, I com to pluck your Berries harsh and crude, And with forc'd fingers rude Shatter your leaves before the mellowing year. **1665** HOOKE *Microgr.* 131 The skin cleaves and at length falls off..and leaves the seed Case to ripen, and by degrees, to shatter out its seed at a place underneath this cap. **1669** WORLIDGE *Syst. Agric.* ii. 13 If the young Cions be..a little sheltered..by shattering a little Straw, Brake, or Hawm lightly over them. **1745** P. THOMAS *Jrnl. Anson's Voy.* 329 They sow almost all Manner of Grain, but Oats and Lentils; but these are..apt to be shatter'd before Harvest. **1844** W. BARNES *Poems Rur. Life* (1848) 178 Nanny..tore the bag wher she'd a-put Her share, an' shatter'd ev'ry nut. **1887** *Kentish Gloss.* **1893** *Wiltsh. Gloss.* Add. 201.

*absol.* **1589** NASHE *Pasquil's Ret.* D iiij, You haue lost your iugling stick, your conueighance is such, that you shatter, and carrie not halfe so cleane as your freends would haue you.

**2. a.** To break in pieces by a sudden blow or concussion; to dash into fragments, disrupt into parts.

*c* **1450** LOVELICH *Grail* xiii. 734 Here helmes he to-Clef A-two, Here Scheldis he Alto-schatered Also. **1564** STOW *Mem.* in *Three 15th Cent. Chron.* (Camden) 130 Y[e] backar partes of y[e] same howsys wer all to blewne and shattard in pecis. **1604** DRAYTON *Moyses* II. 49 The slates fall shatt'red from the roofe aboue. **1634** MILTON *Comus* 799 Till all thy magick structures rear'd so high Were shatter'd into heaps o're thy false head. **1660** BOYLE *New Exp. Phys. Mech.* xxii. 166 Those light and subtle Fumes..into which the Fire it self shatters dry Bodies. **1782** COWPER *Gilpin* 124 The bottles twain behind his back Were shatter'd at a blow. **1816** J. SMITH *Panorama Sci. & Art* II. 228 In this experiment the glasses are often shattered to pieces. **1878** HUXLEY *Physiogr.* 89 A thin glass vessel may easily be shattered by sucking the air from its interior. **1883** *Harper's Mag.* Nov. 946/2 The light.., striking against a series of..prisms, fell shattered and scintillating into a thousand..beams.

**b.** To damage ruinously (a structure, a living organism, a fighting force, etc.) by battery or violent concussion; to damage or destroy by fracture of the parts.

*a* **1513** FABYAN *Chron.* VI. clxxix. (1516) 104/1 He repayred Cyties, townes & Castelles that by the sayd Danys were shatered and broken. **1602** SHAKS. *Ham.* II. i. 95 He rais'd a sigh, so pittious and profound, That it did seeme to shatter all his bulke. *a* **1700** EVELYN *Diary* 20 Feb. 1662, I return'd home to repaire my house, miserably shatter'd by the late tempest. **1735** JOHNSON *Lobo's Abyssinia, Descr.* v. 77 The General had already one Arm broken, and his Knee shatter'd with a Musket-shot. **1748** *Anson's Voy.* II. iv. 167 These Spanish ships..had been greatly shattered by a storm. **1854** TENNYSON *Charge Light Brigade* iv, Cossack and Russian Reel'd from the sabre-stroke Shatter'd and sunder'd. **1863** W. C. BALDWIN *Afr. Hunting* viii. 329 His face was shattered with shot about the upper jaw, nose, and eyes.

**c.** *fig.*, or with immaterial object. Also, to damage or destroy the fortunes of (a person or body of persons).

**1683–4** STILLINGFL. *Serm.* (Job xxiii. 15) (1707) 343 No consideration in the World doth so break in pieces and confound and shatter the Spirit of a Man. **1690** LOCKE *Govt.* I. xi. §147 (1698) 143 When any Monarchy was shatter'd to pieces, and divided amongst revolted Subjects. **1860** EMERSON *Cond. Life, Considerations* Wks. (Bohn) II. 417 The war or revolution..that shatters a rotten system. **1874** GREEN *Short Hist.* viii. §1. 457 The truth against which ecclesiastical dogmatism..must always shatter itself. **1906** PINCHES *Relig. Babyl. & Assyria* iii. 37 An irresistible weapon, which should shatter all his enemies.

**d.** To wreck (a person's constitution, nerves, etc.) by sickness, hardship, or the like. Also, to wreck the health, strength, or spirits of (a person).

**1785** MME. D'ARBLAY *Diary* 14 Dec., Everything shatters her dear feeble frame. **1802** *Med. Jrnl.* VIII. 212 Her constitution, shattered by the frequent attacks it endured, could not long hold out. **1848** DICKENS *Dombey* lxi, Shattered in mind, and perilously sick in body. **1887** *Pall Mall Budget* 21 Apr. 2/2 Continual riding to and fro in the steppes will in time shatter the wiriest constitution.

**e.** To cause (earth) to crumble. ? *dial.*

**1891** MALDEN *Tillage* 58 This land must be stirred in frosts as much as possible; if it once gets baked into a harsh condition, it will have to be allowed to get thoroughly dry, when a rain will 'shatter' it.

**3.** *intr.* To become scattered or dispersed; to be shed or strewn about. Of grain, etc.: To drop out of the husk from over-ripeness. Of a flower: To drop its petals. Also with *out*.

**1577** B. GOOGE *Heresbach's Husb.* I. 36 b, All Pulse..are speedily to be geathered when they be ripe, for they suddaynely shatter. **1669** WORLIDGE *Syst. Agric.* (1681) 150 To gather them [*sc.* hops] before they shatter. **1733** TULL *Horse-hoeing Husb.* xv. 202 The first Crop they let stand till some of the Seed shatter'd. **1904** *Eng. Dial. Dict.* s.v., Those oats are beginning to shatter out. *Kent.*

**4. a.** To become broken suddenly or violently into fragments or separate parts; to fly in pieces or asunder. Also with *up*.

**1567**, **1578** [see SHATTERING *ppl. a.* 1]. **1626** BACON *Sylva* §841 Some Fragile Bodies breake but where the Force is; Some shatter and fly in many Peeces. **1712** J. MORTON *Nat. Hist. Northampt.* 108 A very hard, irregular, lumpish Stone, that does not hew well, but shatters with the Tool. **1858** KINGSLEY *Misc.* (1859) I. 149 To hear that chorus, as it pours round the fir-stems, rings against the roof above, shatters up into a hundred echoes. **1867** AUGUSTA WILSON *Vashti* xvi, Promises, which shatter like crystal under the hammer of the first temptation. **1896** A. E. HOUSMAN *Shropshire Lad* iv, Wake: the vaulted shadow shatters.

**b.** Of a body of men: To suffer disruption.

*a* **1619** FOTHERBY *Atheom.* I. v. §2 (1622) 31 Religion [is] the foundation of euery Citie, both gathering men, and holding them vnanimously together; who else would quickly shatter cleane asunder. **1687** tr. *Sallust, Jug.* (1692) 132 His Army, compos'd of several Nations, having lost their Leader,..shatter'd into several Parties.

**c.** Of earth: To fall or crumble in pieces. Also with *down*. ? *dial.* (Cf. 2 e.)

**1733** W. ELLIS *Chiltern & Vale Farm.* 234 It being a black, fat Mould,..will by the Frosts, Rains, and Winds,.. shatter, crumble, and become hollow. **1891** MALDEN *Tillage* 49 Any pens which have been extra trodden in wet weather should be picked out, and ploughed while frosted, so that they may 'shatter' down on thawing. *Ibid.* Gloss. s.v., Clods shatter into flakes or meal-like particles, when they fall to pieces from the effect of the weather.

**5. a.** To dash or strike noisily against some hard object; to produce sharp sudden sounds by shaking or concussion; to clatter, rattle. *rare.*

**13..** *Gaw. & Gr. Knt.* 2083 Brokez byled, & breke, bi bonkkez aboute, Schyre schaterande on schorez, þer þay doun schowued. ? *a* **1400** *Arthur* 90 Thus they hyw on helmes hye, And schatered on wyþ scheldes. **1623** J. TAYLOR (Water-P.) *World runs on Wheels* Wks. (1630) II. 238/1 The casements shatter, tatter and clatter. **1722** DE FOE *Plague* (1756) 196 Windows stood shattering with the Wind in empty Houses, for want of People to shut them. **1904** *Eng. Dial. Dict.*, *Shatter*, to rattle as the windows of a carriage. *Caithness.* **1912** M. HEWLETT in *Eng. Rev.* Apr. 12 Slantwise comes the rain And shatters at the window-pane To wake the hind.

†**b.** Of the teeth: To chatter. *Obs.*

**1682** CREECH *Lucretius* v. 162 His Teeth all shatter, Limbs all shake with Cold. **1782** [T. VAUGHAN] *Fashionable Follies* I. lxiv. 109 His teeth shattered, his hair stood upright on his head.

**c.** Of birds: To chirp, chatter. *dial. rare.*

**17..** *Bonnie Nancy* i. in Maidment *Ballads* (1844) 13 Nancy's to the Greenwood gain To hear the gowdspink shattering.

**6.** *trans.* and *intr.* To shake, wave, move to and fro. *rare.*

*a* **1530** HEYWOOD *Wether* 513 (Brandl) The wynde is so weyke it..skantely can shatter the shyttyn sayle That hangeth shatterynge at a womans tayle. **16..** MIDDLETON, etc. *Old Law* v. i. (1656) 61 Ist possible these gowty legs danc't lately, And shattered in a Galliard?

**7.** *Comb.*: **shatter belt** *Geol.*, a belt of fractured or brecciated rock formed as a result of faulting; **shatter cone** *Geol.*, a fluted conical structure produced in rock by intense mechanical shock, esp. by that associated with meteoritic impact; hence **shatter-coned** *a.*, characterized by the presence of shatter cones; **shatter-coning** *vbl. sb.*, the formation or presence of shatter cones; **shatter crack** *Metallurgy* (see quot. 1958); **shatter-pate, -wit** = SHATTER-BRAIN; **shatter-pated, -witted** *adjs.* = SHATTER-BRAINED (in Dicts.); **shatter-proof** *a.*, proof against shattering; also *fig.*

**1910** PEACH & HORNE in Murray & Pullar *Bathymetr. Survey Scottish Fresh-Water Lochs* I. 459 *Shatter belts situated along lines of fault or dislocations of the strata have exercised a considerable influence in producing the isolation of these individual masses. **1970** R. J. SMALL *Study of Landforms* iii. 102 Where crustal movement leads to the creation of crushed or brecciated zones ('shatter-belts').., the development of river valleys may be closely guided. **1933** W. H. BUCHER in *Rep. 16th Internat. Geol. Congr.* 1070 In the same vicinity more convincing evidence of the action of an explosive force is seen in the local development of '*shatter cones', innumerable incipient cracks traversing beds of rather coarsely crystalline dolomite in the shape of interpenetrating cones, not unlike cone-in-cone. **1979** *Sci. Amer.* Mar. 43/3 Macroscopic evidence includes 'shatter cones', structures of quartzite that flare outward and downward, away from the direction of impact. **1967** *McGraw-Hill Yearbk. Sci. & Technol.* 110 The Steinheim Basin..is the prototype *shatter-coned structure. **1968** *New Scientist* 28 Nov. 501/2 A really definitive theory of *shatter coning is still lacking. **1975** *Nature* 29 May 394/1 Shatter coning and intense microtwinning of calcite..are indicators of shock metamorphism. **1930** *Jrnl. Iron & Steel Inst.* CXXI. 703 Rapid cooling through the secondary brittle range is believed to cause the formation of *shatter cracks in rails showing secondary brittleness. **1958** A. D. MERRIMAN *Dict. Metallurgy* 315/2 *Shatter cracks*, a name used in reference to fine internal fissures, particularly when found in the heads of steel rails. The cracks lie at random in all directions and occur most frequently in large steel forgings. **1775** ASH, **Shatterpate*, a shatterbrain. **1976** *Times* 7 Dec. 14/5 This poor shatterpate's condition. **1727** *Shatter-pated [see SHATTER-BRAINED]. **1901** *Scotsman* 11 Nov. 9/2 The shatter-pated pulpiteers. **1917** J. B. CABELL *Cream of Jest* (1927) xxi. 115 Everywhere, in every age,..men stumbled amiable and shatter-pated through a jungle of miracles, blind to its wonderfulness. **1938** *Sun* (Baltimore) 18 Feb. 12/2 Ah reckon yo're a mite shatter-pated in yore wit-box. **1936** *Ibid.* 6 Feb. 6/2 Two men who locked the doors of their automobile from the inside..watched State police vainly try to break through *shatterproof glass. **1953** M. MCCARTHY in *Reporter* 3 Mar. 38/2 These people live in shatterproof hierarchical structures. **1978** M. DEWIS *Law Health & Safety at Work* v. 245 The plaintiff relied on a statement that the windscreens were shatterproof and bought one of their cars. **1775** ASH, **Shatterwit*, a shatterbrain, an inattentive young fellow, a giddy girl. **1775** ASH, **Shatterwitted*, inattentive, careless, giddy.

'**shatter-brain**. [See SHATTER *v.* 7. Cf. SCATTER-BRAIN.] A person of 'cracked' brain or wandering wits; a giddy, thoughtless person.

**1719** D'URFEY *Pills* II. 327 Sharks, Shagrags, Shatter-brains. **1788** WESLEY *Wks.* (1872) VI. 448 A petit-maitre,.. or a shatter-brain of any kind. **1853** HAWTHORNE *Eng. Note-Bks.* (1883) I. 459 However, she has undoubtedly a mother's love for this poor shatterbrain.

*attrib.* **1837** MISS MITFORD *Country Stories* 11 A shatter-brain boy who did not know a violet from a nettle. **1839** T. MITCHELL *Frogs of Aristoph.* Introd. p. cxii, A sort of shatterbrain commingling of right and wrong in his intellect.

So '**shatter-brained** *a.* crazy, light-witted; giddy, thoughtless. (Cf. SCATTER-BRAINED.)

**1727** BAILEY vol. II, *Shatter-brain'd*, *Shatter-pated*, scarce *Compos Mentis*, crazy-headed, hare-brain'd, confused, acting without Thought, &c. **1749** LAVINGTON *Enthus. Meth. & Papists* I. (1754) 7 St. Ignatius Loyola, that errant shatter-brain'd visionary Fanatic. **1818** COBBETT *Pol. Reg.* XXXIII. 483 The old, shatterbrained hag who is endeavouring to frighten and murder the people of England.

**1824** SCOTT *St. Ronan's* xxv, This shatter-brained peer was, in other respects, a handsome, accomplished man.

**shattered** (ˈʃætəd), *ppl. a.* [f. SHATTER *v.* + -ED.] **a.** In the senses of the verb.

**1666** DRYDEN *Ann. Mirab.* lxv, His shatter'd Sails with Rigging to restore. **1672** WISEMAN *Wounds* I. x. 101 You must make way to these wounds by removing the shattered flesh. **1707** FREIND *Peterborow's Cond. Sp.* 71 To recruit his shatter'd Cavalry. **1796** MME. D'ARBLAY *Camilla* IX. xi, Her shattered nerves could not bear the interview. **1849** ROBERTSON *Serm.* Ser. I. x. (1866) 182 The languor of shattered health. **1879** FARRAR *St. Paul* (1883) 283 Paul returned from this journey a shattered man.

†**b.** Scattered, not concentrated. *Obs.*

**1687** NORRIS *Misc., Of Seriousness* 171 A man of a loose, volatile and shatter'd humour.

**c.** *colloq.* Extremely distressed or exhausted; upset, overcome.

**1930** A. CHRISTIE *Murder at Vicarage* ii. 14 How tiresome everyone is. I feel shattered... If only I had some money I'd go away. **1968** *Listener* 12 Sept. 337/2, I came in at tea-time, I sat down and I was absolutely shattered. **1978** S. RADLEY *Death & Maiden* viii. 75, I honestly can't tell you anything about Mary. I'm shattered, that's all I know.

ˈ**shatterer.** *rare.* [-ER[1].] One who shatters.

With quot. 1867 cf. De Quincey *Coleridge* Wks. 1863 II. 58 He was called, by one who weighed him well [*sc.* by M. Mendelssohn], the *alles-zermalmender*, the world-shattering Kant.

**1867** J. H. STIRLING in *Fortn. Rev.* Oct. 381 The *Alles-zermalmender*, the shatterer of the world [*i.e.* Kant]. **1923** *Weekly Dispatch* 25 Feb. 2 Stravinsky.. is a disturber of our peace, a shatterer of illusions.

†**shatter-headed,** *a. Obs. rare.* = SHATTER-BRAINED. (Cf. SCATTER-HEADED.)

*c* **1686** in *Brasenose Coll. Quatern. Monogr.* (O.H.S.) II. I. xii. 23 A shatter-headed Fellow of Brasen-nose College. **1713** C'TESS WINCHILSEA *Misc. Poems* 226 Prithee, shatter-headed Fop.

**shattering** (ˈʃætərɪŋ), *vbl. sb.* [-ING[1].] The action of the verb SHATTER; an instance of this. Also *concr.*, a shattered piece or fragment.

**1658** A. FOX tr. *Wurtz' Surg.* II. xxviii. 191 The bone was not black, all kept together, no shatterings nor splinters in it. **1748** *Anson's Voy.* I. x. 100 The violence of the storms, the shattering of our sails and rigging. **1863** *Reader* 31 Oct. 512 Mr. Coxwell's balloon was made by himself.., and he has repaired all the shatterings it has received in the cause of science. **1886** *Athenæum* 6 Feb. 197/1 The sudden shattering of his belief in a miraculous apparition. **1960** *Farmer & Stockbreeder* 16 Feb. 77/1 Some plants produced seed heads which were less susceptible to shattering than others. **1974** E. STACEY *Peace Country* ii. 112 The report said that he lost considerable of the crop from shattering.

ˈ**shattering,** *ppl. a.* [-ING[2].] That shatters.

**1.** That is broken up suddenly or forcibly; falling in pieces or asunder.

**1567** PAINTER *Pal. Pleas.* (1890) III. 431 The foundation ..planted in shattring Soyle. **1578** T. PROCTOR *Gorg. Gallery, Sonnet agst. Detraction* iv. D iv, In weltring waues my ship is tost, My shattering sayles away bee shorne.

**2. a.** Ruinously destructive; that breaks or destroys by a sudden blow or concussion. Also *fig.*

**1577** KENDALL *Flowers of Epigr., Trifles* 27, I shield from shatteryng showers the house. **1805** SOUTHEY *Madoc* II. ix. 65 Till one, or both, Dash'd down the shattering precipice, should feed The mountain eagle! **1847** DE QUINCEY *Joan of Arc* Wks. III. 235 Her answer to this was as shattering as it was rapid. **1903** MORLEY *Gladstone* VI. v. II. 343 Mr. Gladstone's description of a marvellous and shattering hour.

**b.** Of sound: rending the air, ear-splitting.

**1842** TENNYSON *Sir Galahad* 5 The shattering trumpet shrilleth high.

**c.** In trivial use, astounding, upsetting; tiresome.

**1924** WODEHOUSE *Bill the Conqueror* v. 97 Any ordinary disaster she might have coped with, but this was too shattering. **1948** R. LEHMANN *Note in Music* (ed. 2) 114 We don't converse much. But now and then she lets fall a shattering remark. **1958** [see LAVATORIAL *a.* 2]. **1967** *Listener* 16 Nov. 637/3 The hundreds of quotations.. about.. murders, the savage punishments, and slave life in the New World, are shattering.

Hence ˈ**shatteringly** *adv.*

**1818** MOORE *Fudge Fam. Paris* xi. 49 True he.. But raised the hopes of men—as eaglets fly With tortoises aloft into the sky—To dash them down again more shatteringly! **1911** G. K. CHESTERTON *Ballad White Horse* v. 112 On the helm of a high chief Fell shatteringly his brand. **1939** H. J. MASSINGHAM *Countryman's Jrnl.* xxx. 132 The argument applies far more shatteringly to the Purbeck limestone.

**shatterment** (ˈʃætəmənt). *rare.* [-MENT.] The act of shattering, the result of being shattered.

**1841** CARLYLE in T. W. Reid *Life Ld. Houghton* (1890) I. 256 It is above all a new kind of shatterment that I suffer.

**shattery** (ˈʃætərɪ), *a.* [f. SHATTER *v.* + -Y.]

**1.** Of rock, stone or soil: Apt to break in pieces or crumble, friable.

**1728** WOODWARD *Fossils* 7 A brittle Shattery sort of Spar. **1813** BOYS *Agric. Kent* 65 In loose shattery soils. **1884** *Nature* 13 Nov. 34/2 The thin band of shattery quartzite.

**2.** Of furniture, etc.: Loose, rickety. *dial.*

**1844** TUPPER *Crock of Gold* ii. 12 Each room has its shattery casement. **1854** MISS BAKER *Northampt. Gloss.* II. 221 The chairs are very shattery.

**3.** Shatter-brained, giddy. *dial.*

**1820** WILBRAHAM *Cheshire Gloss.*

Hence ˈ**shatteryness.**

**1851-9** MALLET in *Man. Sci. Enq.* 360 The degree of shatteryness or compactness of the rock formations.

**shatterydan:** see SHANDRYDAN.

**shattow,** obs. form of CHATEAU.

**1744** M. BISHOP *Life & Adv.* 186 Then General Webb took two Regiments.. and marched them along in order to beat the French out of a Shattow.

**shattuck,** obs. form of SHADDOCK.

**shattuckite** (ˈʃætəkaɪt). *Min.* [f. the name *Shattuck* (see quot. 1915) + -ITE[1].] A hydrated silicate of copper found as pale blue orthorhombic crystals.

**1915** W. T. SCHALLER in *Jrnl. Washington Acad. Sci.* V. 7 Shattuckite is a blue hydrous copper silicate from the Shattuck Arizona Copper Company's mine at Bisbee, Arizona... Shattuckite forms pseudomorphs after malachite and also occurs as small spherulites. **1928** *Mineral. Abstr.* III. 485 Scalenohedra.. of calcite from Tantara mine, Katanga, are completely changed to dioptase or to a mixture of deep-blue pleochroic shattuckite and pale-blue non-pleochroic plancheite. **1977** *Amer. Mineralogist* LXII. 491 The crystal structure of shattuckite, $Cu_5(SiO_3)_4(OH)_2$ has been refined in the orthorhombic space group *Pcab.*

**shau,** obs. form of SHAW, SHOW.

**shauchle** (ˈʃɑx(ə)l), *v. Sc.* Also 8 shochel, 9 shochle, shachle, (shackle), shaughle. See also SHAFFLE *v.* [Of obscure origin: cf. SHAIL *v.*

The Eng. dial. words *shuckle* (Kent) to shuffle along, or slink along in walking, *shockle* to shuffle, to shake, joggle (see *Eng. Dial. Dict.*), and the G. *schaukel* a swing, *schaukeln* (= MDu. *schockelen*) to swing, rock, in spite of their similarity in form and meaning, appear to be unconnected with this word; they app. belong to the root of SHOCK *v.*]

**1.** *intr.* To shuffle the feet.

**1721** KELLY *Sc. Prov.* 142 Had you such a Shoe on every Foot, you would shochel. *c* **1820** HOGG *Sheph. Wedding* i. Tales & Sk. (1837) II. 152 Off comes Geordie, shaughle shaughlin' wi' a' his pith. *a* **1895** R. McL. CALDER in *Berwicksh. Bard* (1897) 221 Hoo often we'd.. shauchle alang withoot object or aim.

**2.** *trans.* To put out of shape, distort; to shuffle out (shoes).

**1805** JAMIESON, To *Shachle*, to use any thing so as to distort it from its proper shape or direction, S. *He has shachlit aw his schoon*, he has put his shoes quite out of shape [by shuffling]. **1875** G. MACDONALD *Malcolm* I. xiv. 169 'A' heelan' fowk's some kittle aboot their legs'. 'Deil shochle them!' exclaimed the Partaness; 'what care I for 's legs!'

**shauchled** (ˈʃɑx(ə)ld), *a. Sc.* [f. prec. + -ED[1].] Twisted out of shape. (Said chiefly of shoes or the feet.)

**1737** RAMSAY *Sc. Prov.* (1797) 100 Ye shape shoon by your ain shachled feet. **1795** BURNS *Braw Wooer* vii, I spier'd for my cousin.. And how her new shoon fit her auld shachl't feet. **1818** SCOTT *Br. Lamm.* xxviii, Bucklaw was welcome to the wearing of Ravenswood's shaughled shoes. **1898** LD. E. HAMILTON *Mawkin* xi, Richt soon We'se find wha's glinked our scogie-lass, And gar him fill his shackled shoon.

**shauchling** (ˈʃɑxlɪŋ), *ppl. a. Sc.* [f. SHAUCHLE *v.* + ING[2].] Shuffling in gait; infirm, unsteady; *fig.* shuffling, prevaricating, unreliable.

**1755** RAMSAY *To Jas. Clerk* 64 Debts I abhor, and plan to be Frae shochling trade and danger free. **1826** J. WILSON *Noct. Ambr.* Wks. 1855 I. 186 Chiels that would.. look prouder, when taking their forenoon's airing alang Princes Street, on a bit schachlin ewe-necked powney.. than Saladin. *a* **1894** STEVENSON *Weir of Hermiston* iii. (1896) 74 And I would send no man to be a servant to the King.. that has proved such a shauchling son to his own faither.

**shauchly** (ˈʃɑxlɪ), *a. Sc.* Also -ley. [f. SHAUCHLE *v.* + -Y.] Infirm, rickety, shaky. Of a person: Unsteady in gait. (Cf. SHACKLY *a.*)

**1830** J. WILSON *Noct. Ambr.* Wks. 1856 III. 70, I think I see him.. wi' that wee shauchly body the Marquis o' Winchester, and that great big muckle John Bull, Sir William Curtis. **1896** D. S. MELDRUM *Grey Mantle* 272 Hey! for another ride in a shauchly gig, down the pitch-black roads!

Hence ˈ**shauchliness,** unsteadiness.

**1887** WILLOCK *Rosetty Ends* xxi. 162 They had a limp shauchleyness aboot their legs that suggestit [etc.].

**shaugh:** see SHAHI, SHAW, SHEUGH, SHOCH.

**shaugh, shauh:** see SHAH.

**shaughraun** (ˈʃɑːxrɑː, ʃɑːxˈrɑːn). *Anglo-Ir.* and *Newfoundland.* Also **shaughran,** (Newfoundland) **shaugraun** (-g-). [ad. Ir. *seachrán* a wandering, a straying, an error.] **a.** In phrs. ***to go a shaughraun***: to go wrong; ***on*** (or ***in***) ***a*** (or ***the***) ***shaughraun***: in a vagrant or drifting state. **b.** A vagabond.

**1843** W. CARLETON *Traits & Stories Irish Peasantry* I. 5 His speculation was gone a shaughran, as he termed it. *c* **1874** D. BOUCICAULT in M. R. Booth *Eng. Plays of 19th Cent.* (1969) II. 165 (*title*) The Shaughraun. *Ibid.*, Conn, the shaughraun, the soul of every fair, the life of every funeral, the first fiddle at all weddings and patterns. **1892** E. LAWLESS *Grania* I. II. ii. 153 'Tis eight days in the week she'll find herself working.. yes, and going a shaughraun most like at the tail of it all. **1922** JOYCE *Ulysses* 134 We'll paralyse Europe as Ignatius Gallaher used to say when he was on the shaughraun, doing billiardmarking in the Clarence. **1955** L. E. F. ENGLISH *Historic Newfoundland* (St John's Newfoundland Tourist Devel. Div.) 36 *Shaugraun*, a vagabond state. **1961** 'F. O'BRIEN' *Hard Life* v. 34 Well the dear knows I think you are trying to destroy my temper, Father, and put me out of my wits and make an unfortunate shaughraun out of me. **1963** *Amer. Speech* XXXVIII. 300 *Shaugraun*,.. (1) A vagabond state, (2) a person in a vagabond state, a bum. 'He spent his youth in a shaugraun.' 'He was a shaugraun.' [Newfoundland].

**shaul** (ʃɔːl). *dial.* Forms: 6 shawlde, showle, 7–8 shawlé, 9 shaul. [Perh. subst. use of *shalde*, obs. var. of SHOAL *a.*, shallow.]

**1.** A wooden scoop used for winnowing corn.

**1562** WITHALS *Dict.* 16/2 A trey or shawlde to wynowe or wymble corne with, *ventilabrum, pala.* **1674** RAY *S. & E.C. Words* 76 A *Shawle*: a shovel to winnow withall, *Suss.* **1766** *Complete Farmer, Shawle*, a shovel used in winnowing corn. **1884** *W. Sussex Gaz.* 25 Sept. (Advt.), Variety of tools, bushel, shaul, shovel [etc.]. **1908** *Essex Rev.* XVII. 23 The flail has been displaced by a steam threshing-machine, the barn-fan and the shaul by a winnowing-machine.

**2.** A wooden tub with sloping sides used for kneading bread or for washing.

**1600** in W. F. Shaw *Memorials of Eastry* (1870) 226 Ite. in the buntting house one Bunting hutch, Two kneding showles. **1887** *Kentish Gloss., Shaul, Showle*, a wooden tub with sloping sides.

**shaul(d, shauling:** see SHOAL, SHOALING.

**shaulm(e,** obs. forms of SHAWM.

**shault,** obs. variant of SHOLT, cur.

**shault,** variant of SHALT *Sc. dial.* (pony).

**shaume, -melle:** see SHAWM, SHAMBLE *sb.*[1]

**shauneen,** variant of SHONEEN.

**shauntee,** obs. form of SHANTY *a.* (JAUNTY *a.*).

**shaup, shawp** (ʃɑp). *Sc.* [Prob. cogn. w. ON. *skálp-r* scabbard, Du. *schelp, schulp* shell.]

**1.** A pea-pod; a case, wrapper.

**1822** GALT *Sir A. Wylie* I. xxv. 228 But naebody can tell what's in the shawp till it's shelt. **1850** J. STRUTHERS *Poet. Wks.* I. Autobiog. 101 Whether it was sold to be read.. [or] cut.. into squares to be shaups for sweeties, he knoweth not.

**2.** *fig.* An empty person.

**1728** RAMSAY *Archers diverting themselves* 78 Proud shaups, dull coofs, and gabbling gowks.

‖**shauri** (ˈʃaʊriː). Pl. **shauries, shauris.** [a. Swahili, f. Arab. *šūrā.*] Counsel, debate, problem.

**1925** N. K. STRANGE *Wife in Kenya* xvii. 123 Sometimes such strangers came on business intent, to have a grand shauri, or a remunerative deal in posho. **1938** E. HEMINGWAY *Fifth Column* (1939) 121 The gun-bearers.. go with us. It's their *shauri*. You see, they signed on for it. **1970** *Kenya Farmer* Feb. 8/5 Often he can solve a problem by calling a meeting of the staff and obtaining their views and suggestions, not only on their personal *shauris*, but also on improvements in sales and service. **1975** T. DINESEN *My Sister, Isak Dinesen* vi. 79 Sometime in the future, in which we shall remember all the shauries (especially difficult and unpleasant things) as shadows and smile at them.

**shauwe,** obs. form of SHOW *v.*

†**shavaldour.** *Obs.* Also **shavaldwre, schaveldore, -dowr(e, schawa(l)dour, -atour, schalldour.** [Of obscure origin; the form is app. AF. In the *Calendar of Documents relating to Scotland* III. 127 the word is quoted as *schavaldurs* from a document of 1319.] A gentleman brigand of the Scottish border; a border-rider.

The word occurs, chiefly in Latinized forms, in 14th c. chronicles as the appellation of certain marauders in the bishopric of Durham in the reign of Edw. II, some of whom were hanged for plundering two cardinals on their way to Scotland in 1317. Probably on account of the notoriety of this incident, the word seems to have obtained some currency in England in the 15th c.

[*c* **1330** TROKELOWE *Annales* an. 1317 (Rolls) 99 Quidam fatui de Northumbria, qui dicebantur 'Savaldores'. *c* **1335** R. DE GRAYSTANES *Hist. Dunelm.* xxxv. (Surtees) 94 (Bp. Rich. Kellowe, 1310–1316) Schavaldos insurgentes in episcopatu fortiter compescuit... Quidam.. qui portabat robas Episcopi.. occidit quendam schavaldum vel prædonem, Johannem de Wandel nomine, sed Regi familiarem. *a* **1347** MURIMUTH *Contin. Chron.* an. 1317 (Rolls) 27 Et per suos schaveldarios marchiae inter Angliam et Scociam nec voluit R. le Bruys permittere quod ipsi cardinales regnum Scociae intrarent. *c* **1366** KNIGHTON *Chron.* an. 1318 (Rolls) I. 413 Cumque in partes Scotiæ [cardinales] venissent, insultavit eos dominus Gilbertus de Mydelton miles cum aliis elegantibus shavaldres, et eos.. spoliaverunt. *a* **1369** SIR T. GRAY *Scalacronica* (Maitland Club) 147 Les maufesurs estoint appellez schaualdours.]

**1375** BARBOUR *Bruce* v. 205 A knycht.. Said it wes to gret perell, So neir the schavaldwris to ga. *c* **1380** WYCLIF *Wks.* (1880) 210 To ȝeue costly cloþis & manye to riche men & mynstralis or shaualdours for worldly name. *Ibid.* 249 Ydel schaueldowris. *c* **1420** ? LYDG. *Assembly of Gods* 675 Shamefull shakerles, soleyn shaueldores, Oppressours of pepyll. *c* **1425** WYNTOUN *Cron.* VIII. xxvi. 4363[He] gat til hym a company, þat as schawadouris [*v.rr.* schawaldouris, schawatouris] war walkande In til þe wail of Anande. *c* **1440** *Promp. Parv.* 444/2 Schaveldowre, *discursor, vacabundus.* *c* **1440–50** *Brit. Mus. Addit. MS.* 6716 lf. 23 Revera generosi inter nos dicuntur tales Schalldours Ryflours. Tales enim frangunt thalamos magnorum, asportant bona,.. et spoliant religiosos.

Hence †**shavaldry** (schauadry, cheualdre), ?plundering, lawless exaction.

*a* 1400–50 *Wars Alex.* 3371 Þat he [*sc.* a king] schape to na schauadry [*Dubl. MS.* cheualdre] þat shend suld his fame.

**shave** (ʃeɪv), *sb.*[1] Forms: 1 sceafa, sceaba, scafa, 4–5 schave, 7 shaffe, 4– shave. [OE. *sceafa* wk. masc., corresponding to MDu. *schave* (Du. *schaaf*) fem., OHG. *scaba* (MHG., mod.G. *schabe* fem.), Icel. *skafa* fem.:—OTeut. *skabon-, f. root *skab-: see SHAVE *v.* Cf. SHAVE-HOOK.] A name applied to various tools adapted for scraping, paring, or removing the surface of material in very thin slices; a drawing or paring knife; also short for SPOKESHAVE, *hoop-shave*, etc.

Frequently with distinguishing epithet as *cooper's*, *mast*, *round shave*, etc.

*c* 825 *Epinal Gloss.* 853 *Runcina*, locær *vel* sceaba. *a* 1100 *Gerefa* in *Anglia* IX. 263 Æcse, adsan, bil, byrse, scafan. 1352 *Exch. Acc. Q.R.* Bundle 20 No. 27 Pro vi. instrumentis vocatis *Shaues* pro nave praedicta mundanda. 1390 *Earl Derby's Exped.* (Camden) 20 Super officio scutellarie,..pro j hausak, et j schaue. *c* 1400 *Lanfranc's Cirurg.* 127 Euene the brynkis [of a hole cut in the brain-pan] with schauynge. ..Þis schaue schal kutte on þe side þat foldiþ ynward. 1404 *Durham Acc. Rolls* (Surtees) 397 Item in custodia Plumbarii ..2 schaves, cum maliotis, rakis [etc.]. *c* 1440 *Promp. Parv.* 444/2 Schave, or schavynge knyfe, *scalpellum*, C.F. *scalprum*. 1546 LANGLEY tr. *Pol. Verg. de Invent.* III. x. 78 b, The Squire, the Line, the Shaue, the Pricker or Punche were deuised by Theodor a Samian. 1688 HOLME *Armoury* III. viii. 351/1 A kind of a small half round Plain, of which the Fletchers have two sorts; the first is termed a Ripper;.. the next is the Shaffe, or Hollow Shaffe, it worketh the same smooth and round, and fit to be made up into an Arrow. *Ibid.* III. xx. (Roxb.) 249/1 He beareth sable, a Smooth Shave, Argent,..which some call a smooth shaveing Knife. 1780 EDMONDSON *Heraldry* II. Gloss., *Curriers shaves*, or *Paring-knives*. 1842 *Penny Mag.* 12 Nov. 447/1 The skains are thin ribands of willow, produced by passing the splits through a kind of shave or plane. 1859 W. S. COLEMAN *Woodlands* 65 In the manufacture of chip-hats..young branches [of the White Willow] are taken and cut into thin slices by an instrument called a shave. 1875 *Carpentry & Joinery* 13 We now come to the two handed shave or draw knife as it is often called.

**b.** *Comb.*: **shave-iron**, the blade of a shave or drawing-knife.

1872 *Spon's Dict. Engin.* v. 1814.

**shave** (ʃeɪv), *sb.*[2] [f. SHAVE *v.*]

**1. a.** Something shaved off; a shaving, paring, thin slice; †*fig.* a sample, specimen.

Cf. SHIVE *sb.* with which, however, it is not etymologically connected.

1604 T. M. *Black Bk.* F j b, You shall not sticke Benedick, to giue a shaue of your Office [of cut-purse] at Powles Crosse in the Sermon time. 1725 RAMSAY *Gentle Sheph.* I. i, Bannocks and a shave of cheese Will make a breakfast. 1788 PICKEN *Poems* 63 A shave o' cheese. 1875 SEATON *Fret Cutting* vi. 56 Try and take off the smallest possible shaves. 1890 J. SERVICE *Thir Notandums* xi, I got the lassock to fetch me..a saft bile't egg on a shave o' laif.

**b.** '*Theatr. slang.* The proportion of the receipts paid to a travelling company by a local manager' (Farmer *Slang* 1902.)

**2.** An act of shaving the beard.

1838 SOUTHEY *Doctor* cliii. V. 203 And if the daily shavings of one year..could be put into one shave, the operation..would be more than flesh and blood could bear. 1844 DICKENS *Mart. Chuz.* xxix, Being here, I may as well have a shave, and get trimmed close. 1887 TUER & FAGAN *First Year Silken Reign* v. 74 Barbers' shops, where a penny shave had been the staple trade.

**3. a.** An act of swindling or extortion. *clean shave* (*fig.* of sense 1): a complete swindle. Cf. SHAVE *v.* 7.

1834 C. A. DAVIS *Lett. J. Downing* 39 I've got some real shaves myself in that way. 1855 J. R. PLANCHÉ *Discreet Princess* in *Extravaganzas of Planché* (1879) V. 130, I much suspect this is some barbarous 'shave'. 1863 *Once a Week* 7 Feb. 179/1 We doubt if any lady is aware of the very clean shave she is constantly undergoing. 1881 *Harper's Mag.* Sept. 492/2 The benches [on Brighton beach] are in one sense a shave... No sooner is a seat taken than a beach-man ..demands a penny.

**b.** '*U.S. cant.* (*a*) An exorbitant discount on a note. (*b*) A premium paid for an extension of the time of delivery or payment, or for the right to vary a stock contract in any particular' (Webster 1864–96).

**4.** *Mil. slang.* An unauthenticated report.

1813 CAPT. R. M. CAIRNES *Let. to Col. W. Cuppage* 11 June (MS.), The shave of the day is that Burgos is evacuated and destroyed: but this cannot surely be. 1898 SIR G. S. ROBERTSON *Chitral* 322 In every camp in war time, there are curious rumours called 'shaves', which originate no one knows how, and are disseminated with equal mystery. They are sometimes fantastic, but often curiously accurate.

**5. a.** A slight or grazing touch; hence, a narrow escape from touching, more emphatically ***a close, near shave*** and the like. *lit.* and *fig.*

1834 R. H. FROUDE *Rem.* 23 Nov. (1838) I. 381, I seem to myself to have had a shave, if indeed I have weathered the point yet. 1856 KANE *Arct. Expl.* I. vii. 73 We passed clear; but it was a close shave. 1866 DICKENS & HALLIDAY *Mugby Junction* (*All Year Round* Christm. No.) 27/1 The next instant the hind coach passed my engine by a shave. It was the nearest touch I ever saw. 1892 HUXLEY in L. Huxley *Life* (1900) II. xix. 329, I had a narrow shave to get down to Osborne. 1894 ASTLEY *Fifty Yrs. Life* I. 77 Accomplishing the distance..with equally remarkable near shaves of a collision.

**b.** *Univ. slang.*

1840 T. HOOK *Fitzherbert* II. ix. 239 Collegians glorying in a 'pass' (which the Oxford world called a 'shave'). 1840 J. T. J. HEWLETT *P. Priggins* xvi, Getting through his great-go by a shave. 1860 [see SHAVE *v.* 10 c].

**shave** (ʃeɪv), *v.* Forms: *Inf.* 1 scaeban, sceafan, scafan, scæfan, (3 *3rd pres.* scaft, scæft), 4–5 schaf(e, schave, 4 *Sc.* shawe, 5 schavin, schaffe, *Sc.* schaiff, 5–6 scheve, 6 shawe, 7 schaive, 4– shave. *Pa. t.* 1 scóf, 4–5 schove, s(c)hoof(e, (4 shoove, *Sc.* schufe), 5 shufe, schof(e, (schave, shoef), 5–6 shove, (6 *Sc.* schuif); *weak forms* 4 schaved(e, schavyde, 6– shaved. *Pa. pple.* 1 sceafen, scafen, 4–5 schaven, -yn, shavyn, schave, shave, (4 schavun, 5 shavon, 5–6 schavin, 6 *Sc.* schaven, schaiffyn, 7 *Sc.* schevin, 8 *Sc.* schawin, 3– shaven; also 3 ischaven, 3–4 i-schave, 4 y-shave; *weak forms* 4– shaved, (6 *Sc.* schavit). [A Com. Teut. verb (originally strong): OE. *sceafan* str. corresponds to OS. (*scaban) *scavan* (glossing *planare*, *scalpere*), LG., Du. *schaven*, OHG. *scaban*, *scapan* (MHG. *schabun*, *schuop*, *geschaben*, mod.G. *schaben* wk.), ON. *skafa*, *skóf*, *skafenn* (Sw. *skafva*, Da. *skave*), Goth. *skaban*, f. Teut. root *skab-.

It is doubtful whether the pre-Teut. form is *skabh- (= root of L. *scabĕre* to scratch, *scabiēs* itch) or *skap- (= root of Gr. σκάπτειν to dig, σκαπάνη spade).]

**1. a.** *trans.* To scrape, to scrape away the surface of, to cut down or pare away with a sharp tool, thereby removing very thin portions of the surface. Also with *off*. †*to shave on*: to put on by shaving or grating.

*c* 725 *Corpus Gloss.* (Hessels) P 539 *Poleo*, scaebe. *a* 900 tr. *Bæda's Hist.* I. i. (1890) 30 Man scof þara boca leaf þe of Hibernia coman, & þa sceafþan dyde on wæter. *c* 1205 LAY. 22293 Sum scæft horn, sum scaft ban. 13.. *E.E. Allit. P.* B. 1134 Polysed als playn as parchemen schauen. *c* 1366 *Rom. Rose* 941 But they [arrows] were shaven wel and dight. *a* 1425 tr. *Arderne's Treat. Fistula*, etc. 84 Euery day I schoue þe bare bone with instrument preparate þer-to. *a* 1450 MYRC 1822 And schaf hyt after, þat ys be-bled, And do þe schauynge for to brenne. 1542–3 *Act 34 & 35 Hen. VIII*, c. 6 Pinnes..shalbe..wel smethed, the shanke wel shauen. 1584 LYLY *Campaspe* Prol. at Crt., The Persian kings sometimes shaued stickes. *a* 1655 SIR T. MAYERNE *Archimag. Anglo-Gall.* No. 16 (1658) 8 When they are baked, shave on a little sugar. 1688 HOLME *Armoury* III. xx. (Roxb.) 235/2 The Scalpra or Scraping Toole; it is to scrape or shave bones with all. 1784 COWPER *Task* II. 585 A monitor is wood—plank shaven thin. We wear it at our backs. 1856 OLMSTED *Slave States* vi. 395 In the woods I saw a negro..shaving shingles. 1885 *St. James's Gaz.* 2 Jan. 6/2 The shaver, with a few long sweeps of this implement, quickly shaves down his raw material into supple hoops.

**b.** To scrape or pare (a skin, hide, etc.). *spec.* in *Currying*, To pare away the inequalities of and thin down (leather).

1467 in *Eng. Gilds* (1870) 396 Also, that no Sadeler, Bochoʳ, Baker, ne Glover..shave flesh, skynnes, or huydes, but above the Brugge. 1530 PALSGR. 717/1, I shave, as a tanner dothe his leather, *je planie*. Nowe that his hydes be tanned, se howe easely he shaveth them. 1839 URE *Dict. Arts* 378 The currier..next applies the cleaners..to remove or thin down all inequalities. After the leather is shaved, it is thrown once more into water. *Ibid.* 379 Hides intended for covering coaches are shaved nearly as thin as shoe hides.

**c.** *Hat-manuf.* To smooth with pounce, sandpaper, etc. (cf. POUNCE *v.*[3] 1).

1875 KNIGHT *Dict. Mech.*, *Pouncing Machine*, a machine for shaving or rubbing the surface of a hat or hat-body to rid it of shaggy fibres. 1902 [see LURING *vbl. sb.*[2]].

**2.** To remove by scraping or paring; to cut off in thin slices or shavings; also ***to shave off***.

1382 WYCLIF *Ezek.* xxvi. 4 And I shal shaue [Vulg. *radam*] the dust of it [*sc.* Tyre] from it. 1387 TREVISA *Higden* (Rolls) VIII. 129 Gold i-schave of sepulcres and schrynes. 1398 —— *Barth. De P.R.* XIX. xvii. (1495) 874 Yf a man purposyth to shaue other to wasshe the colour Minius out of the perchemyn. 1635–8 *Archdeaconry of Essex* (MS.) Minutes 243 b, The officers found him..in a barne where he is vehemently suspected to be shaving of barke. 1639 O. WOOD *Alph. Bk. Secrets* 46 Take Iuniper thinne shaved, and the Berries bruised. 1680 MOXON *Mech. Exerc.* xiii. 221 Its sharp Edge scrapes or shaves off the little roughness the grosser Tools left upon the Work.

**3. a.** To cut off (hair, esp. the beard) close to the skin with or as with a razor. Also with *away*, *off*.

*c* 1320 *R. Brunne's Medit.* 966 Whan Iewes had dampned hym deþ for to haue, Shamely berde and hede gun þey shaue. 1382 WYCLIF *Lev.* xiv. 8 He shal shaue alle the heeres of the bodi. *c* 1386 CHAUCER *Shipm. T.* 309 With crowne and berde al fressh and newe y-shaue. 1430–40 LYDG. *Bochas* I. i. (1544) 3 Goddes angell shoue away his berde. 1474 CAXTON *Chesse* III. iii. (1883) 93 And the other ought to shaue berdes and kembe the heeris. 1530 PALSGR. 701/2 He hath shavyn away all the heare on his heed. 1535 COVERDALE *2 Sam.* x. 4 Then toke Hanun the seruauntes of Dauid, and shoue of the one halue of their beerdes. 1584 B. R. tr. *Herodotus* II. 88 In what house soeuer there dies a cat, all of the same family shaue their eyebrowes. 1606 SHAKS. *Ant. & Cl.* II. ii. 8 Were I the wearer of Anthonio's Beard, I would not shaue't to day. 1781 GIBBON *Decl. & F.* xix. (1787) II. 140 The ceremony of shaving his beard,..when he first exchanged the cloak of a Greek philosopher for the military habit of a Roman prince. 1843 R. J. GRAVES *Syst. Clin. Med.* vii. 86, I immediately order the hair to be shaved off. 1848 THACKERAY *Van. Fair* xxxii, Take my counsel, and shave off them mustachios, or they'll bring you into mischief. *Ibid.* xxxiv, Mr. Bowls's young man..brought him his hot water to shave that beard which he was so anxiously expecting. 1901 ALLDRIDGE *Sherbro* xx. 197, I observed other women with the wool shaved off just above the forehead.

†**b.** *fig.* ***to shave*** (a person's) ***beard***, to bring to discomfiture. *Obs.*

*c* 1412 HOCCLEVE *De Reg. Princ.* 4340 Hir berdes shaued he right smothe & clene. 1418 *Man, beware!* 53 in *26 Pol. Poems* 62 Er drede and repref þy berde shaue.

**4. a.** To cut off the beard, whiskers, or moustache from (a person, his chin, upper lip, etc.) with a razor.

*c* 1250 *Gen. & Ex.* 2120 Ioseph was sone in prisun ðo hoȝt, And shauen, & clad, & to him broȝt. *c* 1386 CHAUCER *Merch. T.* 582 He kisseth hire..With thilke brustles of his berd vnsofte..ffor he was shaue al newe. *c* 1440 *Alphabet of Tales* 305 Ther was..a passand curios barbur, and for euer-ilk man þat he shufe he tuke a peny. 1522 in *10th Rep. Hist. MSS. Comm.* App. v. 400 No man shalbe made fre unlesse he..shave his upper lipe wicklye. 1611 BIBLE *Gen.* xli. 14 And he shaued himselfe, and changed his raiment. 1618 J. TAYLOR (Water-P.) *Pennyless Pilgr.* C 1 b, This Gentleman ..sent to me his Barber, Who lau'd, and shau'd me. 1650 BULWER *Anthropomet.* 125 Shaving the Chin is justly to be accounted a note of effeminacie. *a* 1722 FOUNTAINHALL *Decis.* (1759) I. 10 As in barbers shops he who is first wet is first shaven. 1748 SMOLLETT *Rod. Rand.* viii, Stepping into a barber's shop to be shaved. 1838 J. H. MERIVALE *Poems* I. 93 Who, were the razor ne'er so bright and keen, Would never think it shaved him clean. 1863 GEO. ELIOT *Romola* I. xvi, To be shaved was a fashion of Florentine respectability. 1872 J. YEATS *Techn. Hist. Comm.* 72 The practise of shaving the chin was commenced in the days of Alexander the Great.

**b.** *transf.* and *fig.*

1589 NASHE *Pasquil's Ret.* Wks. (Grosart) I. 128 And Sprignols man told me (as he trimd me the other day) that there is a new Barber in London, about to shaue the Bible. 1799 HOLCROFT *Mem.* (1816) III. 229 A stiff breeze.. described by a sailor, who swore that it shaved him. 1855 BROWNING *Old Pict. in Flor.* v, The church's..face set full for the sun to shave. 1880 *Encycl. Brit.* XI. 519/1 [Beaver hat making.] The coarse hairs or kemps which may be in the fur are cut off by shaving the surface with a razor.

**5. a.** To remove the hair from (the head, crown, etc.) with a razor. Also (now *rarely*) with the person as object (= to shave the head of).

Shaving the head is often jocularly referred to as a remedial operation for maniacal excitement.

*a* 1225 *Ancr. R.* 422 (MS. C) [ȝe schulen beon] ȝef ȝe wulleð i-schauen, hwase wule ieveset. *a* 1340 HAMPOLE *Psalter, Song Moses* 522 þe whilk [prisoners] was wont to be shauyn þe heuyd, & so solde. *c* 1370 *Robt. Cicyle* 53 Thou art a fole, seyde the aungelle, Thou schalt be schavyn ovyr ylke a dele. 1490 CAXTON *Eneydos* xxiv. (1890) 88 And thenne came out the olde witche of charmouse magyque,..alle her hed shauen. 1596 NASHE *Saffron Walden* Ep. Ded. A 3, There is a..Doctor of late very pittifully growen bald, and thereupon is to be shauen immediately, to trie if that will helpe him. 1600 J. HAMILTON *Facile Traict.* in *Cath. Tract.* (S.T.S.) 235 Wemen with barne..to be set vp in ane opin place with the half of thair haid schevin. 1603 SHAKS. *Meas. for M.* IV. ii. 187. 1685 BAXTER *Paraphr. N.T.* Acts xxi. 22 They [Nazarites] are to shave themselves ceremoniously in the Temple. 1770 LANGHORNE *Plutarch* I. 5 (*Theseus*) He shaved, however, only the fore part of his head. 1819 SHELLEY *Peter Bell* VI. iv, Another [said]—'Let him shave his head! Where's Dr. Willis?' 1886 F. W. ROBINSON *Courting Mary Smith* II. II. xviii. 72, I believe I am nearly off, and they'll be glad to shave my head in a day or two. 1906 W. H. R. RIVERS *Todas* xxviii. 663 The Melgarsol again resemble the Teivaliol in not shaving the head after a funeral.

**b.** *esp.* To tonsure as a cleric. †Frequently with complement, *to shave* (a person) ***a monk, canon, priest, friar***; also, to make (a 'crown') by shaving.

*a* 1400–50 *Wars Alex.* 121 He..Clede him all as a clerke & his croune shauys. *c* 1400 *The Brut* lxvii. 63 This traitoure ..put oppon him an habite of religioun and lete shaue him a brode crone. 1430–40 LYDG. *Bochas* VIII. xix. (1554) 189 b, Constance..forthwith anon Was shaue a Monke. 1481 CAXTON *Reynard* viii. (Arb.) 18 Were ye amonke or an abbot he that shoef your crowne hath nyped of your eeris. 1536 BELLENDEN *Cron. Scot.* (1821) II. 200 He past to the abbay of Sanct Andros, and schuif him thair ane chanoun. 1616 R. COCKS *Diary* (Hakl. Soc.) I. 164 Calsa Same was..to goe to a church neare Miaco..to be shaved a prist. *a* 1691 D. NORTH in R. North *Lives* (1826) II. 312 Who will, may shave himself a friar. 1855 MILMAN *Lat. Chr.* (1864) II. IV. viii. 395 Irene..seized, scourged and shaved into ecclesiastics the chief of her son's adherents.

†**c.** ***to shave*** (a person's) ***crown***: to cut off or gash the head (with jocular reference to clerical tonsure). *Obs.*

13.. *Coer de L.* 4568 Every Sarezen that they mette..by the schuldren they schoof the crown. 13.. *Guy Warw.* 3651 Þou hast a croun schauen to þe bon. 14.. *Beues* 1870 (MS. N), I schaue [*MS. S* schofe] him a kroune of red blode. 1593 SHAKS. *2 Hen. VI*, II. i. 51 *Glost.*..Now by Gods Mother, Priest, Ile shaue your Crowne for this.

**d.** *Proverb.*

1626 T. H[AWKINS] tr. *Caussin's Holy Crt.* I. ix. 77 For if Enuy (according to the prouerbe) will offer to shaue an eg, she will mow in a meadow. [orig. *Car si l'enuie tond survn œuf, que ne fera elle sur vn pré.*] 179. WOLCOT (P. Pindar) *Odes to Kien Long* II. Wks. 1792 III. 299 Curst with an av'rice, some would shave an egg.

**6. a.** *absol.* Of a barber.

*c* 1375 *Sc. Leg. Saints* xxxvi. (*Baptista*) 1020 His barboure tald hym til, gyf he wald haf don þer wil, he had schorne his hals in twa, to schaf þat quhen he suld ga. *c* 1386 CHAUCER *Miller's T.* 140 Wel koude he laten blood and clippe and shaue. 1474 CAXTON *Chesse* III. ii. (1883) 90 He made hys doughters to lerne shaue and kembe. 1689 *Lond. Gaz.* No. 2483/4 He shaves and makes Periwigs. 1718 *Free-thinker* No. 95. 283 A poor Barber who shaves for Two-pence.

**b.** *intr.* for *refl.* To shave oneself.

*a* **1715** BURNET *Own Time* (1766) II. 219 He was quickly dressed, but would lose no time in shaving. **1827** SCOTT *Surg. Dau.* ii, I have seen the Doctor with a langer beard himsell, when he has not had leisure to shave. **1844** DICKENS *Mart. Chuz.* xxvi, Even archbishops shave, or must be shaved, on a Sunday.

**7. a.** *trans.* To strip (a person) clean of money or possessions (? *obs.*); †to treat stingily (*obs.*); to practise exaction or extortion upon; to fleece. Also *absol.* Now *colloq.* or *slang.*

†More emphatically ***to shave to the quick*** (see also QUICK *sb.*[1] 4 b, quot. 1551).

*c* **1399** CHAUCER *Purse* 19 Now purse..Oute of this tovne helpe me..Syn that ye wole nat bene my tresorere, for I am shave as nye as is a Frere. **1540** PALSGR. *Acolastus* II. iv. M iv, He shall be pollyd and shauen by vs, tyll he shal not haue a halfepennye lefte. *a* **1548** HALL *Chron., Hen. VIII*, 143 The religious..were charged with greate sommes of money to the kyng, and now this sodain visitacion or predacion, cleane shaued them. **1606** DEKKER *Seven Deadly Sins* vi. (Arb.) 40 Then haue you Brokers yat shaue poore men by most iewish interest. *a* **1610** HEALEY *Theophrastus* (1636) 48 Hee measureth miserably to his servants; shaving, and pinching them to a grain. **1768** GOLDSM. *Good-n. Man* IV, We should never travel without—a case of good razors... But no matter, I believe we shall be pretty well shaved by the way. **1830** D. BOOTH *Analyt. Dict.* 220 To Shave, in low language, is to strip a person of his property by unfair means. **1861** MRS. H. WOOD *East Lynne* xlix, I bought this rig-out yesterday, second-hand. Two pounds for the lot! I think they shaved me. **1864** *Hotten's Slang Dict.* (1865) s.v., 'To shave a customer', to charge him more for an article than the marked price. Used in the drapery trade. When the master sees an opportunity of doing this, he strokes his chin, as a signal to his assistant.

**b.** *absol.*

**1528** TINDALE *Obed. Chr. Man* 75 b, This..sheringe..of the heare..is to them a remembraunce to shere and shave, to hepe benefice apon benfice [etc.]. **1641** MILTON *Ch. Govt.* II. iii. 50 Thus then the civill Magistrat looking only upon the outward man... Sometimes he shaves by penalty, or mulct... Otherwiles he seres,..and finally..cuts off. *a* **1700** B. E. *Dict. Cant. Crew, He shaves close*, he gripes, squeezes, or extorts very severely. **1816** SCOTT *Let.* in *Lockhart* (1837) IV. i. 7 Economy is the order of the day, and I assure you they are shaving properly close.

**†8.** To steal. *slang. Obs.*

**1585** FLEETWOOD in Ellis *Orig. Lett.* Ser. I. II. 303 *Shave* is to ffylche a clooke, a sword, a sylver sponne or such like, that is negligentlie looked unto. **1719** D'URFEY *Pills* III. 105 The Maidens had shav'd his Breeches.

**9. a.** To cut off cleanly or closely. Also with *off.* † ***to shave out one's way***: to get out by cutting down obstacles.

**1598** SYLVESTER *Du Bartas* I. i. 584 He..Shaves with keen Sythe, the glory and delight Of motly Medowes. **1614** GORGES *Lucan* x. 447 She..from his corps his head did shaue. **1665** *Roxb. Ball.* (1887) VI. 437 Brave Smith in the *Mary* did shave out his way As Reapers do Wheat, or as Mowers do Hay. **1748** *Anson's Voy.* II. vi. 193 The peak [of his cap] was shaved off close to his temple by a ball. **1836** HALIBURTON *Clockm.* Ser. I. xxii, They are afeard to show their noses..lest they should be shaved off by our shots. **1897** MARY KINGSLEY *W. Africa* 164 The Fans, who are very slowly shaving the trees from the top of the hill.

**b.** To cut off closely the growth of (ground, a lawn, etc.); also *transf.* of artillery fire.

**1764** DODSLEY *Descr. Leasowes* in *Shenstone's Wks.* (1793) I. 48 Ground..that before is kept close shaven. **1788** in *Ld. Auckland's Corr.* (1861) II. 98 Our lawn is shaved so close by the goats. **1820** SHELLEY *Witch of Atlas* xlviii, Like a meadow which no scythe has shaven. **1892** BIERCE *In Midst of Life* 56 An artillery fire that will shave the ground the moment they break from cover.

**10. a.** To touch lightly in passing, to graze; hence, barely to escape touching.

**1513** DOUGLAS *Æneis* VIII. i. 137, I am God Tibris..Quhilk..Bettis thir brayis, schawand the bankis doun [L. *stringentem ripas*]. **1667** MILTON *P.L.* II. 634 Som times He [Satan] scours the right hand coast,..Now shaves with level wing the Deep, then soares Up to the fiery concave. **1777** [T. SWIFT] *Gamblers* I. 213 There [at Tennis] Tomkyns shaves the Line; or flying sends The whizzing Globe. **1885** *Field* 7 Feb. 168/1 An attempt of Evelyn's which just shaved the bar. **1888** BARRIE *When a Man's Single* xi. 181 Three hansoms shaved him by an inch. **1890** 'ROLF BOLDREWOOD' *Col. Reformer* (1891) 128 As we turned one corner we hung nearly over the cliff, just shaved it.

**b.** *intr.* ***to shave through***: to get through only by grazing (that which has to be passed); *fig.* to scrape *through*, barely pass (an examination).

**1860** *Hotten's Slang Dict.* (ed. 2) s.v., At Cambridge, 'just shaving through', or 'making a shave', is just escaping a 'pluck' by coming out at the bottom of the list. **1882** FREEMAN in W. R. W. Stephens *Life & Lett.* (1895) II. 256 Another who had barely shaved through his matriculation. **1887** *Poor Nellie* (1888) 45 It would be too late for the straits. You can only shave through at half-tide.

**11.** *trans. U.S. slang.* To discount (a promissory note) at an exorbitant rate of interest; also ***to shave paper.*** (Cf. SHAVER 2 b.)

**1832** WEBSTER s.v., *To shave a note*, to purchase it at a great discount, a discount much beyond the legal rate of interest. (*A low phrase.*) **1833** [S. SMITH] *Lett. J. Downing* xv. (1835) 92 He says..he is makin a good livin in shavin drafts from ½ to 1½ per cent., which the U.S. Bank used to take and collect for nothin. **1834** 'J. DOWNING' *Andrew Jackson* 29 The Pontius Pilates who shave notes and receive niggurs in pawn. **1890** GILDERSLEEVE *Ess. & Stud.* 225 He could not have made both ends meet by 'shaving paper' at thirty-six per cent.

**12. a.** To cut down in amount, to reduce. orig. and chiefly *U.S.*

**1898** *Boston Herald* 23 Jan. 14/3 There are indications that tariff sheets are being secretly shaved. **1941** B. SCHULBERG *What makes Sammy Run?* vii. 141 The studio was having one of its periodic drives to cut overheads—which seemed to mean shaving stenographers' wages first. **1962** WODEHOUSE *Service with Smile* xi. 180 In the hope of making him shave his price a bit? **1972** *Times* 16 Feb. 13/8 This coin enables traders to shave their prices and if it did not exist there would be a considerable rounding up.

**b.** To deduct (a small amount) *from* or *off* (a quantity, time, etc.).

*a* **1961** in *Webster* (1961) s.v., New procedures shave minutes from the unloading process. **1982** *Times* 26 Aug. 15/2 The Bank shaved another 1/8 of a percentage point off the rate at which it buys bills from the discount houses.

**13.** *Comb.*, as **shavecoat**, a man's casual garment resembling a housecoat; **shavetail** orig. *U.S. Mil. slang*, (*a*) an untrained pack animal, identified by a shaven tail; also *attrib.*; (*b*) *fig.* a newly commissioned officer, *spec.* a second lieutenant; also gen., an inexperienced person; also *attrib.*

**1964** *N.Y. Times Mag.* 29 Nov. 73 Weldon makes something like a shavecoat. It's extra comfortable and convenient for shaving. **1970** *Sunday Mail* (Brisbane) 27 Dec. 6D The bridegroom wore a mustard colored shavecoat. But it was a very nice shavecoat. **1846** *New Orleans Delta* 31 Aug. 366/2 [This mule] was followed by Shavetail Kicky, Esq., who, in a few pertinent remarks, expressed his ass-ent to the proceedings. **1891** J. G. BOURKE *On Border with Crook* 153 Officers..are known as 'bell-sharps' and 'shave-tails'..the former being the old captain..and the latter the youngster fresh from his studies. **1908** R. E. BEACH *Barrier* 283 The first shave-tail desperado that meets him will spit in his eye. **1948** F. BLAKE *Johnny Christmas* I. 26 He had..six shavetail Indian ponies packed with articles he had brought down to sell. **1976** L. DEIGHTON *Twinkle, Twinkle, Little Spy* vii. 70, I was a shavetail, just out of pilot training. **1980** *Blair & Ketchum's Country Jrnl.* Oct. 43/1 That last practice started in the mines, where a 'shavetail' was a snaky mule, not to be trusted.

**shaved** (ʃeɪvd), *ppl. a.* [f. SHAVE *v.* + -ED[1].] In the senses of the verb. Cf. SHAVEN *ppl. a.*

**1. a.** Cut off in very thin slices or shavings; *spec.* of ice cut in thin slices or shavings for chilling drinks. Also, trimmed or polished by shaving.

**1688** CLAYTON in *Phil. Trans.* XVIII. 134 She gave him *Oriental Bezoar* shaved. **1747** WESLEY *Prim. Physick* (1762) 96 Half a Pound of fresh shaved Lignum Guiacum. **1855** *Imperial Gazetteer* I. 261/2 He wears..ornaments of shaved sticks in his hair. **1927** E. HEMINGWAY *Fiesta* III. xix. 272, I..had a glass of lemon juice and shaved ice. **1962** *Listener* 16 Aug. 248/2 Snowball, which consists of shaved ice covered with scarlet syrup. **1971** J. PHILIPS *Escape a Killer* (1972) I. ii. 20 The martini shaker in its bed of shaved ice.

**b.** Having the hair, beard, etc. cut closely with a razor. Of the head: Tonsured.

**1786** *Pogonologia* 34 A shaved chin was always a sign of slavery, infamy, or debauchery. **1837** CARLYLE *Fr. Rev.* II. IV. ii, Jurant and Dissident, with their shaved crowns, argue frothing everywhere. **1848** THACKERAY *Van. Fair* lxvi, Gentlemen in shaved heads and yellow jackets. **1888** F. HUME *Mme. Midas* I. ii, A clean shaved chin.

**c.** Of a beaver hat: Having the fur cut close.

**1852** R. S. SURTEES *Sponge's Sp. Tour* (1893) 214 Crowning himself with a shaved white hat. **1861** WHYTE MELVILLE *Mkt. Harb.* ii. 15 The way in which he wore his shaved hat and stuck his hands into the pockets of his wide-skirted grey riding-coat.

**d.** *Leather-trade.* Of a hide: Pared with a shaving-knife.

**1892** *Daily News* 23 Mar. 2/6 The stocks of some articles are short, especially of..shaved hides.

**2.** *U.S. slang.* ***half shaved***, partly intoxicated.

**1834** *Atlantic Club-book* I. 138 (Farmer) When I met him, he was about—yes—just about half shaved. **1836** HALIBURTON *Clockm.* Ser. I. xxii, When he was about half shaved he thought every body drunk but himself.

**shavee** (ʃeɪˈviː). *jocular.* [f. SHAVE *v.* + -EE.] One who undergoes shaving by a barber.

**1826** MISS MITFORD *Village* II. 187 His chin covered with lather, he having been the identical customer—the very shavee, whose beard happened to be under discussion. **1838** SOUTHEY *Doctor* cliii. V. 204 Whether he were..a self-shaver..or merely a shavee.

**shavegrass** (ˈʃeɪvgrɑːs, -æ-). Also 5 **schave-**, 6 **schavi-**, 7 **sheav-**. [f. SHAVE *v.* + GRASS *sb.* Cf. SHAVE-RUSH, SHAVEWORT.] A plant of the genus *Equisetum* (see HORSE-TAIL 2); esp. *E. hyemale.*

*c* **1450** *Alphita* (Anecd. Oxon.) 37 *Cauda equina, cauda caballina idem est. angl.* schauegres. **1548** TURNER *Names of Herbes* (1881) 64 Polygonum femina is called in Englishe thycke Shauegrasse, or short Shaue grasse. **1597** GERARDE *Herbal* II. ccccxlii. 956 This small or naked Shaue grasse, wherewith Fletchers and Combemakers doe..polish their worke, riseth out of the ground like..Asparagus. **1693** *Urquhart's Rabelais* III. li. 408 It is more..hurtful than..the Sheavgrass to the Mowers of Hay. **1773** *Hawkesworth's Acc. Voy.* III. 644 [It] bites upon wood almost as keenly as the shave-grass of Europe. **1839** URE *Dict. Arts* 613 Rubbing with horse's tail (shave-grass) the parts to be yellowed. *Ibid.*, Rubbing the whole work with shave-grass, to remove any granular appearance. **1857** MISS PRATT *Flower. Pl.* IV. 386 Rough Horsetail, Shave-grass, Dutch Rush.

**shave-hook.** [f. SHAVE *v.* + HOOK *sb.*[1]] A plumbers' tool consisting of a blade, commonly triangular, set transversely in a handle, used for scraping metal preparatory to soldering.

**1432** *Muniments Magd. Coll. Oxf.* (1882) 11 Item, j led-knyff;..j shaff-hoke. **1485** *Naval Acc. Hen. VII* (1896) 40 Shaffe hokes xviij. **1486** *Ibid.* 46 Shave hokes..xviij. **1688** HOLME *Armoury* III. 307/1 He beareth Sable, a Cross Staff in Fess, between a Plummers shave Hook, and a Leaden Plummet, proper. **1843** HOLTZAPFFEL *Turning* I. 445 The parts intended to receive the solder are scraped quite clean with the shave-hook.

**shaveling** (ˈʃeɪvlɪŋ), *sb.* (and *a.*). Forms: see SHAVE *v.*; also *Sc.* 6 **scheavelyng, schavel(l)ing, schevel-, schaifl-, schewell-, sc(h)awe-**, 7 **shaweling, shavelling.** [f. SHAVE *v.* + -LING[1].]

**A.** *sb.* **1.** A contemptuous epithet for a tonsured ecclesiastic. (Very common in 16th and 17th c.)

**1529** FRITH *Antithesis* 96 The Pope sayeth..I excommunicate all them that aske eny toll or trybute of me and my shavelinges. *a* **1578** LINDESAY (Pitscottie) *Chron. Scot.* (S.T.S.) I. 385 Monkis and freiris witht all the rest of scawelingis. **1647** TRAPP *Comm.* 1 Tim. v. 1 Ierk him not as ..the Bishops and their shavelings did Henry the 2. of England, till the bloud followed. **1824** BYRON *Deformed Transf.* II. iii, Cleave yon bald-pated shaveling to the chine! **1884** TENNYSON *Becket* I. iii, And that too, perjured prelate —and that, turncoat shaveling! **1911** *Contemp. Rev.* Apr. 492 Counting up the number of shavelings still in France.

**b.** *gen.* A person with shaven head. *rare.*

**1621** BP. MOUNTAGU *Diatribæ* iii. 532 Lycurgus would haue the Spartans weare their hair long..: for slaues were shauelings for the most part.

**2.** A youth, young 'shaver'. *rare.*

**1854** WHYTE MELVILLE *Gen. Bounce* xiv, The very youngest of the shavelings who aspire to dandyism. **1894** WEYMAN *Man in Black* viii, 'He is a runaway!' the voice said. .. 'Rouse up the little shaveling, will you?'

**B.** *adj.* **1.** Of, pertaining to, or characteristic of a tonsured ecclesiastic.

**1577** *Test. 12 Patriarchs* (1581) 24 *margin*, The shauelyng generation. **1581** J. BELL *Haddon's Answ. Osor.* 281 Wheresoever that shavelyng marke of the Romish Prelate is emprinted. **1865** KINGSLEY *Herew.* iv, But they were only honest canons with wives at home, and not shaveling monks.

**2.** Shaven, having the hair cut off.

**1607** TOPSELL *Four-f. Beasts* 283 Those shaueling and short haired Stallions.

**shaven** (ˈʃeɪv(ə)n), *ppl. a.* Forms: see the verb. [Strong pa. pple. of SHAVE *v.*]

**1.** = SHAVED *ppl. a.* 1 b. Chiefly of the head, crown, or of a person; often = tonsured.

*c* **1330** R. BRUNNE *Chron. Wace* (Rolls) 16704 Peres of Langtofte, a chanoun Schauen y þe hous of Brydlyngtoun. *c* **1400** *Apol. Loll.* (Camden) 89 Wil þu hast habit and schauin croun. *a* **1500–20** DUNBAR *Poems* xxvi. 28 Quhill preistis come in with bair schevin nekkis. **1528** TINDALE *Obed. Chr. Man* 60 *margin*, The shaven nacion hath put christ out of his rowme. **1613** PURCHAS *Pilgrimage* (1614) 397 His wiues in blacke, with shauen heads, continually mourne. **1647** TRAPP *Comm. 1 Cor.* i. (1656) 662 Hence it grew to a proverb in times of Popery, That hell was paved with Priests shaven crowns. *a* **1774** R. FERGUSSON *Poems* (1807) 240 Wi' powder'd pow and shaven beard. **1781** COWPER *Charity* 55 Their prince..Died, by the sentence of a shaven priest. **1888** KIPLING *Departm. Ditties* (ed. 3) 24 And red and ever redder grew the General's shaven gill. **1909** J. MCCABE *Decay Ch. Rome* i. 2 Processions of shaven monks.

*absol.* **1528** TINDALE *Obed. Chr. Man* 79 *margin*, The spirte perteyneth vnto the shaven only.

**b.** *Comb.*

**1591** *Troub. Raigne K. John* xi, Yee shamelesse shauen-crowne! **1837** DICKENS *Pickw.* xxix, Which had been called Coffin Lane ever since the days of the old abbey, and the time of the shaven-headed monks. **1897** *Allbutt's Syst. Med.* III. 960 The intestine presents the well-known shaven-beard appearance. **1898** *Syd. Soc. Lex.*, *Shaven-beard appearance*, a peculiar appearance of the enlarged intestinal glands in typhoid fever.

**2.** Of turf, grass: Closely cut.

**1632** MILTON *Penseroso* 66, I walk unseen On the dry smooth-shaven Green. **1716** LADY M. W. MONTAGU *Ep. to Ld. B——t* 15 in Dodsley *Poems* (1748) I. 115 The shaven turf presents a lively green. **1853** WHYTE MELVILLE *Digby Grand* xix, Three short turns on the general's shaven lawn. **1886** CORBETT *Fall Asgard* I. 144 The silvery Gula winding peacefully between the shaven meadows.

**3.** Trimmed or polished by shaving.

**1660, 1812** Shaven latten [see LATTEN 1 b]. **1788** COWPER *Death Mrs. Throckm. Bulfinch* 23 On props of smoothest-shaven wood. **1793** —— *Tale, 'In Scotland's realm'*, 'Twas shaven deal. **1802** WORDSW. *Resolution & Indep.* xi. 72 Himself he propped..Upon a long grey staff of shaven wood.

**shaver** (ˈʃeɪvə(r)). [f. SHAVE *v.* + -ER[1].]

**1.** One who shaves with a razor.

*c* **1425** *Voc.* in Wr.-Wülcker 652/9 *Hic rasor*, shawere. **1483** *Cath. Angl.* 333/2 A Schaver, *tonsor, barbitonsor* (vbi Barbwre A.). **1592** [implied: see 3 below]. **1628** FORD *Lovers Mel.* II. ii, Shall I fetch a Barbour..? He..has not been vnder the Shauers hand almost these foure yeeres. **1777** JOHNSON in *Boswell* (1904) II. 125 Sir, of a thousand shavers, two do not shave so much alike as not to be distinguished. **1844** DICKENS *Mart. Chuz.* xix, The bird-fancier was an easy shaver also, and a fashionable hair-dresser also. **1906** B. CAPES *Loaves & Fishes* 165 And any shaver [will tell you], that his razor, after maltreating..one side of his face, will repent.

*fig.* **1641** MILTON *Ch. Govt.* II. Concl. 64 If they [the Prelatry, likened to Delilah] be such clippers of regal power and shavers of the Laws.

**2. †a.** One who pillages or plunders; an extortioner. ***cunning shaver***: a swindler, sharper.

**1534** WHITINTON *Tullyes Offices* III. (1540) 144, I wyll not speke of murderers,..theues, pollers and shauers in this place. **1606** DEKKER *Seven Deadly Sins* vi. (Arb.) 39 A shauer of yong Gentlemen, before euer a haire peepe out of their chinnes: and these are Vsurers. **1652** J. WRIGHT tr. *Camus' Nat. Paradox* VI. 111 This bred a suspicion..that they were some cunning Shavers that intended to surprise them. *a* **1700** B. E. *Dict. Cant. Crew, Shaver*, a *Cunning Shaver*, a subtil, smart Fellow. **1726** De Foe *Hist. Devil* (1822) 272 The Devil is a cunning shaver. **1785** Grose *Dict. Vulgar T., Shaver*, a cunning shaver, a subtle fellow, one who trims close, an acute cheat. **1800** Weems *Washington* I. (1877) 6 A shaver of farthings from the poor six-penny pay of his own brave soldiers! **1815** W. H. Ireland *Scribbleomania* 242 Those scribes for collectors close shavers. **1823** 'Jon Bee' *Dict. Turf.* s.v., 'He's a shaver'; said of one who charges high for his goods.

**b.** *U.S.* (See quot. 1860.)

**1813** Jefferson *Writ.* (1830) IV. 199 This..the States have..alienated to swindlers and shavers, under the cover of private banks. **1819** H. McMurtrie *Sk. Louisville* 124 (Thornton *Amer. Gloss.*), [The operation of discounting] affords fine sport to shavers. **1849** Hawthorne *Twice-told T., Mr. Higginbotham* 71 As he's a real shaver, I'll have the minister..for an indorser. **1860** Bartlett *Dict. Amer., Shaver*... This word, in the United States, is applied to money brokers, who purchase notes at more than legal interest. Banks, when they resort to any means to obtain a large discount, are also called shavers, or shaving banks.

**3. a.** = 'Fellow', 'chap'; also, a humorous fellow, joker, wag. Now commonly of a youth, with the epithet *young, little*; the wider application seems to be now only *dial.*

**1592** Marlowe *Jew of Malta* II. iii. E, *Itha*... I can cut and shaue. *Bar.* Let me see, sirra, are you not an old shauer? *Ith.* Alas, Sir, I am a very youth. **1602** *2nd Pt. Return fr. Parnass.* I. ii. 264 Locke and Hudson, sleepe you quiet shauers, among the shauings of the presse. **1602** Rowlands *Greenes Ghost* 39 Such iollie shauers haue I knowne..to sit vp all night,..quaffing and swilling at the Tauerne. **1635** Cranley *Amanda* 37 Thou art..not coy..To try the courage of so young a shaver. **1649** Davenant *Love & Hon.* v. iii. 144 Say'st thou so, old shaver? **1698** Farquhar *Love & Bottle* III. i, Who would imagine now, that this young shaver could dream of a woman so soon. **1786** Burns *Dream* xi, There, Him at Agincourt wha shone, Few better were or braver; And yet, wi' funny, queer Sir John, He was an unco shaver For monie a day. **1854** Marion Harland *Alone* ix, I have known him since I was a shaver. **1887** Besant *The World Went* ii, Forty-five years ago I was just such a little shaver as this. **1899** J. Lumsden *Edinb. Poems* 25 Grahame, Campbell, Pollok, Burns, and Tannahill Are worth ten shiploads o' sich shavers still!

*transf.* **1892** Sarah Hewett *Peas. Sp. Devon* Pref. 9 A North Devon Colonel of Militia, on seeing a hare jump up.., exclaimed: 'There 'e go'th, bwoys! a lashing gert shaver!'

†**b.** *mad shaver*: a roysterer. *Obs.*

**1611** Cotgr. s.v. *Enfant, Enfant de la mate*, a ruffin, backster, swash-buckler, swaggerer, mad shauer. *a* **1625** Fletcher *Hum. Lieut.* II. iv, *Leo* [old soldier]. Here's a mad Shaver, He fights his share I am sure... *Lieu.* I learnt it of my Betters. **1651** *Fuller's Abel Rediv.* 63 Erasmus going abroad somewhat early one morning, was met in a narrow lane by a company of madde shavers. **1664** Cotton *Virg. Trav.* 62 My mother's a mad Shaver, no man alive knows where to have her.

**4.** One who shaves hoops; more fully *hoop shaver.*

**1885** *St. James's Gaz.* 2 Jan. 6/1 The chief shaver whistles as he brings his blade down a strip of hazel with a hiss.

**5. a.** A shaving instrument or tool. Now esp. a small electrical appliance with a set of blades working against a perforated guard.

**1558** Warde tr. *Alexis' Secr.* 114b, Fynally, with the saied shaver, or sharp yron, make the sayed pypes or conduites holowe. **1592** *Wills & Inv. N.C.* (Surtees) II. 252, ij cheshels and a shaver. **1597** Middleton *Wisd. Solomon* xiii. 12 As when a carpenter cuts downe a tree,..He pareth all the barke most cunningly, With the sharp shauer of his kniues abuse. **1648** Hexham II., *Een Schaejken*, a small Shaver, or a chiping Axe. *Ibid., Een schrabber*, a Rasour, or a Shaver. **1897** *Sears, Roebuck Catal.* 111/3 A little gem and a dandy shaver, no better steel put in a razor. **1924** *Punch's Almanack for 1925* 3 Nov. p. xxviii/1 (Advt.), The Wilkinson safety shaver with hollow-ground blades is the ideal..gift for men. **1960** N. Mitford *Don't tell Alfred* xviii. 193 'What do you pack?' 'Shavers—you know, razors.' **1980** R. Moody *Devil you Don't* iii. 33 He..took out his shaver and toothbrush.

**b.** A shaving machine.

**1897** C. T. Davis *Manuf. Leather* xvii. 255 With this improved cutter cylinder the Rood shaver is able to shave the best quality skins.

**6.** *colloq.* = *shavecoat* s.v. SHAVE *v.* 13.

**1926** H. Pearson *Whispering Gallery* vii. 106 At a big meeting of hospital directors he turned up..in..un-business-like colours. One of the directors whispered to another: 'He'll be coming in his 'shaver' next.'

**7.** *attrib.*, as **shaver point, socket**, a power point for an electric shaver.

**1971** *Fremdsprachen* XV. 145/1 Shaver point, Trockenrasiersteckdose. **1977** *Western Morning News* 30 Aug. 10/4 (Advt.), Good-sized kitchen; radios, shaver points, &c. all bedrooms. **1965** *Newnes Practical Householder Encycl.* III. 1329/1 The shaver is operated from a special shaver socket unit. **1978** *Cornish Guardian* 27 Apr. 19/2 (Advt.), Strip lights with shaver sockets.

**shaver**, obs. form of SHIVER *v.*

**shave-rush.** *U.S. rare.* [f. SHAVE *v.* + RUSH *sb.* Cf. G. *schaberausch.*] = SHAVE-GRASS.

**1821** T. Nuttall *Trav. Arkansas* 53 *Equisetum hiemale* or Shave-rush.

**shavery** ('ʃeɪvərɪ). *nonce-wd.* [Jocularly formed on SHAVE *v.* + *-ery*, after *slavery*.] Subjection to the necessity of being shaved (*lit.* and *fig.*).

Quot. 1549 refers to the avaricious oppression of tenants.

**1549** Latimer *1st Serm. bef. Edw. VI*, D iiij b, All suche procedynges..do intend plainly, to make the yomanry slauery, & the Cleargye shauery. **1838** Southey *Doctor* cliii, Oh pitiable condition of human kind! One colour is born to slavery abroad, and one sex to shavery at home!

**shaves**, obs. pl. form of SHEAF.

†'**shavester.** *nonce-wd.* [f. SHAVE *v.* + -STER.] A barber.

**1620** Shelton *Quixote* II. i. 7 Well; is this the Tale, Mr. Barber (quoth Don Quixote)..? Ah, goodman Shauester, goodman Shauester [orig. *A Señor rapista, Señor rapista!*]

†**shave-weed.** *Obs.* $rare^{-1}$. [f. SHAVE *v.* + WEED *sb.*] = SHAVE-GRASS, SHAVE-RUSH.

**1691** Aubrey *Let.* 5 Aug. in Ray *Corr.* (Ray Soc.) 237 Shave-weed used by artists (which they have from Holland).

†'**shavewort.** *Obs. rare.* [f. SHAVE *v.* + WORT *sb.*] = SHAVE-GRASS.

*c* **1450** *Alphita* (Anecd. Oxon.) 82 *Hircina,..cauda equina* ..schafwort.

**Shavian** ('ʃeɪvɪən), *a.* and *sb.* [f. *Shavi(us*, the latinized surname of George Bernard Shaw (1856–1950), playwright and critic + -AN.]

**A.** *adj.* Pertaining to, characteristic of, or resembling G. B. Shaw or his works or opinions.

**1904** *Times* 2 Nov. 6/2 Not a play but a thoroughly characteristic 'Shavian' farago. **1935** G. K. Chesterton *G. B. Shaw* 292 The Shavian evolutionist does really want to cast the whole body of man into Chaos. **1960** [see *metabiological* adj. s.v. METABIOLOGY]. **1977** M. T. Bloom *13th Man* vi. 101 Your mother..named you for a Shavian heroine and..you've turned into one.

**B.** *sb.* An admirer or follower of G. B. Shaw. (In quot. 1921, a character of Shaw's.)

**1905** G. B. Shaw *Let.* 10 Feb. (1972) II. 512 Though he is an admirer of Shaw, he is no Shavian. *Ibid.* 18 Feb. 515 Are you going to write a natural history, like a true Shavian? **1921** *Spectator* 28 May 680/2 The poet Eugene Marchbanks is perhaps as near to primary emotion as any Shavian. **1967** O. Lancaster *Eye to Future* I. 8 My mother..always remained a devoted Shavian. **1978** P. Boardman *Worlds of Patrick Geddes* xi. 405 P. G. uses modern socialism as his next example... He names Marx..the Fabians..and the Shavians with income-equalisations.

Hence **Shavi'ana**, objects or texts relating to G. B. Shaw; '**Shavianism**, the tenets or a characteristic saying of G. B. Shaw; also *nonce-wds.* in Shaw's writings, as **Shavia'nismus** = prec.; **Shavi'anity**, the quality or state of being Shavian; '**Shavianized** *a.*, that has been rendered Shavian in character.

**1903** G. B. Shaw *Let.* 2 Sept. (1972) II. 357 Your theme ..is that the book is a mere rechauffée of stale Shavianized Nietzsche. **1905** —— *Let.* 3 Jan. (1972) II. 496 The dawning of Ibsenism & Nietzscheanism & 'Shavianism' seemed to him the coming of chaos. **1920** —— *Shaw on Theatre* (1958) 133 The younger generation, Shavians to a man, demonstrated their Shavianity by scoffing at me as a Back Number. **1927** *Observer* 12 June 15/1 It [*sc.* a foreword to a volume of plays] will be prized by collectors of Shaviana for its friendly and human qualities. **1927** G. B. Shaw *Pen Portraits & Reviews* (1932) 2 The Shavianismus tickled him enormously; and he was never tired of quoting..my jokes. **1958** *Sunday Times* 27 Apr. 8/2 This slender item of Shaviana. **1975** *Listener* 14 Aug. 218/4 A revival of Shavianism.

**shavie** ('ʃeɪvɪ). *Sc.* [f. SHAVE $sb.^{2}$] A trick.

**1767** W. Meston *Poems* 129 And so to fortune I must leave ye, I wish she play not you a shavie. **1785** Burns *Jolly Beggars*, But hurchin Cupid shot a shaft That play'd a dame a shavie. **1785** —— *2nd Ep. to Davie*, The warl' may play you mony a shavie; But for the Muse, she'll never leave ye. **1884** D. Grant *Lays & Leg. North* 97 It played her sic a shavie, Knocked o'er a sauce-pot in her lap.

**shaving** ('ʃeɪvɪŋ), *vbl. sb.* [f. SHAVE *v.* + $-ING^{1}$.]

**1.** The action of scraping or cutting off a thin slice from a surface; an abrasion.

**1390** *Earl Derby's Exped.* (Camden) 22 Pro hedynge iiij doliorum pro floure imponendo, et pro hopes et schauyng dictorum doliorum. *a* **1425** tr. *Arderne's Treat. Fistula*, etc. 84 þe schauyng of þe bone profited noþing. **1595** Duncan *App. Etym.* (E.D.S.), *Intertrigo*, galling, or shauing. **1688** Holme *Armoury* III. 87/1 In the Curriers Art. Shaveing, is the taking down of the thickness of the Leather.

**2. a.** The action of removing the hair from the head or face with a razor; an instance of this.

**138.** *Antecrist* in Todd *Three Treat. Wyclif* (1851) 147 Antecrist makiþ hise [priests] knowen by crowne & berdes schauynge. *c* **1440** *Alphabet of Tales* 306 When I tuke bod a peny for a shavyng, I couthe wele spar som syluer euerilk day. **1528** Tindale *Obed. Chr. Man* 73 *margin*, Shavinge is borowed of the hethen and oylinge of the Jewes. **1613** Purchas *Pilgrimage* (1614) 62 Their Priests vsed shauings of the head and beard. **1823** Byron *Juan* XIV. xxiii, Men for their sins Have shaving too entail'd upon their chins. **1837** Dickens *Pickw.* ii, The operation of shaving, dressing, and coffee-imbibing was soon performed. **1891** Farrar *Darkn. & Dawn* xxxvii, His arrival at full manhood, as marked by the shaving of his beard.

†**b.** = TONSURE *sb.* 2. *Obs.* (? *nonce-use.*)

**1647** N. Bacon *Disc. Gov. Eng.* I. viii. 25 Theodore Archbishop of Canterbury..placed Bishops over each [diocese], every one of them being of the right Roman stampe, as himselfe was of the right Roman shaving.

**3.** *concr.* A thin slice taken off the surface of anything with a sharp tool; esp. a thin slice of wood cut off with a plane. Chiefly *pl.*

*c* **1386** Chaucer *Can. Yeom. T.* 686 What, deuel of helle! shulde it ellis be? Shauyng of siluer siluer is, parde. *a* **1425** tr. *Arderne's Treat. Fistula*, etc. 46 Puttyng in þe shauyng of lard wiþ þe iuse of porres. *Ibid.* 50 Chauyng of lard. *c* **1440** *Promp. Parv.* 444/2 Schavyngys, of boordys or treys, *rasure.* **1575** Turberv. *Faulconrie* 169 You shall not give them..the shaving of a hasell wande. **1592** Nashe *Four Lett. Confut.* Wks. 1904 I. 271 These..might haue beene buried with his bookes in the bottome of a drie-fatte,..amongst the shauings of the Presse. *a* **1661** Fuller *Worthies, Devon* (1662) I. 248 We call the Shavings of Fish (which are little worth) Gubbings. **1680** Moxon *Mech. Exerc.* xii. 212 [It] is only capable to cut a narrow Shaving off of the Work. **1760** R. Brown *Compl. Farmer* II. 68 All shavings of horns..is good manure for land. **1843** Holtzapffel *Turning* I. 151 When the ivory hollows are thin..the material would be turned entirely into shavings. **1859** Geo. Eliot *Adam Bede* I. i, The slanting sunbeams shone through the transparent shavings that flew before the steady plane. **1887** Ruskin *Præterita* II. 361, I worked with a carpenter until I could take an even shaving six feet long off a board.

*attrib.* **1865** J. Hannett *Bibliopegia* (ed. 6) 379 The shaving tub, over which is placed the cutting press..is a frame of wood for holding the shavings, &c., from the cutting of the edges. **1873** J. Richards *Wood-working Factories* 45 The magazine or shavings room should be arranged to allow the dust to pass off at the top.

**b.** (See quot.)

*a* **1700** B. E. *Dict. Cant. Crew, Shavings*, the Clippings of Money.

**c.** *transf.* and *fig.*

**1677** Horneck *Gt. Law Consid.* v. (1704) 298 Is the King immortal..to be put off with the chips and shavings of devotion? **1681–6** J. Scott *Chr. Life* II. iii. Wks. 1718 I. 228 And all the Stock of Learning, they pretend to, is a few shavings of Wit, gathered out of Plays and Romances. **1912** *Engl. Rev.* Sept. 234 Small gleams, shavings and suffusions of light, were escaping from seams in the ship.

**d.** Phrase. ***to a shaving***, completely, exactly.

**1804** *R. Anderson's Cumbld. Ball.* (1808) 90 She'll suit thee till a shavin. **1828** [Carr] *Craven Gloss.* (ed. 2), *Shaving*, a tittle, a nicety. 'It fits to a shaving.' **1843** J. Ballantine *Gaberlunzie's Wallet* 24 The farmer applauded this song.. exclaiming, "od man, ye hae hit aff Peter till a shavin'.

**4.** *slang.* **a.** The action or process of defrauding.

**1606** Dekker *Seven Deadly Sins* vi. (Arb.) 40 Then haue you the Shauing of Fatherlesse children,..and thats done by Executors. The Shauing of poore Clients especially by the Atturneyes. **1841** C. E. Lester *Glory & Shame Eng.* I. 38, I have been very much astonished to find the system of petty shaving so extensively carried on in England.

**b.** *U.S.* The discounting of bills at an exorbitant rate of interest.

**1813** T. Eaton *Rev. N.Y.* 127 Again the broker claims per cent. For he on shaving is attent. **1834** *Niles' Register* (Baltimore) 5 Apr. 85/2 These rates of shaving.

**5.** *attrib.* and *Comb.*, as ***shaving-basin, cream, -cup, customer, -day, dish, foam, -glass, hand, †-house, -jug, -machine, mirror, -mug, -paper, -paste, -pot, -powder, †rag, -shears, -shop, soap, -strop, -tackle, -thing, -tin, utensil, water, whittle***; **shaving-board** (see quot.); **shaving box**, a small round box containing a piece of soap and a lathering brush; **shaving brush**, (*a*) a brush used to put on the lather before shaving; (*b*) (see quot. 1884); **shaving-cloth**, †(*a*) ? emery cloth for shaving wood, etc.; (*b*) a cloth to cover a person's chest when being shaved; †**shaving-grass** = SHAVE-GRASS; †**shaving hat**, ? a hat made of shavings; in quot. *attrib.*; **shaving horse** (see quot.); †**shaving-iron**, (*a*) a razor; (*b*) a plumbers' SHAVING-HOOK; (*c*) a shoemakers' paring knife; **shaving-knife**, (*a*) a paring tool, *spec.* a shoemakers' knife; (*b*) a razor; †**shaving-linen** = *shaving-cloth* (*a*); †**shaving-mill**, *U.S.*, a small privateer used during the Revolutionary war and the war of 1812; **shaving muscle** (see quot.); **shavings room** (see 3); **shaving stick**, a stick of shaving soap; **shaving-tool** (see quot.); **shaving tub** (see 3).

**1488–9** *Durham Acc. Rolls* (Surtees) 282 Pro sowdyng de le *schavyng bassynnys, 6d. **1597–8** *Wills & Inv. N.C.* (Surtees) II. 180 One deepe shaving bason and cover. **1885** *St. James's Gaz.* 2 Jan. 6/1 The rude yet sufficient engines upon which hoops are shaved. Each of these consists of a small slanted beam, the "*shaving board". **1774** J. Woodforde *Diary* 14 Jan. (1924) I. 122 For a *Shaving Box of one Darcy..pd 0.1.0. **1775** *Pennsylvania Even. Post* 27 July 325/2 Brushes, shaving-boxes and black-ball of the best quality. **1841** Thackeray *Gt. Hoggarty Diamond* i, It was about the size of the lid of a shaving-box. **1792** J. Woodforde *Diary* 26 July (1927) III. 364 At D[itt]o for *Shaving Brush and Powder. **1838** Southey *Doctor* clv. V. 210 He shaves..*sans* shaving-brush,..*sans* everything except a razor. **1884** Britten & Holland *Plant-n.* 427 Shaving-brush. *Centaurea nigra*, L. **1427** in Rogers *Agric. & Prices* (1882) III. 476/2 *Shaving cloth. 1 ell..6d. **1483** *Cath. Angl.* 333/2 A Schavynge clathe, *ralla.* **1540** in *Vicary's Anat.* (1888) App. II. 107 Item to Cornelis Hays, that gave a shaving cloth wroght with gold vjs viijd. **1558** *Bury Wills* (Camden) 150 Tenne shavinge clothes. **1851** C. Cist *Sk. Cincinnati in 1851* 226 A. E. Wetherill, manufacturer of..soaps and *shaving creams. **1922** S. Lewis *Babbitt* i. 5 He snatched up his tube of shaving-cream, furiously he lathered. **1976** 'Z. Stone' *Modigliani Scandal* III. iv. 136 Peter Usher put down his safety razor..and washed the remains of the shaving cream off his face. **1871** 'Mark Twain' *Sketches* 258 Noted the numbers on the private *shaving-cups in the pigeon-holes. **1875** Knight *Dict. Mech.*, *Shaving-cup*, a cup with compartments for hot water and soap, for convenience in shaving. **1840** Thackeray *Barber Cox* Nov., Did you not make over your house,..and nine-and-twenty *shaving customers, to me? **1710** Swift *Jrnl. to Stella* 11 Sept., I am rising to go to Jervas to finish my picture, and 'tis *shaving-day, so good-morrow MD. **1879** C. Schreiber *Jrnl.* 17 Sept. (1911) II. 205 An Oriental *shaving dish with the arms of Groningen. **1961** L. G. G. Ramsey *Connoisseur New Guide*

*Antique Eng. Pott. Porc. & Glass* 28 One-handled bleeding bowls, and shaving-dishes with a segment out of the rim. **1974** *Harrod's Christmas Catal.* 11 'His' contains.. deodorant, *shaving foam, soap and talc. **1979** M. PAGE *Pilate Plot* i. 10 A can of aerosol shaving foam. *a* **1817** JANE AUSTEN *Persuasion* (1818) IV. i. 18 Now I am quite snug, with my little *shaving glass in one corner. **1839** [MISS MAITLAND] *Lett. fr. Madras* (1843) 265, I fear it will all end in buying shaving-glasses and penny prints to stick up in his house. **1967** S. BECKETT *Stories & Texts for Nothing* VI. 99 The glass, a round shaving-glass, double-faced. **1538** TURNER *Libellus, Hippuris,* *Shavynge gyrs. **1561** HOLLYBUSH *Hom. Apoth.* 37 Take yᵉ lesse Shauing girss, called also Cattes tayle and Earth yuy of eche two handfull. **1562** J. HEYWOOD *Prov. & Epigr.* (1867) 177 One barber can haue but one *shauyng hande. **1723** *Lond. Gaz.* No. 6192/11 Elizabeth Robinson,..*Shaving Hatmaker. **1841** *Southern Lit. Messenger* VII. 527/2 A receptacle for spinning-wheels, wash-tubs, pitchforks, *shaving horses, and sundry other implements of domestic industry. **1875** KNIGHT *Dict. Mech., Shaving-horse,* a narrow bench or trestle on which the workman sits astride while shaving down work with the drawing-knife or spokeshave. **1930** *Times Educ. Suppl.* 18 Oct. p. iv/1 A few tools for the lathe..a saw, a shaving-horse. **1974** P. BLANDFORD *Country Craft Tools* ix. 128 Most shaving horses still in existence show that all sizes were made. **1401–2** *Durham Acc. Rolls* (Surtees) 300 Sol. pro vitriacione cujusdam fenestre in le *Shavynghous, 12*d.* *c* **1440** *Promp. Parv.* 424/1 Rastyr howse, or schavyng howse,..*barbitondium.* **1352** *Wynnere & Wastoure* 185 in Gollancz *Parl. 3 Ages* (Roxb.) 96 And alle the lethire.. Schynethe alle for scharpynynge of the *schauynge iren. **1541** *Aberdeen Reg.* (1844) I. 176 The steill to scherp the [shoemaker's] schawing jrne. **1858** SIMMONDS *Dict. Trade,* **Shaving jug.* **14..** *Voc.* in Wr.-Wülcker 564/18 *Ansorium,* a *shavyngknyf, or a trenket. **1530–1** *MSS. Duke Rutland* (Hist. MSS. Comm.) IV. 269 For shavinge knyves bought for my Lorde, vjs. viijd. **1647** HEXHAM I, A shaving knife, *een scheer-mes.* **1843** *Knickerbocker* XXII. 386 The rub-a-dub of the cooper's mallet, the creak of his shaving-knife were still. **1512** in Rogers *Agric. & Prices* (1882) III. 483 *Shaving linen..ells. @ /5. **1897** C. T. DAVIS *Manuf. Leather* xvii. 254 *Shaving machine..for shaving the alum, acid and combination tannages. **1781** *Independent Chron.* (Boston, U.S.A.) 19 July 3/3 in *Trans. Col. Soc. Mass.* (1910) XI. 223 A small boat, one of the noted *Shaving-Mills, which continually infest our bay. **1813** *Salem Gaz.* 12 Oct. 4/1 (ibid. 224) The Fairhaven shaving mill..has sailed from Boston on a cruise. **1911** *Daily Colonist* (Victoria, B.C.) 30 Apr. 10/2 In the surrounding staterooms, the rest began to hang up *shaving mirrors and get into deck shoes. **1958** 'R. CROMPTON' *William's Television Show* vii. 187 The double reflection of the dressing-table mirror and the shaving mirror over the hand basin gave her a perfect view of her profile. **1895** *Stores' List,* *Shaving Mugs. **1912** KEITH *Human Body* xii. 188 The skin over the chin has a curious muscle which acts on it, sometimes named the '*shaving' muscle, as it is employed to steady the skin of the chin against the razor. **1839** DICKENS *Nich. Nick.* liv, A few bank notes for *shaving paper. **1808** *Times* 5 Nov., *Shaving Paste, newly invented. **1537** *North Country Wills* (Surtees 1908) 148 A *shavinge potte, a shavinge bason. **1841** THACKERAY *Gt. Hoggarty Diamond* vii, A man..brought me a silver shaving-pot of hot water. **1768** GOLDSM. *Good-n. Man* IV, We should never travel without—a case of good razors, and a box of *shaving-powder. **1796** T. WALE in H. J. Wale *My Grandfather's Pocket-Bk.* (1883) xvii. 341 Wash given out to Mrs. Wheeler... 1 pair under stockings, thread. 3 *shaving wrages. **1814** JANE AUSTEN *Let.* 18 Nov. (1952) 412 The dirty Shaving Rag was exquisite! **1855** BROWNING *Holy-Cross Day* ii, Shame, man! greedy beyond your years To handsel the bishop's *shaving-shears? **1844** DICKENS *Mart. Chuz.* xxvi, Sweedlepipe's easy *shaving-shop. **1790** *Pennsylvania Packet* 19 Apr. 4/2 He has likewise for Sale ..*Shaving soap. **1844** DICKENS *Mart. Chuz.* xxvi, [It] could not remove the smell of shaving-soap. **1886** KIPLING *Departmental Ditties* (ed. 2) 14 Pears's *shaving-sticks will give you little taste and lots of lather. **1915** S. LEWIS *Trail of Hawk* 328, I must go in and get a shaving-stick. **1978** D. BAGLEY *Flyaway* xxviii. 268 I'm old-fashioned enough to use a soap shaving-stick. **1909** H. G. WELLS *Tono-Bungay* III. i. §2. 269 With the name on the..*shaving-strop. **1842** DICKENS *Let.* 3 Apr. (1974) III. 181 My *shaving tackle, dressing case, brushes, books, and papers. **1848** —— *Dombey* xxv, I don't see his shaving tackle. Nor his brushes, Captain. **1980** *Daily Tel.* 16 Feb. 3/1 In some units.. patients are expected to share toothbrushes and shaving tackle. **1797** SCOTT in *Lockhart* (1837) I. viii. 262 A case with *shaving-things, combs, and a knife, fork, and spoon. **1825** J. NICHOLSON *Oper. Mech.* 624 The *shaving-tool is used for getting the slates to a smooth face for skirtings, floors of balconies, &c. **1823** SCOTT *Quentin D.* xxvi, That last remark upon the *shaving utensils. **1837** DICKENS *Pickw.* xxxix. 426 '*Shaving water, Sam,' said Mr. Pickwick. **1853** WHYTE MELVILLE *Digby Grand* xxiii, Shaving-water at seven, breakfast at eight.

**shaving** ('ʃeɪvɪŋ), *ppl. a.* [f. SHAVE *v.* + -ING².] That shaves, in the senses of the verb.

**1611** COTGR., *Frerot,* a shauing, or shifting, fellow. **1789** E. BUTLER *Diary* 12 Jan. in G. H. Bell *Hamwood Papers Ladies Llangollen* (1930) 169 The most bitter Cold I ever remember, cutting shaving wind. **1810** B. HUNT *Diary* 20 Jan. in *Chester County* (Pennsylvania) *Hist. Soc. Bull.* (1898) 17/2 Most shaveing Cold weather. **1860** [see SHAVER 2 b]. **1897** MEREDITH *Amazing Marriage* xxxvi, A shaving Northeaster.

**Shavuoth** (ʃə'vuːəs, ʃɑːvʊ'ɒt). Also **Shavuot, Shevuos, Shevuoth.** [a. Heb. *šābûʿôṯ,* pl. of *šābûaʿ* week.] = PENTECOST 1. Cf. *feast of weeks* s.v. WEEK *sb.* 2 e.

**1892** I. ZANGWILL *Childr. Ghetto* III. xii. 194 He died four years ago come next *Shevuos.* **1941** G. G. SCHOLEM *Major Trends Jewish Mysticism* viii. 297 An incident during the night before the feast of *Shevuoth* in 1665. **1944** M. SAMUEL in M. W. Weisgal *Chaim Weizmann* I. 88 The Jews were more transfigured by *their* celebration of Shavuoth and Sukkoth than the Russian peasants by *their* thanksgiving celebrations. **1962** *New Jewish Encycl.* 442/2 Since the early 1800's Shavuot has been generally the time when annual confirmation exercises are held. **1968** L. ROSTEN *Joys of Yiddish* 338 Synagogues are decorated with greens on *Shevuoth.* **1975** C. POTOK *In the Beginning* i. 63 The last time I had been in the synagogue was about a week ago during the Festival of Shavuoth. **1981** *Amer. Speech* LVI. 13 The word spelled *Shavuot* 'Pentecost' will almost always be read.. with the traditional Yiddish or Ashkenazic pronunciation as if it were spelled *Shevuos.*

**shaw** (ʃɔː), *sb.*¹ Now *arch.* and *dial.* Forms: 1 **sceaȝa, scaȝa,** 2 **scauhe, scawe,** 3–7 **shawe,** 4 **schaȝe,** 4–6 **schawe,** 4–6, 8–9 **schaw,** 5 **scha(ghe,** 6 *Sc. pl.* **shauis,** 8 **shave,** 9 (Kingsley) **shaugh,** 5– **shaw.** [OE. *sc(e)aga* wk. masc., corresp. to NFris. *skage* farthest edge of cultivated land (Outzen), ON. *skage* wk. masc., promontory (cf. sense 3 below), *skaga* to project; related to OE. *sceacga* SHAG *sb.*¹, and (by ablaut) to ON. *skóg-r* wood, SCOGH.]

**1.** A thicket, a small wood, copse or grove.

**755–7** in Birch *Cartul. Sax.* (1885) I. 258 Terra illa juxta silvam quam dicunt Tocca sceaȝa. **987** in Kemble *Cod. Dipl.* (1845) III. 229 Ðis syndon ða landȝæmæro to Westwuda.. of ðære hlywan suð onbutan færs scaȝan on ða dic [etc.]. *a* **1200** *Newminster Chartul.* (1878) 75 Per has devisas, a rivulo propinquiore le Hangande-scauhe versus septentrionem. *Ibid.,* Usque ad rivulum primo nominatum propinquiorem ab Hangandescawe. *a* **1300** *Thrush & Night.* xxi. in *Rel. Ant.* I. 244 Hy beth briȝttore ounder shawe, Then the day, wenne hit dawe. *c* **1325** *Orpheo* 242 In somer he lyveth by hawys, That on hauthorne growth by schawys. **13..** *Gaw. & Gr. Knt.* 2161 At a schaȝe syde. *c* **1386** CHAUCER *Cook's T.* 3 Gaillard he was as Goldfynch in the shawe. **1390** GOWER *Conf.* II. 333 Hou he to love untrewe was..And tok his lust under the schawe Ayein love and ayein his lawe. *c* **1400** *Anturs of Arth.* vi, þei..suwene to þe soueravne within schaghes schene [*v.rr.* undur the scha schene, in cleues so clene]. *c* **1440** *Bone Flor.* 1504 Tymely as the day can dawe, He led her thorow a feyre schawe. *c* **1480** HENRYSON *Mor. Fab., Cock & Fox* 411 Ane lytill fra this foirsaid Wedowis hous, Ane thornie schaw thair wes of greit defence, Quheirin ane Foxe..Maid his repair. **1508** DUNBAR *Tua Mariit Wemen* 516 Beridis schoutit in schaw, with thair schill notis. **1573** G. HARVEY *Letter Bk.* (Camden) 127 In the shawe there lurkes an ilfavorid padd. **1596** DALRYMPLE tr. *Leslie's Hist. Scot.* I. 15 Paslay quhilke is situat amang cnowis, grene woodis, schawis, and forrest fair. *c* **1730** RAMSAY *Eagle & Robin* 57 Straicht to the schaw he spred his wing. **1742** *De Foe's Tour Gt. Brit.* (ed. 3) I. 159 In a Shave belonging to the Estate of Sir John Hales. **1787** BURNS *Let. to W. Nicol* 1 June, A new-blawn plumrose in a hazle shaw. **1816** SCOTT *Old Mort.* xliii, Saddle the gentleman's horse, and lead him..ahint the thorny shaw. **1849** ALB. SMITH *Pottleton Legacy* xvi. 131 The wet cloggy footpaths through the shaws and copses.

*collective.* **1871** KINGSLEY *At Last* ii, Compared with which European parks..are but paltry scrub and shaugh.

*transf.* **1721** RAMSAY *Prospect of Plenty* 21 O'er shaws of coral and the pearly sands.

**b.** In the same sense, ***shaw of wood*** (arch.); also ***greenwood shaw.*** Cf. WOODSHAW (common in ME. verse).

*a* **1400** *Octouian* 355 As he rood be a wodes schawe. **1462** in *Finchale Priory Charters,* etc. (Surtees) 95 An othir parcell o wod also cald the lewod on the estsid, and buttes atte northend apon a shaw o wod of the said William Tillyall, and atte estend apon the more. **1483** *Cath. Angl.* 334/1 A Schawe of wod, *virgultum.* **1562** PHAER *Æneid* VIII. Xiiij, Among the rootes on ground in greenewood shawe A Sowe of syse vnseene..they sawe. **1600** FAIRFAX *Tasso* VIII. lii, Under the greene wood shaw. **1837** R. NICOLL *Poems* (1842) 86 Through yonder greenwood shaw. **1893** STEVENSON *Catriona* xxix. 346 One night in Scotland in a shaw of wood by Silvermills.

**2.** *spec.* A strip of wood or underwood forming the border of a field. Cf. SHAW *v.*¹

**1577** V. LEIGH *Surv.* I ij, What shawes, or good hedge-rowes of wood be about euery fence. **1669** WORLIDGE *Syst. Agric.* (1681) 331 A *Shaw,* a Wood that encompasses a Close. **1736** J. LEWIS *Isle of Tenet* (ed. 2) 38 *Shave,* a small Copse of Wood by a Field Side. **1798** J. MIDDLETON *Agric. Middlesex* 136 Divided into small inclosures by high hedges and broad shaws. **1842** DARWIN in F. Darwin *Life & Lett.* (1887) I. 320 A country..possessing a certain charm in the shaws, or straggling strips of wood, capping the chalky banks. **1859** LUARD in *Archæol. Cant.* II. 6 There had been a shaw partly covering the place where we were digging. **1860** H. AINSWORTH *Ovingdean Gr.* 8 A large close, encompassed by a shaw, or fence of low trees.

**3.** (See quot.)

**1813** J. HOGG *Queen's Wake* Notes 353 *Shaw*..likewise.. denotes the snout, or brow of a hill; but the part so denominated is always understood to be..broad at the base, and contracted to a point above.

**shaw** (ʃɔː), *sb.*² *Sc.* [Of obscure origin; perh. a use of *shaw* SHOW *sb.* with the sense 'what shows above ground'.] The stalks and leaves of certain plants, esp. potatoes and turnips.

**1801** *Farmer's Mag.* Nov. 412, I..made trials as to the effects of cutting the haum, or shaw, as it is commonly called in Scotland, at different stages of its growth. **1812** SIR J. SINCLAIR *Syst. Husb. Scot.* I. 258 The shaws or tops of the plants being removed. **1813** J. HOGG *Queen's Wake* 68 But mine was made of ane humloke schaw, And a stout stallion was he. **1851** *Rural Cycl.* IV. 178 *Shaw,* the haulm of potatoes, beans, and similar plants. **1887** ANNIE S. SWAN *Gates of Eden* xv. 202 The potato fields, with only heaps of sodden shaws and the long, newly-filled pits to tell of what had been.

**shaw,** *sb.*³ *Sc.* [? var. of SHOW *sb.*] (See quot.)

**1844** H. STEPHENS *Bk. Farm* II. 163 The fore legs [of oxen] are usually farther apart than the hind, but the hind at times, when the *shaw* or *cod* is large and fat, is as much and even more apart.

†**shaw,** *v.*¹ *Obs.* [f. SHAW *sb.*¹] *trans.* To fence or border (a field) with a SHAW (*sb.*¹ 2).

**1610** FOLKINGHAM *Art of Survey* II. ii. 49 Collaterage Actiue, as siding, furrowing, balking,..hedging or shawing, immounding, impayling [etc.]. *Ibid.,* Compound Contiguall Boundage is more significant, as side-haying, head-shawing, &c.

**shaw** (ʃɔː), *v.*² *Sc.* [f. SHAW *sb.*²] *trans.* To cut off the tops of (potatoes, turnips, etc.).

**1882** JAS. WALKER *Sc. Poems* 86 She maun shaw the frosty neeps. **1895** CROCKETT *Men of Moss-Hags* lvi, I heard the horrible crunch as of one that shaws frosty cabbages with a blunt knife. **1895** W. C. FRASER *Whaups of Durley* iv. 43 All were busy..shawing turnips.

**shaw,** obs. form of SHAH, SHOW *v.*

‖**shawabti** (ʃə'wæbtɪ). *Egyptology.* Pl. **shawabtiu,** (anglicized) **shawabtis.** [ad. Egyptian *šwꜣbt(y),* prob. f. *šwꜣb* persea-wood, from which the figurines may originally have been made. In later Egyptian this was replaced by *wšbty* USHABTI.] = USHABTI. Cf. SHABTI.

**1922** LD. CARNARVON in *Daily Mail* 18 Dec. 10 Propped against the wall is a most beautiful portrait shawabti of the King. **1923** CARTER & MACE *Tomb of Tut. Ankh. Amen* I. 120 Beside this shrine, there was a large *shawabti* statuette of the king. **1960** *Oxf. Univ. Gaz.* 4 Mar. 805/2 A XXth Dynasty polychrome terracotta shawabti figure of the chantress of Amun, Inhay. **1961** *Ibid.* 10 Mar. 832/1 Eight fragments of royal shawabtiu in various stones inscribed with cartouches of King Akhnaten. **1970** P. R. S. MOOREY *Anc. Egypt* iii. 68 Among a wide variety of other funerary equipment the magical servant figures or *shawabtis* are the most common.

**Shawanese,** obs. var. SHAWNEE *a.* and *sb.*

**shawder,** obs. form of SHADDER *v.*

**1582** in *Trans. Jewish Hist. Soc. Eng.* (1903) IV. 94 The Charges of gettinge, shawdring and carrieing the ure [*sc.* Copper ore].

**shawe,** obs. form of SHAH, SHAVE *v.*

**shaweling,** obs. form of SHAVELING.

†**shaw-fowl.** *Obs. rare.* [f. *shaw* (of obscure origin) + FOWL *sb.*

It is improbable that the first element is *shaw,* the northern form of SHOW *v.* Cf. WFlem. *schuw,* scarecrow, but it is not easy to see how this can be formally connected.]

A scarecrow, also *fig.* Also an artificial bird set up as a mark for shooting at.

**1621** BP. MOUNTAGU *Diatribæ* 323 As Shaw-Fowles are in a Corne-Field, which skarre away the Crowes and Birds at first erecting. **1624** —— *Gagg* To Rdr. 2 Terrible Shawe-fowles to skarre poore Soules. *Ibid.* II. 13 You set up a Shaw foule for a mark and shoot your bolt at it yourselfe alone. **1624** —— *Immed. Addr.* 131 If they vrge Angelicall Reuelation, then that vnanswerable Argument of the Controuerser is but as a Shaw foule, in a Corne field. **1625** in *Cosin's Corr.* (Surtees) I. 45, I feare not those shaw-foules of convention. **1654** TUCKNEY *Death Disarmed* 78 Such shaw-fowls do not scare me. **1678** PHILLIPS (ed. 4), *Shawfowl,* an artificial Bird made on purpose for Fowlers to shoot at.

**shawfron,** variant of SHAFFRON.

**shawgh,** obs. form of SHAH.

**shawhee,** obs. form of SHAHI.

**Shawian** ('ʃɔːɪən), *a. nonce-wd.* [f. the name of George Bernard *Shaw* (1856–1950), playwright and critic, + -IAN.] = SHAVIAN *a.* Also in other *rare* or *nonce* formations, esp. in Shaw's correspondence, as **'Shawism, 'Shawite: 'Shawesque, 'Shawist** adjs., etc.

**1894** G. B. SHAW *Let.* 2 Dec. (1965) I. 466 He resolved to follow up the vein of comedy opened by Henry Arthur Jones ..before venturing upon the Shawian quicksand. **1895** —— *Let.* 27 Aug. (1965) I. 551, I have finished the draft of a one act piece about Napoleon, a very Shawesque curtain raiser. *Ibid.,* I want to write a big book of devotion for modern people..—a gospel of Shawianity. **1897** E. TERRY *Let.* 9 Jan. in *Ellen Terry & Shaw* (1931) 144 His are my sentiments, but how comes it it's all put in a Shawesque manner? **1897** G. B. SHAW *Let.* 14 July (1965) I. 782 If I steal the plot my version will be so Shawified that nobody will recognize it. **1898** *Westm. Gaz.* 15 Jan. 8/1 Mr. Raymond Blathwayt's 'Talk' with Mr. George Bernard Shaw..is full of characteristic Shawisms. **1899** G. B. SHAW *Let. c* 26–30 Dec. (1972) II. 125, I again urge you to make that Marxian column of yours an intelligently Socialist (that is, Shawist) one. **1900** —— *Let.* 27 Jan. (1972) II. 142 The Shawish quality of my characters. **1903** —— *Let.* 26 Jan. (1972) II. 305 [Dr. L. Kellner]..was one of the first German Shawites. **1904** *Times* 2 Nov. 6/2 A rivulet of 'story' meanders through a meadow of 'Shawisms'. **1928** *Weekly Dispatch* 13 May 12/7 Here was a golden opportunity for an exhibition of Shawishness that was instantly forthcoming.

**shawl** (ʃɔːl), *sb.* Forms: 7 **schal, scial, chal,** 8 **shaul,** 8– **shawl.** [a. Pers. *shāl*; the word has been adopted in Urdū and other Indian langs., and hence into all the European langs.: F. *châle* (†*schall*), Sp. *chal,* Pg. *chale,* It. *scialle,* G. *shawl* (from Eng.), Du. *sjaal,* Sw. *schal, sjal,* Icel. *sjal,* Da. *shawl* (from Eng.), Russ. *shalʲ.*

The spurious word *shairl* (also in comb. *shairl-goat* = shawl-goat: see below) which is found in many recent Dicts., is due to a misprint in E. P. Wright *Animal Life* (1879) 165; the index has correctly *shawl* and *shawl-goat.*]

**1.** An article of dress worn by Orientals (commonly as a scarf, turban, or girdle), consisting of an oblong piece of a material manufactured in Kashmir from the hair of the Tibetan 'shawl-goat' (see 4 b).

**1662** J. Davies tr. *Olearius' Voy. Ambass.* vi. 316 The richer sort have.. another rich Skarf which they call Schal, made of a very fine stuff, brought by the Indians into Persia. **1666** Havers *P. della Valle's Trav. E. India* 123 They had such colour'd clothes as in Persia they call Scial, and use for girdles, but the Indians wear them cross the shoulders. **1687** A. Lovell tr. *Thevenot's Trav.* iii. 37 At all times when they go abroad, they were a Chal which is a kind of toilet of very fine Wool made at Cachmir. **1727** A. Hamilton *New. Acc. E. Ind.* II. xxxvi. 50 And when they go abroad, they [women] wear a Shaul folded up, or a Piece of white cotton Cloth lying loose on the Top of their Heads. **1792** tr. *Rochon's Madagascar* in Pinkerton *Voy.* (1814) XVI. 760 There are few oriental travellers who are not acquainted with those fine woollen stuffs known in Bengal by the name of shawls, which the Mahometans use for turbans. **1903** Sir A. H. Layard *Autobiog.* I. iii. 145 A thick shawl in endless folds round their waists.

**2. a.** As the name of an article of clothing worn in Europe and the West, chiefly by women as a covering for the shoulders or, sometimes, for the head; originally applied to the imported 'cashmere shawl' (= sense 1 above: see cashmere), but in later use extended to denote an oblong or square piece of any textile or netted fabric, whether of wool, silk, cotton, or mixtures of these.

The imported 'cashmere shawls' had usually elaborate patterns, in which a prominent feature was a peculiar ornament shaped something like a pear, with the narrow end continued into a curve. These patterns are often imitated in 'shawls' of European manufacture.

**1767** Sterne *Let. to Eliza* x, I dreamt.. that thou camest into the room with a shaul in thy hand.. you folded the shaul about my waist. **1777** *Phil. Trans.* LXVII. 485 The Shauls all come from Cassemire.. [their] material the produce of a Thibet sheep. **1782** *European Mag.* II. 68 Many a lady shrouded in a Shrawl [? *read* Shawl]. **1782–3** W. F. Martyn *Geog. Mag.* I. 44 Those fashionable handkerchiefs, which the English ladies have of late years worn under the name of shauls. **1798** Sophia Lee *Canterb. T., Yng. Lady's T.* II. 544 The servants.. were unfolding for her notice a rich, and remarkable Indian shawl. **1817** Byron *Beppo* lxxxv, The Count was at her elbow with her shawl. **1834** McCulloch *Dict. Comm.* (ed. 2) s.v., The finest Edinburgh and Paisley shawls. **1840** Malcom *Trav.* 9/1 The thin cotton shawls covering not only the whole person but the head, are lent them every morning to wear in school, and kept beautifully white. **1866** G. Macdonald *Ann. Q. Neighb.* xxxii. (1878) 552 Miss Oldcastle appeared in her bonnet and shawl. **1902** Alice Terton *Lights & Shadows Hosp.* ix. 139, I just wropped the baby up in a shawl.

**b.** Worn round the neck as a protection from cold.

**1834** *Baboo* I. xii. 208 (Stanf.) Fold your shawl close round your throat. **1837** Dickens *Pickw.* ix, Emma, give Pickwick a shawl to tie round his neck. **1859** Sala *Gas-light & D.* vii. 85 A gentleman with a very shiny hat, a very long shawl, and an indefinite quantity of thick great-coats.

**3.** [Anglo-Irish.] A common prostitute. Cf. shawlie. *slang.*

**1922** Joyce *Ulysses* 308 Blind to the world up in a shebeen in Bride street after closing time, fornicating with two shawls.

**4.** *attrib.* and *Comb.* **a.** simple attrib., as ***shawl-cloth, counterpane, girdle, goods, kind, -pin, stuff, turban, -weaver, -work, wrap; shawl girt, -shaped*** adjs.; ***shawlwise*** adv.

**1841** Moorcroft *Trav.* II. 169 A strong *shawl-cloth called Patu. **1791** *Trans. Soc. Arts* (1792) X. 196 A *Shawl Counterpane, four yards square. **1844** E. Warburton *Crescent & Cross* (1846) II. xvii. 251 The [Turkish] smugglers gathered round the door of the tent, their *shawl girdles stuck full of pistols and yataghans. **1812** Byron *Ch. Har.* ii. lviii, The wild Albanian kirtled to his knee, With *shawl-girt head, and ornamented gun. **1783** G. Forster *Journ. Bengal to Eng.* xiii. (1798) II. 19 A portion of the revenue of Kashmire is transmitted to the Afghan capital in *shaul goods. **1835** *Court Mag.* VI. p. ii/1 The fronts are trimmed with a lappel of the *shawl kind, of black velvet or silk. **1860** Worcester, **Shawl-pin*, a pin for fastening a shawl. **1873** B. Harte *Fiddletown* 10 Her shawl pin and a soiled cuff. **1898** *Daily News* 2 Apr. 6/5 The *shawl-shaped capes. **1841** Moorcroft *Trav.* II. 186 An immense variety of articles of *shawl-stuff are manufactured in Kashmir, besides the shawls themselves. **1815** Elphinstone *Acc. Caubul* (1842) I. Introd. 31 He wore the Persian dress, with a cap and a *shawl turban over it. **1842** Vigne *Trav. Kashmir* II. 121 A first-rate *shawl-weaver will occasionally earn one small rupi a day. **1897** Mary Kingsley *W. Africa* 223 When they wear anything on their heads it is a handkerchief folded *shawlwise. **1909** *Chamb. Jrnl.* Oct. 640/2 These stitches originally were used for *shawl-work. **1879** Mrs. A. E. James *Ind. Househ. Managem.* 23 You should have your *shawl wraps and rug handy for use on deck when it is chilly.

**b.** Special comb.: **shawl collar** (see quot. 1960); also **shawl-collared** *a.*; **shawl-dance**, a dance originating in the East, in which a shawl or scarf is waved; so **shawl-dancing**; **shawl dressing-gown**, a dressing-gown having a shawl-like pattern; **shawl-goat**, a goat of Tibet (*Capra lanigera*) which furnishes the wool for making the Indian shawls; **shawl-handkerchief**, a handkerchief resembling a shawl; **shawl-loom**, a loom for weaving shawls; also, 'a figure-weaving loom' (Knight *Dict. Mech.* 1875); **shawl-material** (see quot. 1882); **shawl-pattern**, a pattern resembling or characteristic of that of an oriental shawl; also *attrib.*; **shawl-reticule**, ? a reticule made of cashmere bearing a shawl pattern; †**shawl-room**, the room for depositing shawls at a place of assembly; **shawl-strap**, a pair of leather straps joined to a transverse handle, for carrying shawls, etc.; **shawl-waistcoat**, a waistcoat having a pattern resembling that of an oriental shawl; **shawl-wool**, the wool of the shawl goat; also *attrib.*

**1913** *T. Eaton & Co. Catal.* Spring & Summer 4/3 The graceful *shawl collar is edged with whipcord silk. **1960** C. W. Cunnington et al. *Dict. Eng. Costume* 192/2 *Shawl collar*, 1820's on.. a term denoting a broad turn-over collar of a coat or waistcoat, continuous with the lapels, i.e. without a notch between. **1974** *Country Life* 17 Jan. 106/3 Shawl-collar cardigans are the thing to look for. *Ibid.* 107/1 *Shawl-collared, kimono-style cardigan. **1813** *Examiner* 15 Mar. 171/1 A conversation.., which naturally concludes with a *shawl-dance. **1897** 'Ouida' *Massarenes* xxi, She had danced her shawl dance on the brink of exposure and bankruptcy. **1813** *Examiner* 15 Mar. 171/1 There is a lady, whose character is.. marked by her skill in *shawl-dancing. **1837** Dickens *Pickw.* xli, The broken-down spendthrift in his *shawl dressing-gown. **1793** T. Baird *Agric. Middlesex* 39 A *shawl-goat from the East Indies. **1893** Lydekker *Horns & Hoofs* 107 The long-haired shawl goat of Tibet. **1838** Lytton *Alice* vii. iv, The rest of the party.. unmuffled themselves of cloaks and *shawl-handkerchiefs. **1783** G. Forster *Journ. Bengal to Eng.* xiii. (1798) II. 20 The Kashmirians say, that during their subjection to the Mogul dominion, the province contained forty thousand *shaul looms. **1882** Caulfeild & Saward *Dict. Needlework* 445 **Shawl materials.* These are a mixture of silk and wool,.. employed for the partial making and trimming of dresses. **1838** Dickens *O. Twist* xxii, A coarse, staring, *shawl-pattern waistcoat. **1908** *Chamb. Encycl.* IX. 376 A few words may be said about the patterns of Cashmere shawls... The most characteristic feature.. is what has been usually called the 'cone' or 'pine cone'... Sometimes it is simply called the shawl pattern. **1825** T. Hook *Sayings* Ser. ii. *Passion & Princ.* xii. III. 291 An imitation *shawl reticule, as large as a moderate *sac de nuit*, and containing.. pocket-handkerchiefs for the party, hung upon her arm. **1838** Lytton *Alice* viii. ii, The ladies were waiting their carriage in the *shawl-room. **1873** 'Susan Coolidge' *What Katy Did at Sch.* iii. 42 Tucking the railway guide into a *shawl-strap, and closing her bag with a snap. **1840** Thackeray *Shabby-genteel Story* viii, He had a *shawl-waistcoat of many colours. **1774** W. Hastings in C. R. Markham *Mission of Bogle* (1876) 8 The animals called tús, which produce the *shawl wool. **1841** Moorcroft *Trav.* I. 311 The shawl-wool goat. **1879** *Proc. R. Geog. Soc.* I. 449 The export of shawl-wool (*pashm*) to India [from Tibet] has fallen off.

**shawl** (ʃɔːl), *v.* [f. shawl *sb.*] *trans.* To cover with a shawl, put a shawl on (a person). Also *absol.* Hence **'shawling** *ppl. a.* (In quots. *fig.*, of snow.)

**1812** Miss Edgeworth *Absentee* iii, Her son assisted Grace Nugent most carefully in shawling the young heiress. **1820** Byron *Juan* v. cxlvii, His Highness was.. Shawl'd to the nose. **1840** Lady C. Bury *Hist. Flirt* vi, We retired to cloak and shawl ourselves. **1848** Thackeray *Van. Fair* xxvii, George had meanwhile very carefully shawled his wife. **1880** Mrs. L. B. Walford *Troublesome Dau.* I. i. 18 Evelyn beheld a slight feminine form, shawled and wrapped to the chin. **1899** *Blackw. Mag.* Feb. 329/1 She shawled her head and her baby in her sea-blue cloak. **1930** R. Campbell *Adamastor* 72 Around your rocks you furl the shawling snow. *a* **1953** Dylan Thomas *Prospect of Sea* (1955) 97 Our snow was not only shaken in whitewash buckets down the sky, I think it came shawling out of the ground.

**shawl**, obs. Sc. form of shoal *a.*

**shawlde, shawle**, var. ff. shaul *dial.*

**shawled** (ʃɔːld), *ppl. a.* [f. shawl *sb.* (or *v.*) + -ed.] Wearing or covered with a shawl.

**1834** Ht. Martineau *Farrers* ii. 20 Then, while Jane settled herself, aproned, shawled, and mittened, at her desk. **1847** Disraeli *Tancred* iv. ii, Their arms and shawled heads glistened in the silver blaze of the moon. **1876** Whyte Melville *Katerfelto* iii. 27 With a shawled robe of scarlet and orange reaching to her naked ankles. **1902** E. B. Ottley in C. E. Osborne *Father Dolling* iv. (1905) 37 The shawled and hatless East End girls.

**shawlie** ('ʃɔːlɪ). *colloq.* (chiefly *Irish* and *northern*). Also **shawly**. [f. shawl *sb.* + -ie.] A woman (usu. poor or working-class) who wears a shawl over her head.

**1914** F. Niven *Justice of Peace* ii. iii. 258 'Shawlies'— as the girls who are to be seen in the neighbourhood of the Trongate of Glasgow, wearing shawls over their heads, are locally called. **1928** F. T. Jesse *Many Latitudes* 233, I will put a shawl over my head. I will go along the way I was one of them Shawlies from the quays. **1934** S. Beckett *More Pricks than Kicks* 63 A lowly house dear to shawlies. **1947** P. Doncaster *Sigh for Drum Beat* ii. 12 He knew they were the footsteps of a woman. A shawly, with her shawl wound about her body and a baby snuggled into it. **1966** 'L. Lane' *ABZ of Scouse* II. 72 A working-class Liverpool woman usually elderly and of scruffy appearance. Once known as a *shawlie* from the local habit of wearing a shawl. **1980** J. Masters *Heart of War* v. 68 She had been transformed into a typical Dublin shawlie, only more ragged and dirtier than most.

**shawling** ('ʃɔːlɪŋ), *vbl. sb.* [f. shawl *v.* and *sb.* + -ing[1].]

**1.** The action of covering with, putting on, or wearing a shawl.

**1815** Scott *Guy M.* xxix, I should look on his compliments, his bowings, his cloakings, his shawlings, and his handings, with some little suspicion. **1822** Miss Mitford in L'Estrange *Life* (1870) II. 144 His cloakings and shawlings are worse than any cold. **1824** —— *Village* I. 252 The shawlings, the cloakings, the cloggings! the cautions against cold, or heat, or rain, or sun! **1861** Sala *Tw. round Clock* 237 Nor during.. the dancing, the supper, the shawling, the departure, and the drive home to his chambers.

**2.** The material of a shawl.

*c* **1806** Mrs. Sherwood in *Life* xx. (1847) 346 A skull-cap of rich shawling, or embroidered silk.

**shawlless** ('ʃɔːllɪs), *a.* [f. shawl *sb.* + -less.] Without or not wearing a shawl.

**1847** Emily Bronte *Wuthering Heights* ix. (1850) 73 Cathy.. standing bonnetless and shawlless. **1871** Miss Mulock *Fair France* i. 8 What decent English maid-servant would choose to saunter bonnetless, shawlless [etc.]? **1906** *Edin. Rev.* Apr. 469 Mrs. Brown went shawlless.

**shawm** (ʃɔːm), *sb.* Forms: α. 4 **schallemele**, 6 **shamulle, shamble**. β. *pl.* 4–5 **schalmeis, s(c)halmys, shalemeyes, chalemyes**. γ. *pl.* 5 **shalmuse, shalemuse, schalmeuis**, 6 **shalmewes**; *sing.* 5 **sc(h)almuse**, 6 **schalmesse**; *pl.* 5 **s(c)halmuses, schalmoyses**. δ. 5–7 **schalme**, 6 **shaulm(e**, 6–7 **shalme**, 6–9 **shalm**; *pl.* 6 **shalmz, schallmes**. ε. *pl.* 6 **shambes, s(c)hames, schammes**. ζ. 6 **shaume**, *pl.* **schawmys**, 6–7 **shawme**, (7 *pl.* **shawn(e)s**), 7– **shawm**. [The ME. *schallemelle* (whence the other α forms) is a. OF. *chalemel* (mod.F. *chalumeau*):—vulgar L. **calamellus*, dim. of L. *calamus* reed. The β forms (with which cf. MHG. *schalmîe*, MDu. *schalmeye*, *schalmeide*, MLG. *schalmeie*, mod.G. and Du. *schalmei*) are a. OF. *chalemie*, an unexplained derivative of L. *calamus*. The γ forms are a. OF. *chalemeaux*, pl. of *chalemel*, the form of the last syllable being prob. influenced by association with muse *sb.*[3], bagpipe; the pl. was in Eng. early mistaken for a sing., and a new plural *schalmuses* was formed. The reduction of the word to a monosyllable was prob. due to misapprehension of pl. forms like *schalmys*. See also shalle.]

**1.** A mediæval musical instrument of the oboe class, having a double reed enclosed in a globular mouthpiece.

Coverdale, followed by the Prayer-book Psalter, uses *shawmes* in Ps. xcviii. 7 where the original and the ancient versions have 'trumpet' or 'horn'.

α. **1390** Gower *Conf.* III. 358 With Cornemuse and Schallemele [*rhyme* hele]. **1524** *St. Papers Hen. VIII*, IV. 209 And furthwith the trompettes and shamulles did sounde and blewe up mooste pleasauntely. **1572** Bossewell *Armorie* ii. 46 One of them singeth with voice, another with shamble [*Isid.* xi. iii. 59 b, Vna voce, altera tibiis].

β. *c* **1350** *Libeaus Desc.* (Kaluza) 1864 Trompes, hornes, schalmeis [*v. rr.* schalmys, schalmes, schalmuses] Before þe hiȝe deis He herd. *c* **1384** Chaucer *H. Fame* 1218 That maden lowde menstralcies In cornemuse and shalmyes [*v. rr.* chalemyes, shalemeyes] And many other maner pipe.

γ. *c* **1430** *Pilgr. Lyf Manhode* ii. iii. (1869) 117 Reedes and floytes and shalmuses. *a* **1440** *Sir Degrev.* 1086 With trompe and with nakere, And the scalmuse clere. *c* **1440** *Promp. Parv.* 443/2 Schalmuse, pype, *sambuca.* **1480** Caxton *Ovid's Met.* xii. xvi, Gheterns, lutes, shalemuse, recordours. **1481** —— *Reynard* xli. (Arb.) 112 They blewe up trompettis and pyped wyth shalymoyses. *a* **1483** *Liber Niger* in *Househ. Ord.* (1790) 48 Whereof sume use trumpettes, sume shalmuse and small pipes. **1503** *Privy Purse Exp. Eliz. York* (1830) 91 Item to the Kinges mynstrelles with the shalmewes xl s. **1530** Palsgr. 266/1 Schalmesse a pype, *chalmeau.*

δ. *c* **1450** Holland *Howlat* 762 The dulset, the dulsacordis, the schalme of assay. **1513** Bradshaw *St. Werburge* i. 1689 Trumpettes blewe vp shalmes and claryons. **1533** Elyot *Cast. Helthe* ii. xxxiii. (1541) 51 The entrayles.. be exercised by blowyng, eyther by constrainte, or plaiynge on shaulmes or sackbottes. **1542** Udall *Erasm. Apoph.* 223 b, Blowyng on a bagpipe, or a shalme, or on some other facioned pipe. *c* **1560** A. Scott *Poems* (S.T.S.) ii. 45 Trumpettis and schalmis w[t] a schowt Playid or the rink began. **1563–83** Foxe *A. & M.* I. 242/2 A noyse of trumpets and shalmes. **1565** Cooper *Thesaurus*, *Auletes*,.. he that plaieth on the flute or shalme: a pyper. **1575** Laneham *Let.* (1871) 7 This Pageaunt waz clozd vp with a delectable harmony of Hautboiz, Shalmz, Cornets, and such oother looud muzik. *a* **1578** Lindesay (Pitscottie) *Chron. Scot.* (S.T.S.) I. 379 The denner quhair thair was great mirth schallmes draught trumpattis and weir trumpatis. **1578** Lyte *Dodoens* iv. liv. 514 This kinde [of reed] dyd serue to make tongues for pipes, shaulmes, or trumpettes. **1607** *Schol. Disc. agst. Antichr.* i. iii. 144 The douting conscience soundeth heavily like a shalme. **1641** Brome *Joviall Crew* v. (Stage dir.), A flowrish of Shalms. **1705** Motteux *Quix.* (1733) III. 238 The Moors.. only use Kettle-Drums, and a kind of Shaulms like our Waits or Hautboys. **1805** Scott *Last Minstr.* vi. vi, From the lofty balcony, Rung trumpet, shalm, and psaltery. **1837** Carlyle *Fr. Rev.* I. vii. v, Paris.. clasps hands, as the Avengers, with their shrilling drums and shalms tramp by.

ε. **1533** Cranmer in Ellis *Orig. Lett.* Ser. i. II. 317 Tromppets, shambes, and other dyverse instrumentes. **1537** *Lett. & Papers Hen. VIII*, XII. i. 11 Befor y[e] Scotysh gent. Shamis & dyvers oder instrumentes. **1553** Eden *Treat. New Ind.* (Arb.) 14 A great noyse of cimbals, drumslades, timbrelles, shames, pipes, flutes. **1555** in *Burgh Rec. Edin.* (1871) II. 220 James Dromond and his marrowis quha playit befoir Sanct Geill on Sanct Geillis day on the schammes. *c* **1650** *Scottish Field* 320 in *Percy Folio MS.* I. 228 Many shames [15.. *Ibid.* 450 in *Chetham Soc. Misc.* II., shalmes] in that showe: with theire shrill pipes.

ζ. **1513** DOUGLAS *Æneis* IX. x. 67 Wyth tympanis, tawbronis, ȝe war wont to heyr, And bos schawmys of turnyt buschboun tre. **1535** COVERDALE *Ps.* xcvii. 7 With trompettes also & shawmes. **1567** DRANT *Horace de Arte P.* A vij, The shawme [L. *tibia*] was not as it is nowe with copper wrythed in In trumpet wyse but [etc.]. **1590** SPENSER *F.Q.* I. xii. 13 With shaumes, and trompets, and with clarions sweet. **1611** BEAUM. & FL. *Knt. Burning Pestle* Prol., *Cit.* What stately Musick have you? You have Shawnes. *Pro.* Shawns? no. *Cit.* No?.. Ralph plaies a stately part, And he must needs have Shawns. **1675** COVEL in *Early Voy. Levant* (Hakl. Soc.) 211 Their [Turkish] pipe is much the same with our trebble shawme [*printed* shaurne] or Hooboy. **1685** OTWAY *Windsor Castle* 193 The Cornet, Flute and Shawme. **1698** FRYER *Acc. E. Ind. & P.* 30 With the noise of Drum, Shawm, and Fife. **1789** BURNEY *Hist. Mus.* II. iv. 270 *note*, Shawm in old English is a clarinet of low pitch. **1830** TENNYSON *Dying Swan* iii, As when a mighty people rejoice With shawms, and with cymbals, and harps of gold. **1859** R. F. BURTON *Centr. Afr.* in *Jrnl. Geog. Soc.* XXIX. 240 Of these [musical instruments] the most noisy is a kind of shawm, a straight tube of wood bound with palm fibre and opening like a clarionet. **1865** SWINBURNE *Poems & Ball., St. Dorothy* 403 Fair-clothed men that play on shawms and lutes.

**b.** *fig.*

**1637** N. WHITING *Albino & Bellama, Vind. Poesie* H 3, I knew the Roscians feature, not his name, Yet tis engraven on the Shaulme of Fame.

**c.** *transf.* An organ-stop resembling the shawm in quality of sound.

**1852** SEIDEL *Organ* 84 The organ in St. Elizabeth's, Breslau, contains a shalm.

†**2.** A player on the shawm. *Obs. rare.*

**1481–90** *Howard Househ. Bks.* (Roxb.) 207 The same day, my Lord gaff to my Lord Glossetyres schalmevis vj.s. viij.d. **1522** *Ord. King's Ho.* in *Gentl. Mag.* (1834) CIV. I. 48 When it shall please him to have any Schames, Ministrells, or any such other, to come to his presence.

**3.** *Comb.*, as ***shawm-blower, -player, -playing*** (adj.).

**1826** HOR. SMITH *Tor Hill* (1838) I. 260 Scrapers of rebecks, *shawm-blowers, and vagabond pipers. **1540** PALSGR. *Acolastus* II. iii. Mij b, Any trompettours or *shaulme players. **1865** SWINBURNE *Chastelard* V. i. 171 These shawm-players That walk before strange women and make songs! **1894** DU MAURIER *Trilby* II. (1895) 60 A lordly, godlike, *shawm-playing, cymbal-banging hero.

**shawm** (ʃɔːm), *v.*[1] *rare.* In 5 **shalemoyse.** [f. SHAWM *sb.*] *intr.* To play on the shawm.

**1480** CAXTON *Ovid's Met.* XI. iv, There satte Pan.. holdynge a floyte of a rosier, in whiche he shalemoysed & pyped a strange note. **1844** *Blackw. Mag.* LVI. 96 All our talented performers had turned their instruments, scraped, fluted, twanged, jingled, and shawmed to their hearts' content.

**shawm** (ʃɔːm), *v.*[2] *north. dial.* Also **shaum.** [Cf. SCAUM *v.*] *intr.* (See quots. 1855, 1877.) Also *trans.*

**1824** J. HODGSON in J. Raine *Mem.* (1858) II. 49 Keep on our hats and shawm our shins, and be like other Laplanders happy at home. **1855** *Whitby Gloss.*, To *Shawm*, to warm the knees and toes by sitting with them close to the fire. **1877** *Holderness Gloss.*, *Shawm*, to sit in front of the fire, with upraised petticoats, to impart warmth to the legs.

†**shawmer.** *Obs. rare.* In 6 **schawmir, shalmewer, shamuller.** [f. SHAWM *sb.* + -ER[1].] One who plays on the shawm.

**1505** *Acc. Ld. High Treas. Scot.* III. 152 Item, to ane schawmir in Air, xiiij s. **1511** *Lett. & Pap. Hen. VIII*, II. II. 1451 [At Greenwich, to Piers Thoulouse], a minstrel shalmewer, 4*l.* **1527** WHITINTON *Vulgaria* 16 b, Mynstrelles dwelle here and there: as harpers, luters, fydlers, shamullers.

**shawmist** ('ʃɔːmɪst). [f. SHAWM *sb.* + -IST.] One who plays the shawm. (In earlier centuries called a *shawmer* or *shawm-player*.)

**1961** A. BAINES *Musical Instr. through Ages* ix. 233 The European shawmist presses the lips to a wooden 'pirouette'. **1977** *Early Music* July 333/1 The shawmist, perhaps accompanied by the tambourine player, can only have performed monophonic melodies.

**Shawnee** (ʃɔː'niː), *a.* and *sb.* Also †**Savan(n)a, Shawanee, Shaweno, Shawnese, Shonee,** etc. [ad. Munsee *šá:wano:w*, f. Shawnee *ša:wano:ki* people of the south. Early forms in *-ese* prob. represent a hybrid formation with -ESE, later interpreted as the pl. of a stem in *-ee*.]

**A.** *adj.* **1.** Of or pertaining to an Algonquian Indian people, formerly resident in the eastern U.S. and now in Oklahoma; designating a member of this people or its language.

**1674** H. WOODWARD *Let.* 31 Dec. in *S. Carolina Hist. Soc. Coll.* (1897) V. 460 Two days before my departure arrived two Savana Indians. **1714** J. LAWSON *Hist. Carolina* 171 The Savanna Indians, who formerly lived on the Banks of the Messiasippi, and remov'd thence to the Head of one of the Rivers of South-Carolina. **1728** in C. S. R. Hildeburn *Century of Printing* (1885) 94 Two Indian Treaties.. Between the Honourable.. Lieut. Governour of the Province of Pennsylvania.. And The Chiefs of the Conestogoe, Delaware, Shawanese and Canawese Indians. **1737** *Documents Colonial Hist. New-York* (1855) VI. 106, I am very Sorry that there has been any Misunderstanding betwixt Governour Pen & the Shaweno Indians. **1748** C. WEISER *Jrnl.* 10 Sept. in R. G. Thwaites *Early Western Travels* (1904) I. 31, I made a Present to the old Shawonese Chief. **1788** [see MOHICAN, MOHEGAN *a.*]. **1817** *State Papers & Publick Documents U.S.* (1819) (ed. 3) XII. 450 The balance of our men (except five Shonee Indians who had left us several days before),.. came on this side of the first chain of mountains. **1821** T. NUTTALL *Jrnl. Trav. Arkansa* 54 We stopped awhile at a Shawnee camp. **1826** T. FLINT *Recoll.* 231 A rich commandant.. married a Shawnese wife. **1855** A. W. WHIPPLE *Explor. Railway Route* III. 51 [Figure D illustrates] one of a pair of Shawnee ear-drops.. made by a native artist. **1949** *Democrat* 30 June 7/4 Several Shawnee towns were set up in various places over the state [of Alabama]. **1973** A. H. WHITEFORD *N. Amer. Indian Arts* 17 Creek and Shawnee bowls have designs incised around the rims.

**2. Shawnee-haw,** the larger withe-rod, *Viburnum nudum*; **Shawnee salad,** a perennial herb, *Hydrophyllum virginianum*, native to eastern North America and bearing clusters of white or purple flowers; **Shawnee wood** the western catalpa or catawba-tree, *Catalpa speciosa*.

**1780** J. DONELSON *Jrnl.* 29 Mar. in *Three Pioneer Tennessee Documents* (1964) 9 Gathered some herbs in the bottoms of Cumberland, which some of the Company called Shawanee Sallad. **1822** *Trans. Hort. Soc. Lond.* 1st Ser. IV. 445 The *Hydrophyllum Virginicum* is called by the Americans of the Western States, Indian Sallad, or Shawanee Sallad, because these Indians eat it as such, when tender. **1829** LOUDON *Encycl. Plants* 133 Hydrophyllum virginicum is used as a salad, under the name of Shawanese salad in North America. **1866** *Treas. Bot.* s.v. *Hydrophyllum.* **1909** *Cent. Dict. Suppl.*, Shawnee haw. **1931** W. N. CLUTE *Common Names Plants* 31 At least three plants commemorate them: the Shawnee haw.., the Shawnee salad.., and the Shawnee tree, also called Shawnee wood. **1818** W. P. C. BARTON *Compendium Floræ Philadelphicæ* I. 9 Catalpa-Tree, Catawba-Tree, Schawnes-wood. **1931** Shawnee wood [see *shawnee salad* above].

**B.** *sb.* **1.** The name of an Algonquian Indian people; a member of this people.

**1693** *Documents Colonial Hist. New-York* (1854) IV. 43 Wee are glad that the Showannoes.. did make their application to you last fall for protection. **1737** *Ibid.* (1855) VI. 107, I Recommend to you to keep the Shawenoes among your Selves as you have Done the Tuskierores to prevent their Going to the French. **1755** R. DINWIDDIE *Let.* 14 Dec. in S. M. Hamilton *Lett. to Washington* (1898) I. 149 The Cherokees have taken up the Hatchet against the French & Shawnese. **1786** [see HURON]. **1828** M. NEVILLE *Last of Boatmen* in *Western Souvenir 1829* 118 The scout thought it as praiseworthy to bring in the scalp of a Shawnee, as the skin of a panther. **1837** R. M. BIRD *Nick of Woods* I. 15 The Shawanee and the Wyandot still hunted the bear and buffalo in the cane-brake. **1854** *Southern Lit. Messenger* XX. 401 The Shawnese still deserved their chastisement. **1891** H. F. O'BEIRNE *Leaders Indian Territory* p. viii/1 The Shawnees awaited their opportunity until the Tonkaway braves had departed on a big hunt. **1964** B. G. HOFFMAN *Anthrop. Papers of Smithsonian Inst. No. 70* 223 The Shawnee have what may be considered the best claim to having resided in .. the Fort Ancient territory.

**2.** The language of this people.

**1792** H. H. BRACKENRIDGE *Mod. Chivalry* I. v. iii. 61 It would be necessary for him only to talk Irish, which he might pass for the Shawanee. **1940** [see LEXEME]. **1972** *Language* XLVIII. 846 [It] is supposed to be found in.. Tacana, Shawnee.. and Wichita.

†**shaw-net.** *Obs.* [? f. SHAW + NET *sb.*] ? A fowling-net for use in a 'shaw' or coppice.

**1648** HEXHAM II, *Vlowe*, Shaw-nets for Wood-cocks.

**shawp,** variant of SHAUP *Sc.*

**shawy** ('ʃɔːɪ), *a. rare.* [f. SHAW *sb.*[1] + -Y.] Abounding in shaws; woody.

**1848** *Fraser's Mag.* XXXVIII. 186 Through rocky cleugh and shawy glen. *Ibid.* 187, I.. seek some shawy burn. *Ibid.* 317 They wander.. up the shawy braes.

**shay**[1] (ʃeɪ). [A back-formation from CHAISE *sb.* (ʃeɪz) mistaken for a plural. Also CHAY.] = CHAISE *sb.*

**1717** S. SEWALL *Diary* 20 Sept., The Governour went through Charlestown.. carrying Madam Paul Dudley in his shay. **1735** in Corey *Malden* 666 Bought a shay £27 10s. **1806–7** J. BERESFORD *Miseries Hum. Life* xx. (ed. 3) II. 237 Or who'd swelter and stoop Over linen and soap, While each tax-cart and shay To the Fair jolts away? **1841** J. T. HEWLETT *Parish Clerk* I. 71 Some in shays, and others on horseback. **1867** O. W. HOLMES *Guardian Angel* xiv. (1891) 170 It is n't everybody that can ride to heaven in a C-spring shay, as my poor husband used to say. **1873** LD. LYTTON in Lady B. Balfour *Lett.* (1906) I. 298 The Bois.. was full of.. one-horse shays.

**b.** *attrib.*, as ***shay boy, cart.***

**1840** J. T. HEWLETT *P. Priggins* xiv, He gives the coachman or *shayboy twice as much as is usual. **1823** C. M. WESTMACOTT *Points of Misery* 30 [She] puts him in a light *shay cart. **1835** DICKENS *Sk. Boz, Greenwich Fair*, Cabs, hackney-coaches, 'shay' carts.

**Shay**[2] (ʃeɪ). *N. Amer.* The name of Ephraim *Shay* (1813–1916), Amer. engineer, applied to a geared locomotive designed by him in 1874 for hauling timber.

**1894** J. DREDGE *Rec. Transportation Exhibits at World's Columbian Exposition of 1893* 308/1 (*heading*) The Shay Locomotive. *Ibid.* 308/2 The Shay Locomotive Engine No. 75, on the Montana Union Railway, on December 6th, 1890, hauled a train of fifteen loaded cars up the Anaconda high line, a distance of 1½ mile on a 3½ per cent. grade.. at a rate of speed equal to 4 miles per hour. **1936** *ABC Brit. Columbia Lumber Trade Directory* 74 Elk River Timber Co., Ltd... 75 Miles of Track; 5 Locos; 4 Shays. **1942** R. L. HAIG-BROWN *Timber* 253 *Shay*, a geared locomotive, slow but powerful and adapted to heavy hauling. Shays of about 70 tons are commonly used in hauling logs from the landing to the mainline. **1953** *Harmac News* (Vancouver, B.C.) Oct. 8/1 A 42-ton Shay was hauling logs for Wiest logging in 1914. **1962** *Amer. Speech* XXXVII. 135 *Shay*, the most popular of the geared locomotives used in the woods. The several cylinders are upright on the engineer's side of the frame, and the boiler is offset to balance them. A propeller shaft driven by cranks runs along one side of the engine and is geared to the axles. **1974** *Islander* (Victoria, B.C.) 7 July 3/1 The 45-ton Shay (named for designer Ephraim Shay) will be replaced by a 120-ton Baldwin diesel-electric locomotive.

‖**shaya,** variant of CHAY.

**shay-brained,** *a. dial.* Foolish, silly.

**1806** BLOOMFIELD *Wild Fl.*, *Abner* 15 While I take this shay-brained course And like a fool run to and fro.

**shayl, shayr:** see SHAIL *v.*, SHARE *v.*

†**shayth.** *Sc.* [? a. Gael. *seadh.*] Reason, what is reasonable; also, (a person's) rights.

**1542** *Records of Elgin* (New Spald. Club 1903) I. 72 Angnes Stone vrangit in the saying to Necoll Moressone that shayth war it to gadder ane dussane of quyins and gar lesch him quhill tha var ane inch of him togidder. **1546** *Ibid.* 88 Thomas Beyn for the wrangus slaying of ane zoung swyn out of his shayth pertenying to Johne Crokatt.. sall pay to the said Johne four sillingis.

**shazam** (ʃə'zæm), *int. Children's slang.* [Invented word: see quots. 1940 and 1976.] A 'magic' word used like 'abracadabra' or 'presto' to introduce an extraordinary deed or story.

**1940** *Whiz Comics No. 2* 5 'Speak my name!' 'Shazam!'.. As Billy speaks the magic word he becomes Captain Marvel. **1964** *Playboy* May 63 Shazam! **1976** in M. Horn *World Encycl. Comics* 157/1 Captain Marvel was really a homeless orphan named Billy Batson who was taken to see the old wizard Shazam. When Billy spoke his name, he was magically transformed... The lure of simply yelling 'Shazam'—which stood for Solomon's wisdom, Hercules' strength, Atlas' stamina, Zeus' power, Achilles' courage, and Mercury's speed. **1978** *Amer. Poetry Rev.* July/Aug. 44/4 Incantatory rituals are often marked by the repetition of magic formulas. Abbra Cadabra. Enny Meeny Minny Mo. Shazam. A Tisket a Tasket or Hi do Hi do hi de ho.

**shcherbakovite** (ʃɜːbə'kɒvaɪt). *Min.* [ad. Russ. *shcherbakovit* (Es'kova & Kazakova 1954, in *Doklady Akad. Nauk SSSR* XCIX. 837), f. the name of D. I. *Shcherbakov* (1893–1966), Russian mineralogist: see -ITE[1].] A silicate of potassium, sodium, barium, titanium, and niobium, $(K,Na,Ba)_2(Ti,Nb)_2(Si_2O_7)_2$, found as brittle, brown, orthorhombic crystals.

**1955** *Mineral. Abstr.* XII. 569 (*heading*) Shcherbakovite—a new mineral. **1964** *Doklady Acad. Sci. U.S.S.R.: Earth Sci. Sect.* CLI. 129/1 The goniometric measurements were made on small long prismatic crystals of shcherbakovite from an arfvedsonite-feldspar vein in the Khibiny alkalic massif.

‖**shchi** (ʃtʃiː). Also 9 **tschee, stchi, stchie, stchee, shtchee, shtchi, shtshi,** etc. [Russian *shchi* kail.] Cabbage soup.

**1824** J. D. COCHRANE *Narr. Pedestrian Journey through Russia* iv. 105, I never entered a cottage, but shtshee (a cabbage soup), with meat, milk and bread, were.. placed before me unasked. **1833** R. PINKERTON *Russia* 71 A favourite and common dish among them is a kind of broth, called *tschee.* **1855** *Englishwoman in Russia* 46 We get plenty of black bread and salt, and very often stchie. **1901** *Daily Chron.* 14 June 3/4 The delicious and universal cabbage soup is not in English letters *Stchie*,.. but—as nearly as maybe—*Shtchi.* **1904** *Daily News* 14 Apr. 5/3 We won Poltava on stchi (cabbage soup), and beat Napoleon with kasha (buckwheat gruel). **1904** *Westm. Gaz.* 21 Apr. 7/1 The dish of shtchee—fermented cabbage and meat—with vodka, he greatly enjoyed. **1905** *Ibid.* 21 Jan. 16/1 That extraordinary mixture of pickled cabbage, meat broth, and about a hundred other ingredients which goes by the name of *shtshi.* **1906** *Daily Chron.* 28 Aug. 3/1 The fare is disgusting, the 'stchee' uneatable. **1941** A. L. SIMON *Conc. Encycl. Gastron.* III. 18/2 The most popular form of cabbage soup in France is called *Garbure*; the Russian edition of it is known as *Stschi.* **1958** W. BICKEL tr. *Hering's Dict. Classical & Mod. Cookery* 113 *Schtschi*, Russian Cabbage Soup. **1971** *Times* 9 Aug. 5/8 [Soup made from wild sorrel] is a welcome change in the summer and is called *green schchi* (*schchi* being the traditional cabbage soup). **1973** R. MARTIN *Internat. Dict. Food & Cooking* 259/2 *Shchi*, (*Russian*), green vegetable soup of meat *bouillon* and cabbage. **1977** *N.Y. Rev. Bks.* 14 Apr. 10/4 In exchange for a few dissident intellectuals the Ibanskians import from America tons of *shchi*, the Russian national dish of cabbage soup.

**shd, shd.,** abbrev. or contraction of *should* s.v. SHALL *v.*

**1780** H. WOODFORDE *Diary* 9 Dec. (1924) I. 297 Edm[d] also mentions.. that his Father shd say that he had left some shirts behind. **1811** SHELLEY *Let.* 12 Jan. (1964) I. 45, I see no reason why they shd. always continue so. **1885** HARDY *Let.* 13 Mar. (1978) I. 131, I shd say that a married daughter .. who is here, strikes me as a particularly sensible woman. **1930** E. POUND *XXX Cantos* viii. 29 And I shd. like to be party to it, as was promised me. **1962** L. DAVIDSON *Rose of Tibet* 6, I feel strongly we shd go out for a fictional kind of title. **1973** *Black World* Sept. 84 Ever get tired of other people telling you what you shd be doing for yr self?

**she** (ʃiː, ʃɪ), *pers. pron.*, *3rd sing. fem. nom.* Forms: α. 2 scæ, 3 sse, 3–7 sche, 4 shae, 4–5 se, 4–6 che, 4–7, (8) shee, 9 *dial.* zhe(e, sheea, sheh, shey, sha, etc., 3– she; 3 sȝe. β. Chiefly *Sc.* and *north.* 3 sso, 3–5 sco, 3–7, 9 *dial.* scho, 4, 6 schoe, 4–5 schow, 4–7, 9 *dial.* sho, 5 shoy, 6 schew, schw, 5, 9 *dial.* shoo, 6–7, 9 *dial.* shoe, 9 *dial.*

**shou, shu, su,** etc. γ. 4–5 **scheo,** 4–6 **sheo.** δ. Combined with a following verb, as 4 **shere** = she were; 5 **shalighte** = she alight; 6 **shase,** 7 **sh'has,** 8 **sh'as** = she has; 6 **schois,** 7 **shees** = she is; 7 **sh'ad** = she had; 7 **sheele, shele** = she will. See also SH', SH-. [Of difficult etymology; but prob. an altered form of the OE. fem. dem. pron. *síó, séo, síe*: see THE *dem. pron.* A. 1 b.

It would appear that in some dialects of late OE. the diphthong in this word underwent a change of stress, the older pronunciations (si:o) and (si:e) being replaced by (sjo:) and (sje:). The latter of these variants is represented by the spelling *sʒe* of the 13th c.; and the phonetic development so far is exactly parallel to that of the OE. fem. pers. pron. *hío, héo, híe* (see HEO), which in the 13th c. was pronounced in some dialects (hjo:, hje:), as is shown by the written forms *ʒho, ʒhe*. As the combination (sj) is acoustically close to (ʃ), and more difficult (according to English habits of articulation) to produce, it is not surprising that (sje:, sjo:) became (ʃe:, ʃo:), these being the pronunciations expressed by the written forms *scæ* (midland, *c* 1150) and *sco, scho* (northern, *a* 1300).

It has been objected to this view that in ONorthumbrian the fem. sing. of the demonstrative was not *sio, seo,* but *ðeo, ðiu*. Instances of *seo, sio* are, however, found in the Lindisfarne Gospels and the glosses to the Durham Ritual and Hymnarium; and the extant remains of the dialect represent a very small portion of the Northumbrian territory.

With regard to the substitution of the demonstrative pronoun for the original pers. pron., it may be remarked that the phonetic development of various dialects had in the 12th and 13th c. rendered the pronouns *he* (masc.) and *heo* (fem.) almost or wholly indistinguishable in pronunciation. There was therefore where these dialects were spoken a strong motive for using the unambiguous feminine demonstrative instead of the feminine personal pronoun. Further, the districts in which *she* or *sho* first appears in the place of *heo* are marked by the abundance of Scandinavian elements in the dialect and place-names; and in Old Norse the dem. pron. (of all genders) is often used as a personal pron. It is also noteworthy that in OS. and OHG. the fem. pers. pron. nom. sing. was *siu* (mod.G. *sie*, Du. *zij*), corresponding to OE. *sío* (the oblique cases, and the masc. and neut. in the sing., being f. the stems *hi-, i-*); and in OFris. *se* 'she' occurs beside *hiu*.

The conjecture that *she* represents the ON. *sjá* this (nom. sing. masc. and fem.) is untenable: the initial (ʃ) is sufficiently accounted for otherwise, and the vowels do not agree. It is however possible that the change from the falling to the rising diphthong in the development both of *hío* and *sío* may be due to Scandinavian influence, as in ON. the Germanic *eu* and *iu* became rising diphthongs.

Some scholars have maintained that *she* and its dialectal variants descend directly from the pronunciations (hje:, hjo:) of HEO (referred to above); the contention being that (hj) might naturally develop into (ʃ). This development has occurred in some Norwegian dialects, and it is illustrated by the proper names *Shetland* and *Shapinshay* from ON. *Hjaltland* and *Hjalpandisøy*. There is slight support for this view in the existence of north. dialect forms such as SHOOP representing OE *héope* HIP *sb.*[2] Other views are that (ʃ) was substituted for the un-English sound (ç), developed from (hj), and that it arose from the sequence *-s + j-* in such contexts as *was hió*.

The α type (to which the mod. literary form belongs) is in origin East Midland, while the β type is originally northern.]

**I.** As proper feminine pronoun of the third person, nominative case.

**1.** The female being in question, or last mentioned. **a.** Used of persons of the female sex.

α. **1154** *OE. Chron.* (Laud MS.) an. 1140, And te Lundenissce folc hire wolde tæcen & scæ fleh. *c* **1250** *Gen. & Ex.* 1444 Sʒe ne bi-spac him neuere a del. *Ibid.* 1447 Sʒe bar him siðen sex sunen. *Ibid.* 1698 For rachel non birðe ne nam Sʒe bi-taʒte iacob balaam. *Ibid.* 1925 She [see 5]. *Ibid.* 2619 Sche forð-ran. **1297** R. GLOUC. (Rolls) 709 Ȝwan sse wolde imaried be. *c* **1300** *Havelok* 1721 In al denemark nis wimman So fayr so sche, bi seint iohan! *c* **1320** R. BRUNNE *Medit.* 843 Se wende þey wulde so serue here sone. *a* **1340** HAMPOLE *Psalter* Cant. 523 In syngular ioy shae was glad in cryst. *c* **1350** *Will. Palerne* 2317 Ac soþli as che had seide ..þei herd an huge route of horse. *c* **1420** ? LYDG. *Assembly of Gods* 376 Patronesse of plesaunce, be namyd well se myght. *c* **1460** *Towneley Myst.* x. 158 A, hyr body is grete and she with childe! **1567** *Trial Treas.* (1850) 14 Che can make curchy well enowe. **1569** J. ROGERS *Glasse Godly Love* in *Tell-trothes N. Yr's. Gift*, etc. (1876) 180 Aboue all thinges, shee is glad and willinge to suffer for Christes sake. **1611** BIBLE *Gen.* ii. 23 She shalbe called woman, because shee was taken out of man. *a* **1699** LADY A. HALKETT *Autobiog.* (Camden) 4 When she came to my sisters house. **1821** SCOTT *Kenilw.* xx, Yonder be 's her, mon,—yonder be 's her—Zhe will buy changes an zhe loikes stuffs. **1893** F. THOMPSON *Poems* 23 Hers is the face whence all should copied be, Did God make replicas of such as she.

β. **1297** R. GLOUC. (Rolls) 615 So þat sso [þe quene] hadde sone gret poer an honde. *a* **1300** *Cursor M.* 75 Hir luue sco haldes lele ilike. *Ibid.* 20209 Vntil hir chamber scho it bare. *c* **1300** *Havelok* 112 A mayden..þat was so yung þat sho ne couþe Gon on fote, ne speke wit mouþe. **13..** *Cursor M.* 2731–2 (Gött.) Scho said, 'for-soth ne smile i noght'; And if schoe [*Cott.* sco..sco] did it, hir ouerthoght. *c* **1375** *Sc. Leg. Saints* i. (*Petrus*) 64 Quhen men lede hyre to þe stede, quhar schow suld be put to dede, Petir [etc.]. **1436** *Rolls of Parlt.* IV. 498/1 When itt was asked of hir by ye Prist, if shoo wolde agree her to have the said William Pulle to husbond, and sho saide, nay never by hir wille. *c* **1450** *Mirk's Festial* 211 But when þis come to þe qwhene, sco went nyȝ wode wroþ. **1472** *Presentm. Juries* in *Surtees Misc.* (1890) 23 As oft as shoy his fone defectyffe. **1533** GAU *Richt Vay* (1888) 39 And yat schw hayd na payne or trowbel in hir birth as al oder vemen hesz bot schw buir hir sone with Ioi and blythnes. *c* **1560** A. SCOTT *Poems* (S.T.S.) xxiii. 17 For nowdir wald schew rew, Nor beir me at disdane. **1628** in R. M. Fergusson *Alex. Hume* (1899) 274 Margaret Donaldsoune confessed that shoe gave her the sark. *c* **1634** ROW *Hist. Kirk* (Wodrow Soc.) 12 And sho dieing, the work of Reformation prospered. *c* **1730** RAMSAY *Wyfe of Auchtermuchty* iv, Gudeman, quod scho, content am I. **1824** [CARR] *Craven Gloss., Shoe*, she. **1847** EMILY BRONTE *Wuthering Heights* ix. (1850) 75 And Miss Nelly, shoo's a fine lass! shoo sits watching for ye i' t' kitchen.

γ. **13..** *K. Alis.* 151 Kyng Phelippes quene scheo is, Theo fairest woman lyvyng y-wis. *c* **1380** *Sir Ferumb.* 2133, & þan wente sheo þe burde briȝt & tok hem vp anone. *c* **1400** LOVE *Bonavent. Mirr.* iii. (Gibbs MS.), þowe mayste vnderstond [þe] furst ioye þatt scheo hadde. **1440** J. SHIRLEY *Dethe K. James* 15 Sheo is bot a womane.

δ. *c* **1300** *Havelok* 1250 For she wende she were bi-swike That shere yeuen unkyndelike. *c* **1374** CHAUCER *Troylus* v. 189 From hir hors she alighte [*Harl. MS.* shalighte]. **1575**, etc. [see SH-, SH']. **1607** SHARPHAM *Fleire* IV. (1610) G 3 b, Yet in the morning, sheele haue none of them all. **1631** KNEVET *Rhodon & Iris* III. i. E 3, Then to her hips shele have her garments fall. **1637** N. W[HITING] *Albino & Bellama* 4 For having pow're to conquer, being faire, Sh'ad pow're not to be conquerd, being chaste. **1675** SHADWELL *Psyche* III. Wks. 1720 II. 37 To Psyche I haue offer'd my whole heart, Sh'has for no other left me the least part. **1697** VANBRUGH *Relapse* v. ii, Sure there's divinity about her, and sh'as dispensed some portion on't to me. **1724** RAMSAY *Evergreen* (1761) II. 17 Schois fairest payd that gets her Will.

†**b.** With adjective prefixed. *Obs. rare.*

**1589** GREENE *Menaphon* (Arb.) 66 Till proud she repent. **1593** SHAKS. *Lucr.* 1674 Which speechless woe of his poor she attendeth.

**c.** Used of animals of the female sex. Also (esp. in rustic use) of certain animals (e.g. the cat, the hare) the names of which have a quasi-grammatical feminine gender exc. when a male is specifically referred to.

*c* **1386** CHAUCER *Sqr.'s T.* 409 And euere in oon she [the falcon] cryde alwey and shrighte, And with hir beek hir seluen so she prighte, That [etc.]. *c* **1410** *Master of Game* (MS. Digby 182) i, An hare shall dure well iiij. myle or more or lasse, and she be an olde hare mascle. **1486** *Bk. St. Albans, Hawking* c viii, She puttithouer when she Euoidith hir meete owte of hir goorge in to hir bowillis. **1576** TURBERV. *Venerie* lix. 162 Of the subtilties of an Hare, when she is runne and hunted. **1653** WALTON *Angler* vii[i]. 147 The Melter hovers over her all that time that she [the female pike] is casting her Spawn. **1665** J. NORTH in *Extr. S.P. rel. Friends* III. (1912) 234 Tennants and vassalls..who dare not say the Crow is blacke if they say shees white. **1860** READE *Cloister & H.* vii, She [a leopard] was chained to the huntsman. **1891** [D. JORDAN] ('Son of Marshes') *On Surrey Hills* ii. (1892) 44 He [the sparrow-hawk], or 'she', as they say, will fly at anything.

¶ **d.** The misuse of *she* for *I* (also for *you* and *he*) is common in literary representations of Highland English. Cf. NAINSELL, HER *pers. pron.* 2 b, HERSELF 3 c.

*c* **1450** HOLLAND *Howlat* 797 A bard owt of Irland..Said ..'Raike hir a rug of the rost, or scho sall ryiue the'. *c* **1707** in *Scot. Antiquary* (1898) XII. 105 She sall Confin Her nane Speak to te Salt, an te Excise, whilk she far sees will touch Her nane sell Mickle. **1818** SCOTT *Rob Roy* xxix, She'll speak her mind and fear naebody—She doesna value a Cawmil mair as a Cowan, and ye may tell MacCallum More that Allan Iverach said sae. **1819** —— *Leg. Montrose* iv, What the deil, man,..can she no drink after her ain master without washing the cup. *Ibid.*, 'And here she comes,' said Donald, as Captain Dalgetty entered the hall.

**2.** Used (instead of *it*) of things to which female sex is conventionally attributed. **a.** Of a ship or boat. Also (now chiefly in colloquial and dialect use), often said of a carriage, a cannon or gun, a tool or utensil of any kind; occas. of other things.

In quots. *c* 1380 and *c* 1475 the grammatical gender of the Fr. words rendered may have influenced the translators.

**1375** BARBOUR *Bruce* III. 626 And thar schip thai lychtyt sone..And scho, that swa wes maid lycht, Raykyt slidand throw the se. *c* **1380** *Sir Ferumb.* 2182, & þoȝ þe dore were strong & huge, wiþ þe strok sche fleȝ. *c* **1475** *Partenay* 4495 A chambre..full fair wroght & well,..She myght in no wise ..more fairer be. **1483** *Cely Papers* (Camden) 142 Oon Thursday..cam forth a passonger from Dower to Calles ward and sche was chasyd with Frensche men. **1496** *Acc. Ld. High Treas. Scot.* I. 299 Item, to the men that brocht the clos cart furth of the water, quhen scho stude in the watir all nycht. **1561** HOLLYBUSH *Hom. Apoth.* 14 b, Roste a rape upon the fyre till she be all black, and eate her warm. **1594** *Reg. Privy Council Scot.* V. 195 Haveing brocht in thair ship to ane place thair quhair thay thocht sho micht maist convenientlie ly. **1672** J. ROBERTS *Compl. Canonier* 36 To cool a Piece of Ordnance, when she is grown hot with over-much fireing. **1748** *Anson's Voy.* II. iii. (ed. 4) 212 She..was a fine roomy ship. **1821** SCOTT *Pirate* viii, I'll give you my fowlingpiece; she will put a hundred swan-shot through a Dutchman's cap at eighty paces. **1865** DICKENS *Mut. Fr.* III. vii, Mr. Venus..adjusting the kettle on the fire, remarked to himself..'She'll bile in a couple of minutes'. **1869** *St. James' Mag.* III. 309 The certainty of Oriel's bumping Balliol, if she can only hold up as far as the Gut. **1877** *N.W. Linc. Gloss.* s.v., The feminine pronouns *she* and *her* are used for many things, as an oven, a 'stee', a pianoforte, a 'suff', and a church-bell. **1888** LEES & CLUTTERBUCK *B.C. 1887* xxxiv. (1892) 372 A sleeping-car was being prepared here for attachment to the train when she should arrive.

**b.** Of abstractions, etc. personified as feminine; also of the soul, a city, the church, a country, †an army, etc.

*c* **1421** *26 Pol. Poems* xx. 173 She [the soul] is ashamed, now she is wys; Sche lyued in vowtrye so many a day. *c* **1489** CAXTON *Sonnes of Aymon* vi. 136 Whan the cyte vnderstode this, she began to be sore moeved. **1585** T. WASHINGTON tr. *Nicholay's Voy.* I. xiii. 14 b, [He] told the Ambassadour, that the Turkes army was at Malta, and that she had saccaged the towne. *Ibid.* I. xvi. 17 Shee is inhabited & peopled with a great number of..Merchants. **1638** JUNIUS *Paint. Ancients* 21 Phantasie on the contrary doth take in hand also what shee hath not seene. **1760** *Ann. Reg.* III. *Misc. Ess.* 203 With all the pompous titles..bestowed upon France, she is not more than half so powerful as she might be. **1827** SCOTT *Surg. Dau.* i, Nature must not be hurried, and she avenges herself of every attempt to do so. **1845** M. PATTISON *Ess.* (1889) I. 10 The Church cannot be said to have created pilgrimages, or even to have encouraged them—she suffered them. **1871** SMILES *Charac.* i. (1876) 22 South Carolina;.. if that state went out of the world today, she would not have done so much for the world as Socrates. **1900** G. C. BRODRICK *Mem. & Impressions* 252 Stanley had been ridiculing the habit of personifying the Church as a woman, and speaking of it tenderly as *she*.

†**c.** *rarely* of an immaterial thing without personification.

*c* **1380** *Sir Ferumb.* 2359 To morwe we wolleþ..by-gynne þe sege..& fro þat time she ys by-gunne ne schal heo neuere be laft Til þe tour aȝen be wonne.

**d.** Of natural objects considered as feminine, as the moon, or the planets that are named after goddesses; also of a river (now *rare*), formerly of the sea, a tree, etc.

The two examples (quots. 1483, 1588[1]) of *she* used of the sun may possibly be due to misprint; survival of the OE. grammatical gender can hardly be supposed, but Caxton may have been influenced by the fact that the sun is fem. in Flemish.

**1483** CAXTON *Golden Leg.* 112 b/2 The sonne..that day ascended as hye as she is on saynt Iohns day at none. **1588** PARKE tr. *Mendoza's Hist. China* 340 They sayle alwayes towards the west, following the sunne when as she departeth from our hemispherie. **1588** A. KING tr. *Canisius' Catech.* I vj, Conferring..hir [*sc.* the moon's] rising and setting with ye rysing and setting of ye sone..it salbe easie to knaw how longe scho do schyne. **1614** A. ROBERTS *Sacred Septenarie* 169 The Moone cannot shine except shee receiue light from the Sunne. **1657** LIGON *Barbados* 77, I have seen a Negre with two short ropes clyme the tree and gather the fruit, about this time she is 80 foot high. **1673** O. WALKER *Educ.* I. viii. (1687) 73 Demosthenes..strengthened his voice by declaiming near the sea side when she roared. **1823** SCOTT *Quentin D.* xxv, She [*sc.* the harvest moon] shed her yellow influence over rich and deep pastures. **1903** A. ADAMS *Log of Cowboy* ix. 121 The driftwood..indicated what might be expected when she [the river] became sportive or angry.

**e.** Applied *colloq.* to things (both material and immaterial) to which the female sex is not conventionally attributed (esp. in *Austral.* and *N.Z.*). Freq. in idiomatic phrases ***she's jake*** (or ***right***): see JAKE *a.*, RIGHT *a.* 15 d.

**1903** 'T. COLLINS' *Such is Life* (1944) i. 5 You dunno what you're doin' when you're foolin' with this run. She's hair-trigger at the best o' times, an' she's on full cock this year. **1938** N. MARSH *Artists in Crime* vi. 81, I went down to the studio... She was locked, but the key's left on a nail. **1941** J. STREET *Father's House* x. 190 A wet spell would ruin us and she was coming rain before long. **1958** *N.Z. Listener* 18 July 6/2 If you tear the hamstring, in the back of the leg just above the knee, you're gone a million—she's nasty. **1969** *Private Eye* 25 Apr. 12 She's apples Eric—I don't reckon I feel like brekkie! **1973** P. WILSON *N.Z. Jack* xxi. 187 'Fix it all right?' I asked. 'She's jake now, mate,' he said. 'There she is, good as new'.

**3.** Used pleonastically. **a.** In apposition with a *sb.* in the nominative case. Now only *arch.* (*poet.*) and in uneducated use.

*a* **1440** *Sir Eglam.* 110 Upon the morowe the maydyn smalle, Sche wente before hur fadur in halle, Amonge hur byrdys bryght. **1576** *Common Conditions* 243 (Brandl) My sister, she the Juell is. ? *a* **1600** *Beggar's Dau. Bednall-Green* I. xvi. in *Percy Folio MS.* II. 282 Then Bessye shee sighed, & thus shee did say. **1806** JAMIESON *Sir Oluf* 44 The bride she cam' wi' the bridal train. **1892** KIPLING *Barrack-room Ballads* 21 My wife she cries on the barrack-gate, my kid in the barrack-yard. **1896** —— *Seven Seas* 86 The Liner she's a lady by the paint upon 'er face.

†**b.** In apposition with a sb. in the objective case. *Obs.*

**1576** *Common Conditions* 265 (Brandl) Who can but smile and laugh to see the state of Fortune, shee? **1599** *Sir Clyom.* in *Peele's Wks.* (Rtldg.) 501/2 But shall I frame, then, mine excuse by serving Venus she. *Ibid.* 511/1 Yet though unto Neronis she I may not show my mind.

**4.** Used for *her*, as object or governed by a preposition. **a.** in literary use. Now *rare.*

*c* **1530** LD. BERNERS *Arth. Lyt. Bryt.* lxxxi. (1814) 380, I haue no mo chyldren but she. **1588** SHAKS. *L.L.L.* v. ii. 469 The Ladies did change Fauours; and then we Following the signes, woo'd but the signe of she. **1592** DANIEL *Delia* xi, '*Tears, vows & prayers*', Yet will I weepe, vowe, pray to cruell Shee. **1604** SHAKS. *Oth.* IV. ii. 3 You haue seene Cassio, and she together. **1610** —— *Temp.* III. ii. 109, I neuer saw a woman But onely Sycorax my Dam, and she. **1881** OLIVE SCHREINER *Story African Farm* II. xiii. (1889) 284, I want no angel, only she.

**b.** *vulgarly*, as an emphatic objective case.

**1752** FOOTE *Taste* I. (1781) 14 The fat Cook..fell out at the Tail of the Waggon; so we left she behind. **1762** BICKERSTAFFE *Love in Village* III. iv, I have got rid of she. **1856** MISS MULOCK *J. Halifax* x, 'I hope—our presence did not inconvenience—the young lady?' 'Bless your heart, sir! nothing ever inconveniences she'.

**II.** As antecedent pronoun, followed by relative, etc.: cf. HE II.

**5.** The or that woman, or person of the female sex (*that* or *who*...).

Formerly sometimes instead of *her* (objective): cf. 3 b.

*c* **1250** *Gen. & Ex.* 1925 Hu mai ðis sen..ðat ðine breðere, and ic, and she ðat ðe bar, sulen luten ðe? **1390** GOWER *Conf.* I. 46 She that is the Source and Welle Of wel or wo. *c* **1400** *Rule of St. Benet* (Prose) 26 And so þat gas vt of þe wuke, and so þat cumis in, sal recaiue þe benichun at morne at matins. *c* **1489** CAXTON *Blanchardyn* 186 Goo ayen to Tormaday to see the noble lande of that lady, she of whom thou arte amorouse soo moche. *a* **1540** BARNES *Wks.* (1573) 361/2 Faith is shee, whiche by prayer, obtaineth that thing, that the law commaundeth. *c* **1600** SHAKS. *Sonn.* iii, For where is she so faire whose vn-eard wombe Disdaines the tillage of thy husbandry? **1606** —— *Tr. & Cr.* II. iii. 252 Praise him that got thee, she that gaue thee sucke. **1847** TENNYSON *Princess* III. 244 There is nothing upon earth More miserable than she that has a son And sees him err. **1871** R. ELLIS *Catullus* lviii. 2 That bright Lesbia,.. she than whom Catullus Self nor family more devoutly cherish'd.

**III.** As demonstrative pronoun.

**6.** † **a.** ***she and she, she and he***, etc.: this and that, the one and the other, both. *Obs.*

*c* **1374** CHAUCER *Troylus* II. 1747 And though ye wolde han after merye dayes, Than dar ye nought, and why? for she, and she Spak swich a word. **1500–20** DUNBAR *Poems* xviii. 18 Than will thay say, baith scho and hie, That I am jaipit lait and air. **1513** DOUGLAS *Æneis* I. Prol. 317 He or scho Quha takis me nocht, go quhar thai haue ado. **1562** *Aberd. Kirk Sess. Rec.* (Spalding Club) 7 Quhasumeuer within this toun, he or sche, jniuris.. their nychtbour with infamous.. wordis.

**b.** Followed by a prepositional phrase.

**1819** SCOTT *Ivanhoe* xliv, The Church gave her full solemnities, graced with all the splendour which she of Rome knows how to apply with such brilliant effect. **18..** H. G. BELL *Poem, Mary Q. Scots* 29 And there walks she of Medici,.. the haughty Catherine! *a* **1849** POE *The Assignation*, 'Ha!' said he thoughtfully,.. 'the Venus of the Medici?—she of the diminutive head and the gilded hair?'

**IV.** As *sb.* (not changing in the objective).

**7. a.** A female; a woman or girl; a lady-love. (With pl. *shes, she's*, †*shees.*)

**1538** BALE *Thre Lawes* 422 What! sumtyme thu wert an he? Yea but now ych am a she. **1547** SALESBURY *Dict. Welsh*, Banyw, a she. **1575** [see HE 7 b]. **1590** GREENE *Never too late* I. (1600) D 3 b, Bright she was, for twas a she That trac'd her steps towards me. *a* **1592** —— *Jas. IV*, I. iii. 679 Her vertues may compare With the proudest she that waits vpon your Queen. *c* **1600** SHAKS. *Sonn.* cxxx. 14 And yet by heauen I thinke my loue as rare, As any she beli'd with false compare. **1611** —— *Wint. T.* IV. iv. 360, I was wont To load my Shee with knackes. **1648** CRASHAW *Delights of Muses* Poems (1904) 160 Who ere she be, That not impossible she That shall command my heart and me. **1671** *Westminster Drollery* II. (1875) 80 For every he Has got him a she. **1709** MRS. MANLEY *Secret Mem.* (1736) II. 228 The lovely She grew calm and tender. **1752** FIELDING *Amelia* x. ii, The domino began to make very fervent love to the she. *a* **1814** *Forgery* IV. ii. in *New Brit. Theatre* I. 472 The very she who took the bracelets from me. **1819** BYRON *Juan* II. clxxv, The freest she that ever gaz'd on glass. **1840** THACKERAY *Shabby-genteel Story* i, I would not change my condition—no, not to be.. the luckiest she in England. **1881** 'RITA' *My Lady Coquette* xviii, 'She's a friend of yours naturally?' 'How do you know it's a "she"?' **1894** FENN *Real Gold* 40 Those are not shes—they're both men.

**b.** A female animal. [So G. *sie*, Fris. *sy.*]

**1556** *Aurelio & Isab.* G 3, So the moste parte of the sheos [Fr. *des femelles*], aswell of the birdes as of the beastes, will be praide. **1601** BP. W. BARLOW *Eagle & Body* (1609) B 2, A Prey to the Eagles of the Epicene gender, both Hees and Shees. **1604** R. C. *Table Alph.* (1613), *Female*, the shee in mankinde, or other creatures. **1615** SYLVESTER *Job Triumph.* 78 Five hundred yoke of Oxen did hee owe, Five hundred Asse-shees, Camels six times so. **1626** BACON *Sylva* §852 He-Lions are Hirsute, and haue great Maines; the She's are smooth like Cats. **1657** G. THORNLEY *Daphnis & Chloe* 125 The he-goats had battels for the she's, and every one had his own wives. **1677** MRS. BEHN *Adelazer* I. i, He.. Had better snatch the She from the fierce side Of a young amorous lion, and 'twere safer. **1698** FRYER *Acc. E. India & P.* IV. v. 177 The She [= tigress] brings forth but once in Twelve Years. **1759** R. BROWN *Compl. Farmer* 39 Especially the shees which are with kid. **1875** [see HE 7 b].

**8.** Opposed to *he*: Female.

?*a* **1500** *Chester Pl., Noah's Flood* 124 Of cleane fowles seaven alsoe, the hee and shee together. **1567** [see HE 7]. **1613** SHAKS. *Hen. VIII*, v. iv. 25 Any That had a head to hit, either young or old, He or shee, Cuckold or Cuckold-maker. **1634** SIR T. HERBERT *Trav.* 24 These and the Date tree thrive not, except the male and female be united, and have copulation: the she is only fruitfull. **1649** LOVELACE *A Lady with Falcon* vi, For y'are in Falcons Monarchy, And in that just Dominion bred, In which the Nobler is the Shee. **1888** *Sat. Rev.* 20 Oct. 467/1 Any not a poet, whether he or she, might toil [etc.].

**V.** *attrib.* and *Comb.*

**9.** Female. Applied to animals, as in ***she-ass, -bear, -wolf*** (also *fig.*), etc.; **she-dog**, chiefly *transf.* = BITCH 2; **she-dragon**, a female dragon; also *transf.* (cf. DRAGON[1] 6); **she-lion** *slang*, a punning distortion of 'shilling'; **she-stock, -stuff** *U.S.*, female cattle.

**1382** WYCLIF *Gen.* xv. 9 A she gehet of thre ȝeer. —— *Lev.* xxii. 28 Shee oxe other shee sheep. —— *Zech.* ix. 9 Thi kyng shal cume to thee.. sytinge vpon a she asse, and vpon a fole, sone of the she asse. *c* **1386** CHAUCER *Pars. T.* ¶424 A shee ape. **1500–20** DUNBAR *Poems* xxxv. 27 Him meit sall in the air ane scho dragoun. **1508** KENNEDIE *Flyting w. Dunbar* 259 Generit betuix ane sche beir and a deill. **1587** A. DAY *Daphnis & Chloe* (1890) 6 The sucke it receiued from one of his shee-goates. **1596** DALRYMPLE tr. *Leslie's Hist. Scot.* I. 50 The hie Salmonte haueng castne the meltis, and the sche salmonte the Rounis. *c* **1640** J. SMYTH *Hund. Berkeley* (1885) 319 The Conger alias the conger eele, beinge the hee-fish, and the Shee fish is called a quaver. **1692** *Lond. Gaz.* No. 2733/4 A.. She-Ass, with a light coloured She-Foal. **1720** DE FOE *Capt. Singleton* (1906) 100 A chase between a she-lion, or lioness, and a large deer. **1785** GROSE *Dict. Vulgar T.*, *She-Lion*, a shilling. **1821** LAMB in *Coleridge's Lett.*, etc. (1858) 117 'Yet', said Lamb, 'Letitia was only just tinted; she was not what the she-dogs now call an intellectual woman'. **1838** DICKENS *Old C. Shop* xxxiv, She-dragons in the business conducting themselves like professional gentlemen. **1843** MARRYAT *M. Violet* xl, The she-panther lay dead. **1844** H. STEPHENS *Bk. Farm* II. 702 The she-pigs are treated in a different manner. **1856** KANE *Arct. Expl.* I. xxix. 392 A stout Esquimaux.. fired at a she-bear. **1868** J. S. NORTHCOTE *Celebrated Sanctuaries of Madonna* v. 297 The marriage, doomed to so unhappy an issue, between Edward II. of England, and Isabella, the she-wolf of France. **1897** KIPLING *Capt. Cour.* v. 119 Great she-whales slain beside their young. **1923** H. G. EVARTS *Tumbleweeds* 87 The herd would have been worked on the spot,.. the she-stuff.. being allowed to scatter. *Ibid.* 88 There were.. no she-stock on the range. **1936** *Discovery* Nov. 333/2 A figure of the Roman she-wolf is being erected in Addis Ababa. **1937** *Sun* (Baltimore) 15 Nov. 14/6 She stock gathered enough strength to finish around 25c. higher than a week earlier. **1961** *Wranglin' Notes* (Eaton's Ranch, Wyoming) Nov., Our hay crop was cut, baled and stacked early this year. It is fed to the 200 'she stuff' and calves that winter on the lower ranch.

**10.** Female. Applied to persons (now somewhat contemptuous). **a.** Prefixed to sbs. which are otherwise 'common', as in ***she-being, -cousin, dancer, thief***, etc.; †**she-friend**, a female friend, often in bad sense, a mistress; **she-saint**, a female saint; also *transf.* and *fig.*

*c* **1532** DU WES *Introd. Fr.* in *Palsgr.* 918/3 A she thefe, *laronesse.* **1537** tr. *Latimer's Serm. Convoc.* ii. C j b, They swere by al he payntes and she saynts to. **1579** FULKE *Conf. Sanders* 615 S. Vncoulber a she Saint. **1580** HOLLYBAND *Treas. Fr. Tong, Amoureuse*, a shee louer. *a* **1586** SIR H. SIDNEY *Let. to Sir P. Sidney* in *Ussher's Lett.* (1686) App. 25 There is nothing more irksom than a She-Fool. *a* **1592** GREENE *Thieves falling out* (1615) A 3, A Disputation betweene a Hee-Foyst, and a Shee-Foyst. **1594** CAREW *Huarte's Exam. Wits* xiv. (1596) 241 There haue been.. many she Greeks.. specially seen in the Sciences. **1607** DEKKER & MARSTON *Westw. Hoe* II. ii. C 3, She.. is such an intycing shee witch. **1609** B. JONSON *Sil. Wom.* II. ii. (1620) D 2, And for that cause [she will] goe liue with her she-friend, or Cosen at the Colledge. **1623** MIDDLETON & ROWLEY *Sp. Gipsy* IV. ii. (1653) G 3, This young shee Gipsie. **1624** HEYWOOD *Gunaik.* VI. 303 One Pharsalia, a Thessalian shee-dancer. *a* **1625** FLETCHER *Hum. Lieut.* II. ii, He.. Commends his soule to his she-saint and exit. **1664** PEPYS *Diary* 9 Sept., My two she-cozen Joyces. **1668** SEDLEY *Mulb. Gard.* II. ii, And then a Bottle of Wine or two, and a She-Friend is an approv'd Remedy. **1682** MRS. BEHN *City Heiress* I. i. 4, I have an assignation here at Church with the dearest she-saint, and I hope sinner. **1727** LADY M. W. MONTAGU *Let. to C'tess Mar* Apr. (1893) I. 504 Which naturally attracts all the she and he fools in London. **1754** *Gray's Inn Jrnl.* No. 91 (1756) II. 248 She [*i.e.* Elizabeth] had no She-Friends in her Cabinet-Council. **1808** COBBETT *Polit. Reg.* 25 June XIII. 1001, I trust, that mothers and wives and sisters and she-cousins.. will have very little to do in the appointing of generals and other officers. **1823** LAMB *Elia* Ser. II. *Poor Relations*, Your indigent she-relative is hopeless. **1840** THACKERAY *Paris Sk. Bk.* Wks. 1900 V. 87 All the he and she scoundrels of the capital.. rush by you. **1840** BARHAM *Ingol. Leg., Lay St. Odille* Moral, Then let's act like Count Otto, and while one survives, Succumb to our She-Saints—videlicet wives. **1881** G. M. HOPKINS *Sermons & Spiritual Writings* (1959) 170 The woman, that is she-being, not she-man, of the Apocalypse.

**b.** Prefixed to sbs. which naturally or usually denote a male person.

**1530** PALSGR. 266/2 Sche devyll, *diablesse.* **1580** HOLLYBAND *Treas. Fr. Tong, Boulengiére*, a she baker. *c* **1590** MARLOWE *Faust.* iv. 408 There was a hee diuell, and a shee diuell. **1607** R. WILKINSON *Merchant Royall* 17 Christ did call no she Apostles. *a* **1613** OVERBURY *A Wife*, etc. (1638) 45 At first both sexes were in Man combinde, Man, She-Man did with his body breed. *c* **1622** FORD, etc. *Witch Edmonton* IV. ii, [Enter Winnifrede as a page] ..*Frank*... Ah, my She-Page! *a* **1628** F. GREVILLE *Life Sidney* (1652) 188 This She-David [Q. Eliz.] of ours ventured to undertake the great Goliath among the Philistins abroad, I mean Spain and the Pope. **1633** MASSINGER *Guardian* III. vi, Would I were a she-Priapus, Stuck up in a garden to fright away the Crows. *a* **1704** T. BROWN *Walk round Lond., Quaker's Meet.* Wks. 1709 III. III. 22 [She] makes a compleat She-Preacher, fit to denounce Hell and the Devil. *c* **1766** GRAY *Impromptu*, Mrs. Keene the she Bishop of Chester [*i.e.* the bishop's wife]. **1816** *Monthly Mag.* XLII. 202 This she pope. **1840** THACKERAY *Catherine* ii, I don't think I ever saw such a she-devil. **1846** DICKENS *Pictures fr. Italy* 25 A gate, which this She-Goblin unlocked. **1874** LISLE CARR *Jud. Gwynne* I. iii. 73 A flirtation with a she-costermonger or other female. **1881** She-man [see *she-being*, sense 10 a above]. **1892** *Ch. Q. Rev.* July 354 A Salvationist she-captain. **1900** ELWORTHY *Horns of Honour* ii. 91 Cecco d'Ascoli was burnt in 1327.. for having had illicit intercourse with a succuba, or she-devil. **1922** JOYCE *Ulysses* 48 A shefiend's whiteness under her rancid rags. **1937** E. POUND *Fifth Decad Cantos* xlii. 12 By Della Rena and M. Magdalene the She Guardian, *tutrice.*

**c.** Prefixed to masculine nouns in place of the (frequently later) feminine noun in *-ess. rare.*

**1591** PERCIVALL *Sp. Dict., Sacerdotissa*, a shee priest. **1610** HOLLAND *Camden's Brit.* II. 231 A French God, whose shee-priestes, vowing perpetuall virginity, are said to be nine in number. **1656** EARL MONM. tr. *Boccalini's Advts. fr. Parnass.* I. xxii. (1674) 22 [They] admitted the chief She-Poets, or Poetesses, into Parnassus. **1674** BREVINT *Saul Endor* vii. 161 They took her for their Patroness, and consequently for their she God. *a* **1679** EARL ORRERY *Herod Gt.* Prol., Rare Scenes like Opera's, nay, She-Actors too. **1712** W. ROGERS *Voy.* (1718) 279 The other She-Negro (call'd Daphne). **1736** AINSWORTH *Lat. Dict.* IV. s.v. *Cithæron*, It was sacred to Bacchus, and here his she priests were wont to keep their revels. **1809** MALKIN *Gil Blas* II. iv. ¶8 The she-adventurer who had played the part of Camilla.

**d.** Prefixed, with the sense 'that is a woman', to sbs. used *fig.* (chiefly in disparaging use). Also with intensive force, as ***she-woman***. Now somewhat *rare.*

**1582** T. WATSON *Centurie of Love* ix, So shuts or sprouts my ioy, as doth this flow're, When my Sheesunne doth either laugh or lowre. **1591** LODGE *Catharos* 4 b, A filbert is better than a faggot, except it be an Athenian she handfull. **1601** R. JOHNSON *Kingd. & Commw.* (1603) 81 Almost euery common soldier carrying with him his she-baggage, besides his bag and other furniture. **1624** HEYWOOD *Captives* I. i. in Bullen *O. Pl.* IV, Shipp all your goods with these shee-chatteyles. **1638** FORD *Lady's Trial* I. ii, And him have we beleagred to accost This shee-peece, under a pretence of being Grandee of Spain. **1694** MOTTEUX *Rabelais* v. xxi, His Office was to cast anew those She-pieces of Antiquity. **1871** R. ELLIS *Catullus* vi. 4 Some she-malady, some unhealthy wanton, Fires thee verily. **1904** DOWDEN *R. Browning* 246 The lone she-sparrow of the house-top [*i.e.* a poor girl in a garret]. **1931** *Sunday Dispatch* 31 May 12/4, I am one hundred per cent. SHE-woman. **1951** B. RUSSELL *New Hopes for changing World* 162 Correlative to the he-man is the she-woman, who is equally undesirable.

**e.** with names of plants. Cf. HE 8 b. See also SHE-OAK.

**1575** GASCOIGNE *Kenelworth* Wks. 1910 II. 127 Mary there are two kinds of Holly, that is to say, he Holly, and she Holly. **1585** HIGINS *Junius' Nomenclator* 114/1 *Abrotonum mas.* The hee Southernwood. *A. femina.* The shee Southernwood. **1626** [see HE 8 b]. **1705** BEVERLEY *Hist. Virginia* (1722) 127 The other.. looks shrivell'd, with a Dent on the Back of the Grain, as if it had never come to Perfection; and this they call She-Corn. **1756** P. BROWNE *Jamaica* 362 The she-plants throw out their flowers separate. **1884** SARGENT *Rep. Forests N. Amer.* 210 *Abies Fraseri*, Lindley... Balsam. She balsam. **1898** E. E. MORRIS *Austral Engl.* s.v. *Beech*, She Beech, *Cryptocarya obovata. Ibid.* s.v. *She-Oak*, The prefix *she* is used in Australia to indicate an inferiority of timber in respect of texture, colour, or other character; e.g. *She-beech, She-pine.*

**f.** with names of things = FEMALE *a.* 11.

**1816** [see HE 8 c]. **1876** PAPWORTH in *Encycl. Brit.* IV. 472/2 The joint joggles made as at *a*.. is called by workmen a *he*, and that at *b* a *she* joggle.

**11.** With the sense 'effeminate'. *nonce-use.*

**1821** BYRON *Sardanap.* II. i. 48 The she-king, That less than woman, is even now upon The waters with his female mates.

**12.** Of, pertaining to, characteristic of, a woman or women.

**1602** *How Choose Gd. Wife* III. ii. E 3, And since I sware, ..To trust no she tongue, that can name a man. *a* **1625** FLETCHER *Wife for Month* I. Wks. 1907 V. 13 There's no such cure for the she-falling sickness As the powder of a dryed Bawds Skin. **1633** FORD *Broken H.* II. i, But this is but she-newes, I had it from a midwife. *c* **1648–50** BRATHWAIT *Barnabees Jrnl.* I. (1818) 33 Furnish'd with their spritely weapons, She-flesh feeles clarks are no capons. **1655** FULLER *Ch. Hist.* VI. 297 Nunneries also were good shee-schools, wherein the Girles, and Maids of the Neighbourhood, were taught to read and work. *Ibid. marg.*, Conveniency of Shee-Colledges. **1713** ROWE *Jane Shore* Epil., The Poets frequently might move Compassion, And with She Tragedies o'er-run the Nation. **1821** BYRON *Sardanap.* III. i. 220 Lydian Omphale's She-garb. **1831** TRELAWNY *Adv. Younger Son* I. 277 He is as self-willed and obstinate as the she-kind are. **1847** TENNYSON *Princess* Prol. 158 He long'd ..for she-society. **1892** *Daily Chron.* 28 Apr. 3/1 What someone contemptuously phrased as 'she-poetry'. **1978** *N. & Q.* Feb. 85/1 As a 'she-tragedy' and a history play (of sorts), the choice of Banks's play is an interesting move.

**13.** *Comb.*: **She Bible**, the second of the two issues of the Bible printed in 1611 (see quot.); †**she-calends** [tr. L. *femineæ kalendæ*], the calends of March (when the Matronalia were celebrated); †**she-Dunkirk**, a privateer; †**she-flattery**, the act of flattering females; **she-house** *slang* (see quot.); **she-male** (*U.S. colloq.* and *dial.*) = FEMALE *sb.*; †**she-retailing** *a.*, trading in women..

**1878** H. STEVENS *Bibles Caxton Exhib.* 109 This pair.. we shall distinguish by calling the first the Great He Bible, and the other the Great *She Bible, from their respective renderings of Ruth iii. 15. *Ibid.* 111 This [1613–11 ed.] is generally a mixture of the sheets of the He and the She Bible. *a* **1661** HOLYDAY *Juvenal* ix. (1673) 177 A trimme creature, to whom thou might'st send guifts forsooth, such as at the *she-calends they send to women. **1623** MASSINGER *Dk. Milan* III. ii, As he came From a close fight at Sea vnder the Hatches, With a *she Dunckerke. **1637** NABBES *Microcosmus* IV. E 2 b, Melancholy hath been some neglected Courtier; hee's perfect in *she-flattery. **1785** GROSE *Dict. Vulgar T.*, **She House*, a house where the wife rules, or, as the term is, wears the breeches. **18..** in B. A. Botkin *Treas. Amer. Folklore* (1944) I. 8 Davy Crockett's hand would be sure to shake if his iron was pointed within a hundred mile of a *shemale. **1917** S. LEWIS *Job* xv. 246 Course you high-strung virgin kind of shemales take some time to learn to get over your choosey, finicky ways. **1941** E. P. O'DONNELL *Great Big Doorstep* 125 How can that one inside be cruel to dogs like that? If they were she-males always dropping pups, I wouldn't say. **1593** NASHE *Christ's T.* 77 b, These *shee retayling bodie-traffiquers.

**VI.** As adjective.

**14.** Female, feminine. *rare.*

*a* **1300** *Cursor M.* 619 Þe bestes all, bath sco and he, War broght forwit him to see. *a* **1849** H. COLERIDGE *Ess.* (1851) II. 50 He had so little of the woman in him that he could resemble nothing She.

**VII. 15.** In catch-phr. ***who's she—the cat's mother?*** and varr., said to one (esp. a child) who uses the pronoun of the third person singular impolitely or with inadequate reference.

**1897** 'S. GRAND' *Beth Bk.* xx. 204 Don't call your mamma 'she'. 'She' is the cat. **1913** C. MACKENZIE *Sinister St.* I. I. i. 9 'Who's She?' demanded Nurse. 'She's the cat's mother.' **1949** N. STREATFEILD *Painted Garden* ix. 105 'She said so.' Jane looked superior. 'She, my boy, is the cat's mother.' **1959** I. & P. OPIE *Lore & Lang. Schoolch.* iii. 52 To one who keeps saying 'she' in an impolite manner the reproof is: 'Who's *she*, the cat's mother?' **1972** CASSON & GRENFELL *Nanny Says* 21 Who's she? The cat's grandmother?

**she**, var. SE.

**s/he**, written representation of 'he or she', used as nom. sing. third person pron. to include both genders.

**1977** *Gay News* 24 Mar. 6/3 The questionnaire asks congregations whether they would call a minister to their pulpit if s/he were gay. **1978** *Amer. Educator* Winter 65 A child's sexual orientation is determined before s/he enters school. **1982** *Benedicta!* Fall 13 Can s/he figure out your address?

‖**shea** (ʃiː, ˈʃiːə). [Mandingo (Bambara and other dialects) *si*, *se*, *sye*, the tree or its fruit. The current English spelling is due to Park.] A sapotaceous tree of tropical Africa, *Bassia Parkii*, from the kernels of which is obtained ***shea butter*** (also called *galam butter*), a substance resembling butter, used as food by the natives and in Europe for the manufacture of soap, etc. Also ***shea tree***, ***shea-butter tree***.

**1799** PARK *Trav. Africa* xvi. (ed. 2) 202 The people were every where employed in collecting the fruit of the Shea trees. *Ibid.* 203 In clearing wood land for cultivation, every tree is cut down but the Shea. **1846** *Rep. Brit. Assoc.* II. 90 The Shea Butter-Tree. **1846** *J. Bell's Syst. Geog.*, *Guinea* i. IV. 28 The *shea* or butter-tree. **1847** MRS. R. LEE *Afr. Wand.* xiv. (1854) 232 Anointed with vegetable or shea butter. **1905** *Brit. Med. Jrnl.* 26 Aug. 450 Shea butter.. is employed for rheumatism [etc.].

**sheac(k**, var. forms of SHE-OAK.

**sheading** (ˈʃiːdɪŋ). Also 6 **shedding**, 8 **sheeding**. [var. f. SHEDDING *vbl. sb.*] Each of the six administrative subdivisions (three to each 'district') of the Isle of Man.

?**1577** in Mills *Stat. Laws I. of Man* (1821) 12, vj Men of every Shedding of Mann. *Ibid.* 15 In your six Courts of your six Sheadings. **1653** CHALONER *I. of Man* (1656) 17, 6 Coroners or Sheriffs of the 6 Sheadings, into which the Isle is divided. **1894** HALL CAINE *Manxman* 315 The Coroner of the premier sheading began to recite the same titles in Manx.

*attrib.* **1577** in Mills *Stat. Laws I. of Man* (1821) 60 Hereafter follows the Fencing of the Sheading Courts. **1653** CHALONER *I. of Man* (1656) 19 A Jury of six, which is called a Sheading Jury.

**sheaf** (ʃiːf), *sb.* Forms: α. 1 **scéaf**, 4–5 **shef**, **schef**, **scheef**, 4–6 **shefe**, **sheef**, 5 **sheeffe**, (**chyfe**), 5–6 **schefe**, **scheff(e**, **sheff**, 5–7 **sheffe**, 6 **sheaffe**, **schiefe**, *Sc.* **scheiff**, (**teind-)cheif**, 6–7 **sheafe**, 7 **sheave**, **sheive**, 8 *Sc.* **sheaff**, 6– **sheaf**. *Pl.* 1 **scéafas**, (**scéabas**, **scébas**), 3 **sheve**, (*Orm.*) **shæfess**, 4 **schewes**, (**szevis**, **cheves**), 4–5 **schefes**, 4–6 **scheves**, **-is**, **-ys**, **sheves**, **-is**, **-ys**, 5 **shefys**, **shef(f)s**, 5–7 **sheeves**, 6 **sheffes**, **sheiffes**, **sheafes**, 7 **sheaffes**, **shefes**, 6– **sheaves**, 7– **sheafs**. β. *chiefly north.* and *Sc.* 4 **schaf**, (**shafth**), 4–5 **shafe**, 5 **schafe**, **schaffe**, 5–6 **shaffe**, **shayff**, 6 **schaif**, **schayffe**, 5 **shave**, 9 **shaf(f**. *Pl.* 4 **scaves**, **schaffes**, 4–5 **schaves**, 5 **schaiffis**, **shaffis**, 5–6 **schawis**, 6 **shayffs**, 7 **schavis**, **schawes**, **shaves**. γ. 5 **schof(e**, **schoof**, 9 *dial.* **shoaf**, **shofe**, **shoof**. *Pl.* 5 **schovys**, 9 *dial.* **shoves**, **shoofs**, etc. [Com.Teut. (wanting in Gothic): OE. *scéaf* masc. = NFris. *skôf*, WFris. *skeaf*, OS. *skôf* ? sheaf (Gallée), MLG., MDu. *schôf* (mod.Du. *schoof* fem., sheaf), OHG. *scoub* sheaf, bundle or wisp of straw (MHG. *schoup*, mod.G. *schaub* masc., also *schaube* fem., wisp of straw), ON. *skauf* neut., fox's brush:—OTeut. **skaubo-*, app. f. the root **skaub-*: *skeub-*: *skub-*: see SHOVE *v.*[1] From the wk. grade of the root are OHG. *scob*, MHG. *schop*, mod.G. dial. *schob* masc., *schobe* fem., bundle, OHG. *scobar*, MHG., mod.G. *schober* masc., heap of hay, corn, etc.

With the β forms cf. *chap(-man)* beside *cheap*, OE. *céap*. The γ forms are difficult to account for. They may represent an ablaut variant (OE. **scofa* or **scofe*), or they may be due to the influence of continental LG. or Du.; another possible explanation is that locally the original falling diphthong *éa* may have undergone change of stress; but none of these conjectures is quite satisfactory.]

**1. a.** One of the large bundles in which it is usual to bind cereal plants after reaping. Also, a similar bundle of the stalks or blooms of other plants.

α. *c* **725** *Corpus Gloss.* (Hessels) G 15 *Garbas*, sceabas. *c* **1000** ÆLFRIC *Gen.* xxxvii. 7 Me þuhte, þæt we bundon sceafas on æcere and þæt min sceaf arise and stode uprihte omiddan eowrum sceafum. *c* **1000** *Sax. Leechd.* II. 216 Rudan sceafas þry ȝedo on wine croccan. *c* **1200** ORMIN 1481 Þu þresshest tine shæfess, & siþþenn winndwesst tu þin corn. *a* **1250** *Owl & Night.* 455 Hwanne mon howieþ of his sheue. **1485** in *10th Rep. Hist. MSS. Comm.* App. v. 291 Clane whete as it cometh from the shefe. *a* **1490** BOTONER *Itin.* (Nasmith, 1778) 288 Et populi portant anglice shevys de reede segge ad luminandam aulam. **1553** *Cal. Anc. Rec. Dublin* (1889) 433 Brynyng with every pecke two shevis of fyrris. **1621** QUARLES *Hadassa* Introd. B 2, Here lies a new-falne ranke, and there a sheaue. **1717** BERKELEY *Tour Italy* Wks. 1871 IV. 546 Corn reaped and standing in sheaves. **1797** T. HOLCROFT tr. *Stolberg's Trav.* III. lxxxi. (ed. 2) 290 We.. saw barley in sheaf. **1844** H. STEPHENS *Bk. Farm* III. 1053 By practice, he can ascertain by the eye whether sheaves are of the proper size, which is 1 foot of diameter across the band. **1846** J. BAXTER *Libr. Pract. Agric.* (ed. 4) II. 317 It is usual for landlords to pay for the drawing of the reed by the hundred sheaves. **1862** MIALL *Title-deeds Ch. Eng.* 39 *note*, Beans were usually tithed in the sheaf or shock.

β. *a* **1300** *Cursor M.* 4061 Hijs breþer schaues [*Gött.* scheuis, *Fairf.* sheuys] he sagh lutand Til his allan þat was standand. **14..** *Nom.* in Wr.-Wülcker 725/40 *Hec garba*, a schaffe. **1513** DOUGLAS *Æneis* IV. Prol. 14 Of vickit grane quhow sall gud schaif be schorn? **1532–3** *Durham Househ. Bk.* (Surtees) 166 Item 1 stuk et 16 shayffs ordii. **1565** *Reg. Mag. Sig. Scot.* 384 Cum.. 10 garbis vulgo schawis straminum. **1639** MURE *Ps.* cxxvi. 23 Charg'd with shaves.

γ. *c* **1440** *Promp. Parv.* 444/2 Scheffe, or scheef (*S.* schefe or schofe, *K.* schof), *garba*, *gelima*. *Ibid.* 447/2 Schoof or scheef. *Ibid.* Schokkyn schovys, *tasso*, *congelimo*. **1788** W. H. MARSHALL *Yorksh.* II. 35 In these 'reaps',—shoves or open sheaves,—it [*sc.* rape] lies until.. the ripest is ready to open its pods. **1865** W. WHITE *East. Eng.* I. vii. 101 Then we has to lay 'em [the reeds] straight, and tie 'em up into shoofs. **1879** MISS JACKSON *Shropsh. Word-bk.*, Shoves.

*Proverbs.* *c* **1384** CHAUCER *H. Fame* 2140 For alle mote oute, other late or rathe, Alle the sheves in the lathe. *c* **1385** —— *L.G.W.* 2579 The whiche child of hire natyuyte To alle thewis goode I-born was she, As likede to the goddis er she was born, That of the shef she shal be the corn. **1562** J. HEYWOOD *Prov. & Epigr.* (1867) 161, I will take as falth in the sheafe.

†**b.** ***tenth, ninth, third***, etc. ***sheaf***: a specified proportionate part of the annual crop paid to the lord or to the church. Also (in the s.w. counties) ***the sheaf*** = the tenth sheaf, tithe of grain. *Obs.*

*a* **1300** *Cursor M.* 6807 Giue gladli tend And þin offrand, Þe formast scaues of your corn. **1387** TREVISA *Higden* (Rolls) VIII. 335 And þe nynþe scheef [*v.r.* schef] everich glebe of Engelond he ordeyned for his owne iourneys. *c* **1440** *Jacob's Well* 24 Alle þo þat ȝeuyn þe tythe scheef to þe reperys for here hyre,.. & ȝeuyn þe xj. sheef for þe tythe. *c* **1450** *Godstow Reg.* 351 The churche of wygynton takyth all shevis, and halfe of all oþer tythys. *a* **1460** FORTESCUE *Abs. & Lim. Mon.* xii. (1885) 140 When the reaume gaff to thair kyng.. the ix$^{th}$ ffl ese off thair wolles, and also the ix$^{th}$ shefe off þer graynes. **1472** *Rental Bk. Cupar-Angus* (1879) I. 162 Wilȝam sal pay ȝerly for the teynd schafe of standand teyndis.. 20 bollis of vitale. **1552** LYNDESAY *Tragedy* 299 Ye wyll not want teind cheif nor offrandis. *c* **1630** RISDON *Surv. Devon* §309 (1810) 318 The shefe of this place, Walter Stapledon gave to the hospital. **1641** *Will of T. Isaacs* (Somerset Ho.), Whereas the sheaf of sherverton belongs to me. *a* **1687** PETTY *Pol. Arith.* i. (1691) 34 If the Rent of the Land.. be the third Sheaf. **17..** in J. Hammond *Cornish Parish* (1897) 81 The proprietors of the Sheaf [—that is, of the Rectorial tithes —were abated 13*s.* 4*d.*].

**c.** *fig.* in various obvious uses. Also † ***to put on the sheaf***, to crown the feast, add the finishing touch (*Sc.*).

**1600** in *Songs & Poems Costume* (Percy Soc.) 102 Of others take a sheafe, of mee a graine. **1690** LOCKE *Hum. Und.* IV. xii. §12 In the Knowledge of Bodies, we must be content to glean what we can from particular Experiments, since we cannot from a Discovery of their real Essences, grasp at a time whole Sheaves; and in bundles, comprehend the Nature and Properties of whole Species together. **1715** RAMSAY *Christ's Kirk Gr.* II. xx, A kebbuck syn.. pat on the sheaf. **1825** MACAULAY *Ess.*, *Milton* ¶21 Yet the harvest is so abundant that the negligent search of a straggling gleaner may be rewarded with a sheaf. **1885** R. BUCHANAN *Annan Water* xvi, Marriage with a holy man is a sheaf of blessing.

**d.** Applied to a cluster of flowers, leaves, etc.

**1845** BROWNING *Home-thoughts from Abroad* i, The lowest boughs and the brushwood sheaf Round the elm-tree bole are in tiny leaf. **1882** *Garden* 1 July 12/1 The plant shown bore quite a sheaf of large blooms.

**e.** A cluster of jets of fire or water darting up together. (Cf. F. *gerbe*.)

**1811** PINKERTON *Petral.* II. 535 A thousand sheaves of fire blew up into the air, where, breaking and dispersing, they fell like a shower of stars. **1857** DUFFERIN *Lett. High Lat.* 125 A shining liquid column, or rather a sheaf of columns wreathed in robes of vapour, sprung into the air.

**2.** †**a.** A bundle of iron or steel containing a definite number of gads (see quots. 1577, 1597).

[Cf. med.L. *garba*, a bundle of 30 pieces of steel; also MHG. *ein schoup îsens*.]

**1309–10** *Durham Acc. Rolls* (Surtees) 7 In 3 schaffes aceris emp., 12*d.* **1377–8** *Ibid.* 387 In uno shafth calibis pro reparacione securium, 8*d.* **1495** *Naval Acc. Hen. VII* (1896) 150 Payed.. for ij Sheffs of Stelle price the Sheff vij$^{d}$. **1515–16** *Fabric Rolls York Minster* (Surtees) 96, iiij sheiffes de calabe. **1577** HARRISON *England* III. xviii[xi], in *Holinshed*, Our steele.. is not so good for edge toole as that of Cullen, and yet the one is often solde for the other, and lyke tale vsed in both, that is to say thirtie gaddes to the shiefe [**1587** sheffe] and sixe shiefes [twelue sheffes] to the burden. **1597** SKENE *De Verb. Sign.* s.v. *Schaffa*, Ane schiefe of irone containes sexteene gades, ane schiefe of steile containes fourteene gades.

†**b.** ? A certain quantity of timber. *Obs.*

**1534** in Weaver *Wells Wills* (1890) 5 Rych. my son v shefe of tymbre.

†**c.** A certain number of plates of glass. *Obs.*

[Cf. LG. *schoff*, a bundle of six plates of glass (Schiller & Lübben, s.v. *schôf*.]

**1402–3** *Durham Acc. Rolls* (Surtees) 394, 7*s.* 8*d.* pro j pare de lyas et j shafe vitri venditis. *Ibid.* 397 Item de novo vitro colorato 2 scheff. **1476–7** in J. Raine *Auckland Castle* (1852) 54 [For 20] shefs [of new glass for repairing the windows of the manor-house, 13*s.* 4*d.*]. **1482–3** in *Finchale Priory Acc.* (Surtees) p. ccclx, Pro ix shaffis vitri. **1487** *Churchw. Acc. Wigtoft Lincs.* (Nicholls 1797) 83 Paide for a shefe of glass 8$^{d}$. **1488–9** *Durham Acc. Rolls* 99 Pro 5 shaff' vitri empt., 3*s.* 4*d.* **1532–3** *Durham Househ. Bk.* (Surtees) 170 Et in 8 shayff brymmys glasse emptis.

**3.** A bundle or quiverful of 24 arrows.

**1318** *Act Robt. I* c. xxvii, Unum bonum arcum cum uno schapho sagittarum. **1377** LANGL. *P. Pl.* B. III. 324 Half a shef of arwes. *c* **1386** CHAUCER *Prol.* 104 A sheef of pecok arwes brighte and kene Vnder his belt he bar ful thriftily. **1475** *Rental Bk. Cupar-Angus* (1879) I. 200 Bowis and schawis. **1502** *Privy Purse Exp. Eliz. York* (1830) 58 For a sheffe and an half of brode arrowes at ij d. the arrowe vj s. and for a sheef of brode heddes at ij d. the hedde iiij s. **1519** in *Gentl. Mag.* (1864) Apr. 501/1 A boue & a shaffe of arrows, ij$^{s}$. **1590** SIR J. SMYTHE *Disc. Weapons* 20 b, To drawe their arrowes out of their cases and sheafes. **1643** BAKER *Chron.*, *Edw. IV*, 94 The Northern men.. plyed their bowes, till all their Sheaves were empty. **1825** SCOTT *Betrothed* ix, The soldiers.. discharged several sheaves of arrows upon such fugitives, as.. approached too near the castle.

*fig.* **1377** LANGL. *P. Pl.* B. XX. 224 [They] shoten aȝein with shotte many a shef of othes, And brode hoked arwes, goddes herte & his nayles.

**4.** A representation of a sheaf (of corn, arrows, etc.). (In *Her.* the sheaf of corn is called GARB.)

*c* **1420** ? LYDG. *Assembly of Gods* 291 Ceres.. in a garment Of sak clothe.. Embrowderyd with sheues and sykelys bent. *a* **1631** DONNE *Poems*, *To Mr. G. Herbert*, A Sheafe of Snakes used heretofore to be My Seal, The Crest of our poore Family. **1805** SCOTT *Last Minstr.* IV. viii, And hence, in fair remembrance worn, Yon sheaf of spears his crest has borne. **1868** CUSSANS *Handbk. Her.* vii. (1893) 108 A bundle of Arrows bound together in the centre is termed a Sheaf, and consists of three: one in pale, and two in saltire.

**5.** *gen.* **a.** A cluster or bundle of things tied up together; a quantity of things set thick together.

*a* **1728** WOODWARD *Nat. Hist. Fossils* I. (1729) I. 78 A Mineral.. composed of several Sheafs of grey Filaments. **1855** THACKERAY *Newcomes* xlviii, A great palette, and a sheaf of painting-brushes. **1863** GEO. ELIOT *Romola* II. xxii, The sheaves of banners were unfurled at the angles of the Baptistery. **1888** MISS BRADDON *Fatal Three* I. v, He took a sheaf of telegraph-forms from the stand in front of him.

**b.** Emphatically in pl.: A large number, mass, or quantity.

**1865** CARLYLE *Fredk. Gt.* XX. vi. IX. 108 He has sheaves of Letters daily. **1888** HENLEY *Bk. Verses* 123 It falls, in very sheaves, The weary, dreary rain.

**6. a.** *Physics* and *Math.* A bundle of rays, lines, etc. all passing through a given point.

**1863** TYNDALL *Heat* ix. §359. 302 A sheaf of calorific rays. **1885** LEUDESDORF *Cremona's Proj. Geom.* 22 A *sheaf* (*sheaf of planes*, *sheaf of lines*) is a figure made up of planes or straight lines, all of which pass through a given point (the *centre* of the sheaf). **1890** EAGLES *Descript. Geom.* 303 Sheafs of rays which in the case of a source of light.. form a cone of which that source is the vortex.

**b.** *Math.* A topological space each point of which is associated with a structure having all the properties of an Abelian group (e.g. a vector space or a ring) in such a way that there is an isomorphism between the structures on neighbouring points. [The sense is due to J. Leray, who used F. *faisceau* (*Jrnl. de Math.* (1950) XXIX. 5).]

**1955** *Ann. Math.* LXII. 56 The French word 'faisceau' has been translated into English as 'sheaf' or 'stack'. In this paper we use the word 'stack', since 'sheaf' has been used before in mathematics. **1958** R. G. SWAN *Theory of Sheaves* 1 Sheaves are very useful in proving theorems. **1973** R. O. WELLS *Differential Anal. Complex Manifolds* ii. 43 A sheaf.. on a space *X* is a carrier of localized information about the space.

**7.** *Comb.*, as ***sheaf-like*** adj.; †**sheaf-arrow**, an arrow of the kind which was carried in a sheaf (see 3) for warfare; **sheaf-binder**, one who binds sheaves, a machine which does this; **sheaf catalogue** *Librarianship* (see quot. 1976); **sheaf-corn**, corn in sheaves; †**sheaf-iron**, ? iron in sheaves or bundles of rods; **sheaf oats** *U.S.* (now *rare*), oats bound in sheaves; **sheaf-ripe** *a.* (*poet.*), ripe for harvest.

**1474** in Rymer *Fœdera* XI. 838 Sagittas vocatas *Shefe Arowes. **1545** ASCHAM *Toxoph.* II. (Arb.) 126 As concerning sheaffe Arrouse for war. **1627** DRAYTON *Agincourt* 20 A French man back into the Towne doth fall, With a sheafe Arrow shot into the head. **1866** BLACKIE *Homer & Iliad* I. 163 Sowers and reapers and *sheaf-binders. **1880** *Daily News* 10 Dec. 2/4 For many years, the only description of sheaf-binder which was found to work was one which tied with wire. **1902** *Library World* V. 129 Some librarians I know.. are hesitating in their adoption of a ms. catalogue between the card and a new rival—*the sheaf catalogue. **1913** J. H. QUINN *Library Cataloguing* iv. 33 The book-form of catalogues with separate leaves, known as 'sheaf-catalogues'. **1976** *Gloss. Documentation Terms* (*B.S.I.*) 60 *Sheaf catalogue*, a catalogue recorded on slips of paper of uniform size filed in loose-leaf binders. **1785** W. H. MARSHALL *Midl. Counties* (1790) II. 167 *Sheaf corn lies straighter in the cutting box. **1572** *Wills & Inv. N.C.* (Surtees 1835) 364, iiij houndreth lb of *sheff yron j$^{l}$ xij$^{s}$. **1880–1** SAVILLE KENT *Man. Infusoria* I. 249 A *sheaf-like fascicle of rod-like trichocysts. **1765** G. CROGHAN *Jrnl.* 10 June in R. G. Thwaites *Early Western Travels* (1904) I. II. 140 The young reeds being preferable to *sheaf oats. **1894** *Outing* XXIV. 337/1 Ten minutes later the horses were quietly eating their corn and sheaf oats. **1879** BROWNING *Ned Bratts* 3 Corn stood *sheaf-ripe already.

**sheaf** (ʃiːf), *v.* [f. SHEAF *sb.* Cf. SHEAVE *v.*]

**1.** *trans.* To bind into a sheaf or sheaves; also with *up*. Also *absol.*

**1506** *Kal. Sheph.* (Sommer) 18 To laboure in haruest.. To repe and shefe. **1600** SHAKS. *A.Y.L.* III. ii. 113 They that reap must sheafe and binde. **1611** FLORIO, *Affasciare*,.. to sheafe vp corne. **1620** MARKHAM *Farew. Husb.* xiii. 103 Hauing reapt your corne so full of grasse and weeds, you shal by no meanes sheafe it. **1651** W. DURHAM *Maranatha* (1652) 14 Should the tares overlook the wheat here, and hereafter be sheafed up into the barn. **1764** *Museum Rust.* II. viii. 30 When the crop is fully ripe and clear of weeds, 'tis proper to mow inwards, and sheaf it immediately. **1845** *Jrnl. R. Agric. Soc.* V. II. 327 Last harvest Mr. Hudson sheafed part of his barley. **1874** HARDY *Far fr. Mad. Crowd* xxxiii, Maryann.. with some other women was tying the bundles (oats being always sheafed on this farm).

*fig.* **1882** *Fraser's Mag.* Oct. 438 It would be absurd to waste its scholarship and unrivalled opportunities in sheafing up and binding together a puny list of unregistered words. **1891** F. MARY WILSON *Browning Primer* 239 Some ..seem more specially sheafed than others by the binding threads of the *Prologue* and *Epilogue*.

2. To furnish with a sheaf. *rare*.

**1636** R. JAMES *Iter Lancastr.* (1845) 3/69 Who doe bent bowes on their left showlders hould, Their girdle sheaft with arrowes.

**sheaf.** Erroneous form of SHEATH *sb.*

**1697** *C'tess D'Aunoy's Trav.* (1706) 94 These Swords being so long, that they cannot be drawn out, unless a Man has the Arms of a Giant; the Sheaf therefore flies open in laying the finger on a little Spring. **1766** *Complete Farmer* s.v. *Vegetation*, The lateral roots also break forth..from the gaping sheaf which adheres closely to the plant.

**sheaf,** variant of SHEAVE *sb.*

**sheafage** ('ʃiːfɪdʒ). *rare*$^{-1}$. [f. SHEAF *sb.* + -AGE.] Sheaves in the aggregate.

**1885** A. DOBSON *At Sign of Lyre, Masque of Months* viii, Now in wains the sheafage yellow 'Twixt the hedges slow is borne.

**sheafy** ('ʃiːfɪ), *a.* [f. SHEAF *sb.* + -Y[1].] Consisting of or resembling a sheaf or sheaves.

**1712** GAY *Ovid's Met.* VI. *Arachne* 190 Ceres,..Whose golden locks a sheafy garland bear. **1887** BLACKMORE *Springhaven* III. xv. 203 The sun had been ripening his harvest-field of sheafy gold and awny cloud.

**sheah, sheak,** var. ff. SHIAH, SHE-OAK.

**sheakle,** dial. form of SHACKLE *sb.*[1]

**sheal:** see SHEEL *v.*, SHIEL *sb.* and *v.*, SHILL *v.*

**shealing:** see SHEELING, SHIELING, SHILLING.

**sheamble, sheamle,** obs. ff. SHAMBLE *sb.*[1]

**shea-oak,** variant of SHE-OAK.

**shear** (ʃɪə(r)), *sb.*[1] Forms: *sing.* 1 scéar, 3-6 schere, 4 scheere, 4-6 shere, sheere, 6 share, 6-7 sheir, *Sc.* scheir, 7-9 scheer, 8- shear; *pl.* 1 scérero, scéruru, scéroro, scéara, 3 særes, 3-6 scheris, 4 sherys, 4-5 scheres, scherys, sheeris, 4-6 sheris, 4-7 sheres, 5 s(c)herez, schers, shereis, shires, 6 sheires, 6-7 sheyres, sheeres, sheares, 6-9 sheers, 7 shares, 7 shears. [Prob. two formations: (1) OE. *scérero* pl.:—OTeut. type **skærizō*:—pre-Teut. **skēresā*, f. root **sker-*: see SHEAR *v.* (2) OE. *scéar* fem. = MDu. *schaer*, OHG. *scâra* (:—**skærō*), f. the same root. Another declensional variant is represented by OHG. *skâr*, pl. *skâri* (whence the later sing. form MHG. *schære*, mod.G. *schere* fem.), ON. *skǽri* neut. pl. (Norw. dial. *skjæra* fem., *skjære* masc.).]

1. Originally (and still *Sc.* and *dial.*) = SCISSORS. In later use commonly applied to scissors of large size, and to other cutting instruments which similarly operate by the simultaneous action of two blades on opposite sides of the material to be cut.

The various kinds of shears fall into two principal classes: those which are worked in the manner of scissors, and those in which (as in ordinary sheep-shears) the bringing together of the blades is effected by pressure on their stems between the blades and the arched spring by which the stems are connected. Shears of the latter class have now sometimes three or more blades instead of two.

Often with defining word indicating the purpose for which the instrument is intended or some peculiarity of its construction, as *bar-shears*, *clipping shears*, etc. q.v. under the first element; also SHEEP-SHEARS.

**a.** in pl. form, with plural construction, either in sing. or plural sense. When qualification by a numeral or an indefinite article is required, ***pair of shears*** is used.

*c* **725** *Corpus Gloss.* (Hessels) F. 263 *Forfices*, scerero. *Ibid.* 279 *Forfex*, isern, sceruru. *c* **897** ÆLFRED *Gregory's Past. C.* xviii. 138 Ðætte ða sacerdas ne sceoldon no hiera heafdu scieran mid scearseaxum..ac hie sceoldon hie efsian mid scearum. *c* **1050** *Voc.* in Wr.-Wülcker 399/19 *Forficis*, sceara. *a* **1100** *Gerefa* in *Anglia* IX. 263 He sceal..habban.. horscamb and sceara. *c* **1205** LAY. 14215 Whætte his særes alse he scæren wolde. *c* **1300** *Havelok* 857 He tok þe sh[e]res of þe nayl And made him a couel of þe sayl. *c* **1386** CHAUCER *Wife's Prol.* 722 How Sampson loste his heres, Slepynge, his lemman kitte it with hir sheres. **1390** GOWER *Conf.* II. 318 And out he clippeth also faste Hire tunge with a peire scheres. **1473** in *Arnolde's Chron.* (1502) 27 b/1 It is ..enacted, that noo wullen cloth.. be shorne..but yf it be fully wet opon peine of forfetur of the said cloth... The sherar therof shal lese his shereis and pay xx. s' for euery pece cloth. **1527** *Knaresb. Wills* (Surtees) I. 21 Oon pair of sheris and iiij shepe. **1574** in Feuillerat *Revels Q. Eliz.* (1908) 246 Grynding of Sheeres to clypp the Assedue. *a* **1586** SIDNEY *Arcadia* III. (Sommer) 278 The sheares also were at hand to behead the silke. **1628** [P. FLETCHER] *Brittain's Ida* I. ii, His Nimph-like face ne're felt the nimble sheeres. **1686** PLOT *Staffordsh.* 380 Admitting of formation by the Gardiner's sheers. **1783** BURNS *Death of Mailie* 40 So may they [sheep], like their great forbears, For monie a year come thro' the sheers. **1855** DELAMER *Kitchen Garden* 17 A pair of shears, for clipping box-edging and quickset hedges. **1902** MARSHALL *Metal Tools* 44 For cutting thin sheet metal and wire, a pair of hand-shears.

¶ In tavern signs.

**1600** *Sir John Oldcastle* v. v. 12 Yonder at the sheeres. **1826** *Hone's Every-d. Bk.* I. II. 1230 The 'Hand and Shears', a public house [in Cloth-fair].

**b.** in sing. form, = a pair of shears. Now *rare*.

*a* **1300** *Cursor M.* 7240 Quils sampson slepped, sco laght a schere, His hare sco kerf. *c* **1386** CHAUCER *Monk's T.* 66 Ne on his heed com rasour noon ne schere. **1455** in Anstey *Munim. Acad.* (Rolls) II. 664, j. shere to snoffe candels. *a* **1568** *Bannatyne MS.* (Hunter. Club) 396 Thow yeid with elwand, scheir and thymmill, Full mony a day seikand thy craft. **1643** *Orkney Witch Trial* in *Misc. Abbotsf. Club* (1837) I. 184 Laid ane woll scheir on the coggis mouth. **1661** PETTY in T. Birch *Hist. Roy. Soc.* (1756) I. 64 Then the sheer works rank, that is, takes off a deep flock. *Ibid.*, So few men can set and grind a shear exactly.

¶ **c.** in *pl.* form construed as *sing.*

**1649** G. DANIEL *Trinarch., Rich. II*, cclxvii, One Shears must cutt them both. **1842** LOUDON *Suburban Hort.* 141 A shears fixed at the extremity of a long handle, and which clips and holds fast at the same time.

**d.** As used for purposes of divination. Commonly ***sieve and shears***.

**1549** in *Narr. Reform.* (Camden) 334 Sir Robert Brian.. conjureth with a syve and a pair of sheeres. **1570** [see RIDDLE *sb.* 1 b]. **1602-1843** [see SIEVE 2 b].

†**e.** In proverbial use. ***there goes but a pair of shears between them***, they match each other as if cut from the same cloth; they are 'of a piece' (very common in 16-17th c.). ***chalk is not shears*** (Sc.), chalking the cloth is not cutting it. *Obs.*

**1579** LYLY *Euphues* Wks. 1902 I. 195 The *Sympathia* of affections and as it were but a payre of sheeres to goe betweene theire natures. **1603** SHAKS. *Meas. for M.* I. ii. 28. **1632** *Star Chamber Cases* (Camden) 98 There went but a paire of sheeres between a Papist and a Protestant, and not a pinne to choose of what religion a man is. **1643** in W. Macgill *Old Ross-sh.* (1909) 314, I feir me they sall be long in concluding, as we say in the comon proverbe 'Calke is no sheyres'.

**f.** *fig.*, esp. as attributed to the Fates.

**1590** SHAKS. *Mids. N.* v. i. 348 O sisters three, come, come to mee, With hands as pale as Milke, Lay them in gore, since you haue shore With sheeres, his thred of silke. **1637** MILTON *Lycidas* 75 Comes the blind Fury with th'abhorred shears, And slits the thin spun life. **1795** SOUTHEY *Vis. Maid of Orleans* I. 309 Observe how soon..they change Their snowy hue,..Till Atropos relentless shuts the sheers. **1886** CAMPBELL-BANNERMAN *Sp.* 13 May in *Hansard's Parl. Deb.* Ser. III. CCCV. 939 The shears of destiny in the hands of Mr. Jesse Collings were ready.

**g.** *Mech.* In modern use, applied to various machines for cutting metals, more or less analogous to shears in manner of operation.

**1834-6** P. BARLOW *Manuf.* §876 in *Encycl. Metrop.* (1845) VIII. 615 Cut up into narrow slips..by means of a pair of circular shears. **1869** RANKINE *Machine & Hand-tools* Pl. K 1, These shears are so arranged that the long plates can be cut in two or more divisions. *Ibid.* K 6, Fig. 2 is an end view of carriage, showing side views of punch and shear, and front view of drill.

**h.** *Cloth-manuf.* The cutting apparatus of a cloth cropping machine composed of a series of spiral blades on a revolving cylinder which cut against a ledger blade; also each of these blades.

**1839** URE *Dict. Arts* 1323 This wire..being hardened is intended to constitute one edge of the shear or cutter. *Ibid.* 1326 A straight blade of steel..forms the leger blade, or lower fixed edge of the shears. **1846** HOLTZAPFFEL *Turning* II. 913 Revolving shears or 'perpetual shears' are used for shearing off the loose fibres from the face of woollen cloths.

**i.** One of the blades of a pair of shears.

**1794** G. ADAMS *Nat. & Exper. Philos.* III. xxxi. 235 The upper shear is riveted to a couple of strong standards. **1884** *Cassell's Techn. Educ.* II. 19/1 Immediately after the cut of the shear commences the iron must be divided completely across.

**j.** In phr. ***off (the) shears***: of sheep, just shorn. *Austral.* and *N.Z.*

**1888** J. BRADSHAW *N.Z. of Today* vi. 110 The hoggett..in 1882 could be readily sold 'off the shears' at twelve shillings. **1896** T. W. HENEY *Girl at Birrell's* 69 Now and again a buyer visited the stations to get cheap sheep 'off shears'. **1930** L. G. D. ACLAND *Early Canterbury Runs* 1st Ser. viii. 216 He drove them over Porter's Pass off the shears. **1964** T. RONAN *Packhorse & Pearling Boat* 147 The sheep had arrived off-shears.

¶ **2.** Misused for: (*a*) a knife; (*b*) a scythe.

**1382** WYCLIF *3 Kings* xviii. 28 Thei cuttiden hem self.. with sheeris and litil launcis [Vulg. *cultris et lanceolis*]. **1887** MRS. LAFFAN *Song of Jubilee* 58 We could hear The whetstone grate upon the mower's shear.

†**3.** *pl.* Something having the shape of a pair of shears. **a.** ? The clavicles; **b.** = *shear-battle* (see 7); **c.** A pair of wings; **d.** The pincer-like claws of a crustacean. *Obs.*

**1506** *Kal. Sheph.* K 8 b, By the necke betwene the head & the sholders ben .ii. bones named the sheres. **1560** WHITEHORNE *Ord. Souldiers* iv. 7 b, The Sheeres are made with two Triangels ioyned togethers for to receiue betwen them the said battell. **1590** SPENSER *F.Q.* II. viii. 5 Two sharpe winged sheares, Decked with diuerse plumes, like painted Iayes, Were fixed at his backe, to cut his ayerie wayes. **1682** K. DIGBY *Chym. Secr.* II. 195 The black ends of the shares of Crabs. **1714** DERHAM *Phys.-Theol.* IV. xiii. (ed. 2) 234 *note*, Two toothy Cheeks, somewhat like the Sheers of Lobsters.

**4.** *pl.* (Often construed as sing.) A device used upon ships, and in dockyards and mines, for raising and fixing masts, boilers and other heavy gear, consisting of two (or sometimes more) poles steadied (in a sloping position) by guys and fastened together at the top, from which the hoisting tackle depends, and with their lower ends separated as a base and secured to the deck or platform. Often spelt **sheers**. [Cf. G. *scherenkran*.]

*a* **1625** *Nomenclator Navalis* (Harl. MS. 2301) Sheeres. **1644** [see SHEEPSHANKS[2]]. **1739** C. LABELYE *Westm. Bridge* 36 The Sheers and Crab made use of in lifting the Stone. **1834** MARRYAT *P. Simple* xlvii, Then the shears were seen forward. **1859** F. A. GRIFFITHS *Artill. Man.* (1862) 130 The legs or spars for sheers. **1860** *Engl. & For. Mining Gloss., Cornw.* (ed. 2) 22 Shears..for the convenience of lifting out or lowering into the shaft, timber, or other things of great length. **1907** J. H. PATTERSON *Man-Eaters of Tsavo* x. 107, I..improvised a shears made of a couple of thirty-foot rails.

**5.** *pl.* A collector's name for any of several moths of the genus *Hadena* (Schrank), esp. *H. plebeia*; also *H. glauca*, the glaucous shears, *H. leucostigma*, the white-spot shears, *H. ochracea*, the tawny shears.

**1832** RENNIE *Butterfl. & M.* 67. **1869** E. NEWMAN *Brit. Moths* 415.

**6.** *attrib.* and *Comb.* Simple attrib., as ***shear-blade, -handle, -lever, -machine, -mark, rivet, slide, -smith***, (sense 4) ***shear-derrick, -pole***; objective, as ***shear-grinder, -grinding, -maker***; similative, as ***shear-shaped*** adj.

**1812** *Niles' Weekly Reg.* 25 Jan. 390/1 The subscriber at short notice can furnish clothier's *shear blades. **1869** RANKINE *Machine & Hand-tools* Pl. K 1, With shear blades long enough to shear a plate at one cut. **1838** *Civ. Engin. & Arch. Jrnl.* I. 268/1 For the purpose of hoisting the stone to the *shear dericks at the top. **1688** *Rec. Scott. Cloth Manuf. New Mills* (S.H.S.) 178 John Gray *shear-grinder. **1875** KNIGHT *Mech. Dict.*, *Shear-grinding Machine. **1688** HOLME *Armoury* III. 348/1 He beareth Azure, a pair of Clothiers Shears, Argent; and the *Shear handle Or. **1869** RANKINE *Machine & Hand-tools* Pl. K 8, The *shear lever. **1839** URE *Dict. Arts* 720 Two pairs of *shear-machines. **1797** *J. Robinson's Directory of Sheffield* 172 *Shear Makers. **1934** DYLAN THOMAS *Let.* 25 Apr. (1966) 111 There were no *shear-marks visible in my last letter for the reason that I had cut out nothing. **1840** R. H. DANA *Bef. Mast* xxxv, We were obliged to go aloft upon the ropes and *shearpoles. **1859** F. S. COOPER *Ironmongers' Catal.* 63 With *Shear Rivets. **1875** C. C. BLAKE *Zool.* 297 The *shearshaped palps are twice as long as the body. **1869** RANKINE *Machine & Hand-tools* Pl. K 6, *Shear slide. **1623-4** *Act 21 Jas. I*, c. 31 §6 The Occupacion of a Cutler Scissorsmith *Shearsmith or Sicklesmith within..Hallamshire. **1756** PENNECUIK *Hist. Blue Blanket* 42 Shear-smiths.

**7.** Special comb.: †**shear-battle** *Mil.*, a tactical arrangement of forces into two wedge-shaped formations acting in parallel directions toward the same objective; **shear-bill** [tr. F. *bec-en-ciseaux* (Buffon)], the Scissor-bill; **shear board**, a padded board over which the cloth was stretched for cropping with hand-shears; also *attrib.*; **shear-frame** (see quot.); **shear mark**, a mark upon a hide or fleece made when clipping an animal; also *fig.*; also **shear-marked** *a.*; **shear-mast** (see quot.); **shear-tail**, (*a*) *dial.*, a name for the Common Tern (*Sterna fluviatilis*); (*b*) a Peruvian bird (*Thaumastura cora*).

**1598** BARRET *Theor. Warres* 80 Loe here the *sheere battell framed of 4 battallions. **1793** tr. *Buffon's Nat. Hist. Birds* VIII. 412 The *Shearbill. **1562** *Richmond Wills* (Surtees) 156 In the shoppe, shears, *shearborde, and wyrkingere, xjs. *Ibid.* 153 Shearborde handills. **1733** [P. LINDSAY] *Interest Scot.* 110 The cutting on the Shear-board. **1880** F. PEEL *Luddites* 9 While the pair of cropping shears were working across the length of the two pieces fixed and prepared on the shear boards. *Ibid.*, The *shear-frame was one by means of which the two hand-shears could be worked at one and the same time instead of one by the hand cropper. *a* **1586** SIDNEY *Arcadia* II. xxvii. §4 (1912) 321 [They returned home] most of them with *share-marks of their folly. **1844** H. STEPHENS *Bk. Farm* III. 866 The shear-marks are seen to run in parallel bands round the carcass. **1892** *Berwick Advertiser* 16 Sept. 1/6 A Red and White Stirk; one shear mark on near hind quarter. **1696** *Lond. Gaz.* No. 3245/4 A Chesnut Mare about 13 hands high,..*shear marked on the top of the Buttock E.B. **1867** SMYTH *Sailors' Word-bk.*, *Sheer-mast, the peculiar rig of the rafts on the Guayaquil river..having a pair of sheers (instead of a single mast) within which the fore-and-aft mainsail works. **1885** SWAINSON *Prov. Names Birds* 203 *Shear tail. **1899** A. H. EVANS *Birds* vi. 438 The 'Peruvian Shear-tail' is golden-green, with crimson throat shading into blue, and white under surface.

**shear** (ʃɪə(r)), *sb.*[2] Forms: 6 sheere, 6-7 share, sheare, shere, *Sc.* scheir, 7 sheer, sheir, 6- shear. [f. SHEAR *v.*]

I. Action or result of shearing. Now chiefly *dial.*

**1. a.** A mowing of grass or corn, a crop.

**1794** *Har'st Rig* vi, And ay they tell, That, 'a green shear Is an ill shake'. **1813** VANCOUVER *Agric. Devon* 224 Let the shear or swarth be what it may, the average price of mowing is stated..at 2*s.* 4*d.* per acre. **1882** *Cornish Telegraph* 29 June 5 The shear of hay will be a splendid one.

**b.** A shearing (of wool), a fleece.

**1801** W. TAYLOR in *Monthly Mag.* XII. 579 By subdividing multifariously the sorts of wool to which the growers are to attend, the number of competitors in each line of shear will become very small.

**c.** *transf.* A shorn animal.

**1659** *Rec. Baron Crt. Stitchill* (S.H.S.) 16 Ilke sheir without a hird 4d. for ilke fault.

**d.** Used in stating the age of sheep with reference to the number of times the fleece has been shorn. *one shear, two shear*: one, two years old. Also *attrib.* as ***two-shear ram.***

**1614** MARKHAM *Cheap Husb.* III. xxx. 80 If you will know the age of your Sheepe, looke in his mouth, and when hee is one sheare hee will haue two broad teeth afore. **1790** W. H. MARSHALL *Midl. Counties* I. 398, I have seen wedders, of only two shear (two to three years old) so loaded with fat, as [etc.]. *Ibid.*, A loin of mutton of a sheep (ten shear) of twenty-six pounds a quarter, weighed [etc.]. **1799** A. YOUNG *Agric. Lincoln.* 309 He has some shearling tups, and two shear that are good. **1911** *Midl. Counties Herald* 29 June 4/2 Two shear ram.

**2.** The action of shearing or cutting. *Sc.*

**17..** *Jacobite Song, Wee German Lairdie* iv, And we've the trenching blades o' weir, Wad..pass ye 'neath the claymore's sheer, Thou feckless German lairdie! **1809** T. DONALDSON *Poems* 58, I know not but I may come back: To ..help to gie your corn a shear.

**3.** A cut edge.

**1844** H. STEPHENS *Bk. Farm* III. 1038 Moss-sods..laid perfectly close, the shear of each fitted to the other.

**4.** A division, parting. (Cf. SHEAR *v.* 8 b.)

**1876** SKENE *Celtic Scot.* Introd. I. 10 The great wind and water shear which separates the eastern from the western districts.

**5.** *attrib.* and *Comb.*, as *shear-day, -time*; **shear-darg** *Sc.*, a day's work at reaping or shearing; † **shear-mill**, ? = *shear-shop*; **shear-sheep**, a sheep that has passed its first shearing and so more than one year old; † **shear-shop**, a place in which the manufacture of cloth is conducted; **shear wether hog** (see SHEARHOG); † **shear-wool** (see quot.).

**1600** in *Reg. Mag. Sig. Scot.* 1605, 594/2 Lie *scheirdarg. **1689** VISCT. DUNDEE *Sp.* in J. Drummond of Balhaldy *Mem. Lochiel* (1842) 264, I beg leave of yow, however, to allow me to give one 'Shear-darg' to the King, my master, that I may have ane opportunity of convincing the brave Clans that [etc.]. **1717** *Select. Scott. Forfeited Estates Papers* (S.H.S.) Introd. 30 Shear-Dirgs..4 at 5d. each. **1565** in *Reg. Mag. Sig. Scot.* 1581, 58/1, 4 lie *scheir-day-wrokis. *a* **1722** LISLE *Husb.* (1757) 319 Barn-room enough to house my sheep the evening before shear-day. **1607** NORDEN *Survey. Dial.* III. 108 Paper-mill, Sawing-mil, *Shere-mil, or any other kind of Mill. **1503** *Maldon* (Essex) *Crt. Rolls* Bundle 62 no. iv, Defendens conduxit pasturam..pro centum ovibus vocat. *share shepe a festo sancti Michaelis archangeli. **1688** HOLME *Armoury* II. 176/2 A share sheep, at two years old. **1688** *Rec. Scott. Cloth Manuf. New Mills* (S.H.S.) 178 Whearas Mr. Debnams *shearshope is not lairge enowgh for his shearmen to dress ther work in, therfor [etc.]. **1518** *Coventry Leet Bk.* 658 The next *Shear tyme. **1811** T. DAVIS *Agric. Wilts* 260 Wether hogs, chilver hogs, from thence [about Christmas] till shear-time. **1537** in *North Country Wills* (Surtees) 103, I geve unto..John half a hundreth of *share wedder hogges or ewe hogges at his pleasure. **1585** HIGINS *Nomenclator* 173/1 *Tomentum.* *Sheerewooll: flocks, such as clothworkers make in sheering.

**II.** In scientific uses.

**6. a.** *Physics* and *Mech.* (*a*) A kind of strain consisting in a movement of planes of a body that are parallel to a particular plane in a direction parallel to a line in that plane through distances proportional to their distances from that plane. (*b*) The stress called into play in a body which undergoes this kind of strain.

**1850** [see SHEAR *v.* 9]. **1858** RANKINE *Man. Appl. Mechanics* §103. 87 Planes of Equal Shear, or Tangential Stress. **1867** THOMSON & TAIT *Nat. Philos.* I. §171 This kind of strain is called a simple shear. **1869** H. MOSELEY in *Lond.* etc. *Philos. Jrnl.* XXXVII. 230 The unit of shear being the pressure in lbs. necessary to overcome the resistance to shearing of one square inch. **1883** LODGE in *Nature* XXVII. 328 The bound ether inside a conductor has no rigidity; it cannot resist shear. **1885** GLAZEBROOK & SHAW *Pract. Physics* 139 The body is said to undergo a simple shear. **1888** *Lockwood's Dict. Mech. Engin.* s.v. *Shear*, A bar is said to be in shear when it is subject to shearing stress. **1894** TODHUNTER & PEARSON *Hist. Th. Elasticity* II. II. 386 The authors [Thomson & Tait] term it a simple shear. This is unfortunate, for that word was introduced by George Stephenson to denote the transverse stress in rivets, and has been consistently used in this sense of stress by Rankine and the majority of engineers since. Its present confused use partly for stress and partly for strain has been avoided in our own work by the introduction of the term slide for shearing strain. **1906** LOVE *Math. Th. Elasticity* (ed. 2) 532 The word 'shear' has been used in the sense attached to it in the text by Kelvin and Tait. Rankine proposed to use it for what has been called 'tangential traction'.

**b.** *Geom.* The transformation produced in a plane figure by motion in which all the points of the figure describe paths parallel to a fixed axis and proportional in length to their distance from it. (See quot.)

**1885** O. HENRICI *Projection* in *Encycl. Brit.* XIX. 797/2 Such a transformation of a plane figure is produced by a shearing stress in any section of a homogeneous elastic solid. For this reason Sir William Thomson has given it the name of shear.

**7.** *Geol.* Applied to the operation of transverse compression on a mass of rock, resulting in alteration of structure or breach of continuity.

**1888**, etc. [see *shear plane*, sense 8 below]. **1889** O. FISHER *Physics Earth's Crust* xx. (ed. 2) 268 The same amount of shear, which at one locality produces crumpling, may in another..produce schistosity. **1911** [see *shear-zone*, sense 8 below]

**8.** *attrib.* and *Comb.*, as **shear centre**, the point in the plane of a section of a structural member through which a shear force can be applied without producing torsion; **shear flow**, flow which is accompanied by or occurs under the influence of a shearing force: **shear modulus** = *modulus of rigidity* s.v. RIGIDITY 1 b; **shear plane** *Geol.*, a boundary surface between bodies of rock or ice which have experienced relative motion parallel to the surface; **shear strength** = *shearing strength* s.v. SHEARING *vbl. sb.* 8 b; **shear stress**, stress tending to produce shear; **shear-thickening** *sb.* and *a.*, (the property of) becoming more viscous when subjected to shear; similarly, **shear-thinning** *sb.* and *a.*; **shear wave**, an elastic wave which vibrates transversely to the direction of propagation; an S-wave; **shear-zone** *Geol.* (see quot.).

**1937** A. P. POORMAN *Strength of Materials* (ed. 3) vii. 142 This point of application of the load, in order that there shall be no twist of the beam as it deflects, is called the shear centre. **1972** T. H. G. MEGSON *Aircraft Struct.* vii. 247 For cruciform or angle sections..the shear centre is located at the intersection of the sides. **1950** *Phil. Mag.* XLI. 890 (*heading*) The eddy viscosity in turbulent shear flow. **1975** RAUDKIVI & CALLANDER *Adv. Fluid Mech.* iv. 155 A shear flow has non-zero gradients of mean velocity and the fluid is being sheared by the mean motion. **1937** DODGE & THOMPSON *Fluid Mech.* viii. 165 An analogy is often drawn between the coefficient $\mu$ and the shear modulus of elastic materials. **1973** J. G. TWEEDDALE *Materials Technol.* I. iv. 86 The shear modulus may be obtained from experimental values of torsional load and torsional strain measured on a cylindrical test segment. **1888** TEALL *Brit. Petrogr.* 447 *Shearing*, differential movement in a rock-mass. When the movement is concentrated along a plane, this plane is said to be a shear-plane. **1903** E. W. CLAYPOLE in *Amer. Geol.* Aug. 81 (*Cent. Dict.* Suppl.), Some [strata] are completely concealed by others that have been forced over them along shear-planes developed by the enormous pressures to which they have been subjected. **1969** BENNISON & WRIGHT *Geol. Hist. Brit. Isles* xvi. 356 Recent work on the mechanism of ice flow shows that shear planes occur and that these carry material from the sole of the ice sheet to the surface. **1931** LAURSON & COX *Properties & Mechanics of Materials* i. 13 For most brittle materials..the tensile strength is least, the shear strength next, and the compressive strength greatest. **1978** *Sci. Amer.* Apr. 122/3 Under some circumstances molten silicates may not behave like ordinary fluids; they may have a shear strength greater than zero. **1937** DODGE & THOMPSON *Fluid Mech.* viii. 165 There is..an important distinction between the effects of shear stress on solids and on liquids. **1971** J. W. IRELAND *Mech. Fluids* viii. 242 Determine the shear stress at the pipe walls when water flows at the rate of 300 litres/min. through a 7·5 cm diameter pipe 150 m long. **1963** A. J. DE VRIES in P. Sherman *Rheol. Emulsions* 146 (Index), Shear thickening, activation energy. **1966** *Jrnl. Colloid & Interface Sci.* XXII. 554/1 This shear thickening leads to a maximum viscosity beyond which shear thinning occurs as the shear rate is increased. **1978** *Sci. Amer.* Nov. 143/2 The easiest example of a shear-thickening fluid that you can whip up in the kitchen is a simple mixture of water and cornstarch (or any common starch). **1966** Shear-thinning [see *shear-thickening* above]. **1974** P. L. MOORE et al. *Drilling Practices Manual* ii. 25 Most [drilling] muds are shear thinning. **1978** *Sci. Amer.* Nov. 142/3 The advantage of shear-thinning is perhaps most apparent in ink. You want the ink in your ball-point to flow freely (by being sheared) as you write, but you do not want it to flow when the pen is in your pocket. **1936** J. B. MACELWANE *Introd. Theoret. Seismol.* vii. 147 An isotropic elastic solid can transmit two types of waves, compressional and shear waves. **1977** A. HALLAM *Planet Earth* 12 The outer core does not transmit shear waves and so must be liquid. **1911** J. F. KEMP *Min. Deposits* in *Encycl. Brit.* XVIII. 507/2 Sometimes..strains of compression have been eased by local crushing along comparatively narrow belts without appreciable..displacement of the sides such as would be required by a pronounced fault. The word shear-zone has become quite widely used in recent years as ..applicable to these cases.

**shear** (ʃɪə(r)), *sb.*[3] Also sheer. [Of uncertain origin; not easily identified with SHEAR *sb.*[1] or *sb.*[2]] The bar, or one of the two parallel bars forming the bed of a lathe, on which the poppets slide. Also *attrib.*

**1812** P. NICHOLSON *Mech. Exerc.* 364 The bed [of a foot lathe] consists of two parallel parts, called by some shears. **1869** RANKINE *Machine & Hand-tools* Pl. N 1, Two cast iron end standards..upon which is laid the long massive cast iron shear-piece. **1873** J. RICHARDS *Wood-working Factories* 160 The shear, or lathe frame..can be made of wood. **1875** KNIGHT *Dict. Mech.* 1262 The *bar-lathe* has a single beam or shear, generally of a triangular shape. *Ibid.*, The *bed-lathe* is the usual form, and has two parallel shears. *Ibid.*, The bed, sheers, cheeks, sides, on which the puppets slide.

**shear** (ʃɪə(r)), *v.* Pa. t. sheared (ʃɪəd), shore (ʃɔə(r)); pa. pple. sheared, shorn (ʃɔːn). Forms: 1 **sciran, scieran, scyran, scearan, sceoran, sceran, 3 scer, scire, schær, sere, ssere, 3–5 scere, 3–6 schere, 3–7 shere, 4–6 scher, 5 sher, 5–7 scheir, 6 scheer, cheir, shire, (? shore), 6–7 share, sheare, sheere, 7 sheire, 6–9 sheer, 5– shear.** *Pa. t., str.* 1 *pl.* **scǣron**, *subj. sing.* **scéare, 3 sar, scar(e, scher, 3–6 schare, 4 schaar, 4–5 shar, schar, shere, schere, 4–6 schair, schure, 5 share, schayr, 5–6 schewre, 8** *Sc.* **shure, 6– shore.** *wk.* **4 scherde, 5 scharde, scharid, scherid, 6 sheard, 9 sheered, 7– sheared.** *Pa. pple., str.* **1 scoren, 3 soren, 3–4 schoren, 3–5 scorn, schorn, 4 shorun, schorin, sheren, 4–6 schorne, 4–7 shorne, 5 shor, 4–7 shore, 6 shoren, -on, 4– shorn;** also **5 y-schorn(e, y-shore, y-schore, 5, 7 y-shorne.** *wk.* **4 schurd, 4–5 schard, 6 chard, 7– sheared.** [A. Com.Teut. verb, originally strong: OE. *sceran*, pa. t. **scear*, *scǣron*, pa. pple. *scoren*, corresponds to OFris. *skera, schera*, OS. (*bi*)*sceran* (Gallée), LG. *scheren*, MDu., Du. *scheren*, pa. t. *schoor*, pa. pple. *geschoren*, OHG. *sceran*, pa. t. *scar*, pa. pple. *giscoran* (MHG. *scheren, schar, geschoren*, mod.G. *scheren, schor, geschoren*), ON. *skera*, pa. t. *skar*, pa. pple. *skorenn* (Sw. *skära, skar, skuren*, Da. *skjære, skar, skaaret*):—OTeut. **sker-, skar-, skǣr-, skur-* to cut, divide, shear, shave. For Teut. cognates see SHARE *sb.*[1] and *sb.*[2], SHEAR *sb.*[1], SHARD, SCORE, SHORE. Outside Teut. the root appears to be found in Gr. *κείρειν* to shave, Lith. *skirti* to separate, Irish *scaraim*, I separate.]

**1. a.** *trans.* To cut (something) with a sharp instrument. Often with adv. or advb. phrase, as *asunder, in pieces, in two. Obs.* exc. *arch.* †Also *occas.* to pierce, thrust through.

*Beowulf* 1287 (Gr.) Sweord..swin ofer helme ecgum dyhtiȝ andweard scireð. *a* **1000** *Andreas* 1181 Lætað wæpnes spor, iren ecgheard, ea[l]dorȝeard sceoran. *a* **1225** *St. Marher.* 22 Ant tet scharpe sweord..scher hire bi þe schuldren. *a* **1300** *Cursor M.* 8875 Wit ax he wald haf scorn it [þe tre] þan. *Ibid.* 16554 In tua þis tre þai scare. *c* **1320** *Sir Tristr.* 474 Tristrem schare þe brest. *a* **1340** HAMPOLE *Psalter, Cant. Ezech.* 5 Bifore shorne is as of þe wefand my life whils ȝit .i. bigan he sheris me down. **13..** *Coer de L.* 3001 Ther was many gentyl heved, Quykly fro the body weved; Scheldes many schorn in twoo. ? *a* **1400** *Morte Arth.* 1856 They scherde in the schiltrone scheldyde knyghttez. *c* **1400** *Melayne* 1093 And hawberkes sone in schredis were schorne. **14..** *Erasmus* in Horstm. *Altengl. Leg.* (1878) 202 Sheryng his flesshe with cikels. *c* **1450** *St. Cuthbert* (Surtees) 2200 Þe roche away he share. **1563** *Mirr. Mag., Collingbourne* xviii, His grashyng tuskes my tender grystels shore. *a* **1568** *Christ's Kirk Gr.* 68 Throwch baith the cheikis he thocht to cheir him, Or throw the erss haif chard him. **1590** SPENSER *F.Q.* II. vi. 31 Cymochles sword..nigh one quarter sheard away. *a* **1593** MARLOWE & NASHE *Dido* IV. iv, For this will Dido..sheere ye all asunder with her hands. **1596** DALRYMPLE tr. *Leslie's Hist. Scot.* I. 90 At the first straik..it wolde scheir a man in twa. **1793** SMEATON *Edystone L.* §311 As bright as if shorn by a file. **1821** JOANNA BAILLIE *Metr. Leg., Ghost of Fadon* xxxix, His sword shore empty air. **1887** MORRIS *Odyss.* x. 127, I sheared the hawser of my ship.

**b.** *absol.* or *intr.* Now chiefly, To cut *through* (an obstacle) with the aid of a weapon. †Also with cognate obj., to cut (one's way, passage).

*c* **1205** LAY. 14216 Whætte his særes alse he schæren wolde. **13..** *Gaw. & Gr. Knt.* 213 As wel schapen to schere as scharp rasores. *c* **1470** *Gol. & Gaw.* 968 Sa wondir scharply he schare throu his schene schroud. **1535** STEWART *Cron. Scot.* (Rolls) II. 326 Ane small arrow, that scharpe as rasour schair. **1562** PHAER *Æneid* VIII. Z 4 Through yᵉ tydes they [the dolphins] shering glaunst. **1590** SPENSER *F.Q.* III. iv. 42 Then all the rest into their coches clim, And through the brackish waues their passage sheare. **1666** DRYDEN *Ann. Mirab.* lxxviii, So thick, our Navy scarce could sheer their way. **1838** LYTTON *Leila* II. ii, By a back stroke of his own cimeter shore through the cuirass. **1898** STEEVENS *With Kitchener to Khartum* 273 Through the swordsmen they [*sc.* the Lancers] shore without checking.

†**c.** *trans.* To circumcise. (Also with *about.*)

*c* **1250** *Gen. & Ex.* 1200 Ðe eȝtende dai..Circumcised he was, a-buten schoren. *a* **1300** *Cursor M.* 2695 Him self and ismael he scare.

†**d.** To cut for the stone. Const. *of. Sc. Obs.*

*a* **1557** *Diurn. Occurr.* (Bannatyne Club) 77 Henrie bischope of Ross was schorne of the stane. **1572** *Reg. Mag. Sig. Scot.* 529/1 James..hes bene twyis schorne of the stane.

†**e.** To cut up, to chop (a substance) fine, to mince. *Obs.*

*c* **1430** *Two Cookery-bks.* 11 Shere Oynonys, an frye hem in oyle. **1613** J. MAY *Decl. Estate Clothing* v. 29 Flox.. which they can sheare as small as dust. **1725** RAMSAY *Gent. Sheph.* II. i, Small are they shorn.

†**f.** To carve (meat) at table. Also *absol. Obs.*

*c* **1320** *Sir Tristr.* 602 Bifor him scheres þe mes, þe king. **1375** BARBOUR *Bruce* II. 92 Iames off Dowglas, that ay-quhar All-wayis befor the byschop schar. *a* **1440** *Sir Degrev.* 801 All the met that she scharе.

†**g.** To gnaw through, cut in pieces with the teeth. Also *intr.* const. *through. Obs.*

**1530** PALSGR. 702/1 Take hede on hym [a hounde], for he wyl sheare his lyme. **1587** HARRISON *England* III. iv. 225/2 in *Holinshed*, The beuer..will..shere thorough a dubble billet in a night. **1631** MARKHAM *Country Content.* I. x. (ed. 4) 72 They defend the line from shearing or cutting in pieces with the teeth of the Pike.

†**h.** To make (a hole, a wound) by cutting. *Obs.*

*c* **1425** *Noah's Ark* 57 in *Non-Cycle Myst. Plays* (1909) 21 Look that..in her side a door thou shear. *c* **1440** *York Myst.* xlii. 161 Fele the wound þe spere did schere riȝt in his syde. **1617** W. LAWSON *Country Housew. Gard.* x. (1623) 22 Mice ..will in eyther at the mouth [of the hive], or sheere themselues an hole.

†**i.** To rend, tear. Also *intr.* for *refl. Obs.*

*c* **1450** *Mirour Saluacioun* (1888) 93 Jacob..share his clothis vtward. *c* **1500** KENNEDY *Passion of Christ* 1067 The wale full sone [haly] intwa it schure. **1500–20** DUNBAR *Poems* xxxiii. 105 He schewre his feddreme..And slippit owt of it full clene. **1513** DOUGLAS *Æneis* VIII. xii. 70 Wyth mantell rent and schorne men micht hir se.

**j.** To cut (glass, tin-plate, etc.) with shears. Also, to cut (iron or steel bars, etc.) with shears (see SHEAR *sb.*[1] 1 g).

**1837** HEBERT *Engin. & Mech. Encycl.* I. 774 Shearing the Bars.—This rough bar is..put between the jaws of a pair of shears..and cut into lengths of about a foot each. **1850** E. CLARK *Britannia & Conway Bridges* II. 665 The storing away of the plates..as they were sheared and punched. **1869** RANKINE *Machine & Hand-tools* Pl. K 1, Shear blades long enough to shear a plate at one cut. **1883** H. J. POWELL *Princ. Glass-making* 63 The workman heats the severed edge, shears it even, and smooths and rounds it by melting. **1884** *Cassell's Techn. Educ.* II. 19/1 A bar of wrought iron one square inch in section is required to be sheared across.

**2. a.** To remove (a part) from a body by cutting with a sharp instrument. Chiefly with *adv.* to cut *off, out, away*.

*c* **1320** *Sir Tristr.* 1485 His tong haþ he..schorn of bi þe rote. **13..** *Gaw. & Gr. Knt.* 1337 Þen scher þay out þe schulderez with her scharp knyuez. **1483** CAXTON *Golden Leg.* 214/1 Kenelme kyng barn lyeth under a thorn his hede of shorn. **1581** A. HALL *Iliad* v. 78 His right hande at a blow his falchon off did shere. **1614** GORGES *Lucan* VI. 222 He.. with his blade sheares off their wrists. **1740** SOMERVILLE *Hobbinol* II. 58 With its sharpen'd Edge Shear'd both his Ears. **1819** SCOTT *Ivanhoe* xxxi, The plume was partly shorn away. **1837** CARLYLE *Fr. Rev.* I. I. iv, The guillotine-axe, which sheers away thy vainly whimpering head! **1852** KINGSLEY *Androm.* 306 As the vine-hook shears off the vine-bough. **1902** E. PHILLPOTTS *River* 322 He shore off the crust of the heath.

†**b.** *fig.*

*a* **1340** HAMPOLE *Psalter* cxviii. 36 Make my herte meke and lufand,..þat auarice be quytly shorne fra me. *c* **1400** *Rule St. Benet* (Prose) 11 And scere o-way [L. *amputare*] al þe langing of yure fleis. *Ibid.* 36 And for þi þat it es vice of propirte, sal it be scorn als þifte.

†**c.** To fashion by cutting out of a sheet of metal. *Obs.*

**1706** PETTUS *Fodinæ Reg.* xxvi. 79 The Moniers, who are some to sheer the Money, some to forge it [etc.].

**3. a.** To remove (the hair or beard) by means of some sharp instrument (also with *off, away*); to shave (the head or face); to cut (the hair) close or short; to cut or shave the hair or beard of (a person). Now *rare* exc. in pa. pple. *shorn*.

*c* **897** ÆLFRED *Gregory's Past. C.* xviii. 138 Swiðe ryhtlice wæs ðæm sacerde forboden ðæt he his heafod sceare. *c* **1000** ÆLFRIC *Lev.* xix. 27 Ne ȝe eow ne efesion ne beard ne sciron! *c* **1205** LAY. 17663 He scar [*c* **1275** sar] his crune ufenen. **1297** R. GLOUC. (Rolls) 3160 His berd he let ssere verst. *a* **1300** *Cursor M.* 7211 War mi hare schorn [*Gött.* schorin, *Fairf.* shorne], i war noght þan Stranger þan a-noþer man. **1387** TREVISA *Higden* (Rolls) IV. 169 Metridas his secounde wyf schaar hir heed for love of here housbonde. *a* **1450** *Knt. de la Tour* (1906) 92 She share of and cut awey the heres of his hede. **1526** TINDALE *Acts* xviii. 18 He had schorne his heed in Cenchrea. **1596** SPENSER *F.Q.* IV. v. 34 Shagged heare, The which he neuer wont to combe, or comely sheare. **1624** CAPT. SMITH *Virginia* II. 25 His hayre, the one side was long, the other shore close. **1786** *Pogonologia* 97 The preacher drew out a pair of scissars, and sheared the prince's chin. **1821** SOUTHEY *Exped. Orsua* 98 Their hair was sheared in circles. **1850** MRS. BROWNING *Lam. for Adonis* vii, They have shorn their bright curls off to cast on Adonis. **1865** KINGSLEY *Herew.* xv, But I am no monk. I have shorn many a crown, but I have kept my own hair as yet, you see.

†**b.** To give the tonsure to. Usually in passive, *to be shorn a monk*; also occas. *refl.* Also *to be shorn in*, to be initiated to the religious life by the reception of the tonsure. *Obs.* or *arch.*

*a* **950** *Guthlac* (Prose) vii. (1909) 138 Ða ȝelamp hit sume dæȝe þæt se ylca preost com to þam eadiȝan were, þæt he hine wolde scyran. **1387** TREVISA *Higden* (Rolls) VI. 7 He.. was i-schore monk in an abbay. **1565** STAPLETON tr. *Bede's Hist. Ch. Eng.* 165 Being shoren in, he went into a secret cell which the abbot had prouided for him. **1567–9** JEWEL *Def. Apol.* (1611) 372 The King was shorne into an Abbie, and made a Monke. **1591** G. FLETCHER *Russe Commw.* (Hakl. Soc.) 35 Some are put into Abbeyes, and shire themselves friers by pretence of a vowe. **1653** HOLCROFT *Procopius, Pers. Wars* II. xxii. 68 When John was shorne a Priest.

**4. a.** In passive, *to be shorn*: to be deprived *of* some part or appurtenance by or as by cutting. Chiefly *transf.* and *fig.* in certain collocations originally alluding to sense 3, e.g. (of a luminary) *to be shorn of its beams*; *to be shorn of one's strength* (? in allusion to the story of Samson), *of one's authority, privileges*, etc.

**1740** SOMERVILLE *Hobbinol* II. 87 The tall Oak,..shorn of his leafy shade. **1778** JOHNSON *Let.* 3 July in *Boswell*, He cannot bear the thought of living at—in a state of diminution; and of appearing among the gentlemen of the neighbourhood shorn of his beams. **1836** THIRLWALL *Greece* xvii. III. 23 A law, by which the Areopagus was shorn of its authority. *a* **1849** POE *Annie* Poems (1859) 116 Sadly I know I am shorn of my strength. **1875** SCUDAMORE *Day Dreams* 8 It is shorn of its former proportions.

**b.** rarely active (in compound tenses with *shorn*).

**1878** BOSW. SMITH *Carthage* 79 The misgovernment of domestic tyrants had shorn it of much of its grandeur.

**5. a.** To cut the fleece from (an animal); also, to cut off (the fleece, wool, etc.).

**900** in Birch *Cartul. Sax.* (1887) II. 241 And hi sculan waxan sceap and sciran on hiora aȝenre hwile. **1388** WYCLIF *Gen.* xxxi. 19 Laban ȝede to schere scheep. *c* **1440** *York Myst.* xxviii. 141 Lyke schepe þat were scharid A-way schall ȝe schake. **1557** TUSSER *100 Points Husb.* §81 (1878) 231 In June washe thy shepe,..Then share them. **1593** SHAKS. *3 Hen. VI*, II. v. 37 So many yeares, ere I shall sheere the Fleece. **1615** SWETNAM *Arraign. Lewd Women* ii. 29 Is not.. the sheepe sheared for his fleece? **1759** R. BROWN *Compl. Farmer* 81 In some countries they shear their geese. **1867** G. MACDONALD *Poems* 283 He gathered the hemp, and he shore the wool.

*Proverb. c* **1460** FORTESCUE *Abs. & Lim. Mon.* x. (1885) 132 And so his hyghnes shall haue þeroff, but as hadd þe man þat sherid is hogge, muche crye and litil woll. **1654** GAYTON *Pleas. Notes* I. v. 17 The Wooll we shall have is as much as the Devill (God blesse us) got when he shore a hog. **1827** SCOTT *Jrnl.* 24 Feb., It was much cry and little woo', as the deil said when he shore the sow.

*absol. c* **1481** CAXTON *Dialogues* 32/14 He oweth to shere. **1888** 'R. BOLDREWOOD' *Robbery under Arms* (1890) 53 As long as we shore clean..the overseer didn't trouble his head much about our doings.

†**b.** *Phr. to shear against the wool* (fig.): ? to treat roughly. *Obs.*

**1546** J. HEYWOOD *Prov.* (1867) 30 What should your face thus agayne the woll be shorne? *c* **1550** *Song, 'Back & Side'* in *Skelton's Wks.* (1843) I. p. vii, I shall looke lyke one by swete sainte Johnn were shoron agaynste the woole.

**c.** *fig.*

**1570** *Satir. Poems Reform.* xvi. 87, I wald sum man wald scheir ȝow clene. *a* **1628** F. GREVIL *Sidney* (1652) 62 Employing no instruments among the people, but such as devise to sheer them with taxes. **1797** J. LAWRENCE in *Monthly Mag.* (1818) XLVI. 396 It mattered little to them, whether the flock were led by the nose and sheared by a convocation of bishops, or an assembly of divines.

*Proverb.* **1828** SCOTT *F.M. Perth* xiii, He who goes forth to seek such wool should come back shorn.

**d.** To yield (a fleece), to produce by being shorn. †Also *absol.* or *intr.* to be shorn (?). Now *rare*.

**1587** D. FENNER *Song of Songs* iv. 1 Those same goates which doe vpon The mount of Gilhad sheare. **1852** *Trans. Mich. Agric. Soc.* III. 139 An article upon Sheep, describing bucks that shear the big fleeces. **1854** *Jrnl. R. Agric. Soc.* XV. I. 228 The tegs..shear a fleece varying from 5 to 7 lbs.

**e.** *Austral.* and *N.Z.* To own or keep (sheep).

**1930** L. G. D. ACLAND *Early Canterbury Runs* 1st Ser. ii. 35 The homestead..belongs to J. E. Scott who still shears about 3000 sheep there. **1965** J. S. GUNN *Terminol. Shearing Industry* II. 18 *Shear*,..this word is..used by woolgrowers to indicate the size of their flocks, for example, 'I shear about 5000'.

**6.** To cut off (the superfluous nap of woollen cloth) in the process of manufacture; also, in hat-making, to remove (nap) by singeing or scouring.

*c* **1340** *Nominale* (Skeat) 388 Homme drap retounde M. scleruth [*read* scheruth] clothe. **1442** *Eton Coll. Acc.* in Willis & Clark *Cambridge* (1886) I. 382 Robert Falowefeld for the shering of the seid ix yerdes of Ray. **1510** in *10th Rep. Hist. MSS. Comm.* App. v. 394 The said cotteners shall shore a dosen for eight pence of brod cloth. **1583** STUBBES *Anat. Abus.* II. 24 The Clothier also to sheare it very lowe. **1662** *Comenius' Janua Ling. Triling.* 95 From hence they [*sc.* the cloths]..are delivered to the shearer into the shop, who sheareth them being spread upon a table with shears. **1728** CHAMBERS *Cycl.* s.v. *Cloth*, The Cloth..is returned to the Sheerman, who sheers it a second time. *Ibid.*, s.v. *Sheering*, Some use the phrase Sheering of Hats, for the passing of Hats made of Wooll, over the Flame of a clear Fire..to take off the long Hairs. **1844** G. DODD *Textile Manuf.* iii. 105 The nap of the cloth..is 'cut', or 'cropped', or 'sheared'. **1875** *Ure's Dict. Arts* (ed. 7) III. 369 For fine printing, it is by some considered needful to shear the nap of the cloth instead of singeing it.

*absol.* **1474** CAXTON *Chesse* III. iii. (1883) 93 Hit appertayneth to them to cutte cloth shere dighte and dye. **1871** B. TAYLOR *Faust* (1875) I. v. 91 Enjoin upon him..To most exactly measure, sew and shear.

**7. a.** To cut down, to reap (grass, crops, etc.) with a sickle (†formerly also, with a scythe). Now *dial.*

In north midland dialects to *shear* is to cut with a sickle or hook, while to *mow* means to cut with a scythe. In Scotland also to *shear* implies the use of a sickle or hook; for reaping with a scythe the general term *cut* is used.

*c* **1250** *Gen. & Ex.* 1919 His handful stod riȝt up soren. *a* **1300** *Cursor M.* 4057 Him thoght his fader þaier corn schare. **1390** GOWER *Conf.* II. 261 Manye [herbs] with a knyf sche scherth. *c* **1440** *Alphabet of Tales* 118 When he had shorn it [the corn]. **1523–34** FITZHERB. *Husb.* §26 In the later ende of Iuly..is tyme to shere Rye... And in somme places they mowe it. **1594** KYD *Cornelia* IV. i. 9 Lyke cocks of Hay when Iuly sheares the field. **1612** DRAYTON *Poly-olb.* xvi. 48 Where now the sharp-edg'd sithe sheeres vp the spyring grasse. **1745** C. J. HAMILTON in *Academy* 18 Nov. (1893) 440/3 Yᵉ french Put grape shot into their cannon and cut them down just as if they were sheering corn. **1764** *Museum Rust.* I. 440 *note*, In the north of England they call reaping wheat shearing it.

*fig.* **1563** WINȜET *Bk. Quest.* To Rdr., Wks. (S.T.S.) I. 59 We mot also scheir the fruit of the doctrine of quheit.

**b.** *absol.* or *intr.* To cut standing crops; to use a sickle.

*c* **1250** *Gen. & Ex.* 2347 Two ȝer ben nu ðat derke [*read* derðe] is cumen, ȝet sulen .v. fulle ȝer ben numen, ðat men ne sulen sowen ne sheren. *a* **1340** HAMPOLE *Psalter* cxxviii. 6 Of þe whilk he shal not fille his hand þat shal shere. *c* **1400** *Rule of St. Benet* (Verse) 1853 Vnto þe tyme of euynsang, To scher or bind. *c* **1520** NISBET *N.T.* Matt. xxv. 26 Wist thou that I schere [*Wycl.* repe] quhare I sew nocht. *a* **1568** *Bannatyne MS.* (Hunter. Club) 260 Husbandis to saw and scheir. **1616** SURFLET & MARKHAM *Country Farm* v. xiv. 545 In other countries they vse to sheare after the Sunne is risen. **1789** BURNS (*title of song*) Robin shure in hairst. **1883** *Longman's Mag.* Apr. 647 Some years ago cottagers here and there had to 'shear' for their cottage, i.e. to work during harvest time in exchange for a free cottage.

*fig.* **1552** LYNDESAY *Monarche* 5873 Ȝour polit payntit flatterye, Ȝour dissimulat Ypocrasye, That day thay sall be cleirlye knawin, Quhen ȝe sall scheir as ȝe haue sawin.

**c.** *transf.* (*trans.*) To nibble close.

**1609** BIBLE (Douay) *Dan.* iv. 13 Annot., He..did eate grasse as an oxe, putting his mouth to the ground, to shere and swalowe it. **1615** WITHER *Sheph. Hunt.* v. H 1, Our sheepe the short sweet grasse do shear. **1658** ROWLAND tr. *Moufet's Theat. Ins.* 986 This not only tasts of corn or shears it, but breaks and grinds stalk and all.

**d.** To clip, cut, or trim (a tree or bush, a lawn); †to cut off (a branch).

*a* **1300** *Cursor M.* 11713 Iesus..said, 'þou palme, i comand þe þat o þi branches an be scorn'. **1398** TREVISA *Barth. De P.R.* XVII. i. (Tollemache MS.), Tren and herbes of gardenes schulde be wilde, but þey beþ kepte parid and schurde. **1573** TUSSER *Husb.* (1878) 73 Let lop be shorne that hindreth corne. **1693** EVELYN *De La Quint. Compl. Gard.* II. 165 We shear our Palisade's the second time. **1802** W. TAYLOR in Robberds *Mem.* I. 450 A sort of yew-hedge, tangled with luxuriance and sheared into spruceness. **1863** HAWTHORNE *Our Old Home, Lond. Suburb*, The garden.. had been levelled, carefully shorn, and converted into a bowling-green.

**8. a.** To cleave, divide, said esp. of ships, birds, etc.

*a* **1340** HAMPOLE *Psalter* xxviii. 7 Þe voice of lord sherand þe flaume of fire. **1513** DOUGLAS *Æneis* v. i. 5 His navy with north wind scherand the seyis. **1590** SPENSER *F.Q.* II. vi. 5 Her shallow ship away did slide, More swift, then swallow sheres the liquid skie. **1622** MALYNES *Anc. Law-Merch.* 286 Ingots, for to be deliuered to the moneyers to sheire the same by weight into small peeces. **1706** J. PHILIPS *Cerealia* 27 Fame to high Olympus flew, Shearing th'expanse of heaven with active plume. **1864** TENNYSON *Voy.* ii, The Lady's-head upon the prow Caught the shrill salt, and sheer'd the gale. **1885–94** R. BRIDGES *Eros & Psyche* Mar. xxix, Like a plough that shears the heavy land.

**b.** *intr.* for *refl.* ***where*** (or *as*) ***wind and weather*** (or ***water***) ***shears***: on the ridge of a hill, on the highest ground.

**1556** *Reg. Mag. Sig. Scot.* 245/2 Keipand the heid of the Innerhill in propirtie, quhill it cum to the meting of the tua gaittis as wynd and wodder scheris. **1601** *Ibid.* 395/2 Ascendand up to the hill or month heidis thairof as wind and wedder scheirris. **1815** SCOTT *Guy M.* xxxvi, On the tap o' the hill where the wind and water shears.

**9.** *Physics* (also *Mech.*, *Geol.*, etc.). To subject to a shearing stress; to distort or fracture by shear.

**1850** E. CLARK *Britannia & Conway Bridges* I. 389 Examples of this kind of strain occur in the rivet which unites the two blades of a pair of scissors, or the rivet on which the blade rotates in an ordinary pocket-knife. In the former..the evident tendency of the strain is to shear the rivet in one place only, and this is called a single shear; but in the knife the rivet must be sheared in two places before the blade can escape. *Ibid.* II. 517 It is evident that immediate strain from the weight of the structure, close to the piers on which it is supported, will tend to shear off the end of the tube in a vertical line. **1881** O. FISHER *Physics Earth's Crust* x. 120 Yet we may arrive at some conclusion as to whether the material at any given level within the crust will on the average be sheared upwards or downwards by the compression. **1883** LODGE in *Nature* XXVII. 328 The ether may be sheared by electromotive forces into positive and negative electricity. **1911** *Encycl. Brit.* XVI. 669/2 (*Lighting*) The filament after a time breaks up into sections which become curiously sheared with respect to each other.

**shear**: see SHEER.

**shear**, obs. f. SERE *a.*[2], several.

**15..** *Chevy Chase* 12 (Ashm. MS.) Then the wyld thorowethe woodes went on euery syde shear. *Ibid.* 16 On sydis shear.

**shear**, erron. f. *sear*, variant of CERE *v.*

**1688** HOLME *Armoury* IV. xii. (Roxb.) 496/1 First after his departure his body was well sheared and chested, then wrapped in Lead.

**sheared** (ʃɪəd), *ppl. a.* [f. SHEAR *v.* + -ED[1].]

**1.** That has undergone the operation of shearing; shorn. †Of a coin: Clipped.

**1616** *Orkney Witch Trial* in C. Rogers *Soc. Life Scot.* (1886) II. 299 Haveing aft and dyvers tymes desyreit the len of ane scheret sheilling fra James Hunton. **1845** JUDD *Margaret* II. xi. (1874) 334 One greased pole to climb, two sheared pigs to catch, and a silver punch-bowl the prize. **1905** GEIL *Yankee in Pigmy Land* xii. 175 He presented a sheared sheep.

**2.** Subjected to shear; strained or distorted by shearing stress.

**1930** J. S. FLETT in Peach & Horne *Geol. Scotl.* ii. 56 Sheared Granite-Gneiss. This rock belongs to the group of muscovite-biotite-granites, and is rich in alkali felspar.

**shearer** (ˈʃɪərə(r)). [f. SHEAR *v.* + -ER[1].] One who or something which shears.

**1.** A reaper of standing crops.

**1318–9** in *Shropsh. Arch. Soc. Trans.* Ser. III. (1903) III. 51 Rogerus mendepas sherar. **14..** *Nom.* in Wr.-Wülcker 687/11 *Hic messor*, a scherer. *c* **1520** NISBET *N.T.* Matt. xiii. 30 In the tyme of ripe corn I sal say to the scheraris [etc.]. **1641** BEST *Farm. Bks.* (Surtees) 43 Both shearers and binders have neede to be armed with gloves. **1788** PICKEN *Poems* 138 An', hint a' the shearers, wi' Peggy, I bindet the buttles o' grain. **1844** H. STEPHENS *Bk. Farm* III. 1066 Gloves of sheep-skin made on purpose, called shearer's gloves.

*fig. a* **1340** HAMPOLE *Psalter* cxxviii. 6 Aungels are sherers þat gedurs gode frute til god.

*Proverb.* **1668** R. B. *Adagia Scot.* 6 An ill shearer gat never a good hook.

**2.** One who removes the fleece from an animal.

**1388** WYCLIF *1 Sam.* xxv. 11 The fleischis of beestis, whiche Y haue slayn to my schereris. **1523–34** FITZHERB. *Husb.* §52 Take hede of the scherers, for touchynge the shepe with the sheres. **1611** SHAKS. *Wint. T.* IV. iii. 44 Shee hath made me four and twenty Nose-gayes for the shearers. **1637** MILTON *Lycidas* 117. **1883** *Century Mag.* Oct. 817 A good shearer shears seventy or eighty sheep in a day.

*fig.* **1654** M. COKER (*title*) A whip of Small Cords to scourge Antichrist..Whereunto is added, The Sheerer sheer'd and Casheer'd, the Shaver shav'd, and the Grinder ground. **1837** CARLYLE *Fr. Rev.* II. III. iv, Being Shepherd of this indigent People, not Shearer merely.

†**3.** One who removes the nap of cloth by the process of shearing. *Obs.*

**1473** *Acc. Ld. High Treas. Scot.* I. 17 To Sandy Balfoure the scherare, for certane clath schorne be him. **1679** JORDAN *Lond. in Luster* 17 Wool-combers, Sheerers, Dressers [etc.].

†**4.** = INCISOR. *Obs.*

**1610** MARKHAM *Masterp.* II. xxvi. 260 The vpper teeth, which are the shearers in the vpper chappe. **1683** SNAPE *Anat. Horse* v. vi. (1686) 211 The Shearers or Fore-teeth.

**5.** = SHEARMAN 3.

**1881** *Instr. Census Clerks* (1885) 93 Wrought Iron Manufacture..Shearer or Shearman.

**6. a.** A machine designed to cut metal, etc.

**1890** W. J. GORDON *Foundry* 60 Drilling-machines, punchers, squeezers, shearers, all of mighty size.

**b.** A coal-cutting machine that cuts in a vertical plane parallel to the coal face.

**1956** E. MASON *Deputy's Man.* I. xviii. 258 Most of the cutter-loading machines use vertical shearers which make a cut perpendicular to the plane of the seam... Disc shearers have picks attached to a vertical wheel rotating on a horizontal shaft. **1971** *New Scientist* 29 July 260/1 As the shearer cuts its way along the face, coal was automatically loaded on to a conveyor. **1979** *Jrnl. R. Soc. Arts* Jan. 90/1 By far the most common coal-getting machine in use to-day is known as the shearer.., which removes a slice of coal of about two-thirds of a metre in depth from the face by a revolving drum fitted with tungsten carbide tipped picks.

**shear-grass** ('ʃɪəgrɑːs, -æ-). Forms: 5 scher-, 6 sheere-, sher-, 7 sheare-, 8 shar(e-, 9 shere-. [f. SHEAR *v.*] A name popularly applied to several kinds of sharp-edged grass or sedge, which are apt to cut the mouths of grazing animals or the hands of a person gathering them. Now only *dial.*

**1483** *Cath. Angl.* 335/1 A Schergrysse (*A.* Scheregresse), *carex.* **1551** TURNER *Herbal* I. H v, An herbe, whiche we cal in english segge, or shergresse. **1589** A. FLEMING *Virg. Georg.* III. 44 Fed with rough greene leaues, And sheere-grasse sharpe or sedge. **1631** CAPT. SMITH *Advt. Planters* xii. 27 You may have harsh sheare-grasse enough to make hay of. **1790** W. H. MARSHALL *Midl. Counties* II. 442 Sharegrass, *carix hirta*; a species of sedge. **1799** A. YOUNG *Agric. Lincoln.* 168 It makes a soil produce a crop of hay, which naturally would only feed rabbits by shar grass. **1884** W. MILLER *Plant-n.* 57/2 Shear or Shere Grass. *Cladium Mariscus*; also some species of *Carex*.

**shear-head.** [f. SHEAR *sb.*[1] and *sb.*[2]]

**1.** The upper part of the apparatus for hoisting known as 'shears' (see SHEAR *sb.*[1]).

**1769** FALCONER *Dict. Marine* (1776) s.v. *Hulk*, The tackles which extend from the head of the mast to the sheer-heads. **1847** KEY *Recov. H.M. Gorgon* 24 A guy was taken from the sheerhead to the shore.

†**2.** *Mining.* ? A 'fault'. *Obs.*

**1813** VANCOUVER *Agric. Devon* 56 It no where partakes of the regular dip..of the stratum,..but is broken and interrupted with what the miners call shear-heads and saddles.

**shear-hog** ('ʃɪəhɒg). *dial.* Also 6 sharroge, 8 sherrug, 8–9 shar-hog, 9 sharrag. [f. SHEAR *sb.*[2] + HOG *sb.*[1]] A name given to a lamb after the first shearing and until the second.

**1523–34** FITZHERB. *Husb.* §53 The ewes by theym selfe, the share hogges and theyves by them selfe, the lambes by theym selfe. **1558** *Will of Oliv. Leder*, Huntingdon (Somerset Ho.), Ewes or sharrogs. **1736** W. ELLIS *New Exper.* 52 (E.D.S.) The third year a sherrug. **1784** W. H. MARSHALL *Midl. Counties* (1790) II. 27 Fifty 'sharhogs' of the new Leicestershire breed. **1857** GEO. ELIOT *Sc. Clerical Life, Mr. Gilfil's Love Story* i, He thought it a mere frustration of the purposes of language to talk of 'shear-hogs' and 'ewes' to men who habitually said 'sharrags' and 'yowes'.

†**shear-hook.** *Naut. Obs.* [f. SHEAR *v.* + HOOK *sb.*[1]] A sickle-shaped hook intended to destroy the enemy's rigging.

**1338** in Nicolas *Hist. Navy* (1847) II. 475, ii. seilyngnedeles, un dyall, un sherhok, un mykehok. **1485** *Naval Acc. Hen. VII* (1896) 39 Sherhokes for the yerde armes. **1558** W. TOWRSON in Hakluyt *Voy.* (1589) 124 The shippe fell aboorde of vs and with her sheare hookes cut our maine saile. **1619** in Foster *Eng. Factories India* (1906) I. 68 They should be fitted with 'sheere hooks', etc., to keepe off bording. *c* **1635** CAPT. N. BOTELER *Dial. Sea Services* (1685) 289 Sheer hooks are great Hooks of iron about the bigness and in the form of a sickle and they are set into the main-yard-arms. **1704** J. HARRIS *Lex. Techn.* I. **1794** *Rigging & Seamanship* I. 80.

**shear-hulk**: see SHEER-HULK.

**shearing** ('ʃɪərɪŋ), *vbl. sb.* [f. SHEAR *v.* + -ING[1].]

**1.** The action or an act of cutting, clipping, or shaving with shears or some other sharp instrument.

*c* **1315** SHOREHAM I. 1416 þat hys in holy cherche y-cleped wel þe furste scheryngе Of clerke. *a* **1400–50** *Wars Alex.* 2624 Sharpe schudering of schote, schering [*Dubl. MS.* sheryng] of mailes. **1490** *Acc. Ld. High Treas. Scot.* I. 138 Item, for the schereing of xxxiij elne j quartar of clayth. **1523–34** FITZHERB. *Husb.* §51 Beware, that thou put not to many shepe in a penne at one tyme..at the sheryng. **1611** SHAKS. *Wint. T.* IV. iv. 77 Grace, and Remembrance be to you both, And welcome to our Shearing. **1704** POPE *Summer* 64 When swains from shearing seek their nightly bow'rs. **1728** CHAMBERS *Cycl.* s.v. *Cloth*, The Sheerman takes it, and gives it its first cut, or sheering. **1778** [W. H. MARSHALL] *Minutes Agric., Observ.* 92 The Cutting of Wheat is termed Shearing. **1848** J. R. LOWELL *Poet. Works* (1896) 136/2 Your goddess of freedom, a tight, buxom girl..who can sing at a husking or romp at shearing. **1881** RAYMOND *Mining Gloss., Shearing*,..cutting up steel for the crucible. **1890** 'R. BOLDREWOOD' *Col. Reformer* (1891) 122 With spring came all the bustle of washing and shearing. **1891** MORRIS *Poems by Way* (1896) 191 It was Goldilocks woke up in the morn At the first of the shearing of the corn. **1901** M. FRANKLIN *My Brilliant Career* xvi. 136, I was looking forward to the shearing.

†**2.** Cleavage, parting, division. *Obs.*

*c* **1400** *Sc. Trojan War* I. 502 This hede and taill ar for to say A myddle scheryng in þe way Of a cercle þat turnys in hevene.

**3.** Something which is cut off with shears or some other sharp implement. Now only *pl.*

**1536** *Test. Ebor.* (Surtees) VI. 56 To..my shepherde fyve sheipe sheringes. **1558** WARDE tr. *Alexis' Secr.* (1568) 90 A pounde of the shearinge of Scarlet. **1673** F. KIRKMAN *Unlucky Cit.* 287 It was like the shearing of the Hogs, all Bristles. **1712** ADDISON *Spect.* No. 295 ¶10 He would.. have presented her once in three Years with the Sheerings of his Sheep for her Under-Petticoats. **1799** G. SMITH *Laboratory* I. 145 Put the shearings of scarlet cloth upon the coals. **1875** FORTNUM *Maiolica* vi. 55 A certain quantity of the shearings of fine woollen cloth.

**4.** *dial.* A designation for a sheep after the first shearing, a shearling.

**1641** BEST *Farm. Bks.* (Surtees) 2 After they are once shorne, they are called gimmer shearinges. **1781** HUTTON *Tour to Caves* (ed. 2) 95 *Shearing*, a sheep a year old, or once shorn. **1786** CULLEY *Live Stock* (1807) Introd. p. xviii, Then they take the name of shearing, shearling, shear-hog.

**5.** *Mining.* (See quots.)

**1875** KNIGHT *Dict. Mech.*, *Shearing*,..the making of vertical cuts at the ends of a portion of an undercut seam of coal. **1881** RAYMOND *Mining Gloss.*, *Shearing*. 1. The vertical side-cutting which, together with holing or horizontal undercutting, constitutes the attack upon a face of coal.

**6.** *Physics*, etc. See SHEAR *v.* 9.

**1850** E. CLARK *Britannia & Conway Bridges* I. 389 Under these circumstances failure takes place solely from the vertical shearing of the material in a transverse direction. **1858** RANKINE *Man. Appl. Mechanics* §279. 299 The resistance of timber to shearing is in each case that which acts between contiguous layers of fibres. **1869** *Lond.* etc. *Philos. Jrnl.* XXXVIII. 71 On the Fracture of Brittle and Viscous Solids by 'Shearing'. By Sir William Thomson, F.R.S. **1876** F. JENKIN *Bridges* §3 in *Encycl. Brit.* IV. 285/2 There are three kinds of stress, due to tension, compression, and shearing. **1882** GEIKIE *Text-bk. Geol.* III. I. iv. §4 (1903) 428 The planes of sedimentation, or those of cleavage or shearing where these have been developed, being naturally those along which water passes most easily.

**7.** *attrib.* and *Comb.*, as ***shearing-day, -feast, -rent, -season, -time; shearing-floor, -house, paddock, -shed***; esp. in names of tools, weapons, etc. used in the process of shearing, as ***shearing-board, -knife, -machine,*** †***-shaft,*** †***-shears,*** †***-sword, -table.***

**1661** PETTY in T. Birch *Hist. Roy. Soc.* (1756) I. 64 The lower chap [of the sheer] is kept close down to the *sheering-board with weights of lead. **1890** 'R. BOLDREWOOD' *Col. Reformer* xvii, The shearing board would be deserted. **1860** *Indenture* 30 July, *Shearing days fines or *shearing rents and other dues. **1596** SPENSER *Astrophel* 32 Emongst the shepheards in their *shearingfeast. **1829** SCOTT *Anne of G.* vi, Thou shalt have a necklace of jet at next shearing-feast. **1863** R. HENNING *Let.* 26 Nov. (1966) 146 The *shearing floor is made to accommodate twelve shearers. *a* **1914** A. B. PATERSON in *Penguin Bk. Austral. Ballads* (1964) 178 Round the shearing-floor the listening shearers gape. **1614** W. BROWNE *Sheph. Pipe* iii. D 4, Or consuming fire Brent his *shearing-house. **1806** R. CUMBERLAND *Mem.* (1807) II. 145 A very large and commodious shearing-house. **1844** W. BARNES *Poems Rur. Life* Gloss., *Shearen-knife, a thatcher's tool for shearing the roof. **1834–6** P. BARLOW *Manuf.* §1025 in *Encycl. Metrop.* (1845) VIII. 729 *Shearing or cropping machines have now very commonly superseded the hand shearing. **1850** E. CLARK *Britannia & Conway Bridges* II. 665 A steam-engine, with the necessary shafting, for driving the punching and shearing machines. **1977** YIN MING *United & Equal* 70 The commune has gradually mechanized its operations. It now has over 80 items of mechanized equipment—trucks, tractors, diesel engines, fodder-processors, mowers and shearing machines. **1933** L. G. D. ACLAND in *Press* (Christchurch, N.Z.) 25 Nov., **Shearing paddock*, handy paddock to hold sheep during shearing. **1883** *Century Mag.* Oct. 817/1 Organized shearing bands, with captains, that go from ranch to ranch in the *shearing season. **1581** A. HALL *Iliad* v. 87 Iuno..was wounded sore..By triple headed *shearing shafte. **1573** TUSSER *Husb.* (1878) 36 *Sharing sheares readie for sheepe to be shorne. **1857** H. W. HARPER *Let.* 1 Sept. in *Lett. from N.Z.* (1914) 19 He took me to his *shearing shed. **1910** N. MUNRO *Fancy Farm* xiii. 126 The dipping-fold or the shearing-shed. **1707** SIR. W. HOPE *New Method Fencing* vii. 200 A good light *Sheering-Sword. **1875** KNIGHT *Dict. Mech.*, **Shearing-table*, a bench for holding sheep while being sheared. *c* **1520** NISBET *N.T.* Matt. xiii. 30 Suffir ye thaim bathe to grow into *schering-tyme. **1777** BRAND *Pop. Antiq.* 284. **1862** *Rep. Comm. Patents 1861: Agric.* (U.S.) 137 Shearing time..is the month of June. **1953** O. E. MIDDLETON in C. K. Stead *N.Z. Short Stories* (1966) 188 Shearing-time was always a worry for Charlie.

**8. a.** Special comb.: **shearing-darg** *Sc.*, a day's-work performed by a shearer; † **shearing-hook** = SHEAR-HOOK; † **shearing-ram**, a ram past its first shearing and therefore about one year old.

**1550** in *Reg. Mag. Sig. Scot.* 1593, 794/2 Lie *scheringdargis. *c* **1385** CHAUCER *L.G.W.* 641 (Fairf.) In gooth the grapenel so ful of crokes Amonge the ropes and the *sheryng hokes. **1586** *Shuttleworths' Acc.* (Chetham Soc.) 32 Makynge of towe sheryngе houkes x[d]. **1797** *Sporting Mag.* X. 123 The use of some of his *shearing rams..for fifty guineas each.

**b.** in scientific terms (see sense 6 and SHEAR *v.* 9): **shearing plane** *Geol.* = *shear-plane* (SHEAR *sb.*[2] 7); **shearing strain**, a strain of the nature of a shear (SHEAR *sb.*[2] 6 a); **shearing strength**, power of resistance to shearing; **shearing stress**, a stress tending to produce or resist a shear.

**1889** O. FISHER *Physics Earth's Crust* xx. (ed. 2) 263 The throw, that in faulting occurs along a single *shearing plane, the 'fault-' or 'thrust-plane'. **1850** E. CLARK *Britannia & Conway Bridges* II. 517 The strain called by Mr. Stephenson 'the *shearing strain', which rendered thick plates necessary at the extremities of the tubes. **1882** MINCHIN *Unipl. Kinematics* 134 A shearing strain. **1869** SIR E. REED *Shipbuilding* xvii. 333 The *shearing strengths of rivets are proportional to the sectional Areas. **1869** RANKINE *Mach. & Millwork* 497 The ultimate shearing strength..is ..equal, or nearly equal, to the tenacity. *Ibid.* 496 Every *shearing stress is equivalent to a pair of direct stresses of the same intensity, one tensile and the other compressive, exerted in directions making angles of 45° with the shearing stress. **1910** LOVE in *Encycl. Brit.* IX. 143/1 A state of stress in which there is purely tangential traction on a plane, and no normal traction on any perpendicular plane, is described as a state of 'shearing stress'.

**shearing** ('ʃɪərɪŋ), *ppl. a.* [f. SHEAR *v.* + -ING[2].] That shears, in various senses of the verb.

**1375** BARBOUR *Bruce* XVI. 455 Thai seruit thame in sa gret wayne With scherand swerdis and with knyvis. *a* **1586** MONTGOMERIE *Misc. Poems* xxiii. 18 The sheirand shaft soon slippit to my hairt. **1599** SANDYS *Europæ Spec.* (1632) 113 As a sheering wind it kills all in the bud. **1885–94** R. BRIDGES *Eros & Psyche* Nov. 24 Like twin sharks..showing 'bove the water blue Their shearing fins.

**shear-legs.** [SHEAR *sb.*[1]] A device consisting of three poles of wood or iron bolted together at their upper ends and extended below, carrying tackle for raising heavy weights for machinery; cf. SHEAR *sb.*[1] 4.

**1860** *Engl. & For. Mining Gloss., Newcastle Terms* (ed. 2) 62 *Shear-legs.* **1875** J. H. COLLINS *Metal Mining* 49 The boring tools are sometimes worked simply by a rope passed over a shearlegs or triangle. **1900** *Engineering Mag.* XIX. 675 At the Chicago yard there is a steel sheer-legs 100 feet high and of 100 tons capacity.

**shearling** ('ʃɪəlɪŋ). Forms: 4, 6 **scherling**, 5, 7 **sherling**, 6 **sharling, scharlyng, shyrlyng**, 8 **sheerling**, 9 **shearling**. [f. SHEAR *v.* + -LING.]

**1.** A sheep that has been once shorn.

**1378–9** *Durham Acc. Rolls* (Surtees) 587 In 30 pell. de Scherlings empt. de Celer. pro pistrina, 5*s.* **1532–3** *Durham Househ. Bk.* (Surtees) 207 Oves..vocatæ sharlyngs. **1786** CULLEY *Live Stock* (1807) Introd. p. xx, They are not called shearlings until once clipped, which is understood to be the same as one year old. **1833** *Wauldby Farm Rep.* 114 in *Libr. Usef. Kn., Husb.* III, Making up the number by an addition of the finest gimmer shearlings. **1877** BLACKMORE *Erema* lii, I am whiter than yonder shearling.

**2.** The fleece of such a sheep. In recent use, *spec.* the woollen lining or body of a coat, etc. (chiefly *U.S.*).

**1481–90** *Howard Househ. Bks.* (Roxb.) 117, xxij. dousen of scherlinges, and iij. skynnes, prise the dousen xx. d. **1531–2** *Durham Househ. Bk.* (Surtees) 109 Pelles vocati sharlyngs. **1597** *Shuttleworths' Acc.* (Chetham Soc.) 119 Of the glover, for viij shyrlynges, which was kylled before October last, ix[s] iiij[d]. **1680** in Ferguson & Manson *Munic. Rec. Carlisle* (1887) 220 Lamb skins sherlings calfe-skins. **1971** *New Yorker* 16 Oct. 143/2 (Advt.), Suede on the outside, the white shearling on the inside. **1977** L. O'DONNELL *Aftershock* (1979) ii. 31 She shrugged out of her shearling-lined coat and hung it on the rack.

**3.** *attrib.*, as ***shearling-ewe, -ram, -tup, -wether.***

**1861** *Times* 27 Sept., Regular ram-breeders..let *shearling rams by private contract. **1844** H. STEPHENS *Bk. Farm* II. 38 A dinmont or *shearling-tup. **1782** W. H. MARSHALL *Norfolk* (1795) II. 321 Several pens of *sheerling-wedders.

**shearman** ('ʃɪəmən). Forms: 3 sermon, 3–6 scher-, 4–7 shere-, 5–6 s(c)har-, 5–7 sher-, (6 shier-), 6–7 sheare-, 6–8 sheer-, (7 sheere-, share-), 6– **shearman.** [f. SHEAR *v.* + MAN *sb.*]

**1.** One who shears woollen cloth. Now *Hist.*

*c* **1275** in *Shropsh. Archæol. Soc. Trans.* Ser. III. (1901) I. 130 Rogerius le sermon. **1297** *Placita coram Rege* m. 13 (1897) 83 Adam le Scherman. **1379** *Poll-tax W. Riding* in *Yorks. Archæol. Jrnl.* V. 25 Johannes Wykir & Agnes vx. ejus, Shereman. **1415** *Nottingham Rec.* II. 98 Willelmus, filius Thomae Sherman, de Notyngham,..sherman. **1530** in *Archæologia* XXV. 503 The sharman of Snettsham. **1551** T. WILSON *Logic* V. iv, His cote somwhat araied..was dressed at the Shermans [**1580** Shiermans], not past two or thre dayes before. **1593** SHAKS. *2 Hen. VI*, IV. ii. 141 Villaine, thy Father was a Playsterer, And thou thy selfe a Sheareman, art thou not? **1687** *Lond. Gaz.* No. 2224/4 A Sheerman by Trade. **1798** W. HUTTON *Family of Hutton* 97 My great grandfather, was a shearman.

*Comb.* **1463** *Cal. City Lond. Let.-bk.* L. 27 That now person enfraunchesed..take vpon hym to grynde any mennes sheres except Sheremen sherys. **1894** R. S. FERGUSON *Hist. Westmorland* 165 The shearmen-dyers.

**2.** One who conducts the process of shearing metal.

**1881** *Instr. Census Clerks* (1885) 93 Wrought Iron Manufacture..Shearer or Shearman. **1892** *Labour Commission* Gloss., *Shear men*, men who put iron or steel into the shears..and square it and cut it into the required lengths.

**shearn(e,** variant forms of SHARN *sb.*

**shears** *pl.*: see SHEAR *sb.*[1]

**shear-shorie,** variant of SEARCHERY *Sc. Obs.*

**1707** W. BLACK *Privil. Roy. Burrows* App. N 2 b, In.. 1632, a Signature of Foreign Shear-shorie, in favours of Robert Borthwick.. being past in Exchequer [etc.].

**shear steel.** [f. SHEAR *sb.*[1]: see quot. 1837.] Blister steel improved in quality by heating, rolling and tilting.

**1815** J. SMITH *Panorama Sci. & Art* I. 13 The steel which contains the smallest proportion of carbon, for example, shear steel, is the most easily welded. **1837** HEBERT *Engin. & Mech. Encycl.* I. 788 Shear Steel.—This name was given to a steel that was first made by Crowley, of Newcastle, about sixty years ago... Crowley.. stamped his production with the figure of a pair of shears, to indicate its suitable application... Various qualities of shear steel are made, distinguished by the terms half-shear, single-shear, and double-shear, according to the number of times it has been cut, piled, welded, and drawn out. **1857** SCOFFERN, etc. *Usef. Metals* 345 Bar-steel from the converting-furnace is made into single shear-steel and double shear-steel, which will differ in quality and value with the quality of the bar-steel from which it is made, and the judgment and care of the person who selects the steel. This name was given to it because it was the kind used for the blades of shears, formerly employed for cropping woollen cloths. Single shear-steel is distinguished by a single representation of a pair of those shears, and double shear by two. **1861** SIR W. FAIRBAIRN *Iron* 175 Double Shear Steel is single shear steel a second time cut up, piled, heated, and tilted. **1884** LOCK *Workshop Rec.* Ser. III. 293/2 Round the part which is to form the bearing a thick ring of shear-steel must be welded.

†**'Sheart.** *Obs.* Also written 6 shart, 7 s'harte, 's'heart, 8 *erron.* 'sdheart. A euphemistic shortening of *God's heart* (see GOD *sb.* 14), used as an oath or asseveration.

*c* **1596** *Sir T. More* III. ii. 276 Shart, if my haire stand not an end [etc.]. **1604** DEKKER *1st Pt. Honest Wh.* C 3, *Flu...* Sblood why doe you attach vs? *Cast.* Sheart! attach vs! *c* **1615** W. GODDARD *Mastiff Whelp* E 4 b, What crying? s'harte this is ex'lent fine. **1695** CONGREVE *Love for L.* II. vii, 'S'heart, what shou'd he do with distinguishing Taste? **1706** BETTERTON *Amorous Widow* II. 18 *Visc.* 'Sdheart, 'tis impossible!

**Shear Thursday**: see SHEER THURSDAY.

**shearwater** ('ʃɪəwɔːtə(r)). Also 7 shere-, 8 shire-, 8–9 *erron.* sheer-. [f. SHEAR *v.* + WATER *sb.*]

**1.** A bird of the genus *Puffinus*, esp. *P. anglorum*, the Manx Shearwater (see MANX *a.*), and *P. major*, the Greater Shearwater.

*c* **1671** SIR T. BROWNE *Norf. Birds* Wks. 1835 IV. 316 A sea-fowl called a sherewater. **1674** RAY *Coll. Words* To Rdr. A 8, Among some Pictures of Birds which I have received from.. Sr. Thomas Brown.. I find.. A shear-water inscribed *Larus niger*. **1703** DAMPIER *Voy.* III. i. 93 We saw no Fowl but Shear-waters. **1778** *Eng. Gazetteer* (ed. 2) s.v. *Pembrokeshire*, The harry-bird [is] the shirewater of Sir Thomas Brown. **1821** SCOTT *Pirate* iv, The very sheerwaters and bonxies are making to the cliffs for shelter. **1870** GILLMORE tr. *Figuier's Reptiles & Birds* 288 Under the name of Shearwaters.. those species of Petrels are included which have bills as long, and sometimes longer, than their heads.

**2.** *U.S.* The Black Skimmer, *Rhynchops nigra.*

**1794** MORSE *Amer. Geog.* 167 Shear Water or Razor Bill. **1850** F. MASON *Burmah* 300 The sheer-water, or scissors-bill. **1883** *Century Mag.* Sept. 652/2 The black skimmer, or shear-water.

†**'sheary,** *a. Obs. rare*$^{-1}$. [f. SHEAR *v.* + -Y.] Having a hard sharp edge.

**1597** GERARDE *Herbal* I. xv. 16 Cyperus Wood grasse hath many sheary grassie leaues.

**sheat,** *sb. dial.* Also 6 *pl.* shettes, 7–9 sheet, 8 scheat, 9 shet. [Cogn. w. the synonymous SHOAT[2]; the relation between the two forms is obscure.] A pig under a year old.

**1534** *Inv.* in *Lett. & Pap. Hen. VIII*, LXXXIII. lf. 118 (P.R.O.) Yong hogges called Shettes. **1572** in *Pegge's Kenticisms* (E.D.S.) s.v., One sow, two sheetes. **1607** TOPSELL *Four-f. Beasts* 661 In English we call a young swine a Pigge, A weaning Pigge, a sheate, a Yealke, and so foorth. **1653** URQUHART *Rabelais* I. xxxvii, Three hundred barrow-pigs or sheats. **1736** J. LEWIS *Isle of Tenet* (ed. 2) 38 *Scheat*, a little Pig spay'd. **1852** in *N. & Q.* Ser. I. VI. 339/1 They [Kentish men] defined 'sheets' to be 'pigs between the age of six and ten months'. **1875** *Sussex Gloss.*, *Sheat*, a young hog of the first year.

†**sheat,** *a. Obs. rare*$^{-1}$. ? Trim, neat.

*c* **1590** GREENE *Fr. Bacon* vii. (1630) 25 Neat, sheat and fine, As brisk as a cup of wine.

**sheat, sheat(e,** obs. ff. SHEATH[2], SHEET.

**sheat-fish** ('ʃiːtfɪʃ). Also sheath-fish ('ʃiːθ-), sheet-. [The earlier form *sheath-fish* is prob. f. SHEATH[1], after the G. *schaid(e, scheid(e* masc. (now *scheiden* masc.; OHG. had *sceida* fem.), which Gesner *De Piscibus* (1558) regarded as cogn. w. *scheide* fem. SHEATH *sb.*, supposing that the fish was named from some resemblance in shape to a cavalry scabbard. The later *sheat-fish* seems to be ad. G. *scheidfisch* (f. *scheid*: see above), though that compound appears in Grimm only with a reference to Frisch (1741). The etymology of G. *scheid(e, scheiden* is unknown.] **a.** A large fresh-water fish, *Silurus glanis*, common in the Danube and other rivers of eastern Europe.

*a.* **1589** RIDER *Bibl. Scholast.* 1723 A sheath fish, or whale of the river, *stella*. **1601** HOLLAND *Pliny* IX. li. I. 266 The male sheath-fish or riuer-whale Silurus. **1815** ANNE PLUMPTRE tr. *Lichtenstein's Trav. S. Africa* II. 343 A species nearly allied to our *silurus glanis*, or sheath-fish, which in the *systema naturæ* is given as an inhabitant of the Nile.

*β.* **1611** COTGR., *Silure*, the rauening sheat fish, or whall of the riuer. *a* **1672** WILLUGHBY *Hist. Pisc.* (1686) 128 Silurus Rondeletii... The Sheat-fish. **1796** *Phil. Trans.* LXXXVII. 26 At Aleppo, the gall of the sheet fish, Silurus Glanis.. was in particular request. **1853** KINGSLEY *Hypatia* x, A mighty sheat-fish smokes upon the festive board. **1881** ELLEN FREWER tr. *Holub's 7 Yrs. S. Africa* II. i. 30, I succeeded in hooking three large sheatfish.

**b.** In extended use, as a name for the order *Siluridæ* or for a subdivision of it which includes the genus *Silurus*. (See quots.)

*a.* **1881** GÜNTHER in *Encycl. Brit.* XII. 649/2 The electric sheath-fish of tropical Africa (*Malapterurus*).

*β.* **1851** GOSSE *Nat. Hist., Fishes* 227 *Siluridæ.* (Sheat-fishes.) **1854** A. ADAMS, etc. *Man. Nat. Hist.* 106 Mailed Sheat-Fishes (Loricariidæ). *Ibid.*, Naked Sheat-Fishes (Pimelodidæ). *Ibid.* 107 True Sheat-Fishes (Siluridæ) [etc.]. **1883** F. DAY *Indian Fish* 31 Of the sheat-fish, or scaleless siluroids, we have twenty-six genera.

**sheath**[1] (ʃiːθ). Forms: *a.* 1 scéæð, scéað, 1–3 scæð, 2–3 scaþ, 3 shæþ, seaþ, sseþe, 3, (5) seth, 4–6 s(c)hethe, 4–7, (8–9 *dial.*) sheth, 5 scheth, (seeth), 5–6 sheethe, *Sc.* scheith, 6 scheethe, sheeth, 6–7 sheathe, (7 ? *mispr.* skeath, 8 shearth), 6– sheath. *β.* 4–5 schede, 5 shede, 5–6 schete. [OE. *scǽþ, scéaþ* str. fem. = OS. *skêðia*, MDu. *schêde* (mod.Du. *scheede, schee*), OHG. *sceida* (MHG., mod.G. *scheide*), ON. *skeiðir* pl., scabbard (Da. *skede*):—OTeut. **skaiþjō*.

The word app. belongs to the Teut. root *skaiþ-, skaid-*, to separate, divide (see SHED *v.*). The primary notion may have been that of a stick split to receive the blade: cf. the ablaut-variant MSw. *skiþa*, mod.Sw. *skida* a sheath, which appears to be the same word as ON. *skíða* a billet of wood, faggot (see SHIDE *sb.*). The ON. *skauðir* pl., 'sheath' of a horse (see 2 a below) is commonly regarded as cognate, although belonging to a different vowel-series; probably, however, the resemblance in form and sense with the present word is accidental.]

**1. a.** A case or covering into which a blade is thrust when not in use; usually close-fitting and conforming to the shape of the blade, esp. of a sword, dagger, knife, etc. Cf. SCABBARD.

*a.* *c* **950** *Lindisf. Gosp.* John xviii. 11 Send suord in sceæð ..*mitte gladium in uaginam.* *a* **1000** *Cædmon's Gen.* 1992 Handum brugdon hæleð of scæðum hringmæled sweord. *c* **1000** ÆLFRIC *Hom.* I. 482 He awende his swurd into ðære sceaðe. *c* **1200** ORMIN 14675 Abraham.. droh hiss swerd off shæþe. *c* **1205** LAY. 23211 Luken vt of scaþe [*c* **1275** seaþe] sweordes longe. *c* **1375** *Cursor M.* 15795 (Fairf.) Þat dint now gif þou nane In-to þe sheþe [*c* **1425** *Trin.* sheeþe, *earlier texts* forel] þou putt þi squorde. *c* **1450** *Mirk's Festial* 259 Wypyng his blody swerde, and put hit vp ynto his scheþe. *c* **1470** *Gol. & Gaw.* 706 Schort suerdis of scheith smertly thay dreuch. **1530** PALSGR. 266/2 Sheth of a meate knyfe, *gayne.* **1555** EDEN *Decades* 224 He had a longe dager with a hafte of golde, and the shethe of a fayre kynde of carued woodde. **1605** *Shuttleworths' Acc.* (Chetham Soc.) 169 A new sheth for my Mr daggar. **1669** STURMY *Mariner's Mag., Penalties & Forf.* 2 Blades, Handles, Scabbards, Sheaths for Knives. **1715** POPE *Iliad* III. 125 Your shining Swords within the Sheath restrain. **1800** *Med. Jrnl.* III. 195 The lever and cutting blade separated from the handle and sheath. **1809** ROLAND *Fencing* 11 Before drawing the sword from the sheath. **1865** LUBBOCK *Prehist. Times* 29 A bronze sword in a wooden sheath.

*β.* *c* **1385** CHAUCER *L.G.W.* 888 (MS. Gg.) Tysbe.. saw hire wympil & hise emty schede And ek his swerd that hym hath don to dede. *c* **1425** *Seven Sages* (Percy Soc.) 2584 And drew a knyf out of hire schete. *c* **1440** *Promp. Parv.* 444/2 Schede, or schethe, *vagina.* **14..** *Songs & Carols 15th C.* (Warton Club) lxi, Myn baselard haȝt a schede of red, And a clene loket of led. *c* **1500** *Melusine* lix. 359 He putte his swerd vp in the shede. **1518** *Ortus Vocab.*, *Vagina*, a shete [1500 a shethe].

**b.** *transf.* and *fig.*

**1297** R. GLOUC. (Rolls) 2864 Were he mowe þe luþer vortiger witie fram þe deþe þat ich in is Ineward mid suerd make a sseþe. *c* **1393** CHAUCER *Scogan* 39 Ne þynke I neuere of slep to wake myn muse þat rustyþ in myn schede [*Fairf. & Pepys* shethe] stylle in pes. **1592** SHAKS. *Rom. & Jul.* v. iii. 170 (Qo. 1599) O happy dagger This is thy sheath, there rust and let me dye. **1615** HIERON *Three Serm. Necess. Advts.* 14 Some one who is a meere hypocrite, and but as it were the sheath and shadow of a Christian. **1821** SCOTT *Kenilw.* viii, Women.. are occasion for many a blade's exchanging a sheath of neat's leather for one of flesh and blood. **1860** EMERSON *Cond. Life, Fate* Wks. (Bohn) II. 323 Liberation of the will from the sheaths and clogs of organization.. is the end and aim of this world.

†**c.** *by my sheath*, a petty oath. *Obs.*

*a* **1530** HEYWOOD *Love* 1370 (Brandl), The hole faute in fortune by my sheth. **1532** MORE *Confut. Tindale* Wks. 595/2 Yes by my shethe.

†**d.** ***painted sheath***: showy exterior. *Obs.*

[Cf. Fr. '*Dans vne gaine d'or vn cousteau de plomb*: Prov. A leaden sword in a golden sheath; a godlesse heart in a goodly bodie' (Cotgr.).]

**1542** BECON *Pathw. Prayer* li. S iv, Let vs not flatter oure selues nor make to much of our painted shethe, as they saye. **1546** J. HEYWOOD *Prov.* (1867) 22 She maie not beare a fether, but she must breath, She maketh so much of hir peynted sheath. **1576** GASCOIGNE *Steel Glas* Wks. 1910 II. 156 One Which stands so much, upon his paynted sheath.. That he accompts, no Soldiour but himselfe. **1613** HIERON *Abridg. Gosp.* II. iii. Wks. 1614 I. 159 Thou pridest thy selfe .. in thy painted sheath and gay clothing.

**2.** A sheath-like covering. Applied to various animal and vegetable structures.

**a.** The tubular fold of skin into which the penis is retracted, in many animals, as the horse, bull, dog, etc. Also † = PREPUCE.

**1555** EDEN *Decades* I. VIII. 38 The men of this countrey inclose theyr priuie members in a gourde... In other places of that tract, they thrust the synew within the sheethe therof [orig. *intra vaginam mentularem neruum reducunt*]. **1607** MARKHAM *Caval.* I. 70 If, after your foales bee gelt, their cods and sheathes happen to swell exceeding much. *c* **1720** W. GIBSON *Farrier's Guide* I. ii. (1738) 15 Its outer cover, or Sheath, is nothing else but a production of the Scarfskin Hide and fleshy Pannicle. *c* **1800** J. CUNDALL *Sch. Arts* 34 The Cure. First throw him [the bull], and draw his pizzle out of his sheath.

**b.** *Bot.* A tubular or enrolled part or organ of a plant; the part of an expanded organ that is rolled round a stem or other body, as the spathe of a flower, the lower part of the leaves of grasses, etc.

**1671** GREW *Anat. Pl.* I. i. (1682) 10 The Plume in Corn is trussed up within a membranous Sheath. **1720** P. BLAIR *Bot. Ess.* i. 28 Sometimes they are covered with a Vagina or Sheath at the top, which appears blackish in the middle of the Flourish, until it is fully blown, and then the Sheath falls off, and the two Portions separate. **1796** WITHERING *Brit. Plants* (ed. 3) I. 81 *Sheath* (spatha), a species of Calyx, exemplified in the Crocus, the Iris, and the Daffodil. **1832** LINDLEY *Introd. Bot.* I. ii. 95 Occasionally the petiole embraces the branch from which it springs, and in such case is said to be sheathing; and is even called a sheath, or vagina, as in grasses. **1847** TENNYSON *Princess* v. 28, I was.. More crumpled than a poppy from the sheath. **1847** MRS. R. LEE *Afr. Wand.* vii. (1854) 100 He found a large spatha, or sheath, full of cocoa-nuts. **1855** LONGF. *Hiaw.* xiii. 180 The maize-ears full and shining gleamed from bursting sheaths of verdure. **1861** BENTLEY *Man. Bot.* 174 This sheath in all true Grasses terminates above in a membranous appendage. **1876** GEO. ELIOT *Dan. Der.* xx. II. 11 The cheap clothing that moulding itself on her feet seemed an adornment as choice as the sheaths of buds. **1882–4** COOKE *Brit. Fresh-w. Algæ* I. 220 Cells forming a filament (*Trichome*) usually included in a tubular homogenous or lamellate sheath (*vagina*).

**c.** *Bot.* 'A limiting layer of surrounding cellular tissue' (B. D. Jackson *Gloss. Bot. Terms*, 1900). Also 'the lower, longer portion of the cell-wall in division in Oedogonium' (*Ibid.* Add.). ***bundle-sheath***: see BUNDLE *sb.* 4.

**1884** BOWER & SCOTT *De Bary's Phaner.* 6 When a layer (simple or compound) surrounds a tissue, which differs from it, it is termed relatively to the latter a sheath. **1897** tr. *Strasburger's Text-bk. Bot.* (1903) 203 The glucose which is thus produced in the leaves passes out of the mesophyll cells into the elongated cells of the vascular bundle-sheaths. The glucose and maltose are transferred in these conducting sheaths through the leaf-stalks into the stem.

**d.** *Anat.* The connective tissue covering which closely invests a part or elongated organ, and binds it together and holds it in place. Cf. FASCIA 3.

**1805** J. F. D. JONES *Treat. Suppress. Hemorrhage* (1810) 54 A coagulum then, formed at the mouth of the artery, and within its sheath. **1843** R. J. GRAVES *Syst. Clin. Med.* xxx. 404 There was.. no inflammation of it's [i.e. the spinal cord's] membranes or effusion into its sheath. **1872** HUXLEY *Physiol.* i. 10 The sheath is continued at each end into a tendon. **1873** J. ANGELL *Elem. Anim. Physiol.* v. 70 Each primitive fibre is invested with a delicate sheath of fine, tough, elastic, transparent, structureless membrane, termed the *sarcolemma* or *myolemma*. **1897** *Allbutt's Syst. Med.* III. 819 The outermost of the three layers [of the intussuscepted bowel] is known as the intussuscipient, the sheath, or the receiving layer.

**e.** A tube-like case, covering, or protection, e.g. a hair-follicle, the covering of the sting, etc. of an insect.

**1774** GOLDSM. *Nat. Hist.* VIII. 68 The sheath sometimes sticks so fast in the wound, that the animal is obliged to leave it behind; by which the bee soon after dies. **1801** tr. *Haller's First Lines Physiol.* 205 The hair, with both its cylindrical sheaths, arrives at a cutaneous pore, goes out through it, and forces the epidermis into a similar sheath. **1820** SHELLEY *Witch of Atlas* xv, And there lay Visions.. Each in its thin sheath, like a chrysalis. **1828** STARK *Elem. Nat. Hist.* II. 320 Sheath of the sucker [in *Membranaceæ*] with only two or three apparent joints. **1834** MCMURTRIE *Cuvier's Anim. Kingd.* 399 The sheath of this apparatus [the 'sucker' of Hemipterous insects] is at these times frequently bent into an angle. **1885** HALDANE *Workshop Rec.* Ser. II. 369 The softening or destruction of the hair-sheaths either by lime or by putrefaction.

**f.** The covering of certain shell-fish, e.g. the razor-shell.

**1815** S. BROOKES *Conchol.* 156 Sheath. Solen Vagina and Siliqua. **1822** J. PARKINSON *Outl. Oryctol.* 174 Bivalve shells, contained in a tubular sheath distinct from the valves. **1828** STARK *Elem. Nat. Hist.* I. 114 Sheath tapering,.. the valves of the shell elongated.

**g.** The lorica of certain protozoans, etc.

**1841** T. R. JONES *Anim. Kingd.* 34 The Tubiporidæ are enclosed in a calcareous or coriaceous sheath or tube. **1859** J. R. GREENE *Man. Anim. Kingd., Protozoa* vii. 61, Fig. 14 showing animal [*Vaginicola valvata*] contracted within its sheath. **1878** F. BELL *Gegenbaur's Comp. Anat.* 121 Where the proliferating Polyps are provided with a sheath, the generative buds are always enclosed by the same test as the Polyps themselves.

**h.** 'The horny covering of the bill or feet of a bird; esp. a sort of false cere of some birds, as the sheathbills, jägers, etc.' (*Cent. Dict.* 1891).

**1781** PENNANT *Genera of Birds* 43 Upper of the upper mandible lodged in a corneous sheath. **1886** NEWTON in *Encycl. Brit.* XXI. 782/1 *note*, A strange fallacy arose early ..that this case or sheath [of the sheathbill] was movable.

**i.** The elytron or outer hard wing-case of a coleopterous insect.

**1826** KIRBY & SP. *Entomol.* IV. 368 There are some beetles that have neither wings nor sheath. **1854** *Eng. Cycl., Nat. Hist.* II. 62/2 From this character of having the wings in a sheath, the term *Coleoptera* was applied... The superior wings, which form the sheath, are generally called elytra. **1910** D. W. THOMPSON tr. *Aristotle's Hist. Anim.* I. 5 Some are coleopterous or sheath-winged, for they have their wings in a sheath or shard.

**j.** The fold of skin into which the claws of a feline animal are retracted.

**1774** GOLDSM. *Nat. Hist.* III. 200 The cat kind are.. remarkable for the sharpness..of their claws, which thrust forth from their sheath when they seize their prey.

**k.** A contraceptive made of thin rubber worn on the penis; a condom.

**1861** G. DRYSDALE *Elem. Soc. Science* (ed. 4) II. 349 The accessory and sensational part of the venereal act is obtained ..by the use of the sheath (which is..very frequent, but more so on the continent than in this country). **1897** *Science of Generation* xx. 235 The use of various mechanical contrivances, such as French Safes, Condom Sheaths, etc. **1919** M. C. STOPES *Let. to Working Mothers* 14 Some men like to use a sheath, and this is quite a safe method. **1962** *Lancet* 2 June 1194/1 The survey shows that the sheath and coitus interruptus are still the methods most commonly used for contraception in this country. **1977** E. J. TRIMMER et al. *Visual Dict. Sex* (1978) xiv. 134 Careful attention must be taken in the rolling on of the sheath so as not to damage it.

**l.** A long close-fitting dress or skirt, usu. with a slit or pleat on one side. Cf. *sheath dress, gown*, etc., sense 7 a.

**1904** H. O. STURGIS *Belchamber* xx. 273 A sinuous young lady, clad in a sheath of some glittering, shimmering blackness. **1932** in C. W. Cunnington *Eng. Women's Clothes in Present Cent.* (1952) vii. 222 The moulded sheath glorifies the body beautifully. **1958** *Observer* 20 July 9/5 Dresses for day and evening are cut as figure-gripping sheaths to which are added built-out and stiffened hip-pockets of a vast size. **1976** G. MOFFAT *Over Sea to Death* ii. 24 She wore a bright green jersey sheath which emphasised her sharp angles.

**3. a.** *Photogr.* (See quots.)

**1890** WOODBURY *Encycl. Photogr.* 630 *Sheath*, an arrangement for holding the dry plate in detective cameras so that they are protected from the light and can be conveniently changed at will. They are usually made of darkened metal. **1892** *Photogr. Ann.* II. 316 The lens and finders are uncovered by sliding sheaths or covers of the same leather.

**b.** *Electronics.* The anode of a thermionic valve. (Disused.)

**1919** R. D. BANGAY *Oscillation Valve* 57 It [*sc.* the Fleming Valve] consists of a metal or carbon filament (F) and a metal cylinder (S) (usually called the sheath) surrounding the filament..the sheath [thus forming] the anode of the valve. **1922** GLAZEBROOK *Dict. Appl. Physics* II. 880/2 A battery..has its positive terminal connected to the sheath.., and its negative one to the filament.

**c.** *Physics.* A region of charged particles or plasma surrounding an object.

**1923** *Science* 12 Oct. 290/1 Around each negative electrode there is thus a sheath of definite thickness containing only positive ions and neutral atoms. **1955** A. VON ENGEL *Ionized Gases* viii. 194 The anode is therefore covered with a luminous sheath—the anode glow which is sometimes divided into several luminous spots. **1973** KRALL & TRIVELPIECE *Princ. Plasma Physics* i. 46 If the potential of the probe is much larger than the local potential of the plasma, the probe attracts electrons and repels ions, forming a sheath region around the probe, which is electron-rich.

†**4.** The razor-fish or solen. [Cf. 2 f.] *Obs.*

**1722** DIAPER tr. *Oppian's Halieut.* I. 482 Here slender Sheaths, and juicy Oysters hide.

**5.** *Sc.* and *dial.* = KNITTING-*sheath.*

**1893** *Longman's Mag.* Feb. 378 Their straw sheaths tucked into the bands of their tousers [aprons], they clicked merrily away with their needles as they walked along the road.

**6.** A structure or banking of loose stones to prevent the overflow of a river.

**1850** in OGILVIE, and in later Dicts.

**7.** *attrib.* and *Comb.* **a.** Simple attrib. often passing into adj. (applied to dress), as ***sheath dress, gown, model, skirt***, etc.; also ***sheath-like, -maker***; **sheath-knife**, a dagger-like knife encased in a sheath; **sheath-piling** = *sheet-piling* (SHEET *sb.*[1] 12 b).

**1925** in C. W. Cunnington *Eng. Women's Clothes in Present Cent.* (1952) vi. 184 The beltless *sheath dress. **1945** N. L. MCCLUNG *Stream runs Fast* xv. 132 She was a sweet-faced little violet of a woman, in a sheath dress of silver cloth. **1980** 'M. HEBDEN' *Pel under Pressure* xiii. 129 She had one of those sheath dresses on. Fitted like a skin. **1908** *Westm. Gaz.* 12 May 5/1 They were what are called *sheath gowns or skirts *à fourreau*. **1837** CARLYLE *Fr. Rev.* III. IV. i, She purchases a large *sheath-knife in the Palais Royal. **1897** KIPLING *Capt. Cour.* viii. 165 The leather belt with the sheath-knife at the back. **1842** LOUDON *Suburban Hort.* 15 Flowers with *sheath-like bracts. **1899** *Outlook* 7 Jan. 725/2 The skirts cut in a sheath-like scantiness. **1530** PALSGR. 266/2 *Sheth maker, *gaignier*. **1766** ENTICK *London* IV. 357 The third sort were sheath-makers for swords. **1902** *Encycl. Brit.* XXVI. 437/2 This can be accomplished..by careful *sheath-piling to retain the sides of the excavation. **1903** *Daily Chron.* 24 Jan. 8/4 *Sheath-skirts..will still enjoy popularity.

**b.** *Nat. Hist.*, as ***sheath-edge, -leaf***; **sheath bill**, a sea-bird of the genus *Chionis*, having the basal part of the bill ensheathed in a horny case; **sheath cell** *Anat.*, a Schwann cell (SCHWANN b); **sheathclaw**, a lizard of the genus *Thecodactylus*; **sheath-horned** *a.*, having hollow horns enclosing a horn-core; **sheath (razor-) shell**, the razor-shell; †**sheath-scale** *Bot.* (see quot.); †**sheath-stone** (see quot.); †**sheath-wing** = 2 i; **sheath-winged**, having the wings encased in elytra, coleopterous, vaginipennate. See also SHEAT-FISH.

**1781** PENNANT *Genera of Birds* 43 *Sheath-bill. **1854** A. ADAMS, etc. *Man. Nat. Hist.* 47 Sheathbills (Chionidæ). **1902** *Edin. Rev.* Jan. 208 A mother penguin cannot leave her egg for a moment but what a sheath-bill, Chionis, dashes its beak into it. **1906** *Sheath cell [see SCHWANN b]. **1967** D. BODIAN in G. C. Quarton et al. *Neurosciences* 13/1 Axons that are enclosed by a single fold of a sheath cell are referred to as unmyelinated axons. **1850** P. H. GOSSE *Nat. Hist., Reptiles* 90 The Smooth *Sheath-claw..is a native of Jamaica. **1870** HOOKER *Stud. Flora* 411 Carex Buxbaumii ..*sheath-edges filamentous. **1871** DARWIN *Desc. Man* II. xii. (1890) 357 A bull, goat, or other *sheath-horned ruminant. **1766** *Compl. Farmer* s.v. *Vegetation* 7 S 2/2 Above there is a mark of the *sheath-leaf, which was pulled [off the stalk]. **1893** *Jrnl. R. Agric. Soc.* Dec. 821 The spirally twisted sheath-leaves are noticeable when the ear is beginning to form. **1819** TURTON *Conchol. Dict.* 159 *Solen Vagina.* *Sheath Razor-shell. **1796** WITHERING *Brit. Plants* (ed. 3) I. 81 **Sheath-scale*, a membrane found at the top of the sheathes which surround the stem of Grasses, just where the sheath ends, and the proper leaf begins. **1712** *Mus. Thoresby.* (1713) 444 The *Sheath-Shell, as it is commonly called, because of its Form. **1815** BURROW *Elem. Conchol.* 194 Solen. Razor or Sheath Shell. **1681** GREW *Musæum* III. §i. i. 265 The *Sheath-Stone. *Solenites.* Like the petrify'd shell of the Sheath-Fish. **1882** VINES tr. *Sachs' Bot.* 199 A circular projection..on which the *sheath-teeth are formed. **1704** PETIVER *Gazophyl.* II. Tab. xvii, Its Shoulders are yellower than the *Sheath Wings. **1646** SIR T. BROWNE *Pseud. Ep.* III. xv. 141 All vaginipennous or *sheathwinged insects, as Beetles and Dorrs. **1910** D. W. THOMPSON tr. *Aristotle's Hist. Anim.* I. 5 Some are coleopterous or sheath-winged.

†**sheath**[2]. *Obs.* Forms: α. 4 schethe, 6 sheth(e, 7 (? *misprint*) skeath, 7–8 sheath, 9 seath; β. 8 sheat, sheet. [Prob. the same word as SHETH. The specific sense below is in WFlem. *scheeberd, scheidberd* (*berd* = board). It is also one of the meanings of Norw. *skeid*; the form *skeath*, if not a misprint, is prob. Scandinavian.] In ploughs of an old type, the bar connecting the beam and sole in front.

α. **1356–7** *Durham Acc. Rolls* (Surtees) 384 It. in 24 schethes et 24 moldebred cum jugis spakes, 3*s.* 6*d.* **1523–34** FITZHERB. *Husb.* §3 The sheldbrede is a brode pece of wodde, fast pinned to the ryghte syde of the shethe in the ferther ende. **1613** MARKHAM *Eng. Husbandm.* I. Former Pt. iii. B 2, The skeath..is a peece of woode of two foote and a halfe in length, and of eight inches in breadth, and two inches in thicknesse; it is driuen extreamly hard into the Plough-beame, slopewise. **1616** SURFLET & MARKHAM *Country Farm* VII. xvi. 662 Of it [the Ash] also is made all manner of Plow and Cart-timber whatsoeuer, as Beames, Heads, Skeathes [etc.]. **1688** HOLME *Armoury* III. 333/2 The Sheath [of a Plow] is that which holds the Beam and Throck together. **1765** A. DICKSON *Treat. Agric.* (ed. 2) 164 According to the position of the sheath, the earth of the furrow is turned over more suddenly. *a* **1817** W. MUIR *Poems* (1818) 8 (*Elegy on old plough*), The very pettle, riest an' seath, Are pil'd up for a fiery death.

β. **1733** TULL *Horse-Hoeing Husb.* xxi. 301 The Plow-Tail consists of..the Share P., and the Sheat Q. **1766** *Compl. Farmer* s.v. 6 T 1/2 The sheat, or as it is sometimes called the fore-sheat, there being another piece of timber behind it called the hinder sheat, should be..fastened to the beam by a retch. **1791** J. TOWNSEND *Journ. Spain* (1792) I. 229 An English mechanic will not readily conceive how a plough can be made..without any sheets to support the handle and the share.

**sheath**, variant of SEATH *Obs.*, brine-pit.

**1610** HOLLAND *Camden's Brit.* I. 609 (Cheshire) There be two wells of salt water... Sheathes they call them. *c* **1682** J. COLLINS *Salt & Fishery* 2 At Middlewich there are seven Pits or Bryne sheaths, which yield most rich Bryne.

**sheath-anchor**, obs. form of SHEET-ANCHOR.

**sheathe** (ʃiːð), *v.* Also *techn.* **sheath** (ʃiːθ). Forms: 5 schethe, 5–6 shethe, (7 sheate), 6–9 sheath, 6– sheathe. [f. SHEATH[1].]

†**1.** *trans.* To fit or furnish (a sword, etc.) with a sheath. *Obs.*

? *a* **1400** *Morte Arth.* 3853 He schokkes owtte a schorte knyfe schethede with silvere. **1596** SHAKS. *Tam. Shr.* IV. i. 138 Walters dagger was not come from sheathing.

**2.** To put (a sword, dagger, etc.) into a sheath or scabbard. ***to sheathe the sword*** (fig.): to cease hostilities, to put an end to war or enmity.

*c* **1430** *Pilgr. Lyf Manhode* I. xxxii. (1869) 20, I bithouht me what i shulde do..with þilke swerd yshethed, seled, wrapped. **1530** PALSGR. 702/1, I shethe a knyfe or a sworde, I put them in to their shethe... Shethe your sworde, you be man good ynoughe. **1590** GREENE *Orl. Fur.* (1599) 52 Mars come thundring downe, And neuer sheathe thy swift reuenging sword. **1641** J. JACKSON *True Evang. T.* III. 213 Still allowing to Kings and their Senates, and Counsailes, right of drawing or sheathing the sword. *a* **1660** *Contemp. Hist. Irel.* (Ir. Archæol. Soc.) I. 273 The Confederate Catholicks of Ireland were iointly and seuerally sworne,.. neuer to sheate theire sworde untill they see the lustre of religion florish in Ireland. **1737** POPE *Hor. Epist.* II. i. 140 In Days of Ease, when now the weary Sword Was sheath'd, and Luxury with Charles restor'd. **1749** SMOLLETT tr. *Gil Blas* VII. i. (1782) III. 7 Enough (said I to him, sheathing my sword) I am not a brute, to refuse to hear reason. **1812** BYRON *Ch. Har.* II. lxxii, Those scarfs of blood-red shall be redder before The sabre is sheathed and the battle is o'er. **1841** ELPHINSTONE *Hist. India* IX. i. II. 263 He restrained himself sufficiently to sheath his sword. **1849** MACAULAY *Hist. Eng.* v. I. 575 The sword should not be sheathed till he had been brought to condign punishment as a traitor. **1891** MORRIS *Poems by Way* (1896) 210 And then the ancient blade he sheathed.

†**b.** with *up*. Also *transf. Obs.*

**1607** R. TURNER *Nosce Te* C 3 b, Being soundly bangde he sheathde his dagger vp. **1615** HIERON *Dign. Preaching* 9 May I..like Salomons sluggard, sheathe vp my hands into my bosome and renounce husbandrie? **1640** tr. *Verdere's Rom. of Rom.* II. x. 35 But perceiving no body to appear, he presently sheathed up his sword. **1738** WESLEY *Hymns*, '*Long have I view'd*' vi, I will not..beg Thee to sheath up thy Sword.

**c.** *transf.* To bury (a sword) as in a sheath (e.g. *in* an enemy's body). Also with obj. an animal's tusk, claw, etc.

**1584** A. MUNDAY *Fedele & Fortunio* 1255 in *Arch. Stud. neu. Spr.* CXXIII. 72 Attilia tolde me, that her mistresse had made a request, To Crack-stone, to sheathe his sworde in your brest. **1592** SHAKS. *Ven. & Ad.* 617 A churlish swine ..Whose tushes neuer sheathd, he whetteth still. *Ibid.* 1116 The..swine Sheath'd..the tuske in his soft groine. **1593** —— *3 Hen. VI*, v. v. 70 Dispatch me heere: Here sheath thy Sword, Ile pardon thee my death. **1614** GORGES *Lucan* I. 37 Within his [a bull's] throat they sheath'd the knife. **1667** DRYDEN *Ind. Emp.* IV. iv, 'Tis in my breast she sheaths her Dagger now. **1749** FIELDING *Tom Jones* XVI. x, He beat down his guard, and sheathed one half of his sword in the body of the said gentleman. **1858** G. MACDONALD *Phantastes* xxi. 270 The hand of his foe..still grasped the hilt of the dagger sheathed in the wound.

**d.** *fig.* To lay aside, cause to be laid aside (hostility, malice). Now *rare* or *Obs.*

**1598** SHAKS. *Merry W.* II. iii. 88 Sheath thy impatience: throw cold water on thy Choller. **1752** YOUNG *Brothers* I. i, Sheath your resentments in your father's peace. **1773** J. ALLEN *Serm. S. Mary's Oxf.* 16 This ought to sheath plebeian malignity.

**e.** To retract or draw in (the claws).

**1681** GREW *Musæum* I. 12 The Leopard..always keeps the Claws of his fore-feet turned up from the ground, and sheath'd as it were in the Skin of his Toes. **1687** DRYDEN *Hind & P.* III. 270 He sheathes his paws, uncurls his angry mane. **1801** SOUTHEY *Thalaba* IX. xviii, With tranquil eyes and talons sheathed, The ounce expects his liberty. **1813** SHELLEY *Q. Mab* VIII. 126 His [the lion's] claws are sheathed.

**3.** To cover or encase (esp. a person or part of the body) *in* (something, usually protective).

**1632** MASSINGER *City Madam* IV. ii, Thy procurer Shall be sheath'd in Velvet. *a* **1691** BOYLE *Hist. Air* (1692) 140 The [petrifying] spring..sheaths everything with stony cases. **1735** SOMERVILLE *Chase* II. 453 In meet Array, Sheath'd in refulgent Arms, a noble Band Advance. **1816** BYRON *Siege of Corinth* xxiii. 9 Many a bosom, sheathed in brass, Strew'd the earth like broken glass. **1829** SCOTT *Anne of G.* i, Warriors sheathed in complete steel. **1876** GEO. ELIOT *Dan. Der.* lvi, She started impulsively to her full height, sheathed in her white shawl.

*transf.* and *fig.* **1860** EMERSON *Cond. Life, Fate* Wks. (Bohn) II. 311 People seem sheathed in their tough organization. **1885** *Truth* 28 May 850/1 Plumpness sheathes the nerves and gives an impression of good humour.

**b.** To cover from view. *rare.*

**1593** SHAKS. *Lucr.* 397 Her eyes like Marigolds had sheath'd their light.

†**c.** ***to sheathe up***: to envelop so as to confine or obstruct. *Obs. rare.*

**1661** BOYLE *Cert. Physiol. Ess.* (1669) 146 Those active parts of a body which are of differing Natures, when they are as it were Sheath'd up, or Wedg'd in amongst others in the texture of a Concrete. **1764** *Museum Rust.* III. xiii. 64 The rich fat wort sheathes up the pores of the hop, and, as it were, embalms the leaves.

**4.** †**a.** *Med.* To mitigate the acridity or pungency of (a drug) by the use of an emollient vehicle. *Obs.*

**1731** ARBUTHNOT *Aliments* v. (1735) 130 Other Substances..opposite to..Acrimony which are call'd demulcent or mild, because they blunt or sheath those sharp Salts..such as Pease, Beans [etc.]. **1753** *Chambers' Cycl.* Suppl. s.v. *Wine*, It had a pleasing softness that sheathed the acrimony of the spirit, and covered the bitter taste of the hop. **1811** A. T. THOMSON *Lond. Disp.* (1818) 546 Its acrimony requires to be sheathed with some bland powder, as starch.

**b.** *gen.* To mitigate the painfulness of.

**1820** HAZLITT *Lect. Dram. Lit.* 77 The barb of misfortune is sheathed in the mildness of the writer's temperament. **1851** MRS. BROWNING *Casa Guidi Wind.* I. 18 The innumerous Sweet songs which for this Italy outrang From older singers' lips, who sang..with pang Sheathed into music, touched the heart of us So finely, that the pity scarcely pained!

**5.** (Often *sheath.*) **a.** To cover (a ship, a door, roof, etc.) with a sheathing of metal.

**1615** R. COCKS *Diary* (Hakl. Soc.) I. 62 We..brought her agrownd before the English howse to sheath her [the ship]. **1627** CAPT. SMITH *Seaman's Gram.* ii. 13 Barnacles..will eat thorow all the Plankes if she be not sheathed, which is as casing the Hull vnder water with Tar, and Haire, close couered ouer with thin boords fast nailed to the Hull. *a* **1642** SIR W. MONSON *Naval Tracts* III. (1704) 346/2 They Sheath Ships with Lead. **1691** T. H[ALE] *Acc. New Invent.* p. xxviii, There was no occasion for a good while to sheath any of the Kings Ships. **1763** *Brit. Mag.* IV. 332 His majesty's frigate the Alarm..was sheathed with copper, by way of trial. **1849** ROCK *Ch. of Fathers* I. iii. 233 At the more solemn festivals, the high Altar in the richer churches, was sheathed in a gold or silver frontal, studded with precious stones. **1885** CLARK RUSSELL *Strange Voy.* I. ii. 21 The ship..had been newly sheathed, and the yellow metal..gleamed dully, like old gold. **1883** P. H. HUNTER *Story Dan.* ix. 161 The exterior of the dome is sheathed with burnished copper. **1909** *Blackw. Mag.* Sept. 346/2 The doors [of the temple] are sheathed in silver.

**b.** To cover (a tree-trunk) with a 'sheathing'.

**1842** LOUDON *Suburban Hort.* 431 Sheathing the stems of standard trees..should not be neglected.

**c.** To cover a telegraph cable with a protective envelope.

**1884** *Pall Mall Gaz.* 17 Apr. 11/2 These wire-sheathing machines..will sheath fifty miles of cables in a day.

**d.** To place (a photographic plate) in a sheath.

**1892** *Photogr. Ann.* II. 263 With regard to sheaths for the plates—these may be used,..but in the course of several years..no plate has ever been sheathed.

**6.** *Nat. Hist.* To surround with a 'sheath' or covering.

**1664** POWER *Exp. Philos.* I. 36 Those black filaments.. which are sheathed in her [the snail's] horns. **1796** WITHERING *Brit. Plants* (ed. 3) II. 215 Leaves rather longer than the joints of the stem, not at all sheathing it. **1830** LINDLEY *Nat. Syst. Bot.* 154 Leaves alternate, slightly sheathing at the base. **1870** HOOKER *Stud. Flora* 109 Stem.. sheathed below by obtuse leafless stipules. **1872** HUXLEY *Physiol.* i. 10 A mass of red flesh, sheathed in connective tissue. **1882-4** COOKE *Brit. Fresh-w. Algæ* I. 195 A hyaline bristle, which is sheathed at its base.

**sheathe**, bad spelling of SCYTHE.

*a* **1660** *Contemp. Hist. Irel.* (Ir. Archæol. Soc.) III. 125.

**sheathed** (ʃiːθd), *a. Nat. Hist.* [f. SHEATH¹ + -ED².] Having or surrounded by a sheath; put in or capable of being withdrawn into a sheath.

**1664** POWER *Exp. Philos.* I. 16 Mites in Cheese..are sheath'd and crustaceous Animals (as Scarabees and such like Insects are). **1771** J. R. FORSTER *Flora Amer. Septentr.* 4 *Panicum clandestin.* Panic grass, sheathed. Pensylva. Kalm. **1796** WITHERING *Brit. Plants* (ed. 3) I. 81 *Sheathed Fruit-stalk* (spadix), one that is furnished with a sheath. **1835** KIRBY *Hab. & Inst. Anim.* I. viii. 238 The sheathed polype.

*Comb.* **1668** WILKINS *Real Char.* II. v. §2. 127 Sheathed winged Insects, commonly called Beetles or Scarabs. **1863** WOOD *Illustr. Nat. Hist.* III. 460 Coleoptera, a word of Greek origin, signifying sheathed-winged animals.

**sheathed** (ʃiːðd; *techn.* ʃiːθt), *ppl. a.* [f. SHEATHE *v.* + -ED¹.]

**1.** Of a sword, etc.: Put into or encased in a sheath.

**1810** SCOTT *Lady of L.* III. iii, With sheathed broad-sword in his hand. **1825** T. HOOK *Sayings* Ser. II. *Passion & Princ.* v. III. 25 A pair of sheathed scissors. **1848** DICKENS *Dombey* xlii, Softly laying his velvet hand, as a cat might have laid its sheathed claws, on Mr. Dombey's arm. **1903** SIR A. H. LAYARD *Autobiog.* I. iii. 144 His silver-sheathed yataghan.

**2.** Of a ship: Having the bottom covered with sheathing. [SHEATHE *v.* 5.]

**1889** WELCH *Text Bk. Naval Archit.* viii. 105 Passing now to the sheathed ships, the butts of the flat keel plate are double chain riveted.

**sheather¹** (ˈʃiːθə(r)). Also 4-6 shether, 5 schedare, schethare. [f. SHEATH¹ + -ER¹.] A sheath-maker.

**1379** *Poll-tax W. Riding* in *Yorks. Archæol. Jrnl.* VI. 43 Johannes de Breres, Shether vjd. **1419** *Liber Albus* (Rolls) I. 654 Botelmakers et Shethers jurati ad regulandum Misterum suum. *c* **1440** *Promp. Parv.* 444/2 Schedare, or schethare, *vaginarius*. *c* **1515** *Cocke Lorell's B.* 9 Whyte tanners, galyors, and shethers. **1583** *Streat Bk.*, John Cutler, sheather, for riding his mare through the corne, 6d.

**sheather²** (ˈʃiːðə(r)). [f. SHEATHE *v.* + -ER¹.] One who or that which sheathes.

**1761** *Ann. Reg.* IV. *Usef. Proj.* 123 When the salts above described have lost their points, in the absorbing sheather.

**sheathery** (ˈʃiːθərɪ). [f. SHEATH¹ + -ERY.] Sheaths and similar articles collectively.

**1857** *P.O. Directory Yorksh.* 1052 Sheathery Manufacturers.

†**sheath-fish**. *Obs.* [f. SHEATH¹ + FISH *sb.*] The razor-fish.

**1602** CAREW *Cornwall* I. 32 The Sheath, or Rasor-fish, resembles in length and bignesse a mans finger. **1603** OWEN *Pembrokesh.* (1892) 126 Sheth or haft fishe. **1672** *Phil. Trans.* VII. 5022 A Sheath-fish, which is very plentiful in New-England; a delicate fish, cover'd with a thin shell and of the colour of a Musle. **1681** GREW *Musæum* I. §vi. ii. 143 The Sheath-Fish, commonly so called from its similitude to the sheath of a Knife. *Solen. Vnguis.*

†**sheath-fish** *Obs.*: see SAITHE.

**sheath-fish**: see SHEAT-FISH.

**sheathing** (ˈʃiːθɪŋ, ˈʃiːðɪŋ), *vbl. sb.* Also 5 schedynge, 7 shething. [f. SHEATHE *v.* + -ING¹.]

**1. a.** The action of putting into a sheath.

**1499** *Promp. Parv.* 444/2 (Pynson) Schedynge, *vaginatio*. **1596** [see SHEATHE *v.* 1].

**b.** The action of putting on a protective layer to a ship's bottom; also, †the method or manner in which this is done.

**1623** in Foster *Eng. Factories Ind.* (1908) II. 310 Dockes for the sheathinge or carreeninge of theire shipps. *a* **1642** SIR W. MONSON *Naval Tracts* III. (1704) 346/2 Another Sheathing is with double Planks. **1676** J. WOOD *Jrnl.* in *Acc. Sev. Late Voy.* I. (1694) 153 Mr. John Sish took no ordinary Care in Strengthening her, and in her Shething, which was as well performed as in any Ship that ever sailed on the Sea. **1748** *Anson's Voy.* III. vii. 367 Having by that time compleated the new sheathing of the first course..they continued the paying and sheathing the bottom. **1849** LONGF. *Building of Ship* 191 The..seething Caldron, that.. overflowed With the black tar, heated for the sheathing.

**2.** A protective layer or covering laid on the outside of the bottom of a wooden ship, to protect the planks from the borings of marine animals. Formerly of boards, etc., later usually of thin plates of metal (copper). Also a wooden covering sometimes used to protect the submerged parts of iron ships from corrosion by the water.

**1587** in J. S. Corbett *Pap. rel. Sp. War* (1898) 226 Decayed timbers..under the sheathing [*MS.* Shething]. **1633** T. JAMES *Voy.* 32 We saw some of the sheathing swim by vs. **1691** T. H[ALE] *Acc. New Invent.* p. xx, She had her sheathing strip'd at seven Years end to repair the Plank, but not for any defect in the Sheathing it self. **1728** in *6th Rep. Dep. Kpr. Rec.* App. II. 155 A new method for preserving the plank and sheathing of Ships. **1784** J. KING *Cook's 3rd Voy.* VI. v. III. 289 The carpenters..proceeded to rip off the sheathing that had been injured by the ice, from the starboard side. **1849** CUPPLES *Green Hand* ix. (1856) 99 A fathom or two from the bright copper of her sheathing along the water-line. **1886** SIR N. BARNABY in *Encycl. Brit.* XXI. 819/1 The plank, or skin, or sheathing of a ship, both external and internal, is of various thicknesses.

**b.** *gen.* A covering or envelope in which something is encased for protection or ornament; material prepared for use as an envelope or casing. Chiefly in technical applications: e.g. a covering of boards, plates of metal, or other material, fitted to the surface of a wall, roof, or other part of a building, a piece of machinery, or the like.

**1859** *Habits of Gd. Society* iii. 132 A loose covering is both more comfortable and more healthy than a tight sheathing of cloth [*i.e.* tight trousers]. **1867** W. H. SMYTH *Coal & Coal-mining* 116 Upon the upper one the plates or segments of tubbing are built up, sheathing of pitch pine, ⅜ or ½ inch thick, being inserted between all the contact surfaces, and the vertical joints broken, as in stone work. **1868** *Art Jrnl.* 1 Feb. 35/2 Mural sheathings imitative of the finest Persian patterns. **1881** RAYMOND *Mining Gloss., Sheathing*, a close partition or covering of planks. **1909** *Chamb. Jrnl.* Oct. 687/2 The sea-cow..is..skinned—for the back sheathing is thick and hard in texture, rendering it useful for many purposes.

**c.** Sheathing paper.

**1859** *Stationers' Hand-bk.* 81 *Sheathing*, a large thick brown paper, used for ships' bottoms, usually made to order.

**3.** A banking of loose stones to prevent overflowing of a river. Cf. SHEATH¹ 6; also ***camp-sheathing***, var. of CAMPSHEDDING.

**1867** F. FRANCIS *Angling* viii. 246 Working his bait.. behind piles, and under the apron or sheathing [of the weir].

**4.** *attrib.* (sense 2, 2 b), as ***sheathing board, copper, felt, lead, paper***; **sheathing-nail** (see quot.).

**1628** in Foster *Eng. Factories India* (1909) III. 251 Planck, *sheathinge boards, laths. **1773** *Cook's 1st Voy.* III. iii. in Hawkesw. *Voy.* III. 546 We saw by the light of the moon the sheathing boards from the bottom of the vessel floating away all round her. **1800** *Hull Advertiser* 20 Sept. 2/1 Small cordage, sheathing paper, *sheathing copper, and ships stores. **1840** R. H. DANA *Bef. Mast* xxxii. 124 Sheets of sheathing-copper. **1834-6** P. BARLOW *Manuf.* §1064 in *Encycl. Metrop.* (1845) VIII. 763/1 Sheathing felt is applied in coppered ships immediately below the copper. **1691** T. H[ALE] *Acc. New Invent.* 83 The Goodness of *Sheathing-Lead to line the Bread-rooms. **1611** COTGR., *Clou d'estoupe*, a speake, or *sheathing nayle; vsed in ships. *c* **1850** *Rudim. Nav.* (Weale) 134 *Sheathing nails* are used to fasten wood sheathing on the ship's bottom, to preserve the plank and prevent the filling nails from tearing it too much. *Sheathing nails*, for nailing copper sheathing, are of metal cast in moulds, about 1¼ inch long. **1794** MORSE *Amer. Geog.* 214 Writing and printing paper, *sheathing and wrapping paper. **1861** J. SPENCE *Amer. Union* v. 182 Paper is under a prohibitory duty of 30 per cent., but sheathing paper pays only 10 per cent.

**sheathing** (ˈʃiːθɪŋ), *ppl. a.* [f. SHEATHE *v.* + -ING².] That sheathes.

**1847** TENNYSON *Princess* v. 39 And transient in a trice From what was left of faded woman-slough To sheathing splendours and the golden scale Of harness. **1908** *Smithsonian Misc. Collect.* LII. 16 A sheathing projection on occiput, and one above opercle.

**b.** *Bot.*

**1778** *Encycl. Brit.* (ed. 2) II. 1297/1 *Vaginans*, [of a leaf] sheathing, or with its base forming a cylindrical tube investing the stem. **1796** WITHERING *Brit. Plants* (ed. 3) I. 25 This long purplish substance which stands upright within the sheathing conical Calyx. **1847** W. E. STEELE *Field Bot.* 209 The sheathing bases of the leaves. **1861** S. THOMSON *Wild Fl.* I. (ed. 4) 40 The attachment of the leaves of parallel-veined plants is often what is called *sheathing*, as we see in the grasses,..in which the leaf springs from a sheath..which embraces the stem. **1884** BOWER & SCOTT *De Bary's Phaner.* 141 Membranous sheathing layers of a granular substance.

**c.** *Anat.* (See quot.)

**1889** *Century Dict.* s.v. *Canal*, Sheathing canal (*canalis vaginalis*), the communication of the cavity of the tunica vaginalis testis with the general peritoneal cavity of the abdomen.

**sheathless** (ˈʃiːθlɪs), *a.* [f. SHEATH¹ + -LESS.]

**1.** Of a sword, etc.: Not encased in a sheath.

**1717** EUSDEN *Ovid's Met.* IV. *Pyramus & Thisbe* 142 She ..saw his sheathless sword. **1816** BYRON *Parisina* x. 12 A thousand swords had sheathless shone. **1829** SCOTT *Anne of G.* xiv, Francis took up his sheathless sword.

**2.** *Nat. Hist.* Having no sheath.

**1854** WOODWARD *Mollusca* II. 192 Tentacles laminated, non-retractile, sheathless. **1910** D. W. THOMPSON tr. *Aristotle's Hist. Anim.* I. 5 Some are coleopterous or sheath-winged,..others are sheathless.

†ˈ**sheathy**, *a. Obs. rare.* [f. SHEATH¹ + -Y.] Of the nature of a sheath.

**1646** SIR T. BROWNE *Pseud. Ep.* III. xxv. 175 Hee that.. shall with a needle put aside the short and sheathie cases on their [the earwigs'] backe, may extend and draw forth two winges. **1658** ROWLAND *Moufet's Theat. Ins.* 1017 Under their sheathy wings..lye hid their membranous wings.

**shea-tree**: see SHEA.

**sheave** (ʃiːv), *sb.*¹ Forms: α. 4 schive, 5 s(c)hyve, 6 shife, shyfe, 5-6 *Sc.* pl. schyffis, schiffis; β. 4, 8-9 sheeve, 5 shefe, 5-6 sheve, 6 *Sc.* pl. s(c)hawis, 7-8 shaff, 8 shieve, sheff, 9 sheaf, 8- sheave. [Cogn. w. OS. *scîva* fem. (glossing *sphera*), MLG., mod.LG., MDu. *schîve* (mod.Du. *schijf*), OHG. *scîba*, MHG. *schîbe*, mod.G. *scheibe*; also (? from LG.) Icel. *skífa*, Sw. *skifva*, Da. *skive*.

In continental Teut. these words have the senses disk, quoit, wheel, sheave or pulley, pane of glass, flat plate, slice of bread, etc.; their formal equivalent in Eng. is SHIVE (ʃaɪv), which has had most of the senses here enumerated. The etymological relation between the present word and *shive* is hard to determine; the most probable view is that *sheave* represents (with vowel-change as in *week*, *weevil*, etc.) an OE. **scife* or **scifa*, from the weak grade of the root of *scífe* SHIVE. In some of the α forms the quantity of the *i* is doubtful; if it be long, the examples belong strictly to SHIVE *sb.*]

**1.** = SHIVE *sb.*¹, slice of bread.

*c* **1375** *Sc. Leg. Saints* xxx. (*Theodera*) 31 For les þane a schefe of brede. *c* **1475** *Pict. Voc.* in Wr.-Wülcker 772/31, 32 *Hec lesca*, *Hec colirida*, a schefe of brede. **1544** PHAER *Regim. Life* (1553) F iij b, Take a sheaue of bread..toste it, and wete it [etc.]. **1552** HULOET, Cantel or shief of bread, *minutal*. **1586** WARNER *Alb. Eng.* IV. xx. (1592) 85 A Sheeue of bread as browne as Nut. **1603** HOLLAND *Plutarch's Mor.* 57 He cald for shieves of bread to eat.

**2. a.** A wheel having a groove in the circumference to receive a cord passing over it, a pulley; esp. one of the pulleys connected in a block; *U.S.* also, 'the pulley of a window or door-hanger' (*Funk's Stand. Dict.*). Also, a wheel having a groove in the circumference to enable it to run on a rail or bar.

α. **1336** *Acc. Exch. K.R.* 19/31 m. 4 Schiuis et trussis. **1399** in *Fabric Rolls York Minster* (Surtees) 18 Item j par de pulees cum vj shives. **1497** *Acc. Ld. High Treas. Scot.* I. 358 Tua schyffis with xiij puleis. *a* **1515** *Build. Louth Steeple* in *Archæologia* X. 76 Paid to..John Harrison, smith, for one pully shife of brass, 16*d*.

β. **1338** in Nicolas *Royal Navy* (1847) II. 171 Sheeues. [Other terms cited as occurring are 'swivels', 'hawsers for warping'.] **1485** *Naval Acc. Hen. VII* (1896) 36 Sheves of brasse iiij grete & xviij small... Grete sheves of Iren..j. **1511-12** *Rec. St. Mary at Hill* (1904) 278 Paid for shevys of Brasse to hange þe lampe & þe pascall, the on peyre cost xij d, the oþer peire viij d. **1554-5** in *Extracts Burgh Rec. Edin.* (1871) II. 308 Twa faddome and ane half of cords to fessin the shawis to the rufe of the tolbuith, to rais the greit brandrauth togidder. *Ibid.* 311 Thre schawis of brass to the cran, ilk schewe weyand xx pund wecht. **1664** EVELYN *Sylva* vi. (1679) 42 Ash..serves..for..the best blocks for Pullys and Sheffs, as Seamen name them. **1769** FALCONER *Dict. Marine* (1780), *Sheave*, a solid cylindrical wheel, fixed in a channel, and moveable about an axis,..used to.. increase the mechanical powers applied to remove any body. The sheaves are either fixed in blocks, or in channels cut through the masts, caps, cat-heads, or sides of a ship. **1788** *Trans. Soc. Arts* VI. 207 A rope passing over the shieve of a notch block. **1825** J. NICHOLSON *Oper. Mech.* 425 The manner in which the rope goes round, and grasps the sheeves, and occasions their contrary motion. **1841** R. WILLIS *Princ. Mechanism* §211 In each mortise is a friction-pully or sheave, having a groove in its circumference round which the string or cord passes. **1859** *Abridgm. Specif. Patents, Electr. & Magn.* 288 Suspension and insulation of telegraph wires. Non-conducting sheaves or rollers are fixed to the posts [etc.]. **1869** RANKINE *Machine & Hand-tools* Pl. O 2, The barrel and the sheave of the lower block have grooves for the chain to work in. **1888** J. PATON in *Encycl. Brit.* XXIV. 464/1 This eye or mail is placed in the heddle half-way between an upper and a lower wooden sheaf. **1892** KIPLING *Barrack-room Ballads* 205 And the derricks clack and grate, as the tackle hooks the crate, And the fall-rope whines through the sheave.

**b.** An eccentric or its disk.

**1887** D. A. LOW *Machine Draw.* (1892) 47 The eccentric is a particular form of crank... In the eccentric what corresponds to the crank-pin is called the sheave or pulley.

**c.** *attrib.*, as ***sheave-block, -hole***, etc.

**1588** *Churchw. Acc. St. Michael, Oxf.*, Item for makinge a *sheareband [? *read* sheaveband] for the seconde bell. **1590** *Ibid.*, Item for peecing the Shereband [? *read* sheveband] and stirrops to the same bell. **1844** *Civil Engin. & Arch. Jrnl.* VII. 246/2 Using either a simple sling, or *sheave-blocks, for placing the stones, according to their dimensions and weight. **1894** *Times* 26 Feb. 3/6 A sheaf-block to raise up the chain-block. **1769** FALCONER *Dict. Marine* II. (1780), *Trous d'écoutes*, the *sheave-holes,..cut obliquely through a ship's side, wherein the main and fore-sheets are reeved. **1899** F. T. BULLEN *Log of Sea-waif* 148 That third sheavehole..is for the skys'le-halliards. **1883** *Fisheries Exhib. Catal.* 206 *Sheave-roller bushing. Lug-roller bushing. Improved lug-roller... Improved trawl roller. **1939** C. W. TOWNE *Her Majesty Montana* 118 A Butte miner..is lowered to his labors in a steel cage suspended from a heavy wire cable passing over *sheave-wheels on a head-frame. **1971** *Financial Mail* (Johannesburg) 26 Feb. 648/1 They depend upon our equipment—like high speed man cage and skip guide rollers, sheave wheels.

**3.** A layer of a coiled rope.

**1840** F. D. BENNETT *Whaling Voy.* II. 198 It is coiled, continuously, in two tubs, and in neat and compact horizontal layers, or 'sheaves'.

**4.** 'A sliding scutcheon for covering a keyhole' (Knight *Dict. Mech.* 1875).

**sheave** (ʃiːv), *sb.*[2] Now only *dial.* and *techn.* Also 6 sheve. [Variant of SHIVE *sb.*[2] (ʃɪv), with vowel-lengthening: cf. prec. The word corresponds in form and sense to MDu. *scheve* (Du. *scheef*, dial. *scheeft*), G. *schebe*, Da. dial. *skiæv(e.*]

**1.** A fragment, splinter; a particle of chaff; a bit of fluff sticking up on the surface of cloth, etc.; a particle of any hard substance in wool, etc.

*c* **1558** BECON *Gov. Virtue* Wks. 1564 I. 272 Lyke an arthen potte whyche.. breaketh so sore that a man shall not fynde a sheue of it to fetche fyre in. **1696** J. F. *Merch. Wareho. laid open* 8 Hamborogh Dowlas.. this last wears well, but with these faults, which they never fail of, it wears with prickles or sheaves and never wears perfectly white.

**2.** The woody part of flax or hemp.

**1797** A. YOUNG *Agric. Suffolk* 121 The offal [after 'breaking'] is called hemp Sheaves, makes good fuel, and sells at two-pence a stone.

**3.** *Paper-making* = SHIVE *sb.*[2] 2. ? *Obs.*

**1880** J. DUNBAR *Pract. Papermaker* 15 All rags.. contain sheive, which nothing but judicious boiling will remove. **1888** CROSS & BEVAN *Text-bk. Paper-Making* vi. 90 Such impurities as weeds.. if not removed would be liable to appear in the finished paper as dark-coloured specks, technically known as 'sheave'. **1894** G. CLAPPERTON *Pract. Paper-Making* xi. 135 The pressure applied in the super-calender is often such as to cause all the sheave and gritty matters to show up.

**sheave** (ʃiːv), *v.*[1] [f. SHEAF *sb.*, with regular change of *f* into *v.*] *trans.* To bring together, collect, gather or put up (corn, etc.) into a sheaf or sheaves. Hence **'sheaving** *vbl. sb.*

**1579** [implied in SHEAVED *ppl. a.* 1]. **1598** FLORIO, *Affasciare*,.. to sheaue. *a* **1722** LISLE *Husb.* (1757) 180 There is no need to let wheat lie out in gripp before it is sheaved. **1785** W. H. MARSHALL *Midl. Counties* (1790) II. 167 Many oats.. have this year been 'sheaved': namely, mown out-ward, gathered from the swaths, bound, and shucked. **1821** COLERIDGE *Lett.*, etc. (1858) 85 The main portion of my harvest is still on the ground, ripe indeed, and only waiting, a few for the sickle, but a large part only for the sheaving, and carting, and housing. **1830** *Kyle Farm Rep.* 43 in *Libr. Usef. Knowl., Husb.* III, Peas are not sheaved, but left loose, and frequently turned. **1851** MRS. BROWNING *Casa Guidi Wind.* II. 517 While our corn was being sheaved For his own granaries. **1881** DU CHAILLU *Land of Midn. Sun* I. 193 Women and men sheaving the barley. **1893** *Times* 20 May 11/5 Thatching,.. fence-building, mowing and sheaving are, we are assured, becoming lost arts.

*intr.* *c* **1600** DAY *Peregr. Schol.* Wks. (1881) 78, I sawe a little world of people at worke, Some moweinge, some sheaveinge.. some shockeinge, some loadeinge.

*fig.* **1652** ASHMOLE *Theatr. Chem. Brit.* Proleg. 13 As for the whole Worke it selfe, it is sheav'd up from a few gleanings in part of our English Fields. *a* **1711** KEN *Hymnotheo* Poet. Wks. 1721 III. 105 From ev'ry Star Our Maker chose the brightest Beams by far; Which sheav'd up in one Orb, the Sun produce.

**sheave** (ʃiːv), *v.*[2] Forms: 7 (-9) shieve, 9 sheave. [Perh. repr. ME. *schēve*, OE. *scéofan* var. of *scúfan* SHOVE *v.*[1]] *intr.* or *absol.* To back a boat, to work the oars backwards.

**1611** COTGR., *Sier en arriere: C'est aller le derriere devant*, to shieue, or fall a-sterne, (a tearme of Nauigation). **1687** MIEGE *Gt. Fr. Dict.* II, To Shieve, or fall a-stern (a Term of Navigation), *sier*. **1894** R. C. LESLIE *Waterblog.* v. 102 Conant was to take charge of the tiller with one hand and the after-oar in the other, which he used standing in the stern-sheets, and 'sheaving' or shoving with it facing the boat's bow, gondolier fashion. **1895** *Dial. Notes* (Amer. Dial. Soc.) I. 381 (N. Brunswick, etc. word-list) *Sheave*, to hold water with the oar to stop the boat or turn more quickly. (Nfld.) **1911** S. REYNOLDS in *Blackw. Mag.* Feb. 190/2 One man was sheaving—standing up with bent back and rowing forwards—whilst the other man pulled in the ordinary manner.

**sheave**, obs. form of SHEAF *sb.*

**sheaved**, *a. rare.* [f. SHEAVE *sb.*[1] + -ED[2].] Having or containing a (thin, etc.) sheave.

**1800** *Naval Chron.* III. 474 Thin sheaved blocks.

**sheaved** (ʃiːvd), *ppl. a.* [f. SHEAVE *v.*[1] + -ED[1].]

**1.** Of corn, etc., also of arrows: Put up or gathered into a sheaf or sheaves.

**1579** HAKE *Newes out of Powles* vi. (1872) E viij, The fertile soyle that foyson bringes of goodly sheaued graine. **1677** *Lond. Gaz.* No. 1260/4 Lost.., A pair of large Silver Candlesticks.., a Crest upon each Candlestick; at one corner, the Flying-Dragon with a sheaved Arrow in his Claw. **1865** SWINBURNE *Poems & Ball., St. Dorothy* 268 Growth of sheaved wheat. **1892** KIPLING *Barrack-room Ballads* 157 Mingled arrows each one sheaved.

†**2.** ? Made of straw. *Obs. rare*[−1].

**1597** SHAKS. *Lover's Compl.* 31 Her sheu'd hat. [Cf. line 8 Vpon her head a plattid hiue of straw.]

**3.** 'Finished around the top with a flare, like that of a sheaf' (*Cent. Dict.* 1891).

**1867** *Rep. Artisans Paris Univ. Exhib.* II. 134 Time was, when a well sheaved wine glass could be made only in England. *Ibid.*, Wine glasses.. with tops as well sheaved as the best work on the English stalls.

**sheavy** ('ʃiːvɪ), *a. dial.* In 9 sheivy. [f. SHEAVE *sb.*[2] + -Y.] Full of 'sheaves' or 'shivs'. Cf. *shivvy* in the same sense (*Eng. Dial. Dict.*).

**1883** R. HALDANE *Workshop Rec.* Ser. II. 389/1 (Paper making.) There is a considerable difference in the quality and appearance, the rags being thicker and sheivier as the quality deteriorates.

**sheaw, shebandar**, obs. ff. SHOW, SHABANDAR.

**shebang** (ʃɪ'bæŋ). *N. Amer. slang.* Also †chebang, shee-bang. [Of obscure origin.]

**1. a.** A hut, shed; one's dwelling, quarters.

**1862** W. WHITMAN *Jrnl.* 23-31 Dec. in *Specimen Days & Collect* (1882-3) 27 Their shebang enclosures of bushes. **1863** —— *Jrnl.* Jan. in *Ibid.*, The soldiers guarding the road came out from their tents or shebangs of bushes. **1867** W. L. GOSS *Soldier's Story* viii. 153 By common consent, if any one had complaints to make, he carried them to the 'shebang' of Big Peter. **1872** 'MARK TWAIN' *Innoc. at Home* ii. in *Roughing It*, etc. (1882) 270 We've got a shebang fixed up for you to stand behind in No. I's house. **1890** N. P. LANGFORD *Vigilante Days* I. 83 Towards the close of the summer of 1862, the band organized by Plummer [an outlaw] having increased in numbers, he selected two points of rendezvous, as bases for their operations. These were called 'shebangs'.

**b.** Applied to a vehicle.

**1872** 'MARK TWAIN' *Innoc. at Home* i. in *Roughing It*, etc. (1882) 263 You're welcome to ride here as long as you please, but this shebang's chartered. **1877** B. HARTE *Story of Mine* 85 That.. don't fetch me even of he'd chartered the whole shebang. **1899** BINSTEAD *Houndsditch Day by Day* 198 In a four-wheeled fever-box you must take your beaver on your knees or get it hopelessly ruffled against the roof of the old shebang.

**c.** A low drinking establishment, a tavern.

[**1878** C. HALLOCK *Hallock's Amer. Club List & Sportsman's Gloss.* p. x, *Shebang*, any sort of structure from a shanty to a hotel.] **1901** H. G. PARKER *Right of Way* viii. 49 There were people who called the tavern a 'shebang'. **1908** B. W. SINCLAIR *Raw Gold* vi. 68 There was a sort of sheebang—you couldn't call it a hotel if you had any regard for the truth—on the outskirts of Walsh for the accommodation of wayfarers without a camp-outfit. **1963** E. C. GUILLET *Pioneer Farmer & Backwoodsman* I. xix. 314 Less picturesque were the *shebangs* dotted along the rivers, where squaws and whiskey awaited the shanty boys and their winter pay.

**2.** 'More widely, almost any matter of present concern; thing; business; as, tired of the whole shebang' (*Funk's Stand. Dict.* 1895). Freq. in phr. ***the whole shebang*** (see also sense 1 b, quot. 1877).

**1869** 'MARK TWAIN' *Lett. to Publishers* (1967) 26, I like the book, I like you and your style and your business vim, and believe the chebang will be a success. **1904** W. N. HARBEN *Georgians* ix. 88, I sold out my shebang, put the money in my pocket. **1924** H. CRANE *Let.* 5 Dec. (1965) 196, I am growing more and more sick of factions, gossip, jealousies, recriminations, excoriations and the whole literary shee-bang. **1933** E. E. CUMMINGS *Let.* 13 Sept. (1969) 124 Camels placidly nibble the whole shebang, not merely the smallish but the spike thorns. **1948** V. PALMER *Golconda* xiv. 109 I've .. seen him standing up there on one of those outcrops overlooking the company's buildings as if he'd like to call down fire from heaven on the whole shebang. **1967** *Boston Sunday Herald* 7 May IV. 5/2 You can't get rid of the feeling .. that the people in charge of the shebang are far more pessimistic and confused than they were the last time you were here. **1977** R. E. MEGILL *Introd. Risk Analysis* iii. 28 The standard deviation is then calculated by dividing the total number of wells, *N*, into the sum of all the group deviations.. and then taking the square root of the whole shebang.

**Shebat**, variant of SEBAT (Hebrew month).

**shebeen** (ʃɪ'biːn). Also shebean, shibbeen. [Orig. Anglo-Irish; of obscure origin.

The ending is Irish *-in* as in *caubeen, colleen*, etc.; an improbable conjecture is that the word is f. Irish *seapa* ad. Eng. SHOP *sb.* In recent Irish dictionaries it is given as Irish, with the spelling *sibín*.]

**a.** Chiefly in Ireland and Scotland: A shop or house where excisable liquors are sold without a licence (see quot. 1903); any low wayside public-house.

*c* **1787** *Kilmainham Minit* in *Sk. Irel. 60 Yrs. Ago* (1847) 88 With de stuff to a shebeen we hied. **1832** G. DOWNES *Lett. Cont. Countries* I. 382 The hovel, which proved to be a house of entertainment, such as in Ireland we call a shebeen. **1842** LOVER *Handy Andy* xxvi, The money your honour gave me that I spint at the shebeen upon the 'lecthors. **1859** *All Year Round* No. 12. 285 Here we came to a shibbeen, and for the third time the young doctor got down and called for whisky. **1892** *Rev. Reviews* V. 272/1 Twelve hundred shebeens in Cardiff! **1903** *Act 3 Edw. VII*, c. 25 § 107 The word 'shebeen' shall mean and include every house, shop, room, premises or place in which exciseable liquors are trafficked in, by retail, without a certificate and excise licence in that behalf.

**b.** In South Africa, a (usu. Black) illicit establishment where liquor is sold or consumed. In extended sense: a drinking-party, esp. among West Indians.

**1900** *Kruger's Secret Service* vi. 135 In Fordsburg there was a shebeen kept by a certain Pulinski... Pulinski took me inside, where I found the place to be full of Kaffirs. **1931** J. MOCKFORD *Khama* x. 77 So zealous was Khama in enforcing his ban on beer, that he afterwards led raids on shebeens himself and fired the huts of the brewers with his own hand. **1943** *Cape Argus* 13 Jan. 3 Carousals that cannot be described as shebeens, but that are almost as mischievous. **1944** I. D. DU PLESSIS *Cape Malays* v. 81 Shebeens have sprung up in clusters, wine is brought in from Monday to Saturday by 'runners'. **1958** *Times Lit. Suppl.* 22 Aug. 472/5 The flashy, teeming, squalid world of the urban localities.. laughter, gramophones, shebeens, and 'tsotsi' thugs making night excursions dangerous for Africans and police alike. **1962** D. LESSING *Golden Notebk.* I. 57 Peter.. spends his last night in the Colony drunk, and by chance encounters his dark love in some shabby Shebeen. **1975** *New Society* 10 July 71/1 The West Indians [in Southampton], who are more free and easy, and tend to have noisy all night parties and shebeens. **1980** *Times* 31 May 5/1 The South African Government, after years of battling to control illicit drinking dens, known as shebeens, in black townships, has conceded defeat and legalized them.

**c.** *attrib.* as ***shebeen-house, -shop***; also ***shebeen-keeper***; **shebeen queen** *S. Afr.*, a woman who runs a shebeen.

**1798** JOS. HOLT *Mem.* (1838) I. 5, I struck off the road to a shebeen house or cabin in which whiskey is sold without a license. **1800** MAR. EDGEWORTH *Castle Rackrent* Wks. 1848 IV. 53 His Honour.. sent for more spirits from a shebean-house [*note*] *Shebean-house*, a hedge alehouse. Shebean properly means weak small-beer, taplash. *c* **1815** *Song, 'Oh, St. Patrick was a Gentleman'* v, His mother kept a shebeen shop In the town of Enniskillen. **1852** MUNDY *Antipodes* (1857) 29 Every mile or two has some establishment of the kind, ranging between the hotel and the shebeen house. **1922** JOYCE *Ulysses* 443 In the shadow a shebeenkeeper haggles with the navvy and the two redcoats. **1954** R. ST. JOHN *Through Malan's Afr.* xxx. 236 Shebeen queens were warned to stop their liquor selling. **1977** *Time* 10 Jan. 24/1 After the fire-bombing of a few that stayed open, the shebeen queens (women that operate most speakeasies) duly shut up shop, and Sowetoans did their Christmas drinking quietly at home.

Hence **she'beener**, one who keeps or frequents a shebeen. **she'beening**, the keeping of a shebeen; the illegal selling of liquor.

**1870** *Figaro* 14 Dec. (Farmer), Three extensive captures of shebeeners were made in Glasgow on Sunday. One hundred and twenty persons were found in the dens. **1873** *Scotsman* 15 Feb. (ibid.), Grocers, Shebeeners, and others who sell liquors which are consumed on their Premises, and who hold no Licence to do so. **1887** *Scot. Leader* 15 Dec. 4 'Shebeening' by an Edinburgh Publican. **1906** *Daily Mail* 17 Aug. 3/7 A Sheffield barber was fined.. for shebeening. **1942** Shebeener [see *beer-hall* s.v. BEER *sb.*[1] 4]. **1950** Shebeener [see DOP *sb.*[2] 2].

**shebo**, var. SHIVEAU.

**shecarry**, obs. form of SHIKARI.

†**shechanize**, *v. Obs. rare.* [f. Heb. *shākan*, to dwell (the root of SHEKINAH.] *intr.* To dwell as God in a temple.

**1681-6** J. SCOTT *Chr. Life* (1699) V. 225 The Word incarnate, or tabernacled in our flesh, did shechanize, or perform the part of his Father's supreme representative among us full of grace and truth. *Ibid.*, For this is plainly implied in his shechanizing or tabernacling.

**shechinah**, variant form of SHEKINAH.

‖**shechita** (ʃɛ'xita). Also **shecheta, shechitah, shehita(h.** [Heb. *šᵉḥīṭâ*, f. *šāḥaṭ* to slaughter.] The Jewish method of slaughtering animals. Cf. SHOCHET.

**1875** J. PICCIOTTO *Sk. Anglo-Jewish Hist.* xxvii. 217 The Portuguese would willingly join in the formation of a general body for the management of the Shechita (arrangements for slaughtering and preparing cattle for food *more Judaico*). **1891** M. FRIEDLÄNDER *Jewish Relig.* 463 Any deviation from these rules in the act of killing the animal renders the *shechitah* unlawful. **1910** *Jewish Chron.* 14 Jan. 34/1 (*heading*) The Shecheta Board, the Public, and the Butchers. *Ibid.* 1 Apr. 13/2 Fröken von Konow.. constantly describes Shechita as a religious observance, but when it suits her purpose she speaks of it as an act 'practised under the cloak of religion'. **1921** *Dict. Occup. Terms* (1927) § 448 *Slaughterer, Jewish*;.. *shecheta*,.. is employed by Jewish Board of Shecheta. **1939** *Contemp. Jewish Record* II. III. 32 Charges of alleged brutality have been made the basis for the prohibition of *Shehitah* in several European countries. **1941** *Ibid.* IV. 539 The Iron Guards.. bestially murdered them in parody of *shehita*. **1964** E. HUXLEY *Back Street New Worlds* ii. 25 Animals must be killed by a method known as *shechita*, the severing of all veins and arteries in the neck with a single knife-stroke. **1976** C. BERMANT *Coming Home* I. i. 18 Insofar as slaughter can be humane, *shechita* is humane—to the animal. It is, however, inhumane to the *shochet*, for.. he has to face the.. almost pleading eyes of the animal.

**sheck**, obs. form of SHEIKH.

**shecklaton**, variant of CICLATOUN *Obs.*

**sheckle**: see SHACKLE, SHEKEL, SHOCKLE.

**shed** (ʃɛd), *sb.*[1] Forms: 1 (ʒe)scéad, 1-2 scád, 3 schad, *Orm.* shæd, 4-6 schede, shede, 4-7 sched, 5 sced, schade, 5, 8, 9 *dial.* sheed, 6 schedde, sheyde, 6-7 shead(e, shedde, *Sc.* schad, 7, 9 *dial.* shade, 4- shed. [OE. (*ʒe*)*scéad*, altered form of (*ʒe*)*sceád* neut.:—OTeut. type *(*ga*)*skaiđo-m*, f. root **skaiđ-* to divide: see SHED *v.*, where the phonology is explained. Cf. OHG. *sceit*, (MHG. *scheit*) division. In sense 2 the word may represent the cognate OE. *sc*(*e*)*áda* (see SHODE) in the altered form *scēada*.]

†**1. a.** Distinction, discrimination, separation (of one thing from another). *Obs.*

In OE. also in phr. *scád* (*á*)*ʒyldan*, to give account.

*c* **950** *Lindisf. Gosp.* Luke xii. 51 *Separationem*, þæt ʒescead. *c* **1000** *Ags. Gosp.* Matt. xii. 36 Ælc idel word þe menn specað hi aʒyldaþ ʒescead [*c* **1160** scad] be þam on domes dæʒe. *c* **1200** ORMIN 6229 Forr ʒunnc birrþ witenn swiþe wel,.. þatt niss bitwenen ʒunnc & hemm Nan shæd i manness kinde. c 1330 *Spec. Gy de Warw.* 217 Off god and yuel shed to make. *Ibid.* 721 And shed to make in eueri dede Bitwene soþnesse and falshede. 1575 GASCOIGNE *Glasse of Govt.* III. vi. Wks. 1910 II. 59 The Shed is great, and greater then the show, Which seemes to be, betweene the good and bad. 1674 RAY *N.C. Words* 40 No *Shed*: No difference between things. 1703 THORESBY in Ray *Philos. Lett.* (1718) 336 'No Sheds', no difference.

†**b.** The faculty of discerning or distinguishing.

c 1000 ÆLFRIC *Hom.* I. 176/24 Ʒe habbað ʒescead æʒðer ʒe godes ʒe yfeles. c 1200 ORMIN 5534 Þe fifte ʒife iss shæd & skill I weorelldlike þingess. a 1225 *Leg. Kath.* 238 Þat schafte of mon þat he schop & ʒef schad ba of god & of uel. a 1240 *Sawles Warde* in *Cott. Hom.* 255 Warschipe þe haueð wit ant schad bituhhe god and uuel.

**2. a.** The parting made in the hair by combing along the top of the head; also, the part of the head thus indicated, the top of the crown. *Obs.* exc. *dial.* Cf. SHODE.

13.. *Cursor M.* 18837 (Gött.) In heued he had a sched [*Cott.* a clift] biforn. c 1325 *Gloss. W. de Bibbesw.* in *Rel. Ant.* II. 78/1 The shed, *la greve.* a 1380 *Virg. Antioch* 291 in Horstm. *Altengl. Leg.* (1878) 30 Set myn hat vppon þyn hed, To huide þin her and eke þi sched. c 1400 *Destr. Troy* 3023 The shede þurghe the shyre here shone as þe lilly. 14.. *Nom.* in Wr.-Wülcker 674/5 *Hoc discrimen*, the schade of the hede. 1513 DOUGLAS *Æneis* II. xi. 7 For lo! the top of litle Ascanius heid,..fro the sched of his croun, Schane all of lycht wnto the grond adoun. 1519 HORMAN *Vulg.* 25 The shede of the heare goeth vp to the toppe, deuydynge the molde. 1565 COOPER *Thesaurus* s.v. *Diuiduus, Coma diuidua*, heare diuided at the sheade. 1584 HUDSON *Du Bartas' Judith* IV. (1608) 65 Her wav'ring haire disparpling flew apart In seemely shed. 1688 HOLME *Armoury* II. 464/2 Women wear Hair..in shades, when it lieth plain and streight on each side the forehead. 1880 *Antrim & Down Gloss.*, *Shade*, the parting or division of the hair on one's head.

†**b.** Proverb. ***shame is past the shed of*** (*his*) ***hair*** (or ***head***), i.e. (he) has lost all sense of shame.

1382 *Pol. Poems* (Rolls) I. 252 We ben so ful of synne and slouthe, The schame is passed the sched of hede. 1560 ROLLAND *Seven Sages* 37 Schame is past the sched of thair hair, as weill we knaw. 1691 *Contin. Hist. Relat. Gen. Assembly Scot.* 15 But as the Scots Proverb is, Shame is passed the shed of their hair.

**c.** A parting made in the wool of sheep in order to grease or anoint the skin.

1523–34 FITZHERB. *Husb.* §44 Make wyde sheydes in the woll of the shepe, and anoynt them with it. 1641 BEST *Farm. Bks.* (Surtees) 69 In greasinge they beginne usually on the belly, and soe goe rownde aboute by sheddes. 1799 J. ROBERTSON *Agric. Perth* 321 Leaving about an inch betwixt every shed of the wool. 1844 H. STEPHENS *Bk. Farm* III. 1118 Tar-salve..may be..spread along the shed, and worked amongst the wool.

†**3.** A piece cut or broken off, a slice, fragment. (Cf. SHIDE.) Also a clot (of blood). *Obs.* (Chiefly *Sc.* and *north.*)

c 1400 *Anturs of Arth.* xxxix. (Douce MS.), Shaftes in shide wode þei shindre in shedes [*rimes* stedes, ledes, bledis]. 1513 DOUGLAS *Æneis* V. viii. 97 And scheddis of bluid furth spittand throw his lippis [*crassumque cruorem ore eiectantem*]. 1739 A. NICOL *Nature without Art* 74 Asunder I shall hack it [a cheese] In Sheeds this day. 1821 URE *Dict. Chem.* s.v. *Acid* (*Muriatic*), Tinmen's sheds, or old iron, may be employed instead of chalk.

**4.** *Sc.* 'A portion of land, as distinguished from that which is adjacent' (Jam.); a division of land larger than the 'rig'. ? *Obs.* (Cf. SHETH.)

1473 *Rental Bk. Cupar-Angus* (1879) I. 171 Tha sal pairt the toun in twa, gif it ma be, and gif it ma nocht, it salbe partyt in scheddis. 1588 *Reg. Mag. Sig. Scot.* 790/1 Acram terre arabilis continentem 4 *lie lang-riggis* contigue in uno *lie sched.* 1670 LAMONT *Diary* 30 May (Maitland Club) 220 [A great storm of thunder and lightning] att night; it did scorch and spoile some sheads of corne at Lawderdaill.

**5.** A ridge of high ground dividing two valleys or tracts of lower country; a 'divide'. Cf. WATERSHED. (The meaning in quot. 1530 is obscure.)

1530 PALSGR. 266/2 Schedde of an hyll, *tertre.* 1876 A. J. EVANS *Through Bosnia* i. 25 The Styrian mountains seem to form a shed between the areas of German and Italian influences. 1891 *Century Dict.*, *Shed.* 3. The slope of land or of a hill: as, which way is the *shed?*

*Comb.* 1850 OGILVIE, *Shed-line*, the summit line of elevated ground; [1882 adds] the line of the watershed.

**6.** *Weaving.* The opening made between the threads of the warp by the motion of the heddles for the shuttle to pass through.

1792 A. ADAM *Rom. Antiq.* (1801) 523 Which, being alternately raised and depressed by the motion of the feet on the Treadles, raises or depresses the warp, and makes the *shed* for transmitting the shuttle with the weft. 1851 *Art Jrnl. Illustr. Catal.* p. vii**/2 The healds..are situated at the left end, for the purpose of effecting the cross shed. 1888 *Encycl. Brit.* XXIV. 464/1 Treadle number two is next depressed and thereby a new shed is formed.

**b.** *Comb.*, as **shed-rod, -stick**, a device by which the warp is opened.

1968 W. BRAY *Everyday Life of Aztecs* vii. 144 This passage is easy to achieve by means of a roller or shed-rod inserted across the warp under every alternate thread. 1910 L. HOOPER *Hand-Loom Weaving* I. vii. 84 After the weft has been drawn straight, the shed-stick being again in a flat position, its edge may be brought down smartly upon the whole weft in order to beat it together. 1960 G. LEWIS *Handbk. Crafts* 98 Shed sticks, which hold the cross..in place.

**shed** (ʃɛd), *sb.*[2] Forms: 5–6 shadde, 6–7 shad, 7 shedde, 8 sheed, 7–9 *dial.* shade, 6– shed. [app. var. SHADE *sb.*, where cf. the forms OE. *sced*, ME. (Ayenb.) *ssed(e*, 15th c. *shad(de.* The development of the senses explained below was prob. more or less due to association with SHUD (now *dial.*, synonymous with this word).]

**1. a.** A slight structure built for shelter or storage, or for use as a workshop, either attached as a lean-to to a permanent building or separate; often with open front or sides. The special purpose is indicated by a defining word prefixed, as *cow-*, *cart-*, *goat-*, *tool-shed.*

1481 CAXTON *Reynard* v. (Arb.) 10 A yerde..In whiche was a shadde [Du. *een vaste schuere*] where in were six grete dogges. 1502 ARNOLDE *Chron.* (1811) 72 All thoo in the said cite..that ocupye houses not inhabited as shoppis celars shaddys. 1557 TUSSER *100 Points Husb.* §88 (1878) 232 For Tumbrels and cartes, haue a shed redy dight. 1599 NASHE *Lenten Stuffe* 51 A Fisherman of Yarmouth..hung the residue [of his draught of herrings]..in the sooty roofe of his shad a drying. 1615 CHAPMAN *Odyss.* IX. 314 Sheds [Gr. σηκοί] stuft with Lambs and Goates, distinctly kept. 1671 MILTON *P.R.* II. 72 In such a season born when scarce a Shed Could be obtain'd to shelter him or me From the bleak air. 1701 in *10th Rep. Hist. MSS. Comm.* App. V. 517 Three small sheds built against the towne wall. 1723 *Lond. Gaz.* No. 6146/8 The Shops and Sheds in and about Lincoln's-Inn. 1731 *N. Riding Rec.* VIII. 193 The building of a sheed in the Castle of York for the High Sheriffe's coach. 1798 *Hull Advertiser* 30 June 1/1 On the north side stands a work-house and a shade. 1799 J. ROBERTSON *Agric. Perth* 223 The milch cows are generally fed in the house or in a shade. 1816 SCOTT *Old Mort.* xxxiii, They withdrew to the stable, or shed, in order to accommodate their horses. 1870 *Inquiry, Yorksh. Deaf & Dumb* 68 [Employed] in the power-loom shades..as a thrower. 1875 *Encycl. Brit.* I. 7/1 Behind this is a shed..where the cattle are kept before being slaughtered.

**b.** A similar structure, but large and strongly built; often consisting of a roof supported on columns. Also *Austral.* and *N.Z.*, short for WOOLSHED (q.v.).

1855 OGILVIE *Suppl.* s.v., Some sheds, as those connected with railway-termini, wharfs, &c., are most substantial structures. 1857 F. COOPER *Wild Adventures in Austral.* 105 He was bound for the shearing through New England. By this time, most likely, he has set in at some of the sheds on the Namoi. 1887 J. C. HARRIS *Free Joe*, etc. (1888) 254 The passenger-depôt..—it is known as the 'Car-shed' in Atlantese. c 1888 KIPLING *Among Railway Folk* i. Wks. 1900 XVII. 165 On the fourth [side] it is bounded by what are locally known as the 'sheds'; in other words, the station, offices, and workshops of the Company. 1893 H. LAWSON *Coll. Prose* (1972) II. 24 Men tramping in search of a 'shed' are not called 'sundowners' or 'swaggies'; they are 'trav'lers'. 1911 C. E. W. BEAN '*Dreadnought' of Darling* v. 50 They were rich men—shearers—probably making from one big shed to another. 1913 *Times* 3 May 8/2 Last night a disastrous fire broke out at the Trafalgar shed of the Midland Railway Company at Bradford. 1940 F. SARGESON *Man & his Wife* (1944) 47 We got a job picking up fleeces in a big shed. 1955 G. BOWEN *Wool Away!* (1956) 2 Good weather, good shed, good sheep, good boss, and a good gang create an atmosphere of work and action.

**c.** = HANGAR b. ? *Obs.*

1909 *Daily Chron.* 3 Nov. 1/6 They have been watching the great shed gradually nearing completion.., and have been eagerly awaiting the advent of the airship. 1916 H. BARBER *Aeroplane Speaks* 27 The Aeroplane is wheeled out of its shed on to the greensward of the Military Aerodrome.

**2. a.** *poet.* A hut, cottage, poor dwelling.

1600 FAIRFAX *Tasso* II. lviii, The first Aletes, borne in lowly shed, Of parents base. 1634 MILTON *Comus* 323 Courtesie, Which oft is sooner found in lowly sheds With smoaky rafters, then in tapstry Halls. 1700 DRYDEN *Baucis & Philemon* 30 At last an hospitable House they found, A homely Shed. 1750 GRAY *Elegy* 18 The swallow twitt'ring from the straw-built shed. 1764 GOLDSM. *Trav.* 180 He.. Sees no contiguous palace rear its head To shame the meanness of his humble shed. 1783 CRABBE *Village* I. 60 Can poets soothe you, when you pine for bread, By winding myrtles round your ruin'd shed?

**b.** *gen.* A structure that affords shelter or covering; the hiding-place, lair or nest of an animal.

1616 R. COCKS *Diary* (Hakl. Soc.) I. 122 We had greate canes of the China Capt. to make an arbor or shed for a vyne. c 1620 Z. BOYD *Zion's Flowers* (1855) 40, I here doe lye, Without a shed scorch'd with a swelt'ring skye. 1695 CONGREVE *Love for L.* Epil., For still in every Storm, they all run hither, As to a Shed that shields 'em from the Weather. 1821 CLARE *Vill. Minstr.* II. 121 The fields and meadow grass Will gladly hide their [the peewits'] careless shed. *Ibid.* 196 The scouting rabbit seeks her shed.

**3.** A covering; cf. SHADE *sb.* II. †**a.** ? A lid.

1612 in *Antiquary* (1906) XLII. 29/1 Item in the lofte nexte the gatehouse a Troughe, a Tubbe with a Shed, a boultinge hutche [etc.].

**b.** In a telegraph-line insulator, a covering in the form of an inverted cup, a 'petticoat'.

1859 *Abridgm. Specif. Patents, Electr. & Magn.* 236 No sheds or bell coverings are applied, but the wire is varnished [etc.]. 1910 *N. Hawkins' Electr. Dict.*, *Shed of Insulator*, the petticoat of a line wire insulator.

**4.** [By analogy with BARN *sb.* 1 d.] In nuclear physics, a proposed unit of area of nuclear cross-section equal to $10^{-24}$ barn ($10^{-48}$ cm.$^2$).

The unit is impracticably small and appears to have had minimal use.

1956 W. C. MICHELS et al. *Internat. Dict. Physics & Electronics* 820/2 *Shed*, a unit of nuclear cross section equal to $10^{-24}$ barn or $10^{-48}$ square centimetre. 1965 *Guinness Bk. Records* (ed. 12) 80 The smallest unit of area is a 'shed', used in sub-atomic physics. 1968 F. KERTESZ *Lang. Nuclear Sci.* (Oak Ridge Nat. Lab. TM 2367) 20 During the study of the neutrino, a much smaller surface was used in theoretical studies and the area $10^{-44}$ cm$^2$ [*sic*] was quite logically named the shed; however, this latter name did not receive general acceptance. 1979 *New Scientist* 12 July 168/2 The Shed..seems to me to be less witty [than the barn].

**5.** *attrib.* and *Comb.*, as (sense 1 b) ***shed-boss, -hand***; ***shed-smithy***; ***shed-fashion, -wise*** advs.; ***shed-like, -shaped***, adjs.; in sense 'kept, employed, done in a shed', as ***shed-cow, -feeding, -man***; **shed master**, one in charge of a locomotive shed (see quot. 1921); **shed roof**, a roof with only one slope (as in a lean-to shed); hence ***shed-roofed*** adj; **shed-room** *U.S.*, a shed attached to a house and serving as a room.

1892 W. E. SWANTON *Notes on N.Z.* ii. 97 Then there is the '*shed boss', who looks after everything, sees the sheep are shorn properly, takes the tally, looks after pressing etc. 1940 E. C. STUDHOLME *Te Waimate* 110 In the early days the manager acted as shed-boss. 1898 *Jrnl. R. Agric. Soc.* June 415 When an outbreak occurs among a herd of *shed-cows. 1807 P. GASS *Jrnl.* 61 The roofs were made *shed-fashion, rising from the inner side. 1856 MORTON *Cycl. Agric.* II. 841/1 In some trials of *shed-feeding. 1905 W. BAUCKE *Where White Man Treads* 229 The *shed-hands and shearers were mostly Maoris. 1961 *N.Z. Listener* 26 May 8/1 The two shedhands played their unending game of poker. 1835 R. WILLIS *Archit. Mid. Ages* ix. 140 A long, low, *shed-like porch. 1899 RIDER HAGGARD *Farmer's Yr.* 352 The kirk ..is a very plain building, white-washed and shed-like in appearance. 1921 *Dict. Occup. Terms* (1927) §700 **Shed master*, in charge of smaller locomotive shed than that supervised by shed superintendent. 1960 *Times* 2 Sept. 6/6 He should have sent a message to the shed-master. 1978 J. BLACKBURN *Dead Man's Handle* 8 How the shed-master had cursed when he heard the old steamer come clanking home with a fractured bearing. 1857 *Househ. Words* 27 June 605/1 At large stations they [the porters] form two distinct bodies, called technically yardmen and *shedmen. 1736 in *Maryland Hist. Mag.* (1908) III. 45 The *Shead Ruff of Capt Cressap's house. 1805 R. W. DICKSON *Pract. Agric.* I. 61 It is probably the best and cheapest method to make them with shed-roofs. 1817 in *Essex Inst. Hist. Coll.* (1866) VIII. 235 These [carriages] are..built like our mud-scows, with a shed roof over your head, looking like a floating ropewalk. 1907 M. C. F. MORRIS *Nunburnholme* 76 The chancel itself had a shed-roof of mean description. 1976 'O. BLEECK' *No Questions Asked* xii. 130 Above the wall I caught a glimpse of a white-graveled, sloping shed roof. 1836 PARKER *Gloss. Archit.* (1850) I. 432 The body of a church is span-roofed and its aisles *shed-roofed. 1843 *Knickerbocker* XXI. 304, I had in the morning secured a bed in a *shed-room. 1932 H. CRANE *Let.* ? Jan. (1965) 395 We've relegated him to the shed-room in back of the kitchen. 1857 THOREAU *Maine Woods* (1864) 246 A *shed-shaped tent will catch and reflect the heat like a Yankee-baker. 1837 CARLYLE *Fr. Rev.* III. IV. vi, There, in their two-hundred and fifty *shed smithies,.. let them forge gun-barrels. 1650 in *Sussex Archæol. Collect.* XXIV. 280 The said cottage and stable is built *Shedwise against the Castle wall of Tymber and Mudd walles.

**shed** (ʃɛd), *sb.*[3] *rare.* [f. SHED *v.*[1]] Something that is or has been shed: e.g. a silkworm's cocoon; a light fall of snow; the cast shell of a crab.

1648 HERRICK *Hesper.*, *Fairie Temple* 137 And then he dons the Silk-worms shed (Like a Turks Turbant on his head). 1876 BLACKMORE *Cripps* vii, A little powdery shed of flakes had come at noon that very day. 1911 WEBSTER, *Shed* ..5. That which is or has been shed, as the molted shell of a crab or other crustacean. *Colloq.*

**shed** (ʃɛd), *sb.*[4] *local.* [Cf. SCAD[5] and *shad salmon* 'small salmon of from five pounds' to eight pounds' weight' (*Shropshire Word-bk.* 1879).] A young salmon from one to two years old.

1861 *Act 24 & 25 Vict.* c. 109 §4 All migratory fish of the genus salmon, whether known by the names..gravelling, shed, scad,..or by any other local name. 1882 [see SKEGGER].

†**shed**, *sb.*[5] *Obs.* Also **shede, sheade.** Variants of SCHEDE, a written paper.

1510 STANBRIDGE *Vocabula* (W. de W.) C ij b, *Scheda*, a shede. 1590 *Calepini Dict.* (1594) II. 531 *Scheda*..Angl. A sheet or shed of paper. a 1593 H. BARROW *Brief Discov.* To Rdr. p. iij, Where such was the rage of the enimie, as he [the author] might not keepe one sheade by him, whiles he was writinge of an other.

**shed, sched,** Sc. forms of SHADE *sb.*

c 1591 *Rob Stene's Dream* (Maitland Club) 3 A sched, but substance, and no moir. c 1730 RAMSAY *Vision* xxviii, And all as saft and gay appeird As ane Elysion shed.

**shed** (ʃɛd), *v.*[1] Pa. t. and pa. pple. shed. Forms: 1 sc(e)ádan, scēdan, 2–5 shode(n, -scheode(n, 3 scheade(n; 2–3 *Ormin* shædenn, 2–6 shede(n, 3 ssede, 3–5 schede(n, 4–7, 8–9 *dial.* sheed(e, sched, 5 scheed, 5–6 schedde, 6 *Sc.* schad, scheid, 6–7 shedd(e, 6–8, 9 *dial.* shead, 8 *dial.* shade, 4– shed; 3 *sing. pres. ind.* (occas. contracted forms) 1 -scæt, -scát, -sceát, 2 schet, 2–3 shat. *Pa. t.* 1 -scéd, -scēad, 3 sad, 3–6 sched; 1 sc(e)ádde (? scēadde), 2–3 scedde, 2–5 schedde, shadde, 3 scede, chadde, 3–4 ssedde, 3–5 shed(d)e, schadde, 4 scade, 4–5 schad, shad, 5–6 schede, shadd, 6 *Sc.* s(c)hedd, schaid, 6–7 shead, 7 (9 *dial.*) shodd, shod, 4– shed; 1 -sceádade, 4 schedide, 4–5 scheded, 5 scheddet, 5–6 scheddit, 9 *dial.* shedded, sheaded. *Pa. pple.* 1 sceáden (? scēaden), 2 -sceden, 3 scheden, scede, 4–5 schede, shede; 3 sced(d, i-sced, sad(d, 3 (*Ormin*), 5 shadd, 4–5 shad (4 yshad), 4 i-schod, y-ssed, 4–5 schad, yshed, yschad, 5 xad; 4–6 sched (3–5 schedd, isched, 4 isedd, yssed, 4–5 shadde, 5–6 shedde, 6 *Sc.* scheid, 4, 6 *Sc.* schedde (4 yschedde), 9 *dial.* shod, shud, 4– shed; 1 ȝesceádad, 5–6 shedded, 6 sheeded. [A Com. Teut. verb (wanting in Scandinavian), originally str. (redupl.): OE. *sc(e)ádan, scēadan*, pa. t. *sc(e)ád, scēad*, pa. pple. *sc(e)áden* (? *scēaden*), corresponds, either directly or with consonant-ablaut, to OFris. *skêda, skêtha* wk. (mod.Fris. *skiede, schêde*, NFris. *skêr, skial, skias*), OS. *skêdan, skêthan*, pa. pple. *giskêthan*, MLG. *schêden, scheiden*, MDu. *schêden, scheiden, schêen, scheien* (mod.Du. *scheiden*, pa. t. *scheidde*, pa. pple. *geschieden*), OHG. *sceidan*, pa. t. *sciad, scied*, pa. pple. *gisceidan* (MHG. *scheiden*, pa. t. *schiet*, pa. pple. *gescheiden*; mod.G. *scheiden*, pa. t. *schied*, pa. pple. *geschieden*), Goth. *skaidan*, pa. pple. *skaidan-s*; the vb. in all these langs. has the sense to separate, divide; the forms represent two distinct types of the Teut. root, **skaiþ-* (: **skiþ-*) and **skaid-* (: **skid-*); for cognates in Teut. see SHEATH *sb.*, SHIDE *sb.* The pre-Teut. **skeit-*: **skoit-*: **skit-*, from which both the Teut. types descend (with difference due to consonant-ablaut), is not directly represented outside Teut., but is prob. related to the widespread Indogermanic root **sk(h)eid-*: **sk(h)oid-*: **sk(h)id-*, occurring, e.g., in Skr. *čhid-* to split, Lith. *skëdžù* I make thin, separate, divide, *skëda* chip of wood, Gr. σχίζειν to split, σχίζα billet of wood, L. *scindĕre* to cut, cleave.

The original OE. *sc(e)ádan* would normally yield (midland and southern) ME. and mod.E. *shode*, which is occas. found in writings from the 12th to the 15th c. It would appear that by the side of the original form OE. had (presumably in certain districts, but evidence is lacking for localization) an altered form *scēadan*, with change of rising into falling diphthong; from this the modern *shed* (ʃed) descends by a development parallel to that of *bread, dead*, from OE. *bréad, déad*.

The OE. verb retained its strong conjugation in WS., but in Northumbrian occurs only as weak (usually with forms *-scēadade, -scēadad* on the analogy of the *ō* stems; rarely contracted *scēadde*). In early ME. there were forms like *sched* pa. t., *scheden* pa. pple., representing the original strong conjugation; forms like *schedid*, representing the wk. forms of OE.; and forms like *schĕdde, schĕdd*, prob. not repr. ONorthumb. *scēadde*, but new formations due to the analogy of vbs. like *rede* (read), *lede* (lead), etc. The mod. pa. t. and pa. pple. *shed* are prob. to be regarded as representing the last type of conjugation, which was by far the most frequent in ME.]

**1. a.** *trans.* To separate, divide. Now only *dial.*, chiefly in farming uses: To separate (lambs) from the ewes, or (calves) from the cows; to separate (cattle, sheep) from the herd or flock. † ***to shed the shanks*** (Sc.): to set the legs apart.

*c* **1000** *Soul's Addr.* 148 (Gr.) Þonne sceadene beoþ þa synfullan & þa soðfæstan on þam mæran dæȝe. *c* **1200** ORMIN 16865, & forrþi wass þatt name hemm [*sc.* the Pharisees] sett, Forr þatt teȝȝ wærenn shadde, Swa summ hemm þuhhte, fra þe follc þurrh haliȝ lif & lare. *c* **1200** *Trin. Coll. Hom.* 67 Ure louerd ihesu crist..shodeð þe gode fro þe iuele. Et statuet oues a dextris..and shodeð þe rihtwise an his rihthalue. *a* **1225** *Ancr. R.* 270 Þe ȝeteward..ouh forto winden hweate, & scheaden þe eilen & tet chef urom þe clene cornes. *c* **1250** *Gen. & Ex.* 266 Quan al man-kinde..Sal ben fro dede to liue broȝt, And seli sad fro ðe forwroȝt. *c* **1315** SHOREHAM III. 63 Þat doþ þat manye yschoded [*altered to* y-schodred] ben Fram heuene-ryche festes. **1338** R. BRUNNE *Chron.* (1725) 174 He salle sched vs o sonder, fro Acres salle we go. *Ibid.* 305 Þer scheltron sone was shad [Langt. *sevré*] with Inglis þat were gode. **1390** GOWER *Conf.* III. 136 Logique hath eke in his degre Betwen the trouthe and the falshode The pleine wordes forto schode, So that nothing schal go biside. *a* **1400** *Relig. Pieces* (E.E.T.S.) 61 The sonne to schede þe day fra þe nyght. *c* **1470** HENRY *Wallace* v. 77 Wallace mycht nocht a graith straik on him gett: Ȝhett schede he thaim, a full royd slope was maid. **1535** STEWART *Cron. Scot.* (Rolls) I. 15 Schulderis wer schorne and sched the bodie fra. **1550** LYNDESAY *Sqr. Meldrum* 994 Iudge ȝe gif he hir schankis shed. *c* **1553** in Strype *Eccl. Mem.* (1721) III. App. XI. 28 God..myndeth now to..shede out the Gootes from the Shepe. *c* **1560** A. SCOTT *Poems, Ballad Want. Wemen* 30 For conȝie ȝe may chawcht hir To sched hir schankis in twane. **1584** B. R. tr. *Herodotus* I. 60 The mighty river Gyndes being in this sort shed and derived into .360. brookes. **1600** HOLLAND *Livy* VI. XXV. 234 In the view and account taken of the captives there were some of them known to be Tusculanes, who were shed apart from the rest. **1677** W. NICOLSON in *Trans. Roy. Soc. Lit.* (1870) 318 [Cumberl. and Westm.] *Shed*, to part asunder. **1791** LEARMONT *Poems* 276 I've lambs to shed, and sheep a clipping too. **1824** MACTAGGART *Gallovid. Encycl.* 425 *Shed*, to separate; to separate the calves from the cows, we *shed* them. **1844** H. STEPHENS *Bk. Farm* II. 87 The sheep selected for market are the best conditioned at the time, and to ascertain this it is necessary to handle the whole lot and shed the fattest from the rest. **1921** *Kelso Chron.* 26 Aug. 2 A better never lifted paw, To shed or wear off a stell. **1942** R. B. KELLEY *Animal Breeding* xv. 140 The shepherd has to shed or separate these [marked sheep] from the flock of 20. **1949** *Scots Mag.* Sept. 463 Wicket-gates for 'shedding' the sheep into various pens. **1951** N. M. GUNN *Well at World's End* xvii. 131 Some evenings ago, I fell in with a shepherd. I had shed one of his ewes and ultimately run her into a corner. **1977** *Field* 13 Jan. 55/2 The shepherd guided the dog to cut out, or 'shed' the marked sheep. **1981** I. A. GORDON in *N.Z. Listener* 27 June 86 When you shed sheep they are out in the open.

*absol.* **1844** H. STEPHENS *Bk. Farm* II. 618 Those shepherds who dog, force, and shed much about a march, I consider them as bad herds for their masters as for the neighbouring farmer.

†**b.** To set apart, draft off *from* a community. *Obs.*

**1584** B. R. tr. *Herodotus* I. 54 They ioyned felowship with other their countreymen which before tyme were shed from the city to inhabite that place.

†**c.** *refl.* To separate oneself, part *from*; to come apart. Also (of troops) to scatter *asunder*.

*c* **1200** *Ormin* 3200 Forrþrihht anan he..shadde himm all þweorrt ut fra menn. *c* **1400** *Laud Troy Bk.* 7764 He schet aboute him fer & ner..The Gregeis offte In-sunder hem scheded. *a* **1578** LINDESAY (Pitscottie) *Chron. Scot.* (S.T.S.) II. 90 The new wark zeid frome the auld and sched the self.

†**d.** *intr.* for *refl.* To separate, divide, come apart; to part company; to depart; to part *with* a possession. *Obs.*

*c* **1000** *Sax. Leechd.* II. 116 Þonne dæȝ & niht scade, drince þonne þone drenc. **1338** R. BRUNNE *Chron.* (Rolls) 991 Þe Gregeys schadden sone asonder. **13..** *E.E. Allit. P.* A. 411 Þow wost wel when þy perle con schede, I was ful ȝong & tender of age. **1572** MASCALL *Plant. & Graff.* 37 Ye shall binde it so, till the fruites or cliftes be couered..with your sayde hempe, except the oylet and his tayle, the which ye must not couer, for that tayle will shed apart, if the shielde doe take. **1576** GASCOIGNE *Grief of Joy* IV. iii. Wks. 1910 II. 548 Thou showldest foresee, that fagott sticks do hold, Together fast, and seldome list to shedd. **1585** JAS. I *Ess. Poesie* (Arb.) 45 Such was the loue, and reuerence they her bure, Ilk day whill euen, ay whill they shedd at night. **1603** *Philotus* lxxxix, Be Christ I sall thy nurture nip, Richt scharply or wee sched. **1659** W. GUTHRIE *Chr. Gt. Interest* II. (1724) 214 If thou hast a Desire after Jesus Christ,..and cannot think of parting with his blessed Company for ever, or, if thou must shed with him, yet dost wish well to him [etc.].

**2.** *trans.* **a.** To part, or divide (the hair; also the hair or wool of an animal). Also *refl.* of the person. Now *Sc.* and *dial.*

*a* **1300** *Cursor M.* 18848 Metli har was on his chin, And als his hefd was scheud [*Gött.* sched] in tuin. **1387** TREVISA *Higden* (Rolls) V. 369 Þey used to schere of þe heere of hir heed from þe molde to þe nolle, but to fore þey hadde lokkes i-schod [β. ysched; L. *discriminatam*] hongynge doun to þe mouth. **1388** WYCLIF *Judith* x. 3 Sche schedide [1382 platte] the heer of hir heed. **1390** GOWER *Conf.* I. 101 Bot with no craft of combes brode Thei myhte hire hore lockes schode. *c* **1430** *Pilgr. Lyf Manhode* II. lxxiv. (1869) 103, I loue better ..to keembe myn hed, to shode me [Fr. *grauer mon chef*]. **1523–34** FITZHERB. *Husb.* §42 Than take hym, and shede the woll with thy fyngers, there as the scab is, and with thy fynger laye a lyttell terre thervpon. **1530** PALSGR. 717/1 Shede your heare that hangeth so yvell favouredly aboute your eares. **1548** PATTEN *Exped. Scot.* C viij b, A fellowe lyke a man..red hedded, curld rounde about & shedded afore. **1607** TOPSELL *Four-f. Beasts* 411 Make a salue thereof, and with your finger annoint all the sore places, sheading the haire as you go. **1610** GUILLIM *Heraldry* IV. vii. (1632) 296 The Combe is..of most vse with women for shedding and trimming their haire and head-tires. **1621** G. SANDYS *Ovid's Met.* VI. (1626) 111 Her haire She forthwith sheds. **1822** A. CUNNINGHAM *Tradit. Tales, Mother's Dream* (1887) 123 He shed back his long and moistened locks from a burning and bewildered brow. **1832** MOTHERWELL *Poems* 41 Let me shed by your hair. **1844** A. RODGER in *Songs for Nursery* 44 Let me shed your shining hair. **1888** DOUGHTY *Trav. Arabia Deserta* I. 595 He was of goodly great stature, with..hair shed..and hanging down from the midst in tresses.

*intr.* for *refl.* **13..** *E.E. Allit. P.* B. 1690 Faxe fyltered ..þat schad fro his schulderes to his schyre wykes.

**b.** *Weaving.* To divide (the warp-threads), to make a 'shed' in (a web). Cf. SHED *sb.*[1] 6.

**1839** URE *Dict. Arts* 1285 The weaver..thus sheds the warp, by lifting and depressing each alternate thread. **1863** J. WATSON *Weaving* 196 It has been explained how a common Web is shedded, and a few words will show the difference for the shedding in this loom.

†**3. a.** To cleave, divide (something) with a knife, weapon, etc. *Obs.*

**13..** *K. Alis.* 2772 Ac, ar the gate weore y-loke, Mony ponne was to-broke;..And mony brayn was y-schad. **13..** *Gaw. & Gr. Knt.* 425 Þe scharp of þe schalk..scade hit in twynne. *c* **1470** *Gol. & Gaw.* 604 Ane schene scheild and ane schaft, that scharply was sched.

†**b.** *transf.* Of birds, fishes: To 'cleave' (the air, the water) in flight or swimming. *Obs.*

*c* **1480** HENRYSON *Mor. Fab., Preiching of Swallow* vii, The foullis..Scheddand the air with pennis greit and small. **1599** ALEX. HUME *Hymn* ii. 184 The little friand fish in flude, and dentie volatil, Quhilks shedds the waters, & the winds, he traps them at his wil.

†**4. a.** To scatter, sprinkle; in later use only, to sow (seed). *Obs.*

*c* **1000** *Sax. Leechd.* II. 38 Wiþ wyrmum on eaȝum ȝenim beolonan sæd scead on gleda. *c* **1374** CHAUCER *Boeth.* I. met. i. (1868) 4 Heeres hore ben schad [orig. *funduntur*] ouertymelyche vpon myne heued. **1382** WYCLIF *Gen.* xxxviii. 9 He..shede the seed into the erthe. **1608** WILLET *Hexapla Exod.* 535 The seede which was shed the former yeere. **1633** P. FLETCHER *Pisc. Eclogues* v. ii, That primrose there Which 'mongst those violets sheds his golden hair, Seems the sunnes little sonne, fixt in his azure spheare. *c* **1770** HUNTER in Winter *Syst. Husb.* (1797) 173 The drill plow..which by..shedding the seed and covering it, leave[s] the land stocked with plants.

*fig.* **1414** *26 Pol. Poems* (1904) 58 Þan god wil..Drede and stryf among hem shede.

†**b.** To disperse, scatter; to rout, put to flight.

*c* **1250** *Gen. & Ex.* 672 Ðat folc is wide on londe sad. **1387** TREVISA *Higden* (Rolls) VII. 493 Þere sche bode here knyȝtes þat were al i-sched. *c* **1480** HENRYSON *Test. Cress.* (Charteris) 18 The Northin wind had purifyit the Air, And sched the mistie cloudis fra the sky. **1633** P. FLETCHER *Purple Isl.* XII. lxv, His tail, whose folds were wont the starres to shed, Now stretcht at length, close to his belly clings.

**c.** *dial.* To rake out (a fire).

**1873** MURDOCH *Doric Lyre* 26 (E.D.D.), I had shed my fire An' hame was ettlin' to retire.

**d.** To throw off, repel (rain, sunlight, etc.). Now chiefly *dial.*

*c* **1400** *Anturs of Arth.* ii. (Douce MS.), Schurde in a short cloke, þat þe rayne shedes. **1616** SURFLET & MARKHAM *Country Farm* II. lxii. 318 Neither must they be made as some are flat at the top, and shallow, but ascending pyramid wise, smaller and smaller till it come to the top, for thereby it..sheddeth off the raine much better. **1778** [W. H. MARSHALL] *Minutes Agric.* 30 Aug. 1774, The elevation would shed off the rain, and prevent its lodging in the ears. **1818** SCOTT *Hrt. Midl.* xxviii, But it sheds the sun weel aff. **1885** *Harper's Mag.* Apr. 796/2 As a shaggy dog sheds water from his coat. **1886** C. SCOTT *Sheep-Farming* 99 The straw has finally to be raked down on the outside, so as to shed rain well.

†**e.** *refl.* and *intr.* To be dispersed, scatter. *Obs.*

**1456** SIR G. HAYE *Law Arms* (S.T.S.) 61 The bataill of Pompee began to sched and till irk, and toke the flicht. **1535** STEWART *Cron. Scot.* (Rolls) III. 429 Lyke ony scheip tha schudrit all and sched, Quhair euir tha come befoir his face tha fled. **1579** SPENSER *Sheph. Cal.* Oct. 35 Sike prayse is smoke, that sheddeth in the skye. **1589** *Pasquil's Ret.* A iij, The great Empire of..Alexander, like a flame of fire in a heape of flaxe, when it was at the highest, did shed it selfe suddainlie in the ayre. **1650** FULLER *Pisgah* II. v. xviii. 173 That the Pillar of Smoak which ascended from the sacrifice, curled only upwards in direct wreaths to heaven, without any scattering, or shedding it self abroad.

**5. a.** To spill (liquids), let fall (crumbs, etc.) *Obs.* exc. *dial.*

*a* **1225** *Ancr. R.* 344 Of alle kudde & kuðe sunnen, ase of prude..of sum uals word..of schorn leihtre, of scheden crumen oðer ale, oðer leten þinges muwlen oðer rusten. *c* **1380** *Sir Ferumb.* 2296 Schad was al þe wyn. **1526** *Pilgr. Perf.* (W. de W. 1531) 47 The vessell can not holde yᵉ wyne, but anone it breketh, & so shedeth the wyne. **1580** LYLY *Euphues* (Arb.) 455 By carrying water in a siue, not shedding one drop from Tiber to the Temple of Vesta. **16..** *Boy & Mantle* 181 in *Percy Fol. MS.* II. 311 He said, 'there was noe Cuckolde shall drinke of my horne, But he shold itt sheede, either behind or beforne.' **1622** MABBE tr. *Aleman's Guzman d'Alf.* II. 315 In pulling forth my Handkerchiefe, I had shed all my money. **1785** TRUSLER *Mod. Times* II. 83 A bag of tea ..was burst, and a good deal of the tea shed. **1839** STERLING *Alfred the Harper* xviii. Poems 136 Grim sat the chiefs;.. His iron mace was grasped by one, By one his wine was shed. **1847** *Ockley's Hist. Saracens* (ed. 4) 216 *note*, The crafty Harmozanda shed the vase to the ground. **1866** WAUGH *Ben an th' Bantam* iv. 73 His jackass..broke her pitcher, an' sheeded th' milk. *Ibid.* 74 Are yo noan beawn to pay for th' milk 'at wur shed, then?

*absol.* *c* **1430** *Stans Puer* 60 in *Babees Bk.*, Fille not þi spoon lest in þe cariage It scheede bi side.

†**b.** *intr.* Of a liquid: To spill *over*. *Obs.*

**1601** DOLMAN *La Primaud. Fr. Acad.* III. (1618) 769 If one put neuer so little water into a vessell already brimmefull, the vppermost part thereof will shedde ouer.

**6.** *trans.* To pour, pour out. (The ordinary rendering of L. *fundere, effundere*, etc.)

†**a.** Of a personal agent: To pour (water, etc.). Also with *out*. *Obs.*

*a* **1225** *Ancr. R.* 320 'Effunde sicut aquam cor tuum'. 'Sched ut', he seið, Ieremie, 'ase water þine heorte'. **1382** WYCLIF *Exod.* xxiv. 6 And so Moyses took the half parti of the blood, and putte it into chalices: and that other party he shedde [Vulg. *fudit*] vpon the auteer. **1398** TREVISA *Barth. De P.R.* XIX. xxxvi. (1495) 879 Cerusa is gendryd and comyth of vapour of stronge vynegre effusyd and shedde on thynne plates of leed. **1483** CAXTON *Golden Leg.* 247/2 He shadde water on his hede and baptysed hym in the name of Jhesu Crist. **1530** PALSGR. 701/2, I shedde out lycoure out of a vessel. **1595** *Locrine* III. Prol. 11 A subtill Adder..Priuily shead his poison through his bones. **1614** GORGES *Lucan* I. 37 Then doth he take a faire large bull..And twixt his hornes pure wine he sheads. **1621** G. SANDYS *Ovid's Met.* II. (1626) 42 Banefull poyson; which she sheads Into her bones, and through her liuer spreads.

**b.** Of a vessel, receptacle, a fountain, etc.: To pour forth (its contents).

**1430–40** LYDG. *Bochas* VIII. xii[i]. (1494) D j, Which lyke a conducte vpon euery syde Shad out water as any cristall clere. **1668** CULPEPER & COLE *Barthol. Anat.* I. xvii. 47 They are..Veins and Arteries..which end at the Heads of the Caruncles, into which they shed their wheyish humor. **1870** BRYANT *Iliad* XVI. 4 As when a fountain sheds Dark waters streaming down a precipice.

†**c.** *refl.* Of a river, etc.: To discharge itself. Also, to overflow *over* its banks. *Obs.*

**1555** WATREMAN *Fardle Facions* I. iii. 34 Gently sheadyng hymself ouer his bancques, he [Nilus] leaueth in the countrie a merueilous fertilitie. **1610** HOLLAND *Camden's Brit.* I. 696 Coc making no long course sheadeth himselfe into Wherf. *c* **1630** RISDON *Surv. Devon* §28 (1810) 34 The riveret Sid shedding itself into the sea.

†**d.** *fig.* To 'pour out' (one's heart, feelings, prayers, etc.). *Obs.*

*c* **1420** *Prymer* (1895) 67 [*Ps.* xlii. 4], I biþouȝte of þese þingis, & y schedde out in me my soule. **1526** *Pilgr. Perf.* (W. de W. 1531) 137 Ronne to our lorde, & shede forth your herte before hym. **1596** DALRYMPLE tr. *Leslie's Hist. Scot.* I. 111 And throuch thair prayers, quhilkes ydenly wᵗ al diligence thay sched for thair cuntrey, appeir to mitigat the ire of God.

**e.** To emit, give forth, pour out (spawn, eggs, †seminal fluid, etc.).

*c* **1386** CHAUCER *Pars. T.* 503 Vnkyndely synne by which man or womman shedeth hire nature in manere or place ther as [etc.]. **1398** TREVISA *Barth. De P.R.* XIII. xxvi. (1495) 458 Ryuer fysshe and fresshe of marreys sheden more theyr pesen and ofter than other fysshe. *a* **1450** MYRC 1046 Take also wel in mynde. Ȝef þou haue sched þyn owne kynde,

Slepynge or wakynge nyȝt or day. **1538** BALE *Thre Lawes* II. B vj b, I was with Onan not vnacquaynted, Whan he on the grounde hys increase shed. **1584** B. R. tr. *Herodotus* II. 93 These male fishe as they passe still onwarde shed theyr seede by the way. **1617** MORYSON *Itin.* I. 154 There is a Fountaine, or a statua of a woman.. and this statua shed water from all the haires of the head. **1630** in Binnell *Descr. Thames* (1758) 66 Roaches do then shed their Spawn. **1697** DRYDEN *Virg. Georg.* III. 440 From their Groins they shed A slimy Juice, by false Conception bred. **1822–29** *Good's Study Med.* (ed. 3) I. 534 [Polypi] which, if they discharge any thing, shed blood. **1855** BROWNING *An Epistle* 24, I have shed sweat enough, left flesh and bone On many a flinty furlong of this land. **1864** *Rep. Sea Fisheries Comm.* (1865) II. 1189/1 This was fresh spawn just shed. **1880** *Times* 21 Dec. 6/4 The large number of salmon just ready to shed their eggs.

**7. a.** To cause (blood) to flow from the body by cutting or wounding; to let fall (a person's blood) on the ground, etc.

*c* **1205** LAY. 5187 Heo smiten to-gædere.. redde blod scede; rinkas feollen. *a* **1225** *Ancr. R.* 402 Þis blod, for ou i-sched upo þe herde two treon, schal makien ou Sarepciens. *c* **1290** *Beket* 2185 in *S. Eng. Leg.* 169 Forto gaderi of þe blode þat i-sched was on þe grounde. *a* **1300** *Cursor M.* 1129 His blod on erth sced lijs. *Ibid.* 4151 Þat na blod o him be schedd. *c* **1300** *K. Horn* (Laud MS.) 920 Cubert hem broute al honder He schedde of here blode And makede hem al wode. *a* **1325** *MS. Rawl. B.* 520 lf. 50 *Blodwite*, þat is quite of amerciaments for blod isede. *c* **1375** *Sc. Leg. Saints* i. (*Petrus*) 376 Ger wipe myn blud of ȝon stede, quhare I for þe gert it be schede! **1387** TREVISA *Higden* (Rolls) I. 429 Þe blood reed, þat þe mayde Wynefrede Schadde at þat putte. *c* **1400** MAUNDEV. (1839) xxxi. 307 In that Cytee is no man so hardy, to schede Blode of no man. *c* **1400** *Destr. Troy* 7929 My body hath þou brisit, & my blode shed. *c* **1450** *Cov. Myst.* (Shaks. Soc.) 275 ȝe xal drynk myn blood with gret devocyon, Wheche xal be xad ffor mannys love. **1526** *Pilgr. Perf.* (W. de W. 1531) 256 b, After that all his blode was shed. **1705** ADDISON *Italy* 3 Ulysses here the Blood of Victims shed. **1847** MRS. KERR tr. *Ranke's Hist. Servia* 128 Their attendants had already come to blows, and did not separate until blood had been shed.

**b.** With pregnant sense. (*a*) ***to shed the blood of*** (another person or persons): to kill in a manner involving effusion of blood; often *loosely*, to kill by violent means (whether blood is literally shed or not). So ***to shed blood***: to destroy human life by violent means. ***to shed much, little blood***: to destroy many, few lives. (*b*) ***to shed*** (one's own) ***blood***: to undergo wounds or violent death in battle, martyrdom, or the like (*for* some person or cause, one's country, etc.).

(*a*) ? *a* **1100** *Ags. Ps.* xiii. 6 (Spelman) Hrade fot heora to aȝeotenne [*Trin. Coll. MS.* to scedende] blod. *c* **1275** *Passion Our Lord* 346 in *O.E. Misc.* 47 Þe gywes were ful bysie to scheden his blod. *c* **1290** *S. Eng. Leg.* 73 He mid vnriȝhte hadde i-sched mani ane mannes blod. *a* **1300** *Cursor M.* 11805 Hu had he hert to sced þair blod þat neuer did til him bot godd? **1340** *Ayenb.* 239 Moche uolk weren ysslaȝe and moche blod þer y-ssed. **1382** WYCLIF *Ps.* cv. 38 And thei shadden [**1388** schedden] out the innocent blod. **1430–40** LYDG. *Bochas* VIII. x[i]v. (1494) D iij b, And where he rode cristen blode he shadde. **1471** CAXTON *Recuyell* (Sommer) 156 Many ther were that her blood was shedde on the lande. **1500–20** DUNBAR *Poems* lxii. 43 His saikles blude agane thai sched. *c* **1560** A. SCOTT *Ps.* li. 58 Lord God, deliuer me, and gyd Frome schedding blude, and homicyd. **1577** GRANGE *Golden Aphrod.* etc. Q ij, Bloud shall be shedde for bloud, and life shall pay for lyfe. **1596** DALRYMPLE tr. *Leslie's Hist. Scot.* II. 27 That day in that feild was sched mekle scotis blude. **1697** DRYDEN *Virg. Past.* VIII. 65 Relentless Love the cruel Mother led The Blood of her unhappy Babes to shed. **1719** DE FOE *Crusoe* I. 235 The Thoughts of shedding humane Blood for my Deliverance, were very terrible to me. **1823** SCOTT *Quentin D.* xxxv, He is a man of holy church —we may not shed his blood. **1838** JAMES *Robber* ii, I will shed no blood, except in our own defence. **1847** C. BRONTE *Jane Eyre* vi, They shed blood they had no right to shed. (*b*) **12..** *Song. Virg.* 15 in *O.E. Misc.* 194 Bi-sek him.. þat for ous alle sad is blod. *a* **1250** *Owl & Night.* 1616 For heom ich chadde mi blod. *c* **1315** SHOREHAM I. 83 To wesschen ous cryst schedde his blod And water out of hys wonde. *c* **1375** *Sc. Leg. Saints* xxxvi. (*Baptista*) 1009 þat haly nowmir to fulfil, þat sched þare blud for cristis sak. **1471** CAXTON *Recuyell* (Sommer) 624, I my self haue shedde moche of my blood. **1535** FISHER *Ways Perf. Relig.* Wks. (1876) 385 Men and women for his loue haue shead theyr blood. **1586** T. B. *La Primaud. Fr. Acad.* I. (1594) 103 This monarch [Alexander] sustaining infinite labor, and cheerefully sheading his blood. **1707** FREIND *Peterborow's Cond. Sp.* 173 My Subjects are in a disposition to shed the last drop of their Blood for me. **1844** *Mem. Babylonian Princess* II. 63 This spot, where our Saviour shed his blood to save all mankind from everlasting death.

**8.** To emit and let fall in drops.

**a.** With *tears* as obj.

*c* **1175** *Lamb. Hom.* 157 Swiche teres scedde M. Magdalene þa heo wosch ure drihtenes fet. **1423** JAS. I. *Kingis Q.* cxvii, And of my cristall teris that bene schede, The hony flouris growen vp and sprede. **1575** GASCOIGNE *Kenelworth* Wks. 1910 II. 128 Marke what teares they shed. *c* **1610** *Lives of Women Saints* 102/9 Who can recounte what plentie of teares she shodd for her owne sinnes, and the necessities of gods church. **1705** ADDISON *Italy, Pavia* 37 A Tear that our Saviour shed over Lazarus. **1862** MISS BRADDON *Lady Audley* xxxv, He could only shed childish tears of despair and terror. **1908** [MISS E. FOWLER] *Betw. Trent & Ancholme* 45 One [child] was sobbing and shedding tears.

*slang.* **1864** *Hotten's Slang Dict.*, *Shed a tear*, to take a dram or glass of neat spirits... 'Now then, old fellow, come and shed a tear!'

†**b.** *absol.* To shed tears. *Obs. rare*$^{-1}$.

**16..** ? WEBSTER & ROWLEY *Cure for Cuckold* II. iii. (1661) C 4 b, O Urse, give me leave to shed!

**c.** With obj. rain, dew, etc.

**1590** SPENSER *F.Q.* II. iii. 24 And, when she spake, Sweet words like dropping honny she did shed. **1697** DRYDEN *Virg. Georg.* III. 520 Rising Cynthia sheds her Silver Dews. *c* **1730** RAMSAY *Masque* 106 And cease, black clouds, to shed, or wet, or snaw. **1812** J. WILSON *Isle of Palms* III. 293 When evening sheds her dew.

†**d.** *intr.* Of rain, snow, etc.: To fall. *Obs.*

**13..** *Gaw. & Gr. Knt.* 506 Schyre schedez þe rayn in schowrez, ful warme. *Ibid.* 956 Hir brest.. Schon schyrer þen snawe, þat scheder [*read* schedez] on hillez. *c* **1386** CHAUCER *Monk's T.* 843 But swich a reyn doun fro the welkne shadde That slow the fyr. **1616** SURFLET & MARKHAM *Country Farm* II. lxii. 319 If anie raine happen to fall thereupon, yet it may by no meanes sinke into the Hiue, but rather fall off, and shed vpon the earth.

**9.** *trans.* To send forth as an emanation.

**a.** To throw (light) *upon* something. *lit.* and *fig.*

In the figurative use of the phrase *shed* is in our quots. not found before the 19th c.; earlier *throw* or *cast* was used.

*c* **1200** *Trin. Coll. Hom.* 161 Þis edie maiden seinte marie of hire holie licame shedeð þat soðe liht þe lihteð alle brihte þinges on eorðe and ec on heuene. **13..** *Cursor M.* 17883 (Gött.) Þat light es nu apon vs schede þar we sitte in þe schadu of dede. *c* **1402** LYDG. *Compl. Bl. Knt.* 3 And Phebus gan to shede his stremes shene Amid the Bole. **1599** SIR J. DAVIES *Nosce Teipsum* Ded. iv, In euery place as Cynthia sheds her beames. **1775** R. CHANDLER *Trav. Asia M.* viii. (1825) I. 30 The stars shone in a clear blue sky, shedding a calm serene light. **1805** WORDSW. *Prelude* XIV. 279 O capacious Soul! Placed on this earth to love and understand, And from thy presence shed the light of love. **1853** ROBERTSON *Serm.* Ser. III. xxi. (1876) 272 He has been shedding a glory round human life. **1853** KINGSLEY *Hypatia* xix, A lamp of strange form hung from the ceiling, and shed a dim and lurid light. **1860** [see LIGHT *sb.* 6 a]. **1865** DICKENS *Mut. Fr.* III. vi, You come like I don't know what.. shedding a halo all around you. **1912** *Times* 19 Oct. 7/3 The statement ..sheds little light upon a situation still enveloped in mystery.

†**b.** With inverted construction: To suffuse *with* light. *Obs.*

**1412–20** LYDG. *Troy Bk.* I. 2771 Sche.. sawe.. þat þe ferþe parte Of þe mone was schad with newe liȝt.

**c.** To give forth, diffuse (fragrance, sound, heat, etc.); to pour out, impart (influence, blessings, qualities, etc.). Also with advs., *abroad*, †*forth*, †*out*.

*a* **1325** *Prose Psalter* xliv. 3 Grace is shadde in þy lippes. **1412–20** LYDG. *Troy Bk.* I. 2612 And holsomm bawme is schad among þe grene. *c* **1500** *Melusine* iv. 22 This might not be perfightly knowen, yf thou shadd nat vpon the men somwhat of thy full & deuyne grace. **1525** TINDALE *N.T.* Prol., Tyll Christ have.. powred into him that selfe good thynge whych he shedeth forth afterwarde on other. **1526** —— *Rom.* v. 5 For the love that god hath vnto vs is sheed abrod [Gr. ἐκκέχυται] in oure hertes [so later versions] by the holy gost, which is geven vnto vs. **1535** COVERDALE *Acts* x. 45 The gift of y^e holy goost was shed out also vpon the Heythen. **1587** GOLDING *De Mornay* Pref. (ad fin.), Now God vouchsafe to shead out his blessing vpon this worke. *Ibid.* iv. 47 The heate which the Sunne sheadeth into vs from aboue. **1642–7** H. MORE *Song of Soul* III. I. v, Wakend by piercing trump, that farre doth shed Its searching sound. **1709** STEELE *Tatler* No. 130 ¶ 11 All the Prosperity and Success which Heaven ever shed on a Mortal. **1716** GAY *Trivia* II. 443 Now, heaven-born Charity! thy blessings shed. **1760–72** H. BROOKE *Fool of Qual.* (1808) I. 155 For him the stars shine and shed influences upon earth. **1769** GRAY *Ode for Music* 73 Bid it round heaven's altars shed The fragrance of it's blushing head. **1807** MOORE *Ir. Melodies, 'Harp that once'* 2 The harp that once through Tara's halls, The soul of music shed. **1812** CARY *Dante, Parad.* IV. 115 Whose lively words Still shed new heat and vigour through My soul. **1837** CARLYLE *Fr. Rev.* III. III. vi, The waving of it shed terror through the souls of men. **1852** MRS. STOWE *Uncle Tom's C.* xvi, Your piety sheds respectability on us. **1877** R. H. HUTTON *Ess.* (ed. 2) I. Pref. 19 An infinite power shed abroad in the world.

*absol.* **1525** TINDALE *N.T.* Prol., Be faith we receave of god, and be love we shed oute agayne.

**10.** To cast off by natural process.

**a.** To cast off as exuviæ; to undergo the falling of (hair, etc.). Also *absol.*

**1510** STANBRIDGE *Vocabula* (W. de W.) C vj b, *Depennesco*, to multe, or to shede fethers. **1530** PALSGR. 701/2 I shede my heare, my heare falleth. **1594** MARLOWE & NASHE *Dido* I. i. 36 Venus Swannes shall shed their siluer downe. **1721** BRADLEY *Philos. Acc. Wks. Nat.* 91 The Stag and some other sorts of Deer are subject to shedding and renewing their Horns annually. **1732** A. MONRO *Anatomy* (ed. 2) 170 Some more of those [teeth].. are shedded. **1818** SCOTT *Hrt. Midl.* xxxi, A broken and soiled white feather, intersected with one which had been shed from the train of a peacock. **1833** *Hunter's Catal. Physiol. Ser. Comp. Anat. Mus. Coll. Surg.* I. 100 [Elephants] do not shed their teeth as other animals do that have more than one. **1845** JUDD *Margaret* II. xi. (1874) 346 When hens are shedding their feathers they don't lay eggs. **1899** *Allbutt's Syst. Med.* VIII. 537 It is very common for the whole of the nails to be shed in the attack. *Ibid.* 809 The epidermis becoming shed.

*absol.* **1879** *St. Nicholas* Nov. 84/2 He still grows till he is called a 'Buster', and then sheds. Then he is called a 'Soft Crab'. **1974** M. G. EBERHART *Danger Money* (1975) xiii. 139 Her jacket still bore some stray beige hairs from Toby [*sc.* a cat]; doesn't he ever stop shedding? she thought.

*transf.* and *fig.*

**1776** FOOTE *Capuchin* II. (1778) 116 When the sun and summer of plenty returns, I shall shed my coat like a colt. **1853** KANE *Grinnell Exp.* xvi. (1856) 121 The floes.. now shed off dusty wreaths of snow. **1865** SWINBURNE *Chastelard* V. i. 175 The day comes when a woman sheds her sin As a bird moults. **1910** *Spectator* 20 Aug. 269/1 He sheds his bad reputation as a snake its skin.

**b.** Of trees, plants: To lose, cast off (leaves, flowers, bark, etc.).

**1598** BARNFIELD *Poems, Compl. Poetrie* xv, The Trees (for sorrowe) shead their fading Leaues. **1667** MILTON *P.L.* IX. 893 From his slack hand the Garland wreath'd for Eve Down drop'd, and all the faded Roses shed. **1798** SOPHIA LEE *Canterb. T., Yng. Lady's T.* II. 295 The myrtles ..[were] shedding their uncherished blossoms over the perishing works of man. **1819** SHELLEY *Ode to West Wind* 16 Thou on whose stream, mid the steep sky's commotion, Loose clouds like earth's decaying leaves are shed. **1857** LIVINGSTONE *Trav.* xxiii. 462 Some of the bushes and trees are green; others are shedding their leaves.

†**c.** To cause the shedding of (leaves). *Obs.*

**1697** DRYDEN *Virg. Georg.* II. 558 When Storms have shed From Vines, the hairy Honours of their Head.

**d.** Of plants: To let fall, cast (seed) out of the receptacle.

**1523–34** FITZHERB. *Husb.* §35 In some countreys.. they do fan theyr corne, the whiche is.. a great saueguarde for shedynge of the corne. **1573** TUSSER *Husb.* (1878) 128 Hops dried in loft, aske tendance oft, And shed their seedes, much more than needes. **1720** P. BLAIR *Bot. Ess.* Pref. 6 The Apices.. are ready to shed the Dust when it [the Flower] is expanded. **1815** J. SMITH *Panorama Sci. & Art* II. 634 As it is apt to shed its seed when ripe, it is advisable to cut it with the dew upon it. **1862** ANSTED *Channel Isl.* IV. xx. (ed. 2) 476 Owing to a bad habit of leaving the crops till over-ripe, large quantities are shed on the fields.

**e.** *colloq.* To drop, let go; to give away (something of no particular value).

**1855** DICKENS *Dorrit* I. xxi, Whether it had occurred to his good friend, that Society might not unreasonably hope that one so blest in his undertakings,.. would shed a little money in the direction of a mission or so to Africa? **1897** MARY KINGSLEY *W. Africa* 391, I shed a box of lucifer matches on her,.. knowing that one of the great charms of a white man to a black is this habit of shedding things.

**f.** *transf.* To take off (a garment); to doff, divest oneself of. Also *fig.*

**1858** *Lawrence* (Kansas) *Republican* 28 Oct. 1/6 She was compelled to 'shed' her woman's 'fixin's', and put on a man's breeches and hickory shirt. **1884** 'MARK TWAIN' *Huck. Finn* xx. 196 The duke shed his coat and said he was all right, now. **1922** JOYCE *Ulysses* 523 You will shed your male garments, you understand, Ruby Cohen? **1976** *Times* 18 Mar. 1 Cabinet members had been allowed to shed their ministerial cloaks and campaign for their own beliefs.

**g.** Of a share: to fall in price by (an amount). *Financial colloq.*

**1947** *Financial Times* 29 Jan. 1/7 Preferences remained comparatively steady, although B.A.G.S. Sixes shed ½ to 22½. **1981** *Times* 11 Apr. 19/5 Hawker Siddeley added 2p to 266p and Glaxo shed a similar figure at 322p.

**h.** ***to shed*** (***a, the***, etc.) ***load***: temporarily to curtail the electricity supply to an area in order to prevent excessive demand on the generating plant. Cf. *load-shedding* s.v. LOAD *sb.* 8.

**1947** *Times* 27 Feb. 7/3 The alternative was to go on running every day, and to shed the load because they could not carry the peak load. **1952** *Blackw. Mag.* Dec. 483/1 And if the local electrician chose the middle of your party to shed a load—well, where were you then? **1975** *IEEE Trans. Power Apparatus & Systems* XCIV. 360/1, 65% of the companies shed 25% or 30% of their load on underfrequency. *Ibid.* 360/2 Most companies shed load in two or three steps.

**11.** *intr.* for *refl.*

†**a.** Of the hair: To fall off. *Obs.*

**1523–34** FITZHERB. *Husb.* §110 Myllettes.. causeth the heare to sheede. **1530** PALSGR. 701/2 Your heares shede, you wyll waxe balde. **1607** TOPSELL *Four-f. Beasts* 487 The same also being mingled with a certaine oyle and warmed together, and anointed vpon the head of any one, whose hair doth shed,.. doth immediatly helpe and cure the same. **1611** MIDDLETON & DEKKER *Roaring Girl* I 4 b, His haire sheds off. **1644** DIGBY *Nat. Bodies* xxxvii. §4. 326 We see the haire of women with childe, is apt to shedde. **1755** H. BAKER in *Phil. Trans.* XLIX. I. 22 When I saw this man, in the month of September last, they [wart-like growths] were shedding off in several places.

**b.** Of grain: To fall from the ear. Also of leaves or flowers: To drop off.

**1557** TUSSER *100 Points Husb.* §96 The corne, being ripe doe but shead as it stande. **1584** COGAN *Haven Health* xlix. 57 Artichokes.. [are] thought to make euill iuice, especially when the flowers begin to shed. **1606** SHAKS. *Tr. & Cr.* I. iii. 319 The seeded Pride That hath to this maturity blowne vp In ranke Achilles, must or now be cropt, Or shedding breed a Nursery of like euil To ouer-bulke vs all. **1681** R. L'ESTRANGE *Tully's Offices* 103 All Disguises pass away, and shed like Flowers. **1707** MORTIMER *Husb.* 355 The broad leaved Lime.. bears a very fine broad Leaf, only it is apt to shed too soon. **1760** R. BROWN *Compl. Farmer* II. 81 White oats are apt to shed most as they lie, and black as they stand. **1790** W. H. MARSHALL *Midl. Counties* II. 442 To *Shade*, to shed, as corn. **1844** *Jrnl. R. Agric. Soc.* V. I. 284 The wheat ..sheds very easily, that is, the corn or grain falls very readily out of the husk.

**12.** To slope. Now *dial.*

**1530** PALSGR. 702/1, I shedde, as an hyll dothe slopewyse downwardes to the valley... It is a pleasaunt syght to se howe the hylles shedde on eache syde in to the medowes. **1688**, **1747** [see SHEDDING *ppl. a.*[1] 3]. **1826** WILBRAHAM *Chesh. Gloss.* (ed. 2), To *Shead* is also to slope down ground regularly.

**13.** The verb-stem in combination: †***shed-fork***, app. = pitchfork; †***shed-spade***, ? a dungfork or graip.

**1559** *Richmond Wills* (Surtees) 134, ij^o shede forks, ij^o shed spaids. **1706** MRS. CENTLIVRE *Platonick Lady* IV. iv. (1707) 57 All my Rigging hangs as if 'twas zhaked on with a Zhed Vork, as the old Zaying is.

**shed** (ʃɛd), *v.*[2] [f. SHED *sb.*[2] I.] *trans.* †**a.** To roof over. *Obs.* **b.** To place in a shed. Also with *up* (*N.Z. colloq.*).

**1546** WRIOTHESLEY *Chron.* (1875) I. 175 The 15^th daie of September the forreine buchers beganne to keepe their markett in Leeden Hall, which was sheeded rounde aboute for them to stand dry. **1850** *Jrnl. R. Agric. Soc.* XI. II. 419, I have left off shedding my own sheep. **1887** *Pall Mall Gaz.*

21 Mar. 2/1 As to hay feeding and shedding during the winter, that is quite impracticable. **1950** *N.Z. Jrnl. Agric.* Oct. 310 Sheep brought in for shearing should be spelled before shedding up, otherwise the pens in the shed get very dirty and much wool is stained. **1981** I. A. GORDON in *N.Z. Listener* 27 June 86 When you shed-up sheep you put them under cover to prevent their fleeces from getting wet before shearing.

**shed** (ʃɛd), *ppl. a.* [pa. pple. of SHED *v.*[1]]

†**1.** Separated; ? in several ownership. *Obs.*

**1425** in *Rep. MSS. Ld. Middleton* (1911) 107 No man with comyn herd ne with sched herd com on the wold after gresse be mowen to it [be] maked and led away. *Ibid.* 108 Nother comyn herd ne sched herd com' in the qwyte corn feld to the korn [be l]ad awey.

**2.** Fallen; discarded, cast off.

*c* **1430** *Chev. Assigne* 119 Of sadde leues of þe wode wrowȝte he hem wedes. **1847** H. MILLER *Test. Rocks* viii. (1857) 318 It is not credible that all the solid shed antlers of such a species of deer could be carried by the same cause to such a distance. **1892** E. REEVES *Homeward Bound* 43 The shed bark hanging over its branches and clinging to its trunk like a sheeted ghost.

**3.** Of blood, tears (see SHED *v.*[1] 7, 8). Also *dial.* of liquids: Spilt.

**1824** MRS. CAMERON *Pink Tippet* III. 17 'There is no use in crying for shed milk,' answered Betty. **1899** *Allbutt's Syst. Med.* VI. 155 Clots formed in shed blood.

**4.** (See SHED *v.*[1] 2 b.)

**1839** URE *Dict. Arts* 1285 The weaver..drives the fly-shuttle swiftly from one side of the loom to the other, between the shed warp yarns.

**shed**: see SHET.

†**'sheddable**, *a. Obs. rare*[−0]. [f. SHED *v.*[1] + -ABLE.] That can be shed or poured out.

**1570** LEVINS *Manip.* 2/17 Shedable, *fusilis.*

**shedded** ('ʃɛdɪd), *ppl. a.*[1] [f. SHED *v.*[1] + -ED[1]. Cf. SHED *ppl. a.*]

†**1.** Cleft, divided. *Obs. rare*[−1].

*c* **1550** ROLLAND *Crt. Venus* IV. 612 The scheddit scheilds.

**2.** Cast off, fallen. *rare*[−1].

**1818** KEATS *Endymion* IV. 769 Its hazle cirque of shedded leaves.

**3.** Of hair, wool: Parted, separated, divided.

**1844** H. STEPHENS *Bk. Farm* III. 1111 The bath thus made is administered by means of a tin-flask..provided with a long spout, by which to pour it along the shedded wool of the sheep.

**shedded** ('ʃɛdɪd), *ppl. a.*[2] [f. SHED *v.*[2] + -ED[2].] Placed in a shed.

**1850** *Jrnl. R. Agric. Soc.* XI. II. 419 The shedded lot [of sheep] did..best in January, and the folded lot in March.

**shedder** ('ʃɛdə(r)). [f. SHED *v.*[1] + -ER[1].]

**1.** One who sheds, in various senses of the verb.

*c* **1388** in *Wyclif's Sel. Wks.* III. 474 Leste Crist dampne ȝowe for traytouris and monquellers and scheders of his blode. **1555** EDEN *Decades* I. VII. (Arb.) 91 Cruel enemies and sheaders of the Spanyshe bludde. *a* **1625** FLETCHER *Bloody Brother* IV. iii, But your parts in all dues to crying blood For vengeance in the shedder, are much greater. **1712** E. COOKE *Voy. S. Sea* 273 The seventh Inca, whose Name signifies, Shedder of bloody Tears. **1880** MISS BRADDON *Just as I am* xiii, He was never a shedder of blood.

**2.** *spec.* **a.** A female fish of the *Salmonidæ* after spawning.

**1588** LAMBARDE *Eiren.* IV. iv. 450 If any person..haue taken there any Salmons or Trouts, out of season, that is, being kippers, or shedders. **1848** [see KIPPER *sb.*[1] and *a.* 1].

**b.** A name for a crab during the period when it is casting its covering integument or shell.

**1872** SCHELE DE VERE *Americanisms* 390.

**3.** *Comb.* (sense 2), as *shedder-crab*, *-salmon*, *trout.*

**1860** BARTLETT *Dict. Amer.* (ed. 3), **Shedder-crab*, a crab which has recently cast his shell, also called a Soft Crab. **1884** E. P. ROE *Nat. Ser. Story* v. in *Harper's Mag.* Apr. 733/2, I was still..fishing,..and fastened on my hook a peeled shedder crab. **1558** *Act 1 Eliz.* c. 17 §1 That no person..shall..take and kyll any..*shedder Salmons, or *shedder Trowtes. **1787** BEST *Angling* (ed. 2) 139 Any kepper or shedder salmon.

**shedding** ('ʃɛdɪŋ), *sb.* [f. SHED *sb.*[1] + -ING[1].] Sheds collectively; a collection of sheds.

**1883** *Times* 26 July 7/5 Shedding of large capacity will be provided. **1889** SKRINE *Mem. E. Thring* 152 These were.. scheming new bonfires. Whose barns or sheddings were safe? **1898** *Field* 14 May 741/1 Long rows of shedding.

**shedding** ('ʃɛdɪŋ), *vbl. sb.* Also 7 **schiding.** [f. SHED *v.*[1] + -ING[1].] The action or an act of the verb SHED in various senses.

**1. a.** Separation, parting, division. Also *concr.* = SHED *sb.*[1] Now only *dial.*, *spec.* with reference to sheep. Cf. SHEADING.

*c* **1200** ORMIN 16863 Forr Farisew bitacneþþ uss Shædinng onn Ennglissh spæche. **1303** R. BRUNNE *Handl. Synne* 12418 'Dymynucyon'..ys to mene also anoþer þyng, Of þy synne to make shedyng. *c* **1440** HYLTON *Scala Perf.* (W. de W. 1494) II. xxxvi, And this is the yefte of loue that makyth shedynge atwyx chosen soules & reproued. **1598** FLORIO, *Scriminatura*, the shedding or diuiding of a womans haires of a head. **1611** COTGR. s.v. *Greve*, *La greve des cheveux* (&, *les cheveux departis en greve*), the shedding, or shading of the haire; the parting thereof on the forehead (after the old fashion). **1768** ROSS *Helenore* 103 Gin he look'd blyth, the lassie looked mair, For shame was past the shedding o' her hair. **1872** BLACK *Adv. Phaeton* xxix, Then we got out to that 'shedding' of the roads, which marks the junction of the highways coming down from Glasgow and Edinburgh. **1921** *Kelso Chron.* 26 Aug. 2 Test—Hauld between two poles, drive round trainer, and proceed between two other sets of poles before penning, shedding, and wearing. **1942** R. B. KELLEY *Animal Breeding* xv. 140 In Scotland 'shedding' is a special feature of the dog's training. **1956** J. MURRAY *Rural Rhymes* 27 An' them they had a sheep tae pairt Frae a' the rest—ca'ed sheddin'. **1957** *Dumfries & Galloway Standard* 19 Oct. 5/6 Midge had a good run out and the most perfect lift in the competition, perfect fetch, driving and shedding but lost one mark in the penning to total 49 points.

*Comb.* **1609** BIBLE (Douay) *Isa.* iii. 20 Our Lord shal take away..the sheading combes. **1832** *Trans. Highl. Soc.* 295 When gathered to the same fold or shedding-place together. **1959** *Times* 18 Sept. 7/5 He appeared to be well in the lead when he reached the shedding ring. **1977** *Field* 13 Jan. 55/2 Each dog guided a bunch of sheep round the formalized trial course and finished by bringing them to his master in the 'shedding' ring.

**b.** *dial.* (*concr.* in *pl.*). See quot.

**1844** H. STEPHENS *Bk. Farm* II. 39 The lambs, dinmonts, or wethers, that are drafted out of the fat stock, are called the sheddings or tails.

**c.** *Weaving.* The division of the warp threads in such a manner as to permit of the passage between them of a shuttle containing the weft. Also *attrib.*

**1863** J. WATSON *Weaving* 84 The sheding being repeated two times over. **1876** BARLOW *Weaving* 111 Shedding motions may be classed into about six varieties. **1888** *Encycl. Brit.* XXIV. 466/1 The three principal motions, shedding, picking and beating up, are of course the same in both [looms]. *Ibid.*, The treadles called the shedding tappets.

**2. a.** Effusion, pouring out; esp. of blood, tears, †secretions.

*c* **1200** *Trin. Coll. Hom.* 65 Ne bringð no synful man quemere loc þenne teares sheding. *a* **1225** *Ancr. R.* 262 Ȝet nabbe ȝe nout wiðstonden uorte þet þe schedunge of ower blode. **1560** DAUS tr. *Sleidane's Comm.* 465 b, They could not kepe them from sheding of teares. **1657** W. COLES *Adam in Eden* ii. 5 It helpeth..the shedding of the gall. **1760–72** H. BROOKE *Fool of Qual.* (1809) III. 38 Their persons were rendered sacred..by unction, or the shedding of hallowed oil upon them. **1874** O'SHAUGHNESSY *Music & Moonlight* 200 Base sheddings of base blood.

†**b.** Infusion, diffusion. *Obs.*

**1398** TREVISA *Barth. De P.R.* III. ix. (1495) 55 By vertue of sprednge and of shedynge of the spyryte of felynge in to all the synewes, all the makynge of the body is founde able to moeue. *c* **1430** *Pilgr. Lyf Manhode* IV. xix. (1869) 185 In whiche we hadden putte fillinge of þe grete tresores of Paradys, þat was the sweete shedinge of oure grace.

†**c.** *shedding of nature*: gonorrhœa. *Obs.*

**1584** COGAN *Haven Health* xlii. 52 A verie good medicine for the shedding of nature.

**3. a.** Dropping, scattering or letting fall, or parting with something.

**1362** LANGL. *P. Pl.* A. VII. 9 Summe schul souwe sakkes for schedyng of Whete. **1523–34** FITZHERB. *Husb.* §35 [Some] do fan theyr corne, the whiche is..a great saueguarde for shedynge of the corne. **1600** J. PORY tr. *Leo's Africa* I. 38 Unnaturall shedding of haire. **1732** A. MONRO *Anatomy* (ed. 2) 170 This Shedding of the Teeth is of good Use. **1863** A. EWING in A. J. ROSS *Mem.* (1877) 356 Our life has far more in it than is suggested by the growing and shedding of leaves.

**b.** *concr.* in *pl.* Shed leaves, etc.

**1803** WORDSW. *Poems Imag.*, *Yew-trees* 22 Upon whose grassless floor of red brown hue, By sheddings from the pining umbrage tinged Perennially. **1856** AIRD *Poet. Wks.* 294 She trode the dun-brown sheddings of the pine.

**c.** The letting fall of seeds.

**1721** POPE *Let. to E. Blount* 21 Oct., Old Fletcher of Saltoune said one day to me. '..I am like a Tree without a Prop, and without young Trees of my own shedding, to grow round me, for Company and Defence.'

**d.** The premature falling of the young bolls of cotton plants.

**1899** *Yearbk. U.S. Dept. Agric.* 728 Over the eastern portion shedding was reported, with complaints of drought in portions of the Carolinas. **1974** J. W. PURSEGLOVE *Trop. Crops* 348 The first flowering period requires relative dryness, otherwise excessive boll shedding ensues.

**4.** *Electr.* = *load-shedding* s.v. LOAD *sb.* 8. Also *fig.*

**1945** *Electrician* 25 May 457/1 Some shedding of the load may still be unavoidable during next winter. **1958** *Listener* 12 June 990/3 In June there is a shedding of the load of serious drama. **1971** *IEEE Trans. Power Apparatus & Systems* XC. 1460/2 The load selected for shedding will be different for various systems because of geographical, historical, political and reliability factors.

**shedding** ('ʃɛdɪŋ), *ppl. a.* [f. SHED *v.*[1] + -ING[2].] That sheds, in various senses of the verb.

**1.** † **a.** Of liquids: Self-diffusing. *Obs.*

**1587** GOLDING *De Mornay* xv. 272 The bodie is in the Soule, as..a sheading or liquid thing in a thing that is not liquid [orig. *comme..le coulant en ce qui ne coule point*].

**b.** Dropping or casting leaves or petals.

**1687** DRYDEN *Hind & P.* III. 439 The shedding trees began the ground to strow With yellow leaves. **1782** J. SCOTT *Poet. Wks.* 261 And green slopes redden with the shedding rose.

**c.** (See quot.)

**1796** WITHERING *Brit. Plants* (ed. 3) I. 81 Shedding (caducus) continuing but a short time. *Ibid.* 262 Cup 4 leaves, leafits egg-shaped, coloured, shedding.

**d.** *shedding tooth*: any of the primary or milk teeth, which fall out and are replaced by the permanent teeth.

**1799** HOME in *Phil. Trans.* LXXXIX. 258 A view of the grinding surface of a shedding tooth. **1822–29** *Good's Study Med.* (ed. 3) I. 47 The permanent teeth have separate sockets of their own; and..do not lie immediately under the corresponding shedding teeth. **1833** *Hunter's Catal. Physiol. Ser. Comp. Anat. Mus. Coll. Surg.* I. 100 The shedding tooth falls some time before the succeeding tooth can supply its uses.

**e.** *fig.* Of divisions of time: Passing.

**1816** L. HUNT *Rimini* III. 134 The glass that told the shedding hours.

†**2.** Dividing, parting, separating. *Obs. rare.*

*a* **1674** BUNYAN *Reprob. Asserted* i. (1696) 2 These words were shedding words, they sever between Men and Men.

†**3.** Sloping. *Obs.*

**1688** HOLME *Armoury* III. 73/1 A Barn with a sheeding Ridg. **1747** HOOSON *Miner's Dict.* Q 1 b, If a Rock appears to the Day,..where it seems to cut off, and more especially on Sheeding ground.

**shedding, shede**, obs. ff. SHEADING, SHEATH.

**sheder** ('ʃiːdə(r)). *dial.* Forms: 6–7 **shidder**, 7 **shether**, 8 **sheeder**, 9 **sheder.** [f. SHE + ? DEER: cf. HEDER.] A female sheep; spec. a lamb from eight or nine months old to her first shearing.

**1579** SPENSER *Sheph. Cal.* Sept. 211 For, had his wesand bene a little widder, He would haue deuoured both hidder and shidder [*Gloss* He and she. Male and Female]. **1620** T. GRANGER *Div. Logike* 169 As appeares by hether, and shether, *i.* male, and female. **1633** J. FISHER *Fuimus Troes* III. ix. Chorus, Hidder, eke and shidder. **1799** A. YOUNG *Agric. Lincoln.* 325 They are forced to sell their heeders, and joist their sheeders in the spring. **1851** *Jrnl. R. Agric. Soc.* XII. II. 341 The 'heder' hogs being grazed on the seeds, and the 'sheders' on grass.

**shee, Sheeah, sheed(e**: see SHE, SHIAH, SHED.

**sheeding, sheef(fe**: see SHEADING, SHEAF *sb.*

**Sheehan** ('ʃiːən). *Path.* [The name of H. L. *Sheehan* (b. 1900), English pathologist.] *Sheehan's syndrome*: pituitary insufficiency (cf. *Simmonds' disease*) caused by necrosis of the gland as a result of post-partum hæmorrhage and shock.

**1950** R. F. ESCAMILLA in S. Soskin *Progr. Clinical Endocrinol.* x. 529 Case II represents an instance of onset of the disease following a complicated delivery, and is therefore an example of the subclassification of Simmonds' disease described by Sheehan, and called 'Sheehan's syndrome' by some authors. **1973** *Daily Colonist* (Victoria, B.C.) 18 July 2/3 Since the pituitary controls other endocrine glands, Sheehan's syndrome produces symptoms resulting from failure of other glands.

**Sheeite, sheek**: see SHIITE, SHEIKH.

**sheel** (ʃiːl), *v.* Now *dial.* Forms: α. 5 **schel**, 6 **scheill**, 7 **s(c)heele**, **scheil**, 7–9 **sheal**, 8–9 **shiel**, 9 **sheil**, 8– **sheel**; β. 5 **schylle** 6 **shyll**, 6– **shill.** [Related to SHALE *sb.*[1]; the early history is obscure.

The α forms possibly repr. OE. **scielian* (in *ásculian* 'enucleare'), f. *scealu* SHALE *sb.*[1] The β forms, exc. in the northern examples, perh. belong to a distinct though synonymous word, a derivative of SHELL *sb.*]

*trans.* To shell; to take off the husk or outer covering of. Hence **sheeled** *ppl. a.*

α. **1473** *Rental Bk. Cupar-Angus* (1879) I. 182 Payand..ix chalder of vitale of the kyngis met, half beir half meil, the meil twise schelit. **1508**, **1583–4** [implied in SHEELING *vbl. sb.*]. **1605** SHAKS. *Lear* I. iv. 219 That's a sheal'd Pescod. **1615** G. SANDYS *Trav.* II. (1637) 116 *Rosetta*..perhaps deriued of *Ros*, which signifieth *Rice*, and so named for the abundance that it vttereth; (they here shealing monethly three hundred quarters). **1612** in *Trans. Cumb. & Westm. Archæol. Soc.* (N.S.) III. (1893) 155 That the Milner..doe neither sheele nor grinde any Skillinge of any Mans dwelling in another Lordshipp. **1681** *Ibid.* 159 Noe Tennant or Farmer..Shall grinde or Scheele any Wheate, Bigg, Barley, Pease..att any other Mill. **1709** LADY G. BAILLIE *Househ. Bk.* (S.H.S.) 79, 10 stone twist shield meall. **1765** *Museum Rust.* IV. 457 After sheeling, the seed should be well cleansed from bad seeds. **1801** *Farmer's Mag.* Apr. 214 It was first shealed on the barley mill. **1816** SCOTT *Bl. Dwarf* xvii, We took their swords and pistols as easily as ye wad shiel peacods. *a* **1824** G. BEATTIE *John o' Arnha'* etc. (1826) 83 She mussels sheel'd, an' wan her bread. **1861** SMILES *Engineers* II. 105 Barley was shealed by pounding the grains with water in the hollow of a stone until by that means the husks were rubbed off. **1862** HISLOP *Prov. Scot.* 101 He would need to be twice sheeled and ance grund that deals wi' you.

β. *c* **1440** *Promp. Parv.* 446/1 Schyllyn owte, of coddys, *exsi(li)quo.* Schyllyn, or schylle notys, *enuclio.* *Ibid.* 446/2 Schyllyn oysterys, and thyngys closyd yn schellys, *excortico.* **1483** *Cath. Angl.* 336/1 Schylled pyse.., *pise exilique.* **1508** in *Reg. Mag. Sig. Scot. 1510*, 747/1, 4 bollas..albe et bone farrine vulgariter nuncupat. twise schillit mele. *c* **1522** SKELTON *Why nat to Court?* 108 Or pescoddes they may shyll. **1702** LADY G. BAILLIE *Househ. Bk.* (S.H.S.) 66 For Shild pies..2 peck out of 5 p. **1703** THORESBY in Ray *Philos. Lett.* (1718) 336 To *Shill*, as Pease to take them out of the Swads. **1799** J. ROBERTSON *Agric. Perth* 163 When the barley is twice shilled, i.e. put twice through the mill, on purpose to take off the rind more compleatly, and then grinded small. **1862** C. C. ROBINSON *Dial. Leeds* Gloss. s.v. *Shill*, 'Shillin' peis'; 'shillin' beins'—unshelling peas and beans.

**sheel(l, sheeld(e**: see SHIEL, SHIELD.

**sheelah**, var. SHEILA.

‖**sheela-na-gig** ('ʃiːlənə,gɪg). Also **shela-**, **sheila-**, **shiela-**; **-gigg.** [ad. Ir. *Síle na gcíoch* Julia of the breasts.] A medieval carved stone female figure sometimes found on churches or castles in

Britain and Ireland (see quot. 1934[1]). Also *ellipt.*, as **sheela, sheila.**

**1846** *Proc. R. Irish Acad. 1843–4* II. viii. 575 In the church at Dowth there is a shela-na-gig, carved in stone quite different to that which composes the walls of the church. **1861** *Jrnl. Kilkenny Archæol. Soc. 1860–61* VI. 69 This effigy..belongs to that class of sculpturings which in Ireland have extended down to the middle of the sixteenth century... They are known amongst the peasantry of the southern counties by the name of 'Sheela-ni-giggs'. **1882** *Jrnl. R. Hist & Archæol. Soc. Irel. 1879–82* XV. II. 283 The name by which works of this class are generally known is '*Sheelanagigg*'. Our 'Sheela' here measures two feet in length. **1929** *Man* XXIX. 134 A stone..hollowed out to form in relief the rudely carved figure of a woman of the kind known in Ireland as Sheela-na-gig. **1934** *Jrnl. R. Anthropol. Inst.* XXXVII. 97 The more modern examples..are known as the Sheila-na-gig. These are always nude and are represented in the frontal aspect, the legs usually wide apart, and the hands so posed as to call attention to the genitalia. *Ibid.* 98 The Sheila from Blackhall Castle..is represented with breasts and long hair. **1977** *Times* 14 Sept. 5/1 The figures, called Sheela-na-Gig, are not found only in Ireland, ..one of the best preserved is on the corbel of a church in Kilpeck [Hereford and Worcester]. *Ibid.* 5/2 The British Sheelas are slightly older than the Irish.

**'sheeling, 'shilling,** *vbl. sb.* Forms: α. see SHEEL *v.* β. 6 **shillinge**, 6–7 **schilling**, 6, 8–9 **shilling**, 8–9 **shillen**, 9 **shillin**. [f. SHEEL *v.* + -ING[1].]

**1.** The action of SHEEL *v.*

α. **1583–4** *Burgh Rec. Edin.* (1882) IV. 320 That thai diligentlie awaitt vpoun the scheilling of the quheitt pertening to the said nichtbouris of the baxteris. **1606** in *Sel. Rec. Kirk Sess.* etc. *Aberd.* (1846) 198 The haill millers..to absteine from millinge, grindinge or scheilinge on the Sabboth day in tymes cumminge. **1801** *Farmer's Mag.* Apr. 214 It [common barley] produced nearly 21 pecks and a half ..of common barley-flour,..4 lb. of husks from the shealing, and [etc.]. **1844** H. STEPHENS *Bk. Farm* II. 350 The protuberances of the rootlets and woolly ends should not have been rubbed off by any process, such as sheeling.

β. *c* **1440** *Promp. Parv.* 446/2 Schyllynge, of notys. **1906** WOODRUFFE-PEACOCK *Ideal Thoroughbred Stud* 14 'The dry shilling so prevalent in the spring months, which is so serious a throw-back to both plant and animal growth.

**2.** The grain removed from the husk, also the husks of oats, wheat, etc.

α. **1597** in *Spalding Club Misc.* (1841) I. 173 And than the said mylne..grund efter hir auld forme, and made gude meill and scheiling. **1667** *Rec. Baron Crt. Stitchill* (S.H.S.) 46 It is..ordained that the owner of the corne mak their awn sheilling in all tyme cuming. **1844** J. BALLANTINE *Miller of Deanhaugh* x. 177 Rank an' station! bran an' sheelings! exclaimed the miller. **1902** *Ardrossan Herald* 31 Jan. 2/3 The multure is a quantity of grain, sometimes in kind, as wheat, oats, pease, and sometimes manufactured as flour, meal, sheeling.

β. **1508** DUNBAR *Flyting* 147 Thow and thy quene, as gredy gleddis, ȝe gang With polkis to mylne, and beggis baith meill and schilling. *Ibid.* 243 Chitterlilling, ruch rilling, lik schilling in the milhouse. **1546** *Reg. Mag. Sig. Scot.* 7/2 Cum una firlota de lie thirl beir et una firlota de lie ring schilling. **1690** J. MACKENZIE *Siege London Derry* 39/1 There was Oats, Shilling, and Malt in Town, which could not be used for want of Mills. **1681** O. HEYWOOD *Diaries* (1881) II. 286 A stroke of shilling standing on the table. **1729** P. WALKDEN *Diary* (1866) 85 Sent son Thomas towards Preston with a load of shilling to sell. **1795** *Statist. Acc. Scot.* XV. 117 *Shillen*, i.e. shealing, or hulter corn, is measured by the tacksman of the mill, and is paid, not in shealing, but in meal. **1910** G. HENDERSON *Norse Infl. Celtic Scot.* v. 117 In Lowland Scots *shillin*, unhusked grain.

**3.** *attrib.* and *Comb.*, as ***sheeling cylinder, groats, machine, time***, etc.; **sheeling-hill**, a hill or eminence where grain was winnowed by the wind, so **sheeling-mound**; **sheeling-seeds**, the husks of corn, esp. oats, also the grain that has been freed from the husk; **sheeling-stone** (see quot. 1880).

**1844** H. STEPHENS *Bk. Farm* II. 351 The first process which wheat undergoes in grinding is in being put through the *sheeling cylinder. **1585–6** *Shuttleworths Acc.* (Chetham Soc.) 91 A peke of *shillynge grotes. **1597** in *Spalding Club Misc.* (1841) I. 174 The *schilling hill of the Mylne of Fedderet. **1816** SCOTT *Old Mort.* vii, Instead of..waiting patiently for whatever dispensation of wind Providence was pleased to send upon the sheeling-hill. **1840** J. HODGSON *Hist. Northumbld.* II. III. 118 *note*, A shilling-hill, as a place to deet or winnow the groats of oats from the husks that had been shilled off them, before machinery was invented for the purpose, was not an uncommon appendage to a mill. **1911** E. BEVERIDGE *North Uist* i. 11 At a *shieling-mound close to the southern base of Marrival is Tobar Chuithairidh. **1715** PENNECUIK *Wks.* (1815) 87 (E.D.D.) The husks or *shilling seeds are again separated by the farmers. *a* **1867** W. ANDERSON in *Mod. Sc. Poets* Ser. II. (1881) 238 A cushion stuff't wi' sheelin' seeds. **1563** in *Rates Exeter Canal* in *Archæologia* XXVIIII. 18 For everye boate loadinge with beare, *shillingstones, lyme, wood, cole [etc.] iiij.*d.* **1880** *Antrim & Down Gloss.*, *Shilling stones*, the pair of stones in a corn mill which are used for taking the husks off oats. **1895** SIR H. MAXWELL *Dk. of Britain* xix. 281 It is his custom to go frequently up during the *sheiling-time.

†**'sheeling,** *ppl. a. Obs. rare*[−1]. [f. SHEEL *v.* + -ING[2].] That is in process of peeling off.

**1708** tr. *Cowley's Plants* I. C.'s Wks. III. 288 All thy shealing Scabs rub off again.

**sheen** (ʃiːn), *sb.*[1] Forms: 6 *Sc.* scheyne, 6–7 sheene, 7– sheen. [f. SHEEN *a.*, assumed to be connected with SHINE *v.* (The sb. is virtually a verbal noun to *shine.*) Cf. SHEEN *v.*]

**1. a.** Shining, brightness. In recent use chiefly, gleaming, lustre, radiance as of a body reflecting light; a gleam. *rare* before the 19th c.

**1602** SHAKS. *Ham.* III. ii. 167 And thirtie dozen Moones with borrowed sheene, About the World haue times twelue thirties been. **1614** GORGES *Lucan* VI. 240 And modest Cynthias siluer hue Vnto a pallid colour grew... As if the earth had bene betweene To barre her of her brothers sheene. **1629** MILTON *Hymn Nativ.* xv, Thron'd in Celestiall sheen. **1634** —— *Comus* 893 The azurn sheen Of Turkis blew. *Ibid.* 1003 Far above in spangled sheen Celestial Cupid her fam'd son advanc't. **1768** BEATTIE *Minstr.* I. xxii, The southern Sun diffus'd his dazzling shene. **1798** COLERIDGE *Anc. Mar.* I. xiv, And through the drifts the snowy clifts Did send a dismal sheen. **1815** BYRON *Destr. Sennacherib* i, The sheen of their spears was like stars on the sea. **1830** TENNYSON *Song, 'The Lintwhite'* 28 Thy locks are all of sunny sheen. **1881** J. HATTON *New Ceylon* ii. 51 [A pearl] of a peculiarly brilliant sheen. **1879** BLACK *Macleod of D.* I. 178 The beautiful blue sheen on its scales. **1888** ANNIE S. SWAN *Doris Cheyne* ii. 30 Her hair..had a sheen like gold upon it. **1906** WILLIAMSON *Lady Betty across Water* 288 The green of the waving trees seemed to be reflected in their complexions in little sheens and shimmers.

**b.** *transf.* and *fig.*

**1828** COLERIDGE *Gard. Boccaccio* 47 And last, a matron now, of sober mien Yet radiant still and with no earthly sheen. **1831** CARLYLE *Sartor Res.* III. iii, Ever in the dullest existence there is a sheen either of Inspiration or of Madness. **1863** W. PHILLIPS *Sp.* vi. 114 No sheen of official position would ever lead us.

**c.** Gorgeous or bright attire.

[**1631** MILTON *Marchioness of Winchester* 73 With thee there clad in radiant sheen, No Marchioness, but now a Queen.] **1802** MRS. RADCLIFFE *Gaston de Blondeville* Posth. Wks. (1826) II. 348 They saw plainly enough knights, esquires and pages..in all their splendour; and lady-aunts and lady-cousins in the galleries, in all their sheen and joyance. **1812** BYRON *Ch. Har.* I. lxxiv, In costly sheen and gaudy cloak array'd. **1898** NEWBOLT *Isl. Race* 94 Stepped she not with a grace entrancing, Slenderly girt in silken sheen?

**2.** The pupil of the eye. *Sc.* (? *Obs.*)

*c* **1500** KENNEDY *Passion of Christ* 581 For as I writtin into Doctouris fand. He wes mair tender [into] his body, Than is þe scheyne into a mannis e. **1808** JAMIESON, *Sheen* of the eye, the pupil of the eye.

**3.** A very thin film or slick of oil (esp. on water).

**1970** *Daily Colonist* (Victoria, B.C.) 29 Apr. 1/1 Investigators reported four light sheens—the term being used instead of [oil] slicks because the material appears to be spread quite lightly on the water—were sighted from aircraft. **1978** *Daily Tel.* 28 Mar. 1/4 There was 'an extremely thin sheen of oil six to seven miles off Jersey' which was of no danger to marine life or holidaymakers.

**sheen** (ʃiːn), *sb.*[2] *slang.* [Of obscure origin: cf. SHAN.] Base coin. Also *attrib.* or *adj.*

**1839** H. BRANDON in W. A. Miles *Poverty, Mendicity & Crime* 165/1 *Sheen*, bad money. **1864** *Hotten's Slang Dict.* 226 *Sheen*, bad money. **1888** PAYNE *Eavesdropper* II. ii. 80 'Can you smash a thick un for me?' inquired one, handing his friend a sovereign. 'You're sure it ain't sheen?' returned the other, with a diabolical grin. **1890** BARRÈRE & LELAND *Dict. Slang*, *Sheen* (Scotch), bad money. Probably alluding to the 'glitter', or possibly from German *schein*, a bank-bill.

**sheen** (ʃiːn), *sb.*[3] *U.S. slang.* [Prob. abbrev. of MACHINE *sb.* 1 e.] A car; an automobile.

**1968–70** *Current Slang* (Univ. S. Dakota) III–IV. 107 *Sheen*, car. **1975** *Amer. Speech* 1972 XLVII. 153 Hey, look down the street pas' that sheen double-parked. **1980** in S. Terkel *Amer. Dreams* 125 My friends are always talkin' about havin' a nice sheen. That's a nice car or van, something set up real nice on the inside.

**sheen** (ʃiːn), *a.* Now *poet.* Forms: 1 **scíene, scéne, scéone, scíone, scýne,** scíne, 2–4 **seene,** 3 **sceone, sschene,** 3–4 **scen,** (? **schine**), 3–6 **schene,** 3–6, (8–9) **shene,** 4 **schen,** (**sene**), 5 **schenne, sshene,** 6 **shen,** 4–7 **sheene,** 5 **scheene;** 3 **scone,** *Sc.* 4–6 **scheyne,** 5 **sheyn,** 6 **schein(e, schane;** 6– **sheen.** *compar.* 1 **scénra,** 3 **schenre, schennure,** 4 **schenure.** [OE. *scíene* = OFris. *skêne* (mod.Fris. *skjin*), OS. *scôni* (MLG. *schône, schôn*; Sw. *skön*, Da. *skjøn*, prob. from LG.), MDu. *schôn(e* (mod.Du. *schoon*), OHG. *scôni*, earlier *scaoni* (MHG. *schœne, schœn*, mod.G. *schön*), Goth. *skaun-s*:—OTeut. **skauni-*, **skaunjo-* f. root **skau-* to behold: see SHOW *v.*

The Gothic *ibnaskauns* like-formed, *guþaskaunei* likeness of God, suggest that the word may originally have meant 'having (a certain) appearance'. For the development of the eulogistic sense, cf. *sightly, shapely*, L. *forma* form, beauty, *formosus* beautiful.

In English (and app. to some extent in OHG. and OS. where it glosses *lucidus, splendidus*, etc.) the sense was influenced by association with the root of SHINE *v.* In early examples it is often difficult to determine whether the sense is merely 'beautiful', or whether there is some added notion of 'shining, bright'.

The form *scone* in Ormin, which implies the pronunciation ('skoːnə), is unexplained. The identically written form in Layamon, however, seems to be merely an instance of the practice, common in 12–13th c. texts, of writing *o* for *eo*.]

**1.** Beautiful. **a.** Of persons (esp. women), their appearance, features, etc.

*Beowulf* 3017 Mæȝð scyne. *a* **900** CYNEWULF *Crist* 1387 Ic ðe swa scienne ȝesceapen hæfde. *c* **1000** *Genesis* 265 Cwæð, þæt his lic wære leohte & scene. *c* **1200** *Vices & Virtues* 95 Nis ðar non swo god leiȝe se teares: hie makieð scene ansiene. *c* **1205** LAY. 15331, & he haueð to quene mine dohter þa is scone. *a* **1225** *Ancr. R.* 398 And Absalones schene wlite. *a* **1300** *Cursor M.* 24080 His face þat forwit was sa scene [*v. rr.* schen, shene]. *Ibid.* 28505 Gernand i haf oft ben Desird o þire wymmen scen. *c* **1300** *Sir Orfeo* 356 Al þe utmast wal Was clere and schine [*v. rr.* schone, gan schyne] as cristal. *c* **1350** *Will. Palerne* 3296 So schene he was to se in his semli armes. *c* **1374** CHAUCER *H. Fame* III. 446 Graunte vs, lady shene Eche of vs, of thy grace a bone. *c* **1400** *Destr. Troy* 3070 Shulders full shaply, shenest of hewe, Full plesaund & playn. *a* **1450** *Le Morte Arth.* 2612 The mayde was full shene to shewe. *a* **1536** *Songs, Carols*, etc. (1907) 10 Hayle be thou Mary, maydyn shen. *a* **1586** ? MONTGOMERIE *Banks of Helicon* 6 Declair, ȝe bankis of Helicon,..Gif ony of ȝour Muses all, Or nymphes may be peregall Vnto my lady schein? **1589** GREENE *Menaphon* (Arb.) 43, I saw a little one, A bonny prety one, As bright buxsome and as sheene As was shee. **1590** SPENSER *F.Q.* II. i. 10 Her daintie corse so faire and sheene. **1747** MASON *Musæus* 104 Belinda far surpast my beauties sheen.

†**b.** (*the*) *sheen*: used after a woman's name.

*c* **1205** LAY. 3098 þe duc of Cornwaile scal habbe Gornoille & þe Scottene king Regau þat scone [*c* **1275** þe scene]. *c* **1320** *Sir Tristr.* 756 Slawe was rouland þan And ded blaunche þe schene. *c* **1386** CHAUCER *Knt.'s T.* 210 The fresshe Emelye the sheene.

**c.** Of animals, inanimate objects, places, etc.

*c* **1000** *Phœnix* 591 Him folȝiað fuȝlas scyne. *c* **1000** *Panther* 19 (Gr.) Deor wundrum scyne. *c* **1205** LAY. 19767 Vt heo droȝen sone amppullen scone [*c* 1275 six ampulles] ifulled mid attere weten alre bitterest. **12..** *Moral Ode* 340 (Egerton MS.) In þene narewe wei and þene wei grene þer forð-fareð lutel folc ac it is feir and scene. *c* **1275** *Ibid.* 337 (Jesus MS.) in *O.E. Misc.* 70 Go we þene narewe wey þen wey so schene. **13..** *Gosp. Nicod.* 125 (Cott. Galba MS.) þaire armes set on schaftes schene [*Harl. MS.* sene]. *c* **1350** *Will. Palerne* 3411 Many a schene scheld scheuered al to peces. *a* **1352** MINOT *Poems* (ed. Hall) xi. 2 In schawes ful schene. *c* **1400** *Sowdone Bab.* 118 Carrikes, Galeis and shippes shene, vij hundred were gadered al in fere. *c* **1400** *Rom. Rose* 3713 By hir atyre so bright and shene, Men might perceyve..She was not of religioun. *c* **1400** *Destr. Troy* 330 With shotes of shire wode shene to beholde. **1423** JAS. I *Kingis Q.* xcv, His long[e] ȝalow lokkis schene. *c* **1435** *Torr. Portugal* 487 Abowght a facon schene. *c* **1470** HENRY *Wallace* IV. 370 Thar I was born amang the schawis scheyne. *c* **1470** HARDING *Chron.* CCXLII. App. XXX. iv, Four and twentie myles to Lamarke so shene. **1513** DOUGLAS *Æneis* I. vii. 63 Rowmyng about the large temple schene. **1596** DALRYMPLE tr. *Leslie's Hist. Scot.* I. 17 Amang fair forrests and schawis schene. **1785** BURNS *Vision* I. 67 Down flow'd her robe, a tartan sheen, Till half a leg was scrimply seen. **1873** SYMONDS *Grk. Poets* xi. 374 Narcissus will I twine, and lilies sheen.

†**d.** *absol.* (quasi-*sb.*) A fair one; a beautiful woman. *Obs.*

**13..** *E.E. Allit. P.* A. 965 þat schene sayde, þat god wyl schylde, 'þou may not enter with-inne hys tor'. *c* **1400** *Destr. Troy* 8144 The bysshop to his barne barely onswart, And shend to þat schene all in short wordes. *c* **1420** *Avow. Arth.* xl, Thay so a schene vndur schild, Come prekand fast aure the filde, On a fayre stede. **1540** PALSGR. *Acolastus* III. v. R iij, A kisse, my lyght .i. my hart of golde, or my bryght and sheene, this is sweter then honye. *a* **1568** *Bannatyne MS.* (Hunter. Club) 627 Beseik that schene with hummill reuerence The to ressaif.

†**e.** In non-material senses: Beautiful, attractive; noble, illustrious; pure, clean (*from* sin). *Obs.*

*c* **1205** LAY. 24326 To þan..þer com þe king Angel king of Scotlonde mid sceone his folke. *a* **1300** *Cursor M.* 18535 þis hight [*i.e.* promise] þat was sa scene [*v. rr.* shene, schene], Suld tid þam thoru a maiden clene. *c* **1400** *Destr. Troy* 600, I will shunt for no shame of my shene fader, Ne no hede to my heale, þat I thee helpe shall. *c* **1430** *Hymns Virg.* (1867) 18 þi passioun make us briȝt & schene In wil, in worde, in dede & þouȝt! **1460** in *Pol. Rel. & L. Poems* (1866) 254 Fro seuene synnes þou make me schene.

**2.** Bright, shining, resplendent.

In early use this sense may have been merely contextual, the adj. being applied in the sense 'beautiful' to objects (e.g. heavenly bodies, jewels, metals) the beauty of which is dependent on their brightness. In later use, owing to association with SHINE *v.*, SHEEN *sb.*[1], the sense 'shining' is felt as primary.

**900** CYNEWULF *Crist* 695 Hwæt sindan þa ȝimmas swa scyne buton god sylfa? *c* **1200** ORMIN 3431 He sette a steorrne upp o þe lifft Full brad, & brihht, & shene. *a* **1225** *Ancr. R.* 362 In þe ariste of domesdeie, hwon ure vlesches schal blikien schenre þen þe sunne. **13..** *E.E. Allit. P.* A. 1145, I loked among his meyny schene. ? *a* **1366** CHAUCER *Rom. Rose* 1512 He thoughte of thilke water shene To drinke and fresshe him wel withalle. **1377** LANGL. *P. Pl.* B. XVIII. 409 'After sharpe showres', quod pees 'moste shene is þe sonne'. *c* **1402** LYDG. *Compl. Bl. Knt.* 3 In May, whan.. Phebus gan to schede his stremes shene Amid the Bole. **1412–20** —— *Troy Bk.* I. 623 þe schene sonne. **1513** DOUGLAS *Æneis* XII. iv. 40 O thou brycht son, with thy schene bemis glaid. **1535** STEWART *Cron. Scot.* (Rolls) I. 105 And cled thame all..In silk and syper, and in siluer schene. *a* **1542** WYATT *Compl. Absence His Love* 39 in *Tottel's Misc.* (Arb.) 74 Those shene lightes: that wonted for to clere My darked panges of cloudy thoughts. **1590** SHAKS. *Mids. N.* II. i. 28 By fountaine cleere, or spangled star light sheene. **1591** SPENSER *M. Hubberd* 1066 That he might be seene Of the wilde beasts in his new glory sheene. **1591** R. W[ILMOT] *Tancred & Gism.* III. iii. (1592) D 3, But why doth he that sprung from Ioues high head? And Phœbus sister sheene, despise thy power? **1607** WALKINGTON *Optic Glass* 147 To see the Sunne and Moone..in their sheene glory. **1633** P. FLETCHER *Purple Isl.* III. vi, Like rubies sheen. **1748** THOMSON *Cast. Indol.* I. iii, Glittering Streamlets..hurled every-where their Waters sheen. **1798** COLERIDGE *Anc. Mar.* V. vi, The upper air burst into life! And a hundred fire-flags sheen, To and fro they were hurried about. **1808** SCOTT *Marm.* V. viii, His vest of changeful satin sheen. **1817** SHELLEY *Marianne's Dr.* 10 The veiny lids, whose fringe is thrown Over thine eyes so dark and sheen. **1838** BARHAM *Ingol. Leg., Witches' Frolic*, And fairer, I ween, The ivy sheen That thy mouldering turret binds, Than the

Alderman's house. 1839 LONGF. *Voices of Night, Prelude* i. 5 Where, the long drooping boughs between Shadows dark and sunlight sheen Alternate come and go.

**b.** Of a day, the sky, etc.

1503 HAWES *Examp. Virt.* xiv. 296 A daye of gladnes bryght and shene. *a* 1510 DOUGLAS *K. Hart* i. 95 Quhilk hes na craft to knaw the wynter weit, Suppois that sommer schane dois thame reskew. 1577–87 HOLINSHED *Hist. Eng.* II. ii. 8/2 Thou that maist passe aloft in airie skies so sheene. 1599 *Warn. Faire Wom.* II. 341 It is my love. O how the dusky night Is by her coming forth made sheen and bright! 1714 GAY *Sheph. Week, Monday* 3 No chirping lark the welkin sheen invokes. 1839 MRS. BROWNING *Romaunt Page* xxx, 'Look up—there is a small bright cloud..' The page looked up—the cloud was sheen. 1891 F. THOMPSON *Sister-Songs* (1895) 16 There she sat amid her ladies, Where the shade is Sheen as Enna mead ere Hades' Gloom fell thwart Persephone.

†**c.** Bright-coloured. *Obs.*

13.. *Gaw. & Gr. Knt.* 2314 þe schene blod ouer his schulderes schot to þe erþe. 1603 FLORIO *Montaigne* II. xxxiv. 425 Iulius Cæsar.. In his Warres.. was accustomed to weare a verie rich garment and of a sheene and garish colour. 1810 SCOTT *Lady of L.* IV. xii, If pall and vair no more I wear, Nor thou the crimson sheen.

†**d.** absol. *the sheen*: the bright weapon; also, the bright sun. *nonce-uses.*

13.. *Gaw. & Gr. Knt.* 2268 þat oþer schalk wyth a schunt þe schene wyth-haldez. 13.. *E.E. Allit. P.* C. 440 For to schylde fro the schene, oþer any schade kest.

**e.** quasi-*adv.*

*a* 1225 *Ancr. R.* 246 A muchel wind alið mid a lutel rein & te sunne þer efter schineð þe schennure. *c* 1330 R. BRUNNE *Chron. Wace* (Rolls) 11251 Cloþes of golde þat schon so schene. *c* 1400 *Destr. Troy* 1649 The windowes.. [were] shapyn full shene all of shyre stones. 1446 LYDG. *Nightingale Poems* ii. 194 My Ien blynde, that whylom shoone so sheene. 1835 LYTTON *Rienzi* I. xi, The moonlight stole soft and sheen. 1872 HOLLAND *Marble Prophecy* 31 They flash and shine among the flowers While dripping sheen in golden showers.

**sheen** (ʃiːn), *v.* Forms: 4 schen, 4–6 s(c)hene, 6 scheine, *Sc.* scheyne, 6– sheen. [f. SHEEN *a.*]

**1.** *intr.* **a.** = SHINE *v. lit.* and *fig.* Now only *Sc.* and *dial.* (in Sc. the ordinary word.)

*c* 1375 *Sc. Leg. Saints* v. (*Johannes*) 256 Far palacis þat sal leste euirmare, schenand with gemmys oure-alquhare. *Ibid.* xxv. (*Julian*) 54 Fore he wae þane schenand in til halynes. *c* 1420 *Anturs of Arth.* 329 (Douce MS.) þene vnclosed þe cloudes, þe sone con shene. *c* 1470 HENRY *Wallace* III. 119 The sone was rysyne our landis schenand brycht. 1523 SKELTON *Garl. Laurel* 1358 Luna that so bryght doth shene. *c* 1530 *Crt. of Love* 81 No saphir ind, no rube.. There lakked than.. That may the castell maken for to shene. *a* 1542 WYATT *Ps.* xxxvii. 97, I have well seene the wycked sheene lyke goolde lustie and grene as Lawrell lasting aye. 1556 *Chron. Grey Friars* (Camden) 69 Abowte Ester was sene.. three sonnes shenynge at one tyme in the eyer. 1562 in *Sel. Rec. Kirk Sess.* etc. *Aberd.* (1846) 4 That gud lyfe, conversatioun, and maneris may scheyne. *a* 1565 SIR T. CHALLONER tr. *Boeth.* I. met. iii. 15 All sodeynly the Sonne ..sheens the worlde over. 1588 A. KING tr. *Canisius' Catech.* 9 Our lord Iesus thairfor sittis one the rycht hand of the pouer of god,.. scheinand brychtlie with maiestie altogither diuin. 1819 GALL *Poems* 126 Thy ee will wake nae mair, That sheened sae fu' o' glee.

**b.** *poet.* To cast a gleam, glisten.

1812 BYRON *Ch. Har.* I. xvii, This town, That, sheening far, celestial seems to be. 1856 MEREDITH *Shav. Shagpat* (1887) 1 The illusion of rivers sheening on the sands to travellers gasping with thirst.

**2.** *trans.* To cast a sheen upon. *rare.*

1901 H. TRENCH *Deirdre Wed* 31 Who is this woman.. With sun-red hair, entangled as with flight Sheening the knees up to her bosom drawn?

Hence 'sheening *ppl. a.*

*c* 1375 *Sc. Leg. Saints* ii. (*Paulus*) 293 At þe ȝat now com þai In, petir and paule, in clathis shenand. *c* 1470 HENRY *Wallace* VIII. 1201 His schenand schoys, that burnyst was full beyn. 1506 *Kal. Sheph.* (Sommer) 146 The iyes that is blacke as Iete and in the myddes clere and shenynge. 1878 HARDY *Ret. Native* I. x, A great salt sheening sea bending into the land like a bow.

**sheende**, obs. form of SHEND *v.*

**sheene**, obs. form of SEINE *sb.*[1]

1611 FLORIO, *Riuale*,.. a kind of net that reacheth from one side of a riuer to the other called of Fishermen a Sheene-net [1659 Torriano *reads* a Sheere or Shore-net].

**sheened**, (ʃiːnd), *ppl. a.* [f. SHEEN *v.* + -ED[1].] Having a sheen, shining. Freq. in predic. use const. with *with*.

1920 E. SITWELL *Wooden Pegasus* 100 Beneath umbrellas I can see Pink faces sheened with stupidity. 1942 [see KNOLE SOFA]. 1955 *Times* 19 May 12/5 The lady-smocks, 'all silver white', or sheened with lilac.

**sheenless** ('ʃiːnlɪs), *a. rare.* [f. SHEEN *sb.*[1] + -LESS.] Without sheen.

1883 *Brit. Q. Rev.* July 18 The sheenless rays which have lost their power in the struggle through smoke and fumes.

**sheenly** ('ʃiːnlɪ), *adv. rare.* [f. SHEEN *a.*[1] + -LY[2].] Brightly.

1340–70 *Alisaunder* 631 Seuin sterres.. Hee showes forthe the scheenely shynand bright. 1842 *Tait's Mag.* IX. 719 All sheenly barbed, and gaily garbed, With plume and flashing spear.

**sheeny** ('ʃiːnɪ), *sb.*[1] *slang.* Also shen(e)y, sheeney, -ie. [Of obscure origin: cf. Russ. *zhid*, Pol., Czech *žid* (pronounced (ʒiːd)) a Jew.] A Jew. Now only as a term of vulgar abuse.

1816 J. H. LEWIS *Lectures on Art of Writing* (ed. 7) vi. 84 A motley-fool the *thing* I mean is, One of the common puffing sheenies. 1824 in *Spirit Publ. Jrnls.* (1825) 85 Orange Battery among the Sheenes [? *read* Sheenies]. Sketches at Bow-Street.—No. V. 1828 EGAN *Boxiana* Ser. II. I. 632 A good day's play among the Sheenies. 1893 FOREMAN *Trip to Spain* 34 A Portuguese Jew (a 'sheeny', as he is termed by the sailors). 1918 G. FRANKAU *One of Them* x. 75 What cared Jill for Grand Dukes, *Principini*,.. For Russ, Yank, Dago, Teuton, Gaul, or Sheeney? 1946 [see LID *sb.* 1 f]. 1976 *Honolulu Star-Bull.* 21 Dec. E-3/3 Hey mom, there's a couple of sheenies at our door with a turkey.

*attrib.* 1888 KIPLING *Soldiers Three, In Matter of a Private*, You lie, you man-sticker. You sneakin' Sheeny butcher, you lie. 1977 H. FAST *Immigrants* II. 88 Maybe we didn't do so bad for a Dago fisherman and a sheeny storekeeper.

**sheeny** ('ʃiːnɪ), *sb.*[2] [App. a. F. *chiné* ppl. a., woven of threads of different colours.] In full *Pompadour sheeny*: a silk fabric.

1902 *Bladud* (Bath) 26 Mar. 6/3 A very lovely one [dinner jacket].. was of Pompadour sheeny. *Ibid.* 7/1 Our parasols are to be of sheeny with coloured sticks.

**sheeny** ('ʃiːnɪ), *a.* [f. SHEEN *a.* + -Y.] Covered with sheen, full of sheen; having a bright, shiny surface.

1625 MILTON *Death Fair Infant* 48 Or did of late earths Sonnes besiege the wall Of sheenie Heav'n. 1717 FENTON *Odyss.* XI. Poems 103 The sheeny form of Epicaste. 1749 COLLINS *Ode Superst. Highl.* 153 Wreath'd with sheeny gold. 1825 SCOTT *Talism.* ii, His sheeny and crescent-formed sabre. 1830 TENNYSON *Madeline* ii, The silken sheeny woof. 1852 M. ARNOLD *Empedocles* II. i, The eagle.. Droops all his sheeny, brown, deep-feather'd neck. 1871 M. COLLINS *Marq. & Merch.* III. 152 A soft gray sheeny silk. 1893 *Times* 8 July 12/1 A sheeny background of white satin.

*Comb.* 1897 SIR H. JOHNSTON *Brit. Central Africa* 3 Darters with sheeny plumaged bodies of greenish-black.

**b.** *transf.* and *fig.*

1834 DISRAELI *Rev. Epick* II. ix, So in the night Of ages.. riseth some lofty sage The depth of darkness with his sheeny wit Piercing. 1884 *Harper's Mag.* June 149/1 Its sheeny vanes of rhetoric.

**sheep** (ʃiːp), *sb.* Forms: α. 1 scéap, scǽp, scép, 2 sceæp, 2–3 sceap, 2–4 scep, (3 se(e)p, seop), 3–4 scepe, 3–5 (6 in comb.) schep, shep, 3–6 schepe, (4 ssep, schiep), 4–5 scheep, chepe, 4–6 shepe, (5 sheppe, *Sc.* scheipe, 6 sheip(pe, shiepe), 6–7 sheepe, *Sc.* scheip, (7 in comb. shepp), 4– sheep. β. 1 *Northumb.* scíp, 4 schipe, 4–6 schip, 5 schype, 6 shyp(p)e, schyp, shipe, 6–7 shippe, 5, 6–9 *dial.* ship. [OE. (WS.) *scéap*, earlier *scǽp*, (Anglian) *scēp* str. n. = OFris. *skêp*, *schêp* (NFris. *skêp*, *skêap*, *sjip*, *sjapp*, WFris. *skiep*, EFris. *schâip*), OS. *scâp* (MLG. *schâp*, LG. *schaap*), MDu. *schaep* (Du. *schaap*), OHG. *scâf* (MHG. *schâf*, G. *schaf*):—OTeut. **skǣpo-m* (wanting in Gothic and Scand.).

Outside Teut. no certain affinities are known. The prehistoric pl. **skǣpu* normally lost its final vowel in OE., so that nom. and acc. sing. and pl. became identical. (ONorthumbrian, however, had a pl. form *scipo* beside *scíp*.)

The pronunciation (ʃɪp) is specially characteristic of midl. (esp. west-midl.) dialects, but is widely current elsewhere in England, exc. in the north-west.]

**1. a.** Any animal of the ruminant genus *Ovis* (sometimes horned), closely allied to the goats; esp. of the widely domesticated species *Ovis aries*, of which there are many varieties, and which is reared for its flesh, fleece, and skin.

The male of the sheep is a ram, the female a ewe, the young a lamb. The flesh of the adult sheep is mutton. The fleece yields wool, the skin is made into leather or parchment, and the intestines are used for the strings of musical instruments (see CATGUT).

α. *c* 825 *Vesp. Ps.* cxiii. 6 *Velut agniovium*, swe swelomberu scepa. *c* 897 ÆLFRED *Gregory's Past. C.* xvii 122 Ðæt sceap ðæt ðær scancforad wæs. *a* 1000 *Colloq. Ælfric* in Wr.-Wülcker 91 On forewerdne morȝen ic drife sceap mine to heora læse. *c* 1200 *Trin. Coll. Hom.* 37 Ðet oref þe þis deor waneð beð shep and reðeren, and Get, and swin. *c* 1200 ORMIN 12662 Shepess lamb uss ȝifeþþ millc, & flæsh & blod & wulle. *c* 1250 *Gen. & Ex.* 940 A net, and a got, and a sep. *c* 1275 *O.E. Misc.* 41 Beo þe seopheorde aquold..þenne scule sone his seop alle beon to-dreued. *a* 1300 *Cursor M.* 3178 þe angel.. bade him þar biside him tak A scepe [*Fairf.* shepe, *Gött.* schep, *Trin.* sheep] his sacrifice to mak. 1382 WYCLIF *Gen.* iv. 2 Abel was a sheepherd of sheep. 1390 GOWER *Conf.* II. 237 Ther was a Schiep,.. The which his flees bar al of gold. 1422 YONGE tr. *Secreta Secret.* lviii. 221 An hare and a sheppe bene ful gastefull. *c* 1449 PECOCK *Repr.* II. xiii. 225 Whanne Moyses kepte the schep of Ietro. 1538 STARKEY *England* I. iii. 97 Thys inclosyng of pasturys for.. schepe. 1577 B. GOOGE *Heresbach's Husb.* III. (1586) 137b, The champion countrey, breedeth a large and a great sheepe. 1614 MARKHAM *Cheap Husb.* I. 69 If a sheepe be sound.., his eye will be bright. 1629 MILTON *Hymn Nativ.* viii, Perhaps their loves, or els their sheep, Was all that did their silly thoughts so busie keep. 1774 PENNANT *Tour Scot. in 1772*, 79 Verdant grass, the sweet food of the sheep. 1830 TENNYSON *Ode to Memory* 66 The thick-fleeced sheep from wattled folds. 1859 ALLEN *Amer. Farm-bk.* 399 The sheep is sometimes employed.. at the tread-mill or horizontal wheel, to pump the water, churn the milk, or perform other light domestic work. 1889 A. R. WALLACE *Darwinism* 34 Certain mountain varieties of sheep will starve out other mountain varieties.

β. *c* 950 *Lindisf. Gosp.* John ii. 14 Bebycgendo exin & scipo [*Rushw.* scip] & culufro. *c* 1300 *St. Margarete* 39 Hir norice hir sende ofte adai wiþ hire schip afelde. *c* 1310 *St. Brendan* (Bälz) 136 þe vairest scep [*v.r.* scip] þat miȝte be. 13.. *Cursor M.* 6156 (Gött.) Left þai nathing þat þar was, Schip, ne kow, or ox, ne as. *c* 1450 *Godstow Reg.* 127 Pastur for xl schip. *Ibid.*, Pastur for a c schype. *c* 1460 *Promp. Parv.* (Winch.) 395 Scabbyd schyppe, *apica*. *a* 1470 GREGORY *Chron.* in *Hist. Coll. Cit. Lond.* (Camden) 75 Oxyn, kyne, and shippe. *a* 1578 LINDESAY (Pitscottie) *Chron. Scot.* (S.T.S.) II. 266 The cattell and schip pertening to thair enimyes. 1602 *Shuttleworths' Acc.* (Chetham Soc.) 143, iiij wemen for clippinge the shippe xvj[d]. 1848 THACKERAY *Van. Fair* viii, 'What ship was it, Horrocks..?' 'One of the black-faced Scotch, Sir Pitt.'

*pl. with -s.* 1521 in *Visit. Southwell* (Camden) 119, I will that my sheips be soulde. 1588 SHAKS. *L.L.L.* II. i. 219 Two hot Sheepes marie: And wherefore not Ships. 1658 *Topsell's Four-f. Beasts* 504 The skins of other Sheeps [*ed.* 1607 sheep] newly plucked from their backs. 1841 HARTSHORNE *Salopia Antiqua* s.v. *Ship*, Poor grass when ships cannot grase. 1890 *Glouc. Gloss.*, *Ship*, sheep.. Also *pl.* Ships.

**b.** With qualifying word denoting the species as *African*, *broad-tailed*, *Rocky Mountain*, *wild* (see ARGALI, MOUFFLON, MUSMON). Also applied to other genera, as † ***Indian*** or ***Peruvian sheep***, the llama or vicuña; ***mountain sheep***, the ibex.

1604 E. G[RIMSTONE] tr. *D'Acosta's Hist. Indies* I. xxi. 70 Indian sheepe, the which.. do serve them as Asses to beare their burthens. 1607 TOPSELL *Four-f. Beasts* 102 An Indian Sheepe, out of the region of Peru. 1688 HOLME *Armoury* II. viii. 158/1 The Arabian broad tailed Sheep. 1748 [see PERUVIAN]. 1759 [see GO-CART 3]. 1804, 1818 [see ROCKY *a.*[1] 1 c]. 1807 P. GASS *Jrnl.* 143 The Ibex or mountain sheep. 1858 BAIRD *Cycl. Nat. Sci.* s.v. *Oveæ*, The moufflon, or wild sheep of Sardinia and Corsica, and the argali, or wild sheep of India and Siberia. 1875 *Encycl. Brit.* II. 102/1 The Rocky Mountain sheep or goat (*Haplocerus laniger*),.. is closely related to the chamois of Europe. 1879 E. P. WRIGHT *Anim. Life* 161 The Yellow Sheep of Mongolia (*Procapra gutturosa*). 1881 *Scribner's Monthly* May 1/1 The American big horn, or Rocky Mountain sheep (*Ovis montana* Cuv.).

**c.** ***vegetable sheep***: see quot.

1866 *Treas. Bot.* 959/1 The name of Vegetable sheep (!) is given by the settlers in New Zealand to *R[aoulia] eximia*, because, from its growing in large white tufts on elevated sheep-runs, it may be readily mistaken for the sheep.

**2.** Similative (often passing into figurative) uses.

**a.** In allusions to: (*a*) The sheep's timidity, defencelessness, inoffensiveness, tendency to stray and get lost: chiefly in echoes of biblical passages, and sometimes with allusion to sense 4. (*b*) The fabled assumption by a wolf (or other beast of prey) of the skin of a slaughtered sheep. (*c*) The division into 'sheep' and 'goats' (saved and lost) at the Last Judgement. Also *attrib.*, as ***sheep-and-goat***. (*d*) The infection of the whole flock by one sheep. (*e*) The shearing of sheep; with suggestion of 'fleecing' or robbing.

(*a*) *c* 825 *Vesp. Ps.* cxviii. 176 Ic duolude swe swe scep ðæt forwearð. *c* 1175 *Lamb. Hom.* 121 Vre drihten wes iled to sleȝe al swa me dede a scep. *c* 1205 LAY. 1546 Swa þe rimie wulf þan he wule on scheapen [*c* 1275 sẽẽp] scaðe werc wrchen. *c* 1275 *Passion our Lord* 5 in *O.E. Misc.* 37 Al volk wes to dreued so schep beoþ in þe wolde. *c* 1330 R. BRUNNE *Chron. Wace* (Rolls) 13897 As þe wolf chaseþ þe schep, He dide þe Romayns by-fore hym lep. 1546 J. HEYWOOD *Prov.* I. viii. (1867) 16 Subtilly lyke a sheepe thought I, I shall Cut my cote after my cloth. 1552 *Bk. Com. Prayer, Matins* Conf., We have erred and strayed from thy wayes, lyke lost shepe. 1568 GRAFTON *Chron.* II. 737 The Duke.. deliuered the Erle to the Ambassadors,.. not thinking that he deliuered the shepe to the woolfe. 1644 SYMONDS *Diary* (Camden) 67 The rout of soldjers of that regiment prest all of a heape like sheep. 1843 H. BONAR *Hymn*, I was a wandering sheep, I did not love the fold. 1850 DICKENS *David Copp.* xvi, Outside his own domain, and unprotected, he was a very sheep for the shearers. 1862 F. W. FABER *Hymn*, Souls of men! why will ye scatter like a crowd of frighten'd sheep?

(*b*) *c* 950 *Lindisf. Gosp.* Matt. vii. 15 Ðaðe cymes to Iuh.. in wedum scipa Inna-ueard uutedlice sint uulfes.. ferende. 1573 *Tyrie's Refut.* in *Cath. Tractates* 7 Nocht to trow hastelie, that thairbie other thay be lyon or scheip, quhobeit thay weare thair skinnes. 1579 SPENSER *Sheph. Cal.* Sept. 157 They [wolves] gang in more secrete wise, And with sheepes clothing doen hem disguise. 1591 SHAKS. *1 Hen. VI*, I. iii. 55 Thou Wolfe in Sheepes array.

(*c*) *c* 950 *Lindisf. Gosp.* Matt. xxv. 33 He setteð ða scip.. to suiðrum his. 1340 HAMPOLE *Pr. Consc.* 6136 By þe shepe understand we may þe gude men þat sal be saved þat day. *c* 1380 WYCLIF *Sel. Wks.* III. 169 Schepe þat schal be savid schal be on hys riȝt honde. [1810 COLERIDGE in *Lit. Rem.* (1839) IV. 371 How the Ebenezerites would stare to find the Socinians and themselves in one flock on the sheep-side of the judgment-seat]. 1849 W. J. IRONS *Day of Wrath*, With Thy favour'd sheep O place me. 1923 [see *one-nighter* s.v. ONE B. 33]. 1943 J. S. HUXLEY *Evolutionary Ethics* iii. 19 Our ethics will be unrealistic if, after dividing our impulses into sheep and goats, we.. transform the goats into scapegoats. 1954 N. COWARD *Future Indefinite* III. ii. 138, I.. tried repeatedly to analyse my emotions coldly and clearly; to still my anxieties by segregating them, by separating the sheep from the goats. 1962 *Listener* 15 Mar. 469/2 This 'sheep and goats' view, though it may appear plausible, is not to be taken for granted. 1978 K. HUDSON *Jargon of Professions* 13 Is the author using it [*sc.* jargon or propaganda] deliberately as a means of sorting out the sheep from the goats?

(*d*) *c* 960 ÆTHELWOLD *Rule St. Ben.* xxviii. (1885) 53 ðif se ȝetreowleasa ȝewite, he ȝewite, þylæs þe an adliȝ sceap ealle heorde besmite. *c* 1400 *Rule St. Benet* (Prose) 23 A wicke shep may spille al þe flok. *c* 1450, 1798 [see SCABBED 1 d]. *c* 1530 *Songs, Carols*, etc. (1907) 129 On skabbid shepe infectith all the folde. 1894 [see SCABBY 1 b].

(*e*) 142. LYDG. *Horse, Goose & Sheep* 491 What is the sheepe to blame in your sight Whan she is shoorn? *c* 1500 *God Spede the Plough* 35 Thus be we shepe shorne, we may not chese. 1533 GAU *Richt Vay* (1888) 104 Ye blynd giders and pastors quhilk sekis bot the mylk and ye wow of the scheip. **1611** SHAKS. *Wint. T.* IV. iii. 130 If I make not this Cheat bring out another, and the sheerers proue sheepe. **1611** J. DAVIES *Sco. Folly* 164 Hee is as rich as a new-shorne sheepe. **1806** SCOTT in *Lockhart* (1837) II. iii. 89, I will not .. be flayed like a sheep for the benefit of some pettifogging lawyer or attorney. **1900** R. H. SAVAGE *Brought to Bay* vi, A couple of California mine manipulators going over to London to shear those fat-witted sheep, the British investors.

**b.** ***lost sheep***: one who has strayed from the right way. (Cf. 2 a (*a*) and see LOST 2.)

**1611** BIBLE *Jer.* l. 6 My people hath bene lost sheepe. **1633** T. STAFFORD *Pac. Hib.* I. xviii. 106 These fiue (lost sheepe) the children of perdition,.. who lay lurking in desart.. places. **1648** T. VANE (*title*) A Lost Sheep returned home: or, the Motives of the conversion to the Catholike Faith, of Thomas Vane. **1851** RUSKIN *Sheepfolds* 12 There are certain signs by which Christ's sheep may be guessed at. Not by their being in any definite Fold—for many are lost sheep at times: but by their sheep-like behaviour. **1871** R. ELLIS *Catullus* lxiii. 13 Ye sexless eunuchs,.. Lost sheep that err rebellious to the lady Dindymene.

**c.** ***black sheep***: a bad character. Cf. 3.

Prov. ***there is a black sheep in every flock.***

**1792** MACKLIN *Man of World* v. i, O, ye villain! you—you—you are a black sheep; and I'll mark you. **1816** SCOTT *Old Mort.* xxxv, The curates.. know best the black sheep of the flock. **1833** T. HOOK *Parson's Dau.* III. iii, To pick out of the whole mass of English clergy one or two, or one or two and twenty black sheep. **1856** WHYTE MELVILLE *Kate Cov.* xiii, Kate, the 'black sheep' of the family. **1922** JOYCE *Ulysses* 453 He was down and out but, though branded as a black sheep, .. he meant to reform. **1932** R. ALDINGTON *Soft Answers* 76 Every privileged class tries at first to whitewash its black sheep. **1944** W. S. MAUGHAM *Razor's Edge* v. 176 There was a time when the black sheep of the family was sent from my country to America. **1958** 'J. BYROM' *Or be he Dead* viii. 115 I'm the Black Sheep of the family, so if you ever meet any of my relatives, you'll be wise not to mention me. **1979** *Jrnl. R. Soc. Arts* CXXVII. 650/1, I should like to think that they would do this for any black sheep among the countries who tried to defy all reasonable precautions.

**3. a.** Proverbial phrases.

***one might as well be hanged for a sheep as a lamb*** and varr. ***to lose the sheep for a ha'porth of tar***: see HALFPENNYWORTH b.

**1546** J. HEYWOOD *Prov.* II. v. (1867) 58 He loueth well sheeps flesh, that wets his bred in the wul. *c* **1550** *Six Ballads* (Percy Soc.) 4 The blacke shepe is a perylous beast. *a* **1584** T. PROCTOR in Farr *S.P. Eliz.* (1845) II. 400 As soone for to be sold To market cums the yonge sheepe as the olde. **1598** BASTARD *Chrestoleros* IV. xx. 90 Till now I thought the prouerbe did but iest, Which said a blacke sheepe was a biting beast. **1620** [see LAMB *sb.* 1 b]. **1678** J. RAY *Eng. Proverbs* (ed. 2) 350 As good be hang'd for an old sheep as a young lamb. **1748** [see LAMB *sb.* 1 b]. **1836** F. MARRYAT *Mr. Midshipman Easy* II. ii. 58 We may as well be hanged for a sheep as a lamb,.. I vote that we do not go on board. **1859** LEVER *Dav. Dunn* xlvii, 'Just as good for a sheep as a lamb', as the proverb says. **1913** D. H. LAWRENCE *Sons & Lovers* x. 259 It seemed as if she did not like being discovered in her home circumstances... But she might as well be hung for a sheep as for a lamb. She invited him out of the mausoleum of a parlour into the kitchen. **1977** B. PYM *Quartet in Autumn* xv. 133 Letty.. decided that she might as well be hung for a sheep as a lamb and make the most of her meal.

**b.** ***to keep sheep by moonlight***: see quot.

**1898** A. E. HOUSMAN *Shropsh. Lad* ix, [Lads] That shepherded the moonlit sheep A hundred years ago. [*Note*] Hanging in chains was called keeping sheep by moonlight.

**c.** ***to return to our sheep*** [after F. *revenons à nos moutons*]: to return to the matter in hand. (Cf. MUTTON 7.)

**186.** B. HARTE *My Otherself* in *Fiddletown*, etc. (1873) 118 Let us go back to our sheep, which are not all black, thank goodness! **1871** *Athenæum* 12 Aug. 199 'Balaustion's Adventure,'—that we may get to our sheep at last,—is the amber in which Mr. Browning has embalmed the 'Alcestis'. **1890** *N. & Q.* Ser. VII. X. 431/2 But to return to my sheep.

**d.** ***to count sheep***: as a soporific, to count imaginary sheep jumping over an obstacle one by one.

[**1854** S. SMITH '*Way down East* xi. 273 He shut his eyes with all his might, and tried to think of sheep jumping over a wall.] **1920** E. O'NEILL *Beyond Horizon* III. i. 128, I couldn't get to sleep to save my soul. I counted ten million sheep if I counted one. *a* **1922** T. S. ELIOT *Waste Land Drafts* (1971) 27 When restless nights distract her brain from sleep She may as well write poetry, as count sheep. **1977** H. PITCHER *When Miss Emmie was in Russia* x. 75 Nanny.. was trying her hardest to persuade Irina to go to sleep. Did you know that if you count sheep, it is watching the sheep *jump* that sends you off?

**4.** *fig.* In biblical and religious language, applied (as collective plural) to persons, in expressed or implied correlation with *shepherd.* With varying specific reference: said, e.g., of Israel, the Church, or mankind generally, viewed as under the guidance and protection of God, and as owing obedience to Him; of those who are led by Christ as the Good Shepherd (John x. 1-16); and of those who are under the charge of a spiritual pastor, or who are viewed as needing to be spiritually fed or directed. Hence occas. in *sing.*

*c* **825** *Vesp. Ps.* lxxviii. 13 We soðlice folc ðin & scep eowdes ðines. *c* **950** *Lindisf. Gosp.* John x. 16 Oðro scip ic hafo ða ne sint from ðissum plette. *c* **1000** *Ags. Gosp.* Matt. xv. 24 Ne eom ic asend buton to þam sceapum þe forwurdon of israhela huse. *c* **1200** ORMIN 3760 Forr þatt he wollde sammnenn An flocc off menn till Crisstenndom,.. þatt sholldenn wurrþenn hise shep. *c* **1220** *Bestiary* 49 He is hirde, we ben sep. *a* **1300** *Cursor M.* 27451 Sere biscop, ta god kepe, þe wolf es cummen amang þi scepe. *c* **1380** WYCLIF *Wks.* (1880) 32 No curat owiþ to leue his schepe vnkept among þe wolues of helle. *c* **1386** CHAUCER *Prol.* 508 Wel oghte a preest ensample for to yeue, By his clennesse, how þat his sheep sholde lyue. *c* **1400** *Rule St. Benet* (Prose) 22 On alle maner sal þabbes entirmete hir Al maner of sentence at muster til hir sep, þat nan be tint. *c* **1560** A. SCOTT *Poems* (S.T.S.) i. 94 Christis sillie scheip and sobir flok. **1655** MILTON *Sonn.* xv. 6 In thy book record their groanes Who were thy Sheep. **1784** COWPER *Task* VI. 891 All pastors are alike To wand'ring sheep, resolv'd to follow none. **1818** SCOTT *Hrt. Midl.* li, It would ill become me, for the sake of lucre, to leave my sheep in the wilderness. **1850** BROWNING *Christmas Eve* II. ad. fin., I.. found myself.. in Zion Chapel Meeting,.. Which, calling its flock to their special clover, Found all assembled and one sheep over.

**5. a.** A person who is as stupid, timid, or poor-spirited as a sheep.

**1542** UDALL *Erasm. Apoph.* I. 109 Those persones, who wer sely poore solles.. wer euen then.. by a commen prouerbe called sheepes heddes, or sheepe. **1601** SHAKS. *Jul. C.* I. iii. 105, I know he would not be a Wolfe, But that he sees the Romans are but Sheepe. **1692** WASHINGTON tr. *Milton's Def. People* i. 15 You.. That understand so many Languages, turn over so many Volumes, and yet are but a sheep when all is done. **1840** R. H. DANA *Bef. Mast* xx. (1869) 169 They've got a man for mate of that ship, and not a bloody sheep about decks! **1914** G. B. SHAW *Misalliance* Pref. p. lxxiii, Bullied and ordered about, the Englishman obeys like a sheep. **1930** —— *Apple Cart* II. 72 The way you fellows scuttle backward and forward from one mind to another whenever Joe holds up his finger is disgusting. This is a Cabinet of sheep. **1948** WODEHOUSE *Uncle Dynamite* xiii. 226 She looks on you as a.. poor, spineless sheep who can't say boo to a goose.

†**b.** *Sheep* and *shrew* are contrasted as types of wives of opposite characters (see quots.).

**1573-80** TUSSER *Husb.* (1878) 157 Now be she lambe or be she eaw, Giue me the sheepe, take thou the shreaw. **1575** GASCOIGNE *Glasse Govt.* III. i. Wks. 1910 II. 44 It is an olde saying, one shrew is worth two sheep. **1580** LYLY *Euphues* (Arb.) 472 They noted, that although the virgin were somwhat shrewishe at the first, yet in time she myght become a sheepe. *c* **1645** HOWELL *Lett.* (1650) I. 110 It is better to marry a Shrew then a Sheep; for though silence be the dumb Orator of beuty,.. yet a Phlegmatic dull Wife is fulsom and fastidious. **1661** *Tom Tyler & his Wife* 26 To marrie a sheep, to marie a shrow.

**c.** A semi at Aberdeen university.

**1865** G. MACDONALD *Alec Forbes* xxxiii. II. 5 A certain semi (second-classman, or more popularly sheep).

**6.** *ellipt.* (For *sheep leather*; cf. *calf*, *kid.*) Leather made from the skin of the sheep: used in bookbinding.

The term has gone out of use in the bookbinding trade, the material being known under other names, e.g. *roan*, *basil.*

**1705** *Lond. Gaz.* No. 4187/4 Price bound in Sheep 18d. **1727** SWIFT *Further Acc. E. Curll* Wks. 1755 III. I. 156 As to the report of my poor husband's stealing o' calf, it is really groundless, for he always binds in sheep. **1836** *J. R. Smith's Catal. Bks.* Feb. 9/1 Fernandez's Spanish Grammar, 8vo. sheep, 2s. **1879** *Cassell's Techn. Educ.* IV. 90 Sheep may be had white and of all colours. **1911** *Tregaskis' Catal. Bks.* No. 708. 53 One volume in old sheep, the other in calf.

**7.** *attrib.* and *Comb.* **a.** appositive, as ***sheep-cattle***, ***-hog.***

**1552** HULOET, *Shepe cattell, *pecus.* **1596** MASCALL *Cattle, Sheep* 205 There be two sortes of Sheepe cattell, the better sort is those of the soft wooll. **1558** in *Archæol. Jrnl.* V. 317, vj *shepe hogges. **1605** *N. Riding Rec.* (1884) I. 14 Four sheep called sheep hogges, value 20s. **1793** *Carlop Green* II. vii, Mass John, Like sow, or sheep-hog, fat.

**b.** = Of, belonging to, produced by, or concerned with sheep, as ***sheep-dung***, ***-fair***, ***-fell*** (FELL *sb.*[1]), ***-flock***, etc.

**1649** BLITH *Engl. Improver* xx. 121 The most proper soyle for Gardens are your *Sheep-dung, your Hen muck. **1906** C. A. SHERRING *West. Tibet* xiv. 276 Cow-dung and sheep-dung fires. **1473** *Cov. Leet Bk.* 386 That no man occupie their *shepe feyre but between the Gosford yate and the White-frere lane. **1822** in Cobbett *Rur. Rides* (1885) I. 150 The 11th of October is the Sheep-fair. *c* **1400** *Laud Troy Bk.* 791 Medee sayde to Iason than:.. 'I wolde make the that *schepe-fel Wynne to-morwe with-outen perel'. **1562** in *Cal. Anc. Rec. Dublin* (1891) II. 23 That no bowcher.. shall sell any of the shepfell. **1615** CHAPMAN *Odyss.* xx. 3 Vnder him, an Oxe-hide newly flead; Aboue him Sheep fels store. **1398** TREVISA *Barth. De P.R.* XVIII. i. (Bodl. MS.), Swyne flesche and *schepe flesche is better rosted pan sode. **1808** in Shirreff *Agric. Shetl. Isl.* (1814) 56 A common shepherd in each parish.. would tend.. to increase the *sheep flocks. **1876** G. M. HOPKINS *Poems* (1967) 65 And sheep-flock clouds like worlds of wool. **1801** *Farmer's Mag.* Apr. 182 If population was lessened by a general introduction of the *sheep-husbandry in the Highlands. **1846** DICKENS *Pict. Italy, Genoa* 49 Cocks' combs and *sheep-kidney, chopped up with mutton-chops and liver. **1694** *Lond. Gaz.* No. 3000/4 A pair of *Sheep Leather Breeches. **1886** C. SCOTT *Sheep-farming* 43 The use of ensilage overcomes many difficulties in *sheep management. **1779** *Mirror* No. 37 A green hill.. seamed with a winding *sheep-path. **1857** HUGHES *Tom Brown* I. i, The sheep-paths running along their sides like ruled lines. **1858** SIMMONDS *Dict. Trade*, **Sheep-pelts*, the skins of sheep, fresh or salted, intended for leather. **1801** *Farmer's Mag.* Jan. 45 If ever, among the continually changing modes of fashionable follies, *sheep races should happen to become the rage. **1886** C. SCOTT *Sheep-farming* 183 Whether all the present diversities of the sheep race are descended from one original pair or not. **1782** W. H. MARSHALL *Norfolk* (1795) II. 320 Cawston *Sheep-show. *Ibid.* 323 The greatest 'sheep-show' in the country. **1799** J. ROBERTSON *Agric. Perth* 309 *Sheep-stocks have been found more profitable than goats. **1523-34** FITZHERB. *Husb.* §44 Take two pounde of *shepe suet molten. **15..** *Scheip tawcht [see TALLOW *sb.* 1 a]. **1772** GRAVES *Spir. Quix.* (1820) II. 183 Jerry then looked about and found a *sheep-track. **1829** SCOTT *Anne of G.* xv, A path, or rather a sheep-track. **1660** SHARROCK *Vegetables* 92 *Sheep-trotters, and other offal. **1749** SMOLLETT *Gil Blas* I. xv. (1782) I. 84 A huge fricassee of sheep-trotters.

**c.** = Having to do with the rearing, keeping, or feeding of sheep, for the use of sheep, as ***sheep-barn***, ***-boy***, ***-common***, ***crib***, ***down***, ***paddock***, ***ranch***, ***shed***, ***station***, ***wagon***, etc.

**1868** *Rep. U.S. Comm. Agric.* (1869) 42 The remaining twenty-four.. were put in the *sheep-barn. **1842** S. C. HALL *Ireland* II. 81 The *sheep-boy saw him go in. **1859** MEREDITH *R. Feverel* xix, Pipe, happy sheep-boy, Love! **1707** MORTIMER *Husb.* (1721) II. 277 He advised the turning of the Wash of a *Sheep-common to the Roots of the Trees. **1872** *Routledge's Ev. Boy's Ann.* 31/2 Ten thousand acres of first-class *sheep country. **1921** K. S. WOODS *Rural Industries round Oxf.* II. i. 80 Hazel.. is made into wattle or 'flake' hurdles and *sheep cribs. **1946** N. WYMER *Eng. County Crafts* vii. 77 These bands.. also undertake the making of such articles as hen-coops, pump-buckets, sheep-cribs. **1789** G. WHITE *Selborne* i. 2 A vast hill of chalk.. divided into a *sheep down, the high wood, and a long hanging wood. **1805** R. W. DICKSON *Pract. Agric.* I. 108 The inclosures on sheep downs. *Ibid.* II. 777 Where the weld does not succeed, a portion of *sheep-feed may be afforded for winter and spring use. **1523-34** FITZHERB. *Husb.* §18 Thou shalte not nede to bye any hurdels nor *shepe flekes. **1812** SIR J. SINCLAIR *Syst. Husb. Scot.* I. 39 The field may be effectually subdivided by sheep-flakes, or hurdles. **1805** R. W. DICKSON *Pract. Agric.* I. 350 Intended either for a crop of seed, or for *sheep-food. **1560** BECON *Jewel of Joy* Wks. II. fol. xv, What *shepe ground scapeth these Caterpyllers of the commune weale? **1743** *Sel. Trans. Improvers Agric.* 148 The Sheep Ground abounds with many Springs of good Water. **1822-34** *Good's Study Med.* (ed. 4) I. 273 The minute eggs may.. exist in the stagnant atmosphere of the sheep-ground. **1830** *Cumbld. Farm Rep.* 55 in *Libr. Usef. Knowl., Husb.* III, Hay, in *sheep-haicks or cribs, is given along with turnips. **1417-18** *Durham Acc. Rolls* (Surtees) 302 Pro staures emptis pro *shepehekkys apud le Holme. **1856** *Farmer's Mag.* Jan. 28 Lands.. brought into cultivation for the production of *sheep-keep. *a* **1722** LISLE *Husb.* (1757) 339 The *sheep-land at Appleford.. is subject to the staggers. **1606** *Nottingham Rec.* IV. 281 To reduce the *shepe markett thither to a place certayne. **1611** BIBLE *John* v. 2 There is at Hierusalem by the sheep market, a poole. **1930** L. G. D. ACLAND *Early Canterbury Runs* 1st Ser. v. 103 This part of the station is still called the '*sheep paddocks'. **1523-34** FITZHERB. *Husb.* §37 That man, that hath the best *shepe pasture for wynter. **1782** CREVECOEUR *Lett.* 127 Several hundred of sheep-pasture titles have since been divided on those different tracks. *c* **1830** in *Libr. Usef. Knowl., Husb.* III. I. 22 When the land was in poor sheep-pasture. **1851** HELPS *Comp. Solit.* i. 13 The dull *sheep-ponds scattered here and there. **1683** TRYON *Way to Health* 142 The Gospel testifies of a *Sheep-Pool [John v. 2]. **1874** J. G. MCCOY *Hist. Sk. Cattle Trade* i. 1 Thus it is common to hear of a corn ranch, a wheat ranch, a *sheep ranch. **1981** G. MCDONALD *Fletch & Widow Bradley* xviii. 72 She worked six months on a sheep ranch. **1845** BROWNING *Flight of Duchess* ii, Where .. *sheep-range leads to cattle-tract. **1868** *Rep. U.S. Comm. Agric.* (1869) 150 The land is divided as follows: Tilled land, .. roads, pasture, and sheep range. **1600** *Churchw. Acc. Pittington*, etc. (Surtees) 48 For *shepe salve the third of December, iiij d. **1788** W. H. MARSHALL *Yorksh.* II. 351 *Sheep-salve*, tar-and-grease for dressing sheep with. **1946** J. W. DAY *Harvest Adventure* vii. 110 Allus came up to my *sheep-shed, an' if I 'ad people a-watchin' me at work—tourists an' loike—would say, 'Ah! company I zee.' **1834** *Tait's Mag.* I. 411 A *sheep-station in the interior [of Australia]. **1911** C. E. W. BEAN '*Dreadnought' of Darling* i. 8 The long blue-grey galvanised-iron wool-shed of some sheep station. **1944** F. CLUNE *Red Heart* 59 They came to the last outpost of civilisation, at Mount Abundance sheep station. **1733** TULL *Horse-hoeing Husb.* x. 103 Five Pound each (which is but a Third of the Weight of the large size of *Sheep-Turneps). **1909** E. RUPERT *Let.* 24 May in *Atlantic Monthly* (1913) Oct. 434/2 About noon the first day out we came near a *sheep-wagon. **1962** G. MACEWAN *Blazing Old Cattle Trail* xx. 134 The canvas-roofed sheep wagon was the ultimate in household compaction, combining the essentials of kitchen, dining-room, bedroom and sheep dog quarters. **1809** J. LAWRENCE *Treat. Cattle* 294 To every farm yard ought to be attached a *sheep yard, or home fold, completely fenced in. **1842** BISCHOFF *Woollen Manuf.* II. 387, I will only add my testimony in favour of sheep-yard dung. **1634** W. WOOD *New Eng. Prosp.* (1865) 54 In an ill *sheepe-yeare I have knowne Mutton as deere in Old-England.

**d.** objective and objective genitive, as ***sheep-breeder***, ***-clipper***, ***-grazier***, ***-grazing***, ***-rancher***, etc.

**1841** *Penny Cycl.* XXI. 356/2 This is an important consideration with the *sheep-breeder. **1535** COVERDALE *1 Sam.* xxv. 7, I haue herde saye that thou hast *shepe clyppers. **1875** *Jrnl. R. Agric. Soc.* Ser. II. XI. 103 *Sheep-clipping is another part of the piece-work system at Knettishall. **1886** C. SCOTT *Sheep-farming* 30 The Kentish *sheep-graziers of Romney Marsh. **1795** in J. Roberston *Agric. Perth* (1799) 531 The *sheep-holders were persuaded to make a trial of a larger boned stronger sheep. **1875** KNIGHT *Dict. Mech.*, *Sheep-holder*, a cradle or table to hold a sheep while being shorn. *a* **1722** LISLE *Husb.* (1757) 309 That practice.. is common among the *sheep-jobbers. **1688** in *Gentl. Mag.* (1817) LXXXVII. II. 603 Our *sheep-jobing trade. **1604** BABINGTON *Comf. Notes Exod.* iii. 11 Jethro his *Sheepe-keeper. *a* **1578** LINDESAY (Pitscottie) *Chron. Scot.* (S.T.S.) II. 282 Thocht he var nocht leirned.. mair nor he that new come fra the *schip keiping. **1819** REES *Cycl.*, **Sheep-Lamber*,.. the person who has the.. management of the ewe-flocks, which are under the state of lambing. *c* **1830** *Glouc. Farm Rep.* 21 in *Libr. Usef. Knowl., Husb.* III, The dung.. made in the *sheep-lambing fold. **1560** BECON *Jewel of Joy* Wks. II. fol. xv, Howe do the rych men, and specially suche as be *shepemongers oppresse the kynges lyege people by deuouryng theyr commune pastures wyth theyr shepe? **1707** J. SHIRLEY *Triumph of Wit* 205 A *Sheep-napper, whose Trade is so deep, If he's caught in the Corn, he's mark'd for a Sheep. **1841** *Penny Cycl.* XXI. 365/1 This is a view of the case which should never be forgotten by the *sheep-owner. **1865** E. BURRITT *Walk to Land's End* 112 The largest *sheep-raiser in England. **1832** *Encycl. Amer.* XI. 352 *Sheep-Raising. **1880** *Victorian Rev.* I. 660 Had not the soil been well adapted to sheep-raising of the highest order. **1904** *Country Life* July 287/1 The Montana *sheep-rancher figures that the wool will pay all expenses, leaving the increase for his profit. **1976** A. J. RUSSELL *Pour Hemlock* (1979) vii. 61 A sheep rancher who owned vast lands on the Colorado Plateau, in northeastern Arizona. **1611** SHAKS. *Wint. T.* IV. iv. 805 An old *Sheepe-whistling Rogue. **1681** in *Harl. Misc.* (1744) II. 111 They are no more to be reclaimed than a *Sheep-Worrier. **1873** G. C. DAVIES *Mount. & Mere* x. 72 A fierce and savage dog, a confirmed sheep-worrier. **1903** R. BRIDGES *Wintry Delights* 122 That *Sheep-worry of Europe, when pigmy Napoleon enter'd Her sovereign chambers. **1863** W. C. BALDWIN *Afr. Hunting* ix. 417 They hang down their heads like dogs convicted of *sheep-worrying.

**e.** instrumental and adverbial, as ***sheep-bitten***, ***-browsed***, ***-grazed***, ***-proof***, ***-scattered***, ***-white***, etc.

**1917** J. MASEFIELD *Lollingdon Downs* 31 Night is on the downland, on the lonely moorland, On the hills where the wind goes over *sheep-bitten turf. **1870** MORRIS *Earthly Par.* III. IV. 5 The *sheep-browsed slopes. *a* **1887** JEFFERIES *Field & Hedgerow* (1889) 331 Up the round hill, *sheep-dotted, was his way. **1808** BATCHELOR *Agric. Bedford* 450 The other part [*sc.* of a field]..was sown down upon *sheep-fed rye in June. **1925** W. DE LA MARE *Three Sleeping Boys in Broomsticks* 256 The bird-haunted, *sheep-grazed meadows. **1976** *Southern Even. Echo* (Southampton) 2 Nov. (Advts. Suppl.) 3/8 Turfs, good quality, sheep grazed and weed treated, machine cut 3ft. × 1ft. **1812** W. TENNANT *Anster F.* III. ii, Kelly-laws *sheep-nibbled top. **1882** ARMSTRONG & CAMPBELL *Austral. Sheep Husbandry* xvii. 186 This fence can be made still more *sheep-proof..by leaving out the bottom wire, and having..a light embankment thrown up. **1903** 'T. COLLINS' *Such is Life* iv. 134 The fence, much damaged by floods, was repaired merely to the sheep-proof standard. **1950** *N.Z. Jrnl. Agric.* July 74/2, 20 paddocks, all sheep-proof fenced. **1978** I. MURDOCH *Sea* 401 After the bog there was ordinary farm land, *sheep-scattered hillsides. **1894** DU MAURIER *Trilby* II. 147 He went out for a stroll on a *sheep-trimmed down. **1828** HOOD *Town & Country* xv, No *sheep-white hill my dwelling flanks. **1945** DYLAN THOMAS in *Poetry* (Chicago) July 175 The frozen hold Flocked with the sheep white smoke of the farm house cowl.

**8.** Special comb.: **sheep-back** = ROCHE MOUTONNÉE; †**sheep bar**, a kind of hurdle on which sheep are laid to be clipped; **sheep-bell**, a bell hung on a sheep's neck (see BELL-WETHER); **sheep-berry**, the North American tree, *Viburnum Lentago*, or its fruit, which is fancied to resemble sheep-droppings; **sheep blowfly**, a large greenish blowfly belonging to the genus *Lucilia*, esp. *L. coprina*, the larva of which is a pest of sheep in Australia; **sheep-book**, a book of accounts in which are entered the particulars relating to flocks of sheep; **sheep-bot (fly)**, the bot-fly *Œstrus ovis*; †**sheep-brand** = SHEEP-MARK 1; **sheep-bug**, one of the genus *Argas* of mites, infesting sheep; **sheep-bush** *Austral.*, either of two species of *Geijera*, *G. parviflora* or *G. linearifolia*, of the family Rutaceæ, a small evergreen tree sometimes used as fodder for sheep; **sheep-camp**, (*a*) *N. Amer.*, a camp for sheep herders; (*b*) *Austral.* and *N.Z.*, a resting or assembly place of sheep (cf. CAMP *sb.*[2] 4 c); (*c*) *S. Afr.*, a fenced-in enclosure for sheep (cf. CAMP *sb.*[2] 4 e); **sheep cocky** *Austral.* and *N.Z. colloq.*, a sheep-farmer on a small scale (cf. COCKY *sb.*[2] 2); †**sheep-counter**, a counter or token used in counting sheep (cf. Shaks. *Wint. Tale* IV. iii. 38); †**sheep-crook**, a shepherd's crook; **sheep-dip**, (*a*) = SHEEP-WASH 2; (*b*) a place where sheep are washed; also fig. (see quots. 1945, 1976); so **sheep-dipping**; **sheep-dog**, (*a*) a dog that tends sheep; *spec.* one or other of the varieties trained for this purpose, as the Scotch collie, and the bob-tailed English sheep-dog; cf. *shepherd's dog*; (*b*) *fig.* a chaperon; also as *v. trans.*, to urge (someone) on in the manner of a sheep-dog; to direct or 'herd'; also '**sheep-dogging** *vbl. sb.*; **sheep drain**, an open drain cut in grass-land about 18 inches wide by 18 inches deep; †**sheep-drunk** *a.* (see quot. and cf. note s.v. LION-DRUNK); **sheep-fag** (see FAG *sb.*[3]); **sheep-farm**, a tract of land devoted to sheep-rearing; so **sheep-farm** *v.*, **sheep-farmer**, **-farming**; **sheep-fly**, (*a*) = SHEEP-TICK; (*b*) a fly, *Lucilia sericata*, infesting live sheep; **sheep-fodder plant**, a South African plant, *Pentzia virgata* (Miller *Plant-n.* 1884); **sheep-foil** *Hunting*, a foiling (see FOIL *v.*[1] 2) of the track by sheep; †**sheep-furred** *a.*, trimmed with sheep's wool; **sheep gad-fly**, *Œstrus ovis*; †**sheep-garth**, a sheepfold; **sheep-gate**, (*a*) [GATE *sb.*[2] 8] pasturage, or the right of pasturage, for sheep (or a sheep); (*b*) [GATE *sb.*[1]] a gate for the passage of sheep; a hurdle for enclosing sheep; **sheep glue piece** (see quot.); **sheep-heaf**, a sheep-walk; **sheep-herder** *U.S.*, one who herds sheep in large numbers in unfenced country; †**sheep-hound** = *sheep-dog*; **sheep-kill** = *sheep-laurel*; †**sheep-killing pennygrass**, *Hydrocotyle vulgaris*; **sheep-laurel**, a North American shrub, *Kalmia angustifolia*, supposed to be very poisonous to sheep; cf. *lamb-kill*; **sheep-lease** *dial.*, a sheepwalk; **sheep-meat**, (*a*) *Western U.S.*, mutton; (*b*) in mod. trading use: meat obtained from sheep; mutton and lamb; (also written as one word); **sheep-money** = *sheep-silver*; **sheep-net**, a net for confining sheep upon turnips; **sheepnose**, a small cider apple (see quots.); †**sheep-nose-worm**, the larva of the sheep-bot; **sheep-penny** = *sheep-money*; **sheep-pest**, (*a*) a common Australian weed, *Acæna ovina*, the hooked spines of which catch in the wool of sheep (Morris *Austral Eng.* 1898); (*b*) = SHEEP-TICK (*Syd. Soc. Lex.* 1898); **sheep-plant** = *vegetable sheep* (sense 1 c); **sheep-pock**, **-pox**, a form of smallpox to which sheep are subject; **sheep-poison**, (*a*) = *sheep-laurel*; (*b*) *Lupinus densiflorus* (Miller *Plant-n.* 1884); **sheep-rack**, (*a*) a rack from which sheep feed; (*b*) a sheep-house; (*c*) the starling; **sheep-rake**, a sheep-walk or sheep-track; **sheep-ree**, a permanent sheepfold; †**sheep-reeve**, a chief shepherd; **sheep-rot**, (*a*) the rot in sheep, caused by the presence of flukes in the liver; (*b*) a name for plants supposed to cause disease in sheep, as butterwort and marsh pennywort; **sheep-run** orig. *Austral.*, = SHEEP-WALK; **sheep-scab**, a skin-disease of sheep due to an acarus; **sheep-seaweed** (see quot.); **sheep-sick** *a.* (see quot. 1895); **sheep-silver** (see quots.); **sheep-sleight** [SLEIGHT *sb.*[3]] = *sheep-gate* (*a*); **sheep-smearing**, the smearing of sheep with tar to kill vermin; also a kind of tar used for this purpose; **sheep-sorrel** = *sheep's sorrel* (see 9); †**sheep-stead**, **-steading** *Sc.*, a sheep-farm; **sheep-stray**, liberty of sheep to graze on a tract of land; **sheep trot** *nonce-wd.*, a dance as of satyrs; **sheep wagtail**, a bird of the genus *Budytes*; †**sheep-ward**, a shepherd; †**sheep-water** = SHEEP-WASH 2; †**sheep-weald**, sheep-pasture; **sheep-weed**, soapwort, *Saponaria officinalis* (Syd. Soc. Lex.); **sheep-wool** = *sheep's wool* (see 9).

**1877** HUXLEY *Physiogr.* x. 162 The flat-domed hummocks of rock produced in this way are termed *sheep-backs or *roches moutonnées*. **1557** *Richmond Wills* (Surtees) 101, ij. axletrees, withe other *shepe barres and hustlement. **1411** *Nottingham Rec.* II. 86, j. *shepebell, jd. **1794** MRS. RADCLIFFE *Myst. Udolpho* xxxiv, The faint tinkling of a sheep-bell, and..the bleat of flocks. **1872** ELLACOMBE *Bells of Ch.* in *Ch. Bells Devon* ix. 261 [He] was in the habit of tuning, to exact musical scale, the sheep bells of many of his agricultural friends. **1814** PURSH *Flora Amer. Septentr.* II. 709 *Sheep-berry. *Viburnum prunifolium.* **1847** DARLINGTON *Amer. Weeds* (1860) 162 *Viburnum Lentago*... Sweet Viburnum. Sheep-berry. **1932** *Discovery* July 210/2 The *sheep blowfly..is reliably estimated to do £4,000,000 worth of damage every year [in Australia]. **1974** R. D. HUGHES *Living Insects* v. 128 Cool temperatures in autumn can induce a pause in the development of the prepupal larva of the sheep blowfly. **1831** *Sutherland Farm Rep.* 84 in *Libr. Usef. Knowl., Husb.* III, The waste-books, consisting of a corn-book, cash-book, *sheep-book. **1819** *Sheep bot-fly [see BOT *sb.* 3]. **1836–9** *Todd's Cycl. Anat.* II. 871/2 In the larva of the sheep-bot..there are thirteen segments. **1862** T. W. HARRIS *Insects injur. Veget.* (ed. 3) 624 The sheep bot-fly (*Cephalemyia ovis*) lays its eggs in the nostrils of sheep. **1586** FERNE *Blaz. Gentrie* 241 If they be not..agreeing with the conformity..of Blazon..they may vse them as *sheepbrands. **1889** *Sheep-bush [see WILGA]. **1933** *Bulletin* (Sydney) 7 June 25/2 Sheep bush..is tall and ornamental. It has long narrow leaves. **1965** *Austral. Encycl.* IX. 310/2 The smaller related *G*[*eijera*] *linearifolia*, which extends into Western Australia, is called sheep-bush. **1869** J. MUIR *Jrnl.* 25 June in *My First Summer in Sierra* (1911) 85 Though only a *sheep camp, this grand mountain hollow is home. **1921** H. GUTHRIE-SMITH *Tutira* xx. 180 Before the establishment of sheep-camps growing grass and clover, there was nothing to tempt pig from the low grounds. **1931** *Amer. Speech* VII. 120 A *sheep camp*, or the migratory home of a pair of shepherders, consists of a canvas-topped wagon with a stove in it and a *bunk* or bed at the back. **1939** P. A. ROLLINS *Gone Haywire* v. 114 He had stopped at a sheep camp and played casino. **1947** [see CAMP *sb.*[2] 4 e]. **1950** *N.Z. Jrnl. Agric.* May 463/1 The paddock was a sheep-camp paddock or similar place where considerable numbers of sheep were frequently concentrated. **1973** *Kingston* (Ontario) *Whig-Standard* 11 Aug. 7/2 A few miles down-river there was a sheep-camp. **1949** F. SARGESON *I saw in My Dream* II. xiv. 206, I never can teach my wife that a *sheep-cocky's dogs aren't pets. **1647** TRAPP *Comm. 1 John* ii. 18 Children may be easily cozened, and made to take a *sheep-counter for an angel, because broader and brighter. *c* **1420** ? LYDG. *Assembly of Gods* 327 A *shepe-crook in hys hand he sparyd for no pryde. **1600** SURFLET *Country Farm* I. xxv. 158 He must whoop and whistle after them, threatning them with his sheepe-crooke. **1687** NORRIS *Coll. Misc.* 70 Who shall now the royal sheep-crook hold,..who now secure the fold? ? **1873** HARDY *Lett.* (1978) I. 25, I have sketched in my note-book during the past summer a few correct outlines of smockfrocks, gaiters, sheep-crooks, rick-'staddles'..and some other out-of-the-way things that might have to be shown. **1865** *Jrnl. R. Agric. Soc.* Ser. II. I. 51 An 'extract of tobacco', manufactured..for the making of '*sheep-dips'. **1898** MORRIS *Austral Eng.* s.v. *Sheep-wash*, The Place where the sheep are washed, also called the 'sheep-dip'. **1911** W. H. KOEBEL *In Maoriland Bush* v. 93 He was selling a new species of sheep-dip. **1915** *N.Z. Jrnl. Agric.* 20 Nov. 411 Do not economize in the purchase of sheep-dip. **1945** MENCKEN *Amer. Lang.* Suppl. I. 262 Many generic names for alcoholic stimulants..*sheep-dip*, [etc.]. **1968** K. WEATHERLY *Roo Shooter* 118 His seat was an old five-gallon drum that had once held sheep dip. **1976** *New Yorker* 3 May 65/1 'Sheep dip' was what the lumberjacks called their tea. **1852** *Trans. Highl. Soc.* 418 *Sheep-dipping apparatus. **1887** J. COLEMAN *Cattle*, etc. *Gt. Brit.* 281 The value of sheep dipping, both as affecting health, removing vermin, and favouring wool growth. **1915** J. R. MACDONALD *N.Z. Sheepfarming* xxvii. 71 It is needless to set forth all the conditions for complete success in sheep dipping, seeing that..it is the custom to attach directions for use on every packet or drum. **1968** J. ARNOLD *Shell Bk. Country Crafts* 228 The primary use, for a coracle, now, is for fly-fishing and sheep-dipping. *a* **1774** TUCKER *Lt. Nat.* (1777) III. I. 200 The faithful *sheep-dog assists in tending our flocks. **1844** W. C. SPOONER *Sheep* 295 The sheep-owner should never keep a savage sheep-dog. **1848** THACKERAY *Van. Fair* xxxvii, A sheep-dog—a companion! Becky Sharp with a companion! **1897** VIOLET HUNT *Unkist, Unkind!* ix, Philip's sister couldn't manage to get away from Buxton just now, so here I am, without any sheep-dog at all. **1973** *Times Lit. Suppl.* 13 Apr. 418/4 Working with Thomas Jones and *sheep-dogged by vigilant helpers, I entered a new dimension of scholarship. **1981** S. JACKMAN *Game of Soldiers* I. 15 The Group Senior Signals Officer..has done his time..on Coastal Command Sunderlands, sheep-dogging convoys in the Western Approaches. **1969** E. BLISHEN *This Right Soft Lot* I. ii. 40 A surprising number of boys seemed never to have seen the Thames before... So I did a little quick *sheep-dogging, and at last we reached the gallery. **1844** H. STEPHENS *Bk. Farm* I. 497 When the grass is smooth and the soil pretty deep, this is an economical mode of making such drains, which have received the appellation of *sheep drains. **1592** NASHE *P. Penilesse* Wks. (Grosart) II. 82 The fourth [kind of drunkard] is *Sheepe drunke, wise in his own conceipt, when he cannot bring forth a right word. **1789** A. YOUNG in *Encycl. Brit.* (1797) XVII. 348/2 The *hippobosca ovina*, called in Lincolnshire *sheep fagg. **1776** T. PENNANT *Tour Scotl.* II. 400 A letter from Mr. George Malcolm, concerning *Sheep-farms, &c. **1801** *Farmer's Mag.* Apr. 172 The sheep-farms in the higher districts. **1861** *Times* 27 Sept., English farmers who come expressly to till and sheep-farm. **1809** J. LAWRENCE *Treat. Cattle* 314 The least enlightened *sheep farmers of France. *Ibid.*, The various plans of *sheep-farming. **1658** ROWLAND tr. *Moufet's Theat. Ins.* I. xi. 934 The Tick or *Sheep-fly. **1902** *Nature* 7 Aug. 352 The life-history of the sheep-fly (*Lucilia sericata*). **1842** APPERLEY *Life of Sportsman* xiv, For a moment a *sheep-foil now baffles the scent. **1597** BRETON *Wit's Trenchmour* (Grosart) 17/1 His *sheepe-furd short gowne. **1802** BINGLEY *Anim. Zool.* (1813) III. 308 The *sheep gad-fly. **1570** LEVINS *Manip.* 34/17 Y[e] *Sheepgarth, *ouile*. **1537–8** *Cartul. Abb. de Rievalle* (Surtees) 352 Two messes..with all the *shepe-gates and common of pasture. **1535** COVERDALE *2 Esdr.* [*Neh.*] iii. 1 Eliasib the hye prest.. buylded the Shepegate. **1569** T. WILSON *Disc. Usury* (1584) 97 For tillage, [they] vse sheepe-gates, where no men are maintained. **1607** NORDEN *Surv. Dial.* III. 109 What is a Cowe, Oxe, Horse, or sheepe-gate woorth by the yeere, or by the weeke. *c* **1882** JOS. LUCAS *Stud. Nidderdale* iii. 7 'Sheep-gates'..are let..with each farm. **1883** J. Y. STRATTON *Hops & Hop-pickers* 47 A lodging for hoppers.. constructed by means of sheep-gates thatched with straw. **1858** SIMMONDS *Dict. Trade*, **Sheep-glue Pieces* and *Fleshings*, cuttings of sheep skins saved for making glue. **1844** *Min. Evid. Sel. Comm. Commons' Inclosure* 26 The want of accurate knowledge as to the right of stinting in the *sheep-heafs. **1872** SCHELE DE VERE *Americanisms* 210 *Sheepherder. **1890** L. C. D'OYLE *Notches* 25 One melting drift has revealed the body of a frozen sheep-herder. **1891** C. ROBERTS *Adrift Amer.* 244 *Sheep-herding is supposed by those who have never followed it to be an easy, idle, lazy way of procuring a livelihood. **1622** FLETCHER *Sea-Voy.* IV. i, They hang their most dejected heads, Like fearful *sheephounds. **1968** E. R. BUCKLER *Ox Bells & Fireflies* vii. 106 The purple loops of the *sheepkill. **1578** LYTE *Dodoens* I. xxv. 38 Y[e] base Almaignes do call it Penninckcruyt: in English *Sheepe killing Pennygrasse. [**1597** GERARDE *Herbal* II. cxliii. 424 Water Pennywoort..Sheepes killing Penny-grasse, Penny rot,..White rot.] **1810** F. A. MICHAUX *Hist. Arbres Forestiers Amér. Sept.* I. 35 Mountain laurel ..*sheep laurel,..nom secondaire. **1814** PURSH *Flora Amer. Septentr.* I. 296 *Kalmia ovata*.., known by the name of Sheep Laurel, being considered very poisonous when fed upon by sheep. **1954** Sheep laurel [see LAMBKILL]. *a* **1722** LISLE *Husb.* (1757) 324, I am told, that in Dorsetshire the aim of the farmers is, to fold on their *sheep-leases in the middle of July. **1860** BARTLETT *Dict. Amer.*, *Sheep meat. **1975** *Austral. Outlook* XXIX. 298 New Zealand supplies 80 per cent of EEC sheepmeat imports. **1978** *Times* 19 June 17/3 The word 'sheepmeat' with which Brussels refers to mutton and lamb, is translated from the official French term, *Viande ovine*. **1979** *Times* 13 Nov. 17/6 The recent use of the term 'sheepmeat' in place of mutton and lamb is depressing in the extreme and will, I should think, put many people off buying what is one of our most important farm products. *a* **1618** RALEIGH *Prerog. Parl.* (1628) 55 There was nothing new, neither head money, nor *sheepe money, nor escuage. **1822** HIBBERT *Descr. Shetl. Isl.* 321 They pay the ox and sheep money that was granted as a compliment to the Earl of Bothwell. **1794** J. WILSON *Agric. Surv. Renfr.* (1812) 147 (Jam.), [He] has fed annually about 300 or 400 Highland sheep on his turnip fields by using *sheep-nets for folding. **1844** H. STEPHENS *Bk. Farm* II. 72 Sheep-nets run about 50 yards in length, when set, and weigh about 14 lb. **1817** W. COXE *View Cultivation of Fruit Trees* 125 Bullocks Pippin.. is more generally distinguished by the vulgar name of *Sheep-nose, from a supposed resemblance between the form of the apple and that part of a sheep. **1925** C. MORLEY *Safety Pins* 178 We have seen apples of strange shapes, something like a pear (sheepnoses, they call them). **1943** B. DAMON *Sense of Humus* 234 The Sheepnose, for example, had an interesting shape and a name just right. **1753** *Chambers' Cycl.* Suppl., *Sheep-nose-worms..a species of fly-worm, found in the noses of sheep, goats, and stags. **1774** G. LOW *Tour Orkney & Shetl.* (1879) 75 [The Schetlanders] tell us they are subjected to..the *Sheep-penny, the tax on Sheep. **1804** *Med. Jrnl.* XII. 461 Whether the cow-pock will preserve sheep from the *sheep-pock is yet undecided. **1790, 1814** *Sheep poison [see LAMBKILL]. **1846–50** A. WOOD *Class-bk. Bot.* 374 *Kalmia angustifolia*. Narrow-leaved Laurel. Sheep-poison. **1837** *Brit. Husb.* (Libr. Usef. Knowl.) II. 497 The *sheep-pox so closely resembles the scab, that it is not known in this country as a separate disease. **1594** in *Trans. Roy. Hist. Soc.* Ser. III. (1907) I. 266, I suffered..my servant to carrie a *sheeperacke to the pasture on the Sabboth daie. **1600** SURFLET *Country Farm* I. xxv. 153 Setting it [*sc.* the sheephouse] round about with mangers or sheepe-racks of a low pitch for to fodder them in. **1832** *Scoreby Farm Rep.* 18 in *Libr. Usef. Knowl., Husb.* III, A salt-trough, and a sheep-rack for hay, should be found with every flock. **1653** *N. Riding Rec.* V. 139 For unjustly takeinge and driving away fiftie sheep of the Common *sheep-rak of Great Crakeall. **1657** *Burton's Diary* (1828) II. 213 It is a very poor country ..being only mosses and sheep rakes. **1793** *Carlop Green* (1817) 174 The found o' a *sheep-ree. **1824** [see REE *sb.*[3]]. **1894** CROCKETT *Raiders* xli, To be penned like one of a score of hogs in a granite sheep-ree. **1450** (20 Dec.) FASTOLF in *Paston Lett.*, The wrong takyng..my shepe..for declaracioun in whate wyse he dyd it, John Bele my *sheperefe can enforme you best. **1571** GOLDING *Calvin on Ps.* lii. 1 Doeg, who was the Kinges sheepreeve [1 Sam. xxi. 7]. **1641** J. DAY *Parl. Bees* XI. G 3, Keeper of King Obrons Groves, Sheepreeve of his Flocks and Droves. **1552** HULOET, *Shepe rot, *lues ouilis.* **1808** JAMIESON, *Sheep-rot*, butterwort or Yorkshire sanicle. **1844** W. C. SPOONER *Sheep* 401 We cannot limit the cause of rot to eating the sheep-rot weed. **1897** *Allbutt's Syst. Med.* II. 1024 In the sheep *D[istomum] hepaticum* gives rise to the important epizootic known as 'sheep-rot'. **1826** GOLDIE in Bischoff *Van Diemen's Land* (1832) 157 [The land near Circular Head] is..a good *sheep run. **1851** W. FOX *Six Colonies of New Zealand* i. 27 The.. plain..is surrounded by hills which afford excellent sheep-runs. **1862** COLENSO *Pentateuch* I. 59 In Australia, some sheep-runs are estimated to carry one sheep to an acre. **1911** C. E. W. BEAN *'Dreadnought' of Darling* i. 8 The names painted on so many of the railway stations were merely the names of large sheep runs. **1936** A. RUSSELL *Gone Nomad* iv. 23, I even learnt to operate on the lambs myself, and to perform the many other jobs that combine to make up the yard work on a sheep run. **1894** *Act 57 & 58 Vict.* c. 57 §59 Foot-and-mouth disease, sheep-pox, *sheep-scab, or swine-fever. **1895** M. C. POTTER tr. *Warming's Syst. Bot.* 84 *Rhodymenia palmata*..is also used as food for sheep and hence is termed '*Sheep-seaweed'. **1895** *Leader* 3 Aug. 6/1 (Morris *Austral Eng.*), That certain country in which severe losses have occurred in recent years has been too long carrying sheep, and that the land has become what is termed '*sheep sick'. **1962** *Times* 6 June 15/6 Most of it poor land and sheep-sick at that. ?**12..** *Reg. Alb. Bur.* (MS.) 53 in Kennett *Cowel's Interpr.*, De *Schepsilver sc. pro vi. ovibus 1*d.* **1675** SIR W. JONES *Reports* 280 Sheep-silver..is a service now turned into money, which is paid, in respect that anciently the tenants used to wash their lords sheep. **1809** R. KERR *Agric. Berw.* xv. 414 A yearly allowance in money.. from 30*s.* to 40*s.* each, in name of sheep-silver, being a commutation of an ancient permission of keeping a few sheep upon the farm. **1822** HIBBERT *Descr. Shetl. Isl.* 198 The compliment of an ox and twelve sheep from every parish had..been granted to the Earl of Bothwell. It was.. converted into a perpetual tribute, under the name of ox and sheep silver. *a* **1722** LISLE *Husb.* (1757) 328 If they would.. send them abroad for a month..into the vale-lands..and would fold on their *sheep-slates. **1813, 1854** [see SLEIGHT *sb.*[3]]. **1851** *Dorset Gloss.*, *Sheep-slite*, sheep's pasture or walk. **1824** MACTAGGART *Gallovid. Encycl.*, *Rinner*,..butter melted with tar, for *sheep-smearing. **1837** LOCKHART *Scott* I. xi. 408 His hands..bore most legible marks of a recent sheep-smearing. **1884** SARGENT *Rep. Forests N. Amer.* 517 Tar, produced by burning the dead wood and most resinous parts of the long-leaved pine in covered kilns, is graded as follows: 'Rope yellow',..—the highest grade..; 'Roany', or 'Ship smearing'—the next running of the kiln. **1806** P. GASS *Jrnl.* 14 Mar. (1807) xviii. 188 A great quantity of *sheep-sorrel growing in the woods. **1872** OLIVER *Elem. Bot.* II. 225 The diœcious flowers of Sheep-sorrel (*Rumex Acetosella* and *R. Acetosa*). **1581** *Reg. Mag. Sig. Scot.* (1888) 83/2 Lympottis et lie *Scheipsteidis. **1612** *Ibid.* (1892) 239/2 Lie scheipsteidis, pasturas, predia et privilegia pasturarum. **1566–7** *Reg. Privy Council Scot.* I. 501 The twa *scheip stedingis pertening and adjacent thairto. **1891** ATKINSON *Moorland Par.* 10 The tenant is privileged to enjoy the liberty of free *sheep-stray. **1926** E. SITWELL *Elegy on Dead Fashion* 10 The satyrs danced the *sheep-trot all the day. **1869–73** T. R. JONES *Cassell's Bk. Birds* II. 290 The Velvet-headed or *Sheep Wagtail (*Budytes melanocephalus*). **1609** BIBLE (Douay) *1 Kings* xvii, Saul knew not David, being perhaps in a *shepwards habite. **1650** VAUGHAN *Silex Scint.* I. *Mount of Olives* ii, What need The sheep bleat thee a silly Lay, That heard'st both reed And sheepward play? *a* **1722** LISLE *Husb.* (1757) 344 The *sheep-water to kill the scab. **1634** in *Rutland Mag.* (1905) II. 71 For *sheep wealde in fforest of Lee x s. **1851** *Catal. Gt. Exhib.* III. 490/1 Black and blue broad coating, *sheep-wool face, alpaca-wool back. **1883** ADDERLEY *Fisheries Bahamas* 7 The sheep-wool sponge brings quite as high a price in markets as the Turkish variety of same. **1908** *Westm. Gaz.* 30 May 6/3 The strong odour of sheep-wool tells you of the flocks grazing..on its hills and plains.

**9.** Combinations with *sheep's*, †*sheeps(-)* (often varying with combs. of *sheep*, see 7 and 8), as ***sheep's bell, -belly, -dung, -gather*** (see GATHER *sb.*[2]), ***-pelt, -pluck*** (PLUCK *sb.*[1] 6), ***sleight, -tallow, -trotters***; **sheep's bane**, marsh pennywort, *Hydrocotyle vulgaris*, in the West Indies *H. umbellata*; **sheep's beard**, the genus *Urospermum* (*Arnopogon*); **sheep's bit (scabious)** = *sheep's scabious*; †**sheep's-colour**, the colour of unbleached sheep's wool; †**sheep's course**, a sheep-walk; †**sheep's feet** *Naut.*, a kind of stay; **sheep's fescue (grass)**, see FESCUE *sb.* 4; **sheep's foot**, (*a*) the foot of a sheep; †(*b*) a kind of claw-hammer; (*c*) ***sheep's foot roller***, a kind of tamping roller consisting of a steel drum studded with projecting feet; **sheep's grey**, material composed of a mixture of black and white wool; also *attrib.* or as *adj.*; **sheep's gut(s** = CATGUT; **sheep's heart**, put symbolically for 'a timid person'; †**sheep's herd** = SHEPHERD; †**sheep's leather**, leather made from sheepskin; **sheep's nose** = *sheepnose* sense 8 above; **sheep's parsley**, ? hedge parsley; †**sheep's pellet**, sheep's dung; †**sheep's russet**, russet such as was worn by shepherds; **sheep's scabious**, *Jasione montana*; †**sheep's silver**, mica; †**sheep's snout**, a variety of apple; **sheep's sorrel**, *Rumex Acetosella*; **sheep's tongue**, (*a*) the tongue of a sheep used for food; (*b*) a kind of bugloss; **sheep's wool**, (*a*) wool from the fleece of a sheep; (*b*) a West Indian sponge, *Spongia equina*, var. *gossypina*; (*c*) ***sheep's-wool fat***, lanoline (*Syd. Soc. Lex.* 1898). For *sheep's louse, sheepsman, sheep's skin, sheep's tick*, see SHEEP-LOUSE, etc.

**1597** GERARDE *Herbal* II. cxliii. 425 A kinde of Nauelwoort,..which is called of the husbandman *Sheepesbane. **1861** MRS. LANKESTER *Wild Fl.* 61 Marsh Pennywort..known as Pennygrass, White-rot, Fluke-wort, and Sheep's-bane. **1864** GRISEBACH *Flora W. Ind. Islands* 787. **1829** LOUDON *Encycl. Plants* (1836) 666 *Arnopogon*. *Sheep's Beard. **1829** SCOTT *Anne of G.* xxx, Distant and faint tinkling, less loud than that of a *sheep's bell at a mile's distance. **1688** HOLME *Armoury* II. vii. 132/2 *Sheeps Belly, or Intrels, the puddings called strings, or Rope. **1796** WITHERING *Brit. Plants* II. 248 [Iasione montana] Hairy Sheeps Scabious... Scabious *Sheepsbit. **1884** W. MILLER *Plant-n.* 124/2 Sheep's-bit-Scabious. *Jasione montana.* **1551–2** *Act 5 & 6 Edw. VI*, c. 6 §23 Anye other color..then ..watchett *shepes color lyon color. *a* **1562** G. CAVENDISH *Wolsey* (1885) 89 The King being in his doublet and hosen only,..all of sheep's colour cloth. **1623** T. SCOT *Highways of God* 76 Euery Farme, euery trade, euery *Sheepes-course is his. **1552** HULOET, *Shepes dunge or tyrdles, *rudus.* **1669** WORLIDGE *Syst. Agric.* 67 Sheeps-dung is very excellent being dissolved wholly..to steep Grain therein. **1530** PALSGR. 266/2 *Schepes fete, *pied de movton.* **1626** CAPT. SMITH *Accid. Yng. Seamen* 16 Sheeps feet is a stay in setling a top mast, and a guie in staying the tackles when they are charged with goods. **1759** B. STILLINGFLEET *Misc. Tracts* (1791) 390 Hills where the purple and *sheep's fescue,..and the silver hair grasses abound. **1683** MOXON *Mech. Exerc., Printing* xi. ¶20 The *Sheeps-Foot is..of Iron, with a Hammer-head at one end, to drive the Ball-Nails into the Ball-Stocks, and a Claw at the other end, to draw the Ball-Nails out. **1875** KNIGHT *Dict. Mech.*, *Sheep's-foot Trimmer*, a pair of shears or cutting-pinchers to trim the excessive growth of the hoof. **1888** BRANNT *Anim. & Veg. Fats* 266 Sheep's-foot oil is obtained..from the feet of sheep. It resembles neat's-foot oil. **1934** J. H. BATEMAN *Highway Engin.* (ed. 2) xiii. 224 Various types of tamping rollers have been developed..and include sheep's-foot and sectional rollers. **1973** G. E. BERTRAM in Hirschfeld & Poulos *Embankment-Dam Engin.* 1/1 The recent development of heavy vibratory rollers capable of compacting rockfill has produced the most significant change in placement procedures in the construction of earth and rockfill dams since the introduction of the sheepsfoot roller for the compaction of earthen core materials. **1580** HOLLYBAND *Treas. Fr. Tong*, *Corée, ou fressure*, a *sheepes gather. **1852** *Trans. Mich. Agric. Soc.* III. 483 Ten yards or over of *sheep's gray cloth. **1877** *Rep. Vermont Board Agric.* IV. 92 The men and boys' garments of the sheep's grey. **1976** *National Observer* (U.S.) 28 Aug. 13/4 (Advt.), Pullover or Cardigan. Colors: Blue Heather, Natural White, Sheeps Grey. **1599** SHAKS. *Much Ado* II. iii. 61 Is it not strange that *sheepes guts should hale soules out of mens bodies? **1801** BUSBY *Dict. Mus.* s.v. *Viol d'amour*, a viol, or violin, furnished with six brass or steel wires, instead of sheep's-gut. **1600** SHAKS. *A.Y.L.* III. i. 444 And this way wil I take vpon mee to wash your Liuer as cleane as a sound *sheepes heart. **1818** SCOTT *Rob Roy* ix, I tell thee, man, fear nothing, ..Why, thou sheep's heart, how do ye ken but we may can pick up some speerings of your valise? *c* **1200** ORMIN 3595 Daviþþ..þa wass he *shepess hirde. **1474** *Cov. Leet Bk.* 401 No maner of lether but *Shepis lether, Gettes lether. **1596** SHAKS. *Tam. Shr.* III. ii. 58 A headstall of sheepes leather. **1936** *N. & Q.* CLXX. 183/2 *Sheep's Nose, an old-time variety of apple whose name is almost forgotten. **1967** Sheep's nose [see HANG-DOWN *sb.* and *a.*]. **1896** 'J. O. HOBBES' *Herb-Moon* I *Sheep's-parsley—with its long green stems and white delicate flowers. *c* **1440** *Promp. Parv.* 445/2 *Schepys pylett.., *molestra.* **1530** PALSGR. 266/2 Schepes pellet or dong, *fient a brebis.* **1647** TRAPP *Comm. Heb.* xi. 35 Stretched upon the rack, as a *sheeps-pelt is upon a drum-head. **1611** COTGR., *Fressure*,..A *sheepes plucke. **1761** H. WALPOLE *Let. to G. Montagu* 5 May, As if she had just bought a sheep's-pluck in St. James's market. **1589** R. HARVEY *Pl. Percevall* 12, I am no Ape Carrier, I pray you defile not my *sheeps russet Coate, with your dirtie shoes yet. **1624** SANDERSON *Serm.* (1632) 446 All..the richest silkes..are as lawfull for vs, as..sheepes-russet. **1682** BUNYAN *Holy War* 263 They were clothed in sheeps-russet. **1578** LYTE *Dodoens* I. lxxiii. 109 The third [kind of scabious] is called in English *Sheepes Scabious: in French *Scabieuse de brebis.* **1814** JAMIESON *Illustr. Northern Antiq.* 401 The walls and roof, which were..incrusted with *sheeps-silver and spar. **1847** HALLIWELL, **Sheep's-slite*, sheep's pasture, or walk. *Dorset.* **1664** EVELYN *Kal. Hort.* Aug. 72 The Seaming Apple, Cushion Apple,..*Sheeps-snout. **1578** LYTE *Dodoens* v. ix. 558 *Sheepes Sorrel louely dry soyles. **1597** GERARDE *Herbal* II. lxxx. 320 *Oxalis tenuifolia*, Sheepes Sorrell. **1745** *Season. Advice Prot.* (ed. 2) 18 Nothing now appears but loose Stones and Sheeps Sorrel. **1863** BARING-GOULD *Iceland* xi. 242 Among the marshes, I found..both the common and sheep's sorrel (*Rumex acetosa* and *R. acetosella*). *c* **1400** *Schepis talow [see TALLOW *sb.* 1 β]. *a* **1425** tr. *Arderne's Fistula* 92 Þan ow þou for to putte with þe oile as war prid parte of schepez talow. *c* **1450** *M.E. Med. Bk.* (Heinrich) 77 Do þer to þe jus of synygrene and sheps tarowe [*read* talowe]. **1552** HULOET, *Shepes tongue herbe, *agniglossa.* **1578** LYTE *Dodoens* I. iii. 7 The fifth [kind of Bugloss] is the wilde Buglosse, or Sheepes tongue. **1641** MURREL *Cookerie* (ed. 5) 23 A made dish of Sheepes tongues. **1858** SIMMONDS *Dict. Trade* s.v. *Tongue*, Pigs'-tongues, sheep's tongues, calves'-tongues. **1596** NASHE *Saffron Walden* Wks. (Grosart) III. 139 *Sheepes trotters, porknells, and butterd rootes. **1771** SMOLLETT *Humph. Cl.* 10 May (1815) 82 Paunceford once resided in a garret; where he subsisted upon sheep's-trotters and cow-heel. **1888** *Times* (weekly ed.) 11 May 15/1, 3d. worth of sheep's trotters. **1922** JOYCE *Ulysses* 427 A cold sheep's trotter, sprinkled with whole pepper. **1721** AMHERST *Terræ Fil.* App. 297 The bodies..wrap'd up..in *sheeps-wool. **1883** GOODE *Fish. Industr. U.S.A.* 53 The finest quality of American Sponge is the Sheepswool. **1978** S. SHELDON *Bloodline* viii. 105 Samuel huddled into his threadbare sheep's-wool coat.

**10.** Passing into *adj.* **a.** (in early use also *sheep's*; cf. SHEEP'S EYE.) Sheep-like, sheepish.

*a* **1553** UDALL *Royster D.* IV. vi. (1869) 70 Hither will he repaire with a sheepes looke full grim. **1807** SIR R. WILSON 13 May in *Life* (1862) II. 212 With a sheep face and faltering voice.

**b.** In parasynthetic formations (and their derivatives), chiefly with reference to the timidity or stupidity of the sheep, as ***sheep-faced, -headed, -hearted, -spirited, -witted*** adjs.; also †***sheep-hued*** adj., of the colour of a sheep's fleece.

**1583** *Leg. Bp. St. Androis* 1070 in *Satir. Poems Reform.* xlv, A scheip hewit clock to cover his cleathis. **1623** J. TAYLOR (Water P.) *New Discov.* B6b, Those simple Sheepe-headed fooles. **1629** FORD *Lover's Mel.* III. ii, Sheepe-spirited Boy, although he had not married me, He might haue proferd kindnesse in a corner. **1775** SHERIDAN *Rivals* III. i, A vile sheep-hearted blockhead! **1848** THACKERAY *Van. Fair* xxvii, The most modest, silent, sheep-faced and meek of little men. **1852** C. W. HOSKYNS *Talpa* 44 The extraordinary sheep-sightedness of spade-and-mattock-wielding humanity. **1879** F. W. ROBINSON *Coward Consc.* II. vii, General sheepfacedness ensued. **1889** 'MARK TWAIN' *Yankee Crt. K. Arth.* viii, The sheep-witted earl who could claim long descent from a King's leman.

**sheep**, *v. local.* [f. prec. sb.] *trans.* To weed or to dung (land) by pasturing sheep upon it.

**1808** BATCHELOR *Agric. Bedford* 403 Beans..are generally *sheeped*, as it is termed, or weeded by the folding flock. **1856** *Jrnl. R. Agric. Soc.* XVII. I. 136 It [a field] had been sheeped all the summer, but not dunged from the fold. **1898** RIDER HAGGARD *Farmer's Yr.* (1899) 101 The best chance of turning it into a really sound pasture is to sheep it heavily.

**'sheep-,biter.** [Cf. WFris. *skieppebiter* in sense 1.]

**1.** A dog that bites or worries sheep. (Also *attrib.*) ? *Obs.*

**1548** PATTEN *Exped. Scot.* M viij b, Lyke shepe byter curres to snach vp and it wear but a sory lambe for their prey. **1575** tr. *Marlorat's Apoc.* 25 Not shepherds, but sheepe-byters & woolues which spare not the Lords flocke. **1602** BRETON *Mother's Blessing* (Grosart) 9/2 No slouen, sluggard, nor sheep-biter dogge. **1664** *Homer A la Mode* 39 Their eares like sheep-biters they hang'd. **1831** GEN. P. THOMPSON *Exerc.* (1842) I. 418 The public..are running in upon them as at the last hour of a parish sheep-biter.

†**2.** *fig.* **a.** ? A malicious or censorious fellow. **b.** A shifty, sneaking, or thievish fellow. (Cf. SHEEP-BITING *ppl. a.* below.) *Obs.*

**1589** [? NASHE] *Almond for Parrat* 17 b, What say you to that zealous sheepebyter of your owne edition in Cambridge. **1601** SHAKS. *Twel. N.* II. v. 6 Wouldst thou not be glad to haue the niggardly Rascally sheepe-biter, come by some notable shame? **1656** HEYLIN *Surv. France* 40, I was fain sometimes to put on a little impudence, that I might avoid the suspicion of a gelding or a sheep-biter. **1692** R. L'ESTRANGE *Fables* cccxxx. 288 There are Political Sheep-biters as well as Pastoral; Betrayers of Publique Trusts, as well as of Private. *a* **1700** B. E. *Dict. Cant. Crew*, *Sheep-biter*, a poor, sorry, sneaking, ill-lookt Fellow. **1778** SHERIDAN *Camp* I. i, I'll throttle you, you sheep-biter.

†**3.** A great mutton-eater. *Obs.*

**1599** NASHE *Lenten Stuffe* 37 Then the sly sheepe-biter issued into the midst. **1640** *Wandering Jew* 38 The Character of the Glutton..a tormenter of Poultry,..a terrible Sheep-biter; a horrible Mutton-monger.

†**4.** One who runs after 'mutton'; a woman-hunter, whoremonger. *Obs.*

**1611** CHAPMAN *May Day* III. i, I wish all such old sheepe-biters might alwaies dippe their fingers in such sauce to their mutton. **1630** *R. Johnson's Kingd. & Commw.* 56 You shall see an old sheepe-biter..with a slavering lip, a bleare-eye.., courting of a comely Lady. **1719** D'URFEY *Pills* II. 345 You that are plying for Sheepbiters here, And hope to sell your Mutton Loyns so dear.

So **'sheep-,biting** *vbl. sb.* (*rare*); †*ppl. a.*, given to biting or worrying sheep; *fig.* thieving, sneaking (in Scott an echo of Shaks.).

**1603** SHAKS. *Meas. for M.* V. i. 359 Show your sheepe-biting face, and be hang'd an houre. **1620** MIDDLETON *Chaste Maid* II. ii. (1630) 22 Sheepe-biting Mungrels. **1623** FLETCHER *Rule a Wife* v. iv, How like a sheep-biting Rogue taken i'th' manner, And ready for the halter dost thou look now! **1817** J. MAYER *Sportsman's Direct.* (ed. 2) 209 To cure a Dog of Sheep-biting. **1821** SCOTT *Kenilw.* xxix, That pitiful sheep-biting visage of thine.

**sheepcot** ('ʃiːpkɒt). Forms: see SHEEP *sb.* and COT *sb.*[1] = next.

**14..** *Nom.* in Wr.-Wülcker 734/1 *Hec barcaria*, i. *ovile*, a schepcott. **1549** *Compl. Scot.* vi. 43 There faldis, scheip cottis and ludgens. **1609** DANIEL *Civ. Wars* VIII. cii, That Sheepcot,..I rather would my Palace wish to bee, Then any roofe, of proudest Maiestie. **1844** H. STEPHENS *Bk. Farm* II. 61 The utility of sheep-cots on a store-farm. **1872** JENKINSON *Engl. Lake District* 74 A sheepcot at the head of the glen.

**sheepcote** ('ʃiːpkəʊt). [f. SHEEP *sb.* + COTE *sb.*[1]] A slight building for sheltering sheep; a sheephouse.

**1414** *Rolls of Parlt.* IV. 60/2 None housynge left stondynge ther on, but gif it were a Shepecote. **14..** *Tretyce* in *W. of Henley's Husb.* (1890) 48 Make clene your shepcote. *a* **1529** SKELTON *Howe the douty Duke of Albany*, etc. 266 As it were a gote In a shepe cote. **1538** STARKEY *England* I. iii. 72 Wher hath byn many housys and churchys,..now you schal fynd no thyng but schypcotys and stabullys. **1669** WORLIDGE *Syst. Agric.* 201 To pen them up in a Barn or large Sheep-coat. **1785** BURNS *Winter Night* v, The bloodstain'd roost, and sheep-cote spoil'd. **1856** J. H. NEWMAN *Verses on Var. Occas.* (1868) 281 The last are first, the first are last,..These from the sheep-cote sternly cast, Those welcomed to the fold.

†**sheeped**, *ppl. a. Obs.*⁻¹ [f. SHEEP *sb.* + -ED.] ? Made spiritless as a sheep.

**1626** BP. HALL *Contempl., O.T.* XX. ix. *Hezekiah & Sennach.*, With shame and grief enough, is that sheeped tyrant returned to his Nineveh; having left behind him all the pride..of Assyria, for compost to the Jewish fields.

**sheepfold** (ˈʃiːpfəʊld). [f. SHEEP + FOLD *sb.*[2]]

**1.** A pen or enclosure for sheep.

[*c* **1000** *Ags. Gosp.* John x. 1 Se þe ne gæð æt þam gete into sceapa falde]. *a* **1430** *Wyclif's Bible, Num.* xxxii. 16 (MS. C.C.C.) Sheep foldis. *c* **1440** *Alphabet of Tales* 130 þer doggis at kepid þer shepefald. **1523–34** FITZHERB. *Husb.* §18 It is tyme to set out the shepefolde in May. **1611** BIBLE *Judges* v. 16 Why abodest thou among the sheepefolds, to heare the bleatings of the flocks? **1668** COWLEY *Several Disc.* iv. *Hor. Ep.* 52 To pin the sheepfold. **1784** COWPER *Task* I. 290 The sheep-fold here Pours out its fleecy tenants o'er the glebe. **1891** S. C. SCRIVENER *Our Fields & Cities* 142 Sowing barley on a recently-ploughed sheepfold.

*attrib.* **1820** KEATS *Isabella* xxxviii, A sheep-fold bleat.

**b.** *fig.*, esp. in a spiritual sense.

**1579** W. WILKINSON *Confut. Fam. Love* Ep. Ded. *ij b, Many lying seers,..vnder Lambes skinnes, craftely crept into the sheepfold. **1581** J. HAMILTON in *Cath. Tract.* (S.T.S.) 75 The scheipfald of Christ. **1635** A. STAFFORD *Fem. Glory* 136 The Prince of all Shepheards whose sheepefold is the world. **1851** RUSKIN (*title*) Notes on the construction of Sheepfolds [*i.e.* churches]. **1868** E. YATES *Rock Ahead* II. iv, The man who had dared..to invade the sanctity of her sheepfold and carry off one of her pet lambs.

†**2.** A flock of sheep; = FOLD *sb.*[2] 1 c. *Obs.*

**1590** T. WATSON *Eglogue* fin., Poems (Arb.) 175 Lets hence, and shut our sheepfolds in their coat.

Hence †**sheepfold** *v.*, †**sheepfolding** *vbl. sb.*

**1610** FOLKINGHAM *Art of Survey* I. ix. 21 If they be therewithall Sheepe-folded and ground-fedde with ruminant Cattell. *Ibid.* x. 23 The sheepe-folding and foddering.

**sheephead**, obs. var. SHEEP'S-HEAD.

**sheephe(a)rd**, obs. var. SHEPHERD.

ˈ**sheep-hook.** Now *rare.* [See HOOK *sb.*[1] 6.] A shepherd's crook.

Also *fig. esp.*, with reference to a spiritual shepherd; and symbolically (often opposed to *sceptre*) of the shepherd's calling or the office of a bishop.

**14..** *Voc.* in Wr.-Wülcker 562/28 *Agulus*, shephoke. **1523–34** FITZHERB. *Husb.* §41 A shepeherde shoulde not go without..his shepe hoke. **1535** COVERDALE *Ps.* xxii. 4 Thy staffe & thy shepehoke comforte me. *a* **1586** SIDNEY *Arcadia* II. (Sommer) 103 Dametas..was teching him how with his sheephooke to catch a wanton Lambe. **1611** SHAKS. *Wint. T.* IV. iv. 431 Thou a Scepters heire, That thus affects a sheepe-hooke? **1641** MILTON *Reform.* II. 78 The Pastorly Rod, and Sheep-hooke of Christ. **1679** *Establ. Test.* 16 They who were grown so hardened in Mischief, to attempt..upon the Scepter, would never..have scrupled at the Sheephook. **1715** GAY *What D'ye Call It* II. viii, Churns, sheep-hooks, seas of milk, and honey mountains. **1828** S. ROGERS *Italy* II. *A Char.* 29 Inherit they a sheep-hook or a sceptre. **1858** SIMMONDS *Dict. Trade*, *Sheep-hook*, a shepherd's crook for catching sheep by the legs. **1866** G. M. HOPKINS *Jrnls. & Papers* (1959) 143 Beeches..scatter their tops in charming tufted sheep-hooks drooping towards each other and every way.

ˈ**sheep-house.** Now *rare.* [Cf. MDu. *schaep(s)huus*, OHG. *scâfhûs* (G. *schafhaus*).] A covered pen for the housing of sheep.

[*c* **1000** ÆLFRIC *Gloss.* in Wr.-Wülcker 105/12 *Ouile*, sceapahus.] *c* **1410** *MS. Douce 335* fo. 72 b, Ony house, that ony beest vseth out or go oute at..., that is to say swynhouse, nethous, shephous. *c* **1425** *Voc.* in Wr.-Wülcker 670/29 *Hec barcaria*, schepehouse. ? **1545** BRINKLOW *Compl.* xx. F j b, A shepehouse and .ij. or .iij. shepardes. **1577** B. GOOGE *Heresbach's Husb.* III. 141, I haue seene some sheep houses so framed, as they haue had theyr gates toward the South, and towarde the Easte. **1614** J. TAYLOR (Water P.) *Nipping Abuses* F 1, Sheapheard swaines to sheephouse driues their sheep. **1707** MORTIMER *Husb.* (1721) I. 100 Where you cannot fold Sheep, to have a Sheep-house to feed them in. **1844** H. STEPHENS *Bk. Farm* II. 71 The whole have hay..in the sheep-house, on wet..nights. **1906** *Macm. Mag.* Nov. 63 Och, it's only a wee bit of a sheephouse.

ˈ**sheepified**, *pa. pple.* Made sheep-like.

**1812** COLERIDGE *Let. to his Wife* 24 Apr., His legs and hoofs are more than half sheepified.

†ˈ**sheepiness.** *Obs. rare.* [f. SHEEPY *a.* + -NESS.] Meanspiritedness.

**1663** S. PATRICK *Parab. Pilgr.* xi. (1665) 68 Humility then you see is not sheepiness, but loftiness of mind.

**sheepish** (ˈʃiːpɪʃ), *a.* (*adv.*). Also 3 shepiss(h)e, 4 schep-, 4–6 shepishe, 6 sheppeshe, etc. [f. SHEEP *sb.* + -ISH. Cf. MDu. *schaepsch* (Du. *schaapsch*), G. *schäfisch.*]

**1.** †**a.** Of, pertaining to, or concerned with sheep; ovine. *Obs.* **b.** Resembling sheep or their characteristics. Now *rare.*

*c* **1200** *Trin. Coll. Hom.* 37 Sume men..goð eche dai to chirche alse shep to uolde..and beð cleped shepisse men. **1532** MORE *Confut. Barnes* VIII. Wks. 763/2 For al their shepishe semblaunce outwardly, righte rauenous wolues are they within. **1536** in *Lett. Suppress. Monasteries* (Camden) 114 Soche greate ones..in time paste, like bell-wethers, had led the sheppeshe flockes of England against their prince. *a* **1586** SIDNEY *Arcadia* I. (Sommer) 1 b, Some [shepherds were] setting a bell for an ensigne of a sheepish squadron. **1611** STAFFORD *Niobe* II. 218 How to chuse the best tarre:.. how to excell in sheepish surgery. **1847** HELPS *Friends in C.* I. ii. 31 It is not a sheepish tendency, but an independent resolve growing out of our nature.

†**2. a.** Meek, innocent. *Obs.*

*c* **1200** ORMIN 6654 Niss he nohht hinnderrȝæp ne pratt.. Acc iss shepisshe & bilewhit.

†**b.** Simple, silly. *Obs.*

*c* **1380** WYCLIF *Wks.* (1880) 212 Queynte sleiȝtis to disceyue schepische men of worldly goodis. **1592** NASHE *P. Penilesse* 19 b, I haue reade ouer thy Sheepish discourse of the Lambe of God and his enemies, and entreated my patience to bee good to thee whilst I read it. **1613** MARSTON *Insat. C'tess* I. i. 10 Zounds what a sheepish beginning is here?..thou art a simple louer. **1692** WASHINGTON tr. *Milton's Def. People* vii. 169 Would not the English do you a kindness in that, you sheepish Fellow, you?

†**c.** Excessively meek or submissive, fearful or timorous; mean-spirited. *Obs.* exc. as implied in 3.

*c* **1510** BARCLAY *Mirr. Gd. Manners* (1570) F v, While thou would behaue thee demure and pacient, Beware, be not remisse nor sheepish in no wise. **1659** MILTON *Free Commw.* 17 Monarchs..whose aim is to make the people, wealthy indeed perhaps and wel-fleec't..but..not only in fleece, but in minde also sheepishest. **1709** SHAFTESB. *Charac.* I. 93 We are happily tam'd and render'd thus mild and sheepish. **1711** ADDISON *Spect.* No. 13 ⁋3 If the former was too furious, this was too sheepish, for his Part.

**3.** Bashful or awkward in the presence of others, esp. in society to which one is unaccustomed; embarrassed or out of countenance from an excess of shyness or diffidence.

**1693** LOCKE *Educ.* §68 Being used constantly to the same Faces, and little Company, will, when he comes abroad, be a sheepish or conceited Creature. **1773** GOLDSM. *She Stoops* I. i, Sensible, good-natured; I like all that. But then reserved and sheepish; that's much against him. *a* **1774** TUCKER *Lt. Nat.* (1834) II. 124 Bring an unlicked cub into company, and you will find him shy and sheepish;..uneasy in all situations. **1818** SCOTT *Br. Lamm.* xxix, All the sheepish bashfulness common to those who have lived little in respectable society. **1849** MACAULAY *Hist. Eng.* iii. I. 369 Sheepish lads from the Universities. **1876** SMILES *Sc. Natur.* ix. (ed. 4) 170 And away she went, leaving Edward looking rather sheepish.

**4.** quasi-*adv.* and *adv.* = SHEEPISHLY.

**1581** MULCASTER *Positions* xxxix. (1888) 187 It maketh him to shepish bashfull. **1784** COWPER *Task* IV. 629 Sheepish he doffs his hat.

**sheepishly** (ˈʃiːpɪʃlɪ), *adv.* [-LY[2].] In a sheepish manner; †like sheep; †meekly, timorously, or submissively to an excessive degree; with a bashful or embarrassed look or appearance.

**1528** MORE *Dyaloge* IV. Wks. 281/2 We be sure ynough that wolues they be in dede, howe shepishlye soeuer they looke. *a* **1586** SIDNEY *Arcadia* IV. (1598) 414 When the rest (who as sheepe had but followed their fellowes) so sheepishly had submitted themselues. **1612** W. MARTYN *Youths Instr.* 69 Not to bee foolishly desperate, nor sheepishly feareful. **1663** S. PATRICK *Parab. Pilgr.* xxxvii. (1665) 497 Those that are sheepishly led whither confident men will have them. **1697** COLLIER *Ess. Mor. Subj.* II. (1703) 102 Not that men are bound to look as sheepishly as they can, for fear of an imputation. **1714** POPE *Wife of Bath* 183 Billy, my dear, how sheepishly you look. Approach, my spouse, and let me kiss thy cheek. **1830** *Forrester* II. 147 The usual bows were exchanged, stiffly on the part of the peer, and sheepishly by Frederick. **1870** 'A. R. HOPE' *My Schoolboy Fr.* xii, I hung about him, feeling sheepishly grateful.

**sheepishness** (ˈʃiːpɪʃnɪs). [-NESS.] † Simplicity, stupidity; †timorousness; excessive bashfulness or diffidence.

**1577** HELLOWES *Gueuara's Fam. Ep.* 62 To speake something with too much simplicitie..is a sheepishnesse. **1605** CHAPMAN *All Fools* I. ii. 145 Your forged sheepishnes. **1633** G. HERBERT *Temple, Ch. Porch* xvi, Thy Gentrie bleats, as if thy native cloth Transfus'd a sheepishnesse into thy storie. **1647** TRAPP *Comm. 2 Cor.* xi. 3 Simplicity: the world cals it sillinesse, sheepishnesse. **1712** STEELE *Spect.* No. 484 ⁋5 Under the notion of modesty, men have indulged themselves in a spiritless sheepishness. **1814** SCOTT *Wav.* xviii, A natural and rustic grace, with nothing of the sheepishness of an ordinary peasant. **1863** COWDEN CLARKE *Shaks. Char.* vi. 153 He is bashful, even to sheepishness.

ˈ**sheepless**, *a.* [-LESS.] Without sheep.

**1868** W. CORY *Lett. & Jrnls.* (1897) 217 The country was full of blossom, hedgeless, sheepless.

ˈ**sheep-like**, *a.* and *adv.* [-LIKE.]

**A.** *adj.* Resembling a sheep or that of a sheep; *esp.* in an unfavourable sense.

**1596** NORDEN *Progr. Piety* (1847) 123 He did foresee hypocrisy Should lurk in godly weed, And wolves in sheep-like tire to lie. *a* **1653** GOUGE *Comm. Heb.* iii. 6 Believers are subject to wrongs..for their sheep-like and dove-like disposition. **1851** RUSKIN *Sheepfolds* 12 Christ's sheep may be guessed at..by their sheep-like behaviour. **1871** BESANT & RICE *Ready-money Mort.* xiii, Men possess largely themselves the sheep-like propensity of following where one leads. **1891** FARRAR *Darkn. & Dawn* lx, The youth refused to kill himself with the sheeplike docility of so many of his contemporaries.

**B.** *adv.* Meekly, submissively, pusillanimously.

**1582** STANYHURST *Æneis* IV. 84 Shal I dy sheepe lyke, not taking kindlye reuengment? **1590** MARLOWE *2nd Pt. Tamburl.* IV. ii. 3751 See now ye slaues, my children stoops your pride And leads your glories sheep-like to the sword.

ˈ**sheepling.** [-LING.] A young sheep. Also *fig.*

**1654** [J. SPARROW] tr. *Behmen's Myst. Magn.* xxviii. §63 If the sheepling [orig. *Schäfflein*] shall offer to stir, and shew more then a sheepling of Christ. **1859** SALA *Gaslight & D.* xviii, Innocent flocks of more innocent sheeplings.

ˈ**sheep-louse.** Also †sheep's louse: see SHEEP *sb.* 9. [Cf. G. *schaflaus*, Du. *schaapsluis.*] A louse, *Trichodectes sphærocephalus*, which infests the wool of sheep. Also = SHEEP-TICK.

*c* **1440** *Promp. Parv.* 445/1 Schepys lowce, *pego, askarida.* **1530** PALSGR. 266/2 Schepes louce, *pov de moton.* **14..** *Nom.* in Wr.-Wülcker 706/29 *Hec ascarida*, a scheplows. **1523–34** FITZHERB. *Husb.* §44 Brome salue.. shal..kyll the shepe lyce, and it shall not hurte the woll. **1688** HOLME *Armoury* II. ix. 190/1 Insects... Such as have no Wings, but eight Feet, as..Sheep Louse. **1826** KIRBY & SP. *Entomol.* xxxiv. III. 473 *Melophagus*, the sheep-louse. **1844** H. STEPHENS *Bk. Farm* II. 152 Both these vermin are destroyed by the same means as the sheep-louse.

ˈ**sheepman.** Also 6 sheepesman, see SHEEP *sb.* 9. [f. SHEEP *sb.* + MAN *sb.*]

**1.** †A shepherd (*obs.*); orig. *N. Amer.*, a sheep-breeder or -owner; a sheep-tender.

**1591** A. FRAUNCE *C'tess Pembr. Iuychurch*, etc. L 3 b, Pan is good to the sheepe, and Pan is good to the sheepesman. **1620** QUARLES *Feast of Wormes* (1638) 7 In stead of Staffe, he tooke a Sheepmans weede. **1641** BEST *Farm. Bks.* (Surtees) 28 It is an especiall thinge to bee regarded of a sheepman to keepe goode tuppes. **1883** *American* VI. 382 For the small sheepmen, the shepherds, and above all, the herders, it is a terrible life. **1886** C. SCOTT *Sheep-farming* 165 The sheepmen of Great Britain. **1890** HAYDON *Riders of Plains* (1910) 168 This fire is supposed to have been started by sheepmen in the hills. **1924** W. M. RAINE *Troubled Waters* xi. 114 If one sheep-man were permitted to invade the range, dozens of others would drive across into the forbidden territory. **1930** L. G. D. ACLAND *Early Canterbury Runs* 1st Ser. v. 106 D. Oliver, the head shepherd, became manager. He was a very good sheepman from Australia. **1937** *Times Lit. Suppl.* 6 Feb. 86/3 There has never been in Britain the hostility between the cattlemen and the sheepmen. **1950** H. J. MASSINGHAM *Curious Traveller* ix. 168 The communal sheep-men of the mountain parishes only pay half a crown a year to the Lady Marcher if they enclose a mountain pasture. **1966** 'J. HACKSTON' *Father clears Out* 37 A new volume on sheep-raising,..proclaiming to the world that Father was a sheep-man. **1977** F. ORMSBY *Store of Candles* 15 Even the barflies move to corner tables, Mouthing 'Sheepman'.

**2.** ? A sheepstealer, rogue.

**1640** BALFOUR *Sc. Ball.* 13 What change for valiant Cavilers of old To court with sheep-men, rogues, and swinzeours bold.

ˈ**sheep-mark.**

**1.** The mark used by a sheep-owner to distinguish his sheep, and app. formerly by illiterate persons as a substitute for their signature. Also *fig.*

**1534** CRANMER *Let.* in *Misc. Writ.* (Parker Soc.) 291, I have caused one of my secretaries to subscribe for such persons, and made them to write their shepe mark, or some other mark, as they can..scribble. **1632** BROME *North. Lass* II. i, A thumb-Ring with his Grandsirs Sheep-mark, or Grannams butter-print on't. *a* **1644** QUARLES *Sheph. Orac.* ii. (1646) 22 Then brand them with a Crosse, Our Masters Sheepmarke. **1653** BAXTER *Christ. Concord* 98 Have you forgotten your Masters sheep-mark? **1693** O. HEYWOOD *Best Entail* iv, Children of believers are baptized,..and thus have God's sheep-mark set upon them betimes. **1875** *Archæol. Cambrensis* Ser. IV. VI. 94 Sheep-Marks. I. *Bwlch plyg* (folded notch).—This is produced by folding a certain part of the ear, and cutting off with the shears the part thus folded. **1887** *Archæologia* L. 373 *note*, When the commons were unenclosed, it was necessary for every one who had a right of pasture to have a sheep-mark that could be easily distinguished from those of his neighbours.

†**2.** A marking-tool for sheep. *Obs.*

**1580** TUSSER *Husb.* (1878) 38 [Husbandlie furniture.] A sheepe marke, a tar kettle.

ˈ**sheep-master.** [Cf. G. *schafmeister.*] A sheep-owner.

*a* **1520** *Vox Populi* 66 in Hazl. *E.P.P.* III. 270 Withe to many shepemasters, That of erable grounde make pastures. **1611** BIBLE *2 Kings* iii. 4 Mesha king of Moab was a sheepe-master. **1651** in *Hartlib's Legacy* (1655) 167 The great Sheep-Masters usually chuse their Sheeps-Walks, or Pastures, on high dry Lands. **1745** *De Foe's Eng. Tradesm.* xxxvii. (1841) II. 91 The sheepmaster shears and sells the fleece. **1837** YOUATT *Sheep* 540 Mercurial ointment..in frequent use among sheep-masters as a cure for the scab. **1841** *Penny Cycl.* XXI. 357/1 Since the British sheep-master has begun..to look more to the profit to be derived from the carcase.

†ˈ**sheepness.** *Obs.* [-NESS.] Pusillanimity.

*c* **1380** WYCLIF *Sel. Wks.* II. 387 Vertues ben transposid to vices; as mekenes is cowardise,..and myldenesse is shepenesse.

**sheep-o(h** (ˈʃiːpəʊ), *int.* and *sb. Austral.* and *N.Z.* [f. SHEEP *sb.* + -O[2].] **A.** *int.* A shearer's call for a sheep to shear. **B.** *sb.* (Chiefly *N.Z.*) = *penner-up* s.v. PENNER[4].

**1900** H. LAWSON *On the Track* 132 'Go it, you—tigers!' yells a tarboy. 'Wool away!' 'Tar!' 'Sheep Ho!' We rush through with a whirring noise till breakfast time. **1911** W. H. KOEBEL *In Maoriland Bush* viii. 124 The 'sheep-oh' sets to work to fill the nearly emptied pens. **1925** R. REES *Lake of Enchantment* vii. 111 The [shearing] gang [included]..

some boys to act as 'sheep-os'—that is to keep the pens in the shed filled up from the yards outside. **1940**, etc. [see PENNER[4]]. **1949** P. NEWTON *High Country Days* 5 The cry of 'Sheepo!' would rouse the 'penner-up'. **1955** G. BOWEN *Wool Away!* (1956) vii. 96 The 'sheepo' is the man who fills the catching pens. He gets this title from the fact that when a shearer catches the last sheep in his pen, he gives the call of 'sheepo'.

**'sheep-pen.** [f. SHEEP *sb.* + PEN *sb.*[1]; ? partly intended as an analysis of SHIPPON.] A pen in which to keep sheep.

**1649** BLITH *Engl. Improver* xxiii. 139 Hay-Stacks, or Sheep-pens, or places of Shade. *a* **1722** LISLE *Husb.* (1757) 335 Sir Ambrose Philipps's sheep-pen. **1834** MARRYAT *Peter Simple* vii, I inquired for the butcher, whom I found sitting in the sheep-pen with the sheep. **1841** BROWNING *Pippa Passes* iii, Many a valley-thief Caught in the sheep-pens.

**sheep-pick**: see SHEPPECK.

**sheep's eye**(s. (Also 7 sheep-eyes.) [Cf. WFris. *skiepseach*, Du. *schaapsoog*, G. *schafsauge*.]

**1.** Phr. **a.** *to cast* (or *throw*) *a sheep's-eye at* or *upon*, now usually *to cast* (occas. *to make*) *sheep's-eyes at*: to look lovingly, amorously, or longingly at.

*a* **1529** SKELTON *Agst. Garnesche* iii. 54 When ye kyst a shepys ie,..[At] mastres Andelby. *a* **1586** SIDNEY *Arcadia* II. (Sommer) 107 Mopsa throwing a great number of sheeps eyes vpon me. **1614** B. JONSON *Barth. Fair* v. iv, Hero.. seeing Leanders naked legge, and goodly calfe, Cast at him, from the boat, a Sheepes eye, and a halfe. **1726** *Adv. Capt. R. Boyle* 247 Don Manuel cast many a Sheep's Eye at my Wife and his good Lady at me. **1731-8** SWIFT *Pol. Conversat.* 30, I have often seen him cast a Sheep's Eye out of a Calf's Head at you. **1809** MALKIN *Gil Blas* I. iv. (Rtldg.) 9, I could not help casting a sheep's eye at the gold and silver plate peeping out of the different cupboards. **1811** COLMAN *Br. Grins* (ed. 5) 57 He, the beast! was casting sheeps-eyes at her, Out of his bullock head. **1848** THACKERAY *Van. Fair* xxvii, The horrud old Colonel,..was making sheep's eyes at a half-caste girl there. **1888** BRYCE *Amer. Commw.* I. xix. 262 Local leaders cast sheep's eyes at the seat.

†**b.** *to have a sheep's eye*: (*a*) to be timorous; (*b*) see quot. 1711. *Obs.*

**1598** GOSSON *Trump. Warre* D 5 b, Espialles were sent out to discouer the land of Promise, some of them hadde a sheepes eye:..Caleb had a Lions eye. [See *Numbers* xiii. 30, 31.] **1711** *Spect.* No. 250 ¶5 We say such an one has a Sheep's Eye, not so much to denote the Innocence as the simple Slyness of the Cast.

**2.** An amorous glance.

**1604** W. TERILO *Fr. Bacon's Proph.* 283 If a couple kindly kisse, The third thinkes somewhat is amisse. Now sheepes-eies are so watcht, That Lambes can hardly sleepe. **1842** LOVER *Handy Andy* ii, Tom's all ram's horns, and the widow is all sheep's eyes.

So **'sheep's-eye** *v. trans.*, to cast sheep's eyes at.

**1801** COLERIDGE *Let. to R. Southey* 22 July, I should begin to look the damsel Hope full in the face, instead of sheep's-eyeing her.

**sheepshank** ('ʃiːpʃæŋk), *sb.*

**1.** The shank or leg of a sheep.

**1675** COTTON *Planters Man.* 64 The third way [of making pallisados], which is done with Sheep-shancks fastned in the Walls, is doubtless the best..; but the bones must be set so near together, as [etc.]. In mod. Dicts.

**b.** *nae sheepshank* (Sc.): a person or thing of no small importance.

**1785** (Apr. 21) BURNS *Ep. to J. Lapraik* xii, The paughty, feudal Thane,..Wha thinks himsel nae sheep-shank bane, But lordly stalks. *c* **1787** —— *Brigs of Ayr* 91, I doubt na, frien', ye'll think ye're nae sheep-shank. **1806** TANNAHILL *Ep. Jas. Buchanan* 11 Mony a puir, doilt, servile bodie Will ..think himsel nae sma sheepshank.

**2.** *Naut.* In full † *sheepshank(s) knot*: A knot cast on a rope for temporarily shortening it without cutting it or unfastening the ends.

Formed by doubling the rope in three parts and taking a hitch over the bight at each end with the other rope (Voyle).

¶By a printer's or clerical error in Manwayring's *Seaman's Dictionary* (1644), the explanation of *Sheep-shanck* and the heading of the following article *Sheeres* were omitted. Hence Randle Holme *Armoury* III. 166/1 erroneously explains *Sheepshank* as 'two Poles set across where a Block is hung' etc. (= SHEAR *sb.*[1] 4).

**1627** CAPT. SMITH *Seaman's Gram.* v. 26 Sheepshanks Knot. The last is the Shepshanke, which is a knot they cast upon a Runner or Tackle when it is too long to take in the goods, and by this knot they can shorten a rope without cutting it. **1769** FALCONER *Dict. Marine* (1780), *Sheep-shank*, a sort of knot or hitch [etc.]. **1788** *Chambers' Cycl.* s.v. *Knot*, The sheep-shank-knot. **1834** MARRYAT *Peter Simple* vi, Pass that brace through the bull's eye, and take the sheepshank out before you come down. **1870** *Routledge's Ev. Boy's Ann.* 246 When both ends of the rope are fast, the 'sheep-shank' or, as it is sometimes called, the dogshank shortening is used.

Hence **'sheepshank** *v. trans.*, to shorten (a rope) by means of a sheepshank.

**1769** FALCONER *Dict. Marine* (1780) s.v., The runner of the tackle is sheep-shanked. **1886** J. M. CAULFEILD *Seamanship Notes* 4 Shorten up buoy-rope..; this is done by sheep-shanking it.

**sheep's head.** Also *Sc.* sheep-head. [Cf. Du. *schaapshoofd*, G. *schafshaupt*, also WFris. *skieppekop*, LG. *schaapskopp*, Du. *schaapskop*, G. *schafskopf* = simpleton.]

**1.** The head of a sheep; the dish consisting of this.

**1542** BOORDE *Dyetary* v. (1870) 240 Nowe to sende for breade, and by-and-by to sende for a shepes-heade. ? *a* **1550** *Freiris Berwik* 260 in *Dunbar's Poems* 294 Sowsit nolt fute, and scheipheid. **1771** SMOLLETT *Humph. Cl.* 18 July Let. i. (1815) 257 The servants had been informed..that there was nothing to eat in Scotland but oatmeal and sheep's-heads. *c* **1790** BURNS *Ep. Col. De Peyster* 38 Like a sheep-head on a tangs. **1840** THACKERAY *Barber Cox* Apr., I was..set, as is the custom in our trade, to practise on a sheep's-head.. before I was allowed to venture on the human countenance.

*attrib.* **1737** *Ochtertyre House Bk.* (S.H.S.) 102 Sheephead broth. **1817** *Lintoun Green* IX. viii, He'd singed the sheep's heads to the fell, Tæ mak' the sheep-head kale. **1827** SCOTT *Surg. Dau.* v, Sheep-head broth and haggis. **1884** *St. James's Gaz.* 26 Jan. 5/1 Sheep's-head-pie..and other substantial Scotch dishes.

**2. a.** A fool, simpleton. †Also as *adj.*, stupid.

**1542** [see SHEEP *sb.* 5]. **1605** CHAPMAN *All Fools* II. i, Kisse her you sheepes-head. **1624** GEE *Foot out of Snare* App. 108, I suppose..[he] hath better deuices then this simple sheepes-head inuention. **1780** *Mirror* No. 98 What a powdered sheep's-head have we got here? **1878** J. PAYNE tr. *Villon's Poems* (1881) 74 My poor orphans..Are grown in age, and wit likewise. No sheepsheads are they.

**b.** *Cards.* A simple form of skat.

**1886** E. E. LEMCKE *Skat* 4 Skat is of quite recent origin... It bears a great resemblance to the Wendish game of '*Schafskopf*' (Sheepshead) and '*Dreiben*' (three legs). **1913** *Off. Rules Card Games* (U.S. Playing Card Co.) (ed. 17) 205 Schafkopf..(Sheepshead)... Object of the Game—To win in tricks certain cards of counting value as follows: A's, 11, 10, K's 4, Q's 3, and J's 2. **1939** C. ISHERWOOD *Goodbye to Berlin* 186 A group of youths..were playing Sheep's Head. **1951** F. BROWN *Murder can be Fun* iv. 57, I knew he played schaffskopf—sheepshead... It's a three-handed game. **1976** *National Skat & Sheepshead Q.* Dec. 21 Fred Suter always wanted to prove that Sheepshead players will back a Classic Tournament.

**3.** A large and much esteemed food fish, *Archosargus* or *Diplodus probatocephalus* (*Sargus ovis*), abundant on the coasts of the United States. Also applied to similar fishes in N. America, esp. the marine *Archosargus rhomboidalis* of Florida and the fresh-water drumfish, *Aplodinatus grunniens*.

So called from a supposed resemblance of the head to a sheep's.

**1676** *Phil. Trans.* XI. 624 In the Rivers are great plenty and variety of delicate Fish; one kind whereof is by the English called a Sheepshead. **1796** T. TWINING *Trav. Amer.* (1894) 156 The Americans..have given the appellation of sheepshead to the most esteemed fish of their coast. **1836** J. RICHARDSON *Fauna Bor.-Amer.* III. 65 *Sciæna (Corvina) Richardsonii.* The Malasheganè inhabits Lake Huron... It is called 'Sheep's-head' by the Anglo-Canadians. **1885** *Harper's Mag.* Jan. 220/2 The sheep's-head and channel bass abounded. **1888** [see PORGY]. **1897** *Outing* XXX. 435/2 The 'sheeps-head' (freshwater drum), a good-looking, silvery fish. **1924** J. O. LA GORCE *Bk. Fishes* 71/2 The Sheepshead belongs to the Porgy family. **1962** K. F. LAGLER et al. *Ichthyol.* v. 147 In some fishes such as the sheepshead and the sea bream (*Archosargus*) they [*sc.* the cutting teeth] look almost human. **1979** *South Padre Parade* (South Padre Island, Texas) Dec. 6/3 These visiting fishermen caught their limit while fishing locally for speckled trout and sheepshead.

**4.** Short for *sheep's-head clock.*

**1887** *N. & Q.* Ser. VII. III. 285 The square-faced [clocks] were 'sheep's head', and the round-faced 'wag o' th' wall'.

**5.** *Comb.*, as **sheep's-head clock**, a clock having the works exposed to view; **sheep's-head fish** = 3; **sheep's-head gull**, the great tern; **sheep's-head porgy** (see PORGY); † **sheephead sword**, a basket-hilted sword; so *sheep-head hilt.*

**1872** *Routledge's Ev. Boy's Ann.* 9/1 An old Dutch clock, of the kind known as a '*Sheep's-head' clock. **1846** OWEN *Lect. Anat. Vertebrate Anim.* I. *Fishes* 220 The *Sheep's-head Fish (*Sargus*). **1808-13** A. WILSON & BONAPARTE *Amer. Ornith.* (1831) III. 153 The..great tern..by many.. is called the *sheep's-head gull. **1707** W. HOPE *Fencing* v. 158 [Swords] with good, closs, or as they are more commonly termed by the Vulgar, Shell or *Sheep-head Hilts. **1817** *Lintoun Green* 12 A *sheephead sword.

Hence **'sheepshead** *v.*, *U.S.* to fish for sheepshead; **sheeps'headism** *nonce-wd.*, the practice of eating sheep's-head.

**1841** THACKERAY in *Fraser's Mag.* XXIII. 711 Cannibalism in the South Seas, and sheepsheadism in Scotland.

†**'sheep-shear**, *sb. Obs.* [Back-formation f. SHEEP-SHEARING. OE. had *scéapscaru* (*scaru* act of shearing: see SHARE *sb.*[3]).] Sheep-shearing.

**1616** *Rich Cabinet* 54 So is he, neither at season, sheep-sheere, or haruest, beholding to any man. *a* **1635** T. RANDOLPH *Poems* (1668) 76 To morrow morning..Pan's Cornet's blown, and the Great Sheep-shear's kept.

**'sheep-shear**, *v. rare.* In 7 -share. [Back-formation f. SHEEP-SHEARING.] **a.** *intr.* To shear sheep. †**b.** *trans.* To 'fleece', swindle.

**1618** *Owles Almanacke* 45 A cozoning nip shall sheepshare a cunny of his coyne. **1909** *Essex Rev.* XVIII. 170 My poor old father larned many lads to ship-shear in his day.

**'sheep-ˌshearer.**

**1.** One who shears sheep.

**1539** BIBLE (Great) *Gen.* xxxviii. 12 Iudas..went vnto hys shepe sherers to Tymnath. **1688** HOLME *Armoury* II. ix. 176/2 Sheep shearers. **1853** MILBURN *Sheep & Shepherding* 39 The obtaining of servants for shepherds and sheep-shearers. **1898** J. A. GIBBS *Cotswold Village* xvii. 387 First of all there was the sower's feast,..then came the sheep-shearer's feast.

**b.** A machine for shearing sheep.

**1908** *Chamb. Encycl.* IX. 380/1.

†**2.** *Cant.* (See quot.) *Obs.*

*a* **1700** B. E. *Dict. Cant. Crew, Sheep-shearers,* Cheats.

**'sheep-ˌshearing**, *vbl. sb.*

**1.** The act or practice of shearing sheep.

**1607** TOPSELL *Four-f. Beasts* 623 In auncient times there were great feastes at their sheepe-shearings. **1611** COTGR. s.v. *Brebis*, Sheepe-shearing is not euer in season. *a* **1722** LISLE *Husb.* (1757) 319 Two or three days before my sheep-shearing. **1809** J. LAWRENCE *Treat. Cattle* 312 Sheep shearing is performed twice a year in some..countries. **1829** *Chapters Phys. Sci.* 56 The shears used in sheep-shearing.

†**b.** *fig.* Fleecing. *Obs.*

**1632** MASSINGER *Maid of Hon.* I. i, His sheepe sheering, nay shaving to the quicke.

**2.** The season for shearing sheep.

**1688** HOLME *Armoury* II. ix. 176/2 Sheep shearing, is that time wherein the Wooll is cut off them, which..was ever accounted days of Mirth and Feasting. **1771** FOOTE *Maid of B.* III. Wks. 1799 II. 230 *Poul.* That must be a good forty years since. *Flint.* Come sheep-shearing next. **1837** YOUATT *Sheep* ii. 34 The sheep-shearing was the season of peculiar rejoicing.

**3.** The feast held at the shearing-season.

**1611** SHAKS. *Wint. T.* IV. iii. 125, I must go buy Spices for our sheepe-shearing. **1611** *Shuttleworths' Acc.* (Chetham Soc.) 194 Twoe hinder quarters of veale, for provicion against sheepe shearinge. **1655** STANLEY *Hist. Philos.* III. (1687) 108/1, I took a Lute and bid him Sing the Ship-shearing of Simonides. **1797** A. YOUNG in *Autobiogr.* (1898) 276, I went to the Duke of Bedford's sheep-shearing. **1837** *Penny Cycl.* VIII. 223/2 Cumbrian peasantry have various festive meetings, called the kirn, or harvest-home, sheep-shearing, merry nights, and upshots. **1846** BAXTER *Libr. Pract. Agric.* (ed. 4) II. p. xxvii, The sheep-shearing of Woburn or Holkham, in the last century, where nobles, gentlemen, and labourers met together.

**4.** *attrib.* esp. in *sheep-shearing feast.*

**1586** FERNE *Blazon Gentrie* I. 71 If you come, to our sheep-shering veast..yous taste of our cheese cake. **1611** SHAKS. *Wint. T.* IV. iii. 39. **1763** *Museum Rust.* I. 12 It being merry-making time,..like vintage, or sheep-shearing time. **1847** T. MILLER *Pict. Country Life* 58 An old practical farmer, one who..has his sheep-shearing feast and harvest-home. **1886** C. SCOTT *Sheep-farming* 141 A steam sheep-shearing machine.

**'sheep-shears**, *pl.* [f. SHEEP + SHEAR[1]. Cf. NFris. *sjappsjur*, MDu. *schaepschare* (Du. *schaapschaar*), G. *schafschere*.] Shears for shearing sheep.

**1688** HOLME *Armoury* II. ix. 176/2 Sheep shares, or Wooll shares. **1757** *Phil. Trans.* I. 108 It [lightning] melted an old copper skillet, a pair of sheepshears. **1842** S. C. HALL *Ireland* II. 397 Small shears, like the modern sheep-shears. **1875** KNIGHT *Dict. Mech.* III. 2140 A sheep-shears with a six-fingered comb and a revolving bladed disk.

*Comb.* **1797** *J. Robinson's Directory of Sheffield* 116 Edge-tool and sheep sheer maker.

**'sheepskin.** Also sheep's skin. [Cf. NFris. *sjappskann*.]

**1. a.** The skin of a sheep; *esp.* one used as a garment or in the making of a garment.

*c* **1200** ORMIN 3210 Hiss girrdell wass off shepess skinn. *c* **1440** *Jacob's Well* 214 þise schepysskynnes wyth whiche I am wryed were scheep þat I took wrongfully of a wydewe. *c* **1440** LYDG. *Hors, Shepe & G.* 365 Ther is also made of sheepis skyn, Pilchis & glovis. *c* **1500** *Cocke Lorelles Bote* 2 A shepes skyne of a wether. **1526** TINDALE *Heb.* xi. 37 Other ..walked vppe and doune in shepes skynnes [*Rheims, A.V.* sheep-skinnes]. **1596** NASHE *Saffron Walden* K 1, One time shee slept in a sheepes skinne all night. **1738** *Ochtertyre House Bk.* (S.H.S.) 122 For a sheeps skine for the mill .007.

**1411** *Nottingham Rec.* II. 86, j. shepskyn, jd. **1470-85** MALORY *Arthur* I. xvii. 62 He was al be furred in black shepe skynnes. **1562-3** *Act 5 Eliz.* c. 22 §1 To..take away the Wooll of any Shepe skinne or Lambe skinne. **1602** SHAKS. *Ham.* v. i. 123 Is not Parchment made of Sheep-skinnes? **1692** *Capt. Smith's Seaman's Gram.* II. iii. 91 Sheepskins to make Spunges. **1788** GIBBON *Decl. & F.* xli. IV. 149 They promiscuously slept on the ground, perhaps on a sheep-skin. **1850** W. IRVING *Mahomet* xviii. (1853) 81 Garb of coarse woollen patched with sheepskin. **1896** BARRIE *Sentim. Tommy* ii, The floor was bare save for a sheepskin beside the bed.

**b.** in military use.

**1802** C. JAMES *Milit. Dict.* s.v. *Skin*, Sheep skins are made use of to cover the mortars or howitzers between firing. **1833** *Reg. Instr. Cavalry* I. 106 Draw back the sheepskin and shabraque. **1871** *Daily News* 7 Sept., The artillery..were the first to lay their sheepskins aside.

**c.** A coat made of sheepskin.

**1917** W. J. LOCKE *Red Planet* xxi. 270 From the shapeless tam-o'-shanter to the huge boots..[he] was caked in mud. Over a filthy sheepskin were slung all kinds of paraphernalia. **1977** A. SCHOLEFIELD *Venom* II. 83 The policeman made no reply, hunching down again in his sheepskin.

**2. a.** The skin of sheep used for parchment, for the making of drumheads, in bookbinding, etc.

**1340** *Ayenb.* 44 Betere may ech man rede þe ilke zenne, and þe oþre ine þe boc of his inwyt þanne ine ane ssepes scinne. *c* **1412** HOCCLEVE *De Reg. Princ.* 1014 We stowpe and stare vp-on þe shepes skyn, And keepe muste our song and wordes in.

**1567** *Gude & Godlie B.* (S.T.S.) 176 He had to sell.. Remissioun of sinnis, in auld scheip skinnis. **1596** *Raigne K. Edw. III*, II. ii. 50 Poore shipskin, how it braules with him that beateth it! *c* **1613** MIDDLETON *No Wit like Woman's* IV. ii, When did you e'er see a gentleman set his hand to anything, unless it were to a sheep-skin, and receive a hundred pound for his pains? **1771** SMOLLETT *Humph. Cl.* 10 June Let. i, I will find a slip of sheep-skin that will do his business. **1852** DICKENS *Bleak Ho.* xxxii, Where some wise ..conveyancer yet toils for the entanglement of real estate in meshes of sheepskin, in the average ratio of about a dozen of sheep to an acre of land. **1870** *Daily News* 9 Sept. 5 The music of the sheepskin and the trumpets.

**b.** *U.S. slang.* A parchment diploma received on taking a degree; the holder of such a diploma.

**1843** R. CARLTON *New Purchase* (Hall *College Words*), This apostle of ourn never rubbed his back agin a college, nor toted about no sheepskins. *Ibid.*, I can say as well as the best on them sheepskins, if you don't get religion.. you'll be lost, teetotally. **1887** *Lippincott's Mag.* Aug. 299 He has won his sheep-skin; he has, perchance, gained signal honors in his university course.

**3. a.** *attrib.* and *Comb.*, as ***sheepskin-clad***, ***-lined*** adj.; ***sheepskin-gatherer***.

*c* **1645** *Archæologia* LII. 141 A fell monger or Sheepe skin gatherer. **1879** BROWNING *Ivan* Dram. Idyls 63 About him, watched the work his neighbours sheepskin-clad. **1950** C. EDWARDS in *McCall's Mag.* Mar. 68/3 A pair of sheepskin-lined slippers. **1980** *Country Life* 3 July 56/1 The *del* is the colourful Mongolian dress... Winter *dels* are sheepskin-lined (a man's *del* can require up to 40 lambskins).

**b.** *attrib.* passing into *adj.* Made or consisting of sheepskin or parchment; written on parchment.

**1602** DEKKER *Satirom.* F 3 b, This ship-skin-cap shall be put off. **1607** MIDDLETON *Fam. Love* III. i, Wolves that in sheep-skin bands Prey on the hearts to join th' unwilling hands. **1624** J. TAYLOR (Water P.) *Pastorall* C 3 b, So doth a sheepe-skin Bond make money breed. **1823** J. BADCOCK *Dom. Amusem.* 83 Purifying crude mercury.. by passing it through sheep-skin.. leather. **1827** SCOTT *Chron. Canongate* i, A couple of sheep-skin bags, full of parchment and papers. **1833** MARRYAT *Peter Simple* xxxi, To put the sheepskin mat on the stern gratings of my gig. **1837** CARLYLE *Fr. Rev.* I. VII. v, A sheepskin drum! **1850** —— *Latterday Pamph.* vi. 26 A sheepskin Act of Parliament. **1917** *Harrods Catal.* 763/1 Sheepskin rugs 35/0 to 120/0. **1936** 'J. TEY' *Shilling for Candles* xxvi. 278 An atmosphere of marble mantlepieces and sheepskin rugs. **1976** J. BINGHAM *God's Defector* vi. 73 In front of the dressing-table was a white sheepskin rug.

Hence **'sheepskinned** *a.*, clothed in sheepskin (in quot. 1628 with reference to Matt. vii. 15).

**1628** PRYNNE *Brief Surv.* 2 That some should.. watch against deuout and sheepe-skind Wolues. **1879** H. S. EDWARDS *Russ. at Home* I. 202 Their sheep-skinned persons. **1889** 'F. ANSTEY' *Pariah* I. i, Whenever one of the fly-horses.. shook his long-suffering and sheepskinned head.

**sheep-steal**, *v.* [Back-formation f. next.] *intr.* To be a sheep-stealer.

**1820** SHELLEY *Hymn Merc.* xlix, Those Who swindle, house-break, sheep-steal, and shop-lift.

**'sheep-stealer.** One who steals sheep.

**1634** SANDERSON *Serm.* (1674) II. 286 How unequal a thing is it,.. that a sacrilegious church-robber should make a mittimus for a poor sheep-stealer? **1778** JOHNSON *Let.* 13 Oct., in *Boswell*, Pray how many sheep-stealers did you convict? **1829** HOGG *Sheph. Cal.* II. x. 325 A notorious sheep-stealer in the county of Mid-Lothian.

So **'sheep-stealing** *vbl. sb.* and *ppl. a.*

*a* **1578** LINDESAY (Pitscottie) *Chron. Scot.* (S.T.S.) II. 133 For no scheip steilling nor wrangous geir. **1648** JENKYN *Blind Guide* i. 6 Their trade of Sheep-stealing will.. decay. *a* **1704** T. BROWN *Laconics* Wks. 1711 IV. 7 One Sheepstealing Rogue will spoil all the rest. **1824** MISS MITFORD *Village* Ser. I. (1863) 70 We shall be taken up for sheep-stealing presently ourselves.

†**sheepsy-wolvsy**, *a.* *Obs.* A nonsense-compound based on LINSEY-WOOLSEY (q.v. 3 b) to suggest 'wolves in sheep's clothing'.

**1657** J. WATTS *Scribe, Pharisee*, etc. 252 Linsie woolsie, sheepsie woolvsie prophets.

**'sheep-tick**, †**sheep's tick.** [See TICK *sb.*[1] and cf. WFris. *skieppetyk*, G. *schafzeecke*, *schafstieke*.] A horny, bristly, wingless fly, *Melophagus ovinus*, which infests sheep, embedding its head in the skin and extracting the blood. Also = SHEEP-LOUSE.

*c* **1425** *Voc.* in Wr.-Wülcker 642/37 *Hec amittena*, schep-tyke. **1598** *Mucedorus* II. iv. 68 *Ama.* The shepheards force would haue saued thousands more. *Clo.* Aye, shipstickes, nothing else. **1668** CHARLETON *Onomast.* 49 *Reduvius*, the Sheeps Teek. **1837** YOUATT *Sheep* 544 The sheep-tick.. propagates with much rapidity, although not to be compared with the sheep-louse. **1844** H. STEPHENS *Bk. Farm* III. 1109 Sheep are affected by a troublesome insect, the keb or ked, or sheep-tick.

**'sheep-walk.** A tract of grass-land used for pasturing sheep.

**1586** HARRISON *England* II. xix. I. 205/2 Townes pulled downe for sheepe-walks. **1667** MILTON *P.L.* XI. 431 A field, Part arable and tilth,.. the other part sheep-walks and foulds. **1784** COWPER *Task* VI. 111 Sheep-walks populous with bleating lambs. **1810** SCOTT *Lady of L.* II. xxviii, The dales.. Are now one sheep-walk, waste and wide. **1886** C. SCOTT *Sheep-farming* 122 A study of the botany and geology of a sheep-walk is one of the first steps to successful herding.

Hence **'sheep-walker** *Austral.*, a sheep-master.

**1885** *Daily Tel.* 20 Nov. (Cass.), The sheep-walkers of Taranaki will find it to their interest to dispose of their produce by way of Auckland.

**'sheep-wash**, *sb.*

**1.** The washing of sheep before shearing; the place where sheep are washed.

**749** in Birch *Cartul. Sax.* (1885) I. 257 Of þam stane on sceapwæscan. **764–75** *Ibid.* 291 Juxta fluvium qui dicitur Stur ad vadum nomine Scepesuuasce. **1640** BRATHWAIT *Two Lancs. Lovers* 19 (Halliw.) A seed-cake at fastens; and a lusty cheese-cake at our sheepe-wash. **1877** *N.W. Linc. Gloss.*, *Sheep-wesh*, a place in a stream or pond where sheep are washed. **1890** *Melbourne Argus* 9 Aug. 4/2 They would start shearing in three weeks. He would.. get me booked for a good billet in the sheepwash. **1898** TRASK *Norton-sub-Hamdon* 189 The sheepwash was for the use of all who kept sheep.

**2.** A preparation used in washing sheep, sheep-dip.

**1858** SIMMONDS *Dict. Trade*, *Sheep-wash*,.. a mixture of arsenious acid and soft soap in water, in which sheep are dipped. **1882** D. WOOD *Sheep-dipping* (1885) 16 It has.. been customary to employ tobacco-water as a sheep-wash.

Hence **'sheepwash** *v.*, **'sheepwasher**, **'sheepwashing** *vbl. sb.* (also *attrib.*).

**1891** 'R. BOLDREWOOD' *Sydney-side Saxon* x, He can't dig or *sheep-wash or plough there. **1890** —— *Col. Reformer* (1891) 122 Men.. were employed as *sheepwashers. **1826** J. WILSON *Noct. Ambr.* Wks. 1855 I. 174 The murmurs o' the *sheepwashing Yarrow. **1866** *Jrnl. R. Agric. Soc.* Ser. II. II. 371 A sheep-washing day on the Wye. **1899** *Allbutt's Syst. Med.* VIII. 929 Workmen exposed to the use of arsenical pigments.. as in sheep-washing.

**sheepy** ('ʃiːpɪ), *a.* *rare.* [f. SHEEP + -Y[1].]

**a.** Of, pertaining to, or resembling sheep.

**1387–8** T. USK *Test. Love* I. vi. (Skeat) l. 161 It greveth me to remembre these dyvers sentences, in janglinge of these shepy people. *a* **1586** SIDNEY *Ps.* CXLIV. viii, The sheepy prease, The streetes shall scantly hold. **1873** LELAND *Egypt. Sketch-Bk.* 7 The '*La Alláh il Alláh*!'.. is of all human sounds the most like bleating. It is sheep-ier than monotonous; it is absolutely mutton-ous. **1891** MEREDITH *One of our Conq.* I. viii. 131 He called the social English the most sheepy of sheep.

**b.** Full of sheep.

**1934** DYLAN THOMAS *Let.* 25 Apr. (1966) 110, I even go without a coat (sometimes) in this cold weather, & tread be-jumpered over the sheepy fields. **1979** R. BARNARD *Posthumous Papers* viii. 73 The lonely, sheepy expanses of her native land.

**sheer** (ʃɪə(r)), *sb.*[1] *Naut.* Also 7, 9 shear, 8 shere. [f. SHEER *v.*[2]]

**1.** An abrupt divergence or deviation of a vessel from the line of her course; a swerve.

**1670** NARBOROUGH *Jrnl.* in *Acc. Sev. Late Voy.* I. (1694) 61, I was in danger of running the Ship against steep Rocks ..she taking a shear with the Tide. **1725** *Phil. Trans.* XXXIII. 425 A Ship before the Wind will deviate from her true Course, sometimes one Way, sometimes another, in her Yaws and Sheers. **1827** J. F. COOPER *Prairie* II. xvi. 254 Just give the boat a sheer towards yonder low, sandy point. **1849** W. S. MAYO *Kaloolah* i. (1850) 14 The steersman was directed to put the helm up, in order to give her a sheer out of the way. **1897** *Times* 25 Feb. 11 The heavy sheers which such a [rudderless] vessel would take in being towed.

**b.** ***sheer-off***: an act of sheering off (see SHEER *v.*[2] 1).

**1808** *Naval Chron.* XX. 450 This caused such great confusion among them that they got their grapplings unhooked, and took a broad sheer-off.

**2.** An oblique position given to or taken by a vessel when under way or when riding at single anchor.

***to break her sheer***: of a vessel, to be forced by change of wind or current out of the position of sheer in which she was placed.

**1794** *Rigging & Seamanship* II. 247* To break her sheer. *a* **1797** H. TAYLOR in *Encycl. Brit.* (ed. 3) XVII. 370/2 If laying in the aforesaid position, and she breaks her sheer ..[and] recovers.., let the main-yard be again braced about; but if she comes to a sheer the other way.. brace the fore-yard to. **1865** *Cornh. Mag.* Apr. 465 To prevent this, an able master will endeavour to make his vessel 'lie with a sheer'. *Ibid.*, Great care is required in watching the vessel in this position, lest it should fall off or 'break its sheer'. **1867** SMYTH *Sailor's Word-bk.* s.v.

**3.** *Comb.*: **sheer-boom** *Lumbering*, a boom to catch floating logs and turn them in the desired direction; **sheer-line**, in military bridges, the stretched hawser of a flying bridge along which the boat passes.

**1816** H. DOUGLAS *Milit. Bridges* 44 A cable, or sheer line, is stretched across the river. **1875** KNIGHT *Dict. Mech.*, Sheer-boom. **1879** *Lumberman's Gaz.* 1 Oct., A row of piers to which they have attached a sheer-boom 2,500 feet long.

**sheer** (ʃɪə(r)), *sb.*[2] *Naut.* Also 8 shere, 9 shear. [Perh. a use of SHEAR *sb.*[2], or new formation on SHEAR *v.* It is noteworthy that the Fr. synonym is *tonture* (in Fournier *Hydrogr.* ed. 2, 1667), app. identical with *tonture* shearing, clipping.]

**1.** The fore-and-aft upward curvature or rise of the deck or bulwarks of a vessel; the curve of the upper line of a vessel as shown in vertical section.

***straight*** or ***little sheer***, a hardly noticeable rise at the bow and stern. ***quick***, ***high***, or ***great sheer***: a sheer with small radius of curvature.

**1691** T. H[ALE] *Acc. New Invent.* 121 The section of.. the whole Ship.. included between the Plank-sheering, and the Keels, the upper line of which section is called the Sheer of the Ship. **1711** W. SUTHERLAND *Shipbuild. Assist.* 50 The quicker the Sheere is the more it contributes to the strength of the ship. **1779** BARNARD in *Phil. Trans.* LXX. 101, I found her perfectly upright, and her shere (or side appearance) the same as when first built. **1833** T. RICHARDSON *Merc. Mar. Archit.* 1 They likewise should have more sheer in proportion to their length than larger vessels. **1878** W. H. BISHOP *Voy. Paper Canoe* 105 Her great sheer, full bow, and smoothness of hull.. kept her from swamping. **1884** *Pall Mall Gaz.* 5 Sept. 2/1 Boats with a high sheer at each end. **1889** WELCH *Text-bk. Naval Archit.* ii. 41 The considerable sheer (or curve upwards) given to their ends.

**2.** = *sheer-strake* (see 3).

**1841** DANA *Seaman's Man.* 123 *Sheer* or *Sheer-strake.* **1889** R. DOWLING *Isle Surrey* II. xii. 235 His heels, driven by the force of the tide on the sheer of the boat.

**3.** *Comb.*: **sheer-batten**, (*a*) see quot.; (*b*) in ship-building, 'a strip nailed to the ribs to indicate the position of the wales or bends preparatory to those planks being bolted on' (Knight *Dict. Mech.* 1875); **sheer-built** *a.*, built with (little, great, etc.) sheer; **sheer-draught (-draft)**, the sheer-plan; **sheer-line**, the line of elevation of a ship's deck; **sheer-mould** (see also quot. 1846); **sheer-plan, -rail** (see quots.); **sheer-strake**, the uppermost strake of the side planking or plating of a vessel, also *attrib.*; **sheer-wale** = *sheer-strake*.

**1867** SMYTH *Sailor's Word-bk.*, **Sheer-batten*, a batten stretched horizontally along the shrouds, and seized firmly above each of their dead-eyes, serving to prevent the dead-eyes from turning at that part. **1883** JONCAS *Fish. Canada* (Fish. Exhib. Publ.) 11 The boats.. are very *sheer built, and the clinker work is usually of cedar. **1769** FALCONER *Dict. Marine* (1780) C 2 b, The whole length of the ship is represented according to a side view, perpendicular to the keel, and is termed the plane of elevation, or *sheer-draught. **1830** MARRYAT *King's Own* xlix, The dimensions.. I knew by the sheer-draught. **1797** *Encycl. Brit.* (ed. 3) XVII. 383/2 When it is in its proper position, the line WF will be in the same plane with the *sheer line. **1846** A. YOUNG *Naut. Dict.* 245 *Ram-line*,.. a small rope.. for forming the sheer of the ship:.. adjusted on the ship's side by means of a long thin plank, called the *sheer-mould. **1867** SMYTH *Sailor's Word-bk.*, *Sheer-mould*, synonymous with ram-line. **1797** *Encycl. Brit.* (ed. 3) XVII. 377/2 The **sheer plan* or *draught*, otherwise called the *plan of elevation*, is that section of the ship which is made by a vertical plane passing through the keel. **1898** *Encycl. Sport* II. 575/1 (Yachting) The 'sheer plan' or longitudinal elevation, showing the lines of length from stem to stern, that is to say, the sheer-line, water-lines, line of keel, and lines of height from keel to gunwale. **1769** FALCONER *Dict. Marine* (1780), *Rails*.. are likewise nailed upon several planks along the side; one in particular is called the *sheer-rail, which limits the height of the side from the forecastle to the quarter-deck, and runs aft to the stern, and forward to the cat-head. **1846** A. YOUNG *Naut. Dict.*, *Sheer-rails*, a name for the mouldings round a vessel's top sides. **1805** *Shipwright's Vade-M.* 130 **Sheer-strake.* **1874** THEARLE *Naval Archit.* 102 Sheer strakes are the strakes of the plating (generally outer) which are adjacent to the principal decks. **1882** *Daily Tel.* 4 May, A vessel whose sheer-strake plate is half above and half below the line of main-deck beams. **1805** *Shipwright's Vade-M.* 130 **Sheer-wales* or *Middle-wales*, those strakes of thick stuff in the topside of three-decked ships which are wrought between the middle and lower deck ports.

**sheer** (ʃɪə(r)), *a.* and *adv.* Forms: 3 **scere**, 3, 5 **schere**, 4 **schiere**, 6–7 **shere**, **sheere**, **sheare**, (? 6 *Sc.* **schare**), 7 **shier**, **sheir**, 6– **sheer**. [ME. *schēre*:—? OE. **scǣre* = ON. *skǣr-r* (Sw. *skär*, Da. *skjær*):—OTeut. type **skairjo-*, related to the synonymous **skīro-*, SHIRE *a.* It is possible that the ME. word is an adoption from ON., the initial (sk) being modified to (ʃ) by the influence of the related native adj.] **A.** *adj.*

†**1.** Exempt, free (from service or fealty); clear, acquitted (from guilt or crime). *Obs.*

*c* **1205** LAY. 12752 Heo.. habbeð iqueðen us scere nu & auere mare. **14..** T. CHESTRE *Launfal* 429 Fyfty delyverede prysouns, And made ham quyt and schere.

†**2.** Of the wind: ? Blowing steadily in one direction. (Cf. 9.) *Obs.*

*c* **1290** *St. Michael* 25 in *S. Eng. Leg.* 300 Nov was þat a wonder Arewe, and wonder wei heo souȝte.. A wonder schere-wynd heo was on.

†**3.** Of hair: Thin, sparse. *Obs.*

*c* **1400** MAUNDEV. (1839) xxiii. 252 Alle the Tartarienes han smale Eyen and litille of Berd, and not thikke hered, but schiere.

†**4.** Of light: Bright, shining. Of water, crystal, etc.: Clear and pure; translucent. *Obs.*

**1565** GOLDING *Ovid's Met.* IV. 47 b, The water was so pure and shere a man might well haue seene And numbred all the grauell stones that in the bottome beene. *a* **1568** *Bannatyne MS.* (Hunter. Club) 728 Phebus.. Vnto the eist schutand his shaftis schare. **1583** MELBANCKE *Philotimus* Dd iij b, The Chrisolites & gems whereof did geue a sheere and shining light. **1587** GOLDING *De Mornay* xv. 274 The Soule is either a sheere body and of the nature of the Skye [orig. *vn corps luisant et æthere*],.. or els a bodilesse substance. **1600** HOLLAND *Livy* XLIV. xxxiii. 1191 Afterward they began to yeeld sheere and cleere water in great aboundance. **1871** ROSSETTI *My Sister's Sleep* iv, Without, there was a cold moon up, Of winter radiance sheer and thin.

†**5.** Of an article of food: Thin, not containing much substance. Of an animal: Lean. *Obs.*

**1632** *Guillim's Heraldry* III. xxiii. (ed. 2) 241 The Moone is the naturall and secondary cause, that the crabbes of the Sea are either full and plumme, or else sheare and (after a sort) empty. **1735** J. MOORE *Columbarium* 39 The Dutch Tumbler is much of the same make, but larger,.. not unlike a very sheer Dragoon. **1755** *Phil. Trans.* XLIX. 342 The skimmed milk is very thin and sheer.

**6. a.** Of textile fabrics, etc.: Thin, fine, diaphanous. Chiefly *U.S.* (exc. of stockings). [Cf. G. *schier* sb., 'cobweb lawn'.]

**1565** GOLDING *Ovid's Met.* IV. (1567) 49 b, And yet with shere and velume wings [L. *perlucentibus alis*] they houer from the ground. **1641** BEST *Farm. Bks.* (Surtees) 106 Cocke-webbe-lawne, or tiffeny, is the sheirest and cheapest lawne of all. **1706** in Halliwell *Acc. Collect. Bills*, etc. (1852) 31 Shear muslins fit for head dresses and neckcloths. **1727** A. HAMILTON *New Acc. E. Ind.* I. xi. 125 They manufacture

..in Calicoes coarse and fine, sheer and close wrought. **1848** BARTLETT *Dict. Amer.*, *Sheer*,..applied..to fabrics of cotton or silk; as, *sheer muslin*; meaning very thin, clear, or transparent. **1904** *Daily Chron.* 22 Apr. 8/1 So fine (the American girl would say 'sheer') is the batiste or lawn used that a slip lining is necessary. **1911** E. M. CLOWES *On Wallaby* viii. 225 America seems to have taken to fashioning her literature with a crimping-iron and 'sheer-lawn', while Australia hacks hers out with a billyhook from back-block and Bush. **1934** A. WOOLLCOTT *While Rome Burns* 284 Ravishing French peasant girls with high heels, sheer stockings, and a disposition to say 'Ooh, la la' at appropriate intervals. **1951** in M. McLuhan *Mech. Bride* (1967) 95 Ivory Flakes care helps safeguard sheerest nylons. **1977** D. CLARKE *Gimmel Flask* iii. 56 She was..dressed in a tan moygashel suit, sheer nylons on excellent legs.

**b.** *absol.* as *sb.*

**1934** in WEBSTER. **1937** *Jrnl.* (Lincoln, Nebraska) 25 Apr. (Advt.), Saucy sheers for budgeteers. **1943** *Amer. Speech* XVIII. 94 [New Zealand] words like *bobby-pin* (English 'kirby-grip'), *sheer* (dress material), *tubables* (washable frocks), are taken from American, not English, advertisements. **1952** C. W. CUNNINGTON *Eng. Women's Clothes in Present Cent.* vii. 257 Stockings..in service sheers, 4/11 to 6/11. **1966** *Daily Tel.* 26 Oct. 13/3 His curtain sheers..are better than the German Dralon sheers we saw in the shops last winter. **1978** *Lancs. Life* Apr. 85/1 There is..a new range of Swiss sheers and prints with louvred blinds to match.

**7. a.** Of a material substance: Unmixed or unaccompanied with other matter. Esp. of strong drink: (*a*) Undiluted with water; (*b*) taken alone without solid food.

**1596** SHAKS. *Tam. Shr.* Ind. ii. 25 If she say I am not xiiii. d. on the score for sheere Ale. **1601** HOLLAND *Pliny* XXVII. iv. II. 273 Wherof they drinke..the weight of two drams in mead, wine, or sheere water [orig. *aqua pura*]. *c* **1618** FLETCHER *Double Marr.* v, Shall I have no sheere wine then? **1625** MASSINGER *New Way* IV. ii, Thou neuer hadst in thy house to stay mens stomackes A peece of Suffolke cheese, or Gammon of Bacon, Or any esculent,..but sheere drinke only. **1667** *Phil. Trans.* II. 548, 2 or 3 spoonfuls of shier water. **1675** EVELYN *Terra* (1676) 18 Of pure and sheere-Sand, there's white, black, blewish [etc.]. **1755** *Connoisseur* No. 53. 317 She has the gout in her constitution, and whenever she feels a twitch of it, the only thing is sheer Brandy to keep it from her head. **1764** *Museum Rust.* I. 463 Sheer and slight sands. **1802** HEBERDEN *On Gout* in Beddoes *Hygëia* VIII. 154 It has been thought that a large quantity of sheer wine is good for arthritics. **1815** SCOTT *Guy M.* xxxix, Sheer ale supports him under every thing. **1873** J. GEIKIE *Gt. Ice Age* xi. 141 Nothing save sheer till covers the underlying rocks.

¶ Of steel (? misapprehension of SHEAR-STEEL).

**1858** LONGF. *M. Standish* I. 29 This breast-plate..Had it not been of sheer steel, the forgotten bones of Miles Standish Would at this moment be mould.

**b.** Of an immaterial thing: Taken or existing by itself,..alone. Now *rare* or *Obs.*

**1622** MABBE tr. *Aleman's Guzman's d'Alf.* II. 351 When he saw all his former malice could not..doe mee any harme, with sheere money hee went about to purchase out his reuenge vpon mee. *a* **1646** BURROUGHES *Exp. Hosea* i. (1652) 16 That what he shall deliver may be nothing but the word of God in him, sheer word of God, without any mixture of his own. **1836** I. TAYLOR *Phys. Theory Another Life* ii. 22 An unembodied spirit, or sheer mind, is *no where*.

**8. a.** With a descriptive sb., or one denoting a quality, condition, circumstance, etc.: Neither more nor less than (what is expressed by the sb.); that and nothing else; unmitigated, unqualified; downright, absolute, pure. Cf. MERE *a.* 4.

**1583** MELBANCKE *Philotimus* D iij, Which wil be no lesse then sheere beggery. *a* **1680** T. GOODWIN *Expos. Eph.* xxix. Wks. 1681 I. 388 To go out of himself, and by naked and sheer Faith to go to Jesus Christ alone. **1771** *Junius Lett.* lxiii. 324 Out of sheer love and kindness to Lord Chatham. **1789** MRS. PIOZZI *France & It.* I. 99 *note*, I was always a sheer dunce for my own part. **1837** THIRLWALL *Greece* III. xxiii. 269 The conspirators were not strong enough to carry their point by sheer force. **1837** CARLYLE *Fr. Rev.* II. III. iii, Cazalès..said, in a moment of passion, 'the Patriots were sheer Brigands'. **1856** KANE *Arct. Expl.* I. xxxii. 449 Both Peterson and myself..fell asleep through sheer exhaustion. **1879** S. C. BARTLETT *Egypt to Pal.* vi. 145 The railway was closely skirted on the north by a sheer desert. **1885** *Manch. Exam.* 17 Jan. 5/4 It was a sheer mistake on the part of the driver.

†**b.** ***sheer wit***: a fashionable term for some particular form of humour. *Obs.*

**1672** VILLIERS (Dk. Buckhm.) *Rehearsal* III. i. (Arb.) 67 This Scene will make you die with laughing, if it be well acted: it is a Scene of sheer Wit, without any mixture in the world, I gad. [Cf. 71 *infra* is not this pure Wit?] **1682** SHEFFIELD (Dk. Buckhm.) *Ess. Poetry* 269 That silly thing men call sheer Wit avoid, With which our Age so nauseously is cloy'd. **1738** *Gentl. Mag.* VIII. 206/2 The whole Strength of pretended Patriotism lies in Puns, Sheerwit, and a Horse Laugh.

**9. a.** Of a descent or ascent, the face of a wall, cliff, etc.: Continued perpendicularly or very steeply down or up without break or halting-place.

**1800** WORDSW. *Hart-Leap Well* 50 And climbing up the hill—(it was at least Four roods of sheer ascent). **1815** SCOTT *Ld. of Isles* III. xvi, This lake,..whose barriers drear Are precipices sharp and sheer. **1874** SYMONDS *Sk. Italy & Greece* (1898) I. ix. 181 A pedestal of rock..surmounted by a sheer cliff. **1877** BLACK *Green Past.* xxxvii. (1878) 298 The great rapids whirling by at our very feet towards the sudden and sheer descent. **1898** RIDER HAGGARD *Dr. Therne* 25 The precipice, which to our left was quite sheer.

**b.** with *-down* affixed.

**1864** CARLYLE *Fredk. Gt.* XVII. v. (1872) VII. 47 It has cut for itself that mountain gullet, or sheerdown chasm.

**c.** Of a fall or drop: Occurring straight down, happening from top to bottom (of a given height).

**1859** HAWTHORNE *Marb. Faun* xviii, Look over the parapet and see what a sheer tumble there might still be for a traitor.

**10.** Of a blow (or the like): Delivered with full force; (hit or hitting) straight and hard. *poet.*

**1865** SWINBURNE *Atalanta* 1295 And charging with sheer tusk he drove, and smote Hyleus. **1876** —— *Erechtheus* 450 The lord Whose wheels make lightnings of the foam-flowered sea Here on this rock..one sheer blow Struck.

**B.** *adv.*

**1. a.** Completely, absolutely, altogether, quite. Used chiefly to qualify an adv. or prep., or with vbs. expressing removal, separation, cleavage, etc. (Cf. *right, clean.*)

*a* **1600** I. T. *Grim the Collier* IV. (1662) 52 A wily Priest..Intends to bear her shere away from all. **1611** BEAUM. & FL. *Knt. Burn. Pestle* v. i, I..had my feather shot sheere away. **1622** FLETCHER *Span. Cur.* III. i, The prerogative of your crowns will carry the matter, Carry it sheere. **1667** MILTON *P.L.* I. 742 Thrown by angry Jove Sheer o're the Chrystal Battlements. **1706** PHILLIPS (ed. Kersey), *Sheer*, altogether, quite; as This Fancy is Sheer new. **1740** SOMERVILLE *Hobbinol* II. 81 Cautious he crept, and with his crooked Bill Cut sheer the frail Support. **1791** COWPER *Odyss* VII. 113 Sheer from the threshold to the inner house [ἐς μυχὸν ἐξ οὐδοῖο διαμπερές]. **1830** GALT *Lawrie T.* III. ix, I ain't a-going to be 'quivocal but to speak sheer to the point. **1852** MRS. STOWE *Uncle Tom's C.* vii, She vaulted sheer over the turbid current. **1854-5** LONGF. *Hiawatha* vii, Down the trunk, from top to bottom, Sheer he cleft the bark asunder. **1863** MRS. OLIPHANT *Salem Chapel* xvi, She went sheer forward when the door was open. **1896** MRS. CAFFYN *Quaker Grandmother* 324 In climbing over a stile, Miriam blundered, and fell sheer into the arms of John.

†**b.** Qualifying a numeral: Fully, no less than.

**1642** H. MORE *Song of Soul* II. III. iii. 45 That it must fly six hundred thousand sheere Of Germane miles.

**2.** Perpendicularly or very steeply up or down; straight up or down without break or halting-place.

**1829** SCOTT *Anne of G.* i, A platform of rock..from the farther side of which a precipice sunk sheer down. **1831** CARLYLE *Sart. Res.* I. iii, It rose sheer up above the contiguous roofs. **1872** BLACK *Adv. Phaeton* xxvi, The leaden-coloured lake lying sheer below you. **1875** JOWETT *Plato* (ed. 2) III. 681 A lofty cliff, and goes down sheer into the deep sea. **1892** BIERCE *In the Midst of Life* 16 A stone dropped from its outer edge would have fallen sheer downward one thousand feet.

†**sheer**, *v.*[1] *Obs.* In 3-4 schere. [f. SHEER *a.*; cf. SKERE *v.*, SHIRE *v.*]

**1.** *trans.* To clear, free, acquit from blame. In quot. *refl.*; cf. SKERE *v.* 2.

*c* **1250** *Lutel Soth Sermun* 85 (Cott. MS.) in *O.E. Misc.* 190 Euer heo wile hire schere [*Jesus Coll. MS.* skere] ne com hire nomon neh.

**2.** To make bright or pure.

**13..** *E.E. Allit. P.* A. 165 As glysnande golde þat man con schere.

**3.** *intr.* ? Of water: To run bright and clear.

**13..** *E.E. Allit. P.* A. 107, I wan to a water by schore þat scherez.

**sheer** (ʃɪə(r)), *v.*[2] *Naut.* Forms: 7-8 **shere**, 7 **shear(e**, **share**, 7- **sheer**. [Perh. a use of SHEAR *v.*; but the development of the sense is obscure.

In MLG. and mod.LG., MHG. and mod.Ger., mod.Du. (but not MDu.) the vb. *scheren* (etymologically identical with SHEAR *v.*) often occurs intr. and refl. with the sense to withdraw, depart, 'be off' (coincident with sense 1 c below). This sense is commonly regarded by lexicographers as developed from the sense 'to divide'. The word in continental Teut. does not seem ever to have been in use as a nautical term, so that the common view that the Eng. vb. is of LG. or Du. origin is not convincing. The correspondence between the senses below and the Ger. and Du. senses above-mentioned is not sufficiently exact to warrant the assumption that the course of development has been parallel.]

**1.** *intr.* Of a ship: To turn aside, alter its direction, swerve to either side of its course, in obedience to the helm. Chiefly with advs., as *off*, *out*, *away*.

***to sheer alongside, to, up***, to bear up obliquely towards a vessel or other point.

**1626** CAPT. SMITH *Accid. Yng. Seamen* 19 Lash fast your graplins and sheare off. **1670** COVEL in *Early Voy. Levant* (Hakl. Soc.) 104 All ships, if friends, when they meet upon the sea, share up to one another. **1687** A. LOVELL tr. *Thevenot's Trav.* I. 284 The others as they sheared by us, saw no Man above Deck. **1697** *Lond. Gaz.* No. 3318/3 They both sheered out a-stern of us. **1707** *Ibid.* No. 4329/5 She ply'd 'em so warmly, that they were forc'd to sheer off. **1760-72** H. BROOKE *Fool of Qual.* (1809) III. 83 Our guns..obliged two of them to sheer away again. **1834-5** M. SCOTT *Cruise Midge* i. (1836) 6 They sheered-to with an intent to speak him. **1875** BEDFORD *Sailor's Pocket Bk.* vii. (ed. 2) 267 The second boat of each column is to sheer twenty feet out of the wake of her leader. **1890** CLARK RUSSELL *Ocean Trag.* I. ii. 39 The boat then sheered alongside. **1894** *Law Times Rep.* LXXI. 103/1 Suddenly changing her course, and sheering back to the south. **1899** F. T. BULLEN *Log of Seawaif* 218 She sheered in towards us.

**b.** To swerve to either side irregularly or unsteadily, not in obedience to the helm. Also with *round*.

*c* **1635** CAPT. N. BOTELER *Dial. Sea Services* (1685) 289 When a Ship in her Sailing is not steddily steered She is said to go Sheering: Also when a Tide-gate runneth very swift, it will cause a Ship to go in and out, and so not straight forward; and this is called Sheering. **1769** [see SHEERING *vbl. sb.* below]. **1820** W. SCORESBY *Acc. Arctic Reg.* II. 474 The Esk..continued sheering from side to side to the utmost extent that the rope, by which she was towed, would allow. **1848** *Notes of Cases* (1849) VI. 7 The brig was sheering, not drudging. **1860** *Merc. Mar. Mag.* VII. 180 The ship then sheered to her starboard anchor.

**c.** *transf.* and *fig.* Chiefly with *off*: To change one's course; to depart, go away; to go off in a new direction or on the other 'tack'.

In quot. 1865 with irreg. pa. t. *shore* (by confusion with the vb. *shear*).

*a* **1704** T. BROWN *Volunteer's Sp. to Colonel* Wks. 1711 IV. 227, I resolv'd then to shere into the City, to try what luck I could find there. **1710** *Brit. Apollo* III. No. 14. 2/2 [She] has pickt 15 Guineas out of my Pocket, and shear'd off with it. **1778** [W. H. MARSHALL] *Minutes Agric.* 2 May 1776, Letting the points of the coulters hang two or three inches below the shares, to prevent their sheering from side to side. **1810** *Sporting Mag.* XXXVI. 30 They..were obliged to sheer off the ground. **1883** HOFFMAN *Winter Far West* (1835) I. 167 Wheeling my horse suddenly from the trail towards a thicket of dwarf oaks,..he sheered from the bush, and I was thrown upon the spot. **1865** CARLYLE *Fredk. Gt.* XIX. v. V. 509 His captains lagged or shore off. **1875** WHITNEY *Life Lang.* ix. 165 The history of our English, as compared with the Low-German dialects from which it sheered off in the fifth and sixth centuries. **1876** GREEN *Stray Stud.* 118 An age when the interests of popular liberty and of intellectual freedom had sheered off from the church. **1879** JEFFERIES *Amateur Poacher* xii. (1889) 235 The sheep..now sheered out from the hedge, and allowed me to go by.

**2.** *trans.* To cause (a vessel) to sheer; to direct (a vessel) obliquely towards a given point. Also with advs., as *off*.

**1633** T. JAMES *Voy.* 83 Shering the Ship, night and day,..amongst the disperst Ice that came athwart of vs. *Ibid.* 94 We..stood all on the decks to watch the Ices, sheering of the Ship (to and againe), to auoyd it. **1669** STURMY *Mariner's Mag.* I. ii. 20 We will sheer off our Ship, and hoise out our Shallop. **1769** FALCONER *Dict. Marine* (1780) s.v. *Anchor* To sheer the ship to her *Anchor*, is to steer the ship's head towards the place where the anchor lies when they are heaving the cable into the ship. **1797** S. JAMES *Narr. Voy.* 130 The helmsman sheered our ship as close..as it was possible to go. **1816** SIR H. DOUGLAS *Milit. Bridges* IV. 98 Let the boat be sheered off from the bank..by a cable. *Ibid.*, Whenever a current is so strong as to render it unsafe to sheer a boat across with cables.

*transf.* **1880** FITZGERALD *Lett.* (1889) I. 456 Here is a good Warwickshire word—'I sheered my Eyes round the room'. So good that it explains itself.

†**b.** ***to sheer home the anchor***: to drag the anchor by swerving. *Obs.*

**1644** MANWAYRING *Sea-man's Dict.* s.v. *Shearing*, Where a tide-gate runs very swift, the ship will shere in and out, and so much in some places, that they are faine..to sheere her upon the tide, for feare she should shere-home her Anchors (that is, draw them home).

Hence **'sheering** *vbl. sb.* and *ppl. a.*

**1627** CAPT. SMITH *Seaman's Gram.* xii. 58 Shearing off will teare it in peeces if the rope and anchor hold. **1769** FALCONER *Dict. Marine* (1780), *Sheering*, in navigation, the act of deviating or straying from the line of the course, either to the right or left, so as to form a crooked and irregular path through the water. It is commonly occasioned by the ship's being difficult to steer, but very often from the negligence or incapacity of the helmsman. **1896** KIPLING *Seven Seas* 8 We have strawed our best..To the shark and the sheering gull.

**sheer** (ʃɪə(r)), *v.*[3] [f. SHEER *sb.*[2]] *trans.* To give (a ship) a particular sheer or rise.

**1711** W. SUTHERLAND *Shipbuild. Assist.* 49 The Shaping of any Ship upwards, termed Sheering of her. **1909** *Century Dict.* Suppl., *To sheer up* [*aft* or *forward*], to raise the sheer of a vessel.

**sheer** (ʃɪə(r)), *v.*[4] *rare.* [f. SHEER *a.*] *intr.* Of a rock-face: To rise or descend vertically or very steeply; in quot. with *up*. Hence **'sheering** *ppl. a.*

**1851** G. W. CURTIS *Nile Notes* xxvi. 117 Smoothly sheering precipices below gave Hope no ledge to grasp in falling. **1863** BARING-GOULD *Iceland* 134 The rock sheered up some hundred feet above our heads.

**Sheer**, obs. f. SHIAH.

**sheer(e**: see SHEAR, SHIRE.

**Sheeraz**, variant of SHIRAZ (wine).

**sheer cloath**, erron. form of CERECLOTH.

**1711** in Macgill *Old Ross-sh.* (1909) 152.

**sheered** (ʃɪəd), *a. Naut.* [f. SHEER *sb.*[2] + -ED[2].] Of a ship: Built with a (particular kind of) sheer. Usually with defining word as ***moon-***, ***straight-sheered***.

**1769** FALCONER *Dict. Marine* II. (1780), *Vaisseau qui a le côté foible*, a straight-sheered ship. **1852-63** BURN *Nav. & Milit. Techn. Dict.* (ed. 4) II, Sheered, *tonturé*; moon —, *fort enhuché*; round —, *gondolé, fort tonturé, de côté fort*; straight —, low-built ship, *vaisseau ras*, m.; straight—upper works, *accastillage ras*, m.

**sheeregrasse**, obs. form of SHEAR-GRASS.

**sheer-hulk, shear-hulk.** [f. *sheer*, SHEAR *sb.*[1] 4 + HULK *sb.*[2] 3.

The etymologically preferable spelling *shear-hulk* is little used. In the popular figurative use of the word, derived from nautical songs, the first element is often misunderstood as *sheer* adj., and the compound written as two words.]

The hulk or body of an old disused ship fitted with shears, etc., for hoisting purposes; also a vessel specially built and fitted with shears.

**1768** *Phil. Trans.* LVIII. 139 When the Fame Man of War was driven from her mooring in Hamoaze; together with the sheer-hulk on the rocks. **1799** CAPT. PORTLOCK in *Naval Chron.* III. 71 She had been built for a sheer-hulk. *a* **1843** SOUTHEY *Comm.-pl. Bk.* (1851) IV. 385 The S. Raphael.. being too bad for a sheer-hulk was purchased by Mr. Hawker of Plymouth. **1860** WORCESTER, *Sheer-hulk*.. written also *shear-hulk*. **1862** *Catal. Internat. Exhib.* II. XII. 22 Double sheer hulk for raising sunken vessels.
*fig.* **1790** C. DIBDIN *Song, Poor Tom*, Here, a sheer hulk, lies poor Tom Bowling. **1866** SIR P. WALLIS in Brighton *Life* (1892) 213 Then a young lieutenant, but now a worn-out sheer hulk.

**†sheering nail,** ? mistake for *sheathing nail*.
**1686** PLOT *Staffordsh.* 161 Sheering nailes for ships having broad heads and short shanks.

**sheerly** (ˈʃɪəlɪ), *adv.* Also 5 *Sc.* scheirly, 6 sheerely. [f. SHEER *a.* + -LY².]
**†1.** Brightly, clearly. *Obs.*
*c* **1470** *Gol. & Gaw.* 477 With gold and goulis in greyne, Schynand scheirly and scheyne.
**2.** Completely, entirely, wholly; thoroughly; purely, simply. (Cf. SHEER *adv.*)
**1601** *2nd Pt. Return fr. Parnass.* I. iii. 343 This libel of Cambridge.. will sell sheerely vnderhand. *c* **1618** FLETCHER *Mad Lover* v, H'as out-done all, Outstript 'em sheerly. **1786** BURNS *Ep. Major Logan* ix, Eve's bonie squad, priests wyte them sheerly For our grand fa'. **1810** in Dk. Buckingham *Court & Cab. Geo. III* (1855) IV. 430 The cause of the Ministerial majority is.. attributed.. sheerly to their having the better of the argument. **1843** *Blackw. Mag.* LIV. 313 A man is neither a brute, nor a god,.. but simply and sheerly a Man. **1880** BERTHA THOMAS *Violin-Player* I. i. 11 He sheerly frightened the wits out of her comrade.
**3.** Sharply; with sharp cleavage or division.
**1813** SCOTT *Trierm.* III. xxiii, Through gullet and through spinal bone, The trenchant blade had sheerly gone. **1823** —— *Quentin D.* ii, Snares and traps, armed with scythe-blades, which shred off the unwary passenger's limb as sheerly as a hedge-bill lops off a hawthorn-sprig. **1866** W. R. ALGER *Solit. Nat. & Man* II. 70 When he feels the poor atom, self, sheerly contrasted with the vast cold mass of all humanity beside.
**4.** With vertical or very steep ascent or descent.
**1879** STEVENSON *Ess. Trav., Amateur Emigrant* (1905) 23 In the centre the companion ladder plunged down sheerly like an open pit. **1920** C. M. GRIEVE *Northern Numbers* 69 The barrier.. Lifts sheerly.. To the unknowledgeable skies. **1947** E. MEYNELL *Sussex* i. 15 Across the road,.. the chalk drops again almost as sheerly, down to the water-levels and the Ouse valley. **1964** G. B. SCHALLER *Year of Gorilla* (1965) vii. 184 We followed a buffalo trail upward to the base of the huge rock wall that rose sheerly to the peaked summit.

**sheerman,** obs. form of SHEARMAN.

**ˈsheerness.** *rare.* [f. SHEER *a.* + -NESS.] The quality of being sheer (see the adj.).
**1587** GOLDING *De Mornay* iv. 53 Like as the light of the Sunne hath diuers effects through the disposition of mens eyes, and of the sheerenesse of things. **1903** *Edin. Rev.* Oct. 407 There is something of that quality of *sheerness* in this tale of peasant life.. which we find in.. 'A Village Tragedy'... But it is not so grim.

**†sheer-point.** *Obs. rare.* (Origin and meaning obscure.)
Cf. Lisle's expressions on pp. 433–4: 'a hard thundershower, which went to the roots of the corn'; 'a moderate rain.., enough to go to the roots of the corn'; 'one moderate shower.. which went not to the roots of the corn'.
*a* **1722** LISLE *Husb.* (1757) 435 March the 10th, or thereabouts, fell a rain that might possibly go to the sheer-point.

**Sheer Thursday.** *Obs.* exc. *Hist.* Forms: *α.* 3–6 schere, 3–6, 8–9 shere, 4 scer-, scere, 5 scher, chere, 5–6 sher, 5, 7 shear, 6 chare, 7 sheere, 5, 9– sheer. *β.* 4 shir, 4–5 schire, 5 schyre, schyr-, schir-, 6 shyre, shire, shier; 6 *Sc.* chyris. *γ.* 5 schordordai, s(c)hor-, 5–6 shore, 6 shorpthursday. Often written as one word. [The *α* and *β* types correspond respectively to the two Scandinavian forms which are directly represented in Eng. by *Skere Thursday* (SKERE *a.* 4) and SKIRE THURSDAY. The two cognate and synonymous adjs. (ON. *skǽrr* SKERE, SHEER, and *skírr* SKIRE, SHIRE) appear to have been applied to Maundy Thursday with allusion to the purification of the soul by confession (cf. *Shrove Thursday*, F. *jeudi absolu*), and perh. also to the practice of washing the altars on that day. The *γ* forms are corruptions due to the association with words of somewhat similar sound.
Another name for Maundy Thursday, app. of similar meaning, was Du. *witte Donderdag* ('white Thursday'), recorded from the 13th c.; so G. *weisser Donnerstag*.]
The Thursday in Holy Week, Maundy Thursday.
*α.* *c* **1200** *Trin. Coll. Hom.* 99 Gif we bien cumen on bicumeliche wise a shereðursdai to absoluciun. *c* **1275** *Passion our Lord* 89 in *O.E. Misc.* 40 At þe schere þursday. *c* **1290** *St. Brendan* 360 in *S. Eng. Leg.* 229 A-schereþoresday [(1310 ed. Bälz) scere þorsday, *v. rr.* *c* 1300 scerþursday, *c* 1400 scher þursday, 14.. schire þoresday, schordordai, etc.] huy comen þudere in gret trauaile inouȝ. **1398** TREVISA *Barth. De P.R.* IX. xxxi. (1495) 367 The dayе of Cene that we calle Sherethursdaye. *c* **1425** *Processional Nuns Chester* (1899) 6 On sherthursday at the washyng of the auters. *c* **1430** LYDG. *Min. Poems* (Percy Soc.) 253 On sheerthursday. *c* **1450** *Mirk's Festial* 125 Scher þursday; for, in old fadrys dayes, men wold þat day make scher hom honest, and dodde hor heddys, and clyp hor berdys, and so make hom onest aȝeynes Astyr-day. *Ibid.* 169 Chere þursday. **1534** MORE *Answ. Poysoned Bk.* Pref. B b iij b, Yᵉ maundye of Chryste wyth hys apostles vpon shere thursday. **1621** in *Dewsbury Parish Reg.*, Alice daughter of Willm Speight elder baptised the xxix day being Shear Thursdaye.
*β.* *c* **1380** WYCLIF *Sel. Wks.* I. 325 Joon restide on Shir þursdaie in þe soper on Cristis brest. **1387** TREVISA *Higden* (Rolls) VII. 435 In Cene þorsday, þat som men clepeþ Shireþorsday [1432–50 Scherethursday]. *c* **1450** in Aungier *Syon* (1840) 346 A Schirthursday the sustres shal say the seuen psalmes. **1520** *Perth Hammermen Bk.* (1889) 13 For candill upon Chyris Thuirsday in the kirk, iiij d. *c* **1541** in J. Collier *Eccl. Hist.* (1714) II. 197 Shier-Thursday, as we call it.
*γ.* **1456** *Paston Lett.* I. 389, I wold ye wold take avise and counsel of the Preest that had you so long under hand on Shorthursday. *a* **1490** BOTONER *Itin.* (1778) 372 Item quolibet shore-thursday, voluit lavare pedes eorum. **1513** BRADSHAW *St. Werburge* I. 2978 Shorpthursday. **1537** WRIOTHESLEY *Chron.* (1875) I. 62 The 29 daye of March, beinge Shore Thursdaye.

**sheesh kabab,** var. SHISH KEBAB.

**sheeshum,** variant of SHISHAM.

**sheet** (ʃiːt), *sb.*¹ Forms: *α.* 1 scíete, scéte, scýte, scíte, (3 sciet, sced, ssete, 4 schet), 3–6 schete, 4–5 scheete, 4–6 shete, (5 sshete, chete, schett(e, chitte, 6 sheate, shett(e, schett, *north.* scheit, sheyt(t, shite), 5–8 *north.* sheit, 6–7 sheete, 6–8 *north.* sheitt, 7 sheett, 7–9 *dial.* shit, 6– sheet. [OE. *scíete* wk. fem., Anglian *scéte*, later *scýte*:—prehistoric **skautjōn-*, f. root **skaut-*(: *skeut*: *skut-*: see SHOOT *v.*, SHOT *sb.*¹), of which one of the senses was to project.
To the root *skaut-* belong the foll. forms: (1) of the strong declension, OE. *scéat* masc. (which may be partly the source of the mod.Eng. *sheet*) corner, quarter, region, lap, bosom, bay, skirt, cloth, OFris. *skât*, *schât* skirt, lappet (NFris. *skuat*, *skut*, etc. lap, sail-rope), MLG. *schôt*, (M)Du. *schoot* masc. and fem., lap, sail-rope, OHG. (masc., fem., and neut.) *scôz* (MHG. *schôz*, G. *schoss*) skirt, lappet, lap, ON. *skaut* neut., corner of cloth, quarter (of earth, heaven), skirt, bosom, sail-rope (MSw. *sköt* lower corner of a sail, fold in clothing, bosom, lap, Da. *skjød* lap, skirt), Goth. *skaut-s* masc. or *skaut* neut. κράσπεδον, hem of a garment; (2) of the weak declension, OE. *scéata* masc. (see SHEET *sb.*²), OHG. *scôȥa* (MHG. *schôȥe*) fem., (M)LG. *schôte* sail-rope, ON. *skaute* masc., kerchief (Sw. *sköte* bosom, lap, Da. *skjøde* sail-rope).]
**1.** †**a.** A napkin, cloth, or towel. *Obs.* **b.** A broad piece of linen or cotton stuff, canvas, or the like, for covering, swathing, protecting from injury, etc. (Now felt as a transf. use of 3.) *Obs.*
Also with qualifying word, as ***dusting-, winnowing-sheet***.
*c* **725** *Corpus Gloss.* (Hessels) S 57 *Sandalium*, scete, loða. *c* **900** tr. *Bæda's Hist.* III. vii. (1890) 180 Heo.. hire feax ᵹeræddе, & heo mid scytan [*v.r.* scitan] bisweop. *c* **1000** *Ags. Gosp.* Mark xiv. 51 Sum iungling him fyliᵹde mid anre scytan bewæfed nacod & hi namon hine. *a* **1100** *Voc.* in Wr.-Wülcker 427/42 *In sabanis*, on scetum. *c* **1250** *Moral Ode* 367 (Egerton MS.) Ne scal þer beo sced [*v. rr.* sciet, scete] ne scrud. **1297** R. GLOUC. (Rolls) 8962 þis gode mold.. gurde aboute hire middel a uair linne ssete & wess þe meseles vet. **1375** BARBOUR *Bruce* XIII. 236 Schetis that war sum-deill braid Thai festnyt in steid of baneris Apon lang treis. *c* **1386** CHAUCER *Sec. Nun's T.* 536 The cristen folk.. With sheetes han the blood ful faire yhent. *a* **1400** *Leg. Rood* (1871) 216 Oure lady her hede sche schette in a schete. **1434** *E.E. Wills* (1882) 96, Y bequethe a shete to the.. Chirche, to be peynted at the persons coste.., forto hange to-fore ij auteres. *c* **1450** *Mirk's Festial* 219 [He] syȝ an angyl wyth a whyt schete of selke wepe þe sydys of Saynt Laurens. **1523–34** FITZHERB. *Husb.* §122 Set a stole.. nygh vnto the swarme & lay a clene wasshen shete vpon the stole. **15..** *Wowing of Jok & Jynny* 26 in *Bannatyne MS.* (Hunter. Club) 388 Ane blanket, and ane wecht alsо, Ane schule, ane scheit, and ane lang flail. **1577** B. GOOGE *Heresbach's Husb.* I. 40 b, The Wayne or Cart must be lyned with sheetes, lest ..the seede fall thorowe. **1649** *Caldwell Papers* (Maitl. Club) I. 102 Ane new sheitt of tyking to ye lard's horss. **1753** *Chambers' Cycl.* Suppl., *Sheet*, in the manege. **1824** SCOTT *St. Ronan's* xxii, Meddle with your horse-sheets, and leave shawls alone. **1842** ABDY *Water Cure* 61 When the whole skin was thoroughly warm, the sheet was changed for another wet one. **1858** SIMMONDS *Dict. Trade*, *Sheets*, a name given by railway companies to wagon covers, of oiled canvas, made of different qualities and sizes, from 23 to 42 square yards. **1888** *Mrs. Beeton's Househ. Managem.* §3279 She should.. cover up every article of furniture that is likely to spoil with large dusting-sheets.
**c.** In phr. referring to performing penance in a sheet (orig. for fornication).
Cf. 1556, 1797 s.v. PENANCE *sb.* 2, and SHEETEN *a.*
**1587** HARRISON *England* II. xi. 185/1 in *Holinshed*, Harlots and their mates by.. dooing of open penance in sheets, in churches and market steeds are.. put to rebuke. **1597** *Pilgr. Parnass.* v. 546 An honest man that nere did stande in sheete. **1607** MIDDLETON *Fam. Love* IV. iv, I can describe how often a man may lie with another man's wife before 'a come to the white sheet. **1616** R. C. *Times' Whistle* (1871) 104 The standing in a sheet (A punnishment for thy offence moste meet). **1902** W. J. FORD *Hist. Camb. Univ. C.C.* Pref. 11, I am willing to do penance of sheet and candle if I have wounded any one's feelings.
**2.** = WINDING-SHEET (q.v.). Also †***burying-sheet***, †***shrouding-sheet***.
*c* **1000** ÆLFRIC *Hom.* II. 260 Hi bewundon his lic mid linenre scytan. *a* **1300** *Cursor M.* 17288 + 192 Peter come after & in he went.. And saȝe þe schetez spred. **13..** *Medit.* 955 þys body was leyde vpp on a shete. **1450** *Engl. Ch. Furniture* (Peacock 1866) 181 My wreched body to be beryd in a chitte with owte any kiste. **1531** *Rec. St. Mary at Hill* (1904) 42 A beryng sheet with a seme. *a* **1568** *Bannatyne MS.* (Hunter. Club) 56 Quhen thay ar prickit in a scheit Than lost is all thair ryaltie. **1592** SHAKS. *Rom. & Jul.* V. iii. 97 Tybalt, ly'st thou there in thy bloudy sheet? **1633** EARL MANCH. *Al Mondo* 24 Wee come into the world with a sheete about vs, no sooner borne, but going to bee buried. **1721** KELLY *Sc. Prov.* 6 All that you'll get will be a Kist, and a Sheet after all. **1816** C. WOLFE *Burial Sir J. Moore* iii, Not in sheet nor in shroud we bound him.
**3. a.** A large oblong piece of linen, cotton (or, formerly, hempen) cloth, used as an article of bedding, one being placed immediately above and one below the person. ***the sheets***, the pair of sheets belonging to a bed; ***between the sheets*** (colloq.), in bed.
*c* **1250** *Prov. Ælfred* 310 in *O.E. Misc.* 120 Schene vnder schete, and þeyh heo is schendful. *c* **1374** CHAUCER *Former Age* 45 No down of fetheres ne no bleched shete Was kyd to hem. **1377** LANGL. *P. Pl.* B. XIV. 233 Whan he streyneth hym to streche þe strawe is his schetes. **1424** *E.E. Wills* (1882) 56, I wull he haue.. to ilk of þe too beddis too peyre schetys goode. **1462** in Anstey *Munim. Acad.* (Rolls) II. 698 A peyr of schets. **1531** *Rec. St. Mary at Hill* (1904) 42 A payre of shettes of holond. **1611** SHAKS. *Cymb.* II. ii. 16 Cytherea, How brauely thou becom'st thy Bed; fresh Lilly, And whiter then the Sheetes. **1622** BEAUM. & FL. *Beggar's Bush* III. iii, To steal from the hedge, both the shirt and the sheets. **1711** ADDISON *Spect.* No. 90 ¶7, I was laid very decently between a Pair of Sheets. **1790** BURNS *Taylor fell thro' bed* i, The blankets were thin and the sheets they were sma'. **1842** TENNYSON *Vision of Sin* 68 Bitter barmaid, waning fast! See that sheets are on my bed. **1865** MRS. RIDDELL *Max. Drewitt* xxix, When induced to go to bed,.. retiring from view between the sheets in his boots, coat, waistcoat, and trousers.
**b.** *pl.* in phrases with reference to sexual intercourse, e.g. ***between the sheets, lawful sheets***. Also, with allusion to 'the shaking of the sheets' (see SHAKING *vbl. sb.* 1 d), ***to dance (a dance) between a pair of sheets***.
[**1599** SHAKS. *Much Ado* II. iii. 144 O when she had writ it, & was reading it ouer, she found Benedicke and Beatrice betweene the sheete.] **1604** —— *Oth.* II. iii. 29 Happinesse to their Sheetes. **1605** —— *Lear* IV. vi. 118 My Daughters got 'tweene the lawfull sheets. **1612** CHAPMAN *Widow's T.* I. ii, *Tom*... How her honour.. entertained him in very familiar manner. *Ars.* Nay more, that he had alreadie possest her sheetes. **1633** MASSINGER *Guardian* I. i, The delight to meet in the old dance Between a pair of sheets; my Grandame call'd it The peopling of the world. **1683** TRYON *Way to Health* 627 The moderate use of lawful Sheets. *a* **1704** T. BROWN *Aisop's State Conform.* Wks. 1711 IV. 120 You and I can never dance betwixt one pair of Sheets. **1719** YOUNG *Revenge* II. i, Must I then.. Lead to his nuptial sheets the blushing maid? **1871** R. ELLIS *Catullus* lxvii. 30 Truly a noble father.. Thus in a son's kind sheets lewdly to puddle.
**c.** In proverbial phr. ***as white*** (or ***pale***) ***as a sheet***. Cf. WHITE *a.* 5 b.
**1751** FIELDING *Amelia* III. VII. viii. 84 He entered.. with a face as white as a sheet. **1839** W. T. THOMPSON *Chron. Pineville* (1845) 142 He turned pale as a sheet. **1872** HARDY *Under Greenwood Tree* I. I. viii. 125 You'll be white as a sheet to-morrow. **1929** E. RICE *Street Scene* I. 72 Well, there was the three o' them—Mr. Maurrant lookin' at Sankey as if he was ready to kill him, an' Mrs. Maurrant as white as a sheet, an' Sankey as innocent as the babe unborn. **1952** A. J. CRONIN *Adv. in Two Worlds* xxxix. 276 Sitting on a high stool, he seemed little larger than a shrimp, pale as a sheet, with.. big dark eyes.
**4.** A sail. Chiefly *poet.*
Not a nautical use; prob. originating as a misuse of SHEET *sb.*²
**1637** HEYWOOD *Pleas. Dial.* 210 A deeper Sea I now perforce must saile, And lay my sheats ope to a freer gale. **1666** DRYDEN *Ann. Mirab.* lvi, Their folded Sheets dismiss the useless Air. **1712** PARNELL *Spect.* No. 501 ¶3 The Boat was push'd off, the Sheet was spread. **1725** POPE *Odyss.* II. 465 With speed the mast they rear, with speed unbind The spacious sheet, and stretch it to the wind.
**5. a.** An oblong or square piece of paper or parchment, *esp.* for writing or printing; *spec.* one of the pieces of definite size (varying according to the kind) in which paper is made, 24 (formerly also 25) going to a quire. (The 'sheet' of writing-paper was formerly once folded, so as to form two 'leaves'.)
See also BROADSHEET; also *balance-, score-, time-sheet*.
**1510** STANBRIDGE *Vocabula* (W. de W.) C ij b, *Philura*, a shete. **1530** PALSGR. 266/2 Shete of paper, *foyllet de papier*. **1538** LONDON in *Lett. Suppr. Monast.* (Camden) 227 A multitude of small bonys [etc.].. wiche wolde occupie iiij. schetes of papyr to make particularly an inventary of every part thereof. ? **1545** BRINKLOW *Compl.* ix. C iij b, For writing one syde of a shete of paper.. he will haue ij. grotes. **1613** TAPP *Pathw. Knowl.* 62 A Bale containes Reames 10 Quires 200 Sheets 5000. **1623** J. TAYLOR (Water P.) *Praise Hemp-seed* 24 Foure and twenty Sheets doe make a Quire. *a* **1700** EVELYN *Diary* 27 Nov. 1655, He told me of an inke that would give a dozen copies, moist sheets of paper being press'd on it. **1743** JOHNSON *Let. to Mr. Cave* in *Boswell*, I believe I am going to write a long letter, and have therefore taken a whole sheet of paper. **1775** —— *Let.* 27 May *ibid.*, I have returned Lord Hailes's entertaining sheets. **1815** SCOTT *Guy M.* xvi, She.. writes six sheets a-week to a female correspondent. **1833** J. HOLLAND *Manuf. Metal* II. 224 The supply of blank paper, laid upon a table, from whence the sheets are drawn.. by the boy standing upon the platform. **1857** HUGHES *Tom Brown* I. iii, He had.. managed to fill two sides of a sheet of letter-paper. **1894** HALL CAINE *Manxman* v. vii, Pete went out to buy a sheet of notepaper and an envelope. **1895** *Bookman* Oct. 26/2 Plans.. should not be large folded sheets, but single page plans of small districts.
*allusively.* **1691** *Comedy, Win Her & Take Her* II. i. 19 She's a sheet of Rivell'd parchment, on which is Imprest a perpetual Almanack.
**b.** ***in sheets***: lying flat or expanded, not folded.
**1887** *Cassell's Encycl. Dict.*

**c.** A piece of paper on which objects are fixed and arranged in order for sale and use.

**1706** in Halliwell *Acc. Collect. Bills*, etc. (1852) 28 One sheet of pines 4[d]. *Mod.* Several sheets of botanical specimens.

**d.** A piece of paper (or card) which is divided by means of perforations or the like into sections which may be torn or cut away as required.

**1776** *Pennsylvania Even. Post* 2 Mar. 110/2 A Sheet of Continental Money,..containing sixteen bills, being numbered 38019, and 38032. **1852** *Rep. Sel. Comm. Postage Label Stamps* 94 That a sheet of perforated stamps might be charged a penny more than the unperforated one. **1901** *Whitaker's Alm.* (*Postal Guide*), Uncut sheets of half-penny wrappers, 14 on each sheet.

**e.** A dollar bill (*U.S.*) or pound note; the monetary value of this. *slang.*

**1937** *Research Stud. State Coll. Washington* V. 19 What a fellow gets for one sheet from an officer he can sell to the boys..for five and ten sheets. **1958** F. Norman *Bang to Rights* I. 48 Which if it did happen would cost some one half a sheet. **1969** M. Pugh *Last Place Left* xxvi. 191 A sheet the night. Five quid if you last a week. **1978** *Hot Car* June 94 Maserati air horns [have]..a howling, double high-pitched, screaming note... This cacophony can be yours, whatever car you drive, for less than ten sheets.

**f.** *U.S. slang.* = *rap sheet* s.v. Rap *sb.*[1] 7.

**1958** *N.Y. Times Mag.* 16 Mar. 88/3 *Sheet*, a criminal record. **1976** C. Weston *Rouse Demon* (1977) xxvi. 125 Somebody scared him into it. Let's take a look at his sheet, I want to know who.

**6. a.** In printing and bookbinding, a piece of paper (as in 5) printed and folded so as to form pages of a required size (folio, quarto, etc.). Also, a quantity of printed matter equal to that contained in a sheet.

**1589** [? Lyly] *Pappe w. Hatchet* B iij, All his works bound close, are at least sixe sheetes in quarto, and he calls them the first tome of his familiar Epistle. **1659** Bp. Walton *Consid. Considered* vi. 92 When the sheet is past the Correctors hand, and is Printed off. **1683** Moxon *Mech. Exerc., Printing* 218 If it be the First Page of the first Sheet of a Book the Signature is A. **1689** *Gazophyl. Angl.* Pref. A 4 Lest the Book should exceed the quantity of Sheets design'd. **1751** *Chambers' Cycl.* Advt. conc. 2nd ed., A considerable part of the copy was prepared, and upwards of twenty sheets actually printed in that method. **1808** Scott *Let. to C. K. Sharpe* 30 Dec. in *Lockhart*, The fee is ten guineas a sheet. **1824** Johnson *Typogr.* II. *2 Two Sheets in Folio, Quired, or lying one in another. **1844** Dickens *Let.* 3 Apr. A Magazine sheet is sixteen pages. **1885** Lock in *Workshop Rec.* Ser. iv. 228/1 By 'binding' a book is meant the arrangement of the 'sheets' composing it..in proper sequence, within a pair of covers.

**b.** ***in sheets***: (of books) not bound.

**1693** *Lond. Gaz.* No. 2854/4 Numbers of the Books..have been..stolen out of Thomas Basset's Warehouse.., all in Sheets. **1762** Foote *Orator* ii. Wks. 1799 I. 215 Four hundred of News from the invisible world, in sheets. **1880** J. W. Zaehnsdorf *Art of Bookbinding* i. 1 Should the amateur wish to have his books in sheets, he may get them by asking his bookseller for them. **1972** P. Gaskell *New Introd. Bibliogr.* 144 Long books were divided in quires of 12–24 sheets before this folding took place; hence 'books in quires' as a synonym for books in sheets.

**c.** *pl.* With qualifying demonstrative or its equivalent: Pages or leaves of a book; esp. ***these sheets, the following sheets*** = the book now before the reader. Now *rare.*

**1591** Sylvester *Du Bartas* i. i. 122 In sacred sheets of either Testament 'Tis hard to find an higher Argument. **1676** W. Allen *Addr. Nonconf.* 114 What is said..by J. O. in some Sheets intituled, Two Questions [etc.]. **1707** Sir W. Hope *New Method Fencing* Ded., Having of late Discovered the Short and Easy Method of Fencing, contained in the following Sheets. **1710** Wheatly *Bk. Com. Prayer* xv. (1729) 540 It is easy for the Readers to turn to and observe them, without my swelling these Sheets with them here. **1829** Scott *Guy M.* Introd., In changing his plan,..which was done in the course of printing, the early sheets retained the vestiges of the original tenor of the story. **1868** M. Pattison *Academ. Org.* 4 The following sheets assume that the English nation [etc.].

**†d.** A pamphlet. *Obs.*

*c* **1684** in *Harl. Misc.* (1745) V. 348 It is not my Presumption, in this Sheet, to write the Life of this great Statesman. **1726** *Life W. Penn* in *P.'s Wks.* (1782) I. p. cli, About this time [1702]..he wrote a sheet entitled, 'Considerations upon the Bill against Occasional Conformity.'

**e.** A newspaper. Now chiefly *U.S.*

**1749** Foote *Knights* i. (? 1780) 6 Quires of news-papers! now, I reckon, you read a matter of eight sheets every day. *a* **1796** Burns *To Mr. Peter Stuart*, Your sheet, man, (Though glad I'm to see't, man,) I get it no' ae day in ten. **1848** Thackeray *Van. Fair* l, He tried to..read his paper as usual... He chuckled and swore to himself behind the sheet. **1912** *Times* 19 Oct. 5/3 The insinuations of the *Temps* are only taken up by a very few boulevard sheets. **1926** R. Hughes in *Hearst's Internat.* Feb. 44/1 'How come the newspapers keep saying your fights are all fixed?'.. 'Ah, who cares what the doity sheets say!' **1958** *Spectator* 20 June 807/2 A mass-circulation London Sunday sheet. **1977** R. M. Ours in Bond & McLeod *Newslett. to Newspapers* iii. 220 Rivington made it clear that he intended no partisan sheet.

**7.** A continuous extent or 'sweep' of something conceived as hanging, falling, or moving in a certain direction. **a.** Of light, lightning.

**1605** Shaks. *Lear* iii. ii. 46 Such sheets of Fire, such bursts of horrid Thunder. **1795** Coleridge *Lines written at Shurton Bars* 58 When a second sheet of light Flashed o'er the blackness of the night. **1847** De Quincey *Sp. Mil. Nun* x. Wks. 1853 III. 21 A broad sheet of lightning, which, through the darkness of evening, revealed the boat. **1857** Hawthorne *Engl. Note-bks.* (1870) II. 268 There was a broad sheet of daylight in the west. **1882** 'Ouida' *Maremma* viii, The sky was a sheet of lightning.

**b.** Of rain, mist, fog.

**1697** Dryden *Virg. Georg.* i. 437 Oft whole sheets descend of slucy Rain. *a* **1774** Goldsm. *Surv. Exp. Philos.* (1776) I. 327 A sheet of vapour rising from the sea. **1844** Dickens *Let. to T. Mitton* 5 Nov., The water has been falling down in one continual sheet. **1894** *Yachting* (Badm. Libr.) II. 377 A heavy squall with sheets of rain. **1897** G. Allen *Type-writer Girl* i, As one beholds the Paps of Jura on a day of sea-fog through swaying sheets of white cloud.

*transf.* **1892** Bierce *In Midst of Life* 89 Our fellows..sent broad sheets of bullets against the blazing crest of the offending works.

**c.** In an organ, the current (*of* wind) directed through the wind-way against the upper lip of a pipe.

**1881** C. A. Edwards *Organs* xvii. 135 Any movement of the languid would..alter the direction of the sheet of wind.

**8.** A broad expanse or stretch of something lying out flat, presenting a white or glistening surface, or forming a relatively thin covering or layer.

**a.** of water. (In quot. 1593 ? *collect.*)

**1593** *Wills & Inv. N.C.* (Surtees 1860) 219 Eighte shete of the fishinge water of Southe Yarowe. **1687** A. Lovell tr. *Thevenot's Trav.* ii. 83 There you have the Canal and Sheets of Water in the same manner as in the other. *c* **1710** Celia Fiennes *Diary* (1888) 193 A Long as well as Large ffountaine or pond w[ch] is Called a sheete of water. **1727–46** Thomson *Summer* 594 An azure sheet it rushes broad. **1784** Cowper *Task* v. 106 The light and smoky mist That in its fall the liquid sheet throws wide. **1845** *Penny Cycl.* Suppl. I. 35/1 The vast plain..during the greater part of the year..is a sheet of water. **1896** M. M'L. Harper *Rambles in Galloway* i. 23 The loch is a lovely sheet of water.

**b.** of ice, foam.

**1694** *Acc. Sev. Late Voy.* ii. (1711) 172 If it be calm Weather..they stay in the Sea, and fasten themselves to a sheet of Ice, and so they drive along with the Stream. **1807** Wilkinson in Pike *Sources Mississ.* (1810) II. App. 29 The ice had commenced drifting in large sheets. **1833** Tennyson *Lotos-Eaters* 13 A slumbrous sheet of foam below. **1865** Geikie *Scen. & Geol. Scot.* iv. 78 The interior of that tract of country is covered with one wide sheet of snow and ice. **1867** Augusta Wilson *Vashti* xxvi, The surf was..tossing sheets of foam around the stone piers.

**c.** of vegetation, flowers.

**1791** Burns *Lament Mary Q. Scots* i, Now Nature..spreads her sheets o' daisies white Out o'er the grassy lea. **1857** Hawthorne *Engl. Note-bks.* (1870) II. 316 Broad sheets of ivy here and there mantle the headlong rock. **1859** Tennyson *Guinev.* 387 Sheets of hyacinth That seem'd the heavens upbreaking thro' the earth.

**d.** of sediment, gravel, rock, lava, etc.; *spec.* in *Geol.* and *Metal-mining* (see quots.).

**1815** Scott *Ld. of Isles* iii. xxxii, O'er sheets of granite, dark and broad..lay the road. **1818** —— *Hrt. Midl.* i, A mountain, whose sides were covered with heather and sheets of loose shingle. **1877** Huxley *Physiogr.* 203 Sheets of lava are found in the north-eastern part of Ireland. **1880** D. C. Davies *Metallif. Min.* 421 *Sheet* [Australian], a solid body of pure ore filling a crevice. **1897** *Proc. Soc. Antiq.* 17 June 422 A now denuded gravel sheet which once covered the district. **1898** S. H. Cox *Prospecting for Min.* 113 Cave Deposits..might be subdivided into chambers or pockets, flats or sheets, and pipe veins. **1905** Tarr *New Phys. Geog.* 34 A mass of lava thrust between strata forms an intruded sheet or sill.

**e.** *Anat.* and *Path.* of tissue.

**1872** Humphry *Myology* 30 There are four muscular sheets thus arising placed beneath one another and distinct from each other. **1899** *Allbutt's Syst. Med.* VIII. 504 The new epidermis is thrown off..either in sheets or in scales.

**9. a.** A relatively thin piece of considerable breadth *of* a malleable, ductile, or pliable substance.

**1675** Hannah Woolley *Gentlew. Comp.* 132 Lay the Meat round the Dish, on a sheet of Paste. *a* **1700** Evelyn *Diary* 7 Sept. 1666, Where a sheet of lead covering a great space..was totally mealted. **1796** *Mrs. Glasse's Cookery* viii. 143 Lay a sheet of puff-paste at the bottom of your dish. **1827** Faraday *Chem. Manip.* xiv. (1842) 311 A still higher heat may be gained by fanning the upper part of the fire with a sheet of pasteboard. **1856** H. Chance in *Jrnl. Soc. Arts* IV. 226/2 (Glassmaking), The sheets, when annealed, are drawn from the kiln. **1893** J. A. Hodges *Elem. Photogr.* xv. 100 A sheet of plate glass. **1904** Howitt *Native Tribes S.E. Austr.* viii. 462 A sheet of bark is rolled round him.

**b.** A flat piece of tin, used for baking cakes, etc.

**1747** Mrs. Glasse *Cookery* xv. 140 Flower some Sheets of Tin, and drop your Biskets of what Bigness you please. **1769** Mrs. Raffald *Engl. Housekpr.* (1778) 274 Grease your tin sheets, and drop them [the jumbles] in the shape of a macaroon. **1846** Soyer *Gastron. Regen.* p. xxiii, Baking-sheets of various sizes.

**c.** Rubber prepared in thin pieces.

**1900** Brannt *India Rubber* ii. 103 The manufacture of fine cut sheet was invented by Charles Macintosh. **1912** *Times* 19 Dec. 16/3 Vallambrosa smoked sheet realized 4s. 7¾d. and first latex crepe 4s. 4½d. per lb.

**d.** Sheet iron or steel; a length of this.

**1884** W. H. Greenwood *Steel & Iron* x. 211 It is usual to describe all plates of a thickness below No. 4 B.W.G. (Birmingham Wire Gauge)—·238 inch—as 'sheets'. **1897** *Daily News* 12 Apr. 2/5 Sheets of 24 gauge. **1899** *Ibid.* 23 Jan. 8/6 Galvanised corrugated sheets.

**10.** A more or less extensive piece (of a wall). *rare.* (Cf. F. *pan de mur.*)

**1799** *Hull Advertiser* 21 Sept. 4/1 Every shot knocking down whole sheets of a wall.

**11.** *Geom.* A portion of a surface analogous to the branch of a curve.

**1827** H. P. Hamilton *Anal. Geom.* in *Encycl. Metrop.* (1845) I. 730 The conical surface will be composed of two similar portions, one above, and the other below the vertex; each portion is called a sheet. **1859** Cayley *Math. Papers* (1891) IV. 117 An algebraic cone consists..of a closed sheet or sheets.

**12. a.** *attrib.* and *Comb.*, as ***sheet-cloth, -hem, -leaf, -lettering, -maker, -stealer, -whiteness***; ***sheet-like, -pale, -white*** adjs.

**1547** *Test. Ebor.* (Surtees) VI. 256 A *sheite cloithe of my lynne webbe. **1880** *Plain Hints Needlework* 14 The width of a *sheet hem is very different from that on a pocket-handkerchief. **1641** Brome *Jovial Crew* i. Wks. 1873 III. 354 The foul Fiend took him napping with his nose Betwixt the *sheet-leaves of his conjuring Book. **1867** *Ure's Dict. Arts* III. 1044 An expanding comb guides the even and *sheet-like threads on to the weavers' beam. **1883** Moloney *W. African Fisheries* 19 (Fish. Exhib. Publ.), A loose sheet-like body-covering wrapper. **1906** Hardy *Dynasts* II. iii. v. 225 Sir David Baird, still helpless from his wound, was carried in a cot, *sheet-pale and thin. **1611** Cotgr. s.v., *Adventurier, Vn Adventurier vagabond*,..a hedge-creeper, henne-killer, *sheet-stealer. **1891** M. Muriel Dowie *Girl in Karp.* 270 The closed door of a *sheet-white cottage. **1956** H. Gold *Man who was not with It* xxvii. 250 This..creature who was Pauline's dark daughter; but now ice-whiteness, *sheet-whiteness,..in her still and scared face.

**b.** Special comb.: **sheet band** *Printing* (see quot.); **sheet-calender** (see quot.); **sheet-card**, a kind of card used in cotton manufacture (see quot.); **sheet-cow**, *dial.*, a cow having a broad white band round the body [cf. Sheeted 3]; **sheet-delivery** (see quot.); **sheet erosion**, the erosion of soil by rain-water acting more or less uniformly over a wide area; **sheet-fed** *a. Printing*, using paper in the form of cut sheets; **sheet-filled** *a.*, having the sails filled out by the wind; **sheet-flood**, a short-lived expanse of running water that spreads as a continuous film over a large area following sudden heavy rain; **sheet-flow** *Geomorphol.*, a flow that covers a wide expanse of a surface instead of being confined in a channel; **sheet glass**, (*a*) cylinder glass; also *attrib.*; (*b*) a vessel made of this glass; (*c*) in mod. use, a kind of flat glass made by a vertical drawing process (cf. Fourcault); **sheet ice**, ice formed in a thin, smooth layer on water; **sheet lightning**, lightning in a sheet-like form due to reflection by the clouds; **sheet-pile** (see quot. 1862); hence **sheet-pile** *v. trans.*, to protect with sheet-piles; **sheet-piling**, a continuous wall of sheet-piles; **sheet pointing machine** (see quot.); **Sheetrock**, the proprietary name of a plasterboard made of gypsum between heavy paper (also with small initial); **†sheet-shaking** *Sc.*, remains of meal, etc. shaken from the bottom of a sheet; cf. *poke-shaking* s.v. Poke *sb.*[1] 7; **sheet-wash**, sheet erosion; (erosion caused by) a sheet-flood; **sheet-ways**, in single sheets written only on one side; **sheet-wise**, in the form or manner of sheet-work; **sheet-work** (see quot.).

**1946** V. S. Ganderton in H. Whetton *Pract. Printing & Binding* x. 120/2 Carefully set, the *sheet bands hold the sheet up to the cylinder and help to expel air from between the sheet and the cylinder, and thus minimize buckles. **1884** Knight *Dict. Mech.* Suppl., **Sheet Calender*, a machine for pressing paper, rubber, etc., into sheets and giving it surface. **1825** J. Nicholson *Oper. Mech.* 380 Cards are formed in two ways; the one called *sheet-card, is made about four inches wide, and 18 inches long, or of a length corresponding with the width of the main cylinder, which they have to cover; the other, called fillet-card. **1772** in *Mrs. Delany's Autobiogr.* Ser. ii. I. 476 This comes hoping that the *sheet cow will come walking..into the charming domaines of Bulstrode on Wensday next. **1884** Knight *Dict. Mech.* Suppl., **Sheet Delivery*, delivering the printed sheet from the form to the fly. **1917** Mosier & Gustafson *Soil Physics & Management* xxvii. 361 *Sheet erosion is the source of far greater loss than gullying. **1978** W. W. Emmett in M. J. Kirkby *Hillside Hydrol.* v. 171 Rilling is generally considered to be evidence of more accelerated erosion than sheet erosion. **1926** *Sheet-fed [see Rotary *a.* 2 b]. **1973** W. H. Hallahan *Ross Forgery* iv. 52 The paper salesman..sold these people paper in sheets for sheet-fed presses. **1652** Benlowes *Theophila* ix. xxxix, The Poet's Pharos be that sets forth sail, While he steers *sheet-fill'd with a holy gale. **1897** W. J. McGee in *Bull. Geol. Soc. Amer.* VIII. 88 Colloquially a moving water-body of this type is sometimes known as a 'wash'; but since the term is commonly applied primarily to the product and only secondarily to the agency, and since it is usually restricted to limited, though broad channels.., it seems desirable to use some other designation for the water-body; and the term **sheetflood* has come into use in notes and in conversation. **1938** *Bull. Geol. Soc. Amer.* XLIX. 1344 One of the most striking peculiarities of sheetfloods is the shortness of their flow in distance as well as in time. **1977** A. Hallam *Planet Earth* 49 After storms, flow is in the form of sheet-floods, comparatively shallow floods running over a broad area. **1928** *Bull. Geol. Soc. Amer.* XXXIX. 481 The deposit was obviously not a *sheet-flow; it was a stream [of detrital material] of unknown length. **1977** A. Hallam *Planet Earth* 85/2 This leads to preferential weathering at the break in slope, the weathering products being removed by sheetflow, wind and other processes. **1805** *Act 45 Geo. III*, c. 30 Sched., All other Window Glass..commonly called..by the Name of Crown Glass, or German *Sheet Glass. **1846** MacCulloch *Acc. Brit. Empire* (1854) I. 745 Sheet glass furnaces. **1887** *Month* LXI. 162 The reliquary, consisting of two round sheet glasses. **1974** *Encycl. Brit. Macropædia* VIII. 202/1 Sheet glass of admirable flatness for many common purposes, unmarred by glass-to-metal contact, is produced by the continuous vertical draw process. *c* **1900** in *Regional Lang.*

*Stud.—Newfoundland* (1978) VIII. 24 **Sheet ice*, thin ice of one or two nights frost. **1964** H. H. SMITH *Shelter Bay* 123 But even thin ice—what we call sheet ice, could cause us plenty of trouble. **1794** J. B. S. MORRITT *Let.* 24 June (1914) iii. 50 We have beautiful *sheet lightning every evening, and have had for above a week. **1829** *Chapters Phys. Sci.* 472 Lightning of this sort, denominated sheet lightning, is mostly to be seen in the hot sultry evenings of summer or autumn, and is generally unaccompanied with thunder. **1864** TENNYSON *Aylmer's F.* 726 When it seem'd he saw No pale sheet-lightnings from afar, but fork'd Of the near storm. **1841** BREES *Gloss. Civ. Engin.* s.v. *Foundation*, To drive a row of *sheet [*printed* sheep] piles next the foundations of walls adjoining the sea, or rivers. **1862** RANKINE *Man. Civ. Engin.* §404. 605 Sheet Piles are flat piles, which, being driven successively edge to edge, form a vertical or nearly vertical sheet, for the purpose of preventing the materials of a foundation from spreading. **1842** *Civil Engin. & Arch. Jrnl.* V. 58/2 *Sheet-pile it a short space from the wall of the hole. **1789** W. JESSOP *Rep. Thames & Isis* (1791) 23 With some short *sheet piling underneath it at the foot. **1837** *Civil Engin. & Arch. Jrnl.* I. 12/2 The foot of the river wall will be protected by sheet piling of whole timbers 8 feet long. **1884** KNIGHT *Dict. Mech.* Suppl., **Sheet Pointing Machine*, a machine for preparing printing sheets for cutting. **1921** *Official Gaz.* (U.S. Patent Office) 29 Nov. 1065/2 **Sheetrock*.. Plaster Wall-Board. Claims use since Aug. 28, 1917. U.S. Gypsum Co., Chicago. **1924** *Trade Marks Jrnl.* 5 Nov. 2475 *Sheetrock*... Plaster in sheets, for use as wall boards in building or decoration. U.S. Gypsum Co..., Chicago. **1973** R. B. PARKER *Godwulf Manuscript* (1974) ix. 71 It was a tiny office... No windows, sheetrock partitions painted green. **1543** *Extr. Aberd. Reg.* (1844) I. 191 The vittell byaris of the merkat scattis thame grytlie in taking of sampillis, *scheytschakkingis, and sic oder ewill vsit custum. **1561** *Ibid.* 335 Nor na skaiffry, sic as sampill and scheit schakin, to be tane thairof. **1936** FINCH & TREWARTHA *Elem. Geogr.* xxv. 559 One of the most widespread and least noticed kinds of erosion on tilled land is *sheet wash. **1939** *Geogr. Jrnl.* XCIII. 305 If Tibu accounts of the nature of the rainfall are even partially credited, some form of sheet-wash can readily be imagined covering the whole floor of even a broad wadi, and undercutting its sides. **1964** A. HOLMES *Princ. Physical Geol.* (ed. 2) xx. 613 A sudden change of slope seems to be favoured by torrential seasonal rainfalls and by the liberation of only minute amounts of fine debris which can be readily swept away by sheet-wash over the pediment. **1972** J. G. CRUICKSHANK *Soil Geogr.* ii. 39 Fluvial erosion by rivers or sheet wash is the most important present form of transportation of material. **1752** J. LOUTHIAN *Form of Process* (ed. 2) 262 That each Sheet of an Extract, written *Sheet-ways, consist of forty nine Lines,..and, if wrote Book-ways, that it consist of two Pages, and of thirty six Lines in each Page. **1888** JACOBI *Printers Vocab.*, **Sheet work*, applied to works or jobs printed both sides—the reverse of half-sheet or 'work and turn'.

**13.** quasi-*adj.* **a.** Rolled out in a sheet; esp. of metals, as ***sheet iron*** (also freq. attrib.), ***lead, metal, steel.***

**1582** in Feuillerat *Revels Q. Eliz.* (1908) 358 Sheete lead to make A spowte. **1633** T. JAMES *Voy.* 75 The Carpenters-sheet-lead. **1683** MOXON *Mech. Exerc., Printing* xi. ¶21 The Lye-Trough..is Leaded with Sheet-Lead. **1816** J. SMITH *Panorama Sci. & Art* I. 11 Bell-springs are rarely made of any thing else than sheet iron thus managed. **1827** FARADAY *Chem. Manip.* vii. (1842) 209 Sheet caoutchouc, which is about the tenth or twelfth of an inch thick. *Ibid.* iv. 132 A piece of sheet copper. *Ibid.* xxiii. 584 Plates of sheet zinc are often required for the precipitation of metals. **1840** *Civil Engin. & Arch. Jrnl.* III. 290/2 A thin plate of sheet brass. **1842** LOUDON *Suburban Hort.* 323 There are three sizes of the sheet-iron hand-barrow. **1869** MRS. WHITNEY *We Girls* vi, We..sent for the sheet-iron men, and had the stove taken up-stairs. **1869** R. MURRAY *Mar. Engines* 35 Sheet-flue Boilers. **1876** PREECE & SIVEWRIGHT *Telegraphy* 239 The piece of sheet percha that is held in the hand. **1888** RUTLEY *Rock-Forming Min.* 9 A Bunsen's burner..provided with a small chimney of sheet-iron. **1933** *Rep. & Mem. Aeronaut. Res. Comm.* No. 1553. 18 Constructions in thin sheet metal (*e.g.* monocoque fuselage) normally consist of a large area of sheet divided into a number of small panels by a system of stiffeners. **1959** *Motor Man.* (ed. 36) i. 3 The sheet metal forming the front wings and the sides of the bonnet. **1976** LIEBERMAN & RHODES *Compl. CB Handbk.* v. 97 It is fastened securely by two sheet-metal screws that actually screw into the rain-gutter groove of the trunk.

**b.** Hence, pertaining to the manufacture of sheet iron or steel, as ***sheet-mill.*** Also in objective comb., as ***sheet-maker, -worker.***

**1884** W. H. GREENWOOD *Steel & Iron* xvi. 334 The sheet mills of Birmingham and of South Wales. **1885** *Daily News* 5 Oct. 2/5 Certain of the sheet makers are declining to accept further orders... Orders in the sheet trade are very irregularly distributed. **1886** *Ibid.* 20 Sept. 2/5 Sheet prices are without change. **1892** *Labour Comm.* Gloss., *Sheet Makers*, manufacturers who work *sheet mills*, as distinguished from plates and strip mills.

**c.** Of water, etc.: Spread out in a sheet.

**1896** *Idler* Mar. 175/1 At this time it was a sheet-calm. A floating soup-plate would not have filled. **1899** W. M. DAVIS *Phys. Geog.* 314 The water finds no channels; it spreads out in a shallow sheet, called a sheetflood, which gains a breadth of a mile or more, but a depth of only one or two feet. **1904** *Mission Field* June 436 The land is sub-irrigated by what is called 'sheetwater'.

**d.** = Printed on a single sheet or broadside (see sense 5), esp. ***sheet-almanac.*** **sheet music**, music published in sheet form (as opp. to book form).

**1683** in *Lett. Lit. Men* (Camden) 187, I writ to your Lordship for a dozen of your sheet Almanacks for this yeer. **1767** *Ann. Reg., Hist. Europe* 83 There has been lately published a sheet list of changes, said to have happened during the present reign. **1768** TUCKER *Lt. Nat.* (1834) I. 129 She examines the sheet almanack pasted up behind the door, to see what holiday it might be. **1857** *Lawrence* (Kansas) *Republican* 11 June 3 (Advt.), City drug store... Periodicals, lithographs, sheet music, etc. **1881** CROWEST *Phases Mus. Eng.* 146 The pricing of Songs and of Sheet-music generally. **1901** D. B. HALL & LD. A. OSBORNE *Sunshine & Surf* ii. 17 We had a big sheet almanac hanging at one end of the cabin. **1929** J. B. PRIESTLEY *Good Companions* III. iii. 534 Performing rights, sheet music, gramophone records. **1981** J. WAINWRIGHT *Urge for Justice* I. xii. 84 The window of the shop was crammed with sheet music.

**sheet** (ʃiːt), *sb.*[2] Forms: 1 scéata, 4 chete, 4–6 s(c)hete, 5 shet, 6 shit, *Sc.* scheit, 6–7 sheate, 6–8 sheat, 7– sheet. [OE. *scéata* wk. masc., having the meanings of OE. *scéat* (see SHEET *sb.*[1]), also = lower corner of a sail, 'pes veli'; in comb. *scéatlíne* 'propes' (see Wr.-Wülcker 183/26 and 288/24) = MLG. *schôtlîne*, in which sense the simple word is recorded from the 14th c. For the cognate forms and their meanings see SHEET *sb.*[1]; cf. SHOOT *sb.*[2]]

**1.** A rope (or chain) attached to either of the lower corners of a square sail (or the after lower corner of a fore-and-aft sail), and used to extend the sail or to alter its direction. ***false sheet***: see quot. 1644 in sense 4.

See also FORE-SHEET 1, *jib-sheet* (JIB *sb.*[1] 3), MAIN-SHEET 1.

**1336** *Acc. Exch. K.R.* 19/31 m. 4 In xxx. petris cordis de canabo..produobus schetes inde faciendis. **1352** *Excheq. Acc. Q.R.* 20 no. 27 (P.R.O.) Pro ij. cables novis, ij. chetis, j. hauser et quodam bowelyne. **1373** in Riley *Mem. Lond.* (1868) 370 [One sail with] 2 shettes, 2 thurghwalis. *c* **1460** *Pilgrim's Sea-Voy.* 25 Hale the bowelyne! now, vere the shete! **1486** *Naval Acc. Hen. VII* (1896) 13 A payre of takkes & a payr of shets weying dccxlj lb. **1522** *Lett. & Papers Hen. VIII*, III. II. 975 Vyere the shit. **1549** *Compl. Scotl.* vi. 40 Hail eftir the foir sail scheit. **1626** CAPT. SMITH *Accid. Yng. Seamen* 15 The boulespret hath no bow lines, and the misen sheats, are called the starne sheats. **1627** —— *Seaman's Gram.* v. 23 The Sheats..in top sailes..serue to hale them home, that is, to bring the clew close to the yards arme. *a* **1658** CLEVELAND *Wks.* (1687) 293 Vere, vere, more Sheet. **1722** DIAPER tr. *Oppian's Halieut.* I. 367 Let fly the Sheets. **1796** P. HOARE *Song, The Arethusa* 18 Not a sheet, or a Tack, Or a brace did she slack. **1805** E. BERRY 13 Oct. in Nicolas *Disp.* (1846) VII. 118 *note*, The main-top-gallant sheet was carried away. I then let fly the top gallant sheets. **1887** G. B. GOODE, etc. *Fisheries U.S.* v. II. 571 Enough 'sheet' to allow a slow headway. **1891** C. H. PATTERSON *Naut. Dict.* 160 With boom sails sheets are used for controlling the boom.

**b.** † ***betwixt a pair of sheets*** or ***both sheets aft***: said of a ship sailing right before the wind.

**1627** CAPT. SMITH *Seaman's Gram.* ix. 39 A flowne sheat is when shee goes before the wind, or betwixt a paire of sheats, or all sailes drawing. *Ibid.* 42 Well Master the Channell is broad enough; Yet you cannot steare betwixt a paire of sheats; Those are words of mockery betwixt the Cunner and the Stearesman. **1632** LITHGOW *Trav.* VII. 328 Each bulging sayle..begins to swell, betweene two sheetes. **1769** FALCONER *Dict. Marine* (1780), *Both sheets aft* (*entre deux écoutes*, Fr.), the situation of a ship that sails right afore the wind.

**2.** ***three sheets in the wind***: very drunk.

***a sheet in the wind*** (or ***wind's eye***) is used occas. = half drunk.

**1821** EGAN *Real Life* I. xviii. 385 Old Wax and Bristles is about three sheets in the wind. **1840** R. H. DANA *Bef. Mast* xx, He..seldom went up to the town without coming down 'three sheets in the wind'. **1862** TROLLOPE *Orley F.* lvii, A thought tipsy—a sheet or so in the wind, as folks say. **1883** STEVENSON *Treas. Isl.* xx, Maybe you think we were all a sheet in the wind's eye.

**3.** See quots. and FORE-SHEET 2, STERN-SHEET.

**1644** MANWAYRING *Seaman's Dict.* 92 Those plancks under water, which come along the Run of the ship, and are closed to the Sterne-post, are called Sheates, and that part within boord, abaft, in the Run of the ship, is called the sterne-sheates. **1857** P. COLQUHOUN *Comp. Oarsman's Guide* 29 The flooring abaft the stateroom [sitter's seat] is called the *after-sheet*, the forward one the *forward-sheet*, and the next to it (if there be two forward), the *waist-sheet*. *Ibid.* 31 Sheets are the boards used fore and aft, as a floor to the boat, in the same way as the burthens amidships. **1891** C. H. PATTERSON *Naut. Dict.* 160 *Sheets*, the spaces in a rowing boat forward and abaft the thwarts, and named respectively *fore-sheets* and *stern-sheets*. **1898** A. ANSTED *Dict. Sea Terms* s.v., *Head-sheets*, *stern-sheets* (in open boats), the floor-boards covering the space either at the head or the stern of the boat.

**4.** *attrib.*, as ***sheet-bend*** (BEND *sb.*[1] 3), ***-bitt, -block*** (BLOCK *sb.* 5), ***-clip, -pendant*** (PENDANT *sb.* 7), ***-pennant*** (PENNANT[1] 1), ***-rope, -slip*** (see SLIP *sb.*[3] 3 e), ***-stopper***: see quots.

**1841** R. H. DANA *Seaman's Man.* 56 Take your tack under the yard and bend it by a *sheet-bend to the outer clew. **1867** SMYTH *Sailor's Word-bk.*, *Sheet-bend*, a sort of double hitch, made by passing the end of one rope through the bight of another, round both parts of the other, and under its own part. **1891** C. H. PATTERSON *Naut. Dict.* 160 **Sheet Bitts*, bitts near the mast to which the topsail sheets are belayed. **1644** MANWAYRING *Seaman's Dict.* 92 We use to bind an other roape to the clew of the saile above the *Sheate-block, to succour and ease the Sheate, and that roape we call a false Sheate. **1794** *Rigging & Seamanship* I. 225 Sheet-block straps in the lift with a splice. **1841** R. H. DANA *Seaman's Man.* ix. 47 In which case the heavy tack and sheet-blocks may be unhooked. **1898** A. ANSTED *Dict. Sea Terms*, **Sheet clip* (or **sheet slip*), an instrument, the principal agent in which is a sort of drop pawl, by which sheets may be held, while necessary, and instantly released. **1908** *Paasch's Dict. Naval Terms* 422 **Sheet-pendant*, a strong piece of rope attached by one end to the clew of a stay-sail or jib. **1841** R. H. DANA *Seaman's Man.* ix. 53 Having the *sheet pennant hauled amidships. *a* **1642** SUCKLING *Lett.* (1646) 89 Which, like the pulling of a *sheat-rope at Sea, slackens the sail. **1794** *Rigging & Seamanship* I. 226 Sheet-rope splices into the clue of the sail. *Ibid.* 176 Fore-tack, and *Sheet, Stoppers, are for securing the tacks and sheets, till belayed.

**sheet** (ʃiːt), *v.*[1] [f. SHEET *sb.*[1]]

**1.** *trans.* To wrap or fold in or as in a sheet (*lit.* and *fig.*); now *spec.* to cover with a protecting sheet of canvas, tarpaulin, etc.

**1621** T. WILLIAMSON tr. *Goulart's Wise Vieillard* 163 You haue in sleepe the image of death, wherein you are sheeted and wrapped vp euery night. **1835** J. P. KENNEDY *Horse-Shoe Robinson* iv, The pale moon that now sheeted with its light her whole figure. **1837** CARLYLE *Fr. Rev.* II. I. xii, Trees there are all sheeted with variegated fire. *Ibid.* III. IV. i, A fair young creature, sheeted in red smock of Murderess. **1857** *Househ. Words* 27 June 605/2 The truck being now sheeted and ticketted. **1860** WHYTE MELVILLE *Mkt. Harb.* iii, [A racehorse] Clothed and hooded, littered to the hocks, and sheeted to the tail.

**2. a.** To spread a sheet or layer of some substance upon (a surface); to cover with a sheet (e.g. of snow or ice). (Also with *down, up.*)

**1606** SHAKS. *Ant. & Cl.* I. iv. 65 When Snow the Pasture sheets. **1807** J. BARLOW *Columb.* III. 368 The sky-borne waters..Veil the dark deep and sheet the mountain's side. **1863** W. LANCASTER *Praeterita* 85 The amber daffodils, Sheeting the floors of April. **1882** STEVENSON *New Arab. Nts.* II. 106 The flakes were large... The whole city was sheeted up. **1888** —— *Black Arrow* IV. i, The snow was falling,..the whole world was blotted out and sheeted down below that silent inundation. **1912** MASEFIELD *Dauber* V. xli, Is it cold? We're sheeted up, I tell you, inches thick.

**b.** Const. *with* (the substance of which the layer consists).

**1801** MOLLARD *Art of Cookery* (1836) 168 Sheet a mould with paste. **1837** W. IRVING *Capt. Bonneville* II. 218 The river was sheeted with ice. **1845** M. PATTISON *Ess.* (1889) I. 17 Its roof was sheeted, like St. Peter's, with copper. **1893** *Times* 14 July 3/1 The country is green as a meadow and sheeted with flowers.

†**3.** To furnish (a bed) with sheets; usually *pass. Obs.*

**1714** MRS. MANLEY *Adv. Rivella* 119 A Bed nicely sheeted and strow'd with Roses. **1760–72** H. BROOKE *Fool of Qual.* (1809) III. 5 A bed ready sheeted and warmed. **1820** in Southey *Wesley* I. 457 One of the maids, who went up to sheet a bed.

†**4.** *pass.* and *intr.* To bed *with. Obs.*

**1637** WHITING *Albino & Bellama* 72 To be sheeted by Bellama's side. *Ibid.* 90 To sheet with maidens.

**5.** *intr.* To spread or flow in a sheet. Also of rain: to fall in a sheet or sheets (sense 7 b). Freq. with *down.*

**1847** LE FANU *T. O'Brien* 324 High sheets the water round him in glittering spray. **1871** G. MACDONALD *Wks. of Fancy* II. 203 Cataracts sheet..through the air. **1971** D. BEATY *Temple Tree* 9 The monsoon rain was still sheeting down. **1978** *Detroit Free Press* 16 Apr. 2B/1 Bumping over the high noon thunderheads, with rain sheeting across the little round windows, the air passenger over the South Pacific grips the seat arms.

**6.** *trans.* ***to sheet up*** (see quot.).

**1883** R. HALDANE in *Workshop Receipts* Ser. II. 141/1 To Sheet-up.—To rub dry with sheets.

**sheet** (ʃiːt), *v.*[2] [f. SHEET *sb.*[2]] *trans.* ***to sheet home***: to extend the sheets of (the topsails) to the outer extremities of the yards so that the clews are close to the sheet-blocks. Also *absol.* (and in extended sense, see quot. 1867).

**1797** S. JAMES *Narr. Voy.* 227 They sheeted home the topsails. **1833** M. SCOTT *Tom Cringle* xi. (1859) 265 The topsails were let fall and sheeted home. **1837** E. HOWARD *Old Commodore* iv, Let us shake out our reefs, sheet home, and away. **1867** SMYTH *Sailor's Word-bk.*, *Sheet home!*.. Also, when driving anything home, as a blow, &c. **1890** MORRIS *Glitt. Plain* xix, He stepped the mast and hoisted sail, and sheeted home.

Hence **'sheeted** *ppl. a.*

**1821** JOANNA BAILLIE *Metr. Leg.*, *Wallace* xliii, As sheeted sails, torn by the blast, Flap round some vessel's rocking mast.

**sheet**: see SHEATH, SHOOT *v.*, SHUT.

**sheet-anchor** ('ʃiːt,æŋkə(r)). Forms: α. 5 shut(t)e, 6 shut, showte, shoute, shote, 6–7 shoot(e, shot, 7 shott. β. 7 sheath, shed, 7 sheate, 7–8 sheat, 9– sheet. [Origin uncertain.

Perhaps f. ME. *shote*, SHOT *sb.*[2] = cable of two ropes spliced together, but the difference of form (*shott* and *shute*) in quot. 1497 makes this doubtful. The α-forms are parallel with those of SHOOT *sb.*[2], and the substitution of forms of the synonymous SHEET *sb.*[2] in the 17th c. points to association with that word, but the connexion in sense is not obvious.

With regard to the generally accepted derivation from SHOOT *v.* ('an anchor that is shot out'), the formation would be abnormal, it is not supported by the majority of the α-forms, nor is it clear why any anchor in particular should be so designated.]

A large anchor, formerly always the largest of a ship's anchors, used only in an emergency.

α. **1495** *Naval Acc. Hen. VII* (1896) 192 Ankers called Shutte. **1497** *Ibid.* 184 For a Newe Shott of Cables..to the use of the seid Ship for the Shute ankers. **1514** in Oppenheim *Admin. Royal Navy* (1896) I. 378 Ankers called ..Shot ankers j, Caggers j. **1536** *Rem. Sedition* iij, He castethe the shote anker, when he wyll, and not when they bydde hym, that are in his shyp. **1586** J. DAVIS in Hakluyt *Voy.* (1589) 786 The cable of our shut anker brake. **1633** T. JAMES *Voy.* 38 Our shoote-Anker was downe.

β. **1626** CAPT. SMITH *Accid. Yng. Seamen* 16 The greatest in euery ship is called the sheat Anchor. *a* **1647** PETTE in *Archæologia* XII. 275 We broke our best bower, and were forced to let go our sheet anchor. **1690** C. NESSE *Hist. & Myst. O. & N. Test.* I. 292 His shed-anchor to hold fast his floating ship. **1719** DE FOE *Crusoe* I. 10 Our Master order'd out the Sheet Anchor. **1775** *Phil. Trans.* LXVIII. 404 At 4 A.M. found ship drove, veered to a whole cable;..and got sheet anchor overside. **1867** SMYTH *Sailor's Word-bk.* s.v., To a sheet anchor a stout hempen cable is generally bent. **1889** *Daily News* 6 Aug. 5/7 The Howe..went gradually to leeward until she brought herself up with her sheet anchor.

**b.** *fig.* That on which one places one's reliance when everything else has failed.

α. **1524** *St. Papers Hen. VIII* (1836) IV. 228 The next Parlament, which in maner shalbe the shoote anker for thexpedicion of our purpoos. **1532** MORE *Confut. Tindale* Wks. 498/1 Ye shall se what aunswere he maketh, & what he bringeth for the shote ancre of al his shifte. *a* **1553** UDALL *Royster D.* I. i. (Arb.) 11 Of all men he is my chiefe banker Both for meate and money, and my chiefe shoot-anker. **1562** TURNER *Of Bathes* 15 Then shall it be high tyme to go to the bathes as to the shot ancre. **1616** CHAMPNEY *Voc. Bps.* 252 M. Mason cometh now to cast his shott anker, and saith. *a* **1641** BP. MOUNTAGU *Acts & Mon.* (1642) 62 Wherein yet Christ is the Shoot-anker of salvation.

β. **1658** GURNALL *Chr. in Arm.* verse 14. xviii. §2 Casting out his sheat anchour [*ed.* **1669** sheath-anchor] of hope. **1676** MOLLOY *De Jure Marit.* III. vii. (1688) 416 It is Foreign Trade that is the main Sheet-Anchor of us Islanders. **1775** MME. D'ARBLAY *Early Diary* 8 May, The great sheet-anchor, upon which we are to depend in our voyage through life. **1838** LYTTON *Alice* v. ii, The landed interest..is the great stay of this country—the sheet-anchor I may say. **1870** MISS BRIDGMAN *Robt. Lynne* II. iv. 88 Bertie was..the sheet-anchor of her life. **1899** *Allbutt's Syst. Med.* VII. 821 Bleeding is our 'sheet anchor' in this disease.

*attrib.* **1861** HUGHES *Tom Brown at Oxf.* xxxv, As soon as he had his old sheet-anchor friend to hold on to.

**sheet-cable.** *Naut.* [f. *sheet-* in SHEET-ANCHOR.] The cable belonging to the sheet-anchor.

**1611** COTGR. s.v. *Maistre, Vn maistre cable, ou chable,* a sheat-cable. **1642** H. BOND *Boat Swain's Art* 18 Your sheat Cable is commonly so many halfe inches about as your ship is bredth in feete at the midship Beame. **1742** in Hanway *Trav.* (1762) I. II. xxiii. 100 Cutting the sheet cable at the windlass, with great difficulty we wore the ship. **1800** *Asiat. Ann. Reg.* III. 115/2 The sheet cable parted about half after four o'clock.

**sheeted** (ˈʃiːtɪd), *ppl. a.* [f. SHEET *sb.*[1] or *v.*[1]]

**1. a.** Wrapped in a sheet, *esp.* a winding-sheet: applied to the dead and ghosts.

**1604** SHAKS. *Ham.* I. i. 115 (Qo. 2) The sheeted dead Did squeake and gibber in the Roman streets. **1630** H. LORD *Relig. Persees* 50 Shrowded and sheeted carkeyses. **1786** S. ROGERS *Ode Superst.* I. ii. 9 The sheeted spectre, rising from the tomb. **1807–8** W. IRVING *Salmag.* (1824) 88 Church-yard tales of sheeted ghosts. **1876** GEO. ELIOT *Dan. Der.* lv, He saw Gwendolen..pale as one of the sheeted dead.

**b.** Enveloped in a sheet or sheets for protection against injury, cold, etc.

**1766** W. GORDON *Gen. Counting-ho.* 104, 1 sheeted box containing books. **1840** HALIBURTON *Letter Bag* i. 7 Sheeted, blanketed, and quilted, I remain enveloped in the drapery of my bed. **1884** *Longman's Mag.* Apr. 610 A string of some thirty sheeted horses are walking round and round. **1896** *Idler* Mar. 277 The paltry gas-jets on the stage..were just sufficient to show the sheeted boxes and a few of the front rows of stalls.

**2.** In the form of a sheet; expanded or spread out like a sheet: chiefly of rain, snow, lightning.

**1796** *New Ann. Reg.* 164 Thro' plashy glade Where crackles, at each step, the sheeted ice. **1798** COLERIDGE *Wand. Cain* Wks. (1907) 345 The sheeted lightning. **1811** SCOTT *Don Roderick* II. xxxvi, Then sheeted rain burst down. **1847** LONGF. *Evang.* I. v. 100 The sheeted smoke with flashes of flame intermingled. **1851** HT. MARTINEAU *Introd. Hist. Peace* II. i, The two armies lay down amidst the sheeted snow. **1904** R. BRIDGES *Demeter* 551 The useless poppy in sheeted scarlet.

**3.** Of cattle: Having a broad band of white round the body. (Cf. *sheet-cow,* SHEET *sb.*[1] 12 b.)

**1834** YOUATT *Cattle* (L.U.K.) 28 They are called *sheeted* oxen. The head, the neck, the shoulders, and the hind parts appear as if they were uncovered, while there is a sheet fairly and perfectly thrown over the barrel. **1855** KINGSLEY *Westw. Ho!* v, That sheeted heifer of Prowse's. **1858** *Jrnl. R. Agric. Soc.* XIX. II. 389 In colour usually 'sheeted' black and white.

**4.** *Printing.* (See quot.)

**1888** JACOBI *Printers' Vocab.*, *Sheeted,* this expression is used when heavily printed work has to be placed sheet by sheet between other sheets to prevent off-set of ink.

**5.** *Geol.* Of rock (esp. granite) or a rock formation: having been divided into thin laminæ; *sheeted zone,* a belt of highly fissured rock associated with a fault, the fissures freq. being occupied by veins of minerals.

**1903** *Bull. U.S. Geol. Survey* No. 213. 99 The granite is sheeted near the veins, the planes of sheeting being parallel to the veins themselves. **1905** H. RIES *Econ. Geol.* xvii. 339 (*caption*) Ore along sheeted zone. *Ibid.* 340 Composite veins in sheeted basalt dikes. **1939** W. H. EMMONS et al. *Geol.* (ed. 2) xvii. 425 Some veins fill single openings..others fill closely spaced parallel openings, which are sheeted zones. **1943** *Jrnl. Geol.* LI. 82/1 During the glacial epoch these sheeted granites..must have been easily plucked and quarried by the advancing ice. **1974** *Nature* 29 Nov. 375/2 Shattered pebbles and sheeted bedrock are common weathering phenomena in most modern deserts.

†ˈ**sheeten,** *a. Obs.*[−1] [f. SHEET *sb.*[1] + -EN[4].] Consisting of a sheet (see SHEET *sb.*[1] 1 b).

*a* **1618** J. DAVIES *Scourge Paper-persec.* (1624) 11 If..wanton Rig, or letcher dissolute Doe stand at Pauls-Crosse in a Sheeten Sute.

ˈ**sheeter.** [f. SHEET *v.*[1] + -ER[1].] (See quot.)

**1853** URE *Dict. Arts* II. 985 The machine for forming the wool into sheets of a nearly uniform thickness, technically known as the 'sheeter'.

**sheeter,** obs. form of SHOOTER.

**sheet-fish,** variant of SHEAT-FISH.

**sheetful** (ˈʃiːtfʊl). [f. SHEET *sb.*[1] + -FUL.] As much as a sheet will contain.

**1523–34** FITZHERB. *Husb.* §44 Take a shete ful of brome croppes. **1711** ADDISON *Spect.* No. 1 ¶7, I shall publish a Sheet-full of Thoughts every Morning. **1812** *Examiner* 31 Aug. 545/2 A second writes a long uneasy sheet-full of irony. **1825** J. T. COLERIDGE in Ld. Coleridge *Story Devonsh. House* (1906) 287 An hour's talk would be of more help to him than a sheetful of writing.

**sheeth(e,** obs. forms of SHEATH *sb.*

**sheeting** (ˈʃiːtɪŋ), *vbl. sb.* [f. SHEET *sb.*[1] + -ING[1].]

**1.** Stout cloth of linen or cotton, such as is used for bed linen, etc.

**1711** *Lond. Gaz.* No. 4847/3 Irish Sheeting and Ticking. **1796** *Mrs. Glasse's Cookery* xviii. 291 Roll it up tight, bind it round with sheeting, and boil it four hours. **1844** *Ladies' Hand-bk. Haberdashery* 26 Sheeting. This is a strong woven cotton, and is frequently used as a substitute for linen. **1848** KINGSLEY '*Bad Squire*' xv, By dealing out flannel and sheeting A little below cost price. **1853** URE *Dict. Arts* I. 770 Sheetings and towellings. **1877** J. W. HAYES *Draper & Haberdasher* (ed. 4) 96 Sheetings are a stout article, made in Wigans, Croydons, and Double Warps from two or three yards wide. **1910** *Encycl. Brit.* VII. 277/1 *Sheeting* has two meanings in the cotton trade: (1) the ordinary bed sheeting, usually a stout cloth of anything from 45 in. to 120 in. wide ..; (2) a grey calico, heavier than a shirting..usually 36 in. by 40 yd.

**2. a.** A lining or covering of timber or metal, laid on a surface as a protection.

**1776** G. SEMPLE *Building in Water* 32 The sheeting nailed on the Piles. **1870** *Milit. Engin.* I. II. 101 The wooden linings are of two descriptions, viz., cases, or frames and sheeting.

**b.** A layer (of soil or stones).

**1891** *Scott. Leader* 6 Nov., Laying down sheetings of stones in certain districts. **1895** *Outing* XXVII. 236/2 Rocks, which, having lost their thin sheeting of soil.

**c.** A form of batting (Knight *Dict. Mech.*). (See BATTING *vbl. sb.* 2.)

**3.** The action or process of making (lead) into sheets; the action of covering with sheets or laying in sheets.

**1778** *Engl. Gazetteer* s.v. *Mendip,* The lead is..not so proper for sheeting, because, when melted, it runs into knots. **1875** KNIGHT *Dict. Mech., Sheeting,* (*Tobacco*), laying the leaves flat to be piled in books. **1884** *Manch. Exam.* 31 May, 5/1 Clerkage, checking, and weighing, as well as sheeting.

**4.** *Geol.* The occurrence or development of closely spaced, approximately parallel fractures or joints in rock. Freq. *attrib.*

**1899** *Trans. Inst. Mining & Metallurgy* VIII. 67 The multiple fracturing, parallel to the walls of the dyke, is a characteristic feature of such lodes... This feature can be described as a sheeting of the rock. **1903** [see SHEETED *ppl. a.* 5]. **1912** E. C. ECKEL *Building Stones & Clays* iii. 39 Geologists..ascribe some or all sheeting structure to strains induced during the original cooling of the mass, or to the effects of later external stresses. **1934** O. BOWLES *Stone Industries* viii. 108 Widely separated sheeting planes occur at a depth of 250 feet at Quincy, Mass. **1965** A. HOLMES *Princ. Physical Geol.* (ed. 2) ix. 217 The sheeting or sheet structure that is often seen in exposures of granitic and other plutonic intrusions.

**5.** *attrib.*, as (sense 2) ***sheeting deal, plank***; **sheeting-machine** (see quots.); **sheeting-pile** = *sheet-pile* (see SHEET *sb.*[1] 13).

**1837** J. T. SMITH tr. *Vicat's Mortars* 77 *note,* The space on which the foundation is to rest, is first surrounded by sheeting piles. **1838** *Civil Engin. & Arch. Jrnl.* I. 203/1 The 'sheeting' planks, or (in Lancashire phrase) the 'lagging'. **1839** URE *Dict. Arts* 972 This sheeting deal is always applied in pieces laid endwise. **1875** KNIGHT *Dict. Mech., Sheeting-machine,* a wool-combing machine for bringing the fiber into an even sheet. *Ibid., Sheeting-machine,* a machine for smoothing tobacco-leaves.

ˈ**sheeting,** *ppl. a.* [f. SHEET *v.*[1] + -ING[2].] Swathing, enfolding.

**1592** *Arden of Feversham* 1081 Sheeting darkness over-hangs the earth.

ˈ**sheetless,** *a.* [f. SHEET *sb.*[1]] Without sheets.

**1756** *Demi-Rep* 26 Where stand the sheetless bed, the broken chair.

**sheetlet** (ˈʃiːtlɪt). [f. SHEET *sb.*[1] + -LET.] A small sheet; *spec.* in *Philately* (cf. SHEET *sb.*[1] 5 d).

**1934** in WEBSTER. **1971** D. POTTER *Brit. Eliz. Stamps* xi. 123 Three separate editions, 2s, 4s and 6s, contained sheetlets of one stamp. **1978** *Sunday Telegraph* (Colour Suppl.) 29 Jan. 39 (Advt.), A beautifully designed pack containing the unique series of stamps (in sheetlets) to be issued by the Crown Agents.

ˈ**sheetling.** *rare.* [SHEET *sb.*[1]] A little sheet.

**1817** W. WILBERFORCE in *Life* (1838) IV. 310 You would have received a good long letter instead of this sheetling.

**sheet-shot.** *Naut.* [f. *sheet-* in SHEET-ANCHOR + SHOT *sb.*] = SHEET-CABLE. Also *attrib.*

**1750** BLANCKLEY *Naval Expos.* s.v. *Cables,* Cables Allowed for Channel Service, are distributed in this Manner, two being spliced together are called the Sheat-shot; three the Best-bower; one the Small-bower, and one Spare. **1847** MULLER *Polygl. Naut.* 28 Sheet shot cable.

**sheety** (ˈʃiːtɪ), *a.* [f. SHEET *sb.*[1] + -Y[1].] Spreading in a broad sheet: chiefly of a stretch of water.

**1748** COLLINS *Ode to Evening* 29 in Dodsley *Coll.* I. 332 Then lead, calm Vot'ress, where some sheety lake Cheers the lone heath. **1794** GISBORNE *Walks in Forest* vi. (1796) 98 Streams..down the hills Spread sheety o'er the slopes. *c* **1816** FUSELI *Lect. on Art* viii. (1848) 511 Oil, which rounds and conglutinates, spreads less than the sheety medium of fresco. *a* **1834** S. T. COLERIDGE in *Cottle's Early Recoll.* (1837) II. 255 The sheety burst Of lightning o'er the awaken'd midnight clouds.

**sheeve,** obs. form of SHEAF, SHEAVE.

**sheever,** obs. form of SHIVER.

**sheevo,** var. SHIVEAU.

**sheew,** obs. f. SHOW *v.*

**shef,** obs. pa. t. of SHOVE *v.*[1]

**shefe, sheff(e,** obs. forms of SHEAF, SHEAVE.

**Sheffer** (ˈʃɛfə(r)). *Logic.* [The name of Henry M. *Sheffer* (1883–1964), U.S. philosopher.] ***Sheffer('s) stroke***: the symbol |; also, the logical function of non-conjunction (and sometimes non-disjunction) that it represents, described by Sheffer in 1913 (*Trans. Amer. Math. Soc.* XIV. 481–8) (so ***Sheffer stroke function***).

**1932** LEWIS & LANGFORD *Symbolic Logic* ix. 306 The prefixes are analogues of Sheffer's stroke-function $p|q$ in its two interpretations. **1950** L. M. HAMMOND et al. tr. *Hilbert & Ackermann's Princ. Math. Logic* i. 11 Since ∨ and — can be expressed by Sheffer's stroke, the same holds for the other fundamental connectives. **1957** [see NON-CONJUNCTION 2]. **1960** N. R. SCOTT *Analog & Digital Computer Technol.* x. 392 If the low-potential and high-potential signal levels are identified respectively with binary 0 and 1, this circuit performs the Sheffer stroke function. **1972** A. G. HOWSON *Handbk. Terms Algebra & Anal.* i. 2 More basic still are the Sheffer stroke | and the connective ↓ ..since all the other connectives can be defined in terms of | (or ↓) alone.

**Sheffield** (ˈʃɛfiːld).

**1. a.** The name of a manufacturing city of Yorkshire, famous for cutlery, used *attrib.* as ***Sheffield knife, ware, whittle***; **Sheffield plate,** plate made of copper coated with silver by a special process brought to perfection in Sheffield (but now disused).

*c* **1386** CHAUCER *Reeve's T.* 13 A Sheffield [*v. rr.* scheffeld, sheffeld] thwitel baar he in his hose. **1575** LANEHAM *Let.* (1871) 38 A payr of capped Sheffeld kniuez. **1623** DEKKER *Witch of Edmonton* II. ii, The Bridegroom and Bride comes; the new pair of Sheffeild-Knives fitted both to one sheath. **1745** *Life Bampfylde-Moore Carew* 52 Buttons, Knives, Scissars, and other Sheffield Ware. **1821** SCOTT *Kenilw.* xxvii, But thou art sharper than a Sheffield whittle! **1856** GORE in *Orr's Circ. Sci., Pract. Chem.* 92 Old worn-out articles formed of 'Sheffield plate'. **1878** DOWDEN *Stud. Lit.* 37 If a song is to be at all a sword, it must be of finer temper than even the finest Sheffield cutlery.

†**b.** Used predicatively as *adj. Obs.*

**1599** NASHE *Lenten Stuffe* Wks. 1910 III. 178 Tell me if our English sconses be not right Sheffield or no.

**2.** The name of Henry North Holroyd, third Earl of *Sheffield* (1832–1909), used *attrib.* in **Sheffield Shield,** a trophy presented by him in 1892 and contested annually by Australian state cricket teams (freq. *attrib.*).

**1901** *Wisden's Cricketers' Almanack* (ed. 38) 462 The result determined the possession of the Sheffield Shield for the season. **1912** *Dict. National Biogr.* 2nd Suppl. II. 290/2 In 1891–2 Lord Sheffield, at his sole expense, took to Australia a team..under the management of Alfred Shaw. This enterprise greatly stimulated Australian cricket; the earl presented the Sheffield Shield, a trophy to be competed for annually by cricketers of Victoria, New South Wales, and South Australia. **1930** C. G. MACARTNEY *My Cricketing Days* iii. 20 My first season with the new club turned out to be my first in inter-state and Sheffield Shield cricket. **1977** *World of Cricket Monthly* June 19/1 The Australian cricketers we have signed are available to play Test, Sheffield Shield and club cricket when they are not playing in the super Test and other series.

**sheffonier,** rare var. CHIFFONIER, representing the common pronunciation (ʃɛfəˈnɪə(r)).

**1808** MRS. M. T. KEMBLE *Day after Wedding* 3 Furnished with Sofa, Footstools, Sheffoniers.

‖**shefstvo** (ˈʃɛfstvə). Also **chefstvo.** [Russ.] Patronage, sponsorship: variously used (see quots.).

**1937** S. N. HARPER *Govt. Soviet Union* viii. 134 The institution of so-called 'patronage' (*chefstvo*) is extended also to the Red Army and aims to keep those in military service in the everyday life of the community. **1948** J. TOWSTER *Political Power in U.S.S.R.* xiii. 322 Another form of tutelage was the so-called *shefstvo* or patronage by industrial regions over agricultural regions. **1950** B. MOORE *Soviet Politics* viii. 173 Another method, which evidently sprang up in the early thirties and then was permitted to die a natural death, was called 'patronage' (*shefstvo*), usually the patronage of a specific factory or of a specific group of workers over some section of the administration. **1955** H. HODGKINSON *Doubletalk* 120 *Shefstvo,* patronage exercised by a *shef* or 'chief' is the Soviet equivalent of 'empire building' in Western business and service jargon.

**shefte,** obs. f. SHIFT.

**shefure,** obs. f. SHIVER.

**shegger**, misprint for SKEGGER.
1758 BINNELL *Descr. Thames* 175 Little Trout, called a Samlet or Shegger-Trout.

**shegh**, error for *sege*, SIEGE *sb.* (q.v. 2 c).
1688 HOLME *Armoury* II. xiii. 311/1 A Shegh of Herons.

‖**shehecheyanu** (ʃehɛxɛ'jɑːnuː). Also shehechyoni, etc. [Heb., lit. 'that has sustained us'.] A Jewish benediction pronounced on the evening of a principal holy day and on new occasions of thanksgiving.
1892 I. ZANGWILL *Childr. Ghetto* II. xvi. 53 He was wondering whether he ought to say *Shehechyoni*—the prayer over a new pleasure. 1959 R. S. BROOKES *Dict. Judaism* 213 *She'hechiyanu*, a blessing recited on the first evening of festivals, on eating the first fruits of the season and on donning a new raiment [*sic*] for the first time. 1966 L. DAVIDSON *Long Way to Shiloh* xv. 227 When they..told me that the possibility existed, that by some miracle of God's grace, the holy Menorah was still in Eretz Yisroel..I said a *shechayanu*. 1972 C. RAPHAEL *Feast of History* i. 23 The Seder ceremony was an occasion for joy... We thanked God—in the famous *She'heheyanu* prayer—that he had 'kept us alive and sustained us and brought us to this moment'. 1980 *Jewish Chron.* 28 Mar. (Passover Suppl.) p. iii/1 He'd done the kiddush and the *shehecheyanu*.

**shehide**, obs. erron. form of SHAHI.

**shehita(h**, var. SHECHITA.

**shehnai**, var. SHAHNAI.

**sheick**, obs. variant of SAIC.
1775 CHANDLER *Trav. Asia M.* (1825) I. 13 The captain.. made a signal for a scheick or wherry to come along side.

**sheikh** (ʃeɪk, ʃiːk). Forms: 6 siech, 7 sceich, shech, shich, sheicke, shiek, 7–8 sheck, 8 schec(h, shiech, shaik, sheek, 7–9 sheich, scheik, sheick, 9 schiek, shaikh, shaykh, sheykh, 7– sheik, 8– sheikh; 7 cheq, cheke, 8 check, cheik, chiek, 8–9 chaik, 9 cheick; 7–8 xeque. [Arabic *shaikh* properly 'old man', f. *shākha* to grow or be old. Cf. OF. *esceque*, *seic*, F. *cheik*, *scheik*, Sp. *jeque*, Pg. *xeque*.]
**1. a.** The chief of an Arab family or tribe; the headman of an Arabian village; an Arab chief; †an Eastern governor, prince, king. Now also used among Arabs as a general title of respect.
1577 *Eden's Hist. Trav.* 331 b, The kyng of Persia is called Siech Ismael, whom the Italians call Gualizador, or Sophi. 1615 W. BEDWELL tr. *Moham. Impost.* I. §3 The peace of God..be vpon thee my Sheich. 1671 CHARENTE *Lett. conc. Customs Tafiletta* 5 The cheif of each Tribe, who take upon them the Title of Xeque, which is equivalent to Captain. 1687 A. LOVELL tr. *Thevenot's Trav.* II. 160 He sent thither an Arab Scheik with many Arabs. 1727 A. HAMILTON *New Acc. E. Ind.* I. iv. 36 He has the Title of Xeriff given him, to distinguish his Eminency from other Sheeks. 1728 MORGAN *Algiers* I. iii. 32 One of the Numidian petty Princes, called by Greek Authors Philarchs, and by the Arabs, &c. Sheikhs. 1755 *Gentl. Mag.* XXV. 507 Mutavali, the chiek or governor of Mesched. 1788 *Tully's Narr. Resid. Tripoli* (1817) 175 Shaik Alieff, an Arab chief. 1841 KINNEAR *Cairo*, etc. 169 One of the Fellah sheichs. 1882 FARRAR *Early Chr.* I. 457 Abraham..left his home in Ur of the Chaldees to wander as a nomad Sheikh. 1908 MOCKLER-FERRYMAN *Golden Girdle* iii, I knew that the Jelas tribe still existed, and though Sheik Feyzul was dead, his son Faris reigned in his stead. 1908 *Times* 8 July 19/2 As regards the Shaykh's competency as an Arabic scholar, there can be but one opinion.
**b.** (Chiefly in spelling *sheik.*) A type of a strong, romantic lover; a lady-killer. [After *The Sheik*, a novel by E. M. Hull (1919), and its cinematic adaptation *The Sheikh*, 1921, starring Rudolph Valentino.]
1925 *Lit. Digest* 14 Feb. 28/2 We hear almost nothing more of the matinée idol any more... The 'sheik' has taken his place. 1927 *Amer. Speech* II. 202/2 The girl calls the young man..'my sheik'. 1932 S. GIBBONS *Cold Comfort Farm* xviii. 245 The mask smiled..from a great silver screen: 'Seth Starkadder in "Small-Town Sheik".' 1939 'G. ORWELL' *Coming up for Air* I. i. 10 When your last natural tooth goes, the time when you can kid yourself that you're a Hollywood sheik is definitely at an end. 1956 S. LONGSTREET *Real Jazz Old & New* xii. 95 John Held Jr. drew the jazz-flapper and her sheik best... The lad was apple-headed, his hair buttered tight down. He wore bell-bottomed trousers, a racoon coat, drove a Stutz Bearcat and played or danced to jazz a lot. 1980 'L. EGAN' *Motive in Shadow* v. 87 He's sure a handsome sheik, kid.
**2. a.** The head of a Muslim religious order or community; a great religious doctor or preacher; now *esp.* a saint having a local cultus.
1613 PURCHAS *Pilgrimage* (1614) 276 A Nation..which he calleth Hhassissin, which..followed a peculiar Prophet... They called him Sheich [*printed* Hheich] al Hhassissin. 1662 J. DAVIES tr. *Mandelslo's Trav.* 46 The Devotions.. done at the Sepulchre of Schich Sefi at Ardebit. 1682 WHELER *Journ. Greece* II. 199 A Book..written by a Cheke, or Doctor of Grand Cairo. 1753 R. CLAYTON *Jrnl. Cairo to Mt. Sinai* 12 Sept. 1722, As we were passing by a mosch, where a certain shiech Salah was buried,..several of our guides..went thither to receive a benediction. *c* 1850 *Arab. Nts.* (Rtldg.) 674 A convent.., the scheik, or superior of which was a friend of the steward. 1869 TOZER *Highl. Turkey* I. 201 A sheikh's tomb with a tiled roof. 1908 S. A. COOK *Relig. Anc. Palestine* vi. 68 Saints and holy sheikhs of the modern shrines.
**b.** *Sheikh-ul-Islam* (properly *Sheikhu 'l Islam*): the supreme authority in matters relating to religion and sacred law; in Turkey, the mufti. Hence *Sheikh-ul-Islamate*.
1686 tr. *Chardin's Trav. Persia* 261 The Sheikelislam, who is the chief Civil Judge. 1753 HANWAY *Trav.* (1762) I. III. li. 231 The kaziæskar is judge of the army, and the scheichulislam is reputed of equal rank with him. 1902 *Daily Chron.* 26 Apr. 5/4 She went to the Sheikh-ul-Islamate. 1906 *Westm. Gaz.* 3 Sept. 3/2 No political act of the Sultan has any validity without the fetwa of the Sheikh-ul-Islam.
**3.** In India, one of a dissenting sect of Muslims; a general term for Hindu converts to Islam. (Usually *shekh*, *shaikh.*)
[1697 FRYER *Acc. E. India & P.* III. i. 93 All Musselmen ..are distinguished, some according to the Consanguinity they claim with Mahomet... A Shiek is a Cousin..at a distance, into which Relation they admit all new Proselytes.] 1883 *Encycl. Brit.* XV. 185/2 (*Madras*) The Shaikhs number 511,112 the Sayyids 89,219, the Pathans 70,943 [etc.]. 1903 *India Census, 1901* I. i. 451 The converts who call themselves Shekh. 1905 MACPHAIL *K. S. Macdonald* xvi. 243 A Bengali Shekh may be almost anything.
Hence **'sheikhdom, -ship**, the status or office of a sheikh; the territory ruled by a sheikh; **'sheikhling**, a petty sheikh; **'sheikhly** *a.*, pertaining to or characteristic of a sheikh.
1845 E. WARBURTON *Crescent & Cross* II. 254 The Sheikdom is..hereditary in most cases. 1860 TRISTRAM *Gt. Sahara* xiv. 237 The Touareg do not appear to have any subdivided sheikdoms like the Arabs. 1878 *Fraser's Mag.* XVIII. 144 The chief sheikhship is hereditary. 1888 DOUGHTY *Trav. Arabia Des.* I. 98 Of sheykhly blood and noble easy countenance. 1907 EWING *Arab & Druze* iii. 36 He proved to be the son of the sheikhly ruler of Dama. 1914 G. BELL *Let.* 19 Jan. (1927) I. xiii. 326 A young sheikhling of the Sikhur joined us..and spent the night with us as guests. 1974 W. GARNER *Big enough Wreath* iv. 40 Mini-presidents and rich sheiklings seeking advice.

‖**Sheikha** ('ʃeɪkə, 'ʃiːkə). Also Shaikha(h, Sheika, and with small initial. [Arab. *šaika*.] An Arab lady or matron of good family; hence, the (chief) wife of a sheikh. (Also as a title of respect.) Also *transf.*, the consort of a 'sheikh' (cf. SHEIKH 1 b) (*slang*).
1853 J. RICHARDSON *Narr. Mission Cent. Afr.* II. xiv. 247, I had a visit from a great sister of the Sarkee, a woman who is a Sheikha (female Sheikh), and receives the revenues of fifty villages for her own private use. 1926 MAINES & GRANT *Wise-Crack Dict.* 13/2 *Sheika*, Sheik's sweetie. 1949 H. R. P. DICKSON *Arab of Desert* viii. 144 Al Jazi, sister of Khalid al Hithlain..had a will of her own, and was a veritable 'Shaikhah'. 1967 M. CHILDS *Taint of Innocence* iii. 189 The Emir, the Sheika, and a party..had left the palace. 1976 *Times* 22 Sept. 2/3 Shaikha ——, a Saudi Arabian noblewoman, who bought 50 Chepstow Villas, Notting Hill. 1976 L. BLANDFORD *Oil Sheikhs* 256 Sheikha Osheh is.. married to Sheikh Mubarak. 1980 D. CREED *Scarab* xiv. 134 They *are* Arabs—and so are you, sheikha.

**sheil(l, -ing, sheip, sheir, sheire, sheit**: see SHIEL, SHIELING, SHEEP, SHEER, SHIRE, SHEET.

**sheila** ('ʃiːlə). Now *Austral.* and *N.Z. colloq.* Also 9 shaler; sheelah, etc. [Orig. uncertain. Early *shaler* is not formally explained. It may represent a generic use of the (originally Irish) personal name *Sheila*, the counterpart of PADDY *sb.*[2] 1 a (see quot. 1828); in any case, it became assimilated to this at some later stage.] A girl or young woman; a girl-friend. (Playfully affectionate and predominantly in male use.)
[1828 *Monitor* (Sydney) 22 Mar. 1053/2 Many a piteous Shela stood wiping the gory locks of her Paddy, until released from that duty by the officious interference of the knight of the baton.] 1839 H. BRANDON in W. A. Miles *Poverty, Mendicity & Crime* 165/1 *Shalers*, girls (country phrase). 1847 G. W. M. REYNOLDS *Myst. London* III. xxv. 71/1 Cop that young shaler unto thee. 1864 HOTTEN *Slang Dict.* 225 *Shaler*, a girl. Corrupt form of *Gaelic*, *caille*, a young woman. 1895 C. CROWE *Austral. Slang Dict.* 72 *Shaler*, a girl. 1918 *N.Z.E.F. Chrons.* 5 July 252/2, I goes and stays out at Ngaire with my shieler's people. 1919 W. H. DOWNING *Digger Dialects* 44 *Sheila*, a girl. 1928 A. WRIGHT *Good Recovery* 117 Leave the sheilas alone, they're sure to pool a man sooner or later. 1930 V. PALMER *Men are Human* xxvii. 251 There was a sheelah he had working for him once, a lively piece with black eyes. 1940 F. SARGESON *Man & his Wife* (1944) 66 I've got a job in a grocer's shop and I'm trotting a sheila. She's a pearl of a sheila too. 1951 F. HARDY *Power without Glory* (ed. 5) i. 21 'What d'yer expect us to do, just sit around and starve ourselves?'.. 'Please yer bloody self, but you've got to think of yer mother, and that sheila of yours.' 1959 *Woman's Own* 4 July 11/3 They have a daughter—a nice-looking sheila, too. 1962 *Coast to Coast 1961–62* 21 'I know a sheila,' Sonny began. 'A real trimmer.' 1969 *Private Eye* 21 Nov. 14 Don't be shit-scared of these sheilahs who work for me. 1976 *Times Lit. Suppl.* 9 Apr. 418/3 His past would be remythologized by a host of pre-war radio announcers, sepia footballers and nude sheilahs from the master brush of Norman Lindsay. 1977 D. SEAMAN *Committee* 63 They made the usual jokes about the local Sheilas.

**sheila-na-gig**, var. SHEELA-NA-GIG.

**sheirut**, var. SHERUT.

‖**sheitel** ('ʃeɪt(ə)l). Also shaitel. [ad. Yiddish *sheytl*, f. MHG. *scheitel* crown of the head.] Among strictly Orthodox Ashkenazi Jews: a wig worn by a married woman.
1892 I. ZANGWILL *Childr. Ghetto* I. ii. 41 A small, sickly-looking woman, with..the wig without which no virtuous wife is complete... A lower stratum of unmatched brown peeped out in front of the *Shaitel*. 1957 L. STERN *Midas Touch* I. vii. 63 His mother..no longer wore her sheitel, or traditional wig. 1973 *Jewish Chron.* 19 Jan. 22/3 A comely young rebbetzin in a glamorous sheitel and eyelashes long enough to brush dandruff from lapels has been touring American universities to attract straying Jewish youths back to their faith.

**shekar, -ee**, var. forms of SHIKAR, SHIKARI.

**shekel** ('ʃɛkəl). Also 6–7 shekle, shekell, 7 sheicle, sheckle. [a. Heb. *sheqel*, f. *shāqal* to weigh. (The word was adopted in the form SICLE through French and Latin.)]
**1. a.** An ancient unit of weight of the Babylonians, and hence of the Phœnicians, Hebrews, and others, equal to one-sixtieth of a mina (see MINA[1] 1). **b.** A coin of this weight; *esp.* the chief silver coin of the Hebrews.
1560 BIBLE (Geneva) *Exod.* xxx. 13 This shal euerie man giue, that goeth into the nombre, half a shekel, after the shekel of the Sanctuarie. [*But 1 Macc.* x. 42 sicles.] 1597 HOOKER *Eccl. Pol.* v. lxxix. 243 Two thousand and foure hundred shekels of Siluer, an hundred and twentie shekels of Gold, euery shekell waighing halfe an ounce. 1611 COTGR., *Cicle*, a Sheicle. 1614 RALEIGH *Hist. World* II. v. §2. 297 The waight of gold in the incense-Cups [amounted] to 120 sheckles of Gold. 1647 GREAVES *Roman Foot* 76 The Hebrew of Samaritane shekel. 1728 CHAMBERS *Cycl.* s.v., Some are of Opinion, that the Hebrews had two kinds of Shekels. The Common, or Prophane Shekel, call'd Didrachma; and the Shekel of the Sanctuary, which last they will have double the former. 1846 TRENCH *Mirac.* xxviii. (1862) 376 *note*, Before the Babylonian exile, the shekel was only a certain weight of silver, not a coined money.
*attrib.* 1886 CONDER *Syrian Stone-Lore* iv. (1896) 152 In the tenth year of Darius, shekel pieces..are mentioned on inscribed tablets. 1899 *Expositor* Nov. 392 When a shekel ingot was first stamped with a mark of quality or value, it was still called a shekel.
**c.** An Israeli unit of currency introduced in February 1980, equivalent to ten former Israeli pounds; a note of this value.
1980 *Times* 23 Feb. 1/2 From next week the Israeli pound is to be replaced by a new currency named after the Biblical shekel... Each shekel will be purchased with 10 present Israeli pounds. 1980 *Whitaker's Almanack 1981* 979 Israel ..Israeli Shekel of 100 New Agora..[Notes] Shekels 50, 10, 5, 1.
**2.** *fig.* (*pl.*) Coin; money. *colloq.* Also in phr. ***to rake in the shekels***, to make money rapidly or 'hand over fist' (from a venture). Cf. RAKE *sb.*[1] 2 a (*a*).
[1823 BYRON *Age of Bronze* xv, No land of Canaan, full of milk and honey, Nor (save in paper shekels) ready money.] 1883 F. M. CRAWFORD *Dr. Claudius* v, Though he was so rich, he never talked about money except in a vague way as 'lots of shekels', or 'piles of tin'. 1887 [see HIGH *a.* 10 h]. 1915 J. BUCHAN *39 Steps* i. 18 The capitalists would rake in the shekels, and make fortunes by buying up wreckage.

**shekel**, dial. f. SHACKLE *sb.*[1]

**shekere**, var. SEKERE.

**shekest(h)eh**, obs. vars. SHIKASTA.

**shekinah, shechinah** (ʃɪ'kaɪnə). Also 7 shecinah, 8 schecina, -chinah, 9 shekina. [a. late Heb. *shᵉkīnāh*, f. *shākan* to rest, dwell.] The visible manifestation of the Divine Majesty, esp. when resting between the cherubim over the mercy-seat or in the temple of Solomon; a glory or refulgent light symbolizing the Divine Presence.
In the Targums the word is used as a periphrasis to designate God when He is said to dwell among the cherubim, etc., so as to avoid any approach to anthropomorphic expression.
1663 J. STILLINGFLEET (*title*) Shecinah: or a Demonstration of the Divine Presence in the places of Religious Worship. 1681–6 J. SCOTT *Chr. Life* (1747) III. 530 That fiery Shechinah, or visible Glory of the Lord, in which he descended on Mount Sinai. 1708 *Brit. Apollo* No. 101. 1/2 This Light, which in part compos'd the Schechinah is suppos'd to have been Accompanied with a Numerous Retinue of Attending Angels. 1741 WATTS *Improv. Mind* (1801) 187 The Schecina, or bright glory, which is a symbol of God's presence. 1833 *Tracts for Times* No. 13. 4 They murmuring and rebelling with the Shechinah before their eyes. 1858 GEO. ELIOT *Scenes Cler. Life, Mr. Gilfil* vii, The golden sun-light beamed through the dripping boughs like a Shechinah, or visible divine presence.
**b.** *transf.* (*spec.* applied to Jesus Christ.)
1682 HICKES (*title*) The Moral Schechinah: Or a Discourse of Gods Glory. *a* 1684 LEIGHTON *Serm.* (*1 Cor.* i. 30) Sel. Wks. 1823 I. 483 The Shechinah, the habitation of the Majesty, is Jesus Christ; there he dwells as between the cherubim over the mercy-seat. 1739 C. WESLEY *Hymn*, '*Arise, my Soul, arise*' vi, Our Eyes on Earth survey The Dazling Shechinah! Bright in endless Glory bright Now in Flesh He stoops to dwell. 1834 DISRAELI *Rev. Epick* I. xvii. 22 Truth indeed is veiled, But with a Schekinah of dazzling light.

**shekyl**, obs. form of SHACKLE *sb.*[1]

**shekyr**, obs. form of CHEQUER *sb.*[1]
1518 *Cov. Leet Bk.* 653 The bokes of ij leetes euer next afore shall remayn in the counsell howse..on the shekyr.

**shel**, obs. form of SHELL, SHIELD.

**shelaly**, obs. form of SHILLELAGH.

**shelboard.** *dial.* [? f. SHELF *sb.*[1] + BOARD *sb.*: cf. SHELVING *sb.*] An additional framework fixed to the sides of a cart to increase its capacity.

**1569** in T. Phillipps *Wills* (*c* 1830) 84 All my ploughe tymber, and cart tymber, except shelbordes. **1616** SURFL. & MARKH. *Country Farm* VII. xvi. 662 All manner of Plow and Cart-timber whatsoeuer, as Beames, Heads, Skeathes, Hales, Spyndles, Shelboords, Cart or Wayne bodies, rings for Wheeles. **1852** C. W. HOSKYNS *Talpa* xvi. (1854) 137 A sack or two of Wheat that lay not very safely on the near-side shel'-board.

**shelboard, -brede,** obs. ff. SHIELD-BOARD.

**shelburne** (ˈʃɛlbɜːn). (See quot. 1889.)

**1889** DK. BEAUFORT *Driving* 385 Those [landaus] with angular lines are known as 'Shelburne' landaus, from the late Earl of Shelburne, who had the first of that pattern built. **1905** SIR W. GILBEY *Mod. Carriages* 45.

**sheld** (ʃɛld), *a. dial.* Also 6 schell, 9 shell, shelled. [ad. or cogn. with MDu. *schillede* variegated (oftener in comb., as *rootschillede*), = WFlem. *schilde*, f. *schillen* (in mod.Du. *verschillen*) to make different. The existence of the Eng. word at an earlier date is probably implied in SHELDRAKE.] Particoloured, pied, piebald.

**1507** *Will of Crisall* (Somerset Ho.), ij kyne garle & schell. *a* **1672** [see SHELDEN]. **1674** RAY *S. & E.C. Words* 76 *Sheld*, flecked: party-coloured. **1787** W. H. MARSHALL *Norfolk* (1795) II. 388 *Shelled*, pied; party-coloured. **1823** E. MOOR *Suffolk Words* s.v. *Shell*, Shell (or sheld) is pied, of two colours; flecker'd is gay, of more than two. *a* **1825** FORBY *Voc. E. Anglia*, *Shelled*, pie-bald.

**sheld,** obs. form of SHIELD.

**ˈsheld-apple, ˈshell-apple.** *dial.* Also sheldafle, shillaple, etc. [Usually taken to be f. SHELD *a.* + DAPPLE *a.*, but perhaps a metathetic form of **sheldalp*, f. SHELD *a.* + ALP[2] (dial. *alf*), bullfinch.] Applied to two birds remarkable for their variegated plumage.

**1.** The chaffinch, *Fringilla cœlebs.*

**1544** W. TURNER *Avium Præcip.* D6, De Fringilla,.. Anglicè a chaffinche, a sheld appel, a spink. **1611** COTGR., *Berée*, a spinke, sheldaple, chaffinch. **1802** R. ANDERSON *Cumbld. Ball.* (1805) 21, I mind, when he cross'd the deep watter, To get me the shilapple' est. **1813** MONTAGU *Ornith. Dict.* Suppl., Shelly or Shell-apple. **1880** C. H. POOLE *Gloss. Staff.*, *Shell* or *Sheld-apple*, the chaffinch.

**2.** The crossbill, *Loxia curvirostra.*

**1666** MERRETT *Pinax* 172 Loxias, the Shell-Apple. **1668** CHARLETON *Onomast.* 69 *Loxia*..the Cross-beak, or Shell-aple. **1674** RAY *Engl. Birds* 88. **1768** PENNANT *Brit. Zool.* II. 279. **1802** MONTAGU *Ornith. Dict.*, Shell, or Sheld-apple. Vide Crossbill.

**sheldbreath, -brede,** obs. ff. SHIELD-BOARD.

**shelde,** obs. f. SHELLED *ppl. a.*, SHIELD, SHOAL.

†**ˈshelden.** *Obs.* Also -in. [app. f. SHELD *a.* (? + ENDE).] The golden-eye, *Clangula glaucion.*

*a* **1672** WILLUGHBY *Ornith.* (1678) 28 This was sent us from Cambridge by the title of Shelden, I suppose so denominated from its being particoloured of black and white, that is Sheld. **1674** DENT in *Ray's Philos. Lett.* (1718) 21 Some Water Fowl, *viz.* a Pocker, a Smew, three Sheldins.

**shelder,** variant of SHALDER *v.*

**sheldrake** (ˈʃɛldreɪk). Forms: 4 sheldedrake, selddrake, shelledrake, 5 scheldrak, 5–6 -drake, 7–9 shell(-)drake, 8 shel-drake, sheldrach, 8–9 shieldrake, (9 shield-drake), 6– sheldrake. [prob. f. SHELD *a.* + DRAKE[2]. A northern form *skeldraik* (see SCALEDRAKE) is recorded from 1600.

Connexion with SHIELD *sb.* is improbable, since 'spot of colour' is not an established sense of this word, as it is of the cognate G. *schild* and ON. *skjǫldr* (cf. *skjǫldóttr* dappled). The commonly cited ON. *skjǫldungr*, occuring in a late alliterative list of bird-names, is not identifiable (the Icel. names of the sheldrake are *brandgás* and *andakóngur*). The form *scheldrack* given by Gesner (Anim. III. 131) is app. from Eng.]

A bird of the genus *Tadorna* of the duck tribe, frequenting sandy coasts in Europe, North Africa, and Asia, and remarkable for its bright and variegated colouring.

†Occas. applied to the North American canvas-back.

*c* **1325** *Gloss. W. de Bibbesw.* in Wright *Voc.* 164 La herle [*glossed* the selddrake, *v.r.* sheldedrake]. *c* **1340** *Nominale* (Skeat) 802 *Herle*, schelledrake. *c* **1475** *Pict. Voc.* in Wr.-Wülcker 762/39 *Hic umnis*, a scheldrak. **1530** PALSGR. 266/2 Scheldrake a byrde. **1621** BURTON *Anat. Mel.* I. ii. II. i, All those Teales, Curres, Sheldrakes, and peckled Fowles, which come hether in winter. **1668** CHARLETON *Onomast.* 96 *Mergus Harle*..the Shell-drake. *a* **1672** WILLUGHBY *Ornith.* (1678) 28 The Sheldrake, or Borough-Duck: Tadorna Bellonii. *Ibid.* 364 The Swallow-tail'd Sheldrake of Mr. Johnson. **1782** T. JEFFERSON *Notes State Virginia* (1787) 118 Sheldrach, or Canvas back. **1821** SCOTT *Pirate* iv, The shelldrake seems, through the mist, as large as the scart. **1847** LEICHHARDT *Jrnl.* vii. 217 Charley shot the sheldrake of Port Essington (Tadorna Rajah). **1855** F. O. MORRIS *Brit. Birds* V. 137 Ruddy Shieldrake... Collared Duck. *Tadorna rutila.* **1870** GILLMORE tr. *Figuier's Reptiles & Birds* 229 The Shieldrake is the most remarkable of all the Duck tribe, not only from its size, but from its beauty and the elegant variations of its plumage.

**sheldrun,** var. SHELTRON[1].

**shelduck, sheld-duck, shell-duck** (ˈʃɛldʌk). Also shieldduck, shield-duck. [f. SHELDRAKE, by substitution of *duck* for *drake.*] = SHELDRAKE.

**1707** MORTIMER *Husb.* (1721) I. 259 If you would preserve wild Ducks, Teal, Widgeon, Shell-ducks, &c. you should have a place walled in with a Pond in it. **1770** PENNANT *Brit. Zool.* IV. 86 Swallow Tailed Shielduck. **1810** CRABBE *Borough* ix, The sleeping shell-ducks at the sound arise. **1852** MACGILLIVRAY *Brit. Birds* V. 19 *Tadorna Casarca.* The Ruddy Shielduck. **1908** *Zoologist* Apr. 124 Sheld-Duck seen at Fritton by Mr. Buxton. **1925** C. W. R. KNIGHT *Aristocrats of Air* x. 124, I did not succeed in locating a Shelduck's nest. **1939** J. FISHER *Birds as Animals* xi. 190 In ..black skimmer and shelduck, both birds incubate. **1966** E. PALMER *Plains of Camdeboo* xi. 190 Shelduck, well-known for making their nests in holes, often choose ant-bear burrows. **1972** *Country Life* 3 Feb. 274/1 The shelduck is the largest and most striking bird of the English shores.

So **sheld-fowl** (also **s(c)hell-, shield-**), the sheldrake.

? **1593** DRAYTON *Man in Moon* Poems (1619) 480 The greedie Shell-fowle, from whose rape doth flye Th'vnnumbred sholes. **1674** RAY *S. & E.C. Words* 76 *Sheld*..inde Shel-drake & sheld fowle, Suss. **1676** *Phil. Trans.* XI. 626 Cormorants, Brants, Shield-fowl. **1890** BORLAND *Yarrow* 119 Speckled schell-fowl hovering nigh.

**sheldur,** obs. f. SHOULDER *sb.*

**shele,** obs. f. SHIEL.

**shelela,** obs. f. SHILLELAGH.

**shelf** (ʃɛlf), *sb.*[1] Pl. shelves (ʃɛlvz). Forms: 5 schelf(f)e, 5–7 shelfe, 7 shealfe, 5– shelf; *pl.* 4– shelves, (5 schelves, -ys, 6 sylwes); 5 schelfes, 5–7 shelfes, 5–8 shelfs. [app. ad. (M)LG. *schelf* shelf, set of shelves (whence also the northern SKELF), cogn. w. OE. *scylfe* (of uncertain meaning) ? partition or compartment, MDu. *schelve*, (and mod.Du.) *schelf* stack, rick (of hay, etc.), and OE. *scylf* (also *stán-scylf*) rugged rock, crag, pinnacle; ? f. root *skelf-* to split.]

**I. 1. a.** A slab of wood (or other material) fixed in a horizontal position to a wall, or in a frame, to hold books, vessels, ornaments, etc.; one of the transverse boards in a bookcase, cabinet, or the like.

*c* **1386** CHAUCER *Miller's T.* 25 His Augrym stones layen faire a part On shelues [*v.r.* schelfes] couched at his beddes heed. **1422** *Engl. Misc.* (Surtees) 16 Yat the lede pype and the shelfs be the wyfe's of Symond of Stele. **1485** *Rec. St. Mary at Hill* (1904) 28 In the Bottrye iiij schelves. **1505** in *Eng. Gilds* (1870) 327 Yn the spence a tabell planke and ij sylwes. **1566** *Engl. Ch. Furniture* (Peacock 1866) 65 A shelf for to set dishes on. **1615** CHAPMAN *Odyss.* IX. 313 Shelues [ταρσοί] with cheeses heapt. **1719** DE FOE *Crusoe* I. 135, I was full two and forty Days making me a Board for a long Shelf. **1727** SWIFT *Further Acc. E. Curll* Wks. 1755 III. I. 161 Have not I clothed you in double-royal, lodged you handsomely on decent shelves? **1765** J. BROWN *Chr. Jrnl.* 252 Here is the famed surgeon's shop: no doubt his shelfs are planted with pots, vials, and boxes full of useful medicine. **1842** TENNYSON *Talking Oak* 142 She left the novel half-uncut Upon the rosewood shelf. **1856** DELAMER *Fl. Gard.* (1861) 4 A dry airy shelf is a good place for keeping them [*sc.* bulbs]. **1898** G. B. SHAW *You never can tell* III. Stage direct., The bamboo tea table, with folding shelves.

**b.** The gradine of an altar.

**1496–7** *Rec. St. Mary at Hill* (1904) 30 A frontell for the schelffe standyng on the alter.

**c.** *transf.* A shelf with reference to its contents; the contents of a shelf (*esp.* of books).

**1732** BERKELEY *Alciphr.* II. §24 You may confute a whole shelf of schoolmen. **1799** *Monthly Rev.* XXX. 287 This performance cannot be placed on the same shelf with that of Barthelemy. **1818** SCOTT *Hrt. Midl.* xxxi, His works had no place on David Deans's shelf of divinity. **1825** MACAULAY *Ess., Milton* (1897) 2 A few more days, and this essay will follow the *Defensio Populi* to the dust and silence of the upper shelf. **1876** LOWELL *Ode 4th July* IV. ii, Herein they were great Beyond the incredulous lawgivers of yore, And wiser than the wisdom of the shelf.

**d.** fig. phrases. ***on the shelf***: (*a*) On one side, out of the way, in a position or state of inactivity or uselessness; esp. ***to lay*** (***put***, etc.) ***on the shelf***, also † ***to set on shelf***.

**1575** GASCOIGNE *Kenelworth* Wks. 1910 II. 120 Jove in heaven would smile to see Diana set on shelfe. **1815** WELLINGTON in Gurw. *Desp.* (1838) XII. 379 Alava would then be laid upon the shelf, if he had not his situation here to return to. **1816** 'QUIZ' *Grand Master* VIII. 8 He's ever since been on the shelf. **1831** CROKER in *Boswell's Johnson* an. 1740 *note*, His friend General Oglethorpe, who, after acquittal by a court-martial, was (to use a vulgar but expressive phrase) put upon the shelf. **1884** L. J. JENNINGS *Croker Papers* I. vi. 170 The question of Parliamentary Reform could not be perpetually kept upon the shelf. **1893** BEATRICE HARRADEN *Ships that pass* I. vii, Because your career has been checked, and because you have been put on the shelf.

(*b*) Of women: Without prospects of marrying.

**1839** HOOD *I'm not a single Man* v, Mamma, who praises her own self, Instead of Jane or Ann, And lays 'her girls' upon the shelf. **1847** HALLIWELL, *On the shelf*, said of ladies when too old to get married. **1893** *Academy* 25 Nov. 460/3 A worn-out flirt who has run through her chances in the matrimonial market and who is..on the shelf.

(*c*) *slang.* In pawn.

**1859** *Hotten's Slang Dict.*, *On the shelf*, pawned.

**e.** ***off the shelf***: from a supply of ready-made goods. Also (with hyphens) as *adj. phr.*

**1936** *Industr. & Engin. Chem.* Feb. 150/2 The individual customer must generally have his material fabricated to his order and cannot obtain material [aluminium] 'off the shelf'. **1958** *Engineering* 11 Apr. 455/2 Using sets built to a standard pattern which would be available 'off the shelf' and made up of interchangeable parts. **1962** J. GLENN in *Into Orbit* 37 They had to use 'off-the-shelf' items in order to save time. **1978** *Nature* 26 Oct. 784/1 As CAMAC equipment is often sold as individual products to system builders, items are often available either 'off the shelf'.

†**2.** A cupboard or cabinet. *Obs.*

*c* **1440** *Promp. Parv.* 445/1 Schelfe, *epiaster, epilocarium, armarium.* **1570** LEVINS *Manip.* 58/16 A shelfe, *cortinale.*

**3. a.** *Printing.* = TILL *sb.*[1] 3.

**1706** PHILLIPS (ed. Kersey), *Shelf*,..the Till of a Printing-Press. **1808** STOWER *Printer's Gram.* 328 The Till or Shelf. **1834–6** *Encycl. Metrop.* (1845) VIII. 774 The third bar D, called the shelf or till, is intended to guide and keep steady ..the hose, which contains the spindle and screw.

**b.** *Shipbuilding.* A timber on the inner side of the frame to support the deck-beams.

**1834–6** *Encycl. Metrop.* (1845) VI. 396/2 Under the beams of the deck, perpendicularly over the builge-strake, was fixed on its edge a strake of fir along the whole length of the vessel six inches thick, with a score one inch deep for the beams, to which it was bolted, and was called the longitudinal shelf. **1874** THEARLE *Naval Archit.* 35 The several pieces composing the shelf are connected with vertical flat scarphs.

**c.** The charging-bed of a furnace.

**1879** *Spons' Encycl. Manuf.* I. 290 The hopper in which the charge of sulphate, coal, and chalk is contained, is built into the arch over the centre of the 'shelf'.

**4.** A police informer. *Austral. slang.*

**1926** J. DOONE *Timely Tips for New Australians* (Gloss.), *Shelf*, a slang word denoting an informer. **1952** *People* (Austral.) 3 Dec. 8/2 The jail authorities knew such trafficking went on and often set traps for the warders through the good offices of *shelfs* or *trusties* (prisoners who were informers).

**II.** Senses influenced by SHELF *sb.*[2]

**5. a.** A ledge, platform, or terrace of land, rock, etc.

**1809** J. BARLOW *Columb.* III. 170 Torrents of molten rocks ..Lead o'er the shelves of ice their fiery tide. **1818** SCOTT *Hrt. Midl.* l, A huge fragment of stone, which, having fallen from the cliffs above, had..jammed so as to serve for a sloping roof to the farther part of the broad shelf or platform on which they stood. **1833** LYELL *Princ. Geol.* III. 131 These roads or shelves occur in a valley six or seven miles wide. **1872** BLACK *Adv. Phaeton* xxiv, Scrambling up shelves of loose earth and slate.

**b.** ***continental shelf***, the relatively shallow belt of sea-bottom bordering a continental mass, the outer edge of which slopes rapidly to the deep ocean-floor. Also unqualified (freq. *attrib.*).

**1892** H. R. MILL *Realm of Nat.* xi. 201 In many cases it is possible that the continental shelf is the end of a low plain submerged by subsidence; in others a low plain may be an upheaved continental shelf. **1905** *Times* 29 Mar. 10/6 The coast platform and Continental shelf lying off the Norwegian coast. **1913** *Jrnl. Geol.* XXI. 525 The mode of formation keeps the face of the shelf within a certain distance from the sea-surface. *Ibid.*, The shelf zone is..a biologic horizon of the first importance. **1934** C. R. LONGWELL et al. *Outl. Physical Geol.* vii. 125 The shelf beyond the long-quiescent Atlantic coast of North America is 60 to 80 miles wide off the Carolinas. **1964** *Oceanogr. & Marine Biol.* II. 61 The temperature minimum at 150m may be formed, in part, by mixing of winter Bering Sea water with shelf water. **1978** FRIEDMAN & SANDERS *Princ. Sedimentol.* xii. 360/2 (*caption*) Shelf lagoon between margin of a continental block and a reef tract that is situated at the edge of the continental mass.

**6.** *Mining* and *Geol.* Bed-rock: see quots.

**1671** *Phil. Trans.* VI. 2096 The uppermost surface of Mineral Veins or hoads..which is termed by the Miners, the Shelf, Fast Countrey or Ground that was never moved in the Flood. **1839** DE LA BECHE *Rep. Geol. Cornwall*, etc. xiii. 398 We find these pebbles at the base of the whole, resting upon the subjacent rock, commonly termed the shelf. **1852** NICOLAY in *Man. Geog. Sci.* I. 420 Low rocks lying horizontally, especially when laminated, are called Shelves. **1880** D. C. DAVIES *Metallif. Min.* 421 *Shelf*, the uppermost broken surface of the rock under driftal matter.

**III. 7.** *attrib.* and *Comb.*, as † *shelf-board*, *-bracket*, *-load*, *-occupant*, *-press*, *-room*, *-space*; *shelf-like* adj.; **shelf appeal**, the attractiveness to a customer of packaged goods displayed in a shop; **shelf back** *U.S.*, the spine of a book; **shelf-catalogue**, a short-title catalogue of the books in a library arranged according to their location on the shelves and consequently according to their class or subject; **shelf cod**, cod found in inshore waters above the continental shelf; **shelf ice** [tr. G. *schelfeis* (O. Nordenskjöld 1908, in *Zeitschr. der Ges. für Erdkunde zu Berlin* XLIII. 618, following suggestion of A. Penck)], ice which forms a thick level layer on water (usu. the sea) but is attached to land; **shelf life**, the length of time that a commodity may be stored without becoming unfit for use or consumption; **shelf-list** = *shelf catalogue*; so **shelf-lister**, one who compiles shelf-lists; **shelf-mark** = PRESS-MARK; hence **shelf-mark** *v.*, **shelf-marking**; **shelf paper**, paper used for lining shelves; **shelf-piece** = sense 3 b; **shelf-plate**, an iron shelf below the water-line of an armoured ship to support the armour-plate and its backing; **shelf sea**, an expanse of sea overlying continental shelf.

**1933** *Shelf Appeal* July 3 (*heading*) *Shelf Appeal. A monthly publication devoted to the planning, designing, manufacturing & display of the package. **1963** *B.S.I. News* Apr. 20/1 The 'shelf-appeal' pack designed to catch the eye of the ordinary shopper. **1964** *Times Rev. Industry* Feb. 23/1 With the post-war swing to more branded goods, self-service, enhanced hygiene and the need for 'shelf-appeal', the demand for more and better packaging has expanded fast. **1925** J. A. HOLDEN *Bookman's Gloss.* 97 **Shelf-back*, the back of a book, on which the title is lettered. **1931** *Publishers' Weekly* 9 May 2322 It..is strongly bound and has the name of the periodical stamped in gold on cover and shelfback. **1960** G. A. GLAISTER *Gloss. Book* 375/1 *Shelf back*, the spine of a book. **1548** *MS. Acc. St. John's Hosp., Canterb.*, In the kechynne a *shelf bourde. **1859** F. S. COOPER *Ironmongers' Catal.* 10 *Shelf Brackets. **1882** H. BRADSHAW in *Trans. Libr. Assoc.* (1884) 233 He enters the title briefly in the *shelf-catalogue (or class-catalogue as we call it in Cambridge). **1935** L. LUARD *Conquering Seas* 37 Cod... *Shelf Cod. **1976** *Eastern Even. News* (Norwich) 9 Dec. 12/5 Grimsby fish. Poor supply, good demand; six boats landed 1917 kit. Shelf cod £4 to £5. **1910** *Geogr. Jrnl.* XXXV. 726 To this ice formed *in situ* out of snow accumulations in the sea Nordenskiöld gives the name '*shelf-ice'. **1938** *Ibid.* XCI. 511 Of all the glacial features in this region, perhaps the greatest interest attaches to the shelf-ice filling King George VI Sound. **1977** *New Yorker* 20 June 55/1 The river's edges are lined with ice that is stationary—'shelf ice', 'shore ice', the first to freeze at the start of winter and the last to go in spring. **1927** *Manufacturing Confectioner* Jan. 12 (*heading*) What is the *shelf life of your hard candy? **1933** R. A. WATSON WATT et al. *Applications of Cathode Ray Oscillograph in Radio Res.* i. 27 The batteries may..be of very small size; 'shelf-life' and loss through casual leakage..are more important than their actual load current. **1940** *Austral. Jrnl. Dentistry* XLIV. 39 Either copper or copper and zinc must be present in the alloy if it is to possess a reasonable 'shelf life'. **1956** *Visible Packaging of Flour Confectionery* (British Cellophane Ltd.) 3 For small fancy cakes a moistureproof heat-sealing wrap.. should give a shelf-life of several days. **1969** *Observer* 26 Jan. 5/5 The shelf-life of donated blood is about 21 days. **1980** D. FRANCIS *Reflex* viii. 99 Some photographic chemicals lose their power with age. Shelf life, and so on. **1851** H. MELVILLE *Moby Dick* I. iii. 18 On one side stood a long, low, *shelf-like table covered with cracked glass cases, filled with dusty rarities. **1962** *Science Survey* XI. 178 The inner membrane whose shelf-like folds protrude into the interior of the organelle. **1910** A. E. BOSTWICK *Amer. Public Library* 171 The name '*shelf list' is sometimes improperly given to a class list. **1979** *Amer. N. & Q.* June 166/2 Each volume of the shelflist is in four parts, viz., the classification schedule, the shelflist proper (showing shelf mark, author, title, place of publication, and date), the same items (excluding serials) in chronological order, and an author and title index. **1927** W. W. BISHOP *Pract. Handbk. Mod. Libr. Catal.* 21 The catalog room..should be..on the same floor with the order clerks, classifiers and *shelf-listers. **1950** G. GREENE in *Dickens's Oliver Twist* p. vii, We must forget that long *shelf-load of books. **1980** *Jrnl. R. Soc. Arts* Mar. 177/2 Spend how much money you will, apply ten shelf loads of regulations, there is no way of promising that there is no risk of failure. **1842** *Row's Hist. Kirk* (Maitl. Cl.) Introd. Notice 56 A very carefully written MS... Old *shelf mark, W, 6, 30. **1889** H. B. WHEATLEY *How to Catalogue* 233 Printed books are moved and change their shelf-marks. **1897** MACRAY in Burnet *Own Time* Pref. 9 Two folio volumes, now *shelf-marked as 'Bodl. Add. D. 18, 19'. **1842** *Row's Hist. Kirk* (Maitl. Cl.) Introd. Notice 59 Another MS... The old *shelf-marking A. 6, 7. **1878** BROWNING *Poets Croisic* I. lvi, That and my other rare *shelf-occupants. **1895** *Montgomery Ward Catal.* 113/3 *Shelf Paper, pinked in fancy designs, each sheet 8½ inches wide, 33 inches long. **1968** *Listener* 27 June 841/1 Kerouac types *On the Road* on a 120-foot roll of shelf paper but cannot get it published. **1830** HEDDERWICK *Mar. Archit.* 286 A stringer or *shelf-piece bolted edge-ways to the clamp. **1860** H. STUART *Seaman's Catech.* 69 What do the beams rest upon? The shelf pieces, which extend all round the ship. **1869** E. J. REED *Shipbuild.* ii. 20 Armour *shelf-plates like those of the 'Warrior', which are immense angle-irons, in fact. **1898** CROCKETT *Stand. Bearer* v, The little *shelf-press rudely constructed in the wall of four blocks of stone split into faces. **1882** H. BRADSHAW in *Trans. Libr. Assoc.* (1884) 237 They [*sc.* volumes of periodical publications] await better times, when we can afford them proper *shelf-room. **1893** NEWTON *Dict. Birds* s.v. *Kittiwake*, It seems never to breed but on the side of a cliff, and there shelf-room is all it needs. **1913** T. C. CHAMBERLIN in *Jrnl. Geol.* XXI. 523 The waters that rest upon these sea-shelves may be known conveniently as *shelf-seas. **1969** BENNISON & WRIGHT *Geol. Hist. Brit. Isles* ii. 21 Sediments laid down in deeper water..have a quite different faunal content from the shelf-sea deposits. **1954** W. K. HANCOCK *Country & Calling* iii. 95 It became my fate to struggle with a brute documentary mass that has to be measured in miles of *shelf-space. **1978** J. IRVING *World according to Garp* ii. 28 Her books...outgrew the shelf space.

**shelf** (ʃɛlf), *sb.*[2] [Of obscure origin.

The identity of sense with SHELP[1] (recorded a century earlier) suggests that the two words may be in some way etymologically connected. The unexplained variation between *p* and *f* seems to have a parallel in the OE. *scylf* and *scylp*, both used to gloss *scopulus* and *murex* sharp rock, and in SCALP *sb.*[2] bed of oysters (cf. 2 below), which has the variants *scalfe, scalph*. It is not impossible that the word may descend from the OE. *scylf, scylp*, in some unrecorded sense. Some of the later uses show influence from SHELF *sb.*[1]]

**1.** A sandbank in the sea or river rendering the water shallow and dangerous. Also loosely applied to a submerged ledge of rock.

Very common till *c* 1750. See also SHELVE *sb.*[1]

**1545** ELYOT *Dict.*, *Syrtes*, quycke sandes or shelfes [*ed.* 1538 shelpes] in the water made by the dryfte of sande or grauell. **1571** *Act 13 Eliz.* c. 18 §5 The Shyriffes..shall.. after that the said newe Cut shalbe made..cause the same.. to be..clensed of all the Shelfes and Shallowes. **1577–87** HOLINSHED *Chron.* III. 1129/1 A place by the sea side, all of hard stone and pibble, called in those parts [*sc.* Suffolk] a shelfe. **1617** MORYSON *Itin.* III. 138 Before the Rode of Margat lie the dangerous shelfes or flats of sand, whereof the greatest is called Goodwin sand. **1651** DAVENANT *Gondibert* Pref. 19 Coasting Mapps, where the Shelves and Rocks are describ'd as well as the safe Channell. **1691** T. H[ALE] *Acc. New Invent.* p. liv, Deepening the River of Thames, and removing Shelfes therein. **1762** FALCONER *Shipwr.* III. 329 A shore where shelves and hidden rocks abound. **1791** *Selby Bridge Act* 3 To remove any shelves, or other obstructions, in the said river. **1802** *Brooke's Gazetteer* (ed. 12) s.v. *Ladoga*, Quicksands, which..cause several shelves which often prove fatal to the flat-bottomed vessels of the Russians. **1878** BROWNING *La Saisiaz* 34 The every way external stream that now through shoal and shelf Floats it onward.

**b.** *fig.* and in fig. context.

**1560** DAUS tr. *Sleidane's Comm.* Pref. 4b, Whan I somtime doubted, & sticked fast on the rockes & shelves. **1574** HELLOWES *Gueuara's Fam. Ep.* (1577) 186 There is in loue after it is begon, infinite shelues, immeasurable sloughes, daungerous rockes. **1604** EARL STIRLING *Croesus* II. ii, This self-conceit is a most dangerous shelfe. **1612** SIR W. ALEXANDER *Elegie Death Pr. Henrie* 9 Though generall be the losse, one shelfe confounding quyte, The King's chiefe joy, the kingdomes hope, and all the worlds delight. **1616** R. C. *Times' Whistle* (1871) 43 Till i' th' end his pelfe Shipwracks his soule vpon hels rocky shelfe. **1652** BENLOWES *Theoph.* Pref., To divert thee therefore from such Shelves of indiscreet Vice. **1784** COWPER *Tiroc.* 269 Yes—ye are conscious; and on all the shelves Your pupils strike upon, have struck yourselves.

†**2.** ***shelves of margarites, of oysters.*** (Cf. SCALP *sb.*[2])

**1590** GREENE *Fr. Bacon* (1630) 2 Her teeth are shelues of precious Margarites, Richly enclosed with ruddie curroll cleues. **1594** —— & LODGE *Looking Gl.* I. i. 100 I'll fetch from Albia shelves of margarites. **1594** NASHE *Terrors Nt.* G 2b, Great glaring eyes that had whole shelues of Kentish oysters in them.

**3.** *Comb.* †**shelf-spoiled**, rendered dangerous by shoals.

**1627** MAY *Lucan, Pharsalia* IX. Q 8, A shelfe-spoil'd sea.

**shelf**, *sb.*[3] *dial.* (Devon and Cornwall.) Also **shilf**. [? a use of SHELF *sb.*[1] (cf. sense 5).] (See quots.)

[**1602–1778**: ? Implied in SHELFY *a.*[3]] **1849** *Ecclesiologist* IX. 288 *note*, Shilf means broken slate, in small pieces, such as is used for mending roads in parts of Cornwall. **1891** *Hartland Gloss.*, *Shelf*, soft slaty rock.

**shelf** (ʃɛlf), *v.*[1] *Obs.*[−1] [Origin and meaning obscure; cf. OE. *scelfan* to shake; also next vb. (Perh. an arbitrary formation for rhyme: cf. SHELVE *v.*)] *trans.* ? To ruin.

*c* **1425** *Cast. Persev.* 1070 in *Macro Plays*, Euery man þou schalt schende & schelfe, & holde no man betyr þanne þi selfe.

†**shelf**, *v.*[2] *Obs.* [f. SHELF *sb.*[2]] *trans.* To cast on a shelf or sandbank.

**1652** BENLOWES *Theoph.* I. lxxx, Such Saints high Tides n'ere ebbe so low, to shelf Them on the Quicksand of their self.

**shelf** (ʃɛlf), *v.*[3] [f. SHELF *sb.*[1]]

**1.** *trans.* To lay on the shelf, shelve.

**1814** SCOTT *Drama* (1874) 225 He is too often retained for the mere purpose of being laid aside, or shelfed, as it is technically called. **1832** GEN. P. THOMPSON *Exerc.* (1842) II. 285 Trills.., and bravuras, will be shelfed with Mandane's hoop and Alexander's wig. **1863** KINGSLEY *Water Babies* vii. 301 Blind brigadiers shelfed as principals of colleges.

**2.** *Austral. slang.* To inform upon. Cf. SHELF *sb.*[1] 4.

**1953** K. TENNANT *Joyful Condemned* xi. 96 Central has only to lamp you coming in here, and we all go up. Jimmy here shelfed me before. **1958** V. KELLY *Greedy Ones* 104 We were mates in this affair and you don't shelf your mates. And anyone who does shelf a mate has got to take what's coming to him.

**shelfa**, variant form of SHILFA.

ˈ**shelf-ful.** [-FUL.] A quantity sufficient to fill a shelf; the contents of a shelf.

**1876** G. O. TREVELYAN *Life & Lett. Macaulay* (1878) II. xii. 267 A shelf-full of Irish novels. **1912** *Blackw. Mag.* May 700/2 The quarrel of Byron with his wife has furnished forth a shelfful of books.

**shelfy** (ˈʃɛlfɪ), *a.*[1] [f. SHELF *sb.*[2] + -Y. Cf. SHELVY.] Abounding in sandbanks lying near the surface of the water.

**1576** SIR H. GILBERT *Disc. Pass. Cataia* vi, Because all Seas..are maintained by the abundance of the water, waxing more shallow and shelffie towards the ende. **1632** LITHGOW *Trav.* III. 99 We had a shelfie shoare. *Ibid.* v. 228 With dreadfull snares Begirded round, in shelfie gulfes of wracke. **1697** DRYDEN *Æneid* v. 1125 A shelfy coast, Long infamous for ships and sailors lost. **1725** POPE *Odyss.* I. 257 Among a savage race, whose shelfy bounds With ceaseless roar the foaming deep surrounds.

**shelfy** (ˈʃɛlfɪ), *a.*[2] [f. SHELF *sb.*[1] + -Y.] Having ledges or terraces.

**1767** FAWKES *Idyll. Theocr.* XXI. 53 Methought I sat upon a shelfy steep. **1887** BLACKMORE *Cripps* xxxvi, A mighty hedge of beetling brows, and over-hanging shagginess, and shelfy curves, and brambly depths.

**shelfy**, *a.*[3] *dial.* (Devon and Cornwall.) [f. SHELF *sb.*[3] + -Y.] Full of 'shelf' or slaty rock.

The sense 'full of strata of rock' in Webster 1864, to which Ogilvie 1882 adds 'having rocky ledges cropping up' is based on quot. 1602.

**1602** CAREW *Cornwall* 20 The tillable fields are in some places..so shelfie that the Corne hath much adoe to fasten his roote. **1674** FLAVEL *Husb. Spiritualized* vii. 70 Sometimes this plow thin shelfy ground doth turn. **1753** *Chambers' Cycl.* Suppl. s.v. *Sea-sand*, It is sometimes composed of shelly matter alone; but sometimes it is made up partly of this, and partly of broken stones: in this last case it is called shelfy sand. **1778** PRYCE *Min. Cornub.* 74 The Slate, or Shelfy-stone, is always uppermost next the loamy soil.

**sheling**, obs. form of SHILLING.

†**sheliscad.** *Obs.* (See quot.)

*c* **1630** RISDON *Surv. Devon* (1714) II. 394 Shots and Sheliscads, a Fish not unlike the Trout, and said to be peculiar to Devonshire and Cornwall.

**shell** (ʃɛl), *sb.* Forms: 1 **sciell, scel(l, scill, scyll,** 4 **schele, scell, chelle, s(c)hill, (schyl-),** 4–5 **schelle, schylle,** 4–6 **schell, shelle, (schel-),** 4–7 **shel,** 5 **shylle, schull(e,** 7 **shul,** 9 *dial.* **shill, shull,** 4– **shell.** [OE. *sciell, scill*, Anglian *scell* fem. = WFris. *skyl* peel, rind, egg-shell, NFris. *skel, skal* sea-shell, (M)LG. *schelle, schille* pod, rind, fish-scale, eggshell, MDu. *schelle, schille* shell, pod, bark, rind, pl. scurf (Du. *schel, schil*), ON. *skel* sea-shell (Norw. *skjæl*), Goth. *skalja* tile:—OTeut. **skaljō*, f. **skal-*, for other derivatives of which see SCALE *sb.*[1], *sb.*[2], SHALE *sb.*[1] Cf. SKELL, from ON.]

**I.** The hard outside covering of an animal, a fruit, etc.

**1. a.** The calcareous or chitinous outer covering of crustaceans, molluscs, and other invertebrates.

See also COCKLE-SHELL, MUSSEL-SHELL, OYSTER-SHELL, SCALLOP-SHELL.

*c* **725** *Corpus Gloss.* (Hessels) C 863 *Conca*, musclan scel. *a* **1100** *Aldhelm Gloss.* I. 447 (Napier 13/2) *Conca*, musclan scille. *c* **1375** *Sc. Leg. Saints* xxix. (*Placidas*) 518 Ȝet wes lewit hym [*sc.* Job] a schele to schrape his scabbis rycht snel. **1387–8** T. USK *Test. Love* I. iii. (Skeat) l. 78 A muskel, in a blewe shel. *c* **1430** *Two Cookery-bks.* 24 Pyke owt þe Muskele of þe schulle. *c* **1475** *Pict. Voc.* in Wr.Wülcker 765/27 *Hec testa*, a schylle. *c* **1560** A. SCOTT *Poems* (S.T.S.) v. 33 Mussillis in schellis. **1605** SHAKS. *Lear* I. v. 27 Can'st tell how an Oyster makes his shell? *a* **1631** DONNE *Poems* (1654) 38 Let others freez with angling reeds, And cut their legs, with shels and weeds. **1709** STEELE *Tatler* No. 112 ¶3 They used to gather up Shells on the Sea-Shore. **1709** *Lond. Gaz.* No. 4510/7 About 14000 Oysters in the Shells. *a* **1728** WOODWARD *Nat. Hist. Fossils* II. (1729) I. 24 Two Nautiloides, or Bodies form'd in Shells of the Nautilus. **1833–4** J. PHILLIPS *Geol.* in *Encycl. Metrop.* (1845) VI. 684/2 The small bivalve crustaceous shells of cypris. **1834** McMURTRIE *Cuvier's Anim. Kingd.* 272 All the Brachiopoda are invested with bivalve shells, fixed and immoveable. *Ibid.* 468 The..Sea-Urchins..have the body invested by a shell or calcareous crust. **1870** ROLLESTON *Anim. Life* 47 The thickness of the Gasteropodous shell diminishes from its free rim upwards. **1895** KERNAHAN *God & Ant* Apol. (ed. 4) 10 As the grain of sand, which has found its way into his shell, vexes and irks the oyster.

**b.** Allusive uses, with reference to:

(*a*) The formation of pearls within the shells of molluscs. (*b*) The association of a shell with persons of classical mythology (e.g. Venus Anadyomene). (*c*) The sound of the sea heard when a round-lipped shell is placed with the mouth to one's ear.

(*a*) **1390** GOWER *Conf.* III. 346 He hath noght elles, Nomor the perles than the schelles. [**1447** BOKENHAM *Seyntys* (Roxb.) 2 A margerye perle aftyr the phylosophyr Growyth on a shelle of lytyl pryhs.] **1611** B. JONSON *Catiline* I. i. Chorus, Her Women weare The spoiles of Nations, in an eare, Chang'd for the treasure of a shell. [**1813** SCOTT *Trierm.* III. xxvi, See these pearls,..These were tears by Naiads wept..Tritons in the silver shell Treasured them.] **1850** TENNYSON *In Mem.* lii, Thy wealth is gather'd in, When Time hath sunder'd shell from pearl.

(*b*) **1634** MILTON *Comus* 231 Sweet Echo, sweetest Nymph that liv'st unseen Within thy airy shell. **1685** DRYDEN *Albion* I. 8 Venus in her shell. **1823** BYRON *Island* II. vii, A form like Aphrodite's in her shell.

(*c*) **1814** WORDSWORTH *Excurs.* IV. 1141 Even such a shell the universe itself Is to the ear of Faith.

**2.** A shell of this kind (or a vessel resembling one) used for a specific purpose.

**a.** = SCALLOP *sb.* 1 c. **b.** Used as a target. *Sc.*, chiefly with indecent allusion (cf. L. *concha* = cunnus). **c.** *pl.* Seashells used as money. (Cf. *cowry*.) †**d.** A drinking vessel. **e.** A mussel-shell containing pigment to be used by mixing with gum. **f.** = CONCH 3.

**a. 1362** LANGLAND *P. Pl.* A. VI. 12 Signes of Synay and Schelles of Galys. **1507** *Pilton Churchw. Acc.* (Som. Rec. Soc.) 64, iij schellys of Seynt Iame.

**b. 1497** *Acc. Ld. High. Treas. Scot.* I. 360 Item, to the king, to schut at the schell..xvj*d.* **1500–20** DUNBAR *Poems* xxxi. 13 He that..schuttis syne at ane vncow schell,..He wirkis sorrow to him sell. **1536** LYNDESAY *Answ. Kingis Flyting* 45 Tholand ȝow rin schutand frome schell to schell. *a* **1568** *Bannatyne MS.* (Hunter. Club) 392 Few honour wynnis in to that innys For schutting at the schellis.

**c. 1600** J. PORY tr. *Leo's Africa* VII. 288 In matters of smal value they use certaine shels brought hither out of the Kingdome of Persia, fower hundred of which shels are worth a ducate. **1732** LEDIARD *Sethos* II. VII. 65 An office of exchange to receive the shells of foreign savages.

**d. 1577** tr. *Bullinger's Decades* II. x. 243 Some menne there are, which..swallowe..deintie hearbe brothes,..not out of a cup, but out of a shell. **1773** BOSWELL *Tour Hebr.* 5 Oct., Whiskey was served round in a shell, according to the ancient Highland custom.

**e. 1565** COOPER *Thesaurus* s.v. *Concha, Conchæ*, shelles wherin peynters putte theyr colours. **1665** HOOKE *Microgr.* 75 Those several colours they lay on their Shels or Palads. **1666** SPURSTOWE *Wiles of Satan* 12 As a Painter doth his many Colours, that lye..before him in their several Shells. **1895** *Army & Navy Co-op. Soc.* Price List 668 Colours for Illuminating... Tube of Enamel White, Gold Shell, Aluminium Shell.

f. **1634** Milton *Comus* 873 By scaly Tritons winding shell. [**1699** Potter *Antiq. Greece* III. ix. 86 Shells of Fishes.. which they sounded in the manner of Trumpets.] **1823** Byron *Island* II. ii, Ere Fiji blew the shell of war.

**3.** As a rendering of Gr. ὄστρακον, the potsherd or tile used in the ostracism of the ancient Greeks.

The ὄστρακον has been freq. taken by mod. writers for an oyster-shell.

[**1538** Elyot *Dict.*, *Ostracismus*,.. whyche exyle was doone by delyuerynge of oyster shelles.] **1565** Cooper *Thesaurus*, *Ostracismus*, a kinde of banishment amonge the Athenians for .x. yeres space, whiche was done by delieurynge of shelles with the names of the persons condemned wryten in them. **1579–80** North *Plutarch, Aristides* (1595) 353 At a certaine day appointed, euery citizen caried a great shell in his hande, whereupon he wrote the name of him he would haue banished. **1711** Pope *Temple of Fame* 173 He [*sc.* Aristides] whom ungrateful Athens could expell, At all times just, but when he sign'd the Shell. **1770** Langhorne *Plutarch, Nicias* III. 389 The shell was not designed for such wretches as he. **1845** *Encycl. Metrop.* IX. 365/1 If the name of any person was found to be written on six thousand tiles or shells [etc.].

**4.** *pl.* Burnt limestone before it is slaked. †*in shells*: unslaked.

**1743** in R. Maxwell *Sel. Trans. Agric.* 191 Shells will weigh about 25 Stone-weight the Boll. [**1793**: see lime *sb.*[1] 5]. **1799** J. Robertson *Agric. Perth* 282 The farmers endeavour to carry it in shells, while the water is dissipated and the lime light. **1812** Sir J. Sinclair *Syst. Husb. Scot.* I. 178 [He] brings his lime from the kiln, lays it in small heaps, about a firlot of shells in each heap. **1884** F. J. Lloyd *Sci. Agric.* 113 The lumps of burnt and unslaked limestone are known as shells.

**5.** Used as the second element of the name of a particular shellfish, as *acorn-shell*, *razor-shell*; hence (chiefly *pl.*) = shellfish, in referring to classificatory groups.

**1751** *Chambers' Cycl.*, *Balani*... They are commonly called in English, centre-shells. **1840** *Cuvier's Anim. Kingd.* 386 The Balanus or Acorn-Shells. **1858** Baird *Cycl. Nat. Sci.* s.v. *Mollusca*, Conchifera, or ordinary bivalve shells, which breathe by two pairs of gills.

**6. a.** The hard outer calcareous envelope of a bird's egg. (†*in the shell*, of an egg, boiled.) Also, the similar integument of the eggs of other creatures. Cf. egg-shell.

*a* **900** *O.E. Martyrol.* 18 Mar. 40 Se rodor ymbfehð.. sæ & eorðan, swa seo scell utan ymbfehð þæt æg. **13..** *K. Alis.* 571 An ay he laide, so he fleygh,.. That tobrak, Y yow telle: A dragon crep out of the schelle. **1398** Trevisa *Barth. De P.R.* XII. i. (Bodl. MS.), The chikenes comeþ forþe of þe schelle alyue and fulle schape. *c* **1430** *Two Cookery-bks.* 41 Take Eyroun, & blow owt þat ys with-ynne..þan waysshe þe schulle clene. **1599** Sir J. Davies *Nosce Teipsum* 99 When the shell is broke, out comes a chick. **1657** W. Coles *Adam in Eden* xlii, When her food begins once to appear she [the silkworm] comes forth of her shel. **1692** Tryon *Good House-wife* x. 83 Eggs boyled in the Shells. **1719** De Foe *Crusoe* I. 99 The Turtle's Eggs, which I roasted in the Ashes, and eat, as we call it, in the Shell. **1864** *Englishw. in India* 173 Beat the whites of the eggs in a basin... Crush the shells and add them with the wine.

**b.** *in the shell*: (of an egg or a bird, etc.) unhatched; also *fig.*, in embryo.

**1601** Shaks. *Jul. C.* II. i. 34 Thinke him as a Serpents egge,.. And kill him in the shell. **1606** —— *Tr. & Cr.* I. ii. 148 If you loue an addle egge as well as you loue an idle head, you would eate chickens i' th' shell. **1638** Chillingw. *Relig. Prot.* I. ii. §101. 91 Some yet are Embrio's, yet hatching, and in the shell; as the Popes infallibility. **1649** Jer. Taylor *Gt. Exemp.* III. Ad Sec. xvi. 179 Corn for ever in the blade, egges alwaies in the shell. *a* **1659** Osborn *Observ. Turks* Wks. (1673) 278 By the heat of Religion many Vertues are hatched, and more Vices stifled in the shell. **1883** S. C. Hall *Retrospect* II. 71 Embryo poets and artists in the shell. **1897** *Advance* (Chicago) 25 Feb. 242/1 As a writer he is full grown ..but as an evolutionist he is still in the shell.

**c.** In fig. phr. referring to emergence into life; *esp.* in *out of one's shell* (with a negative).

**1551** T. Wilson *Logic* (1580) 58 b, In this worlde a childe shall scant be out of his shell, but he shall be sure to one, or other. **1593** Nashe *Christ's T.* Wks. 1910 II. 86 My young nouice.. not yet crept out of the shell. *Ibid.* 122 If at the first peeping out of the shell a young Student sets not a graue face on it. **1599** *Broughton's Lett.* 27 Those the.. Archbishop.. vnfolded.. at Cambridge, before thou wert crept out of thy Alphabeticall shell. **1670** Baxter *Cure Ch. Div.* 4 The pride of those that run with the shell on their head into the Ministry. **1808** Jamieson s.v., *You're scarcely out of the shell yet*; a phrase applied to young persons, to those especially who affect something beyond their years. **1837** Browning *Strafford* II. i, *Puritan.* His fruit shall be a fiery flying serpent. *Fiennes.* 'Shall be'? It chips the shell, man,—peeps abroad.

**7. a.** = nutshell *sb.*

*c* **1330** R. Brunne *Chron. Wace* (Rolls) 14683 Luytel notes þey toke, & holede þem, þe kerneles out schoke; þey dide y þe schelles fyr & tunder. **1398** Trevisa *Barth. De P.R.* XVII. cviii. (Bodl. MS.), Aschelle oþer aschale þ[t] waxiþ harder & harder & þer w[t]in is þe notte curnel. *c* **1400** *Rom. Rose* 7117 As moche as.. The sunne sourmounteth the mone,.. And the note kernelle the shelle. **1555** Eden *Decades* (Arb.) 342 The halfe shelles of almonds. *a* **1691** Boyle *Hist. Air* (1692) 178 Almonds of a tender Shell. **1699** Dampier *Voy.* II. I. 152 About 100 Nutmegs, which had the Shells on as they grew on the Trees.

*Prov.* *c* **1375** *Cursor M.* 23828 (Fairf.) þaire speche is noȝt worþ a shelle [*Cott.* noght a nute-scell]. **1577** Grange *Golden Aphrod.* I iij b, I see the prouerbe is true: who wil the curnell of the nut must breake the shell. **1611** Cotgr. s.v. *Coque, Nulle noix sans coque*, no nut without a shell.

**b.** *fig.* and in fig. context. (See also shall *sb.*)

**1377** Langl. *P. Pl.* B. xi. 252 After þat bitter barke (be þe shelle aweye), Is a kirnelle of conforte. **1611** Bible *Transl. Pref.* ¶5 Translation it is.. that breaketh the shell, that we may eat the kernel. **1613** Purchas *Pilgrimage* (1614) 490 All are vaine-glorious, and seeke rather the shell then the kernell, the shew then the substance of holinesse. **1621** Laud *Diary* 3 June, He [the King] was pleased to say, he had given me nothing but [the Deanery of] Gloucester, which he well knew was a shell without a kernel. **1650** Hubbert *Pill Formality* 22 Forms are more contended for, then power,.. shel more then kernel.

**c.** The fibre-covered envelope of a coco-nut.

**1638** Sir T. Herbert *Trav.* (ed. 2) 29 The Coco.. is cover'd with a thick rynd,.. the shell is like the skull of man. **1768** Cocoa nut-shell [see coco[1] 4 e]. **1838** Mrs. Browning *Rom. Ganges* iv, Of shell of coco carven, Each little boat is made. **1891** Codrington *Melanesians* xvi. 316 The cream squeezed out from grated cocoa-nut was often cooked over the embers in the shells.

**8. a.** The outer covering of a seed, etc.; a husk, pod (e.g. *pea-shell*); †rind (of pomegranates, etc.); putamen, pericarp.

**1561** Hollybush *Hom. Apoth.* 26 Take the wood of Berberis, fyll the upper shell wyth the leaves from it. **1562** Turner *Herbal* II. (1568) 33 If lentilles be sodden with theyr shelles untaken of. **1607** Topsell *Four-f. Beasts* 389 The powder of vnripe Pomegranat shels. **1611** Cotgr., *Calicules*, .. the rough shells of Chestnuts. **1624** [see gourd[1] 4]. **1631** Widdowes *Nat. Philos.* 24 It may be softened by quenching in juyce of beane shuls or mallowes. **1657** W. Coles *Adam in Eden* xcix, Within which fruit [gourd], lie.. many seeds, having smooth hard wooddy shells. **1707** Mortimer *Husb.* (1721) II. 144 The Scarlet-Bean which has a red Husk, and is not the best to eat in the Shell, as Kidney-Beans are usually eaten. **1745** Pococke *Descr. East* II. i. 233 They fill the shell [of coloquintida] with milk, and let it stand some time. **1796** Withering *Brit. Plants* (ed. 3) I. 66 *Legumen*, or shell; a seed-vessel of two valves. **1861** Bentley *Man. Bot.* 301 A strong shell surrounding the seed, called the *putamen*. **1887** *Ibid.* (ed. 5) 20 The shell or *pericarp*. **1901** Alldridge *Sherbro* ii. 15 A great deal of shell [on palm kernels], which of course is useless.

**b.** The empty case of a fruit.

**1902** H. L. Wilson *Spenders* xxvii. 313 Mr. Milbrey glanced at the two shells of the orange which the butler was then removing. **1974** *Times* 20 Apr. 10/8 Grapefruit mixes well with cottage cheese, and you can use the shell to hold the salad.

**9. a.** The hard covering or 'house' of a snail: cf. snail-shell.

*c* **1400** Maundev. (Roxb.) xxi. 96 Þer er.. so grete snyles þat in þaire schelles three men or foure may be herberd. **1530** Palsgr. 266/2 Schell of a snayle, *cocquille*. **1611** Cotgr., *Caqueroles*, the shels of Snayles, Periwincles, and such like. **1766** [Anstey] *New Bath Guide* vi. (1807) 42 As snug as a hodmandod rides in his shell. **1774** Goldsm. *Nat. Hist.* (1776) VII. 23 In proportion as it grows, the shell encreases in the number of its circles. **1808** *Med. Jrnl.* XIX. 373 The covering or opercle with which they [*sc.* snails] close up their shell in winter.

**b.** In fig. phrases, referring to avoidance of society or to a forbidding and an uncommunicative manner.

**1815** C'tess Granville *Lett.* (1894) I. 73 Madame de Coigny has difficulty in re-uniting people *chez elle*, and if one meets a Frenchman there, he draws into his shell and sits in gloomy silence. **1853** Earl Lytton *Let. to Browning* 26 July, I have long ago crept into my shell for good. **1889** C. F. M. Bell *From Pharaoh to Fellah* xiii. 111 Under the soothing influence of coffee and tobacco, he came out of his shell. **1893** Vizetelly *Glances Back* I. vii. 137 [He] rarely spoke unless personally appealed to, and speedily retired into his shell again.

**10. a.** The hard covering of a tortoise or turtle; the material of which this is composed: cf. tortoiseshell.

**1545** Elyot *Dict.*, *Chelonium*, the shell of a torteyse. **1601** Holland *Pliny* VI. xxiv. I. 134 The Chelonophagi, *i.* such as feed upon the flesh of Tortoises, and the shels of them serve for roufes. **1638** Sir T. Herbert *Trav.* (ed. 2) 25 The Sea Tortoise is not much differing from those at land, her house or shell is only flatter. **1726** G. Roberts *Four Yrs. Voy.* 21 They had nothing to pay me for it, but the Turtle, Oil, and Shell which they had made here. **1844** Thirlwall *Greece* VIII. 353 A tortoise, which is safe only so long as it keeps within its shell.

†**b.** *poet.* [after L. *testudo.*] A lyre (in allusion to the legend that the first lyre was a tortoise shell stringed); occas. (cf. lyre[1] 1 b) put for 'lyric poetry'. *Obs.*

[**1687** Dryden *Song St. Cecilia's Day* ii, When Jubal struck the corded Shell.] **1746** Collins *Ode to Pity* vii, Till, Virgin, Thou again delight To hear a British Shell! **1769** Gray *Ode for Music* 23 'Twas Milton struck the deep-toned shell. **1821** Byron *Diary* Wks. (1846) 423/1 My brethren of the shell. **1821** —— *Sardanap.* III. i. 66 Hast thou thy shell in order? Sing me a song.

**11.** The integument of an armadillo, glyptodon, ostraciont, etc.; the elytron of an insect; the cast skin of a pupa.

**1774** Goldsm. *Nat. Hist.* (1824) II. 112 This animal [*sc.* the armadillo] being covered, like a tortoise, with a shell, or rather a number of shells. **1840** Swainson & Shuckard *Insects* §70. 81 An immense assemblage of insects, having.. four wings, but of which two are converted into cases or shells (*elytra*). **1852** Dana *Crust.* II. 1370 The two elytra-like prolongations of the shell of the third segment of the body [of the Dinematuræ].

**II.** A shell-shaped object; something concave or hollow.

**12. a.** Applied *gen.* to a hollow spherical, hemispherical, or dome-shaped object.

**1599** *Churchw. Acc. Pittington*, etc. (Surtees) 276 Whatsoever shall.. misforten about the clock, viz., shelles or nutes or such like thinges. *a* **1700** Evelyn *Diary* 27 Feb. 1644, That [jetto] which rises over the greate shell of lead, from whence it glides silently down a channel. **1753** *De Foe's Tour Gt. Brit.* (ed. 5) I. 157 There rises above the Roof a semicircular Dome, which has two Shells,.. the outward Shell is Carpentry, covered with Lead. **1759** H. Walpole *Let. to G. Montagu* 2 June, As they were sitting in the shell on my terrace. **1817** Shelley *Rev. Islam* XII. 4630 The boat was one curved shell of hollow pearl. **1850** B. Taylor *Eldorado* iv. (1862) 34 The whole vast shell of the firmament. **1851** Ruskin *Stones of Venice* I. xi. §1 An arch .. is a curved shell of firm materials, on whose back a burden is to be laid of loose materials.

**b.** A thin body bounded by two closely spaced curved surfaces: (*a*) as a concept in *Statics*; (*b*) in *Civil Engin.*, a structural member of this form that has strength by virtue of its shape.

**1877** G. M. Minchin *Treat. Statics* xiv. 432 Hence.. every shell of uniform density and small thickness, bounded by similar, similarly situated, and concentric surfaces produces a constant potential at all points in its interior. **1892** A. E. H. Love *Treat. Math. Theory Elasticity* I. vii. 221 Consider the case of a spherical shell, whose outer and inner surfaces are subjected to hydrostatic pressure. **1952** O. Faber *Reinforced Concrete* xiii. 192 For clear widths of about 150 ft. and over it is found to be economical to provide arched shells spanning direct, with stiffening ribs at about 25 ft. to 35 ft. centres. **1967** H. Kraus *Thin Elastic Shells* p. vii, Sophisticated uses of shells are currently being made in missiles and space vehicles, submarines, nuclear reactor vessels, refinery equipment, and the like. **1972** R. E. Owen *Roofs* vi. 81 A cylindrical shell transmits direct load to its columns.

**c.** *U.S.* A concave structure designed to accommodate a band or orchestra.

**1938** D. Baker *Young Man with Horn* I. vi. 71 At the rear of the room was the orchestra shell, very shell-like, fluted along the upper edge. **1978** *Chicago* June 22/2 Each concert will be given on two evenings, and performances will take place.. in the new James C. Petrillo Music Shell at Jackson and Columbus.

**13. a.** A scale of a balance. *Sc.*

**15..** *Aberd. Reg.* (Jam.), A pair of schellis. **1637** Rutherford *Lett.* (1664) 143 Our Lord (who hath all you the Nobles lying in the shell of his ballance). *c* **1730** Ramsay *Fables, Twa Cats & Cheese* 22 He.. ca's for the scales.. He puts ilk haff in either shell.

†**b.** The bowl (of a chalice). *Obs.*

**1546** *Inv. Ch. Goods* (Surtees) 134 A chalice, the shelle of silver and gilt, waing iiij ounces.

**14.** The semicircular guard of a sword, often elaborately worked.

**1685** *Lond. Gaz.* No. 2050/4 A Rapier Sword, the Hilt of which was made with a whole Shell. **1692** Sir W. Hope *Fencing Master* 3 The Shell is that part of the Hilt next to the Blade. **1707** —— *New Meth. Fencing* iv. §3. 60 The Hilt hath its Pomel, Handle, Shell, and Cross-Barrs. **1748** Smollett *Rod. Rand.* lix, I seized his shell, which was close to my breast, before he could disintangle his point. **1826** Scott *Woodst.* xix. The shell of my rapier struck against his ribs. **1869** Boutell *Arms & Armour* ix. 178 This weapon [the rapier] generally has a kind of small basket or shell.

**15.** The apsidal end of the school-room at Westminster School, so called from its conch-like shape. Hence, the name of the form (intermediate between the fifth and sixth) which originally tenanted the 'shell' at Westminster School, and *transf.* of forms (intermediate between forms designated by numbers) in other public schools; see quots.

**1736** *Gentl. Mag.* VI. 679/2 Near these [forms] y[e] shell's high concave walls appear. **1750** Chesterf. *Lett.* ccxxviii, Observe.. what the best scholars in the Form immediately above you do, and so on, till you get into the shell yourself. **1825** Southey *Life & Corr.* (1849) I. 151 He was floated up to the Shell, beyond which the tide carried no one. **1857** Hughes *Tom Brown* I. v, The lower fifth, shell, and all the junior forms in order [at Rugby]. **1877** Ld. W. P. Lennox *Celebr. I have known* I. 43 The noise grew louder and louder, until the birch was safely deposited in a small room behind the 'shell',—so the upper end of the room was called from its shape [Westminster]. **1884** Forshall *Westm. Sch.* 3 The Headmaster faced all the boys excepting the tenants of the 'Shell'. **1903** *Blackw. Mag.* June 742/2 The third 'shell', a form within measurable distance of the lowest in the school [Harrow].

**16.** The bottom part of a turnip remaining after the root has been scooped out by sheep.

**1802** Willich *Dom. Encycl.* IV. 60/2 The shells of turnips which have been suffered to lie on the ground for some time. **1886** C. Scott *Sheep-farming* 49 An active man will, with the assistance of a boy or woman at picking shells, manage 600 full-mouthed sheep.

**17.** The outer ear; = concha 4 a.

**1847** Youatt *Horse* vi. 122 This cartilage, the conch or shell, is attached to the head by ligaments. **1871** Darwin *Desc. Man* I. i. 21 The whole external shell of the ear.

**18. a.** *U.S.* A light, narrow, racing-boat.

**1867** *Harper's Mag.* Oct. 654/2 Look at these beautiful 'shells', resting one above the other on the brackets on either wall. **1873** B. Harte *What B. Harte Saw* in *Fiddletown*, etc. 98 A shell with its exercising crew. **1894** *Outing* XXIV. 69/2 The first month of rowing in the shell is taken up in coaxing the fractious creature to be steady on its bottom.

**b.** The floating part of a racing boat; the dug-out portion of a West Indian canoe.

**1895** *Westm. Gaz.* 30 Mar. 3/1 After the skin and the ribs, which really constitute the shell of the boat, are finished, we fix the seats and stretchers. **1901** *Daily Tel.* 18 Mar. 7/4 The greater distance between the men necessitated by the slides also involved a longer shell. **1907** C. Hill-Tout *Brit. N. Amer., Far West* vii. 136 The thickness of the shell varies with the size of the vessel, the small [dug-out] canoes being about an inch.

**19. a.** Miscellaneous technical uses.

e.g.: in casting, the outer wall of the mould; a pump bucket or clack before it is grathed; a concave grinding tool; a thin film of copper forming the face of an electrotype, which is backed with type-metal; see also quots.

**1819** REVELEY *Let. to Shelley* 12 Nov., So that the melted metal..may..fill up the..space left between the core and the shell, in order to form the desired cylinders. **1835** URE *Philos. Manuf.* 168 A fluted cylinder called the roller-bowl, encased at its lower and back part within a segment of a hollow cylinder called the shell. **1839** *Civil Engin. & Arch. Jrnl.* II. 311/1 The shells or buckets are fitted with valves opening upwards. *Ibid.* VII. 370 Two 'shells' are to be provided, or what is technically termed the moulding box. **1860** *Ure's Dict. Arts* II. 699 A concave rough grinding tool of cast iron called a shell. **1875** KNIGHT *Dict. Mech.*, *Shell* (*Weaving*), the upper and under shells are the bars of the lay, which are grooved to receive the reed. **1881** MAXWELL *Electr. & Magn.* I. 77 An insulated spherical shell concentric with the globe. **1884** KNIGHT *Dict. Mech.* Suppl., *Shell*, a Russian tool for turning insides of hollow projectiles. **1885** LOCK in *Workshop Rec.* Ser. IV. 215/1 A substantial electrotype or shell should be obtained in 10–15 hours. **1898** *Syd. Soc. Lex.*, *Shells*, a term for tinted spectacles for protecting the eyes from bright light.

**b.** *Physics.* (A set of electrons forming) one of a number of concentric structures around the nucleus of an atom; *spec.* a set of electrons each having the same principal quantum number. Also, (a set of nucleons forming) a corresponding structure within a nucleus.

**1904** J. J. THOMSON in *Phil. Mag.* VII. 255 When the corpuscles [*sc.* electrons] are not constrained to one plane, but can move about in all directions, they will arrange themselves in a series of concentric shells. **1919** *Proc. Nat. Acad. Sci.* V. 252 The electrons in any given atom are distributed through a series of concentric (nearly) spherical shells, all of equal thickness. **1932** *Physical Rev.* XLI. 370/1 For some time, there has been speculation as to whether or not the atomic nucleus can be regarded as consisting of shells of protons, just as the external structure is known to consist of shells of electrons. **1952** *Sci. News* XXIII. 36 Neon has 10 electrons in two complete shells. **1961** G. R. CHOPPIN *Exper. Nuclear Chem.* iii. 30 Frequently, rather than emit a gamma ray, a nucleus will interact with its external electronic shells and cause emission of an electron. **1972** *Sci. Amer.* Oct. 101/1 In nuclei there also is a periodic recurrence of certain properties as nucleons are added to fill successive shells of quantum states. **1974** G. REECE tr. *Hund's Hist. Quantum Theory* viii. 106 The formation of molecules was thus a problem of atomic structure, namely the tendency of atoms to form ions with complete shells.

**III.** An exterior or enclosing cover or case.

**20. a.** A covering (of earth, stone, etc.).

**1667** PRIMATT *City & C. Builder* 4 Coal-mines which are covered with a shell of stone about a fathom or more thick. **1692** BENTLEY *Boyle Lect.* iii. 98 Arched over with an exterior Crust or Shell of Earth.

**b.** The crust of the earth.

*a* **1704** LOCKE *Elem. Nat. Philos.* viii. (1754) 32 Whatever we fetch from under ground is only what is lodg'd in the shell of the earth. **1830** LYELL *Princ. Geol.* I. 35 The separation of the land from the waters, mentioned in Genesis: during which operation some places of the shell of the earth were forced outwards. **1869** PHILLIPS *Vesuv.* xii. 331 The inner as well as the outer surface of the earth's crust or shell must be spheroidal.

**21. a.** A case of metal, etc. in which powder and shot is made up, esp. for use as a hand-grenade.

**1644** NYE *Gunnery* II. (1647) 73 First of all fill these small shels [*i.e.* granadoes for the hand] with fine Gunpowder. **1669** STURMY *Mariner's Mag.* v. xiii. 85 To Load them, fill these small Shells with Gun-Powder. [*marg.*] The Shells are made of Glass, or nelld Clay, or Paper. **1692** *Capt. Smith's Seaman's Gram.* II. xvii. 127 How much Powder will fill that Shell? **1769** FALCONER *Dict. Marine* (1789) Cc 3 b, The shell is a great hollow ball, filled with powder. **1884** *Milit. Engin.* (ed. 3) I. II. 101 Weight of Shell loaded for service.

**b.** Hence, an explosive projectile or bomb for use in a cannon or mortar. Also *collect. sing.*

**164.** *Thomasson Tracts* (Brit. Mus.) CCCCXCII. No. 27. 110 They swear they will never fight more against guns that shoot twice, meaning the two cracks, the mortar and the shell. **1695** LUTTRELL *Brief Rel.* (1857) III. 452, 13 mortars were tryed..and approved of, each of them throwing a shell a mile and half. **1767** T. HUTCHINSON *Hist. Mass.* ii. 181 The bomb-ship..plied the French with her shells. **1806** A. DUNCAN *Nelson* 45 The Thunder..began to throw shells. **1831** SIR J. SINCLAIR *Corr.* II. 391 A single shell bursting, was seen to put an effectual stop to their whole cavalry in a charge. **1854** TENNYSON *Lt. Brigade* iii, Storm'd at with shot and shell.

**c.** A cartridge case of paper or metal.

**1799** G. SMITH *Laboratory* I. 18 Pour it in the paper shells. **1890** LEFFINGWELL *Wild Fowl Shooting* 122 You can get shells at the gunsmith's loaded, or, if you prefer, load them yourself. **1892** GREENER *Breech Loader* 171 In America good paper cases, or 'shells', are dearer than in England.

**d.** *Pyrotechny.* (See quot.)

**1878** T. KENTISH *Pyrotechn. Treas.* 117 Shells are hollow paper globes, fired vertically, from mortars, or iron tubes.

**22.** A wooden coffin, *esp.* a rough or temporary one. Also a thin coffin of lead or other material to be enclosed in a more substantial one.

**1788** *Gentl. Mag.* II. 1045 Great abundance of human bones have been unavoidably dug up, most of which have been put into shells. **1799** SOUTHEY *Engl. Ecl.* Poet. Wks. III. 45 To slave while there is strength, in age the workhouse, A parish shell at last. **1837** RICHARDSON *Brit. Legion* (ed. 2) viii. 212 Their [Spanish criminals] bodies.. were then taken down by the executioner.., and placed in shells. **1855** THACKERAY *Newcomes* lv, Look rather at the living audience standing round the shell;—the deep grief on Barnes Newcome's fine countenance. **1858** SIMMONDS *Dict. Trade*, *Shell*, a rough coffin to be enclosed in another. **1892** *Times* 4 Feb. 12/2 The leaden shell in which the body..is laid was sealed down and this enclosed in a beautiful olivewood coffin.

**23.** Miscellaneous uses.

**a.** *Naut.* The outer casing of a pulley-block; a thimble dead-eye block used to join the ends of two ropes. **b.** See quots. 1802, 1853 and cf. *shell-jacket* (sense 40). Also *N. Amer.*, the unlined body of a coat; *U.S.*, an article of clothing for the upper body, *spec.* a woman's (usu. sleeveless) overblouse or a light all-weather jacket. **c.** The outer plating of a boiler. **d.** *Bridge-building.* (See quot. 1876.) **e.** The body of a car.

**1769** FALCONER *Dict. Marine* (1789), *Shell of a block*, the outer frame or case, wherein the sheave or wheel is contained. **1794** *Rigging & Seamanship* I. 149 The shell is made of elm or ash. **1802** C. JAMES *Milit. Dict.*, *Shell*, a short jacket without arms, which was worn by light dragoons. **1839** R. S. ROBINSON *Naut. Steam Eng.* 114 The chief parts of a boiler are the shell, the flues, the furnaces and the steam chest. **1841** R. H. DANA *Seaman's Man.* viii. 44 A made block consists of..the shell..; the sheave..; the pin..; and the strap. **1853** STOCQUELER *Milit. Encycl.*, *Shell*, a short jacket without tails. **1876** *Encycl. Brit.* IV. 326 *Concrete in a shell* is a name which might be applied to all the methods of founding a pier which depend on the..property which strong hydraulic concrete possesses of setting into a solid mass under water. The required space is enclosed by a wooden or iron shell. **1882** NARES *Seamanship* (ed. 6) 36 Topmast rigging is sometimes spliced round the shell of the dead eye. **1886** *St. James's Gaz.* 22 Dec. 6/1 He had been measured for..tunics and shells and messing-jackets. **1913** *T. Eaton & Co. Catal.* Semi-Annual Sale 17/3 Men's muskrat-lined coat..Collar is genuine Canadian otter; the shell is cut from standard quality black beaver cloth. **1937** *Times* 13 Apr. (Brit. Motor Suppl.) p. xiii/1 The various stages through which the car body shell can pass, therefore, are as follows. **1962** *Mademoiselle* Aug. 276/2 A white cardigan..to show a matching sleeveless shell. **1967** *Boston Sunday Globe* 23 Apr. 5/2 (Advt.), 3-pc. acetate double knit suit with rayon metallic shell. **1972** *Oxford Mail* 13 Oct. 1/5 Output of body shells for the Marina range was halted for a time. **1976** *National Observer* (U.S.) 1 May 7/4 (Advt.), Nylon shell for men and women. Ultra light, all weather sports jacket of tough two-ply coated nylon. **1976** U. CURTISS *Dig Little Deeper* x. 89 Paula came in, wearing a topaz-colored pants suit over a ribbed cream shell.

**IV.** A mere exterior or framework.

**24.** The external part, exterior, or outward aspect, the externals (of something immaterial).

*a* **1652** J. SMITH *Sel. Disc.* I. 10 We must not think we have then attained to the right knowledge of truth, when we have broken through the outward shell of words..that house it up. **1662** STILLINGFL. *Orig. Sacræ* II. iv. §2 It seems somewhat strange that God should take so great care about the shell and outside of his worship. **1707** *Reflex. upon Ridicule* 204 Cullies, that Judge only by the Shell, and Appearance. **1774** *Earnest Addr. Methodists* (ed. 8) 5 The outward form and shell of religion. **1853** KINGSLEY *Hypatia* ii, The old Jewish blood still beat true, under all its affected shell of Neo-Platonist nonchalance. **1875** EARL LYTTON *Lett.* (1906) I. 335 Words are the shells of ideas. **1889** CONAN DOYLE *Micah Clarke* i, Among so many there were some whose piety was a shell for their ambition.

**25. a.** An empty or hollow thing; mere externality without substance.

**1791** COWPER *Yardley Oak* 123 All the superstructure.. a shell Stands now, and semblance only of itself! **1818** CRUISE *Digest* (ed. 2) II. 426 Nothing but the shell of what was intended for the lasting support of a family of honour. **1829** CARLYLE *Misc.* (1857) I. 270 Mere effigies and shells of men. **1846** *New Monthly Mag.* Dec. 410 He piously kissed that shell of a departed being. **1871** SWINBURNE *Songs bef. Sunrise, Halt bef. Rome* 184 How shall the spirit be loyal To the shell of a spiritless thing?

**b.** A company which has ceased to trade but which is still quoted on the stock exchange.

**1964** *Economist* 19 Dec. 1378/2 A company had ceased normal trading and was a pure shell. **1969** 'D. RUTHERFORD' *Gilt-Edged Cockpit* iv. 68 It's called buying a shell. A tax loss company. When you set the Hackforth loss against our profit we're left with practically no tax to pay. **1981** *Times* 27 May 20/6 Mr Alastair Milne..headed a consortium bidding for former cash shell Phoenix Mining two years ago.

**26. a.** The outer part of an edifice or fabric, the interior of which has been removed or destroyed.

**1657** *Docum. St. Paul's* (Camden) 155 The roofe and floore of the w^ch howse is fallen downe to the grownd, and lyeth on a heape w^thin the shell thereof. **1705** JOS. TAYLOR *Journ. Edenb.* (1903) 65 The Shell of Cliffords Tower which was blown up in 1684. **1771** SMOLLETT *Humph. Cl.* III. 6 Sept., Hard by is the shell of a..Gothick palace. **1865** ALEX. SMITH *Summer in Skye* I. 34 The red shell of Tantallon speaks to you of the might of the Douglases. **1866** YOUNG *Fires* 59 Nothing remained but the red-hot skeleton or shell of the building. **1888** BURGON *Lives 12 Gd. Men* I. ii. 288 [She] built herself a stately mansion which was only reduced to a shell in 1794.

**b.** The skeleton or carcass of a building or a ship.

**1705** ADDISON *Italy, Naples* 202 The Shell of a House, which he had not time to finish. **1761** WESLEY *Jrnl.* 29 July (1827) III. 68, I preached..in the shell of the new house. **1814** T. LANE *Guide Linc. Inn* 82 The shells or walls of the several chambers..are insured from fire by the society. **1825** J. NICHOLSON *Oper. Mech.* 580 When the shell of a building is finished, that is, previous to the floors being laid, or the ceilings lathed. **1886** C. E. PASCOE *Lond. of To-day* xxxii. (ed. 3) 295 The shell of the house, of brick, is old; but stone frontages, enlargements, and decorations, were afterwards made. **1900** G. C. BRODRICK *Mem. & Impr.* 53, I was shown the *Great Britain*, then a mere shell on the stocks, one of the first iron ships ever built.

**c.** *U.S.* A rough, wooden structure, without decoration or furniture.

**1852** MRS. STOWE *Uncle Tom's C.* xxxii. 293 They were mere rude shells, destitute of any species of furniture. **1882** HOWELLS in *Longman's Mag.* I. 48 The edifice was what we call a shell; it was not plastered. **1902** WISTER *Virginian* xiii, It [the eating palace] was a shell of wood, painted with golden emblems.

**V.** A scale or scale-like object.

**27.** A scale of a fish or reptile; a hard epidermal excrescence. *rare.*

*c* **893** ÆLFRED *Oros.* IV. viii. 174 Þonne hie mon sloȝ oþþe sceat, þonne glad hit on þæm scyllum, swelce hit wære smeðe isen. *c* **897** —— *Gregory's Past. C.* xlvii. 360 Ælces fisces sciell bið to oðerre ȝefeȝed. *c* **1000** ÆLFRIC *Lev.* xi. 9 Ne ete ȝe nanne fisc buton þa þe habbað finnas and scilla. **1582** N. LICHEFIELD tr. *Castanheda's Conq. E. Ind.* I. xl. 94 [Lagartos] their bodies are couered ouer with shels. **1665** HOOKE *Microgr.* 184 The leggs.. were all of them cover'd with a strong hairy scale or shel.

**28. a.** A scale or lamina (of stone, etc.).

**13..** *Guy Warw.* xciii. (1891) 454 Nas neuer wepen þat euer was make þat o schel miȝt þerof take, Na more þan of þe flint. **1645** *Docum. St. Paul's* (Camden) 144 Whit marble in block and shels 140 fo[ot]. **1833–4** J. PHILLIPS *Geol.* in *Encycl. Metrop.* (1845) VI. 592/1 Such flagstones..are much liable to scale off in irregular 'shells'.

†**b.** A lamina (of bone). *Obs.*

*c* **1400** *Lanfranc's Cirurg.* 86 Neuere þe lattere kynde wole afterward don awey a schelle of þilke same boon, nouȝt aȝenstondynge þi schauynge. **1656** RIDGLEY *Pract. Physic* 171 A Contusion when the bone is pressed down; yet so, that it is not broken into many shells.

†**29.** *pl.* Scurf; = SCALE *sb.*² 2. *Obs.*

*c* **1400** *Lanfranc's Cirurg.* 189 Furfurea ben a maner of squamis .i. schellis þat comeþ of brennyng þat is in þe skyn. **1527** ANDREW *Brunswyke's Distyll. Waters* C iv b, The hede often enointed with the same..withdryveth the shelles from the hede.

**30.** Any of the thin pieces of metal composing scale-armour; = SCALE *sb.*² 7 a.

**1585** T. WASHINGTON tr. *Nicholay's Voy.* IV. iii. 115 b, They had..vppon their bodies curates of shelles of diuers colours. **1849** JAS. GRANT *Mem. Sir W. Kirkaldy* ix. 85 They wore the most splendid armour of the age, with surcoats or hoquetons covered with shells of silver gilt.

†**31.** *Cant.* (*pl.*) Money. *Obs.*

**1592** GREENE *Conny Catch.* I. C 2 The purse, the Bong, The monie, the Shels. *Ibid.* II. D j b, The farmer..mist his purse, searcht for it, but lining and shels & all was gone. **1611** MIDDLETON & DEKKER *Roaring Girl* v. i. L j b, 'Tis a question whether there bee any siluer shels amongst them, for all their sattin outsides.

†**32.** *pl.* Fragments. *Obs. rare.*

**1560** ROLLAND *Seven Sages* 54 The Falcon..russillit & rang hir bellis, Almaist scho had al schakin þame in schellis.

**33.** An epaulette; = SCALE *sb.*² 9.

**1848** THACKERAY *Van. Fair* xxvii, The Captain, with shells on his frock-coat.

**VI.** Attributive uses and Combinations.

**34.** In sense 1: **a.** Simple attrib., as ***shell-colour***, ***-covering***, ***-layer***, etc.

**1865** SWINBURNE *Chastelard* II. i. 67 Bright pink, the *shell-colour. **1890** *Hardwicke's Sci. Gossip* XXVI. 179/1 The evolution of the shell-colour. **1612** DABORNE *Christian turn'd Turke* I. ii. C 2 Poore fishers brat, that neuer didst aspire Aboue a musle boate,..That..didst smell Worse then thy *shell commodity at midsummer. **1854** WOODWARD *Mollusca* 318 The external *shell-layer consists of fusiform cells. **1847–9** *Todd's Cycl. Anat.* IV. 562/2 The various examples of *shell-membrane. **1835–6** *Ibid.* I. 548/2 The inner sides of the *shell-muscles. **1883** *Fisheries Exhib. Catal.* 252 *Shell Net. **1886** A. WINCHELL *Geol. Talks* 193 In Lamellibrachs the *shell-outline is not the same on each side of the beak. **1857** J. G. WOOD *Comm. Obj. Seashore* 24 Upon this leathery mantle are placed eight *shell-plates, which overlap each other. **1854** WOODWARD *Mollusca* 287 The *shell-wall is removed by weathering.

**b.** Objective and objective genitive, as ***shell-cleaner***, ***-eater***, ***-eating***, ***-monger***, etc.

**1858** SIMMONDS *Dict. Trade*, **Shell-cleaner*, a person who makes a business of cleansing and scouring shells. **1774** GOLDSM. *Nat. Hist.* (1776) VII. 17 Our most exact and industrious *shell-collectors. **1880** A. R. WALLACE *Isl. Life* v. 77 Such species as are especially *shell-eaters. **1857** LIVINGSTONE *Trav.* xiv. 252 Clouds of a black *shell-eating bird, called linongolo. **1850** *British Museum* (Chambers) 192 *Shell-engraving, however, under the name of *Conchylie*, is now carried on..in Italy. **1748** CHESTERF. *Let. to Son* 6 Dec., The..tribes of insect-mongers, *shell-mongers, and pursuers and driers of butterflies.

**c.** Parasynthetic, instrumental, etc., as ***shell-borne***, ***-burred***, ***-housed***, ***-wrought***, etc. adjs.

**1818** KEATS *Endym.* III. 237 O *shell-borne Neptune. **1896** KIPLING *Seven Seas, Deep-Sea Cables*, The great grey level plains of ooze where the *shell-burred cables creep. **1835–6** *Todd's Cycl. Anat.* I. 549/1 The *shell-clad Nautilus. **1883** *Good Words* 113 Gorgeous articles of native dress, feather-tasseled, *shell-fringed, coral-beaded. **1600** J. LANE *Tom Tel-troth* 506 The *shell-housde snaile. **1624** QUARLES *Sion's Elegies* (1717) 395 In roughest tides his *shell-prepared brest Untoucht with danger, finds a haven of rest. **1613–16** W. BROWNE *Brit. Past.* II. i. 3 Now with his hands..The Swaine attempts to get the *shell-strewd shores. **1856** STANLEY *Sinai & Pal.* vi. (1858) 261 The *shell-strewn beach. **1741** BOYSE *Patience* 182 Sweet was each *shell-wrought bowl. **1747** MASON *Ode to Water Nymph* 38 Yon shell-wrought terras.

**d.** Similative, as ***shell-curved***, ***-formed***, ***-grey***, ***-pink***, ***-red***, etc.; also ***shell-like*** adj. and adv., ***-wise*** adv.

**1901** LADY DILKE *Fr. Furnit. 18th Cent.* 48 The *shell-curved lines which maintain their decorative value in the Salle à manger. *c* **1800** LEYDEN *Mermaid* liv, The *shell-formed lyres of ocean ring. **1963** *Times* 8 June 12/3 Short dresses of *shell-grey silk with flared skirts. **1692** RAY *Disc.* 132 There are found not only *shell-like stones, but real shells. **1715** LEONI *Palladio's Archit.* (1742) I. 46 Of the .. Rooms..the lesser ones are arch'd shell-like. **1827** HOOD *Bianca's Dream* 242 Her small and shell-like ear. **1899** *Allbutt's Syst. Med.* VI. 917 Shell-like plates of varying size with scalloped margins. **1887** *Daily News* 19 May 5/6 Lined with *shell-pink satin. **1932** J. C. POWYS *Glastonbury Romance* II. xxi. 701 The new silk lining of her ottoman had dyed itself..into an incredible shell-pink. **1951** E. PAUL *Springtime in Paris* xii. 229 Anatole turned shell pink, then a kind of raspberry shade. **1977** 'E. ANTHONY' *Silver Falcon* (1978) 133 The house was..painted shell-pink. **1891** 'O.

THANET' *Otto the Knt.*, etc. 311 Shades of gray and purple and *shell-red. **1835** WILLIS *Pencillings* I. v. 34 The three *shell-shaped squares in the centre of the city. **1552** in Kempe *Losely MSS.* (1836) 88 Makinge the same [feathers] into greate plumes, to stand *shell-wise over-thwarte the hed peces of the worthyes of the Greekes.

**35.** In various senses of branch I, passing into *adj.* **a.** Of an animal, fruit, etc.: Having a shell; see also SHELL-FISH, -SNAIL.

*c* **1440** *Promp. Parv.* 443/2 Schale notys, and oþer schelle frute. **1728** CHAMBERS *Cycl.* s.v. *Shell-fish*, Bonetus observes, That Shell Animals have no Diversity of Sex. **1839** T. MITCHELL *Frogs of Aristoph.* Introd. p. cxviii, The pots containing the seeds or shell-fruits. **1859–62** SIR J. RICHARDSON, etc. *Mus. Nat. Hist.* (1868) II. 353 The genus *Testacellus* or Shell-slug. **1870** KINGSLEY *At Last* xvii, Their shell-fauna is of a Mexican and Central American type.

**b.** Of geological formations or deposits: Consisting wholly or largely of (sea)shells (esp. in a triturated or powdery state, ***shell-gravel, -grit, -marl, -sand***).

(Cf. *shale marl*, 1682, s.v. MARL *sb.*[1] 1 b.)

**1587** MASCALL *Govt. Cattle, Oxen* (1596) 43 The shell stones (that lie in arable landes..) first burnt, and then beaten into fine powder. **1692** A. SYMSON *Descr. Galloway* (1823) 94 As for lime they are supplyed from the Shell-bank of Kirkinner. **1753** *Chambers' Cycl.* Suppl., *Shell-sand*, a name given by the farmers, in some parts of England, to the fragments of shells found on the sea-shores, and ground to a sort of powder, so that they resemble sand. **1759** MILLS tr. *Duhamel's Husb.* I. viii. 29 This author seems never to have seen shell-marle. **1765** J. BARTRAM *Jrnl.* 25 Dec. (1766) 7 This shell-bluff is 300 yards more or less along the river's bank. **1827** G. HIGGINS *Celtic Druids* 138 The coarse shell-limestone, which immediately covers the chalk strata in the neighbourhood of Paris. **1850** ANSTED *Elem. Geol., Min.* etc. Gloss., *Shell marl*, a deposit of clay, peat, and silt, mixed with shells, which collects at the bottom of fresh water lakes. **1850** DANA *Min.* 208 Fire marble or lumachelle is a dark brown shell marble. **1854** A. ADAMS, etc. *Man. Nat. Hist.* 589 Shell-beds are formed of dead and drifted shells, heaped together by tides and currents. **1855** KINGSLEY *Heroes, Perseus* IV, Shell-drifts bleaching in the sunshine. **1882** W. D. HAY *Brighter Britain!* I. xi. 307 A straight, broad path, smooth and white with shell-gravel. **1922** JOYCE *Ulysses* 48 Loose sand and shellgrit crusted her bare feet. **1938** Shell-grit [see ROULETTED *pa. pple.* b]. **1964** *Oceanogr. & Marine Biol.* II. 418 *Spatangus purpureus*..lives in shell-gravel. **1977** *Stornoway Gaz.* 27 Aug. 4/9 These are well worth looking for in June or July in the grassland behind our many shell-sand beaches.

**c.** Of an artificial structure, vessel, etc.: Consisting or formed of a shell or shells; made from a shell or shells; ornamented with shells; (of a road, *U.S.*), having a bed or layer of shells.

**1627** MAY *Lucan* IX. Q8b, Whose shrill shell-trumpett seas and shores doo heare. **1637** NABBES *Microcosmus* IV. F j b, From a rock That weeps a running christall she [*sc.* Temperance] doth fill Her shell cup. **1699** POTTER *Antiq. Greece* III. ix. 87 Triton's Shell-trumpet is famous in Poetical Story. **1753** *Chambers' Cycl.* Suppl. s.v. *Shell*, The effects of this shell-manure. **1756** MRS. CALDERWOOD in *Coltness Collect.* (Maitland Club) 153 The gardens are of great extent, with..shell grottos. **1836** T. POWER *Impressions of Amer.* II. 99 We soon gained the shell road however, and found it as good as the streets of Mobile. **1844** MRS. HOUSTON *Yacht Voy. Texas* II. 17 There are but two drives in the neighbourhood of New Orleans—the old and new 'Shell Roads'... They are..thickly covered..with small sea shells. **1845** J. COULTER *Adv. in Pacific* xiii. 169 Bone or shell ear-rings. **1851** S. P. WOODWARD *Mollusca* I. 46 The makers of shell-cameos avail themselves of this difference [of colour] to produce white or rose-coloured figures on a dark ground. **1853** C. BRONTË *Villette* III. xxxi. 35 Slipping into his hand the ruddy little shell box. **1878** B. HARTE *Man on Beach* 55 Two or three highly-colored prints, a shell workbox, a ghastly winter bouquet of skeleton leaves and mosses. **1888** MRS. CUSTER *Tenting on Plains* ix, The shell drive along the ocean. **1904** WINSTON CHURCHILL *Crossing* III. v, A white shell walk divided the garden. **1976** J. FLEMING *To make Underworld* ii. 21 She makes these shell boxes, y'know..all stuck over with shells.

**d.** Of an implement: Hollow, or having a concave part.

**1823** P. NICHOLSON *Pract. Builder* 254 The Taper-shell-bit is used for widening holes. **1823** J. BADCOCK *Dom. Amusem.* 179 The first tool used is an auger; the shell part.. four inches in diameter. **1875** *Carpentry & Join.* 31 For rough work..the shell augur alone is used.

**e.** Of the shape of a shell; (of material, trimming, etc.) having a shell pattern.

**1774** in *Amer. Hist. Rev.* (1899) V. 311 She is drest in a neat shell Callico Gown. **1780** J. WEDGWOOD *Let.* 21 Oct. (1965) 260, I now expect to sell a good deal of his green shell pattern. **1840** MRS. GAUGAIN *Lady's Assist. Knitting* 142 Shell pattern, or half square for a quilt or counterpane. **1869** MRS. WHITNEY *We Girls* v, Shell-trimmings and flutings. **1882** CAULFIELD & SAWARD *Dict. Needlework* 92 Shell Couching, a Flat Couching, in which the securing stitches are arranged in half curves, and bear some resemblance to the shape of a scallop shell. **1885** W. J. E. CRANE *Bookbinding* xiii. 101 The pattern called large brown French, or shell pattern. **1894** *Daily News* 26 Apr. 9/1 'The shell chair', which is like a scallop shell. **1897** *Private Life of Queen* xxii. 180 The enormous 'shell pattern' service of knives, forks and spoons. **1967** E. SHORT *Embroidery & Fabric Collage* iii. 68 Aluminium templates can be bought in a number of geometric shapes and also a shell pattern.

**f.** Made of tortoise-shell. ? *U.S.*

**1858** SIMMONDS *Dict. Trade*, *Shell-comb*, a lady's comb for the hair, or a toilet comb, made of tortoiseshell. **1884** KNIGHT *Dict. Mech.* Suppl., *Shell-piece*, one of the shields of tortoise-shell or horn, used with spring eye-glasses which clasp the nose. **1896** *Harper's Mag.* XCII. 808/1 She replaced the dagger with a shell pin from her own hair.

**36.** In sense 21: **a.** Simple attrib., as ***shell-burst, crater, -fire, fougasse, -gun, -hole, -madness, -room, -shop, -splinter, -storm, -trap***, etc.; **b.** objective, as ***shell-dodging***, etc.; ***shell-filling, -firing*** adjs.; **c.** advb., as ***shell-pitted, -pocked, -proof, -smitten, -stricken, -torn*** adjs.

**1917** W. OWEN *Let.* 2 Mar. (1967) 440 Did you see any *shell-bursts? **1980** G. M. FRASER *Mr American* xxvi. 556 It wis a shell-burst that Ah stopped. **1916** 'BOYD CABLE' *Action Front* 49 The neutral ground..was a sea of mud, broken by heaped earth and yawning *shell craters. **1977** J. CLEARY *High Road to China* i. 32, I..was trapped in a shell crater with three dead men. **1917** 'CONTACT' *Airman's Outings* 241 Freed from the immediate necessity of *shell-dodging. **1868** *Rep. to Govt. U.S. Munit. War* 31 The carrier-block moves the *shell-drawer and causes it to draw out the discharged shell from the chamber. **1884** *Milit. Engin.* (ed. 3) I. II. 101 A *shell-filling room. **1900** W. S. CHURCHILL in *Morning Post* 25 June 5/7 In spite of an accurate *shellfire they continued to advance boldly against the highest part of the hill. **1977** *Listener* 28 Apr. 559/2 They had had built a reinforced concrete pillbox—a shelter against the shrapnel and the unceasing shellfire. **1858** GREENER *Gunnery* 132 *Shell firing was next tried at a distance of 1,500 yards. **1900** W. S. CHURCHILL in *Morning Post* 1 Jan. 6/1 The shell-firing Maxim continued its work. **1942** *R.A.F. Jrnl.* 16 May 15 These include..constant-speed 3-blade propeller; shell-firing guns; wireless and oxygen equipment. **1834** J. S. MACAULAY *Field Fortif.* 207 *Shell Fougasses. **1875** KNIGHT *Dict. Mech.*, **Shell-gage* (*Ordnance*), an instrument for verifying the thickness of hollow projectiles. **1858** GREENER *Gunnery* 135 The accurate and long-range firing of such rifled *shell-guns. **1940** *Flight* 12 Dec. 522/2 The shell-gun or 'cannon' has been in action mounted in the machines of Fighter Command. **1889** WELCH *Text Bk. Naval Archit.* xii. 132 The *shell hoist..is provided with a cowl. **1916** 'BOYD CABLE' *Action Front* 141 The stretcher-bearers who lifted him from the *shell-hole. **1971** S. HILL *Strange Meeting* iii. 203 Then suddenly they came between the stumps of some trees, dropped down into a shell hole. **1923** KIPLING *Irish Guards in Gt. War* I. 329 A dazed day of '*shell-madness', when all ears and eyes were intolerably overburdened with echoes and pictures. **1918** W. S. CHURCHILL *Let.* 12 Sept. in M. Gilbert *W. S. Churchill* (1975) IV. I. vii. 147 For an hour we ran through devastated, *shell pitted facias—scraggy shreds of woods. **1925** *Scribner's Mag.* Sept. 234/2 Only the 49th lay perforce in the open, on a bleak, *shell-pocked slope. **1864** WEBSTER, **Shell-proof*, capable of resisting bomb shells. **1805** *Shipwright's Vade-M.* 130 **Shell-rooms*, a compartment in a bomb-vessel, fitted up with shelves to receive bomb-shells when charged. **1890** W. J. GORDON *Foundry* 16 The *shell-shop, where they [shells] are taken in and finished. **1917** J. MASEFIELD *Old Front Line* 71 It has been more burnt and *shell-smitten than most parts of the lines. **1910** W. S. CHURCHILL in R. S. Churchill *W. S. Churchill* (1967) I. Compan. II. 1071 The driver..was wounded severely in the scalp by a *shell-splinter almost immediately. **1974** N. FREELING *Dressing of Diamond* 137 He had been ripped by a shell splinter and sewn up casually. **1903, 1914** *Shell-storm [see RAFALE]. **1901** 'LINESMAN' *Words by Eyewitness* iii. (1902) 40 The most *shell-stricken kopje in South Africa. **1891** KIPLING *Light that Failed* ii, A clump of *shell-torn bodies. **1918** W. OWEN *Let.* 4 Jan. (1967) 525 He was badly wounded, and..still wears the shell-torn boots. **1949** S. SPENDER *Edge of Being* 24 Moving in death through shell-torn tenements. **1879** *Encycl. Brit.* IX. 461/2 Such *shell-traps..are scrupulously avoided by modern [military] engineers. **1923** KIPLING *Irish Guards in Gt. War* I. 97 Annequin..had become more than ever a shell-trap. **1890** W. J. GORDON *Foundry* 29 Now that steel is used instead of iron the *shell-wall is much thinner.

**37.** In sense 15.

**1833** *Quart. Jrnl. Educ.* V. 40 Fifth Form... Shell Form. .. Sixth Form. **1857** HUGHES *Tom Brown* II. v, It was the prescribed quantity of Homer for a shell lesson. **1867** W. L. COLLINS *Public Sch., Westm.* viii. 178 At the end of this room [the schoolroom] there is a kind of semicircular apse, in which the 'shell' form were formerly taught.

**38.** In sense 18: Of boats of a light racing form; hence of a race rowed by such boats.

**1858** O. W. HOLMES *Aut. Breakf.-t.* vii, A 'skeleton' or 'shell' race-boat. **1873** *Forest & Stream* 25 Sept. 108/1 A new four-oared shell boat. *Ibid.*, A four-oared shell race.

**39.** In sense 25 b: ***shell company, corporation, game, operation, transaction.***

**1958** *Economist* 15 Mar. 957/1 Shell companies have nothing to do with oil. They are corporate entities empty of their trading assets; they hold only cash or near cash assets in their balance sheets and otherwise have nothing but a stock exchange quotation—which is essential. **1977** *Irish Press* 29 Sept. 7/7 It was in April 1972 that Fitzwilliam Resources, of the same stock that formed Fitzwilliam Securities and Fitzwilton Ltd., (the Irish 'shell' company, which is now a shadow of its former self), took a 6 per cent stake in Tara. **1969** *Wall St. Jrnl.* 3 July 4/2 The Securities and Exchange Commission said it's disturbed by the increasing use of inactive 'shell' corporations as vehicles for distributing unregistered stock to the public. **1974** A. A. THOMPSON *Swiss Legacy* xx. 204 They are shell corporations... They have no assets, no activities, nothing. They are merely conduits for money going elsewhere. **1969** *N.Y. Rev. Books* 2 Jan. 42/3 What becomes almost obscene about such a reactionary shell game..is that these very same corporate chiefs are right now planning an increase in unemployment. **1977** F. BRANSTON *Up & Coming Man* xi. 108 A shell operation, where you buy a dormant or nearly defunct company and inject assets into it. **1958** *Spectator* 11 July 68/3 This should put a stop to 'shell' transactions.

**40. a.** Special comb.: **shell-back**, (*a*) *jocular*, a sailor, *esp.* a hardened or experienced one; also *transf.*; (*b*) a marine turtle; hence **shell-backed** *a.*; **shell-bake** *v.*, to overheat an egg that is being incubated so as to kill (the bird); **shell beach**, a beach composed wholly or predominantly of sea-shells; *spec.* the name of one such on the Channel Island of Herm; **shell-bearing** *a.*, = CONCHIFEROUS 1 and 2; **shell-bird**, (*a*) *Canada*, the red-breasted merganser, *Mergus serrator*; (*b*) *nonce-use*, a tortoise; **shell-blow**, a call blown on a horn made of a large species of shell (e.g. a conch-shell); so **shell-blowing**; † **shell-bread**, a kind of bread or biscuit baked in large mussel-shells; **shell-breaker**, an instrument used in lithotomy; **shell-briar** *a.*, designating a type of tobacco-pipe with a rough, dark-stained stem and bowl; **shell button** (see quots.); † **shell-cap**, ? a lace cap of shell pattern; **shell cocoa**, the husks of cocoa-beans or the drink made from an infusion of these; **shell concrete** *Building*, concrete used in shell construction; **shell construction** *Building*, the use of thin curved shells (sense 12 b above) to roof areas having wide spans; **shell egg**, an egg in its natural state in the shell (opp. to *dried egg*: cf. DRIED *ppl. a.* 1); **shell-fire** *dial.*, phosphorescence or lambent fire seen enveloping or issuing from bodies (see quots.); **shell-flowers**, 'ornaments made with small shells, plain or coloured' (1858 Simmonds *Dict. Trade*); **shell-game** *U.S.*, a sleight-of-hand swindling game in which a small object is concealed under a walnut shell or the like, and bets are made as to which shell the object is under; also *fig.*; **shell-gland**, (*a*) an excretory organ beneath the shell in the lower crustaceans; (*b*) the shell-secreting gland of a mollusc; **shell-gold** [see sense 2 e], gold for painting or writing, laid in a mussel-shell; **shell-gritted** *a. Archæol.*, denoting a ware made of a paste mixed with particles of shell; **shell-heap**, a mound of domestic remains consisting mainly of refuse shells accumulated by aborigines who subsisted on shell-fish; **shell-hearing**, in 'psychical research', the induction of hallucinatory voices by listening with the ear to the aperture of a shell; † **shell-house**, a grotto; **shell ice** *Canad.* = *cat-ice* s.v. CAT *sb.*[1] 18; **shell-jacket**, an undress tight-fitting military jacket, short in the back; **shell-keep**, a form of Norman keep built on a mound (usually the site of an older fortress); **shell-lime**, lime made by burning sea-shells; **shell-man** *U.S.*, a swindler who plays the shell-game; † **shell-meat**, edible shell-fish; **shell midden** *Archæol.* = *shell-heap*; † **shell-mine** (see quot.); **shell model** *Nuclear Physics*, a theoretical description of nuclear structure in which the nucleus is considered to consist of nucleons arranged in shells (sense 19 b); **shell-money** = WAMPUM; **shell-moulding** *vbl. sb.*, in *Founding*, a method of making moulds and cores in which a shell of resin-bonded sand is formed in parts around a heated metal pattern, the parts being joined together after removal of the pattern; so **shell-mould**, a mould made in this way; **shell-mound** = *shell-heap*; † **shell-naked** *a.*, ? as bare as an eggshell; **shell-paste**, thin paste for lining a pie-dish, etc.; **shell-plate**, one of the plates forming the outer shell of a vessel, boiler, etc.; so **shell-plating**; **shell-pump** = *sand-pump* (see SAND *sb.*[2] 10); **shell rock** *N. Amer.*, hard rock consisting largely of compacted sea-shells; **shell-roll** (see quot.); **shell roof**, a roof consisting of a shell (sense 12 b above); **shell-sac** = *shell-gland* (*b*); **shell shock**, (*a*) a name given, esp. during the war of 1914–18, to certain psychological disturbances occurring in conditions of active warfare and supposed to result primarily from exposure to shell-fire; also *fig.*; (*b*) *slang*, cocoa; hence **shell-shock** *v. trans.*, to affect with shell shock; **shell-shocked** *a.*, suffering from shell shock; **shell-shocker**, a sufferer from shell shock; **shell-sickness**, a disease in sheep characterized by shell-like thickenings in the intestines; † **shell-silver**, silver for painting, etc. in the same form as shell-gold; **shell steak**, a steak cut from the short loin; **shell-stick**, a stick with a shell on the end used as a weapon by some Australian aborigines; **shell-stitch**, one of various knitting or sewing stitches producing shell-like patterns; **shell structure** *Physics*, the structure of the atom envisaged as consisting of a number of electron shells (sense 19 b above); **shell-suit**, a suit of clothes consisting of tight-fitting trousers buttoning on to a tunic; † **shell-tooth**, any of the teeth of a horse which bear the mark; also *adj.* = † **shell-toothed** *a.* (see quots.); **shell transformer**, a shell-type transformer (see below); **shell-type** *sb.* and *a.*, (applied to) something having or resembling a shell in any sense; ***shell-type transformer***, a transformer having its windings wholly or largely enclosed within the metal 'core'.

**1853** J. T. DOWNEY *Filings from Old Saw* (1956) vi. 30 Both the nerve of 14 strong armed *shell-backs, and the occasional disbursement of an extra *tot* of whiskey, kept her going. **1883** W. CLARK RUSSELL *Jack's Courtship* i, It takes a sailor a long time to.. get quit of the bold sheer that earns him the name of shell-back. **1891–4** STEVENSON in G. Balfour *Life* (1911) 249 The arrival of strange old shell-back guests out of every quarter of the island world. **1905** A. I. SHAND *Days of Past* iii. 38 The shellbacks from the Caribbean Sea or Ascension floating in the tanks. **1943** A. RANSOME *Picts & Martyrs* xi. 103 He felt as if he was going to sit for an examination and he wanted to make no mistakes with those two old shellbacks, Nancy and Peggy, as examiners. **1959** J. CARY *Captive & Free* 207 The old hulk was full of crabs—there doesn't seem to be anything else in the sub-editor's room. Old shellbacks that have been chewing on Fowler for forty years. **1963** *Listener* 21 Feb. 350/3, I have no doubt a lot of right-wing shell-backs are now conceding, with blimpish magnanimity, that there's really something to be said for these young fellows after all. **1974** *Times* 9 Dec. 13/3 In both division lobbies right-wingers rubbed shoulders with left-wingers, shellbacks with parliamentary apprentices. **1930** R. CAMPBELL *Adamastor* 30 A *shell-backed saint, whom time maroons. **1972** *Daily Tel.* 29 Dec. 7/8 Mr Marcus is always eloquent when he is contrasting innocence with shell-backed experience. **1817** J. MAYER *Sportman's Direct.* (ed. 2) 54 The silk hens are the best for the act of incubation, the heat of the common hens being apt to *shellbake the birds in the eggs. **1835** H. D. INGLIS *Channel Islands* 323 Herm possesses another attraction,.. its *shell beach. **1915** E. R. LANKESTER *Diversions of Naturalist* 144 The shells which are accumulated as shell-beaches have come from animals which lived in quantity at depths of ten or twenty fathoms. **1964** H. MYHILL *Introducing Channel Islands* v. 114 It is possibly the situation of this beach.. which has led to the accumulation there of countless thousands of shells of great variety. There are said to be over five hundred distinct species represented, and they have given it the name of the Shell Beach. **1844** *Athenæum* 5 Oct. 902/3 A species of *shell-bearing annelid, the Ditrupa. **1880** A. R. WALLACE *Isl. Life* 168 Shell-bearing gravels. **1770** G. CARTWRIGHT *Jrnl.* 2 Oct. (1792) I. 40 They returned with three *shellbirds and a saddleback. **1921** D. H. LAWRENCE *Tortoises* 12 Nay, tiny shell-bird, What a huge vast inanimate it is, that you must row against. **1973** E. GOUDIE *Woman of Labrador* II. iv. 102 Shell birds are not very good eating because they taste very fishy. **1828** *Life Planter Jamaica* 50 This mode of working continued till *shell-blow at half past one by the sun-dial. **1861** G. BLYTH *Remin. Miss. Life* ii. 54 At noon or, as it was called, the shellblow time. **1869** *Routledge's Ev. Boy's Ann.* 178 All sounds of *shell-blowing had ceased. **1665** R. MAY *Accomplisht Cook* (ed. 2) 274 To make *Shell Bread. **1830** S. COOPER *Dict. Pract. Surg.* (ed. 6) 815 For small stones.. the '*shell-breaker' only is used. **1972** M. J. BOSSE *Incident at Naha* i. 17 He.. lit a pipe, his largest *shell-briar Apple. **1977** A. SCHOLEFIELD *Venom* v. 203 The chubby face, from which the fragrant bowl of a shell-briar emerged. **1789** *Deb. Congr. U.S.* 29 Aug. (1834) 796 An exclusive patent.. for manufacturing *shell buttons of different dimensions. **1834–6** BARLOW *Manuf.* in *Encycl. Metrop.* (1845) VIII. 608 Shell buttons are those which consist of a back made of bone without any shank but corded with catgut. **1851–4** *Tomlinson's Cycl. Usef. Arts* (1867) I. 263/1 Buttons in which the convex front is closed in behind with another piece of metal, also convex on the outer surface, but less so than the front. These are called shell buttons. **1794** MRS. PIOZZI *Brit. Synon.* I. 359 She gained about 350l. 'tis said, and laid out two hundred of the money instantly in a *shell-cap. **1902** J. T. LAW *Law's Grocer's Man.* (ed. 2) 1170/2 *Shell cocoa. **1909** J. JOYCE *Let.* 21 Aug. (1966) II. 238, I sent Nora a stone of shell cocoa. Pay the duty on it which cannot be high and see that Nora takes it *every morning* and *evening*. **1922** W. B. YEATS *Trembling of Veil* II. xiii. 119 She had lived for many weeks upon bread and shell-cocoa, so that her food never cost her more than a penny a day. **1949** *Archit. Rev.* CVI. 302/2 The boiler house, which has a *shell-concrete roof. **1958** *Times* 23 Sept. 16/3 The structures he [*sc.* Candela] has designed there—mostly in shell-concrete—have begun to attract attention far outside Mexico. **1946** *Archit. Rev.* C. 8 The roofs of the canteen and the concert studio are of *shell construction, 4·8 in. thickness. **1974** *Encycl. Brit. Macropædia* IV. 1078/1 Shell construction, where the strength of a thin curved concrete membrane is used advantageously to produce a light and aesthetic roof capable of bridging wide spaces without appreciable bending. [**1942** *Sun* (Baltimore) 18 Feb. 24/7 There are, according to experts, three kinds of markets for eggs—shell (direct-to-consumer variety), frozen and dried.] **1943** E. OLIVER *Night Thoughts of Country Landlady* viii. 60 Before buying the very small but essential allowance of grain required to make these hens lay, you must hand over your coupons for '*Shell Eggs'. **1949** S. GIBBONS *Matchmaker* i. 11 On Tuesday we have bacon and egg pie, Father, and on Wednesday boiled shell eggs. **1972** *Guardian* 24 Mar. 10/8 Present minimum import prices for shell eggs and for.. dried whole egg are to continue unchanged. **1770** LANGHORNE *Plutarch* (1879) I. 138 A bright flame was always considered as a fortunate omen, whether it were a real one issuing from an altar, or a seeming one (what we call *shell-fire) from the head of a living person. **1787** GROSE *Prov. Gloss.* Suppl., *Fairy-sparks*, or *Shel-fire*, electric sparks, often seen on clothes at night. Kent. **1847** HALLIWELL, *Shell-fire*, the phosphorescence sometimes exhibited in farm-yards, &c., from decayed straw, &c. or touch-wood. **1738–9** MRS. DELANY *Autobiogr.* (1861) II. 37, I wish you could safely send me the antique shell nosegay; I am going to fill a glass case with *shell-flowers. **1890** B. HALL *Turnover Club* 169 Would endeavour to make a collection of Japanese coins, with their cards and a *shell game. **1899** *Philistine* ix. 157 All the people who work the filological shell-game. **1942** *Sun* (Baltimore) 19 Mar. 19/6 The defendant pleaded innocent to charges of operating a shell game. **1972** *Times Lit. Suppl.* 29 Dec. 1570/1 Both memory and history are shell games. **1977** *Rolling Stone* 21 Apr. 88/2 Both of them create with the sleight of hand of a shell-game swindler. **1877** HUXLEY *Anat. Inv. Anim.* vi. 268 At the sides of the latter [carapace], two coiled tubes with clear contents, the so-called *shell-glands, are seen. **1883** E. RAY LANKESTER in *Encycl. Brit.* XVI. 639/2 The embryonic shell-sac or shell-gland. **1573** *Art of Limning* fo. iiij, If you will buye at the Potecaries *shell golde or shell silver, with the which (being tempered with gumme water) you may verye well write with a pen. **1675** A. BROWNE *App. Art of Limning* 25 Cover over the Rais'd Work with the finest Shell Gold. **1758** DOSSIE *Handmaid Arts* 391 When the gold powders are used along with paintings in water colours, it is previously formed into shell gold... This shell gold is prepared by tempering the gold powder with very weak gum water. **1815** J. SMITH *Panorama Sci. & Art* II. 803 When great brilliancy is not wanted, shell-gold may be used instead of gold leaf, to gild upon the size. **1954** S. PIGGOTT *Neolithic Cultures* iii. 108 A bowl of typically 'Abingdon' *shell-gritted ware from Great Ponton in south Lincolnshire. **1965** I. F. SMITH *Windmill Hill & Avebury* v. 50 The heavier rims are decorated more often than the simple and rolled rims, and shell-gritted ware more often than flint-gritted. **1882** E. A. BARBER in *Amer. Antiq.* IV. 201 Mr. Tooker informs me further that he has found perfect clay pipes on *shell heaps and on the sites of aboriginal villages. **1893** *Tablet* 22 July 126 Miss X who is understood to be very gifted.. in crystal vision and in *shell-hearing. *a* **1700** EVELYN *Diary* 27 Feb. 1644, A grotto, or *shell house. **1756** AMORY *Buncle* (1825) I. 46 The operation required in a shell-house. **1875** *United Service Mag.* CXXXIX. 42 [It] is brittle and bad for skating, '*shell-ice' as it is called. **1977** *Globe & Mail* (Toronto) 9 Mar. 36/7 Travel isn't too good. There's shell ice with pockets of water underneath and flooding around the cracks and heaves, but no actual danger yet. **1840** E. E. NAPIER *Scenes & Sports For. Lands* II. iv. 114 As travellers, unprovided with our traps, we appeared there in *shell jackets. **1868** *Queen's Regul. Army* §608 The 'surplus kit'.. being carried in the squad bags,.. viz.: 1 shell jacket, 1 pair socks, 1 shirt, 1 towell [etc.]. **1868** FREEMAN *Norm. Conq.* (1877) II. 197 The true castle of Montgomery.. no square donjon, but a vast *shell-keep on a mighty mound. **1793** SMEATON *Edystone L.* §189 *Shell Lime, that is, Cockle or other shells burnt. **1875** W. MCILWRAITH *Guide Wigtownshire* 39 The antiquity of this very thick old wall is seen from its stones having been run together with hot shell-lime. **1902** *Daily Chron.* 24 Sept. 5/2 The *shell-man whom she hired was the success of the evening, and gallantly handed back the bills of large denominations which the guests passed over to him in making their bets, 'just for fun.' **1642** FULLER *Holy & Prof. St.* v. xi. 402 Sacraments, like to *shelmeats, may be eaten after fowl hands, without any harm. **1924** *Proc. Prehist. Soc.* *1923–24* IV. ii. 206 Directly resting upon the brickearth was a *shell midden. **1971** *Nature* 11 June 397/2 Between 1881 and 1913 three Mesolithic 'shell midden' sites were excavated on the Island of Oronsay in the Inner Hebrides. **1645–52** BOATE *Irel. Nat. Hist.* (1860) 106 The Mine hath the name of.. *Shell-mine for the following reason: for this stuff or Oar being neither loose.. as earth.., neither firm.. as stone, is of a middle substance.. composed of shells or scales. **1946** *Physical Rev.* LXIX. 538 On the *shell model the radius should be equal to Gamow's radius plus the radius of the alpha-particle. **1970** I. E. MCCARTHY *Nuclear Reactions* I. iv. 83 The independent particle model for finite nuclei is the shell model. **1851** J. F. W. JOHNSTON *Notes N. Amer.* II. 465 From the purple interior of this shell the *wampum* or *shell-money of the Indians was prepared. [**1947** *F.I.A.T. Final Rep. No. 1168* (Brit. Intelligence Objectives Sub-Comm.) 2 Such a bed helps the thin mold shell resist the hydrostatic pressure of the influent liquid metal.] **1950** *Materials & Methods* Aug. 45/3 For the investigation of the metallurgical characteristics of the tin bronze alloys as affected by plastic bonded *shell molds, a master pattern plate is being utilized. **1973** J. G. TWEEDDALE *Materials Technol.* II. ii. 39 Since, for simplicity, a shell mould is made up from two, outer shell parts, it is not always possible to build in the best pouring channel system. **1951** *Iron Age* 15 Nov. 111/1 The Builders Iron Foundry has been working with the Croning Process, or *shell molding method of producing castings. **1979** J. NEELY *Pract. Metall. & Materials of Industry* xxiv. 325/2 The advantages of shell molding over other forms of sand casting are that high precision, good finishes, and more complex shapes are possible, and less machining is needed. **1851** D. WILSON *Preh. Ann.* I. i. (1863) 36 Ancient *shell-mounds, the supposed kitchen refuse of the aborigines. **1865** LUBBOCK *Preh. Times* 185 'Shell-mound' axes. **1879** —— *Sci. Lect.* v. 156 The dog is the only domestic animal found in the shell-mounds. **1681** COTTON *Wond. Peak* 33 A Goose.. Which out of Peaks-Arse.. was seen *Shell-naked sally, rifled of her plume. **1764** ELIZA MOXON *Eng. Housew.* (ed. 9) 86 Make a little *shell-paste, and line your tins. **1869** E. J. REED *Shipbuild.* xix. 422 The sides of the poop and forecastle to be one third lighter than the *shell plates amidships. **1899** *Daily Tel.* 18 Jan. 6/6 Shell-plate boilers improve as time goes on. **1894** W. H. WHITE *Man. Naval Arch.* (ed. 3) 333 Iron or steel ships have comparatively thin *shell-plating stiffened by transverse and longitudinal frames. **1875** KNIGHT *Dict. Mech.*, **Shell-pump*, a tube with a clack-valve at its foot, used for removing the detritus from a bored shaft. **1807** J. BARLOW *Columbiad* IX. 321 And mark thy native orb!.. What an age her *shell-rock ribs attest! **1837** J. L. WILLIAMS *Territory of Florida* 56 The bank is formed of concrete shell rock. **1935** H. DAVIS *Honey in Horn* xvi. 261 The road under the horses' feet was black shellrock. **1892** NASMITH *Students' Cotton Spinning* 164 The top rollers are almost universally made for the front line of a drawing frame of the Leigh loose boss type. This is called in America the '*shell roll'. **1954** G. MAGNEL *Prestressed Concrete* (ed. 3) x. 303 (*caption*) Prestressed beams for *shell roof. **1972** R. E. OWEN *Roofs* vi. 91 Most shell roofs are easy to drain to their edges or ends. **1883** E. RAY LANKESTER in *Encycl. Brit.* XVI. 639 In very few instances.. the primitive *shell-sac is retained and enlarged as the permanent shell-forming area. **1915** *Brit. Med. Jrnl.* 11 Dec. 848/2 The necessity of investigating cases of '*shell shock' very carefully in order to differentiate those that are functional from those that are due to organic lesions. **1918** E. A. MACKINTOSH *War, the Liberator* 148 The Corporal.. collapsed suddenly with twitching hands and staring, frightened eyes, proclaiming the shell-shock he had held off while the work was to be done. **1925** FRASER & GIBBONS *Sailor & Soldier Words* 255 *Shell shock*... Since the war, the term has been officially abolished, in favour of the technical term 'Psycho-neurosis'. **1933** J. F. C. FULLER *Generalship* 20 The most rapid way to shell-shock an army is to shell-proof its generals; for once the heart of an army is severed from its head the result is paralysis. **1935** M. HARRISON *Spring in Tartarus* III. 300 The cocoa which Jim sold at a penny the cup, was called 'shell-shock'. **1943** G. GREENE *Ministry of Fear* II. i. 111 There's not a finer shell-shock clinic in the country. **1952** S. KAUFFMANN *Philanderer* (1953) vii. 108 An unfortunate rambling man, supposed to have been shell-shocked in the war. **1959** *Listener* 5 Mar. 406/1 A mug of 'shell-shock'—that is what we call cocoa. **1978** *Ibid.* 9 Feb. 168/2 Seeking relief from this shell-shock, I phone a screenwriter friend. **1978** *Maledicta 1977* I. 121 The student was shell-shocked by the letter. **1918** E. A. MACKINTOSH *War, the Liberator* 146 The man rejected the offer with scorn, as badly *shell-shocked men will. **1973** P. DICKINSON *Green Gene* ix. 180 'How are you?' he said. 'Burnt out,' said Mr. Leary. 'Shell-shocked.' **1918** KIPLING *Debits & Credits* (1926) 65 It appeared that the silent Brother was a '*shell-shocker'. *c* **1794** in Shirreff *Agric. Shetl. Isl.* (1814) App. 47 The water, or *shell sickness, is a disease peculiar to those sheep who feed on the hilly pastures at a distance from the sea shores. **1573** *Shell-silver [see *shell-gold* above]. **1728** CHAMBERS *Cycl.* s.v. *Silver*, Shell-Silver, is made of the Shreads of Silver Leaves, or of the Leaves themselves: Used in Painting and Silvering certain Works. **1968** *Funk & Wagnalls Cook's & Diner's Dict.* 213/2 **Shell steak*, another name for club steak. **1969** R. LOCKRIDGE *Murder in False Face* v. 67 You can watch a tall stranger cutting fat from a shell steak. **1973** *Listener* 19 Apr. 501/1 A landscape of luscious rib roasts, lamb chops, shell steaks, T-bone steaks, sirloin steaks, fillet mignon,.. and so on. **1790** J. WHITE *Jrnl. Voy. N.S. Wales* 194 A convict.. met a party of the natives.. by whom he was beaten, and also slightly wounded with the *shell-stick used in throwing their spears. **1895** *Montgomery Ward Catal.* 291/1 Fascinators, hand made, *shell stitch, made of Shetland floss. **1976** *Woman's Day* (U.S.) Nov. 128/1 Crocheted rainbow afghan in shell-stitch pattern fairly glows with its twelve different colors. **1955** FRIEDMAN & WEISSKOPF in W. Pauli *Niels Bohr* 146 Some years ago when the evidence for the *shell structure was accumulating and some of the inadequacies of the compound nucleus picture were becoming more apparent. **1974** G. REECE tr. *Hund's Hist. Quantum Theory* vii. 92 During this period new facts were discovered which made it possible to understand.. the shell structure. **1893** VIZETELLY *Glances Back* I. ii. 33 The Clapham pedagogue was a great stickler for corporal punishment in the case of small boys, and to the administration of this the *shell suits then worn lent themselves admirably. **1706** *Lond. Gaz.* No. 4249/4 A very strong well-limb'd Punch,.. 6 years old, and *Shell-Tooth. **1826–7** *Encycl. Metrop.* (1845) XVIII. 599/2 As in the centre they [*sc.* corner teeth of a horse] are hollowed like a shell, and contain a kind of fleshy substance, called the mark, they are sometimes called shell teeth. **1726** *Dict. Rusticum* (ed. 3) s.v. *Horse's-age*, A horse is said to be *Shell-toothed, when he has long Teeth, and yet black specks in them. **1753** *Chambers' Cycl.* Suppl., *Shell-toothed*,.. an appellation given to a horse that from five years old to old age naturally, and without any artifice, bears mark in all his fore teeth, and there still keeps that hollow place with the black mark. **1888** G. KAPP in *Jrnl. Soc. Telegr.-Engineers & Electricians* XVII. 96 We may divide transformers broadly into two classes—one in which the copper coils are spread over the surface of the iron core, enveloping the latter more or less completely; and the other in which the core is spread over the surface of the copper coils, forming a shell over the winding. I propose to call the former 'core transformers', and the latter '*shell transformers'. **1902** *Encyl. Brit.* XXXIII. 418/1 Shell transformers have the disadvantage generally of poor ventilation for the copper circuits. **1888** *Jrnl. Soc. Telegr.-Engineers & Electricians* XVII. 113 These figures show that even in stout rings.. the core type [of transformer] is better than the *shell type. **1935** *Discovery* Nov. 333/2 The early pottery lamps of the Ægean, Phœnicia, etc. (known to the British Museum as the 'cocked-hat' type, though 'shell-type' seems much more expressive, both as to shape and origin). **1964** W. L. GOODMAN *Hist. Woodworking Tools* 179 In 1864 the first shell-type chuck with adjustable jaws was patented by Barber. **1922** GLAZEBROOK *Dict. Appl. Physics* II. 911/2 The three-phase *shell-type transformer is a development of the single phase, having three individual sets of coils and the three cores arranged to form one composite core. **1947** R. LEE *Electronic Transformers & Circuits* ix. 239 Lower capacitance obtains with two coils than with a shell-type transformer of the same interleaving.

**b.** In names of animals and plants: **shell-bark**, short for *shell-bark hickory* (occas. *s. walnut*), a North American tree, *Carya* (formerly *Juglans*) *ovata*, having a rough shaggy bark consisting of long narrow plates loosely adhering by the middle; also *C. laciniosa* (Thick Shell-bark); also, the nut produced by one of these trees; **shell-binder**, *Terebella conchilega*, the tube of which is composed of sand and fragments of shells; **shell-cracker** *U.S.*, the red-ear sunfish, *Lepomis megalotis*; **shell-eater**, an African bird, *Anastomus lamelligerus* (cf. OPEN-BILL); **shell-flower**, *Molucella lævis*, the genus *Chelone*, and some species of *Alpinia*; **shell-fly**, a kind of fly; an angler's artificial fly (see quots.); **shell-grinder**, **shell-ibis** (see quots.); **shell-insect**, (*a*) see quot.; (*b*) a name for crustaceans of the group *Entomostraca*; **shell-lettuce** (see quot.); **shell parrakeet**, the Australian species *Melopsittacus undulatus* (Cassell); **shell parrot** = BUDGERIGAR; † **shell-pear** = AVOCADO; † **shell-toad**, nonce-translation of Du. *schildpad* (see SHELLPAD); **shell-worm**, †(*a*) a kind of shell-fish; (*b*) a tubicolous annelid; (*c*) a mollusc of the family *Dentaliidæ*.

**1769** R. SMITH *Jrnl.* 11 May in F. W. Halsey *Tour of Four Great Rivers* (1906) 21 The Timber in these Parts.. consists of.. red Oak Hazel Bushes, Ash and Gum together with Butternut and *Shellbark, Hiccory in plenty. **1785** G. WASHINGTON *Jrnl.* 15 Apr. (1925) II. 362, I planted.. a row of the Shell bark hickory Nutt from New York. **1805** ALEX. WILSON *Foresters* Poems & Lit. Prose (1876) II. 131 In deep glens are groves of Shellbarks found. **1814** PURSH *Flora Amer. Septentr.* II. 637 *Juglans sulcata*.. is called Thick

Shell-bark Hickory, Springfield or Glocester Nut. *Ibid.*, *Juglans alba*.. is known by the name of Shell-bark Hickory, Shag-bark and Scaly-bark Hickory. **1822** *Hortus Anglicus* II. 489 Shell-bark Walnut Tree. **1884** SARGENT *Rep. Forests N. Amer.* 133 *Carya sulcata*,.. Big Shell-bark. Bottom Shell-bark. **1885** *Harper's Mag.* Dec. 78/2 The chipmunk .. [has] his hoard of hazel-nuts and shell-barks. **1948** *N.W. Ohio Q.* Winter 13 Two or three did not get in until dark bearing the big loads of fine shellbarks. **1969** T. H. EVERETT *Living Trees of World* xii. 98/2 The big shellbark hickory.. chiefly inhabits rich, deep, fairly moist soils. **1863** WOOD *Nat. Hist.* III. 701 The *Shell-binder is very plentiful on some of our coasts. **1889** *Cent. Dict.*, **Shell-cracker* **1947** B. W. DALRYMPLE *Panfish* 180 The name 'Shellcracker' comes from his habit of feeding on small crustaceans. **1975** *Southern Living* Aug. 18/3 Fishing is good for bass, crappie, bream, bluegill and shellcracker. **1869-73** T. R. JONES *Cassell's Bk. Birds* IV. 75 The African Clapper-bill, or *Shell-eater. **1845-50** MRS. LINCOLN *Lect. Bot.* App. 129 *Molucella lævis*, *shell-flower. **1856** A. GRAY *Man. Bot.* (1860) 285 *Chelone glabra*,.. called.. Shell-flower, Balmony. **1884** W. MILLER *Plant-n.* 124/2 Shell-flower... Brush. *Alpinia* (*Hellenia*) *cærulea*. Indian. *Alpinia nutans*. **1653** WALTON *Angler* v. 97 There are as many sorts of Flies as there be of Fruits:.. as the dun flie,.. the *shel flie, the cloudy or blackish flie. **1655** *Ibid* v. (1661) 107 The shell-fly, good in mid July, the body made of greenish wool, lapt about with the herle of a Peacocks tail; and the wings made of the wings of the Buzzard. **1741** *Compl. Fam.-Piece* II. ii. 334 The Shell Fly, termed also the Green Fly. **1829** *Glover's Hist. Derby* I. 177 The following list, which are well known to the expert angler: viz. barm fly,.. sand fly, shell fly. **1886** *Encycl. Brit.* XX. 174/1 (*Queensland*), The *shell-grinder, *Cestracion*, is similar to a shark found as fossil in Europe. **1894** NEWTON *Dict. Birds* 655 *note*, Others [*sc.* names given to birds of the genus *Anastomus*].. are Shell-eater, *Shell Ibis, and Snail-eater. **1899** A. H. EVANS *Birds* iv. 97 *Anastomus* is called the 'Shell-Ibis' from its cleverness in extracting *Unio* and other molluscs from their shells. **1753** *Chambers' Cycl.* Suppl., *Shell-gall-insect*, an insect of the gall-insect class, somewhat resembling those which are called the boat-fashioned ones... It has its name of *shell-insect, from the resemblance it bears to a muscle-shell. **1707** MORTIMER *Husb.* (1721) II. 148 The *Shell Lettice, so called from the roundness of its Leaf, almost like a Shell, is the first that will Cabbage at the going out of the Winter; otherwise called Winter Lettice. **1890** 'LYTH' *Golden South* xiv. 127 The tiny budgerigar, sometimes called the *shell parrot. **1954** *Coast to Coast 1953-4* 88 The shell-parrots, in glittering, swerving flights, were shrill over the reaches of the river. **1672** W. HUGHES *Amer. Physit.* 41, I never heard it called by any other name than the Spanish Pear, or by some the *Shell-Pear. **1691-6** PLUKENET *Almagestum* Wks. 1769 III. 39 Shell-Pear (i.e.) *Pyrus corticosus & testaceus.* **1570** FOXE *A. & M.* (ed. 2) 2307/2 He was called Shildpad: that is to say, *Shelltode: for that he beyng a short grundy and of litle stature, did ryde commonly with a great broad hat. **1591** PERCIVALL *Sp. Dict.*, *Escaramugos*, a kind of *shell worm breeding on rocks, and on the sides of ships.

**shell** (ʃɛl), *v.* [f. SHELL *sb.* Cf. MLG. *schellen* to peel; also SHALE *v.*, SHEEL *v.*]

**1.** *trans.* To remove (a seed) from its shell, husk, or pod. Also with *out*.

Shelling peas is put (colloq.) for a type of a simple easy process.

**1562** TURNER *Herbal* II. (1568) 33 Thyrtye granes of Lentilles shelled. *a* **1668** DAVENANT *Play House* I. i, What, Shelling of Beans? 'tis a proper work For the Long Vacation. **1725** P. BLAIR *Pharmaco-Bot.* III. 129 Three Bolls of unshell'd or unhusk'd Oats only yield one Boll of what is shell'd or husk'd. **1796** *Mrs. Glasse's Cookery* iii. 32 Shell your pease just before you want them. **1803** M. CUTLER in *Life*, etc. (1888) II. 125 In bad weather, shell out your corn. **1830** MARRYAT *King's Own* xli, I never.. shelled a pea in my life. **1840** DICKENS *Old C. Shop* xxii, Shelling peas into a dish. **1860** BARTLETT *Dict. Amer.* (ed. 3), *To Shell corn*, to remove the grains of Indian corn from the cob. **1867** AUGUSTA WILSON *Vashti* v, Engaged in shelling some seed-beans.

**b.** *Med.* To extrude, expel (a growth).

**1876** *Trans. Clinical Soc.* IX. 41 The capsule of the glands was opened, and most of them were shelled out without much difficulty. **1879** *St. George's Hosp. Rep.* IX. 384 An elastic moveable tumour.. which was easily shelled after a slight dissection.

**c.** (See quots.)

**1823** CRABB *Technol. Dict.*, *To Shell*, (*Vet.*) is said of a horse that has the teeth completely bare and uncovered, which happens about the fifteenth or sixteenth year. **1886** ELWORTHY *W. Somerset Word-bk.* s.v., Animals and children are always said to shell their teeth—that is, to shed or cast the milk teeth.

**d.** *intr.* Of grain, seed, etc.: To drop out of the shell or husk.

**1828-32** WEBSTER, *Shell*.. 3. To be disengaged from the husk; as, wheat or rye shells in reaping. **1846** *Jrnl. R. Agric. Soc.* VII. I. 71 The oats that shell out on the land at harvest time.

**2.** *trans.* To remove the shell, husk, etc. of.

**1694** MOTTEUX *Rabelais* v. Prol. A 3 They shall shell [orig. *esgoussera*] the Shrub's delicious Fruit, Whose Flow'r they in the Spring so much had fear'd. **1705** in Agnew *Hered. Sheriffs Galloway* (1893) II. xi. 207 That they shell their oats sufficientlie for the first time, and winnow the shelling. **1780** YOUNG *Tour Irel.* I. 139 The oats are dried at home.. they are then sent to a mill to be shelled. **1806** A. HUNTER *Culina* (ed. 3) 228 Some shrimps shelled. **1807** VANCOUVER *Agric. Devon* (1813) 72 Coarse millstones for shelling clover. **1865** TYLOR *Early Hist. Man.* 193 The women who shell almonds in the south of France. **1894** *Century Mag.* XLVII. 851, I remembered that my Lake George neighbors 'shell' out their nuts when they take the 'shucks' off them.

**b.** To bring forth as from a shell. *rare.*

**1890** [MRS. A. MACLEOD] *Austral. Girl* xvi, Creatures that are shelled into life in weltering heaps.

**3.** *intr.* To come away or fall off as a shell, crust, or outer coat; to come *off* in thin pieces, peel or scale *off*.

**1676** WISEMAN *Chirurg. Treat.* IV. iv. 287 By this very method the rottenness of the Bone soon shell'd off. **1686** tr. *Chardin's Coronat. Solyman* 38 There is nothing.. that appears either tarnished or shel'd off [orig. *écaillé*] in any part. **1760** *Phil. Trans.* LI. 636 It did.. damage to the column.. by causing its surface to shell off. **1883** R. HALDANE in *Workshop Rec.* Ser. II. 254/2 (*Whitewashing*) This [mixture] will not shell off.

**4.** *trans.* To enclose in, or as in, a shell; to encase. (See SHELLED *a.* 1.)

**1637** N. WHITING *Albino & Bellama* 9 His body shelled in a Satten skin Of azure dye. *Ibid.* 53 Cupid.. disdaines to dwell In loftie pallace, but does shell Himselfe in straw-thatcht roofe. **1649** G. DANIEL *Trinarch.*, *Hen. V*, lxxiv, They did returne Vnto the King; who Shells himselfe, to see W<sup>th</sup>in himselfe, the Obiect of this Scorne. **1666** [MARVELL] *Third Advice to Painter* 18 Even they (though shell'd in trebble Oak) Will prove an Addle-egg with double Yoalk. **1685** COTTON tr. *Montaigne* xix. (1869) 68 Shell thee with steel or brass,.. Death from the casque will pull thy cautious head. *c* **1822** BEDDOES *Poems*, *Pygmalion* 69 Like a dim mist Shelling a god, it rolled. **1876** GEO. ELIOT *Dan. Der.* xviii, Their faces seemed full of speech, as if their minds had been shelled after the manner of horse-chesnuts.

†**b.** *pass.* (app.) To be fixed close, as a mollusc to its shell.

**1649** G. DANIEL *Trinarch.*, *Hen. IV*, ccxxvi, A Man soe Shell'd in Blood vnto his Beast.

**5. a.** To furnish with shells for collecting spat.

**1885** *Encycl. Brit.* XVIII. 110 Spawning oysters are frequently put down in the spring, two months before the ground is shelled. **1891** W. K. BROOKS *Oyster* 108 Of this vast area a large portion has been cleaned up and shelled.

**b.** To spread oyster-shells on (ground) as a fertilizer; to make up (a road) with shells; *intr.* to deal in or use oyster-shells.

In U.S. Dicts.

**6.** To bombard with shells (also *absol.*); to drive *out of* a place by shelling.

**1856** W. H. RUSSELL *War* xxiii. 227 The Russians now shell vigorously. **1870** *Standard* 16 Nov., A battery was planted, and the chateau was about to be shelled. **1895** *Times* 4 Feb. 5/1 Every gun in the fort had been silenced, and the Japanese were fairly shelled out of it.

*transf.* **1897** 'H. S. MERRIMAN' *In Kedar's Tents* xx, The other soldier was chasing his opponent up the hill, shelling him, as he rode away, with oaths and stones.

*fig.* **1827** SCOTT *Chron. Canongate* i, My quondam doer had ensconced himself chin-deep among legal trenches.. but my two protectors shelled him out of his defences. **1834** DE QUINCEY *Autob. Sk.* Wks. 1853 I. 45 From these.. he was speedily driven, or one might say shelled out, by a concerted assault of my sister Mary's.

**7. shell out.** *colloq.* (*fig.* from sense 1).

**a.** *trans.* To disburse, pay up, hand over. Also (rarely) *to shell down.*

**1801** MAR. EDGEWORTH *Moral T.*, *Forester*, *The Bank-Notes*, One of you.. must shell out your coriander s [see CORIANDER 3]. **1815** —— *Love & Law* I. i, To shell out for me the price of a daacent horse. **1816** SCOTT *Bl. Dwarf* vii, The gold is shelled down when ye command, as fast as I have seen the ash-keys fall in a frosty morning. **1819** MOORE *Tom Crib's Memor.* (ed. 3) 27 Who knows but, if coax'd, he may shell out the shiners? **1863** in Robson *Bards of Tyne* 299 Shell oot yor goold, my collier lad.

**b.** *intr.* To pay up.

**1821** EGAN *Life in London* (1869) x. 265 If you are too scaly to tip for it, I'll shell out and shame you. **1857** HUGHES *Tom Brown* I. vi, I've got a tick at Sally's,.. but then I hate running it high.. towards the end of the half, 'cause one has to shell out for it all directly one comes back. **1889** H. O'REILLY *50 Yrs. on Trail* 254, I had to 'shell out' pretty freely.. it cost me 250 dollars.

**c.** *trans.* To let out, declare. *rare.*

**1862** MRS. H. WOOD *Channings* i, Come, Miss Channing, just shell out what you know.

**shell**, obs. Anglo-Irish form of SELL *v.*

*a* **1660** *Contemp. Hist. Irel.* (Ir. Archæol. Soc.) I. 173 A Judas an Apostat merchant shellinge the same for money. *Ibid.* II. 137 To shell the lives of his abetters.

**shellac** (ʃəˈlæk, ˈʃɛlæk), *sb.* Also 8 **shellack, shel-lack, shell-lake, shell lack,** 8-9 **shell-lac, shell lac.** [transl. F. *laque en écailles* lac (see LAC[1]) in thin plates. (Cf. G. *schalenlack*, beside *schellack* from English.)]

**1.** Lac melted and run into thin plates; formerly used esp. in the manufacture of gramophone records.

**1713** *Mercator* No. 93/4, 1370 l. Shellack. **1716** *Gt. Brit. Weekly Pacquet* No. 17 Gum Shell Lack, Ditto Seed Lack, Ditto Stick Lack. **1725** DE FOE *Voy. round World* (1787) II. 79 Lacks, such as shel-lack, stick lack, &c. **1734-5** *Phil. Trans.* XXXIX. 20 A Cake of Shell-Lake. **1827** FARADAY *Chem. Manip.* xvii. (1842) 476 Varnished with a solution of shell lac in strong alcohol. **1873** SPON in *Work-shop Rec.* Ser. I. 23/1 Shellac is the only cement used by jewellers for jet articles. **1913** *Jrnl. Franklin Inst.* CLXXVI. 192 These modern composition disk records are in reality seals of the human voice, because the substance they are made of is a modified sealing wax,.. containing shellac as a basic substance. *Ibid.*, Shellac is much adulterated, and the mineral and fibrous substances which are added require careful selection. **1933** *Amer. Speech* VIII. 13/1 Professor Jones.. has them [*sc.* cardinal vowels] recorded on shellac. **1962** A. NISBETT *Technique Sound Studio* 266 Formerly, shellac was used for pressing records, and having much greater elasticity was suitable for record materials when only very heavy.. pick-up heads were available.

*attrib.* **1765** T. H. CROKER et al. *Compl. Dict. Arts & Sciences* II. s.v. *Japanning*, The proper japan ground.. is much the best formed of shell-lac varnish. **1816** J. SMITH *Panorama Sci. & Art* II. 792 Shell-lac varnish is rather softer than seed-lac varnish. **1876** *Trans. Clinical Soc.* IX. 12 Carbolised shellac plaster.

**2.** A gramophone record made of shellac.

**1954** *Billboard* 21 Aug. 18/2 Unless a publisher could get hold of an acetate of his song, he had to wait until the shellacs were ready. **1977** G. V. HIGGINS *Dreamland* xvi. 180, I remember the phonograph playing... There was one tune... He played it all the time, scratchy and noisy as the old shellacs were.

**shellac** (ʃɛˈlæk), *v.* orig. and chiefly *U.S.* Also **shellack**; *pa. pple.* **shellacked.** [f. the sb.]

**1.** *trans.* To coat or varnish with shellac.

**1876** *Scribner's Monthly* Feb. 488/1 It is made of plain white pine, brought to a good surface and shellacked. **1881** C. C. HARRISON *Woman's Handiwork* III. 139 Book-shelves have been made of pine, painted in flat color or stained and shellacked. **1917** C. MATHEWSON *Second Base Sloan* 90 Wayne threatened to varnish or shellac the paper so that it would turn the rain. **1969** *Sunday Times* 9 Feb. 58/1 They tend to wear dark blue silken suits or little black dresses and look as if they had been shellacked or sprayed with fixative just before they left home.

**2.** *slang.* To beat, thrash, punish.

**1930** C. F. COE *Gunman* iv. 53 These two bums that Lefty shellacked were members of Red Karfola's gang. **1935** J. HARGAN *Gloss. Prison Lang.* 7 *Shellack*, to punish or beat. **1977** *Time* 8 Aug. 28/2 Pitcher McArdle was shellacked for .. six runs in the first inning.

Hence **she'llac(k)ed** *ppl. a.*, (*a*) coated, varnished, or fastened with shellac; (*b*) *U.S. slang*, intoxicated, 'plastered'.

**1882** *Harper's Mag.* Oct. 688 The bedrooms are shellacked and some are stained of a deep tint. **1884** F. J. BRITTEN *Watch & Clockm.* 88 A piece of sapphire which is .. shellaced to a brass handle. **1902** *Encycl. Brit.* XXXIII. 419 The shellacked cotton, oil, and other materials with which the transformer circuits are insulated. **1922** *Dialect Notes* V. 148 *Shellacked*, stewed, bunned, etc. **1935** J. T. FARRELL *Judgment Day* I. iv. 85 You know, when I first found out about how you'd get shellacked, I thought it was pretty terrible. **1941** WYNDHAM LEWIS *Let.* 17 Oct. (1963) 300 The silly 'toughness' of the Irish immigrant mass, shellacked into a sly, bluff, servility. **1948** H. L. MENCKEN *Amer. Lang.* Suppl. II. 644 When a novelty is obvious it seldom lasts very long, *e.g.*, *shellacked* for drunk.

**she'llac(k)ing**, *vbl. sb.* Chiefly *U.S.* [f. SHELLAC *v.* + -ING[1].]

**1.** A coating of shellac.

**1884** F. J. BRITTEN *Watch & Clockm.* 104 It.. saves time when used instead of waxing or shellacing.

**2.** A beating or thrashing, a 'pasting'; a defeat. *slang.*

**1931** E. H. LAVINE *Third Degree* x. 121 When this method failed, as it invariably did, he would leave the room and the *shellacking* continued. **1941** *Sun* (Baltimore) 18 Sept. 13/1 The main bulk of the Twenty-ninth Division handed the One Hundred and Fifteenth Regimental Combat Team a shellacking on the combat range today. **1956** W. H. WHYTE *Organisation Man* ii. 22 By the time of the First World War the Protestant Ethic had taken a shellacking from which it would not recover. **1960** T. MCLEAN *Kings of Rugby* 56 'Ronnie' left the field to run into the greatest shellacking he had ever had. **1978** H. WOUK *War & Remembrance* xxxiii. 351 The Japs can't recover from the shellacking they took at Midway.

**shellam**, variant of SCHELM *Obs.*

*c* **1619** *Barnavelt* II. i. in Bullen *O.P.* II. 229 The proude Shellams [*printed* Shellains] are paid too well.

**shell-apple, -drake, -duck**: see SHELDAPPLE, SHELDRAKE, SHELDUCK.

**shelled** (ʃɛld), *a.* [f. SHELL *sb.* + -ED[2].]

**1.** Of animals, fruits, etc.: Having a shell.

*shelled insects*, the crustacean group *Entomostraca*: cf. *shell-insect* s.v. SHELL *sb.* 40 b.

**1577** B. GOOGE *Heresbach's Husb.* II. 102 Those fruites that are shelde, as Nuttes. **1649** JER. TAYLOR *Gt. Exemp.* III. Disc. xiv. 29 They are like shelled fish, singing loudest when their house is on fire about their ears. **1730** SOUTHALL *Treat. Bugs* 19 A Bugg's Body is shaped and shelled, and the Shell as transparent.. as the most beautiful.. Turtle. **1752** *Phil. Trans.* XLVII. 510 The juices of shell'd fish. **1812** D'ISRAELI *Calam. Auth.* (1867) 140 Authors must not be thin-skinned, but shelled like the rhinoceros. **1819** SCOTT *Leg. Montrose* iv, He's shelled like a partan. **1854** A. ADAMS, etc. *Man. Nat. Hist.* 370 Shelled-Astacians (*Epipyxididæ*). **1897** *Allbutt's Syst. Med.* II. 1009 The contained eggs, or rather shelled embryos, are minute.

**b.** With prefixed adj.: Having a shell (of a certain kind).

**1611** [see HARD-SHELLED, SOFT-SHELLED]. **1649** Thick-shell'd [see THICK *a.* 12]. **1762** tr. *Busching's Syst. Geog.* V. 626 The corn here is thinner shelled than that which grows in a fatter soil. **1845** GOSSE *Ocean* i. (1849) 58 Some little shelled Mollusk. **1904** P. FOUNTAIN *Gt. North-West* xxi. 249 The eggs.. are very small and delicate shelled.

**2.** Of a beach: Covered with shells.

**1895** *Pall Mall Gaz.* 1 Feb. 11/2 A generous expanse of shelled and sandy beach.

**3.** Of ammunition: Contained in shells.

**1900** *Daily News* 13 June 7/6 Our artillery now poured in common shelled lyddite.

**shelled** (ʃɛld), *ppl. a.* [f. SHELL *v.* + -ED[1].] Deprived of the shell; from which the shell has been removed or shed. Cf. SHEELED. ***shelled corn***: Indian corn removed from the cob. *U.S.*

**1676** in *Maryland Archives* (1884) II. 560 A Peck of Indian shell'd Corn or Oates. **1714** J. GREEN *Diary* in *Essex Inst. Hist. Coll.* (1869) X. 104, I agreed to give Mr. Ganson five bushels of shelled corn at harvest, for ye damage my oxen did ye last night. **1725** P. BLAIR *Pharmaco-Bot.* III. 129 It is of this shell'd Oats that they make the Grotts. **1821** SCOTT *Kenilw.* ii, A shelled pea-cod. **1828** W. COBBETT *Treat. Cobbett's Corn* §136 The Americans call it, and.. we must call it, 'shelled corn'. **1887** *Daily News* 18 July 2/5 Peas ..8d to 1s per shelled pint. **1950** *Chicago Tribune* 20 Mar. IV. 1/3 The class of Illinois shippers primarily affected would be those who consign shelled corn to far western states.

**shelled**, variant of SHELD *a.*

**sheller** ('ʃɛlə(r)). [f. SHELL *v.* + -ER[1].]

**1. a.** One who shells peas, etc.; *spec.* one whose occupation it is to open bivalves.

**1694** MOTTEUX *Rabelais* v. Prol. A 7, Clever Shellers of Beans. **1832** *Scoreby Farm Rep.* 10 in *Libr. Usef. Knowl., Husb.* III, For these long oats, the 'shellers', who buy the largest quantities to convert into oatmeal, will give as much per stone, as they will for the short ones. **1859** SALA *Tw. round Clock* (1861) 43 Some fastidious persons might perhaps object that the fingers of the shellers [of the peas] are some-what coarse. **1887** GOODE, etc., *Fisheries U.S.* v. II. 593 The clams are thoroughly washed before they are given over to the knives of the 'shellers', or 'openers'.

**b.** A machine for rasping or rubbing the grain from the cob.

**1859** *Rep. Comm. Patents 1858* (U.S.) I. 361 The nature of this invention relates..to the form and arrangements of the shellers. **1875** KNIGHT *Dict. Mech.*

**2.** A contrivance for providing an object with a shell or coating.

**1883** *Pall Mall Gaz.* 18 Sept. 12/1 After this it has only to go into the sheller, where it gets its last coat in the shape of a plaster of Paris shell.

**'shellery.** *nonce-word.* [f. SHELL *sb.*[1] + -ERY.] A depreciatory name for: A grotto.

**1737** in Mrs. Delany *Autobiogr.* (1861) I. 608, I have been to see Lady Walpole's shellery (for *grotto* I will *not* call it).

**shellet**, etc.: see SHILLET.

**Shelleyan** ('ʃɛlıən), *a.* (and *sb.*). Also *rarely* **Shellyan, Shelleian.** [f. the name *Shelley* (see def.) + -AN.] Pertaining or relating to, or characteristic of Percy Bysshe Shelley (1792–1822) or his poetry, or the ideas expressed in his works. As *sb.*, an admirer of Shelley.

*a* **1849** POE *Marginalia* Wks. 1864 III. 544 The Shellyan abandon and the Tennysonian poetic sense. **1880** TODHUNTER *Shelley* v. 157 A bit of the Shelleyan philosophy. **1886** *Sat. Rev.* 13 Mar. 374/2 Mr. Wise's reprint of *Adonais* for the Shelley Society is..quite worthy of the attention of Shelleyans. **1886** DOWDEN *Shelley* I. xii. 523 Why Mary was 'Pecksie' must remain a Shelleyan mystery. *a* **1907** F. THOMPSON in *Dublin Rev.* (1908) July 36 Perhaps none of his poems is more purely and typically Shelleian than *The Cloud.* **1930** BLUNDEN *De Bello Germanico* 26 Such a bed is not surpassed by the Shelleian shakedown of roses.

Hence **Shelley'ana** [-ANA *suff.*], books or items relating to Shelley; **'Shelleyism**, thought or action characteristic of Shelley; **'Shelleyist, 'Shelleyite**, an admirer or follower of Shelley; **Shelley'olater**, a worshipper of Shelley; so **Shelley'olatry.**

**1886** *Academy* Mar. 218/2 '*Shelleyana' of all kinds. **1924** P. CRESWICK *Beaten Path* xxxvii. 203 'Had I any books about Shelley?'..'We have considerable Shelleyana,' said I. 'Here is the special shelf.' **1822** LAMB *Lett.* (1888) II. 48 To award his Heaven and his Hell in the presumptuous manner he does, was a piece of immodesty as bad as *Shelleyism. **1934** G. B. SHAW *Prefaces* 506/1 They were *Shelleyists, but not atheists. **1881** *Athenæum* 5 Mar. 329/1 Another sect of devotees..the *Shelleyites. **1898** W. GRAHAM *Last Links* xiii, The infuriated Shelleyan, or rather let me say *Shelleyolater. **1892** W. WATSON in *Bookman* Oct. 23/2 Many a reader, not impeachable on the ground of *Shelleyolatry.

**shell-fish** ('ʃɛlfıʃ). [OE. *scilfisc* = ON. *skelfiskr.*] Any animal living in water whose outer covering is a shell, whether testaceous, as an oyster, or crustaceous, as a crab.

*c* **888** ÆLFRED *Boeth.* xli. §5 Manize sint cwucera zesceafta unstirende, swa swa nu scylfiscas sint. *c* **1374** CHAUCER *Boeth.* II. met. v. (1868) 50 þe blode of a manar shelfysshe þat men fynden in tyrie, wiþ whiche blode men deien purper. *Ibid.* v. pr. v. 21 Oystres and muscles and oþer swiche shelle fysshe of þe see. *c* **1380** WYCLIF *Sel. Wks.* III. 69 Schel fische and scalid fisch. **14..** *Nom.* in Wr.-Wülcker 705/26 *Hoc conchile*, alle maner schelfyche. **1553** EDEN *Treat. Newe Ind.* (Arb.) 22 The shelle fyshe called the Tortoyse of the sea. **1610** HEALEY *St. Aug. Citie of God* v. vi. 204 Crabs..and all shel-fishes. *a* **1691** BOYLE *Hist. Air* (1692) 179 The Clacas, which is absolutely the very best Shell-fish in the World. **1732** ARBUTHNOT *Rules of Diet* in *Aliments*, etc. 255 Shell-fish are nourishing. **1858** SIMMONDS *Dict. Trade, Shell-fish*, the term is chiefly applied in commerce to crabs, lobsters, and cray-fish, oysters, mussels, periwinkles, and whelks, in which a large trade is carried on.

*Comb.* **1837** THACKERAY *Professor* Wks. 1899 XIII. 496 The father of Miss Adeliza Grampus was a shell-fishmonger. **1896** J. LAMB *Ann. Ayrshire Parish* i. 21 A happy hunting-ground for shell-fish gatherers.

**b.** *fig.* of a person.

**1809** MALKIN *Gil Blas* XII. v. (Rtldg.) 430 Open-mouthed and impenetrable shell-fish.

Hence **'shell-ˌfishery, 'shell-ˌfishing.**

**1868** *Harper's Mag.* Dec. 12/2 Our men, some of whom were practiced in the business of shell-fishing,..very soon dug up a very fine feast of clams. **1885** *Encycl. Brit.* XVIII. 108/1 The cultivation of oysters and other shell-fisheries. **1901** *Westm. Gaz.* 31 Oct. 12/1 The shell-fishing..has been wonderfully successful.

**'shellful.** *rare.* [f. SHELL *sb.* + -FUL.] A quantity sufficient to fill a shell; *fig.* a small quantity.

*c* **1450** *M.E. Med. Bk.* (Heinrich) 66 þe juce of cynchen þre schelfulle. **1560** ROLLAND *Seven Sages* 63 Thay will.. gar ȝow traistly trow Quhilk is not worth ane schelfull of credence. **1650** BAXTER *Saint's R.* I. viii. 135 Onely a shell full of Dust, animated with an invisible rational soul.

**shelliness** ('ʃɛlınıs). *rare.* [f. SHELLY *a.* + -NESS.] **a.** The condition of being covered with shells. **b.** Tendency to retire 'into one's shell'.

**1866** G. MACDONALD *Ann Q. Neighb.* xvii, All I have to suggest for myself is simply a certain shyness... I daresay, likewise, that the natural shelliness of the English had something to do with it. **1876** *Macm. Mag.* XXXIV. 336 There are limpid pools..where you may wash your feet free from shelliness.

**shelling** ('ʃɛlıŋ), *vbl. sb.* [f. SHELL *v.* + -ING[1].]

**1.** The action of SHELL *v.*; removal of the shell of peas, nuts, etc. Cf. SHEELING I.

**1725** P. BLAIR *Pharmaco-Bot.* III. 129 The Pains of husking or shelling of it [*sc.* Naked Oats] (as 'tis usually call'd) in a Water Mill. **1892** *Athenæum* 12 Mar. 338/2 A clandestine shelling of peas.

**2.** *concr.* Cf. SHEELING 2. **a.** Husks or chaff.

**1598** FLORIO, *Mondiglia*, cleansings, purifyings, sweepings, parings, shellings. **1629** *Orkney Witch Trial* in *County Folk-Lore* (1903) III. 78 Thair was sevin thrave and ane halff quhairoff he got nothing bot shellings. **1722** P. BLAIR *Pharmaco-Bot.* III. 131 They winnow or fan off the Husk [of oats], call'd in some Places the Shellings. **1812** *Chron.* in *Ann. Reg.* 151 A quantity of wet shellings of oats had been put on the fire. **1830** *Kyle Farm Rep.* 43 in *Libr. Usef. Knowl., Husb.* III, No oats are sold; they are converted into meal for the sake of getting the dust and shelling. **1851** J. F. W. JOHNSTON *Notes N. Amer.* II. 128 The shellings or outer husk of this grain are sent down the stream by the millers.

**b.** Grain, etc. from which the husk has been removed.

**1705** [see SHELL *v.* 2]. **1763** *Chron.* in *Ann. Reg.* 107 Kemp ..brought a peck of shelling to the mill to have it ground. **1815** *Pocklington Canal Act* 52 Flour, shelling, and pearl barley. **1858** SIMMONDS *Dict. Trade, Shelling*, a commercial name for groats, the grain of oats when the shudes are removed.

**3. a.** Manuring with shells. **b.** (See quot. 1796.) **c.** (See quot. 1881.)

**1780** A. YOUNG *Tour Irel.* I. 122 Parts by shelling advanced, from 5s. to 25s. an acre. **1796** —— *Ann. Agric.* XXVII. 189 (E.D.S.) The snow lodging among the tops of the wool, and freezing like an incrustation around [the sheep is called] shelling. **1881** INGERSOLL *Oyster-Industr.* 248 *Shelling*, the spreading of shells upon the bottom to catch spawn.

**4.** The firing of shells, bombardment with shells.

**1860** W. H. RUSSELL *Diary in India* II. 288 We should knock down a few of these fellows' forts, and give them a good shelling. **1870** *Daily News* 29 Aug. 5 After some two hours' shelling the French fire grew slacker.

**5.** The collecting of sea-shells.

**1861** C. P. HODGSON *Resid. Japan* 35 Captain Page..lent me his gig and crew of seven men for a day's shelling. **1876** MORESBY (*title*) New Guinea and Polynesia. Discoveries.. in New Guinea,..a Cruise in Polynesia and Visits to the Pearl-Shelling Stations in Torres Straits.

**6.** (See quot.)

**1897** *Encycl. Sport* I. 341/2 *Kicking*, the old term for the custom of guards to ask travellers for a tip or special fee. Also called *Shelling.*

**7.** *attrib.*, as (= for use in shelling grain) ***shelling machine, mill***; (= pertaining to shell-collecting) ***shelling craft, ground, industry***; (= consisting of shelled grain, etc., cf. SHEELING) ***shelling beans, seeds.***

**1795** PHILLIPS *Hist. Inland Nav.* Addenda 47 Wheat, rye, *shelling beans, pease. **1887** MRS. DALY *Digging & Squatting* 349 Some of the *shelling craft were raising as much as a ton a month. **1896** *Strand Mag.* XII. 356/2 *Shelling ground is usually of coral structure. **1889** H. H. ROMILLY *Verandah in N. Guinea* x. 225 The *shelling industry has very considerably increased. **1803** M. CUTLER in *Life*, etc. (1888) II. 137 Patent for *shelling machine. **1807** VANCOUVER *Agric. Devon* (1813) 179 There being few *shelling-mills, and little or no oatmeal manufactured in the country. **1842** J. AITON *Dom. Econ.* (1857) 241 Cover all with six or eight inches of the *shelling-seeds.

**'shell-less**, *a.* Also **shelless.** [f. SHELL *sb.* + -LESS.] Without a shell or shells.

**1777** G. WHITE *Selborne, Let. to Barrington* 20 May, Myriads of small shell-less snails. **1838** *Penny Cycl.* X. 486/2 In the Frog-tribe the ova..are shelless [*sic*], and generally laid in the water. **1843** *Ibid.* XXVII. 272/2 Shell-less mollusks. **1859–62** SIR J. RICHARDSON, etc. *Mus. Nat. Hist.* (1868) II. 358 *Gymnosomata* (Shell-less Pteropods).

**'shell-out.** *Billiards.* [f. phr. *shell out*: see SHELL *v.* 7.] (See quot. 1884.)

**1866** 'CAPT. CRAWLEY' *Billiard Bk.* xii. 200. **1882** MISS BRADDON *Mt. Royal* x, Jessie joined the revellers at pool or shell-out. **1884** W. COOK *Billiards* 169 Shell out is a game played with the pyramid balls by a number of players. There is a small stake on each ball, and whenever a player pockets a ball he receives one stake from every other player.

**†'shellpad.** *Obs.* Also 6 schell-, 6–7 shel-, 8 **shellpot.** [f. SHELL *sb.* + PAD *sb.*[1] after (M)LG. *schildpadde*, MDu. *schiltpadde* (Du. *schildpad*), lit. 'shield-toad'.] A tortoise.

**1562** WITHALS *Dict.* 9 b/1 A tortes or shell padde, *testudo.* **1570** LEVINS *Manip.* 8/8 A shelpad, *testudo.* **1790** *Massachusetts Spy* 24 June (Thornton *Amer. Gloss.*), A small turtle..known [in Virginia] by the name of shellpot.

Hence **†shell-paddock** *Sc.*

**1565** *Reg. Privy Council Scot.* I. 413 Ane penny..havand on the one syde ane palmetre crownit, ane schell padocke crepand up the schank of the samyn. *c* **1600** in Watson *Coll. Sc. Poems* (1709) II. 54 Shell-padock, ill shapen Shit, Kid-bearded jennet, all alike grit. **1673** WEDDERBURN *Vocab.* 15 (Jam.) *Testudo*, a shel-paddock.

**'shell-snail.** A snail having a shell.

**1600** SURFLET *Country Farm* I. xii. 58 A cataplasme.. made of the muscilage of shell snailes. **1601** HOLLAND *Pliny* XXX. xiii. II. 395 Certaine shell-snailes that creepe in troupes together for to devour the young spring and greene leaves of plants. **1691** RAY *S. & E.C. Words* 102 A Hodmandod, a Shell-snail. **1699** JAS. BARRY *Reviving Cordial.* (1802) 23 Some speckled shell-snails. **1843** *Zoologist* I. 97 Small spiral-shaped shell-snails. **1890** *Hardwicke's Sci. Gossip* XXVI. 239/1 The big shell snails..which lurk, during the day, in crevices of the walls.

**b.** *fig.* A retiring or shy person.

**1585** T. WASHINGTON tr. *Nicholay's Voy.* Ep. Ded., What (think we) may be obiected against those shelsnailes?

**Shelluh, Shelook**, obs. varr. SHILLUK.

**'shell-work.**

**1.** Work consisting of an arrangement of shells in patterns for ornamentation; shells lining the walls of an artificial grotto.

**1611** COTGR. s.v., *Coquillage*, shell-worke; worke made of, or trimd with, shells. **1675** HANNAH WOOLEY *Gentlew. Comp.* 10 All works wrought with a Needle, all Transparent works, Shell-work, Moss-work. *a* **1700** EVELYN *Diary* 27 Feb. 1644, A large..grotto of shell-worke. **1728** GARDINER *Rapin, Gardens* (ed. 3) III. 131 Some Artists will their grotts ..Of Pumice..build; The splendid Roof with shining Shell-work grace. **1773** JOHNSON in *Boswell* (1831) III. 12 She knows French, musick, and drawing, sews neatly, makes shell-work. **1809** MALKIN *Gil Blas* IV. ix. ¶5 A rude front built of pebbles and shell-work. **1836** *Penny Cycl.* VI. 432/1 The delicate petals arranged with the most artificial symmetry, so as to resemble curious shell-work. **1891** FARRAR *Darkn. & Dawn* xxvi, A reticulated shellwork of pale blue was fastened by threads of glass to the opalescent vase within.

**†2.** Shells adhering to a ship's bottom. *rare.*

**1698** FROGER *Voy.* 170 Our Ships being too foul, too full of Herbs and Shell-work, to think of gaining upon Vessels newly careened.

**'shelly**, *sb. nonce-wd.* [f. SHELL *sb.* + -Y.] A shell.

**1611** BEAUM. & FL. *Knt. Burning Pestle* IV. ad. fin., Sluggish snails, that erst were mute, do creep out of their shelies [*rime* bellies].

**shelly** ('ʃɛlı), *a.* [f. SHELL *sb.* + -Y.]

**1.** Abounding in (sea)shells; of a geological formation, consisting wholly or mainly of shells.

**1555** EDEN *Decades* (Arb.) 380 Vpon the coast of Barberie ..there is xv. fadome and good shelly grounde and sande amonge. **1650** S. CLARKE *Eccl. Hist.* I. (1654) 172 Amidst the shelly rocks of the sea. **1662** J. DAVIES tr. *Olearius' Voy. Amb.* 207 We observ'd all along the Caspian Sea, many of these shelly Mountains. **1718** POPE *Odyss.* IV. 555 The shelly shore. **1751** J. BARTRAM *Observ.* 17 The rock consisted of a dark coloured shelly stone. **1776** —— *Jrnl.* 1 Jan. 18 Landed at a high shelly bluff. **1824** G. CHALMERS *Caledonia* III. III. iii. 221 Marle of the shelly kind. **1832** DE LA BECHE *Geol. Man.* (ed. 2) 245 A coarse shelly and sandy limestone. **1877** LE CONTE *Elem. Geol.* (1879) 153 Mollusca which..leave their dead shells..and thus form sometimes pure shelly deposits.

**2.** Consisting of or of the nature of a shell; forming a covering resembling a shell; shell-like.

**1592** SHAKS. *Ven. & Ad.* 1034 As the snaile..Shrinks backward in his shellie caue with paine. **1601** HOLLAND *Pliny* XXXII. VII. 441 The shellie skin of the sea Vrchin. **1662** *Comenius' Janua Ling. Triling.* 27 The slow-pac'd cockle [snail] carryeth about with it its shelly lodge. **1681** GREW *Musæum* I. §ii. i. 18 The fore-part of his Tail is encompass'd with shelly Rings. **1778** MILNE *Bot. Dict.* (ed. 2) 145 The shelly or husky outside incloses a white bitter pulp. **1815** S. BROOKES *Conchol* 96 A subcylindrical shelly or bony body. **1844** DICKENS *Mart. Chuz.* xxi, The very winkle of your country in his shelly lair. **1872** NICHOLSON *Palæont.* 201 In the typical Terebratulæ, the internal skeleton which supports the arms is a short shelly hoop.

**b.** Of coal: see quot.

**1881** RAYMOND *Mining Gloss., Shelly*, the condition of coal which has been so much faulted and twisted that it is not massive, but easily breaks into conchoidal pieces.

**c.** *fig.* Hollow-sounding, empty.

**1648** SYMMONS *Vind.* 132 What they intend by cajol'd, and whom by cabalistical Adversaries, I stand not to argue, for the words are shelly.

**d.** Of a thin, bony, and lanky build.

**1865** SLEIGH *Derbysh. Gloss.* in *Reliquary* VI. 167 *Shelly*, said of a beast which does not carry flesh. **1884** *Live Stock Jrnl.* 1 Aug. 106/3 Darlington Dog Show... Glendale..is rather inclined to be shelly, with drooping quarters. **1893** *Kennel Gazette* Aug. 213/2 Her kennel companion..is too shelly all through.

*Comb.* **1901** *Scotsman* 12 Nov. 8/3 A man of Mr. Maxwell's build cannot get his arms away so freely as a shelly-built player.

**3.** Of an animal: Having a shell; shell-.

**1593** NASHE *Christ's T.* 71 b, In theyr hollowe Caues.. shelly Snayles shall keepe house. **1611** COTGR., *Nautile*, the shellie Pourcountrell. **1774** GOLDSM. *Nat. Hist.* (1776) VII. 65 Of all animals of the shelly tribe, the Pholades are the most wonderful.

**4.** Formed of a (sea)shell; consisting of (sea) shells or shell-fish.

**1716** GAY *Trivia* III. 186 Be sure observe where brown Ostrea stands, Who boasts her shelly Ware from Wallfleet Sands. **1721** D'URFEY *Ariadne* II. i, And loud with quavering Sounds on shelly Hautboys, Tritons shall sing. **1733** BUDGELL *Bee* IV. 400 A pointed Bulrush ev'ry Heroe bears, And ev'ry Head a Shelly Helmet wears. **1753** *Chambers' Cycl.* Suppl. s.v. *Shells*, The great good these shelly fragments do to the lands they are used on. **1759** GRAINGER *Sulpicia* I. 25 Whatever Gems the swarthy Indians boast, Their shelly Treasures [etc.].

**shelly-coat.** *Sc.* Also 8 shellicoat. [f. SHELLY *a.* + COAT *sb.*]

**1.** A water sprite wearing sea-shells which make a clattering noise. Also *attrib.*

**1720** PENNECUIK *Streams from Helicon* 65 No Shellicoat Goblin, or Elf on the Green. **1802** SCOTT *Minstrelsy* I. Introd. 84 Shellycoat, a spirit who resides in the waters, and has given his name to many a rock and stone upon the Scotish coast. **1803** ALEX. BOSWELL *Spirit of Tintoc* To Rdr., Nor Kelpy, nor Shellycoat, nor any of the spirits of the deep. *a* **1869** C. SPENCE *From Braes of Carse* (1898) 90 All the sea and river imps With shelly coats and scaly jimps.

**2.** 'A sheriff's messenger, or bum-bailiff, denominated perhaps from the badges of office on his coat' (Jam.).

*a* **1774** FERGUSSON *Poems* (1807) 304, I dinna care a single jot; Tho' summon'd by a shelly-coat.

So **shelly-coated** *a.* (see 1 above).

**1725** RAMSAY *Gentle Sheph.* I. i, She fled as frae a shelly-coated cow [= goblin; see COW *sb.*[2]].

**shelm**, variant of SCHELM.

†**shelp**[1]. [app. representing OE. *scylp* glossing 'scopulus', 'murex'. Cf. SCALP *sb.*[2]] A sandbank in a river or the sea; = SHELF *sb.*[2]

**1430–31** *Rolls of Parlt.* IV. 381/2 Il y ad si graunde noumbre des schelpes deinz le Ryver de Ley. *c* **1500** *Lib. Rub.* fo. 114 b in *Wells MSS.* (Hist. MSS. Comm.) 145 The water was so lowe and so many shelpes and bayes in the ryver. **1535–6** *Act 27 Hen. VIII*, c. 18 §3 Sande gravell or any other rubbysshe..lieng..uppon any Shelppe or Shelppes within the said ryver of Thamyse. **1538** ELYOT *Dict.*, *Syrtes*, quycke sandes or shelpes [1545 shelfes] in the water made by the dryfte of sande or grauel. **1630** *Lex Londinensis* (1680) 210 At Woolwich shelp two [trinckes], and no more;..At Dagnam shelp six.

†**shelp**[2]. *Obs.* The ribbon-fish.

**1562** WITHALS *Dict.* 8 b/1 A shelpe, *tenia.* **1570** LEVINS *Manip.* 58/34 A shelp, fish, *tenia.*

**s'help:** = so help (cf. S'ELP).

**1904** H. HAWKINS *Remin.* II. xlviii. 76 'S'help me!' said the man..'I'd sooner see the devil.' **1904** E. ROBINS *Magnetic North* vii. 120 A vow that, s'help him, Heaven! it should never happen again.

**shelpit**, variant of SHILPIT *a. Sc.*

**shelt** (ʃɛlt). *Sc.* Also **shalt, shilt, sholt.** [Abbrev. of SHELTIE.] A Shetland pony.

**1774** *Aberdeen Jrnl.* 27 June 4/2 (Advt.), There are Three Shalts, and several Year-olds of very fine Kinds. **1777** J. DUFF *Let.* 1 May in A. & H. Tayler *Lord Fife & his Factor* (1925) iv. 103, I would wish my Horses, My black Shelt, the roan Poney and Smith..to be at Mar Lodge. **1817** J. CHRISTIE *Instructions* 29 We on with our sholts, a jogging and budging. **1880** J. WATT *Poet. Sk.* 59 To wirk some orra beast, or drive a milk shilt. **1920** *Glasgow Herald* 21 Oct. 8 It was the custom of the priest to go about his pastoral duties on a favourite pony..; indeed, he and the 'shelt' were inseparable. **1951** *Scots Mag.* July 278 They have their work cut out for them, those sturdy shelts. **1980** D. K. CAMERON *Willie Gavin* xx. 199 Mettlesome black *shelts* they had been, high-stepping, jingling their bright harness.

**shelta** ('ʃɛltə). Also **shelter.** [Of obscure origin: for the forms of the name that are used in the 'language' itself, see quot. 1891.

Prof. Kuno Meyer conjectured (*Jrnl. Gypsy Lore Soc.* II. 259) that the form *sheldrū* represents the Old Irish *bélre* (mod. *béarla*) language, with arbitrary substitution of initial *sh* for *b.*]

A cryptic jargon used by tinkers, composed partly of Irish or Gaelic words, mostly disguised by inversion or by arbitrary alteration of initial consonants.

**1876** in Leland *Gypsies* (1882) 355 Now Romanes is genteel... But as for this other jib, its wery hard to talk. It is most all Old Irish, and they calls it Shelter. **1882** LELAND *Ibid.* 354 Shelta, the tinkers' talk. *Ibid.* 360 Our informant could give only a single specimen of the Shelta literature. **1891** SAMPSON in *Jrnl. Gypsy Lore Soc.* II. 206 Like all true citizens of the road, the tinkers protect themselves by the use of a secret language, variously known as Shelta, Sheldrū, Shīldru, Shelter, and Shelterox, 'Bog Latin', 'Tinkers' Cant', or 'the Ould Thing'.

†'**sheltbeam.** *Obs.* In 4 scheltbeme. [Partial transl. of MHG. *schaltbaum* (or MLG. *schaldbôm*) pole used as an oar and a rudder, f. *schalten* (MLG. *schalden*) to push, shove + *baum* (see BEAM *sb.*). Cf. SHALTREE.] A pole or beam. Also *attrib.* as ***sheltbeam nail.***

**1336** in Nicolas *Hist. Navy* (1847) II. 470 Timber called scheltbemes. *Ibid.*, Scheltbemnayles. **1366** *Acc. Exch. K.R.* 19/31 m. 1 (P.R.O.), Item in iij lignis vocatis Scheltbemes emptis in grosso de eodem Humfrido viij. s.

**shelter** ('ʃɛltə(r)), *sb.* Also 6 shealter, 7 shelture. [Of obscure origin; possibly f. *sheld* SHIELD *v.* + -TURE in imitation of words like *jointure.*

The common view that the word is an altered form of SHELTRON seems untenable. *Sheltron* became obsolete in the 15th c., and *shelter* has not been found earlier than 1585. Cf., however, the line, addressed to the Virgin Mary, 'Heyle scheltrun schouris to shelde' (SHELTRON 1 *fig.*), which appears to allude to the roof of locked shields implied in the original sense of *sheltron.*]

**1. a.** A structure affording protection from rain, wind, or sun; in wider sense, anything serving as a screen or a place of refuge from the weather.

Now often applied to a small slight building (commonly of wood or iron) erected in a park or other public place to serve as a refuge from the weather.

**1585** HIGINS *Junius' Nomencl.* 181 *Artegiæ* [sic].., thatcht sheds or shelters. **1590** GREENE *Never too late* Wks. (Grosart) VIII. 14 A hat of straw like a swaine, Shealter for the sonne and raine. **1610** SHAKS. *Temp.* II. ii. 40 Alas, the storme is come againe: my best way is to creepe vnder his Gaberdine: there is no other shelter hereabout. **1611** COTGR., *Abri*, a couert, shrowd, shelter, or shadie place. *Ibid.*, *Begude*, a Cote, Cottage, thatched shed, or shelter. **1725** DE FOE *Voy. round World* (1840) 333 Their tent was a sufficient shelter from the rain. **1775** JOHNSON *West Isl.* 162 (Ulinish), They were probably the shelters of the keepers. **1825** SCOTT *Talism.* xxviii, A tent, which..differed little from that of the ordinary shelter of the common Curdman or Arab. **1865** Rock-shelter: see ROCK *sb.*[1] 6. **1877** GEIKIE *Christ* xxix. (1879) 341 The people of Tiberias are glad to sleep in shelters of straw or leaves on their roofs, during the hot months. **1881** *Macm. Mag.* XLIII. 388/2 Copies may be seen occasionally in cabmen's shelters. **1894** *Daily News* 25 July 7/5 The erection of band stands, cricket shelters, refreshment houses, park lodges, and seated shelters.

**b.** Something which affords a refuge from danger, attack, pursuit, or observation; a place of safety; *Mil.* a wall or bank behind which persons can obtain safety from gunshot; an enclosed shelter from air-raids, nuclear fall-out, etc., usu. underground. Cf. ANDERSON, MORRISON.

**1605** SHAKS. *Lear* I. i. 185 The Gods to their deere shelter take thee Maid. **1606** —— *Ant. & Cl.* III. i. 8 Spurre through Media, Mesapotamia, and the shelters, whether The routed flie. **1667** MILTON *P.L.* VI. 843 [They] wish'd the Mountains now might be again Thrown on them as a shelter from his ire. **1724** DE FOE *Mem. Cavalier* (1840) 23 As for the wood, it was a good shelter to save one's life. **1837** CARLYLE *Fr. Rev.* II. II. vi, The Bouillé vanguard..sweeps Mutiny..into shelters and cellars. **1871** FREEMAN *Norm. Conq.* (1876) IV. xviii. 159 She made her way to the old shelter in Flanders, and found a home at Saint Omer. **1906** *Times Hist. War S. Africa* IV. 581 The Colonel had some difficulty in persuading the garrison and townspeople to use the shelters against gun-fire. **1918** *Ann Reg. 1917* I. 175 Much greater public attention was paid to the question of air-raids... Arrangements were made to provide shelters throughout London. **1938** *Times* (Weekly ed.) 29 Dec. 3/1 Sir John Anderson outlined his plans for the provision of shelters against high explosive bombs. **1943** G. GREENE *Ministry of Fear* I. i. 17 The sirens began their nightly wail. .. She was making for her favourite shelter down the street. **1961** E. S. TURNER *Phoney War* v. 50 The authorities had no intention of allowing the Underground to be used as a shelter.., but when the bombing began the people simply bought tickets and took possession of it. **1961** [see FALL-OUT *sb.*]. **1978** L. DEIGHTON *SS-GB* ii. 18 She was killed.. during the air attacks... He was in the shelter that day.

**c.** *transf.* and *fig.*

**1588** SHAKS. *Tit. A.* IV. iv. 22 His fained extasies Shall be no shelter to these outrages. **1597** —— *2 Hen. IV*, IV. iv. 42 And thou shalt proue a shelter to thy friends. **1611** BIBLE *Ps.* lxi. 3 For thou hast bene a shelter for me, and a strong tower from the enemy. **1618** *Owles Almanacke* 42 He that roofes not his wife vnder one of your [haberdasher's] shelters on his marriage day, shall be trust vp. *a* **1650** CALDERWOOD *Hist. Ch. Scot.* (1678) 811 The Government of Prelats is a shelter for damnable Sects. **1855** T. T. LYNCH *Lett. to the Scattered* vi. (1872) 84 The storms of the law may drive men to the shelter of the gospel.

**d.** Protection from the weather; trees, walls, or the like, which afford such protection.

**1613** MARKHAM *Eng. Husbandm.* I. Former Pt. ii. A 4, [Choose a situation] inuironed..with rowes of greater timber,..the shelter will be most excellent to keepe off the bleaknesse of the..tempests in winter. **1664** EVELYN *Kal. Hort.* 59 Covering them [seeds] with sheets and shelter. **1707** MORTIMER *Husb.* (1721) 292, I shall advise the planting of shelter on the West and South West. **1842** LOUDON *Suburban Hort.* 418 The trees..when they grow large.. produce an injurious degree of shelter and shade. **1888** *Law Times* LXXXV. 132/2 If the timber adds beauty or shelter to the mansion-house, the tenant for life must leave it intact.

**e.** A covering to protect an object from injury, 'spec. a box, cage or hut used for the proper exposure of meteorological instruments' (*Funk's Stand. Dict.* 1895).

*a* **1700** EVELYN *Diary* 4 Nov. 1644, A temporary shelter of boards over the most stupendous..Torso of Amphion and Dirces. **1817** J. MAYER *Sportsman's Direct.* (ed. 2) 175 Cover it [*sc.* a trap] with a thin board that the fowls may not spring it in going to roost, then take the board or shelter away. **1827** FARADAY *Chem. Manip.* xiii. (1842) 299 The pressure of the fuel upon the crucible..may be prevented by hanging a shelter over it.

**f.** A place of temporary lodging for the homeless poor.

**1890** W. BOOTH *In Darkest Eng.* II. ii. 97 You come along to one of our Shelters. On entering you pay four-pence, and are free of the establishment for the night. **1895** *Brit. Med. Jrnl.* 22 June 1399/2 Philanthropic Shelters. The establishment of shelters for the class of poor wanderers in the metropolis is in itself praiseworthy. *Ibid.*, A Salvation Army shelter. **1934** *Changing Men* 25 There has been no homelier, happier place than the Woman's Shelter in High Street. **1976** *New Society* 17 June 633/2 All lodging houses, hostels and night shelters in Glasgow were visited on two nights last winter.

**g.** A (temporary) home for animals. *U.S.*

**1971** *New Yorker* 30 Oct. 41/1 The Bide-A-Wee animal shelter in Westhampton. **1979** *Arizona Daily Star* 22 July J 4/4 Lillian Schaaf willed her $1 million estate for a new animal shelter to be built on land she owned outside Worthington, Ohio.

**2. a.** The state of being sheltered; the state of being protected from the elements; security from attack. Chiefly in ***to seek, find, take,*** etc. ***shelter. in, under, shelter. under the shelter of*** = protected by.

**1593** SHAKS. *Rich. II*, II. i. 264 We..seeke no shelter to auoid the storme. **1593** —— *3 Hen. VI*, v. ii. 12 The Cedar ..Whose Armes gaue shelter to the Princely Eagle. **1597** BP. HALL *Sat.* II. vii. D 3, Some breer-bush shewing shelter from the showre, Vnto the hopefull sheepe... The ruthlesse breere..Layes hold vpon the fleece..of the carelesse pray, That thought she in securer shelter lay. **1609** HOLLAND *Amm. Marcell.* XXIV. i. 241 A..tempestuous wind ..had..made such confusion among their places of harbour and shelture. **1653** H. COGAN tr. *Pinto's Trav.* x. 33 Under the shelter of certain packs of Cotton..they one morning assaulted the principal Fortress. **1726** SHELVOCKE *Voy. round World* 68 Where, perhaps, a ship might find good shelter. **1845** DISRAELI *Sybil* IV. vi, Had I needed shelter there was another roof which has long awaited me. **1871** FREEMAN *Norm. Conq.* (1876) IV. xviii. 225 The sons of Harold had..found shelter with the same prince who had once sheltered their father. **1893** STEVENSON *Catriona* I. i, We took shelter under a pend at the head of a close or alley. **1900** DOYLE *Gt. Boer War* xi. 192 Once more it was shown how weak an arm is artillery against an enemy who lies in shelter.

**b.** *fig.*

**1630** CAPT. SMITH *True Trav.* Ded., The shadow of your most noble vertues..under which I hope to have shelter, against all stormes that dare threaten. **1639** S. DU VERGER tr. *Camus' Admir. Events* 46 The way..to set my conscience at rest, and my honour at shelter. **1693** LOCKE *Educ.* §200. 257 Thus under the Shelter and Pretence of a Governour, thinking themselves excused from standing upon their own Legs. **1822** LAMB *Elia* Ser. I. *Modern Gallantry* He [Joseph Paice] took me under his shelter at an early age, and bestowed some pains upon me. **1835** MACAULAY *Ess.*, *Mackintosh* (1854) I. 342/2 The tribunals ought to be sacred places of refuge, where..the innocent of all parties may find shelter. **1866** J. MARTINEAU *Ess.* I. 345 Scientific theology lost the shelter of the mitre.

**3.** *attrib.* and *Comb.*, as ***shelter barrack, belt*** (of trees), ***-camp, -house, -shed;*** (sense 1 b) ***shelter-life, marshal, warden;*** designating conditions and ailments attributed to time spent in air-raid shelters, as ***shelter cough, paralysis, rash, throat*** (all *temporary*); objective, as ***shelter-seeker, -seeking*** (adj.); **shelter-deck**, in a passenger vessel, a light deck more or less closed at the sides but open at the ends; also *attrib.*, as ***shelter-deck vessel;*** **shelter foot**, a painful, swollen foot or leg after a person has slept in a sitting position (*temporary*); **shelter half**, one half of a shelter tent; **shelter leg** = *shelter foot;* **shelterman**, an attendant at a (cab) shelter; **shelter-pit** *Mil.* (see quot.); **shelter tent**, a small ridged tent; a dog-tent; **shelter tree**, *Mil.* (see quot. 1884); also, any tree grown to provide shelter; **shelter-trench** *Mil.* (see quot.); **shelter wood**, trees left standing to provide shelter in which saplings can grow; freq. *attrib.*

**1906** DK. ARGYLL *Autobiog.* I. vi. 144 A *shelter barrack [for the workmen on Skerryvore Lighthouse] was an absolute necessity. **1868** *Rep. U.S. Commissioner Agric.* (1869) 197 For a *shelter belt..this [*sc.* maple] will be found suitable. **1910** MRS. H. WARD *Canadian Born* 335 Epil., The thin background of a few taller trees,—the 'shelter-belt' of the farm. **1940** *New Statesman* 19 Oct. 372/1 In every shelter I have been in during the past six weeks I have heard that hacking '*shelter cough' and the wheezy sleep of the bronchial cases. **1911** *Encycl. Brit.* XXIV. 880/1 The ship is called an awning decked, spar decked, *shelter decked or three decked vessel—according to the details of her construction. **1941** *Lancet* 6 Dec. 690/1 In *shelter-foot the most potent causative factors are venous stagnation and increased capillary permeability. **1942** *Sun* (Baltimore) 23 Apr. 22/2 When the Doaks family goes into a bomb shelter .., Mr. Doaks is likely to say, '..I'll just doze off here in this deck chair'. Next morning Mr. Doaks has a pair of painfully swollen legs and feet—shelter foot. **1911** F. FUNSTON *Mem. Two Wars* 354 Not even *shelter-halves, popularly known as 'dog tents', were carried, and many..a night we stretched out in the rain. **1966** *Sunday Times* (Colour Suppl.) 4 Dec. 73/3 *Shelter half*, half a pup tent, and carried by every GI. **1892** *Daily News* 28 July 6/1 Seated in a small *shelter-house protecting us against the glacier winds. **1899** *Westm. Gaz.* 31 July 2/3 To accommodate these families vestries have established shelter houses. **1940** *Lancet* 7 Dec. 722/1 (*heading*) *Shelter legs. *Ibid.* 722/2 The elderly and obese are loth to make use of bunks in the shelters..and since they are apt to sit about all day as well as all night they readily acquire shelter leg. **1944** *Newsweek* 20 Mar. 97/1 Renewed Nazi raids brought an old ailment back to London—'shelter legs'. **1943** WYNDHAM LEWIS *Let.* 26 Jan. (1963) 342 A sculptor of course cannot exactly be commissioned to do marbles of *shelter-life. **1974** *Times* 21 Jan. 4/3 The Medical Officer of Health reported in 1940 that the increase in deaths from respiratory diseases was at least partially due to shelter life. **1940** *New Statesman* 19 Oct. 372/2 Lord Horder's Committee attaches much importance to the *shelter marshals, who should be paid, whole-time officials, chosen from the wardens' service for their proper human understanding and given a status which would entitle them to the help of the police and authority over the shelterers. **1906** *Daily Chron.* 30 Jan. 3/5 Cab pensioners and *sheltermen. **1942** *Sun* (Baltimore) 23 Apr. 22/2 A similar ailment is called '*shelter paralysis'. **1870** *Instr. Milit. Engin.* §513 It may be necessary [for men skirmishing] to dig small pits, which may be called *shelter pits in contradistinction to the larger pits..called rifle pits. Each shelter pit should be for one man only. **1943** *Our Towns* (Women's Group on Public Welfare) iii. 78 *Scabies* or 'the Itch' has now almost achieved respectability under the name of '*Shelter Rash'. **1864** ATKINSON *Stanton Grange* xxiii, A most complete..drenching to both the *shelter-seekers. **1765** GOLDSM. *Trav.* 162 There..The *shelter-seeking peasant builds his shed. **1861** STEPHENS & BURN *Farm-Buildings* §1376 We give the plan of a *shelter-shed to be placed at the corner of four fields. **1862** O. W. NORTON *Let.* 16 June in *Army Lett.* (1903) 88 Anyone who has lived in these *shelter tents any length of time can appreciate the difficulties of writing in a heavy shower. **1875** KNIGHT *Dict. Mech.* 2534/1 Shelter-tent. **1888** *Encycl. Brit.* XXIII. 183/1 But the humblest tent made—the *tente d'abri* or shelter tent of the French army—is also ridged in form. **1940** *New Statesman* 19 Oct. 372/1 Equally common are the complaints of '*shelter throats', which may mean anything from tonsilitis to diphtheria. **1884** W. MILLER *Plant-n.* 124/2 *Adenostephanus organensis.* Organ Mountain *Shelter-tree. **1891** W. SCHLICH *Man. Forestry* II. ii. 133 They in their turn become mother and shelter trees. **1980** *Garden* CV. 106/1 The Corot-like view of immense weeping willows forming the lake's head must surely have gained by the recent deaths of elms and other shelter trees, though the garden is now more exposed to north-east winds. **1870** *Instr. Milit. Engin.* §512 Artificial cover..can be best obtained by means of small trenches called *shelter trenches. **1974** C. FREMLIN *By Horror Haunted* 12 The kids larking about.. the *Shelter Wardens shouting at them. **1889** W. SCHLICH *Man. Forestry* I. ii. 208 The wood is created, or regenerated, under the shelter of the whole or part of the old crop, which forms the *shelter-wood. **1928** R. S. TROUP *Silvicultural Systems* vii. 82 The original idea underlying the adoption of the shelter-wood strip system was the necessity for working against the prevailing westerly wind, so that the newly exposed edges of mature woods should always be protected from it. **1979** *Sci. Amer.* Feb. 71/3 The final system is called shelterwood cutting, because the mature stand is removed in two or more partial cuts so that the new stand can become established under the shelter of a partial canopy of remaining trees.

**shelter** (ˈʃɛltə(r)), *v.* [f. prec. sb.]

**1.** *trans.* To be or provide a shelter for.

**a.** To screen or protect from rain, wind, cold, the sun, etc. Chiefly of a thing; *rarely* of a personal agent.

**1590** SPENSER *F.Q.* II. xii. 30 A still And calmy bay, on th' one side sheltered With the brode shadow of an hoarie hill. **1593** SHAKS. *Rich. II*, III. iv. 50 The Weeds that his broad-spreading Leaues did shelter..Are pull'd vp. **1671** MILTON *P.R.* II. 73 Scarce a Shed Could be obtain'd to shelter him or me From the bleak air. **1707** MORTIMER *Husb.* xvi. 367, I should advise the planting of other Trees round them to shelter them. **1797** HT. LEE *Canterb. T.*, *Frenchm. T.* (1799) I. 244 Sheltering the light with her hand, she descended the ..stairs. **1860** TYNDALL *Glac.* I. xvi. 111 A wall of rock.. sheltered us from the north wind.

**b.** To screen from pursuit, attack, blows, etc.

**1667** MILTON *P.L.* II. 167 We fled amain, pursu'd..With Heav'ns afflicting Thunder, and besought The Deep to shelter us. *Ibid.* XI. 820 Hee with them of Man and Beast Select for life shall in the Ark be lodg'd, And shelterd round. **1783** WATSON *Philip III*, I. (1839) 51 They were sheltered from the fire of the besiegers, by a dyke. **1862** LD. BROUGHAM *Brit. Const.* xx. 396 Harbours and ports, which may shelter the navy in the operations of war.

**c.** *fig.* To screen from punishment, censure, etc.

**1594** [see SHELTERED *ppl. a.*]. **1648** J. BEAUMONT *Psyche* II. cxlii, Why was not I deform'd, that shelter'd in Sure neglect, I might have scap'd this sin! **1711** PRIOR *Celia to Damon* 10 In vain I strove to..shelter Passion under Friendship's Name. **1818** CRUISE *Digest* (ed. 2) IV. 51 The vendor, who had made use of the act for sheltering fraud. **1818** SHELLEY *Rosalind* 505 Friend, he was sheltered by the grave, And therefore dared to be a liar! **1884** BOSANQUET tr. *Lotze's Metaph.* 444 Many..will make use of his expressions in order to shelter under a great name their favourite doctrine.

**d.** 'To succour with refuge, to harbour' (J.); to take under one's protection. Of a place: To be a secure home or refuge for.

**1663** DRYDEN *Ep. Charleton* 53 These Ruines [Stonehenge] sheltered once His Sacred Head, Then when from Wor'ster's fatal Field He fled. **1814** SCOTT *Wav.* xviii, And do others beside your master shelter him? **1819** SHELLEY *Cenci* I. iii. 105 His children and his wife, whom he is bound To love and shelter. **1825** SCOTT *Betrothed* xxi, Amid the same scenes which had sheltered her infancy and childhood. **1850** TENNYSON *In Mem.* cii. 4 The roofs, that heard our earliest cry, Will shelter one of stranger race. **1868** FREEMAN *Norm. Conq.* (1876) II. vii. 143 The King, instead of bringing them to justice, was sheltering them. **1908** *Blackw. Mag.* July 147/1 When he [Champlain] died in the city which had sheltered him for many years.

**e.** To protect (invested income) from taxation; to invest with this purpose.

**1963** *Vital Speeches* XXIX. 357/2 A tightening of the personal holding company rules, to end the escapes from individual taxation now available through the use of these devices to shelter investment income. **1972** P. C. REID *Corporate & Executive Tax, Sheltered Investments* ix. 125 The prospective investor should always keep in mind that the major objective is to shelter his income. **1973** *Times* 10 Dec. 7/5 False rumours..that I sheltered the income on which my daughter, Tricia, should have paid taxes. **1975** *Tax Shelter Investments* (U.S. Congress Jt. Comm. on Internal Revenue Taxation) III. 22 He sheltered $13,000 with a cattle feeding operation.

†**2.** To ward off. *Obs. rare.*

**1621** LADY M. WROTH *Urania* 337 A place, Rockey, and hilley, nothing but Heath, and some small shrubs to shelter rayne, Sunne, or any thing from one.

**3.** *refl.* **a.** To take shelter; to take refuge from pursuit or attack.

**1611** COTGR., *se Taudir*, to couer, shrowd, shelter, hide himselfe. **1663** *Act 15 Chas. II*, c. 2 Preamb., Great Townes where..such idle and lewd persons doe shelter themselves. *a* **1701** MAUNDRELL *Journ. Jerus.* Ded., To Sir C. Hedges, The only Defence I have, is by shelt'ring my self in the Crowd.

**b.** *fig.* Chiefly, to protect oneself from punishment or censure. ***to shelter oneself under, behind*** — = to use the protection afforded by (what is specified).

**1598** SHAKS. *Merry W.* v. v. 24 Let there come a tempest of prouocation, I will shelter mee heere. **1675** *Essex Papers* (1890) I. 295 My L[d] Newport shelters himselfe under D.M. interest. **1769** *Junius Lett.* xxxv. (1820) 165 You may shelter yourself under the forms of a parliament. **1825** SCOTT *Betrothed* xix, If it is meant..that I have any purpose of sheltering myself behind the Prelate's authority. **1837** THIRLWALL *Greece* xxxii. IV. 225 They..thought it better to purchase the silence of the informer—unless they could shelter themselves by such an expedient.

**4.** *intr.* for *refl.* To take shelter; to find a refuge. *lit.* and *fig.*

**1602** MARSTON *Antonio's Rev.* II. iii, Pigmie cares Can shelter vnder patience shield. **1667** MILTON *P.L.* XI. 223 Hee alone, To finde where Adam shelterd, took his way. **1680** HICKERINGILL *Meroz* Wks. 1716 I. 244 This objection, under which all..opposition of Authority does lurk and shelter to this day. **1727** [E. DORRINGTON] *Philip Quarll* (1816) 14 A company of buccaniers..shelter here. *a* **1774** GOLDSM. tr. *Scarron's Com. Romance* (1775) II. 124 The humane gentry about the country, who permitted their little troops [*sc.* gypsies] to shelter in the villages. **1855** THACKERAY *Newcomes* II. xix. 192 She fled from him and sheltered with the old woman who's dead. **1882** GEIKIE *Geol. Sk.* 110 We sheltered for a little under the lower basalt. **1899** F. T. BULLEN *Way Navy* 79 She also reported our second-class cruiser..out of action and sheltering—I believe in Killery Bay.

**shelterage** (ˈʃɛltərɪdʒ). Also 7 **sheltridge.** [f. SHELTER *sb.* + -AGE.]

†**1.** Sheltering. *Obs. rare*[−1].

**1650** T. BAYLY *Herba Parietis* i. 3 Neither was the Contrivement lesse beneficiall, respecting the three walls sheltridge from the foure winds.

**2.** A place of shelter.

**1632** LITHGOW *Trav.* VI. 273 The remanents of that house ..is turned ouer for a shelterage for sheepe. **1836** *Tait's Mag.* III. 447 His household goods were now removed to more auspicious shelterage.

**sheltered** (ˈʃɛltəd), *ppl. a.* [f. SHELTER *v.* + -ED[1].]

**a.** In the senses of the verb.

**1594** SHAKS. *Rich. III*, III. v. 33 Well, well, he was the couertst sheltred Traytor That euer liu'd. **1671** MILTON *P.L.* IV. 406 Whose branching arms..might shield From dews and damps of night his shelter'd head. **1730–46** THOMSON *Autumn* 1049 There let me sit beneath the sheltered slopes. **1851** HELPS *Comp. Solit.* vi. 85 A garden seat in a sheltered nook. **1912** *Chamb. Jrnl.* Oct. 742/1 The contrast between the sheltered and the shelterless.

**b.** ***sheltered life***, a life protected from the ordinary hazards and hardships of living. Also ***sheltered existence.***

**1888** KIPLING *Plain Tales* 14 There was a Boy once who had been brought up under the 'sheltered life' theory; and the theory killed him dead. **1920** *Ladies' Home Jrnl.* Feb. 185/1 Three thousand dollars and no business experience, thirty-three years of sheltered life, and two children under ten years of age—this was my problem when I was left a widow. **1937** WODEHOUSE *Summer Moonshine* (1938) xix. 221 Hers had been a sheltered life... She had never been brought face to face with tragedy. **1959** J. KIRKUP tr. *S. de Beauvoir's Mem. Dutiful Daughter* II. 117 She led a very sheltered existence in the Basque country, where there were not many eligible young men. **1977** W. H. SAUMAREZ SMITH *Young Man's Country* ii. 35, I had lived a fairly sheltered life in England... Now for the first time in a position of responsibility and power, I was learning how people behave.

**c.** *Econ.* Designating trades, industries, etc., which are not exposed to competition, and the commodities in which they deal.

**1924** *Westm. Gaz.* 18 Aug. 4/5 In the so-called sheltered trades real weekly wages have generally been maintained at at least their pre-war level. **1930** *Economist* 4 Jan. 24/1 The higher Japanese price-level is accounted for largely by such 'sheltered' goods as red beans, miso. **1972** *Wall Street Jrnl.* 9 Aug. 1/5 A number of tax shelter plans are designed to allow investments in sheltered industries like oil.

**d.** Affording relief or exemption from tax; untaxed. *U.S.*

**1955** W. J. CASEY *Tax Sheltered Investments* (ed. 2) xix. 205 Partnership operation allows you a write off of losses, a sheltered return on a quick success by sale of your partnership interest. **1970** *Tax Sheltered Investments* (A. Anderson & Co.) i. 1 All sheltered investments generate one or more of these advantages. **1974** *Los Angeles Times* 13 Oct. III. 9/2 The second $50,000, which was to be 'sheltered income', was to be sent..directly to an insurance company as a payment for an annuity purchased by Hunter.

**e.** Designating places for living or working (or suitable work) provided for the mentally or physically infirm, where special assistance and facilities are available.

**1961** *Oxford Mail* 16 Mar. 4/6 The three-storey house [for patients of a mental hospital in the final stages of readjustment to community life]..was opened last month and is known officially as a 'sheltered hostel'. **1971** *Rand Daily Mail* 3 Apr. 11/4 One of these tenants is a humble man who earns R14 a week in a sheltered employment factory. **1973** *Howard Jrnl.* XIII. 276 Sheltered workshop facilities, industrial training or punitive labour. **1976** *Ilkeston Advertiser* 10 Dec. 16/2 The county council had already decided to stop the grants—towards general improvement areas,..council house adaptation for the handicapped and sheltered housing. **1977** *New Society* 3 Mar. 441/2 Patients leaving Herrison [Mental Hospital] have been 'graded' according to the kind of home they can cope with outside. Those least able to run their own lives are in sheltered accommodation. **1980** *Times* 23 July 12/2 If you are still undecided about sheltered housing or a home, you might investigate the various facilities.

**shelterer** (ˈʃɛltərə(r)). [f. SHELTER *v.* + -ER[1].]

**1. a.** One who takes shelter.

**1725** *Lond. Gaz.* No. 6346/4 For Relief of distressed Shelterers in the Mint. **1856** MISS MULOCK *John Halifax* i, Shivering shelterers from the rain.

**b.** *spec.* One who takes shelter from an air-raid.

**1940** R. MACAULAY *Lett. to Sister* (1964) 116 The Central London tube was so crammed with thousands of shelterers that I couldn't get near the platform. **1944** *Ourselves in Wartime* v. 71 Tiers of bunks, canteens, adequate sanitation and first-aid posts were provided. These amenities helped the shelterers to make the best of a bad job. **1957** R. W. ZANDVOORT in *Wiener Beiträge zur englischen Philologie* LXV. 270 Air raid shelters were a necessary refuge... Books ..were the best means to divert the attention of *shelterers* (as they were called) and others from the pressures and anxieties of life in wartime. **1980** P. FITZGERALD *Human Voices* xi. 163 The LPTB's bunks occupied the walls... Other shelterers had arrived.

**2.** One who shelters another.

**1822** BYRON *Werner* III. iv. 79 In leaving thus His shelterer's asylum to the risk Of a discovery. **1865** KINGSLEY *Herew.* xxxii, She..was liable to punishment herself, and they to punishment also, as her shelterers and accomplices.

**sheltering** (ˈʃɛltərɪŋ), *vbl. sb.* [f. SHELTER *v.* + -ING[1].] The action of the verb. Also *concr.*, a place of shelter (*rare*).

**1674** (*title*) Learn to lye Warm, or, An apology for that Proverb. Tis good sheltring under an old Hedge. **1707** MORTIMER *Husb.* xvi. 367 The sheltring of them with some Litter may do well. **1818** SCOTT *Hrt. Midl.* xlvi, It's better sheltering under an auld hedge than under a new-planted wood. **1901** MEREDITH *Reading of Life* 115 So those numerous tribes from their ships and their shelterings poured forth On that plain of Scamander.

**sheltering** (ˈʃɛltərɪŋ), *ppl. a.* [f. SHELTER *v.* + -ING[2].] That shelters, in the senses of the verb.

**1616** T. SCOT *Philomythie* I. (ed. 2) F6, A ridiculous Mouse For feare of Cats leauing her sheltring house. **1773** [T. DAY] *Dying Negro* 18 And death extends his shelt'ring arms in vain. **1817** SHELLEY *To W. Shelley* 41 Less cruel than the savage slaves Who hunt us o'er these sheltering waves. **1837** CARLYLE *Fr. Rev.* II. IV. ix, They can..stick their head ostrich-like into what sheltering Fallacy is nearest. **1890** R. BRIDGES *Shorter Poems* I. 14 'Twas at this sheltering hour he nightly came.

**shelteringly** (ˈʃɛltərɪŋlɪ), *adv.* [-LY[2].] In a sheltering position or manner; so as to shelter.

**1848** *Fraser's Mag.* XXXVIII. 311/2 The glen lies before you, with its bosky braes and grassy leas shelteringly. **1886** R. A. KING *Shadowed Life* II. i. 8 With one child in her lap, and her arm shelteringly round another.

**shelterless** (ˈʃɛltəlɪs), *a.* [f. SHELTER *sb.* + -LESS.]

**1.** Without a shelter or covering; unprotected from the elements.

**1714** ROWE *Jane Shore* v. i, Now sad and shelterless, perhaps, she lyes, Where piercing Winds blow sharp. **1820** SHELLEY *Prometh. Unb.* II. iv. 54 The unseasonable seasons drove..Their shelterless, pale tribes to mountain caves. **1885–94** R. BRIDGES *Eros & Psyche* Aug. iv, Fainting and shelterless Upon the mountain it were death to bide.

**2.** That affords no shelter; not furnished with a sheltering structure.

**1760–72** H. BROOKE *Fool of Qual.* (1809) III. 113 We were compelled to take up with this shelterless hovel. **1814** [see SHADELESS *a.* 1]. **1839** *Penny Cycl.* XIV. 347/2 At the time of the cession..Malta was almost a shelterless rock. **1881** MISS BRADDON *Asphodel* iii, Even Daphne..blinked a little as she crossed the shelterless promenade.

Hence **ˈshelterlessness.**

*c* **1878–9** in W. J. Fitz-Patrick *Life T. N. Burke* (1885) II. 298 The houselessness and shelterlessness of our Saviour.

**sheltery** (ˈʃɛltərɪ), *a.* Also 8 **sheltry.** [f. SHELTER *sb.* + -Y.] Affording shelter.

**1729** SAVAGE *Wanderer* v. 155 No sheltry Trees invite the Wand'rer's Eye. **1770** G. WHITE *Selborne, To Pennant* 29 Oct., They spend their winters under the warm and sheltery shores of Gibraltar and Barbary. **1826** *Blackw. Mag.* XX. 3 Sheltery groves.

**Sheltie, Shelty** (ˈʃɛltɪ). *Sc.* Also 7 *pl.* **shalties,** 8 *pl.* **schelties, sheltys,** 9 *Sc. dial.* **shaltie, -y, shawltie.** [Prob. repr. the Orkney or Caithness pronunciation of ON. *Hjalti* Shetlander.]

**1.** A Shetland pony; now, any small pony. (In early quots. more fully †***Shelty horse.***)

**1650** in J. C. Lees *Hist. Inverness* vi. (1897) 73 Montrose sat upon a little shelty horse without a saddle. **1654** BLAEU *Atlas* v. (*Scotia*) 144/1 Sunt & eis Equulei (*Shalties* vulgo vocant) specie quidem contemptibiles, sed ad omnes usus, supra quam credi potest, strenui. *a* **1688** J. WALLACE *Descr. Orkney* (1693) 13 Their Horses are but little, Yet strong.., most of which they get from Zetland, and are called Shelties. *c* **1730** BURT *Lett. N. Scot.* (1754) II. xvii. 52 Those Sheltys, being never shod. **1742** *De Foe's Tour Gt. Brit.* (ed. 3) IV. 294 [In Shetland] They have Plenty of little Horses, which they call Schelties. **1793** SYME in *Burns' Wks.* (1800) I. 206, I got Burns a grey Highland shelty to ride on. **1828** SCOTT in *Lockhart* (1839) IX. 273 My smart hack has dwindled into a Zetland shelty. **1895** CROCKETT *Men of Moss Hags* xxvi, My Galloway sheltie..took me bravely over the moss-hags.

**2.** A Shetlander. *rare.*

**1888** EDMONDSTON & SAXBY *Home of Naturalist* 180, I make the acquaintance of other Shelties in the same way. **1967** H. W. SUTHERLAND *Magnie* vii. 94 They were queer, the Shelties, came from nothing... England was heaven to them.

**3.** = *Shetland sheep-dog* s.v. SHETLAND 1 d. Also *attrib.*

**1911** *Our Dogs* 27 Oct. 984/3 (Advt.), Two promising Sheltie pups for sale. **1916** B. THYNNE *Shetl. Sheep-Dog* 5 The origin of the Sheltie is 'wrapt in mystery'. **1950** A. C. SMITH *Dogs since 1900* xii. 248 After the interruption caused by the first war, the Shelties began to assert their charms. **1972** *Times* 19 Sept. 24/6 (Advt.), King Charles and Sheltie Collie, both 2 years old.. free to loving family. **1980** 'T. HINDE' *Daymare* iv. 26 He had been council dust-cart driver till he ran down one Sheltie too many.

**sheltopusik** ('ʃɛltəʊ,puːzɪk). Also sch-. [a. Russ. *zheltopuzik*.] A lizard of the genus *Pseudopus* (*P. pallasii*).

**1841** *Penny Cycl.* XXI. 25/2 Scheltopusik or Sheltopusik, the ordinary name for a genus of *Reptiles*, *Pseudopus* of Merrem. *Ibid.* 72/2 The Scheltopusiks. **1882** GÜNTHER in *Encycl. Brit.* XIV. 735/1 The Glass-Snake (*Pseudopus pallasii*) or *Sheltopusik* (Russ.) is common in Dalmatia, Hungary, southern Russia, and.. Central Asia.

†**'sheltron**[1]. *Obs.* Forms: 1 **scyld-, sciltruma, scyl-, sceltruma,** 3 **sceld-trome, -trume, soltrome, -trume,** 4 **schiltron, -trum, -trun, -t(e)roun, (childrome), scheltroun, (cheltroun), s(c)heltrome, -trun, -trum, scheld(es)trome, (schetrome), sheltrone, shil-, shyltroun, shultrom, scholtrom, -trum,** 4–5 **scheltrom, -tron, sheltron, schiltrom,** 5 **sheltroun, shiltron, shildryme, shyltron, sheldrun,** 5–6 **scheltrone,** (5 **cheltrone,** 6 **seltron),** 6 *Hist.* **schiltron.** [OE. *scieldtruma*, f. *scield* SHIELD *sb.* + *truma* troop.

The original sense is that of a body of men protected by their shields locked so as to form a roof and wall; = TESTUDO 3 b. Cf. the synonymous or nearly synonymous OE. *scieldburg* (= ON. *skjaldborg*), *scieldhrēopa*, *scieldweall*.]

**1.** A close, compact body of troops; troops drawn up in battle array; a phalanx.

The word became obsolete in the 15th c.; all subsequent examples are echoes from early chronicles.

*c* **1000** ÆLFRIC *Gram.* xlvii. (Z.) 274 *Subter densa testudine* under ðiccum scyldtruman oððe randbeaʒe. *c* **1000** in Napier *OE. Glosses* i. 2959 *Testudine*, of scyltruman. *c* **1205** LAY. 16371 He nom his eorles.. & his holdeste men.. & makede his sceld-trume [*c* **1275** one soltrome]. *Ibid.* 27506 Heo comen to þere uerde.. & þene sceld-trume [*c* **1275** sultrome] breken. *c* **1325** *Coer de L.* 5577 They made scheltroun and bataylyde. *Ibid.* 5744 He brak asunder the scheltrome. *c* **1330** R. BRUNNE *Chron. Wace* (Rolls) 3512 þey bere þe launces vp and doun, On þe manere of a scheltroun [*Petyt MS.* cheltroun]. **1375** BARBOUR *Bruce* XII. 429 For all thair battalis sammyn wer In a schiltrum [*Camb. MS.* childrome]. **1382** WYCLIF *Gen.* xiv. 8 And thei dressiden aʒens hem sheltrun in the wodi valey. **1387** TREVISA *Higden* (Rolls) III. 61 þe Romayns wyfes.. wente.. bytwene þe scheltroms, and cryde pees. **1393** LANGL. *P. Pl.* C. XXI. 294 [They] shetep out shot ynowh hus shultrom to blende. **1422** YONGE tr. *Secreta Secret.* xxxi. 174 Haniball.. ordaynyd his shildrymes, steryn battaill he yaue. *c* **1440** *Eng. Conq. Irel.* (Rawl. MS.) 31 Thay brakyn har sheldrun, and wentyn aftyr. *c* **1450** *Merlin* xx. 326 A-gein hem myght endure noon harneys, ne no kynge, ne warde, ne sheltron, were it neuer so clos. *a* **1513** FABYAN *Chron.* VI. ccxvii. (1516) 137/1 (Battle of Hastings.) Than the Seltrons smote togyder with a great noyse and crye, and faught sore. **1530** PALSGR. 266/2 Scheltrone of a batayle. **1577–87** HOLINSHED *Chron.* III. 307/2 The Scots [at Falkirk, 1298] were diuided in foure shiltrons, as they termed them, or as we may saie, round battels.

*fig.* ? **14..** *Salutation Our Lady* 19 in *MS. Cantab. Ff.* 2. 38, fo. 31 b, Heyle, scheltrun schouris to shelde! *c* **1425** *Orolog. Sapient.* ii. in *Anglia* X. 343/39 þe best prevede knihtes sette in þe cheltrone of Criste.

**2.** *transf.* Applied to a compact body of ships.

*c* **1400** *Destr. Troy* 3239 The sheltrun togedur, þat fild were with folke.., Sesit vp þere sailes. *Ibid.* 6033.

¶ The word *jeltron*, *geltron* in the following quot., commonly cited as a form of *sheltron*, is prob. a misprint for **jestron*, *gestron*: see GESTERON.

? **1510** *Hickscorner* (W. de W.) A ij b, No armure so stronge in no dystresse Habergyon helme ne yet no Ieltron [*ed. Waley* (*a.* 1586) geltron].

†**'sheltron**[2]. *Obs.* *rare*[−1]. In 4 **scheltroun, sheltrom, -trun, shyltroun.** [? A corruption of some form of SCANTILLON.

Perh. only a misreading on the part of a scribe; the word *sheltron* in its proper use occurs in the poem.]

A standard, gauge.

**1377** LANGL. *P. Pl.* B. XIV. 81 For-þi mesure we vs wel and make owre faithe owre scheltroun [*v.rr.* as above].

**shelty.** *rare*[−2]. [Prob. some error: cf. *shelter*, *shanty*, *shieling*.] Used for: A hut, shed.

**1834** R. CURZON *Monast. Levant* III. xviii. (1849) 263 We found ourselves at another wretched shelty dignified with the name of khan. **1871** A. R. WALLACE *Nat. Select.* vi. (ed. 2) 212 The Highland stone shelty.

**Shelty:** see SHELTIE.

**shelve** (ʃɛlv), *sb.*[1] [A new sing. evolved from *shelves* pl. of SHELF *sb.*[2]] = SHELF *sb.*[2] Also Comb. † *shelveflat*.

**1582** STANYHURST *Æneis* I. (Arb.) 35 Then sootherne swashruter huffling Flundge vs on high shelueflats, to the rocks vs he buffeted after. **1611** SPEED *Hist. Gt. Brit.* IX. xxiv. §210. 861 Guidelesse she droue with the tyde vpon a shelue in the shoare of Callis. **1662** J. DAVIES tr. *Mandelslo's Trav.* 122 There lies a Shelve a League in length.. at the mouth of the Riuer, which at low water holds not above five or six foot water. **1708** *Brit. Apollo* No. 78. 2/1 The Shelve which stop'd up Sandwich Haven. **1831** SCOTT *Pirate* Introd., The wild cape, or formidable shelve, which requires to be marked by a lighthouse.

*fig.* **1697** C. LESLIE *Snake in Grass* (ed. 2) 120 That desperate Shelve upon which both our Church and State have suffer'd miserable Shipwreck. **1824** SCOTT *St. Ronan's* xx, This plan was wrecked upon the ordinary shelve, to wit, the difficulty of finding performers.

**shelve** (ʃɛlv), *sb.*[2] [f. SHELVE *v.*[1] (sense 1).] A ledge or shelf of rock, or mountain.

*a* **1701** MAUNDRELL *Journ. Jerus.* 28 Mar. (1703) 76 On the left side of it is shewn the Prophet's Bed, being a shelve on the Rock. **1791** NEWTE *Tour Eng. & Scot.* 416 We find the valley or shelve, between the third and the highest mountain,.. covered with a species of oak. **1808** FORSYTH *Beauties Scot.* V. 290 The rapidity and rumbling of the rivers, falling from shelve to shelve. **1814** SCOTT *Ld. of Isles* III. xvi, Precipices.. Yielding no track for goat or deer, Save the black shelves we tread. **1820** KEATS *Hyperion* II. 64 Above her, on a crag's uneasy shelve, Upon his elbow rais'd, all prostrate else, Shadow'd Enceladus.

†**shelve,** *v.*[1] *Obs.*[−1] [perh. an arbitrary alteration of *shelde* SHIELD *v.* for the sake of rhyme. Cf. SHELF *v.*[1]] *trans.* ? To shield, defend.

*c* **1425** *Cast. Persev.* 2576 in *Macro Plays* (1904) 154 Whyl he held hym in þis halle, fro dedly synne we did hym schelue [*rhyme-word* delue].

**shelve** (ʃɛlv), *v.*[2] [f. *shelves* pl. of SHELF *sb.*[1]]

†**1.** *intr.* To project like a shelf, overhang. *Obs.*

**1591** SHAKS. *Two Gent.* III. i. 115 Her chamber is aloft.. And built so sheluing, that one cannot climbe it.

**2.** *trans.* To provide with shelves, esp. to furnish (a library, etc.) with bookshelves.

**1598** in H. Bradshaw *Coll. Papers* 169 Item a studdye desked and shelved rounde. **1727** [E. DORRINGTON] *Philip Quarll* (1816) 52 His barrack.. he shelved round with platted twigs after the manner of his table. **1861** L. L. NOBLE *After Icebergs* 181 You would be delighted, though, with the little vales, notched and shelved with craggy terraces. **1886** *18th Rep. Dep. Kpr. Rec. Irel.* 9 Six bays have been shelved with galvanized iron, instead of.. wooden fittings.

**3.** To place on a shelf or shelves; *esp.* to place or arrange (books) upon shelves.

**1655** FULLER *Cambridge* 79 The.. Libraries.. are bestowed upon Cambridge, and are beautifully shelved. **1801** W. TAYLOR in *Monthly Mag.* XI. 648/1 This.. long expected work, will of course be shelved with eagerness in the libraries of scholars. **1827** SCOTT *Jrnl.* 1 July, I employed myself.. entering all the books.. into a temporary catalogue, so as to have them shelved and marked. **1864** *Reader* 21 May 652/1 To have each book, as it is brought in, registered, shelved, and catalogued.

**b.** *transf.*

**1832** J. H. NEWMAN *Lett.* (1891) I. 288 You knock your head, you bruise your arms, all the while being shelved in a cupboard five feet from the floor. **1847** H. MILLER *First Impress. Eng.* iv. 58 We find it [the bone-bed] shelved high, if I may so speak, in the first storey of the [Upper Silurian] system.

**4.** *fig.* To lay aside as on a shelf, to put away or up as done with. **a.** To remove (a person) from active service. Also *refl.*

**1812** *Sporting Mag.* XL. 131 Defeat, which would tend to annihilate their fame, and what is technically termed shelve them. **1838** LYTTON *Alice* IX. i, [He] being shelved with a plausible excuse of tender compassion for his infirmities. **1850** LD. STANLEY in *Croker Papers* (1884) 18 Aug., Some of the present Government.. will be shelved. **1876** MRS. OLIPHANT *Curate in Charge* viii, To shelve himself in an obscure place like Brentburn. **1885** *Manch. Exam.* 11 June 5/1 To be shelved in a safe place is not what Lord R. Churchill wants.

**b.** To put aside (a question, etc.) from consideration.

**1847** *Illustr. Lond. News* 10 July 27/1 In order that the opera should not be shelved. **1855** DICKENS *Dorrit* I. x, The Circumlocution Office, being reminded that my lords had arrived at no decision, shelved the business. **1877** E. R. CONDER *Bas. Faith* ii. 62 In deliberative assemblies, an expedient is sometimes resorted to for shelving the matter in debate by raising what is termed 'the previous question'. **1890** *Spectator* 29 Mar. 433/2 It was evident.. that the more ambitious part of the original programme would be shelved by common consent.

**shelve** (ʃɛlv), *v.*[3] [Of obscure origin: formation from SHELF *sb.*[1] or *sb.*[2] seems unlikely on account of the sense. Cf. WFris. *skelf* adj., somewhat oblique, not quite straight or level.]

**1.** *intr.* Of a surface: To slope gradually. Also with *away*, *in*, *off*, etc.

**1614** GORGES *Lucan* III. 106 Whose hollow pent-house sheluing steepe Did them from blowes and danger keepe. *Ibid.* VI. 215 That long stretching Malean straine That shelues so farre into the maine. **1657** AUSTEN *Fruit Trees* I. (ed. 2) 129 A loose warme soyle is accompted best if it be shelving upon the sunne. **1726** SHELVOCKE *Voy. round World* 402 The bank shelves away very fast from the Northern shore. **1756** MRS. CALDERWOOD in *Coltness Collect.* (Maitland Club) 122 The first [fish-pond].. was made with no great nicety; it shelved in from all sides. **1823** F. CLISSOLD *Ascent Mt. Blanc* 11 A precipitous declivity, which shelved down, upon our right, in one plane of smooth rock, to the depth of 1000 feet. **1860** tr. *Hartwig's Sea & Wonders* i. 7 The valley of the Atlantic deepens in mid-ocean.., gradually shelving up towards both continents. **1869** TOZER *Highl. Turkey* I. 129 Precipitous banks of wood, which shelved downwards from our feet. **1885–94** R. BRIDGES *Eros & Psyche* May iii, A little hill, whose base Shelved off into the valley all around.

†**2.** To have an inclined position. *Obs.*

**1644** DIGBY *Nat. Bodies* xix. §1. 166 If you hold a sticke in running water, sheluing against the streame. **1763** MILLS *Pract. Husb.* IV. 351 The shoots [of the vine] should be fastened so as that, when they grow beyond the frame, they may go shelving from it, and not hang by their binding.

**3.** *trans.* To tilt or tip up (a cart). *dial.*

**1587** [implied in SHELVER[1] and SHELVING *vbl. sb.*[2]]. **1853** W. D. COOPER *Sussex Gloss.* (ed. 2), *Shelve*, to turn manure, &c., from a cart, by raising its front part and causing it to lie obliquely. E[astern]. **1875** W. D. PARISH *Sussex Gloss.*

**shelvement** ('ʃɛlvmənt). *dial.* Also **shelment, shilment, -mont.** [f. SHELVE *v.*[2] + -MENT.] = SHELVING *vbl. sb.*[1] 3.

**1808** JAMIESON, *Shilmonts.* **1844** H. STEPHENS *Bk. Farm* III. 1088 When the corn is on a level with the frame or shilments of the cart, the sheaves are then laid across the body of the cart in a row along both sides of the frame. *Ibid.* 1172 Three oak standards.. tenoned.. at top into the top rails, or shelvements.

**shelver**[1] ('ʃɛlvɛ(r)). [f. SHELVE *v.*[3] + -ER[1].]

**1.** A workman employed to tilt carts.

**1587** FLEMING *Contn. Holinshed* III. 1544/2 Eight sheluers, which pulled downe the courts as they came to the place where it was needfull to vnlode. *Ibid.* 1545/1 When the taile of the court was turned to the water side, the shelver plucked downe the load.

**2.** (See quot.)

**1891** *Century Dict.*, *Shelver*, a wagon or truck shelving or sloping toward the back.

**shelver**[2] ('ʃɛlvə(r)). *rare.* [f. SHELVE *v.*[2] + -ER[1].] One who shelves or puts aside.

**1881** *Times* 26 Mar. 13/4 The treaty.. was shelved with the avowed intention on the part of the shelvers to get rid of it altogether.

**shelving** ('ʃɛlvɪŋ), *vbl. sb.*[1] Also *dial.* (in sense 3) **shilvin, shilbin, selvin, silvin:** see *Eng. Dial. Dict.* [f. SHELVE *v.*[2] + -ING[1].]

**1.** The action of the verb SHELVE[2].

**1632** in E. B. Jupp *Carpenters' Co.* (1887) 297 The Shelving of all Roomes vnwainscotted and vnpannelled with Seates and bracketts. **1665** BRATHWAIT *Comm. Chaucer* (Chaucer Soc.) 9 From whence he descendeth to the too accurate disposing or shelving of his Books, his Augur stones [etc.]. **1848** *Blackw. Mag.* Sept. 279 Whilst on the subject of shelving, let us remark that the Scottish.. Bills have shared a similar fate.

**2.** Shelves collectively, also material for shelves.

**1817** M. AUSTIN *Let.* 30 June in E. C. Barker *Austin Papers* (1924) I. 316 He has the Plank.. selected,.. as many as is wanted for shelving. **1844** H. STEPHENS *Bk. Farm* I. 214 The best shelving for a milk-house is marble. **1895** SCULLY *Kafir Stories* 18 The counter was high.. and the shelving, sparsely filled with.. bottles.

**3.** *pl.* See quot. 1788. Also *rarely* in *sing.*

**1641** BEST *Farm. Bks.* (Surtees) 16 Lay them in 4 severall rowes, crosse over the shelvinges of the waine. **1788** W. H. MARSHALL *E. Yorks.* II. 351 *Shelvings*, moveable side-rails of a waggon or cart; put on for a top-load, and taken off for a body-load. **1805** R. W. DICKSON *Pract. Agric.* I. 38 By the addition of shelvings.. the different crops can be carried with great facility. **1867** *Gainsburgh News* 23 Mar. in *N.W. Linc. Gloss.* s.v. *Sideboard*, 1 waggon with shelvings and sideboards. **1871** W. ALEXANDER *Johnny Gibb* i, Heely, heely, Tam, ye glaiket stirk—ye hinna on the hin' shelvin' o' the cairt.

**shelving** ('ʃɛlvɪŋ), *vbl. sb.*[2] [f. SHELVE *v.*[3] + -ING[1].]

**1.** The tilting or tipping up of carts to deposit the load.

**1587** FLEMING *Contn. Holinshed* III. 1544/2 Eight men called vntingers, to loose and vndoo the tackle of euerie court immediatlie before the vnloding or sheluing thereof.

**2.** The fact or condition of sloping; the degree of sloping; a sloping surface; a shelve.

**1687** A. LOVELL tr. *Thevenot's Trav.* II. 87 In some places they make a little shelving, that the rain-Water may run off [from the terrace] into wooden Spouts. **1721** MORTIMER *Husb.* (ed. 2) II. 192 To be.. raised a Foot or more higher than the South-side, that by a little shelving the Cover may the better carry off the Rain. **1853** TH. ROSS tr. *Humboldt's Trav.* III. xxix. 170 The great inclination of the shelvings, the smallness of the island,.. may be considered as.. causes of the want of rivers.

**shelving** ('ʃɛlvɪŋ), *ppl. a.* [f. SHELVE *v.*[3] + -ING[2].] That shelves or slopes.

**1615** G. SANDYS *Trav.* III. 192 In the midst of the sheluing roofe, another vpright aspireth. **1621** —— *Ovid's Met.* IX. (1626) 182 A Lake there is, which sheluing margents bound. **1662** GERBIER *Principles* 34 Its usual standing place being so much shelving, accustomes the Horse.. to be more light.. in his Gate. **1725** POPE *Odyss.* V. 564 Where to the seas the shelving shore declin'd And form'd a bay. **1762** COLMAN *Mus. Lady* II. 24 A couple of vile shelving garrets, where I could scarce stand upright. **1788** GIBBON *Decl. & F.* xli. IV. 128 Innumerable arrows glanced without effect from the compact and shelving order of their bucklers. **1839** DICKENS *Nich. Nick.* lxii, The room.. had a shelving roof; high in one part, and at another descending almost to the floor. **1884** J. COLBORNE *Hicks Pasha* 51 We descend a shelving gravelly plain into Berber.

**b.** quasi-*adv.*

**1649** BLITH *Eng. Improv.* iii. 20 If your Lands lye more shelving or descending towards the River. **1657** S. PURCHAS *Pol. Flying-Ins.* xvi. 105 Peeces of Wood.. set shelving, or leaning towards the North. **1683** MOXON *Mech. Exerc.*, *Printing* iii. 20 The Case standing shelving downwards towards them, the Letters.. tend towards the hither side.

**1769** FALCONER *Dict. Marine* (1776) II. s.v. *Talus, Couper en Talus*, to hew a plank shelving, or with a slanting edge.

Hence **'shelvingly** *adv.*, **'shelvingness.**

**1680** H. MORE *Apocal. Apoc.* iv. 46 One [Beast] appeared just in the midst before the Throne, and the spectacle being exhibited to him shelvingly, another appeared beyond the Throne in the same line. **1727** BOYER *Fr.-Eng. Dict., Penchant*, steepness, declivity, bending, shelvingness, bias.

**shelvy** ('ʃɛlvɪ), *a.*[1] [f. SHELVE *sb.*[1] + -Y.] Of a shore: Having shelves or dangerous sand-banks. †Of a brook: Full of sand-banks.

Perh. used by some writers with sense derived from SHELVE *v.*[3]: Sloping down.

**1598** SHAKS. *Merry W.* III. v. 15, I had beene drown'd, but that the shore was sheluy and shallow. **1609** ARMIN *Ital. Taylor* C 4 b, Through sheluie Brooks (by sedgy bancks The shallow and the deepe). **1657** R. LIGON *Barbadoes* 26 The Leeward part of the Iland being rather shelvie then rockie, they seldome or never are cast away. **1746** W. HORSLEY *Fool* (1748) I. 202 The Ship would be certainly wrecked on the shelvy Coast of Holland. **1764** GOLDSM. *Trav.* 84 As well.. On Idra's cliffs as Arno's shelvy side. **1804** SCOTT *Bard's Incant.* 8 The waves.. dash against the shelvy strand. **1872** BLACKIE *Lays Highl.* 2 Uncouth people fishing on a shelvy shore. **1885** A. MUNRO *Siren Casket* 5 He breasts the main And gains, much-spent, a shelvy reef.

**shelvy** ('ʃɛlvɪ), *a.*[2] *rare.* [f. SHELVE *sb.*[2] + -Y.] Projecting like a shelf; overhanging.

**1811** D. BUCHAN in J. Barrow *Chron. Hist. Voyages* (1818) App. I. 8 At noon several difficulties presented themselves in crossing a tract of shelvy ice, intersected with deep and wide rents. **1831** JANE PORTER *Sir E. Seaward's Narr.* I. 148, I deposited the spade under a shelvy rock. **1862** BORROW *Wild Wales* II. xii. 131 The shelvy side of Snowdon rose above me on the left.

**shelynge**, obs. form of SHILLING.

†**shem.** *Obs. rare*⁻¹. [Cheshire pronunciation of SEAM *sb.*[1]] = SEAM *sb.*[1] 6.

**1688** HOLME *Armoury* III. 92/1 A Shem, is when two edges [of lead] are turned one over the other. *Ibid.* 325/2 By these Pincers two Skirts of Lead are turned one over the other, without cutting or bruising the Lead; this kind of Rolling of Lead one within another, is termed a Shem.

So **'sheming** *a.*, that forms a 'shem'.

**1688** HOLME *Armoury* III. 326/1 The Sheming Mallet. *Ibid.* 325/2 A Plummers Pincers or Sheming Pincers.

**Shema** (‖ʃɛ'ma). Also **Shemah, Shemang.** [Heb. *šemaʿ* hear, imper. of *šāmaʿ* to hear.] The first word of the verse Deut. vi. 4 used as a name for three portions of the Scriptures, Deut. vi. 4–9, xi. 13–21, Numbers xv. 37–41, to be repeated twice daily by all adult Jewish males, and used as a Jewish confession of faith.

**1706** I. ABENDANA *Discourse Eccl. & Civil Polity of Jews* iv. 106 Every day we use an office containing three sections of the law, commonly styled *Shemang*, i.e. *Hear.* **1816** J. ALLEN *Mod. Judaism* xix. 331 Another essential part of the daily service.. is the reading of three portions of scripture. The first of these portions beginning with the word *Shema.* .. This term is applied to all the portions taken together, and the recital of them is called *Kiriath Shema*, the *Reading of the Shema.* To recite these passages twice every day they maintain to be expressly enjoined. **1864** *Chambers's Encycl.* VI. 155/1 The first additions to the *Shemah* formed the introductory thanks-giving for the renewed day. **1876** GEO. ELIOT *Daniel Deronda* IV. VII. lxi. 221 The *Shemah*, wherein we briefly confess the divine Unity, is the chief devotional exercise of the Hebrew. **1926** *Brit. Weekly* 5 Aug. 367/3 Esther.. joins in that immemorial declaration of her people the Shemang or Confession of Unity. **1936** E. UNDERHILL *Worship* (ed. 2) I. ii. 28 The Jews' daily repetition of the *Shema*, the Christians' ritual use of the Lord's Prayer, and the Moslems' of the First *Sura*, are all justified by psychology no less than by religion. **1949** W. F. ALBRIGHT *Archaeol. of Palestine* x. 221 In 1902 the Nash fragment containing the Ten Commandments and the Shema ('Hear, O Israel..') was discovered in the Faiyum. **1972** J. CAINE *Hamlet, my Boy* vi. 86 He reminded himself that a Jew was supposed to say the *Shema* in the hour of death. **1977** H. KAPLAN *Damascus Cover* (1978) xii. 123 'Don't you know the Shema?' She was either a Jewess or a highly trained agent.

**shemaul, sheme**, obs. ff. SHAMAL, SEAM *sb.*[2]

**shemeful**, obs. forms of SHAMEFUL.

**shemer**, obs. form of CHIMERE, SHIMMER *v.*

**shemerand**, obs. var. SHIMMERING *ppl. a.*

†**shemewe.** *Obs.* Forms: 6 shamewe, shemew, chemew. [Perh. orig. a misreading of some form of CHIMER[1].] = CHIMER[1].

**1517** in Planche *Cycl. Costume* (1876) I. 450 A 'cote or shamewe'. **1535** *Wardr. Acc. Hen. VIII* in *Archæologia* IX. 245 A shamewe of blacke printed satten. **1548** HALL *Chron., Hen. VIII* (1550) 65 A new fassion garment, called a Shemew, which was in effect a gowne cut in the middle. *Ibid.* 77, I.. perceiued thabiliment royall of the Frenche kynge, his garment was a chemew.

**Shemite** ('ʃɛmaɪt), *sb.* and *a.* [f. *Shem* (Heb. *shēm*, Gr. Σήμ, L. *Sem*), name of the eldest son of Noah (cf. Gen. vi. 10) + -ITE.] = SEMITE *a.* and *sb.*

**1659** GELL *Ess. Amend. Eng. Transl. Bible* 103 The fear, faith, hope, love of God, if we be true Shemites, must inform our whole life. **1791** *Gentl. Mag.* Feb. 107/1 Arabic.. contains a good deal of Persian and Gothic and other Shemite dialects. **1835** KIRBY *Hab. & Inst. Anim.* ii. I. 76 The Shemites in the lapse of ages, passing over to America. **1844** PRICHARD *Phys. Hist. Man.* (ed. 3) IV. 549 Nations of Shemite origin. **1877** R. S. POOLE in *Encycl. Brit.* VII. 722/2 The generous qualities of the Shemite are being perpetually perverted by the inferior impulses of the Nigritian.

Hence **She'mitic** *a.* and *sb.* = SEMITIC *a.* and *sb.* **She'miticize** *v.* = SEMITICIZE *v.* **She-'mitish** *a.*, having Shemitic characteristics. **'Shemitism**, the attributes characteristic of the Shemitic peoples.

**1822** *Malte-Brun's Universal Geogr.* I. XXIII. 570 As most of the nations that speak these languages descend, according to Moses, from Shem, this stock has been distinguished under the general name of the Shemitic languages. **1828** WEBSTER Introd. p. xvi/2 The real original sense of this Shemitic verb is to remove. **1838** W. B. WINNING *Man. Compar. Philol.* 277 The assumptions.. that the Hebrew tongue must necessarily be of Shemitish derivation. **1845** KITTO *Cycl. Bibl. Lit.* s.v. *Harlot*, By a common association of ideas in the Shemitish dialects. *Ibid.* s.v. *Philistines*, The Shemitics gave place to the Hellenics—a change which dates from the time of Minos. **1850** W. IRVING *Mahomet* I. 22 The intellectual attributes of the Shemitic race. **1863** R. S. POOLE in *W. Smith's Dict. Bible* III. 1815/2 The Egyptian words occurring in Hebrew are few, and the forms of some of them evidently Shemiticized. **1873** LELAND *Egypt. Sketch-Bk.* 251 A true Shemitic mania for making money. **1882–3** SCHAFF *Encycl. Relig. Knowl.* I. 665 Far outside of Shemitism one finds serpent-worship.

**shemmal**, var. SHAMAL.

**shemmi**, var. SHIMMY *v.*[1]

**shemozzle** (ʃɪ'mɒz(ə)l). *slang.* Also †chimozzle; s(c)h(e)-, s(c)hi-, s(c)hlemozzle. [Of uncertain origin. In early use (*shlemozzle*, etc.) apparently East End slang: perh. ad. Yiddish *shlimazl* misfortune, unlucky person (see SCHLIMAZEL), with subsequent reduction of *schle-* to *sche-*.] A muddle or complication; a quarrel, row, rumpus, mêlée.

**1899** A. M. BINSTEAD *Houndsditch Day by Day* 23 It was through no recklessness or extravagance that he was in this shlemozzle. **1900** *From Front* xiv. 183 We might look upon this little chimozzle as a kind o' misunderstanding. **1901** J. M. COBBAN *Golden Tooth* xvii. 170 If Will comes out of this shemozzle. **1916** 'PETER' *Trench Yarns* ii. 16 In the ensuing shemmozle Samuel got laid out with the butt-end of a rifle. **1916** 'TAFFRAIL' *Pincher Martin* vii. 120 'We ain't the best o' friends, 'cos me an' 'im 'ad a bit o' a shimozzle—' 'Shimozzle!.. What on earth's that?' 'Bit o' a dust-up, sir.' **1928** *Sunday Dispatch* 29 July 15/2 Those.. who saw so little of war that they still think it to be a gloriously romantic shlemozzle. **1930** S. SASSOON *Mem. Infantry Officer* vi. 156 When I showed the battle-plan to the Sergeant-Major, all he said was 'We'll have a rough house from Ale Alley.' But no one had any idea it was going to be such a schimozzle as it was! **1936** J. G. BRANDON *Pawnshop Murder* i. 9 Has a *schlemozzle*, and takes 'is stuff over to Paris. **1937** G. FRANKAU *More of Us* xv. 160 Then Sophie called; and, brooding, 'Nice schemozzle If that lot stays to feed as well as sozzle.' **1943** T. WORLING *White Ensigns* viii. 146 'How many more shimozzles like yesterday are we going to get?' Mr. Hebard queried. **1949** 'N. BLAKE' *Head of Traveller* xi. 191 Even if it turns out that none of us is implicated in the murder, there's still going to be a shocking shemozzle, I'm afraid, about his original disappearance. **1951** S. KAYE-SMITH *Mrs. Gailey* v. 292 It was in the papers. What a schemozzle! **1955** E. WAUGH *Officers & Gentlemen* 276 There was something of a schemozzle last night but we weren't in that. **1960** I. CROSS *Backward Sex* 167 The whole schmozzle is over. **1966** *Telegraph* (Austral.) 27 Dec. 8/4 The next day saw one of the greatest shemozzles in Australian sport. **1978** L. MEYNELL *Papersnake* ii. 22 There was going to be one hell of an uncomfortable shemozzle in his life if he didn't get his priorities right.

Hence **she'mozzle** *v. intr.*, to decamp, make off, 'scarper'.

**1903** FARMER & HENLEY *Slang* VI. 172/2 *Shemozzle*.. Verb (East End). To be off; to decamp. **1925** FRASER & GIBBONS *Soldier & Sailor Words* 256 *Shemozzle, to*, to make off: to get out of the way—e.g., 'We saw the M.P.'s (Military Police) coming, so we shemozzled.' **1944** AUDEN *For Time Being* (1945) 118 He was caught by a common cold and condemned to the whiskey mines, But schemozzled back to the Army.

‖**shen** (ʃən). Also **Shen, Shin,** etc. [Chinese *shén.*] In Chinese philosophy: a god, person of supernatural power, or the spirit of a dead person.

**1847** W. H. MEDHURST *Dissert. Theol. Chinese* 5 It would appear, that.. Shin and.. Kwei, are terms equivalent to spirit and anima, in the human system. **1901** J. J. M. DE GROOT *Relig. Syst. China* IV. II. 4 Confucius means to say, the shen manifests itself in its full development in man by his khi or 'breath'; indeed, only animated man lives and breathes. **1905** E. H. PARKER *China & Religion* i. 21 The spirits of men were called *kwei*, and those of Heaven and Nature *shên.* **1934** A. D. WALEY *Way & its Power* 29 'If the monarch loses his *shên*,' says *Han Fei Tzŭ*, 'the tigers will soon be on his tracks.' **1955** E. HERBERT *Taoist Notebk.* 43 Thus Mencius in his moral hierarchy posited two grades —the 'spirit-like' (*Shên*), the saint beyond man's power of comprehension. **1978** F. MANN *Acupuncture* (ed. 3) iv. 32 Shen is usually translated as 'spirit', a word which to the Western mind more often than not suggests the supernatural. But Shen.. is a down-to-earth word.

**shenanigan** (ʃɪ'nænɪgən). orig. *U.S.* Also shenan(n)egan, -igan, -gin; shin-; -(c)kin; and other vars. [Origin obscure.] Trickery, skulduggery, machination, intrigue; teasing, 'kidding', nonsense; (usu. *pl.*) a plot, a trick, a prank, an exhibition of high spirits, a carry-on.

Hence **she'naniganning, she'nanigin(g)**, *pres. pple.* and *vbl. sb.*

**1855** *Town Talk* (San Francisco) 25 Apr. 2 Are you quite sure? No shenanigan? **1856** *Spirit of Age* (Sacramento) 30 Apr. 2 These facts indicate that there is some *shenanegan* going on. **1857** C. E. DE LONG *Jrnl.* 15 Aug. in *Calif. Hist. Soc. Q.* (1930) IX. 156 Race came off Whiskey Bill winner, the Mare's rider held in, and Smith pronouncing it shenanigan. **1862** 'MARK TWAIN' *Let.* May (1917) I. iii. 77 Consider them all.. guilty (of 'shenanigan') until they are proved innocent. **1894** M. J. JAQUES *Texan Ranch Life* xiii. 115 He assured me that he was not 'shenan-neganning' me, and that the dish would prove a delicacy. **1897** *Outing* (U.S.) XXIX. 483/1 A man who is firmly kind, but who will stand no shinanigan. **1901** W. S. WALKER *In Blood* xxxi. 332 We're mates all round, an' no more shenannikin. **1902** R. BARR *Victors* v. 81 If I were to pay them they might think there was some shenanigan about it. **1924** J. MASEFIELD *Lord Harker* III. 146 Now, brother, answer me and no damned shinanniking. **1926** E. FERBER *Show Boat* xiv. 305 I'd never had a fight on my boat and wasn't going to begin any such low life shenanigans now. **1928** *Saturday Even. Post* 10 Mar. 11/2 The renunciation of Mr Coolidge was a distinct disappointment to the great mass of the Republican Party, .. and this left the way open for some astute shenanigan in various states. **1930** 'S. S. VAN DINE' *Scarab Murder Case* xv. 212 There's too much shenanigan going on around here to suit me. I want action. **1935** S. O'CASEY *Let.* c 10 Feb. (1975) I. 540 It is really hateful that I should be compelled to turn my thoughts to the pious shinanachin of a few Jesuits & a group of Methodist Preachers. **1936** 'R. HYDE' *Passport to Hell* x. 152 Two more followed him to take care of him and see he didn't lose his pay-roll shenannigin in his Irish way with the mademoiselles. **1938** J. I. RODALE *King's English on Horseback* 137/1 *Mischief*,.. Shenanigins. **1940** DYLAN THOMAS *Portrait of Artist as Young Dog* 122 No shananacking in the old moonlight. **1947** W. GREENWOOD *Cure for Love* I. 23 'Here, listen, you two. No shinanigin'.' .. 'Shinanigin'? What's that?'.. 'Shinanigin'? Well-er-it's. .. Well-er-just shinanigin'... Messing about.' **1948** D. BALLANTYNE *Cunninghams* I. vi. 34 You see you go tomorrow, then... No shinnanicking now. **1960** T. GRIFFITH *Waist-High Culture* II. 81 Readers [of newspapers] do not recognize every shenanigan inflicted upon them. **1969** in Halpert & Story *Christmas Mumming in Newfoundland* 90 The entire household looks on, laughing at the girls' shenanigans. **1973** B. BAINBRIDGE *Dressmaker* 11 They'd all catch their death of cold shenanniging about in the middle of the night. **1973** *Nation Rev.* (Melbourne) 31 Aug. 1448/2 (*heading*) Shennanigans behind the silver screen. **1974** *Ridge Citizen* (Johnston, S. Carolina) 18 Apr. 2/1 We don't condone whatever wrongdoing or shenanigans that may have taken place at Watergate or elsewhere. **1976** R. LEWIS *Witness my Death* ii. 56 There might have been a certain amount of shenanigans going on behind the scenes. **1978** *New York* 3 Apr. 16/2 House Calls—Glenda Jackson, Art Carney, Richard Benjamin, and Charlie Matthau in a film directed by Howard Zieff, about medical shenanigans in and out of a hospital. **1980** *Times* 3 Jan. 10/4 Doubtful political shenanigans.. in the Central Pacific.

†**shench**, *sb. Obs.* Forms: 1, 3 scenc, 2–3 scenche, (senche), 3, 5 schench, 4 sscench. [OE. *scęnc* masc.:—prehistoric **skaŋki-*, related to *scęncan* SHENCH *v.*] A cupful, drink (of liquor). Cf. *noneschenche* NUNCHEON.

*c*950 *Lindisf. Gosp.* Matt. x. 42 Cælc vel scenc [L. *calicem*] wætres caldes. *c* **1000** *Sax. Leechd.* I. 128 Syle drincan on wine, tweȝan scenceas oððe ðry. *c* **1250** *Moral Ode* 331 (Egerton MS.) þes worlð us wule for-drenche Mest alle men he ȝuied drinke, of one deofles scenche [*Trin. MS.* of on euele senche]. *c* **1205** LAY. 9692 þus seide þe King.. þer he sæt mid his scenche An his kine-benche. *Ibid.* 13461 He lette heom bringen schenches of feole cunne drenches. **13..** *Seuyn Sag.* (Weber) 562 He made ther-under a grene bench, And drank ther-under mane a sscench.

†**shench, shenk**, *v. Obs.* Forms: α. 1–2 scencan, scænc(e)an, scencean, 3 scenche, scencche, (ssenche, 3–4 senche), 3–5 schenche, 4 shenche; β. 2–3 *Orm.* shennkenn, 3 senken, 5 schenkyn. [OE. *scęnc(e)an* = OFris. *skenka*, OS. *skenkian* (MLG. *schenken*, whence ON. *skenkja*, Da. *skænke*, Sw. *skänka*), MDu., mod.Du. *schenken*, OHG. *scenken* (MHG., mod.G. *schenken*) :—OTeut. **skaŋkjan.* Cf. SKINK *v.*

For conjectures as to the ulterior etymology see Kluge and Falk & Torp.]

*trans.* To pour out (liquor); to give (a person) drink.

α. *Beowulf* 496 þeȝn nytte beheold se þe on handa bær hroden ealowæȝe scencte scir wered. *a* **1050** *Lamb. Ps.* xxxv. 9 Hiȝ beoþ ȝedrencte.. of burnan þinre wynsumnysse & þu scæncst [L. *potabis*] hiȝ. *a* **1050** *Liber Scintill.* xxviii. (1889) 106 þæt nys coss ræccean ac scencean [L. *propinare*]. *c* **1205** LAY. 8124 I-scængte mid beore. *Ibid.* 20375 He sæið mid his ȝelpe þenne me him win scencche∂. **1297** R. GLOUC. (Rolls) 2526 þe drinke vor to ssenche [*v.rr.* schenche, swenche]. **13..** *K. Alis.* 7581 (Laud MS.) He was.. ysette on heiȝe benche, And wyne & pyement gynneþ shenche. **1390** GOWER *Conf.* I. 263 Envie.. halt taverne forto schenche That drink which makth the herte brenne.

β. *c* **1200** ORMIN 15403, & tu, lef Laferrd Jesu Crist, Ne shennkesst nohht tatt wise. *c* **1250** *Gen. & Ex.* 322 He.. senkede hire hure aldre bale. *c* **1440** *Promp. Parv.* 445/1 Schenkyn drynke, *propino.*

Hence †**'shenker.**

*c* **1440** *Promp. Parv.* 51/1 Bryllare of drynke, or schenkare, (drinkshankere, *P.*), *propinator, propinatrix.*

**shenchipp**, obs. form of SHENDSHIP.

†**shend**, *sb. Obs. rare.* [f. SHEND *v.* Cf. SHOND.] Disgrace, ruin.

*c* **1400** *Laud Troy Bk.* 7304 We ligge here in stormes and schende. *a* **1450** *Le Morte Arth.* 1664 The squyer than was done to shende. *c* **1450** LOVELICH *Merlin* 284 For jlle werk bryngeth a man to evele ende And jn to synne & synneres schende.

**shend** (ʃɛnd), *v.*[1] Now *dial.* and *arch.* Pa. t. and pa. pple. shent (ʃɛnt). Forms: 1 (ȝe-) scendan, (ȝesciendan, -scyndan), 2 sceandan, 3 scanden, scenden, sceind, schiende, s(s)ende, (*Ormin*) shennd, 3–5 schend, 3–7 shende, 4 shind, shynde, scheend, scheind, 4–5 schind, schynde, sheende, 4– 6 *Sc.* schent, 5 sheynd, (schente, 6–7 shent), 2– shend; 3 *pers. sing. Pres. Ind.* 1 (ȝe-) scent, (sciend, ȝesciend, -scind, seynt), 3–4 schent, 4 shent; *Pa. t.* 1, 3 (ȝe-) scent, scende, ssende, 3–4 schende, 3–5 schente, 3–6 schent, 4 shende, shente, 5 shend, 4–6, 9 shent; 3 (*Ormin*) shendedd; *Pa. pple.* 1 ȝe-scend, -scynd, (-sciend), 3 schent, scent, (*Ormin*) shennd, y-scend, (y-)ssent, 3–5 schente, y-schend, -ssend, 3–7 schent, 4 scheint, (chent), 4–5 y-schent, (-chend), (y-)schende, 5 y-shent(e, (e-chent), schend, scheent, 5–6 shend, 5–7 shente, 3– shent; 1 ȝescended, (-sci(e)nded), 5 shendit, 9 shended. [OE. *scęndan* (also *ȝescęndan*), corresp. to OLow Frankish *scendian* (MDu., mod.Du. *schenden*), MLG., LG. *schenden*, OHG. *scentan* (MHG., mod.G. *schänden*):—OTeut. type **skandjan*, f. **skando-*: see SHOND *sb.*

After the 15th c. the word occurs in literary use almost exclusively in the pa. pple. *shent*, and even this form seems already to have been felt as archaic in the latter part of the 16th c. After the pres.-stem had become rare, some writers occas. used *shent* as a present.]

**1.** *trans.* To put to shame or confusion; to confound, disgrace.

*c* **825** *Vesp. Ps.* cxviii. 31 Nyl mec ȝescendan [Vulg. *noli me confundere*]. *a* **1050** *Lamb. Ps.* xxiv. 3 Ealle þa..anbidiaþ þe ne beon ȝescynde. *c* **1205** LAY. 3090 For nauer ich ne wende þþæt þu me woldes þus scanden [**1275** sende]. *c* **1275** *XI Pains of Hell* 362 in *O.E. Misc.* 222 Lest ȝe be chamyd and schend. *a* **1300** *Cursor M.* 16690 'Ihesus nazaren, o Iuus King', þar-on þai wrate,..al for to scend [**13..** (Gött.) schind] his state. *c* **1320** *Sir Tristr.* 3289 Þe wraiers þat weren in halle, Schamly were þai schende. **1426** AUDELAY *Poems* 27 Ellys with chenchip and with chame thai wyll be e-chent. **1436** *Libel Eng. Policy* in *Pol. Poems* (Rolls) II. 183 To shende the olde Englisshe fames. *c* **1570** *Satir. Poems Reform.* xiv. 21 Than, Father slaine, Mother was schent. *c* **1586** C'TESS PEMBROKE *Ps.* CXXIX. iii, Terror shall your mindes amate, Blush and shame your faces shend. **1590** SPENSER *F.Q.* II. vi. 35 Debatefull strife, and cruell enmitie, The famous name of knighthood fowly shend. **1641** J. TRAPPE *Theol. Theol.* v. 198 This serves deepely to shent and shame us for our first brutish ignorance. **1818** KEATS *Endym.* IV. 599 He'll be shent..When he shall hear the wedding lutes a playing.

†**b.** To put to shame by superiority. *Obs.*

**1596** SPENSER *Prothal.* 121 These twaine, that did excell The rest, so far, as Cynthia doth shend The lesser starres.

**2.** To blame, reproach, reprove; to revile, scold. In later use the passive often = to suffer for one's deeds, be punished (cf. sense 3).

*c* **897** ÆLFRED *Gregory's Past. C.* xxxi. 207 Ðone scamleasan mon mæȝ ðy bet ȝebetan ðe hine mon suiður ðreað & sciend [*Cotton MS.* scent]. *c* **1200** ORMIN 1992 Þatt ȝho na were shamedd her, Ne shennd off unnclænnesse. *c* **1230** *Hali Meid.* (Bodley) 454 Chit te & cheoweð þe, & scheomeliche schent te. *c* **1290** *Beket* 975 in *S. Eng. Leg.* 134 "Louerdinges", he seide, 'here ȝe i-seoz hov þis man me schent'. *c* **1394** *P. Pl. Crede* 9 Whan y schal schewen myn schrift schent mote y worþen. *c* **1430** *Hymns Virg.* (1867) 104 Goddis name in ydil take þou not, For if þou do þou schalt be scheent. *c* **1430** *Pilgr. Lyf Manhode* I. cxxxi. (1869) 69, I mihte not endure hem longe swiche withoute sheendinge myself. **1523** LD. BERNERS *Froiss.* I. cclxxviii. 416 Sir Robert Canoll gate in the..voyage..aboue the somme of a hundred thousande frankes, wherof afterwarde he was shente. **1543** in Strype *Cranmer* (1694) App. 66 The Councel said..that the Justices of every shire should be shent, that such things should be. **1548** UDALL *Erasm. Par. Luke* xxii. 35–38 Seyng that Peter was shent because that he drewe his sweorde. **1568** *Jacob & Esau* II. iii, I must in againe, lest perhaps I be shent, For I asked no body licence, when I went. **1600** MARKHAM *Tears of Beloved* (Grosart) 61 This monstrous sinne, for which I thus am shent. **1601** SHAKS. *Twel. N.* IV. ii. 112 Alas sir be patient. What say you sir, I am shent for speaking to you. *a* **1661** FULLER *Worthies, Camb.* (1662) I. 153 Yet was his Loyalty shent, but not sham'd. **1700** DRYDEN *Cock & Fox* 110 Much I fear my Body will be shent. **1742** SHENSTONE *Schoolmistr.* (Imit. Spenser) 18 They..For unkempt hair, or task unconn'd, are sorely shent. **1855** BROWNING *Master Hugues* x, Masters being lauded and sciolists shent.

*Proverb.* **13..** *Minor Poems fr. Vernon MS.* 683/12 Hos seiþ þe soþe, he schal be schent. *a* **1400** in *Songs & Poems Costume* (Percy Soc.) 44 Who seyt trowthe is shent. **1493** *Festivall* (W. de W. 1515) 26 Soo he that wyll saye the trouthe he shall be shente.

**3.** To destroy, ruin, bring to destruction. Also, in milder sense, to injure, damage, spoil.

*a* **900** CYNEWULF *Christ* 1548 Se deopa seað..mid wita fela ..folcum scendeð. *c* **1175** *Lamb. Hom.* 39 Her is ane reowlic bone to biddene bute we inwarliche imilcien and forȝeuen þan monne þe us wreðeð and sceandet. *c* **1205** LAY. 25692 Þe scaðe..þa scendeþ [**1275** sendes] þas leode. *c* **1300** *Harrow. Hell* (Harl. MS.) 130 Þou shalt neuer out wende monkunne forte shende. *c* **1330** *Arth. & Merl.* 450 Mani hauberk was torent & mani þurch þe bodi schent. **1362** LANGL. *P. Pl.* A. Prol. 95 To ben Clerkes of þe kynges Benche þe Cuntre to schende. *c* **1380** *Sir Ferumb.* 523 Þe Sarasyn sayd til him þanne 'þyn heȝ herte wil þee schynde'. **1387** TREVISA *Higden* (Rolls) VII. 347 His navey was nyh [al] adreynt, and his oost i-schend wiþ colde and wiþ honger [L. *fame et frigore contabuit*]. *Ibid.* VIII. 181 [In a hail-storm] men were i-schent [*contriti*], and foules were i-seie flee in þe ayre. *c* **1440** *Gesta Rom.* xxxi. 120 (Harl. MS.) The Oynement, that shendithe the tethe of þe lioune, is almis-dede. **1470–85** MALORY *Arthur* x. xii. 432 They wold not for no good that sire Dagonet were shente, for Kyng Arthur loued hym passynge wel. *c* **1500** *Flower & Leaf* 360 The knightes swelt, for lack of shade ny shent. **1549–62** STERNHOLD & H. *Ps.* lxxiii. 5 And free from all aduersitie, when other men be shent. **1600** FAIRFAX *Tasso* VI. iv, But we must yeeld, whom hunger soone will shend. **1633** HART *Diet of Diseased* II. v. 163 If Physitians should now imitate the Hippocraticall course of dieting, they should be utterly shent. **1697** DRYDEN *Virg. Georg.* II. 621 Tho' shent their Leaves, and shatter'd are their Arms; Yet Heav'n their various Plants for use designs. **1812** BYRON *Ch. Har.* I. xvii, No personage of high or mean degree Doth care for cleanness of surtout or shirt; Though shent with Egypt's plague. **1906** DOYLE *Sir Nigel* v. 52 My papers have been shended and rended and cast to the wind.

*absol.* *a* **1568** *Bannatyne MS.* (Hunter. Club) 648 Quhithir scho schent or scho saif, I am hir serwand.

†**b.** To disfigure, spoil; to corrupt, infect; to defile, soil. *Obs.*

*a* **950** *Durham Ritual* (Surtees) 121/40 Giþyll scendende *aura corrumpens*. **1338** R. BRUNNE *Chron.* (1725) 204 Rise & go þi ways, For þou has wette þi breke, schent is þi hernays. **1340** *Ayenb.* 148 Vor þe leme uorroted ssolde ssende þe hole. *cc* **1386** CHAUCER *Pars. T.* 854 Who so toucheth warm pych it shent hise fyngres. **1387** TREVISA *Higden* (Rolls) VI. 15 Heraclius deide in þe dropesie, and was i-schend [L. *depravatus*] with þat heresy of þe Iacobytes. *c* **1450** *Knt. de la Tour* (1868) 25 She had her nose croked, the whiche shent and dysfigured her uisage. **1530** PALSGR. 717/2 Syt hence, or you shall shende your clothes. **1876** BLACKIE *Songs of Relig.* 145 So with gore they shent His silvery locks.

**c.** In *pa. pple.*: Overcome with fatigue; bewildered, stupefied.

*c* **1400** tr. *Secreta Secret., Gov. Lordsh.* civ. 105 He cryed after him and sayde, 'abide me, I am negh shent of goynge.' **1828** CARLYLE *Goethe's Helena* Misc. 1840 I. 229 Boots not; for amaze hath shent me. **1905** *Outlook* 11 Feb. 194/2, I stood utterly shent and powerless.

†**4.** To discomfit (in battle or dispute). *Obs.*

In ME. confession was often said to 'shend' the devil.

*c* **893** ÆLFRED *Oros.* II. x. § 1 Xersis wæs þa æt twam cirrum on ðæm londe swa ȝescend [*bis victus in terra*]. *a* **1175** *Lamb. Hom.* 21 Þu scalt gan to scrifte and pinian þine licome þe hit þþe makeð don, and scenden þene deofel. *a* **1225** *Ancr. R.* 298 Schrift schent þene deouel & hackeð of his heaued, & to-dreaueð his ferde. **1297** R. GLOUC. (Rolls) 4666 Hengist þoru wan þis lond verst was yssent. *c* **1375** *Sc. Leg. Saints* xxxii. (*Justin*) 241, & þan ware þai fullely schent, & fore rednes fra hyre went. *c* **1385** CHAUCER *L.G.W.* 652 Tyl at the laste..Antonye is schent & put hym to the flyght. *c* **1480** HENRYSON *Mor. Fab.* ix. 2191 The foxe, quhen that he saw the wolf was schent, Said to him selff, 'thir hering salbe myne.' **1643** WITHER *Campo-Musæ* 5 He that armes himselfe to this intent Shall ne're be shamed, though he may be shent. **1829** SOUTHEY *All for Love* IX. xxiii, The Deed is null,..A wicked instrument,..Not to be pleaded in the Courts... Sir Fiend, thy cause is shent!

†**5.** *intr.* = 'to be shent'. *Obs.*

*a* **1366** CHAUCER *Rom. Rose* 1400 And ful of grene leues sytte That sonne myght there none discende Lest the tender grasses shende. *c* **1425** *Cast. Persev.* 283 in *Macro Plays* 85 For schame I stonde & schende. *c* **1560** A. SCOTT *Poems* (S.T.S.) xxxiii. 11 Quhen body, honor, and substance schentis, And saule in perrell.

†**6.** In the *Destruction of Troy* the phrase *to shend of* is app. equivalent to the transitive uses, to dishonour, to destroy, injure. *Obs.*

*c* **1400** *Destr. Troy* 2544 For to shunt vs of shame, shend of our foos. *Ibid.* 5249 He shot thurgh the sheltrons & shent of hor knightes. *Ibid.* 13699 Þen Orestes..schamyt with þe schalke, that schent of his wife, And so dernely hym did dere && dispit.

†**shend**, *v.*[2] *Obs.* [App. a corruption of SHIELD *v.*, arising from confusion with prec. or association with FEND *v.* or DEFEND *v.*] *trans.* To shield, defend. Also *absol.*, ***God shend*** = 'God shield'.

**1530** PALSGR. 717/2, I shall shende hym agaynst all men so longe as I lyve. *Ibid.*, I shende, I forbyd. This verbe they use onely in the potenciall,..'Saye you so Marye God shende'. **1549–62** STERNHOLD & H. *Ps.* cxix. 76 So from all ill me shend. *a* **1597** PEELE *David & Bethsabe* (1599) D iij b, Let Dauids Harpe..sing his praise that shendeth Dauids fame. **1598** BP. HALL *Sat.* v. iii. 73 Vpreare A brazen wall to shend thy land from feare. **1602** R. T. *Five Godlie Serm.* 23 To defend and shend them against all adversaries whatsoeuer. **1614** W. BROWNE *Sheph. Pipe* i. B 2 b, These my harmlesse flocke of sheepe. And through all the day I tend them, And from Wolues & Foxes shend them. **1625** LISLE *Du Bartas* 132 Thou op'nest wide thy lap to shend thy sonne from harm.

†**'shended,** *ppl. a. Obs.* [f. SHEND *v.*[1] + -ED[1]. Cf. SHENT *ppl. a.*] Ruined, injured.

**13..** *E.E. Allit. P.* C. 246 Of þat schended schyp men schowued hym sone.

†**'shendful,** *a. Obs.* Forms: 3–4 schendful, 3–5 schenful, 4 schende-, schent-, schind-, shynful, schentful(e, ssendvol, 4–5 shenful, 5 schent-, schendfol, send-, shendvol, 5–6 shendful, 6 shendefull. [f. SHEND *v.*[1] + -FUL.] Infamous, disgraceful.

*a* **1225** *Ancr. R.* 200 Þe uormest is Cheaste, oðer Strif, þe oðer is Wodschipe, þe þridde is Schenful [*v.r.* schendful] Upbrud. *c* **1305** *St. Kenelm* 366 in *E.E.P.* (1862) 57 Bote hire ending schindful were. *c* **1366** CHAUCER *Rom. Rose* 259 (MS.) If she se any grete lynage Be brought to nought in shynful wise. *c* **1380** *Sir Ferumb.* 1973 Þys day ne wol y on myn halle drynke whit wyn ne red, Til y [haue] seen þe glotouns alle on schentful deþe be ded. *c* **1425** *Seven Sag.* (P.) 3401 Thou schalt dye on schentfol deth. **1566** DRANT Horace, Sat. VI. D v b, That shendful shame through worde or fame did never me oppresse.

†**'shendfully,** *adv. Obs.* [f. SHENDFUL *a.* + -LY[2].] Ignominiously, disgracefully, infamously.

*a* **1225** *Ancr. R.* 316 Spec hire scheome schendfuliche. **1297** R. GLOUC. (Rolls) 6343 Þus senduolliche he him slou. **1362** LANGL. *P. Pl.* A. III. 261 God sende to seye þat [Saul] schulde dye, And al his seed for þat Sunne schendfulliche ende. **1480** CAXTON *Chron. Eng.* XCII. e 6 b, Edelf.. bethought howe that he myȝt..marie hir to a knaue of his kychen..and to hym he thought hir shendfully haue maried for to haue had hir land afterward. *a* **1513** FABYAN *Chron.* v. lxxix. (1533) 32 The enymyes of the lande were shendfully chasyd and vtterly confounded.

†**'shendfulness.** *Obs. rare*[−1]. [f. SHENDFUL *a.* + -NESS.] Vileness.

*a* **1225** *Ancr. R.* 322 Ich chulle..trussen al þi schendfulnesse o þine owune necke.

**'shending,** *vbl. sb. Obs.* exc. *arch.* [-ING[1].] The action of SHEND *v.*[1]; confusion, disgrace.

*a* **1220** *Bestiary* 441 Deuel geld swilk billing wið same and wið sending. *a* **1300** *Cursor M.* 2266 For-þi þat tour hatt babilone, þat schending es wit outen soyne. *c* **1400** *Laud Troy Bk.* 9954 Suche maystry, That the schal lede..In foule schendyng, Al thi lyff to thyn endyng. *c* **1440** *Promp. Parv.* 445/1 Schendynge, or blamynge, *culpacio*... Schendynge, or fulle vndoynge, *confusio*. *c* **1520** NISBET *Epist. Ald Test.* xxxix, Thi pepile ar in schenting to almen [Vulg. *in opprobrium sunt omnibus*] be our cumpas. **1935** J. D. WILSON *What happens in Hamlet* vi. 203 The King at his prayers, the shending of Gertrude, the slaying of Polonius, Hamlet's departure to England.

†**'shendlac.** *Obs. rare.* In 3 schendlac. [f. SHEND *v.*[1]: see -LAIK.] Disgrace, infamy.

*a* **1225** *Leg. Kath.* 1285 Ȝef fifti wimmen..hefden mid wordes ower an awarpen, nere hit schendlac inoh..to alle þæt ȝelpeð of lare? *a* **1225** *Ancr. R.* 188 Þencheð euer inwardliche up o Godes pinen,—..uor his þrelles, þolien swuche schendlakes & hokeres.

†**'shendly,** *a. Obs. rare*[−1]. In 3 sindlice. [Alteration of SHONDLY by association with the vb. SHEND.] Disgraceful, infamous.

*c* **1275** LAY. 2274 Ne sal þe no man silde fram sindlice deaþe.

†**'shendness.** *Obs.* Forms: α. 1 ȝescendnys(s, ȝesceandnys, ȝescyndnys, 3 schend-, ssendnesse, 4 schindnisse, schen(d)nes, (shens); β. 4 schindisse, -esse. [OE. *ȝescęndnyss*, f. *ȝescęnd*, pa. pple. of *scęndan* SHEND *v.*[1]: see -NESS.] The condition of being 'shent'; disgrace, ruin.

α. *c* **1000** ÆLFRIC *Hom.* (Th.) II. 66 Ðone deofol þe ða synfullan..ȝelæt to ȝescyndnysse. Babilonia seo Chaldeisca burh, is ȝereht 'ȝescyndnys'. *c* **1000** *Ags. Ps.* (Spelm.) xxxiv. 30 Syn ȝescrydde mid ȝescendnysse [L. *confusione*]. *c* **1275** *Passion our Lord* 275 in *O.E. Misc.* 45 Muchele schendnesse hi duden vre dryhte. **1297** R. GLOUC. (Rolls) 7030 Astrangled he was riȝt þer & deide atte borde al stif wiþ ssendnesse ynou. *c* **1380** *Sir Ferumb.* 2175 He put hymseluen on a cas whar-for agat a schour, þat turnd him..to schennes && dolour. **1387** TREVISA *Higden* (Rolls) V. 245 Þis man was i-bore to schame and schendnes of nacions.

β. *c* **1300** *Beket* (Percy Soc.) 66 To bring al the land to schindisse and holi churche to spille. *c* **1300** *St. Margarete* 103 Chus weþer þu wold mid schindisse to deþe beon ibroȝt. *cc* **1305** *St. Kenelm* 363 in *E.E.P.* (1862) 57 Þis liþere quene deide siþþe in schindisse ynouȝ.

†**'shendship.** *Obs.* Forms: 4–5 s(c)hend-, s(c)hent-, (5 scend-); 4–5 s(c)hen-, sen- (4 scen, schin-); see also -SHIP. [ME. *schendschipe*, f. *schend*, pa. pple. of *schende* SHEND *v.*[1] + -SHIP.] Disgrace, ignominy; an instance of this. Also, something that is a cause of disgrace.

*a* **1300** *Cursor M.* 17470 Bot wat yll þar-wit quat þai wan Scencip and scam o mani man. *Ibid.* 18172 Wi quat ert þou þþat es sa wight Vr scenscep for to scau to dright? **1303** R. BRUNNE *Handl. Synne* 8250 Þat name Ys our shenshyp and oure shame. **13..** *Guy Warw.* (A.) 3294 And now he me wil sle wiþ schenschipe. **1340** HAMPOLE *Pr. Consc.* 7877 Bot now will I specialy shew yhow mare Of seven maners of blysses þare, And of seven schenschepes in helle alle-swa. *c* **1350** *Will. Palerne* 556 Þat were a schamly schenchip to schende me euer. *c* **1375** *Sc. Leg. Saints* l. (*Katerine*) 306 & at scho mycht sic defence ma þat it war senschepe till hir fa. *cc* **1386** CHAUCER *Pars. T.* 199 To muchel am I peyned for the thynges that I neuere deserued, and to muche defouled for shendshipe that man is worthy to haue. *c* **1425** *Eng. Conq. Irel.* xlv. 114 To-day he wold the wyrshype, tomorow he wold the reue to do shendshype [*c* **1440** shenshipp]. **1426** AUDELAY *Poems* 5 He wold here selle that he had boȝt, And schenschypus here that he hath soȝt. *c* **1450** *St. Cuthbert* (Surtees) 4486 For thing þat meke men oft amendes, God to schrewes to senschipe sends. **1470–85** MALORY *Arthur* XII. xiii. 609 God saue yow this day from senshyp and shame. **1493** *Dives & Pauper* (W. de W.) IV. i. 161/1 His childern sholde be shame & shenshyp to hym.

**b.** = SHAME *sb. rare*[−1].

**1382** WYCLIF *Lev.* xx. 11 He that slepith with his stepdam, and opneth the shenship [Vulg. *ignominiam*] of his fader, thurȝ deth dien thei bothe.

†**'shendshipful,** *a. Obs. rare.* [f. SHENDSHIP + -FUL.] Disgraceful, ignominious.

**1382** WYCLIF *2 Chron.* xxiv. 24 In to Joas also thei enhauntiden schenschipful domys.

Hence †**'shendshipfully** *adv.* [-LY[2].]

**1388** WYCLIF *Ps.* lxxxviii. 52 Whiche thin enemyes, Lord, diden schenschipfuli, for thei dispisiden the chaungyng of thi crist.

**shene**, *v. Obs. rare.* Forms: 1 scǽnan, 3 scanen, scenen, scænen; see also TO-SHENE *v.* [OE. *scǽnan*:—prehist. *skainjan.

Possibly due to an erroneous analysis of *tóscǽnan* (TO-SHENE *v.*):—**tus-kainjan* causative of **tus-kīnan* [MHG. *zer-, zekīnan*) to burst asunder.]

*trans.* To break.

*c* **1000** ÆLFRIC *Hom.* II. 260 þa comon ða cempan, .. and sona ðæra sceaðena sceancan tobræcon... Hi gemetton Crist middaneardе deadne, and his halȝan sceancan scænan ne dorston. *c* **1205** LAY. 5186 Bordes þer scænden. *Ibid.* 19554 Helmes þer scenden. *Ibid.* 26807 Sceldes scenen. *Ibid.* 28552 Sceldes gonnen scanen.

**shene**, obs. rare pa. pple. of SEE *v.*, SHOW *v.*

**shene**, var. SHEEN *a.*; obs. form of SHEEN *v.*

‖**sheng**[1] (ʃʌŋ). *Mus.* Also 8- cheng; 9 sang, sing. [Chinese *shēng*.] A Chinese wind instrument consisting of a set of reed pipes.

**1795** W. WINTERBOTHAM *Hist., Geogr., & Philos. View Chinese Empire* ix. 428 The ancient *cheng* differed in the number of their pipes; those used at present have only thirteen: this instrument appears to have some affinity with our organs. **1839** *Chinese Repository* VIII. 52 The *săng*.. is a collection of tubes varying in length so as to utter sounds at harmonic intervals from each other. **1845** *Encycl. Metropol.* XVI. 579/2 The *Sheng* or *Sing*; the lower half of a gourd, in which a row of pipes is fixed, with a curved and lateral one on which the performer blows. **1937** *Times Lit. Suppl.* 16 Jan. 41/3 The *sheng* is assigned by the notation to a certain level of the voice. **1961** J. HOWARTH in A. Baines *Musical Instruments through Ages* xiii. 321 In 1777,.. Père Amiot.. sent the present of a sheng from China to Paris. **1972** LIU JUNG-EN *Six Yüan Plays* 15 The *shêng*, consisting of thirteen pipes of different lengths forming a circle each with a finger hole and having a mouthpiece through which the musician blows and sucks. **1973** *Times* 11 June 14/2 The concertina was inspired by the Cheng (Chinese mouth organ). **1980** *Early Music* July 355/1 These, the sho of Japan and the sheng of China, are forms of free-reed mouth organ with a rigid wind chest held in the hands, the fingers remaining free to open and close the reeds in the cane pipes.

‖**sheng**[2] (ʃʌŋ). [Chinese *shēng*.] The principal male character in a Chinese opera. Also *attrib.*

**1886** *Jrnl. R. Asiatic Soc.* (*North-China Branch*) XX. 208 The characters in Chinese plays are arranged under five denominations... The hero is *shêng*. He wears a black beard, but his face is not concealed. **1937** ARLINGTON & ACTON *Famous Chinese Plays* p. xxiii, *Shêng* are divided into *Wên*, Civil, and *Wu*, Military. These are the leading actors. **1972** C. P. MACKERRAS *Rise of Peking Opera* i. 2 There were seven types of actors in the *nan-hsi*... Some of these terms can still be found.. in Peking Opera today. For example, the *sheng* and *tan* were—and still are—the principal male and female characters respectively. **1973** R. F. S. YANG in Yuan-li Wu *China* 74/1 Yen was the founder of the Yen school of the 'bearded *sheng*' voice.

**shengle, -yll**, obs. forms of SHINGLE *sb.*

**shenkbeer** (ˈʃɛnkbɪə(r)). *U.S.* [a. G. *schenkbier* draught beer, f. *schenken* to pour, fill (SHENCH *v.*) + *bier* BEER.] A very weak and insipid beer.

**1872** SCHELE DE VERE *Americanisms* 142 *Shenkbeer*, the *Schenkbier* of Germany, is so called because it has to be put on draught (*schenken*) as soon as it is made, for fear of turning sour if not immediately consumed.

**shenshep(e, -ip(e**, etc.: see SHENDSHIP.

†**shent**, *sb. Sc. Obs. rare.* In 4-5 schent. [var. of SHEND *sb.*] Disgrace.

*c* **1375** *Sc. Leg. Saints* I. (*Petrus*) 535 Sic schent and schame at hart had he. *c* **1470** *Gol. & Gaw.* 1077 The sege that schrenkis for na schame, the schent might hym schend.

†**shent**, *a. Obs. rare*⁻¹. [Of obscure origin.] Free, exempt.

*c* **1400** *Destr. Troy* 8119 þi worship is went & wastid for euer, Of shame & shenship shent bes þou neuer.

**shent** (ʃɛnt), *ppl. a.* Now *arch.* Also 5 schent. [pa. pple. of SHEND *v.*[1]] Disgraced, lost, ruined; stupefied.

*c* **1400** *Destr. Troy* 10348 And shamfully a shent mon he shope to the dethe. *c* **1440** *Promp. Parv.* 445/1 Schent, or blamyd, *culpatus, vituperatus*. Schent, ful lost, *confusus, destructus*. **1570** LEVINS *Manip.* 66/21 Shent, *perditus*. **1632** LITHGOW *Trav.* II. 44 Arcadia poore and shent. *a* **1850** ROSSETTI *Dante & Circle* I. (1874) 91 Till, starting up in wild bewilderment, I do become so shent That I go forth, lest folk misdoubt of it.

†**shent**, *v. Obs.* [Of obscure origin: cf. SHUNT *v.* and SHEND *v.*] *intr.* To hesitate.

*c* **1400** *Destr. Troy* 481 As maner is of maydons..: Shentyng for shame to shew furth þere ernd.

**shent**, obs. form of SHEND *v.*

**shenzi** (ˈʃɛnzɪ). [Swahili.] In East Africa, an uncivilized tribesman. In extended sense, a barbarian, a person outside the person's cultural group.

**1910** T. ROOSEVELT *Afr. Game Trails* x. 258 The 'shenzis'—wild natives called in Swahili.. 'wa-shenzi'. **1921** *Blackw. Mag.* Jan. 121/2 He, an askari of G company, ran away from a lot of miserable shouting shenzis! **1926** *Spectator* 3 July 10/2 Local *shenzis*.. had gathered round the gramophone. **1976** K. THACKERAY *Crownbird* vi. 111 The Chinese face was impassive... That he should be.. involved with this bunch of shenzis.. was very confusing.

**she-oak**. *Austral.* Forms: α. 8- she-oak, 9 sheoak; β. 9 shea-oak; γ. quasi-native name 9 sheac(k, shia(c)k, sheak. [See SHE 10 e; cf. *he-oak*, HE 8 b

There is no foundation for the allegation that the word is a corruption of a native Australian or Tasmanian name. Another assertion, that it is a corruption of the name of an American tree, is also baseless.]

**1. a.** A tree of the genus *Casuarina*.

α. **1792** G. THOMPSON *Slavery & Famine* (1794) 18 There are two kinds of oak, called the he and the she oak, but not to be compared with English oak. **1818** OXLEY *Jrnl. Two Exped. N.S. Wales* (1820) 292 That species of casuarina called the beef wood (or she oak) was also seen to-day for the first time. **1875** *Zoologist* Ser. II. X. 4619 Sandal wood, mulga, she oak, all are devoured with apparent relish. **1891** E. KINGLAKE *Australian at Home* 123 Its banks fringed with the dark sheoak and the bending willow.

β. **1842** [see γ]. **1902** 'BESSIE MARCHANT' (Mrs. J. A. Comfort) *Brave Little Cousin* xxiv. 187 Under the shelter of a great Shea oak.

γ. [**1835** J. ROSS *Hobart-town Almanack* 75 *Casuarina torulosa*? She-oak. *C. stricta*? He-oak. *C. tenuissima*? Marsh-oak. The name of the first of these is said to be a corruption of Sheac, the name of an American tree, producing the beef wood, like our She-oak. **1842** *Western Australia* v. 80 The Shea-oak (a corruption of sheak, the native name for this, or a similar tree, in Van Diemen's Land) is used chiefly for shingles.] **1852** S. SIDNEY *Three Colonies of Australia* xxiv. 347 The lowlands.. present a dull scene, sprinkled with funereal shiak or 'she-oak trees'. **1857** W. HOWITT *Tallangetta* I. i. 24 Trees of a peculiar character—the Casuarinas or Shiacks. **1862** G. T. LLOYD *33 Yrs. Tasmania* iii. 32 The 'Sheac' (perverted into she oak) or beef-wood tree, is very abundant. **1891** [see b].

**b.** *attrib.*

**1852** She-oak tree [see above]. **1874** WALCH *Adamanta* I. ii. 16 She-oak Shavings. *a* **1880** D. S. STEWART in Fison & Howitt *Kamilaroi* 168 Sheoak trees. **1891** F. ADAMS *John Webb's End* 223 A few stunted sheak trees.

**2. a.** Slang name for beer.

**1873** J. C. F. JOHNSON *Christmas on Carringa* 1 Able to put away at a sitting a larger quantity of colonial 'sheoak' than any man of his inches. **1888** *Cassell's Picturesque Australia* (1890) III. 83 Their drivers had completed their regulation half-score of 'long-sleevers' of 'she-oak'. **1893** J. A. BARRY *Steve Brown's Bunyip* 282 Hastily finishing his pint of 'sheoak'.

**b.** *attrib.* and *Comb.*, as *she-oak beer*; **she-oak net**, a safety net for sailors boarding ship (see quot. 1898).

**1927** F. H. SHAW *Knocking Around* 106 She-oak beer, the common Australian beverage, was a potent tipple. **1898** MORRIS *Austral Eng.* 415/1 *She-oak nets*, nets placed on each side of a gangway from a ship to the pier, to prevent sailors who have been indulging in *she-oak* (beer) falling into the water. **1925** R. CLEMENTS *Gipsy of Horn* 111 Old Australian traders used to spread a net under the gang-way, called therefrom the sheoke net, whose office it was to save mariners who 'missed stays' when coming aboard from falling into the dock. **1938** W. E. DEXTER *Rope Yarns* 234 A dog.. followed every drunken sailor—never by any chance a sober one—down the pier to his ship. If he managed to get on board safely the dog returned, but if he fell into the she-oak net it would howl until the man was rescued.

**sheogue** (ˈʃiog). Also shee-og. [ad. Ir. *siόg* fairy.] In Ireland: a fairy.

**1852** W. WILDE *Irish Pop. Superstitions* 14 The sheeogue [*sic*] is the true fairy. *Ibid.* 52 The mystic pipers of the sheogues.. are said.. to favour mortals with their melodies. **1892** W. B. YEATS *Countess Kathleen* 26 You poured out wine as the wood sheogues do When they'd entice a soul out of the world. *Ibid.* 50 Brother, where wander all these dwarfish folk, Hostile to men, the sheogues of the fields? **1893** —— *Celtic Twilight* 117 He would not hear of ghosts or sheogues. **1959** D. A. MAC MANUS *Middle Kingdom* i. 20 There are the stories of human encounters with the small spirits, the 'wee folk' of Ulster, the 'little people' of the South, the 'Shee-og' of Gaeldom.

‖**Sheol** (ˈʃiːəʊl, ˈʃiːəl). [Heb. *sheʾōl*.] The underworld; the abode of the dead or departed spirits, conceived by the Hebrews as a subterranean region clothed in thick darkness, return from which is impossible. (Very common in the Revised Version of the O.T., where in the A.V. it was translated 'hell', 'grave', or 'pit'.)

¶In recent slang sometimes jocularly substituted for 'hell'.

**1599** *Broughton's Let.* xiii. 45 *Sheol*, at the best, either is not Heauen,.. or else there is a third place besides Heauen and Hell called *Sheol* for the Saints to rest in. **1642** *Of Article of Creed 'Christ descended to Hades'* 2 Christs soule did *descendere ad Inferos*, or goe to Sheol or Hades. **1822** R. SCOTT *Script. Claims of Devil* 499 We cannot.. interpret the term Sheol, as referring to a Hell of eternal torments. **1873** F. C. COOK in *Speaker's Comm.* IV. 63/1 Nor is the state of the just in Sheol ever represented as one of suffering. **1889** [see RAH *int.* and *sb.*]. **1890** J. FYFE (*title*) The Hereafter: Sheol, Hades, and Hell. **1903** A. M. BINSTEAD *Pitcher in Paradise* v. 117 Briefly, Dickie, I have been out all night and there's sheol to pay. **1920** B. CRONIN *Timber Wolves* vii. 116 Them big bugs are the meanest things this side sheol.

*attrib.* **1910** J. ORR in *Expositor* Nov. 398 Ghostly survival in some Sheol-like condition of semi-existence.

**shep** (ʃɛp). *Obs.* exc. *dial.* Also 4-5 schep, chep. [Short for SHEPHERD.

It is commonly supposed that this word occurs in the second line of *Piers Plowman*, 'I shope me into shroudes as I a *shep* were'. The author's meaning, however, seems to be that the assumption of a hermit's dress by one who was 'unholy of works' was a disguising of himself 'in sheep's clothing'. The sense 'shepherd' seems to be irrelevant; moreover, even if it be intended here, the word with the long vowel indicated by the MS. readings cannot well be of identical formation with the *shep* of the examples below.]

A shepherd.

*c* **1381** *Slaughter Abp. Sudbury* in *Pol. Poems* (Rolls) I. 230 Jak Chep [*v.r.* Schep], Tronche, Jon Wrau, Thom Myllere .. Isti ductores in plebe fuere priores. **14..** LYDG. *Chorl & Bird* xlviii. in Ashmole *Theatr. Chem. Brit.* (1652) 223 A Chepys Croke to the ys better than a Launce. **1877** *N.W. Linc. Gloss.*, *Shep*, a shepherd. 'Cook was shep to Mr. Sorsby then, but he's left now'. **1899** H. D. RAWNSLEY *Life & Nat. Engl. Lakes* 171 Waiting for the late arrival of this or that 'shep', with his contribution of strayed sheep from the fold.

**shep**, obs. form of SHEEP, SHIP.

**shepard(e**, obs. forms of SHEPHERD.

**shepe**, obs. f. SHEEP, SHIP; var. SHIPE *sb. Obs.*

**shepen(e**, obs. forms of SHIPPON.

**shepherd** (ˈʃɛpəd), *sb.* Forms: α. 1 scéaphirde, scéap-, scéphyrde, 2-3 (*Ormin*) shephirde, 3 seopheorde, 4 scheepeherde, shepehurde, 4-5 sheepherde, scheephirde, 5 shepehirde, (sheepperde), 5-6 schepehirde, 6 scheephird, shepeheard, *Sc.* scheipherde, -hird, sheephirde, 7 sheep(e)heard, sheepherd, (8 sheaperd). β. 4-5 schipherd, 5 schipherde, 6 schiphird(e, shiphearde; 4 schipard(e, 5 schippart, 7 shippard. γ. 3-6 schepherde, 4 shephurde, 4-6 shepherde, 5 s(c)hepherde, schepphirde, schephord, chepherd, 6 schephird(e, 7 sheppherd; 3 ssepurde, 3-5 scheperd, 4-5 scheperde, -ard(e, 4-6 shep(p)arde, sheperde, 5 sheppard, 5-7 sheperd, 6 shepperd, 6-8 shepard; 5 schepheerde, 6 schepheird, 6-7 shepheard(e, 7 shepheard; 5 schepeerde; 6- shepherd. [OE. *scéaphirde*: see SHEEP and HERD *sb.*[2] Cf. MLG., MDu. *schâphirde* (mod.Du. has *schaapherder*), MHG. *schâfhirte*, mod.G. dial. *schafhirt*.

The shortened vowel of the first syllable is normal in compounds.]

**1. a.** A man who guards, tends, and herds a flock of sheep (grazing at large); usually one so employed for hire; or one of a pastoral people who herds (his own) sheep, goats, etc.

*a* **1023** WULFSTAN *Hom.* lv. (1883) 288 Swa swa sceaphyrde tosceat sceap fram gatum. *c* **1200** ORMIN 3587 Crist iss all se Daviþþ wass Shephirde, & king, & kemmpe. *c* **1275** *Passion our Lord* 133 in *O.E. Misc.* 41 Beo þe seopheorde aquold and of lyue bireued þenne scule sone his seop alle beon todreued. **1297** R. GLOUC. (Rolls) 7210 Ssepurdes hii beþ luþere vor hii ne witeþ noȝt Her ssep fram þe wolues. **1315** SHOREHAM *5 Joys of Virg.* 135 Out com an aungel wyþ great leem In-to þe feld of bedleem, Amonges þe schepherden, Te telle þat cryst was y-bore. *c* **1450** *Mirk's Festial* 22 Þay.. speken godely and louyngly to pore schephordes þat kepten hor schepe yn þe contre by. **1459** *Inventory* in *Paston Lett.* I. 479 Inprimis, j. clothe of arras, clyped the Schipherds clothe. *Ibid.* 482 Item, j. clothe of arras, of the Schipherds. **1489** CAXTON *Faytes of A.* I. i. 5 The good sheppard exposeth his lyf for his sheep. **1513** DOUGLAS *Æneis* VIII. Prol. 46 Sum schippart slayis the lordis sheip, and sais he is a sant. **1540-1** ELYOT *Image Gov.* 30 Rude sheepeheardes olde and decrepite. **1599** DALLAM in *Early Voy. Levant* (Hakl. Soc.) 87 A foreste-like Cuntrie, wheare we saw nether towne nor villidge, but somtime a shipheardes Hoote. **1606** *Sir G. Goosecappe* v. i. in Bullen *Old Pl.* (1884) III. 77 If the sunne of thy beauty doe not white me like a shippards holland, I am a Iewe to my Creator. **1657** *Penit. Conf.* ix. 283 The next denomination is of a sheepherd and flock. **1815** ELPHINSTONE *Acc. Caubul* (1842) II. 97 The greater part of the tribe is composed of shepherds. **1891** *Spectator* 28 Feb., Every one hastened to turn shepherd, and cultivate wool and mutton.

**b.** Applied to the rustic personages of pastoral poetry. Hence, in poetry more or less adopting the pastoral convention, formerly often used to designate the writer and his friends or fellow-poets.

**1591** SPENSER *Daphn.* 526 And ye faire Damsels, Shepheards dere delights, That with your loues do their rude hearts possesse. *a* **1599** ? RALEIGH in *Pass. Pilgr.* xix. *Love's Answ.*, If that the World and Loue were young, And truth in euery shepheards toung. **1600** SHAKS. *A.Y.L.* III. v. 82 Dead Shepheard, now I find thy saw of might. *a* **1763** SHENSTONE *Elegies* xviii. 2 Near Avon's bank,.. A tuneful shepherd [*note*, Mr. Somerville] charm'd the list'ning wave.

†**c.** = SHEPHERDESS. *Obs. rare.*

**1588** GREENE *Pandosto* Wks. (Grosart) IV. 274 The maide with the garland on her heade was Fawnia, the faire shepheard.

**d.** A representation (in china, etc.) of a youthful shepherd; cf. SHEPHERDESS.

**1866** *Cornh. Mag.* Sept. 358 Like a Dresden shepherd and shepherdess.

**e.** Fr. Hist. ***the Shepherds*** [= Fr. *les Pastoureaux*]: the name applied to those who took part in the peasant insurrections of 1251 ff. and 1320.

**1759** *Universal Hist., Mod.* XIII. 308 The irruption of a band of enthusiastick shepherds, who pretended to work miracles. [*note*] The origin of these shepherds is variously related. **1845** *Encycl. Metrop.* XI. 710/1 *marg.*, [1251] The Crusade of Shepherds. **1874** G. W. COX *Crusades* xv. 215 The outbreak of the Pastoureaux, or Shepherds (so called from their supposed simplicity),.. took place.. while Louis IX. was a captive in Egypt.

**2.** *fig.* **a.** A spiritual guardian or pastor of a 'flock'; = PASTOR *sb.* 2.

*a* **1300** *Cursor M.* 28278 Quare i was scheperd hade sauls to kepe To reckelesly i geit my schepe. **1382** WYCLIF *Ephes.* iv. 11 He ȝaf summe sotheli apostlis,..othere forsoth schepherdis [so Tindale and Coverdale; 1611 pastors] and techeris. *a* **1536** *Songs, Carols*, etc. (1907) 81 The cheff sheperd in this world þat ys, Shuld be the pope. **1588** *Marprel. Epist.* (Arb.) 7 Appointed to be pastors and shepheards to feed others. **1693** PRIOR *To Dr. Sherlock* 68 'Midst thy own Flock, great Shepherd, be receiv'd. **1812** CARY *Dante, Parad.* XXI. 121 Modern Shepherds need Those who on either hand may prop and lead them.

¶ In comic fiction, represented as an official title of the 'pastor' or 'minister' of a sect.

**1837** DICKENS *Pickw.* xxii, 'The kiss of peace', says the shepherd; and then he kissed the women all round. **1889** GRETTON *Memory's Harkback* 52 Then the shepherd read, and supposed that he was explaining a portion of Scripture.

**b.** In Biblical use, applied to God in relation to Israel or the Church; also to Christ (esp. with reference to John x. 12).

**1382** WYCLIF *John* x. 12, I am a good schepherde; a good schepherde ȝyueth his soule, that is, his lyf, for his scheep. **1535** COVERDALE *Ps.* lxxix. 1 Heare o thou shepherde of Israel, thou y[t] ledest Iacob like a flocke of shepe. **1655** EVELYN *Let. to Jer. Taylor* 18 Mar., The shepheards are smitten, and the sheepe must of necessity be scattered, unless the greate Shepheard of Soules oppose. **1738** WESLEY *Ps.* LXXX. i. Shepherd of Souls, the Great, the Good. **1820** SCOTT *Monast.* xxxvii, I have not given to the wolf any of the stray lambs whom the Great Shepherd of souls had intrusted to my charge.

**c.** Applied to temporal rulers. Cf. Gr. ποιμὴν λαῶν (Homer) 'shepherd of the peoples', and similar uses in the Old Testament.

**1577** B. GOOGE *Heresbach's Husb.* III. (1586) 113 b, Poets ..oftentimes call kings and princes by the names of shepheardes, and feeders of the people. Yea the Lorde of the whole worlde doth call himselfe a shepehearde. **1780** J. BROWN *Lett. Toleration* i. (1803) 23 Political shepherds ought never to overdrive their flocks. **1837** CARLYLE *Fr. Rev.* I. I. i, The shepherd of the people has..been put to bed in his own Château of Versailles.

**3.** (With initial capital.) = SHEPHERD KING I.

**1813** PRITCHARD *Phys. Hist. Man* viii. §2. 428 Manetho reckons eighteen years between Sethosis and the exit of the Shepherds from Egypt. The dynasty of Shepherds consists of six monarchs. **1860** R. S. POOLE in *W. Smith's Dict. Bible* I. 509/2 (*Egypt*) There can be no question that he [Pharaoh of Joseph's time] was, if the dates be correct, a Shepherd of the XVth dynasty.

**4.** *Austral.* A miner who holds a claim but does not work it.

**1855** R. CARBONI *Eureka Stockade* 9 The faithful shepherds..were sure to snore in peace a foot and a half under ground from the surface and six score feet from 'bang on the gutter'. **1864** J. ROGERS *New Rush* II. 30 Shame, vagrant shepherds! cast your coat of sloth; other miners.. have ris'n to rule the State, and so may you. **188.** *Argus* in E. E. Morris *Austral Eng.* s.v., Dr. Quick retorted with a declaration that the Grand Junction Company were all 'shepherds', and that 'shepherds' are the worse of the two classes.

† **5.** The shepherd-spider. *Obs. rare.*

**1608** TOPSELL *Serpents* 271 This kind of Spyder.. delighting in the company of Sheepe: and for this cause I take it, that we Englishmen do call her a Sheapheard. **1658** ROWLAND tr. *Moufet's Theat. Ins.* 944 These are called in English *Shepherds*, in Latine *Opiliones*, because they are most often seen where sheep use to feed. **1686** PLOT *Staffordsh.* 238 Those long-legged ones [spiders] we call Shepherds, which never spin any thred.

**6.** = *German shepherd* (*dog*) s.v. GERMAN *a.*[2] and *sb.*[2] 4 a.

**1938** J. STEINBECK *Long Valley* 13 The rangy dog darted from between the wheels and ran ahead. Instantly the two ranch shepherds flew out at him. **1978** R. LUDLUM *Holcroft Covenant* ix. 104 Suddenly, the menacing faces of enormous long-haired black shepherds lunged at the windows on both sides of the car.

**7.** *attrib.* and *Comb.* **a.** Simple attrib., as (appositive) ***shepherd-band, -boy, folk, -girl, -poet***, etc.: (pertaining to a shepherd or shepherds) ***shepherd-care, haunt, life, staff***, etc.

**1902** L. HOUSMAN *Bethlehem* 53 Back to their folds have gone the *shepherd-band. **1802** WORDSW. *To Young Lady* 7 There, healthy as a *shepherd boy. **1819** SCOTT *Ivanhoe* xxxi, As a shepherd boy flourishes his light crook. **1845** G. MURRAY *Islaford* 17 How lamb-like in his *shepherd-care he was. **1900** H. SUTCLIFFE *Shameless Wayne* xix. (1905) 241 Loose-limbed *shepherd folk. **1757** COLLINS *Or. Eclogues* I. 56 Here make thy court amidst our rural scene, And *shepherd-girls shall own thee for their queen. **1600** FAIRFAX *Tasso* VII. v, Swaines and *shepherd groomes. **1807** WORDSW. *White Doe* I. 11 What sprinklings of blithe company! Of lasses and of shepherd grooms. **1860** PUSEY *Min. Proph.* 154 The Prophet's first thought..was towards his own *shepherd-haunts. **1508** KENNEDIE *Flyting w. Dunbar* 254 Put I nocht sylence to the, *schiphird knaif. **1833** TENNYSON *May Queen* I. vii, The *shepherd lads on every side 'ill come from far away. **1591** SPENSER *Daphn.* 316 But now ye *Shepheard lasses, who shall lead Your wandring troupes, or sing your virelayes? **1860** PUSEY *Min. Proph.* 150 The *shepherd-life of Amos. **1807** WORDSW. *Song at Feast of Brougham Castle* 107 The *Shepherd-lord was honoured more and more. **1825** J. WILSON *Poems* II. 310 Quietly slumber *shepherd-men In the silence of some inland glen. **1633** P. FLETCHER *Purple Isl.* XI. xliii, In vain the keeper calls his *shepherd peers. **1835** WORDSW. *Extemp. Effus. Death J. Hogg* 12 And death upon the braes of Yarrow Has closed the *Shepherd-poet's eyes. *a* **1352** MINOT *Poems* (ed. Hall) ix. 20 None letes him þe way to wende whore he will: Bot with *schipherd staues fand he his fill. **14..** *Voc.* in Wr.-Wülcker 564/9 *Angivs*, a shepardstaf. **1867** HAWKER *Pr. Wks.* (1893) 110 A damsel in the bloom of youth stood leaning on her shepherd-staff. **1590** SPENSER *F.Q.* III. vi. 15 The gentle *shepheard swaynes. **1775** MICKLE *Camoens' Lusiad* IV. 163 To the Massylian *shepherd-tents she flies. **1798** SOTHEBY tr. *Wieland's Oberon* (1826) I. 43 Our knight oppress Begs from some *shepherd-wife her simple fare.

**b.** *Egypt. Hist.* [sense 3], as ***Shepherd-invasion, -period, -prince***, etc.; see also SHEPHERD KING.

**1854** W. OSBURN *Mon. Hist. Egypt* II. v. 208 The Shepherd invasion. *Ibid.* 209 When Amosis first attacked the Shepherd kingdom. **1860** R. S. POOLE in *W. Smith's Dict. Bible* I. 509/1 (*Egypt*) The period of Egyptian history to which the Shepherd-invasion should be assigned is a point of dispute. **1863** *Ibid.* III. s.v. *Zoan*, Remains of the Shepherd-period. **1877** J. E. CARPENTER *Tiele's Hist. Relig.* 53 The Arab Shepherd-Princes (the Hyksos).

**c.** Similative, as ***shepherd-hearted***; also ***shepherd-like*** adj. and adv.

**1853** T. T. LYNCH *Self-Improv.* ii. 31 A *shepherd-hearted and royal youth like David. **1591** SPENSER *Ruins of Rome* 251 Peters successor..Who, *shepheardlike,..doth shew, that all things turne to their first being. **1851** MRS. BROWNING *Casa Guidi Wind.* II. 520 Showing now defiled His hireling hands, a better help's achieved Than if they blessed us shepherd-like and mild.

**d.** Special comb.: **shepherd-bird** = PASTOR *sb.* 4; **shepherd-check** = *shepherd's check*; **shepherd-dog** = *shepherd's dog* (see 8 b); † **shepherd fly** (see quot.); **shepherd land**, *Sc.* (see quot.); **shepherd plaid** = *shepherd's plaid* (see 8 c); † **shepherd silver**, ? a tax paid for the keeping of shepherds; **shepherd spider**, the harvest-spider (also *shepherd's*: see 8 b); **shepherd tartan** = *shepherd's tartan.*

**1869** T. R. JONES *Cassell's Bk. of Birds* I. 227 The Rose Starling, or *Shepherd-bird (*Pastor roseus*). **1862** *Catal. Internat. Exhib., Brit.* II. No. 3980, Cloakings, coatings, livery Valencias, *shepherd checks, trouserings, &c. *c* **1425** *Voc.* in Wr.-Wülcker 699/17 *Hic aggregarius*, a *scheperd dog. **1846** E. J. LEWIS *Youatt's Dog* iii. (1858) 105 The descendants of the Spanish shepherd dog, so highly prized in protecting the Merino flocks from the wolves. **1664** POWER *Exp. Philos.* I. 6 The *Shepherd-flye or Spinster-flye, which Muffet calls *Opilionum Muscam*. **1892** C. PATRICK *Mediæval Scot.* ii. 20 '*Shepherd land' seems to have been generally hill pasturage, to which the sheep were sent at suitable seasons. **1940** *Shepherd plaid [see KILLER 7]. **1970** *Globe & Mail* (Toronto) 25 Sept. 3/1 (Advt.), New multiple colored striped worsteds, shepherd plaids and a host of plains are now ready for your inspection. **1665** HOOKE *Microgr.* 198 The Carter, *Shepherd Spider, or long-legg'd spider. **1854** A. ADAMS, etc. *Man. Nat. Hist.* 278 Shepherd-Spiders (*Phalangidæ*). *a* **1377** *Abingdon Rolls* (Camden) 40 Item pro hidagio xijd. Item pro *schepersulfer ijd. q[a]. **1865** D. C. BOYD in Blaikie *Livingstone* xviii. (1881) 362 He wore..*shepherd-tartan trousers.

**8.** Combinations with *shepherd's* (sometimes varying with combs. of *shepherd*, see 7). **a.** Obvious combs. denoting a thing such as is used by or is characteristic of shepherds, as ***shepherd's crook, horn, life, staff***, etc.

*c* **1440** *Promp. Parv.* 445/1 Schepeerdys croke, *pedum. Ibid.*, Scheperdys logge, or cory, *magalis, mapale.* **1530** PALSGR. 266/2 Schepherdes bagge, *pannetiere. Ibid.* Schepherdes staffe, *hovlette.* **1538** ELYOT *Dict.*, *Bardocucullum*, a thrummed hatte, or a shepardes cloke. **1600** SHAKS. *A.Y.L.* III. ii. 11 And how like you this shepherds life M[r] Touchstone? **1688** *Lond. Gaz.* No. 2383/4 Lost... Three Mares, one black,..a Shepherds-hook on the near Hip behind. **1797** MRS. RADCLIFFE *Italian* xiii, Is not that a shepherd's horn sounding at a distance?

**b.** Special comb.: **shepherd's calendar**, a calendar containing weather predictions and seasonable instructions for the use of shepherds (app. proverbially referred to as an unreliable source of information); hence adopted as the title of certain pastoral poems; see also 8 d; **shepherd's chess**, a game, perh. nine-men's morris; **shepherd's club**, two varieties of moth (see quot.); **shepherd's companion** (see quots.); **shepherd's crook arm**, a chair-arm shaped somewhat like a shepherd's crook; **shepherd's crown** = SHEPHERD'S PURSE 2; **shepherd's dog**, a large variety of dog employed by shepherds to control and protect flocks of sheep (cf. *sheep-dog*); † **shepherd's fly** = *shepherd-fly* (7 d); † **shepherd's harp** (see quot.); † **shepherd's hour**, the lover's opportunity (tr. F. *l'heure du berger*); **shepherd's knot** (see quot.); **shepherd's lamp** *dial.*, the evening star; † **shepherd's mastie** = *shepherd's dog*; **shepherd's pie**, a pie consisting of chopped meat and potatoes, covered with a crust of mashed potatoes browned; **shepherd's pipe** (see quot. 1881); † **shepherd's spider** = *shepherd-spider* (7 d).

**1506** *Kal. Shepherdes* (Sommer) 8 These be the contentis of this present Boke of the *Shepeherdes kalender. **1565** JEWEL *Repl. Harding* XVI. vi. 552 His Reader woulde also longe to know..in what Chronicle..thei were recorded. Otherwise he wil suspecte, M. Hardinge founde it in the Shepeheardes Calendare. **1579** SPENSER (*title*) The Shepheardes Calender. **1869** BLACKMORE *Lorna D.* xxxvii, They were..playing at push-pin, or *shepherd's chess, or basset; or some trivial game of that sort. **1832** J. RENNIE *Butterfl. & Moths* 90 The *Shepherd's Club (*Cucullia Thapsiphaga*..) appears in June. *Ibid.* 100 The Shepherd's Club (*Euclidia glyphica*). **1844** LEICHHARDT *Jrnl.* iii. (1847) 80 We also observed..the *shepherd's companion, or fan-tailed fly-catcher (Rhipidura). **1890** *Hardwicke's Sci. Gossip* XXVI. 11/1 The Shepherd's Companion is a curious little bird, which much resembles a wagtail in its habits. **1960** H. HAYWARD *Antique Coll.* 256/2 **Shepherd's crook arm*, chair or settee arm of elegantly curving shape, the end in the form of a shepherd's crook, fashionable during the first three decades of the 18th cent. **1973** *Country Life* 30 Aug. (Suppl.) 74/2 Walnut Queen Anne armchair..has a spoon-back, shepherds' crook arms and graceful cabriole legs. **1893** *Wilts. Gloss.*, *Shepherds'-crown, fossil Echini [see also SHEPHERD'S PURSE 2]. *c* **1440** *Promp. Parv.* 445/1 *Scheperdys dogge, *gregarius.* **1840** BLAINE *Encycl. Rural Sports* § 1415 The shepherd's dog. **1688** HOLME *Armoury* II. ix. 190/2 *Shepherds fly. *Ibid.* III. xvi. (Roxb.) 76/2 An Instrument of Musick, termed a *shepards harpe; it is no other then a Board cut Bevile on both sides, with wyer or bowell strings fastned there on with pins and pegs. **1690** DRYDEN *Amphitryon* IV. *Pastoral Dial.*, Fair Iris and her swain Were in a shady Bow'r, Where Thyrsis long in vain Had sought the *shepherd's hour. **1844** H. STEPHENS *Bk. Farm* II. 33 These ropes are wound round the stakes [of a net enclosing sheep] by a peculiar sort of knot called the '*shepherd's knot'. **1827** CLARE *Sheph. Cal.* 111 The *Shepherd's Lamp, which even children know. **1577** B. GOOGE *Heresbach's Husb.* III. 154 b, *marg.*, The *shepheardes Mastie. **1877** E. S. DALLAS *Kettner's Bk. of Table* 256 In Scotland they produce..such a stew, cover it over with a crust, and call it *shepherd's pie... The shepherd's pie of Scotland is..too farinaceous—potatoes within and paste without. **1896** *Daily News* 30 Nov. 8/5 Shepherd's pie. **1969** R. WOLLHEIM *Family Romance* 228 What I couldn't face was ordering shepherd's pie. **1977** B. PYM *Quartet in Autumn* xviii. 164 Put a shepherd's pie in the oven. *c* **1440** *Promp. Parv.* 445/1 *Scheperdys pype, *barbita.* **1881** W. H. STONE in Grove *Dict. Mus.* III. 486 Shepherd's Pipe, a name given to the pastoral oboe or musette. **1688** HOLME *Armoury* II. x. 215/2 The long legged Spider of the Garden, or Field,..is called the *Shephards-Spider, because they are generally in the grounds where sheepe pasture.

**c.** In certain names of textile fabrics: **shepherd's check, plaid, tartan**, a woollen cloth with a black-and-white check pattern; † **shepherd's cloth**, † **shepherd's velvet** = FEARNOUGHT; † **shepherd's grey**, grey cloth worn by shepherds.

*c* **1640** A. TOWNSHEND *Poems & Masks* (1912) 27 And cast thy purple roabes away, To take a scripp and sheapherds grey. **1791** E. NAIRNE *Poems* 76 A bran new coat Of shepherd's velvet. **1794** *Sporting Mag.* III. 193 The wadding..is made of the cloth called fear-naught or shepherd's cloth. **1834** DICKENS *Sk. Boz, Boarding Ho.* ii, He wore shepherd's-plaid inexpressibles. **1885** 'MRS. ALEXANDER' *Valerie's Fate* i, A large soft shawl of shepherd's plaid. **1896** 'L. KEITH' *Indian Uncle* xvi. 253 Let himself be instantly 'happet' in the sheriff's shepherd-check plaid. **1897** *Westm. Gaz.* 25 Feb. 4/2 Shepherd's check tartan. *Ibid.*, These shepherd's check gowns.

**d.** In the names of plants, chiefly *dial.*: † **shepherd's bag** = SHEPHERD'S PURSE I; **shepherd's beard** = *sheep's beard* s.v. SHEEP *sb.* 9; **shepherd's bedstraw**, *Asperula cynanchica* (Britten & Holland 1886); † **shepherd's bodkin** (see quot.); **shepherd's calendar**, the scarlet pimpernel; **shepherd's clock**, (*a*) = prec.; (*b*) the goatsbeard, *Tragopogon pratensis* (B. & H.); **shepherd's club**, the common mullein, *Verbascum Thapsus*; **shepherd's comb**, *Scandix Pecten* (B. & H.); **shepherd's cress**, the dwarf cruciferous plant, *Teesdalia nudicaulis*; **shepherd's delight, dial, glass**, the scarlet pimpernel, *Anagallis arvensis*; **shepherd's gourd**, the common mullein; **shepherd's hour-glass**, the yellow pimpernel, *Lysimachia nemorum*; **shepherd's joy** (see quot.); **shepherd's knot** = TORMENTIL; **shepherd's myrtle**, *Ruscus aculeatus*; **shepherd's needle**, † (*a*) *Geranium*, (*b*) *Scandix Pecten*; **shepherd's pedler, pouch** = SHEPHERD'S PURSE I; **shepherd's rod**, *Dipsacus pilosus*; **shepherd's root** = TORMENTIL (B. & H.); **shepherd's rose**, ? some species of rose growing in hedges; **shepherd's scrip** = SHEPHERD'S PURSE I; **shepherd's staff**, (*a*) = *shepherd's rod*; (*b*) the common mullein; **shepherd's sun-dial** = *shepherd's dial* above; **shepherd's thyme**, (*a*) the wild thyme, *Thymus Serpyllum*; (*b*) the chalk milkwort; **shepherd's warning, watch**, the scarlet pimpernel (B. & H.); **shepherd's weatherglass**, (*a*) the scarlet pimpernel; (*b*) *Stellaria Holostea* (B. & H.).

**1548** TURNER *Names of Herbs* (E.D.S.) 83 Bursa pastoris is also called in englishe of many Bursa pastoris and of other *Shepherdes bag or Shepherdes purse. **1840** PAXTON *Bot. Dict.*, *Shepherd's Beard, see *Arnopogon.* **1706** PHILLIPS (ed. Kersey), **Shepherds-Bodkin*, a sort of Herb. **1832** MRS. BRAY *Tamar & Tavy* xviii. (1836) I. 318 We have..the *shepherd's calendar, and the one o'clock, the very dial of poetry. **1878** SUSAN PHILLIPS *On Seaboard* 86 We..Read the '*shepherd's clock'. **1790** ALEX. WILSON *Morning* Poet. Wks. (? 1846) 3 *Shepherds clubs hang nodding o'er the steep. *Ibid. Monkey & Bee* 41 O'ertopt with stately shepherds clubs. *c* **1710** PETIVER *Cat. Ray's Eng. Herbal* Tab. 50 *Shepherd's-cress. **1863** *Sowerby's Eng. Bot.* (ed. 3) I. 209 *Teesdalia nudicaulis*..Shepherd's Cress. **1865** *Cornh. Mag.* July 34 The scarlet pimpernel, from its susceptibility to the changes of the weather, is his [the peasant's] '*shepherd's dial'. **1886** BRITTEN & HOLLAND *Dict. Plant-n.*, *Shepherd's glass. *Anagallis arvensis.* **1896** *Garden Work* 4 Mar. 112/1 A young man..called the plant Verbascum Thapsus '*Shepherd's Gourd'. **1909** *Essex Rev.* XVIII. 77

The *Shepherd's Hour-glass. **1884** W. MILLER *Plant-n.* 124/2 *Shepherd's-joy, Australian. The genus *Geitonoplesium*. *Ibid.* 125/1 *Shepherd's-knot. *Tormentilla officinalis*. *c* **1840** W. A. BROMFIELD *Flora Vectensis* (1856) 508 *Shepherd's Myrtle. **1562** BULLEIN *Bulwarke, Bk. Simples* (1579) 42 b, What is the vertue of *Geranium*, called *Sheepherdes needell? **1597** GERARDE *Herbal* II. cccc. 884 *Pecten Veneris, siue Scandix*. Shepheards Needle, or Venus combe. **1805** R. W. DICKSON *Pract. Agric.* I. 564 The *scandix pecten veneris* of botanists, and what is often known to agriculturs by the names of Shepherd's needle, Beggar's needle, &c. **1811** T. DAVIS *Agric. Wilts* 267 *Crowpeck*, Shepherd's purse, or *shepherd's pedler. **1568** TURNER *Herbal* III. 14 Bursa pastoris is called in some places of England *shepherdes pouche. **1633** T. JOHNSON *Gerarde's Herbal* II. 1168 *Dipsacus minor, sive Virga pastoris*. *Shepheards-rod. **1735** KEOGH *Bot. Univ. Hibern.* 122 Wild Teasel, great Shepherds Rod, venus Bason, or carde Thistle. **1796** WITHERING *Brit. Plants* (ed. 3) II. 182 Shepherd's Rod. Shepherd's Staff. Small Teasel. **1817–8** COBBETT *Resid. Amer.* (1822) 43 No *shepherd's rose, no honey-suckle, none of that endless variety of beauties that decorate the hedges and the meadows in England. **1578** *Shepherds scrip [see SHEPHERD'S PURSE 1]. **1760** J. LEE *Introd. Bot.* App. 327 *Shepherd's Staff, *Dipsacus*. **1882** *Trans. Cumb. Assoc. Lit. & Sci.* VII. 142 *Verbascum thapsus*: ..the 'Shepherd's Staff' of the rustic population. **1823** MOOR *Suffolk Words*, *Shepherd's Sun-dial. **1857** MISS PRATT *Flower. Pl.* IV. 168 *Thymus Serpyllum*..*Shepherd's Thyme. **1878** HARDY *Ret. Native* VI. ii. (1890) 395 On the green turf and shepherd's-thyme. **1893** *Wilts. Gloss.*, Shepherds'-Thyme, *Polygala calcarea*,..chalk Milkwort. **1827** CLARE *Sheph. Cal.* 47 Pimpernel, dreading nights and showers, Oft call'd 'the *Shepherd's Weather-glass'. **1872** CHR. ROSSETTI *Sing Song* 86 Scarlet shepherd's-weatherglass Spreads wide open at her feet.

Hence (*nonce-wds.*) **'shepherddom**, the state of shepherds; **'shepherdhood** (in quot.), the personality of a shepherd.

**1905** *Edin. Rev.* Apr. 319 The attributes of shepherddom, milk-jar, crook, pipes [etc.]. **1596** W. SMITH *Chloris* (1877) 30 But that it pleased thy graue shepherdhood The Patron of my maiden verse to bee.

**shepherd** ('ʃɛpəd), *v.* [f. SHEPHERD *sb.*]

**1.** *trans.* To tend, guard and watch (sheep) as a shepherd. Also rarely to keep or breed (sheep).

**1790** [implied in SHEPHERDING *vbl. sb.*]. **1862** RUSKIN *Unto this Last* 43 He must..shepherd his own flocks. **1881** *Cheq. Career* 36 In Australia, sheep..are shepherded and yarded every night. **1885–94** R. BRIDGES *Eros & Psyche* Apr. xiii, Talos..who shepherded the sea-goats on the coast.

*absol.* **18..** *Househ. Words* XXXV. 11 (Flügel) When he used to go shepherding with me on his rough pony. **1884** *Kendal Mercury* 26 Sept. 2/6 Two farmers..were out shepherding, when they were overtaken by an awful storm. **1887** *Pall Mall Gaz.* 26 Oct. 3/1 The Virgin is said to have appeared to two children..who were shepherding up there in the mountains.

**2.** *transf.* and *fig.* To tend, watch over, or guide as a shepherd does his sheep.

**1820** SHELLEY *Arethusa* 6 Arethusa arose From her couch of snows..Shepherding her bright fountains. *a* **1851** *Edin. Rev.* in *Arch. Stud. neu. Spr.* VIII. 276 Shepherding a lady. **1862** H. H. DIXON *Scott & Sebright* (1895) 380 He would put out twenty couple of puppies for him, and go round twice a week to shepherd them. **1868** LOWELL *Dara* 19 So Dara shepherded a province wide, Nor in his viceroy's sceptre took more pride Than in his crook before. **1885** M. ARNOLD *Poor Matthias*, French canary-merchant old Shepherding his flock of gold In a low dim-lighted pen. **1898** G. B. SHAW *You never can tell* II. Stage Dir., The waiter shepherds his assistants along with him into the hotel by the kitchen entrance.

**3.** *Austral.* and *N.Z. trans.* and *intr.* To watch over or guard (a mining claim) by working on it superficially (esp. by digging small pits) so as to retain legal rights.

**1855** R. CARBONI *Eureka Stockade* 8 Here begins as a profession the precious game of 'shepherding', or keeping claims in reserve; that is the digger turned squatter. **1861** T. M'COMBIE *Australian Sk.* 135 Few of their claims, however, are actually 'bottomed', for the owners merely watch their more active contemporaries. *Footnote*, This is termed 'shepherding' a claim. **1863** *Once a Week* VIII. 507 (Farmer), Having sunk their holes, each about a foot, and placed in them a pick or shovel as a sign of ownership, they devoted themselves to the laborious occupation of shepherding. **1864** *Append. Jrnls. House Reps. N.Z.* C. IV. 8 Shepherding forbidden. **1880** D. C. DAVIES *Metallif. Min.* 421 *Shepherding*, Aus., keeping possession of a mining claim by doing the least quantity of work on it allowed by law.

**4. a.** *colloq.* or *slang.* To watch over, to follow closely and watchfully; chiefly *slang*, see quot. 1890; also *Austral. slang*, to follow a person so as to get something out of him or to cheat him.

**1885** *Times* 13 Apr. 5/3 Admiral Dowell is reported to be closely shepherding the Russian vessels in these seas. **1890** BARRÈRE & LELAND *Dict. Slang* s.v., Adversaries opposite each other at football are said to *shepherd* or watch each other. A man may *shepherd* a rich uncle or rich heiress, a detective *shepherds* a criminal whom he suspects of planning a felony. A man *shepherds* one of his own side at football by keeping off adversaries while he is running or kicking. **1893** KIPLING *Many Invent.*, *Lost Legion*, You must know that all along the north-west frontier of India there is spread a force of some thirty thousand foot and horse, whose duty it is to quietly and unostentatiously shepherd the tribes in front of them. **1899** SHEARMAN, etc. *Football* 313 Off goes the ball again; a player seizes it, bouncing it as he goes, 'shepherded' along the way by his friends. **1905** *Sat. Rev.* 10 June 761 He ..should have shepherded at an earlier date the Russian fleet out of French waters.

**b.** *Mil. slang.* To force (a body of the enemy) into an unfavourable position.

**1900** *Daily Tel.* 2 Apr. (Ware *Passing Engl.*), Cronje was shepherded with his army into the bed of the Modder by a turning movement.

Hence **'shepherded** *ppl. a.*, protected, guarded.

**1884** RUSKIN *Fors Clav.* xcvi. 306 To be kept from its evil in shepherded peace.

**shepherdess** ('ʃɛpədɪs). Also 6 *erron.* **shepheardize.** [f. SHEPHERD *sb.* + -ESS.] A female shepherd; a woman or girl who tends sheep; also *fig.* Also in pastoral poetry (see SHEPHERD 1 b).

**1387–8** T. USK *Test. Love* I. ii. (Skeat) l. 86 For me liste.. of al myne a Shepherdesse to be cleped. **1590** GREENE *Never too late* II. Wks. (Grosart) VIII. 216 Consider with your selfe faire Shepheardize, that poore men feele paine as well as Princes. **1591–5** SPENSER *Astrophel* 212 The gentlest shepheardesse that liues this day. **1648** HERRICK *Hesper.*, *Mrs. Eliz. Wheeler*, Tell me, said I, in deep distresse, Where I may find my Shepardesse. **1758** JOHNSON *Idler* No. 71 ¶ 13 He..wondered that he had not seen the shepherdesses dancing. **1859** TENNYSON *Merlin & V.* 608 Percivale.. Then paced for coolness in the chapel-yard; Where one of Satan's shepherdesses caught And meant to stamp him with her master's mark. **1885** RUSKIN *Pleas. Eng.* 137 St. Margaret of Antioch was a shepherdess. **1902** MRS. A. MEYNELL *Later Poems* 9 She walks..A shepherdess of sheep.

**b.** A representation (in painting, etc.; esp. china or earthenware) of a shepherdess.

**1771** H. WALPOLE *Vertue's Anecd. Paint.* (1782) IV. 73 Watteau's shepherdesses, nay, his very sheep, are coquet. **1807** W. IRVING *Salmag.* (1824) 91 Little lacquered earthen shepherdesses. **1870** DICKENS *E. Drood* vi, Her dress is as the dress of a china shepherdess: so dainty in its colours.

**c.** *attrib.* and *Comb.*

**1862** *Catal. Internat. Exhib.*, *Brit.* II. No. 4115, Woollen shawls and cloakings, in clan, shepherdess, and fancy patterns. **1867** MISS BROUGHTON *Cometh Up* xxvi, Her little wild rose-wreathed shepherdess hat.

**shepherding** ('ʃɛpədɪŋ), *vbl. sb.* [f. SHEPHERD *v.* + -ING[1].] The action of tending or guiding (sheep) as a shepherd; an instance of this.

**1790** W. H. MARSHALL *Midl. Counties* I. 446 In the shepherding of sheep, in this country, a few circumstances may be mentioned with propriety. **1866** CARLYLE in Froude *Remin.* (1881) II. 143 The rustic natives..and their shepherdings, huntings (brock and fox) and solitary fishings. **1892** LD. LYTTON *King Poppy* xi. 309 For all His shepherdings were ended. **1905** SIR A. LYALL *Life Dufferin* I. ii. 23 Under Cookesley's shepherding the flock might stray at will.

† **'shepherdish,** *a. Obs.* [f. SHEPHERD *sb.* + -ISH.] Pertaining to or like shepherds; pastoral.

*a* **1586** SIDNEY *Arcadia* I. (Sommer) 10 b, He would also haue drawne her eldest sister..in her shepheardish attire. *Ibid.* 36 The courte could not be visited, prohibited to all men, but to certaine sheapheardish people. **1618** BOLTON *Florus* I. xxii. (1636) 64 That wildnesse which they retained of their shepheardish originall breathed forth somewhat still. **1800** G. CHALMERS *Life A. Ramsay* Wks. 1851 I. 30 A propitious moment for shepherdish poetry.

**shepherdize** ('ʃɛpədaɪz), *v. rare.* [f. SHEPHERD *sb.* + -IZE.] *intr.* To act the part of the shepherd (or shepherdess); to pretend to lead the pastoral life.

**1654** GAYTON *Pleas. Notes* II. vi. 60 Though this life of Shepheardizing be out of fashion. **1773** H. WALPOLE *Let. to C'tess Upper Ossory* 11 June, In the midst of this new prospect must I keep up the tone of the world, go shepherdizing with Maccaronies, sit up at loo with my Lady Hertford [etc.]. **1822** *Examiner* 233/1 Sir W——m C——rt——s, despising the citizens, retreated into the forest, to shepherdize. **1846** *Blackw. Mag.* LIX. 313 [They] sit alone, knit, shepherdise, and stare.

**b.** *trans.* To tend or guide as a shepherd.

**1899** S. LAW WILSON *Theol. Mod. Lit.* 140 The mass of mankind are not just so many sheep which will tamely submit to be shepherdised by him, and coerced into the way chalked out for their feet.

**shepherd king.**

**1.** *pl.* [transl. of Gr. βασιλεῖς ποιμένες, Manetho's rendering of the Egyptian designation which he transliterates as Ὑκσως (Hyksōs).

Modern scholars give the probable Egyptian form of the name as *heqa khoswe* chief of foreign lands, Manetho's rendering being due to a mistake.]

The designation of a succession of kings of Egypt (forming the 15th and 16th dynasties of Manetho), belonging to some foreign people, probably of mixed Semitic-Asiatic stock. (By historians often called HYKSOS.)

**1587** GOLDING *De Mornay* xxvi. 465 Manethon the Historiographer of Egipt setteth vs downe their originall, and their comming downe into Egipt, terming them in his language, Shepherd-kings. **1821** LAMB *Elia*, *Old & New Schoolm.*, I make the wildest conjectures concerning Egypt, and her shepherd kings. **1874** BIRCH *1st & 2nd Egypt. Rooms Brit. Mus.* 7 The monuments of the Shepherd kings.

**2.** *gen.* A king who is a shepherd. (In various nonce-uses: see quots.)

**1727–46** THOMSON *Summer* 402 One, chief, in gracious dignity enthron'd, Shines o'er the rest, the pastoral queen, and rays Her smiles, sweet-beaming, on her shepherd king. *a* **1835** MRS. HEMANS *He Walked with God*, A shepherd-king on Eastern plains. **1856** READE *Never too late* xxxvii, Nomades, shepherd-kings—fellows with a thousand head of horned cattle, and sheep like white pebbles by the sea.

**shepherdless** ('ʃɛpədlɪs), *a.* [-LESS.] Without a shepherd; having no shepherds.

**1648** HEXHAM II, *Herderloose schapen*, Sheepheardlesse, or sheepe without a Sheep-heard. **1778** [W. H. MARSHALL] *Minutes Agric.*, *Digest* 101 He..found a straggling, shepherdless Flock in his own or his neighbour's fields. **1906** G. G. COULTON *St. Francis to Dante* 329 But in fact they [the Middle Ages] felt themselves as shepherdless as we.

† **'shepherdling.** *poet. Obs.* [f. SHEPHERD *sb.* + -LING.] A young or little shepherd.

**1598** SYLVESTER *Du Bartas* II. i. IV. *Handy-crafts* 666 Another valiant Shepheardling [i.e. David], That for a Canon takes his silly sling. **1648** HERRICK *Hesper.*, *To his Muse*, There on a Hillock thou may'st sing Unto a handsome Shephardling, Or to a Girle (that keeps the Neat).

**shepherdly** ('ʃɛpədlɪ), *a.* Now *rare.* [f. SHEPHERD *sb.* + -LY[1].] Pertaining to or befitting a shepherd (*lit.* and *fig.*); that has the characteristics of a shepherd; †that is a shepherd.

**1559** [P. H. PHAYER] *Bk. Presidentes* 5 b, And with a shepherdly reward wytsaue ye hym to fauour. *Ibid.* 6 Other thinges..which to your shepherdly office in this behalf belong. **1579** TWYNE *Phis. agst. Fortune* II. v. 167 a, That shepheardlie founder of the citie of Rome. **1656** W. DU GARD tr. *Comenius' Gate Lat. Unl.* §340. 95 In some places the shepherdly multitude do also carry about their cottages in waines. **1702** C. MATHER *Magn. Chr.* v. iii. (1852) 277 To leave their off-spring under the shepherdly government of our Lord Jesus Christ. **1877** S. A. TIPPLE *Echoes of Spoken Words* 22 The truly high position..is that which enables us to minister richly to our fellows, to shield them, guide them, relieve them and be shepherdly toward them. **1884** J. PARKER *Apost. Life* III. 46 A man with a great shepherdly heart.

†**b.** Pastoral, rural, rustic. *Obs.*

**1579** TWYNE *Phis. agst. Fortune* II. cxiv. 304 This is not only a poetical, but also a shepheardly speech. **1589** PUTTENHAM *Eng. Poesie* I. xi. (Arb.) 41 Their poems were named Eglogues or shepheardly talke. **1656** *Artif. Handsom.* 20 The primitive plainness and shepherdly simplicity of those times. **1743** H. WALPOLE *Let. to Mann* 14 Apr., I hate the country: I am past the shepherdly age of groves and streams.

**'shepherdry.** *rare.* [f. SHEPHERD *sb.* + -RY.] The business of a shepherd. Cf. SHEPHERDY.

**1594** R. ASHLEY tr. *Loys le Roy* 28 Pasturage, grasing, and shepheardrie, were before husbandrie and tillage.

**b.** The affairs of 'the Order of Ancient Shepherds', a benefit society. (After FORESTRY.)

**1900** *Dundee Advert.* 19 July 5 Shepherdry.—At the usual fortnightly meeting of the Maisondieu Lodge of Ancient Shepherds..the balance-sheet..was submitted.

**'shepherdship.** *rare.* [f. SHEPHERD *sb.* + -SHIP.] The office or position of a shepherd.

**1548** UDALL *Erasm. Par. Luke* xxiv. 25–29. 90 His shepherdship leat an other bodye take. **1605** SYLVESTER *Du Bartas* II. iii. III. *Law* 233 While he [Moses] past his sacred Prentiship (In wildernesse) of th' Hebrews Shepheardship. **1874** ABP. BENSON in A. C. Benson *Life* (1899) I. 388 It's the Buckles that ruin the Colonial Church... Men taking Shepherdships for Buckles and Loops.

**shepherd's purse.** [Cf. med.L. *bursa pastoris*, F. *bourse-à-pasteur*, *bourse-de-berger*, G. *hirtentasche*, Du. *herdertasch*.]

**1.** A common cruciferous weed, *Capsella Bursapastoris*, bearing pouch-like pods.

*a* **1400–50** *Stockh. Med. MS.* 172 Shepherdys purs. [*a* **1500** *Gl. Sloane* in *Sax. Leechd.* III. 331 Herdys purse.] *c* **1550** LLOYD *Treas. Health* G vij b, Hold thy handful of sheparders [*sic*] purse. **1578** LYTE *Dodoens* I. lv. 81 *Bursa pastoris*..[is called] in English Shepherds purse, Scrippe, or Pouche. **1597** GERARDE *Herbal* II. xxii. 215 Shepheardes purse staieth bleeding in any part of the bodie. **1657** W. COLES *Adam in Eden* xxxv. 71 In English it is called Shepheards purse or Scrip, from the likenesse the Seed hath with that kind of leatherne bag, wherein Shepherds carry their Victualls into the field. *c* **1710** PETIVER *Cat. Ray's Eng. Herbal* Tab. 49 Ragged Sheaperds-purse. **1882** G. ALLEN *Colour of Flowers* i. 15 The petals of shepherd's-purse (*Capsella bursa-pastoris*) have been observed antheriferous.

**2.** *dial.* The fossil echinus found in the chalk.

**1893** *Surrey Gloss.*, *Shepherd's crown* or *Shepherd's purse*, the fossil Echinus, from the chalk. **1900** A. HARSTON *Let. to Editor*, 'Shepherd's Purse', the common name in some parts of the Country (e.g. Kent) for the Fossil Sea Urchins found in the Chalk formation.

† **'shepherdy.** *Obs. rare.* [f. SHEPHERD *sb.* + -Y.] The profession, practice, or occupation of a shepherd. Cf. SHEPHERDRY.

*a* **1622** AINSWORTH *Annot. Pentat.* Gen. iv. 2 (1639) 21 Abel in shepherdy, as in sacrificing and martyrdome, was a figure of Christ. **1659** GELL *Amendm. Bible* 733 He had his rise, unto the Kingdom, even from keeping sheep, which yet was a kinde of introduction unto a like shepherdie. **1680** J. WOODE (*title*), Shepherdy Spiritualiz'd: or, the improvement of a Shepherd's Life to Soul-advantage. **1702** C. MATHER *Magn. Chr.* II. App. (1852) 221 On the one side of David's coin were to be seen his old pouch and crook, the instrument of shepherdy.

**shepman, shepne,** obs. ff. SHIPMAN, SHIPPON.

**shepp, sheppard(e,** obs. ff. SHIP, SHEPHERD.

**sheppeck, -ick** ('ʃɛpək). *dial.* Also 7 sheppik, -ick, sheep-pick, 9 shuppick, -u(c)k, schoppek. [?

For *sheaf-pick, f. SHEAF sb.[1] + PICK sb.[1] 4. Cf. WFlem. *schoofvorke*.] A pitchfork.

**1602** *Inv.* in *Collect. Archæol.* (1863) II. 102 One save, twoe sheppikes [etc.]. *Ibid.* 104 One sheppick and other od stuffe. *Ibid.* 106 One bill, one spade, and two sheppickes. **1676** *Acc. Exam. Joan Perry* 10 Some..met him..with a Sheep-pick in his hand. **1851** *Glouc. Gloss.*, *Sheppeck*, a fork for lifting hay. *Ibid.*, *Shuppick*, a hay-fork.

†'**sheppend.** *Obs.* Forms: 1 **scippend, scieppend, sceppend, scæpend, 1–2 scyppend, sceoppend, 2 sceoppind, sceappind, scuppend, 2–3 she-, shu-, suppende, shippend, 3 seppande, schuppent, -inde, suppen, suppinde.** [OE. *scieppend*, related to *scieppende*, pa. pple. of *scieppan* to create: see SHAPE *v.*

Hence AF. *sepande*, used by Marie de France as a fem. with the sense 'puissance surhumaine, créateur' (Godefr.).]

The Creator.

*Beowulf* 106 Siþðan him scyppend forscrifen hæfde. *a* **1175** *Cott. Hom.* 219 Hare sceappinde. *Ibid.*, [Lucifer] cweð an his herto þat he wolde and eaðe mihte bien his sceoppende ȝelic. *c* **1200** *Trin. Coll. Hom.* 17 Ic bileue on god, þene almihti fader, suppende and wealdende of heuene and of eorð. *Ibid.* 133 Ure helend is sheppende and wealdende of alle shafte. *c* **1220** *Bestiary* 456 Seftes sop ure seppande, sene is on werlde. *a* **1225** *Leg. Kath.* 366 Heo buheð to him as schafte to his schuppent. *a* **1225** *Ancr. R.* 260 þe heouenliche schuppinde. *c* **1275** *Sinners Beware* 20 in *O.E. Misc.* 72 If we vre suppen herve. [*Ibid.* MS. Digby 86 in Horstmann *Altengl. Leg.* 505 suppinde.]

†'**shepper.** *Obs.* Forms: 2–4 **schuppare, 3 sshipper, 4 shuppare, schepere, ssep(p)ere, shepper.** [Early ME. *schuppare* (ü), *shepper*, f. *schuppen*, *sheppen* to create, SHAPE *v.*: see -ER[1]. Cf. OHG. *skephari* (MHG. *schephære*, mod.G. *schöpfer*), (M)LG., (M)Du. *schepper*.] = prec. Also (*rarely*) one who has control *over*.

*a* **1175** *Cott. Hom.* 217 Ich bileue on god feder al-mihti, schuppare of heouene and of eorðe. *a* **1225** *Ancr. R.* 138 Hire schuppare. *a* **1300** in *Rel. Ant.* I. 57, I bileve in God fadir almichty, sshipper of hevene and of eorþe. **1340** *Ayenb.* 7 To servi þine ssepere. **13..** *Pol. Rel. & L. Poems* (1903) 256 þis time man is mad kniȝth And shuppare ouer alle þinge. **1377** LANGL. *P. Pl.* B. XVII. 167 So is þe fader a ful god formeour and shepper.

**shepperd(e,** obs. form of SHEPHERD *sb.*

**sheppey.** *rare*[−1]. (? quasi-*arch.*) [Perh. some error: cf. SHIPPEN.] A shed for sheep.

**1869** BLACKMORE *Lorna Doone* xlii, I went straight home to the upper sheppey, and set them [the sheep] inside.

**sheppyng,** obs. form of SHIPPING *sb.*

**shepstare** ('ʃɛpstə(r)). *dial.* Also 6, 9 **sheepstare, 7, 9 shepster, 9 shepstey, shepsterd, -ert, shipster, chepster, -stow.** [f. SHEEP + STARE *sb.*[1] The name is said to refer to the bird's habit of perching on the backs of sheep to feed on the ticks.] The starling.

**1563** GOOGE *Eglogs* vi. (Arb.) 54 Sometime I wold betraye the Byrds, that lyght on lymed tree, Especially in Shepstare tyme, when thicke in flockes they flye. **1584** COGAN *Haven Health* clxiii. 135 The Stare or Shepstare. **1660** W. BLUNDELL *Cavalier's Note Bk.* (1880) 296 Observe a flock of stares (or shepsters) when they are ready to lodge themselves in a dovecote. **1681** CHETHAM *Angler's Vade-m.* xxxiv. §14 (1689) 190 Wings of shepstares, stares or starlings. **1802** MONTAGU *Ornith. Dict.* s.v. *Stare*, In the north of England it is called Chepster, or Chep-Starling. **1848** *Zoologist* VI. 2290 The starling [is called in Yorkshire] a 'shepstey' or 'shepster'. **1864** J. C. ATKINSON *Stanton Grange* 225 A pair of shepstares. **1884** A. DOHERTY *Nathan Barlow* 32 The youngling chepstows creaking in the eaves. **1887** E. F. BYRRNE *Heir without Heritage* I. viii. 136 They took wing like a flock of shepsters from a field.

**shepster.** *Obs.* exc. *dial.* Also 4 **shappester, shuppester, shippestere, schipster, 5 shipster, shyppestere,** *pl.* **shappystrys 6 schepstarre** (9 *dial.* **shapster**). [ME. *shepster* (? OE. *scieppestre wk. fem.) fem. agent-noun to *shippen* (OE. *scieppan*) SHAPE *v.*]

**1.** A female cutter-out of material; a dressmaker.

**1377** LANGL. *P. Pl.* B. XIII. 331 Auenge me fele tymes other frete my-selue Wyth-inne, as a shepster shere. **1380** *Poll Tax* in Rogers *Oxf. City Docum.* (1891) 13 De Alicia la Shuppester xijd. *Ibid.*, De Johanna Shippestere xijd. **1387** TREVISA *Higden* (Rolls) VII. 269 A schipster [*mulierculа*] of þat citee. **14..** *Voc.* in Wr.-Wülcker 616/42 *Tonstrix*, a Shyppestere. *c* **1515** *Cocke Lorell's B.* 5 Gogle eyed tomson shepster of lyn. **1517–18** in *Archæologia* XLVII. 311 To dyuerse shepsters for makyng of iij smockes for the seid quene. **1530** PALSGR. 266/2 Schepstarre, *lingiere*. *Ibid.*, Sheres for shepsters, *forces*. **1538** ELYOT *Dict.*, *Sarcinatrix*, a shepster, or seamester. **1855** ROBINSON *Whitby Gloss.* 167 *Shapster*,..a cutter out of apparel. A dress-maker.

†**2.** A female 'shaper' of destinies. *Obs. rare.*

**14..** *Voc.* in Wr.-Wülcker 573/34–5 *Cloto*, on of thre shapsisterys *vel* shappystrys (*vel* an[ce] destynyes).

**shepward:** see *sheep-ward* s.v. SHEEP *sb.* 8.

**shepyng, sher:** see SHIPPING *sb.*, SHIRE.

**sherad,** obs. form of SHRADDHA.

**sheradom,** obs. Sc. f. SHERIFFDOM.

**sheraff(e,** obs. forms of SHROFF.

‖**Sheranino.** *Obs. rare*[−1]. A kind of wine.

**1632** LITHGOW *Trav.* I. 15 The..wine that is drunke in Rome, is..Albano, Muscatello, Sheranino.

‖**Sherant.** *Obs. rare.* Also **sherrant.** [Prob. identical with SCHERAND.] A kind of wine.

**1622** J. TAYLOR (Water-P.) *Farew. Tower-Bottles* A 4 b, With Hollocke, Sherant, Malliga, Canara, I stuft your sides vp with a sursarara. **1623** —— *Praise Hemp-seed* 6 No Gascoyne, Orleance, or the Chrystall Sherrant, Nor Rhenish, from the Rheine would be apparant.

**Sherarat** (ʃɛrə'rɑːt). Also **Shararat, Shererat.** [Arab.] (A member of) a nomadic tribe of northern Saudi Arabia. Also *attrib.*

**1830** J. L. BURCKHARDT *Notes on Bedouins & Wahábys* 17 *El Sherárát*, in the sandy plain S. of the Akabe el Shamye and eastward of the Hadj route. Their numbers are considerable, and all are Wahabys. *Ibid.*, South of the Sherárát on the E. of the Hadj road, as far as the vicinity of Mekka, the whole country is inhabited by Aenezes. **1875** *Encycl. Brit.* II. 247/2 Thirdly, in the northern desert, the Howeytat and Sherarat, comparatively small and savage tribes. **1888** C. M. DOUGHTY *Travels in Arabia Deserta* I. iii. 57 Upon the other hand are..low heights much more distant, in the Sherarát nomad country. **1917** T. E. LAWRENCE *Lett.* (1938) 234 The Arab losses in the fight came to two killed (a Rualla and a Sherarat) and several wounded. **1955** H. ST. J. PHILBY *Sa'udi Arabia* iii. 90 'Abdul-'Aziz now [in 1798] switched his offensive to the north: sending..the Amin of Buraida, to raid the Shararat on the Syrian border with telling effect.

**Sherardia.** [Mod.L., named by Dillenius 1719 after W. *Sherard* (1659–1728), an English botanist.] A genus of gamopetalous rubiaceous plants, comprising one species, *S. arvensis*, the field-madder; a plant of this genus.

**1785** MARTYN *Rousseau's Bot.* xv. (1794) 164 Sherardia and Woodroof have funnel-shaped corollas.

**sherardize** ('ʃɛrədaɪz), *v.* Formerly also **Sherardize.** [f. the name of *Sherard* O. Cowper-Coles (1867–1936), English chemist + -IZE.] *trans.* To coat (iron or steel articles) with zinc by heating in contact with zinc dust at a temperature below the melting point of zinc. So '**sherardized** *ppl. a.*, '**sherardizing** *vbl. sb.*

**1901** *Brit. Pat.* 9927 1 By our process, which we name 'Sherardizing' to distinguish it from galvanizing, the thickness and evenness of the deposit can be regulated..and any description or shape of iron or steel can be..dealt with. **1904** *Athenæum* 21 May 658/3 At Burlington House last Friday week..Mr. Sherard Cowper-Coles..explained..the process which is to be commercially applied under the name of 'Sherardizing'. **1904** *Engin. Rev.* XI. 107/2 In practice Sherardised iron and steel are found to withstand the ordinary corrosive agents galvanised iron is exposed to, to a remarkable degree. *Ibid.*, Bolts which had not been Sherardised. **1909** in *Century Dict. Suppl.* **1935** H. R. SIMONDS *Finishing Metal Products* ii. 12 It is possible to sherardize sash of large size only before it is assembled, as sherardizing is destroyed by welding. **1963** *Times* 22 Apr. (Zinc Suppl.) p. v/1 Sherardizing is excellent for small things like screws, for which only regular and small changes in dimensions can be tolerated. **1977** *Offshore Engineer* June 67 (Advt.), We still sherardize every nut, washer and bolt to cut maintenance to virtually zero.

**Sherari** (ʃɛ'rɑːrɪ), *a.* and *sb.* Also **Sherary.** [Arab.] **A.** *adj.* Of or pertaining to the Sherarat. **B.** *sb.* A member of the Sherarat; also, a dromedary bred by the Sherarat.

**1888** C. M. DOUGHTY *Travels in Arabia Deserta* II. ii. 32 'It is he,' said the Emir, 'Sheráry hound! how durst thou do this violence?' Metaab bade the stranger take the Sheráry's lance. *Ibid.* ix. 239 The thelûls [riding camels] of the Sherarát..are praised above other in Western Arabia: Ibn Rashîd's armed band are mounted upon the light and fleet *Sherâries*. **1926** T. E. LAWRENCE *Seven Pillars* IV. lii. 273 At last the Sherari boy said if we gave him scope he would settle his account and leave him living. *Ibid.* liv. 284 My camel, the sherari racer, Naama, stretched herself out. **1927** —— *Revolt in Desert* xi. 154 It had killed only two of us, one Rueli and one Sherari.

**Sherash,** obs. form of SHIRAZ (wine).

**Sheraton** ('ʃɛrətən), *a.* [f. the name of Thomas *Sheraton* (1751–1806), a furniture maker and designer.] Designating a severe style of furniture developed in England towards the end of the 18th cent., chiefly by Thomas Sheraton. Also *absol.*

**1883** *Mag. of Art* VI. 190 A Sheraton knife-box. *Ibid.* 192 A Sheraton sideboard. **1887** BLACK *Sabina Zembra* I. iii. 33 Sheraton chairs. **1900** 'SARAH GRAND' *Babs* xiii, The lovely Chippendale and Sheraton with which it was furnished.

**Sheraz,** obs. form of SHIRAZ (wine).

‖**sherbaff.** *Obs.* Also 7 **serebaffe, seribaff, serebast, 8 sherbaffe, sherbassee.** [Prob. Persian, f. *shīr* lion (used to denote excellence of quality) + *bāf* stem of *bāftan* to weave. Cf. BAFT.] A kind of silk of Persia. Also ***sherbaff silk***.

**1619** in Foster *Eng. Factories India* 63 Serebaffes. **1624** *Ibid.* 11 Seribaffs. **1629** *Ibid.* 350 Serebasts. **1708** *Lond. Gaz.* No. 4472/4 At the Marine Coffee-house..will be expos'd to Sale..9 Bales Sherbaffe Silk. **1721** C. KING *Brit. Merch.* I. 157 They cannot purchase less..than 22 great Pounds of Sherbassee (or Persia fine Raw Silk). **1753** HANWAY *Trav.* (1762) I. v. lxiii. 289 The first is called Sherbaff, or weavers silk, because the weavers..are supposed to use the best they can procure. *Ibid.* lxix. 314 In regard to the Sherbaff silk, which was bought..in Ghilan,..it was found to be two shillings in a pound better than the Persian Sherbaff imported from Turkey.

**sherbet** ('ʃɜːbɪt). Also 7 **zer-, cer-, sar-, serbet, servet, shurbet, shirbet(t, sherbett(e, -bert, -becke, -pet,** 9 **sherbat, sharbut.** [a. Turkish and Persian *sherbet*, a. Arab. *sharba[h]*, f. *shariba* to drink. Cf. SORBET.]

**1. a.** A cooling drink of the East, made of fruit juice and water sweetened, often cooled with snow. **b.** An European imitation of this; now esp. an effervescing drink made of sherbet powder (see 2).

**1603** KNOLLES *Hist. Turkes* (1621) 833 The guests..dranke..water prepared with sugar, which kind of drink they call Zerbet. *Ibid.* 1203 A beverage, which they call Cerbet, made of the juice of lymons water and sugar. **1615** G. SANDYS *Trav.* I. 12 Not much inferiour in relish to the costly Shurbets of Constantinople. *Ibid.* 65 Yet have they sundry sherbets..some made of sugar and lemons, some of violets, and the like. **1626** BACON *Sylva* §705 They haue in Turkey and the East, certaine Confections which they call Seruetts. **1630** CAPT. SMITH *Trav. & Adv.* xiii. 25 [The Turks'] best drink is Coffa..and Sherbecke which is only honey and water. **1632** LITHGOW *Trav.* IV. 151 Their common drinke is Sherpet. **1668** *Lond. Gaz.* No. 222/1 The Grand Seignior..had sent his Mother a Sherbette. **1675** COVEL in *Early Voy. Levant* (Hakl. Soc.) 239 We..were severall times treated with sherbert of lemmons. **1685** tr. *Gracian's Courtier's Man.* 189 More precious than Chocolate, Coffee or Sarbet. **1753** HANWAY *Trav.* (1762) I. III. xxxiii. 151 There were..plates of comfits, several china basons of sherbets. **1813** BYRON *Bride Abydos* II. viii, A cup too on the board was set That did not seem to hold sherbet. **1817** MOORE *Lalla R.*, *Fire-worshippers* III, The violet sherbets were hastily handed round. *a* **1845** BARHAM *Ingol. Leg.*, *Ld. of Thoulouse*, To bring in sherbet, ginger-pop, lemonade. **1845** COOLEY *Cycl. Pract. Receipts* (ed. 2) 550 *Lemonade*. Syn. Lemon Sherbet, King's Cup. *Ibid.*, Orangeade or Orange Sherbet, for Icing, is made in the same way from oranges. **1845** BREGION & MILLER *Pract. Cook* 336 Indian Sharbut. **1866** LIVINGSTONE in Blaikie *Life* xviii. (1881) 368 After coffee and sherbet we came away.

*fig.* **1728** VANBR. & CIBBER *Provok'd Husb.* III. i, A smart Repartee, with a Zest of Recrimination at the Head of it, makes the prettiest Sherbet!

**2.** In full ***sherbet powder***: A preparation of bicarbonate of soda, tartaric acid, sugar, etc., variously flavoured, for making an effervescing drink.

**1856** COOLEY *Cycl. Pract. Receipts* (ed. 3) 1066 *Powders* (Sherbet). These are made of the same materials as *lemonade powders*, the flavouring ingredient being varied to suit the particular case. **1895** *Stores' Price List*, Sherbet. Per doz. 1 lb. tins, 7/2. **1905** *Macm. Mag.* Dec. 83 The tin of pink sherbet.

**3.** *transf.* **a.** A variously flavoured water-ice (*Cent. Dict.* 1891: and in later Dicts.). **b.** *slang.* (See quots. 1890, 1917.)

**1890** BARRÈRE & LELAND *Dict. Slang*, *Sherbet* (popular), a glass of any warm alcoholic liquor, as grog, &c. A misapplication. **1917** H. LAWSON *Coll. Verse* (1969) III. 214 Beer that *we* called 'sherbet'. **1974** F. ARCHER *Treasure House* i. 18 He had a strident voice and with a few sherbets under his belt you knew he was about.

**4.** *attrib.* **sherbet dabs** (see quot. 1957); **sherbet fountain,** a confection consisting of a bag of sherbet with a liquorice 'straw' through which it is sucked up.

**1675** COVEL in *Early Voy Levant* (Hakl. Soc.) 263 Your little sherbert cups and coffee dishes are made often times of the same earth. **1805** M. WILMOT *Jrnl.* 9 Apr. in Londonderry & Hyde *Russian Jrnls.* (1934) I. 140 Some Sherbet Cups in silver stands. **1966** MRS L. B. JOHNSON *White House Diary* 2 Aug. (1970) 403 My brother Tony Taylor had sent a set of sherbet cups that had belonged to my mother. **1896** *Godey's Mag.* Apr. 446/1 Exquisite little sherbet doilies. **1957** J. KIRKUP *Only Child* 118 Another treat was Sherbet Dabs: we got a caramel-flavoured lollipop which we dipped into a bag of sherbet. **1958** *Listener* 23 Oct. 649/2 The Bonds' shop was not the place for liquorice root, tiger nuts, or sherbet dabs. **1957** R. HOGGART *Uses of Literacy* I. ii. 57 The boy's odder pleasures of taste, not so much..the sherbet-fountains, monkey nuts and aniseed balls, but..a penny stick of licorice or some cinnamon root from the chemist. **1615** SANDYS *Trav.* I. 74 Cookes, sherbet-men (who make the foresaid beurage).

**Sherbro** ('ʃɜːbrəʊ). [ad. a native name.] (A member of) a people of the southern coast of Sierra Leone; also, their language. Also *attrib.* or as *adj.*

**1836** F. H. RANKIN *White Man's Grave* I. ii. 33 The Bulloms of Sherbro, or the Sherbros, pronounced 'Saybras', are to the south of the colony. **1887** *Encycl. Brit.* XXII. 44/2 The following are the more important races that can be distinctly classified:—Mandingos, 1190;..Sherbros, 2882 [; etc.]. **1944** M. GORVIE *Our People of Sierra Leone Protectorate* iii. 20 There is today to be found in the Temne language a large number of Sherbro words. **1957** M. BANTON *W. Afr. City* v. 95 The Sherbro specialize in fishing and water-front work. **1970** J. R. CARTWRIGHT *Politics in Sierra Leone 1947–67* i. 13 It is likely that all these tribes with the possible exception of the Limbas and the Sherbros along the coast, entered Sierra Leone within the past 600 years.

**sherd:** see SHARD *sb.*[1]

**Sherden:** see SHARDANA.

†**sherdoon.** Anglicized spelling of *chardoon*, CARDOON β.

**1661** RABISHA *Cookery Dissected* 4 To pickle stalks of Thessell or Sherdowns. *Ibid.* 143 To make a Sherdoon Pye in the Spring... Put in your Sherdoons [etc.].

†**shere.** *Coining. Obs.* Also 6 shiare, 7 sheere. [Prob. a use of SHEAR *sb.*[2] = REMEDY *sb.* 4; TOLERANCE *sb.* 4a.

**1566** *Acc. Exch. K.R.*, Bundle 305 No. 18 (7) Syluer of xj.oz. ij.d. wᵗ fyne marked wᵗ the portculles 1lb. wᵗ founde at the sheare lx.s... At the assaye Standerd, viz. xj.oz. ij.d. wᵗ fyne. **1617** MORYSON *Itin.* I. 280 The Mint-Master gave account before the Queene's Examiners for the money they coyned, as well by the tale (or number of the pieces) as by the sheere. For the coyning of gold, a certaine proportion of some eight graines in the ounce, was allowed to the Mint-Master in this account by the sheere. **1883** *Encycl. Brit.* XVI. 482/1 The deviation from the standard weight [of coins] permitted by law, now called the 'remedy', and anciently called the 'shere'. *Ibid. note*, Two notable instances are recorded of the use that has been made at various times of the shere, or remedy, as a means of profit.

**shere,** obs. form of SHEAR, SHEER, SHIRE.

‖**shereef** (ʃəˈriːf). Forms: 6 sherife, xarifo, xerifo, serif(f)o, 7 seriph, -iff, zeriff(e, xeriff(e, ceriffe, sheriffe, shreeve, 7- sharif, 7-8 scherif, 7, 9 sherif(f, 7-9 cheriff, 8 shirreff, -eef, cherif(fe, cheref, shariff, xarif, 9 sherriff(e, -eef, sharife, 9- shareef; *pl.* 9 shorfa. [Arab. *sharīf* noble, glorious, f. *sharafa* to be exalted.]

**1.** A descendant of Muhammad through his daughter Fatima. In some of the early quots. taken *spec.* for a Muslim priest.

**1599** HAKLUYT *Voy.* II. II. 104 Wee..tooke a Pangaia of the Moores, which had a priest of theirs in it, which in their language they call a Sherife. **1600** PORY tr. *Leo's Africa* II. 50 A Seriffo or Mahumetan priest. **1687** A. LOVELL tr. *Thevenot's Trav.* I. 30 As for the Kindred of Mahomet, whom they call Scherifs, they wear a green Turban. **1704** PITTS *Relig. & Mann. Mohammetans* vii. 90 The Sultaun of Mecca..is a Shirreeff, *i.e.* one of the Race of Mohammet. **1753** HANWAY *Trav.* (1762) II. IV. ii. 102 *note*, The Cheriffs, successors of Mahommed. **1839** *Penny Cycl.* XV. 309/2 Among them are many sherifs, or pretended descendants of Mohammed. **1860** G. BENNETT *Gatherings Naturalist Austral.* 443 The mosque of El Haibee..contains the tomb of the founder, and from his being a sherriff, is covered with a green silk pall. **1959** *Economist* 3 July 11/2 Even the assorted amirs, sultans and sharifs of south Arabia. **1974** C. MAJUL in Gowing & McAmis *Muslim Filipinos* I. 4 The sultans of Sulu have all claimed descent from this *sharif*.

**2.** Hence used (often with capital initial) as the title of certain Arab princes.

**a.** The sovereign of Morocco; also, the ruler of any of the districts of Morocco.

**1600** PORY tr. *Leo's Africa* To Rdr. 4 The *Xarifo* [*marg.* Or Xerifo, or Serifo] otherwise called the *Miramonin*, or the king of Maroco Sus and Fez. *Ibid.* II. 81, I my selfe was present at this faire in the companie of my Lord the Seriffo for the space of fifteene daies. *a***1618** RALEIGH *War* F iiij, The Seriph in Barbarie. **1632** LITHGOW *Trav.* VIII. 367 Their chiefe Seriff, or Vicegerent, being sent from Morocco. *c***1685** DK. OF BUCKINGHAM *Conf.* Wks. 1705 II. 36 Sultans of Babylon, Caliphs of Ægypt,..and Xeriffs of Morocco. **1753** *Chambers' Cycl.* Suppl., *Cheref*, a title assumed by the emperors of Morocco. **1892** *Blackw. Mag.* Sept. 420/1 The shorfa, or shereefs, had been content to live a pastoral life amongst their flocks and herds... Probably simplicity was the principal feature of the early Shorfa of Wazan.

**b.** The ruler of various other places; esp. the chief magistrate, or local governor of Mecca.

**1603** KNOLLES *Hist. Turks* (1638) 5 And with him [the Sultan] sent the Seriph, a man of great place among the Mahumetans, his Embassador vnto the Emperour. **1622** H. CROSBY *Jrnl.* 10 Mar. in Foster *Eng. Factories Ind.* (1908) II. 2 [At Mohilla] the shreeve that was with him had some of the spice and the chinna trenchers. The King and the shreeve and the Kings two sonns stayed. **1625** PURCHAS *Pilgrims* I. III. xi. 257 The Sheriffe of Mecca. *Ibid.* IV. xvi. 539 Euery night at Sun-set they stand or kneele all towards the Sunne and pray, the Xeriff [of Socatra] throwing water on their heads. **1631** R. H. *Arraignm. Whole Creature* xvii. 300 Others, keeping up their Wives: jayled, and confined to their Prison, as the Zeriffes of Pesia, that none see them. **1694** *Lond. Gaz.* No. 2997/2 The Ceriffe, or King of Mecca,.. had revolted against the Ottoman Government. **1704** PITTS *Relig. & Mann. Mohammetans* vii. 91 The Sultan Shirreef of Mecca. **1734** SALE *Koran* Prelim. Disc. §1. 4 The prince or Sharif has a garden well planted at his castle of Marbaa. **1776** ADAM SMITH *W.N.* v. i. II. ¶7 The authority of an Arabian scherif is very great; that of a Tartar khan altogether despotical. **1805** *Amer. St. Papers* (1832) II. 723 This morning came in two deserters from the enemy's camp, both Levant Turks,..a choux and a cheriff, corresponding with the rank of aid-de-camp and ensign [Tripoli]. **1848** CURZON *Monast. Levant* I. iii. (1897) 22 On entering the tent we found the Cadi; the son of the sheriff of Mecca. **1900** *Q. Rev.* Oct. 348 With the overshadowing Turkish Sultans a dynasty of Shareefs could not well be on amicable terms.

Hence **She'reefate**, the office of Shereef; **she'reefial** *a.* = SHEREEFIAN *a.*

**1917** R. STORRS *Orientations* (1937) x. 244 He [*sc.* the Sultan of Muscat] professes entire satisfaction..with the Sharifial movement. **1920** *19th. Cent.* Aug. 233 It was to the British Government..that the Sherifial family of Mecca addressed their communications during the war. **1924** *Glasgow Herald* 8 Mar. 9 He began his official career by assisting successive Sherifs, and in 1908..was appointed to the Sherifate by the Porte.

‖**she'reefa.** Also sherifa, shareefa, and with capital initial. [Arab. *sharīfaʰ*, fem. of *sharīf*, see prec.] The wife of a Moroccan shereef.

**1906** *Westm. Gaz.* 21 Sept. 2/1 [Morocco] The Sherifa is an Englishwoman. **1911** (*title*) My Life Story. By Emily, Shareefa of Wazan.

**shereefee,** variant of SHERIFI.

**shereefian** (ʃəˈriːfiən), *a.* [f. SHEREEF + -IAN.]

**1.** Of, pertaining to, or designating descent from Muhammad.

**1936** E. WAUGH *Waugh in Abyssinia* 86 The Emir's family claimed high, Sheriffian descent. **1976** *Times Lit. Suppl.* 13 Feb. 164/2 No doubt sultans did issue certificates of 'sherifian' descent. *Ibid.* 164/3 The conversion to the specifically 'sherifian' idiom of prestigious ancestry. **1977** P. RAYMOND *Matter of Assassination* vii. 75 His Sharifian Majesty, exalted of God, received us in his audience chamber.

**2.** *spec.* (With capital initial.) **a.** Of or pertaining to the Shereef of Morocco.

**1887** *Pall Mall Gaz.* 10 Oct. 1/2 Sultan Muley Hassan.. came to the Shereefian throne fourteen years ago. **1890** *Athenæum* 3 May 560/1 Montefiore made his way to Morocco, and obtained from the Sheriffian Sultan the release of the prisoners. **1900** *Q. Rev.* Oct. 354 The Shareefian dynasty.

**b.** Of or pertaining to the Shereef of Mecca. Also as *sb.*, a supporter of the Shereef.

**1921** G. BELL *Let.* 17 Apr. (1927) II. xx. 590, I am therefore identified as a Sharifian. **1926** T. E. LAWRENCE *Seven Pillars* I. xvi. 82 Blood feuds were nominally healed, and really suspended in the Sherifian area. *Ibid.* II. xviii. 93 Garland single-handed was teaching the Sherifians how to blow up railways with dynamite. **1929** W. S. CHURCHILL *World Crisis* V. 462 He came of the Sherifian family which, as guardians of the Holy Places at Mecca, commanded wide veneration throughout the Islamic world. **1935** R. H. KIERNAN *Lawrence of Arabia* viii. 174 He was defeated by the fanatical Wahabis in a fight which resulted in the destruction of a Sherifian force of four thousand men. **1976** *Times Lit. Suppl.* 30 Apr. 519/2 Correspondence which on the Sharifian side was a continuation of the attempts made before the outbreak of the 1914–18 War to enlist the services of Great Britain in Sharif Husayn's resistance to the centralizing policy of the Turkish government. *Ibid.*, To these proposals the Sharifians demanded an answer within thirty days.

**sheref, -efe, -eff,** obs. forms of SHERIFF.

**shereful,** variant of CHEREFUL *a. Obs.*

*c***1475** *Partenay* 829 My ryght doubted and shereful lady.

**sheregrig.** ? *Obs.* [repr. African pronunciation of Arab. *shiriqrāq*.] A green woodpecker or similar bird of Abyssinia.

**1790** BRUCE *Abyssinia* V. 182 Sheregrig. This bird is one of those called Rollier in French. **1790** WOLCOT (P. Pindar) *Compl. Epist. to Bruce* 363 Weasels and polecats, sheregrigs, carrion-crows.

**sheren, shere(y)ve,** obs. ff. SHARN, SHERIFF.

**Shererat,** var. SHERARAT.

**sherge,** obs. form of CIERGE.

*a***1400** *Hom. in Vernon MS.* xii. in *Archiv Stud. neu. Spr.* LVII. 256/1 Hou vr lady gaf a good wyf a sherge.

**Sheriat,** var. SHARIA.

**Sheridanesque** (ˌʃɛrɪdəˈnɛsk), *a.* [f. the name of Richard Brinsley *Sheridan* (1751–1816), British dramatist + -ESQUE.] Of, pertaining to, or characteristic of Sheridan or his plays.

**1931** [see RACINIAN *a.* and *sb.*]. **1933** BLUNDEN *Charles Lamb* ii. 61 He [*sc.* Lamb] ventured to show what he could do independent of the Sheridanesque cleverness around him.

So **'Sheridaniˌana** [-IANA], anecdotes about Sheridan.

**1826** F. REYNOLDS *Sheridaniana* p. iii, The..volume..is intended to comprehend all that is most interesting..about ..Sheridan—a person so eminently qualified to form the subject of such a work, that it seems somewhat singular that the *present* should be the first collection of Sheridaniana. **1931** *Times Lit. Suppl.* 16 Apr. 303/3 Sheridaniana? There is 'at the bottom of this stagnant well' some trace of truth, the misery of a reputation for wit.

**sheridanite** (ˈʃɛrɪdənaɪt). *Min.* [See quot. 1912 and -ITE[1].]

A chlorite, $(Mg,Al,Fe^{2+})_6(Si,Al)_4O_{10}(OH)_8$, chemically similar to clinochlore but containing less silicon.

**1912** J. E. WOLFF in *Amer. Jrnl. Sci.* CCXXXIV. 476 Although it seems hardly permissible to add a new name to the forty or fifty now found under the chlorite group, yet the purity of this material, its peculiar chemical composition and the certainty that it will be available in large quantity, perhaps justifies the name of 'Sheridanite', from the county [in Wyoming] in which it occurs. **1967** *Canad. Mineralogist* IX. 30 The fine white material in the core of the specimen from Zlatoust, Russia... This material gave an extremely sharp chlorite *x*-ray pattern. The structural formula.. classes it as a sheridanite, as defined by Foster (1962).

**sherie,** obs. form of SHERRY.

**Sherif:** see SHEREEF, SHERIFI.

**sherifalty:** see SHERIFFALTY.

**sheriff** (ˈʃɛrɪf). Forms: α. 1 scírȝeréfa, 2 scyrreve, *pl.* scirerevan, sirrefan, 2-3 scirreve, syrreve, 3 schyrreve, 3-5 schir(r)eve, 3-5, (7) shireve, 4-5 schyreve, shirreve, shyr(r)eve, schirrive, schyrryve, (5 *pl.* shirris), 6 shyreeve. β. 3 s(s)erreve, 3-5 scherreve, 4 sschereve, shereyve, 4-5 schereve, sher(r)eve, 5 s(c)heryve, sherreive, shurreve, 7 shearive, 7-8 sherive. γ. 3-6 schirref(f, 4-5 schirrif, schyr(r)eff, 4-6 shiref, shyref, 4-7 schiref(f, 5 schyriffe, shyryf(e, -yffe, shi-, shyrryf, shiriff, -efe, shirrieffe, *Sc.* schirrayf, 5-6 schir(r)effe, shirref, -if, -ef(f)e, 6 schyrriff(e, shyreff(e, shir-, shyreyffe, shirief(f)e, shyrryf(e, -efe, *Sc.* syreff, 6-7 shireff(e, shirif(e, -iffe, shirreff, 7 shierife, shirriff. δ. 4-5 scherref, sherref, -if, -yf, *Sc.* serefe, 4-6 sherreff, 4-7 sheref(f, -if, 5 sherefe, 5-6 schereff(e, -yf(e, sherief(e, -yf(e, 5-7 sherife, scheref, shereffe, 6 scherif, s(c)heryffe, sherrife, 6-7 sheriffe, sherriff(e, 7- sheriff. ε. 4-5 schreve, 5 sherve, schryve, 5-6 shryve, shreve, 6 schreyve, 6-7 shrive, 7-8 shreeve, 5-9 shrieve; ζ. 5 shirffe, 5-6 shreffe, scref(f)e, shryef, 5-7 shrief(e, 6 s(c)hrefe, shreef, shreyfe, shryffe, 6-7 shrife, 7 shrieff, sh'riff, 8 shreif. η. *Sc.* 4-5 schyrray, 5 schirrawe, schirra, schirraye, schyrray, pl. schirrais, 8-9 sherra, 9 shirra, sherry. [OE. *scírȝeréfa*, f. *scír* SHIRE + *ȝeréfa* REEVE. The etymological form *shire-reeve* (q.v. under SHIRE) has occasionally been used by legal antiquaries from the 16th c. downwards.

As the OE. *scír* had, in addition to its specific sense, the general sense of 'district under a person's administration, province', *scírȝeréfa* had also a wider meaning, e.g. when the bishop is called 'Christ's *scírȝeréfa*'. (Cf. sense 3 below.)]

**1. a.** *England* (and *Wales*). In England before the Norman Conquest, the *scírȝeréfa* (also called *scírman*) was a high officer, the representative of the royal authority in a shire, who presided in the shire-moot, and was responsible for the administration of the royal demesne and the execution of the law. After the Conquest, the office of sheriff was continued, that title being retained in English documents, while in Latin and French the usual term was *vice-comes*, *viscounte*, which had been applied to similar functionaries in Normandy.

The functions of the sheriffs of counties have been greatly restricted by successive changes. At the present time the sheriff (more fully called *high sheriff*), appointed for one year by royal patent, is nominally responsible for the keeping of prisoners in safe custody, the summoning of jurors for the High Court, the execution of writs and of the sentence of death. In addition to these duties, which are discharged by the under-sheriff, the high sheriff acts as presiding officer at parliamentary elections for the county, and is required to attend (with the ceremonial state demanded by custom) on circuit judges.

Those boroughs and cities that were, until recently, 'counties of themselves', and also the city of Oxford, have or formerly had a sheriff (or in some instances two) chosen annually by the corporation; the office is now mainly honorary, the specific duties attached to it varying in different towns. The City of London elects annually two sheriffs, who were also Sheriffs of Middlesex until 1888.

In some counties the office of sheriff was formerly hereditary. The last surviving instance of this was in Westmorland; the hereditary shrievalty of that county was abolished in 1850 by the Act 13 & 14 Vict. c. 30.

α. *c***1034** in Kemble *Cod. Dipl.* IV. 54 An scírȝemot sæt æt Æȝelnoðes stane... Ðær wæs Bryning scírȝerefa. *a***1154** *O.E. Chron.* (Laud MS.) an. 963, Ic ȝife þone tun..swa freolice þæt ne king ne biscop ne eorl ne sc[y]rreue ne haue þær nane hæse. *c***1155** in *Anglia* VII. 220 Ealle mine eorlas & ealle mine scirereuan. ? *a***1200** in Kemble *Cod. Dipl.* IV. 192 Eadward king gret..all mine heued men and mine þeȝnes and mine sirrefan. *c***1200** *Moral Ode* 50 in *Trin. Coll. Hom.* 221 Ne mai hit us binime no king ne no syrreue [*other MSS.* scirreue, schirreue, serreue]. *a***1325** *MS. Rawl. B.* 520 lf. 52b, þe king hath igraunted to his poeple þat heo habben election of hoere schirreue þere ase schirreue nis noȝt þoru feo. *c***1386** CHAUCER *Prol.* 359 A shirreue hadde he been and [a] Countour. *c***1460** *Brut* 522 þe yong men of þe mercerie.. held þe Mair & Shyreves stil in Chepe. **1588** FRAUNCE *Lawiers Log.* I. xii. 52 Shyreeve. **1629** COKE *On Litt.* 168 Shireue.

β. **1297** R. GLOUC. (Rolls) 11061 A freinss kniȝt was at gloucetre þe sserreue þoru þe king. *c***1380** WYCLIF *Sel. Wks.* III. 215 Justicis and schereves and stiwardis and bailifis. **1433** *Rolls of Parlt.* IV. 447/1 Retourned by the Shereve of the Shire. *c***1450** *Mirk's Festial* 38 Gylbert, þat was scheryue of London. **1493–4** *Rec. St. Mary at Hill* (1904) 204 Item, payd to þe mayre and to þe ij sheryves. **1619** in *Lismore Papers* Ser. II. (1887) II. 219 Paid the Shearives of Bristoll for the Costome dew to them. **1687** in *Magd. Coll. & Jas. II* (O.H.S.) 102 Whether the Bp. of Oxford was to be put in the presidents Office and yᵗ being a Freehold by any but the sherive.

γ. **1375**, *c***1425** [see b]. *c***1400** *Brut* 218 Sir Symond Ward ..þat þo was shirryf of ȝork. **1415** in *York Myst.* Introd. p. xxxiv, Ye Mair and ye shirefs of yis Citee. *c***1450** *Godstow*

*Reg.* 654 The shyryf of Oxenford-shyre. **1551** *Coventry Leet Bk.* 797 The Shireyffes of the Citie for the tyme beinge. **1559** *Mirr. Mag., Northumb.* xviii, The shirif therof, Rafe Rekesby. **1593** NORDEN *Spec. Brit., Cornw.* (1728) 29 Shirereue, vulgerly the Shiriffe. **1614** SELDEN *Titles Hon.* 226 Shirifes.

δ. *c* **1375** *Sc. Leg. Saints* xl. (*Ninian*) 965 Syne come þe serefe to the ton, &, to hald þe law, set done. *c* **1400** *Gamelyn* 602 (Sloane MS.), Here cometh the Sherryf [*Petw.* sheref] and wil haue oure heedes. **1522** *Coventry Leet Bk.* 680 All Comeners within this Cytte vndur the degre of a Scheryffe. **1554** YAXLEY in Ellis *Orig. Lett.* Ser. III. III. 314 Her Maiestie hath addressed forth her lettres to the Sheriefes of the Sheres. **1676** in *Hatton Corr.* (Camden) 132 Saterday last wase yᵉ day for choosing sherifs in yᵉ city and in yᵉ Hall. *aa* **1700** EVELYN *Diary* an. 1634, My Father was appointed Sheriff for Surrey and Sussex before they were disjoyned. **1710** J. HARRIS *Lex. Techn.* II, *Sherive* or *Sheriff*. **1765** BLACKSTONE *Comm.* I. 178 The county court is a court held every month or oftener by the sheriff. **1769** *Junius' Lett.* xi. (1788) 71 It is admitted, that the sheriffs obeyed the laws, and performed their duty [in returning Mr. Wilkes]. **1788** Encycl. Brit. (ed. 3) II. 209/2 An order was issued..to the sherives of most of the English counties. **1835** *App. Munic. Corpor. Rep.* II. 1165 (Bristol), The two Sheriffs are elected by the common council..for a year. *Ibid.* IV. 2460 (Norwich), Two Sheriffs are chosen yearly; one, who is called the Court Sheriff, by the mayor, sheriffs, and aldermen; and the other by the freemen. **1846** MᶜCULLOCH *Acc. Brit. Empire* (1854) II. 129 Petitions from the city of London..are brought at once to the bar of the House by the sheriffs. **1871** W. M. FAWCETT *Law Land-lord & Tenant* 182 The sheriff must first levy for the rent and then for the execution. **1882** *Act 45 & 46 Vict.* c. 50 §170 The council of every borough being a county of itself, and of the city of Oxford, shall on the ninth of November in every year appoint a fit person to execute the office of sheriff. **1888** *Act 51 & 52 Vict.* c. 41 s. 41(8) The sheriffs of the city of London shall not have any authority except in the city. *Ibid.* s. 46(6) The right of the mayor, commonalty, and citizens of the city of London to elect the sheriff of Middlesex shall cease, and it shall be lawful for Her Majesty the Queen to appoint a sheriff of the county of Middlesex. **1972** *Local Govt. Act* c. 70 s. 219(1) Sheriffs appointed for a county or Greater London shall be known as high sheriffs. **1974** C. A. CROSS *Principles Local Govt. Law* (ed. 5) xxvii. 488 The Queen in granting a charter to preserve the privileges of a city or borough existing prior to April 1, 1974, may confer on the city or borough the power to appoint a sheriff, as opposed to a high sheriff.

ε. **1399** LANGL. *Rich. Redeles* IV. 28 And sente side sondis to schreuys aboute, To chese swiche cheualleris as þe charge wold. **1461** *Paston Lett.* II. 28 The Shreve ys in a dought whedyr he shall make a newe eleccion of knyghts of the shyre. **1463** in *Somerset Med. Wills* (1901) 197 That thoo which were wrongfully hurt when I was Sherve may be recompensid. **1538** in *Lett. Suppress. Monasteries* (Camden) 195 Sir John Russell, schreyve of Wisitor schere. **1559** *Mirr. Mag., Jack Cade* xv, James Cromer shrive of Kent. **1605** *Lond. Prodigal* III. ii. 122 Shreeue, take your prisoner. [**1651** CLEVELAND *Poems* 14 Like Alderman, or Monster-Sheriffs, With Canvas backs, and velvet sleeves.] **1682** OLDHAM *Imit. 3rd Sat. Juvenal* Poems (1684) 192 For Shrieve how oft he has been known to fine. **1748** RICHARDSON *Clarissa* (1811) III. xliii. 252 After condemnation..all will be the king's or the shreeve's. **1796** J. ANSTEY *Pleader's Guide* (1803) 62 But let the Plaintiff, ere he sue In debt or case for money due, Swear to the sum, the writ indorse, And let the Shrieve said writ enforce.

ζ. *c* **1470** HARDING *Chron.* CCV. vii, In Yorkeshyre so the Rokeby with them mette, Shrief of the shyre. **1481** *Coventry Leet Bk.* 495 To þe Maire & shirffes. **1518** *Star Chamber Cases* (Selden Soc.) II. 142 William Dale one of the Shreffes of the Towne of Bristowe. *a* **1548** HALL *Chron., Hen. VIII* 61 b, The Mayre and Shrifes were there present. **1618** J. TAYLOR (Water P.) *Pennyless Pilgr.* C 3, Thus I..Was giu'n from Mayor to Shriefe, from Shriefe to Iaylor. **1691** *New Disc. Old Intreague* xxviii, Nor Shrieffs, nor Mayor, nor Common Halls excus'd. **1771** FOOTE *Maid of Bath* I. (1778) 19 The suit his honour made up twenty years ago comes next Lent, when he was shreif for the county.

**b.** *Scotland.* In early times (from the 12th c.) a high officer of a county with functions more or less analogous to those of the English sheriff of the same period, together with a civil and criminal jurisdiction of very wide extent. The office was commonly held by a noble, and was often hereditary; its judicial duties were performed by the *sheriff-depute*, who was necessarily a lawyer. The Act 20 Geo. II. c. 43 (1747) abolished heritable sheriffships, and in consequence of its provisions the office of sheriff, in the older sense, practically became extinct. The title of sheriff is now given to the sheriff-depute, who is the chief local judge in a Scottish county, and popularly to the sheriff-substitute, who usually hears cases in the first instance, subject to an appeal to the sheriff-depute. Both offices are now held for life, and the appointment rests with the crown

**1375** BARBOUR *Bruce* I. 190 Schyrreffys and bailȝheys maid he then. *c* **1425** WYNTOUN *Cron.* VIII. xxvi. 4110 Schirrayf [*v.r.* Schirref] of Bute and of Cowalle. *Ibid.* 4389 Schir Gotheray þe Rose was..schirrawe of Ayr. *c* **1470** HENRY *Wallace* VI. 791 Schirrais he maid that cruell was to ken. *Ibid.* XI. 1391 A schyrray gart this clerk son fra him pass. *a* **1567** MURE *Ho. Rowallane* 249 The Schereffe of Aire. **1712** FOUNTAINHALL *Decisions* (1761) II. 739 The brewers in and about Edinburgh, conceiving that the Sheriffs of Mid-Lothian had struck the fiars of victual too high. **1816** SCOTT *Antiq.* xx, The shirra sent for his clerk. **1818** —— *Rob Roy* xxix, I desire to be carried before some civil magistrate,..the sherra or the judge of the bounds. **1870** W. R. GREG *Polit. Problems* 114 The then Sheriff of Lanarkshire.

**c.** *Ireland.* A high officer in an Irish county, whose status and functions were closely similar to those of the English high sheriff. There were also sheriffs in certain Irish cities and boroughs: cf. a.

**1542** *Ir. Act 34 Hen. VIII*, c. 1 (1621) 238 The said Sherife of the said Shire [of Meath] for the time being. **1612** SIR J. DAVIES *Why Ireland*, etc. 140 In each of these Counties Palatines, there were two Sheriffes:..As in Meth we find a Sheriffe of the Liberty, and a Sheriffe of the Crosse: And so in Vlster, & so in wexford. **1675** *Essex Papers* (Camden) I. 309 All is forfited and taken up by the Shiriffe or Senescall. *aa* **1687** PETTY *Polit. Anat.* (1691) 36 The Sheriffs of Counties, and of Cities and Counties in Ireland are 40. *Ibid.* 41 [see *sheriff's peer* in 4]. **1817** *Act 57 Geo. III*, c. 68 Whereas it is expedient that the laws relating to Sheriffs in Ireland should be amended.

**d.** *U.S.* (See quot. 1828–32.)

**1662** *Laws of Virginia* xliv. 26 The Sheriffs of James-City ....shall be left to the Governour's free choice. **1788** *Massachusetts Spy* 8 May 3/3 The Mayor, the Sheriff, and some other persons interfered and rescued them, by lodging them in gaol. **1828–32** WEBSTER s.v., The sherif, by himself or his deputies, executes civil and criminal process throughout the county, has charge of the jail and prisoners, attends courts and keeps the peace. *a* **1842** in *Dickens' Amer. Notes* xvii. (1868) 141 A man was suspected, and the Sheriff most probably has possession of him by this time. **1876** 'MARK TWAIN' *Tom Sawyer* xi, The Sheriff was confident that he [the murderer] would be captured before night. *Ibid.* xxiv, Then the judge arrived, and the sheriff proclaimed the opening of the court.

**2. a.** With defining word, as ***deputy sheriff***, ***under-sheriff***, ***vice-sheriff***; ***high sheriff***, the sheriff (in England and Wales, and in some Irish cities) as distinguished from a deputy or subordinate.

**1450** *Paston Lett.* I. 125 The shreve of Kent..sent his under shreve to the juges to wete what to doo. *a* **1455** *Lett. Marg. Anjou & Bp. Beckington* (Camden) 158 Th' occupacion of under sherreive in the countie of Midd. *a* **1500** *Gest of Robyn Hode* xv. in Child *Ballads* III. 57 The hye sherif of Notyingham. **1532** MORE *Epitaph* Wks. 1421/1 Thomas More..being one of the vnder shriefes of London. **1559** AYLMER *Harborowe* L ij, Then must the hyghe Shrife be his frende. **1622** F. MARKHAM *Bk. War* III. vii. 106 The proverbe is, Twise an Under Sherife, euer a knave. *a* **1674** CLARENDON *Hist. Reb.* IX. §9 Colonel Long, the high shrief of the county. **1716** *Act 3 Geo. I*, c. 15 §10 It shall not be lawful..for any Person..to buy, sell, let, or take to Farm, the Office of Under-sheriff, Deputy-sheriff,..or any other Office..pertaining to the Office of High-sheriff of any County or Shire. **1830** *Rep. Sel. Comm. Office High Sheriff* 3 High Sheriffs are nominated by The King in Council, who, with His own hand, according to ancient custom, pricks the person appointed. *Ibid.* 5 The appointment of competent persons as permanent Under Sheriffs, throughout the several counties of England and Wales. **1835** *Tomlins' Law Dict.* (ed. 4) s.v., The under-sheriff usually performs all the duties of the office, a very few only excepted, where the personal presence of the high-sheriff is necessary. **1874** STUBBS *Const. Hist.* (1896) III. xx. 435 In 1319 Matthew of Crauthorn, who had been elected..to be Knight of the shire for Devon, petitioned the council against the undue return made by the vice-sheriff, who had substituted another name.

**b.** Scotland. ***sheriff depute***, ***substitute***: see 1 b. ***sheriff major***, ***principal***: designations formerly given to the sheriff (in the original sense) to distinguish him from the sheriff depute; in mod. use, the sheriff-depute is sometimes called ***sheriff-principal*** in contradistinction to the sheriff-substitute. † ***sheriff wardator***: see WARDATOR.

† ***sheriff in that part***: a person appointed to supply the place of the sheriff for executing process.

**1446** *Registr. Aberdon.* (Maitland Club) I. 244 Sir Alexander of Forbes..scheref depute of Aberdene. **1473** *Acc. Ld. High Treas. Scot.* I. 45 To Adam Bachillur, passande with the Kingis lettres, xvᵗᵒ Octobris, as schiref in that part for the inbringing of Schire William of Rendis gudis. **1489** *Ibid.* 109 The Schirra deput and bailȝeis of Hadington. **1501** *Ibid.* II. 115 Lord Erskin, schiref principale of Selkyrk. **1532** *Ibid.* VI. 116 The Shereffis Deputis of Edinburgh. *a* **1578** LINDESAY (Pitscottie) *Chron. Scot.* (S.T.S.) I. 45 Conflict betwix The Sherrife of Perth and Johne Gormak the Shireff maior. **1597** in *Spalding Club Misc.* (1841) I. 176 Mr. Thomas Leslye, syreff deput of Abirdene. **1671** *Aberdeen Reg.* (1872) IV. 276 Tuo of the baillies..to goe to the Earle Marshell, shirreff-principal. **1752** J. LOUTHIAN *Form of Process* (ed. 2) 249 The said Lords Reverse the foresaid Sentence of the said Sheriff-substitute. **1815** SCOTT *Guy M.* x, The Sheriff-depute of the county arrived at Ellangowan next morning at day-break. *Ibid.* xii, A very decent man, sir; the Sheriff-substitute of the county. **1834** *Tait's Mag.* I. 442/2, 30 Sheriff-Deputeships, varying from £300 to £800 a-year. 48 Sheriff-Substituteships in the gift of the Sheriffs-depute..varying from £150 to £600. **1866** *Cornh. Mag.* Aug. 247 There are two orders of sheriffs—the sheriff-substitutes, who reside each in the locality to which he has been appointed, and the sheriff-deputes (or 'sheriffs' simply), who hold courts at intervals. **1894** *Act 57 & 58 Vict.* c. 40 §7 The expression 'Sheriff' shall not include Sheriff Substitute.

**3.** †**a.** *transf.* Applied to officers (in foreign countries) with functions analogous to those of the sheriff; a governor of a district or city. *Obs.*

*a* **1225** *St. Marher.* 2 Olibrius hehte schirreue of þat lond. *cc* **1290** *St. Leonard* 103 in *S. Eng. Leg.* 459 þe scherreue of leouns feteres made strongue. *c* **1300** *Havelok* 2286 In al Denemark ne was no knith, Ne conestable, ne shireue,..þat he ne com biforn sire Ubbe. **13..** *Seuyn Sag.* (W.) 2564 Hit was a knight, a riche scherreue. **1535** COVERDALE *2 Kings* xxiii. 8 Iosua yᵉ shreue of the cite. **1535** —— *1 Esdr.* iv. 47 Then Darius..wrote a letter vnto all the debytes and shreues. **1545** JOYE *Exp. Dan.* ii. C viij b, Daniel and hys felowes were sought of Arioch the shryue to be slayne. **1562** TURNER *Herbal* II. 51 There was a certayn sherif in Egypt which tooke ij. naughty murtheryng robbers [etc.].

**b.** Short for *sheriff's officer* (sense 4 a); = BAILIFF 2.

**1928** *Daily Mail* 30 July 7/1 You have had the sheriff in your house? *Ibid.*, Who put the sheriff into your house?

**4. a.** *Comb.*: **sheriff's clerk**, *Sc.* **sheriff clerk**, the clerk of the sheriff's court; hence ***sheriffclerkship***; **sheriff's court**, *Sc.* **sheriff court**, a court in which the sheriff or his deputy administers justice; **sheriff fee** *Sc.*, a payment due to the sheriff; **sheriff fiars** *pl. Sc.* (see FIARS); †† **sheriff('s geld (gild, yeld)**, the payment made by the sheriff for the 'ferm' (FARM *sb.* 3) of his shire; † **sheriff('s gloves** *Sc.*, a perquisite of the sheriff levied at a fair; † **sheriff('s house**, ? the official residence of a sheriff (or of a similar official in foreign countries); **sheriff('s mair** *Sc.* [MAYOR 3] = *sheriff's officer*; † **sheriff-man** *Dublin* = *sheriff's peer*; † **sheriff's man** = *sheriff's officer*; also *Shropshire dial.* the goldfinch (see quot. 1796); **sheriff's officer** (*Sc.* also ***sheriff officer***), an official employed to execute the sheriff's writs, to distrain and arrest, etc.; † **sheriff's peer**, one of a class of members of the corporation of Dublin (before 1840) ranking next to the aldermen, and including all ex-sheriffs; † **sheriff roll** *Sc.*, the roll on which the proceedings of the sheriff's court were recorded; **sheriff's sale** *N. Amer.*, a public sale conducted by a sheriff following a court order for seizure and sale of property to satisfy a judgment; † **sheriff silver** = *sheriff geld*; **sheriff('s tourn** (*turn*, *tourney*); see TOURN, TOURNEY *sb.*[2]

**1377** LANGL. *P. Pl.* B. IV. 168 A *schireues clerke. **1564** *Reg. Privy Council Scot.* I. 274 James Makbrok of Campsy, allegit heretabill Sherefclerk of the said Sherefdome. **1679** *Acts of Sederunt* (1790) 144 All Shirriff-clarks to bring in their registers of hornings to be marked by the clark of register. **1875** *Encycl. Brit.* III. 290/1 The counted and rejected papers..are..transmitted by the returning officer to the clerk of the Crown in Chancery in England, or the sheriff-clerk in Scotland. **1564** *Reg. Privy Council Scot.* I. 274 The office of *Sherefclerkschip of the said Sherifdome. *Ibid.* 275 To deliver to the said James Drummond the *Sherefcourt bukis. **1752** J. LOUTHIAN *Form of Process* (ed. 2) App. 264 That no Person shall be obliged to appear before the Sheriff-court, unless he be cited upon a proper Summons. **1835** *Tomlins' Law Dict.* (ed. 4) s.v. *London*, The Sheriffs' Court, holden before their steward or judge. **1894** *Scots Law Times* I. 701 Except in Sheriff Court Cases, the figures refer to the number of the Case, and not to the number of the Page. **1962** T. B. SMITH *Scotland* iv. 102 The sheriff court has jurisdiction to try all crimes committed within the sheriffdom, except treason, murder, attempt to murder, rape, incest, certain offences against the Official Secrets Acts, deforcement of messengers, and breach of duty by magistrates. **1978** *Dumfries Courier* 13 Oct. 2/5 The sequel took place at Dumfries Sheriff Court on Friday when Savage pleaded guilty to the offence. **1603** *Reg. Mag. Sig. Scot.* 515/1 With all uther custumes, *schireff feis, dewteis and exactiones in and about the said burgh. **1765–8** ERSKINE *Inst. Law Scot.* I. iv. §38 Sheriffs were also intitled to the twentieth part of the sums contained in every decree, in name of sheriff-fee. **1689** in *Acts Parl. Scot.* (1875) XII. 55/2 þþᵗ the pryce of victwall payable furth of the shyre of fyfe to the Exchequer for cropt 1688 be payed conforme to the present *shirref fiars of the said shyre. **1301** *Yorksh. Inquisitions* (Yks. Rec. Soc.) III. 145 Rendering annually to the said heiress for Castelward and *Schirefgeld 6*d.* **1376** *Rolls of Parlt.* II. 348/2 Une Rente q'est appelle Shereveyeld q amounte a xiiiili. xixs. id. par an, provenantz des ditz deux Rapes. **1385** *Ibid.* III. 211/2 Shereves-yeld. **1543** *Mem. Fountains* (Surtees) 407 Paid to the exchetor..for the Sherifgylde, ijˢ. **1528** *Burgh Rec. Edin.* (1871) 3 That na *shereff gluiffes be tayne..fra na maner of persoun fra this present fair. **1603** *Reg. Mag. Sig. Scot.* 514/1 Lie schireff-gluiffis. **1641** *Peebles Burgh Rec.* (1872) 104 Thrie frie faires ....togidder with the sherief fie, sheriffis glowes, tolles [etc.]. *aa* **1505** *Chron. Lond.* (1905) 262 Sir William Capell, after his prisonment in the Countour, and *Shryvishouse was..commaundid to the Tower. **1583** STOCKER *Civ. Warres Lowe C.* IV. 6 b, In witnesse whereof, the saied Deputies to this present Treatie haue sette to their handes, in the Sherief house of Gant. **1812** W. TENNANT *Anster F.* II. xxxiii, Sheriffs learn'd, and unlearn'd *Sheriff-mairs, and messengers-at-arms. *c* **1400** *Gamelyn* 583 It ben the *schirrefes men, that hider ben i-come. *a* **1500** *Gest of Robyn Hode* cliii, in Child *Ballads* III. 63 Now is Litell John the sherifes man. **1605** CAMDEN *Rem., Wise Sp.* 226 When he [Sir T. More] was to mount the scaffold, hee saide to one of the Shiriffes men, I pray thee helpe mee vp, as for comming downe I take no care. **1667** DRYDEN *Epil. Tempest* 13 He sends me only like a Sh'riffs man here To let you know the Malefactor's neer. **1796** REV. F. LEIGHTON *MS. Let. J. Boucher* 10 May, I am promised some gleanings of Shropshire words. As to *Sheriff's man* for Goldfinch..the Corbets..were often Sheriffs of the County; their livery was black and yellow, the colour of the goldfinch's penfeathers. **1841** HARTSHORNE *Salopia Ant.* 562 *Sheriff's Man*, the seven coloured linnet, *Carduelis* of Linnæus. **1879** MISS JACKSON *Shropshire Word-bk.*, *Sheriff's-man*, the Goldfinch. **1703** FOUNTAINHALL *Decisions* (1761) II. 196 Here the *sheriff-officers were only brought *pro more*. **1818** SCOTT *Hrt. Midl.* xiii, The warrant's awa to Liberton wi' twa sheriff officers seeking ye. **1837** DICKENS *Pickw.* xl, Giving Mr. Pickwick a friendly tap on the shoulder, the sheriff's officer (for such he was) threw his card on the counterpane. **1843** BETHUNE *Sc. Fireside Stor.* 70 The sheriff's-officers proceeded to take him into custody. **1932** *Encycl. Laws Scotland* XIII. 527 Sheriff Officers are the persons by whom writs are served and executions carried out in the Sheriff Courts. *a* **1687** PETTY *Polit. Anat.* (1691) 41 There are in the City of Dublin a Lord-Mayor, 2 Sheriffs, 24 Aldermen, 48 *Sheriffs Peers, and 96 of the Common-Council. **1534** in *Exch. Rolls Scot.*

XVI. 584 Quhilk charter is registrat on the bak of *schiref roll of this instant yer. **1798** *Pittsburgh Gaz.* 6 Oct. 1/2 (Advt.), *Sheriff's Sales. **1883** *Brandon* (Manitoba) *Daily Mail* 9 Jan. 4/1 There will be a sheriff's sale of goods and chattels belonging to the late firm of Hambly & Miller, barbers, etc., on Saturday next. **1947** *Steamboat* (Colorado) *Pilot* 30 Jan. 2/8 The electric light plant..was sold at sheriff's sale. **1966** *Globe & Mail* (Toronto) 6 Sept. 30/1 Sheriff's Sale of Lands—Under and by Virtue of an Execution issued out of the Ninth Division Court of the County of York to me directed against the lands and tenements of [etc.]. **1324** in *Registr. Monast. de Winchelcumba* (1892) 351 Faciendo insuper annis singulis *Schirreveselver et alia servicia forinseca. **1432** *Rolls of Parlt.* IV. 403/2 Defautes for noun comyng unto ye *Shirrefs tourn. **1451** *Ibid.* V. 217/2 Sheref Tournes. **1536** in *Hexham Priory* (Surtees) App. p. cxxxix, The sade Sir Ingram..as shiref of Northumbeland..kept shiref-turnes at Alnwik. **1648** in J. R. Boyle *Hedon* (1895) App. 47 To the Sheriffturne Jurie 0 4 8.

**b.** In trivial and slang phrases: †**sheriff's basket, tub,** a basket or tub placed outside a prison to receive charitable doles for the prisoners; †**sheriff's posts,** two painted posts, set up at the sheriff's door, to which proclamations were affixed (cf. POST *sb.*[1] 2 b). (See also later quots.)

**1599** B. JONSON *Ev. Man out of Hum.* III. iii. (1600) K j b, How long should I be ere I should put off To the Lord Chancelors tombe, or the Shriues posts? **1600** NASHE *Summers Last Will* 1678 Wks. 1905 III. 286 That's as plentifull almes for the plague as the sheriffes tub to them of Newgate. **1632** MASSINGER *City Madam* I. i. (1658) 5 Did our charitie redeem thee out of prison,..When the Sheriffs basket, and his broken meat Were your Festivall exceedings? **17..** in Grose *Olio* (1792) 232 Dancing on nothing at the Sheriff's ball. *Foot-note,* Sheriff's ball, an execution. **1785** GROSE *Dict. Vulgar T., Sheriff's Bracelets,* handcuffs. *Ibid., Sheriff's Hotel,* a prison. *Ibid., Sheriff's*

**sheriff**: see SHEREEF, SHERIFI.

**sheriffalty** (ˈʃɛrɪfəltɪ). Also 6 **shirevalty, sheryaltie,** 7 **sheralltie, sherivalty, -ifalty, shireveaIty, shirifalty.** [f. SHERIFF + -AL[1] + -TY, after words like *royalty*.] = SHRIEVALTY.

**1518** *Star Chamber Cases* (Selden Soc.) II. 162 The seid Office of Sheryaltie. **1611** SPEED *Theat. Gt. Brit.* xx[i]x. 57/2 The Office of Execution and custody of this County [Huntingdon] is the Sheralfty [? *read* Sherfalty], of old inheritable. **1617** *Shuttleworths' Acc.* (Chetham Soc.) 227 The patent of my M^rs office of y^e sheralltie. **1648** *Persecutio Undecima* 57 Alderman Pennington [chosen] for his knowne zeale by his keeping a fasting Sabboth throughout his Shirifalty. **1682** *Enq. Elect. Sheriffs* 29 The Sherifalty of London. *Ibid.* 41 Sherivalty. **1753** RICHARDSON *Grandison* (1781) I. viii. 35 Sir Rowland Meredith, knighted in his Sheriffalty. **1870** FOSS *Biog. Dict. Judges of Eng.* 54 The Michaelmas solemnities of the sheriffalty of London.

*fig.* **1865** BUSHNELL *Vicar. Sacrif.* III. v. 269 Sending out the rugged sheriffalty of law and penal enforcement.

**sheriffdom** (ˈʃɛrɪfdəm). Forms: see SHERIFF; also *Sc.* 4 **shera-,** 5 **sera-, schirra-, schirre-, serraf-,** 6 **syrefdom(e.** [-DOM.]

**1.** A district or territory under the jurisdiction of a sheriff. *Sc.*

**1385** in *3rd Rep. Hist. MSS. Comm.* 410/1 In the sheradom of Perth. **1453** *Dunfermline Reg.* (Bannatyne Club) 340 Landis..lyand in þe Regalite of Dunfermlyn and the serrafdome of fyff. **1457** in *Acts Parl. Scot.* (1875) XII. 25/1 Quhilke assise [was]..chosin be þar avise of foure seradomes. **1549** *Compl. Scot.* xii. 103 In the schirefdome of galloua. **1662** *Acts of Sederunt* (1790) 84 Lands lyeing in several shirriffdoms. **1769** *De Foe's Tour Gt. Brit.* (ed. 7) IV. 296 The Isle of Arran, which with Bute makes up one Sheriffdom. **1854** *Act 17 & 18 Vict.* c. 91 §37 The sheriff of the sheriffdom in which the offence shall have been committed. **1854** H. MILLER *Sch. & Schm.* (1858) 52 The Hill..had borne the gallows of the sheriffdom on its crest. **1894** *Times* 19 Dec. 8/2 To officiate also as Sheriff-Substitute of the Sheriffdom of Argyll.

*transf.* **1762** tr. *Busching's Syst. Geog.* V. 270 The sheriffdom of Altorf.

**2.** The office of sheriff.

**1596** DALRYMPLE tr. *Leslie's Hist. Scot.* I. 127 This office na vthirwyse dependes than of heritage quhairthrouch vnto thame selfes thay ascriue schirrefdomes. **1610** HOLLAND *Camden's Brit.* I. 578 This Sherifedome was..translated hereditarily into the family of the Beauchamps. **1628** WITHER *Brit. Rememb.* IV. 552 A Couple..that had the Sheriffedome Of London that sad yeare. **1806** SCOTT *Let. to Ellis* 25 Jan. in *Lockhart* xv, The situation is..£800 a-year, besides being consistent with holding my sheriffdom. **1819** *Monthly Mag.* XLVIII. 5 It was thus that the hereditary sheriffdom of the county of Westmoreland came to the family of Tufton. **1877** MISS YONGE *Cameos* II. iii. 31 David bestowed on him the government of the castle, and the sheriffdom of Teviotdale. **1885** H. B. WHEATLEY in *Antiquary* Feb. 48/1 He was afterwards deprived of his sheriffdom and of his aldermanic gown.

**3.** *jocularly.* The realm or order of sheriffs.

**1904** SIR H. HAWKINS *Remin.* II. xliii. 47 All the pomp and splendour, in fact, that Sheriffdom was capable of.

**sheriffe,** obs. f. SHEREEF, SHERIFF, SHROFF.

†ˈ**sheriffess.** *Obs. rare.* [-ESS.] A woman who held the office of sheriff (when hereditary).

*c* **1659** *Inscr. Barden Tower* in *Howitt's Vis. Remark. Places* (1840) 217 Ladie Anne Clifford..High Sheriffesse by inheritance of the Countie of Westmerland. *a* **1661** FULLER *Worthies, Westmerld.* (1662) III. 141, I find Elizabeth the Widdow of Thomas Lord Clifford,..Sheriffess (as I may say) in the sixteenth of Richard the second, till the last of K. Henry the fourth. **1819** *Monthly Mag.* XLVIII. 5 Sir Roger de Clifford was killed in battle..about the year 1280. After his death, his widow sat in person, as sheriffess of the county of Westmoreland,..with the judges.

†ˈ**sheriffhood.** *Obs.* Forms: see SHERIFF. [*-hode,* -HOOD.] The office of sheriff.

*c* **1450** *Godstow Reg.* 70 In-to witnes of þis þinge þe seele of þe foreseid shreuehode was put þer-to. *a* **1470** GREGORY *Chron.* in *Hist. Coll. Cit. Lond.* (Camden) 77 He [Edw. II] grauntyd that sherevehodys sholde goo to ferme for CCC li be yere. **1502** ARNOLDE *Chron.* B iv b, [Charter of London 1384.] We haue graunted..to the Citezens of London the Shorefhode [*read* Sherefhode] of London and of Middelsex. **1556** *Chron. Grey Friars* (Camden) 14 John Briane was drowned in hys shrefehode. **1629** in *Crt. & Times Chas. I* (1848) II. 11 Here Sir Walter Long was brought this day into the Star Chamber, for having at the last election which was made for the parliament left the sheriffhood, which was then in his hands, to become a burgess of the said parliament.

**sheriffian,** variant of SHEREEFIAN.

ˈ**sheriffing,** *vbl. sb.* [-ING[1].] The holding of the office of sheriff, and discharge of its duties.

**1682** T. FLATMAN *Heraclitus Ridens* No. 66 (1713) II. 163 The several Plots and Projects of Exclusion, Association, Sheriffing, Feasting &c. **1896** *Harper's Mag.* Apr. 812/2 'You may think this here sheriffing is mighty funny,' he confided one day to a friend, 'but you ought to try it once, and see the dishonest whelps you have to deal with.'

ˈ**sheriffry.** *rare.* [-RY.] = SHRIEVALTY.

**1610** in *Cal. St. Pap., Irel.* 1608–10, 413 [He..had the] shrifery [of the county bestowed upon him]. **1836** GALT in *Tait's Mag.* III. 511 After my sheriffry.

ˈ**sheriffship.** [-SHIP.] The office of sheriff.

**1473–4** *Acc. Ld. High Treas. Scot.* I. 46 The office of schirefship of Strivelinġ. *a* **1578** LINDESAY (Pitscottie) *Chron. Scot.* (S.T.S.) II. 184 My lord lyndesay tuik possessioun of the Schereffschip of fyffe. **1649** ? EVELYN in *E.'s Diary,* etc. (1852) III. 42 The Scots..have..taken away the hereditary shriefships from the nobility. **1747** *Act. 20 Geo. II,* c. 43 §1 All Sheriffships and Deputy Sheriffships of Districts, being Parts only of Shires. **1884** *Manch. Exam.* 17 Nov. 5/3 It will be exceedingly hard if Mr. M. should be compelled to choose between his fat sheriffship and his political ambition. **1893** AGNEW *Hered. Sheriffs of Galloway* II. 120 The sheriff..was ordered to grant deputations of sheriffship to Grierson of Lagg, Claverhouse, and Earlshall, as his colleagues.

†**sheriff's tooth.** *Obs.* Forms: 3 **schirrefstuthe,** 4 **shirrevestothe,** 5 **sheriffs-tooth,** (8 **sheriff-tooth**). [Cf. phrase 'for one's own tooth' in TOOTH *sb.* 3.] An annual impost (complained of in 1327–77 by Derbyshire tenants as a wrongful exaction) levied by the sheriff on each bovate of land within his county.

**1298** *Yorksh. Inquisitions* (Yks. Rec. Soc.) III. 84, 2*s.* for Waytemete and Schirrefstuthe. **1327–77** *Rolls of Parlt.* II. 401/2 Une torcenouse prise q'est chescun an leve sur eux par Baillifs le Roy q'il appelent Shirrevestothe, c'est assavoir de chescune bove de terre sys deners. **1402** in Leycester *Hist. Antiq.* (1673) 207, & *reddendo per annum de Stothe, alias dictum* Sheriffs-Tooth, *septem Denarios.* **1701** *Cowel's Interpr.* (ed. Kennett) s.v., *Per Sherif-tooth* seems a tenure by the service or duty of providing Entertainment for the Sheriff at his County Turns or Courts.

**sheriffwick** (ˈʃɛrɪfwɪk). Forms: see SHERIFF and -WICK; also 6 **shyrrywyke,** 7 **shirrewicke.**

**1.** The office of sheriff.

**1451** *Rolls of Parlt.* V. 225/1 The offices and occupations of Mairalte, Shirrefwyke, Chaumberleynship. **1520** *Coventry Leet Bk.* 667 Touchyng the office of Shyrrywyke of the Citie. **1542–3** *Act 34 & 35 Hen. VIII,* c. 26 §22 Theyre saide office of Shiriefewike. **1601** MUNDAY *Downf. Earl Huntington* II. C I b, Master Warman, here's your Patent seald, For the high Sheriffewick of Notingham. **1604** in Kempe *Losely MSS.* (1836) 221 There is £500 more unpaide, which they lye in wayte untill I be oute of the Shirrewicke to have of me. *c* **1640** J. SMYTH *Lives Berkeleys* (1883) II. 224 Thomas was..discharged of his Shreevewick of Gloucester^re. **1642** C. VERNON *Consid. Exch.* 26 Extraordinary services done by Sheriffes in the time of their Sheriffwicke. **1884** *Law List* 1299 *note,* The Sheriffwick of London is in the Corporation of London.

**2.** The district over which a sheriff has jurisdiction.

**1535** *Act 27 Hen. VIII,* c. 26 §18 Every misruled and suspecte personne within thir Shireffwik. **1810** BENTHAM *Packing* (1821) 217 Within the Sheriffwick of the Sheriffs of London and Middlesex. **1894** R. S. FERGUSON *Hist. Westmorland* 95 The bailiwick of Westmorland in the sheriffwick or shrievalty, of the whole county of Westmorland.

‖**sherifi** (ʃəˈriːfɪ). Forms: 7 **shariffe, scherifi, sherif,** 7, 9 **scherif,** 8 **sher(r)iff;** 7,9 **xeriff,** 9 **zeriff.** Also (in Dicts.) 9 **shereefee.** [Arab. *sharīfī* (Dozy), f. *sharīf* (see SHEREEF). Cf. SERAPH[2], SERAPHIN.] A gold coin formerly current in the Levant.

**1615** G. SANDYS *Trav.* II. 108 Three millions of Shariffes. **1647** GREAVES *Roman Foot* 121 The Turkish sultani, or Ægyptian sherif. **1687** A. LOVELL tr. *Thevenot's Trav.* I. 262 The Turkish Chequin, which they call Scherif, is worth seventy Maidins, and the Venetian, seventy five. **1690** DRYDEN *Don Sebastian* I. i, I ask Six Hundred Xeriffs for him [*sc.* a horse]. **1696** tr. *Du Mont's Voy. Levant* xix. (1705) 240 His Ransom..was fix'd at 100 Turkish Pieces of Gold, commonly call'd Scherifi, worth 2½ Piasters each. **1785** *Arab. Nts.* II. 203 The necklace was valued at two thousand sherriffs. **1802** *Arab. Nts.* (1815) II. 63, I paid only two scherifs a month for the use of it. **1858** SIMMONDS *Dict. Trade, Xeriff,* a former gold coin, current in Egypt and Turkey, for about 9 s. 6 d. Another name for the ducat in Morocco. *Ibid., Zeriff,* an old Turkish coin worth about 2½ dollars.

**sherish,** obs. form of CHERISH *v.*

**1436** *Libel Eng. Policy* in *Pol. Poems* (1859) II. 188.

‖**sheristadar** (ʃɛˌrɪstəˈdɑː(r)). *Anglo Ind.* Also 9 **serrishtehdar, ser-, sherishtadar.** [Urdū (a. Pers.) *sarishte dār,* f. *sarishte* (properly *sar-rishta*) office, employment + *dār* holder, possessor.] The head clerk or registrar of an Indian court of justice: see quot. 1872.

**1775** in *Min. Evid. Trial W. Hastings* (1788) I. 1033 The Sheristadars have delivered me an Account. **1834** [PRINSEP] *Baboo* I. vii. 110 (Stanf.) The Serishtadar commenced business by informing me that this wretch was a Goreyt. **1872** E. BRADDON *Life in India* vii. 284 The sherishtadar cross-examined witnesses, droned out the proceedings when they were recorded, prompted the decision, and placed the completed case before the judge for signature. **1909** *Ch. Miss. Rev.* Sept. 515 It is not the Englishman who really governs India, but the Brahman sheristadar or deputy collector and the large army of Brahman officials.

**sherivalty**: see SHERIFFALTY.

**sherive, sherk,** obs. ff. SHERIFF, SHIRK.

**sherl,** obs. form of SCHORL.

**1777** FORSTER *Voy. round World* II. v. II. 26 The rocks.. contained volcanic productions, or different kinds of lava, some of which are full of white and greenish sherls.

**Sherlock** (ˈʃɜːlɒk), *sb.* [See HOLMESIAN *a.* and *sb.*, and next.] A person who investigates mysteries or shows great perceptiveness; a private detective.

**1903** G. V. HOBART *Back to Woods* iii. 57 'Down there, eh?' snorted the country Sherlock. **1928** D. L. SAYERS *Ld. Peter views Body* 42 I'm riding with Freddy Arbuthnot,..as you might see by my legs, if you were really as big a Sherlock as you make out. **1932** KIPLING *Limits & Renewals* 178 We aren't exactly first-class Sherlocks. **1967** N. FREELING *Strike out where not Applicable* 27 Mr. van der Valk, my dear, our police Sherlock. **1972** 'L. EGAN' *Paper Chase* xii. 191 You'll have to turn Sherlock and solve the case yourself.

So ˈ**Sherlock** *v. intr.* and *trans.*, to engage in detective work; to investigate (something), to make deductions about; ˈ**Sherlockian,** *sb.* and *a.* (*a*) *sb.* = SHERLOCK *sb.*; (*b*) *adj.* pertaining to or characteristic of Sherlock Holmes; = HOLMESIAN *a.*; ˈ**Sherlockiˌana** [-IANA], things connected with Sherlock Holmes, writings about Sherlock Holmes; ˈ**Sherlocking** *vbl. sb.*, detective work.

**1903** *Bookman* XVII. 5/2 If you decipher this you are a real Sherlockian. **1913** *Manch. Guardian* 15 Jan., Any man with a bundle or package was suspicious, so we 'sherlocked' around for a bit and watched him go into a barber's shop to get disguised by having his hair cut. There we 'pinched' him. **1920** J. GALSWORTHY *Foundations* I, in *Plays* (1929) 468 Don't call in the police!..Let me do the Sherlocking for you. **1934** *Discovery* Sept. 273/2 It is now close on four hundred years since that door was used and sandals trod those steps, but we are able to 'Sherlock' this detail of old times. **1937** STEVENS & SHORTEN *How to watch Football Game* vi. 51 No use in trying to Sherlock the next play. Anything can happen. **1942** H. HAYCRAFT *Murder for Pleasure* xiii. 276 Vincent Starrett's *Private Life of Sherlock Holmes* with its valuable appended bibliography of Sherlockiana. **1957** J. KEROUAC *On Road* (1958) 135 They tried some amateur Sherlocking by asking the same questions twice. **1959** *Listener* 3 Dec. 993/1 A startling piece of detective work, followed up with exact, devoted, Sherlockian tenacity. **1962** W. S. BARING-GOULD *Sherlock Holmes* 263 Late 1895–late 1896 called by many Sherlockian commentators 'The Missing Year', and the subject of much learned speculation. **1963** 'G. CARR' *Lewker in Norway* i. 25 You're really disappointed because you can't go Sherlocking after that young man. **1972** E. ROUTLEY *Puritan Pleasures of Detective Story* ii. 27 This is not a contribution to Sherlockiana, but the..cult of Sherlock Holmes is itself..in the field of our enquiry. **1975** *Daily Tel.* 27 May 14/3 He.. had built up an outstanding collection of Sherlockiana, including such rarities as a copy of the Beeton's Christmas Annual of 1887 in which the first Holmes adventure..was originally published. **1977** *New Yorker* 20 June 71/1 He lights his pipe. It is long and low and looks somewhat Sherlockian.

**Sherlock Holmes** (ˈʃɜːlɒk həʊmz). [See HOLMESIAN *a.* and *sb.*] A person resembling Sherlock Holmes; = SHERLOCK *sb.*

**1896** E. TURNER *Little Larrikin* x. 108 It took her nearly five minutes to wonder sufficiently at him..and call him a Sherlock Holmes. **1914** T. A. BAGGS *Back from Front* xxiv. 118 It needed no Sherlock Holmes to discover where English cavalry had bivouacked for the night. **1957** A. MACNAB *Bulls of Iberia* xvi. 237 The press critics kept very quiet about it, and one need not be a Sherlock Holmes to guess why. **1981** *Times* 22 Apr. 6/5 The doctor becomes a medical Sherlock Holmes.

So **Sherlock Holmes** *v. trans.*, to make deductions about, to assess, to deduce (cf. SHERLOCK *v.*); **Sherlock** ˈ**Holmesian** *a.* = SHERLOCKIAN *a.*; **Sherlock** ˈ**Holmesing** *vbl. sb.* = SHERLOCKING *vbl. sb.*

**1922** JOYCE *Ulysses* 620 He had been meantime taking stock of the individual in front of him and Sherlock-holmesing him up. **1929** C. I. LEWIS *Mind & World-Order* ix. 287 All the Sherlock Holmesing in the world would not help him a bit because he would not be able to recognize evidence when he found it. **1954** E. EAGER *Half Magic* iii. 35 'She just as good as said so,' said Jane, 'and I Sherlock Holmesed the rest.' **1958** *Observer* 16 Mar. 14/3 The stern Sherlock Holmesian K.C. **1958** A. WILSON *Middle Age of*

*Mrs. Eliot* I. 89 All this woman's intuition is just a lot of Sherlock Holmesing. **1972** *Sci. Amer.* Mar. 106/3 He proceeded indeed by a kind of Sherlock Holmesian logic, which presumes that in eliminating the impossible and the more implausible it has arrived at the true.

**Sherman**[1] ('ʃɜːmən). The name of John *Sherman* (1823–1900), U.S. senator, used *attrib.* to designate either of two acts passed by Congress in 1890, one to prohibit combinations in restraint of inter-state or foreign trade, the other to maintain the price of silver by government purchase of silver bullion; also, to designate treasury notes issued under the provisions of the latter act.

**1892** *Dem. Platform* in K. Porter *Nat. Party Platforms* (1924) 162 We denounce the Republican legislation known as the Sherman Act of 1890. **1894** *Harper's Mag.* Jan. 318/1 Mr. Voorhees's substitute repealing the Sherman law was passed by a vote of 43 to 32. **1897** *Money* May 23 Government notes called Treasury notes of 1890, sometimes *Sherman notes*, sometimes *Coin notes*.. were issued in payment of purchases of silver bullion from 1890–93. **1947** *Atlantic Monthly* June 73/1 In 1890 the Sherman Act was passed to 'appease the restive masses', but it would be fifty years before Thurman Arnold would demonstrate, briefly, that the Act could be made to work. **1948** *Duncan* (Oklahoma) *Daily Banner* 1 July 1/3 The U.S. Supreme Court..held that officers of the company and the firm itself had violated the Sherman anti-trust law. **1974** *Encycl. Brit. Micropædia* IV. 303/1 The Bland-Allison Act was superseded in 1890 by the Sherman Silver Purchase Act, which increased the government's monthly silver purchases by 50 percent. Fear that the U.S. was about to abandon the gold standard precipitated the Panic of 1893, causing the Sherman Act to be hastily repealed the same year.

**Sherman**[2] ('ʃɜːmən). The name of W. T. *Sherman* (1820–91), U.S. general, used *attrib.* and *absol.* to designate an American type of medium tank, much used during the war of 1939–45. Also ***General Sherman*** (***tank***).

**1942** *Times* 6 Nov. 6/3 *(caption)* A picture just received from America of General Sherman tanks. **1942** W. S. Churchill *End of Beginning* (1943) 229 This very powerful force.., including all the best tanks, the Grants and the Shermans, was withdrawn from the battle front. **1944** *Sun* (Baltimore) 15 Nov. 11/2 The Sherman tanks jumped off with orders to cross the river. **1965** A. J. P. Taylor *Eng. Hist. 1914–45* xv. 554 To aid Auchinleck, the Americans diverted 300 Sherman tanks to Suez. **1969** Stubbs & Connor *Armor-Cavalry* I. 64 A much improved M3 medium was standardized in 1941 as the M4, better known throughout the war by its British designation, the General Sherman. **1971** E. Luttwak *Dict. Mod. War* 176/1 The Israeli army uses a large number of converted Shermans fitted with a new 105-mm gun.

**sherman, shern(e**, obs. ff. SHEARMAN, SHARN.

**sheroot**, obs. form of CHEROOT.

**1824** Scott *St. Ronan's* xv. (end), I will light my sheroot.

**sherp**, obs. and dial. form of SHARP *v.*

**Sherpa** ('ʃɜːpə). Also 9 **Serpa, Sharpa.** [ad. Tibetan *sharpa*, inhabitant of an eastern country.] **1.** (A member of) a Tibetan people living on the southern slopes of the Himalayas. Also *attrib.* or as *adj.*

**1847** B. H. Hodgson in *Jrnl. Asiatic Soc. Bengal* XVI. 1237 Cis-Himálayan Bhotias vel Tibetans, called..Serpa, &c. *Ibid.* 1238 The sub-Himálayan races..inhabit all the central and temperate parts of these mountains, the juxta nivean or nethermost tracts being left to the Rongbo vel Sérpá. **1874** —— *Ess. on Nepál & Tibet* II. ii. 30 Cis-Himálayan Bhotias vel Tibetans, called Rongbo,..Sérpa or Sharpa etc. **1922** G. H. Leigh-Mallory in C. K. Howard-Bury *Mount Everest* xiv. 224 The Tibetan coolies..were notably less strong than our Sherpas. **1924** *Glasgow Herald* 16 Apr. 10/6 Two of them after a merry-making battered each other in a terrific manner, but the following morning.. they were nursing each other with the greatest care and mutual pity. Such is a Sherpa porter. **1950** T. Longstaff *This my Voyage* iv. 67 He..had not yet shown us that Sherpas could be the mainstay of any Himalayan expedition. **1970** *Daily Colonist* (Victoria, B.C.) 11 Nov. 38/4 Sen Tensing, the sherpa bearer, shuddered in fright. **1979** *Daily Tel.* 17 May 1/4 One of mountaineering's best known Sherpas, Ang Phu, was feared killed yesterday in a fall on Everest after helping a Yugoslav expedition put a second team on the summit.

**2.** *transf.* and *fig.* A mountain guide or porter; a guide; an official who makes the preparations for a summit conference.

**1959** M. Pugh *Chancer* 137 What was the idea of trying that cliff? Did you fancy your chance as a sherpa? **1976** P. Cave *High Flying Birds* iii. 35 'O.K.,' I said. 'Lead the way, sherpa.' **1980** *Times* 23 June 1/2 The seven leaders inevitably based much of their comment on the draft communique drawn up for publication after the meeting by the seven government officials—known as the 'sherpas'—who have been charged with preparing this summit.

†**sherpe.** *Obs. rare*[−1]. Also 5 **shyrpe.** [a. OF. *escherpe*, var. of *escrepe* SCRIP *sb.*[1]] = SCRIP *sb.*[1]

**1426** Lydg. *De Guil. Pilgr.* 5372 Thys bred, pylgrymes eurychon,..In ther sherpe they shold yt bere. *Ibid.* 6220 Shyrpe.

**sherpet, sherrafe**, obs. ff. SHERBET, SHROFF.

**sherrant**, variant of SHERANT *Obs.*

**sherref(f, -eive, -eve, -if(f**, etc.: see SHERIFF.

**Sherriff(e**, variant ff. of SHEREEF, SHERIFI.

**sherris** ('ʃɛrɪs). *arch.* Also 6–8 **sherries**, 7 **ceres.** [a. Sp. (*vino de*) *Xeres* wine of Xeres (see SHERRY *sb.*[1]). The Sp. *x*, now coincident in sound with *j* (x), was formerly pronounced (ʃ).

The name of the town appears in the 17th c. as *Sherries*: e.g. 1626 R. Peeke *(title)* Three to One: Being an English Spanish Combat, performed..at Sherries in Spain.]

= SHERRY *sb.*[1] 1.

[**1540–1** *Will of R. Sowethewarke* (Somerset Ho.), Twenty buttes of sakes of Sherries.] **1597** Shaks. *2 Hen. IV*, IV. iii. 111 The second propertie of your excellent Sherris, is, the warming of the Blood:..the Sherris warmes it, and makes it course from the inwards, to the parts extremes. **1876** Browning *At the 'Mermaid'* ii, The sherris mantling Still about each mouth. **1884** Black *Jud. Shakespeare* xxiv, Lord, Jack, what a sherris that was!

**b.** *attrib.* and *Comb.*: **sherris-sack**, 'sack' imported from Xeres: see SACK *sb.*[3] 1 b.

**1876** Browning *At the 'Mermaid'* xviii, Back then to our *sherris-brewage! **1597** *Sherris sack [see SACK *sb.*[3] 1 b]. **1607** Markham *Caval.* VII. (1617) 36 A pinte of very good Ceres sacke. **1777** W. Dalrymple *Trav. Sp. & Port.* clxviii, Xeres..is famous for..what we call, *sherries wine.

**sherrivalleys**, variant of SHERRYVALLIES.

**sherri-varrie**: see SHIVAREE.

**sherrug**, obs. form of SHEAR-HOG.

**sherry** ('ʃɛrɪ), *sb.*[1] Also 7 **shirry, zerry, shery, sherie**, 8 **sherree.** [A sing. form evolved from SHERRIS, mistaken for a plural.]

**1. a.** Originally, the still white wine made near Xeres (now *Jerez de la Frontera*, a town in Andalusia, near Cadiz); in modern use, extended to a class of Spanish fortified white wines of similar character, and (usually with prefixed word, as ***Californian, Cape sherry***) to wines made elsewhere in imitation of Spanish sherry. Also, a wine of this kind.

**1608** Middleton *Mad World* v. H 1, Some Shirry for my Lords players there. **1614** B. Jonson *Barth. Fair* v. iv, *Cok.* Sack? you said but e'en now it should be Sherry. *Pup. Io.* Why so it is; sherry, sherry, sherry. **1617** *Shuttleworths' Acc.* (Chetham Soc.) 224 One other rundlett of shery. *c* **1645** Howell *Lett.* (1688) II. 350 Those kinds that our Merchants carry over, are those onely that grow upon the Sea-side as Malagas, Sheries, Tents. **1662** Charleton *Myst. Vintners* (1675) 203 They sell decayed Xeres, vulgarly Sherry, for Lusenna wine. **1682** Wheler *Journ. Greece* I. 35 Excellent Wines, especially red Muscatels (which we call Luke Sherry). *a* **1715** Burnet *Own Time* (1766) II. 221 He drunk a little tea and some sherry. **1726** G. Roberts *Four Yrs. Voy.* 331 Some Sherree. **1835** Dickens *Sk. Boz, Public Dinners*, Waiters..are placing decanters of sherry down the tables. **1848** Thackeray *Van. Fair* xxxviii, Most celebrated growths of ports, sherries, and claret wines. **1854** Mrs. Gaskell *North & S.* xxxv, Some rare old sherry. **1897** 'Merriman' *In Kedar's Tents* xiii. 145 The Colonel had an English friend who spoke so—one engaged in the sherry in Xeres. **1958** A. L. Simon *Dict. Wines, Spirits & Liqueurs* 146/1 Sherry is made from the best wine of each vintage, to which some Brandy is added, after which it is kept for many years with the best wine of other vintages. **1967** *Times* 1 Aug. 6/5 'Sherry' means a wine coming from the Jerez district of Spain. The Court, giving judgment,..decided that it would be unjust now to restrain Vine Products Ltd. ..from using the expressions 'British sherry', 'English sherry', 'Cyprus sherry', 'South African sherry', and 'Australian sherry', used for certain wines in England.

*fig.* **1619** *Pasquils Palinodia* title-p., A pleasant pynte of Poeticall Sherry.

**b.** In the names of mixed drinks, ***sherry-and-seltzer, sherry-and-bitters.***

**1881** H. Smart *Race for Wife* I, Men are congregating about the refreshment buffet for another sherry-and-seltzer. **1884** Mrs. C. Praed *Zéro* iii, Will you come in and have a sherry and bitters.

**c.** A glass or drink of sherry.

**1924** Galsworthy *White Monkey* II. ix. 192 Will you have a sherry? **1979** M. McCarthy *Cannibals & Missionaries* i. 19 He had been counting on picking Gus's brains..over a sherry or a bourbon.

**2.** 'A small wine-glass of the size and form commonly used for sherry and similar wines' (*Cent. Dict.* 1891).

**1907** [see PORT *sb.*[7] c]. **1925** [see LIQUEUR *sb.* 2]. **1974** [see PORT *sb.*[7] c].

**3.** *attrib.* and *Comb.* **a.** simple *attrib.*, as ***sherry-bottle, -butt, -case, decanter, -glass, trifle*** [TRIFLE *sb.* 6 b], ***sherry-wine***, also ***sherry-wine colour; sherry-drinker, -grower; sherry-style, -type*** adjs.; **sherry-bar**, a bar at which sherry is the principal drink sold; **sherry morning**, a morning sherry party; **sherry party**, a party at which sherry is the principal drink served.

**1951** G. Greene *End of Affair* v. ii. 181 Waterbury was waiting in a *sherry-bar off Tottenham Court Road. **1848** Thackeray *Van. Fair* xxv, The *sherry-bottle. **1888** *Sat. Rev.* 9 June 688/1 The juice as it runs out is caught and transferred to tubs, sherry hogsheads and *sherry butts. **1853** R. S. Surtees *Sponge's Sp. Tour* (1893) 27 With a formidable looking *sherry-case, in the shape of a horn, at his saddle. **1950** J. Cannan *Murder Included* vii. 164 A tray with two glasses and a *sherry decanter. **1977** G. McDonald *Confess, Fletch* xxiii. 104 There were Scotch bottles, bourbon bottles, gin bottles, sherry and port decanters. **1887** J. R. P. Berkeley in Knapp *Geo. Borrow* (1899) II. 101 Among his peculiarities was his dislike..of *sherry drinkers. **1879** Mrs. A. E. James *Ind. Househ. Managem.* 26 There was only one *sherry-glass broken. **1900** Spielmann *Ruskin* 17 Peter Domecq, the great *sherry-grower of Xerez. **1976** *Milton Keynes Express* 16 July 2/3 A *sherry morning on Sunday brought in £98.32 for Olney Town Cricket Club funds. **1936** *Cherwell* 7 Mar. 158/2 A tendency to throw *sherry parties and get a little drunk. **1977** 'J. le Carré' *Honourable Schoolboy* xi. 239 Christmas was hardly noticed apart from a rather battered sherry party. **1960** *Times* 3 Oct. (Wine Trade Suppl.) p. iv/5 In the United States there is a domestic wine business which last year turned out..20 million gallons of *sherry-style wine. **1951** H. Smith *Master Bk. Dessert Pies & Sweets* viii. 279 **Sherry Trifle*, arrange slices of Swiss roll at the bottom of a round glass dish and sprinkle liberally with sherry. **1979** K. Bonfiglioli *After you with Pistol* xxii. 176 Two helpings of sherry-trifle. **1962** *Times* 3 Feb. 9/4 A glass of *sherry-type wine. **1785** Bentham *Mem. & Corr.* Wks. 1843 X. 160 Good *Sherry-wine. **1832** Marryat *N. Forster* xxxiv, You may have seen the Xerez or sherry wine. **1889** *Anthony's Photogr. Bull.* II. 124 Light sherry-wine color.

**b.** With reference to colour.

**1856** H. H. Dixon *Post & Paddock* 301 Mr. Stirling Craufurd's *sherry-bay horse, The Shaver. **1871** Garrod *Mat. Med.* (ed. 3) 147 A vinous liquid, having a golden *sherry colour. **1878** Abney *Photogr.* xiii. 90 Enough to give a sherry colour to the collodion. **1875** Huxley & Martin *Pract. Biol.* App. (1877) 270 A dark *sherry-coloured solution. **1894** *Season* X. 47/2 Flecked with sherry and rose-coloured strands. **1898** P. Manson *Trop. Diseases* ii. 65 From dark brown to *sherry-red. **1813** *Ann. Reg., Chron.* 102 Boots with *sherry-yellow-tassels.

**c.** In names of drinks: **sherry-negus**, see NEGUS[2]; †**sherry sack**, see SACK *sb.*[3] 1 b, cf. SHERRIS; also *fig.* See also SHERRY-COBBLER.

**1619** *Pasquils Palinodia* A 3, My Muse..weares a Corslet of old Sherry Sacke. **1677** Lady Hatton in *Hatton Corr.* (Camden) 148 All the sherie sack. *c* **1863** T. Taylor *Ticket-of-Leave Man* I. 7 Two sherry negus, two shillings. **1907** *Daily Chron.* 21 Nov. 3/3 Who drank sherry-negus.

†'**sherry,** *sb.*[2] *slang.* In quot. **shirry.** [Cf. SHERRY *v.*[1]] A scurry.

**1821** Haggart *Life* 37 The shirry became general—I was run to my full speed.

†'**sherry,** *a. Obs. rare*[−1]. [f. SHERRY *sb.*[1]] Under the influence of sherry; drunk.

**1770** *Gentl. Mag.* XL. 559/1 To express the Condition of an Honest Fellow, and no Flincher, under the Effects of good Fellowship, it is said that he is..Sherry.

'**sherry,** *v.*[1] *dial.* Also 9 **shirry.** [Perh. a variant of SHEER *v.*] *intr.* To scurry, to run away; retreat hastily. Also with *off.*

**1788** Grose *Dict. Vulgar T.* (ed. 2), *To Sherry*, to run away: sherry off. **1821** Haggart *Life* 36 He went into an entry, as I shirry'd past him. **1866** Brogden *Prov. Words Lincolnsh.* 180 You've been long enough, sherry. *c* **1874** R. E. Leader in *Sheffield Gloss.* (1890) s.v., Now, my lad, sherry. **1877** *Holderness Gloss., Sherry-off*, to run off, or retreat hastily.

'**sherry,** *v.*[2] [f. SHERRY *sb.*[1]]

**1.** *trans.* To supply with sherry, to give sherry to. *nonce-wd.*

**1909** 'Q.' (Quiller-Couch) *True Tilda* xxi. 294 Nursed by a careful butler..a single bottle will sherry twelve guests.

**2.** To add sherry to. Chiefly as '**sherried** *ppl. a.*

**1970** *Guardian* 15 Apr. 10/2 A heavily sherried trifle. **1977** D. J. Elliott in D. Marcus *Best Irish Short Stories* 2 156 They ate prawns in aspic, sherried.

'**sherry-cobbler.** *colloq.* [f. SHERRY *sb.*[1]] A cobbler made with sherry. See COBBLER 3.

**1809** [see COBBLER 3]. **1842** Dickens *Amer. Notes* ix, The bowls of mint-julep and sherry-cobbler. **1855** Haliburton *Nat. & Hum. Nat.* II. 312 He suck in his drink like sherry-cobbler through a straw. **1882** 'Ouida' *Under Two Flags* (1890) 82 He paused to listen till he let the ice in his sherry-cobbler melt away.

**sherryvallies** (ʃɛrɪ'vælɪz), *sb. pl. U.S.* Also 9 **shorrevals, sherrivalleys.** [The proximate history is obscure, but the word must be an adoption of some one of the many forms of a widely diffused word of oriental origin, signifying a kind of trousers: cf. Arab. *sirwāl*, now commonly *sharwāl* (pl. *sarāwīl, sharāwīl*), whence Sp. *zaragüelles* pl., Pg. *ceroulas* pl.), Russian *sharavary*, Polish *szarawary*, Gr. σαράβαρα, late and med.L. *sarabara, saraballa, sarabala, saravara*, etc. (see Du Cange), Syriac *sharbålå*; the ultimate source is by some scholars supposed to be the Persian *shalwār* (see SHALWAR) of the same meaning. The Biblical Aramaic *sarbālīn* pl., which in Dan. iii. 21, 27 is rendered by the like-sounding words in Syr., Gr., and Latin, has been regarded as identical (Eng. Bible 1611 'coats', *margin* 'mantles', 1884 Revised 'hosen'), but this is very doubtful.

Our first quot. might suggest Polish as the probable proximate source for the U.S. word. Gen. C. Lee had been aide-de-camp to the king of Poland.]

(See quot. 1848.)

**1778** Gen. C. Lee *Let.* 20 Dec. in *Mem.* (1792) 430 If you find them to be green breeches patched with leather, and not actually legitimate sherry vallies, such as his Majesty of Poland wears,..I will submit in silence to all the scurrility which [etc.]. **1825** *Springfield Tailor's advt.* in Alice M. Earle *Costume Colon. Times* (1894) 217 Shorrevals and Overalls And Pantaloons he'll make. **1833** C. F. Hoffman *Winter in Far West* (1835) I. 105 Raising his blue cotton frock to thrust his hand into the fob of his sherrivalleys. **1848** BARTLETT *Dict. Amer.*, *Sherryvallies*, pantaloons made of thick velvet or leather, buttoned on the outside of each leg, and generally worn over other pantaloons. They are now chiefly worn by teamsters. Many years ago, when.. journeys were made on horseback, *sherryvallies* were indispensable to the traveller.

**shert**, obs. form of SHORT *adv.*

**shert(e, sherth**, obs. forms of SHIRT *sb.*

‖**sherut** (ʃeɪˈruːt). Also **sheirut**. [Heb., lit. 'service'.] In Israel, a large taxi shared by several passengers.

**1950** G. MIKES *Milk & Honey* 91 Between the two [bus and taxi] there is the communal taxi, the *sherut*. **1968** P. DURST *Badge of Infamy* xiv. 133 He flagged down a *sherut*, one of the ramshackle taxi-cum-buses which plied between Haifa and Tel Aviv. **1977** H. KAPLAN *Damascus Cover* (1978) iii. 21 The *sheirut* drivers, loudly beckoning arriving passengers to share a taxi to Tel Aviv or Jerusalem. **1981** *Daily Tel.* 24 June 11 Jitneys and sheruts should be introduced on the roads to make public transport more efficient.

**sherve**, obs. form of SHERIFF.

**sherville**, obs. form of CHERVIL.

**1689** in *Thanes of Cawdor* (Spalding Club) 353, 4 drop sherville.

**shervon**, obs. f. *shriven*, pa. pple. of SHRIVE *v.*

‖**ˈsherwal.** *rare.* [Arab. *sharwāl*: see SHERRYVALLIES.] A kind of loose trousers worn in various Asiatic countries.

**1844** tr. *Maria T. Asmar's Mem. Babyl. Princess* I. 44 My sherwals, or trowsers, were of crimson silk. *Ibid.* II. 148 Arraying myself in..a sadrieh, or jacket, of golden tissue, rose-coloured sherwals, a turban [etc.].

‖**sherwani** (ʃɜːˈwɑːniː). [Hindi.] In the Indian sub-continent, a knee-length coat, buttoning to the neck, worn by men.

**1911** [see ACHKAN]. **1964** D. N. WILBUR *Pakistan* viii. 168 Among well-to-do Moslems generally, a long coat known as a *sherwani* is worn. **1971** R. RUSSELL tr. *A. Ahmad's Shore & Wave* vi. 54 He gravely took off his *sherwani* and hung it on the coat-hanger.

†**ˈsherwood.** *Obs.* Also 6 **shirwood**. [Perh. from the proper name *Sherwood* in the Robin Hood ballads, taken as a poetic synonym for *greenwood*.] A grove; also, greenwood.

**1562** PHAER *Æneid* VIII. Y iij b, The shirwood great [L. *lucum ingentem*], where saulf defence, and free resort, Duke Romulus vptooke. **1652** LOVEDAY tr. *Calprenede's Cassandra* I. 167 He saw on his right hand near the river side a grove of Sherwood.

**sheshbesh** (ˈʃɛʃbɛʃ). Also **shesh-besh**. [Turk., f. Pers. *shash* six + Turk. *beş* five.] A variety of backgammon played in the Middle East. Also *attrib.*

**1971** L. DAVIDSON *Smith's Gazelle* ii. 37 The sheshbesh players pressed his arm in sympathy. **1975** C. A. HADDAD *Moroccan* (1977) iv. 44 My friends would come over..to play sheshbesh. **1977** H. KAPLAN *Damascus Cover* (1978) vii. 67 In this part of the world we have been playing sheshbesh, what you call backgammon, for nearly three thousand years.

**sheshum**, variant of SHISHAM.

**shet** (ʃɛt), **shed** (ʃɛd), repr. a U.S. dial. and colloq. pronunc. of SHUT *v.* and *ppl. a.*, esp. in phrase ***to get*** **(*be, stay*)** ***shet of*** (see SHUT *v.* 11 a).

**1837** A. SHERWOOD *Gazetteer of State of Georgia* (ed. 3) 70/1 *Get shet of*, for get rid of. **1848**, etc. [see *open-and-shut* s.v. OPEN *a.* 22 c]. **1871** E. EGGLESTON *Hoosier School-Master* (1872) xxxii. 162 I'm glad to be shed of you! **1930** G. B. JOHNSON in B. A. Botkin *Folk-Say* vii. 357 The Negro raises..'great big' hogs, and tries to 'get shet of' his enemies, just as poor white folk have done for hundreds of years. **1935** Z. N. HURSTON *Mules & Men* I. iii. 77 Throw mah trunk out befo' you shet up dat place! **1943** E. CALDWELL *Georgia Boy* 80, I thought you was trying to get shed of it. **1974** *State* (Columbia, S. Carolina) 15 Feb. 1-B/1 A gentleman at the coffee counter began munching his hamburger a whole lot slower yesterday when the waitress admitted she just couldn't 'get shet' of her strep throat. **1976** *Verbatim* Sept. 8/1 The range of his scholarship and the deftness of his intuition..are bound in an engaging prose style that makes a reader grateful to be shet for a while of the orthodox taxonomist. **1978** J. A. MICHENER *Chesapeake* 726 'Turlocks hate us colored,' he warned his daughters, 'so the smart thing, stay shed of 'em... Just you stay clear, like me, an' you find no trouble.

**shet**, dial. var. SHEAT *sb.*[1] (young hog); obs. f. SHEET *sb.*[2], SHUT; obs. pa. t. of SHOOT.

**shete**, obs. form of SHEET, SHOOT, SHUT.

**sheter**, obs. form of SHOOTER.

**sheth** (ʃɛθ). *dial.* and *techn.* Forms: 5 **scheth**, (9 **sheath**), 8– **sheth**. [Cogn. w. WFlem. *schet*, *schette* rail, bar of a gate, palisade, etc.; f. the Teut. root **skaiþ* to divide, split: see SHED *v.*, SHEATH. Cf. also WFlem. *schee* cross-bar, rung of a ladder, one of the laths forming the bottom of a wheelbarrow, etc. See also SHEATH[2].

The etymological sense would be split piece of wood (cf. the cognate SHIDE). The OE. form cannot be inferred from the data, but may possibly be represented by ONorth. *scæþþa*, *sceaþa* (if the vowel in that word be long), which occurs in the Lindisfarne and Rushworth Gospels John xx. 25 in the sense of nail, and as the second element of *hornsceaþ*- 'pinnaculum (templi)' in Matt. iv. 5 (Lind.); a. MDu. *schede* fem., metal pin or peg, appears to correspond to this.]

**1.** A bar or lath, esp. one of a number placed alongside each other so as to form a framework. *spec.* in various applications. **a.** One of the bars or 'ribs' forming the framework for the bottom or sides of a wagon, railway-coach, etc.

**1496** *Acc. Ld. High Treas. Scot.* I. 281 Item..to Will Walkar of Leith, for xxiiij schort treis to be schethis to the cartis,..xxiiij s. **1764** J. BUDDLE in *B. Martin's Gen. Mag.* June 285 The body of the waggon is in form of an inverted prismoid..having strong pieces of oak or ash wood at the bottom called Soals, at the corners and sides called Sheths. **1838** N. WOOD *Railroads* (ed. 3) 208 Upright sheths are placed upon the side frames, and cross sheths as shown in the figures. **1851** GREENWELL *Coal-trade Terms, Northumb. & Durh.* 47 *Sheths*, the ribs of a chaldron waggon. **1894** *Northumbld. Gloss.* s.v., 'Waggon sheth', the group of ribs forming the framework. 'Tram sheth', the cross ties in a tram which connect the soles or main framework.

**b.** In a ladder: Each of 'the broader steps, introduced at intervals, between the rungs, to bind the structure together' (*Northumbld. Gloss.* 1894).

**c.** In a harrow: see quot. 1894. Also *collect.*

**1788** *Encycl. Brit.* (ed. 3) I. 276/1 The bulls are connected by four sheths. **1894** *Northumbld. Gloss.* s.v., 'Harrow sheth', the cross bars of a harrow, intersecting the 'bulls' or longitudinal bars.

**2.** 'A group of parallel rows which stand at right angles to similar and adjoining or intersecting rows' (*Northumbld. Gloss.* 1894). **a.** *Agriculture.* (See quot. 1894.)

**1431** *Munim. de Melros* (Bannatyne Club) 524 Sexten akris of land togithir lyand in þe samyn scheth of land west fra þe said saynte mary rig. **1829** BROCKETT *N.C. Gloss.* (ed. 2), *Sheth*, a portion of a field, which is divided so as to drain off the water by the direction of the ploughings, called *sheths*; i.e. a separated part. **1894** *Northumbld. Gloss.* s.v., In the unenclosed town fields a group of parallel strips of ploughed land, which adjoined a similar group lying at right angles, formed a *sheth*.

**b.** *Mining.* (See quots.)

**1812** J. HODGSON in Raine *Mem.* (1857) I. 95 Till it [the air] traversed the newly-formed sheth or set of workings. **1860** *Eng. & Foreign Mining Gloss.* (ed. 2) *Newcastle* 63 *Sheth of bords*, a district of workings. **1894** *Northumbld. Gloss.* s.v., 'Sheth of boards', a group of cross workings in a coal pit... When a panel or division of a colliery is referred to, the group of parallel excavations which have been driven at right angles to the cleavage of the coal (the boards) are spoken of as a 'sheth of boards'.

*attrib.* **1812** J. HODGSON in Raine *Mem.* (1857) I. 95 The walls which have stoppings in them are called sheth-walls, and those which are open loose-walls. **1816** J. H. H. HOLMES *Coal Mines Durh. & Northumb.* 247 Sheth, Sheth-door, Sheth-stoppings &c.—different means used for regulating the passage of the air through the boards, headways, &c.

**sheth(e, shether**: see SHEATH, SHEDER.

**Shethite**, variant of SETHITE.

**Shetland** (ˈʃɛtlənd). [The name of a group of islands to the north-north-east of the mainland of Scotland.]

**1.** Used *attrib.* (quasi-*adj.*). **a.** ***Shetland pony, horse***, etc. = SHELTIE 1.

**1801** J. ANDERSON *Recreat. Agric.* IV. Index, Shetland pony. **1807** J. HALL *Trav. Scot.* II. 531 The Shetland horses are well known. **1830** LE KEUX *Illustr. Nat. Hist.* I. 34 The Shetland ponies are exceedingly diminutive. **1848** THACKERAY *Van. Fair* xxxvii, On this little black Shetland pigmy young Rawdon's great father was pleased to mount the boy.

*absol.* **1857** HUGHES *Tom Brown* I. ii, Tom rode his little Shetland into the cottage.

**b.** As the designation of a breed of sheep.

**1794** *Statist. Acc. Scot.* XI. 39 The Cheviot sheep are very well made. By crossing the breed of them with the Shetland, ..both the quality of the wool and of the mutton will be improved. **1796** *Ibid.* XVII. 586 Neither the Spanish nor the Shetland sheep has, as yet, been found to thrive here. **1830** LE KEUX *Illustr. Nat. Hist.* I. 139 Shetland Sheep. This breed was formerly a native of the higher parts of Aberdeenshire.

**c.** Applied to a variety of wool, spun in the Shetland Isles, hence to things made of this wool. Also with small initial. ***Shetland floss***, Shetland wool. ***Shetland knitting***, a traditional style of knitting characterized by a distinctive technique and by the following of Scandinavian patterns in 'natural' colours.

**1790** (*title*) Report of the Committee of the Highland Society of Scotland, to whom the subject of Shetland Wool was referred. **1854** *Morning Post* 7 July 1/5 (Advt.), Shetland shawls and veils in great variety. **1856** MRS. PULLAN *Lady's Dict. Needlework* 48 Wools... Shetland. A very fine wool, used for veils, scarfs, shawls, &c. **1856** MORTON *Cycl. Agric.* II. 833/1 Genuine Shetland hose. **1882** CAULFEILD & SAWARD *Dict. Needlework* 446 Shetland Point Lace..is a Needlemade lace, composed of Shetland wool..of sufficiently coarse texture to form babies' shawls [etc.]. **1895** Shetland floss [see *double-knit* adj. s.v. DOUBLE *a.* A. 6]. **1906** E. V. LUCAS *Listener's Lure* 183 Get a Shetland shawl for Mrs. Ring. **1934** W. MOFFATT *Shetland: Isles of Nightless Summer* i. 23 The wool is invariably short, curly and silky... This wool is famous all over the world, and is so valued that unscrupulous people in other lands sell wool called 'Shetland Floss' that was never within a thousand miles of Shetland. **1935** in *Scottish Woollens* (Nat. Assoc. Sc. Woollen Manufacturers) (1956) 55 Shetlanders..still knit a great variety of articles, and the finest Shetland knitting is still unrivalled. **1966** N. FREELING *Dresden Green* I. 17 A beige shetland pullover. **1974** *People's Jrnl.* (Inverness & Northern Counties ed.) 7 Sept. 9/1 They studied island crafts such as silverwork, handloom weaving, carding and spinning, and Shetland knitting. **1979** R. JAFFE *Class Reunion* 5 Plain dark shetland cardigans. **1980** L. BIRNBACH et al. *Official Preppy Handbk.* 107/1 You should be comfortable with a turtleneck,..a button-down shirt and a Shetland sweater.

**d.** ***Shetland sheep-dog***, a small long-coated collie belonging to the breed so called; also ***Shetland collie***.

**1908** *Our Dogs* 27 Mar. 681/2 Shetland Collies.—This variety is at present in the hands of a few fanciers only. **1909** *Ibid.* 15 Oct. 937/1 Shetland Collies or Sheepdogs, the original type and colour. **1960** E. MILLER *Shetland Sheepdog* 5 So much experimenting has gone on with this breed, that the Shetland Sheepdog is still far from being 'typed' like a Poodle or Boxer. **1971** F. HAMILTON *World Encycl. Dogs* 97 The name Shetland Collie was the first choice but the Collie Clubs objected so strongly that the Kennel Club would not allow it. **1977** *Belfast Tel.* 14 Feb. 12/9 (Advt.), Shetland sheepdog puppies.

**2.** *absol.* **a.** A Shetland pony.

**1836** S. C. STEVENSON *Let.* Sept. in E. Boykin *Victoria, Albert, & Mrs. Stevenson* (1957) 30, I cannot tell you how I covet one of these little shetlands for my little nephews. **1975** *Country Life* 6 Feb. 327/1 The ponies shown included Connemaras,..Shetlands and Welsh.

**b.** A Shetland shawl, sweater, etc.

**1870** CROWN PRINCESS OF PRUSSIA *Let.* 18 Mar. in R. Fulford *Your Dear Letter* (1971) 207 In my condition..I.. never am in my own room without a lace shawl or a shetland or black mantilla. **1972** *Vogue* 1 Mar. 57/1 Classic Shetland and cashmere sweaters... Shetlands in 79 colours. **1979** A. V. BADGLEY *Rembrandt Decisions* xi. 156 Stout oxfords, ribbed wool stockings, itchy shetlands.

**c.** A Shetland sheep-dog.

**1945** C. L. B. HUBBARD *Observer's Bk. Dogs* 143 A perfect Collie in miniature, the Shetland is efficient and nimble. **1958** O. GWYNNE-JONES *Shetland Sheepdog Handbk.* i. 8 By 1912 Shetlands were classified at..sixteen shows.

Hence **Shetˈlandic** *a.*, pertaining to Shetland.

**1882** K. BLIND in *Gentl. Mag.* Mar. 353 (art.) New finds in Shetlandic and Welsh. *Ibid.* 356 This Shetlandic word.

**ˈShetlander** (ˈʃɛtləndə(r)), [f. *Shetland* (see prec.) + -ER[1].]

**1.** An inhabitant of the Shetland Isles.

**1807** J. HALL *Trav. Scot.* II. 616 All the labour of the poor Shetlander is under the controul of the landholder. **1882** MISS GORDON-CUMMING in *19th Cent.* Apr. 573 The Shetlanders have a..singularly descriptive word to express it.

**2.** A Shetland pony.

**1875** S. SIDNEY *Bk. Horse* iv. 85 The best Shetlanders come from Unst. **1885** *Mem. D. King* ii. 11 His uncle gave him a pony—a small jet black Shetlander.

**shetle**, obs. variant of SHITTLE *a.*

**shett(e**, obs. ff. SHEET *sb.*[1], SHOOT *v.*, SHUT *v.*

**shettle**, obs. form of SHITTLE *a.*, SHUTTLE.

**shetton, shetyll**, obs. ff. SHITTEN, SHUTTLE.

**sheu**, obs. pa. t. of SHOW *v.*

**sheue**, obs. form of SHOW *v.*

**sheugh** (ʃux), *sb. Sc.* and *north.* Forms: α. 6 **sewch, seuche**, 6–7, 9 **seuch**, 8– **seugh**; β. 7 **shouch**, 8–9 **shough**, (9 **shooch, shaugh, shuch, shugh**, see *Eng. Dial. Dict.*), 9 **sheuch**, 8– **sheugh**. [Northern variant of SOUGH *sb.*[2]]

**1.** A furrow, trench, ditch, drain, etc.

α. **1501** DOUGLAS *Pal. Hon.* III. iv, Ane terribill sewch birnand in flammis reid,..All full of brintstane, pick, and bulling leid. **1513** —— *Æneis* x. xii. 168 Eneas with a pleuch The cetie circulit, and merkit be a seuch. **1520** NISBET *Matt.* xv. 14 Gif a blindman leid a blindman, bathe falle dovn into the seucht. **16..** N. BURNE *Leader-Haughs* x. in Ramsay *Tea-Table Misc.* (1762) II. 181 O'er dub and dyke, o'er seugh and syke. **1818** HOGG *Brownie* II. *Woolgatherer* 147 A deep dry seuch at the back of the garden. **1829** BROCKETT *N.C. Gloss.* (ed. 2), *Seugh*, a wet ditch;..any watery or boggy place—a *sough*.

β. **1665** J. FRASER *Chron. Frasers* (S.H.S.) 164 Riding down the narrow shouch of Corbet Bray. *a* **1779** D. GRAHAM *Jockey & Maggy's Crtshp.* III. Writ. 1883 II. 24 West the hags, an' o'er by Whitehill shough. **1786** BURNS *Twa Dogs* 30 He was a gash an' faithfu' tyke, As ever lap a sheugh or dyke. **1816** SCOTT *Antiq.* xliv, And a' the bonny engines, and wheels, and the coves, and sheughs, doun at Glenwithershins yonder, what's to come o' them? **1830** W. CARLETON *Traits Ir. Peas.* (1843) I. 62 Sometimes one in crossing a stile or ditch would drop into the shough. **1894** T. WATSON *Kirkintilloch* 199 Huge open gutters or 'sheuchs' on either side of the street, received all the sewage.

**2.** A furrow made for the temporary reception of plants: see SHEUGH *v.* 2.

**1844** H. STEPHENS *Bk. Farm* I. 373 The plants are taken from the *sheughs* when wanted.

**sheugh** (ʃux), *v. Sc.* and *north.* Forms: α. **seuch, sewch** (in pr. pple. **sewchquhand**), 7 **seugh**; β. 8–9 **shugh**, 9 **shough**, 9– **sheuch**, 8– **sheugh**. [f. SHEUGH *sb.*]

**1.** *trans.* To plough, make furrows in (also *fig.*); to dig *up*; (see also quot. 1882).

**1513** DOUGLAS *Æneis* V. iii. 76 Thai seuch the fludis. *Ibid.* 102 Now glyde thai baith togiddir furth in front,

Sewchquhand salt fame with thair lang kelis blont. **1606** BIRNIE *Kirk-Buriall* (1833) 31 With shod-shooles to seugh up the sanctuary ground. *a* **1878** H. AINSLIE *Pilgr. Land Burns*, etc. (1892) 334 They're..sheughin' hill an' howe. **1882** JAMIESON, *To Sheuch, Shugh*, to make a ditch or drain; also, to work in a ditch or peat-pit, as *to sheugh peats*, i.e., to cut them from the *sheuch* or pit, West of S[cotland].

**2.** To lay plants temporarily in the earth in order to keep them fresh; also ***to sheugh in***.

**17..** *Jacobite Song, Wee German Lairdie* i, He was delving in his kail-yairdie: Sheughing kail an' laying leeks. **1842** LOUDON *Suburban Hort.* 703 In the nurseries, we have great experience of lifting and shoughing immense quantities of deciduous plants. **1844** H. STEPHENS *Bk. Farm* I. 373 The bundles..should be immediately loosened out on their arrival from the nursery, and *sheughed in*, that is, spread out upright in trenches..and dry earth well heaped against them. **1894** *Northumbld. Gloss.*, *Sheugh*, to 'lay'..trees or plants temporarily in a hastily dug hole.

**b.** *transf.* To cover slightly, bury.

**1742** R. FORBES *Ajax* (1755) 3 Ajax..fase targe was shught In seven fald o' hide. **1832-53** D. WEBSTER in *Whistle-Binkie* Ser. II. 101 The bodies in Mauchlin Wish Meg in her kist, an' as deep sheugh'd as Lauchlan. *a* **1880** in Sir W. Fraser *Red. Bk. Menteith* I. 403 His followers daurna tak his body so far east as Dundurn..so they just shoughed it at the point of Coilmore, whence it was exhumed and placed afterwards in the old chapel.

**sheuk**, obs. Sc. f. *shook* pa. t. of SHAKE *v.*

‖**sheva** (ʃəˈvɑː). Also shewa (ʃəˈwɑː), shva; SCHWA. [a. Rabbinic Heb. *shᵉwā*, app. an arbitrary alteration of *shāw'*, emptiness, vanity. (In German books spelt *schwa*, whence SCHWA.)]

**1.** *Hebrew Grammar.* **a.** The sign ְ placed under a consonant letter to express (what Jewish grammarians regard as) the absence of a following vowel sound. In certain positions the sheva (called ***quiescent sheva***) has really no sound; but in others it is sounded as the neutral vowel (ə), and is then called ***movable*** (or ***vocal***) ***sheva***. ***compound sheva***: any of the signs ֱ, ֲ, ֳ, which represent the neutral vowel with a colouring of ŏ, ă, ĕ respectively. **b.** The sound of 'movable sheva'.

**1582** MULCASTER *Elementarie* xvii. 113 Like to a silent Hebrew Scheua. **1818** P. S. DUPONCEAU in *Trans. Amer. Philos. Soc.* I. 241 A small vacant space, as it were, between the consonants, like the *Sheva* of the Hebrews. **1827** S. LEE *Hebr. Gram.* 19 On *Sheva* and its Substitutes. **1837** G. PHILLIPS *Syriac Gram.* 3 When no vowel is expressed, then as in the Hebrew, a Sheva..will be implied and read accordingly. **1853** J. R. WOLF *Pract. Hebr. Gram.* 10 Hence, when Sheva is placed under such a consonant at the beginning of a syllable, it is sounded like a short *e*, and is called movable Sheva. *Ibid.*, When two Shevas stand in the middle of a word, the first is a resting, and the second a movable. **1914** DAVIDSON & MCFADYEN *Introd. Hebrew Gram.* (ed. 19) 23 The place of shᵉwa vocal, simple or composite, is under the first of two consonants that begin a syllable. **1939** J. WEINGREEN *Pract. Gram. for Classical Hebrew* 9 The shewa is not a vowel. The quick vowel-like sound is like the 'e' in 'because'. **1965** *Language* XLI. 543 The shva is a masoretic grapheme.

**2.** *Phonetics.* The neutral vowel-sound; *esp.* in comparative grammar, the obscure vowel resulting (in primitive Indogermanic) from an original ā, ē, or ō, by loss of accent. More usually SCHWA.

**1818** [see *phonologist* s.v. PHONOLOGY]. **1888** J. B. BURY in *Class. Rev.* Oct. 251/2 The π by labiation for *q*, and the second ᾰ a sheva. **1939** E. PROKOSCH *Compar. Germanic Gram.* 94 IE ə and ь are distinguished as 'shva primum' and 'shva secundum', but the term 'shva' alone always refers to ə.

**sheve**, obs. form of SHEAF *sb.*, SHEAVE *sb.*

ˈ**shevel**, *a. Sc.* In 6 schewill. [Related to SHEVEL *v.*] Distorted, twisted. Also Comb. ***shevel-gabbit***, ***-mouthed*** adjs., having a wry mouth.

**1508** DUNBAR *Tua Mariit Wemen* 106 He schowis on me his schewill mouth, and schedis my lippis. *c* **1785** *J. Thompson's Man* 14 Chandler-chafted, sheavel-gabbed, left-handed. **1866** W. GREGOR *Banffsh. Gloss.*, *Shaivlemoot*, having the mouth distorted.

**shevel** (ˈʃɛv(ə)l), *v. Sc.* and *north.* Also 8 sheavle, 9 shavel, shaivle, sheevil, sheule. (See *Eng. Dial. Dict.*) [App. cogn. w. SHAIL *v.*; a variant common in Sc. dialects is *showl, shool.*] *trans.* and *intr.* To distort, or become distorted. Hence ***sheveling-gabbit*** adj. = *shevel-gabbit* (see prec.); ***sheveling-heeled*** adj., (of a shoe) having a twisted or downtrodden heel.

**1725** RAMSAY *Gentle Sheph.* IV. i, Ye shevelling-gabbit brock! *a* **1779** D. GRAHAM *Jockey & Maggy's Courtship* VI. Writ. 1883 II. 43 An' how think ye the like o' me can wak straight wi' sic auld shevelin heel'd shune as mine. *a* **1779** —— *John Cheap* I. Ibid. II. 92 The deil's on the tap o' the mou', sheavling his mouth at me. **1808** JAMIESON, *To Shevel*, to distort... *To shevel*, to walk in an unsteady and oblique way. **1823** GALT *Gilhaize* iii, That auld shavling-gabbit hielander. **1869** J. P. MORRIS *Furness Gloss.*, *Sheule*, to walk with a shuffling gait.

**shevelled** (ˈʃɛvəld), *ppl. a. rare* and *arch.* Also 7 sheualed, shieveld. [Aphetic form of DISHEVELLED *ppl. a.*] Dishevelled. Also *transf.*

**1613** *Uncasing of Machiav.* 22 While the poore man..May ..wipe his blubbered cheeks with sheualed heares. **1633** T. ADAMS *Exp. 2 Pet.* ii. 5. 592 A shieveld threed is hardly got thorow the needles-eye. **1877** BLACKMORE *Erema* I. xviii. 219 He bowed his tall white head into my shevelled hair. **1886** —— *Springhaven* (1887) I. x. 81 Sandhills shevelled with long rush disarm the western fury.

**shever(e**, obs. forms of SHIVER.

†ˈ**sheveret.** *Sc. Obs.* [Origin and meaning obscure: cf. CHEVEREL.] Some material used for curtains.

**1716** LADY G. BAILLIE *Househ. Bk.* (S.H.S.) 45 For 3 yd. yellow sheveret for a curtine to the Coach 0. 9. 0.

**Shevuos, Shevuoth**, varr. SHAVUOTH.

**shevys** (= *sheuys*), obs. pl. SHOE *sb.*

**shew**, Sc. f. SEW *v.*[1]; var. SEW *v.*[2] *Obs.*

**shew**, variant of SHOW *sb.* and *v.*

†**shewage.** *Obs. rare.* [f. *shew*, SHOW *v.* + -AGE.] An etymologizing alteration of SCAVAGE *sb.*, due to the lawyers of the 15–16th c.

**1500** in *Star Chamber Cases* (Selden Soc.) I. 73 All maner of toll & Shewage oderwise called Skawage amonges oder thynges. **1503-4** *Act 19 Hen. VII*, c. 8 Dyvers Meires..have ..taken of theym a certeyn Costome called Skavage, oderwyse called Shewage. **1641** *Termes de la Ley* (1659) 245 b, Scauage or shewage. **1800** [see SCAVAGE *sb.* 1].

**shewbread** (ˈʃəʊbrɛd). *Jewish Antiq.* Also 6 schew-, shewe- (9 *Dicts.* show-); see also BREAD. [f. *shew*, SHOW *sb.*, after G. *schaubrot* (Luther); the compound seems correctly to represent the sense of the Heb. *'leχem pā'nīm*, LXX ἄρτοι ἐνώπιοι, Vulg. *panes propositionis.*] The twelve loaves that were placed every Sabbath 'before the Lord' on a table beside the altar of incense, and at the end of the week were eaten by the priests alone.

In 16th c. writers sometimes in pl., after the LXX and the Vulgate; the Geneva Bible (1557) has *shewe loues*.

**1530** TINDALE *Exod.* xxv. 30 Thou shalt sett apon the table shewbred before me allwaye. **1535** COVERDALE *Matt.* xii. 4 Haue ye not red..How he [David]..ate the shewe breds. **1563** WIN3ET *Bk. Quest.* lvi. Wks. (S.T.S.) I. 111 Achimelech wold nocht geue the schewbreid to Dauid. **1648** HERRICK *Hesper.*, *Temple* 69 Upon this fetuous board doth stand Something for shew-bread. **1686** HORNECK *Crucif. Jesus* vii. 117 The Shew-bread was to be before the Lord continually. In the original it is called The Bread of Faces. The mystery of it was, to shew, that Christ was to be the great Mediator, who should be always in the presence of God, behold his face [etc.]. **1855** PUSEY *Doctr. Real Presence* (Note S) 413 [tr. St. Ephrem.] The shewbread figures the mystery of our sacrifices which are offered through Christ by the Ministers of the Church.

*attrib.* **1611** BIBLE *2 Chron.* xxix. 18 We haue cleansed.. the shew-bread table.

**shewe**, aphetic form of ESCHEW.

**1502** *Ord. Crysten Men* (W. de W. 1506) I. iii. 34 He ought to put out of us all euyl thoughtes and euyll operacyons to shewe all occasyon the whiche myght stere us unto yll. **1548** H. HART (*title*), A goodly new short Treatyse instructing euery Parson howe they shulde trade theyr Lyues in yᵉ Imytacyon of Vertu, and the shewyng of Vice.

**shewe**, obs. form of SHOW; ? obs. form of SUE *v.*

ˈ**shewel.** *Obs.* exc. *dial.* Forms: α. 3 schawles, s(c)heules, shueles, 5 shewelys; β. 3, 7 sewell, 6 sewelle, sewel, shewelle, 9 shewell, 7–9 shewel. Also SEWIN[2]. [Early ME. *scheules*, perh. repr. OE. **sciewels* = MLG. *schûwelse*, MHG. *schûsel* (mod.G. *scheusal*), a derivative of the vb. which appears as OHG. *sciuhen* (MHG. *schiuhen, schiuwen*, mod.G. *scheuen*) to scare. Cf. SHY *v.*] A scarecrow. Also *Hunting*, something hung up or set up to keep a deer from entering a particular place, or from going in a particular direction. Also *fig.*

*c* **1250** *Owl & Night.* 1648 þu seist þat gromes þe i-foð.. an summe of þe schawles [*v.r.* scheules] makeþ. *Ibid.* 1128 Ac þu art shueles [*v.r.* sheules] suþe god. **1286** in *Select Pleas Forest* (Selden Soc.) 130 Intrare warennam cum rethibus et sewell' et capere volatilia. **1426** LYDG. *De Guil. Pilgr.* 13889 A shewelys enarmyd in the ffeld..Wych ys but A ded ffygure. **1535** LAYTON in *Lett. Suppress. Monast.* (Camden) 71 Getheryng up part of the saide bowke leiffes..therwith to make him sewelles or blawnsherres to kepe the dere within the woode, therby to have the better cry with his howndes. **1576** TURBERV. *Venerie* xxxvii. 98 Any thing that is hung vp, is called a Sewel. And those are vsed most commonly to amaze a Deare, and to make him refuse to passe wher they are hanged vp. *a* **1586** SIDNEY *Arcadia* III. x. ¶4 So are these bugbeares of opinions brought by great Clearkes into the world, to serve as shewelles to keepe them from those faults, whereto [etc.]. **1616** BULLOKAR *Eng. Expos.*, *Sewell*, a Paper, clout, or any thing hanged vp to keep a Deere from entring into a place. **1661** FELTHAM *Resolves* II. lxv. 325 He knows both with what baites to incite them, and with what shewels to drive into the Net and Toyle. **1688** HOLME *Armoury* II. 187/1 Bleinchers, and Sewels, are papers and stick laid cross a Fox-hole, to fear him and make him believe some Gin is set there. **1888** *Berks. Gloss.*, *Shewell*, a scarecrow.

Hence **shewelling** *sb.*, setting up shewels.

**1576** TURBERV. *Venerie*, Terms 242 When they hang vppe any paper, clout, or other marke, then it is to be called Sewelling. **1627** J. TAYLOR (Water-P.) *Armado* D 2, Dewclawes and Dowlcets, drawing the Couerte, Blemishes, Sewelling, Auant-laye, Allaye, Relaye [etc.]. **1688** HOLME *Armoury* II. 188/2 Sewels or S[e]welling, is the setting up of clouts or papers, or the like, for marks, and to fear Deer away from a place. **1902** *Gamekeeper* Dec. 65/1 Sewelling in a piece of cord with rags and feathers fixed at every six inches ..at a reasonable distance in front of the guns will ensure good flying birds.

**shewemaker**, obs. form of SHOEMAKER.

**shewer(e**, obs. f. SEWER *sb.*[2], [3]; SHOWER.

**shewet**, obs. form of SUET.

**shewid**, obs. pa. t. of SHOVE *v.*[1]

**shewin, shewmake**: see SEWIN[1], SUMACH.

**shewre**, obs. form of SHOWER *sb.*

**shewt**: see SHOOT *sb.*[3]

**shewtage**: see SHOOTAGE *Obs.*

**shewter, sheyde**, obs. ff. SUITOR, SHED *sb.*[1]

**sheykh, sheyld**: see SHEIKH, SHIEL.

**sheynd, sheyt(t**, obs. ff. SHEND, SHEET *sb.*[1]

**shiack**, variant form of SHE-OAK.

‖**Shiah** (ˈʃiə). Forms: α. 7 Seaw, Chias, 8 Schia(h, Shiyah, 9 Shiya, Shya, 8– Shia, 9 She(e)ah, Sheer, 8– Shiah; β. 7 Schiai, 7–8 Shii, 8 Shiay. [Arab. *shīʿah* sect, f. root *shāʿa*, in the third conjugation to follow.

The β forms, strictly speaking, represent a distinct word, Arab. *shiyaʿīy* a member of the Shiah sect, a Shiite.]

**1. a.** Properly (but in Eng. somewhat rarely) used as a collective name for that one of the two great Muslim sects (chiefly represented by the Persians) which differs from the Sunnites or orthodox Muslims chiefly in maintaining that Ali (Muhammad's cousin and son-in-law) was the true successor of the prophet, the three first caliphs of the Sunnites being regarded as usurpers. **b.** Commonly, an adherent of this sect, a Shiite.

**1626** METHOLD in Purchas *Pilgrimage* (ed. 4) 995 He is by Religion a Mahumetan, discended from Persian Ancestors, and retayneth their opinions, which differing in many points from the Turkes, are distinguished in their Sects by tearmes of *Seaw* and *Sunnee*. **1668** RYCAUT *Pres. St. Ottoman Emp.* II. xi. 127 The Shii are opposed by the Subjects of the whole Ottoman Empire, as the most heretical of any of the rest. **1687** A. LOVELL tr. *Thevenot's Trav.* II. 107 The Persians call themselves Schiai, because they think it enough to follow the commands of their Law. **1753** HANWAY *Trav.* (1762) II. IV. ii. 106 The sect of Schias includes the Persians and some princes of the Indies, who are followers of Ali, who are also distinguished by the name of Adeliah. **1759** *Universal Hist., Mod.* VI. 34 The two chief sects, named *Sunni* and *Shiay*, into which the Mohammedans are divided. **1798** G. FORSTER *Journ. Bengal to Eng.* II. 129 In contradistinction to the Soonis, who in their prayers cross their hands on the lower part of the breast, the Schiahs drop their arms in straight lines. **1815** ELPHINSTONE *Acc. Caubul* (1842) I. 269 The Sheeahs are more discountenanced than any other religious sect. **1827** BUCKINGHAM *Trav. Mesopot.* II. 483 The mosque of the Imam Hossein, so highly reverenced by the Shiahs. **1830** MEYRICK *Ant. Arms & Armour* II. Pl. 141 He was a Sheer, a religious sect violently opposed to the Sunis. **1874** H. H. COLE *Catal. Ind. Art S. Kens. Mus.* App. 305 The earth is held in superstitious veneration by the Muhammadans, especially the 'Sheahs'. **1883** *Encycl. Brit.* XVI. 593/1 The Shi'a were divided into several sects. **1926** T. E. LAWRENCE *Seven Pillars* II. xxvii. 140 They were Shias, and had been since the days of Kerbela. **1969** *Pioneer* (Lucknow) 13 Aug. 4/8 Syeds are mostly Shias in Lucknow.

**2.** *attrib.* and *adj.*

**1698** FRYER *Acc. E. India & P.* I. iv. 29 His Substitute here is a Chias Moor. **1841** ELPHINSTONE *Hist. India* VII. iv. II. 159 The enthusiasm of the nation for the Shía religion. **1903** SIR A. H. LAYARD *Autobiog.* I. viii. 337 Being of the Shiah sect of Islam. **1955** *Times* 31 Aug. 6/6 The Shia mourning day, Ashura, commemorating the death of Imam Hussein, grandson of the prophet, passed off without incident. **1974** *Educ. & Community Relations* Jan. 5 Celebrated with processions mostly by the Shia sect.

**shiatsu** (ʃiːˈætsuː). Also Shiatsu, shiatzu. [Jap., lit. finger-pressure.] A kind of therapy, of Japanese origin, in which pressure is applied with the thumbs and palms to certain points on the body. Also *attrib.*

**1967** *Tel.* (Brisbane) 4 Dec. 12 A Japanese physiotherapist ..believes that his shiatsu finger massage is good for treating high blood pressure, insomnia and hernia. **1969** T. NAMIKOSHI *Shiatsu: Health & Vitality at your Fingertips* i. 10 Widely practiced in Japan today, shiatsu is described by the Ministry of Welfare as follows: Shiatsu is a treatment in which the thumbs and palms of the hands are used to apply pressure to certain points in order to correct irregularities of the living body. *Ibid.* 13 The thumbs are often used in shiatsu treatment. *Ibid.* iv. 81 Apply strong shiatsu pressure to the eight points on the calf. **1975** *Publishers Weekly* 18 Aug. 29 (Advt.), Shiatzu was developed centuries ago in Japan as a refinement of the acupuncture treatment from China. **1980** *Daily Tel.* 21 June 12/4 There are 13 pressure-points in *shia-tsu*.

**Shibayama** (ʃiːbəˈjɑːmə). Also shibayama. The name of a Japanese family of carvers, used *absol.*

and *attrib.* to denote a distinctive style of inlay work which they originated.

**1928** F. M. Jonas *Netsuké* 174 Shibayama is the name by which all encrusted work is known. **1956** F. Meinertzhagen *Art of Netsuke Carver* III. 45 'Shibayama' work, mostly of poor quality, in the form of vases, jars, trays, etc., was made from the late 19th century up to recent times. **1971** *Country Life* 22 Apr. 941/1 The design is composed of gold lacquer and *shibayama*, that is pieces of ivory, tortoiseshell, mother-of-pearl used to build up the picture. **1982** 'J. Gash' *Firefly Gadroon* iv. 36 A set of Shibayama knife-handles.

**shibboleth** ('ʃɪbəlɛθ). Forms: 4 s(h)ebolech, 6, 7 schiboleth, 7 schibboleth, 7–9 shiboleth, 7– shibboleth. [a. Heb. *shi'bbōleth*; in the Vulgate transliterated *sciboleth*.

The word occurs with the senses 'ear of corn' and 'stream in flood'; in the passage now referred to the LXX and Vulgate give the former rendering; mod. commentators prefer the latter, on the ground that on this view the selection of the word is naturally accounted for, as the slaughter took place 'at the fords of Jordan'. Cf. SIBBOLETH *v.*]

**1.** The Hebrew word used by Jephthah as a test-word by which to distinguish the fleeing Ephraimites (who could not pronounce the *sh*) from his own men the Gileadites (Judges xii. 4–6).

**1382** Wyclif *Judges* xii. 6 Thei askiden hym, Seye thanne Sebolech [**1535** Coverdale Schiboleth, **1611** Shibboleth], .. the which answerde, Shebolech [1388 Thebolech, 1535 Siboleth, 1611 Sibboleth]. **1671** Milton *Samson* 289 In that sore battel when so many dy'd Without Reprieve adjudg'd to death, For want of well pronouncing Shibboleth. **1844** Elphinstone *Hist. India* II. 73 As some endeavoured to conceal their character, recourse was had to a test like the Jewish Shiboleth.

**2.** *transf.* **a.** A word or sound which a person is unable to pronounce correctly; a word used as a test for detecting foreigners, or persons from another district, by their pronunciation.

**1658** Cleveland *Rustick Rampant* 36 They had a Shibboleth to discover them, he who pronounced *Brot* and *Cawse* for *Bread* and *Cheese* had his head lopt off. **1660** Fuller *Mixt Contempl.* xxxviii. 62 It [the word *trespasses*] is a shiboleth to a child's tongue, wherein there is a confluence of hard consonants together. *a* **1661** —— *Worthies, Essex* (1662) I. 335, *R.* was Shiboleth unto him, which he could not easily pronounce. **1827** Scott *Two Drovers* i, In attempting to teach his companion to utter, with true precision, the shibboleth *Llhu*, which is the Gaelic for a calf. **1863** Hawthorne *Our Old Home, Consular Exper.* I. 44 The best shibboleth I ever hit upon lay in the pronunciation of the word 'been'. **1873** Earle *Philol. Eng. Tongue* §138 (ed. 2) 139 The TH with its twofold value is one of the most characteristic features of our language, and more than any other the Shibboleth of foreigners.

**b.** A peculiarity of pronunciation or accent indicative of a person's origin.

**1663** [J. Heath] *Flagellum or O. Cromwell* 123 There were slain [at Worcester] in Field and in Town, .. and in pursuit some 3000, and some 8000. taken prisoners in several places, most of the English escaping by their Shiboleth. **1701** De Foe *Trueborn Engl.* I. 136 The Customs, Sirnames, Languages, and Manners, Of all these Nations.. Whose Relicks.. ha' left a Shiboleth upon our Tongue; By which.. you may distinguish Your Roman-Saxon-Danish-Norman English. **1797** *Encycl. Brit.* (ed. 3) XIII. 112/1 The commonalty [of Northumberland] are.. remarkably distinguished by a kind of *shibboleth* or *whurle*, being a particular way of pronouncing the letter *R*.

**c.** *loosely.* A custom, habit, mode of dress, or the like, which distinguishes a particular class or set of persons.

**1806** A. Hunter *Culina* (ed. 2) 192 Custard and apple-pie is the Shibboleth by which an Alderman may be known. **1837** Howitt *Rur. Life* I. iv. (1862) 40 The sportsman's shooting-dress is a shibboleth, which introduces him alike to his superiors, to his fellows, and his inferiors. **1885** Dodge *Patroclus & Penelope* 10 The newly fledged equestrian who makes them [the English hunting-rig and crop] his shibboleth, and who discards as 'bad form' any deviation upon the road from what is eminently in place after hounds. **1902** Gosse in *Encycl. Brit.* (ed. 10) XXXIII. 819/2 *Joseph and his Brethren* became a kind of shibboleth—a rite of initiation into the true poetic culture.

**3.** *fig.* A catchword or formula adopted by a party or sect, by which their adherents or followers may be discerned, or those not their followers may be excluded.

**1638** E. Norice *New Gospel* 3 His followers sequestring themselves to such as were their own way, .. gave themselves to mirth and jollity, .. as if it were the only Shibboleth whereby to be discerned from the miserable Legalists that held mourning and sorrow for sinne. **1687** Dryden *Hind & P.* IV. 1076 For them.. Their Foes a deadly Shibboleth devise: By which unrighteously it was decreed, That none to Trust, or Profit should succeed, Who would not swallow first a poysonous wicked Weed. **1771** Wesley *Serm.* xliv. Wks. 1829 VI. 63 But here is the shibboleth: Is man by nature filled with all manner of evil?.. Allow this, and you are so far a Christian. Deny it, and you are but a Heathen still. **1784** Cowper *Let. to Newton* 21 Feb., The mere shibboleth of a party. **1809** Scott *Fam. Lett.* (1894) I. v. 146 Knaves and fools invent catch-words and shibboleths to keep them ['honest' persons] from coming to a just understanding. **1862** J. Skelton *Nugæ Crit.* ix. 424 The age .. strives to emancipate itself from the fetters of party shibboleths. **1874** H. R. Reynolds *John Bapt.* vi. §3. 394 Christians were ready to insist upon the insensate Shibboleth, 'Except ye be circumcised.. ye cannot be saved'.

**b.** The mode of speech distinctive of a profession, class, etc.

**1829** Southey *Sir T. More* (1831) II. 231 She has assumed the garb and even the shibboleth of the sect. **1849** Macaulay *Hist. Eng.* iii. I. 400 To that sanctimonious jargon, which was his shibboleth, was opposed another jargon not less absurd. **1884** *Graphic* 25 Oct. 437/3 Not given to talk stable, as is too often the case with racing men, but putting off the shibboleth of the turf with his race-glasses.

**shibol,** obs. form of CHIBOL.

**1546–7** *Cal. Anc. Rec. Dublin* (1889) 416 No persons hensforthe shall syll.. shibols, by Sainct Michels churche.

**shibouk,** variant of CHIBOUK.

**1843** R. J. Graves *Syst. Clin. Med.* xxiv. 303, I soon found the absurdity of asking an Oriental to abandon his shibouk.

‖**shibui** ('ʃibui), *a.* and *sb.* Also **shibu.** [Jap., f. *shibu* an astringent substance.] **A.** *adj.* Tasteful in a quiet, profound, or unostentatious way. **B.** *sb.* Tastefulness, refinement, appreciation of elegant simplicity.

In Japanese the substantival form is *shibu* (the substance) or *shibumi* (its quality); the adj. is *shibui*.

**1947** J. Morris *Phoenix Cup* II. 28 A picture, a piece of pottery, a kimono, or what you will, may be, from the Japanese point of view, in exquisite taste, and yet not *shibui*; to be thus described there must be also some invocation of quietude and austerity. **1958** *Japan: its Land, People & Culture* xxix. 1019/2 As beauty approaches the highest level it becomes a subtle beauty represented by what is known as the *shibu* taste. **1960** E. Mannin *Flowery Sword* x. 166 Vulgarity, and *shibui* side by side. **1965** *This is Japan 1966* 121/2 The sense of appreciation known as *shibui*, which enables Japanese to derive such satisfaction from the drinking of the tea, might seem to the foreigner a type of high, super-refined, even affected taste. **1970** J. Kirkup *Japan behind Fan* 27 That ghastly good taste, common to all modern hotels, that turns the most *shibui* atmosphere into something expensive and pretentious.

‖**shibuichi** (ʃibu'itʃi). [Jap., f. *shi* four + *bu* part(s) + *ichi* one.] An alloy consisting of three parts of copper to one of silver, extensively used by the Japanese on account of its beautiful silver-grey patina. Also *attrib.*

**1880** T. W. Cutler *Gram. Jap. Ornament* 19 The *shibu-ichi* is inlaid with gold and *shakudo*. **1902** *Encycl. Brit.* XXIX. 720/1 Neither metal, when it emerges from the furnace, has any beauty, *shakudo* being simply dark-coloured, and *shibuichi* pale gun-metal. **1911** *Ibid.* XV. 179 On the surface of a shibuichi box-lid we see the backs of a flock of geese. **1977** *Times* 14 Oct. 17/5 The top priced *tsuba* .. is.. made from a Japanese alloy called shibuichi.

**shice** (ʃaɪs), *sb.* and *a.* *slang* (? *Obs.*). Also **shise.** [G. *scheiss*; cf. SHICER.] **A.** *sb.* Nothing; base money; something worthless. **B.** *adj.* Worthless, counterfeit, spurious.

**1859** Hotten *Dict. Slang* 91 *Shice*, nothing; 'to do anything for *shice*', to get no payment. **1877** *Five Years' Penal Servitude* iii. 240, I ascertained while at Dartmoor that a very large 'business' is done in 'shise'. *c* **1890** *Five Years of Prison Life* ii. 62 Seeing how the fellow was acting he sent him two 'shise' notes, which gave him a dose that 'corked him'. **1939** J. B. Priestley *Let People Sing* x. 256 'I keep tellin' Knocker it's a shice,' said Micky earnestly.

**shicer** ('ʃaɪsə(r)). Also **schicer, shiser.** [a. G. *scheisser* 'cacator, peditor'; hence = 1 below.]

**1.** *slang.* A worthless person. Also *Austral.* (? transf. from 2) a welsher, defaulter. Also, something worthless, a failure.

**1846** *Swell's Night Guide* 61 The shiser thinks to bounce us by flashing a shofel quid. **1859** *Hotten's Slang Dict.* 227 *Shicer*, a mean man, a humbug—a person who is either worthless, or will not work. **1874** A. Bathgate *Colonial Experiences* viii. 97 There are, of course, many what may be called technical terms in connection with the pursuit of mining... Such, for example, as 'duffer' or 'shiser', anything that is useless. **1887** 'Hopeful' *Taken in* 135 [New Zealand] If a man isn't 'up to the mark', he is called 'a regular shicer'. **1896** in E. E. Morris *Austral Eng.* s.v., Don't take his bet, he's a regular shicer. **1906** Olive C. Malvery *Soul Market* xvii. 290 A racecourse swindler or welsher is spoken of as a 'shiser'. **1916** J. B. Cooper *Coo-oo-ee* xiv. 203 'The case is a "shicer" already,' replied Jack. 'Hawley has given it up.'

**2.** *Austral.* An unproductive claim or mine.

**1855** *Argus* (Melbourne) 19 Jan. 6/1, 220 feet digging is no plaything just now, with the prospect of a schicer at such depths. **1859** K. Cornwallis *New World* I. 219 We bought a hole.. which those who originally sunk it had determined upon abandoning as a shicer. **1890** 'R. Boldrewood' *Miner's Right* xxxiv, The shaft.. was an old shicer and pretty deep.

**shick** (ʃɪk), Austral. and N.Z. abbrev. of SHICKER *a.*, *sb.* 1.

**1916** C. J. Dennis *Moods of Ginger Mick* 19 The toff's too shick or silly fer to 'eave 'is carkis out. **1941** Baker *Dict. Austral. Slang* 65 *Shick*, drunk. Also (n.) a drunken person. **1966** B. Beaver *You can't come Back* 144 The wonder was we got that far without falling over and breaking them, because we were both pretty shick by then.

**shicker** ('ʃɪkə(r)), *a.* and *sb.* *Austral.* and *N.Z. colloq.* and in Jewish speech. Also **shiker, shikker, shikkur.** [ad. Yiddish *shiker* ad. Heb. *šikkôr*, f. *šākar* to be drunk. Perh. infl. by SHICKERY *a.* and *adv.*] **A.** *adj.* Drunk, intoxicated.

**1892** I. Zangwill *Childr. Ghetto* I. ii. 53 'But I'll get drunk on gingerbeer,' Pesach laughed back. 'You can't,' Fanny said... 'Ha! ha! ha! Can't even get *shikkur* on it. What a liquor!' **1898** *Bulletin* (Sydney) 17 Dec. Red Page, *Shiker*, drunk. **1899** A. Binstead *Houndsditch Day by Day* 46 She comes over shikkur an vants to go to shleeb. **1916** J. B. Cooper *Coo-oo-ee* v. 60 Hickford said the deceased was 'shicker' on the night before his death. **1949** *Hilltop* (N.Z.) I. II. 20 Sid should have some chance to get shicker as everybody else. **1963** 'M. Corrigan' *Why do Women—?* xv. 106 She was shikker and she took it into her head to come here. **1970** *N.Z. Listener* 12 Oct. 12/5 After midnight, Jerry got so shicker that he was quarrelling with everyone.

**B.** *sb.* **1.** A drunk.

**1906** [see *on one's ear* s.v. EAR *sb.*[1] 1 c]. **1938** X. Herbert *Capricornia* xviii. 234 He's the biggest shikker in Town. Now nick off, you old sponge. **1945** A. Kober *Parm Me* 156 Right away they are coming here, the whole bunch!.. Will be Uncle Henry and Uncle Philip—two foist-cless *shikkers*! **1949** D. M. Davin *Roads from Home* I. iii. 41 A shicker. Broke too, by the sound of it. **1964** S. Bellow *Herzog* 135 He drank his pay—a *shicker*. **1970** S. Ellin *Bind* xlvii. 234, I was hunting in the swamps with my *shikker* friend... I dumped my *shikker* off at Flagler Street.

**2.** Liquor; esp in phr. ***on the shicker***. (Only *Austral.* and *N.Z.*)

**1916** C. J. Dennis *Moods of Ginger Mick* 154 *Shicker*, intoxicating liquor. **1918** *N.Z.E.F. Chron.* 27 Feb. 33/1 He saved his strength for shicker. **1928** A. Wright *Good Recovery* 85 'Yes, I've been on the shikker,' he answered huskily. **1945** R. Rene *Mo's Memoirs* 49 One night the magician had been on the shicker, and with a fine disregard for life and limb he let the lion out. **1958** H. D. Williamson *Sunlit Plain* 58 He was on the shicker when I was there last week.

**shicker** ('ʃɪkə(r)), *v.* *Austral.* and *N.Z. colloq.* [f. as prec.] *intr.* To take alcoholic drink, to get drunk.

*a* **1922** H. Lawson *Benno & his Old 'Uns* in *Prose* (1964) III. 230 Her Old 'Un 'shickered' till he got 'mucked' every pay day. **1951** Cusack & James *Come in Spinner* 33 He'd gamble his shirt off on any damn thing that's got a leg to run on, but he doesn't shicker.

**shickered** ('ʃɪkəd), *a.* *Austral.* and *N.Z. colloq.* Also **shikkered.** [f. SHICKER *a.* and *sb.*, or *v.*] Drunk, intoxicated.

**1911** L. Stone *Jonah* I. ix. 124 'E's bin shickered since last We'n'sday. **1911** H. Foston *In Bellbird's Lair* vii. 34 He thinks we're 'shickered'. **1916** C. J. Dennis *Moods of Ginger Mick* 19 There's a shickered toff slings Rosie goo-goo eyes. **1930** A. W. Groom *Merry Christmas* xvi. 123 Every time I get shikkered I sober up after an' say 'Never again, Sandy'. **1934** T. Wood *Cobbers* xvi. 209 He *tole* me he was goin' to get sh-shickered, an' he has... He's sh as drank'sh forty catsh! **1947** D. M. Davin *Gorse blooms Pale* 212 When you're shickered you know.. things aren't really as good as they seem. **1952** J. Cleary *Sundowners* i. 42 He's drunk! Shickered to the eyeballs! **1961** P. White *Riders in Chariot* 261 'I'm gunna get out of this!' he announced at last. 'I'm gunna get shickered stiff!' **1972** C. Drummond *Death at Bar* v. 114 'You look half shickered, love,' said Charlie. 'I'll be right when I've been sick,' said Mrs. Gaukroger.

**shickery** ('ʃɪkərɪ), *a.* and *adv.* *slang* (? *obs.*). [Origin unknown.] **A.** *adj.* Shabby, rickety, shaky; also, drunk. **B.** *adv.* Shabbily, badly.

**1851** H. Mayhew *London Labour* I. 424/1 There's another sort who carry on the crocussing business, but on a small scale; they.. are called hedge crocusses... But as the hedge crocus is shickery togged, he makes poorly out. **1859** Hotten *Dict. Slang* 91 *Shickery*, shabby, badly. **1878** 'R. Boldrewood' in *Town & Country Jrnl.* 26 Jan. 170/1 Old Tom had a goodish cheque this time, and was at it a week afore I come in. He *was* rayther shickerry. **1888** —— *Robbery under Arms* III. xv. 220 Four panels of shickery two-rail fence.

**shickle,** altered f. SHITTLE *a.* *Obs.*, unstable.

**shicksa,** var. SHIKSA.

**shick-shack** ('ʃɪkʃæk). *dial.* Also **shic(k)-sack, shitsack, shig-shag, sic-sac, shuck-shack, shiff-shack,** etc. (See *Eng. Dial. Dict.*) [Perh. a corruption of *shitsack*, an 'opprobrious appellation by which the Nonconformists were vulgarly distinguished' (Granger *Biogr. Hist. Eng.* 1769, II. 224 and index).] App. originally used as a term of abuse for persons who were found not wearing the customary oak-apple or sprig of oak on the morning of Royal-oak day (29 May) which is hence called ***Shick-shack Day***. In some places *shick-shack* appears to have become a name for the oak-apple or sprig of oak itself.

[**1834** G. Roberts *Hist. & Antiq. Lyme Regis* 257 The boys continue to gild their oak apples and apply an opprobrious name to those who have not an oak leaf displayed, or wear it after twelve o'clock.] **1847** Halliwell, *Shick-shack-day*, a term for the 29th of May, or Royal Oak Day. *Surrey. Ibid.*, *Shitsac*, an oak-apple. *Wilts.* **1855** *N. & Q.* Ser. I. XII. 100 *Shig-shag Day.* The working men of Basingstoke, and other towns in Hampshire, arise early on May 29, to gather slips of oak with the galls on: these they put in their hats, or anywhere about their persons... After breakfast these men go round to such houses for beer, &c. Should they not receive anything, the following verses should be said: 'Shig-shag, penny a rag (Bang his head in Crommell's bag), All up in a bundle.' **1891** *Church Times* 13 Feb. 150/2 (E.D.D.) Anybody not decorated was bonnetted, or pinched, and called a 'Shuck-shack'. **1892** Miss Yonge *Old Woman's Outlook* May 105 The 29th.. is called in Hampshire and Sussex, Shik Shak Day. **1896** Ditchfield *Old Eng. Customs* 120 In Wilts it is known as Shitsack or Shick-sack Day, when the children carry shitsack, or sprigs of young oak.

**shickster** (ˈʃɪkstə(r)). *slang* (? *obs.*). [f. SHIKSA: see -STER.] (See quots. 1937, 1965.)

**1839** H. BRANDON in W. A. Miles *Poverty, Mendicity & Crime* 165/1 *Shickster*, a lady. **1846** *Swell's Night Guide* p. iii, The..bully, or cracksman, who would screw a drum,.. collar the shiksters denary, or paste a green-horn. **1882** *Sydney Slang Dict.* 10/2 He got the cant of togs from a *shickster* whose husband's in a bone-box. **1937** PARTRIDGE *Dict. Slang* 755/2 *Shickster*, any (Gentile) woman or girl.. a none too respectable girl or woman. **1965** *English Studies* XLVI. 454 The way for *shyster* in American English is paved by *shickster*..of Yiddish origin; in criminals' cant it designated a respectable girl or lady..but it soon deteriorated to 'prostitute'.

†**shidder**. *Obs. rare.*

**1737** HOPPUS *Salmon's Country Build. Estim.* (ed. 2) 104 The general Sorts [of nails] are..Shidder Hobbs, Thick Hobbs, Clasp Hobbs.

**shidder**, obs. form of SHEDER.

‖**shidduch** (ˈʃɪdəx). Also **shiddach**. [Yiddish, ad. Heb. *šiddūḵ* courtship, arranged marriage.] An arranged marriage, a (good) match. See also SHADCHAN.

**1892** I. ZANGWILL *Childr. Ghetto* I. 108 Every match is a grand *Shidduch* before the marriage; after, we hear another tale. **1968** L. ROSTEN *Joys of Yiddish* 339, I am considering getting married. But I warn you I'll accept nothing but a remarkable *shiddach*! **1976** C. BERMANT *Coming Home* I. i. 16 A *shidduch* was arranged for him and he married the pretty..daughter of a Vitebsk..merchant.

**shide** (ʃaɪd), *sb. Obs.* exc. *dial.* Forms: 1–3 **scid**, 3 **sid**, 4 **szhide, (chide)**, 4–6 **schide, schyde**, 5 **schyd(d, (schudde, chyde)**, 5–6 **shyde, shyyd**, 6 **shyd, (shede)**, 6, 7 **shid**, 4– **shide**. [OE. *scid* (? neut.) = OFris. *skîd*, mod.Flem. dial. *schijd*, OHG. *scît* neut. (MHG. *schît*, mod.G. *scheit*), ON. *skíð* neut. (Norw. *ski*: see SKI):—OTeut. **skīdo-m*, f. root **skīd-* to divide: see SHED *v.*]

A piece of wood split off from timber, esp. such a piece used in building a fire, a block, billet; a board, plank, beam. As a quantity: Half a cubic foot of timber (see quot. for *shide measure* in b).

*c* **725** *Corpus Gloss.* 1817 *Scindulis*: scidum. *c* **825** *Epinal Gloss.* 943. *c* **875** *Erfurt Gloss.* 943. *c* **1050** *Ags. Voc.* in Wr.-Wülcker 266/33 *Incipit de Igne..Scindula*, scid. *c* **1300** *Havelok* 917 Ful wel kan ich cleuen shides. **13..** *K. Alis.* 6421 Mouth they haveth gret, and wide, And a tonge as a schyde. *c* **1325** *Gloss. W. de Bibbesw.* in Wright *Voc.* 170 Les hasteles [*glossed* the chides, szhides] fetez alumer. **1362** LANGL. *P. Pl.* A. x. 160 And com to Noe Anon And bad him not lette Swiþe to schapen A schup of schides and Bordes. *c* **1425** WYNTOUN *Orig. Cron.* III. v. 776 A bale fyre off gret schyddys. *c* **1440** *Promp. Parv.* 446/1 Schyyd, or astelle (*v.rr.* schyd of a astel, schyde wode), *teda*. **1446** *Churchw. Acc. Yatton* (Somerset Rec. Soc.) 86 To I. Parker vor goyng to Thurbbewyll to helpe hewwe the schudde. *Ibid.* 88 Vor vyllyng of a chyde. **1470–73** in *Rec. Andover* 16 Paid for caryng a shide xij[d]. *c* **1512** *Regul. Northumbld. Househ.* (1770) 72 The shedes to be maid of the said Hardwode to be in leinth a Yerde and in thikenes a Spanne. **1533** HEN. VIII in Ellis *Orig. Lett.* Ser. I. II. 31 Item, every mornyng at our Woodeyarde, foure tall shyds and twoo fagotts. **1561** S. WYTHERS tr. *Calvin's Treat. Relics* C ij, And in som places ther are good great shydes [of the Cross]. **1657** LIGON *Barbadoes* (1673) 56 If the fire-man throw great shides of wood in the mouths of the Furnaces. **1677** PLOT *Oxfordsh.* 262 Cutting every shid of tall wood four foot long beside the kerf, and the billet three foot four inches. **1703** T. N. *City & C. Purchaser* 241 *Shides*. The same as *Shingles*. **1793** *Jrnls. Ho. Comm.* 28 Mar. 516/2 A Quantity of Pollard Trees sufficient to make 1,200 Shides of Cleft Wood, containing Half a Foot each.

**b.** *attrib.* and *Comb.*, as ***shide-wood, -yard***; **shide-measure** (see quot.); **shide-wall**, a rampart composed of piles.

**1600** HOPTON *Baculum Geod.* VI. xxxvii. 213 *Shide measure sheweth how many shides of timber is contained in each foote of length: for..a shide of timber is halfe a foote of timber. *c* **1000** ÆLFRIC *Gloss.* in Wr.-Wülcker 146/28 *Uallum*, *scidweallеs eorðbyri. *c* **1205** LAY. 10354 Þe vfenen he makede scid wal. *c* **1420** *Anturs of Arth.* xxxix, Schaftis in *shide wode thay shindre in schides. *c* **1450** *Godstow Reg.* (1911) 422 The which lieth in *shideyerd in Oxenford.

†**shide**, *v. Obs. rare.* Pa. pple. 4 **ischyt**. [f. SHIDE *sb.*] *trans.* To cleave, split.

*c* **1315** SHOREHAM (E.E.T.S.) iv. 178 Þys manere senne nys nauȝt ones, Ac hys ischyt in þry, In þouȝt, in speche, in dede amys. **1513** DOUGLAS *Æneis* VI. iii. 48 With wegis schidit gan the birkis sound.

†ˈ**shider**, *v. Obs. rare*[−1]. [f. SHIDE *sb.*] *trans.* To shatter, splinter.

*a* **1529** SKELTON *Vppon Deedmans Hed* 13 With synnews wyderyd, With bonys shyderyd.

**shie, shiech**, obs. ff. SHY *a.* and *v.*, SHEIKH.

**shiel** (ʃel). *Sc.* and *north.* Forms: α. 3 **sciale**, **shale**, 4–6 **schele**, 5–6 **scheill**, 5, 7 **schell(e**, 6 **shele**, **shile**, 7 **sheale**, **sheel(l**, 7–9 **sheal**, 9 **shill**, **(scheul, schule)**, 8– **shiel**; β. 6–7 **scheild**, 7 **sheyld**, **sheald**, 8–9 **shield**. [Northern ME. *shāle*, *schēle*, of obscure origin.

Prob. connected in some way with the synonymous ON. *skále* wk. masc. (whence SCALE *sb.*[4]). The formal equivalent of this in ONorthumbrian would be **scēla* (= WS. **sceala*), which would yield ME. *schēle* and the later forms. The 13th c. form *shāle* may be an adoption of the ON. form with substitution of initial (ʃ) for (sk), or it may be an alteration of the native word through association with the ON. form.

The β forms arose from confusion with SHIELD *sb.*]

**1.** A temporary building, usually of boards; a shepherd's summer hut; a shanty, shed, SHIELING.

The 'shiels' in quot. 1291 are those from which the town of Shields is named. The place is called 'the shiles by Tinmouth castle' in Bulleyn *Bk. Simples* (1562) 75 b.

α. **1291** in W. S. Gibson *Tynemouth Priory* (1846) II. App. 68 Non fuerunt ibi nisi tres sciales tantum. *Ibid.* 70 Ante prædictum tempus..non fuerunt ibi nisi prædict' tres shales. *a* **1400–50** *Wars Alex.* 4049 Þar þai schewid him in schurrys to schellis & to caues. **1533** BELLENDEN *Livy* III. ix. (S.T.S.) I. 282 To bring his govne fra þe somer schele quhare he duelt. *Ibid.* v. i. II. 142 To mak wynter schelis to defend þame fra wynter stormys. **1502** in *Reg. Mag. Sig. Scot.* 1585, 257/1 To big scheillis and lawis on the hauchis of the saidis landis..for resaweing of the fisch. **1637–50** Row *Hist. Kirk* (Wodrow Soc.) 433 What to doe have the ministring spirits of the Lord with things done in such a contemptible and stinking sheell? *a* **1722** in *W. Macfarlane's Geogr. Collect.* (S.H.S.) II. 36 They..ther live grassing their cattle in litle houses which they build upon ther coming and throwes doun when they come away called sheels. *a* **1756** COLLINS *Ode Superst. Highl.* 48 Whether sitting in the shepherds shiel, Thou hear'st some sounding tale of war's alarms. **1845** *New Statist. Acc. Scot.* II. *Berwick* 159 An alarm is instantly given to the men at the shiel or house where the fishermen lodge.

β. **1688** HOLME *Armoury* II. 36/2 Coats, Sheapards Sheals, or Hovells. **1726** P. WALKER *Life Peden* (1827) 63 He preached in a Shield or Sheep-house, in a desert Place. **1823** J. HODGSON in Raine *Mem.* (1858) II. 9 The floors of a great many shields or circular huts; which had been in it, were rudely paved. **1857** *Act 20 & 21 Vict.* c. cxlviii. §47 To remove from every Fishery, Fishing Shield, and Fishing Ground..all Boats, Oars [etc.].

**2.** A small house, cottage, hovel.

**1338** *Durham Acc. Rolls* (Surtees) 201 Item, idem Elem. [osinarius] adquisivit illam schele in Rokehop que aliquando fuit Roberti de Brandon pro 8 *li.* **1557** *Burgh Rec. Peebles* (1872) 239 Takkand to erd our scheillis and housis. **1605** CAMDEN *Rem.*, *Surnames* 102 Sheal, a cottage or shelter. **1616** *Aberdeen Reg.* (1848) II. 339 And the third voult to be bot ane shell athort the haill hous for the jaylouris duelling. **1728** RAMSAY *Robt., Richy, & Sandy* 127 Come to my shiel, there let's forget our care. **1792** BURNS *Song, Bess & Spinning Wheel* 23 The craik amang the clover hay, The paitrick whirrin' o'er the ley, The swallow jinkin' round my shiel, Amuse me at my spinning-wheel. **1838** J. HODGSON in Raine *Mem.* (1858) II. 379 In the churches they were better sheltered than in their own shiels. **1884** Q. VICTORIA *More Leaves* 62 We stopped at a very picturesque place, surrounded by woods and hills and little shiels.

*transf.* *c* **1470** HENRYSON *Mor. Fab.* II. (*Town & C. Mouse*) vi, It was ane sober wane..Ane sillie scheill vnder ane steidfast stane.

†**3.** A piece of pasture ground having a shepherd's hut upon it; a summer pasturage. *Obs.*

**1532** LD. DACRE in *St. Papers Hen. VIII* (1836) IV. 608 The common brute and voice was to have made a roode upon the Debatable grounde and Liddisdale men, nowe being at the sheles frome their winter houses. **1620** *Reg. Mag. Sig. Scot.* 781/2 Lie insches et shealis super dicta aqua. **1715** PENNECUIK *Tweeddale* 18 Then follows a little Shiel called the Frosthol. **1762** BP. FORBES *Jrnl.* (1886) 144 This place, called the Sheals of Dalquhirn, belongs to Macpherson of Breakachie. **1843** HARDY in *Proc. Berw. Nat. Club* II. 59 *note*, A *shiel* or *shieling* is a shepherd's summer hut, as well as a summer pasturage for flocks. **1857** JEFFREY *Roxburgh.* I. 269 The schules or scheuls, afterwards written Shiels were applied to describe mountain pasture with the huts of the herdsmen.

†**4.** *Comb.*: **shiel-house** = sense 2; **shiel-town** = sense 3.

**1606** *Reg. Mag. Sig. Scot.* 627/1 Lie scheiltounes. **1623** *Ibid.* 151/1 Lie scheildhous. **1804** *Anderson's Cumbld. Ball.* 80 She lives in a shill-house, burns dried sticks, And there has dealins wi' the de'il.

**shiela-na-gig**, var. SHEELA-NA-GIG.

**shield** (ʃiːld), *sb.* Forms: 1 **scild, scyld, sceld**, 3–4 **s(s)eld**, 3–5 **sheld, (cheld)**, 3–6 **scheld**, 4 **sceild, scheeld, (cheeld, schuld)**, 4–5 **scelde, schild(e, schylde, shilde**, 4–6 **s(c)helde, sheeld**, 4, 6 **schield, (childe)**, 4–8 **scheild**, 5 **scheelde, scheyld, shyld, (shulde)**, 5–6 **shild, shylde, sheelde**, 6 **shielde**, 7 **sheild**, 6– **shield**. [Com. Teut.: OE. (**scield*) *sceld* masc. = OFris. *skeld*, *schild*, OS. *scild* (MLG. *schild* masc., neut.), MDu. *schilt*, *schild-* masc. (mod.Du. *schild* neut.), OHG. *scild* masc. (MHG. *schilt*, *schild-* masc., G. *schild* masc., neut.), ON. *skjold-r* (Sw. *sköld*, Da. *skjold*), Goth. *skildu-s*:—OTeut. **skeldu-z*.]

**I. 1. a.** In ancient and mediæval warfare, and still in that of primitive peoples, an article of defensive armour carried in the hand or attached by a strap to the left arm of a soldier, as a protection from the weapons of the enemy. Sometimes applied *spec.* to an article of this kind larger than the BUCKLER, which was usually carried in the hand, and smaller than the PAVIS, which was held by an attendant in front of a knight or archer.

Shields have been made of various materials, as metal, wood, wickerwork covered with skins or leather, etc. The form has varied greatly in different periods and countries; the principal types are (1) the circular shield, usually convex in front, with a boss in the centre; (2) the oblong shield, either flat, or, more commonly, having the form of a portion of a cylinder; and (3) the shield with curved sides tapering to a point at the lower end, which was the prevailing form in Europe during the Middle Ages.

In the Middle Ages the 'armorial bearings' of a knight were depicted on his shield, and decorated shields, made for display and not for warlike use, were often hung on walls in churches or other buildings as a memorial of a knight or noble. Hence sense 3.

*Beowulf* 325 Setton sæmeþe side scyldas,..wið þæs recedes weal. *c* **825** *Vesp. Psalter* lxxv. 4 Ðer ȝebrec hornas boȝan sceld sweord & ȝefeht. **1205** LAY. 23777 Ane scelde gode [**1275** scealde]. *Ibid.* 4212 Heo nomen þa seeldes. *a* **1250** *Owl & Night.* 1713 For mony mon myd speres orde haueþ lutle strengþe & mid his schelde [*Cott.* chelde], Ah [etc.]. **1297** R. GLOUC. (Rolls) 3840 Ȝif he nadde wiþ þe sseld somdel þe dunt yhent Siker he im adde aslawe. *a* **1300** *Cursor M.* 2497 On helme and sceild [*v.rr.* shilde, schild, sheeld]. **13..** *K. Alis.* 693 (Laud MS.) An horne in þe forehede amydward þat wolde perce a shelde hard. *c* **1386** CHAUCER *Knt.'s T.* 1264 And somme woln haue a Pruce sheeld or a targe. **1387** TREVISA *Higden* (Rolls) IV. 97 Scipio sigh ones a childe gayliche arrayed, and seide, 'I wondre nouȝt þat he arrayeþ well his childe [L. *scutum*], for [etc.].' *c* **1418** in *Pol. Poems* (Rolls) II. 244 Hem nedethe nether spere ne shulde. *c* **1420** *Avow. Arth.* xxiv, Take thi schild and thi spere. **1508** DUNBAR *Golden Targe* 151 Than come, Resoun, with schelde of gold so clere. *c* **1550** N. SMYTH tr. *Herodian* II. 22 Lyftynge theyr shyldes and Targettes ouer theyr headеs. **1590** SPENSER *F.Q.* I. viii. 5 His mightie sheld Vpon his manly arme. **16..** *Funeral in Popish Times* in *Q. Eliz. Acad.* 34 The helme, Childe [*elsewhere* shild], sword, the Cote of Armes, to bee layd vppon y[e] bere in dew order. **1699** TEMPLE *Introd. Hist. Eng.* Wks. 1720 II. 531 Their common Arms were small Shields, but very large Swords. **1774** GOLDSM. *Nat. Hist.* (1776) IV. 331 Its skin is thick, and covered with brown hair, and the natives make shields of it. **1867** *Rep. Paris Univ. Exhib.* (1868) II. 489 Two shields, one in iron and one in steel, are the most remarkable of their works.

†**b.** *Phr.* ***under shield***: in battle or combat. ***with spear and shield***: in battle array; by force of arms. *Obs.*

*a* **1300** *K. Horn* 53 Hy smyten vnder schelde [*Laud* selde, *Harl.* shelde]. *c* **1330** *Arth. & Merl.* 3096, vi hundred kniȝtes..þat wele couþe juste in feld wiþ stef launce vnder scheld. *a* **1352** MINOT *Poems* (ed. Hall) iv. 50 Our King and his men held þe felde Stalworthy, with spere and schelde. *c* **1440** *Partonope* 2951 Partonope thatt day vnder hys schelde [*v.r.* sheelde] xx hethen he hathe slayn yn the fylde. **1508** DUNBAR *Poems* liv, Quhai for hir saik, with speir and scheld, Preiffis maist mychtelye in the feld. **1513** DOUGLAS *Æneis* VIII. viii. 111 Of Hetruria the ostis vnder scheild Wyth that word stoppit in the samin feild. **1596** DALRYMPLE tr. *Leslie's Hist. Scot.* II. 129 Baith pairties..cum to Dunfreis, thair tha diuyde it with speir and scheild. **1829** SCOTT *Anne of G.* xxxv, They met, as was the phrase of the time, 'manful under shield'. *Ibid.* xxxvi, We bear no malice for what is done in fair fight under shield.

**c.** In allusion to the custom of suspending a warrior's shield as a memorial of him.

**1817** COLERIDGE *Destiny of Nations* 9 Seize, then, my soul! from Freedom's trophied dome The Harp which hangeth high between the Shields Of Brutus and Leonidas!

**d.** ***two sides of a shield***: two ways of looking at something, two sides to a question; ***the other side*** (or ***reverse***) ***of the shield***: the other side of a question or consideration, the side which is less obvious or which has not been presented (cf. *the reverse of the medal* s.v. MEDAL *sb.* 3 b, Fr. *le revers de la médaille*).

? **1855** A. W. CHAPMAN *Let.* in R. K. Webb *Harriet Martineau* (1960) i. 27, I consider it a great misfortune, in one sense,..a blessing, often times, in another. There are two sides to every shield. **1885** C. M. YONGE (*title*) The two sides of the shield. **1909** P. COLLIER *England & English* i. 16 These beef-eating, port-drinking fellows in Piccadilly..are well enough..but this other side of the shield is distressing to look at. Poor, stunted..denizens of the East End. **1911** H. S. WALPOLE *Mr. Perrin & Mr. Traill* ii. 24 The reverse of the shield is..given in that first letter to his mother.

**2.** *transf.* and *fig.* **a.** Something serving as a defence against attack or injury. Often in echoes of Biblical language referring to metaphorical armour, as *Ephes.* vi. 16.

*c* **1200** *Trin. Coll. Hom.* 193 Habbeð..hope to helme, and soðe luue to shelde, and godes word to swerde. *c* **1220** *Bestiary* 161 Ðis neddre siðen he nede sal, makeð seld of his bodi and sildeð his heued. *a* **1225** *Ancren R.* 52 Heo to þe ȝunge ȝiueð vuel uorbisne, & scheld to werien ham mide. *a* **1300** *Cursor M.* 9972 It [a castle]..standes vs for sceild and targe. **1340** *Ayenb.* 1 Ich bidde þe hit [þin holy blod] by my sseld auoreye þe wycked uend. **1450–1530** *Myrr. our Ladye* 132 For hys passyon is suffycyent shylde to vs. **1567** *Gude & Godlie B.* 107 His trew promeis is thy scheild. *a* **1586** SIDNEY *Arcadia* II. (Sommer) 102 b, What shield [shall I find] against the violent passions of Gynecia? **1771** *Junius Lett.* lix. 305 The favour of his country constitutes the shield which defends him. **1839** FR. A. KEMBLE *Resid. Georgia* (1863) 69 Again the watery shield was interposed. **1853** KANE *Grinnell Exp.* ii. (1856) 20 Strips of heavy sheet-iron ..as a shield against the cutting action of the new ice. **1856** EMERSON *Eng. Traits* xv. *The 'Times'*, No dignity or wealth is a shield from its assault.

**b.** Applied (as a Biblical Hebraism: see, e.g. Ps. xxxiii. 20, lxxxiv. 11) to a personal defender or protector (esp. to God).

**971** *Blickl. Hom.* 29 Þe englas beoþ aa halȝum mannum on fultume swa swa scyld. *a* **1000** *Phœnix* 463 Þam biþ dryhten scyld. *c* **1275** *Five Joys Virg.* 13 in *O.E. Misc.* 87 Beo vre scheld from vre iro. *c* **1374** CHAUCER *Troilus* II. 532 Thow be my sheld for þy benignite. *c* **1380** WYCLIF *Wks.* (1880) 155 Þus lordis ben made schildis of synne for a litel money or worldly seruyce of wickid curatis. **1535** LYNDESAY *Satyre* 3 His Sone, our Sauiour, scheild in necessitie. **1738** WESLEY *Psalms & Hymns, Ps.* iii, But Thou art a Shield for me. *a* **1833** SIR R. GRANT *Hymn, 'O worship the King'*, Our shield and defender, The Ancient of days.

†**c.** Government, sway (of a country). *Obs.*

**1338** R. BRUNNE *Chron.* (1725) 8 þe lond lese þe armes, changed is þe scheld. *Ibid.* 69 Harald, þorgh comon assent, Was corouned nobly, & for kyng þei him helde, Bot þe duke of Normundie to William felle þe schelde.

†**d.** Shelter, protection (in physical sense). *Obs.*

**1615** BRATHWAIT *Strappado* 202 Where being benighted, [he] tooke no other shield, To lodge him and his ware then th'open field. **1618** CHAPMAN *Hesiod's Georg.* II. 331 But then, betake thee, to the shade that lies, In shield of Rocks.

**3.** *Her.* = ESCUTCHEON.

*shield-of-arms*: an escutcheon with armorial bearings. *shield of pretence = escutcheon of pretence* (ESCUTCHEON I c), cf. INESCUTCHEON.

*c* **1320** *Sir Beues* (A) 1322 Tirri on Beues be-held And seȝ þe boiste wiþ a scheld. *c* **1325** *Gloss. W. de Bibbesw.* in Wright *Voc.* 153 L'eskou de gules [*glossed* a reed cheeld] ad porté. **1531** *Rec. St. Mary at Hill* (1905) 48 Item, a lyttell shelde of golde Innamyled with whyt and grene. **1540** *Reg. Mag. Sig. Scot.* 463 Concessit dicto W. et heredibus tallie unum duplex lie tressour auri in eorum lie schield circa eorum arma. *a* **1552** LELAND *Collect.* (1715) I. 234 Syr Maurice bare in a Grene Shild thre Bores of Golde. **1562** LEGH *Armory* 38 b, The fift [worthy] was Iudas Machabeus, whose Shielde was Or, ii. Rauens in Pale proper... The viii. was Charlemaine, & he bare the Ierusalem Shielde, Impaled with the imperiall Cote. **1707** HEARNE *Collect.* 5 July (O.H.S.) II. 24 Persons regard Dr. Woodward's Shield as 'a banter'. **1835** *Penny Cycl.* IV. 110/1 Our author's [Beaumont's] shield may be seen in any *Baronetage*. **1864** BOUTELL *Her. Hist. & Pop.* i. (ed. 3) 4 Such is the origin of Shields-of-Arms. **1868** CUSSANS *Handbk. Her.* iv. (1893) 69 The Inescutcheon, or Shield of Pretence, is [etc.]. **1905** C. DAVENPORT *Jewellery* viii. 142 The three legs in the shield-of-arms of the Isle of Man.

**4.** An ornamental piece of plate (more or less in the form of a shield) offered for competition in an athletic or other contest.

**1868** *Wimbledon Annual* 23 The 'Elcho' Challenge Shield. **1898** *Field* 23 Apr. 625/3 It has now been decided that the clubs shall jointly hold the shield during the ensuing twelve months.

**II.** A protective covering or shelter.

**5.** Applied to certain parts of animal bodies. [= G. *schild*, shield of a boar, a tortoise, etc.]

**a.** The thick, tough skin upon the sides and flanks of the boar; *spec.* an article of food (in full, ***shield of brawn***), made by placing a piece of this skin round the inside of a cylindrical mould and filling up with meat, and cooking until soft and tender. (Cf. BRAWN *sb.* 3.)

[**1337** *Durham Acc. Rolls* (Surtees) 32 Festum Sci. Cuthberti in Sept., In 2 scutis de Braune pro festo empt. a diversis.] **13..** *E.E. Allit. P.* B. 58 Wyth scheldez of wylde swyn. *c* **1400** *Master of Game* (MS. Digby 182) v, þei haue herd skynne and stronge flessh; and specially vpon þe shoulder, þat is called þe shelde. **1486** *Bk. St. Albans, Hunting* f ii b, The sheldys on the sholderis: therof shall .ii. be. *a* **1552** LELAND *Collect.* (1715) I. 231 By eating of a sheelde of a wilde bore he got an appetite. **1625** MASSINGER *New Way* IV. i, Did you not deuoure this morning, A shield of Brawne, and a barrell of Colchester oysters? **1641** MURREL *Cookerie* (ed. 5) 5 A Shield or Collar of Brawne. **1705** *Poor Robin* Observ. Feb., They then look like a Shield of Brawn at Shrovetide out of Date. **1819** SCOTT *Ivanhoe* vii, Wamba.. opposed to the beard of the Jew a shield of brawn, which he plucked from beneath his cloak. **1861** T. L. PEACOCK *Gryll Grange* xxxii, You will always find a piece of cold roast beef and a tankard of good ale; and just now a shield of brawn.

*allusive uses.* **1607** *Lingua* II. i. C 4, If they would vse no other Bucklers in warre, but sheilds of Brawne. **1610** GUILLIM *Heraldry* III. xiv. 135 The shield of a Boare.. is a good Buckler against that cruell Enemy called Hunger.

**b.** *Zool.* A protective plate covering a part; a scute, a carapace, a plastron, or the like.

**1704** *Phil. Trans.* XXVI. 1627 These were the Shields of the Cochineel Flies. **1774** GOLDSM. *Nat. Hist.* (1776) VII. 352 The shield of the breast [of the mole-cricket] is of a firm texture. **1828** STARK *Elem. Nat. Hist.* II. 65 Shell a conical shield, with the summit inclined. **1857** AGASSIZ *Contrib. Nat. Hist. U.S.* I. 255 [In Turtles] The dorsal shield, usually called by the French name 'carapace', is connected by a bridge with another shield, commonly called 'plastron'. **1861** P. P. CARPENTER in *Rep. Smithsonian Instit.* 1860, 234 *Pleurobranchus* has a thin, flat horny shield. **1880** HUXLEY *Crayfish* i. 24 The great shield or carapace is very easily separated from the thorax and abdomen.

†**6.** The seat of a privy; hence, a privy. *Sc. Obs.*

[Cf., for the sense, F. *garde-robe.*]

**1535** STEWART *Cron. Scot.* (Rolls) II. 658 This fals tratour wnder the schield wes set, Quhilk to his cuming tuke gude tent and cuir, With ane lang speit.. Amang the bowellis vpwart in the breist Straik him to deid. **1552** ABP. HAMILTON *Catech.* (1884) 65 Quhen he passit to the scheild to purge his wame. **1566** *Burgh Rec. Edin.* (1875) III. 222 That all personis that hes scheildis clenge the samin or euer thai be full, sua that thai brek nocht furth and rin in the streit. **1582** *Ibid.* (1882) IV. 259 Middingis, scheildes, furrouris [etc.].

**7.** A framework erected for the protection of workmen engaged in boring or tunnelling and pushed forward as the work progresses; also, a watertight case used in submarine tunnelling to keep back quicksands and inrushes of water.

**1837** HEBERT *Engin. & Mech. Encycl.* II. 805 The work [Thames tunnel] was commenced in 1825... To give security to the men in excavating, Mr. Brunel invented a cast-iron shield or frame... This shield [etc.] **1838** *Civ. Engin. & Arch. Jrnl.* I. 290/1 Two rows of close whole timber piles should be driven.. with space sufficient for the shield to travel. **1895** *Daily News* 5 June 7/3 A circular shield with a cutting edge is driven by sheer hydraulic pushing through the soil.

**8. a.** A protective device attached to a field-gun in order to shelter the gunners from rifle-fire.

**1898** E. S. MAY *Field Artillery* 313 Personally I do not believe in shields; if really bullet proof, they are so heavy as to hamper mobility. *Ibid.*, Even without shields men working quick-firing guns would be slightly less exposed than they are at present.

**b.** A protective device in clothing, as a *dress-shield.*

**1884**, etc. [see *dress-shield* s.v. DRESS *sb.* 4 a]. **1897** *Sears, Roebuck Catal.* 321/3 Kleinert pays for the dress if it is ruined by perspiration, if his shields are used in it.

**c.** *Mech.* (See quots.)

**1888** *Lockwood's Dict. Mech. Engin.* 316 *Shield.* (1) A covering employed to protect the bearings and spindles of emery-grinding machines from the action of the gritty dust. (2) A guard placed over or in front of band and circular saws and portions of machinery to protect the workmen from accidents. **1967** J. L. & G. H. F. NAYLER *Dict. Mech. Engin.* 323 *Shield*, a contrivance or covering, protective plate, or screen, to protect machinery or the operator, from damage or accident.

**d.** *Physics.* An electrically conducting cover of a device or apparatus intended to protect it from external electric or magnetic fields or to reduce or eliminate interference radiated by the device or apparatus itself. Cf. SCREEN *sb.*[1] 6.

**1919** J. A. FLEMING *Thermionic Valve* ii. 66 (*caption*) Fig. 34 shows the valve.. with copper-gauze shield for protecting from external electric fields. **1947** R. LEE *Electronic Transformers & Circuits* vi. 174 Multiple shields increase the action.. because eddy currents induced in the shields set up fluxes opposing the stray field. **1975** D. G. FINK *Electronics Engineers' Handbk.* VI. 32 It is often desirable to shield part of the circuit from electromagnetic fields. The shields can absorb, reflect, or degrade (by multiple internal reflections) the electromagnetic energy. The most commonly used shields are braided copper.

**e.** *Physics.* A mass of material, usu. lead or concrete, intended to absorb neutrons and other ionizing radiation emitted by a reactor or accelerator. See also *biological shield* s.v. BIOLOGICAL *a.*

**1933** *Proc. R. Soc.* A. CXLI. 262 The steel shield S prevents the impact of secondary electrons upon the glass walls. **1947** M. D. KAMEN *Radioactive Tracers in Biol.* iv. 93 Protection against γ radiation is best afforded by working with remote control devices behind heavy lead shields at least 2–3 inches thick. **1962** *Newnes Conc. Encycl. Nuclear Energy* 756/2 Such a shield is an iron or barium loaded concrete. The main part of the shield in most reactors, called the bulk or biological shield, is made of such material. **1974** *Encycl. Brit. Macropædia* XIII. 319/1 Typically, a 'core barrel'.. is enclosed in a thermal shield, a pressure vessel, a water shield against neutrons, and a blanket of reinforced concrete for gamma-ray absorption.

**9.** The lower front part of a ploughshare.

**1844** H. STEPHENS *Bk. Farm* I. 415 The share proper, consisting of the shield, terminating in the point *e*, and of.. the feather or cutter. **1875** in KNIGHT *Dict. Mech.*

**III.** Applied to things shaped like a shield.

†**10.** Used to render OF. *escu* as the name of a coin: see ECU. Cf. SCUTE *sb.*[1] 1. *Obs. rare.*

*c* **1386** CHAUCER *Prol.* 278 Wel koude he in eschaunge sheeldes selle. **1599** THYNNE *Animadv.* (1875) 45 The florens in Chaucers tyme.. was of the valewe of thre shillinges, foure pence.. or at the leaste, of two shillinges tenne pence farthinge.. some of them beinge called 'florens de scuto', or of the valewe of the 'shelde', or frenche crowne.

**11.** *Horticulture.* = ESCUTCHEON 3 d, SCUTCHEON *sb.*[1] 4 c.

**1572** MASCALL *Plant. & Graff.* 22 All other maner of trees aforesayde, doe take verye well to be graffed wyth Cyons, and also in the shielde. **1606** RAM *Little Dodeon* D 8, To graffe in the Shield, is to be done in Iune or Iuly, with the rynde. **1707** MORTIMER *Husb.* (1721) II. 262 Sharpen that end of the Bark below the Bud, like a Shield or Escutcheon. **1842** LOUDON *Suburban Hort.* 306 The shield being inserted in the usual manner, another with an orifice in it, to admit the bud of the first, is laid over it.

**12.** *Bot.* **a.** (See quot. 1806.)

**1796** WITHERING *Brit. Plants* (ed. 3) IV. 75 [A Lichen found] about the bodies of old oak.. trees near Holsworthy, Devonshire, abundantly with innumerable shields. **1806** TURTON tr. *Linn. Nat. Syst.* VII. Expl. Terms, *Shield*, the saucer-like fructification of lichens. **1862** *Chamb. Encycl.* III. 352/1 The species of the genus *Lecanora* are crustaceous lichens, with a flat uniform thallus, and unstalked shields.

**b.** (See quot.)

**1840** PAXTON *Bot. Dict.*, *Shield*, a broad table-like process in the flowers of *Stapelia*.

**c.** One of the cells forming the covering to the male organs of *Characeæ*.

**1875** BENNETT & DYER *Sachs' Bot.* 284 Each of these cells forms a segment of the shell of the ball, and they are hence called Shields.

**13.** *Embryology.* (See quot.)

**1913** J. W. JENKINSON *Vertebrate Embryology* 135 There is distinguishable in the blastoderm at the close of segmentation a circular or oval area placed excentrically towards the posterior end; this area is the embryonic shield.

†**14.** ? A sheet of ice. *Obs.*

**1624** *Maldon* (Essex) *Court Deeds* Bundle 108 *fol.* 9 Payd to Willyam Brand and Symon Crauford for breaking the sheilds of ice in the ryver.. this last winter.

**15. a.** A keyhole plate. ? *Obs.* [= G. *schild.*] Cf. ESCUTCHEON 3 c, SCUTCHEON *sb.*[1] 4 e.

**1649** *Caldwell Papers* (Maitland Club) I. 103 For ane lock and sheild to ye new chalmer dore of Cauldwell 3 2 0.

**b.** *Cutlery.* A small metal (usually 'German silver') plate fixed on the handle of a penknife or pocket-knife, for ornament or to be engraved with the owner's name.

**1876** CALLIS *Cutlery* (Brit. Manuf. Industr.) 163 About 1730 engraving of the shields and bolsters of pen and pocket knives.. was commenced.

**c.** (See quot.)

**1870** C. C. BLACK tr. *Demmin's Weapons of War* 369 The flat piece of metal which is sometimes affixed to the bottom of the hilt is called a shield.

**d.** A policeman's badge of office. *U.S.*

**1903** *N.Y. Evening Post* 29 Oct. 3 The ex-policeman who turned in his shield in September. **1956** 'E. MCBAIN' *87th Precinct* (1959) 19 Why don't you turn in your shield? Become a hackie or something? **1970** E. R. JOHNSON *God Keepers* xv. 167 Nobody said that a detective rating.. and a shield provided detectives with all the right answers.

**16. a.** *gen.* A flat or slightly convex surface more or less resembling a shield in shape.

**1849** RUSKIN *Seven Lamps* ii. §21. 53 The shield of stone which, usually supported by a central pillar, occupied the head of early windows. **1873** MISS THACKERAY *Old Kensington* xii. 100 A faded Italian shield of looking-glass.

**b.** A shield-shaped centre of a chair-back.

**1897** [see *shield-back* adj., sense 20 a below].

**17.** A fancy breed of pigeons, of various colours.

**1855** *Poultry Chron.* III. 140/1 (*table*) Toys, or any other Variety [of pigeon] not mentioned above; such as Suabians .., Shields, Swiss, &c. **1868** TEGETMEIER *Pigeons* xxi. 174 The Shields are so termed from bearing on their wings a coloured mark like a shield, on a white ground. **1874–6** *Fulton's Bk. Pigeons* 352 Shields. The colours of these are Black, Red, Yellow, Blue, and Silver. They are invariably plain-headed birds.

**18.** *Physical Geogr.* **a.** A large, seismically stable mass of Archaean basement rock having the form of a flat or gently convex peneplained platform and usu. forming the nucleus of a continent. Freq. with capital initial in proper names, as ***Baltic, Canadian Shield.*** [tr. G. *schild* (introduced in this sense by E. Suess *Das Antlitz der Erde* (1888) II. III. ii. 42).]

In quot. 1968 *ellipt.* for *Canadian Shield.*

**1906** H. B. C. SOLLAS tr. *Suess's Face of Earth* II. III. ii. 30 The whole of the north-east of America, from the mouth of the St. Lawrence to that of the Mackenzie.. belongs to a broad table-land of horizontal Palaeozoic beds, from beneath which the Archaean foundation crops out in the middle of the table-land not unlike a flat shield. This Archaean shield is thus surrounded by a ring of horizontally stratified sediments... It is to the exposed Archaean surface that we give the name of the Canadian shield. **1906** [see BALTIC *a.* 3]. **1915** C. SCHUCHERT *Text-bk. Geol.* II. xxi. 461 Most of the present continents have been formed around ancient protuberances of the lithosphere, the nuclear lands or shields. **1939** A. K. LOBECK *Geomorphol.* i. 4 Suess showed that certain substantial areas of the earth have always been rigid and unyielding, as, for example, the Canadian and Baltic Shields of America and Europe, the eastern Siberia Shield of Asia, [etc.]. **1963** D. W. & E. E. HUMPHRIES tr. *Termier's Erosion & Sedimentation* ii. 40 The ancient shields, which are also called 'old platforms', are none other than peneplains which have almost attained a final form. **1968** *Beaver* Autumn 14/1 He was with the voyageurs somewhere out in the bush covering some historic route over the Shield. **1969** BENNISON & WRIGHT *Geol. Hist. Brit. Isles* iii. 41 Before the break up of the continents the Lewisian rocks were probably contiguous with the Canadian-Greenland shield, one of the original continental cores. **1971** I. G. GASS et al. *Understanding Earth* iii. 55/1 The oldest continental regions, the Precambrian Shields, are often dominated by igneous rocks such as granite or by highly metamorphosed rocks such as gneiss.

**b.** The dome of a shield volcano.

**1937** *Bull. Volcanologique* I. 94 Composite structures resulting from the accumulations of a series of shifting vents of shield type. **1943** *Amer. Jrnl. Sci.* CCXLI. 241 On the north and northwest its great lava shield abuts against the dormant or extinct volcanoes of Mauna Kea and Hualalai, and on its southeastern slope rests the smaller, younger shield of Kilauea volcano. **1976** *Sci. Amer.* Jan. 33/2 Olympus Mons is enormous by terrestrial standards. Its shield is between 500 and 600 kilometers across, some five times larger than the largest shield on the earth.

**IV.** Combinations.

**19.** Obvious combinations: **a.** simple attributive, as ***shield-boss***; denoting a person armed with or carrying a shield, as ***shield-boy***, ***-man***; (sense 15 d) ***shield number***.

**1910** G. HENDERSON *Norse Infl. Celtic Scot.* ii. 42 Sword-axe, *shield-boss and cauldron. **1607** MIDDLETON *Five Gallants* IV. viii. 306 Torch-bearers and *shield-boys. **1892** RIDER HAGGARD *Nada* xxv. 210 Close up, *shield-men—close up! **1972** J. GORES *Dead Skip* i. 8 The policeman.. repeated his name, adding his *shield number.

**b.** objective, as ***shield-maker***; ***shield-bearing***, ***-losing*** adjs.; also ***shield-breaking*** adj. and sb.

**1824** SYMMONS tr. *Æschylus' Agamem.* 64 Many proud *shield-bearing men. **1867** TENNYSON *Passing of Arthur* 109 *Shield-breakings, and the clash of brands. **1870** BRYANT *Iliad* XXI. 485 Shield-breaking Mars began the assault. **1848** B. D. WALSH *Aristoph. Clouds* I. iv, When they saw the *shield-losing Cleónymus. **14..** *Nom.* in Wr.-Wülcker 686/19 *Hic scutarius*, a *scheldmaker. **1908** RIDER HAGGARD *Ghost Kings* xviii. 260, I have sold the hides to the shield-makers.

**c.** similative, as ***shield-form***, ***-formed***, ***-like***, ***-shaped*** adjs.; parasynthetic, as ***shield-backed***, ***-gilled***, ***-headed*** adjs.

**1880** *Shield backed [see REGENCY 7 b]. **1895** COMSTOCK *Study Insects* 115 The Shield-backed Grasshoppers. *Ibid.* 146 The Shield-backed Bugs. **1784** tr. *Spallanzani's Diss. Nat. Hist.* II. 275 The pumpion with *shield-form fruit.

**1835** *Encycl. Metrop.* (1845) XXIII. 640/2 Of the three [laminae] between the eyes, the central is shield-form. **1822** J. PARKINSON *Outl. Oryctol.* 108 *Clipeus.* Round, *shield-formed... *Scutum.* Angular or ovate shield-formed. **1835** *Encycl. Metrop.* (1845) XXIII. 640/1 The central lamina of the three between the edges shield-formed and acuminate. **1861** P. P. CARPENTER in *Rep. Smithsonian Instit. 1860,* 211 Order *Scutibranchiata.* (*Shield-gilled Crawlers). **1854** A. ADAMS, etc. *Man. Nat. Hist.* 307 *Shield-headed Fish-Parasites (*Peltocephala*). **1552** UDALL tr. *Geminus' Anat.* C j, The patyll or the kne bone, called of some men the *shyldelyke bone. **1877** HUXLEY *Anat. Inv. Anim.* v. 227 Flat shield-like processes. **1601** WEEVER *Mirr. Martyrs* C 8 b, If euer *sheild-shapt Comet was portent Of Criticke day, foule and pernitious. **1839** LINDLEY *Introd. Bot.* III. (ed. 3) 448 Shield-shaped (*clypeatus*). **1857** A. GRAY *First Less. Bot.* (1866) Gloss.

**20. a.** Special comb.: **shield-arm**, the left arm (cf. *shield-hand*); **shield-back** *a.*, having a shield-shaped back; †**shield-bone**, a shoulder-blade; **shield-bud**, a bud and a portion of the bark surrounding it used in grafting; hence **shield-budding**, the operation of grafting such a bud; **shield-cartilage, -gristle** = THYROID 1 a; **shield-cell** *Bot.*, one of the component cells of the reproductive organ in *Characeæ*; **shield-guard**, a form of trigger-guard used by some continental manufacturers of shot guns and rifles; **shield-hand**, an alleged ancient designation for the left hand (cf. *shield-arm*); **shield-hedge** = *shield-wall*; †**shield-knave** (= G. *schildknabe*) = SHIELD-BEARER; **shield-leaved** *a.* (*rare*), having peltate leaves; **shield-lion** *nonce-wd.*, a lion emblazoned upon a heraldic shield; **shield-maid, -maiden** = SHIELD-MAY; **shield-money** = SCUTAGE; **shield-pin**, a safety-pin; **shield-plate** *Zool.*, ? = SCUTE *sb.*[1] 4; **shield-ring** = *shield-wall*; **shield-ship** (see quot.); **shield volcano** [tr. G. *schildvulkan* (H. Reck 1910, in *Geol. und palæont. Abhandl.* IX. 84)], a volcano having the form of a very broad dome with gently sloping sides, characteristic of the eruption of basic lavas of low viscosity; **shield-wall** *arch.* [OE. *scildweall*], the interlocked shields of a body of men fighting on foot; †**shield-work**, embroidery in the form of shields.

**1640** tr. *Verdere's Rom. of Rom.* III. xv. 58 A great gash in his *shield arm. **1897** K. W. CLOUSTON *Chippendale Period Eng. Furnit.* 65 In the '*shield back' chair, which is Hepplewhite's favourite shape, the shield and its interior ornament making the splat never touch the seat of the chair at all. **1939** *Country Life* 11 Feb. p. xxvii (Advt.), Fine Antique Hepplewhite Mahogany Shield-back Arm Chair with attractively carved splats. **1978** *Morecambe Guardian* 14 Mar. 9/7 Other new items are shield-back dining chairs and matching carver chairs with loose drop-in seat. *c* **1600** *Leg. Guy Warw.* xxiv, One of his *sheeld-bones to this day Hangs in the citye of Coventrye. **1891** L. H. BAILEY *Nursery-bk.* (1896) 95 This [style of budding] is known as shield-budding.. A *shield-bud is shown natural size. **1842** LOUDON *Suburban Hort.* 301 All the different modes of budding may be reduced to two:—*shield-budding..and flute-budding. **1881** BEHNKE *Mechanism Human Voice* (ed. 2) 51 *Shield (Thyroid) Cartilage. **1881** BENTLEY *Man. Bot.* (ed. 5) 391 The *globule*..consists of eight valves, or, as they have been termed, *shield-cells. **1615** CROOKE *Body of Man* 636 The first is called in Greeke θυρεοειδής the *Shield-Gristle. **1892** GREENER *Breech-Loader* 84 The *shield-guard, or horn before guard. **1891** SIR D. WILSON *Right Hand* 202 The recognition of the *shield-hand..has already been referred to as one familiar to the ancient Greek and Roman. **1892** RIDER HAGGARD *Nada* xxv. 210 Straight at the *shield-hedge drove Umslopogaas. **1627** HAKEWILL *Apol.* (1630) 165 *Shieldknave or armour bearer to Charles the Great. **1860** RUSKIN *Mod. Paint.* V. VI. iii. 11 An outer spray of any *shield-leaved tree. **1872** TENNYSON *Gareth* 1186 Sir Lancelot, having swum the river-loops—His blue *shield-lions cover'd—softly drew Behind the twain. **1851** THORPE *North. Mythol.* I. 156 The Valkyriur..are also called.. Skialdmeyiar (*shield-maids). **1889** R. B. ANDERSON tr. *Rydberg's Teut. Myth.* 192 Shield-maids (amazons) occupy the position which in the original was held by giantesses. **1849** KEMBLE *Sax. Eng.* I. xii. I. 402 The Anglosaxon belief in the *Shield-maidens. **1870** MORRIS *Story of Volsungs* ix, A great company of shield-maidens. **1877** GREEN *Hist. Eng. People* I. 164 To commute their service for sums payable to the royal treasury under the name of 'scutage' or *shield-money. **1883** H. P. SPOFFORD in *Harper's Mag.* Mar. 576/2 They are..*shield-pins, and couldn't prick her if they tried. **1855** GOSSE *Mar. Zool.* I. 99 Cephalana. Segments equally provided with appendages; no *shield-plates. **1892** RIDER HAGGARD *Nada* xxv. 210 The *shield-ring wheels in upon itself. **1875** KNIGHT *Dict. Mech.*, **Shield-ship*, one carrying movable shields to protect the heavy guns except at the moment of firing. [**1911** *Geol. Mag.* VIII. 59 The so-called 'Schild' volcanoes in Iceland.] **1911** *Geogr. Jrnl.* XXXVII. 666 These *shield-volcanoes rise from a roundish base, with a gently convex surface surmounted by an elevated ring surrounding the crater. **1944** A. HOLMES *Princ. Physical Geol.* xx. 457 Hawaii..has been built up from the sea floor by the coalescence of several shield volcanoes. **1977** *Whitaker's Almanack 1978* 1037/1 The Isla Fernandina is the summit of a very large shield volcano rising from the sea floor to 1,495 metres above sea-level. *Beowulf* 3118 þonne stræla storm, strengum ȝebæded, scoc ofer *scildweall. **1880** TENNYSON *Brunanburh* i, He with his brother..Brake the shield-wall. *a* **1661** HOLYDAY *Juvenal* (1673) 22 His gown is all *Shield-work on azure [L. *cærulea indutus scutulata*].

**b.** In book-names (chiefly translations from mod. Latin) of animals, birds and insects, with reference to shield-like markings, or to the shield-like character or form of the scute or carapace. **shield snake**, a venomous southern African snake, *Aspidelaps scutatus*, distinguished by a large scale on its head.

**1854** A. ADAMS, etc. *Man. Nat. Hist.* 371 *Shield-Animalcules (Aspidiscidæ). **1847** *Jrnl. R. Agric. Soc.* VIII. 410 *Cassida nebulosa.* The Clouded *Shield-Beetle. **1854** A. ADAMS, etc. *Man. Nat. Hist.* 196 Shield-Beetles (Cossyphidæ). **1882** *Cassell's Nat. Hist.* VI. 104 Scutata, or *Shield Bugs. **1839** URE *Dict. Arts* 303 Cochineal..was proved by the observations of Lewenhoeck to be.. the female of that species of *shield-louse, or coccus, discovered in Mexico, so long ago as 1518. **1855** J. E. GRAY (*title*) Catalogue of the *Shield Reptiles in..the British Museum. **1850** A. WHITE *List Specim. Crustacea Brit. Mus.* 84 *Apus cancriformis.* *Shield-Shrimp. **1870** NICHOLSON *Man. Zool.* xxxiv. (1875) 253 The *Shield-slaters (*Cassidina*). **1910** F. W. FITZSIMONS *Snakes S. Afr.* iv. 84 This snake is known as the *Shield Snake, because it has a large scale on its nose which is partly detached at the sides. **1973** *Stand. Encycl. S. Afr.* IX. 613/1 The shield-snake is egg-laying. **1863** WOOD *Illustr. Nat. Hist.* III. 70 The Philippine *Shield-tail (*Uropeltis Philippinus*). **1854** A. ADAMS, etc. *Man. Nat. Hist.* 331 *Shield-Urchins (*Scutellidæ*). **1896** tr. *Boas' Text-bk. Zool.* 138 Shield-urchins or *Clypeastridæ*.

**c.** In book-names of plants, as **shield-fern**, various forms of the genus *Aspidium*; **shield-flower**, any plant of the genus *Aspidistra*.

**1814** PURSH *Flora Amer. Septentr.* II. 709 *Shield-fern. *Aspidium.* **1817** PURTON *Brit. Plants* II. 506 *Aspidium filix mas.* Common Hedge Shield-fern. *Ibid.* 508 *Aspidium Thelypteris.* Marsh Shield-fern. *Ibid. Aspidium Oreopteris.* Heath Shield-fern. **1889** *Hardwicke's Sci. Gossip* XXV. 46/2 Male shield fern. **1884** W. MILLER *Plant-n.* 125/1 *Shield-flower. The genus *Aspidistra*.

**shield** (ʃiːld), *v.* Forms: 1–2 **scildan, (ȝescildan),** 1 **sceldan, sceoldan, scyldan,** (2 **sculdan**), 3 **scilden, shildenn, sschild, ssilde, (schuld),** 3–4 **shild, sschilde,** 3–5 **silde, schild(e, scheld, (ssulde),** 3–6 **shelde,** 4 **ssylde, sceild,** 4–5 **scild, shilde, schylde, s(c)held(e, (schulde),** 4–6 **shylde,** 5 **sheelde, (scholde),** 5–6 **scheild,** 6 **sheild, shielde,** 7 **sheeld,** 6– **shield.** [OE. *scildan, ȝescildan,* f. *scild* SHIELD *sb.* Cf. G. *schilden,* ON. *skjalda,* to provide with a shield.]

**1. a.** *trans.* To protect (a person or object) by the interposition of some means of defence; to afford shelter to; to protect (an accused person, etc.) by authority or influence. Const. *from,* †*of,* also (OE. and early ME.) †*with*.

Often used in precatory formulas: cf. 5.

*Beowulf* 1658 Ætrihte wæs guð ȝetwæfed, nymðe mec god scylde. *c* **825** *Vesp. Ps.* xc. 14 Ic..ȝescildu hine [Vulg. *protegam eum*]. *c* **1000** *Sax. Leechd.* II. 238 Scilde hine wiþ cyle. *c* **1175** *Lamb. Hom.* 53 þe feder and þe sune and þe halie gast iscilde us þer wið and wið alle sunnen. *c* **1200** *Vices & Virtues* (1888) 23 Ðe ðie muȝen scilden fram ðese ȝewerȝede gaste(s). **12..** *Moral Ode* 299 (Egerton MS.) Sculde him elc man þe wile he mai, of þos helle þine. *c* **1290** *St. Brandan* 559 in *S. Eng. Leg.* 235 Seint Brendan seide, þoruȝ godes grace we schullen schilde þe. *c* **1330** R. BRUNNE *Chron. Wace* (Rolls) 7355 Mercurius, þat vs saues & schildes, Haþ vs brought vnto þys yldes. *c* **1386** CHAUCER *Sir Thopas* 197 God shilde his cors fro shonde. *c* **1403** CLANVOWE *Cuckow & Night.* 259 And shilde us fro the Cukkow and his lore. **1565** J. PHILLIP *Patient Grissell* 1638 (Malone Soc.) Besechinge God to sheild thee from all in conuenience. **1575** GASCOIGNE *Glasse Govt.* I. v. Wks. 1910 II. 26 So must the father shylde His youthfull Sonnes, that they be not beguylde, By wicked world. **1582** STANYHURST *Æneis* II. (Arb.) 63 Thow shalt bee shielded with my protection alway. **1605** CHAPMAN, etc. *Eastward Hoe* I. A 2 b, And as for my rising by other mens fall; God shield me. **1697** DRYDEN *Virg. Past.* IX. 34 If the kinder Pow'rs Preserve our Plains, and shield the Mantuan Tow'rs. **1797** COLERIDGE *Christabel* 254 O shield her! shield sweet Christabel! **1812** J. WILSON *Isle of Palms* III. 140 For there was a power in the gracious skies To shield their saints from ill. **1861** O. W. HOLMES *Agnes* v. 10 The love that won her girlish charms Must shield her matron fame. **1892** *Photogr. Ann.* II. 406 The sky shade attached, to shield the lens from the sun's rays.

**b.** *Electr.* = SCREEN *v.* 1 c. Const. *from, against.* Also *absol.*

**1922** *Wireless World* 1 July 416/1 The high amplifications possible with multi-stage valve receivers..lead to unexpected results when endeavouring to shield instruments from radio frequency fields. **1935** F. E. TERMAN *Measurements in Radio Engin.* xiv. 342 There are circumstances when it is desirable to shield against electrostatic fields without interfering in any way with the magnetic fields which are present. **1970** J. SHEPHERD et al. *Higher Electr. Engin.* (ed. 2) vii. 226 Sometimes sufficient shielding can be obtained by a few short-circuited copper turns, placed round the object to be shielded in such a direction that the axis of the turns is in the direction of the magnetic field.

**2.** *absol.* To offer a defence, to act as a shield.

*c* **888** ÆLFRED *Boeth.* xviii. §4 Ac siððan he his hispinge ȝehered hæfde, þa scylde he onȝean swiðe unȝeþyldelice. **13..** *E.E. Allit. P.* C. 440 þer he busked hym a bour, þe best þat he myȝt..For to schylde fro the schene, oþer any schade kest. **1822** BYRON *Juan* VIII. cvi, The truly brave, When they behold the brave oppress'd with odds, Are touched with a desire to shield and save. **1849** ROBERTSON *Serm.* Ser. I. xxi. (1866) 348 A desire to shield from pain.

†**3.** To arm with a shield. *Obs.*

*c* **1205** LAY. 4727 Brenne wes swiðe wrað & bannede is ferde scheldede his scalken. **1470–85** MALORY *Arthur* VIII. xxxix. 333 Whan sir Tristram was..wel shelded and swerded. **1667** DENHAM *Direct. Painter* II. ii. 126 But neither riding Pegasus for speed, Nor with the Gorgon shielded at his need.

*fig.* **1576** GASCOIGNE *Droome of Doomesday, Let. Bittern. Death* Wks. 1910 II. 440 Armed with Fayth, shylded with Hope, strengthned with Charitie.

†**4.** To ward off, to keep away. (With material or immaterial object.) Also with *off.* *Obs.*

*a* **1400** *Leg. Rood* viii. 259 God schop me a scheld, schame to schilde. **1596** SPENSER *State Irel.* Wks. (Globe) 631/1 They brought with them theyr usuall weedes, fitt to sheild the cold. **1657** W. RAND tr. *Gassendi's Life Peiresc* II. 253 Whose favours Peireskius made use of only in deprecating and shielding of, the dangers and discommodities of his friends. **1771** GOLDSM. *Hist. Eng.* II. 259 He saw only one method of shielding off the miseries that threatened the state. **1788** *Massachusetts Spy* 23 Oct. 2/1 The reason why the poison did not prove fatal,..is supposed to be owing to her being bit through the cloth, which shielded much of the poison from her hand. **1822** 'B. CORNWALL' *Poet. Wks., Lysander & Ione* i, As though A spirit of goodness peep'd from out the earth To shield decay.

†**5.** In deprecatory phr. ***God shield***, usually with a clause or sentence as direct object, rarely with addition of an indirect object; also *absol.* as an exclamation: = God forbid. *Obs.*

**1297** R. GLOUC. (Rolls) 1347 þat he in þine bendes come god it ssilde me. **13..** *Gaw. & Gr. Knt.* 1776 'God schylde', quod þe schalk, 'þat schal not be-falle!' *c* **1386** CHAUCER *Merch. T.* 20 God shilde that it sholde so bifalle. *a* **1400–50** *Wars Alex.* 3521 Bot me to do slike a dede, driȝtin it schilde! **1579** SPENSER *Sheph. Cal.* July 9 Ah God shield, man, that I should clime. **1589** *Almond for Parrat* E 3, Bishops were the smallest bugs that were aimed at in this extraordinary beneuolence, God shield the court haue escapt their collections. **1602** WARNER *Alb. Eng.* XII. lxxi. (1612) 296 No Clarke will so expound that Text, God shield they should, say I. **1674** BLOUNT *Glossogr.* (ed. 4).

ˈ**shield-ˌbearer.** An attendant who carries the shield of a warrior.

**1603** HOLLAND *Plutarch's Mor.* 427 His [Epaminondas'] esquire or shield-bearer had received a good piece of money for the ransome of a prisoner. **1761** *London & Environs* I. 45 Chaucer..was employed as a shield-bearer to the King. **1852** GROTE *Greece* II. lxxx. X. 479 He first inquired whether his shield was safe and his shield-bearer answering in the affirmative produced it before his eyes. **1875** MORRIS *Æneids* II. 477 Now shield-bearer Automedon and all the Scyrian host Closed on the walls.

*fig.* **1893** GOLDW. SMITH *United States* 165 Jefferson's successor was his shield-bearer, Madison.

**b.** (See quot.)

**1911** *Century Dict. Suppl.*, *Shield-bearer*, any one of the small elachistid moths of the genus *Coptodisca* (formerly *Aspidisca*), as the resplendent shield-bearer.

ˈ**shield-board.** *Obs.* exc. *dial.* Forms: 4 **cheldbrede, scheldbrede,** 6 **shel(d)brede, (sheldbredth),** 7 **shelboard,** 7– **shield-board,** (9 *dial.* **shell-board**). [f. SHIELD *sb.* + BRED *sb.*, afterwards replaced by the cogn. and synon. BOARD *sb.* (Cf. SHILBOARD.) (MHG. had *schiltbret* for wooden shield.)]

**1.** The mould-board of a plough.

*c* **1325** *Gloss. W. de Bibbesw.* in Wright *Voc.* 169 L'eschuchoun [*glossed* the cheld-brede, *v.r.* (Rel. Ant.) *sheldebred*]. *c* **1340** *Nominale* (Skeat) 856 *Vomer et escochoun* Schare and scheldbrede. **1523–34** FITZHERB. *Husb.* §2 In Kente they haue other maner of plowes,..some wyll tourne the sheld-bredth at euery landes ende, and plowe all one waye. **1613** MARKHAM *Eng. Husbandman* I. Introd. B 3 b, The eighth part is called the shelboard. **1652** BLITHE *Engl. Improv. Impr.* (1653) 190 And the Shield-board, some call Breast-board, or Earth-board, or Furrow-board, I shall retaine the Shield board. **1725** *Bradley's Fam. Dict.* s.v. *Plough*, The names of the particular parts of a plough are these..Breast board, throw board, Shield board &c.

**2.** *Antiq.* A wooden shield.

**1872** *Archæol. Cant.* VIII. 223 Piles of shieldboards were found lying one above another..; bundles of arrows [etc.].

**shielded** (ˈʃiːldɪd), *ppl. a.* [f. SHIELD *sb.* and *v.* + -ED.]

**1. a.** Bearing a shield.

**971** *Blickl. Hom.* 221 Tweȝen englas..ȝesceldode and ȝesperode. **1382** WYCLIF *Ezek.* xxxviii. 5 Men..alle sheeldid and helmyd. **1870** BRYANT *Iliad* VIII. 269 Crowded close with steeds and shielded men. *a* **1875** R. S. HAWKER in Byles *Life* (1905) 136 The charm'd and shielded Men.

*transf.* **1830** TENNYSON *Grass-hopper* Poems 109 Clap thy shielded sides and carol. **1883** R. W. DIXON *Mano* I. v. 12 And through the seas the hidden isles they hunt In shielded vessels.

**b.** *Nat. Hist.* In names of various animals characterized by a hard shield-like carapace or scute.

**1662** *Comenius' Janua Ling. Triling.* 42 The shielded tortoise. **1854** A. ADAMS, etc. *Man. Nat. Hist.* 244 Shielded-Bugs (Scutelleridæ). *Ibid.* 265 Shielded-Centipedes (Cermatiidæ). *Ibid.* 289 Shielded-Crabs (Dorippidæ). **1855** J. E. GRAY *Catal. Shield Reptiles Brit. Mus.* Introd., Shielded Reptiles (*Cataphracta*).

**2.** Furnished or hung with shields.

**1805** SCOTT *Hellvellyn* 27 With scutcheons of silver the coffin is shielded. **1876** MORRIS *Sigurd* III. (1910) 274 And thence forth to..the high-built shielded bale. **1892** BROOKE *E.E. Lit.* iv. 113 The shielded hall of Valhalla.

¶**3.** ? Emblazoned. *nonce-use.*

**1820** KEATS *Eve St. Agnes* xxiv, And in the midst..A shielded scutcheon blush'd with blood of queens and kings.

**4.** *techn.* Protected by a 'shield'.

**1855** *Orr's Circ. Sci., Inorg. Nat.* 247 With regard to the relative value of the different safety lamps that have been introduced, the shielded Davy may be said still to keep its place. **1884** *Pall Mall Gaz.* 3 Oct. 12/1 Extremely fast ships, ..mounting shielded guns of very great power. **1927** *Morning Post* 8 Sept. 10/1 The high frequency stage should be screened, and if one of the new shielded valves is used the circuit will be a simple one, easily handled, and cheaply built. **1970** J. SHEPHERD et al. *Higher Electr. Engin.* (ed. 2) vii. 225 For steady (or static) fields, the only method of achieving shielding is to provide a low-reluctance magnetic path for the stray flux, in such a way that this flux bypasses the shielded point.

**shielder** (ˈʃiːldə(r)). [f. SHIELD *v.* + -ER[1].] One who shields or protects another.

*a* **1300** *E.E. Psalter* xxx. 5 Þou salt lede me fra þat snare whilk þai Hid to me, for schilder artou ai. **1902** S. SMITH *Life Work* xiii. 134 He was..a shielder of criminal anarchy.

**shielding** (ˈʃiːldɪŋ), *vbl. sb.* [-ING[1].]

**1.** The action of the verb SHIELD; an instance of this.

**1581** A. HALL *Iliad* I. 3 Whereby [Phœbus] appeasd, some shielding we may haue. **1846** DICKENS *Pict. Italy, Milan* 133 A reforming Pope would need a little shielding, even now. **1883** *Athenæum* 27 Oct. 535/1 The most practical authority on military iron shielding in the United Kingdom.

*Comb.* **1875** MORRIS *Æneids* XII. 491 Æneas stayed, and gathered him behind his shielding-gear.

**2.** *Physics.* Material which protects or shields: **a.** against electric and magnetic fields (cf. SHIELD *sb.* 8 d); also, a shield.

**1930** *Proc. IRE* XVIII. 435 The complete exciter unit is enclosed with a metal grill in addition to the individual shielding compartment for the various stages. **1933** *Practical Wireless* 4 Feb. 962/2 A heavy flexible metal shielding fits tightly over these bakelite shells, and through the shells ordinary rubber-covered lead-in wire is threaded. **1975** D. G. FINK *Electronics Engineers' Handbk.* XVII. 31 The Wagner ground connection..can be used in place of shielding at lower frequencies if the utmost precision is not required.

**b.** against radiation (cf. SHIELD *sb.* 8 e).

**1945** HAWLEY & LEIFSON *Atomic Energy* 185 There was not sufficient radioactive emanation to be dangerous within a radius of fifty feet of the pile; notwithstanding this, precautionary shielding would be necessary in a locomotive unit. **1950** *Chemical Engin. Progress* XLVI. 109/1 To critical size must be added enough shielding to make reactors safe, and the amount of shielding required..is of considerable volume and weight. **1958** W. K. MANSFIELD *Elem. Nucl. Physics* v. 45 The shielding of a reactor will be designed to absorb the $\gamma$-rays rather than $\alpha$ and $\beta$-rays. **1974** *Encycl. Brit. Macropædia* XIII. 319/1 The shielding of the reactor must keep heat losses and radiation levels external to the reactor down to acceptable levels.

**shielding** (ˈʃiːldɪŋ), *ppl. a.* [f. SHIELD *v.* + -ING[2].] That shields or protects.

**1851** G. W. CURTIS *Nile Notes* xxii. 103 In the tropics, the great tree is a great god. Far outspreading shielding arms, he folds his worshippers from the burning sun. **1878** B. TAYLOR *Deukalion* I. ii. 23 And crept for shelter to my shielding arms.

**shieldless** (ˈʃiːldlɪs), *a.* [-LESS.] Having no shield, unprotected by a shield.

*a* **1400** *Octouian* 1131 Now hy beþ scheldles boþ tweyn þese champyouns. **1796** SOUTHEY *Joan of Arc* x. 576 The Frenchman's battle-axe Drove unresisted thro the shieldless mail. **1887** SWINBURNE *Locrine* III. ii. 108 A thing like thee ..Would cast a shieldless soldier forth to death.

**'shieldling.** *nonce-wd.* [f. SHIELD *v.* + -LING[1].] A protected person.

**1885** MEREDITH *Diana* II. xiii. 325 A young actress, like Miss Courtney—Mrs. Warwick's latest shieldling.

**shieldmay** (ˈʃiːldmeɪ). *Teut. Myth.* [f. SHIELD *sb.*[1] + MAY *sb.*[1], after ON. *skjaldmæ-r.*] A maiden warrior, an Amazon. (By some Eng. writers used as equivalent to VALKYRIE.)

**1849** KEMBLE *Sax. Eng.* I. xii. I. 393 The Wælcyrian or Shieldmays were the choosers of the slain. **1870** MORRIS *Story of Volsungs* xxiv. Brynhild answered, '..I am a shield-may, and wear helm on head even as the kings of war'.

**shieldrake,** obs. form of SHELDRAKE.

†**'shieldy,** *a. Obs. rare*[−1]. [f. SHIELD *sb.* + -Y.] Having the form of 'shields' or scales: transl. of mod.L. *scutellaris.*

**1681** GREW *Musæum* II. §iii. iv. 236 The Shieldy Tree Mosse. *Muscus arboreus scutellaris.*

**shieling, shealing** (ˈʃiːlɪŋ). *Sc.* Forms: 6 schæling, schealling, schilling, (scheilding), 6–7 scheilling, 6, 9 scheeling, 7 schel(l)ing, 7–8 shealling, 8 sheelin, 9 sheeling, sheilin(g, shielin, shilling, 7– shealing, 8– shieling. [f. SHIEL + -ING[1].

In the vernacular form the word has not been found earlier than the latter half of the 16th c.; but 13th c. documents show a latinized *scalinga*, which represents either this word (cf. *schale* early var. of SHIEL) or an etymologically equivalent **skāling* (f. SCALE *sb.*[4], ON. *skále*).

**1225** *Registrum Monast. Passelet* (Maitland Club) 212 Cum libertate siccandi retia sua et faciendi domos et scalingas piscatoribus suis. *c* **1230–68** *Cockersand Chartul.* (Chetham Soc.) I. 259 Versus aquilonem infra scalingam quæ fuit Candelani et scalingam quam Ricardus..tenuit.]

**1.** A piece of pasture to which cattle may be driven for grazing.

**1568** in *Reg. Mag. Sig. Scot.* 1575, 628/1 Lie schaelingis, in baroniis de Drumcardny et Bewfort. **1590** *Reg. Mag. Sig. Scot.* 611/1 Cum communi pasturagio lie scheilding infra lie Glen de Glengorf. **1594** *Ibid.* 48/1 Lie outseattis et scheallingis. **1596** *Ibid.* 132/1 Cum communiae et communi pastura ac lie schilling in Glenalmond consueta. **1602** *Ibid.* 481/1 Cum..lacubus, lie scheillingis, montibus [etc.]. **1711** in *Nairne Peerage Evid.* (1874) 138 Shellings grasings woods pasturages. **1806** *Gazetteer Scot.* (ed. 2) 288 The parish.. has been twice inundated by water-spouts, one of which carried off a whole shealing or grazing, with the family and cattle. **1843** HARDY in *Proc. Berw. Nat. Club* II. 59 *note*, A shiel or shieling is..a summer pasturage for flocks. **1884** Q. VICTORIA *More Leaves* 62 Opposite to this, on a place called Ruidh Reinnich, or the 'ferny shieling', a fire was kindled.

**2.** A hut of rough construction erected on or near such a piece of pasture: = SHIEL *sb.* 1.

*a* **1585** POLWART *Flyting w. Montgomerie* (Tullib.) 201 In stoir of lambes and lang taillit wedders..In scheilling, tyit fast in tedderis. **1610** HOLLAND *Camden's Brit.* (1637) 806 Little cottages here and there, which they call Sheales or Shealings. **1673** *Rec. Dingwall Presbyt.* (S.H.S.) 330 [The] Popishe Dishaunters were not cited in reguard that they were dwelling at their sheallings, and therefore [etc.]. **1771** PENNANT *Tour Scot.* I. (1774) 109 We refreshed ourselves with some goats' whey, at a Sheelin. **1791** BOSWELL *Johnson* an. 1773 (1831) II. 373 Little summer huts, called shielings. *c* **1810** TANNAHILL *Poems* (1846) 100 So merrily we'll sing, As the storm rattles o'er us, 'Till the dear sheeling ring Wi' the light lilting chorus. **1815** SCOTT *Guy M.* viii, Ye may stable your stirks in the shealings at Derncleugh. **1819** —— *Leg. Montrose* xviii, Montrose..was laid down to sleep in a miserable shieling. **1860** G. H. KINGSLEY in Galton *Vac. Tourists* (1861) 163 The lassies used to live in sheilings. **1873** BLACK *Pr. Thule* xxiv. 405 Lonely sheilings perched far up on the hills. **1895** CROCKETT *Men of Moss-Hags* xlii. 298 It seemed a hundred miles to the shieling on the hill.

**3.** *attrib.*

**1607** *Reg. Mag. Sig. Scot.* 710/1 Scheilinge-plaices. **1639** *Ibid.* 322/1 Sitting or eating of the scheilling grasse. **1849** WHITTIER *Kathleen* 19 And nightly round the shealing-fires Of her the gleeman sung. **1884** *Spectator* 17 May 642 The shealing feast is a very simple one, each housewife producing a cheese of last year's produce. **1901** *Scotsman* 12 Nov. 8/2 Little has been recorded of shieling life in historical books.

**shier,** variant of SHYER.

**shier, shiere,** obs. ff. SHEER *a.*, SHIRE *sb.*

**shierifewike,** obs. form of SHERIFFWICK.

**shieve,** obs. form of SHEAVE *sb.*[1], SHIVE.

**shife, shifer,** obs. ff. SHEAVE *sb.*[1], SHIVER.

†**shiffer.** *Obs.* [ad. G. †*schiffer*, now *schiefer* slate. Cf. SHIVER *sb.*[1] 3.] Slate.

**1683** PETTUS *Fleta Minor* II. i. 100 The fair Gold that is found..in..a Blew shiffer [orig. Ger. *Schiffer*] streamy and yellow iron.

**shiffer,** obs. form of SHIVER.

**shiffle-shuffle.** *rare.* [Formed by reduplication from SHUFFLE. Cf. SHILLY-SHALLY.] An attempted shuffle or evasion.

*a* **1871** DE MORGAN *Budget Parad.* (1872) 271 Two or three additional shiffle-shuffles towards defence of saying the Athanasian curse in church and unsaying it out of church, are hardly noticed.

**shifle,** obs. form of SHUFFLE *v.*

**shift** (ʃɪft), *sb.* Forms: 3 scift, 4–5 (6–7 *Sc.*) schift, 5–6 shyft, 5–7 shifte, 6 shyfte, schyfte (schiffte, sheft, *Sc.* scheift), 6– shift. [ME. *schift*, related to SHIFT *v.* Cf. ON. *skipti* neut., division, exchange (see SKIFT *sb.*[1]), MSw. *skipt* fem., division of property, *skipte* neut. (? and fem.) division, portion, change (mod.Sw. *skift* neut., spell of work, relay of workmen, *skifte* neut., division of property, change, rotation of crops, spell of work, relay of workmen), NFris. *skeft* division, stratum, *skaft* one of successive parties of workmen.

Many of these senses belong also to MHG., MLG. *schicht(e*, mod.G. *schicht* division of property, stratum, layer, one of several sets of persons or things, period of working time (in mining), one of several successive parties of miners working together for a fixed period of hours. It seems probable that the Ger. word is identical with the Eng. and Scandinavian words, the substitution of (xt) for (ft) being found in other words introduced into standard German from LG. (cf. e.g. G. *sacht* = Eng. *soft*).]

**I.** †**1. a.** A movement to do something, a beginning.

[The form *scift*, however, may possibly represent SKIFT *sb.*[1], which is recorded from *c* 1400.]

*a* **1300** *Cursor M.* 10480 And þus to prai sco gaf a scift.

†**b.** *at one shift*: at one time. *Obs.* [Cf. Icel. *eitt skipti* once (Vigf.).]

*c* **1325** *Metr. Hom.* 26 The faurtend day at a schift Sal bathe brin bathe erthe and lift.

**II.** †**2.** A share, a portion assigned on division. *Obs.* [Cf. MSw. *skipt*, G. *schicht* (Law) 'divisio bonorum'.]

**1461** in *10th Rep. Hist. MSS. Comm.* App. v. 301 The mesuring of salte and corne that sholde long to the shifte of the communes. **1574** *Ibid.* 334 The Maior hath but an Aldermans shift saving onely of every shippe of wyne. **1627** *MS. Acc. St. John's Hosp., Canterb.*, Pittance to help make vpp on of our Shiftes of monye xij d.

**III. 3. a.** An expedient, an ingenious device for effecting some purpose.

**1530** PALSGR. 267/1 Schyfte chevesaunce, *cheuesance.* **1559** *Mirr. Mag., Cambridge* iv, I sought a shift their tenures to vndo. **1595** SHAKS. *John* IV. iii. 7 Ile finde a thousand shifts to get away. **1624** QUARLES *Sion's Sonn.* viii. 5 My Dove, whom daily dangers teach new shifts. **1711** ADDISON *Spect.* No. 44 ¶8 The innumerable Shifts that small Wits put in practice to raise a Laugh. **1725** DE FOE *Eng. Tradesm.* (1732) I. iii. 28 The brickmakers all about London do mix sea-coal-ashes..with their clay..and by that shift save eight chaldron of coals out of eleven. **1842** J. AITON *Dom. Econ.* (1857) 118 A single man..can at any time try all the shifts, from taking land down to breaking stones within the high walls of the county jail. **1878** BOSW. SMITH *Carthage* XIX. 373 Other anecdotes illustrate the thousand shifts and devices of which Hannibal was a master.

**b.** Available means of effecting an end. Often in phrase (*to have*) *no other shift. Obs.* exc. *dial.*

**1523** BERNERS *Froiss.* I. ccccxiv. 293 We knowe all the shyfte in the countre [*nous scauons tous les refuges*] and so do nat they. *c* **1600** ? MONTGOMERIE *Banks Helicon* 105, I have no schift bot to resing All power into hir handis. **1606** G. W[OODCOCKE] *Ivstine* XIII. 60 Which pretense when Eumenes had espied, he had no other shift, but to try the matter against the traitor by the sword. **1639** DU VERGER tr. *Camus' Admir. Events* 74 This old man having no more shift to veile what he had hitherto endeavoured to conceale, declared unto his children that she was his wife.

†**c.** An entertaining or humorous device; a jest. *Obs.*

**1575** GASCOIGNE *Kenelw. Castle* II. iv. Wks. 1910 II. 117 Delight, and pleasures gallant shifts Haue fed your minde with many a Princely sport. **1579** LYLY *Euphues, Anat. W.* 82 Me thinkes that you smile at some pleasaunt shift. **1626** (*title*) The first and best parts of Scoggin's Iests: full of witty Mirth and pleasant Shifts.

**d.** Faculty of contrivance, resourcefulness. *rare.* Cf. SHIFTLESS.

**1542** UDALL *Erasm. Apoph.* 106 And in Menander also.. the housbandes reuile their wiues, calling theim, bliteas, of so small shifte or helpe, that thei wer as good to haue wiues of beetes. **1731–8** SWIFT *Pol. Conversat.* 92 Hang them, say I, that has no Shift. **1865** CARLYLE *Fredk. Gt.* XV. v. (1872) VI. 19 Friedrich's budget is a sore problem upon him; needing endless shift and ingenuity.

†**e.** Manner of livelihood. *to make an honest shift*, to gain one's living honestly. *Sc. Obs.*

**1572** *Reg. Privy Council Scot.* II. 133 Except thay have of thair awin, or sum honest and lauchfull schift quhairupoun to leif. **1596** DALRYMPLE tr. *Leslie's Hist. Scot.* I. 116 The ȝoungest ar put to sum honest schift. **1798** D. CRAWFORD *Poems* 57 (E.D.D.) Will ye compare me to a rogue, I always mak ane honest shift.

**4. a.** A fraudulent or evasive device, a stratagem; a piece of sophistry, an evasion, subterfuge.

**1545** *Act 37 Hen. VIII*, c. 9 §1 Concerninge Usury shiftes corrupt bargaynes and chevysaunces. **1561** T. NORTON *Calvin's Inst.* I. 24 If the Papistes haue any shame, let them no more vse this shift [Fr. *qu'ils n'vsent plus d'oresenauant de ces subterfuges*] to say that images are lay mennes bokes. *c* **1596** *Sir T. More* (Malone Soc.) 757, I conceiue your Lordship, and haue learnde your shift so well, that I must needes be apprehensiue. **1606** SHAKS. *Ant. & Cl.* III. xi. 63 Now I must..dodge And palter in the shifts of lownes, who With halfe the bulke o' th' world plaid as I pleas'd, Making, and marring Fortunes. **1635** R. N. tr. *Camden's Hist. Eliz.* II. 133 This the Queene of Scots delegates rejected as a frivolous shift. **1681** *Trial of S. Colledge* 104 He is a man lives by his Shifts. **1722** WOLLASTON *Relig. Nat.* ix. 207 How many subsist upon begging, borrowing, and other shifts. **1790** BEATSON *Nav. & Mil. Mem.* I. 37 A nobleman, who was not to be put off with ministerial shifts. **1822** HAZLITT *Table-t.* Ser. II. xii. (1869) 253 Their whole life is a succession of shifts, excuses, and expedients. **1870** BRYANT *Iliad* VIII. 116 Ulysses, man of subtle shifts,..whither dost thou flee?

†**b.** *alliterative phrases. Obs.*

**1598** BARCKLEY *Felic. Man* (1631) 111 Those goods that are gotten by shift, are for the most part lost with shame. **1600** A. BOURCHER in R. Edwards *Parad. Dainty Dev.* C iv b, Got with shifts are spent with shame. **1601** MUNDAY *Downf. Earl Huntington* II. D 3 b, You..as yee liu'd by shifts, shall die with shame.

**5. a.** An expedient necessitated by stress of circumstances; a forced measure.

**1647** CLARENDON *Hist. Reb.* II. §102 Cottington..being Chancellor of the Exchequer..had his hand in many hard shifts for money. **1651** HOBBES *Leviath.* II. xxix. 168 Such dammage, or shifts, are all Common-wealths forced to. **1751** JOHNSON *Rambler* No. 141 ¶9 It were endless to recount the shifts to which I have been reduced. **1796** MORSE *Amer. Geog.* II. 20 Being reduced to very extraordinary shifts for supplying the place of bread. **1823** SCOTT *Peveril* xlv, Many of them had shared the wants, and shifts, and frolics of his exile. **1858** J. G. HOLLAND *Titcomb's Lett.* i. 17 That pride of personal independence..that resorts to desperate shifts rather than incur an obligation.

†**b.** *for (a) shift*: as a makeshift; for want of something better. *Obs.*

**1523** HEN. VIII in *St. Papers* (1836) IV. 47 We suppose that many of your souldeours shalbe founden hable to stande in stede of gunners, metely well for a shyfte. **1599** SHAKS. *Much Ado* II. iii. 80 Ha, no, no faith, thou singst well enough for a shift. **1683** in *Phil. Trans.* (1693) XVII. 629 For a shift, common or Sterling Silver will serve the turn.

**c.** *by the shift*: by way of makeshift; 'at a pinch' (*Eng. Dial. Dict.*). So *on a shift.* Now *dial.*

**1665** PEPYS *Diary* 16 Nov., I..had a good bedd by the shift, of Wyndham's. **1842** J. AITON *Dom. Econ.* (1857) 127 Dinners made up on a shift of bread and cheese, and the like, are always the most expensive. **1897** *Leeds Mercury Suppl.* 29 May (E.D.D.), Ah can eyt a pund bi t'shift.

**d.** *one's* (or *the*) *last* (or †*utter*) *shift*: the last resource. *to be at* (†*under*) *one's last shift*(*s*: to be at the last extremity, in the greatest difficulty; so to *put, drive, reduce*, etc. *to the last shifts.*

*a* **1604** HANMER *Chron. Irel.* (1633) 109 You see me..now extremely driven to my utter shifts. **1638** *Hamilton Papers* (Camden) 15 The consideration of thes dangers, and not beeing abill longer to satisfie them with words draufe me to my last shifts. **1733** W. ELLIS *Chiltern & Vale Farm.* 276 Whoever makes use of Chalk for a Dressing, I think, is under the last Shift. **1796** NELSON 18 July in Nicolas *Disp.* (1845) II. 216 They are at their last shifts.

**e.** *to put* or *drive* (*one*) *to one's shifts, to put* or *drive to a* (or †*the*) *shift* or *shifts* (often with adj. as *hard, miserable*, etc.): to bring to extremity.

† *to leave* (a person) *to his shifts*: to leave him to help himself.

**1553** BRENDE *Q. Curtius* I. Bivb, He was driuen to so narrowe shifte, that to furnishe hym selfe of money, he became a Pyrat. **1581** W. S. *Compend.* 15 You draue him to his shiftes. **1589** R. ROBINSON *Golden Mirr.* (1851) 18 Except that Tullie were thy name, Thy pen were put to shiftes. **1617** MORYSON *Itin.* I. 195 These knightes..were much driven to their shiftes, to get money for that journey. **1636** EARL MANCHESTER *Contempl. Mortis* 91 Weake faith lookes for means, and is put to shifts when she sees them fail. **1663** COWLEY *Ess., Of Solitude* ¶3 (1906) 393 It is a deplorable condition, this, and drives a man sometimes to pittiful shifts in seeking how to avoid Himself. **1683** KENNETT tr. *Erasmus on Folly* 125 They are reduc'd to hard shifts, must grapple with poverty [etc.]. **1700** S. L. tr. *Fryke's Voy. E. Ind.* 328 He knew this to be the Elephant, that had put him so hard to his shifts. *a* **1715** BURNET *Own Time* II. (1897) I. 403 Many..who were put to hard shifts to live. **1725** DE FOE *Voy. round World* (1840) 72 The gunner being thus driven to his shifts, made down to the shore. **1775** SHERIDAN *Rivals* V. i, The dear delicious shifts I used to be put to, to gain half a minute's conversation. **1784** BAGE *Barham Downs* I. 173 Two or three bad harvests, a murrain, or a blight, for example might put you sadly to your shifts. **1842** G. S. FABER *Prov. Lett.* (1844) I. 110 When gentlemen resort to such arguments, it shows that they must be sorely put to their shifts. **1849** *Ainsworth's Mag.* XVI. 524 A man likely to be put to the shift in these days would be a fool indeed to marry without it [money]. **1856** MACAULAY *Biog., Goldsm.* (1860) 60 He was still often reduced to pitiable shifts. **1885** 'MRS. ALEXANDER' *At Bay* i, He was put to strange shifts to make out a living.

**6.** ***to make (a) shift.***

**a.** To make efforts, bestir oneself, try all means. Now *dial.* Also † ***to make busy, good, hard shift.***

*c* **1460** *Towneley Myst.* xiii. 285 Bot yit I must make better shyft, And it be right. *c* **1535** LD. J. BUTLER in Ellis *Orig. Lett.* Ser. II. II. 51 But God willing I woll make bessye shifte to sende the said mony in haste unto him. **1570–6** LAMBARDE *Peramb. Kent* 291 They made eache man the best shift for himselfe, that they could. **1600** HOLLAND *Livy* II. x. 50 Euerie man made shift for himselfe. **1675** HOBBES *Odyssey* XVII. 411 And to come hither thence, I made hard shift. **1859** GEO. ELIOT *Adam Bede* ii, I'd make a shift, and fend indoor and out, to give you more liberty. **1882** STEVENSON *Mem. & Portr.* xi. (1887) 175 What they have endured unbroken, we also..will make a shift to bear.

**b.** To attain one's end by contrivance or effort; to succeed; to manage *to do* something. † ***to make shift of***: to manage to secure (some result).

**1504** *Plumpton Corr.* (Camden) 184, I have sent it you with John Walker at this tyme; the which I shall shew you how I mayd schift of, at your comminge. **1594** KYD *Cornelia* I. 87 A Ship vnrig'd Can make no shift to combat with the Sea. **1611** MIDDLETON & DEKKER *Roaring Girl* F1, If I could meete my enemies one by one thus, I might make pretty shift with 'em in time. **1698** FRYER *Acc. E. India & P.* ix. 128 The Horse..made the best shift of all. **1895** 'Q.' (Quiller-Couch) *Wandering Heath* 8 He made shift pretty well till he got to Lowland, and then had to drop upon his hands and knees and crawl.

**c.** To succeed with difficulty, to manage with effort *to do* something. So † ***to make a hard shift.***

**1538** in *Lett. Suppress. Monasteries* (Camden) 194 Thei war not abill to make schiffte to paye for my costis. **1627–8** LAUD *Diary* 5 Feb.–17 Mar., I made a shift to go and christen my Lord Duke's son. **1639** FULLER *Holy War* IV. iii. (1640) 171 Sixty yeares almost did the Latines make a hard shift to hold Constantinople. *a* **1674** CLARENDON *Hist. Reb.* XI. §104 Most of the Foot made a shift to conceal themselves. **1711** BUDGELL *Spect.* No. 77 ¶5, I..can make a shift to command my Attention at a Puppet-Show or an Opera. **1752** FIELDING *Amelia* IV. ii, Booth made a shift to support his lovely burden. **1832** HT. MARTINEAU *Ireland* i. 13 Every year less and less came up, and that which did make a shift to grow yielded less and less meal. **1847** CHARL. BRONTE *Jane Eyre* xi, When she first came here she could speak no English; now she can make shift to talk it a little.

**d.** To do one's best *with* (inferior means), to be content *with*, put up *with*.

**1577** B. GOOGE *Heresbach's Husb.* I. 32 The bread is very drye..but the common people remediyng that with Larde or Oyle, doo make a shift with it as wel as they can. **1629** B. JONSON *New Inn* II. i, Thou must make shift with it; pride feels no pain. **1687** A. LOVELL tr. *Thevenot's Trav.* I. 33 When they have no Spoons, they make an easie shift without them. **1680** MOXON *Mech. Exerc.* xi. 202 Turners seldom use them, but make shift with either of the other [tools]. **1733** SWIFT *Let to Mrs. Cæsar* 30 July, I cannot make shift nor bear fatigue as I used to do. **1770** LUCKOMBE *Hist. Printing* 319 The Press-Stone should be marble, though sometimes Master Printers make shift with purbeck. **1842** J. H. NEWMAN *Paroch. Serm.* V. 71 Act then as persons who are in a dwelling not their own;..who accordingly, make shift and put up with any thing that comes to hand. **1885** *Bookseller* July 650/2 We cannot afford to employ..efficient assistants but have to make shift with cheap labour.

**IV.** Change, substitution, succession.

† **7.** Change or substitution of one thing for another of the same kind. *Obs.*

**1580** TUSSER *Husb.* (1878) 86 Poore cattle craue some shift to haue. **1625** WOTTON *Let. to N. Pey* in L. P. Smith *Life & Lett.* (1907) II. 288 My going to Oxford was not merely for shift of air.

† **8. a.** A plurality of things of the same kind that are or may be used successively. *Obs.*

**1562** BULLEIN *Bulwarke, Bk. Simples* (1579) 30 Let bothe Pease and Beanes bee..tenderly sodden in shifte of waters, before you doe eate theim. **1567–9** JEWEL *Def. Apol.* (1611) 633 It is fit for a Pope to haue shift of mindes. **1592** GREENE *Groatsw. Wit* (1874) 25 He had shift of lodgings, where in euery place his Hostesse writ vp the wofull remembrance of him. **1599** B. JONSON *Ev. Man out of Hum.* II. vi, He hath shift of names, sir: some call him Apple John and some Signior Whiffe. **1611** *Second Maiden's Tragedy* 936 (Malone Soc.) She has her shifte of frendes.

† **b.** A set or suit (of sails, scenes). *Obs.*

**1592** in Hakluyt *Voy.* (1600) III. 845 Being prouided onely of one shift of sailes all worne. **1626** CAPT. SMITH *Accid. Yng. Seamen* 17 A shift of sayles. **1754** A. DRUMMOND *Trav.* i. 15 They had three or four shifts of very good scenes.

**9. a.** Change (of clothing); *concr.* one of several suits of clothing, or of several garments of the same kind belonging to one person. *Obs.* exc. *dial.*

*c* **1570** W. WAGER *The Longer thou livest* 1104 (Brandl) Of rayment he shall haue shiftes twentie. **1600** G. BEST in Hakluyt *Voy.* III. 83 Hee that had fiue or sixe shifts of apparell had scarce one drie threed to his backe. **1657** R. LIGON *Barbadoes* 13 Some passengers of the ship, who had no great store of linnen for shift, desired leave to go ashoare. **1833** *Sel. Comm. Cinque-port Pilots* 11 The men have not a shift of clothes. **1879** MISS JACKSON *Shropsh. Word-bk.* **1886** *S.W. Linc. Gloss.*

† **b.** A player's dressing-room in a theatre.

**1667** PEPYS *Diary* 5 Oct., She took us up..to the women's shift, where Nell was dressing herself. *a* **1704** T. BROWN *Amusem. Ser. & Com., Play-Ho.* Wks. 1709 III. I. 42 If She goes to her Shift, 'tis Ten to One but he follows her.

**10. a.** A body-garment of linen, cotton, or the like; in early use applied indifferently to men's and women's underclothing; subsequently, a woman's 'smock' or chemise. Now chiefly *N. Amer.*

In the 17th c. *smock* began to be displaced by *shift* as a more 'delicate' expression; in the 19th c. the latter, from the same motive, gave place to *chemise.*

**1598** B. JONSON *Ev. Man in Hum.* I. i, I haue knowne some of them, that haue..at length bene glad for a shift (though no cleane shift) to lye a whole winter in halfe a sheete. **1648** WINYARD *Midsummer-Moon* 4 Is the University Pim'd, and therefore must change shifts, or are men turnd out..for being scabby? **1691** *D'Emilianne's Frauds Rom. Monks* 96 They are stript stark Naked in another [room], without suffering them so much as to keep on their Shifts. **1712** ADDISON *Spect.* No. 367 ¶5 A Lady's Shift may be metamorphosed into Billet-doux. **1756** FRANCES BROOKE *Old Maid* No. 34. 204 But remember that Julia and Rosara ..fail not to bring with them checqu'd shifts to appear in at church. **1828** MISS MITFORD *Village* III. 114 Work was lost —even the new shifts of the Vicar's lady. **1853** KINGSLEY *Hypatia* x, A..negress dressed in true negro fashion, in a snow-white cotton shift, a scarlet cotton petticoat, and a bright yellow turban. **1890** SWINBURNE *Stud. Prose & Poetry* (1894) 216 A handsome girl, who was swimming, clothed with a white shift and a short petticoat. **1927** M. DE LA ROCHE *Jalna* xix. 250 He pictured her in a fine embroidered shift, curled softly beneath the silk eiderdown. **1929** W. FAULKNER *Sartoris* 177 The flowers you know are all there, in their shifts and with their hair combed out for the night. **1936** M. DE LA ROCHE *Whiteoak Harvest* xxii. 301 She is such a slack creature that I dare say the poor child doesn't own a clean shift.

**b.** A straight loose dress.

**1957** M. B. PICKEN *Fashion Dict.* 293/1 *Shift,*..loose dress hanging straight from shoulders, with fulness closely belted at waistline. **1965** H. L. BROCKMAN *Theory of Fashion Design* v. 95/2 The shift automatically lengthens the figure at the expense of widening it at the waistline. **1975** D. LODGE *Changing Places* v. 177 Girls in kaftans, saris, skinny sweaters, bloomers, shifts, muu-muus.

**11.** Each of the successive crops in a course of rotation.

**1715** PENNECUIK *Wks.* (1815) 92 (E.D.D.) The adoption in this country of the common course of four shifts, before pasture. **1787** W. H. MARSHALL *Norfolk* (1795) I. 131 An East Norfolk farmer divides his farm into what he calls 'six shifts', to receive his principal crops in rotation. **1812** SIR J. SINCLAIR *Syst. Husb. Scot.* I. Add. 19 By the frequent ploughings given to the turnip break or shift, the land is made perfectly clean. **1880** CHARL. M. MASON *Forty Shires* 222 Sometimes a four-shift, sometimes a five-shift rotation is employed.

**12. a.** A relay or change of workmen or †of horses.

**1708** J. C. *Compleat Collier* (1845) 33 [The] Pit will require..4 shifts of Horses..and indeed you shou'd have a spare Shift, or two Horses more ready. **1812** J. HODGSON in Raine *Mem.* (1857) I. 97 Two shifts or sets of men were constantly employed. **1879** *Print. Trades Jrnl.* XXIX. 9 Working day and night with separate shifts of workmen. **1884** *Manch. Exam.* 22 Feb. 5/2 He would have in all mines which are worked on the double-shift system a fresh examination of the workings..before the second shift goes down. **1912** *Sphere* 28 Dec. 326/1 The night shifts receive so much higher pay for their labour.

**b.** The length of time during which such a set of men work.

**1809** T. DONALDSON *Poems* 132 Like miners, faith, we'll try a shift, An' work by turns. **1825** J. NICHOLSON *Oper. Mech.* 329 It is usual..to divide the men into two classes, one class to relieve the other every 12 hours: these periods are called shifts. **1851** GREENWELL *Coal-trade Terms, Northumb. & Durh.* 47 The payment for off-hand work.., is 3s. per shift of 8 hours. **1862** SMILES *Engineers* III. 25 They worked together for about two years, by twelve-hour shifts. **1913** *Times* 14 May 8/1 An eight hours day, with a standard rate of 5s. a shift.

*transf.* **1860** SMILES *Self Help* i. 17 These men..have often, during the busy season of Parliament, worked 'double shift', almost day and night.

**c.** A quantity (of ore) removed at a time.

**1839** URE *Dict. Arts* 752 The richness of the ore varies from 2 to 20 bings of galena per shift of ore; the shift corresponding to 8 waggons load.

**13.** A change (of wind).

**1594** BLUNDEVIL *Exerc.* VII. xxxi. (1636) 702 At every shift of winde. **1669** STURMY *Mariner's Mag.* IV. ii. 144 Well experienced in Judgment, in estimating the Ship's Way in her Course upon every shift of Wind. **1782** *Ann. Reg.* 91 The season was far advanced for military operations, the shift of the monsoon being at hand. **1820** SCORESBY *Acc. Arctic Reg.* I. 288 The Dundee of London..was suddenly stopped by a shift of wind. **1876** R. H. SCOTT *Weather Charts* 72 In every case it will be seen that the shift from 1 to 3 is *veering*, and from 1′ to 3′ is *backing*, whatever the first direction of the wind may have been.

**V.** Change of position, removal.

**14. a.** A shifting, removal; a change of position or attitude; *dial.* a change of residence or employment. ***to get a shift on*** (colloq.), to get a move on (see MOVE *sb.* 6).

**1831** A. SEDGWICK in *Trans. Geol. Soc.* (1836) Ser. II. IV. 53 If there be any shift of position among the mineral masses in their strike across the valley, it must be of comparatively small extent. **1858** GLENNY *Everyday Bk.* 233/2 Examine every plant as it comes in, to see if the drainage be clear, and whether it wants a shift. **1867** SWINBURNE *Ess. & Stud.* (1875) 150 A suffering which runs always in one groove, without relief or shift. **1871** CARLYLE in Mrs. Carlyle *Lett.* III. 194 A small furnished house should be rented, and a shift made thither. **1906** [see POLE *v.*[1] 8]. **1977** *Times Educ. Suppl.* 21 Oct. 9/2 We could have started certainly a year earlier, even two years earlier if we had got a shift on.

**b.** in immaterial sense, e.g. a shifting or transfer of responsibility, etc.

**1826** E. IRVING *Babylon* v. II. 31 There can be no shift in policy or in power, much less a revolution in them,..without a terrible struggle. **1844** *Min. Evid. Sel. Comm. Commons Inclosure* 27 Many of these commonable meadows have their own peculiar customs as to the shift of the severalty ownership.

**c.** *Physics.* A displacement of a spectral line from the expected position or from some reference position; hence, a change of an energy level in an atom, molecule, etc.; ***chemical shift***, in nuclear magnetic resonance or Mössbauer spectroscopy, the position of a resonance in the spectrum measured relative to some standard signal, the separation being characteristic of the chemical environment of the resonating nucleus. See also RED SHIFT.

**1884** *Phil. Mag.* XVIII. 161 A shift of the lines towards the more refrangible side of the spectrum. **1897** *Astrophysical Jrnl.* V. 210 Here is certainly a *vera causa* for some shift towards the red in molecules causing light. **1932** *Physical Rev.* XLII. 350 The direction of the shift is again such that $Hg^{204}$ has the highest energy. **1945** R. A. SAWYER *Exper. Spectroscopy* v. 118 Changes in temperature and pressure may lead to serious difficulties in prism spectrographs through broadening and shifts of spectral lines. **1952** *Physical Rev.* LXXXVIII. 1070/1 A shift in the nuclear resonance, known as the chemical shift, is due to the effects of diamagnetism and induced paramagnetism in a molecule. **1961** A. D. THACKERAY *Astron. Spectroscopy* xiii. 186 Interpreted as a radial velocity this shift implies that the nebula in question is running away from us at a speed of slightly over 60,000 km/sec. **1966** *McGraw-Hill Encycl. Sci. & Technol.* VIII. 600*a*/1 Chemists have become interested in using the Mössbauer effect because of the isomer shift (also called isomeric or chemical shift); this results from the interaction of the electron density..at the nucleus with the nuclear charge. **1970** G. K. WOODGATE *Elem. Atomic Struct.* viii. 154 Since the perturbing states of opposite parity lie a long way away,..one expects the Stark shift of the ground state to be small. **1978** P. W. ATKINS *Physical Chem.* xix. 625 The two methylene protons are in a different part of the molecule; they therefore have a different chemical shift, and come into resonance at another magnetic field.

**d.** *Philol.* A phonetic change. See also *accent-shift, consonant-shift, sound-shift, stress-shift, vowel-shift*, under the first elements.

[**1875** WHITNEY *Life Lang.* iv. 54 There has been no general shift of the place of the accent as compared with Latin.] **1894** O. F. EMERSON *Hist. Eng. Lang.* xiv. 241 §271 The shift from voiceless to voiced in certain positions has taken place since Teutonic times. **1909** O. JESPERSEN *Mod. Eng. Gram.* (1949) I. viii. 231 In most cases the spelling had become fixed before the shift, which..is one of the chief reasons of the divergence between spelling and sound in English... The shift may be represented graphically. **1934** PRIEBSCH & COLLINSON *German Lang.* II. i. 86 A clean cut was made between those dialects which underwent the shift and those which remained unaffected. *Ibid.* 88 The shift from stop to spirant was carried out over the whole High German area.

**e.** A change of gear in a motor vehicle. *N. Amer.*

**1915** V. W. PAGÉ *Questions & Answers* (rev. ed.) xxvii. 446 The clutch must be disengaged before a shift can be made. **1947** R. F. KUNS in Kuns & Plumridge *Automotive Fundamentals: Chassis & Power Transmission* 164 The overdrive shift is made automatically, by simply lifting the foot from the accelerator for about $1\frac{1}{2}$ seconds.

**f.** *Chem.* A migration of an atom or group, or of electrons, from one point in a molecule to another, or occas. between molecules, in a chemical reaction.

**1932** *Jrnl. Amer. Chem. Soc.* LIV. 3278 The shift of the electron pair includes the atom or group which it holds. **1947** *Ibid.* LXIX. 290/2 On the other hand, the hydrogen atom with its pair of electrons might be transferred by an *inter* rather than an *intra* molecular shift. **1953** C. K. INGOLD *Structure & Mechanism in Org. Chem.* ix. 482 Other rearrangements involve only the shift of a methyl group to an adjoining position. **1968** R. O. C. NORMAN *Princ. Org. Synthesis* xiv. 435 A typical example of a hydride shift occurs in the reaction of a primary aliphatic amine with nitrous acid; e.g. n-propylamine gives iso-propanol, together with propylene, and only a trace of n-propanol. **1975** C. J. COLLINS in R. F. Brown *Org. Chem.* xvi. 535*b* Prior to our explanation it was commonly held that all 1,2-shifts—for example, of hydrogen, alkyl, or aryl during Wagner-Meerwein, pinacol, Demjanov rearrangements and the like—took place with inversion of configuration at the migration terminus.

**g.** *Computers.* The movement of the digits of a word in a register one or more places to left or right, equivalent to multiplying or dividing the corresponding number by a power of whatever number is the base.

**1946** *Ann. Computation Lab. Harvard Univ.* I. 73 The first molding is..used for reset and the second to read out the tens digit of the amount of shift in conjunction with the proper molding of the first column... The shift is counted to the right. **1966** *IFIP-ICC Vocab. of Information Processing* 70 Digits shifted beyond the end of the word or register may simply be dropped, or in a cyclic shift (or end-around shift) they may be returned to the opposite end of the word or register in a circular fashion. **1970** O. DOPPING *Computers & Data Processing* v. 80 Sometimes it is necessary to analyze the individual characters of a word. The computer can do this by means of shift instructions. These are instructions for left shift and right shift.

**15. a.** *Mus.* In violin-playing, a change of the position of the hand on the finger-board.

When the first or ordinary position is quitted, the player is said to be 'on the shift'; the second position is called the 'half shift', the third the 'whole shift', and the fourth the 'double shift'. (Grove *Dict. Mus.* s.v.)

**1771** BURNEY tr. *Tartini* in G. Hart *Violin* (1875) 342 The taking a Violin part..and playing it upon the half-shift, that is, with the first finger upon G on the first string, and constantly keeping upon this shift. **1824** SCOTT *Redgauntlet* Let. x, I..skipped with flying fingers, like Timotheus, from shift to shift. **1884** HOE *Dict. Fiddle.*

**b.** *Pianoforte.* The mechanism for or act of shifting the keyboard action by means of the soft pedal.

**1896** A. J. HIPKINS *Pianoforte* 41 Unless these are directly opposite the strings by a decided shift or return, a snarling quality of tone will be heard. *Ibid.* Up to about 1830 there was a further shift permissible to one string only, the *Una Corda* of Beethoven. **1944** W. APEL *Harvard Dict. Mus.* 778/2 Beethoven..not only calls for a gradation in three steps..but even for a gradual execution of the shift: *poco a poco due corde.*

**16.** *Ship-building.* (See quots.)

**1805** *Shipwright's Vade-M.* 131 *Shift*, a term applied to disposing the butts of the planks, &c. so that they may over launch each other without reducing the length... The planks of the bottom, in British-built ships of war, have a six-feet shift with three planks between each butt... In the bottoms of merchant ships they have a six-feet shift with only two planks between each butt. *Ibid.* 234 The scarphs give shift to the scarphs of the keel and fasten thereto with treenails. *c* **1840** *Encycl. Brit.* (ed. 7) XX. 275/2 *Shift.* This, in its general sense, refers to a certain arrangement among the component parts of a ship. Thus we speak of a shift of plank, a shift of dead-wood, meaning thereby the disposition of the buts of the timber or plank, both with respect to strength and economy. In a more limited sense, 'shift' means the distance apart of two neighbouring buts or scarphs. *c* **1850** *Rudim. Navig.* (Weale) 154 *String*, one or two planks.., giving shift to the scarphs of the sheer-strake. **1867** SMYTH *Sailor's Word-bk.* **1889** WELCH *Text Bk. Naval Archit.* viii. 103 The proper shift of the butts [of the plates] is a question of importance.

**17.** *Mining.* A slight 'fault' or dislocation in a seam or stratum.

**1802** PLAYFAIR *Hutton. Theory* 48 Of this nature are the slips or shifts, that so often perplex the miner in his subterraneous journey. **1830** CARLYLE *Richter again* Misc. 1840 II. 324 What miners call a shift or trouble occurred in it. **1830** LYELL *Princ. Geol.* I. 418 Along the line of this shift, or 'fault' as it would be termed technically by miners, the walls were found to adhere firmly to each other. **1909** *Q. Rev.* Apr. 490 The shift or throw as in the Irwell Valley fault near Manchester.

**18.** Something which effects a shift. **a.** A mechanism for changing gear in a motor vehicle; a gear-lever. Cf. *gear-shift* s.v. GEAR *sb.* IV. *N. Amer.*

**1914** *Automobile* 9 Apr. 771/2 (Advt.), New electric shift. **1926** F. SCOTT FITZGERALD *Great Gatsby* vii. 144 'Shall we all go in my car?' suggested Gatsby... 'Is it standard shift?' demanded Tom. **1968** *Globe & Mail* (Toronto) 13 Jan. 26/1 (Advt.), Mercury Parklane Marauder...radio, bucket seats, floor shift. **1978** J. IRVING *World according to Garp* xii. 224 The gear knob of the Volvo's stick shift came off in her hand.

**b.** = *shift key*, sense 20 below.

**1919** H. ETHERIDGE *Dict. Typewriting* 208 It is usual to provide duplicate keys on each side of the keyboard, so that the shift may be operated with either hand. **1936** A. DVORAK et al. *Typewriting Behavior* x. 260 Really you strike the shift just a tiny fraction of a second before you strike the capital letter. **1957** A. C. LLOYD et al. *Gregg Typewriting for Colleges* 10 A-finger reaches over, to Shift.

**c.** = *shift code*, sense 20 below.

**1957** *Encycl. Brit.* XXI. 886/2 With such a code [as the Baudot code] it is possible to obtain 32 different combinations, 26 of which are assigned to letters of the alphabet, leaving 1 for the idle condition, and 5 for functions such as space, figure shift, letter shift, etc. **1972** *Computers & Humanities* VI. 149 The tape punch would consequently have fewer possibilities than the card punch, if this number of 44 were not doubled by a shift giving an extra punch code to change from lower to upper case, or from upper to lower case. **1980** L. MOORE *Foundations Programming with Pascal* ii. 38 The 5-bit code commonly used by Creed teleprinters had two shift-codes, a 'letter shift' and a 'figure shift'. Each of the remaining thirty codes was mapped to two characters, one belonging to the 'letter' set and the other to the 'figure' set.

**19.** *Telegr.* and *Computers.* A change from one set of characters to another; also, a set of characters indicated by any particular shift code.

**1913** H. W. PENDRY *Baudôt Printing Telegraph System* 2 He adapts therein several elements of the earlier Hughes system—namely, the type-wheel and printing arrangement as well as a similar figure shift device. **1928** A. WILLIAMS *Telegr. & Teleph.* ii. 33 The possible number of permutations is thirty-one, but each of these can be made to signify either of two characters by a 'shift' at the receiving end corresponding to the shift key of an ordinary typewriter. **1960** M. G. SAY et al. *Analogue & Digital Computers* ix. 265 Such an arrangement is very appropriate in telegraphy, where changes from one shift to the other are not common. **1967** D. G. HAYS *Introd. Computational Linguistics* iv. 75 Some of the shifts are capitalization, boldface, superscript, and large. Most alphabets require shifts and diacritics. **1970** O. DOPPING *Computers & Data Processing* ii. 41 We say that the characters are in two shifts, a letter shift and digit shift, in the same way as the characters on a typewriter are in two shifts or cases. **1971** T. C. COLLOCOTT *Dict. Sci. & Technol.* 1064/1 In teleprinters, one shift is capital letters, the other figures and special signs.

**VI. 20.** *attrib.* and *Comb.*: *shift-boss*, *-man*, *-work*, *-worker*, *-working* (sense 12); *shift-sleeve*, *-strap* (sense 10); † *shift-got* adj. (sense 4); *shiftmaker* (sense 6); **shift character, code,** *Telegr.* and *Computers*, a character in a code that indicates that subsequent characters are to be interpreted in terms of a different fount or coding scheme; **shift dress** = sense 10 b; **shift-key**, a key for adjusting the mechanism in a typewriter when characters in a different position on the keys, such as capitals, are to be used; **shift-lever** *N. Amer.*, a gear-lever in a motor vehicle; **shift-lock**, a device for holding the shift-key of a typewriter continuously depressed; also *attrib.*; **shift register** *Computers*, a register specifically intended for subjecting data to a shift (sense 14 g above); **shift-round** *colloq.*, reallocation of positions, a move to another position; **shift-sign** *Phonetics* (see quot. 1939); **shiftsman** (see quot. 1921); **shift-stick** *colloq.*, a gear-lever in a motor vehicle; **shift-terminator** *Computers*, a character introduced into a string of text to cancel the effect of a preceding shift code; **shift valve**, a valve that moves to produce automatic gear-changes in a motor vehicle.

**1877** RAYMOND *Statist. Mines & Mining* 166 Foremen, per day..*Shift-bosses, per day. **1881** —— *Mining Gloss.*, *Shift-boss*, the foreman in charge of a shift of men. **1967** D. G. HAYS *Introd. Computational Linguistics* iv. 75 But there are also 8 *shift characters, that influence the style or position of following graphic characters, and a shift terminator. **1970** O. DOPPING *Computers & Data Processing* ii. 41 After the letter shift character in the teleprinter code, all the following characters are interpreted as belonging to the letter case until there is a digit shift character, and vice versa. **1967** D. G. HAYS *Introd. Computational Linguistics* iv. 70 When we read a *shift code, we must remember what shift we are in until receiving another. **1972** *Computers & Humanities* VI. 149 We get 44 characters which may be preceded by either the upper-case or the lower-case shift code. **1980** Shift code [see sense 18 c above]. **1966** *Shift-dress [see MING sb.² c]. **1970** 'D. HALLIDAY' *Dolly & Cookie Bird* iii. 30, I was wearing a high-necked shift dress. **1598** BP. HALL *Sat.* IV. v. 39 The ding-thrift heyre, his *shift-got summe mispent, Comes drouping like a pennylesse penitent. **1893** *Manual of Typewriter* I. 15 When the machine in use is one with a single keyboard,—that is to say, one with a *shift-key by the depression of which the upper-case characters are brought into play,—the shift-key should be governed by the little finger. **1940** M. CROOKS *Home Instruction Course in Touch Typewriting* 56 You may like to note, whilst on the subject of the shift key, that there is an additional key—usually above one of the shift keys—called the 'Shift Lock'. **1980** *Daily Tel.* 4 Nov. 13/4 Beth Porter as mehitabel (archie couldn't work the shift key) in *the roach and the pussycat.* **1920** F. B. SCHOLL *Automobile Owner's Guide* 7 Place the *shift-lever into the first-speed slot and let up on the clutch pedal. **1973** R. HAYES *Hungarian Game* xlvii. 286 When the engine turned over he jammed the shift lever into reverse and pressed the accelerator. **1899** J. WARDLE *Universal Typewriter Man.* 21 *Shift lock.—When it is desired to write a large number of capital letters or signs, the Cylinder may be brought forward by means of the Lock Handle, and this action will fasten the Cylinder in that position. **1936** M. CROOKS *Bk. of Remington Typewriter* iii. 27 The action of the shift lock key is quite simple. **1977** E. MACKAY *Typewriting Dict.* 195 The shift key should be depressed by the little finger... If a whole word, heading, sentence, etc., is required in capital letters, the typist should depress the shift lock, which 'locks' the typewriter mechanism. **1836** E. HOWARD *R. Reefer* lv, The shifts we were obliged to have recourse to were..amusing, to all but the *shiftmakers. **1880** *Daily News* 10 Sept. 6/1 A survivor (..a *shiftman) gives the following narrative. **1894** *Northumbld. Gloss.*, *Shifter, Shift-man*, a man who prepares the working places at night in a colliery for the men who come in at next shift. **1950** W. W. STIFLER *High-Speed Computing Devices* xiii. 299 A multiplier might be devised using the parallel adder and the *shift register... The product accumulator is twice the length of the operand registers and is also a shift register. **1975** *Nature* 27 Mar. 366/3 A bubble device consists simply of an assembly of a number of integrated circuits each of which carries magnetically activated tracks, that is, shift registers, along which are driven patterns of bubbles and gaps representing binary data. **1940** J. REITH *Diary* 3 Apr. (1975) v. 244 Cabinet changes tonight..a weird *shift-round. *a* **1974** R. CROSSMAN *Diaries* (1975) I. 611 Thursday, the day of my shift-round. **1939** B. BLOCH in H. Kurath et al. *Handbk. Linguistic Geogr. New England* iv. 129 *Shift Signs..In order to avoid the necessity of using special symbols for the innumerable shades of sound intermediate between any two of the vowels shown in the diagram.., the phonetic alphabet of the Linguistic Atlas provides shift signs in the form of small arrowheads, which are placed after a vowel symbol to indicate varieties heard as articulated in a higher, a lower, a more advanced or a more retracted position than the vowel denoted by the unmodified letter. **1970** *Publ. Amer. Dial. Soc.* 1968 L. 5 Shift signs, ∧ raised, ∨ lowered,..are used to show modification of the vowels. *a* **1700** EVELYN *Diary* June 1645, Their sleeves are made exceeding wide, under which their *shift sleeves as wide. **1711** BUDGELL *Spect.* No. 175 ¶2 She came in Shift-Sleeves, and dress'd at the Window. **1921** *Dict. Occup. Terms* (1927) §044 *Shifter, shiftman, shiftsman*..; general terms for labourers assisting repairers, timberers, etc., in building stoppings and clearing falls of stone. *Ibid.* §054 *Shifter, shiftman, shiftsman*,..works at night, when mine workers are absent, repairing roadways, etc. **1924** *Public Opinion* 8 Feb. 127/1 Machinery shall be in charge of a competent shiftsman. **1968** *Autocar* 14 Mar. 25/1 (Advt.), Aussies have better things to do with their arms than glue them to a *shift-stick. **1975** *Publishers Weekly* 17 Mar. 53/1 Even readers who don't know a shiftstick from a lollipop may find themselves caught up in the pace of this exciting inside-story of a veteran Indy 500 racing-car mechanic. **1922** JOYCE *Ulysses* 222 A white petticoatbodice and taut *shiftstraps. **1967** *Shift terminator [see *shift character*]. **1967** D. G. HAYS *Introd. Computational Linguistics* iv. 76 If a whole sentence is in italics, the italic-shift character occurs just once in continuous mode, with a shift terminator at the end. **1949** *Automotive Industries* 1 May 68/3 The mechanism contains other forms of valves designed to perform automatic control functions. Among these are:..*shift valve for direct drive, having a modulator valve at one end. **1955** W. H. CROUSE *Automotive Transmission & Power Trains* vii. 223 The throttle pressure is applied to the spring end of the shift valve. **1970** *AA Bk. Car* 110/3 A system of brake bands and clutches selected by hydraulic shift valves. **1708** J. C. *Compleat Collier* (1845) 36 It is most usual to agree with your Hewers of Coals or Miners, by the Score of Corves,..and not by the Day, or *Shift Work. **1888** W. E. NICHOLSON *Gloss. Terms Coal Trade Northumbld. & Durh.* (E.D.D.). **1942** T. K. DJANG *Factory Inspection in Gt. Brit.* vii. 142 The Home Secretary may require certain conditions for the safe-guarding of *shift workers. **1977** *Rep. Comm. Future of Broadcasting* (Cmnd. 6753) iii. 23 Shift workers wanting more entertainment during off-peak hours. **1937** M. L. YATES *Wages & Labour Conditions in Brit. Engineering* iv. 54 *Shift-working was the subject of a separate Agreement between the Employers' Federation and the Amalgamated Engineering Union in 1920. **1963** *Times* 6 May (Suppl. Electr. Power Brit.) p. iii/7 Because our tempo of life is geared to what we regard as orthodox hours, shift working is a burden and now disrupts family life.

**shift** (ʃɪft), *v.* Forms: 1 sciftan, scyftan, 2 scyfton, 4 schiften, scift, schifte, schyft, schefte, 4–6 schyfte, schift, 4–7 shifte, 5 scifte, schyftyn, 5–6 shyfte, 6 shyft, schyffte, 4– shift. *Pa. t.* 1 scifte, 1–2 scyfte, 3 shiftede, 4 schift, 4–5 shifte, 5 schifte, shift, chefte, 6 shyfted, 6– shifted. *Pa. pple.* 1 scift, 2 scyft, 2–3 iscift, 3 scift, 4 ischyft, shift, scheft, schifted, 4–5 schift, 5 schufte, shyfte, scyfftyd, schiffted, 6 scheftyd, shyfted, -yd, 6– shifted. [OE. *sciftan* wk. vb. corresponds to OFris. *skifta* to determine (WFris. *skifte, skiftsje* to separate, NFris. *skeft* to divide, change), MLG., LG., Du. *schiften* to divide, separate, MHG. (MG.) *schihten* (mod.G. *schichten*) to divide, classify, arrange in order, ON. *skipta* (whence SKIFT *v.*¹) to share, divide, change (Sw., Norw. *skifta*, Da. *skifte*):—OTeut. **skiftjan*, f. Teut. root **skip-* in ON. *skipa* to arrange, assign, etc.]

**I.** To put in order, arrange.

† **1.** *trans.* To appoint, ordain, arrange, assign, dispose in order. *Obs.*

*c* **1000** *Secular Laws Edgar* §7 (Liebermann) 204/3 Scifte [*v.rr.* sceawie, sceapiȝe] man of ðam ȝemote ða ðe him toridan. *a* **1023** WULFSTAN *Hom.* xxxvii. (1883) 176 Moyses ..be godes aȝenum dihte rihte laȝe scyfte. *a* **1122** *O.E. Chron.* (Laud MS.) an. 1046, Þa scyfte man Harold [*read* Beorn] eorl up þæs cynges scipe þe Harold eorl ær steorde. *c* **1200** ORMIN 470 Forr prestess þanne & dæcness ec shifftedenn hemm bitwenenn Whillc here sholde serrfenn firrst. **13..** *K. Alis.* 6714 (Laud MS.), Þe messagers aȝein he shiftes. *c* **1386** CHAUCER *2nd Nun's T.* 278 Witnes Tyburces and Valerians shrifte, To whiche god of his bountee wolde shifte Corones two of floures. **1390** GOWER *Conf.* I. 323 For thou benymst me thilke yifte, Which lith noght in thi miht to schifte. *a* **1400** *Morte Arth.* 2456 Thane the schalkes scharpelye scheftys theire horsez. *c* **1400** *Laud Troy Bk.* 8715 And thus haue thei her armes schiffted, Ther baneres are wel hye lyffted.

**2.** To apportion, distribute; to separate into shares, divide; *rarely* to divide or partition *off from.*

*c* **1000** *Secular Laws Cnut* §78 (Liebermann) 364/3 For þa yrfenuman to lande & to æhtan, & scyftan hit swiðe rihte. *a* **1175** *Cott. Hom.* 237 Ac ȝief ȝe habbeð understande þat we ȝiu er sede eter gate me his scyft and þer me hi to ȝesceodeð. *c* **1200** *Vices & Virt.* 37 Si recte offers, et non recte diuidis, peccasti, 'ȝif ðu right offrest and noht riht ne sciftest, ðu seneȝest mare ðan ðu god do'. *c* **1315** SHOREHAM IV. 178 Þys manere senne nys nauȝt ones, Ac hys ischy[f]t in þry. *c* **1330** *Arth. & Merl.* 1482 A gret schode Of grauel & erþe al so, Þat hem hadde schifted ato. **1390** GOWER *Conf.* III. 294 Al freliche of his oghne yifte His whete, among hem forto schifte. *c* **1425** *Cast. Persev.* 108 in *Macro Plays* 80 To putte his good in gouernaunce..he wolde þat it were scyfftyd a-mongis his ny kynne. *c* **1440** *Promp. Parv.* 446/1 Schyftyn, or partyn, or delyn, *divido, partior.* **1483** in *10th Rep. Hist. MSS. Comm.* App. v. 317 To take..the same hervest corne so boght and to shyfte ond distribute it upon the commynes. **1529** S. FISH *Suppl. Beggars* (Arb.) 5 Nowe let vs then compare the nombre of this vnkind idell sort vnto the nombre of the laye people and we shall se whether it be indifferently shifted or not that they shuld haue half. **1570–6** LAMBARDE *Peramb. Kent* (1826) 477 They of this our Kentish countrie, do yet call their partition of lande (shifting) even by the very same woord that the lawe of

Canutus many yeeres since termed it. **1703** NEVE *City & C Purchaser* 229 A little square corner of a Room, shifted off from the rest of the Room by the Wainscot. **1735–6** PEGGE *Kenticisms*.

*absol.* *c* **1330** *Arth. & Merl.* 2194 King Ban hadde..þe cite of Beuoit & Bohort hadde þe cite of Gaines..& þus þai hadde schift atvo.

†**3.** ***to shift one's hand, one's words***: to act or speak in a particular manner. Also *refl.* *Obs.*

*a* **1300** *Cursor M.* 23390 Als suith mai þou cum þider, Al at þi wil or elles quider, Nu at þe erth nu at þe lift, Or hu sumeuer þou will þe scift. *Ibid.* 23703 And þus-gat sal he schift his hand, þe werld [*read with Gött. MS.* lauerd] þat es ai lastand. **1377** LANGL. *P. Pl.* B. xx. 166 And elde hent good hope and hastilich he shifte [*v.r.* chifte] hym. **1390** GOWER *Conf.* III. 136 And loke wel that he ne schifte Hise wordes to no wicked use. **14..** *Sir Beues* (M.) 502 And he sye, it was no better paye, But shifte hym in the beste way. **1574** W. BOURNE *Regiment Sea* (1577) Introd. 7 b, And to haue capacitie howe for to handle or schift him-selfe in foule weather or stormes.

†**4. a.** *intr.* To manage matters; to deal, bargain, make arrangements *with*; to make provision *for*. ***to let*** (persons) ***shift*** [= F. *laisser faire*]: to let (them) take their own course, not to interfere. *Obs.*

*a* **1300** *Cursor M.* 4440 He ferd ai wit so mikel thrift þat al was don als he wald scift. *c* **1400** *Sowdone Bab.* 2704 With these meyne moste we shifte, To haue parte of here vitailes her. *c* **1489** CAXTON *Sonnes of Aymon* x. 274, I holpe theym not nor I was not agenst theym but wythdrewe me aside & lete the other shyfte [Fr. *laissay faire les autres*] wyth theym and I stode styll. *Ibid.* xii. 301 Lete theym shyfte [Fr. *laissez les faire*] hardely, they two togyder. *Ibid.* xix. 403 Let hym shyfte with the kynge as he wyl. **1490** —— *Eneydos* xxxix. 129 He lete theym shyfte, & fought tyll that the euyn departed theym. **1513** MORE *Rich. III* (1883) 39 And shyfte whoso would with thys busynes afterwarde: for he neuer entended more to moue her in that matter. **1529** RASTELL *Pastyme* (1811) 271 Because they lacked money, they shyfted with the staple of Caleys for .xviii. thousande pounde. **1549** CHEKE *Hurt Sedit.* (1641) 42 Caterpillers destroy the fruit, an hurtfull thing and well shifted for, by a diligent overseer.

†**b.** ? To bestir oneself. *Obs.*

*a* **1400** *Morte Arth.* 3847 And so they schyfte and schove, be schotte to the erthe. *c* **1475** *Partenay* 2792 So he shifte And smote here And ther so faste, That the yren dore persed at the laste.

†**c.** ***to shift in the world***, also quasi-*trans.* ***to shift the world***: to face the chances of life. *Obs.*

**1536** LADY ROCHEFORD in Ellis *Orig. Lett.* Ser. I. II. 68 And I not assuryd of no more..then one hundreth Marke; whyche ys veary hard for me to schyffte the worldd wythall. **1555** W. WATREMAN *Fardle Facions* I. i. 24 They ware banysshed that enhabitaunce of pleasure [Paradise] and driuen to shift the world. **1576** FLEMING *Panopl. Epist.* 386 Chaunge this your perillous purpose, and determine otherwise to shifte in the worlde.

**5. a.** To manage to effect one's purposes, or to make a living, by one's own devices; to succeed, get on (well or ill). *Obs.* exc. *dial.*

*c* **1532** DU WES *Introd. Fr.* in Palsgr. 940 To shyfte, *cheuir*. **1562** BP. PILKINGTON *Abdias* Pref. Aa iv b, Many fishes be raueners, yet the yong fish encreases: the Hawkes be gredy yet shifts the littell byrds. **1568** C. W[ATSON] *Polybius* 61 The inhabitants hauing repaired their walles, shifted well wyth this their lingering off. **1591** SPENSER *M. Hubberd* 660 So well they shifted, that the Ape anon Himselfe had cloathed like a Gentleman. **1620** MIDDLETON *Chaste Mayd* II. 24 She that hath wit, may shift any-where. *c* **1650** *Don Bellianis* 226 Here we can do no otherwise, replied he, but in the city we may better shift. **1719** DE FOE *Crusoe* I. (Globe) 281, I had some Inclination to give them their lives, if they thought they could shift on Shore. **1775** JOHNSON *West. Isl., Coriatachan* 118 The rider then dismounts and all shift as they can.

quasi-*trans.* **1836** CARLYLE *Let.* 16 May in *Atlantic Monthly* (1898) Sept. 295, I have no doubt Robert will shift his way with all dexterity..thro' that Cotton Babylon.

**b.** 'To act or live though with difficulty' (J.); to manage *with* something inferior or *without* something desirable; to make shift.

**1673** TEMPLE *Adv. Trade Irel.* Wks. 1720 I. 116 Common Garrans shift upon Grass the Year round. **1723** DE FOE *Col. Jack* (1840) 128 The first [hard work] I had been an utter stranger to, the last [hard fare] I could shift well enough with. **1793** SMEATON *Edystone L.* Introd. 6 After the public had shifted with having the fire below for the term of ten years. **1815** JANE AUSTEN *Emma* viii, She is left in Mrs. Goddard's hands to shift as she can. **1865** *Cornh. Mag.* Oct. 513 Might not the colonists shift for the present with the southern island? **1900** *Pilot* 7 July 16/2 Congregations were deprived of their pastors, and had to shift as they best could without them.

**6.** To employ shifts or evasions; to practise or use indirect methods; to practise or live by fraud, or temporary expedients.

**1579** LYLY *Euphues* (Arb.) 35 If I be in Crete, I can lye, if in Greece I can shift, if in Italy I can court it. **1586** A. DAY *Eng. Secretary* II. (1625) 20 There be those that will iustifie that by such meanes yᵘ doe shift now and then very cunningly. **1615** J. TAYLOR (Water P.) *Revenge* Wks. 1630 II. 144/1 To Sharke or Shift, or Cony-catch for mony. **1634** LEVETT *Ordering of Bees* 42 They are composed for the most part of yong Bees, who know not how to shift and rob as the old ones do. **1706** PHILLIPS (ed. Kersey), To *Shift*,..to double or dodge, as wild Beasts do when hunted. **1808** SCOTT *Marm.* II. xxix, To Whitby's convent fled the maid, The hated match to shun. 'Ho! shifts she thus?' King Henry cried.

**7. a.** ***to shift for oneself***: to provide for one's own safety, interests, or livelihood (implying either absence of aid, or, sometimes, want of concern for others); to depend on one's own efforts.

*a* **1513** FABYAN *Chron.* v. cxxviii. (1811) 110 The firste was of laufull age, soo that he myght helpe & shyfte for hym selfe. **1529** *Star Chamber Cases* (Selden Soc.) II. 183 He putt the poore man in jepardy of his lyff yff he had nott shyftyd the better for hym self. **1593** *Tell-troth's N.Y. Gift* (1876) 6 The birdes bringe upp the yong untill they can shift for themselves. **1643** BAKER *Chron., Rich. III*, 131 His complices shifted for themselves. **1709** SWIFT *Advancem. Relig.* 32 As if the Physicians should..leave their Patients to shift for themselves. **1808** SCOTT in *Lockhart* (1837) I. i. 5 This occasioned a quarrel between him and his father, who left him to shift for himself. **1877** FROUDE *Short Stud.* (1883) IV. I. x. 123 All..forsook him to shift for themselves.

**b.** *transf.* of inanimate or immaterial things.

**1689** POPPLE tr. *Locke's 1st Let.* L.'s Wks. 1727 II. 248 For the Truth certainly would do well enough, if she were once left to shift for herself. **1788** FRANKLIN *Autobiog.* Wks. 1840 I. 210, I concluded to let my papers shift for themselves. **1859** JEPHSON *Brittany* ii. 16 [Sewage] deposited on the pavement, where it is left to shift for itself.

**c.** ***to shift for one's own safety***, etc.

**1511** *Guylforde's Pilgr.* (Camden) 60 Euery man to shyfte for his escape as Almyghty God wolde yeue theym grace. **1634** SIR T. HERBERT *Trav.* 12 Our Fleet lay a hull..each shifting for its owne safetie. **1858** FROUDE *Hist. Eng.* IV. xviii. 17 They were obliged to shift as they could for their own security.

**II.** To change.

**8. a.** *trans.* To change, to replace by another of the kind. With plural object: To quit one and take another of (the things indicated). *Obs.* exc. (somewhat *arch.*) with obj. a quality or appearance, as ***to shift shapes***.

*c* **1250** *Gen. & Ex.* 1732 Ten siðes ðus binnen .vi. ȝer, Shiftede iacob hirdenesse her. **1545** *Act 37 Hen. VIII* c. 9, §5 The wares..so bargayned, solde, eschaunged or shifted. **1618** CHAPMAN *Hesiod's Georg.* II. 517 The shamelesse Man shifts friends still with his place. **1667** PEPYS *Diary* 3 Oct., There staid..till he shifted his horses. **1697** DRYDEN *Virg. Georg.* IV. 639 Having shifted ev'ry Form to scape, Convinc'd of Conquest, he resum'd his Shape. **1760** T. HUTCHINSON *Hist. Mass.* ii. 212 How many times did..the clergy..change or shift their opinions? **1864** TENNYSON *Voyage* v, The peaky islet shifted shapes.

**b.** *Cookery.* To change (the water in which something is steeped). Also, to change the water for, to transfer to another water. Now *rare* or *Obs.*

**1675** HANNAH WOOLLEY *Gentlew. Comp.* 125 Then steep the [Calves-]Head in fair water warm five hours, in that time shift it twice or thrice. **1747** MRS. GLASSE *Cookery* xi. 122 Shift the Water two or three times. **1769** MRS. RAFFALD *Eng. Housekpr.* (1778) 169 Shift the peel into clean water twice in the boiling.

†**c.** Phrases. ***to shift a mind***: to change one's mind. ***to shift hands***: = 'to change hands'; also, to change one's ground in argument. *Obs.*

**1611** MIDDLETON & DEKKER *Roaring Girl* E 1, But sleepe vpon this once more sir, you may chance shift a minde to morrow. *c* **1680** BEVERIDGE *Serm.* (1729) II. 85 His affections all shifting hands as it were, and changing objects with one another. **1692** WASHINGTON tr. *Milton's Def. People* Pref. 14 Crafty Turn-coat! Are you not asham'd to shift hands thus in things that are Sacred? **1699** BENTLEY *Phalaris* 296 This being the Point he promised to prove, he presently shifts hands, and changes the Question.

†**d.** To change (places). Also *intr.* to change places *with*. *Obs.*

**1691** RAY *Creation* I. (1704) 150 That they should thus shift places, is very convenient for them. **1785** BURNS *Ep. J. Lapraik* 21 Apr. xiii, Wi' cits nor lairds I wadna shift, In a their pride!

†**e.** *Shipbuilding.* (*a*) To replace (old timbers, etc.) with new. (*b*) [? From SHIFT *sb.* 16.] To adjust the 'shift' of (planks, etc.) in building a vessel.

**1691** T. H[ALE] *Acc. New Invent.* 76 She shifted none of her said Rudder-Irons. **1711** W. SUTHERLAND *Shipbuild. Assist.* 47 A Ship's Bottom..wherein are shewed the Shifting, Scarfing or Over-launching the Planks. **1793** SMEATON *Edystone L.* §85 *note*, The term shifting a timber in Ship-wrightry signifies in general the substitution of a piece of new timber in the place of a piece of old. **1805** *Shipwright's Vade-M.* 201 The Wales must be wrought of such lengths, and the butts shifted, so as to give the strongest shift to the ports and each other. **1852** FINCHAM *Ship Building* II. (ed. 3) 39 The butts are properly placed, or what is technically called properly shifted, when they are suitably disposed in relation to the ports and to each other.

**f.** *intr.* To undergo transmutation; to change.

**1605** B. JONSON *Volpone* I. ii, But I come not here, to discourse of that matter,..Or his telling how Elements shift. **1878** B. TAYLOR *Deukalion* I. ii. 24 Let Proteus shift in ocean From shape to shape that eludes.

**9. a.** *trans.* To change (one's own or another's clothing). Now chiefly *dial.* Also *fig.*

*c* **1400** *Rule of St. Benet* (Prose) 36 Tuinnne paire claþis sal ilkain haue for to scifte and for to waisse; yef þai haue mare, it sal be scorn. **1530** PALSGR. 703/1 I shyfte garmentes, *je change*. **1602** MARSTON *Ant. & Mel.* II. Wks. 1856 I. 26 Would'st thou have us sluts, and never shift the vestur of our thoughts? **1605** B. JONSON *Volpone* I. ii, But I Would aske, how of late, thou hast suffered translation, And shifted thy coat, in these dayes of Reformation? **1723** DE FOE *Col. Jack* (1840) 82, I went immediately to shift my clothes. **1844–48** W. BARNES *Poems Rural Life* 185 Poll an' Nan runn'd off up stairs, To shift ther ðings.

†**b.** To change (a person's) clothes; to dress in fresh underclothing. *Obs.*

*a* **1548** HALL *Chron., Rich. III*, 26 They bothe discended to the highe altare and were shifted from their robes. **1579–80** NORTH *Plutarch, Marcus Cato* (1595) 382 His wife did vnswadell the young boy to wash and shift him. **1613** PURCHAS *Pilgrimage* (1614) 611 Neyther may she speake, but by those *Magitæ* is shifted and gallantly adorned. **1754–64** SMELLIE *Midwif.* I. 204 She must then be shifted with a clean, warm, half shift, linen-skirt and bed-gown.

**c.** *refl.* To change one's clothing; to put on fresh clothing, esp. undergarments. *Obs.* exc. *dial.* †Formerly const. *into*, *out of*, *from*, etc. (clothes).

**1530** PALSGR. 703/1 In the sommer season I love to shyfte me often. *a* **1548** HALL *Chron., Hen. VIII*, 64 He shifted hymself into a robe of a Cardinall. **1558** in Kempe *Losely MSS.* (1836) 185 He hath not left hym a shert there to shyft hym with all. **1622** in Foster *Eng. Factories India* (1908) II. 125 Nott leavinge one ragge to shift us. **1719** DE FOE *Crusoe* I. 53, I was wet, and had no Cloaths to shift me. **1839** *Heref. Gloss.* s.v., A man who changes his clothes is said 'to shift himself'.

**d.** *intr.* for *refl.* †Const. *into*.

**1605** SHAKS. *Lear* v. iii. 186 [It] taught me to shift Into a madmans rags. **1728** YOUNG *Love of Fame* VI. 42 She begs you just would turn you, while she shifts. **1834** M. SCOTT *Cruise Midge* xx. (1836) II. 304 We..shifted, breakfasted, and..returned to Ballywindle. **1891** C. ROBERTS *Adrift Amer.* 30 After getting shifted I turned in and was soon asleep.

**10. a.** *trans.* To change (the scene): see SCENE 4.

**1599**, **1611** [see SCENE 4]. **1692** *Scarronides* II. Pref. 3 The Scenes in our publick Theatres are not shifted so often as our thoughts. **1742** YOUNG *Nt. Th.* III. 363 'Tis time, high time, to shift this dismal scene. *a* **1859** MACAULAY *Hist. Eng.* xxiii. (1861) V. 117 The scene of the negociation was again changed. Having been shifted from France to England, it was shifted from England to Holland.

**b.** *intr.* Of a scene: To change. Const. *to*.

**1828** SCOTT *F.M. Perth* i, Gazing on the scene before me as if I had been afraid it would shift like those in a theatre before [etc.]. **1861** PALEY *Æschylus, Eumen.* (ed. 2) Introd., The scene shifts to the latter place.

†**11.** *trans.* To cause (a set of workmen) to change places with another set. Also said of a gang of workmen: To replace (another gang or set) as a relief; also *intr.* for *refl.*

**1673** *Haddock Corr.* 28 in *Camden Miscell.* VIII, I went on bord the R. Charles to shift the men. **1791** SMEATON *Edystone L.* §123 The companies at this time shifted there. *Ibid.* §232 Jessop and company went out to shift Richardson.

**III.** To change the place of, to remove.

* *transitive uses.*

**12.** To transfer from one place to another; to remove; to alter the position of. Const. *from*, *out of*, *to*; also often with adv. or advb. phrase.

**a.** with obj. a person. †Also *refl.* to withdraw.

*c* **1375** *Cursor M.* 24807 (Fairf.) Vn-til ship sone was he shift. *c* **1430** *Syr Gener.* (Roxb.) 9822 And thus this goode knight thei shift Euen to the Citie of Damas. **1575** GASCOIGNE *Hemetes the Heremyte* Wks. 1910 II. 482 Being shifted from yᵉ sighte of yᵗ I sought above all things in the world. **1825** T. HOOK *Sayings* Ser. II. *Passion & Princ.* vi. III. 53 He was shifted to a more commodious apartment.

*refl.* **1555** J. PROCTOR *Wyat's Rebell.* 39 [They] consideringe..their chiefe strength thus tourned vppon them,..shifted them selues awaye. **1643** BAKER *Chron., Eliz.* I 7 He came all in a sweat to the Sheriff Smith's house, who shifteth himself forth at a back door.

**b.** With obj. a material thing. In *Gardening*, to transplant.

*c* **1425** *Cast. Persev.* 2850 in *Macro Plays* 162, I may not onys myn hod up schyfte. **1523–34** FITZHERB. *Husb.* §141 Howe he wolde haue..his cattel shifted out of one pasture into an other. **1588** *Churchw. Acc. Pittington* (Surtees) 27 Item given for bread & drinke when the fonte was shifted, xvj d. **1593** SHAKS. *Rom. & Jul.* I. v. 2 *Ser.* Where's Potpan, that he helpes not to take away? He shift a Trencher? he scrape a Trencher? **1680** SIR C. LYTTELTON in *Hatton Corr.* (Camden) 232 Tother day, in shifting of a cabinet. **1771** SMOLLETT *Humph. Cl.* 1 July (1815) 214 He re-ascends into the apartment by the steps, which had been shifted for that purpose. **1830** GALT *Lawrie T.* II. iii, He showed me how to shift the plants. **1878** HUXLEY *Physiogr.* 209 It is the land and not the sea that has shifted its level. **1879** FROUDE *Cæsar* xxii. 386 Cæsar had shifted his camp continually.

**c.** With immaterial object. Often with reference to a metaphorical burden: To transfer (blame, responsibility, etc.) *from* (a person, oneself) *to* or *upon* another.

*a* **1572** KNOX *Hist. Ref.* Wks. 1846 I. 196 This answer gave he, as mycht appear, to schift ower the argument upon the Freare, as that he did. **1647** CLARENDON *Hist. Reb.* II. §54 Every man shifting the fault from himself. **1774** SIR J. REYNOLDS *Disc. R.A.* 10 Dec. (1778) 204 The name of Genius then shifted its application. **1867** FREEMAN *Norm. Conq.* (1877) I. vi. 498 A feeling of this inconsistency led several later writers to shift the story to a later time. **1869** TOZER *Highl. Turkey* II. 252 The license which is admitted in shifting the accent for purposes of scansion and rhyme. **1885** DUNCKLEY in *Manch. Weekly Times* 7 Feb. 5/5 The burden of taxation has been shifted from articles of necessary consumption to luxuries.

†**d.** To palm off (something) *on* a person; to get rid of by handing *over* (something undesirable) *to* another. *Obs.*

**1634** CANNE *Necess. Separ.* (1849) 289 Some merchants who..will show the buyer a little that is good, and by this means cunningly shift all the rest upon him. **1659** *Clarke Papers* (Camden) IV. 290 The proclamation declaring M. Gen. Egerton, &c., rebells and traytours came..to a petty constable of this towne, who shifted it over to another well-affected constable.

**e.** To change (gear), move (a gear lever). Also *intr.*, to change *from* one gear *into* another; ***to shift up*** or ***down***, to engage a higher or a lower gear. Also *fig.*

**1910** J. E. HOMANS *Self-Propelled Vehicles* (ed. 7) xxix. 381 In shifting from high to low gears, all intermediate speeds were engaged. *Ibid.* xlv. 625 On shifting the transmission lever for the speed changes, if the transmission be of the selective type, the two movements..may offer some difficulty to the beginner. **1946** W. H. CROUSE *Automotive Mech.* xvii. 388 Let us shift into second and note the actions that take place. *Ibid.* 389 Synchromesh devices come into use when gears are shifted into second and high. **1961** WEBSTER, *Shift gears*, to make a change from one method, tempo, or approach to another. **1962** J. D. MACDONALD *Girl* viii. 99 She drove with her brown hands high on the wheel... She shifted up and shifted down. **1965** A. MILLER *Incident at Vichy* 32 For some of us it's difficult to shift gears and go into reverse. **1969** *New Yorker* 6 Sept. 105/2 The Rumanians, having barely paused to shift their ideological gears, began holding the..congress. **1970** D. MACKENZIE *Kyle Contract* (1971) 13 He drove out of Palamos... He shifted into drive and settled back. **1973** R. HAYES *Hungarian Game* liii. 319, I..shifted from second to third and..let my hand linger a while on the gear lever's mahogany knob. **1973** *Sci. Amer.* Apr. 11/2 (Advt.), Once on the valley floor I shifted up into fourth. **1973** *Time* 16 Apr. 53/1 'We're shifting gears,' says Vail, 'and hiring guys with a track record of seven, eight, nine years' experience.' **1976** H. NIELSEN *Brink of Murder* xv. 132 Simon switched on the ignition and shifted into reverse.

**f.** *Computers.* To move (data) to right or left in a register. Also *absol.*

**1946** *Ann. Computation Lab. Harvard Univ.* I. 72 The quotient shift counter..is used to calculate the number of columns the quotient must be shifted to the right upon reading out to the buss in order to conform with the operating decimal position. **1947** A. W. BURKS et al. in *Coll. Wks. J. von Neumann* (1963) V. 44 We do not consider multiplication by 2 as a true product since we will have a facility for shifting right or left in one or two pulse times. **1966** *IFIP-ICC Vocab. of Information Processing* 70 Digits shifted beyond the end of the word or register may simply be dropped. **1968** FOX & MAYERS *Computing Methods for Scientists & Engineers* ii. 21 The first operation 'shifts' $a_2$ to the right by $b_1$-$b_2$ places.

**13.** *Naut.* **a.** To change or alter the position of (a sail, spar, the helm, etc.).

**1667** MILTON *P.L.* IX. 515 As when a Ship..where the Wind Veres oft, as oft so steers, and shifts her Saile. **1669** STURMY *Mariner's Mag.* I. ii. 18 Shift the Mizen tack, hawl bout fore Bowline. **1795** NELSON 13 Mar. in Nicolas *Disp.* (1845) II. 14 Employed shifting our topsails and splicing our rigging. **1825** H. B. GASCOIGNE *Path to Naval Fame* 50 The angl'd Jib with speed they hoist away, Then Shift the Helm to make her cast right way. **1846** A. YOUNG *Naut. Dict.* 150 *Shift the Helm!* to put it from starboard to port, or the reverse.

†**b.** To record the variations of (the tide), the positions of the sun and moon. *Obs.*

*a* **1592** LODGE & GREENE *Looking Gl.* (1598) E 1 b, Lets see the proudest scholler stir his course Or shift his tides as Silly sailers do. **1594** J. DAVIS *Seamans Secr.* (1607) 11 The necessary instrument for the yong practising seamans use, named an Horizontall tyde Table, whereby he may shift his Sun and Moone (as they terme it).

**c.** Of a ship or a navigator: To undergo displacement of (cargo or ballast).

**1854** G. B. RICHARDSON *Univ. Code* v. (ed. 12) 803, I have shifted my ballast. **1880** *Times* 17 Dec. 5/6 The Isabel,..laden with oats, arrived..with cargo shifted.

**14.** To alter the direction of.

**1698** FRYER *Acc. E. India & P.* 3 He not being so often called upon to shift his Course, or hand his Sails. **1781** COWPER *Table T.* 387 Th' inestimable estimate of Brown Rose like a paper-kite, and charm'd the town; But measures, plann'd and executed well, Shifted the wind that rais'd it, and it fell. **1871** B. TAYLOR *Faust* (1875) II. II. iii. 149 As when the winds are shifted Shine snowy sails.

**15.** To change or alter (one's or its position, place); to change (one's lodging, abode, etc.). †Phrase, *to shift place(s.*

In early examples really a contextual application of sense 8.

**1563–83** FOXE *A. & M.* 54/2 Many times he [Origen] was compelled to shift places and houses. **1587** HARRISON *England* II. xix. 205/2 They must needs shift soile, and seeke vnto other countries. **1595** DANIEL *Civ. Wars* I. lxix, Happy confiners you of other landes That shift your soile and oft scape tyrants hands. **1667** PEPYS *Diary* 6 May, At his coming to town again, [he] had shifted his lodgings. **1697** DRYDEN *Virg. Georg.* III. 133 The fiery Courser, when he hears from far..the Shouts of War, Shifts Place. **1774** GOLDSM. *Nat. Hist.* (1776) V. 268 As quails and wood-cocks shift their habitations in winter, so also does the cuckoo. **1860** TYNDALL *Glac.* I. ii. 18 Advancing and retreating as the spray shifted its position.

**16. a.** To get (a person) out of the way. In early use chiefly with *away* (see also 12 a). In later use without adv.: To get rid of (an enemy or rival). Now *slang* or *colloq.*, to dislodge (a body of the enemy); (of a horse) to throw (the rider); also *euphemistically*, to 'put out of the way', murder.

**1604** SHAKS. *Oth.* IV. i. 79 Whil'st you were heere, o'rewhelmed with your griefe Cassio came hither. I shifted him away. **1615** R. COCKS *Diary* (Hakl. Soc.) I. 19 He will be shifted out of his government or kingdom. **1703** DK. QUEENSB. in Ellis *Orig. Lett.* Ser. II. IV. 238 In a short time the Duke of Queensberry was to be shifted out, so as he was to be sole Secretary. **1891** C. ROBERTS *Adrift Amer.* 180 Although the wicked little beast did his utmost to shift me, I managed to frustrate his efforts. **1898** *Daily News* 29 Sept. 3/2 [The enemy] were four to our one, but we shifted them. *Ibid.* 10 Oct. 5/1 That would-be criminals..do sometimes cast about for safe means of 'shifting' inconvenient relatives, or enemies, there is, we fear, little doubt.

**b.** *colloq.* or *slang.* To 'put away', 'dispose of', consume (a quantity of food or drink); to spend (money).

**1896** P. A. GRAHAM *Red Scaur* xvii. 263 Did you ever see her..shiftin' a curran' dumplin'? **1907** H. WYNDHAM *Flare of Footlights* xxii, Lord, but he can shift his liquor! **1923** E. P. OPPENHEIM *Inevitable Millionaires* xiv. 148, I should trip it to Monte. That's the place to shift the shekels.

†**17. a.** To avoid, elude, escape. *Obs.*

**1595** DANIEL *Civ. Wars* III. lxxvii, He..now strikes againe, Then nimbly shiftes a thrust, then lendes a wound. **1667** J. GUTHRIE in *Union Mag.* Oct. (1902) 463 It [a cross] is an affliction man cannot shift except he shift duty. **1678** BUNYAN *Pilgr.* I. (1875) 70 These Beasts range in the night for their prey, and if they should meet with me in the dark, how should I shift them! **1724** A. SHIELDS *Life Renwick* (1827) 60 Whereby they were..convinced of the Evil of these Courses they had taken, to shift and shun Suffering. **1816** SCOTT *Old Mort.* xxxviii, 'Hush! hush!' said Jenny, whose interest lay particularly in shifting further enquiry.

†**b.** To decline, shirk (a duty). *Obs.*

*c* **1611** CHAPMAN *Iliad* XII. 233 This motion, Glaucus shifted not, but (without words) obeyd.

†**c.** To pass, get through (a period of time); to 'kill' time. Also, to put off, defer. Chiefly *Sc.* *Obs.*

*c* **1562** E. UNDERHILL in *Narr. Reform.* (Camden) 149 Ther was..no better place to shifte the Easter tyme in then quene Maryes courte. **1721** RAMSAY *Lucky Spence* 5 When she now faun, That death nae langer wad be shifted, She thus began. **1730** T. BOSTON *View this & other World* (1799) 389 It will be dear-bought ease that is got by shifting to make ready. *Ibid.* 390 These thoughts are shifted, till they force in them-selves by death at the door. *a* **1732** —— *Acc. My Life* (1908) 81 It was suggested..that Langton minded to shift it till Michaelmas was past. **1766** A. NICOL *Poems* I (E.D.D.) Cast wholly on the care of Heav'n I shifted time, toss'd by hard fortune, Till I was near the age of fourteen.

†**d.** To quit or leave (a place). *Obs. rare.*

*a* **1642** SUCKLING *Goblins* I. Wks. 1874 II. 11 Shift, shift the place, the wood is dangerous: As you love safety, follow me. **1822** SCOTT *Peveril* viii, They say he goes to shift the country.

†**18.** To rid *of*. Often *refl.* and *passive.*

**1567** DRANT *Horace, Ep.* I. xiii. E iij, If that my booke be burthenouse shift the of it be tyme. *c* **1610** SIR J. MELVIL *Mem.* (1735) 346, I did what I could to be shifted of the said Commission. **1613** BEAUM. & FL. *Hon. Man's Fort.* IV. i, Shift your house, Lady of 'em, for I know 'em, They come to steal Napkins, and your Spoons. **1657** C. HOOLE *Corderius's School-Colloq.* (1688) 102 He says that he by God's blessing, is now quite shift of his fever.

**19. shift off.** †**a.** To put off, remove (a covering, a garment); *fig.* to remove from oneself or another (a burden). *Obs.*

**1567** FENTON *Trag. Disc.* Ded. (1898) I. 3 Old, not in yeares, wich the moste parte cold be content to shyfte of and forgo. **1635** J. HAYWARD tr. *Biondi's Banish'd Virg.* 157 Deadora..hastily shifted off her gowne. **1673** R. LEIGH *Transp. Reh.* 61 The bishop..would haue declin'd the office, and shifted it off to one of his chaplains. **1786–1805** TOOKE *Purley* Introd. 6 To take upon my shoulders a burthen which you seem desirous to shift off upon me.

†**b.** *colloq.* To get rid of the effects of (drink).

**1660** PEPYS *Diary* 17 Aug., I saw Mr. Creed show many of the strangest emotions to shift off his drink I ever saw in my life.

**c.** To evade, turn aside (an argument); to evade fulfilment of (a duty, a promise).

**1577** tr. *Bullinger's Decades* II. iii. 133 Let vs not lye, nor goe about with subtiltie to shifte off the othe that we once haue made. **1674** HICKMAN *Quinquart. Hist.* (ed. 2) 39 The calling of a Councel had been shifted off by Leo the X. *a* **1768** SECKER *Serm.* (1770) I. iii. 59 Many of them..shift off the Subject, as well and as soon as they can. **1774** REID *Aristotle's Logic* IV. §7 Conceiving that he intended to shift off his second payment.

**d.** To put (a person) off with an excuse or a subterfuge; to get rid of (a person).

*c* **1585** *Faire Em* II. iii, Here commeth Valingford; Shift him off now, as thou hast done the other. **1607** *Lingua* I. vii. B 3 b, Where shall I run? how shall I shift him of? **1748** [? NOBLE] *Voy. E. Indies* (1762) 31 The poor planter..was shifted off with a trifling answer. **1779** JOHNSON *Lives Poets, Denham* ¶42 Now and then the reader is shifted off with what he can get.

** *intransitive uses.*

**20.** To move from one place to another; esp. to change one's lodging.

**1530** PALSGR. 703/1 You can never thrive, you use to shift so often. **1576** FLEMING tr. *Caius' Dogges* I. (1880) 6 To and fro runne they, from place to place shift they, vntil they haue attained to that plot of grounde where they passed ouer. **1577–87** HOLINSHED *Chron.* III. 1149/1 After that he shifted to one James Mower a shipmaster, who dwelt at Milton shore. **1711** SWIFT *Jrnl. Stella* 4 July, Her life passes with boarding in some country town as cheap as she can, and when she runs out, shifting to some cheaper place. **1851** CARLYLE *Sterling* I. iii, On the 20th of March 1815, the family had to shift.

**21. a.** To move about, to move from one position to another, to move slightly. Also with *advs.*

**1595** *Saviolo's Practise* I. E 2, But when the scholler shall giue the mandritta, the maister must shifte a little with his bodye. **1692** R. L'ESTRANGE *Fables* lxviii. 67 A Natural Levity that puts us upon Shifting and Changing. **1815** J. SMITH *Panorama Sci. & Art* I. 598 The nodes shift backwards about 19½° in the ecliptic every year. **1833** TENNYSON *Goose* vii, She shifted in her elbow-chair. **1878** HUXLEY *Physiogr.* 180 Its [the sea's] level is constantly shifting up and down.

**b.** of immaterial things.

**1602** WARNER *Alb. Eng.* IX. lii. (1612) 234 Our Thoughts be shifting to and fro. **1744** ARMSTRONG *Art Pres. Health* II. 244 Happiness..that from stage to stage Invites us still, but shifts as we pursue.

**c.** *Naut.* Of cargo, ballast: To move from its proper position, so as to disturb the equilibrium of the vessel.

**1797** *Encycl. Brit.* (ed. 3) XVII. 377/1 They would have little or no occasion for ballast, and if any was used, could incur less danger from its shifting. **1912** *Times* 19 Dec. 20/5 There is always the risk that a grain cargo may shift.

**d.** Of the wind: To change its direction. Const. *to.*

*c* **1645** HOWELL *Lett.* (1892) II. 659 The wind..begins to sift [*sic*] already. **1687** A. LOVELL tr. *Thevenot's Trav.* I. 14 The wind..shifted to and agen from East to North. **1825** T. HOOK *Sayings* Ser. II. *Passion & Princ.* xiii. III. 311 The wind shifted a point or two to the northward of east. **1885** *Manch. Exam.* 10 Sept. 5/5 The wind has shifted round to due west.

**e.** In playing the violin or other instrument of the viol class, to move the left hand from one position to another on the neck of the instrument.

**1891** LATARCHE *Violin Student's Man.* 7 Shifting... To shift from the fifth to the higher positions, before moving the hand, throw back the thumb until the neck rests on the first joint.

**22. a.** To move away, withdraw, depart; esp. to slip off unobserved. Now only with *away.*

**1590** SHAKS. *Com. Err.* v. 168 Oh Mistris, Mistris, shift and saue your selfe. **1593** —— *Lucr.* 1104 No obiect but her passions strength renewes: And as one shiftes another straight insewes. **1623** BINGHAM *Xenophon* 72 He shifted away by night, leauing his sonne behinde him. **1629** R. L'ESTRANGE *Josephus, Life* (1733) 808 He put himself into a Disguise..and so shifted away till he came to a certain Village of his own. **1862** MISS BRADDON *Lady Audley* xxii, The eyes that had been looking at his shifted away as he spoke.

**b.** *Law.* Of an estate: To pass *away* from one owner to another.

**1844** J. WILLIAMS *Real Prop.* (1877) 292 The lands will shift away from him, and vest in the person next entitled in remainder.

**23.** To move, to travel, esp. quickly; to get a move on. Cf. SHIFT *sb.* 14 a. *colloq.*

**1922** M. ARLEN *'Piracy'* I. i. 21, I am..going to leap on my motor-bike and shift like hell to London. **1968** A. DIMENT *Bang Bang Birds* ix. 170 The speedo needle clawed its way up..to finally flicker over the 180 mark. Kilometres an hour of course but we were still shifting. **1970** M. KENYON *100,000 Welcomes* v. 37 You'll have time for a bite at Murphy's if you shift.

**shifta** ('ʃɪftə). Pl. **shifta, shiftas.** Also with capital initial. [Somali *shúfto* bandit, ad. Amharic.] A Somali bandit or guerrilla, operating mainly in northern Kenya. Also *attrib.*

**1950** *Times* 18 Feb. 5/3 Mr. H. V. Rose, who is in charge of the anti-Shifta operations, has reported a steady decline in the number of incidents this month, as the number of contacts made by 'ferret' forces with the Shifta bands has increased. **1959** *Times* 29 June 11/7 The *shiftas*, although they may relieve the traveller of his goods, seldom harm his person. **1967** *Economist* 27 May 900/3 The Kenyan government warned its Somali neighbours that if they went on supporting the ethnic Somali *shifta* terrorists (freedom-fighters, the Somalis say) in Kenya's north-eastern province, Kenya might hit back. **1972** 'I. DRUMMOND' *Frog in Moonflower* v. 81 Somali *shifta*..were tough and greedy and they had a perverted sense of political mission. **1977** *Time* 23 May 20/2 About 1,000 *shiftas*—armed nomads of the Western Somali Liberation Front—periodically mount hit-and-run attacks along the Somali frontier. **1980** *Daily Tel.* 8 Jan. 1/8 She might have been killed by marauding Somali bandits called 'Shifta', who are blamed for much of the game poaching in Northern Kenya.

**shiftable** (ʃɪftəb(ə)l), *a.* [f. SHIFT *v.* + -ABLE.]

**1.** Capable of being shifted, removable.

**1742** BAILEY (ed. 10), cites *Shaks.* [erroneously]. **1903** J. C. SMITH in *R. Wallace: Life & Last Leaves* 121 To him Gladstone's 'well of truth' seemed to have many shiftable bottoms.

**2.** Able to shift for himself.

**1832** *Let.* 17 Apr. in *J. Constable's Corr.* (1962) I. 269 Abram would have accompanied her on Monday, but as business required *his* going *this day*, we thought it quite unnecessary to alter his plans for so *shiftable a young lady*. **1861** W. B. BROOKE *Out with Garibaldi* xvi. 292 The old soldiers..smoking their pipes quietly, or..helping their less shiftable comrades.

Hence **shifta'bility**, the ability to be shifted.

**1951** [see SELF-LIQUIDATION 1]. **1972** *Linguistic Inquiry* III. 377 (*heading*) On the shiftability of past participles. **1976** *Language* LII. 39 The shiftability of the NP has nothing to do with whether the containing prepositional phrase has or has not originated in a relative clause.

**shifted** ('ʃɪftɪd), *ppl. a.* [f. SHIFT *v.* + -ED[1].] In senses of the verb. †Of a snake: That has changed its skin. Of a ship's ballast or cargo (see quot. 1760).

**1595** SHAKS. *John* IV. ii. 23 Like a shifted winde vnto a saile, It makes the course of thoughts to fetch about. **1648** HERRICK *Hesper., Oberon's Palace* 67 The roome is hung with the blew skin Of shifted snake. **1700** DRYDEN *Ovid's Pythag. Philos.* 389 All Things are alter'd, nothing is destroy'd, The shifted Scene, for some new Show employ'd. **1760** FALCONER *Dict. Marine* (1780), *Shifted*, the state of a ship's ballast or cargo when it is shaken from one side to the other. **1897** F. THOMPSON *New Poems* 132 Even with the shifted Poise and footing of my thought.

**shiften** ('ʃɪftən), *v. Obs.* exc. *dial.* (E. Anglian). [f. SHIFT *v.* + -EN[5].] *trans.* To remove (a thing) from one place to another; to change (one's clothes or garments). Also in knitting (see quot. *a* 1825).

**1544** PHAER *Pestilence* (1553) N viij, It is good for him to shiften his bedde out of one chamber into another. *a* **1825** FORBY *Voc. E. Anglia, Shiften.* 1. To change linen. 2. To shift stitches from one pin to another in knitting.

Hence **'shiftening** *vbl. sb.*, a change of linen.

**1676** in G. N. Godwin *Bits about Bergholt* (1874) 115 Linnen to make shiftnings for the poor. **1691** *Ibid.*, That the shiftnings be cut out at Mr. Robert Woodgate's. *a* **1825** FORBY *Voc. E. Anglia* II. 297 A poor woman begs of the overseer, to give her boy, who is going out to service 'only a shiftening, two of each sort, one on and one off'.

**shifter** ('ʃɪftə(r)). [f. SHIFT *v.* + -ER[1].]

**1.** One who shifts something (in any sense of the vb.); *spec.* a scene-shifter.

**1571** *Act 13 Eliz.* c. 8 §4 All..other Doynges whatsoever for Gayne..whereuppon is not reserved.. to the Lender Contracter Shyfter Forbearer or Deliverer above the Summe of Tenne Poundes for the Loane or Forbearinge of a Hundred Poundes for one yere. **1599** B. JONSON *Cynthia's Rev.* II. iii, He is no great shifter; once a yeare his Apparel is ready to reuolt. **1680** *Reflections on late Libel on Curse-ye-Meroz* 28 The Author had (in all probability) been Lecturer there at this day, (for he is no Starter, nor Shifter, nor Swapper of Livings). **1711** ADDISON *Spect.* No. 42 ⁋3 Two or three shifters of scenes, with the two candle-snuffers, make up a compleat body of Guards upon the English stage. **1761** CHURCHILL *Rosciad* 206 Then came drum, trumpet, hautboy, fiddle, flute, Next, snuffer, sweeper, shifter, soldier, mute. **1887** *Pall Mall Gaz.* 26 Oct. 6/1 The cords.. by which the scenes were raised and lowered were so crossed and entangled that the shifters could not find those belonging to [etc.].

†**2.** *shifter away*: one who eludes, or sets aside.

**1555** RIDLEY in Foxe *A. & M.* (1583) 1451/1 This is a greuous contumely, that you call me a shifter away of the Scriptures, and of the Doctours.

†**3. a.** One who resorts to petty shifts or tricks, or who practises artifice; an idle, thriftless fellow; a trickster, cozener, etc. Also with *for*. *Obs.*

*c* **1562** E. UNDERHILL in *Narr. Reform.* (Camden) 158 Another spitefull enemy att Stepeney, callede Banbery, a shifter, a dycer, a hore-hunter. **1561** AWDELAY *Frat. Vacab.* (1869) 3 The company of Cousoners and Shifters. **1584** G. WHETSTONE *Mirr. Mag. Cities* 26 These expert Shifters, by falce Dice, slipperie castynge, or some other nice Sleight:.. wyll make their Purses as emptie of Money, as the Catte the Mouses headde of Braynes. **1612** BRINSLEY *Lud. Lit.* iv. 40 The great abuse by som shifters, who go vnder the name of Scrieuners. **1670** MILTON *Hist. Brit.* III. 130 In worldly matters, practis'd and cunning Shifters.

*punningly.* (Cf. 1.) **1619** FLETCHER *Bloody Bro.* IV. ii, They have so little [clothes] As well may free them from the name of shifters.

**b.** One who uses evasive reasoning.

**1567–9** JEWEL *Def. Apol.* II. v. (1611) 141 It were hard to say, that Christ, his Apostles, the Prophets and holy Fathers were shifters, and Heretikes. **1648** JENKYN *Blind Guide* iii. 36 Poore shifter!..it seemes the novice hath..driven you to another shift. **1899** *Westm. Gaz.* 23 Dec. 3/2 Shiftings and wrigglings which have made the shifters and wrigglers contemptible in the eyes of all sensible people.

†**4.** *Naut.* (See quots.) *Obs.*

**1704** J. HARRIS *Lex. Techn.* I, *Shifters*, certain Men aboard a Man of War who are employed by the Cooks to shift or change the Water in which the Flesh or Fish is put and laid for some time, in order to fit it for the Kettle. **1750** BLANCKLEY *Nav. Expositor.* **1751** SMOLLETT *Per. Pic.* ii, I have..served all offices on board from cook's shifter to the command of a vessel. **1769** FALCONER *Dict. Marine* (1780), *Shifter*, a person appointed to assist the ship's cook, particularly in..steeping, and shifting the salt provisions.

**5.** *Mining.* (See quots. 1894, 1906.)

**1830** T. WILSON *Pitman's Pay* (1843) 57 Aw gat at furst a shifter's place, And then a deputy was myed. **1880** *Leeds Mercury* 16 Sept. 8 William Hartley, a master shifter said that he worked in No. 2 Hutton or Harvey seam. **1894** *Northumbld. Gloss.*, *Shifter, Shift-man*, a man who prepares the working places at night in a colliery for the men who come in at next shift... *Shifters* work by the day or shift, as distinct from hewers, who work by the ton or yard. **1906** *Daily News* 17 Oct. 7/1 A shifter..is a man whose chief duties are to keep the tunnels clear of falls of coal, and to shore up unsafe places.

**6.** *Mech.* **a.** A contrivance used for shifting. In many applications, e.g. a kind of clutch serving to transfer a belt from one pulley to another; also (see quot. 1875).

**1869** RANKINE *Machine & Hand-tools* Pl. I 5, This shaft actuates a vertical rock shaft,..imparting the required motion to the belt shifter on the top of the machine. **1875** KNIGHT *Dict. Mech.*, *Shifter* (knitting-machine), one of the beardless needles..which..operate to disengage the outer loops of the course and put them on the next inner or the next outer needles for narrowing or widening.

**b.** The gear-change mechanism or control in a motor vehicle. Freq. *attrib. N. Amer.*

**1910** J. E. HOMANS *Self-Propelled Vehicles* (ed. 7) xxix. 378 The arm of the sliding gear shifter meets a raised portion of the reverse shaft. **1915** HOBBS & ELLIOTT *Gasoline Automobile* iii. 67 These two sets [of sliding gears] are operated by two shifter yokes which lead to the gear control lever in the car. **1920** V. W. PAGÉ *Model T Ford Car* (new ed.) vii. 341 To stop the motor close the throttle and turn shifter to the horizontal position. **1946** W. H. CROUSE *Automotive Mech.* xvii. 390 A close-up view of the gear selector and shifter rods. **1972** G. V. HIGGINS *Friends of Eddie Coyle* xiii. 78 'How come you got the automatic?.. I'd want the Hurst shifter in it.' 'You wouldn't want it once you started buying clutches for it.'

**shiftful** ('ʃɪftfʊl), *a. rare.* [f. SHIFT *sb.* + -FUL.] Full of shifts or devices.

**1615** SYLVESTER *Batt. Yvry* 333 The most he fears, is least Some's shift-full feare,..finde out..Som Flat, som Foord, ..To passe the Eure. **1881** GARDINER *Introd. Eng. Hist.* I. iii. 44 If William had not had something more than mere shiftful contrivance in reserve. **1887** FOWLER *Princ. Morals* 219 The general admiration for the wily and shiftful Odysseus.

Hence **'shiftfulness**.

**1865** KINGSLEY *Herew.* i, That hero of 'Arrah', who proved, by his valour, pertinacity, and shiftfulness, not unworthy of his great ancestor Hereward.

**shiftily** ('ʃɪftɪlɪ), *adv.* [f. SHIFTY *a.* + -LY[2].] In a shifty manner.

**1878** P. BAYNE *Purit. Rev.* ii. 49 Williams had intrigued boldly and shiftily. **1887** R. W. DIXON *Lyrical Poems* 22 When the cloud grows luminous and shiftily riven.

**shiftiness** ('ʃɪftɪnɪs). [f. SHIFTY *a.* + -NESS.] The character or quality of being shifty in any sense.

**1839** CARLYLE *Chartism* v. 135 Shiftiness..is a kind of thing that fancies itself..to be talent. **1893** *Times* 11 May 9/4 The shiftiness of the present Government.

**shifting** ('ʃɪftɪŋ), *vbl. sb.* [f. SHIFT *v.* + -ING[1]. Cf. ON. *skipting* division, change.]

†**1.** Used for: A 'course' of the Jewish priesthood. *Obs.*

*c* **1200** ORMIN 467 He wass i þatt shifftinng sett þatt nemmnedd wass Abya [cf. Vulgate: *de vice Abia*].

**2.** The action of the verb SHIFT in various senses.

**a.** Changing, moving.

*c* **1440** *Promp. Parv.* 446/1 Schyftynge, or chaungynge, *mutacio, commutacio, permutacio.* Schyftynge, or removynge, *amocio.* **1579** SPENSER *Sheph. Cal.* Dec. 116, I.. woont to frame my pype, Vnto the shifting of the shepheards foote. **1611** HOBBES tr. *Thucyd.* (1822) 8 After the Trojan war the Grecians continued still their shiftings and transplantations. **1691** T. H[ALE] *Acc. New Invent.* p. lxii, The strange shifting of Tides in this River. **1711** *Lond. Gaz.* No. 4819/2 The sudden..Shiftings of the Weather. **1780** BURKE *Sp. Bristol* Wks. III. 374 Of no use but to indicate the shiftings of every fashionable gale. **1837** CARLYLE *Fr. Rev.* II. I. ii, As in some sudden shifting of the Earth's axis. **1885** BAGGALLAY in *Law Rep. 29 Chanc. Div.* 439 The shifting of the capital of Italy from Florence to Rome. **1901** 'LINESMAN' *Words by Eyewitness* vii. (1902) 155 With their sidelong glances and uneasy shiftings.

*with adverbs.*

**1562** [BP. COOPER] *Answ. Def. Truth* iii. 18 b, It weare but the shiftinge backe of one winge of the battayle. **1575–85** ABP. SANDYS *Serm.* xii. 197 Delatories and shiftings off weare out many a iust cause. **1834–6** P. BARLOW *Manuf.* in *Encycl. Metrop.* (1845) VIII. 736/1 The shifting back of the heddles.

**b.** The action or practice of devising expedients, or of using evasions; a device, expedient; an evasion, shift. Often in *pl.* ? *Obs.* or *dial.*

**1559** BERCHER *Nobil. Women* (Roxb. 1904) 124/2 Ye cannot, for all your shyftinge, denye but man hath the better case. **1616** *Rich Cabinet* 137 b, Shifting is a very poore and troublesome trade, if a man haue no other meanes, to get his liuing. **1691** HARTCLIFFE *Virtues* 177 Men of brave Spirits.. have made no scruple to use these shiftings to save themselves or their Friends.

**c.** *Boxing* and *Fencing.* (See quots.)

**1793** *Sporting Mag.* I. 198/2 Shifting is running from your adversary, whenever he attempts to strike you, or to come near you, or when you have struck him, and is done with a view of tiring him out. *c* **1800** *Mod. Art Boxing* 31 *Shifting*, running from your adversary whenever he attempts to hit you, or to come near you, or when you have struck him. **1821** EGAN *Boxiana* (1830) I. 98 Tom, finding he was over-matched, was obliged..to have recourse to shifting to prevent his being beat straight forward. **1828** *Encycl. Metrop.* (1845) XIX. 85/1 (Fencing), *Caveating, changing, Disengaging*, or *Shifting*, slipping off your adversary's blade to the opposite side, when you feel him endeavouring to *Bind* your own.

**d.** *Ship-building*: (see quots.). Cf. SHIFT *v.* 8 e and *sb.* 16.

**1805** *Shipwright's Vade-M.* 131 *Shifting*, the art of setting off the length of the planks of the bottom, topside, &c. that the butts may over-run each other, in order to make a good shift. Replacing old stuff with new is also called *shifting*. **1830** HEDDERWICK *Mar. Archit.* 272 The first futtock requires to be very long, to make a proper shifting past the floor-head, and extend down to the side of the keel.

**e.** *Philol.* The process of regular phonological change. Cf. SHIFT *sb.* 14 d. See also *sound-shifting* s.v. SOUND *sb.*[3]

**1888** J. WRIGHT *Old High-German Primer* vi. 27 The most striking feature in which High German differs from the other West Germanic languages is the general shifting which certain consonants underwent. **1905** O. F. EMERSON *Hist. Eng. Lang.* 238 There has been no consistent shifting of a considerable number of consonants as in High German. **1938** *Language* XIV. 112 (*heading*) Phonological shifting in American Norwegian. **1954** F. G. CASSIDY in Robertson & Cassidy *Devel. Mod. Eng.* v. 100 Note that though some shifting begins before Chaucer's day, the shift as a whole is subsequent.

†**3.** *concr.* A change of clothes. *Obs. rare*[−1].

**1631** GOUGE *God's Arrows* III. §88. 349 Plagues oft arise.. from noisome savours, from want of cleane shiftings, from unwholsome food.

**4.** *Comb.*: **shifting-boards** (see quot. 1846); **shifting clothes, trousers** *dial.*, clothes, trousers, into which a person changes, esp. after work; †**shifting day**, the day for changing one's clothes or undergarments; **shifting-movement** *Organ-building* (see quot.); †**shifting-room**, an actor's dressing-room.

**1833** POE in *Southern Lit. Messenger* (1835) Dec. 35/2, I therefore thought proper to contrive a hiding-place in the hold. This I did by removing a small portion of the *shifting boards. **1846** A. YOUNG *Naut. Dict.*, *Shifting-boards*, one or more wooden partitions put up fore-and-aft in a vessel's hold..for the purpose of preventing the shifting of a cargo. **1885** F. GORDON *Pyotshaw* 51 Ma guid *shiftin' claes clean spilt. **1957** *Scotland's Mag.* June 46 The first of the noisy band of workers came 'skailing' out of the pithead baths, in their shifting clothes. **1697** VANBRUGH *Relapse* III. iii, And if it was not *shifting Day, let her put on a clean Tucker, quick! **1876** HILES *Catech. Organ* viii. (1878) 56 A *shifting-movement is an old contrivance for shutting off the loud stops [of an organ] by means of a pedal: it..is now superseded by the composition pedals. **1740** CIBBER *Apol.* (1756) I. 272, I haul'd him by the sleeve into my *shifting-room. **1913** D. H. LAWRENCE *Sons & Lovers* viii. 199 She wiped him in a desultory fashion, and went upstairs, returning immediately with his *shifting-trousers. When he was dried he struggled into his shirt.

**shifting** ('ʃɪftɪŋ), *ppl. a.* [f. SHIFT *v.* + -ING[2].]

**1. a.** That shifts or changes position or direction.

**1479** *Office Mayor Bristol* in *Eng. Gilds* (1870) 425 The shyftyng daies of the woke, specially the Wensdaies and Satirdaies, the Maire hath be vsid to walke in the morenynges to the Brewers howses. **1644** MILTON *Divorce* (ed. 2) To Parl. A 4 b, Let him bethink him withall how he will soder up the shifting flaws of his ungirt permissions, his venial and unvenial dispences. **1735** SOMERVILLE *Chase* IV. 70 Nor less the shifting Cur avoid, that breaks Illusive from the Pack. **1791** BURKE *Let. Memb. Nat. Assembly* Wks. VI. 12 The shifting tides of fear and hope. **1814** SCOTT *Diary* 31 July in *Lockhart* (1837) III. iv. 140 A whole parish was swallowed up by the shifting sands. **1859** GEN. P. THOMPSON *Audi Alt.* II. App. 99 In a shifting gale the seaman will do many things, which are the last he would have done an hour before. **1871** FREEMAN *Hist. Ess.* Ser. I. viii. 239 The shifting relations between France and Normandy during the tenth and eleventh centuries.

**b.** Special collocations: **shifting agriculture** = *shifting cultivation*; **shifting backstays, ballast** (see quots.); **shifting bar** *Printing*, 'a cross-bar removably dovetailed into a *chase*' (Knight *Dict. Mech.* 1875); **shifting centre** = METACENTRE; **shifting cultivation**, any of several forms of agriculture in which an area of ground is cleared of vegetation and cultivated for a (usu. small) number of years and then abandoned because of nomadic habits or deliberate fallowing or because the yield of crop has become uneconomic, when cultivation is begun elsewhere; hence **shifting cultivator**; **shifting keyboard** *Pianoforte*, a keyboard action of a grand piano, etc., which is moved by the use of the soft pedal; so **shifting pedal**; **shifting spanner**, an adjustable spanner; **shifting use** *Law*, a use properly created for the benefit of one person, but so as to pass from him upon a specified contingency and vest wholly or in part in another.

**1934** W. FITZGERALD *Africa* III. v. 354 Cocoa-planting necessitated the abandonment of the old system of *shifting agriculture. **1973** W. T. W. MORGAN *E. Africa* iv. 92 In the general absence of fertilisers and lacking any complete rotation system, a system of fallowing was necessary. In the tropics this system has come to be referred to as 'shifting agriculture'. **1867** SMYTH *Sailor's Word-bk.*, **Shifting backstays*,..those which can be changed from one side of a shift to the other, as the occasion demands. **1785** GROSE *Dict. Vulgar T.*, **Shifting Ballast*, a term used by sailors, to signify soldiers, passengers, or any landsmen on board. **1867** SMYTH *Sailor's Word-bk.*, *Shifting ballast*, pigs of iron, bags of sand, &c., used for ballast, and capable of being moved to trim the vessel. Also, a term applied to messengers, soldiers, and live-stock. **1794** *Shifting-centre [see METACENTRE]. **1846** A. YOUNG *Naut. Dict.* 211 *Meta-centre*, sometimes called the *Shifting Centre*. **1922** *Shifting cultivation [see CHENA]. **1952** P. W. RICHARDS *Tropical Rain Forest* xvii. 378 The destruction of the primary forest which gives rise to secondary successions may take place in different ways and for various reasons. By far the most important cause of destruction up to the present has been the system of shifting cultivation (the ladang system of Malaysia and the taunggya system of Burma) which is practised by nearly all the native peoples of the tropics. **1971** J. H. GALLOWAY in Blakemore & Smith *Latin America* viii. 382 Much of the agriculture of Mato Grosso and Goiás is still primitive, unproductive shifting cultivation. **1945** K. J. PELZAR *Pioneer Settlement in Asiatic Tropics* ii. 16 The *shifting cultivator does not use the same piece of land every year; instead, he kills or cuts down at regular intervals—every year, every other year, or every third year—the trees of a small forest patch. **1979** *Nature* 16 Aug. 533/1 Shifting cultivators fell and burn forest land, then plant food crops and raise animals and later move on when soil fertility drops. **1896** A. J. HIPKINS *Pianoforte* 40 In many upright pianos, however, although some are made with *shifting keyboards..a soft pedal is contrived by mechanically dropping a strip of cloth.. between the hammers and the strings. **1922** A. H. LINDO *Pedalling in Pianoforte Music* II. x. 143 The mechanism of the shifting keyboard, which is fitted to many Uprights and to nearly all Grands, is preferable. **1880** GROVE *Dict. Mus.* II. 682/2 The *shifting pedal, first introduced by Stein in his Saitenharmonica. **1962** K. DALE tr. *Riefling's Piano Pedalling* 28 As regards the grand piano at any rate, it is correct to speak of the shifting pedal (*Verschiebung*) because the whole mechanism, keyboard and hammer, is shifted slightly to the right when the left pedal is pressed down. **1829** *Mechanics' Mag.* 31 Jan. 423/2, I send you..a plan of a new *shifting-spanner, which answers better than the wedge-spanner. **1935** J. GUTHRIE *Little Country* ii. 38 I'll let you have my shifting spanner. **1765** BLACKSTONE *Comm.* II. 335 This is sometimes called a secondary, sometimes a *shifting, use. **1844** J. WILLIAMS *Real Prop.* (1877) 293 The establishment of shifting and contingent uses occasioned great difficulties to the early lawyers.

**2.** That uses shifts, tricks, deceit, expedients, subterfuges, or evasions.

**1581** A. HALL *Iliad* I. 7 Among the Kings a coward vile, a slouthful shifting Oxe. **1587** HARRISON *England* II. xi. 186/1 Yoong shifting gentlemen, which oftentimes doo beare more port than they are able to mainteine. **1659** MILTON *Civil Power in Eccl. Causes* 54 Opposing truth to error, no unequal match; truth the strong to error the weak though slie and shifting. **1737** *Gentl. Mag.* VII. 570/1 Nor winged flight, nor shifting wiles, Cou'd save 'em from his deadly toils. **1795** WINDHAM *Sp.* 5 Jan. (1812) I. 261 What course of candour and fair reasoning is a match for this shifting subtlety?

Hence **'shiftingly** *adv.*, **'shiftingness.**

**1573** TUSSER *Husb.* (1878) 17 To hate to liue in infamie, through craft, and liuing shiftingly. **1613** SIR E. HOBY *Counter-sn. Ishmael Rabshacheh* 14 Thus doth he..thinke shiftingly to hide that, which he dares not doctrinally defend. **1624** GATAKER *Transubst.* 109 And this is..when they speake mystically or shiftingly, as hee speaketh. **1866** *Spectator* 8 Dec. 1353 The wonderful variety and shiftingness of the grounds taken by their advocates.

**shiftless** ('ʃɪftlɪs), *a.* [f. SHIFT *sb.* + -LESS.]

†**1.** Helpless for self-defence; void of cunning or artifice. *Obs.*

**1562** BP. PILKINGTON *Abdias* Pref. Aa iv b, Wylde beastes be cruel, yet god defends the shiftles sheepe. **1577** KENDALL *Flowers of Epigr., Trifles* 24 b, I neuer would haue thought The selie simple shiftlesse Bee could haue suche mischief wrought. **1616** R. HILL *Pathw. Prayer, Direct. to live well* 65 Because of my selfe I am shiftlesse to auoid them [occasions of sinne]. **1698** FRYER *Acc. E. India & P.* 122 A Sea-Tortoise..being taken and turned on its back is shiftless.

**2.** Lacking in resource; incapable of shifting for oneself; hence, lazy, inefficient.

**1584** in Neal *Hist. Purit.* (1732) I. 407 Having been either popish Priests or shiftless men, thrust in upon the Ministry. *a* **1697** AUBREY *Lives, Winceslaus Hollar* (1813) II. 402 He was a very friendly good-natured man as could be, but shiftlesse as to the world, and dyed not rich. *a* **1691** WOOD *Fasti Oxon.* I. 871 Joh. Pell..was a shiftless man as to worldly affairs. **17..** ELIZ. CARTER *Lett.* (1808) 118, I hope this shiftless friend of mine was not the very thief that stole your Tasso. **1837** CARLYLE *Fr. Rev.* I. VII. iv, Poor M de Gouvion is shiftless in this extremity. **1865** DICKENS *Mut. Fr.* III. x, Mr. Wrayburn..all idle and shiftless, stood by her bench looking on. **1891** HARDY *Tess* iii, Going to hunt up her shiftless husband at the inn.

**b.** Of actions: Indicating shiftlessness; ineffective, futile.

**1613** PURCHAS *Pilgrimage* I. vi. (1614) 33 Forcing him to his manifold shifts, and shiftlesse remouings. **1678** GALE *Crt. Gentiles* IV. III. iii. 65 How poor and shiftlesse this shift is we have already demonstrated. *a* **1862** THOREAU *Yankee in Canada* ii. (1866) 27 This looked very shiftless, especially in a country abounding in water-power.

†**3.** Not shifted or changed; unvarying. *Obs.*

**1606** WARNER *Alb. Eng.* XIV. xci. (1612) 370 When Canons, Rubrick, Liturgie, and Discipline throughout One shiftlesse Practise had, not to Indifferencie a flout.

**4.** Without a shift or shirt. *rare.*

**1680** OTWAY *Marius* II. ii, He threaten'd me to banish me his house, Naked and shiftless to the world. **1856** MERIVALE *Rom. Emp.* xxxviii. (1865) IV. 336 Actaeon, who had startled the shiftless Diana.

Hence **'shiftlessly** *adv.*, **'shiftlessness.**

**1681** FLAVEL *Righteous Man's Ref.* 265 The misery and shiftlessness of their condition. **1837** EMERSON *Address, Amer. Schol.* Wks. (Bohn) II. 183 In the long period of his [the scholar's] preparation, he must betray often an ignorance and shiftlessness in popular arts. **1847** WEBSTER, *Shiftlessly.* **1888** BRYCE *Amer. Commw.* III. cxii. 608 The larger cities..where recent emigrants, with the shiftlessness of Europe still clinging round them, are huddled together in squalor.

**shiftning,** var. SHIFTENING *vbl. sb.*

**shifty** ('ʃɪftɪ), *a.* [f. SHIFT *sb.* + -Y.]

**1. a.** Full of shifts or expedients; well able to shift for oneself.

**1570** LEVINS *Manip.* 111/21 Shifty, *astutus, prouidus.* **1783** *Maryland Jrnl.* 18 Feb. 3/3 Ran away,..a Negro Man, named Pompey,..very artful and shifty. **1838** 'TEXAN' *Mexico v. Texas* 217 Flambeau, who was extremely shifty, soon built up a nice little booth. **1854** EMERSON *Lett. & Soc. Aims, Resources* Wks. (Bohn) III. 197 What a plastic little creature he [man] is! so shifty, so adaptive! **1859** KINGSLEY *Water-supply Lond.* Misc. II. 218 The canny, shifty, far-seeing Scot, with that mingled daring and caution of his. **1888** BLACK In Far Lochaber xxiii, She was in many ways a shifty and business-like young person, who had early acquired a sense of responsibility.

†**b.** Of a device: Effective, serviceable. *Obs.*

**1585** GREENE *Planetom.* Wks. (Grosart) V. 119 Seeing his troubled minde coulde finde out no shiftie deuise.

**2. a.** Fond of indirect or dishonest methods; addicted to evasion or artifice; not straightforward, not to be depended on.

**1837** CARLYLE *Fr. Rev.* I. IV. iv, A Stanislas Maillard,..one of the shiftiest of men. **1841** KINNEAR *Cairo*, etc. 305 A most shifty old fox he [*sc.* Mehemet Ali] is. **1879** FARRAR *St. Paul* (1883) 554 Their Jewish teachers said that Paul was shifty and complaisant.

**b.** Of a person's attributes, actions, etc. Also *Comb.*, as *shifty-eyed* adj.

**1864** THACKERAY *D. Duval* ii. (1869) 10 A handsome, tall, sallow-faced man, with a shifty eye. **1865** DICKENS *Mut. Fr.* II. vi, I scorn your shifty evasions. **1884** *American* VII. 213 His political methods have been shifty and not straightforward. **1922** H. JENKINS *John Dene of Toronto* i. 11 A shifty-eyed little man. **1977** M. BABSON *Lord Mayor of Death* xiv. 92 He must have looked a right shifty-eyed bastard.

**3.** Changeable or changeful; wavering. *rare.*

**1882** H. S. HOLLAND *Logic & Life* (1885) 294 Principles grow vague, and shifty, and indecisive. **1884** *Manch. Guard.* 22 Sept. 5/4 People of fashion and taste..are so shifty that they do not know their own minds from day to day. **1904** R. BRIDGES *Demeter* 630 Until his shifty mind Became to pity inclined.

**4.** Changing or shifting in position.

**1884** LADY BRASSEY in *Good Words* Mar. 165/1 The wind was shifty, though light and fair. **1891** MEREDITH *One of our Conq.* xxviii, A South-easterly wind blew the waters to shifty gold-leaf prints of brilliance under the sun. **1907** J. G. MILLAIS *Newfoundland* xii. 244 The wind had dropped, and showed signs of being shifty. **1976** *Yachts & Yachting* 20 Aug. 377/1 Weatherwise the 116-strong fleet had mostly light and shifty winds.

**shig** (ʃɪg), *v. Obs.* exc. *dial. rare.* In 5 schyg(ge. [App. related to SHOG *v.*, with difference of vowel symbolic of lighter movement.]

†**1.** *intr.* To jig, trot. *Obs.*

*a* **1400** *Sir Degrev.* 345 He come schygynge ayene.

**2.** *trans.* To shake.

*c* **1440** *Promp. Parv.* 446/1 Schygge clothys or oþer thyngys, *excucio. Ibid.*, Schyggynge, *excussio.* **1893** *Broad Norfolk* (ed. Cozens-Hardy) 27 *Shug* (also *Shig*), shake.

**Shiga.** ('ʃiːgə). *Bacteriol.* The name of Kiyoshi *Shiga* (1870–1957), Japanese bacteriologist, who discovered this bacterium in 1898, used *attrib.* and in the possessive to denote the Gram-negative bacterium *Shigella dysenteriæ*, which causes dysentery in man, and the toxin produced by it.

**1900** *Philad. Med. Jrnl.* VI. 423/1 They proceeded upon the false assumption that Shiga's microorganism was a variety of B[acillus] coli communis. *Ibid.*, Comparison of the Eberth-Gaffky and Shiga bacilli show the criterions of difference are by no means numerous. **1946** *Nature* 10 Aug. 207/2 It supervised the production of typhus vaccine and Shiga toxoid, and made suitable recommendations to the Department of National Defence concerning their use. **1947** *Ann. Rev. Microbiol.* I. 313 The Shiga bacillus is rare except in the Middle East and in India. *Ibid.* 316 There is no evidence that the Shiga toxin plays a significant part in producing the pathology of dysentery. **1976** EDINGTON & GILLES *Path. in Tropics* (ed. 2) vi. 328 *Shigella... Subgroup A:* Ten antigenically distinct serotypes, including Shiga's bacillus.

**Shigella** (ʃɪ'gɛlə). *Bacteriol.* Also **shigella.** Pl. **-ellæ, -ellas.** [mod.L., f. SHIG(A + L. *-ella* (see -EL[2]).] **1.** A member of the genus of Gram-negative, rod-shaped bacteria so called, which includes some causing dysentery in man and other animals.

[**1919** CASTELLANI & CHALMERS *Man. Trop. Med.* (ed. 3) xxxvi. 934 Non-motile—Genus 3, *Shigella* Castellani and Chalmers, 1918.] **1937** M. FROBISHER *Fund. Bacteriol.* xxx. 316 A number of the shigellas..(also commonly known as dysentery bacilli) cause intestinal disturbances. **1969** *New Yorker* 11 Oct. 123/3 A shigella infection produces a rather distinctive kind of damage that can be detected by microscopic examination. **1977** *Lancet* 19 Feb. 409/2 Fæces from 11 children and 3 adults who were ill were examined for salmonellæ, shigellæ, and *Staphylococcus aureus* with negative results.

**2.** = SHIGELLOSIS. Also *Shigella dysentery.*

**1963** G. MAXWELL *Rocks Remain* ii. 21 Immediate veterinary tests showed the presence of liver fluke... When further tests showed the presence of Shigella dysentry [*sic*], we decided to abandon interest in the flukes altogether. **1973** *Daily Colonist* (Victoria, B.C.) 10 May 25/1 Belinda Manybears, three months old, was suffering from shigella, a type of dysentery, at the time of her death. *Ibid.* 1 July 32/2 An intestinal disease doctors have tentatively diagnosed as Shigella swept through the luxury ship. **1977** Shigella dysentery [see SHIGELLOSIS].

**shigellosis** (ʃɪgɛ'ləʊsɪs). *Path.* [f. prec. + -OSIS.] Infection with or a disease caused by shigellæ.

**1944** HARDY & WATT in *Jrnl. Amer. Med. Assoc.* 22 Apr. 1179/1 In line with the accepted use of 'brucellosis' for all Brucella infections, we recommend the adoption of 'shigellosis' for all infections due to pathogenic varieties of shigella. **1977** *Proc. R. Soc. Med.* LXX. 374/1 Shigellosis in monkeys closely resembles Shigella dysentery in humans.

‖**shigram** ('ʃɪgrəm). *Bombay.* [Derived from Hindī *çīghr* (Skr. *çīghra*) quick.] A kind of hack gharry, or palankin-carriage.

**1841** H. MILLER in W. W. Peyton *Life* iv. (1883) 57. **1852** *Life in Bombay* 36 The humble shigram, a strange clumsy-looking article, which bears a striking family-likeness to an English bathing-machine. **1878** G. SMITH *Life J. Wilson* vi. (1879) 105.

**shig-shag,** variant of SHICK-SHACK.

**Shiho,** var. SAHO *sb.* and *a.*

**shih-tzu** ('ʃiːtsuː). Also **shitzu.** [ad. Chin. *shīzigŏu* f. *shī* lion + *zǐ* son + *gǒu* dog, formerly transliterated *shih-tzu kou.*] A small long-coated dog of the breed so called, originally developed in China, often tan or grey and white in colour, with long ears and a tail curling over the back. Also *attrib.*

**1921** V. W. F. COLLIER *Dogs China & Japan* iii. 52 These books [*sc.* the imperial dog-books]..portray dogs closely resembling the 'Pekingese' type, as also the 'Shih-tzu' dog and the 'Pug'. **1934** *Kennel Gaz.* May 385/3 It was decided that dogs might be registered under the heading of A.O.V. Shih-Tzu, and that those now registered as Apsos could be altered without charge. **1948** C. L. B. HUBBARD *Dogs in Britain* xx. 328 The Shih Tzu..is a close relative of the Lhasa Apso with which it has often been confused. **1961** *Guardian* 9 Nov. 10/6 Who,..apart from dog-fanciers, has ever heard of a shih-tzu? **1969** *Queen* 17 Sept. 56/1 She sits ..softly scratching the tummy of one of her Shitzu dogs. **1979** A. CHISHOLM *Nancy Cunard* xxxii. 332 Perhaps she had tripped..trying to avoid one of the Shih Tzu puppies.

**Shiism** ('ʃiːɪz(ə)m). [f. *Shi-* in SHIAH or SHIITE + -ISM.] The doctrines or principles of the Shiahs.

**1883** *Encycl. Brit.* XVI. 592/2. **1915** P. M. SYKES *Hist. Persia* II. xlvii. 43 Persia, where Shiism is the official religion. **1964** W. THESIGER *Marsh Arabs* v. 43 Shiism had started as a political movement among Arabs to advance the claims of Ali and his descendants to the Caliphate... In time, Shiism split Islam as decisively as the Reformation divided the Catholic Church. **1982** *Times* 31 May 6/1 From the Gulf to the Levant, there are 2,000 miles of Shiism, broken only by the irritation of Iraq's survival.

**shiitake** (ʃɪ'tɑːkeɪ). [Jap., f. *shii* a name used for several evergreen trees + *take* mushroom.] A mushroom, *Lentinus edodes*, of the family Agaricaceæ, cultivated in Japan and China on logs from various trees of the family Fagaceæ, esp. *Castanopsis cuspidata* or *Quercus* species. Also *attrib.*

**1877** *Grevillea* V. 103 The Shii-take species..have this peculiar excellence, that though they are all but tasteless in their raw state, when they are dried they have an extremely fine flavour. **1925** *Bot. Mag. Tokyo* XXXIX. 319 The best and most common mushrooms in Japan are Shii-take and Matsu-take. **1936** *Nature* 31 Oct. 746/2 Production of the shiitake has little horticultural similarity to mushroom growing. **1953** J. RAMSBOTTOM *Mushrooms & Toadstools* vii. 74 The cultivation of shii-take in Japan is believed to date back over two thousand years. **1961** R. SINGER *Mushrooms & Truffles* v. 139 Logs with Shii-take mycelium were dragged to a suitable site. **1975** J. GRIGSON *Mushroom Feast* 262 On account of the prolonged and laborious method of cultivation, shiitake are more expensive even on their home ground.

**Shiite** ('ʃiːaɪt). Also 8 **Sciaite,** 9 **Sheeite.** [f. *shi-* in SHIAH + -ITE. (The 18th c. form *Sciaite* seems to be f. Arab. *shiyaʿīy* a Shiite).] A member of the Shiah sect. Also *attrib.* or *adj.*

**1728** CHAMBERS *Cycl.* s.v. *Sonna*, There are also Sectaries among the Mahometans, called *Sciaites*, who reject the Traditions of the *Sonnites.* **1759** *Universal Hist., Mod.* II. 42 The Sonnites make use of the word *Shiites*, or *Shii*, and apply it to their adversaries, as a term of reproach. **1812** T. MOORE *Intercepted Lett.* vi. 24 You know our Sunnites, hateful dogs! Whom every pious Shiite flogs Or longs to flog. **1817** C. MILLS *Muhammedanism* 369 Down to the fifteenth century, the Persians fluctuated between the Sonnite and Shiite sects. **1825** HEBER *Jrnl.* 25 Feb., A furious attack on the Sheeite heresy from the pulpit. **1911** *19th Cent.* Mar. 517 A province which then and for centuries afterward was a stronghold of Yemenite or Shiite.

Hence **Shi'itic** *a.*, of or pertaining to the Shiites.

**1884** H. ETHÉ in *Encycl. Brit.* XVII. 238/1 Purely Shi'itic or Isma'ilitic ideas.

**Shijō** ('ʃiːdʒəʊ). [The name of the street in Kyōto, Japan, where the founder lived.] Used *attrib.* to designate a school of Japanese painting.

**1884** SATOW & HAWES *Murray's Handbk. Japan* (ed. 2) 97 The Shijô art was a compromise, retaining Chinese perspective and ignoring the laws of chiaroscuro, but copying details of form in flowers and animals with remarkable fidelity. **1902** *Encycl. Brit.* XXIX. 717/1 Amongst the associates of the Shijô master was the celebrated Ganku. **1970** *Oxf. Compan. Art* 696/2 A sub-division of the Maruyama School called the Shijo School.

**shikar** (ʃɪ'kɑː(r)), *sb. Anglo-Ind.* Also 7 **sikar,** 8 **shekar.** [Urdū (from Persian) *shikār.*]

**a.** Hunting; sport (shooting and hunting); game. Phr. *on shikar*, on a hunting expedition, out hunting.

*a* **1613** W. FINCH in Purchas *Pilgrims* (1625) I. 430 Whatsoeuer is taken in this inclosure, is called the Kings Sikar or game, whether men or beasts. **1800** WELLINGTON *Let. to T. Munro* 2 Mar. in Gurwood *Disp.* (1834) I. 42 These [horsemen] divided into two or three small parties..would give a proper shekar; and I strongly advise you not to let the Marhatta boundary stop you in the pursuit of your game when you shall once have started it. **1872** 'ALIPH CHEEM' (Yeldham) *Lays of Ind* (1876) 181 They talked..Of divers local matters, acting, racing, and shikar. **1886** KIPLING *Departm. Ditties*, etc. *To Unknown Goddess* 2 A victim of crafty and cautious shikar. **1944** J. CORBETT *Man-Eaters of Kumaon* 186 Of all the men I have been on shikar with Ibbotson is by far and away the best. **1955** *Times* 14 May 10/5 His service in the Indian Army and his periods of leave, which were almost invariably spent on *shikar*, developed his eye for country and his taste for natural history.

**b.** *attrib.* and *Comb.*

**1872** E. BRADDON *Life India* v. 181 He is free to spend his days in the saddle or on the shikar ground. **1883** LD. SALTOUN *Scraps* II. 175 A pair of light cord or dungaree breeches, and long yellow sambur-skin boots, complete the shikar costume. *Ibid.* 241 Followed by my shikar-cart. **1896** MRS. B. M. CROKER *Village T.* 4 About a dozen shikar parties have been got up for his destruction. *Ibid.* 72 You may have the shikar camel.

**shikar** (ʃɪˈkɑː(r)), *v.* [f. prec.]

**a.** *intr.* To hunt animals for sport.

**1872** 'ALIPH CHEEM' (Yeldham) *Lays of Ind* (1876) 155 You may divert your mind with much shikarring. **1905** GLASFURD *Rifle in Ind. Jungle* 344 The more or less hilly country in which the writer has shikar'd.

**b.** *trans.* To hunt (an animal). Also *transf.*

**1882** FLOYER *Unexpl. Baluchistan* 58 My camel was very 'musty', and I involuntarily 'shikarred' three unfortunate individuals whom we met on the road, to their great terror. **1883** *Chamb. Jrnl.* 22 Dec. 808/2 A pretty green lizard used to come every forenoon, shikarring ants and other insects.

‖**shikara** (ʃiˈkaːraː). Also **shikarah, shikari.** [Hind.] A long, swift boat used in Kashmir. Also *attrib.*

**1875** F. DREW *Jummoo & Kashmir Territories* viii. 181 A *shikāri* is the sort of boat that is in daily use with the English visitors; a light boat, manned..by six men, it goes at a fast pace. **1893** E. F. KNIGHT *Where Three Empires Meet* iii. 35 Leaving our slow doongahs to follow us, we hailed some of the gondolas of Srinagur; long, swift canoes known as *shikarahs*, in which we reclined luxuriously on soft cushions. **1933** *Discovery* Nov. 348/2 A *shikara* or river taxi. **1964** V. S. NAIPAUL *Area of Darkness* iv. 103 Their *shikara* boats were a cluster of red and orange awnings and cushions; and in *shikaras* we were ferried over to the houseboats. **1981** S. RUSHDIE *Midnight's Children* I. 14 The thaw had come rapidly... Many of the small boats, the shikaras, had been caught napping. *Ibid.* 16 He floated past the shikara moorings.

**shikara**, var. SHIKHARA.

**shikaree**: see SHIKARI.

**shikari** (ʃiːˈkɑːriː). *Anglo-Ind.* Also **shecarrie, shikaree, shikkaree, -ie, shikarry, -i(e, shikari(e, shickaree, shekary, shekarree, -y.** [Urdū (from Pers.) *shikārī*, f. *shikār*: see SHIKAR *sb*] A hunter or sportsman. **a.** 'A native expert, who either brings in game on his own account, or accompanies European sportsmen as guide or aid' (Yule).

**1827** D. JOHNSON *Ind. Field Sports* 25 Shecarries are generally Hindoos of a low cast. **1832** MUNDY *Pen & Pencil Sk.* I. 119 We got information from some shikkaree (native hunters). **1867** A. L. ADAMS *Wand. Naturalist India* 233 My servants and shickaree were employed in stretching bear-skins. **1881** *Encycl. Brit.* XII. 741/1 Rewards are given by government to native *shikāris* for the heads of tigers. **1885** G. S. FORBES *Wild Life in Canara* 101 The shikari and I entered the jungle in pursuit. **1964** R. PERRY *World of Tiger* i. 8 Peacocks and tigers live together, say Indian shikaris, because the peacock is a thirsty bird and the tiger is a thirsty animal. **1971** *Illustr. Weekly India* 11 Apr. 45/1, I had become a keen shikari; there were few better areas than the country 80 miles round Delhi for small game. **1977** *New Yorker* 27 June 28/2 We're going to use you for bait, as a decoy. The way shikaris stake out a goat in India.

**b.** Applied to a European sportsman.

**1860** (*title*), The Spear and the Rifle; or, Rcollections of Sport in India. By an Old Shekarree [H. A. Leveson]. **1892** H. M. CHICHESTER in *Dict. Nat. Biog.* XXIX. 116/1 His [Jacob's] prowess as a shikarry is perpetuated in native verse. **1907** J. H. PATTERSON *Man-Eaters of Tsavo* App. I. 330 The whole country abounds in game, and there cannot be lack of sport and trophies for the keen shikari. **1936** W. H. SAUMAREZ SMITH *Let.* 21 Nov. in *Young Man's Country* (1977) ii. 43 When they find that I am neither a Blue, nor a brilliant horseman, nor an experienced shikari, nor a bridge-player, they may think twice about offering the appointment to me.

**c.** *attrib.* and *Comb.*

**1887** FIFE-COOKSON *Tiger Shooting* 17 A native merchant in Dehra had a good shikarie or hunting-elephant. **1900** *Absent-minded War* 168 There is a colour known to Indian sportsmen as shikarri mixture, a sort of greenish-grey, which is practically invisible in the jungle or when working among trees.

‖**shikasta** (ʃɪˈkæstə). Also †**shekest(h)eh, shikast, shikasteh,** etc. [Pers., lit. 'broken'.] A late cursive Persian script.

**1771** W. JONES *Gram. Persian Lang.* 15 As to the Shekesteh, it is very irregular and inelegant, and is chiefly used by the idle Indians, who will not take time to form their letters perfectly. **1849** F. MADDEN tr. *Silvestre's Universal Palæogr.* I. 52 For private affairs and official papers, the writing is generally careless and inelegant, destitute of its diacritical marks, and thence named *shekestheh*, or broken. **1889** SACHAU & ETHÉ *Catal. Persian Manuscripts in Bodl. Libr.* 186 Ff. 51–67 is partly written in Shikasta.., partly in Nastaʿlīk. **1901** KIPLING *Kim* xiv. 364 He..tore a leaf from a note-book, and..wrote in gross Shikast—the script that bad little boys use when they write dirt on walls. **1954** A. F. L. BEESTON *Catal. Additional Persian Manuscripts in Bodl. Libr.* 4/2 Ff. 604–5 are pieces of a letter in shikasta. **1966** HOSKING & MEREDITH-OWENS *Handbk. Asian Scripts* ii. 20 The last phase in Persian writing was the evolution of the *Shikasteh* (literally 'broken') script from Nastaʿlīk. **1970** G. UNWIN tr. *Jensen's Sign, Symbol & Script* xi. 331 For correspondence the Persians invariably employ the Sikästä script.

**shikepoke**, var. SHITEPOKE

**shiker**, var. SHICKER *a.* and *sb.*

‖**shikhara** (ˈʃɪkhərə). Also **shikara, śikhara, sikr(a).** [Skr. *śikhara*, point, peak, spire.] A pyramidal tower on a Hindu temple, sometimes having convexly curved sides.

**1829** J. TOD *Ann. & Antiquities Rajast'han* I. 670 The pinnacle or *sikra* rises, like the crown of the Hindú Cybele. **1838** *Penny Cycl.* XII. 238/1 The body of the temple, or sanctuary,.. over which rises a pyramidical *sikr*, or roof. **1891** J. FERGUSSON *Hist. Indian & Eastern Archit.* II. ii. 221 The towers or spires called Sikras.., which invariably surmount the cells in which the images are placed. **1927** A. COOMARASWAMY *Hist. Indian & Indonesian Art* III. 80 In more characteristic examples in the Ganges valley the *śikhara* and cella together form a tower. **1930** K. T. SHAH *Splendour that was 'Ind* viii. 151 Prof. Macdonell is of the view that the *Shikhara* is a natural evolution of the Buddhist Stupa. Later critics of India's art treasures are inclined, however, to hold that the *Shikhara*, with all the symbolism of which it was the concrete and complex expression, was introduced in India by the Vedic Aryans. **1959** HOOYKAAS & CHRISTIE tr. *Frederic's Indian Temples & Sculpture* 297 The temple itself has a *sikhara* of Khajuraho type. **1972** 'E. PETERS' *Death to Landlords* xi. 158 On the outermost platform of rock, its *shikhara* tapering into the air..stood the modern white memorial. **1974** *Daily Colonist* (Victoria, B.C.) 8 Sept. 13/6 But the most noteworthy aspect of the Khajuraho temple is the shikara, or spire. **1977** *Jrnl. R. Soc. Arts* CXXV. 579/1 In the larger temples the *śikhara* tends to be..surrounded by smaller subsidiary *śikharas*.

‖**shikho** (ˈʃɪkəʊ), *sb.* Also **shiko.** [Burmese *shi-hko.*] The posture of prostration with joined hands and bowed head assumed by a Burmese in presence of a superior, or before an object of reverence or worship.

**1886** YULE & BURNELL *Anglo-Ind. Gloss.* s.v., The envoy and his party sat on a carpet, but the attitude had no analogy whatever to that of *shikho.*

‖**shikho**, *v.* Also **shekho, shiko.** [f. prec.] *intr.* To assume the posture of 'shikho'.

**1858** YULE *Narr. Mission to Ava* iv. 82 They..dropt on their knees and *shikhoed* towards the palace. **1882** 'SHWAY YOE' *Burman* II. 206 Another ceremony is that of shekhoing to the spire, the external emblem of the throne. **1890** *Times* 21 Jan. 4/3 The Burmese merely shikoed, by placing their hands on their foreheads and bending forward.

**shikimi** (ʃɪˈkiːmiː). Also **skim(m)i.** [Jap.] A small evergreen tree, *Illicium anisatum*, the Japanese anise, belonging to the family Illiciaceæ, native to Japan and Korea, and bearing aromatic leaves and fragrant white or yellow flowers followed by star-shaped fruits; often associated with funeral rites. Also *attrib.*

**1727** J. G. SCHEUCHZER tr. *Kæmpfer's Hist. Japan* v. xv. 598 He had..a large tub of water standing by him..and some skimmi branches lying by it. **1881** *Jrnl. Chem. Soc.* XL. 918 To this substance.. the author [*sc.* J. F. Eijkman] gives the name of 'shikimine', from the Japanese name of the fruit 'shikimi'. **1889** J. J. REIN *Industries Japan* 136 The fruits of the Skimi, which is consecrated to Buddha and therefore much grown about Buddhist temples and cloisters, made a great stir some time ago. They came to market as a spice, instead of the Star anis, which they closely resemble, and turned out to be poisonous. **1896** L. HEARN *Kokoro* iii. 43 A vase containing *shikimi*—that sacred plant used in the Buddhist ceremony of making offerings to the dead. **1976** E. H. WALKER *Flora of Okinawa & Southern Ryukyu Islands* 472 Shikimi, a variant of *ashiki-mi*, bad (i.e. poisonous) fruits. In Buddhist ceremonies the leaves are burned as incense.

**shikimic** (ʃɪˈkɪmɪk), *a. Biochem.* [ad. F. *shikimique* (J. F. Eijkman 1885, in *Recueil des Travaux chim. des Pays-Bas* IV. 49), f. Jap. *shikimi* Japanese anise (from which it was first isolated): see prec., -IC.] ***shikimic acid***: a hydro-aromatic acid, $C_6H_6(OH)_3(COOH)$, which is formed in many bacteria and higher plants as an intermediate in the synthesis of phenylalanine, tyrosine, and other aromatic compounds from aliphatic precursors.

**1886** *Jrnl. Chem. Soc.* L. 95 Shikimic acid, $C_7H_{10}O_5$,..is a white, crystalline compound, insoluble in alcohol, ether, and chloroform, but readily soluble in water. **1953** FRUTON & SIMMONDS *Gen. Biochem.* xxxi. 742 It would appear..that at least four aromatic compounds can be formed from carbohydrate by mechanisms that involve shikimic acid as an intermediate. **1978** *Nature* 20 July 216/2 The exact nature of the bracken fern 'carcinogen' remains elusive and although various chemicals, such as shikimic acid, which have been extracted from bracken show some oncogenic activity, the major compound responsible has not yet been identified.

**shikkaree, -ie, -y,** variant forms of SHIKARI.

**shikker, -ur,** varr. SHICKER *a.* and *sb.*

**shikkered**, var. SHICKERED *a.*

‖**shikra** (ˈʃɪkrə). Also **shikrah.** [Urdū (from Pers.) *shikra.*] A small Indian hawk, *Astur badius*, sometimes used in falconry.

**1839** JERDON in *Madras Jrnl. Lit. & Sci.* X. 83 *Accipiter dukhunensis*, Sykes..*Chiquera* or *Shikra* H.; the male *chipka.*—Common sparrow-hawk. *Ibid.*, The Shikra is very commonly reclaimed. **1852** R. F. BURTON *Falconry Valley Indus* ii. 15 The Shikrah and her tiercel the Chipak are our common English sparrow-hawks. **1899** A. H. EVANS *Birds* iv. 157 *Astur badius*, the Shikra,..is blue-grey [etc.].

‖**shiksa** (ˈʃɪksə). Also **shicksa, shiksah, shikse(h).** [Yiddish *shikse*, ad. Heb. *šiqṣâ*, f. *šeqeṣ* a detested thing + *-â* fem. suff.] In Jewish speech, a gentile girl. Also *attrib.* or as *adj.* Cf. SHICKSTER.

**1892** I. ZANGWILL *Childr. Ghetto* I. I. vi. 158 We must keep a *Shiksah* to attend to the Shabbos fire. **1928** *Daily Express* 21 Feb. 9/2 There is a suggestion that he has fallen in love with a 'shiksa' (a Christian girl), played by May McAvoy, the 'Ben Hur' star. **1930** E. FERBER *Cimarron* xi. 183 His deep-sunk eyes looked at them. *Shicksas.* **1959** M. LEVIN *Eva* 11 How often as children had we..watched our *shikseh* maids at their prayers, or in moments of closeness with the *shiksehs*..fingered their crosses. **1963** M. McCARTHY *Group* xiv. 318 An Orthodox Jew can't marry a shiksah... They frown on exogamy. **1964** D. GRAY *Devil wore Scarlet* iii. 26 Daisy isn't Jewish, of course. She's a Shicksa. **1969** L. MICHAELS *Going Places* 87 Shikse blonde or purple eggplant, she was his wife. **1978** J. KRANTZ *Scruples* viii. 226 His mother, a lady of the old school, had repeatedly and solemnly warned him that there is a yellow-haired, blue-eyed shiksa lying in wait for every good Jewish boy. **1979** R. JAFFE *Class Reunion* II. iv. 156 She had heard stories that young doctors had affairs with shiksa nurses.

**shilajatu**, var. SILAJIT.

**shilala**, variant of SHILLELAGH.

†**ˈshilboard.** *Obs.* In 5 s(c)hilbord. [The first element is doubtful; cf. SHIELDBOARD.] Meaning uncertain: the conjecture in quot. 1837 seems unlikely, as a plural would be expected. Also in Comb. ***shilboard-clog.***

**1450–1** *Durham Acc. Rolls* (Surtees) 241 Rob. Sawer pro sarracione I shilbordclogge et aliarum bordarum pro molendino de Milneburne. **1476–7** in *Finchale Priory Acc.* (Surtees) p. cccxxxvij, Et sarratoribus pro le shilbord molendini de Coxhowe..xiij$^s$, iiij$^d$. **1477–8** *Ibid.* p. cccxl, Et sarratoribus pro le schilbord et in aliis necessariis x$^s$. [**1837** G. JACKSON *Ibid.* Gloss., Shilboards are the boards or external radii fixed to the rim of an undershot water wheel. **1901** *Durham Acc. Rolls* (Surtees) Gloss., *Shilbordclogge*... Perhaps a shilboard clog is a log of wood suitable for sawing up into shilboards.]

**shild(e,** obs. forms of SHIELD.

**shildre, shildur,** obs. forms of SHOULDER *sb.*

†**ˈshildy,** *a. Obs.* Forms: 1 scyldiȝ, 2 sceldiȝ, sculdiȝ, sculdi, 3 schuldi, (in comb.) -shildiȝ. [OE. *scyldiȝ* = OFris. *skeldech, -ich* (WFris. *skildich*, NFris. *skiljeg*), MDu. *sculdech* (Du. *schuldig*), OS. *skuldig* (MLG. *schuldich*), OHG. *skuldig, -ic* (MHG. *schuldic, -ig*, etc., G. *schuldig*), ON. *skyldug-r, skuldug-r* (Norw. *skuldug*, SW., Da. *skyldig*), f. OTeut. **skuldi-, skuldō* fem. debt, guilt, represented by OE. *scyld*, OS. *sculd*, Du. *schuld*, OHG. *sculd, sculda* (MHG. *schult, schulde*, mod.G. *schuld*), ON. *skuld*: f. root **skal-*: **skul-* to owe: see SHALL *v.*] Guilty.

*Beowulf* 1683 Morðres scyldiȝ. *c* **1000** ÆLFRIC in *Lamb. Hom.* 301 Se bið eall swa scyldiȝ [*c* **1175** *Lamb. Hom.* 113 sculdiȝ] se þe yfel ȝeþafað swa swa þe ðe hyt deð. [*c* **1200** ORMIN 18317 A mann Dæþshildiȝ unnderr sinne.] *a* **1225** *Ancr. R.* 206 Gulche hit ut ine schrifte, utterliche, ase heo hit dude, þeo þet iveleð hire schuldi. *a* **1225** *Leg. Kath.* 2296 þah þu beo schuldi þe ane of alle clane.

**shilela, -agh, -ah,** var. ff. SHILLELAGH.

**shilfa** (ˈʃɪlfə). *Sc.* Also 7 **shoulfall,** 9 **shelfa, shilfy,** etc. [Etymology unknown.] The chaffinch.

**1684** SIBBALD *Scotia Illustr.* II. II. 18 Fringilla, nostratibus *Snowfleck & Shoulfall.* **1792** in *Rutherfurd's Border Almanac 1878* 35 A shilfa's (or chaffinch) nest. **1884** W. C. SMITH *Kildrostan* 47 The shelfa's short bright note.

**Shilha** (ˈʃɪlhə). Also **Shilh, Shilhah, Shleuh, Shluh.** [Native name.] (A member of) a Berber people of southern Morocco; also, the language of this people. Also *attrib.* or as *adj.*

**1713** S. OCKLEY *Acct. S.W. Barbary* i. 28 It is about 30 days journey distant from Macquanes... They also differ from the other Moors in their language, and have a peculiar dialect to themselves, which they call *Shilhah.* **1841** G. BORROW *Zincali* I. I. vii. 113 The tribes who speak the Shilha language, and who are the descendants of the ancient Numidians. *Ibid.* 118 The sect of Sidi Hamed au Muza... Their language is the Shilhah, or a dialect thereof. *Ibid.* II. III. 117 The coast of Northern Africa, where only Arabic and Shilhah are spoken. **1882** [see KABYLE]. **1921** E. SAPIR *Language* 73 The Hamitic languages of Northern Africa, e.g. Shilh. **1951** W. BLUNT *Black Sunrise* iv. 42 The Berber-speaking inhabitants can be further subdivided into Berbers proper, Shluhs, etc. **1972** E. A. NIDA *Bk. Thousand Tongues* (ed. 2) 389/2 Shilha is a Berber language spoken in several dialects throughout southern Morocco. Most Shilha men are bi-lingual in Arabic and their mother tongue. **1973** A. ADAM in Gellner & Micaud *Arabs & Berbers* III. xvii. 325 *Tachelhit*, the language of the Shleuh, who inhabit the western High Atlas, the Anti-Atlas and the plains or valleys of southwestern Morocco. **1976** K. L. BROWN *People of Salé* III. viii. 153 Generally the term used in Salé for those speakers of Berber languages, whether they came from the Rif, Middle Atlas, High Atlas, Anti-Atlas or the valleys of southern Morocco, was Shluh.

**shill** (ʃɪl), *a.* and *adv. Obs.* exc. *dial.* Forms: 1 scyl, 3 sille, 3–5 schille, schulle, 4–5 shyl, shille, schyll(e, shylle, shulle, 4–6 schil(l, 5–6 shyll, shil, 4–7 shill. [ME. *schille* (2 syll.), app. repr. OE. **scielle*, a parallel form of **sciell* (late WS. *scyl*, occurring only once); corresp. to MHG. *schel, schelle* sonorous, quick in movement, luminous, early mod.Du. *schelle* (now *schel*) shrill, ON. *skjall-r* sonorous, resounding; f. OTeut. **skell-*: see SHILL *v.*[1]]

**A.** *adj.* Sonorous, resonant, shrill.

*a* **1000** *Riming Poem* 27 (Gr.) Scyl wæs hearpe, hlude hlynede. *c* **1220** *Bestiary* 572 Mirie ȝe singeð ðis mere, and haueð manie stefnes, manie and sille. *a* **1250** *Owl & Night.*

142 Heo song so lude & so scharpe, Ryht so me grulde schille harpe. *c* **1330** *Arth. & Merl.* 6069 A schille horn þai gun blawe. *c* **1386** CHAUCER *Nun Pr. T.* 575 Certes, he Iakke Straw, and his meynee Ne made neuere shoutes half so shille. **1486** *Bk. St. Albans* d iij, That thay [the hawk's bells] be sonowre and well sowndyng and shil. **1508** DUNBAR *Tua Mariit Wemen* 516 Berdis schoutit in schaw, with thair schill notis. **1597** MONTGOMERIE *Cherrie & Slae* 46 So schill in sorrowe was hir sang, That throwe hir voce the roches rang. **1598** MERES *Pallad. Tam.* 276 As our breath doth make a shiller sound being sent through the narrow channell of a Trumpet then if it be diffused abroad into the open aire. **1885** W. H. SMITH *Walks in Weardale* (ed. 2) 165 *Shill*, shrill. **1892** M. C. F. MORRIS *Yorks. Folk-Talk* 367 *Shill, Shilly* adj. This word is commonly applied to a high wind. .. Its meaning..is clearly 'noisy', 'shrill'.

**B.** *adv.* Sonorously, resonantly, shrilly.

*a* **1250** *Owl & Night.* 1656 Heo..song so schille & so brihte, þat fur & neor me hit i-herde. *a* **1300** *Leg. Gregory* 879 þe winde blewe schille and loude. **1393** LANGL. *P. Pl.* C. VII. 46 Prout of my faire fetours and for ich songe shulle. *a* **1400** *St. Alexius* (Laud 622) 561 þonder dyned shille. *c* **1440** *Promp. Parv.* 446/1 Schylle, and scharpe, *acute, aspere, sonore.* **1570** *Satir. Poems Reform.* xiv. 2 Ane ȝoung King I hard schoutand schill. **1670** NARBOROUGH *Jrnl.* in *Acc. Sev. Late Voy.* I. (1694) 64 The Men..speak ratling in the Throat, and gross; the Women shiller and lower. **1781** BURNS *My Nanie, O* ii, The westlin wind blaws loud an' shill.

Hence **'shilly** *adv.*, **'shillness.**

*a* **1400-50** *Wars Alex.* 929 þen schrikis schilli [*Dublin* shilly] all þe schalkis. **1486** *Bk. St. Albans* d iij, Thay [Dutch bells] be..sonowre of Ryngyng in shilnes. **1538** ELYOT *Dict.*, *Sonoritas*, a shyllenesse, or lowdenesse.

**shill,** *v.*[1] *Obs.* exc. *dial.* Forms: 1 scyllan, 3-4 schill(e, shille, 4 schull(e, 9 shill. [OE. *sciellan (late WS. *scyllan*), prob. a str. vb. = OHG. *scellan* to resound (MHG. *schellen*; mod.G. only in pa. pple. *verschollen* having ceased to resound, hence forgotten), ON. *skjalla* to rattle, f. OTeut. **skell-*(: *skall-*: *skull-*), whence OHG. *scella* fem. (mod.G. *schelle*) bell, OHG. *scal* masc. (mod.G. *schall*) loud sound; see also SHILL *a.*] *intr.* To resound; to sound loudly.

*c* **1000** in Wr.-Wülcker 215/15 *Crepitat, i. resonat*, scylþ, cyrmþ, ræscetteþ. *c* **1300** *K. Horn* (Laud MS.) 220 And þoruuth eche toune Horn him shilleþ soune. **13..** *Guy Warw.* 7286 He grad & ȝelled swiþe loude, þat it schilled into þe cloude. *c* **1380** *Sir Ferumb.* 631 Hure strokes fulle so styþ & sare þay schulde so doþ þe þonder. **1898** BLAKEBOROUGH *Wit, Char.*, etc. *N. Riding* 443 *Shill* v...3. [Of the wind] To make a noise something between a howl and a whistle.

Hence **'shilling** *ppl. a.*

*a* **1225** *St. Marher.* 19 'Cum', quoð þe culure wið schillinde stefne. **1387** TREVISA *Higden* (Rolls) VII. 331 He ..despisede þe smokynge and schillynge speche of mysbyleved men. *c* **1400** *Sege Jerus.* (E.E.T.S.) 528 A schillande schout.

**shill** (ʃɪl), *v.*[2] Now *dial.* Forms: 1 scylian, 4 schille, 5 schyllyn, 7 shel, 7-9 sheal, shill. [OE. *scylian*, **scielian*, ad. or cogn. w. ON. *skilja*, whence SKILL *v.*

App. distinct from *shill* v. to shell, husk: see SHEEL *v.*]

†**1.** *trans.* To separate. *Obs.*

**1049** *O.E. Chron.* (MS. C), On þyson ylcan ȝeare Eadwerd eing scylode .ix. scypa of male. *c* **1325** *Metr. Hom.* 152 Our king, That wic men fra god sal schille. *c* **1440** *Promp. Parv.* 446/1 Schyllyn owte, or cullyn owte fro sundyr, *segrego.* **1641** BEST *Farm. Bks.* (Surtees) 20 If there bee any sheepe that beginne to ragge..yow are to make the sheapheard shill them out. **1788** W. H. MARSHALL *Yorksh.* II. Gloss. s.v., To sever sheep is to shill them. **1790** GROSE *Prov. Gloss.* (ed. 2).

**2.** To curdle (milk). Also *intr.*, to become curdled.

**1691** RAY *N.C. Words* s.v., To *Sheal* Milk is to curdle it, to separate the parts of it. **1695** KENNETT *Par. Antiq.* Gloss. s.v. *Helowe-wall*, In the North to *shel* or *sheal* milk is to curdle it. **1788** W. H. MARSHALL *Yorksh.* II. Gloss. s.v., Turning a small quantity of milk into curds and whey is called shilling it. **1855** *Whitby Gloss.*, *To Sheal or Shill*, to sour milk for curds by the usual process. **1876** *Mid-Yorksh. Gloss.*, *Shill*, v.a. and v.n. to curdle; to scum.

**shill** (ʃɪl), *v.*[3] *slang* (chiefly *N. Amer.*). [f. SHILL *sb.*] **1.** *intr.* To act as a shill.

**1914** L. E. JACKSON *Vocab. Criminal Slang* 75 To 'shill' is to act in the capacity of a hired criminal. **1928** *Amer. Speech* III. 376 *Shill*, to boost for the auctioneer. **1948** F. BROWN *Dead Ringer* 156 She was going to shill on Walter's wheel. **1965** H. GOLD *Man who was not with It* xxv. 236 It's how to get the audience... I shilled for my wife. **1975** *Weekend Mag.* (Montreal) 11 Jan. 9 Canadian advertisers are confined mainly to hockey players when they're looking for an athlete to shill for them.

**2.** *trans.* To entice (a person) as a shill; to act as a shill for (a gambling game, etc.).

**1974** R. B. PARKER *God save Child* xxii. 150 Doctor Croft was the one who shilled old Fraser Robinson onto Vicki's scam. **1978** M. PUZO *Fools Die* x. 96 Diane, the blonde that shills baccarat.

**shill** (ʃɪl), *sb. slang* (chiefly *N. Amer.*). [Perh. abbrev. of SHILLABER.] A decoy or accomplice, esp. one posing as an enthusiastic or successful customer to encourage other buyers, gamblers, etc.

**1916** *Editor* 2 Dec. 518/2 *Shill, copper*:—One who leads the others by patronizing a show or game. **1926** *Amer. Mercury* Dec. 466/1 A wrestler..offered to throw anyone for 500 smacks and a couple of shills accepted his defy. **1935** H. DAVIS *Honey in Horn* xv. 231 She had often thought of renting him out as a shill for some tent-show evangelist. **1955** T. STERLING *Evil of Day* xxi. 208, I used to be a shill in a Reno gambling club. **1971** J. GRAY *Red Lights* vi. 136 The commonest trap was for a shill to haunt Ninth Avenue disguised as a farm hand. **1978** M. PUZO *Fools Die* ii. 19 As a shill she played with casino money... She was subject not to fate but to the fixed weekly salary she received from the casino.

**shill,** Sc. and north. variant of CHILL *a.*

**1599** A. HUME *Hymnes* ii. 108 The shill and freesing frosts. **1876** *Mid-Yorksh. Gloss.*, *Shill*, a weather term—sharply cold.

**shillaber** ('ʃɪləbə(r)). *slang* (chiefly *N. Amer.*). [Origin unknown.] = SHILL *sb.*

**1913** *Collier's* 6 Dec. 29/2 The business men turned out to be 'shillabers', if you know what 'shillabers' are. **1924** G. BRONSON-HOWARD *Devil's Chaplain* vii. 111 One time 'ballyhoo' and 'shillaber', proprietor of 'Chief Bigspoon's..' medicine show. **1940** *Amer. Speech* XV. 122/1 *Shill* or *shillaber*, an accomplice who plays a confidence game so that the *mark* sees him win.

**shillat,** variant of SHILLET.

**shillelagh** (ʃɪ'leɪlə, -'leɪlɪ). Forms: (7 Shelela), 8 shelaly, shillaley, 8-9 shillela, 6 shilala, shillala(h, shilela(h, -elagh, shillely, -aly, shillealah, 8-shillelah, 9- shillelagh. [The name of a barony and village in Co. Wicklow.] An Irish cudgel of blackthorn or oak.

[**1677** YARRANTON *Eng. Improv.* 39 The River Slane.. with that noble great and good Wood called Shelela. **1773** *Batchelor* No. 27 (ed. 2) 183 Shillela's knotted cudgels fail.] **1772** *Town & Country Mag.* 36 'By Jes-s, and that's mine!' exclaim'd I, grasping my shelaly. **1785** GROSE *Dict. Vulgar T.*, *Shillaley*, an oaken sapling, or cudgel, (Irish) from a wood of that name famous for its oaks. *c* **1800** ? LYSAGHT *Song*, '*The Sprig of Shillelah*', With his sprig of Shillelah and shamrock so green! **1827** SIR J. BARRINGTON *Pers. Sketches* I. 74 He bore a shillelagh, the growth of his own estate. **1834** LOVER *Leg. & Stor. Irel.* Ser. II. 297 He bowlted into the cabin wid a murtherin' shillely in his fist. **1862** BORROW *Wales* II. ix. 91 His hat in one hand and his shillealah in the other.

**'shillet.** *s.w. dial.* Also shillot, -at, shillett, shellet, -at, shilt. [Perh. f. SHEEL *v.*; the word may go back to an OE. **scielet*.] = SHALE *sb.*[2] Also *attrib.*

**1777** in *Eng. Dial. Dict.*, Shellet. **1813** VANCOUVER *Agric. Devon* 11 Here the soil is of a good depth upon the shillot. **1841** *Civil Eng. & Arch. Jrnl.* IV. 359/2 The earthy slates.. were interspersed with blue shillat slates. **1859** MURCHISON *Siluria* xiii. (ed. 3) 344 The shillat of Cornwall. **1875** WHYTE MELVILLE *Katerfelto* xxiii, Shilt and shingle glitter on the bare tops above. **1886** *W. Somerset Word-bk.*, *Shillet*,..the disintegrated top layer of the Devonian clay slate so common in West Somerset and North Devon. **1892** H. HUTCHINSON *Fairway Isl.* 20 He..gathered from the road a handful of loose shillett.

Hence **'shillety** *a.* (also *shillotty*, *shellety*, etc.), consisting of shillet.

**1813** VANCOUVER *Agric. Devon* 24 A tender loam of a dark grey cast on a shillotty understratum. **1830** JAS. SAVAGE *Hist. Carhampton* 209 The soil is..a white rag, or as it is here called, a *shellety* soil. **1887** J. W. FORTESCUE *Stag-hunting Exmoor* 181 Our hind has taken advantage of the shillety ground to double about a good deal.

**shillibeer** ('ʃɪlɪbɪə(r)). Also shellibire, -beere. [Named after George *Shillibeer*, coach-proprietor (1797-1866).] **a.** A name given to the omnibus for some time after its introduction into London by Shillibeer in 1829. **b.** A vehicle containing a mourning-carriage and hearse combined, patented by Shillibeer.

*c* **1835** *Song* in *Ludgate* (1897) Feb. 445 You can come to no harm in the safe Shillibeer. **1865** *Chamb. Encycl.* VII. 72/2 (s.v. *Omnibus*) Shillibeer's conveyances, which for some time afterwards were known as *shillibeers* (an epithet still in common use in New York), were of larger size than the French ones, carrying 22 passengers inside, and were drawn by three horses abreast. **1894** *Hereford Times* 28 July 5/3 Washington Cars and Shelliberes for Undertakers.

**shilling** ('ʃɪlɪŋ). Forms: 1 scilling, scylling, (-ingc), 3 ssillinge, 3-6 schillinge, 4 ssyllyng, 4-5 schillyng(e, schelyng(e, shulleng(e, schullyng(e, 4-6 schiling, shill-, shyllyng(e, -inge, silling, 4-7 schilling, 5 schyllynge, shylynge, schilenge, silyn, 5-6 sheling, -yng(e, shellyng(e, 6 scheling(e, schillengge, shealinge, shyllyn, syllyng, 4- shilling. [Common Teut.: OE. *scilling* masc. = OFris. *skilling, skilleng, schilling*, MDu. *schellingh* (Du. *schelling*), OS. *scilling* (MLG. *schillink, schildink*, mod.LG. *schillink, schilling*), OHG. *scilling, skillink, schilling* (MHG., G. *schilling*), ON. *skilling-r* (Icel. also *skildingr*, SW., Da. *skilling*), Goth. *skilliggs*:—OTeut. **skillingo-z*. Adopted in OSlav. as *skŭlęzĭ*, in Sp., Pr., Fr. as *escalin* (13th c. F. *eskallin*, mod.F. also *schelling*), It. *scellino*.

The Teut. word is referred by some etymologists to the root **skel-* to resound, ring (see SHILL *a.* and *v.*[1]). Others assign it to the root **skel-* to divide (whence SKILL *v.*, SHALE *sb.*, SHELL *sb.*, etc.); some have conjectured that the word originally denoted one of the segments of fixed weight into which an armlet of gold or silver was divided, so that they might be detached for use as money. In the bilingual documents of the 6th century, Goth. *skilliggs* corresponds to the L. SOLIDUS; in mediæval Germany the Teut. and the Latin word were commonly used to render each other, but in England the correspondence appears to have been only occasionally recognized until Norman times.

The value of the 'shilling' in continental Teut. countries has varied greatly; its relation to the penny and the pound has also varied, though a widely accepted scale was 1 pound or *libra* = 20 shillings or *solidi* = 240 pennies or *denarii*. See SCHELLING, SCHILLING[1], SKILLING[2].]

**1. a.** A former English money of account, from the Norman Conquest of the value of 12d. or $\frac{1}{20}$ of a pound sterling. Abbreviated s. (= L. *solidus*: see SOLIDUS[1]), formerly also sh., shil.; otherwise denoted by the sign /- after the numeral. No longer in official use after the introduction of decimal coinage in 1971, but still occas. used to denote five new pence.

Before the Norman Conquest the value of the shilling varied in different times and places. It was 5 pence in Wessex and 4 pence in Mercia; the shilling of 12 pence mentioned in two passages *c* 1000 may refer to the continental *solidus.*

*c* **900** *Laws of Ine* §2 (Liebermann) 90 Cild binnan ðritegum nihta sie ȝefulwad. Ȝif hit swa ne sie, xxx scill. ȝebete. *c* **1000** ÆLFRIC *Gram.* l. (Z.) 296 Fif peneȝas ȝemaciað ænne scylling. **1297** R. GLOUC. (Rolls) 7870 To eche chirche of þe lond vif ssillinges me ber. **1377** LANGL. *P. Pl.* B. XII. 146 If any frere were founde þere Ich ȝif þe fyue shillynges. *c* **1440** *Gesta Rom.* xi. 34 That euery man þat were blinde, shuld haue an C[s]. *c* **1483** CAXTON *Dialogues* 3/8 For to lerne rekene By poundes, by shelynges, by pens. **1556** in W. Kelly *Notices Illustr. Drama* (1865) 194 For ix yards of Clothe at fure shyllyns the yarde for the Weyts gownes xxxvj[s]. **1613** TAPP *Pathw. Knowl.* 21 Then 3. shillings from 20. shil. leaues 17. shillings. **1663** PEPYS *Diary* 27 May, Afterwards to ninepins, where I won a shilling. **1856** *Jrnl. Soc. Arts* IV. 361/1 This would be all very well were he to get a shilling's worth for a shilling. **1881** CROWEST *Phases Mus. Eng.* 148 One tradesman could well afford to sell at one penny or so less in the shilling.

**b.** In Scotland, Ireland, America, etc. Also used as a unit of currency (representing variously 12 pence and 100 cents) in other countries, as Kenya, Uganda, Malta, etc.; *freq.* preceded by the name of the issuing country; also, the coin itself.

Through gradual debasement of the coinage the shilling Scots, by the 17th c., was worth only 1d. English.

**1462** *Cal. Anc. Rec. Dublin* (1889) 313 They to les a honderyt schelynges. **1488-91** *Acc. Ld. High Treas. Scot.* I. 167 Hary nobillis gevin for thretty tua schillingis the pece. **1543** *Cal. Anc. Rec. Dublin* (1889) 413 To the Kepere of the Tolsell cloke of Dublin [thirty] five sillings. **1550** *Registr. Aberdon.* (Maitland Club) I. 450 Payand heirfor ȝeirlie allevin schelingis aucht penneis. **1712** *Mus. Thoresby.* (1713) 389 The Proportion betwixt the English and Scotch Pennies, Shillings and Pounds, was then (10 Eliz.) just as one to six, but before he [James I] came into England, it was just doubled; so that the English Penny was exactly the Scotch Shilling, our Twentypence their Pound. **1891** *Century Dict.* s.v., Reckoning by the shilling is still not uncommon in some parts of the United States, especially in rural New England. **1921** W. S. CHURCHILL in *Hansard Commons* 30 May 596 As recommended by the Currency Committee appointed in Kenya in February, 1921, the standard coin will be, not a florin, but a shilling... Rupee contracts..will be construed at the rate of two shillings to one rupee. **1927** W. McG. ROSS *Kenya from Within* xii. 208 The new scheme..was that both florin and rupee should disappear, the shilling be introduced and all existing cental coins be degraded, by edict, to half their value. **1969** *Times* 16 Sept. (Somali Republic Suppl.) p. v/3 The internal value of the Somali shilling has..been relatively stable. **1977** *Times* 24 June 14/8 On the free market in Kenya..100 Uganda shillings usually bring no more than 20 Kenya shillings.

**c.** *a shilling great, a shilling of groats*: see GREAT *a.* 8 e, GROAT 1.

**1593** in *Extracts Rec. Convent. Burghs Scot.* (1870) I. 408 Tuentie schillingis greitt ilk barrell beir.

**d.** unchanged in plural. (Now *vulgar.*)

*a* **1300** *Floriz & Bl.* 126 (Camb. MS.) And for his niȝtes gestinge He ȝaf his oste an hundred schillinge. *c* **1325** *Metr. Hom.* 141 The beggar..sald this corn igain him to, And toc thar for fif schilling. **14..** *Emare* 524 She ȝaf hym for þat tydynge A robe and fowrty shylynge. **1521-2** *Stirling Burgh Rec.* (1887) I. 15 To gife four schilling yeirly..to the dekin of the maltmen. **1752** J. LOUTHIAN *Form of Process* (ed. 2) 263 Item, for each Mile..there shall be paid to him a further Sum of six Shilling.

**e.** Used in emphatic or rhetorical statements, where one wishes to be understood as deliberately reckoning or accounting for every item, however small, of a given sum or expense.

**1737** *Gentl. Mag.* VII. 657/1 This exclusive Privilege cannot be taken from either of them, till every Shilling due to them by the Publick be paid off. **1782** MISS BURNEY *Cecilia* IV. i, He protested..he would pay away every shilling he was worth, rather than witness such injustice. **1815** WELLINGTON in Gurw. *Disp.* (1838) XII. 453, I will not engage to pay one shilling more than the expenses really incurred by Hanover. **1865** TROLLOPE *Belton Est.* i. 9 Every shilling spent in the house did its full twelve pennies' worth of work.

**2. a.** A silver (subsequently cupro-nickel) coin of the value of 12 pence. First issued by Henry VII, in 1503. No longer in official use after the introduction of decimal coinage in 1971, but still occas. used to denote the five-pence piece.

The coin itself was allowed to circulate for some time after decimalization, alongside the new (and equivalent) five-pence piece, which it resembled in shape, size, weight, and composition.

*a* **1513** FABYAN *Chron.* VII. (1533) 233 In the forenamed parlyament [of 1504] was ordeyned a new coyne of syluer, as grotes, half grotes, & shyllynges with half faces. **1549** LATIMER *1st Serm. bef. Edw. VI* (Arb.) 35 We haue nowe a prety litle shilling, in dede a very pretye one. **1639** O. WOOD *Alph. Bk. Secrets* 39 Take so much of this as will lie on a shilling in Anniseed-water fasting. **1678** BUTLER *Hud.* III. i. 688 Still Amorous, and fond, and Billing, Like Philip and Mary on a Shilling. **1799** *Med. Jrnl.* I. 144 One quarter of a grain was sufficient to produce a good blister as large as a shilling. **1857** HUGHES *Tom Brown* I. ii, Two new shillings in his breeches-pockets. **1974** 'J. LE CARRÉ' *Tinker, Tailor, Soldier, Spy* i. 18 Spikely discovered..a draft of the next day's examination paper, and rented it to candidates at five new pence a time. Several boys paid their shilling.

**b.** With defining word indicating a particular coinage.

**1699** NICOLSON *Eng. Hist. Libr.* III. 313 Elizabeth..caus'd indeed some Irish Shillings (call'd Harpers..) to be made of a baser kind than the English, so that they usually pass'd for Ninepence here. **1712** *Mus. Thoresby.* (1713) 365 The Portcluse Shilling [see PORTCULLIS *sb.* 3 b]. **1715** S. SEWALL *Diary* 12 Sept. (1882) III. 56 Gave Mr. Short's daughter a New-England Shilling. **1764** *Mus. Thoresby.* 13 [Lot] 201. Lord Baltimore's Shilling (a Proof Six-pence in Copper) and 3 New England Shillings. **1860** BARTLETT *Dict. Amer.* (ed. 3), *Shilling*, the name given in the State of New York, to the Spanish real; in the neighbouring States it is frequently called a York shilling.

**c.** ***half-shilling, quarter-shilling***, Tudor coins of the value of 6d. and 3d. respectively.

**1561** *Procl. Base Moneys* 15 Nov., There shalbe immediatly coyned in fine sterlyng moneys, halfe shyllynges of six pence, quarter shyllynges of three pence the peece, and a halfe peece thereof called three halfpence. **1695** LOWNDES *Ess. Amend. Silver Coins* 50 Half-shillings, Groats, Quarter-Shillings, Half-Groats.

**d.** ***little shilling***, Cobbett's name for a proposed silver shilling of considerably reduced intrinsic value. Hence used by Macaulay in reference to a similar proposal in 1695.

**1826** COBBETT *Weekly Reg.* 7 Oct. 94/2 This city [Worcester], or this neighbourhood, at least, being the birthplace of what I have called, the 'Little-Shilling Project', and Messrs. Atwood and Spooner being the originators of the project. **1855** MACAULAY *Hist. Eng.* xxi. IV. 640 Montague, after defeating..those who were for the little shilling.

†**3. a.** Used, after L. *solidus*, as a denomination of weight = $\frac{1}{20}$ of a pound. (Cf. SOLID *sb.*[2]) **b.** *Sc.* The weight of twelve silver pennies. *Obs.*

*c* **1000** *Sax. Leechd.* I. 240 Ѣenim of ðysse wyrte petroseline swyþe smæl dust, anes scillinges ȝewihte. *a* **1400** in *Sc. Acts Parl.* (1844) I. 673 Þe pund in King Dauidis dayis weyit xxv. schillingis. Now þe pund aw to wey in siluer xxvi schillingis and iij sterling penijs. **1543** tr. *Stat. Bread & Ale* 51 *Hen. III*, §1 When a quarter of wheate is solde for .xii.d. then wastell bread of a ferthynge shall way .vi. li. and .xvi. s. [orig. *sex libras et sexdecim solidos*]. **1596** *Recorde's Ground of Arts* 319 Therefore here by a shilling you must vnderstand $\frac{1}{20}$ of a pound weight.

†**4.** Used to render or represent the names of various foreign moneys. *Obs.*

***double shilling***, a Dutch florin or guilder.

*c* **950** *Lindisf. Gosp.* Matt. xxvi. 15 Ða ȝesetton him ðrittih scillinga [Vulg. *triginta argenteos*]. *Ibid.* Luke xv. 9 Forðon ic fand þæt scilling [Vulg. *dragmam*] ðæt ic forleas. *c* **1000** ÆLFRIC *Exod.* xxi. 32 Selle þam hlaforde þritiȝ scillinga seolfres [Vulg. *triginta siclos argenti domino dabit*]. *c* **1050** in Wr.-Wülcker 460/17 *Obelus*, scilling. *c* **1050** *Suppl. Ælfric's Gloss.* ibid. 183/21 *Numisma*, scylling. *a* **1225** *Ancr. R.* 398 Two hundred sicles [*v.r.* schillinges] of seolure. *a* **1300** *Cursor M.* 6722 Thritti schiling o siluer again Sal man giue þe lord to mend [Exod. xxi. 32]. **1744** M. BISHOP *Life & Adv.* 140 Each [of the officers] gave me a double Shilling. **1753** [see SCHILLING[1]]. **1776** ADAM SMITH *W.N.* I. iv. I. 32 The French sou or shilling appears upon different occasions to have contained five, twelve, twenty, forty, and forty-eight pennies.

**5. a.** In various proverbial expressions (see quots.).

**1546** J. HEYWOOD *Prov.* II. v. (1867) 54 He maketh his marts with marchantis likely, To bryng a shillyng to .ix. pens quickely. [Cf. NOBLE *sb.*[1] 2 b.] **1677** W. HUGHES *Man of Sin* I. vii. 32 Thus the Cardinal only changeth the Popes shilling into Twelve-pence. **1824** SCOTT *Redgauntlet* ch. x, He will come back again, like the ill shilling—he is not the sort of gear that tynes. **1826** —— *Woodstock* x, Hark ye, good fellow,..I will bestow on thee a shilling wet and a shilling dry if thou wilt go back with me.

**b.** ***to cut off with a shilling***: see CUT *v.* 56 i.

**1700** FARQUHAR *Constant Couple* IV. iii. 43 When I die, I'll leave him the Fee-Simple of a Rope and a Shilling.

**1762** COLMAN *Mus. Lady* II. 27 I'll disinherit him—I won't leave him a groat—I'll cut him off with a shilling.

**c.** ***to take the shilling, the King's*** or ***Queen's shilling***: to enlist as a soldier by accepting a shilling from a recruiting officer (a practice now disused).

**1707** HEARNE *Collect.* 27 Mar. (O.H.S.) II. 2 He did take a shilling, but not with any intent of listing. **1852** THACKERAY *Esmond* III. v, One fellow was jilted by his mistress, and took the shilling in despair. **1886** FARJEON *Three Times Tried* I, I took the Queen's shilling, and became a soldier. **1901** *Scotsman* 4 Mar. 8/1 A contingent of Volunteer Engineers was sworn in for service in South Africa. Each man was presented..with the King's shilling.

†**d.** (See quot.) *Obs.*

**1802** JAMES *Milit. Dict.*, The *Shillings.* A phrase in familiar use among army brokers, to express a certain profit or per centage which they gain in the sale, purchase, and exchange of commissions.

**6.** *attrib.*, with the sense 'of the price or value of a shilling', 'for which a shilling is charged or is due', as ***shilling gallery, ordinary, places, points*** (in a game, hence ***shilling whist***, etc.), ***seats***; (sense 1 b) ***shilling bill***; **shilling dreadful** or **shocker**, a short sensational novel, published at a shilling; **shilling mark** *Typogr.* = SOLIDUS[1] 2.

**1976** K. THACKERAY *Crownbird* viii. 161 Priest..tucked some hundred *shilling bills into his pocket. **1885** *Athenæum* 14 Nov. 638/1 Mr. R. L. Stevenson is writing another '*shilling dreadful'. **1801** *Monthly Mirror* June 421 He grins and looks broad nonsense with a stare, to the vast delight of the *shilling gallery. **1824** SCOTT *Redgauntlet* Let. iii, I heard my varlet of a guide as loud with his blackguard jokes in the kitchen, as a footman in the shilling gallery. **1888** C. T. JACOBI *Printers' Vocabulary* 123 **Shilling mark*, the sign thus / which was used in old books as a 'scratch comma'. **1904** MURRAY & BRADLEY *Hart's Rules for Compositors* (ed. 15) 29 The diagonal sign / or 'shilling-mark'. **1780** *Mirror* No. 91 Their former dinners with him at a *shilling ordinary. **1857** A. MAYHEW *Paved with Gold* III. xi, The *shilling places were packed in half an hour. **1854** GUNNING *Remin. Camb.* I. 22 We played *shilling points, and occasionally half-a-crown was betted on the rubber. **1886** *Pall Mall Gaz.* 20 July 6/2 Given plenty of sensational incident and a certain coherency of plot, and you have all that is necessary to make a '*shilling shocker'. **1893** VIZETELLY *Glances back* I. v. 117 No shilling shockers..to amuse us..during our uncomfortable journey. **1760** MURPHY *Way to keep Him* I. (end), Nobody plays *shilling-whist now.

**7.** With prefixed numerals, forming adjectives of price or value. Also in phrases denoting rate of payment (as 'a shilling an hour'), used *attrib.*

In the attributive use the 's' of the plural is regularly dropped; for a contrary instance see quot. 1683.

*a* **1578** LINDESAY (Pitscottie) *Chron. Scot.* (S.T.S.) II. 198 The xxx schiling peice. **1653** *Ordin. Contin. Excise* 17 Mar. 107 For every Barrel of six shilling Beer or Ale. **1683** TRYON *Way to Health* xiii. 340 Let your Drink at Meals be no stronger than nine shillings Beer. **1695** CONGREVE *Love for L.* II. i, A fellow that has but a groat in his pocket, may have a stomach capable of a ten-shilling ordinary. **1828** SCOTT *F.M. Perth, Chron. Canong.* Introd., Prepared and sold..in five shilling and ten shilling bottles. **1853** *Punch* XXIV. 129/1 It did one good to hear him wither a 'super': his manner of rolling his words at the poor trembling shilling-a-night wretch. **1866** E. YATES *Land at Last* I. x. 192 A model..one of the usual shilling-an-hour victims.

**shillingless** ('ʃɪlɪŋlɪs), *a.* [-LESS.] Not having a shilling; being without (even) a shilling.

**1797** COLERIDGE *Lett. to Estlin* 41 (*Philobiblon Soc. Misc.* XV), At present I am almost shillingless. **1855** HAWTHORNE *Eng. Note-bks.* (1870) I. 342 He told us that the bill was not yet due... As I was almost shillingless, Mr. —— now offered to cash it for me.

**shillingsworth** ('ʃɪlɪŋzwəθ). Formerly **shillingworth.** [WORTH *sb.* The form *shillingworth* (cf. *pennyworth*) is now rare. In the current form the *s* is the sign of the possessive (whether sing. or pl.).] An amount or quantity which is or may be bought for a shilling; as much as is worth a shilling or a (specified) number of shillings.

*a* **1325** *MS. Rawl. B.* 520 lf. 31 b, Þat non ne sal ben i don ..in to ani Iurees þat hath lasse þan a Hundred silling-worth of londe. **14..** *Voc.* in Wr.-Wülcker 612/37 *Solidatus*, a shyllyngworth. *c* **1450** *Godstow Reg.* 87/26, iiij. shillyngworth of Cakys [*quattuor solidatas artocoporum*]. *Ibid.* 158, ij shelynge worthe of rent..yerly to be payde att whytsontyde. **1473–4** *Acc. Ld. High Treas. Scot.* I. 2 Item componit..for the resignacione of a hundreth schilling worth of land callit the Stanly. **1675** TRAHERNE *Chr. Ethics* 528 For a shilling-worth of service a shilling-worth of gratitude is naturally paid. **1857** W. SMITH *Thorndale* IV. ii. 267 My Silver Shilling represents..all possible shillingworths of everything on earth.

**1840** COL. HAWKER *Diary* (1893) II. 175 A few shillingsworth of damage to gear, etc. **1905** *Athenæum* 8 Apr. 432/3 'School-room Humour'..is a capital shillingsworth.

**shilloo** (ʃɪ'luː). *Anglo-Irish.* A loud shouting or outcry. Hence **shi'llooing** *vbl. sb.*

**1842** LOVER *Handy Andy* ix, 'What are you shouting there for?' said the traveller; 'cawn't you wing'. 'Oh, they understand the *shilloo* as well, sir'. *Ibid.* xxxvi, There was a regular shilloo in the house when the thing was found out. **1845** MRS. S. C. HALL *Whiteboy* xi. 91 They'll keep such a shillooing through the country about it.

**shillot**, variant of SHILLET.

**Shilluk** (ʃɪ'luːk). Also †**Chillouk**, †**Shelluh**, †**Shelook**, **Shillook**. [Native name.] The name of a Sudanese people dwelling mainly on the west bank of the Nile: a member of this people; also the Nilotic language of this people. Also *attrib.* or as *adj.*

**1790** J. BRUCE *Travels to discover Source of Nile* IV. VIII. ix. 458 This race of negroes is, in their own country, called Shillook. They founded Sennaar. **1799** W. G. BROWNE *Travels in Africa, Egypt, & Syria* App. II. 453 Shillûk is a town of idolaters... The name *Shillûk* is not Arabic, and its meaning is unknown.—When asked concerning their name or country, the people reply *Shillûk.* **1832** W. M. LEAKE in *Jrnl. R. Geogr. Soc.* II. 26 On the twelfth day they reached the first island of the Shillúks. **1835** *Jrnl. R. Geogr. Soc.* V. 42 Twelve hours farther brought them to the first island of the Shelooks. **1840** *Penny Cycl.* XVI. 232/1 The first island of the Shilluks..is not far from Aleis. **1873** E. E. FREWER tr. *Schweinfurth's Hrt. Africa* I. 261 The jet-black Shillooks, Nueir, and Dinka, native of the dark alluvial flats, stand out in marked distinction to the dwellers upon the iron-red rocks. **1894** [see NUER]. **1913** *Rep. Brit. Assoc.* 633 Dr. Seligmann's discoveries among the Shilluks of the Nile Valley. **1921** E. SAPIR *Language* 80 *Shilluk*, one of the languages of the headwaters of the Nile. **1927** *World Domin.* Oct. 319 All travellers note the Shilluk style of hairdressing. **1927** *Times* (Weekly ed.) 29 Dec. 30/1 Across on the east bank you will see the Shilluk. **1949** [see NUBA]. **1964** E. A. NIDA *Toward Sci. Transl.* iii. 51 Shilluk uses 'break' only with objects such as wood. **1973** *Times* 27 Mar. (Sudan Suppl.) p. viii/3 (*caption*) A Shilluk tribesman with a traditional musical instrument in the Southern Sudan. **1976** D. TOPOLSKI *Muzungu* iv. 56 The Shilluk repeat the cutting process from quite an early age.

**shilly** ('ʃɪlɪ). *north.* Also **shillow, shilla, shelly, shulla**, etc. [? Connected with SHILLET.

Manx has *shillee* 'a mass or assemblage of thin slate, or bits of thin stone' (Cregean), 'a gravelly beach' (Kelly); but the word may be an importation from dialectal English.]

Gravel, shingle; (with *pl.*) a pebble, small stone.

**1675** in Picton *L'pool Munic. Rec.* (1883) I. 307 Every shipp which shall discharge any shilly or stone ballast southwards of the shilly path in this river shall forfeit ten shillings. **1837** THORNBER *Hist. Blackpool* 246 A beach of 'shingle or shulla', the principal portion of which falls from the cliffs. **1869** *Lonsdale Gloss.*, *Shilla*, the loose stones on the sea-beach, the stony sea-beach. **1873** T. E. BROWN *Betsy Lee* 24 A stream ran..down the glen, And soaked through the shilly, and out to the bay. **1878** *Cumberld. Gloss.*, *Shillies, Shilla, Shellies*, shore-gravel. **1901** THEODORA W. WILSON *T'Bacca Queen* xxviii. 261 She turned from the lamp-lighted road on to the wide strand of shillow.

**shilly-shally** ('ʃɪlɪˌʃælɪ), *adv. phr., a., sb.* [At first written *shill I, shall I*, altered form of *shall I, shall I*: see SHALL *v.* B. 7 a (*d*). For the vowel-alteration cf. *dilly-dally, wishy-washy.*]

**A.** *adv. phr.* ***to stand shill I, shall I***: to vacillate, to be irresolute or undecided. Also ***to go shill-I shall-I, to stand at shilly-shally.***

**1700** CONGREVE *Way of World* III. xv. 47, I don't stand shill I, shall I, then; if I say't, I'll do't. **1703** STEELE *Tender Husb.* III. (1705) 34 I'm for marrying her at once— Why should I stand shilly-shally, like a Country Bumpkin? **1709** W. KING *Eagle & Robin* 92 Bob did not shill-I shall-I go, Nor said one word of friend or foe; But flirting at him made a blow. **1823** DE QUINCEY *Fatal Marksman* Wks. 1859 XII. 199, I see no good that comes of standing shilly-shally. **1847** LYTTON *Lucretia* II. ii, Don't stand there shilly-shally. **1873** BROWNING *Red Cott. Nt.-cap* 232 The simpleton who stands ..At shilly-shally, may he knock or no At his own door.

**B.** *adj.* Vacillating, irresolute, undecided.

**1734** CHESTERF. in *Lett. C'tess Suffolk* (1824) II. 95 We were mighty prudent and shilly shally whether to stay or go. **1743** MRS. DELANY *Autobiog. & Corr.* (1861) II. 208, I am shilly-shally about it in my own mind. **1792** JEFFERSON *Writ.* (1830) IV. 470, I had heard him say that this constitution was a shilly-shally thing, of mere milk and water, which would not last. **1869** TROLLOPE *He knew*, etc. lxv. (1878) 363 I'm not going to be stopped by any shilly-shally nonsense. **1886** GOSCHEN in A. D. Elliot *Life* (1911) II. 9 If Gladstone is very shilly shally about the Legislative Union.

**C.** *sb.* **1.** Vacillation, irresolution.

**1755** J. SHEBBEARE *Lydia* (1769) I. 355 Mr. Muckworm.. conceived marriages should be driven like bargains without shilly shally. **1847** DE QUINCEY *Sp. Mil. Nun* v. Wks. 1854 III. 10 She lost not one of her forty-five minutes in picking and choosing. No shilly-shally in Kate. **1876** GEO. ELIOT *Dan. Der.* III. xxv. 212 What I wished to point out to you was, that there can be no shilly-shally now.

**2.** A vacillating, irresolute person. *rare.*

**1834** LANDOR *Exam. Shakesp.* Wks. 1853 II. 271/1 Among the girls in the country there are many such shilly-shallys, who give themselves sore eyes and sharp eye-water. **1883** SAINTSBURY *Dryden's Wks.* VI. 401 The queen [in *The Spanish Friar*] being both bloodthirsty and inconsequent, and Torrismond a vacillating shilly-shally.

**'shilly-ˌshally**, *v.* [f. prec. adv. phr.]

**1.** *intr.* To vacillate, be irresolute or undecided.

**1782** MISS BURNEY *Cecilia* IX. iii, So I suppose he'll shilly-shally till somebody else will cry snap, and take her. **1842** THACKERAY *Miss Tickletoby's Lect.* ix, This Bruce had been for a long time shilly-shallying as to the side he should take. **1879** FARRAR *St. Paul* I. 441 To shilly-shally on the matter, to act in one way today and in a different way tomorrow.

**2.** *trans.* To show indecision in one's dealings with. ? *nonce-use.*

**1864** BP. WILBERFORCE in R. G. Wilberforce *Life* (1882) III. 152 If you go mystifying and shillyshallying them [*sc.* nonconformists].

¶ Occas. analysed into two verbs, 'shilly' and 'shally': see quots.

**1836** T. HOOK *G. Gurney* II. 203 It would be all idleness to go on shillying-shallying with her. **1891** *Daily News* 3 June 2/2 Sir William made the statement..that L. had shillied and shallied, and had then said 'I saw something'.

Hence **'shilly-ˌshallying** *vbl. sb.* and *ppl. a.*

**1842** THACKERAY *Fitz-Boodle's Profess.* i, There shall be no shilly-shallying work here. **1843** —— *Bluebeard's Ghost* in *Fraser's Mag.* Oct. 424/2 Make up your mind what you will ask him, for ghosts will stand no shilly-shallying. **1883** HOWELLS *Woman's Reason* I. 120 If it hadn't been for my wretched shilly-shallying ways, I shouldn't have to write to him at all.

**'shilly-ˌshallyer.** [f. prec. vb. + -ER[1].] One who shilly-shallies.

**1832** J. WILSON *Noctes Ambr.* in *Blackw. Mag.* Apr. 697 Silly shallow shilly-shallyers. **1835** SOUTHEY *Doctor* cv. (1848) 243 He was no shillishallier. **1848** THACKERAY *Contrib. 'Punch'* Wks. 1886 XXIV. 187 Shilly-shallyers are cowards.

**shilment, -mont:** see SHELVEMENT.

**shilpit** ('ʃɪlpɪt), *a.* *Sc.* Also **shilpet, shelpit.** [Etymology unknown; cf. SHIRPIT.

Sc. dialects have also *shilpy* in the same sense, and *shilp* 'a pale sickly girl' (*Eng. Dial. Dict.*).]

**1.** Of persons: Pale and sickly-looking; weak, feeble, puny.

**1813** PICKEN *Poems* I. 79 (E.D.D.) There Care nae shilpit face can shaw. **1818** MISS FERRIER *Marriage* xxiv, The Laird, as he peered at her over his spectacles, pronounced her to be but a shilpit thing. **1820** BYRON *Let. to Murray* 23 Apr., Abstemiousness has made my brain but a shilpit concern for a Scotch sitting 'inter pocula'. **1896** CROCKETT *Grey Man* xxxiv. 230 My puir bit shilpit lassie.

**2.** Of liquor: Insipid, weak, thin.

**1814** SCOTT *Wav.* xi, He pronounced the claret *shilpit*, and demanded brandy with great vociferation. **1824** —— *Redgauntlet* ch. xx, Sherry's but shilpit drink.

**3.** (See quot.)

**1856** J. C. MORTON *Cycl. Agric.* II. 725 *Shilpit* (Scot.), applied to ill-filled ears of corn.

**shilt**, var. SHILLET.

**shily**, obs. var. SHYLY.

**shim** (ʃɪm), *sb.*[1] Also 7 shimm(e. [Represents formally OE. *scima* shadow, gloom.

Cognate forms are OS. *scimo* shade, WFris. *skim*, NFris. *skemm*, MLG. *schême* shade, twilight, ghost, MDu. *schem*, *schim*, *schême* shade, shadow, ghost, shimmer, shine (Du. *schim* shadow, phantom), MHG. *scheme* ghost (G. *schemen*), ON. *skime* or *skíma* gleam, *skíma* glimmer; also OE. *scíma* brightness, light, OS., OHG. *scîmo*, Goth. *skeima*; f. Teut. root *ski-*, for which see SHINE *v.*]

**1.** A streak of white on a horse's face. *dial.*

Cf. SHIMMED.

**1639** T. DE GRAY *Compl. Horsem.* 23 Some commend the shimme or rase downe the face. **1688** *Lond. Gaz.* No. 2459/4 A bright Chesnut Gelding,..a Shim [*printed* Shein] down his Face. **1705** *Ibid.* 4131/4 A Ring of white round each Ear, and a Shim down her Face. **1784** CULLUM *Hist. Hawsted* iii. 173.

**2.** A faint or transient appearance; a glimpse.

*a* **1800** PEGGE *Suppl. Grose's Prov. Gloss.*, *Shim*, appearance, West. A transient view or first sight. **1853** W. D. COOPER *Gloss. Prov. Sussex* 73, I can't be sure it was a partridge, but I saw the shim of something going over the hedge.

**shim** (ʃɪm), *sb.*[2] Also 8 sheim. [Origin unascertained. It is doubtful whether all the following senses belong to one word.]

**I.** *local.* **1.** A piece of iron attached to an agricultural implement for scraping the surface of the soil.

**1723** LEWIS *Hist. Tenet* 9 The furrows..being either howed with a large how, or cleared of weeds and rubbish by what they call a *Shim*. This is a flat piece of Iron, fixed at the end of a slight little plough beam drawn by one horse, and so made that it may be raised up or let down, as occasion serves. [**1736** (ed. 2) 13 *reads*, A Shim or Brake-plough. This is a Piece of Iron, at the Bottom of two Cheeks with Holes in them, which are put thro' a Frame of Timber drawn with one Horse, and with Iron Pins is let up or down as there is Occasion.] **1808** BATCHELOR *Agric. Bedford* 178 A shim, or scraper, might be inserted in the harrow-frame, for cutting thistles and other weeds.

**2.** In full *shim-plough*: A kind of horse-hoe or shallow plough, used in Kent and elsewhere, for hoeing up weeds between rows of beans, hops, etc.

[**1736**: see sense 1.] **1736** PEGGE *Kenticisms* (E.D.S.), *Shim*, an horse-how. **1750** W. ELLIS *Mod. Husb.* III. I. 56 (E.D.S.), The sheim or prong-plough. **1754** POCOCKE *Trav.* (Camden) II. 88 [In the Isle of Thanet] They have a particular way of cleaning the ground sown with beans, with a machine call'd a shim, with irons at such a distance, that two go between the rows, and turn up the earth on each side against the beans. **1792** *Trans. Soc. Arts* (ed. 2) III. 33 Horse-hoed the intervals with a Berkshire shim, which cuts the surface, but turns no furrow. **1805** R. W. DICKSON *Pract. Agric.* II. 880 In the drill-sown lucern some recommend..the passing of a small shim between them. **1892** *Auctioneer's Catal. Farm Sale near Minster, Kent*, 148 Pop shim, 149 Iron single shim, 150 5 furrow corn shim.

**3.** A Dutch hoe.

**1833** *Ridgemont Farm Rep.* 133 in *Husb.* (L.U.K.) III, The Dutch hoe, called in Holderness the 'shim'.

¶ **4.** Used by confusion for SKIM *sb.* (2 b).

So *shim-coulter plough* in some Dicts.

**1805** R. W. DICKSON *Pract. Agric.* I. 470 When the land is of a stiff and lumpy..nature, it may..be necessary to have recourse to *shims*, in order to break down and separate the particles. **1834** *Brit. Husb.* (L.U.K.) I. 348 The shim, or skim, has also been affixed as an additional coulter..to a plough much in use in Oxfordshire. **1837** *Ibid.* II. 18 The skim-plough—or shim, as it is in some places called.

**II.** In wider use. **5. a.** A thin slip, usually of metal, used to fill up a space between parts subject to wear, to align or adjust the level of rails, etc.

**1860** CLARK & COLBURN *Recent Practice Locomotive Engine* 62/2 Where no gibs are employed in the cross-head blocks, 'shims' or thickness pieces of sheet-tin or copper are interposed under the ends of the guide-bars. **1864** in WEBSTER. **1875** KNIGHT *Dict. Mech.*, *Shim*..(*Stone-working*). One of the plates in a jumper-hole to fill out a portion of the thickness not occupied by the wedges or feathers. **1885** WADDELL *Syst. Railroad Bridges Japan* 56 There are two different floor systems..: in the first of these the lower lateral rods pass through the wooden shims. **1887** J. ROSE *Key to Engines* 101 A Liner, Fit-Strip, Distance-Piece, or Shim..is a strip of metal placed between the joint faces of the brasses to hold them the proper distance apart. **1916** R. T. NICHOLSON *Bk. of Ford* viii. 118 Paper 'shims'—that is, slips of paper shaped to the flats—between cap and socket. These 'shims' will prevent your tightening the nuts up too far. **1953** J. LAWRENCE *Questions & Answers on Automobile Transmission & Steering* IV. 90 To rectify the pre-load, adjust the shim pack between the outer bearing cone and the pinion shank or spacer. **1977** *New Yorker* 4 July 33/2 He took out the shims and adjusted them for proper clearance.

**b.** *Criminals' slang* (chiefly *U.S.*). = LOID.

**1968** L. O'DONNELL *Face of Crime* i. 12 The lock was of the deadbolt type that doesn't yield to the opportunist's plastic shim. **1973** R. PARKES *Guardians* i. 8 Had the door fitted flush to the frame, the old perspex shim wouldn't have slipped in. **1977** 'L. EGAN' *Blind Search* x. 172 Denny and I went to Nonie's place, and he used a shim to get us in.

**6.** *U.S.* An imperfect shingle of irregular thickness; also, an imperfect bucket-stave.

In recent U.S. Dicts.

†**shim**, *a.* *Obs.* In 4 schym. [Related to OE. *scima*, *scíma*: see SHIM *sb.*[1]] Bright.

Cf. (Chesh., Shropsh.) *shim-white*, a clear bright white.

**13..** *E.E. Allit. P.* A. 1077 Aboute þat water arn tres ful schym, þat twelue frytez of lyf con bere ful sone.

†**shim**, *v.*[1] *Obs.* [OE. *scímian*, ? also *scimian*, related to *scima* (see SHIM *sb.*[1]): cf. OHG. *scîman*, MHG. *schimmen.*] *intr.* To shine.

*c* **950** *Lindisf. Gosp.* Luke xvii. 24 Scimande of heofnum, *coruscans de sub cælo.* *c* **1000** ÆLFRIC *Gram.* xxiv. (Z.) 138 *Mico*, ic scimiȝe [*v.r.* scine]. *a* **1225** *Juliana* 55 (Bodl. MS.), Schiminde [*Royal MS.* schininde] hire nebscheaft schene as þe sunne. *a* **1225** *St. Marher.* 19 Wið schimmende ant scharp sweord. *Ibid.* 44 Hire foster modres schep, þe schimede ant schan. *a* **1240** [see SHIMMER *v.*[1]].

**shim**, *v.*[2] [f. SHIM *sb.*[2]]

**1. a.** *intr.* To use the shim for hoeing.

**1792**, etc. [see SHIMMING]. **1793** *Trans. Soc. Arts* (ed. 2) IV. 62 The last week in April, shimmed over the surface.

**b.** *trans.* To hoe (crops) with a shim.

**1797** A. YOUNG *Agric. Suffolk* 59 The Kentish method of shimming the stubbles of beans..is unknown in Suffolk. **1799** —— *Agric. Linc.* 128 He..shims them with the expanding horse-hoe. **1833** *Ridgemont Farm Rep.* 138 in *Husb.* (L.U.K.) III, When the land is in good order, an able work-man will shim nearly six roods a day.

**2. a.** 'To wedge up or fill out to a fair surface by inserting a thin wedge or piece of material' (*Century Dict.*). Also const. *out*. Cf. SHIMMER *sb.*[2] and SHIMMING. *N. Amer.*

**1937** H. E. STAFFORD *Troubles of Electr. Equip.* iii. 46 The only permanent way is..by decreasing the air gap by shimming the pole shoes. **1967** E. B. NICKERSON *Kayaks to Arctic* xiv. 126 Each cabin had a single door, well shimmed but still hanging out of plumb. **1974** R. M. PIRSIG *Zen & Art of Motorcycle Maintenance* v. 57 You're going to have to shim those out.

**b.** *Criminals' slang* (chiefly *U.S.*). To open (a lock or door) with a shim. Cf. SHIM *sb.*[2] 5 b.

**1972** J. WAMBAUGH *Blue Knight* (1973) ii. 25 The burglar ..would shim doors which isn't too hard to do in any hotel.

‖**shimada** (ʃɪˈmɑːdə). The name of a town in Honshu, central Japan, applied *absol.* and *attrib.* to a young unmarried ladies' formal hairstyle in which the hair is drawn into a queue and fastened at the top of the head.

**1910** JUKICHI INOUYE *Home Life in Tokyo* ix. 113 Both the *shimada* and the *marumage* are heavy as they require false hair. **1936** K. NOHARA *True Face of Japan* v. 173 The unmarried girl wears the *shimada* coiffure. **1959** R. KIRKBRIDE *Tamiko* vii. 53 A Geisha girl, gorgeous in kimono and shimada hairstyle.

‖**shime-waza** (ˈʃiːmeˈwɑːzə). *Judo.* Also shime waza. [Jap., f. *shimeru* to tighten, constrict + *waza* art, deed, work.] The art of strangulation; a strangle-hold. Also *attrib.*

**1954** E. DOMINY *Teach Yourself Judo* 191 *Shime Waza*, the art of Strangulation. **1956** K. TOMIKI *Judo* iii. 92 There are two methods of strangling, namely necklock and cheeklock. But the latter is excluded from the practice in *judo*, only the former being referred to as *shime-waza*. **1957** *Judo* (Know the Game Series) 26/2 Lastly there is the shimewaza group (strangling and choking techniques)... The definition is as follows: the strangle aims at compressing the common carotid artery just behind the sternomastoid muscle which runs up both sides of the neck... If this pressure is maintained it is only a matter of a few seconds before the man becomes unconscious. **1978** D. STARBROOK *Judo Starbrook Style* vi. 98 A shimewaza is a stranglehold.

**shimiana**, variant of SHAMIANA(H.

**shimiyana** (ʃɪmɪˈjɑːnə). *S. Afr.* Also shimiaan, shimiyane, shimya(a)n. [ad. Zulu *isi)shimeyana.*] An intoxicating home-brewed drink made from treacle or sugar and water.

**1870** A. F. LINDLEY *After Ophir* xix. 306 *Shimyan* and *jwarlar* were produced for our consumption, and we were invited to witness the usual dancing performances at the *kraal* after dark. **1900** J. ROBINSON *Lifetime S. Afr.* 307 'Shimyaan', a concoction of treacle and water allowed to ferment in the sun. This beverage was maddening in its effects, and the parent of much crime. **1934** R. CAMPBELL *Broken Record* 68 You loaf, you drink *shimiaan*. **1946** *Cape Times* 29 Oct. 5 The presiding magistrate called in a number of native spectators to decide whether a drum of brew before the court was shimiyana. **1949** *Cape Argus* 6 Aug. 1/4 Malinga pleaded guilty to being in possession of three gallons of shimiyane which, he said, he brewed for his own consumption. **1961** T. MATSHIKIZA *Chocolates for My Wife* 76 They plug you cockfull of Shimiyana. Some randy home brew.

†**shimmed**, *a.* *Obs.* In 5 schymmid. [app. f. SHIM *sb.*[1] + -ED[2].] Dapple-grey.

*c* **1440** *Promp. Parv.* 446/2 Schymmid, as hors, *scutilatus.*

**shimmer** (ˈʃɪmə(r)), *sb.*[1] [f. SHIMMER *v.*[1] Cf. LG. *schemmer*, NFris. *skimer*, G. *schimmer*, Sw. *skimmer.*] A shimmering light or glow; a subdued tremulous light.

**1821** SCOTT *Kenilw.* vi, Two silver lamps, fed with perfumed oil, diffused..a trembling twilight-seeming shimmer through the quiet apartment. **1847** C. BRONTE *Jane Eyre* xxv, The strange, wraith-like apparel..which, at this evening hour..gave out..a most ghostly shimmer through the shadow of my apartment. **1863** MISS BRADDON *Eleanor's Vict.* i, The first shimmer of the moonlight was silvery on the water. **1899** *Allbutt's Syst. Med.* VIII. 590 The papules..having a wax-like shimmer.

*transf.* and *fig.* **1851** CARLYLE *Sterling* II. iii, A kind of childlike half-embarrassed shimmer of expression, on his fine vivid countenance. **1854** EMERSON *Lett. & Soc. Aims, Poet. & Imag.*, One man sees a spark or shimmer of the truth.

**shimmer** (ˈʃɪmə(r)), *sb.*[2] *U.S.* [f. SHIM *v.*[2] + -ER.] **a.** A workman who inserts shims in cabinet work, etc. **b.** = SHIM *sb.*[2] 5. (In recent U.S. Dicts.)

**shimmer** (ˈʃɪmə(r)), *v.*[1] Forms: 1 scymrian, 3 schimere, 4 schymere, 4–5 s(c)hemere, 6 shy-, shimer, 6– shimmer. [late OE. *scymrian* = WFris. *skimerje*, NFris. *skimere* to shimmer, (M)LG., (M)Du. *schêmeren* to be shaded or shadowy, to glimmer, glitter, G. *schimmern*, Sw. *skimra*; related to SHIM *v.*[1] Cf. the northern SKIMMER.] **1.** *intr.* To shine with a tremulous or flickering light; to gleam faintly. In early use also, to shine brightly, glisten.

*a* **1100** *Chrodegang's Rule* 41 in Napier *Contrib. OE. Lexic.* (1906) 16 Soðlice þa se dæȝredleoma beorhte scymrode, þa Drihten..of helle aras. *c* **1230** [see SHIMMERING *ppl. a.*]. *a* **1240** *Sawles Warde* in *O.E. Hom.* I. 257 Al þat hus schineð ant schimmeð [*v.r.* schimereð] of his leome. **13..** *Gaw. & Gr. Knt.* 772 Hit [a castle] schemered & schon þurȝ þe schyre okez. *c* **1400** *Destr. Troy* 4974 Frut..þat shemert as shire as any shene stonys. **1567** MAPLET *Gr. Forest* 5 b, The Chrusopasse is a Stone of Ethiope, which in the day light shimmereth not. **1582** STANYHURST *Æneis* IV. 82 Thee next day foloing lustring Aurora lay shymring, Her saffrond mattresse leauing to her bedfelo Tithon. **1623**, **1655** [see SHIMMERING *vbl. sb.* and *ppl. a.*].

**1805** SCOTT *Last Minstr.* I. xvii, Twinkling faint, and distant far, Shimmers through mist each planet star. **1860** THACKERAY *Lovel* iv, Often your figure shimmers through my dreams. **1871** GREEN *Let. to W. B. Dawkins* 29 Jan., Blue sea..shimmering with colour. **1874** SYMONDS *Sk. Italy & Greece* (1898) I. xiii. 254 Distant islands shimmering in sun-litten haze. **1877** STOPFORD BROOKE *Fight of Faith* xxiv. 394 The [frozen] ponds..shimmer dark like polished steel.

**2.** *intr.* To move effortlessly; to glide, drift (*by*, *off*, etc.).

**1904** in *Eng. Dial. Dict.* V. 385 [Yorks.] He shimmered by, a piece o' way off. **1923** WODEHOUSE *Inimitable Jeeves* x. 102 Jeeves shimmered off, and Cyril blew in, full of good cheer and blitheringness. **1930** C. WILLIAMS *War in Heaven* xi. 176 'I just want to shimmer up, like Jeeves, not walk,' she said. **1973** M. AMIS *Rachel Papers* 151 Move my hand over her bronze tights, tracing her hip-bone, circling beneath the overhang of her buttock, shimmer flat-palmed down the back of her legs.

ˈ**shimmer**, *v.*[2] [f. SHIMMER *sb.*[2]] = SHIM *v.*[2] 2.

**1908** J. B. DAVIDSON & CHASE *Farm Mach.* 71 (Century Dict. Suppl.), A remedy for this [poor fitting of share and moldboard] is procured by shimmering the share up or down with small pieces of paste-board.

**shimmeriness** (ˈʃɪmərɪnɪs). [f. SHIMMERY *a.*[1] + -NESS.] The condition of being shimmery; a flickering or insubstantial quality.

**1913** D. H. LAWRENCE *Sons & Lovers* II. vii. 153 Only this shimmeriness is the real living. The shape is a dead crust. **1948** M. SCHORER in *Hudson Rev.* I. 76 His [*sc.* Lawrence's] belief in a..poetry in which nothing is fixed, static, or final, where all is shimmeriness and impermanence.

ˈ**shimmering**, *vbl. sb.* [f. SHIMMER *v.*[1] + -ING[1]. Cf. (M)LG. *schêmering*, MHG. *schemerung* twilight, G. *schimmerung* coruscation.] The action of the vb. SHIMMER.

*c* **1386** CHAUCER *Reeve's T.* 377 A litel shymeryng [*v.r.* schemeryng] of a light. **1623** BP. HALL *Gt. Impostor* Wks. (1625) 503 The..blinde man that thought he now saw a shimmering of the Sunne-beames. **1853** KANE *Grinnell Exp.* ix. (1856) 64 Looking toward the shore, I observed a sort of shimmering, as of the heated air above a stove. **1868** HELPS *Realmah* iii, Kissed into ripples by the shimmering of moonlight. **1883** W. S. DUGDALE *Dante's Purg.* I. 9, I discerned the shimmering of the sea.

*fig.* **1880** TODHUNTER *Shelley* vii. 199 It is a weak shimmering of forced fun.

ˈ**shimmering**, *ppl. a.* That shimmers.

*c* **1000** *Gl. Prud.* in *Germania* (N.S.) XI. 401/10 Scymriendes wæles, *cerulei gurgitis.* *c* **1230** *Hali Meid.* 31 Þat eadi trume of schimerinde meidenes. **13..** *E.E. Allit. P.* A. 80 Wyth schymeryng schene ful schrylle þay schynde. *a* **1400–50** *Wars Alex.* 1544 Shemerand shaftis of the shire son. *c* **1440** *York Myst.* I. 69 My schewyng es schemerande and schynande. **1557** PHAER *Æneid* VI. Q 4 In shimring shadowe darck and thinne. **1593** G. HARVEY *Pierce's Super.* 219 If some little shimering light appeare at a little creuise. **1655** GURNALL *Chr. in Arm.* I. 224 There is some shimmering light in all. **1840** ELIZA COOK *Poems* 151 The towering hill, the shimmering rill. **1874** SYMONDS *Sk. Italy & Greece* (1898) I. vii. 124 The plain..basking in the hazy shimmering heat. **1881** *Macm. Mag.* XLIII. 345 The soft brilliancy of her toilet had the look of shimmering plumage.

*fig.* **1880** E. WHITE *Cert. Relig.* 34 The vague and shimmering atmosphere of local and chronological detail.

**shimmery** ('ʃɪmərɪ), *a.*[1] [f. SHIMMER *v.* + -Y[1]. Cf. G. *schimmerig*, WFris. *skimerich*.] Giving out a shimmering light.

**1883** *Harper's Mag.* May 904/2 Some wondrous shimmery cream of brocaded satin. **1890** J. HATTON *By Order of Czar* III. v, The city in the lagoons, with..her shimmery waters.

*fig.* **1893** *Athenæum* 9 Dec. 803/2 'Claudea's Island' has pretty, shimmery touches, natural and human.

**'shimmery,** *a.*[2] 'Shaky.' Also **shimmery-whimmery** *a.*

**1859** MRS. STOWE *Minister's Wooing* xxx, 'How is Mrs. Marvyn?'..'Kinder thin and shimmery, but she is about.' **1894** FENN *Real Gold* xii, Didn't you ever have a set to at school..?..And didn't you feel shimmery-whimmery before you began?

**'shimming,** *vbl. sb.* [f. SHIM *v.*[2] + -ING[1].]

**1.** Hoeing with a shim.

**1792** *Trans. Soc. Arts* (ed. 2) III. 33 The middle of August, repeated the shimming. **1833** *Ridgemont Farm Rep.* 141 in *Husb.* (L.U.K.) III, This 'shimming' is..repeated when the beans have advanced to six inches in height. **1848** *Jrnl. R. Agric. Soc.* IX. II. 557 Horse-hoeing, or what is locally called..'shiming'.

**2.** The insertion of shims; also, a shim, or shims collectively.

**1884** *Car-Builder's Dict.* (Century Dict.), Shimming has been used in fitting on car-wheels when the wheel-seat of the axle was a little too small.

**shimmy** ('ʃɪmɪ), *sb.*[1] Also **shimmey**. *dial.* and *U.S.* corruption of CHEMISE.

**1837** F. MARRYAT *Snarleyyow* xliii. 267 We have nothing but petticoats here and shimmeys. **1839** *Heref. Gloss.*, *Shimmy*, shift; now used by cottagers. **1856** H. H. DIXON *Post & Paddock* x. 176 Two shirts and a 'shimmy' is about the regulation package for a man and his wife. **1889** *Macmillan's Mag.* Sept. 360, I did count on gettin' myself a new shimmy. **1952** *New Yorker* 20 Sept. 35/1 To persuade the young matron to doff her wet shimmy.

**shimmy** ('ʃɪmɪ), *sb.*[2] Also **shimi**. [App. a use of SHIMMY *sb.*[1]]

**1.** A lively modern dance resembling a foxtrot accompanied by simulated quivering or shaking of the body which first achieved wide popularity in the early nineteen-twenties; a performance of this dance. Also in phr. ***to shake a shimmy***. orig. *U.S.*

[**1917** *Variety* 30 Nov. 19/1 The opening number was programed as a combination of 'Strutter's Ball', 'Shimme-Sha-Wabble' and 'Walking the Dog'.] **1918** *Dancing Times* Nov. 35 It is still very, very crude—and it is called 'Shaking the Shimmy'... It's a nigger dance, of course, and it appears to be a slow walk with a frequent twitching of the shoulders. **1920** C. SANDBURG *Smoke & Steel* 223 Shimmying the fast shimmy to the Livery Stable Blues. **1922** *Weekly Dispatch* 31 Dec. 9 'Shimmy' banned in New York... The Chicago camel-walk, scandal, balconnades, and shimmy dances must cease. **1924** P. MARKS *Plastic Age* 275 That music was enough to make a saint shed his halo and shake a shimmy. **1935** J. T. FARRELL *Judgment Day* I. xvi. 387 The building began to waver and dance before his eyes. Funny. The building was doing the shimmy. **1947** M. BERGER in R. de Toledano *Frontiers of Jazz* viii. 96 They did the Virginia reel, slow and fast quadrilles and the shimmy. **1956** B. HOLIDAY *Lady sings Blues* (1973) iv. 41 White people..came to the Cotton Club—a place Negroes never saw inside unless they played music or did the shakes or shimmies. **1975** P. G. WINSLOW *Death of Angel* xii. 232 Frayne..held the towel behind his hips and did what..used to be called the shimmy. **1977** *New Hampshire Times* 27 July 12/2 Glasses in New Hampshire cupboards began to rattle as houses started modest shimmies.

**2.** *transf.* An oscillation or vibration of the wheels, etc., of a motor vehicle or of an aircraft undercarriage; *spec.* = *wheel wobble*.

**1925** *Proc. Inst. Automobile Engineers* XIX. 822 This phenomenon..is variously termed 'wheel flap', 'shimmy', 'goldfishing', 'tramping', 'wobble', according to the nationality and imagination of the writers. **1936** *Aircraft Engin.* July 199/1 With the use of the front castorable wheel another difficulty develops..in the form of wheel shimmy. **1940** G. FRANKAU *Self-Portrait* lxii. 385 'Frankie'.. developed a shimmy in her full elliptic springing that made her solid steering column feel like india-rubber. **1943** F. L. WRIGHT *Autobiogr.* (rev. ed.) v. 411 At high speed it would settle down and shake itself almost to pieces in a perfect frenzy (the garage-doctors called it a shimmy). **1958** H. G. CONWAY *Landing Gear Design* viii. 150 Shimmy can be divided into two basic types: large angle and small angle (or kinematic) shimmy. **1968** K. J. BUNKER in J. G. Giles *Steering, Suspension & Tyres* vii. 132 Shimmy..is usually started by road irregularities. **1977** *Grimsby Even. Tel.* 5 May 5/1 (Advt.), Terrific tyre bargains!.. Wheel balancing. Got the 'shimmy'—Got the 'shakes'? Expert correction.

**3.** *attrib.* and *Comb.*, as (sense 1) ***shimmy dance, dancer, dress***; **shimmy damper**, a device fitted to aircraft undercarriages and motor vehicles in order to prevent or reduce shimmy; **shimmy-fox(trot)** = next; also, (a piece of) music to accompany this dance; **shimmy shake, shiver** = SHIMMY *sb.*[2] 1; hence ***shimmy shaker***.

**1928** *Proc. Inst. Automobile Engineers* XXII. 741 It is important when using a shimmy damper to avoid the use of spring connections..in the steerage linkage. **1946** *Jrnl. R. Aeronaut. Soc.* L. 533/2 In only one aircraft had a hydraulic shimmy damper been used, and that was a direct copy of the damper used in Douglas aircraft. **1958** H. G. CONWAY *Landing Gear Design* viii. 153 (*caption*) A well-known type of American shimmy damper on the rotating vane principle. **1919** *N.Y. World* 17 Jan. 7/5 (*heading*) Shimmy dance is banned in greater New York. **1922** JOYCE *Ulysses* 533 You found me in evil company, highkickers, coster picnic makers, pugilists..and the nifty shimmy dancers. **1967** *Boston Globe* 5 Apr. 59/3 A largely nude shimmy dancer put in all the bumps and grinds with a gyrating G.I. **1919** *Honey Pot* I. I. 8 The Eton collar which, in addition to her plain blue 'shimmy' dress..made her resemble a school-girl of sweet sixteen. **1968** P. OLIVER *Screening Blues* vi. 206 The women dressed exotically and were supported by scantily clad chorus girls wearing the shimmy dresses of the period. **1934** C. LAMBERT *Music Ho!* III. 224 Jannings going to the dogs is not a more melancholy spectacle than some worthy Teutonic fiddler putting a little pep into a 'shimmy-fox'. **1926–7** *T. Eaton & Co. Catal.* 305/1 *Collegiate*—Shimmy Fox Trot. **1928** *Observer* 15 Apr. 12 Instead of a scherzo she has written a shimmy-foxtrot. **1925** INFANTA EULALIA OF SPAIN *Courts & Countries after War* i. 18 The history of dancing during the Revolution repeated itself, with the differences that the Carmagnole of '93 was the Shimmy Shake or the Bunny Hug of 1914. **1920** *Sat. Even. Post* 27 Nov. 42/4 Then they was a pair of young shimmy shakers. **1919** *N.Y. Sun* 16 Jan. 14/4, I was dancing the shimi shiver.

**shimmy,** *v.*[1] orig. *U.S.* Also **shemmi**. [f. prec.]

**1. a.** *intr.* To dance the shimmy.

**1919** J. R. PICKELL *Twenty-Four Days on Troopship* xiv. 74 O, boys, we don't care, If we never get home, If mother will shimmy So long as we roam. **1919** A. J. PIRON (*song-title*), I wish I could shemmi like my sister Kate. **1932** J. LAVER *Nymph Errant* viii. 199 Constantine shimmied until beads of perspiration gathered on his shiny forehead. **1977** *Zigzag* Apr. 28/1 He gyrates, shimmies, shakes his ass.

**b.** *trans.* To dance (the shimmy); to shake (part of the body) as in the shimmy.

**1920** [see SHIMMY *sb.*[2] 1]. **1956** H. GOLD *Man who was not with It* xi. 85 Pauline used to tell me..shimmying her loose bare arms of which she was so proud for their milky flesh, 'like this, like that, and ziggety-zaggety'. **1974** J. IRVING *158-Pound Marriage* vii. 148 She shimmied her fingers the way Tyrone Williams did before the whistle.

**2.** *intr. fig.* and *transf.* To shake, quiver, vibrate, to progress hastily or irregularly.

**1925** C. R. COOPER *Lions 'n' Tigers* ix. 235 Leader Mary was beginning to shimmy slightly with increased flight. **1941** *Picture Post* 3 May 9/2 The gunfire came surging back. .. The floor of the basement shimmied underneath me and the whole house shook like a Chinese lantern in a breeze. **1942** *Jrnl. Aeronaut. Sci.* IX. 400/1 It is impossible for any side force to build up on the tire to cause it to shimmy. **1958** H. G. CONWAY *Landing Gear Design* viii. 152 Aircraft..with less than a certain amount of castoring friction shimmied and those with more did not. **1969** L. MICHAELS *Going Places* 135 She..shimmied up my arm and hung from my shoulder like a bunch of bananas. **1976** *Times Lit. Suppl.* 2 July 814/3 When his wife was asleep, he would shimmy down a pillar to the ground floor. **1980** *Daily Tel.* 29 Nov. 17/3 Palm, shimmying in the warm breezes all along the coasts.

Hence **'shimmying** *vbl. sb.* and *ppl. a.*

**1919** J. R. PICKELL *Twenty-Four Days on Troopship* 73 The star in the heavens, Looked down with a frown, To see mother so shimmied In her shimmeying gown. **1928** GALSWORTHY *Swan Song* II. xiii. 217 He..watched the dancing on deck—funny business nowadays, shimmying, bunnyhugging, didn't they call it. **1942** R. H. BOUND in R. A. Beaumont *Aeronaut. Engin.* xv. 412/2 Main tail wheels have been subject to one very serious defect, namely, shimmying; this consists of violent oscillations of the tail-wheel from side to side when the aircraft is running over the ground. **1972** *Sci. Amer.* Oct. 100/3 Most of the behavior of a nucleus undergoing nuclear fission can be understood as the splitting of a shimmying electrically charged drop. **1977** *Gay News* 24 Mar. 23/1 A mere suggestion of a shimmying hip and you were lectured by a bartender.

**shimmy** ('ʃɪmɪ), *v.*[2] [Alteration of SHIMMER *v.*[1] under infl. of SHIMMY *v.*[1]] *intr.* and *trans.* To 'dance' *in*; to transport (a person) quickly.

**1923** WODEHOUSE *Inimitable Jeeves* vii. 76, I bounded into the sitting-room, but it was empty. Jeeves shimmied in. **1930** G. MACMUNN *Behind Scenes in Many Wars* x. 187 A small destroyer..would shimmy us over to the beaches from Imbros. **1980** G. V. HIGGINS *Kennedy for Defense* x. 104, I just love seeing fat fees shimmy out the door to go elsewhere.

† **shimose** (ʃɪ'məʊseɪ). *Mil. Obs.* [The name of Masachika *Shimose* (1859–1911), Japanese engineer.] A form of lyddite made in Japan. Also † **'shimosite**.

**1904** *Amer. Inventor* 1 June 256/2 An explosive used by the Japanese, and called Shimose, after its inventor,..is said to be more powerful than either dynamite or gun-cotton, and to possess features found in no other high-power explosive. **1915** A. MARSHALL *Explosives* 322 The first satisfactory solution of the problem was the adoption of picric acid by France. This was quickly followed by similar measures taken by practically all the other Powers, each of whom, however, gave the substance a different name; France..Mélinite, England..Lyddite,..Japan.. Shimosite. **1917** *Chambers's Jrnl.* Apr. 258/2 The picric acid compound known as lyddite in England, melinite in France, and *shimose* in Japan.

**shimozzle,** var. SHEMOZZLE.

**'shimper,** *v. local.* [app. corrupt f. SHIMMER *v.* with intrusive *p* (**shimᵖre*).] = SHIMMER *v.*

**1674** RAY *S. & E.C. Words*, To *Shimper*, to shimmer or shine. *Suss.* Dial. **1703** *Art's Improvem.* I. 8 They..stick it full of small pieces of broken Glass, which..adds a Luster to it, Shimpering against the Sun-Beams. **1836** W. D. COOPER *Gloss. Prov. Sussex* s.v., How the carriage-wheels shimper in the sun.

**'shim-sham.** *Obs.* exc. *dial.* Reduplication of SHAM *sb.* and *a.* (Cf. FLIM-FLAM.)

**1797** MRS. A. M. BENNETT *Beggar Girl* (1813) I. 22 To make a parcel of shim-sham ghosts and coffins, and such like blasphemies. **1798** *Geraldina* I. 224 We were served upon plate: none of your shim-shams,..but the real thing. **1823** *Spirit Publ. Jrnls.* 523 His Majesty's real birthday, and none of your George and the Dragon shim shams.

**shimya(a)n,** vars. SHIMIYANA.

**shin** (ʃɪn), *sb.*[1] Forms: 1 **scinu**, 2 **scine, scyne**, 3–4 **s(c)hine**, 4–5 **s(c)hyne**, 5 **schene**, 5–6 **schin, schyn(ne, shyn(ne**, 6 **shinne**, 7 **shinn**, 6– **shin**. [OE. *scinu* str. fem. = WFris. *skine*, NFris. *skenn*, (M)LG., MDu. *schêne* (Du. *scheen*), OHG. *scina, scena, sciena* shin, needle (MHG. *schin(ne*, G. *schiene* thin wooden or metal plate); MSw. *skena* shin, Sw. *skena* shin, Da. *skinne* splint, tire, rail, are from LG. or HG. The fundamental meaning appears to be 'thin or narrow piece'; OE. *scía* shin and MHG. *schîe* hedge-stake are app. related.]

**1. a.** The front part of the human leg between the knee and the ankle; the front or sharp edge of the shank-bone.

Occas. used of analogous parts of birds and insects.

*a* **1000** *Ags. Gloss.* in Wr.-Wülcker 216/3 *Cruscula*, scinu. *a* **1100** *Ags. Voc.* Ibid. 307/27 *Tibia*, scyne, oððe scinban. *a* **1250** *Owl & Night.* 1060 þu were ynume in one grune, Al hit abouhte þine schine [*Cott.* shine]. *c* **1300** *E.E. Psalter* cxlvi. 10 Ne in schines of man queming bes him tille. *c* **1386** CHAUCER *Knt.'s T.* 421 The pure fettres of his shynes grete [*v.rr.* schenys, schinnes]. *c* **1450** LOVELICH *Merlin* 2102 Thanne lefte He vpe His staf Anon and overthwert the Schenys smot him. *c* **1470** HENRYSON *Mor. Fab.* XIII. (*Frog & Mouse*) xxv, This litill mous, heir knit thus be the schin. *a* **1529** SKELTON *E. Rummyng* 494 She..had broken her shyn At the threshold comyng in. **1600** ROWLANDS *Letting Humours Blood* iv. 64 To trie it out at foot-ball by the shinnes. **1658–9** *Burton's Diary* (1828) IV. 10 A Spanish Don that burnt his shins by the fire. **1714** LADY M. W. MONTAGU *Lett.* lxxxv. 140 In..a great crowd..people.. disregard a little kick of the Shins. **1834** MARRYAT *Peter Simple* xxxi, O'Brien, who knew the tender part of a black, saluted Apollo with a kick on the shins. **1871** MEREDITH *Harry Richmond* xv, In mounting [the path] the knees and shins bore the brunt of it.

**b.** The lower part of a leg (of beef), the meat of which is lean and streaked.

**1736** BAILEY *Dict. Domest.* s.v. *Beef*, Take a leg or shin of Beef, strip off the skin and fat. **1872** *Daily News* 5 Sept., An old English proverb says..'Of all joints commend me to the shin of beef, which contains marrow for the master, meat for the mistress, gristle for the servants, and bone for the dog'.

**2.** In fig. phr.: **a.** referring to striking a person over the shins (cf. *a rap over the knuckles*) or wounding his shins.

**1546** J. HEYWOOD *Prov.* I. x. (1867) 20 Priuie nyps or casts ouertwart the shyns. **1589** ? NASHE *Pasqvill & Marforivs* B 4, To come ouer our shinnes with the same rebuke that hee gaue to Phillip. **1590** —— *1st Pt. Pasquil's Apol.* C 2, A wipe ouer the shinnes of the Non Residents. **1598** B. JONSON *Ev. Man in Hum.* I. ii. (1601) 47 It is able to breake the shinnes of any old mans patience in the world. **1651** HOWELL *Venice* 199 He is ready..to throw the Catt at her shinns, to pick a quarrell. [**1795** BURKE *Regic. Peace* iv. Wks. 1812 V. 26 The Author..ought not to have left us in the dark upon that subject, to break our shins over his hints and insinuations.] **1821** LAMB *Elia* I. *All Fools' Day*, Remove those logical forms..that no gentleman break the tender shins of his apprehension stumbling across them. **1884** *St. James's Gaz.* 25 Apr. 7/1 Rubbing down everybody's shins with a brickbat.

† **b.** ***to cut off by the shins***, to leave not a leg to stand on, undermine. *Obs.*

**1592** *Arden of Feversham* D [II. ii. 769], Cut him off by the shinnes, with a frowning looke of your crabed countenance. **1594** NASHE *Unfort. Trav.* H 1, Post-hast letters came to him ..to return as speedily as he could possible..wherby his fame was quit cut off by the shins.

**c.** † ***to cross shins***: see CROSS *v.* 5. ***to set out the shin*** (Sc.), to walk proudly. ***to graze the shins of***, to come very near to.

**1592** NASHE *Strange Newes* M 1, I will crosse shinnes with him though euerie sentence of his were a thousande tunnes of discourses. **1645** [see CROSS *v.* 5]. **1719** RAMSAY *2nd Answ. to Hamilton* ix, Set out the burnt side of your shin, For pride in poets is nae sin. **1786** BURNS *On Dining with Lord Daer* iii, But wi' a Lord!—stand out my shin! A Lord—a Peer—an Earl's son! **1847** DE QUINCEY *Joan of Arc* Wks. 1854 III. 227 The mob of spectators might raise a scruple whether our friend the jackdaw upon the throne, and the dauphin himself, were not grazing the shins of treason.

**d.** ***to break shins*** (slang): to borrow money.

[**1591** G. FLETCHER *Russe Commw.* 45 Whereupon he praued or beat out of their shinnes 7000. rubbels for a mulct. **1606** DEKKER *Seven Sins* I. (Arb.) 17 The Russians haue an excellent custome: they beate them on the shinnes, that haue mony, and will not pay their debts.]

*a* **1700** B. E. *Dict. Cant. Crew*, *Breaking Shins*, borrowing of Money. **1864** *Hotten's Slang Dict.* 227. **1872** SCHELE DE VERE *Americanisms* 632 In financial slang, Americans use the verb *to shin* simply, where the English use *to break shins*, to denote a desperate effort to procure money in an emergency by running about to friends and acquaintances.

**3.** The sharp slope of a hill. *Sc.*

**1817** *Edin. Mag.* Oct. 84 Sometimes on the shin, and some-times in the hollow, of a hill. **1864** CARLYLE *Fredk. Gt.* xv. v. IV. 76 They have climbed the eastern shin of the Harz Range, where the Harz is capable of wheel-carriages.

**4.** Used, after G. *schiene*, for an iron plate or band.

**1747** HOOSON *Miner's Dict.* K 2, The Hack is not made straight but bending a little on either end from the Eye, upon that side the Haum is put in on, yet not too much into the Shins. **1875** KNIGHT *Dict. Mech.*, *Shin*,..a fish-plate.

**5.** *attrib.* and *Comb.*, as ***shin-boot, -cover, -guard, -pad, -pride, -ridge***; † **shin-barker**, a little dog that barks at one's shins; **shin-cracker** *Austral.* (see quots.); **shin-leaf**, the North American ericaceous plant *Pyrola elliptica* (also *P. rotundifolia*); **shin-oak**, applied to dwarf varieties of oak which form thick low-growing underwood, e.g. *Quercus chinquapin*; **shin-plaster**, (*a*) *Hist.* (orig. *U.S.*) a square piece of paper saturated with vinegar, etc., used as a plaster for sore legs; (*b*) a piece of paper money, esp. one of a low denomination, depreciated in value, or not sufficiently secured; (*c*) *Canad.*, a twenty-five cent bill; also *attrib.*; **shin-rapper**, one who disables horses by striking the splint-bone; **shin-scraper**, (*a*) see quot. 1869; (*b*) a contemptuous name for a climber; **shin-splint**, (*a*) *dial.* (see quot. 1893–4); (*b*) *pl.* (const. as *sing.* and *pl.*), any of a number of painful conditions of the lower leg that may be caused by running on hard surfaces; **shin-tangle** *Canad.* (see quot. 1905); **shin wood**, the Ground Hemlock, *Taxus canadensis* (see quot.).

**1645** MILTON *Colast.* 26 Infested, sometimes at his face, with dorrs and horsflies, sometimes beneath, with bauling whippets, and *shin-barkers. **1875** KNIGHT *Dict. Mech.*, **Shin-boot*, .. a horse boot having a long leather shield to protect the shin of a horse. **1845** *Kitto's Cycl. Bibl. Lit.* (1849) I. 228/1 They [*sc.* greaves] consisted of a pair of *shin-covers of brass. **1928** *Wentworth Mag.* (Sydney) June 33 '*Shin-crakers', that is, blows on the shin owing to the rock suddenly breaking off. **1945** S. J. BAKER *Austral. Lang.* 99 *Shin-cracker*, a subsoil of close-grained, brittle sandstone where the potch or silica runs. **1969** E. WALLER *There's Opal out There* 20 Ailments common to the Lightning Ridge, such as shincracker shin. **1971** J. S. GUNN *Opal Terminol.* 42 *Shin cracker.* Also *shincracker*, common name for the fine-grained Coocoran claystone which on exposure at the surface becomes a hard, brittle, siliceous rock that usually has to be dug through to get to the opal ground. Its name is appropriate because, when worked with a sinking pick or jack hammer, pieces shatter or fly off to strike the digger's shins, hence the injury called 'shin-cracker shin'. **1884–5** *Derbyshire Football Guide* 97 (Advt.), **Shin-guards*.. 2s. 6d. **1903** *Daily Chron.* 3 Feb. 3/4 Legs cased in shin-guards. **1845–50** MRS. LINCOLN *Lect. Bot.* App. 151 *Pyrola.. rotundifolia* (*shin-leaf, pear-leaf wintergreen). **1856** A. GRAY *Man. Bot.* 260. **1844** J. GREGG *Commerce of Prairies* II. 200 Black-jacks..[are] intermixed with a very diminutive dwarf oak, called by the hunters '*shin-oak'. **1884** *Encycl. Brit.* XVII. 693/2 *Quercus Chinquapin* or *prinoides*, a dwarf variety, .. forms dense miniature thickets ..; the tree is called by the hunters of the plains the 'shin-oak'. **1895** *Outing* XXVII. 251/2 Neither *shin-pads nor canvas jackets were worn. **1824** *Microscope* (Albany) 15 May (Thornton *Amer. Gloss.*), We advise our friends to exchange their '*shin plasters' for 'solid charms' as soon as may be. **1843** MARRYAT *M. Violet* xxviii, I had taken the precaution in Louisiana of getting rid of my shin-plasters for hard specie. **1878** *N. Amer. Rev.* CXXVI. 170 The 'more money' that is cried for, silver or shinplaster, is not the needed thing. **1887** *Grip* (Toronto) 2 Apr. 10/2, I will give further particulars on receipt of a shin-plaister. **1929** H. COLEBATCH *Story of Hundred Years* xxxvii. 458 The 'shin-plasters' of Connor, Doherty, and Durack, and of many hotel and store keepers, form the regularly accepted currency. **1936** M. MITCHELL *Gone with Wind* xvii. 308, I haven't a cent. Rhett, give me a few shin plasters. Here, Big Sam, buy some tobacco for yourself. **1962** H. GREEN *Time to pass Over* v. 77 Old Josh felt disposed to part with a few of his mouldy shinplasters. **1972** *Tel.* (Brisbane) 10 Nov. 40/1 Some years ago I was working in Boulia, where there wasn't a bank. Shin plasters were issued by Mr. J. P. Howard who owned the hotel at Boulia. **1613** SYLVESTER *Lachr. Lachr.* B 4, Stript .. Of guiddie-Gaudes, .. Of Face-pride, Case-pride, *Shin-pride, Shoo-pride. **1885** *Daily Tel.* 30 Sept. (Cassell), Every great stable in England had the fear of the poisoner, the *shin-rapper, and the nobbler constantly in view. **1889** *Ld. A. Campbell's Celtic Trad.* 87 The sharp *shin-ridge of the greaves. **1869** J. GREENWOOD *Seven Curses Lond.* vi. 87 The treadmill, *shin scraper (arising, it may be assumed, on account of the operator's liability, if he is not careful, to get his shins scraped by the ever-revolving wheel). **1895** *Westm. Gaz.* 11 Oct. 3/1 Although he may be described as a 'shin-scraper', he does not forget that he is first of all a mountaineer. **1812** in J. Bell *Rhymes of Northern Bards* 35, I lost a' my *shin-splints among the great stanes. **1893–4** R. O. HESLOP *Northumberland Words* II. 632 *Shin-splints*, a kind of greave or leg armour worn on the shins by trimmers, etc., to protect the legs in working. **1930** STEDMAN *Med. Dict.* (ed. 11) 951/1 *Shin splints*, myositis and periostitis affecting chiefly the extensor muscles of the lower lateral aspect of the legs. **1938** A. THORNDIKE *Athletic Injuries* xxi. 180 Shin splints in track, cross country and other sports are a very definite injury—a tearing of the origin of the tibialis posticus muscle from the tibia in its lower third. **1977** J. F. FIXX *Compl. Bk. Running* v. 71 Shin splints—pains in the front of the leg that are common in beginning runners. **1905** J. OUTRAM *In Heart Canad. Rockies* 176 A dense undergrowth .. is often designated by the expressive term '*shin-tangle'. **1973** P. GEDDES *Ottawa Allegation* xiv. 181 Nothing else was about except for the birds, making for cover under the shintangle. **1778** CARVER *Trav. N. Amer.* 505 *Shin Wood. This extraordinary shrub .. runs near the ground for six or eight feet, and then takes root again; .. this proves very troublesome to the hasty traveller, by striking against his shins, and entangling his legs.

**Shin** (ʃiːn), *sb.*[2] [Native name.] One of the Dardic peoples inhabiting the Gilgit agency of Kashmir; a member of this people.

**1875** F. DREW *Jummoo & Kashmir Territories* xviii. 428 The table .. shows in what countries the Shīn caste is found. .. The Shīn occur, mixed with Yashkun, along the Indus Valley. **1879** *Encycl. Brit.* X. 598/1 The middle castes, Shin and Yashkun, form the body of the Dard people. The pure Shin looks more like a European than any high-caste Brahman of India. **1910** *Ibid.* XII. 20/1 The dominant race is that of the Shins, whose language is universally spoken. **1913** A. NEVE *Thirty Years in Kashmir* ix. 84 My own impression is that the Rajah families were originally Shins. .. The Shin races (*i.e.*, the Dards) first occupied the eastern Hindu Kush. **1938** R. C. F. SCHOMBERG *Kafirs & Glaciers* xii. 206 The people of Ashret are not Chitralis but Dangariks who speak Palula, a language allied to the Shina spoken at Gilgit... They are probably Shins who came from Chilas.

**Shin** (ʃiːn), *sb.*[3] [Jap., = genuine, authentic.] The name of a major Japanese Buddhist sect which teaches salvation by faith in the Buddha Amida and emphasizes morality rather than orthodoxy. Usu. *attrib.* or as *adj.*

**1877** W. E. GRIFFIS *Mikado's Empire* (ed. 2) I. xvi. 173 The Shin sect hold a form of the Protestant doctrine of justification by faith, believing in Buddha instead of Jesus. **1904** L. HEARN *Japan: Attempt at Interpretation* xiii. 302 Nobunaga agreed to spare the lives of the Shin priests. **1960** B. LEACH *Potter in Japan* ii. 49 Dr. Suzuki is the leading writer on both Zen and Shin Buddhism, both in English and Japanese. **1976** *Education & Community Relations* July/Aug. 8/1 Talks by the Chief Abbot of the Nishi Hongwanji (Shin Sect) of Japan.

**shin** (ʃɪn), *v.* [f. SHIN *sb.*[1]]

**1.** *intr.* (orig. *Naut.*) To climb by using the arms and legs without the help of steps, irons, etc.

**1829** MARRYAT *F. Mildmay* iv, I myself saw him 'shinning' up by the topsail-tie. **1840** R. H. DANA *Bef. Mast* xxxi, We had to .. shin up and down single ropes caked with ice. **1857** HUGHES *Tom Brown* I. ix, Nothing for it but the tree; so Tom laid his bones to it, shinning up as fast as he could. **1888** STEVENSON *Black Arrow* I. iii, As he shinned vigorously down the trunk.

**b.** *trans.* To climb up.

**1891** in *Century Dict.* **1907** *Westm. Gaz.* 8 Apr. 8/1 [He] reached the roof by shinning a water-pipe.

**2.** *U.S.* To 'use one's legs'; to move quickly; to run *round*.

**1838** J. C. NEAL *Charcoal Sketches* 106 Shin it, good man .. shin it as well as you know how! **1840** G. T. STRONG *Diary* 8 May (1952) 138 One banner in particular—representing Matty shinning away from the White House. **1845** *N.Y. Com. Adv.* 13 Dec. (Bartlett 1860), The Senator was shinning around, to get gold for the rascally bank-rags which he was obliged to take. **1864** ATKINSON *Stanton Grange* 267 And then didn't I shin it along the bridge, pretty speedily! **1865** SALA *Diary in Amer.* II. 414, I guess you'll walk down town and show me the stores. I'm tired of shinning around alone. **1887** CONAN DOYLE *Study in Scarlet* II. iii, I guess we had best shin out of Utah.

**3.** To kick (a person) on the shins. Also, to shoot in the shins.

**1819** E. EVANS *Pedestrious Tour* 214 Soldiers are apt to fire too high. He was often heard to say to his troops in battle: 'Shin them, my brave boys!' *a* **1845** BARHAM *Ingol. Leg.* Ser. III. *House-warming*, There's a *pirouette*! .. A ring!—give him room or he'll 'shin' you—stand clear! **1846** *Yale Banger* 10 Nov. (Hall *College Words*), We have been shinned, smoked, ducked. **1864** [HEMYNG] *Eton School Days* xiii, He could not go out of his tutor's .. without some one .. 'shinning' him if he passed near enough.

**4.** *U.S.* To borrow money.

Cf. *break shins*, s.v. SHIN sb. 2 d.

**1855** OGILVIE *Suppl.*, *Shin*, to borrow money. (American cant term.) **1872** [see SHIN *sb.*[1] 2 d].

**shin**, obs. Sc. pl. of SHOE.

**Shina** (ˈʃiːnə). [Native name: cf. SHIN *sb.*[2]] The Indo-Aryan language spoken by the Shin. Also *attrib.*

**1854** A. CUNNINGHAM *Ladák* ii. 37 The Persian character, which all the Dards make use of in writing their own language, of which there are three distinct dialects,—the Shiná, the Khajunah, and the Arniya. The *Shiná* dialect is spoken by the people of Astor, Gilgit, Chelas, Darél, Kohli, and Pálas. **1903** RISLEY & GAIT *Census India 1901* I. I. 310 Shina, one of the non-Sanskrit Indo-Aryan forms of speech. **1936** R. C. F. SCHOMBERG *Unknown Karakoram* I. iii. 39 Shum, which means dog in the Shina tongue. **1977** D. MURPHY *Where Indus is Young* vii. 147 Talking rapidly in Shina, the Gilgit language.

**shinanigan, -gin**, etc., vars. SHENANIGAN.

† **shinbawde.** *Obs.* In 5 schynbawde, -baude, -balde. [The first element is app. SHIN *sb.*[1], the second is obscure.] A greave (leg-armour).

?*a* **1400** *Morte Arth.* 3847 The schadande blode.. schewede one his schynbawde, þat was schire burneste! *c* **1400** *Anturs of Arth.* 395 His schene schynbandes [*read* -baudes, *v.r.* -bawdes], þat sharp were to shrede. **1423** *Test. Ebor.* (Surtees) III. 73 Uno pare de schynbaldes, aliter vamplattes, pro tebiis virorum.

**Shin Bet** (ʃɪn bɛt). Also Shin Beth and as one word. [mod.Heb., f. *šīn* + *bēṯ*, the names of the initial letters of *šērûṯ biṭaḥôn kᵉlālî* (general) security service.] The principal security service of Israel. Also *attrib.*

**1964** L. DEIGHTON *Funeral in Berlin* xlii. 264 Samantha was a Shinbet agent after him for war crimes. **1968** C. LEADER *Angry Darkness* xii. 111 Schererzade was now in the hands of the Shinbeth, the coldly efficient and unemotional Israeli Intelligence Service. **1969** A. MARIN *Rise with Wind* vi. 76 The statement .. went directly to the Shin Beth. **1972** *Guardian* 27 Jan. 3/4 The street always becomes stiff with Shin Bet (Secret Service) men looking studiously unobtrusive. **1981** A. WINCH *Blood Money* xiii. 134 A man .. who has been positively identified by the Israeli Shin Beth.

**shinbin** (ˈʃɪnbɪn). Also -been, -ban, -beam. [Burmese *shin-byin*, f. *shin* to put together side by side + *pyin* plank.] In the teak trade, a thick plank split from a green tree. Cf. SHINLOG[2].

**1791** *Madras Courier* 10 Nov. (Y.), Duggis. Shinbeens. Coma planks. **1821** H. COX *Jrnl. Resid. Burmhan Emp.* 425 Shinban planks.

**shin-bone** (ˈʃɪnbəʊn). Forms: see SHIN *sb.*[1]; also 3 skin-, 4 chine-, shzin-. [OE. *scinbán* = NFris. *skenbiin*, *skennbian* (cf. WFris. *skynbonke*), MLG. *schênebein*, MDu. *schênebeen* (Du. *scheenbeen*), MHG. *schinebein* (G. *schienbein*); (Sw. *skenben*, Da. *skinneben*, from LG.): see SHIN *sb.*[1] and BONE *sb.*[1]] The bone of the shin; the tibia.

*c* **1000** ÆLFRIC *Gloss.* in Wr.-Wülcker 160/19 *Tibiae*, scina uel scinban. *c* **1220** *Bestiary* 359 Oc leiȝeð his skinbon on oðres lendbon. *c* **1325** *Gloss. W. de Bibbesw.* in Wright *Voc.* 148 Mes war le chanel [*glossed* the chine-bon, *Camb. MS.* shzin-bon] de blessure. *c* **1400** *Lanfranc's Cirurg.* 47 In þe boon of þe thie & schene boonys. **1527** ANDREW *Brunswyke's Distyll. Waters* L ij b, It is good for olde sores on the legges upon the shyne bones. **1597** A. M. tr. *Guillemeau's Fr. Chirurg.* 34/1 At three sundry times he tooke away allmost the whole shinne bone. **1650** BULWER *Anthropomet.* xxi. 231 The shin-bone exposed to all encounters, without any defence at all. **1713** CHESELDEN *Anat.* I. v. (1726) 40 The shin-bone is in its middle almost triangular. **1834** MARRYAT *Peter Simple* ix, The great lion was growling and snarling over the shin-bone of an ox, cracking it like a nut. **1862** CALVERLEY *Verses & Transl.* (1894) 86 He barked his shinbone.

**shincke**, Anglo-Irish form of SINK.

*a* **1660** *Contemp. Hist. Irel.* (Ir. Archæol. Soc.) II. 193 The foresaide Conaght armie .. must now shincke or swime.

**shind**, obs. form of SHEND *v.*

† **ˈshinder**, *v. Obs.* In 4 schyndere, s(c)hindre. [? Echoic. Cf. FLINDERS.] *trans.* and *intr.* To shiver or shatter in pieces.

**13..** *Gaw. & Gr. Knt.* 424 þe scharp of þe schalk schyndered þe bones. *Ibid.* 1594 þe mon .. Hit hym vp to þe hult, þat þe hert schyndered. *a* **1375** *Joseph Arim.* 513 Mony swouȝninge lay þorw schindringe of scharpe. *c* **1400** *Anturs of Arth.* 501 Shaftes in shide wode þei shindre in shedes [*v.r.* þay scheuerede in schides].

**shindig** (ˈʃɪndɪg). Also shin-dig. [Of uncertain origin: perh. f. SHIN *sb.* + DIG *sb.*[1], but infl. by SHINDY in later senses.] † **1.** *U.S.* (See quot. 1859.) *Obs.*

[**1849**: see HOE-DOWN.] **1859** BARTLETT *Dict. Amer.*, *Shin-Dig*, a blow on the shins. Southern.

**2.** A country dance; a party, ball, 'knees-up'; a lively gathering of any kind. Also *fig.* orig. *U.S.*

**1871** B. HARTE in *Atlantic Monthly* Sept. 373/1 'Is this a dashed Puritan meeting?' .. 'It's no Pike County shindig.' **1892** *Kentucky Words* in *Amer. Dial. Notes* I. 231 *Shindig*, a dance or party. **1899** *Westm. Gaz.* 31 Oct. 8/3 The natives .. in a number of instances have danced a kind of 'shindig' as soon as released from torture. **1935** C. W. PARMENTER *Kings of Beacon Hill* I. xv. 98 Does everyone attend those shindigs, Sandy, or is a girl invited by some special boy? **1946** [see FURORE 2]. **1956** WALLIS & BLAIR *Thunder Above* (1959) ix. 98 He was killed in an air defence exercise. One of those NATO shindigs. **1959** *New Statesman* 27 June 883/2 The competition among the 'old nobility' to attend what they termed 'Aspers' little shindig' was so fierce that five private detectives were hired to keep out the unwelcome. **1962** E. LUCIA *Klondike Kate* viii. 172 Kate never lacked a date for such shindigs. **1977** C. MCCULLOUGH *Thorn Birds* xi. 267 'What's a ceilidh anyway?' .. 'It's Gaelic for a gathering, a shindig.'

**3.** = SHINDY 3.

**1961** PARTRIDGE *Dict. Slang* Suppl. 1268/2 *Shindig*, an altercation, a violent quarrel, a tremendous fuss. **1966** *Listener* 17 Feb. 255/1 A classic row developed over the half birth of Peter Watkin's film *The War Game*, and this did not wholly distract from the shindig on the other side of the fence about a programme on the police. **1977** 'E. CRISPIN' *Glimpses of Moon* vi. 87 They'd kick up a shindig, naturally, but it was always their husbands they were furious with.

**shindle** (ˈʃɪnd(ə)l), *sb.* [local variant of SHINGLE *sb.*[1] Cf. G. *schindel.*]

**1.** A wooden roofing-tile.

**1585** HIGINS *Junius' Nomencl.* 211/1 *Scandulæ*, .. oke laths: slates or shindles of wood. **1601** HOLLAND *Pliny* XVI. x. I. 461 The bourds or shindles of the wild Oke... The shindles are most easily rent or cloven out of all those trees which yeeld Rosin, .. the housen in Rome were no otherwise covered over head but with shindles, untill the warre with K. Pyrrhus. **1617** MINSHEU *Ductor*, *A Shindle*, Vid. a Shingle. **1728** *Brice's Weekly Jrnl.* 28 June 4 A .. Brick House, cover'd with Shindles. **1872** SCHELE DE VERE *Americanisms* 542 In Pennsylvania the word [*shingle*] is often pronounced *Shindle*, partly, no doubt, under the influence of the numerous Germans in that State.

**2.** A splint.

**1598** FLORIO, *Stecchette*, .. shindles or boordes laid about broken legs or armes.

**3.** In full *shindle-stone*: Thin stone from which slates are cut.

**1669** *Phil. Trans.* IV. 1009 Take the thin cleft stone, slat or shindle. **1725** *Brice's Weekly Jrnl.* 15 Oct. 4 A Parcel of Slate (or Shindle-Stones) for tyling or healing of Houses. **1847** in HALLIWELL. **1882** JAGO *Gloss.*, *Shell-stone*, a slate stone. In Devon, shindle-stone.

†ˈ**shindle**, *v. Obs. rare*⁻¹. In 3 schindle. Origin and precise meaning unknown.

*a* **1225** *Ancr. R.* 186 Nis þet child fulitowen þet schrepeð [*v.rr.* schindleð, scratteð] agean, & bit upon þe ȝerde?

**shindy** (ˈʃɪndɪ). [? Alteration of SHINTY.]

**1.** = SHINTY 1. *local.*

**1846** *Local Act 9 Vict.* c. 29 §41 In case any Person or Persons shall on Shrove Tuesday..play at..Shindy, Football, or any other Game. **1860** BARTLETT *Dict. Amer.* (ed. 3), *Shindy*,..The proper and more usual name is Bandy. **1882** *Lancs. Gloss.*

**2.** A spree, merrymaking. Also, 'a kind of dance among seamen' (Smyth *Sailor's Word-bk.* 1867). *slang.*

**1821** EGAN *Life in London* x. (1869) 248 The Jack Tar is quite pleased with his night's cruise, and is continually singing out, 'What a prime Shindy, my Messmates.' **1848** in Col. Hawker *Diary* (1893) II. 286 All in commotion with the expected grand 'shindy' on Monday. **1866** BALLANTYNE *Shifting Winds* xxv, I want a dance at a wedding, or a shindy of some sort, before setting sail.

**3.** A row, commotion, 'shine'. Phr. ***to cut shindies*** (U.S.), ***to kick up a shindy.***

**1829** B. HALL *Trav. N. Amer.* III. 325, I never saw a more complete row, or as a fellow near me called it, 'a more regular shindy'. **1841** *Sporting Rev.* July 52 The docket of bankruptcy..created, as our polite continental neighbours call it, 'a sensation', or, in downright English, 'a shindy'. *a* **1845** BARHAM *Ingol. Leg.* Ser. III. *Hermann*, He..Joins..in kicking up all sorts of shindies and bobberies. **1850** 'DOW JR.' *Serm.* (Bartlett 1859), You..are..poor, and, therefore, ought to be careful how you cut shindies under the broadsword of justice. **1850** SMEDLEY *F. Fairlegh* i, A chair being the favourite projectile in the event of a shindy. **1882** B. M. CROKER *Proper Pride* I. ix. 189 He and his wife have had no end of a shindy. **1889** [see KICK *v.*[1] 9 a]. **1903** SOMERVILLE & 'ROSS' *All on Irish Shore* vii. 177 There was a frightful shindy, Carew wanting to have his blood, and all the rest of us trying to prevent a row. **1910** MEREDITH in *Fortn. Rev.* June 1055 Irishmen..never satisfied, thirsting for a shindy. **1916** 'TAFFRAIL' *Pincher Martin* vii. 115 If you want to kick up a shindy, Mister Parkin, you'd best do it outside. **1962** L. DEIGHTON *Ipcress File* x. 61 We're not having another Burgess and Maclean shindy, questions in the House and all that. **1976** J. I. M. STEWART *Memorial Service* iv. 53 There was quite a shindy, and there might have been more of it.

**4.** A liking, fancy. (Cf. SHINE *sb.*[2] 4.)

**1855** HALIBURTON *Nat. & Hum. Nat.* xii, They all wondered how..Paddy had taken such a shindy to me.

**shine** (ʃaɪn), *sb.*[1] [f. SHINE *v.* Cf. SHEEN *sb.*[1]

WGer. had a synonymous form derived from the vb.: OS., OHG. *scîn* (Du. *schijn*, MHG. *schîn*, mod.G. *schein*); also OE. *scín* spectre (if the vowel be long).]

**1. a.** Brightness or radiance shed by a luminary or an illuminant.

*a* **1529** SKELTON *P. Sparowe* 1174 Lyke Phebus beames shyne. **1535** COVERDALE *Ecclus.* xlii. 16 The sonne ouerloketh all thinges with his shine. *c* **1590** GREENE *Fr. Bacon* I. i, When heauens bright shine is shadowed with a fogge. **1629** MILTON *Hymn Nativ.* xxii, And mooned Ashtaroth..Now sits not girt with Tapers holy shine. **1683** TRYON *Way to Health* 73 This Fire..sends forth a bright shine and wholsom smell. **1716–8** LADY M. W. MONTAGU *Lett.* II. xliii. 14 Sitting..with the windows open, enjoying the warm shine of the sun. **1844** BROWNING *Colombe's Birthday* IV, Day by day, while shimmering grows shine. **1868** MORRIS *Earthly Par.* (1870) I. II. 460 Their red torches' shine. **1878** HARDY *Ret. Native* v. vii, [Her] bedroom was lighted up, and it was the shine from her window which had lighted the pole.

†**b.** A beam or ray; a halo. *Obs.*

**1581** J. BELL *Haddon's Answ. Osor.* 483 b, You may putt all your winninges in your eyes, and see never a shine the lesse. **1599** B. JONSON *Cynthia's Rev.* v. ii. Masque i, Her deuice within a Ring of clouds, a Heart with shine about it. **1610** G. FLETCHER *Christ's Tri.* iii, The under Corylets did catch the shines, To guild their leaves. **1654** OWEN *Saints' Persev.* i. 5 Such shines of Gods countenance upon them.

**2. a.** Lustre or sheen of an object reflecting light, as metal, water, silk. †*of shine*: lustrous, glistening.

**1599** B. JONSON *Cynthia's Rev.* v. v. (1601) L 3 b, Though we haue now put on no tyre of shine But mortall eyes vndazled may endure. **1648** HERRICK *Hesper.*, *Oberon's Palace* 22 He, and They Led by the shine of Snails. **1667** *Decay Chr. Piety* v. §29 Dazled with the glittering shine of Gold. **1696** TRYON *Misc.* i. 7 This Spirit..loseth its pure Colour, or bright native Shine. **1813** BYRON *Corsair* I. ii, They..to each his blade assign, And careless eye the blood that dims its shine. **1869** 'LEWIS CARROLL' *Phantasmagoria* 92 For it [the hat] had lost its shape and shine, And it had cost him four-and-nine. **1898** MEREDITH *Odes Fr. Hist.* 6 The lurid shine Of seas in the night-wind's whirl.

**b.** Coupled with *shade* (cf. SHINE *v.* 1 c).

**1838** MRS. BROWNING *Seraphim* II, Death upon his face Is rather shine than shade. **1863** 'C. BEDE' *Tour in Tartanland* 179 The mountain is..broken up into shine and shade.

**c.** *Painting* and *Photogr.* Shininess; a shiny patch.

**1880** *Athenæum* 28 Feb. 287/2 [The 'spirit fresco' process] being free from shine, is admirably adapted for mural work on a large scale, which should be seen at any angle. **1889** *Anthony's Photogr. Bull.* II. 37 [The daguerreotype] was full of shines. **1901** E. A. PRATT *Notable Masters of Men* 82 Without shine gold paint was of no value.

**d.** The polish given to a pair of boots by a bootblack; *transf.* a job of boot-blacking.

**1871** *News* (Galveston) 4 May (Schele de Vere), As I left the cars, an imp with smutty face, Said: Shine? **1872** LOWELL *Milton* Writ. 1890 IV. 103 If Mr. Masson never heard a shoeblack in the street say, 'Shall I give you a shine, sir?' his experience has been singular. **1894** *Advance* (Chicago) 27 Dec. 456/1 A little boot-black, who..shivered in the March wind and waited for shines.

**e.** The pupil of the eye. *dial.* (Cf. SHEEN *sb.*[1] 2.)

**1713** *Guardian* No. 58 ¶6 A Gallon of my October will do thee more good than all thou canst get by fine Sights at London, which I'll engage thou mayest put in the Shine of thine Eye. **1868** ATKINSON *Cleveland Gloss.*

**f.** *spec.* The shiny surface of a new cricket ball.

**1950** [see OPENER 1 e]. **1976** J. SNOW *Cricket Rebel* 30 Mike Smith didn't call upon me until Fred Trueman and Rumsey had seen the shine off the new ball.

**3. a.** Sunshine, *esp.* as opposed to *rain*; hence, fine weather. Also, moonlight. Also fig. phr. ***(come) rain or shine***, in any circumstances, come what may.

**1622** WITHER *Philarete* N 3, Or shine, or raine, or Blow, I, my Resolutions know. **1693** LOCKE *Educ.* §9 Heat and Cold, Shine and Rain. **1797** COLERIDGE *Christabel* I. II. 65 Ever and aye, by shine and shower. **1849** BULWER *Caxtons* x. iv, A ceremony which, every night, shine or dark, he insisted upon punctiliously performing. **1888** HENLEY *Bk. Verses* 113 Come storm, come shine, whate'er befall. **1896** A. E. HOUSMAN *Shropshire Lad* lv, And the youth at morning shine Makes the vow he will not keep. **1905** H. A. VACHELL *Hill* vi. 138 With me you're first, rain or shine. **1908** *Sears, Roebuck & Co. Catal.* 1076/2 These overcoats do double service, being adapted for all kinds of chilly weather, rain or shine. **1952** M. R. RINEHART *Pool* vii. 54 She walks everywhere here in the city, rain or shine. **1978** M. BIRMINGHAM *Sleep in Ditch* 115 He said..we'd got to put up with each other for ten years, 'come rain or shine'.

**b.** Abbrev. of MOONSHINE 4.

**1933** *Sun* (Baltimore) 22 July 8/7 You should take a julep made from the wonderful 'shine' made in the hills of Western Maryland. **1938** M. K. RAWLINGS *Yearling* i. 12 'Goin' to Grahamsville allus do make me hongry.' 'You git a snort o' 'shine there, is the reason,' she said. **1969** P. KAVANAGH *Such Men are Dangerous* (1971) iii. 42 Whiskey? A quart of shine, which the Lord loves, it being a natural product. **1977** E. LEONARD *Hunted* (1978) ix. 90 'Hundred-proof pure Kentucky bourbon. How about that.' Like it was a treat and all Davis drank was some kind of piss-poor shine.

**4.** *fig.* **a.** Brilliance, radiance, splendour, lustre. †Also [after G. *schein*], a specious appearance, a 'show'.

**1530** *Proper Dyaloge* in Roy *Rede me*, etc. (Arb.) 131 Vyce cloked vnder shyne of vertuousnes. **1535** COVERDALE *Col.* ii. 23 Which thinges haue a shyne [Luther, *schein*; 1611 shew] of wyszdome. **1586** FERNE *Blaz. Gentrie* 15 The bright shine, and worthines of his auncestors. *a* **1634** ? CHAPMAN *Rev. Hon.* II. i, The glorious shine of your illustrious vertues. **1734** POPE *Ess. Man* IV. 9 Fair op'ning to some court's propitious shine. *a* **1774** GOLDSM. *Hist. Greece* I. 380 The delusive shine of a lively and pompous eloquence. **1867** LOWELL *Fitz Adam's Story* 342 No other face had such a wholesome shine. **1878** BROWNING *Poets Croisic* 53 To bask ..in shine which kings and queens And baby-dauphins shed.

†**b.** Sunniness of disposition. *Obs. rare.*

**1710** STEELE *Spect.* No. 75 ¶4 What can make a Man so much in constant Good-humour and Shine, as we call it?

**c.** A brilliant display, a 'dash'. Phr. ***to cut (make) a shine.***

**1819** *Metropolis* II. 165 His name was well calculated to cut a shine. **1837** CARLYLE *Fr. Rev.* II. I. xii, To celebrate the nuptials with due shine and demonstration. **1847** ROBB *Squatter Life* (Bartlett 1860), To make a shine with Sally, I took her a new parasol.

**d.** Colloq. phr. ***to take the shine out of*** (less freq. ***from***, U.S. ***off***): to deprive (a person or thing) of his or its brilliance or pre-eminence; to outshine, surpass.

**1819** MOORE *Tom Crib* (ed. 3) 34 Shewing such a fist of mutton As..Would take the shine from Speaker Sutton. **1824** LANDOR *Imag. Conv.*, *Southey & Porson* Wks. 1853 I. 73/1, I am inclined to take the shine out of him for it. **1827** DE QUINCEY *Murder* Wks. 1854 IV. 33 The baker jumped up with surprising agility,..but the shine was now taken out of him. **1833** [SEBA SMITH] *Lett. J. Downing* iii. (1835) 43, I am only sorry I didn't bring Seth Sprague along with me, with his pitch-pipe, jest to take the shine off of them 'ere singers. **1842** LOVER *Handy Andy* xxi, The cares of the world..takes the shine out of us.

**5.** An abusive term for a Black. Also *attrib. U.S. slang.*

**1908** J. M. SULLIVAN *Criminal Slang* 24 *Shine*, a colored person. **1929** D. HAMMETT *Dain Curse* iv. 34 How'd you make out with the shine? **1934** J. T. FARRELL *Young Manhood* III. xv. 227 They saw one beautiful blonde girl with a coal-black, sweating nigger, and they said nothing, only because there were too many shines in the place. **1940** R. CHANDLER *Farewell, My Lovely* iii. 13 His voice said bitterly: 'Shines. Another shine killing. That's what I rate after eighteen years in this man's police department.' **1953** W. BURROUGHS *Junkie* v. 51 A Negro sitting opposite us smiled. 'The shine is wise,' said Roy in my ear. 'He is O.K.' **1969** S. GREENLEE *Spook who sat by Door* xiii. 116 He's a shine detective lieutenant.

**shine** (ʃaɪn), *sb.*[2] [perh. uses of prec. sb., but the senses are curiously parallel to those of SHINDY.]

**1.** A party, convivial gathering; usually ***tea-shine***, a 'tea-fight'. *dial.*

**1838** MRS. CARLYLE *Lett.* I. 98 Two tea-shines went off with éclat. **1882** *Jamieson's Sc. Dict.*, *Shine*,..in a good sense the term is generally applied to a social gathering, especially when of a convivial kind, as a wedding..or a merry-making, which is called a grand or great shine.

**2.** A disturbance, row, fuss. *colloq.*

**1832–53** *Whistle-binkie* Ser. III. 53 Siccan shines were there, Siccan noisy peltin'. **1849** CUPPLES *Green Hand* xi, Sich a shine and a nitty as I kicks up. **1852** DICKENS *Bleak House* lvii, There'd be a pretty shine made if I was to go a wisitin them. **1889** 'R. BOLDREWOOD' *Robbery under Arms* vi, What's one horse to make such a shine about?

**3.** *pl.* Capers, tricks. *U.S.* Cf. SHINE *sb.*[1] 4 c.

**1830** N. DANA *Mariner's Sk.* 34 (Thornton *Amer. Gloss.*), Has your skipper begun to cut any shines yet? **1852** MRS. STOWE *Uncle Tom's C.* iv, 'I'll boun you pulled 'em out, some o' your shines,' said Aunt Chloe.

**4.** ***to take a shine to*** (*colloq.*, orig. *U.S.*): to take a fancy for.

**1839** *Crockett Almanac 1840* 14, I wonst had an old flame I took sumthin of a shine to. **1848** LOWELL *Biglow P.* Ser. I. *A Letter*, My gracious! it's a scorpion thet's took a shine to play with't. **1908** W. CHURCHILL *Mr. Crewe's Career* x, He took a shine to you that night you saw him. **1934** F. H. BUSHICK *Glamorous Days* xxiii. 278 Nobody wanted the old corn cutter except this Irishman, who took a shine to it. **1956** P. SCOTT *Male Child* II. iv. 152, I suppose I oughtn't to blame you if Marion's taken a shine to you... You must have a way with women. **1961** *Guardian* 23 Mar. 10/6 Shaw evidently took a shine to the young hero-worshipping woman. **1978** L. MEYNELL *Papersnake* x. 132 He took to you... He took a shine to you. **1980** *Times Lit. Suppl.* 18 July 799/1 If her [*sc.* Barbara Pym's] heroines were married, they were not unfaithful to their husbands, although they might take a shine to the curate.

†**shine**, *a. poet. Obs.* [alteration of SHEEN *a.* by assimilation to SHINE *v.*] Shining, bright.

*a* **1593** MARLOWE *Ovid's Elegies* I. i. 34 Elegian Muse..Girt my shine browe [Ovid *flaventia tempora*] with Seabanke Mirtle praise. **1596** SPENSER *F.Q.* IV. iii. 3 These warlike Champions all in armour shine, Assembled were in field. **1603** FLORIO *Montaigne* II. xii. 259 *Stellisque micantibus Æthera fixum*..the skies with shine-starres fixt to be.

**shine** (ʃaɪn), *v.* Pa. t. and pa. pple. **shone** (ʃɒn). Forms: *Inf.* and *Present stem.* 1 scínan, scȳnan, 2–3 scine(n, 2–4 schine(n, 3–5 scyne, 3–6 schine, 3–8 schyne, (3 sine, 4 schijne, ssine, ssyne, shyyne, 5 schone (?), 6 shynne), 4–6 shyne, 3– shine. *Pa. t.* 1 scán, sceán (*pl.* scinon), 2–3 sc(e)an, 3–5 schon, 4–5 shoon, s(c)hoen, 4–6 schone, (3 scæn, s(c)on, shan, 4 schoon, 4, 7 shon, 6 shoone), 5– shone; *north.* 4 sca(i)n, schan, 4–5 shane, 4–6 schane, 5 chane; *weak* 4 scynde, schyn(e)de, shynede, schinede, 4–6 shyned, 5 schynyd, -it, 6 schynet, schynnit, 6 schyned, 6–7 shinde, 6–8 shin'd, 7 shind, 6– (now *U.S.*, *dial.* and *arch.*) shined. *Pa. pple.* 3 sinen; 4–6 shyned, 7 shin'd, 7– shined; 8 shon, 6– shone. [Com. Teut. str. vb.: OE. *scínan* (pa. t. *scán*, *scinon*, pa. pple. **scinen*) = OFris. *skîna* (WFris. *skine*, NFris. *skiin*), OS. *skînan* (MLG., LG., MDu. *schînen*, Du. *schijnen*), OHG. *scînan* (MHG. *scînen*, *schînen*, G. *scheinen* to shine, to seem, appear), ON. *skîna* (Sw. *skina*), Goth. *skeinan*:—OTeut. **skīnan*, f. root *skī* by means of the present-stem formative *n*, which was carried through into the past tense and pa. pple.

Affinities outside Teutonic are Skr. *chāyā* shade, shimmer, mod.Pers. *sāya*, Gr. σκιά, OSlav. *sěnĭ*, Albanian *hē* shade; for the sense cf. SHIM *sb.*[1] and *v.*[1], SHIMMER *v.*

The regular str. pa. pple. is rare in Eng., being unrecorded in OE. and appearing only once in ME. *sinen*; it was superseded by the weak form *shined*, which was in common use *c* 1300–1800; this was supplanted by the form of the str. pa. t., which first appears as pa. pple. in the second half of the 16th c. (Weak forms are found in some of the continental langs., e.g. (pa. t.) late WFris. *schynd*, MLG. *schynede*, OHG. *scînta*, early mod.G. *schein(e)te*.)]

**1. a.** *intr.* Of a heavenly body or an object that is alight: To shed beams of bright light; to give out light so as to illuminate; to be radiant. Also with *forth*, *out*.

*c* **725** *Corpus Gloss.* (Hessels) A 801 *Ardebat*, scaan. *c* **888** ÆLFRED *Boeth.* ix, þonne seo sunne on hadrum heofone beorhtost scineð, þonne aþeostriað ealle steorran. *c* **1000** ÆLFRIC *Gen.* i. 15 Hiȝ scinon on þære heofenan fæstnysse and alihton þa eorðan. *a* **1122** *O.E. Chron.* (Laud MS.) an. 678, Her ateowede cometa se steorra..& scan .iii. monðas ælce morȝen swilce sunnebeam. *a* **1200** *Moral Ode* 275 Neure sunne þer ne scinð. *c* **1220** *Bestiary* 19 in *O.E. Misc.*, Ne stireð he nout of slepe Til ðe sunne haueð sinen. *c* **1290** *St. Bridget* 41 in *S. Eng. Leg.* 193 þe sonne schon In at one hole. **1390** GOWER *Conf.* I. 323 Hove out of mi Sonne, And let it schyne into mi Tonne. *Ibid.* II. 120 The nyht was derk, ther schon no Mone. *c* **1440** *Alphabet of Tales* 513/5 So he wolde sytt all day to þe son shane on his face agayn. **1500–20** DUNBAR *Poems* xxxv. 1 Lucina schynnyng in silence of the nicht. **1566** GASCOIGNE *Jocasta* II. i, The aultars where the sacred flames haue shone. **1590** SHAKS. *Mids. N.* v. i. 272 Well shone Moone. **1620** T. GRANGER *Div. Logike* 29 It is day: because the Sun shineth above the horizon. **1703** ROWE *Ulysses* I. i, What Sun has shon that has not seen your Insolence. **1704** PRIOR *Celia to Damon* 20 Fires Eternal on Her Altars shine. **1735** JOHNSON *Lobo's Abyssinia*, Descr. iv. 64 When the Storm is over, the Sun Shines out as before. **1815** SCOTT *Guy M.* xxvii, It must surely have been a light in the hut of a forester, for it shone too steadily to be the glimmer of an *ignis fatuus*. **1860** TYNDALL *Glac.* I. xviii. 133 The fog became thin, and the sun shone through it.

*weak pa. t. c* **1305** *Pop. Treat. Sci.* (1841) 133/66 The sonne..that..Maketh hire [the moon] so schyne aboute as heo schynde in crestal. *c* **1385** CHAUCER *L.G.W.* 2194 No man she saw & ȝit shynede the mone. *c* **1450** tr. *De Imitatione* III. lv. 131 Whan þy lanterne shyned upon his hede. *a* **1578** LINDESAY (Pitscottie) *Chron. Scot.* (S.T.S.) I. 229 The sone ..schynnit bright wpoun the saillis. **1645** SYMONDS *Diary* (Camden) 243 This night I saw a rainbow..at five in the morning, and the moone shined bright. **1776** CHANDLER *Trav. Greece* xlv. 201 The moon shined bright.

**b.** Of the day: To be sunny or bright; also, to dawn. Chiefly *poet.*

**1382** WYCLIF *Matt.* xxviii. 1 In the euenyng of the saboth, ..that schyneth [Vulg. *lucescit*] in the firste day of the woke. **1567** *Gude & Godlie B.* (S.T.S.) 95 As the goldin morning schynis bricht. *a* **1578** LINDESAY (Pitscottie) *Chron. Scot.*

(S.T.S.) I. 397 Quhilk at last the daylyght begane to schyne. **1667** MILTON *P.L.* VII. 108 We can..dismiss thee ere the Morning shine. **1742** GRAY *West* I In vain to me the smileing Mornings shine.

**c.** impers. ***it shines***: it is sunny.

*c* **1400** *Beryn* 1317 Thow tokist noon hede whils it shoon hoot. **1577** TUSSER *Husb.* (1878) 43 At noone if it bloweth, at night if it shine. **1622** J. TAYLOR (Water P.) *Water-cormorant* A 4, According to his mood it raines or shines. **1853** HAWTHORNE *Engl. Note-bks.* (1883) I. 436 By and by the sun shone out, and it has continued to shine and shade every ten minutes ever since.

**d.** ***to shine upon***: to look favourably upon, be favourable to, said of a star, or (in biblical language) of the face of God. *arch.*

**1535** COVERDALE *Num.* vi. 25 The Lorde make his face to shyne vpon the. **1568** GRAFTON *Chron.* II. 707 Notwithstanding, that fortune shone on hym in obteyning the victorie agaynst the Erle of Warwike. **1591** SHAKS. *1 Hen. VI*, I. ii. 75 Heauen and our Lady gracious hath it pleas'd To shine on my contemptible estate. **1617** MORYSON *Itin.* II. 51 The Lord Mountjoy, like a good Planet, with a fortunate aspect began to shine thereon. **1648** CROMWELL *Let. to R. Hammond* 25 Nov., We are sure, the good-will of Him who dwelt in the Bush has shined upon us. **1791** BURNS *Lament Mary Q. of Scots* vi, May kinder stars Upon thy fortune shine!

**2. a.** Of a metallic, polished, smooth, or glossy object: To be bright or resplendent; to gleam, glisten, or glitter with reflected light.

*c* **897** ÆLFRED *Gregory's Past. C.* xiv. 88 Swæ swæ on ðæm mæssehræȝle scinð [*Hatton MS.* scienð] onȝemang oðrum bleom ðæt twyðrawene twin. *a* **1000** *Cædmon's Exod.* 125 (Gr.) Scean scir werod, scyldas lixton. *c* **1205** LAY. 27361 Sceldes blikien burnen scinen. *a* **1225** *Juliana* 54 (Royal MS.) Hire nebscheft schininde [*Bodl. MS.* schiminde] al as schene as þe sunne. *c* **1230** *Hali Meid.* 11 Nis hit nower neh gold al þat ter schineð. *a* **1300** *Cursor M.* 8484 Stedfast stode þe marbel stan, On-ferr þe golden letters scan. **1338** R. BRUNNE *Chron.* (1725) I. 148 Of gold schone his coroun. **13..** *E.E. Allit. P.* A. 80 Wyth schymeryng schene ful schrylle þay schynde. *c* **1386** CHAUCER *Prol.* 198 His heed was balled, þat shoon as any glas. *c* **1470** *Gol. & Gaw.* 20 Thair baneris schane with the sone, of siluer and sabill. **1526** TINDALE *Luke* ix. 29 His garment was whyte, and shoone. **1577** T. KENDALL *Flowers of Epigr.* 73 His tongue did lispe, his visage shinde. **1588** SHAKS. *L.L.L.* IV. iii. 246 O 'tis the Sunne that maketh all things shine. **1667** MILTON *P.L.* III. 508 Thick with sparkling orient Gemmes The Portal shon. **1751** LAVINGTON *Enthus. Meth. & Papists* III. (1754) 78 The whole House shined. **1808** SCOTT *Marm.* VI. Introd. 53 The huge hall-table's oaken face, Scrubb'd till it shone. **1860** TYNDALL *Glac.* II. i. 237 A rook's feather may be made to shine with magnificent iridescences. **1888** HENLEY *Bk. Verses* 118 Clear shine the hills. **1974** *Black World* Jan. 57/1 Her shiny black paint shined in the sun.

*indirect passive.* **1737** WHISTON *Josephus, Hist.* IV. x. §1 When they saw the riches of Rome..and found themselves shone round about..with silver and gold.

**b.** To be bright *with*.

**1606** SHAKS. *Ant. & Cl.* I. iii. 45 Our Italy, Shines o're with ciuill Swords. **1733** *Revol. Politicks* v. 37 The Streets in the Evening every where shined very gloriously with Bonefires. **1883** R. W. DIXON *Mano* II. ii. 68 The altar shone With gold and silver.

**3.** To be radiant or brilliant with high colouring, rich array, or the like; to be effulgent with splendour or beauty; to make a brave show. Now *rare*.

**971** *Blickl. Hom.* 7 Seo hwitnes þære lilian scineþ on þe. *c* **1375** *Cursor M.* 23696 (Fairf.) Mani flouris..neuer-mare þe colour tine bot as paradis salle þai shine. *a* **1400** *Pistill of Susan* 106 (MS. I.) Þe chaumpet, þe cheuerell, þat schon opon heyght. *c* **1450** *Mirk's Festial* 132 Þes two woymen þat schynen passyng all oþyr, wer two comyn woymen. **1513** DOUGLAS *Æneis* I. vi. 163 Her nek schane like unto the roise in May. **1577** T. KENDALL *Flowers of Epigr.* 84 b, In all thy body bewty shines, thy forhed shineth fair. *a* **1639** CAREW *To A. L.* 64 When a fair lady's face is pined, And yellow spread where red once shined. **1781** COWPER *Truth* 70 [The pheasant] retreats..To the close copse..And shines without desiring to be seen. **1823** SCOTT *Quentin D.* xxxii, We are somewhat shorn of our train,..but you, cousin, must shine out for us both. **1833** TENNYSON *Œnone* 176 Her light foot Shone rosy-white. **1837** CARLYLE *Fr. Rev.* I. I. ii, Some centennial Cactus-flower, which after a century of waiting shines out for hours! **1878** SUSAN PHILLIPS *On Seaboard* 199 In the golden meadows, where the cowslip and crowsfoot shone.

**4.** In various fig. applications (cf. 5 and 6), with retention of literal phraseology.

*c* **1000** *Ags. Gosp.* Matt. xiii. 43 Þonne scinað ða rihtwisan swa swa sunne on hyra fæder rice. *a* **1225** *Ancr. R.* 246, & te soðe sunne, þet is Jesu Crist, schineð þerefter schennure to þe soule. *a* **1300** *Cursor M.* 12574 Þe clernes self o godds light Schan on him. **1382** WYCLIF *Matt.* v. 16 So shyyne ȝoure liȝt before men, that thei see ȝoure good werkis. *c* **1400** *Rom. Rose* 5357 Whan Richesse shyneth bright, Love recovereth ageyn his light. *c* **1450** CAPGRAVE *Life St. Gilbert* xv, Ther schone, or ellis schyned, in þe soule of þese women a fayr beute of precious perles, of swech goostly richesse. **1526** TINDALE *2 Cor.* iv. 6 It is god..which hath shyned in oure hertes, for to geve the light of knowledge off the glorious god. **1535** COVERDALE *Isa.* ix. 2 As for them that dwel in the londe of the shadowe of death, vpon them shal the light shyne. **1594** MARLOWE & NASHE *Dido* II. i. 481 In whose stern faces shin'd the quenchles fire. **1611** SHAKS. *Cymb.* v. v. 476 The Radiant Cymbeline, Which shines heere in the West. **1654–66** EARL ORRERY *Parthen.* (1676) 212 A Virtue, greater than euer yet had shin'd on earth. **1700** DRYDEN *Fables* Pref. C 2, Chaucer..is a rough Diamond, and must first be polish'd e'er he shines. **1773** R. LOWTH *Serm. Rom. xii. 11* p. 6 Their Learning..was such as could only have shined in dark times. **1837** CARLYLE *Fr. Rev.* I. II. viii, For we shall still find Hope shining..as a mild heavenly light it shone; as a red conflagration it shines. **1849** T. WOOLNER *My Beautiful Lady* xii, How beautiful she is! A glorious gem She shines above the summer diadem Of flowers! **1982** *Chicago Sun-Times* 12 July 65 But Red Smith was a beacon who shined for half a century.

**5.** Of persons: To be conspicuous or brilliant in ability, character, achievement, or position; to be eminent or distinguished, to excel.

*c* **900** tr. *Bæda's Hist.* I. xii. (1890) 44 Se nama ðære Romaniscan þeode, se ðe mid swa lange scean & bryhte. *c* **1375** *Sc. Leg. Saints* xxvii. (*Machor*) 318 A man that schane of halynes. *c* **1400** *Apol. Loll.* 43 If we schyn in þeis vertues. **1474** CAXTON *Chesse* II. v. (1883) 69 Hit was better and more noble thynge to shyne in good maners than in vayssell. **1560** DAUS tr. *Sleidane's Comm.* 202 To shyne before theyr flock with honest examples of lyfe. **1647** CLARENDON *Hist. Reb.* I. §131 He shined in the House of Peers. **1710** STEELE *Tatler* No. 244 ¶1 An Ambition to excel, or, as the Term is, to shine, in Company. **1747** H. WALPOLE *Let. to Mann* 3 July, We shine at sea; two-and-forty sail of the Domingo fleet have fallen into our hands. **1805** T. HARRAL *Scenes of Life* I. 113 That cause in which British valour had so often shined triumphant. **1818** BYRON *Juan* I. xxiii, If there's anything in which I shine, 'Tis in arranging all my friends' affairs. **1836** THIRLWALL *Greece* xvii. III. 2 He..never shone as an orator. **1859** *Habits of Gd. Society* xiv. 349 The people who were stupidest before, suddenly shine out quite brilliantly. **1889** *Harper's Mag.* Mar. 561/1 There was..a special reason which made me resolved to shine at this ball at whatever cost.

**6. a.** Of something immaterial: To appear with conspicuous clearness; to be brilliantly evident or visible; to stand out clearly.

*c* **1340** HAMPOLE *Prose Treat.* 12 In þis gyfte schynes contemplacyone. **1387** TREVISA *Higden* (Rolls) IV. 449 A noble soule schoon by virtues in þat litel body. **1456** SIR G. HAYE *Law Arms* (S.T.S.) 6 His grete beautee schynit sa before all otheris. **1471** CAXTON *Recuyell* (Sommer) 247 Alle good manyeres began to growe and shyne in hym. *a* **1586** SIDNEY *Arcadia* II. (Sommer) 127 b, Then shined foorth indeede all loue among them. **1594** HOOKER *Eccl. Pol.* III. xi. §9 The wisedom of God, which shineth in the bewtifull varietie of all things. **1632** MASSINGER *Maid of Hon.* IV. iv, The reverence and Majesty of Iuno Shinde in her lookes. **1667** MILTON *P.L.* II. 304 Princely counsel in his face yet shon. **1725** POPE *Odyss.* XIV. 204 In all the youth his father's image shin'd. **1853** C. BRONTE *Villette* xx, What fun shone in his eyes as he recalled some of her fine speeches! **1888** 'J. S. WINTER' *Bootle's Childr.* vi, How the aged look faded off her worn face, and the sweet prettiness of former days began to shine out again. **1929** [see CONCORDANCY]. **1948** *Sun* (Baltimore) 18 Oct. 12/5 It was full of adept and memorable phrases... It shined with wit and humor.

**b.** To be clearly evident *through* an outward appearance.

**1590** SHAKS. *Two Gent.* II. i. 40 These follies are within you, and shine through you like the water in an Vrinall. **1605** —— *Macb.* III. i. 128 Your Spirits shine through you. **1628** FELTHAM Resolves II. [I.] xlvii. 138 To see the Countenance, (through which perhaps there shin'd a louely Maiesty..). **1858** HAWTHORNE *Fr. & It. Note-bks.* II. 31 The babe Jesus in her arm, with his Father shining through him. **1859** TENNYSON *Marr. Geraint* 545 Yniol's rusted arms Were on his princely person, but thro' these Prince-like his bearing shone.

†**7.** ***to shine through***: to be transparent. *Obs.*

**1675** ALSOP *Anti-Sozzo* III. ii. 207 This [reasoning] is very thin Stuff; it shines through.

**8.** *trans.* To shed light upon, illuminate. *rare.*

**1398** TREVISA *Barth. De P.R.* VIII. xvii. (1495) 325 The mone is alway halfe shyned of the sonne. *a* **1700** KEN *Hymnotheo* Poet. Wks. III. 355 God shines his Son, the Son God's shine reflects.

**9. a.** To cause (light) to shine, emit (rays). Also *fig.*

**1588** GREENE *Perimedes* H 2 b, Her eyes shines fauour, courtesie, and grace. **1590** —— *Never too late* (1600) E 3, Eyes that lighten and doe shine, Beames of loue that are diuine. **1647** SALTMARSH *Spark. Glory* 118 God..shines forth his wisdom..upon the world. **1661** FELTHAM *Resolves* II. xvi. 211 If it be but by reflection only, the beams are reverberated bright, as is the Sun that shines them. **1852** THACKERAY *Esmond* II. vii, She approached, shining smiles upon Esmond.

**b.** To show the light of (a lantern).

**1895** P. H. EMERSON *Birds*, etc. *Norfolk Broadland* xxxvi. 103 The sparrow-catcher comes of a night and shines his bright lantern, and the foolish birds fly at it like moths at a candle.

**c.** To direct the rays of (a light) *on*, *on to*, *under*, etc.

**1889** *Cent. Dict.* 5573/3 The policeman *shone* his lantern up the alley. **1950** *Sun* (Baltimore) 14 July 8/4 Two men in the office shined a flashlight under the platform. **1967** P. SHAFFER *Black Comedy* 48 The Colonel takes the torch from Harold and shines it pitilessly in Schuppanzigh's face. **1978** J. IRVING *World according to Garp* xi. 210 The policeman shined his light over Garp. **1979** *Sci. Amer.* Mar. 85/2 The intense light from this source was shined on a crystal that served as a frequency doubler.

**10. a.** ***to shine down***: to surpass in brilliance.

**1613** SHAKS. *Hen. VIII*, I. i. 20 The French..like Heathen Gods Shone downe the English. **1866** 'ANNIE THOMAS' *Walter Goring* xxxvii, 'Take it, Walter', she continued, 'give it to her; tell her she shines me down.'

**b.** To drive *away* by shining.

**1884** TENNYSON *Becket* III. i, Not The sun himself.. Could shine away the darkness of that gap.

**c.** ***to shine up to***; to try to please; to make oneself pleasant to. *U.S.*

**1882** *Century Mag.* Oct 827 It was then that David first set out to shine up to her. **1902** S. E. WHITE *Blazed Trail* xlii. 204 You might shine up to Hilda Farrand and join the rest of the fortune-hunters. **1971** C. FICK *Danziger Transcript* (1973) 143, I never saw him sell a single secret..or shine up to a Kraut PW.

**11.** To cause to shine, put a polish on; *orig. U.S.* (inflected *shined*) to black (boots).

**1613** R. C. *Table Alph.* (ed. 3), *Varnish*, shine, set a glosse vpon. **1872** CALVERLEY *Arab* 27 And thou hintest withal that thou fain would'st shine..these bulgy old boots of mine. **1872** O. W. HOLMES *Poet Breakf.-t.* xii, I wonder if they would find the seven-branched golden candlestick... I should like to..shine it up (excuse my colloquialisms). **1872** B. HARTE *Heiress of Red Dog* (1879) 188 Shine your boots, sir? **1892** GUNTER *Miss Dividends* ix, While his large boots have been very brightly shined by the boot-black. **1929** W. FAULKNER *Sound & Fury* 105 He wore a derby and shined shoes.

**12.** *U.S.* (*Hunting.*) To throw the light of a lantern, etc. on (the eyes of an animal); to locate the position of (an animal) in this way.

**1845** [W. T. THOMPSON] *Chron. Pineville* 169 (Bartlett *Dict. Amer.* 1860) You see the way we does to shine the deer's eyes is this—we holds the pan of fire so, on the left shoulder, and carries the gun at a trail in the right hand. **1872** SCHELE DE VERE *Americanisms* 541 Daniel Boone, while fire-hunting, shined a pair of mild blue eyes which struck him as not belonging to the game he was seeking. **1910** ROOSEVELT *Afr. Game Trails* x. 226 We had discovered that the way to get this..nocturnal animal was by 'shining' it with a lantern at night.

**'shineless,** *a.* [f. SHINE *sb.*[1] + -LESS.] Without brightness.

**1882** G. MACDONALD *Princess & Curdie* iii, A dull, shineless twilight filled the place.

**shiner** ('ʃaɪnə(r)). [f. SHINE *v.* + -ER[1].]

**1. a.** An object that shines.

**1398** TREVISA *Barth. De P.R.* VIII. xvi. (1495) 322 The sonne is..shyner of heuen [L. *fulgor olympi*]. **1633** G. HERBERT *Temple, Christmas* 29 Till I finde a sunne Shall stay, till we have done; A willing shiner. **1655** VAUGHAN *Silex Scint.* III. *Thalia Rediv.* 239 O blessed shiner, tell me whither Thou wilt be gone when night comes hither! **1765** J. BROWN *Chr. Jrnl.* 140 Where will yon glow-worms of carnal diversions,..yon shiners in the dark, be? **1844** WILLIS *Lady Jane* I. 326, I cannot shine—but I can see a star —Are there not worshippers as well as shiners? **1859** F. MAHONY *Rel. Fr. Prout* 403 A small twinkling shiner..in the wide canopy of heaven.

**b.** *pl.* Some Russian instrument of torture.

The word in the quotation is perhaps a misprint for *shiver* (pulley).

**1630** [F. CONSTABLE] *Pathomachia* III. iv. 29 Vnlesse thou confesse, the Russian Shiners, the Scottish Bootes,..and Peare of Confession shall torment thee.

**c.** *pl.* Coin, money, *esp.* sovereigns or guineas; occas. *sing.*, a silver or gold coin. *slang.*

**1760** FOOTE *Minor* II. Wks. 1799 I. 251 To let a lord of lands want shiners; 'tis a shame. **1806** SURR *Winter in Lond.* II. 63 So I shows him a shiner. **1838** DICKENS *O. Twist* xix, Is it worth fifty shiners extra, if it's safely done from the outside? **1851** MAYNE REID *Scalp Hunters* ix, I will bring you a mule-load of Mexican shiners. **1887** HAYTER *My Christmas Adv.* 9 Within my purse and pocket scarce a shiner.

**d.** A mirror; *spec.* one used by cheaters at cards. *slang.*

**1812** J. H. VAUX *Flash Dict.*, *Shiner*, a looking-glass. **1819** *Sporting Mag.* (N.S.) IV. 230 He then asked me if I had bought shiners? which means glasses. **1909** *Tit-Bits* 14 Aug. 515/2 The 'shiner' is carried separately in the pocket until needed, while the gambler smokes the pipe.

**e.** *colloq.* A silk hat.

**1867** F. FRANCIS *Bk. Angling* vi. 154 A tall black hat, or one of the genus termed 'shiner'.

**f.** A diamond or other jewel. Usu. *pl. slang.*

**1884** *Queenstown Free Press* 15 Jan. (Pettman), When they dug it up they at once came to the conclusion it was a real shiner. **1928** M. C. SHARPE *Chicago May* 287 *Sparklers, sparks, shiners..*, etc.—diamonds. **1934** D. L. SAYERS *Nine Tailors* 274, I never had those shiners. **1959** [see ICE *sb.* 4 c].

**g.** A black eye. *slang.*

**1904** 'NO. 1500' *Life in Sing Sing* 253/1 *Shiner*, a discolored eye. **1932** [see HECK *sb.* and *int.*]. **1934** A. MERRITT *Burn Witch Burn!* vii. 89 All I can do is..be dignified an' maybe hand out a shiner or two if they get too rough. **1943** C. S. FORESTER *Ship* xviii. 114 That's a rare shiner you've got there, Grant. **1958** C. WILLIAMS *Man in Motion* (1959) iii. 29 At first I thought it was because of the shiner and the bruises on my face, but then I began to wonder. **1967** [see LEFT *sb.* 2 a]. **1977** *Daily Mirror* 16 Mar. 3/5 Annie Walker, Coronation Street's snooty landlady, is about to show up in the snug..sporting a real shiner. But her black eye is not the result of a well-rehearsed punch-up in the taproom.

**h.** *Paper-making.* A glistening particle of a mineral impurity on the surface of finished paper.

**1922** *Manufacture of Pulp & Paper* III. VIII. 3 In colored papers, shiners will not take the dye. **1963** R. A. HIGHAM *Handbk. Papermaking* vii. 197 When super-calendering papers with a high percentage of straw in the furnish, there is a tendency towards shiners and windows.

**2.** One who shines: **a.** One who excels or is eminent.

**1810** *Splendia Follies* III. 106 He was never formed for a shiner through life. **1847** HALLIWELL, *Shiner*, a clever fellow. *North.*

**b.** *pl.* A nickname for the Northumberland Fusiliers, formerly the 5th Foot.

**1891** *Dict. Nat. Biog.* XXV. 3/1 The 5th was..popularly known as the 'Shiners', from its smart appearance and attention to parade details.

**c.** A bootblack.

**1912** *19th Cent.* Nov. 1018 An occasional white face may be seen even among the noisy shiner boys, and the little white shiner works continuously.

**d.** A window-cleaner. *slang.*

**1958** *Listener* 20 Nov. 818/2 His fellow shiners disregarded the L.C.C. by-law, because very few windows are equipped with metal hooks for holding on a safety belt.

**1967** *Sunday Times* 8 Jan. 3/7 Len is widely regarded as London's top 'shiner' (window cleaner). **1977** *Centuryan* (Office Cleaning Services) Christmas 1/1 There we were, shiners and cleaning ladies, surrounding Fred and Dora on the float by the London Wall.

**3. a.** Applied to various small silvery fishes; the young of the mackerel; *U.S.* any of various small freshwater fishes, chiefly cyprinoids as the dace.

***golden shiner***, a fish of the genus *Nometigonus*.

**1836** YARRELL *Brit. Fishes* I. 124 The young Mackerel, which are called Shiners, are from four to six inches long by the end of August. **1836** J. RICHARDSON *Fauna Bor.-Amer.* III. 122 *Cyprinus* (*Leuciscus*) *chrysoleucas*... New York Shiner. **1839** KIRTLAND in *Bost. Jrnl. Nat. Hist.* III. 339 *Luxilus elongatus*... The Red-bellied Shiner. *Ibid.* 341 *L. dissimilis*... The Spotted Shiner. **1844** O. W. HOLMES *Lines Berksh. Jubilee* 46 Oh, what are the prizes we perish to win To the first little 'shiner' we caught with a pin. **1888** GOODE *Amer. Fishes* 99 The 'Sailor's Choice'..bears several other names..as the 'Porgy' and 'Shiner'. **1893** *Outing* XXII. 89/2 A golden shiner about five inches in length.

**b.** = SILVER-FISH 2. (In mod. Dicts.)

†ˈ**shiness.** *Obs. north.* In 1 **scinisse**, 4 **schinnes.** [f. SHINE *v.* + -NESS.] Light, brightness.

*c* **950** *Lindisf. Gosp.* Mark xiii. 24 Ðe mona ne seleð scinisse his [*splendorem suum*]. *a* **1300** *Cursor M.* 23688 þat scene schinnes [*Gött.* þe schene schining] o cristal.

**shiness,** variant spelling of SHYNESS.

**shingle** (ˈʃɪŋg(ə)l), *sb.*[1] Forms: 3 **scincle**, 3–6 **shyngle**, 4 **schingel**, **schingle**, **schyngil**, **scingle**, **shyngel**, **-yl**, **singel**, 4–6 **schyngle**, **shingell**, 5 **chyngle**, **chyngyl**, 5–6 **schyngyl(l**, **shingil(l**, **shyngul(l**, 6 **s(c)hengle**, **shengyll**, **shyngyll(e**, **syngle**, 6–7 **single**, 7 **shingelle**, 4– **shingle**. [ME. *scincle*, *shyngle*, app. representing (? through an AF. modification) L. *scindula*, later form of *scandula*, commonly held to be due to the influence of Gr. σχινδαλμός.

L. *scindula* is represented in Germanic by OHG. *scindala*, *scintila*, MHG. *schintel*, (also mod.) *schindel*, MLG. *schindele*, MDu. *schindel*: cf. SHINDLE. L. *scandula* passed into Romanic as F. *échandole*, It. *scandola*.]

**1. a.** (*a*) A thin piece of wood having parallel sides and one end thicker than the other, used as a house-tile.

*c* **1200** *Vices & Virtues* 95 Ðe faste hope..is rof and wrikð alle ðe hire bieð beneðen mid ðe scincles of holie þohtes. *c* **1305** *Land Cokaygne* 57 in *E.E.P.* (1862) 157 þe scingles alle Of cherche cloister boure and halle. **1335–6** in Bayley *Tower Lond.* (1821) App. I. p. ij, Item in defectibus aulæ domini regis in coopertura, shyngles, coquinæ, pistrinæ. **1398** TREVISA *Barth. De P.R.* XVII. clxviii. (Bodl. MS.), The laþþe..is nailed þwarteouer to þe rafters and theron hongeþ sclattes, tile, and schingels. **14..** *Voc.* in Wr.-Wülcker 610/13 *Scindula*, a shyngul. **1510** STANBRIDGE *Vocabula* (W. de W.) B iv b, *Scandula*, a shyngylles [*sic*]. **1577** B. GOOGE *Heresbach's Husb.* II. (1586) 106 Shingles..are to be cutte betwixte midde Winter, and the beginning of the Westerne Windes. **1591** PERCIVALL *Sp. Dict.*, *Ripia*, a lath, a single. **1669** WORLIDGE *Syst. Agric.* 214 Shingles are to be preferred before Thatch. **1785** *Gentl. Mag.* LV. II. 49 The houses are almost all of wood, covered with the same; the roof with shingles. **1817–8** COBBETT *Year's Resid. Amer.* (1822) 317 Your house..covered with cedar shingles. **1886** RUSKIN *Præterita* I. 299 The Jura cottage..is covered with thin slit fine shingles.

(*b*) *collect. sing.*

*c* **1330** *Arth. & Merl.* 5874 Arthour smot on hem, saunfaile, So on þe singel doþe þe haile. *c* **1340** *Nominale* (Skeat) 481 *Couert oue tiel ou cene*, Hilde with tile or with schyngle. *c* **1440** *Pallad. on Husb.* I. lxxv, Heled weel with shyngul, tile, or broom. **1552** in *Archæol. Cant.* (1872) VIII. 128 For makyng vj thowsen of schyngle & iiij honder xxix s. **1557** in *Shropsh. Par. Docum.* (1903) 58 Re'd of mr Vicar for olde Shengle vi$^{d}$. **1575** *Ibid.* 65 For on thowsand of shyngle xviii$^{s}$. **1872** YEATS *Techn. Hist. Comm.* 132 Their roofs of shingle or of thatch. **1899** BARING-GOULD *Vicar of Morwenstow* ix, The roof was covered with oak shingle.

**b.** fig. phr. (orig. Australian colloq.). ***a shingle short***: 'a tile loose': said of one who is mentally deficient.

**1852** MUNDY *Antipodes* III. i. 17 Let no man having, in colonian phrase, 'a shingle short' try this country. **1885** MRS. C. PRAED *Head Stat.* xviii. II. 6 I've been given to understand that poets are usually a shingle short. **1957** J. FRAME *Owls do Cry* 26 Francie Withers has a brother who's a shingle short. **1966** P. WHITE *Solid Mandala* 82 He accepted Arthur his twin brother, who was, as they put it, a shingle short. **1968** *Southerly* XXVIII. 3 Royal said: 'I reckon we're a shingle short to 'uv ended up on the Parramatta Road.'

**c.** *gen.* A piece of board. (Cf. *shingle-board*.)

**1825** SCOTT *Betrothed* ii, A long low hall, built of rough wood lined with shingles. **1825** J. NEAL *Bro. Jonathan* III. 150 A piece of shingle, which he was pretending to whittle, after the fashion of your 'nait'ral born' Yankee. **1844** *Cath. Weekly Instr.* 114 The hut was low, built of shingles. **1894** MISS E. L. BANKS *Campaigns Curios.* 143, I had neglected to provide myself with a shingle, with small holes, in which to place my flowers, to make them stand upright.

**d.** *U.S.* A small sign-board. ***to hang out*** (or ***set up***) ***one's shingle***, to begin to practise a profession.

**1847** J. M. FIELD *Drama in Pokerville* (Bartlett 1860), The 'No Admittance!' which frowned from a shingle over the door. **1865** HOLLAND *Plain Talk* iv. 131 When a boy changes his roundabout for a coat, he is ready to 'stick out his shingles'. **1879** TOURGEE *Fool's Err.* i. 10 He studied law.. and hung out his shingle. **1944** V. W. BROOKS *World of Washington Irving* xvi. 308 Catlin hung out his shingle as a portrait-painter and made a little money for his next trip. **1963** J. N. HARRIS *Weird World Wes Beattie* i. 8 He had hung up his shingle and commenced the practice of criminal law in the lower courts. **1977** *Time* 22 Aug. 48/2 Any academic can set up his shingle and be a literary critic.

**e.** A style of cutting women's hair short, as in the bob, but with the back hair shingled (cf. SHINGLE *v.*[1] 2 a). Also, hair cut in this way.

**1924** *Hairdressing* Feb. (*caption*), Based on the 'shingle'. **1927** F. E. BAILY *Golden Vanity* xvii. 265 Doris powdered her face, combed her dark shingle, lit a cigarette, and picked up her beef cubes. **1945** N. MITFORD *Pursuit of Love* xx. 172 She had a short canary-coloured shingle (windswept) and wore trousers. **1975** G. HOWELL *In Vogue* 13/1 The small pitted cloche brought in the bob, which became the 'shingle' or the 'bingle' of the twenties.

**2. a.** *attrib.* and *Comb.*, as ***shingle-laden***, ***-laying***, ***-maker***, ***-wise***; ***shingle effect*** (sense 1 e); †**shingle-board** = sense 1, 1 c; **shingle cap, net**, a cap-shaped hair-net for preserving the hair-style in bed; **shingle-nail**, a nail used in fixing shingles in building; **shingle-oak**, (*a*) the laurel oak, *Quercus imbricaria*; (*b*) the she-oak; **shingle-weaver, -wood** (see quots.); **shingle wig**, a short-haired wig cut in a shingle.

Several other compounds are given in Knight's *Dict. Mech.* and the recent U.S. dicts.

*c* **1300** in *Black Bk. Admiralty* (Rolls) II. 192 Menu bord qe lem appele baryl bord ou *shyngel-bord. **1589** HAKLUYT *Voy.* 286 The roofes..are couered with shingle boordes. **1637** HEYWOOD *Royall Ship* 13 Lined with shingle-boards, or wainscot-plankes. **1926** *Vogue* Late Nov. 85 A charming little *shingle cap for night wear. **1934** A. CHRISTIE *Murder on Orient Express* II. xi. 146 She had on a shingle cap and I only saw the back of her head. **1977** 'E. MCBAIN' *Long Time no See* x. 152 Her blond hair was cut in..bangs on the forehead, a *shingle effect at the back of her head. **1881** *Chicago Times* 14 May, The vessel is *shingle-laden. **1866** ROGERS *Agric. & Prices* I. xv. 279 *Shingle-laying is sometimes paid by the thousand. **1792** in E. G. Ingham *Sierra Leone* iii. (1894) 46 Bakers, 4... *Shingle Maker, 1. **1836** HALIBURTON *Clockm.* Ser. I. iii, A shingle-maker's shed. **1303–4** *Acc. Chamberl. Chester* (1910) 42 Bord-nail, *schingelneil, latnail. **1554** in *Shropsh. Par. Docum.* (1903) 55 Half a m of syngle nayle. **1867** LOWELL *Fitz Adam's Story* 417 He had been known to cut a fig in two And change a board-nail for a shingle-nail. **1886** MORSE *Jap. Homes* 79 Bamboo pins..are used as shingle-nails. **1928** R. MACAULAY *Keeping up Appearances* ix. 89 She had bought..three *shingle nets. **1818** T. NUTTALL *Genera N. Amer. Plants* II. 214 *Quercus imbricaria* (*Shingle Oak). **1889** MAIDEN *Native Plants Austral.* 15 *Casuarina stricta*,..'Shingle Oak', 'Coast She-oak'. **1860** BARTLETT *Dict. Amer.* (ed. 3), **Shingle-weaver*, a workman who dresses shingles. **1928** *Times* 19 Dec. 15/7 After bathing the *shingle-wig was slipped over the dishevelled head. **1872** COUES *N. Amer. Birds* 46 Scales ..apt to be imbricated, or fixed *shingle-wise. **1864** GRISEBACH *Flora W. Ind. Islands* 787 *Shingle-wood: *Nectandra leucantha*.

**b.** passing into *adj.* = (*a*) consisting of, covered or built with, shingles, as ***shingle house***, ***roof***; (*b*) used in making shingles, as ***shingle machine***, ***saw***.

**1810** W. IRVING *Life & Lett.* (1864) I. 245 More pleasing in the sight of Heaven..than building a dozen shingle church steeples. **1819–20** —— *Leg. Sleepy Hollow* Sk.-Bk. (1821) 299 The money invested in..shingle palaces in the wilderness. **1848–54** WEBSTER, *Shingle-roofed*, having a roof covered with shingles. *a* **1850** MRS. BROWNING *Runaway Slave* xi, When the shingle-roof rang sharp with the rains. **1858** SIMMONDS *Dict. Trade*, *Shingle-machine*, an American machine for riving, shaving, and jointing shingles, which is capable of making 30,000 per day. *Ibid.*, *Shingle-mill*, a saw-mill for cutting planks or logs into shingles. **1868** *Rep. U.S. Comm. Agric.* (1869) 56 Board and shingle sugar-houses. **1882** R. GRIMSHAW *Suppl. Grimshaw on Saws* 235 One we know of is running a 42-inch shingle saw in heading 1500 revolutions per minute. **1899** BARING-GOULD *Vicar of Morwenstow* ix, A shingle roof he would have or none at all. **1974** D. SEARS *Lark in Clear Air* i. 19 Snoring with a shrill gutter like a shingle-saw slicing knotty cedar.

**shingle** (ˈʃɪŋg(ə)l), *sb.*[2] Forms: α. 6– **chingle**, 6–7 *Sc.* **chyngill.** β. 6– **shingle.** [Of obscure origin; the forms with *ch-*, which are somewhat the earlier and are mainly Sc. and East Anglian, suggest an echoic origin (cf. *chink*). The change of *ch-* to *sh-* is paralleled in the history of SHIVER *v.*[2] The relation of this word to Norw. *singl* coarse sand, small stones, NFris. *singel* (large) gravel, is not clear.]

**1.** Small roundish stones; loose, waterworn pebbles such as are found collected upon the seashore. In New Zealand also loose angular stones in mountain country. **a.** *collect. sing.*

α. **1598** HAKLUYT *Voy.* I. 556 Chingle and great stones being skorched in that fiery gulfe. **1603** *Reg. Mag. Sig. Scot.* 517/2 Arenam et lie chyngill et lapides super ripas dicte aque. **1611** in *Extracts Rec. Convent. Burghs Scot.* (1870) II. 327 To caus the fyscher boits to be ballastet..with chyngill onlie, and nocht with staynes. **1633** J. DONE tr. *Aristeas' Hist. Septuagint* 51 In the Superficies..was represented.. the Flood Meander,..in the Channell of which, one might see a Splendor of Precious Stones, representing his rowling waues, which Chingle was of Carbuncles [etc.]. **1787** W. H. MARSHALL *Provinc. Norfolk* (E.D.S.), *Chingle*, gravel, free from dirt. **1798** *Statist. Acc. Scot.* XX. 27 The surface is not above a foot or 18 inches from the chingle. **1807** HEADRICK *Arran* 232 This stratum is not visible on the sea beach, being probably covered with chingle or stones.

β. **1676** *Phil. Trans.* XI. 627 The shores..are for the most part sandy, but only in some points there is some shingle cast up. **1717** S. SEWALL *Diary* 28 Sept., Not to fetch any more Shingle from the point, to mend the Causey. **1778** *Eng. Gazetteer* (ed. 2), Ramsey, in the Isle of Man,..standing upon a beach of loose sand, or shingle. **1833** LYELL *Princ. Geol.* III. 271 A violent and transient rush of waters which tore up the soil to a great depth, excavated valleys, gave rise to immense beds of shingle. **1867** 'OUIDA' *Cecil Castlemaine*, etc. 239 In dashed the bay through the park-gates, sending the shingle flying up in small simoons. **1882** GEIKIE *Text-bk. Geol.* II. II. §6. 155 In shingle the stones are coarser, ranging up to blocks as big as a man's head or larger. **1894** CROCKETT *Raiders* 116 The swell broke upon a beach of shingle and sand. **1900**, etc. [see *shingle-slip* below]. **1944**, etc. [see *shingle-slide* below]. **1959** *Tararua* XIII. 46 The word *shingle* itself is given an unusual meaning in New Zealand. In standard usage it refers only to the small roundish water-worn stones of the seashore or rivers. We use it also of moderately-sized, angular stones, such as in fact are found in shingle slides.

**b.** *collect. pl.* (Locally the name of a pebbly beach or bank; cf. quot. 1577 in 2 β.)

**1574** W. BOURNE *Regim. Sea* xxii. 60 At the comming from Portland you shall haue .35. fadoms, and small shingles. *a* **1608** DEE *Relat. Spirits* I. (1659) 115 The shingles, through the which the Spring runs. **1706** PHILLIPS (ed. Kersey), *Shingles*,..the Name of a Shelf, or Sand-bank in the Sea, about the Isle of Wight. **1803** SOUTHEY in *Ann. Rev.* I. 9 A neck of land chiefly composed of sand, shingles and drift wood. **1818** SCOTT *Rob Roy* xviii, The way..was a happy interchange of bog and shingles. **1842** SEDGWICK in *Hudson's Guide Lakes* (1843) 188 The overlying..beds of limestone are..separated from the..beds of slate, by masses of conglomerate or cemented shingles. **1848** THACKERAY *Van. Fair* xxv, Just as the nymph..stepped out of the little caravan on to the shingles. **1862** ANSTED *Channel Isl.* I. iv. 79 The shingles here do not afford a landing-place.

**2.** A beach or other tract covered with loose roundish pebbles.

α. **1513** DOUGLAS *Æneis* X. vi. 34 In the schald scho stoppis, and dyd stand Apon a dry chyngill or bed of sand. *a* **1825** FORBY *Voc. E. Anglia*, *Chingly*, abounding in small stones, etc., commonly applied to a newly repaired road. The loose pebbly beach is called the chingle or shingle.

β. **1577** HARRISON *England* I. ix. 22 b, in *Holinshed*, We meete with y$^{e}$ fal of a water neere to S. Catherins chapple as we sailed by y$^{e}$ Shingle. **1674** N. FAIRFAX *Bulk & Selv.* 200 A world of Sea-stones on the shingle. **1822** T. MITCHELL *Com. Aristoph.* II. 182 He has robb'd the sea-shore, And has hived such a store As would give a large shingle its coating. **1856** EMERSON *Eng. Traits*, *Ability* Wks. (Bohn) II. 34 The enchantments of barren shingle and rough weather.

**3.** *attrib.*, as ***shingle-ballast***, ***bank***, ***beach***, ***-bed***, ***-stone***, ***track***, ***trap***; ***shingle-covered***, ***-formed*** adjs.; **shingle slide, -slip** *N.Z.* (see quot. 1944); **shingle-tramper** (see quot.).

**1801** *Naval Chron.* V. 270 The many instances of injury arising from the use of *shingle ballast. **1888** F. COWPER *Cædwalla* i. 15 The scrub on the top of the *shingle bank. **1834** MARRYAT *Peter Simple* xxvi, Oh! with what joy did I first put my foot on the *shingle beach at Sallyport. **1861** C. C. BOWEN *Poems* 76 Ghastly white beneath, Lay stretched the rough, drear *shingle-bed. **1881** *Rep. Geol. Explor. New Zealand* 123 The Dart flows along a wide shingle-bed. **1875** W. M$^{c}$ILWRAITH *Guide Wigtownshire* 51 A narrow, *shingle-covered opening in the cliffs. **1897** MARY KINGSLEY *W. Africa* 116 Masses of *shingle-formed conglomerate. **1944** *Mod. Junior Dict.* (Whitcombe & Tombs) (ed. 7) 365 **Shingle-slide* or *-slip*,..a term used in New Zealand for (steep) mountain-sides covered with loose, sliding stones, in England called 'screes'. **1959** A. MCLINTOCK *Descr. Atlas N.Z.* 32 With the baring of the ground between the tussocks, sheet and wind erosion have taken place and there has been a speeding up of the creep of the mantle of rock waste, resulting in the formation of new shingle slides and an increase in area of old ones. **1900** *Canterbury Old & New* 190 One of the most characteristic features of our Canterbury Alps is afforded by the numerous '*shingle-slips' formed by the weathering of rocks. **1971** *N.Z. Listener* 19 Apr. 56/4 The creek beside the shingle slip just below the confluence. **1614** T. GENTLEMAN *England's Way* 25 Their haven [*viz.* Southwold, Suffolk] is..stopped vp with Beach and *Chingle-stone. **1863** LYELL *Antiq. Man* 31 One of the round shingle stones. **1886** KENDALL *Poems* 201 He camps by the side of a *shingle track. **1867** SMYTH *Sailor's Word-bk.*, **Shingle-tramper*, a coast-guard man. **1839** *Civil Eng. & Arch Jrnl.* II. 85/2 Shingle has a decided tendency to drive eastward, and convert harbours lying in its course into what have been designated '*shingle traps'.

**shingle,** *sb.*[3] Erron. f. SINGLE *sb.* 1 b.

**1660** HOWELL *Parly of Beasts* 51 That lovely white Hinde (though she hath som black spots about her shingle)..she was once a Woman. **1661** MORGAN *Sph. Gentry* I. vi. 81 [The tail] of the Hart is the Tail, and the Ro-buck or Deer the Shingle. **1688** HOLME *Armoury* II. vii. 133/1.

**shingle** (ˈʃɪŋg(ə)l), *v.*[1] [f. SHINGLE *sb.*[1]]

**1.** *trans.* To cover, roof (a house, etc.) with shingles.

**1562** WITHALS *Dict.* 42 b/2 *Scandulo*, to shyngle. **1577** V. LEIGH *Surv.* I ij, Whether..slated, shingled, or thatched. **1638** BP. MOUNTAGU *Art. Enq. Visit.* A 2, Is your Church leaded, tiled, slated, shingled, thatched with straw or reede. **1796** J. ADAMS *Diary* 27 July, I rode up to the barn, which Mr. Pratt has almost shingled. **1833** [SEBA SMITH] *Lett. J. Downing* xxi. (1835) 124 He'll new shingle our old barn for nothin. **1865** 'ARTEMUS WARD' *Trav.* II. xii, When the Lion House was ready to be shingled.

*transf.* **1885** *Harper's Mag.* Mar. 533/1 The..walls and.. roof are shingled with slate. **1891** *Century Mag.* Nov. 61 We constructed a low châlet.., shingling it with swamp grass.

**2. a.** To cut (hair), properly so as to give the effect of overlapping shingles, by exposing the ends of hair all over the head; also *absol.* *U.S.*; to cut (women's hair) so that it tapers from the back of the head to the nape of the neck; also *absol.*, to have the hair so cut.

**1857** HOLLAND *Bay Path* 232 (Thornton *Amer. Gloss.*), I'm great on cutting hair. I don't suppose there's anybody in the settlement can shingle like me... By the way, don't you want your hair cut? I don't know how I'm going to get along, unless you do have it jest shingled. **1864** R. F.

BURTON in *Anthropol. Rev.* II. 51 To 'shingle off' their hair as closely as possible. **1909** KATE WIGGIN *Susanna & Sue* xii, It's kind of pityish to have your hair shingled. **1924** *Punch* 17 Sept. 319 It moves me not if Araminta shingles Her locks, or Evelina has them bobbed. **1926** GALSWORTHY *Silver Spoon* iv. 25 Fully dressed for the evening, she had but little on, and her hair was shingled. *Ibid.*, She had been one of the first twelve to shingle. **1976** M. GREEN *Children of Sun* (1977) v. 207 Women began to bob their hair immediately after the war, were shingling it by 1925.

**b.** To cover like a shingled roof. *U.S.*

**1858** O. W. HOLMES *Aut. Breakf.-t.* 11 A somewhat more than middle-aged female, with a parchment forehead and a dry little 'frisette' shingling it.

**c.** (See quot.) *U.S.*

**1860** BARTLETT *Dict. Amer.* (ed. 3), *To shingle*, to chastise. A shingle applied *a posteriori* is a favorite New England mode of correcting a child.

**shingle,** *v.*[2] *Iron-manuf.* [ad. F. *cingler*, ad. G. *zängeln*, f. *zange* tongs, pincers.] *trans.* To subject (the puddled ball) to pressure and blows from a hammer so as to expel impurities.

**1674**, etc. [see SHINGLING *vbl. sb.*[2]]. **1784** in *Abridgm. Specif., Iron & Steel* (1858) 13 Shingling, welding, and manufacturing iron and steel into barrs, plates, rods, and otherwise. *Ibid.* 365 The slabe, having been shingled..to the sizes of the grooves in my rollers. **1825** J. NICHOLSON *Oper. Mech.* 768 These loops are..brought to a white or welding heat, and then shingled into half-blooms or slabes. **1861** FAIRBAIRN *Iron* 105 The old method of shingling the puddle balls..was to reduce them to shape by a heavy hammer called the forge-hammer or helve.

†**shingle,** *v.*[3] [? f. CINGLE, girdle, with assimilation to SHINGLES.] *trans.* To girdle round.

**1621** T. WILLIAMSON tr. *Goulart's Wise Vieillard* 35 Till the gout is in their knees, or the dropsie doth painefully shingle them round.

**shingled** (ˈʃɪŋg(ə)ld), *ppl. a.*[1] [f. SHINGLE *sb.*[1] or *v.*[1] + -ED.]

**1.** Covered or tiled with shingles; in first quot., ? having the outer timbers overlapping like tiles, clinker-built.

**1362** LANGL. *P. Pl.* A. x. 170 Eihte soules And of vche beest A Couple, þat in þe schynglede schup schullen ben I-saued. **1577** V. LEIGH *Surv.* I ij, Buildinges..whether..Tyled, slated, shingled, or thatched. **1818** J. HASSELL *Rides & Walks* II. 107 The church has a shingled tower. **1881** *19th Cent.* Aug. 306 The prevalence of shingled spires in the wooded districts. **1885** C. F. HOLDER *Marvels Anim. Life* 216 To capture the rain-water from the shingled roof.

**2.** Arranged tile-wise, imbricated.

**1884** COUES *N. Amer. Birds* 94 Individual feathers of the notæum..smoothly shingled or imbricated.

**3.** Of hair: cut with the ends exposed all over the head or in a shingle. Of persons: having hair so cut.

**1889** KIPLING *From Sea to Sea* (1899) I. xxi. 414 The American missionary teaches the Japanese girl to wear bangs—'shingled bangs'—on her forehead. **1924** M. ARLEN *Green Hat* i. 42 Iris Storm was the first English-woman I ever saw with 'shingled hair'. This was in 1922. **1926** R. MACAULAY *Crewe Train* I. iii. 19 She looked..like a Beardsley woman shingled. **1930** W. S. MAUGHAM *Cakes & Ale* xxiii. 231 'Very quiet,' I said to the shingled barmaid. **1953** 'N. SHUTE' *In Wet* vii. 210 He stroked the soft, shingled hair at the back of her head. **1978** *Church Times* 1 Sept. 5/4 Their hair is shingled and rigidly marcel-waved. They stand in Junoesque poses like over-blown flappers.

ˈ**shingled,** *ppl. a.*[2] [f. SHINGLE *sb.*[2] + -ED[2].] Covered with or consisting of shingle or rounded pebbles.

**1802** BLOOMFIELD *Rural Tales* 53 May your days Glide on, as glides the Stream that never stays; Bright as whose shingled bed..May all your..Virtues shine! **1888** HENLEY *Bk. Verses* 156 The shingled shore.

ˈ**shingled,** *ppl. a.*[3] See SHINGLE *v.*[2]

**1884** W. H. GREENWOOD *Steel & Iron* xvi. 305 The shingled blooms will not be uniformly homogeneous if they are produced from different-sized puddled balls.

ˈ**shingler**[1]. [f. SHINGLE *sb.*[1] or *v.*[1] + -ER[1].]

**1.** One who shingles houses, etc.; also *U.S.* 'one who or a machine which cuts and prepares shingles' (Ogilvie 1882).

**1445** in *5th Rep. Hist. MSS. Comm.* 528/1 Paid 2 shyngelers and a boy, mending the old rofe of the church 20d. **1554** in *Shropsh. Par. Docum.* (1903) 55 Paid to the syngler & his man ii[s] vi[d]. **1562** *Act 5 Eliz.* c. 4 §23 Any Persone using or exercising Tharte or Occupation of a..Thatcher or Shingler. **1688** HOLME *Armoury* III. ix. 394/2 There is four sorts of Trades, that formerly used to cover Houses,..*viz.* the Plumer, with Lead;..the Shingler with clift Wood [etc.]. **1865** P. B. ST. JOHN *Snow Ship* ix, Nothing is more necessary to a backwoods-man than to be a good shingler—that is to know how to select the right tree and how to cut it. **1886** MORSE *Jap. Homes* 79 The shingler takes a mouthful of these pegs.

**2.** A woman who has her hair shingled. *transitory.*

**1926** *Glasgow Herald* 11 Nov. 3/4 Was the first shingler a suffragette? **1929** D. MACKAIL *How Amusing!* 337 Though ..Duval has done a certain amount of shingling,..his shop ..has no separate entrance for shinglers.

ˈ**shingler**[2]. *Iron-manuf.* [f. SHINGLE *v.*[2] + -ER[1].] One who or a machine which shingles puddled iron.

**1832** HT. MARTINEAU *Hill & Valley* iv, The shingler who hammers the balls of metals into an oblong form. **1864** WEBSTER, *Shingler*,..a machine for shingling puddled iron, or making it into blooms. **1875** KNIGHT *Dict. Mech.*, *Shingler*, an eccentric..roller revolving within a concave and pressing the dross out of the loop. **1881** GREENER *Gun* 221 The puddler takes the bloom with a pair of tongs, runs with it to the tilt hammer and hands it over to the shingler.

**shingles** (ˈʃɪŋg(ə)lz), *sb. pl.* Also 4 **schingles, 5 cingules, sengles, 5–6 shyngles, 6 chingles.** [Representing med.L. *cingulus* (MS. gloss in Du Cange), var. of *cingulum* girdle, used to render Gr. ζώνη or ζωστήρ in the medical sense.] An eruptive disease (*Herpes zoster*) often extending round the middle of the body like a girdle (whence the name); usually accompanied by violent neuralgic pain.

**1398** TREVISA *Barth. De P.R.* XVII. xciii. (Tollem. MS.), Aȝens icchynge and scabbes wett and drye and aȝens schingles [*Bodley MS.* cingules, *ed.* **1495** shyngles]. *c* **1450** *M.E. Med. Bk.* (Heinrich) 78 Ther ys an euel, þat men callen þe sengles. **1527** ANDREW *Brunswyke's Distyll. Waters* G ij, The onnatural hete named shyngles on the bodye. **1546** PHAER *Bk. Childr.* Bb viij b, Our Englysshe women call it the fyre of Saynt Anthonye, or chingles. **1614** W. B. *Philos. Banquet* (ed. 2) 86 The oyle of Nuttes..helpes the shingles. **1712** SWIFT *Jrnl. to Stella* 10 May, The doctors said that they never saw anything so odd of the kind; they were not properly shingles, but *herpes miliaris*, and twenty other hard names. **1782** W. HEBERDEN *Comm.* xxiii. (1806) 126 The herpes, or shingles..consists of a heap of watery bladders. **1899** *Allbutt's Syst. Med.* VIII. 618 On hearing that it is the 'shingles' and that it is not catching.

**b.** A similar disease in horses.

**1639** T. DE GRAY *Compl. Horsem.* 74 This disease is also called by some the shingles in a horse. **1725** *Bradley's Fam. Dict.*, St. Anthony's Fire, a Disease Horses are subject to,..call'd by some the Shingles.

ˈ**shingling,** *vbl. sb.*[1] [f. SHINGLE *v.*[1] + -ING[1].]

**1. a.** Tiling with shingles or cutting shingles. Also *attrib.*, as ***shingling-hatchet***, etc.

**1703** T. N. *City & C. Purchaser* 243 *Shingling*, the laying on of Shingles. **1859** F. S. COOPER *Ironmongers' Catal.* 157 Shingling Hatchets. **1864** LOWELL *Fireside Trav.* 32 An Indian tomahawk, which had too much the peaceful look of a shingling-hatchet. **1875** KNIGHT *Dict. Mech.*, *Shingling-bracket*, a device to enable a carpenter to stand on a roof while nailing on shingles. *Ibid.*, *Shingling-gage*,..for adjusting shingles in the proper position for nailing. **1910** LADY D. NEVILL *Under Five Reigns* iv, Shingling is a craft quite distinct from ordinary builder's or carpenter's work.

**b.** Arrangement in overlapping layers.

**1903** *U.S. Geol. Surv.* Prof. Paper 13. 48 In numerous sections of these deposits the shingling of the gravels is well marked.

**2.** (See SHINGLE *v.*[1] 2 a.)

**1924** *Chambers's Jrnl.* June 483/2 You do not care for the shingling and bobbed hair styles? **1926** GALSWORTHY *Silver Spoon* iv. 25 'My dear girl,' Michael had said, when shingling came in, 'to please me, don't!' Your *nuque* will be too bristly for kisses.' **1939–40** *Army & Navy Stores Catal.* 901 Hair Clipper... Specially designed for Shingling, Bobbing, and for removing any superfluous hair.

ˈ**shingling,** *vbl. sb.*[2] *Iron-manuf.* [f. SHINGLE *v.*[2] + -ING[1].] The action of SHINGLE *v.*[2]

**1674** RAY *Coll. Words* 128 This Loop they take out with their shingling tongs, and beat it with Iron sledges..that so it may..be in a capacity to be carried under the hammer. Under which they then removing it,..beat it with the hammer very gently, which forces cinder and dross out of the matter, afterwards..they beat it thicker and stronger till they bring it to a Bloom... This operation they call shingling the Loop. **1840** *Civil Eng. & Arch. Jrnl.* III. 298/1 The roasting, smelting, refining, puddling, shingling, balling, and drawing-out. **1881** GREENER *Gun* 222 The loss in the puddling is about 15 per cent., in the shingling and rolling about 14 per cent.

*attrib.* **1674** [see above]. **1839** URE *Dict. Arts* 706 The shingling mill..consists of two sets of grooved cylinders. **1857** G. WILKIE *Iron Manuf.* 108 A 60-horse engine will drive a shingling-hammer [etc.]. **1873** *Iron* 5 Apr. 356/1 The shingling-forge fitted with a 5-ton wrought iron helve.

ˈ**shingling,** *ppl. a.* [f. SHINGLE *v.*[1] + -ING[2].] Used advb.: In a tile-wise arrangement.

**1840** R. H. DANA *Bef. Mast* xxix, As to whether the hides should be stowed 'shingling' or 'back-to-back and flipper-to-flipper'.

**shingly** (ˈʃɪŋglɪ), *a.*[1] [f. SHINGLE *sb.*[1] + -Y.] Covered with shingles or wooden tiles.

**1857** WHITTIER *Last Walk in Autumn* xxi, The..shingly town-house, where The freeman's vote for Freedom falls.

**shingly** (ˈʃɪŋglɪ), *a.*[2] Also *Sc.* 8 **chinlie, chingily,** 9 **chingly;** 9 **shingley.** [f. SHINGLE *sb.*[2] + -Y.] Consisting of or covered with shingle; of the nature of shingle. (For Austral. and N.Z. sense, see SHINGLE *sb.*[2] 1.)

α. **1775** L. SHAW *Hist. Moray* 78 The hard chinlie beach. **1797** *Statist. Acc. Scotl.* XIX. 5 In several parts it [*sc.* the soil] is gravellish or sandy, or chingily. **1807** HEADRICK *Arran* 281 For slight, sandy, or chingly soils.

β. **1789** *Phil. Trans.* LXXX. 91, I landed, within the sound, on a white shingly beach, the stones of which are all chert. **1802** W. FORSYTH *Fruit Trees* xxiii. (1824) 343 Shingly and gravelly soils. **1810** SCOTT *Lady of L.* III. vii, Benharrow's shingly side. **1843** *Chamb. Jrnl.* 45/3 As they stood upon the shingley beach to see him start. **1857** J. T. THOMSON in N. M. Taylor *Early Travellers in N.Z.* (1959) 336 The plains are alluvial and shingly. **1869** TOZER *Highl. Turkey* I. 291 The broad shingly bed of a river. **1870** HAWTHORNE *Engl. Note-bks.* (1879) I. 211 Covered with gray shingly stones. **1878** E. S. ELWELL *Boy Colonists* 182 After a long..climb, they reached the top. It was bare and shingly. **1926** K. S. PRITCHARD *Working Bullocks* v. 52 They rode for hours..along the shingly ledges of steep hill-sides. **1949** A. E. WOODHOUSE in A. E. Currie *Centennial Treasury Otago Verse* 87 The shingly rivers seaward swirling.

**Shingon** (ˈʃɪŋgɒn). Also 9 Singon. [Jap., = true word, mantra, f. *shin* true + *gon* word.] The name of a Buddhist sect founded in Japan in the eighth century and devoted to esoteric Buddhism. Also *attrib.*

**1727** J. G. SCHEUCHZER tr. *Kæmpfer's Hist. Japan* I. II. v. 199 In the 1850 streets of this city, there were..10070 of the sect *Singon.* **1834** *Chinese Repository* Nov. 323 There are now in Japan the following sects which are tolerated by government. 1. Zen... 5. Singon... *Singon* means to repeat true psalms. **1880** E. J. REED *Japan* I. iv. 81 The learned Kobo Daishi..was likewise the founder of the *Shingon* ('True Words') sect of Buddhists in Japan. **1894** *Trans. Asiatic Soc. Japan* XXII. 382 (*heading*) The history of the Shingon sect. **1908** A. LLOYD *Wheat among Tares* iv. 40 Kōbō's faith—the so-called Mantra or Shingon Buddhism—so much resembles Manichaeism that it may be said to be practically the same system. **1931** G. B. SANSOM *Japan* III. xii. 222 The Shingon doctrines are mystical, and not to be explained in words. **1961** *Listener* 31 Aug. 316/1 A Buddhist sect, called Shingon,..is one of the most flourishing sects in Japan today. **1977** T. KASHIMA *Buddhism in America* i. 4 Shingon Buddhism..is based on the *Dainichi* Sutra (the Great Sun Sutra).

**shinily** (ˈʃaɪnɪlɪ), *adv.* [f. SHINY + -LY[2].] With a shiny surface or appearance. So ˈ**shininess,** shiny condition.

**1872** RUSKIN *Eagle's N.* §154 What sort of shininess there is on the end of a terrier's nose. **1874** *Contemp. Rev.* Oct. 760 The utmost shininess that can be got out of it will not replace one-tenth part of the light. **1894** A. MORRISON *Mean Streets* 138 His short hair clung shinily about his bullet head.

**shining** (ˈʃaɪnɪŋ), *vbl. sb.* [f. SHINE *v.* + -ING[1].] The action of the verb SHINE; emission or shedding of light; gleaming, beaming.

*a* **1300** *E.E. Psalter* cix. 3 In schinenges of haliyhes bright [Vulg. *in splendoribus sanctorum*]. **13..** *K. Alis.* 641 (Bodl. MS.) þe erþe shook, þe see bycom grene, þe sonne wiþdrouȝ shynyng shene. **13..** *Cursor M.* 23688 (Gött.) þe schene schining of cristal. **1398** TREVISA *Barth. De P.R.* VIII. xli. (Tollem. MS.), Schinynge is out spryngynge and stremynge oute of þe substaunce of lyȝte. *c* **1400** *Destr. Troy* 919 For chynyng of the chene stone he shont with his hede. *c* **1460** *Towneley Myst.* xxvi. 117 The moyn and starnes of shynyng blan. *a* **1586** SIDNEY *Arcadia* III. (Sommer) 265 b, He..might spie sometimes..the shining of armour, like flashing of lightning. **1613** PURCHAS *Pilgrimage* (1614) 560 Grashoppers doe..come in such quantitie that they intercept the shining of the Sunne like a Cloud. **1725** RAMSAY *Gentle Sheph.* III. iii, I've seen with shining fair the morning rise. **1852** THACKERAY *Esmond* I. v, Harry could see the shining of a steel breastplate he had on. **1852** M. ARNOLD *Self-Depend.* vi, With joy the stars perform their shining. **1905** F. YOUNG *Sands of Pleasure* II. viii, The cold, alert shining of her eyes.

**b.** *transf.* and *fig.*

*c* **1374** CHAUCER *Boeth.* III. pr. ii. (1868) 67 Yif that dignitees lesen hir shyninge by chaunginge of tymes. **1430–40** LYDG. *Bochas* I. vii. (1544) 10 b, Whan his shining was waxt vp to y[e] ful After the chaunge of fortunes lawe His glorye gan discrecen. *a* **1586** SIDNEY *Arcadia* II. (Sommer) 127 Men of vertue suppressed, lest their shining should discouer the others filthines. *Ibid.* III. 249 Our trust is that you yet will not denie the shining of your eies vpon vs. **1656** *Artif. Handsom.* 129 All their Oratorious polishings and shinings are but false beames. **1715** DE FOE *Fam. Instruct.* I. i. (1841) II. 5 We are but as dark as we were before; for we were none of us the better for all your hypocritical shining. *a* **1778** TOPLADY in *Bk. Praise* (1866) 446 The shinings of His grace Soften my passage through the wilderness.

*attrib.* **1748** RICHARDSON *Clarissa* (1768) IV. 64 The time of Adversity is your Shining-time.

**shining** (ˈʃaɪnɪŋ), *ppl. a.* [f. SHINE *v.* + -ING[2].]

**1. a.** That shines; luminous, lustrous, gleaming, beaming; also, of bright or brilliant aspect or exterior; resplendent in dress or equipment.

*a* **900** *O.E. Martyrol.* 22 Nov. 208 Þa stod se engel biȝ hyre myd scynendum fyðerum. *c* **1050** *Voc.* in Wr.-Wülcker 431/23 *Limpidis*, scinendum. *a* **1225** *Ancr. R.* 224 'Demonium meridianum', þet is, briht schininde deouel. *c* **1275** *Serving Christ* 18 in *O.E. Misc.* 91 In schynynde wede. **1382** WYCLIF *Lam.* iv. 7 Whitere is Nazareis than snoȝ, shynyngere [**1388** schynyngere] than mylc. *c* **1475** *Rauf Coilȝear* 559 Bot I the knew, that is sa schynand. **1533** BELLENDEN *Livy* II. xxi. (S.T.S.) I. 215 Þai war iij[c] and vj knichtis in schynyng armoure. **1552** ABP. HAMILTON *Catech.* (1884) 40 The cleir schenand sonne. **1565** J. PHILLIP *Patient Grissell* 702, I nether haue faire Helins shape, nor comly shininge hew. **1626** BACON *Sylva* §352 Shining woods, being laid in a Dry Roome,..lose their Shining. **1664** SIR R. HOWARD & DRYDEN *Ind. Queen* II. i, Showres sometimes fall upon a shining day. **1667** MILTON *P.L.* VII. 401 Fish..with thir Finns & shining Scales. **1719** DE FOE *Crusoe* II. (Globe) 559 Tiles..of a deep shining Black. **1776** GIBBON *Decl. & F.* xiii. I. 377 A bag of shining leather filled with pearls. **1825** HOOK *Sayings* Ser. II. *Passion & Princ.* x. III. 183 A bright shining house-maid. **1845** KITTO *Cycl. Bibl. Lit.* s.v. *Egypt*, The climate is..exceedingly hot; the atmosphere clear and shining. **1852** THACKERAY *Esmond* I. ix, On a shining chestnut horse. *Ibid.* II. iii, That busy, shining scene of the Thames swarming with boats and barges. **1860** TYNDALL *Glac.* I. ii. 21 All covered with shining snow.

**b.** as an epithet of coin. †***shining clay***, gold.

**1668** HOPKINS *Van. World* Wks. (1710) 5 What are Gold and Silver, but diversified Earth, hard and shining Clay? **1677** HORNECK *Gt. Law Consid.* v. (1704) 306 The tears I shed, for being deprived of a little shining clay. **1746** FRANCIS tr. *Hor., Sat.* II. iii. 203 From out his Bags he pours the shining Store.

**c.** *Nat. Hist.*, etc. (See quots.)

**1792** WITHERING *Brit. Plants* (ed. 2) III. 399 Pileus brown, shining, glutinous. **1793** MARTYN *Lang. Bot.*, *Lucidum folium*.. Bright, shining. **1839** LINDLEY *Introd. Bot.* III. (ed. 3) 471 Shining (*nitidus*); having a smooth, even, polished surface; as many leaves. **1850** ANSTED *Elem. Geol.*, *Min.* etc. §310 The degrees of intensity [*sc.* of lustre] are denominated as follows:—..*Shining*, when an image is produced, but not a well-defined image. Ex., Calcareous spar, Celestine. **1871** W. A. LEIGHTON *Lichen-flora* 109 Lobes ascending, glabrous and shining.

**d.** Hence as specific name of animals and plants (rendering L. *lucidus*, *lucens*, *splendidus*, etc.). **shining cuckoo**, a copper-coloured cuckoo, *Chalcites lucidus*, found in New Zealand and other parts of the Pacific.

**1626** BACON *Sylva* §475 The Shining Willow, which they call Swallow-Taile. **1771** J. R. FORSTER *Flora Amer. Septentr.* 7 Potamogeton lucens. Pondweed, shining. **1782** J. LATHAM *Gen. Synopsis Birds* I. II. 528 Shining C[uckow] ..Size of a small Thrush..inhabits New Zealand. **1783** *Ibid.* III. 56 Shining Thrush, *Turdus nitens*. **1784** CULLUM *Hist. Hawsted* App. 232 Shining Dove's-foot cranesbill (*Geranium lucidum*) in hedges. **1809** SHAW *Gen. Zool.* VII. 372 Coppery-green shining Crow. **1865** *Intell. Obs.* VII. 102 The male Satin or Shining Bower Bird. **1888** W. BULLER *Birds N.Z.* (ed. 2) I. 133 A peculiar whistling cry.. announces the arrival in our country of the shining cuckoo. **1965** F. SARGESON *Memoirs of Peon* vi. 155 It was.. something like the call of the shining cuckoo, a sound just in the air.

**2.** Phr. **a.** ***shining light*** (after John v. 35): a person conspicuous for some excellence.

**1526** [see LIGHT *sb.* 5 a]. **1563** WINȜET tr. *Vincent. Lirin.* ix. Wks. (S.T.S.) II. 27 That schyning licht of al the sanctis,.. maist blissit Cypriane. *a* **1796** BURNS *Holy Willie's Prayer* ii, A burnin' an' a shinin' light To a' this place! **1869** TROLLOPE *He knew*, etc. xviii. (1878) 100 Her aunt was regarded as a shining light by very many good people in the county. **1887** *Field* 19 Nov. 790/1 In the opening part of the game, Stadden, Robertshaw, and Brooke had been the shining lights.

**b.** ***to improve the shining hour*** (after Watts, see quot. 1720): to make good use of time.

**1720** WATTS *Div. Songs* xx, How doth the little busy bee improve each shining hour! **1866** 'ANNIE THOMAS' *Walter Goring* ii, Though he had been seeming to improve the shining hours very much to his own satisfaction.

**c.** ***shining armour*** (see quot. 1533 under 1 a, and ***knight in shining armour*** s.v. KNIGHT *sb.* 4 e) (freq. ironic): a sign of preparedness to fight nobly in a good cause, esp. in defence of the weak.

**1910** *Times* 22 Sept. 5/1 The action of an ally in taking his stand in shining armour at a grave moment by the side of your most gracious Sovereign. **1913** S. SHAW *William of Germany* xi. 249 The Emperor's soldiers and his Dreadnoughts, his mailed fist and shining armour, are built and put on in the spirit of precaution and defence. **1919** G. B. SHAW *Inca of Perusalem* 220 What other defence have we poor common people against your shining armor, your mailed fist, your pomp and parade? **1940** E. F. BENSON *Final Edition* xiii. 268 His Field Marshalls took his sabre-rattlings and his stupendous announcements that he was the chosen instrument of the Lord of Hosts at their face value,..and made him keep polishing up the shining armour which he had donned for his secret reassurance. **1960** J. STROUD *Shorn Lamb* xxii. 242 When I first came galloping out of the University, in shining armour..it was To the Rescue of the Deprived Child. **1968** 'M. UNDERWOOD' *Man who killed too Soon* vi. 61, I could tempt him to don his shining armour and try a rescue operation.

**3.** With reference to intellectual or moral qualities: Eminent, distinguished, brilliant. Now *rare*.

*c* **900** tr. *Bæda's Hist.* III. xix. (1890) 210 Se wæs in wordum & dædum beorht & scinende. *c* **1400** tr. *Secreta Secret., Gov. Lordsh.* xxxvii. 69 þe vertu of þy shynynge lyf shal be..gladyd þerby. *c* **1410** HOCCLEVE *Mother of God* 101 Seint Ion Shynynge apostle & euangelist. **1513** *Life Hen. V* (1911) 7 The life and shyninge Acts of this most victorious Kinge. **1593** G. HARVEY *Pierce's Super.* 173 The siluer streaming fountaines of flowingest witt, and shiningest Art. *c* **1665** MRS. HUTCHINSON *Mem. Col. Hutchinson* (1846) 31 Nor was his soul less shining in honour than in loue. **1702** ADDISON *Dial. Medals* i. 11 One that endeavoured rather to be agreeable, than shining in conversation. **1711** —— *Spect.* No. 73 ¶4 Men of the greatest and the most shining Parts. **1761** HUME *Hist. Eng.* II. xxix. 154 Charles duke of Bourbon ..was a prince of the most shining merit. **1781** COWPER *Retirem.* 560 Anticipated rents, and bills unpaid, Force many a shining youth into the shade. **1818** SCOTT *Hrt. Midl.* xxxvii, [His] most shining quality was courage in the field of battle. **1881** M. RALEIGH *Alex. Raleigh* i. 7 [He] was regarded as a boy of good but not shining ability.

**4.** Of looks: Radiant, beaming.

**1821** LAMB *Elia* I. *My relations*, A..shining sanguine face. **1852** THACKERAY *Esmond* I. xiii, Greeting him with one of her shining looks.

**5.** *Comb.*

**1802** SHAW *Gen. Zool.* III. 464 Shining-black Snake. **1822** *Hortus Anglicus* II. 120 Shining-leaved Fig Wort. **1887** G. M. HOPKINS *Poems* (1967) 71 Raced With, along them, cragiron under and cold furls—With-a-fountain's shining-shot furls. **1895** K. MEYER *Voy. Bran* I. 71 A red-eared shining-white cow. **1915** D. H. LAWRENCE *Rainbow* ii. 52 Sometimes, all shining-eyed, she was back at her own home. **1923** KIPLING *Irish Guards in Great War* I. 289 Everything was as shining-new as death.

**'shiningly**, *adv.* [f. prec. + -LY².] In a shining manner; with a shining appearance; brightly, brilliantly.

**1382** WYCLIF *Luke* xvi. 19 Sum man was rich,..and he eet ech day schynyngli [L. *splendide*]. *c* **1440** *Gesta Rom.* lxvi. 305 (Harl. MS.), þe myȝty men and riche men of þis wordle, þat hath golde, and goodis shynyngly. **1556** J. HEYWOOD *Spider & F.* xlii. 17 The show..Upon the ten flies parte showth more shininglie Then on the one spiders side. **1611** SPEED *Hist. Gt. Brit.* IX. xx. §5 Let vs now behold his vertues as they are shiningly deduced into action. **1612** R. SHELDON *Serm. St. Martin's* 15 A God, shiningly appearing in Christ. **1824** GALT *Rothelan* I. II. iv. 181 His eye, which was ever shiningly intellectual. **1836** *Tait's Mag.* III. 447 The silver spoons and forks were laid shiningly side by side in a varnished press. **1859** SALA *Tw. round Clock* (1861) 163 Her ladyship's own private bank is in a shiningly aristocratic street. **1891** 'L. KEITH' *Lost Illus.* II. xix. 208 Shiningly, spotlessly, insolently new.

So **'shiningness**, brightness, brilliance.

**1703** *Phil. Trans.* XXV. 1538 The shiningness being wholly occasioned by the reflexion of the Light from the polisht sides. **1752** 'SIR H. BEAUMONT' *Crito* 41 *note*, The Epithets *marmoreus*, *eburneus*, and *candidus*, are all applied ..to the Shiningness here spoken of. **1837** *New Monthly Mag.* XLIX. 24 Albeit swaying so our thoughts In shiningness and motion.

**shinlog** ('ʃɪnlɒg), *sb.*¹ *Brickmaking.* (See quot. 1703.) Hence **shinlog** *v.*, to close (the mouth of a kiln) with shinlog.

**1703** T. N. *City & C. Purchaser* 48 They damm up the Mouth of the Kiln..with their Shinlog, as they call it (which is pieces of Bricks piled upon each other, with wet Brick Earth, instead of Mortar). This Shinlog they make so high, that there is but just room above it to thrust in a Faggot. *Ibid.*, The Mouth being thus Shinlog'd, they proceed to put in Faggots. **1825** J. NICHOLSON *Oper. Mech.* 534.

†**'shinlog**, *sb.*² *Obs.* [app. f. *shin* in SHINBIN (cf. the form *shinbeam*) + LOG *sb.*¹] = SHINBIN.

**1842** *Penny Cycl.* XXIV. 141/2 Pieces called 'shin-logs', and admirably adapted for ship-timbers.

**shinnanicking**, var. SHENANIGAN.

**shinner**¹ ('ʃɪnə(r)). [f. SHIN *sb.*¹ or *v.* + -ER¹.]

†**1.** A stocking. *Obs. rare*⁻⁰.

**1585** HIGINS *Junius' Nomencl.* 167/1 *Caliga*,.. an hose, a nether stocke, a shinner.

**2.** A blow or kick on the shin. *dial.*

**1835** MARRYAT *Olla Podr.*, *Moonshine*, I'll give you a *shinner* on your lower limb. **1869** *Lonsdale Gloss.*

**3.** *U.S.* 'One who borrows money by the practice of shinning' (Bartlett).

**1840** in Schele de Vere *Americanisms* (1872) 305 Coxcombs and dandies, loafers and nibblers, Shavers and shinners.

**4.** *U.S.* One who 'shins round'; an active person.

**1838** J. C. NEAL in Schele de Vere *Americanisms* (1872) 305 'Shin it, good man!' ejaculated a good-natured urchin, 'shin it as well as you know how!' The qualification was a good one, Berry not being well calculated for a shinner of the first class.

**Shinner**² ('ʃɪnə(r)). Colloq. abbrev. of SINN FEINER (ʃɪn feɪnə(r)).

**1921** *Glasgow Herald* 9 Apr. 12 The sands are running out as Ireland will shortly be ruined. 'Shinners' may be killed daily. **1974** J. JOHNSTON *How Many Miles to Babylon?* 51, I thought I'd heard it about that you were with the Shinners.

**shinnery** ('ʃɪnərɪ). *U.S.* [f. SHIN *sb.*¹ + -ERY.] An area of scrub in which shin-oak predominates.

**1901** *Rev. Reviews* XXIV. 310/1 It [*sc.* 'creeps'] is due mainly to an insufficiency of nourishment in the grass, particularly in pastures where 'shinnery' or dwarf oak trees abound. **1913** W. C. BARNES *Western Grazing Grounds* 268 The scrub oak of the western ranges..forms..great areas called 'shinneries'. **1946** *Oklahoma Game & Fish News* Mar. 4/1 The located crow roosts in the shinnery motts west of Elk City.

**'shinning**, *vbl. sb.* [f. SHIN *v.* + -ING¹.]

**1.** *Football.* The act of kicking an opponent on the shin.

**1873** *Gentl. Mag.* Apr. 388 Mauling, hacking, kicking, shinning, collaring—such are among the terms and rules of the [Rugby] game. **1899** SHEARMAN, etc. *Football* 70 All charging is fair, but no..shinning or back shinning either of the ball or players is allowed.

**2.** *U.S.* (See quot. 1864.)

**1834** A. GREENE *Perils of Pearl Street* i. 16 The exercise of *shinning*. **1864** WEBSTER, *Shinning*, a running about borrowing money temporarily to meet pressing demands. **1872** SCHELE DE VERE *Americanisms* 306 This process of *shinning* is resorted to whenever the merchant or banker is *short*.

**shinny** ('ʃɪnɪ), *sb.*¹ Also shinney, shinnie. [? f. the cry used in the game *shin ye*, *shin you* (also *shin your side*), of obscure origin; cf. *hummie*, a dial. name for shinty, and the cry *hun you*, *shin you* (Sheffield Gloss.); see also SHINTY. Other dial. names of the game are *shinnins*, *shinnock*, *shinnup*; also *shinder* vb.] A (north-country and American) game similar to hockey, played with a ball and sticks curved at one end; also, the stick and the ball used in this game.

**1672** in Maidment *Bk. Scotish Pasquils* (1868) 181 He.. did transub Himself to ball, the Parliament to club, Which will him holl when right teased at ane blow, Or els Sir Patrick will be the shinnie goe. **1794** *Gentl. Mag.* Mar. 216 *Shinney*, a stick rounding at one end, to strike a small wooden ball with. **1810** *Ann. Reg.* 532 Contending parties, in the northern counties of England, exert themselves to drive the shinney to its goal. **1860** J. F. CAMPBELL *Tales W. Highl.* (1890) I. 102 He..gets him to make an iron shinny. **1893** LELAND *Mem.* I. 51 The nose of the [sturgeon] fish.. being greatly coveted by us small boys wherewith to make a ball for 'shinny'.

*attrib.* **1794** *Gentl. Mag.* Mar. 216 *Shinney-hah*, a game so called. **1825** R. CHAMBERS *Trad. Edin.* II. 78 A group of little pensioners, who regularly annoyed him for a shinny ball, or some such article. **1856** KANE *Arctic Expl.* II. xxi. 206 Each of them had a walrus-rib for a..shinny-stick.

**shinny** ('ʃɪnɪ), *sb.*² *Southern U.S.* [Alteration of SHINE *sb.*¹ 3 b: see -Y⁶.] = MOONSHINE 4.

**1934** in WEBSTER. **1944** D. VAN DE VOORT in B. A. Botkin *Treas. Amer. Folklore* v. 686 Wiley went over to the safe and got out his pappy's jug of shinny. **1960** H. LEE *To kill Mockingbird* xiii. 139 Miss Maudie Atkinson baked a Lane cake so loaded with shinny it made me tight. **1972** J. CARR *Second Oldest Profession* xi. 166 There are often regional names by which the illicit distillate is recognized. Some of these are 'cannonball swig'..'preacher's lye'..'shinny' ..'kickapoo joy juice'.

**shinny** ('ʃɪnɪ), *v.* *U.S.* [f. SHIN *sb.*¹]

*intr.* To shin *up* a tree. Also with *down*, *absol.*, and with advb. acc., as ***to shinny one's way***.

**1888** T. STEVENS *Around the World* 307 The trees..are.. swarming with monkeys... Shinnying up the toddy-palms. **1936** J. STEINBECK *In Dubious Battle* vi. 86 Jim shinnied down the tree. **1937** *Sun* (Baltimore) 23 Oct. 12/7 It is difficult to imagine a man over 60 shinnying up a porch post. **1967** 'E. QUEEN' *Face to Face* xiii. 61 Somehow he's managed to shinny his way back into her good graces. **1976** *Daily Tel.* 29 Sept. 15/2 They must..shinny up ropes, and slide down vines. **1977** *Time* 4 Apr. 42/2 Coming on fast is Robert Shaw, Israeli counter-terrorist, who must shinny down a rope from a helicopter.

Hence **'shinnying** *vbl. sb.*

**1906** *Washington Post* 22 May 2 As its girth precluded 'shinnying', Gladden procured a ladder.

**Shinshū** ('ʃɪnʃuː). [Jap., f. *shin* SHIN *sb.*³ + *shū* sect] = SHIN *sb.*³

**1727** J. G. SCHEUCHZER tr. *Kæmpfer's Hist. Jap.* I. IV. i. 264 The monks of the Chinese and other *Sensju* monasteries send also some of the fraternity to go a begging six times a month. **1896** L. HEARN *Kokoro* x. 193 Wealthier sects had established Buddhist schools on the Western plan: and the Shinshū could already boast of its scholars.

**Shinto** ('ʃɪntəʊ). Also Sin-to, Sintu, -oo. [Japanese, f. Chinese *shin tao* way of the gods.]

**1.** The native religious system of Japan, the central belief of which is that the mikado is the direct descendant of the sun-goddess and that implicit obedience is due to him.

**1727** tr. *Kæmpfer's Hist. Japan* I. 203 Sinto..is the Idol-worship, as of old established in the Country. **1829** *Encycl. Metrop.* (1845) XX. 474/2 The first..Faith of the Japanese, is that of the *Sin-to*. **1875** *N. Amer. Rev.* CXX. 282 The abolition of Buddhism and the establishment of pure Shinto. **1906** *Athenæum* 19 May 602/3 Of pure Shinto ancestor-worship was no part, while phallism in a very pronounced form was intimately associated with it.

**b.** *attrib.*

**1727** tr. *Kæmpfer's Hist. Japan* I. 207 The whole System of the Sintos Divinity. *Ibid.*, The Sintosju or adherents of the Sintos Religion. **1829** *Encycl. Metrop.* (1845) XX. 475/2 The Sin-syu, or maintainers of the Sin-to creed. **1880** E. J. REED *Japan* I. 47 The worship of the Shinto gods. **1888** L. OLIPHANT *Epis. in Adv.* 222 Two Buddhist or Sintoo shrines, perched upon pinnacles of rock.

**c.** *adj.* = SHINTOISTIC.

**1904** SLADEN *Playing the Game* I. xii, The idea of the Kami ..was Shinto rather than Buddhistic.

**2.** An adherent of Shinto beliefs.

**1829** *Encycl. Metrop.* (1845) XX. 477/1 The Gods worshipped by the Sin-tos are principally..departed Spirits deified. **187.** RIPLEY & DANA *Amer. Cycl.* IX. 537 (Cass.) The Shintos believe in a past life, and they live in fear and reverence of the spirits of the dead.

Hence **'Shintoism** = SHINTO 1; **'Shintoist** = SHINTO 2; **Shinto'istic** *a.*, belonging to or characteristic of Shinto; **'Shintoize** *v.*, *trans.*, to render Shintoistic.

**1727** tr. *Kæmpfer's Hist. Japan* I. 226 Orthodox Sintoists go in Pilgrimage to Isje once a year. **1857** R. TOMES *Amer. in Japan* xiv. 337 The prevailing religions of the Japanese are Buddhism and Sintooism. **1863** *Chamb. Encycl.* V. 686/1 The minor deities of Sintuism are very numerous. **1875** *N. Amer. Rev.* CXX. 296 Buddhism..and the bakufu were, in the eyes of a Shintoist, all one and the same. **1889** E. ARNOLD *Seas & Lands* xiv. (1895) 218 Pure Shintoism does not admit of any external decoration or images. **1893** in Barrows *World's Parl. Relig.* I. 453 A pilgrimage to various ..Shintoistic and Buddhistic temples. **1895** GRIFFIS *Relig. Japan* vii. 212 Is Japanese Buddhism really Shintoized Buddhism, or Buddhaized Shinto?

**shinty** ('ʃɪntɪ). Also shintie. [Formation obscure; ? for *shin t'ye*, cf. *shin ye* (see SHINNY).]

**1.** = SHINNY.

**1771** PENNANT *Tour Scot.* 167 The shinty, or the striking a ball of wood or of hair. **1793** *Statist. Acc. Scot.* V. 72 On holidays, all the males of a district..met to play at football, but oftener at shinty. **1808** JAMIESON, *Shinty*, the club used in playing [shinty]. **1876** J. GRANT *Burgh Sch. Scot.* II. v. 180 The rough but manly old game of 'shinty' has not yet quite fallen into desuetude. **1882** *Jamieson's Sc. Dict.*, *Shinty*, the ball or knot of wood is called Shintie.

*attrib.* **1863** N. MACLEOD *Remin. Highl. Par.* iii, Few games..demand more physical exertion than a good shinty match. **1865** *Morning Star* 1 Feb., Past your ear whizzes a shinty ball.

**2.** = SHINDY 3.

**1848** THACKERAY *Van. Fair* liv, There's a regular shinty in the house; and everything at sixes and sevens. The landlord's come in and took possession.

**Shinwari** (ʃɪnˈwɑːriː). [Native name.] (A member of) a nomadic people inhabiting areas of Afghanistan around the Khyber Pass. Also *attrib.*

**1875** *Encycl. Brit.* I. 232/1 Lead is found .. in the Shinwari country. **1888** KIPLING *Phantom 'Rickshaw* 85 Would they could have foretold that my *kafila* would have been cut up by the Shinwaris almost within shadow of the Pass! **1958** O. CAROE *Pathans* xv. 234 The Mohmands and Safis formed a tribal confederacy with large numbers of Afridis and Shinwaris to oppose the passage of the royal troops. **1978** 'M. M. KAYE' *Far Pavilions* v. 87 We have a proverb in the country beyond the Khyber, that says 'A snake, a scorpion and a Shinwari have no heart to tame.'

**shiny** (ˈʃaɪnɪ), *a.* Also 6 **shynie**, 6, 9 **shiney**. [f. SHINE *sb.*[1] + -Y.] **A.** *adj.* **a.** Full of light or brightness; luminous; having a bright or glistening surface.

**1590** SPENSER *F.Q.* III. vi. 6 Vpon a Sommers shynie day. **1596** —— *Hymn Heav. Beauty* 51 Affixe thine eye On that bright shynie round still moving Masse. **1606** SHAKS. *Ant. & Cl.* IV. ix. 3 The night Is shiny. **1699** POMFRET *Dies Novis.* 50 Ere ruin blasted from the shiny sky. **1760–72** H. BROOKE *Fool of Qual.* (1809) IV. 126 The evening being calm and shiny. **1846** LANDOR *Exam. Shaks.* Wks. 1853 II. 298/1 Sir Silas looked red and shiny as a ripe strawberry on a Snitterfield tile. **1868** WHYTE MELVILLE *White Rose* xlv, Umbrella, shiny boots, tall hat, go-to-meeting coat. **1874** RUSKIN *Fors Clav.* xlvi. 229 The fattest, shiniest, spottiest trout I ever saw. **1881** C. WHITEHEAD *Hops* 52 The lower sides of the leaves are whitish and shiny.

**b.** *fig.* Beaming, radiant. Also, apparently excellent.

**1876** GEO. ELIOT *Dan. Der.* xlvi, He looked round with shiny gladness. **1915** KIPLING *Fringes of Fleet* 40 'Why didn't you then?' I asked. There were loads of shiny reasons. **1970** *Guardian* 14 Dec. 4/1 The Andean Pact is Latin America's .. shiniest attempt at creating a regional common market, but its gleaming paintwork is likely to take some hard knocks.

**c.** *Comb.* (parasynthetic).

**1882** *Daily News* 7 Jan. 5/4 The shiny-hatted and sealskin-clad rabble. **1898** R. KEARTON *Wild Life at Home* 23 Slugs .. thin little black shiny-skinned .. ones.

**d.** *advb.*

**1596** SPENSER *F.Q.* IV. vi. 20 Goldsmithes cunning could not vnderstand To frame such subtile wire, so shinie cleare. **1903** CONRAD & HUEFFER *Romance* V. ii, His yellow jaws as shiny-shaven as of old.

**B.** *sb.* A shiny or bright object.

***the shiny*** (slang), money.

**1856** READE *Never too Late* i, We'll soon fill both pockets with the shiney in California. **1889** CONAN DOYLE *Micah Clarke* 235 The silk and lace are done in these squares covered over with sacking—a thousand of Mechlin to a hundred of the shiny [i.e. the silk].

**ship** (ʃɪp), *sb.*[1] Forms: 1–5 **scip**, (1, 4 **scipp**, 1–3 **scyp**, 3 **sip**), 3–4 **schup**, **ssip**, 3–7 **schip**, 4–5 **s(c)hyp**, **shipp**, **schype**, **schippe**, (4 **schypp**, **shup**, **scippe**, **shyppe**, **schepe**, 5 **chip(pe**, **schyppe**, **shep**), 4–6 **schipp**, 4–7 **shippe**, 5–6 **shyppe**, **s(c)hipe**, **shype**, **shepe**, 5–7 **shipp**, (6 **sheppe**, *Sc.* **scheip(e)**, 4– **ship**. [Com. Teut.: OE. *scip* str. neut. = OFris. *skip*, *schip* (NFris. *skapp*, *skep*, WFris. *skip*), OS. *skip*, MLG. *schip*, *schêp* (LG. *schipp*), MDu. *sc(h)ip*, *sc(h)eep*, Du. *schip* (oblique *scheepe*, comb. *scheeps-* beside *schip-*), WFlem. *scheep*, OHG. *scif*, *skef* (MHG. *schif*, *schef*, G. *schiff*), ON. *skip* (Sw. *skepp*, Da. *skib*), Goth. *skip*; the ultimate etymology is uncertain. The Germanic word appears in Romanic as F. *esquif*, It. *schifo*, etc., see SKIFF *sb.*[1]]

**1. a.** A large sea-going vessel (opposed to a *boat*); *spec.* (in modern times) a vessel having a bowsprit and three masts, each of which consists of a lower, top, and topgallant mast.

In OE. used also for small craft, as ON. *skip*.

*c* **725** *Corpus Gloss.* (Hessels) S 188 *Scaphum*, scip. *c* **888** ÆLFRED *Boeth.* xxxviii. §1 Ða se Aulixes .. to þam ᵹefiohte for, þa hæfde he sume hundred scipa. *c* **1050** *O.E. Chron.* (MS. C) an. 1048, Eadward cining & þa eorlas foran æfter þam ut mid heora scypun. *c* **1200** *Vices & Virtues* 45 Hlesteð hwat ðe hlauerd seið, ðe ðat scip auh, to ðe stieres-mannen. *a* **1225** *Juliana* (Royal MS.) 32/12 Þu leddest israeles folc þurh þe reade sea buten schip druifot. *c* **1250** *Kent. Serm.* in *O.E. Misc.* 32 And so hi were in þo ssipe so a-ros a great tempeste of winde. *a* **1300** *Cursor M.* 13280 Petre and andreu .. Wit a word þai left þair scipps tuin [*Gött.* schippis]. **1362** LANGL. *P. Pl.* A. x. 160 A schup of schides and Bordes. *c* **1374** CHAUCER *Former Age* 21 No ship yit karf the wawes grene and blewe. *c* **1375** *Sc. Leg. Saints* vii. (*Jacobus Minor*) 370 Quhat schepe þat brokine ware a-pone þat coste. *c* **1400** *Three Kings Cologne* (1886) 84 Þat þey had suffrid hem priuelich to passe ouer þe see in her scheppys. *c* **1485** *Digby Myst.* (1882) III. 1423 Master of þe shepe, a word with the. **1541** *Test. Ebor.* (Surtees) VI. 149, I give to Mathue Wilson my shipe called Marie Janies. *a* **1578** LINDESAY (Pitscottie) *Chron. Scot.* (S.T.S.) I. 355 The skiper of the scheipe. **1596** SHAKS. *Merch. V.* I. iii. 182 My Shippes come home a month before the daie. **1671** MILTON *Samson* 714 A stately Ship Of Tarsus, bound for th' Isles Of Javan or Gadier. **1706** E. WARD *Wooden World Diss.* (1708) 84 There's near as much Stuff drops from his [a sea-cook's] Carcass every Day as would tallow the Ship's Bottom. **1707** *Lond. Gaz.* No. 4380/3 One of the Rocks not being a Ships length to Leeward of her. **1798** COLERIDGE *Anc. Mar.* I. vi, The ship was cheer'd, the harbour clear'd. **1873** LONGF. *Wayside Inn* III. *Elizabeth* iv, Ships that pass in the night, and speak each other in passing. **1889** WELCH *Naval Archit.* viii. 102 The bottom and side plating of all ships is arranged in longitudinal layers or strakes. **1911** *Encycl. Brit.* XXIV. 878/2 Ships with four and five masts were employed by several countries during the 19th century.

¶ Ships are now personified as feminine, but usage has varied (see the following quots.).

The use of the masc. pron. in the 17th and 18th cent. was prob. suggested by the application of *man* to a ship in *Dutchman*, *merchantman*, *man-of-war*. In instances before *c* 1650 *his* may mean 'its'.

**1375**, etc. [see SHE 2]. *c* **1426** *Poem on Agincourt* in Hazl. *E.P.P.* (1866) II. 97 Euery shyp wayed his anker .., They hoysed theyr sayles sayled a lofte. **1588** KYD *Househ. Phil.* Wks. (1901) 278 In a shyppe the Rudder ought to be no lesse then may suffise to direct hys course. **1611** SHAKS. *Wint. T.* III. iii. 93 The Shippe boaring the Moone with her maine Mast. [**1622** *Recov. Exchange* in Arb. *Eng. Garner* IV. 595 'A sail!' 'a sail!': which, at last, was discovered to be another Man of War of Turks. For he made towards us. **1627** CAPT. SMITH *Sea Gram.* xiii. 59 A saile, how beares she or stands shee, to wind-ward or lee-ward, set him by the Compasse; he stands right ahead, or on the weather-Bow, or lee-Bow.] **1635** HAKEWILL *Apol.* (ed. 3) Argt., As a Ship which .. cannot move beyond the length of his Cable. **1676** STREYNSHAM MASTER *Diaries* (1911) II. 93 Wee mett a great Dutch ship neare Nassapore point. He wore a Flagg. **1784** *New Spect.* XIII. 2/1 The last [ship was] drowned and swallowed up, within sight of his own shore.

**b.** Without article, chiefly in dependence on a prep. Also ***to take ship*** (see TAKE *v.* 24 c).

*c* **900** tr. *Bæda's Hist.* IV. i. (1890) 256 Swa eode he in scip & ferde to Breotone. *a* **1122** *O.E. Chron.* (Laud MS.) an. 1046, Hi .. wurpon hine on þone bat .. & reowan to scipe. *c* **1205** LAY. 1098 Brutus nom Ignogen & into scipe [*c* **1275** to sipe] lædde. **1297** R. GLOUC. (Rolls) 1464 Þe emperour bigan to fle mid is folc atte laste To scipes. *c* **1350** *Will. Palerne* 5088 Partenedon passed to schepe & his puple after. *c* **1386** CHAUCER *Miller's T.* 354 Er þat he myghte brynge his wyf to shipe. **1474** CAXTON *Chesse* II. iv. (1883) 45 Guion fledd also in to affricque by shipp. **1568** GRAFTON *Chron.* II. 29 He .. went to Ship, setting aside all perils. **1597** HOOKER *Eccl. Pol.* V. lxvii. (1611) 358 Finding him againe as soone as themselues by shippe were arriued on the contrary side. **1888** [see EX 2]. **1912** *Times* 19 Dec. 20/3 Oats .. American white, ex ship, 18s. 4½d.

**c.** In legal enactments often with greatly extended application, as in the following quot.:

**1870** *Act 33 & 34 Vict.* c. 90 §30 'Ship' shall include any description of boat, vessel, floating battery, or floating craft; also any description of boat, vessel, or other craft or battery, made to move either on the surface of or under water, or sometimes on the surface of and sometimes under water.

**d.** In rowing parlance, applied to the racing eight-oar boat; also used playfully of other craft.

**1878** STEVENSON *Inland Voy.* 14 The bargee is on shipboard—he is master in his own ship—he can land whenever he will. **1888** WOODGATE *Boating* 147 She .. was once specially borrowed by Corpus (Oxon) during the summer eights, and was said by that crew to be a vast improvement on their own ship. **1896** ASHBY-STERRY *Tale of Thames* v, Here they leave their ship and quietly stroll up to the New Inn. **1901** *Daily News* 1 Apr. 5/7 The .. steadiness of their ship .. helped the Oxford men very much.

**e.** *fig.* Applied to the state.

**1675** *Machiavelli's Prince* ix. Wks. 212 But when times are tempestuous, and the ship of the State has need of the help .. of the Subject. **1894** GLADSTONE *Odes of Horace* III. viii. 26 Though the State-ship somewhat heave. **1913** *19th Cent.* Feb. 305 The Ship of the State of China is still labouring in a storm-swept ocean.

**2.** With qualifying word or phrase indicating the kind or use:

**king's ship** (now Hist.), one of the fleet of ships provided and maintained out of the royal revenue; a ship of the royal navy; later, a ship-of-war equipped at the public expense (opp. to *privateer*); so † **ship-royal**. † **great ship**, a ship-of-war.

For *flagship*, *hospital-ship*, *ice-ship*, *line-of-battle ship*, *long ship*, *merchant ship*, *post-ship*, *private ship*, *slave-ship*, *steamship*, *store-ship*, *troop-ship*, *warship*, etc. see the first elements; for *ship of burden*, *of countenance*, *of the line*, *of post*, *of state*, see these sbs.; also SHIP-OF-WAR.

[**1350** in Rymer *Fœdera* (1825) III. I. 195 Johannes Wille, magister navis regis vocatæ La Plente.]

*a* **1400–50** *Wars Alex.* 65 Gales & grete schipis full of grym wapens. **1450** LOMNER *Let. to J. Paston* 5 May, Yn the syght of all his men he was drawyn ought of the grete shippe. **1485–7** *Naval Acc. Hen. VII* (1896) 36 The Kings ship cald the Grace dieu. **1495** *Ibid.* 161 The costes of Kepyng the Kynges Ship Ryall called the Soueraigne. **1512** in Rymer *Fœdera* (1712) XIII. 328/2 All Prisoners, beyng Chieftens .. and one Shippe Royall being of the Portage of Two Hundred Tonnes or above .. Reserved to our said Soveraign Lord. **1568** GRAFTON *Chron.* II. 688 The Easterlynges .. approched the Englishe ship as nere as their great shippes could come at the lowe water. **1660** FULLER *Mixt Contempl.* II. 31, I never did read .. that ever Queen Elizabeth had any Ship-Royal, which .. carried the Memorial of any particular Conquest she got. **1690** C. NESSE *Hist. & Myst. O. & N. Test.* I. 116 The Church here is a mighty Queen, a ship-royal. **1697** DAMPIER *Voy.* I. 50 There escaped but one Kings-ship, and one Privateer. *Ibid.* 357 Captain Swan had his men as much under command as if he had been in a Kings Ship. **1758** J. BLAKE *Mar. Syst.* 45 The commander of the king's ship is obliged to make up his loss by pressing hands from the merchant ships. **1824** HOLT *Shipping & Navig. Laws* (ed. 2) Introd. 36 Foreign seamen, who shall have served in time of war three years on board a king's ship.

**b. ship in a bottle**, a model ship inside a bottle the neck of which is smaller than the ship.

**1949** N. MITFORD *Love in Cold Climate* I. xii. 128 The safes .. were full of treasures .. a carved nut; a ship in a bottle; [etc.]. **1976** *Times* 2 Feb. 16/4 Construction kits are popular .. including a ship-in-a-bottle outfit.

**3. a.** In fig. and allusive phrases, *esp.* where *ship* typifies the fortunes or affairs of a person, etc. or the person himself in regard to them.

***to be in the same ship***, cf. BOAT *sb.* 1 d; ***to give up the ship***, ***to burn one's ships***, see BURN *v.* 9 c. ***when one's ship comes home*** (or ***in***), when one comes into one's fortune.

**1500–20** DUNBAR *Poems* ix. 165 Thow mak my schip in blissit port to arryif, That sailis heir in stormis violent. *a* **1548** HALL *Chron.*, *Hen. VII*, 27 Doubting not to bring his ship to the porte desired. **1643** PRYNNE *Sov. Power Parl.* App. 209 Those who are conversant in the same danger, are said to be in the same Ship. **1680** *Debates Parl.* (1681) 117 Is not all England in danger to be lost? Let us secure the Ship, before we dispose of the Cabbins. **1816** JEFFERSON *Writ.* (1899) X. 4 My exhortation would rather be 'not to give up the ship'. **1820** SHELLEY *Œd. Tyr.* I. i. 245, I drove her—afar! .. From city to city, abandoned of pity, A ship without needle or star. **1851** MAYHEW *Lond. Labour* I. 175 One [customer] always says he'll give me a ton of taties when his ship comes home. **1855** THACKERAY *Newcomes* lxv, That Mr. Ratray who has just come out of the ship, and brought a hundred thousand pounds with him. **1871** HARDY *Desperate Remedies* II. i. 39 He saw the strokes plainly, instantly resolving to burn his ships and hazard all on an advance. **1880** CABLE *Grandissimes* liii, Nobody ever gives up the ship in parlour or veranda debate. **1886** D. C. MURRAY *Cynic Fortune* xii, The wealthy relative .. proposed to supply him with an income of a hundred pounds per annum until the major's next expected ship should come in. **1898** *Allbutt's Syst. Med.* V. 816 It is well in the case of a new patient at any rate to postpone a final diagnosis till the ship is in calmer waters. **1900** MAHAN *War S. Africa* v, Not the courage that throws away the scabbard, much less that which burns its ships.

**b.** ***ship of fools*** [after the title of Sebastian Brant's satirical work *Das Narrenschiff* (1494), translated into English by Alexander Barclay as *The shyp of folys of the worlde* (1509)], a ship whose passengers represent various types of vice or folly.

**1609** DEKKER *Guls Horne-Booke* 3 Any person aforesaid, longing to make a voyage in the Ship of Fools. **1807** W. H. IRELAND (*title*) Stultifera navis; qua omnium mortalium narratur stultia. The modern ship of fools. **1864** TENNYSON *Voyage* x, in *Enoch Arden* 149 'A ship of fools' he shriek'd in spite. **1919** KIPLING *Debits & Credits* (1926) 358 He Who launched our Ship of Fools many anchors gave us. **1975** *Times Lit. Suppl.* 7 Feb. 126/4 The Apocalypse as depicted by Bosch, the upside-down world of Goya, the Ship of Fools having landed its cargo.

**c.** ***ships that pass in the night*** [after the phrase by Longfellow: see quot. 1873], used of people whose acquaintance is necessarily transitory.

**1873** LONGFELLOW *Aftermath in Tales of Wayside Inn* III. iv. 59 Ships that pass in the night, and speak each other in passing... So on the ocean of life we pass and speak one another, Only a look and a voice, then darkness again. **1893** B. HARRADEN (*title*) Ships that pass in the night. **1939** WODEHOUSE *Uncle Fred in Springtime* xiv. 198 The thought that they had met and parted like ships that pass in the night was very bitter to him. **1978** D. BAGLEY *Flyaway* xxv. 235 'Inquisitive, isn't he?' 'Not abnormally so. Chit-chat between ships that pass in the night.'

**d.** ***a tight ship***, a ship in which ropes, etc., are tight; hence a strictly run ship; usu. *transf.* and *fig.*

**1971** 'H. CALVIN' *Poison Chasers* i. 6 Dai liked a tight mainsheet... 'Pull in tighter, boy... I want a tight ship.' **1972** *Sat. Rev.* (U.S.) 24 June 42/1 The two student judges .. ran a tight ship. Firm commands—'There will be no knitting in my courtroom.' **1977** *Times Lit. Suppl.* 13 May 593/3 Dr Kelly runs a tighter ship altogether than Dr Sheeran: her bibliography is a model of both inclusion and exclusion.

**4.** *transf.* Applied to various objects that are, or are conceived to be, navigated.

†**a.** Noah's ark. **b.** a balloon, aircraft, or powered spacecraft. **c.** ***ship of the desert***, ***desert-ship***: the camel. **d.** ***ship of Guinea*** = *Guinea ship* (b) s.v. GUINEA 1.

[*a* **1300** *Cursor M.* 9674 Noe .. in þat scip allan was in.] **1422** YONGE tr. *Secreta Secret.* xxxvii. 193 In Noe's ship he and his wif, har thre sonys and har wiffis sawid were. *c* **1485** *Digby Myst.* (1882) III. 1351 In þe shep of noee. **1526** R. WHYTFORD *Martiloge* 12 b, Saynt Noe that made the shyppe. **1579** T. STEVENS in Hakluyt *Voy.* (1599) II. II. 99 A thing swimming vpon the water like a cocks combe (which they call a ship of Guinea). [**1615** G. SANDYS *Trav.* 138 Camels. These are the ships of Arabia, their seas are the deserts.] **1679** R. HOOKE *Philos. Collections* No. 1. 18 A demonstration, how it is practicably possible to make a ship which shall be sustained by the air, and may be moved either by sails or oars. **1709** *Evening Post* 20–22 Dec. 2 The description of a flying ship, lately invented. **1784**, etc. [see *aerial ship* s.v. AERIAL *a.* 5]. **1823** [see DESERT *sb.*[2] 1]. **1824** [see DESERT *sb.*[2] 5]. **1860** *Brit. Patent 1598* 1 An improved navigable balloon or aerostatic ship. **1878** BOSW. SMITH *Carthage* xxi. 439 Those ships of the desert, the long line of his camels. **1908** H. G. WELLS *War in Air* v. 151 The ships of the German air-fleet rising one by one. **1930** *Sci. Wonder Q.* Spring 352 Both men ran toward the ship .. for if the rocket were destroyed, they would be lost in the icy wastes of Venus. **1980** J. CARTWRIGHT *Horse of Darius* xvi. 251 'O.K. Let's get in the ship.' .. As soon as they were airborne, Teymour told him what had happened.

**5. a.** A vessel, utensil, ornament, etc. shaped like a ship. Also (in first quot.), the noble coined under Edward III, which bore the image of a ship.

*c* **1410** HOCCLEVE *Min. Poems* xvii. 29, vj$^{c}$ shippes grete, To yeue vs han yee grauntid & behight. **1490** CAXTON *Eneydos* v. 22 Cymphes .. ben in maner of lityl bokettis, or lytyl shippes, of a strange stone. **1525** in Ellis *Orig. Lett.* Ser. I. I. 271 A ship of silver for the almes disshe. **1575–6** *New Yrs. Gifts* in Nichols *Progr. Eliz.* (1823) II. 1 A juell of golde, being a shippe, set with a table dyamonde of fyve sparcks of dyamondes.

**b.** An incense boat. Now *Hist.*

**1422** *Rec. St. Mary at Hill* (1904) 14 Also iij sensers of siluer & gilt Also ij sheppis of seluere. **1472** in Swayne *Churchw. Acc. Sarum* (1896) 5 A ship of silver in passel gilt without spone. **1546** S. FISH *Supplic. Poore Commons* 75 Torches, tapurs, shepe, sensoures. **1593** *Rites of Durham*

(Surtees) 8 Two Shipps of silver, parcell gilt, for principall dayes. **1843** Pugin *Apol. Rev. Chr. Arch.* 51 b, Two thuribles, with a ship for incense. **1898** J. Wickham Legg in *Yorksh. Archæol. Jrnl.* XV. 132 *note*, A censer with coals, a ship with incense, and a spoon.

†**c.** The nave (see nave *sb.*²) of a church. *rare.*

**1613** tr. *Mexio's Treas. Anc. & Mod. T.* 713/1 One of his Prophets made a conuocation .. of all the people, in the great Shippe of the great Church.

**d.** *Saltmaking.* The vessel into which the brine runs from the pits. Now *Hist.*

**1669** *Phil. Trans.* IV. 1065 They fill their Panns again with new Brine out of the Ship, (so they call a great Cistern by their Panns sides, into which their Brine runs through the Wooden Gutters from the Pump, that stands in the Pitt). **1674** Ray *Coll. Words* 175. **1753** *Chambers' Cycl.* Suppl. **1981** *Times* 14 July 3/2 Two hollow log 'ships' for boiling brine were found, dating to the sixteenth century.

**e.** *Astron.* The Argo Navis, a southern constellation extending between Canis major and Centaurus from the equator nearly to the pole.

**1599** T. Hill *Sch. Skil* 23 The image named the Ship, hath 45. stars. **1822** Barlow in *Encycl. Metrop.* (1845) III. 508/1 [The milky way] traverses the constellations Cassiopeia, .. Canis Major, and the Ship. **1868** Lockyer *Guillemin's Heavens* (ed. 3) 334.

†**6.** A shipful, shipload. *Obs.*

**1455–6** *Cal. Anc. Rec. Dublin* (1889) 290 A shype of iryn that come yn befor Michalmas. *c* **1595** Carew *Excell. Eng. Tongue* in G. G. Smith *Eliz. Crit. Ess.* (1904) II. 292 When wee would be rid of one, wee vse to saye .. by circumlocution .. another in your steede, a shipp of salte for you.

**7. a.** A ship's company or crew.

**1338** R. Brunne *Chron.* (1810) 170 Do dight & mak ȝow bone, þe schip ere Sarazins alle. **1648** *Hamilton Papers* (Camden) 222 The twelue schipps that haue declared for the King doeth much startill ther former inclinations. **1748** *Anson's Voy.* II. iv. 157 It was not the most eligible place for a ship to refresh at.

**b.** *old ship*, a jocular address to a sailor.

**1849** Cupples *Green Hand* i, 'Come, old ship, give us a Yarn!' said the younger forecastle-men to an old one. *Ibid* vi, 'What's the odds, Harry, old ship?' said Tom.

**8.** *attrib.* and *Comb.*

**a.** Simple attrib. = of or for, pertaining to, or concerning a ship or ships, used or fitted for use on board ship, as ***ship-accounts, -beak, -bell, -canal, -captain, -channel, -crane,* †*-dock,* †*-gun, life, -pump,*** etc. (Cf. the compounds with *ship's*, 9 c.)

**1815** Scott *Guy M.* xliii, *Ship-accounts and other papers. **1613** T. Godwin *Rom. Antiq.* (1614) 9 Those *ship-beakes called in Latine *Rostra.* **1871** Longf. *Wayside Inn* II. *Musician's T.* IV. iv, When the dismal *ship-bell tolled. **1688** Holme *Armoury* III. xv. (Roxb.) 35 The *ship bow or loofe. **1798** I. Allen *Hist. Vermont* 268 A *ship canal would be the means of importing salt, and exporting the preceding articles cheap. **1847** *Niles' Reg.* 13 Nov. 165/2 A ship canal wide and deep enough to float a first-rate man-of-war. **1959** *Chambers's Encycl.* III. 38/1 The great ship canals of modern times have been built to carry large ocean-going vessels; but the earlier ship canals .. can take only small ships and barges. **1858** Simmonds *Dict. Trade*, **Ship-captain*, the master and commander of a merchant-vessel. **1865** W. G. Palgrave *Arabia* II. 195 We fell in with a ship-captain. **1887** J. Ball *Natur. S. Amer.* 356 The passengers .. were resting in their *ship-chairs. **1775** J. Quincy *Let.* 31 Oct. in J. Sparks *Corr. Amer. Revolution* (1853) I. 73 The *ship-channel .. runs between the east head of Long Island and the south point of Deer Island. **1847** *Niles' Reg.* 2 Oct. 70/2 To construct a ship channel, so to speak, to the St. Lawrence. **1676** Marvell *Mr. Smirke* 15, I suspected .. that the Animadverter had been some *Ship-Chaplain. **1699** Dampier *Voy.* II. III. 68 The Planters .. were certain of a Hurricane, and warned the *Ship-Commanders to provide for it. **1932** Auden *Orators* I. 16 Like those *ship-cranes along Clydebank. **1585** Higins *Junius' Nomencl.* 398/1 *Nauale*, a *shipdocke, which is a place where ships are builded and repaired. **1659** Kilburne *Kent* 73 [Deptford] famous for the Shipdock, Storehouse and Corporation there for the Navy. **1552** Huloet, *Shyp drudge, .. *Misonauta.* *c* **1000** *Gl. Prud.* in *Germania* (N.S.) XI. 389/42 *Bellum classicum*, *scypȝefæoht. **1647** Hexham I, A ship-fight, *een schip-vecht.* **1408** tr. *Vegetius' De Re Milit.* (MS. Digby 233) lf. 226/1 *Schipfiȝttynge asketh to haue a loft see & nouȝt rowe see. **1720** De Foe *Capt. Singleton* xvii. (1840) 289 The *ship firing is not at him. **1715** *Lond. Gaz.* No. 5374/2 They placed two *Ship-Guns on the Bridge. **1799** *Hull Advertiser* 7 Sept. 4/3 The thirty two pounder ship-gun. **1644** Manwayring *Seaman's Dict.* 14 *Bracketts.* Are certaine little peeces .. which belong to the supporting of galleries, or *ship-heads. **1904** Sladen *Playing the Game* II. ii, A pair of handcuffs and a pair of *ship-irons. **1867** Smyth *Sailor's Word-bk.*, **Ship-language*, the shibboleth of nautic diction, as *tau'sle, fok'sle*, for topsail, forecastle. **1849** Cupples *Green Hand* ix, It's nouther *ship-law nor shore-law .. as houlds good on a bloody dazart! **1873** *Routledge's Young Gentl. Mag.* 162 Familiar with *ship life. **1485** in *10th Rep. Hist. MSS. Comm.* App. v. 291 The *shippe lofe which is made of clane whete as it cometh from the shefe. *a* **1700** Evelyn *Diary* 1 Nov. 1660, A curious *ship modell. **1655** Marq. Worcester *Cent. Inv.* (1663) 42 A Harquebuss, a Crock, or *Ship-musquet. **1526** *Grete Herball* cccxliii. (1529) T iij, Pytche is of dyuers sortes for there is *shyppe pytche and pytche liquide or thynne, or tarre. *c* **1550** Lloyd *Treas. Health* B 5 Let Shyp Pytche Be dyssolued one whole nyghte in stronge Vyneger. **1610** Holland *Camden's Brit.* I. 17 As it were *ship-planks caught vp from a shipwracke. **1712** J. James tr. *Le Blond's Gardening* 206 Ship-Plank of two or three Inches thick. **1857** Perley *Hand-bk. N. Brunswick* 11 For ship-planks and ship-timber. **1625** K. Long tr. *Barclay's Argenis* II. x. 94 The very Mariners .. tooke heart to snatch vp the *Ship-poles, and to make resistance. **1661** Godolphin *View Admir. Jurisd.* Introd. a 6 He may not sail with other *Ship-provisions then what is good and wholesome. **1847** W. C. L. Martin *Ox* 47/2 A .. breed of cattle .. fed in Basse-Bretagne chiefly for ship-provisions. **1742** W. Ellis *Timber-Tree Improved* II. xxxvii. 181 The Timber is .. of especial Use .. for *Ship-pumps. **1834–6** Barlow in *Encycl. Metrop.* (1845) VIII. 285/2 A good ship pump. **1720** Pope *Iliad* XXIII. *Notes* end, The Naval-Course, or *Ship-Race. **1661** Godolphin *View Admir. Jurisd.* 48 Invoyces, Bills of Lading, *Ship-Roll, with other Instruments and ship-papers. **1698** *Act 10 Will. III*, c. 14 § 1 For building .. or repairing of Stages *Shiprooms Trainfats. **1780** Jefferson *Writ.* (1853) I. 275 Great numbers of negroes .. were left, either for the want of ship-room or through choice. **1841** Dana *Seaman's Man.* III. iii. 212 The contract of passengers with the master is not for mere ship-room .. on board. *c* **1000** Ælfric *Gloss.* in Wr.-Wülcker 167/10 *Rudentes*, *sciprapas. **1675** Hobbes *Odyss.* (1677) 258 [He] shut the utter-gate, And with a ship-rope that lay by it ties. **1688** Holme *Armoury* III. xv. (Roxb.) 48 Other Ship ropes not vsed .. about the masts. **1585** Jas. VI *Ess. Poesie* (Arb.) 39 Since that only wind my *shipsailles blew. **1610** Holland *Camden's Brit.* I. 263 The weaving of .. Ship-sailes. **1485** *Naval Acc. Hen. VII* (1896) 74 *Ship spayres .. iiij. *c* **1300** *K. Horn* 1412 (Laud MS.) He comen out of *scyp sterne. **1688** Holme *Armoury* III. xv. (Roxb.) 27 The Boat rope, is that by which the boat is towed or tyed to the ship stern. **1661** Godolphin *View Admir. Jurisd.* 47 Embezilments of *ship-tackle or furniture. **1647** Hexham I, *Ship-tackling, *scheeps-koorden.* **1688** Holme *Armoury* III. xv. (Roxb.) 32 Two necessary Instruments used much about the ship tacklings. **1836** E. Howard *R. Reefer* lvi, It was pronounced, for *ship-tailoring, excellent. **1717** *Petiveriana* III. 202 Ring-Oak or White-iron .. is esteemed the best for *Ship-use. **1611** Chapman *Iliad* XIII. 370 An Oake, a Poplar, or a Pine, Hewne downe for *shipwood.

**b.** With reference to the Scandinavian and Anglo-Saxon custom of burying a ship in a grave-mound.

**1847** in Madden *Shrines & Sepulchres* (1851) I. 334 Boats, and even large ships, being drawn on shore and turned keel uppermost, the bodies of the slain deposited under them, and stones and earth superimposed, thus forming what may appropriately be termed ship barrows. **1866** G. Stephens *Runic Mon.* I. 196 Mighty Mounds, olden Stone-rings, Ship-settings, .. Grave-cumbels. **1889** Du Chaillu *Viking Age* I. 335 *note*, Other ship-graves, such as that of Tune, Borre, &c., have been found with skeletons of horses. **1899** H. M. Chadwick *Cult of Othin* 43 The ship-funeral .. seems to be a distinctively Scandinavian custom. **1907** —— *Origin Eng. Nation* xi. 288 The launching of the funeral ship really was an ancient custom .. from which both ship-cremation (on land) and ship-burial were derived. **1940** *Burlington Mag.* Dec. 174/1 The great Anglo-Saxon ship-burial at Sutton Hoo .. was excavated in the summer of 1939. **1963** C. Green *Sutton Hoo* ii. 33 (*heading*) The ship-barrow excavation.

**c.** objective and objective genitive, as ***ship-bearing, -jumper, -jumping, -launch, -maker,*** etc.

**1596** Warner *Alb. Eng.* XII. lxxvii. 312 Washt with the once *ship-bearing Ley. **1755** Magens *Insurances* II. 255 Brokers and *Ship-clearers, who would have Goods insured. **1663** Marq. Worcester *Cent. Inv.* Index E j b, A *ship-destroying Engine. **1907** F. T. Bullen *Advance Austral.* xix, It was a fine piece of *ship-handling. **1964** *Punch* 4 Mar. 336/3 Except for a few *ship-jumpers, most come by air. **1959** P. McCutchan *Storm South* xv. 213 Genuine cases of *ship-jumping by men who had had enough of sail. **1832** [Mrs. Traill] *Backwoods of Canada* iv. (1836) 52 At Brockville we arrived .. in time to enjoy .. a *ship-launch. **1552** Huloet, *Ship letter to hyre, *naucularius.* **1483** *Cath. Angl.* 337/1 A *Schyppe maker, *barcarius.* **1858** Simmonds *Dict. Trade*, **Ship-modeller*, .. one who lays down the proposed lines of a vessel. **1762–71** H. Walpole *Vertue's Anecd. Paint.* (1786) III. 101 Simon de Vlieger, an admired *ship-painter. **1839** Ure *Dict. Arts* 253 James Brown, *ship-rigger. **1892** Stevenson & L. Osbourne *Wrecker* 8 Smuggling, *ship-scuttling, barratry, piracy. **1655** Davenport *K. John & Matilda* v. i, From mine eyes, *ship-sincking Cataracts, Whold [*sic*] clouds of waters, .. Shall fall into the Sea of my affliction. **1858** Simmonds *Dict. Trade*, **Ship-surveyor*, an examiner of the condition, fittings, and sea-worthiness of ships. **1806** Wolcot (P. Pindar) *Tristia* Wks. 1812 V. 299 Ship-brokers, or Ship-breakers, or *Ship-swabbers. **1570–6** Lambarde *Peramb. Kent* 86 A most dreadfull gulfe, and *shippe swalower.

**d.** adverbial, esp. instrumental, as ***ship-based, -beset, -borne, -dotted, -forsaken, -laden*** adjs.; similative, as ***ship-fashion*** adv., ***ship-like*** adj.

**1973** J. D. R. Rawlings *Pictorial Hist. Fleet Air Arm* vi. 69 The Navy .. could see a use for the helicopter as a *ship-based submarine spotter. **1870** Morris *Earthly Par.* III. IV. 95 A yellow strand and *ship-beset green sea. **1932** *19th Cent.* Feb. 206 The second [method] is the limitation by agreement of numbers of *ship-borne aircraft. **1978** *Navy News* May 5/2 The Phoebe .. came out of her two-and-a-half year refit with .. shipborne torpedoes fitted. *a* **1835** Motherwell *Poet. Wks.* (1847) 5 The *ship-borne warriors of the North. **1889** Hissey *Tour Phaeton* 216 The far-reaching, *ship-dotted sea beyond. **1771** *Encycl. Brit.* III. 585/1 Pinks sail with three masts, *ship-fashion. **1821** Scott *Kenilw.* xxxii, The chief table was adorned by a salt ship-fashion, made of mother-of-pearl. **1735** Thomson *Liberty* I. 282 The *Ship-forsaken Bay. **1857** Dufferin *Lett. High Lat.* (ed. 3) 6 The yellow, rushing, *ship-laden river. **1842** Faber *Styrian Lake* 239 The *shiplike clouds, which overwhelm The azure sky. **1855** Lynch *Rivulet* XXIV. ii, With a steady will unswerving, Ship-like may we onward press. **1864** tr. *Vambéry's Trav. Central Asia* 198 The camels, the shiplike movements of which I had formerly so much dreaded.

**9. a.** Special comb.: †**ship-agent**, a shipping agent; †**ship-bearer**, one who carries an incense-boat; †**ship-beer** [cf. MDu. *schipbier*, G. *schiffsbier*], beer made for consumption on board ship; **ship('s) biscuit**, hard biscuit prepared for use on board ship, hard-tack; formerly called **ship('s) bread**; †**ship-bridge**, a pontoon bridge; **ship-broker**, a mercantile agent who transacts the business of a ship when it is in port, or is engaged in buying and selling ships, or in procuring insurance on them; **ship-brokerage**, the business performed by a ship-broker; **ship-broking** *vbl. sb.* = *ship-brokerage*; †**ship-burden**, a ship-load; **ship-carver, -caulker** (see quots.); †**ship-chest, -coffer**, a chest used on board ship; **ship('s) company**, the crew of a ship; **ship-contractor, -deliverer** (see quots.); **ship('s) decanter**, a decanter with a base of greater width than the shoulder; †**ship-fare**, (*a*) travelling by ship; (*b*) = *ship-hire*; †**ship-ferd**, a navy; **ship-fever**, a form of typhus fever, called also *gaol fever* and *hospital fever*; **ship float**, (*a*) a lighter; (*b*) the splashers of a paddle-wheel (Knight *Dict. Mech.* 1875); †**ship-fountain** (see quot.); †**ship-fraught, -freight** (see fraught *sb.* 1, freight *sb.* 1) = *ship-hire*; †**ship-governor** = shipmaster; †**ship-gume** = shipman; **ship-hearth** (see quot.); †**ship-hire** [cf. MDu. *schiphure*], the passage money for a sea-voyage; **ship-holder** = ship-owner (Webster 1828–32); †**ship-hook**, ? a grappling iron; **ship-joiner** (see quot. 1858); **ship-keeper**, a man who takes care of a ship when the crew is absent from it; **ship-ladder**, a ladder used in boarding or leaving a ship; also, a kind of embroidery stitch; **ship-lap**, (*a*) a form of joint in carpentry made by halving (see quots. and halving *vbl. sb.*¹ 2 and cf. *half-lap* and *lap-point* s.v. lap *sb.*³ 2 b and 6); (*b*) boards interlocked by rebates, used esp. for cladding; so **ship-lapped** *ppl. a.*, **ship-lapping** (also *attrib.*), and hence **ship-lap** *v.*, to furnish with joints of this kind; **ship-letter**, a letter carried by a private vessel and not by the ordinary mail boat; †**ship-lord** = ship-owner; **ship-mark**, a postmark on a letter carried by a mail ship; **ship-mate**, one who serves with another in the same ship; also in phr. ***to be ship-mates with***, to sail in the same vessel with; hence *transf.*, to be acquainted with, to have knowledge of (*colloq.*); hence **shipmatish** *a.*; †**ship news**, (*a*) news conveyed by ship; (*b*) shipping news; **ship-papers**, now usually **ship's papers**, the documents (passport, muster-roll, charter-party, log-book, etc.) with which a ship is required by law to be provided; **ship-pendulum**, a pendulum with a graduated arc, used in the navy to ascertain the 'heel' of a vessel (Knight *Dict. Mech.*); **ship plane**, an aeroplane specially adapted for operating from an aircraft carrier; **ship-plate**, an inferior grade of wrought iron plate; †**ship-privateer**, a privateer commanded by a captain (cf. *ship-sloop*); †**ship-rae** *Sc.* [see ra¹ and cf. MDu. *schipra*], a sailyard; **ship-railway**, (*a*) an inclined railway running into the water over which a ship may be drawn out on land for repairs, etc.; (*b*) a railway for transporting ships overland; †**ship-rede** *Sc.* [see reid¹], a roadstead; †**ship ren**, a ship's course; **ship-rigged** *a.*, carrying square sails on all three masts; †**ship-road**, (*a*) a sea-voyage; (*b*) a roadstead; †**ship-scot** = ship-money; **ship-scraper**, (*a*) see quot. 1875; (*b*) one whose occupation it is to scrape the keels and decks of ships; an instrument used for this purpose; **shipside**, (*a*) *spec.*, the outside of the hull of a ship; (*b*) the dock adjacent to a moored ship; †**ship sloop**, a sloop of war commanded by a captain, and therefore having the rating of a ship; **ship('s) smith** (see quot. 1858); **ship-spy**, a telescope used on the coast (Halliwell 1847); **ship('s) stores**, (*a*) provisions and supplies for use on board ship; (*b*) sing. (*U.S.*) a shop on board ship; **ship-stuff**, (*a*) inferior wheat flour; (*b*) material for the woodwork of a ship; **ship('s) time**, (*a*) the local mean time of the meridian where the ship is; (*b*) *Canad. local*, (the time of) the arrival of an annual supply ship; †**ship-tire**, a head-dress shaped like a ship or having a ship-like ornament; **ship-to-air**, used *attrib.* to designate a missile fired from a ship at an aerial target; †**ship('s) toll**, passage money, fare for a voyage; **ship-to-ship**, used *attrib.* to designate communications, missiles, etc., directed from one ship to another; **ship-to-shore**, used *attrib.* to designate communications, missiles, etc., directed from a ship to land; also *ellipt.* as *sb.*, a radio-telephone operating in this manner; †**ship-war**, naval warfare; **shipway**, (*a*) a way or bed on which ships are built or laid for examination; (*b*) a ship-canal; **ship-work**, work at a ship or on board ship; ship-building, naval construction; **ship-worker**, one who employs labourers to unload ships; † **ship-writ**, a writ for ship-money.

**1813** *Examiner* 8 Feb. 86/1 O. R. Read and Co...*ship-agents. *c* **1450** in Aungier *Syon* (1840) 337 In festys clepyd *Maius duplex* ther schal be two sensours at euensonge and matyns, and a *schypberer. **1706** E. Ward *Wooden World Diss.* (1708) 85 If ever he [a sea-cook] prays, it's in a Morning fasting, and that is to some Tag-rag, to fetch him a little *Ship-Beer. **1799** *Hull Advertiser* 6 Apr. 1/1 The business of a *ship-biscuit baker. **1823** Adam Clarke in *Life* (1840) xi. 407 Always carry with you some hard or ship biscuit. **1855** E. Acton *Mod. Cookery* (rev. ed.) xxxi. 603 The residents are then compelled to have recourse..to ship's biscuit. **1893** Forbes-Mitchell *Remin. Gt. Mutiny* 27 Twelve ordinary-sized ship's biscuits. **1598** Florio, *Pane biscotto*, bisket bread, *ship-bread. **1748** *Anson's Voy.* III. ii. 310 No ship's bread was expended. **1856** Kane *Arctic Expl.* II. xvi. 169 The ship-bread was powdered by beating it with a capstan-bar. **1663** *Brief Acc. Turks Late Exped.* 11 The River had torn their *Ship-bridges. **1816** *Sporting Mag.* XLVII. 254 Mr. Wild, a *ship broker in the City. **1834** McCulloch *Dict. Comm.* (ed. 2) 188 A ship broker is not within the various acts for the regulation and admission of brokers. **1886** *Daily Tel.* 11 Sept. (Cass.), The question of *ship-brokerage in France had formed the subject of frequent representations to the French government. **1955** *Times* 29 June 14/5 Our *shipbroking department had an active 12 months and profited during the latter part of the year from the substantial rise in tramp freights. **1969** *Daily Tel.* 24 Jan. 5/3 Wigham-Richardson is largely concerned with marine insurance, shipbroking and chartering. **1646** J. Hall *Upon King's Gt. Porter* 22 Wee'l weigh thee by *Ship-burdens not by th' stone. **1858** Simmonds *Dict. Trade*, **Ship-carver*, one who carves figure-heads, and the work on the stern. *Ibid.*, **Ship-caulker*, one whose business it is to stop, with oakum and pitch, the seams of ships' sides and decks. **1494** in *Somerset Med. Wills* (1901) 322, I bequeith to my cousyn William Hill my best bras pott a *ship chest and ij mesers of Ode. **1529** *Reg. Mag. Sig. Scot.* 178 A schip kist 20d. **1534** in *Archæol. Cant.* VII. 285, j olde shyppe cheste without locke. **1557** *Will* in Cullum *Hist. Hawsted* (1784) 126 One great *shipp cofer. **1644** Manwayring *Seaman's Dict.* 2 When Ships meet,..they use to demand how they doe all fore and aft, the reason whereof is, for that the whole *Ships company is devided. **1661** in *Godolphin's View Admir. Jurisd.* App. 174 In the sight and presence of the Ship-Company. **1706** E. Ward *Wooden World Diss.* (1708) 56 To purchase Wine Abroad for the Service of the Ship's Company. **1891** Ship's company [see *ship's writer*, sense 9 c]. **1978** *Cornish Guardian* 27 Apr. 13/5 Shore-based organisations..will be involved..as well as 25 to 35 members of the ship's company. **1867** Smyth *Sailor's Word-bk.*, **Ship-contractor*, the charterer or freighter of a vessel. **1929** W. A. Thorpe *Hist. Eng. & Irish Glass* II. Plate cxxix. (*caption*), *Ship's decanter, four angular rings round the neck. **1976** J. Carroll *Madonna Red* (1977) iii. 93 The ambassador was holding a crystal ship's decanter. **1979** P. Alexander *Show me Hero* vii. 90 A ship decanter and two wine glasses. **1858** Simmonds *Dict. Trade*, **Ship-deliverer*, a person who contracts to unload a ship. *c* **1320** *Sir Tristr.* 926 Bliþe was his bosking, And fair was his *schip fare. **1375** Barbour *Bruce* III. 686 Till our-saile thaim in-to schipfair. *Ibid.* 692 Ankyrs, rapys..And all that nedyt to schipfar. **1648** Hexham II, *Schip-laon*,..ship-hire, Ship-fraught, or Ship-fare. **1661** in *Godolphin's View Admir. Jurisd.* App. 176 The Master..ought to shew them [the company] their Ship-fare, which he may weigh out to each of them. *a* **1122** *O.E. Chron.* (Laud MS.) an. 999, þæt man sceolde mid *scipfyrde & eac mid landfyrde him onȝean faran. *c* **1205** Lay. 2156 Humber king & al his fleote & his muchele scip ferde. **1758** J. Blake *Mar. Syst.* 49 One man labouring under what is called the **Ship Fever*, or the *Goal Distemper.* **1868** *Chamb. Encycl.* X. 721/1 Fleeing in despair, emigrants carried the germs of disease with them; and the so-called ship-fever which followed destroyed its thousands. **1626** *Reg. Mag. Sig. Scot.* 355/2 Instrumentum quo aqua salsa dulcis effecta est, quod πηγοναυτικον vulgo **schip-fontane* appellatum est. *c* **1375** *Schip fraucht [see fraught *sb.* 1]. **1648** [see *ship-fare* above]. **1552** *Ship freight [see *ship-hire* below]. **1526** Tindale *Rev.* xviii. 17 Every *shippe governer, and all they that occupied shippes. *c* **1205** Lay. 4560 Godlac sloh þa *scip-gumen [*c* **1275** sipmen]. **1858** Simmonds *Dict. Trade*, **Ship-hearth Maker*, a manufacturer of the cooking galleys or stoves used on shipboard. **13..** *Metr. Hom.* (Vernon MS.) in *Archiv Stud. neu. Spr.* LVII. 265 For his *schip huyre his wyf he heolde. *c* **1440** *Promp. Parv.* 446/2 Schyphyre, *naulum.* **1552** Huloet, Ship hire or freight, *naulum.* **1648** [see *ship-fare* above]. **1633** Sir J. Burroughs *Sov. Brit. Seas* (1651) 114 With certaine *ship-hookes and other like Instruments [etc.]. **1858** Simmonds *Dict. Trade*, **Ship-joiner*,.. a mechanic who does the neat or fine woodwork in ships and buildings, and is therefore distinguished from the shipwright and carpenter. **1897** *Daily News* 29 Mar. 7/3 The strike of the ship joiners of the River Thames. *c* **1517** in *Archæologia* XLVII. 310 Wages of *Shippekepers in the Thames. **1618** in J. Charnock *Hist. Mar. Arch.* (1801) II. 237 The rigging at the setting forth may bee performed by the ordinary shipp-keepers. **1840** R. H. Dana *Bef. Mast* xxxvi, Not a soul was left on board the good ship Alert but the old ship-keeper. *c* **1050** *Suppl. Ælfric's Gloss.* in Wr.-Wülcker 182/10 *Ponsis*, *sciphlædder. **1611** Cotgr., *Transpontin*, a ship-ladder. *c* **1635** Capt. N. Boteler *Dial. Sea Services* (1685). **1882** Caulfeild & Saward *Dict. Needlework* 187 To work Jacob or Ship Ladder. **1854** Miss A. E. Baker *Gloss. Northants.*, **Ship-lap*, a carpenter's term for a mode of uniting the end of one piece of wood to the side of another, at right angles, by a bevil-shaped bearing on the upper edge. **1939** W. Faulkner *Wild Palms* 15 The flimsy walls (they were not even tongue-and-groove..but were of ship-lap). **1977** *Cornish Times* 19 Aug. 13/2 (Advt.), Our.. plumbing, shiplap claddings and drainage systems are always in stock. **1887** *Home Missionary* (N.Y.) Mar. 432 It [our home] is '*ship-lapped' and partially plastered. **1958** *Archit. Rev.* CXXIII. 327 (*caption*) Northern elevation with ship-lapped pine used as facing for the first floor. **1879** *Cassell's Techn. Educ.* IV. 278/1 The simplest joint is that known as *ship-lapping, in which each end is cut down through half its thickness, and the cut met by a cross-cut, and the piece removed. **1882** Christy *Joints made by Builders* 103 Ship Lapping Joint. *c* **1675** in J. W. Hyde *Post in Grant* (1894) 326 *Ship letter. **1817** Selwyn *Law Nisi Prius* (ed. 4) II. 963 A letter..with the English ship-letter post-mark. **1829** *Parl. Papers* XI. 288 Ship-letter office. **1834** *Ibid.* XLIX. 501 Above 1200 ship-letter mails are forwarded via Liverpool in the course of a year. **1849** Cupples *Green Hand* xxxii, My mother handed Jane a ship-letter. *c* **1050** *Suppl. Ælfric's Gloss.* in Wr.-Wülcker 181/21 *Nauclerus*, *sciphlaford. *c* **1440** *Promp. Parv.* 447/1 Schyplord,..*navarchus.* **1801** S. & Ht. Lee *Cant. T.* IV. 456 The letter had no *ship-mark: I examined that of the post; it was from Hull. **1748** *Anson's Voy.* III. iii. 329 Our Commander and *Shipmates. **1840** R. H. Dana *Bef. Mast* xiii, A handsome, hearty fellow, and a good shipmate. **1876** W. Lamont *Yachting in Arctic Seas* 13 These six Tromsönians were, in seagoing phrase, the *hardest bargains* I was ever shipmates with. **1880** W. Clark Russell *Sailor's Sweetheart* III. ii. 60, I had never been shipmates with an island of this kind before. **1883** Stevenson *Treas. Isl.* ii, 'You know an old shipmate, Bill, surely', said the stranger. **1961** G. Foulser *Seaman's Voice* i. 13, I was never shipmates with a boom mainsail. **1893** W. Clark Russell *Emigr. Ship* II. 84, 'I respect your *shipmatish views', said I. **1712** Luttrell *Brief Rel.* (1857) VI. 723 This being only *ship news, little credit is given theretoo. **1761** *Lond. Chron.* July 2–4, 14/2 Ship News. Falmouth, June 29. Wind N. arrived the King George packet-boat, Bown, from Lisbon. **1661** Godolphin *View Admir. Jurisd.* Introd. a 6 He may not carry counterfeit Cocquets or other Fictitious and Colourable *Ship-papers to involve the Goods of the Innocent with the Nocent. **1753** *Scots Mag.* Mar. 126/2 The ship-papers and depositions. **1853** Maude & Pollock *Law Merch. Shipping* iii. 63 The master is the proper person to have the custody of the ship's papers. **1919** in C. G. Grey *All World's Aircraft* I. 96A The *Beardmore* W.B. III. was evolved from the *Sopwith* 'Pup' in an effort to turn this machine into a *ship-plane. **1922** *Flight* XIV. 126/2 Landplanes designed so as to facilitate their landing on a ship's deck will ordinarily be known as Ship Planes. **1942** *Ark Royal* Aug. 13/2 A ship-plane represents certain constructional problems which entail a sacrifice of speed. **1873** R. Wilson *Steam Boilers* 32 The badly refined, coarse, brittle and uncertain material sometimes sold as *ship plate. **1881** *Instr. Census Clerks* (1885) 93 Ship Plate Maker. **1799** *Naval Chron.* I. 529 A *ship privateer named La Zele, mounting 16 guns and 69 men. **1805** Nelson 23 July in Nicolas *Disp.* (1846) VI. 486 A Ship-Privateer of twenty-two Guns. **1595** Duncan *App. Etym.* (E.D.S.), *Antenna*, a *ship-rae. **1881** *Chicago Times* 12 Mar. *The Times* does not undertake to say that the *ship-railway scheme is impracticable. **1891** *19th Cent.* Mar. 386 No ship railway is at present in operation. **1596** Dalrymple tr. *Leslie's Hist. Scot.* I. 127 Quha is ouir Haevinis and *schipredes thay cal Admiral. **1297** R. Glouc. (Rolls) 341 So þat toward þe west þe *ssiprene [*v.r.* schipreone] drou. **1844** *Civil Engin. & Arch. Jrnl.* VII. 189/2 The vessel was *ship-rigged. *a* **1400** *New Test.* (Paues) *Acts* xxvii. 10, I see þat wiþ iniurye ande myche harme..bigynnes oure *schiprode to be. **1610** Holland *Camden's Brit.* I. 422 To assume unto it the name of a ship-Rode, or Haven. **1640** [H. Parker] *Case of Shipmony* 2 To introduce the legality of the *Ship-scot, such a prerogative hath been maintained, as destroyes all other Law. **1643** *Oath of Pacification* 8 The Kingdome groaned.. under the oppression of the Shipscot. **1884** Knight *Dict. Mech.* Suppl., **Ship Scraper*, a triangular or square piece of steel, handled, and with sharpened edges for scraping the keels and decks of vessels. **1890** *Daily News* 12 June 6/1 The United Shipscrapers' Protection League. **1439** in *Archæologia* (1827) XXI. 37 Men of arms, feyghtyng upon the *shippe syde. **1611** Shaks. *Wint. T.* III. iii. 112, I would you had beene by the ship side, to haue help'd her. **1719** De Foe *Crusoe* I. (Globe) 11 Near the Ship Side. **1887** Morris *Odyss.* x. 172, I cast him adown by the ship-side. **1937** *Sun* (Baltimore) 26 Mar. 26/3 He parked his car in a garage, left orders with an automobile company to have a new machine at shipside [etc.]. **1969** *Jane's Freight Containers 1968–69* 83/3 General cargo facilities..have two shipside tracks. **1972** C. Mudie *Motor Boats & Boating* 93 Most sports fishermen therefore incorporate a section of the cockpit coamings, shipside, or transom which can be removed to help loading. **1867** Smyth *Sailor's Word-bk.*, **Ship-sloop*, commanders were appointed to 24-gun sloops, but when the same sloops were commanded by captains, they were rated ships. **1858** Simmonds *Dict. Trade*, **Ship's-smith*, an iron worker who fits the metal work, bolts, &c. in ships. **1897** *Daily News* 19 Feb. 2/2 All the shipsmiths on the north-east coast. **1785** *Daily Universal Register* 1 Jan. 4/3 Sundry *ships stores, consisting of sails, cables, anchors. **1798** *28th Rep. Sel. Comm. Finance* (1803) XIII. 356 Draught Carts for conveying old Ship's Stores. **1848** Thackeray *Van. Fair* lvii, Disposing of a great quantity of ship stores, claret, preserved meats, and great casks packed with soda-water. **1943** *U.S. Navy Bluejacket's Man.* (ed. 11) 1143 The ship's store, perhaps better known as the 'Canteen', is also under the jurisdiction of the supply officer. **1969** A. R. Bosworth *My Love Affair with Navy* ii. 44 He had been to the ship's store, and he came into the ward with several candy bars. **1793** Washington *Lett.* Writ. 1891 XII. 382 The middlings and *ship stuff may be sold to answer the money calls which you will have upon you. **1884** Sargent *Rep. Forests N. Amer.* 511 Saw oak for shipstuff. **1771** A. Graham *Observations on Hudson's Bay* (1969) ix. 282 How affairs went on last *shiptime I know not. **1869** 'Mark Twain' *Innoc. Abr.* v. 47 Young Mr. Blucher..was a good deal worried by the constantly changing 'ship time'. **1891** Patterson *Naut. Dict.* 303 *Ship Time*, the solar time at the place of the ship—12 o'clock (noon) being made known by eight bells when the sun crosses the meridian. **1956** *Beaver* Winter 52/1 Time to plan the spring work—but why do that; shiptime is far away and now is really the time for that rest. **1598** Shaks. *Merry W.* III. iii. 60 The right arched-beauty of the brow, that becomes the *Ship-tyre..or any Tire of Venetian admittance. **1957** *Times Survey Brit. Aviation* Sept. 2/4 A *ship-to-air weapon. **1972** *Times* 29 Sept. 4/8 The through-deck carriers will carry..the ship-to-air missile, Sea Dart. *c* **1050** *Suppl. Ælfric's Gloss.* in Wr.-Wülcker 182/13 *Naulum*, *sciptol. *c* **1475** *Pict. Voc.* ibid. 805/4 *Hoc naulum*, a schyppes tolle. **1648** Hexham II, *Schip-tol*, Ship-toll, or Custome. **1904** H. W. Wilson in *Cambr. Mod. Hist.* VIII. xv. 482 The battle of Camperdown..was not, as had been planned, a mere *ship-to-ship encounter. **1944** *Proc. IRE* XXXII. 326/2 Ship-to-ship telephone communication. **1977** *Navy News* Aug. 19 (*caption*) H.M.S. Fife, one of four guided missile destroyers in Portsmouth Navy Days, with her new Exocet ship-to-ship missiles mounted just below her bridge. **1923** *Monthly Weather Rev.* LI. 5/1 The cost of radio *ship-to-shore tolls. **1962** K. C. Hutchin *How not to kill your Husband* xlvii. 221 The worst invention of recent years connected with sailing is 'ship-to-shore' radio-telephone. **1971** N. Freeling *Over High Side* III. 197 We've got the ship-to-shore. Couldn't we phone someone? **1977** B. Garfield *Recoil* xiv. 148 'Why the hell don't you ever turn on your ship-to-shore?'..'I go on this boat to get away from telephones.' **1979** *Daily Tel.* 22 Sept. 36/3 Makers of ship-to-shore oil pipes. **1408** tr. *Vegetius' De Re Milit.* (MS. Digby 233) lf. 223/2 þe lawes or hestes of *schep werre. *c* **1440** *Promp. Parv.* 447/1 Schyppe werre, *naumachia.* **1834** *Encycl. Metrop.* (1845) VI. 343 *note*, Constructing buildings for the accommodation of officers of the yards, in storehouses,..and *shipways. **1840** *Hull Docks Comm.* 189 Shipways, a platform of stone-work in the bed of the river, for the purpose of laying the ships on to examine their bottoms. **1884** *Manch. Exam.* 15 Aug. 4/8 The construction of a ship-way from Manchester to the sea. **1408–9** tr. *Vegetius' De Re Milit.* (MS. Digby 233) lf. 224/1 To hewe tymbre as grete bemes for *schip werk. **1503** *Acc. Ld. High Treas. Scot.* II. 283 He gaif to Schir Alexander Makison, to furnis the schip werk, xx li. **1616** in *Compt bk. D. Wedderburne* (S.H.S.) 280, 12 peaceis oak for ship wark. **1904** *Daily Chron.* 9 June 3/4 He might be able to write a good text-book on ship-work. **1881** *Instr. Census Clerks* (1885) 36 Dock Service:..*Shipworker. **1891** *Daily News* 9 Feb. 3/2 The shipworkers and quay foremen. **1640** *Act 16 Chas. I*, c. 14 §1 Diverse Writs..commonly called *Shipwrits for the charging of the Ports Townes..of this Realme respectively to provide and furnish certain Ships for his Majesties Service. **1654** H. L'Estrange *Chas. I* (1655) 140 The Ship-writs having been issued out August the 11. 1635. *a* **1754** Carte *Hist. Eng.* IV. 253 The council who had ..just before the relation issued ship-writs to the inland.

**b.** In the names of animals: **ship-borer** = *ship-worm*; † **ship-halter**, the sucking-fish = remora 1; so **ship-holder**; † **ship-nut** (see quot.); **ship-rat**, a variety of rat found on board ship; **ship-stayer**, a fish of the family *Echeneididæ*; **ship-worm**, any of the worm-shaped mollusks of the genus *Teredo* and allied genera, esp. *T. navalis.*

**1668** Charleton *Onomast.* 125 *Remora*..the Remora, or *Ship-halter. **1860** Wraxall *Life in Sea* v. 111 Many fabulous stories have been told of the small '*Ship-holder', a sucking-fish often met with in the Mediterranean. **1729** Dampier *Voy.* III. I. 420 **Ship-Nuts.* Are hard Shells, which commonly adhere to Ships like the Barnacles. **1860** Wynter *Cur. Civilis.* 132 The *ship-rat must not be confounded with the water-rat, which is an entirely different species. **1890** Stevenson in G. Balfour *Life* (1911) 222 The ship-rats which infest the shores and invade the houses. **1778** Da Costa *Brit. Conchol.* 21 S[erpula] Teredo. The *Ship Worm. **1783** Justamond tr. *Raynal's Hist. Indies* VI. 149 The ship-worm is more apt to injure the vessel in this place than in other parts. **1879** E. P. Wright *Anim. Life* 562 *Teredidæ*, or Ship-worms.

**c.** Combinations with *ship's* (many of which have alternative forms in 8 a; see also 9 a), as ***ship's anchor***, ***apparel***, † ***castle***, ***cook***, ***doctor***, ***log***, ***pump***, ***timepiece***, ***writer***, ***yeoman***; **ship's articles**, the terms according to which seamen take service on board ship; **ship's cousin**, app. humorously modelled on ***ship's husband***; **ship's days**, the days allowed for loading and unloading a ship (*Funk's Stand. Dict.* 1895); **ship's husband** (see husband *sb.* 4 b); **ship's protest** (see protest *sb.* 3); **ship's registry** (see quot.); **ship's time**, the local mean time of the meridian where the ship is.

**1647** Hexham I, A ships anker, *Een schips anker.* **1755** Magens *Insurances* II. 278 The *Ship's Apparel, as Boats, Anchors, Sails, Cordage. **1858** Simmonds *Dict. Trade*, **Ship's Articles.* **1875** Kay *Shipmasters & Seamen* IX. xvii. 704 Which by the special terms of his ship's articles was to cause a forfeiture of wages. **1858** Simmonds *Dict. Trade*, **Ship's-block Maker*, a manufacturer of large blocks for ship's use. **1706** E. Ward *Wooden World Diss.* (1708) 19 These [*sc.* a captain's servants], tho' just pick'd off from a Taylor's Shop-board, are rated able on his *Ship's Books. **1638** Junius *Paint. Ancients* 155 The *ships-castle behinde was most commonly adorned with the picture of one or other God. **1834** *Encycl. Metrop.* (1845) VI. 344 *Ship's Corporal... *Ship's Cook. **1840** R. H. Dana *Bef. Mast* viii, However useful and active you may be, you are but a mongrel,—a sort of afterguard and '*ship's cousin'. **1706** E. Ward *Wooden World Diss.* (1708) 13 The wretched *Ship's Crew..get scarce the very Husk, whilst he [the captain] runs away with the Flower of the Cargo. *Ibid.* 73 He cannot but pity the Surgeon's Simplicity, for calling himself the *Ship's Doctor, when all the World knows, that none but the Carpenter looks to her Wounds. **1974** L. Deighton *Spy Story* xviii. 190 There was the ship's doctor. **1841** *Penny Cycl.* XXI. 405/1 Parts of *ship's furniture. **1835** *Tomlins' Law-Dict.* s.v. *Ship's Papers*, The Log Book, or *Ship's Journal. **1881** *Instr. Census Clerks* (1885) 47 *Ship's Log Maker. **1886** *Pall Mall Gaz.* 29 Jan. 5/2 That comparatively small but highly important section of our sailors generally described as '*ships' officers'. **1846** A. Young *Naut. Dict.* 194 *Ship's protest, which should be compared with the log-book, and certified by the agent. **1875** Knight *Dict. Mech.*, **Ship's Pump*, a suction-pump for freeing a ship's hold from water. **1644** Manwayring *Seaman's Dict.* 100 The standing part of the sheate, is that part which is made fast, by a clinch into a ring of the *ships-quarter. **1867** Smyth *Sailor's Word-bk.*, **Ship's registry and certificate*, an official record of a ship's size, the bills of lading, ownership, &c. *Ibid.*, **Ship's steward*, the person who manages the victualling or mess departments. In the navy, paymaster's steward. **1884** F. J. Britten *Watch & Clockm.* 240 A *Ship's Time-piece has usually a lever escapement. **1881** *Naval Encycl.* 745/2 **Ship's writer*, a petty officer who, under the directions of the executive-officer, does the writing and keeps the watch-, muster-, conduct-, and other books of the ship. **1891** Patterson *Naut. Dict.* 384 *Ship's Writer*,..is a first class petty officer, and his duty is to keep the names and rates of the ship's company. **1969** T. Parker *Twisting Lane* 43 He wasn't a sailor, he was a kind of a clerk on board ship... I believe he was called a ship's writer. **1850** *Ship's yeoman [see YEOMAN 2c]. **1891** PATTERSON *Naut. Dict.* 356 *Equipment Yeoman*, formerly called ship's yeoman.

**ship**, *sb.*[2] *Printing.* A colloquial abbreviation of COMPANIONSHIP 3.

**1875** SOUTHWARD *Dict. Typogr.* 18 The best 'ship' is kept going with work from the others, rather than be suffered to stand still. **1882** —— *Pract. Printing* (1884) 221 The chief of the companionship or 'ship'.. receives the copies from the overseer.

**ship** (ʃɪp), *v.* Forms: 1 **scipian, scypian**, 3-5 **schype**, (3 **ssipe**), 4-5 **schipe, schepe**, 4-6 **schippe, schyppe**, 4-7 **shipe, shippe, shyppe**, (5 **shipp**), 6-7 **schip**, 6- **ship**. [late OE. *scipian*, f. *scip* SHIP *sb.*[1]; cf. MLG. *schêpen*, (M)Du. *schepen*, MHG., G. *schiffen*, ON. *skipa*. In the later senses a new formation directly f. SHIP *sb.*[1]]

†**1. a.** *pass.* To be furnished with a ship or ships.

*c* **900** *O.E. Chron.* (Parker MS.) an. 893, Se micla here.. wurdon ȝescipode. **1594** KYD *Cornelia* v. 298 Seeing himselfe at anchor, slightly shipt, Besieg'd, betraide by winde. **1604** SHAKS. *Oth.* II. i. 47 *Mon.* Is he well ship'd? *Cassio.* His Barke is stoutly Timber'd. **1647** HEXHAM I, Shiped, *Gescheept*.

†**b.** *refl.* To provide oneself with a ship. *Obs.*[−1]

**1627** CAPT. SMITH *Sea Gram.* xii. 55 Euery horseman cannot mount himself alike, neither euery Seaman ship himselfe as he would.

†**2.** To equip or launch (a vessel). *Obs.*

Cf. **1224-5** *Foreign Acc., L.T.R.* No. 1 Municione et Schippatione nauium et galiarum.

**1052** *O.E. Chron.* (MS. C), þa let Eadward cyng scypian .xl. snacca. *c* **1500** *Melusine* 118 He..made fourthwith a galyotte to be shipped redy. *Ibid.* 268 Go make a galyot to be shipped redy with ten oores.

**3. a.** To put or take (persons or things) on board ship; to cause (a person) to embark; to place (goods) in a ship for transportation.

**13..** *K. Alis.* 6062 He schipeth heom in schipes cayvars, In dromondes, and in lumbars. **1425** *Rolls of Parlt.* IV. 276/1 The said Merchantz Englissh, that shippen, or shall shippe any Merchandise. **1465** *Paston Lett.* Suppl. 93 To remember that Guton malt must be shipped at Blakeney. **1513** PACE in Ellis *Orig. Lett.* Ser. III. I. 179 An army.. whiche he affirmith to be nowe schippidde redy to passe the see. **1517** TORKINGTON *Pilgr.* (1884) 67 We shippyd our horses at Caleys. **1582** STANYHURST *Æneis* I. 11 Pigmalions riches was shipt. **1640** YORKE *Union Hon.* 100 King Henry the fifth, was shipping his men for France. **1689** *Lond. Gaz.* No. 2486/3 The Lord Hewit's Regiment of Horse will be shipped to morrow. **1748** *Anson's Voy.* II. xiii. 271 He was shipped on board a vessel bound to Old Spain. **1818** SCOTT *Let.* in *Lockhart* (1837) IV. 216, I rather fear that a quantity of game which was shipped awhile ago at Inverness for the Doctor, never reached him. **1866** CRUMP *Banking* vi. 139 Upon a cargo being shipped, bills of lading..are filled up with the name of the shipper. **1885** *Act 48 & 49 Vict.* c. 41 §17 Any harbour or any works in or at which vessels can.. ship or unship goods or passengers.

*fig.* **1602** MARSTON *Ant. & Mel.* I. Wks. 1856 I. 16 After long travaile through the Asian maine, I shipt my hopefull thoughts for Brittany.

*absol.* **1479** *Cely Papers* (Camden) 18, I wyll nat schepe tyll I have my money hom in lecters of payment. **1482** *Ibid.* 104 Syr thay hawhe begwn to schype at London. **1530** PALSGR. 703/2 We can nat go hence yet, we have nat all shypped.

**b.** said of the ship.

**1800** COLQUHOUN *Comm. Thames* xiii. 374 All vessels shall ship or take in all their cargoes..below the Canal at Blackwall. **1882** 'OUIDA' *Maremma* ii, A little vessel was shipping grain.

†**4. a.** *pass.* Of a person: To have gone on board, to be embarked. *Obs.*

*c* **1300** *Prose Life St. Brandan* (Percy) 37 Whan they were all shypped, sodeynly this yonge man vanysshed away. *c* **1400** *Laud Troy Bk.* 387 Thei are schepped now eche a wyght. *a* **1450** LOVELICH *Grail* lvi. 114 Thike same Nyht.. that In to the See I-scheped they were. **1591** SHAKS. *Two Gent.* I. i. 73 Twenty to one then, he is ship'd already. *a* **1592** GREENE *Jas. IV*, I. i, My royal father is both shipp'd and gone. **1617** MORYSON *Itin.* II. 203 We heard that all the Spaniards..were shipped. **1621** G. SANDYS *Ovid's Met.* VI. (1626) 120 As soone as shipt; as soone as actiue ores Had mou'd the surges.

*Proverb.*

**1570-6** LAMBARDE *Peramb. Kent* 209 Least otherwise the Reader..might be shipped in the boate of this errour. **1575-85** ABP. SANDYS *Serm.* xix. 334 This is the way wherein Christ must bee followed by as manie as desire to be shipped with him, to bee of the number of his people. **1720** DE FOE *Capt. Singleton* (1906) 8 He that is shipped with the devil must sail with the devil.

**b.** *refl.* To go on board ship, embark. Also with *off* (cf. 7b). *Obs.* or *arch.*

*c* **1400** *Destr. Troy* 1783 Antenor..Shippit hym full shortly & his shene folke. **1600** R. CARR tr. *Mahumetan Hist.* 62b, Who..was commaunded to ship himselfe againe in a barque that was prepared. **1607** SHARPHAM *Fleire* II. (1610) E 1, Ile send you to Graues-end, Ile see you in the Tilt-boate, When you are there, ship your selues. *a* **1647** PETTE in *Archæologia* XII. 219, I was constrained to ship myself to sea upon a desperate voyage. **1719** DE FOE *Crusoe* II. (Globe) 505 They shipp'd themselves to serve in the Ship. **1761** HUME *Hist. Eng.* III. lii. 129 The Puritans, restrained in England, shipped themselves off for America. **1831** SCOTT *Cast Dang.* xx, It was thought that the waves had swallowed them when they shipped themselves from the west.

**5.** *intr.* To go on board ship, embark. Now *rare*.

*a* **1122** *O.E. Chron.* (Laud MS.) an. 1091 Se eorl..on Wiht scipode & into Normandiȝ for. *c* **1290** *S. Eng. Leg.* 467/179 Huy schypeden in þe salte se. *c* **1300** *K. Horn* 1013 (Laud MS.) þe page was blyþe And schepede wel swyþe. **1375** BARBOUR *Bruce* III. 575 Then schippyt thai, for-owtyn mar. *c* **1400** MAUNDEV. (Roxb.) viii. 28 þer er many hauens for to schippe at. *c* **1468** in *Archæologia* (1846) XXXI. 327 The Fryedaye next after the Nativite of Saienct John Baptist, she shippid at Margate. **1517** TORKINGTON *Pilgr.* (1884) 1, I shipped at Rye, in Sussex. **1596** DALRYMPLE tr. *Leslie's Hist. Scot.* II. 378 Quhen at Leith tha had shipit in. **1599** DEKKER *Shoemakers Hol.* (1610) B 2 Tis his highnesse will, That presently your cosen shippe for France With all his powers. **1690** *Lond. Gaz.* 2551/3 The 400 Horse..and many Foot..marched to Highlake, where, it's believed, they are Shipping this day. **1891** *Spectator* 17 Jan., People wishing to get from London to New York..ship at Liverpool.

**6. a.** To go by ship *to*, *into*, or *from* a place. Now chiefly *U.S.* Cf. sense 6c below.

**13..** *Metr. Hom.* in *Archiv Stud. neu. Spr.* LVII. 265 Faste he drouh toward þe se For schipen he wolde to oþur þede. **1382** WYCLIF *Acts* xx. 6 We schipiden aftir dayes of therf looues fro Philippis. *c* **1400** *Rowland & O.* 742 þay Schipped ouer at Vertely In to þe landes of lumbardy. **1477** EARL RIVERS (Caxton) *Dictes* 1, I determyned me to take that voyage and shipped from Southampton. **1535** COVERDALE *Matt.* xiv. 34 They shipped ouer, & came in to the londe of Genazereth. **1603** KNOLLES *Hist. Turks* (1638) 247 The Emperour, speedily shipped ouer into Asia. **1654** GATAKER *Disc. Apol.* 79 [They] have slipt away and shipt hence. **1904** H. JAMES *Golden Bowl* II. xxxvii. 279 You regularly make me wish that I had shipped back to American City. **1978** M. PUZO *Fools Die* xvi. 171 By the time Frank and his units left the armory and shipped to Fort Lee there was a lot of bad blood.

†**b.** To sail *about*. *Obs.*

**1387** TREVISA *Higden* (Rolls) VII. 95 He hadde schipped aboute Est Engelonde [*circumnavigata Estanglia*]. *c* **1450** *Mirk's Festial* 260 As I was schyppyng yn þe see, I come to an yle.

**c.** U.S. Mil. slang. ***to ship out***: to depart, to be transported; also *fig.* (cf. *shape up or ship out* s.v. SHAPE *v.* 19e); ***to ship over***: to re-enlist, to volunteer for a tour of duty.

**1908** L. G. TISDALE *Three Years behind Guns* xxiii. 259 Do you want to ship over? **1924** ANDERSON & STALLINGS *What Price Glory?* I. i. 7 When I left China the Yangtse was full of the bodies of virgins that drowned their beautiful selves because I was shipping over. **1948** [see CASH *v.*[2] 2b]. **1953** *CEC Bull.* Jan. 31/1 This outfit shipped out of Davisville 12 September 1943. **1964** G. L. COON *Short End* 223, I wouldn't ship over in Korea, and especially in Pankari. **1978** M. PUZO *Fools Die* xvi. 171 At the end of the month, when everybody shipped out, I bought Frank a present.

**7. a.** *trans.* To send or transport by ship. †***to ship out***: to export.

**1436** *Libel Eng. Policy* in *Pol. Poems* (Rolls) II. 160 Saffron, quiksilver,..Is into Ffiaundres shypped fulle craftylye. **1495** *Halyburton's Ledger* (1867) 12 Bocht in Handwarp and schepit in the Cristoffir of the Fer. **1503-4** *Act 19 Hen. VII*, c. 27 §1 Wolle felles..to be shipped owte of the seid Realme to the seid Staple at Cales. **1602** SHAKS. *Ham.* IV. i. 30 The Sun no sooner shall the Mountaines touch, But we will ship him hence. **1656** TUCKER *Rep. Revenues Scot.* (Bannatyne Club) 26 South Barwick, where the Scots and English both did usually shippe out Skyns, Hides, Wooll. **1719** DE FOE *Crusoe* I. (Globe) 39 One half of the Produce being to himself, and the other to be shipp'd to England. **1725** POPE *Odyss.* XV. 419 Rude pirates seized, and shipped thee o'er the main. **1826** DISRAELI *Viv. Grey* II. i, The third [son] was a Roué, and was shipped to the Colonies. **1861** GOSCHEN *For. Exch.* 127 To ship the silver to England. **1892** KIPLING *Barrack-room Ballads* 53 Ship me somewheres east of Suez. **1912** *Times* 19 Dec. 15/4 Goods shipped in the mail vessels.

**b.** *esp.* with *off*.

**1669** STURMY *Mariner's Mag., Penalties & Forfeitures*, If any Wharfinger..shall..Ship off..any Wares..at any unlawful time. **1706** *Lond. Gaz.* No. 4239/1 They Shipt off 900 of their sick and wounded Men. **1778** *Eng. Gazetteer* (ed. 2) s.v., The inhabitants ship off yearly..seven or eight thousand chaldrons of coal. **1855** MACAULAY *Hist. Eng.* xviii. IV. 195 He would himself send the recusant to prison, or ship him off for Flanders. **1878** BOSW. SMITH *Carthage* 38 Till their numbers became excessive and these were shipped off by the prudence of their rulers to found colonies.

**c.** *transf.* To transport (goods) by rail or other means of conveyance. *U.S.*

**1857** *Harper's Mag.* Sept. 459/2 A few of the more enterprising operators..thought nothing of shipping two or three thousand tons per annum. **1881** *Chicago Times* 17 June, To ship their freight by rail. **1885** *Harper's Mag.* Apr. 663/2 We..shipped our..collection of luggage to the hotel.

**d.** *fig.* To send *off*, send packing, get rid of, dismiss, expel.

**1588** SHAKS. *Tit. A.* I. i. 206 Andronicus, would thou were shipt to hell. **1826** in A. J. C. Hare *Gurneys of Earlham* (1895) II. 31 After a good deal of bustle, all were shipped off, except Aunt Cunningham. **1857** TROLLOPE *Three Clerks* xviii, Old Foolscap says he'll ship me the next time I'm absent half-an-hour without leave.

**e.** *intr.* Of perishable goods: to admit of being transported.

**1867** *Trans. Illinois State Agric. Soc.* VII. 510 It ships well, and is a very good peach. **1927** *Daily Express* 9 Nov. 5/5 Persimmons..will probably be as plentiful and popular as the banana, because it ships well and grows..freely.

**8.** Of a vessel: To take in (water) over the side; to be submerged or flooded with (water) by waves breaking over it; esp. ***to ship a sea***. Said also of the occupants of the vessel.

**1698** FRYER *Acc. E. India & P.* 13 In this Encounter we shipped many a perilous Sea. **1719** DE FOE *Crusoe* I. (Globe) 9 Our Ship rid Forecastle in, shipp'd several Seas. *a* **1734** NORTH *Life Dudley North* (1744) 15 We shipt Seas over our Poop. **1748** *Anson's Voy.* III. v. 342 Baling out the water which she accidentally ships. **1853** KANE *Grinnell Exp.* xx. (1856) 153 Driving before the wind, shipping seas at every roll. **1883** STEVENSON *Treas. Isl.* xvii, The rowing ceased,..and all was so nicely contrived that we did not ship a drop.

**9. a.** To take or draw (an object) into the ship or boat to which it belongs. Also with *up*.

**1630** in Binnell *Descr. Thames* (1758) 65 No Fisherman.. shall at any Time hereafter ship their Draw-Nets (called Shipping a-stern) into their Boats, before such Time as they have laid forth all their whole Net. **1894** *Outing* XXIV. 257/2 As we shipped up our rod the natives began to assemble. **1898** W. W. JACOBS *Sea Urchins* (1906) 213 The visitors went ashore, the gangway was shipped, and..the *Curlew* drifted slowly away from the quay.

**b.** To lift (an oar or scull) out of its rowlock, and (now, in sculling) to bring it into the boat (cf. BOAT *v.* 1 and UNSHIP *v.*). (See also quot. 1898.) Also *absol.* as a command = 'ship oars!'

For another sense of 'ship oars' see 10.

**1700** DRYDEN *Ceyx & Alc.* 92 The Sailors ship their Oars, and cease to row. **1725** POPE *Odyss.* II. 470 And now they ship their oars, and crown with wine The holy goblet to the powers divine. **1857** P. COLQUHOUN *Comp. 'Oarsman's Guide'* 32 To *ship* the oar or scull is to jerk it out of the row-lock, and to *boat* it, to bring it on board. **1861** HUGHES *Tom Brown at Oxf.* ii, The stranger came to the bank, shipped his sculls, and jumped out. **1894** CROCKETT *Raiders* 14, I shipped the oars and lay back thinking. **1896** ASHBY-STERRY *Tale of Thames* xxi, 'Easy all!' says Auntie, following the command by 'Ship!' **1898** *Encycl. Sport* II. 297/2 (Rowing) *Ship*, to lift the handle of the oar when the blade is on the water, and then to allow it to float, with the motion of the boat, alongside.

**10. a.** orig. and esp. *Naut.* To put (an object) in position for performing its proper function; *spec.* to fix (an oar) in the rowlock, in readiness to row; hence, to put in position for any purpose.

**1616** CHAPMAN *Musæus* 352 His faire Limbes of his weede, he strip't: Which, at his head, with both hands bound, he shipt. **17..** *Greenland Voy.* iii. in *Coll. Old Ballads* (1738) III. 173 Each Man ship his Oar, and leave nothing on Shoar That is needful the Voy'ge to advance. **1769** FALCONER *Dict. Marine* (1780) s.v., To ship the oars, *i.e.* to fix them in their row-locks. To ship the swivel-guns, is to fix them in their sockets. **1798** in Nicolas *Disp.* (1845) III. 53 He had a new rudder made upon his own deck, which was immediately shipped. **1833** STURT *Exped. S. Austral.* II. 166 Seven or eight [natives]..crept into the reeds, with their spears shipped to throw at us. **1834** L. RITCHIE *Wand. Seine* 33 Shipping a single oar in the stern, [he] began to scull out with all his might. **1837** MARRYAT *Snarleyyow* xlvii, The skylight was shipped on again. **1845** J. COULTER *Adv. in Pacific* vii. 71 Which mast and sail are..never shipped until required. **1859** F. A. GRIFFITHS *Artil. Man* (1862) 195 No. 3..ships and unships the handspike. **1867** SMYTH *Sailor's Word-bk.* s.v., Ship capstan-bars. **1881** *Daily Tel.* 28 Jan., A hole big enough to ship the mainmast in.

**b.** *intr.* (for *pass.*). To admit of being placed in position; to have a certain position in a contrivance.

**1833** B. SILLIMAN *Man. Sugar Cane* 80 [The pan] is made to ship and unship. **1844** H. STEPHENS *Bk. Farm* III. 1169 The top-sides..which are fitted to ship and unship as occasion may require.

**11. a.** To put on (clothing, etc.); also, to shoulder (a burden).

**1829** MAW *Jrnl. Pass. Pacific* 16 Their regard for new and gay shoes, of which they 'ship' a new pair every Sunday morning. **1831** TRELAWNY *Adv. Younger Son* lxiv, He.. took off his white jacket, and shipped a blue one. **1834** MARRYAT *Peter Simple* xli, I had shipped the swab... I'm lieutenant. **1851** H. MELVILLE *Moby Dick* I. xxxiii. 236 He pauses, ships a new face altogether. **1910** *Blackw. Mag.* Dec. 758/2 The bearers fitted their shoulders under the straps and shipped their burden.

**b.** ***to ship a stripe***: to gain promotion in the navy or air-force. *colloq.*

**1915** H. ROSHER *In R.N.A.S.* (1916) 38, I see in this morning's paper that I have shipped another stripe (Flight Lieutenant). **1924** *Blackw. Mag.* Mar. 333/2 For once his clothes were more interesting than mine for he had 'shipped' his half-stripe, and was a whole degree more important in the world!

**12. a.** *trans.* To engage for service on a ship.

**1643** *Decl. Commons* (*Reb. Ireland*) 50 He..was shipped.. to serve in the said Frigot. **1699** DAMPIER *Voy.* II. I. 150, I was Shipt Mate of the Sloop that came from Malacca with us. **1719** DE FOE *Crusoe* I. (Globe) 15 It was my great Misfortune, that in all these Adventures I did not ship myself as a Sailor. **1840** R. H. DANA *Bef. Mast* xiv, Instead of shipping some hands to make our work easier.

**b.** *intr.* To engage to serve on a ship.

**1829** MARRYAT *F. Mildmay* xxi, We never ask questions when a seaman ships for us. **1845** J. COULTER *Adv. in Pacific* xi. 145 One of the Spaniards shipped on board as an ordinary seaman. **1891** KIPLING *City Dreadf. Nt.* 27 As soon as the money's gone they'll ship, but not before.

**ship, shippe**, var. ff. CHIP *sb.*[2], share-beam.

**1607** J. CARPENTER *Plaine Mans Plough* 115 Next to the Share, is the Shippe. *Ibid.*, The Ship is not only that peece which holdeth the Share, but is placed beneath next the earth.

**-ship** *suffix.* Forms: 1 **-skiepe, -scipe, -scype**, *Anglian* **-scip, -sciop**, 2 **-scep**, 3 **-sip(e**, 3-4 **-scip(e**, 3-5 **-schipe**, 4 **-schupe**, 4-5 **-schippe, -shipe, -schyp, -schepe, -shep(e, -chipe, -chepe**, 4-6 **-schip, -shyp, -shippe**, 5 **-schuppe, -schepe, -chyp, -chep**, 5-6 **-shyppe**, 5-7 **-shipp**, 4- **-ship**. [In OE. **-sciepe*, *-skiepe* (rare), *-scipe*, *-scype*, Anglian *-scip*, (occas. *-sciop*) str. masc. = OFris. *-skipi*, *-skip*, *-schip* (WFris. *-skip*, *-schip*, NFris. *-skep*, *-skap*), OS. *-scepi*, *-scipi*, MLG., MDu. *-sc(h)ip*,

-*sc(h)êpe*, -*sc(h)eep*, -*sc(h)êp*, WFlem. -*schip*, -*schepe*:—OTeut. **skapi-z*, f. *skap-* to create, ordain, appoint (see SHAPE *v.*). The *i* of the stem-syllable of OE. *scipe* and the corresponding continental forms is apparently due to secondary influence of the umlaut, the change being probably favoured by the lack of stress. The related **skapo-z* masc., **skapō* fem., and **skapti-z* SHAFT *sb.*[1], meaning 'creation, creature, constitution, condition', were used in Germanic as the second element of compounds and as such assumed the function and meaning of a suffix equivalent to **skapi-z*; these forms are represented by OS. -*skap* (MDu., Du. -*schap*), OHG. -*scaf* fem., later -*scaft* (MHG., G. -*schaft*), ON. -*skapr* (Da. -*skab*, Sw. -*skap*); the alleged OE. *landsceap* is an error due to misreading.

The abnormal forms of the suffix in Sc. *hussyskap*, -*skep*, -*skip* (see HOUSEWIFESHIP) may have a LG. or Du. origin.]

In certain uses the suffix lends itself more or less freely to the formation of nonce-words; selected instances of these are given below under the divisons to which they belong.

**1.** Added to adjs. and pa. pples. to denote the state or condition of being so-and-so. Such compounds were numerous in OE., and many survived (or were re-coined) in ME., but few have a history extending beyond the 15th century; e.g. OE. *árodscipe* briskness, *dolscipe* folly, *druncenscipe* DRUNKENSHIP, DRUNKSHIP (ME.), *glædscipe* GLADSHIP, *gódscipe* GOODSHIP, *láþscipe* hardship, *prútscipe* pride, SHENDSHIP (ME.), *snelscipe* boldness, WILDSHIP (ME.), *wódscipe* madness. The only survivals of this formation now in common use are HARDSHIP (first in Ancren Riwle), and WORSHIP (OE. *weorþscipe*).

**2.** Added to sbs. to denote the state or condition of being what is expressed by the sb., e.g. OE. *féondscipe* hostility, FIENDSHIP, *fréondscipe* FRIENDSHIP, *þeȝnscipe* THEGNSHIP (cf. THANESHIP); *authorship*, *fellowship*, †*knightship*, *partnership*, *sonship*, *suretyship*.

**1674** N. FAIRFAX *Bulk & Selv.* 89 Supposing that by Almighty power their Sunship and Moonship might be kept by them, without worldship. *a* **1828** *Bentham's Fragm. Govt.* Hist. Pref., Wks. 1843 I. 241 To assume and keep up the tone of junvenility and tyro-ship.

**b.** By extension, compounds of this kind, when the sb. is the designation of a class of human being, assume the sense of the qualities or character associated with, or the skill or power of accomplishment of, the person denoted by the sb.; e.g. OE. *eorlscipe* manliness, *hláfordscipe* domination, supremacy, LORDSHIP, *mannscipe* humanity; *craftsmanship*, *horsemanship*, *housewifeship*, *kingship*, *soldiership*, *workmanship*.

**1858** CARLYLE *Fredk. Gt.* III. x. (1872) I. 198 His wars against the Turks, and his other Hectorships, I will forget. **1879** MORLEY *Burke* vii. 142 The ideas of adventurership.

**3.** Added to sbs. designating an official or person of rank to denote the office, position, dignity, or rank of the person designated, as OE. *ȝeréfscipe* REEVESHIP; *ambassadorship*, *captainship*, *chaplainship*, *clerkship*, *headship*, *laureateship*, *professorship*, *sheriffship*, *stewardship*. In the case of *fellowship*, *scholarship*, *postmastership* and the like, the compound has come to connote not only the office or position itself but the emoluments, etc., pertaining to it.

**1485** *Rolls of Parlt.* VI. 368/2 The Offices of Walstatship of Wydygada. **1568** GRAFTON *Chron.* II. 350 John Fortham Bishop of Durham was discharged of the Treasorer-ship. **1625** in *Buccleuch MSS.* (Hist. MSS. Comm.) I. 262 By virtue of his Cust[os] Rotulorum-ship. **1885** *Pall Mall Gaz.* 9 Apr. 5 There are now four A.R.A. ships vacant. **1895** *Harper's Mag.* Apr. 718/2 The positions they fill are the 'judgeship', the 'searchership', the 'spankership', and general 'juryship'.

**b.** With poss. pron. prefixed, the compounds *ladyship*, *lordship*, *worship*, have passed into honorific designations of the persons who are entitled to the style of 'Lady', 'Lord', 'the Worshipful'. Hence the suffix has been freely employed to form mock titles or humourous styles of address, in which -*ship* is added to the ordinary designation of the person (or animal) or to a word expressing a quality which it is desired to emphasize for the nonce; this use has been extended even to adjs. (e.g. *his uglyship*) and adj. phr. (e.g. *his beyond-sea-ship*).

**1573–80** G. HARVEY *Letter-bk.* (Camden) 94 Wich I knowe not howe your soveraineioyeservantshipp would take. **1611** BEAUM. & FL. *Philaster* IV, I never lov'd his beyond-sea-ship. **1615** W. HULL *Mirr. Maj.* Ep. Ded., One of their Holiships. **1682** SHADWELL *Lanc. Witches* I. 2, I will ..teach your Master of Artship. **1747** W. HORSLEY *Fool* (1748) II. 165 Thus his Grandship open'd. **1767** *Woman of Fashion* I. 143 What a Chace has her Goddessship led me! **1807** MOORE *Mem.* (1853) I. 229, I am beginning to talk too sentimentally for your wag-ship. **1827** FONBLANQUE *Eng. under 7 Administr.* (1837) I. 89 *Non constat*, as the lawyers say, that the voyagers venerated his monkeyship. **1829** T. C. CROKER *Leg. Lakes* I. 230 Down he and the marchioness walk to the kitchen, and her marchionesship sets herself by the fire-side. **1834** M. SCOTT *Cruise Midge* xxi, 'Take that, your owlship', and I made a blow at him with the but-end. **1865** *Public Opinion* 21 Jan. 77/1, I have seen Dyticus rush upon a full-grown smooth newt, and no twistings and writhings of his eftship was of any avail. **1873** *Forest & Stream* I. 148/2 His Uglyship [viz. an alligator], all mouth and squirming tail. **1880** MISS MULOCK *Poems, Dead Czar* 42 You..may parade Your maggotship throughout the wondering world.

**4.** Added to sbs. to denote a state of life, occupation, or behaviour, relating to or connected with what is denoted by the sb., e.g. OE. *béorscipe* feast (lit. 'beer-ship'), *byrdscipe* child-bearing, *werscipe* married state. Compounds of this kind are rare in the later periods; COURTSHIP (first in Shaks.) is the chief instance; COUNTRYSHIP, if it is not merely a shortening of *countrymanship*, may belong here.

**5.** Added to sbs. forming compounds having a collective sense. These were numerous in OE., e.g. *burȝscipe* municipality, *folcscipe* nation, *ȝieldscipe* guild, *þeȝnscipe* body of retainers, *þéodscipe* people, *wæterscipe* piece of water. TOWNSHIP (OE. *túnscipe* the inhabitants of a *tún*) is the one survival from the OE. period; the sense 'domain of ...' which appears in LORDSHIP 2 is not of frequent occurrence.

The following is a nonce-formation after *township*:—

**1768** *Phil. Trans.* LX. 445, I took a jaunt to the Hottentots crawl-ships [= kraal-ships].

**shipboard** (ˈʃɪpbɔəd). Also 3 scipes, 5 shippus bord. [f. SHIP *sb.*[1] + BOARD *sb.*

Cf. WFris. *skipsboard*, MLG. *schêpesbord*, MDu. *schipbort*, *sceeps-*, *scipsbort* (Du. *scheepsboord*), G. *schiff(s)bord*, ON. *skip(s)borð* (Sw. *skeppsbord*, Da. *skibsbord*).]

†**1. a.** The side of a ship (see BOARD *sb.* 12); chiefly in phr.: ***within shipboard*** = on board ship; ***over (the) shipboard*** = OVERBOARD *adv.*; ***to*** or ***from shipboard*** = on to or off a ship. *Obs.*

*c* **1200** *Vices & Virtues* 43 Alle ðe wið-innen scipes borde wuniȝeð. *c* **1205** LAY. 1518 Ne cume ȝe neauer wid vten scipes bord. *a* **1300** *K. Horn* 113 Þe children hi broȝte to stronde..In to schupes borde. ?*a* **1400** *Morte Arth.* 1699 With-in chippe-burdez. *c* **1430** *Syr Gener.* 364 He..bad here lodesman at a word Should cast hem ouer the ship bord. *c* **1440** *Bone Flor.* 1796, I schall hyt hynge on a knagg, At the schypp borde ende. **1470–85** MALORY *Arthur* IV. vi. 125 An C torches sette vpon alle the sydes of the shyp bordes. **1494** *Act 11 Hen. VII*, c. 4 Any Person selling or buying by Water-measure within the Ship-board. **1498** in J. Bulloch *Pynours* (1887) 56 Borne..fra the Schipburd at the Key to ony part of this burghe. **1550** LYNDESAY *Sqr. Meldrum* 174 And euerie man to shipburd drew. **1586** *Reg. Privy Council Scot.* Ser. I. IV. 123 Thay have ressavit within schip-burde a grite quantite of victuallis. **1590** SHAKS. *Com. Err.* V. i. 408 Shall I fetch your stuffe from shipbord? **1596** WARNER *Alb. Eng.* XII. lxxii. 299 In saying which came Stafford in, and wils them to dispatch To ship-board. **1650** T. FROYSELL *Gale of Opport.* (1652) 31 The Marriners they cast him over Ship-board. **1848** THACKERAY *Van. Fair* lvii, His new patient, who had been consigned to shipboard by the Madras practitioner with very small hopes indeed.

**b.** ***on shipboard***: on board ship. (See BOARD *sb.* 14.) Also † ***a shipboard*** (frequent *c* 1620–1720).

*c* **1470** HENRY *Wallace* x. 856 A cruell cowntyr thar was on schipburd seyn. **1556** ROBINSON tr. *More's Utopia* (Arb.) 165 By reason of cold taken, I thinke, a shippeborde. **1568** GRAFTON *Chron.* II. 686 Commaunding his men to go on ship-borde. **1600** HAKLUYT *Voy.* III. 440 We..brought them a shippeboord. **1660–1** PEPYS *Diary* 14 Feb., The first time I ever carried my wife a-ship-board. **1758** J. BLAKE *Mar. Syst.* 18 A Liberty Ticket,..allowing him to follow his occupation unmolested, either on shore or on ship-board. **1848** DICKENS *Dombey* lx, Being then on shipboard, bound for Bengal. **1888** R. GARNETT *Life of Emerson* ii. 43 They were fellow passengers on ship-board back to Charleston.

**c.** Similarly ***of shipboard***.

**1841** LEVER *O'Malley* xxxvi. 198 The escape from the durance vile of shipboard. **1853** KANE *Grinnell Exp.* xxii. (1856) 173 The life of shipboard.

**d.** ***by shipboard***: by ship. *rare.*

**1842** *P. Parley's Ann.* III. 250 My grandfather had a dog which he brought by ship-board to London.

†**2.** A plank of a ship. *Obs.*

**1352** *Exch. Acc. Q.R.* bundle 20 no. 27 (P.R.O.), Bordis magnis et spissis vocatis 'shippebord' emptis pro confeccione navis predicte. **1483** *Cath. Angl.* 337/1 A Schyppe burde, *asser.* **1486** *Naval Acc. Hen. VII* (1896) 15, vij Shipbordes..spent..in repayring..of the Cokke of the same Ship. **1560** BIBLE (Geneva) *Ezek.* xxvii. 5 Thei haue made all thy ship bordes of fyrre trees of Shenir.

**3.** *attrib.* Esp. in phrs. ***shipboard acquaintance***, ***romance***, etc., to denote casual or ephemeral relationships.

**1857** DUFFERIN *Lett. High Lat.* (ed. 3) 147 The innocuous cates which generally compose ship-board rations. **1880** *Plain Hints Needlework* 123 To make mops for shipboard cleaning. **1890** W. CLARK RUSSELL *Marr. Sea* x, What will she have to say to a shipboard wedding? **1916** G. B. SHAW *Overruled* 78 Was it the usual aimless man's lark: a mere shipboard flirtation? **1933** F. BALDWIN *Innocent Bystander* vi. 107 A shipboard romance will do a lot for his ego. **1963** 'W. HAGGARD' *High Wire* iv. 37 I'm a casual pick-up in the snow, a sort of shipboard acquaintance. **1978** 'M. M. KAYE' *Far Pavilions* ix. 148 It had been possible for Mrs Harlowe to introduce both young men as shipboard acquaintances. **1980** J. GARDNER *Garden of Weapons* II. viii. 194 He should be able to treat the business with Miriam like some shipboard romance. But his growing bewitchment would not allow that.

**ship-boat.** ? *Obs.* Now (7–) ship's boat. [See BOAT *sb.*

Cf. MLG. *schêpesbôt*, Du. *scheepsboot* (whence G. *schiff(s)boot*), ON. *skipsbátr* (Sw. *skeppsbåt*, Da. *skibsbaad*).]

The boat carried or towed by a ship.

*c* **1440** *Promp. Parv.* 446/2 Schyppe bot.., *barca.* **1509** HAWES *Past. Pleas.* XXXVI. (1555) 189 When that they were come to us almoste, From their shyppe boate curiously counterfayte. **1555** EDEN *Decades* (Arb.) 111 The greatest vessels..conueighed al theyr vytailes..to lande with theyr shippe boates. **1644** MANWAYRING *Seaman's Dict.* 10 The Boate belonging to a Ship, is either called the Ships-boate, or the Long-boate. **1681** *Lond. Gaz.* 1666/3 Some Ship-boats have been staved and sunk.

**ship-bote, -boot.** *pseudo-arch.* [See BOOT *sb.*[1], BOTE.] Repair of ships.

**1664** EVELYN *Sylva* 103 We have seen how for House-boot, and Ship-boot, Plow-boot, Hey-boot and Fire-boot, the Planting, and Propogation of Timber and Forest-trees is requisite.

**ship-boy.** Also **ship's boy**. A boy who serves on board ship.

**1552** HULOET, Shyp boye, *Misonauta.* **1595** SHAKS. *John* IV. iii. 4 This Ship-boyes semblance hath disguis'd me quite. **1634** SIR T. HERBERT *Trav.* 5 The aduentrous ship-boyes were in perill of those Sharkes. **1661** in *Godolphin's View Admir. Jurisd.* App. 168 The Master ought to set him on shore,..and..to spare him one of the Ship-boyes to look to him. **1839** S. ROGERS *Voy. Columbus* Poems 38 The very ship-boy on the dizzy mast Half breathed his orisons. **1867** SMYTH *Sailor's Word-bk.*, *Ship-boy*, boys apprenticed to learn their sea-duties, but generally appointed as servants. **1883** STEVENSON *Treas. Isl.* ix, 'Here, you ship's boy', he cried, 'out o' that!'

**ship-breaker** (ˈʃɪpbreɪkə(r)). [See BREAKER[1] I.] A person who buys old vessels to break them up for sale. Also, a firm or company engaged in the business of breaking up old vessels.

**1819** *P.O. Lond. Directory* 84 Cristall, Joseph, Sail-maker, Ship breaker, and Dealer in Ship-Stores. **1840** DICKENS *Old C. Shop* iv, On Quilp's Wharf, Daniel Quilp was a ship-breaker. **1888** *Dict. Nat. Biogr.* XIII. 101/2 A ship-breaker, having yards at Rotherhithe, Penzance, and Fowey. **1935** *Sun* (Baltimore) 21 May 12/6 The sale of some of the big outdated ocean liners to shipbreakers (that's the name for companies that take old ships apart with hammers and acetylene torches).

**ˈship-ˌbreaking**, *vbl. sb.* [See BREAKING *vbl. sb.* In sense 1 formed after SHIPBRECHE (cf. MLG., MDu. *schipbrekinge*).]

†**1.** = SHIPBRECHE. *Obs.*

**13..** [see SHIP-BRECHING]. **1398** TREVISA *Barth. De P.R.* XIII. xxi. (Bodl. MS.), ȝif schippes falleþ þerein in anye wise, he scapeþ not þe perille of schipbrekinge. *c* **1440** *Promp. Parv.* 446/2 Schyppbrekynge, *naufragium.* **1493** *Festivall* (W. de W. 1515) 9 b, Saynt poule sayth I haue been..thre tymes in shyppe brekynge.

**2.** The breaking up of old ships; the occupation of a ship-breaker. Also *attrib.*

**1897** *Daily News* 13 May 3/3 The Shipbreaking Company (Limited), of London, has recently purchased from the Admiralty the iron corvette Euryalus [etc.]. **1931** A. HUXLEY *Let.* 6 Aug. (1969) 351 There are bits of Toulon harbour—ship-building and ship-breaking yards..I have always longed to paint. **1976** *S. Wales Echo* 26 Nov. 38/8 The Welshman..has business interests which include farming..and ship-breaking.

**3.** The crime of breaking into a ship for the purpose of committing a felony.

**1901** *Scotsman* 7 Jan. 9/7 Shipbreaking at Aberdeen—..sent..to prison..for breaking into the steam line fishing boat.

†**shipbreche.** *Obs.* Also 1 -bryce, 4 -bruche, -burch. [f. SHIP *sb.*[1] + BREACH, BRUCHE. Cf. WFris. *skipbrek*, MLG. *schipbroke*, MDu. *schipbroke*, -*breuke* (Du. -*breuk*), MHG., G. *schiffbruch*.] Shipwreck.

In late OE. recorded only in the sense 'right to claim what is cast up on the shore in a shipwreck'.

*a* **1067** *Charter* in Kemble *Cod. Dipl.* (1846) IV. 208 Ic habbe ȝeȝeofen Criste and sancte Marie..forestall and hamsocne, griðbryce and scipbryce, and ða sæ upwarp..æt Bramcæstre and æt Ringstyde. ?*a* **1100** *Charter* in Dugdale *Monast.* (1655) I. 237/2 Mundbriche, feardwite,.. infongenthef, sypbriche, tol, & tem. **1387** TREVISA *Higden* (Rolls) II. 369 Schipmen þat seilled in þe see in to shipbruche. *Ibid.*, And þerfore me seide þat þey brouȝte hem to ship-breche. **1398** —— *Barth. De P.R.* XII. xii. (Bodl. MS.), Schipmen trowiþ þat it bodeþ goode ȝif þei mete swannes in perile of schipburch [*ed.* **1495** shippe breche]. *c* **1440** *Gesta Rom.* xiv. 48 Penaunce is þe secunde table aftir Shipbreche.

So †**ship-breching** (in quot. -breging, cf. *bryg* s.v. BREACH *sb.*), †**ship-break** (in quot. -brek).

*a* **1300** *Cursor M.* 20973 Scipbreging [*Gött.* Schip-breking] he suffurd thrise. **1520** NISBET *N.T.* 2 Cor. xi. 25 Thrijse I was at schipbrek [*Wyclif* shipbreche].

**ship-broken** (ˈʃɪpbrəʊk(ə)n), *pa. pple.* and *ppl. a.* Chiefly *Sc.*; now *rare.* Also 5 -broke. [f. SHIP *sb.*[1] + BROKEN, after SHIPBRECHE. Cf. MDu. *schipbroken.*] Shipwrecked; broken or destitute through shipwreck.

**13..** *Metr. Hom.* in *Archiv Stud. neu. Spr.* LVII. 314 A pore schip broken marinere. *c* **1375** *Sc. Leg. Saints* ii. (*Paulus*) 924 Thriis schipe-brokine in þe se. **1474** *Acc. Ld.*

*High Treas. Scot.* I. 72 To iiij pure Franche men.., schipbrokin men,..iij li. 1513 DOUGLAS *Æneis* III. viii. 92 Scillacium quhar schip brokin mony be. 1602 in *Extr. Rec. Convent. Burghs Scot.* (1870) II. 139 Giff ony skipper be schipbrokin. 1623 in *Harl. Misc.* (1809) III. 462 He died ship-broken upon the sea-coast of Ireland. 1661 in *Godolphin's View Admir. Jurisd.* App. 183 The Lord of that place..ought to be aiding..to the said distressed Merchants ..in saving their Ship-broken-goods. 1878 HALL CAINE *Deemster* xxxix, Six or seven poor ship-broken men... In the middle of the night they had come ashore on a raft.

**'shipbuilder.** One whose occupation is to design and construct ships; a naval architect.

*a* 1700 EVELYN *Diary* 10 Aug. 1662, He is esteem'd for the most skilfull ship-builder in the world. 1736 *Gentl. Mag.* VI. 733/1 It will be very hard to prove, that the first Ship-Builders had ever seen that Ark to take a Patern from it. 1855 KINGSLEY *Westw. Ho!* xi, The best shipbuilders from Hull to Cadiz. 1864 *Morn. Star* 12 Jan., The shipbuilders of this country for above a century have built ships for almost every nation on the earth.

**'shipbuilding,** *vbl. sb.* The business or art of building ships; naval architecture.

1717 W. SUTHERLAND (*title*) Britain's Glory, or, Shipbuilding unveil'd. 1777 ROBERTSON *Hist. Amer.* (1783) I. 101 The art of ship-building in the fifteenth century was extremely rude. 1855 MACAULAY *Hist. Eng.* xix. IV. 510 His own yacht, the Peregrine, renowned as the masterpiece of shipbuilding.

*attrib.* 1846 (*title*) The present Ship-building Controversy. 1875 KNIGHT *Dict. Mech.*, *Shipbuilding-dock*, a chamber with a floor and walls of stone masonry, having an opening toward the adjoining harbor, which can be closed when required. 1876 FAWCETT *Pol. Econ.* (ed. 5) IV. vii. 627 The decline of the ship-building trade on the Thames. 1883 *Queen's Printers Aids Bible* 52/2 Cypress, a good ship-building timber.

**'ship-ˌcarpenter.** Also **ship's.** A carpenter employed in the building or repairing of ships.

1495 *Act 11 Hen. VII*, c. 22 §1 An other Ship Carpynter called an Hewer by the day iiij*d*. with mete and drinke. *a* 1583 in Halliwell *Rara Math.* (1841) 33 A litle Boke of Statick. Whiche Booke..hath..helpped the capacityes, bothe of some sea men, and allso shipp carpenters. 1664 EVELYN *Sylva* xxi. 57 There is a way which some Ship-Carpenters in those Countries have us'd to bring their Tar into Pitch for any sudden use. 1748 *Anson's Voy.* II. vi. 200 A ship-carpenter in the yard at Portsmouth. 1798 *31st Rep. Sel. Comm. Finance* App. (1803) XIII. 494 Masters, Boatswains, &c... Ships Carpenters..Sailmakers. 1809 W. IRVING *Knickerb.* (1861) 41 A most gallant vessel..made by the ablest ship-carpenters of Amsterdam. 1840 R. H. DANA *Bef. Mast* iii, A ship-carpenter is kept constantly at work during good weather, on board vessels which are in..perfect sea order. 1862 D. WILSON *Preh. Man* vi, The ancient tools of the prehistoric ship-carpenter.

Hence **'ship-ˌcarpentry**, the business, practice, or art of a ship-carpenter; also, the work turned out by him.

1691 T. H[ALE] *Acc. New Invent.* 127 Ship-Carpentry..is the Art..of composing a Ship, not out of one but several thousand pieces of Wood and Iron. 1862 D. WILSON *Preh. Man* vi, The ancient alluvium of the river Clyde has supplied an unusually rich store of illustrations of primitive ship-carpentry. 1868 BROWNING *Ring & Bk.* VIII. 251 You take ship-carpentry for pilotage.

**'ship-ˌchandler.** [See CHANDLER[1] 3 b.] A dealer who supplies ships with necessary stores.

1642 *Two Orders Lds. & Comm.* 3 Dec. 4 Any Merchants, Ship-chandlers, Grocers. 1755 MAGENS *Insurances* II. 121 The Ship-Carpenters, Ship-Chandlers, and others that have worked at the Ships, or have delivered any Necessaries, Materials or Rigging, for the Use of them. 1858 *Merc. Mar. Mag.* V. 336 Two charts..can..be purchased at any Ship-chandler's.

Hence **'ship-ˌchandlery**, the business of, or goods dealt in by a ship-chandler; also *attrib.*

1663 PEPYS *Diary* 12 Dec., One Abrahall, who strikes in for the serving of the King with ship-chandlery ware. 1798 *31st Rep. Sel. Comm. Finance* App. (1803) XIII. 493/1 Junk, old Rope, old Iron, Canvas, and other species of old Ship Chandlery Wares. 1849 FREESE *Comm. Class-bk.* 14 Trade in Naval Stores and Ship Chandlery. 1900 *Engineering Mag.* XIX. 666 A..ship-chandlery store.

**'ship-craft.** [See CRAFT *sb.* 6. In late OE. *scipcræft* is recorded in the sense of 'strength in ships'.] The art of navigation or of ship-construction.

1387–8 T. USK *Test. Love* I. iii. (Skeat) l. 46 Er I was war, I neyghed to a see-banke; and for ferde of the beestes 'shipcraft' I cryde. 1398 TREVISA *Barth. De P.R.* VIII. xxxiv. (Tollem. MS.), Men þat seyleþ and haueþ schipcrafte [*scientiam navalem habentium*]. 1408–9 tr. *Vegetius' De Re Milit.* (MS. Digby 233) lf. 224/2 Þer nys non gretter peril in schipcraft þanne whenne þe grene tymbre makeþ þe schip to grenne & to gape. *c* 1440 *York Myst.* viii. 67 Of shippe-craft can I right noght, Of ther makyng haue I no merke.

1838 *Fraser's Mag.* XVII. 164 Laertes is a man who finds himself in a storm without knowledge of shipcraft. *a* 1890 R. W. CHURCH *Oxf. Movement* iii. (1891) 36 He..took interest in the niceties of seamanship and shipcraft.

† **shipe,** *sb. Obs.* Forms: 1 scipe, 4 ssepe, shepe, shipe. [OE. *scipe* str. masc.:—prehistoric **skipi-z*, app. something allotted (cf. ON. *skipa* to arrange, ordain, appoint).

The OE. sense of 'dignity, condition' did not survive.]

**1.** Wages; reward.

*c* 1000 ÆLFRIC *Gloss.* in Wr.-Wülcker 114/34 *Stipendium*, scipe, *uel* bigleofa. 1340 *Ayenb.* 33 Huo þe serueþ an naȝt uol-serueþ his ssepe he lyest. *Ibid.* 146 Alle we abydeþ onlepi ssepe þet is þe blisse wiþ-oute ende. *c* 1374 CHAUCER *Anel. & Arc.* 193 Leste that he were proude sheo held him lowe; þus serueþe he withouten mete or shepe [*v.rr.* shep, sheepe]. *c* 1386 —— *Pars. T.* 568 In withholdynge..of the shepe, or the hyre or of the wages of seruauntz.

**2.** *at one shipe*: at one and the same time.

13.. *K. Alis.* 3577 (Laud. MS.), Þe water quyklich hij passe At on shepe, more & lesse.

Hence † **shipe** *v.*, to reward, pay wages to; † **shiping**, wages, remuneration.

*c* 1205 LAY. 13656 Ne mihte ic of þan kinge habben scipinge. *Ibid.* 20012 He heom wolde..scipien heom mid londe mid seoluere & mid golde. 1297 R. GLOUC. (Rolls) 11145 Þe stalwardeste men þat me fond to him vaste he drou & of porchas of neiȝebores ssipede hom wel inou.

**shipentine** ('ʃɪpəntiːn). [f. SHIP *sb.*[1] after BARQUENTINE.] A four-masted vessel, having three square-rigged masts (like a ship) with an additional fore-and-aft rigged mast.

1895 *Even. Post* (N.Y.) 20 July 8 The New York *Marine Journal* suggested the name 'shipentine', on the principle that a barkentine has yards only on the foremast, similar to a brigantine, etc. This term was promptly endorsed by the Liverpool *Journal of Commerce.* 1911 *Encycl. Brit.* XXIV. 878/2 The shipentine clipper 'Great Republic', built in 1853, is noteworthy as being the first ship fitted with double topsails.

**shipful** ('ʃɪpfʊl), †occas. with pl. *ships full.* Also 3 **scipful, sipfol, ssipuol,** 6 *Sc.* **schippill.** [See -FUL.] As much or as many as a ship will hold.

*c* 1205 LAY. 23694 Don he hit nolde for a scip ful [*c* 1275 sipfol] of golde. 1297 R. GLOUC. (Rolls) 917 He mette in þe se þritti ssipuol [*v.r.* schipes fol] of men. *c* 1400 *Laud Troy Bk.* 507 Ther was not a schip-ful of men. 1511 *Acc. Ld. High Treas. Scot.* IV. 306 Ane schippill of tymmer. 1515 *Sel. Cases Star Chamb.* (Selden Soc.) II. 97 If thai had bought a shippful Irne. 1527 TINDALE *Par. Wicked Mammon* Wks. (1573) 62 A C. ton of holy water, a shipfull of pardones. 1535 COVERDALE *Deut.* xxviii. 68 The Lorde shal brynge the agayne in to Egipte by shippe fulles. 1611 COTGR., *Vne Navée de*, a ship full of. [1663 GERBIER *Counsel* 109 Where ships full of lading, may be had besides large Timber.] 1852 H. NEWLAND *Lect. Tractar.* 151 When the people of Ireland by shipfulls go to America. 1856 E. A. BOND *Russia 16th Cent.* (Hakl. Soc.) Introd. 5 Arthur Edwards set out from Yaroslav with a shipful of goods in July 1568. 1910 D. HAY FLEMING *Reform. Scot.* xii. 466 A shipful of the tempest-tossed and starving Spaniards.

**shipless** ('ʃɪplɪs), *a.* [f. SHIP *sb.* + -LESS.]

**1.** Unoccupied by ships.

1719 in Maidment *Scot. Ballads* (1868) I. 25 The Widowit Dame..May lang luke oure the schipless Seis Befoir her mate appears. 1786 S. ROGERS *Ode Superst.* I. iii, The shipless main. 1835 *Fraser's Mag.* XI. 45 Its deserted Exchange, its idle quays, and shipless harbour. 1892 LD. LYTTON *King Poppy* I. 79 Safe over shipless seas.

**2.** Possessing no ships; deprived of one's ship or ships.

1808 MOORE *Sceptic* vi, Let shipless Danes and whining Yankees dwell On naval rights, with Grotius and Vattel. 1819 BYRON *Ode on Venice* ii, The dashing of the spring-tide foam, That drives the sailor shipless to his home. 1904 *Pilot* 9 Apr. 324/1 The wounded and shipless crews of the *Variag* and the *Korietz*.

Hence **'shiplessly** *adv.*, without the aid of a ship.

1865 S. EVANS *Br. Fabian's MS.* 118 Forth to the green-sodded Wilds of Ierne Shiplessly, steedlessly Takes he his journey.

**shiplet** ('ʃɪplɪt). [f. SHIP *sb.* + -LET.] A small ship.

*a* 1552 LELAND *Itin.* (1768) II. 112 An Havenet, or Pere, whither Shippelettes sumtime resorte for socour. *Ibid.* (1769) III. 71 There was begon a fair Pere for Socour of Shippelettes at this Bereword.

So **'shipling** [see -LING].

1866 *Pall Mall Gaz.* 5 Sept. 3 A shipling which has, or is said to have, crossed the Atlantic.

**'ship-load.** A load (of persons or things) carried or capable of being carried by a ship.

1639 *Portsmouth* (Rhode Island) *Rec.* (1910) 10 For men to gett a shipp lood of..pipe stauffes. 1706 E. WARD *Wooden World Diss.* (1708) 85 He had rather have one Bottle of Brandy, than a Ship-Load of Stamford-Air at any Time. 1732 BERKELEY *Alciphr.* II. §22 Half a dozen Shipload of Minute Philosophers might easily be spared upon so good a design. 1799 NELSON 27 Sept. in Nicolas *Disp.* (1845) IV. 31 He will endeavour to send to me two or three ship-loads of corn. 1875 ROBERTSON *Hist. Chr. Ch.* III. 35 He redeemed whole shiploads of captives—Romans, Gauls, Britons, Moors, and especially Saxons from Germany. 1910 D. HAY FLEMING *Reform. Scot.* x. 316 Printed books were sent abroad in shiploads.

So † **ship-lading,** † **-loading.**

1615 G. SANDYS *Trav.* 274 The Emperour Constantine is said to have transported certaine ship-ladings of this sand unto Constantinople. 1641 HAKEWILL *Lib. Subj.* 15 A duty given..upon every shiploading of Wine brought into the kingdom by English Merchants. 1642 *Decl. Lds. & Comm.* 7 Jan. 3 Every ship-lading of Coles exported thence for the use of the City of London. 1719 DE FOE *Crusoe* I. (Globe) 50 A Ship-Loading of Gold.

**shipman** ('ʃɪpmən). Pl. **-men.** [f. SHIP *sb.* + MAN *sb.*[1]

OE. *scipman* = OFris. *skipman*, MLG., MDu. *schipman*, MHG. *schif-*, *schefman* (G. *schiffmann*, also *schiffs-*), ON. *skipamaðr*.]

**1.** A seaman or sailor. Now somewhat *arch.*

*c* 900 tr. *Bæda's Hist.* III. xiii. (1890) 200 Þa ongunnon þa nedlingas & þa scipmen þa oncras upp teon. 1052 *O.E. Chron.* (MS. C), Se cyng hæfde eac mycele landfyrde on his healfe to eacan his scypmannum. 1122 *Ibid.* (Laud MS.), Þær æfter wæron feole scipmen on sæ & on wæter. *c* 1275 LAY. 1335 Brutus iheorde segge of his sipmannen of þan vuele ginne þat cuþe þe mereminne. 1377 LANGL. *P. Pl.* B. XV. 354 Shipmen and shepherdes þat with shipp & shepe wenten. 1406 HOCCLEVE *La Male Regle* 238 So inly mirie syngith shee [the mermaid], þat the shipman ther-with fallith a sleepe. 1497 *Naval Acc. Hen. VII* (1896) 236, xviij shipmen as laborers laboryng..abought..the Kynges dokke. 1563 *Homilies* II. *Agst. Idolatry* III. O o 4 Our Ladye, to whom shypmen synge *Aue maris stella.* 1606 SHAKS. *Tr. & Cr.* V. ii. 172 The dreadfull spout, Which Shipmen doe the Hurricano call. 1623 R. CARPENTER *Consc. Christian* 65 A most ridiculous folly, like to the Shipmans continuall labouring at the pumpe, without any care to mend the leake. 1737 WHISTON *Josephus, Antiq.* XVI. ii. §2 He was seen sailing by the shipmen most unexpectedly. 1791 NAIRNE *Poems* 82 But when the shipmen's boist'rous noise Jan heard, He cried, 'Dant gu no furder—I'm afeard'. 1876 LOWELL *Ode 4th July* IV. ii, They steered by stars the elder shipmen knew.

*fig.* 1564 *Brief Exam.* ***iij b, The wyse shipmen of our Churche haue spyed the rockes.

**2.** A master mariner; the master of a ship; a skipper. Also, a pilot.

*c* 1386 CHAUCER *Prol.* 390 A Shipman was ther, wonynge fer by weste. 1429 *Rolls of Parlt.* IV. 359/2 No oyer shippman yat is bothe Possessour and Maister of any Shippe. *c* 1485 *Digby Myst.* (1882) III. 1395 Shep-man [*loq.*] stryke! skryke! lett fall an ankyr to grownd! *a* 1661 HOLYDAY *Juvenal* (1673) 234/1 The Ship-man, or Pilot, that brings the Ship into harbour. 1912 MASEFIELD *Widow in Bye St.* II. xxxix, The wise shipman puts his ship about Seeing the gathering of those waters wan.

**3.** *attrib.*: † *shipman-craft* = SHIPCRAFT; † **shipman-star**, the pole-star.

1398 TREVISA *Barth. De P.R.* XI. iii. (Bodl. MS.), Vnder þe sterre þat hatte polus articus schyppman sterre. 1418 *26 Pol. Poems* xiv. 43 Þe wyseman his sone forbed..shipman craft.

**b.** Possessive combinations: † **shipman's card**, the mariner's compass; also, a map of the sea; † **shipman's hose** (or **breeks**), a sailor's wide trousers; often *fig.* a statement of wide application that can be turned to fit any case; † **shipman's stone**, the loadstone.

*c* 1400 MAUNDEV. (1839) xiv. 161 The Ademand, that is the Schipmannes Ston, that drawethe the Nedle to him. *c* 1440 *Promp. Parv.* 447/1 Schypmannys stone, *calamita.* 1530 PALSGR. 267/1 Shypmans carde, *carte.* 1540 W. G. *Answ. Smyth* vii, Although a shypmans hose wyll serue all sortes of legges Yet Christes holy scrypture wyll serue no rotten dregges. 1555 EDEN *Decades* (Arb.) 134 Manye of those mappes which are commonly cauled the shipmans cardes, or cardes of the sea. 1562 WINȜET *Cert. Tractates* Wks. (S.T.S.) I. 52 Forgeing thair sermonis for the plesuir of euery auditour, efter the fassoun of schipmenis breiks, mete for euery leg. 1583 STUBBES *Anat. Abus.* II. 79 They make the lawes (as it were) shipmens hoosen,..turning and wresting them at their pleasure. 1592 NASHE *Strange Newes* L 3 The fourth letter of our Orators..is a shipmans hose that will serue any man as well as Green or mee. 1605 SHAKS. *Macb.* I. iii. 17 All the Quarters that they [*sc.* the winds] know, I'th' Ship-mans Card. [1809 MALKIN *Gil Blas* XI. xiv. (Rtldg.) 421 Shafts of malicious wit..were let fly from all the quarters in the shipman's card.]

Hence **'shipmanship**, the art of navigation.

1838 DE QUINCEY in *Tait's Mag.* V. 159 He was respected equally for his seamanship and his shipmanship.

**shipmast** ('ʃɪpmɑːst, -æ-). Also **ship's mast.** [f. SHIP *sb.*[1] + MAST *sb.*[1]] The mast of a ship.

1611 ROWLANDS *Four Knaues* (Percy Soc.) 30 Name any weapon..May-pole, or ship-mast, for to run a tilt. 1612 SELDEN in *Drayton's Poly-olb.* To Rdr. A 2 b, I beleeue much in them as I do the finding of Hiero's Shipmast in our Mountaines. 1796 H. HUNTER tr. *St. Pierre's Study Nat.* I. 244 The Dutch have made many a vain attempt to make the fir grow at the Cape of Good Hope, in order to find a supply of ships-masts. 1842 F. W. FABER *Styrian Lake* 307 The dark sky amid the shipmasts winking.

**b.** *attrib.*

1495 *Naval Acc. Hen. VII* (1896) 158 Parelles to a shippes-mast sayle. 1820 KEATS *Isabella* xvii, The hawks of ship-mast forests. 1837 BROWNING *Forest Thought* i, The builder gazes wistfully Such noble ship-mast wood to see. 1879 —— *Ivan* Dram. Idyls 63 The carpenter, employed On a huge shipmast trunk.

**'shipmaster.** [f. SHIP *sb.*[1] + MASTER *sb.* Cf. MLG. *schifmêster*, MHG., G. *schiffmeister*.]

**1.** The master, captain, or commander of a ship; formerly also, a pilot, steersman.

*c* 1375 *Sc. Leg. Saints* xxix. (*Placidas*) 368 Ay wes þe schipmaster gowand a-pon þe laydy brycht of ble. *c* 1440 *Promp. Parv.* 447/1 Schypmayster, *nauclerus.* *c* 1440 *Jacob's Well* 246 As þe schypmayster redyly sterith þe schyp whan he seeth nede. 1519 HORMAN *Vulg.* 272 The shypmaister pursued vs with a great meyny of shypmen. 1550 COVERDALE *Spir. Perle* vii. (1588) 80 When a great tempest ariseth in the sea, then doth it appeare whether the shipmaster be cunning in ruling the sterne or no. 1577 T. KENDALL *Flowers of Epigr.* 85 b, An Epitaphe, of an excellent Ship-master, or Pilote. 1642 VICARS *God in Mount* 76 The stout-hearted and well-minded Ship-masters and Marriners. 1737 *Gentl. Mag.* VII. 24/2 His Ship-Masters had much more need of..some Knowledge of the Stars.. than the Greeks. 1838 BELL *Dict. Law Scot.* 634 The shipmaster of a British ship must be a British subject. 1878 CUYLER *Pointed Papers* 240 In Great Britain no shipmaster is permitted to use an anchor which has not been tested and stamped with a government mark.

**2.** A man who owns the ship which he commands.

1562 *Act 5 Eliz.* c. 5 §6 Bottoms wherof..Straungers borne then bee Owners Shipmasters or Parte Owners. 1896 *Peterson Mag.* (N.S.) VI. 296/2 Rising to the command of a ship and a ship-master in his adopted city. 1909 GWATKIN *Early Ch. Hist.* II. 60 Marcion of Sinope..was a well-to-do shipmaster.

Hence † **ˈship,mastery**, the art of navigation.
**1593** R. HARVEY *Philad.* 5 Who were long enough after Noahs Arke..to haue some auncestors in shipmastry and many fellowes.

**shipment** (ˈʃɪpmənt). [f. SHIP *v.* + -MENT.]
**1.** The act of shipping (goods or commodities) for transportation.
**1802** ABBOTT *Law Merch. Ships* III. vii. 225 In this country it is not unusual to pay for goods shipped for the East or West Indies, at the time of the shipment. **1833** HT. MARTINEAU *Demerara* xii, I wish you could once witness a shipment for Liberia. **1848** DICKENS *Dombey* vi, Where's that young spark of Dombey's who's been watching the shipment of them goods? **1880** C. R. MARKHAM *Peruv. Bark* 371 The road..winding..past numerous coffee plantations to their port of shipment at Mangalor.
**2.** That which is shipped; a consignment of goods for transportation.
**1861** MAY *Const. Hist.* (1863) II. xvii. 559 A drawback was given them of the whole English duty, on shipments to the American plantations. **1872** RAYMOND *Statist. Mines & Mining* 11 Though the shipments are as yet small, they bid fair to improve rapidly. **1900** *Jrnl. Soc. Dyers* XVI. 6 Shipments are also sent to Europe and to the United States.
**3.** *attrib.* and *Comb.* (esp. in *Commerce* = intended for shipment).
**1887** *Daily News* 15 Oct. 2/4 Shipment jute is easier. **1895** *Ibid.* 3 Oct. 3/3 The floating and forward shipment market. **1897** P. WARUNG *Tales Old Regime* 54 After a seven-days' tramp on the chain from an assize-town to the shipment port.

**ˈship-,money.** Now *Hist.* An ancient tax levied in time of war on the ports and maritime towns, cities, and counties of England to provide ships for the king's service. It was revived by Charles I (with an extended application to inland counties), but was finally abolished by statute in 1640.
**1636** PRYNNE *Rem. agst. Shipmoney* 1 We most humbly represent to Your Excellent Majesty, that this Tax of Shipmoney, is directly contrary to the..Lawes and Liberties of this Your Realme of England. **1640** [H. PARKER] (*title*) The case of Shipmony briefly discoursed, according to the Grounds of Law, Policy, and Conscience. And most hvmbly presented to the Censure and Correction of the High Court of Parliament, Nov. 3, 1640. **1661** COWLEY *Cromwell* Wks. 1710 II. 661 This was done by those Men, who a few Years before had..openly oppos'd the King's regular and formal way of proceeding in the Trial of a little Ship-Mony. **1779** JOHNSON *L. P.*, *Waller* (1868) 99 Waller ..was considered..as a man sufficiently trusty and acrimonious to be employed in managing the prosecution of Judge Crawley, for his opinion in favour of ship-money. **1849** MACAULAY *Hist. Eng.* i. I. 90 Former princes..had raised ship-money only along the coasts: it was now exacted from the inland shires. **1870** T. ROGERS *Hist. Glean.* II. 105 The first writs for ship-money were issued in October of the same year [1634].
*attrib.* **1860** FORSTER *Gr. Remonstr.* 196 The great ship-money lawyer [Mr. Holborne]. **1863** H. COX *Instit.* III. ii. 602 Under ship-money writs..John Hampden was assessed twenty shillings towards providing a ship for his county.

**,ship-of-ˈwar.** ? Now *rare.* A ship equipped for warfare; a man-of-war, warship.
**1479** *Cely Papers* (Camden) 19, I here saye ther schall goe schepys of war to the see. **1568** GRAFTON *Chron.* II. 610 He was encountered with a shippe of warre, appertayning to the Duke of Excester. **1644** MANWAYRING *Seaman's Dict.* 65 A Ship of War (which is called a man of War among Sea-men). **1706** E. WARD *Wooden World Diss.* 107 Our Ships of War are undisputably the best in the World. **1769** FALCONER *Dict. Marine* (1780) s.v. *Ship*, Ships of war are properly equipped with artillery [etc.]. **1800** CHARNOCK *Mar. Archit.* I. Pref. xcv, The custom..of appointing land officers..to the command of ships of war. **1876** BANCROFT *Hist. U.S.* II. xxxiv. 363 A larger ship-of-war from that station joined the expedition.
*attrib.* **1863** P. BARRY *Dockyard Econ.* 4 The thought of permanent ship-of-war construction in the private shipyards was seriously in contemplation.

**shipoo**, var. SHYPOO.

**ˈship-,owner.** One who owns, or has a share in, a ship or ships.
**1530** PALSGR. 267/1 Schypowner, *patron dune nauiere.* **1817** W. SELWYN *Law Nisi Prius* (ed. 4) II. 912 A ship-owner having chartered his ship to J.S. insured the ship and freight with different sets of underwriters. **1861** M. PATTISON *Ess.* (1889) I. 42 As soon as the French trade was again opened, it fell naturally into the hands of English ship-owners. **1872** YEATS *Growth Comm.* 55 Ship-owners and merchants, who had their offices and factories along the whole coasts of the Black Sea and the Mediterranean.
Hence **ˈship,ownering** *vbl. sb.*; **ˈship-,owning** *vbl. sb.* and *ppl. a.*
**1883** *Manch. Exam.* 19 Dec. 5/2 A practice of insuring with a view to wreck would not pay the shipowning community. **1889** STEVENSON *Let. to S. Colvin* Oct., The ship-ownering has rather petered out. **1912** *Times* 19 Oct. 18/6 In shipowning it is quite impossible to stand still.

**ˈshippable**, *a.* [f. SHIP *v.* + -ABLE.]
**1.** Navigable. *rare*⁻⁰
**1483** *Cath. Angl.* 337/1 Schypabylle, *nauiga[bi]lis.*
**2.** That can be shipped.
**1920** *Glasgow Herald* 17 Nov. 11 The Southern Hemisphere promises for 1921 a shippable surplus of 40,000,000 qr. **1979** *Sci. Amer.* Apr. 31/1 This magazine page is a coated stock, several layers of clay filler and white pigment having been rolled onto the moving web during its passage from a wet slurry to a shippable roll.

**ˈshippage.** *rare.* [f. SHIP *v.* + -AGE.] Shipping, shipment.
**1611** in *Essex Rev.* (1906) XV. 154 The Inhabitants..are muche Imployed in Shippage and Navigation. **1754** H. WALPOLE *Lett.* (1845) III. 82 The cutting and shippage would be articles of some little consequence!

**shippe**, obs. form of SHEEP, SHIP.

**shippen**, variant of SHIPPON.

**shipper** (ˈʃɪpə(r)). Also 5 scheper. [late OE. *scipere* (= MLG., MDu. *schipper*, MHG., G. *schiffer*, ON. *skipari*), f. SHIP *sb.*[1] + -ER[1]. In sense 2, representing MLG., MDu. *schipper* (see SKIPPER *sb.*[2]). In sense 3, f. SHIP *v.* + -ER[1].]
†**1.** A seaman. *Obs.*
*c* **1100** *O.E. Chron.* (MS. D) an. 1075, Se cyngc Malcolm ..hine & ealle his scyperan mid mycclan weorðscipe of his gryðe alædde. *a* **1122** *Ibid.* (Laud MS.) an. 1046, His sciperes ʒefengon hine & wurpon hine on þone bat. **1553** BALE *Vocacyon* Pref. 6 As great dyspycyons were among the Iewes at Rome concerning Paule, so were there afterwarde amonge the shyppers in our returne to their shippe concerning vs. **1728** CHAMBERS *Cycl.*, *Shipper*, or *Scipper*, a Dutch Term, signifying the Master of a Ship. We also use the word for any common Seamen.
†**2.** A skipper. *Obs.*
**1496** *Acc. Ld. High Treas. Scot.* I. 300 Dauid Gourlay, schippare of the bark callit the Mary. **1499** *Halyburton's Ledger* (1867) 181 Paid to Rowll the scheper for 2 pety quatris of salt. **1564** *Brief Exam.* ***iij b, A wyse shipper.. wyll not come nygh rockes and flattes. **1581** MARBECK *Bk. Notes* 1118 Yet deserueth not the Maior more grace for gouerning the citie then the Shipper for ruling the Ship. **1603–4** *Act 1 Jas. I*, c. 32 Of which payment the Master Owner and Shipper payinge the same. **1605** VERSTEGAN *Dec. Intell.* iv. (1628) 109 Old shippers of the Netherlands. **1634** BRERETON *Trav.* (Chetham Soc.) 60, I agreed this day with Willm. Wrigtington, the Hull shipper, to carry all my goods to Hull.
**3. a.** One who ships goods for transportation. Also with prefixed sb., as *wine-shipper.*
**1755** MAGENS *Insurances* II. 129 Unless the Names of the Shipper [etc.] are expressed in the Policy. **1789** JEFFERSON *Writ.* (1859) II. 567, I would advise our shippers of oil always to get the certificate of the French consul. **1840** R. H. DANA *Bef. Mast* ii, He..had been in a shipper's counting-room in Boston. **1880** *Times* 26 July 9/5 Shippers of cargo.
**b.** orig. *U.S.* One who transports goods by rail or other means of conveyance.
**1840** *Niles' Register* 4 Apr. 80/2 Principal transportation lines have resolved to give the shipper or owner the full advantage of the reduction of twenty cents per barrel. **1903** H. C. EMERY in *Camb. Mod. Hist.* VII. 706 In the scramble for business the stronger shippers were favoured at the expense of the weaker. **1950** *Times* 28 Feb. 4/5 Charter aircraft have been carrying bulk cargoes... By carrying full loads in each direction low rates have been available to shippers.
**c.** A commodity that is shipped or is suitable for shipping; *spec.* (see quot. 1910).
**1883** KILLEBREW in *Rep. 10th Census U.S.* III. III. 19 Export Tobacco... English shippers consist of leaf and strips. **1884** *Harper's Mag.* July 297/2 We reach..the..pen, where may be gathered one hundred head of choice 'shippers' [*sc.* cattle]. **1910** *Encycl. Brit.* IV. 522/2 *Shippers*, sound, hard-burnt bricks of imperfect shape, obtain their name from being much used as ballast for ships.
**4.** *Mech.* A device for shifting a belt from one pulley to another. Also *attrib.*
**1852** *Trans. Michigan State Agric. Soc.* III. 160 By the shipper the logs may be geared deeper or shallower. **1869** RANKINE *Machine & Hand-tools* Pl. Q 1, This shaft carries a pair of driving pulleys, and is provided with a belt shipper. **1882** *Harper's Mag.* Nov. 889/1 The elevator was operated by means of a lever within the car... The lever took the place of the modern hand rope (or shipper rope).

**shipping** (ˈʃɪpɪŋ), *vbl. sb.* Also 3 scipping, 4–6 **schipp-, schypp-, 5–6 shypping, shepping,** (4 **schepynge, schippyne,** 5 **schuppynge, schipin, schypyng,** 7 **shiping**). [f. SHIP *v.* + -ING[1]. Cf. MLG. *schêpinge* sea voyage, fleet.]
**1.** A ship or ships for the use or accommodation of a person or thing.
**a.** in phrases: † *to do, dight, put to shipping*, to put on board; *to take* (†*one's*) *shipping* (now *arch.*), to embark; occas. pregnantly, to go abroad; also *to deliver to shipping* (? U.S.).
*a* **1300** *Cursor M.* 24815 Elsis to scipping son him did. *c* **1375** *Ibid.* 24828 (Fairf.) þai diʒt him to shipping sone. ? *a* **1400** *Arthur* 339 Eche man hath take his schuppynge. *c* **1440** *Generydes* 4186 Anone thei putt ther horses to shippyng. **1471** CAXTON *Recuyell* (Sommer) I. 153 Another partye peryshyd by swerd and that other toke schyppyng. **1535** BOORDE *Let.* in *Introd. Knowl.* (1870) 56, I was in cathalonya when þe emprowre tok shepyng in-to barbary. *c* **1643** LD. HERBERT *Autobiog.* (1824) 104 My Lord Chandos and myself resolved to take Shipping for the Low Countries. **1691** *Lond. Gaz.* No. 2647/4 'Tis believed he will take Shipping. **1726** SWIFT *Gulliver* II. i, I..took shipping in the Downs on the 20th day of June, 1702. **1771** GOLDSM. *Hist. Eng.* I. 285 Taking shipping for Italy, he was once more wrecked. **1852** THACKERAY *Esmond* II. v, The troops all took shipping. **1856** OLMSTED *Slave States* 48 It is delivered to shipping at Richmond, at fifteen cents a bushel.
†**b.** In general use (sometimes passing into abstract sense = accommodation on board ship, provision of a ship or ships); also *pl.* ships.
**13..** *Cursor M.* 24807 (Gött.) Sone it was his schipping tift wid presand. **13..** *K. Alis* 990 Gold and seolver, and othir thynges, They trussed to heore schepynges. **1375** BARBOUR *Bruce* III. 400 He gat schippyne gud plente. *c* **1400** MAUNDEV. (Roxb.) xx. 92 Bot for he..myght get schipping na ferrere, he turned agayne as he come. **14..** *Beues* 2669 Let vs haue shyppynge to, And we shal to that yle go. *c* **1450** *St. Cuthbert* (Surtees) 772 Bot gif he had shippyng wroght Whilk as nane wer sene beforne. *c* **1468** in *Archæologia* (1846) XXXI. 327 It plesid the kinge to follow aftir hir, and to see her shippinges. **1576** GASCOIGNE *Philomene* xxxiv, But ..Their shipping is preparde. **1579** in *10th Rep. Hist. MSS. Comm.* App. v. 428 He would so bring the one halfe quarter or therd parte in any suche shipp or shippinges coming to Galway. **1620** R. COCKS *Diary* (Hakl. Soc.) II. 119 Yt was agreed Mr. Ed. Sayer shall goe merchant in the shipp *Bull*, and Robt. Hawley and Ric. King..to goe in other shipping. **1641** BEST *Farm. Bks.* (Surtees) 100 This wheate is carryed by shippinge to Newe-Castle. **1819** SCOTT *Ivanhoe* xxxiv, I will..seize on shipping, and embark for Flanders. **1829** —— *Anne of G.* xxviii, I will take care that Blackburn and his cousin-archers have no assistance of shipping from Flanders.
**2.** Ships collectively; the body of ships that belong to a person's or country's fleet, that frequent a particular port or harbour, or that are used for a certain purpose.
**1591** Q. ELIZ. *Procl.* 16 Sept., No Corne nor other Victuall, nor any Ordonance, nor furniture for shipping. *c* **1595** CAPT. WYATT *R. Dudley's Voy. W. Ind.* (Hakl. Soc.) 4 Five of the Queenes shippinge. **1601** HAKLUYT tr. *Galvano's Discov.* 90 From thence vpwards in small shipping he went along the coast of the Abassins and Ethiopia. **1602** CAREW *Cornwall* 27 b, Cornewall is stored with many sorts of shipping. **1669** STURMY *Mariner's Mag.*, *Penalties & Forfeitures* 1 Goods Imported..in Forreign Shipping. *a* **1687** PETTY *Pol. Arith.* (1691) 99 There are employed in the Guinny and American Trade, above forty thousand Tun of Shipping *per annum.* **1725** DE FOE *Voy. round World* (1840) 63 A river very commodious for shipping. **1840** R. H. DANA *Bef. Mast* xxix, He..ventured down toward the shipping, to see if the vessel had sailed. **1846** MᶜCULLOCH *Acc. Brit. Empire* (1854) I. 373 Cork Harbour and Bantry Bay are among the finest asylums for shipping in the world. **1897** HENTY *On Irrawaddy* viii, The British sick were sent away in the shipping to Mergy.
†**3. a.** Navigation. *Obs.*
*a* **1400** *New Test.* (Paues) Acts xxvii. 9 Whanne..was no forþer siker schippynge ande saylynge. **1581** A. HALL *Iliad* II. 37 They little reake for marine worke, and small for shipping care. **1647** N. BACON *Disc. Gov. Eng.* I. iv. (1739) 9 Ireland was nigh, but we find nothing concerning their interest in shipping. *a* **1700** EVELYN *Diary* 4 Feb. 1685, A lover of the sea, and skilfull in shipping.
†**b.** A voyage, a sailing. *Obs.*
***God send you good shipping!*** was used proverbially in the 16th and 17th c. as a wish for success in any venture.
**1483** CAXTON *Gold. Leg.* 183/2 He made a shyppyng into grete brytaygne. *c* **1580** JEFFERIE *Bugbears* IV. ii, God send you good shipping. **1594** NASHE *Unfort. Trav.* B 4, Gone he is; God send him good shipping to Wapping. **1596** SHAKS. *Tam. Shr.* v. i. 43. **1633** T. STAFFORD *Pac. Hib.* II. xxiii. 246 If his said men be sent in two shippings, then he shall goe in the last. **1668** DRYDEN *Even. Love* v. i, My master's in; heavens send him good shipping with his lie. **1688** *Col. Rec. Pennsylv.* I. 236 He believed he should receive his answer by yᵉ ffirst Shipping hether out of England.
**4.** The action of putting persons or things on board ship or transporting them by ship.
**1483** *Cely Papers* (Camden) 144 Item Syr understond that schyppyng ys begon at London. **1499** *Halyburton's Ledger* (1867) 161 Paid for the schipin of my Lordis stan in Brugis ..24s. **1532** *Acc. Ld. High Treas. Scot.* VI. 156 For pynour fee and schipping of the wyne, aill, and gunnis xij d. **1576** FLEMING *Panopl. Epist.* 385 Of the paine in shipping, of the care in conueying your wares..home to your owne house. **1669** STURMY *Mariner's Mag.*, *Penalties & Forfeitures* 3 Goods are forfeited for Undue Shipping or Landing. **1748** *Anson's Voy.* III. x. 410 A licence for the shipping of his stores and provisions. **1821** J. SMYTH *Pract. Customs* 278 Unless the Wine be imported..directly from..the usual port or place of its first shipping. **1884** *Leeds Mercury* 15 Nov. 6/5 The shipping of her *récidivistes* to penal settlements.
†**5.** A ship's company. *Obs. rare.*
**14..** *Beues* 4286 He toke his leve at the kyng And at all his seli shyppyng.
**6. a.** *attrib.* and *Comb.*, as ***shipping-centre, -clerk, company, -crane, house, -interest, lane, line, -place, -point, -port, -trade, -yard.***
**1898** *Jrnl. Sch. Geog.* (U.S.) Oct. 300 *Shipping centers on navigable rivers. **1858** SIMMONDS *Dict. Trade*, **Shipping-clerk*, a merchant's clerk who attends to the shipment of goods. **1897** *Whitaker's Almanack* 709/1 The New Zealand *Shipping Company was established to run steamers direct to New Zealand, Tasmania, and Australia. **1924** *Times Trade & Engin. Suppl.* 29 Nov. 239/1 Shipping companies are complaining that apple shipments are not as heavy as they desire. **1497** *Naval Acc. Hen. VII* (1896) 104 *Shipping crane with a Reysing gynne. **1919** *Brit. Manuf.* Nov. 40/2 The attempt to do away with the *shipping house. **1824** HOLT *Shipping & Navig. Laws* (ed. 2) Introd. 24 This statute has conferred a most solid benefit upon the *shipping interest. **1931** W. G. CARR *By Guess & by God* xii. 194 German submarines which..lurked about the *shipping lanes waiting to attack the Allied merchantmen. **1974** L. DEIGHTON *Spy Story* xii. 122 Ice-breakers keeping two shipping lanes clear all through the winter. **1908** J. R. SMITH *Ocean Carrier* II. iii. 275 The starting of rival *shipping lines is deterred by the certainty of fierce competition. **1981** A. GRAHAM-YOOLL *Forgotten Colony* xviii. 244 The Houlder Brothers shipping line..had been prominent in the meat trade for almost one century. **1766** STORK *Acc. E. Florida* 63 To carry it [*viz.* sugar]..a considerable distance to the *shipping-places. **1874** RAYMOND *Statist. Mines & Mining* 309 The town of Labran is the *shipping-point of the Cañon City coal. **1843** BETHUNE *Sc. Peas. Fireside* 114 One of the *shipping ports on the west coast of Scotland. **1691** T. H[ALE] *Acc. New Invent.* 128 The..Advance of the

*Shipping Trade. **1878** STEVENSON *Inland Voy.* 4 A noisy *shipping yard.

**b.** Special comb.: **shipping-agent**, a licensed agent who transacts a ship's business for the owner; **shipping-articles** = *ship's articles* (see SHIP *sb.* 10c); **shipping-bill**, a bill of lading; **shipping-broker** = *ship-broker* (see SHIP *sb.* 10); **shipping fever** *Vet. Sci.* (orig. *U.S.*), any of several diseases typically contracted by cattle while being shipped from place to place, esp. one caused by bacteria of the genus *Pasteurella*; **shipping-master**, an official who superintends the signing-on and discharging of seamen; †**shipping-money** = SHIP-MONEY; **shipping-note**, a note containing particulars of goods for shipment (Simmonds *Dict. Trade* 1858); **shipping-office**, (*a*) an office where seamen sign on for a voyage; (*b*) 'an office where a shipping-agent receives goods for shipment' (Funk's Standard Dict.); **shipping-order** (see quot.); **shipping ore**, ore suitable for being shipped; **shipping-papers** = *ship's papers*; **shipping tobacco**, tobacco grown for export.

**1844** DICKENS *Mart. Chuz.* xiii, Various *shipping-agents in the city. **1840** R. H. DANA *Bef. Mast* xxix, He went to a shipping-office, where the *shipping articles of the California were open. **1833** *Act 3 & 4 Will. IV*, c. 52 §71 The Person clearing such Goods for Shipment..shall..deliver a *Shipping Bill. **1861** DICKENS *Gt. Expect.* xxxvii, A worthy young merchant or *shipping-broker. **1932** *Jrnl. Amer. Vet. Med. Assoc.* LXXX. 165 The incidence of *shipping fever was greatest during wet, cold weather. **1955** *Sci. News Let.* 15 Oct. 249/3 Shipping fever, the costly cattle disease that strikes like human influenza, makes the movement of cattle from range to feedlot one of the most dangerous activities in the livestock industry. **1970** T. G. HUNGERFORD *Dis. Livestock* (ed. 7) 332/1 Smeal recorded a case which clinically suggested shipping fever. **1840** R. H. DANA *Bef. Mast.* xxix, He was told by the *shipping-master that she was bound to California. **1853** MAUDE & POLLOCK *Law Merch. Shipping* iv. 92 Shipping offices, superintended by persons called shipping masters. **1640** in *3rd Rep. Hist. MSS. Comm.* App. 3/2 The *shipping mony may be putt vigorously vppon collection. **1840** *Shipping-office [see *shipping articles* above]. **1844** FRANCIS *Dict. Trade*, etc., **Shipping Order*, is a written mandate directed by a merchant to his lighterman, ordering him to receive and put on board a certain ship the goods specified in the order. **1877** RAYMOND *Statist. Mines & Mining* 242 The ore-vein yields a large portion of '*shipping' or first-class ore. **1840** R. H. DANA *Bef. Mast* xxix, The *shipping-papers of the *Pilgrim*, from which my name had never been erased. **1883** KILLEBREW in *Rep. 10th Census U.S.* III. III. 194 Dark *Shipping tobacco is generally raised on rich lots.

†**'shippish,** *a. Obs. rare*$^{-0}$. [f. SHIP *sb.* + -ISH.] Nautical.

**1530** PALSGR. 323/2 Shyppisshe belongyng to a shypman, *nautique*.

**shippon, -en** ('ʃɪpən). Now *dial.* Forms: 1 scypen, scipen, scepen, 4 shep(e)ne, s(c)hipne, schepon, 5 shepen, shipun, schepyn, -ene, schyppune, 6 shyppen, 9 shippin, -on, shuppen, -on, 6- shippen. [OE. *scypen* fem.:—OTeut. **skupīnī*, f. *skup-*: see SHOP *sb.* and -EN.[2]] A cattle-shed, a cowhouse.

In quot. 1401 misused, from association with *sheep*.

*c* **900** tr. *Bæda's Hist.* I. i. (1890) 28 þær næniȝ mann for wintres cyle on sumera heȝ ne maweþ, ne scypene his neatum ne timbreþ. *a* **1100** *Gerefa* in *Anglia* IX. 261 Scipena behweorfan and hlosan eac swa. **13..** *E.E. Allit. P.* B. 1076 Was neuer so blysful a bour as was a bos þenne Ne no schroude hous so schene as a schepon þare. *c* **1386** CHAUCER *Knt.'s T.* 1142 The shepne brennynge with the blake smoke. **1401** *Pol. Poems* (Rolls) II. 76 ȝit makist thou to thi sheep a shepen, and to thi hors a stable. *c* **1425** *Voc.* in Wr.-Wülcker 670/26 *Hoc boster*, schyppune. **1570** LEVINS *Manip.* 61/17 A shyppen, *bouile*. **1634** BRERETON *Trav.* (Chetham Soc.) 23 Here is a dainty fine shippen..and hay overhead. *c* **1746** J. COLLIER (Tim Bobbin) *View Lanc. Dial.* Wks. (1775) 41, I gan o glent into th' Shipp'n. **1857** WAUGH *Lanc. Life* 193 When he had to go into the 'shippon' early on a winter's morning. **1859** DICKENS *Haunted House* VII. 44 Atkinson and me will take t'other chap..to th' shippon, and it'll be one piece o' work for to mind them, and the cow. **1881** G. MACDONALD *Mary Marston* xv, The muffled low of a cow from a shippen. **1890** *Westmld. Gaz.* 8 Nov. 4/2 Small Residence and Pleasure Farm..consisting of convenient House, with Stable and Shippon.

*attrib.* **1788** *New Lond. Mag.* 553 Some men who forced the Shippon door by means of iron-crows. **1863** MRS. GASKELL *Sylvia's Lovers* xv, The..shippen door..stood open.

**shippound** ('ʃɪp'paʊnd). Also 6 schip pund, 8 schippound, scheppund, 9 shippund. [ad. MLG. *schippunt* (see also SKIPPOUND) or MDu. *schippond*; whence ON. *skippund*, G. *schiffpfund*, etc.] A unit of weight used in the Baltic trade, varying from 300 to 400 pounds; = 20 lispounds.

**1545** *Rates of Customs* d vj, In Spruce lande..xx. lispoundes facit a shyp pounde. **1560** *Stirling Burgh Rec.* (1887) I. 75 For half schip pund irn. **1615** in *Compt bk. D. Wedderburne* (S.H.S.) 263, 6 schip pund gaid Irone. **1654** WHITELOCKE *Jrnl. Swed. Amb.* (1772) II. 120, 200 shippownd of copper to be brought from the mines to Stockholme. **1753** HANWAY *Trav.* (1762) I. II. xi. 51 The quantity of the hemp is generally about forty thousand schippounds. **1796** MORSE *Amer. Geog.* II. 49 The furnaces and forges [in Sweden] produce yearly 400000 scheppund. **1858** HOMANS *Cycl. Comm.* 423 The commercial weights [of Copenhagen] are, 16 pounds = 1 lispound; 20 lispound = 1 shippound. **1872** YEATS *Growth Comm.* 306, 19,000 ship pounds of iron exported from Gothenburg.

**shippy** ('ʃɪpɪ), *a. rare.* [f. SHIP *sb.*[1] + -Y.] †Suitable for ships (*obs.*); characteristic of ships.

**1632** VICARS tr. *Virgil* I. 16 Some shippy havens contrive. **1898** *Century Mag.* Feb. 531/2 The sour, shippy..odor that hung about the steerages.

**ship-repair** (ʃɪprɪ'pɛə(r)). [f. SHIP *sb.*[1] + REPAIR *v.*[2]] The business or craft of restoring a ship to a sound condition. Usu. *attrib.* So **'ship-repairing** *vbl. sb.*; hence **'ship-repairer**, a firm engaged in the business of repairing ships.

**1941** W. S. CHURCHILL *Secret Session Speeches* (1946) 32 At least another 40,000 men must be drawn into ship-repairing. **1969** *Jane's Freight Containers 1968–69* 198/2 An adjacent yard also provides a ship-repair service. **1976** *Eastern Evening Press* (Norwich) 19 Nov. 1 The Government continued on a collision course..after winning a Commons vote..to retain ship-repairing yards. **1976** *Western Mail* (Cardiff) 22 Nov. 5/2 The ship-repairers don't want to be nationalised. **1976** *Jrnl.* (Newcastle) 26 Nov., The House of Lords refused to back down over 12 ship-repair firms in the old session of Parliament.

**ship-shape** ('ʃɪpʃeɪp), *a.* (*adv.*). Also 7 -shapen. [f. SHIP *sb.*[1] + SHAPEN (which was later reduced to *shape*).] Arranged properly, as things on board ship should be; trim, orderly: orig. *Naut.* but freq. in gen. use. Sometimes passing into *adv.*, in a seamanlike manner, in trim fashion.

**1644** MANWAYRING *Seaman's Dict.* 81 It [*sc.* the rake] being of no use for the Ship, but only for to make her Ship shapen, as they call it. *Ibid.* 113 *Wale-reared*, that is, when a ship is built right up, after she comes to her bearing, this is unsightly, and (as they terme it) not ship shapen. **1769** FALCONER *Dict. Marine* (1789), *Ship Shape*,..in the manner of an expert sailor; as, the mast is not rigged ship-shape; trim your sails ship-shape. **1823** J. F. COOPER *Pioneers* xxiv, It would have been more ship-shape to lower the bight of a rope. **1839** *Nautical Mag.* 165 Neither ship-shape nor Bristol fashion. **1840** R. H. DANA *Bef. Mast* xxii, There was no foolish gilding and gingerbread work,..but everything was 'ship-shape'. **1850** H. BRIDGE *Pers. Recoll. N. Hawthorne* (1893) 122 We..have done a great deal towards making the establishment 'ship-shape' and comfortable. **1864** TENNYSON *En. Ard.* 220 Look to the babes, and till I come again, Keep everything shipshape, for I must go. **1889** H. O'REILLY *50 Yrs. on Trail* 249 In a week..we got shipshape and business commenced.

**b.** in attributive position.

**1847** DE QUINCEY *Sp. Mil. Nun* Wks. 1862 III. 72 She..did it herself in a 'ship-shape', orthodox manner. **1848** DICKENS *Dombey* iv, The shop..seemed almost to become a snug sea-going ship-shape concern. **1855** BROWNING *Bp. Blougram's Apol.* Poet. Wks. 1863 I. 379 Neat ship-shape fixings and contrivances.

So **'ship-shaped, 'ship-,shapely** *adjs.*

**1842** W. IRVING *Let. to Mrs. Grinnell* 30 Sept., Tell him not to cast all his bread upon the water in the shape of ships, however shipshaped they may be. **1843** MRS. ROMER *Rhone* II. 305 A well-appointed yacht, where everything was ship-shapely. **1889** WELCH *Text Bk. Naval Archit.* i. 8 To get the volume of displacement of a ship-shaped vessel when floating at a given water line.

**'ship-,timber.** Timber for shipbuilding.

**1398** TREVISA *Barth. De P.R.* XVII. iv. (1495) 606 And of fer is good shyptymbre made. **1408–9** tr. *Vegetius' De Re Milit.* (MS. Digby 233) lf. 224/1 Loke þat schip tymbre haue þe double tyme to drye. **1503** *Acc. Ld. High Treas. Scot.* II. 282 To the sawaris of the schip tymir. **1625** K. LONG tr. *Barclay's Argenis* v. ii. 332 The place being a vast Countrey, and without ship-timber. **1664** in Marshall *Edwinstow Reg.* (1891) 39 Hodgshon..was killed in the wood..with a peece of shipptimber. **1785** PHILLIPS *Treat. Inland Nav.* 17 Decrease of ship-timber..is a very alarming circumstance to a people whose riches and power depend so greatly upon navigation. **1847** SMEATON *Builder's Man.* 43 The larch..makes excellent ship-timber. **1878** BROWNING *Two Poets of Croisic* I. v, Our log is old ship-timber.

*attrib.* **1854** *Zoologist* XII. 4177 In a ship-timber yard, where he had a yacht building.

**shipton moth.** A noctuid moth, *Euclidea mi.*

**1832** J. RENNIE *Butterfl. & Moths* Index.

**shipun**, obs. form of SHIPPON.

**'shipwards,** *adv. rare.* [See -WARD.] To or towards the ship.

[*c* **1400** *Beryn* 1999 He set hym in ful purpose to his Shippis ward. **1587** TURBERV. *Trag. Tales* 87 b, To the shipwarde on they went.]

**1845** E. WARBURTON *Crescent & Cross* I. 28 Conversing with some of the natives as I rode shipwards.

**shipwreck** ('ʃɪprɛk), *sb.* Also 2–3 wrec(h, 5–6 -wrak, 6 -wre(a)ke, 6–7 -wra(c)ke, 6–8 -wrack, 7 -rack; 6 shipswrack. [f. SHIP *sb.*[1] + WRECK *sb.*

For the form *shiprack* (cf. also 1671 in SHIPWRECKING *ppl. a.*) see RACK *sb.*[5]]

**1.** What is cast up from a wreck; the remains of a wrecked vessel; wreckage. In later use chiefly *fig.*

? *a* **1100** *Charter* in Dugdale *Monast.* (1655) I. 237/1 Cum omni maris projectu, quod nos Anglicè Shipwrec appellamus. *Ibid.* 237/2 Quæcunque maris procellosis tempestatibus in aquam, vel in terram eorum ejecta fuerint, quod Anglicè Shipwrech promulgatum est onomate. **1248** *Libertates Regni Majoricar.* (Du Cange s.v. *Naufragium*), Navim fractam, quæ ad littus a mari ejicitur, quod Angli Shipwrech vocant, id est, wreccum de navibus. **1593** NASHE *Christ's T.* D 2 b, The Sea-monsters,..whom they haue suborned and inspyred to lye in wayte for Shipswrack. **1649** MILTON *Eikon.* ii. 25 Gentlemen indeed;..the spawn and shiprack of Taverns and Dicing Houses. **1667** DAVENANT & DRYDEN *Tempest* II, Heav'n will drive the Shipwracks ashore to make us all rich. **1685** DRYDEN *Alb. & Alb.* Pref., Postscr., By gathering up the shipwrecks of the Athenian and Roman theatres.

**2.** Destruction or loss of a ship by its being sunk or broken up by the violence of the sea, or by its striking or stranding upon a rock or shoal. †*to make shipwreck* (cf. L. *naufragium facere*, F. *faire naufrage*): see MAKE *v.*[1] 64.

*c* **1450** *Mirk's Festial* 70, I haue..þryse ben yn schipwrak on þe see. **1526** TINDALE *2 Cor.* xi. 25, I suffred thryse shipwracke. **1565** COOPER *Thesaurus* s.v. *Naufragium, Pati naufragium*, to haue shipwrecke. **1599** HAKLUYT *Voy.* II. I. 144 If by any casualtie their shippes shall bee driuen on shoare in perill of shipwracke. **1621** BURTON *Anat. Mel.* I. iv. I. i. 277 A ship that is voide of a Pilot, must needs impinge vpon the next rock or sands, and suffer shipwrack. **1694** E. PHILLIPS tr. *Milton's Lett. State* 72 Such Ships and Goods as shall be cast ashore by Shipwrack. *c* **1720** SWIFT *Hist. Eng.* an. 1135, Having..very narrowly escaped shipwreck in his passage from Normandy into England. **1882** *Encycl. Brit.* XIV. 572/1 The wants of sailors and others saved from shipwreck.

*attrib.* and *Comb.* **1611** COTGR., *Naufrageux*,..shipwrack-bringing. **1864** BROWNING *James Lee's Wife* II. i, Is all our fire of Shipwreck wood?

**b.** An instance of this.

*a* **1548** HALL *Chron., Hen. VIII*, 125 Where you say that you haue found landes I say those landes found you by shipwrekes of the sea. **1565** COOPER *Thesaurus, Naufragus*, he that is scaped after a shippewreake. **1633** G. HERBERT *Temple, Ch. Porch* viii, All in a shipwrack shift their severall way. **1692** L'ESTRANGE *Fables* ccccIxxvi. 449 In the Hurry of the Shipwreck,..Simonides was the only Man that appear'd Unconcern'd. **1864** TENNYSON *En. Ard.* 15 A rough sailor's lad Made orphan by a winter shipwreck. **1891** FARRAR *Darkness & Dawn* lx, When some of his precious effects had been lost in a shipwreck, he told his friends that the fishes would bring them back to him.

†**c.** *transf.* of drowning. *Obs.*

**1680** MORDEN *Geog. Rect., Turkey* (1685) 354 Icaria..remarkable for the Shipwrack of Icarus.

**3.** *fig.* Destruction, total loss or ruin: often with literal phraseology retained. †*to make shipwreck*: to come to destruction.

**1526** TINDALE *1 Tim.* i. 19 Havynge fayth and good conscience, which some have put awaye from them, and as concernynge fayth have made shipwracke. **1549** LATIMER *2nd Serm. bef. Edw. VI* (Arb.) 47 After so manifold..shyp wrackes of religion,..whereas the ambitious..prelates..ruleth the sterne [etc.]. **1566** T. STAPLETON *Ret. Untr. Jewel* IV. 144 A generall shipwrake of the Popes uniuersall power. **1591** SHAKS. *1 Hen. VI*, v. v. 8 So am I driuen by breath of her Renowne, Either to suffer Shipwracke, or arriue Where I may haue fruition of her Loue. **1620** GRANGER *Div. Logike* 41 This shipwracke, which Adam brought vpon himselfe, and chiefly his posterity. **1641** QUARLES *Enchir.* II. xxxii. (1654) I 2, Let the Shipwrack of his Understanding be a Sea-mark to thy Passion. **1655** JER. TAYLOR *Guide Devot.* (1719) 120 The only Plank left me in the Shipwrack of my Soul. **1719** DE FOE *Crusoe* II. (Globe) 593 The Shipwreck of our Fortunes. **1850** W. IRVING *Mahomet* II. xi. 102 The..ability with which..he..preserved the scarcely launched empire of Islam from perfect shipwreck. **1891** FARRAR *Darkness & Dawn* xxii, Agrippina was..maddened by the shipwreck of her ambition. **1892** *Speaker* 3 Sept. 289/1 Boys with an unsullied heart, and bright wits like his, have come miserably to ship-wreck before now.

**4.** *to make shipwreck of* (arch.):

**a.** To suffer the loss of.

*to make shipwreck of a good conscience* (with allusion to 1 Tim. i. 19, see quot. 1526 in sense 3) was formerly freq.

**1588** J. UDALL *Demonstr. Discipline* (Arb.) 4 He shalbe molested, till..by your tyrannous dealing, hee haue made shipwrack of a good conscience. **1590** SPENSER *F.Q.* II. xii. 7 Such..Did..make shipwracke violent, Both of their life, and fame. **1631** SANDERSON *Serm.* (1674) II. 14 When we have made shipwrack of our Consciences, we fall into the hands of God. **1683** KENNETT tr. *Erasm. on Folly* 60 They have thrown away their whole Estate, and made shipwrack of all they have. **1784** COWPER *Task* III. 58 Forsaking thee, what shipwreck have we made Of honour, dignity, and fair renown! **1799** HAN. MORE *Fem. Educ.* (ed. 4) I. 14 In the company of certain women of good fashion and no ill fame, he makes shipwreck of his religion. *c* **1800** H. K. WHITE *Rem.* (1837) 348 Lest I should make shipwreck of my hope. **1875** WHITNEY *Life Lang.* xiv. 284 He who..leaves this force out of account, cannot but make utter shipwreck of his whole linguistic philosophy.

**b.** To bring to destruction or total ruin.

**1577–87** HARRISON *England* I. II. vi. 166 It was not long yer open shipwracke was made of this religious obseruation. **1825** SCOTT *Talism.* viii, Worthy were I to die like a dog, did I proceed rashly..and make shipwreck of the weal of Christendom.

**'shipwreck,** *a. rare.* = SHIPWRECKED.

The phr. *to go shipwreck* is probably modelled on *to go bankrupt*.

**1573** *Satir. Poems Reform.* xli. 144 ȝe wer bot schipwrak but reskew. **1598** MARLOWE *Hero & Leander* 164 The shipwracke treasure. **1603** FLORIO *Montaigne* II. xii. 262 Like a shipwracke ship-boy cast from Sease. **1912** D. CRAWFORD *Thinking Black* i. 5 All their colonies have gone shipwreck.

**'shipwreck** ('ʃɪprɛk), *v.* [f. SHIPWRECK *sb.*]

**1. a.** *trans.* To cause (a person) to suffer shipwreck; chiefly *pass.* to suffer shipwreck; also, to cause the loss of (goods) by shipwreck.

**1589** GREENE *Menaphon* (1616) 15 Samela is shipwracked. **1613–16** W. BROWNE *Brit. Past.* II. i. 3 Rockes that vnder water hidden lay, To shipwracke passengers. **1624** SANDERSON *Serm.* (1674) I. 224 Such a storme..hath..shipwrack'd our wares. **1643** SIR T. BROWNE *Relig. Med.*

137, I have been shipwrackt, yet am not enemy with the Sea or Winds. **1703** ROWE *Ulysses* III. i, Shipwrack'd I floated on a driving Mast. **1726** SHELVOCKE *Voy. round World* 367 Those..thus voluntarily shipwrecked themselves rather than fall into our hands. **1823** WORDSW. *Misc. P., To Lady Fleming* 69 Compared With him who..shipwrecked, kindles on the coast False fires, that others may be lost.

**b.** To wreck (a vessel). Now *rare*.

**1624** HEYWOOD *Gunaik.* VIII. 400 It is written of him.. that..he would..by his Inchantments raise stormes to shipwrecke the vessells of his enemies. **1647** COWLEY *Mistr., Resolved to be beloved* iv, Then may my Vessel torn and shipwrackt be, If it put forth again to Sea. **1671** MILTON *Samson* 198, I..Who like a foolish Pilot have shipwrack't, My Vessel trusted to me from above? **1725** DE FOE *Voy. round World* II. 164 Our little Float was shipwreck'd.

**c.** *transf.* and *fig.*

**1599** SIR J. DAVIES *Hymns Astrea* xxii, No doubt our State will Ship-wrackt be. **1613** SHAKS. *Hen. VIII*, III. i. 149 Where are now your Fortunes? Shipwrack'd vpon a Kingdome, where..no Kindred weepe for me? **1631** SANDERSON *Serm.* (1674) II. 14 When our good names are ship-wrackt. **1667** *Decay Chr. Piety* xi. §8 To shipwrack the faith of these weak unstable souls. **1721** AMHERST *Terræ Fil.* xxxi. 167 Men, who have ship-wreck'd their fortunes as well as their reputations upon this rock. **1820** SHELLEY *Witch Atl.* liv, Those wandering isles of aëry dew, Which highest shoals of mountain shipwreck not. **1829** SCOTT *Anne of G.* xiii, The peace which the excellent man desires for the land of his fathers will be shipwrecked. **1875** JOWETT *Plato* (ed. 2) I. 313 The next definition..is shipwrecked on a refined distinction between the state and the act.

**2.** *intr.* To suffer shipwreck. Also *fig. Obs.* or *arch.*

**1607** CHAPMAN *Bussy d'Ambois* I. i, Wee shall shipwracke in our safest Port. *c* **1622** *Interpreter* in Arber *Engl. Garner* VI. 234 A Puritan is he, which grieves to think Religion should in France shipwreck and sink. **1649** JER. TAYLOR *Gt. Exemp.* II. Disc. ix. §34 Like the Apostles in a storme, we should awaken Christ and call to him for aide, least we shipwrack in so violent passions. **1822** SCOTT *Nigel* xiii, Your fortunes shall not shipwreck upon the same coast. **1880** DISRAELI *Endym.* lxv, All the married heiresses I have known have shipwrecked. **1932** J. BUCHAN *Gap in Curtain* iii. 153 His only success was with me, for I..could talk to him about..the inaccuracies of the Greville Memoirs. But the real rock on which the thing shipwrecked was Protection.

**shipwrecked** ('ʃɪprɛkt), *ppl. a.* [f. SHIPWRECK *v.* + -ED[1].] Having suffered shipwreck; destroyed or lost by shipwreck.

**1590** SHAKS. *Com. Err.* I. i. 115 Another ship..Gaue healthfull welcome to their ship-wrackt guests. *a* **1593** MARLOWE *Edw. II*, I. iv, Unless the sea cast up his shipwrack'd body. **1662** DRYDEN *Astræa Redux* 124 His shipwracked vessel. **1702** ROWE *Tamerl.* I. i, Th' approaching Storm may cast thy Shipwreck'd Wealth Back to thy Arms. **1794** MRS. RADCLIFFE *Myst. Udolpho* xv, Soothing the ship-wreck'd sailor's heart. **1855** MACAULAY *Hist. Eng.* xix. IV. 321 A Diving Company which undertook to bring up precious effects from shipwrecked vessels. **1856** LEVER *Martins of Cro' M.* xix, A shipwrecked crew reduced to quarter-rations. **1882** *Encycl. Brit.* XIV. 573 The heroic and dangerous work of saving the shipwrecked.

**b.** *fig.*

**1596** NASHE *Saffron Walden* F 2, Hauing found, by much shipwrackt experience, that no worke of his..would passe. **1643** DIGBY *Observ. upon Relig. Med.* (1909) 10 The losse of Livies shipwracked Decads. **1652** HEYLIN *Cosmogr.* III. 45 That lost and shipwracked Kingdome. *a* **1703** PRIOR *Song, In vain You tell*, Thrown again upon the Coast, Where first my Shipwrackt Heart was lost. **1742** WESLEY *'O Love, I languish'* ii, Haven to take the shipwrecked in, My everlasting rest from sin! **1751** EARL ORRERY *Rem. Swift* (1752) 68 The small remains of the shipwreckt fortune. **1862** DICKENS *Let.* 7 Oct., Through those two harbours of a shipwrecked heart, I..believe..you will..find a peaceful resting-place.

**shipwrecking** ('ʃɪprɛkɪŋ), *vbl. sb.* [f. SHIPWRECK *v.* + -ING[1].] A shipwreck.

**1753** TORRIANO *Gangr. Sore Throat* 2 Voyagers..who having happily escaped many Shipwreckings [etc.].

**shipwrecking** ('ʃɪprɛkɪŋ), *ppl. a.* [f. SHIPWRECK *v.* + -ING[2].] Causing shipwreck.

**1605** SHAKS. *Macb.* I. ii. 26 Shipwracking Stormes, and direfull Thunders. **1671** F. PHILLIPS *Reg. Necess.* 141 Some Ship-racking rock. *a* **1700** KEN *Hymnotheo* Poet. Wks. III. 134 Sailers frighted by Shipwrecking Wind. **1865** SWINBURNE *Atalanta* 814 Shipwrecking reefs.

**'shipwrecky**, *a. rare. colloq.* 'Shaky', weak.

**1857** HUGHES *Tom Brown* II. v, Feeblish, not to say shipwrecky, about the knees.

**shipwright** ('ʃɪpraɪt). Forms: see SHIP *sb.*[1] + WRIGHT *sb.*

**1.** A man employed in the construction of ships.

The Company of Shipwrights was incorporated in 1605.

*c* **1000** ÆLFRIC *Gloss.* in Wr.-Wülcker 112/5 *Nauicularius*, scipwyrhta. **1297** *Coram Rege Roll* m. 23 b, (1898) 149 Thomam le Shipwright. **13..** *K. Alis.* 3665 Hit denned, so ryght, As on nayl doth theo schipwryght. **1474-5** *Durham Acc. Rolls* (Surtees) 645 Thome Witwang, Shipwright, cum 2 famulis operantibus circa reparacionem medietatis de le Fery-bote de Billyngham. **1500-20** DUNBAR *Poems* lxiii. 14 Schip-wrichtis hewand vpone the strand. **1550** J. COKE *Eng. & Fr. Heralds* §156 As touchyng shypwryghtes, there be as good in England as in any other realme. **1656** STANLEY *Hist. Philos.* v. vi. (1687) 184 To make a Helm, is the office of a Shipwright, but to use it rightly of a Pilot. *a* **1700** EVELYN *Diary* 13 June 1680, Old Mr. Shish, master shipwright of his Majesty's Yard here [Deptford]. **1725** W. HALFPENNY *Sound Building* 12 To draw a Shipwright's Arch. **1790** COWPER *Odyss.* IX. 451 As when a shipwright with his wimble bores Tough oaken timber. **1848** LYTTON *Harold* I. i, The hammer of the shipwright shaping strong ribs for the horses of the sea. **1877** MISS A. B. EDWARDS *Up Nile* iv. 90 The ship-wrights are busy on new boats.

**2.** (See quot.)

**1883** DAY *Fishes Gt. Brit.* 306 Spotted ones [*sc.* lings] are taken off Mevagissey and termed shipwrights, having a resemblance to the spilt pitch on the clothes of these mechanics.

Hence **'shipwrighting**, **'shipwrightry**, the art or occupation of a shipwright; shipwright's work.

**1711** W. SUTHERLAND *Shipbuild. Assist.* 22, I was concern'd that Shipwrightry should be utterly neglected. **1793** SMEATON *Edystone L.* §50 The whole of the building was..a piece of Shipwrightry. **1894** A. MORRISON *Mean Streets* 158 Carpentering, ship-wrighting, and engine-fitting.

**shipyard** ('ʃɪpjɑːd). [f. SHIP *sb.*[1] + YARD.]

**1.** A large enclosure, adjoining the sea or a river, in which ships are built or repaired.

*a* **1700** EVELYN *Diary* 17 Sept. 1685, After he had view'd the new fortifications and ship-yard. **1766** ENTICK *London* IV. 439 Blackwall is noted..for a considerable ship-yard. **1863** P. BARRY *Dockyard Econ.* 76 The antiquated labour system of the wooden era would not transplant nor take root in the iron shipyards. **1890** W. J. GORDON *Foundry* 56 The Clyde..is a river of ship-yards.

**2.** *attrib.* as **shipyard eye**, an epidemic form of keratoconjunctivitis caused by a virus.

**1943** *Sun* (Baltimore) 17 June 13/6 The Health Department mentioned the new eye infection, shipyard eye, which appeared last winter. **1974** *Jrnl. Hygiene* LXXIII. 158 Because of this frequent occurrence of the disease among workers in shipyards, the term 'shipyard eye' was coined.

**shir**, obs. form of SIR, SHIRE *sb.* and *a.*

**shiralee** (ʃɪrə'liː). *Austral. slang.* Also **shirallee**. [Origin unknown.] A bundle of blankets or personal belongings, a swag (sense 10).

**1892** G. PARKER *Round Compass in Australia* 49 Let him down easy and slow... Drop in his shirallee and water-bag by him. **1945** BAKER *Austral. Lang.* v. 102 A drum..is the equivalent of *swag*,..*shiralee*,..or *bluey* as the tramp's rolled blanket is variously called. **1955** D. NILAND *(title)* The shiralee. **1955** *Times* 4 Aug. 9/2 The shiralee is the swag, the burden, the Australian swagman carries. **1974** *Sunday Sun* (Brisbane) 5 May 4/2 The fences, the barns, the houses—they're all gone and I'm out on the road with my shiralee.

‖**Shiraz** ('ʃɪəræz). Forms: 7 Sheraz, Shyraz, -as, Sherash, Schiras, (Scherah), 8-9 Schiraz, 9 Sheeraz, Shiraz.

**1.** The name of a city in Persia (formerly the capital); used *attrib.* **a.** as the designation of a wine made in the district; also *absol.* = Shiraz wine. **b.** as the designation of a kind of tobacco. **c.** in *Shiraz lamb*, the trade name of a quality of lamb fur obtained from Persia (1910 W. S. Parker in *Encycl. Brit.* art. *Furs*). **d.** Denoting a rug or carpet made in the district of Shiraz; also *ellipt.*

**a. 1634** SIR T. HERBERT *Trav.* 65 The name of Sheraz Wine is famous farre and neere. **1638** *Ibid.* 78, 20 Camels load of Shyraz [**1677** Shyras] wine. **1837** LOCKHART *Scott* IV. v. 162 An Oriental friend having sent him a butt of sheeraz [etc.]. **1904** T. WRIGHT *Life E. FitzGerald* I. 217 He liked to sit in the Major's snug parlour and talk, over a glass of Shiraz wine, about India.

**b. 1840** N. P. WILLIS *Loiterings of Trav.* II. 224 He politely begged pardon for smoking in the Countess's presence, and filled the enamelled bowl with Shiraz tobacco. **1861** BENTLEY *Man. Bot.* 601 The principal kinds of Tobacco are the American,..the Shiraz or Persian [etc.].

**d. 1900** J. K. MUMFORD *Oriental Rugs* xi. 213 The Shiraz displays unusual features of finish. *Ibid.* 214 The true Shiraz rugs may be known almost invariably by the small checked selvage. **1920** T. E. LAWRENCE *Let.* 16 Feb. (1938) 299 As for the rugs, please take any that seem worthy to you. There were two Afghans in the Arab Bureau, & a big (and not bad but thin) Shiraz, in the Savoy. **1932** P. SELVER tr. *Capek's Tales from Two Pockets* 189 I've got piles and piles of Shiraz, Shirvan..and other common-or-garden carpets. **1968** L. DURRELL *Tunc* III. 153 A small and lovely carpet—an authentic Shiraz according to the label. **1980** G. THOMPSON *Murder Mystery* (1981) xxviii. 215 A large brandy snifter now lay on the floor on the Shiraz rug.

**2.** The name of a variety of grape from which red wine is made, grown orig. in the Rhône valley of France; the wine made from this grape.

The French name for the grape is *syrah* (*scyras, sirrah* are also found). The Eng. form is app. an alteration of this, influenced by the belief that the vine was brought (by Crusaders) from Iran and is therefore to be identified with that from which *Shiraz* (sense 1 a) is made.

[**1908** E. & A. VIZETELLY *Wines of France* 140 For red Hermitage the vine..is the Ciras, Scyras, or Sirrah, a corruption, it is alleged, of Shiraz, the tradition being that the hermit of the mount brought some vine cuttings with him from the East. The Ciras is, at any rate, a distinct variety.] **1927** A. I. PEROLD *Treat. Viticulture* v. 271 Shiraz, the grape of Hermitage,..produces a fine, famous red wine. **1966** *Courier-Mail* (Brisbane) 25 Oct. 2/10 He thought his 1952 shiraz was of such vast quality there was no bottle in a restaurant cellar to equal it. **1973** 'E. FERRARS' *Small World Murder* viii. 102 They drank one of the Lyndon's own wines, a Shiraz. **1977** A. SCHOLEFIELD *Venom* I. 38 Replanting areas with *shiraz* vines.

**shirbet(t**, obs. forms of SHERBET.

**shire** (ʃaɪə(r)), *sb.* Forms: 1-3 scír, (1 sciir, scýr, -scíre, 2 -sir, ? scur, 3 ssire), 3-7 schire, 4-7 schyre, (5 schere, -shir, shyr, sher, chyer), 5-6 schyr, (5-7 sheere), 5-9 shyre, (6 schier, schyir, scyre, shyere, sheyre, 6-7 sh(i)ere, shyer, sheire, 7, 9 *dial.* sheer), 4- shire. [OE. *scír* str. fem. = OHG. *scîra* care, official charge (only in two glosses, *scirono* negotiorum, *scira habat* procurat).

The OTeut. form may have been either **skīrō* or **skīzō*. It has been suggested that **skīzō* may represent a pre-Teut. **skeisā-*, related to OItalic **koisā-* in L. *cūra* care (:—*coira*), Pælignian *coisatens* 'curaverunt'.

The OE. word occurs once (*a* 1030) with wk. declension, in the compound *ȝerefsciran* 'villicationis' (*Rule St. Benet* ed. Logeman, p. 107).]

†**1.** (*OE.* only.) Official charge; administrative office (e.g. that of a steward, bishop, governor etc.).

*c* **725** *Corpus Gloss.* 692 *Dispensatio*, scir. *Ibid.* 1625 *Procuratio*, sciir. *c* **893** ÆLFRED *Oros.* VI. xxxi. 286 þæt him leofre wæs se cristendom to beganne þonne his scira to habbanne. *a* **1100** *Gerefa* in *Anglia* IX. 259 Hede se ðe scire healde þæt he friðige and forðige ælce be ðam ðe hit selest sy.

†**2.** A province or district under the rule of a governor; the see of a bishop, the province of an archbishop, or the like; in wider sense, a country, region, district. *Obs.*

In the later examples *transf.* from sense 3.

*c* **893** ÆLFRED *Oros.* I. i. 19 Ohthere sæde þæt sio scir hatte Halȝoland þe he on bude. **11..** *Fragm. Ælfric's Gloss.* (1838) 3 *Provincia vel pagus*, scur. *a* **1225** *Ancr. R.* 334 And hu biseinte Sodome & Gomorre,..& alle þe nome-cuðe buruhwes, al ane muchele schire, adun into helle grunde. **1338** R. BRUNNE *Chron.* (1725) 299 The bisshop of Canterbire þerof payed was he, For him and alle his schire [Langtoft: *pur ly et sa province*] þis gift gaf fulle fre. *a* **1400** *Octovian* 227 The folk þo com fram eche a schyre Ryȝt ynto Rome. *c* **1440** *Chester Plays* (E.E.T.S.) 386 Goe, echon, to dyvers contray, and preach to Shyre and Citty The fayth. *c* **1470** HENRY *Wallace* VIII. 946 All Mydlame land thai brynt wp in a fyr, Brak parkis doun, distroyit all the schyr. **1574** tr. *Marlorat's Apocalips* 19 Thyatira..is a Citie of Lydia which is a shyre of Asia the lesse. **1590** SPENSER *F.Q.* I. xi. 14 As two broad Beacons, set in open fields, Send forth their flames farre off to euery shyre. **1615** WITHER *Sheph. Hunt.* v. G 2 b, Art not thou hee, that but this other yeere Scard'st all the Wolues and Foxes in the sheere? **1601** HOLLAND *Pliny* v. xxix. I. 107 A third Seignorie or Shire there is that goeth to Apamia. **1824** W. TAYLOR in *Monthly Mag.* LVII. 407 The dame..Was in all Britany the fairest woman, Though 'tis a shire renown'd for handsome ladies.

**3. a.** *spec.* In Old English times, an administrative district, consisting of a number of smaller districts ('hundreds' or 'wapentakes'), united for purposes of local government, and ruled jointly by an ealdorman and a sheriff, who presided in the SHIRE-MOOT. Under Norman rule, the division of England into shires was continued, the AF. *counté*, Anglo-Latin *comitatus*, being adopted as the equivalent of the English term. At the present day *shire* is rare in official use, but is current as a literary synonym for *county* (chiefly restricted to those counties that have names ending in *-shire*). The counties of Wales, and most of those of Scotland, have *-shire* as the ending of their name, but the word is now rarely employed in speaking of them. The counties of Ireland were often called shires in the 16-17th c., but the use is now obsolete.

*England.* ? *a* **1000** *Laws Æthelstan, Lond.* x. (Liebermann) 181 Ðæt ælc ȝerefa name þæt wedd on his aȝenre scire. *c* **1290** *St. Kenelm* 23 in *S. Eng. Leg.* 346 þe schire of gloucestre. **1297** R. GLOUC. (Rolls) 62 Viue & þritti ssiren hii made in engelonde. *c* **1386** CHAUCER *Friar's T.* 103 If that thee happe to comen in oure shire Al shal be thyn right as thou wolt desire. **1414** *Rolls of Parlt.* IV. 57/1 In the shyre of Cambrigge. **1430** *Cov. Leet-bk.* 129, xls. to the collectours of the shire in money and in Costes. **1473** WARKW. *Chron.* (Camden) 8 Thei gadred alle the comons of the schyre. **1549** CHEKE *Hurt Sedit.* (1641) 32 How many suffer injurie, when one hundred of a Shiere is spoiled? **1598** STOW *Surv. Lond.* 305 Then harde by the Barre is one other lane called Shyre lane, because it deuideth the Citie from the Shire. **1599** DEKKER *Shoemakers Holiday* I. (1610) B 1 b, Those companies Mustred in London, and the shires about. **1764** *Oxf. Sausage* 41 The next we heard that in a neighb'ring Shire, That Day to Church he lead a blushing Bride. **1849** MACAULAY *Hist. Eng.* ii. I. 189 The cry of agricultural distress rose from every shire in the kingdom. **1855** HAWTHORNE *Eng. Note-bks.* (1870) I. 279 Lancaster..with taller houses than in the middle shires of England. **1896** A. E. HOUSMAN *Shropshire Lad* xxxvii, As through the wild green hills of Wyre The train ran, changing sky and shire.

*Scotland.* **1529** *Stirling Burgh Rec.* (1887) I. 37 Na flescher within burgh, na within the schier, that bringis ony flecht to the said burgh to sell [etc.]. **1570** *Satir. Poems Reform.* xiii. 99 ȝe wer ay callit for ȝour tyrannie Strypis of the Schyre. *a* **1670** SPALDING *Troub. Chas. I* (Bannatyne Club) II. 247 The schires of Kincardin, Elgyne and Forres.

*Ireland.* *c* **1535** FINGLAS *Breviat* in W. Harris *Hibernica* (1757) 46 The Gentles of the Shires of Myeth and Dublyn. **1542** *Ir. Act 34 Hen. VIII*, c. 1 (1621) 238 Forasmuch as the Shire of Methe is great and large in circuit... The said Sherife of the said Shire for the time being. **1600** in *10th Rep. Hist. MSS. Comm.* App. v. 458 The counties and shyers of the province. **1612** SIR J. DAVIES *Why Ireland*, etc. 256 Next, in reducing the vnreformed partes of Vlster into seauen shires; namely Ardmagh, Monahan, Tirone, Coleraine, Deuegall [*sic*], Fermannagh and Cauan. **1626** [SIR E. CECIL] *Perrot's Govt. Irel.* 41 The Counties thus made in Vlster, were these, Ardmagh, Monahan, Tyrone [etc.]... These circuites thus deuided and setled into Shieres, the Deputy..appointed..Iustices of the Peace.

**b.** Put for: The inhabitants of the shire.

*a* **1122** *O.E. Chron.* (Laud MS.) an. 1010, Ne furðon nan scir nolde oðre ȝelæstan æt nyxtan. **1848** THACKERAY *Van. Fair* xi, You have more brains than half the shire.

†**c.** A shire-court. (Cf. SHIRE-MOTE.) *Obs.*

*a* **1225** *Ancr. R.* 308 Hit nis nout ine Godes kurt ase hit is iðe schire. **1297** R. GLOUC. (Rolls) 11068 Ac sir willam ssire huld in a monenday. *c* **1400** *Gamelyn* 715 Gamelyn came redy to þe next shire. *c* **1450** *Godstow Reg.* 169 He made þys relese & quite clayme in þe shyre of wynchestur. **1461** *Paston Lett.* II. 37, I wold a new dede and letter of atorne were mad owth, .. and that the ded bere date nowh, and that it be selid at the next shire. **1502** ARNOLDE *Chron.* P iij, [tr. Gt. Charter] No shire from hensforth shalbe holden in oure reame but from moneth to moneth.

†**d.** *to be quit from shire and hundred*: to be exempted from taxation levied by the shire and hundred. *Obs.*

**1293** *Rolls of Parlt.* I. 115/1 Sint liberi et quieti ab omni Scotto, Geldo et de .. Tallag', Lestagiis, Stallagiis, Schiris, Hundr' Warda, Wardepeny, Hauerpeny, Hundredespeny. *c* **1450** *Godstow Reg.* 670 And [that their] fre tenauntis ought ther to be quyet fro shire and hundred.

†**e.** *Proverb.* (See HUNDRED 5 c.) *Obs.*

**f.** A rural administrative district in some states of Australia. Freq. *attrib.*

**1909** BRIERLEY & IRISH *Crown Lands Acts New South Wales* (ed. 2) (Advt.), Ordinances for Municipalities or Shires. **1947** K. TENNANT *Lost Haven* iii. 58 A man with any push would form a progress association and devil the shire council about the roads. **1977** *Bulletin* (Sydney) 22 Jan. 46/2 The town also has a shire community centre.

†**4.** A city or town with its liberties to which has been granted a jurisdiction independent of that of the historical shire in which it is situated. *Obs.*

Since the 16th c. the term has been superseded by COUNTY[1] 2 b. Cf. *corporate county*, CORPORATE *ppl. a.* B. 4.

**1433** *Rolls of Parlt.* IV. 425/2 In every Citee or Burgh in this your seide Roialme .. beyng a Shire incorporate. **1485** in *Cov. Leet Bk.* 524 Henry by the grace of God Kyng of Englond and of Fraunce and lord of Irland to oure trusty and wel-beloued the Maire and Justices of our peas within the shire of oure Citie of Couentre .. greting.

**5.** As the terminal element in names of counties (as Berkshire, Derbyshire) and of certain other districts (as Hallamshire, Bedlingtonshire, Islandshire, Norhamshire, Hexhamshire) which have from early times been regarded as separate unities. Pronounced (-ʃə(r)); in dialects often (-ʃɪə(r)).

*a* **1122** *O.E. Chron.* (Laud MS.) an. 1064, Mid Snotingham scire & Deorbi scire & Lincolna scire. *c* **1155** *Newminster Cartul.* (Surtees) 45 Bellingtonesir. **1362** LANGL. *P. Pl.* A. II. 77 Bette þe Budul of Bokynghames schire. *c* **1450** *Godstow Reg.* 637 To here & to ende diuerse transgressions harmis greuis & excessis in wilton sher. **1463–4** *Rolls of Parlt.* V. 503/1 The growyng of the Shires called Alderton Shire, and Richemond Shire, oonly except. **1610** HOLLAND *Camden's Brit.* (1637) 261 The whole shire is expressly named Hanscyre. **1711** STEELE *Spect.* No. 2 ¶ 1 The first of our Society is a Gentleman of Worcestershire. **1893–4** *Northumberld. Gloss.* s.v., Norhamshire, Islandshire, and Bedlingtonshire, are detached portions of the patrimony of Saint Cuthbert.

**6. the Shires. a.** A term applied to other parts of England by the inhabitants of East Anglia, Kent, Sussex, Essex, and Surrey; also *gen.* applied to those counties the names of which end in *-shire*. Also = *shire counties* (see sense 8 b below).

Usually pronounced (ʃɪəz), being a re-stressed form of the unstressed ending (-ʃɪə(r)).

**1796** PEGGE *Anonym.* (1809) 160 The Inhabitants of Kent, to express a person's coming from a great distance .. will say, he comes a great way off, out of the shires. *a* **1825** FORBY *Voc. E. Anglia, Sheres*, pl., a general name for all the counties in England, but Norfolk, Suffolk, and Essex. **1865** W. WHITE *East. Eng.* II. 204 Which do ye like best, master. Essex or the sheres? **1909** A. MORRISON *Green Ginger* 154 'It do seem to me', he said, 'as you'd do better in the shires; I count you make a poor trade in Essex'. **1977** *Daily Tel.* 14 Mar. 2/7 In the shires Labour are defending a rump of seven non-Metropolitan counties they still hold out of 39: Cleveland, Derbyshire, Durham, [etc.].

**b.** *Foxhunting.* As the name of a hunting 'country': see quot. 1910.

**1860** WHYTE MELVILLE *Mkt. Harb.* v. 51 'Excuse me, sir: take the liberty of asking whereabouts you generally hunt'. 'Hunt?' repeated the customer. 'Oh! Leicestershire—Northamptonshire—all about there'... A cloud gathered on the foreman's brow. 'The Shires!' he rejoined, with a perplexed air; 'that increases our difficulties very much indeed'. **1887** *Field* 12 Nov. 731/2 The fleetest pack [of hounds] in all the Shires. **1910** A. E. T. WATSON in *Encycl. Brit.* XIII. 948/2 The 'Shires' is a recognized term, but is nevertheless somewhat vague. The three counties included in the expression are Leicestershire, Rutlandshire and Northamptonshire. Several packs which hunt within these limits are not supposed, however, to belong to the 'Shires', whereas a district of the Belvoir country is in Lincolnshire, and to hunt with the Belvoir is certainly understood to be hunting in the 'Shires'.

**7.** Short for SHIRE HORSE.

**1877** W. GILBEY in *Field* 24 Feb. 225/1 A discussion arose as to the best agricultural stallion to select for use in the district—a 'Clydesdale' or a 'Shire'. **1901** *Q. Rev.* Jan. 7 The Shire, as a distinct breed was not in existence.

**8. a.** *attrib.* and *Comb.* as ***shire-administration***, ***-system***; (sense 6) ***shire-bred***, ***-fattened*** adjs.; (sense 7) ***shire-breed***, ***-class***.

**1874** STUBBS *Const. Hist.* I. vi. 160 A uniform *shire-administration. **1881** *Daily News* 24 Feb. 3/1 In the hope of stimulating the production of *shire-bred horses. **1877** *Field* 17 Mar. 323/2 Good English mares of the '*shire' breed. **1886** P. ROBINSON *Teetotum Trees* 18 Our own *shire-fattened kine. **1874** STUBBS *Const. Hist.* I. v. 117 The general institution of a *shire-system for all England.

**b.** Special comb.: **shire-bishop** (*OE.* and *Hist.*), the bishop of a shire; **shire-borough** (see sense 4); †**shire-clerk** (see quot. 1706); **shire county**, a non-metropolitan county of the U.K., as instituted by the local government reorganization of 1974; †**shire-court** = COUNTY-COURT 1; †**shire-day**, the day upon which a meeting of the shire was appointed to be held; **shire-hall**, †**-house** = *county-hall*, COUNTY 8 b; **shire-jury** *Hist.*, the members of a shire-court; †**shire-knight**, = *knight of the shire*, KNIGHT *sb.* 4 c; **shire-member**, a representative of a shire in Parliament; **shire-oak**, an oak tree marking the boundary of a shire or a meeting place for a shire-court; **shire-reeve**, etymologizing form of SHERIFF; **shire-stone**, a stone serving as a boundary-mark of a shire (also in ***three-***, ***four-shire-stone***); **shire-town**, (*a*) the chief town of a shire, a *county-town*, see COUNTY[1] 8 b; also *transf.*; (*b*) *U.S.* = *county seat* s.v. COUNTY[1] 8 b; †**shire-wyte**, ? a tax paid to a Sheriff for holding a shire-court. Also SHIRE-GROUND, SHIRE HORSE, SHIRE-LAND, SHIREMAN, SHIRE-MOOT, SHIREWICK.

*a* **1023** *Wulfstan* xxxvi. (1883) 173 Bete þæt, swa se *scir-bisceop and eal scirwitan .. deman. **1880** W. H. JONES *Dioc. Hist. Salisb.* 51 We must therefore suppose that occasionally shire-bishops may have been appointed. **1898** F. W. MAITLAND *Township & Borough* 10 One ancient *shire-borough, I mean Nottingham. **1495** *Act 11 Hen. VII*, c. 15 § 1 Shirefs Undershirefs *Shire Clerkis or any other officers. **1706** PHILLIPS (ed. Kersey), *Shire-Clerk*, an Under-Sheriff; sometimes it is taken for a Clerk in the County-Court, or Deputy to the Under-Sheriff. **1972** *Times* 21 Sept. 4/2 The AMC received no guidance whether metropolitan county councils would want to be grouped with '*shire' counties or with district councils. **1977** *Daily Tel.* 25 Apr. 6/8 Britain's great conurbations and the shire counties are preparing for a .. tussle. **1376** *Rolls of Parlt.* II. 348/2 Une novele Court appelle *Shire-court a Arundell. **1503–4** *Act 19 Hen. VII*, c. 24 The Shyre Courte for that Shyre shalbe holden & kepte one tyme at Chichestre aforseid, and the next tyme at the borowe of Lewes. **1542–3** *Act 34 & 35 Hen. VIII*, c. 26 § 58 The Countie or Shyre Courte of the Countie of Radnor. **1482** CAXTON *Policron.* VIII. xxi. in *Higden* (Rolls) VIII. 565 Also at Bedford on a *shyreday were eyghten men murthred withoute stroke by fallynge doune of a steyr. **1796** MRS. INCHBALD *Nature & Art* xl. (1820) 135 The prisoners are demanded at the *shire-hall. **1881** *Instr. Census Clerks* (1885) 30 Shire Hall Keeper. **1759** B. MARTIN *Nat. Hist. Eng.* II. 53 The Guild-hall, the Wool-hall, and the *Shire-house. **1822** *Edin. Rev.* XXXVI. 330 The *Shire-jury was considered as constituting the 'County' or County Court. **1399** LANGL. *Rich. Redeles* IV. 32 And whanne it drowe to þe day of þe dede-doynge, þat soucreynes were semblid and þe *schire-knyȝtis, .. þey begynne to declare þe cause of her comynge. **1910** W. L. MATHIESON *Awak. Scot.* i. 8 *Shire members and burgh members had united to form a House of Commons. **1778** *Eng. Gazetteer* (ed. 2) s.v. *Worksop*, Certain oaks, called *Shire-Oaks. **1879** GREEN *Readings Eng. Hist.* xxiii. 115 During the last half-hour the suiters had been gathering round the shire-oak. **14..** *Langland's P. Pl.* C. IV. 78 Boþe *shire-reues and sergauntes. **1570–6** LAMBARDE *Peramb. Kent* 350 Our Magistrat nowe called a Sherif, or (to speake more truely, Shyrereue). **1765** BLACKSTONE *Comm.* Introd. § 4 I. 112 The sheriff, shrieve, or shire-reeve. **1863** H. COX *Instit.* III. ix. 726 These reeves received in counties the appellation of shire-reeves. **1536** in *Laing Charters* (1899) 108 Fra the said croce lineallie east .. to the *schearstane; fra the scheirsteane lineallie eist [etc.]. **1677** PLOT *Oxfordsh.* Map, Four shire stone .. three shire stones. **1778** *Eng. Gazetteer* (ed. 2) s.v. *Morton in the Marsh*, About one mile from hence, are the 4 shire-stones. **1825** *Gentl. Mag.* June 516 Upon Wreynose Hill are placed the Shire-stones. **1459** *Rolls of Parlt.* V. 368/1 Make open Proclamation in the *Shire Toune of the same Shire or Shires. **1526** TINDALE *Luke* ii. 3 Every man went in to his awne shyre toune, there to be taxed. **1610** HOLLAND *Camden's Brit.* (1637) 396 Then Ouse saluteth Buckingham the Shire Towne. **1648** *New Hampshire Provincial & State Papers* (1867) I. 189 The Court doth think fitt that the *shire town of Norfolke be referred to further consideration. **1708** J. CHAMBERLAYNE *St. Gt. Brit.* I. I. iii. 10 The Shire-Town is Derby. **1717** S. SEWALL *Diary* 13 Jan. (1882) III. 132 Cambridge is the Shire-Town for Middlesex. **1857** PERLEY *Hand-bk. N. Brunswick* 55 The shire town is Richibucto. **1881** *Century Mag.* Dec. 251/1 It was the central town in the county, and yet not the shire-town. **1969** *Bangor* (Maine) *Daily News* 10 July 1/5 (*caption*) This particular sign in Whiting .. has omitted an 'a' from the shiretown of Washington County. **1425** in Kennett *Par. Antiq.* (1695) 573 *Et in solutis pro quadam pensione vocata* *Schire-wyte *annuatim* iv. *sol.*

**shire** (ʃaɪə(r)), *a.* *Obs.* exc. *dial.* Forms: 1 scír, 3 scir, sir, 3–4 shir, 3–5 schir, 4 scire, scirre, schirre, (schyire), 4–5 schyr, 4–6 schire, schyre, 4–8 shyre, 4–9 shire. [Com. Teut.: OE. *scír* = OFris. *skîre*, OS. *skîr*, *skîri* (MLG. *schîre*; hence MHG. *schîre*, *schîr*, mod.G. *schier*), ON. *skír-r* clear, bright, pure (Sw. *skir*), *skýrir* manifest, Goth. *skeir-s* clear:—OTeut. **skīro-*, **skīrjo-*, f. root **skī-* to shine: see SHINE *v.* (Related by ablaut to SHEER *a.* See also SKIRE, SKERE *adjs.*)]

**A.** *adj.*

†**1.** Bright, shining. *Obs.*

In OE. also *fig.* illustrious, noble. In ME. allit. verse sometimes a vague epithet of praise (= beautiful, fine, 'sheen').

*Beowulf* 979 Ðær abidan sceal maga mane fah miclan domes, hu him scir metod scrifan wille. *a* **1000** *Boeth. Metr.* xxx. 9 þeah hio [the sun] sie scir & beorht. *c* **1250** *Gen. & Ex.* 3848 Longe abuten munt seyr folȝede hem ðat skie scir. *a* **1300** *Havelok* 588 She saw þer-inne a lith ful shir. **13..** *Gaw. & Gr. Knt.* 317 þe blod schot for scham in-to his shyre face & lere. *a* **1400–50** *Wars Alex.* 2454 Schalkis scott in-to shipis all in shire mailes. *c* **1400** *Destr. Troy* 2373 In a shadow of shene tres & of shyre floures. *c* **1470** *Gol. & Gaw.* 537 To se that his schire weid be sicker of assay.

†**2.** Of liquids, crystal, etc.: Clear, translucent.

*a* **900** CYNEWULF *Christ* 1282 Swa þæt scire glæs þæt mon ypæst mæȝ eall þurh-wlitan. *c* **1000** ÆLFRIC *Gloss.* in Wr.-Wülcker 163/33 *Limpidus*, scir. *a* **1300** *Cursor M.* 9936 Midward þe heist ture .. springes of scire water o welle. **1340** HAMPOLE *Pr. Consc.* 6934 Als fyssches lyfes in water schyre. *a* **1400** *Stockh. Med. MS.* i. 119 in *Anglia* XVIII. 298 Hony, good & schyre. *c* **1440** *Promp. Parv.* 447/1 Schyre, as water and oþer lycure, *perspicuus*, *clarus*. *a* **1450** *Ratis Raving* I. 1492 Scho berys with hire lycor schyr That slokins syne as vatter fyre. **1513** DOUGLAS *Æneis* III. viii. 48 The sesonable air pipis vp fair and schire. **1776** HERD *Sc. Songs* (ed. 2) II. Gloss. s.v., We call .. clear liquor shire.

†**3.** Pure, unmixed. *Obs.*

*Beowulf* 496 þeȝn .. se þe on handa bær hroden ealowæȝe, scencte scir wered. *c* **888** ÆLFRED *Boeth.* xv, Nalles scir win hi ne druncan. *c* **1200** ORMIN 15383 Forr sippen iss all þeȝȝre spell Shir atter & shir galle Till alle þa þatt herrcnenn itt. *a* **1340** HAMPOLE *Cant.* Psalter 516 þat þa drynke þe shyrest blode of grape [*sanguinem uvae meracissimum*]. *a* **1400–50** *Wars Alex.* 113 He shapis him of shire wax litill schipis many.

†**4.** Morally or spiritually clean; pure. *Obs.*

*a* **1225** *Ancr. R.* 1 þeos riwle is cherite of schir heorte & cleane inwit. *Ibid.* 246 O muchel is .. þe mihte of schir & of clene bone. *c* **1250** *Gen. & Ex.* 518 Metodius, ali martyr, Adde in his herte sigh[ð]e sir. *a* **1300** *Cursor M.* 26200 Scrift sal mak þi saul scirre. *a* **1400** *Rel. Pieces fr. Thornton MS.* 56 When Goddis seruandes hase depely thoghte with schire herte on Gode.

**5.** Complete, perfect, utter; = SHEER *a.* 8. Also (with a negative), mere, bare.

*a* **1225** *Leg. Kath.* 1286 Nere hit schendlac inoh, & schir scheome, to alle þæt ȝelpeð of lare? *c* **1250** *Gen. & Ex.* 3580 He .. dede ðat claf melten in fir, And stired it al to dust sir. **1513** DOUGLAS *Æneis* VIII. Prol. 78 This cuntre is full of Caynis kyne, And sic schyr schrewis. *c* **1520** SKELTON *E. Rummyng* 466 They be wretchockes thou hast brought, They are shyre shakyng nought! **1540** PALSGR. *Acolastus* II. iii. Lj, I wyll not gyue the sole .i. pure or shyre hope, but the thing. **1674** N. FAIRFAX *Bulk & Selv.* 69 As if the outside of the earth were a shire flat or level. **1710** RUDDIMAN *Gloss. Douglas' Æneis* s.v. *Schire*, Scot. we say, *a skire fool*, *a shire knave*, i.e. purus putus nebulo. *c* **1730** RAMSAY *Grub Street nae Satire* 5 He's naething but a shire daft lick. **1836** M. MACKINTOSH *Cottager's Daughter* 59 He was a shire and worthless smaik.

**b.** (See quot.)

**1825** JAMIESON Suppl., *Shire*, *Shyre*, adj. Used in the sense of strait, or S. *scrimp*; as, *shire measure*, that sort of measurement which allows not a hair-breadth beyond what mere justice demands, Teviotdale.

**6.** Thin; tenuous, not dense; sparse, scanty. Of beer: Weak, 'small'.

**1398** TREVISA *Barth. De P.R.* XIX. cxxxi. (1495) 940 The more sadde a body is the more heuy it is; and the more shyre and thynne the more lyght it is founde. *c* **1400** MAUNDEV. (Roxb.) xxii. 101 þe men of þat land has schyre [*Cotton text* (1839) 207 thynne] berdes with few hares in þam. **1513** DOUGLAS *Æneis* IV. v. 188 He vanist far away .. in the schyre air [*in tenuem .. auram*]. **1530** PALSGR. 323/2 Shyre nat thycke, *delie*. **1547** SALESBURY *Dict. Eng. & Welsh*, *Teneu*, Thynne, shyre. **1599** ALEX. HUME *Hymnes* iv. 14 My haires are schyre and gray. **1721** RAMSAY *To Earl Dalhousie* 34 He had rather live on cakes, And shyrest swats. **1776** HERD *Sc. Songs* (ed. 2) II. Gloss. s.v., We call thin cloth .. shire. **1879** MISS JACKSON *Shropsh. Word-bk.*, *Shire*, thin; scanty: said of crops.

†**shire**, *v.*[1] *Obs.* Forms: 1 scíran, scýran, 3 sciren, schire, shire, sire. [OE. *scíran* = MLG., mod.LG. *schiren* to make clear, clarify (whence G. dial. *schieren*), ON. *skíra* to purify, clear (from a charge), Goth. *gaskeirjan* to interpret, f. OTeut. **skīro-*: see SHIRE *a.*]

**1.** *trans.* To declare, make known; to tell, utter.

*Beowulf* 1939 þæt hit sceadenmæl scyran moste, cwealmbealu cyðan. *c* **897** ÆLFRED *Gregory's Past. C.* xxviii. 198 Ac ȝif hie ðonne eallunga forberan ne mæȝen .. ðæt hie hit ne sciren. *c* **1205** LAY. 16822 Nes þer nan swa hæh mon þat durste word sciren. *c* **1250** *Gen. & Ex.* 2036 Ðe wite is hise, ðe right is hire, God al-miȝtin ðe soðe shire. [*a* **1250** *Owl & Night.* 1532 Wan he comeþ ham eft to his wiue, ne dar heo noȝt a word i-schire.]

**2.** To enlighten, purify (the mind or heart).

*a* **1225** *Ancr. R.* 384 Luue, þet schireð & brihteð þe heorte. *c* **1250** *Gen. & Ex.* 327 For is fruit sired mannes mood, To witen boðen iwel and good.

**shire** (ʃaɪər), *v.*[2] [f. SHIRE *sb.*] *trans.* To divide (a country) into shires.

**1810** W. DAVIES *Agric. N. Wales* i. 2 It [North Wales] was shired by Henry the Eighth into six counties. **1867** *Cal. St. Papers, Irel.* 1574–85, 170 The Brenny and Annaly shired. **1885** BAGWELL *Irel. under Tudors* I. 60 Ulster and Connaught were not shired. **1904** *Edin. Rev.* July 215 When .. he [Davies] effected the final shiring of Ulster.

†**shire**, *adv.* *Obs.* [OE. *scíre*, f. SHIRE *a.*]

**1.** Brightly; clearly.

*a* **1000** *Andreas* 835 Oð þæt dryhten forlet dæȝcandelle scire scinan. *a* **1300** *Havelok* 916 [Ich kan] kindlen ful wel a fyr, And maken it to brennan shir. **13..** *Gaw. & Gr. Knt.*

956 Hir brest & hir bryȝt þrote bare displayed, Schon schyrer þen snawe. *c* **1470** *Gol. & Gaw.* 610 The sone in the sky wes schynyng so schir. **1513** DOUGLAS *Æneis* II. v. 14 Quhen the taknyng or the bail of fire Rais fro the kingis schip, wpbirnyng schire.

**2.** With main force, mightily; sheer or straight *down*.

*a* **900** CYNEWULF *Christ* 1141 Scire burstan muras and stanas. *c* **1250** *Gen. & Ex.* 3045 O morȝen, al swilc time al sir, Thunder, and hail, and leuenes fir, Cam wel vnghere. **13..** *Gaw. & Gr. Knt.* 506 Schyre schedez þe rayn in schowrez ful warme. **1508** DUNBAR *Tua Mariit Wemen* 22 Kemmit was thair cleir hair, and curiouslie sched Attour thair schulderis doun schyre, schyning full bricht.

**shire**, obs. form of SIRE *sb.*

**shire clothe**, obs. form of CERECLOTH.

*c* **1450** *Brut* II. 430 Thanne was his body embawmyd..and closid in shire clothe.

**shiref(e**, obs. forms of SHERIFF.

**'shire-ground.** *Hist.* Country divided into shires; a tract of country subject to the control of the authorities of a shire.

**1535–6** *Act 27 Hen. VIII*, c. 26 §24 The said liberties shall continue and be used in every Lordshipp parcell of the said Duchie [of Lancaster] within the Dominion..of Wales, as the liberties of the said Duchie be used in Shire grounde and not Countie Palantyne within this Realme of England. **1536** BP. ROLAND LEE *Let. to Cromwell* in Strype *Eccl. Mem.* I. App. lxxvii. 183 The Proclamations as yet for the Shire grounds be not come: wherby Justice cannot be ministred in Wales. **1556** *Ir. Act 3 & 4 Ph. & Mary* c. 3 (1621) 251 Within sundry Townes, villages and other waste grounds of this Realme, being no shire grounds. **1586** J. HOOKER *Hist. Irel.* 181/1 in *Holinshed*, Sir John Perot..first thought it best to bring the whole land into shire grounds, whereby the laws of England might haue a through course and passage. **1603** OWEN *Pembrokeshire* ii. (1892) 31 And so he continued Earle vntill the xxvij[th] yeere of his Raigne that Wales was reduced to sheere ground. **1612** SIR J. DAVIES *Why Ireland*, etc. 247 All this while, the Prouinces of Conaght and Vlster..were not reduced to Shire-Ground. **1846** MITCHEL *Aodh O'Neill* 226 On O'Neill's part the conditions were that he should.. suffer his country to become 'shire-ground', and admit the functionaries of English government.

**Shire horse.** Also shires horse. [See quot. 1888; cf. SHIRE *sb.*] A horse of a heavy powerful breed, used for draught, chiefly bred in the midland counties of England. Also known as the Old English Black Horse.

**1875** S. SIDNEY *Bk. Horse* xii. 268 The Shire Horse. **1877** *Field* 14 Apr. 447/3 The Shires or Old English Cart Horse. *Ibid.*, Influential breeders of the Shires horse should combine together and [etc.]. [**1888** SIR W. GILBEY *Great Horse* (1899) 52 Arthur Young, in the latter part of the last century,..mentions only two varieties of Cart Horse as deserving attention, namely, the Large Black Old English Horse, 'the produce principally of the Shire counties in the heart of England and the Sorrel-coloured Suffolk Punch'.] **1891** *Spectator* 7 Mar. 340/1 The show of 'Shire horses', as the old breed of the English cart-horse is now generally called.

*attrib.* **1877** *Jrnl. R. Agric. Soc.* 532 Those confined to the 'Shire' horse classes. **1887** *Leamington Spa Courier* 30 Apr. 1/6, 8 grand Shire Horse Colts and Fillies.

**shire-land.** *rare.* [SHIRE *sb.*] **a.** = SHIRE-GROUND. **b.** *transf.* (? *nonce-use.*) A land under regular administration.

**1852** MUNDY *Antipodes* (1857) 19 Lands beyond the shire-land of New South Wales. **1910** *19th Cent.* Mar. 428 Queen Elizabeth turned the country into shireland.

†**'shirely**, *adv. Obs.* [f. SHIRE *a.* + -LY[2]. Cf. SHEERLY.] Brightly, clearly; purely.

*a* **1225** *Ancr. R.* 154 Ase ofte ase heo wolden þencchen schirliche of God, ant makien clene bonen. **13..** *Gaw. & Gr. Knt.* 1880 þere he schrof hym schyrly, & schewed his mysdedez. *c* **1470** *Gol. & Gaw.* 22 Of siluer and saphir schirly thai schane.

**'shireman.** *Obs.* exc. *dial.* (in sense 2). [OE. *scírman, scíreman*: see SHIRE *sb.*, and MAN.]

**1.** *Old Eng. Law.* A sheriff. (Erroneously explained by Lambarde as = *ealdorman*).

In OE. the word had also the sense of 'holder of official charge', 'bailiff', 'steward' (rendering L. *præpositus*, etc.).

*c* **1020** in Kemble *Cod. Dipl.* IV. 9/29 Æðelwine scirman. **1570–6** LAMBARDE *Peramb. Kent* 343 Oure Elders before the conquest, had their trialles for title of land, and other controuersies in each shire, before a Judge, then called Alderman, or Shyreman.

**2.** An inhabitant of the 'shires' (see SHIRE *sb.* 6).

*a* **1825** FORBY *Voc. E. Anglia* II. 296 Aye, I knew he must be a *shere-man* by his tongue. **1874** *Q. Rev.* Oct. 494 To this day also, an East Anglian talks, not without a shade of contempt, of an inhabitant of another county as a *sheeres* man. **1909** A. MORRISON *Green Ginger* 155 [Essex speaker] 'But a shire man allus was a fool'.

**'shire-moot.** *Hist.* [f. SHIRE *sb.* + MOOT *sb.*[1]; after OE. *scírȝemót.*] The judicial assembly of the shire in Old English times.

[*a* **1036** in Thorpe *Diplom. Angl.* (1865) 336 Her swutelaþ on ðissum ȝewrite þæt an scirȝemot sæt æt Ægelnoðes stane be Cnutes dæȝe cinges.] **1614** SELDEN *Titles Hon.* 225 Amongst Knouts Collections, one is, that twise in the yeer, the Scyreȝemot, i. the Shiremote (that which is now called the Shirifes Turne) should be held, and that in it should sit the Bishop of the Diocesse, and the Ealdorman. **1839** KEIGHTLEY *Hist. Eng.* I. 78 The Shire-mote or County Court met twice a year. **1890** HOSMER *Ags. Freedom* 82 The time was coming when the broad suffrage of the shire-moots was also to be greatly curtailed.

†**'shireness.** *Obs.* [f. SHIRE *a.* + -NESS.]

**1.** Clearness, pureness.

*a* **1225** *Ancr. R.* 386 Schirnesse of heorte is Godes luue one. *a* **1300** *E.E. Psalter* cxviii. 130 Schirenes of þi speches lightes wit [*Declaratio sermonum tuorum illuminat*]. *a* **1340** HAMPOLE *Psalter* vi. 2 Sorow for his synn has reft him þe shyrnes of..fleschly lust, as druuynge does watere.

**2.** Thinness, tenuity.

**1398** TREVISA *Barth. De P.R.* XIX. cxxxi. (1495) 940 Also for shyrenesse of partyes in thynne matere ben many poores. **1530** PALSGR. 267/1 Shyrenesse thynnesse, *delievre.*

**shirevalty**, obs. form of SHRIEVALTY.

**shireve**, obs. form of SHERIFF.

†**'shirewick.** *Obs.* [f. SHIRE *sb.* + -WICK.] = SHERIFFWICK.

**1460** *Rolls of Parlt.* V. 382/2 Every Shirref, with the power and myght of his Shirwyk. *a* **1513** FABYAN *Chron.* VII. 327 In this .xi. yere of this Kynge Henry, the shyre-wyke of London & of Myddlesex were lettyn to ferme. **1601** HOLLAND *Pliny* III. v. I. 57 The Shire-wick called Prefecture Claudia, or Foro Clodij. *Ibid.* v. xxix. 107 The free citie Alabanda, whereof that shierewicke or jurisdiction tooke name.

**shirgian, shirif(e**: see SURGEON, SHERIFF.

†**shirk**, *sb.*[1] *Obs.* Also 7 **shirke, sherk, shurk.** [Perh. a. G. *schurke* (earlier *schork, schurk*): see SHARK *sb.*[2]] A needy, disreputable parasite; one who makes a living by sponging on others, cheating at play, swindling, or the like; a sharper. = SHARK *sb.*[2] 1.

**1639** [J. TAYLOR (Water P.)] *Divers Crabtree Lect.* 164 You are an Asse, a Shirke, a Rooke. **1667–8** PEPYS *Diary* 8 Mar., He is a shirke, who owns his owing me 10*l.* for his lady two or three years ago, and yet cannot provide to pay me. **1681** HICKERINGILL *Char. Sham Plotter* 2/1 When Shoals of these Shirks, these Tories and Sham-Plotters appear barefac't in any Land or Nation, they are as Fatal..as Sword-Fishes, Sharks, and Whales, when thrown up in the Thames. *a* **1700** B. E. *Dict. Cant. Crew*, *Shurk*, a Sharper. **1710** *Medley* No. 12 Some..may be reckon'd tame Creatures, such as are those Shirks that ply about Great Tables. **1730** BAILEY (fol.), *Shirk*, a sharping Fellow that lies upon the Catch, as the Shark-fish.

**shirk** (ʃɜːk), *sb.*[2] [f. SHIRK *v.*]

**1.** One who shirks (work, obligations).

**1818** *Blackw. Mag.* III. 402 He..Reviled the Dutchers as Poltroons and shirks. **1883** JESSOPP *Arcady* iv, The shambling and scrofulous shirk whom you may find any night soaking at the pothouse.

**2.** An act or the practice of shirking. *rare.*

**1863** *Sat. Rev.* 29 Aug. 278/1 Small shirks may be apples of Sodom, but they clearly constitute with some people one of the main pleasures of life. **1877** FURNIVALL *Leopold Shaks.* Introd. 85 We saw the many shirks from doing his duty of which Hamlet was guilty. **1897** *Daily News* 3 June 5/7 Leisure—and shirk—have been the characteristics of the proceedings of this remarkable body.

†**shirk**, *sb.*[3] *Obs. rare*[−1]. [Prob. a. Ger. dial. *schirk* (in Nemnich 1793).] The sturgeon.

**1705** HICKERINGILL *Priest-cr.* II. ii. 27 For a Whale's Throat is narrower to my knowledge then a Fish (called a Shirk) but of two Yards long.

**shirk** (ʃɜːk), *v.* Also 7 **sherke, shurk, shirke,** 7–8 **sherk.** [Belongs to SHIRK *sb.*[1]; see SHARK *v.* 1.]

†**1. a.** *intr.* To practise fraud or trickery, esp. instead of working as a means of living; to prey or sponge upon others; *rarely* to pilfer (*from* another). *Obs.* Cf. SHARK *v.*[1] 1 b.

**1633** MARMION *Fine Comp.* IV. i. G 3 b, Thou shalt follow the Court like a Baboone, when a thousand proper fellowes shall sherke for their ordinary. [**1638**: see SHIRKING *vbl. sb.*] **1640** HARBOTTLE GRIMSTONE *Sp. Ho. Comm.* 18 Dec., He [*sc.* Abp. Laud] might have spent his time much better.. than thus sherking and raking in the Tobacco Shops. **1655** tr. *Sorel's Com. Hist. Francion* III. 74 How well he could practice the Lawes of pilfering, by sherking on his Disciples [orig. Fr. *friponant sur ses disciples*], to feast his friends. **1699** E. S——CY *Country Gentl. Vade M.* 77, I utterly lose my Pitty, when I see one of these Wretches shirking about in Rags. **1709** W. REEVES tr. *Apol. Justin Martyr, Tertullian, & Min. Felix* (1716) I. 4 The Platonist Amelius,..upon reading the first Verses of his [S. John's] Gospel, cry'd out, *Per Jovem Barbarus iste cum Platone nostro sentit*, By Jove this Barbarian has been shirking from our Master Plato. **1850** C. MATHEWS *Moneypenny* xviii, He saves him from a house a-fire, and..he sends him off next morning to shirk for himself.

†**b.** *trans.* To obtain by cunning or by sponging. Also *to shirk up. Obs.* Cf. SHARK *v.*[1] 2.

**1634** BP. RAINBOWE *Labour* 39 You that never heard the call of any Vocation..; that shirke living from others, but time from yourselves. **1672** EACHARD *Hobbs' St. Nat. Consid.* 34 Small matter that was shirk'd up in France from some of Cartes's acquaintance, and spoyled in the telling.

**c.** *intr.* To shift or fend *for* oneself. *U.S.*

**1843** C. MATHEWS *Various Writings* 71/1 As for Harvest, let him shirk for himself. **1874** *Rep. Vermont Board Agric.* II. 422 They are then turned into the pasture to shirk for themselves.

**2. a.** *intr.* To go evasively or slyly; to slink, to sneak *away, out,* etc. †*rarely* said of things.

**1681** *Trial of S. Colledge* 25 *Mr. Dugd...* You say that Rowley was gone, the Rogue was afraid of himself, he was shirked away. **1806** J. BERESFORD *Miseries Hum. Life* (1826) IX. xl, Trying often to harpoon a floating pat of butter, which, as often, slips aside, or ducks and shirks under your knife. **1818** G. COLMAN *Two Parsons* Poet. Vagaries (ed. 3) 154 Polyglot Behind the bed-curtain had got, Shirking, and dodging From his Co-Partner. **1850** THACKERAY *Pendennis* lxi, He and his comrades had been obliged to shirk on board at night, to escape from their wives. **1867** MISS BROUGHTON *Cometh Up* xxxiii, Sometimes..I managed to shirk out by myself..and dawdle..about the park. **1874** BARING-GOULD *Yorksh. Oddities* I. 236, I..came shirking round towards t'back door i't' yard.

†**b.** To withdraw or draw *back* through lack of courage *from* one's word or *from* an engagement.

**1778** CRISP *Let. to Miss Burney* 8 Dec., Don't imagine.. that I am retracting or shirking back from what I have said above. **1820** BYRON *Let.* 7 Sept. in Moore *Life* (1839) 453/2 One of the cities shirked from the league.

**3. a.** *trans.* To evade (a person, his conversation, acquaintance, etc.); to avoid meeting, to dodge, 'give the slip' to. Now *rare* or *Obs.*

**1787** MME. D'ARBLAY *Diary* June (1842) III. 378 They have all a really most undue dislike of her, and shirk her conversation, and fly to one another, to discourse on hunting and horses. **1800** MISS EDGEWORTH *Belinda* xvii, To punish her for shirking me, by the Lord, I'd [etc.]. **1815** *Zeluca* I. 393 See, see—he's going to shirk Lady Kitty—he pretends he don't see her coming up. **1837** HT. MARTINEAU *Soc. Amer.* II. 121 Nor would I..throw the slightest obstacle in the way of the escape of any one of the slaves who may be about to shirk their masters. **1851** MAYHEW *Lond. Labour* I. 384/2 Us sailor chaps sometimes shirks the Custom-house lubbers, sharp as they are.

**b.** At Eton: To avoid meeting (a master, a sixth-form boy) when out of bounds. Also *absol.*

**1821** R. DURNFORD *Rashleigh Letter-bag* vi, in *Etonian* (1823) III. 182, I..began to consider..if I could have offended him by not shirking him out of bounds. **1869** BLAKE-HUMFREY *Eton Boating Bk.* Introd. 1 The necessity of all but the Sixth Form being obliged to shirk the Masters, and of all the Lower Boys having to shirk the Sixth Form. **1910** GOLDW. SMITH *Remin.* iii. 38 If you met a master outside the nominal bounds you had to 'shirk', that is, to make a show of keeping out of sight.

**4. a.** To evade (one's duty, work, obligations, etc.).

**1785** GROSE *Dict. Vulgar T.*, *Sherk*, to sherk, to evade; to sherk one's duty. **1835** MARRYAT *J. Faithful* xxxviii, Father says we may, if we do our duty, and I don't mean to shirk mine. **1842** MIALL in *Nonconf.* II. 377 They usually shirk the subject. **1861** GEO. ELIOT *Silas M.* ix, Let him..shirk the resolute honest work that brings wages, and he will presently find himself [etc.]. **1880** L. STEPHEN *Pope* v. 126 This trick..was intended..to shirk responsibility.

**b.** *U.S.* To shift (responsibility, etc.) *on to* or *upon* (another person). Also with *off.*

**1845** LOWELL *Let. to C. F. Briggs* 21 Aug., Lett. 1894 I. 111, I would almost give half the rest of my life if I might shirk off upon somebody else all that is generally considered the pleasant result of a literary reputation. **1863** W. PHILLIPS *Sp.* xvi. 368 Having shirked it on to the North.

**c.** *absol.* To practise evasion of work, one's duties, responsibilities, etc.

**1853** THACKERAY *Eng. Hum.* iii. (1900) 518 He was shirking at the tavern. **1865** J. G. HOLLAND *Plain Talk* iv. 119 The disposition to shirk seems to be constitutional with the human race. **1886** W. H. LONG *Dict. I. Wight Dial.*, 'He's ben and shirked off wi'out dooen his work'. 'He's too windy by half, and he's sure to shirk out on't zomehow or nother'.

Hence **'shirking** *vbl. sb.* and *ppl. a.* Also **'shirker**, one who shirks (duty, work, etc.).

**1634** BP. RAINBOWE *Labour* (1635) 40 Let this shirking generation be cast out. **1638** HOLLAND *1st Disc. Navy* (1896) 54 'Twere safer..to give them a certain competent fee, than by an uncertain reward to expose them to shirking [*Penn MS.* sharking]. **1668** ROLLE *Abridgment* 53 You are a sherking Attorney. **1736** *Disc. Witchcraft* 42 These kind of shirking People, a Generation of impudent Liars. **1799** GEO. [IV] in *Paget Papers* (1896) I. 150, I can safely swear I never flinched one [glass],..& you well know I am not even upon indifferent occasions a Shirker. **1862** *Rep. Publ. Schools Comm.* (1864) III. 283 (Eton) Have you any opinion as to the system of shirking? **1877** FREEMAN *Norm. Conq.* (ed. 3) I. App. 621 Against plain facts and probabilities we have nothing to set except the shirkings and twistings of Dudo's rhetoric. **1883** STEVENSON *Treas. Isl.* I. v, 'Search him, some of you shirking lubbers', he cried. **1884** *Macm. Mag.* Nov. 4/1 Lord Malmesbury..was no shirker of work. **1899** SHEARMAN, etc. *Football* 242 Any shirking..must be suppressed at once.

**shirky** ('ʃɜːkɪ), *a. rare.* [f. SHIRK *v.* + -Y[1].] Characterized by or given to shirking.

**1847** HALLIWELL s.v. *Shirk*, *Shirky*, deceitful. *South.* **1897** [see SCUFFLE *v.*[1] 6]. **1897** *Daily News* 3 June 5/7 Leisure —and shirk—have been the characteristics of the proceedings..and leisurely—and..shirky—they will continue.

†**shirl**, *sb. Obs. rare*[−1]. [f. SHIRL *a.*; cf. SKIRL *sb.*] A shrill cry.

**1598** Q. ELIZ. tr. *Plutarch* iii. 21 Lest stranger..shirles might heare that maiden gaue for Skourge.

**shirl** (ʃɜːl), *a.* and *adv. Obs.* exc. *dial.* Forms: 4 **schirlle,** 5–6 **schyrle,** 6 **shirle, shyrle,** (*compar.* **shirler,** *superl.* **shirllest**), 6, 9 *dial.* **shirl.** [Metathetic form of SHRILL *a.*] **A.** *adj.*

**1.** = SHRILL *a. Obs.* exc. *dial.*

**1418–20** J. PAGE *Siege of Rouen* in *Hist. Coll. Citizen Lond.* (Camden) 45 With that they cryde alle 'Nowe welle', Al so schyrle as any belle. **1530** PALSGR. 726/1, I sownde schyrle, as a mannes or womannes voice that crieth lowd, *je clicque.* *c* **1567** ABP. PARKER *Ps.* F iij b, Of which instruments some as the harpe were lowde and shirle. **1594** PLAT *Jewell-ho.* I. 14

This salt giveth sound.., and without the sounde no mettall will ring in his shirle voyce. **1828** [CARR] *Craven Gloss.* s.v. Her shirl voice rings i my ears. **1869** *Lonsdale Gloss., Shirl*, shrill.

†**2.** Of the hair: Rough. *Obs. rare.*

**1567** GOLDING *Ovid's Met.* VIII. 995 Hir heare was harsh and shirle [*Hirtus erat crinis*]. *Ibid.* XV. 235 With shirle thinne heare as whyght as snowe.

†**B.** *adv.* Shrilly. *Obs.*

*a* **1300** *Leg. Gregory* 415 Rede and sing schirlle. **1583** GOLDING *Calvin on Deut.* viii. 45/2 Gods voyce ought to sounde shirler noweadayes in the Gospell, than it did in the Lawe.

**shirl** (ʃɜːl), *v.*[1] Now *dial.* Also 7 shurl, 9 sherl. [app. an extended form of SHEAR *v.*: see -LE 3.] *trans.* To trim with shears, *spec.* (see quot. 1802–19). Hence **'shirling** *vbl. sb.* Also **shirl** *sb.*, a trimming.

**1688** *Lond. Gaz.* No. 2323/4 Stolen..a bright bay Gelding.., his mane shirled half way. **1688** HOLME *Armoury* II. 252/2 Shurling of a Cock, is to trim the ends of his band, or neck feathers. **1775** J. WATSON *Hist. Halifax* 546 [Vocab.] *Shirl*, to cut with shears. **1802–19** REES *Cycl.*, *Sherling*, or *Shirling Lambs*, in Rural Economy, the practice of cutting or shearing the short woolly coats or coverings of these young animals in the summer season. **1828** [CARR] *Craven Gloss.* s.v., 'To shirl a fleece of wool', to cut off the clotted ends before it be teazed or carded. **1869** *Lonsdale Gloss., Shirlin's*, the fleeces of lambs. **1897** *Leeds Merc. Suppl.* 22 May (E.D.D.), Ah doan't want pollin' cloise; Ah nobbut want shirlin. *Ibid.*, Ah've nobbut hed a shirl this time.

**shirl** (ʃɜːl), *v.*[2] *north.* In 8 shurl. [App. formed (with frequentative suffix: see -LE 3) on a vb. corresponding to G. dial. *schurren, schorren*, to slide on the ice.] *intr.* To slide (see also quot. 1826). Hence **'shirling** *vbl. sb.* Also **'shirler**, one who 'shirls'; **shirl** *sb.*, a slide.

**1790** GROSE *Prov. Gloss.* (ed. 2), *Shurl*, to shurl, to slide, as upon ice. North. **1826** SOUTHEY *Let.* 25 Jan., Lett. 1856 III. 525 My girls are good shirlers... Shirling is neither sliding nor skating, but a sort of intermediate motion, performed in the common clogs of this country [Cumberland]. **1898** *Lakeland Words* in *Penrith Observer* 17 May (E.D.D.), Ther's a grand shirl on t' pond.

**shirl**, obs. form of SCHORL.

**1776** G. EDWARDS *Elem. Fossilogy* 109 Basaltes, or shirl, or cockle. **1789** T. WILLIAMS *Min. Kingd.* II. 178 Shirl is a hard and heavy substance, of a shining jet black.

**shirlcock** ('ʃɜːlkɒk). *dial.* Also shelcock, shircock, shrillcock. [f. SHIRL *a.* + COCK *sb.*] The Missel Thrush, *Turdus viscivorus.*

*a* **1790** PEGGE *Derbicisms, Shirl cock*, a thrush. **1859** W. DICKINSON *Cumberld. Gloss., Shellcock*,.. the missel thrush. **1869** *Lonsdale Gloss., Shircock*, the missel-thrush. **1882** W. DICKINSON *Remin. W. Cumbld.* 21 (Cumbld. Gloss.), I heard a shelcock sing about nine o'clock.

†**shirley**[1]. *Obs.* [The family name of Earl Ferrers, to whom a specimen described by G. Edwards (*Glean. Nat. Hist.*, 1764, III. 276) belonged.] A South American tanager.

**1796** NEMNICH *Polygl. Lex., Eng.* 891/1 *Shirley*, Tanagra. **1828–32** WEBSTER (citing '*Dict.*'). Hence in many later Dicts.

**Shirley**[2] ('ʃɜːlɪ). The name of a district of Croydon, Surrey, used *attrib.* in **Shirley poppy** to designate an annual poppy bearing single or double flowers, usu. red, pink, or white, and belonging to a variety of *Papaver rhœas* developed by William Wilks (1843–1923), vicar of Shirley and secretary of the Royal Horticultural Society. Also *absol.*

**1886** W. WILKS in *Jrnl. Hort.* 21 Oct. 367/1, I call them 'Shirley Poppies', as there seems so much doubt as to their specific name. **1889** *Ibid.* 15 Aug. 126/2, I sent a pinch of seed to a leading firm of London nurserymen last spring for comparison with the Shirley. **1904** *Nature* 25 Aug. 408/1 Many a white-edged poppy may have germinated and perished before Mr. Wilks saved the individual which in a few generations gave rise to the Shirleys. **1932** E. G. WHEELWRIGHT *Garden of Pleasant Flowers* iii. 82 Other common annuals easily raised are godetias,..Shirley poppies, and love-in-a-mist. **1978** R. GORER *Growing Plants from Seed* iv. 53 Shirley and opium poppies transplant very badly.

†**'shirling**, *a. Obs. rare*[−1]. [f. SHIRL *a.* + -ING[2]. Cf. SKIRLING *ppl. a.*] Shrill-sounding.

**1592** WYRLEY *Armorie, Ld. Chandos* 97 There cals A shirling horne, with sharp sownd eccoing.

†**shirlly**, *adv. Obs.* Also 5 shyrly, 6 shirlely. [f. SHIRL *a.* + -LY[2].] Shrilly.

**1470–85** MALORY *Arthur* XVIII. xix. 759 Then she shryked shyrly and felle doune in a swoune. **1565** GOLDING *Ovid's Met.* IV. (1567) 49 b, Bewailing their despight By chirping shirlly to themselues. **1583** —— *Calvin on Deut.*, To Cath. Ch. ¶iiij b, Albeeit that..the praises of God do ring shirlely to mens vnderstanding in the psalms and songs.

**shirmer** ('ʃɜːmə(r)). *local.* (See quots.)

**1823** T. BOND *E. & W. Looe* 77 The pilchards are seen.. playing on the surface of the water, and thereby rendering the spot of a darker colour... Such fish, so appearing, are called Shirmers. **1847** *Zoologist* V. 1645 As the summer advances, the stragglers [*sc.* pilchards] associate into small companies; these again unite into larger ones called 'shirmers'.

**shirp**, *v. Sc.* [Perh. a use of *shirp* SHARP *v.*] *intr.* To wither, shrink, shrivel. Also with *away*.

**1639** MURE *Ps.* cxxix, Be they As grasse vpon the howsses' top, Ere shott which shirps away. *c* **1680** M'WARD *Earnest Contendings for Faith* 146 (Jam.), Even professors sat-up, shirped away, and cryned into a shadow.

Hence **shirpit** *a.*, 'pinched', wasted, shrivelled. [Cf. SHILPIT *a.*]

**1821** GALT *Ann. Parish* xlvii, His nose was shirpit and sharp. **1896** H. JOHNSTON *Dr. Congalton's Legacy* i. 13 Yon shirpet body, the factor.

**shirp**, obs. form of CHIRP *v.*

**shirr** (ʃɜː(r)), *sb. U.S.* Also shir (in Dicts.). [Of obscure origin.]

**1.** Elastic webbing; also, the elastic thread used in its composition.

**1858** SIMMONDS *Dict. Trade, Shirr*, an insertion of elastic cord between two pieces of cloth. **1875** KNIGHT *Dict. Mech., Rubber-cutting Machine*,..for making threads of caoutchouc for shirrs. *Shirr*, (Fabric), an elastic cord inserted in cloth or between two pieces.

**2.** Gathered trimming, gathering. *shirr-string* = shirring string.

**1891** in *Century Dict.* **1895** SARAH M. H. GARDNER *Quaker Idyls* i, The stiff bonnets were relieved by silk shirrs of brown or gray. **1902** *Delineator* Dec. 623 A shirr-string, run through an underfacing, provides the means of closing.

**shirr** (ʃɜː(r)), *v. U.S.* Also shir (in Dicts.). [? Back-formation from SHIRRED *a.*]

**1.** *trans.* To gather or draw up (textile material) by means of parallel threads. = GAUGE *v.*[1] 8.

**1892** *Pall Mall Gaz.* 22 Sept. 1/3 A beautiful gown..of prelate purple velvet made in the loose blouse fashion, shirred into a yoke of gold and gem embroidery. **1896** *Godey's Mag.* Feb. 223/2 Pretty shades may be made by simply taking a piece of crêpe paper..and shirring it several times, leaving sufficient at the top to form a full ruffle.

**2.** *Cookery.* 'To poach (eggs) in cream instead of water' (*Cent. Dict.* 1891).

**shirred** (ʃɜːd), *a. U.S.* [f. SHIRR *sb.* + -ED[2].]

**1.** Having elastic threads woven into the texture.

**1847** WEBSTER, *Shirred*, a term applied to articles having lines or cords inserted between two pieces of cloth, as the lines of India rubber in shirred suspenders. **1875** KNIGHT *Dict. Mech., Shirred Goods*, (Fabric), goods with elastic cords (shirrs) interwoven in suspenders, garters, etc. **1882** [see SHIRRING *vbl. sb.*].

**2.** Gathered; ornamented by or with SHIRRING. Also *fig.*

**1860** SUSAN WARNER *Say & Seal* lxxii, A simply plain shirred spring bonnet of blue and white silk. **1900** ELIZ. L. BANKS in *19th Cent.* XLVIII. 791 A perfectly-fitting gown ..with..ruffles and finely-shirred lace. **1907** KATE D. WIGGIN *Old Peabody Pew* v. 114 Dark-haired Nancy under the shadow of her shirred muslin hat. **1929** S. JAMESON in *Legion Bk.* 105 The waters..in sunshine ruffled and shirred with living light. **1946** C. MCCULLERS *Member of Wedding* I. 29 The March winds banged on the window-panes, and clouds were shirred and white on the blue sky. **1973** P. WHITE *Eye of Storm* viii. 363 A brisk day: the harbour waters slightly shirred, newspaper rising and flapping in gutters.

**3.** *Cookery.* (See quot. 1892.)

**1883** SALA *Amer. Revis.* I. xxii. 302 'That woman's shirred eggs and sugar-cured ham should immortalise her', the sleeping-car 'Cap'n' gravely remarked. **1892** *Garrett's Encycl. Cookery* I. 566/2 *Shirred Eggs.*—Butter the inside of a deep plate, break into it as many Eggs as will cover the bottom, shake a little pepper and salt over them, place bits of butter all over, put them into a moderately hot oven.

**shirrel** ('ʃɪrəl). *Sc.* (Common in the 16th c.) Forms: 6 scherald, -et(t, -att, -ard, cheritt, scheirritt, 8 shirrel, 9 shirrot, shurral. [In 16th c. *scherald*, ? f. *scher-* SHEAR *v.*, to cut. (The final *-ld* developed divergently into *l* and *t*.)] A turf.

**1513** DOUGLAS *Æneis* VIII. iii. 190 And he hym self the Troiane men fut het On sonkis of gresy scheraldis hes doun set. **1554–5** *Burgh Rec. Edin.* (1871) II. 360 Item, for scheratts and devatts ix[s]. *a* **1578** LINDESAY (Pitscottie) *Chron. Scot.* (S.T.S.) I. 336 The fluir laid witht greine cherittis [*v.r.* scheirrittis]. **1597** in *Spalding Club Misc.* (1841) I. 143 Thow..keist a grene truff or scherard, and laid the new calff calff theirvpon. **1755** R. FORBES *Ajax, Jrnl. to Portsmouth* 29 Our..coach-man turned o'er our gallant cart amon a heap o' shirrels, an' peat-mow. *Ibid.* 50 *Shirrels*, turf. **1808** JAMIESON, *Shirrot*, a turf or divot, Banffs. **1826** D. ANDERSON *Poems* (ed. 2) 9 (E.D.D.) Hardly a shurral Even to rest a fire.

**shirring** ('ʃɜːrɪŋ), *vbl. sb.* [f. SHIRR *v.* (? and *sb.*) + -ING[1].] The action of SHIRR *v.*; also *concr.* (see quots.).

**1882** CAULFEILD & SAWARD *Dict. Needlework* 220 Gauging, which, following an objectionable Americanism, is also known as 'shirring', is pulled nearly tight from row to row of the runnings [etc.]. *Ibid.* 447 Shirrings are close Runnings, or cords inserted between two pieces of cloth, as the lines of indiarubber in Shirred Braces or Garters, or the drawing and puckering up any material. **1908** ELIZ. ROBINS *Come & Find Me* v, Miss Mar must have her things made plainer. No puffing, no shirring.

**b.** Comb.: **shirring string** (see quot.).

**1891** *Century Dict.*, *Shirring string*, a string or cord passed between the two thicknesses of a double shirred fabric, so as to make the small gathers closer or looser at pleasure.

**shirrot**, variant of SHIRREL.

**shirrow**, *north.* form of SHREW (mouse).

**shirry** ('ʃɜːrɪ), *a.* [f. SHIRR *sb.* + -Y.] Shirred, puckered.

**1904** *Elect. World & Engin.* 20 Feb. 374 (*Cent. Dict. Suppl.*) The blow of the lay becomes uneven..and 'shirry' cloth is the result.

**shirry**, obs. f. SHERRY *sb.*[1], var. SHERRY *sb.*[2] and *v.*[1]

**shirt** (ʃɜːt), *sb.* Forms: 1 scyrte, 3 s(c)hurte, (schuyrte, scurte, seorte), 4 schirte, sserte, 4–5 schert(e, schorte, 4–6 sherte, 5 schyrt, 5–6 shyrt(e, shurt(e, shirte, shorte, (5 shyrth, 6 shertt, sherth), 6– shirt. [OE. *scyrte* wk. fem. corresponds formally to MDu. *schorte* (mod.Du. *schort* fem.) apron, MLG., LG. *schört(e, schorte* apron (locally also thin gown worn by women), G. *schürze* fem. apron (not found before late 17th c.), ON. *skyrta* shirt (Sw. *skjorta*, Da. *skjorte* shirt; from the ON., with unexplained difference of sense, is Eng. SKIRT *sb.*):—OTeut. type **skurtjōn-*, prob. f. **skurto-* SHORT *a.*, the various senses which the sb. has in the Teut. languages being probably diverse applications of the original sense 'short garment'. A cognate form **skurto-z* is represented by MHG., mod.G. *schurz* masc., apron.]

**1. a.** An undergarment for the upper part of the body, made of linen, calico, flannel, silk, or other washable material. Originally always worn next to the skin (cf. 2 e); now sometimes an undershirt or 'vest' is worn beneath it. Formerly a garment common to both sexes (cf. CHEMISE), but now an article of male attire (cf. sense 3 a) with long sleeves (often terminating in wristbands or cuffs). Also, an infant's undergarment with short body and sleeves.

The meaning of the word in OE. is obscure, as the only instance of its occurrence is a gloss in which the meaning of the Latin word was probably not understood.

***boiled shirt*** (U.S.), a white linen shirt as distinguished from a coloured or flannel shirt. ***coloured shirt***, one made of a coloured material, as distinguished from a ***white shirt***. ***day shirt***, a more emphatic name for the shirt worn during the day time as distinguished from a NIGHT-SHIRT. †***historical shirt***, 'one adorned with worked or woven figures' (Fairholt). ***illustrated shirt***, jocularly used for coloured shirt. Also HAIR-SHIRT, HALF-SHIRT.

[*a* **1000** *Boulogne Glosses* 143 in *Germania* (N.S.) XI. 393 Scyrte *prætexta*, tunecan *togæ*.] *c* **1200** *Trin. Coll. Hom.* 139 He turnde ut of þe burh into wilderne..and ches..stiue here to shurte and gret sac to curtle. *c* **1205** LAY. 23761 Warp he an his rugge..ænne cheisil scurte [*c* **1275** seorte] & ænne pallene curtel. **1340** *Ayenb.* 191 He yaf ofte his kertel and his sserte to þe poure uor god. *c* **1386** CHAUCER *Pars. T.* ¶197 Where been thanne the gaye Robes and the smale shetes and the softe shertes? *c* **1460** J. RUSSELL *Bk. Nurture* 871 Se that youre soueraigne haue clene shurt & breche. **1480** CAXTON *Chron. Eng.* I. (1520) 7 b/1 Hercules..was betrayed by a sherte that Deyanira his wyfe sent hym empoysoned. **1509–10** *Act 1 Hen. VIII*, c. 14 §1 And that no manne undre the degree of a Knyght were any garded or pynshed Sherte. **1530** PALSGR. 267/1 Shirt for a man, *chemise*. **1602** SHAKS. *Ham.* II. i. 81 Pale as his shirt, his knees knocking each other,..he comes before me. **1625** FLETCHER *Cust. Country* ii. i, Having a Mistris, sure you should not be Without a neate historicall shirt. **1705** ADDISON *Italy* 5 (*Monaco*), We here saw several Persons, that in the midst of December had nothing over their Shoulders but their Shirts. **1776** ADAM SMITH *W.N.* v. ii. II. 483 A creditable day-labourer would be ashamed to appear in public without a linen shirt. **1799** H. MITCHELL *Scotticisms* 77 A *shirt* is a man's under garment; a *shift* is a woman's. Many of the Scotch use *shirt* for both. **1851** MAYHEW *Lond. Labour* I. 51/2 Coloured, or 'illustrated shirts', as they are called, are especially objected to by the men [costermongers]. **1854** MCCLURE *Rocky Mts.* 412 (Farmer) In order to attend the Governor's reception I borrowed a boiled shirt. **1869** DICKENS *Mut. Fr.* II. i, Bradley Headstone in his..decent white shirt..looked a thoroughly decent young man. **1896** A. E. HOUSMAN *Shropshire Lad* lxii, They shook, they stared as white's their shirt.

¶ ***shirt of fire*** (poet.): the *tunica molesta* (Juvenal *Sat.* viii. 235), a tunic 'smeared with inflammable materials' (Seneca *Ep.* xiv. 5) in which persons condemned to death by burning were enveloped.

**1852** ALEX. SMITH *Life Drama* ii. 225 Like a pale martyr in his shirt of fire.

**b.** ***bloody shirt***: a blood-stained shirt exhibited as a symbol of murder or outrage. Also *fig.*

*a* **1586** SIDNEY *Arcadia* I. vi. (Sommer) 25 b, People.. hauing no banners, but bloudie shirtes hanged vpon long staues. **1788** GIBBON *Decl. & F.* l. V. 266 The bloody shirt of the martyr was exposed in the mosch of Damascus. **1840** [L. CASS] *France* 44 (Cent.), [Foucher adds] It is by spreading out the miseries of the workmen, the bloody shirt of some victim,..that the people are excited to take arms. **1888** *New York Weekly Times* 21 Mar. (Farmer), It is reprehensible..for the Bourbons of the South to continue to play on the colour line—the Southern bloody shirt.

**c.** ***shirt of hair***: = HAIR-SHIRT.

**1430–40** LYDG. *Bochas* IX. ix. 24 b, Shortes of heer were also layde asyde. *a* **1550** *Image Ipocr.* iv. 222 in *Skelton's Wks.* (1843) II. 441/2 Some were shurtes of heres. **1781**

COWPER *Truth* 81 In shirt of hair and weeds of canvass dress'd, . . See the sage hermit.

**d.** ***shirt of mail*** [= F. *chemise de maille*].

**1522** in *10th Rep. Hist. MSS. Comm.* App. v. 400 No kynde of armor, as shorte of maylle. **1592** STOW *Ann.* 1086, 400 harquebuts in shirts of maile with morins. **1611** COTGR., *Iacquemard*, a coat, or shirt of maile. **1864** SKEAT tr. *Uhland's Poems* 356 How shall a maid's weak hand avail To make thee, my father, a shirt of mail?

**e.** With qualifying word indicating a garment for a specific purpose.

**1756–7** *Keysler's Trav.* (1760) IV. 183 For once bathing one pays six *creutzers*, and five more for the use of a bathing shirt. **1895** *Stores' Price List*, Gentlemen's Lawn Tennis and Cricketing Shirts... Cotton Football Shirts.

**f.** Short for NIGHT-SHIRT.

**1843** ABDY *Water Cure* 140 Shirts and sheets, colder than any unfrozen water can be, are safely worn and lain in by many persons, who, during a hard frost, neither warm their beds nor their shirts.

**g.** Applied to a loose garment resembling a shirt.

**1553** EDEN *Treat. New Ind.* (Arb.) 22 Some [inhabitants of Bornei] weare shertes of gossampine cotton, some beastes skinnes. **1841** ELPHINSTONE *India* I. 313 *note*, The women wear a shirt like that of the men, but much longer. [*Footnote*] They call this shirt Cameess. **1848** CURZON *Monast. Levant* I. ii. (1897) 15 The boat returned with the local authorities, two old villagers, in long blue shirts.

**h.** A shirt of a particular colour worn as the emblem or uniform of a political party or movement. Also *transf.*, the wearer of such a shirt. Cf. BLACKSHIRT, RED SHIRT.

**1864** [see RED SHIRT, REDSHIRT]. **1922** [see BLACKSHIRT, BLACK SHIRT]. **1934** *Times* 28 Feb. 15/5, I beg leave to point out that our election law requires to be brought up to date, since it was framed at a time when the political 'shirt' parties were undreamt of. **1939** H. G. WELLS *Holy Terror* II. i. 114 Two purple shirts who had visited his rooms in his second year. **1940** E. A. WALKER *South Africa* 23 Latterly more than one anti-Semitic 'shirt' movement has arisen owing a good deal to German encouragement and example. **1975** *Times Lit. Suppl.* 11 Apr. 392/1 *Antifalange*, a commentary on an apologia for the old shirts of the Spanish fascist movement.

**2.** Phrases. **a.** †*into*, †*unto*, *to one's* (or *the*) ***shirt***, so as to leave only one's shirt as a covering.

*c* **1290** *Sta. Crux* 489 in *S. Eng. Leg.* 15 His cloþes he caste of euer-ech-on A-non to is schurte and to is briech. *c* **1374** CHAUCER *Troylus* III. 1099 And of he rente vn-to his bare schirte. *c* **1450** *Mirk's Festial* 251 þen þys Emperoure . . dyspoylut hym to his schorte. **1585** T. WASHINGTON tr. *Nicholay's Voy.* I. xx. 25 b, The prease was so greate . . some of them . . were stripped intoo their shyrtes. **1687** A. LOVELL tr. *Thevenot's Trav.* I. 226 [They] were all stript to the shirt as soon as they had been taken. **1692** R. L'ESTRANGE *Fables* cxxvii. 118 A Prodigal Young Fellow that had sold his Cloths to his very Shirt.

**b.** ***in one's shirt***: in one's night attire; without one's outer garments; without one's coat and waistcoat.

*c* **1374** CHAUCER *Troylus* IV. 96 Save of a doghtir þat y left alas Slepyng . . Alas y ne had her broght in her shert. **1470–85** MALORY *Arthur* X. xxiv. 452 And there with al sir Lamorak lepte out of the bedde in his sherte. **1548** HALL *Chron., Hen. VIII*, 63 Then came in the poore younglinges . . bounde in ropes . . one after another in their shertes, & euery one a halter about his neck. **1588** SHAKS. *L.L.L.* v. ii. 704. **1593** —— *2 Hen. VI*, IV. vii. 57. **1592** *Soliman & Perseda* I. iii, Where in a shirt, but with my single Rapier, I combated a Romane. **1615** KYD *Sp. Trag.* III. xii, Bring me foorth in my shirt, and my gowne vnder myne arme. **1744** LOVE *Cricket* 4 The robust Cricketer, plays in his Shirt. **1818** SCOTT *Hrt. Midl.* ii, The officer . . escaped out of his bedroom window, and fled in his shirt. **1837** CARLYLE *Fr. Rev.* II. IV. iv, General Dumouriez . . finds the street covered with 'four or five thousand citizens in their shirts'.

†**c.** ***since, ere***, etc. ***shapen was my shirt***: since or before I was born, esp. with reference to something 'shapen' or decreed before one's birth.

*c* **1385** CHAUCER *L.G.W.* 2629 Syn fyrst that day that shapyn was myn sherte . . So ny myn herte never thing me come As thou. *c* **1386** —— *Knt.'s T.* 1566 That shapen was my deeth erst than my sherte. *c* **1402** LYDG. *Compl. Bl. Knt.* 489 Or I was born, my desteny was sponne By Parcas sustren . .; For they my deth shopen or my sherte. *a* **1542** WYATT *Lover renounces* 2 Alas . . the carefull chaunce, shapen afore my shert.

**d.** (To have) ***not a shirt***, more emphatically (to have, be worth) ***not a shirt to one's back***: no goods or possessions, not even the necessaries of life. (To give away) ***the shirt off one's back***: all one's possessions.

*c* **1386** CHAUCER *Wife's T.* 1186, I holde hym riche al hadde he nat a sherte. **1665** BRATHWAIT *Comment Two Tales* (1901) 91 Admit he be not worth a Shirt to his back, he has Wealth enough, who holds himself content. **1771** SMOLLETT *Humph. Cl., To Mrs. Gwyllim* 28 Apr. (1815) 51 He would give away the shirt off his back. **1781** GIBBON *Decl. & F.* (1787) III. xxxi. 202 *note*, Augustus had neither glass to his windows, nor a shirt to his back. **1925** W. N. BURNS *Saga Billy the Kid* 67 He was a free-hearted, generous boy. He'd give a friend the shirt off his back. **1980** *Times* 7 Oct. 10/5 One day this industry will have the shirt off my back.

†**e.** ***one's shirt***: used as a type of what is nearest to one's person. ***not to tell one's shirt***: to keep a matter strictly secret. ***near is my shirt but nearer is my skin***: a proverb meaning that one's own interests come before those of one's nearest friends. *Obs.*

**1548** HALL *Chron., 3 Hen. IV*, 20 The kyng began . . to muse on this request, and not without a cause, for in dede it touched him as nere as his sherte, as you well may perceiue by the Genealogy. **1579** G. HARVEY *Letter-bk.* (Camden) 67 To have every on in continuall ielouzye, lest he sitt over neere there schirtes or have familiar insighte in ther commendable and discommendable qualityes. **1586** EARL LEICESTER *Let. to Walsingham* 7 June in *Corr.* (Camden) 291, I will warrant him hanged . . but you must not tell your shirt of this yet. **1596** LODGE *Marg. Amer.* 103 My shirt is neare me, my lord, but my skin is nearest. **1625** T. GODWIN *Rom. Antiq.* 155 Close sitteth my shirt, but closer sitteth my skinne. **1654** *Clarke Papers* (Camden) III. 12 The designe is secrett, knowne to the designer onely, whoe saith if hee thought his shirt knew it hee would burne it.

**f.** slang. ***to bet one's shirt, to put one's shirt on*** (a horse) = to bet all one's money on. ***to get*** (a person's) ***shirt out***, to cause him to lose his temper. ***to keep one's shirt on***: to remain calm (orig. *U.S.*). ***to lose one's shirt***: to lose all one's possessions.

**1854** *Spirit of Times* (N.Y.) 4 Nov. 447/3, I say, you durned ash cats, just keep yer shirts on, will ye? **1859** *Hotten's Slang Dict.* s.v. *Shirty*, When one person makes another in an ill humour he is said to have 'got his shirt out'. **1892** *Pall Mall Gaz.* 30 Mar. 6/2 Bet thee my shirt Aunty Jane wins. **1897** BARRÈRE & LELAND *Dict. Slang* s.v., To put one's shirt on a horse. **1904** W. H. SMITH *Promoters* i. 15 I'll tell you how, if you'll keep your shirt on. **1932** WODEHOUSE *Louder & Funnier* 113 Sure he knows you know, Bill... Don't get your shirt out. **1935** E. B. MANN *Thirsty Range* xi. 144 He hit the market . . about the time the bottom dropped out of it. He lost his shirt! **1938** E. BOWEN *Death of Heart* I. i. 25 He had not foreseen ever having to put his shirt on either [woman]. **1945** *Chambers's Jrnl.* Oct. 554/1 Okay, okay—keep your shirt on. Let's see what can be done. **1954** T. S. ELIOT *Confidential Clerk* II. 63 Marriage is a gamble. But I'm a born gambler And I've put my shirt—no, not quite the right expression—Lucasta's the most exciting speculation I've ever thought of investing in. **1981** P. THEROUX *Mosquito Coast* xi. 131 'Keep your shirt on,' Father shouted.

**3. a.** A woman's blouse or loosely-fitting dress-body with a collar, front and cuffs, somewhat resembling a man's shirt; = *shirt-blouse* in 5 c.

**1896** *Westm. Gaz.* 9 Apr. 3/1 There is no need for a shirt to be hard and unfeminine because it is called a shirt. **1913** *Daily Graphic* 24 Mar. 13/2 If a more dressy morning shirt is desired, the chiffon moiré is the favoured fabric.

**b.** ***habit-shirt***, a kind of chemisette: see HABIT *sb.* 12.

**1834**: see HABIT *sb.* 12. **1844**: see CHEMISETTE 2. **1912** ELIN. GLYN *Halcyone* ii. 16 Miss Roberta . . had her thin bones covered with a habit shirt of tulle.

**4.** *transf.* An inner casing or covering. †**a.** = AMNION (*obs.*). **b.** *Comm.* and *Techn.* (See quots.) [Cf. F. *chemise.*]

**1611** COTGR., *Agneliere*, th' inmost of the three membranes which enwrap a wombe-lodged infant; called by some Mid-wiues . . the childs shirt. **1640** in *Court Min. E. India Co.* 12 Aug. (1909) 75 That the Company is much prejudiced by allowing sugars to be 'tared in the gunny' instead of the buyers taking them 'in their shirts'. **1812** J. SMYTH *Pract. Customs* (1821) 211 The Messina package, which consists of three thicknesses, has its lining, or shirt, covered with a smooth oil cloth. **1868** JOYNSON *Metals* 16 The internal lining or shirt of the furnace. **1883** W. M. WILLIAMS in *Knowledge* 25 May 308/2 The fuel should be placed between these [iron bars], and thus form an upright cylindrical ring or shirt of fire, inclosed outside by the bricks.

**5.** *attrib.* and *Comb.*: **a.** simple attrib., as ***shirt-breast, -collar*** (hence ***-collared*** adj.), ***-cuff, pocket, -wrist***; ***shirt-like*** adj. **b.** objective, as ***shirt-ironer, -knitter, -maker, -washer***; ***shirt-making***.

**1847** LYTTON *Lucretia* I. i, The diamond in his *shirt-breast. **1557** SEAGER *Sch. Virtue* 85 in *Babees Bk.*, Thy *shyrte coler fast to thy necke knyt. **1848** THACKERAY *Van. Fair* iv, 'Pooh, pooh, Miss Sharp,' said he, pulling up his shirt-collars. **1895** DU MAURIER *Trilby* VI. 280 *Shirt-collared within an inch of their lives. **1853** WHYTE MELVILLE *Digby Grand* xxiii, Enormous *shirt-cuffs . . called attention to the hands. **1891** *Daily News* 30 Nov. 7/1 An action brought by a *shirt-ironer. **1893** *Laundry Managem.* (ed. 2) 80 Some of the shirt ironers [*sc.* machines] have . . a good-sized iron, heated by steam or gas. **1881** *Instr. Census Clerks* (1885) 75 Hosiery Manufacture... *Shirt Knitter. **1858** SIMMONDS *Dict. Trade*, **Shirt-maker*; a sempstress; a tradesman who employs females to make shirts. **1886** C. E. PASCOE *Lond. of Today* xli. (ed. 3) 355 Hosiers, glovers, and shirt-makers. **1897** *19th Cent.* Aug. 203 Londonderry . . [with] its *shirt-making industry. **1962** L. DEIGHTON *Ipcress File* xxiii. 150 The very young soldier reached into his *shirt pocket. **1977** D. AITKIN *Second Chair* i. 3 My hand in my shirt pocket, tugging at the little diary. **1902** *Daily Chron.* 24 July 9/4 Laundry.—A good *shirt washer wanted. **1909** *Ibid.* 23 Jan. 8/3 Rotary Shirt Washer (Good secondhand, brass cylinder), wanted. **1815** LD. BROUGHTON (J. C. Hobhouse) *Recoll. Long Life* (1901) I. 268 He had long white *shirt-wrists.

**c.** Special comb.: **shirt-band** = BAND *sb.*² 4, also *dial.* the wrist-band of a shirt; **shirt-blouse, -bodice** = sense 3 above; **shirt-bosom** (now *U.S.*) = *shirt-front*; **shirt-button**, a small-sized button of mother of pearl or the like pierced with thread holes, used as a fastening for shirts; **shirt-buttons** (see quot. 1880); **shirt case**, a travelling case for shirts; **shirt cloth**, †(*a*) ? a piece of cloth for a shirt; (*b*) (see quot. 1910); **shirt-cutter**, one who cuts out shirts for the trade; **shirt-dress**, a dress having a bodice styled like a shirt; **shirt-dresser** (see quot.); so **shirt-dressing** (in quot. *attrib.*); **shirt frame** *U.S.* (see quot.); **shirt-frill**, a frill formerly worn on the front and wrist-bands of a shirt; **shirt front** = FRONT *sb.* 9 d; also *transf.* a white patch on the chest (of a dog) or on the breast (of another animal); also *attrib.* of a cricket pitch: very smooth and even (*colloq.*); **shirt gills** *jocular*, the projecting ends of a stand-up collar; **shirt gown** *Sc. dial.*, a bodice; **shirt-jac** = *shirt jacket*; **shirt-jacket** chiefly *U.S.*, a loose-fitting linen jacket; a garment resembling a shirt but worn as a jacket; **shirt-lap**, the tail of a shirt (*obs.* exc. *dial.*); **shirtlifter** *Austral. slang*, a male homosexual; **shirtmaker** = *shirt-waist dress* below; freq. *attrib.* (a proprietary term in the U.S.); **shirt-man**, a name applied to an American colonial rifleman in the war of Independence (see quot. 1788); **shirt-pin**, an ornamental pin used to fasten the shirt at the throat; **shirt ruffle** = *shirt-frill*; **shirt stud**, a stud for fastening a shirt; **shirt-stud-abscess** (see quot. 1898); **shirt-studded** *a.*, wearing (showy) shirt studs; **shirt-tail**, (*a*) the tail of a shirt; (*b*) *U.S.*, used *attrib.* or as *adj.* to designate something small and insignificant, or a remote relationship; freq. as **shirt-tail boy**, a very young boy; **shirt-waist** *orig. U.S.*, a shirt-blouse; also formerly a garment worn by men and boys; freq. *attrib.* as **shirt-waist dress**, a dress having a shirt-waist bodice; **shirtwaister** = *shirt-waist dress*. Also SHIRT-SLEEVE.

**1532–3** *Act 24 Hen. VIII*, c. 13 §1 That no servyngman . . shall weare any shirte or *shirte bande . . made or wrought with Silke Golde or Silver. **1659** *Knaresb. Wills* (Surtees) II. 236, 1 shirt, 1 shirtband. **1907** EDITH RICKERT *Golden Hawk* xx. 160 A gush of . . milk . . trickling in warm currents between his neck and his shirt-band. **1905** *Daily Chron.* 19 May 8/1 Each girl makes . . a *shirt-blouse. **1907** E. M. SELLAR *Recoll. & Impr.* xii. 161 From Brussels I brought home for the little girls red and blue *shirt-bodices and skirts. **1833** J. NEAL *Down-Easters* I. 3 His collar turned back, and his *shirt-bosom all open to the waist. **1856** MISS WARNER *Hills Shatemuc* xiii, If shirt-bosoms gave out, the boys buttoned their coats over them. **1858** SIMMONDS *Dict. Trade* s.v. *Shirt-front*, A dickey, or loose shirt bosom. **1889** GUNTER *That Frenchman* xvi. 204 The champagne . . is shaken . . over his diamonds on his shirt-bosom. **1651** R. VERNEY in M. M. Verney *Memoirs* (1894) III. ii. 38 Blew Thread, *Shirt Buttons and old White . . Buttons. **1742** C. CARROLL *Let.* 24 Nov. in *Maryland Hist. Mag.* (1925) XX. 178 Three or four Papers good shirt Buttons but not made on Wire. **1851** MAYHEW *Lond. Labour* I. 437 Shirt Buttons . . are disposed of in great quantities in the streets. **1978** P. NIESEWAND *Underground Connections* 123 He undid his shirt buttons and stripped to the waist. **1880** *Monthly Packet* N.S. XXX. 409 Local names of plants... *Stellaria Holostea* —*Shirt-buttons, West Kent. **1895** *Stores' Price List*, *Shirt Case to hold 18 Shirts. **1540** *Test. Ebor.* VI. 118 To Thomas Dransfelde a *shirte cloithe, to John Coupe a shert clothe. **1910** *Encycl. Brit.* VII. 277/1 *Shirt-cloth* is the term more commonly applied to what is actually used in the manufacture of shirts. **1881** *Instr. Census Clerks* (1885) 75 *Shirt-cutter. **1909** *Daily News* 7 Jan. 7/1, I was a shirt-cutter by trade. **1943** in C. W. Cunnington *Eng. Women's Clothing Present Cent.* (1952) viii. 273 Necklines avoid the *shirt-dress look which has been so widespread in recent years. **1973** *Country Life* 22 Feb. 492/1 If ever there was a right season to wear a shirt-dress, this is it. **1978** *Detroit Free Press* 5 Mar. D 12/1 A delicate mini-floral two-piece shirtdress. **1867** SIMMONDS *Dict. Trade* (1892) Suppl., **Shirt Dresser*, a laundress who washes and prepares shirts for wear. **1884** KNIGHT *Dict. Mech.* Suppl., **Shirt Frame*, a Guernsey, or shirt knitting machine. **1824** MISS MITFORD *Village* Ser. I. 211 A laundress . . unrivalled in flounces and *shirt-frills. **1838** LYTTON *Alice* II. ii, His black coat, neatly relieved . . by a white under-waistcoat, and a *shirt-front admirably plaited. **1873** *All Year Round* 28 June 203/1 But why is a shirt-front popularly called a dickey? **1877** E. S. DALLAS *Kettner's Bk. of Table* 104 The carp is to be stuffed. . . The skin may be left on his shirtfront. **1893** *Kennel Gaz.* Aug. XIV. 213/3 A liver bitch with a large shirt front. **1920** P. F. WARNER *Cricket* 212 The result of all this work is that the pitch literally shines—and looks as if it had been ironed. 'Shirt-front wickets' they call them. **1963** *Times* 18 May 4/5 By merely bowling accurately, with seam upright, they presented problems which West Indian batsmen, reared on the shirt-front surfaces of their own grounds, found too complicated. **1967** L. EGAN *Nameless Ones* xiii. 158 He [*sc.* the cat] was a handsome sight, his gray tiger stripes smooth and his white shirt front immaculate. **1839** FR. A. KEMBLE *Resid. in Georgia* (1863) 58 One young man . . came to pay his respects to me in . . *shirt gills which absolutely ingulfed his black visage. **1889** A. J. ELLIS *E.E. Pronunc.* v. 725 A brave *shirt-gown. **1964** *Playboy* Nov. 173 The cool, crisp and comfortable *shirt-jac which looks like a shirt, but is worn outside the trousers. **1977** *Guardian Weekly* 10 July 9/1 'Shirt-jacs', as they call tropical suits in Trinidad. **1879** MRS. F. D. BRIDGES *Jrnl. Lady's Trav. round World* 20 Dec. (1883) 231 'Mynheer van Dunk' . . appeared on deck . . in 'pyjamas' . .; a loose white *shirt-jacket . . completed his costume. **1975** *Daily News* (N.Y.) 26 July 12 Many leisure suits have shirt-jackets rather than the traditional jacket. **13 . .** *K. Horn* (Harl. MS.) 1209 His *shurte lappe he gan take & wypede a wey þe foule blake. **1856** GEO. ELIOT *Scenes Cler. Life* ii, Tell the most impassioned orator, suddenly, that his wig is awry, or his shirt-lap hanging out, . . and you would infallibly dry up the spring of his eloquence. **1966** BAKER *Austral. Lang.* (ed. 2) x. 216 **Shirt lifter*, a sodomite. **1974** B. HUMPHRIES in *Bulletin* (Sydney) 19 Jan. 13 When I first seen them photos of him in his 'Riverina Rig' I took him for an out-of-work ballet dancer or some kind of shirtlifter. **1926** *Official Gaz.* (U.S. Patent Office) 15 June 584/2 Best & Co. . . *Shirtmaker frock . . women's and children's dresses. **1960** *Guardian* 27 July 7/3 For this summer they have chosen a shirtmaker in drip-dry cotton. **1976** 'R. ROYLE' *Cry Rape* xx. 91, I chose a simple navy shirtmaker dress.

**1775** *Pennsylv. Gaz.* 16 Aug. 2/3 The damn'd *shirtmen, as they are emphatically called by some of his [the loyal governor's] minions. **1788** W. GORDON *Hist. Independ. U.S.* II. 112 Colonel Woodford had not more than 300 shirtmen (as they call the riflemen, on account of their being dressed in their hunting shirts). **1825** T. HOOK *Sayings* Ser. II. *Passion & Princ.* xiv. III. 344 Presenting him with a *shirt-pin, made of jewellers' gold-wire. **1848** THACKERAY *Van. Fair* xiii, He was attracted by a handsome shirt-pin in a jeweller's window. **1892** A. E. LEE *Hist. Columbus* (Ohio) I. 735 Kneebreeches were abandoned, and the *shirtruffles were reduced. **1851** MAYHEW *Lond. Labour* I. 334/2 In some windows.. shawl-pins, *shirt-studs, necklaces. **1898** *Syd. Soc. Lex.*, **Shirt-stud abscess*, form of abscess having a superficial cavity connected with a deeper one by a sinus. **1855** J. R. LEIFCHILD *Cornwall* 265 Noisy, blustering, *shirt-studded fellows. **1845** J. HOOPER *Adventures Capt. Simon Suggs* 13 From the time he was a '*shirt-tail boy', [his wits] were always too sharp for his father's. **1846** J. W. WEBB *Altowan* I. vi. 174 He.. leaped into the river,.. and made a shirt-tail across the prairie on the other side. **1873** LELAND *Egypt. Sketch-bk.* 47 Rushing madly about, their blue-and-white shirt-tails waving in the wind. **1878** J. C. GUILD *Old Times in Tennessee* 411, I traversed these granite hills and beautiful vales as a shirt-tail boy. **1929** W. FAULKNER *Sound & Fury* 256 My people owned slaves here when you all were running little shirt tail country stores. **1938** M. K. RAWLINGS *Yearling* xxxiii. 421 Nobody but your folks'll bother with a little ol' shirt-tail boy like you. **1941** *Amer. Speech* XVI. 24/2 *Shirt-tail kin*, a remote relationship. **1975** *Publishers Weekly* 8 Sept. 57/2 A shirttail relation of the hotel-owning branch of the family. **1879** *Harper's Bazaar* 14 June 377 Kilt suits made here have the pleats stitched to a belt at the waist, and are then buttoned to a white *shirt waist. **1897** KIPLING *Capt. Cour.* x. 236 The summer-boarder girls in pink and blue shirt-waists. **1902** *Sears Catal.* 819/3 Three hundred dozen men's regular $1·50 shirtwaists to go at 50 cents. **1957** *Observer* 1 Dec. 11/2 This gives the many lovely, tight-belted shirt-waist dresses a heavy look. **1980** *Times* 2 Sept. 10/1 The shirt-waist dress.. is still a basic article of apparel. **1957** *Observer* 1 Dec. 11/2 These *shirt-waisters are lovely, bodices luxuriously bloused [etc.]. **1973** *Country Life* 8 Mar. 633/2 The longer cardigan jacket.. is worn in the daytime over shirtwaisters.

**shirt** (ʃɜːt), *v.* [f. SHIRT *sb.*]

**1.** *trans.* To clothe with or as with a shirt.

**1601** STOW *Ann.* 1291 Friers Capuchins.. girt with hempen cordes, shirted with haire-cloth, and bare footed. **1638** SIR T. HERBERT *Trav.* (ed. 2) 329 The better sort.. shirt their coleblack skins with a pure white cloth. **1691** DRYDEN *K. Arthur* II. i, Souls, as but this Morn' Were cloath'd with Flesh,.. But naked now, or shirted but with Air. **1808** W. WILSON *Dissenting Churches* II. 581 One day shirting himself, he thoughtlessly put his studs between his lips. **1871** B. TAYLOR *Faust* II. iii. (1875) II. 106 Quite naked most, a few are only shirted.

**2.** (See quot.)

**1862** *Jrnl. R. Agric. Soc.* XXIII. 315 'To shirt' hay—that is, to wrap up an inferior quality in prime hay—is such a common practice in the neighbourhood of Paris.

Hence **ˈshirted** *ppl. a.*

**1693** *d'Emillianne's Hist. Monast. Orders* vii. 34 The Congregation of St. John of Lateran.. have a kind of a Surplice.. having the form of a Shirt, for which they are now commonly called in Italy Shirted Fathers, or Fathers of the Shirt. **1880** MEREDITH *Tragic Com.* (1881) 178 Were we to hear all the roarings of the shirted Heracles.

**shirtee** (ʃɜːtiː). *U.S.* [f. SHIRT *sb.* + -EE.] A shirt-front; a 'dickey'.

**1818** *Lancaster* (Pa.) *Jrnl.* 5 Aug. (Thornton *Amer. Gloss.*), A shirt, if you can afford it. But if you can't, then a shirtee, with pretty broad ruffles.

**shirting** (ˈʃɜːtɪŋ). [f. SHIRT *sb.* + -ING[1].] Material for shirts; *spec.* a kind of piece-goods of stout cotton cloth suitable for shirts but also used for other garments.

**1604** DEKKER *Honest Whore* IV. iii. (1635) H, *Cand.* Looke you, here's choice Cambrickes. *Cram.* No sir, some shirting. **1733** P. LINDSAY *Interest Scot.* 128 The Use of Indian Cotton-cloth has been often attempted for Shirting, but to no Purpose. **1792** *Descr. Kentucky* 49 White and checked shirtings. *a* **1879** GEO. ELIOT *Leaves fr. Notebk.* Ess. (1884) 357 His morbid passion for Manchester shirtings. **1882** CAULFEILD & SAWARD *Dict. Needlework* 447/2 *Shirtings*, these are otherwise called Fancy Cotton Shirtings... Dresses are sometimes made of the same.. cloth, which has been sized and glazed... Women's cuffs and collars are made largely in these Shirting-cloths. **1910** *Encycl. Brit.* VII. 277/1 *Shirting*.. has long since ceased to refer exclusively to shirt cloths... Grey and white shirtings are exported to all the principal Eastern markets.

*attrib.* **1882** Shirting cloth [see above]. **1910** *Encycl. Brit.* VII. 277/1 The export shirting trade.

**b.** The material of which a shirt is made. *rare.*

**1872** GEO. ELIOT *Middlem.* xlvi, A troop of.. hatless boys with their galligaskins much worn and scant shirting to hang out.

**shirtless** (ˈʃɜːtlɪs), *a.* [f. SHIRT *sb.* + -LESS.] Without a shirt.

*a* **1613** OVERBURY *Wife*, etc. (1616) G 6, A shirtlesse fellow with a Cudgell vnder his arme. **1728** POPE *Dunciad* III. 116 Grave Mummers! sleeveless some, and shirtless others. **1830** LAMB *Let. to Wordsw.* Lett. 1837 II. 260, I would live in London shirtless, bookless. **1962** J. F. POWERS *Morte d'Urban* 218 Some shirtless youths in an old car rolled up from behind him. **1971** *Daily Tel.* (Colour Suppl.) 16 July 36/1 It had been a long slog up, shirtless, sweating, rucksacks bumping.

*transf.* **1874** HARDY *Far fr. Mad. Crowd* xxii, Away the simple [shorn] dam leaps, panting, over the board into the shirtless flock outside.

Hence **ˈshirtlessness.**

**1829** *Westm. Rev.* X. 371 A timely recollection of the saying might have rescued Augustus from the ridicule of shirtlessness.

**shirt-sleeve, shirtsleeve. 1. a.** A sleeve of a shirt. Chiefly *pl.* Also used *loosely* in pl. with reference to the absence of a coat. Phr. ***in one's shirt-sleeves***, with one's coat off.

*c* **1566** *Merie Tales of Skelton* xi. in *S.'s Wks.* (1843) I. p. lxv, The hostler was in hys ierkyn, and hys shirte sleues wer aboue his elbowes. **1612** PEACHAM *Gentl. Exerc.* viii. 27 [Bathers depicted as] surprized by the enemy, where you might see one putting his head into his shirt sleeue for hast. **1757** *Phil. Trans.* L. 108 His shirt-sleeve, and the upper part of his waistcoat, were reduced to tinder. **1789** J. WOODFORDE *Diary* 30 July (1927) III. 126 The latter was.. working in his garden in his Shirt Sleeves. **1832** F. TROLLOPE *Dom. Manners Amer.* II. xxv. 56, I saw one man.. take off his coat that he might enjoy the refreshing coolness of shirt sleeves. **1837** CARLYLE *Fr. Rev.* III. IV. viii, In their shirt-sleeves, coat flung loosely round the neck. **1859** GEO. ELIOT *Adam Bede* iv, He.. threw off his jacket, and began to roll up his shirt-sleeves again. **1878** EMERSON *Misc. Papers, Fort. Republic* Wks. (Bohn) III. 394 Here is the human race poured out over the continent;.. all mankind in its shirt-sleeves. **1942** D. M. CROOK *Spitfire Pilot* 45 We were flying in shirt sleeves. **1977** *Times* 29 Oct. 5 (*caption*) A Panama hat and shirtsleeves for the Duke of Edinburgh in the tropical sun.

**2.** *attrib.* (in sing. or pl.) **a.** That is in shirtsleeves; usu. *fig.*, hard-working, workman-like; down-to-earth, informal; (see also quot. 1959).

**1864** SALA in *Daily Tel.* 27 Sept., The people are going to elect shirt-sleeve aldermen that work all day. **1908** *Pall Mall Gaz.* 20 Apr. 2/2 The Congressmen have a preference for what they picturesquely describe as 'Shirtsleeve Ambassadors'—men who they think will labour for their country's interests and scorn social fascinations. **1924** LAWRENCE & SKINNER *Boy in Bush* 11 The shirt-sleeves familiarity, the shabby clothes. **1959** *Times* 7 Sept. 16/1 Shirtsleeves weather. **1967** *Boston Sunday Herald* 26 Mar. I. 44/2 (Advt.), A 'self-starter' and a guy who will fit into a small shirtsleeve agency. **1979** G. SEYMOUR *Red Fox* iii. 44 [He] would have given much to have exchanged the brilliance of the surroundings for a shirtsleeves working area.

**b.** ***shirtsleeve(s) diplomacy***, management of political affairs which is characterized by lack of formality or sophistication; ***shirtsleeve order*** (Mil.), the wearing of uniform without a jacket.

**1931** W. F. SANDS *Undiplomatic Mem.* 22, I admit some pride in believing that they acted like gentlemen in the matter, though perhaps it was only shirt-sleeves diplomacy. **1959** *Times* 22 Aug. 9/5 Maximum cartridges are an asset for long-range shots, but perhaps hardly ideal for shirt-sleeve order. **1977** *Listener* 11 Aug. 164/3 Accessibility.. and, in the best sense, shirtsleeve diplomacy are on. **1979** 'J. D. WHITE' *Brandenburg Affair* iv. 37 Colonel Petrov.. was another huge man... Even in shirt-sleeve order.. his massive arms.. gave him an air of permanence.

Hence **shirt-sleeved** *a.*

**1869** LOWELL *Poems, Cathedral* 600 This brown-fisted rough, this shirt-sleeved Cid. **1889** D. C. MURRAY *Dang. Catspaw* 30 Esden, sitting shirtsleeved in his apartments.

**shirty** (ˈʃɜːtɪ), *a.* Also shirtey. [f. SHIRT *sb.* + -Y.]

**1.** Ill-tempered. See SHIRT *sb.* 2f. *slang.*

**1846** *Swell's Night Guide* 54 'I am exceedingly obliged,' grunted Tomkins, in rather a shirty tone, and continued reading. **1856** H. PHILLIPS *Jrnl.* 18 Apr. (typescript) 30 Jem and Mrs R. Shirty. **1859** *Hotten's Slang Dict.*, *Shirty*, ill tempered or cross. **1861** MAYHEW *Lond. Labour* III. 137 They knocked his back as they went over, and he got shirtey. Then came a row. **1892** *Punch* 20 Feb. 88/2 No end of a shirty letter from the Governor. **1911** [see ROUSE *v.*[4]]. **1916** *Chambers's Jrnl.* June 404/2 Please don't get shirty, old chap. **1927** [see RAG *sb.*[1] 3c]. **1934** WODEHOUSE *Right Ho, Jeeves* vii. 73 But don't tell me that when he saw how shirty she was about it, the chump didn't back down? **1960** J. RAE *Custard Boys* I. v. 54 All right; all right; there's no need to get shirty about it.

**2.** Resembling or modelled on a shirt.

**1958** J. KEROUAC *On Road* IV. 288 A sixteen-year-old colored girl.. in her short shirty dress. **1973** *Guardian* 10 Apr. 13/2 Fox-trimmed parka with shirred waist, shirty cuffs.

Hence **ˈshirtily** *adv.*; **ˈshirtiness.**

**1899** *Daily News* 12 Jan. 5/1 With both peoples [French and German].. the whole duty of man includes the duty of getting 'shirty' on the slightest provocation. Till they recognize that 'shirtiness' itself is the real enemy of self-respect, they must infallibly go on boring holes in one another in this fatuous way. **1974** P. CAVE *Mama* (new ed.) xiv. 113 'Seems a bloody con to me,' he mumbled shirtily. **1978** D. FRANCIS *Trial Run* vii. 105 They told us pretty shirtily just now not to bother them.

**Shirvan** (ʃɜːˈvɑːn). The name of a region in the Soviet republic of Azerbaijan, used *attrib.* or *ellipt.* to denote a short-napped rug or carpet made in that area and similar to those of Daghestan.

**1892** CARDINAL & HARFORD *Oriental Carpets & Rugs* 21 Daghestan. This title includes those kinds known as Kazaos, Karabaghs, Cubas, Shirvans, &c. **1913** [see KABISTAN]. **1931** [see DAGHESTAN, DAGESTAN]. **1970** L. DEIGHTON *Bomber* xxiii. 350 Modern Shirvans. They won't interest you, you know too much about carpets.

**shise**, var. SHICE *sb.* and *a.*

**shish** (ʃɪʃ), *int.* Also schisch. Onomatopoeic representation of a prolonged or reiterated hissing sound. Hence also *sb.* and *vb.* Cf. SH *int.*

**1881** MRS. RIDDELL *Alaric Spencely* II. 166 Which startled the wild fowl in Abbey Marsh, and caused them.. to rend the silence of the night with the schisch and schurr of their wings. **1904** 'E. NESBIT' *Phœnix & Carpet* xi. 211 Most of the people [in the theatre] hissed, or said 'Shish!' **1908** *Daily Chron.* 3 June 1/6 [He] was washing himself.. and 'shishing' as he rubbed himself like an ostler with a horse.

‖**shisham** (ˈʃɪʃəm). Also shishim, sheeshum, sisham. [Hindī *çīçam*, cogn. w. Skr. *çinçapā* of the same meaning.] = SISSOO.

**1849** *Dry Leaves* 96, I found it was shisham, a wood of the most valuable kind. **1890** KIPLING *Soldiers Three* 31 We three were comfortably settled under the big *sisham* [ed. 1889 *shisham*]. **1909** *Blackw. Mag.* Sept. 307/1 The wide avenue of the *jhil* road, with its shade of noble *shishams*. **1910** *Ibid.* Aug. 224/2 The 'sheeshum' (*Dalbergia sissoo*) affording excellent timber.

‖**shishi** (ˈʃiʃi). [Jap.] A lion, *spec.* as a decorative motif on Japanese porcelain.

**1970** *Ashmolean Mus. Rep. Visitors 1969* 48 Saucer, with two *shishi* in Kakiemon enamels. **1976** *Daily Tel.* 20 July 12/3 The interior is enamelled in iron-red, blue, turquoise and yellow with a shishi beneath a spray of peony.

**shish kebab** (ˈʃɪʃ kɪˌbæb). Also sheesh kabab, shish-kebab, shishkebab, shushkabab. [a. Turkish *şişkebap*, f. *şiş* skewer + *kebap* roast meat.] **1.** A dish consisting of pieces of meat (usu. lamb) grilled on skewers. Cf. CABOB 1, KEBAB.

**1914** S. LEWIS *Our Mr. Wrenn* ii. 26 I'm sure you'll like shish kebab. **1921** A. C. TRAIN *By Advice of Counsel* 73 Sardi had ordered *sheesh kabab*. **1951** KOESTLER *Age of Longing* I. vii. 153 'What kind of dishes do you really like?' .. 'Shashlik. And shushkabab.' **1960** *Times* 4 June 7/6 Stands of appetizing *shish-kebab* on bamboo skewers. **1976** *Outdoor Living* (N.Z.) I. II. 63 Perfectly suited to barbecue cooking are shishkebabs and the variations are infinite. **1980** P. WAY *Icarus* xli. 180 The cluster of shish kebab stalls.

**2.** *Physical Chem.* A fibrous crystalline structure formed in some flowing or agitated polymer solutions, consisting of many plate-like crystallites (*kebabs*) growing outwards from a long ribbon or rod (a *shish*).

**1966** A. J. PENNINGS in H. S. Peiser *Crystal Growth* 391/2 Most of the fibres exhibit lamellar overgrowth.. and helical structures can also be observed. These structures will be referred to as Shish-kebabs. **1974** J. SCHULTZ *Polymer Materials Sci.* ii. 111 Electron and x-ray diffraction experiments have shown that the polymer chains in both shish and kebab are aligned parallel to the fiber axis. **1975** *Nature* 15 May 195/3 The shish kebab, of overall diameter about 1 μm and length up to several mm, apparently has a central core, the 'shish', about 20 nm diameter skewering lamellar crystals, the 'kebabs'. **1979** *Ibid.* 29 Mar. 440/1 The formation of fibrous precipitates, almost entirely of the shish kebab structure, on the stirrer by stirring supercooled solutions of polyethylene and isotactic polystyrene respectively.

**shism**, obs. form of SCHISM.

**shist, shistose, shistus**: see SCH-.

**shit** (ʃɪt), **shite** (ʃaɪt), *sb.* Not now in decent use. Forms: 1 scitte, 3 schit, 4 schyt, 6 *Sc.* schit, s(c)heitt(e, 6– shit, shite. [f. root of next.

There are prob. two or three different formations: OE. **scite* dung (= MLG. *schite*), *scitte* diarrhœa; also mod.E. dial. *shite* f. the vb. (cf. ON. *skít-r*, MLG. *schit*). The form *shite* now chiefly occurs as an occasional jocular or quasi-euphemistic variant.]

**1. a.** Excrement from the bowels, dung.

*a* *a* **1585** POLWART *Flyting w. Montgomerie* 733 Fond flytter, shit shytter. **1961** F. KING *Custom House* xix. 275 Leave that shit alone! Filthy dog. **1967** P. ROTH *Portnoy's Complaint* (1969) 47 Trying to clear my feet of my undershorts before anybody can peek inside, where.. I always discover in the bottommost seam a pale and wispy brushstroke of my shit. **1973** E. JONG *Fear of Flying* (1974) ii. 25 In general the toilets run swift here and the shit disappears long before you can leap up and turn around to admire it. **1980** K. DOVER *Greeks* ii. 38 We might pick on his revelation of what Greek warfare was like... Blood and shit and pus are the same.. in all ages.

*β* *a* **1732** LD. BINNING *Jolly Hawk* viii. in *North Country Garland* (1824) 52 His s.. te it stinks o' ling! **1971** B. W. ALDISS *Soldier Erect* 137 Do you think Churchill gives a shite for the Fourteenth Army? **1976** *New Musical Express* 17 Apr. 11/4 If you have to spend a lot of time with people who are interested in their chess boards and little card games and shite like that, it can drive you *nuts*.

**b.** A contemptuous epithet applied to a person.

**1508** KENNEDIE *Flyting w. Dunbar* 496 [Thou art] A schit, but wit. *a* **1605** MONTGOMERIE *Flyting w. Polwart* 85 Wanshapen shit. *Ibid.* 365. **1886** *W. Somerset Word-bk.*, *Shit*, a term of contempt. (Very com.) He's a regular shit. Applied to men only. **1889** *N.W. Linc. Gloss.* **1921** D. H. LAWRENCE *Let.* 10 Nov. (1962) II. 673 They are both such abject shits it is a pity they can't be flushed down a sewer. **1922** E. M. FORSTER *Let.* 27 Sept. in P. N. Furbank *E. M. Forster* (1978) II. v. 106, I think that most Indians, like most English people, are shits. **1926** C. CONNOLLY *Let.* 3 Aug. in *Romantic Friendship* (1975) 157 Her son is a complete little shit though.. witty and humorous beyond his years. **1941** J. REITH *Diary* 20 Oct. (1975) v. 281 Beaverbrook—to no one is the vulgar designation shit more appropriately applied —telephoned about park railings. **1956** I. MURDOCH *Flight from Enchanter* xii. 176 'You beastly contemptible shit of a crook,' said Hunter. **1968** *Observer* 29 Sept. (Colour Suppl.) 25/3 We hate the staff here. Keep away from them as much as possible. The shits. **1975** D. LODGE *Changing Places* ii. 67 Is that little shit still shooting his mouth off in there? **1976** J. I. M. STEWART *Young Patullo* viii. 165 She was a third-class harlot who made up for it by being a first-class shit. **1978** J. IRVING *World according to Garp* xii. 217 Oh, I never knew what *shits* men were until I became a woman.

**c.** In negative contexts: Anything. Phr. ***not to give a shit***: not to care at all.

**1922** JOYCE *Ulysses* II. 587 He's a whitearsed bugger. I don't give a shit for him. **1969** W. LABOV in J. E. Alatis *Teaching Standard Eng. to Speakers of Other Languages* (1970) 15 The average whitey out here got everything, you dig? And the nigger ain't got shit, y'know. **1970** *Landfall* (N.Z.) Sept. 218 Nobody gives a shit for nobody. **1973** D. BARNES *See Woman* (1974) I. 19 Don't tell them shit. The skipper is on his way, and he'll decide what to tell them. **1978** K. AMIS *Jake's Thing* iii. 30 An interviewer..being very rude to a politician..and the politician not giving a shit.

**d.** *transf.* Rubbish, trash.

**1930** A. HUXLEY *Let.* 7 Jan. (1969) 326 In every case something precious and lovely had been taken away and replaced by a mound of shit. **1957** I. CROSS *God Boy* (1958) xxii. 192 They just tell me she's in a hospital and that God knows best and all that shit. **1966** L. COHEN *Beautiful Losers* I. 8 Listen, F., don't give me any of your mystical shit. **1976** M. SPARK *Takeover* x. 149 Even if it's shit it gets people thinking about religion. **1977** *Rolling Stone* 5 May 6/2, I enjoyed Simmons' logic that Shakespeare is 'shit' simply because he can't understand it.

**e.** *fig.* Misfortune, unpleasantness. Esp. in phr. ***to be in the shit***: to be in trouble or difficulty.

**1937** PARTRIDGE *Dict. Slang* 758/2 *sh**, in the*, in trouble. **1958** S. BECKETT *Malone Dies* 98 In any case, here I am back in the shit. **1971** B. W. ALDISS *Soldier Erect* 162 We were all in the shit together and it was madness to try and escape it. **1977** *Rolling Stone* 24 Mar. 55/5, I feel really lucky that I've had the opportunity to go through some of the heartaches and shit we've been through the past year.

**f.** An intoxicating or euphoriant drug, *spec.* cannabis, heroin, or marijuana.

**1950** L. RIVERS in *Neurotica* Autumn 45 Senor! You want some shit? How much? Senor, I have great stuff. **1960** J. GELBER *Connection* II. 88 At that time shit was relatively scarce and I had to go out of the city to score. **1972** *Daily Tel.* 3 Apr. 8 Acid (LSD) and 'shit' (cannabis), were on open sale, and..a notice was pinned to a tent stating: 'Anybody with some black shit for sale, ask for Irish Mick.' **1980** S. WILSON *Dealer's War* III. ix. 229 'Hope it's good shit,' I whispered as he swabbed my arm.

**g.** In phrases ***up shit creek***: in an unpleasant situation or awkward predicament (cf. *up the creek* s.v. CREEK *sb.*[1] 2 c); ***shit out of luck***: (see quot. 1942); ***(when) the shit flies*** or ***hits the fan***: alluding to a moment of crisis or its disastrous consequences; ***to beat, kick,*** or ***knock the shit out of*** (someone): to thrash or beat severely; ***to get one's shit together*** (U.S.): to collect oneself, to manage one's affairs.

**1937** J. DOS PASSOS *U.S.A.* I. 70 We're up shit creek now for fair. **1942** BERREY & VAN DEN BARK *Amer. Thes. Slang* §219/10 Unlucky..shit out of luck, (all) washed up. **1966** P. O'DONNELL *Sabre-Tooth* iv. 62 We're all going to be there, where the shit's flying. **1966** L. COHEN *Beautiful Losers* I. 122 Let's beat the shit out of him. **1967** PARTRIDGE *Dict. Slang* Suppl. 1355/2 Wait till the major hears that! Then the shit'll hit the fan! **1968** A. DIMENT *Bang bang Birds* ix. 172 Should the shit hit the fan and the Swedes come over stroppy, he could say..'weren't nothing to do with us, son!' **1969** *Win* 15 May 31/2 We sense the government and its agents daily becoming more ineffective as we get our own shit together. **1971** B. W. ALDISS *Soldier Erect* 260 The Japs ..were meek and respectful... The shit had been knocked out of them. **1973** *Black World* June 62 He sure didn't want a family..to support..just when he was '..gettin' my shit together to finish school'. **1977** H. FAST *Immigrants* III. 171 It's been too quiet. Tomorrow, the shit hits the fan. **1978** M. PUZO *Fools Die* i. 10, I will show you the artist getting the shit kicked out of him for the sake of his art. *Ibid.* xl. 450 So you see, my dear, you're shit out of luck. **1981** *Private Eye* 31 July 11/2 If they'd followed her this far up shit creek it's a long way to walk back.

†**2. a.** Diarrhœa, esp. in cattle. *Obs.*

Cf. the mod. dial. *shoot* with the same meaning (but not etymologically connected).

*c* **1000** *Sax. Leechd.* II. 226 Wiþ þon þe men mete untela melte & ʒecirre on yfele wætan & scittan. *a* **1118** FLORENCE OF WORC. *Chron. ex Chronicis* an. 987 (Thorpe 1848) 148 Lues animalium, quæ Anglice Scitta vocatur, Latine autem fluxus interaneorum dici potest. [Copied by Higden *Polychron.* (Rolls) VII. 50 (with spelling *shitta*). Hence the following quot.] **1387** TREVISA *ibid.* 51 And bestes [had] þe schyt.

**b.** ***the shits***, diarrhœa (in persons). Also *fig.*

**1947** *Amer. Speech* XXII. 305 I'd rather die with the screaming shits. **1967** *Coast to Coast 1965–6* 200 Women have always given me the shits. **1977** *Zigzag* Mar. 8/1 'I've had the shits,' he cried. 'You want to avoid the food.'

**3. a.** Comb.: In terms of abuse, as ***shit-ass, -bag, -breeches, -face, -head, -heel, -pot***; †**shit-word**, abuse; **b. shit-hole** (see quot. 1937); usu. *fig.*; **shit-hot** *a.* (see quot. 1961); also used *loosely* as a term of approbation; **shit-house** a privy; also in *gen.* use as a term of disgust or contempt (freq. *attrib.*); **shit-kicker** *U.S.*, a rustic; **shit-list** (see quots. 1942, 1945); **shit-scared** *a.*, extremely frightened; **shitwork**, (esp. in the language of feminists) work considered to be menial or routine, esp. housework.

**1942** BERREY & VAN DEN BARK *Amer. Thes. Slang* §396 Terms of disparagement..shit-ass. **1971** B. MALAMUD *Tenants* 165 He then cried out, 'Oh what a hypocrite shitass I am to ask a Jew ofay for advice how to express *my* soul work.' **1937** PARTRIDGE *Dict. Slang* 758/2 *Sh**-bag*, the belly; in pl., the guts. **1961** *Ibid.* Suppl. II. 1269/1 *Shit-bag*, ..an unpleasant person. **1968** BETHELL & BURG tr. *Solzhenitsyn's Cancer Ward* I. viii. 121 All he could see was this shitbag wolfing a chicken bone. **1973** Shit-bag [see MENTAL *a.*[1] 1 c]. **1922** JOYCE *Ulysses* 428 Hey, shitbreeches, are you doing the hattrick? **1937** W. L. G. COWAN *Loud Report* II. 97 'Hallo, s—— face.' **1973** M. AMIS *Rachel Papers* 115 'Why,' I wondered, 'did old shitface come round? What was he after?' **1961** PARTRIDGE *Dict. Slang* Suppl. 1269/2 *Shit-head*, an objectionable person. **1971** J. MICHENER in *Reader's Digest* Apr. 240 Again the girls were particularly abusive, taunting the guards, calling them 'shit-heads', 'half-ass pigs'. **1979** P. NIESEWAND *Member of Club* viii. 56 You lying shithead! **1935** J. HARGAN *Gloss. Prison Lang.* 7 *Shitheel*, an inmate who considers himself superior to all the others. **1939** J. STEINBECK *Grapes of Wrath* 212 And Mae, when she is alone with Al, has a name for them. She calls them shit-heels. **1977** H. FAST *Immigrants* VI. 359 You could have sent a registered letter, or that little shitheel of an errand boy, Clancy? **1937** PARTRIDGE *Dict. Slang* 758/2 *Sh**-hole*, the rectum. **1969** A. CORNELISEN *Torregreca* v. 176, I made up my mind early I wasn't going to..spend my life..in one of those shit-holes. **1977** *Zigzag* June 28/3 John went to a Catholic school in Caledonian Road—'a right shit-hole'. **1961** PARTRIDGE *Dict. Slang* Suppl. 1269/2 *Shit-hot*, unpleasantly enthusiastic,..very skilful, cunning, knowledgeable. **1973** M. AMIS *Rachel Papers* 199 They've elected a new guy... I don't know anything about him. Except that he's shit-hot. **1976** *Sounds* 11 Dec. 29/2 Chuck Leavell's pretty damn good all the time, and the rhythm section's still shit-hot. **1795** in G. MacGregor *Coll. Writings of Graham* (1883) II. 247 For honour of the Scots, we have his [Wallace's] effigy in the shite-houses to this very day. **1922** JOYCE *Ulysses* 335 Cute as a shithouse rat. **1972** G. MORLEY *Jockey rides Honest Race* 173 You're probably right ..but I still feel shithouse about it. **1973** J. WAINWRIGHT *Devil you Don't* 46 Have you explained all this shithouse philosophy to the rate-payers? **1976** P. CAVE *High flying Birds* ii. 19 'Nothing wrong with it—safe as a brick-built shithouse,' I assured her. **1977** *Zigzag* Aug. 5/2 If you're banned in town A and then banned in town B, well then town C has just got to ban you or it's, 'well what kind of shithouse place are you running there, councillor?' **1966** *Publ. Amer. Dial. Soc. 1964* XLII. 29 The commonplace generic term for any rustic, *shit kicker*. **1969** L. MICHAELS *Going Places* 23, I was a city boy. No innocent shitkicker from Jersey. **1969** *Rolling Stone* 28 June 14/1 Saturday nights the avid shitkicker can whoop it up. **1942** BERREY & VAN DEN BARK *Amer. Thes. Slang* §336/2 *Blacklist*,..shit or stink list. **1945** *Amer. Speech* XX. 263 In the vulgar talk of the barracks, soldiers uninhibitedly use the phrase *shit list*, for a list of men whom one dislikes and is anxious to see embarrassed or inconvenienced. **1965** *Liberator* Aug. 23/1 Sweet Mac is on my shit list. **1970** R. D. ABRAHAMS *Positively Black* i. 8 Moynihan had made it onto the black shit-list in spite of his obvious sympathies. **1937** PARTRIDGE *Dict. Slang* 758/2 *Sh**-pot*, a thorough or worthless humbug (person); a sneak. **1971** B. MALAMUD *Tenants* 132 Lesser, don't think you so hot, You got the look of a shit-pot. **1958** P. SCOTT *Mark of Warrior* 169 I'm shit-scared stuck up there with all my men gone. **1977** *Rolling Stone* 13 Jan. 12/4 Stewart was 'shit scared' about opening night. *a* **1250** *Owl & Night.* 286 Ʒif ich mid chauling..Hom schende & mid fule worde So herdes doþ oþer mid schit worde. **1968** *No More Fun & Games* Oct. 43 Along with their equal integrated position they can equally misuse their less political sophisticated sisters to do their shitwork. **1972** *Guardian* 30 Mar. 13/3 They call it..'shit work' and they equate it with emptying dustbins and crawling on your belly in a coal mine... The resentment against housework came up like a great surging wave. **1980** D. SPENDER *Man Made Lang.* i. 48 Because of its parallels with housework, Fishman argues that women do the shitwork in conversation.

**c.** *attrib.* or as *adj.*

**1968** H. DAVIES *Beatles* ix. 66, I think it [*sc.* jazz] is shit music, even more stupid than rock and roll. **1971** B. MALAMUD *Tenants* 104 He sat on the bed with a shit smile on his mouth. **1973** BOYD & PARKES *Dark Number* v. 55 'Look, so you've got a crippled leg.'..He winced at that and turned away. 'That was a shit thing to say.'

**shit** (ʃɪt), **shite** (ʃaɪt), *v.* Not now in decent use. Forms: 4 **schite, schete,** 5 **schyte, -yyte,** 4–6 **shyte,** 6 **shyt,** 4– **shite,** 7– **shit;** *Pa. t.* 4 **schoot, schote, shyt,** 5 **shote,** 7— **shit, shat, shitted,** 9– **shit;** *Pa. pple.* 1 **-sciten,** 4 **i-schete, schetun,** 4–8 **shitten,** 9– **shat, shit.** [The form *shite* represents OE. **scítan*, pa. t. **scát*, pa. pple. *-sciten* (in *be-sciten*), corresponding to OFris. **skíta* (NFris. *skĭtj*, pa. t. *skäd*, pa. pple. *skedden*), MLG. *schîten*, Du. *schijten*, OHG. *scîzan* (MHG. *schîzan*, mod.G. *scheissen*), ON. *skíta* (MSw. *skíta*, Da. *skide*), f. OTeut. root **skīt-*. The now more common form *shit* is influenced by the pa. pple. or the related sb.]

**1.** *intr.* To void excrement.

*c* **1308** in *Rel. Ant.* II. 176 Hail be ʒe, skinners, with ʒure drenche kive,..Whan that hit thonnerith, ʒe mote ther in schite. **1387** TREVISA *Higden* (Rolls) IV. 329 Þey wolde.. make hem a pitte..whan þey wolde schite..; and whanne þey hadde i-schete þey wolde fille þe pitte aʒen. *c* **1400** *Lanfranc's Cirurg.* 12 If he may not schite oones a day, helpe him þerto..with clisterie. *c* **1425** *Castle Persev.* 1969 in *Macro Plays* 136 Þei schul schytyn for fere. **1484** CAXTON *Fables of Æsop* v. xv, The wulf..shote thryes by the waye for the grete fere that he had. **1538** BALE *Three Laws* IV. E v b, Whan ye haue hym in hys graue, Stampe hym downe tyll he shyte. ? **1677** VILLIERS (Dk. Buckhm.) *Instalment* Wks. 1705 II. 88 You're such a scurvy..Knight, That when you speak a Man wou'd swear you S——te. *c* **1720** GIBSON *Farrier's Guide* II. xlvii. (1738) 159, I have known a hide-bound Horse shit often, and his excrement soft. *c* **1784** W. BLAKE *Island in Moon* in *Compl. Writings* (1966) 46 'The trumpeter shit in his hat,' said the Epicurean. **1787** BURNS *Death & Dr. Hornbook* xix, Just sh—— in a kail-blade, and send it. **1929** C. CONNOLLY *Let.* Nov. in *Romantic Friendship* (1975) 329 It [*sc.* a kinkajou]..had a genius for sitting where it shat. **1952** M. LOWRY *Let.* 24 Nov. (1967) 323 A seagull has shat on the roof of the convent. **1975** R. HOBAN *Turtle Diary* xlix. 199 Their dogs shitted on the paths. **1976** *Listener* 22 Jan. 92/1 The titillation of finally finding out that great men and women spat and shat and had piles. **1979** *Guardian Weekly* 4 Nov. 21/2 Shat in his pants with fear.

**2.** *trans.* To void as excrement. *lit.* and *fig.*

**13..** *K. Alis.* 5670 The addres shiteth preciouse stones. **1387** TREVISA *Higden* (Rolls) V. 152 [He] sched out his bowels and his lyf wiþ þe dritt þat he schoot [*v.r.* schote]. **1393** LANGL. *P. Pl.* C. x. 264 Þe wolf shiteþ woolle:..lupus lanam cacat. *c* **1450** *Mankind* 561 in *Macro Plays* 21 *Tityuillus*. Mankynde was besy in hys prayere..; I haue sent hym forth to schyte lesynges. **1484** CAXTON *Fables of Æsop* x. xv, I dyde shyte thre grete toordes. **1527** L. ANDREW *Brunswyke's Distill. Waters* C iv b, An ounce for them that spetteth blode, pysseth blode, or shyteth blode. **1659** N. R. *Prov., Eng. Fr.* etc. 68 It is not all butter that the cow shites. **1691** MRS. D'ANVERS *Academia* 5 But that the Devil shites Disasters. *c* **1730** *Round abt. Coal-Fire* 17 He was taken with a sharp griping Pain, which made him sh—t Pins and Needles as he thought. **1978** T. L. SMITH *Money War* (1979) I. 149 The planes..had shit a neat stream of Day-Glo orange bricks.

**3. a.** To defile with excrement. Esp. in phr. ***to shit oneself***: (*a*) to defile oneself with excrement; (*b*) *fig.*, to be afraid.

**1877** *N.W. Linc. Gloss.*, *Shit your breetches*, common redshank; *Totanus calidris*. So called from the cry it makes. **1914** LD. FISHER *Let.* 14 Aug. in M. Gilbert *Winston S. Churchill* (1972) III. *Compan.* I. 35 The French Admiral shot himself. The English Admiral 'shit' himself. **1968** A. DIMENT *Bang Bang Birds* iv. 51 You can shit yourself. I'm not working for you. **1977** *Spare Rib* May 8/3, I was shitting myself before I came, looking for all kinds of excuses. **1980** *Sunday Times* 27 Apr. 42/3, I can easily arrange not to be diverted by knowing when a sorry old man shat himself.

**b.** In slang phrases ***to shit (someone)***: to tease or attempt to deceive; ***to shit a brick***: (see quot. 1961); also as *int.*

**1934** H. MILLER *Tropic of Cancer* 61 Carl looks at me in despair. 'Is he shitting me, that bastard?' **1961** PARTRIDGE *Dict. Slang* Suppl. 1269/1 *Shit*, esp. *be shitting, bricks*, to be really worried,..to be thoroughly frightened. **1965** M. SHADBOLT *Among Cinders* x. 83 'A queer thing. Something psychological.' 'Shit a brick,' he said. **1971** B. W. ALDISS *Soldier Erect* 187 You're shitting me, Jock! You never did it! **1976** H. FERGUSON *Confessions Long Distance Acid Head* 48 By the time I got back to the hospital they were all shitting bricks. **1978** J. KRANTZ *Scruples* vii. 216 'Prince will shit a brick,' Billy said with a giggle. **1979** C. KILIAN *Icequake* iii. 47 Didja see the wave comin' across the Shelf?.. There was a wave. I'm not shittin' you.

**4.** Comb.: **shit-abed**, † (*a*) a term of abuse; (*b*) *dial.* a name for the dandelion (E.D.D.); **shit-breech**, an epithet of abuse applied to a person, also *attrib.*; hence ***shit-breeched*** adj.; **shit-fire**, a contemptuous epithet applied to a hot-tempered person; †**shite-rags, -sticks** (see quot. 1659); †**shit-sack**, an opprobrious name applied to nonconformists (see SHICK-SHACK).

**1690** *Pagan Prince* x. 29 But the Arragonian Bakers..also gave them ill Language, calling them Tooth-Gapers, Sherks, *Shittabeds, Slubber-degullions, [etc.]. **1648** HEXHAM II, *Een Schijt-broeck*, a *Shit-brich. **1675** COTTON *Scoffer Scoft* 92 A Scurvy shit-breech Lad. *Ibid.* 130 Nay even me dost [thou] so enflame Who (Shit-breech) thy own Mother am. **1680** AUBREY in *Lett. Eminent Persons* (1813) III. 383 He..did call the neoteriques s..t-breeches. **1664** COTTON *Scarron.* I. 97 But with a Bow the *Shit-breech'd elfe [Cupid] Would shoot like Robin-Hood himself. **1598** FLORIO, *Cacafuoco*, a hot violent fellow, a *shite-fire. **1659** TORRIANO, *Caca-fuoco*, a shite-fire, by Met. a hot-spur, a rash-headed fellow. **1704** E. WARD *Helter Skelter* 7, I say, Sir, you're a meer Shite-fire. **1598** FLORIO, *Cacastraccie*, a *shite-rags, an idle, lazie, loobie fellow. **1659** TORRIANO, *Caca-sodo, Caca-stecchi, Caca-stracci* [etc.],..a shite-sticks, a shite-rags, that is to say, a miserable pinch-pennie. **1769** J. GRANGER *Biog. Hist. Eng.* Index, *Sh——t Sacks; the occasion of that appellation. **1785** GROSE *Dict. Vulgar T.*, *S——t sack*, a dastardly fellow. **1598** FLORIO, *Cacastecchi*, a hard chuffe, a *shite-sticks.

Hence **ˈshitting, shiting** *vbl. sb.* (also *attrib.*) and *ppl. a.*; **ˈshitter, shiter,** (*a*) one who, or that which, shits; (*b*) a privy; a lavatory pan.

**1386** *Will R. Huberd* (Somerset Ho.), Meliorem patellam meam vocatum schetyngpanne. **1398** TREVISA *Barth. De P.R.* VII. lxix. (1495) 288 That the matere..may be ladde oute..by spewing other by shityng, other by swete. *c* **1440** *Promp. Parv.* 447/1 Schytynge, *stercorizacio*. Schyytynge, or kukkynge vesselle,..*lassarium*. *a* **1585** [see SHIT *sb.* 1]. **1648** HEXHAM II, *Een Schijter*,..a Shiter. **1663** WOOD *Life* June (O.H.S.) I. 477 Sir Charles Sedley being fined 500 *li.* he made answer, that he thought he was the first man that paid for shiting. *a* **1704** T. BROWN *Lett. fr. Dead* II. (1707) 68 Knocking a shiting Porter down..backwards into his own Surreverence. **1952** *Amer. Speech* XXXIII. 270 Here I bring together all the current terms [for 'horse']. The most common are *pony, cayuse, shitter,* and *scate*. **1967** M. SHULMAN *Kill 3* II. iv. 77 You bastard! You shitting little bastard! **1969** R. FERNANDEZ in A. Chapman *New Black Voices* (1972) 380 Markings on a shitter wall. **1971** B. W. ALDISS *Soldier Erect* 168 The blokes say Calcutta's got more whore-houses than it has shitters. **1971** *Black Scholar* Sept. 46/2 He lit a square and sat down on the shitter and tried to collect his thoughts. **1980** L. COOPER *Desirable Residence* xlii. 160 That shitting girl looks at me as if I was dirt.

**shit** (ʃɪt), *int.* Also **shee-y-it, she-it** (emphatic forms), **shite.** [f. the sb. and vb.] **1.** A coarse exclamation of annoyance or disgust.

**1920** JOYCE *Let.* 3 Jan. (1957) I. 134 O shite and onions! When is this bloody state of affairs going to end? **1922** E. E. CUMMINGS *Enormous Room* xi. 219 My father is dead! Shit! Oh, well. The war is over. Good. **1925** D. H. LAWRENCE *Let.* 7 Nov. (1962) II. 865 Why doesn't somebody finally and loudly say Shit! to it all! **1959** 'E. MCBAIN' *87th Precinct* xix. 138 'When I came back, he was gone.' 'Shit,' Willis said. **1969** 'J. MORRIS' *Fever Grass* xvii. 150 'Shit!' Scully said disgustedly. 'Oh, shee-y-it!' **1977** *Time* 14 Nov. 66/3 Aw, she-it, as the street kids say.

2. In trivial use.
**1937** J. Dos Passos *U.S.A.* I. 73 Shit, let's try pick 'em up. **1969** *Private Eye* 23 May 14 Shit! What a lovely scene. **1976** P. Cave *High flying Birds* iii. 42 'Aw, shit. It was nothing,' she muttered, writing the matter off casually.

**shit**: see SHEET *sb.*[1] and *sb.*[2], SHUT.

**shitan, shite**, obs. ff. SHAITAN, SHEET.

**shite-hawk** ('ʃaɪthɔːk). [f. SHIT(E) *sb.* + HAWK *sb.*[1]] **1.** In India, a name used for a kite of the genus *Milvus*. (This sense probably much earlier in oral use.)
**1967** Partridge *Dict. Slang.* Suppl. 1356/2 Shite-hawk. .. A vulture: British Army in India: ca. 1870–1947. **1971** B. W. Aldiss *Soldier Erect* 75 The universal kite-hawks—universally known as 'shite-hawks'—had been plentiful in Kanchapur; in Vadikhasundi, they were two a penny. Like the fly, the shite-hawk was one of India's essential scavengers.
**2.** *transf.* = SHIT *sb.* 1 b.
**1958** M. K. Joseph *I'll soldier no More* iv. 95 That shitehawk... Why can't a man like that be shot like a sick horse. **1981** J. B. Hilton *Playground of Death* v. 64, I liked the man... And yet he was a shite-hawk. He was a journalist.

**shitepoke** ('ʃaɪtpəʊk). *U.S.* Also **shikepoke.** [f. *shite*, SHIT *v.* + POKE *sb.*]
**1.** The small green heron of North America, *Butorides virescens*; also, the black-crowned night heron, *Nycticorax nycticorax*, or the bittern, *Botaurus lentiginosus*.
**1775** *First Bk. Amer. Chron.* ii. 19 They drummed with their drums,..running too and fro like shite-pokes on the muddy shore. *c* **1850** 'Dow Jr.' in Jerdan *Yankee Hum.* (1853) 48 Seagulls, shitepokes, cranes. **1913** [see HOP-TOAD]. **1942** W. Faulkner in *Sat. Even. Post* 28 Mar. 11/3, I..went to the barn and got the slingshot and the shikepoke egg. **1966** *Publ. Amer. Dial. Soc.* XLII. 17 The green heron... Another widely-used name is shitepoke (or shikepoke). **1972** G. Beine *Land of Coyote* 88 A shitepoke waded about searching for frogs.
**2.** (See quot. 1926.)
**1926** in H. Wentworth *Amer. Dial. Dict.* (1944) 550/2 *Shitepoke*,..applied opprobriously to a person. **1936** D. Lutes *Country Kitchen* 19 I'll return it—when they've returned all the molasses and sugar and eggs and everything else they've borrowed in the last year—the old shitepoke.

†**shiterow.** *Obs.* In 4 **schiterow**, 9 *dial.* **shederow.** [f. SHITE *v.*; cf. prec. The latter part may be a corrupt form of HERON.] The heron.
¶ In the Sc. Acts of James VI the word occurs (in a list of game birds prob. repeated from some older enactment) under various corrupt forms as *schidderems*, *schildernes*, *schiwerines*.
**13..** *Nominale* (Skeat) 824 *Un beuee de herouns* A hep of schiterowys. *a* **1827** J. Poole *Gloss. Forth & Bargy, Wexford* (1867) 67 *Shederow*, the heron: a thin weakly person.

**shitless** ('ʃɪtlɪs), *a. coarse slang.* Alluding to a state of extreme fear or physical distress. Esp. in phr. *to be scared shitless.*
**1936** L. Durrell *Spirit of Place* (1969) 42, We're scared shitless because if there's any place Benito wants more than Ethiopia it's Corfu. **1964** L. Auchincloss *Rector of Justin* x. 158 You're scared shitless this little affair will do you out of old Tanager's dough, aren't you? **1971** B. Malamud *Tenants* 62 On my first solo gig I was..beaten shitless, and dumped in jail. **1976** *New Musical Express* 12 Feb. 24/1 The self-appointed custodians of public morality who campaign against pornography because they're simply scared shitless by it.

‖**shittah** ('ʃɪtə). *rare*⁻¹. [Heb. *shiṭṭāh*.
The *ṭṭ* is for prehistoric *nṭ*; cf. Arab. *sanṭ*, OEgyptian *sonṭ*, acacia.]
*shittah tree*: a tree belonging to some species of Acacia, from which SHITTIM wood was obtained.
**1611** Bible *Isa.* xli. 19, I will plant in the wildernes the Cedar, the Shittah tree [1884 (*Revised*) acacia tree].

**shitte, shittell**, obs. ff. SHUT, SHUTTLE.

**shitten** ('ʃɪt(ə)n), *a.* [pa. pple. of SHIT *v.*]
**a.** Defiled with excrement.
*c* **1386** Chaucer *Prol.* 504 And shame it is, if a prest take keepe A shiten [*v.rr.* schetyn, schiten] shepherde and a clene sheepe. **1557** *Welth & Helth* B iij b, I ran my way and let hym syt Smoke and shitten arse together. **1575** *Gamm. Gurton* II. ii. 1 Fy, shytten knaue! and out vpon thee! **1694** Motteux *Rabelais* v. xv. (1737) 58 A shitten Clout. **1738** Swift *Pol. Conversat.* Wks. VI. 276 Why, Miss, you shine this Morning like a sh—— Barn-Door. ? **1750** *Birth*, etc. *John Franks* 18 He came crying into the parlour in his shitten condition,..complaining..that he had beshit himself, and Mary Dover would not clean him.
*Comb.* *a* **1500** *Chester Plays, Innocents* 157 A vyllany it were, I-wisse for my fellow and me, to slay a shitten-arsed shrew. **1694** Motteux *Rabelais* iv. ix. 36 A little shitten-ars'd Girl.
**b.** *transf.* and *fig.* Disgusting, contemptible.
**1546** Bale *Eng. Votaries* I. (1550) 48 b, As though to be a kynge were a farre vyler..offyce, than to be a pylde shytten nonne. **1592** Nashe *Strange News* H 2, Thou grosse shifter for shitten tapsterly iests. **1616** B. Jonson *Epigr.* cxxxiii. *On Famous Voy.*, And all his followers, that..in so shitten sort, so long had vs'd him. **1656** *Choyce Drollery* 34 'Twas shitten luck to perish so. **1702** *Mouse grown a Rat* 24 You and I are in a shitten Condition. **1846** *Swell's Night Guide* 49 Which of us had hold of the crappy (sh-ten) end of the stick? **1931** [see LORD *sb.* 12 d].

Hence †'**shittenly** *adv.*
**1598** Florio, *Cacatamente*,..shittenly.

**shitticism** ('ʃɪtɪsɪz(ə)m). *joc.* [f. SHITTY *a.*, after *witticism*.] A scatological figure of speech.
**1936** R. Frost *Let.* 9 May (1964) 277 My contribution was the witticisms: yours the shitticisms. **1977** *N.Y. Rev. Bks.* 10 Nov. 21/1 On his deathbed Frost forgave Pound his shitticisms.

**shittim** ('ʃɪtɪm). Forms: α. 4 **sychym, sichym, sechym,** 5 **cetyne,** 6 **sethin, (seathin),** 6–7 **sethim,** 7 *Dicts.* **setim, sittim.** β. **shittim.** [a. Heb. *shiṭṭīm*, pl. of *shiṭṭāh*: see SHITTAH. The α forms are from the L. *setim* (Vulg.), appearing in many corrupt forms in the MSS.]
**1.** (More fully ***shittim wood.***) The wood of the shittah-tree, acacia wood.
Sometimes erroneously used for SHITTAH *tree*.
α. **1382** Wyclif *Exod.* xxv. 5 And trees of Sychym [1388 Sechym]. **1398** Trevisa *Barth. De P.R.* xvii. cl. (1495) 704 Sechym is a name..of a tree that is lyke to white thorne in leuys. **1481** Caxton *Reynard* xxxii. (Arb.) 84 The tree in whiche this glas stode..was named cetyne hit sholde endure euer er it wold rote. **1588** Greene *Alcida* (1617) G 2 b, The Sethim wood wil neuer be eaten with wormes. **1616** Bullokar *Eng. Expos.*, *Sethim*, a kinde of tree like a white Thorne. **1656** Blount *Glossogr.*, *Sethim* or *Setim. Sittim.*
*attrib.* **1592** Lodge *Euphues* B j b, Her tongue of a Sethin leafe, that neuer wagges but with a Southeast winde. **1592** Greene *Philomela* (1615) F 3, As if he had..eaten of the seathin roote, that maketh a man to be as cruell in heart, as it is hard in the rynde. **1594** —— *Friar Bacon* III. i, In Frigats bottomd with rich Sethin planks.
β. **1611** Bible *Exod.* xxv. 5 And shittim wood. **1635–56** Cowley *Davideis* II. 330 Near this Halls end a Shittim Table stood. **1856** Stanley *Sinai & Pal.* i. 68 The shittim-wood of the Tabernacle. **1862** —— *Jew. Ch.* (1877) I. vii. 141 The Ark was of shittim, or acacia.
**2.** *U.S.* (See quots.)
**1884** Sargent *Rep. Forests N. Amer.* 41 *Rhamnus Purshiana*,..Shittim wood. *Ibid.* 102 *Bumelia lanuginosa*,.. Shittim wood.

†'**shittle**, *a. Obs.* Forms: 5 **schytylle, -ttyl, schityl,** 6 **shyttell, -ttle,** 6–7 **shittle, shet(t)le,** (9 *dial.*) **shuttle** (see SHUTTLE *a.*), 7 **shickle.** [App. repr. an OE. **scytel*:—prehist. **skutil*, f. **skut-* wk. grade of the root of SHOOT *v.*] **a.** Of persons and their faculties: Inconstant, variable, wavering; fickle, flighty.
*c* **1440** *Promp. Parv.* 444/2 Schey, or skey, as hors, or sty3tyl (*S.* schyttyl, *P.* styrtyll). Schytylle, styrtyl, or hasty (*K.* schityl, on stabyl), *preceps.* **1530** Palsgr. 323/2 Shyttell nat constant, *variable.* **1563** *Mirr. Mag.*, *Collingbourne* iii, We passe not what the people saye or thynke, Theyr shyttle hate maketh none but cowardes shrinke. **1576** Newton *Lemnie's Complex.* II. ii. 97 All which do signify a shuttle waueryng nature, & a mynde subiect to great mutability and vnconstancy. **1583** Golding *Calvin on Deut.* cviii. 662 But our wits are so shettle that we be stil hearkening after this and that. **1589** Nashe *Pasquil's Ret.* D iij, A lyer must haue no shettle memory. **1603** H. Crosse *Vertues Commw.* (1878) 61 There be some that haue such wandring wittes and shittle heads, that neuer rest till they haue assaied all meanes. **1610** R. Tofte *Honours Acad.* To Rdr. ¶ 5 Who knowes not when ought well is, or amis, Of shallowe shickle Braine, a token is. **1617** Moryson *Itin.* III. I. i. 6 The dull brain, the shickle memory. **1638** Heywood *Wise Wom.* III. i, To have my shittle-wits runne a wooll-gathering already? **1650** H. More *Observ.* 79 Did your Sculler, or shittle Skull ever arrive at that Rock of Crystall you boast of?
**b.** Of things: Shaky, unstable.
**1601** Holland *Pliny* xviii. xiv. I. 571 The stalke is very shittle in mowing, and therefore flyeth from the edge of the syth. *a* **1623** W. Pemble *Salomon's Recant.* (1627) 5 The Waters, a shuttle and running substance.
**c.** Comb.: **shittle-brained, -headed, -witted** *adjs.*
**1681** W. Robertson *Phraseol. Gen.* (1693) 277 A light or *shuttle-brained fellow. **1580** Hollyband *Treas. Fr. Tong*, *Volage*, a *shittle headed fellow, an inconstant man. **1583** Golding *Calvin on Deut.* xxiii. 137 If wee goe this way to worke..we shall not be so shettleheaded as wee bee. **1607** Middleton *Five Gallants* iv. vii. G 3, Was euer mistris so plaugd with a shetle-headed seruant. **1448** Marg. Paston in *P. Lett.* I. 69, I am aferd that Jon of Sparham is so *schyttyl wyttyd, that he wyl sett hys gode to morgage. **1577** tr. *Bullinger's Decades* III. v. 330 They therfore are very fooles ..or to vse a more gentle terme, they are shuttle witted. **1613** Tapp *Pathw. Knowl.* 36 See how shittle witted I am, for..I had forgotten it till now.
Hence †'**shittleness.**
**1530** Palsgr. 267/1 Shyttelnesse, *uariableté.* **1573** Baret *Alv.* S 321 The vaine Shittlenesse of an vnconstant head. **1647** Hexham I, Shittlenesse, *ongestadigheyt.*

**shittle, -cock**: see SHUTTLE, -COCK.

**shitty** ('ʃɪtɪ), *a. coarse slang.* [f. SHIT *sb.* + -Y[1].]
**a.** = SHITTEN *a.* b.
**1924** E. Hemingway *Let.* 19 July (1981) 119 In all other arts the more meazly and shitty the guy, i.e. Joyce, the greater the success in his art. **1952** S. Kauffmann *Philanderer* (1953) iv. 65 The first thing we do is change the looks of *Hearts Today.* We keep the same size but we get rid of that shitty confession look. **1970** *Guardian* 18 Nov. 11/6 You keep asking shitty questions that are irrelevant. **1977** *Spare Rib* Sept. 4/3 All the shitty jobs that most women.. do every day of their lives.
**b.** = SHITTEN *a.* a.
**1935** in A. W. Read *Lexical Evidence from Folk Epigr. in W.N. Amer.* 75 This Shithouse stinks like shit Because it is so shitty. **1977** C. McCullough *Thorn Birds* i. 7 If I catch you flaming little twerps touching that doll again I'll brand your shitty little arses!

**shitzu**, var. SHIH-TZU.

**shiur** ('ʃiːuː(r)). [Heb. *šiʻūr* measure, portion.] A lesson in Jewish traditional sources.
**1959** D. D. Runes *Conc. Dict. Judaism* 206/2 *Shiur*, fixed measure; generally used to designate Talmudic study hour. **1967** [see RAV]. **1973** *Jewish Chron.* 9 Feb. 21/4 Like other fortnightly meetings..it began with a shiur on the sidra of the week given by Rabbi Rosin.

**shiv** (ʃɪv), *sb.* Also **shive.** = CHIVE *sb.*[3] Also *attrib.*
**1915** *N.Y. World* 9 May (Suppl.) 14/3 *Shive*, a razor. **1926** J. Black *You can't Win* (1927) vii. 87 'Better get busy with your 'shive', kid.' I started cutting on the side opposite the boarding house. **1926** *Clues* Nov. 162/2 *Shiv*, a knife. **1930** *Sat. Even. Post* 5 Apr. 46/1 Those he does not shoot he sticks with his shiv—which is a knife. **1951** F. Brown *Murder can be Fun* viii. 120, I won't use no shiv. I'll take him apart with my bare hands. **1959** 'M. Ainsworth' *Murder is Catching* vi. 72 Has he any criminal connections...could he get hold of shiv-boys, for instance? **1959** H. Hobson *Mission House Murder* xiii. 88 He held a white-handled open razor... "Strewth!" he said, 'a shiv!' **1972** *Daily Progress* (Charlottesville, Va.) 17 Feb. B. 11/5 The guards even planted a 'shive'—a tableknife—in McKinney's cell. **1976** L. Deighton *Twinkle, twinkle, Little Spy* ix. 89, I never heard of the K.G.B. using a shiv artist who hit the wrong target, and..let them grab the knife.

**shiv** (ʃɪv), *v.* Also **shive.** = CHIVE *v.*
**1926** [see JAM *sb.*[1] 1 b]. **1959** 'M. Ainsworth' *Murder is Catching* xv. 163 The boys been shiving you? **1967** 'E. Queen' *Face to Face* xxx. 136 'When was that?' 'The night they found Spotty shivved.' **1980** J. Wainwright *Venus Fly-Trap* 165 Two guys. So much hatred—eh? One shivs the other.

**shiva(h** ('ʃɪvə). [Heb. *šibʻâ* seven.] A period of seven days' mourning for the dead, beginning immediately after the funeral; *to sit shiva*, to observe this period. Also *attrib.*
**1892** I. Zangwill *Childr. Ghetto* I. 177 If you had come round when he was sitting *Shivah* for Benjamin—peace be upon him!—you would have known. **1910** *Jewish Chron.* 29 Apr. 15/2 As an orthodox family we 'sat shiva'; and we took to the low seats with great heaviness of heart and in utter distress. **1938** *Ibid.* 10 June 15/2 The mourners requested that three 'shiva' chairs be sent to the house. **1959** B. Kops *Hamlet of Stepney Green* II. i. 33 The Shiva is starting soon. Oh, those seven days of mourning. **1964** D. Gray *Devil wore Scarlet* vi. 41 For seven days from the day of the funeral onwards a Jewish family sits Shiva. They sit on low stools in the drawing-room..and they sort of receive their friends and relations and get their sympathy. **1976** B. Williams *Making of Manchester Jewry* xi. 279 Members paid..4*d* a week, which entitled them..to *shiva* benefits, and to free burial. **1977** *New Yorker* 23 May 38/3 Elka's husband, Yontche, died, but Elka didn't observe shivah.

**Shivaism, -ite**, var. ff. SIVAISM, SIVAITE.

**shivaree** (ʃɪvə'riː), *sb. U.S.* and *Cornwall.* Also **shiveree.** Corrupt form of CHARIVARI *sb.* Also *fig.*
**1805** J. F. Watson in *Amer. Pioneer* (1843) May 229 When a *sherrie-varrie* is announced, it is done by a running cry through the streets. **1843** 'R. Carlton' *New Purchase* II. lv. 231 The musicians..letting off at each repetition of the demand peals of shiver-ree. **1876** 'Mark Twain' *Old Times* 55, I started such a rattling 'shivaree' down below as never had astounded an engineer in this world before. **1881** —— *Tramp Abroad* xxxii, She turned on all the horrors of the 'Battle of Prague', that venerable shivaree, and waded chin-deep in the blood of the slain. **1883** *Cassell's Sat. Jrnl.* I. 76 It was a shiveree—that is, the kind of serenade they give to a newly-married couple. **1926** Galsworthy *Silver Spoon* III. v. 251 And now came the usual 'shivaree' about such and such a case. **1942** A. L. Rowse *Cornish Childhood* 9 The most splendid of 'shivarees' given at Tregonissey was for the wedding of Eliza Dyer to Eneas (pronounced Enas) Kellow. **1966** G. E. Evans *Pattern under Plough* xi. 115 It was called the *Kiddly Band* in Cornwall..and it took part in the *shivaree* or wedding junketings there until the 'twenties. **1977** *Western Morning News* 30 Aug. 6/4 There was another word for a shallal: perhaps imported, or re-imported, from America. This is a shivaree, probably a corruption of charivari.
Hence **shiva'ree** *v. trans.*, to greet or serenade with a 'shivaree'.
**1805** J. F. Watson in *Amer. Pioneer* (1843) May 229 Edward Livingston, esq., was *sherri-varried* here; on which occasion the parties came out promptly to the balcony and thanked the populace for their attention. **1872** E. Eggleston *End of World* xlvi. 294 Among the manly recreations which they have proposed to themselves is that of shivereeing 'that Dutchman, Gus Wehle'. **1879** G. W. Cable *Old Creole Days* (1883) 132 'What is it you call this thing where an old man marries a young girl, and you come out with horns and ——' '*Charivari?*' asked the Creoles. 'Yes, that's it. Why don't you shivaree him?' **1910** *Guide* July 139/1 A crowd of the more riff-raff and ignorant foreigners..started out to 'shivaree' (mob and din to madness) the dreaded old man.

**shive** (ʃaɪv), *sb.*[1] Chiefly *dial.* Forms: 3 **schive,** 4–6 **shyve,** 5 **schyfe, schyve,** 4– **shive.** [ME. *schīve* (? repr. OE. **scīfe* wk. fem.) = OFris. *skîve* (only in *knê-skîve* knee-cap), OS. *scîva* (glossing *sphera*), MLG., MDu. *schîve* (mod.Du. *schijf*) fem., OHG. *scîba* (MHG. *schîbe*, mod.G. *scheibe*); also (prob. from LG.) Sw. *skifva*, Da. *skive*, Icel. *skífa.* The senses in mod. continental Teut. are quoit, disc, knee-cap, pulley, window-pane, slice of bread, etc. Cf. the str. vb. MHG. *schîben* (early mod.G. *scheiben*) to roll, to spin on an axis; but this is prob. f. the sb. The weak grade *skib- of the root is represented by SHEAVE *sb.*[1]

Affinities outside Teut. are uncertain. The Gr. σκοῖτος (Hesych.) is often cited as cognate, but the alleged sense 'potter's wheel' is a mistake; the gloss appears to mean 'the projecting part of the beams supporting roof-tiles'.]

**1.** A slice (of bread; rarely of other edible).

**a 1225** *Ancr. R.* 416 Gif heo mei sparien eni poure schreaden [MS. T. schiue], sende ham al derneliche ut of hire woanes. **c 1330** *Spec. Gy de Warewyke* 970 Bring me wid þe a shiue bred! **c 1440** *Alphabet of Tales* 525 þe preste bad hym cut shyvis of bread and fyll a kyste þerwith and lokk it. **1562** TURNER *Herbal* II. 23 The rootes [of Iris]..are cut in litle shiues or cakes. **1581** DERRICKE *Image Irel.* II. F ij, And with the same [stabbers] thei slashe me out, good God what preatie shiues. Not shiues of bread I meane..But gobbes of fleshe. **1607** T. D[EKKER?] & WILKINS *Jests* 12 Michaelmas tearme you know is like a great houshold loafe, you may cut out a good many shiues, and yet feede vpon it well too. **1703** THORESBY in Ray *Philos. Lett.* (1718) 336 A Shive of Bread, cut off the Loaf. **1825** *Blackw. Mag.* XVIII. 155 A mere wafer of fatless ham, between the finest shives of bread. **1851–61** MAYHEW *Lond. Labour* II. 227 Thick 'shives' of bread.

†**2.** The knee-cap, patella. *Obs.*

**1597** A. M. tr. *Guillemeau's Fr. Chirurg.* 12/3 The shive of the knee, Lat. *Patella.*

†**3.** A pane of glass. [? After LG. *schîve.*] *Obs.*

**1527** ANDREW *Brunswyke's Distyll. Waters* B j, The great rounde shyves of Venys glas.

**4.** A thin flat cork for stopping a wide-mouthed bottle; also a thin bung for a cask.

**1869** W. MOLYNEUX *Burton-on-Trent* 247 [The cask] is then closed with a wooden 'shieve' or bung. **1876** *Encycl. Brit.* IV. 275/2 Ales intended to be stored some months should have a porous vent peg placed in the shive.

*attrib.* **1901** *Daily Chron.* 3 Dec. 10/6 Advt., Shive Turner wanted by a leading London brewery.

†**5.** A piece (of wood) split off, a billet. [? Confused with SHIDE or SHIVER.] *Obs.*

**1661** BOYLE *Scept. Chym.* VI. 401 The shavings..differing from those shives or thin and flexible pieces of wood that are obtain'd by Borers. **1786** COWPER *Odyss.* XIV. 518 Then lifting a huge shive [Gr. σχίζῃ δρυός] that lay beside The fire, he smote the boar, and dead he fell.

**shive** (see below), *sb.*[2] Also 9 shiv. See also SHEAVE *sb.*[2] [= WFlem. *schif* (for other cognates see SHEAVE *sb.*[2]), f. Teut. root *skif- to split, whence SHIVER *sb.*[1]]

**1.** With pronunc. (ʃɪv). A particle of husk; a splinter; a piece of thread or fluff on the surface of cloth, etc.; *pl.* the refuse of hemp or flax. *Obs.* exc. *dial.*

**1483** *Cath. Angl.* 337/2 Schyfes (*A.* schyffes) of lyne, *stupa, napta.* **1601** HOLLAND *Pliny* XIX. i. II. 4 What shall bee done with all the hard refuse [of the Flax], the long buns of the stalkes, the short shuds or shives. **1672** HOOLE *Comenius' Visible World* lix. 121 Where the Shives [*cortices*] fall down, then they are heckled with an Iron Heckle. **1695** WOODWARD *Nat. Hist. Earth* II. (1723) 81 The Shiv's or Chaff of the *Juli* of Trees and Shrubs. **1855** *Whitby Gloss.*, *Shivs*, husks of grain and such like particles.

**2.** With pronunc. (ʃaɪv). *Paper-making.* A dark particle in finished paper resulting from incomplete digestion of impurities in the raw material; such particles collectively. Cf. SHEAVE *sb.*[2] 3.

**1922** *Manuf. Pulp & Paper* III. VIII. 1 The difference between shives and slivers should be clearly understood. **1937** E. J. LABARRE *Dict. Paper & Paper-Making Terms* 207/2 *Sheave*, also spelt *shive*..are dark specks in the finished paper, due to impurities in raw materials, rags and esparto grass, [etc.]..., hence 'shivery' or 'shivey' paper. **1952** F. H. NORRIS *Paper & Paper Making* xx. 291 Shives are usually light in colour..and..shaped like a minute splinter. **1968** R. R. A. HIGHAM *Handbk. Papermaking* (ed. 2) ii. 79 Shive, knots..and similar impurities, cause breaks in the web.

**3.** *Comb.*: **shivelight** *nonce-wd.*, a sliver of light.

**1888** G. M. HOPKINS *Poems* (1967) 105 Shivelights and shadowtackle in long lashes lace, lance, and pair.

†**shive**, *v.*[1] *Obs.* [f. SHIVE *sb.*[1] Cf. ON. *skífa.*] *trans.* To cut (bread) into slices.

**1570** LEVINS *Manip.* 152/39 To shiue, *dissecare.* **1629** GAULE *Holy Madn.* 343 He shiues out his Bread by weight or measure.

†**shive**, *v.*[2] *Obs.*$^{-0}$ [f. SHIVE *sb.*[2]] *trans.* To 'break' (hemp, flax).

**1483** *Cath. Angl.* 337/2 To schyfe, *extupare.*

**shive**, variant of CHIVE *sb.*[2] *Obs.*

**1599** A. M. tr. *Gabelhouer's Bk. Physicke* 58/2 Heerof thou shalt alwayes after meales eate a discided shive of Fennelle. **1639** O. WOOD *Alph. Bk. Secrets* 92 Adding..three shives of Saffron undried.

**shive**, see SHIV *sb.*, *v.*

**shiveau** (ʃɪ'vəʊ). *dial.* Now *rare* or *Obs.* exc. as SHIVOO. Also 8 **chevaux**, 9 **chiveau**, **shebo**, **sheevo**. [Origin unknown.] = SHIVOO.

**1798** C. CATHCART *Let.* 6 May in Fraser & Gibbons *Soldier & Sailor Words* (1925) 255 We have just left Gibraltar... Sir John Orde gave a grand chevaux to which he was so good as to invite me. **1828** 'JON BEE' *Living Pict. Lond.* ii. 83 A pressing invitation to what he calls a '*Chiveau*', or merry dinner. **1849** A. HARRIS *Emigrant Family* I. vii. 114 A 'shiveau' at the hut. **1862** C. C. ROBINSON *Dial. Leeds* 402 *Sheevo*, a shindy. 'A bonny sheevo thuh wor.' **1877** F. Ross et al. *Gloss. Words Holderness* 123/2 We'd a meetin i vesthry las' neet aboot a new cess, and them at didn't want yan kick'd up a riglar *shebo.* **1880** M. A. COURTNEY *Gloss. W. Cornwall* 50/2 *Shee-vo*, a disturbance; a row. 'There was such a grand *shee-vo.*'

**shiver** ('ʃɪvə(r)), *sb.*[1] Forms: **3 scifre, scivre, 4 schivere, 4–6 shyver, 5 schyver(e, schevyre, schyvyr, 5–6 shever, 6 shyvere, shiever, 6– shiver.** [Early ME. *scifre*, cogn. w. OHG. *scivero* wk. masc., splinter (MHG. *schiver(e, schever(e* splinter, mod.G. *schiefer* slate, short for *schieferstein*), f. Teut. root *skif- to split, whence SHEAVE *sb.*[2], SHIVE *sb.*[2]]

**1.** A fragment, chip, splinter. Now *rare* exc. in phrases: see b.

**c 1205** LAY. 27784 Sceld aȝein scelden sciuren þer wunden. **c 1400** *Ywaine & Gaw.* 3234 It was na wapen that man might welde Might get a shever out of thair shelde. **1525** BERNERS *Froiss.* II. lxxviii. 234 Syr Raynolde du Roy brake his spere in iiii. peces, and ye sheuers flewe a grete hyght into ye ayre. **1576** NEWTON *Lemnie's Complex.* I. vii. 53 A splint or shyuer of a broken speare. **1723** *Present St. Russia* I. 119 They use no Candles, but long Shivers of Wood. **1810** SCOTT *Lady of L.* III. iv, A heap of withered boughs was piled, Of juniper and rowan wild, Mingled with shivers from the oak. **1885** TENNYSON *Balin* 108 Thorns of the crown and shivers of the cross.

*fig.* **1649** JER. TAYLOR *Gt. Exemp.* III. Ad. Sect. 16. 180 The Church gathering up..the shivers of the broken heart may reunite them.

**b.** Phrases. ***in shivers***, broken, in small fragments (so ***to break, burst***, etc. ***in*** or ***into shivers***); ***(all) to shivers***, into small fragments; †***to go shivers***, to be shattered to pieces.

**c 1205** LAY. 4537 Scip ærne to-ȝen scip þa hit al to-wonde to scifren. **13..** *Guy Warw.* 7213 Wiþ þe spere he him smot smertliche..þat alto schiueres it to-fleye. **1470–85** MALORY *Arthur* II. v. 82 The Irysshe knyght smote Balyn on the sheld that alle wente sheuers of his spere. **1589** GREENE *Tullies Love* Wks. (Grosart) VII. 109 The boult rebounded and brake into a thousand shiuers. **1626** BACON *Sylva* § 10 If you strike or pierce a Solid Body, that is brittle,..it breaketh not onely, wher the immediate force is; but breaketh all about into shiuers. **1769** GRAY *Let. to Wharton* 18 Oct., The rocks at top deep-cloven perpendicularly, by the rains, hanging loose and nodding forwards, seem just starting from their base in shivers. **1823** SCORESBY *Jrnl.* 443 The other ship..endeavouring to set his main-top-sail, it blew to shivers. **1883** LD. R. GOWER *Remin.* II. xxix. 303 The thunder crashed and tore itself into shivers overhead.

*fig.* **1658** CLEVELAND *Rust. Ramp.* 2 And had not Providence held back the hand, the blow had faln, the Government had broke into shivers then. **1852** H. ROGERS *Ecl. Faith* (1853) 135 Yet this faculty uniformly yields—goes into shivers in the encounter!

**c.** *spec.* A flake or splinter of stone (e.g. one knocked off in stone-dressing). Now *Sc.* and *dial.*

**1600** SURFLET *Country Farm* III. xlvi. 517 Put in the clefts some shiuers of hard stone. **1708** J. C. *Compleat Collier* (1845) 22 The Shivers or Splints of the Whin or hard Stone. **1861** STEPHENS & BURN *Farm-Buildings* 243 A ditcher's shovel is also useful to him in putting the shivers of the stones together into heaps.

†**2.** ? A loose fibre or filament in undressed hemp. *Obs.* Cf. SHIVE *sb.*[2]

**1440** *Wyclif's Bible, Josh.* ii. 6 [Forsothe sche made the men to stie in to the soler of hir hows, and hilide hem with stobil] or schyueres [of flex, that was there]. **1615** MARKHAM *Eng. Housew.* iii. 97 You shall beate out all the loose buns and shiuers that hang in the Hempe or Flaxe. **1794** *Rigging & Seamanship* I. 56 *Shivers*, the foul particles taken from the hemp when hatchelling.

**3.** Any kind of stone of a slaty or schistous character. [Perh. a. G. *schiefer*; cf. SHIFFER.]

**1729** WOODWARD *Attempt Nat. Hist. Fossils* I. I. 18 Shiver, of a dark Ash-Colour, near Black. **1789** J. WILLIAMS *Min. Kingd.* II. 10 Some varieties of the schists or shivers are of the same colour and quality as the slates. **1829** *Glover's Hist. Derby* I. 46 Shale or shiver..A black laminated clay, much indurated. **1881** RAYMOND *Mining Gloss.*, *Shiver.* 1. Shale; a hard argillaceous bed. 2. See *Sheave.*

*attrib.* **1804** JAMESON *Syst. Min.* I. 9 Slate spar, or shiver spar. [Ger.] Schieferspath.

**shiver** ('ʃɪvə(r)), *sb.*[2] Forms: **4 schivere, shyvere, schever, 4–5 schiver, schevere, 5 schevyr, schevre, schyver(e, shefure, 5–6 shyver, 5–8 shever, 6 shiffer, 7 shivar, shivor, 7–9 sheever, 6– shiver.** [ME. *schivere*, f. Teut. root *skib- of SHEAVE *sb.*[1], SHIVE *sb.*[1]]

†**1.** = SHIVE *sb.*[1] 1. *Obs.*

**13..** *Sir Beues* (A) 1826 Now ich wolde ȝeue hit [i.e. Arondel] kof For a schiuer of a lof! **c 1386** CHAUCER *Sompn. T.* 132 'Now dame' quod he,..'Haue I nat of a capon but the lyuere And of youre softe breed nat but a shyuere'. **c 1430** *Two Cookery-bks.* 40 Whan it is cold, larde it, & schere on schevres. **1525** *Test. Ebor.* (Surtees) V. 209 An halpeny white loffe and a shiffer of chese. **1656** W. DU GARD tr. *Comenius' Gate Lat. Unl.* 269 Rolls of bread taken out of the basket, or shivers cut out of the loaf. **a 1721** PRIOR *Erle Robert's Mice* 50 Therein eke may Both be fed With Shiver of the Wheaten Bread. **1753** *Phil. Trans.* XLVIII. 87 [It] left large spots..on that side whence the shivers were taken off.

**b.** *fig.* and in fig. context.

**1594** O. B. *Quest. Profit. Concern.* 4 b, The Moncks and Abbots of my knowledge, cut large shivers of the loafe for which they neuer sweate, to make themselues strong in the peoples favour and opinion. **1655** FULLER *Ch. Hist.* III. 55 His [*sc.* the Pope's] intolerable extortions; which, how great soever, were but a large shiver of that loaf, which he had given into the Kings hand.

**2.** A pulley: = SHEAVE *sb.*[1] 2.

**1485** *Cely Papers* (Camden) 176 For brassyn schyver for the schype, xxiiij d. **1495** *Naval Acc. Hen. VII* (1896) 192 Snache poleyes with oon shever of brasse to ye same. **1514** in Oppenheim *Adm. Royal Navy* (1896) I. 373 Ramehedes with ij shevers of Brasse. **1578** *Nottingham Rec.* IV. 52 An ironmonger of smale made wares, *videlicet*, of nayles, horse shues, slyppes, shyuers, spade shoes [etc.]. **1615** R. COCKS *Diary* (Hakl. Soc.) I. 94 To have had his advice about bras shivers. **1800** *Trans. Soc. Arts* XVIII. 232 The pulleys, or shivers. **c 1850** *Rudim. Navig.* (Weale) 147 Shivers to stand nearly athwartships.

†**3.** The breastplate of a plough. *Obs.*

**1652** W. BLITH *Eng. Improver Improved* II. xxviii. (1653) 192 [Parts of a Plough.] 1. The Share, 2 the Coulter, 3 the Shield or Breast-plate (as some call them) Shivers. *Ibid.* 194 A Shiver [*printed* Shiner] or Breast-plate.

**shiver** ('ʃɪvə(r)), *sb.*[3] [f. SHIVER *v.*[2]]

**1.** An act or a condition of shivering; a quivering or trembling, esp. of the body under the influence of cold, emotion, etc. Phrase, ***(all) in a shiver.***

**1727** [E. DORRINGTON] *Philip Quarll* 163 High Mountains of Ice, which echo'd with Shivers. **1835** *Comic Almanack* Jan. (1870) 4 When you first go to bathe, gentle Sir, in a river, If you dip in one foot, it will give you a shiver. **1852** MRS. STOWE *Uncle Tom's C.* viii, You are cold, and all in a shiver. **1863** MRS. OLIPHANT *Salem Chapel* x. 161 Shivers of restrained emotion ran through the astonished audience. **1876** HARDY *Ethelberta* xliv, She closed her eyes in a white shiver.

**b.** *transf.* and *fig.*

**1860** MOTLEY *Netherl.* ii. I. 31 Germany was in a shiver at every breeze from East and West. **1876** GEO. ELIOT *Dan. Der.* xxxix, With a sort of mental shiver.

**2.** *(the) shivers*: an attack of shivering; often spec. the ague.

**1861** DICKENS *Gt. Expect.* iii, I'll beat the shivers so far, I'll bet you. **1882** MISS BRADDON *Mt. Royal* xxx, I only know that I get the shivers every time I sit in your drawing-room. **1888** *Century Mag.* May 28/2 It gives me the cold shivers when I think what might have become of me. **1899** *Allbutt's Syst. Med.* VIII. 658 The beginning [of hydroa gestationis] is sometimes marked by shivers, illness and fever.

**shiver** ('ʃɪvə(r)), *v.*[1] Forms: α. **3 shivre, 4 schiver(e, 4–5 schyver, 5 shifer, 4–6 shyver, shiever, 6– shiver**; β. **4–5 schever, 5 schevere, scheffer, (chever), 4–6 shever, 7 shevire, shaver.** [f. SHIVER *sb.*[1] Cf. MDu. *scheveren*, MHG. *schiveren* (G. *schiefern*).]

**1.** *trans.* To break or split into small fragments or splinters.

α. **c 1200** [see TO-SHIVER *v.*]. **c 1350** *Will. Palerne* 3411 Mani a spere spacli on peces were to-broke, & many a schene scheld scheuered al to peces. **c 1400** *Ywaine & Gaw.* 3539 Thair sheldes war shiferd and helms rifen. **1530** PALSGR. 704/1, I whyl shyver this blocke into small chyppes. **c 1586** C'TESS PEMBROKE *Ps.* LXXVI. i, Their bow, and shaft, and shield, and sword he shivered. **1621** G. SANDYS *Ovid's Met.* III. (1632) 82 What would haue..shiuered towres, doth giue no wound at all. **1711** STEELE *Spect.* No. 32 ¶2 How many impartial Looking-Glasses had been censured and calumniated, nay, and sometimes shivered into ten thousand Splinters. **1815** J. SMITH *Panorama Sci. & Art* II. 227 The glass, under this management, is generally shivered into small pieces. **1837** CARLYLE *Fr. Rev.* I. VII. vii, Or rusty firelocks belch after him, shivering asunder his—hat. **1843** —— *Past. & Pr.* IV. iv. 369 Ye have shivered mountains asunder. **1876** *Jrnl. Franklin Inst.* Jan. 30 The mail cars were completely crushed and shivered.

β. **a 1400** *Morte Arth.* 1813 Schotte thorowe the schiltrouns, and scheverede launcez. **a 1548** HALL *Chron., Hen. VI*, 105 b, The sonne of the Master gonner..fired the gonne, whiche brake & shevered ye yron barres of the grate. **1598** *Mucedorus* Induct. 22 Ile thunder musicke shall appale the nimphes, And make them sheuer their clattering strings. **1688** R. HOLME *Armoury* III. xvii. (Roxb.) 113/2 A Lance broken, or shavered in the middle.

**b.** *fig.* and in fig. context. Also with *out.*

**a 1593** MARLOWE tr. *Lucan* I. 85 O Roome thy selfe art cause of all these euils, Thy selfe thus shiuered out to three mens shares. **1631** LENTON *Charact.* C 4 b, Diseases at last dry vp her marrow, and rottennesse so shiuers her, that shee drops asunder on a sudden, and wretchedly dyes without pitty. **1639** FULLER *Holy War* IV. viii. (1640) 181 He found the Christians there shivered into severall factions. **1871** FREEMAN *Hist. Ess.* Ser. I. vii. 197 At last the might and the hopes of Charles were shivered beneath the halbert of the free Switzer.

**c.** ***shiver my timbers***: a mock oath attributed in comic fiction to sailors.

**1835** MARRYAT *J. Faithful* ix, I won't thrash you Tom. Shiver my timbers if I do.

**2.** *intr.* To fly in pieces; to split.

α. **c 1330** R. BRUNNE *Chron. Wace* (Rolls) 13829 þeir schaftes schiuered, & fleye in feld. **c 1386** CHAUCER *Knt.'s T.* 1747 Ther shyueren shaftes vpon sheeldes thikke. **c 1430** *Chev. Assigne* 315 þe speres..shyuereden to peces. **1581** J. BELL *Haddon's Answ. Osor.* 34 b., Will at lenth bryng all his other buildyng to ruine, and cause it to shiuer in peeces to the grounde. **1605** SHAKS. *Lear* IV. vi. 51 Had'st thou beene ought But Gozemore, Feathers, Ayre, (So many fathome downe precipitating) Thoud'st shiuer'd like an egge. **1768** GRAY *Fatal Sisters* vi, Ere the ruddy sun be set Pikes must shiver, javelins sing. **1837** CARLYLE *Fr. Rev.* I. VII. x, The panels shivering in, like potsherds. **1879** FROUDE *Cæsar* xxvi. 460 As he crossed the hall, his statue fell, and shivered on the stones.

β. **c 1402** LYDG. *Compl. Blk. Knt.* 46 So loude songe that al the wode ronge, Lyke as hyt sholde sheuer in pesis smale. **1523** BERNERS *Froiss.* I. ccxix. 282 The two knyghtes mette rudely togeyder, soo that their speares sheuered all to peaces.

*fig.* **1638** MAYNE *Lucian* (1664) 2 Since my works are as frail, and brittle as their pots, and are ready to shiver and break, upon the least dash of a stone. **1645** MILTON *Colast.* 10 His eighth Argument shivers in the uttering.

†**b.** To send *down* (débris) by crumbling. *Obs.*

**1759** B. MARTIN *Nat. Hist. Eng.* II. 235 This Hill is almost perpetually shivering down Earth and great Stones.

**3.** *intr.* Of stone: To split along the natural line of cleavage. [? After G. *schiefern.*]

**1728** CHAMBERS *Cycl.* s.v. *Vein*, Veins, in stones, are often a defect, proceeding usually from an inequality.. which makes the stone crack, and shiver in those parts. **1826** W. A. MILES *Deverel Barrow*, etc. 51 Its [*i.e.* Kimmeridge coal money's] great tendency to destructibility and of shivering laminally, would be a bar to its ever having been a coinage intended to pass from hand to hand.

**shiver** (ˈʃɪvə(r)), *v.*$^{2}$ Forms: α. 3–4 chivere, chievere, 5–6 chyver, chever; β. 5–6 shyver, shever, 6 shiever, 8 schiver, 6– shiver. [Early ME. *chivere*, of obscure etymology.

It may be doubtfully suggested that the word may originally have had reference to the chattering of the teeth from cold (cf. *to chevere with the chin*, quot. *c* 1475 below), and that (with the app. synonymous CHIVEL *v.*) it is connected with early ME. *cheovele, chefle* to wag the jaws, chatter (see CHAVEL *v.*), f. OE. *ceafl* jaw (see JOWL). The ending *-el* may have been assimilated to the suffix -ER$^{5}$, common in verbs expressing tremulous movement; cf. however MHG. *kiver* (G. *kiefer*) beside *kivel* jaw. The change of *ch* to *sh* may have been due to the frequent association with *shake.*]

**1.** *intr.* To tremble, shake, quiver; esp. to tremble with cold or fear.

α. *c* **1250** *Death* 142 in *O.E. Misc.* 176 For ich schal bernen in fur, and chiuerin in ise. **1390** GOWER *Conf.* III. 9 Thanne comth the blanche fievere With chele and makth me so to chievere. *a* **1400** *Leg. Rood* (1871) 144 Þe temple walles gan chiuere and schake, Veiles in þe temple a-two þei sponne. *c* **1475** *Rauf Coilȝear* 96 My Gaist and I baith cheueris with the chin, So fell ane weddir feld I neuer. **1530** PALSGR. 483/2, I chever, as one dothe that is in an axes whan the colde cometh on hym.

β. *c* **1402** LYDG. *Compl. Blk. Knt.* 230 With hote and colde my acces ys so meynt, That now I shyuer for defaute of hete. *c* **1489** CAXTON *Sonnes of Aymon* x. 259 All his body shevered all sodenly for grete ioye. **1562** A. BROOKE *Romeus & Iuliet* 370 And now for feare she sheuereth, and now for loue she burnes. **1667** MILTON *P.L.* x. 1003 Why stand we longer shivering under feares That show no end but Death? **1749** SMOLLETT *Gil Blas* VII. i. (1782) III. 7 He drew his long rapier, which made me shiver. **1833** HT. MARTINEAU *Charmed Sea* i. 3 The pines are stooping and shivering on all the hills around. **1866** GEO. ELIOT *Felix Holt* I. i. 44 Under the cold weight of these thoughts Mrs. Transome shivered. **1878** SUSAN PHILLIPS *On Seaboard* 185 Where the sea-pinks grow, And the dry rushes shiver in the sand.

**b.** *fig.* or in fig. context.

**1649** MILTON *Tenure Kings* 4 [They] begin to swerve and almost shiver at the majesty and grandeur of som noble deed, as if they were newly enter'd into a great sin. **1878** J. S. CAMPION *On Frontier* (ed. 2) 27 The air shivered with noise; the earth trembled under our feet.

**2.** *trans.* (causative.) †**a.** To give a sensation of chill to, to cause (a person or object) to shiver.

*c* **1200** [see SHIVERING *ppl. a.*$^{2}$ 1]. **1797–1805** S. & HT. LEE *Canterb. T., Old Woman's T.* I. 354 A waking dream of horrors, not unlike that which had disturbed his sleep, seemed to shiver his senses.

**b.** †To cause (one's jaws) to tremble (*obs.*); to pour out or give forth with a trembling motion.

*a* **1693** *Urquhart's Rabelais* III. xx. 167 Diddering and shivering his Chaps, as Apes use to do. **1821** CLARE *Vill. Minstr.* II. 167 Where tiny blossoms with a purple bell Shiver their beauties to the autumn-gale. *a* **1861** T. WOOLNER *My Beautiful Lady, Storm* ii, Quiet are the birds In ghostly trees that shiver not a sound.

**3.** *Naut.* **a.** *intr.* Of a sail: To flutter or shake (in the wind).

**1769** FALCONER *Dict. Marine* (1780) s.v. *Tack*, The head-sails are immediately made to shiver in the wind. **1809** BYRON *Bards & Rev.* liii, The sail.. is shivering in the gale. **1891** *Patterson's Naut. Dict.* I. s.v., A vessel's sails are said to shiver when she is luffed so close that the wind is spilled out of them.

**b.** *trans.* To cause (a sail) to flutter or shake in the wind, to bring a sail edge-on to the wind.

**1769** FALCONER *Dict. Marine* II. (1780), *Déventer les voiles*, to shiver the sails, or brace them so as to shiver in the wind. **1875** BEDFORD *Sailor's Pocket-bk.* iii. (ed. 2) 59 Shiver the mizen topsail or brail up the spanker.

**4.** To quiver, to tremble with a shrinking movement.

*c* **1869** ADM. PAGET *Autobiog.* (1896) 221 The gory head of a Greek just decapitated, the trunk still shivering. **1905** *Brit. Med. Jrnl.* 27 May 1147 Time and again, I have seen the skin 'shiver' at the touch of the knife.

**ˈshivered,** *a. rare*$^{-1}$. [f. SHIVER *sb.*$^{2}$ + -ED$^{2}$.] Fitted with a shiver or pulley (of a specified size or kind).

**1775** FALCK *Day's Diving Vessel* 27 A single eight-inch shivered block was bound in a strong iron strop.

**shivered** (ˈʃɪvəd), *ppl. a.* [f. SHIVER *v.*$^{1}$ + -ED$^{1}$.] Broken, shattered.

*a* **1542** WYATT *Poems, 'The furious gun'*, The furyous gonne.. cracketh in sonder: and in the ayer doeth rore the shevered peces. **1621** G. SANDYS *Ovid's Met.* v. (1626) 90 And through his flesh the shiuered bones arise. *c* **1764** GRAY *Welsh Fragm., Conan* 8 As the thunder's fiery stroke, Glancing on the shiver'd oak. **1815** SCOTT *Ld. of Isles* III. xii, Where Coolin stoops him to the west, They saw upon his shiver'd crest The sun's arising gleam. **1897** F. THOMPSON *New Poems* 221 Like shivered moonlight on long waters.

**shivereens** (ʃɪvəˈriːnz), *sb. pl. dial.* [f. SHIVER *sb.*$^{1}$, after SMITHEREENS.] Fragments, small pieces.

**1855** *Sheffield Ann.* 6 (E.D.D.) Nock it ta shivereens. **1893** CROCKETT *Stickit Min.* 191 Kelly could 'lick him into shivereens'.

**shiverer**$^{1}$ (ˈʃɪvərə(r)). [f. SHIVER *v.*$^{1}$ + -ER$^{1}$.] One who breaks (something) into small pieces.

**1834** *Tait's Mag.* I. 311 Chosen ground for the shiverers of lances and the lovers of courtly splendour.

**shiverer**$^{2}$ (ˈʃɪvərə(r)). [f. SHIVER *v.*$^{2}$ + -ER$^{1}$.]

**a.** One who trembles or shakes.

**1883** MEREDITH *Poems of Joy of Earth* 103 Ere you follow nature's lead, Of her powers in you have heed; Else a shiverer you will find You have challenged humankind.

**b.** *dial.* (See quots.) Cf. SHIVERING *vbl. sb.*$^{2}$ 2.

**1888** *Sheffield Gloss., Shiverer*, a horse which has a lameness in the loins. **1899** *Daily News* 13 Apr. 3/5 Another horse was sold.. it fell down in the street the first time it was harnessed, and was proved to be a 'roarer and a shiverer' of long standing.

**ˈshiverine.** *Sc. Obs.* Also 6 schiverone, shivering, 6–7 schiverene. [? Some kind of derivative of F. *chèvre* goat.] **a.** ? A goat-skin. **b.** *pl.* ? Goatskin or kid gloves (? or breeches).

**15..** *Customs* in *Balfour's Practicks* (1754) 87 For ane hundreth lamb skinnis, I. d. For ane hundreth schiveronis, iiij d. **1598** in Beck *Gloves* (1883) 151 For each dozn shewing [? *read* shivering] shewed with silk, six shillings; each dozen shivering shewed with threed, five shillings. **1663** in *Maitland Club Misc.* (1840) II. 502 For a pair of shiverines to my Lord and drink money to the boy. **1664** *Ibid.* 508 A pair of schiverines.

**ˈshivering,** *vbl. sb.*$^{1}$ [f. SHIVER *v.*$^{1}$ + -ING$^{1}$.]

**1. a.** The action or an act of SHIVER *v.*$^{1}$

*c* **1400** *Sege Jerusalem* (E.E.T.S.) 31/548 For schyueryng of sche[l]des, & schynyng of helmes. *a* **1548** HALL *Chron., Hen. VIII*, 146 b, By chaunce of shiueryng of the spere. **1625** BACON *Ess., Viciss. Things* (Arb.) 574 Vpon the Breaking and Shiuering of a great State and Empire, you may be sure to haue Warres. **1647** HEXHAM I, A shivering, or a rieving, *Een klievinge, ofte een scheuringe.*

**b.** *Pottery.* Peeling and splitting of the glaze.

**1921** A. B. SEARLE *Clayworkers' Hand-bk.* (ed. 3) xi. 208 Shivering is a variety of 'peeling' which may be produced by adding flint which has been too finely ground or an excess of fine silica to a body. **1947** J. C. RICH *Materials & Methods of Sculpture* ii. 51 Another cause of shivering is firing at too low a temperature. **1964** H. HODGES *Artifacts* ii. 52 Peeling .. or shivering of a glaze usually results from a failure to fit the glaze to the body, the contraction of the glaze being less than that of the body.

**2.** A fragment, splinter. *rare.*

**1599** HAKLUYT *Voy.* II. I. 270 In stead of Occam they vse the shiuerings of the barke of the sayd trees.

**shivering** (ˈʃɪvərɪŋ), *vbl. sb.*$^{2}$ [f. SHIVER *v.*$^{2}$ + -ING$^{1}$.]

**1. a.** The action or an act of SHIVER *v.*$^{2}$

**1398** TREVISA *Barth. De P.R.* VII. xxxix. (1495) 253 A feuer Terciane greuyth euery daye fyrste wyth sheueringe and thenne wyth heete. *c* **1440** *Promp. Parv.* 75/1 Chymerynge or chyuerynge, or dyderynge, *frigutus.* **1597** A. M. tr. *Guillemeau's Fr. Chirurg.* 17/3 Ther is a chillnes and shiueringe therwith associated. **1681** BELON *New Myst. Phys.* Introd. 1 A Tertian that comes with a cold Shivering. **1741** WESLEY *Jrnl.* 25 Oct., About two in the afternoon just as I was set down to dinner, a shivering came upon me, and a little pain in my back. **1873** *Lancet* 27 Dec. 900/1 Every day she had shiverings, which came on after 4 o'clock P.M.

**b.** *Comb.*, as *shivering attack, fit.*

**1816** SCOTT *Bl. Dwarf* vii, The poor goat stretched out her limbs with the twitches and shivering fit of the last agony. *a* **1859** MACAULAY *Hist. Eng.* xxv. V. 305 Headaches and shivering fits returned on him almost daily. **1899** *Allbutt's Syst. Med.* VIII. 169 The patient frequently feels cold all over, and may have a sharp shivering attack.

**2.** *Vet. Sci.* A pathological condition of horses in which certain muscles undergo rapid spasms, most commonly those in the hindquarters.

**1847** *Vet. Record* III. 4 'Shivering', an affection of the stifle-joint, associated with luxation of the patella. **1907** J. W. AXE *Horse* VIII. 374 During this test it will be noticed whether the action is close,.. and whether there are any indications of stringhalt or shivering. **1978** C. GEDDES *Horse* 218 The most common conditions are:... Shivering, a condition of the hind limbs, characterized by shaking movements of the hind limb and tail when the leg is flexed and lowered to the ground.

**shivering** (ˈʃɪvərɪŋ), *ppl. a.*$^{1}$ [f. SHIVER *v.*$^{1}$ + -ING$^{2}$.] That shivers (in various senses of the verb); shattering, breaking, splintering.

*a* **1400–50** *Wars Alex.* 789 Sone in scheuerand schidis schaftis ere brosten. *c* **1470** HENRY *Wallace* VIII. 771 Our schefferand harnes schot the blud so scheyn. **1775** MICKLE tr. *Camoens' Lusiad* IX. 115 The shivering trumpets tear the still-voiced air. **1824** G. CHALMERS *Caledonia* III. III. i. 221 The soft shivering argillaceous stone which easily yields to the weather.

Hence **ˈshiveringly** *adv.*$^{1}$ *rare*$^{-1}$.

**1631** GOUGE *God's Arrows* IV. *Extent of God's Provid.* §15. 400 The maine Summier of the other floore that fell was much stronger... Yet that also failed.., and that more shiveringly, and with a longer rent.. then the other.

**shivering** (ˈʃɪvərɪŋ), *ppl. a.*$^{2}$ [f. SHIVER *v.*$^{2}$ + -ING$^{2}$.]

**1.** That causes to shiver with cold, chilly.

*c* **1200** *Vices & Virtues* 63 And ðu, earme saule, on ðe wallende brene of ðe hote fiere, and eft, embehwile, on ðe chiuerinde chele. **1786** *Har'st Rig* xc, Cold shiv'ring blasts do not dismay The Celtic race. **1830** G. COLMAN *Random Rec.* xii. II. 63 My companion's lower habiliments appear'd somewhat shivering for the season. **1894** BLACKMORE *Perlycross* 238 It was truly a shivering and a shuddering night.

**2.** Trembling with cold, fear, etc.

**1577** GRANGE *Golden Aphrod.* I iv b, The crampe ouertooke hir feeling, hyr sheuering nayles started. **1697** DRYDEN *Virg. Georg.* III. 488 Their Camelots.. shield the shiv'ring Mariner from Cold. **1754** GRAY *Poesy* 57 To chear the shiv'ring Natives dull abode. **1806** SURR *Winter in Lond.* III. 71 The shivering wretch turned up a narrow court in Holborn. **1891** FARRAR *Darkn. & Dawn* l, The shivering throngs whom the flames had driven from their homes.

*jocularly.* **1822** LAMB *Elia* Ser. II. *Det. Thoughts on Bks.*, A tithe of that good leather would comfortably re-clothe my shivering folios.

**b.** of feelings, and the like.

**1562** A. BROOKE *Romeus & Iuliet* 907 Of shyuering care and dred I haue felt many a fit. **1632** J. HAYWARD tr. *Biondi's Eromena* 23 Awaking with a shivering feare, caused by his imagination and passion. **1747** MALLET *Amyntor & Theodora* III. 420 Thro shivering joy and doubt. **1898** MEREDITH *Odes, Napoleon* xiii, His nature with her shivering faith ran yoked.

**c.** *shivering-Jemmy* (see quot.). Also a dial. name for *Briza media*, also known as *shivering-grass* (Britten and Holland).

**1864** *Hotten's Slang Dict., Shivering-Jemmy*, the name given by street folk to any cadger who exposes himself half naked, on a cold day to obtain alms.

**3.** Of things: Trembling, shaking, fluttering.

**1762–9** FALCONER *Shipwr.* II. 151 The shivering sails descend; the yards are square. **1849** NOAD *Electricity* 290 Large extraordinary movements of the needle, in which it traverses frequently, with a shivering motion, an arc of several degrees on both sides of its usual position. **1865** SWINBURNE *Chastelard* III. i. 103 Shivering soft eyelashes. **1870** O'SHAUGHNESSY *Epic of Women* 57 The swaying pine and shivering fir.

**b.** Of sound: Tremulous.

**16..** tr. *Strada* in Flavel *Husb. Spirit.* (1669) 236 And closing up his layes, Like a full Quire, a shivering consort playes. **1891** *Spectator* 23 Mar., That wants nothing but the shivering music to make a grand sensation on any boards.

Hence **ˈshiveringly** *adv.*$^{2}$

**1825** MRS. HEMANS *Forest Sanctuary* xlvi, Some like the leaf swept shiveringly along. **1856** *Chamb. Jrnl.* VI. 349 'Ah', he continued shiveringly, 'how very cold it is!' **1889** GUNTER *That Frenchman* xx. 266 Vassilissa enters timidly, and gazes shiveringly at the head of secret police.

**shiversome** (ˈʃɪvəsəm), *a.* [f. SHIVER *sb.*$^{3}$ + -SOME$^{1}$.] Causing shivers.

**1930** *Observer* 28 Sept. 8 As shiversome a phase of sociology as the world has known. **1948** I. BROWN *No Idle Words* 53 Fever is a hideous paradox, being cold heat and shiversome ardour. **1970** *Daily Tel.* 17 Nov. 12/4 As brilliantly shiversome a film as I have seen for years.

**shivery** (ˈʃɪvərɪ), *a.*$^{1}$ [f. SHIVER *sb.*$^{1}$ + -Y$^{1}$.] Apt to split into flakes, brittle, flaky.

*shivery salt*: ? a salt exhibiting a laminal texture.

**1683** PETTUS *Fleta Min.* I. 87 Cause a small Ballance to be forged out of the blade of an old Sword, that it may have.. nothing ruff or shivery [orig. Ger. *schifferig*].. on it. **1748** BROWNRIGG *Art of Making Salt* 72 In making a kind of salt called shivery salt they use yet more gentle fires. **1794** SCHMEISSER *Syst. Min.* I. 145 Its texture is rather shivery or fibrous. **1797** ROBISON in *Encycl. Brit.* (ed. 3) XVI. 280/2 Shivery angular stones of the size of an egg. **1858** GEIKIE *Story Boulder* x. 198 This rock is worthless as a source of lime, nor from its irregular laminations and shivery structure has it much value in any other way.

**shivery** (ˈʃɪvərɪ), *a.*$^{2}$ [f. SHIVER *v.*$^{2}$ + -Y.]

**1.** Characterized by a shaking, quivering motion, or appearance of motion.

**1747** MALLET *Amyntor & Theodora* III. 532 His frame with shivery horror shook. **1817** KEATINGE *Trav.* I. 59 The shivery appearance his engravings convey, totally misrepresents the features of this extraordinary mass. **1852** MRS. STOWE *Uncle Tom's C.* xiv, The shivery canes, and the tall, dark cypress, hung with wreaths of dark, funereal moss, glow in the golden ray.

**2.** Inclined to shiver. Also *shivery-shaky*.

**1837** MARRYAT *Dog-Fiend* xliii, I'm all wet and shivery. **1864** *Derby Day* iv. 50 He's all shivery shakey as if he'd got the staggers or the cold shivers. **1898** *Allbutt's Syst. Med.* V. 826 She turns a little shivery and pale, at times even ashy. **1934** J. JOYCE *Let.* 13 Aug. (1966) III. 317, I have a fit of ague for the past 24 hours... O Lord, the one day I feel so shivery-shaky!

**3.** Causing a shivering feeling, chilly.

**1839** HOOD *Ode for Ninth Nov.* 15 Was there no better day To fix on, than November Ninth so shivery? **1905** J. B. FIRTH *Highw. Derbysh.* iii. 44 It was a shivery place and gave her headaches.

**shivey** (ˈʃɪvɪ), *a.* Also shivvy (*Eng. Dial. Dict.*) and SHEAVY. [f. SHIVE *sb.*$^{2}$ + -Y$^{1}$.] Full of shives (see also quot. 1884).

**1884** W. S. B. MCLAREN *Spinning* (ed. 2) 189 In the wool-sorting a good deal can be done, but when wool is full of burrs, seeds, etc., and is what is generally called 'shivey', sorting and shaking can do little. **1937** [see SHIVE *sb.*$^{2}$ 2].

**shivoo** (ʃɪˈvuː). *Austral. colloq.* Also chivoo. [Var. SHIVEAU.] **a.** A celebration, a party, a spree. **b.** A disturbance, a row.

**1889** J. I. HUNT *Hunt's Bk. Bonanzas* 82 Jones had been to a lodge night shivoo, and he and the boys had a gay old time. **1919** W. H. DOWNING *Digger Dialects* 16 *Chivoo*, a celebration. **1924** LAWRENCE & SKINNER *Boy in Bush* i. 15 There was a chivoo. They held me on their shoulders and I smashed the principal's windows. **1933** *Bulletin* (Sydney) 18 Oct. 11/3 Calling for a juvenile descendant at a children's birthday party, I thought of my own similar shivoo 50 years ago. **1940** F. D. DAVISON *Woman at Mill* 59 Wally had a head full of the bush balladists and aspirations toward performing at bush shivoos. **1961** P. WHITE *Riders in Chariot* ix. 314 Friday is the big shivoo, when the swells begin to swell. **1979** *Sunday Mail Mag.* (Brisbane) 14 Jan. 6/5 More than 200,000 revellers packed the forecourt of Sydney's Opera House for the big shivoo on New Year's Eve.

**Shkyipetar, Shkypetar**, varr. SHQIPETAR.

**shl-**, var. *schl-* in many words (mostly German or Yiddish), qq.v. under this latter spelling.

**shlanter**, var. SCHLENTER *sb.* and *a.*

**shlemozzle**, var. SHEMOZZLE.

**Shl(e)uh**, varr. SHILHA.

**shlinter**, var. SCHLENTER *sb.* and *a.*

**shloke**, var. SLOKE[2].

**shm-**, var. *schm-* in many words (mostly German or Yiddish), qq.v. under this latter spelling (cf. SCHM-).

**shmear**, var. SCHMEER.

**shmock**, var. SCHMUCK.

**shmoo** (ʃmuː). *U.S.* [Invented word.] A fabulous animal invented by the U.S. cartoonist Al Capp in 1948. It is small and round, and ready to fulfil immediately any of man's material wants. Also, a model or toy version of this animal. Also *Comb.*, as ***shmoo-like*** adj.

**1948** *Newsweek* 12 July 56/3 Scheduled for appearance in August, the nature of the 'Shmoo' is a well-kept Capp secret. **1948** *Times-Herald* (Washington, D.C.) 25 Aug. 32/2 Too bad this fine, young specimen done heard th' call o' th' shmoo. **1948** *Sun* (Baltimore) 9 Dec. 16/3 The Berlin airlift ..has ferried everything from coal to shmoos. **1964** R. T. PETERSON et al. *Birds* i. 13 Certainly they [*sc.* kiwis] are the most unbird-like of all birds, shmoo-like creatures shaped like large, hairy footballs. **1978** *Washington Post* 8 Sept. A. 13/1 Cloning would..even put an end to world hunger. Those who can discuss these things make them sound like Al Capp's 'shmoos'.

**shmoos**, var. SCHMOOZE *v.*, *sb.*

‖**sho** (ʃoː), *sb.*[1] Pl. sho. [Jap.] A Japanese unit of capacity equal to ten *go*; equivalent to approximately 3·18 pints (1·80 litres).

**1876** W. E. GRIFFIS *Mikado's Empire* (1877) II. Notes & App. 609 Measures of capacity. The unit is the *masū* or *shō*, a wooden box, usually with a transverse bar of iron across the top for a handle. **1902** L. HEARN *Kottō* xii. 148 No less than five shō—that is to say about one peck—of dead fireflies. **1938** D. T. SUZUKI *Zen Buddhism & its Influence on Jap. Culture* II. iii. 243 Half a *shō* (less than one quart) of rice.

‖**shō** (ʃoː), *sb.*[2] [Jap.] A small Japanese organ, made from seventeen vertical bamboo pipes, which is held in the hand and blown into.

**1888** L. A. SMITH *Music of Waters* 281 The 'shô'..seems to correspond to our organ, but only in so far as it has pipes. **1936** K. SUNAGA *Jap. Music* 27 The *shō* is an instrument of which there seems to be no equivalent outside oriental music, though it is sometimes spoken of as a mouth organ. **1972** *Times* 18 Sept. 5/4 The head priest showed the instruments to Mr Heath, who took special interest in the sho pipes... He watched closely as a musician demonstrated the sho.

‖**sho** (ʃɔː), *sb.*[3] [Tibetan.] A former Tibetan unit of currency; a coin of this value.

**1902** S. C. DAS *Journey to Lhasa & Central Tibet* vii. 182 Shopkeepers and pedlars pay five *sho* (1¼ rupee) annually. **1970** R. D. TARING *Daughter of Tibet* ix. 107 Ten *sho* made one *sang*.

**sho, sho'** (ʃɔː), repr. U.S. Blacks' pronunc. of SURE *adv.*

**1893** H. A. SHANDS *Some Peculiarities of Speech in Mississippi* 56 *Sho*.., the common negro pronunciation for *sure*. *Sholy* is likewise used for *surely*. *Sho* is sometimes used for *surely*. **1926** N. N. PUCKETT in A. Dundes *Mother Wit* (1973) 7/2 A person who eats too fast 'will sho marry too young'. **1942** S. KENNEDY *Palmetto Country* 144 Sho nuff there was the preacher's buggy. **1966** *Massachusetts Rev.* VII. IV. 664 Sholey. Sho, hit'll be jes fine. Yo' done real good. **1973** E. BULLINS *Theme is Blackness* 99, I sho feel sorry for you when Cliff gets here, Bummie.

**sho**: see SHE, SHOE, SHOO *int.*[1] and [2].

**shoad, shode** (ʃəʊd). *local.* Forms: 7–9 shod, (8 shoald), 7– shoad, 8– shode; also 7 shadd, 7–8 shade. [Prob. a derivative of OE. *scádan* to divide, separate: see SHED *v.* Cf. SHODE. The genuineness of the forms *shadd*, *shade* is doubtful.] Loose fragments of tin, lead, or copper ore mixed with earth, lying on or near the surface and indicating the proximity of a lode. Also (with pl.) one of these fragments.

**1602** CAREW *Cornwall* I. 8 b, They discouer these workes, by certaine Tynne-stones, lying on the face of the ground, which they terme *Shoad*. **1670** PETTUS *Fodinæ Reg.* 3 They [Metals] are discovered to us..by Moles which cast up their shade or glittering earth. *Ibid.* 79 [Quotes (from Holland's *Camden*) the passage of Carew given above (quot. 1602), but with *shadd* substituted for *shoad*]. **1674** RAY *Coll. Words, Preparing of Tin* 120 The Tinners find the Mine by the Shoad (or as they call it Squad) which is loose stones of Tin mixed with the Earth. **1681** GREW *Musæum* III. §i. v. 306 A Shod. *Spuma Lupi.* The forerunner of the Load or Mother of the Tin-Ore. **1778** W. PRYCE *Min. Cornub.* 126 Copper and Lead Shodes are very seldom met with. **1789** J. WILLIAMS *Min. Kingd.* I. 406 The shoad of lead is always either coated or tarnished. **1809** A. HENRY *Trav.* 230 Examining the shods, or loose stones, in search of minerals. **1855** J. R. LEIFCHILD *Cornwall* 200 This stream-tin is..met with..in separate stones called *shodes*.

**b.** *attrib.*, as ***shade earth, shoad-ore, -stone.***

**1735** *Dict. Polygraph.* s.v. *China*, To Gild China. You must first grind some *shade-earth on a marble, with linseed-oil,..with which trace out your figures. **1789** J. WILLIAMS *Min. Kingd.* I. 362 There is a very material difference between float and *shoad ore, although they are both found upon the surface of the rock. Shoad ore..is always found in loose masses of all sizes, either in or under the upper soil. *a* **1728** WOODWARD *Fossils* I. (1729) I. 202 A *Shoad-stone, found near the Surface of the Earth... *Cornwall.*

Hence **ˈshoader** (see quot. 1882). **ˈshoading**, the process of searching for shoad-ore by digging small pits (hence ***shoading-heap, -pit***).

**1778** W. PRYCE *Min. Cornub.* 124 Another and very ancient method of discovering Tin Lodes, is by what we call Shodeing, that is, tracing them home by loose Stones, fragments, or Shodes. **1880** *W. Cornw. Gloss.*, *Shoading-heaps*, heaps from pits sunk in search of veins of metal. **1882** JAGO *Anc. Lang. & Dial. Cornwall* 263 *Shoaders*, miners engaged in shoading. *Ibid.*, *Shoading pits*, pits dug in the search for a lode. **1893** *Northumbld. Gloss.* s.v., To 'go a shoading' is to go prospecting for shoad-ore.

**shoal** (ʃəʊl), *sb.*[1] Forms: α. 4–5 shelde. β. (Chiefly *Sc.*) 4–6 schald, 5 schauld, 6 schalde, shaulde, (9 *dial.* shall, shad); 6 *pl.* shawllys. γ. 5–7 sholde, 6–7 shold, should(e, 7 showld, shoald, (9 *dial.* shod, shoad). δ. 6 shol, shoel(l, 6–7 shole, 7 shoule, (schoole), 7–8 shoale, 7– shoal. [Absolute use of SHOAL *a.*] A place where the water is of little depth; a shallow; a sand-bank or bar.

α. **13..** *Coer de L.* 2054 The mariners unneth it withhelde, That shyppe left in the shelde.

β. *c* **1375** *Sc. Leg. Saints* xvii. (*Martha*) 113 Quhare þe body lay, to ryvine al castine one a schald. *c* **1470** HENRY *Wallace* x. 44 Bot ix or x he kest a gait befor, Langis the schauld, maid it bath dep and schor. **1529** RASTELL *Pastyme* Prol. (1811) 5 The passage [is] so strayte and daungerous that they must nedis come thorow many straytis and shawllys. **1583** *Leg. Bp. St. Androis* 161 in *Satir. Poems Reform.* xlv, His schip come never on the schalde, But stak still on the ancker halde. *c* **1585** in *Early Naval Ballads* (Percy Soc.) 16 When shauldes and sandie bankes apears What pillot can direct his course?

γ. **1414** *26 Pol. Poems* xiii. 146 On see, on lond, on sholde, and depe. **1555** PHAER *Æneid* I. A ij b, And three the Easterne winde also..Out of the deepe into the sholdes and quicksands made to sinke. **1594** BLUNDEVIL *Exerc.*, *Plancius' Map* (1597) 277 Deapthes, sands, showlds and rocks. **1633** T. JAMES *Voy.* 24 This was nothing but shoalds to the land. **1669** STURMY *Mariner's Mag.* IV. i. 137 Knowledge of Depths and Shoulds.

δ. **1555** EDEN *Decades, 2nd Voy. Guiana* 351 The sholes of the ryuer cauled Rio Grande. **1582** N. LICHEFIELD *Castanheda's Conq. E. Ind.* 24 b, She strake vpon a shoel. **1589** BIGGES *Summarie Drake's W. Ind. Voy.* 47 The shols appearing daungerous. **1624** CAPT. SMITH *Virginia* VI. 215 A long and dangerous shoule of rocks and sand. **1634** SIR T. HERBERT *Trav.* 21 We were cast vpon the shoales or flats of Mozambique. **1697** DRYDEN *Æneid* v. 285 Wedg'd in the Rocky Sholes, and sticking fast. **1769** BANCROFT *Guiana* 357 On the east side is a sandy shoal. **1853** SIR H. DOUGLAS *Milit. Bridges* (ed. 3) 169 Among the shoals and eddies with which the Sutlej abounds. **1871** TYNDALL *Fragm. Sci.* (1879) I. vi. 200 There is a dangerous shoal in the harbour.

**b.** *fig.*

**1605** SHAKS. *Macb.* I. vii. 6 Vpon this Banke and Schoole of time. **1613** —— *Hen. VIII*, III. ii. 437 Wolsey, that once ..sounded all the Depths, and Shoales of Honor. **1815** BYRON *Stanzas for Music*, '*There's not a joy*' 6 Then the few whose spirits float above the wreck of happiness Are driven o'er the shoals of guilt or ocean of excess.

**c.** *attrib.*, as ***shoal-bank, -ground, -rock***; **shoal-mark**, a buoy or other mark set to indicate a shoal.

**1712** W. ROGERS *Voy. round World* 51 There are..some Shoal-Banks between them, but no Shoal-Ground before we come to this Cove. **1883** 'MARK TWAIN' *Life Mississippi* xi. 112 He..then began to work her warily into the next system of shoal marks.

**shoal** (ʃəʊl), *sb.*[2] Forms: 6–7 shoale, 6–8 shole, 7 shoole, showl, 9 shool, 7– shoal. [Late 16th c. *shole*; the earlier history is uncertain. The word is etymologically identical with OE. *scolu* str. fem., troop, division of an army = OS. *scola* multitude (MLG. *schole*), MDu. *schole* multitude, flock, shoal of fishes (Du. *school*, WFris. *skoal*, NFris. *sköl*, shoal of fishes) :—OTeut. type **skulō*, f. **skul-* wk. grade of **skel-* to divide (whence SHALE *sb.*, SHELL *sb.*, SKILL *sb.* and *v.*, etc.).

It is possible that the OE. word may have had the sense of shoal of fishes, and in this sense may have continued in nautical use ever since, though unrecorded in ME. and early mod.E. The simpler hypothesis is that the 16th c. *shole* was a re-adoption of the Du. form (see above) which in the 14–15th c. had been taken into English as *scole* (see SCHOOL *sb.*[2]). The initial (ʃ) may be an English sound-substitution for the Du. (sx), or it may come from one of the Flemish dialects in which *sch* is pronounced (ʃ).]

**1.** A large number of fish, porpoises, seals, whales, etc. swimming together; = SCHOOL *sb.*[2] 1. Phr. ***in a shoal, in*** or ***by shoals.***

**1579** [see 3]. **1601** R. JOHNSON *Kingd. & Commw.* 69 Sholes of fish frisking and playing. **1653** MILTON *Ps.* viii. 22 Fish that through the wet Sea-paths in shoals do slide. **1774** PENNANT *Tour Scot. in 1772*, 333 Herrings offer themselves in shoals. **1835** MARRYAT *J. Faithful* viii, The shoals of seals would follow the ship if you whistled. **1836** *Uncle Philip's Convers. Whale Fishery* 286 The ship..came upon a large shoal of whales. **1899** BARING-GOULD *Bk. West* II. *Cornw.* xix. 314 As the season advances the shool, or shoal, comes nearer the shore. **1905** D. SMITH *Days of His Flesh* l. 515 Supposing..that the stranger had skill in fisher-craft and had perhaps observed indications of a shoal, they obeyed.

**b.** Hence occas. used of a number of aquatic animals or floating objects.

**1593** NASHE *Christ's T.* 31 b, The waters..bare the whole shole of them [*sc.* dead carcasses] before them. **1660** BOYLE *New Exp. Phys. Mech.* xxiv. 190 The bubbles ascended in this Liquor, as it were in sholes. **1692** R. L'ESTRANGE *Fables* xxvii. 26 A Whole Shoal of Frogs. **1839** THIRLWALL *Greece* I. VI. 198 A shoal of boats now came off from the harbours filled with people. **1840** *Ibid.* VII. 219 The scaly monsters of the Nile..flocked in shoals to the place.

†**2.** A flock of birds. *Obs.*

**1579–80** NORTH *Plutarch, Cicero* (1595) 935 From thence there came a great shole of crowes. **1584** R. SCOT *Discov. Witchcr.* XIII. xxx. (1886) 278 To make a shoale of goslings drawe a timber log. **1659** HAMMOND *On Ps.* cvi. 15 He sent them whole sholes of quails. **1801** HUNTINGTON *God Guard. Poor* 98 Like a shoal of eagles.

**3.** *transf.* **a.** A large number of persons thronging together or classed together; a troop, crowd.

**1579** SPENSER *Sheph. Cal.* May 20, I sawe a shole of shepeheardes outgoe. **1579** E. K. *Gloss*, ibid., A shole, a multitude taken of fishe, wherof some going in great companies, are sayde to swimme in a shole. *c* **1610** G. HERBERT *Sonn. to his Mother*, Wherewith whole showls of martyrs once did burn. **1625** BACON *Ess.*, *Viciss. Things* (Arb.) 574 When there be great Shoales of People, which goe on to populate. **1749** SMOLLETT *Gil Blas* VII. viii. (1782) III. 67 The actors and actresses..poured upon me in shoals. **1791** BOSWELL *Johnson* an. 1763, The shoals of Scotchmen who flocked about him. **1848** DICKENS *Dombey* ix, I see people going up and down the street in shoals all day. **1876** TREVELYAN *Macaulay* II. viii. 91 The adherents of the Government.. who sate for the counties were turned out by shoals. **1901** *Scotsman* 6 Apr. 9/7 A shoal of injured people were brought for treatment to the Royal Infirmary.

**b.** A large number (of inanimate things).

**1639** FULLER *Holy War* V. x. (1640) 246 Infinite are the sholes of miracles done by Christs Crosse in Jerusalem. **1688** *Clear Proof Certainty Protest. Faith* 7 We may expect Shoals of Texts. **1858** CARLYLE *Fredk. Gt.* I. v. (1872) I. 42 Never-ending shoals of small troubles. **1891** 'J. S. WINTER' *Lumley* xii, Notes and telegrams, which came in by shoals from morning till night. **1900** *Jrnl. Soc. Dyers* XVI. 12 A shoal of novelties in machinery.

**4.** *Comb.*: **shoal-cod** (see quot.; cf. *school-cod*); **shoal-net**, a net for catching seals; **shoal-wise** *adv.*, in shoals or crowds.

**1836** J. RICHARDSON *Fauna Bor.-Amer.* III. 241 *Gadus arenosus*, Shoal-cod, Smith. **1792** G. CARTWRIGHT *Jrnl. Labrador* I. 181 The sealers put out two more shoal-nets, and another stopper. **18..** BLACKIE (Ogilvie 1882), When he goes abroad, as he does now shoalwise, John Bull finds a great host of innkeepers, etc.

†**shoal**, *sb.*[3] *Obs.* [a. Du. *schol* in the same sense (earlier also clod, lump of metal) = MLG. *scholle*, *schulle* clod, sod, OHG. *scolla* fem., *scollo* masc. (MHG., mod.G. *scholle*) clod, mass of ice; perh. f. root **skul-*: see SHOAL *sb.*[2]] A mass of floating ice; an iceberg or floe.

**1648** HEXHAM II, *Een Schoole van ys*, a Shoole of yce. **1713** *Cal. Treas. Papers* 537 The great shoals of ice that came down in the winter often damaged it [Berwick bridge]. **1760** *Ann. Reg.* III. 67/1 Near 100 sail have been drove from their anchors and moorings by the shoals of ice.

**shoal** (ʃəʊl), *a.* (and *adv.*) Forms: α. 1 (in proper names) sceald, 4 schealde, 5 scheld(e. β. (Chiefly *Sc.*) 5–7 schald, 5 schalde, shald, schawlde, schaulde, 6 schauld, 7 shalde (9 *dial.* shald, etc.); 5 schawd, 6 schaud, 6 schaud(e (9 *dial.* shawd, shoad, etc.); 6 schaule, 8 (and 9 *dial.*) shaul, shawl. γ. 4 schoold, schoolt, 5 schold(e, scold, 5–7 shold(e, shoald, 7 should. δ. 6–7 shoale, showle, 6–8 shole, 7 should, 7– shoal. [OE. *sceald*:—prehistoric **skalda-*; a parallel formation, differing only in the suffix, appears to be the synonymous SHALLOW *a.*:—OE. **scealu*:—**skalwa-*. The import and affinities of the base **skal-* of these formations are not easy to determine; possibly it may be 'thin layer' as in OTeut. **skalō* SHALE *sb.*; this supposition would fairly well account for the sense of the English adjs.

Some etymologists have compared G. *schal* insipid, vapid (of liquors; hence *fig.* of discourse, thoughts, etc.); but the sense has little real affinity. The LG. *schol* (Fris. *skol*) shows remarkable identity in sound and meaning with the Eng. adj. (*schol water* shallow water, *schol plögen* to plow shallow), but its etymology is dubious.]

**1. a.** Of water, etc.: Not deep; = SHALLOW *a.*[1] 1.

**839** in Birch *Cartul. Saxon.* I. 593 Æt Scealdan fleote. *c* **1440** *Jacob's Well* 65 ȝif þi scope of penaunce be to scheld, it takyth no water of sorwe.

β. **1375** BARBOUR *Bruce* IX. 354 He spyit, and slely gert assay Quhar of the dik the schawdest [*v.r.* shaldest] was.

*c* **1425** WYNTOUN *Cron.* VII. v. 769 Than Trent and Temys war sa schawlde [*v.rr.* schaulde, schald]. **1513** DOUGLAS *Æneis* V. xi. 56 Sa huge wilsum rolkis and schald [*Camb. MS.* schaud] sandis. *Ibid.* VII. xiii. 57 Inhabitand the schauld flude Vulturnus. **1577–95** *Descr. Isles Scot.* in Skene *Celtic Scot.* (1880) III. App. 429 Thair is na great waters nor rivers in this Ile [of Lewis], but small schaule burnis. **1597** MONTGOMERIE *Cherrie & Slae* 1544 The watter allso is sae schald We sall it pass, evin as we wald. **1606** BIRNIE *Kirk-Buriall* (1833) 28 Which the Lord has set on the shalde shoare, lyke beakens to warne. **1736** RAMSAY *Prov.* xxxi. (1750) 84 Shawl waters make maist din.

γ. **1387** TREVISA *Higden* (Rolls) III. 131 He wolde make þat greet ryuer so schalowe [*v.rr.* schoolt, schoold] þat þe water schulde nouȝt reche to women kneen. *c* **1440** *Promp. Parv.* 447/2 Schold, or schalowe, noȝte depe, as water or oþer lyke, *bassa.* *c* **1460** *Ibid.* (Winch.) 165 Flew, or scold . . *bassus.* *a* **1554** SIR H. WILLOUGHBY in Hakluyt *Voy.* (1589) 269 After that we sounded againe, and found but 7 fadome, so shoalder and shoalder water. **1556** J. HEYWOOD *Spider & Fly* xxxi, Holes, sides and toppes, brode, narrow, depe and sholde. **1633** T. JAMES *Voy.* 23 The shouldest water . . was 7. fad[omes].

δ. *a* **1554** SIR H. WILLOUGHBY in Hakluyt *Voy.* (1589) 269 The boat could not come to land the water was so shoale. **1589** IVES *Fortif.* 35 The ditches are narrow and showle. *a* **1599** SPENSER *F.Q.* VII. vi. 40 This Molanna, were she not so shole. **1624** CAPT. SMITH *Virginia* I. 2 The second of July they fell with the coast of Florida in shoule water. **1666** PEPYS *Diary* 15 Aug., Our shipps running all a-ground, it being so shoal water. **1719** DE FOE *Crusoe* I. 50 What the Shore was, whether Rock or Sand, whether Steep or Shoal we knew not. **1748** *Earthquake Peru* i. 23 Having fourteen Fathom Water in the sholest Part. **1840** *Evid. Hull Docks Comm.* 113, Q. What has been the effect of that extension upon the mud? A. It is much shoaler than it was before. **1858** MAURY *Phys. Geog. Sea* vii. §430 In the Straits . . the depth across the shoalest section is not more than one hundred and sixty fathoms. **1894** *Law Times Rep.* LXXI. 103/2 The available waterway of the cut is . . greatly reduced in width by shoal water on the north.

**b.** The phr. ***shoal water*** used attrib.

**1874** J. W. LONG *Amer. Wild-fowl* Introd. 15, I shall . . separate them into . . deep-water and shoal-water varieties. **1888** CLODD *Story Creation* iv. 34 The fossils are shown to resemble present shoal water deposits.

**c.** The phr. ***shoal water*** used *fig.*

**1884** 'MARK TWAIN' *Huck. Finn* xxviii. 284 It jolted her up like everything, of course; but I was over the shoal water now, so I went right along . . and told her every blame thing. **1941** J. MASEFIELD *In Mill* 105, I had . . plenty of money in the bank to tide me over the shoal-water.

**2.** *fig.* Of intellect, etc. (Cf. SHALLOW *a.*[1] 6.)

**1728** RAMSAY *Gen. Mistake* 65 The sumphish mob of penetration shawl. **1785** BURNS *Twa Herds* x, There's Duncan, deep, and Peebles, shaul, But chiefly thou, apostle Auld, We trust in thee.

*Comb.* **1844** LOWELL *Columbus* 264 One day more These muttering shoalbrains leave the helm to me.

†**3.** *Naut.* Of a sail or a bonnet: Narrow, not wide. *Obs. rare*$^{-1}$.

**1688** HOLME *Armoury* III. xv. (Roxb.) 44/2 The Main saile showler, is the main saile made narrower or skant. *Ibid.* 45/1 A showler or shoule Bonnett, is to haue it shallow, or narrow.

**4.** *adv.* [ME. *schealde.*] To or at a slight depth. Also *fig.*

*c* **1315** SHOREHAM *Poems* III. 116 Ac many man desceyued hys, . . And weyneþ þat he be out of peryl, Oþer ine senne so schealde, þat hym ne douteþ of no breche Of godes hestes healde. **1817–8** COBBETT *Resid. U.S.* (1822) 150, I went very shoal with the plough, because deep ploughing would have turned up the sods.

Hence †**scheldhed** [-HEAD], shallowness.

*c* **1440** *Jacob's Well* 168 A skete also, sumdel in þe heuyd, is raysed & reryd on bothe sydes; for ellys it myȝt noȝt receyvin but lytel wose, for scheldehed, for to castyn it out.

**shoal,** *v.*[1] *Obs.* exc. *dial.* Forms: 6 shole, shool(e, shoule, 6–7 shoal(e, 7 sholl. [Of obscure origin.

Formally, it could represent an OE. **scálian* equivalent to ON. **skeila* suggestd as a possible origin for SKAIL *v.*]

†**1.** *trans.* To separate. Usually with *out.*

**1571** GOLDING *Calvin on Ps.* lxviii. 26. 254 The hypocrites . . should bee sholed from the good and holy ones. **1574** tr. *Marlorat's Apocalips* 43 In this exhortation John treateth of the difference between the good and the bad, and of the sholing of the one from the other by the rigor of Justice. **1581** LAMBARDE *Eiren.* I. v. (1602) 23 Labouring . . to increase their iurisdictions, & to shoale out themselues from the ordinarie gouernment. **1583** GOLDING *Calvin on Deut.* xxvii. 164 In that he hath so shooled vs out from among the vnbeleeuers. **1642** D. ROGERS *Naaman* 358 With such caution and encouragement as shall both sholl out the dogs, and welcome the children, whose bread it is. **1647** TRAPP *Comm.* Rev. ii. 24 Here Christ comes with his fan, shedding and shoaling out his own from others.

**2.** To divide into classes. ? *Obs.*

**1805** *Ann. Reg.* 62 One of the reforms . . was that of shoaling or classing the workmen. . . As to the practice of shoaling the shipwrights, as it had proved so advantageous in the merchants' yards, there was reason to conclude that it would prove equally so in those of his majesty.

**3.** *dial.* (See quot.)

**1887** *Kent. Gloss.*, *Shoal-in*, to pick sides at cricket or any game.

**shoal** (ʃəʊl), *v.*[2] Forms: 6 shald, should, 7 showlde, shoald, shold, showl(e, 7, 9 *dial.* shool, 8 shole, shaul, 7– shoal. [f. SHOAL *a.*]

**I.** *intr.*

**1.** Of water, a watercourse, harbour, sounding, etc.: To become shallow or more shallow.

**1574** [implied in SHOALING *vbl. sb.*[2] 2]. **1584–5** *Act 27 Eliz.* c. 21 The Haven of Orforde . . is greatelie shoulded and decaied. **1633** T. JAMES *Voy.* 19 Now the water begins to showlde. **1779** FORREST *Voy. N. Guinea* 178 It shoals suddenly from ten to two fathoms. **1841** W. A. BROOKS *Treat. Navig. Rivers* 57 The soundings shoal gradually also up the Rio de la Plata. **1883** *Science* I. 368/1 The sea . . had so far shoaled as to bring up the land within 65 feet of its present level. **1897** H. NEWBOLT *Admirals All* 6 He anchored them fast where the Texel shoaled.

**b.** With *out*: To become gradually more shallow until no water is to be seen.

**1889** *Universal Rev.* Nov. 428 The limpid reedy thoroughfares shoal out To glinting silt-beds where the minnows lie. **1894** *Law Times Rep.* LXXI. 102/2 The water of the cut . . gradually shoals out until it reaches a mud bank.

†**2.** ? To slant, slope. *Obs.* Cf. SHORE *v.*[1] 3.

**1621** MARKHAM *Hungers Prev.* 18 Then for the vpper side of the Net, you shall place it slantwise shoaling against the water. *Ibid.* 21 They [the sticks] shall be prickt a little shoaling or slantwise.

**II.** *trans.*

**3.** *Naut.* To find (one's soundings) gradually more shallow; to pass from a greater into a less depth of (water), as shown by sounding.

**1670** NARBOROUGH *Jrnl.* in *Acc. Sev. Late Voy.* I. (1694) 60 As I shoaled my soundings I had 22, and 18, and 16 . . Fathoms. **1731** CAPT. W. WRIGLESWORTH *MS. Log-bk. of the 'Lyell'* 3 Jan., When we sholed the Water as per Logg. **1748** *Anson's Voy.* I. vi. 60 We . . kept shoaling our water, till at length we came into twelve fathom. **1839** *Nautical Mag.* 237 The lead should be kept constantly going, and the Ship tacked to the eastward as soon as the water is shoaled to 22 or 20 fathoms. **1852** CONYBEARE & HOWSON *St. Paul* II. xxiii. (1862) 356 The alarm of the sailors was great when they perceived how rapidly they were shoaling the water.

**b.** *absol.* Of a ship: To come into shallow water. *rare.*

**1898** HARDY *Wessex Poems* 100 He gained the beach, where Yeomen, . . With Regulars in thousands, were enmassed to meet the Foeman Whose fleet had not yet shoaled.

**4.** To cause (a piece of water) to become shallow; also, to obstruct by shoals.

**1864** G. P. MARSH *Man & Nat.* 430 The maritime approaches to river harbors frequented by the ships of Phenicia . . are shoaled to a considerable distance out to sea. **1865** J. H. INGRAHAM *Pillar of Fire* III. xii, He pursued with the idea that the sea had been shoaled by the wind.

†**5.** To drive (a plough) less deeply in the soil.

**1670** EVELYN in *Phil. Trans.* V. 1061 According to this proportion the husbandman must govern himself deepning or showling the Plough, as the condition of the land shall require.

**6.** *Otter-hunting.* (See quot.)

**1897** *Encycl. Sport* I. 583/2 *Shoal*, verb, to drive the otter down to the shallows.

Hence **shoaled** *ppl. a.* (see quot. 1867). '**shoaling** *ppl. a.*, growing shallow.

**1859** TENNYSON *Enid* 1536 Where like a shoaling sea the lovely blue Play'd into green. **1867** SMYTH *Sailor's Word-bk.*, *Shoaled-harbour*, that which is secured from the violence of the sea, by banks, bars, or shoals to seaward. **1892** STEVENSON *Vailima Lett.* xix. 181 The four . . set off in the boat across that rapidly shoaling bay of the lagoon.

**shoal** (ʃəʊl), *v.*[3] Also 7 shoole, shole. [f. SHOAL *sb.*[2] Cf. Fris. *skoalje*, Du. *scholen.*]

**1.** *intr.* Of fish: To collect or swim together in a shoal or shoals.

**1610** HOLLAND *Camden's Brit.* I. 718 About Midsommer they [*sc.* herrings] shoole out of the deep and vast Northen-sea to the coasts of Scotland. *c* **1611** CHAPMAN *Iliad* XXI. 191 The waue-sprung entrailes, about which, Fausens, and other fish, Did shole. **1774** GOLDSM. *Nat. Hist.* (1776) VI. 279 Gesner even asserts . . that he has seen them [*sc.* sturgeon] shoal together, at the notes of a trumpet. **1901** S. GWYNN *Mater Severa, Queen's Chron.* 28 The mackerel shoaling in each bay.

**2.** *transf.* Of persons, birds, things: To crowd together, assemble in swarms. Also with advs., as *together, in, up.*

*a* **1618** RALEIGH *Maxims* (1642) 21 Men of the same quality, tongue and condition, doe easily shole, and combine themselves together. **1638** WOTTON *Let. to Sir E. Bacon* 5 Dec. in *Reliq.* (1672) 472 Whereupon the Women . . do flock to St. Maries in such troops . . that the Masters of Art have no room to sit; so as the Vice-Chancellor and Heads of Houses were in deliberation to repress their shoaling thither. **1647** PAGITT *Heresiogr.* (ed. 4) B iij b, You have power to keep these Hereticks . . from . . sholing together to infect one another. **1667** MILTON *P.L.* x. 288. **1817** T. L. PEACOCK *Melincourt* xxx, The distracted multitude, who were shoaling in from all quarters. **1825** J. NEAL *Bro. Jonathan* III. 399 About him, on every side, were the white winged water-fowl . . shoaling up in the van of the sea breeze. **1863** *Reader* 12 Sept. 284/1 In England there are none of those pamphlets and mediocre romances which shoal in France.

Hence '**shoaling** *vbl. sb.*[2]

**1799** W. TOOKE *View Russian Emp.* III. 148 When the shoaling of the beluga has ceased. **1884** *Publ. Opinion* 12 Sept. 330/1 When this has happened during a great shoaling, the herrings have in subsequent years refused to pass over the spot.

†**shoal,** *v.*[4] *dial. Obs.* [Of obscure origin: cf. SHALDER *v.*] *intr.* Of soil: ? To crumble, become disintegrated.

**1733** W. ELLIS *Chiltern & Vale Farm.* 237 These stiff, cold Grounds, being of the most surly Nature, will not shoal, shatter nor crumble. **1750** —— *Mod. Husb.* V. iii. 7 (E.D.D.) The top of this land will shoal and run into a fine hollowness, even by very small frosts.

†'**shoalen,** *v. Obs. Naut.* [f. SHOAL *a.* + -EN[5].] *trans.* = SHOAL *v.*[2] 4.

**1731** CAPT. W. WRIGLESWORTH *MS. Log-bk. of the 'Lyell'* 2 Jan., When we sholened the water at 1, 2 and 3 this morning I judge wee were off of Fire Island. **1867** SMYTH *Sailor's Word-bk.* s.v. *Shoal*, A vessel is said to shoalen, or shoal her water, when she comes from a greater into a less depth.

**shoaler** ('ʃəʊlə(r)). ? *U.S.* [f. SHOAL *sb.*[1] + -ER[1].] (See quot.)

**1891** *Century Dict.*, *Shoaler*, a sailor in the coast-trade; a coaster: in distinction from one who makes voyages to foreign ports. *Shoaler-draft*, light draft: used with reference to vessels.

'**shoaliness.** *rare*$^{-1}$. [f. SHOALY *a.* + -NESS.] The state of being shoaly.

**1670** *Acc. Sev. Late Voy.* I. (1694) 122 He could not get higher with the Boat, by reason of the . . shoaliness in the Water. **1727** BAILEY vol. II, *Sholiness*, Fulness of Flats in the Sea, &c. **1755** JOHNSON, *Shoaliness*, shallowness; frequency of shallow places. [Hence in later Dicts.]

**shoaling** ('ʃəʊlɪŋ), *vbl. sb.*[1] [f. SHOAL *v.*[2] + -ING[1].]

**1.** The process of becoming shallow or more shallow; an instance of this.

**1633** T. JAMES *Voy.* 30 The shoalding of the Western shoare. **1832** LYELL *Princ. Geol.* II. 276 The shoaling continued until the river water prevailed. **1886** *Pall Mall Gaz.* 9 Dec. 1/1 As the shipowner is precluded from delivering his cargo by a blockade or a sudden shoaling up of the port of discharge.

**2.** *concr.* A place where the water becomes shallow.

**1574** W. BOURNE *Regiment for Sea* xxii. (1577) 61 Some sandes or daungers there be hauing fayre or good soundings or shaldings, that they may borrow of & on at their pleasure. **1644** MANWAYRING *Sea-mans Dict.* 94 When they say there is very good showleing, it is meant that the water doth grow shallower, by degrees, and not suddenly. **1689** *Lond. Gaz.* No. 2456/4 All the Sands, Shoalings, and Depths of Water, upon the said Coasts. **1887** HALL CAINE *Deemster* xxvi. 167 The ground swell among the shoalings before the storm comes to shore.

**3.** *Sc.* Spearing fish in shallow water.

**1792** *Statist. Acc. Scot.* II. 15 This [*sc.* spearing fish] is also called shauling; as it is generally practised, when the tide is almost spent, and the waters turned shallow.

**shoaling,** *vbl. sb.*[2]: see SHOAL *v.*[3]

**shoalness** ('ʃəʊlnɪs). For forms see SHOAL *a.* [-NESS.] Shallowness (of water).

**1552** HULOET, Shallownes or sholenes in water, *uadum.* **1588** HICKOCK tr. *C. Frederick's Voy.* 4 b, No great ships come thether, by reason of the sholdnes of the water thereabouts. *c* **1685** [see INTERCURRENT *a.* 1 a]. *c* **1725** *Torrington Mem.* (Camden) 104 In regard of the shoalness of the coast in that bay. **1862** DUPONT *Desp.* 4 Mar. in *Times* 27 Mar., The difficulties arising from the indirectness of the channel and from the shoalness of the bar.

**shoaly** ('ʃəʊlɪ), *a.* Also 7 sholy, 8–9 shoally. [f. SHOAL *sb.*[1] + -Y.] Full of shoals or shallows.

**1612** DRAYTON *Poly-olb.* xv. 235 [The river] hasting to his fall, his sholy grauell scowr's. **1697** DRYDEN *Æneid* V. 1130 The watchful Heroe felt the knocks: and found The tossing Vessel sail'd on shoaly Ground. **1707** *Lond. Gaz.* No. 4378/3 The Place . . being very narrow and shoally. **1820** *Q. Rev.* XXIII. 77 The basin is navigable, but shoally for about eight miles. **1892** *Cornhill Mag.* Dec. 570 To steer in a shoaly sea.

**shoar(e,** obs. forms of SHORE.

**shoat**[1]. *Obs.* exc. *dial.* Also 7 shote, shoate, shoot, 7, 9 shott, 9 shot. [Prob. repr. OE. *sceota* trout (? f. root of *scéotan* to shoot, with reference to its swift movement).] A fish resembling the trout, but smaller, found in Devon and Cornwall. (See also quots. 1865 and 1894.)

*a* **1000** *Colloq. Ælfric* in Wr.-Wülcker 94 *Tructos*, sceotan. **1602** CAREW *Cornwall* I. 26 The Shote [is] in a maner peculiar to Deuon and Cornwall, in shape and colour he resembleth the Trowt: howbeit in bignesse and goodnesse, commeth farre behind him. **1613–16** W. BROWNE *Brit. Past.* I. ii. 23 The Shoates with whom is Tauie fraught. *c* **1630** RISDON *Surv. Devon* §301 (1810) 312 This brook . . aboundeth with shoots and sheliscads, a fish not unlike the trout, and said to be peculiar to Devonshire and Cornwall. *a* **1636** WESTCOTE *View Devonsh.* (1845) 39 Scad. Salmon. Shott. Seal. **1865** COUCH *Brit. Fishes* IV. 225 Common Trout. [Syn.] Shot. **1880–84** F. DAY *Brit. Fishes* II. 104 *Salmo fario.* Shot (Westmoreland). **1894** *Trans. Woolhope Nat. Field Club* 204 Mr. Matthews caught a good many 'shotts' [app. a local term for grayling] in the Monnow above Monmouth Cap.

**shoat**[2] (ʃəʊt). *dial.* and *U.S.* Forms: 5 schoyth, 6 schot, shoit(e, shoitte, shoyte, shoyite, 7 shott, shoate, 5–9 shote, 6–9 shot, 7– shoat; 6–7 shoote, 7–9 shoot; 7 shutt, 8 shute, 8–9 shut. [Cf. WFlem. *schote, schoteling*, a pig under one year old.]

**1.** A young weaned pig.

**1413** *Durham Acc. Rolls* (Surtees) 54 In 1 porcell. de x$^{ma}$, 4d. In 1 Schoyth empt., 22d. **1465** *Mann. & Househ. Exp.* (Roxb.) 296 For vij. yonge shotes. v.s. **1509** in Stocks *Market Harb. Rec.* (1890) 230 A Boere Fedde v shots and A Sowe. **1567** *Richmond Wills* (Surtees) 203 Of old swyne xij. Two shoits, v piggs, iiij$^{s}$ viij$^{d}$. **1611** COTGR., *Marson*, a shoat; a hog thats a yeare, or vnder a yeare, old. **1618** WEBSTER & ROWLEY *Cure for Cuckold* II. iii, You have a brave Boy of your own wifes; Oh tis a shot to this pig. *c* **1640** J. SMYTH *Lives Berkeleys* (1883) I. 155 Hoggs, porkets, shootes and piggs. **1668** R. B. *Adagia Scot.* 54 The shots overgoes the old swine. **1669** WORLIDGE *Syst. Agric.* (1681) 331 *Sheat*, or *Shutt*, a young Hog. **1697** DAMPIER *Voy.* I. 411 We killed a small Shote, or young Porker. **1707** [E. WARD] *Barbacue Feast* 5 A Hoggard coming by with a Drove of young Shoats. *a* **1722** LISLE *Husb.* (1757) 403 Spayed and gelt shutes. **1787** W. H. MARSHALL *Norfolk* (1795) II. 388 *Shots*, young store swine. **1811** T. DAVIS *Agric. Wilts* 260

Shoots, young pigs of three or four months old. **1904** G. H. LORIMER *Old Gorgon Graham* vi. 120 Like a six-months shoat at the trough.

**2.** *transf.* An idle worthless person.

**1800** WEEMS *Life of Washington* vi. (1877) 40 The poorest shoat. **1840** HALIBURTON *Clockm.* Ser. III. xi. 153, I am the poorest shot in the world. Poorest shote, said he, you mean, for you have no soul in you. **1862** LOWELL *Biglow P.* Ser. II. iii, Long'z you elect for Congressmen poor shotes thet want to go Coz they can't seem to git their grub no otherways than so.

**shoat-fish**, error for SHEAT-FISH.

**1705** S. DALE *Pharmacol.* Suppl. 341 De Siluro... The Shoat-Fish.

**shoch** (ʃɒx), *sb.* *Anglo-Irish.* Also **shaugh, sheoch, shock, shough.** [a. Irish *seach* 'a turn; *seach tobac*, a smoke of a pipe' (Dinneen).] A draw at a tobacco-pipe, a smoke.

**1831** LOVER *Leg. & Stor. Irel.* Ser. I. 199 Afther gitten' an air o' the fire and a shaugh o' the pipe. **1900** *19th Cent.* July 79 Now 'herself'— as the [Irish] husband calls her—rarely indulges in a *shock* of the pipe. **1901** W. BARRY *Wizard's Knot* 53 (E.D.D.) We'll.. take the sheoch of a dudeen to clear our mouths of Davy Roche.

**shoch** (ʃɒx), *v.* *Anglo-Irish.* [f. prec.] *intr.* To draw at a tobacco-pipe, to smoke.

**1898** MACMANUS *Bend of Road* 107 An' himself an' the Playboy *shoughed* out o' the same pipe!

**shochel**, obs. form of SHAUCHLE *v.* *Sc.*

‖**'shochet.** *Judaism.* Pl. **shochetim.** [Heb. *shōḥēṭ*, pr. pple. of *shāḥaṭ* to slaughter.] A Jewish slaughterer, a person officially certified as competent to kill cattle and poultry in the manner prescribed by Jewish law.

**1889** HALL CAINE *Scapegoat* v, Within the gate of the Mellah, a shochet was killing fowls and taking his tribute of copper coins. **1892** ZANGWILL *Childr. Ghetto* I. 88, I don't believe the Shochetim kill the animals properly. **1907** —— *Ghetto Comedies* 386 The *Shomer* and the *Shochet* are the official twain of ritual butchery. **1961** A. W. MOSS *Valiant Crusade* vi. 81 In Shechita, the Shochet, or official who actually does the killing, has to be specially trained. **1972** *Daily Tel.* 8 June 18 Before the Shochet can use his knife the animal has to be got into the correct position.

**shochle**, var. SHAUCHLE, SHAUGHLE *v.* *Sc.*

‖**shochu** ('ʃoːtʃuː). [Jap.] A rough Japanese spirit distilled from various ingredients, including sake dregs. Also *attrib.*

**1938** BUSH & KAGAMI *Japanalia* 143/1 *Saké* contains 12 to 14 per cent. alcohol... *Shōchū*, distilled from *saké* dregs contains up to 60 per cent. alcohol. **1964** I. FLEMING *You only live Twice* x. 124 The herdsman.. handed Bond a bottle of what appeared to be water. Tiger said, 'This is *shochu*. It is a very raw gin.' **1970** J. KIRKUP *Japan behind Fan* 80 Cheap Japanese spirits known as *shochu*. **1980** 'J MELVILLE' *Chrysanthemum Chain* 88 A bottle of cheap *shochu* rotgut.

**shock** (ʃɒk), *sb.*[1] Forms: *α.* (4 ? **schoke**), 4–5 **schock, shokk,** 5 **s(c)hokke,** 6 **schocke, shoke,** 6–7 **shocke,** 4– **shock.** *β.* 8–9 *dial.* **shuck,** 9 **shook.** [Corresponds to OS. *scok* neut., some definite number of sheaves, MLG., LG. *schok* shock of corn, group of 60 units (see next), NFris. *skukke, skok* shock of corn, MDu. *schok* shock of corn, sixty (Mod.Du. only the latter), MHG. *schoc, schoch* heap, crowd, multitude, also sixty (mod.G. *schock* sixty), MSw. *skokk* crowd, flock (so Sw. *skock*, also sixty), Norw. *skok* flock, Da. dial. *skok* six sheaves.]

**1.** A group of sheaves of grain placed upright and supporting each other in order to permit the drying and ripening of the grain before carrying. Phrase, *in shock.*

*α.* *c* **1325** *Gloss. W. de Bibbesw.* in Wright *Voc.* 154 Les javeles en garbes lieet, En tresseus [*glossed* in schekes; ? *read* schokes] les garbes mettet. **1387–8** T. USK *Test. Love* I. Prol. 105 And al-though these noble repers,.. han al drawe and bounde up in the sheves, and mad many shockes, yet [etc.]. *c* **1440** *Promp. Parv.* 447/2 Schokke, of corne, *congelima.* **1490** CAXTON *Eneydos* xxi. 74 A shokke of whete or other corne. **1573** TUSSER *Husb.* (1878) 130 Corne tithed (sir Parson) to gather go get and cause it on shocks to be by and by set. **1621** BP. MOUNTAGU *Diatribæ* 170 The lightest sheafe in all the shocke,.. good enough for God. **1651** tr. *Kitchin's Jurisdict.* (1653) 87 The Lord cannot distrain shocks of Corn. **1670** J. WIGHTWICK in *O. Sansom's Acc. Life* (1710) 79 We having reaped two Acres of Wheat, and set it up in Shock, Lodowick came and threw it all down. **1746** *Brit. Mag.* 109 He found Three hundred Shock of Corn in the Fields. **1798** *Monthly Mag.* Mar. 192/2 They bind it [wheat] up in small sheaves, and place them in what they call shocks, ten together, five on each side. **1829** *Glover's Hist. Derby* I. 182 Whole fields of corn, both standing and in shock. **1891** MORRIS *Poems by Way* (1896) 192 So 'tis wellaway for Goldilocks, As he left the land of the wheaten shocks.

*β.* **1775** JOHNSON *West. Isl., Lough Ness* 68 A small spot of ground on which stood four shucks, containing each twelve sheaves of barley. **1784** W. H. MARSHALL *Midl. Counties* (1790) II. 15 In this country, 'sheaf corn' is universally 'hooded'—covered with two sheaves inverted,—as it is set up in 'shuck'. **1823** A. SMALL *Rom. Antiq. Fife* 135 Any piece of ground.. in which the stooks or shooks of corn stood thick after being reaped. **1892** P. H. EMERSON *Son of Fens* xv. 146 As I pitched on the two shooves to make up the shuck—that be twenty shooves.

**2.** *transf.* A crowd (of persons); a heap, bunch, bundle (of things).

*c* **1430** LYDG. *Paternoster* 306 Lyk as a glenere on a large lond Among shokkys plentyvous of auctours. **1567** GOLDING *Ovid's Met.* VII. (1593) 154 Folke by heaps did flocke To Marsis sacred field, and there stood thronging in a shocke. **1806** BERESFORD *Mis. Hum. Life* (1826) xii, We have both been equally busy.. in gleaning up such.. tortures.. as we had left behind at our general harvest. For my own share, I have cocked up a tolerable shock of 'em.

**3.** *Comb.* (See quots.)

**1865** *Trans. Illinois Agric. Soc.* V. 27 So long as the present system of.. placing shock-corn on the ground.. shall prevail. **1925** R. R. SNAPP *Beef Cattle* xv. 179 Before the silo became common, corn fodder or shock corn was used extensively for wintering cattle. **1845** W. SEWALL *Diary* 10 Dec. (1930) 280/2 Shucked out a little shock fodder. **1949** H. HORNSBY *Lonesome Valley* i. 12 Chester was up in the cornfield, getting a sledload of shock fodder. **1856** MORTON *Cycl. Agric.* II. 725/3 *Shock-fork* (Suff.) a large three-tined fork, used in gathering barley and clover into heaps for the pitchers. **1759** BROWN *Compl. Farmer* 47 Those pigs that are reared on stubble, are call'd shock pigs.

**shock** (ʃɒk), *sb.*[2] *Comm.* Now only *Hist.* Forms: 4 **schok, (scok)** 4–6 **shok,** 7 **shocke,** 6– **shock.** [a. G. (LG., HG.) *schock*, Du. *schok*; prob. a special use of *schock* = SHOCK *sb.*[1]]

**1.** A lot of sixty pieces. (Used with reference to certain articles of merchandise originally imported from abroad.)

[**1391** *Earl Derby's Exped.* (Camden) 72 Et per manus eiusdem pro ij schok bykeres per ipsum emptis ibidem, xx scot.] **1583** *Rates of Custome ho.* F j, Trayes the shock [1545 flocke] contayning lx. x, s. **1660** *Act 12 Chas. II*, c. 4 Sched. Rates, s.v. Boxes, Sope boxes the Shocke containing three-score boxes. **1674** JEAKE *Arith.* (1696) 65 Many small Wares called Habberdashery.. are sold by Dozens, Scores, Shocks. **1724** *Act 11 Geo. I*, c. 7 Addit. Bk. Rates, Platters of Wood, the Shock, containing sixty.

‖**b.** A German money of account = 60 groschen.

**1617** MORYSON *Itin.* I. 288 In Bohemia.. Merchants reckoned two hallers for a pfenning, and six pfenning for a grosh, and sixty grosh for a shocke.

†**2.** A roll of cloth containing twenty-eight ells. *Obs. rare*[−1].

**1612** *Sc. Bk. Customs* in *Halyburton's Ledger* (1867) 318 Poldaveis the shok contening xxviii elnis.

**shock** (ʃɒk), *sb.*[3] Forms: *α.* 6–7 **shocke** (6 **shocque**), 7 **shok,** 7–8 **shoke;** *β.* 6 **chok, choke,** 7 **choc, chock, chocke,** 7–8 **choque.** [app. a. F. *choc*, noun of action f. *choquer*: see SHOCK *v.*[2]

First adopted as a military term; the wider use is partly due to development in Eng., and partly to the readoption of the Fr. word in specific applications.

The *β* forms present difficulties. The *choc, choque* of the late 17th and early 18th c. were obviously viewed by the writers as adoptions from French; but in some of the earlier instances there are three possibilities: (1) the word may have been adopted orally with (ʃ), but spelt *ch* after the Fr.; (2) the word may have been originally a graphic adoption, and the *ch* have been pronounced in Eng. fashion as (tʃ); (3) the Fr. word may have been confused with an etymologically unrelated word *chock.*

The following examples, where *chocke* has the sense 'light blow', 'chuck (under the chin)' probably represent a different word (cf. similar examples under SHOCK *v.*[2]):

**1607** MARKHAM *Caval.* II. v, 82 Giue him the euen stroke with both your spurres, & a good chocke in the mouth with your brydle hand. **1611** (see CHUCK *sb.*[3] 1).]

**1. a.** *Mil.* The encounter of an armed force with the enemy in a charge or onset; also, the encounter of two mounted warriors or jousters charging one another.

*α.* **1565** COOPER *Thesaurus, Coitio militum*, the shocke. **1583** STOCKER *Civ. Warres Lowe C.* III. 106 The saide Englishe Men abode the first Shocque or charge. **1594** SHAKS. *Rich. III*, v. iii. 93 This doubtfull shocke of Armes. **1621** in Kempe *Losely MSS.* (1836) 462 Ye best men for yᵉ shock of yᵉ warr. **1634** PEACHAM *Compl. Gentl.* xix. (ed. 2) 242 But the Pikes when they are to give or receive a shocke, are to be commanded [etc.]. **1758** *Ann. Reg.* 52 The Prussian infantry, which had often stood, and often given, so many terrible shocks. **1814** SOUTHEY *Roderick* xxv. 166 Anon the hosts met in the shock of battle. **1881** BELL tr. *C. von Schmidt's Instr. Training Cavalry* 129 We thus obtain the moral effect of surprise, in addition to the physcial effect of the shock and sabre, &c. **1897** 'O. RHOSCOMYL' *White Rose Arno* 210 To retreat without coming to the shock.

*β.* **1584** HUDSON *Du Bartas' Judith* v. (1608) 78 Scarsly they could keep them in their bound, Till pype, or Cymball, or the trumpets sound, Denounce the choke. **1585** JAS. I *Ess. Poesie* (Arb.) 17 Syne Phifers, Drummes, and Trumpets cleir do craue The pelmell chok.

**b.** *transf.* and *fig.*

*α.* **1638–56** COWLEY *Davideis* III. Poems (1905) 341 Long had the patient Adriel humbly born The roughest Shocks of her imperious Scorn. **1683** D. A. *Art of Converse* 87 It happens.. that we either understand not, or mistake what is said in opposition to what we advance..; we think only on't when the shoke is past, that we could have easily return'd this or that answer. **1879** B. TAYLOR *Germ. Lit.* 285 The shock and encounter of thought.

*β.* **1665–6** PEPYS *Diary* 14 Feb., Sir G. Carteret had prepared himself to answer a choque of Sir W. Coventry, by offering of himself to shew all he had paid, and what is unpaid [etc.].

**2. a.** A sudden and violent blow, impact, or collision, tending to overthrow or to produce internal oscillation in a body subjected to it; the disturbance of equilibrium or the internal oscillation resulting from this. Also, a sudden large application of energy other than mechanical energy, esp. thermal energy (cf. *thermal shock*); a shock wave.

**1614** GORGES *Lucan* VI. 219 The rams, the engines, and the slings,.. Whose often shockes did make such wrack, That tower and rampart gins to crack. **1653** H. COGAN tr. *Pinto's Trav.* xxiii. 81 He.. running her on the starboard side gave her so terrible a shock that they sank both together. **1741** A. MONRO *Anat.* (ed. 3) 302 To prevent too great a Shoke of the Fabrick of the Body in walking. **1813** SCOTT *Trierm.* III. xxxix, Fierce and frequent were the shocks. **1842** TENNYSON *Godiva* 74 With twelve great shocks of sound, the shameless noon Was clash'd and hammer'd from a hundred towers. **1865** TYNDALL *Fragm. Sci.* (1879) I. ii. 66 Millions of shocks are received every second from the calorific waves. **1889** SIR E. ARNOLD *Seas & Lands* ii. (1895) 17 The colossal block [of consolidated snow] capsizes with a second shock, startling the ocean for leagues around. **1904, 1907** [see SHOCK WAVE a]. **1932** *Trans. Amer. Soc. Mech. Engineers* LIV. 310/2 The actual deflection can be estimated.. from the location of the strong compression shock waves which follow the shock between the convergent streams. **1950** D. Q. KERN *Process Heat Transfer* xx. 733 While scale may be loosened by thermal shock, the shock does not necessarily cause it to drop off the tubes. **1955** K. F. HERZFELD in F. D. Rossini *Thermodynamics & Physics of Matter* H. ii. 686 In this method a shock travels down a shock tube. Behind it, the gas is adiabatically.. compressed and is at higher temperature. The shock itself is only a few mean free paths thick. **1966** *McGraw-Hill Encycl. Sci. & Technol.* XIII. 552/1 Such shock arises when a body at one uniform temperature is suddenly accelerated to or decelerated from high supersonic or hypersonic speeds. **1974** *Acustica* XXX. 260 A reproducible acoustic shock pulse is generated in an aluminium bar by means of a transducer of the electro-magnetic induction type.

*β.* **1603** FLORIO *Montaigne* I. xix. 32 Hast thou not seene.. one of his ancestors die miserably by the chocke of an hog [orig. *chocqué par un pourceau*]. **1684** WALLER *Ess. Nat. Exper.* 59 As soon as ever the Bubbles rise above the Vinegar, and by the chock of the Air break, their Covering is curiously scattered about. **1726** SWIFT *Gulliver* III. iii, A sudden fall might endanger the bottom or under surface of the island, which.. might happen to crack by too great a choque.

**b.** *spec.* (= *earthquake shock*). A sudden and more or less violent shake of a part of the earth's surface; a single movement of the series of movements constituting an earthquake.

**1692** T. ROBINSON in Ray *Disc.* II. v. (1693) 211 Some Machines were.. retarded by the Choc [of the Earthquake]. **1719** DE FOE *Crusoe* I. 95 After I.. found still no more Shocks of the Earthquake follow, I began to be more compos'd. **1767** *Ann. Reg.* 67 They had felt thirty-six shocks of the earth. **1869** PHILLIPS *Vesuv.* ix. 253 Vibrations in the land—suddenly excited and rapidly passing on, so as to be described as 'shocks'.

**3.** *transf.* and *fig.* **a.** A sudden and violent effect tending to impair the stability or permanence of something; a damaging blow (to a condition of things, a person's health or constitution, an institution, a belief, etc.).

**1654** tr. *Scudery's Curia Pol.* 92 Griefe did not seize upon her reason.. and it is fit then that joy should not now give a chock to mine. **1736** BUTLER *Anal.* I. i. 21 The great shock and alteration, which we shall undergo by death. **1794** MRS. RADCLIFFE *Myst. Udolpho* i, It gave a severe shock to his constitution. **1833** HT. MARTINEAU *Berkeley* I. viii. 152 The shock given to commercial credit. **1885** TEMPLE *Relig. & Sci.* iv. 109 In spite of these shocks belief in revelation is strong still in men's souls.

†**b.** Opposition, clashing, conflict. (Cf. SHOCK *v.*[2] 1 c.) *Obs.*

**1664** MARVELL *Corr.* Wks. 1872–5 II. 172 Your Majesties Sovereign Power is free from all shock and competition.

**4. a.** A sudden and disturbing impression on the mind or feelings; usually, one produced by some unwelcome occurrence or perception, by pain, grief, or violent emotion (occas. joy), and tending to occasion lasting depression or loss of composure; in weaker sense, a thrill or start of surprise, or of suddenly excited feeling of any kind. Also *ironically* in apposition with *horror*; so ***shock-horror*** used *attrib.*

**1705** COLLIER *Ess. Mor. Subj.* III. *Pain* 12 He that can't stand the Shock of Pain.. can never be firm in his Duty, nor true to his Engagements. **1782** MISS BURNEY *Cecilia* x. x. (1882) II. 463 When Cecilia was a little recovered from the shock of the first interview. **1812** CRABBE *Tales, Arabella* 28 But (though her young companions felt the shock) She studied Berkeley, Bacon, Hobbes, and Locke. **1848** THACKERAY *Van. Fair* xxxix, So Mrs. Bute, after the first shock of rage and disappointment, began to accommodate herself as best she could to her altered fortunes. **1879** GEO. ELIOT *Theo. Such* x. 180 Invigorating shocks of laughter. **1885** 'MRS. ALEXANDER' *At Bay* v, It gives me a kind of shock to think you are obliged to be on your guard in your own home. **1977** *Gay News* 7–20 Apr. 15/3 The message must have got through: certainly there were no shock-horror reactions and fun was had by all. **1980** *Times Lit. Suppl.* 31 Oct. 1240/4 The shock-horror world of the media men. **1981** *Brit. Med. Jrnl.* 18 Apr. 1312/2 The shock-horror *TV Eye* of recent weeks.

**b.** Used for: An occurrence, discovery, etc. that occasions a shock.

**1841** B'NESS BUNSEN in Hare *Life* (1879) II. 18 The death of my Father was a great shock to me. **1902** R. BAGOT *Donna Diana* xiv. 161 It had been somewhat of a shock to the Cardinal when Monsignor Tomei had frankly informed him that [etc.].

**c.** A feeling of being shocked (see SHOCK *v.*[2] 4); a pained sense of something offensive to morality or decorum.

**1876** TREVELYAN *Macaulay* I. iv. 159 He was still quite young when the concession of Catholic Emancipation gave a moral shock to the Tory party. **1874** H. R. REYNOLDS *John*

*Bapt.* v. §2. 321 It occasioned no moral shock for Him to believe in the gospel of the kingdom.

**d.** (*a*) ***culture*** (or ***cultural***) ***shock***: a state of distress or disorientation brought about by sudden subjection to an unfamiliar culture; (*b*) ***future shock***: an analogous state brought about by too rapid a pace of social or technological change.

(*a*) **1940** J. B. Holt in *Amer. Sociol. Rev.* Oct. 744 All these citations suggest the 'culture shock' arising from the precipitation of a rural person or group into an urban situation. **1952** *Human Organization* Spring 16 (*heading*) The Papuan Ovokaiva vs Mt. Lamington: Cultural shock and its aftermath. **1960** [see *culture shock* s.v. CULTURE *sb.* 5 d]. **1970** A. Toffler *Future Shock* i. 12 Culture shock is the effect that, immersion in a strange culture has on the unprepared visitor... Culture shock is what happens when a traveler suddenly finds himself in a place where yes may mean no, where a 'fixed price' is negotiable, where to be kept waiting in an outer office is no cause for insult, where laughter may signify anger. **1978** *Lancashire Life* July 43/3 To see a defender in a protective helmet playing at cover point can cause culture shock in newcomers to the game. (*b*) **1965** A. Toffler in *Horizon* Summer 109/1 Culture shock is relatively mild in comparison with a much more serious malady that might be called 'future shock'. Future shock is the dizzying disorientation brought on by the premature arrival of the future. It may well be the most important disease of tomorrow. **1972** *Newsweek* 17 July 34 Fortunately, Japan's innate self discipline and sense of harmony have cushioned much of the 'future shock'.. and so far Japan is relatively free of the.. disorders so prevalent in other industrialized societies. **1975** *Whig-Standard* (Kingston, Ontario) 7 Jan. 6/3 Canada's foreign policy is in poor health these days—suffering from a severe case of future shock complicated by a crippling inferiority complex.

**5.** *Med.* **a.** A sudden debilitating effect produced by over-stimulation of nerves, intense pain, violent emotion, or the like; the condition of nervous exhaustion resulting from this. Now used more precisely for a condition whose principal characteristic is low blood volume (see quot. 1968); also *ellipt.* for *shell shock* s.v. SHELL *sb.* 40. ***in shock***, in a state of shock; incapacitated by very low blood pressure and associated symptoms, or debilitated by ill-treatment or bad news; so ***into shock, out of shock***.

**1804** Abernethy *Surg. Observ.* 218 The shock of the operation. **1867** E. Morris (*title*) A practical Treatise on Shock after Surgical Operations and Injuries. **1889** *Amer. Jrnl. Med. Sci.* XCVII. 282 For the purpose of stimulating a patient in shock it is more rational to give ether than to give alcohol. **1898** *Allbutt's Syst. Med.* V. 430 The condition known as 'shock', which is apt to supervene, to a greater or less degree, on serious injuries and on surgical operations. **1912** *Standard* 20 Sept. 8/4 She suffered severely from inflammation of the eyes and nervous shock. **1917** W. Owen *Let.* 23 May (1967) 463 Sorrel was mentioned for Shock [in the Casualty List]. **1928** *Jrnl. Amer. Med. Assoc.* 9 June 1859/2 The blood pressure.. suddenly fell to 52 systolic and 44 diastolic as he went into shock. **1958** J. Cannan *And be Villain* vi. 137 Mrs Hallow was subjected to quite an ordeal this morning and is practically in shock. **1959** *Woman's Own* 27 June 44/2 She's in shock, of course, but we're giving her a transfusion. **1968** Passmore & Robson *Compan. Med. Stud.* I. xxviii. 41/1 Loss of blood volume is an important but not the only cause of shock; a similar state of shock occurs in acute heart failure and in severe infections in which the responsible haemodynamic mechanisms are different. **1975** *Publishers Weekly* 21 July 67/2 When Joe signed his first pro contract, Rose.. went into shock. **1980** M. Russell *Death Fuse* xvi. 149, I think she's able to talk. She's out of shock.

**b.** A paralytic seizure or stroke. Chiefly *Sc.* and *U.S. dial.*

**1794** J. Woodforde *Diary* 13 Oct. (1929) IV. 143 Mr. Whitmell had a kind of Paralytic Shock this last Spring. **1896** H. Johnston *Dr. Congalton's Legacy* xxiv. 315 The mistress of Windy-yett had taken 'a terrible turn—a shock or something'. **1903** K. D. Wiggin *Rebecca of Sunnybrook Farm* xxvi. 279 We had three o' the worst shocks in our family that there ever was.. and I know every symptom of 'em better 'n the doctors. **1951** E. Graham *My Window looks down East* xi. 96 That was when he came the nearest to the stroke. (In Maine we call them 'shocks'.) **1955** W. P. Milne *Eppie Elrick* xxx. 284 Haein teen a shock an' soocht awa in 'is sleep. **1981** M. Cantwell in *N.Y. Times Mag.* 9 Aug. 6/4 One cause of my future demise might be that I 'took a shock.' In other places, a person in that condition would be said to have suffered a paralytic stroke.

**c.** ***anaphylactic shock***: see s.v. ANAPHYLAXIS.

**6.** A momentary stimulation of a nerve. Also, a stimulation of nerves with resulting contraction of muscles and feeling of concussion; *spec.* = *electric shock* (see ELECTRIC *a.* 2 b).

**1746** W. Watson *Sequel to Experiments in Electr.* 10 He receives a violent shock through both his arms. **1818** Bostock *Galvanism* 24 Volta.. found that forty pairs of the metallic disks, with the proper number of pieces of moistened card interposed, were sufficient to produce a shock, which was very distinctly felt in the hands and arms. **1857** Hughes *Tom Brown* II. iii, He.. had made unto himself an electric machine from which it was his greatest pleasure and glory to administer small shocks to any small boys who were rash enough to venture into his study. **1899** *Allbutt's Syst. Med.* VIII. 828 The needles should not touch one another or shocks are produced, very harmful to young infants.

**7.** ellipt. for *shock-absorber*. Chiefly *U.S.*

**1961** in Webster. **1968** *Hot Car* Nov. 14/2 (Advt.), These are the shocks to end all shocks. **1977** *Transatlantic Rev.* LX. 22 He told her that the car would also need new shocks, brakes, a muffler, a starter and an engine job. **1979** *Guardian* 4 June 6/7 Shock-absorber people who will swop your worn-out shocks.

**8.** *attrib.* and *Comb.*, as ***shock effect, -value***; ***shock-like, -resistant, -resisting, -seasoned*** adjs.; also, of things that startle or shock, as ***shock headline, language, news, story***; **shock-action** *Mil.*, a method of attack by a charge of cavalry, in which the force of the impact is principally relied upon; †**shock-bottle**, a humorous designation for an electric jar; **shock cone** *Aeronaut.*, a nose cone or other conical fairing which serves to streamline an aircraft for supersonic flight; **shock cord**, heavy elasticated cord designed to absorb or resist mechanical shock; a length of this; **shock excitation**, the excitation of natural oscillations in a system by a sudden impulse of energy from an external source; so **shock-excited** *ppl. a.*; **shock front**, the wave front of a shock wave; **shock measure**, a severe or exceptional measure taken usu. to deal with an emergency; **shock-mount** *sb.*, a mounting designed to absorb or resist mechanical shock; also as *v. trans.*, to attach by means of such a mounting; **shock-mounted** *ppl. a.*, **shock-mounting** *vbl. sb.*; **shock police**, in Spain, a republican force of specially armed police for use in assault operations; **shock-proof** *a.*, proof against damage by mechanical shock or by a surge of electrical power; also *fig.*; hence **shock-proofing** *vbl. sb.*, the process of rendering shock-proof; **shock stall** *Aeronaut.*, a stalling condition undergone by an aircraft at a speed close to that of sound, involving increased air resistance and loss of lift and control; also **shock stalling** *vbl. sb.*; **shock strut** *Aeronaut.*, a strut containing a shock absorber in the landing gear of an aircraft; **shock-tactics** *Mil.*, tactics in which shock-action forms a principal part; also *transf.* and *fig.*; also occas. **shock-tactic**; **shock test**, a test in which an object is subjected to mechanical shock; hence **shock-testing** *vbl. sb.*; **shock therapy, treatment**, treatment by means of artificially induced shock, whether anaphylactic, electrical, or drug-induced; *spec.* electro-convulsive therapy; also *fig.*; **shock tube**, an apparatus for producing shock waves by making a gas at high pressure expand suddenly into a low-pressure tube or cavity.

**1884** M. H. Hayes *Man. Tactics* iv. 25 The distinguishing characteristics of cavalry are its great mobility and *shock action. **1827** in *Hone's Every-day Bk.* II. 1077 Taking from *Shock-bottles shocks. **1947** *Shell Aviation News* No. 112. 6/3 Republic is building a fighter aircraft with a needle-nose *shock cone to permit supersonic speed. **1961** *Aeroplane* CI. 548/1 The 'shock cones' are merely fairings over the boundary-layer bleed, which brings the intakes proud of the fuselage. **1930** P. White *How to fly Airplane* xx. 279 (*caption*) Two boys at the rear are holding against the pull of the *shock cord. **1980** *TWA Ambassador* Oct. 32/3 Secure all gear, such as the coffee-cans, in the canoe with rope or shock cord. **1959** *N. & Q.* CCIV. 36/2 The most intense *shock effects come from the imposition of war's horrible destruction upon familiar places usually associated with quiet and peace. **1977** A. Giddens *Stud. in Social & Polit. Theory* ix. 317 Suicide attempts do appear to have a 'shock' effect on relatives and friends. **1920** E. W. Stone *Elem. Radiotelegr.* iii. 54 Exciting a vibratory circuit into oscillation is variously termed impulse excitation, *shock excitation, and whip-crack excitation. **1930** A. B. Wood *Textbk. Sound* 213 A single explosion impulse is often sufficient to set a resonator into vibration, thereby producing a musical note or a noise by shock excitation. **1967** R. F. Graf *Mod. Dict. Electronics* 138/2 *Free oscillations*, commonly referred to as *shock-excited oscillations. **1975** D. G. Fink *Electronics Engineers' Handbk.* XIX. 17 The sound levels of shock-excited tones are more difficult to specify because they vary so much during decay and can be excited over a very wide range. **1949** L. M. Milne-Thomson *Theoret. Hydrodynamics* (ed. 2) xx. 577 If the *shock front is sufficiently oblique to the oncoming air, the conditions behind may still be supersonic. **1969** *New Scientist* 28 Aug. 434/2 The boom signature appears to coalesce at a relatively short distance from the flightpath into two shockfronts. **1977** M. Walker *National Front* iii. 60 *Shock headlines like 'Five Million Coloured Asians now in Britain?' (*RPS News*). **1959** *Listener* 13 Aug. 253/1 One is reminded more of the *shock-language of the *avant-garde* Russian poets of the time. **1899** *Allbutt's Syst. Med.* VII. 865 The muscular contractions differ from those which occur in ordinary chorea by being sudden and *shock-like. **1962** *Daily Tel.* 13 Dec. 10/2 Mr. Marples's *shock measures.. will be more than justified if this savage record [of death and injury on the roads] can be substantially improved. **1939** *Interavia* 5 Dec. 10 Two sets of *shock mounts on either side of the blades are employed. **1947** B. W. Pike et al. in A. Roberts *Radar Beacons* xvi. 361 The beacon should be either internally *shock-mounted or carried in a padded case. **1976** *National Observer* (U.S.) 1 May 3/4 (Advt.), Precision, shock-mounted lucite level. **1942** P. C. Sandretto *Princ. Aeronaut. Radio Engin.* i. 10 *Shock mounting in the past consisted of certain rubber shock absorbers mounted to the radio units; however, the trend is toward the use of shock-mounted shelves permanently installed in the airplane. **1964** R. F. Ficchi *Electr. Interference* iv. 40 Since many equipments are presently being installed on shock mountings so they will not be affected by vibration, it is important to bond adequately across shock mounts. **1973** *Times* 31 Oct. (Suppl.) p. viii, His company believe they can avoid fatigue failure.. by overdesign of various components and by shock-mounting valves, pipes and other equipment. **1974** *Times* 3 Apr. 1/1 (*heading*) *Shock news is broken to EEC ministers. **1937** *Ann. Reg. 1936* 249 The murder, on July 12, of Lieutenant Castillo of the *Shock Police (known to have Socialist sympathies) by gangsters of the Right. **1957** P. Kemp *Mine were of Trouble* i. 16 Shock Police (*Guardias de Asalto*), posted in side streets on motor cycles. **1911** T. Dreiser *Jennie Gerhardt* xviii. 138 He was.. curiously elated beneath a sturdy, *shock-proof exterior. **1925** *Wireless World* 8 Apr. 280/3 (*heading*) Shock-proof valve holder. **1930** R. Macaulay *Staying with Relations* xiv. 203 They needed a shock-proof screen between them, to deaden the assaults of each on the other's strained nerves. **1952** H. R. Clauser *Pract. Radiogr. for Industry* iii. 37 Protection is obtained by immersing the [X-ray] tube in oil inside a shockproof casing. **1971** J. Wainwright *Dig Grave & let him Lie* 20 He was shockproof—the ultimate example of what bobbying can do to a man. **1978** R. Good *Watches in Colour* viii. 116 Shock-proof bearings for the balance pivots. **1952** H. R. Clauser *Pract. Radiogr. for Industry* iii. 37 *Shockproofing of x-ray tubes can be done by enclosing the tube in a casing which is at ground potential. **1946** D. de Carle *Practical Watch Repairing* (1947) xx. 262 The *shock-resistant watch cannot be looked upon as a novelty, in the sense that it is a passing phase. **1963** *New Yorker* 7 Dec. 136/1 (Advt.), Self-winding, thin, water- and shock-resistant. **1842** *Civil Engin. & Arch. Jrnl.* V. 285/2 We have reduced the blow or *shock-resisting quality of the iron. **1863** Patmore *Angel in Ho.* II. I. ix, My lonely faith, like heart-of-oak, *Shock-season'd. **1938** *Proc. R. Soc.* A. CLXIX. 188 This critical speed at which the sound wave condenses into a single pressure discontinuity is probably the *shock stall or compressibility stall. **1948** *Sci. News* VII. 30 The use of swept-back wings raises the critical Mach number for the aircraft and allows the higher speeds to be reached without the danger of shock stall. **1966** D. Stinton *Anat. of Aeroplane* vi. 103 The buffeting and sharp loss of lift (Shockstall) caused by compressibility gave rise to the early misconception of a 'sound-barrier', beyond which man might not fly. **1937** *Flight* 4 Nov. 450/1 The elliptic cylinder ..has a lower maximum velocity..and therefore presumably a higher *shock stalling speed. **1952** W. J. Duncan *Princ. Control & Stability of Aircraft* xiii. 310 The separation of the shock stalling and critical Mach numbers may vary from almost zero to about 0·2. **1946** *Sun* (Baltimore) 5 Nov. 9/6 (Advt.), You'll see the *shock story of the year. **1931** F. D. Bradbrooke *Light Aeroplane Man.* vi. 92 When the advantages of the divided undercarriage began to compel attention the shock-absorbing gear had to be incorporated in the compression or *shock strut. This was done by having a telescopic strut, generally with projections in each portion which were lashed with rubber cord in such a way that a shortening of the strut stretched the cord. **1949** J. W. Vale *Aviation Mechanic's Aircraft Man.* xii. 343 The fluid used in the Pneudraulic shock struts.. may be used for initial filling or for partial refilling. **1895** Sir E. Wood *Cavalry Waterloo Camp.* i. (ed. 2) 2 The most successful 'Nation in Arms', believing thoroughly in the use of *shock tactics, has adopted the lance, not only for 'Medium', but also for 'Light' Cavalry. **1919** *Manch. Guardian* 4 Feb. 5/1 It was the 'shock Tactics' of labour warfare. **1954** *Essays & Studies* VII. 84 To judge from the vehement reactions of the critics, the revolutionary shock-tactics seem in this aim to have succeeded remarkably well. **1959** *Listener* 19 Nov. 895/2 This definition of Zen as a kind of natural mysticism whose shock-tactic and other techniques are designed to stimulate the intuitive and.. religious awareness. **1960** G. E. Evans *Horse in Furrow* xx. 239 His initial shock tactics were successful: he gained control of the horse. **1961** *Encounter* Apr. 56/2 This shock-tactic had by no means the same general appeal as his witch being burnt at the stake. **1977** R. Barnard *Blood Brotherhood* ix. 92 There was a hidden design behind.. Chief Inspector Plunkett's questions, or perhaps..he was trying shock tactics. **1904** *Proc. Inst. Mech. Engineers* 1135 Considerable movement has been made of late towards the establishment of a *shock test for steel. **1949** J. F. Blackburn *Components Handbk.* xiii. 516 In certain cases the shock tests resulted in permanent mechanical damage to the relays, often without opening the contacts. **1974** *Jrnl. Soc. Environmental Engineers* XIII. 17/1 Maximum displacement during a shock test can be obtained in several ways, one of the simplest is to measure the deformation of a piece of plasticine. **1917** *Jrnl. Iron & Steel Inst.* XCVI. 65 The regularity of the results which can be obtained with carefully manipulated *shock-testing machines. *Ibid.*, A system of calibrating apparatus for the shock-testing of metals. **1963** C. T. Morrow *Shock & Vibration Engin.* I. v. 114 The advantages of an asymmetrical pulse shape in shock testing. **1917** *Jrnl. Exper. Med.* XXVI. 699 The mechanism of recovery following the so called 'protein *shock therapy'. *Ibid.* 705 Bacterial infection not confined to the lymph spaces will not be influenced by shock therapy to the same extent. **1939** *Jrnl. Amer. Med. Assoc.* 16 Sept. 1170/2 Dislocations and fractures occur in insulin and metrazol shock therapy. *Ibid.* 2 Dec. 2100/2 The author recommends the use of electric shock therapy for old cases of depressive psychosis in which other therapeutic methods have failed. **1953** H. Read *True Voice of Feeling* I. viii. 149 There may be more sense in [Ezra] Pound's shock-therapy. **1973** W. Barlow *Alexander Principle* i. 13 The psychiatrists.. treated her with shock therapy and anti-depressant drugs. **1979** *Tucson Mag.* Jan. 24/1 The shock therapy that was Simon's murder induced a spirited public outcry. **1938** M. Sakel (*title*) The pharmacological *shock treatment of schizophrenia. **1939** *Jrnl. Amer. Med. Assoc.* 16 Sept. 1170/2 (*heading*) Faradic shock treatment of 'functional' psychoses. **1945** Koestler *Yogi & Commissar* III. iii. 202 That diplomatic shock-treatment of which they have so far only had a faint foretaste. **1947** *Sun* (Baltimore) 20 Jan. 7/1 We believe that the 'shock treatment' of prompt action is needed to halt the insane spiral of mounting costs and rising prices. **1974** *Listener* 24 Jan. 124/3 Munch suffered a complete breakdown, received shock treatment at a clinic in Copenhagen. **1949** *Sci. Amer.* Nov. 18/2 These pictures illustrate the great potentiality of the *shock tube in observing and recording supersonic flow patterns. **1977** I. M. Campbell *Energy & Atmosphere* v. 105 In the shock tube these conditions are produced by the rapid adiabatic compression of air or $N_2$–$O_2$ mixtures across the shock front created by the sudden release of high-pressure driver gas at one end of the tube. **1933** *Archit. Rev.* LXXIV. 68/1 The

*Daily Mail*, drawn naturally to the new medium by its tradition of public-spirited interest in aviation and its awareness of the *shock-value of surprise. **1959** *Encounter* Nov. 59/2 He had never dreamt that his [ballet] company would have such shock-value.

**b. shock troops** [tr. G. *stosstruppen*], forces of selected and specially armed men trained for deployment in assault operations, especially against strong positions or large numbers; (rarely) *sing.*, such a force. Also *fig.* and *attrib.* (in *sing.*). Hence **shock trooper**.

**1917** *Times* 20 June 5/5 The second shock-troop battalion of the Third Army. **1918** E. S. Farrow *Dict. Mil. Terms* 553 *Shock Troops*, troops especially selected for assault work. They usually wear steel breastplates and other protection strong enough to turn a bullet at 50 or 60 feet. **1927** *Daily Express* 14 July 9/4 The G.P.U. troops..in..a war against Poland and Britain..would be used as shock troops. **1928** *Dict. Amer. Biogr.* I. 382/2 A master of strategy usually stays behind the lines. Not so Bishop Asbury. He asked no more of his skirmishers and shock troops than he was himself prepared to undergo. **1934** W. A. Edwards in F. R. Leavis *Determinations* 155 Swinburne, like some Soviet shock-trooper exhorting feeble comrades, batters and bullies us into thinking every playwright a demi-god. **1938** Auden & Isherwood *On Frontier* I. i. 30 As for the Shock Troops.. the whole organization's rotten from top to bottom. *Ibid.* II. i. 61 Such a nice boy! And quite high up in his shock-troop already. *Ibid.* ii. 84 My Peace Speech. I shall stand before my shock troopers and I shall tell them [etc.]. **1940** *Ann. Reg. 1939* 225, 54 front-line divisions..of which 14 divisions represented shock troops. **1940** *War Illustr.* 12 Apr. 353 Those who man the submarines may well be called the 'shock troops' of the sea, for of all the seafaring men their task is surely the most arduous and the most dangerous. **1952** C. Day Lewis tr. *Virgil's Aeneid* II. 48 At the Scaean gate, panoplied Juno Heads the shock-troops. **1955** M. Banks *Commando Climber* i. 6 As the war developed, the general trend of commando operations had been..towards the amphibious shock-troop variety of fighting, usually on a brigade or at least on a commando scale. **1955** A. Galland *First & Last* xii. 91 The fighter supporting land operations of the army is exclusively a tactical arm, a kind of 'flying shock-troop', for attacking at low level enemy positions and troop movements in the front line, even with bombs, rockets and small arms. **1959** *Listener* 10 Dec. 1031/1 The main line of Chartist stock in the north is poorly represented. Where are those shock troops of Feargus O'Connor, from whose enduring loyalty his influence in the movement was derived? **1962** *Daily Tel.* 14 Sept. 24/5 While Mr. Macmillan was having longish talks with Mr. Menzies of Australia and Mr. Diefenbaker of Canada and others, his shocktroop Ministers, Mr. Sandys and Mr. Heath were standing up to all comers. **1968** *Economist* 16 Nov. 67/1 The National Union of Mineworkers' leaders voted to accept exactly the same percentage pay rise for their men, once the shocktroops of the wage struggle. **1973** R. L. Fox *Alexander* iv. 78 The Shield Bearers..served as shock troops on night raids, hill climbs and forced marches. **1975** *Guardian* 21 Jan. 14/1 The cliché about the Jesuits as the 'Pope's shock troops'. **1977** *Times* 21 Nov. 15/6 Many members of the Waffen SS..were used simply as shock troops during Hitler's War.

**c.** Applied to a worker in the U.S.S.R. who voluntarily exceeds the production quotas and is regarded as exemplary, and to a brigade formed by such workers and used for the achievement of arduous or urgent tasks; also to such methods of work.

**1931** S. N. Harper *Making Bolsheviks* iii. 52 The so-called 'shock-brigade movement' among workmen, which is interpreted by the Communists as an illustration of a new attitude and as a new and vital force produced by the Revolution. *Ibid.* 53 The shock-brigade of a given factory or mine is a voluntary organization of workmen who have come together to fulfil and, if possible, exceed the quota of production assigned to the factory under the Five-Year Plan of expansion. **1931** *Times Lit. Suppl.* 9 July 536/4 'Cultural work' is still in effect a kind of propagandist 'shock work'. **1931** *Morning Post* 11 Aug. 11/7 Three hundred and fifty Russian 'shock workers' landed in London from the S.S. Ukraine yesterday for a two days' 'holiday'. **1934** *Spectator* 26 Oct. 615/2 The 'shock-brigaders' and star 'go-getters'. **1938** *Times* 25 July 13/6 The other projects undertaken by the groups include organization of labour to help in times of special agricultural pressure (like the Shock Brigades in Russia). **1939** R. Campbell *Flowering Rifle* v. 124 Each grim, shock-working Stakhanov. **1946** —— *Talking Bronco* 16 For us mere Shock-workers of the Camp and City Whose sweat, and life-blood, is their beer. **1949** F. Maclean *Eastern Approaches* I. xi. 157 From what I had heard of Soviet 'shock' methods a group of Stakhanovites or shock-workers should be able to put any paddle boat in order in an hour or two. **1962** E. Snow *Red China Today* (1963) lviii. 441 By intensive cultivation, luck and shock-brigade methods, we brought in a rich harvest in record time. **1981** I. Boland tr. *Ginzburg's Within Whirlwind* I. x. 84 The management did not want to use force... These girls were shock workers.

† **shock**, *sb.*[4] *Obs.* [See shough.] A dog having long shaggy hair, *spec.* a poodle. See also shock-dog.

**1638** Nabbes *Bride* v. i, My neighbour is very skilfull; he cured my little shock of the mange. **1685** Tate *Cuckolds-Haven* I. ii. 5 Dear delicate Madam, I am your little Paraquit, your Sparrow, your Shock, your Pugg, your Squirrel. **1709** Steele & Swift *Tatler* No. 70 ¶15 The Bones are pick'd clean by a little French Shock that belongs to the Family. **1719** D'Urfey *Pills* II. 331 Neat Spanniel 'Squires and combing Shocks,..Were at her Leve early. **1800** Shaw *Gen. Zool.* I. 280 Maltese Dog... In some of its varieties the hair is extremely long, as in the Skock [? *read* Shock] and the Lion-Dog.

**shock** (ʃɒk), *sb.*[5] [? Formed as next adj.] A thick mass (of hair).

**1819** 'R. Rabelais' *Abeillard & Heloisa* 70 Each Blood, who all day capers, At night puts up his shock in papers. **1847** Longf. *Evang.* I. iii. 3 Shocks of yellow hair, like the silken floss of the maize. **1883** Stevenson *Silverado Sq.* 140 He would toss back his shock of hair and laugh hoarsely. **1894** *Geog. Jrnl.* III. 479 They are beardless, and usually wear a shock of unkempt hair.

*transf.* **1888** Stevenson *Black Arrow* I. vi, The pit was sandy and dry; a shock of brambles hung upon one edge.

**shock** (ʃɒk), *a.* [? Back-formation from shock-dog.]

**a.** Having rough thick hair. Of hair: Rough and thick, shaggy. (See also shock-head.)

**1681** T. Flatman *Heraclitus Ridens* No. 39 (1713) I. 255 A certain little shock Whig. **1707** Mortimer *Husb.* (1721) I. 253 The white shock Turky Rabbet. **1771** Franklin *Autobiog.* Wks. 1840 I. 30, I reached through the water to his schock pate and drew him up. **1862** Borrow *Wales* xxv. I. 294 He was a fellow with red shock hair and very red features. **1865** Alex. Smith *Summer in Skye* II. 205 There were quick and nimble brains under the shock heads of the lads you saw.

**b.** *Comb.*, as ***shock-bearded, -haired, -maned, -pated*** adjs.

**1908** *Blackw. Mag.* Sept. 408/2 *Shock-bearded peasants. **1862** Calverley *Verses & Transl.* (1894) 89 Bob the *shock-haired knifeboy. **1922** *Shock-maned [see *shaggy-chested* s.v. shaggy *a* 3]. **1830** Miss Mitford *Village* Ser. iv. 281 A handy, good humoured, *shock-pated fellow.

† **shock**, *v.*[1] *Obs.* In 5 schokke. [Before the 16th c. found only in *Morte Arthure*; cf. shog *v.*, and MLG., MHG. *schocken* to swing, wag, quiver; also G. *schaukeln* to swing.]

**1.** *intr.* To go swiftly and suddenly; to dart, rush; to make a rapid or forced march. Chiefly with adv., *away, down, in, on.*

? *a* **1400** *Morte Arth.* 1759 Thay..Schokkes in with a schakke, and schontez no langere. *Ibid.* 4235 He..schokkes in scharpely in his schene wedys. **1553** Brende *Q. Curtius* iv. 104 They shocked away in divers companies. **1581** A. Hall *Iliad* iv. 62 An enterprise it selfe presentes, whereto if so you shocke, Men shal thee cal the happiest this side the Ocean firre. **1583** Stocker *Civ. Warres Lowe C.* iv. 62 There came out..about thirtie horsemen, shockyng firste on towardes Eastwike Trenche, and anon towards Westwike. **1603** Knolles *Hist. Turks* (1621) 246 And so shocking downe towards the straits of Bosphorus, by his embassador concluded a league with Emanuell the Greeke Emperour.

**2.** *trans.* To move suddenly and swiftly.

? *a* **1400** *Morte Arth.* 3816 In he schokkes his schelde, schountes he no lengere. *Ibid.* 3852 He schokkes owtte a schorte knyfe schethede with siluere.

**shock** (ʃɒk), *v.*[2] Forms: α. 6 shok, 6–7 shocke, 6– shock; β. 6 chock, 7 chocke, chocque, 8 choak. [app. a. F. *choquer* (13th c.) = Sp. *chocar*, of obscure origin.

Some regard the vb. as an adoption from Germanic, comparing OHG. *scoc* swing, MHG. *schocken* to swing. But an early OF. *ch* can hardly represent G. *sch*, and the affinity of sense is not close. Others suppose that the original sense is 'to stumble, knock against', the vb. being f. OF. *choque* tree-stump; cf. OF. *choper* to stumble, f. *chope* tree-stump.

The senses below are all from Fr. *choquer*, and were introduced at different periods: see note to sense 4. The older shock *v.*[1] appears to be unconnected.

¶The form *chock* (prob. to be regarded as a distinct word) occurs (in the 16–17th c.) in various senses of Fr. *choquer*. *trans.* (a.) To knock about, buffet. (b.) To give a blow to; to 'chuck' under the chin. (c.) To knock one against the other, to jingle (coins).

(a.) **1567** Turberv. *Epit.*, etc. 128 Now, now the churlish chanell me doth chock, Now surging Seas conspire to breede my carke.

(b.) **1583** [see chuck *v.*[2]]. **1607** Markham *Caval.* iv. vi. 29 The verie manner of bringing a horse vnto it, which is by chocking him in the mouth. *Ibid.* viii. 38 You shal neither chock him in the mouth, nor [etc.]. **1658** [see chuck *v.*[2] 1].

(c.) **1627** Drayton *Agincourt* 63 In the Tauerne, in his Cups doth rore, Chocking his Crownes.]

**1. a.** *intr.* To come into violent contact, to collide, clash *together*; esp. to encounter in the shock of battle. Now only *arch.* or as a Gallicism.

**1576** Turberv. *Venerie* xvii. 45 They beginne then both of them to vault, and to scrape the grounde with their feete, shocking and butting one against another. **1584** Hudson *Du Bartas' Judith* III. (1608) 46 Together soone they shock with hatefull yre. **1640** tr. *Verdere's Rom. of Rom.* I. xxv. 116 One would have said, that four towres torn from their foundations, by so many whirlwinds, had shocked together. **1742** Hume *Ess., Parties* (1817) I. 54 Two men, travelling on the highway, the one east, the other west, can easily pass each other, if the way be broad enough: but two men, reasoning upon opposite principles of religion, cannot so easily pass, without shocking. **1774** Goldsm. *Nat. Hist.* (1862) I. 49 Two mountains shocked against each other, approaching and retiring with the most dreadful noise. **1832** Tennyson *Love thou thy Land* 78 If New and Old, disastrous feud, Must ever shock, like armed foes. **1872** —— *Gareth* 939 All at fiery speed the two Shock'd on the central bridge. **1888** *Chamb. Jrnl.* 6 Oct. 626/2 Carriage after carriage shocked fiercely against the engine and the compartments in front of it.

† **b.** *trans.* To collide with, jostle. *Obs.*

**1783** Justamond tr. *Raynal's Hist. Indies* V. 151 It is necessary to fix them with several anchors, to prevent their shocking each other. **1794** *Rigging & Seamanship* II. 268 The rudder is shocked by the water.

† **c.** To run counter to, to oppose. *Obs. rare.*

**1667** Dryden *Ind. Emp.* I. ii, That Monarch sits not safely on his Throne, Who bears, within, a power that shocks his own. **1676** —— *Aurengz.* II. i, Advise him not to shock a Father's Will.

† **2.** To assail with a sudden and violent attack, to charge (an enemy) with troops, etc. *Obs.*

**1614** Gorges *Lucan* III. 110 But whosoever of the foes Did shocke their sides, or changed blowes With Brutus shippe, him grappling fast, He boords. **1699** *Relat. Sir. T. Morgan's Progr. France* 7 Major-General Morgan demanded of his Excellency, whether he would Shock the whole Army at one dash, or try one Wing first? **1767** *Ann. Reg., Acc. Bks.* 276/1 The Christians rowed forwards..and shocked the enemy's gallies with the spurs or beaks of theirs.

**3.** † **a.** To throw (troops) into confusion by an onset or charge; to damage or weaken by impact or collision; to destroy the stability of. Also *fig.*

**1568** Grafton *Chron.* II. 1364 The Countie Egmond.. recharged vpon them with all his forces together so terribly that he shokt all their battayle. **1674–5** Stillingfl. *Serm.* 24 Feb., Wks. 1710 I. 215 They who could not be shocked by persecution were in danger of being overcome by flattery. **1726** G. Roberts *Four Yrs. Voy.* 351 That Sea that shock'd the Vessel, was a Forerunner of a greater. **1770** Langhorne *Plutarch* (1879) II. 770/1 It carried down trunks of trees.., which much shocked and weakened the pillars of his bridge.

† **b.** To shake (a building, etc.) with an earthquake shock. *Obs.*

**1731** [see raise *v.* 4 a]. **1742** Plant *Earthquakes* in *Phil. Trans.* XLII. 34 It continued roaring, bursting, and shocking our Houses all that Night.

**c.** To subject to or transform by mechanical shock. Cf. shocked *ppl. a.* 3.

**1950** D. Q. Kern *Process Heat Transfer* xiv. 382 Hard scale which can be shocked from the tube. **1965** *Ann. N.Y. Acad. Sci.* CXXIII. 602 Salt shocked by a chemical explosion adjusted mainly by plastic glide along close-spaced slip planes. **1968** Ahrens & Rosenberg in French & Short *Shock Metamorphism of Natural Materials* 59/2 The Hugoniot curve is defined as the locus of pressure-volume-energy states that may be achieved within the material by shocking it from a given initial state.

**4. a.** In early use, to wound the feelings of, offend, displease. In later use, with stronger sense: To affect with a painful feeling of intense aversion or disapproval; to scandalize, horrify; to outrage (a person's sentiments, prejudices, etc.). Often in passive, to be scandalized or horrified *at*.

The prevalent 17th c. spelling (see β) shows that the sense was then regarded as a use of the F. *choquer*.

α. **1694** Congreve *Double Dealer* v. xvii, Thy stubborn temper shocks me, and you knew it would. **1711** Steele *Spect.* No. 6 ¶2 They are no more shocked at Vice and Folly, than Men of slower Capacities. **1767** Lady S. Bunbury in Jesse *Selwyn & Contemp.* (1843) II. 178 I am shocked to death to see you must be back by the end of September. **1815** Scott *Guy M.* iv, They durst not at once shock the universal prejudices of their age. **1849** Macaulay *Hist. Eng.* ii. I. 188 Every moderate man was shocked by the insolence, cruelty, and perfidy with which the nonconformists were treated. **1867** Smiles *Huguenots Eng.* x. (1880) 164 The priests who visited the slaves at the galleys were horribly shocked at the cruelties practised on them. **1880** L. Stephen *Pope* vii. 175 Pope..was terribly shocked when he found himself accused of heterodoxy.

β. **1656** Cowley *Odes, 2nd Olympique* Introd., The Reader must not be chocqued to hear him speak so often of his own Muse. **1663** Sir G. Mackenzie *Relig. Stoici* x. (1685) 97 To abrogate, by our practice, whatever chocks our present humor. **1708** Swift *Abol. Christianity* Misc. (1711) 174 The Gentlemen of Wit and Pleasure are apt to murmur, and be choqued at the sight of so many daggled-tail Parsons.

**b.** *absol.* Also *intr.* for *pass.*, to suffer shock.

**1820** Belzoni *Egypt & Nubia* I. 109 Those [customs] which shock at first sight, lose their effect on him. **1959** N. Clad *Love & Money* (1960) 15 She liked to say things to shock Clarence, partly because he shocked so easily. **1967** *Listener* 5 Oct. 448/3 Triana's play does shock.

**5. a.** To impart a physical shock to, to cause (a person or a part of the body) to suffer a nervous shock.

**1733** Belloste *Hosp. Surg.* ii. 17 Mercury produces its effect..by its shocking and disengaging the fibres. **1747** tr. *Astruc's Fevers* 213 The corresponding parts of the medullary substance are so shocked, that the animal spirits there contained are more vigorously protruded into the nerves. **1841** J. T. Hewlett *Parish Clerk* I. 271 The nervous system was so much shocked. **1900** *Brit. Med. Jrnl.* 3 Feb. 257/2 The state of the patients, as to collapse, when first seen varied enormously..: some were absolutely 'shocked', others not at all so.

**b.** To give (a person) an electric shock.

**1746** Watson in *Phil. Trans.* XLIV. 741 It remains now, that I endeavour to lay before you a Solution why our Bodies are so shocked in the Experiments with the electrified Water. **1769** E. Bancroft *Guiana* 196 The Torporific Eel, caught by a hook, violently shocks the person holding the line. **1882** *Nature* XXVI. 260, I got severely shocked [by lightning] when sending my report.

**shock** (ʃɒk), *v.*[3] Now *dial.* [f. shock *sb.*[1]]

**1.** *trans.* To arrange (sheaves) in a shock. Also with *up*.

*c* **1440** *Promp. Parv.* 447/2 Schokkyn schovys or oþer lyke, *tasso*. **1526** *Pilgr. Perf.* (W. de W. 1531) 23 After that he wedeth it, repeth it, bindeth it, and shocketh it, and at the last caryeth it home to his barne. **1584** *Act 23 Eliz.* c. 10 §2 Before..suche Corne and Graine shalbe shocked, cocked, hiled or copped. **1657** Trapp *Comm.* Job v. 26 Corn when ripe is reaped, shockt up, and carried into the barn. **1764** *Museum Rust.* II. 107 Some shock their sheaves, setting them up in traves of six sheaves of a side, and two to cap them. **1836** *Backwoods of Canada* 188 The ripe corn is either shocked as beans..or the cobs pulled and braided on ropes. **1899** Rider Haggard *Farmer's Yr.* 325 We finished cutting, tying, and shocking the wheat on Baker's.

*absol.* **1599** BRETON *Praise Virtuous Ladies* (Grosart) 59/1 If he can shocke, shee can binde sheafes.

†**b.** *transf.* and *fig. Obs.*

*c* **1450** LYDG. & BURGH *Secrees* 354 In sondry konnynges I Can Remembre noon,..But ye haue parcel of hem euerychoon, And shokkyd hem vp in Ordre by and by. **1519** HORMAN *Vulg.* 19 Valantynys be put and shocked in a close vessell as is a cappe. **1555** WATREMAN *Fardle Facions* Pref. 6, I haue shocked theim [stories] vp together, as well those of aunciente tyme, as of later yeres.

†**2.** *refl.* and *intr.* To crowd together. *Obs.*

*c* **1400** MAUNDEV. (1839) xxiii. 252 And whan thei wil fighte, thei wille schokken hem to gidre in a plomp. [Fr. *ils sount si sarres ensemble que..*]. *a* **1548** HALL *Chron., Hen. VIII* 33 Sodaynly the Frenchmen shocked to their standarde and fled. **1622** F. MARKHAM *Bk. War* IV. viii. 151 He shall also see that when they march in Battalia, then they shocke close together and as it were ioyne Cush to Cush.

**shockability** (ʃɒkəˈbɪlɪtɪ). [f. SHOCKABLE *a.*: see -ITY.] The capacity for being shocked. Also *attrib.*

**1929** G. GOULD *Democritus* 89 What we want is to preserve the precious gift of shockability while remaining too intelligent to be shocked. **1963** O. STEWART in C. Irving *Scandal '63* xix. 213 In England shockability is primarily sexual. **1969** J. ELLIOT *Duel* III. iii. 259 She had a low shockability threshold when it came to language. **1977** *Zigzag* Aug. 5/2 The new wave audiences have been beaten into applauding what they can get while ignoring any new trends that don't quite fit the Sunday People blueprint for shockability.

**shockable** (ˈʃɒkəb(ə)l), *a.* [f. SHOCK *v.*[2] + -ABLE.] Easily shocked. Also *absol.* in pl. sense (with *the*). Hence **ˈshockableness** = SHOCKABILITY.

**1893** COLLINGWOOD *Ruskin* I. 27 His parents were not of the shockable sort. **1929** M. ARLEN *Babes in Wood* 254 How ..nice I think you are—to be so shockable. How different from your books! **1939** H. G. WELLS *Holy Terror* III. i. 207 Shockableness is still high. Reverence is something that survives belief. **1965** *Listener* 1 July 12/1 Experimental plays, full of loose living and talk..should be put on at a rather late hour at regular intervals, so that the shockable know not to look. **1976** S. BARSTOW *Right True End* III. xii. 183, I think she's shockable. I'm not certain how her loyalty to me would stand the strain if she knew I was knocking off a colleague's wife.

**shock-absorber.** [SHOCK *sb.*[3]]

**1.** A device, esp. on a motor vehicle, aircraft undercarriage, etc., which serves to absorb mechanical shock and to damp vibration.

**1906** *Daily Chron.* 20 Oct. 2/7 It is this reactionary shock, of course, which..has brought into use the various forms of shock-absorbers. **1929** *Times* 31 Oct. 21/3 The considerable number of cars which were fitted with the Luvax hydraulic shock absorbers. **1931** *Henley's ABC of Gliding & Sailflying* 193 If the landing gear is not provided with shock absorbers, it is desirable to pad the pilot's seat well. **1945** CROCKER & KING *Piping Handbk.* (ed. 4) xviii. 1319 Hydraulic piping can be supported in box guides so as to permit free longitudinal movement except as restrained by the shock absorbers. This arrangement is..effective in cushioning shocks which are due to water hammer. **1951** *Engineering* 26 Oct. 533/2 Long semi-elliptical reverse-camber springs of conventional design are used for the rear suspension, which is..controlled by double-acting hydraulic shock absorbers. **1973** *Times* 15 Oct. 21/8 British Leyland have admitted that fires have occurred in 18 of the new buses and shock-absorber brackets have broken off.

**2.** *fig.* Something which (or someone who) reduces or mitigates the worst effects of a new and unpleasant occurrence or experience. Also *attrib.*

**1924** *Foundry* 15 Feb. 105 (Advt.), Where lower production costs are necessary our products are real shock-absorbers. **1954** KOESTLER *Invisible Writing* iv. 52 The elastic shock-absorbers of my Party training began to operate at once. **1954** B. & R. NORTH tr. *M. Duverger's Pol. Parties* I. ii. 83 Stable and stabilizing communities, playing some part as political shock-absorbers. **1957** *Economist* 28 Sept. 1003/1 The process..would close when the promised elections set up an all-Korean government—perhaps with a degree of regional autonomy, and with shock-absorber clauses written into the constitution to cushion the losers. **1969** *Listener* 15 May 666/1 They cannot rely on help from friends or families in emergency—they are people without shock-absorbers. Often a single misfortune gives the push towards disintegration. **1977** *Time* 15 Aug. 13/1 Black labor acts as a shock absorber enabling Italy to survive economic crisis.

Hence **shock-absorbent** *a.*, **shock-absorbing** *ppl. a.* and *vbl. sb.*

**1909** *Westm. Gaz.* 23 Mar. 4/2 The under-part of the aeroplane is fitted with wooden runners, independent of the shock-absorbing suspension. **1946** D. DE CARLE *Pract. Watch Repairing* xx. 262 Had the balance been fitted with some shock absorbent device the damage would not have occurred. **1958** *Listener* 30 Oct. 683/1, I think you want a car that has adequate shock absorbing. **1973** *Times* 13 July 9/1 Each [crash-helmet] has a shock-absorbent liner as well as ear and cheek pads. **1973** J. G. TWEEDDALE *Materials Technol.* II. iii. 56 Drums..may be lined with shock-absorbing material, to minimise wear of the drum and to reduce noise.

**shockatory,** variant of SHACKATORY *Obs.*

†**shock-dog.** *Obs.* [f. SHOCK *sb.*[4]] = SHOCK *sb.*[4]

**1673** SHADWELL *Epsom Wells* I. 9 We [women] are already so pester'd with gay Fools, that have no more sense than our Shock-dogs. **1780** H. WALPOLE *Vertue's Anecd. Paint.* (1782) IV. Advert. 13 Her shock dog, large as life, and only not alive, has a looseness and softness in the curls that seemed impossible to terra-cotta. **1845** YOUATT *Dog* iv. 104 The Shock-dog is traced by Buffon, but somewhat erroneously, to a mixture of the small Danish dog and the pug.

**shocked** (ʃɒkt), *ppl. a.*[1] [f. SHOCK *v.*[2] + -ED[1].]

**1.** Shaken violently.

**1642** *Iacke Puffe* 16 in Hazl. *E.P.P.* IV. 315 The women did..quake, As did the people, in old Æsops time, At the shockt mount, whereforth a Mouse did clime. **1904** KIPLING *Things & the Man* 17 in *Times* 1 Aug. 7/6 The peace of shocked Foundations flew Before his ribald questionings.

**2.** Scandalized, horrified.

**1840** QUEEN VICTORIA *Let.* 21 Jan. in B. Connell *Regina v. Palmerston* (1962) i. 20 A letter..which she has kept near three years, she is shocked to say. **1861** PALEY *Æschylus* (ed. 2) *Agam.* 1555 *note*, He..is with difficulty pacified by the more collected and shocked, if not now repentant Clytemnestra. **1883** MISS BROUGHTON *Belinda* II. 191 'She is making him [the Prince] shake hands with her!' says Sarah, in a shocked voice. **1884** *Harper's Mag.* Oct. 692/1 Agnes put on a shocked face.

**3.** Subjected to mechanical shock, esp. by the passage of a shock wave.

**1962** E. M. SHOEMAKER in Z. Kopol *Physics & Astron. Moon* viii. 317 Part of the kinetic energy of the meteorite engulfed by shock is converted to internal energy in the meteorite, and part is transferred as kinetic and internal energy to the shocked rock ahead of the meteorite. **1973** *Nature* 27 July 211/2 Hypervelocity impact cratering studies have shown that about ninety-nine volumes of crushed and shocked rock are formed and ejected for each volume of liquid melt (glass) that is formed and ejected. **1976** *Ibid.* 11 Nov. 114/3 This ionisation front is preceded by a shock front, and after a time there is a shocked layer of neutral gas between these two fronts.

Hence **shockedly** (ˈʃɒkɪdlɪ, ˈʃɒktlɪ), *adv.*; **ˈshockedness.**

**1895** MRS. W. K. CLIFFORD *Flash of Summer* xxvi, 'Perhaps you will come into the dining-room, sir', Elizabeth said, with a little air of shockedness at Mr. Belcher's manner. **1926** FOWLER *Mod. Eng. Usage* 531/2 *Shockedly*. A bad form. **1963** D. HUGHES in Sissons & French *Age of Austerity* 93 Then, rather shockedly, a knight's name figured in court.

**shocked** (ʃɒkt), *ppl. a.*[2] [f. SHOCK *v.*[3] + -ED[1].] Of corn: Heaped in shocks.

**1839** CLOUGH *Early Poems* iii. 7 And glimmering grain Standing or shocked through the thick hedge espied. **1884** *St. James's Gaz.* 22 Aug. 14/2 Fields of shocked or stooked corn.

**shocker**[1] (ˈʃɒkə(r)). [f. SHOCK *v.*[2] + -ER[1].]

**1.** Something which shocks or excites; esp. a work of fiction of a sensational character. Also, something or someone shockingly bad. Also *attrib.*

**1824** [CARR] *Craven Gloss., Shocker*, a person of infamous character. **1886** [see SHILLING 6]. **1890** *Athenæum* 7 June 734/3 'For so Little' has some of the qualities one looks for in the 'shocker'; but the greatest of these is brevity, and that it has not got. **1907** *Daily Chron.* 20 Nov. 3/4 The reader must often be in doubt whether he is being treated to genuine biography or mere 'shocker' fiction. **1954** M. CROFT *Spare Rod* I. ix. 62 A lot of people believe that to be a good writer a man must have a well-nigh perfect character... On the contrary, many of them have been perfect shockers. **1958** *Manch. Guardian* 7 June 4/7 The 'musical' is still in the ascendant. I caught one real shocker—'Jamaica'. But the others..were fun. **1960** J. STROUD *Shorn Lamb* xxiii. 248, I remember a girl we had..an absolute shocker, never settled anywhere. **1965** MRS. L. B. JOHNSON *White House Diary* 17 June (1970) 291 Then Lyndon delivered the shocker of the evening. **1973** *Express* (Trinidad & Tobago) 9 Apr. 1/3 The series will be the sort of shocker that should cast out smug complacency. **1976** *Daily Times* (Lagos) 12 Oct. 1/3 This is the shocker for teachers in Bomo State. **1977** *Time* 17 Jan. 9/1 What began as a shocker killing has grown steadily more sensational. **1977** *Horse & Hound* 10 June 8/2 Lucky Sovereign ran a shocker, presumably either unable or unwilling to give his true running on this firm ground and/or the Epsom course. **1977** *Time* 8 Aug. 39/1 Then on Wednesday came a shocker from Bethlehem Steel, which reported an operating loss of $75·4 million for the first half. **1978** *Chicago* June 119/2 The jury found the guy guilty on only one count. A real shocker, and entirely due to Sullivan's work.

**2.** A shock-absorber. *colloq.*

**1949** PARTRIDGE *Dict. Slang* (ed. 3) 1168/1 *Shocker*,..a shock-absorber: motorists': since ca. 1925. **1969** *Guardian* 23 Aug. 5/8 The models with worn shockers were thrown from side to side. **1977** *Caravan World* (Austral.) Jan. 19/2 Incorrect loading on the tow-ball..results in overloaded tyres, springs and shockers if the weight is forward.

**shocker**[2] (ˈʃɒkə(r)). [f. SHOCK *v.*[3] + -ER[1].] One who piles sheaves in shocks.

**1786** G. WASHINGTON *Diaries* 15 July (1925) III. 91 For every two Cradlers to allow 4 rakes, 1 shocker, and two Carriers. **1827** CLARE *Sheph. Cal.* 71 Some o'er the rustling scythe go bending on; And shockers follow where their toils have gone. **1895** *Voice* (N.Y.) 28 Nov. 7/4 He rides a harvester, and rapidly tumbles his wheat sheaves..into convenient bunches for the one lone shocker to set up and cap.

**shock-head.** [f. SHOCK *a.*] A head covered with a thick crop of hair.

**1818** SCOTT *Rob Roy* xxxii, A shock-head of red hair.

**b.** *attrib.* or *adj.* (in quot. *transf.*).

**1842** TENNYSON *Amphion* v, The shock-head willows.

So **shock-headed** *a.*; ***shock-headed Peter*** = STRUWWELPETER.

**1818** SCOTT *Rob Roy* xxii, He was a wild shock-headed looking animal. **1848** tr. *H. Hoffmann's English Struwwelpeter* (ed. 4) 2 Any thing to me is sweeter Than to see Shock-headed Peter. **1860** GEO. ELIOT *Mill on Floss* I. xi, Two small shock-headed chidren were lying prone and resting on their elbows. **1895** R. STEPHENS *Cruciform Mark* ix. 47 'Shock-headed Peter', as he was familiarly dubbed.. was a very interesting personality... Red-haired and red-bearded, his head was a perfect burning bush. **1899** R. BRIDGES *Idle Flowers* Poems (1912) 353 Shock-headed Dandelion, That drank the fire of the sun. **1905** C. MACKENZIE *Diary* 23 May in *My Life & Times* (1964) III. 224 Went to see Martin Harvey as Hamlet... He looked like ..shock-headed Peter. **1926** D. L. SAYERS *Clouds of Witness* vii. 159 Shaking her head so angrily that she looked like shock-headed Peter.

**shocking** (ˈʃɒkɪŋ), *vbl. sb.*[1] [f. SHOCK *v.*[2] + -ING[1].] The action of SHOCK *v.*[2] in various senses.

**1692** R. L'ESTRANGE *Josephus, Wars Jews* VI. xii. (1733) 754 Upon the Shocking of the two Bodies, it rais'd such a Dust and Clamour, that there was nothing distinctly to be seen or heard. **1739** HUME *Hum. Nat.* I. IV. v. (1874) I. 529 'Tis absurd to imagine..That the shocking of two globular particles shou'd become a sensation of pain. **1828** [H. BEST] *Italy as it is* 89 Foot walkers, spreading over the whole, have not found the necessity for a rule to prevent shocking which we experience on our crowded trottoirs.

**b.** *attrib.* in ***shocking-coil, -machine***, names of apparatus for giving electric shocks.

**1882** *Knowledge* 17 Mar. 434/2 Would any reader give.. particulars for making a powerful shocking coil. **1894** BOTTONE *Electr. Instr.* 90 The 'Shocking' Machine.

**shocking** (ˈʃɒkɪŋ), *vbl. sb.*[2] [f. SHOCK *v.*[3] + -ING[1].] The action of piling sheaves in shocks.

**1657** W. COLES *Adam in Eden* cclxxxi, Concerning the gathering, shocking, threshing, watering..and spinning of Hemp. **1764** *Museum Rust.* II. lxxv. 249 Shocking, or stooking, is only a temporary preservative.

**shocking** (ˈʃɒkɪŋ), *ppl. a.* Also 8 chocquing, choquing, choqueing. [f. SHOCK *v.*[2] + -ING[2].] That shocks, in various senses of the vb.

†**1.** Of troops: Meeting in the shock of battle.

**1697** DRYDEN *Virg. Georg.* IV. 115 The shocking squadrons meet in mortal fight. **1716** POPE *Iliad* VIII. 75 And now with Shouts the shocking Armies clos'd.

**2.** That gives offence; offensive. Also, causing unpleasant surprise. Now *rare* or *Obs.*

[It is noteworthy that in the earliest quot. the Fr. spelling is used. A little earlier we find the actual Fr. word:

**1691** NORRIS *Pract. Disc.* IV. 392 This is the Drift of my Meaning,..than which I think nothing could be more innocent or inoffensive in it self, how choquant or distastful soever it may appear as our Reverend Author has been pleased to dress it up.]

**1703** FLEETWOOD *17 Serm.* (1717) 359 Such different images would have crowded in upon the mind, as must have occasion'd a confusion, horrible and chocquing. **1709** STANHOPE *Paraphr.* IV. 534 This was the Choqueing Principle to the Jews. **1710** ADDISON *Whig Exam.* No. 1 ¶1 There is such a shocking familiarity both in his railleries and civilities. **1740** RICHARDSON *Pamela* (1824) I. 163, I could tell twenty pleasant stories; but my lady is too nice to hear them; and yet I hope, I should not be shocking neither. **1774** tr. *Chesterf. Let. to Son* 29 Oct. 1739, Nothing is more shocking and disgustful than presumption and impudence. **1782** COWPER *Alex. Selkirk* 16 They are so unacquainted with man, Their tameness is shocking to me. **1855** MACAULAY *Hist. Eng.* xvii. IV. 29 His rude doctrines were polished into a form somewhat less shocking to good sense and good taste.

**3. a.** In stronger sense: Revolting to the feelings; exciting intense horror or repugnance.

*a* **1704** T. BROWN *Sat. agst. Woman* Wks. 1730 I. 57 The tale's too black and shocking to be told. **1749** POINTER *Oxon. Acad.* 70 Brazen-nose College... The fine, though shocking, Statue of Cain and Abel in the middle of the Quadrangle. **1769** *Junius Lett.* v. 28 The charge..is of so shocking a complexion that I sincerely wish you may be able to answer it. **1828** SCOTT *Aunt Marg. Mirror* ii, The shocking tidings were brought from Holland, which fulfilled even her worst expectations. **1849** MACAULAY *Hist. Eng.* iii. I. 418 A state shocking to humanity. **1891** FARRAR *Darkn. & Dawn* xxx, It is shocking enough to see noble beasts ruthlessly mangled.

**b.** *absol.*

**1893** LELAND *Mem.* I. 129 Even the Old Testament, with all its stores of the 'shocking', really does very little harm.

**c.** In colloquial use often *hyperbolical*: cf. 4 and SHOCKINGLY 2.

**1842** BROWNING *Pied Piper* iii, And as for our Corporation —shocking To think we buy gowns lined with ermine For dolts that [etc.].

**d.** ***shocking pink***: a vivid, garish shade of pink.

**1938** *Encycl. Brit. Bk. of Year* 248/2 Only one new colour arrived; it is 'Shocking Pink', introduced by Schiaparelli in Feb. 1937, then taken up by other designers, with the result that the vanguard of fashionable women everywhere are now seen wearing this crude, cruel shade of rose. **1939** *Archit. Rev.* LXXXV. 305/3 There it is, in its gay 'shocking pink' cover, compact, comprehensive and invaluable. **1954** E. SCHIAPARELLI *Shocking Life* ix. 97 My friends and executives..began to say that I was crazy and that nobody would want it because it was really 'nigger pink'... The colour 'shocking' established itself for ever as a classic. Even Dali dyed an enormous stuffed bear in shocking pink. **1960** M. STEWART *My Brother Michael* x. 136 They [*sc.* socks] were luminous, and of a startling shade of shocking pink. **1977** C. MCCULLOUGH *Thorn Birds* xix. 520 An involuntary grimace at first sight of her shocking-pink slipper satin.

**4. a.** 'Shockingly' bad, 'execrable'.

**1798** FORESTER in *Paget Papers* (1896) I. 115 Shocking Weather since you left. **1824** W. C. TAYLOR *Anc. Hist.* xvii. §2 (ed. 3) 496 His [Vespasian's] first care was to restore the discipline of the army, which he found in a shocking state of demoralization. **1872** BLACK *Adv. Phaeton* vii, The shocking way those boys spell.

**b.** quasi-*adv.* = SHOCKINGLY. *vulgar.*

**1831** SURTEES *Jorrocks's Jaunts* (1838) 36 *foot-note*, 'Vot a shocking bad hat!'—the slang cockney phrase of 1831. **1833** [S. SMITH] *Lett. J. Downing* xvii. (1835) 102 As soon as I saw what a shocking big place New York was. **1857** HUGHES *Tom Brown* I. i, A shocking bad road.

**shockingly** ('ʃɒkɪŋlɪ), *adv.* [f. SHOCKING *ppl. a.* + -LY².] In a shocking manner or degree.

**1.** So as to shock the feelings; revoltingly.

**1741** RICHARDSON *Pamela* IV. 106 There is not one Character in it, but what is shockingly immoral. **1816** J. SCOTT *Vis. Paris* (ed. 2) Pref. 68 We are shockingly treated by the Prussians. **1858** *Househ. Words* 28 Aug. 241/1 A shockingly rude article.

**2.** *colloq.* Often, in depreciatory sentences, without any special reference to the sensibilities, equivalent to 'very', 'extremely'.

**1777** MISS BURNEY *Early Diary, Let.* 27 Mar., Dr. Johnson..is shockingly near-sighted. **1782** —— *Cecilia* I. iv, To be sure she's shockingly dear, that I must own. **1840** HALIBURTON *Letter Bag* iv. 57, I feel so shockingly nervous. **1901** W. R. H. TROWBRIDGE *Lett. her Mother to Eliz.* xiii. 61 Two rather pretty, but shockingly badly-dressed girls.

**b.** = *shockingly ill*; 'abominably'. †*to look shockingly*: to appear to be much out of health.

**1768** GOLDSM. *Goodn. Man* I, You look most shockingly to-day, my dear friend. **1772** *Ann. Reg.* 59/2, I could perceive that his eyes looked quite shockingly. **1825** T. HOOK *Sayings* Ser. II. *Doubts & F.* vii. II. 218 How shockingly he looks. **1881** W. G. MARSHALL *Through Amer.* i. 47 Many of the principal streets are shockingly paved.

**3.** So as to cause a shock of surprise.

**1883** STEVENSON *Treas. Isl.* iv, This sudden noise startled us shockingly.

**shockingness** ('ʃɒkɪŋnɪs). [f. SHOCKING *ppl. a.* + -NESS.] The quality or condition of being shocking; †repulsiveness.

**1753** RICHARDSON *Grandison* I. xix. 128 It softened the shockingness of his expression. **1885** *American* IX. 215 The shockingness of intrusion at such a time. **1900** MISS BROUGHTON *Foes in Law* xx, The phrase strikes her as crude, even to shockingness.

**shockle** ('ʃɒk(ə)l). *Sc.* and *north.* Now *rare.* Forms: 6 schokle, (7 sheckle), 9 schochle, shoggle. [Shortened from *ice-shockle*, ICICLE.] A lump of ice; an icicle.

**1596** DALRYMPLE tr. *Leslie's Hist. Scot.* I. 46 First in thay ryde into this riuer..to thow the pypes and schokles of yce, frosin vpon thame. **1639** SIR R. GORDON *Hist. Earld. Sutherl.* (1813) 208 The ground wes ful of ronns, or sheckles of yce. *a* **1859** WATT in *Mod. Scott. Poets* Ser. II. 54 The shochles, like crystal, hing clear frae the rocks. **1871** WADDELL *Ps.* lxxviii. 47 He dang doun their plane trees wi shoggles o' ice.

**Shockley** ('ʃɒklɪ). The name of William B. *Shockley* (b. 1910), British-born U.S. physicist, used *attrib.* to designate concepts and devices he invented, as **Shockley diode**, a semiconductor diode consisting of four regions of alternate conductivity types (*n* and *p*), with the anode and the cathode connected to the end ones; **Shockley partial (dislocation)**, a partial dislocation in which the lattice displacement, as represented by the Burgers vector, lies in the fault plane, so that the dislocation is capable of gliding.

**1962** *Instrument Pract.* XVI. 1466/2 The arrangement will then have the characteristics of the Shockley or four layer diode which has only two terminals. **1965** *Wireless World* Aug. 397/2 Transistors, unijunction transistors or Shockley diodes can be used. **1975** T. D. TOWERS *Semiconductor Circuit Elements* xii. 146 A Shockley diode represents a switch with an off resistance of megohms and an on resistance of ohms. **1953** W. T. READ *Dislocations in Crystals* vii. 98 The Shockley partial is one of the three types of partial dislocations associated with plane faults in f.c.c. **1969** [see PARTIAL *sb.* 2]. **1976** M. T. SPRACKLING *Plastic Deformation Simple Ionic Crystals* iv. 51 Shockley partial dislocations can glide in the fault plane; Frank partial dislocations cannot.

**shock wave.** Also 'shock-wave, 'shockwave. [f. SHOCK *sb.*³; cf. F. *onde de choc* (common in early 20th-cent. Fr. writings on fluid dynamics).]

**a.** A disturbance that travels through a fluid as a narrow region in which there is a large, abrupt change in pressure and related quantities, esp. one separating regions of subsonic and supersonic fluid flow such as is created by an object moving faster than sound or by an explosion; *loosely*, any pressure wave of large amplitude.

[**1904** *Sci. Abstr.* A. VII. 646 Quasi-waves of shock propagating a dilatation in accordance with Hugoniot's law.] **1907** *Chem. Abstr.* I. 1470 The explosive wave is a shock wave accompanied by a decided combustion. **1931** *Proc. Nat. Acad. Sci.* XVII. 534 Let us regard a plane discontinuity or 'shock wave' from the point of view of the observer moving with it, so that the shock wave will appear to us stationary. **1945** *Times* 8 Nov. 2/2 When the oncoming aeroplane is travelling at, say, 600 m.p.h. or more the steadiness of the air-flow over the wing then breaks down with the result that what is known as a shock-wave occurs at the thickest part of the wing. **1950** *Sci. News* XV. Plate 5 (*caption*) The segmented appearance of the flame is due to the shock wave which is formed in the jet as it leaves the nozzle and which is reflected to and fro within the jet. **1958** *N. & Q.* CCIII. 139/1 Aside from other factors in nuclear explosions, the shock-wave, or blast, is possibly the greatest source of danger. **1973** C. MASON *Hostage* v. 65 The building was meanwhile hit by a shockwave so severe it felt like an earthquake. **1979** *Jrnl. R. Soc. Arts* CXXVII. 403/1 A small explosive charge is detonated in the ground and the resulting shock waves picked up by sensitive microphones called geophones.

**b.** *fig.*

**1969** *Harper's Mag.* Dec. 125 The last writer who sent shock waves through Western literature. **1974** I. MURDOCH *Sacred & Profane Love Machine* 145 The shock wave had not yet really come... Awful grief and pain hovered somewhere near to her. **1979** P. HARCOURT *Sleep of Spies* I. iv. 56 The question caused shock waves round the room.

†'**shocky,** *a. Obs. rare*⁻¹. [f. SHOCK *a.* + -Y.] Having a thick head of hair.

**1698** TYSON *Opossum* in *Phil. Trans.* XX. 114 Nierembergius, in his Figure..represents him as Shocky, and, as it were, with Curly Hair.

**shod** (ʃɒd), *sb. Sc.* and *north.* [f. SHOD *ppl. a.*]

**1.** A plate of iron fastened upon the heel of a shoe to protect it from wear; a heel-tip; more fully *heel-shod.*

*c* **1840** in A. Trotter *E. Galloway Sk.* (1901) 102/1 There's a' things in the Jangle Box, Brass, airn, and tin, and shods o' shoon. **1912** A. MCCORMICK *Words from Wild Wood* viii. 128 He had never seen heel shods like them.

**2.** A skid in the form of a shoe; = SHOE *sb.* 5 f.

**1893** CROCKETT *Stickit Minister* 198 The great iron curved shods which the lorrymen used to stop their coal waggons on the steep streets.

**shod** (ʃɒd), *ppl. a.* For forms see the vb. See also SHOED. [pa. pple. of SHOE *v.*]

**1.** Wearing shoes. Chiefly with qualifying adv., *well, neatly*, etc. Also DRY-SHOD, HIGH-SHOD, SLIPSHOD *adjs.*

**1382** WYCLIF *Isa.* xi. 15 So that thei passe thurȝ hym shod men [1388 schood men]. *c* **1384** CHAUCER *H. Fame* I. 98 Dreme he barefote, dreme he shod [*Caxton, Thynne* shood]. *c* **1400** *Rom. Rose* 7463 And alle freres, shodde and bare. *c* **1440** *Promp. Parv.* 447/2 Schod, as men, *calceatus.* Schod, as hors, *ferratus.* **1537** in Brand *Hist. Newcastle* (1789) I. 129 *note*, The Blake-Friers otherwise called the Shode Freers. **1782** COWPER *Gilpin* 82 But, finding soon a smoother road Beneath his well-shod feet. **1840** DICKENS *Old C. Shop* v, A pair of very imperfectly shod feet. **1888** 'J. S. WINTER' *Bootle's Childr.* i, Neatly shod feet.

**2. a.** Of things: Furnished with a shoe of metal, etc.; tipped, edged, or sheathed with metal. † *shod shovel*: see SHOVEL *sb.*

**1565** COOPER *Thesaurus* s.v. *Aeratus*, *Pila ærata*, shadde [*sic*] or poynted with brasse. **1578** *Knaresb. Wills* (Surtees) I. 134 A shod dunge forke. **1840** J. ROWAND *Let.* 8 July in G. P. de T. Glazebrook *Hargrave Corr.* (1938) 317 A couple of blood Indians got afighting..which ended by driving two shod arrows through one fellows body. **1903** KIPLING *Five Nations* 39 Where a man may bask and dream To the click of shod canoe-poles.

**b.** Of cart wheels: Furnished with tyres. Hence of a cart: Having 'shod' wheels. Of a motor vehicle: having tyres of a certain quality, as *well shod.* Cf. SHOE *v.* 2.

**1481** *City Letter Bk. L.* 163 b, No shod cart laden be suffred to passe over the said Brigge. **1535** in *Archæol. Cant.* VII. 304, j pece of shoyd whelys, the other onshoyd. **1563** *Bottesford Manor Rec.* in *N.W. Linc. Gloss.*, A shod-wayne or carte. **1631** WEEVER *Anc. Funeral Mon.* 516 Diuers great Nailes of Iron were there found, such as are vsed in the wheeles of shod carts. **1728** *Act 1 Geo. II*, Stat. II. c. 22 §3 The Duty..on Shod Carts, payable to the said City [of Edinburgh]. **1831** J. HOLLAND *Manuf. Metal* I. 157 Wheels, considerably increased in breadth on their shod surface,.. are not uncommon. **1967** PARTRIDGE *Dict. Slang* Suppl. 1356/1 *Shod.* 'Colloquially applied to motor vehicles. A car with good tyres is described as '*well shod*' (B.P.): Australian: since ca. 1945. **1977** *Horse & Hound* 14 Jan. 44/2 (Advt.), Bedford T.K. diesel, 1964, horse/cattle box... Well shod.

**shod:** see SHUD *dial.*, shed.

**shodden** ('ʃɒd(ə)n), *a. rare.* [Badly f. SHOD *ppl. a.*, on the supposed analogy of *sod, sodden, trod, trodden*, etc.] = SHOD *ppl. a.*

The form also occurs for the pa. pple.: see SHOE *v.*

**1829** J. F. COOPER *Borderers* vi. 74 His beast hath had a shodden hoof. **1844** R. M. MILNES *Palm Leaves* 20 The floor ..unstained by touch of shodden feet. **1859** H. KINGSLEY *G. Hamlyn* xix, 'Black fellow', I said to myself; but no, those were shodden feet that swept along so wearily.

**shodder,** obs. form of SHUDDER *v.*

**shoddy** ('ʃɒdɪ), *sb.* [Of obscure origin.

It is possible that sense 4 may be the original meaning; if so, the word may be a derivative of SHOAD *sb.*]

**1. a.** Woollen yarn obtained by tearing to shreds refuse woollen rags, which, with the addition of some new wool, is made into a kind of cloth (see 2).

**1832** [see *shoddy-grinder* in 6]. **1836** G. HEAD *Home Tour* 146 The 'shoddy' as it is called may be, as occasion requires mixed with new wool in any proportion. **1884** G. DODD *Textile Manuf.* iv. 138 Shoddy, or woollen rags torn up fibre from fibre. **1851** MAYHEW *Lond. Labour* II. 30/1 To this stuff [*sc.* cotton rags ground up] the name of 'shoddy' is given, but the real and orthodox 'shoddy' is a production of the woollen districts. **1881** *Leicestersh. Gloss.*, *Shoddy*, waste from worsted spinning mills. **1904** *Tailor & Cutter* 4 Aug. 480/1 Shoddy: The fibres of wool of the softer makes of old cloth after it has been torn to pieces.

**b.** *Yorksh. dial.* (See quot.)

**1857** C. B. ROBINSON *Best's Farm. Bks.* (Surtees) 183 Gloss., *Scudde*, 95. The dirt and grease from a fleece when washed, called in the factories 'mouts'; the entire substance that falls on the floor being called 'shoddy' or 'food', and being sold at a high rate for top-dressing grass land.

**2.** A cloth composed of shoddy wool (see 1); more fully *shoddy cloth.* (See quot. 1911.)

**1847** MCCULLOCH *Brit. Empire* (ed. 3) I. 661 Formerly, shoddy cloth was used only for padding and such like purposes; but now flushings, druggets,..&c., are either wholly or partly made of shoddy. **1865** J. G. HOLLAND *Plain Talk* iv. 128 He clothed our troops with shoddy. **1884** MCLAREN *Spinning* (ed. 2) 187 Shoddy is the worked-up waste of soft woollen goods which have not been milled and felted. **1903** *Times* 12 Mar. 11/3 Berlin Textiles... Shoddies have been active and strong. **1911** *Encycl. Brit.* XXIV. 992/2 The term 'shoddy' is sometimes applied to all fabrics made of such remanufactured materials,..but strictly it should be confined to a cloth produced from fabrics originally made from English and the longer cross-bred wools... Upon the whole the 'cheap and nasty' idea usually associated with the term 'shoddy'..is quite a mistake. Some most excellent cloths are produced.

**3.** *transf.* and *fig.* Worthless material made to look like what is of superior quality; what is worthless and pretentious in art, manufactures, ideas, etc.; the class of persons characterized by the endeavour to pass for something superior to what they really are, with respect to wealth, birth, culture, or refinement. Also (*U.S.*), a 'shoddy' person (see SHODDY *a.* 1).

**1862** LOWELL *Biglow P.* Ser. II. vi, 'You think thet's ellerkence,—I call it shoddy, A thing,' sez I, 'wun't cover soul nor body, I like the plain all-wool o' common-sense.' **1864** SALA in *Daily Tel.* 10 June, Shoddy wears its sapphire, or its diamond, or its signet ring outside its glove. **1873** L. STEPHEN *Free Thinking* v. 156 He calmly retailed his lengths of theological shoddy,—old fragments of decaying systems woven into a web of the usual polish and flimsiness. **1879** GEO. ELIOT *Theo. Such* xi. 195 A syntactical shoddy of the cheapest sort. **1904** *Boston* (Mass.) *Sunday Her.* 29 June 8/5 They like the old families best, the families that have always had money and servants... To use the language of the girls themselves, they have 'no use for the shoddies'.

**4.** *dial.* **a.** 'The smaller stones at a quarry' (*Antrim & Down Gloss.*, 1880); also *pl.* stones of this kind. **b.** Inferior coal (*Eng. Dial. Dict.*).

**1893** *Building News* 10 Feb. 195 [The house] is built of shoddies quarried from the hill behind.

**5.** = *reclaimed rubber.* Now *rare.*

**1892** *Sci. Amer.* 7 May 293/2 Mould work of the lower grades is often made of shoddy with no addition of pure rubber. **1898** *India-Rubber & Gutta-Percha & Electr. Trades' Jrnl.* XVI. 190/2 It is not surprising..that the volume of mechanical 'shoddy' should be placed by the best estimates at not above one-sixth of the total production of reclaimed rubber in the United States. **1974** K. F. HEINISCH *Dict. Rubber* 428/2 *Shoddy*, jargon formerly used for reclaim; now rarely used.

**6.** attrib. and Comb., as *shoddy dust, flock, merchant, metropolis, mill, trade*; *shoddy-wards* adv.; objective, as *shoddy dealer, grinder, manufacturer, shoddy-making* adj.; instrumental, as *shoddy-robed* adj.; **shoddy dropper** *Austral.* and *N.Z. slang*, a pedlar of cheap or falsely described clothing; a hawker; **shoddy fever** (see quot. 1851); **shoddy-hole,** a place in which rubbish is deposited, a dust-hole; also *fig.*

**1857** *P.O. Directory Yorksh.* 1053 *Shoddy Dealers... Shoddy Merchants. **1941** BAKER *N.Z. Slang* vi. 52 We have [this century]..acquired some underworld slang of our own ..[e.g.] **shoddy dropper*, a seller of cheap serge; [etc.]. **1964** *Australasian Post* 28 May 38/3 The 'shoddy droppers' (Indian hawkers) always carried a supply of patent medicines..with them on their rounds. **1972** *Telegraph* (Brisbane) 30 Aug. 24/6 The operators were known as dudders and professional shoddy-droppers. **1860** PIESSE *Lab. Chem. Wonders* 31 You who breathe *shoddy dust. **1851** MAYHEW *Lond. Labour* II. 31/2 The disease popularly known as '*shoddy fever'..is a species of bronchitis, caused by the irritating effect of the..dust. **1862** *Catal. Internat. Exhib., Brit.* II. No. 4040, *Shoddy flocks. **1832** THACKRAH *Effects of Arts*, etc. *on Health* (ed. 2) 67 *Shoddy-grinders.. are persons employed..in picking and tearing woollen rags, and afterwards manufacturing them, with the addition of new wool..into yarn. **1845** DISRAELI *Sybil* IV. iv, It's a pretty go this, that I should be toiling in a *shoddy-hole to pay the taxes for a gentleman what..stretches his legs on a Turkey carpet. **1895** M. MATHER *Lanc. Idylls* III. iii. 150 But durnd yo' think, doctor, that..we's be turnin' th' Church into a shoddy hoile? **1851** MAYHEW *Lond. Labour* II. 30/2 The stuff which even the *shoddy-making devil rejects, is packed off to the agricultural districts for use as manure. *Ibid.*, The *shoddy manufacturer. **1857** *Shoddy merchant [see *shoddy dealer* above]. **1868** *Q. Rev.* Apr. 338 Batley and its neighbourhood, in Yorkshire, the great *Shoddy metropolis. **1837** MCCULLOCH *Brit. Empire* II. 51 In the neighbourhood of Batley and Dewsbury are..*shoddy mills. **1886** POLLOCK *Oxf. Lect.* etc. iv. (1890) 107 You will refuse to fall down and worship the *shoddy-robed goddess Banausia. **1847** MCCULLOCH *Brit. Empire* (ed. 3) I. 661 Dewsbury is at the head of what is called the *shoddy trade. *a* **1882** A. TROLLOPE *Autobiogr.* (1883) II. 210 Their [*sc.* Carlyle and Ruskin's] lamentations..over a world which is supposed to have gone altogether *shoddy-wards.

Hence **'shoddy** *v. trans.*, to convert into shoddy. **'shoddydom,** the shoddy class. **'shoddyism,** pretentious vulgarity of style. **'shoddyite,** one who deals in shoddy; also, one of the shoddy class.

**1851** MAYHEW *Lond. Labour* II. 33 While woollen and even cotton goods can be 'shoddied'..no use is made of the refuse of silk... There is little doubt that silk, like cotton, could be shoddied. **1865** *Daily Tel.* 18 Apr. 5 This..will bring about a genuine prosperity, not the fictitious glare of contractors and shoddyites. **1865** *Three Years among*

*Working Classes in U.S.* vi. 124 Shoddyism among a large class of the people, corruption in official stations, an absorbing passion for making money..are the prevailing characteristics of the day. **1868** M. H. SMITH *Sunshine & Shad. N. York* 61 A marble palace that would make all Shoddydom red with envy. **1877** D. M. WALLACE *Russia* (ed. 2) I. 269 The Russian merchant's love of ostentation is ..something entirely different from English snobbery and American shoddyism. **1883** *Harper's Mag.* Nov. 820/2 Unfortunately no part of the world..is absolutely free from the shoddyite, the cockney, and the snob.

**shoddy** ('ʃɒdɪ), *a.* [attrib. use of SHODDY *sb.* 3.]

**1.** Of a person: That pretends to a superiority to which he has no just claim; said esp. of those who claim, on the ground of wealth, a social station or a degree of influence to which they are not entitled by character or breeding.

In the U.S. the word seems to have been first used with reference to those who made fortunes by army contracts at the time of the Civil War, it being alleged that the clothing supplied by the contractors consisted largely of shoddy.

**1862** *Cong. Globe* 3164/1 (Thornton *Amer. Gloss.*) The anxiety of the 'shoddy' politicians to assail that address. **1863** *Boston* (Mass.) *Sunday Her.* 15 Feb. 2/3 There are shoddy lawyers, shoddy doctors,..shoddy husbands and shoddy wives, and, worse than all, there are shoddy newspapers whose especial business it is to puff up all the shoddy in the world and endeavor to make the people believe that it is the genuine article. **1865** *Reader* 8 July 36 Those who have become rich by swindling the United States Government during the Civil War compose the 'shoddy' aristocracy. **1896** How & LEIGH *Hist. Rome* 434 That shoddy saviour of society, called L. Cornelius Cinna.

**2.** Of a thing: Having a delusive appearance of superior quality. Also, cheap, inferior; displaying signs of use, shabby, dilapidated.

**1882** *Daily Tel.* 27 Nov. 5 A fleet of ships, shoddier by a hundredfold than the shoddiest of those now afloat. **1891** S. C. SCRIVENER *Our Fields & Cities* 16 When they built the shoddy cottages away down the hill—mere traps to catch rent. **1927** *Melody Maker* Apr. 305/1 The great majority of dance bands have settled down to a very stereotyped and shoddy sort of music. **1929** V. WOOLF *Room of one's Own* v. 133 She will still wear the shoddy old fetters of class on her feet. **1932** E. WAUGH *Black Mischief* vii. 255 The royal box was still there, shoddy sort of affair, but it provided a platform. **1952** *Manch. Guardian Weekly* 31 July 7/2 Because Stevenson was the man to beat, and Kefauver was their man, they had to fall back on the shoddy pretence that Stevenson was the tool of the big city machines.

**3.** Of, pertaining to or dealing in shoddy goods.

**1864** SALA in *Daily Tel.* 26 Feb., Some shoddy upholsterer has here evidently had *carte blanche*, and the result is..gaudy ugliness. **1874** COUES *Birds N.W.* 197 Felting..made by some shoddy contractor for the supply of army clothing. **1895** BARRETT *Surrey* viii. 194 Nor is the furniture unworthy of the room... There is no shoddy antique about this.

Hence **'shoddily** *adv.*, **'shoddiness**.

**1886** J. R. REES *Divers. Book-worm* 122 We began by talking of the 'shoddiness' of the age. **1899** E. CALLOW *Old Lond. Taverns* I. 59 The foundations were so shoddily constructed that to prevent its falling down, it had to be pulled down.

†**shode.** *Obs.* Forms: 1 scáda, 4 schod(e, school, 4- shode. [OE. *scáda* wk. masc.:—prehistoric **skaidan-*, f. Teut. root **skaid-* to divide: see SHED *v.* From the same root (or the parallel form **skaiþ-*) are MDu. *scheide* (mod.Du. *schei*), OS. *scêthlo*, MDu. *scheidel* (mod.Du. *scheel*), OHG. *sceibila* (mod.G. *scheitel*) crown of the head.]

**1.** The crown of the head; the parting of the hair. Cf. SHED *sb.*[1] 2.

*c* **1000** *Ags. Ps.* lxvii. 21 Feaxes scadan [L. *verticem capilli*]. **13..** *Guy Warw.* 7229, & smot him in þe heued schod. *c* **1325** *Gloss. W. de Bibbesw.* in Wright *Voc.* 144 La greve de moun cheef [*glossed* the schod of my eved]. *c* **1386** CHAUCER *Knt.'s T.* 1149 The nayl ydryuen in the shode [*v.rr.* schod, school, schode] a nyght. **14..** *Voc.* in Wr.-Wülcker 578/40 *Discrimen*, þe shode of the hed.

**2.** A dividing ridge.

*c* **1330** *Arth. & Merl.* 1480 To stones þicke þai founde.. Hem bitven a gret schode. Of grauel & erþe al so, þat hem hadde schifted ato.

**shode**, variant of SHOAD.

**shoder** ('ʃəʊdə(r)). *Gold-beating.* [ad. F. *chauderet, chaudret.*] The packet of skins into which the gold taken from the 'cutch' is placed and beaten out before its final beating in the 'mould'. Hence **'shodering** *vbl. sb.*, in ***shodering-hammer***.

**1763** W. LEWIS *Commerc. Philosophico-Techn.* 47 Three hammers are employed..: the first, called the cutch hammer ..: the second, called the shodering hammer..: the third, called the gold hammer, or finishing hammer. **1851-4** *Tomlinson's Cycl. Useful Arts* (1867) I. 793/2 These [pieces of gold] are put between the leaves of another tool, called a shoder, made of gold beater's skin. **1911** *Encycl. Brit.* XII. 202/1 Each leaf is then..cut into four pieces, and put between the skins of a shoder..containing about 720 skins.

**shoder**, obs. form of SHOULDER, SHUDDER.

†**'shoding**, *vbl. sb. Obs.* In 5 schodynge. [repr. OE. *sc(e)ádung*: see SHEDDING *vbl. sb.*] Separation; parting of the hair.

*c* **1440** *Promp. Parv.* 447/2 Schodynge, or departynge, *separacio, divisio.* Schodynge, of the heede.., *discrimen.*

**shodur**, obs. form of SHUDDER *v.*

**shoe** (ʃuː), *sb.* Pl. shoes (ʃuːz); *dial., poet.*, and *arch.* shoon (ʃuːn). Forms: *sing.* 1 scóh, scó, sceó, 2 sceoh, 2-6 sho, 3 sco, 4 sso, 3-6 scho, 4-6 schoo, 4-7 shoo, (4 show), 6 showe, shue, (shough), 6-7 shew, 6-8 shooe, 6- shoe. *pl.* α. 1 scós, 1-2 sceós, 4-7 shoos, 4 schos, 5 schoz, schoys, schoez, schewis, 5-6 shoys, shewes, show(e)s, showys, shooys, shues, shuse, shuez, 6-8 shooes, 4- shoes. β. 3-5 schon, 3-6 schone, (3 scheon, son, sson), 4-7 shon(e, 4-6 schoon(e, 4-8 shoone, (4 *Sc.* schoyne, 5 shoyn, *Sc.* schoune), 5-6 shoen, 6 schoun(e, (*Sc.* schwyne), 6-8 shune, shooen, (7 *Sc.* shin), 4- shoon. [Com. Teut.: OE. *scóh* masc. = OFris. *scô* (NFris. *skog, skuch*, WFris. *skoech*), OS. *scôh* (MLG. *scô*, LG. *schô*), MDu. *scoe* (mod.Du. *schoen*), OHG. *scuoh, scuah* (MHG. *schuoch, schuo*, mod.G. *schuh*), ON. *skó-r* (Sw., Da. *sko*), Goth. *skōh-s*:—OTeut. **skōho-z* or *skōhwo-z*.

Some scholars refer the word to the root **skōhw-*: **skǣw-* to walk (Goth. *skēwjan* to take a walk, ON. *skǽva* to stride). Others, on account of the alternation of vowel in ON. *skór* pl. *skúar*, assume a pre-Teut. **skōuko-s*, f. **skeu-* to cover.

In OE. the collective *ȝescý* was often used for the plural.]

**1. a.** An outer covering for the human foot, normally made of leather (but often of other materials) and consisting of a more or less stiff sole and a lighter upper part. Chiefly in more specific sense, distinguished from *boot.*

The original distinction was that the *boot* covered a part or the whole of the leg together with the foot, while the *shoe* covered the foot only. In the U.S. *boot* is still commonly applied only to an article of footgear reaching at least to the middle of the calf, one which ends at or below the ankle or just above it being called a *shoe.* In modern British use, the term *boot* is extended to include what were formerly called 'half-boots' or 'high shoes', i.e. 'shoes' (in the older sense) which cover the whole foot including the ankle; hence *shoe* is taken to mean specifically a 'low shoe', which leaves part of the foot covered only by the stocking; a shoe in this sense may either be fastened with laces, buttons, or the like, or (as in 'dancing shoes') it may differ from a slipper only in being suited for more ceremonious wear.

*sing. c* **950** *Lindisf. Gosp.* John i. 27 Ðæs ic ne am wyrðe þætte ic undoe his ðuong scoes. *c* **1050** *Ags. Voc.* in Wr.-Wülcker 283 *Calcarium*, scoh. *c* **1200** ORMIN 10438 Annd tiss dæþshildiȝ mann..Wass uss..ȝa þurrh þe sho ȝa þurrh þe þwang bitacnedd. *c* **1250** *Long Life* 29 in *O.E. Misc.* 156 Ac deþ luteþ in his scho, Him stilliche to for-do. **1340** *Ayenb.* 220 Zuiche fourme ase þe sso takþ ate ginnynge: he halt euremor ine þet stat. *c* **1440** *Promp. Parv.* 447/2 Schoo, mannys fote hyllynge, *sotularis, calceus.* Schoo, for buschopys, *sandalium.* **1449** PECOCK *Repr.* II. xiv. 231 If he haue on him his scho, his slyue, his coot. **1535** FISHER *Serm.* Wks. (1876) 402 If you be ashamed for a foule myrie shoo, and not of a foule stinking soule. **1697** POTTER *Antiq. Greece* I. iv. (1715) 18 A kind of Shooe that fitted both Feet. **1864** PUSEY *Lect. Daniel* (1876) 314 [The custom] of giving the shoe in witness of a covenant.

*pl. c* **950** *Lindisf. Gosp.* Matt. x. 10 *Calciamenta*, scoea [*c* **975** *Rushw.* scoas, *c* **1000** ȝe-scy]. *c* **1050** *Byrhtferth's Handboc* in *Anglia* (1885) VIII. 322/19, & habbað eowre scos on eowrum fotum. *c* **1175** *Lamb. Hom.* 37 Do..wrecche men sceos and claðes. **12..** *Prayer to our Lady* 42 in *O.E. Misc.* 193 Inne wel sittende schon. *a* **1225** *Ancr. R.* 362 Two þongede scheon. *c* **1250** *Gen. & Ex.* 2781 Moyses, moyses, do of ðin son. ? *a* **1366** CHAUCER *Rom. Rose* 843 And shod he was with greet maistrye, With shoon decoped, and with laas. **1377** LANGL. *P. Pl.* B. xx. 218 Proude prestes come with hym..In paltokes & pyked shoes. *c* **1470** HENRY *Wallace* VIII. 1201 Wallace can him aray, In his armour,..His schenand schoys, that burnyst was full beyn. **1508** FISHER *7 Penit. Ps.* xxxviii. Wks. (1876) 79 The hunter therfore wyll laye a payre of shoon in his wayе, and whan he perceyueth the hunter doynge on his shoes he wyll doo the same. **1577** KENDALL *Flowers of Epigr.* 4 b, With patche on patche like loutishe lob, he cobled oft his shues. **1602** SHAKS. *Ham.* III. ii. 288 With two Prouinciall Roses on my rac'd Shooes. *Ibid.* IV. v. 26 By his Cockle hat and staffe, and his Sandal shoone. **1634** MILTON *Comus* 635 The dull swayn Treads on it daily with his clouted shoon. **1688** HOLME *Armoury* III. 14/2 Laced shooes, have the Over Leathers and edges of the Shooe laced in orderly courses. **1712** ADDISON *Spect.* No. 317 ¶4 Put on my double-soaled Shoes. **1786** BURNS *To J. Smith* ii, Ye've cost me twenty pair o' shoon Just gaun to see you. **1818** SCOTT *Rob Roy* ix, Our immortal deliverer from papists and pretenders, and wooden shoes and warming pans. **1911** *Encycl. Brit.* XXVII. 1058/1 In the 11th century the use of liturgical shoes and stockings was reserved for cardinals and bishops.

**b.** Explicitly distinguished from *boot.*

*c* **1400** *Rom. Rose* 2264 Of shoon and botes, newe and faire Loke at the leest thou have a paire. **1521** *Stirling Burgh Rec.* (1887) I. 13 Ane pair of buttis and ane pair of schoun. **1617** MORYSON *Itin.* III. 165 They..delight to have their boots and shoos shine with blacking stuffe. **1823** SCOTT *Quentin D.* Introd., His sedulous attachment to shoes and stockings, in contempt of half-boots and pantaloons. **1847** J. S. HALL *Bk. Feet* (ed. 2) 138 Shoes are now very little worn: boots of some kind or other being the general wear.

**c.** ***high shoes***, boots with high uppers. Hence, one who wears high shoes: see HIGH-SHOE.

**1387** TREVISA *Higden* (Rolls) V. 369 þey usede hiȝe schone unto þe kne, i-slitte to fore [L. *calcei usque ad poplites fissi*], and i-laced wiþ þwonges. *c* **1400** *Rom. Rose* 7260 But Beggers with..high shoos knopped with dagges,..Or bootes revellyng as a gype. **1553** LATIMER *Serm. Lincolnsh.* iii. (1562) 82 When a man shall goe to battaile..for the nether parte he hathe high shoen. **1597** SHAKS. *2 Hen. IV*, I. ii. 44 The horson smooth-pates doe now weare nothing but high shoes. **1603** [see HIGH-SHOE 1].

**d.** as the lowest portion of one's attire.

**1616** B. JONSON *Ev. Man in Hum.* II. i, Whilst they.. mocke me all ouer, From my flat cap, vnto my shining shooes.

*Proverbial phrase.* **1887** MRS. OLIPHANT *Son of Father* xiv. 242 [She] felt..her heart sink to her shoes.

**e.** ***shoes of swiftness***: the magic shoes of the giant in the tale of Jack the Giant-killer: occas. used allusively.

**1787** *Hist. Jack & Giants* 12 Jack soon put on his coat of darkness, with his shoes of swiftness. **1837** CARLYLE *Fr. Rev.* I. v. v, Surely also Punishment, this day, hitches..after Crime, with frightful shoes-of-swiftness!

**2.** Phrases and figurative uses.

**a.** ***old shoe***: a type of something discarded as worn out, useless or worthless. Also, ***to cast, fling***, etc. ***an old shoe after*** (a person): *lit.* as a means of bringing good luck (e.g. at a wedding); also *fig.* to wish (a person) good luck. †***go meddle with (thy) old shoes***: mind your own business.

*c* **1386** CHAUCER *Wife's Prol.* 708 The clerk whan he is oold and may noght do Of Venus werkes worth his olde sho. **1538** BALE *Thre Lawes* 1670 What is that to the? go meddle thee with olde shone! **1546** J. HEYWOOD *Prov.* I. ix. (1562) C, Nowe for good lucke, caste an olde shoe after mee. **1679** *Hist. Jetzer* 25 Thou Traytor..meddle with thy Old shooes! ..Go about thy business, Goodman Fool! **1663** KILLIGREW *Pars. Wedding* IV. vii, *Pars.* I, with all my heart, there's an old shooe after you. **1842** TENNYSON *Will Waterproof* 216 And wheresoe'er thou move, good luck Shall fling her old shoe after.

**b.** ***another pair of shoes*** (predicatively): quite a different matter or state of things. ***the shoe is on the other foot***: the facts are otherwise, the position is reversed. Cf. *the boot is on the other leg* s.v. BOOT *sb.*[3] 1 b.

**1861** DICKENS *Gt. Expect.* xl, We'll show 'em another pair of shoes than that, Pip; won't us? **1865** [see PAIR *sb.*[1] 1 b]. **1895** MRS. CROKER *Village Tales* (1896) 10 'Ah! and you'll find a tiger is quite another pair of shoes', I assured him impressively. **1933** *Mystery* May 122/1 Inspector Queen has not been able to discover our man-about-town's source of income. A gigolo? Gigolos do not pay for ladies' apartments; the shoe is rather on the other foot. **1939** B. K. HARRIS *Purslane* 179, I tell him if he had the waitin' on him to do the shoes would be on the other foot. **1953** J. S. HUXLEY *Evolution in Action* ii. 49 All the objections to a selectionist explanation of evolution that are based on the improbability of its results, simply fall to the ground. In fact the shoe is now on the other foot. Improbability is to be *expected* as the result of natural selection. **1976** *Times Lit. Suppl.* 2 Jan. 13/4 Most obviously, the shoe is on the other foot. Anyone who knows what rigour is will find it lacking in most of Hegel's transitions.

**c.** ***in one's shoes, without shoes***, as a condition of measurement of stature. ***in their shoes***: (of soldiers) fully equipped.

For *to shake in one's shoes*, see SHAKE *v.* 4.

**1724** *Lond. Gaz.* No. 6308/3 John Cockran,..5 Foot 10 Inches one quarter without Shoes. **1815** WELLINGTON in Gurw. *Desp.* (1838) XII. 323 We are getting on in strength, I have now 60,000 men in their shoes. **1859** MEREDITH *R. Feverel* xlii, 'You're afraid of ghosts'. 'Belike I am when they're six foot two in their shoes'.

**d.** ***to die in one's shoes***: to meet with a violent death, esp. to be hanged. Also allusively.

**1694** MOTTEUX *Rabelais* IV. xlv. 174 Whoever refus'd to do this, should presently swing for't, and die in his Shoes. **1712** [see DIE *v.*[1] 3]. **1837** BARHAM *Ingol. Leg.* Ser. I. *Execution*, All come to see a man 'die in his shoes!'

**e.** ***over (the) shoes***: deeply immersed or sunk (*in* something). *lit.* and *fig.* See also OVER ***prep.*** 3 and OVER-SHOE. Similarly ***up to the shoes.***

*over shoes, over boots*: see BOOT *sb.*[3] 1 b.

**1518** *Star Chamber Cases* (Selden Soc.) II. 137 They.. thrust the same Antony ouer the showys in the myre. **1590** GREENE *Menaphon* (Arb.) 45 The countrey maides themselues fel in loue with this fair Nimph, and could not blame Menaphon for being ouer the shooes with such a beautifull creature. **1590** SHAKS. *Mids. N.* III. ii. 48. **1594** —— *Rich. III*, V. iii. 326. **1600** ABP. ABBOT *Jonah* xxvi. 541 Being in vp to the shooes he will on to the shoulders. **1601** [? MARSTON] *Jack Drums Entert.* I. B 2, *Enter Flawne. Kathe.* It seemes he can scarce carry himselfe. *Drum.* Hee's ouer the shooes, yet heele hold out water, for I haue liquor'd him soundly. **1615** V. ALSOP *Anti-sozzo* iii. 124, I find our Author over the shoes in Love.

**f.** ***to know best where one's shoe pinches***: see PINCH *v.* 1 b. Also in many other similar phrases.

*c* **1386** CHAUCER *Merch. T.* 309 But I woot best where wryngeth me my sho. —— *Wife's Prol.* 492 He sat ful ofte and song Whan þat his shoo full bitterly hym wrong. **1500-20** DUNBAR *Poems* xc. 54 Thow knawis best quhair bindis the thi scho. **1639** [J. TAYLOR (Water P.)] *Divers Crabtree Lect.* 96 No man can tell where his shooe wrings him, but hee that weares it. **1749** SMOLLETT *Gil Blas* VIII. vi. (1782) III. 161 He defrayed the expence of every body; so that there I did not feel where the shoe pinched. **1890** W. E. NORRIS *Misadventure* xlviii, Only after the deed has been done does the shoe really begin to pinch.

**g.** ***to put the shoe on the right foot***: to put the blame on the real offender. (In mod. Dicts.)

**h.** ***to kiss*** (a person's) ***shoe*** (in token of servility or abject submission).

*c* **1395** *Plowman's Tale* lii. in *Pol. Poems* (Rolls) I. 317 A king shall kneele and kisse his show. **1599** SHAKS. *Hen. V*, IV. i. 47 *Pist.* The King's a Bawcock..: I kisse his durtie shooe. **1819** SHELLEY *Peter Bell* VII. vii, There was a bow of sleek devotion..; each motion Seemed a Lord's shoe to kiss.

†**i.** ***to win one's shoes*** (*on* or *upon* an adversary): to achieve renown by a victory. Cf. *to win one's spurs.* Common in the 15th century.

*a* **1400** *Sir Perc.* 1595 Ther salle other dedis be done, And thou salle wynne thi schone Appone the sowdane. ?*c* **1475** *Sqr. lowe Degre* 174 And other dedes of armes to done, Through whiche ye may wynne your shone.

**j.** ***to waste one's shoes***: to wear out one's shoes to no purpose.

**1509** Barclay *Shyp of Folys* (1570) 85 Another on his fiste a Sparhawke..and so, wasting his shone, Before the aulters he to and fro doth wander.

**k.** ***to be in*** (another person's) ***shoes***: to be in his position or place. Chiefly in negative form = in his unenviable condition or plight. ***to place*** (a person) ***in the shoes of*** (another person): to give (him) the position vacated by (another). ***to step into the shoes of*** (another person): to occupy the position vacated by him. ***to wait for dead men's shoes***: to wait for the death of a person with the expectancy of succeeding to his possessions or office.

**1546** J. Heywood *Prov.* I. xi. (1867) 37 Who waitth for dead men shoen, shall go long barefoote. **1609** *Old Meg of Herefordsh.* (1816) 12 It were no hoping after dead mens shooes, for both vpper-leather and soles would bee worne out to nothing. **1767** Bedingfield in *Lett. Lit. Men* (Camden) 404, I would rather chuse to stand in his Sardinian Majesty's shoes than his; who [etc.]. **1776** *Pennsylvania Even. Post* 29 June 325/2 Volunteers, with the rank of officers (who are impatiently waiting at 'the pool' for the death and old shoes of commissioned officers). **1777** J. Adams in *Fam. Lett.* (1876) 304, I judge, I should put more to risk if I were in his shoes. **1822** Scott *Nigel* x, But then, in order to secure the lender, he must come in the shoes of the creditor to whom he advances payment. 'Come in his shoes!' replied the Earl... 'It is a law phrase, my lord'..said Heriot. **1842** Sir H. Taylor *Edwin the Fair* III. viii, Them that were placed by Edred in the shoes Of Seculars that by Edred were expulsed. **1860** Reade *Cloister & H.* i, Cornelis ..stuck to the hearth, waiting for dead men's shoes. **1864** Trollope *Small Ho. at Allington* xxviii, I must be the first to congratulate you on the acquisition of my old shoes. **1880** J. Payn *Confid. Agent* III. 130, I wish I was in your shoes. **1908** *Times* 21 July 3/1 The respondents were interested in the success of Mme. Bovet..but that could never put them in her shoes in vindicating her rights against wrongdoers.

†**l.** ***to tread*** (***her***) ***shoe awry*** (rarely ***amiss***): to make a lapse from virtue. *Obs.*

*c* **1422** Hoccleve *Minor P.* xxiv. 66 No womman..But swich oon as hath trode hir shoo amis. **1560** Daus tr. *Sleidane's Comm.* 187 Where the king had maried her for a mayde, he founde that she had troden her showe awrye. **1693** *Urquhart's Rabelais* III. xxviii. 241 His Wife did tread her Shooe awry. **1828** [Carr] *Craven Gloss.* (ed. 2) s.v. *Shoe*, 'To tread one's shoes straight', to behave with propriety, to be circumspect in our conduct.

**m.** Proverbial phrases.

**1546** J. Heywood *Prov.* II. v. (1562) G iiij, Folke say of olde, the shoe will holde with the sole. **1591** Lambarde *Archeion* (1635) 78 To apply one generall Law to all particular cases, were to make all shooes by one last. **1622** Mabbe tr. *Aleman's Guzman d'Alf.* II. 163 As arrant a villaine, as euer trode vpon a shooe of leather. *a* **1700** B. E. *Dict. Cant. Crew*, *One Shoe will not fit all Feet*, Men are not all of a Size, nor all Conveniences of a Last. **1752** Foote *Taste* I. (1781) 9 Twenty as fine Babes as ever trod in Shoe of Leather. **1825** Brockett *N.C. Gloss.* s.v. *Old-Shoe*, As easy as an old shoe. **1887** *S. Chesh. Gloss.* s.v. *Shoe*, 'Too big for one's shoon', used of a person whose notions are too high for his station, a conceited person.

**3.** in the names of plants (see quots.).

*a* **1825** Forby *Voc. E. Anglia*, *Shoes and stockings*, the variety of primrose and polyanthus which has one flower sheathed within another. **1838** W. Holloway *Dict. Provinc.*, *Shoes and stockings*, [also] a wild flower of the cypripedium genus. **1878** Britten & Holland *Plant-n.* s.v. *Boots*, Boots and Shoes (1) *Lotus corniculatus*, L.—*Suss.* (2) *Aquilegia vulgaris*, L.—Corn. **1882** Friend *Devonsh. Plant-n.*, Boots and shoes,..(2) *Cypripedium Calceolus*, L., often called 'Lady's-slipper'. **1893** *Rep. Provinc.* (E.D.D.), On seeing the *Linaria vulgaris* in blossom [she], Cornish by birth,..replied, 'We always call it "Shoes and Stockings".'

**4. a.** A plate of metal, usually iron, nailed to the under-side of the hoof of a horse as a protection from injury: = horseshoe 1. Also occas. a similar plate nailed to the hoof of an ox or some other animal.

**1387** Trevisa *Higden* (Rolls) VII. 127 He made..þe mule ..to be schodde uppon wiþ gold, forbedyng al his men þat when þe schone fel awey þat non schulde gadre þaym up. **1430-40** Lydg. *Bochas* VII. v. (1554) 169 b, This Nero.. Made his mules be shod with siluer shone. **1523-34** Fitzherb. *Husb.* §6 Oxen..haue no shoes, as horses haue. *Ibid.* §114 Lyttel stones, that goth in betwene the shough and the herte of the fote. **1540** *Coventry Leet-bk.* 745 [That] no Smyth within this Cetie shoo no horse with forest shoyes. *a* **1674** Clarendon *Hist. Reb.* XIII. §101 [The smith observed] that he was sure that his four shoes had been made in four several counties. *a* **1720** W. Gibson *Diet of Horses* viii. (1726) 135 Their Shooes should never be suffer'd to wear too smooth. **1818** Scott *Br. Lamm.* xxx, You can never ride beyond the village but your horse will cast a shoe. **1828** [Carr] *Craven Gloss.* (ed. 2) s.v. *Shoon*, 'To addle his shoon', is when a horse rolls on his back from one side to the other. **1844** H. Stephens *Bk. Farm* II. 697 The first shoes of a young horse should be light, with no heels.

**b.** See quot. (Cf. horseshoe 1 b.)

**1801** Strutt *Sports & Past.* II. ii. §9. 60 Formerly..the rustics not having..quoits to play with, used horse-shoes and in many places the quoit itself..is called a shoe.

**5.** Something resembling a shoe (sense 1 or 4) in shape, position, or function.

†**a.** The iron blade or an iron cutting edge fastened upon the wooden blade (of a spade or shovel). *Obs.* †**b.** The piston (of a pump). *Obs. rare.* **c.** A metal rim, ferrule, casing or sheath, esp. for the end of a pile, pole, rod, or the like. **d.** The receptacle beneath the hopper of a mill. **e.** The short section which turns out the water at the foot of a water pipe. **f.** A kind of drag or skid for a wheel of a vehicle; also the concave part of a brake, which acts upon the wheel (more fully ***brake shoe***). **g.** A strip of iron, steel, etc. fastened upon that part of a vehicle, machine, etc. which is liable to be worn out by friction. **h.** A socket for the reception of a bolt, pin, or the like. **i.** *Naut.* (See quot. 1769). **j.** A block, plate, etc. which serves as a socket or bearing for the foot of a pole, the legs of sheers, etc. to prevent slipping or sinking. **k.** An iron plate shaped to receive the end of one or more pieces of timber in roof-construction. **l.** (See quot. 1881.) **m.** That part of the breech which carries the breech block in a converted rifle. **n.** (See quot.) **o.** *Electr. traction.* A block attached to an electric car in such a position that it slides upon a conductor-wire or rail and collects the current for its propulsion. **p.** An ingot of precious metal, somewhat in the form of a Chinese shoe, but more like a boat, formerly current in the trade of the Far East and current until the early 20th c. in silver in China. **q.** A tyre. *slang.* **r.** A box for dealing the cards in baccarat or *chemin de fer*. Also, a game of baccarat. **s.** On a camera, a socket or other mounting for the temporary attachment of an accessory.

**a.** *c* **1440** *Jacob's Well* xxx. 193, I lykenyd satysfaccyoun to a schouele... I telde ȝou þat þe scho of þe schouell was almes-dede. **1578** [see shiver *sb.*[2] 2]. **1688** Holme *Armoury* II. 331/1 He beareth Vert, a Spade Iron, Argent (some call it a shooe for a Spade). *Ibid.* III. 393/1 The Bottom, or Shooe of a Trenching Spade. It is all Iron and put on the Staffe.. with a..Socket.

**b.** **1576** *Churchw. Acc. St. Michael, Oxford* (MS.), Item payd to William Williams for a showe for the plumpe xvij[d]. **1593** *Ibid.*, It'm payd to Oven for settinge a shooe & a staff in ye plompe xxij[d]. **1599** *Acc. Balliol Coll., Oxford* (MS.), Imprimis, a shooe for the plumpe, xvi[d].

**c.** **1495** Pyles shone [see pile *sb.*[1] 5 d]. **1580** *Reg. Privy Council Scot.* III. 320 The quhelis garnesit with schone and two virollis only. **1791** Smeaton *Edystone Lightho.* §81, I had a wooden measuring rod..this was shod with a rounded end or shoe of iron. **1837** *Civ. Engin. & Arch. Jrnl.* I. 33/1 All the piles are to be shod with proper wrought-iron shoes. **1857** P. Colquhoun *Comp. Oarsman's Guide* 30 The boat-hook consists in the staff and shoe. **1972** L. M. Harris *Introd. Deepwater Floating Drilling Operations* ix. 90 The shoe of the foundation pile is equipped with a breakaway guide frame. **1976** *Offshore Platforms & Pipelining* 8/2 Deviation will begin about 100 ft below the conductor shoe.

**d.** **1688** Holme *Armoury* III. 340/2 The parts of a Wind-Mill... The Shoo or Shough, the Corn by its shaking drops down into the Mill. **1839** Ure *Dict. Arts* 749 Below the hopper there is a small bucket called a shoe, into which the ore is shaken down.

**e.** **1769** *Phil. Trans.* LIX. 166 The bottoms of these pipes ..terminate with a shoe of lead. **1899** *Daily News* 10 Oct. 6/6 Water-pipes with heads and shoes.

**f.** **1837** Hebert *Engin. & Mech. Encycl.* II. 377 The shoe or skid ought to be somewhat broader than the tire of the wheels. **1875** Knight *Dict. Mech.*, *Shoe*, that part of a car-brake which is brought in contact with the wheel in the act of stopping a train. **1910** Hobart *Dict. Electr. Engin.*, *Brake shoe*, a cast-iron or wooden block which is pressed against the rim of a car wheel, or against the track rails..to retard the motion of the car.

**g.** **1837** Hebert *Engin. & Mech. Encycl.* II. 805 Each division [of Brunel's tunnelling shield] was supported by two strong cast-iron plates, called shoes, and which rest upon gravel at the base. **1855** in *Harper's Mag.* (1884) Jan. 232/2 Her bow was raised out of the water three or four feet, her shoe taken off her keel, and her keel itself cut through. **1879** *Encycl. Brit.* IX. 246/2 The lower part of the trawl-head..is straight and flat... It is called the 'shoe', and is the part which slides over the ground.

**h.** **1858** *Skyring's Builders' Prices* 9 Shutter shoes with screws. **1878** Dixon Kemp *Yacht & Boat Sailing* 368 *Shoe* or *Shod*, iron plates rivetted to the ends of wire rigging to receive shackle bolts.

**i.** **1750** Blanckley *Naval Expos.*, Shoe for an Anchor is made of a Piece of Baulk,..one End cut with a Hole for the Bill...and the other with a triangular Notch to receive the Stock. **1769** Falconer *Dict. Marine* (1789), *Shoe of the anchor*, a small block of wood..having a small hole, sufficient to contain the point of the anchor-fluke... It is used to prevent the anchor from tearing..the planks..when ascending or descending. **1867** in Smyth *Sailor's Word-bk.*

**j.** **1843** *Rep. Brit. Assoc.* 112 The frames stand upon legs resting upon capacious shoes. **1882** Nares *Seamanship* (ed. 6) 62 A shoe is a piece of wood about four feet long, two feet wide, and nine inches thick, with a hole in the centre for the sheer to step in. **1894** *Times* 26 Feb. 3/6 There were no 'shoes' to prevent poles from slipping.

**k.** **1842** *Civ. Engin. & Arch. Jrnl.* V. 242/2 The principals [rafters] are fitted into cast iron shoes resting on the walls. **1879** *Cassell's Techn. Educ.* I. 156 The straining pieces [of a truss]..at their lower end..are fitted with a wrought iron shoe. *Ibid.*, A cast-iron double shoe, or housing for the reception of the upper ends of the principals.

**l.** **1874** Raymond *6th Rep. Mines* 410 Every casting, such as a shoe or die, in the battery is full of flaws. **1881** —— *Mining Gloss.*, *Shoe*. A piece of iron or steel, attached to the bottom of a *stamp* or *muller*, for grinding ore. The shoe can be replaced when worn out.

**m.** **1866** *Cornh. Mag.* Sept. 348 It is now found more convenient to make the whole of the breech arrangement separately, and this 'shoe' is screwed into the back end of the barrel. **1881** Greener *Gun* (1888) 141 The shoe of the breech carries within it the cylinder or breech-piece. *Ibid.* 142 An iron frame or shoe is screwed on to the barrel. The breech block is placed in this shoe.

**n.** **1883** Gresley *Gloss. Coal-mining*, *Shoes*, steel or iron guides fixed to the ends and sides of cages, to fit and run upon the conductors. **1894** *Northumbld. Gloss.*

**o.** **1891** *Times* 28 Sept. 13/6 The pulley has been abandoned in America as being inferior to the trolley or sliding shoe.

**p.** **1702** in J. T. Wheeler *Madras in Olden Time* (1861) I. 397 One Hundred shoes of gold, or so many thousand Pagodas or Rupees. **1711** C. Lockyer *Trade in India* v. 132 Gold-makers..cast all the Gold, that comes through their Hands, into Shoos of about 10 Tale weight, 12 oz. 2 dwt. 4 gr. **1911** *Contemp. Rev.* Nov. 705 A Chinese high offical said ..'I cannot obtain an audience at Court unless I send a number of 'shoes' of silver..to an Imperial Prince'.

**q.** **1917** E. E. Cummings *Let.* 2 Aug. (1969) 32 The rear axle looked like a mosquito's beak, and there were 2 shoes blown. **1934** R. Blaker *Night-Shift* vii. 87 If the tyres were worn to the fabric smooth as an egg, he could dismiss this outlay as 'a set of new shoes'.

**r.** **1923** W. J. Locke *Moordius & Co.* xi. 149 Moordius dealt from the shoe. One card to the right, one to the left, one to himself. **1930** D. Byrne *Golden Goat* i. 8 They were only interested in the passing of the 'shoe' as the *chemin-de-fer* box is called. **1960** O. Manning *Great Fortune* I. 54 Hadjimoscos took his place before the shoe. As soon as he had drawn cards, he became serious and businesslike. **1964** A. Wykes *Gambling* xiii. 324 Zographos could remember every card that was played throughout a game (or 'shoe') of baccarat. **1965** D. Francis *Odds Against* iv. 52 He kept his side of the bargain by digging out the chemmy shoe. **1976** 'J. Welcome' *Grand National* iv. 54 The bank passed and the polished walnut and silver shoe slid along the table to a gaunt, henna-haired woman.

**s.** **1953** A. Matheson *Leica Way* 47 The Leica If and Ic models carry a detachable brilliant viewfinder..in one of the two accessory shoes. **1971**, etc. [see *hot shoe* s.v. hot *a.* 12 c]. **1979** *SLR Camera* Feb. 74/1 The modification consists of adding an extra contact to the shoe of the sensor lead.

**6.** ***attrib.*** and ***Comb.*** **a.** simple attrib., as (sense 1) ***shoe-bag***, ***-clasp***, ***-factory***, ***heel***, †***-knot***, †***market*** (Sc.), ***ribbon***, ***-rose*** (rose *sb.* 15), ***-shop***, ***-sole***, ***-store*** (*orig.* U.S.), ***-strap***, ***-thread***, ***-tip***, ***-top***, ***-trade***; also in the names of shoemakers' tools, as ***shoe nippers***, ***pincers***, ***pliers***; (sense 5) ***shoe-seat***.

**1873** S. Coolidge *What Katy did at School* vii. 139 Hang your dresses up..and put your shoes in the *shoe-bag. **1972** J. Wilson *Hide & Seek* i. 7 The children began to pour out into the playground. Alice was..dragging her shoe bag along after her. **1797** *J. Robinson's Directory of Sheffield* 52 *Shoe-clasp, and seal maker. **1855** J. Holbrook *Ten Years among Mail Bags* 276 How many persons are employed in that *shoe factory? **1960** M. Spark *Ballad Peckham Rye* vi. 111 She told him all of her life in the shoe factory. **1716** *Lond. Gaz.* No. 5466/4 A middle sized Man.., Lame of his Left Leg, his Left Foot *Shoe-heel half a Quarter of a Yard high. **1766** *Compl. Farmer* s.v. *Shoeing* 6 U 4/2 Strong shoe-heels are an ease to the weak heels, and fetlocks of horses. **1777** Sheridan *Trip to Scarboro* IV. i, That which they call pin-money, is to buy everything.., down to their very *shoe-knots. **1756-7** tr. *Keysler's Trav.* lxxxii. (1760) IV. 186 His *shoe ribbons are also embroidered. **1796** Jane Austen *Pride & Prej.* xvii, The very *shoe-roses for Netherfield were got by proxy. **1844** *Civ. Engin. & Arch. Jrnl.* VII. 112/1 The '*shoe seat' or base of the frame is more deeply imbedded in the wood than is usual. **1824** Miss Mitford *Village* Ser. I. 8 The fair nymph of the *shoe-shop. **1387** Trevisa *Higden* (Rolls) IV. 395 Nero..usede *scho soles of silver. **1862** Lowell *Biglow P.* Ser. II. Introd. *The Courtin'*, For she felt sartin-sure he'd come Down to her very shoe-sole. **1789** *Boston Directory* 175 Bond and Bryant, *shoe-store. **1813** *Boston* (Mass.) *Rec.* (1908) XXXVIII. 84 The old Town house adjoining his shoe store. **1976** *Milton Keynes Express* 11 June 12/2 The shoe store of Leslie Wheeler at New Bradwell. **1775** Ash, **Shoestrap*, a shoe string. **1573** Tusser *Husb.* (1878) 123 Vse ton for thy spinning, leaue Mihel the tother, for *shoo thred. **1609** B. Jonson *Silent Wom.* IV. ii, She has a peruke, that's like a pound of hempe, made vp in shoo-thrids. **1858** Simmonds *Dict. Trade*, *Shoe-thread Maker*. **1897** Flandrau *Harvard Episodes* 64 From the bit of white ribbon twisted through her hair..to the non-committal exposure of *shoe-tip. **1689** *Rector's Bk., Clayworth* (1910) 89 Y[e] 27[th] o' March was a snow to y[e] *shoe-tops. **1850** Ogilvie, **Shoe-trade*, the trade of making boots and shoes.

**b.** Objective and obj. genitive, as ***shoe-clouter*** (Sc.), ***-factor***, ***-repairer***, ***-rivetter***, ***-stitcher***, ***-vamper***, ***-wearer***, ***-worker***; ***shoe-soling***, ***-wearing***; also ***shoe-embossing***, ***-eyeleting***, ***-pegging***, ***-sewing*** (machines): see Knight *Dict. Mech.* 1875-84.

**1581** N. Burne *Disput.* 188 Quhais fals prophetes ar maid of Tinklaris, *schocloutaris [etc.]. **1858** Simmonds *Dict. Trade*, **Shoe-factor*, a wholesale dealer in shoes. **1933** *Radio Times* 14 Apr. 127/1 The well-known Kensington *Shoe Repairers. **1976** M. Hinxman *End of Good Woman* vii. 94 Shoe repairer, now that was 'poshe' if you like! **1887** *Pall Mall Gaz.* 19 Nov. 6/2 Boot and *shoe rivetters and finishers. **1842** A. Raleigh *Rec. Life* iii. (1881) 19, I have had to pay a good deal in books, *shoe-soling, medicine, etc. **1891** S. C. Scrivener *Our Fields & Cities* iii. 26 Further, over the Huntingdonshire ground, where the *shoe-stitchers have extended. **1838** Dickens *O. Twist* xxvi, Here, the clothesman, the *shoe-vamper, and the rag-merchant, display their goods. **1657** J. Watts *Scribe & Let. Answ.* Ep. Rdr. A 3 b, Thou Histiæus wast the Shoemaker, but Aristagoras was the *Shoewearer. **1902** *Munsey's Mag.* XXIV. 854/2 After a year of constant *shoe wearing, the gravel hurt her feet. **1888** *Philadelphia Ledger* 23 Nov. (Cent.), The *shoe-workers' strike and lock-out.

**c.** Special comb.: **shoe-beak** = *shoe-bird*; **shoe-bench** *U.S.*, a shoemaker's bench; **shoe-bill**, (*a*) = *shoe-bird*; so *shoe-bill(ed) stork*; (*b*) a kind of nail used in shoemaking; **shoe-binder** (see quot. 1858); so *shoe-bindery*, *binding*; **shoe-bird**, a bird, *Balæniceps rex*, found in Central Africa; **shoe-block** (see quot.); **shoe-board**, (*a*) a shoe-cleaner's bench; (*b*) a pedal of a silk-winding machine; **shoe-boy**, a shoeblack; **shoe-brush**, a brush for cleaning and polishing shoes; also *attrib.* of an object shaped like a shoe-brush; **shoe buckle**, a fastening for a shoe, in the form of a buckle, also an ornamental buckle worn on the front of a shoe; **shoe-butt**, thick leather (see butt *sb.*[11]) for making the soles of shoes; **shoe-button**, a button used for fastening a boot or a shoe; freq. *attrib.* of a small expressionless eye; **shoe-case**, a saddle case in which one or more spare horseshoes are carried; **shoe-cleaner** = shoe-black; so **shoe-cleaning**

*sb.* and *a.*; † **shoe clout**, a cloth for wiping shoes; **shoe-deep** *a. U.S.*, deep enough to cover a person's shoes; **shoe-finder** *U.S.*, one who deals in shoemakers' tools and appliances; **shoe findings** *pl.*, tools and material for shoemaking; **shoe-flower** *Anglo-Indian*, the flower of the *Hibiscus Rosasinensis* (Yule); **shoe hairs** *pl.*, prepared bristles for shoemakers' use; **shoe-hammer**, a shoemakers' hammer with a broad convex face and wide thin peen; **shoe-hand**, a shoemaking operative; **shoe-knife**, a shoemakers' knife; **shoe-lace**, a lace used to fasten a shoe by passing it in and out through eyelet-holes; **shoe-last** = LAST *sb.*[1] 2; also *fig.*; also used *attrib.* in *Archæol.* to designate or with reference to polished stone implements, flat on one side and curved on the other, found in the area of neolithic Danubian culture; **shoe-latch, -latchet** = LATCHET I c; **shoe-licker** *fig.*, an abject sycophant or toady; **shoe-lift** = SHOE-HORN *sb.* I; **shoe-lifter** = prec.; hence *shoe-lifter-like* adj.; **shoeman**, (*a*) see quot. 1841; (*b*) one who makes or deals in shoes; **shoe mercer**, one who deals in shoemercery; **shoemercery**, laces, buttons, and other small wares of a boot and shoe dealer; **shoe-nail**, a nail used in fastening on the soles of shoes, also a projecting nail put in the soles of shoes to prevent slipping; **shoe peg** = PEG *sb.*[1] 2 d; **shoe-piece**, (*a*) (see quot. 1867); (*b*) a piece of wood at the back of a chair, supporting the splat; **shoe pin** = *shoe-peg*; **shoe-plate** (see quot.); † **shoe-pride**, ostentatious foot-wear (*nonce-use*); **shoe-rag** = *shoe-clout*; **shoe-scraper** = SCRAPER 5; **shoe-shine, shoeshine** (orig. and chiefly *U.S.*), a polish given to shoes, esp. by a shoe-shiner; freq. *attrib.*; **shoe-shiner**, one who polishes shoes for money; **shoesmith**, a shoeing-smith (*obs.* or *arch.*); **shoe-stirrup**, a stirrup shaped like a shoe (*Cent. Dict.* 1891); **shoe-stone** (see quot.); **shoe-stretcher** (see quot. 1875); † **shoe-thong**, a leathern shoe-latchet; **shoe-tie** = *shoe-string*; **shoe-tree** = *boot-tree* (see BOOT *sb.*[3] 8); † **shoe-turner**, the workman who 'turns' or cuts to shape the soles of shoes; **shoe-valve** (see quot.); **shoeward** *adv.*, towards the shoe; *adj.* directed towards the shoe; **shoe whang** *dial.* = *shoe-thong*; **shoe-wiper**, a servant who cleans shoes. Also SHOE-BLACK, SHOE-HORN, SHOE LEATHER.

**1869-73** T. R. JONES *Cassell's Bk. Birds* IV. 59 The Whale-headed Stork, or *Shoe-beak (*Balæniceps rex*). **1841** *Knickerbocker* May 362 A few weeks' rumination on the *shoe-bench, or cogitation on the tailor's board. **1891** *Harper's Mag.* June 57/1 An express wagon was..loaded with the old shoe bench. **1861** GEO. ELIOT *Let.* 20 Feb. (1954) III. 381 There is a *shoe-bill, a great bird of grotesque ugliness. **1874** tr. *Brehm's Bird-Life* 191 *Balæniceps Rex*, the Boot-bill, or Shoe-bill, as the Arab tribes of East Soudan call it. **1881** *Instr. Census Clerks* (1885) 91 Nail manufacture... Shoe Bill, Cutter. **1957** *Bull. Brit. Mus.* (*Nat. Hist.*): *Zool.* V. 111 (*heading*) The Pelecaniform characters of the skeleton of the Shoe-bill Stork. **1964** E. A. NIDA *Towards Sci. Transl.* iii. 40 A person points to the beak of a shoe-billed stork and says *That's a big bill.* **1975** *Daily Colonist* (Victoria, B.C.) 17 Dec. 6/3 Shoebill stork..is one of only eight. **1809** *Longworth's New York Directory* 227 *Shoebinder. **1858** SIMMONDS *Dict. Trade*, *Shoe-binder*, a female who attaches the leather or ribbon binding to a shoe. **1848** in *Amer. Industrial Soc.* (1910) VIII. 200 *Shoe-bindery. **1835** DICKENS *Sk. Boz*, *Charac.* iv, Miss Evans.. had adopted in early life the useful pursuit of *shoe-binding. **1861** PETHERICK *Egypt*, etc. 475 Six *shoe-birds, so called by the Arabs, or royal balaeniceps. **1794** *Rigging & Seamanship* I. 156 **Shoe-blocks* are two single blocks, cut in a solid piece, transversely to each other. **1845** *Glance at Interior of China* (Shanghae) 82 A couple of grooves, on which the *shoe-board is to rest. **1857** HUGHES *Tom Brown* II. ix, Tom..sat down on the shoe-board, while the old man told his tale. **1724** SWIFT *Drapier's Lett.* vii. Wks. 1755 V. II. 137 If I employ a *shoe-boy, is it in view to his advantage, or to my own convenience? **1820** HOGG in *Blackw. Mag.* VI. 392 He makes your homebred coxcomb look a shoeboy. **1740** E. PUREFOY *Let.* 8 Mar. (1931) II. x. 248, I received Mr Robotham's letter..with half a dozen of oranges, a dozen of Delft plates, & 2 *shoe Brushes. **1775** *Phil. Trans.* LXVII. 12 This was done..with water and a stiff shoe-brush. **1968** J. ARNOLD *Shell Bk. Country Crafts* 185 For use in difficult angles an extra leggat is used, having a shoe-brush handle to make it easy to use in those awkard places. **1482** in *York Myst.* Introd. 40 [Those that] maketh ffisshe-hukes or *shobakilles. **1848** THACKERAY *Van. Fair* xxxix, A large pair of paste shoe-buckles. **1858** SIMMONDS *Dict. Trade*, **Shoe-butts*, stout leather suited for soles. **1895** *Montgomery Ward Catal.* Spring & Summer 525/2 Button Machine... No family should be without this machine..for putting on their own *shoe buttons. **1928** E. O'NEILL *Strange Interlude* v. 170 Lust ogling me for a dollar with oily shoe-button Italian eyes! **1973** 'A. GILBERT' *Is she Dead Too?* (rev. ed.) ii. 29 Her eyes round and hard as shoe buttons. **1854** R. S. SURTEES *Handley Cross* xxxii, A sandwich-case for one side, and a *shoe-case for t'other. **1725** DE FOE ['A. Moreton'] *Every-Body's Business* title-p., A Proposal..for clearing the Streets of those Vermin call'd *Shoe-Cleaners. **1716** GAY *Trivia* Index, *Shoe-cleaning Boys. **1821** SCOTT *Kenilw.* xxii, That very cloakbrushing, shoe-cleaning fellow..my lord's lackey. *c* **1425** ? LYDG. *Assembly of Gods* 1274 Syr ye do me wrong ..to put thys creature..to be her vnderlowte, As hit were a castaway or a *shoo clowte. **1702** C. MATHER *Magn. Chr.* III. IV. vii. (1852) 613 Some greasy dish-clout, or some dirty shoe-clout. **1773** P. V. FITHIAN *Jrnl.* 28 Dec. (1900) I. 75 Last night there fell a snow, which is about half *Shoe-deep. **1891** M. E. WILKINS *New England Nun* 174 There had been a light fall of snow..but it was not shoe-deep. **1909** *Boston* (Mass.) *Transcript* 19 July 14/5 The National Leather and *Shoe Finders' Association. **1836** in *Amer. Industrial Soc.* VI. 37 *Shoe findings. **1814** J. LUNAN *Hortus Jamaicensis* I. 176 They are also put to a use which seems little consistent with their elegance and beauty, that of blacking shoes, whence their names of *rosæ calceolariæ* and *shoe-flower. **1834** G. BENNETT *Wanderings* II. 203 The Malays use the flowers of this shrub for cleansing shoes... This is probably the cause of its being called the shoe-flower. **1859** F. S. COOPER *Ironmongers' Catal.* 160 *Shoe Hairs... Shoe Knives. **1875** KNIGHT *Dict. Mech.*, **Shoe-hammer*. **1859** *Shoe-knife [see *shoe hairs* above]. **1647** HEXHAM I, A *shoe-lace, *een schoe-lint, ofte schoe-riem. Ibid.*, A *shoe-last, *een schoe-leest*. **1832** BABBAGE *Econ. Manuf.* xi. (ed. 3) 102 An instrument..proposed for the purpose of making shoe-lasts. **1879** G. M. HOPKINS *Lett. to R. Bridges* (1955) 76 Look upon them [*sc.* suggestions] as shoelasts on which to shape your final handiwork. **1927** PEAKE & FLEURE *Priests & Kings* vi. 126 They had..stone celts or hoes, among which is a type, not unlike that found in the Danube basin, known as the shoe-last celt. **1961** G. CLARK *World Prehist.* vi. 126 Boian pioneers..used a variety of stone tools, including adze-blades of bevelled and shoe-last form. **1970** BRAY & TRUMP *Dict. Archaeol.* 210/2 *Shoe-last adze* or *celt*, a long thin stone adze employed by the Danubian farmers of the Early Neolithic, possibly as a hoe for cultivating their fields. **1884** ANNIE S. SWAN *Carlowrie* i. 19 She was neat and smart, down to the very *shoe-latch. **1526** TINDALE *Mark* i. 7 Whos *shue latchett I am not worthy to stoupe doune and vnlose. **1535** COVERDALE *Gen.* xiv. 27 A shue lachet. **1611** BIBLE *Ibid.* **1826** COBBETT *Rur. Rides* (1885) II. 192, I challenge all his *shoe-lickers, all the base worshippers of twenty thousand acres, to show me [etc.]. **1862** *Catal. Internat. Exhib.* II. xxvii. 55 This golosh..is put on without the aid of a *shoe-lift. **1846** W. KING in *Ann. & Mag. Nat. Hist.* XVIII. 86 In this species [of *Terebratula*] the condyle plates are attached to a process, which, to use a homely comparison, resembles a *shoe-lifter. **1850** —— *Permian Fossils* 136 The shoe-lifter-like process. **1841** *Penny Cycl.* XXI. 410/2 [Shoemaker's workmen:] The *shoeman or maker of the sole part of the shoe. **1899** HOWELLS *Ragged Lady* 59 The shoeman, turning with a pair of high-heeled bronze slippers in his hand from the wagon. **1881** *Instr. Census Clerks* (1885) 76 *Shoe Mercer, Shoe Mercery Manufacturer. **1862** *Catal. Internat. Exhib.* II. xxvii. 48 Elastic webs, and *shoe mercery. *c* **725** *Corpus Gloss.* (Hessels) C 480 *Clauus caligaris* *scohneȝl. **1860** WORCESTER, *Shoe-nail*, a nail used in making shoes. **1860** TYNDALL *Glac.* I. iii. 28 My guide first tried the slope alone; biting the ice with his shoe-nails. **1854** GRACE GREENWOOD *Haps & Mishaps* 13 The Yankee having whittled a large lot of unsaleable *shoe-pegs into melon seeds. **1867** SMYTH *Sailor's Word-bk.*, **Shoe-piece*, a board placed under the heel of a spar or other weighty mass, to save the deck. In some cases intended to slip with it. **1923** J. C. ROGERS *Eng. Furnit.* II. ii. 63 The splat..rose from a shaped shoe-piece planted on the rear seat rail. **1969** J. GLOAG *Short Dict. Furnit.* (rev. ed.) 607 *Shoe-piece*, the shaped projection that rises from the back rail of a chair seat, into which the base of the splat is socketed. **1723** MANDEVILLE *Fable of Bees* (ed. 2) 275 A Cobler,..if he runs of Errands when he has no work, or makes but *Shoepins,..he deserves the Name of Industrious. **1904** A. C. HOLMS *Pract. Shipbuild.* I. viii. §75. 79 In coasting vessels..the bottom of the keel gradually wears away... It is remedied by fitting *shoe plates, *i.e.* U-shaped plates embracing the keel. **1613** SYLVESTER *Lachr. Lachr.* B 4, Stript from Top to Toe, Of guiddie-Gaudes,.. Of Face-pride,..*Shoo-pride. **1594** NASHE *Unfort. Trav.* K 1, Taffatie..which serueth him..for a *shoo-rag. **1842** LOUDON *Suburban Hort.* 169 Portable *shoe-scrapers of cast-iron. **1911** H. P. FAIRCHILD *Greek Immigration to U.S.* vii. 127 In 1904 there were but three *shoe-shine parlors in the hands of Greeks in the city. **1931** *Kansas City Times* 29 Oct., Cecil, the Negro shoe shine boy at the City barber shop, has organized a band. **1957** *New Yorker* 5 Oct. 35/1 President Romano,..resting tensely in his shirtsleeves, getting a shoeshine. **1958** X. FIELDING *Corsair Country* i. 20 Where's the nobility in..these importunate shoe-shine boys? **1976** *National Observer* (U.S.) 21 Feb. 4/2 Complaints about the all-female shoeshine parlors in Salt Lake City may diminish... The commissioners said that the parlors..must not allow the shoe shiners to mingle with the customers or sit on their laps. **1910** *Chambers's Jrnl.* July 431/1 The hotel will not be bothered with boot-cleaning, that service being performed by the '*shoe-shiner' in the basement. **1976** Shoe shiner [see *shoe-shine* above]. **1625** *Nottingham Rec.* V. 103 Wee present Francis Levys, laborer, for vsinge the trade of a *shoesmithe..and nott being Apprentice. **1896** A. AUSTIN *England's Darling* II. iii, Woodcraft and masonry, Shoesmith or wheelwright, all are one to him. **1858** SIMMONDS *Dict. Trade*, **Shoe-stones*, sharpening or setting-stones..for the use of shoe-makers, book-binders,..&c. **1875** KNIGHT *Dict. Mech.*, **Shoe-stretcher*, an expansible last for distending shoes. *c* **1000** *Ags. Gosp.* John i. 27 Ne eom ic wyrðe þæt ic unbinde his sceo-þwang. *c* **1200** ORMIN 10387 Þatt he ne wass nohht god inoh Cristess shoþwang tunnbindenn. *c* **1200** *Trin. Coll. Hom.* 137 Ac ich nam noht ne forðen wurðe þat ich un-cnutte his sho þuong. **1599** B. JONSON *Ev. Man out of Hum.* Induct. (1600) B, But that a Rooke in wearing..A yarde of *shooe-tie, [etc.]..should affect a Humor, O, 'tis more than most rediculous. [**1603** SHAKS. *Meas. for M.* IV. iii. 18 Then haue we heere..braue M[r] Shootie the great Traueller.] **1611** —— *Wint. T.* IV. iv. 611 Gloue, Shooe-tye, Bracelet. **1851** HAWTHORNE *Twice-told T.* I. ii. 29 [She] blushes from topknot to shoetie, one universal scarlet. **1827** DRAKE & MANSFIELD *Cincinnati* viii. 60 In the third story the manufacture of *shoe trees is carried on. **1862** *Catal. Internat. Exhib.* II. xxvii. 56 Boot and shoe trees. **1486** *Bk. St. Albans* f. vii, A Plocke of *Shoturneris. **1858** *Skyring's Builders' Prices* 100 Long Spindle, or *Shoe Valves. **1875** KNIGHT *Dict. Mech.*, *Shoe-valve*, a valve at the foot of a pump-stock, or at the bottom of a reservoir. **1607** MARKHAM *Caval.* VI. 60 Assoone as any naile is driuen in, you shall turne the point backe againe, downe to the *shooeward. **1852** *Meanderings of Mem.* I. 163 He looked submission with a shoeward eye. **1691** NICHOLSON *Gloss. Northanhymbr.* in Ray *Coll.* 148 *Shoe-whang, *corrigia*. **1894** *Northumbld. Gloss.*, *Shoe-whang, shough-whaing*, a boot lace, a shoe tie. Usually called a whang or whaing simply. **1706** E. WARD *Wooden World Diss.* (1708) 19 Every Thing at free Cost, from a Steward, down to a *Shoe-Wiper.

**shoe** (ʃuː), *v.* Pa. t. and Pa. pple. **shod** (ʃɒd), *rarely* **shoed** (ʃuːd). Forms: *Inf.* 1 **scóȝan, scóȝean, sceóȝan, scóan, sceón, sceóian**, 3 **scheo**, 3, 6 **sho**, 4 **schoye**, 4–7 **shoo**, 5 **scho**, 5–6 **show**, (5 **schoyn**), 6–7 **shooe, shoue**, (6 **shu, schoe, schue, sue, sew**), 6– **shoe**. *Pa. t.* 1 **scóde**, 3 **scoide, soide**, 4 **schodde**, 9 **shoed**, 6– **shod**. *Pa. pple.* 1 **(ȝe)scód, (ȝe)sceód**, 3 **scod, sod, i-schud, iscod**, 4 **ischood**, 3–4 **i-schod**, 3–6 **schod**, 4–6 **shodd(e**, (4–5 **shood, schood**), 5 **y-shood, y-schod, schodde**, 5–6 **shode**, 6 **shoode, showed, shoyd**, 7 **shoad, shoud**, 7–9 **shoed**, (7, 9 *erron.* **shodden**), 4– **shod**. [OE. *scóȝan*, corresp. to MLG. *schoigen, schoien, schoen*, Du. *schoeien*, OHG. *scuohôn, scuohan* (MHG. *schuohen, schuon*, mod.G. *schuhen*), ON. *skúa* (MSw. *skoa*, Sw., Da. *sko*):—OTeut. **skōhōjan*, f. **skōho-* SHOE *sb.*

The doubling of the *d* and the consequent shortening of the vowel in ME. *schodde* pa. t., *schodd* pa. pple. (whence the mod. *shod* pa. t. and pa. pple.) are anomalous. (An OE. example occurs in Wulfstan *Hom.* p. 173, Unsceoddum fotum.) Cf. MSw. *skodde* pa. t., and Sw. *skodd* pa. pple. The case is parallel to that of *fledde, fledd* from FLEE *v.* (where Sw. also has the corresponding gemination).]

**1.** *trans.* To put shoes on (one's feet); to put on (one's) shoes; to clothe or protect the feet with shoes; to provide (a person, oneself) with boots or shoes.

*c* **897** ÆLFRED *Gregory's Past. C.* v. 44 Sceoȝeað eowre fett. *c* **1000** ÆLFRIC *Gram.* xxvi. (Z.) 158 *Calceo* vel *calcio* ic scoȝe me. *c* **1000** —— *Hom.* (Th.) II. 382 Se engel cwæð, Begyrd þe, and sceo þe, and fyliȝ me. *a* **1225** *Ancr. R.* 16 Þer efter scheoinde ou & cloðinde, siggeð Pater Noster & Credo. *a* **1300** *Havelok* 1138, I ne may hire fede, ne cloþe, ne sho. *c* **1366** CHAUCER *Rom. Rose* 842 And shod he was..With shoon decoped, and with laas. **1387** TREVISA *Higden* (Rolls) I. 411 They..gooþ i-hosed and i-schod. **1398** —— *Barth. De P.R.* XVIII. xcvi. (1495) 842 Ofte apes shoo themself wyth shoon that hunters leue in certen places slyly. **1530** PALSGR. 704/1, I shoo one, I put shoes upon his fete. **1599** THYNNE *Animadv.* 13 [Chaucer's name] signyfyinge one who shueth or hooseth a manne. **1794** C. PIGOT *Female Jockey Club* 195 Government..cannot spare wherewithall to keep the poor fellows feet properly shoed. **1846** MRS. KIRKLAND *West. Clearings* 10 The shoemaker..travels from house to house, shoeing the family. **1855** LONGF. *Hiawatha* xv. 24 Shod with snow-shoes..Forth to hunt..went Chibiabos. **1910** *Nation* 30 July 644/1 Women never learned to shoe themselves till they took to playing outdoor games with men.

*Proverbial.* **1546** J. HEYWOOD *Prov.* I. xi. (1867) 32 But who is wurs shod, than the shoemakers wyfe. **1581** PETTIE tr. *Guazzo's Civ. Conv.* I. (1586) 20 He ought to stop his eares ..and to walke amongst them (as the saying is) shood amongest the thornes.

**2. a.** To provide (a horse, etc.) with a shoe or shoes. †Also with *up*. ***shod all round***: completely shod.

*c* **1205** LAY. 22291 Heo wipeden hors leoue..heo sceren heo scoiden [*c* **1275** and soide hire stedes]. **1387** TREVISA *Higden* (Rolls) IV. 395 He..schodde his mules wiþ silver. **1435** *Coventry Leet-bk.* 185 The smythes..shall..show straungers horsies as-well on Sondais as on othur weke-days,..apon the payn of xld. **1523–34** FITZHERB. *Husb.* §142 Gyue thy horse meate, se he be showed well. **1605** SHAKS. *Lear* IV. vi. 188 It were a delicate stratagem to shoo A Troope of Horse with Felt. **1639** T. DE GRAY *Compl. Horsem.* 290 You may shooe him up, but drive no naile at that place. *a* **1648** LD. HERBERT *Autobiog.* (1886) 205 He staid in the highway..until my horse was shoed. **1776** *Pennsylvania Even. Post* 27 June 320/2 A Bay Mare,..a natural trotter, shod all round, remarkably bad to shoe behind. **1870** THORNBURY *Tour rd. Eng.* II. xxiii. 139 The forge of the blacksmith who shoed Tyrrell's horse. **1889** F. E. GRETTON *Memory's Harkback* 149 He shod her all round, and she never kicked once.

*fig.* **1731–8** SWIFT *Pol. Convers.* i. 95 *Lady Smart.* This is his Fourth Wife; then he has been shod round. **1788** GROSE *Dict. Vulg. T.* (ed. 2) s.v. *Shod*, A parson who attends a funeral is said to be shod all round, when he receives a hat-band, gloves, and scarf.

**b.** Phrases. ***to shoe the goose, gosling***: see those words; similarly ***to shoe the gander***, † ***the daw***. Also, † ***to shoe the goose*** (slang): to get drunk. ***to shoe the wild mare***: see MARE[1] 2 b.

**1566** DRANT *Horace, Sat.* I. ix. E iij, All the reaste mighte blow their nayles, or go to shough the dawe. **1594** NASHE *Unfort. Trav.* C 2 b, Galen might goe shooe the Gander for any good he could doo. **1611** COTGR. s.v. *Bertrand*, *Deschausser Bertrand*, to be drunke,..to whip the cat, shoo the goose.

**c.** To provide (a motor vehicle) with tyres of a specified type or quality. Cf. SHOE *sb.* 5 q.

**1925** *Morris Owner's Man.* p. lxx (Advt.), Every car is turned out in sound order and condition, shod with good tyres. **1971** *Drive* Summer 121/1 The test car was shod with radial tyres. **1976** *Southern Even. Echo* (Southampton) 2 Nov. 15/3 Braking is by servo-assisted discs at the front and rear drums, with radial tyres as standard shoeing equipment.

**3. a.** To protect (the point, edge or face of a thing, esp. something made of timber) with a plate, rim, ferrule or sheath of metal, etc.

*c* **1205** LAY. 7831, & þa Bruttes..nomen longen ræftres.. mid stronge irene heo weoren i-scod. **1496** *Acc. Ld. High Treas. Scot.* I. 290 Item, for..irne to Johne Lam, to scho the quhelis..xxvjs. **1531** *Lett. & Papers Hen. VIII*, V. 183 To John Locker for sewing moulddes with ireon for the brykmakers. **1565** COOPER *Thesaurus, Aries*,..a great peece of timber shodde with brasse, in facion like a rammes heade. **1585** T. WASHINGTON tr. *Nicholay's Voy.* IV. xiii. 126b, Bootes.. shodde vnderneath with yron. **1601** *Shuttleworths' Acc.* (Chetham Soc.) 134, ij speades shoud with iren, ij[s]. **1618** in Charnock *Mar. Archit.* (1801) II. 205 Shovells steele shodden. **1789** BURNS *Capt. Grose's Peregr.* vii, A broomstick o' the Witch of Endor, Weel shod wi' brass. **1823** P. NICHOLSON *Pract. Build.* 303 The ends of the piles are cased or shoed with pointed iron. **1829** *Chapters Phys. Sci.* 138 In the processes of hooping barrels, and shoeing wheels. **1869** RANKINE *Machine & Hand-tools* Pl. P. 21 These bars..are shod at their lower cutting ends with serrated or notched steel faces for chipping the stone. **1911** *Act 1 & 2 Geo. V*, c. 45 §2 (4) The driving wheels of a locomotive..shod with diagonal crossbars of not less than three inches in width.

**b.** Naut. *to shoe the anchor*: (see quot. 1644).

**1644** MANWAYRING *Sea-mans Dict.* 3 The ground may be soft and ozie; In such places we use to shooe the Anchor, that is, to put boords to the flooke..and make it much broader. **1769** FALCONER *Dict. Marine* (1789). **1867** in SMYTH *Sailor's Word-bk.*

**4.** *transf.* To cover or protect as with a shoe or shoes.

**1639** FULLER *Holy War* IV. xiii. (1640) 191 The shores there being not shod against the sea with huge high rocks. **1807** *Prize Ess. & Trans. Highl. Soc.* III. 448 The surface turfs are carefully laid aside, and after the peats are taken out, these turfs are brought back..and placed upon the part that was made bare. This operation is called shoeing the moss. **1837** LONGF. *Frithiof's Homestead* 24 On a bear skin (the skin it was coal-black, Scarlet red was the throat, but the paws were shodden with silver), Thorsten sat.

**shoe** (ʃuː), *a.* *U.S. slang.* [Origin obscure.] Conforming to the dress, behaviour, or attitudes of students at exclusive educational establishments; acceptable to or commended by such people.

**1962** *Punch* 13 June 895/3 A girl at these institutions [*sc.* schools] must prove herself to be 'shoe'—and woe betide her if her dress and manner don't manifest..'shoeness'. **1973** *N.Y. Times Mag.* 17 June 38/3 Perhaps it is significant that one favourite mode of protest in the fifties was satire. We—a lot of us—were cool, ironic, 'shoe'. **1980** L. BIRNBACH et al. *Official Preppy Handbk.* 222/2 *Shoe, adj.* Top-drawer. Very acceptable.

**shoe**, obs. form of SHOW *sb.* and *v.*, SOW *v.*

**shoeblack** (ˈʃuːblæk). [f. SHOE *sb.* + BLACK *v.*]

**a.** One who cleans boots and shoes for a livelihood.

**1778** FOOTE *Trip to Calais* I. (1778) 21 As I live, a couple of shoe-blacks. **1831** CARLYLE *Sart. Res.* II. ix, Will the whole Finance Ministers..of modern Europe undertake to make one Shoeblack happy?

*attrib.* **1862** G. H. TOWNSEND *Man. of Dates* s.v. *Shoeblacks*, The existing ragged school shoeblack brigade was founded in 1851.

**b.** *shoe-black plant* = *shoe-flower* (SHOE *sb.* 6c). Also *ellipt.*

**1837** J. MACFADYEN *Flora Jamaica* I. 66 The flowers, from the mucilaginous juice they contain, are employed to give a polish to the leather of shoes; and hence the plant has received the name of the shoe-black. **1858** SIMMONDS *Dict. Trade, Shoe-black*,..a name in Jamaica for the *Hibiscus rosa sinensis*. **1866** *Treas. Bot.* I. 589/1 *Hibiscus Rosa sinensis*... These flowers..are used..in Java for blacking shoes, whence the plant is frequently called the Shoe-black Plant. **1965** *Harper's Bazaar* Feb. 18/3 The scarlet blossoms of the bush they [*sc.* Jamaicans] call the Shoe-Black.

So †**shoe-blacker**, a shoeblack. **shoe-blacking**, (*a*) = BLACKING *vbl. sb.* 3b; (*b*) the blacking and polishing of shoes.

**1755** JOHNSON *Dict., Japanner*..2. A shoeblacker. **1843** M. A. RICHARDSON *Local Hist. Table Bk., Hist.* II. Index, Shoe blacker. **1890** L. C. D'OYLE *Notches* 13 They were.. the only persons possessed of shoe-blacking. **1902** ALICE TERTON *Lights & Shadows in Hosp.* x. 166 His interest in the shoe-blacking soon waned.

**shoe-box, shoebox** (ˈʃuːbɒks). [SHOE *sb.*]

**1.** A box in which a pair of shoes is packed.

**1860** EMERSON *Cond. Life* viii. Wks. (Bohn) II. 439, I cry you mercy, good shoe-box. **1897** *Westm. Gaz.* 16 Feb. 12/1, I gathered a bunch large enough to nearly fill an ordinary shoe-box. **1930** J. DOS PASSOS *42nd Parallel* I. 101 A small house like a shoebox. **1970** J. EARL *Tuners & Amplifiers* i. 14 A modern stereo amplifier capable of yielding 20 watts..is nowadays barely larger than a shoe box.

**2.** *fig.* A building or part of a building resembling a shoe-box. Also *attrib.*

**1968** *Listener* 1 Aug. 134/2 Leeds hasn't changed much. There are a few changes. Some of those glass shoe-boxes have been plonked down at random in the city centre. **1972** *Times* 8 June (Birmingham Suppl.) p.v/4 The mandatory shoe-box buildings. **1978** N. FREELING *Night Lords* xxxiii. 153 Bianchi..waved casually at the building; the usual pile of open shoe-boxes. **1979** M. A. SHARP *Sunflower* iii. 29 Shoebox buildings, nestled together like children's blocks.

**shoed** (ʃuːd), *ppl. a.* [f. SHOE *sb.* or *v.* + -ED.] Furnished or protected with a shoe or shoes; shod.

See also SLIP-SHOED *a.* and *high-shoed* var. of HIGH-SHOD.

**1601** *Will of W. Snawdon of Winterton, Lincs.*, One shoed waine with the furniture belonging to it. **1612** *Inv.* in *Antiquary* (1906) Jan. 28 A shoed shovel, a shoed spade. **1902** *Edin. Evening News* 14 July 2 [He] kicked her with his shoed feet.

**shoef**, obs. pa. t. of SHAVE *v.*

**shoe-goose**: see SYAGUSH.

**shoe-horn** (ˈʃuːhɔːn), *sb.* In 5, 6 *Sc.* schone-, shone-, ? -schune.

**1.** A curved instrument of horn, metal, etc. used to facilitate the slipping of one's heel into a shoe by placing it between shoe and heel; a shoeing-horn.

**1589** *Burgh Rec. Edin.* (1882) IV. 540 Ane schone horne 30d. **1612** *Sc. Bk. Rates* in *Halyburton's Ledger* (1867) 315 Shone hornes the dozen vis. **1874** BURNAND *My time* xxiv. 213 Giving his back the graceful outward bend of a shoe-horn.

**2.** *fig.* = SHOEING-HORN 2.

**1630** BP. G. GRÆME *Let.* in *Miscellany S.H.S.* (1904) II. 255 Sone, cum not in such termis, for..I fear that if more be offered it will be takin, be warie, ye be no schurehorne [? *read* schunehorne]. **1869** *Lonsdale Gloss.*, *Shoe-horn*, a puffer at an auction. **1894** *Northumberld. Gloss.*, *Shoe-horn*, a helper on. One employed to bid for the sellers at sales.

**3.** = SHOEING-HORN 3.

**1864** ATKINSON *Prov. Names Birds*, *Shoe-horn.* Avocet—*Recurvirostra avocetta.* **1895** P. H. EMERSON *Birds Norfolk Broadland* lxxxvi. 281 And you know 'tis an avocet, or 'shoe-horn', as the old Broadsmen call him.

**ˈshoe-horn**, *v.*

†**1.** *trans.* To cuckold. (Cf. HORN *v.* 2.) *Obs.*⁻¹

*c* **1650** BRAITHWAIT *Barnabees Jrnl.* II. xvi. H6, Venus swore it, She'd shooe-horn her Vulcans forehead.

**2. a.** To put or thrust (a thing) *upon* (a person) or (a person) *into* (a position) by means of an 'instrument' or 'tool' for the purpose.

**1859** W. CHADWICK *Life De Foe* v. 292 A penny trash, shoe-horned upon the public for buyers, by the addition of the Shortest Way with Daniel De Foe. **1901** *North Western Daily Mail* (Barrow) 6 Mar., A non-expert..who is shoehorned into a position like that of the War Secretary.

**b.** To manœuvre or compress (someone or something) *into* (*in*, *on to*) an inadequate space (occas. *into* an inadequate period of time).

**1927** D. L. SAYERS *Unnatural Death* vi. 64 He shoe-horned himself into his seat [in a motor car]. **1954** *Archit. Rev.* CXVI. 212/1 For the second edition he shoehorned in material on Eiffel, Maillart and Alto, thus playing havoc with his illustration numbers. **1968** *Economist* 18 May 69/1 Big aircraft are shoe-horned on to small landing strips with only elementary navigation aids. **1969** J. WAINWRIGHT *Take-over Men* iii. 37 Lewis..was shoe-horning himself behind the steering wheel. **1972** *Real Estate Rev.* Winter 107/1 The logical-thought input might be assumed to have been forcibly pressed and shoe-horned into a preconceived formal framework. **1974** *Daily Tel.* (Colour Suppl.) 23 Aug. 7/2 In order to shoe-horn in more people airlines and aircraft manufacturers have given up any interest at all in comfort. **1978** *Science* 17 Mar. 1161/2 Nearly 140 symposia and almost 1000 speakers shoehorned into five days and nights. **1979** R. L. SIMON *Peking Duck* ii. 19 The houses were..shoe-horned onto thirty feet of beachfront land.

**3.** *intr.* To act as a 'shoe-horn' at a sale. *dial.* (Cf. SHOE-HORN *sb.* 2.)

**1904** *Eng. Dial. Dict.*

**shoeing** (ˈʃuːɪŋ), *vbl. sb.* Forms: 4–6 shoyng(e, (4 ssoinge), 4–7 shoing, 5 schoynge, schoing, 5–6 scho(w)yng, 6 showing, showyng(e, shouing, (schevyng, 7 schewing), 6–8 shooing, 7– shoeing. [f. SHOE *v.* + -ING¹.]

**1.** The action of SHOE *v.*; the action of putting shoes on a person or animal, or of furnishing a pile, wheel, etc. with a shoe.

*c* **1440** *Promp. Parv.* 447/2 Schoynge, of menn, *calceacio*. Schoynge, of hors, *ferracio*. **1458** *Nottingham Rec.* II. 366 For vj. powls schoyng and þe powls ij s. **1515** *Acc. Ld. High Treas. Scot.* V. 32 Item..for..the schoyng of gun cartis.. iij li. x s. **1523–34** FITZHERB. *Husb.* §109 Enterfyre is a sorance, and cometh of yll shoynge. **1657** W. COLES *Adam in Eden* cxii, Laid or bound to a Horses foot that is grievously pricked with shooing. **1707** FLEETWOOD *Chron. Prec.* v. 149 For Hay, Oats, Litter and Shooing. **1840** THACKERAY *Catherine* vii, My horse wants shoeing. **1883** 'ANNIE THOMAS' *Mod. Housewife* 67 The only broad rule that can be laid down for the successful shoeing of children is [etc.].

**2.** *concr.* **a.** Shoes collectively.

*a* **1340** HAMPOLE *Psalter* cvii. 10 In til ydumy i sall streke my shoynge. **1382** WYCLIF *Exod.* iii. 5 But lowse thow thi shoyng [*v.r.* schone] fro thi feyt. *c* **1450** *Godstow Reg.* 394 And..the forsaid hugh shold fynde the forsaid Anneys..in vitaile clothyng and shoyng. **1480** CAXTON *Chron. Eng.* ccxxvi. 233 They were more lyche to tormentours and deuels in hir clothyng and shoyng. **1483** *Cath. Angl.* 337/2 A schoynge, *ferramentum*. *Ibid.*, Schoynge of a byschope (*v.r.* schon of a bischoppe), *sandalia*. **1530** PALSGR. 267/1 Schowyng of an horse, *ferrure*.

**b.** The protective casing or covering with which a thing is shod.

**1805** R. W. DICKSON *Pract. Agric.* I. 378 A strong lever, shod with iron, and having the iron shoeing bent a little upwards. **1806** MORISON *Decis.* XXXIII. 14296 The shoeing or causewaying in the river..must be taken away. **1870** *2nd Rep. Dep. Kpr. Irel.* 20 The sides of the tray are fitted with a light shoeing of wood. **1892** R. C. LESLIE *Sea-Boat* 162 *Shooing*, an iron band to protect the keel.

**3.** *attrib.* and *Comb.*, as *shoeing forge*, *-hammer*, *-shed*, *-stool*, *-trade*; **shoeing smith**, a smith who shoes horses.

**1889** *Harper's Mag.* June 13/2 Outside the town you find the *shoeing forges. **1753** *Chambers' Cycl.* Suppl., **Shoeing-hammer*. **1833** LOUDON *Encycl. Archit.* §418 The *shoeing-shed ought to have rings in the walls for the..halters of the horses being shod, to be fastened to. **1809** *Sporting Mag.* XXXIII. 41 Mr. Goodwin, *shoeing-smith. **1861** DICKENS *Gt. Expect.* I. ix. 146 'Should you, Pip?' said Joe, drawing his *shoeing stool near the forge. **1865** H. KINGSLEY *Hillyars* I. ii. 11 His business was..what we call a good *shoeing trade, principally with the omnibus horses.

**ˈshoeing-horn.** [SHOEING *vbl. sb.*]

**1.** = SHOE-HORN *sb.* 1.

*c* **1440** *Promp. Parv.* 447/2 Schoynge horne, *parcopollex*. **1523–34** FITZHERB. *Husb.* §142 Shoyng horne, boget, and shoes. **1614** B. JONSON *Barth. Fair* II. ii, Oyly as the Kings constables Lampe and shining as his Shooing-horne. **1713** SWIFT *Elegy Death Partridge* Misc. (1727) 100 The Horned Moon, which heretofore Upon their Shoes the Romans wore..And whence we claim our Shoeing-Horns. **1825** T. HOOK *Sayings* Ser. II. *Man of Many Fr.* I. 250 A pair of pumps into which, with the assistance of..a shoeing-horn, the old gentleman had compressed his proper proportions. **1855** DICKENS *Dorrit* xxii, A little instrument like a shoeing horn for serving it [snuff] out.

*attrib.* **1623** FLETCHER *Rule a Wife* IV. i, Here's a shooing-horn Chain gilt over.

*Proverbial.* **1508** STANBRIDGE *Vulgaria* (W. de W.) Bv, His nose is lyke a shoynge horne. **1659** HOWELL *Lex., Prov.* 4/1 Every one cannot have a nose like a shooing-horn.

**2.** *fig.* **a.** An appetizer for food or drink.

**1536** *Remedy for Sedition* 19b, We haue to many sawces, to many showying hornes to drawe in meate. **1575** *Gammer Gurton* I. i, I..caught a slyp of bacon..Which..Shall serue for a shoinghorne to draw on two pots of ale. **1622** MABBE tr. *Aleman's Guzman d'Alf.* II. 275 The hungry sauour of our porrige was a shooing-horne to drawe downe the hardnesse of our bread. **1737** OZELL *Rabelais* I. 152 *note*, Thus we say, a Red Herring is a shoing-horn to a Pot of Ale. **1815** SCOTT *Guy M.* xxiv, This [conversation] served as a 'shoeing-horn' to draw on another cup of ale.

**b.** Something serving to facilitate a transaction, to bring on a condition, or to procure acceptance for something else.

**1584** D. FENNER *Def. Ministers* (1587) 71 This was nothing but a shoing-horne, to pull on a page or two more. **1621** BURTON *Anat. Mel.* I. ii. II. vi. 115 Voluntary solitarinesse..gently brings on as a Siren, a shooing-horne, or some Sphinx to this irrevocable gulfe [Melancholy]. **1759** FRANKLIN *Ess.* Wks. 1840 III. 198 It appeared..that a treaty and a purchase went on together, that the former was a shoeing-horn for the latter. **1819** SCOTT *Leg. Montrose* v, A long story, my lord,..is..the best shoeing-horn for drawing on a sound sleep. **1864** SIR T. SEATON *From Cadet to Colonel* xvii. 358 An occupation that was a certain shoeing horn for cholera.

*attrib.* *a* **1704** T. BROWN *Walk round London, Tavern* Wks. 1709 III. III. 6 As soon as that [his money] begins to fail, then her Shooing-horn Looks and Freedoms, are turn'd into moody Pouts.

**c.** A person used as a tool by another; esp. one who is employed as a decoy.

**1602** *Narcissus* 441 O, that same youthe's the scummer of all skorne, Of surquedry the very shooing horne. **1606** SHAKS. *Tr. & Cr.* v. i. 61. **1692** WOOD *Ath. Oxon.* II. 494 Oliver had made him..his shooing horn, merely to serve his turn. **1712** ADDISON *Spect.* No. 536 ¶5 Most of our fine young Ladies..retain in their Service..supernumerary and insignificant Fellows, which they..commonly call *Shoeing-Horns*. These are..designed..when a good Offer comes, to whet and spur him up to the Point. **1864** CARLYLE *Fredk. Gt.* XVI. vii. IV. 335 D'Arnaud—once Friedrich's shoeing-horn and 'rising-sun' for Voltaire's behoof.

†**3.** The Avocet: = SHOE-HORN *sb.* 3. *Obs.*

**1668** SIR T. BROWNE *Let.* Wks. 1836 I. 400 A shoeing-horn or barker, from the figure of the bill and barking note.

†**4.** A cuckold's horn: see HORN *sb.* 7. In quot. *attrib.* (Cf. SHOE-HORN *v.* 1.)

**1663** KILLIGREW *Pars. Wedding* v. iv, Fine y' faith, none but the small Levites brow to plant your shooing-horn-seed in? How now?

Hence †**ˈshoeing-horn** *v.* = SHOE-HORN *v.* 2.

**1658–9** *Burton's Diary* (1828) IV. 77 This House does not intend to trepan, or shoeing-horn, any body.

**ˈshoekin.** *nonce-wd.* [-KIN.] A small shoe.

**1844** THACKERAY *Contrib. Punch, Wand. Fat Contrib.* ii. Wks. 1898 VI. 60 A Belgic child..in little wooden shoekins.

**shoel**, obs. form of SHOAL *sb.*¹

**shoe-leather.** Leather for the making of shoes; the leather of which (one's) shoes are made.

**1660** BOYLE *Spring of Air* 13 A sucker,..upon which is nail'd a good thick piece of tan'd shoe Leather. **1818** LADY MORGAN *Autobiog.* (1859) 119 As good a lad as ever stepped in shoe-leather. **1828–32** WEBSTER, *Shoe-leather*, leather for shoes. **1889** JESSOPP *Coming of Friars* ii. 89 The poor man's loaf was..as tough as his shoe-leather.

**b.** put for the wear of shoes in walking.

**1576** FLEMING *Panopl. Epist.* 319 He counteth me..such a one as is altogether unworthy of a litle shoe leather, when he is sent for. **1675** V. ALSOP *Anti-sozzo* iii. 114 No need to look out, if they had sufficient at Home, they might save Shooe leather. **1874** RUSKIN *Fors Clav.* IV. xliv. 166 He walked to Ulverstone; spent nothing but shoe-leather on the road.

**shoeless** (ˈʃuːlɪs), *a.* [f. SHOE *sb.* + -LESS.] Without shoes.

**1627** DRAYTON *Agincourt* 59 A shoolesse Souldier there a man might meete. **1825** LAMB *Elia* Ser. II. *Barbara S——*, And then came staring upon her the figures of her little stockingless and shoeless sisters. **1875** JOWETT *Plato* (ed. 2) I. 134 He found that the other animals were suitably furnished, but that man alone was naked and shoeless.

Hence **ˈshoelessness.**

**1843** [G. P. R. JAMES] *Commissioner* xxxvi. 220 She had found her shoelessness not very pleasant.

**shoemack, -make**, obs. forms of SUMACH.

**shoemaker** (ˈʃuːmeɪkə(r)). Forms: see SHOE *sb.* and MAKER; also 6 *north.* shounemaker (from the *plural*).

**1.** One whose trade it is to make shoes.

**1381** *Rolls of Parlt.* III. 112/2 Johannes Stotesbury, Childe-shomakere. *c* **1440** *Alphabet of Tales* 164 A philosophur.. þat boght a payr of shone on a tyme of a shomaker. **1519** *Presentm. Juries* in *Surtees Misc.* (1890) 32 That the shounemaker sewe well thayre shown. **1621** in Kempe *Losely MSS.* (1836) 430 To yᵉ shoo maker for boots and shooes..4ˡⁱ. 3s. **1824** MISS MITFORD *Village* Ser. I. 5 Our shoemaker..employs three journeymen. **1865** DICKENS *Mut. Fr.* I. vii, His expression and stoop are like those of a shoemaker.

**b.** in Latin proverb (cf. LAST *sb.*[1] 2 c.).

**1587** GOLDING *De Mornay* (1592) 155 The Shoomaker ought not to presume aboue the Pantople. **1768–74** TUCKER *Lt. Nat.* (1834) II. 173 Carrying the shoe-maker beyond his last, and encroaching upon the province of divines.

**2. a.** In the names of various fishes.

[**1688** HOLME *Armoury* II. 377/2 Table, Shoomaker fish 15 16. *Ibid.* II. xv. 350 The Hollanders call it [the Tench] a Schoemaker]. **1836** J. RICHARDSON *Fauna Bor.-Amer.* III. 120 *Cyprinus* (*Catastomus*) *nigricans.* (Le Sueur.).. This species is..an inhabitant of Lake Erie, where it is known to the fishermen by the names of 'Shoemaker', and 'Black Sucker'. **1884** GOODE *Nat. Hist. Aquatic Anim.* 326 The Threadfish, *Blepharis crinitus*.., also known as the 'Shoemaker-fish'. *Ibid.* 332 The Runner, *Elagatis pinnulatus*.., known..at Pensacola as..'Shoemaker', is..abundant on the..coasts of Florida. **1891** *Century Dict.* s.v. *Coral*, Coral shoemaker, a fish of the family *Teuthididæ* and genus *Teuthis* or *Acanthurus*, living in the coral reefs of the Seychelles. **1904** *Eng. Dial. Dict.*, *Shoemaker*, the lesser weever, *Trachinus vipera*; also in comb. *Master shoemaker.*

**b.** A name for the bird *Skua antarcticus.*

**1867** SMYTH *Sailor's Word-bk.*, *Egmont*, or *Port Egmont Fowls*, the large Antarctic gulls with dark-brown plumage, called *shoemakers.*

**3.** *Comb.* † **shoemaker-loo** *U.S.*, some game at cards.

**1813** R. B. THOMAS *Farmer's Alm.* (Boston, U.S.) Dec. in Kittredge *Old Farmer & Almanack* (1904) 95 Tom Teazer, well known at the grog shops for a dabster at shoe-maker loo.

**b.** Combinations of possessive, as ***shoemaker's craft***, but chiefly in the names of tools and appliances, as ***shoemaker's awl***, ***black*** (BLACK *sb.* 1 b), ***end*** (END *sb.* 6 c), ***hammer***, ***knife***, ***nippers***, ***paste***, ***rasp***, ***thread***, ***wax***; also **shoemaker's bark-tree** (see quot.); **shoemaker's holiday**, † (*a*) see quot. 1607; also applied to Monday (see Dekker *Shoemaker's Holiday* III. i); (*b*) used jocularly (after the title of Dekker's play, *a* 1600) for a day's holiday or 'outing' in the country; **shoemaker's spasm**, a synonym given to tetany because of the liability of shoemakers to be affected by it; † **shoe-maker's stocks** *slang*, shoes which pinch the feet.

**1647** HEXHAM I, A *shoe-makers aule. **1874** *Treas. Bot.* Suppl., *Shoemaker's bark-tree, a Montserrat name for *Byrsonima spicata.* **1563** HYLL *Art Garden.* (1593) 91 The seedes..being mixed with *shoemakers blacke, doth take away warts. **1530** PALSGR. 267/1 *Shoomakers crafte, *cordovanerie.* **1540** *Maldon* (Essex) *Liber B.* 158 Idem Andreas in arte sive occupacione de shomakerscrafte bene et fideliter serviret dictum Cornelium. **1598**, etc. *Shoemaker's end [see END *sb.* 6 c]. **1895** P. N. HASLUCK *Boot Making* 18 A *shoemaker's hammer, knife, nippers, glazing iron, and rasp. *Ibid.* 27 *Shoemaker's Rasp. **1607** *Christmas Prince* III. (1816) 47 *Tuesday* [loq.]..Bouzer I am not, but mild, sober Tuesday..if I light not on St. Hewsday. *Footnote.* The *Shoemakers holy-day. **1768** GOLDSM. in *European Mag.* (1793) Sept. 172/1 And now my dear boy, if you are not better engaged, I should be glad to enjoy a Shoemaker's holiday with you. **1822** SCOTT *Let.* 23 June in *Lockhart* (1837) V. 189 Castle Street is bad enough, even with the privilege of a hop-step-and-jump to Abbotsford, by way of shoemakers' holiday. **1647** HEXHAM I, A *shoemakers knife. **1842** DICKENS *Amer. Notes* vii, [He] would have gladly stabbed me with his shoemaker's knife. **1688** HOLME *Armoury* III. 349/2 These..*Shoo-makers Nippers ..having a sharp point in the end of one [shank]; and a slit in the other, to strain up a Tack. **1866** *Athenæum* Feb. 243/3 The paste to be used for all prints..should be *shoemakers' paste. **1899** *Allbutt's Syst. Med.* (1910) VIII. 578 Of 399 cases [of Tetany]..174 occurred in shoemakers ('*shoemaker's spasm'). *a* **1700** B. E. *Dict. Cant. Crew*, **Shoemakers-stocks*, pincht with strait Shoes. **1607** TOPSELL *Four-f. Beasts* 420 Fasten on each side of the hole, two ends of *Shoomakers thread. **1603** DEKKER *Wonderf. Yr.* Wks. (Grosart) I. 132 *Shooemakers waxe being laide to a byle. **1885** LENO *Boot & Shoemaking* 221 Shoemakers' Wax..is composed generally of..pitch and resin, with 10 per cent. of tallow.

Hence **ˈshoemakeress**, a female shoemaker. **ˈshoemakerish** *a.*, resembling that of a shoemaker.

**1860** *All Year Round* Sept. 523/2 They all bought their shoes of a woman who was called Mother Rousselle... The shoemakeress [etc.]. **1866** HOWELLS *Venetian Life* xiv. 204 With bead-black eyes and of a shoemakerish presence.

**shoemaking** (ˈʃuːmeɪkɪŋ), *vbl. sb.* [f. SHOE *sb.* + MAKING *vbl. sb.*] The making of shoes.

**1611** COTGR., *Cordouannerie*, Shoo-making. **1859** DICKENS *T. Two Cities* I. vi, The white head that bent low over the shoemaking. **1910** MRS. H. M. TIRARD *Bk. of Dead* i. 18 All the trades are also represented, shoe-making, boat-building, pottery-making [etc.].

**shoepack** (ˈʃuːpæk). *N. Amer.* Also **shoepac**, **shupac.** [ad. Delaware Jargon *seppock*, *sípack* shoes, f. Unami Delaware *čipahko* moccasins, infl. by SHOE *sb.*] Orig., and still locally, a moccasin with an extra sole; more recently, a commercially manufactured oiled leather boot, usually with a rubber sole. Cf. PAC.

**1755** in S. M. Hamilton *Lett. to Washington* (1898) I. 99 It would be a good thing to have Shoe-packs or Moccosons for the Scouts. **1824** J. HALL *Sketches* (1835) I. 75 Gentlemen dressed in shoepacks, mocassons, leather breeches [etc.]. **1853** S. STRICKLAND *Twenty-Seven Years in Canada West* II. 286 Shoe-packs, a species of mocassin peculiar to the Lower Province, cow-hide boots, and a *bonnet rouge* for the head, complete the costume of the Canadian lumber-man. **1882** J. M. LEMOINE *Picturesque Quebec* 201 He came pounding along Notre Dame street, in Montreal, in his red shirt and tan-colored *shupac* boots, all dripping wet. **1903** S. E. WHITE *Forest* x. 120 He brought to light..oil-tanned shoepacs, with and without the flexible sole. **1940** R. MARSHALL *Arctic Village* 101 It is only in the fall and the spring that the snow is soggy, and in those seasons shoepacks with rubber bottoms and leather uppers replace the moccasins. **1977** *New Yorker* 20 June 69/2 After the cast comes off, I can walk with a shoepac and a cane.

**shoer** (ˈʃuːə(r)). Forms: 1 scóere, scóehere, 5 schoer, 6 shooer, 9- shoer. [OE. *scóere*: see SHOE *v.* and -ER[1].] One who shoes. In OE. a shoemaker; later usually, one who shoes horses, etc.

*c* **725** *Corpus Gloss.* (Hessels) S 696, *Sutrinator*, scoere. *a* **900** *Leiden Gloss.* 122 in *O.E. Texts* 115 *Sutrinator*, scoehere. **1483** *Cath. Angl.* 337/2 A Schoer, *ferrarius.* **1562** J. HEYWOOD *Prov. & Epigr.* (1867) 159 We should haue as many goose shooers as geese. **1861** OLMSTED *Journ. Cotton Kingdom* I. 111 He tells Prior that if he can find a first rate shoer..not to lose him. **1902** *19th Cent.* Aug. 313 The mystic shoer Wayland Smith.

**shoerl**, variant of SCHORL.

**1789** *Phil. Trans.* LXXX. 81 Indurated clay and shoerl.

**ˈshoe-string, shoestring. 1.** A string or tie used to fasten or lace a shoe.

**1616** R. COCKS *Diary* (Hakl. Soc.) I. 157 A peare silk garters, with gould fring, and shewstring same. **1755** SMOLLETT *Quix.* I. IV. iii. (1803) II. 40 She is not worthy to tie her majesty's shoe-strings.

**2.** A small or inadequate amount of money; a very little capital; a small margin. Chiefly in phr. ***on a shoe-string.*** *colloq.* (orig. *U.S.*).

[**1882** *Century Mag.* Apr. 884/2 [He] could draw to a shoe-string, as the saying went, and obtain a tan-yard!] **1904** *Cosmopolitan* May 89 He..speculated 'on a shoe-string'—an exceedingly slim margin. **1926** J. BLACK *You can't Win* viii. 90 The new owners had no bankroll, just opened up on a shoestring. **1932** *Atlantic Monthly* Mar. 310/1 Every business man who has made a big success of himself started on a shoestring. **1957** *Listener* 28 Nov. 893/3 Reformative efforts have to be..as they say, 'run on a shoe-string'. **1977** C. MCCULLOUGH *Thorn Birds* xvii. 441 Australians in England, youth-hostelling on a shoestring.

**3.** = *shoe-string potato*, sense 4 c below.

**1931** B. STARKE *Touch & Go* x. 156, I..found that the word 'shoe-strings' on the menu really meant Julienne potatoes. I ate every last shoe-string.

**4.** *attrib.* and *Comb.* **a.** *attrib.* Narrow (*lit.* and *fig.*).

**1878** *Congress. Rec.* App. 13 June 478/2, I will promise to meet him on the northern border of 'the shoe-string district'. **1897** *Pop. Sci. Monthly* L. 309 Bad roads and shoestring paths..fringe them. **1953** *Times* 30 July 7 A shoe-string majority.

**b.** *attrib.* Operating on a shoe-string, costing or spending little; cheap, informal; petty.

**1890** J. P. QUINN *Fools of Fortune* 494 The gamblers, aside from a lot of 'hangers on', known as 'shoestring' or 'tin horn' gamblers, do not figure in the criminal records. **1923** 'B. M. BOWER' *Parowan Bonanza* xi. 137 The little shoestring propositions that go broke and leave empty houses behind them. **1936** *Sun* (Baltimore) 20 Nov. 1/5 The governors of the Federal Reserve System today proposed steps to plug up loopholes through which 'shoe-string' and other operators have been able to trade extensively without even posting margins. **1941** B. SCHULBERG *What makes Sammy Run?* vi. 123 A shoe-string producer..had bought the stock shots from *Hell's Angels* and *Wings* and needed an airplane story. **1958** *Vogue* Oct. 203 Winter after winter ski-crazy students flock to the snow for shoestring holidays which have been planned to the last farthing. **1959** 'M. NEVILLE' *Sweet Night for Murder* i. 17 She talked, thought, dreamed clothes. On a shoe-string allowance, however, she could do little about them. **1977** *S. Wales Guardian* 27 Oct. 1/3 The Education Committee was being penny wise and pound foolish by giving some contracts to small private contractors running on a shoe-string budget and using non-union labour. **1978** J. KRANTZ *Scruples* iii. 78 The ad that launched Spider was for a new type of fingernail hardener, put out by a shoe-string company.

**c.** Special comb.: **shoe-string catch** *Baseball*, a running catch made close to the ground; **shoe-string fungus** = *honey fungus* s.v. HONEY *sb.* (*a.*) 7 b; **shoe-string potato** *U.S.*, a julienne potato (see JULIENNE 2) (chiefly *pl.*); **shoe-string (root) rot**, the disease caused by shoe-string fungus; **shoe-string tie**, a very narrow neck-tie.

**1926** *N.Y. Times* 11 Oct. 25/2 Haley ran up on it and tried to make a shoestring catch of it. **1957** *New Yorker* 13 July 17/1 Like a shoestring catch in center field, make it and you're the hero. Muff it and you're a dope. **1926** F. D. HEALD *Man. Plant Diseases* xxvi. 794 The causal fungus is generally referred to as the 'honey agaric'..or the 'shoestring fungus'. **1978** T. A. TATTAR *Diseases of Shade Trees* xxiii. 315 The shoestring-fungus..and the two-lined chestnut borer..are the most common organisms of secondary action. **1906** 'H. MCHUGH' *Skiddoo!* ii. 30 The next course was French fried potatoes with some shoe-string potatoes on the side. **1940** *Amer. Mercury* Sept. 72 Old Fred Harvey started turning a shoestring potato into a 2500-mile of railroad eating-places. **1976** U. CURTISS *Birthday Gift* xv. 141 As fruitless as looking for shoestring potatoes in strange supermarkets. **1978** T. A. TATTAR *Diseases of Shade Trees* x. 140 Shoestring root rot affects a wide range of shrubs and trees. **1931** E. E. HUBERT *Outl. Forest Pathol.* ix. 417 Shoestring rot is a disease well known to the forest pathologist. **1903** F. NORRIS *Pit* 337 His shoestring tie straggled over his frayed shirt front. **1961** *Sunday Express* 29 Jan. 15/6 A short, dark Frenchman in a shoe-string tie.

**shoey** (ˈʃuːɪ). *slang.* [f. SHOE *v.* + -Y[6].] A shoeing-smith in a cavalry regiment.

**1919** in *War Terms* in *Athenæum* 1 Aug. 695/2. **1925** in FRASER & GIBBONS *Soldier & Sailor Words* 256. **1969** S. MAYS *Fall out Officers* xii. 93 Shoey..Slap some shoes on my new horse.

**shof(e, shoff(e**, obs. forms of SHOVE *v.*[1]

‖**shofar** (ˈʃəʊfə(r)). *Jewish ritual.* Also **shophar.** [Heb. *shōphār.*] An ancient Hebrew musical instrument usually made of a curved ram's horn, still used in Jewish religious services.

**1833** *Children's Mag.* V. 113 The crooked trumpet, or *shophar*, was appointed by the Law of Moses to be blown.. when the year of jubilee was proclaimed. **1864** ENGEL *Mus. Anc. Nat.* 292 The Shophar is..the only Hebrew instrument which has been preserved to the present day in the religious services of the Jews. **1887** *Pall Mall Gaz.* 5 May 11/1 The trumpet—or shophar, as it is technically called—is used in the Jewish ritual on certain festivals 'to call the hearers to repentance'. **1891** M. FRIEDLANDER *Jewish Relig.* 403 The *shofar* is intended to awaken us. **1892** ZANGWILL *Childr. Ghetto* I. vii, The minister refused to blow the Shofar three minutes too early. **1931** *Times Lit. Suppl.* 24 Sept. 722/2 The blowing of the Shofar turns out to have been originally the imitation of the voice of the dying God. **1973** *Synagogue Light* Sept. 41/2 Every morning at the conclusion of the service a blast of the shofar reminds us of the approaching Day of Judgment.

**shoffle, shofful**, obs. ff. SHUFFLE, SHOVEL.

**shoful** (ˈʃəʊfʊl). *slang.* Also **showfull, shouful, schofell, shofle, schoful, shofel.** [a. G. *schofel* worthless stuff, rubbish (primarily Yiddish, and thence adopted in London slang, though it has long been in ordinary German use), subst. use of G. *schofel* base, mean, worthless, repr. the German-Jewish pronunciation of Heb. *shāphēl* low.]

**1.** Counterfeit money. Also *attrib.* or *adj.*, counterfeit. *Comb.* **shoful-man, -pitcher**, one who passes counterfeit coin; so ***shoful-pitching.***

**1828** *Sessions' Papers Old Bailey 1827–28* 602/2 The twenty counterfeit shillings were found on me; the sister came to me and asked if I had any *shofle* about me, if I had to put it away. **1846** *Swell's Night Guide* 61 The shiser thinks to bounce us by passing a shofel quid. **1851** MAYHEW *Lond. Labour* I. 24/1 [Costermonger's slang] Showfulls, Bad money. **1856** —— *Gt. World London* 47 The '*shoful-men', or those who plunder by counterfeits; as coiners and forgers of checks, and notes, and wills. **1859** *Hotten's Slang Dict.*, **Showfull-pitcher*, a passer of counterfeit money. **1860** *Ibid.* (ed. 2), **Showfull-pullet*, a 'gay' woman. **1863** W. B. JERROLD *Signals of Distress* 106 The passers of base coin, shofulmen,..will be sensibly strengthened. **1891** CAREW *Autobiog. Gypsy* 417 Got down and heaved the sack-ful o' shoful into the water.

**2.** A hansom cab. Also (rarely) ***shoful-cab.***

[Possibly a distinct word; the explanation in quot. 1851 does not seem altogether certain.]

**1851–61** MAYHEW *Lond. Labour* II. 488/2, I don't think those 'shofuls' (Hansoms) should be allowed. *Ibid.* III. 351/1 Hansom's..are always called 'showfulls' by the cab-men. 'Showfull', in slang, means counterfeit, and the 'showfull' cabs are an infringement on Hansom's patent. **1854** *Househ. Words* VIII. 76 A hackney cab is a shoful. **1862** *Offic. Catal. Internat. Exhib.* I. No. 1444 Original builders of the shofle or gentleman's Hansom. *Ibid.* No. 1367 New brougham 'shofle'. **1869** *St. James' Mag.* III. 285 There ought to be other conveyances beyond the 'Growler and Shofle'.

**3.** A low-class tavern. ? *rare.*

**1851** MAYHEW *Lond. Labour* I. 259/1 'A rackety place, sir, ..one of the showfuls; a dicky one; a free-and-easy'.

**shog** (ʃɒg), *sb.* Now only *dial.* and *arch.* Forms: 6 schogg, 7–8 shogg, 7– shog. [f. SHOG *v.*]

† **1.** A shaking condition. *Obs. rare.*

**1596** DALRYMPLE tr. *Leslie's Hist. Scot.* II. 141 Gif thir tua landis he ma vanquis, Scotland, he thinkis, will be in a schogg. **1689** N. LEE *Princess of Cleve* IV. iii, I feel a gorgeing pain..A shog of Blood and Spirits.

**2.** A shake, jerk.

**1611** COTGR., *Bransle*,..a shake, shog, or shocke. **1669** STURMY *Mariner's Mag.* V. xii. 68 Thrust in the Ladle, being full, give it a shog, then strike off the heaped Powder. **1709** STEELE *Tatler* No. 39 ¶2 My learned friend assured me further, that the earth had lately received a shogg from a comet. **1724** HEARNE *Collect* (O.H.S.) VIII. 280 He warned her to hold by the ropes..that so she might not fall, if there happened any greater shog than ordinary.

*transf.* **1728** RAMSAY *Fox & Rat* 20 Thus thou, great King, hast by thy conqu'ring Paw, Gi'en Earth a Shog, and made thy Will a Law. **1785** BURNS *Address to Deil* xvi, Ye cam to Paradise incog,..An' gied the infant world a shog. **1888** STEVENSON *Black Arrow* Prol. 11 This will be a rare shog to poor Sir Oliver; he will turn paper-colour.

**3.** A shogging gait. Cf. SHOG *v.* 3.

**1885** DODGE *Patroclus & Penelope* 25 In early days, horses were mainly ridden on a canter or a gallop. If perchance a trot, it was a mere shog.

**shog** (ʃɒg), *v.* Now chiefly *dial.* Forms: 4-7 **shogge**, (5 **shogke**), 5-6 **schog(ge**, 6 **shugge**, (**shougge**), 7-8 **shogg**, 8 **shogue**, (**shug**), 5- **shog**. [ME. *shogge*, prob. related to OHG. *scoc* (pl. *scocga*) oscillation, swinging, a swing, MHG. *schock*, *schocke* swing, see-saw, MDu., Du. *schok* shake, jolt, MLG., MDu., MHG. *schocker* to swing, oscillate, shake. The word was doubltess felt as phonetically symbolic of the character of the movement denoted; cf. JOG *v.* See also SHOCK *v.*[1]]

**1. a.** *trans.* To shake or roll (something heavy) from side to side; to rock (a cradle); to shake, agitate (a liquid or the vessel containing it); to jolt or jar (some one or something). Also, to shake *off* a load. *rare.*

**1388** WYCLIF *Matt.* xiv. 24 The boot.. was schoggid with wawis [Vulg. *jactabatur fluctibus*]. *c* **1420** *Chron. Vilod.* 3015 þey houe, þey drawe, þey shogkeden hit [*sc.* the shrine] also. *c* **1440** *Pallad. on Husb.* XI. 322 Of wynys soure is taught to make swete Wit barly floure... And oon doth dregge of swete wyn therto; Of gliricide [*read* gliciride] a part he hath infuse Al drie, & longe yshogged it wol vse [L. *utuntur, cum diu vasorum commotione miscuerint*]. *c* **1550** *Droichis Part of Play* 38 in *Dunbar's Poems* 315 He, quhen he dansit, the warld wald schog. **1625** PURCHAS *Pilgrims* II. 1659 Now their [children's] Couch hangs in the Aire, within little Beds of coard, or little Chaires, where they shogge and rocke them. **1665** HOOKE *Microgr.* 31 If care be taken that the tube in erecting be not shogged. **1787** W. H. MARSHALL *Norfolk* (1795) II. 388 To *Shug*, to shake; as hay, &c. **1949** D. L. SAYERS tr. *Dante's Divine Comedy* I. xvii. 178 Having shogged our burden off.. away he bounded.

†**b.** To shake (a person) in order to cause pain or annoyance, or to rouse from sleep; to jog (a person) in order to attract attention. Also rarely *to shog upon* in the same sense. *Obs.*

*c* **1440** *York Myst.* xl. 100 They schogged hym and schotte hym his lymes all in sondir. *c* **1495** *Epitaffe*, etc. in *Skelton's Wks.* (1843) II. 389, I shogged him, I shaked him. **1530** PALSGR. 705/1 Shougge nat so upon him to wake hym out of his slepe. *Ibid.* 706/1 Shugge. **1534** MORE *Comf. agst. Trib.* II. Wks. 1189/2 Rudely and boystuously shogge hym & wake him. *c* **1613** MIDDLETON *No Wit like Woman's* II. ii. 107 *Philip.* May I crave one word, madam? [*stage-direction.*] Shogs his Mother. **1651** H. MORE *Enthus. Tri.* (1656) M 2, You onely mutter against the present disturbance, as one shogged while he dreams upon his pillow.

†**c.** *fig.* To 'shake' mentally; to upset, discompose; to irritate, annoy. *Obs.*

**1639** CADE *Serm.* 50 The deadly arrow sticks in his flesh, and shogs and galls him. **1688** PENTON *Guardian's Instruct.* (1897) 47 His Brains have become so shogged, he cannot think in a fortnight. **1701** STEELE *Chr. Hero* (1711) 16 Cæsar .. a little shogg'd with reiterated ill Omens.

**2.** †**a.** *refl.* (obs.) and **b.** *intr.* To jerk or jolt; to shake to and fro, to rock; †to be shaky or insecurely fixed, to get shaken *out*.

**a.** *a* **1400-50** *Wars Alex.* 5018 þan schogs hire þe sontree & schoke hire schire leues.

**b.** *c* **1450** *Mirk's Festial* 174 As he hyet on his way .. þe box schoget out of his bosome. **15..** in Boys *Sandwich* (1792) 365 For amendyng of a chalys foote y[t] schoggyd ij d. **1609** HOLLAND *Amm. Marcell.* XVI. x. 63 Neither was he seene so much as to give a nod with his head, when the wheele shogged. **1658** ROWLAND tr. *Moufet's Theat. Insects* 900 Let there be two handfuls distance between every Hive, that one shogging or shaking, the next may stand unmoved. **1841** R. CHAMBERS *Pop. Rhymes Scot.* (1870) 337 Big it [the castle] in a bog Where 'twill neither shake nor shog.

†**c.** *intr.* Of troops: To waver, become unsteady.

**1642-4** VICARS *God in Mount* 147 All the enemies Horse began to shogge a little.

**3. a.** To walk, ride or move with a succession of bumps or jerks; to jog along. Now usually, to advance at a steady easy pace, to travel steadily on.

*c* **1400** *Destr. Troy* 11089 Restorit full stithly opon strong wise, Shot into sheltrons shoggend full þicke. **15..** *Scot. Field* 94 in *Chetham Soc. Misc.* II, Shott into a sure shipp, and shoggeth over the water, Into Scotland. **1530** PALSGR. 704/1 The carte shogged so faste that I went ever I shulde have fallen downe. **1719** RAMSAY *Ep. Hamilton* Answ. iii. 20 Be blythe, and let the Warld e'en shog, as it thinks fit. **1857** KINGSLEY *Two Y. Ago* xxviii, They shog on side by side. **1893** J. A. BARRY *Steve Brown's Bunyip* 12 Shogging steadily on.. I at length reached the creek.

**b.** To go away, begone. Usu. with *off*.

**1599** SHAKS. *Hen. V*, II. i. 47 Will you shogge off? *Ibid.* II. iii. 48 Shall wee shogg? *a* **1625** FLETCHER *Coxcomb* II. i, Come, prethee let's shogg off, and browze an hour or two. **1884** C. M. YONGE *Armourer's Prentices* I. x. 192 Bolt.. bade him shog off, and not come sneaking after other folks' shoes. **1929** J. C. POWYS *Wolf Solent* vii. 154 Lob began to swagger slowly away. 'I knows why you wants me to shog off,' he called back. *Ibid.* ix. 208 Wolf shogged off by himself. **1962** L. R. BANKS *End to Running* I. v. 71 I'll just say to hell with her, to hell with the money and the house and everything else—I'll just shog off.

†**4.** Of troops: To move gradually to one side. Also *trans.* of a commander, to cause (troops) to move gradually to one side. *Obs.*

**1650** CROMWELL *Let.* 4 Sept. in *Carlyle* (1845) II. 45 The Enemy drew down to the right wing..; shogging also their foot and train much to the right. **1654-66** EARL ORRERY *Parthen.* (1676) 691, I gave strict order to all my Army to shog still toward the right hand.

Hence '**shogged** *ppl. a.*

**1594** R. CAREW *Tasso* (1881) 73 Nor shogged earth so euer bideth throwes, When bigge in wombe she doth the vapours close.

**shogging** ('ʃɒgɪŋ), *vbl. sb.* [-ING[1].] The action of SHOG *v.*; a shaking, jolting, jerking, etc.

*c* **1440** *Promp. Parv.* 447/2 Schoggynge,.. *agitacio.* **1563-83** FOXE *A. & M.* 1492/1 Rogers.. being found a slepe, scarse with much shogging could be awaked. **1600** HOLLAND *Livy* XXVII. xxix. 650 Scarce able to endure the shogging and shaking of the horselitter. **1725** *Bradley's Family Dict.* s.v. *Shoeing*, So as the Heads of the Nails may enter in, and fill the same, appearing somewhat above the Shoe, and then they will stand sure without shogging, and endure Danger.

**b.** *spec.* in *Lace manuf.* (See quots.)

**1839** URE *Dict. Arts* 732 One of these two combs, in the double bolt machine, has an occasional lateral movement called shogging. **1878** A. BARLOW *Hist. Weaving* 336 This motion of the comb-bar is technically called 'shogging', and by its means the diagonal arrangement is given to the threads. *Ibid.* 362 The 'shogging' motion of the combs.

'**shogging**, *ppl. a.* [-ING[2].] That shogs.

**1581** STUDLEY tr. *Seneca's Hippol.* 61 The shogging carte made crake with swagging sway. *a* **1800** PEGGE *Suppl. Grose* s.v. *Shog*, A shogging horse. *a* **1881** J. CRAIG in *Mod. Scott. Poets* Ser. II. 123 The mavis will sing to me,.. Aff the shoggin' boughs o' the sauchen tree. **1897** 'O. RHOSCOMYL' *White Rose Arno* 272 A sort of shogging amble.

**shoggle** ('ʃɒg(ə)l), *v.* Chiefly *dial.* Also 8 **schogle**, 9 **shoogle**, **shogle**, **shuggle**. [Frequentative f. SHOG *v.*: see -LE. Cf. G. *schockeln*, *schuckeln* to shake, jostle, walk unsteadily.]

**1.** *trans.* To shake, to cause to move; to shake (something or somebody) *off*.

**1577** GOOGE *Heresbach's Husb.* IV. 159 b, You must in no wise shake them, or shoggle them..: by shaking of the egges, the Chickins haue been hatched lame. **1822** GALT *Sir A. Wylie* xxxiv, If, by ony mischance, she had been shooggled aff [the coach] whar would I hae been then? *a* **1844** W. MILLER in Whitelaw *Bk. Scott. Song* 6/2 Stravagin' wuns begin To shoggle and shake the window-brods. **1855** ROBINSON *Whitby Gloss.*, To *Shoggle*, to joggle.

**2.** *intr.* To shake; to swing about, to dangle; to shake or settle *down*.

*c* **1730** RAMSAY *Vision* v, A braid-sword schogled at his thee. **1896** CROCKETT *Cleg Kelly* xxix, I'll just lock them in and they'll [soon] hae shuggled doon as quaite as a session.

**3.** To walk unsteadily.

**1884** *Reports Provinc.* (E.D.D.), The old cat was shuggling about in the hole. **1896** B. MITFORD *Sign of Spider* xxvii. 268 It stood for a moment in rigid immobility, then.. it shoggled over the ridge. *Ibid.* 274 The fearful Thing.. shoggled away in the direction whence it had come.

'**shoggy**, *a.* [f. SHOG *sb.* + -Y.] Shaky, insecure.

**1866** D. MITCHELL *Hist. Montrose* 22 Sandy Fullerton.. ascended to the narrow shoggy scaffold at the top of the spire.

‖**shogi** ('ʃoːgi). Also **Sho-gi**, †**Sho-Ho-Ye**, **Shongi.** [Jap.] A Japanese board game resembling chess.

**1858** *Japan Opened* (Relig. Tract Soc.) vii. 267 The game is called *Sho-Ho-Ye*, and is a great favourite among the Japanese. **1884** tr. *J. J. Rein's Japan* II. ii. 430 Among those of which adults of all classes.. are very fond, the most conspicuous at present are Shôgi, or chess, and Go. **1890** B. H. CHAMBERLAIN *Things Japanese* 66 Japanese chess (*shōgi*) was introduced from China centuries ago. **1905** CHO-YO *Japanese Chess (Shō-ngi)* 27 The governing class of people valued the chessological Art or Science of struggles, commonly known as *Shōngi* (Chess). **1969** R. C. BELL *Board & Table Games* II. ii. 38 There are about ten million Sho-gi players in Japan. **1975** *Way to Play* 50/1 There have been many forms of shogi since its introduction in about the eighth century.

‖**shogun** ('ʃəʊgʊn). Now only *Hist.* Forms: 7 **shongo**, 8-9 **seogun**, (9 **djogoun**), **s(h)iogoon**, **sjogun**, 9 **ziogoon**, 9- **shogun**. [Jap. *shōgun*, short for *sei-i-tai shōgun*, 'barbarian-subduing great general', bestowed on the first holder of the office in 1192. *Shōgun* is a Japanese sound-substitution for Chinese *chiang chün* (*chiang* to lead, *chün* army).] The hereditary commander-in-chief of the Japanese army, until 1867 the virtual ruler of Japan. Also called TYCOON.

By successive usurpations of power, the Shogun or Tycoon had become the real ruler of Japan, though nominally the subject of the Mikado, and acting in his name. This state of things was misunderstood by Europeans, and it was erroneously supposed that there were two emperors in Japan, the Mikado (who was the object of a loyalty of the nature of religious devotion) being called 'the spiritual emperor', and the Shogun 'the temporal emperor'. In 1867, with the abolition of the feudal system, the Mikado assumed the actual sovereignty, and the reign of the Shoguns came to an end.

**1615** R. COCKS *Diary* (Hakl. Soc.) I. 5 His wife is sent back to her father Shongo Samme, King of Edo and to succeed in the Empire. **1727** SCHEUCHZER tr. *Kæmpfer's Japan* App. I. 65 It was thought expedient, that the Seogun, or Crown-General, should be sent against them at the head of the imperial army. **1863** ALCOCK *Capital of Tycoon* II. 233 The Seogun, or Dai-Seogun. **1875** *N. Amer. Rev.* CXX. 281 The fall of the shogun's (tycoon's) government. **1879** AUDSLEY & BOWES *Keramic Art Japan* I. Pref., The difficulty which modern writers have found in deciding upon the correct mode of spelling the single word Shôgun; in the Japanese Government Reports we find it written Shogun; Mr. F. Ottwell Adams.. writes it.. Shôgun; Mr. Dickson, Shiogoon; Mr. Mossman, Siogoon; Mr. Mitford, Shogun; Dr. Siebold, Sjôgun; and Mr. Satow.. Shôgun.

**b.** *attrib.* as designating fashions or art belonging to the Japanese feudal period.

**1889** SIR E. ARNOLD *Seas & Lands* xiv. (1895) 226 A seated figure, which might have been taken at first for the chief triumph of the Shogun carvers' work. **1904** D. SLADEN *Playing the Game* I. vi, Tied in the elegant and fantastic Shogun knots which are the formal way of fastening up presents in Dai Nippon.

Hence '**shogunal** *a.*, pertaining to a shogun, the shoguns, or the shogunate; '**shogunate**, the office or dignity of a shogun or the shoguns; '**shogunite** (*rare*), a partisan of the shogunate; '**shogunship** = *shogunate*.

**1841** *Mann. & Cust. Japanese* 357 The Annals begin to tell.. of rival heirs contending for the ziogoonship. **1871** A. B. MITFORD *Tales Old Japan* I. 99 After.. the abolition of the Shogunate, he accompanied the last of the Shoguns in his retirement. **1873** MOSSMAN *New Japan* 333 The despotic rule of the Mikados before the Siogoonate was established. **1883** E. M. THOMPSON *R. Cocks' Diary* (Hakl. Soc.) I. 5 *note*, Iyéyasu held the Shogunate only two years. **1890** SIR E. ARNOLD *Seas & Lands* xxii. (1895) 364 The rebels, or Shogunites, were defeated. **1899** C. J. HOLMES *Hokusai* 14 His artistic reputation had even spread to the Shogunal court.

**Shoho**, var. SAHO *sb.* and *a.*

**shoir**, obs. form of SHORE *sb.* and *v.*

**shoit(e**, **shoitte**, obs. forms of SHOAT.[2]

‖**shoji** ('ʃoːdʒi). [Jap.] **1.** In Japanese architecture, a sliding outer or inner door made of a latticed screen covered usu. with white paper.

**1880** I. L. BIRD *Unbeaten Tracks in Japan* I. 90, I closed the sliding windows, with translucent paper for window panes, called *shōji*. **1922** J. STREET *Mysterious Japan* ii. 24 Children glimpsed through the open wood and paper *shoji* of their matchbox houses. **1959** R. KIRKBRIDE *Tamiko* iv. 28 He swung himself over the sill and dropped into her room, closing the shoji behind him. **1979** H. MCCLOY *Smoking Mirror* Inside the house there were.. sliding partitions like the panels on a Japanese shoji.

**2.** *attrib.* or as *adj.*

**1886** J. LA FARGE *Let.* 1 Sept. in *Artist's Lett. Japan* (1897) 217 To look out of the *shoji* screens into the garden. **1896** L. HEARN *Kokoro* ii. 19 The light *shōji* frames serving at once for windows and walls, and repapered twice a year. **1958** R. GANNON *New Ways with Dried Flowers* x. 126 (*caption*) Shoji type screen decorated with a variety of pressed leaves. **1967** M. M. PEGLER *Dict. Interior Design* 407 The shoji panels are used as screens, dividers, doors that slide behind one another on a track (Japanese style), or as window coverings. **1977** *Time* 24 Jan. 17/1 The hero tears his way through the hard paper covering of a shoji screen.

**shok**, obs. f. SHOCK *sb.*; obs. pa. t. of SHAKE *v.*

**shoke**, obs. f. SHOCK; obs. pa. t. of SHAKE *v.*

**shokinge**, obs. pres. pple. of SUCK *v.*

**shokk(e**, obs. forms of SHOCK *sb.*

‖**shokku** ('ʃɒkuː). [Jap., f. SHOCK *sb.*[3]] Used *joc.* to denote a shock or surprise in political or economic affairs concerning Japan.

**1971** *Time* 4 Oct. 36/1 The President had convulsed Japan .. with the 'Nixon *shokku*'—his spectacular policy shifts on China and the economy. **1973** *Time* 3 Sept. 18 Indeed, the Nixon Administration's diplomatic *shokkus* in 1971 did lasting damage to Japan's relations with the U.S. **1978** *Encounter* Sept. 56/2 The Japanese were able to cope with their frightful '*oil shokku*' with far more self-restraint than marked the response of other countries to the oil embargo.

‖**shola**[1] ('ʃəʊlə). [Hindī *sholā* (*çolā*) = Bengalī *solā*.] = SOLA[1].

**1836** FANNY PARKS *Wand. Pilgr.* (1850) II. 100 Each float was formed of eight pieces of sholā... When this light and spongy pith is wetted, it can be cut into thin layers, which, pasted together, are formed into hats. **1884** *Sunday at Home* June 373/2, I cannot but grieve to see the graceful shola disappearing fast before the planter's axe.

*attrib.* **1876** J. H. BALFOUR in *Encycl. Brit.* IV. 100/2 Æschynomene aspera (Shola plant, the Rice-paper plant of India). **1887** BENTLEY *Man. Bot.* (ed. 5) 726 They are not so durable as the Sola or Shola hats of Calcutta.

‖**shola**[2] ('ʃəʊlə). Also **sholah**. [Tamil *çolāi*.] A thicket or jungle, in Southern India.

**1862** MARKHAM *Trav. Peru & India* xxiii. 38 A wooded ravine or *shola*. *Ibid.* 383 There are many *sholas* which will be found equally well adapted for the growth of the hardier chinchonas. **1863** SIR V. BROOKE in O. L. Stephen *Mem.* (1894) 109 She [the tigress] got weaker and weaker, let go the boar, and slunk off to the *sholah*.

**shold(e**, obs. forms of SHOAL.

**sholdarry**, variant of SHOOLDARRY.

**sholder(e**, **sholdre**, obs. forms of SHOULDER.

**shole** (ʃəʊl). *Naut.* [Of obscure origin. Cf. SHOE *sb.* 5 j.] (See quots.)

**1711** W. SUTHERLAND *Shipbuild. Assist.* 26 The Transoms ought to be level, but especially the Wing Transom, securing all very well with Shores, which ought to be plac'd on Timber Foundations, called Sholes. **1805** *Shipwright's Vade-M.* 131 *Sholes*, pieces of oak or plank, placed under the soles of the standards; or under the heels of the shores, in docks or slips where there are no groundways, to enable them to sustain the weight required without sinking.

**shole**, obs. form of SHOAL, SHOVEL.

**sholt.** *Obs.* exc. *dial.* Also 6 shault, 9 shoult (*E. Angl. Gloss.*, 1895). A cur.

**1587** HARRISON *England* III. vii. 231/2 in *Holinshed*, Besides these also we haue sholts or curs dailie brought out of Iseland. **1592** GREENE *Conny-catch.* Wks. (Grosart) XI. 65 The Boy..neuer saw a Dog nor Bitch, but a little prickeard Shault, that kept the Mil doore. *a* **1825** FORBY *Voc. E. Anglia, Sholt*, a cur.

**sholve**, obs. var. SHOVEL *sb.*

**sholy** ('ʃəʊlɪ). Also **sholey**. Representation of U.S. Black and Southern dial. pronunc. of SURELY *adv.*

**1929** H. W. ODUM in *Amer. Mercury* Sept. 48/1 Camp sholy was roughish place. **1940** W. FAULKNER *Hamlet* I. ii. 56 'You brought it to me?' 'Sholy,' Ratliff said. 'Take it.' **1966** M. THELWELL in A. Chapman *New Black Voices* (1972) 140 Sholey. Sho, hit'll be jes fine.

**shomach, -acke**, obs. forms of SUMACH.

**shomaker(e**, obs. forms of SHOEMAKER.

† **shome.** *Obs. rare.* In 4 schome. ? Some kind of adornment for horses. Hence (?) **schom** *v. trans.*, to adorn with this.

*a* **1310** in Wright *Pol. Songs* (Camden) 239 Nou beth capel-claweres With shome to-shrude; Hue boskeþ huem with botouns, Ase hit were a brude. **1500–20** DUNBAR *Poems* lxi. 3 Quhy sould not palfrayis thane be prowd, Quhen gillettis wilbe schomd and schroud.

**shome**, obs. form of SHAME *sb.*

‖ **shomer** ('ʃəʊmə(r)). Pl. **shomrim**. [ad. Heb. *šōmēr* watchman.] **1.** (See quot. 1971.)

**1909** *Cent. Dict.* Suppl., Shomer. **1923** H. TRAGER *Pioneers in Palestine* II. iii. 147 The other passengers talk of the killing of one of the Shomrim by an Arab. **1935** *Zionist Review* Mar. 10/2 At 4-30 a.m...pounded the shomer (night watch) on my door. **1938** *Ibid.* Feb. 35/1 The renowned old Jewish watchmen..have been in the country for twenty-five years and more, having been members of the '*shomrim*' organisation. **1944** M. SAMUEL *Harvest in Desert* xiii. 121 From Gomel came the members of first group of *Shomrim* ('Guards') who organized in Palestine. **1971** *Encycl. Zionism & Israel* I. 462 *Hashomer* (*Shomer*) Self-defence organization of Jewish pioneers..established in Palestine in 1909 to protect Jewish settlements there... Each..colony.. was supplied with Shomrim (watchmen).

**2.** An inspector who verifies that food is prepared in accordance with Jewish religious laws.

**1909** *Cent. Dict.* Suppl., Shomer. **1923** H. M. LAZARUS *Ways of her Household* I. i. 8 There is need for a special supervisor—*shomer*—to be appointed for licensed butcher-shops. **1954** A. H. HYAMSON *London Board for Shechita* vi. 33 The shomer visited the community in Paris..and was given every facility to investigate the methods of porging. **1980** *Times* 28 May 14/4, I am quite happy to accept supervision of our food supplies by a shomer appointed by the local Jewish authorities.

**shon**, obs. form of SHUN.

**Shona** ('ʃəʊnə). = MASHONA *sb.* and *a.*

**1930** C. M. DOKE *Rep. Unification Shona Dialects* 61 The Language Committee..hope to unify..the dialects of the area..known as Mashonaland and the name for the language should..be one which indicates this width of range. No name but 'Shona' has been suggested which can do this. **1930** C. G. SELIGMAN *Races of Africa* viii. 187 The Shona peoples of Southern Rhodesia and of Portuguese East Africa immediately south of the Zambesi as far as the Sabi River. **1936** *Discovery* June 179/1 The Shona..were the later or perhaps the military occupiers of the Hill which we call Mapungubwe. **1955** G. FORTUNE (*title*) An analytical grammar of Shona. **1976** *Times* 26 Aug. 12/6 The Shona.. comprise about 75 per cent of the..population. *Ibid.* 12/7 Mr. Joshua Nkomo..is apparently a Kalanga..one of the smallest Shona groups..whose language is furthest from basic Shona. **1979** *Financial Times* 29 Jan. 16/4 The right wing says there is still time to negotiate a three tier federal solution which would avoid domination of the minority Ndebele and the minority Whites by the majority Shonas.

† **shond**, *sb.*[1] *Obs.* Forms: 1 sceand, sceond, scond, 1–2 scand, 2–3 *Ormin* shande, 3 scond(e, sond(e, ssonde, 3–5 schonde, 4 schounde, schond, 4–5 shonde, (5 shont). [Com. Teut.: OE. *scand*, *scǫnd* fem. corresponds to OFris. *skonde*, (M)Du., (M)LG. *schande*, OHG. *scanta* (MHG., mod.G. *schande*), Goth. *skanda* :—OTeut. **skandō*, f. **skando-* ashamed (OHG. *scant*, OE. as subst. masc. *scand*: see next) :—**skamdo-* pa. pple. of **skam-*: see SHAME *sb.*] Shame, disgrace, infamy, ignominy; scandal. *to do* (someone) *shond*, to treat with indignity; *to bring, make to shond*, to disgrace, ruin.

*a* **900** CYNEWULF *Crist* 1274 þonne is him oþer earfeþu swa some scyldȝum to sconde. *c* **1100** *O.E. Chron.* (MS. D.) an. 1076, Sume ȝe tawod to sconde. *c* **1200** ORMIN 11956 Forr þatt wass..Hiss aȝhenn shame & shande. *c* **1205** LAY. 7032 þe ȝunge wifmen & þe ælde he makeden to sconde. *c* **1250** *Gen. & Ex.* 2714 Ðat ðhuȝte moyses michel sond. **1297** R. GLOUC. (Rolls) 1493 To spousy þe emperours doȝter hit nere him no ssonde. *c* **1315** SHOREHAM 7 *Deadly Sins* 45 Wyth schame and eke wyth schounde. *c* **1384** CHAUCER *H. Fame* 88 And shelde hem fro pouerte and shonde. *c* **1400** *St. Alexius* 80 (Laud 463) þou most þole shame & shonde, al for my sake. *c* **1450** LOVELICH *Grail* xiv. 28 With his Ax he wrowhte hem Mochel schonde.

† **shond**, *sb.*[2] *Obs.* Forms: 1 sceand, scond, 3 sconde. [OE. *scand*, *scǫnd*: see prec.] An infamous person, a deceiver, charlatan, recreant.

*c* **725** *Corpus Gloss.* (Hessels) S 165 *Scurra*, scond. *c* **1000** ÆLFRIC *Saints* xvii. 159 Ac þyllice sceandas sceolan siðian to helle. *c* **1205** LAY. 23668 Beon he in ælche londe iqueðe for ane sconde.

† **shond**, *v. Obs. rare.* [f. SHOND *sb.*[1] Cf. SHEND *v.*] *trans.* To harm, injure.

**1338** R. BRUNNE *Chron.* (1725) 226 þe Sarazins do grete wreche, þe Cristen for to schond. *c* **1450** LOVELICH *Grail* xiii. 886 For Erthly Man was non leveng In londe That so moche he hated, ne wolde schonde.

† **'shondful**, *a. Obs.* [OE. *sceandfull*, f. OE. *sceand* SHOND *sb.*[1] + -FUL.] Shameful, disgraceful; infamous. Hence † **'shondfully** *adv.*

*a* **900** *O.E. Martyrol.* 29 Aug. 156 He [John Baptist] wæs heafde becorfen for scandfulra wifa bene, and for.. scondfulles ȝebeorscypes hleahtre. *c* **1175** *Lamb. Hom.* 31 þis him wule þunche swiðe strong and swiðe scondful þet he [etc.]. *c* **1330** *Arth. & Merl.* 9198 Better is to sterue worþ-schipliche þan long to liuen schandfulliche.

† **'shondly**, *a. Obs.* Forms: see SHOND *sb.*[1] Also 2 sandlice. [OE. *sceandlíc*: see SHOND *sb.*[1] and -LY[1].] Shameful, disgraceful, vile.

**888** ÆLFRED *Boeth.* xiv. §3 Ðif hit ær scandlic wæs, he bið hit no ðy fæȝerre. *a* **1175** *Cott. Hom.* 239 Wat sceol se wrecce don þe þufon iseȝð his hlaford..him selfe bi sandlice senne beswapen. *c* **1205** LAY. 2274 Ne scal þe nan man scilden wið scondliche deaðe. *c* **1330** *Arth. & Merl.* 4276 We no haue pouer Arthour oȝen..No for Merlin,..þat can so michel schandliche werk.

**shone**, pa. t. and pa. pple. of SHINE *v.*

**shone**, obs. pl. of SHOE; obs. f. SHUN *v.*

**Shonee**, var. SHAWNEE *a.* and *sb.*

**shoneen** (ʃəʊ'niːn). *Anglo-Irish.* Also **shauneen.** [f. mod. Irish *Seón*, ad. Eng. *John* + *-ín* diminutive suffix.] (See quot. 1910.) Used (esp. *attrib.*) to indicate a person's inclination towards English rather than Irish standards and attitudes in cultural life, sport, etc. Hence **sho'neenism.**

*c* **1840** KEEGAN *Leg. & Poems* (1907) 67 The likes of him, a bandy-legged shoneen. **1889** *Times* 30 Jan. 6/5, I hope to hear of ye shooting Hubert Davis..the shauneen of a landlord. **1909** *Ibid.* 21 Jan. 6/6 What difference did it make whether a man got a 'shoneen' education in Belfast or in Oxford so long as he was not educated an Irishman. **1910** P. W. JOYCE *English as we Speak it in Irel.* 321 Shoneen, a *gentleman* in a small way: a would-be gentleman who puts on superior airs. Always used contemptuously. **1918** F. HACKETT *Ireland* iii. 65 West Britonism makes us what we are, shoneenism and toadyism, so it is, they're the curse of Ireland. **1920** B. MACNAMARA *Clanking of Chains* iv. 44 But the shoneenism of Ambrose was in more perfect keeping with the shoneen heart of Ballycullen... The songs which he sang were out of the English music halls, the books which he read were English drivel. **1922** JOYCE *Ulysses* 311 Irish sport and shoneen games. **1927** [see *pro-Britisher* s.v. PRO-[1] 5 b]. **1958** B. BEHAN *Borstal Boy* III. 326 Now, there was a lot of shoneen writing and playing up to the herrenvolk by Rugby writers. **1960** *20th Cent.* Oct. 324 This aunt practically invented the whole concept of shoneenism... She believed that God was Anglo-Saxon, Protestant.

† **shongable.** *Obs. rare.* [f. *shon* pl. of SHOE *sb.* + *-gable* in imitation of older compounds: see GAVEL *sb.*] A tax on the making of (a particular kind of) shoes.

*a* **1400** in *Eng. Gilds* 359 Euerych sowtere þ[t] makeþ shon of newe roþes leþer, shal bote..twey pans, in name of shongable.

**shonicker** ('ʃɒnɪkə(r)). *U.S. slang.* Also **shoniker, shonniker.** [Orig. uncertain: see quots. 1966, 1970.] An offensive name for a Jew (see also quot. 1914).

**1914** JACKSON & HELLYER *Vocab. Criminal Slang* 75 *Shoniker*, current among cosmopolitan thieves, especially Jews. A neophyte or inexperienced hand at the game. **1927** *Dialect Notes* V. 462 *Shonniker*, n., a Jewish pawn-broker. **1932** J. T. FARRELL *Young Lonigan* vi. 269 Two hooknoses ..did come along. Andy and Johnny O'Brien..stopped the shonickers. **1966** *Publ. Amer. Dial. Soc. 1964* XLII. 45 Thus folk etymology derives *shonicker* from Yiddish *schnozzle*... My colleague..suggests a derivation from Hanukkah. **1970** L. M. FEINSILVER *Taste of Yiddish* 338 Shon, shonk, shonky, shoncker, shonniker. These opprobrious terms for a Jew in England are supposed to have come from Yiddish *shoniker* (petty trader or peddler).

**shonie**, obs. form of SHUN *v.*

† **shonk**, *v. Sc. Obs. rare.* In 5 schonk. [Of obscure origin.] **a.** *trans.* To shatter. **b.** *intr.* To burst forth. Hence † **'shonkand** *ppl. a.* (*Sc.*)

*c* **1470** *Gol. & Gaw.* 619 Thair speris in splendris sprent, On scheldis schonkit and schent. *c* **1470** HENRY *Wallace* III. 147 The shafft to schonkit off the fruschand tre. *Ibid.* 156 Vpon the flouris schot the schonkan blude.

**shonk** (ʃɒŋk), *sb. slang.* [Shortened form of SHONICKER.] An offensive name for a Jew. Hence **'shonky** *a.*[1] (see quot. 1951).

**1938** W. MATTHEWS *Cockney Past & Present* v. 153, I diffidently suggest the following words as the most familiar slang terms rarely used except by cockneys..*shonk*, nose, Jew. **1940** R. POSTGATE *Verdict of Twelve* I. v. 75 Let's have a bit of fun with the shonks. **1951** PARTRIDGE *Dict. Slang* (ed. 4) Add. 1168/1 *Shonky*, adj., mean; money-grubbing: late C. 19–20. **1981** 'W. HAGGARD' *Money Men* xv. 174 'Brighton? .. It's full of shonks.'.. 'Which means there are hotels with night clerks.'

**shonke, shonne**, obs. ff. SHANK, SHUN.

**shonkie**, var. SHONKY *a.*[2]

**shonkinite** ('ʃɒŋkɪnaɪt). *Geol.* [f. *Shonkin*, Indian name for the Highwood Mountains, Montana + -ITE[1].] A dark granular form of syenite consisting largely of augite and orthoclase. Hence **shonki'nitic** *a.*, having the character or consisting of shonkinite.

**1895** WEED & PIRSSON in *Bull. Geol. Soc. Amer.* VI. 415 For this type of rock, then, we propose the name of shonkinite,..and shonkinite we define as a granular plutonic rock consisting of essential augite and orthoclase, and thereby related to the syenite family. **1900** *Bull. Geol. Soc. Amer.* XI. 395 The relations of the 'fine grained' (shonkinitic) syenite to the leucite-porpyhry are uncertain. *a* **1928** PEACH & HORNE *Chapters Geol. Scotl.* (1930) iv. 112 A discontinuous zone of fine-grained shonkinite and pulaskite. **1943** S. J. SHAND *Eruptive Rocks* (ed. 2) xiv. 259 There are no lavas of shonkinitic composition. **1951** TURNER & VERHOOGEN *Igneous & Metamorphic Petrology* viii. 169 The syenite undoubtedly is a differentiate derived from a parent shonkinite magma. **1978** S. R. NOCKOLDS et al. *Petrology for Students* v. 61 Other shonkinites from the Highwood Mountains and from the Bearpaw Mountains, Montana, may have a little plagioclase.

**shonky**, *a.*[1]: see SHONK *sb.*

**shonky** ('ʃɒŋkɪ), *a.*[2] *Austral. slang.* Also **shonkie.** [Perh. f. SHONKY *a.*[1]: see SHONK *sb.*] Unreliable, dishonest, 'crooked'. Hence as *sb.*, one engaged in irregular or illegal business activities.

**1970** R. BEILBY *No Medals for Aphrodite* 116 You shonkie sod! **1976** *Sunday Mail* (Brisbane) 2 May 8/4 Queensland has some 'shonky' charities. I cannot name them because of libel. **1979** *Financial Rev.* (Sydney) 25 July 11/6 Mr Groom is right when he refers to the building industry as being characterized by initiative and drive, but unless something is done to eliminate these 'shonkies' quickly, then such qualities will be characteristics of the past. **1981** *Australian* 2 Feb. 7/7 The woman..was forthright about the cut-price air fares... 'We call these tickets shonky,' she said.

**shont(t**, obs. forms of SHUNT *v.*

**sho' nuff**: see NUFF b.

**shoo** (ʃuː), *v.* Forms: 7 shough, 8–9 shue, 9 schue, sheugh, 8– shoo. [f. SHOO *int.*[1] Cf. It. *scioiare* (Florio).]

**1.** *trans.* **a.** To scare or drive away (fowls, etc.) by calling out 'shoo' or by means of movement or gestures. Also with *away*, *from*, *off*, *out* (*of*). Also *transf.*

**1622** BRETON *Strange News* (Grosart) 12/2 With that the Cock-master came in..and shought away the Hen. *c* **1798** T. BROWN *Awd Daisy* 40 Ah waved my hat an' shoo'd 'em all away. **1819** W. TENNANT *Papistry Storm'd* iii. (1827) 106 Think alswa How to rebut and schue awa Thir damnit faes. **1872** 'SUSAN COOLIDGE' *What Katy did* viii, 'Shue'-ing away the other children. **1912** CHESTERTON *Manalive* 161 'Get inside! get inside!' cried Moon hilariously, with the air of one shooing a company of cats. **1919** CONRAD *Arrow of Gold* I. i. 9 Shells were falling all round till a tiny French gunboat ..shooed the *Numancia* away out of territorial waters. **1938** W. DE LA MARE *Memory* 14 She shoo'd it away with her gloves. **1959** D. BEATY *Cone of Silence* ii. 25 Then she shooed cups and plate away from her. **1959** *Listener* 15 Jan. 113/2 He shakes or nods his head to shoo the flies away. **1973** 'H. CARMICHAEL' *Too Late for Tears* viii. 108 Hope you won't mind if I shoo you out now. I've got work to do. **1977** *Time* 22 Aug. 10/1 Israeli artillery regularly fires into south Lebanon to shoo away Palestinian guerrillas from Lebanese Christian enclaves in the border area.

**b.** To drive or urge (a person, animal, etc.) in a desired direction.

**1903** *N.Y. Sun* 17 Nov. 12 The police shoo everybody to the south side of the loops. **1923** 'B. M. BOWER' *Parowan Bonanza* xiii. 151 You're supposed to shoo a lady gently before you down the aisle. **1946** M. DICKENS *Happy Prisoner* xi. 267 The first pony had already been shooed into the ring. **1973** M. AMIS *Rachel Papers* 150, I do not churlishly flatten her on to the sofa nor shoo her downstairs.

**2.** *intr.* To cry out 'shoo' in order to frighten or drive away fowls, etc. Const. *at.*

*c* **1746** J. COLLIER (Tim Bobbin) *View Lanc. Dial.* (1806) 22 Still they kept shuing. **1881** MRS. MOLESWORTH *Adv. Herr Baby* 120 It was very funny to see the way the little footman went 'shoo-ing' at the poor cat.

**3.** To hasten away, as after being 'shooed at'.

**1851** STERNBERG *Northampt. Gloss.* 95 Lady lock, lady lock! shoo all the way home. *a* **1869** C. SPENCE *Fr. Braes of Carse* (1898) 192 The fairies..beat the beldames blank and hollow, And sent them sheughing down the Ballo'. **1882** P. ROBINSON *Under the Sun* III. v. 213 If the domestic says *shoo* to her [the cat] she shoos at once.

**4.** *trans.* With *in*, to allow a racehorse to win easily. *U.S. slang.* Cf. SHOO-IN.

**1908** G. E. SMITH *Racing Maxims & Methods of 'Pittsburgh Phil'* ix. 123 There were many times presumably that 'Tod' would win through such manipulations, being 'shooed in', as it were. **1935** D. RUNYON *Money from Home* 128 They are going to shoo in Never Despair. **1976** *New Yorker* 22 Mar. 85/2 To be sure, Shoemaker's confreres could have shooed him in long before this, but jockeys never, never do such things.

Hence **'shooer**, in comb. *bird-shooer.*

**1849** HALLIWELL *Pop. Rhymes* 179 This is the universal bird-shooer's song in the midland counties.

**shoo** (ʃuː), *int.*[1] Forms: 5 schowe, ssou, 7 shooe, shooh, shue, shoogh, 7–8 shough, 9 shu(h, shue, sho (etc.: see Eng. Dial. Dict.), 9– shoo. [An instinctive exclamation; cf. LG. *schu*, MHG. *schu*, *schuo* (mod.G. *schu*), F. *shou*, It. *scioia*.] An exclamation used to frighten or drive away poultry, birds, or other intruders. Also as *sb.*

**1483** *Cath. Angl.* 338/1 Schowe ssou, *jnterieccio est.* **1611** FLORIO, *Scioiare*, to cry shooe shooe, as women do to their hens. **1623** FLETCHER & ROWLEY *Maid in Mill* v. i, Shough, shough, up to your coop, Pea-Hen. **1639** J. CLARKE *Paræmiologia* 145 He cannot say shooh to a goose. **1675** HOBBES *Odyss.* xv. 139 An eagle..seis'd a great white tame goose grazing near: The standers-by shouted and cri'd, Shue! shue! But yet away the eagle bore him clear. **1681** OTWAY *Soldier's Fort.* IV. (1683) 49 Shoogh, shoogh, get you into a corner when I bid you, shoogh, shoogh, shoogh, what there already? **1822** T. MITCHELL *Aristoph.*, *Wasp* I. ii. II. 191 Shuh! shuh! foolish bird, must I stone 'ee? **1829** J. HUNTER *Hallamsh. Gloss.*, *Shoo*, the interjection used in frighting away birds from their prey. **1852** DICKENS *Bleak Ho.* xxxix, Shoohoo! Get out, you goblin! **1891** J. L. KIPLING *Beast & Man India* ii. 44 The servant shows the master a fowl standing on one leg. The master crows sho! and the fowl runs away with two. **1894** CROCKETT *Raiders* xxxvii. 311 An owl flew by..and I heard him say, 'Shoo, you beast!' **1896** JANE BARLOW *Mrs. Martin's Comp.* 41 A..burly man, who says 'shoo-shoo' to a..cluster of tiny yellow ducks.

**shoo** (ʃuː, ʃʊ), **sho** (ʃɔː), *int.*[2] *dial.* and *U.S.* Also **shuh, shah.** [Instinctive: cf. prec.] An exclamation indicating impatient or contemptuous rejection of a statement. Cf. PSHAW.

**1845** S. JUDD *Margaret* I. xi, 'Sho! it's humans you are speaking of', replied Nimrod. **1856** P. THOMPSON *Hist. Boston* 722 *Shoo* or *Shah.* Pshaw! a peevish reply. **1883** J. C. HARRIS in *Century Mag.* May 139/2 Shoo! won't my ole 'oman holler! **1900** WEYMAN *Sophia* xiv, 'Sho!' Lady Betty cried contemptuously.

**shoo**, obs. form of SHE, SHOE, SHOW *v.*

**shooba, shoobe**, variant forms of SHUBA.

**shooch**, dial. variant of SHEUGH *sb.*

**shood, shude** (ʃuːd). *dial.* Also 7 shud, 9 shewd. [Prob. cogn. w. MLG. *schode*, MHG. *schôte*, mod.G. *schote* husk, pod of peas or beans, f. **skeu-* to cover; the OE. form may have been **scéod* (*sceōd*) corresponding formally to ON. *skjóð* fem., skin bag.] The husk of oats after threshing. Usually in *pl.* Also †= SHIVE *sb.*[2]

**1601** HOLLAND *Pliny* XIX. i. II. 4 But what shall bee done with all the hard refuse [from the flax],..the short shuds or shives that are either driven from the rest in the knocking, or parted in the hetchelling. **1691** RAY *N.C. Words* (ed. 2) 62 *Shoods*, Oat-hulls; *Darbish.* **1829** J. HUNTER *Hallamsh. Gloss.*, *Shewds*, the outer coat of oats, sometimes called *shiffs.* **1879** MISS JACKSON *Shropsh. Word-bk.*, *Shoods*, husks of oats,—'this wutmil's full o' shoods'. **1886** *Cheshire Gloss.*, *Shudes*, husks of oats, sifted from the meal. Bacon is often stowed away in a chest amongst shoods.

**shood, shooe**, obs. ff. SHOD *a.*, SHOE.

**shoof(e**, obs. pa. t. of SHAVE *v.*, SHOVE *v.*[1]

**shooffell, shoof(f)le**, obs. ff. SHUFFLE *v.*

**shoo-fly** (ˈʃuːflaɪ), *vbl. phr.* and *sb.* *U.S.* Also **shoofly, shoo fly.** [f. SHOO *int.*[1] + FLY *v.*[1] and *sb.*[1]]

**A.** *vbl. phr.* A catch phrase, popularized by a song, used as an exclamation of annoyance. *Obs.*

**1867** *Chicago Republican* 24 July 8/1 [Baseball] players invariably say 'Shoo-fly', when they make a miss. **1889** FARMER *Americanisms* 484/2 *Shoo! fly! don't bother me!* An exclamation of impatience is *shoo* and *fly* are both common ejaculations in country districts when driving wandering fowls or cattle from gardens etc., to legitimate pastures... The full phrase is now familiarly colloquial. **1919** MENCKEN *Amer. Lang.* 311 *Shoo-fly* afflicted the American people for at least two years, and '*I don't* think' and *aber nit* quite as long.

**B.** *sb.* †**1.** A device or structure intended to afford protection from flies. *Obs.*

**1879** *Glendale* (Montana) *Atlantis* 28 Dec. 4/4 A Dutchman drove rapidly along Main Street, with a new shoo-fly attached to his wagon, making forty flips a second and striking back and forth with the vigor of a hewgag. **1896** J. RALPH *Dixie* iv. 126 In many cases they order great pavilions like giant nests built around their trees, and..they call them 'shoo-flies', a name utterly without significance in that connection.

**2.** A policeman, usu. in plain clothes, whose duty is to watch and report on other policemen. *slang.*

**1877** *Daily Graphic* May 1 A 'shoofly' is the term applied by a policeman to another officer who is detailed to watch him. **1903** H. HAPGOOD *Autobiogr. Thief* (1904) xii. 265, I was gathered in to make a reputation for those two shoo-flies. **1931** *Detective Fiction Weekly* 27 June 790/2 A force of 'shoo flies'—roundsmen in civilian clothes—were sent out regularly from headquarters to sweep into a precinct and look over the men. **1952** *Sun* (Baltimore) 10 May (B ed.) 2/2 Evans said he spent eighteen months on 'shoo-fly duty'—on the chief inspector's squad that worked out of headquarters keeping other policemen in line and honest. **1980** 'E. MCBAIN' *Ghosts* vii. 127 'You want a beer?.. Officially I'm still on duty, but fuck it.' 'Shooflies are heavy around the holidays.'

**3.** A rocking horse in which the seat is placed between two rockers representing the animal. Freq. *attrib.* as ***shoo-fly rocker***.

**1887** *Chicago Tribune* 27 Nov. 16/7 (Advt.), Shoo fly hobby horse, 75 c. **1895** *Montgomery Ward Catal.* Spring & Summer 563/2 Shoo-fly rockers... Shoo-fly 12 × 40 inches; painted and dappled. **1947** *Chicago Tribune* 30 Dec. 15/1 The Teaneck, N.J., library has installed something called a shoo-fly, an enclosed rocker in which little Elmer..can rock his head off.

**4.** A temporary railway track constructed for use while the main track is obstructed or under repair. Also *transf.* (see quot. 1907).

**1905** *N.Y. Even. Post* 29 July 1 The Southern Pacific Company's 'shoo-fly' around the tracks now submerged will be completed in a few days. **1907** *Dialect Notes* III. 249 *Shoo-fly, n.*, suburban railway train. **1929** *Macon* (Georgia) *Tel.* 2 July, There comes into Macon every morning on the Eatonton Shoo Fly a very old white woman named Mary Loring. **1937** *Highway Mag.* Jan. 9/1 Beginning in the spring of 1936 the railroad built two temporary 'shoo fly' tracks about 75 feet west of the existing tracks. **1961** *Washington Post* 17 Feb. B4 (*caption*) Workers on top of a construction train adjust the overhead wires for a bypass—or 'Shoo-fly' in railroad parlance—of the main railroad tracks serving the area to the south of Washington.

**5.** *Printing.* In some flat-bed presses, a set of narrow strips which lift the edge of the sheet off the cylinder ready for delivery. Also ***shoofly finger***.

**1908** *Inland Printer* XL. 551/2 Where the delivery construction uses shoo-fly fingers to give the forward edge of the sheet a lift as it passes out onto the delivery, the proper setting of these fingers or shoo-flies, as they are usually called, is of prime importance. **1927** E. ST. JOHN *Pract. Hints Presswork* ii. 10 When farthest open the shoofly fingers should be five-sixteenth of an inch away from the drawsheet. **1962** *Theory & Practice of Presswork* (U.S. Govt. Printing Office) (rev. ed.) xxviii. 170 The shooflies, stripper fingers, and tape delivery have all been eliminated on the newer chain-delivery Miehle presses.

**6.** In needlework, a traditional patchwork design.

**1931** R. S. MCKIM *One Hundred & One Patchwork Patterns* 84/1 As shoo fly is one of the simplest of old-fashioned patchworks, both to cut and to piece, it would be a good choice for one on which a little girl could learn sewing. **1977** E. Y. WOOD *Amer. Patchwork Quilts* 15 Four-patch designs are here, such as the classic 'Shoo Fly'.

**7.** *attrib.* and *Comb.* **a.** In various unspecified senses.

**1870** *North Alabamian & Times* (Tuscumbia, Alabama) 21 Apr. 2/7 The gentlemen can gratify their taste by ornamenting themselves with the latest style of 'Shoo Fly' Hats. **1886** M. B. BUCKLEY *Diary Tour in Amer.* viii. 223 There were 'Shoo fly neckties' and 'Shoo fly hats'. **1891** O. WISTER *Jrnl.* 17 June (1958) 106 That's a terrible plain woman Hank's got. All driven and dried up. Looks like a picture on one of these shoo-fly boxes. **1897** *Sears, Roebuck Catal.* 35/3 Shoo-fly flasks..½ pints..pints..quarts. **1946** C. RICHTER *Fields* 278 Huldah had gone with Amy MacMahon, a red shoofly ribbon low on both their necks.

**b. shoo-fly pie**, a rich tart made of molasses baked in a pastry case with a crumble topping; **shoo-fly plant**, a large annual herb, *Nicandra physalodes*, belonging to the family Solanaceæ, native to Peru, and bearing pale blue flowers followed by berries enclosed in the enlarged calyx.

**1935** *Esquire* Dec. 200/1 'Shoo-fly pie'—a brown-and-white crumb-cake, faintly spiced. **1971** *Daily Colonist* (Victoria, B.C.) 9 July 3/4 The pair is helping their father sell shoo-fly Pie and other Pennsylvania items. **1979** *United States 1980/81* (Penguin Travel Guides) 48 Vermont cheese and maple syrup,..and shoofly pie and pretzels in the Pennsylvania Dutch country are all specialties of their respective regions. [**1902** L. H. BAILEY *Cycl. Amer. Hort.* IV. 1664/1 Shoo-fly plant. A name proposed by one seedsman for Physalis.] **1949** L. H. BAILEY *Man. Cultivated Plants* (ed. 2) 871 N[*icandra*] *Physalodes*..Apple-of-Peru, Shoo-fly Plant. **1973** *Times* 20 Oct. 16/7 Left-over seeds thrown out for the birds from special mixtures..are responsible for appearances of casual weeds like..the Apple of Peru, or 'shoo-fly plant', and its pale blue flowers that are succeeded by swollen, green berry-enclosing lanterns.

**ˈshoo-in.** *N. Amer.* [f. vbl. phr. *to shoo in*: see SHOO *v.* 4.] **1.** In *Horse-racing*, a predetermined or 'fixed' race, or the winner of it. Hence *loosely*, a horse which is a certain winner.

**1928** *National Turf Digest* (Baltimore) Dec. 929/2 A 'skate' is a horse having no class whatever, and rarely wins only in case of a 'fluke' or 'shoo in'. **1937** *Collier's* 11 Sept. 11/3 Sharp Practice wins by so far it looks like as if he is a shoo-in. **1950** *Sun* (Baltimore) 1 June 22/4 Some horsemen wondered whether Chris Chenery's Virginia flyer would be such a shoo-in for the Belmont Stakes..after all. **1969** R. LOCKRIDGE *Risky Way to Kill* xii. 152 Got two hunters entered in the Ridgewood show... One of them doesn't like wet going... Figuring him to be pretty much of a shoo-in for the..hunter championship.

**2.** *transf.* (esp. *Pol.*). A certain or easy winner; a certainty, a 'walk-over'.

**1939** *News* (San Francisco) 30 Jan. 15/5 (*heading*) Bear cagers appear shoo-in for southern division title. **1948** *Tuscaloosa* (Alabama) *News* 30 July 4/2 This type of registration might endanger their balloting in the local elections, where Democratic candidates are usually chosen on a 'shoo-in' basis. **1962** K. ORVIS *Damned & Destroyed* (1966) xxv. 183 The rest was a shoo-in. The house dick nailed the room number, then waltzed down and checked the register. **1968** *Economist* 20 Jan. 29/1 Governor Rockefeller became the Republicans' leading presidential hopeful for 1964. The press thought him a shoo-in for the nomination. **1976** *Islander* (Victoria, B.C.) 10 Oct. 15/3 From then on, in spite of the fog, it [*sc.* the sailing] was a shoo-in. **1981** *Time* 13 May 68/1 If they gave a good sport Oscar, she would be a shoo-in.

**shook** (ʃʊk), *sb.* Now chiefly *U.S.* [? f. SHOOK *ppl. a.* Cf. SHAKEN *cask.*] 'A set of staves and headings sufficient for one hogshead, barrel, or the like, prepared for use and bound up in a compact form for convenience of transport. Boards for boxes prepared or fitted for use and packed in the same way bear the same name' (*Cent. Dict.* 1891).

[**1768, 1794**: see SHOOK *ppl. a.*] **1796** MORSE *Amer. Geog.* (ed. 3) I. 250 [Exports of U.S.] Shooks. **1860** *Merc. Mar. Mag.* VII. 120 Shooks are free of duty. **1894** *Times* 16 Aug. 6/5 Casks and barrels, empty, sugar-box shooks and packing boxes and packing box shooks, of wood.

**b.** 'Furniture made in parts and not set up, but shipped in packs' (Knight *Dict. Mech.* 1875).

Hence **shook** *v. trans.*, to pack in shooks.

**1847** in WEBSTER; and in later Dicts.

**shook** (ʃʊk), *ppl. a.* [pa. pple. of SHAKE *v.*]

**1.** = SHAKEN *ppl. a.* In educated use only *arch.*

**1695** BLACKMORE *Pr. Arthur* III. (1696) 68 And the shook Sphears, with loud Hosannahs ring. **1768** *Massach. Gaz.* in Thornton *Amer. Gloss.* s.v., A few large shook hogs-heads. **1794** MORSE *Amer. Geog.* (ed. 2) 206 [Exports of U.S.] Wood ..Shingles, Shook Casks, Casks, Laths. **1897** F. THOMPSON *New Poems* 25 Reversing the shook banners of their song.

**2.** *colloq.* **a.** *to be shook on*: to be enamoured of or enthusiastic about. *Austral.* and *N.Z.*

**1888** 'R. BOLDREWOOD' *Robbery under Arms* II. iii. 46 He was awful shook on Mad; but she wouldn't look at him. *Ibid.* xix. 291 I'm regular shook on the polka. **1926** J. DEVANNEY *Butcher Shop* iv. 43 She had but fallen victim to the state of mind described by girls she knew as being 'shook' on a man. **1965** S. T. OLLIVIER *Petticoat Farm* vii. 100 Tom said he wasn't too shook on makin' a public fool of himself. **1975** *Sunday Tel.* (Sydney) 29 June 49 Like Chappell, I'm not all that shook on cocktail parties myself.

**b.** Emotionally or physically disturbed, discomposed, upset. Usu. const. *up*. orig. and chiefly *U.S.*

**1891** KIPLING in *Macmillan's Mag.* Oct. 473/2 He took my 'and an' pulled me up, an' I was pretty shook. **1897** —— *Captains Courageous* ii. 31 You was shook up and silly. **1914** *Dialect Notes* IV. 79 *Shook, p.a.*, startled, shocked, grieved. 'Jed was pow'ful shook when Minervy pegged out.' **1953** *Sun* (Baltimore) 24 Apr. (B ed.) 20/2 Ken Jackson..should qualify for the nickname Stonewall... Ken..fell two floors down a freight elevator shaft and as he said was only 'shook up'. **1959** H. SALISBURY (*title*) The shook-up generation. **1960** *Washington Post* 25 May 1 'Elva behaved all the way through it just like a good policeman,' Liverman said of his wife's role in the chase. 'But she still gets a little shook thinking about the ride.' **1976** *Daily Mirror* 11 Mar. 1/1 Rock superstar Rod Stewart was all shook up last night after a lovers' tiff with..Britt Ekland.

**shool** (ʃuːl), *v. dial.* and *slang.* Also 8–9 shule, 9 shoal. [Of obscure origin; hardly identical with *shool* var. of SHOVEL *v.* In Ireland it seems to have been associated with Irish *siubhail* to go, travel; *shooler* (see below) seems to correspond to Irish *siubhlach* vagrant.] *intr.* To go about begging; to sponge, to acquire some advantage by insidious means; also to skulk.

**1736** J. LEWIS *Isle of Tenet* (ed. 2) 38 *Shooling*, begging, to go a Shooling. **1748** SMOLLETT *Rod. Random* xli, When they found my hold unstowed, they went all hands to shooling and begging. **1785** GROSE *Dict. Vulgar T.*, *Shoole*, to go skulking about. **1842** LOVER *Handy Andy* xxxiv, 'Throth, you do me wrong', said the beggar, 'if you think I came shooling'. *a* **1876** M. & FR. COLLINS *Village Comedy* (1878) I. xxii. 297 As we watch these daring damsels starting to 'shool', we cannot help wishing them some lively adventures. **1899** 'MARTELLO TOWER' *At School & Sea* 73 Hullo, Dil, at it again, shooling (that is, getting things) on the youngsters.

**b.** *trans.* To impose on (a person).

**1745** *Life Bampfylde-Moore Carew* 158 One Day he met with an English Doctor, whom he shuled as a cast-away Seaman.

**c.** To carry as a pretence.

**1820** CLARE *Rural Life* (ed. 3) 125 Who takes delight To shool her knitting out at night.

Hence **ˈshooler**, one who 'shools'.

**1830** CARLETON *Traits Irish Peas.* (1843) I. 62 What tribes of beggars and shulers. **1856** P. THOMPSON *Hist. Boston* 722 *Shooler*, one who intrudes upon his neighbour, and forces an invitation to dinner, &c.

**shool**, obs. and dial. form of SHOVEL.

**shool**, var. SHUL.

‖**shooldarry** (ʃuːlˈdærɪ). *Ind.* Also shoaldarree, sholdarry. [Urdū *chholdārī*, of obscure origin.] 'A small tent with steep sloping roof, two poles and a ridge-piece, and with very low side walls' (Yule).

**1808** ELPHINSTONE in Colebrooke *Life* (1884) I. 182, I have now a shoaldarree for myself, and a long paul for my people. **1902** T. W. WEBBER *Forests Upper India* v. 46 The baggage consisted of a small sholdarry tent, 6 feet square.

**shoole**, obs. form of SHOAL *sb.*

**shoomack, -ak(e**, obs. forms of SUMACH.

**shoon**, pl. f. SHOE; obs. pa. t. of SHINE *v.*

**shoone**, obs. f. pa. t. of SHINE *v.*

**shoop** (ʃuːp). *north.* Forms: 5 schowpe, 8–9 shoup, showp, 9– shoop. See also CHOOP. [The forms *shoop*, *choop* perh. represent aberrant pronunciations of ON. **hjúpa* (MSw. *hiupa*, Norw. dial. *hjupa*, Da. *hybe*) = OE. *héope* HIP *sb.*[2]]

The fruit of the rose; = HIP *sb.*[2]

**1483** *Cath. Angl.* 338/1 A schowpe, *cornum.* A schowpe tre, *cornus.* **1721** *MS. Cook Book* in *Girl's Own Paper* (1886) VII. 729 How to Candy Shoups. **1781** J. HUTTON *Tour to Caves* (ed. 2) 95 *Shoup*, an hep. **1804** *Europ. Mag.* XLV. 326/2 [Shaped] like a hip or a shoup on a rose-tree. **1878** *Cumberld. Gloss., Choop, Shoop*, the fruit of the wild rose.

**shoop**, obs. pa. t. of SHAPE *v.*

**shoope, shoore**, obs. ff. SHOP *sb.*, SHORE.

**shoot** (ʃuːt), *sb.*[1] Forms: 6 s(c)hute, 6 schote, 5 schoyt, 6 shote, 6 showt, 6–7 shoote, 7 shout, 5– shoot. [f. SHOOT *v.*

In early examples it is sometimes difficult to distinguish this word from certain other derivatives of the same root. In the early 16th c. the spellings *shote* and *shoot(e* are both ambiguous, so that only the shade of meaning can determine whether the word is *shoot* (rhyming with *root*) f. the pres.-stem of the vb., or the older SHOTE (rhyming with *throat*). The 16th c. examples of the spelling *s(c)hute* belong to the present word, but down to the 14th c. this spelling (with *u* = *ü*) represents the OE. *scyte*: see SHUTE *sb.*]

**1. a.** An act of shooting (with fire-arms, a bow, etc.); a discharge of arrows, bullets, etc.: = SHOT *sb.* Now only *arch.*

**1534** MORE *Comf. agst. Trib.* I. Wks. 1157/2 This marke.. we shal nowe meate for the shoote and consider.. how farre of your arrowes are from the prik. **1545** ASCHAM *Toxoph.* I. (Arb.) 89 The strongest men, do not drawe alwayes the strongest shoote. *Ibid.* II. 107 For in a rayne and at no marke, a man may shote a faire shoote. **1546** *Plumpton Corr.* (Camden) 250 Tomorrow.. I must.. ride to Tankerslay.. & mete my Lord of Shrewsburry, who will be thear tomorrow by ij of the clock, & se a showt at a stage [= stag]. **1565** COOPER *Thesaurus* s.v. *Conficere*, He killed twelue at .xii. shootes. **1583** MELBANCKE *Philotimus* R iv b, O that I mighte haue a shoote at one of the Deares in his Parke. **1629** WADSWORTH *Pilgr.* iv. 35 In 12 shootes more they strooke downe our maine Mast. **1676** SHOTTEREL & DURFEY *Archerie reviv'd* 78 If in measuring a Shoot, the Mark be stirred out of its place, he loseth the Shoot that removed it. **1692** R. L'ESTRANGE *Fables* lxvi. 65 As a Country Fellow was making a Shoot at a Pigeon. **1775** *Pennsylvania Even. Post* 30 Nov. 551/1 The riflemen.. declare that they can hit a man every shoot if within two hundred and fifty yards. **1801** T. ROBERTS *Engl. Bowman* 293 A *Shoot*, an arrow shot. **1888** STEVENSON *Black Arrow* Prol. 8 How many a rogue would give his two crop ears to have a shoot at either of us! *Ibid.* v. vi. 306, I have two score men at my whistle, and with one shoot of arrows I could answer for you all.

*fig.* **1590** *Cobler of Canterb.* 2 All men.. saide, that he [Chaucer] shot a shoote which many haue aimed at but neuer reacht to. **1682** DRYDEN & LEE *Dk. Guise* I. i, *Pol.* But one prime Article of our holy League, Is to preserve the King, his Power and Person *Cur.* That must be said, you know, for Decency; A pretty Blind to make the Shoot secure.

†**b.** Range, distance or reach of a shot; shooting distance. *Obs.*

**1530** SIR D. LYNDESAY *Test. Papyngo* 941 They haue ane Boumbard.. Within quhose schote there dar no Enimeis Approche thare place. **1545** ASCHAM *Toxoph.* I. (Arb.) 33 There was nothing within his retche and shote. **1613** BEAUM. & FL. *Hon. Man's Fort.* IV. ii, Hence, and take the wings of thy black Infamy, to carry thee beyond the shoot of looks, Or sound of curses. **1641** EARL MONM. tr. *Biondi's Civil Warres* IV. 64 Chartier brings the two Armies face to face within the shoote of a Culverin. **1676** *Acc. Exam. Joan Perry* 3 He went again with him about a Bows shoot into the Fields. *a* **1700** EVELYN *Diary* Apr. 1646, Nor could we any where see above a pistol shoote before us. **1719** DE FOE *Crusoe* I. (Globe) 236 So that I might come within shoot of them before I should be discover'd.

†**c.** Weapons for shooting, firearms. *Obs.*

**1469** *Paston Lett.* III. 372 That, with ther gret multitude of gannes [sic], with other shoot and ordynaunce, ther shall no man dar appere in the place.

†**d.** A charge (of powder). *Obs.*

**1645** SYMONDS *Diary* (Camden) 276 Their ammunition was so spent that the enemy gave the soldjer many shootes of powder to make the conditions good.

**e.** A game-shooting expedition; the result of such an expedition.

**1852** VISCOUNTESS CANNING in Hare *Story Two Noble Lives* (1893) I. 360 The Prince is much pleased with his shoot this year. One day he killed five stags. **1877** 'WILDFOWLER' *Shooting Trips* Ser. II. II. 99 We should arrive at Ford in time for a stroll and a 'shoot' along the river Arun. **1895** SIR W. W. HUNTER *Old Missionary* iii. 59 Their return.. was celebrated by a big shoot in the jungle.

**f.** A shooting party.

**1885** *Field* 4 Apr. 446/1 At a big shoot in Warwickshire. **1894** 'J. S. WINTER' *Red Coats* 69 Miss Dawson.. gave big dinners and big shoots.

**g.** The right to shoot game in a given area; also the area itself.

**1861** MRS. JENKIN *Who Breaks Pays* II. 93, I hear Sir Frederick a taken the shoot hisself, and bought Bill Fordham's black hunter. **1892** GREENER *Breech-Loader* 221 The sportsman whose shoot is small and the game.. scarce and wild, will be unable to practise driving to any advantage. **1900** *Field* 29 Sept. Advt. p. vi/2 Wanted, a good rough shoot, commencing season 1901–1902, on Lease; plenty of rabbits essential; 2000 to 5000 acres.

**h.** A shooting match or contest; a round of shots in such a contest.

**1892** GREENER *Breech-Loader* 102 Some men who attend second-rate pigeon shoots and do not take their own guns. **1892** *Times* 23 July 6/1 Volunteer Aggregate... One shoot at 200, one at 500, and three at 600 yards. Seven shots at each. **1894** *Daily News* 12 June 8/6 The full scores of the first 'shoot' for places in the 'English Twenty' at Bisley.

**i.** *transf.* The action of shooting a film. Cf. SHOOT *v.* 22 f.

**1929** *Morning Post* 24 May 12/7 A Wembly 'Shoot' Described... A 'talkie' sequence is being 'shot' in the studio. **1978** *Broadcast* 13 Nov. 24/1 Had you crewed in features or television productions and then suddenly found yourself part of a commercial shoot?

**j.** *Mil.* An act of bombardment; esp., an exercise in which anti-aircraft drill is practised.

**1941** *Hutchinson's Pictorial Hist. War* July–Sept. (*caption*) 162 Bofors guns, of proved efficiency against low-flying aircraft, are included in Malaya's defence programme... A practice shoot is in progress. **1961** B. FERGUSON *Watery Maze* xiv. 344 The prize shoot was executed by *Ajax* and *Argonaut* on a troublesome battery at Longues. **1977** *R.A.F. News* 8–21 June 11/2 Such blank days, and other times when 'shoots' are cancelled.. can be as disappointing and frustrating to the range team as to the fliers and their units.

**2. a.** The action of shooting, sprouting, or growing; the amount of growth (also *concr.* the new wood, etc. produced) in a certain period. Also †the mounting or rising (of the sap).

**1572** MASCALL *Plant. & Graff.* (1592) 9 For to set the Pine tree, ye must set or plant them of Nuts, in March, or about the shoote of the sappe. **1661** BOYLE *Certain Physiol. Ess.* (1669) 92 Others content themselves to chuse a hazel rod (which some will have to be all of the same years shoot). **1664** EVELYN *Kal. Hort.* Jan. (1679) 8 Cut off all the shoot of August, unless the nakedness of the place incline you to spare it. **1733** W. ELLIS *Chiltern & Vale Farm.* 266 The Clover makes a quick Shoot, and will get a large second Head. **1832** *Boston Herald* 8 May 3/5 The shoot of Spring grass is also unusually late, and slow in vegetation. **1896** *Daily News* 19 Sept. 2/5 The crops presented at harvest what to agriculturists is known as 'two shoots', i.e., a crop composed of ripe and also unripe grain.

**b.** A young branch which shoots out from the main stock of a tree, plant, etc.

*a* **1450** *Fysshynge w. Angle* (1883) 8 Take a feyr schoyt of blake thorne. **1578** LYTE *Dodoens* I. liv. 80 This plante [*Linaria*] hath diuers small shutes or scourges bearing small narrow leaues. **1634** MILTON *Comus* 296, I saw them under a green mantling vine.. Plucking ripe clusters from the tender shoots. **1720** P. BLAIR *Bot. Ess.* i. 10 If it be put into a Pot, and all its Stolones or Shoots be taken off. **1796** WITHERING *Brit. Plants* (ed. 3) I. 81 Shoot (*surculus*) the branch of a Moss. **1812** *New Bot. Gard.* I. 6 The French in Canada eat the tender shoots in spring as Asparagus. **1842** LOUDON *Suburban Hort.* 497 Cut smooth the lower end of the shoot or cutting, and stick it into fine leaf or other rich mould about an inch deep. **1863** GEO. ELIOT *Romola* viii, The fresh shoots among the darker green of the oak. **1909** J. G. FRAZER *Psyche's Task* iv. 38 The shoots of the sweet potato had flowered and withered long ago.

**c.** *fig.* An offshoot; a growth or sprout from a main stock.

*c* **1610** *Women Saints* 71 Kinesburge and Kineswide were daughters to Penda, a Pagan thoughe king of Mercia, holie shootes of a dead stocke or truncke. **1749** SMOLLETT *Gil Blas* XII. v. (1782) IV. 237 His excellency.. immediately sent for his equivocal heir, and new shoot from the trunk of the Guzmans. **1833** LONGF. *Outre-Mer, Sexagenarian*, Monsieur d'Argentville was a shoot from a wealthy family of Nantes. **1882** CHILD *Eng. & Sc. Pop. Ball.* I. 51/1 The ballad we are dealing with is a wild shoot from the story of Judith and Holofernes. **1899** J. MATHEW *Eagle Hawk & Crow* ii. 9 Upon the aboriginal Australian stock there was grafted a strong Malayo-Dravidian shoot.

**d.** *transf.*

**1611** SHAKS. *Wint. T.* I. ii. 128 Thou want'st a rough pash & the shoots that I haue To be full, like me. **1671** GREW *Anat. Pl.* I. iv. (1682) 28 Those Fibrous Shoots which run along the Pith in the Root. **1822–29** *Good's Study Med.* (ed. 3) I. 531 It is better.. to distinguish by the phrase polypous tumours, caruncles, or shoots, such adscititious productions as may have a resemblance to them [i.e. to nasal polypi] in other organs. **1847** PRESCOTT *Peru* III. i. (1862) II. 14 Ridges of barren land, that seemed like shoots of the adjacent Andes. **1851** S. P. WOODWARD *Mollusca* I. 18 The oyster continues enlarging his shell by annual 'shoots' for four or five years. **1861** *The Oyster* 35 These [overlapping plates forming an oyster-shell] are technically termed 'shoots', and each of them marks a year's growth.

**e.** Applied to the forms of crystals ? likened to those of a plant. Cf. SHOOT *v.*

*a* **1728** WOODWARD *Nat. Hist. Fossils* I. (1729) I. 158 Spar of a yellow Hue, shot into numerous trigonal pointed Shoots of various Sizes. *Ibid.*, Hexangular Sprigs or Shoots of Crystal of various Sizes. **1748** *Phil. Trans.* XLV. 364 He tried Alum, which fully answered everything he proposed; for it restored the Salt to its natural cubical Shoot.

**3. a.** A motion or movement (of a thing) as though shooting or being shot in a particular direction; also the space or distance covered by such a motion or by a push; *spec.* (see quot. 1903).

*c* **1596** *Sir T. More* IV. iii. 20 Thence some slight shoote Being carried by the waues, our boate stood still Iust opposite the Tower. *a* **1658** LOVELACE *The Falcon* x, The Falcon charges at first view With her brigade of Talons; through Whose Shoots, the wary Heron beat, With a well counter-wheel'd retreat. **1863** HAWTHORNE *Old Home, Up Thames* II. 130 [The journey by river is] far preferable to the brief, yet tiresome shoot along the railway track. **1869** 'WAT. BRADWOOD' *The O.V.H.* xxx, They have nearly completed the shoot to the Middlesex shore [in the University boat-race]. **1881** MACDONALD *Mary Marston* II. xiii. 223 Into those eyes she would call up her soul and there make it sit, flashing light, in gleams and sparkles, shoots and coruscations. **1894** *Times* 25 June 7/2 Both [yachts] had a long shoot up in the eye of the wind. **1903** EDWARDS-MOSS in A. E. T. Watson *Eng. Sport* 178 In order then to give the same shoot (*i.e.* pace between the strokes) when the oars are coming forward for the next stroke, there must be greatly increased power put into each stroke.

**b.** Of an immaterial thing: A sudden advance.

**1752** JOHNSON *Rambler* No. 200 ¶4, I felt at his sudden shoot of success an honest and disinterested joy. **1752** HUME *Ess. & Treat.* (1777) I. 125 The sciences.. were enabled to make.. considerable shoots. **1837** CARLYLE *Fr. Rev.* I. VII. i, Many things too, especially all diseased things, grow by shoots and fits. **1839** HALLAM *Lit. Europe* II. iv. §16 We find it near the end of Elizabeth's reign, when our literature made its first strong shoot.

**c.** A sharp short twinge (of pain).

**1756** FOOTE *Engl. fr. Paris* II. Wks. 1799 I. 122, I burn, I burn—Ah, there's a shoot. **1822–29** *Good's Study Med.* (ed. 3) IV. 320 The lancinating shoots darted both downward.. and upward. **1892** SWINBURNE *Sisters* II. i. 36, I thought, Between the shoots and swoonings, off and on, How hard it was. **1899** J. HUTCHINSON in *Arch. Surg.* X. 126 The shoots of pain were like those of an electric discharge.

†**d.** = THRUST *sb.* 3 (*a*). *Obs.*

**1772** C. HUTTON *Bridges* 58 The weight of the pier ought ..to.. exceed in effect the shoot of the arch. **1823** P. NICHOLSON *Pract. Build.* 340.

**e.** A detachment and falling away or tumbling down (as of part of a cliff); a landslip.

**1820** SCORESBY *Acc. Arctic Reg.* I. 104 Various heaps of broken ice denoted recent shoots of the seaward edge [*sc.* of an iceberg]. **1889** W. RYE *Cromer* 68 In 1832, there was so heavy a shoot of the cliff.. that [etc.].

**f.** In slang phr. ***to give*** (a person) ***the shoot***: to dismiss from employment, sack; also *transf.* So ***to get the shoot***. Cf. BOOT *sb.*[3] 1 c.

**1846** *Swell's Night Guide* 50 'You nasty old man,' said she, 'and your doss gorger cracked a wid about you to me, and said she must give you the shoot.' **1906** [see MOVE *sb.* 6].

**g.** = SHOT *sb.*[1] 7 h. *U.S.*

**1959** *Time* 5 Jan. 24/2 Another 20 or 30 Atlas shoots must be made. **1961** *N.Y. Times Mag.* 5 May 28/2 (*caption*) In a recent 'shoot' the capsule was picked up at sea fifty-six minutes after take-off.

**4.** *Weaving.* One movement or throw of the shuttle between the threads of the warp; the length of thread thus placed; also, the weft.

**1717** PARNELL *Homer's Battle of Frogs & Mice* II. 114 Along the Loom the purple Warp I spread, Cast the light Shoot, and crost the silver Thread. **1731** MORTIMER in *Phil. Trans.* XXXVII. 107 Wherefore they fasten a Loop or *Potlart* to as many of these simple Chords as there are Threads of the Warp to be pull'd up at every Shoot, or every Throw of the Shuttle; by which means the Shoot shews itself on the right Side, where the Warp is pulled up. **1736** *Act 9 Geo. II*, c. 37 §7 The Shoot Yarn.. shall be.. close struck with four Shoots of treble Threads at the Distance of every two Feet. **1810** J. T. in *Risdon's Surv. Devon* Introd. p. xxv, The other yarn, of a softer twist, is called the abb or shoot. **1831** G. R. PORTER *Silk Manuf.* 231 The commoner sorts of ribands, are composed altogether, both warp and shoot, of Bengal silk. **1840** *Civil Engin. & Arch. Jrnl.* III. 139/2 An improved method of preparing shoot or weft to be used in weaving woollen cloth. **1844** G. DODD *Textile Manuf.* vi. 201 Plain silks, as well as most woven fabrics, consist of threads crossing each other at right angles; the 'long-threads' being technically called the warp, and the 'cross-threads' the shoot or weft. **1888** J. PATON in *Encycl. Brit.* XXIV. 464/1 A new shed is formed, the last made pick or shoot being enwrapped between the intersecting warp sheds.

**5. a.** A heavy and sudden rush of water down a steep channel; a place in a river where this occurs, a rapid. (Confused with CHUTE *sb.*[1] 1; cf. SHUTE.)

*a* **1613** DENNIS *Secrets Angling* II. xxvi, At the Tayles, of Mills and Arches small, Whereas the shoote is swift. **1725** DE FOE *Voy. round World* (1840) 287 Gulleys.. where.. great shoots of water had been used to run. **1792** G. CARTWRIGHT *Jrnl. Labrador* I. Gloss. p. xiv, *Shoot in a River*, a place where the stream, being confined by rocks which appear above water, is shot through the aperture with great force. **1818** SCOTT *Hrt. Midl.* l, A single shoot carried a considerable stream over the face of a black rock. **1869** BLACKMORE *Lorna D.* xlv, The 'shoot' as we called our little runnel of everlasting water, never known to freeze before. **1870** D. MACRAE *Amer. at Home* xli. II. 161 At these points it [the Mississippi] sooner or later makes a new channel for itself across the neck of land. This is called a shoot.

**b.** An artificial channel for conveying water by gravity to a low level; or for the escape of overflow water from a reservoir, etc.; also for forcing water into a railway engine in rapid motion.

**1707** MORTIMER *Husb.* (1721) II. 82 By maintaining of the leaden Shoot. **1765** TUCKER *Lt. Nat.* (1834) I. 32 The miller of an overshot mill.. has shoots lying over every one of his wheels, stopped by flash-boards at their upper ends, against which the water lies bearing, always ready to drive the wheels whenever it can find a passage. **1813** VANCOUVER *Agric. Devon* 320 Immediately below the weir, there is an outlet regulated by another flood-hatch, and conducted through a shoot, formed of oak-plank, from the leat. **1833** LOUDON *Encycl. Archit.* §85 To paint the whole of the external wood-work, and the gutters, and shoots (spouts). **1843** *Civil Engin. & Arch. Jrnl.* VI. 90/1 A form of gully hole and shoot, constructed with radiated bricks, the shoot being half a brick in substance. **1865** *Morn. Star* 5 Apr., To make provision for draining the water from the surface, and having shoots on each side to carry it off. **1875** W. D. PARISH *Sussex Gloss.*, *Shoot*, a gutter round a roof for shooting off the water.

†**c.** ? The flow of water (from a hill). *Obs.*

**1799** A. YOUNG *Agric. Lincoln.* 275 The catch-water drain runs all winter, taking the shoot from an extensive range of hills, and bringing in floods much of the finer and richer particles.

**6. a.** A sloping channel or conduit for letting down coal, ore, wheat, etc. into a lower receptacle.

**1844** H. STEPHENS *Bk. Farm* II. 137 It is always desirable that the frame below should contain a *shoot* formed of light boarding, that will receive the broken cake from the rollers. **1862** *Chamb. Jrnl.* Apr. 216 [Mining] The shoots are iron gratings or screens, placed at a considerable incline, and as the coal runs down, the dust falls through on to heaps below. **1869** RANKINE *Machine & Hand-tools* Pl. P 20, The bullet, now finished, is delivered through a shoot into a wooden box. **1884** SIR R. COUCH in *Law. Rep.* 9 App. Cases 426 The *Westport*.. made fast to the coalstaiths.. with the forehatch under No. 1 shoot. **1899** BARING-GOULD *Bk. West* II. xviii. 290 Above the door is a shoot for melted lead.

**b.** *U.S.* 'A passage-way on the side of a steep hill or mountain down which wood and timber are thrown or slid' (Bartlett 1848). Also SHUTE *sb.*

**1881** [see CHUTE *sb.*[1] 2].

**c.** *U.S.* 'An enclosed steep passageway for animals to pass, as from one corral to another or to railway-cars' (*Funk's Stand. Dict.* 1895). *Austral.*, an opening and ramp leading from one pen to another in a sheep-shearing shed. Cf. CHUTE *sb.*[1] 3 b.

**1873** J. H. BEADLE *Undevel. West* xxii. 432 About a quarter section of cattle-yards and 'shoots' extend around the depot. **1880** *Harper's Monthly* Jan. 203 (Funk) There were.. three corrals connected by 'shoots' or narrow passages. **1900**, **1905** [see PEN *sb.*[1] 1 c]. **1955** STEWART & KEESING *Austral. Bush Ballads* 239 The shearers squint along the pens, they squint along the shoots; The shearers squint along the board to catch the Boss's boots.

**d.** A place where rubbish may be 'shot'; = TIP *sb.*[5] 4 b.

**1851** MAYHEW *Lond. Labour* II. 286/2 Each particular district appears to have its own special 'shoot' for rubbish. **1894** *Daily News* 27 Dec. 5/3 It [the dust] is taken to 'shoots' on vacant land.

**7.** *Mining.* A considerable and somewhat regular body or mass of ore in a vein, usually elongated and vertical or inclined in position. Also 'a vein branching at a small angle from and reentering a main vein' (*Funk's Stand. Dict.* 1895).

**1850** ANSTED *Elem. Geol., Min.* etc. Gloss., *Shoot* (in mining), a vein parallel [? *erron.*] to the stratification. **1880** H. R. NICHOLLS in *Victorian Rev.* I. 657 Gold is not distributed uniformly through the quartz, but exists in 'shoots' and bands. **1890** *Goldfields of Victoria* 14 As a rule, as soon as the shoot of stone carrying gold runs out, the reef is abandoned. **1894** A. ROBERTSON *Nuggets* 31 The rich shoot of gold he had come upon.

**8.** ***the whole (entire) shoot***: the entire lot. ***to go the whole shoot***: to risk all. *slang* and *colloq.*

**1884** *Longman's Mag.* Feb. 382 The Colonel responded by declaring his intention of paying for the whole shoot. **1896** *Pall Mall Mag.* Nov. 380, I interviewed the entire shoot. They were all strangers to me. **1899** E. PHILLPOTTS *Human Boy* 197 To mothers he never talked about 'pupils'; but called the whole shoot of us 'his lads'.

**9.** *dial.* A cross-bar connecting the parts of an old-fashioned plough; = SHEATH[2].

**1733** TULL *Horse-Hoeing Husb.* xxii. 351 My Plow.. being composed of four rough Pieces of Planks.. held together by three shoots, or Pieces of Wood. **1811** T. DAVIS *Agric. Wilts.* 263 Parts of a Plough... Fore-shoot, backward-shoot, two pieces of wood immediately behind the coulter.

**10.** *attrib.* and *Comb.*, as ***shoot-bud***, †***-graft*** (in quot. *fig.*), ***-structure***; ***shoot-producing*** adj.; **shoot-board** = *shooting-board* (Knight *Dict. Mech.* 1875); †**shoot-serpent** = DART *sb.* 4; **shoot-thread** (see quot. and sense 4); †**shoot-tobacco** (see quot.); **shoot-trough**, a trough placed under a 'shoot' (sense 5 b); †**shoot-yarn** = *shoot-thread.*

**1786** ABERCROMBIE *Gard. Assist.* 142 To disbud or rub off the useless *shoot-buds of the year, now fast advancing. **1610** HOLLAND *Camden's Brit.* I. 109 From hence it is, that the *shoot-grifts of iniquitie.. sprout and put forth in our soile. **1909** *Contemp. Rev.* Apr. 446 Analogous to the case of the *shoot-producing plant is that of certain ascidians. **1731** MEDLEY *Kolben's Cape Good Hope* II. 163 The Eye-Serpent .. is likewise call'd the Dart- or *Shoot-Serpent, on Account of her darting her self very swiftly either at or from an Enemy. **1906** *5th Rep. Carnegie Trust Scot.* 18 William Macrae..—Correlation of *shoot-structure and root-structure in plants with relation to their environmental conditions. **1844** G. DODD *Textile Manuf.* vi. 203 A *shoot-thread is thrown over the pile threads, and also over one-half of the warp-threads. **1666** J. DAVIES tr. *Rochefort's Caribby Isles* 191 It is called by some *Shoot-Tobacco, or Sucker-Tobacco, or Tobacco of the second cutting or growth. **1831** in Mrs. Bray *Descr. Tamar & Tavy* (1836) I. vii. 119 It is now used.. as a *shoot-trough, in which they wash potatoes, &c. **1736** *Act 9 Geo. II*, c. 37 §7 The Wharp and *Shoot Yarn.

†**shoot**, *sb.*[2] *Naut. Obs.* Also 5 shutt, 6 shute, shoutt. [a. (M)LG. *schôte* or (M)Du. *schoot* (see SHEET *sb.*[1], etym. note), whence WFris. *skoat*, G. *schote*, Sw. *skot*, also AF. *escote* (whence 14th c. Eng. SCOTE *sb.*[1]), MF. *ecoucte* (mod.F. *écoute*, dial. *escôte*), †*scot(t)e* (Cotgr.), It. *scotta*, Sp., Pg. *escota.*] = SHEET *sb.*[2]

**1495** *Naval Acc. Hen. VII* (1896) 188 Mayne shuttes olde and ffeble.. ij. **1514** in Oppenheim *Admin. Royal Navy* (1896) I. 375 Shutes with iiij shevers of Brasse. **1531** in J. Strutt *Mann. & Cust. Eng.* (1776) III. 53 A bonnet haulf worren, with shoutts, tacks, and bollyngs;.. two top sayll shouts;.. foer sayll shoutts. **1582** LICHEFIELD tr. *Castanheda's Conq. E. Ind.* I. xxviii. 71 Other belying the shootes both great and small. **1633** T. JAMES *Voy.* 30 We ouer-looked our Tacks and Shoots, with other Riggings of stresse.

**shoot**, *sb.*[3] Forms: 6, (8–9) shewt, 8 shut, 9 shoote, shute, 9– shoot. [app. a special use of SHOOT *sb.*[1]] A species of colic or diarrhœa in cattle.

**1587** MASCALL *Bk. Cattell* I. (1596) 44 To helpe the shewt of bloud in cattell. The shewt of bloud commonly is, to those beastes which haue bin euil kept. **1725** *Bradley's Fam. Dict.*, Shewt of Blood. *c* **1800** J. CUNDALL *Sch. Arts* 34 For Shut, or Flux in Calves. *Ibid.* 35 For a gut foundered, or Shut in Cows. **1834** YOUATT *Cattle* 356 A disease of this character [*i.e.* of inflammatory fever], but known by a number of strange yet not inexpressive terms, is occasionally prevalent, and exceedingly fatal among cattle in every district. It is termed black-quarter, quarter evil, joint murrain, blood-striking, shewt of blood, &c. **1839** *Compl. Grazier* (ed. 7) VI. ii. 309 The Shoote or Dysentery in calves. **1886** *Cheshire Gloss.*, *Shute*,.. diarrhœa in cattle.

**shoot** (ʃuːt), *v.* Pa. t. and pa. pple. shot (ʃɒt). Forms: Present-stem. *α.* 1 scéote, 2–3 sceote, 3 sceate, 3–4 scheote, 3–5 schete, shete, 3 ssete, 4 sscete, 5 scheete, 4–5 sheete. *β.* 4–6 schote, shote, 4 schut(e, 4–6 schut, 5 schwt (*Sc.*), shutte, 6 shutt, 6–7 shut, 6–8 shute, 4 schout, 6–7 shoute, 6 *Sc.* schuit(e, shuit, schoit, 6–7 shoote. *γ.* [1–3 scotie, 3 scote,] 3–6 schott, 4 schot, 6 shot. *3rd sing. pres.* (contracted forms) 1 scíet, scíat, scȳt(t, 3 scheot, 4 schut, schit, 4–5 schet. *Pa. t. α. sing.* 1 scéat, scǽt, scét, 3 sceat, scæt, scheat, sset, set, 3–5 schet, 4–5 scheet, 4 ssat, 5 shate; *plur.* 1–2 scuton, 1 sceoton, 3 scuten, soten, 3–4 schoten, 3–5 shoten, 4–5 shotten, 4 schotten, 5 shotyn, shottyn, -on. *β.* 4– 6 shotte, 4–5 schott, 5 schoote, shote, 7 shotted, 6 (9 *rare*) shooted, 4–6 schot, 4– shot. *Pa. pple. α.* 1 (ȝe)scoten, 3 (i-)scote(n, (hi-sote, i-scote, i-ssote), 3–4 i-schote, y-schote, 4 (y-)schoten, 4–5 (y-)shoten, -in, -on, 5 schottyn, 6–9 shotten, 7 shoote, 5 y-schott(e, y-schot, 4– shot. *β.* 5 *rare* schett. [A Com. Teut. strong verb: OE. *scéotan* (*scéat*, *scuton*, *scoten*) corresponds to OFris. *skiata* (WFris. *sjitte*, EFris. *sjôt*, *schjôte*, NFris. *sjit*, *skjit*, etc.), OS. (Gallée), OLowFrankish *skietan* (LG., Du. *schieten*), OHG. *sciozzan* (MHG. *schiezen*, mod.G. *schiessen*), ON. *skjóta* (Sw. *skjuta*, Da. *skyde*), f. OTeut. **skeut-*: *skaut-*: *skut-*, for other derivatives of which see SHEET *sb.*[1] and *sb.*[2], SHOT *sb.*, SHUT *v.* The affinities outside Teut. are doubtful.

The form-history in Eng. is to some extent parallel with that of CHOOSE *v.*, the only other surviving verb which has the series *éo*, *ǽ* (*éa*), *u*, *o* preceded by a palatal consonant.

In the present-stem, the forms *shete*, *sheete*, etc., directly representing the OE. *scéot-*, became obsolete in the 15th c. (cf. *chese*, which survived into the 16th c.). The spelling *s(c)hote*, which, like the corresponding *chose*, occurs first in the 14th c., is phonetically ambiguous, and possibly represents two distinct formations: (1) ME. *shōte* with close *o*, the antecedent of the mod. *shoot*, and prob. descending from an OE. pronunciation with altered diphthongal stress, *sceōt-*, *scᵉōt-*; and (2) ME. *shǭte* with open *o* (the mod.Eng. form of which, if it had survived, would have been **shote* or **shoat*), descending from OE. *scotian* to shoot (chiefly, with arrows), a weak verb f. the ablaut-form *scot-* of the root (cf. *scot* SHOT *sb.*, *scota* shooter, archer). The form *s(c)hute*, prob. representing a pronunciation (ʃjuːt) or (ʃiwt), earlier perhaps (ʃuːt), is in chronology parallel with *chuse*; the vowel was probably in some dialects the regular phonetic descendant of OE. *ēo* or *eō* when preceded by (ʃ). It is noteworthy that Ben Jonson (*Gram.* xviii) says that to pronounce *chewse*, *shewt*, 'is Scottish-like'.

The OE. pa. t. *scéat* is normally represented by the 15th c. form *scheet*; the contemporary forms *schet*, *shate* (14th c. *ssat*) perh. had the vowel-shortening which is common before a final dental. The modern form *shot* is of uncertain and probably mixed origin. It may partly represent the 14th c. weak form *schotte*, which itself admits of a twofold explanation, as it may have been evolved from the originally strong pl. *schotten* (repr. OE. *scuton*), or it may descend from OE. *scotode*, pa. t. of *scotian*. The ME. *schōt* (spelt *schote* in the 15th c.), with which cf. *chose*, pa. t. of *choose*, may descend from OE. *sceāt*, and by vowel-shortening may be one of the sources of the modern form. Further, the influence of the pa. pple. may, as in many other vbs., have affected the form of the pa. t.

The pa. pple. *shotten* normally represents OE. *scoten* (for the short vowel cf. *gotten*); *shot* is prob. a shortening of this, though it may also be partly a weak form as in the pa. t. Rare weak forms are *schett* (15th c.) from pres.-stem *schete*, and *shooted* (16th c.).]

**I.** To go swiftly and suddenly.

**1. a.** *intr.* Of an inanimate thing (or of a living being moving involuntarily): To go or pass with a sudden swift movement through space; to rush, be precipitated; to fly as an arrow from a bow. Also with adv. expressing direction of movement, as *up*, *down*, *forward*, etc.

*a* **1000** *Ælfred's Blooms* in *Shrine* (1864) 201 þonne þa wolcnan sceotað betweon hyre [the sun] & þe. *c* **1000** ÆLFRIC *Deut.* ix. 21 On ðа burnan ðe of ðam munt scytt [Vulg. *qui de monte descendit*]. *a* **1225** *Juliana* 71 [The boiling pitch] smat up aȝein þeo þe iȝarket hit hefden & for schaldede of ham as hit up scheat. *c* **1290** *St. Michael* 529 in *S. Eng. Leg.* 314 Liȝtingue.. scheot þoruȝ þe cloude. *c* **1305** *Pilate* 255 in *E.E.P.* (1862) 118 And as an arewe schet of a bwe þat bodie [*i.e.* of Pilate] schet þerinne. þe roche schet togadere anon þo þat bodie was wiþ-inne. *c* **1330** *Arth. & Merl.* 9159 Also þicke þe arwe schoten, In sonne bem so doþ þe moten. **1338** R. BRUNNE *Chron.* (1725) 170 þe galeie þer þorght [*i.e.* through the enemy's ship] schete, &.. þe schip þat was so grete, it dronkled in þe flode. **15..** *Scot. Field* 206 in *Chetham Soc. Misc.* II, The sonne shott up full sone, and shone over the hilles. **1569** T. PRESTON *Cambises* 1166 As I on horse back up did leap, my sword from scabard shot. **1602** MARSTON *Ant. & Mel.* i. Wks. 1856 I. 16 Keen lightning shot Through the black bowels of the quaking ayre. **1632** G. FLETCHER *Christ's Vict.* I. i, And how the rising Morne, That shot from heav'n, did backe to heaven retourne. **1727–46** THOMSON *Summer* 1700 The lambent lightnings shoot Across the sky. **1829** *Chapters Phys. Sci.* xvii. 201 The water will shoot forwards within it. **1848** AYTOUN *Lays Scott. Cavaliers* (1849) 77 Thicker, thicker grew the swarm, And sharper shot the rain. **1860** TYNDALL *Glac.* I. ii. 12 The heavier masses.. shoot forward like descending rockets. **1863** BARING-GOULD *Iceland* 113 The Buthera shoots over a rock in a pretty cascade. **1864** TENNYSON *A Dedication* 4 As the rapid of life Shoots to the fall. **1889** CONAN DOYLE *Micah Clarke* 82 The weary creature stumbled, and the rider came perilously near to shooting over its head. **1899** *Allbutt's Syst. Med.* VI. 244 The blood at once shoots in from the arteries with great rapidity and distends the vessels.

**b.** Of a 'star' or meteor: To dart across the sky. Cf. SHOOTING STAR.

*c* **1290** *St. Michael* 517 in *S. Eng. Leg.* 314 Ase ȝe mowe.. I-seo a wonder siȝte, Scheote as þei it a steorre were bi þe lofte an heiȝ. **1590** SHAKS. *Mids. N.* II. i. 153 Certaine starres shot madly from their Spheares, To heare the Sea maids musicke. **1609** B. JONSON *Masq. Queens* Wks. 1616 I. 954 Neuer a starre yet shot? **1630** DEKKER *2nd Pt. Hon. Wh.* II. i, A Starre may shoote, not fall. **1712** POPE *Rape of Lock* II. 82 The stars that shoot athwart the night. **1810** SOUTHEY *Kehama* XII. vii, Gone like.. A star that shoots and falls, and then is seen no more.

**c.** Of light, etc.: To be emitted in rays, to dart. Also with advs., as *out*, *up*. Of a glance: To dart.

**1693** DRYDEN *Juvenal* Ded. (1726) p. v, I was as soon sensible as any Man of that Light, when it was but just shooting out, and beginning to travel upwards to the Meridian. **1810** SCOTT *Lady of L.* IV. xviii, There shot no glance from Ellen's eye To give her steadfast speech the lie. **1825** SCOTT *Talism.* xxii, When the very first level ray shot glimmering in dew along the surface of the desert. **1825** —— *Betrothed* xvi, A gleam of anger shot along his features. **1845** GOSSE *Ocean* iv. (1849) 175 Not a cloud tempers the fierce burning rays of the sun, which shoot directly on our heads. **1853** KANE *Grinnell Exp.* xv. (1856) 111 From these, acicular rays shoot out in every direction. **1860** TYNDALL *Glac.* I. xx. 137 [The sun's] rays,.. shot more and more deeply into the valley. **1908** R. BAGOT *A. Cuthbert* iii. 27 From the north-eastern horizon broad streams of light were shooting up into the centre of the heavens.

**d.** *fig.* Of thoughts, etc.: To pass suddenly *into*, *across*, etc. a person's mind.

**1542** UDALL *Erasm. Apoph.* 307 He could none other but folowe every soodain guerie or pangue that shotte in his braine. **1791** MRS. RADCLIFFE *Rom. Forest* v, A thousand apprehensions shot athwart her busy thought. **1826** SCOTT *Woodst.* xvii, It shot.. across my mind, that [etc.] **1832** L. HUNT *Sir R. Esher* (1850) 400 It shot across me.. that I was doing the very thing I described him as wishing not to be done. **1842** LOVER *Handy Andy* xxxvii, 'Am I to see nothing but the evidences of death's doing this night?' was the mental question which shot through Edward's over-wrought brain. **1870** E. PEACOCK *Ralf Skirl.* II. 236 A ray of light had shot into his mind.

†**e.** Of fluids, tears, blood, etc.: To issue suddenly, stream out. *Obs.*

*c* **1470** HENRY *Wallace* III. 156 The Scottis.. With suerdis schar throuch habergeons full gude, Vpon the flouris schot [*ed.* 1570 schot out] the schonkan blude, Fra hors and men throw harnes burnyst beyne. *c* **1470** *Gol. & Gaw.* 639 Schire teris schot fra schalkis. *Ibid.* 690 Fra schalkis schot schire blude our scheildis so schene.

**f.** Of a person's feet: To slip suddenly. Now only with phrase or adv.

*c* **1430** *Syr Tryam.* 1547 Hys fote schett and he felle downe. **1889** GRETTON *Memory's Harkback* 153 At a specially slippery place all my mare's feet shot from under her.

**g.** Of a wall, cliff, etc.: To fall precipitately.

**1589** IVE *Pract. Fortif.* 21 But the discommoditie a wall receiueth of that so greate scarpe, is, that oft times through the great waight of the top, it looseth it foote and shooteth. **1754** T. GARDNER *Hist. Dunwich* 93 The Serges playing against the Foot, easily undermines the Cliff, which shoots in abundance.

**h.** *Naut.* Of ballast: = SHIFT *v.* 21 c.

**1678** PHILLIPS (ed. 4) s.v., The ballast is said to shoot, when it runs from one side of the Ship to the other. **1711** *Milit. & Sea Dict.* (ed. 4), The Ballast shoots: That is, runs over from one Side to the other; for which Reason all kind of Grain is dangerous Lading, as being apt to shoot. **1867** SMYTH *Sailor's Word-bk.* s.v., The ballast shoots on one side.

**i.** Of a ball: To move with accelerated speed after its first impingement; esp. in *Cricket.* Of a bowled ball: To move rapidly close to the ground after pitching.

**1816** W. LAMBERT *Instructions & Rules of Cricket* 29 When a ball is pitched short of its usual and proper length ..it may cut or shoot on the ground. **1833** NYREN *Yng. Cricketer's Tutor* 29 When you see the ball shoot, play the bat back as near to the wicket as possible. **1851** LILLYWHITE *Guide Cricketers* 15 Try every manœuvre to make the ball twist and shoot after it touches the ground. **1873** BENNETT & CAVENDISH *Billiards* 371 The effect of which ['side'] is to make it shoot.. as soon as it touches the cushion. **1888** A. G. STEEL *Cricket* (Badm. Libr.) 184 The ball which, after the pitch, never rises, but shoots along the surface of the ground ..is commonly called a 'shooter'. **1901** R. H. LYTTELTON *Cricket & Golf* 31 A ball pitching on that spot would sometimes shoot, sometimes hang.

**j.** ***to shoot on***: in immaterial sense, to make rapid progress.

**1871** GREEN *Lett.* (1901) 281 My physical strength has shot on wonderfully.

**2. a.** Of a person or living thing: To pass swiftly and suddenly from one place to another; to precipatate oneself, rush, dart. Also with advs., esp. *off*, *out*.

*c* **1000** *Ags. Gosp.* John xxi. 7 Petrus..scet [Vulg. *misit se*] innan sæ. **1297** R. GLOUC. (Rolls) 7455 His folc quicliche to þe bataile sscet [*v.rr.* schet, schette]. **13..** *Coer de L.* 7025 Kyng Richard..gan to crye: 'Turne arere Every man with his banere!' And many thousand before hym schete, With swerdes and with launses grete. **1375** BARBOUR *Bruce* IX. 387 Arayit weill in all his geir, [he] Schot in the dik. *Ibid.* XI. 596 For sum vald schut out of thar rout. *c* **1380** *Sir Ferumb.* 3962 Wyþ is riȝt hond þan blessede he hym, And þoȝ þe ryuere were styf & grym, Wyþ boþe hors in a schet. *a* **1400** *Sir Beues* (Sutherl. MS.) 2388 Iosian into þe caue gan shete. *c* **1400** *Destr. Troy* 5933 He..Shot thurgh the sheltrons, shent of þe pepull. **14..** *Sir Beues* (Camb. MS.) 1811 Beues smot is hors, þat he can shete In to þe se. *c* **1430** *Syr Gener.* (Roxb.) 4598 Into the thikkest anoon he shet Ful redilie with his swerd draw To make wey for his felow. *c* **1470** HENRY *Wallace* IV. 552 Rycht stark he was, and in to souir ger, Bauldly he schott amang thai men of wer. **1615** MARKHAM *Pleas. Princ.* ii. (1635) 11 This Corke..will float till the hooke be fastned, and that the Fish beginneth to shut away with the bayte. **1666** DRYDEN *Ann. Mirab.* cviii, She [the eagle] stops, and listens, and shoots forth again. **1712** STEELE *Spect.* No. 498 ¶3 A lively young fellow in a fustian jacket shot by me. **1748** RICHARDSON *Clarissa* VI. 258 She shot to the stairs-head to receive him. **1823** SCOTT *Quentin D.* xx, The Scot shot back to the castle with the speed of the wind. **1828** W. CARR *Dial. Craven* (ed. 2) II. 121 *To shoot off*, to go off precipitately. **1840** DICKENS *Old C. Shop* xlv, Animated with a ray of hope, the child shot on before her grandfather. **1853** WHYTE MELVILLE *Digby Grand* xvi, Captain Black judiciously lets him out for a few strides, and shoots forward some five or six lengths in front of his companions. **1871** L. STEPHEN *Playgr. Eur.* v. (1894) 114 We shot out of the long tunnel..and descended into the valley. **1877** MARY M. GRANT *Sun-Maid* ii, Finally they shot round a sharp corner. **1930** J. DEVANNY *Bushman Burke* xii. 72 Whatja shoot off for? Had great time after you left. **1946** [see COAST *sb.* 4 c].

†**b.** To rush *on* or *upon* (with intent to attack or devour). *Obs.*

*a* **1300** *Havelok* 1838 þey drowen ut swerdes, ful god won, And shoten on him, so don on bere Dogges, þat wolden him to-tere. *Ibid.* 2431 The Kinges men hwan he þat sawe, Scuten on hem, heye and lowe, And euerilk fot of hem slowe. *c* **1330** *Arth. & Merl.* 3868 þer miȝt men se þe baners roten, þe stedes forþ wel ȝern schoten. **1338** R. BRUNNE *Chron.* (1725) 94 Opon þe rode he schete. **1375** BARBOUR *Bruce* VII. 390 He suld schute on hym sodanly.

**c.** To slide *down* a slope at full speed.

**1738** GRAY *Tasso* 19 Swift shoots the Village-maid in rustic play..adown the shining way. **1860** TYNDALL *Glac.* I. xxvii. 216 Once, while shooting down a slope, he incautiously allowed a foot to get entangled.

**d.** *colloq.* To depart, go away. Freq. *int.*

**1897** *Leeds Mercury* 19 June Suppl., Nah, then, shooit, or ah'll mak yo! **1970** G. F. NEWMAN *Sir, You Bastard* viii. 230 I'll shoot then, if it's all right. Nothing else? **1974** H. L. FOSTER *Ribbin', Jivin', & Playin' Dozens* v. 203 Two of them said, 'Shoot.' They all turned and walked away.

**e.** ***to shoot through***: to escape, abscond; to depart, leave. *Austral.* and *N.Z. slang*. Cf. GO *v.* 91 d.

**1947** *Pix* 20 Sept. 15 *Shoot through*, escape, abscond. **1951** S. MACKENZIE *Dead Men Rising* 37 I'm shooting through—my woman's sick and I've waited longer than I should have. **1965** M. SHADBOLT *Among Cinders* xviii. 168 'Well,' I said... 'I guess I'd better be shooting through. Thanks for the sausage.' **1978** *Telegraph* (Brisbane) 11 Jan. 28/1 I've been advised to shoot through and forget about the debts.

**3. a.** Of a vessel (hence of its commander or crew): To move swiftly in a certain direction. ***to shoot to***: to 'shoot' into the desired position. (Cf. sense 12 b.)

*c* **1400** *Destr. Troy* 6033 Thaire shippis in sheltrons shotton to lond. **1579** T. STEVENS in Hakluyt *Voy.* (1589) 161 Our Pilot..thinking himselfe to haue wind at will, shot so nigh the land, that [etc.]. **1670** NARBOROUGH *Jrnl.* in *Acc. Sev. Late Voy.* I. 23, I concluded we had shot past Port Desier Harbour in the Fog. **1716** GAY *Trivia* II. 167 She downward glides, Lights in Fleet-ditch, and shoots beneath the tides. **1815** SCOTT *Guy M.* v, She fired three guns as a salute..and then shot away rapidly before the wind. **1849** M. ARNOLD *Mod. Sappho* 34 'Tis..the boat, shooting round by the trees! **1850** SCORESBY *Cheever's Whalem. Adv.* xii. (1859) 178 We shot past him like a meteor. **1856** MISS WARNER *Hills Shatemuc* viii, Again clearing the rocks the little boat..shot off down the stream. **1887** GOODE, etc. *Fish. Industr. U.S.* IV. 132 When speaking another vessel it is customary to pass by her stern and shoot to alongside of her.

**b.** ***to shoot ahead***: of a vessel, to increase speed suddenly, so as to pass accompanying or competing vessels; hence *fig.* Also, to be carried forward by momentum.

**1669** STURMY *Mariner's Mag.* I. ii. 20 Brace too the Fore-top-sail, that we may not shoot ahead. **1840** DICKENS *Sk. Yng. Couples* 29 We were suffered to shoot a-head, while the second boat followed ingloriously in our wake. **1867** SMYTH *Sailor's Word-bk.* s.v., A ship shoots ahead in stays.

**4. a.** *trans.* With obj. denoting what is passed through, over, or under by 'shooting': (*a*) To pass quickly under (a bridge) in a boat; (*b*) to descend (a rapid or cataract) swiftly in a boat or other vessel; so ***to shoot a river***; (*c*) to 'coast' down (a hill) in cycling; (*d*) *nonce-use*, to pass swiftly over (a distance).

(*a*) **1570** FOXE *A. & M.* (ed. 2) 2290/1 They could not shoote the Bridge. **1617** MORYSON *Itin.* I. 74 Having shot two or three small bridges..we came to the Village Lizzafusina. **1679** ALSOP *Melius Inq.* II. i. 179 To withdraw from Apparent Duty for fear of uncertain Danger is but like his, that would not shoot the Bridge, because it might fall on's Head. **1729** FIELDING *Author's Farce* III, When one day, among other frolics, our ship's-crew shooting the bridge, the boat overset. **1835** MARRYAT *J. Faithful* vi, In half an hour I had shot Putney Bridge. **1877** FOLEY *Rec. Eng. Province S.J.* I. 496 *note*, This was the old London Bridge... It was always a dangerous thing to 'shoot' the arches when it was running.

*transf.* **1706** E. WARD *Hud. Rediv.* I. IV. 3, I shot the Porch that bears the Name of good king Lud.

(*b*) **1613** R. HARCOURT *Voy. Guiana* 49 Wee turned downe the riuer, shooting the ouerfalles with more celerity then when wee came vp. **1686** GOAD *Celest. Bodies* II. i. 141 The Boat..sometimes shoots the Cataract. **1703** *La Hontan's Voy. N. Amer.* I. 143 Another River..has six or seven Water-falls that we commonly shoot. **1776** C. CARROLL in Kate Rowland *Life* (1898) I. 393 All our batteaux which shoot the rapids and go down the Sorel to Chamblay. **1829** SOUTHEY *Sir T. More* II. 18 It must have been a grand sight to have seen them shoot the falls! **1861** HUGHES *Tom Brown at Oxf.* ii, There were probably not three men..who would have dared to shoot the lasher in a skiff in its then state. **1872** SCHELE DE VERE *Americanisms* 104 The..voyageurs..prefer ..shooting a river, that is to say, dashing over the rapids in the swift current. **1877** BLACK *Green Past.* xxxiv, You would have fancied that Bell had..spent her life in shooting rapids.

*fig.* **1842** DE QUINCEY *Cicero* Wks. 1858 VII. 226 A man might shoot a whole series of divorces, still refunding the last dowry, but still replacing it with a better.

(*c*) **1878** *Athletic World* 3 May 57/2 Mr. Godlee..having ..taken a header while shooting a hill with legs over the handles [of his cycle].

(*d*) **1898** MEREDITH *Odes Fr. Hist.* 26 Who..Spurred a blood-mare immeasurably fleet To shoot the transient leagues in a passing wink.

**b.** *Naut.* To succeed in sailing through (a dangerous strait, passage, gulf, etc.). Hence ***to shoot the gulf*** (fig.): proverbially for any daring enterprise. (See GULF *sb.* 2 c.)

The fig. phrase appears to have originally had reference to sense 1 of GULF *sb.*, but prob. was often associated rather with sense 2 or 4.

**1622** R. HAWKINS *Voy. S. Sea* xli. 95 Sir Francis Drake told me, that having shott the Straites, a storme tooke him first at North-west. **1628** GAULE *Pract. Theories* (1629) 319 So neither will I feare to shoot that great Gulfe. *c* **1645** [see GULF *sb.* 2 c]. **1682** WHELER *Journ. Greece* I. 28 We stood out to Sea, that we might shoot the Gulph of Londrin. **1687** A. LOVELL tr. *Thevenot's Trav.* II. 173 Ships sometimes shoot that passage. **1751** R. PALTOCK *P. Wilkins* xi. (1884) I. 107, I never had one hour's rest together since I shot the gulf till this. **1773** *Cook's 1st Voy.* III. v. in Hawkesw. *Voy.* III. 606 While we were shooting this gulph, our soundings were from thirty to seven fathom.

†**c.** ***to shoot the pit***: of a fighting cock, to rush out of the cockpit from cowardice. Often *fig.* *Obs.*

**1675** [see PIT *sb.*[1] 5]. **1681** T. FLATMAN *Heraclitus Ridens* No. 31 (1713) I. 204 Two or three more such stroaks will make them shoot the Pit. *a* **1734** NORTH *Exam.* II. v. ¶19 (1740) 327 Which made the whole Party shoot the Pit and retire, as not caring to be pointed at with ill-favoured Reflections.

**d.** ***to shoot the moon***: to remove household goods by night in order to avoid seizure for rent. (Cf. the older phrase in SHOVE *v.*[1] 10 c.)

**1836** *Comic Almanack* Sept. (1870) 63 And lack-a-day! here's Quarter Day; It always comes too soon; So we by night must take our flight, For we must shoot the moon! **1844** ALB. SMITH *Mr. Ledbury* iii, Gradually moving all his things away, and shooting the moon to a friend's lodging. **1882** BESANT *All Sorts* iv, I let his houses... I warned him when shooting of moons seemed likely.

**e.** *Racing.* To dash past (a competitor). ***to be shot on the post***: see quot. 1897.

**1868** *Field* 11 July 29/2 Cannon..just managed, after a fine specimen of riding between the two, to shoot Fordham by a head. **1897** *Encycl. Sport* I. 62/1 (Athletics) A man is said to be 'shot on the post' when a competitor just dashes by him as he eases for the finish, or falls from exhaustion.

**f.** U.S. ***to shoot the chute***(*s*: = *to chute the chute*(*s* s.v. CHUTE *v.* 1. Also ***shoot-the-chute*** used as *sb.*

**1895** *N.Y. Dramatic News* 30 Nov. 17/4 Shooting the Chutes, the latest craze that has struck the town, is.. drawing large crowds. **1920** R. FROST *Let.* 23 July (1964) 116 This man's island..will be full of divers and entertainment dives such as movies, con games, and shoot-the-chutes. **1946** E. O'NEILL *Iceman Cometh* III. 165 We're goin' to beat it down to Coney Island and shoot the chutes. **1977** *Time* 4 July 26/2 They are the not-so-spiritual descendants..of the Parisians who in 1817 rode the original shoot-the-chute.

**5. a.** *intr.* Of a pain: To pass in a sudden paroxysm along the nerves; to dart. Hence of a part of the body, a wound, etc.: To have darting pains.

*a* **1000** [see SHOOTING *ppl. a.* 3]. **1602** MARSTON *Antonio's Rev.* IV. i, I should want sense to feele The stings of anguish shoot through every vaine. **1633** G. HERBERT *Temple, Misery* viii, These preachers make His head to shoot and ake. **1667** DRYDEN & DAVENANT *Tempest* V. ii, Alas! I feel the cold air come to me; My wound shoots worse than ever. **1718** POPE *Iliad* XVI. 638 Pierc'd with Pain, That thrills my Arm and shoots thro' ev'ry Vein. **1818-20** E. THOMPSON *Nosologia* (ed. 3) 198 Pain in the region of the kidnies, often shooting along the course of the ureter. **1875** W. S. GILBERT *Tom Cobb* II, *O'Fi.* Ye wouldn't have a major-gineral with corns that couldn't shoot? **1895** R. W. CHAMBERS *King in Yellow* (1909) 148 Then again something struck my ankle, and a sharp pain shot through me. **1899** *Allbutt's Syst. Med.* VI. 742 The pain may dart and shoot.

**b.** *fig.*

**1611** *2nd Maiden's Trag.* (Malone Soc.) 860 His very name shootes like a feaver throughe me. **1786** BURNS *Vision* II. xvi, When youthful Love, warm-blushing, strong, Keen-shivering shot thy nerves along. **1848** DICKENS *Dombey* l, A pang of hopeless love visibly shooting through him, and flashing out in his face. **1869** LECKY *Europ. Mor.* I. iii. 492 One brief spasm [of persecution] indeed..shot through the long afflicted Church of Asia Minor. **1895** R. W. CHAMBERS *King in Yellow* (1909) 238 A pang of homesickness shot through him.

**6. a.** Of a plant, bud, etc.: To emerge from the soil (also with *up*) or from the stem, etc.; to sprout, grow.

**1483** *Cath. Angl.* 338/2 To Schute as corne dose [*v.r.* Schott os corne dose], *spicare*. **1523-34** FITZHERB. *Husb.* §21 Let hym beware, that he trede not to moche vppon the corne, and specyallye after it is shotte. **1583** MELBANCKE *Philotimus* F ij b, The greene blade that shooteth too earely is soone bitt with a black frost. **1695** J. EDWARDS *Perfect. Script.* 60 Others imagin'd they shooted out of trees. **1678** MOXON *Mech. Exerc.* vi. 108 The Bough or Branch that shoots out of the Trunk of a Tree. **1732** POPE *Ess. Man* I. 7 A Wild, where weeds and flow'rs promiscuous shoot. **1779** *Mirror* No. 61 There they [plants] have room to shoot out at will. **1830** *Kyle Farm Rep.* 39 in *Libr. Usef. Knowl., Husb.* III, Rib grass..puts out its foliage very early.., and as it is always shot before they can be admitted to pasture, it is rather injurious. **1834** YOUATT *Cattle* 566 Fungus shooted up. **1847** W. C. L. MARTIN *Ox* 40/2 When the spring grass is beginning to shoot luxuriantly. **1866** SHUCKARD *Brit. Bees* 223 A thick and prodigious quantity of the common mustard plant shot up.

**b.** *fig.*

**1596** SPENSER *F.Q.* IV. xi. 26 That faire City, wherein make abode So many learned impes, that shoote abrode, And with their braunches spred all Britany. **1663** PATRICK *Parab. Pilgr.* xii. (1687) 74 All these grow upon this single root, or rather are but Love shooting forth in divers shapes. **1728-46** THOMSON *Spring* 1149 Delightful task! to rear the tender thought, To teach the young idea how to shoot. **1751** JOHNSON *Rambler* No. 166 ¶12 When we find worth faintly shooting in the shades of obscurity, we may let in light and sunshine upon it. **1768** TUCKER *Lt. Nat.* (1834) II. 281 Charity, though shooting most vigorously from rational self-love, yet, when perfectly formed, has no tincture remaining of the parent root. **1825** LAMB *Elia* Ser. II. *Superann. Man* (end), They tell me, a certain *cum dignitate* air, which has been buried so long with my other good parts, has begun to shoot forth in my person.

**c.** Of parts of animal bodies, teeth, hair, morbid growths.

**1607** TOPSELL *Four-f. Beasts* 403 The rift being closed in the top, draw him [the horse] betwixt the haire and the hooue with a hot yron ouerthwart that place, to the intent that the hooue may shoote al whole downeward. **1739** S. SHARP *Oper. Surg.* Introd. 31 When the Surface of the Ulcer begins to yield thick Matter, and little Granulations of red Flesh shoot up. **1753** J. BARTLET *Gentl. Farriery* xxv. 226 This last, applied early, will prevent a fungus, or proud flesh, from shooting out. **1796** MORSE *Amer. Geog.* I. 206 Sea Cow tusks, which shoot from the upper jaw. **1799** UNDERWOOD *Dis. Childhood* (ed. 4) I. 189 From..the very first shooting of the teeth within the jaw. **1826** S. COOPER *First Lines Surg.* (ed. 5) 326 The hairs fall off, and when they grow again, they shoot in a wrong direction.

**7. a.** To put forth buds or shoots, as a plant; to germinate. †Formerly often with advs., *forth*, *out* (const. *with*, *into*); also *transf.* of an animal, to put out limbs.

*c* **1560** A. SCOTT *Poems* (S.T.S.) xxxv. 11 He sall haiff brute, as tre on rute Endlang the rever plantit; To burge and schute, and sall gif frutt In tyme, as God hes grantit. **1607** WALKINGTON *Opt. Glass* 10 They neither shotte out right, nor hardly have any blowne blossoms. **1611** BIBLE *Luke* xxi. 30 Behold the figge tree, and all the trees, Whan they now shoot foorth, [etc.]. **1627** HAKEWILL *Apol.* (1630) 303 When it sprang up *Proserpina*, *Nodolus* when it shut into a blade. **1697** DRYDEN *Virg. Georg.* IV. 439 Shooting out with Legs, and imp'd with Wings, The Grubs proceed to Bees with pointed Stings. **1710** W. KING *Heathen Gods* xiii. (1722) 53 The Cypress Tree..when cut down, never shoots again. **1713** ADDISON *Guardian* No. 156 ¶6 The Corn that is laid up by Ants would shoot under Ground, if those Insects did not take care to prevent it. **1756-7** tr. *Keysler's Trav.* (1760) IV. 447 It is the property both of the walnut and olive-tree, that after a severe frost they shoot out with fresh vigour. **1773** *Phil. Trans.* LXIII. 398 As I could not directly contrive a total section of this large species [of Sea-Anemone], I tried it upon the young ones; and these shooted out again after the operation. **1786** ABERCROMBIE *Gard. Assist.* 212 Always cut close, not leaving any stump to shoot again. *c* **1792** *Encycl. Brit.* (ed. 3) IX. 744/1 Plants stript of any of their leaves, cannot shoot vigorously. **1877** JEFFERIES *Gamekeeper at H.* vi. (1890) 145 For although furze and fern soon shoot again, yet animal life is not so quickly repaired. **1908** [MISS E. FOWLER] *Betw. Trent & Ancholme* 362 They shoot, and bud, and their tendrils and branches reach far around.

**b.** *transf.*

**1711** ADDISON *Spect.* No. 16 ¶2 The young People of both Sexes are so wonderfully apt to shoot out into long Swords, sweeping Trains, bushy Head-dresses. **1791** H. WALPOLE *Let. to Miss Mary Berry* 8 June, Bath shoots out into new crescents, circuses, squares every year.

**8. a.** To increase rapidly in growth (sometimes, with inclusion of sense 6, to sprout and grow rapidly); to advance to maturity. Now only with *up* or equivalent adv. or phrase: To grow quickly tall, 'spring up' to a height (said of plants, young persons, buildings, etc.; also of immaterial things). Also of prices, sales, etc.: to rise sharply.

**1538** AUDLEY in *Lett. Supp. Monast.* (Camden) 246 He [the infant prince] shotyth owt in length. **1577** GRANGE *Golden Aphrod.* L iij, Intermingled with all kinde of sweete and fragrant floures, the growth whereof shotte vp in heigth aboue the lower grasse..two foote. **1607** CHAPMAN *Bussy d'Ambois* III. i, Great D'Ambois (Fortunes proud mushrome shot vp in a night). **1621** FLETCHER *Wild Goose Chase* I. iii, I am none of those that, when they shoot to ripeness, Do what they can to break the boughs they grew on. **1626** BACON *Sylva* §653 Such Trees..are (commonly) Trees that shoot vp much. **1654** J. SHEFFIELD *Rising Sun* 259 As there is in all dying or departed persons a great shooting in their stature observed; so is there in the soul much more. The least Infant shoots in the instant of Dissolution to that perfect knowledge of God. **1711** ADDISON *Spect.* No. 98 ¶1 About ten Years ago it [ladies' head-dress] shot up to a very great Height. **1721** AMHERST *Terræ Fil.* No. 11 (1754) 51 The sumptuous edifices which of late years have shot up in Oxford. **1750** JOHNSON *Rambler* No. 55 ¶11 Having, she said, never seen any body shoot up so much at my age. **1812** *Ann. Reg., Gen. Hist.* 109/2 They ought not to tax Ireland as this country—she was shooting, and, if not oppressed, would come to maturity. **1818** MISS FERRIER *Marriage* II. iii, A perfect dwarf..till she took a shooting... But she'll shoot no more. **1828** SCOTT *F.M. Perth* xxxiii, I have often..seen a raw young fellow, shoot up after his first fight, from a dwarf into a giant-queller. **1861** M. PATTISON *Ess.* (1889) I. 39 Our commercial relations with the Baltic cities..soon shot up into one of our leading national objects. **1862** MISS BRADDON *Lady Audley* xv, Four or five bare and over-grown poplars, that had shot up too rapidly for their strength. **1880** MRS. RIDDELL *Myst. Palace Gard.* ix, She had shot up into a woman all in a minute. **1905** L. WHIBLEY *Companion to Grk. Studies* ii. §2. 70 Tragedy had not yet passed its prime when the old comedy shot up to maturity. **1968** *Listener* 27 June 826/3 The sales of vodka in Moscow shot up by 25 per cent. **1977** *Evening Gaz.* (Middlesbrough) 11 Jan. 1/6 The pound shot up two cents against the dollar.

**b.** conjugated with *to be*. Also in pa. pple., **(*well*) *shot in years*** (rare), advanced in life.

**1530** PALSGR. 705/1 Se howe this corne is shotte up within this senyght. **1549** COVERDALE, etc. *Erasm. Par. Heb.* xi. 24–26 After he was shotte vp towardes mannes state. **1596** SPENSER *F.Q.* v. vi. 19 Well shot in yeares he seem'd. *c* **1610** *Women Saints* 80 This happie branch of that vertuous stemme being shott vp beyond infancie, began to attempt workes of maturitie. **1799** HT. LEE *Canterb. T., Poet's T.* (ed. 2) I. 48 Little Henry was now shot up beyond his years. **1886** BURTON *Arab. Nts.* (abr. ed.) I. 176 The Wazir of Bassorah, a man shot in years.

†**c.** ***to shoot up*** (with complement): To become by sudden growth. *Obs.*

**1692** DRYDEN *Cleomenes* I. i. 4 Let me but live to shadow this young Plant, From Blites and Storms; He'll soon shoot up a Heroe.

**9. a.** Of a solution: To produce crystals. Also said of the crystals. Of a salt: To crystallize from solution or evaporation. [So G. *schiessen*.]

? *a* **1626** MEVEREL in *Bacon's Physiol. Rem.* Baconiana (1679) 126 If the Menstruum be overcharged,..the Metals will shoot into certain Crystals. **1666** BOYLE *Orig. Formes & Qual.* Wks. 1772 III. 54 The exact and curious figures, in which vitriol and other salts are wont to shoot. **1670** W. CLARKE *Nat. Hist. Nitre* 7 Nitre shoots long in Needles, but Salt shoots in tesseras, or squares. *a* **1697** AUBREY *Surrey* (1718) IV. 57 There is also here a Boyling-House, where the Salt-Petre is made, and shoots. **1732** *Hist. Litteraria* IV. 35 This Solution, when rich, shoots into a Vitriol by standing. **1789** A. CRAWFORD in *Med. Commun.* II. 355 A solution of the..salt shoots by evaporation into thin octagonal plates. **1807** T. THOMSON *Chem.* (ed. 3) II. 272 Crystals again shoot as the solution cools.

**b.** *trans.* To form (crystals); of a solution, to deposit in the form of crystals. Also *refl.* and *pass.*, to crystallize; in wider sense, of a substance, to assume some definite form by internal movement.

**1662** MERRETT tr. *Neri's Art of Glass* i. 5 Till you see it thicken, and shoot its salt. **1688** CLAYTON in *Phil. Trans.* XVII. 795 Parts of natural Rock shot in those Figures. **1695** WOODWARD *Nat. Hist. Earth* IV. 172 Tis usual to meet with the very same Metall or Mineral, naturally shot into quite different Figures. **1719** HAUKSBEE *Phys.-Mech. Exper.* (ed. 2) Suppl. 258 The various Forms the new made Ice had shot it self into. **1732** *Hist. Litteraria* IV. 23 It shoots a Tartar by standing. It has a vinous Taste.

**10. a.** *intr.* To project, jut out; to extend in a particular direction. Often with advs., esp. *out*. †Of a road (OE.): To go in a particular direction.

*c* **1000** ÆLFRIC *Gen.* xxiv. 62 Eode Isaac on þam weȝe, þe scytt to þam pytte. **1387** TREVISA *Higden* (Rolls) I. 305 Þe ilond Corsica is cornered wiþ many forlondes schetynge [*Caxton* stretchyng] in to the see. **1584** B. R. tr. *Herodotus* I. 56 b, The partition of the walles made by the intercourse of yᵉ riuer, shootes vppon the bankes on eyther syde. **1607** *B.N.C. Documents* (MS.) Bundle A 3. f. 19, 3 half acres of Errable land..shouting South and North. **1610** HOLLAND *Camden's Brit.* (1637) 183 That Region [Cornwall].. shooteth out farthest into the West. *Ibid.* 542 The shore shutteth forth with a mighty swelling bent into the German Sea. **1679** in J. C. Blomfield *Heyford* (1892) 85 A land by Oxford way side shooting north and south. **1684** T. BURNET *Theory Earth* I. ix. 110 The Promontories and Capes shoot into the Sea. **1688** BUNYAN *Heavenly Footman* (1886) 155 Though the way to heaven be but one, yet there are many crooked lanes and by-paths shoot down upon it, as I may say. **1700** J. BROME *Trav. Eng.* 245 From hence the Shore, after several crooked flexures, shooteth forth into the Sea. **1705** ADDISON *Italy, Tirol* 532 This long Valley of the Tirol lyes enclos'd on all Sides by the Alps, tho' its Dominions shoot out into several Branches that lye among the Breaks and Hollows of the Mountains. **1726** in W. Wing *Ann. Steeple Aston* (1875) 54 And one other land shooting into Oxford way. **1759** in *Q. Jrnl. Economics* (1907) Nov. 79 Where the furlong shoots up the brook to be mownded by the two outside hides. **1815** ELPHINSTONE *Acc. Caubul* (1842) I. 137 The next branch..shoots out from the south-eastern side of Suffaid Coh. **1831** SCOTT *Ct. Robt.* xxviii, Where the private gardens..shot down upon and were bounded by the glassy waters. **1847** W. C. L. MARTIN *Ox* 58/1 The horns..first sweeping outwards and downwards, shot forward at the points.

**b.** With *up* or equivalent phrase: To extend vertically upwards; to tower, 'rise' into the air.

**1648** HEXHAM II. s.v. *Schieten, In de locht Schieten*, To Shoote up into the Aire or Sky. **1726** SWIFT *Gulliver* III. iii, One even regular plate of adamant, shooting up to the height of about two hundred yards. **1757** W. WILKIE *Epigoniad* VII. 213 A promontory..Whose rocky brow..Shoots high into the air. **1810** SCOTT *Lady of L.* I. xi, Many a rocky pyramid, Shooting abruptly from the dell. **1851** MAYNE REID *Scalp Hunters* xxxv, Mountains, whose tops shot heavenward in fantastic forms and groupings. **1871** L. STEPHEN *Playgr. Eur.* iii. (1894) 79 We could see..the sharp pyramid of the Finsteraarhorn shooting upwards. **1878** SMILES *Robt. Dick* i. 3 It shoots up into a tall rocky point.

**II.** To send forth, esp. swiftly or by sudden impulse.

Some of the senses under this head are in modern use often coloured by the specific sense 21.

**11. a.** *trans.* To throw suddenly or with violence. Also with advs., *out*, *down*, etc. *Obs.* exc. as *transf.* from sense 21.

*c* **1075** *O.E. Chron.* (Cott. MS.) an. 1040, He let draȝan up þæne deadan Harald & hine on fen sceotan. *c* **1205** LAY. 5081 He scæt [*c* 1275 caste] his riche sceld feor ut in þene feld. *a* **1300** *Cursor M.* 21043 Þat Imperur wend [John] to mat In a tun was welland hat Fild of oyle he did him schott, But noþer him harmd, hefd ne fott. *a* **1340** HAMPOLE *Ps.* cxxxv. 15 And he shot out pharao and his vertu in the reed see. *c* **1375** *Sc. Leg. Saints* xxvii. (*Machor*) 981 Suddanly þai ware all deide, & schot in till gong stinkand. *c* **1400** *Destr. Troy* 1408 Þe Grekes..Shottyn into shippes all þe shene godis. *c* **1450** METHAM *Wks.* (E.E.T.S.) 37/993 The sperehed lefft in hys brayn, And so schet hym ouer his hors on the pleynne Dede. **1533** BELLENDEN *Livy* v. xxiii. (S.T.S.) II. 225 The gaule be his pride & Insolence schot in his swerde in þe leif of þe ballance. **1600** *Reg. Privy Counc. Scot.* VI. 129 [They] maist dispitfullie expellit and schoit him oute of the said kirkyaird be the schoulderis. **1600** *Gowrie's Conspiracy* C 1 b, He tooke the said Maister Alexander by the shoulders, and shotte him down the staire; who was no sooner shotte out at the doore, but [etc.]. **1700** DRYDEN *Ovid's Met.* I. 930 The liquid Air his moving Pinions wound, And, in the moment, shoot him on the ground. **1835** DICKENS *Sk. Boz, Making a Nt. of it*, [They] found themselves shot with astonishing swiftness into the road [out of the theatre]. **1858** R. S. SURTEES *Ask Mamma* xxvi. 107 A more fractious horse..had finally shot him over his head.

**b.** To empty out (gold, grain, earth, etc.) by overturning or tilting the receptacle; to dump (rubbish); to send (goods, débris, etc.) down an inclined plane or 'shoot'. Also, to discharge the contents of, empty (a sack) by overturning. Often with adv., as *down*, *out*.

*a* **1400** *Sir Perc.* 2114 Percevelle..schott owte alle the golde. *c* **1412** HOCCLEVE *De Reg. Princ.* 4248 What doth þan þis fel man & right prudent, But out þis golde on a tippet hath shotte, That in þe bagges lefte þere no grotte. **1592** GREENE *Conny Catch.* 22 There at the back gate [he] causeth him to vnloade, and, as they say, shoot the coles down. **1604** N. F. *Fruiterers Secrets* 13 Also haue a care, that they be poured or shot downe very gently, laying euery sort by themselues. *Ibid.* 18 Haue a great care also in shooting or pouring them out. **1712** ADDISON *Spect.* No. 511 ¶3 Upon opening the Sack, a little old Woman popped her Head out of it; at which the Adventurer was in so great a Rage, that he was going to shoot her out into the River. **1765** *Museum Rust.* IV. 210 If the farmer has sold, so as to deliver soon, he shoots not the sacks. **1821** *Acc. Peculations Coal Trade* 11 He found the men shooting his coals in their master's warehouse. **1865** DICKENS *Mut. Fr.* I. iv, A tract of suburban Sahara, where..carpets were beat, rubbish was shot,..and dust was heaped by contractors. **1876** J. FERGUSSON *Hist. Ind. Archit.* IV. ii. 338 To chip away 50,000 yards of rock, and shoot it to spoil (to borrow a railway term) down a hill-side. **1885** *Law Times* 16 May LXXIX. 46/2 Bales were shot from the top to the bottom floors by means of zigzag inclined planes. **1892** *Labour Commission* Gloss. *s.v.*, The flour is emptied down the shoot through the floor [of the flour loft]..into the troughs in which the dough is made. This operation is universally termed shooting flour.

*transf.* (*jocular*.) **1860** W. H. RUSSELL *Diary India* I. 135 After a..tedious journey..the train shot us out amid a heap of cinders, and a wooden station at its terminus.

†**c.** To throw or pull *down*, overthrow. *Obs.*

*c* **1375** *Sc. Leg. Saints* xxi. (*Clement*) 254, & quhene he wend scho wod had bene, he schot hyre to þe erde in tene. *c* **1470** HENRY *Wallace* II. 126 Atour the dike thai ȝeid on athir side, Schott doun the wall. **1513** DOUGLAS *Æneis* XII. v. 154 Sum schot doun wyth thar hand The altaris markyt for the sacryfys.

**d.** *refl.* To throw or precipitate oneself; to rush. Also †*fig.* Now *rare*.

**1587** HOLINSHED *Chron.* (ed. 2) III. 1259/2 A monstrous fish or whale of the sea did shoot himselfe on shore. **1641** MILTON *Reform.* II. 73 Hee that flying from degenerate and traditionall corruption, feares to shoot himselfe too far into the meeting imbraces of a Divinely warranted Reformation, had better not have run at all. **1679** A. LOVELL *Indic. Univ.* 28 A Serpent that casts and shoots himself on passengers. **1697** DRYDEN *Virg. Georg.* Ded. ¶2, I have laugh'd sometimes..when I have reflected on those Men, who from time to time have shot themselves into the World. **1700** S. L. tr. *Fryke's Voy. E. Ind.* 316 The Man shoots himself up to fetch breath. **1705** BEVERLEY *Hist. Virginia* II. v. (1722) 133 The poor Fish is no sooner loosed from the Hawk's Talons, but the Eagle shoots himself, with wonderful Swiftness, after it, and catches it in the Air. **1705** ADDISON *Italy, Pesaro* 158 This is the Gulf thro' which Virgil's Alecto shoots her self into Hell. **1889** BADEN-POWELL *Pigsticking* 114 When the pig 'shoots' himself (as only a pig can do) over a mud wall, she follows.

**e.** To throw (rain, or running water) *from*, *off* (the surface); also with *off*, †*down* advs.

**1573** TUSSER *Husb.* (1878) 111 Where houses be reeded.. The iuster ye driue it, the smoother and plaine, more handsome ye make it to shut off the raine. **1650** FULLER *Pisgah* IV. iv. 68 The latter [Badgers-skins] no doubt had the fur upon them, the lubricity of the hair thereof being excellent gutters and spouts to shoot down the rain thereby. **1719** DE FOE *Crusoe* I. (Globe) 136 A great Cap for my Head, with the Hair on the Outside to shoot off the Rain. **1764** *Museum Rust.* III. 334 As it [straw used in thatching] is not bruised by the flail, it shoots off the wet better. **1814** T. HAYNES *Treat. Strawberry*, etc. (ed. 2) 100 Then reduce the embankment..by throwing away the earth, the more readily to shoot off all wet. **1855** KINGSLEY *Westw. Ho!* xxv, 'The Lord has stood by me' panted he, as he shot the water from his ears. **1882** CHRISTY *Joints used by Builders* 76 It is ..important that the pitch should not be so steep as to shoot off heavy rain with too much velocity for the gutters to properly discharge.

†**f.** ***to shoot forth, out, away***: to drive out or away, to banish, expel. (Chiefly *Sc.* and *north.*)

*a* **1300** *Cursor M.* 13658 Wit þis þai scott him als a dog Right vte o þair synagog. **13..** *K. Alis.* 5968 Thou shalt there fynde kynges felouns,..That in Babiloyne made the toure,..That fele mylen in heightte stood, And thorough Goddes wreche shoten away, Into that vile countreye. *c* **1400** MAUNDEV. (Roxb.) vi. 19 He tuke þe citee of Acoun and schotte oute of it all þe Cristen men þat ware þerin. *c* **1400** *Privity of the Passion* in *Hampole's Wks.* (Horstm.) I. 214 And here was it þat þey schot hym forthe so felly & so cruelly and spytte in his face, and garte hym hye so fast. *a* **1500** *Battle of Otterburn* xxxii. in Child *Ballads* III. 297/1 He lyghted dowyn vpon his foote, And schoote hys horsse clene awaye. **1533** BELLENDEN *Livy* II. vi. (S.T.S.) I. 148 He commandit ane large nowmer of bestial to be schot furth on þe nixt day at porte aquillye. *Ibid.* IV. xx. II. 125 Ȝit he wan þe castell at þe first assalt, and schot furth all þame þat war fundin þareintill. **1535** COVERDALE *Ps.* xlii[i]. 2 Why hast thou shot me from the? **1562** WINȜET *Cert. Tractates* i. Wks. (S.T.S.) I. 8 Or of the schuiting of honeste men fra thair native roumes. **1581** *Satir. Poems Reform.* xliii. 97 Sicklyk was Sipio saiklesly schot furth. **1596** DALRYMPLE tr. *Leslie's Hist. Scot.* I. II. 144 He repudiat, forsuke, and frome him, as vnworthie, schott [Lat. *repudiavit*] her [his wife] away. **1605** B. JONSON *Volpone* I. v, Now, is he gone; we had no other meanes, To shoote him hence, but this.

**g.** To separate (the worst animals) from a drove or flock. Cf. SHOT *sb.*³

**1824** MACTAGGART *Gallovid. Encycl.* **1828** [CARR] *Craven Gloss.*, *Shoot* v. 2 To draw the worst cattle out of a drove. 'I'll gee ye ten apiece for thur hundreds yows, and you'll let me shoot ten'.

**h.** To put hurriedly and carelessly. Also, to dispatch (a thing) rapidly.

**1833** HT. MARTINEAU *Loom & Lugger* I. iii. 27 He rose from his knee and shot his instrument into its case. **1844** ALB. SMITH *Adv. Mr. Ledbury* vii, The dirty cups and saucers were shot away into the drawers, and the table turned outside the door. **1926** *S.P.E. Tract* XXIV. 126 If the article is ready, shoot it in. **1942** *Tee Emm* (Air Ministry) II. 129 You have grumbled at the amount of bumph the Group has shot at you. **1971** *Black Scholar* June 54/2, I don't have a picture at this time, but when I get one I will shoot it to you.

†**i.** ***to shoot*** (something) ***on fire***: to cause to burst into flame. *Obs.*

*c* **1400** *Destr. Troy* 9509 The shippes on a shene fyre shot þai belyue, That the low vp lightly launchit aboute.

**j.** To discard, get rid of; orig. in ***shoot that hat***, etc., as a mild imprecation. Also ***to shoot trouble*** = TROUBLE-SHOOT *v. slang* (orig. *U.S.*).

**1877** in Bartlett *Dict. Amer.* (ed. 4) 586 One lady..with derisive scorn..observed in the language of the day, 'Oh, shoot that hat!'.. The slang the gang is using now, You'll hear from every lip; It's *shoot the hat!* and get it boiled; And don't you lose your grip. **1884** J. HAY *Bread-Winners* xvi. 249 If I had all the cash he takes in to-night, I'd buy an island and shoot the machine business. **1902** FARMER & HENLEY *Slang* VI. 188/1 *Shoot that* (*hat, man*—anything)!.. a mild imprecation, 'Bother!' **1928** *Sunday Express* 18 Mar. 9/2 'Tell him to shoot that song-and-dance outfit'.., and jump into some plain overalls. **1965** 'W. HAGGARD' *Hard Sell* xiv. 154 When there was trouble..then Marco Monti shot it. Political trouble especially. **1980** P. HARCOURT *Tomorrow's Treason* I. v. 72, I want you to shoot trouble for me till the conference is over.

**k.** *Cricket.* To bowl (a side or part of one) *out* quickly and cheaply.

**1900** P. F. WARNER *Cricket in Many Climes* IV. ii. 159 Next day Ainsworth and 'Bos' shot the opposing side out for 30. **1976** J. SNOW *Cricket Rebel* 112 Half the Warwickshire side had been shot out for 46.

**l.** Slang phr. ***to shoot a card***: to leave a visiting card. ? *Obs.*

**1901** *Captain* V. 7/2 The second-year man is always careful to 'shoot' his card when the fresher is abroad. **1924** 'SAPPER' *Third Round* vi. 139 He may have heard that Mrs. Goodman is here, and has come to shoot a card.

**12. a.** To launch (a vessel); to cast forth or let down (an anchor); to lower and place in position (a fishing net). Now also *spec.* in *Angling*, to allow a quantity of (line) to run out through the hand at the forward motion of the rod in casting. Also *absol.*

**1375** BARBOUR *Bruce* IV. 629 Than in schort tym men mycht thaim se Schute all thair galais to the se. *a* **1529** SKELTON *Col. Cloute* 1257 Shote anker, and lye at rode, And sayle not farre abrode, Tyll the cost be clere. **1552** in *Select Pleas Admiralty* (Selden Soc.) II. 21 That no person nor persons from hensfurthe doo shote any wyddenett within x fathom of his next felowe by estimacon in the day tyme... Thesterly man to begynne first and so every man to shote in order. **1583** *Reg. Mag. Sig. Scot.* 225/2 To haill, schutt, peill and draw nettis on all pairtis usit and wont within the said boundis. **1600** HOLLAND *Livy* XXVIII. xlv. 706 The ships were finished, rigged, armed, and furnished with all things, and shot into the water. **1630** in Binnell *Descr. Thames* (1758) 65 No fisherman..shall shute any Draw-Net, Cord-Net, or other Net or Engine..after Holyrood Day is past. **1776** *Act 16 Geo. III*, c. 36 §3 Unless the Boat..do in the mean Time shoot or cast out into the Water her.. Seyne Net. **1873** *Act 36 & 37 Vict.* c. 71 §14 Any person who shall shoot or work any seine or draft net for salmon in a river across the whole width. **1894** Hall Caine *Manxman* v. iii. 286 The nets were shot over the starboard quarter. **1931** *Hardy's Anglers' Guide* 13 In Figs. 1 and 2 the left hand gathers slack line, while in Fig. 3 this line is released during the forward stroke. This is termed 'shooting' line. **1977** *Chicago Tribune* 2 Oct. III. 10/2 The current will pull on the line, making casting and 'shooting' of fly line on the next cast extremely difficult.

**b.** To cause (a vessel) to move forward suddenly or swiftly. *to shoot* (a vessel) *to*: to bring it by 'shooting' to a required position. †*to be shot*: of a vessel, to have advanced (a certain distance or to a certain point). Cf. sense 3.

**1408** tr. *Vegetius' De Re Milit.* (MS. Digby 233) lf. 226/2 þei scheten here schippes to gedre & casteth out planckes or brygges.. & fiȝteþ hand at hand. **1555** Eden *Decades* (Arb.) 382 When yow reken yowre selfe as farre shotte as cape de las Palmas. **1574** W. Bourne *Regim. Sea* xxii. (1577) 60 You ..shall be well shotte towardes the banke of Silley. **1588** Fenner in *Defeat Sp. Armada* (Navy Rec. Soc.) I. 242 Being shot some ten leagues off South and by West of Ushant. **1793** Smeaton *Edystone L.* §137 A north-west wind would shoot the sloop clear of the house reef. **1794** *Rigging & Seamanship* II. 316 Her sails tend to shoot her a-head. **1849** W. S. Mayo *Kaloolah* vi. (1850) 50 With a sweep of his paddle he turned the bow of his boat from us, and with a few vigorous strokes shot it ahead. **1887** Goode, etc. *Fish. Industr. U.S.* iv. 132 Shooting to. This evolution is peculiar to fore and aft rigged vessels... To shoot a schooner to, it is only necessary, when sailing by the wind, to put the wheel part way down, and as she comes head to wind to keep her in that position by the management of the helm until her headway is stopped.

**13. a.** To push or slide (a bar or bolt of a door or the like) into or out of its fastenings. Also to force (a lock).

*c* **1000** *Gosp. Nicodemus* xxvii. 15 in Thwaites *Heptat.* (1698), Belucaþ ða..ærenan gatu & toforan on sceotaþ þa ysenan scyttelsas. **1573** *Satir. Poems Reform.* xxxix. 209 Thay schot na keyis to brek the coffiris than, Ane day of blythnes for the men of weir. *a* **1617** Bayne *On Eph.* (1658) 104, I have Power to shoot the bolt and lock it. **1637** Rutherford *Lett.* (1664) 343, I know now.. how to shut the lock & unbolt my welbeloved's door. **1696** Cibber *Love's last Shift* III, If you have lost it [the key] we must shoot the lock, I think. **1797** Mrs. Radcliffe *Italian* xii, I fear we are betrayed; the second lock is shot. **1833** Marryat *P. Simple* ix, One of the midshipmen shot the bolt of the door. **1886** J. Paton in *Encycl. Brit.* XXI. 144/2 Safe bolts are shot not by the key, as in an ordinary lock, but by the door handle. **1894** A. Robertson *Nuggets* 92 Annie ran to the stable, shot the wooden bolt, and went in.

**b.** *intr.* Of a bolt: To slide *into* its fastenings; to admit of being shot.

**1886** J. Paton in *Encycl. Brit.* XXI. 144/2 The frame.. into which the bolts shoot is made of great strength. *Ibid.*, In all Chubb's safes bolts shoot both to front and back.

**14.** *trans.* **a.** *Weaving.* To pass (the shuttle, the weft) between the threads of the warp. Also in figurative context.

**1603** Holland *Plutarch's Mor.* 337, I suppose that a weaver will say that his worke is to make a web,.. and not to ..lay his warpe, shoot oufe, or [etc.]. **1612** Beaum. & Fl. *Coxcomb* v. i, An honest Weaver, and as good a work-man as ere shot shuttle. **1839** Hallam *Lit. Eur.* iv. v. §46 Lines of consummate excellence are frequently shot, like threads of gold, through the web. **1849** Robertson *Serm.* Ser. i. xxi. (1866) 351 The woof of life is dark.. but.. shot through a web of brightness. **1888** J. Paton in *Encycl. Brit.* XXIV. 464/1 A clear way is thus provided for picking or shooting the shuttle. **1895** R. W. Frazer *Silent Gods* (1896) 58 The weaver still sang as he quickly shot the shuttle with the weft through the warp.

**b.** To variegate by admixture of different coloured threads in the woof. Hence, in wider sense, to variegate (an expanse of colour) by interspersing streaks or flecks of some other colour.

**1532–3** *Act 24 Hen. VIII*, c. 2 The same wollen clothes [shall].. be perfectly boyled grayned or maddered vppon the wodde and shotte, with good and sufficient corke or orchall. **1566** *Churchw. Acc. St. Dunstan's Canterb.* in *Archæol. Cant.* XVII. 120 One couerlyt shot wyth blew and red. **1684** *Lond. Gaz.* No. 1944/4 A Petticoat of Musk coloured Silk, shot with Silver on the right side. **1751** Johnson *Rambler* No. 116 ¶8 Carnation shot with white. **1856** H. H. Dixon *Post & Paddock* xiii. (1860) 272 Mundig's stock are nearly all chestnuts, many of them shot with white hairs. **1860** Sala *Baddington Peerage* I. i. 26 His stiff, black hair a little shot with gray. **1863** B. Taylor *H. Thurston* xv. 192 The canes of maize shot the brown fields with points of shining green. **1882** *Garden* 7 Oct. 312/2 Of older flowers we have.. Burgundy, rich dark puce, shot and suffused with light purple [etc.]. **1895** *Jrnl. R. Inst. Brit. Architects* 14 Mar. 347 The Saviour was dressed in a purple tunic shot with gold.

*fig.* **1850** *Fraser's Mag.* Sept. 244/2 Vague theory shot with technicalities. **1874** L. Stephen *Hours in Libr.* (1892) II. iv. 109 The texture of Disraeli's writings is.. ingeniously shot with irony.

**15.** Formerly, to send out, dispatch (persons) (now *dial.*: see *Eng. Dial. Dict.*). Now *colloq.*, to convey or transfer (a person) with speed. Also *to shoot* (a person) *about*: to hurry (him) from place to place.

**1542** Becon *Pathw. Prayer* xxix. M vij, Therfore sayth Christ, praye vnto the Lorde of yᵉ Heruest, that he may shote forth workemen into his Heruest. **1895** Mrs. B. M. Croker *Village Tales* 71 You, as an officer's wife.. are shot about from Colombo to Peshawar. **1919** F. Hurst *Humoresque* 200 Come; I'll shoot you to the club. **1921** E. B. White *Let.* 15 Sept. (1976) 24, I go to one person and he says hello and shoots me on to another. **1972** T. Stoppard *Jumpers* i. 50 I'll shoot him in here... You can try your charms on him.

**16. a.** To emit swiftly and forcibly (rays, flames, etc.).

*c* **1375** *Sc. Leg. Saints* x. (*Mathou*) 157 Twa dragonyse, þat awful ware one to luke,.. & blessis of fyre with brynt-stane at nese and mowthe þai schote owte. **1596** Dalrymple tr. *Leslie's Hist. Scot.* II. viii. 90 A maruellous gret Comet, quhilk toward the South schot fyrie stremes terrabillie. **1690** T. Burnet *Theory Earth* iii. xii. 105 At the first opening of the Heavens, the brightness of his Person will scatter the dark Clouds, and shoot streams of light throughout all the Air. **1712–14** Pope *Rape of Lock* i. 13 Sol thro' white curtains shot a tim'rous ray. **1727–46** Thomson *Summer* 1371 The sun has lost his rage: his downward orb shoots nothing now but animating warmth And vital lustre. **1792** S. Rogers *Pleas. Mem.* ii. (1801) 55 A cool, sequester'd grot, From its rich roof a sparry lustre shot. **1812** Cary *Dante, Parad.* iii. 22 My sweet guide, who, smiling shot forth beams From her celestial eyes. **1823** Scott *Quentin D.* iv, His keen eyes.. shot forth occasionally a quick and vivid ray. **1833** N. Arnott *Physics* (ed. 5) II. 187 A ray.. Shot from *a* to the point *c*, in the surface of a piece of glass *g h*, would reach directly across to *o* and *b*. **1839** J. Sterling *Sexton's Dau.* i. xxxii, As if it were the cloven sky.. Shot out its glory suddenly.

**b.** To put forth, utter (words, sounds); chiefly with adv., *out, forth.* Now only as *transf.* from sense 21.

*a* **1225** *Leg. Kath.* 812 Scheoteð forð sum word, & let us onswerien. *a* **1250** *Owl & Night.* 23 (Jesus MS.), Bet þuhte þe drem þat he were Of harpe & pipe þan he nere, Bet þuhte þat heo were i-shote Of harpe & pipe þan of þrote. *c* **1470** Henryson *Mor. Fab.* v. (*Parl. Beasts*) viii, He.. Schot out his voce, full schill, and gaif a schout. **1546** J. Heywood *Prov.* ii. iii. (1867) 48 But shoote out some woordes, if she be to whot. **1602** Marston *Ant. & Mel.* ii. D 2 b, I would shoot some speach forth, to strike the time, With pleasing touch of amorous complement. **1657** J. Smith *Myst. Rhet.* 143 *Acclamo* to cry out or shoot forth the voice. **1848** Thackeray *Van. Fair* lx, Even Dobbin would shoot out a sudden peal [of laughter] at the boy's mimicry. **1848** Dickens *Dombey* iii, Shooting out whatever she had to say in one sentence, and in one breath, if possible. **1886** Stevenson *Kidnapped* iii, From time to time.. he shot out one of his questions.

**c.** To cause (a pain, an emotion, etc.) to pass rapidly *through.*

**1842** Tennyson *Godiva* 58 Her palfrey's footfall shot Light horrors thro' her pulses. **1852** Mrs. Stowe *Uncle Tom's C.* xxxiii, This question shot a gleam of joy and triumph through Tom's soul.

**17. a.** To thrust (one's hand, a limb, a weapon, etc.) *into* something. Also to thrust *out, forth, up,* etc.

*c* **1205** Lay. 1876 Heo scuten [*c* **1275** soten] heora sconken [in wrestling]. **1375** Barbour *Bruce* iii. 117 With that ane othir gan him ta Be the lege, and his hand gan schute Betuix the sterap and his fute. **1533** Bellenden *Livy* ii. vi. (S.T.S.) I. 151 He schot his hand in þe fire. **1567** *Satir. Poems Reform.* iii. 81 Unles ȝe now sharplie shuit out ȝour handis. **1596** Dalrymple tr. *Leslie's Hist. Scot.* II. ix. 186 Ilk schuteng his rapper in vtheris bellie. **1648** Winyard *Midsummer-Moon* 1 His head is shot up, as if it would only converse with the Prince oth'aire. *c* **1730** Ramsay *Boy & Pig* 4 A greedy Callan.. Shot his wee nive into the pot. **1774** Goldsm. *Nat. Hist.* (1776) VIII. 174 They will be found to shoot forth their arms in every direction. *c* **1850** *Croodin Doo* in Chambers *Pop. Rhymes Scot.* (1870) 53 O it shot out its feet and died.

**b.** *to shoot out*: To protrude (the tongue, the lips), usually as an expression of mockery.

**1535** Coverdale *Ps.* xxii. 7 They shute out their lippes. **1688** Boyle *Final Causes* ii. 69 The camelion.. was to take his prey, by shooting out his tongue at the flies he was to live upon. **1840** Macaulay *Ess., Ranke* (1851) II. 146 A sect laughing at the Scriptures, shooting out the tongue at the sacraments. **1857** Livingstone *Trav.* i. 18 Away she would go with her lips shot out. **1865** Swinburne *Chastelard* ii. i. 56 As at my Lord the Jews shot out their tongues. **1893** Stevenson *Catriona* i. 12, 'I thoucht ye had been a lad of some kind o' sense', he began, shooting out his lips.

**c.** *to shoot one's eyes*: to gaze eagerly. *rare.*

**1602** Marston *Antonio's Rev.* iv. i, I should not shoote mine eyes into the earth, Poring for mischiefe.

**d.** *to shoot one's cuffs* or (formerly) *linen* (*colloq.*): to pull one's shirt cuffs out so that they project beyond the cuffs of one's coat. Also *fig.*

**1878** Yates in *World* 16 Jan. (Farmer), Adjust your curls, your linen shoot, your coat wide open fling. **1887** *Poor Nellie* (1888) 104 He 'shot his linen' in style. **1889** 'J. S. Winter' *Harvest* 168 Major Pottinger.. shot his linen till the bystanders.. wondered if it was a new kind of conjuring entertainment. **1909** M. Beerbohm *Yet Again* 230 The large young man, shooting his cuffs, strode forward. **1929** W. Deeping *Roper's Row* iii. 25 You felt that you had shot your cuffs and scored a point when you wiped Moorhouse's stately eye. **1942** L. A. G. Strong *Unpractised Heart* 27 The millionaire pulled out a gold pencil and shot his cuff. **1974** S. Coulter *Château* i. xvii. 133 He shot his cuffs and walked resolutely towards Mademoiselle Aurélie. **1977** J. Cheever *Falconer* 129 He shot his cuff to check the time.

**18.** To eject from the body. †**a.** To eject (venom). Also of a spider: To eject (its thread).

*c* **1400** Maundev. (Roxb.) xxxi. 143 þai er euermare gapand, redy for to schote þaire venym. **1775** G. White *Selborne, To Barrington* 8 June, Every day in fine weather.. do I see those spiders shooting out their webs and mounting aloft. *Ibid.*, Those filmy threads, when first shot, might be entangled in the rising dew.

†**b.** To discharge (excreta); also (see quot. 1688). Also *to shoot one's belly, bowels. Obs.*

**1594** Nashe *Unfort. Trav.* Wks. (Grosart) V. 160 So swelled Zadoch [with rage] and was readie to burst out of his skinne, and shoote his bowels like chaine-shot full at Zacharies face for bringing him suche balefull tidings. **1634–5** Brereton *Trav.* (Chetham Soc.) 179 My mare chanced to eat some green corn, which did occasion her to shoot her belly, and purge so stour intolerably. **1688** R. Holme *Armoury* ii. 252/1 Terms in feeding cocks... Shuting the Body, is to purge it from its groser dung. **1737** Bracken *Farriery Impr.* (1757) II. 84 It is a Sign, if he shoot off his Food very fast, that he gets too little Corn.

†**c.** *absol.* To have a looseness in the bowels.

**1641** Best *Farm. Bks.* (Surtees) 5 A weake lambe.. will shoot and scowre allmost for the space of two dayes.

**d.** *trans.* Of a fish: To discharge (spawn). Also *absol.* (Cf. shot *ppl. a.* 1, shotten 3.)

**1609** Holland *Amm. Marcell.* 201 Fishes flocke.. to this nooke of the Ocean, to breed and shut their spawne. **1884** Goode *Nat. Hist. Aquatic Anim.* 409 The Sea-Bass, when they come into the pounds in the spring, are full of spawn, ready to shoot.

**e.** *intr.* To ejaculate; orig. in phr. *to shoot one's roe. slang.*

**1879–80** *Pearl* (1970) 217 And the little creatures found, When they dragged him to the ground, That, while lecturing, he'd shot his noble roe, roe, roe. **1922** Joyce *Ulysses* 553 Bloom: (*His eyes wildly dilated, clasps himself*). Show! Hide! Show! Plough her! More! Shoot! **1969** [see come *v.* 17]. **1972** H. C. Rae *Shooting Gallery* iii. 191, I wanted him to shoot and get it over.

**19. a.** Of a plant: To put forth (buds, leaves, branches, etc.). Chiefly with *forth* or *out.* Also *fig.*

**1526** *Pilgr. Perf.* (W. de W. 1531) 109 To shote forth yᵉ braunches of murmure, grudge [etc.]. **1535** Coverdale *Luke* xxi. 30 Whan they now shute forth their buddes. **1611** Bible *Mark* iv. 32 It.. shooteth out great branches. **1657** W. Coles *Adam in Eden* cx, Colts-foot shooteth up a slender stalk, with small yellowish Flowers. **1663** Patrick *Parab. Pilgrim* xxix. (1687) 349 Rosemary and Sweet-Brier,.. which shoot flowers, and dart forth Musk. **1719** London & Wise *Compl. Gard.* 143 When a fine Fruit Branch shoots many others. *a* **1766** *Complete Farmer* s.v. *Turnep* 7 P 2/1 Apt to make the wheat shoot fresh ears. **1853** M. Arnold *Scholar Gipsy* i, Nor let.. the cropp'd grasses shoot another head. **1908** [Miss E. Fowler] *Betw. Trent & Ancholme* 20 The largest round Lavender bush, soon to shoot forth buds and blossoms generously.

**b.** *transf.* Chiefly of an animal, etc.: To put forth (limbs, etc.); also *fig.* of immaterial things. *to shoot the red*: of a turkey-cock (see red *sb.*[1] 1 d).

**1596** Dalrymple tr. *Leslie's Hist. Scot.* I. iv. 238 Quhen this Pelagian hæresie.. appeired to schute out the hornes ay wyder and wyder. **1739** S. Sharp *Oper. Surg.* Introd. 31 The callous Edges softening, will, without any great Assistance, shoot out a Cicatrix. **1865** *Englishm. Mag.* Feb. 155 He throbs and tingles as the new wings shoot their feathers. **1899** *Allbutt's Syst. Med.* VIII. 875 These.. masses of epithelium.. do not shoot downwards the root-like processes so characteristic of epithelioma of the malignant type.

**c.** To cause to grow or 'shoot'; to make to spring *up. rare.*

**1610** Fletcher *Faithf. Sheph.* ii. i, All the verdant grass The spring shot up, stands yet unbruised here Of any foot. **1821** Clare *Vill. Minstr.* II. 107 The Power.. Who rules the year, and shoots the spindling grain.

**20.** With reference to stationary position: To throw out as a projection or protuberance; *refl.* to stand out, protuberate in a particular direction. †Also in passive, to appear as if thrust down.

**13..** *K. Alis.* 5953 He ne had noither nekke, ne throte, His heued was in his body y-shote. **1533** Bellenden *Livy* i. xvii. (S.T.S.) I. 97 Throw quhilk þe wallis war schot out with mare magnificent boundis þan afore. **1603** Owen *Pembrokeshire* i. (1891) 5 Carmarthenshere that waye shooteinge it selfe on the Northeast. **1635** Person *Varieties* i. 19 Where the mouth of a large valley endeth at the Sea.. shooting as it were it selfe forth into the said Sea.. there it should be more shallow. **1784** Cowper *To Mem. Halibut* 17 Where Hibernia shoots Her wondrous causeway far into the main.

**III.** To send missiles from an engine.

(A Com. Teut. specialization of branch II.)

**21. a.** *trans.* To send forth, let fly (arrows, bolts, etc.) from a bow or other engine, or (bullets or shot) from a firearm. Const. *at,* †*against,* †*to.*

*a* **900** *O.E. Martyrol.* 15 Nov. 206 Hiȝ sceoton hyra strælas on twa healfa tosomne. *c* **1205** Lay. 6487 þa his flæn weoren iscoten þæ iwærd his boȝe to-broken. *c* **1330** *Arth. & Merl.* 317 þer was mani arwe yschote. **1338** R. Brunne *Chron.* (1725) 178 Oft tille our Inglis men was schewed a mervaile grete, A darte was schot to þem, bot non wist who it schete. *c* **1386** Chaucer *Pars. T.* ¶ 500 If a man, by caas or aventure, shete an arwe or caste a stoon with which he sleeth a man, he is homicyde. *c* **1450** *Merlin* xi. 167 Than he shette a-nothir bolte, and slowgh a malarde. **1471** Caxton *Recuyell* (Sommer) 94 Tho was drawen & shotte many an arowe. **1549** *Compl. Scot.* xv. 131 Siklyik ane preist of turque callit deruis schot ane bolt befoir the port of tempil contrar basit. *c* **1643** Ld. Herbert *Autobiog.* (1824) 6 The principal outlaw shot an arrow against my grandfather. **1756–7** tr. *Keysler's Trav.* (1760) III. 396 A third [cannon ball].. said to have been shot into the wall at the siege of Padua. **1769** Pennant *Tour Scot.* (1774) 101 Elf-shots.. are supposed to be weapons shot by fairies at cattle. **1819** Scott *Ivanhoe* xxxi, The Templar's retreat was rendered perilous by the numbers of arrows shot off at him and his party.

**b.** *fig.* and in fig. context. *to have shot one's bolt*: to have done all that one can do. Proverb, *a fool's bolt is soon shot*: see bolt *sb.*[1] 1.

*a* **1100** *Prudentius* in *Zeitschr. f. deutsches Alterthum* (1876) VIII. 38 Ða wæpna.. ðe þæt yrre scet [*miserat*]. *a* **1225** *Ancr. R.* 60 Erest heo [lechery] scheot þe earewen of þe liht eien, þet fleoð lichtliche uorð, ase earewe þet is iviðered, & stikeð iðe heorte. *Ibid.* 62 Sikerliche vre vo, þe weorreur of helle, he scheot.. mo cwarreaus to one ancre þen to seouene &

seouenti lefdies iðe worlde. c 1400 *Rom. Rose* 1800 The thridde arowe he [the God of Love] gan to shete,.. Into myn herte he did avale. 1586 Stanyhurst *Descr. Irel.* i. 11 in *Holinshed*, But if I may craue your patience till time you see me shoot my bolt. 1621 T. Williamson tr. *Goulart's Wise Vieillard* 89 Many others haue shot forth the like bolts and censures, whereof this is the totall summe and substance. 1652 Benlowes *Theophila* ix. iii. 127 Hope be thy Bowe, thy Hand Love, Faith the Shaft; Let Hope shoot Faith to God with Loves strong Draft. 1852 *Househ. Words* V. 577 [The winds] never cease to shoot at us their arrows barbed with the poison of rheum. 1901 *Daily Express* 28 Feb. 4/5 The home players had shot their bolt, and in thirty minutes the Birmingham team added two goals.

**c.** With cognate object, *to shoot a shot* (or †*a shoot*). Now *rare*.

1297 R. Glouc. (Rolls) 11103 An carpenter þat hii sede þat sset þe ssute [*MS. Add.* þane schote] hii nome. c 1400 *Pilgr. Sowle* (Caxton) iv. xxix. (1859) 61 But, soothly, they sheten neuer shotte. 1545 Ascham *Toxoph.* ii. (Arb.) 107 For in a rayne and at no marke, a man may shote a faire shoote. 1590 Barwick *Disc. Weapons* 17 *marg.*, The archer dooth require more time then dooth the firy weapon to shoot the first shoot. 1633 T. Stafford *Pac. Hib.* ii. xiii. 208 All this while the Enemy shot not a shot. 1642–4 Vicars *God in Mount* 193 They forced all the Musketeers.. to.. shroud themselves within their pikes, not daring to shoot a shoot. 1816 Scott *Old Mort.* xxxii, May the hand be withered that shot the shot!

†**d.** To hurl or throw (a spear, etc.). *Obs.*

a 1100 *Prudentius* in *Zeitschr. f. deutsches Alterthum* (1876) VIII. 38 þæt yrre scyt his spere onȝean þæt ȝeðyld. c 1205 Lay. 5690 And þa oðere hem scuten [c 1275 sote] to scærpe gares. 1393 Langl. *P. Pl.* C. xxi. 50 '*Aue, rabbi*', quaþ þat ribaud and reodes shotte at hus eyen. 1585 T. Washington tr. *Nicholay's Voy.* i. viii. 8 Their weapons are three dartes or long Iauelins, whyche they.. doe shoote and throw with wonderfull dexteritie.

**e.** *transf.* To discharge, send forth like an arrow or a shot. Also *fig.* with obj. a glance, question, etc.

1612 Drayton *Poly-olb.* ii. 69 When sharp Winter shoots her sleet and hardned hail. 1622 Massinger & Dekker *Virg. Martyr* iv. i, Doe thine eyes shoote daggers at that man That brings thee health? 1642 Fuller *Holy & Prof. St.* v. i. 358 She hurts most with those glances which are shot from a down-cast eye. a 1700 Evelyn *Diary* 2 Oct. 1658, A porcupine, of that kind that shoots its quills. 1816 Scott *Old Mort.* xxxiii, The sullen and indignant glances which they shot at them. 1881 *Scribner's Monthly* XXI. 268/2 She shot the question at him with a force which took away his breath. 1889 Conan Doyle *Micah Clarke* 229 A wild race of fishermen.. who.. shot some rough West-country jest at me as I passed.

**22.** *absol.* and *intr.* To send forth missiles from a bow, firearm, or similar engine. †Also with *forth*.

993 *Battle of Maldon* 270 Hwilon he on bord sceat, hwilon beorn tæsde. c 1205 Lay. 12574, & Bruttes weoren igærede & þene wal weoreden; heo scuten in, heo scuten ut, scalkes þer feollen. 1297 R. Glouc. (Rolls) 11218 Hii mette wiþ þis burgeis & bigonne to ssete vaste I wounded þer was manion. c 1330 R. Brunne *Chron. Wace* (Rolls) 858 An herde of hertes sone þey met, Al a triste to schete, Brutus was set. 1387 Trevisa *Higden* (Rolls) I. 91 þey techiþ besiliche here children to ride and to schete. c 1400 tr. *Secreta Secret., Gov. Lordsh.* cxi. 111 Ordeyne þy wenges, on þe right syde of hem þat stryken and assayllen, and of þe left syde hem þat shoten. c 1422 Lydg. *Serpent of Division* (1911) 59 And somme with firye dartes and scharpe hokid arwis schetynge in þe eire. 1471 Caxton *Recuyell* (Sommer) 66 Than the archers of kynge saturne began to drawe & shote. 1569 T. Preston *Cambises* 879 [Venus to Cupid] Shoot forth, my son; now is the time that thou must wound his hart. 1595 Shaks. *John* v. vi. 2 Whose there?.. speake quickly, or I shoote. 1668 R. Steele *Husb. Calling* ix. (1672) 223 If a man stand on a tower and shoot downward, he that stands at the bottom of it and shoots upward, may fly above him. a 1700 Evelyn *Diary* 15 Oct. 1650, Sir Tho. Osborn.. and Lord Stanhop shot for a wager of 5 Louis. 1753 Jago *Elegy on Blackbird* in *Adventurer* No. 37 O! had he chose some other game, Or shot as he had used to do! 1899 T. M. Ellis *Three Cat's-eye Rings* 123 They turned round to shoot, and a bullet from one of their muskets shrieked past Clayside's ear. 1907 Galsworthy *Country Ho.* i. i. 2 Foxleigh; he's no good... But can't he shoot just! That's why they ask him.

**b.** *intr.* To engage in archery (in mod. use occas. in rifle-practice, etc.) as a sport or contest. †*to shoot compass* (*obs.*): see compass *adv.* 3 b.

c 1205 Lay. 24698 Summe heo gunnen lepen summe heo gunnen sceoten [c 1275 sceate] summe heo wræstleden. c 1412 Hoccleve *De Reg. Princ.* 651 No more I hadde set þerby or roght, A wif or mayde or nune to deffoule, Than scheete, or pleyen at þe bal or boule. 1589 *Hay any Work* A iij b, When the wether is foule, that men cannot go abroad to boules, or to shoote. 1801 T. Roberts *Engl. Bowman* 293 To shoot down the butts, to begin at the furthest, and end at the shortest butt.

**c.** *well shot!* an applauding exclamation when a shooter hits the mark. Also used in sports involving the scoring of goals. Cf. sense 27. Also *fig.*

1640 Sir E. Dering *Carmelite* (1641) 41 Your promise is of thoughts within, and your proof still of things done without. Well shot. Go to your Book again and study the point better. 1655 Fuller *Ch. Hist.* vii. i. 425 One day being shooting at Butts,.. He hit the very mark. The Duke of Northumberland, being present,.. Well shot my Liege, quoth he. 1981 E. North *Dames* xiii. 255 'Well shot! Well shot!' Some feeble cheering on the touchline.

**d.** Constructions. (*a*) *to shoot at* (†also *after, against, on, unto, to*) the mark or object aimed at.

*to shoot at rovers*: see rover[1] i.

c 1250 *Gen. & Ex.* 474 Lamech.. wurð bisne, and haued a man ðat ledde him.. To scheten after ðe wilde der. c 1290 *St. Sebastian* 47 in *S. Eng. Leg.* 179 [The emperor] let archers to him scheote: ase it were to one marke. 1340 *Ayenb.* 45 An archer uor þet he hedde ylore ate geme: nom his boȝe and ssat an heȝ aye god. c 1400 *Laud Troy-bk.* 7779 To schote at him so was he prest. c 1450 *Mirk's Festial* 64 But euer deþe sewyth hym wyth his bow drawen and an arow þeryn redy to choton at hym. 1471 Caxton *Recuyell* (Sommer) 147 He entryd among tharchers of the troians that shotte thikke on hym. 1496 [see prop *sb.*[1] 2 b]. 1497 [see shell *sb.*[1] 2 b]. 1538 Starkey *England* i. iv. 105 Euer as a marke to schote vnto. 1576 Gascoigne *Spoyle of Antwerp* Wks. 1910 II. App. 591 They of the Towne did not shote at the prince of Orenges Shippes. 1611 Bible *Gen.* xlix. 23 The archers haue sorely grieued him, and shot at him. 1673 [R. Leigh] *Transp. Reh.* 97 They fought for his crown when they shot at his person. a 1715 Burnet *Own Time* (1724) I. 242 Van Gheudt.. shot against Bruntisland without doing any mischief. 1774 Goldsm. *Nat. Hist.* (1776) VI. 96 They have stood to be shot at in flocks, without offering to move. 1816 Scott *Bl. Dwarf* ii, Willie of Winton whom you shot at? 1908 E. M. Gordon *Indian Folk Tales* ix. (1909) 85 A young man.. asked me to shoot at an owl.

(*b*) *to shoot with* (also †*in*) a bow, gun, etc.; also rarely *with* an arrow.

[c 1205 Lay. 16555 Nu ich hine [Hengest] ȝiue þe.. & þet þine hired-childeren.. scotien mid heore flan & his cun scenden anon.] 1297 R. Glouc. (Rolls) 7735 He wolde.. ssete [*v. rr.* schute, schete] also mid bowe & arblaste. c 1440 *Promp. Parv.* 445/2 Schetyn yn a bowe (*v.r.* shotyn with bowes) *sagitto*. 1530 Palsgr. 704/2, I shote in any bowe, crosse bowe, or longe bowe. 1546 J. Heywood *Prov.* ii. vi. (1867) 61 But many a man speaketh of Robyn hood, That neuer shot in his bowe. 1610 Holland *Camden's Brit.* (1637) 633 Sirnamed Strongbow, because hee shot in a bow of exceeding great bent. 1644 Nye *Gunnery* (1647) 35 It is as easie to shoot in a great Gun as in a Musket. c 1665 Mrs. Hutchinson *Mem. Col. Hutchinson* (1846) 22 He shot excellently in bows and guns, and much used them for his exercise. a 1700 Evelyn *Diary* Sept. 1646, Here I first saw huge balistæ or crosse-bows shot in.

(*c*) *to shoot at* (†*to*, etc.) an object *with* a bow, gun, etc.; also *with* an arrow.

971 *Blickl. Hom.* 199 þa ȝenam he his boȝan.. & ða mid ȝeættredum stræle ongan sceotan wiþ þæs þe he ȝeseah þæt hryþer stondan. c 1290 *St. Cristopher* 204 in *S. Eng. Leg.* 277 With bouwe and Areblast þare schoter to him four hondret knyȝtes and mo. c 1440 *Gesta Rom.* ii. xix. 335 (Addit. MS.) The knyght.. shotte to [*Cambr. MS.* shot at] hym with an arowe, and slough hym. 1613 Purchas *Pilgrimage* (1614) 740 They shoot at the Fish with their darts. 1873 B. Harte *What B. Harte Saw* in *Fiddletown*, etc. 100 There was a mark at which a few credulous people shot with a toy rifle.

(*d*) With adv. or phrase, *to shoot beside, far from, near the mark*; *to shoot short, straight*, etc. Often *fig.*

1471 Caxton *Recuyell* (Sommer) 256 Hercules and many other shotte at most strayt and next the marke. 1545 Ascham *Toxoph.* i. (Arb.) 101 But to shoote wyde and far of the marke is a thynge possyble. 1546 J. Heywood *Prov.* i. vi. (1867) 12 Ye mary (quoth he) nowe ye shoote nie the pricke. 1577 Harrison *England* iii. i. [ii. vi.] 95 b in *Holinshed*, Wherein they [*sc.* foreign writers] haue shot so farre wyde as the quantity of ground was betweene themselues and their marke. 1585 Q. Eliz. *Let. to Jas. VI* (Camden) 17 Who seaketh two stringes to one bowe, he [*printed* the] may shute strong, but neuer strait. 1658 Gurnall *Chr. in Arm.* verse 15. iii. 335 Man he lets flie against God (though against his will he shoots short) whole vollies of sinnes and impieties. a 1704 T. Brown *Ess. on Women* Wks. 1711 IV. 155 But alas! how far do you shoot from the mark? [in answer to a question]. 1862 'F. G. Trafford' *City & Suburb* iii. (1869) 22 He had shot wonderfully near the truth.

(*e*) In phr. *to shoot to kill* (cf. kill *v.* 6 c), implying the desire or intention to kill, rather than frighten or wound, a living target. Also *shoot-to-kill* adj. phr.

1867 *Harper's Mag.* Feb. 274/2 Wild Bill with his own hands has killed hundreds of men... 'He shoots to kill', as they say on the border. 1949 N. Marsh *Swing, Brother, Swing* iii. 48 Plays like he shoots an' he shoots to kill. 1956 'J. Christopher' *Death of Grass* v. 79 'Must you shoot to kill?' He began to say: 'It's a matter of safety.' 1973 *Black Panther* 7 Apr. 10/3 LEAA was the liberal establishment's attempt to modernize police techniques as a substitute for 'shoot to kill' repression. 1977 *New Yorker* 15 Aug. 67/1 A Cuban businessman.. recalled favorably Mayor Richard Daley's calling for the National Guard and giving the police shoot-to-kill orders because of the Chicago riots.

(*f*) *to shoot it out*: to settle (a dispute) by shooting or by the exchange of military fire. Cf. fight *v.* 8.

1912 W. M. Raine *Brand Blotters* xii. 327 Had he shown any sign of indecision, they would have taken a chance and shot it out. 1939 *War Illustr.* 18 Dec. 458/3 Two gangsters have temporarily joined hands to plunder the wealthier citizens, on the understanding that they will 'shoot it out' between them later. 1949 F. Maclean *Eastern Approaches* ii. iv. 221 To try and shoot it out with them would bring the whole place about our ears.

**e.** quasi-*trans.* *to shoot a match*: to engage in a shooting-match. Also *to shoot off a tie*: to decide a tie in a shooting-match by a supplementary contest.

1840 Blaine *Encycl. Rur. Sports* §2763 Captain R. and Mr. S. then shot the tie off. *Ibid.*, Two matches were then shot by Capt. Ross and Mr. Osbaldeston. 1859 'Stonehenge' *Shot-gun* ii. 7 Lord Huntingfield,.. and Mr. Bateson having repeatedly shot matches at Hornsey Wood House. 1861 *Temple Bar* III. 266 This target was chosen for shooting off the ties at the long distances.

**f.** *transf. intr.* and *trans.* To take a snapshot (of) with a camera; to photograph (a scene, action, person, etc.) with a cinematographic camera; to take (cinematographic film), to film; occas. with the actor as subject.

1890 *Anthony's Photogr. Bull.* III. 3 Beside him is another sort of shutter operator with an ordinary camera and fairly good shutter... Does he shoot when his companion did? 1892 *Photogr. Ann.* II. 51 We at first tried the other method, namely, looking at the object and shooting at the critical moment. 1896 *Punch* 30 May 264/2, I even bless the Kodak now With which, dear Nell, you 'shot' me. 1916 'B. M. Bower' *Phantom Herd* ii. 22 He.. debated whether it should be 'shot' with two cameras or three. 1919 *Conquest* Dec. 70/2 First, the camera man 'shoots' on the tank containing the fishes with one half of the lens open. 1930 E. Waugh *Vile Bodies* ix. 156 'All right,' said one of the men with megaphones... 'We'll shoot the duel now.' 1953 *Manch. Guardian Weekly* 27 Aug. 7/1 While the big-city exhibitors were pondering this expensive outlay a small studio in Hollywood shot a poor film with two interlocking lenses. 1962 Montagu & Leyda tr. *Nizhny's Lessons with Eisenstein* iii. 66 Could the set-up be so changed as to shoot past Dessalines' back? 1976 *Observer* (Colour Suppl.) 9 May 10/2 She has also shot the odd film here. 1978 J. Krantz *Scruples* iii. 77 If anyone was going to go down to the Virgin Islands and shoot three models in next year's monokinis.. it was Hank.

**g.** *to shoot a profile*: see profile *sb.* 4 e.

**23.** *fig.* and in figurative context.

**a.** With reference to metaphorical arrows or darts, e.g. of love, temptation, affliction.

a 1000 *Minds of Men* 35 He.. hyȝegar leteð, scurum sceoteþ. c 1200 Ormin 3839, & ȝiff he [the devil] seoþ þe mann forrdredd, He wile himm skerren mare, & ræfenn himm his rihhte witt, & shetenn inn hiss heorrte. c 1386 Chaucer *Pars. T.* ¶714 An ydel man is lyk to a place that hath no walles; deueles may entre on euery syde and sheten at hym at discouert, by temptacion on euery syde. c 1400 *Rom. Rose* 1777 And whanne that love gan nyghe me nere, He.. shette at me with all his myght. 1895 R. W. Chambers *King in Yellow* (1909) 255, I think.. that he [Cupid] does shoot fairly—yes, and even gives one warning.

†**b.** *to shoot at*: to assail with censure or contempt. *Obs.*

c 1586 C'tess Pembroke *Ps.* lii. vi, The just shall.. shoote at thee With scornfull glances. c 1640 H. Bell *Luther's Colloq. Mens.* (1652) 113 The Turks and Jews do acknowledg God the Father, but it is the Son that they shoot at. 1643 Baker *Chron., Eliz.* 57 The Queen conceiving, that through the sides of the Prelates, she her self was shot at, suppressed them what she could. c 1660 South *Serm.* (1715) I. 28 If it is a Pleasure to be envyed and shot at, to be maligned standing,.. then it is a Pleasure to be great.

**c.** *to shoot at* (with express or implied reference to a metaphorical mark or target): (*a*) to aim at, to seek to have or accomplish; to aspire to, strive after (now *arch.*); †(*b*) to 'drive at', mean, to have reference to; †(*c*) to aim at imitating, follow the example of.

(*a*) c 1407–10 Hoccleve *Min. Poems* (1892) 58 But myn herte is euere bent To sheete at yow good wil in soothfastnesse. 1528 Tindale *Par. Mammon* 30 The same is blynde and wotteth not what he dothe: erreth and shoteth at a wronge marke. a 1568 Ascham *Scholem.* ii. (Arb.) 127 Thou, that shotest at perfection in the Latin tong, think not thy selfe wiser than Tullie was. 1635 R. N. tr. *Camden's Hist. Eliz.* iii. 266 The Queene of Scots.. easily understood that her destruction was shot at by this Association. 1647 Trapp *Mellif. Theol.* 652 Their evil dissembled ambitious desires plainly declared.. that they both shot at one and the same mark. 1888 Stevenson *Black Arrow* iii. iii. 163, I shoot at no advantage to myself.

(*b*) 1577 tr. *Bullinger's Decades* i. ix. (1592) 84 For to this ende shoote all the exhortations of the Prophets and Apostles. 1583 Babington *Commandm.* viii. (1590) 331 An equalitie of commodities present is plainely shot at in this law. *Ibid.* 347, I might recite the lawes of God,.. which directly shoote at the shame of this sinne. 1629 H. Burton *Truth's Tri.* 307 The maine thing Vega shootes at in this chapter.

(*c*) 1515 *St. Papers Hen. VIII*, II. 15 Bycause the Deputye useyth the said wrongfull extortion, all the noble folke of the lande shotes at hym, folowyth his wayes in that behalf, asmuche as in them is.

†**d.** To have an aim or reference (*beyond* something mentioned). *Obs.*

1680 H. More *Apocal. Apoc.* 66 This part of the Vision therefore shoots beyond the Pergamenian and Thyatirian Interval of the church, and begins with the Sardian.

†**e.** *to shoot over*: to overshoot the mark. *Obs.*

1605 Bacon *Adv. Learn.* ii. xxiii. §20. 96 b, And certaynelye, it is an errour frequent, for men to shoot ouer, and to suppose deeper ends, and more compasse reaches then are.

†**f.** in certain proverbial phrases. *Obs.*

1530 Palsgr. 704/2, I shote at all adventures, or at the unhappyest, *Je tire a la volée*. 1577 *F. de L'isle's Legendarie* G iij b, Now in making warre against the Protestants, they shote sundry wayes with owne selfe arrowe. 1624 Massinger *Renegado* v. iii, Neither can I Be wonne to thinke, but if I should attempt it, I shoote against the Moone.

**g.** *slang* (orig. *U.S.*). *to shoot off one's mouth*: to talk indiscreetly or abusively; to talk unrestrainedly or at length, to assert one's opinions; to boast or brag. Also *to shoot one's mouth off* and similar phrases.

1864 *Rocky Mountain News* (Denver, Colorado) 3 Aug. 4/2 A Dutch married woman.. was taxed $17·80 for 'shooting off her mouth' against the virtue and morality of a neighbouring maiden. 1880 *News & Press* (Cimarron, New Mexico) 8 Apr. 1/5 Nobby, you've.. never yit shot off yer mouth on the marryin' biz. 1890 N. P. Langford *Vigilante Days* I. 295 Why, you fool; there you go, shooting off your mouth to me the first thing. Didn't I caution you not to tell any one? 1896 S. Crane *Maggie* xi. 86 Youse fellers er lookin' fer a scrap, an' its like yeh'll fin' one if yeh keeps on shootin' off yer mout's. 1919 O. W. Holmes *Let.* 5 Apr. (1964) iii. 184 They make me want to write a letter to ease my mind and shoot off my mouth; but of course I keep a judicial silence. 1933 D. L. Sayers *Murder must Advertise* x. 165 That don't prove nothing... Not without you know 'ow long it took Mr. Tompkin to shoot 'is mouth off. **1946** E. O'NEILL *Iceman Cometh* II. 99 He ought to do it, and not just shoot off his old bazoo about it. **1954** WODEHOUSE *Jeeves & Feudal Spirit* xiii. 123 So this was how the woman was accustomed to shoot off her bally head about me in my absence. **1967** *Boston Globe* 5 Apr. 51/5 The only way we can keep Red..quiet is to beat Boston... I'm tired of hearing him shoot off his mouth. **1973** W. J. BURLEY *Death in Salubrious Place* i. 24 With Matthew Eva shooting his mouth off about Peters it could turn ugly.

**h.** *trans.* and *intr.* To inject by means of a hypodermic syringe (used esp. with reference to the taking of addictive drugs). Also *refl.* Freq. const. *up. slang* (orig. *U.S.*).

**1914** JACKSON & HELLYER *Vocab. Criminal Slang* 75 *Shoot*, verb, current amongst hypodermic habitues. To inject morphine or other drug with a syringe. Example; 'How many times do you shoot a day?' **1926** J. BLACK *You can't Win* xii. 161 They grew so despondent over their plight ..they decided to 'shoot up' the small portion of white stuff they had left. **1951** *Life* 25 June 120/1 But furnishes hypodermics and other paraphernalia so he may 'shoot himself' on the spot. **1953** W. BURROUGHS *Junkie* i. 23 He shot another syrette. *Ibid.* iii. 36, I began shooting in the main line to save stuff and because the immediate kick was better. **1969** H. WAUGH *Young Prey* iv. 65 The junkies.. need a place to go where they can shoot themselves and where an expert can shoot the novices. **1971** *Oz* May 5/2 They were using those needles man, they were shooting up. **1979** R. JAFFE *Class Reunion* (1980) II. iv. 204 He [*sc.* a dermatologist] would be the magician who would..peel off wrinkles, shoot silicone into laugh lines.

**i.** *intr.* To proceed, go ahead (with a speech, question, etc.), to 'fire away'. Usu. *imp.*, as an invitation to introduce a topic. Also *trans.* to direct (words); to say, speak; occas. *imp.* with *it*, and *to shoot back*, to riposte, retort. *colloq.* (orig. *U.S.*)

**1915** *Dialect Notes* IV. 235 *Shoot, imper.*, continue; go ahead. **1917** ADE *Let.* 12 June (1973) 64 The other day a harelipped man working for me stopped me and said he wished to ask a question. I told him to shoot. **1920** S. LEWIS *Main Street* 121 'Shall we try 'The Idylls of the King?' They're so full of color.' 'Go to it. Shoot.' **1934** J. M. CAIN *Postman always rings Twice* ii. 9, I shot it right close to her ear, almost in a whisper. 'How come you married this Greek, anyway?' **1935** W. D. HUBBARD *Thousandth Frog* 157 'Well,' said Gratton. 'Shoot it.' **1942** *Amer. Mercury* July 90 Dat what you shooting ain't worth a damn! **1951** J. G. FENNESSY *Sonnet in Bottle* VII. iii. 259 'I want to ask your advice about something.'.. Rupert said, 'Well, shoot.' **1974** 'E. LATHEN' *Sweet & Low* xi. 112 'Where's Amory?'... 'How do I know?' Yeoman shot back. **1978** H. WOUK *War & Remembrance* xxxvii. 388 'Can I pick your brain on one more point?' 'Shoot.'

**j.** Chiefly *U.S. slang. to shoot the works*: to effect something to the fullest extent; *spec.* to discharge the necessary business; to tell the truth, reveal all; *to shoot the bull*: to talk nonsense (cf. BULL *sb.*[4] 3); *to shoot a line*: see LINE *sb.*[2] 13 g.

**1922** E. O'NEILL *Hairy Ape* vii. 74 Can't youse see I belong? Sure! I'm reg'lar. I'll stick, get me? I'll shoot de woiks for youse. **1930** *Amer. Speech* V. 197 (*heading*) Shooting the bull. **1946** MEZZROW & WOLFE *Really Blues* i. 5 We had a yen..to strut and act biggity and shoot the works. **1951** W. STEVENS *Let.* 27 Dec. (1967) 735 We have people who seem to hand a list of names to a stenographer and tell her to shoot the works. **1972** *Maclean's Mag.* Mar. 41/2 'Writes all my speeches,' he'd say and slap me on the back. 'Smart boy! He can sure shoot the bull.'

**k.** *Bridge.* To play abnormally in a tournament in order to achieve a high score, e.g. one needed to win a tournament.

**1957** M. MILES *How to win at Duplicate Bridge* vii. 318 Why do people invariably overbid when they are shooting? There are many better opportunities to shoot by underbidding. **1972** *Times* 3 June 8/6 It was the 98th deal of a 100 board match and North South were 'shooting' for top scores.

**l.** To strive *for*, to aim at. *U.S. colloq.*

**1967** *Technology Week* 23 Jan. 15/3 The space agency is currently shooting for a nuclear engine that would operate for 1,000 hours before refueling. **1976** *Billings* (Montana) *Gaz.* 20 June 6-E/2 Mississippi College long jumper Larry Myricks is shooting for a jump of 27 feet.

**24.** Of a bow, engine, or firearm: **a.** *trans.* To send forth (a missile).

?*a* **1366** CHAUCER *Rom. Rose* 989 That bowe semede wel to shete These arowis fyve. **1547** in *Archæologia* LI. 262 Brode fawcons shotinge iij shotte. **1679** BLOUNT *Anc. Tenures* 3 *Catapulta*, was an ancient warlike Engine to shoot Darts.

**b.** *intr.* To send forth missiles; to 'carry' a certain distance. Also, of a gun, to be discharged, go off (e.g. in a salute).

*a* **1575** GASCOIGNE *Posies, Weedes* Wks. 1907 I. 374 A peece which shot so well, so gently and so streight. *a* **1578** LINDESAY (Pitscottie) *Chron. Scot.* (S.T.S.) II. 124 Quhan thir proclamatiounis war endit..than the trumpattis and schalmes blew and so did the arteilʒerie schuit and bellis rang. **1598** SHAKS. *Merry W.* III. ii. 34 This boy will carrie a letter twentie mile as easie, as a Canon will shoot point-blanke twelue score. **1655** MARQ. WORCESTER *Cent. Invent.* §67 To make Guns shoot. **1669** STURMY *Mariner's Mag.* v. xii. 68 The Piece directed by her Metal, will shoot above twice as far as when..set by a Dispert. **1846** GREENER *Sci. Gunnery* 406 We have seen American rifle-barrels, which were far from the straight..yet they shot well.

**25.** *trans.* To discharge (a bow, catapult, etc.), to fire (a gun or other firearm); also with *off out.* Const. *at*, †*against*, etc. *spec.* in gun-making (see quot. 1886).

**1482** *Cely Papers* (Camden) 113 All the gonnes yn the colle warkys and abowte the marttes were schett for joye. *c* **1500** *Melusine* xxi. 116 Oure galeyes..bygan of al partes to shutte theire gonnes. **1506** *Acc. Ld. High Treas. Scot.* III. 203 To the pynouris of Leith quhilk carying the irn gun to the sandis to schut hir thair before the King. **1530** PALSGR. 704/2 They have shotte fourscore peces agaynst this towre in lesse than halfe an houre. **1557** *Peebles Burgh Rec.* (1872) 240 The counsall ordanis gif thair cum ony sodane fray to the toun..to James Frank to schoit ane goone. **1619** W. PHILLIP tr. *Schouten's Wonderf. Voy.* 11 We shot two peeces, an houre betweene each shot, to call her. *c* **1643** LD. HERBERT *Autobiog.* (1824) 69 Then you may shoot off a Pistol in the Stable. **1826** SCOTT *Woodst.* xvii, The malignants shooting their wall-pieces at us. **1833** [SEBA SMITH] *Lett. J. Downing* iii. (1835) 42 Says he, 'Can you shoot a rifle, Major?' 'Pretty considerable,' says I. **1886** WALSINGHAM & PAYNE-GALLWEY *Shooting* I. 71 The gun is now stocked and screwed, and then in the rough state is sent to the ground to be shot and regulated. *Ibid.* 75 A high-class gunmaker will spend days in shooting a gun in order to get its pattern and force up to the mark he considers requisite to make it a perfect weapon.

*transf.* **1681** DRYDEN *Span. Friar* v. ii, But man..should make Examples; Which like a Warning-piece must be shot off, To fright the rest from Crimes.

**26. a.** To propel (a marble, pellet, etc.) as from the thumb and forefinger. Also *U.S.*, to throw a die or dice; to play at dice. *colloq.*

**1820** W. IRVING *Sketch Bk.* (1821) I. 47 Rip Van Winkle ..taught them to fly kites and shoot marbles. **1857** HUGHES *Tom Brown* I. v, Some of whom were..shooting pellets, or digging their forks through the tablecloth. **1909** WEBSTER 526/1 The caster throws or 'shoots' the dice, and wins if the throw is 7 or 11. **1929** *Amer. Mercury* Sept. 49/2 We got to stop shootin' dices. **1932** W. FAULKNER *Light in August* 34, I would have thought that maybe shooting dice would be the one thing he could do. **1940** —— *Hamlet* 258 Vagrancy or razor fights or shooting dice for ten or fifteen cents.

**b.** *U.S. colloq.* To play (a game), as in *to shoot pool, casino*, etc. Cf. *to shoot crap(s)* s.v. CRAP *sb.*[4] 1, CRAPS.

**1926** E. HEMINGWAY *In our Time* 183 They talk and tell stories and shoot pool. **1935** A. SQUIRE *Sing Sing Doctor* xiv. 207 Perhaps he goes for a walk, or attends a movie, or shoots a practice game of pool. **1949** A. MILLER *Death of Salesman* I. 48 Come in later, we'll shoot a little casino. **1979** R. JAFFE *Class Reunion* (1980) II. ii. 187 He liked to dance, play golf, drink, shoot skeet, and laugh.

**27. a.** *Sport.* To kick, hit, drive (the ball) at goal. Also with *goal, basket*, etc. as object.

**1882** *Daily News* 4 Mar., The last-named shot it [the football] between the posts. **1885** *Field* 24 Jan. 108/2 On restarting Marlow again shot the ball through the posts. **1900** *Springfield Daily Republican* 4 Dec. 3/1 Both teams warmed up slowly and played open polo. Curtis shot the first goal in from the side. **1901** A. FARRELL *Ice Hockey & Polo Guide* 54 This sudden movement surprises the man and he is liable to shoot the puck inaccurately. **1908** in H. A. Fisher *Basket Ball Guide 1908–9* 67 It was he who shot Williams' two baskets in the first overtime period. **1935** F. HEWITT *Down Ice* (rev. ed.) iv. 88 The best play is to shoot the puck at the boards and jump ahead to receive the carom. **1975** *New Yorker* 7 Apr. 112/2 He went over to shoot some baskets by himself, and while he was doing this it suddenly hit him that the game meant too much to him to give up.

**b.** *intr.* To kick or drive the ball at goal. Also in *Croquet*, to aim *at* a ball from a long distance.

**1874** J. D. HEATH *Croquet-player* 65 But Yellow is confident of hitting, so he shoots at Blue, and roquets him. **1890** *Field* 1 Nov. 671/2 Hewitt soon after had a chance to equalise but shot over. **1900** H. C. NEEDHAM *Croquet* 50 When thinking of taking a bisque, instead of shooting hard, shoot so as to hit, if possible,..but to lie quite handy if you miss. **1901** *Daily Express* 18 Mar. 8/1 Both sides being too excited to shoot straight. **1917** *N.Y. Times* 4 Feb. VIII. 1/5 The Aggies won the game in the final period when D. Ross shot at random from the centre of the rink. **1929** J. G. BUSS *Basketball* vi. 71 *Shoot high*—and do not aim at the rim of the basket. **1951** *Netball* ('Know the Game' Series) 28/2 The player..must..aim directly at the goal... If she shoots and then catches the ball again, she must not shoot again directly. **1978** *Washington Post* 26 Oct. A 19/5 The 'problem' is that the girls' game has only forwards and guards, and the three guards do not shoot.

**c.** *Golf* (orig. *U.S.*). *trans.* To record (a score) for a round or part of one; also *to shoot a birdie*, to achieve a score of one under par for a hole. Also *intr.*

**1922** *Golfers Mag.* Aug. 28/1 This class of golfers, the fellows who shoot from 90 up, make golf possible in this country. **1923** [see BIRDIE *sb.* 2]. **1933** *Amer. Golfer* July 34/1 How about birdies and eagles?.. In order to shoot a birdie, you'd have to play the hole in 3.3 strokes. **1941** *Sat. Even. Post* 19 Apr. 118/3 They shot a twelve-under-par score in winning their first match. **1977** *Rolling Stone* 5 May 47/5 He played a round every day, shooting in the low 100s.

**IV.** To assail, wound, or kill with a shot.

**28. a.** *trans.* To wound or kill with a missile from a bow or firearm (in early use, occas. with a spear or javelin). Const. *with.* †Also, to assail with arrows or gunshot: = *to shoot at* (see 22 d).

The simple verb is now often used where formerly the fuller expression 'to shoot dead' or 'to death' would have been preferred (see b); e.g. with reference to the infliction of death as a penalty.

*c* **893** ÆLFRED *Oros.* IV. vi. §7 Ac þonne hie [the serpent] mon sloᵹ oþþe sceat. **993** *Battle of Maldon* 143 Ða he oþerne ofstlice sceat. *c* **1205** LAY. 313 He wende to sceoten [*c* **1275** sceote] þat hea der. *a* **1250** *Owl & Night.* 1121 If þu art i-worpe oþer i-scote [*Cott. MS.* i-shote], þenne þu myht erest to note. **1297** R. GLOUC. (Rolls) 242 As he wolde seste [*v.r.* scheten] an hert al aȝen is wille, To deþe he sset [*v.r.* scheet] his owe fader. **13..** *K. Alis.* 6345 They buth archeris with the beste, And scheoteth [*Laud MS.* shoten] theo gryp in his neste. *a* **1340** HAMPOLE *Ps.* x. 2 That thai shote in myrke the right of hert. *a* **1400** *Sir Perc.* 213 He wolde schote with his spere Bestes and other gere. *c* **1460** *Frere & Boye* 84 in Ritson *Anc. Pop. Poetry* 38 Than sayd the boye..It is best that I haue a bowe, Byrdes for to shete. **1561** S. WYTHERS tr. *Calvin's Treat. Relics* H j, But they muste also make reliques of the arrowes wher with he was shotten. **1617** MORYSON *Itin.* II. 49 My Lord himselfe had his horse shot under him. **1650** CROMWELL *Let.* 25 Sept. in *Carlyle*, They have done us no harm, except one soldier shot (but not to the danger of his life). **1678** SIR G. MACKENZIE *Crim. Laws Scot.* I. xix. §15. 208 It should be unlawful to kill or shoot them, as it is to shoot or hunt other wild beasts. **1709** LAWSON *Voy. Carolina* 151 The bald, or white Faces are a good Fowl. They cannot dive and are easily shotten. **1765** LD. HOLLAND in Jesse *Selwyn & Contemp.* (1843) I. 382 But there is no use in the D. of Bolton's shooting himself. **1807** J. HALL *Trav. Scot.* II. 425 A variety of other beautiful birds which we shot with water, not to spoil their plumage. **1809–10** COLERIDGE *Friend* (1865) 211 Do you hesitate to shoot a mad dog? **1838** *Murray's Handbk. N. Germ.* 482/1 The duke was inhumanly shot, 6 days after. **1842** TENNYSON *Audley Court* 40 Oh! who would fight and march and counter-march, Be shot for sixpence in a battle-field. **1848** THACKERAY *Van. Fair* xlv, Mr. James, the Colonel, and Horn, the keeper, went and shot pheasants. **1873** *Chamb. Jrnl.* 20 Dec. 802/2 A man who was shot on leaving a ballroom told me that he could not guess who was his assailant. **1896** A. E. HOUSMAN *Shropshire Lad* lvi, Fly I would, for who would not? 'Tis sure no pleasure to be shot.

**b.** Amplified with *dead* or *to death* added.

*c* **1205** LAY. 254 For his ahne sune seoþen hine sceat [*c* **1275** set] to deaþe. *c* **1290** *St. Christopher* 203 in *S. Eng. Leg.* 277 To a piler he let him binde faste and knyȝtes a-boute him go, For-to scheoten him to deþe with Mani a kene flo. *a* **1578** LINDESAY (Pitscottie) *Chron. Scot.* (S.T.S.) I. 3 Sum Invyand vthir with maist crewell feid with sword and dag to schut him to the deid. **1617** MORYSON *Itin.* II. 37 Condemning to bee shot to death an Irish Lieutenant. **1697** DAMPIER *Voy.* I. 2 We gave out, that if any man faultred in the Journey over Land he must expect to be shot to death. **1719** OZELL tr. *Misson's Mem. & Observ.* 226 Deserters are shot to Death. **1836** J. RICHARDSON *Jrnl. Brit. Legion* IV. 116 A priest..was publicly shot to death without the walls of that city. **1863** W. C. BALDWIN *Afr. Hunting* viii. 317, I shot him dead in two bullets. **1863** TWISTLETON in W. Smith *Dict. Bible* III. s.v. *Zidon*, He betrayed into the king's power one hundred of the most distinguished citizens of Sidon, who were all shot to death with javelins.

**c.** To hit or wound with a shot *in* (or †*into*) or *through* a part of the body.

**1297** R. GLOUC. (Rolls) 7483 Þe ssetare donward al uor noȝt vaste slowe to gronde So þat harald þoru þen eie issote [*v.r.* shotte] was deþes wounde. **14..** in *Hist. Coll. Cit. Lond.* (Camden) 58 At the Castelle Gaylerde in Normandy he was schottyn thorowe the hedde. *c* **1440** *Gesta Rom.* I. i. 3 (Harl. MS.) He hath y-schotte him selfe in þe lungen, and lyeth ded. **1596** DALRYMPLE tr. *Leslie's Hist. Scot.* I. IV. 250 The king passing furth to do his eise..in the heid he is schott. **1647** CLARENDON *Hist. Reb.* VII. §80 Hambden.. being shot into the shoulder with a brace of bullets. **1649** HEYLIN *Relat. & Observ.* II. 255 A party of Horse..shot an old Woman into the head. **1761** HUME *Hist. Eng.* lxi. III. 323 Tromp..was shot through the heart with a musket ball. **1771** GOLDSM. *Hist. Eng.* I. 133 Harold..was shot into the brains by an arrow. **1816** TUCKEY *Narr. Exped. R. Zaire* iv. (1818) 141 He had been taken..by a slave catcher, who had shot him in the neck with a ball.

**d.** *to shoot flying*: to shoot (birds) on the wing. Now usually *absol.*, as denoting a sportsmanlike accomplishment.

**1698** FRYER *Acc. E. Ind. & P.* 291 Flocks of Water Fowl, which the Persians are skill'd..to shoot flying. **1707** FARQUHAR *Recruiting Officer* I. ii, I can do every thing with my father, but drink and shoot flying. **1852** THACKERAY *Esmond* I. xi, He had learned to ride, and to drink, and to shoot flying.

†**e.** To hit (a thing) with shot. *Obs.*

**1662** J. DAVIES tr. *Olearius' Voy. Ambass.* 218 He also, with a Fire-lock, shot an Apple, which he had caus'd to be cast into the Air.

**29.** *intr.* To engage in or practise the sport of killing game with a gun (formerly with a bow or the like).

*a* **1300** *K. Horn* 939 Til o dai þat he ferde To wude for to schete. **1687** A. LOVELL tr. *Thevenot's Trav.* I. 13 This Island, as all the rest of the Archipelago, being full of Game, we went a shore to shoot. **1766** EARL MARCH in Jesse *Selwyn & Contemp.* (1843) II. 82 Cadogan and Thomond are gone into the country to shoot. **1820** J. W. CROKER *Diary* 27 Jan. in *C. Papers* (1884) I. 156 Huskisson, Peel and I were to have gone to-day to shoot at Sudbourne with Lord Yarmouth. **1862** *Lillywhite's Cricket Scores & Biogr.* I. 303 He also shot with a license for fifty years, which can be recorded of few sportsmen. **1908** R. BAGOT *A. Cuthbert* xviii. 225, I have read of your English country life—and of how the women ride and shoot.

**30.** *trans.* With advs. and advb. phrases.

**a.** With *away, off, out*: To remove or separate from its place or environment by shooting; to carry away, destroy, or break off by a shot. Also *to shoot to pieces* and similar phrases. Cf. BLOW *v.*[1] 24.

**1340–70** *Alisaunder* 277 A schaft with a scharp hed shet oute his yie. **1615** R. COCKS *Diary* (Hakl. Soc.) I. 63 A Duch marener..had his hand shott offe and his face all batterd. **1632** LITHGOW *Trav.* II 62 We shot away their middle mast. **1706** E. WARD *Wooden World Diss.* (1708) 73 He will..fix ye a Couple of new [Ship's] Knees, when the old ones are shot to the Devil. **1849** W. S. MAYO *Kaloolah* vii. (1850) 65 People had been shot all to pieces and survived. **1859** C. KNIGHT *Pop. Hist. Eng.* V. xx. 309 His..equerry had his head shot off by a cannon ball. **1901** D. B. HALL & LD. A. OSBORNE *Sunshine & Surf* v. 55 The man-of-war fired fifteen shots before they shot away the flagstaff. **1939** R. G. COLLINGWOOD *Autobiogr.* vi. 49 A philosophical doctrine was stuck up and shot to pieces by the 'realistic' criticism. **1946** W. H. AUDEN in *Harvard Alumni Bull.* 15 June 707 And nerves that never flinched at slaughter Are shot to pieces by the shorter Poems of Donne. **1955** E. POUND *Section: Rock-Drill* xcii. 81 Semele's personality shot to atoms. **1973** *Black Panther* 31 Mar. 2/1 These same pilot officers..are now being encouraged to avenge their injured pride which was shot to hell because many of the anti-war enlisted men were Black. **1979** *Homes & Gardens* June 81/1 The Season has been shot to pieces this century.

**b.** *to shoot* (a person, thing) *through*: to pierce with a shot. *to shoot..through and through*: to riddle with shot; also †*fig.* to overwhelm with exactions.

**1535** COVERDALE *Exod.* xix. 13 There shal no hande touch it, but he shall either be stoned, or shot thorow. **1599** HAKLUYT *Voy.* II. II. 106 We..at last shooting her maine-yard through, she came to an anker and yeelded. *c* **1643** LD. HERBERT *Autobiog.* (1824) 19 The English shot her [the Spanish ship] through and through so often that she run herself aground. **1690** WOOD *Life* 31 Dec. (O.H.S.) III. 348 Complayning..against the salaries and pensions paid to great persons, officers, etc. who pay no taxes,..while the country is shot thro and thro.

**c.** *to shoot* (a person) *down*: to kill by a shot (usually with suggestion of merciless cruelty or determination); to bring down (an aircraft, hence a pilot, etc.) by shooting; (freq. in phr. *to shoot down in flames*). Also *fig.*, to overwhelm (a person) in argument, to destroy (an argument or theory); to assail with objections; to bring down to size.

**1845** J. COULTER *Adv. in Pacific* xiii. 175, I have witnessed several of their battles, and it appears to be the first object to shoot down, or otherwise kill a man. **1897** SIR G. T. GOLDIE in *Times* 23 Jan. 13/1 It is more humane to shoot down promptly a few running carriers than to sacrifice the lives of some 2,000 men of a column. **1918** W. A. BISHOP *Winged Warfare* xii. 160, I turned on the nearer of the two-seaters and..managed to shoot him down. **1928** E. WALLACE *Tam* iii. 29 Captain Muller shot down his twenty-seventh aeroplane. **1943** N. BALCHIN *Small Back Room* 5 'Just army conservatism,' he said wearily. 'Just the army's usual trick of shooting things down.' **1943** C. H. WARD-JACKSON *It's a Piece of Cake* 54 *Shot down in flames*, hopelessly beaten at anything. **1948** *Daily Tel.* 26 May 4/5 Another enemy aircraft was shot down in flames. **1958** *Times* 18 Dec. 11/4 To be shot down in flames may be an exaggerated description of getting the worse of an argument. **1959** *Listener* 3 Sept. 351/1 This is the way in which we shoot down cosmological theories. **1962** J. F. POWERS *Morte d'Urban* iv. 98 He had no choice but to shoot the woman down. **1969** M. O'BRINE *Mills* xi. 43 She, herself, had been a little shocked by his answer, but had secretly enjoyed seeing Eileen shot down in flames. **1977** *R.A.F. News* 11–24 May 8/6 He saw..Baron von Richtofen, shot down. **1981** J. B. HILTON *Playground of Death* vi. 81 Please shoot me down in flames if you think I'm making a bloody idiot of myself.

**d.** Naut. *to be shot by the board*: of masts, etc. (see quot. 1706). *to be shot between wind and water*: of a vessel, to receive a shot causing a dangerous leak; also *slang* (see quot. *a* 1700).

**1613** BEAUM. & FL. *Philaster* IV. i. (1620) 40 The wench has shot him betweene wind and water, and I hope sprung a lake. **1623** MASSINGER *Dk. Milan* III. ii, A she Dunckerke, that was shot before Betweene winde and weather. **1655** MARQ. WORCESTER *Cent. Invent.* §12 A Ship not possible to be sunk though shot an hundred times betwixt wind and water by Cannon. **1692** *Capt. Smith's Seaman's Gram.* I. xvi. 82 If a Ship lose her Masts in Fight, we say, *her Masts were shot by the Board.* *a* **1700** B. E. *Dict. Cant. Crew, Shot 'twixt Wind and Water* Clapt, or Poxt. **1706** PHILLIPS (ed. Kersey), *Shot by the Board*, a Sea-Phrase, us'd when a Mast or Yard is broken by the Enemies Shot, in a Fight.

**e.** *colloq.* (orig. *U.S.*). *to shoot up*: to assail (a person, thing) by shooting; to terrorize or rampage around (a place). Also *R.A.F. slang* of an aircraft or its pilot: to dive over (a person, thing) as if or in order to attack.

**1890** *Stock Grower & Farmer* 18 Jan. 5/2 This so enraged the boys that they began shooting up the town. *Ibid.* 21 June 3/1 Three cowboys shot each other up. **1909** *Chambers's Jrnl.* Feb. 104/1 Armed and masked men..took entire possession of it [*sc.* Princeton], 'shot it up' until opposition subsided. **1926** *Daily Colonist* (Victoria, B.C.) 22 July 15/7 Paul Davis..wounded after 'shooting up' rooming houses here early yesterday morning, died in hospital today. **1937** *New Statesman & Nation* 20 Feb. 288/2 Mr. Partridge is not quite so strong with regard to the slang of flying... I think ..to *shoot-up*, to dive onto, and the *wind-sock* should all find a place. **1946** D. HAMSON *We fell among Greeks* xvii. 180 When he had finished unloading his parachutes and parcels, he would take a long circle round and 'shoot us up', i.e. dive and roar over us at less than fifty feet, and, as he zoomed up, dip his wings left and right in salute. **1973** L. M. BOSTON *Memory in House* iv. 40 A squadron would roar over the house from which one plane swooped down to shoot us up. **1976** *Daily Tel.* 5 July 1, The Air France airbus which was skyjacked..a week ago, was also 'shot up'.

**f.** With *out*: to render (something) useless with a shot; *spec.* to puncture (a tyre), extinguish (a lamp) by shooting.

**1972** *Daily Tel.* 9 Feb. 4/5 The vehicle was halted when police shot its tyres out. **1976** D. BARNES *Yesterday is Dead* (1977) II. 267 Couple of cut-'em-up family disputes and a guy that shot out fourteen street lights. **1977** J. CARTWRIGHT *Fighting Men* viii. 102 He was sorely tempted to shoot out the plane's tyres.

**31.** *slang* or *vulgar*. *I'll be shot* (occas. shortened to *shot!*) *if* ——: used as a strong expression of denial or refusal. Similarly, *I'll see you shot first.*

**1761** STERNE *Tr. Shandy* IV. xiv. 85 Can'st thou carry *Trismegistus* in thy head... If she can, I'll be shot, said my father. **1803** J. KENNEY *Raising Wind* II. i. 24 What a fine seal; and I'll be shot if it [*sc.* a letter] don't feel like a bank note. **1826** BUCKSTONE *Luke the Labourer* III. i, *Bob.* He, he he! I'll be shot if Lunnun temptation be onything to this. **1852** DICKENS *Bleak Ho.* vii, I'll be shot if it ain't very curious how well I know that picture! **1860** F. W. ROBINSON *Grandmother's Money* II. iii, Shot, if I have not forgotten him too. **1894** 'J. S. WINTER' *Red Coats* 56 Then..let me tell you straight, I'll just see you shot first.

**32.** Transferred uses. **a.** To injure or kill by witchcraft. (Cf. ELF-SHOOT *v.*)

*c* **1000** *Sax. Leechd.* III. 54 Ȝif ðu wære on fell scoten oððe wære on flæsc scoten, oððe wære on blod scoten, oððe wære on lið scoten. **1790** BURNS *Tam o' Shanter* 167 For mony a beast to dead she shot.

**b.** *fig.* Of Cupid, love, etc.

**1471** CAXTON *Recuyell* (Sommer) 621 Than was Achilles shoten with the darte of loue. **1852** THACKERAY *Esmond* II. x, One poor gentleman, who had been shot by her young eyes two years before. **1885–94** R. BRIDGES *Eros & Psyche* Feb. xxvii, Whom gently Eros shooteth.

**c.** *to shoot the sun*: see quot.

**1867** SMYTH *Sailor's Word-bk.*, *Shoot the sun, To*, to take its meridional altitude; literally aiming at the reflected sun through the telescope of the instrument.

**d.** slang. *to shoot the cat*: To vomit. *shot in the neck* (*U.S.*): drunk. *to shoot one's grandmother* (*U.S.*): see quot. 1855. *to shoot the breeze* (*U.S.*): to chat, talk idly. *to shoot the crow* (*Sc.*): to steal away without paying one's bill; to depart hurriedly, abscond, 'do a bunk' (see *S.N.D.*).

**1785** GROSE *Dict. Vulgar T.*, *Shoot the Cat*, to vomit from excess of liquor, called also catting. **1830** *Cherokee Phoenix* (New Echota, Georgia) 21 Apr. 4/3 *Counsel.* What do you mean by *corned? Witness.* I mean, pretty well *shot in the neck.* **1855** HALIBURTON *Nature & Hum. Nat.* xxii. II. 297 You showed her she had shot her grandmother. *Footnote.* Shooting one's granny, or grandmother, means fancying you have discovered what was well known before. **1855** *Brooklyn Jrnl.* 18 Apr. (Bartlett 1860), Mr. Schumacher defended his client by observing that some of the prisoner's attorneys got as often 'shot in the neck', as the Under-Sheriff in the head. **1887** *Fun* 8 June 246/2 A canny Scot was recently sentenced to ten days' hard for shooting the crow —*i.e.* ordering half-a-quartern of whiskey, drinking it rapidly, and neglecting to pay. **1941** *Guide to U.S. Naval Academy* 149 *Breeze, shoot the*, to refight the Civil War, etc. **1943** *Sun* (Baltimore) 4 June 30/2 He can..walk across the camp to meet some friend in another outfit, and 'shoot the breeze'. **1971** R. K. SMITH *Ransom* (1972) III. 113 There were other negative signs, too. No one had come by to shoot the breeze, to have a cup of coffee. **1973** 'J. PATRICK' *Glasgow Gang Observed* xi. 97 He had been serving a sentence of twenty-eight days detention in the last week of which he had 'shot the crow' and 'jolted', i.e. absconded. **1977** W. MCILVANNEY *Laidlaw* xliv. 206 There'll only be his mother in the house. His father shot the crow years ago.

**33. a.** *intr. to shoot over* or *to* (a dog), to train by use on a shooting expedition. *to shoot over* (a cover, a tract of country), to kill game upon.

**1868** *Field* 4 July 22/1 For Sale, a Brace of..Spaniels..; they..have been thoroughly broken and shot to by an experienced breaker. **1888** *Century Mag.* Mar. 671/2 This holiday he was about to spend in shooting over his two handsome young setters. **1894** *Times* (weekly ed.) 19 Jan. 58/1 During his stay the Belvoir covers were shot over.

**b.** *trans.* To go over (a piece of country) shooting game. *to shoot one's way*: to shoot game as one goes along. *to be shot out*: of a district, to have its supply of game exhausted through overshooting.

**1833** T. HOOK *Parson's Dau.* II. vi, As the [shooting-] party at Colonel Bradfield's were shooting their way home. **1857** G. A. LAWRENCE *Guy Livingstone* vi, We shoot an outlying cover after luncheon. **1865** LD. MALMESBURY *Mem.* (1884) II. 333 We shot the park, and the Miss Jolliffes accompanied us. **1900** ISABEL SAVORY *Sportsw. India* 234 Gaggai was a sportsman's paradise, but it has been shot out. **1903** SIR M. G. GERARD *Leaves fr. Diaries* v. 107, I shot my way through the Bheel country, from Ahmedabad..to Mhow.

**34.** In *Mining*, to blast. In the *Oil Industry*, to detonate an explosive charge in (a well) in order to increase the flow of oil or gas.

**1830–60** *Eng. & For. Mining Gloss.* 23 (Cornwall terms). *c* **1870** *Scribner's Mag.* III. 576 (Cent.), They [explosives] are used in the petroleum industry to shoot the wells, so as to remove the paraffine which prevents the flow of oil. **1872** J. H. COLLINS *Mining & Quarrying* 112 *Shutting* or *Shooting*, blasting. **1903** *Dialect Notes* II. 344 *Shoot (the well)*, to cause an explosion of several quarts of nitro-glycerine at the depth of the *pay-streak*..so as to break and crack the oil rock, enabling the oil to flow faster from the pores. **1921** *Daily Colonist* (Victoria, B.C.) 11 Mar. 12/3 The report states that in Ironville No. 1 a good showing of thick oil was obtained at various depths... It was decided to shoot this well, but owing to water it was not yet known what result this would have. **1949** *Our Industry* (Anglo-Iranian Oil Co.) (ed. 2) ii. 52 Some rocks..containing oil are.. compact and 'tight'... In such cases the well is often 'shot' in order to shatter the rock.

**V.** Senses of uncertain position.

†**35. a.** In OE.: To refer (a case) *to* a person or court; also *absol.* **b.** In early ME.: To trust, to submit oneself *to* a person's mercy. *Obs.*

*a* **1000** in Thorpe *Dipl. Angl. Sax.* (1865) 288 Ða nolde he, butan hit man sceote to sciregemote. *c* **1000** ÆLFRIC *Hom.* (Th.) II. 306 Ðus wrat Hieronimus..ȝif hwa elles secge, we sceotað to him. *c* **1205** LAY. 977 Ȝif we sceoteð to heora mæðe þat bið ure imone deað.

†**36.** *trans.* (or const. *dative*). To fall to the lot of. *Obs.*

*c* **1200** ORMIN 19952 Forrþi þatt he Ne wollde nohht forrbuȝhenn To seggenn soþ biforr þe king, þohh þatt himm shollde shetenn To þolenn forr his soþe word Full grimme dæþess pine.

**37. † a.** To avoid, escape. *Sc. Obs.*

**1543** SADLEYR in *St. Papers Hen. VIII*, V. 321 The misdemeanour and evill behaviour of the Wardens of Scotland on the Borders towardes thobservation of the peax, with their delayes of redresse, shoting their dayes of meating, and continuall rodes and forreys made into England. **1685** PEDEN *Let.* in P. Walker *Life* (1827) 98, I am confident, the safest Way to shoot the Shower, is, to hold out of God's Gate, and to keep within his Doors, until the Violence of the Storm begin to ebb.

**b.** *colloq.* (orig. *dial.*). In passive, to be rid *of*. Cf. SHUT *v.* 11.

**1802** R. ANDERSON *Cumbld. Ball.* (*c* 1850) 47 He'd gi'e aw his gear to get shot o' the gout. **1818** SCOTT *Br. Lamm.* xxxii, Are you not glad to be fairly shot of him! **1837** CARLYLE in Froude *Life Lond.* (1884) I. 95 One infallible truth, precious for us all, is that I am shot of it [a book just finished], and you are shot of it. **1866** *Morn. Star* 22 Dec. 3, I thought, when I came out, I would do this [murder], and so get shot of my life. **1891** HARDY *Tess* x, 'Jump up behind me', he whispered, 'and we'll get shot of the screaming cats in a jiffy!' **1952** 'R. GORDON' *Doctor in House* i. 9 His love for his old hospital, like one's affection for the youthful homestead, increased steadily with the length of time he had been shot of it. **1976** *Daily Tel.* 22 Sept. 16/1 Advising its members to make haste to get shot of unsuitable employees.

**38.** To splice (a rope); to mend (a bar); †to fit (boards) *together* by a mortise or the like (*obs.*); to weld (metals). *Obs.* exc. *dial.*

Cf. SHUT *v.* 6. In this use the vbs. *shut* and *shoot* seem to have been more or less confused.

**1499** *Church-w. Acc., Yatton* (Somerset Rec. Soc.) 124 To Antony for schothyng the clapyr xiij[d]. **1545** *Luton Trinity Guild* (1906) 232 For shotynge of the tapers of the awtere ageynst relyk Sonday [o o] 2. **1548** *Ludlow Church-w. Acc.* (Camden) 33 For shottynge the belle rope ij tymes iiij d. **1569** *Ibid.* 134 For shutting and mending of the clapper of the santes bell, iiij d. **1573–4** in *Fabric Rolls York Minster* (Surtees) 116 For shootinge and mendinge certeyne barres to the glasse wyndowes, 4 d. **1608** WILLET *Hexapla Exod.* 605 These regals serued to shoot the boords together. *Ibid.*, One boord should have been shot within another. **1888** *Sheffield Gloss.*, *Shoot*, to weld a piece of iron to the blade of a table knife. **1892** [see SHOOTING *vbl. sb.* 6].

**39.** *Carpentry* and *Joinery*. To plane accurately (the edge of a board), esp. with the aid of a shooting-board.

**1667** PRIMATT *City & C. Builder* 61 For plaining the boards, and shooting them for a Square, two shillings. **1678** MOXON *Mech. Exerc.* iv. 59 Two Pieces of Wood are Shot (that is Plained)... They are Shot or Pared..so exactly straight, that when they are set upon one another, light shall not be discern'd betwixt them. **1793** SMEATON *Edystone L.* §146 Slips of deal board..shot straight upon the edges by a plane. **1846** HOLTZAPFFEL *Turning* II. 502 In squaring or shooting the edges of boards, the shooting board..is very much used. **1881** YOUNG *Every Man his own Mechanic* §384. 167 The Amateur unless he has a trying-plane will use his jack-plane for shooting the edges of boards.

**VI. 40.** The verb stem in combination: **shoot-hole**, a hole through which to shoot; **shoot-rail** (see quot.); † **shoot-serpent** (see quot.). Also **shoot-off**, the subsequent competition between tied contestants in a shooting-match.

**1850** R. G. CUMMING *Hunter's Life S. Afr.* (1902) 36/2 Having constructed a *shoot-hole..I took up my position for the night. **1892** W. W. GREENER *Breech-Loader* 250 The tie was immediately shot off at 25 birds each, Captain Brewer killing all his birds while Mr. Fulford scored 24, leaving Mr. Brewer..the winner of the *shoot-off by a single bird. **1900** *Westm. Gaz.* 16 July 6/3 Three competitors tie with 34..the shoot-off takes place to-morrow. **1856** P. THOMPSON *Hist. Boston* 722 *Shottles*, *shoot-rails. Rails easily removed in a fence, to make an entrance into an inclosure, and then *shot* (thrust) back again into their places. **1731** MEDLEY *Kolben's Cape G. Hope* II. 163 She is likewise call'd the Dart- or *Shoot-serpent, on account of her darting herself very swiftly either at or from an enemy.

**shoot,** *int. U.S. slang.* An arbitrary alteration of SHIT *int.*

In some instances this may perh. be regarded as an imp. use of SHOOT *v.* 11 j.

**1934** WEBSTER 2319/2 *Shoot..*, *interj.* Pshaw! Bother! —often with *it.* **1941** E. WELTY *Curtain of Green* 42 Oh, shoot, that was about three and a half years ago. **1950** R. MOORE *Candlemas Bay* 301 'Oh shoot,' she told Jen, when Jen suggested they'd better write the next batch of boarders not to come. **1979** *Tucson Mag.* Feb. 42/1 Back in high school, I tried other so-called sports, but I always went back to rodeo. Shoot, that's the only sport there is.

**shoot,** obs. f. SHEET *sb.*, SHOUT, SHUT.

**shoot,** variant of SHOAT[1] and [2].

**shootable** (ˈʃuːtəb(ə)l), *a.* [f. SHOOT *v.* + -ABLE.] That may be shot; suitable for shooting.

**1852** M. W. SAVAGE *R. Medlicott* IV. iv, I rode everything rideable, shot everything shootable. **1908** *Blackw. Mag.* July 108/2 The binoculars disclosed the three to be 'shootable' beasts.

**shootable,** vulgar pronunciation of SUITABLE.

**1831** MISS FERRIER *Destiny* xlviii, The lady's fortune is *shootable*; indeed, I may say, pretty handsome.

†**'shootage.** *Obs. rare*$^{-1}$. In 6 shewtage. [f. SHOOT *v.* + -AGE.] The art of shooting.

**1546–7** in Leland *Collect.* (1774) IV. 320 Take Bow and Shaft in Hand, learn Shewtage to frame.

**shoot-an(c)ker,** obs. forms of SHEET-ANCHOR.

**shoote,** obs. form of SHOUT *sb.*

**shooted** (ˈʃuːtɪd), *a.* [f. SHOOT *sb.*[1] + -ED[2].] Of a building: Supplied with 'shoots' or spouts.

**1853** *Jrnl. R. Agric. Soc.* XIV. II. 408 The farm buildings ..are shooted to carry off the drip.

**shootee** (ʃuːˈtiː). [f. SHOOT *v.* + -EE.] The person shot, or shot at.

**1837** *New Monthly Mag.* LI. 205 The shooter very commonly expresses much regret to the shootee. **1867** HALES *Introd. to Rob. Hood Ball.* in *Percy Folio MS.* I. 9 He [Robin Hood] is as regularly represented as a shooter as St. Sebastian in the old pictures is as a shootee.

**shoot-'em-up** (ˈʃuːtəmʌp). *slang* (orig. *U.S.*). Also **shoot-em-up, shootemup.** [f. vbl. phr. *to shoot them up*: see SHOOT *v.* 30 e.] A fast-moving story or film, esp. a Western, of which gun-play is a dominant feature. Also *attrib.* (or as *adj.*) and *Comb.*

**1953** *Variety* 11 Feb. 6/2 A standard outdoor action plot is unfolded in 'Gunsmoke' to make it a Western feature for the shoot-'em-up market. **1958** *Washington Post* 30 July A25/7 That doesn't leave much room for anything except shoot-'em-ups. **1968** *Listener* 18 July 86/1 A racetrack-gang, shoot-em-up-bang plot and one of Mr Hawkes's disturbingly discontinuous surfaces of experience are yoked by violence together. **1973** *N.Y. Times* 10 June VII. 28/2 The new or free-form Western has several choice entries ..'Oklahoma Crude', a splendid shootemup about a lady wildcatter in the oil fields. **1976** *Publishers Weekly* 15 Mar. 50/2 Her decision to put expediency ahead of love nearly costs Corey his life when the shoot-'em-up finale swings the action back to North Africa.

**shooter** (ˈʃuːtə(r)). Forms: α. 3 **ssetare**, 4 **ssyetere, schetor, scheotere, sheter, shetere**, 5 **schetare, scheter(e, sheter**; β. 4 **schot(t)er**, 4–6 **shoter**, 5–6 **schuter**, *Sc.* **schutar**, 6 **shewter**, *Sc.* **schuiter, schutur**, 7 **shootter**, 6– **shooter**. [f. SHOOT *v.* + -ER[1].]

I. One who shoots.

**1. a.** One who shoots with a bow or with firearms; in early use, an archer; now chiefly applied to a sportsman who shoots game.

α. **1297** R. GLOUC. (Rolls) 7482 þe ssetare [*v.rr.* ssetares, schetors, scheoteres, scheters, scheteres] donward al uor noȝt vaste slowe to gronde. **1382** WYCLIF *2 Kings* xi. 24 And the sheeters dresseden dartis to thi servauntis fro the wal above. *c* **1400** *Promp. Parv.* 445/2 Schetare, or archare, *sagittarius.* **1450** *Gesta Rom.* i. 3 Whenne he sawe the sheter drawe his bowe.

β. *a* **1300** *Cursor M.* 3607 þou ert schotter wit þe beist, Bath in feild and in forest. **1398** TREVISA *Barth. De P.R.* v. vi. (1495) 111 Shoters close the one eye for to shote the more euyn. **1471** CAXTON *Recuyell* (Sommer) II. 506 The whiche was.. the best shoter and drawer of a bowe. **1499** *Exch. Rolls Scot.* XI. 394 Gif thare be.. within.. forestis.. schutaris. **1540** PALSGR. *Acolastus* I. iii. G j b, As the archer or shoter in a crossebow directeth his eie towardes his marke. **1598–99** *Aberd. Acc.* in *Spalding Club Miscell.* V. 71 Appoyntit for calling and accusing of schuturis with gwnnis. **1611** BIBLE *1 Sam.* xxxi. 3 The archers [*marg.* shooters, men with bows] hit him. **1634** SIR T. HERBERT *Trav.* 101 He sends a shooter or footman to him. **1676** SHOTTEREL & DURFEY *Archerie reviv'd* 10 Mark what Grace Sits in each line of every Shooters Face. **1778** JOHNSON in *Boswell* 9 Apr., Where there are many shooters, some will hit. **1821** *Examiner* 105/1 A vigorous shooter of woodcocks. **1842** LACY *Mod. Shooter* 113 Some shooters nearly always, others but seldom, kill their game in style. **1865** 'CUTHBERT BEDE' *Rook's Garden*, etc. 232 The heads of the slaughtered sparrows would have to be produced.. to the secretary, who would note their number, and record it against the name of the shooter. **1908** B. MALLET *Life Earl Northbrook* 276 Joining the shooters at lunch.

†**b.** *transf.* (appositively). *Obs.*

*c* **1381** CHAUCER *Parl. Foules* 180 The saylynge fyr, the cipresse deth to pleyne, The shetere [*v.rr.* sheter, shoter, scheter] Ew, the Asp for shaftys pleyne.

†**c.** The constellation Sagittarius. *Obs.*

**1386** *Almanack* 1 The Schoter es þe principal howce of Saturne. **1601** WEEVER *Mirr. Mart.* C ij b, Then From Scorpio, Saturne to the Shooter's straide.

†**d.** The guard of a coach. *Obs.*

The 'guard', as the name implies, was originally armed for the protection of the passengers: see GUARD *sb.* 7 b.

**1840** THACKERAY *Shabby-genteel Story* i, A nod for the 'shooter' or guard, and a bow for the dragsman. **1897** *Encycl. Sport* I. 342/1 (Driving), *Shooter*, a name given to coach guards in the olden time.

**2. a.** The man who 'shoots' a seine-net.

**1855** LEIFCHILD *Cornwall* 13 The men who cast this net are termed the 'shooters'.

**b.** *Sport.* One who kicks or drives a ball at goal; also in extended use in *Basketball, Netball*, etc.

**1901** A. FARRELL *Ice Hockey & Ice Polo Guide* 54 The goaler.. may skate out to meet him, being careful that he is directly in line between shooter and goal. **1922** W. E. MEANWELL *Basket Ball for Men* vii. 68 Line throwing is the chief fault with most shooters. **1957** *Encycl. Brit.* III. 181/1 Previously, a star shooter could attempt all free throws for his team. **1963** C. GLYN *Don't knock Corners Off* xxi. 178, I stood and shivered as Miss Pratt picked people for the netball teams... 'You can be Shooter.' **1978** T. L. SMITH *Money War* (1979) III. 218 The only gambit he could think of was darts. He was the fifth best shooter in the very active St. Louis league.

**c.** One who throws a die or marble. Cf. also *crap-shooter* s.v. CRAP *sb.*[4] 2.

**1910** A. BENNETT *Clayhanger* I. i. 9 The bearded shooter, pleased by this tribute.. twisted his white apron. **1926** [see *little Joe* s.v. LITTLE *a.* 13]. **1969** R. C. BELL *Board & Table Games* II. v. 84 When any pair is thrown and the third die is 2, 3, 4, or 5, the number of the third die becomes the shooter's point.

II. Something that shoots or is used for shooting.

†**3.** A bolt. *Obs. rare*$^{-1}$.

**1632** SHERWOOD, The shooter of a locke, *verrouil.* **1681** W. ROBERTSON *Phraseol. Gen.* 1123 The shooter of a lock; *obex seræ versatilis.*

†**4.** A shooting star. *Obs.*

**1633** HERBERT *Temple, Artillerie* iii, I have also starres and shooters too.

**5.** With qualifying adj.: A plant that shoots (vigorously, etc.).

**1731** MILLER *Gard. Dict.* s.v. *Espalier*, For vigorous Shooters, twenty Feet are little enough. *c* **1791** *Encycl. Brit.* (ed. 3) VIII. 32/2 Robust but moderate shooters. **1981** *Country Life* 18 June 1772/1 Sappy shooters, from which to take cuttings now.

**6.** 'A board placed between cheeses under a press' (*Eng. Dial. Dict.*). Also, in a cider press, a board laid flat on the top of the pile of must.

**1586** *Shuttleworths' Acc.* (Chetham Soc.) 29 Fyffe cheffates [*read* chesfats = *cheese-vats*].. and one shewter vj[s] viij[d]. **1833** LOUDON *Encycl. Archit.* §1316 [Cider-press], A square board, termed a shooter.

**7.** A contrivance for shooting or discharging the contents of sacks.

**1880** J. W. HILL *Guide Agric. Implements* 469 An efficient Sack Lifter, Loader, Unloader, and Shooter.

**8. a.** With qualifying word: A gun, pistol, etc. that shoots (well or ill). Cf. SIX-SHOOTER. **b.** *colloq.* or *slang.* A shooting instrument, a gun or pistol, *esp.* a revolver.

**1812** COL. HAWKER *Diary* (1893) I. 64 The barrel was a bad and weak shooter. **1840** R. H. DANA *Bef. Mast* iv, We got our shooters in order. **1877** BLACK *Green Past.* xiii, Then Jack drew his shooter out and shot Billy Bill through the head. **1931** E. O'NEILL *Hunted* IV, in *Mourning becomes Electra* 156 Easy goes, shipmate! Stow that pistol!.. Not that I'm skeered o' you or your shooter! **1970** G. F. NEWMAN *Sir, you Bastard* v. 138 Why did you pull the shooter on the two detectives? **1972** L. HENDERSON *Cage until Tame* ix. 77 We'll need a shooter, one barrel into the ceiling straight off.

**9.** *Cricket.* (See quot. 1897.)

**1843** 'WYKHAMIST' *Pract. Hints Cricket* 7 Another advantage of this mode of holding the Bat close to the ground, is the greater facility the player has in stopping 'shooters'. **1856** HUGHES *Tom Brown* II. viii, The Captain stumped the next man off a leg-shooter. **1884** *Q. Rev.* Oct. 469 Lumpy's favourite achievement was to bowl 'shooters'. **1897** *Encycl. Sport* I. 246/2 (Cricket) *Shooter*, a ball which on touching the ground keeps very close to the turf, often with an increase of pace.

**10.** *Public School slang.* A black morning coat. ? *Obs.*

**1870** *Harrovian* 9 Apr. 134/2 Although the use of slang words and phrases has now become almost universal among the greater portion of the community, we generally find that each University or School possesses a dialect peculiar to itself... *Shooter*, a shooting coat. **1920** GALSWORTHY *In Chancery* II. vii. 181 'I suppose I'd better change into a 'shooter',' he muttered, escaping to his room. He put on the 'shooter', a high collar, a pearl pin, and his neatest grey spats.

**11.** *U.S. slang.* A measure or drink of spirit, esp. whisky.

**1971** *Car & Driver* Jan. 75/1 He made his famous call for 'shooters'. Now in case you haven't heard, a 'shooter' is a Turner variation of the word 'shot', as in a 'shot of likker', and.. refers to a shot of Canadian Club mixed into a few fingers of 'Co-cola'. **1973** W. MCCARTHY *Detail* i. 61 Let's have a shooter and a beer. **1981** W. SAFIRE in *N.Y. Times Mag.* 2 May 16/4 The word coming up fast for a *straight shot* is a *shooter.* 'A shooter is a shot of liquor swallowed in one quick gulp,' says Jeff Dee.

**shootherly**, obs. form of SOUTHERLY.

**shooting** (ˈʃuːtɪŋ), *vbl. sb.* Forms: see the vb. [ME. *scheotunge*, later *schoting*, f. *scheote, schote* SHOOT *v.* + -ING[1]. OE. had *scotung*, f. *scotian* to shoot: see etymological note under SHOOT *v.*] The action of SHOOT *v.*

**1. a.** The action or practice of discharging missiles from a bow or gun.

[*c* **1000** ÆLFRIC *Saint's Lives* xxxii. 180 þa wunda þe þa wælhreowan hæþenan mid ȝelomum scotungum on his lice macodon.] *a* **1225** *Ancr. R.* 60 Also ase men weorreð mid þreo kunne wepnen, mid scheotunge, mid speres ord, & mid sweordes egge [etc.]. *a* **1352** MINOT *Poems* (ed. Hall) v. 49 It semid with þaire schoting als it war snaw. *c* **1450** LOVELICH *Merlin* 11564 These kynges hadden beholden ful wel the schetyng of this cherl Every del. **1549** LATIMER *6th Serm. bef. Edw. VI* (Arb.) 161 The arte of shutynge hath ben in tymes past much estemed in this realme. **1572** *Nottingham Rec.* IV. 141 Matches of showttyng. **1601** R. JOHNSON *Kingd. & Commw.* (1603) 89 Shoting in peeces, crosbowes, longbowes &c. **1692** LUTTRELL *Brief Rel.* (1857) II. 526 Much shooting with cannon and musquet was heard. **1727** [E. DORRINGTON] *Philip Quarll* (1816) 57 He daily practised shooting at a mark. **1880** MAITLAND *Gunmaking* in *Encycl. Brit.* XI. 294/1 When this [windage] is considerable, it is a principal cause of error in shooting.

†**b.** Discharge (of a bow), firing (of a gun).

**1426** LYDG. *De Guil. Pilgr.* 12071 Yiff I koude wysly provyde.. Fro shetyng off croos bowes. **1530** LYNDESAY *Test. Papyngo* 439 Throuch reakles schuttyng of one gret cannoun. **1625** *Peebles Charters*, etc. (1872) 414 Gewine to John Frank for schiwting of the tua goineis in the steippell. **1637–50** ROW *Hist. Kirk* (Wodrow Soc.) 363 Shooting of canons.

**c.** The sport of killing game with the gun.

**1642** FULLER *Holy & Prof. State* III. xiii. 185 Shooting.. provides food when men are hungry. **1740** GRAY *Let. to Mother* 2 Apr., The two boys.. go a-shooting almost every day. **1823** SYD. SMITH *Game Laws* Wks. 1859 II. 28/2 There are certainly many valuable men brought into the country by a love of shooting. **1823** BYRON *Juan* XIII. xlviii, But there's no shooting (save grouse) till September. **1833** T. HOOK *Parson's Dau.* II. ii, The Squire was invited to a day's shooting at Colonel Bradfield's. **1903** MCNEILL *Egregious English* xix. 174 Grouse-shooting, pheasant-shooting, pigeon-shooting, and even rabbit-shooting. **1908** R. BAGOT *A. Cuthbert* i. 3 Every November the coverts at Cuthbertsheugh afforded four days' shooting.

¶ ***shooting flying***: used as noun of action to the vbl. phrase to *shoot flying* (28 d). ? *Obs.*

**1727** MARKLAND (*title*) Pteryplegia: or, the Art of Shooting Flying. **1766** PAGE (*title*) The Art of Shooting Flying. **1814** DOBSON *Kunopædia* title-p., With Instructions for attaining the Art of Shooting Flying.

**d.** An exclusive right to shoot game on a particular estate or tract of country. Hence also, a tract of country on which a person has such an exclusive right. Often *collective plural.*

**1848** CLOUGH *Bothie* I. 64 Hither from lodge and bothie in all the adjoining shootings. **1854** *Act 17 & 18 Vict.* c. 91 §42 The expression 'lands and heritages' shall.. include.. shootings, and deer forests, where such shootings or deer forests are actually let. **1879** *Daily News* 12 Aug. 5/1 The southern shootings are reported to be very poorly stocked with birds. **1884** *Pall Mall Gaz.* 12 Aug. 4/1 The man who takes a shooting with the intent of enjoying sport upon it until he is snowed off the premises. **1896** EARL SELBORNE *Memor.* I. xv. 236 He rented, for two or three years, the shooting of Mixbury.

**e.** An incident in which a person is shot with a firearm.

**1873** 'MARK TWAIN' *Gilded Age* xlvi. 425 What some of the journals lacked in suitable length.. they made up in encyclopaedic information about other similar murders and shootings. **1977** *Whitaker's Almanack 1978* 590/2 During the election campaign 50 people were reported killed in shootings and bombings.

**f.** *Oil Industry.* Detonation of an explosive charge in a well to increase the flow of oil or gas. Cf. SHOOT *v.* 34.

**1914** F. A. TALBOT *Oil Conquest of World* v. 64 'Shooting' is undertaken only when the limestone or sandstone is of such a nature that it restricts the flow of oil. **1937** *Amer. Speech* XII. 154/1 *Shooting a well*, using nitro-glycerine to make oil flow. **1946** [see OIL WELL]. **1969** *Times* 2 May 25/1 The international oil companies are stepping up their interest in the Irish Sea in search for oil and gas... The area involved covers at least 15,000 miles and although the 'shooting' will be selective, the cost will.. be.. high.

**2.** The feeling of a sudden pain; a thrill or dart of pain.

**1528** PAYNELL *Salerne's Reg.* E j, Mylke.. doth mitigate the shotynge or prickynge of the longes. **1640** HABINGTON *Castara* (Arb.) 107 The shootings of a wounded conscience. *c* **1702** in *Cath. Rec. Soc. Publ.* IX. 375 It seemed to her she felt.. most violent shewtings in her back. **1710** *True Acc. Tom Whigg* I. (ed. 2) 12 The shooting of my Corn. **1758** J. S. *Le Dran's Observ. Surg.* (1771) 152 He felt frequent Throbbings or Shootings in the Tumour. **1818** *Art Pres. Feet* 27 Some, on the approach of rain, experience what is called a shooting of the corns. **1825** SCOTT *Betrothed* xxx, I was but grieved with the shooting of an old wound.

**3. a.** Sprouting, beginning to grow (of plants, also of the teeth, etc.); sudden or rapid growth. Also ***shooting up.***

**1579** W. WILKINSON *Confut. Fam. Love* Ep. Ded. *ij b, To shew that shootyngs vp and encrease of God's Church beyng but from a feeble and weake begynnyng [etc.]. **1615** CROOKE *Body of Man* 344 The shooting of Stagges hornes which euery yeare fall and grow againe. **1765** *Museum Rust.* IV. 227 Hot manures.. will bring on a speedy shooting. **1799** UNDERWOOD *Dis. Child.* II. 121 The shooting up of a soft fungus. **1801** *Med. Jrnl.* V. 569 That is what they call the shooting of the teeth. **1901** 'ZACK' *Dunstable Weir* 23 What wi' the shooting o' the crops, and birds calling one to t'other, there was a wonderful lot of nature about.

**b.** *concr.* A shoot or collection of shoots.

**1653** BELLINGHAM *Plat's Gard. Eden* 66 [Carrots.] You must pare off the shooting at the upper end of the root and then lay them in sand. **1790** A. WILSON *Poems & Lit. Prose* (1876) II. 254 Beneath an old hedging for shelter he crawled And clung by a shooting of birch. **1886** W. J. TUCKER *E. Europe* 100 A wild undergrowth of rank weeds and acacia-shootings.

**4.** The sending out of shoots or spicules in crystallization.

**1665** HOOKE *Microgr.* 92 The shootings of Ice on the top of Water. *a* **1728** WOODWARD *Nat. Hist. Fossils* I. (1729) I. 114 Of the Stellar Shootings upon the Surface of the Regulus of Antimony. **1788** BLAGDEN in *Phil. Trans.* LXXVIII. 134 The shooting of the ice. **1855** KINGSLEY *Glaucus* (1878) 35 The shooting of salts intermixed with mineral particles.

**5.** *Football.* The kicking the ball at a goal. Also in extended use in other sports, as *Basketball, Netball, Hockey*, etc.

**1885** *Field* 31 Jan. 135/2 Any shooting that the centres attempted was very defective. **1897** *Encycl. Sport* I. 518/2 The goalkeeper should run forward.. so as to attempt to tackle him [*sc.* the hockey player] before he can get within shooting range. **1901** *Daily Express* 18 Mar. 8/1 The football was.. except for poor shooting most enjoyable. **1935** *Encycl. Sports* 436/1 It [*sc.* the game of netball] proceeds when.. the ball.. is received by one standing within the shooting circle. **1961** *Netball* ('Know the Game' Series) (ed. 5) 20 (*heading*) Footwork for throwing and shooting. **1974** *Plain Dealer* (Cleveland, Ohio) 26 Oct. 4-D/1 This system paid off in the team's shooting this week.

**6. a.** In various senses of the verb.

**1464** *Nottingham Rec.* II. 374 For shotyng of the same spyndelle. **1603** *Reg. Mag. Sig. Scot.* 530/1 Cum.. privilegio lie haling, schutting, landing, peilling, drawing of nettis, [etc.]. **1609** HOLLAND *Amm. Marcell.* a 1 b, The shooting of London bridge at an ebbe or low water. *Ibid.* 166 The shooting of starres. **1694** *Marten's Voy. Spitzbergen* in *Acc. Sev. Late Voy.* II. 120 Some are propagated by the shooting of their Row. **1711** ADDISON *Spect.* No. 7 ¶2, I have known the shooting of a Star spoil a Night's Rest. **1821** *Acc.*

*Peculations Coal Trade* 17 Wall's-end coals, 47*s*...free of expence, except the trifling expence for metage and shooting. **1825** J. NICHOLSON *Oper. Mech.* 586 The operation of making the edge of a board straight is called shooting. **1846** DICKENS *Pict. Italy, Rome* 173 Now and then, a swift shooting across some doorway or balcony, of a straggling stranger in a fancy dress. **1888** *Encycl. Brit.* XXIV. 464/1 The 'picking' or shooting of the weft. **1892** *Labour Commission* Gloss., *Shooting*, the operation of emptying the sacks of coal into the consumer's cellars or stores. *Ibid.*, *Shooting*, the process by which the iron which is to form the 'bolster' and 'tang' in a genuine hand-forged table blade is welded to the steel of the blade.

**b.** The action or process of taking film with a cinematographic camera.

**1920** I. P. GORE in *Stage Year Book* 56 Many companies are paying trips to the Continent for the 'shooting' of certain scenes in the actual 'locations'. **1941** B. SCHULBERG *What makes Sammy Run?* xi. 284 A director exhausted from the day's shooting. **1955** *Times* 31 May 10/3 Mr. Orson Welles, for one, has shown..the methods of 'shooting' which lay emphasis on rehearsals. **1979** *Beautiful Brit. Columbia* Spring 4 Victoria was one of the shooting locations for Harry in Your Pocket.

**c.** The action or process of injecting an (addictive) drug intravenously. *slang* (orig. *U.S.*).

**1951** *Evening Sun* (Baltimore) 27 Mar. 4/1 A powerful combination of 'bernice snorting' and heroin 'shooting' was called 'blowing speed balls'. **1953** W. BURROUGHS *Junkie* 8 You don't wake up one morning and decide to be a drug addict. It takes at least three months' shooting twice a day to get any habit at all. **1971** *Black Scholar* Apr.-May 46 Mugging, theft, pimping and shooting dope are not themselves political actions.

**7.** ***shooting forth***: **a.** an outburst; †**b.** *concr.* a projection, prominence.

**1601** HOLLAND *Pliny* I. xxii. I. 88 The shooting forth of the Promontorie aforesaid some have reported to be 60 miles, others 90. **1722** QUINCY *Lex. Phys.-Med.* (ed. 2) 16 *Ancon*, is the top of the Elbow, or the backward and greater Shooting-forth of the *Ulna*. **1837** CARLYLE *Fr. Rev.* I. VII. i, The first grand fit and shooting forth of sansculottism.

**8.** *attrib.* and *Comb.* **a.** Simple attrib., as (sense 1 c) ***shooting-party***, ***-season***; (sense 1 d) ***shooting-place***, ***-tenant***; (sense 6 b) ***shooting schedule***, ***script***. Also designating clothing worn or equipment used by a person engaged in shooting, as ***shooting-boot*** (also (*fig.*) in sense 5), ***-canoe***, ***-coat***, ***dress***, ***-gear***, ***-horse***, ***-jacket***, ***shoe***, ***-stocking***, ***-suit***.

**1855** 'C. IDLE' *Hints Shooting & Fishing* 34 To return from this digression on *shooting boots. **1894** *Country Gentleman's Catal.* 154 Fagg Brothers,...makers of shooting boots to *H. R. H. The Duke of Saxe-Coburg*. **1947** *Sporting Mirror* 7 Nov. 11/3 Grimsby were having a sad and sorry season until the unexpected revival at Manchester United when Cairns found his shooting boots. **1948** C. DAY LEWIS *Otterbury Incident* 26 Everyone knows he's a deadly shot when his shooting-boots are on. **1978** *Cornish Guardian* 27 Apr. 5/5 Tintagel found their shooting boots in the second half of their game. **1842** LACY *Mod. Shooter* 443 Going afloat in a *shooting-canoe for the first time. **1840** *John Bull* 3 Oct. 469/2 Advt., A superb Collection of *Shooting Coats. **1884** J. HATTON in *Harper's Mag.* Feb. 337/1 An old velvet shooting coat. **1794** J. WOODFORDE *Diary* 27 Oct. (1929) IV. 149, I met Mr. Stoughton..in a *Shooting Dress. **1852** J. R. PLANCHÉ *Day of Reckoning* III. i. 30 *Claude*..in a shooting dress, is seated on the steps of the terrace, examining the lock of his gun. **1555** in *Richmond Wills* (Surtees) 106, I beqweth unto John Cawrew..all my husband's *shotyng gere. **1850** R. G. CUMMING *Hunter's Life S. Afr.* (1902) 14 These drove their *shooting-horses loose behind the waggon. **1893** F. C. SELOUS *Trav. S.E. Africa* 16 A splendid shooting horse. **1796** JANE AUSTEN *Let.* 5 Sept. (1952) 11 Let me know..how many of the Gentlemen, Musicians & Waiters, he will have persuaded to come in their *Shooting Jackets. **1831** COL. HAWKER *Diary* (1893) II. 28, I slipped on my shooting jacket. **1776** EARL CARLISLE in Jesse *Selwyn & Contemp.* (1844) III. 154, I was only absent two days from home on a *shooting-party. **1848** THACKERAY *Van. Fair* lxii, There were shooting-parties and battues. **1819** SCOTT *Let.* in *Lockhart* (1837) IV. ix. 308 He really thought of getting some *shooting-place in Scotland. **1950** 'E. CRISPIN' *Frequent Hearses* i. 36 'It would be possible for me to meet her?'.. 'That depends on the *shooting schedules. The film's on the floor.' **1976** M. MAGUIRE *Scratchproof* i. 11 Shooting schedules were being delayed and people were beginning to say the film was jinxed. **1929** I. MONTAGU tr. *Pudovkin's On Film Technique* vi. 176 The **Shooting-script* is the scenario in its final cinematographic form. **1933** A. BRUNEL *Filmcraft* 141 Here follow two sequences of the actual shooting script of 'A Light Woman'. **1976** H. OREL in M. Drabble *Genius of T. Hardy* 103 Perhaps John Wain exaggerates by describing the entire work [*sc. The Dynasts*] as a shooting script. **1781** G. SELWYN *Let.* 19 May in *15th Rep. R. Comm. Hist. Manuscripts* App. VI. 484 in *Parl. Papers 1897* (c. 8551) LI. 1 Boothby proposes to go to you in the *shooting season, that is near Christmas. **1818** SCOTT *Hrt. Midl.* xlviii, To spend the shooting-season in Scotland. **1981** C. MILLER *Childhood in Scotland* 54 The opening of the shooting seasons varied with the type of game. **1839** A. MATHEWS *Mem. Charles Mathews* III. vii. 162, I had them made after a plan of my own, for *shooting-shoes. **1976** *Shooting Times & Country Mag.* 18-24 Nov. (Advt.), The golden boot—our famous shooting shoe. **1893** KIPLING *Day's Work* (1898) 43 The Rao Sahib, in tweed *shooting-suit and a seven-hued turban. **1891** *Daily News* 9 Apr. 2/2 That objectionable person, the *shooting tenant.

**b.** Special comb.: **shooting-block**, **-board**, an appliance to facilitate the accurate planing of the edge of a board or stereotype plate, consisting of a board or block, upon which the material is laid, furnished with a rebate to guide the plane; **shooting booth**, a booth at a fair in which shooting for prizes is carried out (cf. *shooting gallery* (*a*)); **shooting box**, a small country house in or adjacent to a shooting locality used as a residence while shooting; **shooting brake**, an estate car, now *rare*; orig. a light, horse-drawn wagonette designed to accommodate passengers and goods (cf. BREAK *sb.*[2]); **shooting-fish** = ARCHER 5; **shooting-gallery**, (*a*) a long room, or a booth at a fair, fitted with a target and other appliances for the practice of shooting; also *fig.* in colloq. phr. ***the whole shooting gallery*** = *the whole shoot* s.v. SHOOT *sb.*[1] 8; (*b*) *U.S. slang*, a place where addictive drugs may be obtained and 'shot' or taken by injection; **shooting-glove** *Archery*, a glove worn to protect the hand in drawing a bow; **shooting-ground**, (*a*) = sense 1 d; (*b*) that part of a gun-factory where rifles, etc. are tested; (*c*) a place where rubbish is shot; **shooting-hole**, a pit made by a sportsman for purposes of concealment; **shooting-iron**, a fire-arm, esp. a revolver; **shooting-lodge** = *shooting-box*; **shooting match**, a competition testing skill in shooting; also *fig.* in colloq. phr. ***the whole shooting match*** = *the whole shoot* s.v. SHOOT *sb.*[1] 8; **shooting phaeton** = *shooting brake* (orig. sense) above; **shooting-plane**, a plane used with a shooting-board for squaring or bevelling the edges of stuff (Knight *Mech. Dict.* 1875); **shooting-range**, a place used for the practice of shooting, having the various ranges or distances marked off between the respective firing points and the targets; **shooting seat** = *shooting stick* (*c*) below, now *rare*; **shooting-stick**, (*a*) *Printing*, a piece of hard wood or metal which is struck by a mallet to loosen or tighten the quoins in a chase; (*b*) *slang* = *shooting iron* (obs.); (*c*) a walking-stick with a handle that may be opened to form an impromptu seat, first used by shooters; **shooting-tool** *Mining*, a tool or implement used in blasting; **shooting war**, hostilities involving armed conflict, as opposed to *cold war* s.v. COLD *a.* 19; first used with reference to U.S. involvement in the war of 1939-45.

**1812** P. NICHOLSON *Mech. Exerc., Joinery* §63 The *Shooting Block is two boards fixed together, the sides of which are lapped upon each other, so as to form a rebate for the purpose of making a short joint. **1885** LOCK *Workshop Rec.* Ser. IV. 217/1 [Electrotyping] A shooting-block must be made. **1846** HOLTZAPFFEL *Turning* II. 502 In squaring or shooting the edges of boards, the *shooting board..is very much used. **1900** *Times* 7 July 10/1 We may soon expect swings erected in the practice-ground, *shooting booths under..the big stand. **1970** R. LOWELL *Notebk.* 202 The shags Flying in straight lines like duck in a shooting booth. **1812** SIR R. T. WILSON *Priv. Diary* (1861) I. 42 Rode to La Favorita, the king's private *shooting-box, about three miles from Palermo. **1837** LOCKHART *Scott* IV. xi. 350 John Ballantyne, who had at this time a shooting or hunting-box a few miles off in the vale of the Leader. **1912** H. J. BUTLER *Motor Bodies & Chassis* iv. 48 Wagonettes, *Shooting Brakes, and Luggage Cars.—This type of body fulfils the requirements of the sporting dogcart, and generally has sufficient capacity to replace two of these horsed vehicles. **1934** A. G. STREET *Endless Furrow* xvii. 301 After a few minutes occupied with introductions and drinking a glass of sherry James found himself in the shooting brake, and soon the four-in-hand swept through the gates into the town. **1948** H. MCCAUSLAND *Eng. Carriage* iv. 77 A very neat, very sporting little brake..intended for private use in the country with a team or pair, was the Shooting Brake, which had, behind its high box, a strong suggestion of the dog-cart in its bodywork. **1958** *Times* 13 Aug. 4/5 One man was killed and 11 people were injured when a shooting brake and a motor coach were in collision at Holcombe Brook, Bury, to-night. **1802** BINGLEY *Anim. Biog.* (1813) III. 34 The Beaked Chætodon or *Shooting-fish. **1836** DICKENS *Sk. Boz, Gt. Winglebury Duel*, The Pall-mall *shooting-gallery. **1897** CROCKETT *Sir Toady Lion* xix. 151 The Aunt-Sallies, the shooting-galleries, and the miscellaneous side-shows [at the fair]. **1951** *Life* 11 June 120/1 Sometimes he runs a 'shooting gallery', an establishment which not only sells the addict dope but furnishes hypodermics. *a* **1966** 'M. NA GOPALEEN' *Best of Myles* (1968) 323 Put the whole shooting gallery into a saucepan of cold water. **1972** J. WAMBAUGH *Blue Knight* (1973) ii. 36 He knows this boss dyke, a real mean bull dagger. Her pad's a shooting gallery for some of us. **1973** R. BUSBY *Pattern of Violence* v. 79 'Did you call in?'.. 'Yeah. .. The whole shooting gallery 'll be here in a few minutes.' **1545** ASCHAM *Toxoph.* II. (Arb.) 107 Bracer, *shotyng-gloue, stryng, bowe & shafte. **1801** T. ROBERTS *Engl. Bowman* 294 *Shooting-glove*, a glove used on the *shaft-hand* in drawing the String. **1835** J. J. AUDUBON *Ornith. Biogr.* III. 37 There is no lack of *shooting grounds, for every creek of salt-water swarms with Marsh Hens. **1859-61** RAMSAY *Remin.* vi. (1870) 187 A young Englishman had taken a Scottish shooting-ground. **1868** *Rep. to Govt. U.S. Munitions War* 37 The shooting-grounds of the Woolwich Arsenal. **1884** *Pall Mall Gaz.* 24 May 11/1 Australia has been for too many years already the shooting ground of Europe's rubbish. **1897** *Outing* Mar. 536/2 A shooting friend..and myself were staying at a farmhouse, near the shooting-grounds. **1850** R. G. CUMMING *Hunter's Life S. Afr.* (1902) 21 At night I took up a position in an old *shooting-hole beside the vley. **1775** S. ADAMS *Let.* 31 Jan. in *Writings* (1907) III. 172 It puts me in mind of what I remember to have heard you observe, that we may all be soon under the necessity of keeping **Shooting Irons*. **1793-9** J. GERROND *Advertisement* v. Wks. (1815) 109 Dear brother sportsmen, crack the springs Of these things I call shooting-irons. **1891** E. PEACOCK *N. Brendon* I. 149, I shall keep this shooting-iron tonight. **1859** Q. VICTORIA *Leaves Jrnl. Highl.* (1868) 127 Inchrory (a *shooting-lodge of Lord H. Bentinck's). **1750** *Acts Assembly Pennsylv.* (1762) II. 33 Horse races, *Shooting-matches, or other idle Sports. **1813** *Niles' Weekly Register* IV. 35/1, I..gained their applause for my activity at our shooting matches. **1896** [see CON b]. **1922** D. H. LAWRENCE in *N. Y. Times* 24 Dec. 9/4 What a lively shooting match will go on between all the Jacks and the Juans! **1953** K. REISZ *Technique Film Editing* II. 76 The final chase..was best presented as a 'battle of wits', instead of a wild action-packed shooting match. **1974** *BP Shield Internat.* Oct. 2/4 This had the effect of tilting up the whole shooting match. **1890** *Coach Builders' Jrnl.* 15 Nov. 181/2 Another of this firm's exhibits was a *shooting phaeton... It was furnished with luncheon basket. **1898** *Carriage Builders' Jrnl.* Dec. p. ix/2 (Advt.), Four-wheel shooting phaeton; varnished walnut; pigskin cushions, brass mounts and lamps, mat, and gun-box complete. **1908** J. WELLS *Stewart of Lovedale* vi. 41 One of his amusements was to practise at the *shooting-range. **1895** *Army & Navy Co-op Soc. Price List* 15 Sept. 954 Cane *shooting seat. *Ibid.*, Wood, folding Shooting Seat, can be used as a Walking Stick. **1917** *Harrods Gen. Catal.* 1089/2 Mills' Patent Shooting Seats. Strongly recommended as being the lightest and best seat, it is also telescopic. **1683** MOXON *Mech. Exerc., Printing* IX. §2 The *Shooting-stick must be made of Box. **1845** E. J. WAKEFIELD *Adventure N.Z.* I. xi. 319 Every article of trade with the natives has its slang term,—in order that they may converse with each other respecting a purchase without initiating the natives into their calculations, thus pigs and potatoes were respectively represented by '*grunters*' and '*spuds*', guns..by '*shooting-sticks*'. **1866** 'F. KIRKLAND' *Pictorial Bk. Anecdotes* 237/2 Sambo..fell back in confusion when the 'shooting stick' was brandished toward his own breast. **1882** SOUTHWARD *Pract. Printing* (1884) 68 The shooting-stick..transmits the pressure from the mallet to the quoin. **1926** E. P. OPPENHEIM *Golden Beast* I. xvii. 163 Judith had already disappeared, swinging her shooting stick in her hand. **1967** *Guardian* 23 May 2/6 The shooting sticks will prod the roots of every stately garden. **1855** LEIFCHILD *Cornwall* 112 The blasting or *shooting tools of the miner. **1941** *Time* 4 Aug. 15/3, 55%..are ready to risk some kind of *shooting war at once. **1956** F. CASTLE *Violent Hours* vi. 51, I got into the real shooting war towards the close, at Okinawa. **1978** L. HEREN *Growing up on The Times* iii. 86 Pat had joined me before the end of the shooting war, and was almost killed in Jerusalem.

**shooting** ('ʃu:tɪŋ), *ppl. a.* [f. SHOOT *v.* + -ING[2].] That shoots.

**1.** Moving swiftly, darting.

**1535** COVERDALE *Isa.* xxx. 6 The waye that is ful of parell and trouble, because of the lyon and lyones, of the Cockatrice and shutynge dragon. *c* **1710** J. HUGHES *Ode to Creator* iv, The shooting flame obeys th' eternal will, Launch'd from his hand. **1798** WORDSW. *Poems Imag.*, '*Five years have past*' 118, I..read..My former pleasures in the shooting lights Of thy wild eyes. **1887** MEREDITH *Ballads & P.* 151 A pool of scum for shooting flies.

**2.** Sprouting, growing.

**1702** POPE *Dryope* 47 The shooting leaves are seen to rise And shade her. **1798** W. LESLIE *Surv. Moray* iii. 278 A luxuriantly shooting grove of different species of trees.

**3.** Of pain: Sharp and sudden, darting, lancinating. Also of a diseased part, a corn, etc. (see SHOOT *v.* 5).

*c* **1000** *Sax. Leechd.* II. 324 Wiþ sceotendum wenne. **1710** SWIFT *Tatler* No. 238 ¶3 A coming Show'r your shooting Corns presage. **1752** BERKELEY *Tar-water* Wks. III. 497 The shooting pains that precede a cancer. **1898** P. MANSON *Trop. Dis.* xxiii. 354 Among the sympathetic pains [in liver abscess] may be mentioned shooting pains radiating over the chest. **1899** *Allbutt's Syst. Med.* VIII. 618 Pain is usually present from the first, it is shooting in character.

**4.** *Cricket.* (See SHOOT *v.* 1 i.)

**1833** NYREN *Yng. Cricketer's Tutor* 72 Bowling a wicket down with a shooting ball.

**5.** Addicted to the sport of shooting.

**1891** L. B. WALFORD *Mischief of Monica* xiv, She was expecting guests from the North, 'shooting men'.

**shooting star.** [SHOOTING *ppl. a.*; cf. G. *schiessender stern.*]

**1.** A meteor resembling a star, that darts across the sky. (Cf. FALLING STAR.)

**1593** SHAKS. *Rich. II*, II. iv. 19. **1607** *Lingua* II. vi, The shooting Starres Which in an eye-bright euening seem'd to fall. **1667** MILTON *P.L.* IV. 557 Thither came Uriel, gliding ..swift as a shooting Starr In Autumn thwarts the night. **1857** *Rep. Brit. Assoc.* I. 152 This instance, the rare one of an *ascending* shooting star. **1872** PROCTOR *Ess. Astron.* xi. 151 The November shooting-stars.

*attrib.* **1886** BALL *Story of Heavens* xviii. (1897) 378 The periodic shooting star shower known as the Leonids.

**2.** *U.S.* A Western name for the American Cowslip, *Dodecatheon Meadia*.

**1856** A. GRAY *Man. Bot.* 272 *Dodecatheon Meadia*... In the West called Shooting-Star. **1882** *Garden* 13 May 324/2, I send you..two varieties of Dodecatheon. These 'Shooting Stars', as they are called, are very effective.

**shootist** ('ʃu:tɪst). *slang.* [f. SHOOT *v.* + -IST.] One who shoots game, or who competes in a shooting-match; one skilled in shooting. Chiefly *jocular* or *disparaging*.

**1864** *Gold Hill* (Nevada) *News* 15 Jan. 3/1 (*heading*) A Shootist. **1872** SCHELE DE VERE *Americanisms* 657 The man whose rifle brought down the largest amount of game became known as a famous shootist. **1899** F. V. KIRBY *Sport E.C. Africa* iv. 47 Unfortunately it would not be the shootist and his party who would suffer. **1976** *National Observer* (U.S.) 4 Sept. 18/2 J. B. Books, the protagonist of Wayne's new movie, *The Shootist*,..not only restores the legend but expands it, giving the man and his memory grace and dignity. A shootist is a man good with a gun, and J. B. Books is a retired marshal who was good enough to kill 30 men.

**'shootlet.** [f. SHOOT *sb.* + -LET.] A small shoot.
**1889** *Sunday Mag.* Mar. 208/1 We see the field that was all black or brown become green with little shootlets coming up.

**'shoot-out.** orig. *U.S.* Also **shootout.** [f. vbl. phr. *to shoot it out*: see SHOOT *v.* 22 d (*f*).]
**1.** A sustained exchange of shooting, a gun-fight. Also *fig.*, a dispute or competition.
**1953** *N.Y. Times* 5 July VII. 13/2 The justly famous shoot-out between the Earps and the Clantons in the O-K Corral. **1968** 'R. MACDONALD' *Instant Enemy* xxx. 188 The last thing needed was the kind of shoot-out in which innocent people could get hurt. **1969** *Daily Tel.* (Colour Suppl.) 17 Jan. 15/3 In one 'shoot-out' that developed, Oakland police killed a 17-year-old Panther, Bobby Hutton, while he was unarmed. **1975** *Atlanta Jrnl.* 20 Jan. 1/2 In the ensuing shootout Sunday, the man who fired the shot was killed. **1976** *Washington Post* 19 Apr. A4/1 Church's strategy is to have the decisive shoot-out on the Senate floor in a major public debate. **1978** *Fortune* 31 Dec. 59 In the quick-draw tradition of the Old Wild West stagecoach, the two major lines have responded to adversity.. by taking on one another in a fierce and profitless shootout over passenger fares. **1981** *Economist* 8 Aug. 34/1 The normal run of muggings, burglaries and rapes has been exacerbated by shootouts.. among 'cocaine cowboys'.
**2.** *transf.* In *Football*, a tie-breaker (see quot. 1978).
**1978** *Guardian Weekly* 16 June 19/4 If the match is still tied.. the teams resort to a shoot-out. Five different members of each team take a free shot at goal, starting from the 25 yard line and having five seconds to dribble the ball before shooting. If even these ten shots fail to produce a decision, they play a sudden death shoot-out until one side wins. **1979** *Globe & Mail* (Toronto) 1 May 48/9 Johann Scharmann converted the deciding shot in a shootout to win it for Detroit Express.

†**'shootress.** *Obs. rare*⁻¹. [f. SHOOTER + -ESS.] A female shooter.
**1600** FAIRFAX *Tasso* XI. xli.

**'shoot-up.** [f. vbl. phr. *to shoot up*: see SHOOT *v.* 30 e.] **1.** A furious exchange of shooting, a gun-battle, a shoot-out; also, an assault by gun-fire.
**1922** *Blackw. Mag.* Oct. 441/2 A favourite form of amusement of the I.R.A. used to consist in what was commonly called 'shooting up' a district: these outrages took the form of shooting at every Loyalist who appeared within range for a whole evening... Before one of these shoot-ups you might search every house in the district to be shot-up till dusk, and not find any arms..; but soon after dusk.. men would.. distribute arms to the gunmen. **1942** BERREY & VAN DEN BARK *Amer. Thes. Slang* §348/4 *Gun battle*,.. shoot-up. **1962** *Listener* 20 Sept. 438/3 A shoot-up in Alcatraz. **1972** P. DICKINSON *Lizard in Cup* ix. 122 The cops in New Jersey got him in a shoot-up with the Black Panthers. **1978** *New York* 3 Apr. 10/2 Were the Egyptian commandos killed by Cypriot soldiers—as the Cyprus government claims—or by the PLO? Was the shoot-up at Larnaca airport a 'misunderstanding' or a well-conceived plan?
**2.** The act of flying low over a target as if to or actually to attack. *R.A.F. slang.*
**1942** I. GLEED *Arise to Conquer* vi. 62 We do a gentle shoot-up of our billets.

**shoove,** obs. pa. t. of SHAVE *v.*; obs. f. SHOVE.

**shoovelle, shoowre,** obs. ff. SHOVEL, SOUR.

**shop** (ʃɒp), *sb.* Forms: 1 sceoppa, 3 ssoppe, 4-5 schopp, 4-6 schop(p)e, shope, 4-7 shoppe (q.v. also as main entry), 5-6 schop, 5-8 shopp, 6 schoop, shoope, 5- shop; *Sc.* and *north.* 5 shapp, 5-6 chope, 6 choipp, 8 shap, 9 chop. [ME. (*c* 1300) *schoppe* (*ssoppe*):—OE. *sceoppa* wk. masc., occurring only in *Ags. Gosp.* Luke xxi. 1 as rendering of *gazophylacium* treasury (of the temple):—prehist. **skuppan-*, cogn. w. OE. *scypen* SHIPPON (:—**skuppinjō*) and OHG. *scopf* masc., porch, vestibule (MHG. *schopf* str. masc., *schopfe* wk. masc., early and dial. mod.G. *schopf* porch, lean-to building, cart-shed, barn, etc.), MLG. *schoppe*, *schuppe* fem., also *schoppen*, *schuppen* masc. (adopted in mod.G.) shed. The Teut. word was adopted into OF. as *eschoppe*, *escope* (mod.F. *échoppe*), a lean-to booth, cobbler's stall.]
**1. a.** A house or building where goods are made or prepared for sale and sold.
**1297** R. GLOUC. (Rolls) 11222 Þe bowiares ssoppe hii breke & þe bowes nome echon. *c* **1386** CHAUCER *Cook's T.* 52 He [a prentice] loued bet the Tauerne than the shoppe. **1420** *Cov. Leet-bk.* 21 William Oteley, wich kept a cart & horses for clensyng of the stretys, shuld haue quarterly of euery hall dorre jd., & euery schop ob. **1554** *Edin. Burgh Rec.* (1871) II. 288 The cordineris choippis. **1592** *Arden of Feversham* II. i. 23 You are a gouldsmith and haue a lytle plate in your shoppe. **1600** J. PORY tr. *Leo's Africa* II. 315 Among the artizans whosoever is the first inventour of any new and ingenious devise is.. carried.. as it were in triumph from shop to shop. **1752** HUME *Ess. & Treat.* (1777) I. 318 One man erects a shop, to which all the workmen and all the customers repair. **1859** FITZGERALD *Omar* lix, One Evening .. In that old Potter's Shop I stood alone.
†**b.** *banker's shop*: a bank. (Originally, the shop of a goldsmith or other tradesman who practised banking.) *Obs.*
**1752** HUME *Ess. & Treat.* (1777) I. 371 It would be.. imprudent to give a prodigal son a credit in every banker's shop in London. **1796** [see BANKER² 1 c].

**2. a.** A building or room set apart for the sale of merchandize. *to keep shop*: to exercise the calling of a shopkeeper; also *occas.* to take charge of a shop in the shopkeeper's absence. *shop!* an exclamation used to summon an attendant or shopkeeper.
**1362** LANGL. *P. Pl.* A. II. 189 Marchaundes.. Bi-souȝten him in heore schoppes to sullen heore ware. **1435** *Nottingham Rec.* II. 362 A nother comon graund with a draper chope on it. *c* **1440** *Alphabet of Tales* 108 A yong man .. went vnto a fayre; and when he had.. sene many shappis & mekull chafir to sell, at þe laste he come vnto a shop þer ane old man [st]ude. **1515** *Star Chamber Cases* (Selden Soc.) II. 96 Thewe.. bought.. all maner of merchandise.. and kept ane oppin Schoopp for Retailling of the same. **1560-70** J. DAVIS in *Narr. Reform.* (Camden) 63, I have kept the at the gramer skoole a great while, and am minded to have you to keepe the shopp. **1605** CHAPMAN, etc. *Eastw. Hoe* I. A 2 b, Keepe thy shoppe, and thy shoppe will keepe thee. **1682** DRYDEN *Medal* 192 Their Shops are Dens, the Buyer is their Prey. **1712** J. MORTON *Nat. Hist. Northampt.* 405 That Spungy Ball.. call'd.. in the Shops *Bedeguar*. **1770** LUCKOMBE *Hist. Printing* 61 He first kept shop at the sign of our Lady of Piety. **1809** KENDALL *Trav.* I. xii. 136 There are one or two other bookseller's shops.. where books at least are sold. **1848** DICKENS *Dombey* xxiii, Rob was despatched for a coach, the visitors keeping shop meanwhile. **1888** KIPLING *Plain Tales from Hills* 242 A little wife to call 'shorp!' 'shorp!' when the door-bell rung. **1898** *Punch* 4 June 255/2 Millionaire (who has been shown into fashionable Artist's studio, and has been kept waiting a few minutes). 'Shop!'
**b.** *transf.* and *fig.*
**1450-1530** *Myrr. Our Lady* 139 Saynte Ambrose sayeth, that this psalme ys.. a shoppe full of spyces of the holy gooste. **1600** S. NICHOLSON *Acolastus* (1876) 63 The shop where Nature gets her art to showe, Where crimson Roses, sleepe in beds of snowe. **1630** R. JOHNSON *Kingd. & Commw.* 94 Our England is the very shop of the World, and Magazine of Natures dainties. **1677** GILPIN *Dæmonol.* III. i. 6 Temptation is the Shop of Experience.
**c.** The contents of a shop. In quot. *humorously*.
**1906** CHARL. MANSFIELD *Girl & Gods* xix, A fat Jewess with a jeweller's shop on her fingers.
**d.** Used to express the status or characteristics of a retail tradesman. (Cf. 8 b.)
**1848** CLOUGH *Amours de Voy.* I. 125 Middle-class people .. not wholly Pure of the taint of the shop.
**e.** [Back-formation f. SHOP *v.* 4.] An act of shopping for purchases. *colloq.*
**1960** *Housewife* May 121/2 You should find it possible to have one big 'shop' a week with a small mid-week 'shop' for perishables. **1978** D. MURPHY *Place Apart* ix. 198 It was a Saturday morning, when many go into the city centre to do their weekly 'big shop'.
**f.** *shop-within-a-shop*, a shop which functions independently within the premises of a larger store, usu. dealing in the goods of one manufacturer.
**1962** E. GODFREY *Retail Selling & Organ.* i. 5 Another practice.. is that of opening a shop-within-a-shop, selling the manufacturer's goods and staffed by his employees. **1978** *Country Life* 5 Oct. 1054/1 Mulberry Company.. makers of.. high fashion accessories are opening shops-within-shops at nine Nieman Marcus stores.
**3. a.** A building or room set apart and fitted up for the carrying on of some particular kind of handiwork or mechanical industry; a workshop. Now often, a building or room in a factory, appropriated to some particular department or stage of the work carried on there. *the shops*: the workshops of a factory, as distinguished from the counting-house, offices, etc.
**14..** *Voc.* in Wr.-Wülcker 599/10 *Operarium*, a shoppe or a werkehouse. **1587** HIGINS *Mirr. Mag., Author's Induct.* iii, I gate mee strayght the Printers shops unto. **1647** A. ROSS *Mystag. Poet.* xviii. (1675) 415 [Vulcanus] his shop was in Lemnos, where.. he makes Jupiter's thunder. **1728** RAMSAY *Robt., Richy & Sandy* 68 He bad them.. pap Their crazy heads into Tam Tinman's shap. **1869** KOHN *Iron & Steel Manuf.* 23 Extensive engineering and repairing shops are added to these works. *c* **1888** KIPLING *Among Railway Folk* ii. Wks. 1900 XVII. 177 Four-and-twenty engines in every stage of decomposition stand in one huge shop.
**b.** spec. (in full *shop of frames, looms*): a building or apartment fitted with frames or looms and rented by workers in the weaving industries.
*a* **1779** 'J. H. ST. JOHN DE CRÈVECŒUR' *Sk. 18th-Cent. Amer.* (1925) 143 The truly economical farmer has always what we call a shop, that is, a house big enough to contain a loom. There.. our wives can.. weave. **1843** *Penny Cycl.* XXVII. 181/1 Other persons are renters of what is termed a 'shop of frames', containing eight or ten frames. **1844** G. DODD *Textile Manuf.* iv. 142 There are in various parts of the town [Paisley] 'shops' of looms.
†**c.** *fig.* (Chiefly after L. *officina*.) A place where something is produced or elaborated, or where some operation is performed. Often said of the heart, liver, or other internal bodily organs.
**1545** RAYNALD *Byrth Mankynde* I. ix. (1552) 14 b, The lyuer (which is the bloud shop, wher the bloud is engendred). **1579** G. HARVEY *Letter-bk.* (Camden) 83 The very worlde itselfe.. was predestinate to be a schoolehowse and shopp of all villanyes. **1590** SPENSER *F.Q.* II. i. 43 Then gan softly feele Her feeble pulse,.. Which when he felt to moue, he hoped faire To call backe life to her forsaken shop. **1668** CULPEPER & COLE *Barthol. Anat., Man.* II. v. 320 That the fore-parts, the shops of generation.. might be neerer the great Artery. **1737** WHISTON *Josephus, Hist.* IV. iii. §7 The sanctuary was now become.. a shop of tyranny.

**d.** *Glass-making.* A team or gang of workers (see quots.).
**1889** *Harper's New Monthly Mag.* July 259/1 Generally four [glass factory workers] constitute a shop, the most skilful workman (the blower) at the head, the gatherer (a young fellow) next, and two boys, one handling moulds or tools, and the other carrying the products to the annealing oven. **1905** *28th Ann. Rep. New Jersey Bureau Statistics of Labor* III. 201 A case in point.. is the change from single blower method of doing work, which prevailed previous to 1870, to what is now known as the 'shop system'; that is to say, three men now work together, two of them gathering glass and blowing the ware, while the third makes the neck smooth. **1949** P. DAVIS *Devel. Amer. Glass Industry* x. 230 The operation was performed by a three-worker shop composed of a gatherer, a blower, and a crimper. **1970** *Awake* (Austral.) 8 Jan. 23/1 The glassblowers function as a 'shop' of six or seven men.
**e.** *N. Amer.* A schoolroom equipped for teaching the arts of the workshop; this study as a classroom discipline. Cf. *shop class*, sense 9 d below.
**1914** J. S. TAYLOR *Handbook of Vocational Education* iii. 54 The school shop now resembles the abode of the cabinet maker. *Ibid.* v. 65 The student learns much of what industrial life is like.. in the successful operations of.. the school shop. **1941** *School Shop* Oct. 2/2 *School Shop* has been established to serve shop teachers. **1948** G. O. WILBUR *Industrial Arts in General Educ.* ix. 127 There is some evidence which seems to indicate a close correlation between the atmosphere of the school shop and the type of learning which takes place there. **1974** J. HELLER *Something Happened* 224 The new teachers, the old teachers,.. the shop teacher, and the science teacher (he has always been leery of shop teachers and science teachers. Perhaps because they are men.) **1978** *Detroit Free Press* 2 Apr. 3D/1 A school ..cannot prevent a girl from taking shop or a boy from taking home economics.
**4. a.** *colloq.* or *slang.* A place of business; the place where one's ordinary occupation is carried on. Also used jocularly for 'place'. *the Shop* (*Army slang*): the Royal Military Academy, Woolwich; also (*Austral. slang*), the University of Melbourne.
**1779** E. GIBBON *Let.* 15 May (1956) II. 215 So much remains to be done, that I can hardly spare a single day from the Shop. **1827** T. SURR *Richmond* II. i. 5, I hurried off with Bucks to the office, or *shop*, as he called it. **1841** THACKERAY *Gt. Hoggarty Diamond* ii, At the shop, as we called it (it wasn't a shop, but as splendid an office as any in Cornhill) he was always talking about Vestris and Miss Tree. **1848** —— *Van. Fair* xxxiv, Senior Wrangler, indeed; that's at the other shop. **1889** *Centennial Mag.* II. III. 218 It related how 'a medical student came up to the Shop' as a freshman, and 'thought through exams. he would speedily pop'. **1899** KIPLING *Stalky* 199 They're goin' up for Sandhurst, or the Shop, in less than a year. **1918** G. WALL *Lett. of Airman* 15, I would be quite glad to get the Shop exam results. **1964** G. JOHNSTON *My Brother Jack* 260 The years at the Shop gave me nothing except a worthless B.A. and the privilege of being thrown into the University lake. **1978** G. M. FRASER *Flashman at Charge* 110 We treated each other decently, and weren't one jot more incompetent than this Sandhurst-and-Shop crowd.
**b.** *Stage slang.* An engagement, a 'berth'. Also in gen. use (*rare*).
**1885** J. K. JEROME *On Stage & Off* 126 After that it was next to impossible for him to get a shop (this expression is not slang, it is a bit of local colour). **1892** *Cassell's Sat. Jrnl.* 28 Sept. 27/2 In the long summer months,.. the artiste is frequently out of a 'shop', as he terms his engagement. **1922** E. WALLACE *Flying Fifty-Five* xxx. 178 Fired, are you?.. Well, what are you going to do? Get another shop? **1978** G. MITCHELL *Wraiths & Changelings* xii. 128 He was an out-of-work actor and was very anxious to get a shop, as he called it.
**5.** Matters pertaining to one's trade or profession; discourse on matters of this kind, esp. as introduced unseasonably into general conversation; chiefly in phrase *to talk shop* (see TALK *v.* 7).
*a* **1814** *Last Act* I. iii. in *New Brit. Theatre* II. 379 Come, Tom, no shop now. **1856** KINGSLEY *Let.* May (D.), Three hours useless (I fear) speechifying and shop. **1860** C. FOX *Jrnl.* 28 Sept. (1972) 232 Holman Hunt.. does not talk 'shop', but is perfectly willing to tell you anything you really wish to know of his painting. **1902** *Brit. Med. Jrnl.* 12 Apr. 924 Nurses are given to talking 'shop'.., and the gruesomeness of their 'shop' makes it and them a terror to their friends.
**6.** *slang.* †**a.** A prison. *Obs.* **b.** The mouth. Hence phr. *shut your shop*: be silent, hold your tongue.
**a.** *a* **1700** B. E. *Dict. Cant. Crew*, *Shop*, a prison.
**b.** **1868** J. HARTLEY *Budget* 32 (E.D.D.), Th' maister oppened sich a shop 'at aw thowt th' top ov his heead had come off.
**7.** *Stock Exchange.* The inside influences affecting or controlling a company by the exercise of special knowledge; also a name for the South African gold market.
**1889** *Rialto* 23 May (Farmer), The latest name for the South African gold market is the Shop. **1906** *Westm. Gaz.* 24 Nov. 15/1 The account.. has not been barren of business in a good many of the departments of the House, although a good deal was of the speculative kind, engineered by the 'shops'.
**8.** *Phrases.* **a.** With sbs.: *shop and job* (attrib.): ? formed by an association of permanent and temporary workers. *shop to shop*: carried on from shop to shop in succession.
**1891** *Daily News* 24 Nov. 3/3 A specially summoned 'shop and job' delegate meeting of carpenters and joiners was held

last night. **1898** *Westm. Gaz.* 28 Apr. 10/1 A general inquiry and shop-to-shop visit.

**b.** With verbs. †*to break up shop*: to become bankrupt. *to come to the right* (or *wrong*) *shop*: to apply to the right (or wrong) person in order to obtain something. *to live over the shop*, to live on the premises where one works. *to mind the shop*: see MIND *v.* 11. *to set up shop*: to start a business; also *fig.* *to shut up shop*: to close business premises; hence, to withdraw from or bring to a close any business. *to smell of the shop*: (*a*) to indicate the spirit characteristic of a shopkeeper; (*b*) of remarks or expressions, to savour unduly of the speaker's profession or calling. †*to stick to the shop*: to continue a business (in quot. with ref. to sense 4).

*c* **1570** *Wyfe in Morrelles Skin* 596 in Hazl. *E.E.P.* IV. 204 He set vp his shop with haberdash ware. **1599** DEKKER *Shoemakers Holiday* v. ii. (1610) I 4, We may shut vp our shops, and make holiday. **1650** VAUGHAN *Silex Scint., Faith* 19 Stars shut up shop, mists pack away, And the Moon mourns. **1659** N. R. *Prov., Eng. Fr.* etc. 58 He that hath not his Craft let him shut up shop. **1712** ARBUTHNOT *John Bull* II. iv, And to have these Usurers transact my Debts at Coffee-Houses, and Ale Houses, as if I were going to break-up Shop. **1826** J. BANNISTER *Let.* in *Sotheran's Catal.* No. 12 (1899) 1, I shall 'stick to the shop' till I quit the stage of life. **1831** MRS. SHERWOOD *Henry Milner* III. xvi. 320 Provided such double dealings did not smell too much of the shop, or indicate too much of the spirit of the common tradesman. **1837** DICKENS *Sk. Boz, Drunkard's Death*, And what does he want?..money? meat? drink? He's come to the wrong shop for that, if he does. **1838** —— *Nich. Nick.* iv, They have come to the right shop for morals. **1860** GEN. P. THOMPSON *Audi Alt.* III. 95 The Royal Society might as well be invited to shut up shop, because Newton made huge discoveries. **1880** PAYN *Confid. Agent* II. 207 To use a vulgar image, it smells of the shop. **1930** D. L. SAYERS *Strong Poison* i. 23 'He's put her into a house somewhere round about, I fancy,' said Freddy, 'with a typewriting office to look after and live over the shop and run those comic charity stunts of his.' **1963** A. HUXLEY *Let.* 27 Mar. (1969) 952, I..heard of his plans for an LSD institute... He may be more successful in setting up shop within the US. **1976** H. WILSON *Governance of Britain* iv. 83 In 1964–70 I lived in No. 10. In 1974 I decided that I did not want to live over the shop again, and I slept each night in my home in Lord North Street.

**c.** Adverbial phr. *all over the shop*: scattered about the place, spread out in every direction; following an erratic and undefined course; in a state of confusion.

**1874** HOTTEN *Slang Dict.* 288 In pugilistic slang, to punish a man severely is 'to knock him all over the shop'. **1886** *Pall Mall Gaz.* 29 July 1/2 Formerly, the authorities associated with our fisheries were 'all over the shop', if a vulgarism of the day be permissible. **1893** KIPLING *Many Invent.* 109 To go sailing all over the shop never knowing where they'd fetch the land. **1916** 'TAFFRAIL' *Pincher Martin* xiv. 267 'Wagglin' about a bit,' the coxswain answered, gazing at his compass-card... 'She's all over the shop. Up to sou'-east one minute, an' back to south-eighty the next.' **1926** G. B. SHAW *Intell. Woman's Guide* lxxi. 345 The unconventional ones are all over the shop with all sorts of opinions. **1935** F. M. FORD *Let.* 15 Oct. (1965) 245 He is in the greatest danger of going slack all over the shop. **1978** J. I. M. STEWART *Full Term* ix. 93 At one of Anthea Gender's [parties] one was substantially although not too obtrusively in the presence of grandees drawn from all over the shop.

**9.** *attrib.* and *Comb.* **a.** Simple attributive with various notions. (*a*) Forming a part or an adjunct of a shop, as *shop-bell*, *-counter*, *-door*, *-front* (also *attrib.* and *fig.*), *-shutter*, *sign*, †*-stall*, *-till* (also attrib. in fig. sense). (*b*) Used in a shop, as *shop-coat*, *-ledger*, †*-thread*, †*-tool*. (*c*) Sold or kept in a shop (†sometimes = 'officinal'), as *shop-goods*, †*preparation*, *wares*. (*d*) Performed or carried on in a shop; belonging to or connected with a shop; as †*shop-business*, *-club*, †*-craft*, *hours*, †*-shift*. (*e*) Of persons: Belonging to a shop; employed in or about a shop; as *shop-boy*, *-clerk*, *-folk*, *-girl*, †*-maid*, *-mate*, †*-merchant*, *-people*, *-wife*, *-woman*, *-worker*.

**1853** MRS. GASKELL *Cranford* xv. 299 She..was only extricated from her dilemma by the sound of the *shop-bell. **1972** J. THOMSON *Not One of Us* viii. 90 The tinkle of the shop bell severed the conversation and she went through to serve. **1813** JANE AUSTEN *Pride & Prejudice* I. xv. 166 Mr. Jones's *shop boy..had told her that they were not to send any more draughts to Netherfield. **1834** HT. MARTINEAU *Farrers* iii. 39 Sam the shop-boy. **1903** G. B. SHAW *Man & Superman* III. 132, I breathe an atmosphere of sweetness, like a confectioner's shopboy. **1977** *Daily Times* (Lagos) 25 Dec. 22/4 (Advt.), Drivers—Houseboys, Shopboys, Shopgirls, Housegirls. **1767** S. PATERSON *Another Trav.* II. 157 No further *shop-business could be transacted that day. **1911** H. S. HARRISON *Queed* xiii. 151 There is your public ..*shop-clerks, stenographers [etc.]. **1921** *Dict. Occup. Terms* (1927) §939 *Shopclerk*.., keeps record of amount of work done by piece workers for purpose of calculating cost and wages. **1902** *Act 2 Edw. VII*, c. 21 title, An Act to prohibit compulsory Membership of Unregistered *Shop Clubs or Thrift Funds. **1852** DICKENS *Bleak Ho.* x, He stands at his door in his gray *shop-coat. **1822** D. WORDSWORTH *Jrnl.* 21 Sept. (1941) II. viii. 361 One a gentlemanly, middle aged man; the other rather younger, with a dash of the *shop-counter. **1972** *Listener* 23 Nov. 690/1 'Voluntary price control'..has certainly not worked over the shop counter where it was most needed. **1691** *Siege & Surrender of Mons* III. iii. 25 O Priest-Craft, *Shop-Craft! how do ye Effeminate The Mind of Man. **1477–9** *Rec. St. Mary at Hill* 85 For a key to William Blases *shoppe door. *a* **1745** SWIFT *Works* (1766) XIII. 47 Our shop-doors will be no longer crowded with so many thieves and pick-pockets. **1832** *Chambers's Edin. Jrnl.* I. 277/1 Transported, he through the shop-door pops his head. **1977** A. HUNTER *Gently Instrumental* v. 60 The hour of the lunchtime siesta when every shop door was closed. **1823** J. BADCOCK *Dom. Amusem.* 176 Persons who have..taken the oxalic acid, under the appalling mistake of *shopfolk serving it for Epsom salts. **1835** DICKENS in *Evening Chron.* 14 July 3/3 He..got his butcher to skewer them up on conspicuous joints in his *shop-front. **1838** —— *O. Twist* v, A great many of the tenements had shop-fronts. **1873** BROWNING *Red. Cott. Nt.-cap* 2 Bound for some shop-front in the Place Vendôme. **1934** *Times Lit. Suppl.* 25 Jan. 61/1 (*title*) Modern shopfront construction. **1961** D. HOLBROOK *Eng. for Maturity* 15, I never knew how much shop-front is behind—or perhaps in front of—teaching. **1975** *Sunday Times* 3 Aug. 24/6 The keening nature of the sounds resembles so often the seizing music one has heard in shop-front gospel churches all over America. **1820** M. EDGEWORTH *Let.* 21 May (1979) 134 The fishwomen, criers and *shopgirls whose manners to customers are in general a curious mixture of the affected indifference..and of the real anxiety for your custom. **1824** W. IRVING *Tales Trav.* II. vii. (1848) 152 A hint to all haberdashers who have pretty daughters for shop-girls. *c* **1855** GEO. ELIOT in J. W. Cross *George Eliot's Life* (1885) I. vi. 364 She looked like a shop-girl who has donned a masquerade dress impromptu. **1951** A. BARON *Rosie Hogarth* 176 She forced herself to speak calmly, in her precise shopgirl's voice. **1686** *Lond. Gaz.* No. 2147/4 Remnants of Cloth and Serges, seeming to be *Shop-Goods. **1796** J. WOODFORDE *Diary* 2 Apr. (1929) IV. 268 Betty Cary went wth. him, to bring home some Shop Goods. **1875** [see ABUSEFULLY *adv.*]. **1972** *Morning Star* 11 Oct. 1 Wage earners might receive more in their pay packets than they do at present but might pay more than they gained in the extra tax paid on shop goods. **1892** *Act 55 & 56 Vict.* c. 62 §1 This Act may be cited as the *Shop Hours Act, 1892. **1967** *Observer* 14 May 28/7 Shop hours are 10–7 p.m. **1782** MISS BURNEY *Cecilia* IX. i. (1882) II. 281 They know no more of reasoning and arguing than they do of a *shop ledger. **1659** BROME *Eng. Moor* III. iii, The streight spiny *Shop-maid of St. Martins. **1851** MAYHEW *Lond. Labour* I. 343/1 Two of my *shopmates were boys. **1619** PURCHAS *Microcosmus* lv. 521 The Haberdasher of Hats (the *Shop-Merchant). **1854** MRS. GASKELL *North & South* xi, The pretence that makes the vulgarity of *shop-people. **1723** P. BLAIR *Pharmaco-Bot.* I. 12 Lavender Cotton is but seldom us'd in *Shop-Preparations. **1616** B. JONSON *Devil an Ass* III. v. 4 There's a *shop-shift! plague on 'hem. **1851** THACKERAY *Eng. Hum.* v. (1853) 257 'Milksop!' roars Harry Fielding, clattering at the timid *shop-shutters. **1876** *Remin. Old Draper* 6, I used to take down the shop shutters and put them up at night. **1930** *Daily Express* 6 Oct. 3/5 A great flame which lit up the whole sky..and clearly illuminated the *shop signs. **1969** E. H. PINTO *Treen* 410/2 Trade labels on London goods sold between 1765 and 1770, are sometimes printed with the old shop sign. **1614** RALEIGH *Hist. World* v. i. §1. 312 The things performed..by our common English Souldier, leauied in haste, from following the Cart, or sitting on the *shop-stall. **1635** *Roxb. Ball.* (1890) VII. 141 Nay, if a Shoomaker me wed, his *Shop-Thread I can spin. **1835** DICKENS *Sk. Boz, Priv. Theatres*, The sums extracted from the *shop-till. **1599** DEKKER *Shoemakers Holiday* III. i. (1610) D 2 b, Master, ile stay no longer, heres a vennentorie of my *shop tooles. **1661** *Knaresb. Wills* (Surtees) II. 249 All my shopp tooles and instruments belonging to my trade. **1877** RUSKIN *St. Mark's Rest* i. §12 These mighty gaseous illuminations by which Venice provides for your seeing her *shop-wares by night. **1863** J. THOMSON *Poems, Polish Insurgent* viii, These rich *shopwives who stare. **1753** *World* No. 4. 20 She enquired of the *shop-woman if she knew the gentleman. **1861** *Sat. Rev.* 30 Nov. 556 Plain men are quite right to do all they can for ragged boys and young shopwomen. **1896** *Shop Assistant* Aug. 11/2 Manchester may again be counted as a stronghold of unionism amongst *shop workers, eager and ready for the fray..which shall emancipate the shop slaves from slavery. **1966** *Listener* 25 Aug. 264/2 Shop-workers' union is to join the opposition to the Government's wage freeze.

**b.** Objective and obj. genitive, as *shop-holder*, *-shutting*; locative, as *shop-bought* adj.; *shop-done* adj. (*nonce use*).

**1894** BOTTONE *Electr. Instr.* 26 In *shop-bought instruments glass handles are generally seen. **1888** G. M. HOPKINS *Let.* 1 May (1956) 291, I may be able to send you one [*sc.* a photograph] of me, not *shop-done but artistically better. **14..** *Mercers' Oath* in Blades *Caxton* (1882) 146 Vnto suche tyme as that ye have ben..for *shopholder amytted sworn and entred. **1880** A. MᶜKAY *Hist. Kilmarnock* (ed. 4) 247 He was a friend to the system of early *shop-shutting.

**c.** Applied to food, goods, etc., produced commercially for sale, as (often unfavourably) opposed to home-made or made to order, as *shop-bread*, *cake*, etc.; shop-bought.

**1859** GEO. ELIOT *Adam Bede* II. I. xx. 95 A cloth made of homespun linen... None of your bleached 'shop-rag' that would wear into holes in no time. **1876** C. M. YONGE *Three Brides* II. i. 304 I'm sent for one of Herbert's shirts... I believe their hearts would break outright if he took to shop ones. **1928** E. G. MILLAR *Eng. Illuminated MSS. of XIVth & XVth Cent.* iii. 38 Sarum Horae... These are seldom of more than mediocre quality, and are merely 'shop' copies. **1949** D. SMITH *I capture Castle* xii. 203, I had..two slices of cake (real shop cake) and milk. **1957** J. BRAINE *Room at Top* xxi. 180 It must have seemed that she was offering me a good home-cooked dinner and that I was rejecting it in favour of a slice of chalky shop bread spread with factory-made meat paste. **1975** *Times* 22 Nov. 11/6 As late as the 1930s the better-off continued to look down on those who..spread 'shop' jam on their bread. **1978** D. MURPHY *Place Apart* xi. 229 She brought out a slice of Christmas cake... 'It's only shop,' she apologised.

**d.** Special comb.: **shop assistant**, a salesman or saleswoman in a retail shop or store; **shop-bill** = *shop-card*; **shop-book**, a shopkeeper's or mechanic's account book; *spec.* (U.S.) see quot. 1856; **shop-breaker**, a burglar who breaks into a shop; **shop-breaking**, the offence committed by a shop-breaker; †**shop-bulk** [BULK *sb.*²], a shop-front; **shop-card**, a written or printed advertisement of the contents of a shop; **shop class** *N. Amer.*, a class in which the arts of the workshop are taught (cf. sense 3 e above); †**shop-cloth**, a cloth laid upon the boards of a butcher's stall; **shop committee** *U.S.* (see quot. 1923); †**shop-conscience**, a venal conscience; **shopcraft** *N. Amer.*, an association of railway employees working in repair shops, etc.; †**shop-divine** *nonce-wd.*, a divine who keeps a stock of approved spiritual medicines; **shop-dropper** *local Austral. colloq.* (see quot. 1957) (cf. DROPPER 1 d); †**shop dust**, the refuse of a shop; †**shop-fellow**, an intimate; **shop-finish**, the professional finish of an article produced in a commercial workshop (sometimes depreciatory); also *transf.*; hence **shop-finished** *ppl. a.*; **shop-fitting**, (*a*) *pl.*, the fitments (as counters and shelves) with which a shop is equipped; (*b*) the action or process of fitting out a shop with these; hence **shop-fitter**; **shop-gaze** *v. intr.*, to window-shop; **shop-house**, in S.E. Asia, a shop opening on to the pavement and also used as the residence of the proprietor; †**shop-light**, ? a fan-light, a window giving entrance to light from the top of a room or building; **shop-like** *a.*, †(*a*) venal, meretricious; (*b*) resembling a shop; **shop-list** = *shop-card*; †**shop-magistral** = *shop-medicine*; **shop-mark**, a private mark placed by a dealer upon his goods; †**shop-medicine**, an officinal medicine; †**shop-note**, a credit note exchangeable for goods at a shop; †**shop-pad** [PAD *sb.*² 3], a thief who steals from a shop; †**shop-price**, a wage paid to a permanently engaged worker in a factory or workshop; †**shop-purger**, see *shop-medicine*; †**shop-rid** *a.* [after *bed-rid*], worn out by lying in a shop; †**shop-slop**, used contemptuously for *shop-medicine*; **shop-soiled** *a.*, depreciated in value and appearance by being exposed for sale in a shop; also *fig.*; **shop steward**, a person elected by his or her fellow-workers in a factory, etc., or a branch of it as their spokesman on conditions of work, etc.; **shop-talk**, see sense 5; **shop-thief**, †(*a*) a dealer who carries on his business dishonestly; (*b*) a thief who steals from a shop; **shop-ticket** = *shop-note*; **shop-walker**, an assistant exercising general supervision over a department of a shop; an attendant who directs customers to that part of the premises where the goods they wish to inspect or purchase are to be found; so **shop-walk** *v. intr.*, to act as a shop-walker; **shop-work**, work done in a shop or workshop; **shop-worn** *a.* = *shop-soiled*, (orig. *U.S.*) also *fig.* See also SHOP-BOARD, etc.

**1880** *Girl's Own Paper* 25 Sept. 612/1 There are two great enemies for the *shop assistant—the severe shop-walker.. and the inconsiderate lady-customer. **1921** *Dict. Occup. Terms* (1927) §775 *Shop assistant*.., serves customers with goods in retail shop or store, makes out bill or docket. **1977** D. JAMES *Spy at Evening* xii. 86 They were mostly school kids..or young shop assistants and working boys. **1780** *Mirror* No. 89 Much of the employment a shop-keeper gets, is owing to the attraction of a happy-fancied sign, advertisement, or *shop-bill. **1890** *N. & Q.* Ser. VII. IX. 432 The late Mr. Anderson..had collected a great number of engraved shop-bills as specimens of the engraver's art. **1609–10** *Act 7 Jas. I*, c. 12 §1 No Tradesman..shall..be allowed..to give his *Shoppbooke in Evidence in any Accion for any Money due for Wares [etc.]. **1798** HUTTON *Course Math.* (1807) II. 251 My plumber has set me up a cistern, and his shop-book being burnt, he has no means of bringing in the charge. **1856** BOUVIER *Amer. Law Dict.* (ed. 6), *Shop Book*, a book in which a merchant, mechanic, or other person, makes original entries of goods sold or work done. **1585** HIGINS *Junius' Nomencl.* 424 *Directarii*..night-theeues: *shopbreakers: robbers by night. **1907** *Daily Chron.* 29 Nov. 5/5 They found wounds upon his body corresponding with the blows delivered upon the shop breaker. **1906** *Ibid.* 23 Jan. 6/2 A charge of *shop-breaking. **1586** LUPTON *1000 Notable Things* (1675) 288 Dr. Butler.. went close to the *shopbulks to keep himself drie. *a* **1843** SOUTHEY *Comm.-pl. Bk.* (1851) IV. 258/1 A song or sonnet on an upholsterer's *shop card. **1948** G. O. WILBUR *Industrial Arts in General Educ.* xiv. 212 If students go home enthusiastic about the work in their *shop classes, a general approval of the whole school program by the parents is apt to follow. **1962** A. LURIE *Love & Friendship* iv. 70 On the last day of school he would take home the present he had made for his mother in shop class. **1978** M. PUZO *Fools Die* xxxix. 435 In the shop class of the asylum school I made myself such a hat. **1501** *Maldon* (Essex) *Court-Rolls* Bundle 60 No. 4 b, Attachiatus est per xiiii pecias beff et mete precii xvii *d.* et 1 *shopcloth in custodia servientis. **1908** *Mod. Business* Aug. 69/1 With a good *shop committee the men will not be afraid to ventilate their grievances. **1923** J. D. HACKETT *Labor Terms* in *Managem. Engin.* May 344/2 *Shop Committee*, a committee appointed by members of a works committee for the consideration of some special labor problem. **1954** C. E. DANKERT *Introd. Labor* x. 187 In many labor organizations there are structural units smaller than, and subordinate to, the locals. These are the so-called shop committees, which are under the leadership of shop stewards. **1973** S. Aronowitz in G. Hunnius et al. *Workers' Control* I. 105 The impulse to dual forms of struggle—shop committees, wild cat strikes, steward movements—may become important in the labor movements of the future. **1683** Dryden *Dk. Guise* I. i, *Shop-Consciences, of Proof against an Oath. **1919** W. Hines *Let.* 10 Nov. in *Official Proc. 5th Biennial Convention Railway Employees Dept. Amer. Fed. Labor* (1920) 133 The fullest cooperation of.. the national officers of the *Shop Crafts organizations. **1942** H. E. Jones *Wages & Labor Relations in Railroad Industry 1900–1941* 14 For shop craft employees, annual compensation stood at $1,754 in 1922. **1973** *Daily Colonist* (Victoria, B.C.) 7 Sept. 1/4 Latest union flareup occurred.. as members of Canadian National Railways shopcraft unions walked off the job. **1672** Marvell *Reh. Transp.* II. (1673) 22 Some doubt there is that his *Shop-Divines have not the right Composition of that Medicine. **1957** *Courier-Mail* (Brisbane) 26 Nov. 2 '*Shop-droppers' are truck owners who buy large quantities of fruit and vegetables at the market and sell them to shopkeepers in and around Brisbane. **1967** *Sunday Mail* (Brisbane) 12 Feb. 18 The suppliers—known as 'shop-droppers'—have been operating for several years. **1592** Nashe *P. Penilesse* A 4 b, Greedinesse .. busies himselfe.. in syuing of Muck-hills and *shop-dust. **1579** Northbrooke *Dicing* To Rdr. A 4, A good companion and a *shopfellowe. **1923** *New Statesman* 6 Oct. 738/1 They [*sc.* early plays by Somerset Maugham] had the handy compactness, *shop-finish and alluring shinyness of a new dressing-case. **1931** R. Fry in W. Rose *Outl. Mod. Knowl.* 914 This last perfection of finish, for which craftsmen have adopted the excellent term 'shop-finish'. **1938** R. G. Collingwood *Princ. Art* xv. 329 The slick shop-finish of a ready-made article. **1932** R. Fry *Characteristics French Art* II. 43 Elsheimer's pictures are so tight, so horribly *shop-finished and over-polished. **1885** *List of Subscribers, Classified* (United Telephone Co.) (ed. 6) 188 (*heading*) *Shop fitters. **1921** *Dict. Occup. Terms* (1927) §483 *Shop fitter*, receives wooden parts or sections of counters, desks, ..and other shop-fittings.. fits and joins these parts or sections together. **1951** A. Baron *Rosie Hogarth* 13 Fred was an engineer and Jack a shopfitter by trade. **1978** *Detroit Free Press* 16 Apr. (Parade Suppl.) 21/1 The 33 indicted.. included.. a shopfitter. **1858** P. L. Simmonds *Dict. Trade Products* 342 **Shop-fittings*, the counters, desks, shelves, gas-burners, and other fixtures of a shop. **1911** *Rep. Labour & Soc. Cond. Germany* III. vi–vii. 29 The building and shopfitting trade. **1939** C. Vernon *Sweet Shop* xii. xlix. 178 We give in this chapter some general hints on shop fitting and decoration. **1959** R. Buckner *Design for Selling* ii. 14 So many bakers are altering their shop fittings to comply with the hygiene regulations. **1977** *Centuryan* (Office Cleaning Services) Christmas 2/4 The firm was concentrating too much on shopfitting for one client. **1876** L. Troubridge *Life amongst Troubridges* (1966) 143 Shopped the whole morning—*flanéed* down Regent Street, *shop-gazing with true country zeal. **1946** S. Spender *European Witness* 21 Crowds who a few years ago were shop-gazing in their city. **1949** *Malayan Pictorial Observer* Aug. 9 *Shop-houses line the main street. **1957** G. W. Skinner *Chinese Society in Thailand* iii. 107 By the 1880's.. the junk bazaar was.. a thing of the past... The former floating population of Chinese tradesmen moved to the two-story shop-houses built in rows along the new streets. **1966** 'A. Hall' *9th Directive* i. 7 Where the trishaw had dropped me.. was a narrow street of shop-houses. **1978** L. Heren *Growing up on The Times* v. 182 The shophouse had four small rooms. The front room, or shop, was given over to a dispensary... Behind were two small bedrooms and a kitchen. **1631** A. Townshend *Alb. Tri.* Poems & Masks (1912) 65 Is not your studdy backward? with a *shop-light in it, where one can see nothing but the skye? **1636** B. Jonson *Discov.* (1640) 92 Some love any Strumpet (be shee never so *shop-like, or meritorious) in good clothes. **1849** Rock *Ch. Fathers* I. 222 A church is built N. and S. merely for the sake of showing itself well, shoplike, from the street. **1780** *Mirror* No. 89, I ..am resolved to bestow more than common pains in furnishing out as elegant a *shop-list as possible. **1665** Nedham *Med. Medicinæ* 312 Treacle-water, a few Syrups, and 1 or 2 *Shop-Magistrals. **1592** *Act 35 Eliz.* c. 10 §1 That eche Weaver should weave his *Shopmarke in eche Dozen. **1801** Mar. Edgeworth *Pop. Tales, Contrast* Tales 1832 V. 120 His sisters unpacked them.. to set shop-marks upon each article. **1756** Law *Lett. Important Subj.* 170 If your physician be for your purpose, he will not load you with *shop-medicines. **1740** W. Douglass *Disc.* 23 The Shopkeepers giving a great Advance in Consideration of a very long Credit, and to be drawn out in *Shop Notes. **1705** Dunton *Life & Errors* (1818) I. vii. 261, I verily think, without restitution, such *shop-pads cannot be saved. **1838** in *Rep. Comm. Hand-loom Weavers* iv. (1840) 334 The few under-journeymen who.. receive from them the full *shop-price for their labour. **1665** Nedham *Med. Medicinæ* 89 Nor is it thus only with the *Shop-purgers, but even by the ordinary Diet-Drinks used in Families. *c* **1610** Beaum. & Fl. *Philaster* v. i, May their false lights.. discover presses, holes, stains, and oldness in their Stuffs, and make them *shop-rid. **1706** Baynard *Cold Baths* ii. 267 Swallowing Bolus upon Bolus, together with a Scavengers Cart full of all their other *Shop-slops. **1898** *Cycling* 11 In the fall of the year '*shop-soiled' machines are often to be bought for a couple of pounds or so less than at the beginning of the season. **1926** T. E. Lawrence *Seven Pillars* (1935) v. lix. 333 Beyrout was the door of Syria, a chromatic Levantine screen through which cheap or shop-soiled foreign influences entered. **1927** M. Arlen *Young Men in Love* ii. 137 Always together... That shop-soiled man and the tall girl with the curly gleaming hair. **1977** J. Wainwright *Day of Peppercorn Kill* 33 Not the love of a wife... A shop-soiled love—which.. he'd reject. **1904** *Rules Amalg. Soc. Engineers* 46 Committees may also appoint *shop-stewards to.. keep the committee posted with all events occurring in the various shops. **1928** *Britain's Industr. Future* (Liberal Industr. Inquiry.) iii. xviii. 226 The shop-steward movement, which reached such magnitude during the War, was essentially an attempt to base the struggle for better conditions upon the natural unit of the factory. **1950** A. P. Herbert *Independent Member* 251 At Short's works at Rochester.. the shop-stewards threatened a strike. *a* **1974** R. Crossman *Diaries* (1975) I. 478 This is the first big event of this election campaign—the revelation of a so-called kangaroo trial by shop stewards at the B.M.C. works. **1881** *Scribner's Monthly* XXII. 864/2 The continual *shop-talk of three passengers opposite. **1922** S. Lewis *Babbitt* x. 143 The shop-talk roused Paul Riesling... He was.. a very able salesman. **1971** D. E. Westlake *I gave at Office* 76, I must have given her my complete life story.. and virtually tons of shoptalk about my job. **1692** T. Watson *Body Divin.* 377 The *Shop-Thief, he steals in selling [etc.]. **1913** *Everyman* 21 Feb. 582/2 The spies and detectives.. watch not only for the shop-thief but seek to catch the poor assistant tripping. **1867** *Rep. Paris Univ. Exhib.* (1868) VI. 272 Are there any sources of profit besides the annual dividend? e.g. by *shop tickets or other advantages of a similar kind. **1905** H. G. Wells *Kipps* i. vi. 135 Buggins, whose place it was to *shopwalk while Carshot served, shopwalked with quite unparalleled dignity. **1825** in A. Nicoll *Hist. Eng. Drama 1660–1900* (1959) VI. 459 (*title of play*) The *shop-walker. **1861** Sala *Dutch Pict.* xv. 235 A sort of shop-walker, whose duty it was to pace the galleries. **1896** Wells *Wheels of Chance* ii. 13 The shop-walker brings up parallel to the counter. **1899** W. James *Talks to Teachers* v. 35 Laboratory work and *shop work engender a habit of observation, .. a knowledge of the difference between accuracy and vagueness. **1932** O. E. Saunders *Hist. Eng. Art in Middle Ages* xiii. 157 Countless lesser Books of Hours were turned out all through the fifteenth and sixteenth centuries for private patrons, but they represent mere shop-work. **1974** J. Burnett *Useful Toil* ii. 141 Girls could now go into shop work, into the new light factory trades and into.. clerical work. **1838** *Amer. Comic All-I-Make for 1839* 7 The piece of goods got kinder *shop worn, and the old man thought he'd never get her off his hands. **1849** Thoreau *Week Concord Riv.* 220 He is even envied by his shop-worn neighbours. **1871** P. T. Barnum *Struggles & Triumphs* 40 A large quantity of tin ware which had been in the shop for years and was considerably 'shop-worn'. **1901** *N. Amer. Rev.* Feb. 168 One can get shop-worn kings for less. **1909** Vachell *Paladin* 112 Peace with honour.. has become slightly shop-worn.

**shop** (ʃɒp), *v.* [f. shop *sb.*]

**1. a.** *trans.* To shut up (a person), to imprison. Of an informer, evidence, etc.: To cause to be imprisoned, to 'get (a person) into trouble'. Also with *up*. Now only *slang* or *dial.*

**1583** Stocker *Civ. Warres Lowe C.* iv. 52 b, [They] onely shopped vp some of the Catholikes within their owne house. **1678** [? Winstanley] *Four for a Penny* 8 A main part of his Office [a bum-bailiff's] is to swear and bluster at their trembling Prisoners, and cry, Confound us, why do we wait? Let's Shop him! **1701** Sedley *Grumbler* iii. i, He talks like a fool, and was presently shopp'd up. **1771** Smollett *Humph. Cl.* 11 June (1815) 182 He did not at all doubt but that they would find matter enough to shop the evidence himself before the next jail-delivery. **1838** Dickens *O. Twist* xvi, It was Bartlemy time when I was shopped. **1899** *Tit-Bits* 20 May 150/1 [He] volunteered for a fiver to 'shop' his pals.

*refl.* **1548** Patten *Exped. Scot.* B viij, Thei had likewise shopt vp themselfes in yᵉ highest of their house.

**b.** To dismiss (a person) from a position or post. *rare.*

**1864** Hotten *Slang Dict.* 228 *Shop*, to discharge a shopman. **1915** H. L. Wilson *Ruggles of Red Gap* xvii. 308, I would have shopped the fellow in an instant, .. had it been at any other time. He was most impertinent.

†**2.** To instal in a shop as a merchant. *nonce-use.*

**1652** Benlowes *Theoph.* x. xx, Where Prideis coacht, Fraud shopt and Taverns drown the Soul.

**3.** To bring or take (an article) to a shop; to expose for sale in a shop.

**1688** Holme *Armoury* iii. iii. 102/2 Shop the Candles, is to hang them by pounds, dozens, two or three on the two ends of a strong staff, and so a Man.. brings them to the place where they are to be. **1727** A. Hamilton *New Acc. E. Ind.* I. xviii. 206 When our Goods are in a Readiness, we send them to the accustomed Place to be shopt. **1890** *Charity Organis. Rev.* Jan. 14, I ask my man whether he will have.. 2s., when he 'shops' the boots [etc.].

**4. a.** *intr.* To visit a shop or shops for the purpose of making purchases, or examining the contents. Also *transf.*

**1764** Zeal *Seasonable Alarm London* 13 *note*, Ladies are said to go a Shoping, when, in the Forenoon, sick of themselves, they order the Coach, and driving from Shop to Shop [etc.]. **1799** *Monthly Rev.* XXX. 265 Venus and all the little loves, A shopping went for ring and gloves. **1845** Disraeli *Sybil* vi. iv, I thought Joan was going with you, and that you would be shopping. **1886** C. E. Pascoe *Lond. To-day* xxxii. (ed. 3) 290 Shopping, or making pretence to shop. **1951** M. McCarthy in *Holiday* May 47/2 He determined to attach his name to some lasting benevolent enterprise and settled on woman's education after cautious shopping and advice-seeking. **1973** *Times* 27 Feb. 16/3 The National Portrait Gallery went shopping at Phillips sale room yesterday.

**b.** With *around*. To visit different shops examining the prices of comparable goods offered for sale before making a purchase; to make purchases at different shops according to which offers the best price. Freq. *transf.* and *fig.*

**1922** *Management Engineering* Feb. 89/1 During the war, although orders greatly exceeded production, absenteeism increased. Men took days off to 'shop around', knowing that if unsuccessful they would be welcomed back. **1936** D. Powell *Turn, Magic Wheel* ii. 195 Can't you just see those little embryos shopping around for security. **1948** *Economist* 31 July 171/2 It is impossible to shop around for cheaper raw materials. **1952** A. Huxley *Let.* *c* 20 July (1969) 647 Since success depends on a satisfactory relation between the hypnotised person and the operator you must be prepared to 'shop around' until you find someone sympathetic as well as skilful. **1960** W. Taplin *Advertising* iv. 83 We have.. noticed the.. case.. of the people who buy advertised products and in effect accept the advertiser's persuasion rather than spend time 'shopping around'. **1976** J. I. M. Stewart *Memorial Service* ii. 35 It's usual to shop around a little. To send in a list of three or four colleges.

**c.** *trans.* To shop at (a store); to examine goods on sale in (a shop). *N. Amer.*

**1955** in H. Galinsky *Amerikanisches und Britisches Englisch* (1957) 49 Shop the store that gives you more. **1961** *Ford Times* Mar. 28 (*heading*) Shopping the southern roadside. **1974** S. Marcus *Minding Store* iv. 85 One man who had shopped the entire store complained that he hadn't found what he was looking for. **1980** 'E. McBain' *Ghosts* ii. 18 Maybe all the burglars.. were out shopping the department stores.

**5.** *trans.* To give (a person) a situation, to give (a person) work.

**1808** *Rules of Journeymen, Hat-Makers & Finishers of Stockport* in A. Aspinall *Early Eng. Trade Unions* (1949) iv. 110 And when any person comes wishing to be asked for, the person that goes and asks for him, to take his ticket, and in case that man is shopped, he must leave his ticket at the place he is shopped. **1855** [Burn] *Autobiog. Beggar-boy* 119, I travelled 1400 miles upon this occasion ere I could obtain work. At last I got shopped in Sherborne, in Dorsetshire. **1867** *All Year Round* 13 July 56/1 There are many men who would regard themselves as ingrates, were they not to celebrate their being 'shopped', after having been out of collar, by a 'spree'.

**shop**, obs. form of chop *v.*[1]

**1591** R. Bruce *Serm. Edin.* i. B 5, There are verie few that haue their heart free when the Lord shoppeth.

**'shop-board.** [f. shop *sb.* + board *sb.*[1]]

**1.** A counter or table upon which a tradesman's business is transacted or upon which his goods are exposed for sale.

**1524–5** *Rec. St. Mary at Hill* 328 Paid for a shopp borde in partriches shopp in Estchepe, vj s viij d. **1602** *2nd Pt. Return fr. Parnass.* i. iii. 345 When all these bookes of Exhortations and Catechismes, lie moulding on thy shop-board. **1705** Dunton *Life & Errors* (1818) I. vi. 72 He may starve behind his Shop-board, for want of subsistence. **1861** Sala *Dutch Pict.* xxi. 233 On every merchant's shopboard similar heaps.. are tumbling out of similar sacks.

**2.** A table or raised platform upon which tailors sit when sewing.

**1589** *Pappe w. Hatchet* in *Lyly's Wks.* (1902) III. 412 One seeing all sortes of his shreddes, would thinke he had robd a taylors shop boord. **1599** Dekker *Shoemaker's Holiday* iv. ii. (1610) G 1 b, Enter Hodge at his shop boord, Rafe, Firke, Hans, and a boy at worke. **1762** Foote *Orators* ii. (1780) 46 One day as I was sitting cross-legged on my shop-board, .. I felt the spirit within me moving. **1837** Hawthorne *Twice-told T., Toll-gatherer's Day*, A dashingly dressed gentleman .. from a tailor's shop-board.

**3.** *attrib.*

*a* **1658** Cleveland *Puritan* iii, With Shop-board Breeding and Intrusion.

**Shope** (ʃəʊp). *Biol.* The name of Richard Edwin *Shope* (1902–66), U.S. physician, used *attrib.* to designate a transmissible papilloma of rabbits described by him in 1932 (*Jrnl. Exper. Med.* LVI. 793, 803), and the DNA virus which causes it.

**1934** *Jrnl. Exper. Med.* LX. 756 The Shope papilloma, as occurring in nature, manifestly falls into the group of infectious warts, condylomas, and papillomas. **1935** *Proc. Soc. Exper. Biol. & Med.* XXXIII. 193 Shope virus from some sources gives rise to progressively enlarging papillomas, and that from others to growths which tend to disappear. **1938** *Ann. Reg. 1937* 349 A high molecular weight protein apparently associated with the viral activity was isolated from the Shope rabbit papilloma. **1961** R. D. Baker *Essent. Path.* xiii. 311 Carcinogenic viruses are known to produce the Rous sarcoma in chickens and the Shope papilloma of rabbits. **1970** *New Scientist* 29 Jan. 194/1 The Shope virus.. induces warts on the skins of rabbits.

**shop floor.** [f. shop *sb.* + floor *sb.*[1]]

**1.** The floor of a workshop or factory, where the operatives work; the part of a factory or workshop concerned with productive as opp. to administrative work. Freq. (with hyphen) *attrib.* Also in phr. ***on the shop floor.***

**1951** E. Jacques *Changing Culture of Factory* iii. xii. 316 The workers' representatives.. were regarded as a more reliable source of information about shop floor matters. **1956** *Nature* 18 Feb. 300/2 It is difficult to see how, in a Handbook of this kind, the real challenge and opportunity which shop-floor industry presents could be presented. **1962** *B.S.I. News* Apr. 17/2 Polymethyl-methacrylate might be understood by a chemist but 'Perspex' (a trade name) would be understood at shop-floor level. **1962** *Listener* 12 July 44/2 The lack of participation on the shop floor may be one of the underlying causes of malaise. **1967** C. Margerison in Wills & Yearsley *Handbk. Management Technol.* 31 The worker on the shop floor does not tend to identify himself either with the values or the goals of the manager. **1970** *Guardian* 11 July 11/6 The unanimous decision of a dockers' delegate conference—shop floor democracy at its most democratic. **1977** M. Walker *National Front* vi. 156 The new trade union policy did not focus solely on the exploitation of racialism on the shop floor.

**2.** By extension, the workers on the shop floor considered *collect.*

**1958** *Listener* 30 Oct. 680/2 A dispute between management and shop floor about the number of men to be employed upon a machine. **1977** *Times* 20 Apr. 4/7 They have decided to cancel... The shop floor is upset about it.

**shopful** (ˈʃɒpfʊl). [See -ful.] As much or as many as a shop will hold.

**1638** Baker tr. *Balzac's Lett.* (vol. III) 231, I could wish you would bring me a shopfull. **1901** *Spectator* 12 Oct. 510/2

One 'shopful' of customers may complete their purchases.. before another is admitted.

**shophar**, var. SHOFAR.

**'shopkeeper.** [f. SHOP *sb.* + KEEPER *sb.*]

**1.** One who carries on business in a shop.

**1530** PALSGR. 267/1 Schoppe kepar. **1626** B. JONSON *Staple of News* I. iii. 44, I say 'tis nobly done, to cherish Shop-keepers, And pay their Bills, without examining thus. **1768** TUCKER *Lt. Nat.* (1834) II. 142 A shopkeeper will never thrive who despises small profits. **1817** J. SCOTT *Paris Revis.* 3 An elderly London shop-keeper.

**b.** *a nation of shop-keepers*: applied disparagingly to a nation whose chief interest and concern lies in commerce (now often, to England).

Cf. quots. 1766, 1769 s.v. SHOPKEEPING *a.*

**1776** ADAM SMITH *W.N.* IV. vii. (1828) III. 41 To found a great empire for the sole purpose of raising up a people of customers, may at first sight appear a project fit only for a nation of shopkeepers.

**c.** *attrib.*

**1776** ADAM SMITH *W.N.* IV. vii. (1828) III. 43 A clause in the famous act of navigation established this truly shopkeeper proposal into a law.

**2.** *slang.* An article that has remained long in the shop unsold.

**1649** G. DANIEL *Trinarch., Hen. V*, cccviii, Blunt Reason, as an vseless Toole they give; Old Shopkeeper, with rusted Conscience! **1764** *Low Life* 76 Petty Booksellers.. looking out their imperfect and antient Shopkeepers, that they may expose them to Sale.

Hence **'shopkeeperess** *nonce-wd.*, a female shopkeeper. **'shopkeeperish** *a.*, having the nature of a shopkeeper. **'shopkeeperism**, the characteristics of shopkeepers as a class. **'shopkeepery**, the body of shopkeepers.

**1828** MISS MITFORD *Village* III. 55 The whole farmerage and shopkeepery of the place. **1843** CARLYLE *Jrnl.* in Froude *Life Lond.* (1884) I. 331 The boundless element of twaddle, dilettantism, shopkeeperism. **1858** *Chamb. Jrnl.* X. 261 No tight, prim, pale, eager shopkeeperesses. **1858** CLOUGH *Poems*, etc. (1869) I. 120 Extremely shopkeeperish and merchantish.

**'shopkeeping**, *sb.* The keeping of a shop, the business of a shopkeeper.

**1631** T. POWELL *Tom of All Trades* 32 Little Skill, Art or Mystery, shall a man learne in Shop-keeping. **1753** *Scots Mag.* Aug. 374/2 If naturalized foreigners should set up shopkeeping. **1847** GROTE *Greece* II. xxxii. IV. 268 He advised Cyrus.. to enforce upon them.. habits of playing on the harp and shopkeeping. **1912** *19th Cent.* Jan. 61 His Majesty will make his rule in India a real government and not shop-keeping on the largest scale.

**'shopkeeping**, *a.* [f. SHOP *sb.* + *keeping* pr. pple. of KEEP *v.*] Having the characteristics of a shopkeeper; pertaining to a shopkeeper's business.

**1622** ROWLANDS *Good N. & Bad N.* 7 Her worship highly scorn'd shop-keeping trade. **1766** J. TUCKER *Four Tracts* III. (1774) 132 A Shop-keeper will never get the more Custom by beating his Customers: and what is true of a Shop-keeper, is true of a Shop-keeping Nation. **1769** FRANKLIN *Let.* 27 Apr., Wks. 1838 VII. 441 This handicraft, shopkeeping state will, for its own sake, learn to behave more civilly to its customers. **1865** *Sat. Rev.* 7 Oct. 461/2 Nothing less suited than they are to the shopkeeping mind can be imagined.

**'shopless**, *a.* [-LESS.] Destitute of shops.

**1888** DRUMMOND *Trop. Africa* 5 This shopless.. land.

**'shoplet.** [-LET.] A little shop.

**1872** S. BUTLER *Erewhon* vii. 54 Even on this ledge of human society there was a stunted growth of shoplets.

†**shop-lift**, *sb.* *Obs.* [f. SHOP *sb.* + LIFT *sb.*[2] (sense 6).] = SHOPLIFTER.

**1673** R. HEAD *Canting Acad.* 106 *Of the Shop lift.* She is commonly well clad. *Ibid.* 191 The tenth is a Shoplift that carries a Bob, When he ranges the City the Shops for to rob. **1692** *Scarronides* II. 1 How Grecian Shop-lifts.. Brake open honest Trojans doors. **1762** BRIDGES *Hom. Trav.* I. (1797) 297 Thus shoplifts see their brothers taken.

**shoplift**, *v.* [Back-formation f. SHOPLIFTING *vbl. sb.*] To steal from a shop while pretending to be a customer. **a.** *intr.*

**1820** [see SHEEP-STEAL *v.*]. **1843** *Punch* 8 Apr. 150/1 Policeman, here's a wench Shoplifting, take the customer to jail. **1959** *Times* 9 Mar. (Britain's Food Suppl.) p. ix/3 The temptation to shop-lift is one facet of the principle on which every self-service store depends. **1971** *Guardian* 22 Feb. 9/1 When Mrs Brown gets depressed, she starts to shoplift.

**b.** *trans.*

**1922** JOYCE *Ulysses* 741 A whore always shoplifting anything she could. **1979** K. CONLON *Move in Game* I. iii. 39 She'd shoplifted a bottle of nail varnish remover.

**'shoplifter.** [f. SHOP *sb.* + LIFTER.] A person who steals from a shop, a shop-thief.

**1680** [KIRKMAN] *Eng. Rogue* IV. xvii. 232 Towards Night these Houses are throng'd with People of all sorts.. Shoplifters, Foilers, Bulkers. **1770** BARETTI *Jrnl. Lond. to Genoa* II. xxxiv. 2 A shop-lifter was once hang'd in England. **1881** A. LANG *Library* 47 The papers call lady shoplifters 'Kleptomaniacs'.

**'shoplifting**, *vbl. sb.* [f. SHOP *sb.* + LIFTING *vbl. sb.*] The action of stealing from a shop.

**1698** *Act 10 Will. III*, c. 12 Preamble, The Crime of stealing Goods privately out of Shops and Warehouses, commonly called Shop-lifting. **1850** HT. MARTINEAU *Hist. Peace* (1877) III. 136 A lady was convicted for shop-lifting.

**shopman** ('ʃɒpmən). [f. SHOP *sb.* + MAN *sb.*]

**1.** The owner of a shop. Now *rare.*

**1591** in W. M. Williams *Ann. Founders' Co.* (1867) 74 Leaden Waits ar and have been used time out of mynd by all Shoppmen and Sellers of smaller Wares. **1860** RUSKIN *Unto this Last* iv. §76 *note*, He [the consumer] pays, probably, an intermediate ship-owner, velvet merchant, and shopman. **1888** MEREDITH *Stave of Roving Tim* vi, The shopman piles a heap While I perhaps am fasting.

**2.** An assistant in a shop.

**1758** JOHNSON *Idler* No. 15 ¶2 My wife, though she could be of as much use as a shopman to me, if she would put her hand to it, is now only in my way. **1828** *Ann. Reg.* 370/2 William Noble, shopman with Mr. Rymer, Portsburgh, knew the prisoner Burke. **1892** [W. H. WHITE] *Mark Rutherford's Deliv.* (ed. 5) 175 A shopman was at the counter.

*Comb.* **1826** MISS MITFORD *Village* II. 193 Home I returned,.. laden.. with huge packages,.. papered and pack-threaded in shopmanlike style.

**3.** A man employed in a railway workshop.

**1926** *Times* 8 Mar. 9/4 He was glad to be able to state that the case of the railway shopmen had been advanced. **1960** *Listener* 18 Aug. 250/1 They were trainmen, shopmen, telegraph operators, and so on, all highly specialized in their respective callings.

**shopocracy** (ʃɒ'pɒkrəsɪ). [f. SHOP *sb.*: see -CRACY.] Shopkeepers as a class aspiring to social importance; a wealthy or influential body of shopkeepers. So **shopocrat** ('ʃɒpəkræt) [-CRAT], a member of the shopocracy; also *attrib.*

**1832** *Poor Man's Guardian* 9 June 419 'The Shopocracy' in the neighbourhood.. were somewhat alarmed. *Ibid.* 29 Dec. 658/2 A shopocrat Parliament. **1841** *Blackw. Mag.* L. 63 We have left behind the regions of the great merchants, and of the shopocrats. **1881** [see TERRITORIALISM 1].

**shoppe** (ʃɒp, 'ʃɒpɪ), an archaic form of SHOP *sb.* now used affectedly (as in the names of tea-shops, etc.) to suggest quaint, old-world charm. Cf. OLDE *a.*

**1933** J. BETJEMAN *Ghastly Good Taste* 138 Arts and Crafts. Gentle folk weaving and spinning; Modern Church Furnishing; Old Tea Shoppes. **1948** [see *gift shop* s.v. GIFT *sb.* 9b]. **1957** E. POUND tr. *Rimbaud* 15 What lures the aintient truss-maker from his shoppe whose luxury Sucked in the passers-by. **1979** L. KALLEN *Introducing C. B. Greenfield* i. 10 This is a business office, not a tea shoppe.

**shopper** ('ʃɒpə(r)). [f. SHOP *v.* + -ER[1].]

**1. a.** One who frequents a shop or shops for the purpose of inspecting or buying goods.

**1860** MRS. GASKELL *Let.* 27 Aug. (1966) 632 She is very dainty-fingered, a beautiful ready workwoman, a capital shopper &c. **1862** *Guardian* 3 Sept. 847/2 It [Paris] is a city not only of pleasure seekers, but of keen and indefatigable shoppers. **1910** ANNIE THORNTON *Leaves Afghan Scrapbk.* 170 This was [Queen] Ulya Hazrat's messenger and chief shopper.

**b.** An advertising sheet or newspaper.

**1958** PALMER & GILMORE in W. C. Clark *Journalism Tomorrow* iii. 32 The little advertising sheet, often called a shopper... In a few cases, the shopper can be converted into a fine-looking, profitable weekly newspaper. **1976** *National Observer* (U.S.) 16 Oct., He would junk a lot of the expensive radio and TV commercials, spend the money instead in shoppers and small town weeklies, where you can buy the whole back page for $65.

**c.** A shopping bag or trolley.

**1968** H. C. RAE *Few Small Bones* II. v. 113 He bought enough tinned food.. to last him a full week, then lugging the laden shopper, set out along the main street. **1970** *Kay & Co.* (Worcester) *Catal.* 1970–71 Autumn/Winter 934 (*caption*) Giant size trolley shoppers. *Ibid.*, Tartan shopper. Novelty-shaped large capacity zip-top Shopping bag in Black Watch Tartan. **1978** H. R. F. KEATING *Long Walk to Wimbledon* IX. 137 The wheels of Marigold's shopper squeaked.

**2.** *slang.* An informer.

**1924** E. WALLACE *Room 13* xxxi. 300 Jeffrey's going to shop you sooner or later, because he's a natural born shopper. **1955** P. WILDEBLOOD *Against Law* 105 'Shoppers'. .. people who go to the cop-shop and squeal on their friends.

**shoppie** ('ʃɒpɪ). *Sc.* [f. SHOP *sb.* + -IE.] A little shop.

**1872** QUEEN VICTORIA *Jrnl.* 13 June in D. Duff *Victoria in Highlands* (1968) 260 At half-past ten drove out in the waggonette.. and drove beyond Mrs. Patterson's 'shoppie' a little way. **1887** W. CARNIE *Waifs of Rhyme* 17, I ken a winsome wifikie that keeps a snug bit shoppie.

**shoppie**, var. SHOPPY *sb.*

**shoppin**, obs. f. CHOPINE.

**1663** GERBIER *Counsel* 31 Some Venetian Ladies, must have their Shoppins to stand on.

**shoppiness** ('ʃɒpɪnɪs). [f. SHOPPY *a.* + -NESS.]

**1.** Tendency to talk 'shop'.

**1865** *Cornh. Mag.* XI. 492 The followers of literature should be less tainted with the vice of 'shoppiness' than the members of any other profession.

**2.** Abundance of shops.

**1881** MISS BRADDON *Asphodel* xvi. 180 So delighted with Torquay, in its increased towniness and shoppiness.

**shopping** ('ʃɒpɪŋ), *vbl. sb.* [f. SHOP *v.* + -ING[1].]

**1. a.** The action of visiting a shop or shops for the purpose of making purchases or of examining the goods exposed for sale. Also with *around.* Freq. *transf.*

**1764, 1799** [see SHOP *v.* 5]. **1782** CHARL. BURNEY in *Mme. D'Arblay's Early Diary* (1889) II. 300 They spent at one shopping £20 in Gauzes two or three years ago! **1848** THACKERAY *Van. Fair* xii, The delightful round of visits and shopping which forms the amusement, or the profession as you may call it, of the rich London lady. **1872** HOWELLS *Wedd. Journ.* (1892) 311 They also had done a little shopping. **1940** *Sun* (Baltimore) 16 Feb. 24/2 By the simple expedient of 'shopping around' before making a deal, Walter N. Kirkman.. has succeeded in saving the State $13,300 a year in office rent here. **1971** *Nature* 10 Dec. 368/1 An author does much better by bargaining hard and honestly with almost any single good publishing house than by 'shopping around'.

**b.** *transf.* The goods that have been purchased (in quot. 1934, 'something that has been purchased').

**1934** *Punch* 2 May 489/1 Thank you so much, darling, for those marvellous Shoppings... The pyjamas are divine. **1948** P. WENTWORTH *Traveller Returns* i. 6 There were three people in front of her—a very stout woman with a basket full of shopping.., and a stooping elderly man. **1975** *Oxford Consumer* June 4 There are those, i.e. the elderly, the infirm, people with shopping,.. for whom cycling is not always possible.

**c.** = SHOP *sb.* 2e. *colloq.*

**1934** *Punch* 2 May 489/1 Would you think me the most terrific pest if I asked you to do yet another shopping for me? **1980** M. FORSTER *Bride of Lowther Hall* xviii. 272, I could perhaps go to Wigton and do a mammoth shopping.

**2.** *attrib.* and *Comb.* Simple attrib.: ***shopping bag, basket, day, expedition, hours, spree, tour, trip***; in the names of places where shopping is performed, as ***shopping arcade, area, centre, complex, mall*** (chiefly *N. Amer.*), ***parade, plaza*** (chiefly *N. Amer.*), ***precinct, street***; **shopping-bag lady** *U.S.*, a vagrant woman carrying her possessions in shopping bags; **shopping cart** orig. *N. Amer.*, a large wire basket on wheels provided for the use of supermarket customers; **shopping net**, a shopping bag made of string or plastic net; **shopping service**, a department or organization offering advice or assistance with shopping; **shopping tray**, an open wire receptacle for shopping designed to fit over the chassis of a pram; **shopping trolley**, (*a*) a shopping bag set on a wheeled frame; (*b*) = *shopping cart* above. See also SHOPPING LIST.

**1933** *Radio Times* 14 Apr. 72/2 Dear Covent Garden.. we hear, alas, that you are soon to.. make way for shopping-arcades. **1977** J. BINGHAM *Marriage Bureau Murder* xvi. 184 There was a shopping arcade... He often shopped there. **1959** *Manch. Guardian* 11 Aug. 6/5 More shopping areas for pedestrians only. **1974** A. MORICE *Killing with Kindness* ii. 18 You have to pass through the shopping area to get to the main road. **1886** S. COOLIDGE *What Katy did Next* ix. 247 In her shopping-bag one or two of the Carnival bonbons still remained. **1973** J. STRANGER *Walk Lonely Road* xiii. 97 Millie came in with a brimming shopping-bag. [**1972** S. R. CURTIN *Nobody ever died of Old Age* vi. 85 Letty the Bag Lady.. would pack all her valuables in two large shopping bags and carry them with her.] **1976** *N.Y. Times* 30 Sept. 43/5 The chief thing about Sally, the former 'shopping bag lady', is that she has personality. **1978** *Harper's Mag.* Mar. 104 On a nearby bench, apparently keeping an intermittent vigil on the vigil, were two shopping-bag ladies. **1979** *N.Y. Times* 10 Jan. B7 An elderly 'shopping bag lady',.. one of the legion of homeless, independent, often eccentric women who live on the city's streets. **1923** E. BOWEN *Encounters* 166 She had forgotten her shopping basket and her purse. **1977** *Times* 29 June 5/7 She arrived at the court by bus carrying a shopping basket containing her dressing gown. **1956** *Sun* (Baltimore) (B ed.) 19 Jan. 14/1 A feature of the supermarket is the now familiar shopping cart, a contraption of recent invention. **1958** M. DICKENS *Man Overboard* v. 83 A woman with a shopping cart bumped into him. **1976** G. A. BROWNE *Slide* (1977) ix. 74 The shopping cart somehow getting fuller than intended. **1898** Shopping centre [see CENTRE *sb.* 6a]. **1933** L. E. NEAL *Retailing & Public* v. 25 There is.. great competition between multiple branch organisations.. to acquire the best positions in the popular shopping centres. **1944** H. G. WELLS *'42 to '44* 136 In Welwyn Garden City to-day there is a single 'shopping centre' associated with one bazaar. **1971** P. GRESSWELL *Environment* 183 Very few shopping centres are imaginatively designed. **1977** B. GARFIELD *Recoil* v. 62 Caruso.. drove him.. to a shopping center in Santa Monica. **1970** *Times* 27 Feb. 19/7 Fram Gerrard, of Manchester, has won the building contract for the £1·5m. shopping complex in Leicester. **1861** C. M. YONGE *Young Step-Mother* xxix. 439 This was a grand shopping day, an endless business. **1973** D. MILLER *Chinese Jade Affair* xxiii. 220 'Only thirty Shopping Days to Christmas!' advised the big department stores. **1847** A. BRONTË *Agnes Grey* xxv. 358, I took a little more pains with my attire than if I had merely been going on some shopping expedition alone. **1885** RUSKIN *Præterita* I. vi. 184 He [the courier] invariably attended the ladies in their shopping expeditions. **1979** L. MEYNELL *Hooky & Villainous Chauffeur* xi. 139 What with cooking.. and the necessary shopping expeditions she didn't have much time over. **1964** A. ADBURGHAM *Shops & Shopping* i. 7 There were no stated shopping hours. **1967** *Canad. Ann. Rev. 1966* 137 Its proposals for.. restriction of billboards, abolition of overhanging signs and overhead wires, closed pedestrian shopping malls, [etc.]. **1972** *N.Z. News* 26 Jan. 7 (*caption*) This scene is taken from the Cuba Street shopping mall, Wellington. **1979** *Jrnl. R. Soc. Arts* July 505/1 Shopping malls are the nearest thing to the market place which you could find in North America. **1955** T. STERLING *Evil of Day* i. 1 Within the cabin, women with shopping nets and men with folded newspapers awaited their turns. **1969** P. HIGHSMITH *Tremor of Forgery* xxi. 195 Adams had a shopping net in his hand. He was putting things away in the kitchen. **1969** *Morning Star* 1 Dec. 4/1 There will be various amenities when Stage 1 and Stage 2 are completed, [including] a shopping parade. **1957** *Ottawa Jrnl.* 6 Aug. 1/1 The break-ins were compared with the noisy June 3 'tow-truck' robbery at another grocery store in the shopping plaza. **1981** P. THEROUX *Mosquito Coast* vi. 44 We came to a shopping plaza, where we parked. **1958** Shopping precinct [see PRECINCT *sb.* 4]. **1980** A. AUSWAKS *Trick of Diamonds* iii. 75 At the end of the High Street stood a new shipping precinct. **1925** *Eaton's News Weekly* 26 Sept. 18 When Ordering by Mail..Address Letter to *Shopping Service.* **1972** S. ELLIN *Mirror, Mirror on Wall* 79 The lady happens to work for a shopping service... If you want to do some shopping for your wife..these people take you to the right places and pick the right stuff. **1962** M. SUMMERTON *Nightingale at Noon* (1963) iv. 55 A shopping spree to purge a memory. **1976** 'S. WOODS' *My Life is Done* 69 Ana had been on a shopping spree. **1914** A. BENNETT *Price of Love* xiv. 283 Her first apparition in the shopping streets of the town..as Mrs. Louis Fores, married woman. **1975** P. MOYES *Black Widower* ii. 19 The great shopping street that bisects the area. **1878** *Masque of Poets* 249 She dressed herself to start upon a fashionable shopping-tour. **1970** *Kay & Co.* (Worcester) *Catal.* 1970–71 Autumn/Winter 227 Leeway shopping tray provides secure storage space and is readily adaptable to most prams. **1977** *Cornish Times* 19 Aug. 7/3 (Advt.), Silver Cross pram, detachable body..with shopping tray. **1969** G. LYALL *Venus with Pistol* xviii. 116 Henri has been *killed*... Doesn't that mean more than this—shopping trip? **1976** *Economist* 17 Apr. 79/3 A motorised pram-cum-shopping-trolley would arguably be the most egalitarian form of transport. **1978** *Green Shield Stamp Catal.* Feb. 113 *Shopping trolley.* Adjustable telescopic handle. Detachable shopping bag. **1979** *Criminal Appeal Reports (Sentencing)* (1980) I. 255 On the morning of January 25, 1979 at Brent Cross Shopping Centre she went into a Waitrose Supermarket and loaded up a shopping trolley with groceries.

**shopping list.** [f. SHOPPING *vbl. sb.* + LIST *sb.*[6]]

**1.** A list of purchases to be made or shops to be visited.

**1913** *Vanity Fair* Sept. 7/2 You can easily clip half a dozen and attach them to your own shopping list. **1921** *Daily Colonist* (Victoria, B.C.) 31 Mar. 6/5 We have a beautiful selection of Oriental Rugs and Jewels. Put our name on your shopping list. **1947** W. STEVENS *Let.* 5 Sept. (1967) 567 But now that the weather is growing cooler, I begin to look at my shopping list. **1977** 'E. CRISPIN' *Glimpses of Moon* xii. 256 He went to investigate, finding a message..scribbled on a sheet torn from a Shopping List pad.

**2.** *transf.* and *fig.* A list of items to be considered, acted upon, etc.; *spec.* a list of weaponry sought for purchase.

**1959** *Manch. Guardian* 8 July 3/3 He..did not want to put down a shopping-list of industries to be nationalised. **1963** *Times* 21 Feb. 11/3 Ground-to-air missiles were on the 'shopping list' of defence equipment taken to Moscow by the Secretary-General of the External Affairs Ministry. **1969** *Nature* 2 Aug. 436/2 The council should say which fields of medical and biological research come at the top of its shopping-list—biological organization, arterial disease, population control and drug dependence. **1970** *Cape Times* 28 Oct. 26/5 His shopping list will include a full-back..and a creative mid-field player. **1975** *N.Y. Times* 8 Sept. 1/3 The Israeli sources said negotiations had resumed on a shopping list that includes..F-15 fighter planes to match the MIG-23's deployed by Egypt and Syria. **1977** *Times* 10 June 17/1 The [French] left have indeed a fearsome shopping list for nationalization.

**shoppish** ('ʃɒpɪʃ), *a.* [SHOP *sb.* + -ISH.] Characteristic of persons connected with a shop; also = SHOPPY *a.* 1.

**1815** *Sporting Mag.* XLVI. 122 To use a shoppish simile. **1860** *Leader* 25 July, This piece of revenge was about as shoppish an act as ever any shopkeeper..could be capable of.

Hence **'shoppishness**, professionalism.

**1882** *Fraser's Mag.* XXV. 533 His profession stamped upon every movement, yet without the least nautical assumption or 'shoppishness'.

**'shoppism.** *nonce-wd.* [f. SHOP *sb.* + -ISM.] 'Shoppy' talk and behaviour; professionalism.

**1872** J. H. NEWMAN in W. Ward *Life* (1912) II. 387, I have a great dislike of this shoppism personally.

**shoppy** ('ʃɒpɪ), *a.* [f. SHOP *sb.* + -Y[1].]

**1.** Of the nature of 'shop' or professional concerns or conversation.

**1840** HALIBURTON *Letter Bag* i. 4 Still my attention was riveted (I fear that word is shoppy). **1900** *Macm. Mag.* Jan. 222 A novel of clerical life written by a clergyman is apt to be what is vulgarly called shoppy.

**2.** Characterized by having a number of shops, forming a centre for business.

**1851** MAYHEW *Lond. Labour* I. 292/1 Thoroughfares which are well-frequented, but which..are not so 'shoppy' as others. **1892** *Pall Mall Gaz.* 6 Oct. 1/2 The innumerable shades of colour in all the drapers' windows make the 'shoppy' part of town more fascinating than usual.

**3.** Belonging to retail trade.

**1854** MRS. GASKELL *North & South* ii, I don't like shoppy people. **1890** HATTON *By order of Czar* (1891) 388 Critics in the press..who characterize both his manner and his work [paintings] as commercial and shoppy. **1914** W. OWEN *Let.* 10 May (1967) 249 Miss H—— who, you confess, is 'shoppy'. Now that is distressing. The fact of being employed in a shop does not matter; but shoppiness does matter.

**shoppy** ('ʃɒpɪ), *sb. slang.* Also **shoppie.** [f. SHOP *sb.* + -Y[6].] A shop assistant.

**1909** P. WEBLING *Story of Virginia Perfect* i. 6 Her manner towards him..had none of the affectation of the ordinary 'young lady in business', or the vulgar intimacy of a poorer class of 'shoppie'. **1916** 'TAFFRAIL' *Pincher Martin* vii. 114 She's in Skeets the draper's... Never could stand them shoppies; they give themselves such airs. **1934** H. A. VACHELL *Disappearance of Martha Penny* i. 20 Her sparkling eyes, her fine figure, were gifts rarely bestowed upon urban 'shoppies'.

**shop-window.**

**1. a.** A window of a shop, in which goods are displayed for sale.

*c* **1447–8** *Shillingford Lett.* (Camden) 85 Yn the whiche walle buth diverse shoppez wyndowes of olde tyme hadde. **1531–2** *Rec. St. Mary at Hill* 359 For xvj staples to the shope windowes ij s viij d. **1632** in E. B. Jupp *Carpenters' Co.* (1887) 296 All Sorts of Shopp Windows that are made for ornament or beautie. **1798** JANE AUSTEN *Northang. Abb.* vi, I saw the prettiest hat you can imagine, in a shop-window. **1863** J. MACGREGOR in Lady Fr. Balfour *Life* (1912) 132 As plainly as you see those men in some shop-windows in Glasgow go through the mysteries of hat-making.

**b.** *transf.* In the phrases: *to open* or *shut* (*one's*) *shop-window*, to begin or close the business of the day; also, to begin or give up business.

**1477** in *Eng. Gilds* (1870) 304 Whereupon fell and folowed greate trobles and enemitie: for some were disfraunchised, some imprysoned, some theire shop windows shutt downe. **1529** *Barber-Surg. Draft Rules* §13 in *Vicary's Anat.* (1888) 254 That no persone presume to opyn his Shoppe wyndowes before he hath presented hymself to & before the Maysters or Gouerners of the sayde Mystere for the tyme beyng. **1646–7** *Nottingham Rec.* V. 248 The shopp windowes of all persons that trade in this Towne whoe are not sworn burgesses shalbee forthwith shutt vpp. **1661** HICKERINGILL *Jamaica* 80 It never makes him sell his land, nor shut Shop-windows up.

**2.** *transf.* and *fig.* A display of anything, resembling the display of goods by a tradesman, intended to catch the attention.

**1905** *Times Lit. Suppl.* 31 Mar., This..may surprise some who have seen the shop-window of American education, and have not looked behind it. **1929** C. CONNOLLY *Let.* Nov. in *Romantic Friendship* (1975) 328 [In America] a wife is a man's shop window. **1933** P. GODFREY *Back-Stage* iii. 34 A 'shop-window' is a part which carries a low salary, but which, nevertheless, is likely to enhance his acting reputation. Certain small theatres are also 'shop-windows', like the Everyman Theatre in its early days. **1954** [see END *sb.* 7 c]. **1961** *Radio Times* 6 Apr. 4/2 Once a year the BBC..stages a couple of all-star concerts as a shop-window for the kind of 'pop' programmes that it broadcasts..during the rest of the year. **1977** *Listener* 17 Mar. 347/3 London was to be a city of individuals..rather than a shop-window of state, monarchy and empire.

Hence **shop-'windowful**, as much or as many as a shop-window will hold.

**1898** G. B. SHAW *Mrs. Warren's Prof.* IV. 231, I shouldn't enjoy..being bored at the opera to shew off a shop windowful of diamonds.

**shor** (ʃɔː(r)). [Turki *shōr.*] In Turkistan, an elongated saline depression in desert sand.

**1888** *Encycl. Brit.* XXIII. 512/1 A feature distinctive of the Turcoman desert is seen in the very numerous *shors*, or elongated depressions, the lower portions of which are occupied mostly with sand impregnated with brackish water. **1898** *Geogr. Jrnl.* XII. 308 The *shors*..are seen on the southern border of the Kara-kum sands. **1951** N. T. MIROV *Geogr. of Russia* xv. 155 Lower depressions, so-called sor or shor, equally extensive, are occupied with alkaline soil of the solonchak type.

†**'shorage.** *Obs.* Also (in Dicts.) shoreage. [f. SHORE *sb.*[1] + -AGE. (Perh. formed by Cotgrave as a rendering of *rivage.*)] (See quot. 1611.)

**1611** COTGR. s.v. *Droict, Droict de Rivage*, Shorage, or Boatage; the Custome, or Toll for wine, or other wares, put vpon, or brought from, the water, by boats. **1706** PHILLIPS (ed. Kersey), *Shorage*, a Duty paid for Goods brought on Shore. [So in later Dicts.]

**shoran** ('ʃɔə-, 'ʃɒræn). orig. *U.S.* Also **Shoran.** [f. the initial letters of *sho*rt-*ra*nge *n*avigation.] A secondary radar system, used for precision navigation and for distance measurement, in which an aircraft or ship determines its distance from two widely-spaced ground stations which it interrogates alternately with radio pulses. Freq. *attrib.* Cf. LORAN.

**1946** *N.Y. Times* 28 Apr. 1/3 Those who have..tested shoran call it 'perhaps the greatest single invention of its type for long-range mapping to come from the family of radar in the war'. **1946** *Trans. Amer. Geophys. Union* XXVII. 459 Basically, the shoran equipment consists of three main units, the airborne transmitter-receiver-indicator and the two ground station transponders. **1949** *Sun* (Baltimore) 2 Mar. 13/2 What prompted the use of the Superforts was the belief that the development of Shoran (Short Range Navigation) equipment had reached the point where it could be put to work for the astronomer. **1966** *McGraw-Hill Encycl. Sci. & Technol.* IX. 18/2 The single-path round-trip system is the basis of distance determination in all radars. It is the system employed by Benito, Condar, Oboe, shoran, and the distance-measuring portion of Tacan equipment. **1970** *Canad. Cartographer* VII. 23/1, 12 shoran ground stations. **1977** *Sci. Amer.* Oct. 92/3 At each one a transponder was set up for a shoran radio-positioning system.

**shorde**, obs. form of SWORD.

**shore** (ʃɔə(r)), *sb.*[1] Forms: 4–7 **schore**, 5 **schor**, 5–7 *Sc.* **schoir**, 6 **shawre**, *Sc.* **schoyr**, 6–7 **shoare**, *Sc.* **shoir**, 6–8 **shoar**, (7 **shoore**), 5– **shore**. [ME. *schore* a. or cogn. w. MLG. *schore, schare* shore, late MDu. *schore, schor*, also *schaer* shore, sea-marsh, mod.Du. *schoor* masc., *schor, schorre* fem., land washed by the sea, sea-marsh.

Prob. f. the root of SHEAR *v.*, but the etymological notion is not easy to determine; it may perh. be 'division' (between land and water). The OE. *scoren clif* 'shorn cliff', precipice, commonly cited as illustrative of the etymology, seems hardly relevant, as the LG. and Du. equivalents of *shore* are applied only to low-lying shores.]

**1. a.** The land bordering on the sea or a large lake or river. Often in a restricted sense more or less coinciding with the legal definition (see b).

**13..** *E.E. Allit. P.* A. 230 On wyþer half water com doun þe schore. **13..** *Gaw. & Gr. Knt.* 2083 Brokez byled, & breke, bi bonkkez aboute, Schyre schaterande on schorez. *c* **1470** HENRY *Wallace* x. 797 Thai saylyt furth by part off Ingland schor. *c* **1489** CAXTON *Blanchardyn* xxvi. 97 Where as the sayd mast and Blanchardyn vpon it was cast of the wawes vnto the shores. **1513** DOUGLAS *Æneis* VII. iii. 7 At the schoyr, wndir a gresy bank, Thair navy can thai ankir fast and hank. **1582** N.T. (Rhem.) *Acts* xxvii. 39 They spied a certaine creeke that had a shore [Vulg. *littus*]. **1591** SPENSER *Vis. Worlds Vanitie* 29 Beside the fruitfull shore of muddie Nile. *c* **1600** SHAKS. *Sonn.* lx. 1 Like as the waues towards the pibled shore. **1601** —— *Jul. C.* I. ii. 101 The troubled Tyber chafing with her Shores. **1670** MILTON *Hist. Eng.* VI. 272 Canute..caus'd his Royal Seat to be set on the shoar, while the Tide was coming in. **1703** *Lond. Gaz.* No. 3955/4 A Piece of Ground of about 40 Acres in Fulham Parish, and lies upon a clean Gravelly Shore. **1797–1805** S. & HT. LEE *Canterb. T.* I. 349 The sharp promontories and rocky shores of Greece. **1821** SCOTT *Pirate* xxv, As he entered the little bay, on the shore and almost on the beach of which the ruins are situated. **1856** EMERSON *Eng. Traits* ii. Wks. (Bohn) II. 14 There lay the green shore of Ireland, like some coast of plenty. **1876** *Nature* 7 Dec. 128/1 On the Swiss shore of the Rhine.

**b.** In *Law* usually defined as the tract lying between ordinary high and low water mark, but see quots. Similarly in *Geomorphol.*

**1622** CALLIS *Stat. Sewers* (1647) 221, I then landed at the shore, which in definition containeth those grounds which extend from the lowest Ebb to the highest Flood. *a* **1676** HALE *De Jure Maris* I. iv. (1787) 12 The shore is that ground that is between the ordinary high-water and low-water mark. This doth *primâ facie* and of common right belong to the king. *Ibid.* I. vi. 25 There seem to be three sorts of shoars, or *littora marina*, according to the various tides, viz. (1st.) The high spring tides... (2d.) The spring tides... (3d.) Ordinary tides or nepe tides. **1856** BOUVIER *Amer. Law Dict.* (ed. 6) s.v., Land on the side of the sea, a lake, or a river, is called the shore. Strictly speaking, however, when the water does not ebb and flow, in a river, there is no shore. **1919** D. W. JOHNSON *Shore Processes & Shoreline Devel.* iv. 160 The most important of the four zones extends from low water mark to the base of the cliff,..which usually marks the landward limit of effective wave action. This is the zone over which the water line, the line of contact between land and sea, migrates; and it will here be called the shore. **1968** R. W. FAIRBRIDGE *Encycl. Geomorphol.* 62/1 The shore is technically the coastal zone extending from the low tide limit to the maximum swash line. **1978** A. L. BLOOM *Geomorphology* xix. 437 The shore zone, or simply shore, is the zone affected by wave action.

**c.** In vague or rhetorical use (*sing* or *pl.*): A sea-coast or the country which it bounds.

**1611** SHAKS. *Wint. T.* V. i. 164 My best Traine I haue from your Sicilian Shores dismiss'd. **1691** TATE *Petty's Pol. Anat.* Ded., You have since accompanied our Royal Master to other Shores. **1796** MORSE *Amer. Univ. Geog.* II. 546 Their religion seems to forbid them [*sc.* Hindoos] to quit their own shores. **1820** BYRON *Juan* III. lxxxvi. ii, The Scian and the Teian muse,..Have found the fame your shores refuse. **1871** R. ELLIS *Catullus* lxviii. 97 Now on a distant shore, no kind mortality near him.

**d.** *transf.* and *fig.*

**1599** SHAKS. *Hen. V*, IV. i. 282 The Tyde of Pompe, That beates vpon the high shore of this World. **1603** —— *Meas. for M.* III. ii. 266, I haue labour'd for the poore Gentleman, to the extremest shore of my modestie. *a* **1639** WOTTON *Surv. Educ.* Introd. *Reliq.* (1651) 317 But before I lanch from the shoars, let me resolve a main question which may be cast in my way. **1742** BLAIR *Grave* 709 Thrice welcome Death! That..lands us safe On the long-wish'd for Shore. **1814** WORDSW. *Excurs.* VII. 28 Deposited upon the silent shore Of memory. **1871** MORLEY *Voltaire* (1886) 10 The full flood on which the race is borne to new shores.

†**e.** *common shore*: app. = 'shore' simply. (Cf. SHORE *sb.*[4]) *Obs.*

*a* **1568** ASCHAM *Scholem.* II. (Arb.) 152 As one caried in a small low vessell him selfe verie nie the common shore, not much vnlike the fisher men of Rye [etc.].

**f.** *dial.* The edge of a ditch.

**1602** *Peramb. Great Park of Fastern* in *Wilts. Gloss.*, A Mearstone lyinge within the Shoore of the Dyche. **1879** JEFFERIES *Amateur Poacher* (1903) 235 A large hawthorne bush growing on the 'shore' of the ditch.

**2.** In prepositional phrases without article, as *on shore*, on the shore, ashore, on land (indicating either position or direction); *in shore*, near or nearer to the shore (from the water).

In the first quot. *upon shore* seems to be used for 'on the ground'.

**13..** *Gaw. & Gr. Knt.* 2332 The haþel heldet hym fro, & on his ax rested, Sette þe schaft vpon schore, & to þe scharp lened. **1585** T. WASHINGTON tr. *Nicholay's Voy.* I. ii, [We] returned on shore certaine vnfit eaters. **1590** SHAKS. *Com. Err.* III. ii. 153 If the winde blow any way from shore. **1599** —— *Much Ado* II. iii. 66 One foote in Sea, and one on shore. **1611** BIBLE *Matt.* xiii. 48 Which, when it was full, they drew to shore. —— *Acts.* xxvii. 40 They..made toward shore. **1719** DE FOE *Crusoe* I. (Globe) 23 Resolving to swim on Shore as soon as it was dark. **1835** SIR J. ROSS *Narr. 2nd Voy.* xi. 173 Part of the crew was sent on shore for exercise. **1836** MARRYAT *Midsh. Easy* xxxviii, Steer in shore of them.

**3. a.** *Sc.* A part of the sea-shore built up as a place for lading and landing; a landing-place.

**1512** *Acc. Ld. High Treas. Scot.* IV. 292 Item, to the said James, for kepin of the schoir of Dunde in the custumez, v li. **1603** *Stirling Burgh Rec.* (1887) I. 104 The grete decay of thair shoir and heavin upon the watter of Forthe. **1603** *Reg. Mag. Sig. Scot.* 515/1 Radum et stationem de Leyth, cum propugnaculis (the peiris, schoiris and bulwarkis) ejusdem. **1747** in *Nairne Peerage Evid.* (1874) 151 The..peir and shore of Leith. **1836** *Brit. Cycl., Nat. Hist.* II. 737/2 Any one who chose to go to the shore, meaning thereby the harbour of Crail.

**b.** *local.* A place at the side of a river built for a special purpose (see quot.).

**1649** W. G. *Surv. Newcastle* 28 There is many Ballist shoares made below the water, on both sides of the river. *Ibid.* 29 Below East is many shores built for casting of Ballist out of Ships.

**4.** = *shore wainscot*: see 5 b.

**1832** J. Rennie *Butterfl. & Moths* 87 The Shore (*Leucania littoralis*, Stephens) appears on the sea coast.

**5. a.** *attrib.* and *Comb.*, as ***shore-cliff*, *clothes*, *duty*, *-fishing*, *-ice*, *-sands*, *-suit*, *-water***; *shore-based* adj.; **shore-anchor** (see quot.); **shore-boat**, a small boat plying near the shore, or between the shore and large vessels farther out; **shore break** *Surfing* (see quot. 1962); †**shore-creeper**, one who sails close in to shore; **shore dinner** *U.S.*, a dinner consisting mainly of sea-food; **shore-due** *Sc.*, a toll paid for making use of a 'shore' or port; a harbour-due; **shore-end**, †(*a*) the end of a 'shore' or landing-place; (*b*) that end of a rope, net, etc., which is on the shore or nearest the shore; **shore face** (see quots.); **shore-fast** *Naut.* (see quot.); **shore fishery** *N. Amer.* (see quot. 1948); **shore-fowler, -fowling** = *shore-shooter, -shooting*; **shore-grape** = SEA-GRAPE 4; **shore grass**, a grass, or grass-like plant, growing on the shore; *spec.* = *shore-weed*; **shore-gun**, a gun for shore-shooting; **shore-gunner, -gunning** = *shore-shooter, -shooting*; **shore-land**, land bordering on a shore; **shore leave**, leave of absence granted to a sailor to go on shore; **shore-levy** *Sc.*, a duty on ships entering a harbour; **shore liberty** = *shore-leave*; **shore-line**, (*a*) the line where shore and water meet; (*b*) = *shore-rope*; **shore-loafer** *Naut. slang*, a civilian; †**shore-mail** *Sc.* = *shore-due* (see MAIL *sb.*²); **shore-master** *Sc.*, a harbour-master; **shore-oil**, the finest kind of cod-liver oil (see quot.); **shore party**, (*a*) *N.Z.*, a body of whalers using a land-based station (*obs.*); (*b*) a body of persons going ashore from a ship; *spec.* a body of soldiers sent ashore; **shore patrol** *U.S.*, a naval police organization responsible for the conduct of sailors on land; hence **shore patrolman**; **shore platform**, a horizontal or gently sloping platform cut at about sea level in a cliff by wave action; **shore-popper**, used contemptuously for *shore-shooter*; **shore-reef** = *fringing reef*: see FRINGING *ppl. a.*; **shore-rope**, a rope connecting a net with the shore; **shore seine**, a seine used near the shore; **shore-shooter**, one who shoots birds on the shore; **shore-shooting**, the sport of shooting birds on the shore (as distinguished from punt-shooting); †**shore-silver** *Sc.* = *shore-due*; **shore station**, a base on land used for shore-whaling; **shore-weed**, a weed growing on the shore; spec. *Littorella lacustris*; **shore-whaling**, whale-fishing near the shore in open boats; also *spec.* = *bay whaling* s.v. BAY *sb.*² 5; hence **shore whaler**, a person engaged in shore-whaling; **shore zone**, the intertidal zone, or the zone affected by wave action; = SHORE *sb.*¹ 1 b.

**1867** Smyth *Sailor's Word-bk.*, **Shore-anchor*, that which lies between the shore and the ship when moored. **1927** *Daily Tel.* 22 Mar. 10/7 The limitation of air armaments shall be effected by limiting the number of *shore-based aircraft of service type maintained in commission. **1950** A. Lee *Soviet Air Force* 34 Its naval force was shore-based except for a few reconnaissance machines on cruisers. **1980** *Jrnl. R. Soc. Arts* July 521/2 The professional mariner currently gives cautious approval to shore-based information services. **1829** Marryat *F. Mildmay* xi, No *shore-boat was near. **1886** Stevenson *Treas. Isl.* ix, The last man or two came off in a shore-boat. **1962** T. Masters *Surfing made Easy* 65 **Shore break*, waves which break close to the beach. **1965** J. Pollard *Surfrider* ii. 20 The next one you might take right to the 'shore break', the waves breaking on the very edge of the beach. **1972** Y. Maley in G. W. Turner *Good Austral. Eng.* iv. 77 Drouyn gets it on,..hangs five, re-enters the shore break, then steps off onto the sand. **1838** Longf. *Beowulf's Exped. Heort* 67 So that the sailors The land saw, The *shore-cliffs [*Beowulf* 222 brimclifu] shining. **1859** Tennyson *Enid* 1013 The long shore-cliff's windy walls. **1862** E. Hodder *Mem. N.Z. Life* 24 *Shore clothes were unpacked, the ship was made tidy. **1922** E. O'Neill *Anna Christie* I. 100 He is dressed in a wrinkled, ill-fitting dark suit of shore clothes. **1599** Nashe *Lenten Stuffe* 29 Discrediting our countrymen for *shorecreepers, like these Colchester oystermen. **1895** *Outing* XXVI. 408/2 Happy-Go-Lucky Beach is proud of their achievements..in the ordering of and presiding at a good *shore-dinner. **1947** E. H. Paul *Linden on Saugus Branch* 267 It was arranged for the party to eat at the Massasoit a shore dinner cooked by Jeff. **1692** in *Extracts Rec. Convent. Burghs Scot.* (1880) IV. 565 *Shoar dewes at Leith 7,700 marks. **1881** *Library Universal Knowl.* XI. 408 Pay-masters..on *shore-duty are employed in the naval purchasing agencies. **1901** *Chambers's Jrnl.* Aug. 551/2 Four keepers are employed in connection with the lighthouse, three being in constant attendance while the fourth is on shore-duty. **1577–87** Holinshed *Chron.* III. 1224/1 At the blacke *shore end, before the said floud, no bote could passe further than the shore end. **1865** Bertram *Harvest of Sea* 160 The shore-end [of the cord] is generally anchored to a stone. **1900** *Law Rep.* App. Cases 415 At the point where the water is shallow, the shore-end of the net is generally a good way out, perhaps 300 to 400 yards. **1912** J. Barrell in *Bull. Geol. Soc. Amer.* XXIII. 385 The *shore face is the relatively narrow slope developed by the breaking waves, a slope which separates the subaerial plain above from the subaqueous below. **1944** A. Holmes *Princ. Physical Geol.* xiv. 291 In appropriate circumstances some of the sediment in transit across the wave-cut platform accumulates in the deeper water beyond, to form a shoreface terrace which grows forward like a broad embankment with its upper surface in smooth continuity with the platform. **1972** *Gloss. Geol.* (Amer. Geol. Inst.) 654/2 *Shoreface*,..the narrow, rather steeply sloping zone seaward or lakeward from the low-water shoreline, permanently covered by water, and over which beach sands and gravels actively oscillate with changing wave conditions. **1867** Smyth *Sailor's Word-bk.*, **Shore-fast*, a hawser carried out to secure a vessel to a quay, mole, or anchor buried on shore. **1767** T. Hutchinson *Hist. Province Mass.-Bay* II. iv. 445 In what they call a sedentaire and we a *shore fishery we shall always outdo them. **1948** R. de Kerchove *Internat. Maritime Dict.* 671/1 *Shore fisheries.* Under this head are included all those fisheries prosecuted from small boats or from the shore without the aid or use of vessels. **1971** E. R. Seary *Place Names Avalon Peninsula* iv. 65 [The Killigrews] either settled permanently or had a summer plantation at Killigrews for the shore fishery. **1865** Wilcocks *Sea-Fisherman* 20 *Shore Fishing.—Fishing from shore with rod and line from the following spots. **1882** Payne-Gallwey *Fowler in Irel.* 348 *Shore-fowlers. **1841** J. T. Hewlett *Parish Clerk* I. 263 They had gone down to *shore-fowling the night before. **1871** Kingsley *At Last* xi, The *Shore-grapes with their green bunches of fruit. **1863** Prior *Plant-n.*, **Shore-grass*, or Shore-weed. **1893** *Scribner's Mag.* June 796/1 Covered with the long pendent shore-grass. **1841** J. T. Hewlett *Parish Clerk* I. 262 He should go and get Davy's *shore-gun. **1859** Folkard *Wild-Fowler* liv. 285 Punters have, generally, a great antipathy to *shore-gunners. *Ibid.* 287 He intended having a night's punting at Ted's expense, by way of change from *shore-gunning. **1752** J. Robson *Acct. Six Years Residence in Hudson's Bay* 58 At Yorkfort and Churchill-river I have observed that the ice did not break off close at the shore, but gradually; the first field leaving the *shore-ice two or three miles broad, the second less, and so on till it was cleared away. **1856** Kane *Arctic Explor.* I. vi. 56 The absence of shore or land ice to the south in Baffin's Bay. **1953** *Beaver* June 22 They walked across the shore ice, perhaps as far as two miles. **1977** *New Yorker* 10 June 55/1 The river's edges are lined with ice that is stationary—'shelf ice', 'shore ice', the first to freeze at the start of winter and the last to go in spring. **1807** J. Barlow *Columbiad* II. 178 Migrant tribes these fruitful *shorelands hail. **1862** R. H. Story *Life R. Story* iii. 61 The hill lying behind the level shorelands of Rosneath. **1888** E. L. Dorsey *Midshipman Bob* 205 They set about making the most of their *shore-leave. **1941** C. S. Forrester *Captain from Connecticut* xv. 216 Shore leave..meant rum and women. **1974** M. Hastings *Dragon Island* iv. 37 Darley was leaning on the rail. 'Shore leave?' he asked. **1593** in *Extracts Rec. Convent. Burghs Scot.* (1870) I. 406 The..supplicatioun..for licence to haue ane impoist and *schoir leiwe within thair harbery..of all schippis arryueand to and fra the samyn. **1906** J. London *Let.* 17 Nov. (1966) 220 You can depend upon me giving good opportunities for *shore-liberty. **1971** S. E. Morison *European Discovery Amer.: Northern Voy.* ix. 287 *La Dauphine* almost always anchored in an uncomfortable roadstead, and they had shore liberty but once in the entire voyage. **1852** Henfrey *Veget. Europe* 187 The *shore-line along the edge of the hilly ridges. **1866** Lowell *Seward-Johnson Reaction* Writ. 1890 V. 299 The levels and shore-lines of politics are no more stationary than those of continents. **1900** *Law Rep.* App. Cas. 409 When the coble has paid out the net in the usual way, it curves down the stream, and the Bermoney boat begins to haul down the shore-line. The man moves the boat down hand over hand. In that way the shore-rope is taken down. **1916** 'Taffrail' *Carry On!* 25 If an ordinary '*shore-loafer', as a bluejacket sometimes calls a civilian, were suddenly transported to one of His Majesty's battleships he would probably spend his first few days on board in a state of hopeless bewilderment. **1603** *Stirling Burgh Rec.* (1887) I. 104 Tua penneis of *schoir maill [to be paid]. **1619** in *Compt Bk. D. Wedderburne*, etc. (S.H.S.) 302 Androw painter *schoir maister. **1833** Cunningham *Lives Painters* VI. 21 David Allan..was born..at Alloa,..where his father held the situation of shore-master. **1875** H. C. Wood *Therap.* (1879) 407 In the manufacture of the so-called *shore oil, the only variety usually employed in medicine, the fish caught near land are brought at once to the shore, and the oil is obtained from the fresh livers. **1841** H. W. Petre *Acct. Settlements N.Z. Co.* iv. 77 System of '*shore-parties'..is much more economical than the pursuit of the whale by ships equipped for the purpose. **1901** G. B. Shaw *Caesar & Cleopatra* III. 160 My men at the barricades are between the sea party and the shore party. **1974** M. Hastings *Dragon Island* v. 42 Tallander's concern regarding any shore parties from our ship. **1917** *Blue Jacket's Man.* (ed. 5) 644 Perhaps the establishment of the *Shore Patrol has done more than any other one institution to make petty officers realize their duty as a class. **1973** H. Gruppe *Truxton Cipher* xvii. 176 The phone rang urgently in Shore Patrol headquarters at the fleet landing. **1944** *Bull. Bur. Naval Personnel Information* (U.S.) Sept. 12/1 The *shore patrolman could have barged in to break up the argument. **1973** H. Gruppe *Truxton Cipher* xx. 208 Dieter leaped..straight into the arms of two waiting Shore Patrolmen. **1895** J. D. Dana *Man. Geol.* (ed. 4) 220 Besides battering and degrading cliffs, wave-action makes *shore-platforms, by shearing away the rocks of coasts down to a horizontal surface near low-tide level. **1978** A. L. Bloom *Geomorphology* xix. 448 Shore platforms are developed by water-level weathering at various heights, relative to tide level, depending on structural factors..and also on wave energy, tidal range, and climate. **1826** Col. Hawker *Diary* (1893) I. 291 Spoiled by some rascally *shore popper. **1886** Payne-Gallwey *Shooting* (Badm. Libr.) II. 225 A shore-shooter—or 'shore-popper', as he is rather contemptuously called by the punter. **1842** Darwin *Coral Reefs* iii. 51 Fringing reefs, or, as they have been called by some voyagers, *shore reefs. **1900** *Shore-rope (see *shore-line*). **1626** Bacon *Sylva* §613 The Ancients report of a Tree, by the Persian Sea, vpon the *Shore-Sands, which is nourished with the Salt-Water. **1884** G. B. Goode et al. *Fisheries & Fishery Industries of U.S.* I. 289 It seems..absurd that the Massachusetts people should have supposed that the use of *shore-seines was exterminating the Mackerel on the coast of Massachusetts. **1973** W. Elmer *Terminol. Fishing* ii. 69 The shore seine is worked with a boat and a shore party. **1880** 'Wildfowler' *Mod. Wildfowling* 422 It must not be imagined that the *shore shooter bags only shore birds. **1829** G. Griffin *Collegians* III. xxxi. 2 He had gone down to the Dairy farm, for the purpose of *shore-shooting. **1876** 'Wildfowler' *Shooting & Fishing Trips* II. 259 Shore-shooting, Fresh-water Angling, and Sea-fishing near Yarmouth. **1589** in *Extracts Rec. Convent. Burghs Scot.* (1870) I. 299 Sic dewty of *schoir syluer sall..be vplifted att thair particular poirttis of sic gudes as salbe..transported furth thairof. **1966** *Austral. Encycl.* IX. 276/2 In 1947 a small chaser fed a *shore station at Albany. **1966** *Encycl. N.Z.* III. 639/1 Hunting, therefore, occurred from vessels ranging considerable distances off shore, from others at bay anchorages, and also from a large number of open boats based on shore stations. **1885** W. D. Howells *Rise S. Lapham* xxiii. 415 A young fellow in the shabby *shore-suit of a sailor. **1924** J. Masefield *Sard Harker* I. 30 Steward, will you have the goodness to set out my shore-suit presently? **1856** Kane *Arctic Explor.* II. xiii. 134 They are still found in groups..disporting in the leads and *shore-water. **1796** Withering *Brit. Plants* (ed. 3) II. 195 *Littorella*..Plantain *Shoreweed. **1871** R. Ellis *Catullus* lxiv. 60 From amid shore-weeds [*ex alga*]. **1872** *Trans. & Proc. N.Z. Inst.* V. 156 The females visit the bays and inlets round the coast to calve..where they are captured by the *shore whalers. **1966** *Encycl. N.Z.* III. 640/1 Hundreds of right whales killed by pelagic whalers off shore and in the bays where ships' boats were often in direct competition with those of the shore whalers. **1841** S. Revans *Lett. to H.S. Chapman* (typescript) II. 163 If no *shore whaling were allowed the cow would rear the calf and get fat. **1851** H. Melville *Moby Dick* II. xxxix. 273 In the Shore Whaling.., when a Right Whale gives token of sinking, they fasten buoys to him. **1852** Mundy *Antipodes* 104 What is called shore-whaling, in contradistinction to deep sea-fishing. **1922** E. C. Starks *Hist. Calif. Shore Whaling* 6 Whaling may be classified under three heads:..Third.—For want of a better term we may call the third form modern shore whaling. The whales are not taken from small boats, but from a seaworthy steam whaler... The whaler stays out until it has secured one or more whales, which it tows to a whaling station on shore. **1959** A. H. McLintock *Descr. Atlas N.Z.* p. xvii, Today there is a shore whaling station at the seaward entrance to Tory Channel. **1921** A. W. Grabau *Textbk. Geol.* I. xvii. 518 This [littoral] district naturally falls into two zones, (*a*) that of the shore between high and low tide (*shore zone) and (*b*) that permanently submerged..(neritic zone). **1978** A. L. Bloom *Geomorphology* xix. 444 Where the postglacial rise of sea level has created a shoreline on a former hill slope, shore-zone processes cut a cliff and bench.

**b.** with names of animals: **shore-beetle**, a beetle of the family Pimeliidæ; **shore-bird**, a bird that frequents the sea-shore or estuaries; *spec.* the sand-martin, *Cotile riparia*; **shore-bug**, a bug belonging to the family Saldidæ; **shore-crab**, the common small crab, *Carcinus mænas*; **shore finch** (see quot.); **shore-fish**, a general name for fish whose habitat is near the shore; **shore fly**, a small black fly of the family Ephydridæ, found in damp or marshy places; **shore-hopper, -jumper**, a small crustacean of the genus *Orchestia*; **shore lark**, *Otocorys* (formerly *Alauda*) *alpestris*; **shore pipit**, the rock pipit, *Anthus obscurus*; **shore sandpiper**, the ruff, *Machetes pugnax*; **shore snipe**, (*a*) the common sandpiper, *Totanus hypoleucus* (Swainson *Names of Birds*); (*b*) *U.S.* the grey plover, *Squatarola helvetica*; **shore swallow**, the sand-martin, *Cotile riparia*; **shore wainscot**, a night-moth, *Leucania littoralis*, found among sandhills.

**1854** A. Adams, etc. *Man. Nat. Hist.* 195 Burrowing *Shore-Beetles (Pimeliidæ). *a* **1672** Willughby *Ornith.* (1676) 156 *Hirundo riparia* Aldrov. The Sand-Martin or *Shore-bird. **1888** [see *shore-snipe*]. **1895** J. H. Comstock *Man. Study Insects* 134 Some of the *Shore-bugs dig burrows, and live for a part of the time beneath the ground. **1968** *Oxf. Bk. Insects* 28/2 The most common and widespread British shore bug..lives around the margins of ponds, ditches, and semi-stagnant streams and lakes. **1850** A. White *List Specim. Crustacea Brit. Mus.* 12 *Carcinus Mænas.* Common *Shore-Crab. **1869–73** T. R. Jones *Cassell's Bk. Birds* I. 184 The *Shore Finches (*Ammodromus*) are likewise included in the family of Bunting Finches. **1802** Bingley *Anim. Biog.* (1805) II. 249 [The raven] eats *shore-fish, and shell-fish. **1880** Günther *Study of Fishes* xix. 260 The Shore-fishes of the extremity of Africa. **1942** E. O. Essig *College Entomology* xxxv. 743 (*Shore Flies, Ephydrid Flies.) Ephydridæ. **1954** Borror & DeLong *Introd. Study Insects* xxvii. 633 The shore flies are small to very small; most of them are dark coloured. **1979** *Nature* 29 Nov. 501/2 Eighty per cent of their diet comprises three insect species, the shore fly, *Ephydra riparia*, the waterboatman, *Trichocorixa reticulata*, and the mosquito, *Aedes dorsalis.* **1863** Wood *Illustr. Nat. Hist.* III. 623 The *Shore-hopper (*Orchestia littorea*) is also plentiful on sandy coasts. **1850** A. White *List Specim. Crustacea Brit. Mus.* 48 *Orchestia littorea.* The common *Shore-Jumper. **1771** J. R. Forster *Catal. Anim. N. Amer.* 12 *Shore Lark. *Alauda* *alpestris.* **1893** NEWTON *Dict. Birds* 512 The Shore-Lark is in Europe a native of only the extreme north. **1839** MACGILLIVRAY *Brit. Birds* II. 194 *Anthus aquaticus.* The *Shore Pipit. **1785** PENNANT *Arctic Zool.* II. 481 *Shore Sandpiper. *Tringa Littorea.* **1888** TRUMBULL *Names of Birds* 191 *note,* The term 'shore-birds'.. means such species as the curlews, plovers, sandpipers, &c... On Long Island, and in its vicinity, 'bay snipe' and '*shore snipe'. **1869–73** T. R. JONES *Cassell's Bk. Birds* II. 111 The Mountain or *Shore Swallows (*Cotyle*). **1869** E. NEWMAN *Brit. Moths* 263 The *Shore Wainscot (*Leucania littoralis*).

**†shore,** *sb.*² *Sc. Obs.* Forms: 4–5 schor, schoyr(e, schoire, 4–6 schore, schoir, (7 showre). [Related to SHORE *v.*²] Menace, threatening.

*c* **1375** BARBOUR *Bruce* VI. 621 The fif.. Com vith gret schoyr and mannasyng. *c* **1470** HENRYSON *Mor. Fab.* XII. *Wolf & Lamb* vi, Swa thy father before Held me at bait, baith with boist and schore. **1513** DOUGLAS *Æneis* XI. Prol. 105 Stand at defens, and schord him for a schore. **1535** STEWART *Cron. Scot.* (Rolls) II. 10 This Victoryn thame manassit with grit schoir. **1567** *Gude & Godlie B.* (S.T.S.) 60 For weill, for wo, for boist, or zit for schoir, Quhair I am set, I sall lufe euer moir. *c* **1650** *Eger & Grime* in *Percy Fol. MS.* (1867) I. 375 Alas, he may make great boast and showre.

**shore** (ʃɔə(r)), *sb.*³ Forms: 5–6 schore, 6–7 shoare, 7–9 shoar, 9 *dial.* shoor, 5– shore. [Late ME. *schore*, a. or cogn. w. MLG., MDu. *schōre*, *schāre* (Du. *schoor* masc.) prop, stay; cf. ON. *skorða* (Norw. *skorda*, *skor*) of the same meaning. The ulterior etymology is obscure.]

**1.** A piece of timber or iron set obliquely against the side of a building, of a ship in dock, etc., as a support when it is in danger of falling or when undergoing alteration or repair; a prop or strut.

*c* **1440** *Promp. Parv.* 448/1 Schore, undur settynge of a thynge þat wolde falle,.. *suppositorium.* *c* **1450** *Brut* 577 And after, vndermynet þe walles and þe toures, and sette shores vndernethe, And after, sette þe same shores on fyre, and brent hem. **1496** *Naval Acc. Hen. VII* (1896) 175 Certayn shorys occupied abought the shoryng of the Soueraigne leing in the dokke. **1587** FLEMING *Contn. Holinshed* III. 1545/2 They were faine to susteine the tide thereof with shores. *a* **1647** PETTE in *Archæologia* XII. 242 To take the dimensions of the ship, to deface the works by striking aside the shores. **1719** DE FOE *Crusoe* I. (Globe) 75, I.. got two Shores or Posts, pitch'd upright to the Top. **1748** *Anson's Voy.* III. v. 341 The mast itself is supported by the shore and by the shrowd. **1823** P. NICHOLSON *Pract. Builder* 593 *Shoar,* an oblique prop, acting as a brace upon the side of a building. **1848** ARNOULD *Mar. Insur.* III. ii. II. 798 The tide .. knocked away the shores which supported the ship. **1882** C. H. STOCK *Shoring & Underpinning* 3 The ordinary use of raking shores.

**b.** *fig.* (Now *rare*; common in the 16th c.)

**1534** JOYE (*title*) The subuersion of Moris false foundation: wher vpon he sweteth to set faste and shoue vnder his shamles shoris, to vnderproppe the popis chirche. **1580** FULKE *Dang. Rock* v. 214 Peter the Apostle is a rocke and a shoare of the Churche. **1603** KNOLLES *Hist. Turks* (1621) 1127 The true shoares of the unstable wheele of fortune. **1831** CARLYLE *Sart. Res.* III. i, He too stands on the adamantine basis of his Manhood, casting aside all props and shoars.

**2.** A prop or stake used for various purposes.

**1601** HOLLAND *Pliny* XVII. xxii. I. 530 As touching props and shores to support vines, the best.. are those of the Oke or Olive tree. **1672** HOOLE *Comenius' Vis. World* liii. 109 The Hunter hunteth wild-beasts, whilest he besetteth a Wood with Toyls, stretched out upon Shoars. **1808** JAMIESON, *Shore,* The prop or support used in constructing *flakes* for inclosing cattle. **1847** HALLIWELL, *Shoars,* stakes set at a distance to shoar or bear up toils or nets in hunting. *Ibid., Shore,* a post used with hurdles in folding sheep. *Dorset.*

**†3.** A slope. *Obs. rare.*

**1546** J. HEYWOOD *Prov.* II. ii. (1867) 47 Ye leane (quoth he) to the wrong shore. **1681** COTTON *Wond. Peak* 61 Where once again the Roof does sloping rise In a steep craggy, and a lubrick shoar.

**4.** *attrib.*

**1867** SMYTH *Sailor's Word-bk., Shore-cleats,* heavy cleats bolted on to the sides of vessels to support the shore-head, and sustain the ship upright.

**shore** (ʃɔə(r)), *sb.*⁴ Also 7 shower, shoare, 7–8 shoar. [Usually regarded as a variant of SEWER *sb.*¹, but probably a use of SHORE *sb.*¹; 'the common shore' being originally the 'no-man's-land' by the water-side, where filth was allowed to be deposited for the tide to wash away. Cf. the use of *common shore* in SHORE *sb.*¹ 1 e; also SHORE *sb.*¹ 3 b.] = SEWER *sb.*¹ 2. Orig. in ***common shore*** = common sewer (see SEWER *sb.*¹ 2); cf. SHORE *sb.*¹ 1 e.

**1598** FLORIO, *Fogna,*.. a common shore iakes or sinke. **1608** SHAKS. *Per.* IV. vi. 186 Emptie olde receptacles, or common-shores of filthe. **1612** DABORNE *Christian turn'd Turke* F 4 b, Here's a vault leads to the common shower. *a* **1667** SKINNER *Etymol. Ling. Angl.* (1671) s.v., The common Shore, *corruptum pro* common Sewer. **1687** DRYDEN *Hind & P.* II. 558 Our sayling Ships like common shoars we use. **1705** ADDISON *Italy* (1733) 196, I need not mention the old common-shore of Rome. **1708** *Brit. Apollo* No. 25. 3/2 The Shores.. stink.. When foul Weather does come. **1792** A. YOUNG *Trav. France* 262 What, in point of beauty, has London to do with the Thames.. any more than with Fleet-ditch, buried as it is, a common shore? **1818** *Blackw. Mag.* May 202/1 Her Luckenbooths now choak the common shore. **1884** *Irish Times* 28 Nov., The fox.. was.. dug out.. seventeen yards from the mouth of the shore.

**b.** *transf.* and *fig.*

*a* **1642** GATAKER *Bale* in Fuller *Abel Rediv.* (1867) II. 260 Lo, here the man that stirred Rome's common shore. **1692** SOUTH *12 Serm.* (1697) I. 512 The Ungratefull person is a Monster which is all Throat and Belly; a kind of thoroughfare, or common-shore, for the good things of the world to pass into. **1705** HICKERINGILL *Priest-cr.* II. v. 51 After the Pope had call'd her all to naught.. the common shore of all Wickedness, and the sink of Perdition. **1733** CHEYNE *Eng. Malady* II. vii. §2 (1734) 186 Carries it into the Guts (the common Shore, to be thence carry'd out of the Habit).

**c.** *attrib.*, as ***shore-man, -worker.***

**1851** MAYHEW *Lond. Labour* II. 150/2 The persons who are in the habit of searching the sewers, call themselves 'shore-men' or 'shore-workers'. *Ibid.* 151/2 The shore-workers, when about to enter the sewers, provide themselves.. with a canvas apron [etc.].

**Shore** (ʃɔə(r)), *sb.*⁵ *Metallurgy.* The name of Albert F. *Shore* (fl. 1907), U.S. manufacturer, used *attrib.* with reference to the SCLEROSCOPE he invented and to a scale of relative hardness associated with the use of this instrument, as ***Shore hardness, Scleroscope, test,*** etc.

**1908** *Iron Age* LXXXII. 555 (*heading*) The Shore Scleroscope. **1908** *Jrnl. Iron & Steel Inst.* LXXVIII. 639 Maurer also gives an account of his investigations on the Shore hardness test. **1924** JEFFRIES & ARCHER *Sci. of Metals* i. 21 The Shore numbers are more representative of the yield point than of the tensile strength. **1937** R. T. ROLFE *Steels for User* vi. 110 Thus a Brinell hardness of 131 should be equivalent to a Shore figure of.. 22, which is the same as the Shore hardness determined. **1967** E. CHAMBERS *Photolitho-Offset* xv. 226 The Shore hardness of the rubber stock should be between 8 to 16. **1979** J. NEELY *Pract. Metall. & Materials of Industry* vi. 71/2 Elastic hardness is measured by an instrument called a Shore Scleroscope.

**†shore,** *a.* Chiefly *Sc. Obs.* Also 4, 5 schore, 6 schoir. [Possibly repr. OE. *scoren* (pa. pple. of *sceran* SHEAR *v.*) in *scoren clif* precipice. More prob. a derivative from the same root, corresp. to Du. *schor* (WFris. *skor, skoar,* NFris. *schōr, skor*) harsh, rough, steep; cf. also OHG. *scorro* (MHG. *schorre*) rugged rock.] Steep, precipitous; rugged.

**1375** BARBOUR *Bruce* x. 22 A schoir crag, hye ande hydvouss. **14..** *Sailing Directions* (Hakl. Soc. 1889) 16 The groundes on the southir side lyen ferr oute, and arne shore too, for ye may come no nere them than vii fadome. **1513** DOUGLAS *Æneis* I. iv. 15 In ane braid sownd.. Flowis the schoir deip. *a* **1585** MONTGOMERIE *Cherrie & Slae* 314 The craig was high and schoir.

**shore** (ʃɔə(r)), *v.*¹ Also 4 ssore, schore, 7 shoar(e. [f. SHORE *sb.*³ (which, however, is not recorded so early). Cf. (MLG., (M)Du. *schoren.*)]

**1.** *trans.* To prop, support with a prop. Often with *up*. Also *fig.*

**1340** *Ayenb.* 207 Holy bene is wel mi3[t]vol avoreye God, vor hi is yssored mid uour þinges ase mid uour posstes. [**1393** LANGL. *P. Pl.* C. XIX. 47 Ne were hit vnder-shored certes hit sholde nat stande.] **1534** BERNERS *Gold. Bk. M. Aurel.* (1546) Cc vij b, If that the house begin to falle, shore and staie it not with pieces of sclender tymbre. *a* **1548** HALL *Chron., Hen. VII,* 34 b, The Easterlynges.. so strongly shored and fortefied them selves that they could not prevayle. **1581** MULCASTER *Positions* xxxvii. (1887) 142 Learning hath some strength to shore vp the person. **1633** P. FLETCHER *Purple Isl.* XI. xxxi, As when a hunted Stag, now welnigh tir'd, Shor'd by an oak, 'gins with his head to play. **1663** GERBIER *Counsel* 29 To shoare the middle part of the head of the Windowes. **1680** C. NESSE *Church Hist.* 340 Christ might stand upon his own legs onely, and not be any longer shored up by the Baptist. **1773** BERRIDGE *Wks.* (1864) 78 The second.. would fall to pieces, unless shored up by sincere obedience. **1792** G. CARTWRIGHT *Jrnl. Labrador* I. Gloss. p. xiv, *Shore up a Boat.* When a boat is placed upon the blocks, and set upright, several shores are placed on each side; to prevent its falling either to one side or the other. **1841** *Peter Parley's Ann.* II. 48 He would have.. shored up the sea-wall as usual. **1884** STEVENSON *Across the Plains* (1892) 135 The old inn, long shored and trussed and buttressed. **1892** 'MARK TWAIN' *Amer. Claimant* xxii. 219 This prop shored him up and kept him from floundering back into democracy and re-renouncing aristocracy. **1959** *Listener* 10 Dec. 1021/1 These are all signs that local authorities are likely to shore up their position for the time being. **1978** *N.Y. Times* 30 Mar. D9/4 The Carter Administration was not contemplating any emergency measures to shore up the dollar.

**†2.** To lift up, raise (the eyes). *Obs.*

**1579** FULKE *Heskins' Parl.* 128 Wee may well bid him shore vp his eyes, & see. **1607** MIDDLETON *Fam. Love* III. iii, Shore up your eyes, and lead the way to the goodliest people that ever turned up the white o' th' eye. **1617** COLLINS *Def. Bp. Ely* II. x. 421 Therfore shore vp your eyes, good Mr. Adioynder.

**†3.** *intr.* To lean, slope, shelve. *Obs.*

**1521** FISHER *Serm. agst. Luther* Wks. 1876 323 The sonne [in winter] shooreth so lowe by the grounde that his bemes thanne sklaunteth vpon the grounde. **1555** WATREMAN *Fardle Facions* I. iii. 34 Afrike.. is shorter than Europe, but broader toward the Occean, where it riseth into mounteigne. And shoryng toward the Weste, by litle and litle waxeth more streighte. **1610** MARKHAM *Masterp.* II. xlix. 293 The horse will.. stand shoaring or leaning alwaies on that side that he is hurt. **1611** SPEED *Theat. Gt. Brit.* II. xiii. 121 That side of the Country vpward, that lieth shoaring vnto the top. **1621** MARKHAM *Hungers Prevent.* 224 These Lime-roddes must bee prickt sloapewise and crosse, shoaring alongst the ground.

**shore,** *v.*² *Sc.* and *north.* Forms: 4–6 schoir, 5–6 schore, 6– shore. [Belongs to SHORE *sb.*²; of obscure origin; perh. cogn. w. SHORE *a.*]

**1.** *trans.* To threaten. Also *absol.* or *intr.* to use threatenings.

*c* **1375** *Sc. Leg. Saints* xlii. (*Agatha*) 58 Syne vthir tyme þai wald hir schore vith visage bald. *c* **1400** *Apol. Loll.* 85 His forbeding to worschip hem is opunly found: & many veniaunces are schorid to her worschipars. *c* **1475** *Rauf Coilȝear* 733 Than the Coilȝear quoke.. Quhen he hard the suith say how he the king schord. *a* **1500–20** DUNBAR *Poems* xiv. 36 This to correct, thay schoir with mony crakkis. **1516** *Caldwell Papers* (Maitland Club) I. 53 Ye and your foresaidis.. come furth.. and wᵗʰ great manissing wordis, schoiring [*printed* schowing] ye said Johne and his servand .. for to slay them perforce. **1597** MONTGOMERIE *Misc. Poems* xv. 65 Thy absence also shores To cut my breath. **1638** R. BAILLIE *Lett. & Jrnls.* (Bannatyne Club) I. 51 The wives railed, and shored him with stones, and were some of them punished. *Ibid.* 76 A number of women waits on, and did shoare him with strookes. ? **1721** RAMSAY *Robt. Richy & Sandy* 134 Yon sooty Cloud shores Rain. **1786** BURNS *To Gavin Hamilton* 3 May, Ye'll catechise him every quirk, An' shore him weel wi hell. **1891** 'H. HALIBURTON' *Ochil Idylls* 66 The freits that were begun To shore us ill.

**2.** To offer. (Cf. similar dialectal use of *threaten*: see *Eng. Dial. Dict.*)

**1787** BURNS *Petition Bruar Water* 22 A panegyric rhyme, .. Even as I was he shor'd me. **1832–53** *Whistle-binkie* Ser. III. 21 A compliment kindly and decently shored.

**†shore,** *v.*³ *Obs.* [App. a variant of SCOUR *v.*² If the source of *scour* be MDu. or MLG. *schūren,* the variation in the initial may be due to dialectal difference of pronunciation of the continental word. For the vowel cf. the form *score* under SCOUR *v.*²]

*trans.* To scour or cleanse by rubbing.

*c* **1460** *Promp. Parv.* (Winch.) 192 Glacyng, or shoryng of harneys, *pernitidacio.* **1531** *Luton Trinity Guild* (1906) 201 Payde to Edwarde Treket for shorynge of the candylstykes. **1564** in *Brit. Mag.* (1834) VI. 148 It'm pd for shoreinge the egoll, vjᵈ.

**shore** (ʃɔə(r)), *v.*⁴ [f. SHORE *sb.*¹]

**1.** *intr.* To go ashore. Of a vessel: To run aground.

*a* **1600** JANE in Hakluyt *Voy.* III. 848 The ship.. shot past that rocke, where wee thought shee would haue shored. **1645** RUTHERFORD *Tryal & Tri. Faith* (1845) 43 They think they are sailing to heaven, and know nothing till they shore, sleeping in the land of death.

**2.** *trans.* To put ashore; to land (passengers or goods); to beach, run aground (a vessel).

**1611** SHAKS. *Wint. T.* IV. iv. 869, I will bring these two Moales, these blind-ones, aboord him, if he thinke it fit to shoare them againe.. let him [etc.]. **1611** CHAPMAN *Odyss.* XVI. 98 Set him where his heart would haue bene shor'd. **1859** SALA *Tw. round Clock* (1861) 18 Two pence per draft is paid for shoreing or landing the fish from the vessels. **1899** J. SPENCE *Shetland Folk-Lore* 126 The boat was temporarily shored on the beach.

**3.** To border as a shore, be the shore of.

**1832** J. BREE *St. Herbert's Isle* 2 A little garden.. Just shored the river in its broomy pride. **1865** MASSON *Rec. Brit. Philos.* iv. 273 Clearing.. the whole periodicity of its materialistic horror.. its dread of being shored by a Nothingness.

**4.** *intr.* To sail *along* (a coast).

**1632** LITHGOW *Trav.* VII. 334 Shoaring along for foure hundred miles, the higher and lower Calabrian Coast,.. we landed at Naples. **1725** DE FOE *Voy. round World* (1840) 169 They had been *shoring,* as they called it, that is to say, coasting along the shore, to see if they could find anything worth their labour.

**†b.** *trans.* To pass by the side of (a hill). *Obs.*

**1592** WYRLEY *Armorie, Capital de Buz* 124 Shoring a hill, we plainly do appear By a little wood, and to our enimies neere.

**shore** (ʃɔə(r)), repr. *colloq.* or (in *U.S.*) *dial.* pronunc. of SURE *a.* and *adv.*

**1890** *Dialect Notes* I. 71 *Shore,* sure. **1898** G. B. SHAW *Candida* I. 97 Glad to meet you, I'm shore. **1932** V. RANDOLPH *Ozark Mountain Folks* ix. 163 Hit shore was a bad night at our place. Yas, sir, hit *shore* was! **1938** M. K. RAWLINGS *Yearling* vii. 62 Well, stay, then, if these folks is shore you're welcome. **1973** R. HOBAN *Lion of Boaz-Jachin & Jachin-Boaz* xviii. 100 It's a proper thing for a man to do —not like running a restaurant or some shore thing like that. **1979–80** *Verbatim* Winter 14/1 My cousin Sharon, a University of Missouri homecoming queen, shore did look pretty, and her mother shore could fry chicken.

**shore,** obs. f. SHOWER *sb.*; pa. t. of SHEAR *v.*

**shored** (ʃɔəd), *ppl. a.*¹ *Sc.* [f. SHORE *v.*² + -ED¹.] Threatened.

**1668** R. B. *Adagia Scot.* 7 A shored Tree stands long. **1818** SCOTT *Rob Roy* xxix, Shored folk live lang.

**shored** (ʃɔəd), *ppl. a.*² [f. SHORE *v.*¹ + -ED¹.] Propped up, supported by shores.

**1563** *Mirr. Mag., Dk. Somerset* xv, Shored houses can not long continue. *a* **1600** *Battle of Flodden* 510 Saint Andrew with his shored cross.

**shorefhode,** obs. form of SHERIFFHOOD.

**'shore-going,** *vbl. sb.* Going ashore (from the sea); living on shore. (Cf. SEA-GOING.)

**1900** *Daily News* 13 June 8/4 Everything was ready for shore-going when it was discovered there were no boats. *attrib.* **1846** *Knickerbocker* XXVIII. 64 He rigged himself in his 'shore-going togs' after supper. **1887** B. HARTE *Crusade of 'Excelsior'* 63 Captain Bunker.. wore a shore-going suit of black broadcloth. **1895** *Times* 19 July 11/2 The half-rater in yachting should exactly fill the position which the gun, the rod, and the hunter hold in shore-going sport. **1898** KIPLING *Fleet in Being* v. 53 When you sit on a man's bunk..with..the shore-going walking sticks slung up overhead.

**'shore-going**, *a.* Going, living, etc., on shore. (Opposed to *sea-going*.)

**1833** DARWIN in *Life & Lett.* (1887) I. 248 This is a curious life for a regular shore-going person such as myself. **1860** *All Year Round* No. 67. 404 A shot came in and took off the truck (or, as a shore-going person would say, 'the wheel').

**shoreless** ('ʃɔəlɪs), *a.* [f. SHORE *sb.*[1] + -LESS.] Having no shore. **a.** Of a sea, or what is compared to a sea: Boundless.

**1628** FELTHAM *Resolves* I. v. 10 One will haue him one that liues religiously, and will not reuell it in a shorelesse excesse. **1643** HERLE *Answ. to Ferne* 21 We shall be no longer lost upon that shorelesse Sea. **1764** GRAINGER *Sugar Cane* II. 275 Can she unappall'd,..The shoreless deluge stem? **1789** E. DARWIN *Bot. Gard.* II. (1791) 53 So on the shoreless air the intrepid Gaul Launch'd the vast concave of his buoyant ball. **1837** CARLYLE *Fr. Rev.* I. v. vi, The crowd seems shoreless. **1863** I. WILLIAMS *Baptistery* I. Imag. i. (1874) 10 An atom in the shoreless infinite. **1891** KIPLING *Light that Failed* xi. (1900) 189 He was adrift on the shoreless tides of delirium.

**b.** *nonce-uses.* Of a vessel: Having no shore in sight. Of a coastline, etc.: Having no low ground adjacent to the sea; precipitous.

*a* **1848** O. W. HOLMES *Parting Word* 6 Ere this shining day grow dark, Skies shall gird my shoreless bark. **1869** TOZER *Highl. Turkey* II. 9 The shoreless cliffs of Ossa. **1892** LORD LYTTON *King Poppy* iii. 306 A shoreless, steep, surf-beaten island rose.

**shoreman** ('ʃɔəmən). Also *U.S.* (sense 2) **shoresman.** [f. SHORE *sb.*[1] + MAN *sb.*]

**1.** A dweller on the seashore.

**1643** TRAPP *Comm. Gen.* xlix. 13 Shore-men are said to be *horridi, immanes.* **1783** *Ann. Reg.* 120 A little army was formed..composed of 80 American rangers,..of 500 shore-men, white and negroes, and 600 Musquito Indians. **1839** *Times* 2 Sept. 4/1 The enthusiasm of the Kentish shoremen spread rapidly into the adjacent districts.

**2.** One who is employed on shore in the business of a fishery: see quot. 1883.

See also quot. 1690; but it is doubtful whether the explanation there given is correct.

**1690** CHILD *Disc. Trade* (1698) 227 There being employed in that Trade two hundred and fifty Ships, which might carry about ten thousand seamen, fishermen and shoremen, as they usually call the younger persons, who were never before at Sea. **1761** *Ann. Reg., Chron.* 188/2 Who are the chief people among the fishermen and shoremen, being the catchers and curers of fish. **1792** G. CARTWRIGHT *Jrnl. Labrador* I. Gloss. p. xiv, *Shoremen*, the people who are employed on shore, to head, split, and salt the codfish. **1872** TALMAGE *Serm.* 56 Some plain shoresman in rough fishing smack..brings them ashore in safety. **1883** G. B. GOODE *Fish. Indust. U.S.* 22 (Fish. Exh. Publ.) To the class of 'shoresmen' belong (1) the capitalists who furnish supplies and apparatus for the use of the active fishermen; (2) the shopkeepers from whom they purchase provisions and clothing; and (3) the skilled labourers who manufacture for them articles of apparel [etc.].

**3.** One who makes his living by shooting on the shore; a shore-gunner.

**1882** PAYNE-GALLWEY *Fowler in Irel.* 348 Once offend the shoremen,..and your sport is spoilt in that locality for years to come.

**4.** A landsman.

**1888** STEVENSON *Black Arrow* III. iv, We are not like shore-men, we old, tough tarry-Johns!

**shore-man**: see SHORE *sb.*[4] c.

**shoren**, obs. form of SHORN.

**shorer** ('ʃɔərə(r)). Also 4-5 **shorier, shoryere.** [f. SHORE *v.*[1] + -ER[1].] A thing (rarely a person) that shores up; a shore, prop. Now only with *up*.

**1387-8** T. USK *Test. Love* II. vii. in *Chaucer's Wks.* (1532) 342b, But if the shorers ben wel grounded, the helpes shullen slyden and suffre the charge to fal. **1393** LANGL. *P. Pl.* C. XIX. 20 Hit hadde shoriers to shoue hit vp, þre shides of o lengþe. **1532** MORE *Confut. Tindale* Wks. 473/2 Nowe thys shorer is so surely sette, that it is shortlye blowen downe quite, if a man saye no more but what than. *a* **1680** T. GOODWIN *Unreg. Man's Guilt.* v. iii. Wks. 1692 III. 207 God is the foundation, and prop, and shoarer up of all being in the World. **1855** BAILEY *Mystic* 113 Mööoi, stretched Full length, gigantic shorer up of earth.

**shoreside, shore-side**, *sb.* (*a.*) **a.** The edge of the shore; the part either of the land or sea adjacent to the shore.

**1571** in *Reg. Mag. Sig. Scot.* 1580, 11/1 Apud lie Schoir-syid de Almond. **1590** WEBBE *Trav.* (Arb.) 33 Fishes.. swimming neere the shore side. **1605** BACON *Adv. Learn.* I. viii. §5 It is a view of delight to stand or walke on the shoare side and to see a Shippe tossed with tempest upon the sea. **1653** WALTON *Angler* I. vii[i]. 155 And if you would have this ledger bait to keep at a fixt place, undisturbed by wind or other accidents, which may drive it to the shoare side [etc.]. **1667** in *Extr. St. Papers rel. Friends* Ser. III. (1912) 270 Shee ..left her 4 small Chilldren weeping on the shoare side. **1869** LYNCH *Ch. & St.* 19 When a larger company was gathered by the hillside, or the shoreside, there was a Church. **1885** PATER *Marius* vi. I. 112 Every one walked down to the shore-side to witness the freighting and launching of the vessel.

**b.** *attrib.* passing into *adj.*

**1883** STEVENSON *Treas. Isl.* xiii, The bow [of the boat] had struck among the shore-side trees. **1937** *Sun* (Baltimore) 4 Sept. 3/1 Harry Bridges, leader of the longshoremen, proclaimed his union's aim of a 'march inland'—to organize all shoreside transportation and commodity handling under the stevedores. **1966** *Economist* 25 June 1439/3 Norway makes sure of a flow of young men into the merchant service. Bachelors pay half the income tax of workers ashore; married men pay a little more, though still less than the shoreside worker. **1979** D. LOWDEN *Boudapesti 3* xxx. 160 Buildings going up... Shoreside villages, without a fishing boat in sight.

Hence as *adv.*, to the shore, to land (*rare*).

**1948** PARTRIDGE *Dict. Forces' Slang* 168 Are you coming shore-side this afternoon? **1949** *Sun* (Baltimore) 6 July 10/2 A desolate peninsula in Venezuela, expected to become the Western Hemisphere's largest oil port, needed facilities for seamen going 'shoreside'.

**Shore Thursday**, obs. f. SHEER THURSDAY.

**shoreward** ('ʃɔəwəd), *adv.* and *a.* [f. SHORE *sb.*[1] + -WARD.]

**A. 1.** *advb. phrase. to* (*the*) *shoreward*: in the direction of the shore. †*from the shoreward*: from the direction of the shore.

**1582** N. LICHEFIELD tr. *Castanheda's Conq. E. Ind.* I. vii. 18b, He retourned to shore ward agaíne, carrieng with him the Pilot of Monsambicke. **1592** in Hakluyt *Voy.* (1600) III. 845 But missing him towards night, we stood to the shoare-ward. **1632** J. HAYWARD tr. *Biondi's Eromena* 11 The Galley slaves being eased by a little gale that blew from the shoreward. **1633** T. JAMES *Voy.* 49 We..put an Anker to shoareward. **1692** in *Capt. Smith's Seaman's Gram.* I. xvi. 80 Her head [lies] to the shoreward. **1887** BOWEN *Æneid* I. 87 Huge waves under them roll to the shoreward.

**2.** *adv.* In the direction of or towards the shore.

*a* **1691** FLAVEL *Sea-Deliv.* Wks. 1716 II. 195 The Danger being equal on every Side, whether we stood Seaward, or Shoreward. **1762** FALCONER *Shipwr.* II. 736 That bids us.. shoreward steer. **1833** TENNYSON *Lotos-Eaters* 2 This mounting wave will roll us shoreward soon. **1901** E. PHILLPOTTS *Striking Hours* 259 Shoreward the crag was connected with..the cliffs by a narrow razor-edge of stone.

**3.** *shoreward of*: towards the shore in respect of; on the shoreward side of.

**1941** *Sun* (Baltimore) 12 July 7/3 All interested parties are urged to be present, particularly those engaged in fishing or operating boats shoreward of or adjacent to existing authorized fishing areas. **1974** R. ADAMS *Shardik* xvi. 110 They came ashore..close to..the cluster of storage huts and servants' quarters lying shoreward of the Sindrad.

**B.** *adj.* Situated or directed towards the shore.

**1804** GRAHAME *Sabbath* 519 Sweet sounds Came slowly floating on the shoreward wave. **1862** MEREDITH *Mod. Love, Cassandra* iv, The deep's long shoreward roll. **1883** STEVENSON *Treas. Isl.* xix, The rear, or shoreward side, of the stockade.

**'shorewards**, *adv.* = SHOREWARD 2 *adv.*

**1837** MACDOUGALL tr. *Graah's E. Coast Greenland* 114 There is a considerable suction, so to say, of this current shorewards. **1849** M. ARNOLD *Forsaken Merman* 4 Now the great winds shorewards blow. **1889** C. EDWARDES *Sardinia* 349 It tends shorewards.

**Shorfa**, Arabic plural of SHEREEF.

**Shorfftyd**, obs. form of SHROVE-TIDE.

**shorge, shorier**, obs. ff. SCOURGE *v.*, SHORER.

**shoring** ('ʃɔərɪŋ), *vbl. sb.*[1] [f. SHORE *v.*[1] + -ING.]

**1. a.** The action or an act of propping up or supporting. Also *shoring up.* **b.** *concr.* The shores or props with which a building, vessel, etc. is held up.

**1496** *Naval Acc. Hen. VII* (1896) 175 The shoryng of the Soueraigne leing in the dokke. **1603** KNOLLES *Hist. Turks* (1638) 324 Things ready to fall, need shoaring. *a* **1639** WOTTON *Surv. Educ.* Reliq. (1651) 316 Where young tender trees..would yet little want any after-underproppings and shoarings. **1688** HOLME *Armoury* III. xxi. (Roxb.) 254/1 He beareth Or, a plaine wall..with a Tower vpon it Battled, with chambers conioyned therevnto, after the maner of shourings. **1768-74** TUCKER *Lt. Nat.* (1834) II. 417 These our discerning artificer considers as shorings to sustain the upper story. **1828** *Examiner* 129/1 The Church wanted shoring up. **1832** *John Bull* 13 Feb. 56/1 The shoring up of the south-west wall of St. Alban's Abbey is being proceeded with. **1878** F. S. WILLIAMS *Midl. Railw.* 357 The miners are protected by immensely strong shorings. **1882** C. H. STOCK (*title*) A treatise on Shoring and Underpinning.

†**2.** A slope. *Obs.*

**1567** GOLDING *Ovid's Met.* VIII. (1593) 187 And orderly he knits A rowe of feathers one by one..That on the shoring of a hill a man would think them growe. **1603** T. M. *True Narr. Entert. Jas. I*, D 1, A pleasant Castle..stands on the shoring of a hill.

**'shoring**, *vbl. sb.*[2] *Sc.* [f. SHORE *v.*[2] + -ING[1].] Threatening.

**1573** TYRIE *Refut.* To Rdr. (beg.), All the writtinges of those quha defendes ane euill caus..vsis to be stufit..with schoring and hedinfull saingis. **1582** in Calderwood *Hist. Kirk* (Wodrow Soc.) III. 670 As the vaine and bloodie minassing, and shoring of his counsels in France and England did oft times testifie.

**shoring** ('ʃɔərɪŋ), *vbl. sb.*[3] [f. SHORE *v.*[4] + -ING[1].] (See quot.)

**1742** *De Foe's Tour Gt. Brit.* (ed. 3) I. 353 Several Mornings after it had blown something hard in the Night, the Sands were covered with Country People, running to and fro to see if the Sea had cast up anything of value. This the Seamen call *going a shoring*; and it seems they often find good Purchase.

**'shoring**, *ppl. a.*[1] [f. SHORE *v.*[1] + -ING[2].]

**1.** Propping, supporting.

**1622** BACON *Hen. VII*, 145 There was also made a shoaring or underpropping Act for the Benevolence.

**2.** Sloping. Also quasi-*adv.*, awry.

*a* **1502** in *Arnolde's Chron.* (1811) 189 And than set your turfe or your erthe ayen the fyre, and set it shoring ayen the fyre. **1567** GOLDING *Ovid's Met.* VI. (1593) 140 The river.. In very deepe and shoring banks to seaward runnes apace Through Phrygia. **1594** BLUNDEVIL *Exerc.* VIII. *Terms Cosmogr.* (1597) 364b, The Zodiake is a great, broade, and slope, or shoring Circle, carrying the 12 signes. **1607** MARKHAM *Caval.* IV. 37 This plate must from the very toe of the shoe forward, rise a little shoaring from the ground. *a* **1825** FORBY *Voc. E. Anglia, Shoring*, awry; aslant. From the oblique or slanting position of a shore or buttress.

Hence **'shoringness**, slantingness.

**1567** GOLDING *Ovid's Met.* VIII. (1593) 202 A tilesherd made it even And tooke away the shoringnesse.

†**'shoring**, *ppl. a.*[2] *Obs.* [f. SHORE *v.*[2] + -ING[2].] Threatening.

**1513** DOUGLAS *Æneis* VIII. iv. 13 First, do behald ȝone schorand hewchis brow, Quhair all ȝone craggy rochis hingis now.

**shoring** ('ʃɔərɪŋ), *ppl. a.*[3] [f. SHORE *v.*[4] + -ING[2].] Forming a shore.

**1581** A. HALL *Iliad* IV. 72 Like as the waues within the sea, ..Forst by some flaw, yeelds whushing noise and shoring banks do sweepe.

†**'shorling.** *Obs.* Forms: 5-6 **shorlyng**, *Sc.* **schorling**, 6-7 *Sc.* **schoirling, scorling**, 6 **shorelinge, -lynge**, 9 **shortling**, 6-9 **shorling.** [f. *shor-*, SHORN *ppl. a.* + -LING.]

**1.** The skin of a sheep that has been recently shorn; the wool taken from such a skin.

**1429** *Rolls of Parlt.* IV. 352/1 Wolle icalled Lambeswolle, shorlyng and scaldyng. **1435** *Exch. Rolls Scot.* IV. 604 De custuma 1155 pellium qui dicuntur schorlingis. **1503-4** *Act 19 Hen. VII*, c. 27 §1 Ther wolles and wolle felles and felles called Shorlyng and Morlyng. **1603** *Reg. Mag. Sig. Scot.* 515/1 All custumes paying of salt and schoirlingis, skaddyngis [etc.]. **1660** *Act 12 Chas. II*, c. 32 §1 Any Woollfells Mortlings or Shorlings. **1688, 1833** [see MORLING].

**b.** (See quot.) *rare*[-0].

**1753** *Chambers' Cycl.* Suppl. s.v., In some parts of England, they understand by a shorling, a sheep whose fleece is shorn off.

**2.** A tonsured person, a shaveling. Also *attrib.*

**1538** BALE *Thre Lawes* v. Fivb, And now I perseuer, amonge y[e] ranke rable of papystes Teachyng ther shorlynges, to playe the Antichrystes. *c* **1550** COVERDALE *Exhort. Cross* vi. 82 That is the prerogatyue of the pryestes and shauen shorelynges. **1560** BECON *Catech.* v. Wks. I. 454b, Swarmes of smeared, spyrituall shorlyng Sorcerers.

**shorn** (ʃɔən), *ppl. a.* Forms: see the verb. [Pa. pple. of SHEAR *v.*]

**1.** Shaven, tonsured.

*c* **1050** *Voc.* in Wr.-Wülcker 507/34 *Rassis* [*read* rasis], scorenum. **1398** TREVISA *Barth. De P.R.* v. lxvi. (1495) 183 Heer shorne is callyd Cesaries, heer vnkytte is callyd Coma in Grewe. **1530** *Compend. Treat.* in Roy *Rede me* (Arb.) 170 Many a shoren crowne. **1600** J. LANE *Tom Teltroth* 114 Bald pate Priests and shoren Friars. **1798** D. COLLINS *Acc. N.S. Wales* I. 583 With..scars upon their shorn heads.

*absol.* **1565** CALFHILL *Answ. Martiall* iv. 111 Therefore ye doe wrong to your shorne and annoynted, to forbyd them mariage.

†**2.** Of gold: Newly cut, so as to have a bright surface. *Obs.*

**13..** *E.E. Allit. P.* A. 213 As schorne golde schyr her fax þenne schon.

**3.** Of corn: Cut with a sickle. Of grass: Cut close.

*c* **1440** *Promp. Parv.* 448/1 Schoryn, or repyd, *messus.* **1523-34** FITZHERB. *Husb.* §26 And also it [mown corn] wyll not kepe nor saue it selfe frome rayne or yll wether, when it standeth in the couer, as the shorne corne wyll do. **1735** SOMERVILLE *Chase* III. 102 Smooth as Swallows skim The new-shorn Mead, and far more swift we fly. **1819** SCOTT *Ivanhoe* xxxix, They are trampled down like the shorn grass. **1885** PATER *Marius* x. I. 172 There was still a glow along the road through the shorn cornfields.

**4.** Of sheep, etc.: Having undergone shearing. *shorn lamb*: also applied to the dressed fur of the sheep used in garment-making.

*c* **1515** *Cocke Lorell's B.* 1 The nexte that came was a coryar..As ryche as a newe shorne shepe. **1602** *2nd Pt. Return fr. Parnass.* IV. ii. (1886) 132 And hauing lost their fleeces, [they] liue afterward like poore shorne sheepe. **1768** [see TEMPER *v.* 2]. **1913** *Times* 13 Sept. 18/6 While shorn skins and lambs are quoted ½d. higher. **1945** N. MITFORD *Pursuit of Love* xxi. 183 Linda..comes back covered with rich furs, while you and I..get..three-quarter-length shorn lamb. **1968** J. IRONSIDE *Fashion Alphabet* 153 *American broadtail.* This was the trade-name for the fur of the very young Argentine lamb... The name is now prohibited in the U.S.A. and the fur is sold under its true name of 'shorn lamb'. **1978** *Lancashire Life* Oct. 101/1 (*caption*) The 'Rambler' jacket in shorn lamb with leather piping all round and on the pockets, plus leather belt, is about £130.

**5.** *Sc.* †**a.** Carved (*obs.*). **b.** Chopped up.

**1547** *Reg. Mag. Sig. Scot.* 20 *note*, Ane Scottis comptar of aik, schorne werk, with the furmis of the samyn. **1597** in *Spalding Club Misc.* (1841) I. 115 Thow gawe him ane drink, mixt with certaine shorne herbis. **1837** CARLYLE *Fr. Rev.* III. VII. vi, Plates containing each three grilled herrings, sprinkled with shorn onions. **1842** J. AITON *Dom. Econ.* (1857) 265 Hard eggs, chopped fine with crumbs of bread, or shorn nettles and oatmeal.

**6.** Lessened in extent, deprived of splendour, etc.: see SHEAR *v.* 4.

**1853** M. ARNOLD *Sohrab & Rustum* 894 For many a league The shorn and parcell'd Oxus strains along Through beds of sand and matted rushy isles. **1868** Lowell *Pict. Appledore* vi, The great shorn sun as you see it now, Across eight miles of undulant gold That widens landward. **1902** *Daily Chron.* 28 July 5/1 Lord Lister has spoken with confidence of the King's ability to go through the shorn ceremonial at the end of next week.

**shorn**, variant of SHARN.

† **shorned**, erroneous form of SHORN *ppl. a.*

**1600** Breton *Pasquils Foolscap* (Grosart) 20/1 She that is neither noble, faire, nor wise, Nor scarce so rich as a newe shornèd Eawe.

**Shorpthursday**, obs. f. SHEER THURSDAY.

**short** (ʃɔːt), *a. sb.* and *adv.* Forms: 1–3 sceort, (1 *compar.* scyrtra, *superl.* scyrtest, scortost), 1–5 scort, 3 shorrt, scheort, (sort), 3–4 ssort, 3–8 schort, (4 schorth, chort), 4–5 s(c)hert, 4–6 shortt, schorte, 4–7 shorte, (5 schorthe, sorte), 5–6 schortt, 3– short. [OE. *sc(e)ort* = OHG. *scurz*:—OTeut. type **skurto-* (compar. **skurtizon-*, OE. *scyrtra*), whence Du. *schorten*, ON. *skorta* to lack; for other derivatives see SHIRT, SKIRT *sbs.*

The Teut. adj. is commonly regarded as a popular L. **excurtus* (f. L. *ex-* + *curtus*). On this view it would be parallel in origin with the synonymous OFris., OS. *kurt*, Du. *kort*, OHG. (MHG., mod.G.) *kurz*, a WGer. adoption of L. *curtus*. The Rom. langs., however, afford no evidence of a popular Latin **excurtus*, and it is unlikely that such a form existed. It is possible that Teut. **skurto-* may be an altered adoption of L. *curtus*, with prefixed *s* either due to some Teut. analogy or attracted from the ending of a preceding word in some Latin context. Some scholars, however, regard **skurto-* as a native Teut. word, f. a root **skert-* (supposed to be evidenced in MHG. *scherze*, *scherzel* small piece):—pre-Teut. **skerd-*, an extension of **sker-* to cut (see SHEAR *v.*).]

A. *adj.* I. With reference to spatial measurement.

**1. a.** Having small longitudinal extent; measuring little along its greatest dimension, or from end to end. Opposed to *long*.

*c* **888** Ælfred *Boeth.* xxxix. §3 Forþy hi habbað swa sceortne ymbhwyrft [etc.]. *c* **1000** *Sax. Leechd.* III. 252 Se winterlica mona..hæfð scyrtran sceade þonne seo sunne. **1154** *O.E. Chron.* (Laud MS.) an. 1137, An cæste þat was scort & nareu. *c* **1205** Lay. 28624 þat wes an sceort bat liðen. *c* **1290** *S. Eng. Leg.* 9/284 þo was it bi a fote to schort. *c* **1386** Chaucer *Knt.'s T.* 1686 No man ther fore..No maner shot polax ne short[e] knyf In to the lystes sende. **1390** Gower *Conf.* I. 99 Hire Necke is schort. *c* **1475** *Rauf Coilȝear* 864 Ilk ane schort knyfe braidit out sone. **1545** Ascham *Toxoph.* I. (Arb.) 28 The corne commeth thinne vp: the eare is short, the grayne is small. **1577** B. Googe *Heresbach's Husb.* I. 45 b, Some do vse short Sythes. **1596** Dalrymple tr. *Leslie's Hist. Scot.* I. 19 Thay beir verie schorte tailis, als schorte as the tail of ane hyne. **1735** Johnson *Lobo's Abyssinia, Voy.* ii. 11 Surrounded by his Courtiers who had each a Stick in his Hand, which is longer or shorter, according to the quality of the Person admitted into the King's Presence. **1796** Withering *Brit. Plants* (ed. 3) I. 81 Short (abbreviatus), a cup is said to be short, when it is shorter than the tube of the blossom. **1840** Lardner *Geom.* 146, PF must be the shortest line which can be drawn from the point P to the line AB. **1871** Farjeon *Joshua Marvel* xlii. III. 263 George Marvel.. having by this time got used to the short clays..had just declared that he enjoyed a short pipe as well as a long one. **1895** A. J. C. Hare *Gurneys of Earlham* I. i. 7 A short staircase leading to an ante room.

**b.** of grass, wool, hair, down, etc. ***to get by the short hairs***: see HAIR *sb.* 8 o. Also, in same sense (*slang* (orig. *Mil.*)), ***to get*** or ***have*** (a person) ***by the short and curlies***.

**1398** Trevisa *Barth. De P.R.* xvii. lxxvi. (1495) 650 Herbes of mountaynes and of hye places ben thynner and shorter than herbes of valeyes and of meedys. **1523–34** Fitzherb. *Husb.* §25 Shorte hey, and leye-hey is good for shepe. **1607** Topsell *Four-f. Beasts* 603 The salt and short pasture. **1620** *Westward for Smelts* (Percy Soc.) 55 She felt by the short haire on his head, that it was the priest. **1796** Withering *Brit. Plants* (ed. 3) I. 95 The pyramidal Seed, crowned by the short down. **1823** Irby & Mangles *Trav.* viii. (1844) 149/2 The short woolly hair of the Africans. **1859** *Habits of Gd. Society* i. 114 Nothing..makes the face look so unlovely as a chin covered with short stubble. **1870** Yeats *Nat. Hist. Comm.* II. (1872) 200 The long silk staple of Georgia, and the short cottons of Egypt. **1948** Partridge *Dict. Forces' Slang* 168 *Short and curlies*, the short hairs, in the phrase 'He got me by the short and curlies'—he caught me out properly. **1956** P. Scott *Male Child* III. i. 191 'Is there any point in going on, if you can't fool yourself?'..'Of course not. That's where we're got by the short and curlies. We cling on.' **1969** J. Gardner *Founder Member* iv. 72 'Stalemate?'..'Looks like it... Got us hard by the short and curlies. I wouldn't try arguing.' **1971** D. Francis *Bonecrack* xii. 153 Suppose..that I abducted Alessandro... I would then have Enso by the short and curlies. **1976** P. Hill *Hunters* xi. 164 There is no need for kid gloves now, we've got him by the short and curlies.

**c.** of a garment.

*c* **1386** Chaucer *Prol.* 93 Short was his gowne with sleues longe and wyde. *c* **1440** *Promp. Parv.* 448/1 Schort or stukkyd garment, *nepticula*. *a* **1548** Hall *Chron., Hen. VIII*, 7 A certayne number of gentelmen..apparayled all in one sewte of shorte garmentes. **1607** [see PANED *ppl. a.*]. **1821** Scott *Kenilw.* xxvi, A close jerkin of scarlet velvet, looped with gold, with short breeches of the same. **1859** *Habits of Gd. Society* iv. 168 Tight dresses and short waists. **1892** W. S. Gilbert *Foggerty's Fairy* 225, I see no reason why a governess in a vicarage should not wear short petticoats if she has good legs. **1893** Leland *Mem.* I. 92, I was sixteen years of age and six feet high before I was allowed to leave off short jackets.

**d.** Const. *in*: Having a specified part short.

**1800** *Med. Jrnl.* III. 425 Not peculiarly short in the neck. **1837** Dickens *Pickw.* ii, 'Rather short in the waist, an't it,' said the stranger. **1841** Thackeray *Gt. Hoggarty Diamond* v, But my coat was..very high in the waist and short in the sleeves.

**e.** Of distance: Not great. Of a journey, flight, etc., Extending over a short distance. †Hence of a passenger, a train: Travelling a short distance.

**1597** Hooker *Eccl. Pol.* v. lxvii. §10 The way which they take to the same Inne is somewhat more short but no whit more certaine. **1604** E. G[rimstone] *D'Acosta's Hist. Indies* IV. xxxv. 305 Birdes..whose flight is shorte. **1697** Dryden *Virg. Georg.* IV. 283 Nor dare they stray,..Nor Forrage far, but short Excursions make. **1774** Goldsm. *Nat. Hist.* (1776) IV. 171 Their blood, without entering their lungs, takes a shorter passage through the very partition of the heart. **1785** Trusler *Mod. Times* I. 30 'Tis true we get a shilling or two occasionally, by a short passenger, or for the carriage of a parcel that is not booked. **1844** *Civil Engin. & Arch. Jrnl.* VII. 288/1 To what are called short passengers, this delay is a most serious inconvenience. **1858** *Rep. Sel. Comm. Rlwy. Accid.* 72 First of all, there are short trains. **1886** C. E. Pascoe *Lond. To-day* xx. (ed. 3) 201 A shorter and more economical trip would be to take the train at King's Cross for Muswell Hill. **1889** *Infantry Drill* 217 Firing distances with the rifle may be classified as follows:—Up to 400 yards, 'Short Distances'; From 400 to 800 yards, 'Medium Distances'; [etc.].

†**f.** ***short weapon***: ? a weapon for hand-to-hand fighting (or perh. a sword, dagger, etc. as opposed to a lance or pike). Also a soldier bearing such a weapon. *Obs.*

**1600** Dymmok *Ireland* (1843) 32 The forelorn hope consisting of 40 shott and 20 shorte weapons. **1821** Scott *Kenilw.* xvi, Retainers or followers, armed with short, or with long weapons.

**g.** *fig.* In Biblical expressions, said of a person's 'hand' or 'arm', implying inadequacy or limited range of power.

**1549** *Compl. Scot.* ix. 75 Behold, the hand of the lorde is na scheortar nor it vas. [**1593** Shaks. *2 Hen. VI.* I. ii. 12 Put forth thy hand, reach at the glorious Gold. What, is't too short? Ile lengthen it with mine.] **1611** Bible *Num.* xi. 23 And the Lord said vnto Moses, Is the Lords hand waxed short? **1656** Bp. Hall *Solil.* 28 If thou hast given me but a private and short hand, yet give a large and public heart. **1705** Stanhope *Paraphr.* I. 10 They whose Hands are shortest, may yet have Hearts as large as the greatest Monarch upon Earth.

**h.** Of action, vision, etc.: Reaching but a little way. (See SHORT SIGHT.) Hence *fig.* of mental powers, ideas, etc.: Contracted in range.

*c* **1386** Chaucer *Prol.* 746 My wit is short ye may wel vnderstonde. **1665** Boyle *Occas. Refl.* IV. vi. (1848) 207 How short and dim a knowledge must they have of him, that have no other than these Corporal Instructers. **1702** Rowe *Ambit. Step-Mother* I. i. 174 Their own short understandings reach No farther than the present. **1714** Young *Force of Relig.* I. 225 Oh! mortals, short of sight. **1736** Butler *Anal.* Diss. II. 319 Our short Views. **1837** Carlyle *Fr. Rev.* II. III. ii, Cradled in hope and short vision.

**i.** As complement. ***to cut, trim***, etc. ***short***: to make short by cutting, trimming, etc.

This use is difficult to distinguish from the advb. use in *to cut short* (= F. *couper court*): see C. 9.

**1545** Ascham *Toxoph.* II. (Arb.) 109 The fingers [of a shooting glove] muste be cut short. **1840** Dickens *Old C. Shop* iii, Hair..cut short and straight upon his temples.

**2. a.** Of persons: Low in stature: opposed to *tall*. Phr. † ***shorter by the head***: beheaded.

*short by the knees* (nonce-use): said of a person kneeling.

*a* **900** Wærferth *Gregory's Dial.* 46 Swa sceort man & swa unfæger on ansyne. **1297** R. Glouc. (Rolls) 8532 Vor he was somdel ssort he clupede him courtehese. *c* **1386** Chaucer *Wife's Prol.* 624, I..euere folwed myn appetit Al were he short or long or blak or whit. **1483** *Cath. Angl.* 337/2 Schorthe, *argutus, vt corporis arguti surgit pigmeus*. *a* **1548** Hall *Chron., Hen. IV*, 14 The Duke of Exceter..was.. there made shorter by the hed. **1713** Rowe *Jane Shore* I. i. 5 Her brother Rivers Ere this lies shorter by the head at Pomfret. **1746** Francis tr. *Horace, Epist.* I. xii. 38 Short by the Knees [L. *genibus minor*] the haughty Parthian kneels. **1891** Farrar *Darkn. & Dawn* xliii, A man..somewhat short of stature.

*absol.* **1377** Langl. *P. Pl.* B. XIV. 243 Louely layke was it neuere bitwene þe longe and þe shorte.

†**b.** *rarely* of a hill. *Obs.*

**1596** Dalrymple tr. *Leslie's Hist. Scot.* I. 43 This is the last and hindmest hil in Scotland, and thairfor the schortest.

**3.** ***short dung, manure, muck***: manure containing short straw and in an advanced state of fermentation. (Cf. branch IV.)

**1618** W. Lawson *New Orch. & Gard.* ii. (1623) 3 Good short, hot, and tender mucke. **1778** W. Marshall *Minutes Agric.* Observ. 111 The ordinary distinction of Long-Dung and Short or Spit-Dung, have likewise been observed. **1812** Sir J. Sinclair *Syst. Husb. Scot.* I. 199 In situations, where much alluvial compost, or short town manure, can be procured. **1830** *Cumb. Farm Rep.* 58 in *Lib. Usef. Knowl., Husb.* III, Short dung is unquestionably most suitable for turnips. **1884** L. F. Allen *New Amer. Farm Bk.* 70 The comparative advantages of long and short manure (the fermented and unfermented).

**4.** Of the sea, etc.: Having short waves; choppy.

**1834** H. Miller *Scenes & Leg.* xxviii. (1857) 420 The sea rose tremendously—at once short, high, and irregular. **1838** FitzGerald *Let. to Barton* Apr., *Lett.* (1889) I. 42 One labours through it [a book] as vessels do through what is called a short sea. **1903** Kipling *Five Nations* 40 Do you know the shallow Baltic where the seas are steep and short, Where the bluff, lee-boarded fishing-luggers ride?

**II.** With reference to duration or serial extent.

**5. a.** Of a period of time, of a process, state or action considered as extending over a period of time: Having little extent in duration, lasting but little time, brief. Also said of duration. ***at short intervals***: at times separated by brief intervals. ***in short order***: see ORDER *sb.* 27 d.

*c* **888** Ælfred *Boeth.* iv, þu þe ðam winterdagum selest scorte tida & þæs sumeres dahum langran. *c* **1055** *Byrhtferth's Handboc* in *Anglia* VIII. 306 Forþam he [*sc.* February] ys scyrtest ealra monða. *c* **1200** *Vices & Virtues* 9 Al swo we forlieseð ðis scorte lif ðurh unhersumness. *c* **1380** Wyclif *Wks.* (1880) 38 Men be nowe of lesse wittis & schortere tyme & feblere of complexion. *c* **1381** Chaucer *Parl. Foules* 1 The lyf so short, the craft so long to lerne. **14..** in *Rel. Ant.* I. 318 The xij day of December ys the shortest day of the yere. *c* **1450** Holland *Howlat* 112 That ȝe wald cry apon Crist,..To schape me a schand bird in a schort space. **1539** Cromwell in Merriman *Life & Lett.* (1902) II. 213 The kinges maiestes will is that ye shal make the shortiest abode there ye can. **1588** Shaks. *L.L.L.* I. i. 181 Three yeeres is but short. **1684** Norris *Poems* 21 Like Angels visits, short and bright. **1696** Whiston *Theory Earth* II. (1722) 209, I shall shew..that the Antediluvian Year was shorter than the present Year. **1742** Blair *Grave* 589 Its Visits Like those of Angels short, and far between. **1751** Jortin *Serm.* (1771) I. ii. 17 The death of Isaac would be only a short sleep. **1771** Smollett *Humph. Cl.* 3 Oct. (1806) VI. 341 The short intervals betwixt every heave he employed in crying for mercy. **1807** *Med. Jrnl.* XVII. 143 The fever is of shorter duration. **1842** Mrs. Kirkland *Forest Life* II. 19 The short remainder of his stay at Mr. Hay's, say him eat his meals like a Trappist. **1859** *Habits of Gd. Society* xiv. 348 Ices handed at short intervals throughout the evening. **1885** 'Mrs. Alexander' *At Bay* vii, Is it possible that on so short an acquaintance you were so severely hit? **1895** *Law Times* XCIX. 499/2 Days are considerably shorter at this time of year [Oct.].

**b.** Occas. applied to conditions, qualities, etc. not usually described in terms of duration: Not lasting a long time, soon over, short-lived. Somewhat *arch.*

**971** *Blickl. Hom.* v. 65 Cuþlice þæt wuldor þysses middanȝeardes is sceort & ȝewitende. *c* **1200** *Trin. Coll. Hom.* 19 And mid his shorte deaðe he lesde hem ut of eche deaðe. **1340** *Ayenb.* 81 Uayrhede..is þing uals ssort and ydel. **1570** T. Norton *Nowell's Catech.* 17 Doest thou say, that vnaduised and sodeine desires, and short thoughtes that come vpon the very godly are sinnes? **1620** Granger *Div. Logike* 107 A short inclination, setling, or apt entrance to an habite. **1697** Dryden *Virg. Georg.* III. 474 Where basking in the Sun-shine they may lye, And the short Remnants of his Heat enjoy. **1768** Sterne *Sent. Journ.* (1778) I. 52 (*Remise Door*) The triumphs of a true feminine heart are short upon these discomfitures. **1787** 'G. Gambado' *Acad. Horsem.* (1809) 34 Your attachment to your horse may be as short as you please.

**c.** ***to make short work of*** (occas. ***with***): to deal summarily with, to dispose of quickly.

**1577** Grange *Golden Aphrod.* I ij b, He desirous to make shorte worke thereof, sayd. **1686** W. Hopkins tr. *Ratramnus* Dissert. v. (1688) 84, I might make short work of it, by alledging all those Authors who [etc.]. **1728** Cibber & Vanbr. *Prov. Husb.* IV. i. 63 This was making short Work on't. **1834** *Tracts for Times* No. 22. 12 When they made such short work with the Prayer-Book. **1885** Clodd *Myths* I. vii. 123 Criticism has made short work of the romancing chronicles which so long did duty for sober history.

†**d.** Qualifying *days* as collect. pl. = time. Also ***short days*** used advb. for 'in a short time'. *Sc.*

**1533** Bellenden *Livy* I. vi. (S.T.S.) I. 37 Schort dayis following king Tacius past to lavyne. *a* **1578** Lindesay (Pitscottie) *Chron. Scot.* (S.T.S.) II. 87 They war beguild withtin schort dayis.

**e.** ***short prescription*** (Law): a prescription established by a short period of user.

**1838** W. Bell *Dict. Law Scot.* 770 The object of the shorter prescriptions, in truth, is, generally speaking, to protect parties against the consequences of negligence in the preservation of vouchers. **1911** *Encycl. Brit.* XXII. 297/2 There are certain short prescriptions recognized by Scots law—corresponding to the limitations of English law... There are also other shorter prescriptions limiting rights of action in different matters.

**f.** Qualifying a sb. denoting a period of time, to indicate a pleased or regretful sense of its brevity. (Cf. 15 b.)

**1715** Pope *Iliad* II. 357 One short month. **1807** Crabbe *Par. Reg.* III. 953 A few short years,..A few, still seeming shorter, and we hear [etc.]. **1837** Carlyle *Fr. Rev.* II. v. i, Seven short weeks of quiet. **1855** Tennyson *Maud* II. IV. iii, Ah Christ, that it were possible For one short hour to see The souls we loved.

**g.** ***short while***, used advb. (now only preceded by *a*) with the sense 'during a short time'. (In OE. as adverbial genitive.)

*c* **897** Ælfred *Gregory's Past. C.* xxxvi. 255 Ðæt wæs to suiðe scortre hwile. *a* **1300** *Cursor M.* 6683 Scort quile or lang. **1340** Hampole *Pr. Consc.* 632 Whether he lyf lang or short while. **1635** J. Hayward tr. *Biondi's Banish'd Virg.* 161 The King (after having jeasted a short while with some of the Ladies). **1613** Drumm. of Hawth. *Tears Death Mœliades* 9 O short-while-lasting Ioy! Of Earth-borne Man. **1828** Scott *Aunt Marg. Mirror* Introd., The adventurous spirit of times short while since passed.

†**h.** ***to make*** (***it***) ***short***: to lose no time, hasten.

**1490** Caxton *Eneydos* xx. 73 Hie the, and make it shorte, mounte vpon the see, and tarye no lenger. **1523** Berners *Froiss.* I. xxv. 15/2 Within a certayn day lymitted, to auoyde out of his countrey the erle of Artoyse, & to make shorte.

**i.** Of a person's memory: Not long retaining anything.

**1340** Hampole *Pr. Consc.* 774 His mynde es short when he oght thynkes. **1607** Chapman *Bussy d' Ambois* I. i. 209 You call'd me lately D'Ambois; has your Worship So short a head? **1731–8** SWIFT *Pol. Conversat.* Introd. 32 Whose Memories may be too short. **1839** HALIBURTON *Letter Bag* Ded. (1840) p. vii, Great men are apt to have short memories.

**6. a.** Of an appointed date in the future: Allowing but a short time, early, near at hand. Chiefly in phrases ***a short day*** (Law), (a bill) ***at short date*** or ***sight*** (Comm.).

? *a* **1400** *Arthur* 213 þu schalt be tawȝt at a schort day for to make suche aray. *c* **1450** in Kingsford *Chron. Lond.* (1905) 117 þe day þt þei askyd was to shorte. **1472–3** *Rolls of Parlt.* VI. 51/2 A corpus cum causa, retournable..at a certeyn short day to come. **1523** BERNERS *Froiss.* I. cxv. 136 They wolde fayne haue had a short day, but it wolde not be. **1682** SCARLETT *Exchanges* 42 If the Bill be at short sight. **1683** *Lond. Gaz.* No. 1864/8 As soon as the whole Sum is paid in, a short day will be appointed,..for the drawing thereof. *a* **1715** BURNET *Own Time* (1724) I. 441 They were bound..to commit the person so impeached, and then give a short day for his trial. **1747** RICHARDSON *Clarissa* (1811) I. 311 You must not wonder that a short day is intended. **1912** *Times* 19 Dec. 19/4 Exchange on London, sight..Do., 60 days' sight..Do., Berlin, short sight.

**b.** Of notice: Given not long beforehand.

**1811** *Regul. & Orders Army* 23 Prepared..on the shortest notice. **1850** KINGSLEY *Cheap Clothes* 6 So that an order may be executed 'at the shortest possible notice', if requisite.

†**c.** Phrase. ***at short hand***: for immediate needs only. *Obs.*

**1825** T. JEFFERSON *Autobiog.* Wks. 1859 I. 28 What matters it whether a landlord, employing ten laborers on his farm, gives them annually as much money as will buy them the necessaries of life, or gives them those necessaries at short hand?

†**7.** Quick, speedy, immediate. *Obs.*

**1480** *Coventry Leet Bk.* 436 Yf the shorter remedy be not had therin, be liklihode it woll growe to gret Inconvenience. **1535** HARVEL in Ellis *Orig. Lett.* Ser. II. II. 75, I thinke to go shortely to Ancª. but I wil made shorte retorne by Godds grace. *a* **1578** LINDESAY (Pitscottie) *Chron. Scot.* (S.T.S.) I. 62 This sudand accis to heigh feliecietie sould haue ane schort decay. **1596** SPENSER *State Irel.* Wks. (Globe) 663/2 The shorte decaye of that governement. **1780** BURKE *Corr.* (1844) II. 364 There is no short remedy for our disease.

**8. a.** Of a speech, sentence, book, word, etc.: Having a small extent from beginning to end; brief. Phrase, ***to make a long story short***. Also †***in short words***: in few words, briefly. ***the short answer to*** (something) ***is*** (and variants) (*colloq.*), used to introduce a straightforward, immediate, or peremptory response or solution; also *transf.* and *fig.*

*c* **1000** ÆLFRIC *Saints' Lives* I. iv. 140 We hit sæcȝað eow on þa scortostan wisan. **1340** *Ayenb.* 98 þe bezechinge þet he ous made of his uayre ylblessede mouþe uayre guode wordes an cleuiynde. *c* **1375** *Sc. Leg. Saints* ii. (*Paulus*) 8 Hillarius, In schorth spech sayand þus [etc.]. *c* **1380** WYCLIF *Sel. Wks.* III. 221 Jesus Crist made it [the Paternoster], and comaundid it in schorte wordis. **1300** GOWER *Conf.* I. 190 And forto make schorte tales, Ther cam [etc.]. **1411** *26 Pol. Poems* 40 At a sarmon wil bid a frere Make it short, or ellys be stylle. **1484** CAXTON *Fables of Alfonce* viii, Thre fables wel shorte. **1526** *Pilgr. Perf.* (W. de W. 1531) 7 A shorte recapitulacion. **1575** GASCOIGNE *Glasse of Govt.* II. v. Wks. 1910 II. 40 Short tale to make, I [etc.]. **1577** B. GOOGE *Heresbach's Husb.* III. 156 Fit names for Dogges. Their names that you geue them, must be short. **1651** HOBBES *Leviath.* II. xxx. 182 When I consider how short were the Lawes of antient times. **1687** A. LOVELL tr. *Thevenot's Trav.* I. Pref. a 2 b, They are only not so full as they would have been, had the Author liued to decipher the Short Notes. **1747** in *Nairne Peerage Evid.* (1874) 150 A full double of the said summons with a short copy on the foot thereof. **1750** GRAY *Elegy* 32 The short and simple annals of the poor. **1815** SCOTT *Guy M.* ii, A short rent-roll. **1848** THACKERAY *Van. Fair* xii, Osborne's were short and soldier-like letters. **1891** OLVER & O'REILLY *Imperial Tariff* 262 When it is complete he makes a short copy. **1905** R. BAGOT *Passport* ii. 8 To make a long story short, certain loans [etc.]. **1908** [MISS E. FOWLER] *Betw. Trent & Ancholme* 275 Important letters or short notes. **1955** *New Statesman* 24 Dec. 851/1, I suppose the short answer is money. **1962** *Times* 24 Nov. 4/6 The short answer is that they seem to indicate a far less cavalier attitude to viewers' wishes on the part of the television companies than has previously been manifest. **1966** W. COOPER *Memoirs of New Man* I. iv. 47 'The short answer to that, my dear, is No.' 'But what about the *long* answer?' **1968** *Guardian* 10 June 7/6 There's no short answer. We have tried..to persuade our dealers that giving service increases sales. **1978** A. PRICE *'44 Vintage* vi. 69 We don't get captured, Jack—that's the short answer. **1980** *N.Y. Times Book Rev.* 23 Mar. 11/3 The short answer is: yes, it is ill will.

**b.** ***short story***: a prose work of fiction, differing from a novel by being shorter and less elaborate; a novelette. Also *attrib.* Hence ***short-storyist***. Also ***short short story***, a very short story; also *ellipt.* as ***short-short***.

**1877** *Independent* 17 May 9/2 His various books have been eminently readable, in the highest sense of the adjective, and some of his short stories have been almost without a flaw in their glittering beauty. *a* **1882** TROLLOPE *Autobiogr.* (1883) I. viii. 182, I had..written from time to time certain short stories, which had been published in different periodicals. **1898** *Daily News* 13 Oct. 6/2 Any really good short story writer. **1902** H. BELLOC *Path to Rome* 140 Terror..is half the plot of their insane 'short stories'. **1923** J. M. MURRY *Pencillings* 82 Mr H. G. Wells's definition of the short story as a fiction that can be read in a quarter of an hour. **1929** *Science Wonder Stories* Nov. 485/1 A few years ago, a short story was anywhere from ten thousand to twenty thousand words. Of late the short, *short* story has gained ascendency in a number of magazines. A short, *short* story is one that runs to not more than fifteen hundred words. **1936** E. BOWEN *Faber Bk. Mod. Short Stories* 17 H. E. Bates has, as a shortstoryist, already a substantial body of work to his name. **1940** G. V. MARTIN *For our Vines have Tender Grapes* iv. 32 Unemployed unemployables..typing endlessly the Great American Saga..cannot sell a short-short to the *Chicago Daily News*. **1957** R. HOGGART *Uses of Literacy* vi. 166 The magazines go beyond the stories to the 'short short stories' or the 'one-minute stories'. **1962** E. LACY *Freeloaders* vi. 106 An airmail letter from my agent telling me he'd sold a short-short of mine. **1972** J. SYMONS *Bloody Murder* xiii. 164 The 'short short story' of 2,000 words or less. **1977** V. S. PRITCHETT *Gentle Barbarian* vi. 90 From a short-story writer's point of view, the timing..is perfect... Turgenev is a master of his craft.

**c.** Phrase. ***short and sweet***: brief and pleasant; now usually more or less ironically, of an expression that is brief and severe or decisive, or that is excessively or unusually brief.

**1539** TAVERNER *Erasm. Prov.* (1552) 68 The Englysh prouerbe is thus pronounced. Short and swete. **1589** PUTTENHAM *Eng. Poesie* III. xxiii. (Arb.) 272 Great princes..who haue little spare leisure to hearken, would haue speeches vsed to them such as be short and sweete. **1624** HEYWOOD *Captives* III. i. in Bullen *Old Plays* IV. 153 'Tis short and sweete, wryte this in your own hand. **1694** MOTTEUX *Rabelais* IV. xlix, Short and sweet, I pray you. **1809** MALKIN *Gil Blas* VII. viii, After a conversation short and sweet, I left the steward. **1866** *Harper's Mag.* Oct. 674/2 The letter-book was consulted, and there stood, short and sweet, and right to the point: 'Dear Sir' [etc.]. **1882** H. MUNBY *Let.* 9 June in D. Hudson *Munby* (1972) 408, I don't like burning your letters & I don't like to *keep* them either—short & sweet is what I like from you. **1970** W. SMITH *Gold Mine* xxxv. 92 Reasons first. I'll make it short and sweet, right?

†**d.** ellipt. ***to make short***: to cut one's speech short. Also as inf. phrase: 'to make a long story short'; to be brief. Const. *of*. *Obs.*

**1556** in W. H. Turner *Select. Rec. Oxford* (1880) 246 Whereby the lord Williams cried, Make short, make short. **1585** T. WASHINGTON tr. *Nicholay's Voy.* I. viii. 9 And to make shorte,..this tower was made..for the garding and keeping of the fountayne. **1600** LYLY *Love's Metam.* IV. ii. 9 (Bond), To make short, a good wind caused him to goe I know not whither. *a* **1687** PETTY *Pol. Arith.* viii. (1691) 109 To make short of this matter. **1679** MOXON *Mech. Exerc.* viii. 142 But to make short of this Argument. **1738** *Gentl. Mag.* VIII. 640/1 To make short of my Story: In order [etc.]. **1823** *New Monthly Mag.* IX. 200/1 To make short of the story, Celso..is put in possession.

**e.** Of a speaker: Brief, occupying little time. Now *rare*.

**1515** DK. SUFFOLK in Mrs. M. A. E. Wood *Lett. Ladies* (1846) I. 201 The queen was in hand with me the first day [after], and said she must be short with me, and shew to me her pleasure and mind. **1631** *Star Chamber Cases* (Camden) 30 My Lords,..I shall be shorte. **1713** ADDISON *Trial Count Tariff* 7 Goodman Fact was very Short but Pithy. **1783** BURKE *Sp. Fox's E. Ind. Bill* Wks. 1842 I. 292, I will endeavour to be a little shorter upon the countries immediately under this charter-government. **1839** LANE *Arab. Nts.* I. 81 Be short in thy words. **1840** DICKENS *Old C. Shop* lxvi, To be short with you, then, it leads me to this. If the truth has come out [etc.].

**9. a.** Of style of writing or speaking, hence of a writer or speaker: Concise.

**1487** CAXTON *Bk. Gd. Manners* IV. vii. (W. de W. *c* 1515) K j, The langage of a mayde oughte to be prudent attempred and ryght shorte without habondaunce of wordes. **1530** PALSGR. 323/2 Shorte compendyouse, *compendieux*. *Ibid.*, Shorte in communycacions, *succint*. *c* **1532** DU WES *Introd. Fr.* in *Palsgr.* 898 In all workes one ought to be shorte. **1815** SCOTT *Guy M.* xxxv, Let me pray you to be short and explicit in what you have to say.

†**b.** ***to be short*** (inf. phrase) = 'in short'.

**1544** BETHAM *Precepts War* Ep. Ded. A vij, But nowe to be shorte, I take them beste englysshe men, which folowe Chaucer, and other olde wryters. **1611** BIBLE *Transl. Pref.* 2 To be short,..what thanks had he? **1784** P. WRIGHT *New Bk. Martyrs* 806/1 To be short, he has left the character, amongst his neighbours, of an honest man.

**10. a.** Of utterances (occasionally of gestures, etc.): Rudely, angrily, or sternly brief or curt. Of persons (chiefly predicative): Rudely or angrily curt in expression; returning short answers; snappish (const. *with* a person).

**1390** GOWER *Conf.* I. 308 Sche no merci on me leith Bot schorte wordes to me seith [etc.]. **1480** *Coventry Leet Bk.* 446 They gyven hem schort langage. *a* **1586** SIDNEY *Arcadia* II. (Sommer) 102 Sorie for his short answere. **1588** SHAKS. *Tit. A.* I. i. 409 You are very short with vs, But if we liue, weele be as sharpe with you. **1591** LYLY *Endim.* III. i. 8 What make you Tellus to bee so short? **1686** tr. *Chardin's Trav. Persia* 33 No other answer but only a short *yes*. **1706** ESTCOURT *Fair Example* v. i. 56 *Flora*. She gave me a thousand short Words whilst I dress'd her this Morning, nothing wou'd please her. *a* **1726** VANBRUGH *Journ. Lond.* IV. i. 45 You are very short, Sir. **1855** DICKENS *Dorrit* I. xix, To-night he was quite—quite short with me. **1894** SIR J. ASTLEY *Fifty Yrs. Life* I. 32, I got a trifle short with him.

†**b.** Not 'long-suffering'; prompt to condemn. *Obs. rare*$^{-1}$.

**1483** [see LONG *a.* 11 c].

**c.** Hasty in temper, easily provoked, irascible. Said also of the temper.

**1599** HAKLUYT *Voy.* II. I. 73 But the deuill..had so blinded the eyes of his thought, that..at euery purpose that was spoken afore him, hee was short and might not dissemble. **1637** RUTHERFORD *Lett.* (1664) 225 If Christ had ..been as wilfull and short as I was, my faith had gone over the brae and broken it's neck. **1818** SCOTT *Hrt. Midl.* v, A wee bit short in the temper. **1885** *Manch. Exam.* 6 Mar. 5/3 Prince Bismarck's short temper.

**11.** Of breath, breathing: Coming in hurried gasps, impeded. Of a cough: Abrupt, checked; recurring abruptly at frequent intervals, dry, fast. Of a pulse: Making short beats, quick.

*a* **1400–50** *Stockh. Med. MS.* 34 For schort onde. **1591** DELONEY *Maiden's Choice* 8 Wks. (1912) 363 Ages breath is short. **1748** RICHARDSON *Clarissa* VII. 208 Her breath being very short, she desired another pillow. **1799** HT. LEE *Canterb. T., Poet's T.* (ed. 2) I. 185 The short and sudden cough..instantly recalled his reason. **1820** KEATS *Eve St. Agnes* viii, Anxious her lips, her breathing quick and short. **1822–29** *Good's Study Med.* (ed. 3) I. 614 *Dyspnœa chronica*. Short breath. [**1843** GRAVES *Syst. Clin. Med.* xiv. 173 The pulse..changed its character from a short and small to a full soft stroke.] **1845** BUDD *Dis. Liver* 316 A short dry cough. **1870** DICKENS *E. Drood* ii, Mr. Jasper's breathing was so remarkably short. **1898** *Allbutt's Syst. Med.* V. 929 In regurgitation, on the contrary [we have] a short pulse not slowed.

**12. a.** Of a series or succession: Of small extent, having few members or terms. ? *Obs.*

**1681** DRYDEN *Abs. & Achit.* 817 In this short File Barzillai first appears. **1788** PRIESTLEY *Lect. Hist.* II. vi. 55 Out of a short collection of medals, he has given us an entire chronicle of the kings of Syria. **1825** C. M. WESTMACOTT *Eng. Spy* I. 9 A short edition.

**b.** ***short hour***: an hour indicated by a few strokes of the clock. (Cf. *small*.)

**1837** CARLYLE *Fr. Rev.* I. II. i, The short hours of night. **1861** HUGHES *Tom Brown at Oxf.* xxxvi, Soda-water and brandy, and cigars, into the short hours. **1865** KINGSLEY *Hereward* xxvi, The monks of Peterborough prayed in the minster till the long hours passed into the short.

**c.** ***a short purse***: a purse soon exhausted; scanty resources. So ***a short kennel***: a small pack of hounds.

*a* **1548** HALL *Chron., Hen. VI*, 148 Kyng Reyner..for al his long stile had to short a purse, to sende his doughter honorably to the kyng her spouse. **1827** *Sporting Mag.* XXI. 142 All gentlemen who have but a short kennel should look to the sort of hound they are to keep. **1835** T. MITCHELL *Acharn. of Aristoph.* 46 *note*, A man with a long pedigree, and a very short purse.

**13.** *Phonetics* and *Prosody*. Applied to a vowel (less frequently to a consonant) when its utterance has the less of the two measures of duration recognized in the ordinary classification of speech-sounds. Also, in *Prosody*, of a syllable: Belonging to that one of the two classes which is supposed to be distinguished from the other by occupying a shorter time in utterance. ***short*** †***accent, mark***: the mark ˘ placed over a vowel letter to indicate short quantity.

For various inaccurate uses see LONG *a.* 13 a.

*c* **1000** ÆLFRIC *Gram.* ix. (Z.) 32 Seo forme ȝeendung is on scortne *a*. **1412–20** LYDG. *Troy-bk.* II. 184, I toke non hede nouþer of schort nor long, But to þe trouþe, and lefte coryouste Boþe of makyng and of metre be. **1573** BARET *Alv.* To Rdr., The last sillable saue one is short. **1585** JAS. I *Ess. Poesie* Pref. (Arb.) 55 Abone the heid of the shorte fute, I haue put this mark ∪. *c* **1620** HUME *Brit. Tongue* I. ii. §17 If this argument reached as wel to i short as i lang. **1704** J. HARRIS *Lex. Techn.* I, *Short-Accent*, in Grammar, shews that the time of Pronounciation ought to be short, and is marked thus ˘. **1770** LUCKOMBE *Hist. Printing* 252 Vowels with the marks of Short and Long over them. **1827** TATE *Grk. Metres* in *Theat. Greeks* (ed. 2) 443 Which do not permit the short vowel precedent to form a short syllable. **1845** *Proc. Philol. Soc.* II. 138 The short *u* continues to represent the Gothic *u*. **1861** PALEY *Æschylus* (ed. 2) 7 *agst. Thebes* 488 *note*, The vowel is properly long, but made short by position. **1952** [see CHECKED *ppl. a.*¹ 1 b]. **1962** [see DURATION 1 c].

**14.** colloq. **a.** ***something short***: undiluted spirits. ***short drink***: a small measure of liquor; a drink which is relatively strong in alcohol and hence drunk in small measures; a dram of spirits or the like.

Perh. originally from having a short name: e.g. 'brandy', not 'brandy and water'.

[**1823**: see B 4 f.] **1837** DICKENS *Pickw.* xlvi, If you'll order the waiter to deliver him anything short. **1844** HOOD *Anacreontic* iv, A drop of summut short. **1883** *Daily Tel.* 2 July 5/3 All these are short drinks—that is to say, drams. **1898** W. W. JACOBS *Sea Urchins, Money-changers* (1906) 224 I've got a bundle o' cigars an' a drop o' something short in my pocket. **1937** A. J. CRONIN *Citadel* II. vii. 155 Challis..was successfully and cheerfully despatching his third short drink. **1957** M. SPARK *Comforters* iv. 85 Caroline and Laurence had been on short drinks, and both were rather lit up. **1973** J. AIKEN in V. Whitaker *Winter's Crimes* 5 22 A large Whisky Mac—his favourite short drink.

**b.** *Comm.* (See quots.)

**1841** G. ROBERTS *Terms Trade & Comm.* 43 Short; an expression of bankers when a cheque is cashed, not in small notes or gold, but by a short or ready method of giving one or more large notes. **1860** *Hotten's Slang Dict.* s.v., Upon presenting a cheque, the clerk asks, 'how will you take it?' *i.e.* in gold or in notes? Should it be desired to receive it in as small a compass as possible, the answer is, 'short'.

**III.** Not reaching to some standard.

**15. a.** Of things: Not coming up to some standard of measure or amount; inadequate in quantity. ***short measure, weight***: defective quantity by measure or weight; also, a measuring rod, vessel, etc., or a scale-weight, which defrauds the purchaser. ***short commons***: see COMMONS; also *fig.*; so ***short allowance, rations***, etc. Also ***short change*** (CHANGE *sb.* 7 b). Phr. ***in short supply***: inadequate to demand.

**1390** GOWER *Conf.* II. 59 It were a schort beyete To winne chaf and lese whete. *c* **1430** *Freemasonry* 192 Suche a mon, throȝe rechelaschepe, Myȝth do the craft schert worschepe. **1596** RALEIGH *Discov. Guiana* 47 We made but a short breakfast aboord the Galley in the morning. *c* **1610** *Women Saints* 80 Short and simple food. **1615** G. SANDYS *Trav.* 12

Some cottons here grow; but short in worth to those of Smyrna. **1662** GREENHALGH in Ellis *Orig. Lett.* Ser. III. IV. 282 Many short meals. **1668** in *10th Rep. Hist. MSS. Comm.* App. v. 72 We conceive the said certifycate to be short and expect that the same in that point be supplied. **1681** FLAVEL *Meth. Grace* xi. 242 The Law accepts no short payment. **1705** STANHOPE *Paraphr.* II. 273 Report is seldom short on the Reflecting Part. **1745** P. THOMAS *Voy. S. Seas* 3 We went to short Allowance of all Species. **1748** *Anson's Voy.* II. xi. 257 Our water being now very short. **1753** *Scots Mag.* Feb. 98/1 The money..was short by 3d. **1789** BENTHAM *Princ. Legisl.* xi. §24 You have detected a baker in selling short weight. **1820** SOUTHEY *Wesley* I. 227 They had been long upon short allowance. **1831** *Lincoln Herald* 16 Dec. 2/2 There was a very short attendance. **1837** CARLYLE *Fr. Rev.* I. VII. iv, A Baker who has been seized with short weights. **1852** DISRAELI in *Hansard Commons* 9 Feb. 303, I cannot, however, help congratulating Parliamentary reformers on the content with which they have accepted the repast provided for them; the voracity of their appetites seems to me satisfied with very short commons. **1871** *Routledge's Ev. Boy's Ann.* 301 An excellent method of securing a prisoner when cord is short. **1874** Short change [see FLUFF *sb.*[1] 3 a]. **1901** 'L. MALET' *Sir R. Calmady* VI. vii, He's certain to take them home short money. **1908** U. B. SINCLAIR *Metropolis* 351 Three times in a single day in another of these great caravansaries, Montague was offered short change. **1928** FOY & HARLOW *Clowning through Life* 81 Our Peanut and juice vendors were all short change artists. **1942** *Times Rev. 1941* 3 Jan. p. v/4 There has been an exemplary pooling of machine tools and of other requisites in short supply. **1943** *Sun* (Baltimore) 7 Jan. 24/2 The State's lawmakers are going to be on 'short commons' and the employes are going to be comparatively flush. **1951** D. HOWARTH *Shetland Bus* xi. 150 Larsen..now found himself in urgent need of bootlaces, so he tried to take the opportunity to buy some; but they were 'in short supply', and he had to make do with string. **1970** *Observer* 13 Sept. 38/5 It's shortcommons for tourists unless they're white.

**b.** Qualifying a sb. denoting a period of time, distance, number, quantity, etc., to indicate an extent less than that expressed by the sb. ***short ton***: see TON[1] 4.

**1702** *Lond. Gaz.* No. 3773/2 Within a short Mile. **1842** BORROW *Bible in Spain* xxiv, A short league distant. **1913** *Times* 9 Aug. 19/2 Short tons.

**c.** Qualifying a noun of action. ***short delivery, shipment*** (*Comm.*): delivery or shipment of goods less in quantity than agreed on or invoiced.

**1884** *Weekly Notes* 9 Feb. 32/1 There was a counter claim for short delivery and defective packing. **1891** OLVER & O'REILLY *Imperial Tariff* 267 A certificate of short shipment from the searcher. **1901** *Scotsman* 13 Mar. 10/7 Loss.. sustained..in consequence of short delivery of a contract for coal.

**d.** Said of a book which has been cut down or cropped in the binding. (Cf. TALL *a.* 7 b.)

**1864** *Reader* No. 88. 304/3 The folio..is quite perfect, but 'short'.

**16.** Of a throw, a missile, etc.: Travelling too short a distance, not reaching the mark. Chiefly in *Archery* and *Bowls*: see quots. 1801, 1897. In *Cricket*: see 26 d.

**1545** ASCHAM *Toxoph.* I. (Arb.) 36 Escheweing shorte, or gone, or eithersyde wide. **1659** N. R. *Prov., Eng. Fr.*, etc. 90 Short shooting loseth the game. **1801** T. ROBERTS *Engl. Bowman* 294 *Short arrow*, an arrow which falls short of the mark. **1897** *Encycl. Sport* I. 129/2 (Bowls) *Short bowl*, one that does not reach the jack.

**17. a.** ***short of*** or †***from*** (in predicative use, also qualifying a preceding sb. or neuter indefinite pronoun): Not fully attaining or amounting to (some condition or degree); not equalling (some other person or thing); inferior to; less than (a specified number or quantity). Also, †inadequate to, not fully worthy of (*obs.*). Often with limiting adv. (*far, little, much, nothing*, etc.) or an expression of number or quantity used advb., indicating the extent of the deficiency.

In mod. use, the original adjectival character of *short* in this application is much obscured, *short of* tending to be felt as a preposition. Occasionally the word governed by *of* is an adj. (e.g. in quot. 1837); cf. the similar use of (*little, nothing*) *less than*.

**1560** GRESHAM in Burgon *Life* (1839) I. 322 If it is discovered, there is nothing short of death with the searcher, and with him who enters it at the custom-house. **1579** FULKE *Heskin's Parl.* 125 A long saying.., but not so long in wordes, as short of his purpose. **1581** J. BELL *Haddon's Answ. Osor.* 494 b, Having regard rather to make manifest.. how much you were short yet of a true and perfect knowledge in the true doctrine of Divinitye. *a* **1586** SIDNEY *Arcadia* II. (Sommer) 172 b, Those immoderate praises, which the foolish Louer thinkes short of his Mistres, though they reach farre beyond the heauens. **1634** SIR T. HERBERT *Trav.* 48 [Gombroon] was a dozen yeares agoe, so short from the title of a Citie, that it could not boast of twelue houses. **1665** J. SERGEANT *Sure Footing* 163 Let my Reader..see how far they are short from..even an Attempt of Evidence. **1693** C. MATHER *Wonders Invisible World* (1862) 16 It will be a thing little short of Miracle. *a* **1700** EVELYN *Diary* Apr. 1646, Cheese little short of the best Parmeggiano. **1747** RICHARDSON *Clarissa* (1811) I. 47 Disgust little short of affrightment. **1748** *Anson's Voy.* II. xii. 265 The Spaniards were not much short of two hundred. **1762** KAMES *Elem. Crit.* i. (1774) I. 30 Words are so far short of the eye in liveliness of impression. **1780** WARNER in Jesse *Selwyn & Contemp.* (1844) IV. 398 Phil. has been unlucky at Sudbury, as he was one short of Marriot. *a* **1792** SIR J. REYNOLDS in Malone *Wks.* (1797) I. p. xxxi, A refined taste, which could not acquiesce in any thing short of a high degree of excellence. **1801** *Farmer's Mag.* Jan. 81 A crop, one fourth short of an average. **1806** J. BERESFORD *Miseries Hum. Life* vi. (ed. 3) 102 Nothing short of a full gallop will save your time. **1818** BYRON *Juan* I. lxii, Ladies..Prefer a spouse whose age is short of thirty. **1837** CARLYLE *Fr. Rev.* I. VI. iv, And such a Constitution, little short of miraculous. **1862** STANLEY *Jew. Ch.* (1877) I. xiv. 280 It could be compared to nothing short of the day when Israel passed through the desert. **1879** MCCARTHY *Own Times* xxix. II. 401 He had everything short of genius. **1880** *Encycl. Brit.* XIII. 194/1 Short of war, certain preliminary measures of hostility are recognized. **1892** *Law Times' Rep.* LXVII. 199/2 Nothing short of that will do.

**b.** In expressions like ***little, nothing short of***, the adj. is occas. used *absol.*

**1838** F. A. P[ALEY] tr. *Schömann's Assemb. Athen.* Introd. 7 The archons were invested with little short of kingly power. **1879** B. TAYLOR *Germ. Lit.* 53 The colossal affectation of his career seems to us little short of idiocy. *Mod.* Little short of £1000 will be required.

**18.** In predicative use, chiefly of persons:

**a.** Defaulting in payments.

**1586** A. DAY *Eng. Secretorie* II. (1625) 7 Divers summes wherein you were short in reckoning. **1864** *Hotten's Slang Dict.* s.v., A conductor of an omnibus, or any other servant is said, to be short when he does not give all the money he receives to his master.

†**b.** Lacking in performance. Of an author: Defective in information. *Obs.*

*a* **1697** SOUTH *Serm.* III. 306 Very large in Pretence and Promise, but short in Performance. **1653** RAMESEY *Astrol. Restored* To Rdr. 25, I have endeavoured to compare one Author with another..and where one hath been short, I have inlarged with another. **1662** PEPYS *Diary* 20 June, I do perceive that I am very short in my business by not knowing many times the geographical part of my business.

†**c.** Below the truth in one's estimate or calculation. *Obs.*

**1669** STURMY *Mariner's Mag.* IV. xvii. 203 In two Voyages I differ but two Leagues, and that I was short.

**d.** Having an insufficient supply of money, food, or something else implied by the context; *spec.* not having the means to meet one's engagements. ***to go short***: to suffer privation, have less than enough.

**1762–71** H. WALPOLE *Vertue's Anecd. Paint.* (1786) III. 65, I am so short in cash, that I am not able to pay my workmen. **1830** GALT *Lawrie T.* II. ii, I have to settle for my coffee spec., and may be short. **1840** DICKENS *Old C. Shop* lxiv, 'They kept me very short,' said the small servant. '.. So I used to come out at night..and feel about in the dark for bits of biscuit.' **1872** SCHELE DE VERE *Americanisms* 306 *Short*, that is, in want of the necessary means to comply with his obligations. **1894** G. W. APPLETON *Co-Respondent* I. 106 I'm always short..Would a loan of 100l. be of any service to you? **1895** *Cornh. Mag.* Dec. 603 'So you goes short, Sarann?' 'I be used to 't', said Mrs. Bradley. **1901** *Essex Herald* 9 Apr. 5/5 Please cash the orders I enclose:.. don't go short when you want any.

**e.** ***short of***: having an insufficient quantity of. Also, not possessing, lacking (something necessary or desirable); in want of (something to complete the desired number).

**1697** DRYDEN *Virg. Georg.* III. 679 Their defenceless Limbs the Brambles tear; Short of their Wool, and naked from the Sheer. **1700** FARQUHAR *Constant Couple* II. v, I am very short of Mony at present. **1721** AMHERST *Terræ Fil.* No. 33. 176 Young men, having been kept short of money at school. **1794** NELSON 8 July in Nicolas *Disp.* (1844) I. 425 They will, from using as many again as is necessary, be soon short of that article, which probably cannot be supplied them. **1855** DICKENS *Dorrit* I. xxv, Allow me to take your hat—we are rather short of pegs. **1866** CRUMP *Banking* xi. 246 As it gives rise to the opinion that he is short of funds. **1897** FLOR. MARRYAT *Blood of Vampire* xii, No one in this 'ouse is kept short of food. **1905** ELIN. GLYN *Viciss. Evangeline* 93 He might be useful to us, if we are short of a gun. **1908** *Westmorld. Gaz.* 21 Nov. 3/2 They were short of bailiffs.

**f.** Preceded or followed by a sb. or an expression of quantity, indicating what is lacking of the required number or amount. ***a shingle short***: see SHINGLE *sb.*[1] 1 b.

**1873** TROLLOPE *Phineas Redux* in *Graphic* 22 Nov. 486/2 He did take the key with him... We were a key short at the time he was away. **1893** E. F. BENSON *Six Common Things* 217 We are a lady short. Shall I tell her to come down to dinner? *a* **1914** *Mod.* The clerk was two pounds short in his cash. **1923** KIPLING *Irish Guards in Great War* I. 1 They were short one officer. **1944** M. PANETH *Branch Street* 97 Our last warden left us... Now we were two people short. **1976** J. SNOW *Cricket Rebel* 43 We were more than 150 short when Derek joined me at the wicket. **1977** *Cork Examiner* 6 June 10/1 Cork..were short three of their regulars.

**g.** *U.S. Stock Exch.* Having sold as yet unacquired stock which the seller hopes can be bought at a lower price before the time fixed for delivery. Also *short of* (such stock). Cf. SHORT *adv.* 11.

**1849** *Merchants' Mag.* (U.S.) XXI. 118 If he does not own the stock he is 'short', or what is the same thing, a 'bear'. **1865** *Harper's Mag.* Apr. 616/2 If he has sold 500 Hudson for future delivery, expecting it to fall, he is pronounced 'short of Hudson'. **1884** A. DALY *Big Bonanza* 20 The market opened lively with a demand for speculative shares by those who have been 'short' of the leading stocks.

**h.** ***short on***: having an insufficient quantity of, deficient in respect of.

**1922** P. A. ROLLINS *Cowboy* iii. 54 The actual 'bad man' was 'short on conversation'. **1942** E. WAUGH *Put out More Flags* ii. 113 It's just this kind of influence these children need... They're rather short on culture at the moment. **1959** *Omaha World-Herald* 20 Dec. D 18/3 Many a gypsy, short on funds and long on nerve, is a master at avoiding inspections. **1977** *Lancet* 13 Aug. 357/1 Dr Bartsch's comment, though interesting, is short on facts.

**i.** *U.S.* Of a race-horse, not in top form. Also in *attrib.* use.

**1942** *Sun* (Baltimore) 1 May 17/1 Ben would prefer to pass the Derby altogether and point his guns at the Preakners' $50,000 the following week, rather than take a chance on setting a 'short' horse back farther in the Derby. **1960** *Washington Post* 23 May A 22 He said..that Venetian Way was 'short', meaning the horse wasn't quite ready for the $1\frac{1}{8}$ mile race. **1977** *Time* 20 June 51/2 Horsemen were quick to point out that he was slightly 'short'—not in peak form—for the Kentucky Derby.

**19.** ***to run short***. **a.** Of persons, etc.: To become short *of*, 'run out' *of* (something). Also without const.

**1752** in *Scots Mag.* (1753) Sept. 452/1 Being run short of money. **1809** *Naval Chron.* XXII. 189 In consequence of running short of water. **1884** C. READE in *Harper's Mag.* Sept. 603/1 I've purchased this cutlery in case she may run short. **1890** S. LANE-POOLE *Barbary Corsairs* I. vii. 81 Coron was running short of supplies.

**b.** Of supplies: To become or prove insufficient in quantity; to become exhausted.

**1850** *Jrnl. R. Agric. Soc.* XI. I. 143 Turnips sometimes run short. **1894** WOLSELEY *Marlborough* II. 99 There was a great dearth of arms..and the supply in the Tower soon ran short.

*transf.* **1890** IZA D. HARDY *New Othello* III. vi. 131 The time was running very short.

**IV.** Not tenacious in substance, friable, brittle.

[Prob. connected with branch I through the notion 'having little length of fibre': cf. sense 3.]

**20.** Of edible substances: Friable, easily crumbled. Phrase, ***to eat short***: to break up or crumble in the mouth. **a.** of crust, pastry, etc. Cf. SHORTBREAD, SHORTCAKE, SHORT CRUST.

*c* **1430** *Two Cookery Bks.* 52 Þan take warme Berme, & putte al þes to-gederys, & bete hem togederys with þin hond tyl it be schort & þikke y-now. **1594** *Good Huswife's Handmaid* 17 b, To make short paste in Lent. **1700** CONGREVE *Way of World* III. xv. 46 You may be as short as a Shrewsbury Cake, if you please. **1888** EDMONDSTON & SAXBY *Home Nat.* 99 A thick cake, which may be made of either flour or oatmeal, and may be rendered 'short' by the use of fat.

**b.** of fruit, meat, etc.

**1648** GAGE *West Ind.* 143 This is the Venison of America, whereof I have sometimes eaten, and found it white and short. **1655** MOUFET & BENNET *Health's Improv.* xix. 186 Salmons are of a fatty, tender, short and sweet flesh. **1699** EVELYN *Acetaria* 57 The bigger Roots..should..eat short and quick. **1706** LONDON & WISE *Retir'd Gard.* I. I. vii. 35 Its Pulp eats short, and its Juice is sugar'd. **1856** *Orr's Circ. Sci., Pract. Chem.* 337 Vinegar makes the meat short, short meat being easy of digestion.

**21.** *gen.* Wanting in tenacity; friable, brittle. Phrase, ***to work short***: to break or crumble when being worked. Of metals: cf. COLD-SHORT, RED-SHORT.

**1607** MARKHAM *Caval.* I. (1617) 57 Lest..it burne and drie vp their hoofes, making them short and brittle. **1682** GREW *Anat. Plants, Anat. Roots* 86 All Piths and more simple Parenchyma's, break short. **1725** *Bradley's Fam. Dict.* s.v. *Corn-land*, Some mix it [dung] with Sand, which causes it to work short. **1766** *Compl. Farmer* s.v. *Mould* 5 P 4/1 And this will be the better yet, if it..does not stick obstinately, but is short, tolerably light, breaking into small clods. **1800** tr. *Lagrange's Chem.* II. 139 Bismuth..renders gold short and brittle. **1839** URE *Dict. Arts* 300 Pure clay.. affords a very short paste. **1859** *Stationers' Hand-bk.* (ed. 2) 105 *Short*, the technical term for the absence of strength in paper. **1883** GRESLEY *Gloss. Coal-mining* s.v., Coal is 'short' when of a very friable or tender nature.

†**22.** Of liquids: Not viscous. (Cf. LONG *a.* 4.)

**1612** PEACHAM *Gentl. Exerc.* I. xxii. (1634) 69 Let it be thoroughly dry, then take the glaire of eggs, and straine it as short as water.

**V.** In Combination.

**23.** In concord with sbs., forming combinations used attributively or quasi-adj., as ***short-arm, -date, -distance, -form, -grain*** (see also sense 26 below), ***-haul*** (HAUL *sb.* 1 c), ***-hay, -hole, -leaf, -life, -line, -notice, -persistence, -range, -stroke, -take-off, -time, -vowel, -water***.

**1902** *Daily Chron.* 3 May 8/6 As if he were going to do a *short-arm balance on the parallel bars. **1908** *Installation News* II. 45/2 Used for concealed work, in conjunction with a screwed shortarm bend or tee. **1909** *Q. Rev.* Oct. 358 British railways offer facilities for cheap, *short-date bookings. **1898** *Daily News* 15 July 5/1 These *short-distance races are ruinous in their effect upon the breed of horses. **1947** *Sun* (Baltimore) 15 May 2/8 The bill carries a new set of tables for the so-called *short-form taxpayers—those with adjusted gross incomes of $5,000 or less. **1961** R. B. LONG *Sentence & its Parts* x. 234 The Appalachians, the Rockies..are short-form phrasal proper names. **1972** *Accountant* 19 Oct. 487/2 The position [should] be clarified by an appropriate reference in the short-form report. **1947** L. P. DE GOUY *Gold Cookery Bk.* xi. 766 There are many varieties of rice produced in the United States. They are.. of three general types, long grain, medium grain, and *short grain. **1970** SIMON & HOWE *Dict. Gastronomy* 326/2 Rice generally can be divided into long, medium and short grain types. **1895** *Funk's Stand. Dict.* II. 1658/1 The interstate commerce law forbids a greater charge in the aggregate for a shorter than for a longer distance over the same line..and is commonly called the long and *short haul clause. **1939** *Jrnl. R. Aeronaut. Soc.* XLIII. 900 This figure represents about 3 lbs. per rated h.p. of the engines, which is appreciably better than the figure for most modern short-haul air liners. **1960** *Times* 14 Nov. 13/6 The most popular aircraft in use for short-haul work is the Bristol Freighter. **1976** P. R. WHITE *Planning for Public Transport* ix. 190 Increased fuel costs affect short-haul operations more radically than long-haul. **1979** *Arizona Daily Star* 5 Aug. I. 3/1 It's mainly on short-haul trains. **1843** A. R. WALLACE in *Life* (1905) I. xiv. 208 The '*short-hay meadows', as they are called [in South Wales]. **1901** *Scotsman* 8 Mar. 6/6 A *short-hole golf course in the park. **1796** B. HAWKINS *Let.* 4 Dec.

in *Coll. Georgia Hist. Soc.* (1916) IX. 24, I..came..to oak and *short leaf pine. **1911** *Encycl. Brit.* XXVII. 634/2 Short-leaf pine. **1969** T. H. Everett *Living Trees of World* iv. 51/1 The shortleaf pine..is found from New York to Florida and Texas and has dark bluish-green foliage. **1966** M. Woodhouse *Tree Frog* xix. 144 A self-contained *short-life powerplant. **1973** *Guardian* 16 Feb. 6/1 Foods classified by the Ministry as 'short-life'—that is with a storage capacity after packing of less than three months—would eventually all be stamped with a 'sell by' date. **1977** *Spare Rib* July 40/3 (Advt.), Willing to expand the project into emergency and shortlife housing and building coops. **1941** L. MacNeice *Poetry of W. B. Yeats* vi. 114 Yeats..is outstanding among modern poets for his mastery of the *short-line poem with three or four stresses to a line. **1974** *Aiken* (S. Carolina) *Standard* 24 Apr. 1-B/1 (*caption*) Train enthusiast Larry Raid, Denmark, Iowa, stands on the tracks of a shortline railroad that he has rebuilt from Keithburg, Ill., to Oakville, Iowa. **1853** R. S. Surtees *Sponge's Sp. Tour* xvii. (1893) 88 We are rather badly off for neighbours just here—at least for *short-notice neighbours. **1965** *Math. in Biol. & Med.* (Med. Res. Council) iv. 192 The 1·5-mil-spot cathode ray tube..produces the *short-persistence flying spot, with a swept diameter of 10 cm. **1973** *Gloss. Electrotechnical, Power Terms (B.S.I.)* i. vi. 16 *Short-persistence screen*, of a cathode ray tube. A screen whose luminance decays rapidly after the stimulus has been reduced or removed. **1869** Lowell *Let.* 16 July in Ogden *Life E. L. Godkin* (1907) II. 84 'Tis an honest old-fashioned piece of straight-forward *short-range notions and carries an ounce ball. **1900** *Daily News* 23 May 5/6 A desperate short-range fight followed. **1838** *Civil Engin. & Arch. Jrnl.* I. 394/2 The *short stroke engines are propelling the boats ..faster than long stroke ones. **1921** A. W. Judge *Automobile & Aircraft Engines* iv. 167 Tests..show that at low piston speeds the short stroke engine has a somewhat better thermal efficiency. **1977** D. Bastow *W. O. Bentley —Engineer* xx. 337 The short stroke engine would be at least no worse off in terms of specific weight per horse-power. **1959** *Times Lit. Suppl.* 27 Feb. 115/2 The Army pressed for ample supplies of vertical or *short take-off aircraft to move troops on the battlefield. **1973** *Lebende Sprachen* XVIII. 69/1 Britain's aircraft manufacturers also have in mind a new medium size short take-off aircraft to replace the Hawker Siddeley 748. **1877** Spurgeon *Serm.* XXIII. 130 In the army they have *short-time soldiers and long-time soldiers. **1898** *Daily News* 26 July 5/7 It was too large for such a short-time contract. **1965** *Language* XLI. 25 We can posit for Proto-Germanic a *short-vowel system consisting of four phonemes. **1791** R. Mylne *2nd Rep. Thames* 20 In *short-water Time, or dry Seasons.

**24.** Parasynthetic derivatives in -ED[2], unlimited in number, as ***short-armed, -barrelled, -billed, -bodied, -frocked, -handled, -leaved,-necked, -nosed, -vowelled***, etc.

**1606** Shaks. *Tr. & Cr.* ii. iii. 15 *Short-arm'd ignorance. **1649** G. Daniel *Trinarch., Hen. V*, ccxviii, Now a nearer Thirst Rages, and Short-arm'd Struggles makes 'em feel't. **1833** Nyren *Yng. Cricketer's Tutor* (1902) 35 This is a puzzler to a short-armed batsman. **1847–9** *Todd's Cycl. Anat.* IV. 20/2 The *Hydra viridis* or short-armed polype. **1832** J. Rennie *Butterfl. & Moths* 159 The *Short-barred White (*Ditula scriptana*)..The Short-barred Grey (*D. semifasciana*). **1978** R. Ludlum *Holcroft Covenant* xxxi. 365 He withdrew a small, *short-barreled revolver and handed it to Tennyson. **1752** J. Hill *Hist. Anim.* 148 The *short-beaked Purpura. **1891** Moullin *Surg.* 1248 An instrument shaped like a short-beaked lithotrite. **1835–6** Owen in *Todd's Cycl. Anat.* I. 292/1 The *shorter-billed birds. **1872** Coues *N. Amer. Birds* 88 Short-billed Marsh Wren. **1677** *Lond. Gaz.* No. 1257/4 A brown bay Gelding,..strong made, *short bodied. **1877** Huxley *Anat. Inv. Anim.* vi. 366 In the short-bodied *Læmodipoda*. **1858** Hawthorne *Fr. & It. Note-bks.* (1872) I. 22 *Short-breasted coats. **1819** Samouelle *Entomol. Compend.* 425 *Botys cucullatalis*. The *Short-cloaked Moth. **1751** G. Edwards *Birds* IV. 248 The *Short-eared Bat. **1820** Scott *Monast.* Answ. Introd. Ep., The *short-faced president of the Spectator's Club. **1859** Darwin *Orig. Spec.* i. (1872) 15 Compare the English carrier Pigeon and the short-faced tumbler. **1915** G. Frankau *Tid'apa* ii. 17 Perched sideways, *short-frocked, on the mattress, he thought her a child in the gloom. **1933** Dylan Thomas *Let.* Nov. (1966) 52 My only sister passed through the stages of..short-frocked flappery and social snobbery into a comfortable married life. **1622** T. Stoughton *Chr. Sacrif.* xii. 169 Of such *short haired Gentlewomen I find not one example either in Scripture or elsewhere. **1698** *Phil. Trans.* XX. 330 Carinated, short-hair'd stiff Pods. **1906** Olive C. Malvery *Soul Market* viii. 140 A thick-set, short-haired man. **1851** H. Melville *Moby Dick* II. xxxvi. 241 A *short-handled sharp spade being sent up to him, he diligently searches for the proper place to begin breaking into the Tun. **1964** W. L. Goodman *Hist. Woodworking Tools* 29 The T- axe was gradually superseded from the middle of the 14th century onwards by the short-handled version of type 3. **1715** Ramsay *Christ's Kirk Gr.* ii. xii, A *short-hought man. **1592** Shaks. *Ven. & Ad.* 295 This Horse..Round hooft, *short iointed, fetlocks shag, and long. **1846** J. Baxter *Libr. Pract. Agric.* I. 260 Cuttings are taken from the most fruitful, well-ripened, short-jointed boughs in autumn. **1748** M. Catesby *Nat. Hist. Carolina* App. p. xxii, The *short-leav'd Pine is usually a small tree. **1884** Sargent *Rep. Forests N. Amer.* 200 Short-leaved pine. **1597** Shaks. *2 Hen. IV.* v. i. 28 A couple of *short-legg'd Hennes. **1886** Dufferin in Lyall *Life* (1905) II. 114 Our poor little short-legged Goorkhas. **1647** C. Harvey *Schola Cordis* x. 52 The *short-lin'd circumference Of that three-corner'd figure. **1768** Sterne *Sent. Journ.* (1778) I. 66 (*Remise Door*), She walk'd..with the slow, *short-measur'd step of thoughtfulness. **1663** Boyle *Usef. Exp. Nat. Philos.* i. ii. 42 Having with the same liquor filled other small crystalline viols, though *short-necked. **1845** Youatt *Dog* ii. 33 In the act of seizing the hare the short-necked dog may lose the centre of gravity and fall. **1849** D. Campbell *Inorg. Chem.* 286 The sulphide is introduced into a short-necked Florence flask. **1955** *Archaeol. News Let.* VI. 15 Professor Piggott proposed the replacement of the alphabetical classification by descriptive terms... Classes A and C should be known as 'necked beakers'... Abercromby.. suggested that Class C—short necked beakers—was derived from Class A. **1970** Bray & Trump *Dict. Archaeol.* 36/2 The international bell-beakers are uncommon in Britain, where they are replaced by local variants, the long-necked (formerly A) beakers of eastern England and the short-necked (formerly C) beakers of Scotland. **1693** Tate *Dryden's Juvenal* ii. (1697) 38 In vain, O Rome! thou dost thy Conquest boast Beyond the Orcades *short-nighted Coast. *c* **1440** *Promp. Parv.* 59/2 Cammyd, or *schort nosyd, *simus*. *a* **1652** Brome *Queen & Concubine* ii. iv. (1659) 31 Short-nos'd Dogs. **1681** Grew *Musæum* i. §vi. i. 128 The Short-Nos'd Snail. **1910** *Blackw. Mag.* Feb. 287/1 The Jumna, like all Indian rivers, is full of crocodiles both of the short- and long-nosed descriptions. **1948** C. L. B. Hubbard *Dogs in Britain* 3 Such breeds as the Pug and short-nosed dogs. **1839** T. Beale *Nat. Hist. Sperm Whale* Introd. (ed. 2) 7 A row of widely separated, *short-pointed, conical teeth. **1687** *Lond. Gaz.* No. 2287/8 A bright bay, thick *short quartered. **1807** W. Irving *Salmag.* (1824) 193 A pair of short-quartered high-heeled shoes. **1862** *Rem. Golf* 15 The Putter..is a *short-shafted, stiff club, with a large flattish head, and square face. **1681** Grew *Musæum* i. §vii. ii. 169 The *Short-Shell'd Beetle. **1647** Ward *Simple Cobler* 24 To borrow a little of their [women's] loose-tongue Liberty, and mispend a word or two upon their long-wasted, but *short-skirted patience. **1901** C. Holland *Mousmé* 40 My shortskirted, somewhat tomboy niece. *a* **1661** Holyday *Juvenal* (1673) 157 When Rome was burn'd By *short-slop'd Gauls and the Senonian brood. **1575** Turberv. *Venerie* vi. 14 The head..is more to be esteemed when it is long than when it is *short snowted. **1815** Kirby & Sp. *Entomol.* vi. (1818) I. 177 A short-snouted weevil. **1896** H. Woodward *Guide Fossil Reptiles Brit. Mus.* 6 The Crocodiles..are divided into a *brevirostrine*, or short-snouted section [etc.]. **1800** Shaw *Gen. Zool.* II. 7 *Short-spined Porcupine. **1836** Yarrell *Brit. Fishes* I. 60 Short-spined Cottus. **1682** *Lond. Gaz.* No. 1768/4 A *short statured Man,..broke into a House near Basingstoke. **1840** Dickens *Old C. Shop* xlvi, Travellers jogging past on little *short-stepped horses. **1694** *Lond. Gaz.* No. 2946/4 Flat hoofed, very *short strunted. **1874** Lubbock *Wild Flowers* ii. 34 A *short-styled plant. **1684** *Lond. Gaz.* No. 1910/4 A Dun coloured Mare..*short tailed. **1774** Goldsm. *Nat. Hist.* (1776) IV. 75 The short tailed field mouse. **1848** Gould *Birds Austral.* VII. Pl. 39 Short-tailed Albatros. **1900** H. Lawson *On Track* 139, I was very *short-tempered. **1598** Marston *Sco. Villanie* i. ii, A *short term'd tenancie. **1680** Otway *C. Marius* v. ii, The short-term'd Life Of one old Man. **1935** G. O. Curme *Gram. Eng. Lang.* II. xii. 307 In early Modern English there was alongside of the long-voweled *bete* or *beat* the *short-voweled *bett*. **1611** Cotgr. s.v. *Autour*, A *short-winged hauke. **1668** Charleton *Onomast.* 63 The short-winged Eagle. **1687** Dryden *Hind & P.* iii. 473 In fine, short-wing'd, unfit himself to fly, His fear foretold foul weather in the sky. **1828** Sir J. S. Sebright *Hawking* (1828) 46 A short-winged hawk. **1869–73** T. R. Jones *Cassell's Bk. Birds* III. 287 Short-winged Cursorial Birds. **1653** R. Sanders *Physiogn.* 41 The *Short wristed, cut, and dissected, signifies Weakness of Body and Minde.

**25.** Combinations with participles in which *short* is used as a complement, as ***short-bitten, -cropped, -drawn, -growing***, etc.

*a* **1586** Sidney *Arcadia* i. Ecl. (1598) 84 *Short-bitten grasse. **1884** Birch *Kouyunjik Gallery Brit. Mus.* 89 The horse has a *short-cropped mane. **1680** *Lond. Gaz.* No. 1561/4 A Sorrel Mare..her Foretop cut off, and *short Dock'd. **1816** Scott *Old Mort.* xxxviii, She could discover by his *short-drawn sobs that it was a paroxysm of mental agony. **1889** *Hardwicke's Sci. Gossip* XXV. 195/1 The Morello and many *short-growing varieties of similar habit. **1794** *Rigging & Seamanship* 56 **Short-laid*, implies *short-twisted. **1869** Tozer *Highl. Turkey* I. 212 Men with tails.. are always *short-made and broad-shouldered. **1677** *Lond. Gaz.* No. 1170/4 A *short-truss'd Nag.

**26. a.** Special collocations and combinations: **short-arc** *a.* (see quot. 1972); **short-arm** *a.*, (*a*) designating a punch thrown with the arm not fully extended; also *ellipt.* as *sb.*; (*b*) *slang* (orig. and chiefly *Mil.*), designating an inspection of the penis for venereal disease or other infection; also *ellipt.* as *sb.*; **short-arse, -ass** *slang*, a person of small stature; a person of little account; hence **short-arsed, -assed** *a.*, of small stature; **short back and sides**, a haircut in which the hair is cut short at the back and sides of the head; also *attrib.*; **short ballot** *U.S.*, a ballot in which only the more important offices are held up for election, the minor offices being filled by appointment; *spec.* (see quot. 1940); also, a form for such a ballot; also *attrib.*; **short bath** *Dyeing* (see quot.); †**short-board** (see BOARD *sb.* 15); **short cards** *U.S.*, one of various card games played for money (see quots.); also *attrib.* in *sing.*; **short chain** *Chem.* [CHAIN *sb.* 5 g], a relatively small number of atoms (usu. of carbon) linked together in a line; usu. *attrib.* (with hyphen); **short-cloak**, a cloak coming down only to the elbows; **short clothes**, an infant's short-coats (see SHORT-COAT *sb.* 2); also *fig.*; **short con** *U.S. slang*, a small-scale confidence racket; also (with hyphen) *attrib.*; **short corner** *Hockey*, a penalty hit taken from a spot on the goal-line up to within ten yards of the goal-posts, a penalty corner; **short-cross**, (*a*) *Printing*, 'the shortest and also the broadest bar that divides a chase into quarters' (Savage *Dict. Printing*, 1841); (*b*) *Numism.*, a cross with arms extending only to the inner circle of the coin; also *attrib.*; **short-cycle(d** *adjs. Bot.*, (of a rust fungus) not having a complete life cycle; **short-day** *a.*, (of a plant) not flowering until the period of light each day falls below some limit; **short-eat** *Sri Lanka*, a snack; **short end**, (*a*) *pl.* odds and ends (cf. END *sb.* 6 c); (*b*) see quot. 1844; (*c*) a remnant of cloth; (*d*) *U.S. slang*, the inferior part or share (*of* something), the losing end, a bad deal; (*e*) *Comm.* that part of a stock market which deals in short-term stocks; †**short-ended** *a. Sc.* [f. *end* var. of ANDE breath], short-winded; **short-eyed** *a.*, short-sighted (in quot. *fig.*); **short focus**, a focal point that is near to the lens; chiefly *attrib.*, esp. in ***short-focus lens***, spec., a photographic lens whose focal length is less than the length of the diagonal of the negative or plate with which it is used; **short-frock**, a short garment usually worn in childhood, hence *fig.* in *pl.* habits, etc. associated with childhood; **short fuse** *U.S. slang*, a quick temper; hence **short-fused** *a.*; **short game** *Golf*, the style of golf played at the approach to and on the green; **short gown**, a dress with a very short skirt, worn by women engaged in house-work; also †a night-gown worn by a person of rank; also *attrib.*; **short grain**, a condition of the fibres which gives rise to brittleness in wood (cf. SHORT-GRAINED *a.*); **short-grass**, (*a*) grass grown and trimmed as a lawn; (*b*) used, usu. *attrib.*, to designate the vegetation of certain prairies; **short-hairs** pl. *U.S. slang*, a name given to a branch of the Democratic Party in the Western States who show discontent with the administration; also *attrib.* in *sing.*; **short head**, (*a*) *Anthropology*, a brachycephalic person; (*b*) *Racing*, a distance less than the length of a horse's head; a horse that has lost by a short head; also *attrib.* and *fig.*; hence **short-head** *v. trans.*, to defeat by a short head; also *transf.* and *fig.*; **short-headed** *a.*, having a short head, *spec.* in *Anthropology*, brachycephalic; hence ***short-headedness***; **short heeled** *a.*, having a short heel; *fig.* wanton; hence **short-heels**, a wanton person; **short horse** *U.S.*, (*a*) = QUARTER-HORSE; also *attrib.*; (*b*) (see sense 18 i above); **short-line** *Rackets* (see quot.); **short linseed**, ? a trade name for a kind of linseed-meal; **short-long**, (*a*) *Med.* a technical name for a variety of Cardamom; (*b*) an iambic verse (*nonce-use*); **short-lunged** *a.* = SHORT-WINDED; in quot. *fig.*; **short measure**, an arrangement of the keyboard of a spinet in which advantage is taken of the 'short octave'; **short metre**, a form of stanza used in hymn-writing, consisting of four lines of which the first, second, and fourth are of six syllables and the third of eight, usually expressed by the symbol S.M.; also *vulgarly* as *adv. phr.* quickly, soon; **short octave** *Mus.* (see quot. 1801); also in keyboard instruments other than the organ; **short order** *U.S.*, an order for food to be prepared and served up quickly; a dish so served; also *attrib.*; **Short Parliament**, the Parliament which sat from 13 April to 5 May, 1640; **short-period** *a.*, extending over or lasting for a brief period of time; recurring at short intervals; **short-pipe**, ? a kind of musket with a short barrel; **short-punt** *v. intr. Rugby Football*, to punt the ball a short distance; **short-rest** *Billiards* = JIGGER *sb.*[1] 5 g; **short rib**, (*a*) a popular name for any of the lower ribs which do not attach to the sternum; also a piece of butcher's meat, esp. of pork, containing one or more of such ribs; (*b*) *Printing*, = CRAMP-IRON 3; †**short sail** (see quot.); **short sauce**: see SAUCE *sb.* 4 a; **short score** *Mus.* (see quots. 1876, 1954); **short-sea(s)** *a.*, of or pertaining to short sea crossings; **short-service**, military service limited to a prescribed short period; also *attrib.*; **short shorts** *U.S.*, very short drawers or trousers; briefs; †**short shouldered** *a.*, thick-set; **short-silk**, cotton having a short staple; †**short-six**, (*a*) = SIX *sb.* 3 h; (*b*) *U.S.*, a type of cigar (cf. LONG NINE); **short sleeve**, a sleeve which does not reach below the elbow; also *attrib.*; hence **short-sleeved** *a.*, having short sleeves; **short-snorter** *U.S. Mil. slang*, (see quot. 1954); also, a person who collects a short-snorter; also *attrib.*; †**short speaking**, brevity in speech, 'brachylogy'; **short-spirited** *a.*, lacking forbearance or perseverance; **short-splice** (see quots.); **short spoon** *Golf*, a short wooden club (see SPOON *sb.* 4 c); **short-staff**, a short cudgel, also a contest between two persons armed with such cudgels; **short-staffed** *a.*, not adequately provided with staff, understaffed; **short-stage** *a.*, with short distances between stopping places; also *ellipt.* as *sb.*, a coach travelling in this way (*obs.* exc. *Hist.*); **short staple** *a.*, having a short fibre, a commercial term applied to cotton of an inferior grade, also known as 'upland cotton'; also *absol.*; **short-stapled** *a.*, having a short staple (= prec. adj.; said also of wool); **short stepper**, a horse equally lame in all its legs; **Short Street**, an imaginary street where people in financial difficulty are supposed to reside; **short suit** *Cards*, a suit of which a player has few cards; also *attrib.*; hence **short-suited** *a.*, having a short suit; also *fig.*; **short sweetening** *U.S. dial.*, (*a*) cane sugar (as opposed to molasses); (*b*) maple sugar (as opposed to cane sugar); † **Short-thigh** *Hist.* = CURT-HOSE; † **short-thinker**, a person whose thought does not carry him far into a subject; **short-title**, the abbreviated title by which an Act of Parliament is officially designated; an abbreviated form of the full title of a book; also *attrib.*; **short turn** *a.*, (of a wagon) constructed so as to turn easily in a short space; **short-waisted** *a.* (of a person or a garment) short in the waist; also † *fig.*; **short-warp** (see quot.); **short-weight** *v. trans.*, to give short weight to (see sense 15 a) (*U.S.*); **short whist**: see WHIST *sb.*³ a; † **shortwindiness** = SHORT-WINDEDNESS; **short-wise** *adv.*, in the shortest direction; **short-witted** *a.*, lacking intelligence.

**1955** *Sci. News Let.* 27 Aug. 136/2 Use of xenon and platinum eliminates the usual warm-up period required before today's signaling searchlights can be used. The bulb, called a *short-arc mercury-xenon lamp, was developed by Westinghouse Electric Corporation. **1972** *Gloss. Electrotechnical, Power Terms* (*B.S.I.*) IV. iii. 14 *Short-arc lamp*, discharge lamp in which the distance between the electrodes is small (of the order 1 mm to 10 mm). **1906** 'H. MCHUGH' *Skiddoo!* 10 To the Bury Little Bunch of Newspaper knockers who have so assiduously plied hammer and harpoon since this series began, I want to say that 575,000 John Henry books were sold up to March 1st, 1906. There is your answer, O Beloved of the *Short Arm Jab! **1911** J. MASEFIELD *Everlasting Mercy* 11 Billy bats Some stinging short-arms in my slats. **1919** in *Wine, Women & War* (1926) 307 Short arm inspection between vomits. Doctor sicker than patients. **1953** *Sun* (Baltimore) 5 Jan. (B ed.) 12/5 At the Gay street station you are taken to the second floor for a brief physical check, the army 'short-arm', given in this case to see if anything has turned up since your preinduction physical. **1975** C. ALLEN *Plain Tales from Raj* xv. 159 Periodical medical checks, known as 'short arm inspections', ensured that any man who availed himself of the 'tree rats' or 'grass *bidis*' was properly dealt with. **1978** M. PUZO *Fools Die* xl. 450 Before you go to bed with a guy, give him a short arm... You strip down his penis, you know, like you're masturbating him, and if there's a yellow fluid coming out like a drippage, you know he's infected. **1706** *Short-arse [see SPUD *sb.* 4]. **1949** D. M. DAVIN *Roads from Home* 212 That little shortarse tried to report him. **1962** H. HOOD in R. Weaver *Canad. Short Stories* (1968) 2nd Ser. 203 'Now this Pearson,' said one of the revellers, 'he's just a little short-ass. He's just a little fellow without any brains.' **1973** M. AMIS *Rachel Papers* 54 'What's her real name?' I implored. 'Jean.' 'Oh. The short-arse? Yeah, she's all right. Boring dress.' **1951** PARTRIDGE *Dict. Slang* (ed. 4) 1168/2 **Short-arsed*, (of a person) that is short. **1962** *Canadian Jrnl. Linguistics* Autumn 49 Short-ass(ed). **1973** M. AMIS *Rachel Papers* 114 He was a short-arsed little bastard—about five-five. **1965** M. ALLINGHAM *Mind Readers* xxii. 241 A bony young man who..wore '*short back and sides'. **1972** N. BENTLEY *Events of that Week* 72 The gents, in tweed caps or with their silvery short-backs-and-sides exposed to the unrelenting sun. **1974** 'G. BLACK' *Golden Cockatrice* v. 81 Mr Long favoured short back and sides hair-cuts for his personnel. **1982** *Observer* 16 May 4/3 Bejeaned teenagers seemed to outnumber the elderly short-back-and-sides 'sweats'. **1909** R. S. CHILDS in *Outlook* 17 July 638/2 On such a *short ballot basis the entry of our best men into public life becomes possible. **1914** *Cycl. Amer. Government* I. 104/2 A short ballot is any voting paper which requires the selection of only a few important candidates. **1940** *Amer. Pol. Sci. Rev.* Oct. 955 The term 'presidential short ballot' is applied to the ballot form in which the names of candidates for presidential electors are omitted, and only the names of the candidates for president and vice-president appear. **1952** R. RIENOW *Introd. to Government* IV. xix. 362 A suggested reform would limit the offices upon which people vote to those which..have a broad policy-making function. The plan is called the short ballot. **1968** *Economist* 27 July 33/3 As for the electors themselves, they could scarcely be more anonymous. In fact, thirty-five states have abandoned any attempt to tell the voters who they are. Instead these states only use what is called 'the short ballot'. **1911** *Encycl. Brit.* VIII. 753/1 '*Short bath', *i.e.* a bath containing a minimum amount of dye liquor. **1644** MANWAYRING *Seaman's Dict.* 13 A *short-boord, is when you stand-off but little. **1772–84** [see BOARD *sb.* 15]. **1845** J. J. HOOPER *Some Adventures Simon Suggs* 134 Thar never were a *peaceabler* or more *gentlemanlier* game o' *short cards played. **1876** *Scribner's Monthly* May 45 It is worthy of a short-card sharp and a keno flopper. **1935** A. J. POLLOCK *Underworld Speaks* 105/2 *Short card player*, a gambler who plays all card games well except draw poker. **1938** H. ASBURY *Sucker's Progress* 286 Short card games predominated, the favorites being Brag, Poker, Seven-Up and Whist. **1942** BERREY & VAN DEN BARK *Amer. Thes. Slang* §743/1 *Short-card player*, a poker player, esp. a cardsharp. **1940** *Jrnl. Dairy Sci.* XXIII. 1054 The *short chain fatty acids are by products of this synthesis. **1961** *Lancet* 12 Aug. 343/1 There was a high content of short-chain acids and unidentified long-chain..acids in the cholesterol esters. **1972** *Jrnl. Chromatogr.* LXXIV. 335 Measurement of short-chain fatty acids in various biological materials is becoming increasingly important in the physiology and taxonomy of microorganisms and in the dairy, food, and beverage industries. **1837** CARLYLE *Fr. Rev.* I. IV. iv, 'In his rustic farmer-clothes'; which he will wear always; careless of *short-cloaks and costumes. **1816** E. WEETON *Jrnl. of Governess* (1969) II. 140, I have been.. making *short-clothes for Mary... I think of having her weaned in a few weeks. **1843** C. RIDLEY *Let.* Nov. in *Cecilia* (1958) xii. 138, I believe it is much better for children to be put early into short clothes if they are well. **1921** J. BUCHAN *Path of King* xii. 246 He held that the country had grown up and couldn't be kept much longer in short clothes. **1932** *Detective Fiction Weekly* 6 Feb. 126/1 Little tricks known as the '*short con'. **1948** MENCKEN *Amer. Lang.* Suppl. II. 667 Short-con workers operate on a modest scale, and are usually content with whatever money the victim has on him at the time he is rooked. **1965** H. GOLD *Man who was not with It* viii. 67 This was better than..any of the other short-con moments of which Grack had told. **1967** J. POTTER *Foul Play* i. 10 His team had failed to score from the resulting *short corner. **1976** *Southern Even. Echo* (Southampton) 2 Nov. 22/5 Yateley..reduced the arrears from a short corner. **1683** MOXON *Mech. Exerc., Printing* IX. §6. 35 [The Chase] hath two Crosses belonging to it, viz., a *Short-Cross..and a Long-Cross. **1870** HENFREY *Eng. Coins* II. 23 Not many years ago there was much discussion whether these 'short-cross pennies', as they were called, belonged to the last coinage of Henry II, or the first issue of Henry III. **1904** STAINER *Oxf. Silver Pennies* (O.H.S.) 55 Short cross voided, each limb terminating in incurved segment of a circle. **1915** H. C. TRAVELBEE in *Proc. Indiana Acad. Sci. 1914* 231 We note the teliospores of a *short-cycled rust appearing on the æcial host of a long-cycled heterœcious rust. **1926** Short-cycle [see MACROCYCLIC *a.* 1]. **1950** E. A. BESSEY *Morphol. & Taxon. Fungi* xii. 396 Another anomaly in the life cycle of a short-cycle rust. *Ibid.* 397 In most of the short-cycled rusts studied..it has been shown that the mycelium is of monocaryon type until the telium or aecium is formed, when dicaryon cells appear. **1920** GARNER & ALLARD in *Jrnl. Agric. Res.* XVIII. 559 It will be convenient to use the expressions 'long day' as meaning exposure to light for more than 12 hours and '*short day' as referring to an exposure of 12 hours or less. *Ibid.* 576 It [*sc. Aster linearifolius*] is a typical 'short-day' flowering perennial. **1947** *Sci. News* IV. 129 By and large, short day plants flower if they receive 8–9 hours of light a day, and long day plants flower if they receive 14–16 hours of light a day. **1980** *Sci. Amer.* May 105 (*caption*) The cocklebier is a short-day plant and will flower only if it receives at least 8·5 hours of continuous total darkness each day. **1962** *Housewife* (Ceylon) Feb. 25 (Advt.), Order your:—*Short Eats..Cakes & Pastries From Grosvenor Caterers. **1971** *Times Weekender* (Ceylon) 3 Oct. 4/7 She wanted to go to a creamery and after looking at the short-eats on display, ordered a special bun. **1560** DAUS tr. *Sleidane's Comm.* 252 Certen ryche men..had packed up theyr *short endes, & were gonne out of the Citie. **1635** in Foster *Crt. Min. E. Ind. Comp.* (1907) 95 What Gosnell may have brought home in 'short ends' he knows not. **1844** H. STEPHENS *Bk. Farm* II. 489 Lengthening the plough-chains by short-ends, that is, short pieces of chain, which are hooked in a similar manner. **1860** Short end [see BALK *sb.*²]. **1904** ADE *True Bills* 14 Each Partner naturally believed that he was getting the Short End of the Arrangement. **1942** BERREY & VAN DEN BARK *Amer. Thes. Slang* §371/2 Lose,.. get the short end. **1960** *Lebende Sprachen* V. 35/1 Left-overs, remnants, *short-ends*. **1964** *Financial Times* 10 Feb. 9/1 A fair business was done in temporary funds in the Local Authorities loans market last week. Rates tended to move erratically at the short end. **1976** *Scottish Daily Express* 24 Dec. 12/1 At the short end of the market prices were clipped by £1/8. **1977** *Time* 8 Aug. 28/2 *Annie* went back to Broadway on the short end of a 6–2 score. **1979** E. NEWMAN *Sunday Punch* xxiii. 205 You're getting the very short end of the purse. **1595** DUNCAN *App. Etym.* (E.D.S.), *Anhelus*, pursie, or *short-ended. **1721** SOUTHERNE *Loyal Brother* I. i, No, no, Arbanes, no; thou'rt *short-ey'd here. **1845** *Encycl. Metrop.* IV. 408 Another..method is to substitute for the sun its image formed in the focus of a convex lens of *short focus. **1862** *Illustr. Catal. Internat. Exhib., Industr. Dept., Brit. Div.* II. No. 3154 The same camera can be used for either short-focus portrait or long-focus landscape lenses. **1882** *Encycl. Brit.* XIV. 580/2 The sun's image formed by a lens or burning glass of short focus is our best mode of attempting to realize the conception of a luminous point. **1935** *Discovery* Jan. 25/1 The picture [*sc.* the oldest existing photograph] was taken on sensitised paper, probably with a small short-focus camera having a large-aperture lens. **1973** *Focal Dict. Photogr. Technol.* 559 Short focus lenses of normal angle are used in macrophotography at natural size or larger scales of reproduction. **1885** KIPLING in *Pioneer* 27 Jan. 5/2 Clad in *short frocks in the West, Are you growing the charms that shall capture and ravish the heart from my breast? **1900** G. SWIFT *Somerley* 37 The literary short-frocks of Jules Verne and Henty. **1968** *N.Y. Times* 13 Oct. IV. 10 Tully, a fellow notorious around Sausalito for his *short fuse. **1980** G. THOMPSON *Murder Mystery* xix. 149 Postel's first-rate but he's got a short fuse. You lie to him.. and he'll walk off your case. **1979** *Observer* 16 Dec. 9/1 He's quite *short-fused, but he knows how to control his temper. **1858** *Chambers's Jrnl.* 4 Sept. 157/2 The '*short game'—coming into play when the ball lies from a hundred to one hundred and fifty yards from the hole. **1903** H. G. HUTCHINSON et al. *Bk. Golf* IV. ii. 238 Treat the combination of mashies (sometimes irons) and putting together, calling it the short game. **1976** *Webster's Sports Dict.* 386/2 *Short game*..., the aspect of play in which control of relatively short shots (as approach shots or putts) is of primary importance. **1473** *Acc. Ld. High Treas. Scot.* I. 13, j½ elne of blac to lyne a *schort gowne to the King. **1489** *Ibid.* 135 For xj elne of rede dammysk to lyne a lang gowne and the schorte gowne..xxij li. **15..** *Christ's Kirk* 34 in *Bannatyne MS.* (Hunter. Club) 283 Sa schamefully his schort goun set him. **1818** SCOTT *Hrt. Midl.* x, Her brown russet short-gown set off a shape, which time, perhaps, might be expected to render too robust. **1851** [see *long-short*, LONG *a.* 18]. **1861** J. BROWN *Horæ Subs.* Ser. II. 132 Her bright young careless face, her tidy shortgown, and her dark eyes. **1947** J. C. S. BROUGH *Timbers for Woodwork* iv. 30 *Short grain means that the fibres lie in such a direction that the timber may snap or fracture with practically no splintering. **1956** F. W. JANE *Struct. Wood* xi. 254 Where this type of grain occurs it is clearly impossible to produce lumber which is straight grained—the wood must, inevitably, have short grain and suffer from the defects associated with such a structural peculiarity. **1826** COBBETT *Rural Rides* (1885) II. 52 *Short-grass very neatly kept. **1916** *Jrnl. Ecol.* IV. 49 This *Bouteloua* mixed consocies, representing the most radical departure from the typical short-grass, really differs mainly in the possession of a derived element. **1929** WEAVER & CLEMENTS *Plant Ecol.* xvii. 401 The short-grass plains extend over areas in western Nebraska and include much of the western half of Kansas, eastern Colorado, [etc.]. **1961** *Listener* 7 Sept. 346/2 The short-grass plains of the Serengeti. **1867** *Ball Players' Chron.* 4 July 2/1 Being assisted by their brutish followers of the *short-hair grade, they generally manage to make large hauls of plunder. **1875** *Nation* 1 Apr. 218 A very real division of the Democratic party in this city into two sets of politicians known familiarly as 'Short Hairs' and 'Swallow Tails'—the former comprising the rank and file of voters, and the latter 'the property owners and substantial men'. **1886** *Chicago Tribune* in Barrère & Leland *Slang* (1890) s.v., They did not resign, as had been hoped by the short-hairs. **1888** BRYCE *Amer. Commw.* II. App. 642 Dudes and roughs, civil service reformers and office-holding bosses, short-hairs and college presidents. **1894** STEAD *If Christ came to Chicago* 36 Mayor Hopkins was elected by the silkstockings on the one hand and the shorthairs on the other. **1883** J. GREENWOOD *Odd People in Odd Places* 107 Fancy him having that horribly anathematized '*short head' all his own and in hand to do as he likes with—to revile it, and punch it. **1892** *Athenæum* 3 Dec. 781/3 The long-headed race kept up a desultory warfare with the short-heads for many years. **1898** A. E. T. WATSON *Turf* 133 There are legends of judges having made mistakes in short head verdicts. **1922** *Weekly Dispatch* 12 Nov. 7 Danny caught him napping and shortheaded him on the post. **1932** A. J. WORRALL *Eng. Idioms* VII. 55 Teckla took the lead on the straight and won by a short-head from Bomba II. **1935** N. MITCHISON *We have been Warned* I. 55 She successfully short-headed a wool merchant for the bath. **1963** J. PRESCOT *Case for Hearing* iii. 44 The favourite was beaten on the post... I was short-headed out of a fiver. **1976** LD. HOME *Way Wind Blows* xiii. 186 Had these two pulled their weight, I have no doubt at all that our short-head defeat would have been converted into a narrow victory, and a win at that time for the Conservative Party could well have smashed the Socialists. **1977** *Irish Times* 8 June 2/1 Frozen Tiger beat the flying outsider, Poppy Fields, by a diminishing short head. **1802** SHAW *Gen. Zool.* III. 170 *Short-headed Toad. **1854** A. ADAMS, etc. *Man. Nat. Hist.* 68 Short-headed Serpents. **1863** LYELL *Antiq. Man* 26 It exhibits..a type..which is intermediate between the long-headed and short-headed form. **1883** *Academy* 17 Mar. 190/1 That Turanian admixture is the cause of relative *short headedness must for the nonce be relegated to the background. **1591** ? NASHE *Wond. Strange Prognost.* B 1 b, Some shalbe so *short heeld & so quesie stomackt, that [etc.]. **1600** SURFLET *Country Farm* II. xlix. 322 This kind of meate [apples of love] is good for such men as are inclyned to dallie with..short heeld huswiues. **1785** GROSE *Dict. Vulgar T.*, *Short heeled Wench*, a girl apt to fall on her back. **1839** MACGILLIVRAY *Brit. Birds* II. 188 Short-heeled Field Lark. **1599** PORTER *Angry Wom. Abington* (Percy Soc.) 35 Mistresse flurt, yon [*sic*] foule strumpet, Light a loue, *shorte heeles! **1922** *Breeders' Gaz.* 24 Aug. 212/4 There is little doubt he came from Southern Illinois, the home of many well-known '*short-horses'. **1971** *Amer. N. & Q.* Apr. 127/2 They..have had many and strong infusions of thoroughbred blood through the years, but not such that the prized short horse characteristics were lost. **1898** *Encycl. Sport* II. 244/2 (Rackets) **Short-line*, the line on the floor at the distance of about 39 feet from the front wall and parallel to it. **1726** *Act 13 Geo. I*, c. 26 §2 Any Lintseed commonly called or known by the Name of *Short Lintseed. **1871** GARROD *Mat. Med.* (ed. 3) 333 Cardamoms are distinguished according to their lengths by the respective names of shorts, *short-longs, and longs. *a* **1881** O. W. HOLMES *Old Vol. Life* ix, The first two in iambics, or short-longs. *a* **1687** 'AUSON' *On Elegy to Cleveland* 4 in *C.'s Wks.* 279 Elegiacks..too *short-lung'd to parallel thy Fame. **1911** *Encycl. Brit.* XXI. 562/1 Three and two-third octaves, E to C—which by the '*short measure' would be four octaves, C to C. **1718** *Short metre [see COMMON *a.* 19 b]. **1848** LOWELL *Biglow P.* Ser. I. ii, Ef it worn't fer wakin' snakes, I'd home agin short meter. **1801** BUSBY *Dict. Mus.*, **Short-Octaves*. An appellation given to some of the lower octaves of an organ, because from the omission of some of the intermediate notes, the extreme keys lie nearer to each other than those of the full octaves. **1880** GROVE *Dict. Mus.* II. 588/1 In the short octave two of the natural keys were omitted, and the succession stood thus:—CC (on the EE key), FF, G, A, B, C. **1961** A. BAINES *Musical Instruments through Ages* iv. 77 The earlier instruments [of the harpsichord family] very generally had a 'short' or 'broken' octave in the bass. **1980** *Early Music* Apr. 215/1 In my own field of keyboard instruments, the important questions used to be how the jack mechanism worked and how the short octave was tuned. **1906** 'O. HENRY' *Four Million* 103 The clatter of steel, the screaming of '*short orders', the cries of the hungering and all the horrid tumult of feeding men. **1927** *Amer. Speech* II. 414/1 The nomenclature of the short-order restaurant. **1928** S. LEWIS *Man who knew Coolidge* I. 31 We plan to have a restaurant there serving short-orders twenty-four hours a day. **1956** J. POTTS *Death of Stray Cat* vii. 75 Working..as a short-order cook in his diner. **1978** J. UPDIKE *Coup* (1979) iv. 137, I..worked as waiter and short-order cook in various eating establishments. **1653** CROMWELL *Sp.* 4 July in *Carlyle* (1845) II. 188 The state of affairs as they were before the *Short, that is the last, Parliament. **1884** GARDINER *Hist. Eng.* IX. xci. 117 The Short Parliament..had sat for three weeks. **1887** *Encycl. Brit.* XXII. 509/1 *Short-period fluctuations between a maximum and minimum, within the limits of each single stroke [of a piston]. **1895** *Knowledge* 1 May 111/2 There is no longer any reason to doubt that all 'short-period variables' are really close binaries. **1900** *Ibid.* 1 Dec. 285/2 Brorsen's Comet... This interesting short-period comet. **1923** P. B. BALLARD *New Examiner* 107 For..an overwhelming majority, short-period testing, when properly carried out, is as sound and as valid as long-period testing. **1962** L. S. SASIENI *Optical Dispensing* viii. 195 A second pair of lenses for special purposes, or for short-period use. **1967** *Oceanogr. & Marine Biol.* V. 128 Such a rise is a normal aspect of the short-period low-amplitude, climatic oscillations of the Holocene epoch. **1844** *Queen's Regul. Army* 99 For *short-pipe 3*d.* **1937** C. DAY LEWIS *Starting Point* I. iii. 48 The next time he received the ball, he *short-punted ahead. **1954** J. B. G. THOMAS *On Tour* 184 Morgan was half through before he short-punted. **1910** *Encycl. Brit.* III. 935/2 The '*short rest' (or 'jigger'). **1592** TIMME *Ten Eng. Lepers* K 3 b, Joab..stabbed him under the *short ribbes, and killed him. **1769** E. Bancroft *Guiana* 242 A little below the short ribs. **1912** *Standard* 20 Sept. 8/7 Bacon, Short Rib Sides. **1710** J. Harris *Lex. Techn.* II, **Short Sails*, in a Man of War, are the same with the Fighting-sails, and are the Fore-sail, Main-sail, and Fore-topsail. **1876** Stainer & Barrett *Dict. Mus. Terms* 388/2 A *short or compressed score is when all the parts are arranged or transcribed so that they shall appear in two staves... In transcribing four-part music into short score, the two upper parts are arranged in the treble stave. **1946** A. Hutchings in A. L. Bacharach *Brit. Music* xvi. 207, I do not think that, even now, Rubbra finds it easy to bring off the orchestration conceived in his mind's ear while writing his 'short score'. **1954** *Grove's Dict. Music* (ed. 5) VII. 765/1 *Short score*, a term meaning either (*a*) a condensation of a vocal or instrumental full score for pianoforte or organ for use at rehearsal or (*b*) a composer's first draft of a full score in which a large orchestral lay-out is reduced to a few staves. **1980** *Early Music* July 414/3 The collection is most unusual in that it..has..a fully notated 'short-score' keyboard accompaniment. **1952** J. W. Day *New Yeomen of England* iii. 40 The bargemen were a race apart, born and brought up to the *short-seas trade. **1966** *Guardian* 28 Feb. 16/7 The coastal and short-sea container services. **1976** *Daily Tel.* 9 Sept. 1/2 All cross-Channel and short-sea vessels crewed by union members will be affected immediately the strike starts. **1882** E. W. Hamilton *Diary* 19 Nov. (1972) I. 361 What struck him [*sc.* Mr. Gladstone] most was the magnificent appearance of the line regiments—an unanswerable proof against the charges of *short service. **1897** *Daily News* 9 Feb. 6/3 A sufficient short-service home army, and a really effective reserve force. **1905** Arnold-Forster in *Parl. Deb.* 29 Mar. 1582 If we were allowed to take the Militia and make them the short-service Army. **1946** *Sun* (Baltimore) 24 Apr. 7/2 'What are briefs,' asked Senator Millikin... Cheney dug into his satchel, came up with a pair, and waved them at Millikin. 'Oh,' said the senator. '*Short shorts.' **1964** [see Jamaica b]. **1976** *Billings* (Montana) *Gaz.* 2 July 2-A (Advt.), Coordinate your tops with shorts from the great selection of short shorts cuffed or uncuffed and jamaica length shorts. *c* **1386** Chaucer *Prol.* 549 He was *short sholdred, brood, a thikke knarre. **1870** Yeats *Nat. Hist. Comm.* II. (1872) 200 Cottons may be divided into the long silk and *short silk. *Ibid.*, The United States generally furnish the short silks in the greatest quantity. **1831** H. J. Finn *Amer. Comic Ann.* 219, I wus drest all in white, and lookt like a *short-six goin to be dipt. **1838** W. E. Burton *Burton's Comic Songster* 188 Give me some short six's. **1843** [see six *sb.* 3]. **1865** C. F. Browne *A. Ward: his Trav.* 57 Tom Slink, who used to smoke short-sixes and get acquainted with the little circus boys. **1885** *Pioneer* 19 Aug. 5/1, I buy me not twelve-button gloves, 'short sixes' eke, or rings. **1890** J. Jefferson *Autobiogr.* 146 The very cornerstone of Juliet's balcony contained twenty pounds of the best 'short sixes'. **1639** in *Rec. Governor & Co. Massachusetts Bay* (1853) I. 274 No garment shalbee made w[th] *short sleeves, whereby the nakedness of the arme may be discovered. **1847** Dickens *Dombey* (1848) xxxv. 354 Mrs Skewton..in a very youthful costume, with short sleeves. **1931** *Mod. Woman* Feb. 46 Length of short sleeve seam, 4¼ ins. **1969** *Sears Catal.* Spring/Summer 11/1 Short sleeve tops in windowpane printed plaid. **1976** *Lady's Mag.* Dec. 564/2 Short sleeves in small plaits. **1839** C. Brontë *Caroline Vernon* in W. Gérin *C. Brontë* (1967) viii. 133 [A] *short-sleeved frock, worked trousers and streaming sash that would better have suited the age of 9 or 10 than that of 15. **1973** D. E. Westlake *Cops & Robbers* 7 With the heat the way it was, I was glad the Police Department let its people wear a short-sleeved shirt in the summer. **1944** *Sun* (Baltimore) 1 May 13/5 A '*short-snorter' made up of 18 pieces of currency. *Ibid.*, The short-snorter fellowship consists of persons who have flown over salt-water. Its 'membership card' is a piece of currency signed by other short-snorters. **1954** Berrey & Van den Bark *Amer. Ther. Slang* (ed. 2) §896/1 *Short snorter*, an autograph list on a string of attached bills, usually of the currency in the countries visited. **1976** R. M. Stern *Will* ii. 15 On the study wall in a plain wood frame were the connected, signature-scrawled dollar bills..called short-snorters, or some such silly name. 'They were the in thing,' his father had told him. .. 'You carried them with you..and got as many signatures as you could... If there ever was a reason, I've forgotten it.' **14..** *Voc.* in Wr.-Wülcker 568/35 *Braciologia*, a *shortspekynge. **1647** Trapp *Comm. Epist.*, *Marrow Gd. Authors* 672 If God should be as *short spirited, what would soon become of all? **1673** Janeway *Heav. Earth* (1847) 149 God is not like short-spirited man. **1769** Falconer *Dict. Marine* (1789) Nn1, The *short-splice is made by untwisting the ends of two ropes, or the two ends of one rope, and, having placed each of the strands of one..in the interval between two strands of the other, to draw them close together; and then interweave the strands of one into the alternate strands of the other. **1858** *Chambers's Jrnl.* 4 Sept. 157/1 The names of the wooden-head clubs..*short-spoon. **1901** *Encycl. Sport* II. 459/2 The long spoon, mid spoon, short spoon and baffing spoon..are now rarely seen, having been supplanted by the brassy, and the modern irons and mashies. **1970** F. C. Avis *Golf Dict.* 196 Long spoon, the No. 3 wood; short spoon, the No. 4 wood. **1775** Sheridan *Rivals* iv. i, A bout at boxing, quarter-staff, or *short-staff. **1953** K. Tennant *Joyful Condemned* xxxiv. 334, I should get my patients to bed. They're very *short-staffed. **1968** 'M. Carroll' *Dead Trouble* ii. 27 They've got a room but they're short-staffed. I said we'd take our cases up. **1977** J. Sherwood *Honesty will get you Nowhere* i. 16 Matron..was short-staffed, at her wits' end to keep the place going. **1837** Dickens *Pickwick Papers* xxxii. 339 Numerous cads and drivers of *short stages. **1903** W. Gilbey *Early Carriages & Roads* 56 It seems..certain that the year 1662 saw a great increase in the number of 'short stages'—that is to say, coaches running between London and towns twenty, thirty, forty miles distant. **1963** *Times* 24 May (London Underground Suppl.) p. vi/4 Local transport in and around the Metropolis was by short-stage carriages, which ran from point to point (usually an inn). **1969** J. E. Tuffs *Essex Coaching Days* vii. 63 Spreading out from London in all directions was the net-work of short-stage coach routes. **1802** J. Simons *Let.* 15 Dec. in *Steele Papers* (1924) I. 341 *Short Stable [*sic*], or Green seed Cotton if the best Quality, 16 cents. **1858** Homans *Cycl. Comm.* s.v. *Cotton* 437/2 The 'Georgian', or 'short-staple', is [believed to be] the sea-island [variety of cotton] carried into the interior. *Ibid.* 438/1 The short staple cotton is more or less cultivated all the way from the southern borders of Virginia, to the southwestern streams of the Mississippi. **1834** McCulloch *Dict. Comm.* s.v. *Cotton* (ed. 2) 436 [Cottons] are usually classed under the denominations of long and *short stapled. **1835** Ure *Philos. Manuf.* 126 Short-stapled, or cloth-wool, is valued by the fineness..and whiteness of its fibres. **1836** Head *Home Tour* 101, I perceived him to be what is technically called 'a *short stepper'. **1920** in *Further Lett. from Man of No Importance* (1932) 79 Soldiering is an honourable but not a profitable profession, and landed property is apt to land the owner in '*Short Street'. **1938** *Daily Tel.* 25 July 9/1 She was finally unable to help Wilde, then penniless, for his defence: and having lived in 'Short Street' myself, I quite understood. **1876** A. Campbell-Walker *Correct Card* p. xiii, **Short suit*, one of which you hold originally not more than three cards. **1893** 'L. Hoffman' tr. *Hertefeld's Game of Skat* 8 As..a suit consists of seven cards only, three or more constitute a long suit; and two or less a short suit. **1931** E. Culbertson *Contract Bridge at Glance* 43 With an Ace, a King, or honours not in sequence in one or two suits, and a *worthless* doubleton or a singleton in the third suit, lead the short suit. **1964** Frey & Truscott *Official Encycl. Bridge* 499/1 The short-suit lead is also indicated when there is a bidding inference that this is partner's suit. **1935** Auden & Isherwood *Dog beneath Skin* II. ii. 82 Hullo, you *short-suited? Here, let's see your hand. **1940** C. Woolrich in *Ellery Queen's Magicians of Mystery* (1976) 281 Did I say she was beautiful? Double it in spades, and you're still short-suited. **1850** *Quincy* (Illinois) *Whig* 19 Nov. 2/2 He put..all the money she had in *short sweetening, and left her without a cent. **1883** [see *long sweetening* s.v. long *a.*[1] 18]. **1914** B. T. Washington *Selected Speeches* 218 This good lady asked whether we wanted long or short sweetening in our coffee. **1948** E. N. Dick *Dixie Frontier* 291 'Short sweetening', or maple sugar, was also obtained in its raw state from the trees. **1596** Drayton (*title*) The Tragicall Legend of Robert Duke of Normandye surnamed *Short Thighe. **1711** Shaftesb. *Charac.* III. 302 They..being necessitated thus to become *Short-thinkers, are contented to go no further than they are led by those to whom..they apply themselves for Cure and Comfort. **1869** *Act 32 & 33 Vict.* c. 42 §1 *marg.*, *Short-title. This Act may be cited..as The Irish Church Act, 1869. **1892** *Act 55 Vict.* c. 10 §2 The Short Titles Act, 1892. **1896** in A. H. Chester *Dict. Names Minerals* 1 (Advt.), Short-Title Catalogue of..Publications... Arranged under subjects. **1945–51** D. Wing (*title*) Short-title catalogue of books printed in England, Scotland, Ireland, Wales, and British America.., 1641–1700. **1978** *Amer. N. & Q.* XVI. 151/1 The short-title lists..ought to be based on meticulous bibliographical descriptions. **1686** *Lond. Gaz.* No. 2188/4 Lost.., a *short turn Waggon. **1590** Sir J. Smyth *Disc. Weapons* 46 Collars, light and *short wasted cuirasses and backes. **1592** Nashe *Strange Newes* M 1 b, This thy short-wasted Pamphlet. **1756** C. Smart tr. *Horace*, *Sat.* I. ii. (1826) II. 21 But..she is low-hipped, short-waisted [L. *brevi latere*], with a long nose, and a splay-foot. **1851** H. Melville *Whale* lx, The *short-warp—the rope which is immediately connected with the harpoon. **1932** T. S. Stribling *Store* vii. 73 It is much mo' dangerous to accuse a white man of *shawt-weightin' you when he ain't 'an when he is. **1952** *Sun* (Baltimore) 8 Apr. (B ed.) 30/5 Many Harford county coal dealers apparently are short-weighting their customers. **1977** *Time* 7 Nov. 72/3 A leading Catholic contractor short-weights the church. **1545** Raynald *Byrth Mankynde* 116 The cough: and distillation of the heade: *short wyndynesse [etc.]. **1562** Turner *Baths* 8 b, They are good..for shortwindines. **1865** *Daily Tel.* 22 Aug. 6/5 The bullocks' half of the square..is divided *shortwise, by the wooden barriers to which I have alluded. **1477** Norton *Ordin. Alch.* vi. in Ashm. 93 All *short-witted Men and mutable. *a* **1656** Hales *Golden Rem.* (1688) 255 Piety doth not require at our hands, that we should be either short-witted or beggerly. **1809–10** Coleridge *Friend* (1865) 9 The more pitiable asthma of a short-witted intellect.

**b.** In names of animals, as **short bill**, a Brazilian bird, *Phibalura flavirostris*; **short diodon**, a species of sunfish, *Cephalus brevis*; **short-eared owl**, a light-coloured owl flecked with brown or black, *Asio flammeus flammeus*, distinguished by short ear-tufts and found in Europe, northern Africa, and North America; **short-hair**, one of a breed of short-haired cats; also *attrib.*; **short-head**, a name given by sailors to the young of the whale; **short-sheep**, a name given to a short-woolled sheep of the black-faced Scotch variety; **short-tail**, (*a*) a bird of the genus *Pitta*; (*b*) a name given to a small family of snakes, *Tortricidæ*, found in India and America; **short-wing**, a diving bird of the group *Brachypteri*.

**1820–1** Swainson *Zool. Illustr.* I. Pl. 31 *Phibalura cristata*. Crested *Shortbill. **1776** Pennant *Brit. Zool.* III. 115 *Short Diodon... Sun-fish, from Loo. **1766** T. Pennant *Brit. Zool.* I. 71 The *Short eared Owl..is found in the mountanous [*sic*] wooded parts of our island. **1833** Jardine *Humming-B.* 50 The short-eared owl. **1974** *Times* 20 Mar. 18/4 Twenty short-eared owls have settled on a Humber nature reserve. **1903** *Ladies' Field* 7 Nov. 347/1 Woodkirk Prince was pronounced the best *short-hair in the [cat] show. **1903** F. Simpson *Bk. Cat* vii. 99 The ranks of short-hair breeders. **1725** Dudley *Whales* in *Phil. Trans.* XXXIII. 257 At a Year old, when they are called *Short heads, they are very fat. **1805** Forsyth *Beauties Scotl.* II. 155 The black-faced sheep are short-legged, [etc.]. Hence they are often called *short sheep, in contradiction to the Cheviot, which are much longer bodied. **1816** Scott *Bl. Dwarf* i, 'Aweel, aweel, maister,' said the attendant, 'short sheep had short rents, I'm thinking.' **1792** tr. *Buffon's Nat. Hist. Birds* III. 373 The *Short Tail. **1879** E. P. Wright *Anim. Life* 395 The Short-tails are a small family [*Tortricidæ*], the species of which are about six in number. **1839** Jerdon in *Madras Jrnl. Lit. & Sci.* X. 250 Black-headed *short wing. **1865** T. R. Jones *Anim. Creation* 459 The Short-wings (*Brachypteres*) exhibit considerable relationship with the Water-hens.

**c.** In names of plants or vegetable products, as † **short-neck**, a variety of pear having a rounded form; † **short-shank**, † **-start**, a variety of apple having a short stalk (so ***short-started*** adj.); **short-top**, a kind of radish; also *attrib.*; (so ***short-topped*** adj.).

**1707** Mortimer *Husb.* (1721) II. 295 The Rosewater Pear, the *Shortneck, so called from the shortness of its Form and Tail. **1611** Cotgr. s.v. *Cour-pendu*, *Pomme de cour-pendu*, the *short-start, or *short-shanke; (an excellent apple). **1707** Mortimer *Husb.* (1721) II. 294 The Short-start, the Chesnut Apple, and the Great Belly are in many Places Apples of esteem. **1600** Surflet *Country Farm* I. xii. 56 After the head beginneth to be ill, to eate one or two *short started apples, or some bitter almonds. **1786** Abercrombie *Gard. Assist.* Dec. 335 Radishes.—sow a few early *short-tops. *Ibid.* Jan. 6 Radishes—sow early short-top kinds on warm borders, in open weather. **1842** Loudon *Suburban Hort.* 653 The *short-topped scarlet [radish] is the best for a cottage garden.

**d.** In Cricket: **short ball**, a ball which pitches short of a length (see length *sb.* 10); **short hit**, a ball which when hit does not travel far from the wicket; **short leg** (see leg *sb.* 6 c); **short notch** = *short run* (*b*); **short pitch**, the pitch of a short ball (q.v.); **short slip** (see slip *sb.*[3] 14); **short square (leg)**, a square leg standing close in to the wicket; **short stop** = *short slip* (see also in Baseball, below). In Baseball: **short field**, that part of the field in which the short stop plays; also, = *short fielder*; **short fielder**, **short stop** (see quots.); also *fig.*; see also in Cricket, above.

**1911** *Encycl. Sport.* (Cricket) I. 495/2 **Short ball*, a ball which pitches too far from the batsman to be a good length. **1856** *Spirit of Times* 6 Dec. 229/1 *Adams*, as *short field has for many years, been deservedly distinguished. **1948** *N.Y. Times* 25 Apr. 51/6 Jack Conway was shifted to the short field. **1961** J. S. Salak *Dict. Amer. Sports* 397 *Shortfield*,.. area around shortstop position, between second and third bases. **1857** *Spirit of Times* 18 July 309/3 He is a splendid *short fielder. **1874** H. Chadwick *Base Ball Man.* 27 The Short Fielders. In the present position of the game there is but one 'short-stop', and he stands to the left of the in-field between the second and third base positions. Ultimately however, a 'right-short' will be introduced. **1833** Nyren *Young Cricketer's Tutor* (1902) 76–7 John Small..was the best short-runner of his day, and indeed I believe him to have been the first who turned the *short hits to account. **1843** 'Wykhamist' *Pract. Hints Cricket*, (*caption*) *Short leg or Middle On. **1851** J. Pycroft *Cricket Field* x. 191 Short-leg is often a very hardly used personage, expected to save runs that seem easy, but are actual impossibilities. **1877**, **1894** [see leg *sb.* 6 c]. **1963** *Times* 14 Jan. 8/3 Jarman over-balanced in pushing the first ball he received to forward short leg. **1774** *Laws of Cricket* in Lillywhite *Scores & Biogr.* (1862) I. 17 If the strikers run a *short notch, the Umpire must call No Notch. **1877** Box *Eng. Game Cricket* 457 **Short Pitch*, in this the ball has a greater parabola than the half volley. **1860** *Baily's Mag.* Aug. 364 Willsher, too, made a rare catch at *short square leg. **1963** *Times* 1 May 4/5 (*caption*) M. J. K. Smith (M.C.C.), at short square leg, ducks as P. J. Sharpe (Yorkshire) hooks a ball from J. A. Flavell during the match at Lord's yesterday. **1977** *Sunday Times* 30 Jan. 30/4 He made it strike like a snake and Fletcher was caught at short square. *c* **1837** W. Martin *Bk. Sports* vi. 104 *Order of the Players*... 4 Long stop. 5 *Short Stop. **1857** *Spirit of Times* 25 July 324/3 Second Nine Fahys, pitcher;..Smith, short stop. **1860** in H. T. Peters *Currier & Ives* (1942) Pl. 162, I thought our fusion would be a 'short stop' to his career. **1874** Short-stop [see *short-fielder*]. **1875** *Encycl. Brit.* III. 406/2 Latterly [at Base-ball], an additional man has been introduced as right short-stop. *Ibid.* 407/2 The catcher, pitcher, first and third basemen, and short-stop comprise the in-field; the remainder the out-field. **1877** *London Soc.* XXXI. 533/1 Dorrington was almost as good at cover as Hillyer was at short-stop. **1912** *Australasian* 6 Jan. 21/2 Hobbs..was caught at short-stop by Carter. **1950** *Nature Mag.* Mar. 131/2 A sudden lunge with the net will often cut off its escape. If the net misses, a lucky shortstop may nab the lizard in passing. **1977** *Time* 8 Aug. 28/3 Andrea played shortstop and first base. **1978** *Verbatim* Feb. 2/2 If a batter hits safely between the shortstop and second, or second and first, the announcer will call that 'a seeing-eye base hit'.

**e.** *Comm.*, as **short bill**, a bill having less than ten days to run; **short-exchange**, exchange having a short time (commonly thirty days or less) to run; also the rate for collecting short bills; **short-loan**, a loan repayable at an early date; **short-money**, money to borrow or to lend upon short-time loans; **short-paper**, short bills; **short-payment**, payment at any early date after the completion of a transaction; **short price**, a low price (in *Betting*, low odds). Designating or pertaining to transactions in which a seller sells stock or goods that he does not at the time possess (cf. senses A. 18 g and C. 11), as ***short operation***, ***position***, ***sale***, ***selling***, ***side***; **short covering**, the buying in of stock or goods to cover a short sale; **short interest** (see quot. 1900); **short market** (see quot.).

**1808** Scott *Let.* in *Lockhart* (1837) II. v. 175, I will get him a *short bill for the copy-money the moment Constable returns. **1861** Goschen *For. Exch.* 86 The discount, which has to be deducted from the long bill before it can become equally available with the short bill. **1912** *Times* 19 Dec. 16/4 The Bank of England, which did a fairly large business in short bills at the official minimum. **1930** *Daily Express* 22 May 2/6 In late dealings the downward trend was more pronounced, but finally sporadic *short covering resulted in some improvement from the day's levels. **1937** *Sun* (Baltimore) 17 Feb. 15/5 Steels, after putting on a draggy performance during the morning, whittled down part of the early losses with the aid of what brokers described as short covering. **1973** *Times* 13 July 21/8 Prices by now were really moving. Record after record was smashed. Massive short covering helped to keep prices on the boil. **1866** Crump *Banking* vii. 154 Between Paris and London the *short exchange is the most prominent. **1866** *Comm. & Fin. Chron.* III. 75/2 During the week a moderate *short interest has been drawn out by the dullness of the market. **1900** S. A. Nelson *ABC of Wall St.* 159 *Short interest*, that interest in the market which is represented by the aggregate sales of men who have sold at a price with the expectation of buying in at a cheaper price. **1949** *Time* 30 May 73/1 By mid-May, the short interest had risen 130,058 in a month to 1,628,551 shares. **1865** *Standard* 2 Sept. 2/1 The terms for *short loans in the early part of the day were 2½ to 3. **1900** S. A. Nelson *ABC of Wall St.* 159 **Short market*, an oversold market, with the aggregate contracts for the delivery of stocks exceeding the supply at a certain range of prices. **1865** *Standard* 2 Sept. 2/1 A variety of parcels of *short money afloat. **1899** *Truth* 23 Feb. 477/2 Short money is quoted at from 1½ to 2 per cent. **1870** J. K. Medbery *Men & Mysteries Wall St.* 202 A sale profit either in a 'long' or '*short' operation. **1912** *Times* 19 Dec. 19/5 Sterling exchange has ruled strong for *short paper at 20 to 35 points advance in posted rates. **1884** *Times* (weekly ed.) 10 Oct. 13/2 Corn for long payments; bread for *short payments. **1931** *Daily Express* 22 Sept. 2/1 Short selling in the present circumstances would demoralise the market. Consequently all *short positions carried must be reported in detail each day. **1638** Cotton *Tower Rec.* 15 Security of payment at a long day and a *short price. **1856** H. H. Dixon *Post & Paddock* viii. 126 He was a fine large horse..and was purchased as a yearling, for a short price. **1885** *Field* 7 Feb. 157/2 Although quoted at so short a price, Mineral Water [a greyhound] has not been backed by his owner. **1870** J. K. Medbery *Men & Mysteries Wall St.* 175 With..realizations upon *short sales, Jerome felt rich enough to dissolve partnership. **1911** *Amer. Year Bk. 1910* 385/2 All of these bills were directed against the use of 'options', 'short sales', and transactions in 'futures'. **1930** *Daily Express* 23 May 2/6 *Short-selling in Case Threshing Machine, which declined more than 18 points, was an unsettling factor. **1966** 'H. MacDiarmid' *Company I've Kept* iii. 71 We find..fantastic spectacles which, like short-selling, are, as the late Otto Kahn stigmatised that operation, 'inherently repellent to a right-thinking man'. **1902** A. D. McFaul *Ike Glidden* xviii. 139 He bought and sold on the *short side for cash and sold on the long side for credit.

**B.** Quasi-*sb.* and *sb.*

**I.** The neuter adj. used *absol.* **1.** With prepositions, forming adverbial phrases.

**a.** ***in short*** (also *Sc.* †***at short***): briefly, concisely. From the 18th c. onwards used only as parenthetical phrase, introducing or accompanying a summary statement of what has been previously said. †***in short and plain***: briefly and plainly.

*c* **1386** Chaucer *Clerk's T.* 521 He tolde him point for point, in short and playn. **1513** Douglas *Æneis* xi. x. 79 Thus said he, and with sic wordis at schort Mesapus to the fycht he did exhort. **1556** Lauder *Tractate* 266 Att schorte, ȝe daylie do aduert To serue ȝour God with faithfull hert. **1575** Badger in *Gascoigne's Kenelworth Castle* Wks. 1910 II. 93 Though haste say on, let sute obtaine some stay,..While that in short my state I doe display. **1660** Barrow *Euclid* Pref. (1714) 1, I shall here explain it to you in short. **1665** Boyle *Occas. Refl.* v. i, Upon philosophical Disquisitions or Experiments, or (in short) upon some such other thing as seems extrinsecal to the Doctrine that is according to Godliness. **1666** C'tess of Warwick *Diary* 19 Aug., I overslept myself in the morning, and was fain only in short to recommend myself to God for that day. **1690** W. Walker *Idiomat. Anglo-Lat.* 413, I shall not think much to tell you in short what I think. **1748** Chesterf. *Let. to Son* 17 May, And, in short, [they] put themselves in every attitude but the right. **1833** Ht. Martineau *Fr. Wines & Pol.* iv. 61 These were, in short, the Orleans mob. **1846** Dickens *Cricket on Hearth* ii, The Blind Girl..never knew that Tackleton was Tackleton, in short. **1847** C. Brontë *Jane Eyre* xi, Nothing in short was wanting to complete the beau ideal of domestic comfort. **1907** J. A. Hodges *Elem. Photogr.* (ed. 6) 13 In short, my object is to instruct those who desire to become photographers.

†**b.** ***in short*** (? also *Sc.* ***at short***): in a short time, quickly. *Obs.* (The Sc. example may belong to sense a.)

**1513** Douglas *Æneis* ii. xli. 82 Quhen na hoipe of reskew at schort is, My purpose I left, obeyand destanye. *Ibid.* iii. ix. 36 Gif that I perishe it is ȝit sum confort That I of mennis handis deis at schort. *c* **1550** Rolland *Crt. Venus* iii. 584 His kin and freindis, and Father but mercie Was put at schort till exterminioun. **1560** —— *Seven Sages* 12 And sa at schort the barne delyuerit he. **1599** Sir J. Harington *Nugæ Ant.* (1804) I. 276 For want of th' artillerie, whiche coulde not arrive in shorte, the same beinge onlie drawen by the force of menne.

**c.** ***for short***: as an abbreviation.

*a* **1845** Barham *Ingol. Leg., Blasphemer's Warning*, Father Dick—so they called him for short. **1870** J. White *Sk. America* 284 He's Attorney-general for Colorado, and we call him 'general' for short. **1896** Mrs. Hungerford *Lonely Girl* i, Carrig Castle—The Castle, as it is called 'for short' by the peasantry.

**2.** ***the short***: the total, the result, upshot; a brief summing up of something which has been previously explained in full. Now only *dial.* (Cf. *the long and the short*, long *sb.* 3). †***short is***: 'to speak briefly', 'the short of the matter is'.

*a* **1586** *Answ. to Cartwright* 2 This is the short of M. Harrisons longer discourse. **1607** S. Collins *Serm.* (1608) 181 The short of it is, my deere brethren, though the Papists bee troublesome, yet the Puritans must not looke to goe vncontrolled. **1649** G. Daniel *Trinarch., Hen. IV*, cccxliii, Short is: the Sheriffe of Yorkeshire by his Power Attach't the Earle if it may be exprest Soe, to his Office. **1674** *Govt. Tongue* viii. 147 The short is, wherever this game is plaied there is alwaies a fool in the case. **1694** Norris *Refl. Locke's Hum. Underst.*, etc. 51 The short of Mr. Lock's reasoning in that part is this [which follows]. *a* **1761** Law *Comf. Weary Pilgrim* (1809) 75 The short is this: the kingdom of self is the fall of man. **1777** Wesley *Wks.* (1872) XI. 398 The short of the matter is this. **1804** M. Cutler in *Life*, etc. (1888) II. 162 This is the short of the story. **1874** L. Carr *Jud. Gwynne* I. v. 165 The short on it's this.

**3.** Phr. ***to draw short and long***: to draw lots by means of straws, etc. of different lengths.

**1870** Morris *Earthly Par.* III. 287 We shared the spoil by drawing short and long.

**II.** *sb.* **4.** Something that is short.

†**a.** *Mus.* A short note. ***short and long*** (see quot. 1597). *Obs.*

**1591** Cockaine *Treat. Hunting* (Roxb.) D 3 b, To blow to seeke. Two windes: The first a long and a short, the second a long. *Ibid.* D 4 b, One short conteineth three quauers. **1597** Morley *Introd. Mus.* 78 The first is called short and long, when we make one note alone and then two of the same kinde bound togither, and then another alone.

†**b.** *Dancing.* A short step. *Obs.*

*a* **1652** Brome *City Wit* iv. i, Your traverses, Slidings,.. Closings, Openings, Shorts, Turns, Pacings, Gracings.

**c.** *Prosody.* A short syllable. ***longs and shorts***: see long *sb.* 5.

*a* **1795** S. Bishop *Poet. Wks.* (1796) II. 194 With longs and with shorts all our heads are so full. **1837** C. P. Brown *Sanscrit Prosody* 3 A foot of four shorts.

**d.** ? The narrow part (of a boat).

**1800** *Hull Advertiser* 15 Nov. 4/3, I..tied them round the short of the boat.

**e.** *Electr.* = short circuit. (Cf. short *v.*[2])

**1906** *Daily News* 27 Jan. 7/5 In technical language, there was a 'short'. **1909** *Installation News* III. 80/1 Strange to say, it is a very rare thing for a dead short to occur on a good earthed pipe system.

**f.** = ***something short, short drink*** (see A. 14 a).

**1823** *Grose's Dict. Vulgar T.* (ed. Egan), *Short*, a dram unlengthened by water. 'I'll take a drop of short.' **1851** Mayhew *Lond. Labour* I. 52 Saveloys, with a pint of beer, or a glass of 'short' (neat gin) is with them another common week-day dinner. **1898** Henley *Lond. Types, Bus-driver*, He arrogates a special taste in short. **1953** *Word for Word* (Whitbread & Co.) 32/1 *Short*, a colloquial name for a gin or whisky drink, usually taken before a meal. **1973** J. Wainwright *Touch of Malice* 89, I wouldn't have thought ..you were a beer man. I'd have said shorts. **1978** R. Barnard *Unruly Son* xvi. 176 There was a man and his wife. .. Didn't talk much, just sat and drank shorts. **1980** G. Mitchell *Whispering Knights* i. 7 They only drank shorts. .. Gin, and doubles at that.

**g.** A contraction of a name or phrase.

**1873** L. Troubridge *Life amongst Troubridges* (1966) vi. 53 We..have *names* for some of our relations... Uncle Tum and Aunt Kitty are Tumbo and Kitginx. *Of course* these names we never tell *anybody*..but only use them as *shorts*. **1879** Grove *Dict. Mus.* I. 332/2 *Change*..the word used as the short for change of key or *Modulation*. **1885** *Athenæum* 31 Oct. 567/3 'Nuttie' may be a local contraction for 'Ursula', though we should hardly have supposed that the name was common enough..to have its own 'short'. **1914** H. Stretton *Alone in London* iii. 28 Dolly was the short for Dorothy, and in early times he had often called his wife by that name. **1920** *Black's Domestic Dict.* 28/2 Bouquet is the short for 'Bouquet garni'.

**h.** In the Morse code, a dot (opp. 'long'); a short buzz, etc., sounded as a signal.

**1875**, etc. [see long *a.*[1] B. 4 b]. **1978** P. Niesewand *Underground Connection* 91 Ziad pressed the bell for flat 23, two shorts, a long and a short, and waited for the entrance buzzer to sound. **1978** J. H. Bentley in *Islands* (N.Z.) Aug. 79 'I was waiting for the proper knock,' I said. Three shorts, one long.

**i.** A short story or article.

**1912** E. A. Parry *What Judge Saw* xiv. 245 For many years I wrote dramatic criticism and reviewed books, and wrote 'shorts' and occasionally full-dress leaders for the *Manchester Guardian*. **1937** D. L. Sayers *Busman's Honeymoon* xiv. 297 That was a special effort. Three five-thousand-word shorts at forty guineas each for the *Thrill Magazine*. **1965** *Listener* 10 June 873/1 How many 'shorts' appear in comparable circumstances in this country today? Two dozen a year? The others have to make their bows between hard covers.

**j.** *U.S. slang.* A street-car; a car.

**1914** Jackson & Hellyer *Vocab. Criminal Slang* 76 *Short*, ..a street car. Derived from the limited extent of a street car ride compared with the distances negotiable by railroad transportation. **1932** *Literary Digest* 9 Apr. 36 *Short*, an automobile, used especially in the phrase 'hot short', for a stolen car. **1961** 'D. Shannon' *Ace of Spaces* vi. 70 This perfectly good almost brand new Caddy I got for him, a *present*, an' he says he can't handle it..comes back with this piece of old junk, my God, pickin' up a thing like—stickin' me with a hot short to get rid of! **1975** W. McCarthy *Fourth Man* i. 26 Everybody brings him hot cars..shorts, we get up north, he fixes 'em up and then sells 'em.

**k.** *Mil.* A shot that falls short of its target.

**1922** [see ladder *sb.* 3 c]. **1969** I. Kemp *Brit. G.I. in Vietnam* vii. 150 We were watching the shells bursting among them when a 'short' exploded right in front of us.

**l.** A short film for cinema or television.

**1929** *N.Y. Times* 20 Oct. ix. 8 *Shorts*, short, audible pictures. **1930** *Times* 26 Mar. 14/2 The production of several multilingual talking pictures and a series of talking comedy 'shorts'. **1935** *Life & Letters* Sept. 195 This film is actually an advertising short. **1961** *Sunday Express* 2 Apr. 19/6 A half-hour 'short'..made by a brand-new director. **1980** A. Cornelisen *Flight from Torregreca* i. 19 A young actor, who was in town making a television short.

**m.** *U.S.* A pair of shorts (see B. 7 d).

**1936** *Institute News* (Underwear Institute, N.Y.) 15 Dec. 11/2 The knitted trunk short has done very well indeed. **1956** *Amer. Speech* XXXI. 109 *A short* (a pair of drawers). **1974** *State* (Columbia, S. Carolina) 28 Mar. 2-a (Advt.), Western jean short with pockets and belt loops in navy cotton denim.

**5.** *Comm.* A broker who sells more stock than he has in his hands at the time of sale, intending to take advantage of a possible drop in prices to obtain the remainder.

**1849** G. G. Foster *N.Y. in Slices* 19 Some wild-looking 'short'..rushes down and hysterically inquires of his obliging neighbour, Mr. Smith, whether he hasn't a few hundred over. **1881** *Chicago Times* 4 June, The May deal in white mixed [corn] is not yet settled, the shorts refusing to pay the closing price. **1891** *Boston* (Mass.) *Jrnl.* 27 Nov. 6/4 Some outside short was badly rattled. **1913** *Daily Mail* 31 Mar. 3/5 A sharp 'squeeze' of shorts in March contracts by spot houses.

**6.** *Baseball.* = *short stop* (see A. 26 d).

**1856** *Spirit of Times* 4 Oct. 86/1 The Eagle Club now made a very judicious change by placing..Mr. Place as short, which effectually prevented their opponents from making any more such scores as was done in the first innings. **1897** *Outing* May 203/1 Chandler at short is being very hard pushed. **1967** C. Potok *Chosen* i. i. 34 The first one hit a single, and the second one sent a high fly to short, which Sidney Goldberg caught without having to move a step. **1976** *National Observer* (U.S.) 14 Aug. 6/5, 'I try to imagine what I'd throw to get the guy out,' says Stone. 'You know, to get him to ground out to short or something.'

**7.** In various uses of the *pl.*

**a.** A mixture of the bran and coarse part of meal.

**1765** *Museum Rust.* IV. 402 Neither grains (drains), peas, barley, gurgins (shorts),..grew thereon. **1793** Washington *Let.* Writ. 1891 XII. 389 Now, if the midlings, ship stuff, shorts and bran does not amount to this difference, all short of it is loss. **1856** P. Thompson *Hist. Boston* 722 *Shorts*, the finer sort of bran left in coarse flour. **1868** *Rep. U.S. Commissioner Agric.* (1869) 439 Poor pastures, poor meadows, hay, and a few shorts or cob-meal.

**b.** *Rope-making.* 'The toppings and tailings of hemp, which are dressed for bolt-ropes [etc.]... The term is also employed to denote the distinction between the long hemp, used in making staple-ropes and inferior hemp' (Crabb *Technol. Dict.* 1823).

*c* **1790** *Encycl. Brit.* (ed. 3) VI. 175/1 A large machine for spinning shorts or backens into candlewicks.

**c.** Short whist. (See whist *sb.*)

**1825** T. Hook *Sayings* Ser. ii. *Man of Many Fr.* II. 9 It was suggested that a rubber of shorts would be extremely seasonable. *a* **1874** *Pop. Author's Miseries* in *Casq. Lit.* V. 109/2 My father-in-law abhors me because I play shorts.

**d.** Trousers reaching only to the knees or higher (*orig.* knee-breeches). In the U.S. also *spec.* underpants. ***rowing shorts***: short drawers worn by oarsmen; similarly ***football shorts***.

**1826** Disraeli *Viv. Grey* i. iii. 7 Another..wanted to act the ghost, which he proposed doing in white shorts and a nightcap. **1837** Dickens *Pickw.* xlvii, The gentleman who condescended to appear in plush shorts and cottons for a quarterly stipend. **1859** *Habits of Gd. Society* iii. 150 You may dress like a bargee, in shorts and grey stockings. **1865** P'cess Alice *Mem.* 7 June (1884) 100 Uncle Louis received us in shorts! **1913** *Blackw. Mag.* Apr. 520, I..stood outside in football 'shorts', nailed boots and sweater. **1927** *Amer. Speech* II. 278/1 *Shorts*, athletic trousers. **1933** *Sun* (Baltimore) 29 Sept. 14/3 Too long has man..allowed himself to be made miserable by a summer garb which is anything but summery. We thrill to the bold challenge issued by A. Van Dyke.., 'Shorts for men!' **1941** B. Schulberg *What makes Sammy Run?* x. 253 He was stripped down to his silk shorts. **1965** H. Gold *Man who was not with It* i. 6 He..plucked a tricksie in shorts as she wiggled by. **1973** G. Robyns *Wimbledon* xx. 137 In the thirties Wimbledon abounded in beauty... Eileen Bennett ..was the girl who dared to wear shorts for the first time in public. **1974** *Caribbean Contact* Mar. 10/5 Bishop's wife came to my hotel and reported that her husband had spent the night in his 'shorts' (or underwear)..after being stripped.

**e.** Short clothes.

**1836** Marryat *Midsh. Easy* iii, Six months passed in these innocent amusements, and then he [the baby] was put into shorts.

**f.** Cuttings of tobacco.

**1840** Marryat *Poor Jack* xv, Two penn'orth of pigtail and a paper of shorts. **1883** Dodge in *Rep. 10th Census U.S.* III. iv. 27 When a manufacturer desires to sell his shorts, clippings, [etc.]..to another manufacturer, he is required to apply to the collector..stating..the kind and quality of tobacco he wishes to sell.

**g.** What is 'short' or lacking. (*a*) *Printing.* 'The copies that have been or should be reprinted to make full a deficient edition' (*Cent. Dict.*). (*b*) That amount of stock which a broker who 'sells short' needs to cover his deficiency. (*c*) *Mining.* (See quot. 1886.)

**1868** *Territorial Enterprise* (Virginia, Nevada) 11 Feb. 3/2 We believe..this rise is attributable to 'cornering' of the 'shorts' below. **1886** Barrowman *Sc. Mining Terms* 60 *Shorts*, term applied to the amount that the sum of Lordships in one year is under the minimum or fixed rent payable. **1901** *Munsey's Mag.* XXV. 433 He could easily take in his shorts at seventy-five.

**h.** *Comm.* Short-dated securities.

**1932** *Manch. Guardian* 28 Jan. 15/1 The 'shorts' are all due for repayment at par at various dates between 1933 and 1936. **1940** *Economist* 13 July 48/2 If the above sequence of interest rates reveals an artificially wide gap, it is between the yields on medium shorts and the irredeemables. **1963** H. D. Berman *Stock Exch.* (ed. 4) v. 40 U.K. Government loans with less than five years to go to the final redemption date (known as 'shorts') are always dealt in plus accrued interest. **1980** *Times* 15 Jan. 14 Gains of up to £2 were seen in long gilts and of up to ⅝ in shorts.

**C.** *adv.*

**1.** Of a manner of speaking: Briefly, concisely, curtly. Now *rare* in educated prose use.

*a* **1300** *Cursor M.* 8347 Bot elles scilwisli and scort he tald þat him lai apon hert. *c* **1374** CHAUCER *Troylus* IV. 890 This, shorte and pleyne, þeffect of my message. **1575** GASCOIGNE *Kenelworth Castle* I. i. Wks. 1910 II. 108 Then Engistes lande as Chronicles do write Now England short, a land of worthy fame. **1610** HOLLAND *Camden's Brit.* (1637) 277 Bistleham, now called short, Bisham. **1681** R. L'ESTRANGE *Tully's Offices* 96 Now to speak short and plain. *a* **1715** BURNET *Own Time* (1724) I. 328 He spoke short, but with life. **1729** G. ADAMS tr. *Sophocles, Oedip. Colon.* II. ii. II. 121 How short and seasonable thou speakest this? **1859** TENNYSON *Elaine* 882 Then if the maiden..spoke, he answer'd not, Or short or coldly.

†**2.** *to set short by, to tell short of*: to hold in low estimation. *Obs.*

**1377** [see SET *v.*[1] 91 e]. **1399** LANGL. *Rich. Redeles* III. 194 For wolde they..dryve out the dagges and all the Duche cotis, And sette hem a-side, and scorte of hem telle.

**3. a.** For a brief while. *Obs.* in the positive.

**1611** MURE *Misc. Poems* i. 54 Lyk to a blooming meadow, Quhose pryd doth schort remaine. *c* **1730** RAMSAY *Wyfe of Auchtermuchty* i, But schort the storm wald let him stay. **1875** *Ure's Dict. Arts* III. 307 Resinous woods, like the pine, last much shorter than the oak.

†**b.** In a brief space of time, soon. *Obs.*

**1556** LAUDER *Tractate* 30 Thir kyngs yai ar bot kyngs of bane; And schort wyl heir yare tyme be gane. **1590** *Satir. Poems Reform.* xix. 47 With schot of gunne yai murdreist him fra hand, Schort ouer twa yeiris quhen he had rung in deid. **1643** *Orkney Witch Trial* in *Abbotsford Club Miscell.* I. 178 And shortefter, the said Annabell Murray contractit ane lingring disease.

**4. a.** In various uses relating to size or distance: With short garments, appendages, etc.; to a short distance.

**1706** *Lond. Gaz.* No. 4212/4 When he trots out he over-slips, and is shod short before for it. **1847** *Infantry Man.* (1854) 8 On the words Step Short,..each recruit will step as far as the ball of his toe, and no farther. *c* **1850** *Rudim. Navig.* (Weale) 153 The..bolts are driven short. **1887** GUNTER *Mr. Barnes* xi. 76 A plain, round-faced girl..big enough to be sixteen, and dressed short enough to be eleven.

**b.** *to break, snap* (etc.) *short* (*off*): to break straight across, so as to leave nothing beyond the plane of fracture; to break *off* close to the point of attachment.

**1679** MOXON *Mech. Exerc.* vii. 124 It may cut or brake it short asunder. **1709** STEELE *Tatler* No. 48 ¶2, I..pretended that I had broken my Wooden-Leg..but I snap'd it short off on purpose. **1745** P. THOMAS *Jrnl. Anson's Voy.* 145 The Gloucester's..Fore-top-mast broke short. **1790** BURKE *Fr. Rev.* Wks. 1808 V. 401 This weapon will snap short. **1850** SCORESBY *Cheever's Whalem. Adv.* xii. (1859) 178 His first effort broke it short at the lock. **1863** W. C. BALDWIN *Afr. Hunting* vi. 212 He broke almost every tooth short off upon this chain, in his furious efforts to bite it through. **1865** MILTON & CHEADLE *N.-W. Passage by Land* ii. (1867) 31 We ..saw..great trees blown down, or trunks snapped short off. **1898** *Blackw. Mag.* Jan. 17 Her wheel stood in the corner with the thread snapped short in the heck.

**5. a.** Abruptly, suddenly: esp. in phrase *to turn short* (*round*).

**1579** GOSSON *Sch. Abuse* (Arb.) 24 Dogs..drinke running [in the Nile] lest they bee snapte short for a pray too Crocodiles. *c* **1643** LD. HERBERT *Autobiog.* (1824) 83 Finding that I had almost overtook him, he turned short. **1666** *Lond. Gaz.* No. 55/4 The wind coming short upon them off of Scheveling, they were forced to put back. **1707** MORTIMER *Husb.* (1721) I. 360 Such Waggons as seldom have occasion to turn short, as Carriers Waggons, and such like. **1815** SCOTT *Guy M.* xli, Bertram turned short round upon Glossin at the distance of two yards only. **1841** DICKENS *Barn. Rudge* xl, 'You catch me up so very short.' 'You will be caught up much shorter, my good friend—infinitely shorter—one of these days.' **1888** BURGON *Lives 12 Gd. Men* I. iv. 434 After a considerable pause, the Provost turned short round.

**b.** *to take* (a person) *short.* (*a*) To take by surprise, at a disadvantage; to come suddenly upon; esp. *Naut.* (of wind or bad weather), or *colloq.* (in passive) to have an urgent need to urinate or defecate.

**1553** T. WILSON *Rhet.* (1560) 100 He spent once a groate at good ale, being forced through companie, and taken short at his worde. **1584** B. R. tr. *Herodotus* II. 77 b, They were suddenly surprised and taken short by a company of little dwarfes. **1609** BIBLE (Douay) *2 Macc.* viii. 26 But they returned being taken short with the time. **1691** *Lond. Gaz.* No. 2674/4 The Wind taking them short..they came to an Anchor in Torbay. **1760** C. JOHNSTON *Chrysal* II. I. ii. 10 [He] was taken short after dinner, and died in his chair! **1818** COBBETT *Pol. Reg.* XXXIII. 302 Our Prince Regent has his chaplains..amounting to several scores in number; so that he can never be at a loss. He can never be taken short. **1823** *New Monthly Mag.* IX. 113/1 They may have been taken short by the climate before reaching the Pacific. **1837** DICKENS *Pickw.* lii, I wos took up wery short by this, Samivel. **1890** *Funk's Stand. Dict.* s.v., *To be taken short* (colloq.), to be pressed with the need of evacuation of feces. **1928** R. CAMPBELL *Wayzgoose* i. 30 'Tis Nature's whim that dogs, when taken short, Still to the loftiest monument resort. **1967** 'J. ASHFORD' *Forget what you Saw* xx. 180 Simon was in such a terrible state of nerves that he had already been taken short twice and had to rush for the lavatory. **1977** *Private Eye* 11 Nov. 10/2 Taken badly short when on his way to work, and finding that both of the public lavatories in Putney were closed, Mr. Peter Herring entered a police station and asked if he could use their convenience.

(*b*) To interrupt with a reply; not to allow to complete his speech or offer explanations. Often with *up*.

**1565** JEWEL *Repl. Harding* (1611) 228 If M. Harding had not taken S. Ambrose vp so short, by the words that immediately follow, he might well haue knowen his meaning. **1586** STANYHURST *Descr. Irel.* ii. 17 in *Holinshed*, Sir, you take me verie short. *a* **1647** PETTE in *Archæologia* XII. 257 His majesty, taking it ill that my lord should [etc.] ..took him short with a sharp reprehension. **1711** ADDISON *Spect.* No. 34 ¶3 Sir Andrew Freeport took him up short. **1815** SCOTT *Guy M.* xxxv, But, my dear sir, you take me so very short. **1865** DICKENS *Mut. Fr.* IV. xiii, 'But bless ye, my beauty!' cried Mrs. Boffin, taking him up short at this point.

†**6. a.** At close quarters, closely, tightly. *to fight short*: to engage in a hand to hand struggle. *to ride short*: to ride with a tight rein. *Obs.*

*a* **1530** J. HEYWOOD *Play of Wether* (Brandl) 487 Byr lady these knauys muste be tyed shorter. **1600** HOLLAND *Livy* VII. x. 255 A light footman's shield he takes unto him, and a Spanish blade by his side, as being more handsome to fight short and close. **1689** T. R. *View Govt. Europe* 54 They undertook likewise to loosen his power, or tye it up short. *a* **1700** EVELYN *Diary* 24 Jan. 1682, They [Moors] rid very short, and could stand upright at full speede.

†**b.** *to hold* or *keep* (a person) *short* [= F. *tenir court*]: to press (him) hard in a contest; to keep rigidly confined or under strict discipline; to keep *from* something; in later use, to keep (a horse) tightly reined in. *Obs.*

*c* **1425** ? LYDG. *Assembly of Gods* 1307 'Kepe hym short', he seyde, 'tyll hys lust be spent.' **1470–85** MALORY *Arthur* IX. xxx. 385 And euer sir tristram held them passynge shorte, and euer sir Bleoberys was passynge besy vpon syre Tristram. **1530** PALSGR. 597/2 Lette men holde hym very shorte... If youth be nat kepte shorte it wyll be marred anone. **1565** COOPER *Thesaurus, Cohibeo*..to keepe shorte. **1568** GRAFTON *Chron.* II. 12 The king helde them so short, that in processe of tyme they were faine to yelde. **1581** PETTIE *Guazzo's Civ. Convers.* (1586) 131 b, They perswade themselues, that if they doe not keepe them [their wives] short, they keep them not as they ought to doe. **1600** SURFLET *Country Farm* Table, Girles must be kept short. **1632** BP. HALL *Hard Texts* Luke vi. 25 The time shall come wherein ye shall bee held short of all worldly comforts. **1674** FLAVEL *Husb. Spirit.* iii. 216 Oxen for use are daily yoaked and kept short, whilst those that are designed for the shambles are let loose to feed at pleasure. **1792** OSBALDISTONE *Brit. Sportsm.* 416 When your horse attempts to be vicious..hold him very short.

**7. a.** On the hither side of the point aimed at or contemplated. Also, †lagging behind, in the rear (*of*). Const. *of*. †*to lie short*: to pass the night at a place short of one's journey's end.

*c* **1588** in *Defeat Sp. Armada* (Navy Rec. Soc.) I. 13 The next morning..there was a great galleon of the Spaniards short of her company to the southwards. **1634** SIR T. HERBERT *Trav.* 67 Three miles short of the great Citie. **1644** SYMONDS *Diary* (Camden) 49 The foot army lay short of the hill all night. **1669** STURMY *Mariner's Mag.* I. ii. 14 Coming to the same Point and Degree where she [the moon] was in Conjunction with the Sun last, she is short of the Sun. **1676** MARVELL *Mr. Smirke* 24 Another Exposer..would rather have turn'd out of the Road, and lay'd short all night somewhere by the way. **1684** NORRIS *Poems* 35 I'm flush'd with silent joy, and smile to see The Shafts of Fortune still drop short of me. **1698** FRYER *Acc. E. India & P.* 130 He met me..in a Garden short of the Town. **1726** SHELVOCKE *Voy. round World* 21 He came to an anchor short of us. **1751** ELIZA HAYWOOD *Betsy Thoughtless* IV. 309 He had lain the night before eight miles short of Sir Ralph's seat. **1816** *Sporting Mag.* XLVIII. 180 Ford frequently hit short. **1862** *Chamb. Encycl.* III. 320/1 Misconception of this may lead to overthrowing the ball, or throwing it short. **1855** KINGSLEY *Westw. Ho!* xiv, There's not such a piece in London;..nor short of Calicut, where it came from. **1888** *Daily News* 7 Sept. 5/2 The trout has 'risen short'.

**b.** *to fall short* (*of*): see FALL *v.* 97, 98. Hence *falling short*, a failure in attainment, a deficiency.

*a* **1680** T. GOODWIN *Govt. Ch. Christ* VI. xii. Wks. 1697 IV. IV. 402 His Disciples..had..great fallings short. **1856** MRS. BROWNING *Aur. Leigh* IX. Poet. Wks. (1904) 539/1 Shine out for two, Aurora, and fulfil My falling-short that must be!

**c.** *to stop short of*: not to go the length of (some extreme action).

**1818** SCOTT *Rob Roy* xii, I had but just stopped short of insulting the beautiful..being by whom it was proffered. **1865** DICKENS *Mut. Fr.* I. vii, But stop short of any compunction for the people who would lose the same.

**8. to come short.** †**a.** To arrive too late. *to come short of*: to arrive too late for, or later than.

**1569** W. FORREST *Joseph* I. in *Grisild the Second* (Roxb.) 167 To aske their [*sc.* Gower and Chaucer's] counsaylles I came all to shorte. **1597** MORLEY *Introd. Mus.* 116 Remembring that this morning..I hied me out thinking that if I had staied for you, I should haue come short. **1646** SUCKLING *Aglaura* v. i, After't, like a man that's come too short o' th' ship And's left behind upon the land. **1688** HOLME *Armoury* III. 177/1 If any [Monk] come short to Prayers or his Meat, he is to stand apart by himself.

†**b.** To be 'taken short', be taken by surprise.

*c* **1611** CHAPMAN *Iliad* v. 553 Lions..Rush out, and prey on sheepe, Steeres, Oxen; and destroy mens stals, so long that they come short, And by the Owners steele are slaine.

**c.** To be imperfect or inadequate.

**1579** W. WILKINSON *Confut. Fam. Love* B i b, They will all come to short in their reconing. **1589** PUTTENHAM *Engl. Poesie* III. ix. (Arb.) 169, I consider..how short the Latines come to expresse manie of the Greeke originals. **1601** SHAKS. *All's Well* v. iii. 176 Your reputation comes too short for my daughter, you are no husband for her. **1605** BACON *Adv. Learn.* I. iv. §12. 23 In arts Mechanicall, the first deuiser coms shortest, and time addeth and perfecteth. **1677** MILTON *P.L.* VIII. 414 To attaine The highth and depth of thy Eternal wayes All human thoughts come short, Supream of things. **1690** LOCKE *Hum. Underst.* II. xi. §11 A faculty which we see Beasts come short in. **1881** JOWETT *Thucyd.* I. 121 Even those who come short in other ways may justly plead the valour with which they have fought for their country.

**d.** *to come short of*: (*a*) to fail to reach (a standard); not to equal *in* some quality; to be something less than, not to amount to; †(*b*) not to extend to (a place) (*obs.*); †(*c*) to fail to get; also, to lose; (*obs.*).

**1570** DEE *Math. Pref.* 2 Surmountyng the imperfection of coniecture..; and commyng short of high intellectuall conception. **1587** HARRISON *England* II. i. 139/1 in *Holinshed*, Some bishops, &c. in our time doo come short of the ancient gluttonie & prodigaltie of their predecessors. **1611** BIBLE *Rom.* iii. 23 For all haue sinned, and come short [Gr. ὑστεροῦνται, *Revised Version* fall short] of the glory of God. **1623** LISLE *Ælfric on O. & N.T.* To Rdr. 33 Giotto came far short of Dominico. **1638** JUNIUS *Paint. Ancients* 30 Whatsoever beareth the similitude of any other thing, must of necessitie come short of the thing it doth resemble. **1681** W. ROBERTSON *Phraseol. Gen.* 346 He comes short of none for bravery. **1696** WHISTON *Theory Earth* II. (1722) 181 I cannot well perceive how this Proposition comes short of Physical Demonstration. **1745** PASCOE *Jrnl.* 196 The Chinese come far short of us in the Magnificence of their Houses. **1889** SWINBURNE *Study B. Jonson* i. 6 [They] came short of the triumph which might have been theirs.

(*b*) **1615** G. SANDYS *Trav.* 217 The higher mountaines now comming short of the sea, do leaue a narrow leuel between.

(*c*) **1632** LITHGOW *Trav.* IX. 420 Who Religiously feast upon the Corps of their aged Parents..for indeed the Wormes come short among the dead Tartars of their foode. **1690** W. WALKER *Idiomat. Anglo-Lat.* 412 My Master is like to come short of his wife.

†**e.** *to come short home*: to return from an expedition in reduced numbers or with loss of men. Hence, to be missing on the return of an expedition; to fail to return. *Obs.*

In the first quot. perh. = to reach home too late; cf. a.

*a* **1548** HALL *Chron., Hen. VI,* 175 b, The erle of Warwicke had come to short home, to tel these tidynges if the duke of Excester..might haue had his awne will. **1577** *F. de L'isle's Legendarie* G iv, Fiue of them came short home, and the most doulte of all remained behinde. **1677** W. HUBBARD *Narrative* (1865) II. 93 Many of the young Men.. did, Sundry of them, come short Home. **1713** WARDER *True Amazons* 54 And will venture in, tho' they come short home. **1721** DE FOE *Mem. Cavalier* (1840) 189 He had not always ..success in these enterprises; for sometimes we came short home.

**9. to cut short** [= F. *couper court* (where *court* is uninflected as adv.); cf. A. 1 i]: to put a sudden end to (a person's life or career, a course of events, an action, speech, etc.). Hence, to stop (a person) abruptly in a course of action or speech; to interrupt and not allow to proceed. Also *rarely* †to disappoint (a person) *of* something.

**1593** SHAKS. *2 Hen. VI*, IV. iv. 12 Rather then bloody Warre shall cut them short. **1647** WARD *Simple Cobler* 15 The Rule..cuts the work short and sharpe. **1706** A. BEDFORD *Temple Mus.* viii. 163 The Chanters did Cut their Notes Short. **1712** STEELE *Spect.* No. 534 ¶1, I love to ask Questions when I fall into such Conversation; but I am cut short with something or other about my bright Eyes. **1732** BERKELEY *Alciphr.* v. §7 Wks. 1871 II. 179 To cut this matter short, I shall borrow an allusion to physic. **1760–72** H. BROOKE *Fool of Qual.* (1809) I. 48 We may cut them short of their desires. **1780** *Mirror* No. 88 It would be a pity to cut short a boy of my genius. **1818** BYRON *Juan* I. clxiii, Wise Antonia cut him short. **1837** CARLYLE *Fr. Rev.* I. i. i, A malady which threatened to cut short his days. **1840** DICKENS *Old C. Shop* lix, An exclamation..cut the lawyer short. **1886** BARING-GOULD *Court Royal* II. xxx. 78 The young man cut her short with—'You may go'. **1891** E. PEACOCK *N. Brendon* I. 114 His reverie was cut short by the castle clock striking a quarter to five.

**10.** *to breathe short*: to take short breaths.

**1826** DISRAELI *Viv. Grey* III. iv, She looked pale and breathed short.

**11.** *to sell short*: (*a*) to effect a sale of stock or goods which the seller does not at the time possess, but hopes to buy at a lower price before the time fixed for delivery; (*b*) *fig.* to undervalue; to belittle.

**1852** *Hunt's Merch. Mag.* XXVI. 738 The writer of the *Aurora* phillipic complains of the practice of 'selling short'. **1861** in *Rebellion Rec.* (1862) I. III. 27 When one of the members of the Board offered to sell Government Stock 'short' on time, he was instantly hissed down. **1881** *Daily News* 1 Mar. 5/1 A speculator will sell bacon 'short'. **1883** *Century Mag.* July 329/1 When crude oil..goes down to fifty cents, times are hard, and nobody wears a cheerful face save the speculators who have sold 'short'. **1936** B. & S. SPEWACK *Boy meets Girl* I. 35 Larry: You can't act with a baby. They steal every scene—Law: Are you selling motherhood short? **1959** *Times* 1 Sept. 3/5 Brown, the man who knocked out the present British featherweight champion..has been sold short before. **1972** *Guardian* 21 June 1/2 Who, throughout the Labour Government, spent his time 'selling sterling short' in speeches both at home and abroad? **1974** J. CLEARY *Peter's Pence* x. 281 *Domine, non sum dignus*... Martin would always sell himself short. **1980** *Times Lit. Suppl.* 24 Oct. 1194/5 It is poetry that is being sold short by such determined efforts to be funny and clever.

**12.** *Comb.*, with pples., as *short-breathing*, *-fetched*, *-lasting*, *-living*, *-pitched* adjs.; with agent-n., as *short-liver*; also **short-acting** *a. Pharm.*, relatively transient in effect; **short-manned**, insufficiently manned; **short-running**, (*a*) *Coursing*, of a hound or hare, running with short strides, slow in pace; (*b*) making short runs; **short-set**, of short build, stumpy; **short-shipped**, lacking from an intended shipment; **short-spoken**, laconic in speech; **short-weighting**, giving short weight; **short-working**, *Coursing*, of a greyhound = *short-running* (*a*).

**1951** A. GROLLMAN *Pharmacol. & Therapeutics* vi. 143 In insomnia, where there is difficulty in falling asleep, the *short acting drugs are indicated. **1978** *Price's Textbk. Practice of Med.* (ed. 12) III. 260/1 The short-acting barbiturates are apt to cause profound depression. **1701** ROWE *Ambit. Step-mother* III. i, *Short breathing sighs heav'd in my panting breast. **1612** DRAYTON *Poly-olb.* I. 493 Their *short-fetcht troubled breath a hollow noise doth make. *c* **1400** *Rom. Rose* 3283 The Ioye it is so *short-lasting. *a* **1683** OLDHAM *Charac. Old P[riest]* Rem. (1684) 125 Par and John of the Times were *short-Livers to him. **1637** RUTHERFORD *Lett.* (1664) 372 Ye know this world is but a shadow, a *short-living creature, under the law of time. **1830** MARRYAT *King's Own* xxxii, Captain M—— did not like to have the frigate *short-manned. **1867** G. H. SELKIRK *Guide to Cricket Ground* ii. 36 A ball which grounds nearer the bowler than a length ball is '*short-pitched'. **1977** *World of Cricket Monthly* June 32/2 Some pointless, short-pitched bowling by Imran and Sarfraz. **1855** LEIFCHILD *Cornwall* 6 The people patronised the vans to such an extent that *short-running coaches were few. **1853** 'STONEHENGE' *Greyhound* ix. 194 A good Wiltshire *short-running dog. *Ibid.* x. 211 A short-running, yet strong hare. **1883** *Good Cheer* 36, I remembered a *short-set young chap. **1891** OLVER & O'REILLY *Imperial Tariff* 306 The requirement for the return of *short shipped goods into bond. **1865** KINGSLEY *Herew.* xxxii, *Short-spoken, hard-headed, hard-swearing warriors. **1837** CARLYLE *Fr. Rev.* I. VII. iv, The official persons have to smuggle forth the *short-weighing Baker by back doors. **1853** 'STONEHENGE' *Greyhound* ix. 198 A dog got by a racing sire out of a little *short-working dam.

†**short**, *v.*[1] *Obs.* Forms: 1 sceortian, 1–2 scortian, 2–5 scort, 4–6 schort(e, 5 schortyn, shorte, shortt, scorte, (sorth), 4–7 short. [OE. *sc(e)ortian* to grow short, f. *sc(e)ort* SHORT *a.* Cf. Du. *schorten*, ON. *skorta* to be lacking. In the trans. sense OE. had the cognate (*ȝe*)*scyrtan*.]

**1.** *intr.* To grow short or shorter.

*c* **1000** *Sax. Leechd.* III. 250, & se dæȝ þonne sceortað, oð þæt seo sunne cymð eft suð to þam winterlican sunnstede. **1387** TREVISA *Higden* (Rolls) II. 185 In his elde þe stature boweþ..þe breþ schorteþ. *a* **1400–50** *Wars Alex.* 3298 Loke to þine ende, For die þe bose, quen all is done & ay þi day scortis. *c* **1450** *Brut* II. ccxxxviii. 334 Wherefor..his lyff shorted þe sonner. **1500–20** DUNBAR *Poems* lxix. 46 3it, quhone the nycht begynnis to schort, It dois my spreit sum part confort. **15..** *Pol. Rel. & L. Poems* (1866) 44 So schortithe my brethe.

**2.** *trans.* To make short or shorter; to shorten.

**a.** To shorten the duration of (a person's life, a period of time, a condition); *occas.* to bring nearer (an appointed date). Also, *to short* (a person) *of* (life, suffering).

*c* **1175** *Lamb. Hom.* 25 þenne cumeð..þe deofel..and him scorteð his daȝes. *a* **1300** *Cursor M.* 22214 For his derlinges ..vr lauerd sal do scort þe dais, for if þe dais ne scorted were unnethes suld ani flexs be fere. **1338** R. BRUNNE *Chron.* (1725) 49 þorgh Edrike's conseile, scho [quene Emme] scorted his life. **1340–70** *Alex. & Dind.* 401 We ne liȝthe noht our lif wiþ no luthur dede, Where-fore we scholde with schame be schorted of daies. *c* **1350** *Will. Palerne* 1549 þow hast lengþed my lif & my langour schortet. *c* **1386** CHAUCER *Pars. T.* 653 Wherfore swich sorwe shorteth ful ofte the lif of man. **1387–8** T. USK *Test. Love* III. iv. (Skeat) 119 Than saye I that no man may shorte ne lengthe the day ordayned of his dying. **1422** YONGE tr. *Secreta Secret.* ix. 139 The foly company of women destrueth the body, sorthyth the lyuedayes [etc.]. *c* **1440** *Jacob's Well* 174 þi sorwe may be so gret & so parfyȝt, þat it schal don awey synne, & schortyn þe peyne, as it dyde þe theef on þe crosse. *a* **1500** *Abraham* 309 in *Brome Bk.* 63 Fader, I prey ȝow hartely, schorte me of my woo. *a* **1533** BERNERS *Huon* xxi. 60 To sende me in to strange countres to thentent to short my dayes. *c* **1590** GREENE *Fr. Bacon* III. i. 1026 Then, Edward, short my life and end her loues. **1599** SHAKS., etc. *Pass. Pilgr.* xv, Short, night, to-night, and length thyself to-morrow. *a* **1615** MONTGOMERIE *Sonn.* iii. 14 Sen conscience, love, and cheritie all laiks, Lord, short the season, for the chosens saiks.

**b.** To shorten (a discussion, narration, process, etc.); to curtail by omissions, abbreviate; to make an abridgement of (a literary work).

*a* **1300** *Cursor M.* 22305 The Iuus sal scort þam þair consail. *a* **1390** *Prol. Job* in *Wyclif's Bible* II. 670 Seuene hundrid almest or eiȝte hundrid vers failen; with the whiche the boc shortid..sheweth openli to the rederes his foule defaute. *c* **1400** MAUNDEV. (Roxb.) xxii. 103 Many oþer meruailes..at þis tyme I speke noȝt of, by cause of schortyng of my buke. **1450–1530** *Myrr. Our Lady* 17 And therfor yt ys not semely that they [words & notes] shulde be shorted. **1483** CAXTON *Gold. Leg., Justyn*, The which hystorye saint Justyn abreuyd or shorted. **1529** MORE *Dyaloge* IV. Wks. 287/2 If I hadde seen so muche before, it had been likely to haue shorted much part of our long communicacion. **1570** *Satir. Poems Reform.* xii. 147, I flait not to offend ȝow In sempill veirs, this Schedull that I send ȝow; Beseikand ȝow to schort it gif ȝe may.

**c.** To reduce the length of (a material object, a journey); to cut short. ***to short*** (a person) ***by the head*** or ***knees***: to decapitate or cut off the legs (cf. SHORT *a.* 2, SHORTEN *v.* 1 d).

**1398** TREVISA *Barth. De P.R.* v. xxiv. (Bodl. MS.), þe tunge is so schorted þat vnneþe it is idrawe oute or neuer. **1412–20** LYDG. *Troy Bk.* III. 3017 With a stroke he rofe his nose a-two, And shortid it by þe haluendel. **1470–85** MALORY *Arthur* v. viii. 173 He shorted hym and smote of bothe his legges by the knees. *a* **1500** *Nutbrowne Maid* xx. in *Arnolde's Chron.* (1502) 76 b, To short my here, a bowe to bere. **1523** BERNERS *Froiss.* I. cclxxxv. 426 Howbeit, their way was shorted, for..the frenchmen and they met togyder sodenly. **1545** ASCHAM *Toxoph.* II. (Arb.) 117 With shorting and pikynge your bowes..[you] can neuer haue done vntyll they be starke nought. *a* **1548** HALL *Chron., Edw. IV* (1550) 3 His body was shorted, by the length of his hed.

*fig.* *c* **1550** BALE *K. Johan* 227, I se now they be at to mych lyberte; we wyll short ther hornys.

**3.** To make to appear short, to beguile (the time, the way) with sport or stories. Hence *refl.* To amuse oneself (*Sc.*). (Cf. SHURT *v.*)

*c* **1400** [see SHORTING *vbl. sb.*]. *c* **1450** METHAM *Wks.* (E.E.T.S.) 14/406 And thus with myry songys and talys, day be day, They schortyd the tyme with myrtht and with play. **1513** DOUGLAS *Æneis* VI. x. 37 Thai fall to wersling on the goldin sand, Assaying honest gemmis thaim to schort. *Ibid.* VIII. v. 75 With sindry sermondis schortis he the way. **1528** LYNDESAY *Dreme* 75 3it fure I furth..Towarte the see, to schorte me on the sandis. **1530** TINDALE *Gen.* To Rdr., As the maner is to prolonge the tale to shorte the tyme with all.

**4.** To cause to go short *of*.

**1620** J. TAYLOR (Water-P.) *Praise Hemp-seed* (1623) 5 The Draper of his wealth would much be shorted.

**5.** To make of no effect. *nonce-use.* Cf. SHORTEN *v.* 3 b.

**1611** SHAKS. *Cymb.* I. vi. 200, I shall short my word By length'ning my returne.

**6.** *intr.* To come short in one's reckoning.

*a* **1641** BP. MOUNTAGU *Acts & Mon.* (1642) 141 Three years, which indeed should be five, or he shorts in his account.

**7.** *Naut.* = SHORTEN *v.* 5 b. *absol.*

*c* **1557** S. BURROUGH in Hakluyt *Voy.* (1599) I. 277 For as we shorted vpon yᵉ said warpe the anker came home.

**short**, *v.*[2] *trans.* and *intr.* = SHORT-CIRCUIT *v.* (Cf. SHORT *sb.* 4 e.) Also with *out*, and *fig.* Hence **'shorting** *vbl. sb.*[2] and *ppl. a.*

**1904** *Electr. Rev.* 3 Sept. 341 Should any line become 'shorted' or 'grounded'. **1907** *Motor Boat* 4 July 440/2 The battery must be disconnected and the magneto 'shorted'. **1907** *Daily Chron.* 27 July 9/2 The coil went wrong, and the accumulators 'shorted' internally. **1912** *Motor Manual* Advt. facing p. iii, The separators allow the plates to be placed closer together and yet make 'shorting' impossible. **1957** *Practical Wireless* XXXIII. 734/1 A 150Ω resistor with a shorting switch. **1971** B. W. ALDISS *Soldier Erect* 87 Both men were immediately sympathetic, and Di made a lot of clicking noises like a shorting Morse key. **1971** P. O'DONNELL *Impossible Virgin* x. 198 I'll take the Land-Rover and short out the ignition. **1974** *Sumter* (S. Carolina) *Daily Item* 24 Apr. 2A/6 The fire was started by an electric fence shorting out. **1976** *National Observer* (U.S.) 14 Aug. 9/2 A calcium-lead battery requires an inorganic sack around the lead grids to prevent materials of erosion from shorting out the battery. **1979** *N.Y. Rev. Bks.* 8 Feb. 12/2, I cannot see for the life of me why Miss Renault, that dedicated Hellenophile, should choose to live anywhere rather than the Aegean—unless she is anxious to avoid shorting out the overloaded circuits of fantasy by the insistent presence of the real world.

**shortage** ('ʃɔːtɪdʒ). Orig. *U.S.* [f. SHORT *sb.* + -AGE.] Deficiency in quantity; the amount by which a sum of money, a supply of goods, or the like, is deficient. Also *attrib.*

**1868** *Amer. Newsp.* Apr. The 'shortage war' [at Chicago] between the shippers of grain and the skippers who carry it, is practically over. **1873** *Wisconsin Rep.* XXIX, The plaintiff must recover damages for any shortage. **1898** RIDER HAGGARD *Dr. Therne* 184 When there was any shortage of the party funds..I posed as the friend round the corner. **1901** *Scotsman* 9 Apr. 5/3 The actual shortage was £545,000.

**shortall** ('ʃɔːtɔːl). *U.S.* [f. SHORT *a.* + OVER)ALL *sb.*] Freq. *pl.* A child's one-piece suit with short sleeves and short trouser legs.

**1966** *N.Y. Times* 17 Apr. I-97/2 (Advt.), Both dress and shortalls have the fresh-from-the-laundry look of striped cotton seersucker that survives even after a hard day's play. **1969** *Sears Catal.* Spring/Summer 23 Shortall with soil release. **1976** *Billings* (Montana) *Gaz.* 5 July 3-B (Advt.), Infants & Toddler shortalls, Orig. 4.00.

**'short-bread.** [SHORT *a.* 20 a.] An article of food, in the form of flat (usually round) cakes, the essential ingredients of which are flour, butter, sugar, mixed in such proportions as to make the cake 'short' when baked.

**1801** *Farmer's Mag.* Apr. 217 It can be used for biscuit, bunns, and particularly for short-bread. **1853** MRS. CARLYLE *Lett.* II. 226 A decanter of wine..and a plateful of shortbread. **1891** BARRIE *Little Minister* (1892) 201 Two of those pans, that could be broken in the hands to-day like shortbread.

**short-breathed** (ʃɔːt'brɛθt), *a.* [f. SHORT *a.* + BREATH *sb.* + -ED[2].] Short of breath; suffering from difficulty of breathing, dyspnœic.

**1470–85** MALORY *Arthur* VIII. xxxix. 333 Sir Lamorak was so sore brysed and shorte brethed that he tracyd and trauercyd somwhat abak. **1620** VENNER *Via Recta* vi. (1650) 100 It is very profitable for such as be asthmaticke or short-breathed. **1753** J. BARTLET *Gentl. Farriery* ix. (1754) 89 The horse..turns short-breathed with the least exercise. **1805** J. WHITAKER in *Polwhele's Tradit.* (1826) II. 551 The air of London..is so loaded with sulphur..as to be almost pestilential to a short-breathed man. **1809** MALKIN *Gil Blas* x. iii. (Rtldg.) 343 The deuce and all! stammered out my secretary, short-breathed with sudden admiration. **1911** *Blackw. Mag.* Sept. 306/2 Being short-breathed and unable to go up even a gentle hill without panting and puffing.

**b.** *fig.* (Cf. SHORT-WINDED.)

**1845** MRS. BROWNING *Lett.* (1899) I. 255 One should not be grateful for kindness only while it lasts: that would be short-breathed gratitude.

**'short-cake.** [SHORT *a.* 20 a.] A cake made short or crisp with butter or lard.

The specific application varies according to locality; in some English districts the word means a cake of shortbread; elsewhere in England, and in the U.S., it is applied to a rich tea-cake, and to a cake of pastry enclosing a layer of fruit.

**1594** *Good Huswife's Handmaid* 52 To make short Cakes. [**1598** SHAKS. *Merry W.* I. i. 211 Booke of Riddles? why did you not lend it to Alice Short-cake vpon Allhallowmas last.] **1804** R. ANDERSON *Cumbld. Ball.* (1850) 90 There wur snaps, yell, nuts, gingerbread, shwort-keakes, and brandy. **1820** IRVING *Leg. Sleepy Hollow* Sketch Bk. (1821) II. 286 Sweet cakes and short cakes. **1826** MRS. DODS *Cook & Housew. Man.* 316 Derby Short-Cakes. **1829** *Frugal Housew.* 61. **1884** 'E. GARRETT' *At Any Cost* iii. 51 She had scarcely realized that there were so many jam-pots and tea-boxes and short-cakes to be seen together anywhere in the wide world. **1902** *Strand Mag.* Jan. 69/2 We are promised to-day a Strawberry Shortcake.

**short-'change**, *v.* orig. *U.S.* [f. *short change*: see SHORT *a.* 15 a.] *trans.* To rob by giving insufficient change. Also *fig.*, to deprive (a person) of his due; to cheat, deceive. So **short-'changed** *ppl. a.*; **short-'changer**; **short-'changing** *vbl. sb.*

**1903** ADE *People you Know* 30 Brad was out in the back Townships short-changing the Farmers. **1914** [see GYP *sb.*[1] 3]. **1920** C. R. COOPER *Under Big Top* 205 The gambling and the graft of the side shows, the short-changers in the 'connection', the constant form of Temptation ever beckoning! **1928** L. NORTH *Parasites* 304 The girl at the cash-register short-changed him. **1946** *Richmond* (Va.) *Times-Dispatch* 14 Feb. 4/1 Henry C. Clausen..told Pearl Harbor investigators tonight that the Navy in the South Pacific was 'short-changing' the Army right up to the latter months of the war on the information it received from decoding Japanese messages. **1958** *Photoplay* Oct. 33/2 As a child, I felt that life had short-changed me. **1959** J. BRAINE *Vodi* vii. 108 He'd never bought a drink for a barmaid in his life; he said that..the bitches always short-changed you anyway. **1962** A. LURIE *Love & Friendship* xiv. 278 Short-changing in the stores. **1964** D. FRANCIS *Nerve* i. 9 He probably shot himself because that whey-faced bitch short-changed him in bed. **1976** 'D. HALLIDAY' *Dolly & Nanny Bird* i. 14 The cultural circuit for short-changed minorities. **1978** J. A. MICHENER *Chesapeake* 788 My mom and pop have worked fourteen hours a day, six days a week for more than fifty years... From birth to death they've been short-changed.

**short circuit**, *sb.* *Electr.* A circuit made through a small resistance, esp. one that acts as a shunt to a circuit of comparatively large resistance. Also *attrib.* and *fig.*

**1854** *Q. Rev.* XCV. 146 If the insulator should happen to get wet, the electric fluid will sometimes..run down the post to the earth, and make a short circuit home again to its battery. **1876** PREECE & SIVEWRIGHT *Telegraphy* 37 A cell is said to be on 'short circuit' when the plates are directly connected by means of a conductor. **1893** SLOANE *Electr. Dict., Short Circuit*, a connection between two parts of a circuit, which connection is of low resistance compared to the intercepted portion. **1900** HOBART *Dict. Electr. Engin.* I. 98/2 A short circuit occurs when connection takes place, generally through a fault, between two conductors... When the short circuit is one of extremely low resistance it is known as a dead short circuit. **1920** *Whittaker's Electr. Engineer's Pocket-bk.* (ed. 4) 253 The short-circuit test consists in measuring the voltage and power required to send current through the windings of the machine, and results in ascertaining..the power lost in heat during the passage of the current through them. **1937** KOESTLER *Spanish Testament* II. 311 True, at least once a day there is a short-circuit in my consciousness. **1970** J. SHEPHERD et al. *Higher Electr. Engin.* (ed. 2) xvii. 547 The circuit-breakers.. must be capable of dealing with the maximum possible short-circuit current that can occur at their points of connexion. **1972** D. BLOODWORTH *Any Number can Play* xvi. 149 You could both only be relied upon to play it straight if you didn't know everything about each other? As soon as you get a security short-circuit and double agents giggling..someone is bound to give the game away.

**short-circuit**, *v.* [f. prec. sb.]

**1.** *Electr.* (*trans.*) **a.** To connect by a short circuit; to establish a short circuit in (an electric system).

**1867** R. S. CULLEY *Handbk. Practical Telegr.* (ed. 2) viii. 166 *To short circuit a battery*, to connect the poles by a wire. **1873** F. JENKIN *Electr. & Magn.* xiii. §15. 203 If any two coils touch or are connected through the silk, they are, in technical language, said to be short-circuited. **1886** CUMMING *Electricity treated experimentally* 236 We find on short-circuiting the battery a deflection of 73°. **1893** SLOANE *Electr. Dict.*, To short circuit a lamp. **1896** FOSTER & ATKINSON *Electr. & Magnetism* §345. 420 When the plug is placed at O, the galvanometer is 'short-circuited'.

**b.** Of a conducting body: To be traversed by (a current) by way of short circuit. Also *refl.* of a current: To make a short circuit.

**1882** *Nature* 16 Nov. 59/1 If one of the machines drops in speed the currents from the other machines short-circuit themselves through the one. **1884** P. HIGGS *Magneto- & Dynamo-Electric Mach.* 172 Care should be taken that these bed-plates do not short-circuit the magnetic lines of force from pole to pole of the field-magnets. **1908** *Athenæum* 28 Mar. 392/1 The patient..can be brought back to life, even after having 'short-circuited' a current of 2,000 volts.

**c.** To cut off the current from (part of an apparatus) by establishing a short circuit.

**1882** *Nature* 27 July 289/2 Moreover, we doubt whether 'the happy idea of *filling up* the space between the lead plates used by Planté with red lead', would by any means produce the result of 'vastly increasing the usefulness of that excellent apparatus: it would rather destroy it by short-circuiting it.

**d.** *intr.* Of electrical apparatus: to fail or cease working as a result of a short circuit occurring in it.

**1902** *Electr. Rev.* 31 Oct. 732/1 Many a motor.. condemned for short-circuiting when it is really the fault of the brakes. **1975** *New Yorker* 21 Apr. 34/2 It was a gutsy performance,..recalling Margo's near-rendezvous with Rock 'n Roll Heaven last September, when another jump-suit-cum-guitar short-circuited during an impromptu hailstorm in Louisville. **1976** *Evening Post* (Nottingham) 15 Dec. 5/3 The machine short-circuited with a bang when it was switched on.

**2.** *Surg.* To form a direct communication between two portions of an intestine above and below an obstruction; to make a direct passage from (an organ) *into* some other part when the normal passage is obstructed; to avoid (an obstruction) or establish (circulation) by this means.

**1897** *Brit. Med. Jrnl.* 13 Mar. 645 As an alternative the gall-bladder may be short-circuited into the intestine. **1905** ROLLESTON *Dis. Liver* 259 The portal circulation through the liver is short-circuited. **1901** *Brit. Med. Jrnl.* 2 Feb. 261 Wherever adhesions are very extensive and likely to recur it is better to short-circuit the obstruction.

**3.** *fig.* To interrupt, to cut short; to bypass by taking more direct action. Also *absol.*

**1899** *Educat. Rev.* Dec. 475 The omnibus-institutions are to short-circuit the college. **1924** J. BUCHAN *Three Hostages* iii. 48 If you had happened to look at that rag you might have short-circuited your inquiry. **1938** *Ann. Reg. 1937* 159 The Council decision naturally short-circuited much of the debate which might have been expected in the Assembly. **1953** E. M. FORSTER *Hill of Devi* 40 Dewas and King-Emperor! In Dewas it often seemed that they might have much in common. Could one but short-circuit, all might yet be well. **1978** D. BLOODWORTH *Crosstalk* v. 40 It was.. essential to have a secure means of short-circuiting the usual channels. **1979** D. CUPITT in M. Goulder *Incarnation & Myth* iii. 32 Here is matter for a great deal of controversy. I propose to short-circuit it by simply stipulating that [etc.].

Hence **short-'circuited** *ppl. a.*; **short-'circuiting** *vbl. sb.*

**1896** [see *entero-enterostomy* s.v. ENTERO-]. **1919** H. E. PENROSE *Wireless Telegr.* IV. 75 Examine the band of the magnetic detector, the magnets, and the short-circuiting contacts of the manipulating key. **1949** KOESTLER *Insight & Outlook* iv. 39 The concept of bisociation implies a short-circuiting of two separate mental patterns. **1951** M. MCLUHAN *Mech. Bride* 145/2 A kind of streamlined or short-circuited version of the usual success pattern. **1972** *Jrnl. Social Psychol.* LXXXVIII. 247 It may be postulated that the more empathic two people are with one another, the more short-circuited or 'efficient' their communication.

**short cloth.** A kind of cotton cloth or calico manufactured in short pieces. Also a length or piece of such cloth.

**1545** [see LONG CLOTH]. **1641** HAKEWILL *Libertie Subj.* 93 The custom upon a short cloth was fourteene-pence, and.. a sack of Wool did commonly make foure short clothes. **1753** HANWAY *Trav.* (1762) I. v. lxxi. 322 Cloth exported to Turkey the five preceding years..short cloths.

**short-coat,** *sb.* [In sense 1, f. SHORT *a.* + COAT *sb.*; in sense 2 derived from SHORT-COAT *v.*]

**1.** A person wearing a short coat. Also *attrib.* in † **short-coat vicarage** (meaning obscure).

**1649** BLITHE *Eng. Improv.* xii. 68 Where those great Impropriations are that devoure all the Profits, and have all to a short-coat Vicaridge. **1847** DISRAELI *Tancred* II. x, There was a strong feeling against the shortcoats [*i.e.* 'two tall footmen in short coats'].

**2.** *pl.* The garments in which an infant is clothed when the long clothes are laid aside.

**short-coat,** *v.* [f. SHORT *adv.* + COAT *v.* Cf. quot. 1650 under COAT *v.* 1.]

*trans.* To dress (an infant) in short clothes.

**1799** UNDERWOOD *Dis. Childhood* (ed. 4) III. 107 It will be adviseable, in order to inure infants to the air, that they be short-coated as early as the season of the year will permit. **1888** MAUDE BRADSHAW *Ind. Outfits* 32 It is best to short-coat babies in the Plains, after the first month. **1897** *Allbutt's Syst. Med.* III. 746 Infants when first short-coated often suffer in this way [from chill].

**b.** *fig.* in *passive.* To emerge from babyhood.

**1890** *Athenæum* 22 Feb. 238/1 The North-West Territories are waiting to be shortcoated.

Hence **short-coating** *vbl. sb.* used *collect.* for the various articles required when a child is short-coated.

**1895** *Stores Price List.*

**short-coated,** *a.* [f. SHORT *a.* + COAT *sb.* + -ED[2].]

**a.** Wearing a short coat. **b.** Of animals: Having a short coat as opposed to 'shaggy'.

**1813** MOORE *Post Bag* vi. 12, I [*sc.* a Turk in London] saunter on—the admiration Of this short-coated population. **1890** *Daily News* 10 Dec. 2/3 One of Mr. Smith's short-coated prize-winners.

**'short-comer.** One who comes short of duty.

**1865** W. G. PALGRAVE *Arabia* I. 410 The undevout short-comer is quickened into new fervour. **1868** H. LAW *Beacons* (1869) 131 As sanctified, they are miserable shortcomers.

**'shortcoming,** *vbl. sb.* [f. phrase *to come short*: see SHORT *adv.* 8 c, d. In 1847 censured by De Quincey as a Scotticism (*Protestantism* Wks. 1858 VIII. 89).]

The condition or fact of coming short; an instance of this. **a.** Failure to come up to a standard of excellence or to fulfil a duty; a defect. (Chiefly in *plural*). **b.** Failure to reach the required or expected amount, a deficiency.

*c* **1680** M'WARD *Contendings* (1723) 222 (Jam.), A just sensibleness..of our unworthy shortcomings. **1801** *Farmer's Mag.* Nov. 441 A short-coming of the proprietor's rent. **1837** CARLYLE *Fr. Rev.* III. VI. vi, He sounded..the note of Jacobinism, to hide past shortcomings. **1845** GLADSTONE *Glean.* (1879) II. 10 He had no eye for our faults and shortcomings. **1848** DICKENS *Dombey* lviii, There were no shortcomings anywhere, in anything but money. **1860** —— *Lett.* (1880) II. 113 The shortcomings of representative government. **1885** SWINBURNE *Victor Hugo* vi. (1886) 84 Such..shortcomings as will probably be detected in a work which at least lays no claim to completeness. **1889** *Standard* 17 Apr., How can this shortcoming be made good? **1898** L. STEPHEN *Stud. Biogr.* I. iv. 106 A confession of shortcoming.

So **'shortcoming** *a.*, defective.

**1889** BRYDALL *Art in Scot.* xii. 246 His works are carefully finished and drawn, but rather shortcoming in colour.

**short copy,** *v. nonce-wd.* [f. *short copy*, SHORT *a.* 8.] *trans.* To make a short copy of.

**1891** OLVER & O'REILLY *Imperial Tariff* 262 The landing books should be sent in..short copied as far as possible.

**short crust.** In sense b also **shortcrust.** [SHORT *a.* 20 a.] **a.** A crust of pastry made short with butter or other fat. **b.** (Also ***shortcrust pastry.***) A type of short pastry.

**1747** MRS. GLASSE *Art of Cookery* iv. 60 Make a short Crust, roll it thick. **1868** M. JEWRY *Warne's Model Cookery* 411/1 (*heading*) To make a short crust with dripping. **1951** *Good Housek. Home Encycl.* 586/1 Lard is suitable for shortcrust and flaky pastry. **1970** SIMON & HOWE *Dict. Gastronomy* 290/2 Shortcrust (basically 1 lb. flour to ½ lb. fat) is crumbly when cooked.

**short cut, short-cut,** *sb.*[1] [CUT *sb.*[2] 16.]

† **1.** A short passage or journey. Also *fig. Obs.*

*a* **1568** ASCHAM *Scholem.* II. (Arb.) 151 In the short cut of a priuate letter..small shew of difference can appeare. **1579** LYLY *Euphues* (Arb.) 198 If the winde sende him a short cut you shall in the second part heare what newes he bringeth. **1631** MAY tr. *Barclay's Mirr. Mindes* I. 270 From thence is but a short cut to Swethland. **1673** *S' too him Bayes* 25 Both sayls and reason insufficient for so short a cut.

**2.** A path or a course taken between two places which is shorter than the ordinary road. (In early use almost exclusively *shorter* or *shortest cut.*)

**1618** BOLTON *Florus* (1636) 169 Out-stripping the Enemy by shortest cuts [L. *occupatis compendiis*]. **1643** TRAPP *Comm. Gen.* xxxiv. 21 They should take a shorter cut to Dan and Bethel. *a* **1774** GOLDSM. *Surv. Exp. Philos.* (1776) II. 279 [A ray of light] takes a shorter cut in passing through diamond than glass. **1796** MME. D'ARBLAY *Camilla* I. 309 The baronet..declared that if there was a short cut, they should not part company, for he could walk it himself. **1820** KEATS *Cap & Bells* xxiii, He 'knew the city', as we say, of yore, And for short cuts and turns, was nobody knew more. **1889** *Spectator* 14 Dec. 837 Those for making ocean short-cuts behind the backs of peninsulas and angles of land. **1890** 'R. BOLDREWOOD' *Col. Reformer* (1891) 126 By-tracks and short cuts, by..which the road was materially shortened.

**b.** *fig.* A compendious method of attaining some object.

**1589** MARLOWE *Faustus* 287 Therefore the shortest cut for coniuring Is stoutly to abiure the Trinitie. **1637** RUTHERFORD *Lett.* (1862) I. 208 He is the short cut (as we used to say) and the nearest way to an outgate of all your burdens. **1790** BURKE *Fr. Rev.* 246 The degenerate fondness for tricking short-cuts, and little fallacious facilities, that has in so many parts of the world created governments with arbitrary powers. **1807** SOUTHEY *Espriella's Lett.* III. 314 In England they..have made many short cuts to philosophy for the accommodation of ladies and gentlemen. **1873** SPENCER *Study Sociol.* (1882) 402 Between infancy and maturity there is no shortcut by which there may be avoided the tedious process of growth and development. **1891** KIPLING *Light that Failed* vii. (1900) 115 What will you give me if I tell you a sure short-cut to everything you want.

**c.** *attrib.*

**1885** *Daily Tel.* 10 Sept. (Cass.), Men who have been to the University..have been known before now to take the short-cut road to their meaning which swearing unhappily supplies. **1903** *Critic* XLIII. 382/2 To make war the short-cut solution of the existing difficulties.

**short cut, short-cut,** *a.* and *sb.*[2] [CUT *pa. pple.*]

**A.** *adj.* Cut to a short length. (See SHORT *a.* I. i.)

**1596** NASHE *Saffron Walden* Ep. Ded. B 1, Content..to trauerse the subtile distinctions twixt short cut and long taile. **1786** *Jackson's Oxf. Jrnl.* 8 July 2/3 A grey Poney, with a short cut Tail, broken winded. **1873** SPON *Workshop Rec.* Ser. I. 83/2 The curls or knots [should be] formed by turning a short-cut hair pencil.

**B.** *sb.* (*ellipt.*)

**1.** A kind of tobacco.

**1789** G. PARKER *Life's Painter* (*c* 1800) 140 Part swig'd barley swipes, As short-cut they were smoking. **1839** 'J. FUME' *Paper on Tobacco* 119 About forty years ago short cut was the favourite with those for whom the common shag was too strong.

**2.** A ham that is cut short or round.

**1906** *Times* 2 June 12/6 A parcel of hams, 'short-cuts' called in the trade.

**'short-cut,** *v.* Also **shortcut** and as two words. [f. SHORT CUT *sb.*[1]]

**1.** *trans.* **a.** To overtake by taking a short cut. **b.** To traverse by a short cut.

**1915** J. LONDON *Let.* 26 Jan. (1966) 443 If I could short-cut men to such success, I'd quit writing for a living. *a* **1951** H. G. LAMOND in *Austral. Short Stories* (1951) 211 But he short-cut her on one circle. **1960** *Times* 19 Sept. 3/5 An attempt to short-cut the way to success.

**2.** *intr.* To take a short-cut. Also const. *it.*

**1925** M. ARLEN *May Fair* 210 You'll go short-cutting alone... I've heard enough tales about Carmion Wood to last me a life-time. **1933** J. STEINBECK *Red Pony* in *N. Amer. Rev.* Nov. 425/1 They crossed a stubble-field to shortcut to the barn. **1960** E. BOWEN *Time in Rome* v. 137 He rushed up ..the Janiculum hill, short-cutting from level to level. **1970** K. GILES *Death in Church* i. 11 He knows London... He's short-cutting it towards the South Bank all right. **1977** *S. Wales Echo* 18 Jan., 'This way,' says Dai Dogs. 'We'll short cut.' The short cut is through Abertridwr's dead pit.

So **'short-cutting** *ppl. a.*

**1901** KIPLING *Kim* xiii. 330 Though low-lying clouds might be a hindrance to a short-cutting stranger, they made no earthly difference to a thoughtful man.

**short-'dated,** *a.* [f. SHORT *a.* + DATE *sb.* + -ED[2].]

† **1.** Lasting a short time. *Obs.*

**1632** BP. H. KING *Poems, Elegy on Gust. Adolphus* (1843) 69 Who, clos'd in thy cold lead, Dost from thy self a mournful lecture read Of Mans short-dated glory. **1637** RUTHERFORD *Lett.* (1664) 253 Clipped and short-dated crosses.

**2.** Of bills, notes of hand, etc.: Falling due at an early date.

**1815** SCOTT *Guy M.* v, Duncan Robb, the grocer at Kippletringan, who has aye a sum to make up, and either wants ready money, or a short-dated bill. **1900** *Westm. Gaz.* 3 Jan. 9/1 It was thought the Government might have allotted shorter-dated paper now, seeing the unpropitious rates.

† **'shorted,** *a. Obs. rare.* [f. SHORT *v.* + -ED[1].] Shortened, cut short.

**1483** *Cath. Angl.* 338/1 Schortyd, *correptus, breuiatus.* **1769** GOLDSM. *Hist. Rome* (1786) I. 208 The Roman General ..marched directly by the shorted road.

**shorten** ('ʃɔːt(ə)n), *v.* [f. SHORT *a.* + -EN[5].]

**1.** *trans.* To make shorter, to diminish the length of, to abridge, curtail.

**a.** With reference to duration.

***to shorten*** (a person's) ***life***: in early use sometimes † to kill.

**1513** MORE *Rich. III* (1883) 6 The king his brother (whose life hee loked that euil dyete shoulde shorten). **1614** SIR H. SPELMAN *Law Terms* xvii. (1684) 44 Trinity-Term was altred and shortned by the Statute of 32 Hen. 8 chap. 21. **1697** DRYDEN *Virg. Georg.* I. 420 When Autumn weighs The Year, and adds to Nights, and shortens Days. **1733** DUCHESS QUEENSBERRY *Let. to Swift* 21 Feb., As you can-not lengthen your friend's days, I must beg you, in your own words, not to shorten your own. **1824** MISS L. M. HAWKINS *Annaline* II. 79 [They] could not make any excuse for shortening their stay at the castle. **1849** MACAULAY *Hist. Eng.* v. I. 665 She calmly disposed the straw about her in such a manner as to shorten her sufferings. **1885** *Spectator* 25 July 978/2 We may blame him for shortening a valuable life by inflicting needless hardships upon himself.

**b.** To make to appear shorter; to beguile (time, a journey, etc.) by conversation or pastime.

**1579** MONTGOMERIE *Misc. P.* xlviii. 216 With *Pro* and *Contra*, so shortnit we the way. **1663** PATRICK *Parable Pilgrim* xxviii. (1687) 323 In such delightful and useful talk as this they beguiled the time, and shortned the length of the ways. **1733** FIELDING *Quix. Eng.* I. vii, When a lover suffers his mistress to come first to the place of appointment, he cannot blame any innocent amusement with which she would shorten his absence. **1829** SCOTT *Anne of G.* xii, The tale, which had shortened the way in so interesting a manner. **1867** *All Year Round* 13 July 56/2 Narrations of adventures met with on previous tramps..serve to shorten the road.

**c.** With reference to compositions, speeches, discussions, etc.

**1530** PALSGR. 704/2 Shorten your mater, for it is to longe for this audyence. **1672–5** COMBER *Comp. Temple* (1702) 35 But (as is done in our Common Prayer) he shortned it because of his weakness. **1709** STEELE *Tatler* No. 107 ¶7 To shorten my Story, she was married to another. **1850** W. R. WILLIAMS *Relig. Progr.* iii. (1854) 50 The Jesuits..who lengthened the creed and shortened the commandments. **1912** J. M. THOMSON *Reg. Mag. Sig. Scot. 1306–1424*, Pref. 8 The custom grew up of shortening it [a list of witnesses] to *ut in aliis cartis* [etc.].

**d.** With reference to linear measurement. † ***to shorten up***: to contract, draw together.

† ***to shorten by the head***: to behead (cf. SHORT *a.* 2, SHORT *v.* 2 c).

**1530** PALSGR. 704/2 A tall man may shorten hym selfe so moche that he shall nat seme so hye as a childe. **1555** EDEN *Decades* (Arb.) 273 They had shortened the course of the landes he had discouered. **1568** GRAFTON *Chron.* II. 662 There his body was shortned, by the length of his hed. **1610** SHAKS. *Temp.* IV. i. 260 Goe, charge my Goblins that they.. shorten vp their sinewes With aged Cramps. **1791** G. WALLIS *Motherby's Med. Dict.* (ed. 3) s.v. *Musculus*, A muscle..can contract itself so as to be shortened one third. **1798** SOPHIA LEE *Canterb. T., Yng. Lady's T.* II. 106 The tour..they must now necessarily shorten. **1860** TYNDALL *Glac.* I. xvi. 107 This we crossed in order to shorten our way. **1883** *Manch. Guard.* 15 Oct. 5/7 To shorten the course of the river from London Bridge to Gravesend by 2¼ miles. **1912** T. D. ATKINSON *Cathedr.* 179 Shortening the total length of the church by about 37 feet.

**e.** *fig.* In Biblical phrase, ***to shorten the arm*** or ***hand of***: to limit the power of.

**1535** COVERDALE *Num.* xi. 23 The Lorde sayde vnto Moses: Is the Lordes hande shortened then? **1583** STUBBES *Anat. Abus.* II. (1882) 97 Doe they thinke that his arme is shortened, or his power weakened? **1645** HARWOOD *Loyal Subj. Retiring-room* 28 Why should we think his hand will be shortned towards any of us? **1647** TRAPP *Comm. Rev.* xx. 3 God will shorten your hand of cruelty. **1833** LYTE *Hymn, 'When at thy Footstool,'* Thine arm can never shorten'd be.

**f.** To diminish in working length; to tighten (a rein), in quot. *fig.*; to hold (a weapon) nearer to the middle, in order to deal a more effective blow or thrust.

**1597** HOOKER *Eccl. Pol.* v. xliii. §4 They shorten somewhat the reynes of their censure. **1821** SCOTT *Kenilw.* iv, He closed with him, shortening his own sword at the same time, with the purpose of despatching him. **1857** HUGHES *Tom Brown* I. ix, Shortening the rod in his hand, and preparing for battle. **1888** F. HUME *Mme. Midas* I. xii. 84 Villiers.. shortened his stick to give her a blow on the head. **1898** *Encycl. Sport* II. 298/1 (Rowing) *Shorten oars,* to draw the handle of the oar in-board, in order to avoid an obstacle in the river, or to pass through a narrow place such as a lock.

**g.** With reference to phonetic quantity.

**1589** PUTTENHAM *Eng. Poesie* II. xii[i]. (Arb.) 131 He that first shortned *ca,* in this word *cano,* and made long *tro,* in *troia,* and *o,* in *oris,* might haue aswell done the contrary. **1861** PALEY *Aeschylus* (ed. 2) *Eumen.* 996 *note,* Homer shortens the α in δαΐδος. **1871** ROBY *Lat. Gram.* I. II. xviii. §/583 The imperative-forms in Plautus and Terence often shortened the final vowel.

†**h.** To diminish in number or quantity. *Obs.*

**1598** DALLINGTON *Method Trav.* L 2 b, The Nobilitie of France is exceedingly shortned in number. **1611** *Second Maiden's Tragedy* 2385 (Malone Soc.) Thy glories shalbe shortend.

**i.** *Hort.* To cut back in pruning. Also *to shorten in, back.*

**1706** LONDON & WISE *Retir'd Gard.* I. II. ii. 110 We.. only shorten the young shoots. **1842** LOUDON *Suburban Hort.* 457 The short lateral shoots, which are shortened in at the winter pruning to two or three buds. *Ibid.* 475 The shoots on the upper or farther extended branches may be shortened back to half or one-third of their lengths.

**j.** To clip (coin).

**1857** BORROW *Rom. Rye* xli, My grandfather.. sometimes shortened money, and at other times passed off what had been shortened by other gentry.

**2.** *intr.* To grow shorter. **a.** To diminish in length (either of duration or measurement).

**1568** GRAFTON *Chron.* II. 369 Thus euer the time passed, and the dayes shortened. **1663** GERBIER *Counsel* 36 The third story of Columns would shorten so much. **1676** MARVELL *Mr. Smirke* 21, I am glad to see my labour shorten. **1821** LAMB *Elia* Ser. I. *New Yr.'s Eve,* In proportion as the years both lessen and shorten, I set more count upon their periods. **1850** MISS WARNER *Wide Wide World* xxxvi, Ellen's face shortened considerably. **1899** E. E. HALE *Lowell & Friends* ii. 17 As the days shortened, morning prayers came later.

†**b.** To become less diffuse. *Obs. rare*$^{-1}$.

**1727** WODROW *Corr.* (1843) III. 299 After this interruption, Mr Grant shortened.

†**c.** Of the breath: To become shorter.

**1765** J. BROWN *Chr. Jrnl.* 78 My breath shortens; my pulse beats high.

**d.** Of a price, odds: To be lowered or lessened.

**1884** H. SMART *Post to Finish* xliv, The odds shortened rapidly. Still the fielders continued to lay the lessening price. **1891** N. GOULD *Double Event* xl. 302 The horse's price shortened. **1913** *Engl. Rev.* May 301 To use the bookmaker's parlance, the prices shorten somewhat.

**3.** *trans.* †**a.** To hold in check, restrain. *Obs.*

**1596** SPENSER *State Irel.* Wks. (Globe) 663/2 They should not be able once to styrre or murmure, but that it shoulde be knowen, and they shortened according to theyr demerites. **1700** DRYDEN *Fables* Ded. B 2 b, Here, where the Subject is so fruitful.. I am shorten'd by my Chain.

†**b.** To render (an intention) ineffectual. (Cf. SHORT *v.* 5.) *Obs.*

**1605** SHAKS. *Lear* IV. vii. 9 Yet to be knowne shortens my made intent.

**c.** To keep from the attainment *of.*

**1837** CARLYLE *Fr. Rev.* I. III. vii, Whereon the Parlement, shortened of its prey, would look with yellow despair. **1850** BLACKIE *Æschylus* I. 234 Of thy due honours shortened.

†**4.** To cause to go short, to supply insufficiently. Const. *of, in. Obs.*

**1599** *Life Sir T. More* in Wordsw. *Eccl. Biog.* (1853) II. 51 So shortened of money.. he was rid of many occasions that hinder good proceedings. **1621** R. COCKS *Diary* (Hakl. Soc.) II. 149, I knew they had.. shortned thenglish in all they demanded, contrary to the kinges promis.

**5.** *Naut.* **a.** *to shorten sail(s*: to take in some of the sails of a vessel in order to slacken speed.

**1627** CAPT. SMITH *Seaman's Gram.* ix. 44 As you approach the shore, shorten your sailes. **1748** *Anson's Voy.* I. iv. 35 We shortned sail for her to come up with us. **1805** NELSON in Nicolas *Disp.* (1846) VII. 107 The Ships of the Fleet are directed, particularly in the night, to shorten sail. **1884** *Times* (weekly ed.) 25 Feb. 15/3 Sail is being shortened all round.

*transf.* **1824** SCOTT *St. Ronan's* xxx, 'You are a gay old gentleman!' said Jekyl, relaxing his pace; 'and if we must be fellow-travellers.. I must even shorten sail for you.'

**b.** *to shorten in*: to heave in (the cable) so that a shorter length remains overboard. Also *absol.*

**1854** G. B. RICHARDSON *Univ. Code* v. (ed. 12) 1284 Shorten in cable. *Ibid.* 4981 Shorten in tow-lines. **1867** SMYTH *Sailor's Word-bk.* s.v., *Shorten in,* when alluding to the anchor, by heaving in cable.

**6.** To make 'short' or friable. Also (of manure) *intr.* for *refl.*

**1733** W. ELLIS *Chiltern & Vale Farm.* 24 The Chalk or Sand will shorten and crumble the Clay before the Plough. *Ibid.* 30 They as carefully take care to clamp up their Yard Dungs.. in order to rot and shorten against the next Wheat or Barly Season. **1883** *Harper's Mag.* Apr. 659/1 The crust being shortened with.. suet.

**7.** To put (a child) into short clothes.

**1871** *Punch* 9 Dec. 240/1 An authentic fragment of the blue sash he wore the day he was shortened. **1897** HALL CAINE *Christian* I. i. 6 At the end of the first year she wrote: 'I have shortened our darling'.

Hence **'shortened, 'shortening** *ppl. adjs.*

*c* **1000** *Sax. Leechd.* III. 252 Se sceortiȝenda dæȝ hæfð liðran ȝewederu þonne se langienda dæȝ. **1597** A. M. tr. *Guillemeau's Fr. Chirurg.* 57/3 The dissease of a shortened tunge. **1621** G. SANDYS *Ovid's Met.* IX. (1626) 194 Her shortning curles scarce hang beneath her eares. **1645** MILTON *Passion* i, In Wintry solstice like the shortn'd light Soon swallow'd up in dark and long out living night. **1700** DRYDEN *Pal. & Arc.* III. 509 That none shall dare With shortned Sword to stab in closer War. **1785** BURNS *Cotter's Sat. Nt.* ii, The short'ning winter-day is near a close. **1805–17** R. JAMESON *Char. Min.* (ed. 3) 199 Shortened heavy-spar. **1825** SCOTT *Talism.* xxii, His red and inflamed eye, his heated hand, and his shortened respiration. **1857** KINGSLEY *Two Y. Ago* ii, Ships.. driving fast to the eastward with shortened sail. **1874** GLADSTONE *Corr. Ch. & Relig.* (1910) I. 397 The Bills for Clerical Subscription.. and the Shortened Services. **1887** RUSKIN *Præterita* II. 263 In the shortening days of 1845. **1913** CHESTERTON *Victorian Age* 30 Tom Moore,.. a shortened shadow of Lord Byron.

**'shortener.** [-ER[1].] One who or something which shortens (in various senses of the vb.).

**1565** J. PHILLIP *Patient Grissell* 715 (Malone Soc.) Oh dyrfull daye, oh haples hap, oh shortner of my yeares. *a* **1636** G. WILLIAMS *Best Relig.* viii. 183 Sin is an epitomizer or shortner of every thing. *c* **1710** SWIFT *Inq. Behav. Queen's Last Ministry* ii, The gout, which is not usually reckoned a shortener of life. **1878** SPURGEON *Treas. Dav.* Ps. cix. 8. V. 183 Sin the great shortener of human life.

**shortening** ('ʃɔːt(ə)nɪŋ), *vbl. sb.* [-ING[1].]

**1.** The action or an act of the verb SHORTEN.

*a* **1542** WYATT *Poems, Epitaph Sir T. Gravener* 12 No sickness could him from it let; Which was the shortening of his days. **1603** KNOLLES *Hist. Turks* (1638) 160 Hee should neuer seeke to attempt any thing to the shortning or hurt of his Grandfathers life or empire. **1796** C. MARSHALL *Garden.* xii. (1813) 149 The rule for shortening is this: Consider the strength of the tree [etc.]. **1868** *Rep. U.S. Commissioner Agric.* (1869) 249 As in the case of shortening back to induce the growth of fruit spurs in the apple tree. **1886** MAGEE in *Contemp. Rev.* Jan. 15 Oaths of allegiance, supremacy and abjuration have shrunk, after many lengthenings and shortenings, into the brief and simple form [etc.].

**2.** *concr.* A fat or oil used to make pastry, etc., short.

**1796** A. SIMMONS *Amer. Cookery* 34 *Loaf Cakes* No. 2 Rub 4 pound of sugar, 3 and a half pound of shortning, (half butter and half lard) into 9 pound of flour. **1823** MOOR *Suffolk Words, Shortning,* suet or butter, in cake, crust, or bread. **1854** SEBA SMITH *Way down East* 333 We have n't got a bit of shortnin' in the house. **1883** *Cassell's Fam. Mag.* Nov. 758/2 The very reason for boiling the 'shortening' with water is that by liquefying the fat a minimum quantity of water can be used. **1970** SIMON & HOWE *Dict. Gastronomy* 347/2 *Shortening,* a culinary term used more in the United States than in Britain and it applies to fats used in making breads, cakes, pastry etc. All fats, even oils, come under this nomenclature and are used because they make mixtures 'short' or tender. **1980** *Blair & Ketchum's Country Jrnl.* Oct. 34/3, 2 tablespoons shortening.

**shorter** ('ʃɔːtə(r)). *slang.* [f. SHORT *v.* + -ER[1].] A clipper of coin.

**1857** BORROW *Rom. Rye* xli, My grandfather was a shorter, and my father was a smasher. **1864** *Hotten's Slang Dict.* s.v., From a crown piece a shorter could gain 5*d.*

†**'shortestness.** *Obs. rare*$^{-1}$. [f. *shortest,* superl. of SHORT *a.* + -NESS.] Minimal length.

**1674** N. FAIRFAX *Bulk & Selv.* 32 And though a point be the least of boak, and a nowt the shortest of time, yet they may speak everlastingness and allfillingness.. for all their shortestness and leastness, as well as the longest or the biggest.

**'short-fall.** Also short fall, shortfall. [From the phrase *to fall short*: see FALL *v.* 97.] A falling short; the amount by which a supply falls short, shortage, deficiency. Also, a decline; a shortcoming, a fault; a deficit, a gap; a loss. Also *attrib.*

**1895** *Johannesburg Standard* 23 Nov. 5/2 The best that could be expected this year from the harvest was an eight months' crop, and the shortfall would be some million-and-a-half bags of grain. **1906** *Macm. Mag.* Aug. 793 From the very beginning the shortfall in the labour-supply had been the principal factor in the slow development of these colonies. **1928** *London Mercury* May 4 We notice in Mr. Churchill's Budget Speech the repeated use of the word 'shortfall'. The word is used to indicate the difference between the amount estimated and the amount received, when the difference is on the wrong side. **1941** W. S. CHURCHILL *2nd World War* (1950) III. 748 We cannot afford losses on that scale in view of the short fall of the American bomber programme. **1953** *Economist* 3 Jan. 35/1 The Exchequer return as a whole.. showed a deficit of £951 million, in contrast with one of £602 million in the first nine months of 1951/52. These comparisons, moreover, understate the extent of the shortfall. **1960** *Times Rev. Industry* Mar. 99/3 The report estimates that the changes in American shares of these markets alone cost just over $500m. in 1958. This total is called a shortfall, for want of a better name, but is the equivalent value in 1958 of the net change in the United States share of these six markets for a list of 45 classes of manufactured goods. **1960** *Catholic Herald* 1 Apr. 3/3 He has.. no illusions about her [*sc.* France's] immediate shortfall from that high level of being. **1960** *Washington Post* 16 Nov. A 16 West Germany is now running a foreign payment surplus about half the size of the country's deficit, which in view of the disparity in gross product suggests a considerable shortfall by the Federal republic in the assumption of common obligations. **1966** *Economist* 28 May 970/3 Lord Moran's apology for his [*sc.* Churchill's] shortfalls in world and domestic decisions is based too often on a too simple fallacy. **1969** *Times* 14 Feb. 25/4 The shortfall between exports and imports in January was $216m. **1971** 'D. HALLIDAY' *Dolly & Doctor Bird* ii. 23 A scene of continuous short-fall pandemonium. **1976** *Ann. Rep. Manpower Services Comm. 1975–76* iii. 25/2 To make good the shortfall in employers' recruitment into long-term training occupations ITBs made available 'training awards' where the level of recruitment overall into long-term training was likely to fall below the particular industry's long-term needs. **1981** *Times* 4 Aug. 16/5 Half year figures from Standard Telephone & Cables revealed a profits shortfall.

†**'shortford.** *Law. Obs.* [Appears in med.L. and AF. documents as *sortfort, shortford, shartfort, shatford, schotford*; of obscure origin.

It is noteworthy that in the *Statutum de Gaveleto in London* (prob. 13th c.) a tenement forfeited to the lord 'for default of service' is said to be designated by a term which appears under the various forms *forshard, forshot, forthot, forsshott* (the early printed edd. have *forschoc, forchoc, forschoke*): see *Stat. of the Realm* (Record ed.) I. 222 and *Liber Albus* (Rolls) I. 63, 469. Some of these forms look like transpositions of the syllables of *shortford, shartfort,* etc.; but it is possible that they arose from progressive corruption of A.F. *forclot* = *forclos* pa. pple. of *forclore* to FORECLOSE.]

An ancient process by which the lord could obtain possession of a tenement when the tenant had failed to render the services due, and there were no effects on which a distraint could be levied.

**1291** in G. Oliver *Hist. Exeter* (1861) 309 Adjudicatum est ei sortfort. **1335** in Izacke *Antiq. Exeter* (1677) 48 Adjudicatum fuit Decano & Capitulo beati Petri Exoniensis quoddam Tenementum scituatum in vico Australi Civitatis Exoniensis secundum Consuetudinem Civitatis prædictæ & dicitur Shortford. **1419** *Liber Albus* (Rolls) I. 186 Solonc le jugement appelle 'Shartfort' [*v.r.* Shatford (*Cowel's Law Dict.* 1727)] par custome de la cite suisdite. ? *a* **1500** in G. Oliver *Hist. Exeter* (1861) 309 *note,* Schotford, quod gallicè dicitur forclot. **1701** *Cowel's Interpreter* (ed. Kennett) s.v. [cites Izacke].

**short-grained,** *a.* [f. SHORT *a.*; cf. GRAINED *ppl. a.*[2]]

**1.** Of wood: Having a short fibre rendering it liable to snap easily. Hence *transf.* of a bone.

**1670–1** NARBOROUGH *Jrnl.* in *Acc. Sev. Late Voy.* I. (1694) 107 White Cedar and such like Wood.. are very heavy and short-grained, and will break short. **1776** G. SEMPLE *Building in Water* 86 Bog Oak Timber is.. dozed and short grained. **1835–6** *Todd's Cycl. Anat.* I. 441/1 The presence of .. phosphate of lime rendered the bone short-grained.

**2.** Of rice: having a relatively short grain.

**1953** N. HEATON *Cassell's Cooking Dict.* 422 Rice may be short-grained.., or long-grained and brightly polished.. The former is used chiefly for puddings. **1978** J. PASSMORE *All Asian Cookbk.* (1979) 8 Chinese like their rice reasonably dry, short-grained.

**shorthand** ('ʃɔːthænd). Also **short hand** (*rare*), **short-hand.** [f. SHORT *a.* + HAND *sb.*]

**a.** A method of speedy writing by means of the substitution of contractions or arbitrary signs or symbols for letters, words, etc., brachygraphy, stenography.

**1636** *Jeffrey Hudson's New Yeeres Gift* title-p., With a Letter as it was penned in short-hand. **1639** MAYNE *City Match* I. iii, Shall I not learn Arithmetic too, sir, and Short-hand. **1724** R. FALCONER *Voy.* (1769) 98 His Journals were mostly taken in Short-Hand. **1864** *Soc. Sci. Rev.* 220 A species of shorthand was practised in the time of Cicero. **1909** *Athenæum* 13 Mar. 1/3 The training includes Indexing, Shorthand, Type-writing, Stenotypy.

**b.** *transf.* and *fig.*

**1697** COLLIER *Ess. Mor. Subj.* II. (1709) 126 Tis the Short-hand of the mind and crowds a great deal into a little space. **1801** BUSBY *Dict. Mus.* p. xxxii, These abbreviations form a musical Brachygraphy, or Short Hand. **1827** HARE *Guesses* Ser. I. (1873) 4 To address the prejudices of our hearers is to argue with them in short-hand. **1894** H. DRUMMOND *Ascent of Man* 232 To save time the objects were drawn in shorthand—a couple of dashes for the limbs and one across, as in the Chinese for man. **1897** KIPLING *Capt. Cour.* v. 124 The *We're Here* rang her bell thrice, using sea shorthand. **1931** E. A. ROBERTSON *Four Frightened People* ii. 57 Arnold Ainger spoke exactly the same language as we did.. It is possible to talk from the first in mental shorthand with such an acquaintance. **1960** N. MITFORD *Don't tell Alfred* xiv. 158 Americans.. need the dissertation; the kind of shorthand that we talk would be useless to them. **1970** *Guardian* 10 July 10/6 'Oxfash' is undergraduate shorthand for the establishment of councillors, planners, shopkeepers, and dons.

**c.** *attrib.* as in ***shorthand clerk, minute, note, notebook, pad, report, reporter, teacher, writer, writing***; †**short-hand-man,** a short-hand writer; **shorthand typist,** one who takes down dictation in shorthand and then types out the text.

**1647** J. BIRKENHEAD *Assembly-Man* (1662–3) 17, I admire the *Short-hand-men, who have the patience to write from his Mouth. **1682** OWTRAM *Serm.* A 2 b, They were taken from the author by a Short-hand-man. **1822–29** *Good's Study Med.* (ed. 3) I. 420 Copying my *short-hand minutes of medical lectures. **1709** *Female Tatler* No. 4/2, I took *Short-hand-Notes. **1903** G. B. SHAW *Man & Superman* I. 2 He has no secretary with a *shorthand notebook. **1977** A. MORICE *Scared to Death* xxiii. 154 A single page of lined paper, perforated at the top and obviously torn from a shorthand notebook. **1960** C. MORRIS *Unloved* 463 Janet is making notes on a *shorthand pad. **1977** M. BABSON *Lord Mayor of Death* iv. 36 The recording officer began noting the words in his shorthand pad. **1831** D. E. WILLIAMS *Sir T. Lawrence* I. 401 The following is the *short-hand report of his evidence. **1881** 'MARK TWAIN' *Lett. to Publishers* (1967) 147 A *short-hand reporter to travel with us in the spring. **1887** LD. ROSEBERY in *Standard* 27 Sept. 2/4 The first authorised shorthand reporter in a Court of Law. *a* **1704** T. BROWN *Laconics* Wks. 1711 IV. 12 'Tis wisely done..of a *Short-hand teacher [to live next door] to a Meeting-house. **1901** *Phonetic Jrnl.* 24 Aug. 541 To a large extent the occupation of the *shorthand-typist has hitherto been synonymous with the lady typist. **1926** I. PITMAN *Dictation Practice in Bus. Corr.* Pref. p. i, In addition to business correspondence, the shorthand-typist is frequently called upon to complete forms. **1973** J. R. L. ANDERSON *Death on Rocks* i. 21 She had worked as a shorthand typist. *a* **1734** NORTH *Exam.* III. viii. §76 (1740) 642 The Party Men attended with their *Short-hand Writers at their Elbows, to take what might incauteously..slip from the Mouths of the Judges, for Matter of Accusation. **1904** SPENCER *Autobiog.* II. 292 The amanuensis was a short-hand-writer. **1922** JOYCE *Ulysses* 140 There was not even one shorthandwriter in the hall. **1964** T. L. KINSEY *Audio-Typing & Electric Typewriters* ii. 7 Any audio-typist can transcribe audio-dictation—the dictation is never lost, as can be the case with written notes recorded in an absent shorthand-writer's notebook. **1641** WILKINS *Mercury* xii. (1707) 52 This *Short-hand Writing is now so ordinary in Practice [etc.]. **1747** RICHARDSON *Clarissa* I. xii. 68 He is a complete master of shorthand writing.

**d.** quasi-*adj.* Of the nature of shorthand; compendious.

**1822** W. IRVING *Braceb. Hall* (1823) II. 26 Every new short-hand mode of doing things. **1844** DE QUINCEY *Logic Pol. Econ.* Pref. 8 A short-hand expression for the relation between the quantity offered for sale, and the quantity demanded. **1887** SAINTSBURY *Hist. Elizab. Lit.* vii. (1890) 275 The recourse to dumb show..looks like a kind of short-hand indication of scenes that might have been worked out.

Hence **'shorthand** *v.*, (*a*) *trans.*, to transcribe in shorthand; also *fig.*; (*b*) *intr.*, to use shorthand; †**'short-handed,** *a.*[1] competent to write shorthand; **'shorthander,** a writer of shorthand, a stenographer.

*a* **1658** CLEVELAND *Count. Com. Man* Poems (1677) 99 A new blew stockin'd Justice..with a short-handed Clerk, tack'd to the Rear of him to carry the Knapsack of his Understanding. **1738** THYER *Byrom's Rem.* (1856) II. I. 198 We arrive at Hartley's where we accidentally find a party of shorthanders. **1898** L. STEPHEN *Stud. Biogr.* I. iii. 86 The meetings of the shorthanders naturally took place at taverns. **1928** *John Blunt* 11 Aug. 1/3 (*heading*) Shorthand it! **1936** *Punch* 15 Jan. 60/1 All I wanted..was a secretary—just an ordinary girl who could shorthand and typewrite and answer a telephone and so on. **1975** *Times Lit. Suppl.* 28 Feb. 210/4 The urbanized cluster of inlets and coastal fringe the Venetians shorthanded as *La Dominante.* **1975** I. K. MARTIN *Regan & Manhattan File* 37 One of Broughton's silent colleagues had a notebook out, shorthanding Regan's words. **1977** *Monitor* (McAllen, Texas) 17 July 5F/6 'Shorthand' has also become quite popular in what is jocularly referred to in Hollywood as the 'creative community'. Ask a producer what his show is all about and he'll never say, 'I don't know.' He says instead, 'There's no way to shorthand that.'

**short-handed,** *a.*[2]

†**1.** ? Niggardly, mean; inefficient, ineffective.

**1622** MABBE tr. *Aleman's Guzman d'Alf.* II. 228 My Hostesse was not short, either handed, or witted. **1643** TUCKNEY *Balm of Gilead* 10 Our thoughts and hopes are too short sighted and handed to reach to all that salvation.

**2.** Lacking a full complement of 'hands', undermanned, understaffed.

**1794** NELSON 29 July in Nicolas *Disp.* (1845) I. 461 He would be satisfied with an indifferent Carpenter, but he could not with propriety go to sea without one: that he would not ask for any one in lieu of the other, but he was very short-handed. **1802** C. JAMES *Milit. Dict.* s.v. *Gun,* Ships that go to sea short-handed. **1897** MARY KINGSLEY *W. Africa* 202, I think the Ogowé Protestant mission sadly short-handed. **1912** TREVELYAN *Geo. III & Fox* I. v. 143 Ships..in far superior condition to his own short-handed and woefully provided vessels.

**b.** *spec.* in *Ice Hockey,* having fewer players on the ice than the opposing team because a penalty has been imposed; also, of a goal: scored while a team is short-handed.

**1939** R. F. VAUGHAN *Hockey* 364 *Short handed,* a team with one or more players in the penalty box. **1951** L. PERCIVAL *Hockey Handbk.* iv. 126/2 The fundamental weapons are..aggressive use of the body, getting the puck into the opposing defensive zone and keeping it there with five men up, forcing the game (even though shorthanded), and generally keeping the pace of the play high. **1969** *Official Rule Bk. & Schedule of National Hockey League 1969–70* 30 'Short-handed' means that the team must be below the numerical strength of its opponents on the ice at the time the goal is scored... Thus coincident minor penalties to both teams do *not* cause either side to be 'short-handed'. **1970** B. ORR *Orr on Ice* 96 Our men attempt to get the puck down to the other end and keep it, for even a possible shorthanded score. **1976** *Washington Post* 19 Apr. D3/1 Serge Savard scored a short-handed goal..to lead the Montreal Canadians to a 4-1 victory over the Chicago Black Hawks.

Hence **short'handedness.**

**1886** *Sat. Rev.* 6 Feb. 173 The combination [of offices] now, had Mr. Gladstone repeated it, would rather be forced on him by shorthandedness than taken of free-will.

†**'shorthead.** *Obs. rare*[−1]. In 4 ssorthede. [f. SHORT *a.* + -HEAD.] Shortness, brevity.

**1340** *Ayenb.* 99 Þis bene pasep alle opre ine þri þinges, ine dignete, in ssorthede, an ine guodnesse.

**shorthorn** ('ʃɔːthɔːn). [f. SHORT *a.* + HORN *sb.*]

**1. a.** One of a breed of cattle having short horns, originally bred in the north-eastern counties of England and now widely distributed over Great Britain and exported to other countries.

[**1826** SOUTHEY *Vind. Eccl. Angl.* 376 A Sockburn Short-horns from Grassy-hook which should put the best bull of Basan out of the field.] **1847** W. C. L. MARTIN *Ox* 61/2 They have succumbed before the superiority of the short-horns. **1911** B. HOLLAND *Life Duke Devonshire* I. ix. 213 A famous breed of shorthorns.

**b.** *attrib.*

**1862** BURTON *Bk. Hunter* I. 24 The pedigrees and physical characteristics recorded in stud-books and short-horn books. **1877** *Field* 17 Feb. 191/2 A society similar to the Shorthorn Society. **1909** *Carlisle Jrnl.* 27 Apr. 3/4 The splendid selection of shorthorn stirks.

**2.** A small round carrot belonging to the variety so called. Also *attrib.*

**1873** *Young Englishwoman* Oct. 499/1 There are several sorts of carrots: the earliest of which are generally termed short-horn. **1885** W. ROBINSON tr. *Vilmorin-Andrieux's Veg. Garden* 162 French Horn, or Early Short Horn, Carrot. .. Root almost globular, or slightly top-shaped. **1930** *Times Educ. Suppl.* 26 Apr. (Home & Classroom Suppl.) p. iv/3 Attend to the successional sowing of such crops as peas, spinach,..short-horn carrots, and lettuces. **1976** *Publishers Weekly* 19 Apr. 77/1 Such virtually unknown and unavailable items as perennial broccoli and short horn carrots.

**3.** *U.S. slang.* A new arrival, a greenhorn.

**1888** *Outing* Nov. 129/2 Besides a few snipe killed at a swamp called by Shorthorns 'cineky', from the Spanish *sienica,* we still depended upon Uncle Sam's subsistence stores for our daily bread. **1905** A. H. LEWIS *Sunset Trail* ii. 34 Don't let no shorthorn have my room. **1907** J. LONDON *Road* 173 Gay-cats are short-horns, *chechaquos,* new chums, or tenderfeet. A gay-cat is a new-comer on The Road who is man-grown, or, at least, youth-grown. **1942** BERREY & VAN DEN BARK *Amer. Thes. Slang* §456/1 Inexperienced person;..*shorthorn.*

**'short-horned,** *a.* Having short horns.

**1707** MORTIMER *Husb.* (1721) I. 227 The long-legg'd, short-horn'd Cow of the Dutch-breed. **1854** A. ADAMS, etc. *Man. Nat. Hist.* 254 Short-horned Flies.

**short-hose. a.** A kind of stocking reaching only a short distance up the leg. †**b.** Used as a rendering of CURT HOSE. *Obs.*

*a* **1513** FABYAN *Chron.* VII. ccxxii. 245 Robert, the eldest sone of Kynge Wyllyam, the whiche was surnamed Curthose, or Shorthose. **1530** PALSGR. 267/1 Schorte hose, *chausse courte.* **1880** J. HAY *Pike Co. Ballads* 61 Women that shorthose wore.

**Shorthursday,** obs. form of SHEER THURSDAY.

**shortia** ('ʃɔətɪə). [mod.L., f. the name of Charles W. *Short* (1794–1863), American botanist + -IA[1].] A small stemless evergreen herb of the genus so called, belonging to the family Diapensiaceæ, native to eastern North America and temperate parts of Asia, and bearing glossy leaves and white, pink, or blue flowers.

*Shortia galacifolia* was first described by Asa Gray from a dried specimen seen in Paris in 1839, which had been collected by André Michaux in 1798. The plant was not rediscovered in the wild until 1878.

[**1839** A. GRAY *Jrnl.* 8 Apr. in *Lett. A. Gray* (1893) I. iii. 178 As this is a good North American genus and comes from near Kentucky, it shall be christened Shortia, to which we will stand as godfathers.] **1877** *Field & Forest* Sept. 40 More than once I was greeted with the query 'Found "Shortey" yet?' By which I suppose was meant the mythical Shortia of Michaux, for which any enthusiastic young or old botanist is at liberty to hunt. **1948** *Hyde Park Shopper* (Chicago) 29 Apr. 8/5 The rare flower, shortia, is found only in the mountains of North Carolina and Japan. **1962** *Times* 8 Dec. 11/3 The shortias, too, do well in a moist..position. **1974** *Country Life* 12 Dec. 1896/1 American woodlanders, such as shortias, schizocodons,..and erythroniums especially revel in it [*sc.* beech leaf-mould].

**shortie,** var. SHORTY *sb.* and *a.*

**'shorting,** *vbl. sb.*[1] [f. SHORT *v.* + -ING[1].] The action of the vb. SHORT in various senses.

*a* **1390** tr. *St. Jerome's Prol. Jer.* in *Wyclif's Bible* (1850) III. 342 But more riȝt it were, to the shorting of euel, to putte mesure to the wodnesse of them bi my silence. *c* **1400** *Beryn* 209 That euery man shuld, by the wey, with a tale glade Al the hole company in shorting of þe wey. **1490** *Act 7 Hen. VII,* c. 1 §1 If any Captain..give not them their full Wages without shorting as he shall receive of the King.

**shorting,** *vbl. sb.*[2]: see SHORT *v.*[2]

**shortish** ('ʃɔːtɪʃ), *a.* [f. SHORT *a.* + -ISH.] Rather short. Also in comb.

**1800** SHAW *Gen. Zool.* I. 24 Shortish-tailed brown Baboon. **1817** J. SCOTT *Paris Revisit.* (ed. 4) 253 He was a stout, shortish, compactly-made fellow. **1835** HOOD *Poetry, Prose, & Worse* xxxvi, To tenants but shortish at present, When Michaelmas comes with its day. **1871** W. A. LEIGHTON *Lichen-Flora* 146 Laciniæ shortish. **1882** BLACKMORE *Christowell* xxii, A shortish old man with hedger's gloves on.

**shortite** ('ʃɔːtaɪt). *Min.* [f. the name of Maxwell N. *Short* (1889–1952), U.S. mineralogist + -ITE[1].] A double carbonate of sodium and calcium, $Na_2Ca_2(CO_3)_3$, found as colourless to pale yellow wedge-shaped, orthorhombic crystals that are strongly pyroelectric.

**1939** J. J. FAHEY in *Amer. Mineralogist* XXIV. 514 Crystals of shortite..were found in cores of clay shale from Sweetwater County, Wyoming, at depths between 1258 and 1805 feet. *Ibid.,* Shortite is named in honor of Dr. Maxwell N. Short, Professor of optical mineralogy at the University of Arizona..and widely known for his contributions to the study of opaque minerals. **1973** *Jrnl. Geol.* LXXXI. 229 Shortite..occurs in the groundmass of micaceous kimberlite dikes from the Upper Canada Gold Mine, Ontario.

**short list.** [f. SHORT *a.* + LIST *sb.*[6]] A list of selected names, *esp.* of candidates for a post, from which the final selection is to be made. Hence **'short-list** *v. trans.,* to put on a short list; **'short-listing** *vbl. sb.*; **'short-listed** *ppl. a.*

**1927** W. E. COLLINSON *Contemp. Eng.* 124 Selection committees to University posts first familiarised me with the meaning of the short list. **1929** J. VAN DRUTEN *Young Woodley* ii. 28 He dreamed of a Headship elsewhere, always pulling wires and toadying to achieve it. He had applied for six, and lost them all; in only one case had he ever been on the Short List. **1955** M. GILBERT *Sky High* ii. 26 The police have got a short list of suspects. **1955** *Times* 12 July 2/3 Further particulars may be obtained from the Registrar, with whom applications (five copies) and the names of two referees, must be lodged not later than 23rd July, 1955. Candidates short-listed will be interviewed on 27th July, 1955. **1958** *New Statesman* 3 May 559/3 It is said that there is a Catholic majority on the party executive which did the short-listing. **1961** *Guardian* 4 Feb. 6/4 A documentary film ..has been shortlisted for a 1961 British Academy award. **1962** *Listener* 4 Jan. 23/2 The mass of short-listed poems was taken to Farringford. **1974** *Country Life* 17 Jan. (Suppl.) 25 Discussions..in England will 'short list' the properties that should interest you. **1977** *Wandsworth Borough News* 7 Oct. 2/2 The local party's General Management Committee will vote for their choice next Monday evening after hearing each of the short-listed candidates give a 10-minute talk. **1979** *Financial Rev.* (Austral.) 3 July 26/1 A two-ship shortlist for the Melbourne aircraft carrier replacement.

**short-lived** (ʃɔːtlaɪvd; the stress is variable), *a.* Also -**lif'd.** [f. SHORT *a.* + *live,* LIFE + -ED[2]. Often apprehended as f. *lived* pa. pple. of LIVE *v.* (cf. *smooth-spoken*) and pronounced (-lɪvd).]

**1.** Having a short life.

**1588** SHAKS. *L.L.L.* II. i. 54 Such short liu'd wits do wither as they grow. *c* **1608** B. JONSON *Hymenæi* Wks. (1616) 911 So short-liu'd are the bodies of all things, in comparison of their soules. **1645** QUARLES *Sol. Recant.* ii. 3 The short lif'd days of flesh and blood. **1707** *Curios. Husb. & Gard.* 336 The Plants indeed were short-liv'd, and continued no longer than the Heat of the Vessels lasted. **1842** LOUDON *Suburban Hort.* 591 The peach being a short-lived tree. **1871** NAPHEYS *Prev. & Cure Dis.* I. vi. 168 Gymnasts are short lived. **1875** E. WHITE *Life in Christ* I. i. (1878) 13 The million species of organisms of which he [man] is the short-lived lord.

**2. a.** *transf.* Lasting only a short time, brief, ephemeral.

**1588** SHAKS. *L.L.L.* IV. i. 15 O short liu'd pride. **1645** WALLER *Poems, To Amoret* 60 Then smile on me, and I will prove Wonder is shorter liv'd then Love. **1711** ADDISON *Spect.* No. 256 ¶5 Admiration is a very short-liv'd Passion. **1848** DICKENS *Dombey* liii, I was made a short-lived toy, and flung aside more cruelly and carelessly than even such things are. **1888** BURGON *Lives 12 Gd. Men* II. v. 18 He afforded a short-lived triumph to the enemies of Religion.

**b.** *Metallurgy.*

**1884** LOCK *Workshop Rec.* Ser. III. 22/1 Sulphur..makes molten iron 'short-lived'.

**c.** Of a radioisotope or sub-atomic particle: having a relatively short half-life.

**1926** R. W. LAWSON tr. *Hevesy & Paneth's Man. Radioactivity* xxiii. 170 Short-lived thorium isotopes like uranium X, radiothorium, etc. **1947** *Radiology* XLIX. 286/2 The tracer and therapeutic studies with 'short-lived' artificially produced radioactive isotopes were not directed toward the study of the more general biologic effects. **1973** L. J. TASSIE *Physics of Elem. Particles* ix. 91 Since the weak interaction causing the decay of the neutral kaon does not conserve *CP,* the short-lived neutral kaon and the long-lived neutral kaon are not necessarily eigenstates of *CP.*

Hence **short'livedness,** brief duration.

**1817** BENTHAM *Parl. Reform* Introd. 69 In proportion to the short-livedness of the power, diminishes, both to purchasers, and thence to sellers, the venal value of it. **1875** STUBBS *Const. Hist.* I. i. 6 The shortlivedness of their organisations.

†**short livy,** *a. Obs. rare*[−1]. In 3 sort leui (? error for *-liui*). [f. SHORT + LIFE *sb.* + -Y. Cf. OE. *langlife* long-lived.] Short-lived.

*c* **1250** *Gen. & Ex.* 712 Aram bi-gat loth, and sarray, And melcham, and was sort leui In lond caldea.

†**'shortly,** *a. Obs. rare.* [f. SHORT *a.* + -LY[1].] Brief, not long (in time).

*a* **1050** *Liber Scintill.* lxxx. (1889) 214 Se apostol sæde þæt soþlice þæt on andwerdum sceortlic oþþe hwilendlic [L. *momentaneum*] ys. *a* **1340** HAMPOLE *Psalter* i. 2 His wil is in godis lawe..and þat will is noght ydell na shortly. *a* **1513** FABYAN *Chron.* VII. 664 When both hoosts were met within shortly space, such offers of a pease were proferid by the Frenshe Kynge, that fynally both prynces agreed vpon a pease.

**shortly** ('ʃɔːtlɪ), *adv.* [f. SHORT *a.* + -LY[2].]

**1.** Briefly, concisely, in few words.

*c* **893** ÆLFRED *Oros.* I. i. §5 Scortlice ic hæbbe nu ȝesæd ymb þa þrie dælas ealles þises middanȝeardes. *c* **1200** ORMIN 12788 Ta seȝȝde Filippe Shorrtlike till Natanaæl; Cum nu þe sellf, & loke. *a* **1300** *Cursor M.* 8520 For he þat mikel has for to tell þe scortliker he aght to spell. **1340** *Ayenb.* 252 þeruore ich paci þe ssortlaker. **1390** GOWER *Conf.* I. 99 And schortly to descrive hire al, Sche hath no lith withoute a lak. **1472** *Paston Lett.* III. 71 He can telle yow more shortlyer then I shuld wryte. **1581** W. Charke in *Confer.* iv. (1584) E ej, Answere shortly. **1624** Bedell *Lett.* x. 136 It would require a iust volume to shew it, though but shortly. *a* **1676** Hale *Prim. Orig. Man.* i. i. 1 The instances thereof,.. shall be only these two, which I shall but shortly touch. **1805** *East's Rep.* V. 254 The Attorney General was heard shortly in reply. **1886** *Act 49 Vict.* c. 22. §4 (1) (a), An advertisement describing shortly the object for which the land is proposed to be taken.

†**b.** In short, 'to speak briefly'. Also more fully, ***shortly (the sooth) to say, to say shortly***, etc.

*a* **1300** *Cursor M.* 22203 Scortli to sai. **1303** R. Brunne *Handl. Synne* 6007 And, shortly, ȝow for to telle, þys lady wulde nat hem selle. *c* **1386** Chaucer *Prol.* 30 And shortly.. I was of hir felaweship anon. *c* **1400** *Beryn* 836 And for to seye shortlych, in Room was noon hym lych. **1483** Caxton *G. de la Tour* g v b, And shortly to say he lost alle that he had. **1535** Coverdale *Eccl.* ii. 8 (Shortly) I was greater in more worshipe, then all my predecessours in Ierusalem. **1641** 'Smectymnuus' *Vind. Answ.* §14. 175 Shortly, resolve us but this one thing.

**c.** Abruptly, curtly, sharply.

*c* **1815** Jane Austen *Persuasion* iv, 'I think very differently', answered Elizabeth, shortly. **1857** Hughes *Tom Brown* i. viii, 'I won't sell a bit of him', answered Tom, shortly. **1872** H. Kingsley *Hornby Mills* I. 26, I am not the only person who ought to be taken up shortly. **1885** 'Mrs. Alexander' *At Bay* iii, I wish I hadn't been obliged to send that cad Vincent to the right-about so shortly.

**2.** In a short time; not long after the present or the point reached in a narration; soon. †In early use also: With little delay, speedily, quickly: often in *compar.* or *superl.*

*a* **1050** *Lamb. Ps.* xxxvi. 10 & is nu ȝyt vel scortlice vel lytel fæc & ne byð se synfulla. *a* **1100** *Gloss.* in *Haupt's Zeitschrift* IX. 527 *Maturius*, scortlicor. *a* **1300** *Leg. Rood* (1871) 38 Þo þe giwes i-somned were hi [hadde] schor[t]liche gret fere. **13..** *E.E. Allit. P.* B. 519 For-þy schal I neuer schende so schortly at ones. *c* **1386** Chaucer *Knt.'s T.* 519 And shortly turned was al vp so doun Bothe habit and eek disposicioun Of hym this woful louere daun Arcite. **1483** *Cely Papers* (Camden) 138 Ȝe schall be payd be Easter and schorttlyer. **1512** *Act 4 Hen. VIII*, c. 1. §1 Grete multitude of people can not shortly resort to put theym of at theire landyng. **1523** Berners *Froiss.* I. ccxxxviii. 344 The shortlyer y[t] ye do it, the gretter thanke we shall gyue you. **1568** Grafton *Chron.* II. 600 The drawe Bridge could not be shortly drawen vp. **1596** Shaks. *Merch. V.* iii. v. 31, I shall grow iealous of you shortly Lancelet, if you thus get my wife into corners? **1632** Lithgow *Trav.* x. 448 A French ship.. shortly bound for Alexandria. **1798** Sophia Lee *Canterb. T.*, *Yng. Lady's T.* II. 84 [They] only invited her from knowing the consequence she would shortly have a right to. **1836** *J. R. Smith's Catal. Bks.* Feb. 32 Shortly will be published, in one vol. 8vo.. Bibliotheca Cantiana. **1861** M. Pattison *Ess.* (1889) I. 34 Very shortly a treaty is on foot for a matrimonial alliance between the houses of Plantagenet and Hapsburg. **1871** Blackie *Four Phases Morals* i. 14 Socrates.., after saying a prayer to the sun, shortly retired.

†**b.** quasi-*sb.* *odd shortly* = *odd-come-shortly*: see odd *Comb.* 2.

**1681** T. Flatman *Heraclitus Ridens* No. 26. 2/2 We'l give him as good as he brings one of these odd shortlies, I warrant him.

**3.** At a short time *after*, *before*, †*syne*.

**1548** Hall *Chron.*, *Hen. VIII*, 158 And so ye viscount Rochforth retorned into England, and so did the bishop of Bathe shortly after. **1593** *Knaresb. Wills* (Surtees) I. 198 Shortlie after my deathe. *c* **1643** Ld. Herbert *Autobiog.* (1824) 145 And so returning shortly after to his Excellency [I] related to him the success of my journey. **1752** *Scotland's Glory* 19 Some hundred of our ministers They shortly syne silenced. **1832** W. Palmer *Orig. Liturg.* I. 29 Shortly before, probably about the end of the fourth century, Jerome.. said [etc.]. **1886** C. E. Pascoe *Lond. To-day* xviii. (ed. 3) 162 On a given morning.. shortly after noon. **1902** R. Bagot *Donna Diana* xxviii. 353 Perhaps you will.. ask him to meet us here shortly before four o'clock.

**4.** For a short time. *rare.*

**1809** Campbell *Gertrude* ii. vii, And see thee once again whom I too shortly saw! **1815** Scott *Guy M.* xxvi, He's been but shortly in office. **1836** E. Howard *R. Reefer* xxi, A lady whom she knew but shortly.

**5.** In a small compass.

**1567** *Satir. Poems Reform.* iii. 30 Dartis about him swyftlie could he fling, And rin ane rais and shortlie turne ane steid. **1833** Darwin *Jrnl.* 15 Oct., It has the power of turning very shortly in the air.

**6.** At a short distance. *rare.*

**1908** *Blackw. Mag.* Aug. 205 Shortly south of Donabyu the river Irrawaddy dissolves its main stream.

**7.** *Comb.* Qualifying an adj. with the sense 'having little length'. (Chiefly in *Botany*.)

**1840** Paxton *Bot. Dict.*, *Shortly-acuminated*,.. *Shortly-bifid*, *Shortly-two-cleft*. **1875** Bennett & Dyer *Sachs' Bot.* ii. v. 558 More often the cotyledons remain thin like shortly stalked foliage-leaves of simple form.

**shortness** (ˈʃɔːtnɪs). [f. short *a.* + -ness.]

**1.** The quality or fact of being short in duration, linear magnitude, serial extent, etc.; absence of length, brevity.

*c* **1000** Ælfric *Gram.* xliv. (Z.) 266 Maneȝa synd ȝyt *Coniunctiones*, þe we ne maȝon nu secȝan on ðissere sceortnysse. *c* **1380** Wyclif *Wks.* (1880) 44 Wiþ schortnesse of sermon. **1496–7** *Act 12 Hen. VII*, c. 2 The seid Statutes for shortnes of tyme syn the making of theym.. as yet may not be perfitely knowen. **1588** Shaks. *L.L.L.* iii. i. 378 Such as the shortnesse of the time can shape. **1660** Heylin *Hist. Ref.*, *Mary* (1849) II. 222 [Mary's reign] was only commendable in the brevity or shortness of it. **1774** Goldsm. *Nat. Hist.* (1776) VI. 47 The shortness of the legs in the web-footed kinds. **1782** Miss Burney *Cecilia* ii. vi, The shortness of our acquaintance. **1841** Latham *Eng. Lang.* ii. vii. 136 The comparative shortness of Vowel *u*. **1885** *Law Times* LXXVIII. 295/2 The shortness of the title might not have been a sufficient objection.

†**b.** Brevity or conciseness in speech or writing.

*c* **1450** in Aungier *Syon* (1840) 297 Withe a quyet schortenes, they schal say that is to be seyde. **1576** Fleming *Panopl. Epist.* 104 Therfore must I vse so much the more shortnesse at this present. **1596** Shaks. *Tam. Shrew* iv. iv. 39 Your plainnesse and your shortnesse please me well.

**c.** *for shortness*: for the sake of brevity, to save time or distance. Now *rare.* †Also *for the sake of, because of shortness*, etc.

*c* **1450** *St. Cuthbert* (Surtees) 931, I leeue þe prolog for shortnes. **1599** Hakluyt *Voy.* II. i. 84 And many other were wounded, whose names be not rehearsed here, because of shortnesse. **1710** in *Nairne Peerage Evid.* (1874) 153 Under the reservations provisions and declarations above exprest (which are here holden as sett down for shortnes sake). **1837** Carlyle *Fr. Rev.* II. iv. vii, Taking side-roads, for shortness, for safety.

†**d.** (*a*) A short period (of time). (*b*) Short stature. *Obs.*

**1596** Shaks. *1 Hen. IV.* v. ii. 83 The time of life is short; To spend that shortnesse basely were too long. **1650** *Don Bellianis* x. 56 Don Bellianis, whose shortnesse reached not to the others middle. **1684** *Contempl. St. Man* i. ii. (1699) 12 Most of those things.. even during the shortness of Time which they last, have a thousand changes.

**2.** Defective reach (of vision, memory, etc.).

**1635** R. N. tr. *Camden's Hist. Eliz.* iv. 586 The Queene made answer with shortnesse of minde. **1661** Cowley *Cromwell* Ess. etc. (1906) 361 A little mistake of the shortness of his sight. **1704** Swift *T. Tub* iii. 74 Yet has the unhappy shortness of my Memory led me into an Error. **1837** Carlyle *Fr. Rev.* III. iii. iv, Their fatal shortness of vision. **1904** H. Paul *Hist. Mod. Eng.* II. ix. 192 The extreme shortness of his sight would have interfered with his efficiency as a soldier.

†**3.** Defectiveness, imperfection; *pl.* defects, shortcomings. *Obs.*

**1644** Digby *Nat. Bodies* 346 Since his raigne was but at the beginning of sciences, he could not chose but haue some defects and shortenesses. **1662** Stillingfl. *Orig. Sacræ* i. i. §9. 10 Which.. through the shortness of their own reason doth appear to them to be so. **1736** Butler *Anal.* ii. iii. Wks. 1874 I. 181 The shortness of our faculties.

**4.** ***shortness of breath***: a dyspnœic condition, breathlessness.

**1577** Googe *Heresbach's Husb.* iv. (1586) 190 The water thereof distilled and drunke.. helpeth the cough, and shortnesse of breath. **1898** *Allbutt's Syst. Med.* V. 350 The dyspnœa of pleurisy without liquid effusion is chiefly shortness of breath.

**5.** The condition of being 'short *of*' something; deficiency, want (esp. of money, food, etc.); also, scantiness (of a supply, a crop, †a meal).

**1669** Woodhead *St. Teresa* ii. 265 The meanness, and shortness of their Dinner. **1763** Scrofton *Indostan* i. (1770) 20 The poor and middling sort are only curbed by the shortness of their finances. **1831** Sir J. Sinclair *Corr.* II. 28 The shortness of the crop, will assist in reducing the price of lands still lower. **1838** *Civil Engin. & Arch. Jrnl.* I. 174/2 The shortness of water in the boiler had the effect of over-heating the plates. **1882** Mrs. J. H. Riddell *Prince's Garden-Party* 205 There was no shortness of money.

**6.** The quality of being 'short' in texture or substance; friability, brittleness.

**1655** Moufet & Bennet *Health's Improv.* (1746) 271 The Head of the Carp, the Tail of a Pike, and the Belly of a Bream are most esteemed, for their Tenderness, Shortness, and well relishing. **1758** Reid tr. *Macquer's Chem.* I. 363 The brittleness and shortness of Pig-iron. **1861** W. Fairbairn *Iron* 175 Metallic manganese has been used by Mr. Mushet to correct red shortness or cold shortness in steel.

**short run**, *sb.* and *a.* [f. short *a.* + run *sb.*[1]]

**A.** *sb.* **1.** *Cricket* **a.** A run made when the ball does not travel far enough to give time for an easy run. **b.** One which does not count by reason of a batsman not having technically completed the run.

**1830** *Laws of Cricket* in Nyren *Young Cricketer's Tutor* (1902) 23 If the striker run a short run, the umpire must call 'One short'. **1833** Nyren *Young Cricketer's Tutor* (1902) 76–7 His decision was as prompt as his eye was accurate in calculating a short run. **1921** P. F. Warner *My Cricketing Life* xi. 203 One of the features of his [*sc.* J. B. Hobbs's] long partnerships with Rhodes was the number of short runs they ran.

**2.** A relatively brief passage of time within a sequence of events (opp. long run, long-run), usu. in phr. ***in the short run***.

**1879** Geo. Eliot *Let.* 18 Oct. (1956) VII. 212 Mrs. Healy's marriage is surely what you expected in the long or short run. **1928** *Britain's Industr. Future* (Liberal Industr. Inquiry) iv. xxvii. 396 But we do not believe that in anything but the very short run industry benefits from displacing adult workers by successive relays of young boys and girls. **1940** F. Pickersgill *Let.* 19 Jan. (1948) 151 Chamberlain is of course succeeding in the short run in getting rid of all the energetic and intelligent people in the Party. **1952** Isard & Whitney *Atomic Power* ix. 185 The question arises whether the economic benefits of atomic power may be greater for such a country as Russia in the short-run and middle-run as well. **1965** *New Statesman* 7 May 718/3 In the long run you will obtain substantial benefit from professional business schools like the one at Harvard... In the short run—well, I don't envy George Brown. **1971** D. C. Hague *Managerial Econ.* ii. v. 112 In economic theory, the short run is defined as that period of time during which the physical capacity of the firm is fixed.

**3.** *Theatr.* A short period of being represented on the stage. Also *attrib.*

**1922** H. Granville-Barker *Exemplary Theatre* vi. 260 To replace the long run by the short run.. or the hastily concocted 'repertory' season, is no remedy. *Ibid.* 262 Most of the 'short-run' theatres.. by misplaced courtesy are dubbed 'repertory'. **1961** *Twentieth Century* Feb. 101 The short-run system of provincial repertory. **1967** *Oxf. Compan. Theatre* (ed. 3) 797/1 In Stratford-upon-Avon plays are now introduced into the bill one at a time, and given a short run before being merged in a changing bill.

**4.** A class or line of goods produced in limited quantity. Also *attrib.*

**1957** *Times* 4 Nov. 13/1 The blot on the British copy-book is the complaint from a number of stores that most manufacturers [of furniture] will not consider what are known in the trade as short runs. **1959** *Times* 14 Jan. 12/4 Printing short-run quality bookwork. **1967** V. Strauss *Printing Industry* x. 660/1 Foot-operated wire stitchers.. are used for short runs or for jobs that cannot be handled on more automatic machinery. **1970** *Publishers' Weekly* 8 June 152 Many speakers complained about printing short-run jobs: price is too high, quality is not good, and.. deliveries are too slow. **1976** *Scotsman* 25 Nov. 4/3 (Advt.), Craft Bookbinding. Contemporary style bindings in leather and cloth: short-runs re-backing and general restoration.

**B.** *adj.* (With hyphen.) Occurring in or relating to the short run; = short-term *a.*

**1947** *Partisan Rev.* XIV. 240 There is certainly a short-run tendency in critical situations toward reliance on reactionaries as counter to communists. **1958** *Listener* 9 Oct. 548/1 A combination of short-run and long-term programming on two different political and geographical levels. **1966** *Philos.* XLI. 294 Any cyclical view of history can harbour only a short-run optimism. **1979** *Internat. Jrnl. Sociol. of Law* VII. 308 Larceny, some of it responsive to short-run price changes.

Also **short runner**, one skilled in making short runs (sense 1 a).

**1833** Nyren *Young Cricketer's Tutor* (1902) 76–7 John Small.. was the best short-runner of his day.

**short sight.** [short *a.* 1 h.] The defect of sight by which only near objects are seen distinctly; myopia.

**1822–29** *Good's Study Med.* (ed. 3) IV. 211 *Paropsis propinqua*. Short sight. **1879** Harlan *Eyesight* vi. 79 Dr. Cohn, of Breslau,.. found the percentage of short-sight increasing from year to year.

**b.** *fig.*

*a* **1888** H. D. Rawnsley in W. Knight *Shairp & Friends* 384 Invective against the modern shortsight of commercial utilitarianism.

**short-sighted**, *a.* [Cf. prec. and sighted *a.*]

**1.** Having short sight; having the focus of the eyes at less than the normal distance; unable to distinguish objects clearly at a distance; myopic.

*a* **1649** Drumm. of Hawth. *Jas. V* Wks. (1711) 105 The other, who was short-sighted, had broken his ponderous sword. **1710** Berkeley *Princ. Hum. Knowl.* §5 Wks. 1871 I. 139 He who is short-sighted will be obliged to draw the object nearer. **1856** *N. Brit. Rev.* XXVI. 165 Two lenses of this kind, one for cylindrical and short-sighted eyes.. and another for long-sighted eyes. **1875** Jowett *Plato* (ed. 2) III. 238 A short-sighted person had been requested by some one to read small letters.

**b.** *absol.*

**1856** *N. Brit. Rev.* XXVI. 181 The observations which we have made on spectacles for longsight, are, generally speaking, applicable to the shortsighted.

**2.** *fig.* Lacking in foresight or in extent of intellectual outlook.

**1622** Mabbe tr. *Aleman's Guzman d'Alf.* i. 216 Those that are yong, are very short-sighted in your choyser sort of things. **1740** J. Clarke *Educ. Youth* (ed. 3) 198 The giddy short-sighted Minds of young Men. **1830** D'Israeli *Chas. I*, III. 8 So short-sighted are politicians in power. **1902** R. Bagot *Donna Diana* xxx. 396 He.. cursed himself for a short-sighted fool.

*absol.* **1648** Denham *Cato Major* iv. (1669) 50 The foolish and short-sighted die with fear, That they go no where, or they know not where. **1837** Ht. Martineau *Soc. Amer.* II. 107 The march of circumstance has become too obvious to escape the attention of the most short-sighted.

**3.** Characterized by or proceeding from want of foresight or limited mental vision.

**1736** *Gentl. Mag.* VI. 314/2 [Discoverers] whose Geography was so weak, and so short-sighted, that [etc.]. **1858** Froude *Hist. Eng.* III. xiii. 92 The laws which we call shortsighted, against engrossers of grain. **1864** Kingsley *Roman & T.* i. (1875) 10 A shortsighted and suicidal policy. **1891** *Speaker* 11 July 36/1 The pitiable display of short-sighted greed over the Factory Bill.

Hence **short-ˈsightedly**, *adv.*; **short-ˈsightedness** *lit.* and *fig.*

**1670** Cotton *Espernon* ii. vii. 320 The short-sightedness of humane Wisdom. **1715** *Pope's Iliad* Notes iv. 503 The divine Boldnesses which in their very Nature provoke Ignorance and Short-sightedness to shew themselves. **1853** 'C. Bede' *Verd. Green* i. xii, Verdant.. was short-sightedly peering at the celebrated 'Charles the First' of Vandyck. **1884** R. W. Church *Bacon* iii. 63 The apparent shortsightedness of the policy. **1887** Moloney *Forestry W. Afr.* 55 Rash and short-sightedly premature gatherings of crop.

**short-stay**, *a.* [f. short *a.* + stay *sb.*[3]]

**1.** *Naut.*, in phr. ***short stay apeek*** (see quot. 1867).

**1837** Marryat *Snarleyyow* ix, Short stay apeak was the anchor. **1867** Smyth *Sailor's Word-bk.* s.v. *Apeek*, A ship drawn directly over the anchor is *apeek*: when the fore-stay and cable form a line, it is *short stay apeek*; when in a line with the mainstay, *long stay apeek*.

**2.** That makes a short stay, *spec.* in a hospital or other institution providing care or treatment;

providing accommodation for a short stay; of or pertaining to those who make a short stay.

**1946** *Nature* 26 Oct. 578/2 It is proposed to establish a diagnostic and research centre at the teaching hospital..to deal with short-stay in-patients and out-patients. **1952** C. P. BLACKER *Eugenics: Galton & After* xi. 316 These mainly consist of nursery services (long- and short-stay residential nurseries; part and full-time day nurseries; nursery schools). **1960** J. STROUD *Shorn Lamb* i. 14 A short-stay case..[is] a case where..the children are only going to be In Care for a very short time. **1965** J. POLLITT *Depression & its Treatment* vi. 85 Out-patient treatment and short-stay admission is now widely practised for all psychiatrically ill patients. **1976** *Howard Jrnl.* XV. I. 45 Readers working with homeless alcoholics will appreciate the accounts of the birth and growth of two long-stay hostels and a short-stay house. **1981** D. KAVANAGH *Fiddle City* ii. 31 Short-stay car parks, long-stay car parks.

**short-sword.** *Obs.* exc. *Hist.* A sword with a short blade.

*c* **1470** *Gol. & Gaw.* 706 Schort suerdis of scheith smertly thay dreuch. **1865** INGRAHAM *Pillar of Fire* I. xviii. (1872) 295 A thousand men in iron helmets, round shields, and heavy short-swords. **1881** J. TAYLOR *Sc. Covenanters* 81 The old-fashioned Scottish short-sword.

**shortsyne,** *adv. Sc.* [f. SHORT *adv.* + SYNE *adv.*] A short while ago, lately.

**1768** Ross *Helenore* 62 Shortsyn unto our glen, Seeking a hership came yon unko' men. **1832** RODGER *Poems* (1838) 298 She promis'd shortsyne she would soon be my ain.

**short-term,** *a.* [f. SHORT *a.* + TERM *sb.*] Lasting for, pertaining to, or involving a relatively short period of time; maturing or becoming effective after a short period. Also quasi-*advb.*

**1901** *Scotsman* 3 Apr. 10/1 Mr. Gage has bought in New York 2,000,000 dols. worth of short term bonds for the Sinking Fund. **1901** *Westm. Gaz.* 25 July 2/1 In the matter of remission of sentence the short-term prisoner has now been raised to an equality with the convict. **1932** *Ann. Reg. 1931* 194 The withdrawal of French short-term credits has given the impetus to the original crisis, and other foreign creditors had followed suit. **1943** J. S. HUXLEY *Evolutionary Ethics* iv. 31 All existing societies manifest considerable ethical disunity, and..this is an expression of the conflicts and contradictions inherent in the situation—conflicts between classes and groups, between long-term and short-term good, [etc.]. **1948** 'N. SHUTE' *No Highway* 2 Short-term *ad hoc* experiments to solve a particular problem. **1956** *Planning* XXII. 41 The short-term forecasts, up to one year, are the basis for current production and buying and sales planning. **1959** *Times* 20 Jan. 9/3 It will not be enough, however, for the Government to solve the problems short-term. **1970** *Money Which?* Mar. 56/3 A gain counts as a short-term gain if, in general, you had held the asset for a year or less. **1972** *New Scientist* 24 Feb. 428 This type of memory is referred to as short-term memory because the number of events we can hold in this fashion is strictly limited, and forgetting is extremely rapid once our attention is diverted. **1980** *Daily Tel.* 28 June 16 The Minister of the Environment is seeking ways to control local high-spending by councils such as Manchester. Short-term, his powers are fairly limited.

**short time.** Also (attrib.) short-time. [f. SHORT *a.* + TIME *sb.*] **1.** The state or condition of working less than the regular number of hours per day or of days per week. Also *attrib.* and quasi-*advb.*

**1848** W. FAGAN *O'Connell* II. 561 A supporter of 'short time' work for children in the Factories. **1861** J. S. MILL *Let.* 1 Mar. (1910) I. 245 The equality, if not superiority,.. of the short-time pupils. **1861** J. WARD *Diary* 16 Nov. in J. Burnett *Useful Toil* (1974) I. 80 The manufacturing districts ..are all running short time through the scarcity of cotton. **1864** R. A. ARNOLD *Hist. Cotton Famine* iii. 84 Short time means short wages. **1906** *Daily Colonist* (Victoria, B.C.) 1 Jan. 13/2 Disorderly scenes were witnessed recently in Newcastle-on-Tyne..owing to an intimation that fifty [employees] would be put on short time. **1930** *Economist* 22 Feb. 411/1 Several watchmaking factories are working short time. **1955** *Times* 14 May 5/6 Three years ago more than 80,000 textile and clothing workers were flung out of work, and thousands more were on short time. **1961** *Ann. Reg. 1960* p. xix, Unemployment was at a low level but in the latter half of the year there was much short-time working particularly in the motor-car industry. **1978** P. BAILEY *Leisure & Class in Victorian England* iv. 80 In the early 1870s...the success of the Short Time agitation encouraged further campaigns to cut working hours.

**2.** *slang.* A brief visit to a prostitute; a brief sojourn in a hotel for sexual purposes. Also *attrib.*

**1937** PARTRIDGE *Dict. Slang* 763/1 *Short time*, a visit to a prostitute for one copulation only. **1939** G. GREENE *Confidential Agent* I. ii. 48 It's no bother. It's the 'short times' that are the bother. In and out three times in a night. **1961** R. SETH *Anat. Spying* ii. 30 Ninety-five per cent of any ship's company, as soon as they are able to get ashore,.. make straight for the nearest bar for a 'quick one', and then on to the nearest brothel for what is known in the jargon as 'a short time'. **1971** *Guardian* 8 July 3/1 Miles of girlie bars, short time hotels. **1979** J. WAINWRIGHT *Take Murder* i. 23 Three hours. Not the proverbial 'short time'... It means a bed somewhere.

**short-'timer.** [f. SHORT *a.* + TIMER 4.]

**1.** A child who is allowed to attend school for less than the full number of hours daily (cf. *half-timer*). *Obs.* exc. *Hist.*

**1863** DICKENS *Uncommercial Traveller* in *All Year Round* 20 June 400/2 The Short-Timers, in a writing competition, beat the Long-Timers of a first-class National School. **1883** MRS. A. E. BARR in *Chr. Union* 22 Nov., A 'short-timer' is a child who works half the day at the mill.

**2.** *U.S. Mil. slang.* One nearing the end of his period of military service.

**1906** T. BEYER *Amer. Battleship in Commission* 73 In most cases..'short-timers' are sent home before their enlistment expires. **1918** L. E. RUGGLES *Navy Explained* 132 Any man who has less than six months to do on his enlistment is called a 'short timer'. **1952** M. RUSS *Last Parallel* (1957) 16 Being what is known as a short-timer..I'm at peace with service life. **1977** *Chicago Tribune* 2 Oct. II. 4/6 An inspecting officer discovered a 'short-timer's calendar' centrally positioned in a foot-locker display.

**3.** *slang.* One serving a short prison sentence.

**1915** J. LONDON *Jacket* iv. 25 He was a pallid-faced, little dope-fiend of a short-timer.

**4.** *slang.* One who makes a brief sojourn in a hotel for sexual purposes; one who visits a prostitute. Cf. SHORT TIME 2.

**1923** J. MANCHON *Le Slang* 267 *Short-timers*,..un couple (amoureux) qui loue en meublé pour peu de temps. **1939** G. GREENE *Confidential Agent* I. ii. 87 The shabby hotel to which 'short timers' come. **1960** *Amer. Speech* XXXV. 120 When the GI visited a *movie star*, it was usually for a *short-time. Short-time*..also..had an agent noun, a *short-timer.*

**short-toed,** *a.* [SHORT *a.* 24.] Having short toes; esp. in ***short-toed lark***, any of various larks of the genera *Calandrella* and *Spizocorys*, which comprise small gregarious birds widely distributed in Europe, Africa, and Asia, esp. in deserts and steppes.

**1837** GOULD *Birds Europe* IV. Pl. 256 Short-toed Ptarmigan. **1863** T. C. JERDON *Birds of India* II. I. 425 The short-toed Lark appears in India in October and November, in flocks. **1869–73** T. R. JONES *Cassell's Bk. Birds* I. 198 The Short-toed Lark. **1933** *Discovery* July 224/1 The short-toed lark, whose protective colouring makes him almost invisible on sandy soil. **1963** *Times* 27 Feb. 11/6 Overhead range the 14 species of birds of prey, which breed here or within everyday range, including the imperial, short-toed and booted eagles. **1972** ALI & RIPLEY *Handbk. Birds India* V. 21 Short-toed Larks become excessively fat before emigration and are then netted everywhere in vast quantities. **1980** HOWARD & MOORE *Compl. Checklist Birds of World* 347/1 *Spizocorys starki* (Stark's Short-toed Lark). Angola to W. Transvaal.

**short-tongued,** *a.* Having a short tongue; hence (now *dial.*) inarticulate, stammering, lisping. Also *occas.* taciturn, unready in speech.

*c* **1575** GELSON in *Durham Depos.* (Surtees) 289 The said Sir Richard..wilbe some tyme mery and light with drink, and short tonged, but nott dronken. **1865** DICKENS *Mut. Fr.* II. v, If I am a short-tongued fellow. **1874** LUBBOCK *Wild Flowers* iii. 68 The honey which is accessible even to beetles, and short-tongued flies.

**'shortwall.** *Mining.* [f. SHORT *a.* + WALL *sb.*[1]] A short coalface. Freq. *attrib.*, denoting (equipment designed for) a method of mining in which shortwalls are worked. Cf. *longwall* s.v. LONG *a.*[1] 18 a.

**1912** F. D. POWER *Coalfields & Collieries Austral.* 409 *Shortwall machine*, a coal cutter for use in bords, which, when once the cutting part has made the sumping cut, is drawn across the face automatically by ropes, under-cutting as it proceeds. **1931** *Trans. Inst. Mining Engineers* LXXXI. 474 The thin seams are extracted on a 'shortwall' (retreating) method. **1942** *Ibid.* CII. 42 The shortwall is antagonistic to the basic principle that the maximum area of seam should be won with the minimum of roadway consistent with roadway costs. **1958** I. C. F. STATHAM *Coal Mining Pract.* I. vii. 298 Mechanised methods are now generally adopted for the coal-cutting in these narrow opening-up places, using either a shortwall coal-cutter, a Universal coal-cutting machine or in some cases a long-wall machine. **1964** A. NELSON *Dict. Mining* 406 A shortwall face may be any length between about 5 and 30 yd and is generally employed in pillar methods of working. **1973** L. J. THOMAS *Introd. Mining* vii. 258 A group of shortwalls are mined adjacent to each other with rib-pillars left between.

**shortward(s** ('ʃɔːtwəd(z), *adv.* [f. SHORT *a.* + -WARD, -WARDS.] Towards shorter wavelengths; on the short-wavelength side *of.*

**1972** *Science* 1 Sept. 789/3 Figure 4c..shows features shortward of Lyman-α, which are attributed to the Birge-Hopfield bands of $N_2$. **1974** [see LONGWARD(S *adv.*]. **1978** *Nature* 5 Oct. 414/1 IUE provides an excellent way for acquiring UV spectra in the wavelength region shortwards of the Earth's ozone cutoff (about 3,100 Å).

**short wave.** Also 'short-wave, shortwave. [f. SHORT *a.* + WAVE *sb.*] **a.** An electromagnetic wave of relatively short wavelength, *spec.* a radio wavelength of less than about 100 metres, corresponding to a frequency of more than 3000 kilohertz; radio communication or broadcasting employing such waves. Usu. *attrib.* or as *adj.*; also in adverbial use.

**1839** [see *long wave* s.v. LONG *a.*[1] 18]. **1902** *Encycl. Brit.* XXVIII. 68/2 With very fine wires the condition *na* small can be fulfilled with quite short waves. **1907** J. ERSKINE-MURRAY *Handbk. Wireless Telegr.* i. 5 Short-wave Hertzian telegraphy has never been successful at distances beyond a mile or two. **1928** D. BRUNT *Meteorology* v. 40 We have thus to picture a beam of short-wave light from the sun reaching the outer boundary of the earth's atmosphere. **1928** *Daily Mail Year Bk.* 240/2 The B.B.C.'s slowness to recognise the importance of short-wave Empire broadcasting. **1941** J. STEINBECK *Sea of Cortez* i. 7 In all the crackle and noise of the short-wave one of our men made contact with another boat. **1943** D. POWELL *Time to be Born* xiii. 308 They.. drove to N.B.C. studios where he broadcast short-wave to London. **1961** *Ann. Reg. 1960* 447 The mass-produced short-wave transistor. **1972** *Sci. Amer.* Sept. 109/1 Finally it was discovered that 'shortwave' frequencies (from three to 30 megahertz) can travel halfway around the earth and more by being repeatedly reflected between the *F* layer and the earth. **1978** W. F. BUCKLEY *Stained Glass* xviii. 182 The Director rose and turned off the impressive short-wave speaker that had brought in the press conference.

**b.** *Med.* Used *attrib.* or as *adj.* to denote diathermy in which energy is applied to the tissues by means of oscillating electric fields having frequencies within the short-wave radio range.

**1935** R. KOVÁCS *Electrotherapy & Light Therapy* (ed. 2) xviii. 306 Short-wave diathermy comprises wave lengths from 12 to 30 meters... Ultra short-wave diathermy comprises wave lengths below 12 meters. **1935** WILSON & DOWSE tr. *Holzer & Weissenberg's Found. Short Wave Therapy* 160 Short wave therapy has been used for about eight years, and..not a single case of irreparable injury has been published. **1965** E. D. R. CAMPBELL in C. W. H. Havard *Fund. Current Med. Treatment* xvi. 596 Short-wave diathermy causes heat to be more evenly distributed through the bulk of a limb by two distinct processes. **1965** N. FREELING *Criminal Conversation* I. ii. 18 Dr. Hubert van der Post, neurologist, specialist in short-wave and other electrical treatments.

**short-winded,** *a.* [f. SHORT *a.* + WIND *sb.* + -ED[1].]

**a.** Short of breath; suffering from or liable to difficulty of breathing; that soon becomes out of breath with any exertion.

*c* **1450** *Merlin* xv. 245 And whan thei saugh the saisnes well chased and short wynded, thei lete renne at hem. *c* **1593** JANE in Hakluyt *Voy.* (1600) III. 852 Captaine Cotton and my selfe swolne and short winded. **1656** RIDGLEY *Pract. Physick* 81 Forestus often prescribeth to short-winded people in a Consumption. **1793** T. BEDDOES *Obesity* 101 Short-winded persons are very often corpulent. **1840** DICKENS *Barn. Rudge* li, The short-winded locksmith had no chance against a man of Sim's youth and spare figure. **1891** C. ROBERTS *Adrift Amer.* 166, I was wretchedly weak and short-winded, only being able to walk a few yards at a time.

**b.** *fig.*

**1596** SHAKS. *1 Hen. IV*, I. i. 3 Finde we a time for frighted Peace to pant, And breath shortwinded accents of new broils To be commenc'd in Stronds a-farre remote. **1656** TRAPP *Comm. 2 Cor.* viii. 11 Their shortwinded wishes. **1688** BUNYAN *Heav. Footman* (1886) 165 They went to the work at first pretty willingly, but they were very short-winded, they were quickly out of breath, and in their hearts they turned back again into Egypt. **1934** C. LAMBERT *Music Ho!* I. 36 His [*sc.* Debussy's] melodies may be a little short-winded. **1976** *Gramophone* May 1772/3 The first movements, if short-winded for Bach, have an easy fluency.

Hence **short-'windedness**, a state or condition of being short-winded, dyspnœa. Also *fig.*

**1614** T. ADAMS *Divells Banket* vi. 303 Balme taken fasting ..is very good against short-windednesse. **1753** TORRIANO *Non-Naturals* 52 It begets..pulmonary Humours, (especially Short-windedness,) and Death. **1934** C. LAMBERT *Music Ho!* II. 102 His [*sc.* Stravinsky's] melodic style has always been marked by extreme shortwindedness.

**short wool.**

**1.** Wool having a short staple or fibre.

**1728** CHAMBERS *Cycl.* s.v. *Woollen Manufactory*, A Pack, or 240 Pounds Weight of short Wool. **1841** *Penny Cycl.* XXI. 358/2 In 1828 the number of packs of short wool had diminished to 2800. **1912** *Times* 19 Dec. 20/3 The finer varieties of short wools.

**2.** (Hyphened.) A sheep producing such a wool.

**1837** YOUATT *Sheep* ix. 351 A few of the short-wools were left. **1844** W. C. SPOONER *Sheep* 72 [The South Down breed] ranks with the Leicester—the former first among the short-wools.

**3.** *attrib.*

**1824** BANKS in Bischoff *Woollen Manuf.* (1842) II. 55 Any drawback so obtained must operate as a bounty to the English short-wool grower. **1841** *Penny Cycl.* XXI. 358/1 Various breeds of short-wool sheep still prevail on the hills of Devonshire and Cornwall.

Hence **short-woolled** *a.*

**1787** *Young's Ann. Agric.* VIII. 199 The South Downs.. are, for that point, the best short-woolled sheep which I know in England. **1841** *Penny Cycl.* XXI. 359/2 One other breed of short-woolled sheep must be mentioned.

**†short-writing.** *Obs.* = SHORTHAND.

**1620** W. FOLKINGHAM *Brachigr.* To Rdr. A 4, Applying my Letters to those formes of Short-writing, which intimate regionarie Vowels by contiguitie of Consonants. **1650** SHELTON (*title*) Zeiglographia or A New art of Short-writing never before published. **1691** WOOD *Ath. Oxon.* I. 269 His most dextrous and incomparable faculty in short-writing. **1715** S. LANE (*title*) The Art of Short Writing made lineal and legible as the Common long Hand.

**shorty** ('ʃɔːtɪ), *sb.* and *a. colloq.* or *slang.* Also shortie. [f. SHORT *a.* + -Y[6], -IE.] **A.** *sb.*

**1.** *Sc.* (spelt *shortie.*) Shortbread; a piece of shortbread.

**1882** in JAMIESON, s.v. Short-Bread. **1919** C. ORR *Glorious Thing* i. 11 Home wouldn't be home to Minnie without your shorties, Jenny. **1974** *Sunday Post* (Glasgow) 27 Oct. 17/5 Shortie made with butter and browned real good is sold in St. Andrews.

**2.** A person of short stature; freq. with capital initial as a nickname or form of address.

**1888** *Texas Siftings* 7 Jan. 10/3 One boy yelled out: 'Go it, Shorty!' **1908** S. FORD *Side-Stepping with Shorty* xix. 306 'Hello, Shorty!' says he, in that little squeak of his. **1914** 'BARTIMEUS' *Naval Occasions* xxiii. 213 Your middle watch,

Shortie? *a* **1935** T. E. LAWRENCE *Mint* (1950) 152 The figure gives a large surplus of shorties. **1960** V. NABOKOV *Invitation to Beheading* vi. 70 The door of this cell was wide open, and inside, the likable shorty whom he had seen before ..was standing on a chair. **1978** *Oxford Times* 20 Oct. 13/2 A reader who is 5ft 1½in tall has sent me a delightful document entitled 'Reflections of a Suicidal Shortie'.

**3.** A drink of spirits; a short drink. orig. *U.S.*

**1931** *Amer. Speech* VII. 83 *Shorty*, and *apple-jack* are illicit drinks. **1942** BERREY & VAN DEN BARK *Amer. Thes. Slang* §99/8 Strong liquor,..*shorty* (esp. hard, illicit liquor). *Ibid.* §101/2 *Shorty*, a straight gin with a ginger ale chaser. **1963** *Freedomways* III. 523 Yarborough..yelled, 'Bartender. Give the professor another shorty of gin there.' **1971** *Scope* (S. Afr.) 19 Mar. 77/2 Also popular are the tall cylindrical tumblers for long drinks, and the chunky tumbler for 'shorties'.

**4.** A short story, article, film, etc.

**1934** M. H. WESEEN *Dict. Amer. Slang* 151 *Shorties*, short motion picture films. **1968** *Listener* 4 July 22/1 Half the time we wanted to kill its crippling name and start on a new formula, with nudes and shorties to rival the money-making *Lilliput* and *Men Only*. **1976** 'K. ROYCE' *Bustillo* x. 137, I read rather an interesting article. Just a shortie. About your man Warton.

**5.** A short article of clothing; pl. *spec.* shorts.

**1942** BERREY & VAN DEN BARK *Amer. Thes. Slang* §87/37 Underwear,..*shorties*, shorts. **1945** *Richmond* (Va.) *News Leader* 2 Mar. 19 (Advt.), Shorties: More popular than ever this spring! 100% wool Shetlands, in a belted all-around style. **1957** M. B. PICKEN *Fashion Dict.* 151/1 *Shortie*, glove, either slip-on or having one button; extending to wrist or a little beyond. **1958** *Vogue* Jan. 2 Jackets..just right for spring..like the jaunty shortie. **1959** 'D. BUCKINGHAM' *Wind Tunnel* xix. 157 She was already in her nightdress—a silly little nylon shorty. **1962** *Times* 19 Nov. 14/4 Among modern 'shorties' and light-weight garments in my wardrobe. **1963** [see PEEP-HOLE].

**B.** *adj.* Designating products which are shorter than the norm.

**1949** *Sun* (Baltimore) 19 Mar. 7/7 (Advt.), Short and sugary..cool and comfy..these delicious Rayon Jersey Shortie Pajamas in pastel shades. **1952** *N.Y. Times* 6 May 33/8 A black suede shorty glove. **1954** *Wall St. Jrnl.* 16 Apr. 1/1 Promoters of Florida tourist attractions are energetically courting a new, inexpensive and very rewarding publicity medium. It's the 'shortie' TV feature—films which Floridians make and which the networks admit they're eager to show without charge. **1956** J. POTTS *Diehard* x. 165 Her bright-green shortie coat was spotted with rain. **1960** *News Chron.* 5 July 1/7 They were sacked..after a party in which they staged their own version of Florence Nightingale in the nurses' home, dancing about in 'shortie' nighties waving lighted candles. **1971** *Scope* (S. Afr.) 19 Mar. 64/1 The girls changed into shortie cat-suits. **1972** D. HASTON *In High Places* v. 69 To go anywhere in the winter you have to be able to ski, so I had borrowed a pair of shorty skis from Grahame Tiso. **1980** *Dirt Bike* Oct. 64/3 Both bikes are using Oakley II grips and DeHandler shorty levers.

†**'shory**, *a. Obs. rare*⁻¹. [f. SHORE *sb.*¹ + -Y¹.] Of or pertaining to a shore.

**1684** T. BURNET *Theory Earth* I. 89 At the same time were made the shory rocks and mountains which are the bars and boundaries of the sea.

‖**shosagoto** (ʃosa'goːto). [Jap., f. *shosa* acting, conduct + *koto* matter, affair.] In Japanese Kabuki drama: a dance play; a mime performed to music.

**1911** *Encycl. Brit.* XV. 170/1 Mimetic posture-dances (*Shosagoto*) were always introduced as interludes. **1957** *Oxf. Compan. Theatre* (ed. 2) 412/2 The Japanese theatre recognizes three main classes, the *jidaimono* or histories..; the *sewamono* or melodramas; and the *shosagoto* or dances. **1967** 'J. H. ROBERTS' *February Plan* I. iii. 92 The play today was a *shosagoto*, a Kabuki drama adapted from a Noh play. **1975** J. R. BRANDON *Kabuki* 5 In the late seventeenth century, three major divisions of kabuki drama were recognized: *sewamono*..*jidaimono*; and dance pieces, called *shosagoto*.

**Shoshone** (ʃəʊ'ʃəʊniː), *sb.* and *a.* Also 9 **Shoshonee, -ie**; 9- **Shoshoni**. [From an unidentified American Indian language; the folk-etymology given in quot. 1918 is rejected by scholars.]

**A.** *sb.* **1.** (A member of) a North American Indian people of Wyoming, Idaho, Nevada, and neighbouring states.

**1805** M. LEWIS *Jrnl.* 19 Aug. in *Orig. Jrnls. Lewis & Clark Exped.* (1904) II. xv. 370 The Shoshonees may be estimated at about 100 warriors. **1830** *Western Monthly Rev.* III. 562 The Shoshonee are a numerous and powerful tribe of Indians. **1834** A. PIKE *Prose Sketches & Poems* 200 The Shoshones are the Snakes. **1836** W. IRVING *Astoria* II. xi. 132 The Shoshonies are a branch of the once powerful and prosperous tribe of the Snakes. **1884** W. SHEPHERD *Prairie Exper.* 59 The Crows..came down to visit the Rapahoes, Shoshones, and other tribes. **1918** J. E. REES *Idaho Chronol., Nomenclature, Bibliogr.* 111 The name comes from two Indian words, 'Shawnt', meaning 'abundance', and 'shaw-nip', 'grass', which was etymologically changed to the euphonious name 'Shoshoni' and in English conveys the thought of 'abundance of grass'. **1938** *Bull. U.S. Bureau Amer. Ethnol.* No. 120. 238 Shoshoni and Ute were periodically at grips. **1959** E. TUNIS *Indians* 91/1 In time, the Shoshone in the far west were following social patterns that had been folk-ways along the Missouri. **1977** J. GUNN in Hill & Gunn *Individual in Prehistory* ix. 190 If it is assumed that Shoshoni ware is truly diagnostic of Shoshoni population movement, these data are incongruent with the proposed 1000-year-later migration of the Shoshoni into the Great Basin.

**2.** The language of this people, a member of the Uto-Aztecan family (formerly also applied to a grouping of languages including Shoshone).

**1843** F. MARRYAT *Travels & Adventures of Monsieur Violet* xiv. 33/2, I addressed him in Shoshone, which beautiful dialect is common to the Comanches, Apaches, and Arrapahoes. **1933** [see PAIUTE *sb.* b]. **1977** *Language* LIII. 459 The correlations with Cupan *yax* 'to be', Shoshoni *yikʷi* 'to sit (pl.)', and a present-tense suffix in Southern Paiute are improbable.

**B.** *adj.* Of or pertaining to the Shoshone or their language or a former grouping of languages to which this language was assigned.

**1805** M. LEWIS *Jrnl.* 17 Aug. in *Orig. Jrnls. Lewis & Clark Exped.* (1904) II. xv. 364, I was to bring on the party and baggage to the Shoshone Camp. **1837** W. IRVING *Adventures Capt. Bonneville* I. xvi. 260 There was but little chance of meeting the Shoshonie bands. **1886** *Outing* Dec. 198/2 Dick had..a Shoshone woman for his wife. **1926** D. BRANCH in J. F. Dobie *Rainbow in Morning* (1965) 128 The precarious, abject living of the Shoshone Diggers. **1956** J. WHATMOUGH *Lang.* xii. 221 A Shoshoni dialect spoken in southwestern Utah. **1976** *Billings* (Montana) *Gaz.* 16 June 1-A/6 What more fitting tribute to those who fought and died in this struggle, U.S. soldiers, Sioux, Cheyenne, Crow and Shoshone warriors, than to protect it for those who follow us?

**Shoshonean** (ʃəʊ'ʃəʊnɪən), *a.* and *sb.* Also **-ian**. [f. prec. + -AN.] (Designating) a branch of the Uto-Aztecan languages including Shoshone; of or pertaining to speakers of these languages.

**1891** J. W. POWELL in *Ann. Rep. U.S. Bureau Amer. Ethnol.* VII. 109 Very likely much of the area occupied by the Atsina was formerly Shoshonean territory. **1893** A. F. CHAMBERLAIN in *Rep. Brit. Assoc. Adv. Sci. 1892* 589 A seeming similarity in a few points of general structure to the Shoshonian and to the Siouan tongues. **1904** *Rep. U.S. Nat. Museum 1901–2* 472 All the Shoshonean types of weaving, all their forms of baskets, and most of the patterns on them are ancient. **1921** A. F. HALL *Handbk. Yosemite Nat. Park* 51 The Mono..are an offshoot from the Paiutes and other Shoshoneans of Nevada and the Great Basin country. **1929** E. SAPIR in *Encycl. Brit.* V. 138/1 *Shoshonean*..occupies the greater part of the Great Basin area and contiguous territory in southern California and the southwestern Plains. **1932** [see PIMA]. **1940** M. J. ROGERS in E. C. Jaeger *California Deserts* xi. 117 In historic times the Mohave Desert had fallen almost entirely into the hands of the Shoshoneans. **1950** F. EGGAN *Social Organization of Western Pueblos* i. 13 By comparing the Hopi system with other Shoshonean systems, he came to the conclusion that 'linguistic conservatism has been of slight importance in the history of the present Hopi nomenclature'. **1974** *Amer. Anthropologist* LXXVI. 11 (*heading*) An archaeological perspective on Shoshonean bands.

**shoshonite** (ʃəʊ'ʃəʊnaɪt). *Petrogr.* [f. the name of the *Shoshone* River, Wyoming (cf. SHOSHONE) + -ITE¹.] A type of basaltic rock varying quite widely in composition and distinguished by containing, in addition to augite, labradorite, and usu. olivine, significant amounts of potassium feldspar.

**1895** J. P. IDDINGS in *Jrnl. Geol.* III. 938 The classes will be described in the order just given under the names: *Absarokite, Shoshonite* and *Banakite*. *Ibid.* 943 The rocks classed as shoshonites are more numerous than the absarokites, and embrace a somewhat wider range of composition. They occupy the middle ground, as it were, in the series. **1937** HOLMES & HARWOOD *Volcanic Area of Bufumbira* (Mem. Geol. Survey Uganda No. 3) xii. 269 The xenoliths of the shoshonites of Sabinyo include aggregates referable to kentallenite and olivine-monzonite. **1976** *Nature* 12 Feb. 472/1 The calc-alkaline lavas..range from 'normal' basalts, basaltic-andesites and andesites to highly potassic varieties having all the compositional and modal characteristics of shoshonites.

Hence **shosho'nitic** *a.*, resembling or consisting of shoshonite.

**1937** HOLMES & HARWOOD *Volcanic Area of Bufumbira* (Mem. Geol. Survey Uganda No. 3) ii. 16 These rocks are more feldspathic than the shoshonitic absarokites of Muhavura and Mgahinga. **1964** G. A. JOPLIN *Petrogr. Austral. Igneous Rocks* vii. 90 The different shoshonitic rocks show many common characteristics.

**shot** (ʃɒt), *sb.*¹ Forms: 1 sc(e)ot, ȝesc(e)ot, 2, 4-7 schot, 3 scott, 4-7 schott, shotte, (5 shet), 5-6 schotte, 5-7, (8) shott, (6 shutt, 6-7 shote), 5- shot. [OE. *sc(e)ot, ȝesc(e)ot* neut. (the prefix, as usual in sbs., fell away—in this instance not surviving beyond OE.—so that the forms with and without prefix fell together) = OFris. *skot* neut., OS. *-scot* in *sîlscot* 'balista', MLG. *scot, gescot*, OHG. *scoz* neut. (MHG. *schoz* masc., mod.G. *schoss* masc.), also *giscoz* neut. (MHG. *geschoz*, mod.G. *geschoss*), ON. *skot* neut. :—OTeut. *skuto-, *gaskuto-m, f. root *skŭt-: see SHOOT *v.*]

**I.** The action of shooting.

**1. a.** A rapid movement or motion; †a rush, dash or onset. *rare.*

*a* **1000** *Menologium* 272 Leax sceal on wæle mid sceote scriðan. **1375** BARBOUR *Bruce* XII. 77 A gret schot till thame can thai mak. **1859** MEREDITH *R. Feverel* xxiii, 'You needn't to ask, sir—ye know', said the farmer, with a side shot of his head.

**b.** A sudden sharp pain; also *dial.* 'a sudden attack of illness or disease'. *rare.*

*a* **1400-50** *Stockh. Med. MS.* 101 For þe schottes & þe prikkynges in sydes. **1527** ANDREW *Brunswyke's Distyll. Waters* C v, The hede enoynted with the same water.. withdryveth the payne and shotte in the hede comynge of hete. **1899** *Cumberld. Gloss.*, *Shot*,..a sudden attack of illness or disease... A shot of rheumatics.

**c.** A rush (of colour) over a person's face, etc. ? *nonce-use.*

**1895** MEREDITH *Amazing Marr.* I. xi. 123 A shot of colour swept over Henrietta.

†**d.** A rush of water. *Obs.*

*c* **1400** *Destr. Troy* 3300 And þou drunkyn hade dewly as mony du sopis, As shottes of shire water has shot fro þin ene. **1673** RAY *Journ. Low C.* 8 In process of time..all the Hills and Mountains..would by Floods and Shots of Rain be quite washed away.

**e.** A sheet (of ice). *Obs.* exc. *dial.*

*a* **1650** CALDERWOOD *Hist. Kirk* (1843) II. 248 The rain falling freezed so vehementlie, that the ground was like a shott of yce.

**2.** A discharge, flux or issue. (Cf. SHOOT *sb.*³)

*c* **1500** *Rowlis Cursing* 67 in Laing *Anc. Poet. Scot.*, The kanker and the kattair, And never to be but schot of blude. **1841** DICK *Man. Vet. Science* (1862) 148 Cattle and sheep.. after indulging..in luxuriant pastures, take what is called a Shot of Blood. **1844** H. STEPHENS *Bk. Farm* II. 226 There is a complaint called a *shot of grease*, arising from a different cause from the common grease.

**3.** *Fisheries.* **a.** The spread or cast of a net; the throw and haul-in of a fishing-net.

**1859** ATKINSON *Walks & Talks* (1892) 322 A second shot of the net produced eleven more [mullet]. **1864** *Rep. Sea Fisheries Comm.* (1865) II. 1188/1, I believe I got the second shot of trawled fish that was ever fished in this country. **1873** *Act 36 & 37 Vict.* c. 71 §14 Within 100 yards from the nearest point in the line of shot of any other seine or draft net worked in like manner.

**b.** *Sc.* A place where nets are shot. *Obs.* exc. *Hist.*

**1452** in *Reg. Monast. Passelet* (Maitld. Club) 250 Tertiam partem totius piscarie de le Crukytshot. **1584** *Reg. Mag. Sig. Scot.* 354/1 Beginnand at the schott of the fisching callit the Hoilschott. **1882** J. F. S. GORDON *Hist. Moray* III. 228 The proprietor of the Friars' Shott salmon fishings.

**4.** The shooting of a bolt.

**1905** 'H. HALIBURTON' *Excursions* i. 5 The shot of the lock caught the ear of Beenie.

**5. a.** A passage of the shuttle across the web; *concr.* 'one thread of each colour or kind of yarn' (*Eng. Dial. Dict.*).

**1834-6** P. BARLOW *Manuf.* in *Encycl. Metrop.* (1845) VIII. 739/1 If a shot of blue and a shot of white be thrown alternately, a corresponding check will be produced. **1864** T. BRUCE in *Poets of Ayrshire* (1910) 232 Sad and slow the shots he threw And slow he trod the treddles.

**b.** (See quot.)

**1875** F. J. BIRD *Dyer's Hand-bk.* 90 When satins..or silks of any kind are found to contain shots—that is, warp and weft of different qualities—they must be prepared as follows.

**6.** The course of a plough.

**1843** *Jrnl. R. Agric. Soc.* IV. I. 34 It is usual to cut the drains directly across the shot, as we term the course of the plough.

**7. a.** The action of shooting with the bow, catapult, or firearms; the mechanical discharge of arrows or other projectiles as a means of attack; shots or discharges of missiles collectively. Now only *arch.* †Const. *of* (bows, guns, etc., also arrows or other projectiles).

*c* **1386** CHAUCER *Nun's Pr. T.* 529 Whan thy worthy kyng Richard was slayn With shot. *c* **1471** *Arriv. K. Edw. IV*, (Camden) 29 Sore annoyed..as well with gonnes-shott, as with shot of arrows. **1568** GRAFTON *Chron.* II. 279 The shot of the Scottes endured but a short space: But the shot of the Englishmen was long and fierce. **1639** DRUMM. OF HAWTH. *Consid. to Parlt.* Wks. (1711) 185 By shot of pistols. **1759** HUME *Hist. Eng., Tudor* I. 87 Their admiral lost an eye by the shot of an arrow. **1819** SCOTT *Ivanhoe* xxiv, At which a few archers might be stationed for defending the turret, and flanking with their shot the wall of the castle on that side. **1855** KINGSLEY *Westw. Ho!* vii, Which bark..was taken without shot or slaughter.

*fig.* **1377** LANGL. *P. Pl.* B. xx. 224 And so seide sexty of þe same contreye, And shoten aȝein with shotte many a shef of othes. **1567** TURBERV. *Epit.* etc. 12 The surest shielde Against the dreadfull shot of wordes that thousandes had beguilde. **1662** HIBBERT *Body of Div.* II. 29 We cannot be at peace with God, and therefore lie ever open to the shot of general dangers. **1718** T. GORDON *Cordial Low Spirits* 27, I must be obliged to stand the shot of his noise and nastiness for perhaps an hour or two together.

**b.** An act of shooting, an individual discharge of a bow, gun, etc. Phrases, ***to fire***, also (now *arch.*) ***to make, shoot a shot*** (see SHOOT *v.* 21 c).

*to fire a shot* is used also in senses 13, 14 b, and 17.

*c* **1000** in Napier *O.E. Glosses* (1900) 214 *Iactibus*..*uacuis*, mid idelum ȝescotum. *c* **1435** in Kingsford *Chron. Lond.* (1905) 96 In this same yere..was slayn sir Thomas Movntagu..thruh a shotte off a gonne. **1585** T. WASHINGTON tr. *Nicholay's Voy.* II. i. 31 b, Notwithstanding wee had giuen them a shot of assurance, [they] began to prepare themselues to the fight, thinking we had bin Coursaries. **1629** *Capt. Smith's Trav. & Adv.* iii. 5 She stood to her defence, and made shot for shot. **1721** DE FOE *Mem. Cavalier* (1840) 130 Several regiments..never..fired a shot. **1818** SCOTT *Hrt. Midl.* lii, They heard a shot. *c* **1850** *Arab. Nts.* (Rtldg.) 693 Prince Houssain..took his bow and made the first shot.

*fig.* **1576** LAMBARDE *Peramb. Kent* (1826) 416 He had directed his shot at the crowne of England.

†**c.** uninflected plural (with numeral). *Obs.*

**1642-4** VICARS *God in Mount* 193 After many shot of Cannon, which did very little hurt among us.

**d.** Phrases. (*a*) ***a shot between wind and water***, also *slang* (cf. SHOOT *v.* 30 d). (*b*) colloq. ***like a shot***: at once, with rapidity. Also, without hesitation, most willingly. (*c*) colloq. ***a shot in the eye***: an ill turn.

(*a*) **1695** CONGREVE *Love for L.* III. xv. Ballad, And then he let fly at her, A shot 'twixt wind and water, That won this Fair Maids Heart. **1706** E. WARD *Wooden World Diss.* vii. (1708) 62 Sometimes his Captain, being disabl'd by some unlucky Shot 'twixt Wind and Water, repairs to him for a Refitment.

(*b*) **1809** MALKIN *Gil Blas* v. i. ¶6, I went off like a shot, in the direction of our inn. **1843** DICKENS *Chr. Carol* v. 156 The boy was off like a shot. **1894** W. E. NORRIS *St. Ann's* I. 72 If I could hear of any chance of employment elsewhere, I'd take it like a shot.

(*c*) **1897** *Pearson's Mag.* Sept. 254/1 He thought he saw the means of getting square with the millionaire who had done him such an unscrupulous 'shot in the eye'.

**e.** *transf.* (*a*) *Naut. slang.* A meridional altitude taken (cf. SHOOT *v.* 32c). (*b*) A snapshot (cf. SHOOT *v.* 22f); a picture (or sequence of pictures) continuously shot by a single film or television camera; the action or process of taking such a picture.

**1867** SMYTH *Sailor's Word-bk.* s.v. *Shoot the sun*, 'Have you obtained a shot?' applied to altitudes of the meridian, as for time, lunar distances, &c. **1889** *Brit. Jrnl. Photogr.* XXXVI. 605/2, I developed some instantaneous shots. **1895** *Outing* XXVI. 33/2, I must have a camera shot at this. **1923** 'B. M. BOWER' *Parowan Bonanza* xxvi. 303 Bill and Tommy were both below examining the effect of their 'shots' of the evening before. **1937** *Discovery* Nov. 330/2 For each unit of programme transmission, called a shot, on account of similarity with sound-film technique, several electron cameras may be in use. **1957** W. ALWYN in Manvell & Huntley *Film Music* 9 Chapter 4 shows the various dramatic forms film music takes, and analyses in each case shot-by-shot and phase-by-phase a particular sequence [etc.]. **1963** *Movie* Jan. 8/1 The sequence in the Albert Hall auditorium ..lasts about twelve minutes, 124 shots without any dialogue. **1972** *Listener* 21 Dec. 852/1 Sequence of calls before a shot. Production Assistant: 'Quiet. Going for a take. Standing by.' Director: 'Right.' **1979** D. GURR *Troika* i. 2 The first picture is on the screen... He never told me they had that shot.

**f.** *Mining.* An explosion of a blasting charge. Cf. 17.

**1881** RAYMOND *Gloss. Mining* s.v. *Shoot*, A *shot* is a single operation of *blasting*. **1900** *Daily News* 25 July 2/1 Every shot is improving the appearance of the ore chute.

**g.** (*a*) A hypodermic injection of a narcotic, hallucinogen, or the like, or of a vaccine; a measure of a substance for injection. Also *fig. colloq.* (orig. *U.S.*).

**1904** *San Francisco Chron. Suppl.* 30 Oct. 4/1, I varied hardly a minute each day in the time of taking my injection. My first shot was when I awoke in the morning. **1921** S. LEWIS *Let.* 12 July in C. Mackenzie *My Life & Times* (1966) V. 199 Your book..was..at once a Social Document, and an opiate—or, as we say in the States, a shot of dope! **1936** L. C. DOUGLAS *White Banners* xviii. 373 That reminds me —I've to take some typhoid shots. **1948** G. H. JOHNSTON *Death takes Small Bites* iv. 81 If you've never had a plague shot and you've been here for five hours you might have contracted the disease. **1953** W. BURROUGHS *Junkie* viii. 74 About fifteen minutes later the attendant called, 'Shot line!' Everyone in the ward lined up. **1957** *London Mag.* Sept. 40 They were persons of a kind needing shots of the notion of art as others need shots of insulin. **1969** A. LURIE *Real People* 154 A doctor had come and given Charlie a shot and put him to bed. **1978** G. A. SHEEHAN *Running & Being* x. 136 We begin to hear about Butazolidine and cortisone shots.

(*b*) In *fig.* phr. ***a shot in the arm***, a much needed stimulant or encouragement. *colloq.* (orig. *U.S.*).

**1922** S. LEWIS *Babbitt* viii. 108 All afternoon he snorted and chuckled and gurgled over his ability to 'give the Boys a real shot in the arm tonight'. **1939** I. BAIRD *Waste Heritage* xii. 157 He saw the thing because he recognized it and knew how the shot-in-the-arm worked. **1949** *Hansard Commons* 27 Sept. 82 The brake..will lead rapidly to that dollar competition..in which we..and the Belgians will use this 'shot-in-the-arm' only for the purpose of making our positions worse. **1951** M. MCLUHAN *Mech. Bride* (1967) 47/1 Their masters, who then decided what sort of shot in the arm the public needs. **1961** *Daily Tel.* 11 May 20/6 A 'shot in the arm' will be given to Minehead if Mr. Billy Butlin is allowed to build a holiday camp there. **1976** 'A. GARVE' *Home to Roost* i. 21 Everyone felt better for seeing her. She was a shot in the arm.

(*c*) A measure of lubricant injected into the petrol tank of a motor vehicle.

**1965** L. SANDS *Something to Hide* v. 82 'Four gallons, Will, and four shots.'.. The shots were squirted in. **1978** *Reader's Digest* Sept. 130 (Advt.), Regular shots of Redex can save you well over £30 a year at current petrol prices... Add one shot of Redex for every gallon of petrol you buy.

**h.** (See quots.) Cf. *moon-shot* s.v. MOON *sb.* 16; *space shot* s.v. SPACE *sb.*[1] 20.

**1934** *Scoops* 19 May 456/1 Shot..a rocket flight. **1957** WILLIAMS & EPSTEIN *Rocket Pioneers* viii. 188 The last moments before a rocket shot are always tense. **1959** F. D. ADAMS *Aeronaut. Dict.* 152/2 *Shot*, an act or instance of firing a rocket, esp. from the earth's surface.

**i.** ***to call the shots***, to make the decisions; to exercise control over events. *colloq.* (orig. and chiefly *U.S.*).

**1967** E. LIEBOW *Tally's Corner* v. 157 Sea Cat made no secret of the fact that Gloria was calling the shots in this relationship. **1972** *N.Y. Times* 3 Nov. 38/3 It is the majority party which calls the 'shots' on the rules and legislative policies affecting our city. **1978** S. BRILL *Teamsters* v. 164 They stand off in a corner as if to say, 'I'm calling the shots here.' **1981** *Sunday Tel.* 5 July 8/5 They felt that an anti-Old Etonian cabal was calling the shots.

**8. a.** The range of a shot, or distance to which a shot will go. ***in(to), within, out of shot***: in, within, out of shooting distance; also *Photogr.*, *Cinemat.*, and *Television*, in(to) or out of view of the camera. †***to have open shot***: to have unobstructed range of shooting.

**1455** [see FLIGHT-SHOT 1.] *c* **1489** CAXTON *Sonnes of Aymon* vii. 180, I bode behynde well the shotte of a bowe. **1513** [see *arrow-shot* s.v. ARROW *sb.* IV. 2]. **1513** *Life Hen. V*, (1911) 111 They of the Towne had from euery place open shott w[th] there gonns into the hoast. **1635** *Long Meg of Westminster* xii. (1816) 21 While the Dolphins army lay in view..there was a French-man that sundry times would as on a brauery come within shot and tosse his Pike, and so goe his way. **1670** NARBOROUGH *Jrnl.* in *Acc. Sev. Late Voy.* I. (1694) 3 The Ships ride in shot of Ordnance of the City. **1719** DE FOE *Crusoe* I. (Globe) 237 And that then I should be within half Shot of them. **1882** PAYNE-GALLWEY *Fowler Irel.* 431 To find..that the pole has slipped just as you are getting well in shot, is no joke. **1958** *Spectator* 18 July 87/1 One Coco-Cola-clutching teenager..darting little glances at the camera to see if he was still in shot. **1960** N. KNEALE *Mrs. Wickens in Fall* 174 The maid Cecile hurried into Shot with a tray heaped with cut bread. **1960** I. MACCORMICK *Small Victory* 69 Thompson looks at each of them disgustedly, then he turns away and moves out of shot. **1969** J. ELLIOT *Duel* III. iii. 248 You'll have to move the mike up... Unless you want it in shot. **1976** M. MAGUIRE *Scratchproof* iii. 40 The camera pulled back as she dashed into shot. **1980** D. FRANCIS *Reflex* x. 120 [He] told me it was important that he should be included in my photographs..prominently in shot.

**b.** *transf.* Range or reach of anything likened to a shot. (Cf. EARSHOT.)

**1602** SHAKS. *Ham.* I. iii. 35 Keepe within the reare of your Affection; Out of the shot and danger of Desire. **1611** BIBLE *Transl. Pref.* ¶1 A man would thinke that Ciuilitie, holesome Lawes..should be as safe as a Sanctuary, and out of shot [*marg.* ἔξω βέλους], as they say, that no man would lift vp the heele..against the motioners of them. **1822** SHELLEY *Chas. I*, iv. 15 Beyond the shot of tyranny.

**c.** ***to run into shot***: Of a sporting dog: to run into the line of fire.

**1884** T. SPEEDY *Sport Highl.* iii. 25 The faults..of being gun shy, springing their game, running into shot [etc.].

**9. a.** An attempt to hit with a projectile discharged from a gun. Phrase, ***to exchange shots***: said with reference to a skirmish or a duel.

**1653** HANE *Jrnl.* (1896) 2 Wee made all the resistance wee could, changing some shotts with him for the space of halfe an houre. **1669** STURMY *Mariner's Mag.* v. xii. 46 A good Shot may be made out of a bad Piece. **1817** J. MAYER *Sportsman's Direct.* (ed. 2) 25 You will be able to take shots at them, before they reach the high slope. **1820** *John Bull* 17 Dec. 5/2 A duel was fought on Saturday..when some shots were exchanged. **1847** MARRYAT *Childr. N. Forest* v, It was a good shot that you made. **1898** *Field* 2 Apr. 509/3 Seeing a large buck..I sat down, prepared to have a long shot at him. **1908** R. BAGOT *A. Cuthbert* xxix. 377 Six rabbits in six shots with my pea-rifle.

**b.** *fig.* A remark aimed at some one, esp. in order to wound. Sometimes with mixture of sense 14b. Also ***cheap shot*** (*N. Amer. colloq.*).

**1841** THACKERAY *Gt. Hoggarty Diam.* ix, The shot told. Your aunt bounced up at once, and in ten minutes more was in my carriage, on our way back to London. **1878** B. HARTE *Man on Beach* 27 This last shot was from the gentle Maria, who bit her lips as it glanced from the immovable man. **1973** W. JUST *Congressman who loved Flaubert* 97 He tells me it's going to be a sympathetic show... No cheap shots. **1979** R. JAFFE *Class Reunion* (1980) II. xi. 288 'Every time you come back from those faggots you hang around with in New York you act like a bitch.'.. A cheap shot.

†**c.** *fig.* (A person's) ***great shot***: chief aim. *Sc.*

**1644** R. BAILLIE *Lett. & Jrnls.* (1841) II. 230 The great shott of Cromwell and Vane is to have a libertie for all religions. *a* **1658** DURHAM *Comm. Rev.* iv. III. (1660) 281 The Lords great shot in all this is to get praise to Himself.

**d.** Phrases: ***by a long shot***, by a considerable amount, by far; freq. negative in emphatic use. *colloq.* (orig. *U.S.*). ***a long shot***: a wild guess or venture, a bet at long odds.

**1848** in Bartlett *Dict. Americanisms* 215 Mr. Divver offered a resolution summarily removing the superintendent, and was quickly told..that he was going too fast by a long shot. **1861** M. B. CHESNUT *Diary* 26 Aug. in C. V. Woodward *M. Chesnut's Civil War* (1981) 163 'They dont pay the soldiers every week.' 'Not by a long shot,' cried a soldier laddie. **1884** in I. M. Tarbell *Hist. Standard Oil Co.* (1904) II. xiii. 114 They are not the Democracy of Ohio by a long shot. **1888** EGGLESTON *Graysons* i. 12 He didn' wear uz good close in them days 's 'e does now, by a long shot. **1897** A. R. MARSHALL *Pomes* 27 (Farmer) So Zippy went in for a long shot. **1931** WYNDHAM LEWIS *Apes of God* 17 If those were my last wishes as they are not by a long shot, would they be perfectly clear or not? **1957** W. SAROYAN *Whole Voyald* 17 It wasn't only to have pretty women swarm around that I hustled my first book into print. It wasn't that alone by a long shot.

**10. a.** A random guess attempting to 'hit' the right answer. ***to make a shot***: to attempt an answer by guessing. Also, ***a shot in the dark***, a guess, a random attempt. Cf. DARK *sb.* 5.

**1840** J. T. J. HEWLETT *P. Priggins* xvii, After waiting for a little while [in construing], Ninny..made a shot, and went so near the mark, that [etc.]. **1847** ALB. SMITH *Chr. Tadpole* Prelude, 'Do you want a bed here to-night, Sir?' asked the waiter..making a shot at the sex of the blue serge bundle. **1887** *Times* (weekly ed.) 19 Aug. 4/3, I do not believe that yesterday when she was supposed to be doing 15 knots she was really running more than 13. This, however, is only a shot. **1895** G. B. SHAW in *Sat. Rev.* 9 Feb. 183/1 Never did man make a worse shot in the dark. **1935** C. ISHERWOOD *Mr. Norris changes Trains* xii. 184, I could no longer resist trying a shot in the dark. 'But you get paid from Paris?' I had scored a bull. **1950** G. GREENE *Third Man* iv. 39 'There's something queer about Harry's death.' It was a shot in the dark, but already he had this firm instinctive sense that there was something wrong. **1963** *Listener* 7 Mar. 420/2 It can have been nothing more than a 'shot in dark' [*sic*], but it was a strange prediction none the less.

**b.** An attempt or try.

**1756** W. DODD *Fasting* (ed. 2) 30 The random shots of second causes. **1878** E. FITZGERALD *Lett.* (1889) I. 422, I cannot understand why I have not yet taken to Hawthorne, ..I will have another Shot. **1912** *Throne* 7 Aug. 227/1 Pinks is going to have a shot at the Wingfield Sculls.

**c.** Something which has a chance to succeed (as a racehorse, etc.); usu. preceded by the odds. *colloq.*

**1923** WODEHOUSE *Inimitable Jeeves* iv. 49, It was one of those occasions about which I shall prattle to my grandchildren—if I ever have any, which at the moment of going to press seems more or less of a hundred-to-one shot. **1931** *Daily Express* 23 Sept. 17/6 Mick..will be a neat shot for anybody when the St. Leger is run. **1936** WODEHOUSE *Laughing Gas* i. 9 As far as my chances of ever copping the title went, I don't suppose I was originally more than about a hundred-to-eight shot, if that. **1941** *Sun* (Baltimore) 14 Aug. 13/6 I've seen 10-to-1 shots that I knew were better horses in certain races than 2-to-1 shots. **1977** *New Yorker* 10 Oct. 174/1 Proud Birdie, a lightly weighted, 4-1 shot in the betting, was next to last going down the back-stretch.

**d.** *U.S. Billiards.* ***to call one's shot***, to announce which ball one intends to shoot into which pocket; also *fig.* (Properly distinguished from sense 7i above.)

**1953** *Official Rule Bk. Pocket & Carom Billiard Games* 27 Player does not have to 'call his shot' on opening stroke. **1954** BERREY & VAN DEN BARK *Amer. Thesaurus Slang* (ed. 2) §179/4 Call one's shot,..*to guess or predict rightly*. **1959** N. MAILER *Advts. for Myself* 22 It will be fine if I can write so well and so strongly as to call my shot. **1962** WODEHOUSE *Service with Smile* vi. 83 In making this statement, he called his shots correctly. **1976** *Billings* (Montana) *Sunday Gaz.* 20 June 1-A/3 There was no question in my mind that Nixon was calling his own shots.

**11. a.** An aim or stroke, esp. in a game, as tennis, golf, billiards, etc.

**1868** *Field* 8 Aug. 106/3 (Croquet) Mr. Whitmore distinguished himself by his long shots, one of which came off at thirty-six yards. **1902** W. W. JACOBS *Lady of Barge* 83 Wilfred Carr..taking a cue from the rack, bent over the board and practiced one or two favourite shots.

**b.** A throw of a ball, stone, or other thing aimed with the hand.

**1852** THACKERAY *Esmond* I. iv, Fling another shot [*i.e.* potato] at that carriage..and by the Lord I'll send my rapier through you! **1868** 'S. DARYL' *Quoits & Bowls* 54 (Bowls) The game is thirty shots—ten Guarding, ten Riding, ten Drawing.

**c.** In *Football*, *Hockey*, *Lacrosse*: an attempt to drive the ball into goal.

**1868** *Field* 28 Nov. 446/2 Several well intended, though badly misjudged, shots were fired at the School goal. **1912** *Oxford Mag.* 14 Nov. 75/1 Essex reduced the lead by means of a good shot from the inside left.

**d.** In *Boat-racing*: an attempt to 'bump' the boat in front. (Cf. BUMP *sb.*[1] 2 and *v.*[1] 3.)

**1868** *Field* 28 Nov. 445/2 Owing to his pulling his wrong scull, he managed to miss his shot at him, and Lowe went away easily. **1890** *Eng. Illustr. Mag.* Apr. 501 Ah! they have made a shot in the Gut and missed.

**e.** In *Curling*: (see quots. 1835, 1897).

*a* **1772** GRAEME in Anderson *Poets* XI. 447 (Jam.) Of many a bonspeel gain'd, Against opposing parishes; and shots, To human likelihood secure, yet stormed. **1835** H. HAREWOOD *Dict. Sports* s.v. *Curling*, When the stones on both sides have been all played, the one nearest the tee counts one; and if the second, third, fourth, &c. belong to the same side, all these count so many shots. **1897** *Encycl. Sport* I. 264/2 (Curling), *Shot*, (1) the unit of scoring, each stone nearer to the tee than any opponent counting one. (2) The delivery of a stone.

**f.** In *Cricket*, *Tennis*, *Golf*, etc.: ***(oh,) shot!***, an applauding exclamation used when a player makes a good stroke, or on an accurate throw; also used when a boxer delivers an effective blow. Freq. ***good shot!***

**1906** WODEHOUSE *Love among Chickens* 311 Oh, shot, sir! Shot, indeed! **1907** 'I. HAY' *Pip* x. 309 Here are two young men worth watching. Number One is addressing his ball for an approach shot... 'Good shot!' remarks Number Two. **1922** WODEHOUSE *Clicking of Cuthbert* ix. 218 He drove a perfect ball, hard and low with a lot of roll. Even Eunice was impressed. 'Good shot, partner!' she said. **1933** D. L. SAYERS *Murder must Advertise* xviii. 310 He always hits out. I like to see a batsman hitting out, you know. There! Good shot! Good shot! **1940** E. F. BENSON *Final Edition* iii. 52 Everybody chorused 'Good shot, my lord' on the smallest excuse. **1972** J. BURMEISTER *Running Scared* vii. 95 The resonant bonk of a tennis racket..a distant cry of 'Oh, shot!'

†**12.** A result of shooting. **a.** A wound or pain in the body caused by witchcraft. (Cf. SHOOT *v.* 32a, and ELF-SHOT.) **b.** A gunshot wound. *Obs.*

**1597** in *Spalding Club Misc.* (1841) I. 131 Thow said.. thow suld put ane schot in his syde, within xlviij houris, that suld do him gryter harme nor that schot did the;.. immediatly thairefter, he contractis sic ane deidlie seiknes, be ane schot in his syde vnder his oxtar. **1599** A. M. tr. *Gabelhouer's Bk. Physicke* 329/1 Squirte heerof into the shot,..and thrust into the wounde a peece of Larde of a reasonable longitude.

**II.** That which is discharged in shooting.

†**13. a.** That which is discharged from a bow, an arrow or arrows; also in early use stone or other projectiles thrown by a catapult, or other engine; ammunition for such an engine. *Obs.*

*c* **893** ÆLFRED *Oros.* III. ix. §15 þær forwearþ micel Alexandres heres for ȝeætredum ȝescotum. *a* **1300** *Cursor M.* 10036 þe berbikans seuen þat es a-bute..wel tas kepe to þat castell, For aro, scott, and for quarel. **1387** TREVISA tr. *Higden* (Rolls) III. 239 þe sonne is derked wiþ þe arwes and schot of Perses. **1601** HOLLAND *Pliny* VIII. xiv. I. 199

Arrowes, quarrels, stones, bullets, and such like shot. **1664** BUTLER *Hud.* II. ii. 856 The Law of Arms doth bar The use of venom'd shot in War.

†**b.** *fig.*

*c* **897** ÆLFRED *Gregory's Past. C.* lvi. 431 Ða diȝlan ȝescotu [*jacula*] ðæs sweocolan feondes. *c* **1374** CHAUCER *Troylus* II. 58 Pandarus,.. Felte eek his part of loves shottes kene. *c* **1460** SIR R. ROS *La Belle Dame* 145 And of his eyen the shot I knew anon Which federed was with right humble requestes. *c* **1586** C'TESS PEMBROKE *Ps.* LXIX. iv, The shott of piercing spight Bent at thee, on me doth light.

**14. a.** Projectiles (esp. balls or bullets, as distinguished from explosive 'shells') designed to be discharged from a firearm or cannon by the force of an explosive. Often with qualifying word as *bar-*, *chain-*, *grape-shot*, etc. See the first words. ***hollow shot***: 'empty shells, with metal screw plugs, sometimes used in the navy' (Brande & Cox *Dict. Sci.* 1866 s.v.).

**1474** *Acc. Ld. High Treas. Scot.* I. 69 To bring again.. artilzery, powder, schot and sic thing. **1513** *Life Henry V*, (1911) 80 Masons to hewe stones for shott to breake walls. *Ibid.* 111 Then the Frenchmen, perceauinge there shott to be spent in vaine, imagined a newe manner of shott instead of stones; they shott great peeces of steele fire-hott. **1669** STURMY *Mariner's Mag.* v. xiii. 84 The Shot of great Mortar-Pieces are.. one tenth part lower than the Bore. **1704** *Milit. Dict.* (ed. 2), *Shot*, all sorts of Bullets for whatsoever Fire-arms, from the Cannon to the Pistol. Those for Cannon are of Iron, those for Musket, Carabine, and Pistol, of Lead. **1854** TENNYSON *Lt. Brigade* v, Storm'd at with shot and shell. **1862** *Catal. Internat. Exhib.* II. xi. 23 Hollow shot are treated in a similar manner and then filled in the same manner as the ordinary spherical shells.

**b.** A cannon-ball. Also (with numerals) as *collect. sing.* or uninflected plural.

(*not*) ***a shot in the locker***: see LOCKER *sb.*[1] 5 b.

**1622** R. HAWKINS *Voy. S. Sea* xvii. 39 Not to suffer.. Pitch to be heate in the Ship, except it be with a shott heate in the fire, which cannot breed daunger. **1669** STURMY *Mariner's Mag.* v. xii. 48 Diameter of the Shot $3\frac{3}{8}$, weight of the Shot 4 pound 12 ounces. **1770** G. FARMER *Let.* 22 Sept. in *Ann. Reg.* (1772) 232/2 The Spanish frigate fired two shot, which dropt to leeward of the Favourite.

**c.** Hence, an iron globe like a cannon ball, used in the sport of 'putting the shot' (or 'weight'): see PUT *v.*[1] 2. Also *occas.* the sport of putting the shot.

**1881** *Cassell's Bk. Sports* (1886) 114 Putting the Weight. Sixteen pounds is the full-size shot for this feat. **1895** MANSON *Sporting Dict., Putting the Shot.* **1895** *Outing* XXVI. 460/2 The list of events will include.. high jump, broad jump, shot and hammer.

**d.** ***small shot***: †(*a*) musket bullets, in distinction from cannon-balls (*obs.*); (*b*) small pellets of lead (= sense 15), as distinguished from bullets. †***great shot***: cannon-balls; also occas. bullets as distinguished from 'small shot' (*b*).

**1593** G. HARVEY *Pierce's Super.* 12 This Termagant.. fighteth not with.. the small shott of contention, but with the maine ordinaunce of fury. **1632** LITHGOW *Trav.* II. 61 A long and doubtfull fight, both with great and small shot. **1727** BOYER *Dict. Royal* II, s.v. *Shot*, Small shot, used to shoot with a Birding-piece. **1727** A. HAMILTON *New Acc. E. Ind.* II. xli. 106 We gave them a Volley of great Shot in return of their Volley of small. **1803** SCOTT *Let.* in *Lockhart* (1837) I. xi. 390 A volley of small shot fired through the window.

*attrib.* **1834–6** P. BARLOW *Manuf.* §961 in *Encycl. Metrop.* (1845) VIII. 677/2 Small Shot Manufacture.

**15. a.** Lead in small pellets, of which a quantity is used for a single charge of a sporting gun. Also (less frequently), a single pellet, a shot-corn (plural *shot*, esp. with numerals; sometimes *shots*).

Shot is assorted by sizes distinguished by numbers (usually 1 to 10 or 12), or by letters (as *BB* called *double-B*), or by specific names (as *swan-shot*, etc.).

**1770** *Phil. Trans.* LX. 185, I would not recommend shooting them.. with shot smaller than common partridge shot, or No. 5. **1827** FARADAY *Chem. Manip.* ii. (1842) 40 Besides sheet lead, shot of different sizes are often used for this purpose. **1833** J. RENNIE *Alph. Angl.* 126 A strong silk-worm gut, with a shot or two on it. **1884** LOCK *Workshop Rec.* Ser. III. 361/2 The manufacture of shot is almost universally conducted in tall brick towers with iron frames. **1895** R. W. CHAMBERS *King in Yellow* (1909) 265 He ornamented each line with four split shot, a small hook, and a brilliant quill float.

**b.** Used by horse-copers as a dose to give a horse a temporary appearance of sound-windedness.

**1857** DICKENS *Dorrit* xii, Taking into account the shot he [a gelding] had been made to swallow for the improvement of his form.

**c.** *transf.* in ***Indian shot***, the plant *Canna indica* (see INDIAN *a.* 4). Also ***plantain***, ***flowering shot*** applied to the same or other species of the genus.

**1760** J. LEE *Introd. Bot.* App. 327 Shot, Plaintain, *Canna*. **1884** W. MILLER *Plant-n.* 47/2 Flowering Shot. The genus *Canna*. *Ibid.* 67/2 Indian Shot. The genus *Canna*.

†**16.** A charge (of powder); also a charge (of small shot) for discharge from a gun. *Obs.*

**1708** *Lond. Gaz.* No. 4479/5 The Garrison is to march out .. with loaded Arms,.. and are to have 12 Shots of Powder and Ball each. **1752** MACCOLL in *Scots. Mag.* (1753) Aug. 401/1 There was a shot of drops in it [the gun].

**17.** *Mining.* The charge of powder sufficient for a blast in a mine (esp. a coal-mine); also the bored hole into which the charge is put.

**1851** GREENWELL *Coal-trade Terms, Northumb. & Durh.* 47 *Shot.*—The cartridge or portion of gunpowder used in blasting... A pound of gunpowder will make five 6-inch shots. **1874** DUFFERIN in Lyall *Life* (1906) I. vii. 245 They had bored with a steam drill.. some fifty or sixty 'Shots', as they are technically termed, i.e. deep holes in the rock, which are then filled with gunpowder and exploded. **1886** [see *shot-firer* in 31].

†**18.** A bolt or bar for securing a door, etc. (Cf. SHOOT *v.* 13.) *Obs.*

*c* **1430** *Syr Gener.* (Roxb.) 196 The shottes of the gates opened she, And sett open the gates wide. **1595** in *Scott. Hist. Rev.* (1913) X. 302 Closit wit ane key be ane shott.

**19.** = WHALE-SHOT (spermaceti).

In recent Dicts.

[Spermaceti was supposed to be the spawn of the whale. Cf. SHOOT *v.* 18 d.]

**III.** That which shoots.

†**20. a.** Weapons for shooting; firearms. *Obs.*

**1579** *Proclam. agst. Dagges* etc. 26 July, The common carying of Dagges, Pistolles and such other short pieces of shot. **1596** DANETT tr. *Comines* Supply iii. (1614) 229 The people had planted shot against the castell. **1727** BOYER *Dict. Royal* II. s.v. *Shot*, Great and small Shot (great Guns and Muskets), *le Canon & la Mousqueterie*.

†**b.** A shooting weapon, a cannon or musket.

*a* **1578** LINDESAY (Pitscottie) *Chron. Scot.* (S.T.S.) I. 251, iij[c] schott of small artaillzie. *Ibid.* II. 185 Quhilk schip.. had xx gret brassin schottis in hir. **1599** MINSHEU *Span. Dict.*, What armes serue you with, a pike or shot? *con pica, o arcabúz.*

†**21. a.** *collect. sing.* Soldiers armed with muskets or other firearms (rarely with bows). ***small shot***: troops furnished with small arms as distinguished from artillerymen. *Obs.*

**1572** WALSINGHAM in D. Digges *Complete Ambass.* (1655) 314 To send under.. the Marquis de Maine 1000 shot,.. who shal land at a place called Aier. **1590** SIR W. WILLIAMS *Brief Disc. War* 46 To prooue Bow-men the worst shot vsed in these daies. **1617** MORYSON *Itin.* II. 118 His Lordship.. had lodged in a trench some foure hundred shot, charging them not to shoot till the rebels approached neere. **1706** PHILLIPS (ed. Kersey) s.v. *Tower*, Hollow Tower.. where the Small-Shot are plac'd that they may not be too much expos'd to the Enemies View.

†**b.** A soldier armed with a firearm. *Obs. rare.*

**1597** SHAKS. *2 Hen. IV*, III. ii. 294. **1598** BARRET *Theor. Warres* III. ii. 71 Hee is but a foolish shot, that shooteth at.. light skirmishers. **1611** COTGR., *Harquebusier*, an Arquebusier, or small shot.

**22. a.** One who shoots; an expert in shooting. Often with qualifying adj., ***good***, ***bad shot***. ***dead shot***: see DEAD *a.* 31 b.

**1780** *Mirror* No. 69 As I am a good shot, I spend great part of my time in shooting. **1823** COBBETT *Rur. Rides* (1885) I. 367 A professed shot is, almost always, a very disagreeable brother sportsman. **1826** DISRAELI *V. Grey* II. ix, No, I am no shot. **1882** SIR R. TEMPLE in *Proc. R. Geog. Soc.* N.S. IV. 460 He was taught to be a splendid shot with the gun and with the bow.

*transf.* **1897** *Encycl. Sport* I. 420/2 (Assoc. Football) Half-backs should be good shots at goal, for they frequently have chances of scoring.

**b.** ***queer shot*** (dial.): an 'odd customer'.

**1900** 'SARAH GRAND' *Babs* xl, 'You're a queer shot, Tinney,' she remarked.

**c.** ***big shot*** (formerly also ***great*** or ***high shot***), an important person; a prominent member of a profession, organization, etc. Also *attrib.* Chiefly *U.S.*

**1861** G. MEREDITH *Let.* 9 July (1970) I. 91 The great 'shots' of Stanz parade the town with their prizes in their hats. **1929** *Cincinnati* (Ohio) *Enquirer* 5 Oct. 10/3 One of them is just as likely to win the series as one of the 'big shots'. **1933** D. RUNYON in *Collier's* 28 Jan. 41/1 Many of these guys are very high shots during the gold rush. **1935** C. ODETS *Waiting for Lefty* in *3 Plays* (1936) iii. 135 Sure, the big shot money men want us like that. **1941** AUDEN *New Year Letter* II. 33 Unlike the big-shots of the day. **1957** H. ROOSENBURG *Walls came tumbling Down* iii. 74 Who are these new prisoners? Are they all the big-shot Nazis? **1960** *New Statesman* 9 Jan. 31/1 On arrival I was asked to dine with Thomas Lamont, along with a number of big-shots in the American newspaper world, including.. Henry Luce of *Time-Life*. **1974** K. MILLET *Flying* (1975) III. 300 He would still go for his man in an interview. Used the program to get the big shots.

**IV.** Payment, share. [Cf. OE. *scéotan* (= SHOOT *v.*) to pay, contribute.]

**23. a.** The charge, reckoning, amount due or to be paid, esp. at a tavern or for entertainment; a or one's share in such payment. Now only *colloq.* ***to stand shot*** [perh. with allusion to sense 7], to meet the expenses, pay the bill (for all).

*c* **1475** *Songs & Carols* (Percy Soc.) 94 On cast down her schott and went her wey. Gossip, quod Elenore, what dyd she paye? Not but a peny. **1617** MORYSON *Itin.* III. 84 The shot demanded must be paid without expostulation. **1732** *Tricks of Town* 3, I could stand it no longer, but paid my Shot.. and came away. **1821** SCOTT *Kenilw.* xix, Are you to stand shot to all this good liquor? **1891** MRS. RIDDELL *Mad Tour* 107, I was to make enough to.. 'pay my own shot'.

**b.** *transf.* and *fig.* Also in fig. context.

*a* **1533** BERNERS *Gold. Bk. M. Aurel.* (1546) A a viij b, She .. wil not be paied, but with the shotte of our lyfe. **1612** DAY *Festivals* ii. (1615) 50 Our Saviour hath paid al the shot. **1677** W. HUBBARD *Narrative* II. 26 The Indians invited themselves to breakfast with him, making the poor Fellow pay the shot.. with the loss of his life.

†**c.** ***to have free shot***: to have gratuitous entertainment. *Obs. rare.*

**1585** T. WASHINGTON tr. *Nicholay's Voy.* III. xviii. 104 [They] go roging alone.. following the bathes, tauernes and assemblies, for to haue free shot and cheare.

†**d.** A levy or contribution of so much a head from the members of a company for some common purpose. Also, a banquet to which each guest contributes his share (tr. Gr. ἔρανος). *Obs.*

**1519** HORMAN *Vulgaria* 283 Let vs gether or make a schotte or a stake for the mynstrels rewarde or wagis. **1615** CHAPMAN *Odyss.* XI. 545 As when you see At any rich mans nuptials, shot, or feast, About his kitchin, white-tooth'd swine lie drest.

†**e.** ***the whole shot***: the 'sum and substance'.

**1628** T. SPENCER *Logick* 151 These words.. doe containe the whole shot, or generall summe that ariseth from all the precepts, belonging to this part of Logicke. **1642** FULLER *Holy & Prof. St.* III. xx. 208 Ancient Fathers made the Creed *symbolum*, the shot and totall summe of Faith.

†**f.** A supply or amount of drink. *Obs.*

**1676** O. HEYWOOD *Diaries* (1882) I. 339 A company of fellows would needs drink *2d* a peece.. their vain way of drinking shots. **1691** MEEKE *Diary* 23 Jan. (1874) 34 About noon we returned, had a shot of ale at Slathwaite.

**g.** A dram of spirits.

**1928** WODEHOUSE *Good Morning, Bill* II. 72, I think *I'll* take a shot in a glass. **1935** J. T. FARRELL *Judgment Day* II. xviii. 449 Near White City he stopped in front of a speakeasy, deciding that one good, stiff shot would jack him up. **1955** 'A. GILBERT' *Is She dead Too?* vi. 112 Edwin.. produced a very little whisky in a bottle. Lamb.. gave himself a generous shot in the cup of tea. **1979** R. JAFFE *Class Reunion* (1980) II. v. 235 He poured two shots of vodka, one for her and one for himself.

†**24.** ***shot and lot*** = ***scot and lot***: see SCOT *sb.*[2] 4.

**1100** *Charter Hen. I* in *Liber Albus* (Rolls) 128 Item, quod cives Londoniarum sint quieti de Schot et Loth, et de Danegelde. **1459** *Cal. Anc. Rec. Dublin* (1889) 301 They schall ber lot and schot with the citte to all maner workys. **1668** in Jeake *Chart. Cinque Ports* (1728) 168 Rationabil. & ratabil. taxationes, scott. shott. & lott. tallag. & rationabil. taxationes communiter vocat. common fines.

**V.** Senses of doubtful position.

**25.** A division of land.

*a* **1490** BOTONER *Itin.* (1778) 152 Englysh stonys et le rok vocat. Trogy, anglice le shotes. **1523** FITZHERB. *Surv.* 40 b, This medowe lyeth in dyuers shotes of length somtyme in two shotes of length somtyme in one & somtyme in thre. **1743** R. MAXWELL *Sel. Trans. Agric. Scot.* 32 The Infield is divided into three Shots or Parts, much about eighteen Acres in all. *a* **1805** A. CARLYLE *Autobiog.* iii. (1860) 138 That part of it [the plain] which belonged to Preston estate was divided into three shots, as they were called, or rigg lengths, the under shot, the middle, and the upper. **1822** SCOTT *Pirate* xxx, He claps down an enclosure in the middle of my bit shot of corn. **1854** J. M. KEMBLE *Surrey Provinc.* in *Trans. Philol. Soc.* 84 *Shot*, a portion of land... 'Will you let the upper shot be laid up for hay?' **1887** S. H. A. HERVEY *Wedmore Chron.* I. 181 (E.D.D.) [Somerset] Each of these fields was divided into shots or furlongs. **1907** *Times* 15 June 24/2 Nineteen Plots or 'Shots' of Freehold and copyhold land.. in Bearfield and Hamfield.

**26.** *Shetland.* (Also *shott.*) A compartment in the stern of a boat (see quots.).

**1834** G. & P. ANDERSON *Guide Highl.* 709 Another extricates the fish from the hooks, and throws them in a place near the stern, named the shot. **1899** J. SPENCE *Shetl. Folk-Lore* 127 The old *haf* boat.. was divided into six compartments, viz., fore-head,.. shott [etc.]... The shott.. formed a sort of hold in which the fish were carried.

**27.** = SHOT-WINDOW. *Sc.* ? *Obs.*

**1513** DOUGLAS *Æneis* VII. Prol. 138 The schot [cf. *shot wyndo* above, line 129] I clossit and drew inwort in hy. **1638** R. BAILLIE *Lett. & Jrnls.* (1841) I. 91 Some out of shotts cryed rebels on the readers. **1722** WODROW *Hist. Suff. Ch. Scot.* III. vii. II. 286 With Windows called Shots, or Shutters of Timber, and a few Inches of Glass above them.

**28.** A corpse disinterred by body-snatchers.

App. from the expression 'a good shot for the doctors'.

**1828** *Ann. Reg.* 377/2 Burke.. asked witness to go down to his house, to see the shot he had got to take to the doctor's. .. Understood by the word shot that he was going to murder the woman. *Ibid.* 380/1 M'Dougal came and said to witness, there was a shot in the house. She did not say what she meant by a shot. **1867** *All Year Round* 16 Mar. 285/1 Burke .. told him he had got an old woman off the street, who would be a good shot for the doctors (that was the phrase of these men for a person they had fixed on to murder). **1882** SALA *Amer. Revis.* (1885) 206 Servants.. who, for the consideration of so many dollars per 'shot', or human body, undertake to supply subjects for dissection to the anatomical schools throughout the States.

**29.** ***that's the shot!*** and varr.: in expressions of approval, that's a good idea, or the 'very thing'. *Austral. colloq.*

**1953** T. A. G. HUNGERFORD *Riverslake* 142 That's the shot. Buy a bit of land and grow things. **1958** R. STOW *To Islands* ii. 46 Cattle's the shot... They worked it before. **1963** J. CLEARY *Flight of Chariots* 370, I think a good strong cuppa brew would be the shot. **1976** D. IRELAND *Glass Canoe* 227 'That's the shot,' said Mick. 'Stick around and guard the place.'

**VI.** *attrib.* and *Comb.*

**30.** simple attributive, as ***shot-belt*** (also *attrib.*), so ***shot-belted*** adj., ***-box***, ***-cartridge***, ***-gauge***, ***-like*** adj., ***-mould***, ***-proof*** adj., ***-range***, ***-wound***, etc.; objective, as ***shot-casting***, ***-sorter***; instrumental, as ***shot-shivered***, ***-swept*** adjs.

**1805** *Times* in *Spirit Publ. Jrnls.* (1806) IX. 310 *Shot-belts, pouches, powder-flasks [etc.]. **1823** SYD. SMITH *Game Laws* Wks. 1859 II. 30/1 A feeling not only among Reviewers, who never see nor eat game, but among the double-barrelled, *shot-belted members of the House of

Commons. **1829** MARRYAT *F. Mildmay* viii, Sitting on a *shot-box. **1875** KNIGHT *Dict. Mech.*, **Shot-cartridge*, a round of ammunition for a shot-gun. **1907** J. H. PATTERSON *Man-Eaters of Tsavo* App. I. 319, 500 12-bore shot cartridges of, say, the 6 and 8 sizes. **1835** URE *Philos. Manuf.* 59 Granulating and *shot casting. **1841** TOTTEN (Webster 1847) *Shot-gauge. **1805** *Shipwright's Vade-M.* 131 **Shot-lockers*, or *Garlands*, apartments built up in the hold to contain the shot. **1842–63** BURN *Nav. & Mil. Techn. Dict.* I, *Coquille à boulets*, *shot-mould consisting of two cubes of iron with a hemisphere hollowed in each. **1859** F. S. COOPER *Ironmongers' Catal.* 38 Bullet and Shot Moulds. **1599** B. JONSON *Cynthia's Rev.* V. x, Aretes fauour makes any one *shot-proofe against thee, Cvpid. **1863** TREVELYAN *Compet. Wallah* (1866) 84 A shot-proof screen of boards. **1862** *Catal. Internat. Exhib.* II. XII. 17 *Shot proofing for ships and batteries. **1837** CARLYLE *Fr. Rev.* I. VII. vii, Were it not well to draw back out of *shot-range? **1636** PRYNNE *Rem. agst. Shipmoney* 10 To provide fourty, five and fourty, and fifty *shot round of powder and bullets, for every peece in the Ships set out. **1806** J. GRAHAME *Birds Scot.* 76 Then.. flies To some *shot-shivered branch. **1842–63** BURN *Nav. & Mil. Techn. Dict.* I. s.v. *Coup*, [*Coup de feu*] shot, *shot-wound. **1854** DK. NEWCASTLE in J. Martineau *Life* (1908) 161 Sir George Brown's horse received no less than six shot-wounds.

**31.** Special comb.: **shot-borer**, a beetle, *Xyleborus dispar*, which bores small round holes in the bark of trees; **shot bort** (see quot.); **shot-corn**, a small shot, a grain of shot; **shot-drill**, an obsolete form of military punishment in which the soldier punished had to carry a cannon-ball; **shot effect** [tr. G. *schroteffekt* (W. Schottky 1918, in *Ann. der Physik* LVII. 547), f. *schrot* small shot], the fluctuation in the magnitude of the anode current in a thermionic valve due to the random character of electron emission; also *transf.*, any fluctuation having a similar stochastic character; **shot-firer**, (*a*) a man employed to fire the shot (sense 7 f) in blasting; (*b*) an electrical device for detonating the shot; hence **shot-firing**; †**shot-flagon** *dial.* (see quot.); **shot-glass**, (*a*) [see 5] *Weaving*, a cloth-prover (Ogilvie, 1882); (*b*) *U.S.* a glass for holding a short drink; **shot gold** orig. *U.S.*, gold occurring in the form of small spheres like lead shot; **shot-lighter**, the man who fires the 'shot' in a mine; **shot line** = *shot rope* below; **shot list** *Cinematogr.* and *Television*, a list of shots made by a camera; **shotmaking** *U.S.*, in golf, tennis, etc.: the playing of (esp. successful or attacking) strokes; also **shotmaker**; **shot-mark**, †(*a*) a mark to aim or shoot at; (*b*) a mark made by a shot; **shot-metal** (see quot. 1875); **shot noise** = *shot effect* above; **shot-peening** [see PEEN, PENE *v.*], the use of a stream of hard metal particles directed against a metal part to harden and strengthen its surface; so **shot-peen** *v. trans.*; **shot-peened** *ppl. a.*; **shot-pepper**, (see quots.); **shot-plug**, a tapered cone of wood to stop a shot-hole in a vessel's side, to prevent leakage (Smyth *Sailor's Word-bk.* 1867); †**shot-pot**, ? = *shot-flagon*; **shot-prop** [? after Du. *geschutprop* = G. *schusspropfen*: cf. PROP *sb.*[2]] = *shot-plug* (Knight *Dict. Mech.* 1875); **shot-putter**, one who puts the shot in athletic sports, so ***shot-putting***; **shot-rack** (see quot. 1867); **shot rope**, a weighted rope hung over the side of a boat and used to guide the descent and ascent of divers; †**shot-shark**, a tavern waiter; **shot soup** (see quot. 1847); **shot-tower**, a tall round tower in which small shot are made by dropping molten lead from the top into water; †**shot-whaip** *Sc.*, a variety of curlew. See also SHOT-BOARD, -BUSH, -CLOG, etc.

**1890** MISS E. A. ORMEROD *Injur. Insects* (ed. 2) 331, I found that the cause of the injury was the '*Shot-borer' Beetle. *Ibid.* 334 The Shot-borer frequents stumps or fallen trees. **1910** *Encycl. Brit.* IV. 276/2 The typical bort occurs in small spherical masses... These masses..are often called '*shot bort' or 'round bort'. *c* **1792** *Encycl. Brit.* (ed. 3) X. 39/1 A middling sized *shot-corn. **1794–6** E. DARWIN *Zoon.* (1801) II. 62 As large as shot-corns. **1869** E. A. PARKES *Pract. Hygiene* (ed. 3) 385 The *shot-drill which military prisoners perform. **1936** 'R. HYDE' *Passport to Hell* xv. 232 Either he didn't know I was supposed to be in Le Havre doing shot drill, or he'd forgotten. [**1921** *Sci. Abstr.* A. XXIV. 759 The object is the measurement of the spontaneous current variations in high-vacuum discharge tubes, a subject which has been previously dealt with theoretically by Schottky and called by him the 'Schrot effect' (literally, the small shot effect).] **1923** *Chem. Abstr.* XVII. 924 (*heading*) The present state of the *shot effect problem. **1930** *Proc. IRE* XVIII. 243 In the absence of space charge the noise has been termed by Schottky the 'schroteffekt', or 'small shot effect', from the analogy which the flight of electrons from the filament to the plate of a vacuum tube bears to the spattering of small shot fired from a shot gun. The simple term 'shot effect' will be used in this paper to denote this noise either with or without space charge. **1947** *Electronic Engin.* XIX. 82/1 Shot effect is more pronounced when the negative grid bias is greater than the usual value. **1964** N. WIENER *God & Golem* 41 There are.. cases..where these irregularities are just what we wish to produce, and there are commercial devices for producing them. These are known as shot-effect generators. **1968** P. A. P. MORAN *Introd. Probability Theory* ix. 423 Campbell's theorem originally arose in the study of the 'shot effect' in thermionic vacuum tubes. **1883** W. S. GRESLEY *Gloss. Terms Coal Mining* 219 **Shot firer*, a man specially appointed by the manager of a mine to fire off every shot in a certain number of stalls or heads during the shift. **1886** J. BARROWMAN *Sc. Mining Terms* 60 *Shot firer*, the person appointed to fire shots in fiery workings. **1891** C. PAMELY *Colliery Manager's Handbk.* xiv. 472 Shots are fired by the aid of litter straws, paper squibs.., safety fuze or by an electric shot-firer. **1939** G. HEYER *No Wind of Blame* xvi. 315 'What's that thing called that they use in mines when they want to blast? Electrical thing they touch off the dynamite with?' 'A shot-firer, do you mean?' **1973** 'J. PATRICK' *Glasgow Gang Observed* xvii. 140 He began work as a shot firer in a factory close to the approved school. **1884** *Engineering* 31 Oct. 420/2 (*heading*) *Shot-firing in mines. **1959** *Times Rev. Industry* Feb. 14/1 For many years the infusion of coal *in situ* by water under pressure has been employed to reduce the dust hazard. Recently this procedure has been combined with that of shot-firing. **1691** RAY *N.C. Words* (ed. 2) 62 The **Shot-flagon* or *Come again*; which the Host gives to his guests of [*read* if] they drink above a Shilling, *Darbish*. **1955** A. MILLER *Mem. Two Mondays* in *View from Bridge* 43 Enter Bert, carefully carrying a *shotglass of whisky. **1970** A. MALING *Lambert's Son* (1972) xxxviii. 157, I put the lemon twists in a shot glass. **1858** *Pike's Peak Guide Book* 222 Those who have prospected over in the parks..say that they find the *shot gold there. **1929** E. J. DUNN *Geol. Gold* xvii. 185 Spherical grains and small pieces of gold are found in the alluvial wash at Creswick... They are often quite spherical, generally of small size, but occasionally up to several dwts. in weight, and are known as 'shot gold'. **1971** A. P. MCINNES *Dunlevy* 113 Shot gold..is always considered a coarse gold prospect, indicating coarser gold lower down. **1881** *Instr. Census Clerks* (1885) 84 Miners... *Shot-lighter. **1897** *L'pool Courier* 10 Mar. 3/8 A colliery shotlighter,..was summoned by his employers. **1968** A. P. BALDER *Compl. Man. Skin Diving* xiii. 248 A *shot line..should be used from a boat when diving in bad visibility. **1976** ZANELLI & SKUSE *Sub-Aqua Illustr. Dict.* 84/2 *Shot line*, a line to which a very heavy weight (or 'shot') is fixed. It is used to guide the descent and ascent of divers. It must not be used as an anchor, because shot lines should be hung vertically. **1969** J. ELLIOT *Duel* III. ii. 233 She..learned how to make production breakdowns, set out commentary scripts, type *shot lists. **1971** P. PURSER *Holy Father's Navy* xxi. 101 The film was back from the labs, the shot list neatly typed up, the editing facilities booked. **1974** *Union* (S. Carolina) *Daily Times* 23 Apr. 9/5 The best five *shot-makers in each team. **1969** *New Yorker* 14 June 45/1 My style is playmaking—consistent, percentage tennis—and his style is *shotmaking. **1977** *Ibid.* 8 Aug. 48/3 These statistics..give no indication of the absolutely superb shotmaking that Bolt produced on an exceedingly narrow, fast, and exacting course. **1610** HEALEY *St. Aug. Citie of God* VIII. viii. 309 They beleeued that his [*sc.* man's] cheefe good must..therein subsist; as the finall end standing as the *shot-marke of all their actions. **1828** *Trial W. Dyon at York Assizes* 9 There were two shot marks on the left side. **1875** KNIGHT *Dict. Mech.*, **Shot-metal*, an alloy of lead, 56 parts; arsenic, 1. Used for making bird-shot. **1930** *Proc. IRE* XVIII. 255 The solid line curve *D* is the sum of the calculated *shot and thermal noises. **1978** *Nature* 8 June 432/1 Individual QSO continuum magnitudes, which are also affected by the added uncertainty introduced by shot noise were generally accurate to ±7%. **1944** *Proc. Soc. Exper. Stress Analysis* II. 172/2 These pieces..were *shot-peened on both flat faces. **1944** H. F. MOORE *Shot Peening & Fatigue of Metals* (Amer. Foundry Equipment Co.) 5/1 The metal just below the *shot-peened layer is somewhat affected by the *shot peening. **1956** F. H. KEATING *Chromium-Nickel Austenitic Steels* v. 70 Well substantiated claims have been made for improvement in fatigue-resistance by shot-peening, which introduces compressive stresses in the surface layers. **1962** *Engineering* 23 Mar. 403/2, 85 per cent of the metal is machined away on electronically controlled milling machines before being curved by press or shot-peening. **1972** L. M. HARRIS *Introd. Deepwater Floating Drilling Operations* xii. 138 Each weld should be ground inside and out, and the transition area and weld shotpeened. **1972** H. T. JENSEN in Mann & Milligan *Aircraft Fatigue* 156 We established an allowable strength of two-thirds of the strength of the machined and shot-peened strength for components that retain their as-forged surfaces. **1890** *Century Dict.* s.v. *Pepper*, **shot-pepper*, the heavier kinds of Sumatra pepper. **1898** SENN *Culin. Encycl.* 86 *Shot Pepper*. This is mignonette pepper, which is made from white peppercorns. It is broken into grains or granulated about the size of mignonette seed. **1829** *Shot-plug [see SHOT-HOLE 1]. **1664** COTTON *Scarron.* IV. 111 Straight to the Wharff repairs the hot-shot, Without once calling for his *shot-pot. **1882** *Tales Mod. Oxford* 99 Lord, the *shot-putter. **1894** *Outing* XXIV. 444/2 *Shot-putting had been his favourite game. **1834** MARRYAT *P. Simple* xi, I did contrive to crawl up the ladder to the main deck, where I sat down on the *shot-racks. **1867** SMYTH *Sailor's Word-bk.*, *Shot-racks*, wooden frames fixed at convenient distances to contain shot. There are also, of recent introduction, iron rods so fitted as to confine the shot. **1909** *Man. Seamanship* (Admiralty) II. vi. 116 As soon as the diver sees anything he can signal for *shot rope to be lowered. **1940** 'N. SHUTE' *Landfall* 257 Then in slow motion he [*sc.* a diver] reached out and grasped the shot-rope, stepped off the ladder and was gone. **1960** BROOKES & BROADHURST *Diving Manual* (ed. 2) 105 A shot rope should be very heavily weighted so that it will hang vertically in the water, uninfluenced by tides and currents. **1599** B. JONSON *Ev. Man out of Hum.* V. iv, Holla: where be these *shot-sharkes? **1847** H. MELVILLE *Omoo* iii, What English seamen call '*shot soup'—great round peas, polishing themselves like pebbles by rolling about in tepid water. **1835** URE *Philos. Manuf.* 59 A shower of drops, which congeal in the course of their descent from the top of the *shot-towers into the water-cistern. **1639** SIR R. GORDON *Gen. Hist. Earld. Sutherld.* (1813) 3 Routs, whaips, *shot-whaips, woodcok, larkes, [etc.].

†**shot**, *sb.*[2] *Naut. Obs.* Forms: 4 **shote**, 5 **shott**, 7– **shot**. [Of uncertain origin; perh. a use of prec.; see SHOOT *v.* 38. But cf. SCOTE *sb.*[1]] Two cables spliced together.

**1316** *Exch. Acc. Army* Bundle 15 No. 3 Vna cabula vocata shote. **1497** *Naval Acc. Hen. VII* (1896) 184 A shott of Newe Cables. *a* **1625** *Nomencl. Navalis* (Harl. MS. 2301) 72 Shot of Cabell. Two Cabells spliced together make a Shot. *a* **1642** SIR W. MONSON *Naval Tracts* III. (1704) 375/2 Never Ships..were better fitted with Ground Tackle, or whole Shots of Cables. **1750**, **1847** [see SHEET-SHOT].

**shot**, *sb.*[3] Also **shott**. [subst. use of SHOT *ppl. a.* (Cf. SHOOT *v.* 11 g.)] An ill-grown ewe; a refuse animal left after the best of the flock or herd have been selected.

**1796** *Statist. Acc. Scot.* XVIII. 569 A few of the worst ewes called shotts, are likewise sold every year about Martinmas. **1865** A. SMITH *Summer in Skye* II. 140 The inferior qualities [of ewes]—shots, as they are technically called—occupied a place by themselves.

*attrib.* **1878** *Cumberld. Gloss.*, *Shot sheep or cattle*, *Shots*, the refuse; the leavings; the worst. **1886** C. SCOTT *Sheep-farming* 109, 62 Shot ewe and wedder lambs at 5/-.

**shot** (ʃɒt), *sb.*[4] [SHOT *ppl. a.*, used ellipt.] A 'shot' silken or other fabric.

**1883** *Daily News* 10 Oct. 7/5 The new Tissu for Costumes, 'Poil de Bison', in broché, in stripe, and in shot, all made to match. **1893** *Pall Mall Gaz.* 9 Jan. 2/1 Shots and stripes will be in fashion.

**shot** (ʃɒt), *v.* [f. SHOT *sb.*[1]]

†**1.** *intr.* ? To participate or consort *with*. *Obs.*

*a* **1250** *Prov. Alfred* 411 in *O.E. Misc.* 126 Ne gabbe þu ne schotte ne chid þu wyth none sotte.

**2.** *trans.* To load (a fire-arm) with shot.

**1681** R. KNOX *Hist. Ceylon* 119 His order to me was, to see the top Chains put upon the Cables, and the Guns shotted. **1781** in Nicolas *Disp. Nelson* (1846) VII. Add. p. iii, Firing twenty-six nine-pounders, and one eighteen-pounder, shotted at her. **1863** W. PHILLIPS *Sp.* vi. 106 The guns are shotted to their lips.

**b.** *transf.* and *fig.*

**1822** SCOTT *Pirate* xxxiv, It was the gracious custom of this commander to mix his words and oaths in nearly equal proportions, which he was wont to call *shotting* his discourse. **1861** L. L. NOBLE *Icebergs* 163 A pudding of rice well shotted with raisins. **1884** SHARMAN *Hist. Swearing* i. 20 Their every word was shotted with an oath.

**3.** To weight by attaching a shot or shots, so as to cause to sink in water.

**1857** W. SMITH *Thorndale* III. iv. 230 With this in my pocket, I was shotted for a sailor's grave. **1910** *Spectator* 23 Apr. 664 The line is shotted carefully so as to sink the bait to the right depth.

**4.** To supply with shot.

**1886** *Pall Mall Gaz.* 21 Aug. 2/2 This other fleet—how differently armed, how differently shotted.

**5.** To wound or hit with shot.

**1855** BAILEY *Mystic* 75 Who..fell Shotted with three times Cæsar's trickling wounds.

**6. a.** *slang.* To give (a horse) a dose of small shot so as to make it appear sound-winded. (Cf. SHOT *sb.*[1] 15 b.)

**1890** BARRÈRE & LELAND *Dict. Slang* s.v. **1902** FARMER & HENLEY *Slang*.

**b.** To clean (bottles) by partially filling with shot and shaking.

**1895** in *Funk's Stand. Dict.*

**7.** To variegate in weaving.

**1847** TALFOURD *Vacation Rambles* I. 218 It was shotted, like wavy silk, with the pale violet crocus.

**shot** (ʃɒt), *ppl. a.* [pa. pple. of SHOOT *v.*[1]]

**1.** Of a fish: having discharged its spawn. (Cf. SHOTTEN *ppl. a.* 3.)

**1414** in Riley *Mem. Lond.* (1868) 599 [All manner of fish called] shotfisshe [taken in the Thames]. **1618** BRAITHWAITE *Rem. Death* E 7 b, Darted, He runnes as swift as euer ran, Shot-herring made. **1865** J. SLEIGH *Derbysh. Gloss.* (E.D.D.), As lean as a shot-herring.

**2.** Of a stalk, blade, etc.: that has grown or sprouted. ***shot-blade***, that part of the corn-stalk which encloses the ear.

**1629** Z. BOYD *Last Battell* 726 (Jam.), The sunne.. maketh..the cornes to come vp at the first with small green points, and after that to shoote vp to the shot bled, and after that to come to the seede. **1799** J. ROBERTSON *Agric. Perth* 196 Weeds are taken from the oats and barley when they are in the shot blade. **1830** *Kyle Farm Rep.* 83 in *Libr. Usef. Knowl., Husb.* III. The only grass sown in this district is perennial rye grass, the very worst for pasture, as cattle reject its shot stalks.

**3.** Of a bullet, arrow, etc.: that is discharged. Also of a bolt: that has been pushed into or out of the lock.

**1863** *Leisure Hour* Jan. 2 The rusty sockets of a shot-bolt. **1908** *Edin. Rev.* Oct. 364 The spiral ascent, the shot-arrow precipitation earthwards.

**4. a.** Hit, wounded or killed by a projectile discharged from a gun or bow. Also with *down*: of an aircraft or its crew.

**1837** CARLYLE *Fr. Rev.* I. VII. x, Other women lift the corpse of shot Jerôme. **1881** TYNDALL *Floating Matter in Air* 103 A shot hare will remain soft and limp for a day. **1943** 'M. COLES' *Without Lawful Authority* ix. 115 'The 'plane.. crashed in flames just this side of the Polish frontier... One of our fellows..says there were bullet-holes in the wings.' 'Shot down, eh?' **1957** H. ROOSENBURG *Walls came tumbling Down* 7 A local resistance group..concentrated on picking up shot-down Allied pilots. **1968** *Listener* 26 Dec. 858/2 He was also the source of her story..of the shot-down pilot who told his captors that his sister in the States was a rich '*industrielle*'. **1980** E. BEHR *Getting Even* x. 120 Organising escape routes for shot-down R.A.F. and U.S. air crews on the run.

**b.** Drunk. *slang* (chiefly *U.S.*, *Austral.*, and *N.Z.*). Cf. SHOOT *v.* 32 d.

**1864** *Harper's Mag.* May 856/2 He again sat down by the fire..by which time he was pretty well 'shot'. **1896** W. C.

GORE in *Inlander* Jan. 146 *Shot*, a. Intoxicated. **1930** *Sat. Even. Post* 26 July 145/2 'I'm half shot,' he said... 'An' so are you. You're just as drunk as I am.' **1943** N. MARSH *Colour Scheme* x. 187 The chap was half-shot... He smelt of booze. **1957** *Nelson* (N.Z.) *Even. Mail* 18 May 7 He asked the man: 'Are you shot?' The man said: 'Yes.'.. It was ascertained that he had fallen down while intoxicated. **1972** T. LILLEY *K Section* ix. 43 He was well shot last night. Staggering.

**c.** In fig. phr. ***shot through*** (also ***to hell*** or ***pieces***), in a state of ruin or collapse. *colloq.* (chiefly *U.S.*).

**1926** E. HEMINGWAY *Fiesta* (1927) III. xix. 277 That meant San Sebastian all shot to hell. **1932** L. GOLDING *Magnolia St.* I. iv. 67 The old man was all shot to pieces... He had fallen into a sort of torpor. **1937** H. G. WELLS *Brynhild* xi. 243 To-day I feel shot through. I feel shot to pieces. **1977** M. BABSON *Murder, Murder, Little Star* vii. 50 Look at the price I pay. My private life is shot to hell.

**d.** Of things: worn out, ruined, used up, spent. *slang* (chiefly *U.S.*).

**1933** C. K. STEWART *Speech Amer. Airman* (Univ. Akron thesis) 89 *Shot*, an adjective meaning 'useless' 'gone', or 'worn out'. **1960** *Analog Science Fact/Fiction* Oct. 136/1 With him gone, the interstellar drive project would've been shot. **1970** I. PETITE *Meander to Alaska* I. vii. 66 At that point they discovered that the transmission bearings were 'shot'. **1981** G. V. HIGGINS *Rat on Fire* vii. 54 Your boiler is one of those old things... I think it's about shot.

**e.** With *up*, severely wounded or damaged by shooting. Also *fig.* (*colloq.*) and *transf.* drugged (*U.S. slang*).

**1934** V. M. YEATES *Winged Victory* I. xviii. 146 If he tried to do anything on his own he would probably get himself shot down, or at least shot up. **1938** [see POLLUTED *ppl. a.* b]. **1945** *Richmond* (Va.) *Times-Dispatch* 22 May 2/8 The Forty-fifth Division's 'most shot up soldier to return alive' is back in the States. **1964** L. NKOSI *Rhythm of Violence* 63 Stop Shouting!.. Are you all shot up or something! **1978** *Detroit Free Press* 2 Apr. (Detroit Suppl.) 8/1 Starting up the stairs, she steps around a recently shot-up addict who is just nodding off.

**f.** Of people: exhausted. *slang* (chiefly *U.S.*).

**1939** [see COSY *v.* 2]. **1945** G. CASEY *Downhill is Easier* IV. 183 Late at night you could easily walk the twelve miles.. without seeing a vehicle. I realized I was shot. **1951** E. B. WHITE *Let.* 11 Dec. (1976) 346 Ross died last week and we have been in something of a scramble here, as well as feeling quite shot. **1967** 'V. SILLER' *Biltmore Call* 120, I thought she was shot and her nerves had given out. **1972** J. GORES *Dead Skip* (1973) xii. 83 He..[was] literally too tired to move... Shot. Utterly shot.

**5. a.** Of a textile fabric: Woven with warp-threads of one colour and weft-threads of another, so that the fabric (usually silk) changes in tint when viewed from different points. Also, applied to mixed fabrics (esp. of cotton and silk), dyed by a process which produces a variegated effect similar to that of 'shot silk'.

**1763** CHURCHILL *Ghost* IV. 847 A slight shot silk. **1843** *Penny Cycl.* XXVII. 177/2 This produces the peculiar effect called shot patterns. **1847** C. BRONTË *Jane Eyre* I. vii. 117 A spread of shot orange and purple pelisses. **1870** ROCK *Text. Fabr.* Introd. i. 91 Shot, or, as they were then called, changeable silks, were fashionable in England during the sixteenth century. **1882** *Artist* 1 Feb. 55/1 Shot velvets are being worn for visiting dresses.

**b.** ***shot-silk***: used *attrib.* or *adj.* = made of or resembling shot silk.

**1850** THACKERAY *Pendennis* lxv, Feathers, and flowers, and trinkets, and a shot-silk dress, and a wonderful mantle. **1882** *Garden* 7 Jan. 7/2 The whole forming one of the finest 'shot silk' bed arrangements that can be conceived.

**c.** Of a colour, etc.: Changeable, variable, resembling that of 'shot silk'.

**1824** HEBER *Jrnl.* 31 July, An ape.. covered with long silky hair generally of a rusty lead colour, but on his breast a fine shot blue. **1877** HUXLEY *Anat. Inv. Anim.* viii. 519 The peculiar play of 'shot' colours, which pass like blushes over their [*sc.* Cephalopoda] surface, in the living state.

**6.** Of copper: Short for *bean-* or *feather-shot*.

**1877** GEE *Silversmith's Handbk.* 68 We have recommended the employment of shot copper [cf. p. 44 bean-shot] in the manufacture of silver alloys.

**7.** Of metal: Welded. (Cf. SHOOT *v.* 38, SHUT *v.* 6.)

**1810** *Table Blade Forger's Statem.* (Sheffield Gloss. 1888) Shot chicken carvers. **1833** J. HOLLAND *Manuf. Metal* II. 38 Shot scissors;—consisting of steel blades, and iron shank and bows.

**8.** Comb.: **shot-brae, -heuch** (†*pl.* **-houis**), *Sc.* a landslip. See also SHOT-FARE, SHOT-NET, SHOT STAR.

**1574** *Cal. Laing Charters* (1899) 225 Fra the said stane downe throuch the schothouis direct north to the burne of Awchlansky. **1822** *Blackw. Mag.* Feb. 181/1 With every here and there the recent scar of some extensive 'shot brae', or 'avalanche', which had rushed into the flood below. **1825** JAMIESON Suppl., *Shot-heuch.*

**shot**, variant of SHOAT[1], [2].

**shot-anchor**, obs. form of SHEET-ANCHOR.

**'shot-bag.** Chiefly *U.S.* [SHOT *sb.*[1]] A bag for carrying shot; a shot-pouch. Also *transf.* a purse.

**1638** in *Archives of Maryland* (1887) IV. 32 It[em] one fowling piece & shott bagge. **1756** P. HOG *Let.* 14 May in S. M. Hamilton *Lett. to Washington* (1898) I. 260 Going to Load he missed his Shot Bag which had been Carried away by one of the Shots. **1800** A. HENRY *Jrnl.* 4 Oct. (1897) I. iii. 111 The Indians were standing in the fort with nothing on but their breech-clouts, powder-horns, shot bags, and guns in their hands. **1872** 'MARK TWAIN' *Roughing It* ii. 5 We also took with us a little shot-bag of silver coin. **1946** *Aircraft Engineering* XVIII. 109/2 The time-honoured method of loading with shot bags the structure to be tested in an inverted position is still current practice across the Atlantic.

**'shot-blast.** [SHOT *sb.*[1]] A high-speed stream of steel particles directed at a surface to clean and roughen it.

**1923** *Foundry* 1 Feb. 13 Have you noticed how the modern shot-blast and grit-blast are replacing the old dust breeding sand-blast? **1934** *Foundry Trade Jrnl.* LI. 340 The barrel.. is essentially a contrivance for mechanically exposing every part of the casting or forging to be cleaned to the effect of the shot-blast. **1958** *Engineering* 21 Mar. 382/3 An airless type shot-blast plant has been installed, to deal with 35 tons of castings a day.

Hence **shot-blasting**, the use of a shot-blast; also **shot-blast** *v. trans.*, to subject to shot-blasting; **shot-blasted** *ppl. a.*; **shot-blaster**, a person using a shot-blast.

**1934** F. W. PARTINGTON *G. F. Charnock's Mech. Technol.* (ed. 2) xxxi. 415 Steel castings are frequently cleaned of both sand and scale by subjecting them to shot-blasting. **1937** *Jrnl. Iron & Steel Inst.* CXXXV. 160A (*heading*) Buick shotblasts large castings automatically. **1941** W. K. WILSON *Pract. Solution Torsional Vibration Problems* (ed. 2) II. vii. 146 Shot-blasted springs are very susceptible to rusting. **1946** *Engineer* 15 Feb. 152/1 A large-capacity dust extractor, coupled to the shot-blasting chamber, exhausts all the fine dust and sand. **1959** *Times* 27 Apr. (Suppl.) p. xi/4 It has first to be shot-blasted to provide an absolutely clean surface. **1961** *Evening Standard* 26 July 18/5 (Advt.), Shot blasters & metal sprayers..reqd. **1964** S. CRAWFORD *Basic Engin. Processes* iii. 87 Prior to bronze welding the joint faces or edges are cleaned by shot blasting. **1975** *Offshore Engineer* Sept. 143/4 A new version of their shot-blaster's helmet has been introduced by Martindale Protection. **1977** *Exchange & Mart* (South) 24 Feb. 19 M/3 One bodiless chassis, stripped, shotblasted, etc. partly reassembled.

†**'shotboard.** *Obs.* In 4 schote bord, 7 shot-boord. [? Cf. Du. *schot* partition.] ? A board of wainscot.

**1310** in Riley *Mem. Lond.* (1868) 75 [Four] schotebordes [value 8d.]. **1633** T. JAMES *Voy.* 70, I made a shot-boord to be naild on it: and to be made as tight as might be.

**shot-bush.** *U.S.* [SHOT *sb.*[1]; 'from its shot-like fruit' (*Cent. Dict.*).] A name for two species of *Aralia*: the small prickly tree Hercules' club, *A. spinosa*, and the Wild Sarsaparilla, *A. nudicaulis*.

**1785** [see *pigeon-weed* s.v. PIGEON *sb.* 6]. **1845-50** MRS. LINCOLN *Lect. Bot.* App. 75/2 *Aralia..spinosa* (shot-bush, angelica tree). **1872** SCHELE DE VERE *Americanisms* 414 In the South the *Tear-Coat* (Aralia spinosa), also humorously called *Shot-Bush*, rises almost to the dignity of a tree, its prickles being quite formidable to the hunting-shirts and Indian blankets.

†**shot-clog.** *Obs. rare.* [f. SHOT *sb.*[1] + CLOG *sb.* Cf. SHOT-LOG.] An unwelcome companion tolerated because he pays the shot for the rest.

**1599** B. JONSON *Ev. Man out of Hum.* v. vi, If you be out [of humour] keepe your distance, and bee not made a Shot-clog no more. **1601** —— *Poetaster* I. ii. **1626** —— *Staple of N.* IV. i. 47.

†**shote.** *Obs.* Also 4-6 schote. [ME. *schote*, in the 14th c. disyllabic and rhymed with words with long open *o*, seems to point to an OE. **scotu*, **scote*, or **scota*, cognate and synonymous with *scot* SHOT *sb.*[1] In some or all of the later instances, the word may be a mere graphic or dialectal variant of SHOOT *sb.*[1] or SHOT *sb.*[1]]

**1.** A rush or rapid motion.

*c* **1330** R. BRUNNE *Chron. Wace* (Rolls) 1738 Al holyke com þer flote In Dertemuthe, at o schote. *Ibid.* 15700 Cadwalyn was ofte on ffote Wyþ many fair[e] schip on schote, & wel þe wynd gan hym dryue.

**2.** The action or an act of shooting with a bow, gun, etc., also the missiles discharged. Cf. SHOT *sb.*[1]

Phrase, *all at one shote*, in a volley, all at once.

*c* **1330** R. BRUNNE *Chron. Wace* (Rolls) 861 Wyþ þat schote his ffader he slow. *c* **1400** *Laud Troy-bk.* 7722 Al was of man bothe nese & throte, And fyngres als for his schote. *c* **1425** *Cast. Persev.* 1957 in *Macro Plays* 135 Schete we all at a schote. **1481-90** *Howard Househ. Bks.* (Roxb.) 273 Perrin hath a cest ful of schote for crosbowes. **1541** *Act 33 Hen. VIII*, c. 6 No person..shall..shote..with any handgunne ..vpon peine for forfaite for euery such shote .x. li. **1596** DALRYMPLE tr. *Leslie's Hist. Scot.* v. (S.T.S.) I. 297 Sche subtilie, to flie the schotis of that Ingine, slipis intil a nuik neir by.

**3.** A crick in the neck, ? a spasm of pain.

*c* **1440** *Promp. Parv.* 448/1 Schote, or crykke, *tetanus.*

**shote**, variant of SHOAT[1], [2].

**shoter**, obs. form of SHOOTER, SHUDDER *v.*

**'shot-fare.** *dial.* Also 8 shotver. [Contracted from *shotnet fare*: see SHOT-NET.] A mackerel-fishing expedition (also *attrib.*); the mackerel season.

**1736** PEGGE *Kenticisms* (E.D.S.), *Shotver men*, the mackerel fishers at Dover. *a* **1798** PENNANT *Journ. I. of Wight* (1801) I. 137 The Shotfare season, or time of catching mackrel. **1887** *Kent. Gloss.*, *Shot-fare*, the mackerel season, which is the first of the two seasons of the home fishery.

**shot-free,** *a.* [f. SHOT *sb.*[1] (senses 7 and 23) + FREE *a.* Cf. M.Du. *schotvrî* = sense 2 below; mod.Du. *schotvrij*, G. *schussfrei* = sense 1.]

†**1.** Safe from shot, shot-proof. *Obs.*

*a* **1586** MONTGOMERIE *Misc. Poems* xl. 19 Last, Reson rais, ay shotfrie vnder sheeld. **1591** SYLVESTER *Du Bartas* I. vi. 184 What shot-free Corslet,..'Gainst th'angry Aspick could assure them safety? *a* **1661** FULLER *Worthies, Wilts* (1662) III. 157 Such Officers being commonly shot-free by their place, as not exposed to danger. **1778** *Arminian Mag.* I. 198 A receipt to make us shot-free, sword and pistol proof.

**b.** *fig.*

**1602** B. JONSON *Poetaster* Apol. Dial. 25 Whilst I, at whom they shot, sit here shot-free, And as vn-hurt of enuy, as vnhit. **1736** J. SERCES *Popery an Enemy to Script.* 96 As long as our Adversaries level no other Arrows at our Heads we are Shot-free. **1820** W. TOOKE *Lucian* I. 317 Why are the Muses invulnerable to you and shot-free?

**2.** Free from payment of 'shot'; hence also, unpunished; = SCOT-FREE. Now *rare*.

**1596** SHAKS. *1 Hen. IV*, v. iii. 30 Though I could scape shot-free at London, I fear the shot heere: here's no scoring, but vpon the pate. **1598** R. BERNARD tr. *Terence, Phormio* II. i, To come shot free [L. *asymbolum venire*] anointed and washed from the bathes. **1620** J. TAYLOR (Water-P.) *Praise Hemp-seed* (1623) 32 Bread, Beere, and Oysters is their meat, Which freely, friendly, shot-free all doe eat. **1736** AINSWORTH *Lat. Dict.* 1, Shot free (unpunished) *impune.* **1892** H. V. MILLS *Lake Country Romances* 169 Thou shalt not go shot-free this time.

†**b.** Of a meal: at which no payment is made.

**1697** POTTER *Antiq. Greece* IV. xi. (1715) 288 A shot-free Banquet, or a Marriage-Feast, Not such as is by Contribution made.

**shot-garland.**

†**1.** *Naut.* (See quot.) *Obs.*

**1769** FALCONER *Dict. Marine* (1780) s.v. *Garland, Shot-Garland*,..a piece of timber nailed horizontally along the ship's side from one gun-port to another, and used to contain the round-shot ready for charging the great guns in battle. For this purpose it is furnished with several semi-globular cavities, corresponding to the size of the cannon-balls which it is employed to contain.

**2.** 'In land-batteries, an iron or wooden stand on which shot and shell are piled in order to preserve them from deterioration' (*Cent. Dict.* 1891).

**shot-gun, 'shotgun.** Originally *U.S.*

**1. a.** A smooth-bore gun (fowling-piece) used for firing small-shot, as distinguished from a rifle for firing a bullet.

**1828** J. HALL *Lett. fr. West* 86 Luck's like a shot-gun, mighty uncertain. **1835** W. IRVING *Tour Prairies* xi. 86 The lads of the West holding 'shot-guns', as they call them, in great contempt, thinking..the rifle the only fire-arm worthy of a hunter. **1892** GREENER *Breech-Loader* 220 The sportsmanlike use of the shot-gun.

**b.** *ellipt.* for (*a*) a shotgun building (sense 3 b below); (*b*) = *shotgun formation* (U.S. Football), sense 2 below.

**1945** B. A. BOTKIN *Lay my Burden Down* 98 They had to go out and live in sod houses and little old boxed shotguns and turn their Negroes loose. **1966** [see *shotgun formation* below]. **1976** *Time* 19 Jan. 43 Staubach's talent is throwing from the shotgun. **1977** *New Yorker* 10 Oct. 178/2 Buckley, operating from the shotgun, threw some forty, of which some twenty were valid.

**2.** *attrib.* as ***shotgun barrel***; **shotgun formation** *U.S. Football* (see quot. 1966); also *fig.*; **shotgun marriage** orig. *U.S.* = *shotgun wedding* below; also *fig.*; **shotgun microphone** (or *colloq.* **mike**), a highly directional microphone with a long barrel that is pointed at a distant source of sound; **shotgun prescription** *Medical slang*, a prescription containing a great number of drugs of various properties; **shotgun wedding** orig. *U.S.*, a wedding made in haste or under duress by reason of the bride's pregnancy; also *fig.*

**1892** GREENER *Breech-Loader* 8 The strain to which a *shot-gun barrel is ordinarily subjected. [**1966** ROTE & WINTER *Lang. of Pro Football* III. 137 *Shotgun*, offensive formation where quarterback sets four or five yards behind center with other backfield men split out as flankers or slot backs; an offensive formation designed to facilitate sending out as many pass receivers as possible while passer is in safer position to throw.] **1967** *Wall St. Jrnl.* (Eastern ed.) 30 Jan. 8/5 Mr. Hornung's argument [that his accomplishments consituted educational, artistic, scientific and civic achievements] constitutes 'a *shotgun formation', the court said. **1972** J. MOSEDALE *Football* vi. 91 Hickey installed the shotgun formation, putting the quarterback at tailback where he could pass or run. **1929** E. W. HOWE *Plain People* xxix. 267 Two people cordially disliked me for years because I thought it best to mention very briefly and respectfully their *shot gun marriage. **1958** *Manch. Guardian* 22 Mar. 4/6 There were references to..the possible shotgun marriage of the 'Daily Herald' and the 'News Chronicle'. **1973** 'H. CARMICHAEL' *Too Late for Tears* xv. 179 Shot-gun marriages went out with the advent of the Pill. **1968** J. M. ULLMAN *Lady on Fire* (1969) viii. 111 Even if they walked around Curley..could pick up the conversation with a *shotgun microphone. The device had a range of several hundred feet. **1972** *Jrnl. Social Psychol.* LXXXVI. 30 A shotgun microphone was located to one side of the group to record the verbal interactions. **1978** T. GIFFORD *Glendower Legacy* (1979) 187 We used that miserable shotgun mike and believe me, Brennan was watching television and sneezing. **1891** *Century Dict.*, *Shotgun prescription. **1898** *Syd. Soc. Lex.* **1913** *Times* 13 Aug. 4/4 The old 'shotgun' prescriptions so justly condemned by modern physicians. **1927** S. LEWIS

*Elmer Gantry* ix. 134 There were, in those parts and those days, not infrequent ceremonies known as '*shotgun weddings'. **1946** *Sun* (Baltimore) 29 Oct. 1/1 Charges that the veto system was a 'shotgun wedding' forced upon the small nations. **1974** E. HUXLEY *Gallipot Eyes* (1976) 61 She can't have been more than fourteen when she married. A shot-gun wedding, clearly.

**3. a.** Passing into *adj.* Made or done hastily or under pressure of necessity.

**1937** *Sun* (Baltimore) 18 Aug. 8/2 Shotgun legislation... Measures pushed through in a last-hour rush. **1962** *Economist* 7 Apr. 73/1 Mr Sandys's shot-gun reorganisation of the aircraft industry. **1977** *Observer* 13 Mar. 13/2 By the end of last year, 464 men had been forced to quit, 74 after formal proceedings, the remainder in shotgun resignations.

**b.** Designating a house or other building with rooms set in a line on either side of a long central hallway. *U.S.*

**1938** J. STUART *Beyond Dark Hills* vi. 156 Their faces wore the blank expression of the Armco plant's shotgun dwelling houses. **1944** T. D. CLARK *Pills, Petticoats & Plows* iii. 56 There was no wiser spot on earth than the porches which jutted out from the long shotgun buildings. **1950** *Penguin New Writing* XL. 67 Your Riverbottom Nigras lived in little shotgun houses. **1964** *Amer. Folk Music Occasional* I. 92 De Ole souf unroll... Dog-trots and shotgun shantys. **1974** *Times* 14 Jan. 12/3 The American South is still unmistakably southern.. grits at breakfast, blacks living in shotgun shacks.

**c.** quasi-adv. *to ride shotgun*: see RIDE *v.* 1 m.

**shot-hole.** [SHOT *sb.*[1]]

**1. a.** A hole made by the passage of a shot.

**1745** CAPT. DURRELL *Jrnl.* 20 May in J. S. McLennan *Louisbourg* (1918) 177 We had several Shott holes in all our sides. **1801** NELSON 22 Apr. in Nicolas *Disp.* (1846) VII. p. ccvii, The Inforđestein.. was desired to be sunk, which she soon was as no person stopped her shot-holes. **1907** J. H. PATTERSON *Man-Eaters of Tsavo* v. 55 They had..induced one of their fellow workmen to make a few holes like shot holes in their backs.

**b.** *transf.* 'A hole made in wood by a boring insect' (Webster 1911).

[**1889** E. A. ORMEROD *Rep. Observations Injurious Insects* 94, I found that the injury [to the tree] began by a small hole like a shot-hole in the side of the attacked stem.] **1946** *Nature* 13 July 52/2 Dry rot.. is the result of the operations of fungi, and not of insects—the attacks of the latter being usually discernible by the presence of small pin or 'shot' holes in the wood. **1972** *Gloss. Terms Timber (B.S.I.)* 17 *Shothole*, a worm-hole usually more than 1·5 mm and not more than 3 mm in diameter.

**c.** A small round hole made in a leaf by a fungus or bacterium; also, a condition in which such holes occur.

**1897** [implied in sense 4 below]. **1902** D. MCALPINE *Fungus Dis.* iii. 33 There is a very familiar appearance in the leaves of many of our stone-fruit trees, where they are more or less punctured with round holes, as if riddled with shot; hence the name 'shot-hole' applied to the injury. **1926** F. D. HEALD *Man. Plant Dis.* ii. 33 Some varieties are more prone to shot hole whenever localized areas of leaf tissue are killed. **1946** H. WORMALD *Dis. Fruits & Hops* 143 The chief agent of leaf spotting in plums is the organism which causes Bacterial Canker... Eventually the infected parts are killed and drop out, leaving 'shot holes'. **1976** A. HELLYER *Collingridge Encycl. Gardening* 259 Small round holes appear in the leaves, a symptom which is sometimes known as shot-hole and was once believed to be a separate disease [from bacterial canker caused by *Pseudomonas morsprunorum*].

**2.** *arch.* A small hole in a fortified wall through which to shoot. (Often in Scott.)

**1818** SCOTT *Br. Lamm.* x, A small projecting window, or shot-hole, through which, in former days, the warders were wont to reconnoitre those who presented themselves before the gates. **1845** STOCQUELER *Handbk. Brit. India* (1854) 236 The whole having, in addition to shot-holes, embrasures, &c., an abundance of glazed windows.

**3.** *Mining.* A hole bored in the rock in which to insert a blasting-charge.

**1875** J. H. COLLINS *Metal Mining* 58 Boring machines.. for the purpose of boring these 'shot-holes'.

**4.** *Comb.*, as **shot-hole borer**, a small bark beetle of the family Scolytidæ, esp. *Anisandrus dispar* (cf. SCOLYTID); **shot-hole disease**, a plant disease characterized by shot-holes in the leaves; **shot-hole fungus**, a fungus which causes shot-holes, esp. in certain fruit trees.

[**1890** E. A. ORMEROD *Man. Injur. Insects* (ed. 2) 331, I found that the cause of the injury was the 'Shot-borer' Beetle (as it is called in America).] **1916** *Farmers' Bull.* (U.S. Dept. Agric.) No. 763. 2 The shot-hole borers or barkbeetles burrow into the bark. **1968** *Oxf. Bk. Insects* 190/2 The Shot-hole Borer.., one of the Ambrosia Beetles, is found locally in southern England. **1926** F. D. HEALD *Man. Plant Dis.* xx. 511 The disease [*sc.* cherry leaf spot] is known by various common names, such as 'leaf blight', 'leaf spot', 'yellows', 'yellow leaf', and the 'shot-hole disease'. **1946** Shot-hole disease [see ABSCISSION 3]. **1897** W. G. SMITH tr. *von Tubeuf's Dis. Plant* II. 463 *Phyllosticta persicae*... The name 'shot-hole fungus' has sometimes been applied to this and allied forms. **1906** M. C. COOK *Fungoid Pests* 131 A shot-hole fungus has been found lately, several times affecting Peach leaves in this country.

**shotil**, obs. form of SHUTTLE.

**'shotless** ('ʃɒtlɪs), *a. rare.* [f. SHOT *sb.*[1] + -LESS.] Without shot.

**1798** BLOOMFIELD *Farmer's Boy, Autumn* 197 Exert thy voice, and wield thy shotless gun.

**† shot-log.** *Obs. rare*$^{-1}$. = SHOT-CLOG.

**1618** FIELD *Amends for Ladies* III. iv, For the reckoning there's some of their cloakes: I will be no shot-log to such.

**'shotman, 'shotsman.** [f. SHOT *sb.*[1]]

**1.** A shooter.

**1897** *Westm. Gaz.* 21 Aug. 1/3 No, 'tain't shotsmen; 'tis a nasty hedge-creeper of a devil, with nets and ferrets. **1900** MORLEY *Cromwell* II. i. 117 The shotmen, the musketeers, and harquebusiers.

**2.** *Mining.* (See quot. 1905.)

**1905** *Daily News* 29 July 5/2 The shotman, whose special duty is to charge the shot-hole ready for firing. **1908** *Daily Chron.* 15 Jan. 6/7 A shotsman's assistant at the Llanbradach Colliery.

**shot-net.** *dial.* [SHOT *ppl. a.* + NET *sb.*] A mackerel net. Also *attrib.* **† shotnet-fare** (see quots.).

**1320** in Rogers *Agric. & Prices* (1866) I. xxiv. 611 [180 fathoms of] shotnet. **1419** *Liber Albus* (Rolls) I. 577 Shotnet, Shof-net, et Kydels, sount defenduz. **1736** PEGGE *Kenticisms* (E.D.S.) *Shotver-men*, the mackarel fishers at Dover. Their nets are called *shot-nets*.

*attrib.* **1580** in *Sussex Archæol. Collect.* (1849) II. 43 [The fishermen proceeded to set down their ancient fishing customs under certain heads, called fares,..such as those used in] Tucknett Fare, Shotnett Fare, [etc.].

**shot-pouch.**

**1.** A sportsman's pouch or bag, usually of leather, for carrying shot.

**1732** *Inventory Sir R. Sutton's Goods* 6 Two Powder Flasks and four Shot-Pouches. **1842** LACY *Mod. Shooter* 89, I have already expressed my dislike of shot-belts; the fact is, I prefer shot-pouches.

**2.** *Local U.S.* The ruddy duck, *Erismatura rubida*: so called in allusion to the quantity of shot often required to kill it.

**† 'shotship.** *Obs. rare*$^{-1}$. [f. SHOT *sb.*[1] + -SHIP.] A party or assembly paying 'shot' or pecuniary contribution or reckoning.

*a* **1300** *Havelok* 2099 Betere is i go miself, and se: Hweþer he sitten nou, and wesseylen, Or of ani shotshipe to-deyle.

**shotsman**: see SHOTMAN.

**shot star.** [f. SHOT *ppl. a.*]

**1.** A shooting star.

**1633** T. BANCROFT *Gluttons Fever* C 1, (Like a shot starre,) from prides high turrets throwne To Stygian deepes. **1818** KEATS *Endym.* III. 597 As shot stars fall, She fled ere I could groan for mercy.

**2.** The alga *Nostoc commune*, vulgarly supposed to be of meteoric origin.

**1811** MCSKIMIN *Hist. Carrickfergus* 202 Common Heron ..is believed to disgorge that gelatinous substance called *Shot-star*.

‖**shott** (ʃɒt). Also **shat, shot, chott.** [NAfrican Arab. *shaṭṭ* 'lac salé' (Belkassem *Dict. Arabe-fr.*).] A shallow brackish lake or marsh in Northern Africa, usually dry in the summer and covered with saline deposits. Cf. SABKHA.

**1878** A. K. JOHNSTON *Africa* ii. 20 A long series of brackish lakes, here called *Sebkha* or *Shott*. **1891** PLAYFAIR in *Rep. Brit. Assoc. 1890* 876 Some parts of the Sahara are below the level of the sea, and here are formed what are called *chotts* or *sebkhas*, open depressions without any outlets, inundated by torrents from the southern slopes of the Atlas in winter and covered with a saline efflorescence in summer. **1898** *Geogr. Jrnl.* June 604 The shats, or salt lakes, of the south of Tunis are rather a disappointment to the traveller. **1902** *Encycl. Brit.* XXXIII. 482/1 These shats.. are, strictly speaking, not lakes at all at the present day. **1926** A. HUXLEY *Essays New & Old* 7 Beyond the oasis we could see the chotts, glittering in the sun. **1957** G. E. HUTCHINSON *Treat. Limnol.* I. i. 136 In north Africa there is a series of inland drainage basins or shotts between the Greater and Lesser Atlas Mountains. **1969** J. MAVOR *Voyage to Atlantis* ii. 46 Paul Borchardt, in 1927..placed the lesser island of Atlantis..a few miles inland of the gulf of Gabès in Tunisia in the region of 'shotts'.

**shott**, variant of SHOAT[1], [2].

**shotte**, obs. form of SHOT.

**shotted** ('ʃɒtɪd), *ppl. a.* [f. SHOT *v.* and *sb.*[1] + -ED.]

**1.** Loaded with shot or ball as well as powder.

**1800** COLQUHOUN *Comm. Thames* xii. 346 The firing of shotted guns. **1884** *Law Times* LXXVIII. 2/1 Substituting a shotted for a blank cartridge.

**2.** Weighted with 'shot'; having a shot attached; chiefly of a fishing-line or net, and of a corpse for burial at sea.

**1850** TENNYSON *In Mem.* VI. iv, His [the sailor's] heavy-shotted hammock-shroud Drops in his vast and wandering grave. **1866** DICKENS, etc. *Mugby Junction, No. 5 Branch Line*, The serge cap and shotted chain of any galley-slave. **1889** *Century Dict.* s.v. *Line*, *Shotted line*, a fishing-line to which split shot are attached as sinkers. Shotted casting-lines are also used in special cases for fly-fishing.

**3.** Of metal: (see quot. 1796).

**1796** PEARSON in *Phil. Trans.* LXXXVI. 422 *note*, By shotted copper is meant copper which has been poured when melted into cold water, by which it is divided into small globular pieces and grains. **1859** BESSEMER in *Min. Proceed. Inst. Civil Engin.* XVIII. 532 To pour the fluid steel into water and afterwards to remelt the shotted metal in a crucible.

**shotten** ('ʃɒt(ə)n), *ppl. a.* [pa. pple. of SHOOT *v.* Cf. SHOT *ppl. a.*]

**† 1. a.** Of an arrow: Shot from a bow. *Obs.*

*a* **1225** *Juliana* 73, & tet beali blencte & breid him aȝeinwart bihinden hare schuldren as for a schoten [*vr.* ischoten] arewe.

**† b.** Of a wound: Produced by gunshot. *Obs.*

**1597** A. M. tr. *Guillemeau's Fr. Chirurg.* 6/2 Commonlye, shotten woundes doe not enter right, or liniallye, into the bodye, but turninge.

**† 2.** Of tin: ? = SHOTTED 3. *Obs.*

**1414** *Rolls of Parlt.* IV. 56/1 Diverses autres Marchantz.. achatent et envoyent Estayn founduz, appelle Shotentyn. **1429** *Ibid.* 359/1 No manere Wolle.., Lede, ne Tynne, hoole ne shoten.

**† b.** ? Crystallized. (Cf. SHOOT *v.*)

**1766** BORLASE in *Phil. Trans.* LVI. 38 The granulated surface, and shotten edge, of the metal, pronounce it..to be native tin.

**3.** Of a fish (esp. a herring): That has spawned.

[Cf. Du. *schoten haringh* (1661 in Boekenoogen *Zaansch Volkstaal* s.v. *Ropziek*).]

**1451** in T. Gardner *Hist. Dunwich* (1754) 148 Rec. of Thomas Comber 2500 full Heryns 200 schotyn. **1593** G. HARVEY *Pierce's Super.* 74 His conceit [was] as lank as a shotten herring. **1596** *Nottingham Rec.* IV. 243 Prysez of Heryngés Whyte ful v. for ijd.; shutten iij. for jd. *c* **1682** J. COLLINS *Salt & Fishery* 154 The Shoal begins to be lean, shotten, and sick. **1863** *Rep. Sea Fisheries Comm.* (1865) II. 419/1 We have caught shotten fish one night, and the next they have been full of spawn. **1864** J. M. MITCHELL *Herring* 114 Full herrings..and..empty or shotten herrings.

**b.** *transf.* and *fig.* In ***shotten herring***, applied to a person who is exhausted by sickness or destitute of strength or resources (*arch.*) Hence *gen.*, †Thin, emaciated; worthless, good-for-nothing.

**1596** SHAKS. *1 Hen. IV* II. iv. 143 If manhood, good manhood be not forgot vpon the face of the earth, then am I a shotten Herring. **1617** *Let.* 31 Jan. in *India Office Rec.* (MS.) O.C. No. 442 [The factories] ad to their rotten and shotten [goods] and demynish (or take away) such as is vendable. **1618** FLETCHER *Women Pleas'd* II. iv, What Penurio, My shotten friend, what winde blew you? **1662** R. MATHEW *Unl. Alch.* 14 He looked shotten and wan, as one that had been sick. **1826** COBBETT *Rur. Rides* (1885) II. 2 Come and look at this poor, shotten-herring of a creature.

**4.** Blood-shot. quasi-*arch.* (Cf. BLOOD-SHOTTEN.)

*c* **1460** *Compl. Criste* 401 in *Pol. Rel. & L. Poems* (1903) 218 They [my eyes] been shotyn [*earlier text* blood-schoten] with ffleschely luste. **1858** KINGSLEY *Real King* 36 His eyne were shotten, as red as blood.

**5.** *dial.* Of milk: Sour, curdled.

*a* **1667** SKINNER *Etymol. Ling. Angl.* (1671), Shotten milk, *nobis Lac vetustate Coagulatum.* **1886** *S.W. Linc. Gloss.*, *Shotten-milk*, milk turned sour and curdled... Still understood here, but almost out of use.

Hence **† shottenly** *adv.*

**1661** K. W. *Conf. Charac., Covetous Usurer* (1860) 73 But as shottenly as he looks, he's a notable crafty fox in his way.

**† 'shotter**[1]. *Obs. rare.* [f. SHOT *sb.*[1] + -ER[1].]

**1.** A missile weapon.

**1585** JAS. I *Ess. Poesie* viii. (Arb.) 68 A shaft, a shotter, that our harts hes slane.

**2.** A large sea-fishing boat.

**1580** in *Sussex Archæol. Collect.* (1849) II. 44 [Shotnett fare is applied to larger vessels] called shotters of diverse burthens between six and twenty-six tonn, going to sea from Aprill to June for macrell.

‖**shotter**[2] ('ʃɒtə(r)). *Geol.* [ad. G. *schotter.*] Pebbles and sand deposited in layers by a river.

**1911** SOLLAS *Anc. Hunters* i. 19 To these deposits the Germans give the name of shotter (schotter), a term we shall find it convenient to adopt. The shotter have evidently been deposited by swiftly running water. *Ibid.* 20 A sheet of shotter, over a hundred feet in thickness.

**† 'shotterel.** *Obs. rare.* Also 6 shotrel. [Of obscure origin: cf. SHOAT and *cockerel*, *pickerel* etc.] A young pike of the first year.

**1566** GASCOIGNE *Supposes* II. iv, As though sixe mouthes ..bee not sufficient to eate an harlotrie shotterell, a pennieworth of cheese, and halfe a score spurlings. *c* **1620** LAWSON *Dennis' Secrets of Angling* (1885) 49 The Shotrell, 1 year, Pickerel, 2 year, Pike, 3 year, Luce, 4 year, are one.

**shottle**, variant of SHUTTLE *sb.*[4]

**shotty** ('ʃɒtɪ), *a.* [f. SHOT *sb.*[1] + -Y.] Resembling shot or pellets of lead; hard and round. *spec.* of gold: in the form of small, roundish lumps.

**1860** *Mining Surveyors' Rep.* (Mining Dept., Victoria) Aug. 236 There were also some very good patches of shotty gold and small nuggets found in the vicinity of this nugget. **1875** *Ure's Dict. Arts* III. 185 Weathered barley has a dull and often a dirty appearance, quite distinct from the bright shotty character of good samples. **1876** BRISTOWE *Th. & Pract. Med.* (1878) 248 These [points] soon increase in size, ultimately perhaps attaining the bulk of peas, and feeling hard and shotty between the fingers. **1880** *Tea Advt.*, This tea..is brisk,..shotty in leaf, and heavy. **1929** E. J. DUNN *Geol. Gold* xix. 222 Pounds weight of 'shotty' gold..were washed from a dish of gravel. **1959** *Observer* 17 May 8/3 Odd old prospectors still fossick in the hills in search of shotty gold.

**shot-window.** Now only *Sc.* [Prob. f. SHOT *sb.*[1] The precise sense of the first element is difficult to determine. Some have thought that the word originally meant a window for shooting from; but there is no trace of this in the examples. Cf. MDu. *schotdore* sliding door, *schotpoorte* portcullis.] A window that can be opened and shut by turning on its hinges, like a door or shutter, a casement; a shutter with a few panes of glass at the top. (Cf. quot. 1722 s.v. SHOT *sb.*[1] 27.)

In quot. 1836 app. used for *outshot window*.

*c* **1386** CHAUCER *Miller's T.* 172 He..dressed hym vp by a shotwyndowe That was vp on the Carpenteris wal. **1513** DOUGLAS *Æneis* VII. Prol. 129 Ane schot wyndo vnschet a lytill on char. **15..** *Adam Bel* 85 in Hazl. *E.E.P.* II. 142 Alyce opened a shot wyndow, And loked all a bout. **1821** SCOTT *Kenilw.* xxiv, She hath jumped out of the shot-window of old Gaffer Thackham's grange. **1836** J. STRUTHERS *Dychmont* Poet. Wks. (1850) II. 64 Its braw shot window, where to th' e'e Shines Snuff, Tobacco, and Bohea.

**shou** (ʃuː). [Alleged Tibetan *çu* stag; according to Jäschke *Tibetan-Eng. Dict.* known only from 'Cunningham and other English authorities', and probably a blunder due to mishearing of *çaba*.] A Tibetan species of deer, *Cervus affinis*.

**1850** HODGSON in *Jrnl. Asiatic Soc. Beng.* XIX. 466 On the Shou or Tibetan Stag. **1910** LYDEKKER *Deer* in *Encycl. Brit.* VII. 923/1 Another Asiatic species is the great shou (*Cervus affinis*) of the Chumbi Valley.

**shou**, dial. form of SHE.

**shouful**, variant of SHOFUL.

†**shough.** *Obs.* Also 6 **shaugh**, 7 **showgh**, **shogh(e**. [Perh. the same word as SHOCK *sb.*; but the relation between the two forms is obscure.] A kind of lap-dog, said to have been originally brought from Iceland.

**1599** NASHE *Lenten Stuffe* 29 They are for Vltima Theule the north seas or Island, and thence yerke ouer..a trundle-taile tike or shaugh or two. **1605** SHAKS. *Macb.* III. i. 94 Spaniels, Curres, Showghes. *a* **1630** J. TAYLOR (Water-P.) *Dog of War* B 1 b, No Mungrell Cur or Shogh. **1688** HOLME *Armoury* II. 185/2 An Island Dog,..curled and rough all over... These Curs are much set by with Ladys, who..trim of all the hair of their hinder parts... Some call them Shoughs.

**shough**, var. SHEUGH; obs. form of SHOO *int.*

†**'shoughtering**, *vbl. sb. Obs. rare*$^{-1}$. [Of obscure origin; perh. an error for **floughtering* (see FLICHTER, FLAUGHTER *vbs.*] Flapping or agitation of the wings.

*c* **1440** *Pallad. on Husb.* I. 628 A shoughturyng [*Colchester MS.* shuddering], a flusshyng, & a fray He [*sc.* the pea-cock] maketh then.

**should** (ʃʊd), *sb. nonce-wd.* An utterance of the word *should*. Also, what 'should be'.

**1604** SHAKS. *Ham.* IV. vii. 123 (Qo. 2) And then this should is like a spend thrifts sigh, That hurts by easing. **1854** EMERSON *Lett. & Soc. Aims* Wks. (Bohn) III. 151 All writings must be in a degree exoteric, written to a human *should* or *would*, instead of to the fatal *is*.

**should**, pa. t. of SHALL *v.*; obs. f. SHOAL.

**shoulda, shouldda** ('ʃʊdə), repr. colloq. or vulgar pronunc. of *should have* (see SHALL *v.* 18).

**1933** [see JUNK *sb.*[2] 1 e]. **1943** C. HIMES *Black on Black* (1973) 194 Man, you shoulda seen them cats. **1956** 'E. MCBAIN' *Cop Hater* in *87th Precinct* (1959) 77 The kid was a Junior... Nobody shoulda given him a reefer. **1967** V. S. NAIPAUL *Mystic Masseur* iv. 55, I shoulda get married long before now. **1978** J. IRVING *World according to Garp* xviii. 393, I guess I shoulda *knocked*.

**shouldarye**, obs. form of SUDARY.

**should-be** ('ʃʊdbiː), *sb.* and *a.*

**a.** *sb.* What should be. **b.** *adj.* That should be.

**1790** ANNA SEWARD *Lett.* (1811) III. 35 What says Prior, when he describes the should-be of artists' conduct to each other! **1878** W. JAMES in *Jrnl. Speculative Philos.* XII. 14 The interest of survival..has hitherto been treated as an ideal *should-be*. **1885** G. M. HOPKINS *Let.* 24 Apr. (1938) 107 God grant it may not be..that the should-be receiver was dead. **1887** *19th Cent.* Aug. 210 His should-be helpmate. **1951** [see IS *sb.*].

**shoulde**, obs. form of SHOAL *sb.*[1]

**shoulder** ('ʃəʊldə(r)), *sb.* Forms: 1 sculdur, sculdor, sculder, scyldur, 3 sculder, (solder), scholdur, 3–4 shuldre, 3–5 schuldre, 3–6 scholder, 4–5 schuldur, -dyr, 3–8 sholder, 4–6 s(c)hulder, schuldir, schuldere, sholdre, 4 s(c)holdere, (soldre), 5 schuldire, -dyre, s(c)hildur, shuldur, shuder, (6 shoder, schodyr, showlder), *Sc.* schowder, 7 souldiour, *Sc.* sulder, shuldeir), 8–9 *Sc.* shouther, 6– shoulder. *Plural.* α. 1 sculdru, -o, -a, (*north.* dat. scyldrum), 3 shulldre (Ormin), 4 shuldre; β. sculderen, schuldren, ssoldren, 3–5 scholdren, shuldren, 6 shouldren; γ. 3 sculdres, 3–5 shuldres; 4 shuldris (chuldris, schylderez, *Sc.* schuldrys), 4–5 schuldris, shulderis, scholdres, 4–6 schulderis, sholdres, schulder(e)s, 5–6 schuldiris, 5 s(c)hildres, soldrys, 6 schouldiris, *Sc.* schildris; also 5– as sing. + -s. [OE. *sculdor* masc. corresponds (exc. in declension and gender, app. evidenced only in one passage) to OFris. *skulder*, *skolder* (WFris. *skouder*, Hindelopen *skoalder*, NFris. *skoller*), MLG. *schulder*, MDu. *schouder(e* masc. (mod.Du. *schouder* fem.), OHG. *scultarra*, *scultirra* fem. (MHG., mod.G. *schulter* fem.); not found in ON.; the MSw., Sw. *skuldra* fem., Da. *skulder*, are prob. early adoptions from LG. As the OE. pl. *sculdru* is anomalous for a masculine sb., it has been suggested that it may represent a dual. The ONorthumbrian *scyldr-* seems to represent the WGer. **skuldrja* fem. which is indicated by the OHG. forms.

The affinities of the WGer. word are disputed: see Heyne in Grimm *Deutsches Wb.* s.v. Some scholars (e.g. Kluge, Brugmann) hold that **skuldr-* is a dissimilated form of **skurdr-*, related by ablaut to **skard-* in OHG. *scarti* shoulder.]

**1. a.** Each of the two corresponding portions (right and left) of the human body, including the upper joint of the arm with its integuments and the portion of the trunk between this and the base of the neck; esp. the curved upper surface of this; in *pl.* often including the part of the back between the two. In quadrupeds, the upper part of the fore-limb and the adjacent part of the back.

*a* **700** *Epinal Gloss.* 963 *Scapula*, sculdur. **971** *Blickl. Hom.* 127 Is þonne on westan medmycel duru þæt mannes heafod ȝe þa sculdro maȝan in. *c* **1000** *Sax. Leechd.* II. 198 & of þære stowe ofer ealle þa sidan astihð..oþ ðone swiþran sculdor þæt sar. *c* **1200** ORMIN 4776 All samenn, brest..& shulldre, & bacc, & side. **1297** R. GLOUC. (Rolls) 7449 Hou longe ssolle hor luþer heued aboue hor ssoldren be. **1375** BARBOUR *Bruce* I. 386 Bot off lymmys he wes weill maid, With banys gret & schuldrys braid. **1423** JAS. I *Kingis Q.* xcvi, Venus..that had A mantill cast ouer hir schuldris quhite. **1523–34** FITZHERB. *Husb.* §57 If thou shalte bye fatte oxen..se that they be soft..behynde the shulder, and vpon the hindermost rybbe. **1576** TURBERV. *Venerie* lviii. 161 You shall know him [a male hare] if you marke his shoulders well before he ryse, for they are redder than a female Hares be. **1596** NASHE *Saffron Walden* P 3, I, euen from a childe.. replide Scarlet, and made a mouth at him ouer his shoulder. **1611** BIBLE *1 Sam.* xvii. 6 And he had..a target of brasse between his shoulders. **1722** RAMSAY *Three Bonnets* II. 16 That braw blue stringing That's at your houghs and shuthers hinging. **1753** *Chambers' Cycl.* Suppl. s.v. *Horse*, The part from the withers to the top joint of the thigh, is called the shoulder. **1774** FOOTE *Cozeners* II. (1778) 37 Shoulders back, Toby; and chest a little more out! **1832** TENNYSON *Œnone* 58 A leopard skin Droop'd from his shoulder. **1845** BUDD *Dis. Liver* 84 A gnawing, aching pain, about the top of the shoulder. **1897** *Encycl. Sport* I. 329/2 (Dogs) *Shoulder*, the top of the shoulder blade, the point from which the height of a dog is measured.

**b.** In fishes (*sing.* and *pl.*), the upper part of the trunk, adjoining the head.

*cod's head and shoulders*: see COD'S HEAD 2.

**1820** *Q. Rev.* May 277 Here's a cod's head and shoulders With soles for upholders. **1839–47** R. JONES *Pisces* in *Todd's Cycl. Anat.* III. 958/1 The anterior extremity or pectoral fin comprehends the shoulder, which is an osseous semicircle composed of many bones, suspended at the upper part to the cranium or spine. **1859** *Habits Gd. Society* v. 222 The shoulder is the best part [of a fish], and should be first helped.

**c.** The upper part of the wing or wing-case of a bird, beetle, butterfly, etc. adjoining the point of articulation; of a bird, *spec.* the carpal joint.

**1735** J. MOORE *Columbarium* 49 The Chain does not come down so low to the Shoulders of the Wings. **1753** *Chambers' Cycl.* Suppl. s.v. *Scarabæus*, The reddish beetle with two spots on the shoulders. **1832** T. BROWN *Bk. Butterflies & M.* (1834) I. 174 The upper wings [of the butterfly] are.. marked with two acute triangular patches of crimson on the shoulders. **1899** D. SHARP *Insects* II. vi. 316 In some Sphingidae there is the unusual condition of a highly-developed shoulder coexisting with a perfect frenulum and retinaculum.

**d.** = SHOULDER-JOINT *lit.* and *fig.*; chiefly in *to put one's shoulder out*.

**1611** COTGR., *Espauler*, to burst a shoulder, to put a shoulder out of ioynt. **1847** HALLIWELL s.v., A young lady who has unfortunately listened to the persuasions of the other sex, is said to have a slip of the shoulder. **1886** *Cheshire Gloss.* s.v. *Shoother*, 'To put one's shoulder out' is an idiom meaning to take offence.

**2.** Phrases. †**a.** *to be more, lower by the shoulders*: to be head and shoulders taller or shorter in stature. *Obs.* (Cf. HEAD *sb.*[1] 50.)

*a* **1300** *Havelok* 982 þan was hauelok bi þe shuldren more þan þe meste þat þer kam. **1470** *Paston Lett.* II. 394 He is.. lower then my lytell Tom by the schorderys [*sic*].

**b.** *over the shoulder*, †*over (the) shoulders*: †(*a*) indicating that what is said is meant ironically for the reverse; 'over the left'; (*b*) said of a remark aimed indirectly at some one.

(*a*) **1596** NASHE *Saffron Walden* O 2 b, By these complots ..Wolfe could not choose but bee a huge gainer, a hundred marke at least ouer the shoulder. **1611** COTGR. s.v. *Espaule*, *Par dessus l'espaule*, ouer the shoulder,..and hence; *Riche, ou vertueux, par dessus l'espaule*; (signifies) a verie begger, or, an arrant knaue. **1631** R. H. *Arraignm. Whole Creature* x. § 1. 74 They prove not bread unto them, as they thought, but Huskes which they thought not: they gaine over shoulders by them, when all their Cards are cast. **1675** V. ALSOP *Anti-Sozzo* iii. 194, I think our Author has either lost money by his Discourse, or got it over the shoulders.

(*b*) **1847** HELPS *Friends in C.* I. vii. 105 That which may be called criticism over the shoulder.

**c.** *to put an old head on young shoulders*: to make a young person as staid or experienced as an elderly one; similarly *to have an old head on young shoulders. to have a head upon one's shoulders*: to have good sense.

**1824** SCOTT *St. Ronan's* i, 'They were daft callants,' she said, '..ye could not put an auld head upon young shouthers.' **1837** MARRYAT *Perc. Keene* xix, You appear to have an old head upon very young shoulders. **1883** STEVENSON *Treas. Isl.* xxxii, 'Well, that's so,' he said. 'You've a head upon your shoulders, John, and no mistake.'

**d.** *shoulder to shoulder*: lit. of soldiers, so as to shoulder one another, in close conflict; also, in rank, in close formation; hence *fig.* of persons, with united effort, with mutual co-operation and support.

*a* **1586** SIDNEY *Arcadia* III. (Sommer) 293 So as both the horses & men met shoulder to shoulder. **1625** MARKHAM *Souldiers Accid.* 5 A Ranke..is a Row of men placed Pouldron to Pouldron, or Shoulder to Shoulder. *a* **1627** HAYWARD *Edw. VI* (1630) 32 The Scots..closed and in a manner locked themselues together, shoulder to shoulder. **1889** JESSOPP *Coming of Friars* iii. 118 We are..strongest when we are labouring shoulder to shoulder for some common object. **1894** DONOVAN *With Wilson in Matabeleland* 301 That band of heroes who died shoulder to shoulder.

**e.** *Horsemanship.* (Cavalry.) *shoulder forward! right* (or *left*) *shoulders* (*in*)*!* orders given for a rider to 'bend' his horse so that he moves obliquely to the right or left for alteration of position or direction in marching; also, the performance of this order.

**1796** *Instr. & Regul. Cavalry* (1813) 136 The officer.. gives a word, *Shoulder* (the outward one) *forward!* on which the man next to himself gradually turns his horse so as to arrive in the new line perfectly square in his own person. **1833** *Ibid.* I. 80 When he is properly bent in 'Shoulder-in', his whole body from head to tail is curved, and he will move in two lines parallel to the sides of the manege. **1844** *Ibid.* 18 Bending Lesson. The Ride being in file... 'Right Shoulder in.' The horses' heads to be brought into the school with the (inward) or right rein [etc.]. *Ibid.* 107 When the change [of direction] is to be made to the Pivot hand, the Leader of the Head of the Column..will give the word 'Right (or Left) shoulders'.

**f.** (*straight*) *from the shoulder*: (of a blow) with the fist brought to the shoulder and then swiftly sent forward; (of pulling or other movements) with the arm kept straight, not 'from the elbow'; also *fig.*

**1856** READE *Never too late* xv, No! give me a chap that hits out straight from the shoulder. **1859** *Lillywhite's Guide to Cricketers* (ed. 12) 17 Wriggling and twisting your body instead of letting your arms go from the shoulder. **1864** *Bohn's Handbk. Games* 516 The stroke should be made freely from the shoulder, and not in a cramped manner from the elbow. **1904** W. H. SMITH *Promoters* v. 103 You'll..be in a shape to talk business, right from the shoulder. **1911** R. D. SAUNDERS *Col. Todhunter* ix. 118 A man that talks old-fashioned American Democracy straight from the shoulder. **1926** N. COWARD *Easy Virtue* I. 10, I must..have a talk to her... A straight-from-the-shoulder chat might make her see things in a better light. **1947** L. P. HARTLEY *Eustace & Hilda* xi. 182 That letter had been written straight from the shoulder, or the heart. **1963** V. NABOKOV *Gift* iv. 214 He subsequently wrote it right down, straight from the shoulder, in three nights. **1977** *Gramophone* Aug. 291/3 As to the power and authority, he takes Beethoven at his word when he sees an *ff* mark and lets you have it right from the shoulder.

**g.** *to rub shoulders with*: see RUB *v.* 5 b.

**h.** *to weep* (or *cry*) *on* (a person's) *shoulder*: to pour out one's troubles to a person; also in phr. *a shoulder to cry on*, a sympathetic and consoling listener to a person's troubles.

**1935** H. L. ICKES *Diary* 10 Feb. (1953) I. 292, I called Tugwell yesterday afternoon to tell him that if he wanted any shoulder to weep on, mine was a broad one. **1942** T. BAILEY *Pink Camellia* iii. 19 She likes to talk of her troubles and weep on people's shoulders. **1966** L. DEIGHTON *Billion Dollar Brain* xvi. 163 I'm always weeping on your shoulder. **1974** 'J. LE CARRÉ' *Tinker, Tailor, Soldier, Spy* xviii. 158, I asked 'What did he want?' And Ann said 'A shoulder to cry on.' Bill..wanted to pour out his heart, she said.

**i.** *off-the-shoulder* (attrib. phr.): of a dress, blouse, etc., that leaves the shoulders bare.

[**1813** JANE AUSTEN *Let.* 15 Sept. (1932) 322 Stays now are not made to force the bosom up at all... I was really glad to hear that they are not to be so much off the shoulders as they were.] **1952** S. KAUFFMANN *Philanderer* (1953) xiv. 232 She was wearing an off-the-shoulder white blouse. **1960** *Guardian* 5 Jan. 6/7 A golden off-the-shoulder evening dress of only eight years ago. **1974** *Country Life* 17 Jan. 106/3 Off-the-shoulder and square necklines.

**3. a.** As the part of the body on which burdens are carried; also, as the seat of muscular strength employed in carrying, pushing, etc.

*c* **950** *Lindisf. Gosp.* Luke xv. 5, & miððy ȝemoetað hia on-settað on scyldrum his ȝefeande. *a* **1300** *Cursor M.* 12033 Wit scholdur gaf he him a scou. **1600** J. PORY tr. *Leo's Africa* IX. 343 The shee apes carrie their whelpes vpon their shoulders. **1697** DRYDEN *Virg. Georg.* III. 800 He Yokes himself, and..With his own Shoulders draws the Waggon's Weight. **1697** —— *Æneid* II. 659 Then all their Shoulders ply, 'Till from the Posts the brazen Hinges fly. **1842** TENNYSON *Morte d'Arth.* 164 Make broad thy shoulders to receive my weight, And bear me to the margin.

**b.** *transf.* Of things quasi-personified.

**1602** SHAKS. *Ham.* I. iii. 56 Aboord, aboord for shame, The winde sits in the shoulder of your saile. **1849** LONGF. *By Seaside, Lightho.* xi, And steadily against its solid form Press the great shoulders of the hurricane. **1901** H. TRENCH *Deirdre Wed* 33 So a swimmer is uplifted Horsed on a streaming shoulder of the Sea.

**c.** *fig.* and in fig. context.

*c* **950** *Lindisf. Gosp.* Matt. xxiii. 4 Hia ȝebindas uutedlice byrðenna hefiȝa..& settas in scyldrum *vel* bæccum monna. **1382** WYCLIF *Isa.* x. 27 And it shal be in that dai, shal be don awey his berthene fro thi shulder. **1533** TINDALE *Supper of the Lord* B vij, Syr ye..haue taken to great a burden vpon your weke shoulders. **1593** SHAKS. *3 Hen. VI*, II. vi. 100 *Ed.* Euen as thou wilt sweet Warwicke, let it bee: For in thy shoulder do I builde my Seate. **1671** MILTON *P.R.* II. 462 A Crown..Brings..sleepless nights To him..When on his shoulders each mans burden lies. **1775** EARL CARLISLE in Jesse *Selwyn & Contemp.* (1844) III. 133 Thus this affair is off my shoulders for a little time. **1841** THACKERAY *Gt. Hoggarty Diam.* x, All the debts are put upon my shoulders, on account of my known wealth. **1860–70** STUBBS *Lect. Europ. Hist.* I. viii. (1904) 97 Charles..was desirous..to rid his own shoulders of the pressure of imperial business.

†**d.** Phrases (all *Obs.*). ***to go to shoulder with***: to set about pushing. ***to lend a shoulder, to put under one's shoulder***: to help to lift or carry something. ***to set shoulder against, to set one's shoulder against***: to oppose strongly or forcibly. ***narrow in the shoulders***: incapable of bearing ridicule.

**1551** ROBINSON tr. *More's Utopia* (1895) 10 An other is so narrow in [ed. 2, betwene] the sholders, that he can beare no iestes nor tawntes. **1577** tr. *Bullinger's Decades* IV. viii. (1592) 725 That the doctrine of godlinesse should be spred thoroughout the whole worlde,..maugre the might of the whole worlde, setting shoulder against the same all in vaine. **1583** GOLDING *Calvin on Deut.* xvi. 94 That hee..shoulde not forbeare..to put vnder his shoulder (as they say) to beare a peece of the burthen. *c* **1630** RISDON *Surv. Devon* §330 (1810) 341 All such whose wives have the sovereignty, should go to shoulder with that stone. **1647** SANDERSON *Serm.* (1674) II. 200 It may be..they will..lend a shoulder, yea, and sweat, to lift us up yet higher. *a* **1663** *Ibid.* 306 Though all the powers in earth and hell should..set to all their shoulders and strength against it.

**e.** ***to put*** (occas. ***lay, set***) ***one's shoulder to the wheel***: (literally) so as to extricate the vehicle from the mire; hence *fig.* to set to work vigorously. So also ***to put, set one's shoulder to*** (work, a task, etc.)

**1678** MARVELL *Growth Popery* 39 If it had hitherto seemed to go up-hill, there was a greater cause to put the whole shoulder to it. **1692** R. L'ESTRANGE *Fables* ccxlvi. 213 Lay your Shoulder to the Wheel, and Prick your Oxen. **1792** MME. D'ARBLAY *Diary* June, We must all put our shoulders to the work. **1837** CARLYLE *Fr. Rev.* III. II. v, They.. instead of pushing on all shoulders at the wheel, will stand idle there.

**f.** ***to open the shoulders***: to give free play to the muscles of the shoulders in making a stroke; to 'let out'.

**1882** [see OPEN *v.* 3]. **1892** E. V. LUCAS *Songs of Bat* 7 But the batsman knows a finer joy When he opens his shoulders and drives!

**4. a.** The fore-leg and adjacent parts cut from the carcass of a deer, sheep or other animal; a joint consisting of this prepared for the table.

*c* **1320** *Sir Tristr.* 497 Þe forster for his ri3tes þe left schulder [of a hart] 3af he. **1382** WYCLIF *Exod.* xxix. 27 And thou shalt halwe..the shuldre that thow seuerdist fro the wether. **1428–9** *Rec. St. Mary at Hill* (1905) 71 Also payd for..a sholdere & a brist of moton iiij d ob. **1583–4** *Shuttleworths' Acc.* (Chetham Soc.) 19 Vnto a mane wch broughte a shoulder of a stagge frome Lyme xij d. **1641** MURREL *Cookerie* (ed. 5) 6 A Shoulder of Mutton with Oliues and Capers. **1731–8** SWIFT *Pol. Conversat.* 122 I'll help myself to a Slice of this Shoulder of Veal. **1848** THACKERAY *Van. Fair* vi, The knife-boy was caught stealing a cold shoulder of mutton. **1913** *Times* 13 Sept. 18/6 Bacon continued fair... Shoulders were sparingly offered at full prices.

**b.** ***cold shoulder***: see COLD SHOULDER *sb.* and *v.*

**c.** ***shoulder of mutton***, used

†(*a*) proverbially. ***as good, wholesome***, etc. ***as a shoulder of mutton to a sick horse***: no good at all. ***one shoulder of mutton draws down another***: eating induces eating. ***a shoulder of mutton for a sheep's head***: something of worth *for* a substitute of comparatively little value. *Obs.*

**1546** J. HEYWOOD *Prov.* (1867) 70 Thou art..As holsome a morsell for my comely cors As a shoulder of mutton for a sicke hors. **1687** MIEGE *Gt. Fr. Dict.* II. s.v. *Shoulder*, One Shoulder of Mutton draws down another, (Prov.) *en mangeant l'Appetit vient.* **1700** T. BROWN *Amusem. Ser. & Com.*, *Marriage* Wks. 1709 III. I. 66 As two Shoulders of Mutton drive down one another, so two powerful Griefs destroy one another. **1725** BAILEY tr. *Colloq. Erasmus* (1878) I. 228 Ho! I find I was out in my Notion; to leave a Shoulder of Mutton for a Sheep's Head [orig. *Hem! pro thesauro carbones*].

(*b*) *attrib.* with similative notion. ***shoulder of mutton fist***: a large, heavy, fleshy fist; hence ***shoulder-of-mutton fisted*** adj. ***shoulder of mutton sail***: a triangular sail attached to a mast; hence ***shoulder of mutton rig***.

**1694** MOTTEUX tr. *Rabelais* IV. xv. 64 The crippled Bum had struck him such a horrid thump with his Shoulder-of-Mutton-Fist. **1719** DE FOE *Crusoe* I. (Globe) 232, I..made a Three-corner'd vgly Thing, like what we call in England, a Shoulder of Mutton Sail, to go with a Boom at Bottom. **1831** TRELAWNY *Adv. Younger Son* III. 228 What sailors call, a shoulder-of-mutton rig, the larger part..being in the body of the boat. **1880** *Harper's Mag.* LXI. 350/2 But the Hampton boat—a modified pink-stern, with shoulder-of-mutton sails on its small masts—was the 'abler'..to stand the exigencies of all sorts of weather. **1900** F. T. BULLEN *With Christ at Sea* x. 194 A great raw-boned, shoulder-of-mutton fisted fellow. **1961** F. H. BURGESS *Dict. Sailing* 187 *Shoulder-of-mutton sail*, name given to the triangular Bermudan sail.

**5. a.** That part of a garment which covers the wearer's shoulder.

**1473–4** *Acc. Ld. High Treas. Scot.* I. 25 Item..iij quarteris of blac for the Kingis gowne schulderis. **1696–7** *Act 8 & 9 Will. III*, c. 30 §2 Upon the Shoulder of the right Sleeve of the uppermost Garment. **1855** LADY E. FINCH *Sampler* (ed. 2) 103 Gather the shoulders and the back.

**b.** *Leather trade.* The portion of a hide between the butt and the cheeks. Also, see quot. 1858.

**1858** SIMMONDS *Dict. Trade*, *Shoulders*, a name in the leather trade for tanned or curried hides and kips, as well as for English and foreign offal. **1885** H. R. PROCTER *Text-bk. Tanning* viii. 155 A piece called a 'middle' is sometimes taken between the butt and the shoulder.

**6. a.** A projection or protuberance resembling the human shoulder in shape, position or function; that part of a thing where it widens or swells out to greater bulk from what may be viewed as its head or neck.

**1545** ASCHAM *Toxoph.* II. (Arb.) 137, I call that the shoulder in a heade [of an arrow] whyche a mans finger shall feele afore it come to the poynte. **1587** MASCALL *Govt. Cattle* (1596) 157 A nayle well made should haue no shoulder at all, but still lesser and lesser toward the poynt. **1680** MOXON *Mech. Exerc.* xi. 197 The Rowler must also be so long between its Shoulders, that it may conveniently contain so many Diameters of String as shall be necessary. **1794** *Rigging & Seamanship* I. 157 The pin..with a shoulder on the upper side. **1839** F. A. GRIFFITHS *Artil. Man.* 39 [Plate] Shoulder of the Trunnion. **1857** BIRCH *Anc. Pottery* (1858) II. 79 The neck [of the amphora] is not cylindrical, but slopes upon the shoulders. **1873** BENNETT & CAVENDISH *Billiards* 339 To make the hazard, play at the shoulder of the pocket. **1910** R. P. SPIERS in *Encycl. Brit.* VIII. 420 The lintel of the Greek doorway projected on either side beyond the dressings, constituting what are known as the shoulders or knees.

**b.** A sudden inward curvature in the outline of something, from which it tapers to a point.

**1618** W. LAWSON *New Orch. & Garden* x. (1623) 27 The Graft is..with a sharpe knife fitted in the knot..with shoulders an ynch downeward, and so put into the stock. **1688** HOLME *Armoury* III. xv. (Roxb.) 20/2 The end [of a pen] in which the slit is, is called the cheeks; and the shoulders is the highest cut. **1834** D. LOW *Elem. Pract. Agric.* iv. 150 [In ploughing] it is important that the ridge be formed with a uniform curvature, so that it shall not have what is technically termed a shoulder, or hollow part on each side of the crown. **1873** TRISTRAM *Moab* i. 3 Skirting the coast of the Dead Sea till they passed the shoulder of the Peninsula of the Lisan.

**c.** A rebate which serves as an abutment; a projection which serves as a support.

**1669** STURMY *Mariner's Mag.* v. xiii. 83 Then turn a Foot thereto with a Shoulder to put the Trunk upon. **1799** J. ROBERTSON *Agric. Perth* 272 The middle space is cut down ..and well cleaned out, so that it has..six inches of firm ground for shoulders on each side. On these shoulders or abutments sods..are laid. **1812** P. NICHOLSON *Mech. Exerc.* 172 To form the tenon; cut the shoulders in with the drawing knife. **1857** COLQUHOUN *Comp. Oarsman's Guide* 30 Those timbers which come up to strengthen the row-locks are called shoulders.

**d.** *Fortif.* = EPAULE.

**1672** A. TACQUETT *Milit. Archit.* iv. 7 The Bulwork will be very much straitned..and the Angle of the shoulders made so much the less.

**e.** The flat surface below the letter, etc. on the shank of a type.

**1683** MOXON *Mech. Exerc.*, *Printing* 369 Beard of a Letter, is the outer angle of the Square Shoulder of the Shank. **1882** SOUTHWARD *Pract. Printing* (1884) 12 Certain small capital letters..have nicks at the back of the stem near the shoulder.

**f.** The projection between the blade and the tang (of a knife, chisel, etc.) which abuts on the handle.

**1683** MOXON *Mech. Exerc.*, *Printing* xxi. ¶4 A short piece of a Knife broken off about two Inches from the Sholder. **1810** C. JAMES *Milit. Dict.* (ed. 3), *Shoulder*, the upper part of the blade of a sword is so called. **1884** R. F. BURTON *Bk. Sword* 124 The tang,..the thin spike which projects from the shoulders or thickening of the blade.

†**g.** Each of the two stones adjacent to the keystone of an arch. *Obs.*

*a* **1734** NORTH *Life Dudley North* (1744) 198 To secure a Compass Arch, it was necessary by weight, or some other Means, to keep down the Shoulders, which, rising, let the Crown, or Key, fall in.

**h.** A comparatively gentle slope on the side of a hill and near the top.

**1817** *Blackw. Mag.* Oct. 84/2 Millar..brought his drove over the shoulder of Wallace's hill. **1885–94** R. BRIDGES *Eros & Psyche* June xii, The road, Which from the mountain shoulder o'er the plain Led to the city.

**i.** *pl.* The broadest part (of a bunch of grapes).

**1838** *Penny Cycl.* XI. 357/1 A bunch [of grapes].. upwards of 21 inches in length, and 19 inches across the shoulders.

**j.** The edge of a road; *spec.* a strip at the side of the main carriageway on which vehicles may stop in an emergency. Cf. *hard shoulder* s.v. HARD *a.* 23 b; *soft shoulder* s.v. SOFT *a.* 29. orig. *U.S.*

**1933** *Sun* (Baltimore) 27 Dec. 8/7, I..stayed well over on the shoulder. But..only one of the numerous cars.. bothered to move nearer the middle of the road. Repeatedly, I stepped back into the bushes and mud. **1942** *Short Guide Gr. Brit.* (U.S. War Dept.) 32 *Shoulder*, (of road)—verge. **1965** 'E. MCBAIN' *Doll* (1966) x. 127 The road was winding and narrow... The shoulders were muddy and soft. **1979** G. SEYMOUR *Red Fox* xii. 185 The engine coughed and died, barren of petrol... They were about to stop on the hard shoulder.

**k.** A poorly resolved subsidiary maximum interrupting a part of a graph otherwise having a fairly uniform or smoothly varying slope.

**1956** *Jrnl. Exper. Med.* CIII. 657 The existence of the shoulder in the survival curve..is unequivocal and constitutes evidence for a multiple hit killing mechanism. **1964** *Physics in Med. & Biol.* IX. 167 If the log of the surviving fraction is plotted against dose on a linear scale, after an initial shoulder, a straight-line graph is obtained. **1977** *Nature* 17 Feb. 660/2 The asymmetry evident in the low resolution scan is revealed to be a shoulder at $\sim$ 10 cm$^{-1}$ to lower energy than the main band which occurs at 1,528 cm$^{-1}$.

**l.** *Surfing.* (See quots.)

**1962** T. MASTERS *Surfing made Easy* 65 *Shoulder*, the unbroken section to the side of a breaking wave. **1965** J. POLLARD *Surfrider* ii. 20 Take this one near the 'shoulder', the unbroken part of the wave reached at the end of a slide. **1968** *Surfer Mag.* Jan. 65/1 Positively the shoulder-hoppers paradise.

**7.** An arched piece of wood or metal, or a frame of metal rods, placed under the shoulders of a coat or cloak to be hung up in a wardrobe, a shop-window, etc.

**1899** *Westm. Gaz.* 31 July 1/3 Clothes hung about on wooden 'shoulders'. **1903** *Daily Chron.* 23 Nov. 4/4 A 'shoulder', the technical term for the wooden frame upon which ladies' mantles are hung by linen drapers.

**8.** Short for *shoulder-moth* (see 9 c).

**1803** HAWORTH *Lepidoptera Brit.* 226 *Noctua plecta* (the flame Shoulder).

**9.** *Combinations.*

**a.** simple attrib., 'pertaining to the shoulder' as ***shoulder band, belt, blanket, brooch, -fin, garment, hackle, harness, pad, plaid, sack, -socket***; with the meaning 'having a shoulder' (sense 6), as ***shoulder-block, bolt, screw, spike***.

**1688** HOLME *Armoury* III. 97/2 [Seamsters terms] *Shoulder Band. **1968** *N.Y. Times* 15 Sept. I. 46 A new safety seat, with built-in *shoulder belts, is being developed by the General Motors Corporation. **1976** *Billings* (Montana) *Gaz.* 24 June 7-A/5 Ontario on Jan. 1 became the first jurisdiction on the North American continent to require the wearing of available lap or shoulder belts. **1973** A. H. WHITEFORD *North Amer. Indian Arts* 69 *Shoulder blankets, worn by males, have checkered or tartan patterns. **1794** *Rigging & Seamanship* I. 156 *Shoulder-block is a large single block, left nearly square at the lower end, or arse of the block. *Ibid.*, Mast-making Plate, *Shoulder bolt. **1902** *Cassell's Encycl. Dict.* Suppl., **Shoulder brooch*, the large brooch worn in the Highland costume, fastening the plaid on the left shoulder. **1681** GREW *Musæum* I. §v. i. 97 The Scate, or Angel-Fish. His *Shoulder-Fins..expanded. **1608** WILLET *Hexapla Exod.* 651 The ephod or *shoulder garment. **1867** F. FRANCIS *Angling* x. 299 [In a salmon fly] ..*g.* the *shoulder hackle. **1968** *Time* 5 Apr. 38 Padded roll bars and *shoulder harnesses are standard on the Shelby Cobra. **1974** HAWKEY & BINGHAM *Wild Card* xxxii. 180 Wallcroft unfastened his seatbelt and shoulder harness and got out [of the car]. **1868** C. L. EASTLAKE *Hints on Household Taste* iii. 80 The 'Cromwell' chair..is..copied from examples of the seventeenth century... Both the seat and *shoulder-pad are stuffed..with horsehair. **1904** *Sci. Amer.* 21 May 406/1 Every coat has a shoulder-pad of various thicknesses made of wadding. **1951** *Sport* 16–22 Mar. 14/3 A slight 'teacup storm' occurred in Yorkshire Rugby Union circles because a Leeds team were alleged to be wearing shoulder pads. **1979** R. PERRY *Bishop's Pawn* iii. 51 He ripped seams, split shoulder pads and carved up shoes. **1831** J. LOGAN *Scott. Gaël* I. 246 The *shoulder plaid is worn by the present Highlanders chiefly for ornament. **1923** D. H. LAWRENCE *Captain's Doll* 232 Alexander was putting the bread back into his *shoulder-sack. **1953** *Scrutiny* XIX. 289 He pulls out the picture from his shoulder-sack. **1747** *Gentl. Mag.* 223 The bar..must be fixt to the plate..by a *shoulder screw, allowing a little play between. **1921** D. H. LAWRENCE *Birds, Beasts & Flowers* (1923) 81 Shall great wings flame from his *shoulder-sockets Assyrian-wise?

**b.** Objective, as ***shoulder cutting***; ***shoulder-shrugging*** adj.; locative, as ***shoulder-fired, galled, -launched*** adjs.

**1883** GRESLEY *Gloss. Coal-mining*, **Shoulder Cutting* (South Staffordshire), cutting the sides of the upper lift of a working place in a Thick-coal colliery next the rib, preparatory to falling the coal. **1967** J. S. TOMPKINS *Weapons of World War III* viii. 105 There is also a *shoulder-fired descendant of the bazooka called the LAW, or Light Antitank weapon. **1694** *Lond. Gaz.* No. 3010/4 A strong grey Gelding..*Shoulder-gal'd. **1974** *Times* 5 Mar. 6/8 Guards now are equipped with the General Dynamics Redeye infra-red-guided, *shoulder-launched anti-aircraft missile. **1977** *Belfast Tel.* 22 Feb. 17/4 Our new Blowpipe shoulder-launched missile which is in service with the armed forces of both the United Kingdom and Canada. **1840** THACKERAY *Cruikshank* Wks. 1900 XIII. 293 A villainous race of *shoulder-shrugging mortals are his Frenchmen indeed.

**c.** Special comb.: **shoulder angle** *Fortif.* (see quot.); **shoulder-bag**, a bag carried by a strap or straps slung over the shoulder; **shoulder belt** = BANDOLEER; **shoulder board** chiefly *U.S.*, each of the two stiffened pieces of material worn at the shoulders of military uniform and bearing the insignia of rank; **shoulder-brace** (see quot.); **shoulder-butt**, a pistol butt shaped for firing from the shoulder; **shoulder cap**, (*a*) *Antiq.* a piece of armour covering the point of the shoulder (= EPAULET 3); (*b*) *Surg.* see quot. 1895; **shoulder charge**, a charge in which the shoulder is directed at the target; hence as *v. trans.*; **shoulder-clapper**, an officer charged with the arrest of an offender, a bailiff, sheriff's officer; so *shoulder-clapped, -clapping* adjs.;

**shoulder-cover** *Ent.* = PATAGIUM c (*Cent. Dict.* 1891); †**shoulder-dash**, a sharper's trick of throwing his liquor over his shoulder instead of drinking it; **shoulder-girdle** *Anat.* (see GIRDLE *sb.*[1] 4); **shoulder-grafting** (see quot. 1842); **shoulder gun**, a gun which is fired from the shoulder, as distinguished from a stancheon or punt gun; †**shoulder-head** = SHOULDER STRAP 1; **shoulder-height** *adv.*, as high as one's shoulder; **shoulder-high** *adv.* = prec.; *adj.*, that is up to one's shoulder in height; **shoulder-hitter** *colloq. U.S.*, one who hits from the shoulder; hence a pugilist, a bully, rough; **shoulder holster**, a holster suspended from a shoulder-strap; †**shoulder-knife**, a huntsman's knife used to take out the shoulder in cutting up a deer; **shoulder-lappet** *Ent.* (see quot.); **shoulder-length** *a.*: of hair, etc., that reaches down to the shoulders; †**shoulderlin**, *lit.* shoulder-linen, i.e. shoulder-piece (of the ephod); **shoulder line**, (*a*) a line drawn on the shoulder (of an object); (*b*) the line of a woman's garment over the shoulders; **shoulder-lyar** *Sc.*, a piece cut from the upper part of the fore-leg of a carcass of beef; **shoulder moth**, a collectors' name for certain moths of the family *Noctuidæ* (Cent. Dict.); **shoulder net**, a fishing-net with a long pole which slides over the shoulder of the user; **shoulder note** *Typogr.*, a marginal note inserted at the top corner of a page; **shoulder patch**, a patch attached to the shoulder of a garment and bearing an emblem or insignia; **shoulder-pegged** *a.* (see quot.); †**shoulder pight** *a.* = *shoulder pitched*; †**shoulder-pinched**, †**pinching** (see quots.); **shoulder pit** [after *arm-pit*], the hollow under the shoulder of a sheep; †**shoulder pitch** = ACROMION; †**shoulder pitched** *pa. pple.* and *ppl. a.*, (of animals) having the shoulder dislocated; **shoulder plane** *Woodworking* (see quot. 1954); **shoulder plate** = SHOULDER PIECE 1; **shoulder pod** [cf. TRIPOD *sb.*], a support for a camera that rests against the shoulder; †**shoulder point**, (*a*) the point of the shoulder; (*b*) a shoulder-knot (= AGLET 2c); **shoulder-pole**, a pole, each end of which rests upon a carrier's shoulder, the load being slung from the centre; **shoulder-rest**, a rest for a rifle in experimental firing; †**shoulder-shake** *v. trans.*, to shake the shoulders of; **shoulder-shaken** *a.* (of a beast) strained in the shoulder; **shoulder shield**, a shield-shaped piece of armour used to protect the shoulder; **shoulder-shot** *sb.*, a shot fired into the shoulder (of an animal); **shoulder-shot, -shotten** *adjs.*, (of an animal) having a strained or dislocated shoulder (*arch.*); **shoulder sling** *dial.*, a yoke for carrying (milk) pails; **shoulder slip**, a strain or dislocation of the shoulder-joint; hence ***shoulder slipped*** *a.*; †**shoulder-splate**, †**-splating** *sbs.* = *shoulder-slip*; †**shoulder-splate**, †**splated**, **-splayed** *adjs.*, = *shoulder-shotten* adj.; **shoulder stand**, a position in which the body and legs are held up in the air and supported on the shoulders; †**shoulder-stick**, a coach passenger carried by the method called 'shouldering' (see SHOULDER *v.* 14); **shoulder-striker** *U.S.* = *shoulder-hitter*; **shoulder-stripe**, a collectors' name for a variety of moth; **shoulder-stripe, -striped** *adjs.*, having a stripe of colour on the shoulder (indicating a species of moth); **shoulder tab**, each of the two pieces of material worn at the shoulders of military or other uniform and bearing insignia of rank; **shoulder-tap**, the action (of a bailiff) of tapping a person on the shoulder; hence ***shoulder-tapping***; **shoulder throw** *Judo* (see quot. 1968); **shoulder-tippet** *Ent.* = PATAGIUM c (*Cent. Dict.*); †**shoulder-torn** *a.* = *shoulder-shotten*; **shoulder-tuft** *Ent.* = *shoulder-lappet*; **shoulder-wedge** *Building* (see quot.); **shoulder wing**, a monoplane wing mounted high on the fuselage but not in the highest position; usu. *attrib.*; **shoulder-work**, carrying of burdens; also, continuously hard work; **shoulder-wrench** (see quot. 1898); **shoulder-yoke**, a yoke for carrying pails. Also SHOULDER-BLADE, -BONE, -JOINT, -KNOT, -PIECE, -STRAP.

**1835** *Penny Cycl.* IV. 16/2 The angles formed by the faces and flanks which are denominated **shoulder angles.* **1912** D. H. LAWRENCE *Let.* 19 Aug. (1932) 49 We walked from the Isarthal down here—F. and I—with our German *shoulder-bags on our backs. **1960** L. DAVIDSON *Night of Wenceslas* ii. 32 She was wearing a gaily coloured cotton frock and a shoulder bag. **1977** P. THEROUX *Consul's File* 48 She sat down and threw her shoulder-bag on a side-table. **1668** PEPYS *Diary* 17 May, Up, and put on my new stuff-suit, with a *shoulder-belt according to the new fashion. **1856** KANE *Arct. Expl.* I. viii. 85 Our track-lines and shoulder-belts replaced the warps. **1949** J. STEINBECK *Russian Jrnl.* 20 The uniforms were without insignia and without *shoulder boards. **1980** 'J. LE CARRÉ' *Smiley's People* xxv. 295, I saw no shoulder-boards, the guards wore plain clothes. **1875** KNIGHT *Dict. Mech.*, **Shoulder-brace* (Surgical), an appliance for treating round shoulders or unconfirmed curvatures of the spine. **1810** *Sporting Mag.* XXXVI. 273 A rifle pistol..furnished with a pistol *shoulder-but. **1830** SKELTON *Arms & Armour* I. Pl. xxii, Fig. 3. The gorget with *shoulder caps. **1895** *Arnold's Catal. Surgical Instrum.* 777 Shoulder Cap, moulded leather for the after treatment of dislocation. **1930** *Daily Express* 6 Oct. 16/2 They exchanged good *shoulder charges, and honours were about even. **1971** *Sunday Australian* 8 Aug. 3/4 Twice outside the motel where the Springboks were staying they were *shoulder-charged by police. **1973** *Weekly News* (Glasgow) 11 Aug. 7/2 He shoulder-charged the door pushing it open. **1590** SHAKS. *Com. Err.* IV. ii. 37 He's in Tartar limbo..: A back friend, a *shoulder-clapper [hath him]. **1621** J. TAYLOR (Water-P.) *Praise Beggery* B2, He's free from *shoulder-clapping Sergeants clawes. **1796** GROSE *Dict. Vulgar T.* (ed. 3), *Shoulder Clapper*, a bailiff, or member of the catch club. **Shoulder-clapped*; arrested. **1711** PUCKLE *Club* 19 These brethren in iniquity using finger-shade, mouth-spirt, or *shoulder-dash, drank little 'til the company were mellow. **1868** W. K. PARKER (*title*), A Monograph on the structure and development of the *shoulder-girdle and sternum in the Vertebrata. **1669** WORLIDGE *Syst. Agric.* 108 The third way ..that is made use of..is *shoulder or Whip-grafting. **1842** LOUDON *Suburban Hort.* 291 Sometimes also the scion is prepared with a shoulder..and this mode is called shoulder-grafting. **1824** COL. HAWKER *Instr. Young Sportsm.* 298 *Shoulder duck-guns. **1842** LACY *Mod. Shooter* 103 A thin coat of olive oil is the best external application for a shoulder-gun. **1688** *Shoulder-head [see SHOULDER-STRAP 1]. **1825** SCOTT *Betrothed* xxiii, Many a fair knight would leap *shoulder-height for leave to look on you as free as the brook may! **1837** CARLYLE *Fr. Rev.* I. III. v, No crowds now to carry you, *shoulder-high, to the immortal gods. **1897** MARY KINGSLEY *W. Africa* vi. 119 As I walk on through the now shoulder-high grass. **1856** J. HOLBROOK *Mail Bags* 27 *Shoulder-hitter, who strikes from the shoulder, ruffian. **1864** LOWELL *Rebell.* Writ. 1890 V. 126 We remember our own roughs and shoulder-hitters at the beginning of the war. **1895** *Montgomery Ward Catal.* 481/2 *Shoulder Holster, with breast and shoulder strap to wear under coat on left side. **1935** M. M. ATWATER *Murder in Midsummer* xxi. 193 Mr. Henry Smith..buckled on his shoulder-holster, weighted by his old six-shooter. **1973** 'I. DRUMMOND' *Jaws of Watchdog* xiii. 166 Sandro's own gun was in its shoulder-holster. **1576** TURBERV. *Venerie* xlii. (1908) 129 This beyng done, he shall first take out the right shoulder [of the deer] with his *shoulder knyfe. *Ibid.* xliii. 135. **1899** D. SHARP *Insects* II. vi. 312 These appendages [the tegulae] are frequently erroneously called patagia, but have also been called scapulae,..and shoulder-tufts, or *shoulder-lappets. **1951** *Shoulder-length [see CUT *sb.*[2] 17a]. **1976** C. DEXTER *Last seen Wearing* xxix. 202 Long shoulder-length hair..brushed forward over her face. *c* **1200** ORMIN 954 Off þatt preostess *shulldrelin, & off hiss breostlin baþe. **1916–17** *T. Eaton & Co. Catal.* Fall & Winter 414/2 Semi-porcelain dinner set has..gold edges and green *shoulder line. **1931** *McCall's Mag.* Sept. 74 A significant self-fabric cuff and a very notable shoulder line. **1979** *Guardian* 13 June 12/4 The best of this year's T-shirts ..are loose with a dropped shoulderline. **1844** H. STEPHENS *Bk. Farm* (1855) II. 693/1 The *shoulder-lyar is a coarse piece, and fit only for boiling fresh to make into broth or beef-tea. **1793** *Statist. Acc. Scot.* IX. 322 Salmon, grilse and sea trouts, are caught in the night time, by what they term the fishing with the *shoulder-nets. **1882** J. SOUTHWARD *Pract. Printing* (1884) 248 *Shoulder notes are placed at the top of a page. **1909** P. VIVIAN *Campion's Wks.* 373 The custom is fully explained in a shoulder-note. **1947** A. P. GASKELL *Big Game* 82 He recalled their first issue of *shoulder-patches. **1970** N. ARMSTRONG et al. *First on Moon* v. 101 An Apollo 11 shoulder patch..would be left on the moon. **1753** *Chambers' Cycl.* Suppl., *Shoulder-pegged horses, called in French *chevillées*, are such as have their shoulders gourdy, stiff, and almost without motion. **1565–6** BLUNDEVIL *Horsemanship* IV. cxiii. (1580) 52 Of the *shoulder pight. That is when the shoulder point or pitch of the shoulder is displaced. **1728** BAILEY *Dict.* (ed. 4), **Shoulder Pincht*, a Disease in Horses. **1810** C. JAMES *Milit. Dict.* (ed. 3), **Shoulder-pinching*, a misfortune which befals a horse by labouring or straining when too young. **1607** TOPSELL *Four-f. Beasts* 650 The greasie wooll which groweth in the *shoulder pits of sheepe. **1585** HIGINS *Junius' Nomencl.* 36/1 *Acromium*,..the *shoulder pitch or point. **1695** *Lond. Gaz.* No. 3081/4 One of her Coach Geldings.. hath been *shoulder Pitch'd. **1935** N. R. ROGERS *Technol. Woodwork & Metalwork* I. iv. 56 The *Shoulder Plane is intended, as its name implies, for trueing tenon shoulders (end grain). **1954** W. E. KELSEY *Carpentry, Joinery & Woodcutting Machinery* i. 16 Shoulder planes..are metal rebate planes with a narrow mouth and a low-pitched cutter. .. They are used chiefly for planing against the end grain and are specially suitable for hardwoods. **1979** A. B. EMARY *Woodworking* xxviii. 121 The bevelled portion of the mouldings can be made with a shoulder plane or a badger plane. **1846** FAIRHOLT *Costume* Gloss., *Epauliere, epaullets*, *shoulder-plates. **1847** LEITCH tr. *C. O. Müller's Anc. Art* §257.238 The splendid shoulder-plates of a suit of armour. **1963** D. BOTTING in A. Smith *Throw out Two Hands* 263 It was possible to make hand-held movie shots (using pistol-grip or *shoulder pod) with lenses of longer focus than usual. **1981** *Birds* Autumn 18/3 With miniaturisation and the wide use of telephoto lenses,..the stalking technique evolved, using shoulderpods rather than tripods. **1510** STANBRIDGE *Vocabula* (W. de W.) Aiij, *Hec scapula*, the *shoulder poynt. *a* **1625** FLETCHER *Nice Valour* III. i, [He] has hir'd meer rogues..To beat the Soldier..for wearing Shoulder-points, With longer taggs than his. **1740** SOMERVILLE *Hobbinol* I. 316 Then with quick Wheel oblique, his Shoulder-point Beneath his Breast he fix'd. **1910** D'A. W. THOMPSON tr. *Aristotle's Hist. Anim.* I. 12 The part to the back of the neck is the epomis, or 'shoulder-point'. **1888** *Century Mag.* Nov. 35/1 A couple of fettered convicts carrying water in a large wooden bucket slung between them on a *shoulder-pole. **1868** *Rep. Munitions War* 44 That two rifles at a time should be shot for accuracy from two *shoulder-rests, one on the right, the other on the left of the shooting-stand. **1649** CLEVELAND *Chron. Decoll. Car.* iii, Charles our dread Sovereign's murdered!—tremble and View what Convulsions *shoulder-shake this Land. **1844** H. STEPHENS *Bk. Farm* II. 158 When the roads become very hard, they [beasts] are apt to become *shoulder-shaken. **1824** MEYRICK *Ant. Armour* I. Introd. p. xvi, Their [*sc.* the retiarii's] left arms were protected by padded linen..out of which issued a *shoulder-shield high enough to guard the face. **1830** SKELTON *Arms & Armour* I. Pl. ix, Fig. 6. The shoulder shield which rendered unnecessary a grande-garde on the breast plate. **1900** POLLOK & THOM *Sports Burma* vi. 212, I gave this [bison] the *shoulder-shot with the remaining barrel of my rifle. **1600** SURFLET *Country Farm* I. xxiii. 126 Oxen..being either *shoulder-shot [orig. F. *espaulez*] or brused,..are fatted. **1596** SHAKS. *Tam. Shr.* III. ii. 56 His horse hip'd..and *shoulder-shotten. **1894** K. GRAHAME *Pagan P.* 108 He [a horse] seems sorely shrunk and shoulder-shotten. **1813** ST. J. PRIEST *Agric. Bucks* 297 in Marshall *Rev. Rep. Board Agric.* (1814) IV. 545 [The milk is] carried home in pails hanging upon a wooden *shoulder sling (as it is called). **1729** SWIFT *Direct. Serv.* v. (1745) 71 The Horse will probably take so much Care of him self, as to come off with only a Strain or a *Shoulder-slip. **1898** *Syd. Soc. Lex.* **1695** *Lond. Gaz.* No. 3100/4 Lost.., a black Nag above 13 hands,..lately *shoulder slip'd. **1872** TENNYSON *Gareth & Lyn.* 740 They shock'd, and Kay Fell shoulder slipt. **1621** J. TAYLOR (Water-P.) *Motto* A4b, The necke-cricke, spauins, *shoulder-splat, and aches. *c* **1720** W. GIBSON *Farrier's Guide* II. lxvii. (1738) 222 It is called a Shoulder Splait. **1639** T. DE GRAY *Compl. Horsem.* 309 If your horse be *shoulder splat. **1725** *Bradley's Fam. Dict.*, *Soldiers Ointment*, an Ointment..for a Horse that is *Shoulder Splaited. **1708** KERSEY *Dict.*, **Shoulder-splaiting.* **1882** OGILVIE, **Shoulder-splayed.* **1956** KUNZLE & THOMAS *Freestanding* iv. 44 *Inverted *shoulder stand.* Start from back lying and raise the legs and hips until vertical. **1977** 'M. YORKE' *Cost of Silence* iv. 32 Sarah was practising the shoulder stand upstairs. **1828** *Sporting Mag.* XXI. 324 'Why do they call the opposition [coach] the Regulator?' asked Joe Walton's *shoulder-stick one day. **1860** O. W. HOLMES *Prof. Breakf.-t.* ix, No '*shoulder-striker' hits out straighter than a child with its logic. **1819** SAMOUELLE *Entomol. Compend.* 251 Genus *Leucania*... Sp. 1. *Phalæna comma* (*shoulder stripe wainscot). **1869** E. NEWMAN *Brit. Moths* 165 The *Shoulder Stripe (*Anticlea badiata*). *Ibid.* 264 The *Shoulder-striped Wainscot (*Leucania Comma*). **1966** D. FRANCIS *Flying Finish* v. 66 Gold-braided *shoulder tabs on his navy uniform jacket. **1881** BESANT & RICE *Chapl. Fleet* II. i, There was no street..where I did not fear..the unfriendly *shoulder-tap of a bailiff. **1842** LOVER *Handy Andy* xlv, If I could get on the press I'd quit the *shoulder-tapping profession. **1956** K. TOMIKI *Judo* iii. 73 *Seio-nage* (*Shoulder-throw). **1960** *Oxford Mail* 10 Mar. 8/3 Milsom scored a half-point for a shoulder throw then full points for a hip throw and a stranglehold. **1968** K. SMITH *Judo Dict.* 186 *Shoulder throws*, those made from a standing position and using principally the action of the hands and arms. **1610** MARKHAM *Masterp.* II. lix. 311 Of splayting the shoulder, or of *shoulder torne. **1899** *Shoulder-tuft [see *shoulder-lappet*]. **1887** *Dict. Archit.* (Arch. Publ. Soc.), **Shoulder wedge*..the block of wood secured to the upper side of the principal rafter of a roof truss, to sustain the purlin. **1941** R. A. SAVILLE-SNEATH *Aircraft Recognition* I. ii. 15 Variants of the *high-wing* type are..**Shoulder-wing*, a type in which..the wing-roots join the fuselage at the 'shoulder', i.e. lower than the normal high-wing but appreciably higher than the mid-wing position. **1962** L. DEIGHTON *Ipcress File* v. 33, I noticed a twin-engined shoulder wing Grumman S2F-3. **1969** K. MUNSON *Pioneer Aircraft 1903–14* 149/1 The Type A was a single-seat, warp-controlled, shoulder-wing monoplane with a 50 h.p. gnome rotary. **1660** SOUTH *Serm.* (1727) IV. 61 It is observed of the Levites, though much of their Ministry was only *Shoulder-work, that they had yet a very considerable Time for Preparation. **1886** *Cheshire Gloss.*, *Shoother-wark* (shoulder-work), any work that is continuously hard. **1708** KERSEY *Dict.*, **Shoulder-wrench*, a Strain in a Horse's Shoulder. **1898** *Syd. Soc. Lex.*, *Shoulder wrench*, a wrench, sprain, or dislocation of the shoulder. **1862** J. SAUNDERS *Abel Drake's Wife* x, He..adjusted the *shoulder-yoke, hooked on the pails, and rose.

**shoulder** ('ʃəʊldə(r)), *v.* Forms: see the sb. [f. SHOULDER *sb.* Cf. Du. *schouderen*, LG. *schuldern*, G. *schultern* (dial. *schullern*).]

**1. a.** *trans.* To push against (a person or thing) with the shoulder; (of a crowd) to push shoulder against shoulder; hence, to push roughly, unceremoniously, or insolently; to thrust aside with the shoulder; to hustle, jostle. Now *rare* or *Obs.* exc. as in b.

*c* **1300** *Havelok* 1056 þe chaunpiouns..Shuldreden he ilc oþer, and lowen. *c* **1375** *Cursor M.* 12034 (Fairf.) Wiþ þat þer come a childe in hy and shulderred ihesu with grete enuy. *c* **1450** in Aungier *Syon* (1840) 259 If any schulder pusche or threten to smyte another. **1523** BERNERS *Froiss.* I. cccxlii. 537 And in the passyng by, Bernarde sholdred sir Langurantes horse in suche wyse, that the lorde fell out of the sadell. *c* **1590** *Faire Em* II. ii. 35 *Sir Rob.* Lord Marques, you offerd me disgrace to shoulder me. **1621** QUARLES *Argalus & P.* (1678) 115 So that both men and horse, Shouldring each other, with a double force Fell to the ground. **1713** ROWE *Jane Shore* v. i, Around her, numberless, the rabble flowed, Shouldering each other, crowding for a view. **1802** BLOOMFIELD *Rural Tales* 5 You shoulder'd me; then laugh'd to see Me and my Gotch spin down the Hill.

*fig.* **1549** LATIMER *2nd Serm. bef. Edw. VI*, Ciiij, Thys byshoppe was a great man borne, and dyd beare suche a stroke, that he was able to shoulder the Lorde Protectour. **1606** J. CARPENTER *Solomon's Solace* xv. 64 Albeit the lande hath been sometimes resisted and shouldered by Adoniah.

**b.** With adv. or advb. phrase expressing the result of the action.

*c* **1375** *Cursor M.* 13741 (Fairf.) Ne wiste þai neuer quat to say ilkan shuldered oþer a-way. **1573** G. HARVEY *Letter Bk.* (Camden) 50 Momus him self wil sooner be shouldrid out of heaven. **1607** MARKHAM *Caval.* viii. 48 Now for the rules of foule play [in horse-racing], as..the striking your adversaries horse thwart the face.., the shouldring him vp into vneuen pathes..whereby you may indanger to ouerthrowe him. **1624** T. SCOTT *Belg. Souldier* 31 They haue.. by maine force shouldred open the Castillian gates. **1815** SCOTT *Guy M.* xxxvi, The stranger..divided the press, shouldering from him..both drunk and sober passengers. **1835** L. HUNT *Town* iii. (1848) 160 Here at all events he [Dr. Johnson] walked and talked and shouldered wondering porters out of the way. **1846** DICKENS *Pict. Italy, Rome* 171 Ecclesiastics..having their humility gratified to the utmost, by being shouldered about. **1848** THACKERAY *Van. Fair* vi, 'Be off, you fools!' said this gentleman—shouldering off a great number of the crowd. **1850** KINGSLEY *Alton Locke* xxviii, He skipped up by the speaker's side, and gently shouldered him down. **1887** SHEARMAN *Athletics & Football* 349 Trying to shoulder him round and send him staggering off the ball. **1889** F. E. GRETTON *Memory's Harkback* 178 A French Marshal met an English Colonel in the street, and shouldered him off the causeway.

*fig.* **1579** W. WILKINSON *Confut. Fam. Love* 6 b, For all his ..shouldring out the sonne of God. **1617** tr. *M. A. de Dominis on Rom. xiii. 12*, 15, I conceiue not to what purpose Aristotle..troubled naturall Philosophie, by Shouldring in after Matter and Forme, Priuation for a third principle of naturall bodies. **1638** MEDE *Rem. Pass. Apocal.* iii. Wks. (1672) 586 A Probability stands in place of a Demonstration, till a greater Probability can be brought to shoulder it out. **1784** COWPER *Task* VI. 839 Custom and prejudice..That govern all things here, should'ring aside The meek and modest truth. **1880** MCCARTHY *Own Times* III. xxxii. 56 The..Briton began to monopolise the officers' posts everywhere. The natives were shouldered out of the high positions.

**c.** To 'rub shoulders' with, mix with. *rare.*

**1851** MAYNE REID *Scalp Hunters* lvii, I had shouldered society..enough to render me slightly sceptical of its sincerity.

**2.** *transf.* of inanimate things.

**1590** SPENSER *F.Q.* I. xi. 21 The rolling billowes beate the ragged shore, As they the earth would shoulder from her seat. **1603** DRAYTON *Bar. Wars* VI. xxiv, Like to some low Brooke..By waste of Waters that is ouer-flow'd, Is sated, till it shouldreth downe the Mound. **1625** N. CARPENTER *Geog.* I. ii. (1635) 23 The Water being the most ponderous and waighty,..shoulders out the Aire. **1630** *R. Johnson's Kingd. & Commw.* 494 Shouldering all the Northerne shore of the Caspian, it runneth along..by the high looking walls of China. **1644** DIGBY *Nat. Bodies* xix. §9. 175 The latter graines were shouldered of by others that already besieged the superficies. **1796** *Hist. Ned Evans* I. 220 Neither could he conceal his indignation at the vile watch-house shouldering King William's statue. **1817** COLERIDGE *Biog. Lit.* (Bohn) 15 Walls of rock..shouldering back the billows. **1866** ALGER *Solit. Nat. & Man* I. 19 From the equator to the poles the waves shoulder their fellows. **1867** SMYTH *Sailor's Word-bk.* s.v., When a seaman..gives his ship too little cable to ride by, she may be thrown across tide, lift or shoulder her anchor, and drift off.

**3.** Of troops: To push, force, drive back (an opposing force); to manœuvre or turn.

**1581** STYWARD *Martial Discipl.* I. 21 This battaile [*i.e.* disposition of troops] is of great force to shoulder and beate downe the enimie. **1887** *Athenæum* 24 Sept. 398/3 Thus rendering it possible two days later to shoulder the French off the direct road to Berlin.

**4. a.** *absol.* and *intr.* To push with the shoulder; to use the shoulders (in a struggle or contest). Const. *against, at.* Also *to shoulder it.*

*a* **1440** *Found. St. Barth. Hosp.* II. Prol. (1886) 77 And menne presydde hydder thykly for variawnte causys, and shuldrid to gider. *a* **1568** ASCHAM *Scholem.* II. (Arb.) 128 And soch runners, as commonlie, they shoue and sholder to stand formost. **1688** BUNYAN *Jerus. Sinner Saved* (1886) 82 They shoulder and crowd, and say, Pray give way,.. wherefore up and shoulder it, man; say: Stand away, devil. **1818** SCOTT *Rob Roy* v, All tramped, kicked, plunged, shouldered, and jostled. **1894** BLACKMORE *Perlycross* 403 Some working at his legs, and some shouldering at his loins.

*fig.* **1579** TOMSON *Calvin's Serm. Tim.* 76/1 It is a sinne.. for a mortall man to..shoulder against God, and fight against his glorie. **1603** KNOLLES *Hist. Turks* (1621) 409 Not contented with such possessions..hee began to shoulder for more roome.

**b.** To make one's way by pushing with the shoulders; more fully *to shoulder one's way*; also *refl.* With various prepositions and advs. Also *transf.* and *fig.*

**1581** J. BELL *Haddon's Answ. Osor.* 383 b, [He] lyke a false Prophet shouldreth forewardes. **1615** T. ADAMS *Black Devil* 27 Hee [Satan] shoulders to the barre, and pops in a forged evidence. **1720** AMHERST *Epist.* 9 On me they never cast an Eye, But take their Snuff and shoulder by. *c* **1800** H. K. WHITE *Rem.* (1837) 375 The design of shouldering himself into notice. **1835** W. IRVING *Tour Prairies* xxix, As the ground was level, they [buffaloes] shouldered along with great speed. **1842** TENNYSON *Audley Court* 8 Then we shoulder'd thro' the swarm. **1879** L. STEPHEN *Hours in Libr.* III. 323 The Englishman..goes on trampling upon acuter sensibilities, but somehow shouldering his way successfully through the troubles of the universe. **1893** KIPLING *Many Invent.* 12 A couple of junks came shouldering through from the north.

**c.** To 'rub shoulders', stand shoulder to shoulder *with.* ? *Obs.*

**1692** DRYDEN *Don Sebast.* IV. i, What, shall the people know their godlike prince Headed a rabble, and profaned his person, Shoulder'd with filth?

†**5.** Of a hare: To crouch in her form. *Obs.*

*c* **1486** *Bk. St. Albans* f vij b, An haare in her forme shulderyng or leenyng.

†**6. a.** *trans.* To put (soldiers) shoulder to shoulder in close rank. Also *transf.* Also with *up.* **b.** *intr.* To stand shoulder to shoulder. *Obs.*

**1591** SPENSER *Ruins of Rome* 213 Like as ye see the wrathfull Sea from farre, In a great mountaine heap't.. Eftsoones of thousand billowes shouldred narre. **1598** BARRET *Theor. Warres* III. i. 40 The which [files] being shouldred vp close together. **1603** KNOLLES *Hist. Turks* (1621) 200 The Christians..shouldering close together in their charge, would be like a rock of yron. **1604** DRAYTON *Moyses* III. 61 Which by the stroke of that commaunding wand, Shoulder the rough seas forcibly together. **1781** COWPER *Table-t.* 137 If guards, mechanically form'd in ranks,..Should'ring, and standing as if struck to stone.

**7. a.** *trans.* To support with, bear up or carry on the shoulder or shoulders; to take or place on one's shoulder to be carried. Also *spec.* of a racehorse, to carry (a specified weight) on the back.

**1611** COTGR., *Espauler*,..to shoulder; to support with, or beare on the shoulders. **1698** FRYER *Acc. E. India & P.* 180 They cut a whole Tree down, and..shoulder'd it with great Clamours. **1845** COULTER *Adv. in Pacific* viii. 93, I determined..to shoulder my gun, and walk right round the island. **1851** W. W. COLLINS *Rambles beyond Railways* vii. (1852) 122 We shouldered our knapsacks, and started for the Lizard. **1865** R. S. HAWKER in *All Year Round* XIII. 154/2 The people..gathered up fragments of the wreck for fuel, and shouldered them away. **1883** STEVENSON *Treas. Isl.* xxxii, Hearing no further sound, they shouldered the tools and set forth again. **1939** *Country Life* 11 Feb. 156/2 Last year, when shouldering 10st. 2lb., he fell at Becher's Brook on the second circuit. **1977** *Western Morning News* 30 Aug. 11/7 The six-year-old was returning to the course of his previous success this season, and for that win was shouldering a 7lb. penalty.

**b.** *fig.* †To forward; to help or push on; to prop *up*; to second (*obs.*). Also to take upon oneself as a burden (expense, responsibility, etc.).

**1582** STANYHURST *Æneis* II. (Arb.) 49 Thee Greeks assurauNce in Pallas whoalye remayned And with her assistaunce theyre wars were shouldered always. **1586** J. HOOKER *Hist. Irel.* 98/1 in *Holinshed*, She began to incline to hir wooer his request, to the end hir nephue should haue beene the better by his countenance shouldered. **1614** RALEIGH *Hist. World* V. iii. §15 II. 511 The yong Nephew.. regarded only..the much monie that his grand-father had laied out in vaine, to shoulder vp a falling house. **1685** COTTON *Montaigne's Ess.* I. I. xli. 501 The greatest of Scipio's acts were in part due to Lelius, whose constant practice it was to advance and shoulder [orig. F. *seconder*] Scipio's grandeur and renown. **1900** *Westm. Gaz.* 14 Nov. 2/2 The local Progressives are public-spirited enough to shoulder the expense.

†**c.** *transf.* Of a thing: To prop up. *fig.* Of the terms of an argument: To back up. *Obs.*

**1674** N. FAIRFAX *Bulk & Selv.* 99 And though the 'may be' in the Argument came starveling alone without any thing of proof to back it, yet the 'may not be' in the Answer shall be thus shoulder'd up. **1675** COTTON *Planters Man.* 16 It is good also to shoulder or clod up the Tree for three foot about, and some four foot high.

**8.** *Mil.* To place (a weapon, etc.) upon the shoulder. Also *absol.* †Also in *passive* of a soldier: To have his musket shouldered.

***to shoulder one's*** or ***a rifle*** etc., is often used for: to join the ranks, to enlist as a soldier.

**1595** SIR J. SMYTHE *Instr. Milit.* 5 They are then to say to the first ranke: Shoulder your piques and march; which is as much to say: Lay your piques vpon your right shoulders and march. **1625** MARKHAM *Souldiers Accid.* 24 Shoulder your Musquet, and carry your Rest in the right hand. **1635** W. BARRIFFE *Milit. Discipline* i. (1639) 4 Thus being armed, with Muskets shouldered, some account their Postures to begin from this place. *Ibid.* 5 Thus having charged some men will shoulder and so from thence make ready. **1672** VENN *Milit. Observ.* 37 The Musquetteer being shouldered Command..Unshoulder your Musquet, and Poyse. **1770** GOLDSM. *Des. Vill.* 158 The broken soldier..shoulder'd his crutch. **1837** CARLYLE *Fr. Rev.* II. I. xi, They have shouldered, soldier-wise, their shovels and picks. **1847** *Infantry Man.* (1854) 40 *a*, Wait for the word of command of the officer to shoulder. **1859** JEPHSON *Brittany* xiv. 234 Many a poor gentleman finds himself obliged to shoulder a musket.

**b.** *to shoulder arms* (esp. *imper.* as a word of command): to hold one's rifle in a nearly vertical position, the barrel resting against the shoulder and the butt in the hollow of the hand; also *fig.* in *Cricket* (see quot. 1966); hence *at shoulder arms*, at the position directed by this word of command.

**1844** *Queen's Regul. Army* 260 Shoulder Arms. **1847** *Infantry Man.* (1854) 30 Serjeants..will remain steady at *Shoulder Arms.* **1853** WHYTE MELVILLE *Digby Grand* vii, The brigade 'shoulder arms' preparatory to receiving..the time-honoured hero who is to inspect them. **1966** *Armchair Cricket 1966* 111 *Shoulder arms*, an expression used to describe a batsman's action when he holds the bat aloft over his shoulder as he allows the ball to go by on the off-side without attempting a stroke. **1975** *Daily Mirror* 16 Aug. 28/2 Ross Edwards immediately walked into the next ball, shouldered arms and was leg before. **1977** *Sunday Times* 30 Jan. 30/3 The next ball hit Gaekwad on the pad as he shouldered arms.

†**9. a.** To cut up the carcass of (a lamb, kid, etc.). Cf. *shoulder-knife* (SHOULDER *sb.* 8 c). *Obs. rare.*

*c* **1486** *Bk. St. Albans* f vij b, [Termys..of breekyng or dressyng of dyverse beestis..] a Lambe shulderide, a Kidde shulderide.

**b.** (See quot. 1844 in SHOULDERING *vbl. sb.* 1).

†**10.** *pa. pple.* Strained or dislocated at the shoulder. *Obs.* [? after F. *épaulé.*]

**1565–6** BLUNDEVIL *Horsemanship* IV. iii. (1580) 2 b, As when a Horse is shouldered by meanes of some outward cause, or his backe galled with the saddle.

**11. a.** To furnish (a thing) with a shoulder; to cut shoulders or a shoulder on; to fit *into* with a shoulder. Also with *down, up.*

**1438** [see SHOULDERING *vbl. sb.* 1]. **1733** TULL *Horse-Hoeing Husb.* xxiii. 355 The Tenon is also shoulder'd on each side. *a* **1734** NORTH *Life Dudley North* (1744) 198 At Powis House..they shouldered and keyed the Portico Arches with Pieces of Stone. **1778** [W. H. MARSHALL] *Minutes Agric.* 9 May 1776, I shouldered the spikes,.. leaving a small triangular shoulder at each angle of the square stump. **1879** *Cassell's Techn. Educ.* IV. 206/1 The spokes are then shouldered down slightly taper-wise. **1884** R. F. BURTON *Bk. Sword* 142 The Sword should be tightly mounted and well shouldered-up before and behind. **1901** *J. Black's Carp. & Builder, Scaffolding* 35 The staves must now be fitted..by shouldering them at the marks made.

**b.** *Slating.* (See quot.)

**1833** LOUDON *Encycl. Archit.* §1122 The roofs to be covered with the best dark blue slate.., to be well shouldered in haired lime (the upper part of each row bedded in lime).

**12.** *intr.* Of inanimate things: To form a shoulder, project as a shoulder, or spread out into a shoulder; also with *up.*

**1611** COTGR. s.v. *Espaulette, Maçonnerie à espaulettes*,.. walls..left..shouldering, bearing, or standing out in one place more then in another. **1677** MOXON *Mech. Exerc.* i. 5 Because the Chaps [of the Square Nos'd Hand-Vice] do not stand shouldering in the way. **1858** HAWTHORNE *Fr. & It. Note-bks.* (1871) I. 46 Farther off we could see blue hills, shouldering high above the intermediate ones. **1870** *Daily News* 12 Nov., The hill shoulders up very steeply for three-fourths its height.

**13.** *trans.* (*Horticulture.*) To tie out the 'shoulders' of (bunches of grapes).

**1842** LOUDON *Suburban Hort.* 461 Finished shouldering the Hamburgh, and thinning the Sweetwater and St. Peter's (neither of the two latter wants shouldering much).

**14.** *slang.* (See quots.)

**1823** 'JON BEE' *Slang* s.v. *Shouldering*, Among stage-coachmen, to shoulder, is to take up passengers on own account, without consulting the proprietors. **1865** *Hotten's Slang Dict.* (ed. 2), *Shoulder*, when a servant embezzles his master's money, he is said to shoulder his employer.

**shoulder-blade.** [Cf. MLG. *schulderblat*, Du. *schouderblad*, MHG. *schulterblat* (mod.G. *-blatt*).] Each of the two flat triangular bones articulated with the humerus, and lying over the ribs in the upper part of the back in all mammals; the scapula.

*a* **1300** *Havelok* 2644 Bi þe shu[l]dre-blade þe sharpe swerd let [he] wade, þorw the brest unto þe herte. *c* **1470** HENRY *Wallace* V. 823 Baith cannell bayne and schuldir blaid in twa, Throuch the myd cost, the gud suerd gert he ga. **1572–3** *Reg. Privy Council Scot.* I. 205 Stevin Urde.. straik the said Jonet upoun hir schulder blaid with the kavill of ane mylne. **1611** SHAKS. *Wint. T.* IV. iii. 77 Oh good sir, softly, good sir: I feare (sir) my shoulder blade is out. **1763** 'THEOPHILUS INSULANUS' *Second Sight* 77 There is another kind of divination, by looking in the shoulder-blade of a sheep, goat, &c. as in a book. **1840** CARLYLE *Heroes* ii. 101 Mahomet's followers found the Koran..as it had been written down at first promulgation; much of it, they say, on shoulder-blades of mutton. **1875** SIR W. TURNER in *Encycl. Brit.* I. 826/2 The Scapula, or Shoulder Blade..lies at the upper and back part of the wall of the chest, reaching from the second to the seventh rib.

**b.** *transf.*

**1608** TOPSELL *Serpents* 65 [Bees] haue 4 wings..growing to their shoulder-blades. **1826** KIRBY & SP. *Entomol.* III. xxxv. 662, I propose calling these pieces by names.. appropriated to the arm in the higher vertebrate animals: thus..I call the whole fore-leg the *brachium* or arm, and.. the trochanter [becomes] the *scapula* or shoulder-blade.

**shoulder-bone.** = SHOULDER-BLADE.

*c* **1320** *Sir Beues* 4217 His riȝt arm & is scholder bon He made fle to gronde anon. *c* **1325** *Gloss. W. de Bibbesw.* in Wright *Voc.* 146 Les espaules ount blasouns [*glossed* chuldel-bones; *v.rr.* the soldre-bon, scholder-bon]. *c* **1386** CHAUCER *Pard. Prol.* 22 Thanne haue [I] in laton a sholder boon Which that was of an hooly Iewes sheepe. *c* **1460** *Towneley Myst.* xxiii. 260 Godys son..hase not where apon his hede to rest Bot on his shuder bone. **1548–77** VICARY *Anat.* vii. (1888) 48 In the shoulder there be two bones,.. the Shoulder bone, and the Cannel bone. **1691** R. KIRK *Secret Commw.* i. (1815) 17 The minor Seers prognosticat many future Events,..from the Shoulder-bone of a Sheep. **1858** W. ELLIS *Madagascar* v. 125 The sides..were edged.. with the shoulder-bones of oxen stuck in the ground, the broad part upwards.

**shouldered** ('ʃəʊldəd), *ppl. a.* [f. SHOULDER *sb.* and *v.* + -ED.]

**1.** Having shoulders; furnished with shoulders. Chiefly with qualifying adv. or advb. phrase. Also ROUND-SHOULDERED.

**13..** *K. Alis.* 4968 Another folk there is biside:.. Ben y-shuldred as an fysshe, And clawed after hound, i-wisse. *c* **1386** CHAUCER *Prol.* 551 He was short sholdred, brood, a thikke knarre. *c* **1430** *Pilgr. Lyf Manhode* I. cxxxiv. (1869) 70 It is nouht for that thou ne art sholdred ynowh, and boned. *c* **1440** *Pallad. on Husb.* IV. 701 Take oxon yonge..Yshildred wide is good. *a* **1533** [see CROOKED *a.* 5]. **1591** [see BROAD D. 1]. **1697** [see HIGH *a.* 22 b]. **1740** in *Scott. Hist. Rev.* (1905) Apr. 303 [Recruits] must be straight, well limbd and shouldered. **1860** RUSKIN *Mod. Paint.* V. IX. iii. 220 Thighed and shouldered like the billows.

**2.** Having a shoulder or projection; made with a shoulder or with shoulders.

**1671** PHILLIPS (ed. 3), *Shouldred-head* (a term in Archery) the best made Heads of an Arrow..being..made with shoulders. **1750** BLANCKLEY *Nav. Expos.* 81 That shouldered Part of all Masts over which the Shrouds are put. **1805** R. W. DICKSON *Pract. Agric.* I. Plate xlviii, Fig. 1. Represents a shouldered turf-drain. **1847** MRS. J. W. LOUDON *Amateur Gard. Cal.* (1857) 152 When the upper branches of the bunch [of grapes] are large, and almost as strong as the main stem, it is said to be shouldered. **1861** P. P. CARPENTER in *Rep. Smithsonian Instit.* 1860, 214 In *Gibbula*..the whirls are shouldered, and the pillar-lip is plain. **1862** *Catal. Internat. Exhib., Brit.* II. No. 5169

Cardboard pill boxes;..plain and shouldered. **1882** CHRISTY *Joints* 103 Shouldered Joint occurs between two timbers when one is strengthened by being shouldered or thickened out to reinforce its abutting..powers.

**b.** Arch. ***shouldered arch***: a form of head for an opening (not properly an arch) somewhat resembling the outline of a man's shoulders and part of the neck.

**1853** *Turner's Dom. Archit.* (ed. Parker) II. vi. 230 Several of the smaller doorways [of Bolton Castle] have the 'shouldered arches' of the Carnarvon form. *Note.* This name has been proposed by the duchess of Northumberland for this peculiar form... It is commonly called the square-headed trefoil arch. **1866** PARKER *Gloss. Archit.* 20.

**3.** Placed and carried at, on or over the shoulder; spec. *Mil.* (see SHOULDER *v.* 7), *to stand shouldered*: to stand with shouldered arms.

**1760** *Cautions & Adv. Officers of Army* 173 Be sure to make your Men march with shouldered Arms. **1811** *Regul. Army* 13 The Officer is..to make his Men stand shouldered. **1844** *Queen's Regul. Army* 30 Their own Guards are to turn out with shouldered Arms, once a Day.

† **'shoulderer.** *Obs.* [-ER[1].] One who shoulders.

**1500–20** DUNBAR *Poems* lxiii. 49 Bot..on ȝour hienes followis eik..Schulderaris, and schowaris, that..can non vthir craft nor curis Bot to mak thrang, Schir, in ȝour duris.

**shouldering** ('ʃəʊldərɪŋ), *vbl. sb.* [f. SHOULDER *v.* + -ING[1].]

**1.** The action of the verb; an instance of this.

**1438** in Willis & Clark *Cambridge* (1886) I. 11 Schulderying de le gystes. **1590** SPENSER *F.Q.* II. vii. 47 Some thought to raise themselves to high degree..by close shouldring; some by flatteree. **1844** H. STEPHENS *Bk. Farm* II. 239 Care being taken that the point of the knife does not ..go between the shoulder-blade and the ribs. This error.. in slaughtering pigs..is called shouldering. **1856** KANE *Arctic Expl.* I. xvii. 208 There may have been something of discourtesy in the occasional shoulderings and hustlings. **1897** *Encycl. Sport* I. 342/1 (Driving) *Shouldering*, of the horse, pushing sideways upon pole or partner.

**b.** Amount of 'shoulder' or projection.

**1683** MOXON *Mech. Exerc., Printing* xiii. ¶4 The..Face thus finished, he considers what Sholdering the Shank of the Punch makes now with the Face, round about the Letter.

**2.** *concr.* Something which projects or supports as a shoulder. †Also = EPAULEMENT.

**1388** WYCLIF *1 Kings* vii. 30 And bi foure partis weren as litle schuldryngis [Vulg. *humeruli*] vndir the waischyng vessel,..*Margin*, Schuldryngis; that is, schort pileris to susteyne the waschyng vessel. **1545** ASCHAM *Toxoph.* II. (Arb.) 149 Therfore to drawe easely and vniformely..vntil you come to the rig or shouldring of ye head [of the shaft], is best. **1669** WORLIDGE *Syst. Agric.* 108 Cut the Graff.. with a shouldring but not deep. **1704** J. HARRIS *Lex. Techn.* I, *Shouldring*, in Fortification, is a Retrenchment opposed to the Enemies, or a Work cast up for a Defence on one side. **1886** *Encycl. Brit.* XX. 583/1 When there is not a kerb there should be a 'shouldering' of sods..to keep the road materials in place.

**3.** *attrib.* and *Comb.*, as **shouldering file**, a kind of file for shaping a shoulder; † **shouldering piece**, a corbel or a buttress.

**1585** HIGINS *Junius' Nomencl.* 210 *Mutuli*..Corbeaux, modillons, peeces of timber in building called braggers, or shouldering peeces. **1611** COTGR., *Espaulette*,..a buttresse, shore post, or shouldering peece. **1846** HOLTZAPFFEL *Turning* II. 825 French pivot and shouldering files which are small, stout, and have safe-edges.

**shouldering** ('ʃəʊldərɪŋ), *ppl. a.* [f. SHOULDER *v.* + -ING[2].] That shoulders.

**1535** STEWART *Cron. Scot.* II. 335 Thair raiss greit murmour..With sic ane schout, and sic ane schouder and [? *read* schouderand] schow, That euirilk one that tyme ȝeid other throw. [**1590** SPENSER *F.Q.* II. xii. 23 Spring-headed Hydraes, and sea-shouldring Whales.] **1747** COLLINS *Ode to Liberty* iii. 16 This pillar'd earth..was push'd aside, And down the shoul'dring billows born. **1824** W. IRVING *Tales Trav.* II. 233 The current is violently compressed between shouldering promontories. **1846** H. G. ROBINSON *Odes of Horace* II. xiii, The shouldering crowd.

**shoulder-joint.** The joint of the shoulder; the articulation by which the arm or foreleg is connected with the trunk.

**1726** POPE *Odyss.* XIX. 520 Ulysses..Soon..the wound repay'd; To the right shoulder-joint the spear apply'd. **1875** SIR W. TURNER in *Encycl. Brit.* I. 838/2 The Shoulder Joint is a ball-and-socket joint, the ball being the head of the humerus, the socket the glenoid fossa of the scapula.

**shoulder-knot.**

**1.** A knot of ribbon or lace, sometimes enriched with jewels, worn on the shoulder by men of fashion in the 17th and 18th c.; also a knot, formerly of ribbons of the family colours, subsequently of lace, worn on the shoulder by some livery servants; a knot or bow of ribbon worn at the shoulder by a woman or child; also *Mil.* = AGLET 2 c.

**1676** *Lond. Gaz.* No. 1075/4 Went away from his Master ..in a cloth Sute..his Shoulder-knot and Hatband of Twelve-penny broad Ribon figured. **1700** FARQUHAR *Const. Couple* I. i. 7 *Clinch*... Sir, (to Wildair) I admire the mode of your Shoulder-knot. **1704** *Lond. Gaz.* No. 3998/4 A light-grey Cloth Livery lined with yellow, a yellow Shoulder-knot. **1781** COWPER *Table-T.* 44 Better..Then grace the bony phantom..With the king's shoulder-knot and gay cockade. **1861** *Ladies' Gaz. Fashion* July 6/1 Three-quarter length sleeves, with ribbon shoulder-knots. **1862** *Macm. Mag.* May 17, I have seen..an officer with his shoulder-knots sewed on to a common plain frock-coat.

**2.** *attrib.*

**1772** FORSTER *Hudson's Bay Birds* in *Phil. Trans.* LXII. 393 Shoulder-knot Grous. **1819** STEPHENS in *Shaw's Gen. Zool.* XI. 300 Shoulder-knot Heathcock. (*Bonasa Umbellus.*) **1848** THACKERAY *Van. Fair* xiv, The Park Lane shoulder-knot aristocracy.

Hence **shoulder-knotted** *a.*

**1818** G. COLMAN *Two Parsons* Poet. Vagaries (ed. 3) 144 A shoulder-knotted Puppy..let him in. **1831** CARLYLE *Misc. Ess., Schiller* 1840 III. 4 Such valets as are too genuine, as are shoulder-knotted..in soul as well as in body.

**'shoulderless,** *a.* [f. SHOULDER *sb.*] Without a shoulder or shoulders, esp. of garments.

**1928** PEAKE & FLEURE *Steppe & Sown* vi. 78 Keller figures two shoulderless sleeves from Meilen, which Schenk placed in the third or Morgienne period. **1963** C. R. COWELL et al. *Inlays, Crowns, & Bridges* vi. 62 Shoulderless crowns present fewer difficulties in fitting than those with shoulders. **1979** *N.Y. Times Mag.* 30 Sept. 68/3 Giorgio Armani..has put together a take-off on classic men's wear that may be the most significant look to come out of Italy this season: the 'shoulderless' suit.

**shoulder-piece.**

**1. a.** *Antiq.* A piece of armour covering the shoulder.

**1580** HOLLYBAND *Treas. Fr. Tong.*, *La haute piece*, the shoulder peece of an harneis. **1611** COTGR., *Espauliere*, a showlder peece; the peece of armour, or apparell that serues for the shoulder. **1869** BOUTELL *Arms & Armour* iv. 58 The shoulder-pieces [of the Roman cuirass] formed of four plates..pass over the shoulders like straps.

*transf.* **1681** GREW *Musæum* I. §ii. i. 20 The Weesle-headed Armadillo... His Shoulder-piece consisteth of several Ranks or Rows of such like square pieces.

**b.** A piece or each of the pieces of material composing the shoulders of a garment.

**1611** BIBLE *Exod.* xxviii. 7 It shall haue the two shoulder pieces thereof, ioyned at the two edges thereof. **1632** MASSINGER *Fatal Dowry* IV. i, With a haire breadth's errour, ther's a shoulder piece cut [of a new suit of clothes]. **1861** *Engl. Wom. Dom. Mag.* III. 117 It was made with shoulder-pieces cut out in the shape of a pelerine... The shoulder-pieces were trimmed with brown ribbon.

†**2.** = BUST *sb.*[1] 1. *Obs. rare*[−1].

**1692** WOOD *Ath. Oxon.* II. 262 Before this play is a shoulder-piece of the author standing on a pedestall.

**3.** The piece forming the shoulder (of a tool, etc.).

**1811** *Self Instructor* 28 The cheek or shoulder-piece [of a pen]. **1904** WINDLE *Rem. Prehist. Age* xi. 285 By the extension of the pin-trough, which is bent backwards towards the shoulder-piece.

**b.** A piece of the fore-hock (of bacon).

**1888** *Leeds Mercury* 18 Feb. 5 Beautiful bread, and a large thick piece of shoulder-piece in addition to real coffee.

**shoulder-strap.**

**1.** Each of the two short straps which go over the shoulders, connecting and supporting the fore and back parts of a garment.

**1688** HOLME *Armoury* III. 94/1 In a Woman's Gown.. The Shoulder heads, or Shoulder straps; are two peeces that come over the Sholders. **1727** BOYER *Fr. Dict.* s.v. *Epaulette*, *Shoulder Strap*, a part of a Bodice or Stays. **1808** *Lady's Econ. Assist.* 23 Men's Shirts..Cut off ten inches and a half for the six pair of shoulder-straps. **1855** LADY E. FINCH *Sampler* (ed. 2) 95 Tack the shoulder-straps upon the shift.

**b.** *Antiq.* Each of the straps connecting the front and back parts of body armour.

**1830** SKELTON *Arms & Armour* I. Pl. xxxix, Fig. 2. The back-plate with its shoulder straps guarded with steel. **1900** A. S. MURRAY *Catal. Sculpt. Parthen. in Brit. Mus.* 91 He wears a cuirass, of which the shoulder straps terminate in panther's heads.

**2.** Each of the narrow straps fastened upon the shoulders of a military tunic; esp. an ornamental strap distinguishing the corps and grade of an officer.

**1840** *Addenda Gen. Regul. Army* 1 Approved Patterns of the Shoulder Straps, for the Staff Serjeants of Infantry.. have been sealed. **1861** O. W. HOLMES *Sweet Little Man* 12 You with the waist made for sword-belts and sashes, Where are your shoulder-straps, sweet little man? **1864** *Regul. Dress Officers of Army* 45 First Life Guards... Aiguillette and Shoulder-Strap of twisted gold cord, with gilt engraved tags, worn on the right shoulder; a gold twist cord strap similar to that of the aiguillette worn on the left shoulder. **1895** R. W. CHAMBERS *King in Yellow* 49 He rattled on.., calling my attention to his captain's shoulder-straps, and the triple gold arabesque on his sleeve.

**3.** A strap to go over one shoulder across the body and under the other arm as a support for some article to be carried.

**1870** W. M. BAKER *New Timothy* 203 (Cent.) He then mends the shoulder-strap of his powder-horn and pouches.

**'shoulderwise,** *adv.* [See -WISE.] So as to form a shoulder.

**1618** W. LAWSON *New Orch. & Garden* x. (1623) 29 And first of incising, which is the cutting of the barke..of a tree ..shoulderwise with two gashes.

**shoule,** obs. form of SHOAL.

**shouler, -erd:** see SHOVELLER, SHOVELARD.

**shoulfall,** obs. form of SHILFA.

**shoull,** obs. f. SHOVEL.

**shoult,** var. SHOLT.

**shount,** obs. f. SHUNT *v.*, to avoid, escape.

**shoup,** var. SHOOP.

**'shoupiltin.** *Shetland.* ? *Obs.* Also 9 **shoupeltin, shoopiltee, -ie.** [Derivative of ON. **sjó-piltr*, f. *sjó-r* sea + *pilt-r* boy.] (See quots.)

**1711** SIR R. SIBBALD *Descr. Orknay & Zetland* 9 Sometimes they catch with their Nets and Hooks Tritons, they call them *Shoupiltins* and Mermaids. **1821** SCOTT *Pirate* xvi, The Tritons..called by Zetlanders of that time, Shoupeltins, were represented by young men grotesquely habited. **1822** S. HIBBERT *Descr. Shetl. Isl.* 526 In Shetland, the same deity [Neptune], the Shoopiltee, assumes the form of a beautiful shelty, inviting some one to mount him, when he immediately runs into the sea and drowns his rider.

**shour(e,** obs. ff. SHOWER.

**shouse** (ʃaʊs). *Austral. slang.* [Syncopated form of *shit-house* (SHIT *sb.* 3).] A privy.

**1941** S. J. BAKER *Dict. Austral. Slang* 66 *Shouse*, a privy. **1951** D. STIVENS *Jimmy Brocket* 214, I seen that now as plain as a country shouse. **1957** 'N. CULOTTA' *They're a Weird Mob* (1958) 43 Yeah, chuck 'em ter the shouse. **1968** T. KENEALLY *Three Cheers for Paraclete* 84 I'd like some trees on it, pines and gums, so you don't have to see your neighbour's shouse first thing each morning. **1975** L. RYAN *Shearers* 98 Dewlap, who had been standing at the back of the ring, all alone like a country s'house, now sidled up.

**shout** (ʃaʊt), *sb.*[1] *Obs.* exc. *dial.* (Lincs.): see Eng. Dial. Dict. Forms: 4 s(c)houte, 4–5 showte, 4–5, 9 shute, 4, 9 shout; 7 scuyt, scutte. [ME. *schoute*, *shute*, prob. a. MDu. *schûte*: see SCHUIT, SCOUT *sb.*[3]] A flat-bottomed boat.

**13..** *Coer de L.* 4785 Berges, schoutes, crayeres fele, That were chargyd with al weel. **14..** *Piers of Fullham* in Hartshorne *Metr. Tales* (1829) 120 Com there nat dayly out off fflaunders Off ffat elys full many a showte? **1464** *Rolls of Parlt.* V. 569/2 Trowes, Botes, Cobles and Shutes. **1842** LACY *Mod. Shooter* 365 The Lynn and Boston gun-boat, or shout.

*Comb.* **1395** *Acc. Manor Savoy* in *Archæologia* XXIV. 304 [Paid to divers mariners, called] shoutemen.

**shout** (ʃaʊt), *sb.*[2] Forms: 4 **schoute,** 4–6 **shoute, schowte,** 4–7 **showt(e, schout,** 6 **schowt,** 7 **shoot(e,** 6– **shout.** [This and the related SHOUT *v.* first appear in the 14th c. The sb. corresponds formally to ON. *skúta*, *skúte*, a taunt: see SCOUT *v.*[3]; derivation from the root of SHOOT *v.* is probable.]

**1. a.** A loud, vehement cry expressing joy, grief or pain, fear, triumph, warning, encouragement, etc.; a loud cry to attract attention at a distance; a tumultuous uproar by a large body of people.

**1375** BARBOUR *Bruce* VI. 158 With that all haill a schout thai [geve]. *c* **1450** *Merlin* xiv. 223 Than a-roos the showte and the noyse of the saisnes. *c* **1513** MORE *Rich. III.* Wks. 66/2 With this there was a great shout, crying kyng Richarde kyng Rychard. **1594** SHAKS. *Rich. III.* III. vii. 39 This generall applause, and chearefull showt, Argues your wisdome, and your loue to Richard. **1616** J. LANE *Contn. Sqr.'s T.* XI. 195 So great weare th' peoples shootes, y[t] thearth it startes. **1667** MILTON *P.L.* I. 542 A shout that tore Hells Concave. **1737** WHISTON *Josephus, Antiq.* VI. ix. §5 The intire army of the Hebrews made a shout, and rushed upon them. **1809** MALKIN *Gil Blas* x. viii. (Rtldg.) 358 An involuntary shout of laughter. **1871** L. STEPHEN *Playgr. Eur.* (1894) vi. 143 We heard a faint shout.

†**b.** ***shout and hoyes*** (= OYEZ), ***shout and cry*** = HUE AND CRY. *Sc. Obs.*

**1609** SKENE *Reg. Maj.* IV. xv. 69 b, Gif ane man steilles cattell, or anie moueable gudes, and the shout and cry of neighbours follow him [etc.]. **1609** *Ibid.* tr. *2 Stat. Robt. I*, xx. 32 b, They sall raise the schout, and hoyes vpon him. *Ibid.*, The Lord of the land or the creditour with schout, and hoyes, may follow him.

**c.** *transf.* Applied to any loud noise or cry forcing itself upon the attention.

In quot. 1660 'shout' may be a misspelling of SHOOT *sb.* **1503** DUNBAR *Thistle & Rose* 183 All the birdis song with sic a schout, That I annone awoik. *c* **1560** A. SCOTT *Poems* (S.T.S.) ii. 45 Trumpettis and schalmis w[t] a schowt Playid or the rink began. **1660** PEPYS *Diary* 9 Apr. Great was the shout of guns from the castles and ships. **1802** WORDSW. *Cuckoo* ii, Thy twofold shout I hear. **1855** R. S. HAWKER in C. E. Byles *Life* (1905) 257 The shout of the trumpet.

**d.** *U.S.* Among American Blacks, a form of dancing accompanied by much loud singing, of religious origin (cf. *ring-shout* s.v. RING *sb.*[1] 19); a song of the type sung during such a performance. Also *attrib.*

**1862** in E. W. Pearson *Lett. from Port Royal* (1906) 27 As we walked home we asked Cuffy if they considered the 'shout' as part of their religious worship. **1908** *Sears, Roebuck Catal.* 199/3 *Negro Shouts.* Songs with laughing and whistling choruses. **1937** [see *praying band* s.v. PRAYING *ppl. a.* b]. **1938** *Mississippi* (Amer. Guide Ser.) 24 Soon a woman leaps out into the aisle. She is 'moved by the spirit', she cries, and slowly, rigidly, she begins 'the shout', or if it is a Holiness meeting, the 'Holy Dance'. It is shuffling, intricate; her heels thud on the floor. **1955** KEEPNEWS & GRAUER *Pictorial Hist. Jazz* xii. 127 Stomping variations of rags, known as 'shouts', were the show-pieces most often used in competition. **1972** *Listener* 10 Aug. 187/1 A musical innovator with tremendous vocal power, he brings gospel and shout singing to the blues.

**e.** ***shout-up***, a noisy argument. *colloq.*

**1965** G. MELLY *Owning Up* ix. 107 Whenever one of us was describing to the other some drunken shout-up with a third party. **1973** *Times* 3 Nov. 11, I didn't mention it until it seemed to become a pattern and then we had a good old shout up.

**2.** *slang* (orig. *Colonial*). A call to a waiter to replenish the glasses of a company; hence, a turn in paying for a round of drinks. Also, a free drink given to all present by one of the company; a drinking party.

***to go on the shout***: to drink immoderately. ***to stand (a) shout***: to stand treat all round.

**1854** F. FYANS *Let.* in T. F. Bride *Lett. fr. Victorian Pioneers* (1898) 127 Do you forget the shout you stood—the shout for all hands? **1863** H. SIMCOX *Outward Bound* (1864) 81 Many a 'shout' they're treated to. **1886** H. BAUMANN *Londinismen* 177/1 *It's my shout*, jetzt will ich euch traktieren. **1887** 'HOPEFUL' *Taken in* 135 [New Zealand] There is a great deal of standing 'shout' in the Colonies. **1892** KIPLING *Barrack-room Ballads, Yng. Brit. Soldier*, Don't go on the shout. **1911** C. E. W. BEAN '*Dreadnought' of Darling* xxxii. 282 'Boys,' he says, 'help yourselves. This is my shout.' **1914** *Bulletin* (Sydney) 17 Dec. 44/2 The..bloke ..ses t' me: 'Your shout mate.' **1954** S. MACKENZIE *Refuge* 16 Come up and have a cup of coffee—my shout. **1977** D. BAGLEY *Enemy* xxvii. 212 Honnister addressed the landlord. 'Hi, Monte: a large scotch and a pint of Director's.' 'My shout,' I said.

†**3.** *Comb.*: **shoutcry**, a loud, piercing shout.

**1582** STANYHURST *Æneis* I. (Arb.) 28 Soom mayden coompany..Rearing with shoutcry soom boare.

**shout** (ʃaʊt), *v.* Forms: 4 schoute, 4–6 schowt, shoute, showte, 4–8 schout, 5 (schuot), schowte, 6–7 showt, 4– shout; 4–5 shote, 7, 9 (*dial.*) shoot. [See SHOUT *sb.*[2]]

**1. a.** *intr.* To utter a loud call, to make a loud outcry expressive of joy, exultation, etc. or to raise an alarm, to incite to action, etc.

**13..** *E.E. Allit. P.* A. 877 Naupeles þaȝ hit schowted scharpe & ledden loude al-þaȝ hit were A note ful nwe I herde hem warpe. *c* **1385** CHAUCER *L.G.W.* 635 And in the se it happede hem to mete—Vp goth the trompe—& for to schoute & schete. **1470–85** MALORY *Arthur* v. viii. 173 The batails approached and shoue and showted on bothe sydes. **1597** SHAKS. *2 Hen. IV*, IV. ii. 87 The word of Peace is render'd: hearke how they showt. **1611** BIBLE *Job* xxxviii. 7 When the morning starres sang together, and all the sonnes of God shouted for ioy. **1687** LOVELL tr. *Thevenot's Trav.* I. 236 The People..all shouted, and wished him a thousand Blessings. **1726** SWIFT *Gulliver* III. i. 181, I called and shouted with the utmost strength of my voice. **1821** SHELLEY *Hellas* 931 Shout in the jubilee of death! **1863** GEO. ELIOT *Romola* II. i, He..shouted in her ear.

**b.** ***to shout at***, †***on*** (a person): to assail with shouts, *esp.* of derision or anger.

*c* **1384** CHAUCER *H.F.* 1808 That euery wight gan on hem shout. **1617** MORYSON *Itin.* I. 57 The common people, as if they had never seene a stranger before shouted at mee after a barbarous fashion. *c* **1730** RAMSAY *Wyfe of Auchtermuchty* xv, On hir to cry, on hir to schout. *c* **1850** *Arab. Nts.* (Rtldg.) 576 They ran and collected round him, hooting and shouting at him.

†**c.** To vote by acclamation *for* (a candidate for Parliament). (Cf. SHOUTING *vbl. sb.* 1 c.) *Obs.*

**1679** O. HEYWOOD *Diaries* (1881) II. 104 Rode to York.. found them shouting for knights of the Shire.

†**d.** Said of animals making loud cries. *Obs.*

*c* **1435** *Torr. Portugal* 570 Me thynkythe, I here my dragon schowt. *a* **1568** *Bannatyne MS.* (Hunter. Club) 661 The mirthfull maveiss mirriest Schill schowttit throw the schawis.

**e.** Of a place: To resound with shouts. Of an inanimate thing: To make a loud uproar. *rare.*

**1513** DOUGLAS *Æneis* VIII. v. 67 Euery schaw Schouttis agane of thair clamour and dyn. **1871** MACDUFF *Mem. Patmos* xx. 275 The valleys shouting with summer joy. **1880** HOWELLS *Undisc. Country* x. 139 The fire shouted and roared within.

**f.** quasi-*trans.* (*refl.*) with complement.

**1898** 'MERRIMAN' *Roden's Corner* ii. 14 He waved his silk hat and shouted himself hoarse.

**g.** *U.S. slang.* Of things: To be unmistakably significant. Also in phrase ***now you're shouting*** = 'now you are speaking to the purpose'.

**1876** *Scribner's Monthly* Nov. 142/1 'Then why prevaricate?' Said he perversely, 'Now yer shoutin'!' **1892** HOWELLS *Mercy* 420 Northwick said simply, 'Yes, I will go with you.' 'Well, now you're shouting,' said Pinney. **1892** *Pall Mall Gaz.* 25 July 3/1 Figures which, to use an Americanism, fairly 'shout'.

**h.** *Indirect passive.*

**1837** CARLYLE *Fr. Rev.* I. v. ii, Necker, for not being at the *Séance*, shall be shouted for.

†**i.** To be loud in support of a candidate. Cf. ROOT *v.*[2] 1 d. *U.S. Obs.*

**1875** [implied in SHOUTER[2] 1 b]. **1907** *N.Y. Evening Post* (semi-weekly ed.) 21 Nov. 4 Federal office-holders in various Southern States have been dutifully shouting for Roosevelt.

**2. a.** *trans.* To utter (something) with a loud voice.

**1500–20** DUNBAR *Poems* xxvi. 112 Be he the correnoch had done schout. **1607** SHAKS. *Cor.* I. i. 218 They threw their caps As they would hang them on the hornes a'th Moone, Shooting their Emulation. **1718** ROWE tr. *Lucan* I. 250 He.. lov'd to hear the Vulgar shout his Name. **1872** MORLEY *Voltaire* i. 8 Industriously shouting the cry of a church, the more effectually to reduce the faith to a vague futility.

**b.** With clause or quoted words as object.

*c* **1374** CHAUCER *Troylus* II. 614 With that gan al here meyne for to shoute 'A go we se, cast vp þe yates wyde'. **1595** SHAKS. *John* v. ii. 103 Haue I not heard these Islanders shout out *Viue le Roy*. **1760–72** H. BROOKE *Fool of Qual.* (1809) IV. 97, I heard a voice, at my side, shout out, in once-loved accents, O, my dearest mamma. **1887** HALL CAINE *Son of Hagar* II. i, 'A canny morning, Mr. Christian', he shouted.

**c.** *fig.* To indicate plainly.

**1931** E. F. BENSON *Mapp & Lucia* ii. 30 Red-brick houses with tiled roofs, that shouted Queen Anne and George I in Lucia's enraptured ears. **1976** D. FRANCIS *In Frame* iii. 48 From laquered hair via crocodile handbag to gold-trimmed shoes she shouted money.

†**3. a.** To insult with a clamorous outcry; = *to shout at* (see 1 b). **b.** To welcome with shouts, acclaim. *Obs.*

**1375** BARBOUR *Bruce* IX. 366 Thai schowtit hym and scornyng maid. *c* **1560** A. SCOTT *Poems* (S.T.S.) ii. 122 This still for bargan Sym abyddis, And schowttit Will to schame. **1706** I. WATTS *Horæ Lyr.* (1743) 76 While our Hosannas all along the Passage Shout the Redeemer. **1784** COWPER *Task* VI. 698 The statesman of the day..comes. Some shout him, and some hang upon his car.

**4.** (in senses a–e *dial.*) **a.** To call, summon (a person). **b.** To publish the banns of marriage of (persons): = CRY *v.* 5 d. **c.** To call *in* (assistance). †**d.** ***to shout*** (a person) ***up, out of bed***: to 'call' (a person) in the morning, to awaken (some one, from sleep by calling loudly. *Obs.* **e.** To urge *on* (an animal) to the attack by a vehement outcry.

**1797** T. WRIGHT *Autobiog.* (1864) 189 We therefore shouted the landlord out of bed. **1812** *Ann. Reg., Chron.* 38 After a while, the servant girl, Hannah Evans, came up to him to shout him up. **1864** CARLYLE *Fredk. Gt.* II. xii. I. 121 He stood obstinate siege from the Kaiser's people.., shouted-in Denmark to help. **1888** MRS. RIDDELL *Nun's Curse* I. vi. 106 He broke into a great laugh, and shouted the dogs on to her. **1895** *Longman's Mag.* Aug. 394 To goo an' get the lass shouted afore thou knowed if hoo were willin' to wed thee or not. *Mod.* (N.E. Derbyshire) I've got to go home; my mother's shouting me.

**f.** To howl *down* or reduce to silence by shouts of disapproval. Also *fig.*

**1924** G. B. SHAW *St. Joan* vi. 89, I know that there is no faith in a Frenchman. [*Tumult, which he shouts down.*] **1965** M. SPARK *Mandelbaum Gate* iii. 59 Freddy's thoughts whispered on, refusing to be shouted down by any other voice that might arise in his brain to hush them up. **1967** N. FREELING *Strike out where not Applicable* 36 Francis forces things sometimes by simply shouting her down. **1978** P. MOORE *Man, Woman, & Priesthood* xi. 171 This challenge may be not only right, but vindicated; it cannot, however, be ignored and shouted down.

**5.** *Australian* and *N.Z. slang.* **a.** *intr.* To stand drinks, to treat a crowd of persons to refreshments.

**1855** R. CARBONI *Eureka Stockade* 68 You shouted nobblers round for all hands—that's all right; it's no more than fair and square now for the boys to shout for you. **1856** H. W. HARPER *Lett. from N.Z.* (1914) 10 The first person in New Zealand to 'shout' for me, which here means to ask you into a house of call and stand treat. **1859** H. KINGSLEY *G. Hamlyn* xxxi, So I shouted for him and he for me. **1873** J. H. H. ST. JOHN *Pakeha Rambles through Maori Lands* v. 82 Our friend set to work pumping him, and 'shouted' liberally till the old fellow's tongue was unloosed. **1896** KIPLING *Seven Seas, Lost Legion* iii, We've shouted on seven-ounce nuggets. **1916** J. B. COOPER *Coo-oo-ee* iii. 36 Passing that stage of drunkenness, they started to quarrel over the question as to whose turn it was 'to shout'. **1963** N. HILLIARD *Piece of Land* 32 'Going to shout, Horace?' Clarrie pulled out some change. **1981** *National Times* (Austral.) 25–31 Jan. 23/1 The tightwad..wouldn't shout if a shark bit him.

**b.** *trans.* To call for (refreshments, drinks, etc.) in order to treat the bystanders. Also ***to shout*** (a person) ***to*** (a treat) and with indirect obj.

**1855** [see sense a above]. **1867** A. L. GORDON *Sea-spray, Credat Judæus* 139 You may 'shout' some cheroots, if you like. **1881** *A Chequered Career* 205 He then 'shouted' champagne, and assumed the most pompous airs. **1906** E. DYSON *Fact'ry 'Ands* xiv. 185 He gave up beer..in order to have it in his power to shout the young lady to 2 s. seats at the Royal. **1940** F. SARGESON *Man & his Wife* (1944) 64 If he had a win he'd shouts us plenty of beer and cigarettes. **1964** V. M. GRAYLAND *Grave-Digger's Apprentice* xx. 119 If my luck's in..I'll shout you to the pictures tonight for helping me out. **1965** S. T. OLLIVIER *Petticoat Farm* vii. 98 'Mingy old skinflints!' hissed Jane. 'They could have shouted us an ice-cream!' **1977** *Caravan World* (Austral.) Jan. 35/1 On meeting an old friend a miner would shout him, not a drink as in other places, but a bath.

Hence **'shouted** *ppl. a.*

**1870** MORRIS *Earthly Par.* IV. 280 The gates swung backward at his shouted word. **1906** BELLOC *Hills & Sea* 113 We heard..the shouted order to mount.

†**'shouter**[1]. *Obs. rare.* [f. SHOUT *sb.*[1] + -ER[1].] The master of a 'shout' or flat boat.

*c* **1325** in Grose *Antiq. Repert.* (1808) II. 407 Pour les Gages de ses vij Shouters.

**shouter**[2] ('ʃaʊtə(r)). [f. SHOUT *v.* + -ER[1].]

**1. a.** One who shouts or cries out loudly; one who acclaims or applauds.

**1692** DRYDEN *Cleomenes* I. i, A peal of loud applause rang out, And thin'ed the Air, till even the Birds fell down Upon the Shouters Heads. **1820** MME. D'ARBLAY *Let.* 15 Aug., The heroine passed..surrounded with shouters and vociferous admirers. **1908** *Academy* 13 June 878/1 The English labourers in the Papal vineyard..are silent, prayerful persons rather than shouters or sensation-mongers.

†**b.** One who loudly supports a particular candidate. Cf. SHOUT *v.* 1 i. *U.S. Obs.*

**1875** *Weekly New Mexican* 13 Oct. 2/1 The Carleton and Perea 'shouters', got up a procession with banners, transparencies and noise. **1904** *Rochester* (N.Y.) *Post-Express* 26 May 4 The canvass..was very thorough, Hearst shouters being busily engaged in every city.

**2. a.** A name applied to some Methodist congregations in the north of Ireland who used to leap and shout in their ecstasies. (Cf. Hampson *Mem. Wesley*, 1791, II. 75.)

**1820** POLWHELE *Lavington's Enthus. Methodists* Introd. p. cxii, Of a similar description with the Welsh Jumpers were the Irish Shouters.

**b.** In the West Indies, a member of a Baptist sect influenced by African religious practices.

**1950** *Caribbean Q.* II. II. 17 The Shouters and Shakers.. may practise a pseudo Christianity strongly influenced by African cult practices. **1956** M. STEARNS *Story of Jazz* (1957) iii. 30 The northern religion did not make much headway except with a small group of converts to the Baptist faith in Toco, a village in the northeastern part of the island. They are called Shouters with some accuracy, for they generated enough excitement and noise to be officially banned. **1974** *Encycl. Brit. Macropædia* III. 906/1 Charismatic leaders frequently organize distinctive local variants of Christianity, such as the Baptist sects graphically termed 'Shouters' or 'Jumpers'.

**3.** *Australian* and *N.Z.* One who stands drinks.

**1863** *Lyttelton* (N.Z.) *Times* 31 Dec. 4/1 Perhaps some of our readers do not know the extent to which the practice of 'shouting', or of inviting to drink at the 'shouter's' expense, is carried even here. **1885** SLADEN *In Cornwall*, etc. 156 (*title*) The sigh of the shouter.

**4.** One who participates in a shout (SHOUT *sb.*[2] 1 d); a gospel-singer; a type of blues-singer. *U.S.*

**1867** *Nation* 30 May 433/1 A band, composed of the best singers and of tired shouters stand at the side of the room to 'base' the others. **1931** R. W. GORDON in A. T. Smythe et al. *Carolina Low-Country* 199 The shouters form a circle and proceed around and around in a sort of slow processional. **1946** R. BLESH *Shining Trumpets* xiii. 311 In barrel-house vein are his records..with vocals by Joe Turner, then an unspoiled shouter. **1976** A. MURRAY *Stomping Blues* ix. 169 Joe Turner..has long been considered the Big Daddy of traditional blues shouters.

**shouther**, variant of SHOULDER.

**shouting** ('ʃaʊtɪŋ), *vbl. sb.* [f. SHOUT *v.* + -ING[1].] The action of the vb. SHOUT.

**1. a.** Loud crying, uproar, clamour; vociferous applause, acclamation; an instance of this.

*c* **1386** CHAUCER *Knt.'s T.* 2095 Ne how the grekes..Tries riden al the place aboute..with a loud shoutynge. **1535** COVERDALE *Job* xxxix. 25 Yᵉ noyse, the captaynes and the shoutinge. **1828** EGAN *Boxiana* IV. 174 Cy..fell on him so heavily that the shoutings were—'He cannot come again.' **1848** THACKERAY *Van. Fair* xliii, Dobbin..kept up a great shouting.

†**b.** Applied to the song of birds. *Obs.*

**1508** DUNBAR *Gold. Targe* 26 The skyes rang for schoutyng of the larkis.

†**c.** An election carried out by acclamation.

[**1660** MILTON *Free Commw.* Wks. 1851 V. 438 Not committing all to the noise and shouting of a rude Multitude, but permitting only those of them who are rightly qualifi'd, to nominate as many as they will.] **1679** O. HEYWOOD *Diaries* (1881) II. 139 Captain Pockly fell ill at the shouting at York.

**d.** Phr. ***it is all over bar*** (†***but***, occas. ***except***) ***the shouting***: said when the result of a contest or the outcome of an action appears certain.

**1842** APPERLEY *Life Sportsman* xvi. 332 It's all over but shouting..Antonio's as dead as a hammer. **1869** A. L. GORDON *How We beat Favourite* in *Poems* (1912) 140 The race is all over, bar shouting. **1897** *Nat. Police Gaz.* (U.S.) 26 May 7/4 It was all over 'bar' the shouting, but the youngster refused emphatically to give way. **1909** A. BENNETT *What Public Wants* IV. 54 If I wasn't sure that it's all over except the shouting, I wouldn't touch it. **1959** *Times* 12 June 5/3 In the absence of rain or miracles it was all over bar the shouting at Romford last evening. **1976** *Western Morning News* 25 Sept. 8/2 But if the Rhodesia affair is all over bar the shouting, can the same be said about South Africa?

†**e.** Loud support for a particular candidate. *U.S. Obs.*

**1904** *Minneapolis Times* 29 May 6 Thus far most of the enthusiastic shouting for Gorman can be traced to the Gorman press bureau.

**2.** Standing drinks, treating. *Austral.* and *N.Z.*

**1862** E. HODDER *Memories N.Z. Life* 123 Among this class, going to these [public houses] and 'shouting'..is considered the acmé of pleasure. **1874** A. BATHGATE *Colonial Experiences* viii. 99 One of the greatest social evils in the gold-fields is the system of 'shouting'. **1883** *Longman's Mag.* June 180 *Shouting*, a colonial expression for standing treat to strangers, is a common form of hospitality. **1911** E. M. CLOWES *On Wallaby* iv. 106 Of course, men still go 'on the bust', cheques are planked down, and 'shouting'—the Australian equivalent for 'treating'—indulged in till all the money is finished. **1963** *Evening Post* (Wellington, N.Z.) 10 July 13/5 Costs incurred by licensing trusts in dispensing free liquor or 'shouting' ostensibly for the purpose of encouraging patronage are under fire.

**3.** The performing of a shout (SHOUT *sb.*[2] 1 d); a declamatory style of singing among American Blacks.

**1871** in *Rep. 42nd U.S. Congress 2 Sess. Joint Select Comm. Condition of Affairs Late Insurrectionary States: Georgia*

(1872) I. 306, I have attended what they call their religious meetings; and they have what they call 'shouting'. **1927** *N.Y. Times Mag.* 24 Apr. 4/1 The type of song used in shouting is peculiar and has had much to do with molding and changing spirituals. **1946** R. BLESH *Shining Trumpets* (1949) v. 109 The rhythmic style of singing which we shall call *shouting*, a style clearly derived from, or related to, the declamatory sermons of the rural preacher.

4. *Comb.*, as **shouting distance** = *hailing distance* s.v. HAILING *vbl. sb.* b; chiefly in phr. ***to be within shouting distance*** (*of*) (also *fig.*); **shouting match**, a loud altercation.

**1930** E. H. YOUNG *Miss Mole* iii. 29 She must be within shouting distance of the rich old gentleman who was going to leave her a fortune. **1958** L. A. G. STRONG *Light above Lake* 11 This is not to say that.. O'Hara was an angel, or within shouting distance of one. **1961** *Guardian* 20 Jan. 22/7 Different ways of making..thermo-nuclear weapons cheaply are already within shouting distance. **1977** R. GADNEY *Champagne Marxist* xiii. 83 I'll station two men outside... One will be within shouting distance. **1970** M. BRAITHWAITE *Never sleep Three in Bed* vi. 68 We would begin a full-scale debate on which way we should have turned. Soon it would develop into a shouting match. **1981** V. GLENDINNING *Edith Sitwell* xv. 189 Edith was able to field, in this shouting match, one impressive new ally—John Sparrow.

**shouting** ('ʃaʊtɪŋ), *ppl. a.* [f. SHOUT *v.* + -ING².]

1. That shouts.

**1600** SIR W. CORNWALLIS *Ess.* II. xxx. (1631) 48 Patrone of the vulgar whose..showting allowance hath such an operation with mans frailtie. **1716** POPE *Iliad* v. 627 And now the god..Produced Æneas to the shouting train. **1849** MACAULAY *Hist. Eng.* v. I. 576 The hedges were lined with shouting spectators. **1892** KIPLING *Barrack-room Ballads, L'Envoi* ix, Where..the shouting seas drive by.

2. *U.S.* Denoting religious sects whose congregations express themselves by shouting, esp. in phr. ***shouting Methodist***.

**1851** T. A. BURKE *Polly Peablossom's Wedding* 87 Forgeron was from that time 'a shouting Methodist'. **1876** J. BURROUGHS *Winter Sunshine* I. 23 About the only genuine shouting Methodists that remain are to be found in the coloured churches. **1941** W. C. HANDY *Father of Blues* (1957) xi. 158 My mother was a 'shouting Methodist'. **1959** [see *religio-musical* s.v. RELIGIO-].

Hence '**shoutingly** *adv.*, vociferously. Also *fig.*

**1827** POE *Tamerlane* 220 The dwindled hills, whence.. Gush'd shoutingly a thousand rills. **1866** *Athenæum* 3 Nov. 562/3 He seems to lift his voice shoutingly. **1894** 'MARK TWAIN' *Those Extraordinary Twins* ii. 335 The new lodger, rather shoutingly dressed.

**shove** (ʃʌv), *sb.*¹ Forms: α. *north.* 3 scou, 4 chou, 5–6 schow; β. 5 shoffe, 6 shuffe, 6– shove. [f. SHOVE *v.*¹]

1. An act of shoving; a strong thrust or push to move a body away from the agent.

*a* **1300** *Cursor M.* 12033 Wit scholdur gaf he him a scou [*Gött.* chou]. *c* **1475** *Rauf Coilȝear* 698 As he gat ben throw He gat mony greit schow. **1581** A. HALL *Iliad* II. 21 They labor stil with heaue and shoue. **1762** in T. Mortimer *Ev. Man own Broker* (ed. 5) 93 *note*, An united shove commences, by which others, as well as I, have measured their length in a very dirty place. **1812** H. & J. SMITH *Rej. Addr.* II. xi, But Mr. Thing-um bob, the prompter man, Gave with his hand my chaise a shove. **1871** MEREDITH *H. Richmond* v, Mr. Rippenger added a spurning shove on my shoulder to his recommendation.

b. *fig.* In various uses: An impulse given to make a person or thing move or act more quickly; a 'push' or exertion of influence to get a person through a difficulty or further him in his career; in schoolboy phrase, a hint or prompting to one who is backward with an answer.

**1724** CALAMY *Howe's Wks.* I. Life 7 Sir, said he [Fuller to Howe],..I am a pretty corpulent Man, and I am to go thro a Passage that is very strait, I beg you would be so kind as to give me a shove, and help me thro. **1784** COWPER *Task* IV. 210 With all the tricks That idleness has ever yet contriv'd ..To..give time a shove. **1857** HUGHES *Tom Brown* I. viii, Whose parsing and construing resisted the most well-meant shoves. **1873** MISS BROUGHTON *Nancy* vi, It would be such a fine thing for all the family: I could give all the boys such a shove.

†2. An onset, attack. *Obs.*

*c* **1450** *Merlin* xiv. 219 Thei threwe down CCC at the firste shoffe in theire comynge. *c* **1470** HENRYSON *Mor. Fab.* IX. (*Wolf & Fox*) iv, Thow can..mak ane suddane schow vpoun ane scheip.

†3. Phr. ***all at a shove***: by a single act. *Obs.*

**1555** WATREMAN *Fardle Facions* I. v. 51 Their maner of ordres, is not to make seuerally, for euery Goddesse and God, a seuerall priest, but al at a shoue, in generall for all.

4. *slang.* a. ***a shove in the mouth***: a drink. b. ***the shove***: dismissal from employment.

**1821** EGAN *Life in London* x. (1870) 265, I vished to be a little nutty upon Dirty Suke..so I gov'd her 'a shove in the mouth'. **1899** R. WHITEING *5 John St.* x, Did you get the shove to-day? *Ibid.* xxi, If it warn't ready, he give the shove to the 'ole shoot.

5. *Canadian.* A forward movement of packed and piled ice in a thawing river.

**1865** [see *ice-shove*, ICE *sb.* 7 a]. **1890** *Montreal Witness* 19 Mar. 8/2 The shove may be expected every day.

**shove** (ʃʌv), *sb.*² [app. a corruption of *shiv*, SHIVE *sb.*², perh. assimilated to prec.] The woody core of flax or hemp. Also, a fragment of the stems of flax or hemp broken off when 'scutching'. Cf. SHEAVE *sb.*², SHIVE *sb.*², SHOW *sb.*²

**1688** HOLME *Armoury* III. 285/2 Both Flax and Hemp are first broken from the strong Stalks into large Shoves or Shivers. **1780** YOUNG *Tour Irel.* I. 164 They scutch it to separate the heart or the shoves from the rest. **1855** ROYLE *Fibrous Pl. India* 129 A layer of wood-like matter, which in some plants is called boon, or shove. **1910** *Encycl. Brit.* X. 486/1 When it is found that the fibre [of flax] separates readily from the woody 'shove' or core.

**shove** (ʃʌv), *v.*¹ Pa. t. and pa. pple. **shoved** (ʃʌvd). Forms: see below. [A Com. Teut. (originally strong) verb: OE. *scúfan* (*scéaf*, *scufon*, *scofen*) corresponds to OFris. *skûva* (NFris. *sküüw*, *skōw*, WFris. *skouwe*), MDu. *schûven* (mod.Du. *schuiven*), MLG. *schûven* (mod.LG. *schuven*), OHG. *sciuban* (MHG., mod.G. *schieben*, early mod.G. also *schauben*), Goth. (*af*)*skiuban*; also with weak conjugation, ON. *skúfa*, more commonly *skýfa*; f. OTeut. root **skeub*-: *skaub*-: *skŭb*-. As there are traces of a variant with *f* instead of *b* (see SHOVEL *sb.*), the pre-Teut. form is prob. **skeup*-.

The Gothic and HG. forms have the normal grade (*eu*) of the present-stem; the other forms have an 'aorist-present' with *ū* as the root-vowel. The occasional OE. *scéofan* is generally regarded not as a descendant of OTeut. **skeub*-, but as a late WS. phonetic development from *scúfan*; another possibility is that it resulted from the analogy of other verbs of the same conjugation; that it had a falling diphthong seems clear from its representation in later Eng.

The phonetic development, OE. *scúfan*, mod.E. *shove* (ʃʌv) may be compared with OE. *dúfe*, mod.E. *dove* (dʌv). In Sc. and north. dial. the OE. word regularly became in the 14–16th c. *schowe*, and should be represented in mod.Sc. by *shoo* (cf. Sc. 14–16th c. *dowe*, mod. *doo*, dove), but this has not survived (unless it be in SHUE to swing), being superseded by the Eng. *shove*.]

A. Illustration of Forms.

1. *Pres.-stem.* α. 1 sc(e)úfan (3 *sing. pres. ind.* **scúfeð, -ið, scýfð, scífð, scýft), 3 sc(h)uven, (shufe), 3–4 schouve, (4 schowf, s(c)howve, schowe, shouwe), 4–5 schove, (5 showe, schowwyn, xowyn, schoffe, 5–7 shuff, 6 schow, sowe, 7 shoove), 5– shove**; β. 1 **scéofan, 3 seve, 4 scheve, 5 schyve**; see also SHEAVE *v.*²

α. *a* **900** Scufan [see B. 1]. *c* **1000** ÆLFRIC *Gram.* xxiv. (Z.) 137 *Præcipito* ic sceufe. *c* **1205** Scuuen [see B. 2.]. *a* **1225** *Ancr. R.* 314 Schuueð hit ut. *a* **1300** *E.E. Psalter* lxi. 5 Mi worth þai thoght to schouue awai. *c* **1320** *Beues* 2592 Whan þe beschop him scholde in schoue. *c* **1386** CHAUCER *Reeve's T.* 58 Leueful is with force force of showue. *c* **1403** Shove [see B. 7]. *c* **1440** *York Myst.* xxxvi. 297 In Jesu side schoffe it þis tyde. *c* **1440** *Promp. Parv.* 105/1 Showen [*later v.rr.* xowyn, shoue], *impello.* **1449** *Rolls of Parlt.* V. 152/1 Hevyng and shuffyng of her Chaffare out and home. **1508** DUNBAR *Tua Mariit Wemen* 106 He schowis on me his schewill mouth. **1653** HOLCROFT *Procopius, Goth. Wars* III. x. 93 To shoove it down.

β. *c* **1000** ÆLFRIC *Gram.* xxviii. (Z.) 171 *Trudo*, ic sceofe. *c* **1275** [see B 3 b]. *c* **1320** [see B. 7]. *c* **1440** *Wyclif's Bible, Judges* xvi. 19 To caste [*MS.* I., schyue] hym awei.

2. *Pa. t.* a. *1st* and *3rd sing.* α. 1 **scéaf**, (3 **scæf, sef, 3–4 schef, 4 shyf, scef), shoofe, shoif, s(c)hofe, shoff, schove, 4–5 s(c)hof, shoof, 5 shoef, shoove, (sheef, 6 schew)**; β. *weak* 4 **shufte, schuft, schovede, 5 showved, showvyt, schufte, shofed, showed, 6 shoffed, 5– shoved.**

**993** *Batt. Maldon* (Gr.) 136 He sceaf þa mid þam scylde. *c* **1205** LAY. 9366 He þa scipen vt scæf [*c* **1275** sef]. *c* **1275** [see B. 1 c]. *c* **1290** *St. Brendan* 412 in *S. Eng. Leg.* 231 After heore schip so swyþe he schef [*v.rr.* scef, schof, showved]. *c* **1300** *Havelok* 871 Hauelok shof dun nyne or ten. *c* **1350** *Will. Palerne* 3290 & schuft his scheld on is schulder. *c* **1381** CHAUCER *Parl. Foules* 154 Til African my gyde Me hente and shofe [*v.rr.* shof, shoff, schofe, shoofe, shoif] yn at the gatys wyde. *c* **1400** *Sowdone Bab.* 1578 Floripe..shofed hire oute in to the flode. *c* **1440** *Alphabet of Tales* 144 He showed hym oute att þe dure. **1470–85** MALORY *Arthur* XIII. ix. 624 Syr Bagdemagus..sheef hym thorou the ryght sholder. **1481** CAXTON *Reynard* xxxiii. (Arb.) 95 How I shoef and stack. *a* **1578** LINDESAY (Pitscottie) *Chron. Scot.* (S.T.S.) I. 67/31 The bischope..schew out his toung.

b. *plur.* α. 1 **scufun, sceufon, 1–2 scufon, -sceofon, 2–3 scufen, 3 scuven, (soven), ssove, 3–4 schoven, 4 shoven, schowen**; etc. β. *weak* (see *sing.*).

*Beowulf* 215 [see B. 3 b]. *Ibid.* 3131 [see B. 2 b]. *c* **1000** *Ags. Gosp.* Luke iv. 29 Hiȝ arison & scufon [**1160** *Hatton Gosp.* scufen] hine of ðære ceastre. *c* **1205** LAY. 7859 Heo scuuen [*c* **1275** souen] ut heore lof. *Ibid.* 20925 He scufen [*c* **1225** souen] from þan stronde scipen. **1297** R. GLOUC. (Rolls) 3103 Hii..uaste ssone [*v.r.* schofe] & drowe.

3. *Pa. pple.* α. 1 **sc(e)ofen, -scoben**, *North.* **-scyfen, 2 i-scoven, 3 i-schuven, 4 schoven, 4–5 y-)s(c)hove, 4– shoven**; β. *weak* **4 s(c)hufte, schowved, 5 shuftyd, schowid, 5–6 shuffed, 7 shooved, 6 shoved.**

α. *Beowulf* 918 (Gr.) Ða wæs morgenleoht scofen and scynded. *c* **1175** *Lamb. Hom.* 129 Heo weren iscouen. *a* **1225** *Ancr. R.* 316 Hit is..iðe schrifte ischuuen ut. *c* **1250** *Gen. & Ex.* 107 Watres ben her ðer-under suuen. *c* **1385** CHAUCER *L.G.W.* 726 Thus by report was hir name I-shoue [*v.rr.* y-shove, yshoue, y-schoue, shoue]. **1390** GOWER *Conf.* III. 202 He..Was schoven out of his empire. **1470–85** MALORY *Arthur* XVII. vii. 699 The shyp was anone shouen in the see. **1764** *Oxf. Sausage* 197 Here..The mouldy old Crust, Of Nell Batchelor lately was shoven. **1829** LANDOR *Imag. Conv., Wallace & Edw. I*, Wks. 1853 I. 450/1 To be thrust and shoven.

β. **13..** *E.E. Allit. P.* B. 44 He schulde be..harde þer-oute schowued. **1398** TREVISA *Barth. De P.R.* VIII. xliii. (Tollemache MS.) A ly3t beme is broke oþer schufte [**1582** shuft] aside. *a* **1400–50** *Wars Alex.* 4759 He wald haue schowid on þat schene. *c* **1450** tr. *De Imitatione* III. xliv. 115 þei ben shuftyd [*v.r.* shuffed] from oon to a noþer. **1529** MORE *Dyaloge* III. Wks. 1226/1 They shal bee pushed and shoued in by vyolence.

B. Signification. (Generally equivalent to *thrust*, *push*; but now less dignified in use, often suggesting some notion of rough, careless, or hasty action.)

1. a. *trans.* To thrust away with violence; to precipitate; to 'cast' (into prison, etc.). *Obs.* exc. *arch.*

*Beowulf* 3131 Dracan ec scufun, wyrm ofer weallclif. *a* **900** CYNEWULF *Elene* 692 (Gr.) Scufan scyldiȝne..in dryȝne seað. *c* **1050** *Voc.* in Wr.-Wülcker 471/8 *Precipitate*, scufað. **13..** *E.E. Allit. P.* B. 1029 If any schalke to be schent wer schowued þer-inne. *c* **1380** *Sir Ferumb.* 1369 By þe legges lifte he þe schrewe þan & schef hur out ech del. **1529** MORE *Dyaloge* III. Wks. 1226/1 He that gathereth treasures shall be shoued into the grynnes of death. *a* **1568** *Bannatyne MS.* (Hunter. Club) 210 Suthle he will ye schow Vnto the grund. **1844** HOOD *Forge* II. xii, All at once he is seized and shoven ..Headlong into the blazing oven.

†b. ***to shove out***: to force oneself to utter.

*a* **1225** *Ancr. R.* 314 Al so schal þe þet schriueð him, efter þe greate, schuuen ut þet smele.

†c. To thrust (a weapon, etc.) *into* or *through* a body. *Obs.*

*c* **1275** *Passion our Lord* 499 in *O.E. Misc.* 51 He schef hit myd strenkþe þat to his heorte hit com. **1387** TREVISA *Higden* (Rolls) III. 451 He wrapped a cloþ aboute his hond, and schove it in [to] þe leon his mowþe. *c* **1440** *Alphabet of Tales* 288 He drew his knyfe & shewid it in his throte & kyllid hym. *a* **1586** SIDNEY *Astr. & Stella* xiii. (1591) A 4 b, In verde fieldes, Mars beares a golden Speare, Which through a bleeding heart, his point did shoue. **1589** WARNER *Alb. Eng.*, Addit. to 2nd Bk. 166 Then Æneas..shoffed his Sworde through his [*sc.* Turnus'] Breaste.

†d. To reject, banish; to eject from an office or dignity, from a society, etc. *Obs.*

*c* **1200** *Trin. Coll. Hom.* 53 He erneð here, þat ure louerd ihesu crist him shendeð and wile shufe fro him a domes dai. *a* **1300** *E.E. Psalter* cxviii. 10 Fra þine bodes schouue [Vulg. *repellas*] noght me. **13..** *E.E. Allit. P.* B. 1740 þe medes schal be maysteres here, & þou of menske schowued. *c* **1412** HOCCLEVE *De Reg. Princ.* 4940 Chesith eke gode men; and awey shoue The wykked. *c* **1421** *26 Pol. Poems* 111 From worldis worschipe y am shoue. **1657** J. WATTS *Scribe, Pharisee*, etc. I. 177 So some hasty man would be heaving and shoving out the wicked from the godly.

†e. To impart, communicate. ? *nonce-use.*

*c* **1626** W. BOSWORTH *Arcad. & Sepha* I. 544 Her lips that oft did shove Life to the hearts of those that saw them move.

2. a. To move (a heavy or resisting object) forward by the application of muscular strength from behind; to push along with effort.

*c* **1205** LAY. 17396 ȝe mote..scuuen & hebben mid hæȝere strenðe treon græte & longe. *c* **1290** *St. Edward* 167 in *S. Eng. Leg.* 51 Huy schouen it [*sc.* a horse] faste forthþe-ward and drowen. **1440** CAPGRAVE *Life St. Kath.* v. 1846 Take to thin behoue Thyng that this bocher may not hale ne shoue, Take þou my soule. **1481** CAXTON *Reynard* xii. (Arb.) 26 He shoof the table from hym. **1760** R. BROWN *Compl. Farmer* 11, The breast-plough, which a man shoves before him. **1873** BLACK *Pr. Thule* xxiv. 404 He was the first to shove the gangway on to the vessel. **1887** MORRIS *Odyss.* XI. 596 With hands and feet for ever against the stone did he [Sisyphus] strain Up o'er the bent to shove it.

*fig.* **1858** HAWTHORNE *Fr. & It. Note-bks.* (1872) I. 300 Their events seem to come in great masses, shoved along by the agency of many persons.

b. To force (a person, etc.) onwards by pushing. Also, to cause to fall *over* (a cliff, etc.) or *out of* (a place) by a push.

**1387** TREVISA *Higden* (Rolls) VI. 89 Hunulphus..bete hym with his feest, and schuft [*v.rr.* schufte, schyf] hym, and putte hym forþ þoruȝ þe myddel of þe citee anon to þe walles. **1481** CAXTON *Reynard* xii. (Arb.) 27, I..shooue him forth so ferre that he fylle doun vpon the floer. **1579** *Rastell's Expos. Terms Laws* s.v. *Manumission*, The Lorde.. therewith shewed [*edd.* **1592** ff. shoued] him forward out of his handes [= *& oue ceo il luy mise auant hors de ses maines*]. **1780** *Ann. Reg.* 196 Mr. Gough, turned round, and shoved Atkins over the bannister. **1809** MALKIN *Gil Blas* XI. x. (Rtldg.) 412, I should stand a very good chance of being shoved by the shoulders out of doors. **1865** KINGSLEY *Herew.* iii, My master shoved the fellow over after he had stabbed him.

c. To throw *down* with a push.

**13..** *K. Alis.* (W.) 4250 He schof him quycly adoun. **1390** GOWER *Conf.* I. 165 Part of the bank he schof doun riht. **1681** R. KNOX *Hist. Relat. Ceylon* 22 It is their constant practice to shove down with their heads great Trees.

†d. Of winds or other natural forces: To drive, propel, impel. *Obs.*

*c* **1374** CHAUCER *Boeth.* II. pr. i. (1868) 32 þou shalt be shouen not þider þat þou woldest: but whider þat þe wynde shoueþ þe. *c* **1386** —— *Frankl. T.* 553 He knew ful wel how fer Alnath was shoue [*v.rr.* schoue, y-schoue, yshoue] Fro the heed of thilke fixe Aries aboue. **14..** tr. *Higden* App. (Rolls) VII. 525 There come a whirlewynde..and schufte in the body anone to the ynner wal of the chirche. **1614** GORGES *Lucan* II. 66 Like as when whistling Southerne winde.. Shoouing the seas before his blast. **1705** ADDISON *Italy, Pesaro* 168 [tr. Claudian], The Seas..shove the loaden Vessels into Port.

†e. *fig.* To bring into prominence. Also, to impel, urge *forward* in a course of action. *Obs.*

*c* **1385** CHAUCER *L.G.W.* 1381 If that I live, thy name shal be shove In English, that thy sleighte shal be knowe! **1572** tr. *Buchanan's Detect. Mary Q. Scots* G ij, Causis..sic as are able to shooue forward and to push hedlang a hart for outrage nat able to gouerne it selfe.

**f.** To urge (a horse) to a leap.

**1869** 'WAT. BRADWOOD' *The O.V.H.* xii, He shoved his horse at the rail.

**3.** *spec.* To propel (a boat or other vessel) either by pushing at the stern or with a pole worked from the inside. Also *absol.*

**1513** DOUGLAS *Æneis* VI. v. 15 Hymself the cobil did with his bolm furth schow. **1649** OGILBY *Æneis* v. (1684) 222 Old Portunus with his mighty Hand Shov'd him along. **1726** SWIFT *Gulliver* I. viii, The seamen towed, and I shoved. **1802-19** REES *Cycl.* XXXII, *Set*, a term used for a pole or shaft, used to shove boats along a canal, &c. **1837** MARRYAT *Snarleyyow* ix, I shoved on shore.

**b.** With *out*, *off*, or const. *from*. (*a*) *trans.* To launch (a boat) by means of a steady push applied at the stern. (*b*) *absol.* To push one's vessel away from the bank. Also *transf.* of the boat.

(*a*) *Beowulf* 215 (Gr.) Guman ut scufon..wudu bundenne. *a* **1122** *O.E. Chron.* (Laud MS.) an. 1048, & ȝewende þa Godwine eorl & Sweȝen eorl to Bosenham & scufon ut heora scipu. *c* **1205** LAY. 21590 Heo wenden þa scipen stronge to sculuen [*read* scuuen; *c* **1275** seue] from þan londe. **1660** F. BROOKE tr. *Le Blanc's Trav.* 287 As we endeavoured with strength to shove her off, the vessel overturned. **1839** MARRYAT *Phant. Ship* xvii, The boats were shoved off.

(*b*) **1513** DOUGLAS *Æneis* v. iv. 95 He and he Inforcis of to schowin the schip to saif. **1600** HOLLAND *Livy* XLI. iii. 1098 Others shove off from the wharfe. **1834** MARRYAT *P. Simple* xvi, The boat was not ordered to shove off. **1858** LONGF. *M. Standish* v. 103 Into the boat he sprang, and in haste shoved off to his vessel.

**c.** *intr.* Of persons: to depart, go away. Const. with advbs., as *off*, †*out*, etc. Cf. PUSH *v.* 1 h. *colloq.* (orig. *U.S.*).

**1844** *Spirit of Times* 24 Aug. 302/2 As we shoved off from Fort P. our boys made the welkin ring, and away we dashed down the Apalachicola. **1856** 'MARK TWAIN' *Adv. T. J. Snodgrass* (1928) 31, I shoved out for the Massasawit House. **1904** 'O. HENRY' in *McClure's Mag.* Apr. 612/1 When dark came we fagged 'em a batch of bullets and shoved out the back door for the rocks. **1909** J. R. WARE *Passing Eng. Victorian Era* 223/1 *Shove off* (Navy), to quit, go, flee, depart—from shoving off a boat from land or ship. **1916** 'TAFFRAIL' *Pincher Martin* vii. 105 'Ere, 'arf a mo'!..Don't shove orf. **1922** JOYCE *Ulysses* 591 Well, I'll shove along. **1936** J. STEINBECK *In Dubious Battle* viii. 133 Them deputies knew we was goin' to shove off before daylight. **1956** P. SCOTT *Male Child* III. ii. 206, I wouldn't dream of telling you to shove off. You're there by Alan's invitation. **1979** D. ANTHONY *Long Hard Cure* xiv. 113 My, look at the hour. I'd better shove off.

**d.** Similarly without adv.

**1866** 'MARK TWAIN' *Lett. from Hawaii* (1967) 43, I then took what small change he had and 'shoved'. **1884** —— *Huckleberry Finn* xl. 409 We just unfurled our heels and shoved. **1944** *Sat. Even. Post* 9 Dec. 82/3 Well, I guess I'll shove. Good-by. **1954** C. WILLIAMS *Touch of Death* vii. 61 I'm going to shove. I can get away. **1975** N. FREELING *What are Bugles blowing For?* iv. 17, I have to ferry you down to the office... Let's shove, shall we?

**4. a.** Without the notion of difficulty. To push (something) so as to make it slide along a surface or in a groove or channel; also to move *up* or *down* by pushing.

**1633** P. FLETCHER *Purple Isl.* v. xxvi, Six bands are set to stirre the moving tower: The first the proud band call'd, that lifts it higher; The next the humble band, that shoves it lower. **1725** T. THOMAS in *Portland Papers* (Hist. MSS. Comm.) VI. 123 The bread..was shoved along the table on platters. **1770** LUCKOMBE *Hist. Printing* 357 Lest when he Runs in his Second Pull, the Face of the Plattin rub upon the Tympan, and shoves the sheet upon the Face of the Letter. *c* **1826** LAMB *Elia* Ser. II. *Wedding*, He did not once shove up his borrowed locks. **1830** HERSCHEL *Study Nat. Phil.* II. vii. (1851) 193 A sheet of blank paper is placed upon a frame and shoved forwards. **1902** VIOLET JACOB *Sheep-Stealers* xv, He shoved the paper away impatiently.

†**b.** To put surreptitiously or improperly: const. *in*, *on*, *under*, *out of*. *Obs.*

*c* **1374** CHAUCER *Troylus* III. 1026 Folk now..wolde a busshel venym al excusen For þat o greyn of loue is on it shoue. **1412-20** LYDG. *Troy Bk.* 2876 Doubilnes so sliȝly was in schoue, As þouȝ he hadde sothly ben allied With trewe menyng. **1534** JOYE *Subv. More's False Found.* title-p., He sweteth to set faste and shoue vnder his shameles shoris, to vnderproppe the popis chirche. **1612** T. TAYLOR *Comm. Titus* i. 6 (1619) 93 He setteth himselfe in all ages to shove in, and hold in the Ministerie such persons as are too base for the dunghil. **1642** MILTON *Apol. Smect.* Wks. 1851 III. 295 Which conceit of the man cleanly shoves the King out of the Parlament. **1773** J. BERRIDGE *Wks.* (1864) 74 To shorten man's duty..by shoving a commandment out of Moses's tables.

**c.** (Chiefly *colloq.*) To put or thrust (carelessly or hastily) into a place or receptacle; also to thrust *aside*, *away*.

**1827** SCOTT *Surg. Dau.* iv, Dick Middlemas, on his appearance, shoved into his bosom a small packet. **1861** HUGHES *Tom Brown at Oxf.* iv, All the characteristics are shoved away into the background. *a* **1864** HAWTHORNE *Sept. Felton* (1879) 78 My meditations are perhaps of a little too much importance to be shoved aside. **1911** MARETT *Anthropol.* vi. 156 You need never allow yourselves to be shoved away into such an inhospitable region.

**d.** To push *out of* a position, *away*, by gradual encroachment.

**1629** *Leather: a Discourse* 11 As darknesse shoues away Light. **1768-74** TUCKER *Lt. Nat.* (1834) II. 645 Whoever bears this reflection in mind will not..be so apt..to complain of seeing the rising generation grow up to shove them out of the world. **1789** T. WILLIAMS *Min. Kingd.* I. 271 The gash vein..is frequently crossed and intersected by whin dykes or bars of hard stone, which generally shoves it a little to one side, off the true line of bearing. **1814** D'ISRAELI *Quarrels Auth.* (1867) 538 The wit gradually shoved the antiquary off the end of the bench. **1860** MAURY *Phys. Geog.* (Low) xvi. §711 The land-wind..shoves away the calms which preceded it from the hills to the coast. **1870** MOZLEY *Univ. Serm.* iii. (1877) 54 The most visibly flourishing and busy department shoves the others out of sight.

**e.** To put or place. (In *colloq.* and casual use without notion of effort.) Also with *up*, *down*.

**1902** WODEHOUSE *Pothunters* v. 93 You might shove up the list to-night. **1927** W. E. COLLINSON *Contemp. Eng.* 23 At Dulwich..we plunked things down, we shoved down notes or we shoved up lists. **1938** N. STREATFEILD *Circus is Coming* vi. 76 He threw an envelope across to Santa. 'Shove yours to Mr Stibbings in there, and lick it up.' **1974** A. FOWLES *Pastime* ii. 12 Shove your coat on the chair.

**5.** *absol.* and *intr.* **a.** To push, to apply force against an object in order to move it from its position.

*a* **900** *O.E. Martyrol.* 13 Dec. 218 Sume scufon, sume tuȝon..and seo godes fæmne hwæðre stod. *c* **1290** *St. Lucy* 109 in *S. Eng. Leg.* 104 Huy schoue and drowe al þat huy miȝhte ake huy ne miȝhten hire anne i-winne. **13..** *K. Alis.* (W.) 5889 The kynges oost..broughtten gynnes to the walle, Houen, shouen, and drowen alle. ?*c* **1366** CHAUCER *Rom. Rose* 534 Ful long I shof, and knokkide eke,..Til that dore of thilk entre A mayden curteys openyde me. *c* **1425** *Sev. Sages* (P.) 1411 At hys dore he wolde inne, And hit was stoken with a pyne. He schof ther-onne. *c* **1450** *Merlin* xiii. 199 He hitte Agrauayn with his spere so sore that it preced two folde thurgh his haubreke, and therto he shof ther-on so harde that Agravayn fill to the erthe.

**b.** *to shove at*: to push against (an object) in order to displace or overthrow; †*fig.* to apply one's energies to (a task); also, to make an attack on, try to overthrow (a person). (Also in *indirect passive.*) †*to shove at the cart* (fig.): to lend a helping hand (also *ironical*).

**1421-2** HOCCLEVE *Dialog* 617 Now, good freend shoue at the cart, I yow preye. **1471** *Paston Lett.* III. 15 Iff ye be cleer owt off Doctor Aleyn danger, kepe yow ther, and her afftr ye maye schoffe as well at hys carte. **1542** PAGET in *St. Papers Hen. VIII*, VIII. 705 Lay your heddes all three to gidre, and shove at the treatye, that it may take effect. **1577** STANYHURST *Descr. Irel.* vi. 22/2 in *Holinshed*, This Erle now liuyng, as hys Auncesters before hym, haue beene shrewdly shooued at by his euill willers, saying that [etc.]. **1607** TOURNEUR *Rev. Trag.* I. i, Tis a maruaile thourt not turnd out yet! *Hip.* Faith I haue been shooud at. **1639** AINSWORTH *Ps.* lxii. 4 Ye shall be a bowed wall, as a fence that is shooved at.

†**c.** of inanimate agencies. *Obs.*

*c* **1400** R. GLOUC. (Rolls) App. A. 14 Whar so hit bifalleþ þat þe erþe is so fast þat þe wynd ne passez he schoueuþ & þrast þat al þe erþe quakiȝeþ.

†**6. a.** *intr.* To push one's way forward or onward, to press on. Chiefly with adv., *on*, *along*, etc. *Obs.*

*c* **888** ÆLFRED *Boeth.* Met. xiii. (1895) 298 Swa deð eac sio sunne þonne hio on siȝe weorþeð..merecondel scyfð on ofdæle. *c* **1374** CHAUCER *Troylus* III. 487 He shof ay on, he to and fro was sent. *c* **1400** *Destr. Troy* 11804 An Erne..Braid vp the bowels, & bere hom away, And showvet to the shippes of the shene grekes. **1520-30** CORNYSH in *Anglia* XII. 238 The dere shoffe on the mede. **1563** GOOGE *Eglogs*, etc. (Arb.) 121 They..forwarde shoue. **1581** A. HALL *Iliad* IX. 152 To supper let vs get vs nowe, sith night so farre on shoues. **1721** DUDLEY in *Phil. Trans.* XXXI. 167 A Moose ..shoves along side-ways.

†**b.** To make an attack with violence, to make a charge or onset. *Obs.*

**13..** *Gaw. & Gr. Knt.* 1454 Schalkez to schote at hym schowen to þenne. **1415** HOCCLEVE *To Knts. Garter* 36 In honour of his name Shoue on & putte his foos to the outraunce! **1470-85** MALORY *Arthur* v. viii. 173 Thenne the batails approuched and shoue and showted on bothe sydes.

†**c.** *to shove down*: to fall with force. *Obs.*

**13..** *Gaw. & Gr. Knt.* 2083 Schyre schaterande on schorez, þer þay doun schowued.

†**d.** *to shove and heave*: to move tumultuously.

The vbs. were commonly coupled also in other uses: see, e.g., quot. *c* 1205 in 2, 13.. in 5, 1449 in A. 1 a; and cf. quot. 1581 under SHOVE *sb.*[1] 1 and quot. 1568 under SHOVING *vbl. sb.*[1]

**1638** W. LISLE *Heliodorus* VII. 101 Diuers passions in her shoue and heaue. **1680** OTWAY *Orphan* III. i, Thy little breasts, with soft compassion swelled, Shove up and down, and heave like dying birds.

**e.** *transf.* To protrude, project. *rare.*

**1849** CUPPLES *Green Hand* xvi. (1856) 157 The huge sharp green notched aloe-leaves and fern shoving here and there out of it [the water].

**7. a.** To push about or jostle in a crowd; to make one's way by jostling or elbowing.

*c* **1290** *Beket* 2217 in *S. Eng. Leg.* 170 Faste heo [wormes] schouen and cropen al-so ase ametene al a-boute. *c* **1320** *Sir Beues* 1407 So fast hii gonne aboute him scheue, As don ben aboute þe heue. **13..** *Gaw. & Gr. Knt.* 2161 Thenne gyrdez he to Gryngolet, & gederez þe rake, Schowuez in bi a schore, at a schaȝe syde. *c* **1403** LYDG. *Temple Glas* 534 Gret pres of folk,..To croude and shove—the tempil was so ful. **1530** PALSGR. 705/1 It is no good maner to shove in a dores a this facyon. **1633** P. FLETCHER *Purple Isl.* v. xxxvi, An hundred shapes that through flit ayers stray, Shove boldly in. **1714** LADY M. W. MONTAGU *Let. to W. Montagu* 24 Sept., There's a little door to get in, and a great crowd without, shoving and thrusting who shall be foremost. **1849** CUPPLES *Green Hand* xiii. (1856) 127 Her want of actual headway making the Indiaman sag dead away to leeward, as she shoved into the force of the sea-stream. **1897** MRS. E. L. VOYNICH *Gadfly* (1904) 60/2 The crowd of holiday masqueraders, laughing and shoving.

**b.** *refl.* With adv. or phrase: To make one's way by shoving.

*c* **1489** CAXTON *Sonnes of Aymon* xxiv. 515 Reynaude.. shoved himself among the thickest. **1671** tr. *Marten's Voy. Spitzbergen* in *Acc. Sev. Late Voy.* II. (1694) 105 They shove themselves along just like an Eel. **1842** LOVER *Handy Andy* viii, Biddy..had shoved herself well before the door.

**8.** *trans.* To push (a person) with one's body or elbows; to knock against, jostle.

**1530** PALSGR. 705/1, I shove one, I pusshe hym, *je pousse*. I pray the, shove nat whyle I am writyng. **1667** PEPYS *Diary* 15 Sept., I did step back, and clap my breech to our pew-door, that she might be forced to shove me to come in. **1805** MAR. EDGEWORTH *Mme. de Fleury* i, I shoved Victoire, and she pushed at me again. **1853** KINGSLEY *Hypatia* iii, Laughing and shoving each other about.

†**9.** To prop *up*. *Obs. rare*$^{-1}$. (The reading is doubtful.)

**1393** LANGL. *P. Pl.* C. XIX. 20 Hit hadde shoriers to shoue [MS. I. schyuyn; MS. T. schyue; MS. G. schule] hit vp.

**10.** *slang.* **a.** To pass (counterfeit money); also ***to shove (the) queer***. Now *Obs.* or *rare.* †**b.** ***to shove the tumbler*** (see quot. *a* 1700). †**c.** ***to shove the moon*** (see quot. 1809). **d.** *intr.* (*U.S.*) To set out for home. **e.** ***to shove it***: to depart; to desist from a course of action. Usu. in *imp.*, as an expression of contemptuous dismissal. Cf. STICK *v.*[1] 18 d.

*a* **1700** B. E. *Dict. Cant. Crew*, *Shove the Tumbler*, to be Whipt at the Cart's Tail. **1809** G. ANDREWES *Dict. Slang*, *Shoving the moon*, to steal your goods away without paying the rent. **1859** MATSELL *Rogue's Lex.* 79 *Shove queer*, pass counterfeit money. **1859** [implied in SHOVER[1] b]. **1873** G. W. PERRIE *Buckskin Mose* ii. 36 If I had been detected in 'shoving the queer',..they wouldn't have cared one red cent. **1885** LELAND *Brand-new Ballads* (ed. 2) 35 The one [note] I shoved was never worth a continental dam. **1915** A. CONAN DOYLE *Valley of Fear* II. ii. 189 This man Pinto helped me to shove the queer... It means to pass the dollars out into circulation. **1941** BAKER *Dict. Austral. Slang* 71 *Stick it!*, a contemptuous ejaculation. Also, '*shove it!*' **1956** B. HOLIDAY *Lady sings Blues* (1973) viii. 84 It wasn't long after I left that he told them to shove it like I had. **1973** J. WAINWRIGHT *Devil You Don't* 18 'What say we pick one?'.. McGuire said: 'Shove it. It's not why we're here.' **1978** L. STEWART *Same Time, Next Year* (1979) xiii. 145 If he doesn't like it he can shove it, but don't worry—he won't.

**11.** *intr.* (*Canadian.*) Of river-ice: To move forward so as to become more compact. Cf. SHOVE *sb.*[1] 5.

**1836** *Montreal Transcript* 29 Dec. 2/2 About one it [*sc.* the ice] shoved for the second time, when it remained stationary till dark. **1878** BOYD in *Bartlett's Dict. Amer.*, When the St. Lawrence at Montreal has frozen over, it is not safe to cross it until the ice has shoved.

**12.** *Comb.*: **shove-halfpenny, -ha'penny,** a game similar to shovel-board; †**shove-pike** [PIKE *sb.*[5]], ? a weapon used in fighting at close quarters; †**shove-up** *a.* in ***shove-up socket***, a contrivance forming part of a candlestick and designed to allow a candle to be burnt out to the end.

**1841** *Punch* 27 Nov. 232/2 The favourite game of *shove-halfpenny was kept up till a late hour. **1894** SIR J. ASTLEY *50 Yrs. Life* I. 50 The aristocratic and bewitching game of shove-halfpenny. **1915** T. BURKE *Nights in Town* 126 She shot knife, fork, and spoon across the table with a neat shove-ha'p'ny stroke. **1942** *R.A.F. Jrnl.* 3 Oct. 5 Moving from bar to shove ha'penny table. **1969** *Listener* 20 Mar. 381/3 The Camley Arms sounded such a nice pub, with piano on most nights and darts and shove-ha'penny in the public bar. **1763** FOOTE *Mayor of Garrat* I. Wks. 1799 I. 167 We could get you a *shove-pike. **1751** RICHARDSON in Mrs. Barbauld *Corr.* (1804) VI. 118 Her farthing candle blinking in its *shove-up socket.

**shove** *v.*[2]: see SHOVER[2].

**shove,** dial. form of SHEAF *sb.*; obs. pa. t. of SHAVE *v.*

†**shove-board.** *Obs. rare.* [f. SHOVE (after next) + BOARD *sb.*] = SHOVEL-BOARD.

**1522** in F. A. Inderwick *Cal. Inner Temple Rec.* (1896) I. 63 [None of the society shall play at the game called] Shoffe boorde [or] slypgrote. **1532** *Ibid.* 100 Shobebord [? *read* shovebord]. **1616** T. SCOT *Philomythie* I. (ed. 2) M1 b, Their idle houres..They spend at shoue-boord. **1623** in Simpkinson *Washingtons* (1860) App. p. xlvii, To Hartopp 3 daies making the new shove bord table 00 02 06.

**shove-groat.** *Obs.* exc. *Hist.* [f. stem of SHOVE *v.*[1] + GROAT *sb.*] = SHOVEL-BOARD. (Cf. SLIDEGROAT, SLIP-*groat*.)

**1488** in W. Kelly *Notices illustr. Drama* (1865) 181 [All persons were forbidden to play at]..checker-in-the-mire, or shove grote. **1541-2** *Act 33 Hen. VIII*, c. 9 §1 Slyde-thrifte otherwise called shovegrote. *c* **1640** J. SMYTH *Lives Berkeleys* (1883-5) II. 363 The hours..spent..at bowles tenis Cockpit Shufgrote cards and dice. **1801** STRUTT *Sports & Past.* IV. i. §19. 225. **1855** KINGSLEY *Westw. Ho!* ii, Playing at shove-groat with Spanish doubloons.

**b.** *attrib.*, as ***shove-groat table***; **shove-groat shilling**, a shilling used in the game.

**1597** SHAKS. *2 Hen. IV*, II. iv. 206 Quoit him downe (Bardolph) like a shoue-groat shilling. **1598** B. JONSON *Ev. Man in Hum.* III. ii. [v], [They] made it runne as smooth of the toung, as a shoue-groat shilling. **1628** WITHER *Brit. Rememb.* 210 A Shove-groat table.

Hence **'shovegroating**, playing at shove-groat.

**1601** HAKEWILL *Van. Eye* xxix. (1615) 140 Bouling, shooting, coiting, shoufgrating, and the like.

**shovel** ('ʃʌv(ə)l), *sb.* Forms: α. 1 scofl, -scobl, 3 ssofle, 3–5 schovele, 4–5 schovel, 5 schofylle, schovyl(le, schowulle, -elle, shofful, showele, shovele, shoville, 5–6 schovell, shovill, 5–7 shovell, 6 schovyll, shoffell, choffell, shoovell, shovull, shovelle, showel, 6–7 showell, 7–8 shufle, 5– shovel; β. chiefly *north.* 3–6 schole, 4, 6 schule, 5 schoyll, schwll, 5–6 schowle, sholl, 5–6, 9 (*dial.*) shole, 5–7 schuill, 6 showll, schull, shoull, showle, 6–7 s(c)hoole, shoule, 6–9 shule, 8 shull, 8–9 (*dial.*) shool, shoo, 9 shoul, showl, shul; γ. 1 ? scolf, 6 chollve, 6, 9 (*dial.*) sholve. [OE. *scofl* fem. corresponds to NFris. *skofel* digging shovel, MLG., LG. *schuffel*, shovel, weeding hoe, MDu. *schofel*, *schoffel* shovel (mod.Du. *schoffel* weeding hoe, whence SCUFFLE *sb.*); the MSw. *skofl*, *skofwel* (Sw. *skofvel*), Da. *skovl*, Norw. *skufl*, are prob. from LG.; parallel forms with long root-vowel are OHG. *scûvala* fem. (MHG. *schûvel*, mod.G. *schaufel*) shovel, early mod.Du. *schuivel*, dial. *schoefel* shovel; the OTeut. type **skûflō* is app. f. the root **skūf-*, **skŭb-* of SHOVE *v.*[1]]

**1. a.** A spade-like implement, consisting of a broad blade of metal or other material (more or less hollow and often with upturned sides), attached to a handle and used for raising and removing quantities of earth, grain, coal or other loose material. (In some dialects the word is applied to a spade.)

*baker's shovel* = PEEL *sb.*[2] 2; *coal-shovel*, see COAL *sb.*[1] 15; *malt-shovel*, see MALT *sb.*[1] 4 b; *paring-shovel*, see PARING *vbl. sb.* 4; also FIRE-SHOVEL.

α. *c* **725** *Corpus Gloss.* 2051 *Trulla*: cruce, turl, scofl. *Ibid.* 2081 *Vatilla*: isern-scobl. *c* **825** *Epinal Gloss.* 1022 *Trulla*: scofl. *a* **1100** *Gerefa* in *Anglia* IX. 263 He sceal habban spade, scofle, wadspitel [etc.]. **1297** R. GLOUC. (Rolls) 2197 Vor ȝe beþ men bet iteiȝt to ssofle [*v.rr.* schouele, shouell] & to spade.. þan [etc.]. **1377** LANGL. *P. Pl.* B. VI. 192 An heep of heremites.. wenten as werkemen with spades and with schoueles. *c* **1440** *Jacob's Well* 189 A schouyl hath iij. thynges; a scho, an heued, & an handyl. **1531** *Rec. St. Mary at Hill* 37 A lityll fyer choffell. **1602** SHAKS. *Ham.* V. i. 110 Why doe's he suffer this rude knaue now to knocke him about the Sconce with a dirty Shouell. **1718** HICKES & NELSON *Kettlewell* I. xv. 107 The Apprentice-Boys would soon knock them on the Head with their paring Shovels. **1848** THACKERAY *Van. Fair* xiii, The cashier (whose benevolent occupation it is to.. dispense sovereigns out of a copper shovel). **1906** PETRIE *Relig. Anc. Egypt* xiii. 84 The winnowing shovels and rakes stuck upright.

β. *a* **1300** *Holy Rood* 42 (Ashm. MS.) þo nome hi spade and schole. *c* **1340** *Nominale* (Skeat) 519 *Trobile beche furche fymere* Schole spade mouke-forke. **1453–4** *Durham Acc. Rolls* (Surtees) 150, ij sholez ferro ligat. **1545** *Acc. Ld. High Treas. Scot.* VIII. 360 For ane dousan of schulis, xs. **1612** *Sc. Bk. Rates* in *Halyburton's Ledger* (1867) 326 Schooles vngarnished the hundreth xli. **1785** BURNS *Ep. to J. Lapraik* xi, What sairs your grammars? Ye'd better taen up spades and shools. **1823** SCOTT *Quentin D.* xxxi, A beard like a baker's shool. **1894** CROCKETT *Raiders* xv. 137 We made a grave.. and I went for spades and shools.

γ. *c* **875** *Erfurt Gloss.* 1022 *Trulla*: scolf. **1504–5** *Rec. St. Mary at Hill* (1905) 255 Payde for a chollve [*cf.* sholve *ibid.* 381] to pare the Chyrche iiij d. **1573** TUSSER *Husb.* (1878) 35 A.. wheelebarrow, sholue and a spade. **1583** *Wills & Inv. N.C.* (Surtees 1860) 78, j grape, and sholve, iij spades, and iiij irrone forkes 4s. **1858** SPURDENS *Suppl. to Forby*, *Sholve*, a shovel.

**b.** In fig. context.

*c* **1440** *Jacob's Well* 199 A skeet of contrycyoun, wyth a scauell of confessioun, wyth a schouyl of satysfaccyoun. *Ibid.* 203 þe schouyl, I telde ȝou, was satysfaccyoun, þe scho þer-of is almes-dede, þe heuyd is preyere, þe handyll is restitucyoun.

†**c.** *shod-shovel*: a shovel of wood edged or tipped with metal. *Obs.*

**1465** in *Finchale Priory Acc.* (Surtees) p. ccxcix, j schoyd schoyll. **1526–7** *Rec. St. Mary at Hill* 339 For a Shod-shovill for the Church iiijd. **1606** BIRNIE *Kirk Buriall* (1833) 31 With shod-shooles to seugh up the sanctuary-ground.

**d.** Occas. used for: A shovelful.

**1881** C. WHITEHEAD *Hops* 8 The plant centres being covered with a few shovels of earth.

**e.** *Phr. to be put to bed with a shovel*: to be buried (Grose *Dict. Vulgar Tongue*, 1785).

**f.** *transf.* The cue used in the game of SHOVEL-BOARD (sense 2).

**g.** *shovel and broom*: rhyming slang for 'room'. Chiefly *U.S.*

**1928** M. C. SHARPE *Chicago May* 288/2 *Shovel and broom*, room. **1929** [see LINE *sb.*[2] 13 f]. **1938** *Detective Fiction Weekly* 23 Apr. 75/1 In Australian slang.. a house is a 'rat and mouse' and a room a 'shovel and broom'.

**2.** ? = SHOVELLER[2].

**1580** HOLLYBAND *Treas. Fr. Tong*, *Pale* or *cuellier*, a bird called shouell.

**3.** The flat portion of the horn of a moose-deer.

**1908** *Blackw. Mag.* Aug. 230/1 The brows were very good indeed, and the shovels cupped and broad.

**4.** = SHOVEL HAT.

**1841** J. B. MOZLEY *Let.* in Purcell *Life Manning* (1895) I. 194 The straight-cut coat and the gentlest shovel. **1854** THACKERAY *Newcomes* xxv, She managed the hat shop... My uncle the Bishop had his shovels there.

**5.** A person using a shovel.

**1834–7** J. S. MACAULAY *Field Fortif.* (1851) 54 Four shovels are placed on the berm,.. and the remaining 4 shovels and rammers on the parapet. *c* **1890** *Engineer* LXVII. 344 (Cent.) In the early days after the Crimean War, the engineers in the Navy.. were technically known as shovels.

**6.** *Mil.* A contrivance fitted to a field-gun to act as a brake to lessen the recoil.

**1899** *Daily News* 8 Mar. 4/3 They intend that a 'shovel' shall be fixed to our field guns... This 'shovel', or break, was described to me by several officers.

**7.** *attrib.* and *Comb.* **a.** simple attrib., as *shovel hilt*, † *iron*; similative, as *shovel-beaked*, *-beard*, *-bladed*, *-ended*, *-footed*, *-handed*, *-headed*, *-mouthed*, *-shaped* adjs.; objective, as † *shovel-cheaper*, *-maker*.

**1896** *Roy. Nat. Hist.* (ed. Lydekker) V. 516 *marg.* *Shovel-Beaked Sturgeons. **1864** SALA in *Daily Tel.* 26 Feb., Those bushy locks, that *shovel beard. **1901** *Ibid.* 18 Mar. 7/4 An Eton crew.. with *shovel-bladed oars. *c* **1515** *Cocke Lorell's B.* 11 *Schouyll chepers. **1841** PUGIN *Pres. St. Eccles. Archit.* (1843) 7 A *shovel-ended stole. ? *a* **1400** *Morte Arth.* 1098 *Schovelle-fotede was þat schalke. **1836** E. A. POE in *Southern Lit. Messenger* Aug. 595/2 Not a shovel-footed negro waddles across the stage. **1860** EMERSON *Cond. of Life* vii. *Consid.* Wks. (Bohn) II. 414 No *shovel-handed, narrow-brained, gin-drinking million stockingers. **1859** R. F. BURTON *Centr. Afr.* in *Jrnl. Geog. Soc.* XXIX. 161 Their huge *shovel-headed spears. **1888** BURT *Stand. Timber Meas.* 279 *Shovel Hilts. **1395** *Cartular. Abb. de Whiteby* (Surtees) 606 Pro ij *schole iryn, ij d. **1638** *Canterb. Marriage Licences* (*MS.*), Elias Tonge of Charing, *shouell-maker. **1763** *Ann. Reg.*, *Chron.* 106/2 A *Shovel-mouthed or cow-bellied shark. **1879** E. O'DONOVAN *Merv Oasis* (1882) I. 314 Queer long *shovel-shaped oars.

**b.** Special comb.: **shovel-bill** = SHOVELLER[2]; **shovel-cultivator** *U.S.* = *shovel-plough*; † **shovel dog-fish** ? = *shovel-fish*; **shovel-duck** *dial.* = SHOVELLER[2]; **shovel-fish**, a fish of the genus *Scaphirhynchus*, esp. *S. platyrhynchus*; † **shovel-groat** = SHOVE-GROAT; **shovel head**, (*a*) = *shovel-fish*; (*b*) the bonnet-headed shark, *Reniceps tiburo* (also *attrib.*); **shovel-man**, a labourer who uses a shovel; **shovel-nose**, a nose having the shape of and fulfilling the functions of a shovel, also *attrib.* in the names of certain animals and fishes having this characteristic; hence *shovel-nosed* adj., also *transf.*; **shovel pass** *U.S. Sports*, an underarm, forward pass made with a shovelling movement of the arms; so as *v. trans.* and *intr.*; **shovel-penny** = SHOVEL-BOARD; **shovel-plough**, an implement for clearing cornland of weeds; **shovel-stirrup**, a stirrup with a broad rest for the foot, extending behind the heel; **shovel-sturgeon** = *shovel-fish*; **shovel-tree** (see quot.); † **shovel-wood** = *shovel-tree*.

**1864** ATKINSON *Prov. Names of Birds*, *Shovel-bill.. *Anas clypeata*. **1868** *Rep. U.S. Commissioner Agric.* (1869) 236 They are sometimes very expeditiously covered.. with the mold-board or the *shovel cultivator. **1664** HUBERT *Catal. Rarities* 13 A *Shovell Dogge fish. **1893** in Cozens-Hardy *Broad Norfolk* 47 *Shovel Duck. **1863** WOOD *Illustr. Nat. Hist.* III. 200 The two smaller figures represent the *Shovel-fish, so called from the curious form of its head. **1825** JAMIESON s.v., *Slide-thrift*. A species of draughts in which the winner is the one who first gets his men off the board; also called *Shovel-groat. **1881** *Cassell's Nat. Hist.* V. 45 The second genus called the *Shovel-head (*Scaphirhynchus*), is represented by a single species. **1882** JORDAN & GILBERT *Synopsis Fishes N. Amer.* 25 Shovel-head Shark. **1559** in Boys *Hist. Sandwich* (1792) 738 Every spade and *shovell man muste have.. iii laborers with wheale barrowes. **1898** H. KIRKE *25 Yrs. Brit. Guiana* iii. 37 The late Mr. W. R. once described him as 'a good shovel man spoiled'. **1709** LAWSON *Voy. Carolina* 153 One being called a Bottle-Nosed Whale, the other a *Shovel-Nose. **1768** SOLANDER in *Ann. Reg.* (1769) *Chron.* App. 188/2 Shovel nose sharks. **1882** JORDAN & GILBERT *Synopsis Fishes N. Amer.* 88 Shovel-nose Sturgeon. **1885** C. F. HOLDER *Marvels Anim. Life* 180 The shark.. running its shovel nose into the sand. **1707** FUNNELL *Voy.* v. 120 The *Shovel-nos'd-Shark. **1837** J. F. COOPER *England* (ed. 2) I. 185 A shovel-nosed hat and a wig. **1948** *News-Age-Herald* (Birmingham, Alabama) 31 Oct. C-5/2 Frank Tripucka.. then *shovel-passed to Sitko. *Ibid.*, Frank Tripucka.. faked a handoff to Bill Gay then shovel-passed it to Sitko. **1976** *Honolulu Star Bull.* 21 Dec. H-1/1 Alabama trotted out such gimmicks as.. an underhand *shovel pass for a key 19-yard gain and an unbalanced line. **1887** *Cassell's Encycl. Dict.*, *Shovel-penny. **1801** *Farmer's Mag.* Apr. 209 An implement for cleaning corn land is also used, called the *shovel plough. **1812** SIR J. SINCLAIR *Syst. Husb. Scot.* I. 96 Cast-metal rollers, and scrapers, or shovel-ploughs. **1883** V. STUART *Egypt* 33 Most of the party were mounted on horses with carpet housings and *shovel stirrups. *a* **1894** LAYARD *Autobiog.* (1903) II. 34 Heavy shovel stirrups which served for spurs. **1875** E. D. COPE *N. Amer. Batrachia & Rept.* 87 The *shovel-sturgeon (*Scaphirhynchops*). **1887** DARLINGTON *Folk Speech S. Chesh.*, *Shovel-tree, the handle of a spade. *c* **1615** *MS. Acc. St. John's Hosp., Canterb.*, Payd for a *shoufell wood v d and setting of it ane [sic] viij d.

**shovel** ('ʃʌv(ə)l), *v.*[1] Forms: see the sb. Also 9 (*dial.*) shulve. [f. SHOVEL *sb.* Cf. MLG. *schuffelen*, MHG. *schûveln*, *schûfeln* (mod.G. *schaufeln*), Sw. *skofla*, Da. *skovle*, Norw. *skufla*, *skovla*.]

**1.** *trans.* To take up and remove with a shovel. Chiefly with adv. or advb. phrase. Also *fig.*

*c* **1440** *Promp. Parv.* 448/2 Schovelyn, wythe a schowelle, *tribulo*. *c* **1440** *Jacob's Well* 193, I lykened satysfaccyoun to a schouele to schouell out wyth þe crommys of þe wose of dedly synne. **1590** in Harwood *Lichfield* (1806) 527 Payd.. for shollynge snowe off the Churche. **1626** A. SPEED *Adam out of Eden* xiv. (1659) 107 Shovelling the Corn from the sides of the roomes. **1791** *Gentl. Mag.* 24/2 The men that shovel the dirt out of the road. **1816** SCOTT *Antiq.* xxv, Tak the shule a bit, and shule out the loose earth. **1891** SMILES *J. Murray* I. vii. 141 The labourers were at work shovelling away the snow.

†**b.** *to shovel down*: to destroy by shovelling away. *Obs.*

**1563** WINȜET *Cert. Tractates* Wks. (S.T.S.) II. 5 To schuil doun thir wallis to the ground.

**c.** *transf.* (With adv.) To remove as rubbish; to move about roughly and without consideration.

**1816** SCOTT *Antiq.* xxv, I haena lived sae lang in the warld neither, to be shuled out o't that gate. **1837** CARLYLE *Fr. Rev.* I. II. i, In such sort are poor mortals swept and shovelled to and fro. **1863** HAWTHORNE *Old Home, Recoll. Gifted Woman* I. 184 A great amount of rubbish, which any competent editor would have shovelled out of the way.

**2.** To excavate, dig up (the ground, etc.), dig (a hole, etc.) with a shovel.

*c* **1470** HENRYSON *Mor. Fab.* VIII. (*Preach. Swallow*) xxxii, In the snaw he schuillit hes ane plane. *a* **1785** *Ulysses' Answ. Ajax* in *Poems Buchan Dial.* 37 The gutter's sheeled. **1857** *Jrnl. R. Agric. Soc.* XVIII. I. 105 A man will 'shool' about one-eighth of an acre per diem.

**3.** To throw (quantities of some material) *into* a receptacle, to cast (earth, dust, etc.) *on* or *upon* something or somebody.

**1611** SHAKS. *Wint. T.* IV. iv. 469 Some Hangman must.. lay me Where no Priest shouels-in dust. *c* **1800** '*Broom blooms bonnie*' x. in Child *Ballads* I. 184/2 It was nae wonder his heart was sair, When he shooled the mools on her yellow hair. **1869** E. A. PARKES *Pract. Hygiene* (ed. 3) 98 The powder is shovelled into sacks. **1913** *Blackw. Mag.* Sept. 356/2 One of them.. was shovelling tipsy cake into his ample mouth.

*fig.* **1749** FIELDING *Tom Jones* x. iii, Partridge likewise shovelled in his share of calumny. **1864** BURTON *Scot Abr.* 269 Thousands.. unshipped on the desert shore, shovelled as it were, into a strange land.

**4.** To gather (something) *up* in quantities as with a shovel.

**1685** PENN *Further Acc. Pennsylv.* 9 Herring.. swarm in such shoales.. in little Creeks, they almost shovel them up in their tubs. **1713** DERHAM *Phys.-Theol.* IV. xi. Note *n* (1727) 187, I have seen.. Ducks shovel them up as they swim along the Waters. **1879** *Daily News* 22 Mar. 6/2 Storekeepers.. are simply shovelling up money.

**5.** *intr.* To use a shovel.

**1685** TRAVESTIN *Acc. Siege of Newheusel* 30 No one offered to put out the fire, till the Duke of Lorrain came and began himself to shovel upon it. **1864** CARLYLE *Fredk. Gt.* XV. ii. V. 280 In relays, 3,000 of the Militia-men dig and shovel night and day.

*transf.* **1815** SCOTT *Guy M.* xlvi, Is that all? thought Sampson, resuming his spoon, and shovelling away manfully. **1882** PAYNE-GALLWEY *Fowler in Irel.* 39 You can discern.. the rippling bills as they shovel greedily along the ooze.

**6.** *transf.* To turn (something) over with a shovel.

**1775** W. WILLIAMSON *Trials at York* 29/2, I shoveled it [the earth] over, and threw it into that corner. **1868** *Rep. U.S. Commissioner Agric.* (1869) 425 The salt and lime were.. mixed about three months before use and afterward shoveled over several times.

**7.** *to shovel out*: to distribute in shovelfuls. *fig.*

**1858** CARLYLE *Fredk. Gt.* V. iii. (1865) II. 85 George I shovelling out his English subsidies as usual.

**8.** *trans.* and *intr.* To intrude. *Obs.* exc. *dial.*

**1540** PALSGR. *Acolastus* II. iii. L iij b, I wyll sowe me in i. I wyll thrust me in, or schole in [orig. *a tergo me hinc inseram*]. **1861** C. C. ROBINSON *Dial. Leeds* 403 He'll shool in onnywhear, whear ther's owt to be gotten. **1876** *Mid. Yorks. Gloss.*, *Shool*, v.a. and slightly as a v.n. to intrude. *Shovel* is also in occasional *active* use with this meaning.

**shovel** ('ʃʌv(ə)l), *v.*[2] Now *rare*. Also 5 schovel, 9 *dial.* shool, shulve. [app. a frequentative f. SHOVE *v.*[1] Cf. SHUFFLE *v.* In mod. use app. associated with SHOVEL *v.*[1]] *intr.* To make movements *with* the feet, without raising them from the ground; to walk languidly or lazily. (Cf. SHUFFLE *v.* 1.)

*c* **1430** *Wyclif's Bible* Job xi. 10 (MS. S.) Shoueling forth [*v.rr.* stumblynge, hirtynge, Vulg. *offendens*] with his feet. *c* **1450** in Aungier *Syon* (1840) 381 They schal euer haue warnes.. that they schouel not withe ther fete up on the pament, wherby the reder may the wers be herde. **1549** LATIMER *6th Serm. bef. Edw. VI* (Arb.) 169 They hard hym quietly, with out any shouelynge of feete or walkynge vp and downe. **1674** N. FAIRFAX *Bulk & Selv.* 29 When I walk, that assignable.. part of my soul, which was in my leg, comes shoveling after me. **1824** CARLYLE in Froude *Life* (1882) I. 222 In walking he does not tread, but shovel and slide. *a* **1825** FORBY *Voc. E. Anglia*, *Shool*, *Shulve*, to saunter, with such extreme laziness, as if the saunterer did not mean to walk, but to shovel up the dust with his feet.

†'**shovelard.** *Obs.* Forms: α. 5 schovelerd, schevelard, 6 s(c)hovelarde, 6–7 shovelard; β. 5 scholard, 6 sholard, 7 shoulerd. [f. SHOVEL *sb.* + -ARD; ? after MALLARD, POPARD; cf. the form *poplerd* = POPELER.] The SPOONBILL, *Platalea leucorodia*. (Cf. SHOVELLER.)

α. *c* **1440** *Promp. Parv.* 448/1 Schovelerd, or popler, byrd. **1533–4** *Act 25 Hen. VIII*, c. 11 §4 For every egge of every byttour heroune or shovelard eight pence. **1646** SIR T. BROWNE *Pseud. Ep.* VII. xiv. 368 So have Cranes, Hernes, Storks, and Shovelards long necks.

β. *c* **1460** *Promp. Parv.* (Winch.) 400 Scholarde, or poplerd, bryd: *populus*. *c* **1512** *Regul. Northumberld. Househ.* (1770) 106 Item Sholardes to be hadde for my Lordes owne Mees. **1626** BRETON *Fantasticks* (Grosart) 10/2 The yong Herne and the Shoulerd are now fat for the great Feast.

**shovel-board** (ˈʃʌv(ə)lbɔəd), **ˈshuffleboard.** Forms: α. 6 shovillabourde, shovelaborde, 7 shovell a board, shouleaborde, shovelabord, showlibord, shovellabord. β. 6–7 shovelboord, 7 shovell-boord, sholven borde, shovell board, shuel board, 7– shovel-board. γ. 6 shoffle-, shoofle-, 7 shufle-, 8 shuffell-. [The earliest form *shovill-, shovelabourd*, is an unexplained alteration of SHOVE-BOARD. There does not seem to be any connexion with *shovel* or *shuffle*.]

**1. a.** A game in which a coin or other disk is driven by a blow with the hand along a highly polished board, floor, or table (sometimes ten yards or more long) marked with transverse lines. The game is out of use in England, but is still played (with some modifications of form) in the U.S. Cf. SLIDE-GROAT, SHOVE-GROAT, SHOVE-BOARD.

The modern game as played in the U.S. is always called *shuffleboard*; in historical references to the older game the usual form is *shovel-board*.

α. **1532** *Privy Purse Exp. Hen. VIII* (1827) 188 Paied to my lord Wylliam for that he wanne of the kinges grace at shovillaborde ix li. **1575** in W. H. Turner *Select. Rec. Oxford* (1880) 364 All unlawfull games, as..tables, bowlls, shovelaborde. **1656** in *Verney Mem.* (1907) II. 40 That you ..keep showlibord playing..on sondaies contrary to order. **1688** *Nottingham Rec.* V. 352 Wee present William Finn for keeping men plaing att shouell-abord in his seller.

β. **1613** BEAUM. & FL. *Cupid's Rev.* III. i, How haue you sped heere at home at shouelboord? **1672** SHADWELL *Miser* III. i. Wks. 1720 III. 47 He has already lost his Edward Shillings that he kept for Shovel-board. **1708** J. CHAMBERLAYNE *St. Gt. Brit.* I. III. vii. (1710) 205 The Citizens and Peasants have..Cricket, Skittles, or Nine-Pins, Shovel-board, [etc.]. **1873** BENNETT & 'CAVENDISH' *Billiards* 3 Before the introduction of Billiards the fashionable game on a board was shovel-board.

γ. **1577–86** STANYHURST *Chron. Irel., Hen. VIII*, 86/2 in *Holinshed*, Plaieng at slidegrote or shoofleboord. **1736** CARTE *Ormonde* II. 178 The Marquis chose to sit up all night at shuffleboard with four Suffolk malsters. **1884** *Harper's Mag.* Jan. 235/2 Checkers and shuffle-board were in requisition.

†**b.** = *shovel-board shilling*. *Obs.*

**1598** SHAKS. *Merry W.* I. i. 159 Seauen groates in mill-sixpences, and two Edward Shouelboords [Qo. 1602, Two faire shouell boord shillings].

**c.** The table upon which the game was played.

**1603** *Inv.* in Gage *Hengrave* (1822) 22 Itm, one long table for a sholven borde. *a* **1660** *Prince d'Amour*, etc. 163 A new shuel board whereon never stood food. **1666** WOOD *Life*, etc. (O.H.S.) II. 96 Dice, cards, sketells, shuffle-boards, billiard tables. **1724** J. MACKY *Journ. Eng. & Scot.* II. iii. 40 [In] the Hall..is a Marble Shuffleboard. **1843** LYTTON *Last Bar.* II. iii, He was laughing loud with a knot of young men by the shovel-board.

**2.** *transf.* A game played (*orig.* on shipboard, now also on a court) by pushing wooden or iron disks with a cue (called a *shovel*) so that they may rest on one of nine squares of a diagram chalked on the deck or marked on the court.

The usual form is now *shuffleboard*.

**1836** T. POWER *Impressions of Amer.* I. 14 Shuffle-board, chess, and backgammon, with exercise and pleasant converse, will while away the intervening hours. **1851** J. D. LEWIS *Across Atlantic* 6 That ignominious game called shovel-board, which consists in stooping down and projecting flat slabs of wood at figures chalked on the deck. **1877** BLACK *Green Past.* xxviii. 224 There were rope quoits got out too; and the more energetic shovel-board. **1886** R. C. LESLIE *Sea-painter's Log.* vi. 115 The long afternoon game of shuffle-board was interrupted by a break, in that clear sea-line to windward. **1932** E. WAUGH *Cruise* in *Work Suspended* (1949) Papa is very good at the deck games especially one called shuffle board. **1967** *Boston Sunday Herald* 26 Mar. VI. 7/7 (Advt.), 500-ft. sandy beach, 3 pools, putting green, tennis, shuffleboard, supervised Kiddie Playground. **1977** 'J. LE CARRÉ' *Hon. Schoolboy* iv. 90 Sometimes she stayed for old-tyme dancing or a game of shuffleboard.

**3.** *attrib.* and *Comb.* as † ***shovel-board piece***, † ***play***, † ***room***, † ***table***; † **shovel-board shilling,** a shilling (sometimes of Edw. VI; see 1 b) used in the game of shovel-board.

**1622** MABBE tr. *Aleman's Guzman d'Alf.* II. 145 He might ..strike me, like a *shovell-board peece (being now a ledger) into the box. **1679** *Lond. Gaz.* No. 1435/4 Six or eight Shovel board peices of Silver. **1691** WOOD *Ath. Oxon.* I. 19 The game called *Shovel-board play. **1631** *Minute-bk. Archd. Essex* 16 June, Others of the companye..ran into the *shovell board roome. **1653** ROWE *Tragi-Comœdia* *3 b, A Shufle-board-roome. **1602** *Shovel board shilling [see 1 b]. **1611** MIDDLETON & DEKKER *Roaring Girl* K 2, Away slid I my man, like a shouell-board shilling. **1634** in Simpkinson *Washingtons* (1860) App. p. lxvii, Mending the covers of the *shovleaborde Table. **1686** PLOT *Staffordsh.* ix. 383 The Shuffle-board table tho' ten yards, 1 foot, and an inch long is made up of about 260 pieces. **1719** D'URFEY *Pills* III. 273 A new Shuffle-board-table. **1738** EARL OF OXFORD in *Portland Papers* (Hist. MSS. Comm.) VI. 176 A fine table of white marble of a great length, made use of for a shovel board table.

**shovelful** (ˈʃʌv(ə)lfʊl). Also -full. [f. SHOVEL *sb.* + -FUL.] A quantity that fills a shovel; as much as a shovel can hold or take up at one time.

**1533** J. HEYWOOD *Johan* (1903) 654 This shovyll full of colys. **1658** EARL MONM. tr. *Paruta's Wars Cyprus* 117 One shufle-full of earth. **1711** ADDISON *Spect.* No. 26 ¶3, I entertain'd my self with the digging of a Grave; and saw in every shovelful of it that was thrown up, the Fragment of a Bone or Skull. **1856** MISS YONGE *Daisy Chain* I. viii, He stood over her, counted her shovelsfull of tea, and watched the water into the tea-pot. **1894** SIR J. ASTLEY *50 Yrs. Life* I. 100 Shovelsful of sand and sawdust.

*fig.* **1622** MABBE tr. *Aleman's Guzman d'Alf.* II. 256 Throwing out lies and scandals by shouell-fuls. **1858** CARLYLE *Fredk. Gt.* VII. iii. (1865) II. 263 Riddling or screening certain cartloads of heavy old German printed rubbish..we obtain the following shovelful of authentic particulars.

**shovel hat.**

A stiff broad-brimmed hat, turned up at the sides and projecting with a shovel-like curve in front and behind, worn by some ecclesiastics.

**1829** CARLYLE in Froude *Life* (1882) II. 73 Does not the very sight of a shovel-hat in some degree indispose me to the wearer thereof? **1848** THACKERAY *Van. Fair* xxxii, If he could have got a shovel-hat he would have worn it. **1871** *Fair France* ii. 58 The priest..in shovel hat and cassock appeared a pleasant gentleman enough. **1889** W. S. GILBERT *Gondoliers* II. 35 And Bishops in their shovel hats Were plentiful as tabby cats.

**b.** *transf.* A wearer of such a hat.

**1859** LEVER *Dav. Dunn* lxvii, A regular don amongst the shovel-hats.

Hence **shovel-ˈhatted** *a.*, wearing a shovel hat; *transf.* of or pertaining to the ideas or opinions of a wearer of a shovel hat.

**1832** CARLYLE *Misc., Boswell* (1857) III. 50 A cleanly, Shovel-hatted look. **1848** THACKERAY *Van. Fair* xi, A tall, stately, jolly, shovel-hatted man.

**shoveller**[1] (ˈʃʌv(ə)lə(r)). Forms: α. 5 schoveler, 9 shoveller (*U.S.* shoveler); β. 9 shooler. [f. SHOVEL *v.* + -ER[1].] One who shovels.

α. *c* **1440** *Promp. Parv.* 448/2 Schoveler..*tribularius.* **1833** HT. MARTINEAU *Charmed Sea* iv. 60 She..stood dripping with her load in the presence of the shoveller. **1884** *Milit. Engin.* I. II. 27 It is advisable to provide one shoveller to each two diggers in the third relief.

β. **1857** *Jrnl. R. Agric. Soc.* XVIII. I. 105 The labourer with the spade—or 'shooler', as he is called—commences his work by throwing out a furrow.

**shoveller**[2] (ˈʃʌv(ə)lə(r)). Forms: α. 5 shovelere, schoveler, 6 schofler, shovelor, (shoovelar), 6–7 shovelar, 7 shovler, 7–8 shuffler, 6– shoveler, shoveller; β. 7 shouler. [Alteration of SHOVELARD, with substitution of -ER[1] for -ARD. Cf. G. †*schufler* (1582 in Gesner-Heusslin), *schaufler* (Nemnich).]

†**1.** = SHOVELARD.

α. *c* **1460** J. RUSSELL *Bk. Nurture* 541 Also for bustard betowre & shovelere, gamelyn is in sesoun. *a* **1529** SKELTON *P. Sparowe* 408 The shouelar with his brode bek. **1577** V. LEIGH *Surveying* D j b, The like Rente, maie be and in some Mannours, is of Herneshawes, Shouelors, &c. **1603** G. OWEN *Pembrokeshire* (1892) 131 The Shovler. **1612** PEACHAM *Gentl. Exerc.* I. xvi. (1634) 54 Waterfowle, as the Mallard, Shoveller, Sheldrake. **1668** CHARLETON *Onomast.* 103 *Ardea Alba*..the white, and spoon-bill'd Heron, or Shoveler. **1796** STEDMAN *Surinam* II. xxviii. 343 The shoveler, or spoon-bill (which has some affinity to the cranes) is about the size of a goose.

β. **1622** DRAYTON *Poly-olb.* xxv. 353 The Shouler which so shakes the ayre with saily wings.

**b.** ¶Erroneously applied to the Pelican.

**1552** COOPER *Elyot's Dict.*, *Pelicanus*, a byrde called a pelicane, or shouelar.

**2.** 'From the latter half of the 17th century' (Newton *Dict. Birds* 841) applied to the Spoonbill Duck, *Spatula* (or *Rhynchaspis*) *clypeata*, a bird with a broad shovel-like beak. Also ***shoveller duck***.

**1674** RAY *Coll. Words, Water Fowl* 96 The Shoveler: *Anas platyrynchos, sive clypeata.* *a* **1700** B. E. *Dict. Cant. Crew*, *Shuffler*, a Bird like, but not so big as a Duck, having a broader Bill. **1732** MORTIMER in *Phil. Trans.* XXXVII. 449 The Blue-wing'd Shoveler. **1768** PENNANT *Brit. Zool.* (ed. 4) II. 467 Red Breasted Shoveler. **1838** J. J. AUDUBON *Ornith. Biogr.* IV. 241 Shoveller Duck. *Anas clypeata*, Linn. **1859** DARWIN *Orig. Species* vii. (1873) 184 The beak is thus very inferior as a sifter to that of the shoveller. **1878** *Proc. U.S. Nat. Museum* I. 446 *Spatula clypeata* (Linn.). Shoveller; Spoon-bill Duck.

**3.** *Her.* A representation of a 'shoveller'.

[**1572** BOSSEWELL *Armorie* III. 25 Beareth to hys creste a shouelard Argente (*misprinted* a shouelar d'Argente).] **1780** EDMONDSON *Heraldry* II. Gloss., *Shoveller*, a species of water-fowl, somewhat like the duck.

†**ˈshoveller**[3]. *Obs. rare*$^{-1}$. [f. SHOVEL *sb.* + -ER[1].] ? The Shovel-head Shark.

**1664** HUBERT *Catal. Rarities* 13 Whole Fishes. A Shoveller or Blew Sharke.

**shovelling** (ˈʃʌv(ə)lɪŋ), *vbl. sb.* [f. SHOVEL *v.*[1] + -ING[1].]

**1.** The action or an act of SHOVEL *v.*

α. *c* **1440** *Promp. Parv.* 448/2 Schovelynge, *tribulatus.* **1827** STEUART *Planter's Guide* (1828) 192 Two spits deep, with two intermediate shovellings. *a* **1832** S. WARREN *Diary Physic.* xvi, Shovelling *in* was surprisingly easier than shovelling *out!*

**2.** Something which is shovelled up. Usually *pl.*

α. **1653** BLITHE *Eng. Improv. Impr.* (ed. 3) 145 The shovelling of Streets and Yards, and Highwaies..is very good both, of it self, and compounded with other Soyl, Manure, Mud, or Straw. **1733** W. ELLIS *Chiltern & Vale Farm.* 277 Parings of Turf, or Shovelings of Highways may be mix'd with Lime and Chalk. **1805** R. W. DICKSON *Pract. Agric.* I. 129 The shovelings from the ditches in road sides.

β. **1523–34** FITZHERB. *Husb.* §17 And if it [the dung] be medled with erthe, as sholynges and suche other, it wyll laste the longer.

**shove-net** (ˈʃʌvnɛt). Forms: 5 schofnet(t, shofnet, 6 shovenette, shuffnet, 7– shove-net. [f. SHOVE *v.*[1] + NET *sb.*] A fishing-net with a broad mouth expanded by means of a frame, worked by pushing along the bed of a river, etc., or through shallow sea-water.

**1418** *Court Roll Gt. Waltham Manor*, Piscavit sine licencia cum diversis instrumentis videlicet spertes, lammes, et schofnetts et pisces cepit. **1419** *Liber Albus* (Rolls) I. 577 Shotnet, Shofnet, et Kydels, sount defenduz. **1464** *Maldon* (Essex) *Court-Rolls* Bundle 40 No. 7 Debet sibi xviii d. pro rethe vocato a schofnet. **1523** FITZHERB. *Surv.* 10 b, The lordes tenantes haue lybertie by customer to fysshe with shouenettes. **1539** in *Archæologia* XLIII. 212, iiij potyngers; and j shuffnet. **1611** COTGR., *Sauve*, a shoue-net to fish withall. **1742** *De Foe's Tour Gt. Brit.* (ed. 3) I. 327 They throw in a Net on a Hoop at the end of a Pole, the Pole going cross the Hoop, which, in some Places, they call a Shove Net. **1841** J. T. HEWLETT *Parish Clerk* I. 27 The use of the shove-net to entrap the prawns and shrimps. **1874** HOLDSWORTH *Deep-Sea Fishing* 218 Shrimps are fished for with the common hand or 'shove'-net.

*attrib.* **1861** HUGHES *Tom Brown at Oxf.* xxxvi, 'Tis only our shove-net traps as I wur a-telling you of.

**shover**[1] (ˈʃʌvə(r)). [f. SHOVE *v.*[1] + -ER[1].]

**a.** One who or something which shoves, in senses of the vb.

**1500–20** DUNBAR *Poems* lxiii. 49 Schulderaris, and schowaris that hes no schame. **1893** *Cycl. Rev. Current Hist.* III. 287 A difference between the lumber shovers and the lumber-men. *Ibid.*, The lockout of the shovers continued. **1901** *Daily Chron.* 12 Dec. 6/3 The Cambridge forwards were 'shovers' and nothing else.

*Comb.* **1876** *Life Cheap Jack* (ed. Hindley) 232 A pair of the best brass candlesticks, with a patent shover-up and a good pusher-down.

**b.** *slang.* One who passes base coin.

**1859** *National Police Gaz.* (U.S.) 14 May 4/3 A 'shover' named Flynn,..obtained a quantity of 'queer' and went with it to Mrs. Beemer's house and left it on her table. **1889** *Harper's Weekly* 21 Sept. 768/1 Eight persons, mostly 'shovers' or passers, were arrested in Russo's gang.

**shover**[2] (ˈʃəʊvə(r)). Also shovver, shuv(v)er. Jocular alteration of CHAUFFEUR. Hence (as back-formation) **shove** *v.*[2] *intr.*, **ˈshoving** *vbl. sb.*[2]

**1905** S. A. BARNETT *Let.* 17 Aug. in H. Barnett *Canon S. A. Barnett* (1918) II. xli. 192 Dick Batston had to leave us and we are waiting here till a 'shover' comes from London. .. Dick drives splendidly. **1912** *World* 5 Nov. 707/2 She can drive as well as any 'shuver'. **1914** *Professional Chauffeurs' Club Jrnl.* May 15/2 When Tommy, the bad boy of the family, has received the Order of the Boot..his fond mama ..says, 'Let us make him a shuvver.' **1925** *Chambers's Jrnl.* Feb. 146/1 Joseph—our 'shover'—was in the back of the car. **1932** E. M. KEATE *Mimic* vi. 77 'Paulett come and shove for me on Monday... My shover's ill.' Timothy enjoyed 'shoving'. **1953** J. TRENCH *Docken Dead* ix. 127 Sir R. went out first to tell the shuvver to bring the car round to the front. **1974** E. LEMARCHAND *Buried in Past* v. 95 It was class, for one thing. His Dad had been shovver to old Mrs P's mother and father. **1976** 'J. CHARLTON' *Remington Set* xiii. 63 Rabbiting on with the Pritchards' shover.

**shoveshim** (ˈʃʌvʃɪm). *local.* [f. SHOVE *v.*[1] + SHIM *sb.*[2]] (See quot.)

**1846** *Jrnl. R. Agric. Soc.* VII. II. 591 The peas are cut by Dutch hoes or shoveshims.

**shoville**, obs. form of SHOVEL *sb.*

**shoving** (ˈʃʌvɪŋ), *vbl. sb.*[1] [f. SHOVE *v.*[1] + -ING[1].] The action or an act of SHOVE *v.*[1]

**1297** R. GLOUC. (Rolls) 4313 Þer was pultinge & ssouinge [*v.rr.* ssouyng, schuuing, schowynge, schowyng]. *c* **1386** CHAUCER *Manciple's Prol.* 53 Ther was greet showving bothe to and fro To lifte him up. **1489** CAXTON *Faytes of A.* I. ix. 23 The strengthe of shouing is at the lifte syde of men. **1568** GRAFTON *Chron.* II. 382 There was great heauing and shouyng, and many people vp. **1609** HOLLAND *Amm. Marcell.* 111 Antoninus..set his course against our State and Common-wealth, not (as they say) with spret nor oare, with shooving, or haling. **1766** GOLDSM. *Vic. W.* ix, However, after a little shoving and dragging, they at last went merrily on. **1837** CARLYLE *Fr. Rev.* II. III. v, Accelerated by ignominious shovings from sentry after sentry. **1875** BEDFORD *Sailor's Pocket Bk.* vi. (ed. 2) 214 In shoving off, when the ship is not head to wind, pull well clear of her before making sail. **1889** H. VASSALL *Rugby Football* 31 Turning now to the other great branch of forward play, namely, scrummage work, it must not for a moment be supposed that shoving is all that is wanted.

**show** (ʃəʊ), *sb.*[1] Forms: 3 (in comb.) shæw-, 4 sceu, 4–5 schewe, 4–6 *north.* schawe, 6 sheaw, sheow, shoe, shue, *Sc.* schaw, s(c)hau, 6–7 shewe, showe, 7 sho, *Sc.* schew, shaw, 6–9 shew, 6– show. [f. SHOW *v.*: cf. MLG., MDu. *schowwe* fem. (mod.Du. *schouw*), OHG. *scou* fem. (MHG. *schou*, *schow(e* fem. and masc., mod.G. *schau* fem.) looking at, inspection.]

**I. 1. a.** The action or an act of exhibiting to view or notice. Now *rare*, exc. in specific use or phrase (see 1 c, 1 d, 1 k).

*a* **1300** *Cursor M.* 28616 Lele script agh be thre-fald, Wit reuth of hert, wit sceu to preist, Betyng of sin þe thrid þer neist. *c* **1320** *Sir Tristr.* 2253 Tristrem hir bar þat tide And on þe quen fel he Next her naked side, þat mani man miȝt y se San schewe. **1399** LANGL. *Rich. Redeles* IV. 56 Some had ..schewed ffor þe shire and here schew lost. **1530** PALSGR.

267/1 Shewe of a thyng to sale, *lustre*. **1568** GRAFTON *Chron.* II. 763 The Dukes themselues entended for the shewe of their diligence, to be the first that should attend that day vpon the kinges highnesse. **1582** N. LICHEFIELD tr. *Castanheda's Conq. E. Ind.* I. ii. 7 Yᵉ next day then following (upon shew of himselfe to them) there came about the number of fifteene of his Countrey men. **1598** STOW *Surv. Lond.* 349 Two publique houses for the acting and shewe of Comedies, Tragedies, and Histories. **1600** SURFLET *Country Farm* I. ii. 2 A briefe show of that which shall more largely be described in that which followeth. **1712** ADDISON *Spect.* No. 412 ¶3 We are indeed so often.. tired out with so many repeated Shows of the same Things, that whatever is new or uncommon contributes a little to vary human Life.

†**b.** The fact of being presented to view or displayed. ***at the first show***: at first sight. *Obs.*

**1555** EDEN *Decades* (Arb.) 364 Fyrst bryngynge it [gold] furth to the open shewe. **1563** GOOGE *Eglogs, To W. Louelace* (Arb.) 24 The grosenes of my Style: whiche thus commytted to the gasynge shewe of euery eye shuld forth with disclose ye manifest foly of the Writer. **1565** T. STAPLETON *Fortr. Faith* 58 God hath placed his church in the sight and shew of the worlde. **1574** A. L. *Calvin's 4 Serm.* I, These things at the first shew seeme very straunge.

**c.** A demonstration or display of military strength or of intention to take severe measures. †Also *transf.* a manifestation of divine power. Chiefly in phr. ***to make a show***.

*a***1548** HALL *Chron., Hen. VIII*, 24 All the countrey of Arthois and Picardie, fortified their holdes and made shewes as the Englishe army passed, but thei durst not once assaile them. *c***1586** C'TESS PEMBROKE *Ps.* CXXXV. iv, Ægipts first borne in one night [God] overthrew: And yet not so his dreadfull showes he ceas'd, But did them still in Ægipts mid'st renew. **1726** SHELVOCKE *Voy. round World* 412 They made no manner of show of their arms to us. **1853** DICKENS *Child's Hist.* xx. II. 115 [Henry IV.] began his reign by making a strong show against the followers of Wickliffe. *Ibid.* xxii. 169 Jack Cade.. having made a show of his forces there.

**d.** Phr. † ***to set in show, set to show***: to exhibit to view, display (*obs.*). ***on show*** (formerly † ***in show***, † ***upon a*** or ***the show***): in process of being shown or exhibited; on view.

*a***1533** BERNERS *Gold. Bk. M. Aurel.* (1546) G ij, To sell suche marchaundyse, sette it not in so yll a shewe. **1576** GASCOIGNE *Steel Glas* (Arb.) 69 These things (my Lord) my glasse now sets to shew. *c***1590** MARLOWE *Jew of Malta* II. ii. 748 On this condition shall thy Turkes be sold. Goe Officers and set them straight in shew. **1595** A. DAY *Engl. Secretorie* Ded. A 2, In signification of the will I haue to do vnto your Lordship any acceptable seruice, [I have] no other matter in shew, then a fresh renouation of the selfe same title by a second presentment. **1681** DRYDEN *Abs. & Achit.* I. 688 His joy conceal'd, he sets himself to show. **1711** ADDISON *Spect.* No. 255 ¶8 His Actions.. lose their Lustre when they are drawn at large, and set to show by his own Hand. **1737** BRACKEN *Farriery Impr.* (1757) II. 34 They generally buy Horses when upon a Shew (as it is called) in the Dealer's Hand, which is the Way to be deceived. *Ibid.* 35 As to his Spirit which appears upon the Shew, it is all forced. **1890** *Spectator* 22 Nov. 733/2 We proceed to look at the tables and chairs and other things on show.

†**e.** ***to make*** or ***give show of***: to manifest, display, indicate. *Obs.*

**1596** DANETT tr. *Comines* (1614) 222, I haue seene his pourtraiture.. the lineaments whereof made shew of an excellent wit. **1607** TOPSELL *Four-f. Beasts* 152 The good and aproued hounds.. when they haue found the Hare, make shew therof to the hunter. **1642** H. MORE *Song of Soul* I. I. xx, Those parts the eye is near give not the shew Of any colour. **1697** DAMPIER *Voy.* I. 288 Shaking their Lances at us, [they] made all the shew of hatred that they could invent.

†**f.** ***in show of***: by way of indicating or expressing, in token of. *Obs.*

**1653** H. COGAN tr. *Pinto's Trav.* xix. 68 Vailing their two top sails in shew of obedience.

**g.** ***to give*** (*one*) ***a show of***: to let (one) see (and partake of). *Sc.*

**1788** PICKEN *Pooms* 58 Come tak' a seat, an' gies a shaw O' your snuff-horn.

**h.** ***show of hands***: the holding up the hand above the head, as a means by which the members of an assembly indicate their vote or judgement upon a proposition.

**1789** SCOTT in J. Haggard *Rep. Consist. Crt.* (1822) I. 13 It often happens that on a shew of hands, the person has the majority, who on a poll is lost in a minority. **1837** DICKENS *Pickw.* xiii, There was a show of hands; the Mayor decided in favour of the honourable Samuel Slumkey.. Horatio Fizkin, Esquire.. demanded a poll. **1912** *Times* 19 Dec. 18/5 At each of the meetings the scheme appeared to be approved on a show of hands.

**2. a.** The external aspect (of a person or thing). Now *rhet.* or *poet.* in this gen. sense.

**1555** WATREMAN *Fardle Facions* I. iv. 39 Dyuers peoples.. monstruous and of hugly shewe. **1566** DRANT *Hor. Sat.* II. vii, I ij b, His master, goes in sage attyre: that geues a sober shue. **1594** WILLOBIE *Avisa* xlvii. (Grosart) 96 Say, 'twas her wit & modest shoe, That made you like and loue her so. **1602** SHAKS. *Ham.* I. ii. 85 But I haue that Within, which passeth show; These, but the Trappings, and the Suites of woe. **1611** BIBLE *Isa.* iii. 9 The shew of their countenance doeth witnesse against them. *a***1781** WATSON *Philip III*, III. (1793) I. 296 Under the simple show.. of a citizen, he concealed all the qualities of a hero. **1799** WORDSW. *Poems Sentim., Poet's Epit.* 45 The outward shows of sky and earth, Of hill and valley, he has viewed. **1840** CARLYLE *Heroes* iii. (1841) 136 Men worship the shows of great men; the most disbelieve that there is any reality of great men to worship.

**b.** ***in show***, in appearance. Often with the idea that the reality behind is different (cf. 6, 7): In appearance only, ostensibly, seemingly. Also (rarely) ***with show***.

*a***1586** SIDNEY *Arcadia* I. ii. §7 While hee was speaking, there came a boy in shew like a Merchants prentice. **1597** HOOKER *Eccl. Pol.* v. xlviii. §10 Otherwise they are but in shew opposite and not in truth. **1597** GERARDE *Herbal* I. xxxv. 48 The small Flower de-luce of Dalmatia is in shew like to the precedent. **1614** GORGES *Lucan* v. 187 With shew the Vrne the lots decides. **1647** N. BACON *Disc. Govt. Eng.* I. lviii. (1739) 108 The place of the Chief Justice was in shew but one Office. **1732** LEDIARD *Sethos* II. x. 365 She had let the council of state.. subsist in shew. **1817** JAS. MILL *Brit. India* III. VI. i. 51 To have two governing bodies; the one real, the other only in show. **1871** FREEMAN *Norm. Conq.* xvii. (1876) IV. 54 The King by the edge of the sword changed himself in all outward show into a King according to the laws of England.

†**c.** ***to the show***: to outward view or appearance, as far as appearance goes. *Obs.*

**1556** ROBINSON *More's Utopia* I. (Arb.) 44 This iustice is more beautiful in apperaunce, and more florishynge to the shewe, then either iuste or profitable. **1609** BIBLE (Douay) *Isa.* vi. 13 She.. shal be to the shew [Vulg. *in ostensionem*] as a terebinth, and as an oke.

**d.** ***to have*** (†***bear***, †***carry***) ***a*** (or ***the***) ***show of***: to wear the appearance of; to appear to be, appear to partake of; to look like, resemble. *arch.* or *Obs.*

**1581** CAMPION in *Confer.* III. (1584) T iij, He gaue them that which had the name of wine, and had the shewe of it, but.. was not in deede wine. **1581** *Act 23 Eliz.* c. 9 § 2 Which Coulers.. carrye a shewe of a good true and perfitte couler of woaded and mathered Blacke. **1611** BIBLE *Col.* ii. 23 Which things haue in deed a shew of wisedome. **1613** DAY *Festivals* v. (1615) 124 Even of those that beare the shew of the purest Professors amongst us. **1625** BACON *Ess., Simulation* (Arb.) 510 Simulation and Dissimulation, commonly carry with them a Shew of Fearfulnesse.

†**e.** ***for show***: to save appearances, 'for the look of the thing'. *Obs.*

*a***1700** DRYDEN *Cymon & Iph.* 637 The Kindred of the Slain forgive the Deed; But a short Exile must for Show precede. *a***1715** BURNET *Own Time* (1897) I. ix. 398 They were not to be surprised, if the Danes seemed at first to talk high: that was to be done for shew: but they would grow calmer when they should engage.

**f.** *Theol.* and *Philos.* Used occas. as an equivalent for 'accident', 'phenomenon', 'species'.

**1560** JEWEL *Serm. at Paul's Cross* C viij, The accidents of the bread, (that is to say) the whitenes or roundenes, or other sutch outward fourmes or shewes of breade, as he seeth with his eye. **1678** CUDWORTH *Intell. Syst.* I. i. §5. 7 Intentional Species or Shews, propagated from the Objects to our Senses.

**3. a.** With qualifying word: A (fine, striking, etc.) appearance; an appearance which makes a strong impression on the beholder. Usu. in phr. ***to make*** (†***bear***, †***yield***) ***a*** (fine, etc.) ***show***. Also without qualification, a fine or striking appearance, imposing display. Also ***to put up a*** (good, etc.) ***show***: to give (such) an account of oneself.

*c***1550–80** *Robin Consc.* in Hazl. *E.P.P.* III. 239 Bvt and I liue another yeer, I will haue a better showe; I will not goe thvs slvttishly, I trowe. **1592** BABINGTON *Notes Gen.* vii. 32 b, About the beginning of May, when all things flourished and yeelded show. **1610** HOLLAND *Camden's Brit.* (1637) 277 Windesore beareth a goodly shew. **1686** tr. *Chardin's Trav. Persia* 263 And all to make a shew and dazle the world. **1743** J. MORRIS *Serm.* ii. 34 They rather affected to exercise those gifts, which make a great shew. **1840** THACKERAY *Barber Cox* July, Their names made a famous show in the bills. **1881** WESTCOTT & HORT *Grk. N.T.* I. 548 After Eusebius they [i.e. Western quotations] make no show in Greek theology. **1905** R. BAGOT *Passport* xxi. 205 The furniture.. made a sorry show of comfort in the huge rooms. **1934** A. P. HERBERT *Holy Deadlock* 265 They've got to run the thing as they find it; and I think they put up a jolly good show. **1941** 'G. ORWELL' in *World Rev.* (1950) June 41 Impossible to guess what kind of show the Russians can put up.

†**b.** ***to have some show***: to present a specious or plausible appearance; to have weight with, or commend itself to, others; also, to appear likely, 'promise' (*to* do something). *Obs.*

**1560** DAUS tr. *Sleidane's Comm.* XI. 151 b, At the fyrst, he covered his mynde craftely, that his writte myght have some shewe [*ut aliquam haberet speciem diplomа*]. **1574** WHITGIFT *Def. Answ.* III. ii. 143 The places of the 44. of Ezechiel haue some shew in them. **1606** KNOLLES tr. *Bodin's Commw.* I. v. 34 These arguments haue some good show to proue that seruitude is naturall, profitable, and honest.

**c.** (Now only *U.S.*, *Austral.*, and *N.Z.*) An opportunity for displaying or exerting oneself; a chance, 'opening'. Phr. ***to give*** (a person) ***a show; to have*** or ***stand a*** (or ***no***) ***show***. Const. *for*, *to* (do something).

Continuity of the mod. use with that in quot. 1579 is hardly possible, but the notion seems to be closely similar.

**1579** LYLY *Euphues* (Arb.) 41 Education can haue no shewe, where the excellencye of Nature doth beare sway. *Ibid.* 62 Where loue beareth sway, friendship can haue no shewe. **1864** 'MARK TWAIN' in Harte & 'Twain' *Sk. Sixties* (1926) iv. 141 Give him another show. **1866** H. W. HARPER *Lett. from N.Z.* (1914) 102 There was a general response: 'We'll be there, and give you a show', a bit of diggers' slang, which I found meant—'Here's your chance, can you use it?' **1876–7** 'R. BOLDREWOOD' *Colonial Reformer* (1890) II. xvi. 42 As he's a gentleman, he's bound to give you a show. **1884** *Lisbon* (Dakota) *Star* 22 Aug., He stood no show of securing the nomination for the legislature. **1888** *Boston* (Mass.) *Jrnl.* 10 Dec. 2/3 Must we found an O'Brien dynasty to convince outsiders that men of Celtic blood have a fair show in Boston? **1891** N. GOULD *Double Event* 70 He thought Caloola had a big show for the Sydney Derby.

**d.** *dial.* Applied to the display made by an animal when at its best; e.g. the plumage of a cock-bird at pairing-time, the udder of a cow.

**1886** NEWTON in *Encycl. Brit.* XXI. 54/2 (*Ruff*), The cock-bird, when out of his nuptial attire, or, to use the fenman's expression, when he has not 'his show on'. **1886** *Sale-catalogue* in *W. Somerset Word-bk.* s.v., Grand heifer, splendid show.

**4. a.** In generalized sense: Ostentatious display.

**1713** ADDISON *Trial Count Tariff* 14 The Court.. upon Examination found him a True Spaniard: Nothing but Show and Beggary. **1817** MAR. EDGEWORTH *Ormond* i, Sir Ulick.. loved shew and company. **1859** *Habits Gd. Society* v. 233 Yet it [the zither] is not calculated for large concerts: we English must have noise and show.

†**b.** ***of show***: suited for display; fine, splendid.

**1573–80** TH. M. *To Rdr.* xi. in *Baret's Alv.* A vj/2 These floures of shewe.. Are here in Hiue. *a***1668** LASSELS *Voy. Italy* (1698) II. 119 They shewed me.. curious saddles, harness, liveries of show embroidered with gold and silver. **1789** MRS. PIOZZI *Journ. France* II. 169 Wealth diffused makes all men comfortable, and leaves no man splendid... Objects of show are therefore unfrequent in England.

**c.** ***for show***: for the sake of mere appearance or display, as opposed to utility.

*a***1700** EVELYN *Diary* Aug. 1641 (Haarlem), A faire payre of organs, which I could not find they made use of in divine service,.. but only for shewe. **1849** DK. RUTLAND in *Croker Papers* (1884) III. 195, I apprehend that for night use they [the pillows] were large, and were replaced by small ones for show during the day. **1886** RUSKIN *Præterita* I. vi. 184 My father.. never would have paid the cost of an extra horse for show.

**5. a.** An appearance or display (*of* something, a quality, activity, sentiment, etc.) to which there is at least some degree of reality to correspond. Chiefly in negative contexts or with a limiting word (*some, some little*).

**1581** LAMBARDE *Eiren.* I. v. (1602) 26 It hath some shew of question. **1604** E. G[RIMSTONE] *D'Acosta's Hist. Indies* v. xxvii. 408 In other things their customes and ceremonies have some shew of reason. **1668** DRYDEN *Secret Love* Pref. a 1 b, If this with any shew of reason may be defended. **1841** THACKERAY *Gt. Hoggarty Diam.* xii, Whereupon, that gentleman, with some little show of alarm, told her that [etc.]. **1872** BLACK *Adv. Phaeton* xviii. 244 When she is in the house, I am treated with some show of attention.

**b.** An indication, sign or token *of* something; a trace or vestige *of*. Now only in negative contexts.

**1563** *Homilies* II. *Inform.* II. Vvvj, Yet let vs not be scorners.. for that is the vttermost token & shewe of a reprobate. **1600** HAKLUYT *Voy.* III. 394 Here are many mountaines that beare shewes of mettals, but they went not to see them. **1604** E. G[RIMSTONE] tr. *D'Acosta's Hist. Indies* I. xxv. 79 These markes and shewes of a deluge. **1611** SPEED *Hist. Gt. Brit.* IX. xv. (1623) 810 Vexation of mind and distemperature of body carried apparant shewes in his face. **1718** HICKES & NELSON *Kettlewell* I. i. 2 It fell into Decay, and now hath no Shew of its ancient Grandeur. **1821** SCOTT *Kenilw.* xvi, No show or sign of greeting passed between the Earls.

**c.** (*a*) *U.S.* and *Austral.* An indication of the presence of metal in a mining ground, of oil in a well, etc.

[**1600**: cf. 5 b]. **1756** W. FAIRFAX *Let.* 26 Apr. in S. M. Hamilton *Lett. to Washington* (1898) I. 231 Prospect of great Wealth from his Share of a Copper Mine.. which has a Show of much rich Ore. **1864** *Harper's Mag.* Dec. 60/2 A young farmer.. was eloquent upon the 'show' the new well had made. **1870** CONE & JOHNS *Petrolia* 144 (Cent.) The depth to which a well is drilled is.. regulated.. sometimes by the show, as it is called, of the oil in the well. **1876–7** VENNOR in *Geol. Survey of Canada* 304 The best *shows* of the mineral [apatite] occur on the first part of lot nineteen. **1916** *Daily Colonist* (Victoria, B.C.) 29 July 4/3 The copper deposits which have been examined have not advanced beyond the stage of prospectors' shows. **1949** *Amer. Speech* XXIV. 34 *Black gold, crude, crude oil,.. show,* and *showing* are synonyms. **1975** *North Sea Background Notes* (Brit. Petroleum Co.) 19 Ten days later a more encouraging show was found at a deeper level, but it was two months before the company was able to announce that it had indeed made the first commercial discovery of gas in the North Sea.

(*b*) *Austral.* A mine.

**1931** V. PALMER *Separate Lives* 186 He's sitting on twelve thousand since he got rid of his cobalt show, and he can't spend that here. **1942** [see NEVER *adv.* 9]. **1948** V. PALMER *Golconda* ii. 9 During the war they had rehabilitated themselves by carting wolfram on camels from a show they had discovered on the Western Australian border.

**d.** An appearance or 'promise' *of* or *for* something that is to come. *Obs.* exc. *dial.*

**1648** GAGE *West Ind.* 90 The Indians comforted us with the shews of fair weather. **1768** *Ann. Reg., Hist. Europe* 133/1 The season seems critical and the shew for plenty not yet to be relied upon. **1886** *W. Somerset Word-bk.* s.v., There's a fine *show* for apples—*i.e.* prospect or appearance of a crop.

**6. a.** An unreal or illusory appearance (*of* something); an appearance with little or no reality behind it.

**1547** *Homilies* I. *Good Wks.* I. C ij b, They be but shadowes & shewes of liuely and good thynges, & not good and liuely thynges in deede. **1639** N. N. tr. *Du Bosq's Compl. Woman* I. 8 There is a shew onely of good in these kinde of Pamphlets. **1700** ROWE *Amb. Step-Mother* I. i. 215 Disdain those shews of Danger. **1873** SYMONDS *Grk. Poets* vii. 227 True: for it gives a show of seeming health; And shows are good, although there be no substance.

**b.** In generalized sense: Empty appearance without reality.

**1583** MELBANCKE *Philotimus* C j b, They scatter the meate they haue in their mouthes, while they scratch for the shadowe which deludes them with shew. **1856** MISS YONGE *Daisy Chain* xiv. 139 'Ah!' she thought, 'if he knew how ill I behaved! It is all show and hollowness with me'.

**7. a.** An appearance (*of* some quality, feeling, activity, etc.) assumed with more or less intention to deceive; a feigned or misleading appearance; a simulation or pretence. Also, a half-hearted or inchoate attempt or 'offer' (*of* doing something). Formerly often *pl.*

*c* **1526** TINDALE *Introd. Ep. Rom.* a iij, Though their be.. never so glorious an outewarde shewe and apperance off honeste lyvynge. **1596** DRAYTON *Leg. Robt. Norm.* 473 To cloath Treason in a vertuous show. **1611** BIBLE *Luke* xx. 47 Which deuoure widowes houses, and for a shew [προφάσει] make long prayers. **1725** POPE *Odyss.* IV. 966 Ill suits it with your shews of duteous zeal, From me the purpos'd voyage to conceal. **1827** SCOTT *Highl. Widow* v, Whether he purposed by a show of resistance, to provoke them to kill him on the spot. **1849** MACAULAY *Hist. Eng.* ii. I. 267 [They] were heard, if not with approbation, yet with the show of acquiescence. **1867** FREEMAN *Norm. Conq.* (1876) I. vi. 449 His refusal was cloked under a show of feudal loyalty. **1885** *L'pool Daily Post* 7 May 5/3 It was instructive to witness Mr. John Hughes rise, and with great show of indignation, gibe at his leader.

**b.** ***to make* (*a*) *show***, to assume an appearance which is more or less deceptive; to make a pretence or feint, pretend. Const. *of*, †*for*, †*to* with inf.; †also with *as though*, *as if* and clause. Also, to make a half-hearted beginning or attempt at doing something; const. *of* with n. of action.

**1559** FECKNAM in Strype *Ann. Ref.* (1709) I. II. App. ix. 25 Every Booke made a shewe to be set furthe accordinge to the syncere Word of God. **1568** GRAFTON *Chron.* II. 340 Such as were wicked and maliciously mynded, would not depart, but made a shewe as though they would do somewhat. **1611** BIBLE *Gal.* vi. 12 As many as desire to make a faire shew in the flesh. **1635** R. N. tr. *Camden's Hist. Eliz.* III. 268 Whatsoever he revealed, the Queene made shew as if she understood it all before. **1640** tr. *Verdere's Rom. of Rom.* II. l. 195 Trasiclea.. peradventure is not so much displeased, as she makes shew for. **1653** H. COGAN tr. *Pinto's Trav.* x. 30 They made shew as though they would be gone. **1653** HOLCROFT *Procopius, Pers. Wars* I. 3 The Ephthalites made shew to be much affraid. *a* **1674** CLARENDON *Hist. Reb.* XI. §98 They made great shows of being mutually glad to see each other. **1819** SCOTT *Leg. Montrose* xv, The Lowland cavalry made a show of charging. **1863** DICKENS *Let. W. Collins* 24 Sept. in *Pall Mall Gaz.* (1891) 23 Oct. 3/1 Two little men, who did nothing, made a show of doing it all.

**c.** ***by show of*, *under a show of***: under pretence or pretext of, by alleging as a pretext or authority.

**1625** BACON *Ess., Judicature* ¶1 And by Shew of [*ed.* 1612 by colour of] Antiquitie, to introduce Noueltie. **1681** W. ROBERTSON *Phraseol. Gen.* 1119/2 Under a shew of friendship, *per simulationem amicitiæ*.

**d.** ***to put on* (or *up*) *a show***: to present a good appearance that conceals the reality; to put a good or brave face on something.

**1953** B. GORDON-CUMMING *Gentle Rain* 140 'It was encouraging to see her looking so nice, wasn't it?'.. 'I expect she was putting on a show for our sakes.' **1960** O. MANNING *Great Fortune* III. xviii. 215 He had learnt to 'put up a show'. He had hidden his fears and uncertainties.

**II.** *concr.* Something shown or presented to view.

**8. a.** A person or thing exhibited or gazed at as an object of admiration, curiosity, mockery, or the like. ***to make a show of***, to exhibit to public view; to expose to public contempt.

**1535** COVERDALE *Col.* ii. 15 And hath spoyled rule and power, and hath made a shewe of them openly. **1560** DAUS tr. *Sleidane's Comm.* x. 136 b, The kyng and his two fellowes were caried hither and thither vnto Prynces, for a shewe and mockery. **1605** SHAKS. *Macb.* v. viii. 24 Then yeeld thee Coward, And liue to be the shew, and gaze o' th' time. **1618** BOLTON *Florus* III. iii. (1636) 170 Theutobocchus,.. being apprehended.. was single an whole shew himselfe. **1791** 'G. GAMBADO' *Ann. Horsem.* x. (1809) 109, I could have sold my horse for a hundred guineas, as a show. **1810** CRABBE *Borough* ii. 97 That marble arch, our sexton's favourite show. **1818** BYRON *Ch. Har.* IV. xviii, [Venice] Perchance even dearer in her day of woe, Than when she was a boast, a marvel, and a show. **1842** *Murray's Hand-bk. N. Italy* 17/2 The *Armeria Regia*.. is considered as one of the principal *shows* of Turin.

**b.** Something mechanically contrived or put together as an object for exhibition or display.

**1587** MASCALL *Cattle, Sheep* (1596) 236 Others set vp shewes of dead Dogges heades, which is to feare any wilde beast in comming to the folde. **1590** E. WEBBE *Trav.* (Arb.) 29 In which shew or Arke there was thirteene thousand seuerall peeces of fire worke.

**c.** *transf.* A person whose appearance is likely to attract notice for its oddity, etc.; a 'sight'; an object of contemptuous pity.

**1700** T. BROWN *Amusem. Ser. & Com., Lond.* 28 That Wheezing Sickly Shew.. is the Devil's Broker. **1749** JOHNSON *Van. Hum. Wishes* 318 And Swift expires a Driv'ler and a Show.

†**9.** Something put forward or exhibited as a specimen or sample. *Obs.*

**1572** N. LICHEFIELD tr. *Castanheda's Conq. E. Ind.* I. xxix. 72 b, With this Caruel he sent a man of that Countrey for a shew, by what kinde of people the same was inhabited. **1639** S. DU VERGER tr. *Camus' Admir. Events* A iiij, This booke is so little, that it is but a shew, which breeds a wish for an ampler piece.

**10. a.** *gen.* A sight, spectacle. Usually with qualifying word.

**1577** HANMER *Anc. Eccl. Hist., Euagrius Schol.* II. xiii. 437 This lamentable destruction reached.. from Constantines market vnto the market of Taurus, a pitiefull shewe and dredfull to behold. **1639** ROUSE *Heav. Univ.* iii. (1702) 24 So neither are they presented to us as bare sights, Shews, and Spectacles. **1673-4** GREW *Anat. Plants* III. ii. (1682) 127 In the Leaves of Pine, they [the Pores] are likewise through a Glass a very Elegant Show. **1712** ADDISON *Spect.* No. 412 ¶6 We no where meet with a more glorious or pleasing Show in Nature than what appears in the Heavens at the rising and setting of the Sun. **1806** WORDSW. *Addr. Child* 27 That one upright twig.. Studded with apples, a beautiful show! **1908** [MISS E. FOWLER] *Betw. Trent & Ancholme* 28 The golden Alyssum grows, a beautiful show in the spring.

**b.** *dial.* A picture or print in a book.

*a* **1837** MRS. PALMER *Dial. Devon. Dial.* I. (1839) 1, I.. was looking to zee if there be any shows [*footn.* prints or pictures] in en. **1901** F. E. TAYLOR *Folk-Sp. S. Lancs.* (E.D.D.), Aw loike a book wi' plenty o' shows in it.

**11.** A phantasmal appearance; an apparition.

**1611** SHAKS. *Cymb.* v. v. 428 As I slept, me thought Great Iupiter vpon his Eagle back'd Appear'd to me, with other sprightly shewes Of mine owne Kindred. **1645** USSHER *Body Div.* 117 What mean you by Visions? Their appearing ..to the mind and inward senses, either in the night by dreams.. or in the day by some strange shows, as they did to the Prophets. *a* **1700** DRYDEN *Flower & Leaf* 481 What you saw, was all a Fairy Show.

**12. a.** A display on a large scale of objects for public inspection; esp. a temporary exhibition in a particular place and under special regulations of objects (e.g. flowers, cattle, motor-cars) arranged so as to facilitate inspection, comparison or purchase.

**1816** JANE AUSTEN *Emma* III. xviii. 338 You were both talking of other things; of business, shows of cattle, or new drills. **1837** YOUATT *Sheep* 317 From the 1st to the 8th of June the members shall not show their rams, except to one another. They shall begin their general show on the 8th of June. **1840** *Jrnl. R. Agric. Soc.* I. p. lviii, The show of live-stock [at the Oxford Meeting] was numerous. **1864** *Field* 2 July 8/2 Show of Horses at the Agricultural Hall, Islington. *Ibid.* 71/3 The aristocratic shows of the Royal Horticultural Society. **1913** *Illustr. Lond. News* 22 Feb. 260/1 In previous years the Aero Show.. has utterly failed to attract the general public.

**b.** A display *of* objects casually brought or found together.

**1695** WOODWARD *Nat. Hist. Earth* VI. (1723) 295 July, and August.. exhibit a still different Shew of Vegetables. **1885** *Field* 7 Feb. 147/3 The chief feature of the day was the fine show of foxes at Gumley.

**13. a.** A spectacle elaborately prepared or arranged in order to entertain a number of spectators; a pageant, masque, procession, or similar display on a large scale.

Often used, esp. in *pl.*, for the displays of the theatre and circus in ancient Rome (*spectacula*, *ludi*). Not applied to a regular dramatic performance (but see 15, and cf. DUMB SHOW). For *Lord Mayor's Show* see LORD MAYOR 1.

**1561** [see DUMB SHOW]. **1575** LANEHAM *Let.* (1871) 1 Too bee prezent at any sheaw or spectacl. **1588** SHAKS. *L.L.L.* v. i. 118 The King would haue mee present the Princesse.. with some delightfull ostentation, or show, or pageant. **1629** HOBBES *Thucyd.* II. 90 All the dedicated vessels belonging to the Shewes and Games. **1770** LANGHORNE *Plutarch, Sylla* (1879) I. 515/1 A few months after, he presented the people with a shew of gladiators. **1797** BURKE *Regic. Peace* iii. Wks. VIII. 393 It is a shew, and a spectacle, not a play, that is exhibited. **1849** MACAULAY *Hist. Eng.* iv. I. 474 It is surely the height of absurdity to shut out the populace from a show of which the main object is to make an impression on the populace. **1911** T. S. HOLMES *Orig. Chr. Ch. Gaul* ii. 43 It was the last day of the shows.

**b.** In generalized sense: Pageantry.

**1912** *Stage Year Bk.* 9 Without stage show Shakespeare would not be so popular.

**14. a.** In more trivial use: An exhibition of strange objects, wild beasts, dancers, acrobats, etc., held usually in a booth or portable building, with a small charge for admission. (A number of these are often set up side by side at a fair, or within the enclosure of a large 'exhibition'. Cf. SIDE-SHOW.)

Often with defining word: cf. PEEP-SHOW, PUPPET-SHOW, RAREE-SHOW.

**1760-72** H. BROOKE *Fool of Qual.* (1792) IV. 198 All were obliged to pay treble prices, on account of the unprecedented novelty of the shew [a lion and dog in one cage]. **1825** HONE *Every-Day Bk.* I. 1175 Atkin's Menagerie ..one of the largest shows in the fair. *Ibid.* 1185 Another penny show: 'The Wonderful Children on the Tight Rope, and Dancing Horse'. **1835** DICKENS *Sk. Boz, Greenwich Fair*, The travelling menageries, or to speak more intelligibly, the 'Wild-beast shows'. **1855** BARNUM *Life* x. (Low) 252 We concluded to take a tour through the 'penny shows', the vans of which lined one side of the [race-]course. **1862** 'ARTEMUS WARD' *His Bk.* (1865) Note before title-p., At the Door of the Tent. Ladies and Gentlemen, the Show is about to commence. **1886** *W. Somerset Word-bk.*, *Show*, an exhibition of any kind; a performance, whether circus, wild-beast show, wax-work, or theatricals.

**b.** The booth or building (with its contents).

**1840** DICKENS *Old C. Shop* xix, At his heels went Thomas Codlin, bearing the show as usual. *Ibid.*, Short was.. knocking the characters in the fury of the combat against the sides of the show. **1874** T. FROST *Old Showmen* 22 The practice of displaying in front of the shows large pictures of the wonderful feats, or curious natural objects, to be seen within.

**15. a.** Applied to any kind of public display; e.g. an exhibition of pictures, a dramatic performance in a theatre, *colloq.* or *jocularly* to a fashionable ceremony or gathering, a speech-making, etc.

**1830** J. CONSTABLE *Let.* (1965) III. 26, I have laid by my Wood, to enable me to pay some old and just debts, to Smith, to Woodburn, & others—which I shall have ready for the 'show' I hope. **1844** J. COWELL *Thirty Years passed among Players* xvii. 42/2, I consented to become his guest for a week, and 'show my show' in the town-hall. **1863** SALA in *Temple Bar* VIII. 278 It has been my vocation to see shows. First nights of new pieces; private views of picture exhibitions;.. royal marriages and funerals;.. layings of first stones; openings of railways. **1886** *Stage Gossip* 69 The theatre itself is invariably in slang parlance, alluded to as the 'show'. **1896** *N.Y. Dramatic News* 4 July 12/1 [The circus] well merited its title of the 'greatest show on earth'. **1907** H. WYNDHAM *Flare of Footlights* viii, 'I hate matinées', exclaimed Miss Assherton. 'Giving two shows in one day quite tires me out'. **1912** W. OWEN *Let.* 23 June (1967) 142 Methought I was treating you to a Show at a Picture Palace! **1935** J. REITH *Diary* 4 July (1975) 121 This was a very good show, interesting people, plenty of room, and plenty to eat. **1963** *Listener* 31 Jan. 210/1 That these painters were not a handful of isolated figures was made plain by the Whitechapel show devoted to recent Australian painting. This show.. was, however eclectic it may have been, still an intelligent reflection of one man's taste. **1978** *Lancashire Life* Sept. 89/2 My favourite Blackpool show? Unhesitatingly, I nominate *No, No, Nanette*.

**b.** *Mil. slang.* An engagement, battle, or raid; a war. Also ***big show***, a major campaign. Cf. DO *sb.*[1] 2 b.

**1892** KIPLING *Barrack-Room Ballads* 59 What was the end of all the show, Johnnie, Johnnie? Ask my Colonel, for I don't know. **1914** R. BROOKE *Let.* Dec. (1968) 644, I entered this show (Sub-lieutenant R. Brooke R.N.D. at your service) in September and by the end of the month was in a trench. **1915** T. E. LAWRENCE *Let.* 29 Aug. (1938) 199 This Dardanelles show lags all the time... The big show must go wrong or go right first. **1918** E. A. MACKINTOSH *War, the Liberator* IV. 129 'Oh, God,' he whispered, 'don't let us get casualties before we start the show.' **1924** J. GALSWORTHY *White Monkey* II. xi. 205, I should very much dislike being blown up.. but I should still more dislike missing the next show. **1939** A. B. CALLAWAY *With Packs & Rifles* ii. 20 With less than a month's training I was on my way across to the big show. **1942** *R.A.F. Jrnl.* 18 Apr. 10 At the end of the show I flew to Mosul. **1944** V. G. GARVIN tr. *Gary's Forest of Anger* xxvi. 110 The convoy was strongly guarded... Scenting 'a big show', the three Zborowski brothers spent their nights prowling round the lorries. **1977** *Daily Tel.* 15 Mar. 12/6 He was there in '98, I think, for the Malakand show. **1980** P. FITZGERALD *Human Voices*. ix. 135 The pale pink smoke of London's fires.. reminded him of a quiet sector of the line in the last show.

**c.** In radio and television, a light entertainment programme; more generally in the U.S., any kind of broadcast.

**1932**, etc. [see *radio show* s.v. RADIO *sb.* 7]. **1937** *Amer. Speech* XII. 101 *Show* is used to designate nearly every type of broadcast. **1949** [see SERVICE *sb.*[1] 31 c]. **1956** B. HOLIDAY *Lady sings Blues* (1973) xv. 124 If you're an American citizen and unless you go to bed early these nights, you're liable to see me on the late-late show. **1964** MRS L. B. JOHNSON *White House Diary* 22 Apr. (1970) 116 In a few minutes I got a call from Lyndon's office saying, 'Turn on TV and watch the David Brinkley Show.' **1972** *Listener* 22 Jan. 124/3 If we do get breakfast television, the chat show will flourish.

**16. a.** *slang* (*fig.* use of senses 14, 15). A matter or affair, a 'concern'. Also with qualifying word (esp. *good*, *bad*). Also, a body or collection of persons. ***to boss*** or ***run the show***: to assume chief management or control. ***to run one's own show***: to be independent. ***to give the show away***: to blab; to betray the deficiencies, pretentiousness, etc. of an affair in which a number of persons are concerned.

**1797** H. W. FOSTER *Coquette* 138 The show is over, as we yankees say; and the girl is my own. **1851** N. KINGSLEY *Diary* 29 Jan. (1914) 171 He got 500 dollars for his share, which takeing the show as we now have it I think was a plenty. **1879** L. TROUBRIDGE *Life amongst Troubridges* (1966) 152 Tanner [the maid] was tweaked up in a cap as our 'Aunt'. She rather gave the show away by dashing forward to open the cab door! **1889** *Daily News* 9 Feb. 6/1 The U.B. endeavoured.. to control the funds and operations of the League—to 'boss the show', as Sir Charles suggested, making use of a familiar American expression. **1898** DAVITT *Life & Progr. Australia* I. iv. 15 Compared with the working and machinery at 'Bayley's Reward' [a mine] the Lord Fingall concern appeared a very small show. **1899** DELANNOY *Nineteen Thous. Pounds* xxx, I didn't want to give the show away. **1900** W. S. CHURCHILL in *Morning Post* 12 Apr. 5/7 'Yes,' replied the subaltern laconically, 'shoulder smashed up.' We expressed our sympathy. 'Oh, that's all right; good show wasn't it? The men are awfully pleased.' **1901** *Essex Weekly Herald* 8 Mar. 3/3, I do not wish to be tried by this court, because I have never had any pity from this show. **1922** 'R. CROMPTON' *More William* ix. 156 Life was a rotten show. **1927** E. M. FORSTER *Aspects of Novel* viii. 205 James.. has.. a very short list of characters. .. For so fine a novelist it is a poor show. **1932** *Sun* (Baltimore) 23 Sept. 1/5 Farm representatives viewed the decision as another victory for the banker element which they fear intends to 'run the show'. **1946** L. P. HARTLEY *Sixth Heaven* iv. 95 You made a mistake.. to absent yourself from the 'rag'—it was a really good show. **1955** *Times* 15 Aug. 6/1 They wanted to be independent... The Sudanese people wanted to 'run their own show'. **1957** J. BRAINE *Room at Top* vii. 61 The accountants and the engineers run the show no matter who's in charge. **1959** *Listener* 5 Nov. 766/1 He.. came back with the bowl empty, which was taken by his mother as a jolly good show. **1969** *New Yorker* 12 Apr. 115 The astronauts.. like to think they are running their own show. **1974** D. SEAMAN *Bomb that could Lip-Read* xi. 92 It's a bad show, Dickie... Why didn't you go straight in to clobber those terrorists?

**b.** ***bad*** (also ***poor***) ***show!***: an expression of dismay or disapprobation. Opp. ***good show!*** = an excellent performance or production! fine! splendid!

**1916** H. YOXALL *Jrnl.* 18 Sept. in *Fashion of Life* (1966) iv. 37 They intend to do nothing to provide us with battle hdqrs. Bad show. **1936** 'M. INNES' *Death at President's Lodgings* x. 187 'Poor show,' said Horace. 'Distinctly where we step off,' said Mike. **1940** 'GUN BUSTER' *Return via Dunkirk* II. xvi. 195 The Battle of All Time is about to commence. Probably shan't get back. Jolly good show, chaps. Jolly good show. **1956** J. SYMONS *Paper Chase* iv. 12 Transport definitely not laid on to time. Bad show. **1963** N. MARSH *Dead Water* (1964) v. 123 'Bad show,' he said. 'Apologise. Not myself.'

**c.** ***the show must go on***: things (orig. a circus or theatrical peformance) must carry on as planned despite difficulty, calamity, etc.; ***to get the show on the road***: to get started (*colloq.*); ***to steal the show***: see STEAL *v.*[1] 4h; ***to stop the show***: see STOP *v.* 23c.

**1941** E. HOLDING *Speak of Devil* xvii. 281 The hotel business is like the theatre. No matter what happens, the show must go on. **1943** *Amer. N. & Q.* Jan. 159/1 The Show Must Go On..is still primarily a circus slogan, although it can certainly be regarded as an axiom, in a lesser degree, of any form of show business, including the theatre. **1957** J. BLISH *Fallen Star* II. vii. 88 They came trooping into the thawing shack... 'That's enough,' Jayne said at last. 'Let's get this show on the road.' **1957** 'GYPSY ROSE LEE' *Gypsy* xxxiv. 309 Gertrude Lawrence, with a true show-must-go-on attitude had accepted my degree *in absentia*. **1961** L. MUMFORD *City in History* viii. 231 For the Roman the whole routine of the spectacle became a compulsive one: *The show must go on!* **1973** M. RUSSELL *Double Hit* ix. 67 Now we can start to make plans... There's no harm in getting the show on the road. **1978** R. HILL *Pinch of Snuff* i. 10 How'd she look at the end of the film? I've heard that the show must go on, but this is ridiculous.

**d.** ***all over the show*** = ***all over the shop*** s.v. SHOP *sb.* 8c.

**1947** 'A. P. GASKELL' *Big Game* 24 Is he very shickered? Yes; he's all over the show. **1980** M. DRABBLE *Middle Ground* 171 The district's not what it was... Arabs, all over the show. Shocking, isn't it?

**III.** Technical uses.

**17.** *Med.* A sanguino-serous discharge from the vagina prior to labour. Also, the first appearance of a menstrual flow. (*Syd. Soc. Lex.*)

**1753** R. RUSSELL *Diss. Sea Water* 385, I was called to a young Lady, who had a Shew of the Menses at twelve Years old. **1822–29** *Good's Study Med.* (ed. 3) V. 40 The mucous fluid, secreted in the beginning of labour..and hence vulgarly denominated show, or appearance. **1893** *Brit. Med. Jrnl.* 30 Sept. 55 A lady aged 42 had never seen any vaginal 'show' for thirteen years.

**18. a.** *Piquet.* (See quot. 1889.)

**1744** HOYLE *Piquet* i. 6 But if on the contrary you are to be younger-hand, and are eighty-six to fifty or sixty, never regard the losing two or three Points for the gaining of one, because that Point brings you within your Shew. **1889** H. JONES ('Cavendish') *Piquet* (ed. 6) 132 The *Show*, elder hand (when small cards are counted in play), is twenty-eight; younger hand is fourteen. That is, it is about an even chance the elder hand will score twenty-eight or more, and that the younger hand will score fourteen or more.

**b.** *U.S. horse-racing.* The third place in a race. Freq. *attrib.*

**1925** W. L. COMFORT in *Sat. Even. Post* 11 July 13/3 He had broken into show money this afternoon. Yesterday he had won and placed. *Ibid.* 124/4, I wouldn't back Black Ball right now for any better than place or show. **1944** *Sun* (Baltimore) 14 Apr. 14/1 Rougemont won by three lengths. .. So Bluesteel took the place and Sea fight, the favorite, got the show award. **1964** A. WYKES *Gambling* viii. 197 There is no 'show' betting in England. **1975** *Cleveland* (Ohio) *Plain Dealer* 23 Mar. 13-C/2 Hail to Springtime was moved into the show spot and Top of the Morn dropped to fourth.

**19.** *Mining.* A lambent blue flame appearing above the ordinary flame of a candle or lamp when fire-damp is present.

**1851** GREENWELL *Coal-trade Terms, Northumb. & Durh.* s.v. **1872** J. H. COLLINS *Mining & Quarrying* 112.

**IV.** *attrib.* and *Comb.*

**20.** Simple attrib. (= of or belonging to a show or exhibition), as ***show-bench***, ***field***, ***-ground***, ***jump***, ***-keeper***, ***-line***, ***-ring***, ***saddle***, ***-world***.

**1715** *Lond. Gaz.* No. 5329/3 Shew-keepers of Wild Beasts. **1843** W. DYOTT *Diary* Sept. (1907) II. 374 Both attended in the show field, and afterwards at the dinner. **1846** *Amer. Agriculturist* V. 333/1 The show-ground was located in the heart of the village. **1865** 'C. BEDE' *Rook's Gard.* 190 Much the same sort of thing existed in the Show world. **1870** H. H. DIXON *Saddle & Sirloin* iv. 89 When they met in the show-ring. **1888** *Times* 10 Oct. 5/5 Barnaby [a bloodhound] is better known on the show benches. **1901** *Munsey's Mag.* XXIV. 567/1 Have you been in the show-line ever since you left home. **1930** J. L. M. BARRETT *Pract. Jumping* ix. 94 Blinks..admitted to having had a whole set of show-jumps..made by the local carpenter. **1931** *Times Lit. Suppl.* 29 Oct. 840/4 The chapter on The Hound, with its warning against over-estimating the importance of success in the show-ring. **1955** *Times* 4 July 5/7 The showground, extending over 166 acres,..will be fully occupied by the trade stands..and the livestock lines, judging rings, and the pavilions. **1963** E. H. EDWARDS *Saddlery* xvii. 126 The English show saddle, confined in its use purely to the show ring, approximates more nearly to the dressage saddle than any other type, but its design is directed at displaying the horse's conformation rather than giving the rider any assistance in showing off the action of the horse. **1973** *Country Life* 8 Mar. 654/2 Large assortment of B.S.J.A. Show Jumps. All brightly painted and bolted construction. **1976** T. HEALD *Let Sleeping Dogs Die* v. 100 'Judging of the Dog-lovers' League Dog of the Year will commence..in the main ring.'.. The crowds were already gathered round the main show-ring. **1977** *Western Morning News* 1 Sept. 8/5 This year a vast number of traders throughout the area will be displaying their goods in the large marquee on the showfield.

**21.** *attrib.* or quasi-*adj.* **a.** In sense 'characterized by show or display', 'fitted for display or striking effect', 'that is made a show or exhibition of', 'chosen or put forward as a choice or effective specimen'. Of animals and plants: Bred or grown for display or for 'points'.

**1573** G. HARVEY *Letter-bk.* (Camden) 48 As he is marvelously given to be popular for a show matter. **1614** B. JONSON *Barth. Fair* III. ii, A delicate show-pig. **1809** MALKIN *Gil Blas* v. i. ¶1 There is a show article or two for public exhibition. **1819** KEATS *Otho* I. ii. 167 For, without thee, this day I might have been A show-monster about the streets of Prague. **1826** MACAULAY in Trevelyan *Life* (1880) I. 148 He [Sydney Smith] is not one of those show-talkers who reserve all their good things for special occasions. **1831** TRELAWNY *Adv. Younger Son* I. 131 My horse and I became a shew-lion to the sober natives. **1849** *Bentley's Misc.* Dec. 583 The *Flâneur* gazed for the first time upon this famed show-stream of the Continent. *a* **1855** C. BRONTË *Emma* in *Cornhill Mag.* (1860) I. 480 To judge whether the acquisition now offered was likely to answer well as a show-pupil. **1861** HUGHES *Tom Brown at Oxf.* i, This quadrangle is the show part of the college. **1862** [F. W. ROBINSON] *Owen* II. iv, Owen was the show-boy now when visitors came. **1869** S. R. HOLE *Bk. about Roses* ix. 138 *Paul Ricaut*..is not reliable as a show Rose, expanding rapidly.. on his arrival at the exhibition. **1886** S. SCOTT *Sheep-farming* 163 So long as the show sheep pay their own way they do very well. **1901** *Edin. Rev.* Oct. 433 That tendency to display, fostered by the vanity of parents, which is the hall-mark of what has been, in late years, designated the show-child. **1915** W. B. YEATS *Reveries* 173 My friend, now in his last year at school, was a show boy, and had beaten all Ireland again and again. **1941** F. THOMPSON *Over to Candleford* xiii. 200 She was the show pupil of the school; good at every subject. **1950** BLUNDEN *John Keats* 33 His friends..cultivated him with vague praise, as though they were raising the most scented, gorgeous show-rose ever exhibited. **1952** A. G. L. HELLYER *Sanders' Encycl. Gardening* (ed. 22) 159 Sweet Williams, Show-type—smooth-edged petals with dark centres. **1961** C. H. D. TODD *Popular Whippet* iv. 54 The exact type of brood bitch for which I was seeking in preference to the most brilliant show-type bitch.

**b.** In sense 'merely spectacular', 'existing only in appearance', 'pretended', 'unreal'.

*a* **1734** NORTH *Life Dudley North* (1744) 65 *marg.* He had a Shew-Audience before the Grand Signor. **1819** SHELLEY *Lett.* Pr. Wks. 1888 II. 285 Hobhouse, Eustace, and Forsyth, will tell all the shew-knowledge about it. **1856** MISS YONGE *Daisy Chain* I. ix, It would be hollow, show-goodness.

**22.** Special comb.: **show band**, a jazz band which performs with verve and theatrical extravagance; **show-bill**, a bill or placard announcing a show, public sale, etc.; **show-board**, a sign-board; **show-bottle**, a large glass bottle containing coloured liquid, to make a show in a druggist's window; so **show-carboy**; **show-card**, a card containing a tradesman's advertisement of goods, etc.; also, a card on which patterns are exhibited in a shop; **show-cart**, a cart forming part of a travelling menagerie, etc.; †**show-cloth**, a cloth hung up in front of a booth and painted with a highly-coloured representation of the show within; †**show-ern** [OE. *ærn* place, house], a show-house (an interpretation of 'Ephratah' in Micah v. 2); †**show-fellow**, a strolling player; **show flat**, a flat decorated and furnished for exhibition as an advertisement, usu. for others of similar construction (cf. SHOW HOUSE 2b); **show-folk**, showmen and others connected with a show; †**show-hall**, a theatre; **show-people** = *show-folk*; **show piece**, an item of work presented for exhibition or display; freq. *transf.*; **show-shop**, (*a*) a contemptuous term for a show or exhibition; (*b*) a shop in which an attractive display is made, esp. of cheap goods; †**show-stone**, a crystal used as a magic mirror for gazing in; **show-stopper**, an item (esp. a song or other performance) in a show that wins so much applause as to bring the show to a temporary stop; also *fig.*; hence **show-stopping** *a.*; **Show-Sunday**, (*a*) the Sunday before the Oxford Commemoration, on the evening of which a kind of University parade used to be held in the Broad Walk of Christ Church; (*b*) among artists, the Sunday before 'sending-in day'; †**show-token**, a sign, portent; †**show-trade**, a trade in cheap and showy goods; **show trial**, a judicial trial attended by great publicity: usu. used with specific reference to a prejudged trial of political dissidents by a Communist government; **show tune**, a popular tune from a light musical entertainment; **show-window** orig. *U.S.*, a shop-window in which goods are displayed; also *fig.*; **show-woman**, a woman who conducts a show (cf. SHOWMAN), or who is employed to display goods, etc.; also, a female guide in a show-place; **show wood**, the exposed wood of the frame of an upholstered chair (chiefly *attrib.*); †**show-worthy** *a.*, ? deserving of display, fine or splendid in appearance; **show-yard**, an enclosure in which live stock, machinery, and other large objects are exhibited; also *attrib.* See also SHOW BIZ, -BOAT, -BOX, -BUSINESS, -GLASS, HOUSE, SHOWMAN, SHOW-PLACE, -ROOM, etc.

**1927** *Melody Maker* Aug. 759/2 (*heading*) South African *show band in England. **1933** *Fortune* Aug. 48/1 Ellington has never compromised with the public taste for..'show bands' combining music with scenic effects, low comedy, and flag drills. **1952** B. ULANOV *Hist. Jazz in Amer.* (1958) xiv. 162 The Cotton Pickers were best known as a show band. **1970** J. WAINWRIGHT *Freeze thy Blood less Coldly* 55 He could be corner-man in any showband in the country. **1801** STRUTT *Sports & Past.* III. vi. §23 The following *show-bill [announcing an exhibition of sword-play]. **1837** HAWTHORNE *Twice-told T.* (1851) I. xvi. 248 The immense showbill of a wandering caravan. **1806** *Sporting Mag.* XXVII. 42 Lines painted on a *shewboard lately put up in Barrack-street in the city of Norwich. **1862** *Catal. Internat. Exhib., Brit.* II. No. 5263 Show-boards of all kinds. **1848** *Mech. Mag.* May 454/2 Improvements in..*show-cards. **1862** *Catal. Internat. Exhib., Brit.* II. No. 5289 Samples of coloured labels, show cards, &c. **1817** COLERIDGE *Biog. Lit.* xxiii. (1907) II. 181 Polito's (late Pidcock's) *show-carts. **1758** H. WALPOLE *Let. to G. Montagu* 24 Oct., I am a little sorry that my preface, like the *show-cloth to a sight, entertained you more than the bears that it invited you in to see. **1825** HONE *Every-Day Bk.* I. 1172, I..examined the promising show-cloths and inscriptions on each show. *c* **1200** ORMIN 7025 Effrata bitacneþþ uss *Shæwerrne onn Ennglissh spæche. **1756** *Life E. T. Bates* 38 Intimate with a vagabond *Shew-fellow. **1962** *Guardian* 7 Feb. 8/2 Those *show flats where colour seems to have been interpreted on a liquorice all-sorts plan. **1974** *Country Life* 14 Mar. 602/1 The first five-storey block of 20 flats is expected to be completed at the end of the year... A show flat is expected to be ready in the summer. **1755** C. CHARKE *Life* vii. 252 The very chairmen had something to say, by way of exultation, on the misfortunes of the poor *show-folk, as they impudently and ignorantly termed them. **1819** F. MOORE (*title*) The Age of Intellect, or, clerical Showfolk and wonderful Layfolk. **1856** R. W. PROCTER *Barber's Shop* xviii. (1883) 177 Barnum, whose book of confessions is sufficient to make one doubt the veracity of all show-folk. **1562** TURNER *Herbal* II. 51 The theues war brought into the great theatre or *shewhall agayn. **1853** *Diogenes* 9 Apr. 159/2 Here is a description of the President's inauguration costume, to which we call the attention of Tussaud, Springthorpe, and other waxwork *show-people. **1954** *Encounter* Feb. 63/2 Arthur Helliwell..treats it [*sc.* society] as a kind of *demi-monde*, dominated by show-people and speculators. **1962** 'K. ORVIS' *Damned & Destroyed* xii. 82 I'm showpeople. Well, anyway, I was once. I headlined in vaudeville for fifteen years. **1838** DICKENS *Sk. Young Gentlemen* 52 He likes to place implicit reliance upon the play-bills when he goes to see a *show-piece. **1885** [W. H. WHITE] *Mark Rutherford's Deliv.* i. (1892) 14 They evidently considered the prayer merely as an elocutionary show-piece. **1928** W. DE LA MARE *Come Hither* (ed. 2) 773 The sampler..the show-pieces on canvas or linen of a little girl (aged six or upwards) to prove her skill and diligence with the needle. **1941** BLUNDEN *Thomas Hardy* iv. 84 The poet John Clare..had become a sort of show-piece in a lunatic asylum. **1978** G. HOUSEHOLD *Last Two Weeks Georges Rivac* ii. 23 He looked suspiciously international.. a show piece to impress the foreigner. **1818** COBBETT *Pol. Reg.* XXXIII. 431 How the fellow's *show-shop would be crowded! **1848** KINGSLEY *Alton Locke* x, The public ran daily more and more to the cheap show-shops. **1850** BIGSBY *Shoe & Canoe* I. 109 Some of the show-shops [of Montreal] rival those of London in their plate-glass windows. *a* **1608** DEE *Relat. Spir.* I. (1659) 6, I had..set the *shew-stone with the mystery in it on the Table. **1693** I. MATHER *Cases Consc.* 66 How often have they..been known..to shew in a Glass or in a Shew-stone persons absent? **1926** *Variety* 18 Aug. 63/1 The first half [of the programme] held two *show-stoppers in the Dixie Four..who stopped the show..with their 'itch' dance finish, and Dave Apollon and Co., who stopped it, closing the first half. **1945** [see GASSER 2]. **1953** N. COWARD *Noël Coward Song Bk.* 76 'The Stately Homes of England' was what is colloquially known as a 'show stopper'. **1960** *Sunday Express* 18 Dec. 14/3 A show-stopper of shimmering silver lamé. **1967** T. STOPPARD *Rosencrantz & Guildenstern are Dead* II. 50 *Rosencrantz*: I can't remember how I did it. *Guildenstern*: It probably comes natural to you. *Rosencrantz*: Yes, I've got a show-stopper there. **1981** *Times Lit. Suppl.* 20 Feb. 202/3 Despite the inclusion of..other operatic items, and the Handel and Mendelssohn oratio arias which Lind loved to sing, the real show-stoppers were the 'Bird Song', [etc.]. **1962** *Times* 7 Dec. 8/7 There are few *show-stopping solos of any length. **1975** *Listener* 2 Jan. 25/3 The song..is one of the few heart-seizing, if not show-stopping, moments in Western theatre. **1854** 'C. BEDE' *Verdant Green* II. xii, In the evening they attended the customary '*Show Sunday' promenade in Christ Church Broad Walk. **1886** C. E. PASCOE *Lond. To-day* xiv. (ed. 3) 128 'Show-Sunday' is the day on which artists who exhibit, or hope to exhibit, at the Royal Academy and elsewhere, receive their friends and friends' friends at their studios. **1535** COVERDALE *Ezek.* xii. 6 I haue made the a *shewtoken vnto the house of Israel. **1597** J. PAYNE *Royal Exch.* Pref. 7 Beinge suche a shew token to patrons of benefices. **1848** KINGSLEY *Alton Locke* x, Our young employer intended to enlarge his establishment, for the purpose of commencing business in the '*show-trade'. **1937** E. LYONS *Assignment in Utopia* (1938) III. x. 370 The Ramzin affair..in my mind.. figures as the classic example of the demonstration trial—those attributes which set the *show trial off from ordinary trials..seem..sharply delineated. *Ibid.* 373 Sitmin..was the one whose young son had demanded his death... This was by now a standardized piece of business in important show trials. **1949** KOESTLER *Promise & Fulfilment* I. vii. 87 The Administration resorted to the eccentric and rather un-British expedient of staging several show-trials. **1966** M. WOODHOUSE *Tree Frog* viii. 63 The Russians had U2 sorted out... They were able to go to town on it, show trial, the lot. **1978** P. P. READ *Train Robbers* viii. 145 Because it was a show trial..many of the best barristers in England were retained. **1981** *Ann. Reg. 1980* 302 Jiang Qing constantly harangued witnesses and shouted defiance at the court—to such effect that she was forcibly removed on two occasions. Thus the trial was not equivalent to the Stalinist show trials of the 1950s. **1962** J. HELLER *Catch-22* vii. 59 He was a short-legged, wide-shouldered, smiling young soul who whistled bouncy *show tunes continuously. **1977** *New Yorker* 10 Oct. 177/1 The Brown band..opened up its offensive with one of those breezy, quickstep middle-period Jule Styne show tunes. **1826** 'N. NONDESCRIPT' *The* —— I. III. 30 Have you not noticed a **shew window* full of pictures, and a sign with the words 'visiting cards for sale'? **1855** 'Q. K. P. DOESTICKS' *Doesticks, what he Says* xiv. 118 Those.. ladies who used to perform their perpetual gyrations in the show-windows. **1880** CABLE *Grandissimes* xlviii, A nameless fellow in the throng..dropped two bricks through the glass of the show-window. **1905** WHITMAN in *Westm. Gaz.* 16 Oct. 4/2 Dr. Japp's intellectual stock-in-trade would have gone far to fill up the mental show-window of half a dozen 'popular' reputations. **1914** 'B. M. BOWER' *Flying U Ranch* 33 Where do you keep him when he ain't in the show window? **1958** S. SPENDER *Engaged in Writing* 125 The glass-making was a show-window of Venice. **1965** *Navy News* Apr. Suppl. 2/5 Yeovilton is the most suitable and convenient venue for show window air displays throughout the country. **1820** M. EDGEWORTH *Let.* 26 Dec. (1971) 231 A holy family by Leonardo da Vinci which the woman who shewed the pictures told us was by *Vincy* Ma'am... A cabinet brought from Italy by the 3d Duke of Beaufort as said *shew-woman always carefully told us. **1825** T. HOOK *Sayings* Ser. II. *Man of Many Fr.* I. 181 Look at..my Lady Frances, a shew-woman—like Madam Catharina, with watchwork under her hoop! **1825** HONE *Every-day Bk.* I. 1194 It [the head] looked sufficiently terrific, when the lady show-woman put the candle in at the neck. **1848** MRS. GASKELL *Mary Barton* I. iii. 37 Her beauty would have made her desirable as a show-woman. **1877** G. M. HOPKINS *Let.* 15 Aug. in *Further Lett.* (1956) 147 Mary's photographs are of Snowdon, Cadair Idris, and Valley Crucis Abbey: in the foreground of the last is the show-woman Miss Lloyd in her green shade, a quaint old character. **1898** *Daily News* 7 May 8/4 The beautiful girls who are secured as show-women by the West-end shops. **1919** V. WOOLF *Night & Day* xxiv. 335 While Katharine went on steadily with her duties as show-woman, Rodney examined intently a row of little drawings. **1909** WELLS & HOOPER *Mod. Cabinet Wk.* 368 **Show wood*, applied to stuffed chairs with part of the frame showing. **1921** F. PALMER *Pract. Upholstering* xii. 39 In some show-wood frames the whole surface is polished. **1958** *House & Garden* Mar. 5 The showwood legs can be polished to any shade. **1976** *Canadian Collector* (Toronto) Sept.-Oct. 16/2 The show-wood in this piece [*sc.* a sofa] is mahogany and the frame is birch. **1542** UDALL *Erasm. Apoph.* 283b *marg.*, What triumphe is honourable and *shewe woorthie. **1840** *John Bull* 19 July 346/2 Nearly 1,500 l., it is said, were taken at the *Show-yard in the course of the day. **1847** *Illustr. Lond. News* 10 July 27/2 The Race-course, which is set apart as a show-yard for the exhibition of prize-cattle. **1877** *Jrnl. R. Agric. Soc.* 533 His handsome chestnut colt..seems to have a deal of Showyard mettle in him.

**show**, *sb.*[2] *Sc.* and *dial.* Also **shoe, shough, shove**, etc. (see *Eng. Dial. Dict.*). [var. of SHOVE *sb.*[2]] = SHOVE *sb.*[2]

**1765** *Museum Rust.* IV. 459 When the flax is sufficiently watered, it feels soft to the grip, and the harle parts easily with the boon or show. **1827** STEUART *Planter's G.* (1828) 494 'Shows', as the refuse of a Flaxmill is usually called, in this part of the kingdom. **1900** *Scotsman* 23 Oct. (E.D.D.), The shows being now removed, the heckling process followed.

**show** (ʃəʊ), *v.* Pa. t. showed (ʃəʊd). Pa. pple. shown (ʃəʊn). Forms: α. 1 scéawian, 2-3 sceawen, sheawen, 2-4 sewe(n, 2-6 shewen, 3 scæwen, scewen, seawen, scheauwen, (*imp.* scheau), *Ormin* shæwenn, 3-4 scheawe(n, schewi, -y, scewi, ssewe, -i, -y, sceu, (cheu), 3-5 scheu, sheu(e, 3-6 schew(e, (3-5 -en, 4-5 -yn), 3-8 shewe, 4 sschewe, sseawe, -y, scewe, (*imp.* scheuȝ), 5 sheew, 6 sheaw, sew(e, 4- shew. β. Chiefly *northern* and *Sc.* 2-4 scawe(n, 3-4 scau, scawin, shauwe, 3-6 scaw, shawe, schaw(e, (3-5 -in), 3-7 schau, (3-4 -en, 7 schaue), 5-6 saw(e (?), 5-7 shau, 3- shaw. γ. 3 seowen, showen, ssow, 3-4 schowi, 4-6 schow(e, 5 schou- 5, 7 scho, 5-7 showe, 6 sho(e, sheowe, 6, 9 *dial.* shoo, 5- show. *Pa. t.* α. In regular forms 1 scéawede, -ode, etc.; 3- shewed, 5- showed; also 2 sceaude, 2-3 sheude, 3-4 schued, 6 schuyd, shoyd. β. Strong forms *Sc.* 4-6 scheu, schew(e, 6 sheu, shewe, 6- (also *Eng. dial.*) shew (ʃuː). *Pa. pple.* α. In regular forms 1 ȝescéawod, etc.; 4- shewed, 5- showed; also 5 shued, -yd. β. Strong forms 3 *Ormin* shawenn, 3-4 schaun, scaun, scawin, 4-6 shawen, -in, 5-6 schau-, schawen, -in, -yn, 6 shaune, s(c)hawne, (*erron.* schaw); 4-5 shene (?), 5-6 s(c)hewin, 6-7 shewen, 7- shewn; 6 schowin, shoun, 6-7 showen, showne, 7 schowne, 7- shown. [A common WGer. weak verb: OE. *scéawian* = OFris. *skawia, skowia, schoia, skua* (WFris. *skoaije, skôgje, skouje*), OS. *skawon* (MLG. *schowen*), MDu. *scauwen, schauwen* (mod.Da. *schouwen*), OHG. *scauwôn, scouwôn* (MHG. *schouwen, schawen*, mod.G. *schauen*) :—WGer. **skauwôjan*, f. OTeut. **skau-* to see, look, whence Goth. *skaun-s* beautiful (see SHEEN *a.*); other alleged cognates in Gothic are spurious. In all the continental WGer. langs., as in OE., the verb means 'to look at'; the sudden change in Eng. (*c* 1200) from this to the causative sense 'to cause to see, exhibit, manifest', is difficult to account for. (The existence of the causative sense in OE. is not really proved by the rare *áre ȝescéawian* to show mercy, *grið scéawian* to grant a safe-conduct, as these uses may be explained as developed from the sense 'to look out, provide'.) From early ME. the verb has had a strong conjugation (after KNOW *v.*, etc.) by the side of the original weak conjugation; in the pa. t. this survives only in dialects; but for the pa. pple. *shown* is now the usual form; the older *showed* is still sometimes used in the perfect tenses active (chiefly with material object), but in the passive it is obs. exc. as a deliberate archaism. The spelling *shew*, prevalent in the 18th c. and not uncommon in the first half of the 19th c., is now obs. exc. in legal documents. It represents the obsolete pronunciation (indicated by rhymes like *view*, *true* down to *c* 1700) normally descending from the OE. *scéaw-* with falling diphthong. The present pronunciation, to which the present spelling corresponds, represents an OE. (? dialectal) *sceāw-* with a rising diphthong.

The OTeut. root **skau-* represents an Indogermanic **sqou-* found in Gr. θυο-σκό(ϝ)ος 'one who attends to sacrifices', a priest; cognates without the initial *s* are Skr. *kavi* wise man, Gr. κοεῖν to feel, observe, L. *cavēre* to take precautions.]

†**I. 1. a.** *trans.* To look at, gaze upon, behold, view; to inspect, review; to reconnoitre, spy (a land, etc.); to look at mentally, consider, examine; to 'see', read, find (in a book). *Obs.*

Also (OE.) to look with favour upon, have respect to.

*Beowulf* 132 Syðþan hie þæs laðan last sceawedon. *c* **1000** *Ags. Gosp.* Luke xii. 27 Sceawiaþ þa lilian hu hi wexað. *O.E. Chron.* an. 1086, Se cyng ferde to Winceastre & sceawode þæt madme hus. *c* **1200** ORMIN 7032, & sen & shæwenn þurrh innsihht..All þatt tatt erþliȝ mann maȝȝ sen þurrh clennsedd sawless eȝhe. *c* **1205** LAY. 4815 He scawede þa wuodes & þa wildernes. *c* **1300** *Havelok* 2136 þe knithes þouth of hem god gamen, Hem forto shewe, and loken to.

†**b.** *intr.* To look or gaze *upon*. *Obs.*

*c* **1250** *Gen. & Ex.* 2661 Quiles he seweden him up-on.

†**c.** (*for*) *to show* used epexegetically after an adj. = to look upon, to behold, to see. *Obs.*

*a* **1400-50** *Wars Alex.* 601 þe fax on his faire hede was ferly to schawe. *c* **1400** *Destr. Troy* 1550 þat were shene for to shew & of shap noble.

**II.** To cause or allow to be seen or looked at.

* Uses implying intentional action.

**2. a.** *trans.* To bring forward or display (an object) in order that it may be looked at; to expose or exhibit to view. Const. *to* or dative of person.

*a* **1225** *Ancr. R.* 292 Hold hit [*sc.* the cross] up aȝean þe ueonde and scheau hit him witterliche. *c* **1275** *Passion of our Lord* 610 in *O.E. Misc.* 54 He schewede heom his honde and so he dude his fet. *a* **1300** *Cursor M.* 19889 And quen þis wessel thris was scaun, Again it was til heuen draun. *a* **1400** *Minor Poems fr. Vernon MS.* 491 Whon he was schewed to þe siht. **1563-83** FOXE *A. & M.* 1398/2 Sir John..sheweth the people the empty chalice. **1656** COWLEY *Mistress, Gazers* i, To shew such stores, and nothing grant, Is to enrage and vex my want. **1774** GOLDSM. *Nat. Hist.* (1776) V. 210 A partridge is shewn him, and he is then ordered to lie down. **1833** T. HOOK *Parson's Dau.* III. xii, Show me your tongue—let me feel your pulse. **1888** 'J. S. WINTER' *Bootle's Childr.* i, Taking the pups indoors..to show little missie.

†**b.** With advs. *to show forth*: to put forth or bring out to be seen. *to show up*: to hold up to view. *Obs.*

*c* **1320** *Sir Tristr.* 3097 þi finger forþ þou schawe. *a* **1533** BERNERS *Huon* lx. 209, I pray you shewe hym forth that ye speke of. **1563-83** FOXE *A. & M.* 1938/2 Thirdly, that the Priest sheweth vp an Idoll at masse.

**c.** *refl.* To present oneself to a person or persons in order to be looked at. (Cf. sense 10.)

*c* **1200** *Trin. Coll. Hom.* 71 *Ite et ostendite uos sacerdotibus* ..goð and sheweð ȝiu ȝiuwer prest. *a* **1225** *Ancr. R.* 250 Efter his ariste, þo he com & scheawede him. **1340** *Ayenb.* 13 He aros uram dyaþe to liue and sseawede him to his deciples. *a* **1700** EVELYN *Diary* 29 Aug. 1695, The King went a progresse into the North, to shew himselfe to the people against the elections. **1760-2** GOLDSM. *Cit. W.* v, Yesterday the new king shewed himself to his subjects.

**d.** With complement (rarely †acc. and inf.): To display in a (specified) condition or with a (specified) appearance. Also *refl.* †Also, to cause to appear or look (such and such).

*c* **1275** *Serving Christ* 13 in *O.E. Misc.* 91 I-seon vre louerd crist..Showen his wunden so blodi to-bleden. **13..** *Seuyn Sag.* (W.) 833 And sschewede his child hol and sound. *c* **1375** *Sc. Leg. Saints* xxxvii. (*Vincencius*) 73 þai schew þaim fere starkare & glad, þane quhen to presone he þaim had. **1483** CAXTON *G. de la Tour* (1906) 167 One ought not to coynte her body for to shewe it small and better shapen. **1584** R. SCOT *Discov. Witchcr.* XIII. xxxiii. (1886) 282 Then ..he would shew you everie leafe to be painted with birds. **1882** *Century Mag.* I. 589 She showed herself much more lavishly..bangled and bugled than the Americans.

**e.** To hold up or place (a light) where it can be seen (as a signal, to point out the way in the dark, etc.). Also *fig.*

**13..** *Cursor M.* 18196 (Gött.) And þu þaim scheus sua selcuth light? *a* **1533** BERNERS *Huon* lxi. 212, I pray you.. make no fyer, nor shewe no lyght. **1567** *Gude & Godlie B.* (S.T.S.) 173 Schawand till vs thy perfite lycht. **1831** SCOTT *Ct. Robt.* xxiii, The Prince of Otranto had orders to show certain lights..so as to indicate danger. **1838** DICKENS *O. Twist* xliv, 'Light him down' said Sikes,..'show him a light'. **1895** *Law Times Rep.* LXXIII. 623/1 Neither did Judges..stand by the line and show a light, as it was his duty to do.

**f.** To exhibit (a sign, token). *lit.* and *fig.* Hence, in Biblical language, to exhibit (a 'sign' or marvel), to work (a miracle); but cf. sense 3. †Also, to make (a dream or vision) appear to a person.

*c* **1200** ORMIN 15586 Whatt takenn shæwesst tu till uss þatt dost tuss þise dedess? [Cf. John ii. 18]. *a* **1225** *Leg. Kath.* 1573 þe cwen..cleopede to hire Porphire,..& seide him a sweuen þet hire wes ischawet. *c* **1330** R. BRUNNE *Chron. Wace* (Rolls) 1349 On fele maners scho scheweid hem syngne. *c* **1400** *Destr. Troy* 11791 Two meruellis on mold maynly were shewid. *a* **1533** BERNERS *Huon* lxxxi. 246, I haue sayd nothynge but he shal shew tokens that my sayenge is trewe. **1526** TINDALE *Mark* xiii. 22 For falce christes shall aryse..And shall shewe [δώσουσι] myracles and wonders. **1526** —— *Acts* vii. 36 Shewynge [ποιήσας] wonders and signes in Egipte. **1535** COVERDALE *Neh.* ix. 10 And hast ..shewed tokens and wonders [**1611** And shewedst signes and wonders] vpon Pharao.

**g.** To display (goods, wares, for sale or in an exhibition).

**1340** *Ayenb.* 44 þe vifte manere is, oþer þing zelle þanne me heþ y-sseawed beuore. *c* **1400** *Destr. Troy* 1581 There were stallis by the strete..Werkmen into won, and þaire wares shewe. **1517** *Star Chamber Cases* (Selden Soc.) II. 120 For his licens there to shewe his seid heryng & sparlyng to sell. **1884** *Stationers' & Booksellers' Jrnl.* 3/1 A goodly quantity of soft and silky curl-papers, neatly shown. *Mod. Advt.*, Messrs. A. B. are showing to-day a large stock of new fancy goods.

**h.** To display, hang out, unfurl (a banner, ensign, etc.) †Also with *out, up. to show the flag*: see FLAG *sb.*[4] 1 c.

*c* **1470** *Gol. & Gaw.* 474 Ilka souerane his ensenye shewin has thair. **1596** DALRYMPLE tr. *Leslie's Hist. Scot.* II. 108 The kings bluddie sark vp tha schawe for thair ansinȝie. **1604** SHAKS. *Oth.* I. i. 157, I must show out a Flag and signe of Loue. **1698** FRYER *Acc. E. India & P.* 36 The Colours the Fort shewed us, was St. George's Flag. **1815** SCOTT *Guy M.* x, The chase then shewed Hamburgh colours, and returned the fire.

**i.** To exhibit (a spectacle, some interesting object) for the amusement of the public; to make a show of. †Also (cf. sense 3), to perform (a stage-play, tricks, etc.).

?*a* **1500** *Mankind* 78 in *Macro Plays* 4 Xall I breke my neke to schow yow sporte? **1574** in Feuillerat *Revels Q. Eliz.* (1908) 238 My Lord Chamberlens players did show the history Phedrastus. **1575** GASCOIGNE *Kenelworth Castle* Wks. 1910 II. 95 At which time there wer fireworks shewed upon the water. **1619** in W. Kelly *Notices illustr. Drama* (1865) 254 Item, given to the Playors that shewed Etalion Motion x[s]. **1662** J. DAVIES tr. *Olearius' Voy. Ambass.* 392 This Calenter..diverted us in our way, by..shewing tricks with a half-pike. **1701** EVELYN *Diary* Apr., A Dutch boy.. was carried about by his parents to shewe. **1726** SWIFT *Gulliver* II. ii, I was shown ten times a-day, to the wonder and satisfaction of all people. **1840** DICKENS *Old C. Shop* xvi, 'Good!' said the old man, venturing to touch one of the puppets,.. 'Are you going to shew 'em to-night?' **1862** 'ARTEMUS WARD' *His Bk.* (1865) 28, I showed my show in Uticky.

**j.** To exhibit threateningly. Hence *jocularly*, to make the slightest possible application of.

**1833** *Reg. Instr. Cavalry* I. 75 Great care must be taken not to press the horse too suddenly up to the snaffle by showing the whip. **1839** HOOD *Lost Heir* 67 As for hair, tho' it's red it's the most nicest hair when I've time to just show it the comb.

**k.** *to show one's hand*: to display one's cards face upwards; *fig.* to allow one's plans or intentions to be known.

**1879** MEREDITH *Egoist* xxxvi, Her intrepid lead had shown her hand to the colonel. **1887** RIDER HAGGARD *Jess* xiii, What are you driving at, Frank Muller? You don't show me your hand like this for nothing. **1895** *Bookman* Oct. 23/1 He was perilously near showing his whole hand to the other side.

**l.** To exhibit (an animal) in a show or display.

**1854** *Poultry Chron.* I. 572/2 The best [birds] should never be shown more than once a month. **1976** T. HEALD *Let Sleeping Dogs Die* i. 25 The best dog I ever had..went to a Count in Florence. He paid £3000 and never showed him.

**m.** To display (a slide, film, etc.) on a screen by projection for public viewing. Also *absol.* for *pass.*

**1911** [see FILM *sb.* 3 c]. **1931** B. BROWN *Talking Pictures* xii. 290 Some of the first talking pictures to be shown in this country were from Fox Movietone News. **1942** E. WAUGH *Put out More Flags* iii. 219 A film was showing in the Ministry theatre: it dealt with otter-hunting. **1964** G. MCDONALD *Running Scared* (1977) I. ii. 22 It was Sunday and there would be a new film showing. **1976** *Oxf. Compan. Film* 118/2 Local councils..gradually accepted the principle that a film passed by the Board could be shown without fear of prosecution under the 1909 Act.

**n.** *absol.* Of an artist, fashion designer, etc.: to hold an exhibition of one's work.

**1912** R. FRY *Let.* (1972) I. 357 I'm delighted that [Augustus] John wants to show. **1958** *Listener* 28 Aug. 310/3 Mr. Pooley, a young painter showing at the Hammersmith Gallery..is worth watching. **1960** *Guardian* 21 July 7/7 The autumn collections of the Incorporated Society of London Fashion Designers began yesterday... John Cavanagh and Lachasse showed on this the first of the three days. **1972** E. LUCIE-SMITH in Cox & Dyson *20th-Cent. Mind* II. xiv. 486 Other American artists who showed there included Robert

Motherwell. **1977** *Times* 24 Feb. 8/1 Emanuel Ungaro was showing in the hotel.

†**3.** To perform openly (a deed, feat, exploit); to put in overt act (something declared or purposed).

**1382** WYCLIF *John* x. 32, I haue schewid to ȝou manye goode werkis of my fadir. **1474** CAXTON *Chesse* IV. viii. (1883) 184 That thou darst not doo and shewe that thou saist. **1477** EARL RIVERS (Caxton) *Dictes* 22 If thou wylt correcte eny man shewe it not by vyolence. **1581** A. HALL *Iliad* v. 91 Wherefore some worthy deede of Armes, it you behoooues to shoe. **1737** WHISTON *Josephus, Hist.* I. iv. §5 Alexander's mercenaries shewed the greatest exploits, both in soul and body.

**4.** To produce or submit for inspection (something in one's possession). **a.** To produce (a legal document, etc.) for official inspection; to exhibit (something) in proof that one possesses it.

*a* **1325** *MS. Rawl.* B. 520 lf. 64 þe desturbour sal aperen bi fore Justises ant sewen his chartre. **1426** *Cov. Leet Bk.* 106, I neuer relesed ne made dede except oon shued afore all the seyd wurthy men. **1509** *Star Chamber Cases* (Selden Soc.) I. 199 They desire that the seid abbot may schow his charterys & Evidence. **1617** MORYSON *Itin.* I. 68 Wee rode a mile..to the village Treviso, where the Dutchmen shewed a pasport. **1662** in *Extr. St. Papers rel. Friends* (1911) Ser. II. 145 Hugh Tickell hauing the letter shown beleiues it to be the hand of John Dixon. **1866** *Chamb. Encycl.* VIII. 91/1 (*Railways*) A call by the guard to 'shew tickets' previous to starting.

**b.** ***to have*** (something) ***to show for*** (one's labour, expenditure, etc.): to be able to exhibit as a result.

**1727** GAY *Begg. Op.* I. vii, I have this watch and other visible marks of his favour to show for it. **1826** SCOTT *Jrnl.* 6 Sept., Here is a fine spate of work—a day diddled away, and nothing to show for it. **1853** LYTTON *My Novel* III. x. xxiv. 217 The Great Commoner had, indeed, 'something to show' for the money he had disdained and squandered. **1976** J. R. L. ANDERSON *Redundancy Pay* i. 11 He had been earning quite a lot of money, but had nothing real to show for it... They spent his salary as it came in.

†**c.** To produce for inspection with a view to military service; to muster. In *Cock-fighting*, to make an array of (cocks) on either side. *Obs.*

**1655** FULLER *Ch. Hist.* VIII. 39 The Queen priviledged them from shewing their Horses with the Laytie; yet so as they should muster them up for the defence of the Land under Captains of their own choosing. **1716** *Lond. Gaz.* No. 5436/4 There will..be 31 Cocks shewed of a side. **1730** CHENY *Hist. List Horse-matches*, etc. 167 Mr. Ruston fought Mr. Newton showing 21 Cocks aside for 2 Guineas a Battle.

**d.** *fig.* (Often of things quasi-personified). To (be able to) present to (physical or mental) view.

**1611** *Second Maiden's Tragedy* 623 (Malone Soc.) The only enemye that my life can showe me. *a* **1700** EVELYN *Diary* 21 Nov. 1679, Such an hospitable costume and splendid magistrature dos no city in the world shew. **1705** ADDISON *Italy, Monaco* 13 Perhaps there is no House in Europe that can show a longer Line of Heroes. **1802** WORDSW. *Misc. Sonn., Composed upon Westm. Bridge*, Earth has not anything to show more fair. **1805–6** CARY *Dante's Inf.* XXIX. 119 Sure not France herself Can show a tribe so frivolous and vain. **1886** C. E. PASCOE *Lond. Today* xxxi. (ed. 3) 288 White's can show a record of more than a century.

**e.** ***to show up***: To hand up (a school-exercise, etc.) for inspection by a teacher or examiner.

**1803** *Pic Nic* No. 14 (1806) II. 247 Shewing up our exercises to the Assistant of the form. **1912** MARG. F. MOORE *Two Sel. Bibliogr.* Pref. 16 Students are encouraged to show up exercises in the transcription and extension of facsimiles.

†**5. a.** To bring or put forward for some purpose or use; to present (an object) *to* a person in order that he may take it or use it. ***to show water***: to produce a fee. *Obs.*

*a* **1300** *K. Horn* 1461 Harpe he gan schewe. *a* **1300** *Cursor M.* 12405 To me þou scau þar-of þe tan ende for to drau And þou þe toþur. *a* **1375** *Joseph Arim.* 587 Scheuȝ me myn hache, and I schal note hit to-day. *c* **1450** *Mirk's Festial* 90 þen sayde Crist: 'Schew me þy hond'; and toke hur hond, and put hit ynto hys syde. **1632** MASSINGER *Maid of Honour* I. i, If you have a suite, shew water, I am blinde else.

†**b.** To fire (a broadside). Const. *to*. *Obs.*

**1624** MASSINGER *Renegado* v. viii, As a farewell they shewed a broad side to vs.

†**c.** Naut. ***to show canvas***: to spread sail *to* the wind.

**1874** BEDFORD *Sailor's Pocket Bk.* iv. 57. 12 [denotes] Hurricane To which she could show No canvas.

**6.** To let (a person) read or examine (a book, writing); to bring (it) to his notice.

**1677** H. SAVILE in *12th Rep. Hist. MSS. Comm.* App. v. 43 The Grantham verses you sent me I shewd Sir Robert Carr, and asked him if he made them. **1848** THACKERAY *Van. Fair* xlv, I showed Lord Steyne your pamphlet on Malt. **1855** BROWNING *Gramm. Funeral* 48 'What's in the scroll', quoth he, 'thou keepest furled? Shew me their shaping, Theirs, who most studied man, the bard and sage.'

**7.** To represent in sculpture or graphic art. Also in film.

**1660** BLOOME *Archit.* Cj, 10 parts, shewed on the right side. **1700** T. BROWN *Amusem. Ser. & Com.* 105 This Picture does not shew them to Advantage. **1854** in *Orr's Circ. Sci., Org. Nat.* I. 254 The saltatorial modification of the..skeleton is here shewn in that of..*Macropus elegans*. **1904** R. C. JEBB *Bacchylides* (Proc. Brit. Acad.) 6 Here is the ship..but the painter could not also show us Minos throwing the ring, or Theseus diving. **1905** L. WHIBLEY *Companion Grk. Studies* iv. §3. 247 The western frieze shows the horsemen preparing. **1963** *Movie* June 29/1 The early part of the film shows their reactions to the death of Toni's wife.

**8. a.** To display deliberately or ostentatiously in order to attract notice or win admiration.

**1509** BARCLAY *Shyp of Folys* (1874) I. 221 Or to be sene, and to showe his gardyd cote. **1693** *Humours Town* 114 A Throng of Fools, of both Sexes, walking up and down to shew their new Cloaths. **1848** THACKERAY *Van. Fair* xliii, She curled her hair and showed her shoulders at him, as much as to say, Did ye ever see such jet ringlets and such a complexion? **1853** KINGSLEY *Hypatia* v, Taking care to show the most lovely white heel and ankle.

**b.** ***to show off***: to display ostentatiously.

**1820** W. IRVING *Sketch Bk., Christmas Day*, He turned over the leaves..with something of a flourish; possibly to show off an enormous seal-ring. **1848** THACKERAY *Van. Fair* l, To show off before them his new wealth and splendour. **1879** M. PATTISON *Milton* 192 An opportunity for an author to show off his powers of writing.

** Uses in which the being seen is an unintended or incidental result.

**9.** To allow (a part of the body) to be seen.

**a.** ***to show one's head, face***, etc.: to allow oneself to be seen, make an appearance. Also jocularly ***to show one's nose***.

*a* **1225** *Ancr. R.* 90 Scheau þi neb to me. *a* **1225** *Leg. Kath.* 915 He..schawde us his nebscheft & weolc..bimong worldliche men. **1500–20** DUNBAR *Poems* xxxiii. 2 As ȝung Awrora..In orient schew hir visage paile. **1551** T. WILSON *Logic* (1580) 49 This manne..durst not once for his life shewe his hedde. **1635** *Long Meg of Westminster* xviii. (1816) 30 He was ashamed to shew his face in the streetes. **1648** J. BEAUMONT *Psyche* VI. clx, No Weed presum'd to shew its roitish face On this fair stage. **1746** FRANCIS tr. *Hor., Sat.* II. vii. 18 Where a clean slave would blush to show his face. **1841** THACKERAY *Gt. Hoggarty Diam.* x, My aunt had so frightened him, that he never once showed his nose in the place all the time we lived there. **1843** CARLYLE *Past & Pr.* II. x, Jew and Christian creditors, pouncing on him..wherever he showed face. **1888** 'J. S. WINTER' *Bootle's Childr.* vii, Let him show his ugly mug anywhere hereabouts, and I'll grease all the steps that he may break 'is neck.

†**b.** To display (a countenance, looks, etc.) of a specified sort. ***to show a red pair of cheeks***: to blush. ***to show tears***: to weep. *Obs.*

*c* **1450** *St. Cuthbert* (Surtees) 2098 In what disees þat he war stadd He shewed ay countenance gladd. *c* **1470** HENRY *Wallace* VI. 57 Fortoune him schawit hyr fygowrt doubill face. **1542** UDALL *Erasm. Apoph.* 249 Cæsar shewed a redde paire of chekes. **1553** T. WILSON *Rhet.* (1580) 17 Fewe..spake of these two gentlemen, but thei shewed teares. **1585** T. WASHINGTON tr. *Nicholay's Voy.* I. vii, I alwaies shewed an assured countenance. **1590** GREENE *Never too late* II. (1600) O 3, She shewes thee kinde lookes.

**c.** ***to show*** (a person) ***one's heels, a clean*** or ***fair pair of heels***: to flee (from him). (Cf. F. *montrer les talons*.) Also *transf.* of a ship. Similarly † ***to show*** (a person) ***the back***, etc.

***to show*** (one) ***the cold shoulder***: see COLD SHOULDER *sb.*

*a* **1400–50** *Wars Alex.* 928 Philip..Braidis on his blonke toward þe burȝe & þaim þe bak schewis. **1523** [see HEEL *sb.*[1] 3 c]. **1546** J. HEYWOOD *Prov.* II. vii. (1867) 64 Except hir maide shewe a fayre paire of heeles. **1595** *Hasleton's Trav.* in Arb. *Garner* VIII. 394 Shewing them a clean pair of heels, [I] took my way over the mountains. **1675** *Machiavelli's Prince* (1883) 256 He should..show them a light pair of heels. **1863** SPEKE *Source Nile* xii. 334 Her majesty..rose from her seat, and showing her broad stern to the company, walked straight away. **1887** FLOR. MARRYAT *Driven to Bay* xi, She..would have held her own with most ships, and shown her heels to not a few.

**d.** ***to show the cloven foot*** (***hoof***): to betray something diabolic or sinister in one's character or motives.

**1841** THACKERAY *Gt. Hoggarty Diam.* x, It was especially about my wife's fortune that Mr. B. showed his cloven foot. **1885** [see HOOF *sb.* 1 b]. **1896** *Pall Mall Mag.* Mar. 399 Mrs. Mac showed me the cloven foot just now.

**e.** ***to show foot***: ? to get ready *for*. *U.S.*

**1825** J. NEAL *Bro. Jonathan* I. 269 Carter..began to 'show foot' for another, and more active demonstration.

**f.** ***to show a leg***: see LEG *sb.* 2 a.

**10.** *refl.* **a.** To appear, make an appearance, allow oneself to be seen. Cf. 2 c.

*a* **1300** *Cursor M.* 17039 þar scheud he him for mighti godd. *a* **1400–50** *Wars Alex.* 3429 Bathe Besan & Anabras..baldly þam shawis. ? *a* **1550** *Freiris of Berwik* 529 in *Dunbar's Poems* 302 And vnto ws thow schaw the oppinlie. **1589** BIGGES *Summarie Drake's W. Ind. Voy.* 37 Our men..seeing no man of the Spaniards to shew them selues, aboorded the Spanish barkes. **1824** MISS L. M. HAWKINS *Mem.* II. 197 *note*, The Sovereign of Great Britain has only to show himself to be adored. **1859** TENNYSON *Enid* 240 They..climb'd upon a fair and even ridge, And show'd themselves against the sky.

**b.** Of a thing: To be or become visible.

**1578** LYTE *Dodoens* II. xl. 198 The flowers of these strange plantes doo shewe them selues commonly in June. **1856** MISS WARNER *Hills Shatemuc* iv, Here and there..the lighter green of an oak showed itself.

**11. a.** Of plants, the seasons, etc.: To bring forth to view, display (fruit, flower, etc.).

*c* **1330** *Arth. & Merl.* 1711 Floures schewen her borioun. *Ibid.* 8657 Mirie is June, þat scheweþ flour. **1820** *Trans. Hortic. Soc.* (1822) IV. 393 The suckers of inferior strength will not shew fruit in the same season. **1842** LOUDON *Suburban Hort.* 674 As soon as the plants have shown the third leaf.

**b.** Of animals or plants: To display (their colours, beauties, etc.).

**1667** MILTON *P.L.* VII. 406 Part..sporting with quick glance Show to the Sun their wav'd coats dropt with Gold. **1742** GRAY *Spring* 29 Some shew their gayly-gilded trim Quick-glancing to the sun. **1788** PICKEN *Poems* 55 How fine to range owre meadows wide, Whan flowers their charms are shawan!

**c.** Of a luminous body: To display (its light).

**14..** LYDG. in *Pol. Rel. & L. Poems* (1903) 73 Charbunclys, rubeys..Shew in derknes lyght. **1544** BETHAM *Precepts War* I. cci. I vij b, The lyghte, and also..the false vmbrage whych the Moone doth shewe fourthe. **1752** YOUNG *Brothers* I. i, Like a bold star, that shews its fires by day. **1818** SCOTT *Br. Lamm.* xxxv. The sun..showed its broad disk above the eastern sea.

**12. a.** Of a thing: To be the means of displaying, revealing to sight, or allowing to be seen; to serve to exhibit or indicate.

**1398** TREVISA *Barth De P.R.* x. iv. (1495) 375 In shewynge of himself fyre sheweth other thynges that ben presente. **1614** GORGES *Lucan* IX. 386 Thy sight the North-starre vndergoes, And Vrsa Maior to thee showes. **1790** BURNS *Tam o' Shanter* 126 Coffins stood round, like open presses, That shaw'd the dead in their last dresses. **1859** *Habits Gd. Society* iv. 169 Very short petticoats, only not showing the knees. **1897** MAX PEMBERTON *Queen of Jesters* iii. 104 For one short instant a window showed him the city.

**b.** ***to show off, out***: to display in relief or by contrast; to set off, enhance in appearance. *rare.*

*c* **1380** WYCLIF *Wks.* (1880) 470 For, as þei seyen, þer staat wolde perische but ȝif siche richesse shewide it out. **1611** SHAKS. *Wint. T.* v. iii. 21, I like your silence, it the more shewes-off Your wonder. **1874** H. H. COLE *Catal. Ind. Art S. Kens. Mus.* 230 The very roughness of the embroidery..shows out the intention of the design.

**c.** To be in such a state or position as to allow (something) to be seen. ***to show up*** (rare): to expose (something underneath). ***to show daylight***: to have holes or openings through which light can be seen.

**1848** THACKERAY *Van. Fair* xx, His coat..was white at the seams, and his buttons showed the copper. **1850** *Habits Gd. Society* v. 199 The man who 'shows daylight' between himself and his saddle is a bad rider. **1871** *Chamb. Jrnl.* 28 Jan. 49 While it [the material] is equally suitable for tropical wear, it does not show the traces of soil so soon. **1874** H. H. COLE *Catal. Ind. Art S. Kens. Mus.* App. 289 Then cutting out certain parts of the pattern which showed up the copper as a ground. *Mod.* This colour shows the dirt more than the other.

**13. a.** To have visibly (some external feature or mark); to have (a part of itself) in a position exposed to view.

*a* **1585** POLWART *Flyting w. Montgomerie* 570 His shaven shoulders shawes the marks, no dout, Of teugh tarladders. **1611** COTGR., *Perpins*..stones made iust as thicke as a wall, and shewing their smoothed ends on either side thereof. *a* **1700** EVELYN *Diary* Sept. 1646, The Alps..shewing their aspiring tops. **1822** J. PARKINSON *Outl. Oryctol.* 227 This shell, though round, shows five angles. **1883** BESANT *Captains' Room* ii, Her planks show signs of age. **1890** *Goldfields of Victoria* 18 This run of stone..shows payable gold. **1907** J. A. HODGES *Elem. Photogr.* (ed. 6) 101 Sometimes bromide prints..show stains.

**b.** Of a list, record, a recording instrument: To be found on inspection to indicate.

**1866** LIVINGSTONE *Last Jrnls.* (1874) I. 162 The barometers had shown no difference of level from about 1800 feet above the sea. **1883** *Stubbs' Merc. Gaz.* 8 Nov. 982/2 Grey shirtings show a falling-off of over 90,000 yards. **1910** 'MARK RUTHERFORD' *Pages fr. Jrnl.* (ed. 2) 329 His watch showed 7.30 p.m. *Mod.* The thermometer showed ten degrees below zero.

**III.** To guide another person's sight to (an object).

**14. a.** To enable a person to discover or identify (a visible object) by pointing to it, or by conducting him to a place where it can be seen. Also, to direct a person's observation to the various parts or features of (a country, town, building, or any complex object). † ***to show with one's finger*** (= L. *monstrare digito*): to point to.

*c* **1175** *Lamb. Hom.* 41 Seodðan he him sceaude an ouen on burninde fure. *a* **1300** *Cursor M.* 12979 þat warlau..bar him forth..Apon þe heist fell he faand, And þare he scaud him þe land. **1340–70** *Alex. & Dind.* 59 þanne þei caire wiþ þe king hur cauus to schewe. **1387** TREVISA *Higden* (Rolls) V. 289 His buriel is ȝit i-schewed in þe est side of Kent. *c* **1450** *Merlin* xxi. 371 Nascien..seide '..lo, hym yonde..', and shewde hym with his fynger. **1456** SIR G. HAYE *Law Arms* (S.T.S.) 10 Quhen he schewe with his fyngir the sone of God in figure of a lambe. **1569** UNDERDOWNE *Heliodorus* VII. 94 b, Therefore folowe this woman (shewing them Cibele). **1582** N. LICHEFIELD tr. *Castanheda's Conq. E. Ind.* I. vii. 18 b, The Pilot..did then foorthwith shew them the water. **1596** SHAKS. *Merch. V.*, IV. ii. 11, I pray you shew my youth old Shylockes house. **1632** LITHGOW *Trav.* I. 24 They shew me the Crub or Stall where he was borne. **1705** ADDISON *Italy, Brescia* 60 A Stranger is always shown the Tomb of Pope Lucius. *a* **1734** R. NORTH *Autobiog.* Lives 1890 III. 171 I walked them all over the house to shew the rooms and buildings. **1781** COWPER *Hope* 221 Conscience..Shows, with a pointing finger..A pale procession of past sinful joys. **1814** SCOTT *Diary* 19 Aug. in *Lockhart* (1837) III. vi. 217 Mr. Anderson showed me the spot where the Norwegian monarch, Haco, moored his fleet. **1848** THACKERAY *Van. Fair* xxxix, I can show you her room, Mum, and the press in the housekeeper's room.

**b.** *fig.*

**1818** SCOTT *Br. Lamm.* ii, The adage 'Shew me the man, and I will shew you the law', became as prevalent as it was scandalous. **1848** THACKERAY *Van. Fair* xxviii, Show me a cavalry chief like him now that Murat is gone. *a* **1869** M. ARNOLD *Urania* v, Yet show her once, ye heavenly Powers, One of some worthier race than ours!

**c.** With mixture of sense (cf. 22 c): To point out or indicate a place *where* (etc.).

*c* **1450** *Merlin* xxi. 371 We praye yow that ye will vs shewen where he is that we may hym knowen. **1742** GRAY

*Eton* 58 Ah, shew them where in ambush stand To seize their prey the murth'rous band! **1877** TALMAGE *Serm.* 337 God shows them where to fall.

**15. a.** ***to show*** (one) ***the way***: to guide a person in a required direction, by leading or accompanying him, or by giving him instructions; also *fig.* In *Racing* and *Hunting*, to lead; ***to show the way from***, to draw away from, get before (in a race).

**1530** PALSGR. 703/1, I shewe him the way. **1796** MME. D'ARBLAY *Camilla* IV. 285 'O never mind shewing me the way'..and [he] sallied into the apartment. **1863** W. C. BALDWIN *Afr. Hunting* vi. 195 The captain..would send no one with us to show the road. **1869** M. ARNOLD *Culture & Anarchy* 192 So, too, one who wants to be a painter or a poet cannot help loving and admiring the great painters or poets who have gone before him and shown him the way. **1871** LEGRAND *Camb. Freshm.* 251 No time was lost about the start; Mr. Pokyr, Mr. Fitzfoodel, and several other high-flyers showing the way, which at first lay through a grass field. **1887** *Daily News* 1 Dec. 2/4 Merry Maiden, at a good pace, showed the way from Ballot Box and Great Paul. **1891** 'J. S. WINTER' *Lumley* xii, Show me the way upstairs.

**b.** ***to show*** (one) ***the door***: to order (a person) to leave the room or house; to turn out of doors.

**1778** MISS BURNEY *Evelina* xxi, I shall make bold to show you the door. **1809** MALKIN *Gil Blas* I. v. (Rtldg.) 12 Don Rodrigo..showed the goddess of my devotions the outside of the door. **1866** W. COLLINS *Armadale* v. iii, In your place, I should have shown him the door.

**16. a.** (With inverted const.) To guide or conduct (a person) *to*, *into* a particular place, room in a house, etc., *over* or *through* the rooms of a house.

*a***1400–50** *Wars Alex.* 4049 And þar þai schewid him in schurrys, to schellis & to caues. **1594** NASHE *Unfort. Trav.* Wks. 1904 II. 309 Go, maid, shewe him to the farther chamber. **1596** SHAKS. *Merch. V*, IV. ii. 19 Come good sir, will you shew me to this house. **1748** SMOLLETT *Rod. Rand.* li. (1760) II. 139 The grim janitor..shewed me into a parlour. **1848** THACKERAY *Van. Fair* ii, You may be sure that she showed Rebecca over every room of the house. **1891** E. PEACOCK *N. Brendon* I. 287 She was shown into Mr. Stutting's private room. **1891** 'J. S. WINTER' *Lumley* xiii, So as to be ready when Mrs. Hope should require showing to her carriage.

**b.** ***to show up, upstairs***: to conduct (a person) upstairs. ***to show out***: to take (a person) to the exit door; to turn out of doors. ***to show in***: to bring (a person) into a house or room. ***to show round***: to show (a person) over a place, show the 'sights'.

**1693** CONGREVE *Old Bach.* II. iv, *Aram.* [to *Footman*] Be ready to shew 'em up. **1777** SHERIDAN *Sch. Scand.* IV. ii, Oh, gentlemen, I beg pardon for not showing you out. **1843** MRS. CARLYLE *Lett.* I. 274 As there was no fire in the room below, they had to be shown up to the library. **1874** ALDRICH *Prudence Palfrey* xv. 287 Wants to see me?.. Show him in, Fanny. *a***1885** 'H. CONWAY' *Living or Dead* xi, Now, sir, listen before I ring for you to be shown out. **1896** KIPLING *Seven Seas* 42 *M'Andrews' Hymn*, I showed him round last week.

**IV.** To exhibit or manifest by outward signs.

**17.** To exhibit, allow to be seen (some inward quality, feeling, condition, etc.) by one's outward appearance; occas. said of the appearance. Also with obj. clause. Also ***to show a sign*** or ***signs*** (*of, that*..).

*c***1275** *Passion of our Lord* 618 in *O.E. Misc.* 54 Vre louerd nom and et þer-of to-uore heom euervychone, And sewede þat he wes a-ryse myd fleysse and myd bone. **1597** MONTGOMERIE *Cherrie & Slae* 265 My hew so furth schew so The dolour of my woundis. **1697** DRYDEN *Virg. Georg.* III. 119 The Colt that for a Stallion is design'd, By sure Presages shows his generous Kind. **1831** SCOTT *Cast. Dang.* xx, Douglas and De Walton..began to show some signs that their human bodies were feeling the effect of the dreadful exertion. **1863** GEO. ELIOT *Romola* x, He showed all the outward signs of a mind at ease. **1884** W. BLACK *Jud. Shakespeare* xxxiv, On the awakening she might show that the crisis was over.

**18. a.** To display (a quality, condition, feeling, etc.) by one's action or behaviour; to give proof of possessing. Also ***to show a sign*** or ***signs*** (*of*).

*c***1200** *Vices & Virtues* 49 Þurh his mannisnesse, and ðurh ðare michele eadmodnesse ðe he mid hire sceawede. **1297** R. GLOUC. (Rolls) 9318 Vor vre prowesse we mote nede ssewe to day ywis. **1375** BARBOUR *Bruce* II. 367 The Bruyss folk full hardely Schawyt thar gret chewalry. *c***1550** LYNDESAY *Tragedie* 80, I schew my Lordlye Lyberalitie, In Banketting, playng at cartis, and Dyse. **1575** GASCOIGNE *Philomene* 85 She shewed great skil, for tunes of unisone. *c***1643** LD. HERBERT *Autobiog.* (1824) 60 A man's Wit is best shewed in his Answer. **1675** COVEL in *Early Voy. Levant* (Hakl. Soc.) 216 There was..a middle-sized squad fellow, who shew a vast strength in tossing about weights. **1751** JORTIN *Serm.* (1771) I. i. 6 Every behaviour which shews inhumanity. **1857** BUCKLE *Civiliz.* I. xi. 642 In the preliminary work of accumulating the facts, great energy was shown. **1886** C. E. PASCOE *Lond. To-day* xl. (ed. 3) 337 A lady's maid will frequently show far better taste than her mistress. **1887** *Field* 5 Nov. 718/3 Rogers..showed a great turn of speed.

†**b.** with *forth. Obs.*

*c***1400** *Sowdone Bab.* 424 Shewe forth here nowe your crafte. **1565** J. PHILLIPS *Patient Grissell* 138 (Malone Soc.) Now Polliticke perswasion shoe forth thy skyll.

**c.** With object-clause: To make it plain in regard to oneself (*that*).

*a***1225** *Leg. Kath.* 1036 In þis an þing he schawde..þet he wes soð godd. *c***1380** WYCLIF *Sel. Wks.* III. 311 To..schewe in dede þat þei seken more profit and savynge of Cristene soulis þanne here owene wynnynge or worschipe. *a***1600** MONTGOMERIE *Misc. P.* xxxiv. 6 Becaus no signe is shaune That ȝe held me ȝour aune. **1706** E. WARD *Wooden World Diss.* (1708) 26 He would..shew he had one Ounce better Blood than his Leader. **1766** PITT *Sp.* in Walpole *Mem. Geo. III* (1845) II. 267, I have done all in my power to shew I hate distinctions. *Mod.* In both transactions he showed he was no fool.

†**d.** To make a fictitious show of. *Obs.*

*c***1200** ORMIN 393 Forrþi þatt teȝȝ forr idell ȝellp..Shæwenn biforenn oþre menn Godnesse & rihhtwisnesse. **1297** R. GLOUC. (Rolls) 6294 He..assailede edmond vaste Mid al þe strengþe þat he miȝte & ssewede more þer to.

**19.** *refl.* **a.** With compl. (adj. or sb., also with *for* prefixed) or inf.: To exhibit oneself in a (specified) light or character; to manifest or exemplify a (specified) quality, etc., in one's behaviour.

*c***1200** ORMIN 16520, 16522 Forr Godd himm shæweþþ towarrd te Aȝȝ o þatt illke wise, þatt tu þe shæwesst towarrd himm I þohht, i word, i dede. *a***1548** HALL *Chron.*, *Hen. VIII*, 161 Shewe your selfe an aide, a defendour of the Church, and god shall reward you. *c***1590** MARLOWE *Jew of Malta* II. iii. 797 Now will I shew my selfe to haue more of the Serpent Then the Doue. **1615** R. COCKS *Diary* (Hakl. Soc.) I. 31 He shewed hym selfe a fermer frend to Zanzaber..then to me. *a***1657** SIR J. BALFOUR *Ann. Scot.* Hist. Wks. 1825 II. 170 By this acte of his he shew himselue to be a stoute souldier, rather then a wysse generall. **1837** CARLYLE *Fr. Rev.* III. IV. vii, Anxious to show himself Patriot. **1873** BLACK *Pr. Thule* xix. 302 He had shown himself..inconsiderate to the verge of cruelty. **1888** 'J. S. WINTER' *Bootle's Childr.* xi, Mrs. Halliday had shown herself to possess a dainty taste.

†**b.** To profess (truly or falsely) to be... *Obs.*

*c***1200** *Vices & Virtues* 15 Oðer ic habbe ibien ðanne ic habbe me i-sceawed. *c***1450** *Mirk's Festial* 194 Al þay þat schoth hom holy to man syght, forto be praysyd of hom. **1484** CAXTON *Fables of Æsop* III. ii, Euery body oughte to shewe hym self suche as he is.

**c.** Of a quality, condition, etc. To manifest itself; to become evident by signs or tokens.

**1340** *Ayenb.* 21 Þis zenne him sseaweþ ine uele maneres. *a***1768** SECKER *Serm.* ix. (1770) I. 214 To hinder any other Distemper..from shewing itself by its common Effects. **1831** SCOTT *Ct. Robt.* ix, The same bold and arrogant disposition showed itself in occasional quarrels with their unwilling hosts. **1864** BRYCE *Holy Rom. Emp.* xv. (1875) 242 The tendency was one which shewed itself in various..directions.

**20. a.** To display (kindness, mercy, courtesy, malice, neglect, etc.) *to* a person by one's acts or behaviour; to accord or grant (favour, honour, grace; a courtesy, †pleasure, etc.). Const. *to*, *towards* (†*till*, †*on*) or dative.

[*a***1000** *Cædmon's Gen.* 1581 Þær he freondlice on his agenum fæder are ne wolde ȝesceawian.] *c***1200** ORMIN 1041 *Propitiari*, þatt maȝȝ onn Ennglissh nemmnedd ben Millcenn, & shæwenn are. *c***1275** *Orison of our Lord* 52 in *O.E. Misc.* 140 Þe muchel þoleburne[sse]..þat þu schawedest mon-kunne. *a***1300** *Cursor M.* 14303 Mikel luue he hir sceud þar. *c***1330** *Spec. Gy de Warw.* 263 Merci nele he shewe non. *c***1460** FORTESCUE *Abs. & Lim. Mon.* v. (1885) 119 To shew rigoure þer as fauour awght to be shewid. **1526** TINDALE *Acts* xxiv. 27 Felix willynge to shewe the Iewes a pleasure. **1535** COVERDALE *Ecclus.* x. 10 And though the phisician shewe his helpe neuer so longe. **1590** SPENSER *F.Q.* I. iv. 15 But to Duess' each one himselfe did paine All kindnesse and faire courtesie to shew [*rimes with* crew, knew]. **1653** HOLCROFT *Procopius*, *Pers. Wars* I. 5 That onely is pure gratitude, which is shewen to the dead. **1667** PEPYS *Diary* 9 Oct., He is troubled that my wife shows my sister no countenance. **1772** JOHNSON 21 Mar. in *Boswell*, Else we should have shewn his lady more civilities. **1799** NELSON 23 Sept. in Nicolas *Disp.* VII. p. cxcii, I feel much for the neglect showed him. **1870** ROGERS *Hist. Gleanings* Ser. II. 20 The king shows favour to the Lollards.

†**b.** Similarly, ***to show*** (one) ***a sign, token, semblance of.*** Also, ***to show the fruits of.*** *Obs.*

*a***1450** *Knt. de la Tour* 76 She shewed hym..signes and semblauntz of fals loue. **1565** J. PHILLIP *Patient Grissell* 273 (Malone Soc.) Shewyng to you the fruites of true obedience.

†**c.** *occas.* To inflict (shame, a judgement).

**1508** KENNEDIE *Flyting w. Dunbar* 311 And gar me schaw thy antecessouris schame. *a***1700** DRYDEN *Life Lucian* (1711) 16 To deter others from Satyrizing the new Dogma's of Christianity by the Judgment shown on Lucian.

†**d.** To set or offer (an example) in one's own person. Also of a thing. *Obs.*

**1340** HAMPOLE *Pr. Consc.* 1027 Yhit þe bodys of þe world in þair kynde, Shewes us forbisens to haf in mynde, How we suld serve God in our kynde here, Als þai do þar. **1405** *Bidding Prayer* in *Lay Folks Mass Bk.* 64 So for to reuel the popil, and swilk ensaumpil for to tak or scheu thaim. **1484** CAXTON *Fables of Avian* iii, He that wylle teche other ought to shewe good ensample.

†**21. a.** To put forth, exert (one's power, strength). Also of things. Const *on*, *against*. *Obs.*

**1398** TREVISA *Barth. De P.R.* XI. ii. (1495) 385 Whan the wynde fyndyth obstacle and lette thenne he showuyth his myghte the stronger. **1456** SIR G. HAYE *Law Arms* (S.T.S.) 47 The Romaynis..schew sik power agaynis thame that thai slewe thair king. **1575** GASCOIGNE *Kenelworth Castle* Wks. 1910 II. 106 Syr Bruse shewing a great power upon the land. *c***1595** CAPT. WYATT *R. Dudley's Voy. W. Ind.* (Hakl. Soc.) 14 That night the winde began to shew his force on us, drivinge us back againe to Palma.

**b.** To offer, attempt (resistance). ***to show fight***: to display pugnacity or readiness to fight. (Properly of animals.)

**1634** SIR T. HERBERT *Trav.* 185 The Ionas men..without cause beat the miserable Blacks that shewed no resistance. **1827** COL. HAWKER *Diary* (1893) I. 315 The..birds showed such fight against the dogs. **1863** [see FIGHT *sb.* 4]. **1907** J. H. PATTERSON *Man-Eaters of Tsavo* xvii. 189 The second rhino..showed considerable fight as we attempted to approach its fallen comrade.

**V.** To make known by statement or argument.

**22. a.** To point out, reveal, make known; to make evident or clear, explain, expound. In ME. to confess (one's sins). Also with *forth*, *out*.

*c***1200** *Trin. Coll. Hom.* 73 And for þat gult he solde his sunnes at srifte sheawen. *c***1200** ORMIN 1114, & nu icc wile shæwenn ȝuw All þatt whatt itt bitacneþþ. *c***1230** *Hali Meid.* 3 (Titus MS.) As þu scheawest forð al þat god þunckeð, & helest al þat bitter bale þat ter lið under. *a***1300** *Cursor M.* 6662 A tabernacle all for to dight, þarof he sceud þam þe slight. *Ibid.* 27293 [To] sceu his sinnes vte. **14..** *Tundale's Vis.* 212 (Wagner) Thy wykked thoughtes in thy breste Woldest þou never schewe to þe preste. **1500–20** DUNBAR *Poems* xc. 32 Gif thow can nocht schaw furth thi synnes perqueir. **1601** SHAKS. *All's Well* IV. i. 93 O let me liue, And all the secrets of our campe Ile shew. **1666** C'TESS OF WARWICK *Diary* 28 Aug., When I had showed before God all my trouble. **1725** POPE *Odyss.* x. 363 The sovereign plant he drew,..And shew'd its nature, and its wond'rous pow'r. **1772** J. H. MOORE *Pract. Navig.* (1794) 116 All traverses are worked in the manner shown above. **1832** W. PALMER *Orig. Liturg.* I. 141 No material difference can be shewn between them. **1861** PALEY *Æschylus* (ed. 2) *Pers.* 706 *note*, To show the syntax more clearly, Πέρσαις ὡς θεὸς has been marked off by commas.

*indirect passive.* **1651** HOBBES *Leviath.* II. xxx. 179 It is necessary they be shewed the evill consequences of false Judgment. **1779–81** JOHNSON *L.P.*, *Gray* ¶4 In a short time many were content to be shown beauties which they could not see.

**b.** said of a thing.

*c***1200** ORMIN 6645 Affterr þatt uss Latin boc þurrh haliȝ lare shæweþþ. **13..** *Cursor M.* 1162 (Gött.) Caym sau his sinne was knaued, And þat þe erde had it schauede. **1375** BARBOUR *Bruce* I. 566 The endentur till him gaf he, That soune schawyt the iniquite. **1542** UDALL *Erasm. Apoph.* 223 b, The same beeyng unfolded & spred abrode shewed some high mysticall mater. *a***1586** *Satir. Poems Reform.* xxxvii. 6 The suythe sall schaw it selffe out to þair schame. *a***1700** EVELYN *Diary* 27 June 1653, Monsieur Roupel sent me a small phial of his *aurum potabile*, with a letter shewing the way of administering it. *Ibid.* 20 May 1688, The consequences of which a little time will shew. **1875** JOWETT *Plato* (ed. 2) V. 15 Words are aggregated in a manner which fails to show their relation to one another.

**c.** With a relative pron. or adv. and clause. (Often with indirect obj. of the person informed.) Said also of a thing.

*c***1175** *Lamb. Hom.* 49 Nu we sculen heow sceawen hwilc hit is heom for to heren [etc.]. *a***1225** *Leg. Kath.* 2121 Ich schal schawin hu mi sweord bite i þi swire. *c***1290** *S. Eng. Leg.* 32/104 To tweie Monekus at Ierusalem him-sulf he cam bi niȝhte And schewede heom ȝware is heued lay. **1340** HAMPOLE *Pr. Consc.* 6437 Bot first I wille shew whare es helle. **1382** WYCLIF *Acts* ix. 16, I schal schewe to him, how manye thingis it bihoueth him for to suffre for my name. **1471** CAXTON *Recuyell* (Sommer) 296 The seconde booke, where shall be shewyd how troye was reedyfyed. **1697** J. LEWIS *Mem. Dk. Glocester* (1789) 38 He was then very busy shewing how he would have me build a ship. **1736** BUTLER *Anal.* I. i. Wks. 1874 I. 30 Reason does not at all shew us, in what state death naturally leaves us. **1779** *Mirror* No. 1 (1787) I. 4 Time alone can show whether I be qualified for the task I have undertaken. **1839** THACKERAY *Fatal Boots* Jan., The following letter from mamma to a friend..will pretty well show you what a poor foolish creature she was. **1848** —— *Van. Fair* vi, Suppose we had shown how Lord Joseph Sedley fell in love.

**d.** With indirect obj.: To inform, instruct, teach (a person) *how to* or †*to* (do something). Also with ellipsis of the inf.

**1567** *Gude & Godlie B.* (S.T.S.) 61 Thow lytill bill,..Thow schaw thame till Beleue in Christ. **1607** SHAKS. *Timon* III. iv. 17 Ile shew you how t'obserue a strange euent. *c***1643** LD. HERBERT *Autobiog.* (1824) 42 Those parts of Logic which..show men to distinguish betwixt truth and falsehood. **1697** J. LEWIS *Mem. Dk. Glocester* (1789) 78 She asked who shewed him? he said, Lewis. The princess ordered Mrs. Wanley to tell me not to shew him any more, as she intended to have him taught regularly. **1916** 'B. M. BOWER' *Phantom Herd* vii. 112 As to the break I made in getting those boys out here, you'll have to show me—that's all. **1976** J. E. TAYLOR in L. Wing *Early Childhood Autism* (ed. 2) viii. 209 He [*sc.* the autistic child] should not be shown how to perform, since this strengthens his dependence on other people.

†**e.** To teach (a lesson). [Cf. F. *montrer.*]

**13..** *Cursor M.* 6861 (Gött.) Suilk was þe lessoun and þe lare..þat vr lauerd scheud to moysen. **1377** LANGL. *P. Pl.* B. x. 36 Litel is he loued þat suche a lessoun scheweth. **1576** GASCOIGNE *Droomme of Doomes Day* Wks. 1910 II. 226 One night sheweth and teacheth carefulnesse to another.

†**f.** ***to show one's mind***: to reveal one's thought or intention; to express one's opinion or judgement. Also with *forth. Obs.*

*c***1520** SKELTON *Magnyf.* 1646 To shewe you my mynde I wolde haue the lesse fere. **1562** TURNER *Herbal* II. (1568) 54 Now will I shewe yow my mynde whych of all these myntes semeth unto me to be it. **1565** J. PHILLIP *Patient Grissell* 75 (Malone Soc.) Speake on my knightly knightes, eche one shewe forth your mind. **1611** BIBLE *Lev.* xxiv. 12 That the minde of the Lord might bee shewed them.

**g.** Used as an expression of defiance or self-assertion. With ellipsis of obj. clause.

**1894** MRS. H. WARD *Marcella* I. I. ii. 28 'They shall see—I will show them!' she said to herself with angry energy. **1910** A. BENNETT *Clayhanger* I. ii. 16 'I'll show 'em!' he muttered. And he meant that he would show the world. **1921** H. WILLIAMSON *Beautiful Years* 170 My aunt, what a riff-raff of new bugs, Spotty. We'll show 'em, eh? **1935** C. S. FORESTER *African Queen* vi. 116 They hadn't believed anyone would try to get down those gorges... Well, this'd show 'em. **1952** M. LASKI *Village* xvi. 215 Never did I think I'd live to hear my friends making excuses for me... I'll show them, she thought, I'll show them. **1974** M. BABSON *Stalking Lamb* iv. 32 Perhaps she wouldn't come back and collect her at all—that would show her!

**23. a.** To communicate, announce, declare, narrate, state, tell (a fact, story, news, etc.); to describe, give an account of. †Also with *forth*. Now *arch.*

*a* **1300** *Ten Commandm.* 15 in *E.E.P.* (1862) 16 God commandid to ysay . . hou he ssold þe folke tech and to ssow ham god-is defens: of þe .x. commandemens. *c* **1325** *Metr. Hom.* 30 That he suld schew him openly . . Of his felaw state sum tithand. *c* **1330** *Arth. & Merl.* 7615 Lete we hem now at þis segeing & schewe werres & wo. **1450–1530** *Myrr. our Ladye* 81 And my mouthe shall shew thy praysynge. **1456** Sir G. Haye *Law Arms* (S.T.S.) 11 He send his Apostlis . . to ger schawe the cristyn faith. **1530** Palsgr. 717/2, I shewe tydinges, or a message, *je annonce*. **1535** Coverdale *Judg.* xiv. 13 Shewe forth hy ryddle, let vs heare it. **1549** *Bk. Com. Prayer, Mattins*, My mouthe shall shewe forth thy prayse. **1637** Rutherford *Lett.* (1664) 224, I know ye desire news from my prison & I shall shew you news. **1657** Austen *Fruit Trees* I. 86 Having shewed some profitable Instructions. **1723** Ramsay *Fair Assembly* ix, These modest maids inspire the muse In flowing strains to shaw Their beauties. **1883** R. W. Dixon *Mano* I. viii. 21 For friendship's sake I may not all declare, Nor more than fits the story shall be shown.

†**b.** with *that* or *as* and clause, or with complement. Also said of a book, writing, etc. *Obs.*

*a* **1300** *Cursor M.* 699 Als scheus þe bok. *a* **1400–50** *Wars Alex.* 608 And he wald-eȝed was, as þe writt schewys. *c* **1440** *Jacob's Well* 14 We denounce & schewe acursyd . . þat is to say, we schewe hem dampnyd . . And we schewe hem to be takyn to þe powere of sathan. *c* **1505** in *Surtees Misc.* (1890) 31 He schewyd hus that he had spokyn wt John Cauthorn. **1529** More *Dyaloge* III. Wks. 223/2 Frere Hierom . . came to hym . . shewing him that he wold cast of his abite. **1632** Lithgow *Trav.* III. 83 Iohn Smith . . shewing me that all the Officers . . were in searching . . for me.

**c.** To set forth, allege (in a legal document). Often in petitionary formulae.

**1425** *Munim. de Melros* (Bannatyne Club) 544 Schawand and pretendand þair rychtis and clamys on ilke syde. **1425** *Rolls of Parlt.* IV. 289/1 Shewyn and besechyn full benignely, your trew humble Liegies the Comens of this present Parlement. **1480** *Cov. Leet Bk.* 443 These ben the compleyntes of the Iniuries & wronges don to Tho. Deram, . . shewed & deliuered be this present bill vnto Will. Shore, Mair of Couentre. **1531** *Star Chamber Cases* (Selden Soc.) II. 184 Most humbly Shewen and Complayn vnto your good lordship your daily Oratours. **1683** *Col. Rec. Pennsylv.* I. 64 The Peticion was read shewing that the Mr. of said ship deney'd to pay them their wages. **1709** Steele *Tatler* No. 118 ¶10 The humble petition of Penelope Prim, widow, Sheweth, That your petitioner was bred a clear-starcher and Sempstress.

**d.** To state, allege, plead (a cause, reason, etc.). Now chiefly in *Law*: see cause *sb.* 3 b.

*a* **1225** *Ancr. R.* 112 þe reisuns hwui beoð her efter suteliche ischeawede. **1340** Hampole *Pr. Consc.* 1052 þan wil I after shew . . Skille why men a man world calles. *c* **1374** Chaucer *Boeth.* IV. pr. ii. (1868) 114, I shal shewe þe more þikke and continuel resouns. **1535** Coverdale *Josh.* xx. 4 He . . shal . . shewe his cause before the Elders of the cite. **1568** Grafton *Chron.* II. 707 Shee declared and shewed the cause, why she could not come to them in tyme. **1597** Montgomerie *Cherrie & Slae* 1045 Hope and Curage did . . Schaw skild and pithie resouns quhy That Danger lap the dyke. **1625** Gill *Sacr. Philos.* 223 Thus have I very briefly showen not many reasons, but rather how many reasons may be showen for this Christian assertion.

†**e.** ***to show law***: to plead (*for* a suitor). *Obs.*

**1362** Langl. *P. Pl.* A. VIII. 53 He þat . . spekeþ for þe pore . . Coueiteþ not his goodes, Bote for vr lordes loue lawe for him scheweþ. **1377** *Ibid.* B. II. 134 Ledeth hire to londoun, þere lawe is yshewed.

†**f.** *absol.* To tell, declare, expound; to speak as a representative *for*; to speak, tell, give an account *of*. With indirect obj.: To inform or apprise *of*. *Obs.*

*c* **1230** *Hali Meid.* 13 þis mihte is þat an þat i þis deadlich lif scheaweð in hire estat of þe blisse undeadlich i þat eadi lond. *a* **1300** *Cursor M.* 119, I sal yow schew . . Bre[fl]i of aiþere testament. **1362** Langl. *P. Pl.* A. iv. 145 þe kyng . . rehersede þat Reson hedde Rihtfoliche I-schewet. **1399** —— *Rich. Redeles* IV. 30 To chese . . cheualleris . . To schewe ffor þe schire in company with þe grete. *c* **1400** *Rule St. Benet* (Verse) 205 Of swilk sufferance god schewes til vs In his godspel. *c* **1470** Henry *Wallace* III. 319 He schew thaim of hys deide. *c* **1500** *Melusine* 295 And shortly to shewe, he came & recountred hys brother. **1585** T. Washington tr. *Nicholay's Voy.* I. xvii. 19 [He] was sent to shewe the Bascha of our comming.

†**24.** To decree, award, assign (*to* a person) in a legal or formal manner; to fix or appoint authoritatively; to declare, make an award (*that*). In later use *Sc. Obs.*

*a* **1122** *O.E. Chron.* (Laud MS.) an. 1048, þa . . sceawede him mann .v. nihta grið ut of lande to farenne. *a* **1300** *Cursor M.* 26196 On seke man agh na scrift be laid, Bot þus gat o þe preist be said, sli scrift sceuid þan sal þou driue if þou war couerd to liue. **1387** Trevisa *Higden* (Rolls) VII. 125 þis William often tymes fauȝt wiþ þe kyng of Fraunce, nevere sodenly, . . but þe day of batayle i-schewed and assigned byfore. **1524** *Registr. Aberdon.* (Maitland Club) I. 390 This court wardis and schawis for law that [etc.]. **1540** *Aberd. Reg.* (1844) I. 171 The court wardis and schawis for law, and it wes gewine for dome, that [etc.].

**25. a.** To prove, demonstrate (a fact, statement) by argument, reasoning, allegation of evidence or instances, experiment, etc.

*c* **1330** *Spec. Gy de Warw.* 399 þat is preued and ishewed. **1390** Gower *Conf.* I. 264 And that . . I schal be reson prove and schewe. **1560** Daus tr. *Sleidane's Comm.* Pref. 4 Unlesse they could first shewe his erroure, he coulde not chaunge his opinion. **1626** W. Sclater *Expos. 2 Thess.* (1629) 200 It sufficeth to shew inualidity of the inference. **1793** Beddoes *Math. Evid.* 105 What is shewn to us by anatomy, we are just as sure of, as of that which is shewn to us by geometry. **1880** Driver *Hebr. Tenses* App. III. (ed. 2) 260 This can be shewn inferentially from Hebrew itself.

**b.** With *that* and clause (or *as* . .).

*c* **1200** Ormin Pref. 30 Jesuss iss Amminadab, Swa summ icc hafe schæwedd. **1297** R. Glouc. (Rolls) 6975 God aþ vaire issewed þat we gultelese beþ. *c* **1450** *Mirk's Festial* 40 But forto schew þat God suffrede hym specyaly, þus ensampull I tell. **1584** *Leycesters Commw.* (1641) 64 Every falling out must have an attonement againe . . as I have shewed before. **1651** Hobbes *Leviath.* II. xxiv. 127 As hath been already shewn. **1765** Blackstone *Comm.* I. viii. 303 Sir Edward Coke hath clearly shewn, that [etc.]. **1861** Paley *Æschylus* (ed. 2) *Supplices* 836 *note*, As Wilkinson shows from Aelian. **1875** Jowett *Plato* (ed. 2) IV. 238 Many arguments are used to show, that motion is the source of life. **1893** W. B. Smith *Introd. Mod. Geom.* 120 Show that tangents from two points on a centre ray form a kite.

**c.** With complementary obj.: To prove, make out (a person or thing) to be (something). Also with accus. and inf.

**1563** Winȝet *Wks.* (S.T.S.) II. 5 Gif the trew citienaris . . war recouncelit . . be sik meanis as we scheu Nehemias to hef bene. **1883** R. W. Dixon *Mano* I. xv. 48 But here to my intent it is not main In that concern to show him right or wrong. **1893** W. B. Smith *Introd. Mod. Geom.* 262 The student may easily show it to be a rectangle.

**d.** ***to go to show***: see go *v.* 42; freq. absol. in colloq. phr. ***it just*** (or ***only***) ***goes to show***. Also simply ***it just*** (or ***only***) ***shows***. Occas. with indirect obj.

**1926** F. Scott Fitzgerald *Great Gatsby* ix. 209 It just shows you, don't it? . . Jimmy was bound to get ahead. **1937** M. Sharp *Nutmeg Tree* xiv. 182 'Do you care for Galsworthy?' asked Julia. . . Sir William replied that he did. Which just showed. **1945** E. Waugh *Brideshead Revisited* II. i. 222 My wife's in a terrible way. She's an experienced sailor. Only shows, doesn't it. **1952** M. Laski *Village* iv. 68 An elementary school-teacher, that's what she was. . . Well, it just shows. **1977** J. Bingham *Marriage Bureau Murders* xi. 140, I was a little worried about you . . but . . here you are safe and sound, well, well, it just shows!

**26. a.** Of a thing: To be a proof, evidence, sign or indication of.

*c* **1330** *Arth. & Merl.* 1575 We seiȝen . . her aboue Ouer ous a sky houe, þat ous schewed þe biȝate Of swiche a þing on erþe late. *c* **1380** Wyclif *Sel. Wks.* III. 175 Her workes schewes þis wel, howevere þei speke by syde. *c* **1430** *Pilgr. Lyf Manhode* II. cxlviii. (1869) 135 Bi which disioynct is ysawed þe onhede of bretherhed. **1596** Shaks. *1 Hen. IV*, III. i. 181 You must needes learne, Lorde, to amend this fault: Though sometimes it shew Greatnesse, Courage, Blood. **1673** O. Walker *Educ.* (1677) 97 Huffing, and swaggering . . commonly shews want of spirit. **1750** Gray *Long Story* 138 Her air and all her manners shew it. **1848** Thackeray *Van. Fair* lvii, Having undergone such a process of blood-letting and calomel as showed the strength of his original constitution. **1859** *Habits Gd. Society* xi. 314 Nothing showing worse taste than to load your plate. **1884** *Q. Rev.* Jan. 215 Misprints, showing . . carelessness on the part of the corrector.

**b.** Const. clause with *that*, *as*, etc.

*a* **1225** *Leg. Kath.* 450 Ah þi schene nebscheft & ti semliche schape schaweð wel þet tu art freo monne foster. **1338** R. Brunne *Chron.* (1725) 70 þat þe lond is þin, þi helm schewes it þe. *c* **1380** Wyclif *Wks.* (1880) 145 As here wickid lif scewiþ. *a* **1704** T. Brown *Misc.*, *Match for Devil* Wks. 1711 IV. 147 His Habit, Cane, and formal Face, Shew'd he was of Geneva Race. **1847** Helps *Friends in C.* I. vi. 98 All of it only goes to show how little we know of each other. **1861** Paley *Æschylus* (ed. 2) *Agam.* 1261 *note*, 'Go on faring as you now fare', viz. prosperously, as the context shows. **1868** Lockyer *Elem. Astron.* vi. (1879) 234 That nebulæ are masses of glowing gas is shown by the fact that their light consists merely of a few bright lines.

**c.** Const. obj. with compl., or accus. and inf.

**1560** *Ovid's Narcissus* Dj, For who dothe count [*printed* couet] him selfe of wyser skole Then dedes him showe, doth proue him selfe a fole. **1751** Labelye *Westm. Bridge* 77 Considerable Openings in the Joints shewed those Arches in some Danger. **1828** Duppa *Trav. Italy*, etc. 114 The walls of the city are now sufficiently entire to shew their extent to have been about three miles. **1871** Meredith *H. Richmond* xlvi, Their maxims show them to direct all their acuteness upon obtaining quality for their money.

**27. show up. a.** In school language: To report (a scholar) for punishment.

**1845** *College & T.B. Life at Westm.* 25 Oct., I went into School not having done my Verses. . . I was therefore *Shown-up*, and . . pleaded my first fault.

**b.** To disgrace or discredit by a thorough exposure; to exhibit as an impostor or an imposture; to expose (a person's faults, ignorance, misdeeds, etc.).

**1826** *Blackw. Mag.* Aug. 325/2 A long article in the Quarterly Theological Review has fairly *shown up* the Yankee divine. **1829** *Examiner* 476/1 He threatened to 'show up' my brother in the *Age*. **1865** Mill *Exam. Hamilton* 478 That mathematical mysticism, so mercilessly shown up by Berkeley. **1884** *St. James's Gaz.* 17 Oct. 3/1 The unpleasing process of 'showing-up' an unscrupulous adversary.

**VI.** *intr.* To be seen, be visible, appear.

**28. a.** To be or become visible; to make an appearance. Said of persons and things. Also *transf.*, of a woman: to manifest visible signs of pregnancy (*colloq.*).

*a* **1300** *Cursor M.* 17288 + 254 þis was þe first time þat iesus, . . Schewed til anyman after his vp-risyng. **1393** Langl. *P. Pl.* C. XI. 159 þe sonne som tyme for cloudes May nat shyne ne shewe on shawes on erthe. **1399** —— *Rich. Redeles* II. 52 þanne comeþ . . Anoþer proud partriche . . and houeth þe eyren . . and ffostrith and ffodith, tille ffedris schewe. *c* **1400** Maundev. (1839) iv. 23 Sche lyeth in an olde Castelle . . and schewethe twyes or thryes in the ȝeer. *c* **1450** *Merlin* iii. 56 Than shewde the signe in the ayre that Merlin hadde seide. **1470–85** Malory *Arthur* XVI. ii. 666 They sawe an hand sheuyng vnto the elbowe. **1573–80** Tusser *Husb.* (1878) 92 Rowle after a deaw, when barlie doth sheaw. **1599** T. M[oufet] *Silkwormes* 50 Til you can attaine wherwith to feed your guests when first they shew, Haste not their hatching. **1607** Shaks. *Timon* I. i. 23 The fire i' th Flint Shewes not, till it be strooke. **1862** Ansted *Channel Isl.* I. iv. (ed. 2) 61 One of the most dangerous rocks . . only shows within two hours of low water. **1887** A. E. Housman *Shropshire Lad* i, It dawns in Asia, tombstones show, And Shropshire names are read. **1891** 'J. S. Winter' *Lumley* vi, Where the lily-buds were just beginning to show. **1892** Bierce *In Midst of Life* 97 He showed against the sky, he and his horse, sharply defined . . as an equestrian statue. **1936** M. Mitchell *Gone with Wind* xxxviii. 681 Comforting herself . . with the belief that she did not show at all when thus covered. **1957** [see mistake *sb.* 1 d]. **1966** B. Askwith *Step out of Time* vi. 95 How the old lady knew, miss, we have no idea. Rose certainly hadn't begun to show. **1979** R. Rendell *Make Death love Me* iii. 25 In that field Christopher was conceived. . . Pam would marry before she began to 'show'.

**b.** Of a thing: To be seen (*through*, *over*, *under*, etc.) something that partly covers or conceals it. Also, to be visible as a fault or defect.

**1842** Browning *Soliloquy Sp. Cloister* iv, Can't I see his dead eye glow . . That is, if he'd let it show! **1844** Mrs. Browning *Lost Bower* xii, Few and broken paths showed through it. **1852** Mrs. Stowe *Uncle Tom's C.* xxvi, Take care, don't spoil the looks of it! cut underneath, where it won't show. **1886** *Manch. Exam.* 13 Jan. 3/2 Were the paper a little better it would be perfect. As it is the type shows through the page. **1908** R. Bagot *A. Cuthbert* v. 39 The walls and towers of Warkworth, barely showing above the woods surrounding them. **1907** J. A. Hodges *Elem. Photogr.* (ed. 6) 88 Markings . . which would show in the prints.

**c.** of immaterial things.

**1390** Gower *Conf.* I. 31 Wherof the sothe schewe may, At Rome ferst if we beginne. *Ibid.* 308 Hate is a wraththe noght schewende. **1542** Udall *Erasm. Apoph.* 29 The disposicion of a manne dooeth not shewe so clere in his face. **1585** T. Washington tr. *Nicholay's Voy.* IV. xxxvi. 158 b, True religion . . began to shew and take root. **1886** Stevenson *Kidnapped* ix, It was plain he meant more by the words than showed upon the face of them.

†**d.** *impers.* = (it) is seen or shown, appears, is plain. *Obs.*

*c* **1386** Chaucer *Pars. T.* ¶331 As sheweth here by the naddre. **1390** Gower *Conf.* I. 63 It scheweth ek how he can werche Among tho wyde furred hodes. *c* **1391** Chaucer *Astrol.* II. §32 As shewith by the canoun of thi kalender. **1509** Barclay *Shyp of Folys* (1874) I. 35 Unstable is your mynde: that shewes by your garment. **1556** *Chron. Grey Friars* (Camden) 78 As it shalle shoo after. **1570** *Satir. Poems Reform.* xiii. 101 As schawis weill be ȝour Genalogie.

**e.** ***to show forth***: to come forth to view. ***to show ahead***: to take a position ahead (in a race).

**1375** Barbour *Bruce* IV. 121 The pomp of pryde ay furth shawis. **1500** *Ortus Vocab.*, *Compareo*, to shewe forth. **1884** *Cambr. Rev.* 10 Dec. 132 At the start, Bristowe's crew at once shewed ahead by about three feet.

**f.** Of an oil well: to give an indication of the presence of oil. Cf. show *sb.*[1] 5 c.

**1904** *Dialect Notes* II. 389 *Show*, v., to promise oil. **1977** *Times* 2 Nov. 3 Almost five years ago to the day, Beryl [*sc.* an oil well] showed.

**g.** In catch phr. ***your slip*** (etc.) ***is showing*** (cf. slip *sb.*[3] 10, 4 c), addressed to someone thought to be unwittingly exposing a fault. Also in similar contexts.

**1943** D. Powell *Time to be Born* v. 103 Pardon me, lady, your slip is showing. **1958** *Spectator* 1 Aug. 174/2 There were still standards, and hypocrisy, the homage of vice and virtue, was the duty of all public figures. But in a gratifying number of cases the slip showed and the shocked and gratified public learned that 'Anything Goes'. **1968** [see *credibility gap* s.v. credibility c]. **1971** C. Fick *Danziger Transcript* (1973) 33 Your defense mechanisms are showing, Mr. Danziger. **1976** A. Miller *Inside Outside* vii. 83, I see in you a new broom, though your slip is still showing in places.

**29. a.** To appear in public, make a display in public. In mod. use chiefly *colloq.* (cf. b): To appear in company or society; to make an appearance in an assembly, among guests, etc. Also in weakened sense, an *ellipt.* use of sense 35 c, to put in an appearance, 'turn up'.

**1625** B. Jonson *Staple of N.* Prol. for Stage 14 To know How many Coaches in Hide-parke did show last spring. **1671** in *12th Rep. Hist. MSS. Comm.* App. v. 22 All the troopes are to show in Hide Parke beefore the Prince of Orange.

**1825** C. M. Westmacott *Engl. Spy* I. 215 He *shows* in Park. **1833** T. Hook *Parson's Dau.* III. x, The breakfast party did not assemble till noon, and then Lady Catherine did not 'show'. **1848** Thackeray *Bk. Snobs* vii, Marian has a hump-back and doesn't show. **1858** Trollope *Dr. Thorne* II. v. 91 He'll be in presently. I believe he never shews till just before dinner. **1864** Dickens *Mut. Fr.* (1865) I. I. xiii. 127 What if I . . take a look round? . . None of you need show. **1889** H. F. Wood *Englishm. Rue Cain* ix, I'll show against him for any object of value. Sing? What do you think of this note . . ? **1898** Jean A. Owen *Hawaii* iii. 65 If the king was in the cabin of a vessel no subject might show on deck. **1907** B. M. Croker *Company's Servant* xxxiii. 335 'Gojar never shows by day,' explained Talbot. **1951** T. Sterling *House without Door* vii. 81 Big-shots like that didn't come to the police. . . The guy would never show. **1969** W. Garner *Us or Them War* xxxvii. 276 Jagger said flatly, 'I'm staying until she shows.' **1974** 'J. le Carré' *Tinker, Tailor, Soldier, Spy* vii. 56 She didn't show. . . It was the first time she'd broken a date.

**b.** *Pugilism.* To enter the ring as a combatant.

**1813** *Sporting Mag.* XLI. 99 He *showed* with seeming reluctance about an hour after the appointed time. **1818** *Ibid.* (N.S.) II. 279 Johnson . . first *showed* and threw his hat in the ring. **1828** Egan *Boxiana* IV. 169 Turner . . was far more likely to make his *exit*, than ever be made able to *show* again in the Prize Ring.

**c.** *colloq.* To exhibit oneself for money.

**1898** DAILY NEWS 2 Apr. 6/1 He got a living by 'showing' in the various public-houses in the neighbourhood at entertainments got up for his benefit.

**d.** *Comm.* Of a commodity: To appear or be prominent in the market.

**1913** *Times* 11 Dec. 10/2 In insurance phraseology, 'a good deal of radium has lately been showing.' **1982** *Times* 13 July 16/1 Glaxo showed strongly, moving up 12p on revised profit forecasts. *Ibid.* 17 July 12/1 Mixconcrete showed very firm.

**e.** *N. Amer. Horse-racing.* To finish third or in the first three in a race.

**1903** J. ULLMAN *What's the Odds?* 129 The customary limit of the handbooks around Chicago was twenty, eight and four, to win, place and show. **1936** [see PLACE *v.* 5 f]. **1968** *Globe & Mail* (Toronto) 13 Feb. 27/1, I myself.. usually bet $200 to show, or $50-$100-$200 across the board. **1977** *New Yorker* 16 May 130/1 In the OTB betting shops..he paid three dollars straight, three dollars to place, and three dollars to show.

**30. a.** With complement (*adj.* or †*sb.*): To look, seem, appear. *arch.*

**1340** *Ayenb.* 44 Huanne þo þet zelleþ be wyȝte purchaceþ and makeþ zuo moche þet þet þing þet me ssel weȝe ssseweþ more heuy. **1399** LANGL. *Rich. Redeles* III. 368 þe sonne þat so briȝte schewed. *c* **1430** LYDG. *Minor Poems* (Percy Soc.) 22 All is not golde that outward shewith bright. **1479** *Paston Lett.* III. 267 That my Lord of Ely is and shal be bettyr lord to me then he hathe shewyd as yet. **1513** *Act 5 Hen. VIII*, c. 4. §1 If the same Worsted..taketh any Wet, incontinent it will shew spotty and foul. **1572** in Bercher *Nobility Wom.* (1904) 31 Hitherto he hath shewid an Obstinate and a Fole. **1592** TIMME *Ten. Eng. Lepers* E 3 A Woolfe in a sheepes skinne sheweth a dead sheepe. **1635** PAGITT *Christianogr.* I. ii. (1636) 82 The Pope to make his Jurisdiction to shew greater then it is, giveth many titles. **1671** tr. *Marten's Voy. Spitzbergen* in *Acc. Sev. Late Voy.* II. (1694) 19 These Snow-Mountains show very strange to those that never saw them before. **1726** LEONI *Alberti's Archit.* II. 17b, Lead.. shews very handsome, and is not very expensive. **1747** DR. HOADLY *Suspicious Husb.* II. iv, Why, how dull and phlegmatick do you shew to me now? **1812** *Examiner* 11 May 292/1 Poor..soils..show..very thin. **1863** COWDEN CLARKE *Shaks. Char.* iv. 101 How daintily epicurean the fellow shows. **1893** *Oxford Mag.* 1 Nov. 40/2 The wood when cut showed sound as a bell.

**b.** With adv. or advb. phrase: To present an appearance (specified by the adv.); to make a (good, bad, etc.) show or display.

*c* **1375** *Sc. Leg. Saints* xxxvi. (*Baptista*) 645 Lowing in-to kine wel scheuis, þat is enhornit with gud thewis. **1602** MARSTON *Ant. & Mel.* II. Wks. 1856 I. 27 They showe as well as if they were new. **1631** MASSINGER *Emperor East* V. iii, The falling out, and in, Betweene the husband and the wife showes rarely. **1632** SIR T. HAWKINS tr. *Mathieu's Unhappy Prosp.* 243 Great wealth shews ill without honours. **1764** REID *Inquiry* i. §6 Wks. I. 103/1 It [a puppet] shews tolerably by candle light. **1802** MAR. EDGEWORTH *Moral T., Forester* viii, The lady-patronesses..contenting themselves with seeing the charity-children *show well* in procession to Church. **1823** SCOTT *Quentin D.* xi, Her imperfect and unequal gait, which shewed to peculiar disadvantage as she traversed this long gallery. **1851** J. H. NEWMAN *Catholics in Eng.* 19 Here, again, things would show very differently, if Catholics had the painting. **1877** FROUDE *Short Stud.* (1883) IV. I. iv. 48 Becket never showed to more advantage than in moments of personal danger. **1912** *Times* 19 Dec. 13/5 He [a prize dog] moved and showed well and deserved his honours.

**c.** To look *like*. *arch.*

**1578** LYTE *Dodoens* IV. lii. 510 A white substance or pith, the whiche being drawen out, sheweth like long, white.. threds. **1605** SHAKS. *Lear* I. iv. 265 This our Court infected with their manners Shewes like a riotous Inne. **1697** DRYDEN *Virg. Georg.* IV. 805 Like a large Cluster of black Grapes they show. *a* **1700** EVELYN *Diary* 14 July 1675, Holmby House, which being demolish'd in the late civil warrs, shews like a Roman ruine. **1877** BLACKIE *Wise Men Greece* 137 We shall show like an army of crows marching against eagles.

†**d.** With *to* and inf.: To appear or seem (to be, to do something); to affect, profess, pretend; to be seen evidently (to be or do). *Obs.*

*c* **1386** CHAUCER *Melib.* ¶2386 Whan he sheweth to doon a thyng openly and werketh priuely the contrarie. **1402** *Friar Daw Topias* in *Pol. Poems* (Rolls) II. 109 And ȝit ȝour sect susteynes wommen to seie massis, shewyng to trete a sacrament as preestes that thei were. **1575** GASCOIGNE *Hemetes* Wks. 1910 II. 481 W[th] all semblaunt that mighte be, he shewed to sett by her but litle. *c* **1580** SIDNEY *Ps.* IX. xi, Then the Lord in judgment showes to raign. **1588** PARKE tr. *Mendoza's Hist. China* 334 There are many mountaines which shewe to haue mettals. **1632** BP. HALL *Hard Texts, Matt.* xii. 33 Be good, and shew to be such by the fruits which ye beare. **1653** H. COGAN *Scarlet Gown* 60 The Pope ..received him very graciously, and shewed to be glad of his recovered liberty.

†**e.** With *as though*, *as if*: To have an appearance which suggests that —. *Obs.*

**1526** *Pilgr. Perf.* (W. de W. 1531) 78 Pretendynge and shewynge outwardly as though it were of very mekenes. **1582** N. LICHEFIELD tr. *Castanheda's Conq. E. Ind.* I. vii. 18b, Skirmishing with their dartes, and showing as though they..wold defende the water. **1657** EARL MONM. tr. *Paruta's Pol. Disc.* 102 The Romans..in all their actions shewed as if they desired nothing but glory. **1670–1** NARBOROUGH *Jrnl.* in *Acc. Sev. Late Voy.* I. (1694) 67 The Wood shews in many places as if there were Plantations. *c* **1710** CELIA FIENNES *Diary* (1888) 214 It makes all the houses shew as if they were cover'd with snow. **1725** POPE *Shaks. Wks.* I. Pref. 12 Which shows as if the friendship had continued thro' life.

**f.** With ppl. adj. *to show willing*, to display readiness to please or satisfy. *colloq.*

*Willing* is sometimes construed as a noun, in which case the verb belongs to branch IV.

**1957** *Loneliness* (Women's Group on Public Welfare) iii. 29 The older woman..must 'show willing' and be adaptable. **1959** P. BULL *I know Face* i. 11 My father wanted me to be a chartered accountant... However, in order to show willing, I did settle for 'journalism'. **1964** A. WILSON *Late Call* iii. 121 Luckily the poor creature was very willing, and there was one rule Sylvia always made—never turn off anyone who shows willing. **1973** J. WILSON *Truth or Dare* x. 121, I feel I've got to go, Claire, just to show willing.

**31.** *to show for—*. †**a.** To claim to be, have, or do (something). *Obs.* **b.** To give promise of, portend, 'look like'. *dial.*

**a. 1577** tr. *Bullinger's Decades* III. v. (1592) 330 Let this labour of mine not seeme to any man to bee..lesse profitable than it sheweth for. **1628** FELTHAM *Resolves* I. xxvi. 83 Hee would make vs beleeue, Divinity is much short of what it shewes for. **1680** FILMER *Patriarcha* ii. §3. 36 As this Argument comes not home to our Point, so it is not able to prove that Title which it shews for.

**b. 1778** [W. H. MARSHALL] *Minutes Agric.* 2 Oct. 1776, The other evening shewed for rain. **1876** *Surrey Gloss.*, *Show for*, to look like; e.g. 'It shows for rain uncommon'. **1886** *W. Somerset Word-bk.* s.v., The wind's up again, and I sim do show vor fine weather.

†**32. show away** = *show off* (33 a). *Obs.*

**1759** GOLDSM. *Bee* No. 1 ¶14 The French player..begins to show away by talking nonsense. **1760–72** H. BROOKE *Fool of Qual.* (1809) III. 38 He paraded and shewed away, at a vast rate, concerning the divinely inherent right of monarchs. **1770** C. JENNER *Placid Man* III. ix, Lord B. shewed away in all his glory.

**33. show off. a.** To act or talk for show; to make a deliberate or ostentatious display of one's abilities or accomplishments. *colloq.*

*a* **1793** G. WHITE *Nat. Cal., Observ. Birds* (1795) 79 A fern-owl this evening..showed off in a very unusual.. manner. **1815** LADY GRANVILLE *Lett.* (1894) I. 69 She puts me in mind of Miss Berry when she is showing off. **1894** D. C. MURRAY *Making Novelist* 201 He was tempted to swagger and 'show off' as children say.

**b.** *Pugilism.* ? To begin the attack, start a round.

**1812** *Sporting Mag.* XL. 66 His antagonist shewed off at his head. **1821** EGAN *Boxiana* (1830) I. 261 Dan *showed off* in good style..and finished the round by knocking down his opponent.

**34. show out. a.** ? To become visible, emerge from obscurity or concealment; *fig.* to exhibit one's true character.

**1839** M. WALKER *Diary* 9 Feb. in C. M. Drury *First White Women over Rockies* (1963) II. 143 Mrs. W. on first reaching us seemed in good humor & I hoped she had made her a better heart. But at supper table & even before she began to show out. **1846** DE QUINCEY *Syst. Heavens* Wks. 1862 III. 179 Description of the nebula in Orion as forced to show out by Lord Rosse. **1859** —— *Mackintosh* Wks. XIII. 75 Rarely has a false idea been more suddenly caused to founder and show out. **1888** 'R. BOLDREWOOD' *Robbery under Arms* vi, The horse held up his head and snorted as he came abreast of us, and we showed out.

**b.** *U.S.* = *show off* (33 a).

**1889** MARY E. WILKINS *Far-away Melody*, etc. (1890) 258 See that old lady trailing her best black silk by... Ain't it ridiculous how she keeps on showing out?

**35. show up. a.** To appear conspicuously or in relief.

**1883** *Truth* 31 May 768/2 A brocade on which..yellow marguerites..showed up upon a ground of scarlet. **1891** BAX *Outlooks fr. New Standpoint* iii. 171 Most persons are afraid of something, but they, at times, show up brave on the background of persons who are afraid of something else.

**b.** To become prominent, to catch the eye.

**1885** *Field* 31 Jan. 135/2 Some scrummaging took place at the half way till Ekin showed up with a good run, which brought the play to the North lines.

**c.** *colloq.* To put in an appearance; to be present or 'turn up' (at an appointed time or place).

**1888** *Lisbon* (Dakota) *Star* 3 Feb. 4/1 Will Worden is expected to show up next week. **1890** 'R. BOLDREWOOD' *Col. Reformer* (1891) 167 Paul did not show up at the office next day. *c* **1895** *Thompson St. Poker Club* 131 The regular members showed up, however, in force.

**VII.** The verb-stem in combinations.

**36. show-and-tell.** *N. Amer.* A method used in teaching young children, who are encouraged to bring objects to school and describe them to their classmates. Usu. as *attrib. phr.*

[**1948** *Q. Jrnl. Speech* XXXIV. 361/1 Those who volunteered to speak during the regular classroom share-and-tell period.] **1950** *Amer. Childhood* Sept. 18/1 Woodridge Elementary School in Austin, Texas, along with many other schools in the nation, began solving this problem three years ago through a 'Show and Tell' period, conducted almost every day in the first, second, and third grades. *Ibid.* 18/3 Pictures cause a great sensation at 'Show and Tell'. **1958** J. E. LEAVITT *Nursery-Kindergarten Educ.* xi. 235 The virtues of 'show and tell' are too often dissipated in either agonies of shyness, or frantic last minute panics at home to 'find something for show and tell'. **1962** P. BRACKEN *I hate to housekeep Bk.* (1963) vi. 62 The children might, at their Show-and-Tell sessions at school. **1980** in S. Terkel *Amer. Dreams* 112 No courses in show-and-tell and personality adjustment.

†**37. show-away** *a.* (Cf. 32.) Given to display, ostentatious.

**1775** S. J. PRATT *Liberal Opin.* liii. (1783) II. 137 Those shew-away fellows are mere pick-pockets. **1795** HAN. MORE *Sheph. Salisb. Pl.* I. Wks. 1834 I. 265 A plain frugal man, who..was remarked to give away more than any of his show-away neighbours.

**38. show-through.** *Printing.* The fact of print on one side of a sheet of paper being visible from the other side. Cf. PRINT-THROUGH 2, *strike-through* s.v. STRIKE *v.* 88.

**1947** *New Book Faces* (Lanston Monotype Machine Co., Philadelphia) 3/2 The 'show through' which is the result of printing in heavy color on thin or semi-transparent papers results in a loss of visibility and thereby affects readability. **1961** *N. & Q.* Apr. 160/2 A comparison of the facsimile with the original has shown that the fascimile is not so clear, but it has an adequate definition and the show-through, which occurs on several pages, does not seriously interfere with the reproduction. **1971** *British Printer* Jan. 80/2 The show-through is slight enough to permit printing both sides.

**39. show up. a.** (Cf. 27 b.) The act of 'showing up' or exposing to ridicule, censure, or the like. Also, an instance of this; an exposé.

**1830** 'JON BEE' *Ess. Foote* p. lxxvii, (Cent.) Treading closely on the heels of a threatened show up. **1840** *Fraser's Mag.* XXII. 372 We cannot muster up impudence enough to continue our show-up of Wightwick's naughtiness. *a* **1854** MILL *Early Draft Autobiogr.* (1961) ii. 93 In my father's article the detailed shew-up of the Edinburgh Review had been left unfinished. **1854** *Fraser's Mag.* L. 253 Mr. Disraeli was to make a show-up of Mr. Gladstone's finance. **1937** W. H. S. SMITH *Let.* 30 Oct. in *Young Man's Country* (1977) ii. 97, I am beguiling myself..by reading Sinclair Lewis's *Elmer Gantry*, a show-up of American Nonconformists. **1949** 'G. ORWELL' *Let.* 16 June in *Coll. Essays* (1968) IV. 502 My recent novel is *not* intended as an attack on Socialism..but as a show-up of the perversions to which a centralised economy is liable. **1961** *Guardian* 9 June 9/2 One of those tough, sexy, ostensibly moralistic show-ups.

**b.** A police identification parade. *U.S. slang.*

**1929** M. A. GILL *Underworld Slang* 11/1 *Show-up*, where suspects are viewed by the police. **1932** *Sun* (Baltimore) 12 Dec. 1/3 The authorities conducted a mysterious 'show up' today for De Larm..police endeavoring to learn whether he had been seen in the vicinity..at the time of the killing. **1949** *Penguin New Writing* XXXVI. 96 They were real cops though. I had..to stand the showup..and to put in twenty days at Juvenile. **1955** *Sun* (Baltimore) 22 Nov. 3/1 Lyman Brown.. picked Graham out of a 'showup' of seven jail inmates.

**showable** (ˈʃəʊəb(ə)l), *a.* Also shew-. [f. SHOW *v.* + -ABLE.]

†**1.** Demonstrative, able to prove. *Obs. rare*$^{-1}$.

*c* **1400** tr. *Secreta Secret., Gov. Lordsh.* 96 And þanne comes to him a strengh shewable, or Philosophable, þat byholdys shappys vndirstandable. *Ibid.* 103 þat he be knowynge..in arsmetyk, þat is ful soth and shewable.

**2.** Demonstrable, provable. *rare*$^{-1}$.

**1617** HIERON *Penance for Sin* iv. Wks. 1619 II. 103 This ..is shewable by Scripture.

**3.** That can be shown or presented to view.

**1813** F. BURNEY 15 July *Let.* (1978) VII. 157 It was most fortunate that bit was shewable, for it gave propriety to the Measure. **1823** LAMB *Lett. to J. H. Payne* 23 Jan., Mary.. says you must write more *showable* letters about those matters. **1838** P'CESS ELIZABETH *Lett.* (1898) 347, I have so bad a swelled face I am not shewable.

**showance** (ˈʃəʊəns). *rare.* [f. SHOW *sb.* + -ANCE.] Showing, display, appearance.

**1898** HARDY *Wessex Poems* 3 Sole the showance those of my onward earth-track—never transcended. **1908** —— *Dynasts* VII. ix. 346 My only course To make good showance to posterity Was to implant my line upon the throne.

**show biz.** Also show-biz and as one word.

**a.** Colloq. (orig. *U.S.*) abbrev. of SHOW BUSINESS.

**1945** *Variety* 13 June 25/4 Big-league baseball already had rearranged its team travel schedules to a minimum. However show biz has done nothing about this yet. **1948** *N.Y. Times* 18 July 2E/7 Jack Pulaski..helped coin much of *Variety's* lingo, such as 'show biz'. **1953** [see IMPRESSION *sb.* 6 d]. **1959** R. LONGRIGG *Wrong Number* iv. 60 Got to extemporise in show biz. **1960** M. T. WILLIAMS *Art of Jazz* p. i, A strange branch of big-time show biz. **1960** *New Left Rev.* May–June 33/2 They have their 'Pop Page'..their key to Showbiz. **1971** 'A. BURGESS' *MF* xv. 162 A lot of science gets turned into showbiz as they call it. **1976** *Liverpool Echo* 23 Nov. 6/4 Blackpool remains..the heartland of Northern showbiz.

**b.** *attrib.*

**1945** *Variety* 30 May 28/3 (*heading*) Cantor's Showbiz tribute. **1946** J. B. PRIESTLEY *Bright Day* viii. 243 Wouldn't it be heavenly if you could mix them up—..the retired majors..and the Show Biz boys. **1959** *News Chron.* 17 Oct. 4/2 Skirmishes with showbiz brigands. **1976** A. DAVIS *Television: First Forty Years* 42 Many of the public had misgivings, for the word 'newscaster' suggested a show-biz American approach.

Hence **show-bizzy** *a.*

**1969** *Listener* 9 Jan. 62/2 The first night..was a show-bizzy occasion. **1973** S. COHEN *Diane Game* (1974) xvii. 149 After the welcoming speeches and..show-bizzy, bouquet-throwing speeches, the stage was cleared. **1981** *Times* 20 May 14/5 Even more controversial, however, is Cardin's idea to make Maxim's more showbizzy with a series of monthly soirees starring international artists.

**show-boat.** *U.S.* [SHOW *sb.*[1]] A river steamer on which theatrical performances are given.

**1869** *Atlantic Monthly* July 85/1 The little steamer Banjo, a show-boat belonging to Dr. Spaulding, the manager of the Floating Palace, was advertised to be at Cape Girardeau. **1909** A. C. RICE *Mr. Opp* vii. 98 A new and handsome Show Boat will tie up at the Cove. **1926** E. FERBER *Show Boat* i. 13 Eager for entertainment as the dwellers were along the little Illinois and Missouri town,..they came sparsely to the show boat. **1952** M. ALLINGHAM *Tiger in Smoke* v. 88 Lighted buses crawling by looked as big as showboats. **1977** N. ADAM *Triplehip Cracksman* xii. 124 They were a mixed bunch..drinker..showboat gambler.

**ˈshowboater.** *U.S.* [f. prec. + -ER[1].] An actor on or manager of a showboat. Also *fig.*, one who performs (in other contexts) in the theatrical style characteristic of a showboat player.

**1951** P. GRAHAM *Showboats* ii. 15 Green River..was in later years to become showboaters' paradise. **1952** *Times Lit. Suppl.* 4 Apr. 239/4 The show that Mr. Chapman, the first 'showboater', presented to the Mississippi Valley. **1968** 'G. BAGBY' *Another Day* iii. 45 'What was wrong with him?' 'He was a clown. He was a showboater. He had a big mouth.' **1969** *Wall St. Jrnl.* 10 Oct. 14/1 Some of the best umpires in baseball today are almost unknown to the fans... They're not the showboaters. **1977** *Time* Jan. 56/2 Streisand is a showboater, a sort of one-woman Hippodrome whose roots are in the brassiest tradition of the American musical theatre.

Also **ˈshowboating.**

**1951** P. GRAHAM *Showboats* vii. 66 The years 1884–1889 were important..to the growing institution of showboating. **1972** D. RAMSAY *Little Murder Music* 71 Maybe there's some other reason behind the recent tendency towards showboating. The fact is, there have been a lot of gimmicks lately. **1975** W. SAFIRE *Before Fall* vi. 384 The proposal was what Nixon would call..'showboating', presented primarily for its political impact in the States..with little chance of its acceptance by the North Vietnamese.

**ˈshow-box.** [SHOW *sb.*[1]] A box in which objects of curiosity are exhibited; esp. a box containing a peep-show.

**1748** LADY LUXBOROUGH *Let. to Shenstone* 28 Apr. (1775) 19 But were you to present me with the Views of the Leasowes, I own I should not put them into my show-box without pain. **1779** WARNER in Jesse *Selwyn & Contemp.* (1844) IV. 312 A Savoyard with a show-box. **1842** HAWTHORNE *Twice-t. T.* Ser. II. *Seven Vagabonds* (1883) 125 Rescuing the showbox of such a couple from a mob of great double-fisted countrymen.

*fig.* **1789** BURNS *Fragm. inscribed to C. J. Fox* 23 Mankind are his show box.

**show business.** orig. *U.S.* [SHOW *sb.*[1]]

**1. a.** The entertainment industry, esp. light entertainment (formerly, always with *the*). Occas., people engaged in show business collectively. Cf. SHOW BIZ.

**1850** T. FORD *Peep behind Curtain* vii. 26 This gentleman has been engaged..in the show-business, and is, beyond all question, the best. **1870** D. J. KIRWAN *Palace & Hovel* v. 65 I've been in the show business for sixteen years... I fust began jumpin', as a hacrobat in the penny gaffs. **1886** [see PERFORMING *ppl. a.* 2]. **1903** *Century Mag.* Apr. 819/1 General Grant..declined to remain in town for the occasion, saying that he had had enough of 'show business'. **1911** G. K. CHESTERTON *Innoc. Father Brown* v. 126 He happened to be picked up by some travelling show, and..got on quite well in the show business. **1936** 'P. QUENTIN' *Puzzle for Fools* iv. 26 He was crazy to get into show business; stunts and strong-man acts. **1956** H. GRISEWOOD in A. Pryce-Jones *New Outl. Mod. Knowl.* 426 The cinema and broadcasting to a large extent are part of what is called show-business. **1962** J. MCCABE *Mr. Laurel & Mr. Hardy* i. 28 He had a great opening. All show business on the British Isles came to it. **1978** M. MUGGERIDGE in R. Trevivian *So you're Lonely* 11 The Religious Broadcasting Department of the BBC..itself a curious no-man's-land lying between show business and evangelism.

**b.** In catch-phr. ***there's no business like show business.***

**1946** I. BERLIN (*song-title*) There's no business like show business. **1956** B. HOLIDAY *Lady sings Blues* (1973) vi. 62 It's like they say, there's no damn business like show business. You have to smile to keep from throwing up. **1972** *Guardian* 24 June 11/7 There is, as they say, no business like show business.

**2.** *attrib.*

**1958** *Punch* 26 Feb. 278/1, I was delighted to see that Frankie Vaughan had been selected as Show Business Personality of the Year. **1961** *Radio Times* 6 Apr. 53/2 No.. illusions about the permanence of show-business reputations. **1976** M. BUTTERWORTH *Festival!* xi. 187 Feature stories on the show business stars.

**showcase,** *sb.* (*a.*) [f. SHOW *sb.*[1] + CASE *sb.*[2]]

**1.** A glass case for exhibiting delicate or valuable articles in a shop or museum.

**1835** F. LIEBER *Stranger in Amer.* II. ii. 64, I..found there ..all the companions of my earliest youth, the show-cases.. with their old Nuremberg prints. **1879** *Print. Trades Jrnl.* XXVIII. 12 Put up in inexpensive little show-cases. **1897** R. M. STUART *In Simpkinsville* 121 Old Dr. Jenkins stood behind the showcase in his drug-store. **1935** D. L. SAYERS *Gaudy Night* vi. 124 What a blessing I hadn't put the Folio Chaucer and the other valuables in the show-cases. **1952** P. WENTWORTH *Brading Collection* xii. 69 Round the sides there were glass-topped show-cases. **1970** J. S. HARDMAN tr. *R. Boulanger's Turkey* 201 In the showcases against the wall ..are various glass objects.

**2.** *fig.* A place or medium for presenting (esp. attractively) to general attention (freq. in Theatr. contexts). Chiefly *U.S.*

**1937** 'M. INNES' *Hamlet, Revenge!* II. iii. 131 Scamnum is ..simply a Crispin show-case, dukedom and all. **1958** D. EWEN *Compl. Bk. Amer. Musical Theater* 79 It [sc. *Walk a little Faster*]..deserves to be remembered if only because it was the showcase for..Duke's most popular song, 'April in Paris'. **1967** N. FREELING *Strike out where not Applicable* i. 7 Its park has been turned into a landscaped garden which is a showcase for the bulb industry. **1976** M. BUTTERWORTH *Festival* xi. 173 The entertainment world fell over itself to get into this, the biggest 'showcase' on earth. **1978** S. BRILL *Teamsters* x. 364 Gibbons' local was becoming a showcase of progressive unionism.

**3.** *attrib.* or as *adj.* Freq. *fig.*

**1903** A. H. LEWIS *Boss* 189 He's no show-case proposition!.. To look at him folks might take him for a fool. **1934** *Architect. Record* Sept. 189 Show case height for standard selling. **1937** 'M. INNES' *Hamlet, Revenge!* II. iii. 131 The Duke has a show-case role. He's an Elder Statesman. **1955** *Times* 10 May 3/5 The London Philharmonic Orchestra has broken out for the summer season with some showcase programmes. **1975** B. GARFIELD *Death Sentence* (1976) vi. 36 The First Ward [of Chicago].. included the showcase hoop.

Hence as *v. trans.* (orig. *U.S.*), to place in or as in a showcase (chiefly *fig.*).

**1945** H. L. MENCKEN *Amer. Lang.* Suppl. I. v. 387 A few of its [sc. *Variety*'s] characteristic inventions will suffice: *to ash-can, to angel, to showcase* [etc.]. **1949** *Jrnl.* (Baltimore) 20 July 2/1 They showcase new acts, who want to be on TV. **1959** *Spectator* 14 Aug. 192/1 It [sc. the Festival Ballet] has show-cased any number of notable performers. **1961** *Times* 4 Feb. 11/5 An album which introduces a new verb to the English language. It has been recorded 'to showcase' 10 different bands at a *Jazz Festival in Hi-Fi*. **1982** *Time Out* 16 July 39/5 The film..showcases both sides of Young's music.

**show-down.** [f. SHOW *v.* + DOWN]

**1.** *Card-playing.* The act of laying down one's cards with their faces up; also, the name of a game similar to poker. Also **show-down poker** (see quot. 1901).

**1892** W. J. FLORENCE *Handbk. Poker* 42 If a player miscalls his hands, innocently, and on the show-down has enough to win the pot, it remains his. **1898** W. C. MORROW *Ape, Idiot*, etc. 159 Never disclose your hand except on a showdown. **1901** R. F. FOSTER *Poker* 16 If the limit is ten cents only, and the blind is one, the game becomes 'showdown Poker' because a player will bet the limit on anything and everything. **1902** WISTER *Virginian* xvi, Whatever hand he's been holdin' up, this is the show-down. **1908** *Westm. Gaz.* 1 Feb. 14/1 It is usual to have a 'show down' unless at least a three by tricks declaration has been arrived at. **1973** D. WESTHEIMER *Going Public* v. 79 How about one hand of showdown poker?.. Low man does the job?

**2.** *fig.* An open disclosure of plans, means, etc.; also, a declaration or trial of one's strength or position; a final confrontation, a reckoning (intended to be conclusive).

**1904** F. LYNDE *Grafters* ix. 131 'You don't mean to say there is any doubt about our ability to do it?' 'Oh, no; I suppose not, if it comes to a show-down.' **1909** *E. Suffolk Gaz.* 12 Jan. 7/5 When it comes to an academic show-down, we'll make some of those rivals of ours sit up. **1916** *Daily Colonist* (Victoria, B.C.) 9 July 4/4 It is quite time that there should be what is vulgarly known as a 'show down', and this 'show down' is what I have been endeavoring to bring about. **1927** *Glasgow Herald* 19 Aug. 10 An opportunity of 'forcing a show-down' concerning British flights in China. **1936** M. ALLINGHAM *Flowers for Judge* ix. 143 Salley has been stewing up for a row with his critics for some time and is spoiling for a show-down. **1945** E. WAUGH *Brideshead Revisited* 241 If he has a show down with the old gang, they'll just disappear. **1950** T. S. ELIOT *Cocktail Party* III. 161, I believe, Henry, if I may put it vulgarly, That Lavinia has forced you to a show-down. **1962** A. LURIE *Love & Friendship* xvi. 310 When it comes to a showdown, women stick to their husbands. **1977** J. CROSBY *Company of Friends* xvii. 113 Never had she told him her code name. Some things a woman needed—for the final showdown.

**3.** *Comb.*, as **showdown inspection** *U.S. Mil.*, a surprise inspection of kit. Also *ellipt.*

**1920** in H. S. Duell *Hist. 306th Field Artillery* 4/1 First of numerous 'show-down' inspections for the missing 'Laces, shoe, russet, pair, extra'. **1928** L. H. NASON *Top Kick* 27 When we get back to billets they'll have a show-down, an' anyone that's shy, finds it on the payroll. **1943** *Yank* 2 Apr. 19 The Army custom of show-down inspection is unnerving. **1963** J. O. KILLENS *And then We heard Thunder* ii. 14 Showdown Inspection with all of your equipment spread out before you to be checked by the pink-cheeked officers.

**showe,** obs. form of SHOE, SHOVE *v.*[1]

**showel(l,** obs. forms of SHOVEL.

**shower** (ˈʃaʊə(r)), *sb.*[1] Forms: 1 scúr, sceór, scyur, 3 sur, shur, 3, 5 scur, 3–4 schur, 3–7 showre, 4 shor, 4–6 schour, 4–7 schoure, shour(e, 5 *pl.* scoures, shure, shwre, schowr, 5–6 schowre, 5–7 shewer, 6 schower, schouer, 6–7 shewre, 7 showr, shore, 5– shower. [OE. *scúr* str. masc. (also once *scúran* wk. pl.) corresponds to OS. *skûr* masc., OFris. *skûr* fit of illness (NFris. *skŷr* shower, caprice), MDu. *schuur* (mod.Du. *schoer* with dialectal vowel), OHG. *scûr* (MHG. *schûr*, mod.G. *schauer*), OTeut. **skûro-z*; also ON. *skúr* fem. (but in early texts sometimes masc.), Goth. *skūra* fem. storm:—**skūrō*. The suggested affinities are uncertain: see Uhlenbeck and Falk and Torp.]

**1. a.** A fall of rain, of short duration and (usually) comparatively light. Also, a similar fall of sleet or hail, rarely of snow. See also HAIL-*shower*, RAIN-SHOWER, SNOW-*shower*.

In various dialects the word may be applied to a continuous fall of rain lasting for many hours.

*c* **950** *Lindisf. Gosp.* xii. 54 Scyur [*Rushw.* scur] cymeð. *a* **1000** *Andreas* 512 (Gr.) þonne sceor cymeð. *a* **1000** *Lambeth Psalter* lxxvii. 44 Heora scuras [*imbres eorum*]. *c* **1200** *Trin. Coll. Hom.* 175 Storm..werpeð þat water upward and arereð shures fele. *c* **1374** CHAUCER *Troylus* IV. 751 The teres from hir eyen two Doun fille, as shour in Aperill. *c* **1407** LYDG. *Reason & Sens.* 6310 Holsom as the Aprile shour Fallyng on the erbes newe. **14..** *Voc.* in Wr.-Wülcker 588/48 *Imber*, a shure. *c* **1550** CHEKE *Matt.* vii. 25 Y[eer] fell a greet schower. **1576** GASCOIGNE *Droome of Doomes day* Wks. 1910 II. 248 The Lord God rayned from the Lorde, (even from him selfe) not shewers nor dewe, but fyre and brimstone. **1618** J. TAYLOR (Water-P.) *Pennyless Pilgr.* C 2 b, All the day long it rayned but one showre. *a* **1700** EVELYN *Diary* 21 May 1645, After a showre has fall'n. **1759** JOHNSON *Idler* No. 49 ¶5 A shower beating against his windows. **1817** G. ROSE *Diaries* (1860) I. 42, I was overtaken by a shower. **1907** W. EWING *Arab & Druze* v. 63 A light shower drifted down the valley.

*fig.* *c* **1580** SIDNEY *Ps.* VII. i, O, save me from this persecutions show'r. **1663** PATRICK *Parab. Pilgrim* xxx. (1687) 351 It pleased God so to order it, that this cloud [of indisposition] was cast about him without any showre. **1868** MORRIS *Earthly Par.* Prol. (1890) 19/2 We..knew the lot of all men should be ours, A chequered day of sunshine and of showers.

**b.** Followed by qualification *of rain*, *of hail*, etc.

*a* **1300** *Floriz. & Bl.* 272 He..gan Blauncheflur bimene Wiþ teres rive as a scur of rene. *c* **1320** *Sir Tristr.* 1937 Of snowe was fallen aschour. **1570** *Satir. Poems Reform.* xv. 15 With schouris Of hailstaines, snaw, and sleit! *c* **1620** A. HUME *Brit. Tongue* 10 A shour of hael. **1678** WOOD *Life* (O.H.S.) II. 412 A vast shore of raine. **1807** P. GASS *Jrnl.* 181 Some showers of snow fell in the course of the day. **1825** T. HOOK *Sayings* Ser. II. *Passion & Princ.* ix. III. 153 Strong gusts of wind, accompanied by fleeting showers of rain.

**c.** In extended use: A copious downfall of anything coming or supposed to come from the clouds or sky: in recent use often of meteors.

**13..** *E.E. Allit. P.* B. 227 So fro heuen to helle þat hatel schor laste. **1562** LEGH *Armorie* (1591) 16 b, Son of the high Ioue begotten vppon Danae shadowed in the golden shower. **1643** BAKER *Chron., Hen. II*, 79 A showre of Blood Rained in the Isle of Wight two houres together. **1829** *Chapters Phys. Sci.* 433 The sky was overcast at mid-day with clouds of ashes, the showers of which covered every thing to the depth of several inches. **1835, 1856** Meteoric showers [see METEORIC *a.* 3]. **1878** HUXLEY *Physiogr.* 189 The solid materials are shot forth into the air and fall in showers around the mouth of the orifice.

**d.** A dust-storm: freq. qualified by a place-name. *Austral.*

**1898** E. E. MORRIS *Austral Eng.* 115/1 *Darling Shower*, a local name in the interior of Australia, and especially on the River Darling, for a dust storm, caused by cyclonic winds. **1903** 'T. COLLINS' *Such is Life* (1944) 329 (*heading*) Wilcannia shower. *Ibid.* 331 The steady intensity of the shower augmented as I went on... The increasing broadside pressure, with the sand and dust, was becoming too much for the horses. **1933** A. B. PATERSON *Animals Noah Forgot* 36 The Bogan shower, that is mostly dust. **1949** *Geogr. Mag.* Feb. 373 Duststorms are called, in various parts of the country as indicated by the change in operative names, *Darling shower*, *Cobar shower*, *Bedourie shower* and *Wilcannia shower*.

**e.** In prov. phr. ***I didn't come down in the last shower***, indicating that one is not inexperienced, or not so raw as to be easily fooled. Chiefly *Austral.*

[**1906** 'T. COLLINS' *Rigby's Romance* (1946) 256 *He* didn't come down with the las' rain. Pity that sort of bloke ever dies.] **1944** L. GLASSOP *We were Rats* 51 I'm awake-up, I am... I didden come down in the last shower. **1951** F. HARDY *Power without Glory* 259 'It's no use lying to me, Arty,' John West said. 'I didn't come down in the last shower.' *a* **1966** 'M. NA GOPALEEN' *Best of Myles* (1968) 277 No damn fear. I didn't come down in the last shower. **1971** B. VERNON *Big Day at Bellbird* 135, I didn't come down in the last shower, and neither did you.

**f.** A group or crowd (of people). Usu. *derog.*, a pitiful collection or rabble. *slang.*

**1942** G. KERSH *Nine Lives Bill Nelson* ii. 13 I've seen him with some of the lousiest showers of rooks you ever saw in your life. **1958** A. HACKNEY *Private Life* xiv. 139 That unit was an absolute shower. **1962** 'H. CALVIN' *System* xiii. 176, I bet none of your shower ever even looked at Challen and his mob. **1967** M. PROCTER *Exercise Hoodwink* xiv. 100 'Have you still got the same shower in your lot?' 'Mainly. One or two new faces.' **1973** *Observer* 1 Apr. 13/3 Some of the people who go out with the hounds these days are a shower... We can't have people turning up as if they have been wearing the same pyjamas for a month. **1978** L. DAVIDSON *Chelsea Murders* I. v. 29 It's a group. What I was thinking..the Manson shower.

**g.** A term of mild abuse used of one person as opp. to a group. *slang.*

**1949** M. LEIGH *Cross of Fire* iv. 71 You bat-eyed, buttock-brained..shower! **1959** S. GIBBONS *Pink Front Door* ii. 23 Hasn't he [*sc.* a baby] lain down *yet*? He is a little shower. **1966** O. NORTON *School of Liars* iv. 63 I'm of finer stuff, personally. I don't know why I waste my time playing with a shower like you. **1973** 'P. ALDING' *Field of Fire* xv. 123 'You're a right shower,' said Welland.

**2. a.** *transf.* A copious fall or discharge of water or other liquid in drops. Often of tears; hence *poet.* a shower of *grief*, *sorrow*, etc. † ***to make showers***: to weep.

*a* **1400–50** *Wars Alex.* 2048 Sike scoures were of blude ..þat foles ferd in þe flosches to þe feterlakis. **1538** HEYWOOD *Wise Wom.* IV. ii. G 2, Shall I the shower of all my griefe at once Power out before you? **1663** PATRICK *Parab. Pilgrim* xxvii. (1687) 302 It was not possible so to repress them [tears], but that all concluded in a plentiful showre. **1818** SHELLEY *Rosal.* 1271 Rosalind..wept A shower of burning tears, which fell upon His face. **1846** MRS. KIRKLAND *West. Clearings* 25 This brought only another shower of tears. **1859** R. HUNT *Guide Mus. Pract. Geol.* (ed. 2) 233 This is effected by passing showers of water through the flue by which the [lead] fumes escape. **1874** CROOKES *Dyeing & Calico-Printing* 655 Stuffs, previous to finishing, are moistened with an extremely fine shower, produced by allowing water to descend through a sieve of silk.

**b.** *poet.* Of light, sound, etc.

**1781** COWPER *Retirem.* 350 The stars that, sprinkled o'er the vault of night, Seem drops descending in a show'r of light. **1820** SHELLEY *To Maria Gisborne* 70 When from the moist moon rains The inmost shower of its white fire. **1840** R. S. HAWKER *Cornish Ballads*, etc. (1908) 73 What showers of gold the sunbeams rain!

**c.** Short for SHOWER-BATH. (Now the more usual term.)

**1873** 'MARK TWAIN' & WARNER *Gilded Age* xxxiii. 308 He has fell back on hot foot-baths at night and cold showers in the morning. **1889** GUNTER *That Frenchman* iii. 24 You forgot to put the ice in the shower, François; it is hardly bracing enough. **1930** P. MACDONALD *Link* xi. 218, I had a shower and rammed on some clothes. **1953** R. LEHMANN *Echoing Grove* 48 Must have a shower. I've been in a muck sweat all day. **1973** J. WAINWRIGHT *Pride of Pigs* 59 The bathroom..was small, but lush..with..a bidet and a corner shower.

**d.** *Pyrotechny.* A device for producing a shower of small slow-burning 'stars', which fall from a rocket.

**1839** [see GOLDEN *a.* 10]. **1866** *Chamb. Encycl.* VIII. 35/2 Yellow stars and yellow showers are made of nitre [etc.].

**e.** *N.Z.* (See quot. 1943.)

**1943** J. A. W. BENNETT in *Amer. Speech* XVIII. 86 A *shower* is..a light decorated covering spread over cups and saucers set out on a tray or table. **1957** J. FRAME *Owls do Cry* I. vi. 24 Parcels from the handwork sale, tablerunners and tea-showers in lazy-daisy and chain and shadow stitch. **1967** F. SARGESON *Hangover* xiv. 108 All was out of sight beneath a large and snowy fabric..—the kind of gossamer thing he could remember his mother had coveted many years ago in a shop window and described as a shower.

**3.** *fig.* **a.** A copious or liberal supply bestowed.

**13..** *K. Horn* 334 (Harl.) Shame þe mote by shoure ant euel hap to vnderfonge. *c* **1460** *Play of Sacrament* 664 in *Non-Cycle Mystery Plays* 78 Of thy gret mercy lett vs receyue þe showre. **1616** BRETON *Invect. agst. Treason* (Grosart) 3/2 Our gratious King, on whome yᵉ King of Grace, hath rayn'd a shewre of his æternall graces. **1748** GRAY *Alliance* 18 Light golden Showers of Plenty o'er the Land. **1751** *Affect. Narr. of Wager* 39 The Sailors,..poured upon them a very plenteous Shower of hard Names and Execrations. **1803** WORDSW. *To Highland Girl*, Sweet Highland Girl, a very shower Of beauty is thy earthly dower! **1817** JAS. MILL *Brit. India* VI. i. III. 21 The revenues, from which so many showers of emolument fell. **1888** BURGON *Lives 12 Gd. Men* I. iv. 405 Hawkins's election ..was the signal for a shower of interesting letters of hearty congratulation.

**b.** An abundance of gifts of a similar kind presented by guests at a party to celebrate esp. a wedding or birth; a party given for this purpose. Also *attrib.* Also as second element in *kitchen shower* s.v. KITCHEN *sb.* 7, *linen shower* s.v. LINEN *sb.* 5, *wedding shower*, etc. *U.S.*

**1904** *Grand Rapids* (Michigan) *Even. Press* 22 June 4 The 'shower parties' that through mistaken hospitality the wedded couple are forced to attend. **1926** *Publishers' Weekly* 26 June 2031/1 First comes June, then the showers, the wedding and after the honeymoon the settling down to a home life. **1949** *Los Angeles Times Home Mag.* 8 May 14/3 Wedding showers..are a particularly warmhearted American custom. **1958** *Even. Standard* 10 Apr. 8/2 A shower..is really a gift-giving party centred round a luncheon, tea or supper party. **1978** J. CARROLL *Mortal Friends* IV. ii. 394 She didn't explain, but implied that she wanted to discuss her trousseau and her silver and china patterns and the sort of showers she would want.

**4. a.** A copious fall or flight of solid objects, esp. of missiles. Also of blows.

*a* **1000** *Judith* 221 (Gr.) Hie ða fromlice leton forð fleogan flana scuras. *a* **1000** *Elene* 117. **1375** BARBOUR *Bruce* XIII. 43 The arrowis als so thik thai flaw,..That thai ane hydwiss schour can ma. **1508** DUNBAR *Golden Targe* 195 The schour of arowis rappit on as rayn. **1570–6** LAMBARDE *Peramb. Kent* 291 They..made it raine suche a shoure of clubbes and coulestaues vpon the Monks Copes, cowles, & Crownes, that [etc.]. **1687** A. LOVELL tr. *Thevenot's Trav.* I. 283 We could hear showers of Bullets batter against the Ships sides. **1736** GRAY *Statius* i. 18 Batter Cadmus' walls with stony showers. **1827** FARADAY *Chem. Manip.* vi. (1842) 184 The breaking of the bubbles will throw up a shower of particles. **1849** MACAULAY *Hist. Eng.* vi. II. 115 They were received with a shower of stones. **1852** MRS. STOWE *Uncle Tom's C.* xxxiii, A shower of blows. **1877** MARY M. GRANT *Sun-Maid* viii, And the leaves were falling in a crimson and russet shower all over the ground.

**b.** *Physics.* A number of high-energy particles appearing together; *spec.* a group generated in the atmosphere by cosmic radiation.

**1933** *Proc. R. Soc.* A. CXXXIX. 702 Particles of great energy are thrown backwards in a direction nearly opposite to that of the incident shower. **1947** *Sci. News* IV. 125 Sixty-five Geiger-Muller counters have been used to follow the direction of some of the rays and establish the width of one shower. **1966** *McGraw-Hill Encycl. Sci. & Technol.* III. 498/1 The electrons and photons of such showers are referred to as the soft component of the atmospheric (secondary) cosmic rays, reaching a maximum intensity at an atmospheric depth of 150–200 g/cm². **1977** J. NARLIKAR *Struct. Universe* iii. 99 These showers contain particles produced after the cosmic rays have interacted with the atoms of the atmosphere.

†**5. a.** A conflict, combat, battle, assault, attack. Also, an attack of pain; a pang, throe. *Obs.*

Very common in ME.

*c* **1220** *Bestiary* 281 We sulen hunger hauen and harde sures. *c* **1330** R. BRUNNE *Chron. Wace* (Rolls) 6820 Þer myghte men se on boþe partys A scharp schour by-twyxten enemys. *c* **1412** HOCCLEVE *De Reg. Princ.* 3939 In bataile.. Hym leuere is to suffre dethes schour, Than cowardly and schamefully flee. *c* **1420** ? LYDG. *Assembly of Gods* 732 For he was lyke to endure that day A gret mortall shoure..With Vyce. *a* **1513** FABYAN *Chron.* VII. (1811) 399 The Englisshmen susteyned many harde showres in Gascoyne & Guyan. *c* **1570** *Satir. Poems Reform.* (S.T.S.) 117 ȝe, hardest ..To him has felt of deith the schouris. **1637** RUTHERFORD *Lett.* (1664) 257 It cost Christ and all his followers sharp showers and hot sweats, ere they won to the top of the mountain.

†**b.** *spec.* in *pl.* Labour-pains. *Obs.*

**14..** *Athelston* 636 (Zupitza) Harde schourys þenne took her stronge Boþe in bak and eek in wombe. *a* **1598** ROLLOCK *Lect. Passion* xx. Wks. 1844 II. 230 It shall come upon them suddenly, even as the showres and dolor come on a woman who is travailing in birth. *a* **1800** *Fair Janet & Sweet Will.* iii. in Child *Ballads* II. 105/1 Till sharp, sharp showers fair Janet took, She grew sick and like to die.

**6.** *attrib.* and *Comb.*, as **a.** *shower-cloak, -coat; shower-like, -producing,* †*-raised, -shedding,* †*-swelled* adjs.; **shower-bouquet**, 'a large bouquet from which many small bouquets depend by ribbons of various lengths' (Webster 1911); **shower-cloud**, a cumulo-nimbus cloud (see quot. 1910); see also SHOWER-BATH. **b.** (sense 2 c) *shower-cap, shoe*; **shower box** *N.Z.*, = next; **shower cubicle**, a cubicle containing a shower; **shower curtain**, a waterproof curtain separating the shower from the rest of the room; **shower head**, a rose or nozzle from which the water issues in a shower; **shower-room**, a room housing one or more showers; **shower stall** *U.S.* = *shower cubicle* above; **shower unit**, a shower or the principal apparatus of a shower.

**1892** *Star* 25 Feb. 1/7 They carried *shower bouquets composed entirely of lilies of the valley. **1965** F. SARGESON *Memoirs of Peon* vii. 201 Beyond that a *shower-box of such microscopic dimensions. **1977** *N.Z. Herald* 5 Jan. 2–16/8 (Advt.), Must be good value, with..shower box, basement garage plus carport. **1964** *Punch* 19 Feb. 289/1 *Shower-cap and bath-towel. **1972** R. K. SMITH *Ransom* III. 125 She.. stepped into the shower, remembering only at the last minute to slip on a shower cap. **1893** *Daily News* 29 June 6/1 Her grey *shower-cloak hid her dress. **1886** A. W. CLAYDEN in *Q. Jrnl. R. Meteorol. Soc.* Apr. 102 On the Thickness of *Shower Clouds. **1910** —— in *Encycl. Brit.* VI. 559/1 *Cumulo-nimbus* (Cu.-N.), The Thunder-cloud; Shower-cloud—Heavy masses of clouds, rising in the form of mountains, turrets, or anvils, generally having a sheet or screen of fibrous appearance above (false cirrus) and underneath a mass of cloud similar to nimbus. **1964** *Punch* 14 Oct. p. xiii, Rainwear shop..includes velvet *showercoats. **1976** *Evening Standard* 29 Dec. (Advt.), Quelrayn showercoats, fleecey lined. **1966** P. O'DONNELL *Sabre-Tooth* iii. 56 She..padded into the big *shower-cubicle. **1938** L. BEMELMANS *Life Class* II. iv. 158 He was inside his *shower-curtain, whistling. **1974** HAWKEY & BINGHAM *Wild Card* xviii. 145 She pulled aside the shower curtains and leaned out. **1967** *Gloss. Sanitation Terms* (*B.S.I.*) 44 **Shower head*, a water fitting, for use in a shower bath, from which water issues as a film or spray. **1978** R. NIXON *Mem.* 369 The shower in the President's private bathroom in the Residence..consisted of half a dozen different jets and showerheads. **1893** *Times* 8 May 10/5 Weather dull and *shower like. **1621** G. SANDYS *Ovid's Met.* VII. (1626) 136 Men, if Fame say true, Here at the first from *shower-raysed mushrumps grew. **1939** 'E. QUEEN' *Mind Over Matter* in *Blue Book* Oct. 21/2 The crowd was so dense it overflowed into the adjoining *shower-room. **1951** *Good Housek. Home Encycl.* 20/2 The ideal is of course to have a separate 'shower room'. **1965** F. SARGESON *Memoirs of Peon* iv. 90 He..was washing his hands at a basin in the far corner of the shower-room. **1975** W. CRAIG *Strasbourg Legacy* (1976) i. 8 Hoess, the commandant at Auschwitz,..refused to take credit for killing three million inmates. He had been on leave of absence while a portion of them died in the shower rooms. **1800** HURDIS *Fav. Village* 122 The cloud immense, whose *shower-shedding folds Have all day dwelt upon a deluged world. **1960** *Amer. Speech* XXV. 264 From the verb *edewa* [*sc.* 'come here'], sandals or *shower shoes were generally called *edewa shoes.* **1978** *Sat. Even. Post* July/Aug. 105/1 (Advt.), Swim sneaks. All-rubber bathing and shower shoes. Sure-footed protection on rocks, decks, or shower floors. **1956** 'E. MCBAIN' *Cop Hater* (1958) ix. 81 The café still served as a sort of no-man's-land..served the same purpose as the *shower stall does in a honeymoon suite. **1975** J. F. BURKE *Death Trick* (1976) ii. 12 He took a quick look in the bathroom, noted that the shower stall was wet. **1627** MAY *Lucan* I. (1631) 8 The streame *showre-swell'd The marches ore. **1973** *Times* 15 Dec. 3/1 (Advt.), *Shower Units, Taps, Mixers, Splashbacks.

**shower** ('ʃəʊə(r)), *sb.*² Forms: 1 **scéawere, scéawre, (scéware)**, 2 **scawere**, 3 **scheauware**, 3–4 **shewere**, 4 *Kent.* **sseawere**, 4–5 **schewer(e**, 5– **schewar, schoer, scewre**, 6 *Sc.* **scheware, (schawar)**, 4–9 **shewer**, 6– **shower**. [OE. *scéawere*, agent noun from *scéawian* to SHOW; cf. OHG. *scawâri* (MHG. *schouwære*, mod.G. *schauer*) looker, spectator, watchman, etc. In later times formed afresh on SHOW *v.* + -ER¹.]

†**1.** One who looks out, observes, or inspects; an observer; a scout or spy; a watchman. *OE.*

*Beowulf* 253 Lease sceaweras. *c* **1175** *Lamb. Hom.* 117 Episcopus is grekisc noma..and is on englisc scawere.

†**2.** A mirror. *Obs.*

*c* **1000** *Homily* in Napier *Contrib. OE. Lexicogr.* 55 Nu we men geseoð swylce þurh sceawere & on rædelse [= *1 Cor.* xiii. 12]. *c* **1200** *Trin. Coll. Hom.* 29 Þe wimman bihalt hire sheawere and cumeð hire shadewe þaronne. *a* **1225** *Ancr. R.* 92 Ȝe schulen, ase ine scheauwere, iseon ure Lefdi mid hire meidenes. **13..** *Poem Times Edw. II*, xvi. (Percy Soc.) 8 He putteth in hys pawtener A kerchyf and a comb, A shewer, and a coyf.

**3.** One who shows, points out, or exhibits.

**13..** *K. Alis.* 18 For Caton seith, thes gode techere 'Other monis lif is owre schewere [*Laud. MS.* shewer, Lat. *magistra*]. *c* **1400** *Apol. Loll.* (Camden) 60 Noyþer þe deposing of þe witnes, nor þe sentens ȝeuing of þe juge,.. makiþ not man synful, ne worþi to be dead; syn þei are but schewars & witnessars. *c* **1450** *Mirk's Festial* 187 God toke hom to hym yn ensampull to al oþer, and made hom as a schoer to al oþer synfull. **1484** *Certificate* in *Surtees Misc.* (1890) 41 Where trewth is..set oparte froym the scewres of right. **1511–2** *Act 3 Hen. VIII*, c. 10. §1 The oder halfe to the taker fynder or shewer of the same. **1586** J. MELVILL in *Calderwood's Hist. Kirk* (1843) IV. 522 The rebooker and shower thee of thy vice. **1680** H. MORE *Apocal. Apoc.* 333 It is the Angel that is the shower of the whole scene of this vision. **1810** LAMB *Let. to Hazlitt* 9 Aug., Perhaps they [*sc.* the pictures] are shown separately to put another fee into the shower's pocket. **1859** BOYD *Recreat. Country Parson* ii. 61 In compassion for human weakness, the Great Director and Shower of events practises the Art of Putting Things. **1868** *Jrnl. R. Agric. Soc.* Ser. II. IV. II. 283 The breeders of Herefords have always been keen showers. **1899** *Daily News* 11 Apr. 6/3 Deceased..was for some time a shower in the State apartments [at Windsor Castle].

**b.** *Scots Law.* One of the two men who are appointed by the court to accompany the jurors or viewers when a view of the property which the cause relates to is allowed.

**1838** W. BELL *Dict. Law Scot.* s.v. *Viewer*, The premises are pointed out to them by two persons, named by the Court, usually on the joint suggestion of the parties, and technically called shewers.

**c.** With *off.*

**1823** COBBETT *Rur. Rides* (1885) I. 384 Mr. Buxton figured here, also Lord Suffield, who appear to have been the two principal actors, or showers-off.

†**4.** Something which shows; an indicator; an indicative symptom (of a disease). *Obs.*

**1377** LANGL. *P. Pl.* B. XII. 153 (Rawl. MS.), It [the star] schon to [þe] schepherdes a schewer [**1393** C. XV. 96 shewere] of blisse. **1532** MORE *Confut. Tindale* Wks. 383/2 He meaneth yᵗ..ye sacrament is no cause thereof..nor instrument therin, but only a bare signyfier and a shewer therof. **1561** EDEN tr. *Cortes' Art Navig.* III. xi. 78 In the ioynte of the two halfe cyrcles..muste be a poynte (called the Index or shewer) whiche shall shewe..the degrees that the pole is raysed aboue the Horizon. **1572** J. JONES *Bathes of Bathes Ayde* Ep. Ded. 3 Withall the signes shewers of the state of the sicke and whole. **1668** CULPEPER & COLE *Barthol. Anat.* IV. i. 160 The second [finger] is cal'd Index and Demonstrator, the shewer, or pointer.

**5.** An animal that 'shows' well or otherwise, that makes a (good or bad) display of its qualities.

**1893** *Kennel Gaz.* Aug. 215/2 An indifferent shower. *Ibid.* 217/3 He is a smart shower, and a well-made dog.

**shower** ('ʃaʊə(r)), *v.* Also 6 **shoure, shewre**, 6–7 **showr(e**, 7 **shou'r**. [f. SHOWER *sb.*¹]

**1.** *intr.* To rain in a shower, or in showers. †Also with *out.* Chiefly *impers.*; occas. said †of a cloud.

**1573** TUSSER *Husb.* (1878) 30 If great she [the moone] appereth, it showreth out, If small she appereth, it signifieth drout. **1590** SPENSER *F.Q.* II. viii. 48 The cloudes..fiercely then begin to shoure. **1687** A. LOVELL tr. *Thevenot's Trav.* II. 193 It continued showring by intervals, with great Thunder-Claps, till half an hour after six. **1891** STEVENSON *Vailima Lett.* (1895) 75 It showered all afternoon and poured heavy and loud all night.

**2.** To fall down in a shower or showers, or as a shower of rain. **a.** Of water (esp. tears), or other material things. Often with *down, on*, etc.

**1582** STANYHURST *Æneis* IV. (Arb.) 108 At my tears showring dyd he sigh? dyd he winck with his eyelyd? **1601** WEEVER *Mirr. Mart.* E iij, Teares from her eies did shower. **1683** *Apol. Prot. France* ii. 12 Instead of having the Heavenly Mannah shower down at the Doors of their Tabernacles. **1717** BERKELEY *Vesuvius* in *Phil. Trans.* XXX. 711 Ashes continually shower'd on us all the way from the Sea-Coast. **1830** TENNYSON *Sea-Fairies* 10 Down shower the gambolling waterfalls From wandering over the lea. **1890** W. J. GORDON *Foundry* 155 The sparks showering off as if from a catherine-wheel. **1910** J. AITKEN in *Encycl. Brit.* VIII. 714/2 These [dust particles] when showering down as rain tend to wash the others out of the atmosphere.

**b.** *fig.* Of immaterial things.

**1596** SHAKS. *1 Hen. IV*, v. i. 47 It rain'd downe Fortune showring on your head. **1633** BROME *North. Lass* v. ii. K 3, Sir, all the accumulations of honour showre downe vpon you. **1732** BERKELEY *Serm. to S.P.G.* Wks. III. 249 The Divine grace will no longer shower down on our obdurate hearts. **1821** J. W. CROKER *Diary* (1884) 4 Aug., Visits and invitations shower upon one. **1912** *Standard* 20 Sept. 7/6 Thousands of congratulatory messages have showered upon the happy pair from all parts of the world.

**3. a.** *trans.* To pour down or discharge in a shower or showers; to send down or pour out in abundance and rapidly. Often with *down*, †*out*, etc.

**1582** STANYHURST *Æneis* II. (Arb.) 52, I..salt tears dolfulye showred. **1594** DANIEL *Cleopatra* I. ii. 73 And vp they hoise the swounding body there Of pale Antonius showring out his blood. **1635** A. STAFFORD *Fem. Glory* (1869) 147 Presume not thou to number what her eyes Showre forth in tears. **1665** SIR T. HERBERT *Trav.* (1677) 43 The Clowds shower there continually an insalubrious moisture. **1788** GIBBON *Decl. & F.* l. V. 198 A miraculous flight of birds, who showered down stones on the heads of the infidels. **1807** J. HALL *Trav. Scot.* II. 458 They would have hissed him, and showered rotten eggs at his head. **1832** TENNYSON *Godiva* 42 She shook her head and shower'd the rippled ringlets to her knee. **1860** TYNDALL *Glac.* I. x. 65 The clouds..showered their liquid spheres down upon us. **1869** TOZER *Highl. Turkey* II. 331 Sugar-plums..are showered..by friends over the bride. **1878** SUSAN PHILLIPS *On Seaboard* 109 Does the crab-tree shower down Perfumed snow for treading?

**b.** *fig.* With immaterial obj: To bestow lavishly.

*c* **1586** C'TESS PEMBROKE *Ps.* CXXXIV, All blessing you accompany, From him in plenty showered. **1613** SHAKS. *Hen. VIII*, I. iv. 63, I showre a welcome on yee: welcome all.

**1741** WATTS *Improv. Mind* I. v. (1801) 56 Let not little critics ..shower down their ill-nature upon him. **1838** THIRLWALL *Greece* xl. V. 124 The royal bounty was largely showered upon him. **1889** GODKIN in Ogden *Life* (1907) II. 156 They all showered invitations upon me which, alas! I cannot accept.

†**c.** *absol.* To weep; to shed tears. Also to bestow gifts in abundance. *Obs. rare.*

**1592** SHAKS. *Rom. & Jul.* III. v. 131 What still in teares? Euermore showring..? **1667** MILTON *P.L.* V. 637 Th' all bounteous King, who showrd With copious hand.

**4. a.** To water with or as with a shower; to wet copiously with rain or with water in drops or spray; *transf.* to cover or strew as with rain. Also *fig.*

**1667** MILTON *P.L.* IV. 152 When God hath showrd the earth. *Ibid.* XI. 879 Or serve they as a flourie verge to binde The fluid skirts of that same watrie Cloud, Least it again dissolve and showr the Earth? **1819** KEATS *Otho* V. v. 89 Ladies..bright In silks, with spangles shower'd. **1891** *Century Dict.* s.v., To shower plants from a watering-pot; to shower one's head in bathing; to shower a convict as a punishment. **1895** R. W. CHAMBERS *King in Yellow* (1909) 128 The gorse scraped against my leggings..showering the brown earth with blossoms. **1900** A. BLACK *Even. & Morn.* iii. 60 In the midst of our hot and dusty world this garden stands and heaven itself showers it and fans it.

**b.** *intr.* To have a shower. Rarely *refl.* or *trans.*, to give (oneself or someone) a shower (SHOWER *sb.*[1] 2 c).

**1930** U. PARROTT *Strangers may Kiss* 196 He..asked if he could do anything helpful about dinner, and when she said 'no', went to shower himself. **1939** R. CHANDLER *Big Sleep* xxii. 213, I shaved and showered and dressed. **1948** *Sun* (Baltimore) 1 Oct. 15/4 Jockeys..had to shower before donning silks for their next riding assignment. **1956** K. HULME *Nun's Story* viii. 128 Time to shower and put on a fresh guimpe. **1966** T. PYNCHON *Crying of Lot 49* v. 115 The executive undressed, showered and hung his suit out on the line to dry. **1977** *Listener* 7 Apr. 446/2 The condemned man ..will have been showered and then been dressed in his brown burial suit. **1978** R. LUDLUM *Holcroft Covenant* xiii. 153 Holcroft showered, shaved, put the soiled clothes in a hamper outside the door, and called the car-rental agency.

Hence **'showered** *ppl. a.*

**1848** W. R. WILLIAMS *Lord's Prayer* iv. (1854) 251 Stephen praying for his murderers amid the showered stones that fall and bruise him. **1953** A. UPFIELD *Murder must Wait* xxiv. 209 Shaved, showered and dressed, Boney sat at his desk. **1971** D. E. WESTLAKE *I gave at Office* (1972) 139 Dressed in..new clothes..showered, fed beef stew and beer, my basic optimism..began slowly to rise.

**shower**, obs. variant of SEWER *sb.*[2]

**shower-bath.**

**a.** A bath in which water from above is poured in a shower upon the person. Also an apparatus for producing a bath of this kind. (Now a somewhat old-fashioned term.)

Also *U.S.* a form of punishment for convicts.

**1803** *Med. Jrnl.* IX. 209 A slight delirium..subsided immediately on the use of the shower bath. **1815** tr. *Duc de Levis' Eng. 19 Cent.* I. 211 They have invented a machine.. which is now very much in use; it is called a shower-bath. It is like a sentry-box. **1853** A. R. WALLACE *Amazon & Rio Negro* 30 In the morning, after a refreshing shower-bath under the mill-feeder, we shouldered our guns [etc.]. **1859** F. S. COOPER *Ironmongers' Catal.* 3 Hand Shower Baths. **1868** B. J. LOSSING *Hudson* 303 Severe punishments are becoming more and more rare, and the terrible Shower Bath ..is now seldom used. **1899** *Allbutt's Syst. Med.* VIII. 380 Shower baths in the young, when they can be borne, are most efficacious.

**b.** *transf.* and *fig.* Also in *fig.* phr. ***to pull the string of the shower-bath***, to cause (something concealed) to be released or made known suddenly. *colloq. rare.*

**1824** SCOTT *St. Ronan's* iv, He was soused with a deluge of water... [A threat] induced him to retreat in all haste from the repetition of this shower-bath. **1889** SWINBURNE *Study B. Jonson* 25 The character of Captain Pantilius Tucca, which seems to have brought down on its creator such a boiling shower-bath or torrent of professional indignation. **1928** KIPLING *Limits & Renewals* (1932) 20 If I pull the string of the shower-bath in the papers..Castorley might go off his veray parfit gentil nut. **1937** V. WOOLF *Years* 441 Why can't he flow? Why can't he pull the string of the shower bath? Why's it all locked up, refrigerated? Because he's a priest, a mystery monger.

**showerer** ('ʃaʊərə(r)). [f. SHOWER *v.* + -ER[1].] One who showers or pours down abundantly.

**1882** G. RAWLINSON *Relig. Anc. World* iv. 129 Indra..is ..'the showerer of benefits'.

**showerful** ('ʃaʊəfʊl), *a. nonce-wd.* [f. SHOWER *sb.*[1] + -FUL.] Abounding in showers.

**1872** TENNYSON *Gareth & Lynette* 2 Gareth, in a showerful spring Stared at the spate.

**showeriness** ('ʃaʊərɪnɪs). *rare.* [f. SHOWERY *a.* + -NESS.] The state of being showery.

**1855** HAWTHORNE *Eng. Note-bks.* (1870) I. 388 After a slight showeriness. **1890** *Blackw. Mag.* CXLVIII. 361/1 A suspicion of April showeriness.

**showering** ('ʃaʊərɪŋ), *vbl. sb.* [f. SHOWER *v.* + -ING[1].] The action of SHOWER *v.*; also *concr.*, that which is showered.

**1592** WYRLEY *Armorie, Ld. Chandos* vii, Led onward with hope of long assurance We neuer thinke of fortunes frowning, But high honors plant as if perdurance had promised continuall showring. **1653** RUTHERFORD *Lett.* (1836) II. 282 The dewings and showerings of Him that every moment watereth his vineyard. **1862** MEREDITH *Shemselnihar* Poet. Wks. (1912) 171 Like a rose by the fountain whose showering we hear.

**'showering,** *ppl. a.* [f. SHOWER *v.* + -ING[2].]

**1.** That sends down in or as in showers.

**1609** C. BUTLER *Fem. Mon.* (1634) 60 *note*, Xantippe, that thundring shouring Queen of shrews. *c* **1620** Z. BOYD *Zion's Flowers* (1855) 12 With sad showring eyes, Cry to thy God. **1669** WORLIDGE *Syst. Agric.* 166 If the Spring be mild, calm, and showring, then is it good for Swarms. **1892** W. WATSON *Poems* Prel. 5 Not mine the rich and showering hand, that strews The facile largess of a stintless Muse.

**2.** That falls in or as in a shower or showers.

**1622** J. TAYLOR (Water-P.) *Farew. Tower-Bottles* A 4 b, When showring hayleshot..Nor blustering Gusts..Could holde me backe. **1817** SHELLEY *Marianne's Dream* xiv, She Was borne towards the showering flame By the wild waves heaped tumultuously. **1818** BYRON *Juan* I. cxxiv, Sweet is the vintage, when the showering grapes In Bacchanal profusion reel to earth. **1860** PATMORE *Faithf. for Ever* I. vii, For all the showering tears that soak This paper.

Hence †**'showeringly** *adv.*

**1621** LADY M. WROTH *Urania* 362 A Fountaine..out of which..the water came so..showringly,..as [etc.].

**'showerless,** *a. rare.* [f. SHOWER *sb.*[1] + -LESS.] Without a shower or showers.

**1744** ARMSTRONG *Art Preserv. Health* I. 257 Scarce in a showerless day the heavens indulge Our melting clime. **1801** COLERIDGE *Lett., To Southey* (1895) 357, I will be Supreme Bey of that showerless district.

**'showerproof,** *a.* (*sb.*) [f. SHOWER *sb.*[1] + PROOF *a.*, after *rainproof*, etc.]

**1.** Resistant to light rain.

**1895** *Stores Price List*, Shower proof cloaks. **1907** *Army & Navy Stores Catal.* 751 A Large Variety of Showerproof Garments in all the Newest Shapes. **1923** *T. Eaton & Co. Catal.* Spring & Summer 214/4 There is no coat more popular than the English Gabardine. It is stylish, light in weight, yet firm in the weave, making it showerproof. **1960** *Farmer & Stockbreeder* 9 Feb. Suppl. 5/2 (Advt), Shower-proof coat..is in a simulated leather material. **1969** A. J. HALL *Stand. Handbk. Textiles* (ed. 7) v. 333 Silicones..are now much used for making textile fabrics shower-proof. **1973** *Times* 9 Apr. 6/1 Within the trade, 'shower-proof' apparently means only that the garment will not soak through at the first hint of drizzle.

**2.** As *sb.*, a showerproof garment, esp. a raincoat.

**1972** *Guardian* 6 June 13/3 Showerproofs will stand up to short sharp showers... But they are not for the drenching downpour. **1974** M. BIRMINGHAM *You can help Me* i. 14 A slight girl in a short off-white shower-proof, a crimson scarf at her neck.

Hence as *v. trans.*, to render showerproof; **'showerproofed** *ppl. a.*, **'showerproofing** *vbl. sb.* and *ppl. a.*

**1933** *Dyer* 28 Apr. 450/3 Where a shower proofing effect is desired, many of the difficulties..are less in evidence. **1951** *Good Housek. Home Encycl.* 314/2 It is sometimes advisable to showerproof outer garments. **1958** *Vogue* Apr. 104 Reversible coat in showerproofed poplin. **1962** J. T. MARSH *Self-Smoothing Fabrics* ix. 123 With urea-formaldehyde and Velan..the latter can act as a catalyst as well as the shower-proofing agent or softener. **1970** *UK Trade Names* 73/3 Marriner Hand-knitting Wools.. Halyard showerproofed, nylonised, chunky. **1973** *Country Life* 23 Aug. 529/1 Alligator are still shower-proofing melton cloth.

**showery** ('ʃaʊərɪ), *a.* [f. SHOWER *sb.*[1] + -Y.]

**1.** Raining in showers; abounding with or characterized by frequent showers of rain.

**1591** PERCIVALL *Sp. Dict.*, *Lloviznar*, to drizle, to be showry. **1626** BACON *Sylva* §548 In a Showry Season. **1652** HEYLYN *Cosmogr.* IV. 138 The Aire hereof is very shewery. **1773** COOK *2nd Voy.* II. xi. (1777) I. 317 On the 23d showery weather. **1854** HAWTHORNE *Eng. Note-bks.* (1870) I. 140 It continued showery all day. **1885** H. FINCH-HATTON *Advance Australia!* 173 The weather..had been, as they say in the west of Scotland, 'showery and rain atween whiles'.

**b.** *fig.* Tearful.

**1847** TENNYSON *Princess* Concl. 33 She fixt A showery glance upon her aunt.

**2.** Causing or producing showers; bringing showers. Said of a cloud, wind, constellation, etc.

**1697** DRYDEN *Æneid* IX. 909 Like the Storm that flies From Westward, when the Show'ry Kids arise. **1858** HAWTHORNE *Fr. & It. Note-bks.* II. 200 The showery clouds that haunt a hill-country. **1871** R. ELLIS *Catullus* xxvi. 2 'Tis not showery south, nor airy wester.

**3.** Pertaining to, produced by or resembling a shower or showers.

**1667** MILTON *P.L.* VI. 759 Inlaid with pure Amber, and colours of the showrie Arch. **1729** SAVAGE *Wanderer* II. 70 Bright It collects the Beams, which, trembling All, Back from the God, a show'ry Radiance, fall. **1791** COWPER *Iliad* IV. 509 The waves..scatter far the show'ry spray. **1833** TENNYSON *Lotos-Eaters* 17 Dew'd with showery drops, Upclomb the shadowy pine above the woven copse. **1853** O. W. HOLMES *Poem Amer. Med. Assoc.* 78 The selfsame founts her chalice fill With showery sunlight running over.

**4.** Falling in showers.

**1841-6** LONGF. *Rain in Summer* ix, Aquarius old.. Scattering every where The showery rain.

**showful**, variant of SHOFUL *slang*.

†**'showfully,** *adv. Obs.*[−1] [f. SHOW *sb.*[1] + -FUL + -LY[2].] Gaudily, showily.

**1613** CHAPMAN *Maske Inns Court* A 3, All showfully garnisht with seueral-hewd fethers.

**'showgirl.** [SHOW *sb.*[1]]

**1. a.** An actress whose role is decorative rather than histrionic.

**1836** G. SOANE (*title*) Lilian, the show girl. *Ibid.* (Duncombe ed.) I. ix. 8 The tinsel dress of the poor show girl. **1903** 'C. E. MERRIMAN' *Lett. from Son* xv. 208 Not quite all the modern Venuses have been corralled for the 'show-girl' department of musical comedy. **1923** A. TRAIN *Children's Children* xv. 192 He found it hard to believe that she was an actress, and a show-girl at that. **1936** J. BEYNON *Planet Plane* viii. 73 Give a show-girl smile, and everyone is only too glad to have you along. **1960** 'N. SHUTE' *Trustee from Toolroom* i. 5 She had gone with a party of show girls ..to the Queen's Hotel after the performance. **1977** W. M. SPACKMAN *Armful of Warm Girl* 38 A leathery cousin of his own who when divorced had set up this show girl in a little flat.

**b.** *transf.* A mannequin.

**1929** *Punch* 17 Apr. 444/3 Not the least interesting thing about these parades is that among the show-girls are many well-known titled heiresses, doing it purely for cigarette-money. **1936** J. B. PRIESTLEY *They Walk in City* i. 16 Mannieekin. One o' them show girls in the big shops.

**2.** A girl in charge of a booth at a fair. *rare.*

**1912** A. BENNETT *Matador of Five Towns* 91 The showmen and the showgirls and the showboys were titivating their booths.

**'show-glass.** [SHOW *sb.*[1]]

**1.** A glass case for exhibiting valuable or delicate goods.

**1709** *Lond. Gaz.* No. 4574/4 Elizabeth Mechin..did.. feloniously break open several Locks of Drawers, Press-show-Glasses, and other places. **1733** *Read's Wkly. Jrnl.* 24 Nov. 3/2 Some Rogues carry'd away a Shew-Glass from the Shop of..a Goldsmith.., with Plate to the Value of 15*l.* **1854** *Zoologist* XII. 4189 Confectioners' show-glasses. **1862** *Catal. Internat. Exhib.* II. x. 13 They are especially adapted for show-glasses..where safety and protection from dust are essential.

**2.** A glass in which something is seen; a mirror; a magic mirror.

**1855** in OGILVIE Suppl. **1891** in *Century Dict.*

**show house.** [SHOW *sb.*[1]]

†**1.** A shop or other building in which wares are displayed. *Obs.*

**1527** in *Chron. Calais* (Camden) 107 All persons having shewehouses or packhouses. *c* **1600** in *Trans. Roy. Hist. Soc.* (1902) XVI. 35 No..Merchant Adventurer..shall..keepe open shoppe or shewhouse.

**2. a.** A house conspicuous and celebrated for architectural beauty, splendid furniture, or the like; esp. one over which the public are at certain times admitted to be shown.

**1806** J. BERESFORD *Miseries Hum. Life* VI. xxviii, In seeing what is called a 'Shew-house',—keeping pace, whether you will or not, through all the rooms, with another party. **1880** MISS BRADDON *Just as I am* ii, Fairview was not a grand house, or a show house.

**b.** A house specially finished for exhibition as an advertisement, usu. for others of similar construction (on a housing estate). Also *fig.* Cf. *show flat* s.v. SHOW *sb.*[1] 22.

**1962** *Listener* 15 Nov. 799/1 It [*sc.* the Labour Party] wished, as it were, to paddle its own canoe—to build in Britain a show-house of democratic socialism which the rest of Europe might inspect and then draw the lesson. **1963** *Times* 9 May 9/4 The first showhouse of a new private development which will ultimately provide 800 low-cost homes was opened here today. **1970** *Times* 4 Mar. 15/1 (Advt.), Don't miss the 'House and Garden' showhouse. **1974** *Country Life* 19 Dec. Suppl. 19 Family houses to be constructed... Showhouse available for visiting. **1978** J. SHERWOOD *Limericks of Lachasse* iii. 34 Frau Hoffmann's got the place looking like a show house in an exhibition.

**3.** A building used for staging theatrical performances; a travelling theatre.

**1920** D. H. LAWRENCE *Lost Girl* vi. 105 A certain wooden show-house..an old travelling theatre. **1930** I. GOLDBERG *Tin Pan Alley* 217 The showhouses, too..are taxed for this privilege, on the basis of their seating capacity.

**showily** ('ʃəʊɪlɪ), *adv.* [f. SHOWY *a.* + -LY[2].] In a showy manner; with display.

**1789** MRS. PIOZZI *Journ. France* I. 286 Trapped showily in various colours. **1825** SCOTT *Betrothed* xviii, His garments, of various colours, and showily disposed, were none of the newest. **1870** 'OUIDA' *Held in Bondage* 22 Wild young Cantabs, mounted showily from livery-stables.

**showiness** ('ʃəʊɪnɪs). [f. SHOWY *a.* + -NESS.] The quality of being showy.

**1813** *Examiner* 18 Jan. 35/2 The shewiness of their [the soldier's] profession. **1816** COLERIDGE *Statesm. Man.* App. 31 Which gave a sickly and hectic shewiness to the latter half of the last century. **1869** SPURGEON *Treas. Dav.* Ps. xvi. Introd. I. 240 There is much showiness, and may be some solidity in the suggestions.

**showing** ('ʃəʊɪŋ), *vbl. sb.* [f. SHOW *v.* + -ING[1]; in OE. *scéawung, scéawing.*]

**1. a.** The action of displaying, exhibiting, manifesting, etc.; the fact of being displayed, etc.; with *pl.*, an instance of this.

*c* **950** *Lindisf. Gosp.* Mark xii. 40 Under sceawung longes ȝebeddes [*sub obtentu prolixae orationis*]. *a* **1300** *Cursor M.* 26110 Scrift es opin scheuing o breist Laufulli mad be-for þe preist. *c* **1325** *Metr. Hom.* 29 Of this openlic schauing Hauis Godd schawed many taking. **1526** *Pilgr. Perf.* (W. de W. 1531) 25 By the ostencyon or shewynge of grace. **1568** GRAFTON *Chron.* II. 225 There were great embracynges and shewynges of frendship on both sydes. **1709** HEARNE *Collect.* 13 Mar. (O.H.S.) II. 176 Mr. Lhuyd..made what he could by Shewing. **1765** *Treat. Dom. Pigeons* 11 When you observe the hen to sweep her tail to the cock..which is termed shewing. **1837** CARLYLE *Fr. Rev.* III. I. vii, In one of those wheelings and shewings of new front.

**b.** with adv., as *showing off, up.*

**1874** GARROD in *Proc. Zool. Soc.* 471 On the 'showing-off' of the Australian Bustard. **1887** 'F. ANSTEY' in *Graphic* 31 Dec. 727/3 He was annoyed with them for what he considered was 'showing off'. **1923** 'K. MANSFIELD' *Doves' Nest* 143 She detected that morning just the very faintest boyish showing off. **1962** N. STREATFEILD *Apple Bough* xviii. 255 Wolfgang put on his showing-off voice... 'I'm starring in this new picture.' **1973** J. PATRICK *Glasgow Gang Observed* vi. 64 Tim summed up..the boy's loss of face: 'Whit a showin' up in front o' aw the boays.'

†**c.** *to make showing of*: to exhibit, display, reveal; to tell of, describe, relate. *Obs.*

*a* **1300** *Cursor M.* 22298 þar sal he..sceuing make of his maistris. *c* **1330** *Arth. & Merl.* 7626 Of whom y made bifore scheweing. **1477** *Cov. Leet Bk.* 422 To make a clere shewing of the same before certen oure..Counsellours.

**d.** *Cinemat.* and *Television.* The projection of a film on to a screen; the exhibition or broadcasting of a film. Also, an instance of this.

**1947** *Ann. Reg. 1946* 376 British films..have brought $8,000,000 back to this country in 1946 from their American showings. **1967** *Listener* 6 July 15/1 The first London showings of..*New Faces* filled a cinema in Tooting with a stream of unaccustomed patrons. **1972** 'E. FERRARS' *Breath of Suspicion* iii. 45 They had arrived just as the earlier showing of the film was ending.

**e.** A public exhibition of the work of an artist or fashion designer; an art or fashion show.

**1967** 'T. WELLS' *Dead by Light of Moon* (1968) i. 8 Wouldn't you know something like this would happen at my first important showing? All the big art critics here, and somebody has to jinx the lights! **1969** 'H. PENTECOST' *Girl Watcher's Funeral* (1970) III. i. 136 It's about my showing on Friday... The fashion writers and the trade journals haven't given me much of a play. **1982** *Times* 3 Aug. 6/1 A decade or so ago, the couture salons of Paris were filled with American store buyers. At the showings this week, there weren't any store buyers.

†**2.** A sight, spectacle. *Obs.*

**971** *Blickl. Hom.* 187 Neron..bead þæt eall þæt folc come to þisse sceawunga. *c* **1450** *Brut* 426 The meyre and aldremen..lete..make many diuerse shewyngis and sightis.

**3.** *Old English Law.* A duty or toll payable for the right of displaying goods for sale; = L. *ostensio.*

In spurious charters of Edward the Confessor and William I; see Kemble *Cod. Dipl.* IV. 213, 215, Thorpe *Diplom.* 359, 411.

? **1121** *Charter Hen. I* in *New Palæogr. Soc.* I. (1903) pl. 20(1) Cum saca et soca..et miskenninge et sceawinge. **12..** *Annales de Burton* in *Ann. Monast.* (Rolls) I. 247 Liberi sint ab omni scoto et geldo..et stallagio, schewinge, mischenninge. **1387** TREVISA *Higden* (Rolls) II. 95 Schewynge, settynge forþ of marchaundise.

**4.** Manner of putting a case: in phrases *on this showing* (= if the facts be as thus represented), *on one's own showing*, etc.

[**1408** tr. *Vegetius De re milit.* (MS. Digby 233) lf. 183 b/2 After wyse mennys schewyng.] **1857** MILL *Pol. Econ.* III. xii. §7 (ed. 4) II. 70 On this showing, the notes at least of private banks are not money. **1868** FREEMAN *Norm. Conq.* II. x. 502 The revolt could not be justified on any showing. **1869** LATHAM, s.v., This is proved even by your own showing. **1883** *Manch. Guard.* 17 Oct. 5/2 The st p which the United Kingdom Alliance wants Parliament to take is on their own showing a momentous one.

**5.** A statement or presentation of figures, accounts, or the like. Chiefly *U.S.*

**1868** *Rep. U.S. Commissioner Agric.* (1869) 51 This is a very meager showing, but an export of ten times the amount would be worse. **1877** RAYMOND *Statist. Mines & Mining* 453 We have been unable to obtain any data that justifies a showing so favorable. **1902** *Westm. Gaz.* 31 July 9/1 On the whole it is not at all a bad 'showing', and shareholders need not fidget.

**6.** *U.S.* An appearance or display of a specified kind. Phrases *to make a* (good or bad) *showing.*

**1890** in Leffingwell *Upland Shooting* 459 [The greyhounds] made a very sorry showing in the public contests. **1901** *N. Amer. Rev.* Feb. 240 Like all officers, I was intensely interested in the showing made by the different forces.

**7.** Outward appearance. †*fair showing*, fair appearance or seeming; persuasiveness (of speech).

**1340** *Ayenb.* 36 Huanne þet hi [corn and vines] byeþ of uaire ssewynge. *c* **1400** *Rom. Rose* 4041 Than, al abawid in shewing, Anoon spak Dreed. *c* **1412** LYDG. *Reas. & Sens.* 3917 [Apples] Delytable in shewyng, But wonder bitter in tastyng. **1470–85** MALORY *Arthur* XVIII. ii. 728 The quene outward made no maner of sorowe in shewynge. **1903** R. KIPLING *Five Nations* 1 Who hath desired..His Sea in no showing the same—his Sea and the same 'neath each showing.

**8. a.** Something that is shown or appears; a manifestation, revelation (*of*); a sign or token; a dream or vision. *book of showing(s*: the Apocalypse. *Obs.* exc. *Hist.*

*a* **1225** *Ancr. R.* 268 Ase lease swefnes, & false scheauwinges. *a* **1300** *Cursor M.* 10707 þat he þam suld sli sceuing scau, þat þai moght wit sum taknyng knau Quat þai suld do. *Ibid.* 21039 þe bok o scheuing þer he wrat. ? *a* **1400** *Morte Arth.* 3401 Thow has a schewynge, sir kynge, take kepe ʒif the lyke! **1450–1530** *Myrr. Our Ladye* 16 With meruaylous tokens and shewynges. *c* **1485** *Digby Myst.* III. 1621 A mervelows shewyng In my slep I had. **1859** GEO. ELIOT *Adam Bede* III. I. 224 It is a vain thought to flee from the work that God appoints us... But now, I believe, I have a clear showing that my work lies elsewhere. **1978** F. BEER *Julian of Norwich's Revelations* 28 These four shewings seem without question to fall into the first of Julian's 'thre partyes'.

†**b.** An appearance or indication *of* (something).

*c* **1491** *Chast. Goddes Chyld.* (Caxton) 50 Whether there be in hym ony sheweng of vaynglory.

**c.** = SHOW *sb.*[1] 5 c.

**1926** *Daily Colonist* (Victoria, B.C.) 28 July 7/2 The work now in progress at the property consists in the stripping downwards of the showings in these workings, which will afford..an idea of the character of the ore showings over a depth of 900 feet. **1977** J. B. HILTON *Dead-Nettle* ii. 20 'I'll drive deep. Happen there's another seam.' 'Then your first job is to collect your showing.'

**'showing,** *ppl. a.* [f. SHOW *v.* + -ING[2].]

**1.** That displays, exhibits, indicates, etc.

† *showing finger*, the forefinger or index.

*c* **1425** tr. *Arderne's Treat. Fistula*, etc. 22 þan at first putte the leche þe schewyng fynger of his left hande..in-to þe lure of þe pacient. **1522** VAUS *Rudimenta* B 6 b (Jam.) *Indicatiuo modo*, schawand mode. **1551** T. WILSON *Logic* (1580) 27 b, The first called a demonstratiue, or shewyng reduction [= *reductio ostensiva*], is made by conuersion of the Propositions. **1568** GRAFTON *Chron.* II. 125 It is written at the length, and in most shewyng maner, to their honour and worship.

†**2.** That appears; seeming; evident. *Obs.*

*c* **1374** CHAUCER *Boeth.* IV. pr i. (1868) 109 þe þinges þat þou hast seid me hider to ben to me so clere and so shewyng [*patuerunt*]..þat þei ne mowe nat ben ouercomen. **1579** J. STUBBES *Gaping Gulf* A 2, Deceiued by theyr lusts to embrace a shewing and false good.

**3.** *Hort.* Of fruit: Beginning to appear.

**1794** MCPHAIL *Treat. Cucumber* 155, I..picked off several of the showing and set fruit where they were too thick.

**4.** With advbs., as *showing-up. rare.*

*a* **1941** V. WOOLF *New Dress* in *Haunted House* (1943) 49 The looking-glass..that dreadfully showing-up blue pool.

†**'showish,** *a. Obs.* (Very common in the 18th c.) [f. SHOW *sb.*[1] + -ISH.] = SHOWY *a.*

**1675** J. DANCER *Agrippa* Ded. A ij b, This Play in it self is not at all calculated to the humour of the present times..: nor is it (to speak Modishly) showish enough. **1710** T. FULLER *Pharm. Extemp.* 393 This Age produces a set of idle shallow shewish Men. **1747** CHESTERF. *Let. to Son* 3 Apr., A showish binding attracts the eyes. *a* **1768** SECKER *Serm.* (1770) II. 52 The outward Act being a Matter of great Form and Punctuality..they easily persuaded themselves..that a scrupulous Performance of such troublesome and shewish Duties would certainly be sufficient.

**showitt,** obs. form of SUET.

**'show-jumping,** *vbl. sb.* [SHOW *sb.*[1]]

Competitive jumping on horseback over a prepared course of hurdles or show jumps (also with horse as subj.).

**1929** G. BROOKE *Way of Man with Horse* xvii. 235 Show jumping is a thing apart from steeplechasing... Riding over the ordinary English show-jumping course,..necessitates a horse that will not rush. **1936** [see *show-jumper* below]. **1958** S. WILLCOX *Three Days Running* xii. 141 Chips led after the dressage and did a clear round of show-jumping. **1963** E. H. EDWARDS *Saddlery* xvi. 121 Recently there has been much correspondence as to whether..the National Hunt jockeys, should employ a saddle incorporating the features of a show-jumping saddle and so conform to something approaching a show-jumping seat. **1973** *Country Life* 13 Sept. 697/1 The second fence, to him, was simply a show jumping fence.

Hence [as a back-formation] **'show-jump** *v. intr.*, to compete in show-jumping; **show jumper**, a horse or rider that competes in show-jumping competitions.

**1929** G. BROOKE *Way of Man with Horse* xvii. 236 A large percentage of show jumpers are half-bred horses. **1936** P. RODZIANKO *Mod. Horsemanship* xi. 193 A horse that has hunted is usually more successful as a show jumper than a horse that has never hunted... Hunting helps show jumping. **1943** R. S. SUMMERHAYS *Elements of Riding* (ed. 2) xix. 91 The method I have described is universally accepted as being the true way to show-jump. **1954** I. TOPTANI *Mod. Show Jumping* ii. 41 No normally trained show jumper will make for every single jump it encounters on its way. **1966** M. CATTO *Bird on Wing* iii. 58 I've show-jumped at the Tivoli. **1974** *Radio Times* 14 Mar. 4/2 Olympic silver medallist show jumper Ann Moore. **1977** N. MARSH *Last Ditch* v. 145 Dulce fancied it, though. Thought she'd make a show-jumper of it. **1980** 'E. ANTHONY' *Defector* iii. 69 She used to show-jump as a teenager.

**showl, showld(e,** obs. forms of SHOAL.

**showle,** obs. form of SHOAL, SHOVEL.

**'showler.** [Of obscure origin.] A local name for the DACE.

**1681** CHETHAM *Angler's Vade-m.* xx. §1 (1689) 136 The Dace or Dare in some Places called a showler. **1816** BAINBRIDGE *Fly Fisher's Guide* 91 The Dace, Dare, or as it is sometimes called the Showler.

**showll,** obs. form of SHOVEL.

**showman** ('ʃəʊmən). [SHOW *sb.*[1]]

**1. a.** One who exhibits a show; the proprietor of a show.

*a* **1734** NORTH *Life Ld. Keeper Guilford* (1742) 280 An enormous Rhinoceros, to be sold to Shew-men for Profit. **1787** M. CUTLER in *Life*, etc. (1888) I. 309 There are constant exhibitions from rope-dancers, mountebanks, jugglers, and show-men. **1833** LONGF. *Outre-Mer* Pr. Wks. 1886 I. 129 Staring in stupid wonder at the miracles of a showman's box. **1840** DICKENS *Old C. Shop* xvi, Itinerant showmen—exhibitors of the freaks of Punch.

**b.** *gen.* and *transf.*: (in sports, politics, etc.), one who performs with a display of style or panache.

**1774** COOK *2nd Voy.* II. xii. (1777) I. 324 He was conducted all over the ship... On this occasion Otoo was the principal shew-man. **1861** *Sat. Rev.* 30 Nov. 568 The showmen who hurry the..parties of visitors round the eastern chapels. **1964** *Guardian* 2 Mar. 7/6 There's two kinds of workers in the game, shooters and showmen. The shooter's the real wrestler... The showman's in there to make a splash, do the theatricals. **1967** C. SETON-WATSON *Italy from Liberalism to Fascism* xii. 547 In politics he [*sc.* D'Annunzio] was never more than a dilettante and a theatrical showman. **1977** *Irish Press* 29 Sept. 13/2 Meanwhile, showman Brian Barnes, was giving the small crowd their money's worth by nominating to them the type of shots he was going to play.

**c.** *attrib.*

**1880** W. CORY *Lett. & Jrnls.* (1897) 455 The garrulity and the showman proclamations of Thackeray and Trollope. **1899** *Pall Mall Gaz.* 11 Oct. 4/3 The shares of the 'show-man' class exhibited their true nature.

†**2.** (See quot.) *Obs.*

**1797** *Times* 23 Nov. in Ashton *Old Times* (1885) 336 It was the custom of Publicans, when they want to let their houses, to get a number of people together, whom they treat with beer. They call them show-men, and this is done for the purpose of deceiving the persons who come to view their house, and to make them suppose it has good custom.

Hence **'showmanism, 'showmanry,** (*nonce-wds.*); **'showmanship** (chiefly *transf.* and *fig.*).

**1859** SALA *Gas-light & D.* xvi. 178 One touch of showman-ship makes the whole world kin. **1874** G. H. LEWES *Let.* 19 Feb. in *Geo. Eliot Lett.* (1956) VI. 20 The story is very well told... But there is a chorus of objection against the excessive *showmanship* of the commentary. **1886** *Sat. Rev.* 15 May 675/2 Charles Lamb would have delighted in one of their effects as he delighted in the showmanry of Elliston. **1886** PETRIE *Tanis* II. *Nebesheh* (1888) Pref. 6 To reject anything [from a museum] because it is not popularly attractive is a concession to mere showmanism. **1926** A. BENNETT *Ld. Raingo* II. lxiv. 287 He had made a fine display of courage and wit on the doctor's declaration of his malady, but it was only a display, a proud piece of showmanship perhaps unworthy of so solemn an occasion. **1927** *Daily Express* 12 Aug. 9/3 She held a great reception yesterday, sitting in her red caravan, and chatted of the olden times and the present conditions of showmanship. **1966** *People* 13 May 4/5 But Tony, no slouch when it comes to show-manship, helped it along by wearing..a rose brocade dinner jacket. **1972** *Newsweek* 10 Jan. 8/1 Pragmatism—coupled with some of the showmanship for which he has long been known—stood as the hallmark of Bhutto's first fortnight as President.

**show-me,** *attrib. phr. U.S.* [SHOW *v.*] That demands demonstration; believing only on clear evidence, extremely sceptical. (Orig. used to describe the people of Missouri: see MISSOURI 2.)

**1909** *N.Y. Even. Post* (semi-weekly ed.) 19 Apr. 88 Everything indicative of the 'show-me' State of Missouri. **1909** R. A. WASON *Happy Hawkins* 283 He belonged to the show-me club. **1933** *Sun* (Baltimore) 29 July 6/1 These administrators are going to spend a great deal of their time ..trying to get money from Secretary Ickes, who appears to be a show-me man. **1949** *Manch. Guardian Weekly* 20 Oct. 2 A typically materialistic 'show-me' American. **1978** J. UPDIKE *Coup* (1979) i. 37 The premature gray and show-me squint of these Yankees is muddled in with their something eternally puerile, awkward, winning, and hopeful.

**shown** (ʃəʊn), *ppl. a.* [pa. pple. of SHOW *v.*] Exhibited, presented to view, etc.

**1892** GREENER *Breech-loader* 135 The pattern is the *shown* shooting of a gun, the only visible proof of a gun's powers. **1897** F. THOMPSON *New Poems* 37 Hidden stars by the shown stars' wings.

**show-off,** *sb.* (*a.*) [f. vbl. phr. *to show off*: see SHOW *v.* 8 b, 33.]

**a.** A display, exhibition or exposure *of* (something).

**1776** S. J. PRATT *Pupil of Pleas.* II. 14 He allots to each of us such a share of fortune in our own hands as is sufficient to the display and shew-off of the natural disposition. **1783** —— *Liberal Opin.* (ed. 3) Pref. 20 It appears to have been.. the..effort of the author..to display the..inconsistencies of human opinion respecting Happiness; and, (after this shew off of folly, delusion, and absurdity) [etc.].

**b.** *Pugilism.* A public display.

**1828** EGAN *Boxiana* IV. 168 We believe it was the first *show-off* of the latter with the *mufflers.*

**c.** An imposing or specious display; an opportunity for display. Also, in generalized sense, display, showiness.

**1843** S. BAMFORD *Passages in Life of Radical* II. iii. 18 After some show off, by Mr Hunt, without which indeed, he scarcely knew how to get out of any matter, we left the dock. **1856** MISS YONGE *Daisy Chain* II. i, A bazaar—a field for her trumpery, and a show-off for all the young ladies. **1856** LEVER *Martins of Cro' M.* xxvi, In all the glitter and show off of fashionable acquirement poor Molly is the inferior. **1893** W. WALKER *Three Churchmen* 173 He considered it an unreality and too much of a show-off. **1896** BADEN-POWELL *Matabele Campaign* xviii. 136 Our Colonial expansion..is not undertaken with any idea of show-off.

**d.** A person given to showing off. (The principal sense.)

**1924** G. E. KELLY (*title*) The show-off. **1925** [see GO *v.* 58 g]. **1932** W. S. MAUGHAM *For Services Rendered* II. 42 Lois: Well, I've always looked upon you as rather a show-off. **1943** D. POWELL *Time to be Born* ii. 52 We..don't like to show off. Our women aren't show-offs. **1954** C. ARMSTRONG *Better to eat You* iv. 34 He knew how to deflate the show-offs and encourage the shy. **1960** T. GRIFFITH

*Waist-high Culture* I. ii. 24 Grateful for an adult audience.. we must have been unbearable showoffs. **1972** 'E. FERRARS' *Breath of Suspicion* vii. 102 That honey-moon couple... What show-offs they both are, acting as if no one else had ever had a love affair before them.

**e.** *attrib.* or *adj.* Given to display; ostentatious, showy.

**1818** S. FERRIER *Marriage* II. xxii. 298 Colonel Lennox was evidently not a shew-off character. **1837** [MISS MAITLAND] *Lett. fr. Madras* (1843) 154 He was a conceited, show-off sort of person. **1843** *Punch* Feb. 79/1 We never see this show-off style of living. **1934** T. N. WILDER *Heaven's my Destination* iii. 48 He was one of that loud show-off kind. **1954** KOESTLER *Trail of Dinosaur* (1955) II. 89 The perfect symbol of it all is the show-off TV aerial on the roof of suburban houses. **1977** H. INNES *Big Footprints* IV. i. 317 You stupid show-off bastard.

Hence **show-offish, show-'offy** *adjs.*

**1942** H. HAYCRAFT *Murder for Pleasure* ix. 189 He has too often stooped to merely show-offish quotation-spouting. **1952** S. KAUFFMAN *Philanderer* (1953) iii. 54 My sweet, dear husband. My darling, show-offy, gentle husband. **1971** LAVER & COLLINS *Educ. Tennis Player* xxv. 292, I hadn't jumped a net in a dozen years. I thought it was a bit show-offish for one thing. **1978** A. MALING *Lucky Devil* xxix. 155 He just came along to write the check. And he was kind of show-offy about it.

**'show-place.** [Cf. G. *schauplatz* = sense 1.]

†**1.** A place for public shows or spectacles; a theatre. (Used to render *θέατρον*, *circus*, etc.)

**1579–80** NORTH *Plutarch*, *Antonius* (1595) 994 He assembled all the people in the shew place, where young men doe exercise themselues. **1603** HOLLAND *Plutarch's Mor.* 96 Whither men flocke to heare, as at the Theaters and shew places. **1647** R. STAPYLTON *Juvenal* (1670) 49 Circus, the great show-place neer mount Aventine.

**2.** A place (e.g. a large mansion or estate) which is regularly exhibited to visitors; a place much visited for its beauty, antiquities, or the like.

**1794** J. B. S. MORRITT *Let.* 19 Mar. (1914) i. 10 This [*sc.* Dresden] I hear is a very fine show-place, particularly for pictures. **1817** MAR. EDGEWORTH *Harrington* vi, Mamma.. generally leaves her at the Priory, to take care of all the old trumpery, and show the place—you know it's a *show place*. **1853** 'C. BEDE' *Verdant Green* I. v, They soon found a guide, one of those wonderful people to which show-places give birth. **1888** PAYN *Myst. Mirbridge* xvii, 'A show-place'—as country mansions important enough for exhibition are called. **1893** MATHESON *About Holland* 44 Flushing is not a show place by any means.

**showrde,** obs. form of SWORD.

**showroom** ('ʃəʊru:m). [f. SHOW *sb.*¹]

**1.** A room used for the display of goods or merchandise.

**1616** R. COCKS *Diary* 2 Jan. (Hakl. Soc.) 95 To keepe the shopp or shew rowme. **1617** *Ibid.* 23 July 283 We delivered divers sortes merchandiz to Jno. Japon to sell in the shopp or shew roome over the way. **1839** DICKENS *Nich. Nick.* x, Madame Mantalini's showrooms were on the first floor. **1879** F. W. ROBINSON *Coward Consc.* II. xxi, From the busy workshops into the great show-room.

*fig.* **1829** CARLYLE *Misc.*, *Voltaire* (1840) II. 163 Voltaire's knowledge is not a mere show-room of curiosities, but truly a museum for purposes of teaching. **1833** H. COLERIDGE *Biogr. Bor.* Introd. 6 It.. is deposited in the shew-room of the memory.

†**2.** A room in which a show is exhibited. *Obs.*

*c* **1714** ARBUTHNOT etc. *Mem. M. Scribl.* I. xiv. (1741) 51 The Dwarf who kept the gates of the Show-room.

**3.** *pl.* The rooms in a large mansion which are regularly shown to visitors. Occas. in *sing.*

**1820** T. CREEVEY *Let.* 23 Jan. in J. Gore *Creevey* (1948) xiii. 179 She is like one of her numerous gold and silver musical dickey birds, that are in all the show rooms of this house. **1820** D. WORDSWORTH *Jrnl.* 29 Sept. (1941) II. 322 Having paced through every show-room of the palace, we surveyed again the exterior. **1863** HAWTHORNE *Our Old Home, Near Oxford* II. 12 We were guided through the show-rooms [at Blenheim] by a very civil person.

**showse,** obs. variant of CHOUSE *sb.*

**showt(e,** obs. forms of SHOUT.

**showve,** obs. form of SHOVE *v.*¹

**showy** ('ʃəʊɪ), *a.* [f. SHOW *sb.*¹ + -Y. Cf. the earlier SHOWISH *a.*] Characterized by show.

**a.** Of visible objects: Presenting an imposing or striking appearance; making a good display.

**1712** ADDISON *Spect.* No. 434 ¶6 The Men would make a Present of every thing that was Rich and Showy to the Women whom they most admired. **1746** W. THOMPSON *R.N. Adv.* (1757) 40 They do not always Weigh six Hundred Weight,..tho' large shewy Oxen. **1777** MISS BURNEY *Early Diary* (1889) II. 168 A very showy striped pink and white Manchester. **1779** G. KEATE *Sketches Nat.* (ed. 2) I. 8 Rather a showy than a pretty woman. **1826** P. POUNDEN *France & Italy* 186 Hung with chintz of a shewy pattern. **1832** BABBAGE *Econ. Manuf.* xv. (ed. 3) 139 Inferior but showy watches are made at a cheap rate. **1839** THACKERAY *Fatal Boots* Oct., A showy black-haired woman with one eye. **1882** *Garden* 15 July 41/1 One of the showiest of hardy border flowers. **1893** F. T. RICHARDS in Traill *Social Eng.* i. 23 Showy market places, and fine houses.

**b.** Of immaterial things, qualities, etc.: Brilliant, striking, 'effective'. Of persons: Displaying brilliant talents, etc.

**1728** MORGAN *Algiers* I. List Subscribers (*ad fin.*), Had I been fond of borrowed Plumes this List had been considerably more Showy than it is. **1782** MISS BURNEY *Cecilia* II. vi, Forming friendships with every shewy adventurer that comes in your way. **1824** SCOTT *St. Ronan's* v, His manners, without being showy, were gentleman-like and pleasing. **1836** J. H. NEWMAN *Par. Serm.* xxxii. (ed. 2) II. 448 The showy talents, in which the present age prides itself. **1872** BAGEHOT *Physics & Pol.* ii. (1876) 44 The progress of the military art is the most conspicuous, I was about to say the most *showy*, fact in human history. **1912** *Eng. Hist. Rev.* Oct. 817 Dr. McGiffert is..inclined to let generalities—more or less showy—do duty for concrete statements of fact.

**c.** *Nat. Hist.* In names of plants and birds.

**1817** *Shaw's Gen. Zool.* X. 466 Showy Tanager (*Tanagra ornata*). **1880** BESSEY *Bot.* 460 *Lilium speciosum*, the Showy Lily, from Japan. **1890** *Century Dict.* s.v. *Orchis*, The common American species is *O[rchis] spectabilis*, the showy orchis.

**d.** Comb.: ***showy-dressed, -looking.***

**1788** MRS. HUGHES *Henry & Isab.* III. 80 A tall, plain, showy dressed, affected woman. **1821** HAZLITT *Table-t.*, *Living to one's-self* (1869) 125 A showy-looking girl.

**showyll,** obs. form of SHOVEL.

**showyng(e,** obs. forms of SHOEING *vbl. sb.*

**shox** (ʃɒks), *sb. pl.* [Re-spelling of *shocks* (chiefly in advertising and trade journalism).] Shock absorbers.

**1976** *Hot Car* Mar. 20/2 (Advt.), Full range of automatic adjusting shox for American and European cars. **1977** *Custom Car* Nov. 13/1 The Fiesta 1·3S feels like a dry-sprung Mini on competition shox.

‖**shoya** ('ʃɔ:ja). = SOY¹, SOYA.

**1883** N. OKOSHI *Fisheries Japan* (Fish. Exhib.) 24 The sauce known here under the name of Japanese shoya, properly called shoyu.

**shoy-hoy**¹, **shoyhoy** ('ʃɔɪhɔɪ). [Imitative of the cry used for scaring birds.] One who scares away birds from a sown field. Also *transf.*

**1819** COBBETT *Weekly Pol. Reg.* 14 Aug. 22 These bird-scarers, or, as we call them in Hampshire, *Shoy-hoys*. *Ibid.* 23 Look at the conduct of these shoy-hoys during this present session... The shoy-hoy Chamberlaine from Southampton; the shoy-hoy Palmer,..the two shoy-hoys from Nottingham. **1835** *Fraser's Mag.* XII. 211 Waithman the pride of the senate became Waithman the empty shoyhoy; Hunt the patriot degenerated into Hunt the greatest of liars.

**shoy-hoy**². App. jocularly used for HOY *sb.*¹

**1840** HOOD *Up Rhine* 17 In the old shoy-hoy times I was once at sea three days and two nights between London and Ramsgate, now a certain passage of a few hours.

†**shoyn(e.** *Obs. rare.* [Of obscure origin; perh. some error.] (See quot.)

**1527** ANDREW *Brunswyke's Distyll. Waters* I v b, Water of Cardes.. is good agaynste the sore named the shoyne. *Ibid.* K ii b, Clothes wet in the same water and layd vpon the shoyne.. is very good for the shoyn which commeth with hote brenyng blaynes.

‖**shoyu** ('ʃɔ:ju). Also sho-yu, †soeju. [Jap.: see SOY¹.] = SOY¹ 1. Freq. *attrib.* as ***shoyu sauce.***

**1727** J. G. SCHEUCHZER tr. *Kæmpfer's Hist. Japan* I. ix. 121 What they call Soeju, is also made of it, which is a sort of an *Embamma*, as they call it, which they eat at meals to get a good stomach. **1880** I. L. BIRD *Unbeaten Tracks in Japan* I. 232 Eels and other dainties are served with soy (*shô-yu*), the great Japanese sauce. **1920** *Japan Advertiser* 22 Aug. 5/1 The eel is laid out flat and broiled over a charcoal fire with a special shoyu sauce. **1936** K. W. COLEGROVE *Militarism in Japan* iv. 45 He came from a most humble home, and he worked as a boy for a manufacturer of *shoyu* (a Japanese sauce). **1960** B. LEACH *Potter in Japan* vi. 132 We ate it first with shoyu sauce. **1976** *Sci. Amer.* Sept. 172/1 Tempeh, ragi, sufu, shoyu, ang-kak, tea fungus and mizo are among those [fermentation products] eaten in Asian countries.

**Shqip** (ʃkjɪp). Also **Shqup, Shqyp.** [Alb.] = ALBANIAN *sb.*² 2. Cf. next.

**1969** 'R. STARK' *Blackbird* xxv. 169 In Albania, they speak Shqyp... And in Shqyp,..Albania is Shqipenija. That means eagle country. **1974** *Encycl. Brit. Macropædia* I. 422/1 The origins of the general name Albanian.. and of the current official name Shqip or Shqipëri, which may well be derived from a term meaning 'pronounce clearly, intelligibly', are still disputed. **1976** W. H. CANAWAY *Willow-Pattern War* iii. 25 'From now on we speak only Shqyp'—which is what Albanians call Albanian.

**Shqipetar** (ʃ'kjɪpətɑ:(r)). Also **Shkyipetar, Skipitar,** etc. [Alb.] = ALBANIAN *sb.*² 1. Cf. prec.

**1833** *Penny Cycl.* I. 256/2 The Albanian.. calls himself Skipitar, and his native land Skiperi. **1860** *Chambers's Encycl.* I. 104/2 The *inhabitants*, estimated at 1,900,000, form a peculiar people, the Albanians or Arnauts; they call themselves Skypetars. **1876** [see LATIN *sb.* 3 c]. **1902** *Encycl. Brit.* XXV. 246/2 The Albanians, both Ghegs and Tosks, call themselves *Shkyipetar*, and their land *Shkyipenia* or *Shkyiperia*, the former being the Gheg, the latter the Tosk form of the word. **1935** *Chambers's Encycl.* I. 122/2 The name Shkypetar is derived by some from *shkip*, a rock, and thus signifies Hillmen; while others derive it from *shkyup*, an eagle, signifying Sons of the Eagle. **1971** *Guardian* 10 Aug. 4/5 Shquiptars prefer folk songs..rather than the Internationale.

‖**shrab** (ʃrɔ:b). *Anglo-Indian.* Also [7 sharab, scherab], 9 shraub. [Urdū a. (through Persian) Arab. *sharāb* wine, or any beverage, f. *shariba* to drink. Cf. SHERBET, SHRUB *sb.*²] Wine, spirits, or a drink prepared with them.

[**1662** J. DAVIES tr. *Mandelslo's Trav.* 6 To treat his friends with Schiras Sharab. **1662** —— tr. *Olearius' Voy. Amb.* 175 A Bottle of Scherab or Persian Wine.] **1867** SMYTH *Sailor's Word-bk.*, *Shrab*, a vile drugged drink prepared for seamen who frequent the filthy purlieus of Calcutta. **1886** YULE & BURNELL *Hobson-Jobson* s.v. *Sherbet*, Port-shraub, Sherry-shraub, Lall-shraub, Brandy-shraub, Beer-shraub. **1888** *Nature* 19 July 269, I take brandy shrab, and get drunk like you.

**shradd,** obs. form of SHRED *sb.*

‖**shradh, shraddha** ('ʃrɑ:d(ə)). Also 8 †seradeh, sherad, 9 shraad, sradh, s(h)raddha, sraddha, 20 shradh. [Skr. *çrāddha* (whence Hindī *çrāddh*, Urdū *shrāddh*, *srāddh*), f. *çraddhā* faith, trust.] A Hindu ceremony in honour and for the benefit of a deceased relative, at which water and food are offered; the offerings thus made.

**1776** N. B. HALHED tr. *Code Gentoo Laws* ii. 73 Who, after his Father's Death, performs not the *Seràdeh* (religious Offices to his Father's Memory). **1787** in Seton-Karr *Select. Calcutta Gaz.* (1864) I. 209 Nemoo Mullick, the rich Banker, is said to have spent lately three lacks of Rupees in the sherad or funeral ceremonies at his mother's death. **1832** H. H. WILSON in *Asiatic Res.* XVII. 276 *Sràddhas*, obsequial ceremonies at stated periods. **1845** STOCQUELER *Handbk. Brit. India* (1854) 215 He..performs the obsequies, or *shraad*, of his deceased ancestors. **1887** W. J. WILKINS *Mod. Hinduism* 463 At Shrādhas, Manu and other writers distinctly enjoin eating of flesh. **1969** *Hindu Weekly Mag.* (Madras) 3 Aug. p. ii/4 Nimai performed the necessary rituals and ceremonies—tarpan, shradh, ablution, offering of oblations. **1971** *Illustr. Weekly India* 4 Apr. 13/2 Females and children whose *yagyopavit* has not been done are not permitted to perform the *shradh* ceremony.

**shraep,** obs. variant of SHRAPE *sb.*

**shraf,** obs. pa. t. SHRIVE *v.*

**shraff, shraffage,** obs. var. SHROFF, SHROFFAGE.

**Shraftyde,** obs. form of SHROVETIDE.

**shrag** (ʃræg), *sb. Obs.* exc. *dial.* Also 5 schragge, 6–7 shragge. [A parallel form to SCRAG *sb.*² (see SCR-). Cf. SHRIG, SHROG.]

†**1.** A rag, tatter. *Obs.*

? *a* **1400** [see SHRED *sb.* 3].

**2.** A twig; a branch lopped off; also, *occas.* a bush or low tree. *dial.*

**1552** HULOET, Shragge of trees, *sarmenta.* **1605** VERSTEGAN *Dec. Intell.* ix. 285 A kynd of breach or valey down a slope from the syde of a hill, where comonly shragges and trees do grow. **1642** D. ROGERS *Naaman* 23 Absolon is snatcht up by his long head locks, by a shrag of an oake. *Ibid.* 185 If they lose their hooke upon a shrag of triall and temptation. **1823** E. MOOR *Suffolk Words*, *Shrags*, the ends of sticks—of the birchen twigs in a broom; or of whins or furze... The clippings of live fences.

**shrag** (ʃræg), *v.* Also 5 schragge, schregge, 6 shragge, 9 shreg. [f. SHRAG *sb.*] *trans.* To lop, trim, prune.

*c* **1440** *Promp. Parv.* 448/2 Schredyn, or schragge trees, *sarculo.* **1552** HULOET, Twygges or boughes of trees cut of, or shragged, *sarmenta.* *Ibid.*, Shragge vnder so that the sunne maye come to the ground, *subluco.* **1647** HEXHAM I, To Shrag, *lubben ofte snijden.* **1847** HALLIWELL, *Shreg*, to lop trees. *Somerset.*

Hence †'**shragger,** a trimmer or pruner of trees; '**shragging** *vbl. sb.*, that which is lopped off (also *attrib.*).

*c* **1440** *Promp. Parv.* 449/1 Schreggare, *sarculator.* *Ibid.*, Schreggynge, *idem quod* schredynge [*putamen*]. *c* **1460** *Ibid.* (Winch. MS.) 401 Schraggyng, *idem quod* schreggyng. **1900** *Oxf. Times* 1 Dec. 2/3, 1,500 shragging fagots.

**shrager:** see SAGGAR.

†**shragged,** *a. Obs.* In 4 shragid. [f. SHRAG *sb.* + -ED².] Having ragged or jagged edges.

**13..** *MS. Arundel Coll. Arms* 27 f. 130, A red hod on hir heved, shragid al of shridis.

**shram** (ʃræm), *v. dial.* Also shramp, shramb. [A parallel form to SCRAM *v.*¹ (see SCR-). Cf. SHRIM, SHRIMPED.] *trans.* To benumb or paralyse with cold. Chiefly *pass.*

**1787** GROSE *Prov. Gloss.*, *Shram'd*, chilled. I am shram'd to death, I am dead with cold. W. **1865** *Daily Tel.* 15 Nov. 5/2 Being 'shrammed with cold', as they say in Wiltshire. **1873** *Gentl. Mag.* X. 326 A bitter..wind..'shramming' the loungers in Palace Yard. **1892** *Pall Mall Gaz.* 22 Nov. 6/3 In the open yard amidst all the fog, where he should have been 'shramped' with cold. **1898** HARDY *Wessex Poems* 207 Half shrammed to death.

Hence **shrammed** *ppl. a.*, numbed.

**1874** LADY HERBERT *Hübner's Ramble* III. ii. (1878) 473 The sun has been pleased to unstiffen our shrammed bodies.

**shrame,** variant of SHREAM *v. Obs.*

†**shrank,** *a. Obs.* [Related to SHRINK *v.*] Of seed: Parched, shrivelled. Hence †'**shrankness.**

**1651** in *Hartlib's Legacy* (1658) 93 Then the Grain is purest and the perfectest, without Smut, Mildew, Shrankness, or other imperfections. **1686** PLOT *Staffordsh.* ix. 347 That [seed] which is thin and shrank (as they [Staffordshire people] call it).

**shrap** (ʃræp). Colloq. abbrev. of SHRAPNEL.

**1918** in Hamilton & Corbin *Echoes from Over There* (1919) xi. 125 They come fast at times too... I mean shrap and heavies. **1920** *Amer. Legion Weekly* 4 June 15 Top kicks whose skulls no shrap could dent. **1944** *Yank* 7 Apr. 3 The shrap is flying like rain.

**shrape**, *sb. Obs.* or *dial.* Also 6 **shraep**, 6– **shrap.** [A parallel form to SCRAPE *sb.*[2] (see SCR-).]

**1.** A bait of chaff or seed laid for birds; the place where such bait is laid. Hence *gen.* a snare.

**1532-3** *Act 24 Hen. VIII*, c. 10 §2 A Shrape made with Chaffe or other thing. **1592** NASHE *P. Penilesse* 8 Casting foorth silken shraps to catch Woodcocks. **1594** PLAT *Jewell-ho.* III. 55 After you haue procured the pigeons to haunt a place, by making of a shrap. **1618** S. WARD *Jethro's Just. Peace* 48 The Diuell as well as the Briber laieth his hookes in this shrap. **1624** BEDELL *Lett.* iii. 59 The most chaffie shrap that euer was set before the eyes of winged Fowle. **1669** WORLIDGE *Syst. Agric.* 197 They [sparrows] being so easily induced to come to a Shrape or Place baited for them. **1817** J. MAYER *Sportsman's Direct.* (ed. 2) 160 To trap a fox in cover, make a shrape with some free moulds where the hares' paths meet. **1895** *E. Angl. Gloss.*, *Shrap or Scrap*, a bait of chaff laid in the winter season to attract sparrows, &c., which are then netted with a contrivance called a 'shrap net'.

†**2.** ? The enclosure in a cockpit, within which the cocks fight.

**1575** CHURCHYARD *Chippes* I. 99 Loe heer how soen, the strong becoms full weak And out of shraep, fly cocks and so crie creak. **1599** —— *Fort. Farewel* A 2 A crauen cock .. Will run about, the shraep and daer not stand, When cocks of gaem, comes in to giue a bloe.

†**shrape**, *v. Obs.* Forms: 1 **scrapian**, 3 **schreape**, 3–4 **schrape**, 4–6 **shrape.** [OE. *scrapian* (see SCRAPE *v.*).] *trans.* and *intr.* To scratch, scrape (*lit.* and *fig.*).

*c* **1000** in *Techmer's Internat. Zeitschrift* (1885) II. 124 Ʒyf þu æȝera beþurfe, þonne scrapa þu mid þinum fingre up on þinne wynstran þuman. *a* **1225** *Ancr. R.* 116 Heo schulden schreapien eueriche deie þe eorðe up of hore putte þer heo schulden rotien ine. *Ibid.* 82 (MS. C.), þeose beoð all ischrapede ut of ancre riule þæt swich fulðe spit ut. **13..** [see SHAB *sb.* 1]. **1362** LANGL. *P. Pl.* A. v. 215 þenne was he a-schomed .. and schraped his eren. *c* **1380** WYCLIF *Serm.* Sel. Wks. II. 27 Take ȝe out litil foxis þat schrapen doun þe vines. *c* **1430** LYDG. *Min. Poems* (Percy Soc.) 184 Herly in the morowe to shrapyn in the vale, To fynde my dyner amonge the wormes smale. **1509** BARCLAY *Shyp of Folys* 24 Youth brought vp in lewdnes and in syn Shall skant it shrape so clene out of his mynde.

**shrapnel** ('ʃræpnəl), *sb.* Also *erron.* **-ell.** Orig. with capital initial. [f. the name of Gen. H. *Shrapnel*, who invented this shell during the Peninsular War.] **1.** A hollow projectile containing bullets and a small bursting charge, which, when fired by the time fuse, bursts the shell and scatters the bullets in a shower.

The term *Shrapnel shell* was adopted officially (instead of *spherical case shot*) in accordance with the Report of a Select Committee at Woolwich dated 11 June, 1852. Used in forms ***Shrapnel's*** or ***shrapnel shell***, ***shot*** or as collect. sing.

(*a*) **1806** CAPT. J. F. OGILVIE in Shrapnel *Petit. Ho. Lords* 14 The excellent effect of your Spherical Case (Shrapnel Shells). **1807** SIR R. WILSON in *Life* (1862). II. 148 If we had only some of Shrapnell's shot. **1812** LIEUT. BOUCHER in Shrapnel *Petit. Ho. Lords* 10 The French complained much of the 'Shrapnel Case Shot'. **1870** *Daily News* 31 Aug. 2 The new Indian gun .. throwing a nine-pound shrapnel shell. **1890** *Nature* 4 Sept., The efficiency of a projected shrapnel shell is materially altered by an increase in the velocity. **1940** [see sense 3 below]. **1944** *Daily Tel.* 22 Feb. 4/6 Most people know what a shrapnel shell (now temporarily obsolete) used to be.

(*b*) **1812** LIEUT. H. HOUGH *Diary* 27 June (MS.), Our batteries cracking shrapnells over their ears. **1858** MAJ. SINGLETON in Shrapnel *Petit. Ho. Lords* 21, I ordered Shrapnel to be fired, which did great execution. **1877** *Field Exerc. Infantry* 384 A slight earthen parapet is sufficient to protect men from the effects of Shrapnel.

*attrib.* and *Comb.* **1854** F. A. GRIFFITHS *Artil. Man.* (ed. 6) 82 The Shrapnell fuze. **1909** DEHAN *Dop Doctor* xxx, A dusty stretch of shrapnel-raked ground. **1918** G. FRANKAU *Judgement of Valhalla* 7 And floundered, torn and bleeding, Over trenches, through the wire, With the shrapnel-barrage leading To the prey of our desire. **1923** KIPLING *Irish Guards in Gt. War* I. 222 A shrapnel-barrage fell also on the supports. **1939** AUDEN & ISHERWOOD *Journey to War* 71 If you looked closely you could see dull red shrapnel bursts.

**2.** *Austral.* and *N.Z. Mil. slang.* Small change, notes, or coins of low denominations.

**1919** W. H. DOWNING *Digger Dialects* 44 *Shrapnel*, .. tattered French bank notes of small denominations. **1977** *Camera & Ciné* Nov. 24 'I don't suppose you'd have a bit of shrapnel?' .. I shook fifty cents out of my purse and handed it to him.

**3.** Fragments from shells or bombs (see quot. 1940[1]).

**1940** *N. & Q.* CLXXIX. 278/1 The public has chosen to ignore the facts that shrapnel shell has become obsolete and that anti-aircraft guns fire high-explosive only. In consequence the shell fragments which are at present descending upon its devoted head are unhesitatingly referred to by the public as 'shrapnel' and the correct expression, 'shell fragments', has begun to verge on pedantry. **1940** W. S. CHURCHILL *Secret Session Speeches* (1946) 20 Our barrage will be firing, and .. great numbers of shell splinters usually described most erroneously as shrapnel, will be falling in the streets. **1946** *Chambers's Jrnl.* May 228/2 A viciously singing piece of shrapnel put his helmet straight for him. **1976** *Times* 18 Aug. 12/5 What journalists and other non-gunners call shrapnel are in fact fragments from high explosive bombs or shells. **1982** *Times* 21 June 4/5 One found a piece of shrapnel from the bomb in the pocket of his overalls.

Hence (*rare*) **'shrapnel** *v.*, to shell with shrapnel; **'shrapnelize** *v.* (*transf.*).

**1837** T. HOOK in *New Monthly Mag.* L. 156 They were sweeping up the mud, and spooning it into a cart with an almost inevitable certainty of Shrapnelizing the 'passing villagers'. **1901** *Westm. Gaz.* 2 Dec. 7/1 Our guns shrapnelled their advance.

**shraum** (ʃrɔːm). *rare*$^{-1}$. [ad. Ir. *sream* corrupt matter, phlegm, running from the eyes.] A mucous deposit.

**1922** JOYCE *Ulysses* 241 He wiped away the heavy shraums that clogged his eyes.

**shrave** (ʃreɪv). *local.* (See quots.) Hence **shrav(e)y** *a.*

**1793** A. YOUNG *Agric. Sussex* 12 This land is provincially called Shravey, stoney, or gravelly. **1850** *Jrnl. R. Agric. Soc.* XI. I. 81 Shravy land, flinty and gravelly. **1858** *Ibid.* XIX. I. 187 The subsoil varies from a stiff yellow clay to what is called shrave, which consists of innumerable fragments of flaky pieces of mixed clay and sand.

**'shravel.** *local.* Small refuse wood or faggots.

**1732** in Cullum *Hist. Hawsted* (1784) 216 [In 1732 the tenant was allowed] shravel wood.

**shrdlu** ('ʃɜːdluː). Also **shrdlu etaoin** ('ɛtəɔɪn). A sequence of letters appearing on the keyboard of a type-setting machine, used as an example of an absurd or unintelligible utterance. Cf. QWERT, QWERTY.

**1943** D. POWELL *Time to be Born* xii. 290 She read .. the words... For all the sense they made to Vicky they might have been a trail of 'shrdlu etaoin's'. **1970** *New Statesman* 25 Dec. 863/2 Those witty literals, exotic printers' pies and secret messages in the *shrdlu* code.

**shread head.** *Archit.* [Cf. next.] = JERKIN-HEAD.

**1842** GWILT *Archit.* Gloss. 1032.

**'shreadings**, *sb. pl. Building.* ? *Obs.* Also 8 (*rare*) **shreedings**, 9 **shredding.** = FURRING 3 b.

**1668** LEYBOURN *Platform for Purchasers* 133 Furrings or Shreadings [of a roof]. **1679** MOXON *Mech. Exerc.* ix. 172 *Shreadings*, .. the lower end of the Principal Rafters markt *rr* are called *Shreadings*, or *Furrings.* **1812** P. NICHOLSON *Mech. Exerc.* 88. **1842** GWILT *Archit.* Gloss., Shreddings or Furrings. **1850** PARKER *Gloss. Archit.*, *Furrings*, or *Shreadings*, short pieces attached to the feet of the rafters of a roof, making a small angle outwards and downwards, for the purpose of carrying the eaves beyond the line of the wall.

**shreak**, obs. variant of SHRIEK.

†**shreake.** *Obs.* Of obscure meaning and origin.

Perh. a misprint; cf. *streak* dial., strip.

**164.** HERRICK *Oberon's Palace* 57 Ribands, and then some silken shreakes The virgins lost att barlye breakes.

†**shream**, *v. Obs. rare.* Forms: 3 **schreamen**, 6 **shrame**, 7 **shream(e.** [A parallel form to SCREAM *v.*] *intr.* To scream. Hence †**'shreamer**, a screamer; **'shreaming** *ppl. a.*

*c* **1230** *Hali Meid.* 52 þet wif .. þe ihereð, hwen ha kimeð in, hire bearn schreamen [*v.r.* screamen]. **1561** DAUS tr. *Bullinger on Apoc.* (1573) 204 b, Clamorous cryers, shrekers, shramers, or yellers. **1565** GOLDING *Ovid's Met.* IV. (1593) 91 They heard about them round Of tubbish timbrels perfectly a hoarse and jarring sound, With shraming shalms and gingling bels. **1567** *Ibid.* VIII. 184 She shraming cried out aloud. **1681** HICKERINGILL *Sin Man-catching* I. 16 The little Peacocks shreame [*ed.* 2 shream] out and yawle amain.

**shreawd**, obs. form of SHREWD.

**shred** (ʃrɛd), *sb.* Forms: 1 **scréade**, *pl.* **scréada, -an**, 3 **schreade, shrade**, 3–6 **shrede**, 4–5 **schrede**, 6 **shredd, shradde**, 6–7 **shredde**, 7, 9 **shreed**, 7–9 **shread**, (9 **shrid**), 6– **shred.** [OE. **scréad* str. fem. (pl. *scréada*), *scréade* wk. fem. = OFris. *sc(h)rêd* hair-cutting, clipping of coin, MLG. *schrôt*, *schrât* neut., cut, cut-off piece, width of linen, also *schrôde*, *schrâde* wk. masc. (LG. *schraad*), MDu. *schrôde* fem. (WFlem. *schroode*, *schroo* fem., Du. *schroot* neut., from G.), OHG. *scrôt* str. masc. (MHG. *schrôt*; G. *schrot* neut., in dial. masc.), f. OTeut. **skrauđ-* (:*skreuđ-*, *skrŭđ-*, to cut, for other derivatives of which see SHROUD, SHRIDE *v.*[1]). Cf. SCREED *sb.*

The OTeut. **skreuđ-* is commonly viewed as an extended form of **skreu-*, which is itself an extension of **sker-*: see SHEAR *v.*]

**1.** A fragment cut or broken off; a strip; a scrap.

In late use apprehended as transf. from sense 3.

*c* **1000** ÆLFRIC *Gloss.* in Wr. Wülcker 151/20 *Praesegmina*, *praecisiones*, screadan. *Ibid.* 164/6 *Sceda*, screade. *a* **1225** *Ancr. R.* 416 Ʒif heo mei sparien eni poure schreaden [*MS. C* schraden, *T* schiue], sende ham al derneliche ut of hire woanes. *c* **1300** *Havelok* 99 Hauede he non so god brede, Ne on his bord non so god shrede. þat he ne wolde þorwit fede Poure. *c* **1330** *Arth. & Merl.* 1540 þe white [dragon] brent þan rede, þat of him nas founden a schrede, Bot dust. *c* **1400** *Laud Troy Bk.* 4455 Thei hadde ben hewen euery a schrede. **1564-78** BULLEIN *Dial. agst. Pest.* (1888) 102 There is a fletyng Island... Sume saied it was a shred of the bankes of Paradise. *a* **1701** MAUNDRELL *Journ. Jerus.* (1732) 106 A small shred of ground twelve yards long, and one broad. **1860** THACKERAY *Lovel* iii, He munched a shred of toast. **1860** PUSEY *Min. Proph.* 65 One of those little shreds which float in countless numbers on the surface of the water. **1863** KINGLAKE *Crimea* (1876) I. x. 140 It would be well to set apart one small shred of ground.

**b.** = SHERD. *rare.*

**1613-6** W. BROWNE *Brit. Past.* II. i. (1625) 17 Carrying my pot as Maids vse on their heads, I fell with it, and broke it all to shreads. **1865** KINGSLEY *Herew.* xxx, He .. sorted his pots, kept the whole ones, threw the shreds at the rabbits.

**2.** In OE., *pl.* Parings (of fruit, etc.); in mod. use, a narrow strip (of peel, vegetable, root, etc.) shaved so thin that it curls.

*c* **1000** ÆLFRIC *Gloss.* in Wr.-Wülcker 118/1 *Quisquiliæ*, æppelscreada, *uel* cornæsceda. **1741** *Compl. Fam.-Piece* I. ii. 119 Put shreds of Lemon-peel into some of the Glasses. **1840** THACKERAY *Shabby-genteel Story* iii, Three shreds of celery in a glass. **1842** LOUDON *Suburban Hort.* 307 The part of the stock which projects over the ring of the bark is next split into shreds. **1846** J. BAXTER *Libr. Pract. Agric.* I. 469 The root [horse-radish] scraped into shreds is the well-known accompaniment of 'the roast beef of Old England'.

†**b.** *pl.* Parings of leather or parchment. *Obs.*

**1551-2** *Act 5 & 6 Edw. VI*, c. 15 §3 Everie Girdler .. maye .. sell their Neckes Wombes and Shreddes of tanned Leather, to anye person. **1553** *Inv. Ch. Goods* (1885) 19 Pd. for a bag of glover's shreds xij d. **1687** *Lond. Gaz.* No. 2240/2 Glovers Clippings, Parchment Shreds.

**3.** A fragment or strip of textile material cut or torn off; one or more fibres torn from a piece of cloth; a small piece of cloth, a fragment of clothing; *pl.* scanty or ragged garments.

? *a* **1400** *Morte Arth.* 3473 Manye schredys and schragges at his skyrttes hynnges. *c* **1400** *26 Pol. Poems* 2 God wole haue rekenyng, .. Of men and cloth the leste shrede. *c* **1430** *Syr Gener.* (Roxb.) 6118 Generides than cut his shirt .. And with the shredes hem he bond. *c* **1450** *Pol. Rel. & L. Poems* 137 Nakede with outen clath or schrede. **1589** NASHE *Martin's Months minde* 45 The shreddes that fall into the Tailors hell, neuer come backe to couer your backe. **1615** G. SANDYS *Trav.* 56 Some of them going almost starke naked: others clothed in shreds of severall colours. **1661** BOYLE *Style Script.* (1675) 72 A fair suit of Arras, of which .. a shread may assure you of the fineness of the colours, and richness of the stuff. **1735** BERKELEY *Querist* §505 The very shreds shorn from woollen cloth. **1848** THACKERAY *Van. Fair* xvii, They have hung a shred of carpet out of an upstairs window. **1850** MRS. JAMESON *Leg. Monast. Ord.* 324 Her clothes became ragged, and she mended them with shreds of any colour. **1881** O'SHAUGHNESSY *Christ will Return, Songs of Worker* 23 Clothed withal In shreds, the greatest beggar, yea in all The world.

**b.** *pl.* Strips of cloth used for nailing up plants or fruit trees.

**1796** C. MARSHALL *Gardening* xii. (1798) 136 The proper use of nails and shreds is necessary to the beauty of the tree. **1840** DICKENS *Old C. Shop* xli, The old gentleman handed up the nails and shreds of cloth as he wanted them. **1842** LOUDON *Suburban Hort.* 353 Shreds will last two or three years.

**c.** ***of shreds (and patches)***: made up of rags or scraps. Hence used *allusively.*

**1602** SHAKS. *Ham.* III. iv. 102 A King of shreds and patches [*1st Qo.* A king of clowts, of very shreads]. **1649** G. DANIEL *Trinarch.*, *Rich. II*, xxxiii, Led by a Rascall, made of shreds. **1827** CARLYLE *Misc.*, *Richter* (1869) 4 That this thing of shreds and patches has been vamped together for sale only. **1885** W. S. GILBERT *Mikado* I, A wand'ring minstrel I, a thing of shreds and patches.

†**d.** A cant term for a tailor. *Obs.*

**1599** B. JONSON *Cynthia's Rev.* v. iv. Wks. (1616) 246 You slaue, you lift, you shreds. **1632** MASSINGER & FIELD *Fatal Dowry* III. i, That poore shred Can bring more to the making vp of a man. *a* **1700** B. E. *Dict. Cant. Crew*, *Shred*, a Tailer.

**e.** *transf.* (of cloud, mist, etc.).

**1834** M. SCOTT *Cruise Midge* xxiii, These fibres, or shreds of clouds. **1877** BLACK *Green Past.* xxxiv, The windy shreds of cloud. **1912** *Engl. Rev.* Nov. 514 Some shreds [of mist] are caught among the topmost trees.

**f.** (See quot. 1898.)

**1846** G. E. DAY tr. *Simon's Anim. Chem.* II. 2 Membranous shreds are sometimes observed [in the saliva]. **1897** *Allbutt's Syst. Med.* III. 923 Loose motions containing much mucus or 'shreds' or 'casts', or even blood. **1898** *Syd. Soc. Lex.*, *Shreds*, patches of filmy material passed with the fæcal discharges in some cases of enteritis and diarrhœa.

**4.** A length or end of gold or silver thread or lace. *arch.*

*a* **1450** *Le Morte Arth.* 2359 Launcelot and the quene were cledde In Robes of A Riche wede, Off Samyte white, with syluer shredde. **1583** STUBBES *Anat. Abus.* II. 39 Neuer so litle scraps or shreds or short ends of lace. **1765** GOLDSM. *Double Transform.* 36 Half the charms that decked her face Arose from powder, shreds, or lace. **1845** JAMES *Arrah Neil* ii, His doublet .. displayed a great number of ornamented buttons, and shreds of gold lace.

**5.** Phr. ***in, into shreds***: in or into small fragments. ***to tear to shreds*** (also, ***shred by shred***): to rend into small pieces; *fig.* to destroy, annihilate.

*c* **1400** *Melayne* 1093 Hawberkes sone in schredis were schorne. **1762** FALCONER *Shipwr.* II. 28 'Brail up the mizen quick!' the Master cries: 'Mann the clue-garnetts, let the main-sheet fly!' In thousand shiv'ring shreds it rends on high! **1813** SCOTT *Rokeby* VI. xvii, 'Give Oswald's letter'— Bertram read. And tore it fiercely, shred by shred. **1819** KEATS *Why did I laugh to-night?* 12 Yet would I .. the world's gaudy ensigns see in shreds. **1837** CARLYLE *Fr. Rev.* I. VI. iii, A Townhall torn to shreds. **1855** BROWNING *Fra Lippo* 61 Into shreds it went, Curtain and counterpane and coverlet. **1878** LECKY *Eng. in 18th C.* I. i. 25 Lewis tore to shreds the treaty he had signed. **1903** TALLENTYRE *Voltaire* xxxix. II. 217 It tore Vernet's reputation to shreds.

**6.** A fragment, small piece, little bit, scrap (of something immaterial).

*c* **1400** *Brut* cxcvii, Allas! Holonde me haþ bitraiede! Ay is in þe rede [? = red-haired man] of somme euel shrede. *a* **1529** SKELTON *Sp. Parrot* 94 Suche shredis of sentence, strowed in the shop Of auncyent Aristippus. **1593** G. HARVEY *Pierce's Super.* Wks. (Grosart) II. 115 The dregges of common scurrilitie, the shreds of the theater. **1607** SHAKS. *Cor.* I. i. 212 They said they were an hungry, sigh'd forth Prouerbes ..: With these shreds They vented their Complainings. **1642** MILTON *Apol. Smect.* 18 This was a shred in his common place-book. **1645** G. DANIEL *Poems* Wks. (Grosart) II. 39 A despis'd Shred of mankind. **1742** R. BLAIR *Grave* 225 As if a slave was not a shred of nature. **1768** TUCKER *Lt. Nat.* (1834) I. 504 It is a shred torn off from the substance. **1834** H. MILLER *Scenes & Leg.* viii. (1857) 105 Shreds of heretic sermons would be whispered over their ale. **1868** NETTLESHIP *Ess. Browning* iv. 113, I must preserve a shred of independence in my inner self. **1885** *Times* (weekly ed.) 9 Oct. 2/2 Not a shred or shadow of truth.

†7. A twig. (Cf. SHRED *v.* 2.) *Obs.*

**15..** *Guye of Gisborne* i. in Furniv. *Percy Folio* II. 227 When shales beeene [*sic*] sheene, and shradds full fayre, and leeues both Large and longe. **1599** T. M[OUFET] *Silkwormes* 72 To view vppon one birchen shredde Some hundred Clewes to hang like clustred peares.

**shred** (ʃrɛd), *v.* Forms: 1 scréadian, 3 scradien, *Ormin* shrædenn, 3-5 schrede, 4-5 schredde, 4-6 shrede, 5 schred, 6 shreade, shrid, 6-8 shread, 6- shred. *Pa. t.* 4 s(c)hredde, schradde, 4-5 shradde, 5 schrede, 6 shrede, 9 shredded. *Pa. pple.* 1 ȝescréadod, 4 schrede, schradde, 5 yshrad, yschredyd, schrad, 5-6 shredd(e, 6-8 shreaded, shread, 6- shredded, 4- shred. [OE. *scréadian* wk. vb. = OFris. **skrêda* (whence *skrêdere* clipper of coin). The other WGer. langs. have a redupl. str. vb. (later partly conjugated weak) of the same meaning: MLG. *schrôden*, *schrâden*, MDu. *schrôden* (mod.Du. *schrooien*, *schroeien*, W.Flem. *schrooden*), OHG. *scrôtan* (MHG. *schrôten*, G. *schroten*); f. OTeut. **skrauđ-*: see SHRED *sb.*]

†1. a. *trans.* To rid (a tree, vine, vineyard) of superfluous growth; to prune. *Obs.*

*c* **1000** ÆLFRIC *Hom.* (Th.) II. 74 Ðif se winȝeard..ne bið onriht ȝescreadod. **1398** TREVISA *Barth. De P.R.* IX. xxx. (Bodl. MS.), In lente vynes and oþer treen beþ ikutte & pared, and ischred of superfluitees. *c* **1440** *Jacob's Well* 26 Alle paryschenys þat..schredyn, or croppyn, ony treen in cherche-ȝerde. **1523-34** FITZHERB. *Husb.* 42 b, If yᵉ haue any trees to shrede loppe or croppe for the fyre wode. *Ibid.* 43 It is the comun vse to begynne at the toppe of yᵉ tree whan he shall be shred or cropped. **1570** GOLDING *Justin* XLIII. 175 They lerned to shred their vynes. **1620** J. WILKINSON *Courts Leet* 119 Trees and hedges which hang over the kings high waies must be cut and shredded. **1707** MORTIMER *Husb.* (1721) II. 73 As for Timber-Trees, it is best not to head them at all, but to shred them up to one single Bough. **1762** in *Jrnls. Ho. Comm.* 13 Feb. 1792, 254/1 The Shreddings of all such Trees [that]..have heretofore been used to be lopped, cut, or shred.

*absol.* **1571** JEWEL *On 1 Thess.* (1611) 72 To plant, to weed, to graffe, to shrid.

**b.** *fig.* To strip (a person) *of* his wealth or some possession; to fleece. (Cf. SHREDDED b.) *Obs.*

**1548** PATTEN *Exped. Scot.* F ij, A good fellowe,..that hath cum to a dycyng boord..and hath soon bene shred of al that euer he brought. **1579** HAKE *Newes out of Powles* ii. (1872) B vij, To shred him cleane from all his wealth. **1643** TRAPP *Comm. Gen.* xviii. 19 He that hid his talent, was soon shred of it.

**2.** †**a.** To lop *off* (branches), esp. in pruning. In first quot. *fig. Obs.*

*c* **1000** ÆLFRIC *Hom.* (Th.) II. 74 Buton ða lareowas screadian symle ða leahtras þurh heora lare aweȝ, ne bið þæt læwede folc wæstmbære. **1390** GOWER *Conf.* I. 138 Hew doun this tree..And let of schreden every braunche. **1540** ELYOT *Image Gov.* (1556) 127 Yf the boughes be rotten or seare, the owner will shredde theim. **1568** WITHALS *Dict.* (1644) 124 The superfluous and wast sprigs of Vines, beeing cut and shreaded off. **1633** BP. HALL *Occas. Medit.* §116 If thou shouldest deale with me as I deserue, thou shouldst not only shred my boughs, but cut downe my stocke. **1662** *Comenius' Janua Ling. Triling.* 76 He loppeth (shreddeth) off the suckers. **1707** MORTIMER *Husb.* (1721) II. 32 Though they will grow amongst other Wood provided you shred up the side Boughs. **1725** *Bradley's Fam. Dict.* s.v. *Walnut-Tree*, You must by no means, in the Removal of them cut the Head, only shred up the side Branches.

†**b.** To cut or strip *off*; to cut (a piece) *from* or *out of*. *Obs.*

**1580** T. M. *Baret's Alv.* To Rdr. A vj/2 And there with floures he stuffeth first his Hiue, From which he Honie from the best hath shred. **1583** MELBANCKE *Philotimus* F j b, Too much drought doth shred the leaues. **1591-5** BRYSKETT *Thestylis* 75 in Spenser *Astrophel*, Purple flowre, Which languisheth being shred by culter as it past. **1614** GORGES *Lucan* II. 52 One pares his eares from off his head, Another doth his nostrels shred. *Ibid.* III. 111 This maister with his brasse-beake head, Out of a Roman ship had shred A mighty planke. **1649** G. DANIEL *Trinarch.*, *Hen. IV*, v, Th' vnguided Rage Of an Insultinge Conquerour, who shreds Maiesty like the mounting Poppie-Heads. **1823** SCOTT *Quentin D.* ii, Traps, armed with scythe-blades, which shred off the unwary passenger's limb.

*fig.* **1581** MULCASTER *Positions* xxxvii. (1887) 148 The retained [religion] must pitch the defence of her truth, in some paucity of choice: seeing the liuinges are shred, which should serue the great number. **1596** NASHE *Saffron Walden* S 2 b, I know what you are about to saye, but Ile shred you off three leaues at one blowe.

**c.** To cut off (a lock of hair).

**1808** SCOTT *Marmion* III. xvii, They durst not, for their island, shred One golden ringlet from her head. **1856-9** *Novels & Tales fr. Household Wds.* (Tauchn.) I. 339 (Flügel) Where [a haircutter] had once shred their locks.

†**3. a.** To pare, peel. *Obs.*

*c* **1000** ÆLFRIC *Hom.* (Th.) I. 88 Þa het he him his seax aræcan to screadiȝenne ænne æppel. *c* **1200** ORMIN 8118 He badd himm brinngenn ænne cnif An appell forr to shrædenn. **1639** O. WOOD *Alph. Bk. Phys. Secrets* 197 Then shred off the inner bark of a white Bullas tree.

**b.** *transf.* To cut away a part of, cut down, shave away. *Obs.*

*c* **1205** LAY. 5866 Kerueð eowre spere longe, & makiet heom scorte..scradieð eower sceldes al of þe smal enden.

**4. a.** To cut into shreds or small thin strips or slices; esp. in *Cookery*, so that the shreds curl.

*c* **1386** CHAUCER *Clerks's T.* 227 Wortes or othere herbes.. The whiche she shredde and seeth. **1388** WYCLIF *2 Kings* iv. 39 He gaderide therof gourdis of the feeld..and schredde in to the pot of potage. *c* **1440** *Pallad. on Husb.* VIII. 139 A pound and vncis sixe yshrad be do. **1584** COGAN *Haven Health* l. (1636) 64 Take unset Leekes..shread them small and distill them. **1648** GAGE *West Ind.* vi. 19 Had they beene but that night with the Indians, doubtlesse they had beene shred for their Suppers. **1656** MARNETTÉ *Perf. Cook* 115 Grate or shred fat Bacon or lard with a grater or knife. *a* **1756** ELIZA HAYWOOD *New Present* (1771) 197 Shred very fine a pound of suet. **1836** MARRYAT *Japhet* x, We were employed by Fleta in shredding vegetables. **1884** F. BOYLE *Borderland* 371, I shredded some Spanish moss, bound up his wounds,..and set out for home. **1908** *Motor Boat* 5 Mar. 133/2 To shred up some best yellow soap and dissolve it in water.

**b.** To cut or tear (textile stuff) into shreds or narrow strips; to reduce to shreds; also, to tear (paper, etc.) into shreds; *spec.* to reduce (documents) to unreadable strips or fragments by means of a shredder (cf. SHREDDING *vbl. sb.* 4).

**1613** J. MAY *Decl. Estate Clothing* v. 24 The vse of short thrums is likewise so ordered, that they take and shred into short length, and then lay it in steepe. **1810** in Risdon *Surv. Devon* p. xxiii, The..Serges are shredded or cut up into small pieces. **1890** HOSIE *Three Yrs. W. China* 19 There is an entire absence of machinery for washing and shredding rags. **1906** CONAN DOYLE *Sir Nigel* v, With his own hands he had shredded those august documents. **1950** *Paper-Maker* Aug. 151 (Advt.), The 'Watford' Shredder and Duster..gives most excellent results in shredding and dusting waste papers. **1974** BERNSTEIN & WOODWARD *All President's Men* xiii. 267 People became afraid that the newspapers might be discovered, so someone said, 'Shred them.' **1980** *Daily Tel.* 3 Nov. 1/4 One of his jobs was to check and shred hundreds of bundles of secret and confidential papers.

†**5.** To cut or hack in pieces; to cut *down*. *Obs.*

*c* **1275** *Sinners Beware* 328 in *O.E. Misc.* 83 Þe feondes heom forþ ledeþ Boþe lychom and saule And beteþ heom and schredeþ. ? *a* **1400** *Morte Arth.* 2688 Thoffe my schouldire be schrede. *a* **1440** *Sir Degrev.* 293 Schyre scheldus they schrede. *a* **1450** *Le Morte Arth.* 2563 Than shall we oute vppon them Ryde And shredde them downe as shepe in folde. *a* **1548** HALL *Chron.*, *Hen. V*, 59 b, The capitaines of Roan..cut doune trees, shrede the bushes, destroyed the vines. **1627** DRAYTON *Agincourt* 30 Another wafts his Blade about his head, And shewes them how their hamstrings he will shread. **1633** B. JONSON *Tale of Tub* IV. iii, This sword shall shred thee as small unto the grave, As minced meat for a pye.

**6. a.** To divide *into* small portions.

**1660** T. LYE in J. Nichols *Morn. Exerc.* (1845) V. 285, I shall not stand to shred the words into any unneccessary parts. **1674** N. FAIRFAX *Bulk & Selv.* 145 Indivisibles, such as can't be shread. **1859** DICKENS *T. Two Cities* I. v, Hunger was shred into atomies in every farthing porringer of husky chips of potato.

**b.** *intr.* To be reduced to shreds; to become divided or scattered into small portions.

**1646** J. HALL *Poems* I. 21 May these Roses here To palenesse shred, And Lilies stand disguised in new Red. **1889** 'MARK TWAIN' *Yankee at Crt. K. Arthur* xliii, At last it [smoke] began to shred away lazily. **1891** CONAN DOYLE *White Company* x, The forest began to shred out into scattered belts of trees.

**7. a.** *trans.* To cut in two, sever, as with scissors: chiefly with reference to severing the thread of life. Now *rare.*

**1565** J. PHILLIP *Patient Grissell* 1887 Possesse thou myne while death deuide, & shred my File in twain. **1575** GASCOIGNE *Posies, Dan Barth.* Wks. 1907 I. 118 O sheare that shreadst the seemerent sheete of shame. **1596** SPENSER *F.Q.* IV. ii. 52 When ye shred with fatall knife His line. **1614** GORGES *Lucan* I. 4 When..Atrops knife Shall shred in twaine thy time of life.

**b.** To divide into two parts, cleave.

**1765** *Museum Rust.* III. lxxxix. 371 [The shepherd] must shred or open the wool. **1881** *Daily Tel.* 28 Jan., To see the beautiful hull shredding the water.

**shred** (ʃrɛd), *ppl. a.* [pa. pple. of prec.]

**1.** = next.

**1665** HOOKE *Microgr.* 147 The stinging of shred Hors-hair. **1764** ELIZA MOXON *Eng. Housew.* (ed. 9) 173 Put to 'em a little shred lemon-peel. **1806** A. HUNTER *Culina* (ed. 3) 85 As much..shred onion, as will lie upon a quarter guinea. **1897** MARY KINGSLEY *W. Africa* 470 Shred-up palm-leaves.

†**2.** Pruned. *Obs.*

*c* **1648-50** BRATHWAIT *Barnabees Jrnl.* IV. (1818) 155 Sweet briers, shred vines, privet bushes.

**shredded** ('ʃrɛdɪd), *ppl. a.* [pa. pple. of SHRED *v.*] **a.** Divided, cut, or torn into shreds.

*shredded wheat*: the grain of wheat cut by machinery into long filaments freq. eaten as a breakfast cereal. Often written with capital initials as if a proprietary term.

**1577** HANMER *Anc. Eccl. Hist.* IX. viii. 178 Others gnawing the small shreded tops of greene grasse..vsed them for foode. **1656** MARNETTÉ *Perf. Cook* 241 Adde your shredded herbs thereunto. **1662** J. DAVIES tr. *Olearius' Voy. Amb.* 305 The ordinary Forrage for Horses is..Rice mixt with shredded Straw. **1713** C'TESS WINCHELSEA *Misc. Poems* 249 Ye shredded clouds that fall in Snow. **1864** R. A. ARNOLD *Cotton Famine* 514 The bleached waste of flax, or of shredded cotton-goods. **1891** MRS. MARSHALL *Cookery Bk.* s.v., Blanched and shredded pistachio nuts. **1899** *T. Eaton & Co. Catal.* Spring & Summer 171/3 Shredded wheat drink, 1-lb. package. **1906** *Mrs. Beeton's Bk. Househ. Managem.* lxvii. 1721 Menus for simple breakfasts.. Buttered shredded wheat. **1911** GALSWORTHY *Patrician* II. iv. 199 A grape fruit, which, with a shredded wheat biscuit, constituted her first meal. **1944** [see PUFFED *ppl. a.* c]. **1980** *Times* 6 Feb. 13/8 The arrival of a truck loaded with packets of Shredded Wheat.

†**b.** Stripped of one's wealth, fleeced. *Obs.*

**1596** NASHE *Saffron Walden* 38 Like a swearing shredded gamester, that looseth at one set all that euer he is worth.

†'**shredden**, *a. Obs. rare.* [f. SHRED *sb.* + -EN⁴.] Made of shreds; patchwork.

**1581** J. BELL *Haddon's Answ. Osor.* 433 b, I do shuffle together a number of raggs of auncient writers scraped together, to make upp a poore shredden coverlett, to cover the nakednes of their Idolatry.

**shredder** ('ʃrɛdə(r)). [f. SHRED *v.* + -ER¹.

Cf. OFris. *skrêdere* clipper of coin, MLG. *schrôder*, *schrâder* (LG. *schröder*) pruner, etc., also tailor (whence Da. *skrædder*, Sw. *skräddare*), MHG. *schrôtære* (mod.G. *schröter*) now chiefly in sense 'stag-beetle'.]

†**1.** A lopper or pruner of trees. *Obs.*

**1589** FLEMING *Virg. Ecl.* i. *note* i, The lopper or shredder of trees. **1631** ANCHORAN *Comenius' Gate Tongues* 69 A lopper or shredder seates and putteth young graffs, sciences, shootes and twigges to a seed plot.

†**2.** One who utters 'scraps'. *Obs.*

**1592** NASHE *Strange Newes* K 1 b, The short shredder out of sandy sentences without lime.

**3.** An instrument for shredding; †a pruning-knife; a machine for reducing a substance to shreds; *spec.*, a machine for reducing documents to small unreadable fragments.

**1572** in *Midland Counties Hist. Coll.* II. 363 Item two billes & a shredder iiijᵈ. **1887** *American* XIV. 24 The use of a shredder for reducing the canes to a pulp. **1950** [see SHRED *v.* 4 b]. **1962**, **1973** [see *paper shredder* s.v. PAPER *sb.* 12]. **1977** *New Yorker* 27 June 23/1 Papers were discussed behind sealed doors..and tossed into shredders.

†**4.** A front tooth, an incisor. *Obs.*

**1650** BULWER *Anthropomet.* 138 The Fore-teeth or Shredders. **1683** SNAPE *Anat. Horse* v. vi. (1686) 210 The *Incisores*, Cutters or Shredders.

**shredding** ('ʃrɛdɪŋ), *vbl. sb.* Also 5 s(c)hredyng(e, 6-9 shridding, 7 shreading. [OE. *scréadung*: see SHRED *v.* and -ING¹.]

†**1.** Pruning or lopping of trees. *Obs.*

*c* **1000** ÆLFRIC *Gloss.* in Wr.-Wülcker 149/11 *Putatio*, screadung. *c* **1380** WYCLIF *Sel. Wks.* III. 264 Scredynge of trees. *c* **1440** *Promp. Parv.* 448/2 Schredynge, of trees and oþer lyke, *sarmentacio*, *sarculacio*. **1486** *Nottingham Rec.* III. 255 Felling and shredyng of wode. **1567** in F. J. Baigent *Crondal Records* (1891) 172 In shreddinge of bussheѕ, heathe or fearne. **1601** HOLLAND *Pliny* XVII. xxiii. I. 538 In lopping and shredding of trees. **1664** EVELYN *Sylva* 114 It may take root, and hasten..to a sudden Tree; especially, if seasonable shreading be appli'd.

**2.** *concr.* **a.** A fragment; a shred. Now *rare.*

*c* **950** *Lindisf. Gosp.* Matt. xiv. 20 Tuoelf ceawlas vel foðer screadunga fullo, *duodecim cophinos fragmentorum plenos.* **1594** HOOKER *Eccl. Pol.* v. xxvii. (1611) 241 It [the Common Prayer] hath a number of short cuts or shreddings which may bee better called wishes then prayers. **1672** EACHARD *Let. to B. D.* (1705) 15, I knew of no better instance to represent the vanity of such kind of idle shreddings. **1821** CLARE *Vill. Minstr.* II. 112 The cloak and hat..worn to shreddings. **1853** RUSKIN *Stones Venice* III. iii. 136 An artistical pottage composed of nymphs, cupids, and satyrs, with shreddings of heads, and paws of..beasts, and nondescript vegetables. **1867** MORRIS *Jason* VII. 183 She.. cast therein Shreddings of many herbs.

†**b.** *pl.* or *collect. sing.* Prunings or loppings (of trees). *Obs.*

**1398** TREVISA *Barth. De P.R.* XVII. cii. (1495) 667 The Arabees makith fyre of shredynge of the mirtus tree. *c* **1440** *Promp. Parv.* 449/1 Schredynge, or schrub.., *putamen.* **1529** in J. H. Glover *Kingsthorpiana* (1883) 70 Almaner of laufull loppe and schreddyng of trees. **1553** *Respublica* 102 The windefalles, the shriddinges, the flycinges. **1649** in T. West *Antiq. Furness* (1774) 178 Any shredings, lops, crops, under woods, and other woods. **1762** in *Jrnls. Ho. Comm.* 13 Feb. 1792, 255/1 A competent Quantity of Browsing of the Shredding of the Trees.

†**3.** ? Trimming with shreds of gold lace. *Obs.*

**1766** GOLDSM. *Vic. W.* iv, I do not know whether such flouncing and shredding is becoming even in the rich.

**4.** Reducing to shreds; *spec.* the reducing of documents to small strips or fragments by a machine esp. for reasons of security.

**1954** *Paper-Maker* Dec. 94 (Advt.), Watford Shredder and Duster. A speedy and efficient method of shredding, dusting and cleaning. **1966** *Punch* 15 June 864/3 The special executive type shredder involved the user in actually removing pins from documents before shredding. **1973** *Times* 18 May 11/4 Mr Odle said he did not know what documents Mr Liddy was destroying in the paper shredder but in retrospect he conceded that the shredding had been very significant.

**5.** *attrib.*, as ***shredding-hook***, ***-knife***, ***machine***, ***-scythe***.

*c* **1000** ÆLFRIC *Gloss.* in Wr.-Wülcker 106/15 *Surculus*, winȝeardes screadungisen. **1548** UDALL *Erasm. Par. John* xv. 97 An unprofitable braunche, when it is cut of with a shreadyng hooke. **1577** GRANGE *Golden Aphrod.*, etc. S iij b, Come Atropos therefore in haste On me to vse thy shredding knyfe. **1586** in Farr *S.P. Eliz.* (1845) I. 209 Time attendes with shredding sithe for all. **1615** MARKHAM *Engl. Housew.* II. 40 Take a good quantity of blaunch't Almonds, and with your shredding knife cut them grosly. **1890** *Glouc. Gloss.*, *Shriddin' Bill or Hook*, a tool used for cutting out grass, briars, etc., from a ditch. **1975** R. L. SIMON *Wild Turkey* xii. 77, I was in my office..when I heard someone at the shredding machine. **1980** P. KINSLEY *Vatchman Switch* xvii. 115 He switched on the shredding machine.

**shredding** ('ʃrɛdɪŋ), *ppl. a.* [f. SHRED *v.* + -ING².] Breaking up into shreds.

**1883** 'MARK TWAIN' *Life on Mississippi* li. 501 Spectral trees, dimly glimpsed through the shredding fog. **1904** DOWDEN *Browning* 304 These change like the shifting and shredding clouds before our eyes.

**shreddings**, variant of SHREADINGS.

**shreddy** ('ʃrɛdɪ), *a.* [f. SHRED *sb.* + -Y¹.] Consisting of or resembling shreds; hanging in shreds, ragged.

**1835-6** *Todd's Cycl. Anat.* I. 61/2 An ash-coloured, fetid, semifluid pulp, mixed with shreddy filaments. **1855** *Chamb. Jrnl.* III. 49 His vest.. sombre-hued and shreddy with long service. **1897** *Allbutt's Syst. Med.* IV. 142 [The hepatic substance] is found projecting in shreddy masses into the pus.

**shredless** ('ʃrɛdlɪs), *a.* [-LESS.] Of which not a shred remains.

**1816** BYRON *Ch. Har.* III. xlvii, Those [Banners] which waved are shredless dust ere now.

**shredlet** ('ʃrɛdlɪt). [-LET.] A small shred.

**1840** *Tait's Mag.* VII. 183 We'll 'bide by its tatter'd shredlets, While leaf or breath remains.

†**'shredling.** *Obs. rare*⁻¹. In 7 shread-. [-LING.] A minute portion.

**1674** N. FAIRFAX *Bulk & Selv.* 105 That puzling Question, Whether a bulky Being be made up of a throng of cleaveless shreadlings?

**shred-pie.** *Hist.* Also shrid-. [prob. f. SHRED *ppl. a.* (cf. MINCED-PIE).] A mince-pie.

**1580** TUSSER *Husb.* XXXI. iii, Shred pies of the best,..and turkey well drest. **1651** S. SHEPPARD *Epigr.* 121 Christmasse Day. No matter for Plomb-porridge, or Shrid-pies. **1655** FULLER *Ch. Hist.* IV. 182 How King Henry the sixth..sent this Arch-Bishop, for a New-years-gift, a shred-pie indeed, as containing pieces of cloath and stuff, of several sorts and colours, in jeer. **1834** SOUTHEY *Doctor* viii, A shred pie, which is a coarse north country edition of the pie abhorred by puritans. **1884** BESANT *Dorothy Forster* xiii, The tables were covered with Yule-cakes..not to speak of goose-pies, shrid or mince pies.

**shreechowl**: see SHRITCH-OWL.

**shreed, shreek**, obs. ff. SHRED *sb.*, SHRIEK.

**shreevalty**, obs. f. SHRIEVALTY.

**shreeve**, obs. f. SHERIFF, SHRIVE *v.*

**shref**, obs. pa. t. SHRIVE *v.*

**shrefe**, obs. f. SHERIFF.

†**shreitch.** *Obs. rare.* [? Representing dialectally OE. *scríc*, *scréc* 'turdus': see SHRIKE *sb.*²] The missel-thrush, SHRITE.

Cf. the local names *holm-screech*, *screech-thrush*, *shrike-cock*.

**1668** CHARLETON *Onomast.* 83 *Turdus Viscivorus*..the Misletoe-Thrush, or Shreitch.

**shreitch**: see SHRITCH.

**shreive**, obs. f. SHERIFF.

**shrelle**, obs. f. SHRILL *v.*

†**shrench**, *v.*¹ *Obs.* Also 2-3 screnche, 3 schrenche, *Ormin* scr-, skrennkenn, 4 chrenche. [OE. *screncan* = (M)LG. *schrenken* to place crosswise, MDu. *schrencken* to ensnare, hinder, deceive, OHG. *screnchan*, *screnken* to lay crosswise, deceive (MHG. *schrenken*, G. *schränken*):—prehistoric **skraŋkjan*.

From the root *skraŋk-* oblique, awry, are also MLG. *schrank* neut., barrier, hedge, OHG., MHG. *schranc* masc., bar, barrier, limit, enclosed space, deception, also MHG. *schranke* fem., G. *schrank*, *schranke*; MLG. *schranken* to shamble, stutter, MDu. *schranken* to sit cross-legged, waver, totter, OHG. *scranchôn*, MHG. *schranken* to be crossed, waver, stagger.]

*trans.* To put a stumbling-block in the way of; to overthrow; to entrap; to deceive.

*c* **897** ÆLFRED *Gregory's Past. C.* ix. 59 Healden hie ðæt hie ..ða ne screncen ða ðe gað on ryhtne weȝ toweard ðæs hefonrices. *Ibid.* lix. 453 Ne screnc ðu ðone blindan. *c* **1000** *Ags. Ps.* (Splm.) xvii. 41 þu ȝescrenctyst on arisende on me, *supplantasti insurgentes in me.* *c* **1200** *Trin. Coll. Hom.* 209 Ute we..bidden god þat he us..shilde þer-wið þat he us ne schrenche. *c* **1200** ORMIN 2618 Þe deofell, þatt..stanndeþþ inn To scrennkenn ure sawless. *Ibid.* 11467 Þatt te deofell næfre Ne blinneþþ off to skrennkenn þa þatt haffdenn himm forrworrpenn. *a* **1225** *Leg. Kath.* 1189 He bicherde þene feont, & schrenchte þen alde deouel. *a* **1225** *Juliana* 34 þat weneð me to schrenchen ant schunchen of þe weie. **13..** in *Archiv Stud. neu. Spr.* LXXXII. 348 He hatied wommen.. he seyde hit weren paunceris [*read* paunteris] mannus soule to chrenche.

†**shrench**, *v.*² *Obs.* [OE. *screncan*, causative of *scrincan* to SHRINK.] *trans.* To cause to shrink or shrivel with heat.

*c* **950** *Lindisf. Gosp.* Matt. xiii. 6 Weron ȝescrencde, *aruerunt.* *c* **1290** *S. Eng. Leg.* 316/589 Men I-seoth ofte liȝtingue brenne hous and schrenche. **13..** in *Archiv Stud. neu. Spr.* LXXXII. 342 Brondis me dedin to his sydus his fel for to schrenche.

**shren(c)k**, obs. form of SHRINK *v.*

**shrene**, obs. form of SHRINE *sb.*

†**shrepe**, *v. Obs.* [app. repr. OE. *screpan* str. vb.: see SCREPE *v.*] *intr.* To scratch.

*a* **1225** *Ancr. R.* 186 And nis þet child fulitowen þet schrepeð [*v.rr.* schindleð, scratteð] aȝean, & bit upon þe ȝerde?

**shreud(e**, obs. f. SHREWD.

**shrevalty, shreve**, obs. ff. SHRIEVALTY, SHERIFF.

**shrew** (ʃruː), *sb.*¹ Forms: α. 1 screuua, screauua, scraeua, 6 shreaw, 6-7 shrewe, 6- shrew. β. 6 shrowe, schro, 8 shrow. γ. 6 shyrewe, 9 *dial.* shirrow, sheroo, shorrow. [OE. *scréawa*, *scrǽwa*, not found elsewhere in Teut.

Some scholars refer the word to the OTeut. **skreu-* to cut (see SHRED *sb.*), comparing, for the sense, MHG. *schermûs* 'sorex', 'glio', 'talpa' (mod.G. *schermaus* mole, also a kind of mouse), OE. *scirfemús* 'sorex' (related to *sceorfan* to cut). See, however, SHREW *sb.*² With the β forms cf. *strow* STREW *v.* It is possible that in the γ forms there may be some mixture of the (? synonymous) OE. *scirfe(mús)*: cf. the dial. *sarrow* = SERVE *v.*

The absence of evidence for the word between the OE. period and the 16th century is remarkable; its place may have been supplied locally in ME. by *erdshrew* (i.e. earth-shrew), though this, with its apparent corruptions *hard-shrew*, HARDISHREW, *harvest-shrew*, *nossro*, *nursrow* (with prefixed N 3), is not recorded before the 17th century.]

**1.** Any of the small insectivorous mammals, belonging to the genus *Sorex* or the family *Soricidæ*, much resembling mice but having a long sharp snout; a SHREW-MOUSE.

The common European shrew is *Sorex vulgaris*. For *elephant*, *house*, *jumping*, *marsh*, *mole*, *musk*, *otter*, *pygmy*, *rat-tailed*, *river*, *tree*, *water shrew*, see the qualifying words; also HARDISHREW. The shrew was popularly held to be venomous and otherwise injurious; cf. *shrew ash*, *-bitten*, *-run* below.

*c* **725** *Corpus Gloss.* M 336 *Musiranus*, screauua. *c* **825** *Epinal Gloss.* 649 *Musiranus*, screuua. *a* **900** *Leiden Gloss.* 226 *Musiranus*, scraeua. **1538** ELYOT *Dict.*, *Scytala*, a lytel beaste callyd a shyrewe. **1545** *Ibid.*, *Mus Araneus*, a kynde of myse called a shrew, whyche yf it goo ouer a beastes backe, he shall be lame in the chyne. **1551** TURNER *Herbal* 169 The poyson of..the feld mouse called a shrew. **1578** LYTE *Dodoens* 622 The poison of the Scorpion and Shrowe and such like venemous beastes. **1595** DUNCAN *App. Etym.* (E.D.S.), *Sorex*, a rotton, a schro. **1600** SURFLET *Country Farm* I. xxviii. 195 The shrew by her biting of the horse maketh him oftentimes to die. **1797** *Encycl. Brit.* (ed. 3) XVII. 610 The tucan, or Mexican shrew. **1813** J. C. PRICHARD *Phys. Hist. Man* iii. 92 The proper Shrews, of which there are ten species. **1825** JAMIESON *Dict.* Suppl., *Shirrow*,..the shrew, Roxb. **1859** DARWIN *Orig. Spec.* xiii. 414 The external similarity of a mouse to a shrew. **1904** J. G. MILLAIS *Mammals Gt. Brit.* I. 145 In still summer evenings, when lying in the woods waiting for rabbits to come out, I occasionally catch a momentary glimpse, of the restless, excitable Common Shrew.

*Proverb.* **1562** J. HEYWOOD *Prov. & Epigr.* (1867) 41 When all shrews haue dind, Chaunge from foule weather to faire is oft enclind. **1674** N. FAIRFAX *Bulk & Selv.* 73 It does likely hold up, as we say, by that time the Shrews have dined. **1849** *Literary Gaz.* Apr. 266 It will be fair weather when the shrews have dined.

**2.** *attrib.* and *Comb.*, as ***shrew-bitten***, ***-faced***, ***-like*** adjs.; **shrew-afflicted** = *shrew-struck*; **shrew-ash** (see quot. 1776); **shrew-mole**, a mole of either of the genera *Scalops* and *Scapanus*; **shrew-run**, paralysed (as was supposed) as the result of being overrun by a shrew-mouse; so †**shrew-running** (see quot.); **shrew-stroke**, the fact or condition of being shrew-struck; **shrew-struck** = *shrew-run*.

**1841** *Penny Cycl.* XXII. 263 If a person or animal, thus *shrew-afflicted, was passed through the arch of a bramble [etc.]. **1776** G. WHITE *Selborne*, *To Barrington*, 8 Jan., A *shrew-ash is an ash whose twigs or branches, when gently applied to the limbs of cattle, will immediately relieve the pains which a beast suffers from the running of a shrew-mouse over the part affected... A shrew-ash was made thus:—Into the body of the tree a deep hole was bored with an auger, and a poor devoted shrew-mouse was thrust in alive, and plugged in, no doubt, with several quaint incantations. *a* **1845** MRS. BRAY *Warleigh* xiii, So long as I hold in my hand this wand of shrew ash there is nothing to fear. You are safe from the spirit in this chamber. **1614** MARKHAM *Cheap Husb.*, *Bull*, etc. xxxix. 61 Of being shrew runne, or *shrew bitten. A Shrew Mouse..is a venemous thing [etc.]. **1913** D. H. LAWRENCE *Sons & Lovers* iv. 97 A tall, thin *shrew-faced woman. **1898** *Guide Mammalia Brit. Mus.* 108 The *shrew-like *Tarsipes*. **1823** GODMAN *Amer. Nat. Hist.* (1836) I. 61 The *shrew-mole is found abundantly in North America, from Canada to Virginia. **1607** MARKHAM *Caval.* VII. 80 If your horse be *shrew-runne, you shall looke for a briere which growes at both endes, and draw your horse thorow it and he will be well. *c* **1720** W. GIBSON *Farrier's Guide* II. xvi. (1722) 61 Many of the Country People..when they see a Horse or a Bullock have his Limbs suddenly taken from him,..believe him to be either Planet-struck or Shrow-run. **1726** *Dict. Rusticum*, *Planet-Struck*, or **Shrew-Running*; (in Horses) is a deprivation of Feeling or Motion. **1872** *Routledge's Ev. Boy's Ann.* 131 The curative power which alone could heal the *Shrew-stroke lay in the branches of a Shrew-ash. **1850** KINGSLEY *Alton Locke* xxi, When my vather's cows was *shrew-struck, she made un be draed under a brimble as growed together at the both ends.

**shrew** (ʃruː), *sb.*² and *a.* Forms: α. 3-4 screwe, ssrewe, shreu, (4 schreawe, srewe), 4-6 shrewe, schrew, (6 shreaw, 7 shreue), 4- shrew. β. 4 *Sc.* schraw, 6 shrowe, shroe, srow, 6-7 shrow. γ. 4 sherewe, s(s)cherewe. [Generally held to be a figurative use of SHREW *sb.*¹, the transference of meaning being accounted for by the superstitions as to the malignant influence of the animal: see e.g. quot. 1545 under SHREW *sb.*¹ 1. This appears possible; on the other hand, SHREW *sb.*¹ may be a specific application of this word in the sense 'malignant being'; cf. MHG. *schröuwel* devil.]

**A.** *sb.* **1.** †**a.** A wicked, evil-disposed, or malignant man; a mischievous or vexatious person; a rascal, villain.

Sometimes emphasized by *cursed*, *false*.

*c* **1250** *Owl & Night.* 287 Ne lust me wit þe screwen chide. *c* **1290** *Beket* 1917 in *S. Eng. Leg.* 161 Þe foure þat mest schrewes weren biþouȝten hem of guyle. **1297** R. GLOUC. (Rolls) 3020 Þe ssrewen dude seþþe to þis lond suiþe moche wo. *a* **1300** *Cursor M.* 14825 Þan come þai to þe phariseus, Of all þai war þe maister schreus. **1387** TREVISA *Higden* (Rolls) IV. 321 That schrewe Pilatus. **1390** GOWER *Conf.* I. 353 For o schrewe which he spareth A thousand goode men he grieveth. *c* **1400** *Destr. Troy* 12547 All a company is cumbrit for a cursed shrewe. *c* **1400** *Gamelyn* 230 While þou were a ȝong boy a moche schrew þou were. *c* **1400** *St. Alexius* (Laud MS.) 572 For þat tyme were þe folk of Rome þe mest shrewen of cristendome. **1461** *Paston Lett.* II. 4 These fals shrewes that are of an oppynion contrary to the Kyng. *a* **1529** SKELTON *Bouge of Court* 525 Who deleth with shrewes hath nede to loke aboute. **1563** *Homilies* II. *Serm. Rogat. Wk.* II. Qqqqj, Now are they taken from me by euil chaunces, and false shrewes, by naughty wretches. **1587** HARRISON *England* II. xvi. in *Holinshed* I. 199/2 These are some of the policies of such shrewes or close booted gentlemen. **1609** DEKKER *Rauens Alm.* Wks. 1873 IV. 264 Such as were shrewes to their wiues. *a* **1650** *Merline* 1571 in Furniv. *Percy Folio* I. 471 Then said Merlyn thoe, 'hee was a shrew that told you soe'.

β. *c* **1375** *Sc. Leg. Saints* xl. (*Ninian*) 459 Al þai schrawis euire-ilkane. *c* **1570** *Pride & Lowl.* (1841) 36 To trye a true friend from a shrow. *a* **1650** *Merline* 1221 in Furniv. *Percy Folio* I. 460 Thou cursed srow, thou goe vs froe!

γ. **13..** *Beues* (A.) 1211 Hii lowe, þe scherewes, þat him gan wreie. *c* **1386** CHAUCER *Melib.* ¶232 Dauid seith blisful is that man þat hath nat folwed the conseilyng of sherewes.

†**b.** Applied to the Devil. *Obs.*

[*c* **1315** SHOREHAM VII. 470 Þaȝ god soffrede such a schreawe Al for to spylle.] **1362** LANGL. *P. Pl.* A. x. 209 Þei don vuele and þe deuel plesen, And aftur heore deþ day schul dwelle wiþ þe schrewe. *c* **1386** CHAUCER *Can. Yeom. T.* 364 Though þat the feend noght in oure sighte hym shewe I trowe he with vs be þat ilke shrewe. **15..** *New Notbroune Mayd* 13 in Hazl. *E.P.P.* III. 2 Yet yf that shrewe To hym pursue That clepyd is Sathan.

†**c.** Applied to a malignant planet. *Obs.*

*c* **1391** CHAUCER *Astrol.* II. §4 þat he be nat retrograd ne combust, ne ioigned with no shrewe in the same signe.

†**d.** Used as a term of abuse: Wretch, villain.

**1362** LANGL. *P. Pl.* A. VII. 143 To Pers þe plouh Mon one profrede his gloue,..And bad go pisse him with his plouh, pillede screwe [*v.rr.* s(c)hrewe]! *c* **1460** *Towneley Myst.* xiii. 221 Shrew, Iape! Thus late as thou goys, what wyll men suppos? **1508** DUNBAR *Tua Mariit Wemen* 110 That auld schrew, schame him betide!

**e.** *pseudo-arch.* In a weakened use, to express playful reprobation.

**1888** STEVENSON *Black Arrow* I. i, Take me this old shrew softly to the nearest elm, and hang him tenderly by the neck. *Ibid.*, Our poor shrew of a parson is, by some mad soul, accused of slaying him.

†**2.** A thing of evil nature or influence; something troublesome or vexatious. *Obs.*

*c* **1315** SHOREHAM IV. 207 And ase god dyȝt þeawes In alle gode men, þe feend a-rayeþ þe schreawes In wykken þer a-ȝen. *c* **1450** *Godstow Reg.* 629 That this his yifte sholde not fro that tyme be reuoked by ony machynacion or shrew. *c* **1450** *Merlin* 568 Than seide Dodinell the sauage that it were a shrewe to go, for in this foreste is noon rescettes. *a* **1500** *Brome Bk.* (1886) 12 Take iij schrewys. [A waspe, a wesill, a woman.] **1535** COVERDALE *Ecclus.* xxxi. 12 Remembre, that an euel eye is a shrew. **1581** MULCASTER *Positions* xxxvii. (1888) 166 If to great a multitude making to great a state do not proue a shrew, then am I deceyued. **1620** T. GRANGER *Div. Logike* 223 Enmitie, hatred, and ill will is a shrew.

**3. a.** A person, *esp.* (now only) a woman given to railing or scolding or other perverse or malignant behaviour; freq. a scolding or turbulent wife.

For the proverbial collocation of *sheep* and *shrew* see SHEEP *sb.* 5 b.

α. **13..** *Minor Poems fr. Vernon MS.* 547/380 He þat his tonge con not holde, In cumpaygnye a schrewe is tolde. *c* **1386** CHAUCER *Merch. T.* Epil. 10 But of hir tonge a lobbyng shrewe is she. *c* **1400** *Beryn* 1282 For now, I am in certen, I have a Stepmodir: They been shrewis som. *a* **1450** MYRC 59 Wymmenes speche that ben schrewes, Turne ofte a-way gode thewes. **1508** DUNBAR *Tua Mariit Wemen* 251, I schaw ȝow, Sisteris in schrift, I wes a schrew euir. **1546** J. HEYWOOD *Prov.* II. vi. (1867) 61 Euery man can rule a shrewe, saue he that hath her. **1589** PUTTENHAM *Eng. Poesie* III. xxiv. (Arb.) 299 To be a shrewe in the kitchin, a saint in the Church. **1609** C. BUTLER *Fem. Mon.* I. (1623) Cj, They [bees] are like vnto incorrigible shrews: there is no dealing with them but by patience. *a* **1720** SEWEL *Hist. Quakers* (1795) I. III. 200 His wife who was a wicked shrew. **1820** W. IRVING *Sketch Bk.* I. 59 Those men are most..conciliating abroad, who are under the discipline of shrews at home. **1839** —— *Wolfert's Roost* (1855) 183 He brought home with him a wife, who seemed to be a shrew, and to have the upper hand of him.

β. **1581** A. HALL *Iliad* I. 12 Iuno Dame that shrowe. **1584** PEELE *Arraignm. Paris* IV. iii, *Vul.* A harletrie I warrant her. *Bac.* a peeuish eluish shroe [*rime* so]. **1596** SHAKS. *Tam. Shr.* v. ii. 193 Now goe thy wayes, thou hast tam'd a curst Shrow. **1603** FLORIO *Montaigne* III. x. (1632) 575 Happy he..[that]

Pan and old Sylvan knowes, And all the sister shrowes. **1608** [Tofte] *Ariosto's Sat.* iv. (1611) 51 Silence cuts a shrow worse then a sword. **1659** *Lady Alimony* v. iii. Kj, He that wil practise the art of swinging in a Halter, either to please or cross a Shrows humour.

*fig.* **1731-8** Swift *Pol. Conversat.* 83 Marriage is honourable, but House-keeping is a Shrew. **1742** Young *Nt. Th.* iii. 356 To love, and hate, The same vain world; to censure, and espouse, This painted shrew of life.

†**b.** *jocularly* for: A wife. *Obs. rare.*

*a* **1626** Breton *Post with Packet of mad Letters* (Grosart) 40/1 With commendations to your kind Son, your selfe, and your good Shrew.

**4.** *attrib.* and *Comb.*, as ***shrew-tamer***, ***-wife***; ***shrew-ridden*** adj.; †**shrew-shake(n** *a.*, ? cured of shrewishness.

*c* **1530** *Songs, Carols*, etc. (E.E.T.S.) 110 þe wyff was sum-what shrew shake. **1551** T. Wilson *Logic* O vj b, To be obedient, to be shrewshaken, to bring vp her children well [etc.]. **1808** Mrs. M. T. Kemble *Day after Wedding* 8 Accomplish that, and I'll acknowledge you the Prince of Shrew-tamers. **1911** *Chamb. Jrnl.* Dec. 774/2 The snappish utterances of his shrew-wife. **1922** Joyce *Ulysses* 425 We have shrewridden Shakespeare and henpecked Socrates.

**B.** *adj.* = shrewd (in various senses); wicked, evil-disposed; bad; shrewish, ill-tempered.

**1297** R. Glouc. (Rolls) 2091, & so þei sserewe robeours abbe hor wille. *Ibid.* 6718 A ssrewe & luþer dom. *c* **1305** *St. Kenelm* 202 in *E.E.P.* (1862) 53 þis quene..schrewe leuedi bicom ynouȝ. **13..** *Beues* (A.) 398 Go hom, truant!.. Scherewe houre sone. *c* **1481** Caxton *Dialogues* 44/27 Pieryne his doughter Is the shrewest [F. *la pieure*] ghyrle That I knowe on this side the see. **1638** R. Baillie *Lett. & Jrnls.* (1841) I. 76 He of Liberton does us a very shreue turne.

†**shrew**, *v.* *Obs.* Forms: α. 4-6 shrewe, schrew(e, 7 'shrew, 5- shrew. β. 4 schrowe, 6 shrow, *Sc.* schir(r)o, 6-7 *Sc.* schro. [app. f. shrew *sb.*², q.v.; cf. beshrew *v.*]

**1.** *trans.* To curse; = beshrew 3. Chiefly in imprecations *I shrew*... (occas. with *I* omitted).

α. *c* **1386** Chaucer *Nun Pr. T.* 606, I shrewe vs bothe two And first I shrewe my self bothe blood and bones If thou bigyle me. *c* **1386** —— *Sompn. T.* 519 O vile proude cherl I shrewe his face. **1393** Langl. *P. Pl.* C. vii. 75, [I] Venged me fele tymes..and shrewede myn emcristyne. *c* **1403** Clanvowe *Cuckow & Night.* 250, I shrewe al hem that been of love untrewe. *c* **1460** *Towneley Myst.* ii. 341 Here will I lig thise fourty dayes And I shrew hym that me fyrst rayse. *a* **1553** Udall *Royster D.* i. iii. (Arb.) 21, I shrew them that say nay, and that shall not be I. *a* **1568** *Bannatyne MS.* (Hunter. Club) 269, I wait nocht gif thir lawis be gud, I schrew thame first thame fand. **1611** Shaks. *Wint. T.* i. ii. 281 'Shrew my heart. **1611** —— *Cymb.* ii. iii. 147.

β. **1338** R. Brunne *Chron.* (1810) 236, I schrowe alle þer maners, þat lufes þer partie. *a* **1529** Skelton *Agst. Garnesche* iv. 127 To know thy selfe yf thow lake grace, Lerne or be lewde, I shrow thy face. *a* **1568** *Bannatyne MS.* (Hunter. Club) 377 Ye hurt me now, schirro your fais. **15..** *Wowing of Jok & Jynny* 15 in *Ibid.* 388, I schro the, lyar, full leis me yow. **1668** R. B. *Adagia Scot.* 48 Shro the ghuest the house is the war of.

**2.** To deprave; = beshrew 1. *rare*$^{-0}$.

*c* **1440** *Promp. Parv.* 449/1 Schrewyn, *pravo.*

**3.** To treat shrewishly; to scold. *rare.*

*a* **1687** Cotton *Joys of Marriage* 31 If too wary, then she'll shrew thee. **1883** Miss Braddon *Golden Calf* xx, She shrewed me so abominably..that my pride was roused.

†'**shreward.** *Obs.* Also 3 ssreward, 4 schrew-, -art, scherewarde. [f. shrew + -ard.] A scoundrel.

**1297** R. Glouc. (Rolls) 5441 Vor pur hate aȝen is broþer held as a ssreward. *a* **1325** *Names of Hare* in *Rel. Ant.* I. 134 The fusttart, the pollart, His hei nome is srewart. **1338** R. Brunne *Chron.* (1810) 262 In Wales is a schreward to werre risen on.

**shrewd** (ʃruːd), *a.* Forms: α. 4-5 schrewid(e, shrewid, schrewd(e, 4-6 schrewed(e, 4-7 shrewed(e, shrewde, shreude, 5-6 schrewyd, (4 schreuyt, 6 shreawd, schrewit), 5-8 shreud, 6-8 shrew'd, 5- shrewd. β. 5 schrod, 5-6 schrode, 5-7 shrode, 6 schroyd, 6-7 shroud, shrowd(e, shrow'd, shroad, 9 *dial.* srode. γ. 4 scherewed, 5 sherewd. [ME. *schrewed-e*, etc., prob. orig. f. shrew *sb.*² (? or *sb.*¹) + -ed². Cf. *crabbed*, *dogged*, *wicked* (all early ME.); the two former suggest the possibility that the animal (*sb.*¹) is alluded to. This formation coincided with the pa. pple. of shrew *v.*, which may be the source of some of the senses; cf. the similar use of *cursed*.]

**1. a.** Of persons, their qualities, actions, etc.: Depraved, wicked; evil-disposed, malignant. Passing into a weaker sense: Malicious, mischievous. *dial.*

α. **1303** R. Brunne *Handl. Synne* 4904 Ryche men haue shrewed sonys,—Shrewys yn dede and yn sawe. **13..** *Lay Folks Catech.* (MS. L) 139 Envye to oure neyȝbore with oþer schrewde castys. *c* **1380** Wyclif *Sel. Wks.* II. 349 Sclaundris and oþir shrewid wordis. *c* **1400** *Beryn* 1079 Fawnus..Was set oppon a purpose to make his sone leue All his shrewde tacchis. *c* **1450** *St. Cuthbert* (Surtees) 7330 þe schrewed sonn of þe fende. *Ibid.* 7742 A schrewyd counsaile toke þai þan. **1470-85** Malory *Arthur* ix. xviii. 366 Whan he dyd ony shrewd dede they wold bete hym with roddes. **1483** Caxton *Gold. Leg.* 35/1 Thenemye the fende with his angellis cursed and shrewd. *c* **1490** —— *Rule St. Benet* 122 Kepe euer your tongue from euyll and shrewde langage, & speke lytyll & well. **1548** Cranmer *Catech.* 165 Our owne euyl workes and shrewed wylles. **1570** *Satir. Poems Reform.* xviii. 62 Schrewit is that seruice ȝe haif schawin to ȝour King. **1590** Shaks. *Mids. N.* ii. i. 33 That shrew'd and knauish spirit Cal'd Robin Good-fellow. **1612** Day *Festivals* ii. (1615) 29 How do they pule & cry? nay, how wil they shew a shrewd stomach or ever they can go or speake? **1634** Milton *Comus* 846 All urchin blasts, and ill luck signes That the shrewd medling Elfe delights to make. **1879** Miss Jackson *Shropsh. Word-bk.*, *Shrewd* (s'roa·d),.. (shr'oa·d), ..badly-disposed; wicked; vicious. ''E's gwun a despert srōde lad.'

β. **1547** Boorde *Brev. Health* cccxxix, Beware of anger, for it is a shrode hert that maketh al the body fare the worse. **1606** Dekker *Seuen Deadly Sinnes* iii. Wks. (Grosart) II. 48 Drunkards, Vnthriftes and shrode Husbonds.

γ. **13..** *Beues* (A.) 4498 þar was a Lombard in þe toun, þat was scherewed & feloun. **14..** *Chaucer's H. Fame* 275 (Caxton), Ther may be vnder goodlyhede Couerd many a sherewd vyce.

†**b.** Of children: Naughty. *Obs.*

[**1526** *Pilgr. Perf.* (W. de W. 1531) 91 b, These ben called ..capytall vyces, bycause other shrewde children ryseth of them.] *a* **1548** Hall *Chron.*, *Hen. IV*, 9 Experience teacheth, that..of a shreude boye, proveth a good man. **1584** Cogan *Haven Health* cii. 89, I haue knowen..many a shreude boye for the desire of Apples, to haue broken into other folkes orchardes. **1588** Shaks. *L.L.L.* v. ii. 12 He [Cupid] hath beene fiue thousand yeeres a Boy. *Kath.* I and a shrewd vnhappy gallowes too. **1645** Bp. Hall *Treat. Content.* 77 The best of us are but shrewd children.

†**c.** Of animals: Of evil disposition, bad-tempered; vicious, fierce; = cursed 4 b. *Obs.*

**1509** Watson *Ship of Fools* vi. (1517) B vij, Oftentymes a mylde bytche bryngeth forth shrewed whelpes. ? *a* **1533** Frith *Another Bk. agst. Rastell* (1829) 242 And may be likened to a shrewd cow, which, when she hath given a large mess of milk, turneth it down with her heel. **1546** Heywood *Prov.* i. x. (1867) 22 God sendth the shrewd coow short hornes. **1547-50** Bauldwin *Mor. Philos.* iv. Q iv, As to a shrewde horse belongeth a sharpe brydle: so oughte a shrewde wyfe to be sharpely handeled. **1607** Markham *Caval.* ii. 96 The practice of some Horse-men..to tie a shrewd Cat to a Poale, with her heade and feete at libertie, and so thrusting it vnder the horses bellye,..to make her.. clawe him. **1630** Drayton *Noah's Flood* 319 [They] together sat By the shrewd Muncky, Babian, and the Ape.

†**2.** Of material things (*esp.* animals): Mischievous, hurtful; dangerous, injurious. *Obs.*

*c* **1380** *Sir Ferumb.* 4431 An Axe had he þan an honde, A shrewedere wepene for to fonde Was neuere non yfounde. **1387** Trevisa *Higden* (Rolls) I. 335 Wel schrewed mys [*mures nocentissimos*]. **1398** —— *Barth. De P.R.* v. xxviii. (Bodl. MS.), Blaynes..comeþ of schrewed and corrupt humours. **1399** Langl. *Rich. Redeles* iii. 20 þoru busschis and bromes þis beste.. Secheth and sercheth þo schrewed wormes. *c* **1400** Maundev. (1839) v. 46 Egipt is a strong Contree: for it hathe manye schrewede Havenes, because of the grete Roches. *c* **1450** *Robyn & Gandeleyn* vi. (Child *Ball.*), There cam a schrewde arwe out of þe west. **1493** Festyvall 31 b, They wyll slee theym with a shrewed knyfe. That is with the euyll and cursed tonge. **1593** Shaks. *Rich. II*, iii. ii. 59 To lift shrewd Steele against our Golden Crowne. **1607-12** Bacon *Ess.*, *Of Wisdome for a Mans selfe* (Arb.) 182 An Ant..is a shrewd thing, in an Orchard, or a garden. **1621** Donne *Serm.* xv. (1640) 148 The Buls of Babylon, the shrewdest Buls of all, in temporall, in spirituall persecutions.

†**3. a.** Of things (chiefly immaterial): Of evil nature, character, or influence; ill-conditioned, bad, vile. *Obs.*

**1382** Wyclif *Luke* iii. 5 Schrewide thingis [*prava*] schulen be in to dressid thingis. **1387-8** T. Usk *Test. Love* ii. vi. (Skeat) l. 72 Right so he is a shrewe, on whom shreude thinges and badde han most werchinge. *c* **1400** *Beryn* 2613 They have a custom, a shrewid for the nonys, Yf [etc.]. *c* **1470** Henry *Wallace* ii. 94 At thi shrewed ws thow wenys me to leid. **1513** Douglas *Æneis* ii. viii. 57 The eddir, with schrewit herbis fed. **1519** *Interl. Four Elem.* (ed. Pollard) 438 Though he loke never so well, I promyse you he hath a shrewde smell. *c* **1535** *Frere & Boy* 283 The good wyffe sayd, wer hast thou be? In schrewyd plas as thynkys me. **1644** Milton *Areop.* 16 There are shrewd books, with dangerous Frontispices set to sale. **1678** in *Lauderdale Papers* (1885) III. 140 His Maj^tie did highly signify his displeasure against Sir William Lowther... The shreud effects whereof he has since tasted.

**b.** Of reputation, opinion, meaning: Evil, bad, unfavourable. *Obs.*

*c* **1384** Chaucer *H. Fame* 1619, Y graunte yow That ye shal haue a shrewde fame And wikkyd loos. **1527** in Froude *Hist. Eng.* (1881) I. 523 *note*, Some of them, as Master Dean hath known a long time, hath had a shrewd name. **1565** Cooper *Thesaurus* s.v. *Commode*, To be ill reported of: to haue a shrewde name. **1598** Shaks. *Merry W.* ii. ii. 232 Shee enlargeth her mirth so farre, that there is shrewd construction made of her. **1621** T. Williamson tr. *Goulart's Wise Vieillard* 82 Many men..giue good things a shrewd vnhappie, and wrong name. **1664** H. More *Apology* 491 That spirit is not of God, but in some shreud sense or other is the spirit of Antichrist.

**c.** Poor, unsatisfactory. *Obs.*

α. **1426** Lydg. *De Guil. Pilgr.* 21126 Thow hast..Mad a shrewde marchaundyse. **1470-85** Malory *Arthur* ix. xxiv. 375 There is shrewde herberowe,..lodge where ye will, for I wille not lodge there. **1525** Ld. Berners *Froiss.* II. viii. 17 They will make a shrewde marchaundyce for vs. ? **1537** *Thersytes* 146 (Pollard) He that should medle with me shall have shrewde rest! **1565** Cooper *Thesaurus*, *Coenare malum* .., to suppe with sorow and shrewde rest. *a* **1586** Sidney *Arcadia* i. (Sommer) 26 b, The Helots..would haue giuen a shrewd welcome to the [invading] Arcadians.

β. **1593** *Tell-Troth's N.Y. Gift* (1876) 8 You might haue tooke better heede, and It was your owne fault, are two shrode plasters for a greene wound. **1616** *Marlowe's Faustus* (ed. Brooke) 990 By Lady sir, you haue had a shroud iourney of it.

**d.** In bad physical condition (the precise meaning varying with the application); in bad order; ugly; tough. *Obs.*

*c* **1430** *Pilgr. Lyf Manhode* ii. cxxvi. (1869) 123, i can with good vynture enoynte a shrewede wheel that cryeth. **1526** Skelton *Magnyf.* (E.E.T.S.) 1155 With a shrewde face *uilis imago.* **1571** Golding *Calvin on Ps.* xviii. 26 A shrewd knot must haue a shrewd wedge [*malo nodo quærendum esse malum cuneum*]. **1593** *Tell-Troth's N.Y. Gift* (1876) 34 The young tree will stoup, when the old shrewd cannot bend.

†**4.** Of events, affairs, conditions: Fraught or attended with evil or misfortune; having injurious or dangerous consequences; vexatious, irksome, hard; (of a task) difficult, dangerous. *Obs.*

α. **1508** Stanbridge *Vulgaria* (W. de W.) B vj, It is shrewed to Iape with naked swerdes. **1513** Douglas *Æneis* v. ix. 64 The feirfull spa men therof pronosticate Schrewit chancis to betyde. **1531** Frith *Judgm. upon Tracy* Wks. (1572) 79 Those holy fathers were in shreud cause, which continuing in long penurie, scant lefte at theyr departing, a halfe pennie. **1563-83** Foxe *A. & M.* 1936/2, I aduise thee beware of the fire, it is a shrewd matter to burne. **1595** Shaks. *John* v. v. 14 Ah fowle, shrew'd newes. **1613** Purchas *Pilgrimage* (1614) 711 Strangers haue more shrewd entertainment, and scarsely in twentie daies..can shake off this Shaker [ague]. **1623** Middleton *More Dissemblers* iii. ii, By'r Lady a shrewd business, and a dangerous. **1627** Donne *Serm.* xxii. (1640) 222 The King, that comes after a good Predecessour, hath a shrewd burthen upon him. **1632** Rowley *New Wonder* iii. i. E 3, Sir, 'tis a shrewd taske. **1821** Joanna Baillie *Metr. Leg.*, *Lady G. B.* liv, The times are shrewd, my treasures spent.

β. **1482** *Cely Papers* (Camden) 108 Wee fere here that ther weil be schrode passage to thys Balling martt. **1536** *St. Papers Hen. VIII*, II. 355, I promes you I am in a schroyd case, oneles the Kinges highe Majestie..do see redresse in suche causes. **1538** Starkey *England* i. iii. 79 Yf the yeomanry of Englond were not, in tyme of warre we schold be in schrode case. **1573** G. Harvey *Letter-bk.* (Camden) 11 This singulariti in philosophi is like to grow to a shrode matter.

**5.** ***shrewd turn***: **a.** a mischievous or malicious act (*arch.*); †**b.** a piece of misfortune, an accident (*obs.*).

**1464** *Paston Lett.* 29 Feb., He wold do Debenham a shrewd turne and he coud. **1530** Palsgr. 712/2, I provoke.. him to do a shreude tourne. **1565** Cooper *Thesaurus* s.v. *Fero, Infortunium ferre*,..to haue a shrewde turne. **1593** *Passionate Morrice* (1876) 76 As a dogge doth that is crept into a hole, hauing done a shroude turne. **1612** Brinsley *Lud. Lit.* 9 They are..sent to the schoole to keepe them.. from danger, and shrewd turnes. **1642** D. Rogers *Naaman* 282 The nurses eie attends the feeble infant, for feare of shrewd turnes. **1660** Jer. Taylor *Duct. Dubit.* ii. i. rule 5 § 3 They can doe a good turne or a shrewd. **1702** *Engl. Theophrastus* 204 No enemy is so despicable but some time or other he may do a body a shrewd turn. **1724** De Foe *Mem. Cavalier* (1840) 211 That town owed us a shrewd turn for having handled them coarsely.

**6.** As an intensive, qualifying a word denoting something in itself bad, irksome, or undesirable: Grievous, serious, 'sore'.

†**a.** of injury, loss, disease, etc. *Obs.*

α. **1387** Trevisa *Higden* (Rolls) VI. 357 þe evel þat hatte ficus, þat is a schrewed evel. **1461** *Paston Lett.* II. 4 Ther was shrewd rewle toward in this cuntre. **1542** Udall *Erasm. Apoph.* i. 132 b, He gaue a shrewd checke to y^e vnmeasurable praiser. **1592** *Soliman & P.* 426 A shrewd losse, by my faith, sir. **1593** Shaks. *2 Hen. VI*, ii. iii. 41 Humfrey, Duke of Gloster, scarce himselfe, That beares so shrewd a mayme. **1606** Chapman *Gent. Usher* ii. i. 25, I have been hanted..with a shrewd fever. **1609** G. Archer in Purchas *Pilgrims* (1625) IV. 1734 Some three or foure dayes after her, came in the Swallow,..and had a shrewd leake. **1626** B. Jonson *Staple of News* i. Interm. 73 O, but the poore man had got a shrewd mischance, one day. **1658** A. Fox *Wurtz' Surg.* iii. x. 248 A Wound closed up, where a piece of the vein is yet unhealed,..will cause shrewd Imposthumes. **1713** C'tess Winchelsea *Misc. Poems* 180 Meeting with a shrew'd mischance. **1819** Scott *Ivanhoe* xxxi, That is a shrewd loss.

β. **1482** *Cely Papers* (Camden) 112 Hytt woll be a shrode losse. **1610** Holland *Camden's Brit.* 441 With shrowde fines eftsoones redoubled, if not answered. **1612** N. Field *Woman is a Weathercock* ii. i, *Mrs. Wag.*...Haulke, hauke. [Coughs and spits.] *Page.* Shee has a shrowde reach, I see that. **1623** Bradford *Plymouth Plant.* (1856) 150 His father suffered a shrowd check.

†**b.** of temptation. *Obs.*

**1601** *Death Rob. Earl Hunt.* iv. ii. in Hazl. *Dodsley* VIII. 297, I know thou shalt be offer'd wealth, Which is a shrewd enticement in sad want. **1650** Fuller *Pisgah* iii. ii. 437 A shroud bait to tempt his hungry souldiers to sacriledge. **1696** Whiston *Theory Earth* 61 They were under a shrewd Temptation of thinking very meanly of the Bible it self.

†**c.** Qualifying an agent-noun. *Obs.*

**1576** Fleming *Panopl. Epist.* 171 *marg.*, Timorousnesse a shrewd hinderer of enterprises. **1591** Shaks. *1 Hen. VI*, i. ii. 123 These women are shrewd tempters with their tongues.

¶**d.** 'Hard to beat', formidable. *rare*$^{-1}$.

**1851** Borrow *Lavengro* xii, I was now a shrewd walker, thanks to constant practice.

†**e.** As a vague intensive. *Obs.*

*a* **1643** W. Cartwright *Ordinary* iv. i, *Caster.* He threw twice twelve. *Credulous.* By'r lady, a shrewd many!

†**7.** Of persons and their actions: Severe, harsh, stern. *Obs.*

**1387** Trevisa *Higden* (Rolls) I. 379 Oure men beeþ schrewed and angry inow to hem self, but in Goddes seruauntes þey leye neuere no hond. *c* **1470** Henry *Wallace* ix. 1424 The captane than a schrewed ansuer him gaiff. *a* **1586** Sidney *Arcadia* ii. xvi, She being sharp-set vpon the fulfilling of a shrewde office in over-looking Philoclea. **1600** Holland *Livy* xxvii. xxxiv. 654 The hard and shrewd dealings of a mans countrie. **1654** Bramhall *Just Vind.* vi. 133 The Bishop..gave him..such a shrew'd remembrance, partly with words, and partly with his crosier staffe.

**8.** Severe, sharp, hard. **a.** Of a blow, wound. *arch.*

1481 CAXTON Reynard (Arb.) 27 They.. gauen hym many a shrewde stroke. a 1500 Brut 593 This shal be þe shrewdest bofet þat euer thow yovyst. 1596 LODGE Wit's Misery (1879) 92 Hee [the devil] will giue a shroud wound with his tongue. 1597 SHAKS. 2 Hen. IV, II. iv. 228 Me thought hee made a shrewd thrust at your Belly. 1647 CLARENDON Hist. Reb. I. 39 Many.. were drowned, or forced on shore with shrewd hurts, and bruises. a 1713 ELLWOOD Hist. Life (1714) 237 He struck her with the Stick, a shrewd Blow over the Breast. 1872 MORLEY Voltaire (1886) 9/1 The shrewd thrusts, the flashing fire, with which the hated Voltaire pushed on his work of 'crushing the Infamous'. 1885 V. L. CAMERON Across Africa xvi. (ed. 2) 224 One or two got some shrewd knocks.

†**b.** Of conflict or effort. *Obs.*

1576 FLEMING Panopl. Epist. 43 To abide other bitter bruntes and shrewde skirmishes of aduersitie. 1630 R. Johnson's Kingd. & Commw. 111 Foure thousand men would have made a shrewd adventure to have taken his Indies from him. 1682 BUNYAN Holy War (1905) 412 Many a shrewd brush did some of the Townsmen meet with from them. 1698 FRYER Acc. E. India & P. 21 They adventure with better force, and in shrewder Battels.

**9.** Sharp, piercing, keen. **a.** Of a weapon or the like; also of pain. *arch.* (After Shaks.: see quot. 1593 in 2.)

1842 TENNYSON St. Sim. Styl. 195 A sting of shrewdest pain Ran shrivelling thro' me. 1871 R. ELLIS Catullus lxxxiii. 5 A shrewder stimulus arms her, Anger. 1878 BROWNING Poets Croisic 107 Sharpest shrewdest steel that ever stabbed To death Imposture.

**b.** Of the air, wind, weather.

1642 D. ROGERS Naaman 96 There comes a shrewd right winde, and gets into the hollow of the tree. 1784 COWPER Task III. 581 All plants.. that can endure The winter's frown, if screen'd from his shrewd bite. 1824 W. IRVING T. Trav. I. 23 The night was shrewd and windy. 1849 ROSSETTI Ruggiero & Angelica 9 The sky is harsh, and the sea shrewd and salt. 1864 LOWELL Fireside Trav. 337 That shrewd Yorkshire atmosphere. 1894 CROCKETT Raiders xviii, The air was shrewd as it breathed from the north.

*advb.* 1603 SHAKS. Ham. (Qo.) 400 The ayre bites shrewd [Qo. 1604 shroudly]; it is an eager and An nipping winde.

**c.** Of sound: Harsh. *rare.*

1876 SWINBURNE Erechtheus 10 The song-notes of our fear, Shrewd notes and shrill, not clear or joyful-sounding.

†**10. a.** Of a sign, token, etc.: Of ill omen, ominous; hence, strongly indicative (of something unfavourable).

1577 B. GOOGE Heresbach's Husb. IV. (1586) 177 Be sure to marke them well.. whether they go all out or no: for if they doe, it is a shrewde signe they will away. 1619 T. TAYLOR Titus ii. 8 Bitternesse [is] a shrewd signe of a bad cause. 1630 DONNE Serm. xiii. (1640) 135 If our own heart.. condemne us, this is shrewd evidence, saies S. Iohn. 1691 NORRIS Pract. Disc. 186 'Tis a shrewd Symptom of an ill habit of Body. 1692 BP. PATRICK Answ. Touchstone 262 We hear not a word of Fathers to countenance this Doctrine, which is a shrow'd sign it is so far from being Ancient, that they speak directly against it. 1732 BERKELEY Alciphr. VI. §17 When a man is against reason, it is a shrewd sign reason is against him.

**b.** Of probability, etc. *Obs.*

1542 UDALL Erasm. Apoph. I. 149 A good plain maner of knowelage geuyng it was & a shrewd likelyhood. 1619 SCLATER Expos. 1 Thess. v. 554 To array our selues.. aboue our Calling [is] no lesse then Pride; at least a shrewd species and appearance of it. 1709 SHAFTESB. Moralists II. 52 If Pain be Ill.. we have.. a shrewd Chance on the ill side, but none at all on the better.

**11.** Of a piece of evidence: Hard to get over, 'awkward', damaging. *arch.*

1606 HOLLAND Sueton. Annot. 4 If his Questour or Treasurer had beene condemned, it would haue beene a shrewde precedent for his conviction also in the same cause. 1633 LAUD in Strafford Lett. (1739) I. 213, I am afraid that many of them will be found Guilty: You give me one shrewd Instance in the Bishop of Waterford. 1692 Vindiciæ Carol. ii. 31 The pinching Article against him [Strafford] was the Twenty third... A shrewd Article no doubt, and sufficiently evidences their Crime. 1849 H. MILLER Footpr. Creator xv. 310 A shrewd fact, which they who expect most from the future of this world would do well to consider.

†**12. a.** Given to railing or scolding; shrewish. *Obs.*

α. 1387 TREVISA Higden (Rolls) III. 285 Tweie schrewed [ligitiosissimas] wifes þat wolde alway chide and stryve. 1483 CAXTON G. de la Tour D vij b, The tale and matere of the euylle and shrewde wyues. 1550 COVERDALE Spir. Perle xv, His [Socrates'] curst and shrewd wife. 1599 SHAKS. Much Ado II. i. 20 Thou wilt neuer get thee a husband, if thou be so shrewd of thy tongue. 1605 CAMDEN Rem. (1623) 250 Somewhat shrewd to her Seruants. a 1661 FULLER Worthies, Shropsh. (1662) 2 The Poets faining Juno, chaste and thrifty, qualities which commonly attend a shrewd nature.

β. a 1500 Brome Bk. 11 The properte of a schrod qwen ys to have hyr wyll. ?c 1530 in Pol. Rel. & Love Poems, etc. (1903) 58 Thowe shalte bettyr chastise a shrode wyfe with myrthe, then with strokes or smytyng. 1596 SHAKS. Tam. Shr. I. ii. 70 As old as Sibell, and as curst and shrow'd As Socrates Zentippe.

**b.** Of words, language: Scolding, railing, abusive. *Obs.*

1538 CROMWELL in Merriman Life & Lett. (1902) II. 128 If ye had.. sowght fully to instructe me in the matier, then thus to desire to conquer me by shrowde wordes. 1565 COOPER Thesaurus s.v. Confero, Maledicta in aliquem, to rayle at one; to geue shrewde woordes. 1606 HOLLAND Sueton. 191 She had reviled him & given him shrewd words. 1632 LITHGOW Trav. x. 488 With shrew'd Acerbious speech, you Anathematize. a 1661 FULLER Worthies, London (1662) 197 Shrewd words are sometimes improved into smart blows betwixt them.

**13. a.** In early use: †Cunning, artful (*obs.*). Now only in favourable sense: Clever or keen-witted in practical affairs; astute or sagacious in action or speech. (The chief current sense.)

α. 1520 Calisto & Melib. in Hazl. Dodsley I. 60 Seeming to be sheep, and serpently shrewd. 1589 PUTTENHAM Engl. Poesie III. xxi. (Arb.) 257 Least with their shrewd wits, when they were maried they might become a little too phantasticall wiues. 1638 JUNIUS Paint. Ancients 47 By acting sharpe old men, shrewd servants,.. and all such parts as did require some noise and stirre. a 1700 EVELYN Diary 15 June 1675, His lady had ben very handsome, and seem'd a shrewd understanding woman. 1706 STANHOPE Paraphr. III. 331 The Men of the World are abundantly more shrewd in the Business of it, than even Good Men are in the Management of their great and eternal Concern. 1807-8 W. IRVING Salmag. (1824) 228 A shrewd old gentleman, who stood listening by with a mischievously equivocal look. 1867 SMILES Huguenots Eng. ii. (1880) 25 Palissy was.. by nature a shrewd observer and an independent thinker. 1880 L. STEPHEN Pope iv. 102 A woman of shrewd intellect and masculine character. 1884 TENNYSON Falc. I. i. 468 Lady, I find you a shrewd bargainer.

*absol.* 1867 LOWELL Fitz Adam's Story 360 Hard-headed and soft-hearted, you'd scarce meet A kinder mixture of the shrewd and sweet.

β. 1594 NASHE Unfort. Trav. B 4 b, They told the King he was a foole, and that some shrowd head had knauishly wrought on him. 1605 CHAPMAN All Fools IV. i. H 2, Rinal. Y'aue gotten a learned Notarie Signior Cornelio. Corn. Hees a shroad fellow indeed. 1606 SHAKS. Tr. & Cr. I. ii. 206 He has a shrow'd wit.

**b.** Of action, speech: †Cunning, artful (*obs.*); characterized by penetration or practical sagacity.

1589 ? NASHE Pasquill & Marforius B 1, Whereuppon they presume to make a shrewde scruple of their obedience. 1649 MILTON Eikon. xxvi. 502 The shrewdest and the cunningest obloquie that can be thrown upon thir actions. 1761 HUME Hist. Eng. II. xxvii. 120 Empson made a shrewd apology for himself. 1781 COWPER Table-T. 205 The cause.. may yet elude Conjecture and remark, however shrewd. 1824 W. IRVING T. Trav. II. 259 An eminent man, who had waxed wealthy by driving shrewd bargains with the Indians. 1882 J. H. BLUNT Ref. Ch. Eng. II. 113 Taking shrewd advantage of the Lord Chancellor's unlucky mistake. 1884 R. W. CHURCH Bacon iii. 59 He liked to observe, to generalise in shrewd and sometimes cynical epigrams.

**c.** Of the face or look.

1816 SCOTT Antiq. i, A shrewd and penetrating eye. 1877 MRS. FORRESTER Mignon i, Fred Conyngham.. has a plain, shrewd face. 1877 BLACK Green Past. iii, The shaggy, dark brown eyebrows gave shadow and intensity to the shrewd and piercing grey eyes.

**14.** Of a suspicion or guess: Coming 'dangerously' near to the truth of the matter. (? Partly arising from sense 10.)

1588 J. HARVEY Disc. Probl. 127, I denie not but the wisest .. politiques may.. giue a shrewd gesse, and go neare the marke. 1599 Warn. Faire Women II. 1025 Should you be guilty of this fact, As this your flight hath given shrewde suspition. 1604 SHAKS. Oth. III. iii. 429 'Tis a shrew'd doubt, though it be but a Dreame. 1653 H. MORE Antid. Ath. III. xii. §3 It is a shrewd presumption that he doth lie with them indeed. 1848 THACKERAY Van. Fair li, I have a shrewd idea that it is a humbug.

**15.** *Comb.*, as ***shrewd-eyed***, ***-headed***, †***-hearted***, ***-looking***, ***-pated***, ***-tongued***, †***-wit***, ***-working*** adjs.; **shrewd-head** *Austral.* and *N.Z. slang*, a cunning person.

c 1440 Promp. Parv. 449/1 Schrewyd hertyd, pravicors. 1582 STANYHURST Æneis II. (Arb.) 47 The priest Calchas was broght by the shrewdwyt Vlisses. 1607 HIERON Wks. I. 197 A shrewd-tongued woman. 1628 FORD Lover's Mel. IV. ii, A shrewd-braine Whorson; there's pith In his vntoward plainenesse. 1629 MAXWELL tr. Herodian (1635) 199 A notable shrewd-pated Fellow. 1827 LYTTON Pelham xvi, She was a pretty, fair, shrewd-looking person. 1856 J. G. WHITTIER Panorama 9 The shrewd-eyed salesman, garrulous and loud. 1865 KINGSLEY Herew. ix, The.. shrewdest-headed.. Berserker in the North Seas. 1916 C. J. DENNIS Songs Sentimental Bloke 43 Now this 'ere gorspil bloke's a fair shrewd 'ead. 1946 J. MORRISON in Coast to Coast 163 Some shrewd-head overseas will get the blame for that pillaged case. 1959 Daily Tel. 20 May 17/1 A smiling, shrewd-eyed woman. 1960 N. HILLIARD Maori Girl III. i. 177 Only the shrewd-heads go for that hard stuff: the shysters the takes.

**shrewd** (ʃruːd), *sb. rare.* [f. the adj.]

**1.** A shrewd or cunning person (see also quot. 1954).

c 1858 E. DICKINSON Poems (1955) I. 14 Could a shrewd advise me We might e'en divide—Should a shrewd betray me—Atropos decide! 1954 Picture Post 2 Jan. 34 The word 'Spiv', it seems, is out of date. The new word, we are reliably informed, is 'Shrewd' —and it is used as a noun, adjective and verb... The 'shrewd' is not an American by-product. He is home-bred and thoroughly English, in style and slang.

**2.** Shrewdness, sagacity, cunning.

1977 F. BRANSTON Up & Coming Man xii. 126 All you needed was some capital and a lot of shrewd and you couldn't go wrong.

**shrewd**, obs. form of SHROUD *v.*

†**'shrewdhead.** *Obs.* [f. SHREWD *a.* + -HEAD.] Wickedness, depravity.

13.. Guy Warw. (1891) 510 For his scherewdhed sir Berard þemperour haþ made him his steward. c 1315 SHOREHAM VII. 574 Ryȝt deuelen so for screawed-hede Euer mo forse scholle brede. 14.. R. Glouc. Chron. 5676 (MS. γ), His schrewedhede [see quot. 1297 s.v. SHREWHEAD].

**shrewdie** ('ʃruːdɪ). *colloq.* (orig. *Austral.* and *N.Z.*). Also **shrewdy**. [f. SHREWD *a.* + -IE.]

**1.** A shrewd or cunning person.

1916 A. WRIGHT Under Cloud 35 Look here, Wilson, you're not such a shrewdie as you imagine. 1933 E. PARTRIDGE Words, Words, Words! III. 199 Flankenheinrich, to build a 'flank(ing) Henry', to show oneself a 'shrewdy'. 1949 F. SARGESON I saw it in my Dream 116 Johnny's a shrewdy. 1956 D. M. DAVIN Sullen Bell II. viii. 161 There'd been none of the shrewdies who dug themselves into good hospital jobs. 1967 'E. QUEEN' Face to Face xx. 95 She couldn't have kept it under wraps indefinitely. Not with a shrewdie like Geegee Guild to account to. 1970 Daily Tel. 14 May 13/5 In the train of each social upheaval in America, like jackals at a carcase, come the shrewdies and hucksters in search of a quick dollar. 1979 J. DRUMMOND I saw him Die ii. 16 'A shrewdie, would you say?' 'Very shrewd.'

**2.** A cunning trick. *rare.*

1961 B. CRUMP Hang on a Minute 27 Everything was as good as he said it was, but I knew he was pulling a shrewdie on me somewhere.

**shrewdish** ('ʃruːdɪʃ), *a.* [f. SHREWD *a.* + -ISH.] Somewhat or fairly shrewd.

1823 Spirit Publ. Jrnls. 485 We have a shrewdish suspicion. 1872 'ALIPH CHEEM' (Yeldham) Lays of Ind (1876) 33 Lieutenant Rudge was a shrewdish lad, Not easy to be cajoled. 1873 C. M. DAVIES Unorth. Lond. (1876) 162 Some shrewdish forecasting of events.

**shrewdly** ('ʃruːdlɪ), *adv.* Forms: see SHREWD *a.*; also 6 **scrodely**, 6-7 **shrodly**. [f. SHREWD *a.* + -LY[2].]

†**1.** Evilly, ill; wickedly; maliciously. *Obs.*

13.. Pol. Songs (Camden) 326 He bithenketh him hu he may shrewedelichest worche. c 1380 Sir Ferumb. 2860 Alle wiþ herte grete, & shrewed-liche þai dede hym kulle. 1382 WYCLIF Isa. i. 16 Resteth to do shreudely, lerneth to do wel. c 1450 Godstow Reg. 324 He was ful ignorant wilfulli & shrewdeli. c 1450 Merlin xx. 313 To dye as cowardes shrewdely oon with-oute a-nother. 1523 SKELTON Garl. Laurel 620 Fals flaterers that.. speke fayre before the and shrewdly behynde. 1532 MORE Confut. Tindale Wks. 528/2 They may seme repentaunt openlye, and yet thinke in their heartes ful shrewdly.

†**2.** Of wounding, hurting, cutting: Sharply, severely. Often in fig. context. *Obs.*

c 1375 Sc. Leg. Saints xlviii. (Juliana) 80 Quhene we do nocht all his wil, he gerris dynge ws schreuytly. c 1440 Alphabet of Tales 431 He.. was shrewidlie wowndid with waspis & fleis. 1576 GASCOIGNE Steel Glas Wks. 1910 II. 147 My battred braynes, (which now be shrewdly brusde). 1600 HOLLAND Livy VI. 224 Deepe debts are sharpe goads, and prick shreawdly. 1602 SHAKS. Ham. I. iv. 1 The Ayre bites shrewdly: is it very cold? 1606 —— Tr. & Cr. II. iii. 228, I see my reputation is at stake. My fame is shrowdly gored. 1613 W. B. tr. Michaelis' Hist. Magic. 337 A stone.. fell vpon his head, and did shrewdly cut him. 1658 A. FOX Wurtz' Surg. III. ix. 244 A Gentleman had a fall with his horse, was shrewdly bruised on his left side. 1699 DAMPIER Voy. II. II. 99, I knew one shrewdly gor'd by a Bull.

†**3.** Sharply, severely, harshly. *Obs.* **a.** Of speech.

c 1386 CHAUCER Sompn. T. 530 Lo yet how shrewedly Vn-to my confessour to day he spak. c 1412 HOCCLEVE De Reg. Princ. 3514 A man.. to Iulius Cesar ones Crabbidly seid, and schrewdly [etc.]. 1483 CAXTON Gold. Leg. 134/3 The mynysters answerden thou spakest shrewdly to y[e] wymen. 1513 DOUGLAS Æneis VII. vii. 134 Oft and richt schrewitly wald scho clepe and cry. 1593 NASHE Christ's T. To Rdr., This word Mummianiz'd in the beginning of my first Epistle is shrewdly called in question. a 1661 FULLER Worthies, Somerset (1662) 16 Sir Roger.. urged it [falsehood] shrewdly against the Person, who in that place, first revived the Aspersion.

**b.** Of treatment.

c 1489 CAXTON Sonnes of Aymon x. 257 He was a ferde lest he sholde be yet more shreudely handlyd. 1589 GREENE Tullies Loue Wks. (Grosart) VII. 203 If I write sharpely, blame me not that am vsed so shrowdlie. 1601 DENT Pathw. Heaven 244 Some of Gods children.. are shrewdly handled ..and brought very low, euen vnto deaths doore. 1697 POTTER Antiq. Greece I. ix. (1715) 46 Being of Opinion, that he had been shrewdly handled by the Divine Vengeance.

†**4.** Badly, ill, poorly. *Obs.*

c 1430 Pilgr. Lyf Manhode II. xviii. (1869) 82 Thei.. passen the gospel that j haue herd seyd in oure toun, and keepen it shrewedeliche. 1523 SKELTON Garl. Laurel 1210 Shroudly it doth accorde, To pyke out honesty of suche a potshorde. 1541 St. Papers Hen. VIII, I. 658 Ordre must be taken in tyme for the payment of the workmen, or elles they shal worke but shrewdly.

**5.** Qualifying a word or phrase expressive of a painful or adverse condition, menacing or disquieting action, violent or oppressive treatment; passing into a mere intensive: Grievously, intensely, seriously.

α. 1551 ROBINSON tr. More's Utopia II. viii. (1895) 245 Most florishing and wealthie peoples beyng some of them shrewedely shaken. a 1553 UDALL Royster D. IV. iv, Then Truepenny's fire-fork will him shrewdly fray. 1601 SHAKS. All's Well III. v. 91 He's shrewdly vext at something. c 1610 Women Saints 57 A greate number of birds alighting in her fields of corne, and deuouring it shrewdlie. 1652 HEYLIN Cosmogr. I. F 2 A Famine, which shrewdly raged among the Commons. 1661 BOYLE Style Script. (1675) 220 To be shrewdly tempted to be a partial relator of them. 1687 Good Advice 43 Shrewdly against the will of the high Churchmen. 1687 DRYDEN Hind & P. III. 133 Yet seem'd she not to winch, though shrewdly pain'd. 1710 SHAFTESB. Soliloquy III. §2. 146 Shrewdly disappointed. 1848 C. C. CLIFFORD Aristophanes, Frogs 4 My shoulder acheth shrewdly. 1856 BOKER Anne Boleyn I. i, We shall be shrewdly cuffed. 1863 WHYTE-MELVILLE Gladiators xliv, The attack of yesterday ..must have shaken them shrewdly.

β. c 1533 SIR W. FITZWILLIAM in Ellis Orig. Lett. Ser. III. II. 284 Which happenyng shulde shrowdly discomfort her. 1596 NASHE Saffron Walden O 4 b, I haue brought him lowe, and shrowdly broken him. 1599 SHAKS. Hen. V, III. vii. 163 These English are shrowdly out of Beefe. c 1600 DAY Begg. Bednall Gr. IV. ii. (1881) 83 He's shrowdly frighted by this violence. 1622 in Foster Eng. Factories Ind. (1908) II. 57 Hee threatned us shrodly. 1633 T. JAMES Voy. 78 The Ice did driue against the Ship, and shake her shrowdly. 1650 FULLER Pisgah II. 56 Shroudly shrubbing their branches.

**1673** MARVELL *Reh. Transp.* II. 73 Otherwise he would be shrowdly disappointed.

†**b.** Intensely, immensely. *Obs.*

**1663** KILLIGREW *Parson's Wedding* IV. i, I like her shrewdly; I hate a wench that is all whore and no company.

**6.** See SHREWD *a.* 14 and 10 b.

**a.** qualifying *suspect, suspicious, guess, fear, mistrust.*

**1559** *Mirr. Mag., Warwick* vi, This made the French king shrewdly to suspecte. **1576** FLEMING *Panopl. Epist.* 273, I mistrust yᵉ present case of Democritus so shrewdly. **1588** J. UDALL *Diotrephes* (Arb.) 22 He gesseth shrewdlie..our intent. **1662** STILLINGFL. *Orig. Sacræ* I. v. §1 Which may make it shrewdly suspitious that their intent is only to impose on our understandings. **1674** N. FAIRFAX *Bulk & Selv.* 73 'Tis shrewdly to be mistrusted, that something a great deal further off..has some kind of tamperings here. **1757** CHESTERF. *Lett.* cccxxiii, I shrewdly suspect that his Royal Highness has been the dupe of that sentiment. **1813** SCOTT *Rokeby* VI. x, 'Tis shrewdly guess'd That Redmond rules the damsel's breast. **1847** C. BRONTE *Jane Eyre* xiii, She coined pretexts to go downstairs, in order, as I shrewdly suspected, to visit the library.

†**b.** qualifying *probable. Obs.*

**1659** H. MORE *Immort. Soul* II. i. 120 It is shreudly probable, that fluid perceptive Matter will not fail to find the colours tinctured from one another. **1664** POWER *Exp. Philos.* I. 72 Is it not shrewdly probable, that..Colours are nothing else but a various modification of this motion?

**7.** With keen insight or perception; with shrewd intelligence or discrimination; astutely, sagaciously.

**1599** SHAKS. *Much Ado* II. i. 84 Cosin you apprehend passing shrewdly. **1719** WATERLAND *Vind. Christ's Div.* xxi. 310 The..Author observes, very shrowdly, that..it is to Him a Mystery. **1782** J. BROWN *Nat. & Rev. Relig.* I. ii. 35 The Spartans held theft to be innocent, if it was but shrewdly committed. **1825** SCOTT *Talism.* ix, 'Shrewdly replied', said the monarch. *a* **1859** MACAULAY *Hist. Eng.* xxiii. V. 110 He shrewdly propounded a dilemma which silenced Pomponne and Torcy. **1870** E. PEACOCK *Ralf Skirl.* II. 258 Shrewdly he kept the secret to himself.

**b.** Cleverly, skilfully. *rare.*

**1851** T. T. LYNCH *Lett. to Scattered* (1872) 194 Many a rough stone..will take a fine polish..if it be shrewdly cut and carefully rubbed.

**shrewdness** ('ʃruːdnɪs). Forms: see SHREWD *a.*; also 5 schredenes. [f. SHREWD *a.* + -NESS.]

†**1.** Wickedness, depravity; evil disposition, ill nature; malignity; maliciousness. *Obs.*

*c* **1315** SHOREHAM VII. 376 He [*sc.* Lucifer] hys heaued of schrewednesse, As god hys cheaf of alle godnesse. *c* **1384** CHAUCER *H. Fame* 1853 As gret a fame han shrewes..for shrewdenesse, As good folke han for godenesse. **1422** YONGE tr. *Secreta Secret.* xl. 199 He passet in shrewetnesse and malice al the Paganesse and mysbelewynge men. *c* **1450** *Godstow Reg.* 646 That hys graunt shold not by ony shrewdnes be destroyde, he confirmyd hyt with hys seele. **1484** CAXTON *Fables of Auian* vi, The shrewdness and malyce of the dogge. **1533** MORE *Apol.* xxxvi. Wks. 902/2, I purpose to purchace suche a proteccion for them, that I wyl leaue my selfe lesse then the fourth part, euen of shrewdnes rather then euer I wyl pay them. **1535** *Goodly Primer, Prime & Hours* Ps. cxxv, Them that swerve from the right way unto shrewdness. **1540** HYRDE tr. *Vives' Instr. Chr. Wom.* (1541) 79 If the housbande were yll, yet oughtest thou to suffer hym, nor stryue with him by shrewdenes.

†**b.** An instance of this. *Obs.*

*c* **1374** CHAUCER *Boeth.* IV. pr. iv. (1868) 124 þat þei (shrewes) ben constreyned by þre vnselynesses þat wolen and mowen and performen felonyes and shrewednesses. *c* **1386** —— *Pars. T.* 442 In hire houses been iniquitees and shrewednesses. *a* **1533** LD. BERNERS *Gold Bk. M. Aurel.* (1546) D, The shrewdenes and cruelties, that Domician did to the virgins Vestales.

†**c.** Naughtiness, mischievousness. *Obs.*

**1567-9** HARDING in Jewel *Def. Apol.* (1611) 344 They..be subiect to all shrewdnesse of the boies of the streets, who vse commonly to mocke and reuile them. **1612** BRINSLEY *Lud. Lit.* 9 If they bee apt much before fiue yeeres of age, to learne shrewdnesse.

†**d.** A pretended term for a 'company' of apes.

*a* **1452** *Termys of venery, &c.* (Egerton MS. 1995) in J. Hodgkin *Proper Terms* (1909) 52 A Schrewdenys of Apys. **1486** *Bk. St. Albans* f vi b, A Shrewdenes of Apis. [Hence in various later works.]

**2.** Sagacity or keenness of mental perception or discrimination; astuteness in practical affairs.

**1606** SHAKS. *Ant. & Cl.* II. ii. 69 Her Garboiles..Made out of her impatience: which not wanted Shrodenesse of policie to. **1676** RAY *Corr.* (1848) 126 Shrewdness in inventing and discovering, is a particular gift of God. **1770** LANGHORNE *Plutarch, Agis* ¶10 With his shrewdness and capacity he had a proper mixture of spirit. **1816** SCOTT *Bl. Dwarf* iv, Some..requested advice upon other matters, which he delivered with an oracular shrewdness. **1864** TENNYSON *En. Ard.* 250 Not being bred To barter, nor compensating the want by shrewdness. **1878** GLADSTONE *Prim. Homer* 120 Natural shrewdness was the guide of the people in the business of exchanges.

†'**shrewdom.** *Obs.* [f. SHREW *sb.*² + -DOM.] Wickedness.

**13..** *Pol. Songs* (Camden) 340 That shrewedom that regneth in the lond.

†'**shrewdship.** *Obs.* [f. SHREWD *a.* + -SHIP.] = prec.

**13..** *E.E. Allit. P.* B. 580 þat schamez for no schrewedschyp schent mot he worthe! *c* **1425** *Seven Sages* (P.) 1737 [Scho] bythout hire al by the way Vppon a schrewydschyp or tway.

†'**shrewhead.** *Obs.* In 3-4 schrewe-, ssrew-, schreuhede, schr-, ssrewede. [f. SHREW *sb.*² + -HEAD.] = prec.

*c* **1290** *St. Lawrence* 4 in *S. Eng. Leg.* 340 Decius þe Aumperour..And is Iustise Valerian þat to alle schrewehede drovȝ. **1297** R. GLOUC. (Rolls) 5676 Ȝut for alle ssrewede [*v.rr.* schrewede, schrewehede, schrewedhede]..is soule com in to blis. *c* **1315** SHOREHAM VII. 638 [He] dede hym in an addre wede, þat best was of mest schreuhede.

**shrewing** ('ʃruːɪŋ), *vbl. sb. rare*⁻¹. [f. SHREW *sb.*² + -ING¹.] ? A scolding.

**1847** MRS. CARLYLE *Lett.* II. 1 If I had waited patiently..I might have spared you a shrewing.

†'**shrewing,** *ppl. a. Obs. rare*⁻¹. In 4 shrewende. Used to render L. *refrenantem.*

**1382** WYCLIF *Isa.* ix. 14 The Lord shal scatere fro Irael the hed and the tail, the inbowende and the shrewende [? *error for* þeschewende (ESCHEW *v.*); 1388 bischrewynge].

**shrewish** ('ʃruːɪʃ), *a.* [f. SHREW *sb.*² + -ISH.]

†**1.** Wicked, ill-disposed, malignant. *Obs.*

*c* **1375** *Sc. Leg. Saints* iv. (*Jacobus*) 262 þat name [sc. *lupa*] gaynyt hyr til, for scho wes schrewis, feloun & Il. **1481** CAXTON *Myrr.* I. xiv. d j b, That one shal happen to be wyse and discrete & that other folissh or shrewyssh. **1481** —— *Reynard* (Arb.) 23 Thowgh my eme were twyes so bad and shrewessh.

**2.** Of a woman: Pertaining to or resembling a shrew; having the character or disposition of a shrew; given to or characterized by scolding.

**1565** J. PHILLIP *Patient Grissell* 1619 Therbe a nomber liuinge that Grissills haue to name, But yet very shrewishe by naturall dispocisyon. **1577** GRANGE *Golden Aphrod.* etc. Riij, A shrewishe tongue. **1599** NASHE *Lenten Stuffe* G 4, Shee was a shrewish snappish bawd, that wold bite off a mans nose with an answere. **1603** DEKKER *Batch. Banquet* iv. Wks. (Grosart) I. 195 Not caring to prouide ought for his supper, but contrariwise taunts him with sharp and shrewish speeches. **1641** J. JACKSON *True Evang. T.* III. 225 The Mistris is a good Huswife, but of shrewish condition. **1818** SCOTT *Hrt. Midl.* x, 'Good woman', said the magistrate to this shrewish supplicant,—'tell us what it is you want, and do not interrupt the court.' **1824** W. IRVING *T. Trav.* II. 42 My wife became more and more shrewish and tormenting the more I wanted comfort. **1840** DICKENS *Barn. Rudge* vii, Slender and shrewish,..and though not absolutely ill-looking, of a sharp and acid visage. **1891** *Athenæum* 3 Oct. 447/3 Her vigorous, if somewhat shrewish dismissal of the Council's envoys.

**b.** In wider sense: Ill-natured, ill-tempered; of a sharp or cross-grained nature.

**1596** NASHE *Saffron Walden* E 3, *Scelarata sinapis,* shrewish snappish mustard, as Plautus calls it.

**1816** SCOTT *Antiq.* xix, He threw his coral and bells at my head for refusing him a bit of sugar—and you have too much sense to mind such a shrewish boy. **1824** MISS MITFORD *Village* Ser. I. (1863) 194 His little dog Viper,..sleek, sharp, and shrewish. **1888** STEVENSON *Black Arrow* I. i, Y'are the shrewishest old dolt in Tunstall Forest.

*transf.* **1863** R. F. BURTON *W. Africa* I. 1 The shrewish gusts tore to pieces the very strongest showers. **1882** HOWELLS in *Longman's Mag.* I. 43 It was a shrewish afternoon late in April... The season was very dry.

Hence '**shrewishly** *adv.*, '**shrewishness.**

**1590** SHAKS. *Mids. N.* III. ii. 301, I was neuer curst: I haue no gift at all in shrewishnesse. **1602** —— *Twel. N.* I. v. 170 He is verie well-fauour'd, and he speakes verie shrewishly. *a* **1661** FULLER *Worthies, Shropsh.* (1662) 2 How much shrewishness may be allowed in a Wife? **1826** MISS MITFORD *Village* Ser. II. (1863) 268 Elvira we chose for her especial gift in scolding, her natural shrewishness. **1855** MOTLEY *Dutch Rep.* VI. i. (1866) 779 These and similar sins of omission and commission were sharply and shrewishly set forth in the Queen's epistle. **1884** H. S. WILSON *Stud. Hist.* 169 The hair red, the face rather pointedly oval, with an expression of some shrewishness.

**shrewly** ('ʃruːlɪ), *adv.* [f. SHREW *a.* + -LY².] = SHREWDLY (for which, in some instances, it may be a misprint).

*a* **1529** SKELTON *Sp. Parrot* 439 Ryn God, rynne Devyll! yet the date of ower Lord And the date of the Devyll dothe shrewlye accord. *a* **1652** BROME *Queenes Exch.* II. i, Your Lady wants The furious sharpnesse of the nose, which here My Queen has very shrewly. **1677** W. HUGHES *Man of Sin* III. iii. 83 One is shrewly out, but neither was Pope: therefore both fallible. **1706-7** NORTH *Let. Mrs. Foley* 13 Jan. in *Lives* (1890) III. App. 256, I am both inclined and shrewly solicited, which is a civil word for commanded, by one of no small authority here [*viz.* his wife]. **1858** *Times* 30 Mar. 6/1 The north wind which whistles shrewly at night.

**shrewmouse** ('ʃruːmaʊs). (Also with hyphen and as two words.) Pl. **-mice.** Also 6-7 shroue-, 8-9 shrove-. [f. SHREW *sb.*¹ + MOUSE *sb.*] Any of the small insectivores of the genus *Sorex* or family *Soricidæ*; = SHREW *sb.*¹

**1572** HULOET, Shrewmous, *mus araneus, Mus cæcus.* **1587** MASCALL *Govt. Cattle, Oxen* (1596) 74 The shroue-mouse is an ill beast, and doth trouble and hurt mens cattell. **1607** TOPSELL *Four-f. Beasts* 535 This Shrew mouse is a little and light creature, which like a Spider climeth vp vpon any small threed, or vpon the edge of a sword. *Ibid.* 536 The places where the Shrew-mice hanteth. **1614** MARKHAM *Cheap Husb., Bull,* etc. xxxix. 61 A Shrew Mouse, which is a Mouse with short vneven legges, and a long head, like a Swines, is a venemous thing. **1768** PENNANT *Brit. Zool.* I. 113 The shrew mouse inhabits old walls, heaps of stones, or holes in the earth. **1835** BROWNING *Paracelsus* v. 433 Strangling rushes,..Where the shrew-mouse with pale throat Burrows. **1849** [DINSDALE] *Teesdale Gloss., Shrove-mouse,* the field mouse. **1872** CALVERLEY *Sad Mem.* 7 The shrewmouse eyes me shudderingly, then flees;..why was I born a cat?

†'**shrewness.** *Obs. rare.* [f. SHREW *a.* + -NESS.] Wickedness.

*c* **1425** *Seven Sages* (P.) 1739 And anoon in the stude A great schrewnes he dude.

**Shrewsbury** ('ʃruːz-, 'ʃrəʊzbərɪ).

**1.** The name of the county town of Shropshire, used as the specific appellation of articles manufactured there. ***Shrewsbury cake***: a flat round crisp biscuit-like cake. ***Shrewsbury simnel***: see SIMNEL 1 b.

**1728** E. SMITH *Compl. Housew.* 129 To make Shrewsbury-Cakes. **1831** *Lincoln Herald* 7 Oct. 4/4 Gingerbread buttons and Shrewsbury cakes. **1840** BARHAM *Ingol. Leg.* Ser. II. *Bloudie Jacke* xxxii, She has given him..a Shrewsbury cake, Of Pailin's own make. **1844** *Ladies' Hand-bk. Haberdashery* 45 White or broad Reel-thread, Scotch Thread, Shrewsbury Thread. **1883** C. S. BURNE *Shropsh. Folk-L.* 325 'Shrewsbury Simnels'..are eaten by many who do not heed the pious habit of 'mothering' which they were intended to celebrate.

**2.** In phrases. ***by Shrewsbury clock***: added (in allusion to quot. 1596) to statements of duration as a proverbial phr., esp. to indicate exaggeration; ***as exact*** (or ***regular***) ***as Shrewsbury clock***: very exact or regular.

[**1596**, SHAKS. *1 Hen. IV* v. iv. 151 We rose both at an instant, and fought a long houre by Shrewsburie clocke.] **1681** *Poor Robin Almanack* Mar. 12 A great many people shall feed (according as Sir John Falstaffe used to sight) three hours together by Shrewsbury Clock. **1784** H. COWLEY *More Ways than One* I. i. 1 My master is as exact as Shrewsbury clock. **1796** J. WHITE *Orig. Lett. Sir J. Falstaff* 17 Fifteen minutes, as thou say'st, by Shrewsbury clock. **1835** J. KINCAID *Random Shots from Rifleman* xiii. 332 Sir Arthur, in all his movements for twenty years, had been as regular as Shrewsbury clock. **1891** R. L. STEVENSON *Let.* in *Wks.* (1923) XXII. xi. 386, I remember, when I first saw this, laughing for an hour by Shrewsbury clock. **1901** G. B. SHAW *Admirable Bashville* III. 324 On the impenetrable sarcolobe That holds his seedling brain these fists have pounded By Shrewsb'ry clock an hour.

**shrewyd,** obs. form of SHREWD.

‖**Shri, Sri** (ʃriː). [Skr. *Srī,* the name of Lakshmī (goddess of prosperity or beauty and the wife of Vishnu); hence, as an honorific title.] In India, a title prefixed to the names of deities and distinguished persons (and to the titles of sacred books, etc.) as a mark of respect; also, more recently, used as the Indian equivalent of Mr.

**1799** *Asiatick Researches* VI. 475 *Sitá* was an incarnation of *Devi*: for *Sri-De'vi* the wife of Daisha, and daughter of *Adima* and *Iva,* entreated the Goddess, to give her one daughter exactly like herself. **1832** *Ibid.* XVII. 178 The *Kerala Utpatti*..calls him [*sc.* Sankara] the offspring of adultery, for which his mother *Sri Mahádevi* was expelled her caste. **1924** E. M. FORSTER *Passage to India* xxxiii. 289 Infinite love took upon itself the form of Shri Krishna, and saved the world. **1938** M. K. GANDHI in D. G. Tendulkar *Mahatma* (1952) IV. 348 The readers will remember that in the heyday of non-co-operation, the terms 'Mr.' and 'Esquire', were dropped by Congressmen and the nationalist press, and 'Shri' was the title largely used for all, irrespective of religion. **1969** 'E. PETERS' *Mourning Raga* iii. 44 'We are looking for the house of Shri Satyavan Kumar.'..'Yes, this is house of Mr Kumar.' **1981** S. RUSHDIE *Midnight's Children* I. 77 My cousin, Shri Ramram Seth, is a great seer.

**shriche,** variant of SHRITCH.

**shrick(e)-owle:** see SHRIEK-OWL.

**shrid,** obs. form of SHRED.

†**shride,** *v.*¹ *Obs.* Forms: 1 scrȳdan, scridan, scrēdan, 2-3 scrude(n, 3 shridenn, screde(n, sride(n, 3-4 s(c)hrude(n, 4 schride, scruyde, schrede, ssrede, shride; *3rd sing. pres. ind.* (contracted) 1 scrȳt(t, 2 scred, 3 shrut. *Pa. t.* 1 scrȳdde, 2 scridde, scredde, 3 schrudde, srid, sredde, 4 shrudde, schredde, schred(e, schridde. *Pa. pple.* 2 ȝescrid, 2-3 iscrud, 3 ischrud, shrid(d, 3-4 schred, 4 ischrid, yshred, yssred, shred, shrud. [OE. *scrȳdan* = ON. *skrýða*:—OTeut. **skrūdjan,* f. *skrūd-* (see SHROUD *sb.*¹).]

**1.** *trans.* To clothe, provide with clothes.

**971** *Blickl. Hom.* xviii. 213 He wolde..earme frefran..& nacode scrydan. *c* **1000** *Ags. Gosp.* Matt. xxv. 36 Ic wæs nacud & ȝe me scryddon [*c* **1160** *Hatton Gosp.* scredden]. *a* **1175** *Cott. Hom.* 225 Hi were mid þon fellen ȝescridde. *Ibid.* 233 He us fett and scred. *c* **1200** ORMIN 137 Shridd wiþþ haliȝ shrud ȝede he till Godess allterr. *a* **1225** *Ancr. R.* 66 Monie cumeð to ou ischrud mid lombes fleose, & beoð wode wulues. *c* **1250** *Gen. & Ex.* 379 Ðor-wið he ben nu boðen srid. **13..** *K. Alis.* 6803 (Bodl. MS.), In a lyouns skyn he was yshred. *c* **1386** CHAUCER *Clerk's T.* 322 þis mayde bright of hew Fro foot to heed þay schredde han al newe. *c* **1400** *St. Alexius* 565 (Laud 463) þat liche þei let wake & shride, wiþ pal & wiþ oþer pride.

*refl. c* **1000** ÆLFRIC *Deut.* xxii. 5 Ne scride nan wif hiȝ mid wæpmannes reafe ne wæpman mid wifmannes reafe. *c* **1200** *Trin. Coll. Hom.* 193 Mid þos wapnes dauid shrude him. *a* **1225** *Ancr. R.* 302 þis was bitocned þuruh þet Iudit schrudde hire mid helidawene weaden. *a* **1300** *K. Horn* 840 Cutberd ros of bedde Wiþ armes he him schredde. **1340** *Ayenb.* 258 þe queade riche þet zuo ofte ham ssredeþ. *a* **1400** *Launfal* 416 Launfal yn purpure gan hym schrede.

**b.** *transf.* and *fig.*

*c* **1000** *Ags. Gosp.* Luke xii. 28 Ʒyf god scrytt [*c* **1160** *Hatton* scrit] þæt hiʒ..swa mycele ma god scryt eow. *c* **1200** ORMIN 3673 He þat all þiss middellærd Onn alle wise shrideþþ. *c* **1250** *Gen. & Ex.* 23 Til god srid him in manliched. *Ibid.* 1878 Salamon findin is [*viz.* idols and gold rings] sal, And his temple sriðen wið-al. **13..** in *Pol. Rel. & L. Poems* (1903) 269 Wite blisse in heuene I schal þe scruyde.

**2.** ? To ward off.

*c* **1400** *Anturs of Arth.* 20 (Thornton MS.) Schruedede in a schorte cloke, þat the rayne schrydes.

Hence † **'shriding** *vbl. sb.*

**1340** *Ayenb.* 258 O moche is he fol..þet of his ssredinge is proud. *Ibid.*, þe ssredinge of his bodye.

† **shride**, *v.*² *Obs.* Also 4-5 schride, schryde. [? repr. OE. **scrýdan* (:—**scrúdjan*), f. **scrúd* SHROUD *sb.*³] *trans.* To lop or prune (trees). Chiefly in *vbl. sb.*, *concr.* = prunings, loppings. Cf. SHROUD *v.*²

**1388** WYCLIF *Song of Sol.* ii. 12 Flouris apperiden in oure lond, the tyme of schridyng is comun. *c* **1440** *Promp. Parv.* 242/1 Hooke to hewe wode, or schrydynge. **1450** *Yatton Churchw. Acc.* (Som. Rec. Soc.) 90 Schrydyng of treyes yn church hay jᵈ. **1457** *Ibid.* 99 To the chorchemen for schryde wode yn the chorchehay, jᵈ. **1553** BECON *Reliques of Rome* (1563) 248 *b*, [Gifts] of shriding of trees, and of al manner of vnderwoode. **1825** JENNINGS *Obs. Dial. W. Eng.*, *Shride*, to cut off wood from the sides of trees; to cut off wood from trees generally.

† **shridels.** *Obs.* In 4 schrydeles. [app. f. SHRIDE *v.*² + -ELS. Cf. MLG. *schratele* piece cut off, LG. *schradels*, *schrodels* bruised corn for cattle, G. *schrotel* shreds, parings.] Loppings of trees.

**1399-1400** in Worth *Tavistock Par. Rec.* (1887) 5 [Bought] de la schrydeles [to the said timber belonging ijᵈ].

**shrief(e, shrieff,** obs. forms of SHERIFF.

**shriek** (ʃriːk), *sb.* Also 6-7 shreek(e, shreik, (6 *Sc.* shraich, 7 schrick, 7 shrieck, shrieke, 8 shreak). [f. SHRIEK *v.* Parallel to SCREAK *sb.*; cf. SHRIKE *sb.*] **a.** An act of shrieking; a shrill, piercing, or wild cry expressive of terror or pain. Also, an utterance of loud high-pitched laughter.

**1590** SPENSER *F.Q.* I. vi. 6 The pitteous maiden..Does throw out thrilling shriekes, and shrieking cryes. **1594** KYD *Cornelia* 144 Whose mournfull cryes and shreekes to heaven ascend. **1632** MILTON *L'Allegro* 4 In Stygian Cave forlorn 'Mongst horrid shapes, and shreiks, and sights unholy. **1642** FULLER *Holy & Prof. St.* IV. xviii. 332 They..lift up a panick schrick which pierced the skies. **1757** GRAY *Bard* 55 The shrieks of death, thro' Berkley's roofs that ring, Shrieks of an agonizing King! **1812** BYRON *Ch. Har.* II. lxxii, The shrieks of the conquer'd, the conqueror's yell. **1837** CARLYLE *Fr. Rev.* I. II. iv, One shriek of indignation and astonishment. **1892** *Photogr. Ann.* II. 513 It will prove a great attraction and provoke shrieks of laughter.

**b.** Applied to the wild cry of birds, etc.

**1765** J. BROWN *Chr. Jrnl.* (1792) 301 The shrieks of the owl. **1813** SHELLEY *Q. Mab* VIII. 97 The sea-bird's harrowing shriek. **1864** TENNYSON *En. Ard.* 579 The myriad shriek of wheeling ocean-fowl.

**c.** The loud high-pitched piercing sound produced by an instrument of music, the whistle of a locomotive, etc.

**1599** ALEX. HUME *Hymns & Sacred Songs* 59 The shraichs of deadly clarions. **1847** *Literary Gaz.* 28 Aug. 631/1 An apparatus to produce..a scale or gamut of whistle shrieks. **1853** KANE *Grinnell Exp.* xxix. (1856) 244 The low whine which the ice gives out when we cut it at right angles with a sharp knife, rising sometimes into a shriek. **1865** SWINBURNE *Chastelard* III. i. 98 The shriek of slipping swords. **1882** O. W. HOLMES *In Twilight* 35 A locomotive's shriek.

**d.** *fig.* A hysterical exclamation; an outcry of alarm, surprise, or reproof. *colloq.*

*c* **1853** KINGSLEY *Misc.* I. 47 One of the stock-charges..at which all biographers..break into virtuous shrieks of 'flattery', 'meanness',..and so forth. **1929** 'SEAMARK' *Down River* i. 22 'Yet this man is getting through?' 'Yes—and with bags of it, too, judging from the shriek we got from the Yard.'

**e.** *colloq.* A note of exclamation (!). Also ***shriek-mark***.

**1864** H. ALFORD *Queen's Eng.* §128. 93 A note of admiration consists..of a point with an upright line suspended over it... These shrieks, as they have been called, are scattered up and down the page by the compositors without mercy. **1864** *Ibid.*, Our friend the compositor is sure to write '*Oh*' with a shriek (!) and to put another shriek after 'Sir'. **1933** BLUNDEN & NORMAN *We'll shift our Ground* 16 It remained only to add the shriek-marks and to discover a heroine. **1969** A. GLYN *Dragon Variation* i. 9 In her mind's eye she saw the printed score-sheet, 'N × P!!', shriek-mark, shriek-mark. **1977** *Times Lit. Suppl.* 29 Apr. 521/1 He reviewed *Principia Mathematica*... He was the only man at the college who could read its curlicues, shrieks, and hooks.

**shriek** (ʃriːk), *v.* Also 6 shreak, shreke (*pa. t.* shrekt), 6-7 schrick, shrieke, shreek(e, 7 schreek, shreik, 8 schriek. [Parallel to SCREAK *v.*; cf. SHRIKE *v.*]

**1.** *intr.* To utter a loud sharp shrill cry. **a.** of a human being in pain or terror; also, said of loud high-pitched laughter.

**1577** T. KENDALL *Flowers of Epigr.*, *Trifles* 31 b, The Prince, the peeres, the people shreke, in Death to see thee sleepe. **1601** SHAKS. *Jul. C.* II. ii. 24 Ghosts did shrieke and squeale about the streets. **1671** MILTON *P.R.* IV. 423 Infernal Ghosts, and Hellish Furies,..some howl'd, some yell'd, some shriek'd. **1681** DRYDEN *Span. Friar* IV. i, *Gom.* Why did you shriek out, Gentlewoman? *Elvi.* 'Twas for Joy at your Return. **1798** COLERIDGE *Anc. Mar.* VII. xi, The Pilot shrieked And fell down in a fit. **1848** THACKERAY *Van. Fair* xxix, Mrs. Major O'D., taking the compliment to herself, returned the salute with a gracious smile, which sent that unfortunate Dobbin shrieking out of the box again. **1891** KIPLING *Light that Failed* x, She used to shriek with rage when Dick stared at her between half-closed eyes.

**b.** of the characteristic cry of certain animals, *spec.* of the badger in rutting-time (cf. SHRIKE *v.*).

**1567** MAPLET *Gr. Forest* 94 A certaine Shrickowle or Owlet which when she crieth, she shricketh. **1593** SHAKS. *Lucr.* 307 Night wandring weezels shreek to see him there. **1593** —— *3 Hen. VI*, v. vi. 44 The Owle shriek'd at thy birth. *a* **1700** B. E. *Dict. Cant. Crew*, *Shrieketh*, the Noise a Badger makes at Rutting Time. **1807** CRABBE *Par. Reg.* III. 242 The bat shrill shrieking woo'd his flickering mate. **1830** TENNYSON *Mariana* 64 The mouse Behind the mouldering wainscot shriek'd.

**c.** of inanimate things.

**1596** SPENSER *F.Q.* VI. viii. 46 Then gan the bagpypes and the hornes to..shrieke aloud. **1840** DICKENS *Old C. Shop* xlv, [Engines] shrieking in their rapid whirl..as though in torment unendurable. **1848** *New Monthly Mag.* LXXXIII. 472 The whistle shrieked, and Pemberton was whirled rapidly along the rail. **1860** RUSKIN *Mod. Painters* V. VI. 82 The winter wind, which shrieks through the bare branches. **1879** *Organ Voicing* 18 The upper notes of..all mutation stops, have..a tendency to shriek.

**d.** *fig.*

**1837** CARLYLE *Fr. Rev.* II. III. vii, Moralities not a few must shriek condemnatory over this Mirabeau. **1847** EMERSON *Repr. Men, Montaigne* Wks. (Bohn) I. 344 Montaigne..never shrieks, or protests, or prays.

**2.** *trans.* To utter (a shriek); to utter (words) with a shriek or shrieks.

**1592** SHAKS. *Ven. & Ad.* 531 The owle (nights herald) shreeks, tis verie late. **1597** —— *Lover's Compl.* 18 Often reading what contents it bears; As often shrieking undistinguish'd woe. **1603** DRAYTON *Bar. Wars* v. xli, Berckley,..Let thy faire buildings shreeke a deadly sound. **1725** POPE *Odyss.* III. 321 Nor earth had hid his carcase from the skies, Nor Grecian virgins shriek'd his obsequies. **1828** SCOTT *F.M. Perth* xxvii, The coronach was again..shrieked, as the body was carried into the interior of the church. **1864** TENNYSON *En. Ard.* 33 Then would Philip..Shriek out 'I hate you, Enoch'. **1885** W. S. GILBERT *Mikado* II. Trio, O never shall I Forget the cry Or the shriek that shriekèd he.

**3.** To bring (oneself) into a certain condition by shrieking.

**1642** DENHAM *Sophy* I. ii, In a dreadful dream I saw my Lord so near destruction,..Then shriekt my self awake. **1837** CARLYLE *Fr. Rev.* I. VI. i, Much less shalt shriek thyself hoarse, cursing it. **1893** *Nat. Observer* 29 Apr. 593/2 Liberals shrieked themselves hoarse with impious horror.

**4.** *fig.* **a.** *trans.* To indicate clearly or blatantly. **b.** *intr.* To provide a clear or blatant indication *of*.

**1920** 'O. DOUGLAS' *Penny Plain* xii. 127 The ospreys in her hat seem to shriek money. **1938** E. AMBLER *Cause for Alarm* xiv. 225 That hat of yours..shrieks English to high Heaven. **1944** M. LASKI *Love on Supertax* v. 57 In that gathering her dress, she felt with a hot rush of shame, simply shrieked of Grosvenor Street. **1972** K. BENTON *Spy in Chancery* xi. 106 The furniture was old, well-worn and miscellaneous, fairly shrieking of 'furnished let'.

**'shrieker** ('ʃriːkə(r)). Also 8 schrieker. [f. SHRIEK *v.* + -ER¹.] One who shrieks or utters a shriek.

**1708** OZELL tr. *Boileau's Lutrin* 42 Fruitful of evil Fate the Schrieker cries. **1819** CRABBE *T. of Hall* VII. 141 The shriekers lack a friend. **1837** CARLYLE *Fr. Rev.* III. I. vii, To seize the first shriekers and ring-leaders. **1882** *American* V. 135 The 'revenue only' shriekers.

**b.** The black-tailed godwit, *Limosa limosa*.

**1855** F. O. MORRIS *Brit. Birds* IV. 233.

**'shriekery.** *nonce-wd.* [f. SHRIEK *v.* + -ERY.] Shrieking, shrieking noise.

**1865** CARLYLE *Fredk. Gt.* XXI. iv. VI. 491 Mendacious shriekeries from an ill-informed Public. **1866** —— *Remin.* (1881) II. 289 As I journeyed and tumbled along amid the shriekeries and miseries.

**'shriekily,** *adv.* [f. SHRIEKY + -LY².] In shrieky tones. So **'shriekiness**.

**1881** *Sci. Amer.* XLIV. 288 The *Western Rural*..demands as shriekily the overturning of the patent system. **1881** *Scribner's Mag.* XXII. 150 He had become a common scold;..gone all to shriekiness and dyspepsia.

**shrieking** ('ʃriːkɪŋ), *vbl. sb.* [f. SHRIEK *v.* + -ING¹.] The action of the verb SHRIEK.

**1601** B. JONSON *Poetaster* v. ii, The nymphs, with shreekings, doe the region fill. *a* **1700** EVELYN *Diary* 3 Sept. 1666, The shreiking of women and children. **1845** J. H. NEWMAN in W. Ward *Life* (1912) I. 105 The shrieking and screaming of the keyhole and casements. **1901** W. R. H. TROWBRIDGE *Lett. her Mother to Eliz.* xxi. 100 Mrs. Dorking said she stuffed her handkerchief into her mouth to keep from shrieking.

**shrieking** ('ʃriːkɪŋ), *ppl. a.* [f. SHRIEK *v.* + -ING².] **1.** That shrieks or utters shrieks; accompanied by shrieks.

*a* **1586** SIDNEY *Arcadia* I. Ecl. i. (1633) 93 Out shreaking Pipe, made of some witched tree. **1590** [see SHRIEK *sb.* 1]. **1596** DRAYTON *Mortimeriados* N 2, The vgly shreeking Owles. **1604** —— *Moyses* III. 81 The shrill screame the shrieking people gaue. *a* **1649** DRUMM. OF HAWTH. *St. Peter* 9 Wks. (S.T.S.) II. 214 The shrieking Bird that courtes the Night. **1810** SCOTT *Lady of L.* III. x, A sharp and shrieking echo. **1855** TENNYSON *Maud* I. VI. viii, The shrieking rush of the wainscot mouse. **1892** *Speaker* 3 Sept. 289/2 The high road, with its shrieking steam-tram.

**2.** *fig.* **a.** Great, excellent, splendid. **b.** Of colours: excessively bright; lurid, glaring.

**1926** N. COWARD *Queen was in Parlour* I. i. 15 My first experience was such a shrieking success. **1958** P. POLLACK *Pict. Hist. Photogr.* xii. 155/1 Satin blouses of shrieking colors. **1966** [see CAPRI 2].

Hence **'shriekingly** *adv.*, with a shriek or shrieks.

**1641** BRATHWAIT *Engl. Gentlew.* 278 The needy cry, and shreekingly complaine unto us. **1877** BROWNING *Agamemnon* 29 The old men..Shriekingly wail the death-doom of their dearest. **1888** MEREDITH *Poet. Wks.* (1912) 367 Shriekingly the timber cracks.

† **shriek-owl.** *Obs.* Also 6 schrick-, 7 scrick-, 7 shreike-. [f. SHRIEK *v.* + OWL *sb.* Cf. SCREECH-OWL, SHRITCH-OWL.] The screech-owl.

**1567** [see SHRIEK *v.* 1 b]. **1591** SPENSER *Teares Muses* 283 Fowle Goblins and Shriekowles, With fearfull howling do all places fill. **1616** T. SCOT *Philomythie* II. B 4 b, The Rauen and Shreikeowle there did build their neasts. **1623** WODROEPHE *Marrow Fr. Tongue* 399/2 Wee are with Men our Brothers, and not with Stockes, Wood, Wolues and Scrick-Ooles. *a* **1764** LLOYD *Progr. Envy* Poet. Wks. 1774 I. 145 Shriek-owls and ravens, whose fell croaking bodes Approaching death to miserable wight. **1913** SIR R. ROSS in *Engl. Rev.* Sept. 168 No sound; Save haply the shriek-owl cryes.

*attrib.* **1748** RICHARDSON *Clarissa* VI. 383 Thou liftest up thy shriek-owl note.

**shrieky** ('ʃriːkɪ), *a.* [f. SHRIEK *sb.* or *v.* + -Y.] Characterized by a shriek or shrieks; of a loud sharp shrill pitch; *fig.* hysterical.

**1858** CLOUGH *Poems*, etc. (1869) I. 132 The four days of June I dare say you have heard spoken of in a somewhat shrieky account. **1864** CARLYLE *Fredk. Gt.* XVI. vii. IV. 355 Be judicial,..not shrieky, mobbish, and flying off into the Infinite! **1871** —— in Mrs. Carlyle *Lett.* II. 328 Reciting or reading in a high shrieky tone.

**shrieval** ('ʃriːvəl), *a.* [f. *shrieve*, obs. var. SHERIFF + -AL¹.] Of or belonging to a sheriff.

**1681** DRYDEN *Abs. & Achit.* I. 618 Chaste were his Cellars; and his Shrieval Board The Grossness of a City Feast abhor'd. *a* **1734** NORTH *Life Dudley North* (1744) 157 When all the Forms of this shrieval Instalment were over. **1837** LOCKHART *Scott* (1839) II. 181 The Lord Lieutenant of Selkirkshire complained of Scott's military zeal as interfering sometimes with the discharge of his shrieval functions. **1884** *Manch. Exam.* 9 Feb. 5/3 The City Remembrancer has always by no means an easy task in inducing members to accept the shrieval hospitality.

Hence **'shrievaldom, 'shrievalry** = next.

**1679** in *Spirit of Popery* 72 When the Ancient Nobility..cannot enjoy their Royalties, their Shrievaldoms, and their Stewardaries. *a* **1715** BURNET *Own Time* (1724) I. 592 During his Shrievalry in London.

**shrievalty** ('ʃriːvəltɪ). Also 6 shreav-, shreev-, (shrevaltry), 6-7 shrev-, 7 shrief(f)-, shriv-, shreiv-. [f. *shrieve* (see prec.) + *-alty*, representing OF. *-alte* (F. *-auté*):—L. *-alitātem*, as in *admiralty*, *principalty*.] The office or dignity of sheriff; a sheriff's jurisdiction or term of office.

**1502** ARNOLDE *Chron.* (1811) p. xlii, This yere Robert Johnnson was dismissyd of his shreualtee. **1596** *Sir T. More* (Malone Soc.) Add. ii. 165 Shall we heare shreef moor speake. *Doll.* Letts heare him a keepes a plentyfull shrevaltry. **1633** HEYWOOD *Engl. Trav.* IV. i, In time Sir, you may keepe your Shreualtie; And I be one oth' Seriants. **1663** PEPYS *Diary* 28 Sept., Sir R. Ford beginning his shrievalty to-day. *c* **1683** T. HUNT *Def. Charter Lond.* 38 The Shriefalties had not been before granted in Fee. **1692** LUTTRELL *Brief Rel.* (1857) II. 590 Sir Thomas Cook has laid by 10,000£ to spend in his shreivalty. **1771** *Junius Lett.* l. 259 Your next appearance in office is marked with his election to the shrievalty. **1870** LOWELL *Among my Bks.* Ser. II. (1873) 52 The shrievalty of the county of Cork. **1887** *Law Rep.* Weekly Notes 215/2 The vacancy of the shrievalty by reason of the decease of the sheriff.

*attrib.* **1810** BENTHAM *Packing* (1821) 124 In the shrievalty year 1807-8.

**shrieve:** see SHERIFF, SHRIVE.

**shrife,** obs. form of SHRIVE *v.*

**shrift** (ʃrɪft), *sb.* Now *arch.* or *Hist.* Forms: 1-5 scrift, 2-5 scrifte, 3-6 schrift, (2 scrifft, 3 srift, shrifft, scryf ?, 4 shreft, shruft, ssrifþe, ssryft(e, ssrifte, 4-5 scrif ?, 5 scheryft), 4-5 schrifte, shryfte, schryft(e, 4-6 shryft, shrifte, 3- shrift. [OE. *scrift* m., corresp. to OFris. *skrift* m. and f., MDu. *schrift* (*schricht*) f. and n., (Du. *schrift*), OHG. *scrift* f. (MHG., G. *schrift*), ON. *skript*, *skrift* f. (Sw., Da. *skrift*), vbl. n. f. SHRIVE *v.*

The meanings 'penance', 'confession' are confined to English and Scandinavian, arising app. from an original meaning of 'prescribed penalty'. The other languages have only the senses 'writing', 'graphic art', 'scripture', 'written character'.]

† **1.** Penance imposed by the priest after confession; chiefly in phr. as ***to take, nim shrift***; ***to do shrift***; ***to give shrift***. *Obs.*

*c* **1030** *Laws Cnut* II. lxviii. (Liebermann) 354 Æʒþer man sceal ʒe on godcundan scriftan ʒe on woruldcundan doman þas þingc tosceadan. *c* **1030-50** *Eccl. Compensations* iii, Twa pund to bote mid godcundan scrifte. *c* **1175** *Lamb. Hom.* 17 þet þu scalt gan to bote and niman scrift þer of al swa þe proest þe techet. *Ibid.* 9 ʒif hwa is swa sunful..þet nulle for his ouermoð..his scrift ihalden. *c* **1200** *Vices & Virtues* 19

Wandeð to me,..and nemeð and doð scrift. *c* **1200** ORMIN 9262 To wurrþenn fullhtnedd att hiss hannd, & forr to takenn shriffte. *a* **1300** *Cursor M.* 9090 Sin i haf serued to haue þe scam, Gis me mi scrift. *Ibid.* 26194 On seke man agh na scrift be laid. *Ibid.* 28300, I brake my scrifte vmquile mai falle. *c* **1400** *Rule St. Benet* (prose) 21 Lauerd giue vs sua vre scrifte at do, þat we may hys rengne cum to. *a* **1425** *Cursor M.* 23297 (Trin.) For þei wolde no shrifte take And at her ende amendes make.

**2.** The imposition of penance implying absolution, *shrift* came to be apprehended in certain contexts as = absolution.

*a* **900** *Poenitentiale Ecgberti* I. iii. in Thorpe *Anc. Laws* (1840) II. 172 ðif he ȝewitnysse hæfð..þæt he scriftes ȝyrnde & husles. *c* **1030–60** *Laws Northumb. Priests* viii, ðif preost fulluhtes oððe scriftes forwyrne. **1297** R. GLOUC. (Rolls) 8661 He..deide wiþoute speche Wiþoute ssrift & hosel. *c* **1300** *Havelok* 1829 [Havelok] smot him sone ageyn the brest, That hauede he neuere schrifte of prest. *c* **1400** *Rule St. Benet* (prose) 6 Scrif sal he do on þaim, þare sinnis for to les. **1603** SHAKS. *Meas. for M.* IV. ii. 223, I will giue him a present shrift, and aduise him for a better place. **1628** WITHER *Brit. Rememb.* II. 1684, I leave it to the shrift Of their owne consciences. **1635** QUARLES *Embl.* III. x. 161, I need no other shrift Than mine owne conscience. **1828** SCOTT *F.M. Perth* iii, Father Francis the Dominican, from whom she had her shrift to-day. **1867** *Month* VI. 21 When the words of shrift had been uttered.

†**3.** A confessor. *Obs.*

*c* **897** ÆLFRED *Gregory's Past. C.* xvi. 105 He ðonne ondette ælce costunge þe him on becume ðæm mode his scriftes beforan ðæm temple. *a* **900** CYNEWULF *Crist* 1307 Ne mæȝ þurh þæt flæsc se scrift ȝeseon on þære sawle. *c* **1175** *Lamb. Hom.* 19 þu scalt hit ibeten al swa þin scrifte þe tachet. *a* **1225** *Ancr. R.* 418 Ne mid breres ne ne biblodge hire sulf wiðuten schriftes leaue. **1638** *New Litany* in *Bk. Sc. Pasquils* (1868) 57 From bussie Bishops without orders, As master shrifts in ther borders [etc.]. [**1860** HOOK *Lives Abps.* I. vii. 407 If a man will..confess his sins to the shrift.]

**4.** *to go, come to shrift*: to resort to confession, seek the ministry of a priest in the sacrament of penance. Also † *to seek to shrift.*

**1008** *Laws Æthelred* V. xxii, ðyme his Cristendomes ȝeorne & ȝewuniȝe ȝelomlice to scrifte. *a* **1023** WULFSTAN *Hom.* xxxix. (1883) 181 Ga man to scrifte. *c* **1175** *Lamb. Hom.* 25 Ic wulle gan to scrifte for scome alswa doð oðer men. *c* **1250** *Kent. Serm.* in *O.E. Misc.* 32 Comeþ to srifte, forleted yure sennen, and þer of bieþ a-soiled. *c* **1315** SHOREHAM I. 948 Wanne he ne may to schryfte come. *c* **1400** *Rule St. Benet* (verse) 988 To be swift Eftir our sin to seke to schrift. **1583** FULKE *Def. Tr. Script.* vi. 192 To make the ignorant beleeue that the people went to auricular shrift. **1590** *Tarlton's Newes Purgatory* 13 The next time Lisetta came to shrift, after she had made her confession, and had receiued absolution. **1592** SHAKS. *Rom. & Jul.* II. iv. 192 Bid her deuise some meanes to come to shrift this afternoone. **1630** DEKKER *2nd Pt. Honest Wh.* I. i. K 4, Let the Gentlewoman alone, she's going to shrift. *a* **1680** BUTLER *Rem.* (1759) I. 259 In the Church of Rome to go to Shrift Is but to put the Soul on a clean Shift. **1880** T. E. WEBB *Goethe's Faust* III. vii, [He] goes To shrift with nothing to disclose.

**5.** Confession to a priest; auricular confession; also, the sacrament of penance.

More explicitly, †*shrift of mouth.*

*c* **1175** *Lamb. Hom.* 11 Muchel is us þenne neod..sod scrift. *c* **1200** *Trin. Coll. Hom.* 73 Drede letteð þe mannes shrifte. *a* **1300** *Cursor M.* 25749 He..mak to preist his costes cuth, Wit reuth of hert and scrifte o mouth. *Ibid.* 27444 It es als vnder sel o scrift him sceud al to consail. **1340** *Ayenb.* 14 Cristninge, conferminge, þe sacrement of þe wyefde, ordre, spoushod, þe holy ssrifte, and the laste anoylinge. *c* **1369** CHAUCER *Dethe Blaunche* 1114 Me thynketh ye haue suche a chaunce As shryfte wythoute repentaunce. *c* **1450** *Mirk's Festial* 279 Apon scheryft wyth mowthe and satysfaccyon yn dede. **1528** TINDALE *Obed. Chr. Man* 96 b, Shrifte in the eare is verely a worke of sathan. **1567** ALLEN *Def. Priesthood* 215 Priuate shrifte, which they call nowe auricular confession. **1603** DRAYTON *Heroic. Ep.* III. 92 As I should joy t'absolve thee after Shrift. **1652** GATAKER *Antinom.* 40 Some Popish Priest, pressing men to shrift. **1662** PETTY *Taxes* 6 When every particular sheep was.. drest and shorn three or four times per annum by Shrift. **1849** MACAULAY *Hist. Eng.* i. I. 54 Shrift was no part of her system. Yet she gently invited the dying penitent to confess his sins to a divine.

**b.** Phrases.

†(*a*) *under* or *in shrift*: in a state of penitence.

*c* **1175** *Lamb. Hom.* 7 Ȝef we beod under sod scrifte. *c* **1200** ORMIN 10473, & tær [uss clennseþþ] þatt fir ȝiff þatt we rihht Her endenn unnderr shriffte. *c* **1205** LAY. 18435 Ælc mon forð rihte dude hine vnder scrifte. *c* **1250** *Gen. & Ex.* 422 An hundred ȝer after is dead Adam fro eue in srifte abead. *c* **1400** *Rule St. Benet* (prose) 4 þat here liuis in clene scrift ..þai sall haue part wid him.

†(*b*) *at, in shrift*: at, in confession.

*c* **1175** *Lamb. Hom.* 27 Hwet wule mon et scrifte bute he wulle forleten his misdede? *a* **1225** *Ancr. R.* 46 Scheaweð ofte ine scrifte ower ȝemeleaste her abuten. *c* **1330** *Spec. Gy de Warewyke* 796 þat þu hit nilt in shrifte seie. *c* **1450** *Mirour Saluacioun* (Roxb.) 58 When we in shrift reherce oure synnes. **1579** LYLY *Euphues* 28 Dost thou not laugh Liuia, to see my ghostly father keepe me heere so long at shrifte? *c* **1592** MARLOWE *Jew of Malta* III. ad fin., 'Twas told me in shrift, Thou know'st 'tis death and if it be reueal'd. *a* **1625** FLETCHER *Love's Pilgr.* I. ii, I have called my conscience to confession, And every sillable that might offend I have had in shrift. **1793** *Minstrel* II. 144 Crimes so enormous that they dared not confess them in shrift.

†(*c*) *transf.*

**1596** WARNER *Alb. Eng.* XII. lxix. (1602) 291 Let this be spoken in Shrift, so was it spoke to me.

†(*d*) *shrift's even*: Shrove Tuesday.

**15..** *Colkelbie Sow* 943 in *Bannatyne MS.* (Hunter. Club) 1048 At schriftis evin sum wes so battalouss That [etc.].

**6.** An instance of this; a confession on a particular occasion.

Phr. *to make one's shrift, to hear a shrift.*

*c* **1275** *Passion our Lord* 549 in *O.E. Misc.* 52 þat we mote at vre scrift þane veond schende. *a* **1300** *Cursor M.* 27490 Ar he [a priest] ga to scriftes here þat he may þus first his praier. *c* **1375** *Sc. Leg. Saints* iii. (*De Sancto Andrea*) 896 Til hym þi schrift þu ma! *c* **1385** CHAUCER *L.G.W.* 745 With a sown as softe as ony shryfte. **1534** MORE *Comf. agst. Trib.* II. Wks. 1183/2 When it came to the penance geuing, the Foxe found yᵗ the most weighty synne in all hys shryft was glotony. **1622** WOTTON in *Reliq.* (1672) 314 He took occasion at the next shrift, to confer certain doubts with his Confessor. **1828** SCOTT *F.M. Perth* ii, For the purpose of making their several shrifts in the confessionals. **1839** J. P. KENNEDY *Rob of Bowl* xxxiii, In this temper he had made his shrift, and abjured the lawless life..into which his passions had plunged him. **1865** KINGSLEY *Herew.* iii, He said..that..your shrift should be as short and as clean as David's.

†**b.** A thing confessed. *Obs. rare.*

**1596** WARNER *Alb. Eng.* XII. lxix. (1602) 292 Blab'd be our Shrifts to women, of simplicitie, or spight.

†**c.** A place of confession, confessional. *rare.*

**1604** SHAKS. *Oth.* III. iii. 24 My Lord shall neuer rest... His Bed shall seeme a Schoole, his Boord a Shrift.

**7.** In a wider sense: Confession (*of* sin or wrong); admission (*of* guilt); revelation (*of* something private or secret).

*a* **1340** HAMPOLE *Psalter* vii. 18 þis shrift is noght of synne, bot of rightwisnes of god. **1390** GOWER *Conf.* II. 173 Upon the schrifte of thi matiere. **1508** DUNBAR *Tua Mariit Wemen* 251, I schaw ȝow, Sisteris in schrift, I wes a schrew euir. **1598** B. JONSON *Ev. Man in Hum.* I. i, Ile studie..To call my sonne vnto a happier shrift. **1633** FORD *'Tis Pity* III. F 3, His Vnkle..Will hinder all, and call his Couze to shrift. **1668** R. L'ESTRANGE *Vis. Quev.* (1708) 133 If this Gallant were taken to shrift. **1678** —— *Seneca's Mor.* I. To Rdr., etc. 39 Then do I Recollect all that I have said, or done that day, and take my self to shrift. *Ibid.* II. vi. 80 Our Vices will abate of themselves, if they be brought every day to the Shrift. **1865** S. EVANS *Br. Fabian's MS.* 88 A dread Grew up between them such as those may tell Who have made shrift of love.

†**8.** Rendering *confessio* of the Vulgate: Acknowledgement of the power and glory of God. *Obs.*

*a* **1300** *E.E. Psalter* xli. 5 In steuen of gladschip and ofe schrifte. *c* **1380** WYCLIF *Sel. Wks.* III. 71 þis song of þes children, where we maken an opin schrift þat God is passingli blessid. **1382** —— *3 Esdras* ix. 8 And now ȝiueth shrifte, and gret doing to the Lord God of oure fadris. *a* **1400** *Prymer* (1891) 23 Entrith his ȝatis in schrift.

**9.** *short shrift*: orig. a brief space of time allowed for a criminal to make his confession before execution; hence, a brief respite; *to give short shrift to*, to make short work of.

[**1594** SHAKS. *Rich. III*, III. iv. 97 Make a short Shrift, he longs to see your Head.] **1814** SCOTT *Ld. of Isles* V. xxxii, Short were his shrift in that debate... If Lorn encounter'd Bruce! **1823** —— *Quentin D.* viii, They are like to meet short shrift and a tight cord. **1879** W. H. DIXON *Windsor* II. xxxi. 315 Short trial, shorter shrift, had been given to the chief criminals. **1887** *Times* 15 Feb. 4/3 Every argument..tells with still greater force against the present measure, and it is to be hoped that the House of Commons will give it short shrift to-night. **1889** JESSOPP *Coming of Friars* ii. 82 If he were brought to his trial he would have a short shrift and no favour.

**10.** *attrib.*: †**shrift child**, one who goes to confession to a certain priest, a penitent; **shrift-district** *Hist.* = *shrift-shire*; † **Shrift Monday** = *Shrove Monday*; **shrift-shire** *Hist.* [representing OE. *scriftscír*], the district in which a priest exercised his functions; †**shrift-silver**, a fee paid on receiving priestly absolution; **shrift-time** *pseudo-arch.*, Lent; †**Shrift Tuesday** = *Shrove Tuesday*.

**1577** tr. *Bullinger's Decades* 580 By those confessions the confessours coulde cunningly..robbe theyr *shrift-children ..of theyr substaunce. **1625** tr. *Gonsalvius' Sp. Inquis.* 125 That anie other ghostly Father had dealt in anie such like sort with anie of his shrift children. **1872** E. W. ROBERTSON *Hist. Ess.* 196 The secular priest..was not expelled from his '*shrift-district'. **1587** in *Cath. Rec. Soc. Publ.* V. 133, I came on *Shrift Munday last to Mr. Pawlet of Heryote. **1838** SOAMES *Anglo-Saxon Ch.* (ed. 2) 262 *note*, Right is it that no priest do any of those things that belong to another, either to his minister, or in his *shrift-shire. **1844** LINGARD *Anglo-Saxon Ch.* (1858) I. iv. 144 *note* 2, These districts allotted to priests were called priestshires, shriftshires, and kirkshires. **1402** *Reply of Friar Daw Topias* in *Pol. Poems* (Rolls) II. 46 Thi paroche preest, Jacke,..that nyl not.. assoilen hem of her synne withouten *schrift silver. **1853** ROCK *Ch. of Fathers* III. II. xii. 223 All through *shrift-time or Lent. **1542** *Will of J. Dowdynge of Cannington* (MS.), On *Shryfte Twesdaye.

**shrift,** *v. rare.* [f. prec.] *trans.* To shrive.

**1611** CORYAT *Crudities* 33, I saw a gray Frier shrift a faire Gentlewoman, which I..mention because it was the first shrifting that euer I saw. *a* **1683** OLDHAM *Wks.* (1686) 129 Thus I have made my shrifted Muse confess. **1699** R. L'ESTRANGE *Fables* II. vii, A New-marry'd Couple had a Toy took them in their Heads,..to Shrift one another before they came together. **1849** ROCK *Ch. of Fathers* II. vii. 461 The soul might wing its flight for its doom before God, shrifted, assoiled, aneled, and houseled.

**'shrift-,father.** *Obs.* exc. *arch.* Also 4 schrefvader, 5 schryffader. [f. SHRIFT *sb.* + FATHER *sb.* (sense 6 a). Cf. ON. *skriptafaðer.*] A confessor.

*a* **1225** *Ancr. R.* 316 Inouh hit is to siggen so þet þe schrift feder witterliche understonde hwat tu wulle menen. **1340** *Ayenb.* 38 Hi ssollen do be þe rede of holy cherche oþer be hire ssrifte-uaderes. **1387** TREVISA *Higden* (Rolls) VI. 457 Kyng Edredus..sente to his schriftfader [*MS.* γ schrefvader] Donstan. *c* **1430** *Pol. Rel. & L. Poems* (1903) 229 To do such penaunce..As þi schrift-fadir þee councellis. *a* **1450** MYRC 233 How and where he doth þat synne, To hys schryffader he mote þat mynne. **1533** GAU *Richt Vay* (1888) 3 Quhou thay sal rekkine al thair sinnis to thair schrift fader. **1600** FAIRFAX *Tasso* XI. ix, In close and priuate cell, Where (but shrift fathers) neuer mankinde treades. **1853** ROCK *Ch. of Fathers* III. II. xi. 19 The penitential, a book which only shrift-fathers..might read. **1882** F. J. CHILD *Ballads* I. 26/1 Louise then tries her shrift-father.

†**'shriftness.** *Obs. rare*$^{-0}$. [f. SHRIFT *sb.* + -NESS.] Confession.

*c* **1460** *Promp. Parv.* 401/1 (Winch. MS.) Schryftnesse, *confessio.*

**shrig** (ʃrɪg), *v. dial.* [Cf. SHRAG.] *trans.* To lop off (branches), strip off (leaves); to strip (a tree, root, etc.) of its branches or foliage; *fig.* to strip (a person) *of* his possessions.

**1601** HOLLAND *Pliny* XVII. xii. I. 514 If the braunches thereof, or of any tree within-forth be shrigged. *Ibid.* XIX. vi. II. 21 Having their uppermost leaves lightly shrigged off. *Ibid.* XXVII. vi. 275 The same root..staieth a laske, in case it be first shrigged from the hairie strings thereof. **1609** —— *Amm. Marcell.* XIX. x. 137 If all men were shrigged of their goods. **1873** W. P. WILLIAMS & W. A. JONES *Gloss. Prov. Som.*, *Shrig*, to shroud or trim a tree.

†**shright,** *sb. Obs.* [Corresponding to SCRIGHT = OFris. *skrichte*, MLG. *schricht(e*; but perhaps (in the 16th c.) suggested by some passage like the following, where *forshright* = wearied with shrieking:—

*c* **1374** CHAUCER *Troylus* IV. 1147 (Harl. MS.), With brokyn vois al hois [*v.r.* hors] for shright [*v.r.* forshright] Criseyde To Troilus thise ilke wordes seyde.]

Shrieking; a shriek.

**1556** PHAER *Æneid* IV. Kj, And mountaynes hie they fill with shright. **1590** SPENSER *F.Q.* II. vii. 57 With their pitteous cryes, and yelling shrights. **1596** *Ibid.* VI. iv. 2 Drawne with that Ladies loud and piteous shright.

†**shright,** *v. Obs.* [Either f. prec., or the pa. t. of SHRITCH taken as inf.] To shriek.

*a* **1542** WYATT in *Tottel's Misc.* (Arb.) 38 And ye so ready sighes, to make me shright, Then are ye slacke, when that ye should outstart.

**shrike,** *sb.*[1] *Obs.* or *dial.* [f. SHRIKE *v.* Cf. SKRIKE *sb.*] = SHRIEK *sb.* (In first quot., a shrill note.)

*c* **1400** *Destr. Troy* 346 Small briddes..With shrikes full shrille in the shire bowes. *c* **1450** *Merlin* i. 15 Whi made the childe this shrike? wilt thow slen it? *a* **1547** SURREY *Æneid* II. (1557) C j b, The palace within confounded was..with ruful shrikes and cryes. **1592** SHAKS. *Rom. & Jul.* IV. iii. 47 Loathsome smels, And shrikes like Mandrakes torne out of the earth. **1613** HEYWOOD *Silver Age* II. i, Acrisius heares their clamours and their shrikes [*rhyme* strikes]. **1651** JER. TAYLOR *Serm. for Year* II. ix. 109 The air became full of shrikes of the desolate mothers of Bethlehem for their dying Babes.

**shrike** (ʃraɪk), *sb.*[2] Also 6–7 shreek(e. [app. representing OE. *scríc, scréc* (glossing L. 'turdus'), which was perhaps used generally for birds having shrill cries; *shrike* and *shrike-cock* are dial. names for the missel-thrush. Cf. SHREITCH, SHRITE.

ON. *sólskríkja*, which has been compared, means 'snowbunting', not 'shrike'.]

Any of the birds of the numerous species of the family *Laniidæ*, characterized by a strong hooked and toothed beak; the majority of them are insectivorous, but several species, as the (Great or European) Grey Shrike, *Lanius excubitor*, prey upon mice and small birds; = BUTCHER-BIRD. **b.** Applied to similar birds of other families (e.g. *Prionopidæ*), e.g. CUCKOO, DRONGO, SWALLOW *shrike*.

Red-back(ed Shrike, *Lanius collurio*.

**1544** TURNER *Avium Præcip.* F 8, De Mollicipite.. Anglicè a shrike, a nyn murder. **1598** FLORIO, *Gazza sparuiera*, a kinde of lanaret hauke called a shreeke, or nine murther. **1678** RAY *Willughby's Ornith.* 87 Of the Europæan Rapacious birds it is the least... In English it is called a Shrike. **1776** PENNANT *Brit. Zool.* II. 604 The Flusher, or red back Shrike, and the great Shrike, breeds with us. **1851** F. O. MORRIS *Brit. Birds* I. 229 Great Shrike. [Syn.] Grey Shrike. Great Grey Shrike. Ash-coloured Shrike. Greater Butcher bird. Murdering Pie. Shrike. Shreek. **1855** TENNYSON *Maud* I. IV. iv, The Mayfly is torn by the swallow, the sparrow spear'd by the shrike. **1860** G. BENNETT *Gatherings Natur. Austral.* 283 The Australian Shrike or Butcher-bird, also called Rain-bird by the colonists (*Vanga destructor*). **1883** *Cassell's Nat. Hist.* IV. 29 The Helmeted Wood Shrikes (*Prionops*).

**shrike,** *v. Obs.* exc. *dial.* Also 4–5 schrike, schryke, 4–6 shryke. [Parallel to SCRIKE *v.* (see SCR-); perhaps representing an OE. **scrícan* (cf. SHRIKE *sb.*[2]) = Norw. *skrika*, Da. *skrige.*] = SHRIEK *v.* †Of birds: To pipe.

*c* **1200** *Trin. Coll. Hom.* 181 Elch wimman..þan hie beð mid childe bistonden..shrike) and reuliche biginneð. *c* **1300** *Pol. Songs* (Camden) 158 Heo biginneth to shryke, ant scremeth anon. *c* **1400** *Destr. Troy* 12973 Shene briddes in shawes shriked full lowde. **1471** CAXTON *Recuyell* (Sommer) II. 485 The ladies..shryked and cryed dolorously. **1530** PALSGR. 705/2 She shriked so loude that a man myght her her tenne houses of. **1576** TURBERV. *Venerie* 238 [At rutting time] a Badgerd shriketh. **1593** SHAKS. *Rich II*, III. iii. 183 Night-Owls shrike. **1629** GAULE *Holy Madn.* 283 To shrinke and shrike, at euery push and pricke. **1676** HOBBES *Iliad* XXI. 15 Grievous 'twas to hear them groan and shrike. **1828** CARR *Craven Gloss.* **1895** *Lakeland Gloss.*

Hence †'**shriking** *vbl. sb.* and *ppl. a.*

*c*1374 Chaucer *Troylus* v. 382 As Rauenes qualm or shrykyng [*v.r.* schrychynge] of þese owlys. *c*1440 *Promp. Parv.* 449/1 Schrykynge. 1530 Palsgr. 267/2 Schrikyng or roring out, *escry.* 1579 E. K. *Gloss. to Spenser's Sheph. Cal.* May 54 Piteous outcryes, and dreadfull shriking. 1583 Babington *Commandm.* 14 Christ..dooth crie vppon vs with shriking sounde. 1648 Gage *West Ind.* 89 Judging every cry, every howling & shriking as an alarm to my death. 1650 Howell *Giraffi's Rev. Naples* i. 70 Shrikings, and howlings, with horrid curses.

**shrikelet** ('ʃraɪklɪt). [f. shrike *sb.*[2] + -let.] A bird of the genus *Vireolanius.*

1866 P. L. Sclater & Salvin *Exotic Ornith.* 13 *Vireolanius melitophrys* (Honey-browed Shrikelet).

**shrill** (ʃrɪl), *sb.* [f. shrill *v.* Cf. shirl *sb.*] A shrill sound, cry, whistle, etc.

1591 Spenser *Ruins of Time* 581, I heard a voyce, which loudly to me called, That with the sudden shrill I was appalled. 1833 Brewster *Nat. Magic* viii. 179 The wiry shrill of the Jew's harp. 1893 *Month* Sept. 19 The ceaseless shrill of the Cicala. 1904 Macnaughtan *Gift* i. vi, The Gillie-Callum ended with a final shrill of the pipes.

**b.** Comb.: **shrill-vein** = *shrilling-organ.*

1880 Swinton *Insect Variety* 163 In *Odontura Fischeri*.. the shrill-vein [is] simply bowed instead of S-shaped.

**shrill** (ʃrɪl), *a.* and *adv.* Also 4 **shrille**, 4–5 **schrylle**, 5 **shrille, shrylle, scrylle**, 6 **shryll**, *superl.* **shrilst**, 6–7 **shril**, 7 **schril**. (See also shirl *a.*) [ME. *shrille*, related to LG. *schrell* of sharp tone or taste, G. *schrill* (late 18th cent.). Cf. shrill *v.*] **A.** *adj.*

**1.** Of voice, sound: Of a sharp high-pitched piercing tone.

*c*1386 Chaucer *Nun Pr. T.* 575 (Hengwrt MS.), Ne made he neuere showtes half so shrille [*MSS. Ellesm.* & *Lansd.* s(c)hill(e)] When þat they wolden any flemyng kille. *c*1400 [see shrike *sb.*[1]]. 1545 Ascham *Toxoph.* (1904) 15 All voyces, great and small, base & shril, weke or softe. 1596 Shaks. *Tam. Shr.* Ind. ii. 48 Thy hounds shall..fetch shrill ecchoes from the hollow earth. 1661 Lovell *Hist. Anim. & Min.* Isagoge, That [*sc.* the noise] of the bee is humming, but it's shrill in the grassehopper. 1667 Milton *P.L.* v. 7 The shrill Matin Song Of Birds. 1742 Collins *Ecl.* iv. 72 Loud along the vale was heard A shriller shriek. 1860 Tyndall *Glac.* ii. i. 229 The shrill chirruping of innumerable insects. 1885 'Mrs. Alexander' *At Bay* i, A sweet, slightly shrill soprano.

**2. a.** Emitting or producing a sound of this kind: of persons or animals, their throats, etc.

1508 Stanbridge *Vulgaria* (W. de W.) B v b, My brest is shryll. *Vox mea est sonora.* 1601 Shaks. *Jul. C.* i. ii. 16, I heare a Tongue shriller then all the Musicke Cry, Cæsar. 1605 *1st Pt. Jeronimo* iii. i, Weele be as shrill as you: strike a larum, drum. 1738 Wesley *Ps.* cxlvii. x, Let the shrill Birds his Honours raise. 1784 Cowper *Task* iv. 569 The first larum of the cock's shrill throat. 1837 Carlyle *Fr. Rev.* III. i. vii, Shrill women cry shame on us. 1866 *Mysteries of Isis* 207 Churl and noble, fair lady and shrill fish-wife. 1901 *Macm. Mag.* Apr. 447/1 One of his colleagues became shrill on the subject.

**b.** of an instrument or other inanimate object.

1567 R. Edwards *Damon & Pithias* (1571) B ij b, Whose vertue, the shrill trump of fame so farre hath blowne. 1603 E. Fairfax *Ecl.* iv, Ambling along the meads and rivers shrill. 1604 Shaks. *Oth.* iii. iii. 351 Farewell the neighing Steed, and the shrill Trumpe. 1704 Pope *Windsor Forest* 96 Wind the shrill horn. 1819 Scott *Ivanhoe* xxx, The blast of a shrill bugle. 1835 Marryat *Jacob Faithful* xxxviii, The shrill whistles of the boatswain and his mates piping all hands to unmoor.

**3.** Characterized or accompanied by sharp high-pitched sounds.

1725 Pope *Odyss.* iv. 1013 Shrill ecstasies of joy. 1812 Byron *Ch. Har.* i. xiii. iv, Let winds be shrill, let waves roll high. 1837 Carlyle *Fr. Rev.* III. iii. vi, A shrill scene, but a brief one. 1844 Kinglake *Eothen* i, In a shrill and busy hotel. 1865 Dickens *Mut. Fr.* i. vi, The night was black and shrill. 1893 Pater *Plato* 209 A single day of somewhat shrill gaiety, between two days of significant mourning.

**4.** In various transf. applications: Keen; sharp; pungent; poignant. Also of colours: bright, glaring.

1608 Topsell *Serpents* 57 A shrill and quicke sence of hearing. 1650 Vaughan *Silex Scint.* Admission, How shrill are silent tears! 1864 Tennyson *Voyage* 12 The Lady's-head upon the prow Caught the shrill salt. 1904 M. Hewlett *Queen's Quair* i. viii, The Court went thither [*i.e.* to St. Andrews] with various great affairs in train, whose conduct throve in that shrill air. 1973 D. Lessing *Coll. Afr. Stories* II. 117 She wore a tight shrill green dress.

**5.** *Comb.*, as *shrill-accented, -mouthed, -sounding, -toned, -tongued, -voiced* (also *transf.* and *fig.*) adjs.; †**shrill-bated**, with a shrill sound as of voices in strife; †**shrill-breasted**, †**-gorged**, shrill-voiced, shrill-throated.

1896 Kipling *Seven Seas* 162 Inopportune, *shrill-accented, The acrid Asiatic mirth. 1582 Stanyhurst *Æneis* i. 13 Gates with the metal dooe creake in *shrilbated harshing. 1594 Nashe *Unfort. Trav.* H 2 b, As many sortes of *shrill breasted birdes as the Summer hath allowed for singing men in hir siluane chappels. 1855 Tennyson *Maud* i. i. iv, The *shrill-edged shriek of a mother. 1605 Shaks. *Lear* iv. vi. 58 The *shrill-gorg'd Larke. 1658 Rowland tr. *Moufet's Theat. Ins.* 953 It maketh a *shrill-like noise as the other kindes of Gnats do. 1621 Quarles *Argalus & P.* (1678) 84 The *shrill-mouth'd Musick. 1838 Poe *Narr. Arthur Gordon Pym* xxiii. 188 A *shrill-sounding and phantom voice screamed within my ears. 1813 Walker *Poems* 90 (Jod.) Thro' night's dim arch the *shrillton'd Ezzan rings. 1848 Thackeray *Van. Fair* liv, The shrill-toned bell of the..clock. 1592 Shaks. *Ven. & Ad.* 849 Like *shrill-tongu'd Tapsters answering euerie call. 1743 Blair *Grave* 532 The shrill-tongu'd Shrew. 1879 Morley *Burke* viii. 176 The eager, bustling, shrill-tongued crowd of the Voltairean age. *a*1649 Drumm. of Hawth. *Poems* Wks. (1711) 37 The gawdy hunts-man winds his *shrill-tun'd horn. 1593 Shaks. *Rich. II*, v. iii. 75 What *shrill-voic'd Suppliant, makes this eager cry? 1628 R. H. *Owen's Epigrams* iv. No. 156. 33 The World's so full of shrill-voyc'd iangling. 1728–46 Thomson *Spring* 590 The lark, Shrill-voiced and loud. 1895 Mrs. Wilson 5 *Yrs. India* 271 'My husband' is the shrill-voiced reply. 1920 A. Huxley *Leda* 15 The sky Was full of strange tumult suddenly—Beating of mighty wings and shrill-voiced fear. 1960 R. Campbell tr. *Paço d'Arcos's Nostalgia* 44 The voiceless city of the shrill-voiced lights.

**B.** *adv.*

**1. a.** With a shrill voice or tone; shrilly. Now *rare.*

13.. *Coer de L.* 3999 For scorne he gan to lawghe schrylle. *a*1450 *Le Morte Arth.* 1376 'Mercy!' she cryed loude and shrylle. *c*1515 *Cocke Lorell's B.* 14 The bote swayne blewe his whystell full shryll. 1592 Kyd *Murther I. Brewen* Wks. (1901) 287 The blood of the iust Abel cried most shrill in the eares of the righteous God. 1632 Milton *L'Allegro* 56 Through the high wood echoing shrill. 1742 Collins *Ecl.* ii. 10 Shrill roar'd the winds. 1821 Scott *Kenilw.* xxv, Men laughed loud, and maidens giggled shrill. 1829 —— *Anne of G.* xii, I promise you the wind blew shrill.

**b.** Qualifying a ppl. adj. used attrib. (often hyphened).

1562 J. Heywood *Prov.* (1867) 152 A shryll whystlyng wenche. 1599 Shaks. *Hen. V*, iii. iii. 35 Your shrill-shriking Daughters. 1602 —— *Ham.* i. i. 151 The Cocke..with his lofty and shrill-sounding [Qo. 1603 shrill crowing] Throate. 1652 Benlowes *Theoph.* i. lxii, Shall Larks with shrill-chirpt Mattens rouze from Bed..Sols orient Head? 1867 Morris *Jason* ii. 298 While the harp-string and shrill-piping reed Still sounded. 1878 *Masque of Poets* 105 The shrill-blown trumpets.

†**2.** Clearly, brightly. *Obs.*

13.. *E.E. Allit. P.* A. 80 Wyth schymerynge schene ful schrylle þay schynde.

**shrill** (ʃrɪl), *v.* Also 4 **schrille**, 4–6 **shrille**, 5 **shrelle, [skrille]**, 6–7 **shril**. [f. shrill *a.* Cf. G. *schrillen.*]

**1.** *intr.* Of a voice, cry: To sound shrilly. Hence of noises, the wind, or the like, or a place echoing with sound.

13.. *K. Alis.* 777 Bulsifal neied so loude, That hit schrillith into the cloude! 1582 Stanyhurst *Æneis* ii. 35 The inner lodgins dyd shrille with clamorous howting. 1591 Spenser *Virg. Gnat* 518 Their mightie strokes so shrild, As the great clap of thunder. 1647 H. More *Song of Soul* ii. App. iii, Its tearing noise so terribly did shrill, That it the heavens did shake. 1782 Mickle *Proph. Q. Emma* iv, When the female scream ascended, Shrilling o'er the crowded lawn. 1811 Scott *Don Roderick* ii. xix, First shrill'd an unrepeated female shriek! 1842 Tennyson *Morte d'Arth.* 201 A wind, that shrills All night in a waste land. 1884 L. Wallace *Ben-Hur* iv. iv. 166 His voice shrilled with passion.

**2.** To speak, cry, or sing with a shrill voice; to make a shrill noise.

**a.** Of persons or animals.

[*c*1400 *Anturs of Arth.* xlviii, þene his lemmane one loft skrilles and skrikes.] *c*1440 *Floriz & Bl.* (MS. T) 756 þe mayde, al for drede, Bygan to shrelle [*earlier MSS.* crie, schrichen] and to grede. 1595 Spenser *Epithal.* 82 The Ouzell shrills, the Ruddock warbles soft. 1598 Florio, *Querulare*..to shril, to..chirp. 1639 H. Ainsworth *Annot. Ps.* v. 12 To showt, shrill, or cry aloud for sorrow. 1837 Carlyle *Fr. Rev.* III. ii. vi. (1872) 81 The Tribune drones, ..the whole Hall shrilling up round it into pretty frequent wrath and provocation. 1896 A. Austin *England's Darling* i. ii, The misselthrush That shrilled so gleefully.

**b.** Of an instrument of music, whistle, etc.

1579 Spenser *Sheph. Cal.* Nov. 71 Breake we our pypes, that shrild as lowde as Larke. 1590 —— *F.Q.* ii. iii. 20 A horne, that shrilled cleare Throughout the wood. 1710 Philips *Pastorals* iv. 56 Thro' all the Wood his Pipe is heard to shrill. 1842 Tennyson *Sir Galahad* 5 The shattering trumpet shrilleth high. 1879 E. Gosse *New Poems* 100 The first sharp snow is shrilling through the trees. 1903 Kipling *5 Nations* 114 The whistle shrills to the picket.

**3.** *trans.* To utter, give forth (a sound, cry, words) in shrill tones; to exclaim or proclaim with a shrill voice. Also with *out.*

1595 Spenser *Epithal.* 129 Harke, how the Minstrels gin to shrill aloud Their merry Musick. 1606 Shaks. *Tr. & Cr.* v. iii. 84 Harke..How poore Andromache shrils her dolour forth. 1613 Heywood *Silver Age* iii. i, Through all th' Abysse, I haue shril'd thy daughters losse. 1613 —— *Brazen Age* ii. ii, What better can describe his shape and terror Then all the pittious clamours shrild through Greece?

1801 *Lusignan* I. 173 The terror of the feathered tribe, shrilled in the omens of an approaching tempest. 1817 Coleridge *Biog. Lit.* xxi. (1882) 205 Gnats, beetles, wasps, ..may shrill their tiny pipes..unchastised and unnoticed. 1837 Carlyle *Fr. Rev.* I. v. ii, 'Messieurs', shrills de Brézé. 1904 M. Hewlett *Queen's Quair* i. vii, Lethington likened her to Diana on Taygetus shrilling havoc. 1947 A. Ransome *Great Northern?* i. 16 Roger's voice shrilled out, 'Sail HO!' 1975 *New Yorker* 16 June 97/3 It was a lapse on Miss Sills' part to shrill out a high E flat at the end of the first finale, but otherwise she was tender, touching, and sensitive.

**4.** To render shrill. *rare*$^{-1}$.

1772 Foote *Nabob* Prol. Wks. 1799 II. 285 If age contracts my muscles, shrills my tone.

**5.** To summon with a shrill sound. *rare*$^{-1}$.

1859 Masson *Brit. Novelists* iii. 204 The pibroch shrills them to the work they do.

**shrilled** (ʃrɪld), *ppl. a. rare.* [f. shrill *v.* and *a.* + -ed.] **a.** Sounded shrilly. **b.** Made shrill.

?1598 Marlowe *Ovid's Elegies* ii. vi. 6 For long shrild trumpets let your notes resound. 1880 L. Wallace *Ben-Hur* 446 Look at my wrinkled face..listen to my shrilled voice.

'**shrilling**, *vbl. sb.* [f. shrill *v.* + -ing[1].] The utterance of shrill sounds, shrill crying, whistling, chirping, etc.

1639 H. Ainsworth *Annot. Ps.* xlvii. 2 Shout trimphantly to God with voice of shrilling. 1777 Mountain *Poet. Reveries* (ed. 2) 27 Th' excursive shrillings of some Eunuch's throat. 1778 G. White *Selborne* xlvi. (1789) 252 The shrilling of the field-cricket. 1887 D. C. Murray & Herman *Trav. Returns* xvii. 254 The maidens..fled..with clamorous shrillings. 1892 Tennyson *Death of Œnone* 21 A wailing cry..Thin as the batlike shrillings of the Dead. 1901 W. Clark Russell *Ship's Adv.* v, The shrilling of the fife.

**b.** *Comb.* **shrilling-organ**, the sound-producing organ of a male cicada (Webster Suppl. 1902).

'**shrilling**, *ppl. a.* [f. shrill *v.* + -ing[2].] Uttering or producing shrill sounds; sounding shrill, stridulous.

1566 Adlington *Apuleius* xxii. 46 Shrilling Zephyrus. 1590 Spenser *F.Q.* i. v. 6 A shrilling trompett. *Ibid.* iii. viii. 29 With shrilling shriekes. 1633 P. Fletcher *Pisc. Ecl.* i. ii, The lads, Whose shrilling pipe, or voice the sea-born maiden glads. 1714 Gay *Sheph. Week* Friday 102 Shrilling crickets in the chimney cried. 1766 Goldsm. *Vic. W.* xxii, No sounds were heard but of the shrilling cock, and the deep-mouthed watch-dog. 1808 Scott *Marm.* iv. xxvi, The horses' tramp and tingling clank,..And charger's shrilling neigh. 1875 Jowett *Plato* (ed. 2) III. 259 The soul with shrilling cry, passed like smoke beneath the earth. 1908 *Academy* 23 May 809/1 The thorn-bushes began to rustle before a shrilling wind.

**shrillish** ('ʃrɪlɪʃ), *a.* [f. shrill *a.* + -ish.] Somewhat shrill.

1583 Babington *Commandm.* 141 Crie rather vp to heauen with shrillish shrike. 1587 M. Grove *Pelops & Hippod.* (1878) 68 With shrillish notes I would ne stay nor stent of warbuling. 1863 Reade in *All Year Round* 12 Dec. 163 'Come in', said a shrillish voice. 1886 Mrs. C. Praed *Miss Jacobsen* vii, Miss Croyle's shrillish tones crossed the lawn.

'**shrillness.** [f. shrill *a.* + -ness.] The quality or condition of being shrill.

1581 Pettie tr. *Guazzo's Civ. Conv.* ii. (1586) 58 b, Those of Piemount, who with the shrilnesse of their wordes goe thorow ones eares. 1664 H. More *Myst. Iniq.* 239 The shrilness and asperity of the noise they make. 1709 *Tatler* No. 157 ¶6 The Shrilness and Sharpness of the Sound. 1837 Carlyle *Fr. Rev.* III. ii. vi, This shrillness getting ever shriller. 1856 Kane *Arctic Expl.* I. vii. 69 'Twang, twang!' came a second report. I knew it was the whale-line by the shrillness of the sing. 1903 Morley *Gladstone* vi. v. II. 339 Cardwell adding with a certain shrillness that [etc.].

**shrilly** ('ʃrɪlɪ), *a.* Chiefly *poet.* [f. shrill *a.* + -y.] = shrill *a.*

1594 R. C[arew] *Tasso* (1881) 93 So spake he, and with him his fellowes all, Concording iangle in a shrilly sound. 1776 Mickle tr. *Camoens' Lusiad* 126 The trumpet's shrilly clangor sounds alarms. 1826 Hood *Mermaid of Margate* xxvii, The wild bird about him flew, With a shrilly scream. 1847 Brontë *Jane Eyre* xx, A sharp, a shrilly sound that ran from end to end of Thornfield-Hall. 1887 Morris *Odyss.* xii. 408 There came upon us at last The shrilly west loud piping with the rush of a mighty blast.

**shrilly** ('ʃrɪllɪ), *adv.* [f. shrill *a.* + -ly[2].] With a shrill sound or utterance; in shrill tones.

1582 Stanyhurst *Æneis* ii. 23 Thee vauts haulf shrillye rebounded With clush clash buzing. 1587 Turberv. *Trag. Tales* 17 A dolefull noyse, Of one that in the groue full shrilly cryde. 1607 Shaks. *Timon* iv. iii. 155 That he may neuer more..sound his Quillets shrilly. 1642 H. More *Song of Soul* ii. ii. iii. xl, Mount up aloft, my Muse, and now more shrilly sing. 1799 Coleridge *Lines in Concert-Room* vi, The gust pelting on the out-house shed Makes the cock shrilly in the rainstorm crow. 1818 Keats *Teignmouth* ii, The pipes go shrilly, the libation flows. 1910 *Edin. Rev.* Jan. 103 His enemies were shrilly protesting.

**shrim** (ʃrɪm), *v.* Now *dial.* [OE. *scrimman* (only once); cf. shram, scrimp *a.* and *v.*] *intr.* and *pass.* To shrink or shrivel; now chiefly in *pa. pple.*, chilled, benumbed.

*c*1000 *Sax. Leechd.* II. 6 Ȝif monnes fot to hommum scrimme & scrince. 1846 [W. Sandys] *Spec. Cornish Dial.* 18 He squinnied, tell I were nigh shrimmed with his look. 1847 Halliwell, *Shrimmed*, chilled. Corn. 1890 *Glouc. Gloss.*, *Shrim* or *Srim*, to shiver; shrink or shrivel up with cold or fright; also of shrinkage in cooking.

**shrimp** (ʃrɪmp), *sb.* Forms: 4–5 **schrympe**, 4–6 **schrimpe, shrympe**, 4–7 **shrimpe**, 5 **schrymp, scrympe, srympe, shyrympe**, 6 **schriemp**, 6– **shrimp**. [Prob. cogn. w. MHG. (MG.) *schrimpen* str. vb., to shrink up: see scrimp *a.* and *v.*; cf. also prec.

Sense 2 is prob. directly from the etymological sense 'shrunken creature', but is now felt as *transf.* from 1.]

**1. a.** Any of the slender, long-tailed, long-legged (chiefly marine) crustaceans of the genus *Crangon* and allied genera, closely related to the prawns; esp. *C. vulgaris*, the common shrimp, which inhabits the sand on the coasts of Great Britain and is a common article of food.

Also, in a wider sense, applied to various similar crustaceans, as the families *Mysidæ* and *Gammaridæ*; see *brine, fairy, opossum shrimp*, etc.

**1327** *Wardrobe Acc. 20 Edw. II*, 31/18 Shrimpis, 3d. *c***1430** *Two Cookery-bks.* 42 Take þe Luce, an þe Perche, & þe Schrympe, & seþe hem. *c***1440** *Promp. Parv.* 449/1 Schrymp, fysche, *stingus*. *c***1450** *Brut* 447 Grete Scrymppys. *c***1460** J. Russell *Bk. Nurture* 646 in *Babees Bk.*, Shrympes welle pyked þe scales awey ye cast. **1553** Belon *De Aquatilibus* 273 Anglorum..pisces ex Tamesi & aliis Britanniæ fluminibus..Roches, Daces, Tenche, Ruff, Schriemp, Prans. **1622** Drayton *Poly-olb.* xxv. 190 The Periwincle, Prawne, the Cockle, and the Shrimpe, For wanton womens tasts, or for weake stomacks bought. **1674** Flatman *Belly God* 97 An ore-charg'd Stomack roasted shrimps will ease. **1770** Pittman *Europ. Settlem.* 5 Shrimps are found in the Mississippi as far as Natches. **1802** Bingley *Zool.* (1813) III. 389 The Shrimp is much smaller than the Prawn, and is by no means so much esteemed as food. **1848** Dickens *Dombey* vi, She partook of shrimps and porter. **1890** *Hardwicke's Sci. Gossip* XXVI. 280/1 The phantom shrimp (*Caprella linearis*) of S. Australia.

*collect. sing.* **1867** Augusta Wilson *Vashti* viii, The boy.. whose sublimest idea of heaven consists in the hope that its blessed sea of glass is brimming with golden shrimp.

†**b.** Applied to a scaly monster. *Obs.*

?*a***1400** *Morte Arth.* 767 His scoulders ware schalyde alle in clene syluere, Schreede ouer alle the schrympe with schrinkande poyntez.

**c.** A shrimp or prawn used as a bait in angling.

**1856** 'Stonehenge' *Man. Brit. Rural Sports* 236/2 *Shrimps* are used for angling in docks and canals, and are good baits for perch, if used alive. **1910** *Encycl. Brit.* II. 29/1 Odd attractions such as boiled shrimps, caddis-grubs, small frogs, maggots, wasp-grubs, &c. are sometimes successful. **1924** *Blackw. Mag.* Apr. 489/1, I would not trust the most experienced salmon with Michael Lydon and a Galway 'shrimp'. **1931** *Hardy's Anglers' Guide* 31 The shrimp will wake the lazy dozer, and he'll take it or your fly with a rush. *Ibid.* 180 Prawn and Shrimp Tackles. **1962** *L. L. Bean Catal.* 52 Bean's shrimp fly is an excellent imitation of the natural food for trout.

**d.** A colour resembling that of a cooked shrimp, a bright shade of pink.

**1895** *Montgomery Ward Catal.* Spring & Summer 12/1 Colored Surah silks..in the following colors: green.. shrimp, wine. **1927** T. Woodhouse *Artificial Silk* 81 The particulars of the colours and patterns are as under—No. 1. A shrimp ordinary crochet pattern. **1975** *New Yorker* 26 May 81 (Advt.), This plain white steerhide belt reverses to cool summer shades including seafoam green, shrimp, bone.

**2. a.** A diminutive or puny person (*rarely* thing). Chiefly *contemptuous*.

*c***1386** Chaucer *Monk's Prol.* 67 We borel men been shrympes. **1581** J. Bell *Haddon's Answ. Osor.* 384b, He would have been a notorious Goliath over these little moathes, and simple shrimpes. **1582** Stanyhurst *Æneis* III. 61 On a suddeyn we behold a windbeaten hard shrimp, With lanck wan visadge. **1588** Shaks. *L.L.L.* v. ii. 594 When he [*sc.* Hercules] was a babe, a childe, a shrimpe, Thus did he strangle Serpents. **1602** *Narcissus* (1893) 167 Thou art my mother, I thy sonne, thy shrimpe. **1615** *Exchange Ware Second Hand* (ed. 2) C1b, Alas poore shrimpe, thou art nothing in my hands. **1768** Tucker *Lt. Nat.* II. 142, I wondered how such a shrimp as you could dragg about such a great carcass as mine. **1840** Barham *Ingol. Leg.* Ser. II. *Aunt Fanny*, And all for a 'Shrimp' not as high as my hat —A little contemptible 'Shaver' like that!! **1863** Hawthorne *Our Old Home, Near Oxford* II. 35 Poor little shrimp that he was [*sc.* Pope]. **1905** Elinor Glyn *Viciss. Evangeline* 85 He did look such a teeny shrimp climbing after me!

*fig.* **1634** S. R[owley] *Noble Soldier* III. ii, The small ones [*sc.* poets] are but shrimpes of Poesie.

**b.** *a shrimp of a* —: a diminutive, a very minute or tiny —.

*a***1774** Tucker *Lt. Nat.* (1834) II. 574 By continual ruminating upon this shrimp of a possibility. **1834** Marryat *Peter Simple* xxiv, If it bears me, it will not condescend to bend at your shrimp of a carcass. **1884** 'H. Collingwood' *Under Meteor Flag* 258 A little shrimp of a fellow named Fisher.

**3.** *attrib.* and *Comb.*

**1611** Cotgr., *Escruoëlle*, a little Shrimp-resembling worme. **1736** Bailey *Dict. Domest.*, A Shrimp Pye. **1747** Mrs. Glasse *Cookery* 61 To make Shrimp Sauce. **1758** Johnson *Idler* No. 33 ¶7 The shrimp-sauce not so good as Mr. H...and I used to eat. **1762–71** H. Walpole *Vertue's Anecd. Paint.* (1786) IV. 191 The Shrimp-girl, a head, by Bartolozzi. **1791** Huddesford *Salmag.* 111 Shrimpscalders and bugkillers, taylors and tylers. **1828** Davy *Salmonia* 62 Small shrimp-like aurelia. **1855** Dickens *Dorrit* I. xiii, A butter-boat of shrimp sauce. **1859** A. J. Munby *Diary* 18 July in D. Hudson *Munby* (1972) 39 She stood there leaning on her shrimp net (for she had been fishing). **1882** *Cassell's Fam. Mag.* 236/1 Shrimp-pink with white is one of the happiest and latest combinations. **1883** [see shrimping]. **1888** *Pall Mall Gaz.* 20 Sept. 11/2 She was dressed in a shrimp pink. **1888** Goode *Amer. Fishes* 192 They are sometimes taken by hook and line, with shrimp-bait. **1889** 'Mark Twain' *Connecticut Yankee* ii. 34 An airy slim boy in shrimp-colored tights. **1918** Shrimp paste [see *Gentleman's Relish* s.v. gentleman 7c]. **1923** D. H. Lawrence *Kangaroo* vii. 137 The different shells, their sea-colours of pink and brown and rainbow and..shrimp-red. **1932** A. Huxley *Brave New World* iii. 38 Two shrimp-brown children emerged from a neighbouring shrubbery. **1973** J. Rossiter *Manipulators* viii. 90 A shrimp-pink shirt. **1976** *Western Living* (Vancouver, B.C.) June 50/2 A fishing village, processing salt fish, making shrimp paste, and doing a bit of duck-farming.

**b. shrimp-boat**, a boat engaged in fishing for shrimps; **shrimp cocktail** [cocktail *sb.* 4], a dish of boiled shrimps served cold in a sauce; **shrimp cracker**, a light, crisp cracker flavoured with shrimp and served as an accompaniment to Oriental food; **shrimp-fixer**, (see quot. 1850); **shrimp gumbo** *U.S.*, a shrimp soup thickened with okra pods; **shrimp-hearted** *a.*, pusillanimous; **shrimp-louse**, (see quot. 1850); **shrimp plant**, an evergreen shrub, *Justicia brandegeana* (formerly *Beloperone guttata*), belonging to the family Acanthaceæ, native to Mexico, and bearing small white flowers hidden in clusters of pinkish-brown bracts.

**1872** B. Jerrold *London* p. viii, Smacks, barges shrimp-boats. **1979** *Guardian* 22 Oct. 26/7 The size of mesh permitted on shrimp boats in British waters. **1937** *America's Cook Bk.* 180 Lobster or shrimp cocktail... Chill thoroughly and serve in cocktail glasses. **1977** J. Wainwright *Nest of Rats* I. vi. 38 It was a nice meal. Shrimp cocktails, followed by a good mixed grill. **1969** *Listener* 12 June 814/1 The village chief himself asked us to a dinner of dried deer and shrimp crackers, chicken and lettuce. **1975** J. van de Wetering *Outsider in Amsterdam* (1976) vi. 79 He..broke a piece of shrimp-crackers and grabbed the noodles. **1850** A. White *List Specim. Crustacea Brit. Mus.* 82 *Bopyrus squillarum*. Shrimp-fixer. [**1805** Shrimp gumbo: see gumbo 1b.] **1885** L. Hearn *La Cuisine Creole* 21 (*heading*) Maigre shrimp gombo for Lent. **1889** J. Whitehead *Steward's Handbk.* IV. 337/2 Shrimp-gumbo.. not boiled after gumbo is in. **1938** C. H. Matschat *Suwanee River* 255 The supper was fresh shrimp gumbo, hot and highly spiced. **1796** Mrs. M. Robinson *Angelina* II. 187 You shrimp-hearted lubber. **1850** A. White *List Specim. Crustacea Brit. Mus.* 81 *Ione thoracicus*. Mud shrimp-louse. **1941** L. H. & E. Z. Bailey *Hortus Second* 101 [*Beloperone*] *guttàta*. Shrimp-plant. **1946** M. Free *All about House Plants* xvii. 153 The Shrimp Plant..is a comparatively new introduction to the house-plant scene. **1956** X. Field *Housewife Bk. House Plants* III. 74 The Shrimp Plant has always been a favourite of mine. I delight in its prawn-like flowers. **1975** J. van de Wetering *Tumbleweed* (1976) ii. 18 There were plants on all window-sills..the shrimp plant with a pink growth at the end of each stalk.

**shrimp** (ʃrɪmp), *v.* [f. the sb.] **a.** *intr.* To fish for shrimps. **b.** *trans.* To fish (a pool, etc.) with shrimp as a bait.

**1844** M. Hole *Diary* 26 Aug. in B. Massingham *Turn on Fountains* (1974) ii. 39 Making the most of our last day at old Blackpool... Loafed. Shrimped. **1926** R. Macaulay *Crewe Train* II. v. 119 Torquay wasn't bad. One could shrimp and prawn and fish. **1931** *Hardy's Anglers' Guide* 31 And remember too that you may shrimp a pool in this manner and revert to fly without any fear of your pool being disturbed. **1938** *Mississippi* (U.S. Works Progress Admin.) 169 In many instances, however, boats are oystering at one season and shrimping at another.

**shrimped** (ʃrɪmpt), *pa. pple.* Now *dial.* [f. **shrimp*, parallel form to scrimp *a.* or *v.* + -ed.] Shrivelled, withered, shrunk; huddled *up* with cold.

**1638** Rous *Diary* (Camden) 85 His hands were both shrimped and lame. **1670** Eachard *Cont. Clergy* 36 Such things as these go for Wit so long as they continue in Latin; but what dismally shrimp'd things would they appear, if turn'd into English. **1837** Mrs. Palmer *Devon. Dial.* I. 19 Seeing Batt a shrimp'd up, her nadded and mean'd to en, that a shud come by the vire.

**shrimper** (ˈʃrɪmpə(r)). [f. shrimp *sb.* + -er[1].] One who catches shrimps; also, a vessel engaged in shrimping.

**1851** W. Collins *Rambles bey. Railways* ii. (1852) 14 We ..found ourselves in a small room, filled with shrimpers, sailors. **1864** *Daily Tel.* 11 Aug., A shrimper stranded. **1872** Calverley *Fly Leaves* (1884) 34 Has she wedded some gigantic shrimper, That sweet mite with whom I loved to play? **1879** *Encycl. Brit.* IX. 265/1 Leigh is the head-quarters of the Thames shrimpers.

†ˈ**shrimpet.** *Obs.* [f. shrimp *sb.* + -et[1].] (See quot.)

**1688** Holme *Armoury* II. xiv. 344/2 A Sea Prane, or Sea Shrimpet, or Shrimplet. It is somthing bigger then those of the river or fresh waters.

ˈ**shrimping,** *gerund* and *vbl. sb.* [f. shrimp *sb.* + -ing[1].]

**1.** Catching shrimps.

**1848** Maunder *Treas. Nat. Hist.* 617 Shrimp-catching, or Shrimping, as it is termed. **1862** Ansted *Channel Isl.* I. vi. 128 Shrimping is carried on by many of the women. **1876** 'Ouida' *Winter City* iii, The women..who go shrimping or oyster-hunting on fashionable sea-shores.

*attrib.* **1883** *Fisheries Exhib. Catal.* 14 Model Shrimping Boat, showing how four shrimp nets are worked. **1886** Fenn *Master Cerem.* xxi, Fisherman Dick did his work with a shrimping net.

**2.** Fishing with shrimp as a bait.

**1931** *Hardy's Anglers' Guide* 31, I have had splendid sport, owing to this way of shrimping.

**shrimpish** (ˈʃrɪmpɪʃ), *a.* [f. shrimp *sb.* + -ish.] Diminutive, puny, insignificant.

**1549** Chaloner *Erasmus on Folly* Div, What will suche shrimpysshe bodies dooe..whan it cometh to handstrokes? **1567** Golding *Ovid's Met.* xiii. (1575) 161b, Those same shrimpish armes of his. **1655–87** H. More *App. Antid.* vi. 330 How shrimpish he is and unfit to fill this place. **1664** *Comenius' Janua Ling.* 278 Slender, shrimpish, lean. **1881** Mrs. C. Praed *Policy & P.* II. ix. 145 A shrimpish sprig of nobility.

Hence ˈ**shrimpishness**, insignificance.

**1651** H. More *Enthus. Tri.*, etc. (1656) 255 The shrimpishnesse of the second part of Eugenius his Answer.

ˈ**shrimplet.** [-let.] A little shrimp.

**1688** [see shrimpet]. **1884** *Jaunt in Junk* xv. 252 Some annoyingly nimble shrimplet.

**shrimpy** (ˈʃrɪmpɪ), *a.* [f. shrimp *sb.* + -y.] Abounding in shrimps.

**1859** Sala *Tw. round Clock* (1861) 58 Margate the shrimpy, Ramsgate the asinine, Canterbury the ecclesiastical. **1875** Miss Braddon *Hostages Fort.* III. ii. 42 Margate's crowded jetty or Pegwell's shrimpy bay.

**shrinal** (ˈʃraɪnəl), *a.* [f. next + -al[1].] Containing or forming a shrine.

**1884** *N. & Q.* 29 Mar. 251/1 The four daughters..of whom one has left her name, St. Sidwell, in a shrinal church on the blood-stained spot.

**shrine** (ʃraɪn), *sb.* Forms: 1–2 scrin, scryn, 3 s(c)hrin, ssrin, ssryn, 4–5 shryn, 4–6 schrine, schryne, 4–7 shryne, 5 schryn, schrene, shrene, 6 shreene, 6– shrine. [OE. *scrín* str. n., corresp. to OFris. *skrîn* (WFris. *skryn* chest, *skrine* coffin), MLG. *schrîn*, MDu. and WFlem. *schrîne* f., Du. *schrijn* n., OHG. *scrîni*, *scrîne* n. (MHG. *schrîn* n. and m., G. *schrein* m.), ON. *skrín* n. (Sw., Da. *skrin*); ad. L. *scrīnium* case or chest for books or papers.

Unexplained variants with *e* occur in OFris. *skrên*, MLG., MDu. *schrein*, LG. *schrên*, WFlem. *schrêne*.

L. *scrīnium* is represented in Romanic by OF. *escrin* (see scrine), F. *écrin*, Pr. *escrin*, It. *scrigno*, Sp., Pg. *escrinio*, and in OSl. *skriniya*, *skrina*, Lith. *skrine*, Russ. *skrin*.]

†**1.** A box, coffer; a cabinet, chest. (Cf. scrine.)

In OE. and ME. applied to the ark of the covenant.

*c***1000** Ælfric *Josh.* iii. 8 þa sacerdas, þa þe þæt scrin [Vulg. *arcam*] beraþ. *c***1000** *Ags. Gosp.* John xii. 6 Forþam þe he wæs þeof & hæfde scrin [Vulg. *loculos*]. *c***1150** *Voc.* in Wr.-Wülcker 546/29 *Archa*, scrin. **1387** Trevisa *Higden* (Rolls) III. 109 þe schryne of þe testament [*arcam testamenti*]. **1398** —— *Barth. de P.R.* xiii. ix. (Tollem. MS.), þe schryne of oure lorde [*ed.* 1582, the Arke]. **1516** *Burgh Rec. Edin.* (1869) I. 161 Item, in the compertas of Craufurdis ane standand bed, and ane schryne. **1560** *Stirling Burgh Rec.* (1887) I. 75 Ane schryne but the lid. **1658** Phillips, *Shrine*, a chest or cabinet.

**2. a.** The box, casket, or other repository in which the relics of a saint are preserved. Also, a tomb-like erection of rich workmanship, enclosing the relics of a saint.

*c***1000** Ælfric *Saints' Lives* xi. 275 þa ȝebrohte se bisceop ealle þa halȝan ban on ȝelimplicum scrynum. *c***1000** —— *Hom.* (Th.) II. 426 þa wolde se casere wyrcan him eallum gyldene scryn. *a***1122** *O.E. Chron.* (Laud MS.) an. 1070 Hi namen þære twa gildene scrines & .ix. seolferne. *c***1290** *S. Eng. Leg.* 37/125 þulke daye is bodi was in-to schrine i-bore. **1297** R. Glouc. (Rolls) 9851 þulke ȝer al so Seint egwine at euesham in ssrine was verst ido. **1362** Langl. *P. Pl.* A. vi. 48, I nolde fonge a ferþing for seynt Thomas schrine. *a***1400–50** *Wars Alex.* 5592 Of schene schemerand gold as it a schrine ware. *c***1420** *Chron. Vilod.* 4265 Byfore hurre shrene mekeliche he knelede doune. *c***1450** Capgrave *Life St. Gilbert* xxxviii, þe schrine..is..born a-boute on þe schulderis of princes and lordis. **1551** Sir J. Williams *Accompte* (Abbotsf. Club) 1 The defacinge and takinge downe of shrynes. **1593** Shaks. *2 Hen. VI*, II. i. 63 A blinde man at Saint Albones Shrine,..hath receiu'd his sight. *a***1638** Mede *Wks.* (1672) 677 The Miracles at the Shrines and Sepulchres of the holy Martyrs. **1788** Gibbon *Decl. & F.* xlv. IV. 455 The shrines of the apostles were guarded by miracles and invisible terrors. **1834** L. Ritchie *Wand. by Seine* 217 The exhibition of the relics took place..and as each shrine was elevated, every knee touched the earth. **1849** Macaulay *Hist. Eng.* i. I. 24 It was a national as well as a religious feeling that drew great multitudes to the shrine of Becket.

*Prov. phr.* *c***1374** Chaucer *Troylus* v. 553 Fare-wel shryne of whom þe seynt is oute.

**b.** In extended application: A receptacle containing an object of religious veneration; occas. a niche for sacred images.

**1526** Tindale *Acts* xix. 24 A goldsmyth, which made silver schrynes [Gr. ναούς, Vulg. *ædes*; *Wyclif* housis] for Diana. **1756–7** tr. *Keysler's Trav.* (1760) III. 58 On certain days of the year this crucifix is..exposed to public view;.. seven persons having in their custody as many different keys of the shrine in which it is kept. **1797** Mrs. Radcliffe *Italian* vi, She passed several shrines and images half hid among the shrubs and the cliffs. **1894** J. T. Fowler *Adamnan* Introd. 43 The bell of any famous saint..was enclosed in a shrine, made in its own form.

†**c.** *fig.* An object of veneration. *Obs.*

*c***1400** *Beryn* 1114 So excellent of bewte, þat she myȝt be shryne To all othir vymmen.

**d.** The part of a church in which a shrine stands. Cf. feretory 3.

**1833** Raine *Brief Acc. Durham Cath.* 50 Let us now enter the shrine. **1850** *Parker's Gloss. Terms Archit.* I. 427 Modern writers often erroneously apply the word shrine to the chapel or church in which the real shrine is deposited.

**3.** A case or casket for a dead body; also, a tomb or cenotaph of an elaborate kind.

*c***1385** Chaucer *L.G.W.* 672 Sche..made hire subtyl werkemen make a schryne Of alle the rubyis & the stonis fyne..that sche coude espie. **1613** Purchas *Pilgr.* (1614) 660 They cast their dead into the Riuer, others reserued them at home in glasse shrines. **1613** R. C. *Table Alph.*, *Shrine*, a remembrance for the dead. **1720** Pope *Epit. Harcourt* 1 To this sad shrine, whoe'er thou art! draw near. **1824** W. Fowler *List Subj. Engravings*, The Percy Shrine (Beverley). **1829** Scott *Old Mort.* Introd., This peculiar shrine of the Whig martyrs is very much honoured by their descendants.

**4.** *transf.* **a.** That which encloses, enshrines, or screens, or in which something dwells.

*a***1400** Chaucer *To Rosemounde* 1 Madame, ye ben of al beaute shryne As fer as cercled is the mapamonde. *a***1586** Sidney *Arcadia* II. iv. (1912) 172 You living powres enclosed in stately shrine Of growing trees. *a* **1649** DRUMM. OF HAWTH. *Hist. Jas. III*, Wks. (1711) 60 Favourites are shrines to shadow princes from their people. **1667** MILTON *P.L.* VII. 360 Of Light by farr the greater part he [*sc.* God] took, Transplanted from her [*sc.* moon's] cloudie Shrine, and plac'd In the Suns Orb. **1813** BYRON *Giaour* 106 Clime of the unforgotten brave!..Shrine of the mighty! **1874** O'SHAUGHNESSY *Music & Moonlight* 127 The heart was a shrine For that memory to dwell in divine.

†**b.** Used for: An enclosing membrane. *Obs.*

**1398** TREVISA *Barth. De P.R.* v. xxxvi. (Bodl. MS.), Aboute þe herte is a manere cloþing þat hatte thee schryne and þe coofer of þe herte.

**5. a.** A place where worship is offered or devotions are paid to a saint or deity; a temple, church.

**1629** MILTON *Hymn Nativ.* xix, Apollo from his shrine Can no more divine. **1697** DRYDEN *Virg. Past.* VII. 43 This tusky Boar Young Mycon offers, Delia, to thy Shrine. **1698** FRYER *Acc. E. India & P.* 78 Seva Gi was departed thence to Purtaabgur, to visit the Shrine of Bowany. **1738** GRAY *Propertius* I. 2 Before the Goddess' shrine we too, love's vot'ries, bend. **1841** ELPHINSTONE *Hist. India* I. 163 The pilgrims [distinguished] by bearing some symbol of the god to whose shrine they are going. **1880** L. OLIPHANT *Land of Gilead* iii. 80 In the East it is a common thing for the same shrine to serve the purpose of many succeeding religions. **1891** FARRAR *Darkn. & Dawn* i, Behind this temple was the shrine of Vesta. **1905** BYLES *Life R. S. Hawker* v. 42 The position of the Church, like that of all ancient Shrines in England, was chosen and fixed on certain principles.

¶**b.** In the following quots. commonly explained as 'an image (of a saint or god)'. The passages seem, however, to be merely somewhat strained figurative applications of sense 5. Cf. 2 c.

**1593** SHAKS. *Lucr.* 194 Offer pure incense to so pure a shrine. **1596** —— *Merch. V.* II. vii. 40 From the foure corners of the earth they come To kisse this shrine, this mortall breathing Saint. **1611** —— *Cymb.* v. v. 164 For Feature, laming The Shrine of Venus, or straight-pight Minerua.

**c.** *fig.* in contexts referring to the veneration or idolizing of some person or thing.

**1575** GASCOIGNE *Kenelworth* Wks. 1910 II. 109 It can not be that such a Saint to see Can long in shrine her seemely selfe so shroude. **1595** *Caxton's Blanchardyn* liv. 210 The neighboring Princes, which long had bent their deuotions to the sweet Saint which kept her shrine in Tormaday. **1605** B. JONSON *Volpone* I. i, Good morning to the day; and, next, my gold: Open the shrine, that I may see my saint. **1690** TEMPLE *Ess.* II. *Poetry* 1, The Two common Shrines, to which most Men offer up the Application of their Thoughts and their Lives, are Profit and Pleasure. **1712–14** POPE *Rape Lock* IV. 105 Honour forbid! at whose unrivall'd shrine Ease, pleasure, virtue, all our sex resign. **1750** GRAY *Elegy* 71 To ..heap the Shrine of Luxury and Pride With incense kindled at the Muse's flame. **1808** W. WILSON *Hist. Diss. Ch.* II. 57 He was too consciencious to sacrifice his principles at the shrine of worldly advantage or emolument. **1853** 'DOW JR.' in Jerdan *Yankee Humour* 88 Ye grey-haired worshippers at the shrine of Mammon! **1904** PAUL *Mod. Eng.* I. Introd. 13 He [*sc.* Mill] kept the lamp burning in the Benthamite shrine.

**6.** *attrib.* and *Comb.*

**1582** STANYHURST *Æneis* I. 13 Hee throngs in shryne clowd [*infert se sæptus nebula*]. *Ibid.* IV. 67 The slip Ascanius (for sainct thee shrinecase adoring) Shee cols for the father. *a* **1661** HOLYDAY *Juvenal* (1673) 240 If these [*e.g.* crowns] Be wanting, a less Shrine-robber will seize On a gilt Hercules his thigh. **1869** BROWNING *Ring & Bk.* XI. 572 'Such was its virtue!' twangs the Sacristan, Holding the shrine-box up. **1876** J. S. BREWER *Engl. Studies* (1881) 107 The exquisite tracery of their screens and shrine-work.

**b.** With reference to the Order of Nobles of the Mystic Shrine. Cf. SHRINER.

**1968** *Chicago Tribune* 7 July I. 1/1 More than 2,500 Shriners gathered..to kick off the 94th annual Shrine convention. **1974** *Sunday Advocate-News* (Barbados) 3 Mar. 11/4 [The] Prime Minister..received members of the Manito Shrine Club. **1976** *Columbus* (Montana) *News* 27 May 6/3 Tom participated in the clown unit of the Shrine Ceremonial parade.

**shrine** (ʃraɪn), *v.* Forms: 3 ssryne, ssrine, 3–4 schrine, 4–5 schryne, 4–6 shryne, 7 chrine, 6– shrine. [f. prec.]

**1.** *trans.* To enclose (relics) in a shrine; to provide (a saint or deity) with a shrine or sanctuary. Now *rare.*

*c* **1290** *Beket* 376 in *S. Eng. Leg.* 117 In þulke ȝere seint thomas schrinede seint edward At westmunstre. *Ibid.* 175/2406 Seint thomas..onder eorþe he lay, Are þat he I-schrined were, wel mani a long day. *c* **1386** CHAUCER *Pard. T.* 627, I wolde I hadde thy coillons in myn hond In stide of Relikes... They shul be shryned in an hogges toord. *c* **1440** *Alphabet of Tales* 69 þe fame þerof come vnto þe monasterie þer Saynt Austyn was shrynyd. **1526** R. WHYTFORD *Martiloge* 49 Theyr two bodyes were ioyned bothe togyder, & so shryned at rome by myracle. **1550** BALE *Engl. Votaryes* II. L ij b, Saint Wyllyam of Norwyche, a martyr, whych was ther shryned in Christes church abbeye. **1635** PAGITT *Christianogr.* III. (1636) 93 To take up the body of Edith.. and to shrine it. **1702** POPE *Dryope* 87 Believe a Goddess shrin'd in ev'ry tree. **1803** SOUTHEY *Queen Orraca* 60 Our brother Pedro brings them here, In Coimbra to be shrined.

†**b.** phr. *to shrine* (a person) *for a saint*: to venerate or proclaim him as a saint. Also *fig.*

**1530** TINDALE *Pract. Prelates* C vij, Shryninge them alwaye for saynctes which purchased them preuileges or fought for their libertyes. **1591** LYLY *Endym.* v. iii, You must nowe tell who Eumenides shrineth for his Saint. **1599** SANDYS *Europæ Spec.* (1632) 27 Setting forth Lady Ignorance for a great Sainct..and shrining her unto them for the true mother of Devotion.

†**c.** To canonize (*fig.*). *Obs.*

*a* **1400** CHAUCER *Agst. Women Unconst.* 15 Ye might be shryned, for your brotelnesse, Bet than Dalyda, Creseide, or Candace. **1878** W. C. SMITH *Hilda among Broken Gods* II. 177 What, if heaven should be wroth at my shrining and sainting a man, Sinful and mortal as I?

†**d.** To set up as a sacred offering. *Obs.*

*c* **1611** CHAPMAN *Iliad* x. ad fin., Poore Dolons spoiles Vlysses had; who shrin'd them on his sterne.

†**2.** To entomb. *Obs.*

**1567** R. EDWARDS *Damon & Pithias* (1571) D j b, Shrine me in clay aliue, some good man stop mine eye. **1567–8** *Gismond of Salerne* v. iii. 40 (Cunliffe), And in one tombe our bodies bothe to shrine. **1570–1** in *B.L. Ball. & Broadsides* (1867) 35 The Nortons' bones should be so shrynd That now hanges wauering in the wynd. **1610** HOLLAND *Camden's Brit.* I. 703 His ashes..were carried to Rome and shrined there in the monument of the Antonines.

**3.** To enclose, envelop, engird, as a shrine or sanctuary does the body or the image of a saint.

**1577** GRANGE *Golden Aphrod.* F iv, Ye Muses nine With grace deuine My wittes to shrine Giue not consent. **1582** STANYHURST *Æneis* Ded. A ij, Thee pyth, that is shrind vp wythin thee barck and bodye of so exquisit..a discourse. **1597–8** BP. HALL *Sat., Defiance to Envie* 21 Nor earthen pot wont secret death to shrine. **1648** CRASHAW *Delights of Muses* Wks. (1904) 140 So sweet the Temple was that shrin'd The Sacred sweetnesse of his mind. **1667** MILTON *P.L.* VI. 672 Th' Almightie Father where he sits Shrin'd in his Sanctuarie of Heav'n secure. **1728** POPE *Dunc.* III. 263 Booth in his cloudy tabernacle shrin'd [as Harlequin]. **1820** KEATS *Lamia* II. 190 Thus loaded with a feast the tables stood, Each shrining in the midst the image of a God. *a* **1851** MOIR *Poems* (1852) II. 363 A patch of sky..shrining a star Magnificent. **1871** R. ELLIS *Catullus* lxiv. 286 Tempe, shrined around in shadowy woods o'erhanging. **1871** ROSSETTI *Poems, Portrait* iii, In painting her I shrined her face Mid mystic trees.

**b.** To enclose, shut *up* (an object) in a case; †hence, to treasure.

**1586** A. DAY *Engl. Secretorie* II. (1625) 82 What auaileth it to shrine so much this vaine beautie, which..is euery day in danger? **1662** HIBBERT *Body of Div.* I. 115 A liveless peece of earth [*viz.* money] is his master, yea his God, which he shrines up in his chest. **1886** CONDER *Syrian Stone-Lore* iv. (1896) 166 The oldest [copy of the Pentateuch], shrined in its silver case and bound in green.

†**c.** To enfold, embrace. *Obs. rare.*

**1605** CHAPMAN *All Fooles* III. 17 Ist possible that I.. Should shrine within mine armes so bright a goddesse?

†**d.** *refl.* To conceal oneself. *Obs. rare.*

**1570** T. PRESTON in *Old Ballads* (Percy Soc.) 71 Loth was I [a fly] to go out, And shrind my selfe under a brome.

†**e.** ? To cover with rich ornament. *Obs. rare*

**1582** STANYHURST *Æneis*, etc. 95 An armoure..With gould ritchlye shrined [Aen. VIII. 436 *arma..auroque polibant*].

†**f.** To bury (a sword) in a person's body.

**1614** GORGES *Lucan* VII. 276 If any should his kinsman finde, And in his breast his sword hath shrin'd.

**4.** To enshrine in one's heart or thoughts.

**1579** LYLY *Euphues* 32, I haue shrined thee in my heart for a trustie friende. **1587** TURBERV. *Trag. Tales* 15 b, The idoll that was shrinde within his brest. *c* **1590** GREENE *Fr. Bacon* vi. (1630) C 4 Loue..straight diued into my heart, And there did shrine the Idea of your selfe. **1607** B. BARNES *Divils Charter* III. ii. F 1 He that aliue was shrined in my brest, Now dead liues yet intombed in my thoughts. **1817** SHELLEY *Rev. Islam* I. xxiv, When that majestic theme Shrined in her heart found utterance. **1822** HAZLITT *Table-t.* I. iv. 88 The man of real genius..has the feeling of truth already shrined in his own breast. **1863** MRS. GASKELL *Sylvia's Lovers* xi, It was waste of time and life to keep her shrined in the dearest sanctuary of his being.

†**5.** *refl.* and *intr.* To dwell as in a shrine; to be 'tabernacled'. *Obs.*

*c* **1400** *Langland's P. Pl.* A. I. 162 (Univ. Coll. MS.), Chastite wiþouten charite wurþ schryned in helle. **1592** KYD *Sp. Trag.* III. vi, The soule, that shoulde be shrinde in heauen. **1602** *Thomas Ld. Cromwell* v. v, My soule is shrinde with heauens celestiall couer. **1614** GORGES *Lucan* IX. 387 Fild with grace diuine, That in his secret soule did shrine [*tacita quem mente gerebat*].

**shrined** (ʃraɪnd), *a.* [f. SHRINE *sb.* + -ED[2].]

**1.** Containing a shrine or shrines.

**1589** FLEMING *Virg. Georg.* IV. 76 Reare vp..foure altars ..Neere to the shrined temples of the goddesses.

**2.** Contained in a shrine.

**1849** ROCK *Ch. of Fathers* II. 395 He swore upon the shrined relics of their common patron saint.

'**shrineless**, *a.* [-LESS.] Having no shrine.

**1892** MEREDITH *Poet. Wks.* (1912) 382 Showing her shrineless, not a temple, bare. **1898** A. AUSTIN *Lamia's Winter-Quarters* 55 And through your shrineless pilgrimage you make Unending moan.

'**shrinelet.** [-LET.] A little shrine.

**1884** M. M. MACMILLAN *Lett.* (1893) 102 The panels of St. Laurence's Vatican shrinelet.

**Shriner** ('ʃraɪnə(r)). orig. and chiefly *U.S.* [f. SHRINE *sb.* + -ER[1].] A member of the Order of Nobles of the Mystic Shrine, established in the U.S. in 1872. Also **Shrinite**.

**1884** *Proc. Imperial Council Anc. Arabic Order Nobles of Mystic Shrine* 54 His brother..was a Noble of the Shrine, and well up in all that makes an efficient and sincere Shrinite. **1886** *Ibid.* 85 The Walee..was made a Shriner in 1883. **1927** E. O'NEILL *Marco Millions* II. i. 95 This costume is a queer jumble of stunning effects that recall the parade uniforms of our modern Knights Templar, of Columbus, of Pythias, Mystic Shriners, the Klan, etc. **1966** *Economist* 24 Dec. 1332/2 It appears that the celebrated Shriners are a sub-class of masons. **1979** P. THEROUX *Old Patagonian Express* xii. 193 It was Club-going Hour. At the officers mess and the VFW,..the Shriners Club, the Masons..the day's work was done.

'**shrining**, *vbl. sb.* [f. SHRINE *v.* + -ING[1].] Enclosing in or as in a a shrine; enshrining, encasing.

**1574** tr. *Josselin's Life 70 Abp.* To Rdr. E 2 b, Their deathes, entermentes, entombinges, translations, and shryninges. **1581** MULCASTER *Positions* xxxviii. (1888) 181 If she be an honest woman..were she not worth the wishing, and worthy the shryning? **1622** WITHER *Philarete* F 4 b, Tis found, that costly shrining Did but hinder tothers shining.

'**shrining**, *ppl. a.* [f. SHRINE *v.* + -ING[2].] Embracing, enveloping.

**1826** A. A. WATTS *Love's Wealth* i, Whilst my shrining arms enfold, love,..a prize like thee.

**shrink**, *sb.* [f. SHRINK *v.*]

**1. a.** An act of shrinking, flinching, cowering, etc.: †a shrug.

**1590** SIR J. SMYTHE *Disc. Weapons* 23 b, After the first shrinck at the entring of the bullett. **1594** DANIEL *Cleopatra* (Bang) 1729 Not a yeilding shrinke, or touch of feare Consents now to bewray least sence of paine. *c* **1645** HOWELL *Let. to Capt. T. P.* 1 Aug. 1622, He [the Spaniard] never speaks of her [Queen Elizabeth] but he fetcheth a shrink in the shoulder. **1702** C. MATHER *Magn. Chr.* III. Introd. 11, I saw a visible shrink in all Orders of Men among us, from that Greatness..which was in the first Grain, that our God brought from Three sifted Kingdoms, into this Land. *a* **1728** WOODWARD *Nat. Hist. Fossils* (1729) I. I. 230 A Shrink, or Contraction, in the Body since 'twas first form'd. **1832** L. HUNT *Poems* 179, I..almost wish with sudden shrink, That I had less to praise. **1880** L. WALLACE *Ben-Hur* 178 The shiver and shrink with which the sitter caught sight of him.

**b.** *spec.* in *Textiles*, the reduction in dimension of a fibre or fabric, usu. caused by treatment with water.

**1947** J. T. MARSH *Introd. Textile Finishing* ix. 244 Modern anti-shrink treatments are based on..two methods.

**2.** A psychiatrist. Cf. *head-shrinker* s.v. HEAD *sb.*[1] 66. *slang* (orig. *U.S.*).

**1966** T. PYNCHON *Crying of Lot 49* i. 16 It was Dr Hilarius, her shrink or psychotherapist. **1969** C. YOUNG *Todd Dossier* 78 What you've written may prove helpful. That's what the man said, the shrink. **1973** *Nation Rev.* (Melbourne) 31 Aug.–6 Sept. 1434/1 A number of value judgments were offered..by a couple of the shrinks. **1978** M. WALKER *Infiltrator* iii. 39 He could have gone to a pricey shrink who would have certified him too delicate for the Army. **1980** *Times Lit. Suppl.* 3 Oct. 117/2 It does not take a shrink to see that a man so humanly flawed and artistically inept has got to be a loser.

**3.** *attrib.* and *Comb.*, as (sense 1) ***shrink-proofing***, **-resistance**, ***treatment***; ***shrink-controlled***, **-*proof***, **-*resist***, **-*resistant***, adjs.

**1967** KARCH & BUBER *Offset Processes* ii. 31 Controlled sheets of rubber with shrink-controlled material in the centre of the plate. **1969** *Sears, Roebuck Catal.* Spring/Summer 44/2 Shrink-controlled..core. **1928** Shrink-proof [see *colour-fast* s.v. COLOUR *sb.*[1] 19]. **1965** A. J. HALL *Stand. Handbk. Textiles* (ed. 6) v. 307 In recent years three important shrinkproof treatments have come into use. **1962** J. T. MARSH *Self-Smoothing Fabrics* ii. 11 The work is based fundamentally on the shrinkproofing of wool. **1963** A. J. HALL *Textile Sci.* v. 236 (*heading*) Shrink-resist finishes for cellulose fibre fabrics. **1958** *Times* 20 Oct. 13/2 This tweed has been woven for the school..and tested for washability, shrink-resistance. **1967** SHAW & ECKERSLEY *Cotton* xv. 131 (*heading*) Dimensional stability (shrink resistance). **1946** A. J. HALL *Stand. Handbk. Textiles* v. 275 (*caption*) Sanforising machine for making fabric shrink resistant in washing. **1973** *Times* 9 Apr. 6/3 The main terms covered by the new standard will be..'shrink resistant', 'crease shedding'. **1954** A. J. HALL *Standard Handbk. Textiles* (ed. 4) v. 280 The well-known London shrink treatment is widely used to remove residual stretch in a wool fabric.

**shrink** (ʃrɪŋk), *v.* Pa. t. shrank (ʃræŋk), pa. pple. shrunk (ʃrʌŋk). Forms: 1 scrincan, 2–3 scrinke(n, 3–5 schrinke, 4–6 schrynke, shrynke, 5–6 s(c)hrynk, schrenk(e, (4 scrynke, schryngke, scherenke, shrynge, 6 shren(c)k(e, shryng, shrinck, shrike, schrink, scrincke), 6–7 shrinke, 6– shrink. *Pa. t.* 1 scranc (*pl.* scruncon), 4 schrank, 5 schranke, 6–7 shranke, 7– shrank; 4 schronk, 5–7 shronke, 6 shroncke, shroonke, shrounke, 6–7 shronk, shrun(c)ke, 7– shrunk; *wk.* 6 *Sc.* schrinket, -it, 6– (now *dial.*) shrinked. *Pa. pple.* 1 (ʒe)scruncen, (-scrungen), 2 scrunken, 4 schrunken, 4–5 shronken, 7 shruncken, 6– shrunken; 5–6 shronke, 6 shroonke, shruncke, 6–7 shroncke, shrunke, 6– shrunk; *wk.* 6 *Sc.* schrenkit. [OE. *scrincan* (pa. t. *scranc*, *scruncon*, pa. pple. *ʒescruncen*) = MDu. *schrinken* (only in Kilian as obs. Flem.; ? from Eng.), Sw. *skrynka* to wrinkle (MSw. *skrunkin* pa. pple. shrivelled, wrinkled), Norw. *skrekka*, *skrøkka* (pa. t. *skrakk*, *skrokk*, pa. pple. *skrokken*, *skrokket*). The causative is SHRENCH *v.*[1]

The pa. t. originally had vowel change *I shrank, we shrunke(n*, but, as early as the 14th c., the properly plural form is found with a singular subject, and *shronk*, *shrunk* becomes frequent in the 15th c.; *shrunk* is the normal pa. t. in the 18th c., and still survives. The pa. pple. *shrunken* is now rarely employed in conjugation with the vb. 'to have'; see also SHRUNK, SHRUNKEN.]

**I.** Intransitive senses.

†**1. a.** To wither or shrivel through withdrawal of vital fluid or failure of strength. *Obs.*

[*c***893** ÆLFRED *Oros.* III. ix. §3 þa for þæm ciele him ȝescruncan ealle þa ædra.] *c***1000** *Sax. Leechd.* I. 204 Hy [male and female pennyroyal] blowaþ ðonne nealice oþre wyrta scrincaþ & weorniað. *Ibid.* III. 48 Seonuwa fortoȝene & ða tan scrinceð up. **1387** TREVISA *Higden* (Rolls) III. 411 þanne his senewes gonne to schrynke [*MS. γ* schryngke]. **1471** CAXTON *Recuyell* (Sommer) II. 497 His synewis shronke and withdrewe them. **1540** PALSGR. *Acolastus* II. i. H ij, My chekes that hanged syde downe, do shrynke awaye. **1573–80** TUSSER *Husb.* (1878) 40 Fruit gathred too timely.. wil shrink. **1611** BIBLE *Gen.* xxxii. 32 The children of Israel eate not of the sinewe which shranke.

**b.** To pine away. *Obs. rare.*

*c***1205** LAY. 2278 þer fore þu scalt scrinkin [*c* 1275 deȝe]. *a***1586** SIDNEY *Ps.* XL. vii, Though I in want be shrinking, Yet God on me is thinking.

**2. a.** To become reduced in size, volume, or extent; *esp.* to contract through heat, cold, or moisture. Also with *up*, *away*.

*c***1275** *Sinners Beware* 245 in *O.E. Misc.* 80 Heo schule in helle Euer schrinke and swelle. *c***1449** PECOCK *Repr.* III. xi. 347 If..the lethir..were of such kinde that it wolde daili schrinke. **1530** PALSGR. 705/2 If these bordes shrinke, all my purpose is marred. **1616** R. COCKS *Diary* (Hakl. Soc.) I. 143 The grownd on the W. side our new gadong did shrink with the extreme rayne. **1666** DRYDEN *Ann. Mirab.* cclxvi, We.. shrink like parchment in consuming flame. **1684** T. BURNET *Th. Earth* I. ii. 19 After these waters had rag'd for some time on the Earth, they began to lessen and shrink. **1742** tr. *Heister's Surg.* (1768) II. 10 Those [polypuses] which are recent will sometimes shrink and disappear by repeated Punctuation. **1816** J. SMITH *Panorama Sci. & Art* II. 337 The pyrometric pieces of clay..the more they are heated, the more they shrink in all their dimensions. **1856** STANLEY *Sinai & Pal.* vi. (1858) 270 The modern town has very much shrunk within its ancient limits. **1877** HUXLEY *Physiogr.* 151 When a body of water is cooled, it shrinks in bulk. **1887** HALL CAINE *Deemster* xl, Sometime a house had stood there, but..it had shrunken in some settlement of the ground.

**b.** Of a textile fabric: To contract when wetted. Phr. ***to shrink in the wetting*** (chiefly pass.): app. orig. said proverbially of cloth manufactured in some northern counties; hence allusively and fig. of anything that is damaged or depreciated in value.

**1483** *Act 1 Rich. III*, c. 8 *Preamble*, Whiche Clothes so shorn er they be wett..most of werrey necessite shrynk. **1511–2** *Act 3 Hen. VIII*, c. 6 §1 Cloth..which when it shalbe full wette shall shrynke more than oon yerd in all the lenght. **1540** PALSGR. *Acolastus* IV. vi. U iv, It is peryshed .i. it is shrunk in the wetynge. **1577–87** HARRISON *England* II. v. 158 in *Holinshed*, Their..ambitious titles are now decaied and worthilie shroonke in the wetting. **1583** MELBANCKE *Philotimus* R iij b, To perswade you not to shrinke in the wetting, but like a Kentish cloth..stande inuiolated. **1592** NASHE *Strange Newes* D I Three of his sonnes universally ridiculouslie reputed of... The fourth is shrunke in the wetting, or else the Print shoulde haue heard of him. **1616** R. C. *Times' Whistle* (1871) 63 The first is merry drunk,.. although his braines be somewhat shrunk I' th' wetting. **1653** R. CARPENTER (*title*), The Anabaptist washt and washt, and shrunk in the washing. **1682** N. O. *Boileau's Lutrin* III. 28 'Tis York-shire Cloath, you know, that shrinks i' th' wetting! **1727** BOYER *Dict. Royal* s.v., A Stuff that shrinks. **1879** *Encycl. Brit.* IX. 292/1 Patent flannel, which does not shrink in washing.

**3.** To draw the limbs together, bring the body into a small compass; to cower, huddle *together*; (of the body) to contract as with pain or cold; (of a plant) to shrivel or curl *up* under a blasting or withering influence.

*c***1000** ÆLFRIC *Hom.* II. 436 þa wearð se cyning [*viz.* Belshazzar] to ðan swiðe afyrht, þæt he eal scranc. *c***1300** *Pol. Songs* (Camden) 158 Heo cometh by modered ase a mor-hen, Ant scrynketh for shome. *c***1440** *Promp. Parv.* 449/1 Schrynkyn, *rigeo.* **1530** PALSGR. 705/2 Be nat a frayde, I shall shrinke so lowe that he shall nat spye me. *c***1572** GASCOIGNE *Hearbes* Wks. 1869 I. 382 The tender plant..In winter shrinks and shrowdes from euery blast. **1592** BRETON *Pilgr. Parad.* xiv, An vnwildy trunke..With weight whereof, their shoulders often shruncke [*printed* thruncke]. **1600** SHAKS. *A.Y.L.* II. i. 9 Till I shrinke with cold. **1601** W. LEIGH *Soules Solace* (1617) 18 At last shrinking downe againe, he [the sick man] gaue a sigh. **1621** G. SANDYS *Ovid's Met.* II. (1626) 29 Distressed Atlas shoulders shrinke with payne. **1680** *Revenge* IV. ad. fin., I'll make him shrink with fear, ere I have done. **1782** COWPER *Poet, Oyster, & Sens. Plant* 35 When I bend, retire, and shrink. **1819** SCOTT *Ivanhoe* xxxiii, Isaac shrunk together, and was silent. **1841** T. R. JONES *Anim. Kingd.* (1871) 115 If..any point of its surface be rudely touched, the whole animal does not immediately shrink. **1847** TENNYSON *Princess* v. 444 Her small goodman Shrinks in his arm-chair. **1891** KIPLING *Light that Failed* xiv, Bessie remained in his arms shrinking.

**4. a.** In immaterial sense: To be contracted or reduced in extent; to be drawn together *into* certain limits.

*c***1449** PECOCK *Repr.* III. xi. 347 Bicause that thilk lijflode wolde continueli schrinke. **1566** GASCOIGNE *Jocasta* II. i, When disdayne is shrunke or sette asyde. **1601** SHAKS. *Jul. C.* III. i. 150 Are all thy Conquests, Glories, Triumphes, Spoiles, Shrunke to this little Measure? **1667** DRYDEN *Maiden Queen* I. ii, When, after all his Eagerness of two Minutes before, he shrinks into a faint Kiss, and a cold Compliment. **1671** MILTON *P.R.* II. 223 All her Plumes Fall flat and shrink into a trivial toy. **1742** BLAIR *Grave* 728 Each Earth-born Joy grows vile, or disappears, Shrunk to a Thing of Nought. **1796** BURKE *Regic. Peace* i, To make England, inclined to shrink into her narrow self, the arbitress of Europe. **1856** KINGSLEY *Misc.* (1859) II. 36 How the poor soul would shrink back into nothing before that lion eye. **1911** T. S. HOLMES *Chr. Ch. Gaul* iii. 66 This influence increased as the extent of the imperial authority in Gaul steadily shrank.

†**b.** To fail. *Obs. rare.*

**1608** WOTTON in *Cal. St. Papers, Irel.* 655 He has done well to bring her to Rome, in case all other means should shrink.

**5. a.** To move *backward*, retire, or retreat *into* a cavity, shelter, or place of refuge; to draw oneself or itself *in*. In first quot. app. †to sink deep.

**13..** *Gaw. & Gr. Knt.* 2313 þe scharp schrank to þe flesche þurȝ þe schyre grece. **1426** LYDG. *De Guil. Pilgr.* 1837 Lych hornys of a lytell snayl, Wych..for a lytel strawh wyl shrynke. **1513** MORE *Rich. III* (1883) 48 Another let flee at the lorde Standley, which shronke at the stroke..as shortely as he shranke yet ranne the blood aboute hys eares. **1521** FISHER *Serm. agst. Luther* ii. Wks. (1876) 323 The trees whan they be wydred and theyr leues shaken from them and all the moystour shronke in to the rote. **1570–6** LAMBARDE *Peramb. Kent* (1826) 325 This done our Lady shranke againe into her shrine. **1606** MARSTON *Parasit.* iv. G 4 b, Her sometimes enuious lips, now shrink in, and giue her nose and her chin leaue to kisse each other. **1613** PURCHAS *Pilgrimage* (1614) 710 A twigge..growing vp to a yong tree: which when they offered to pluck vp, it shrunke downe into the ground. **1627** W. HAWKINS *Apollo Shroving* III. i. 37 Shrinke in while I buckle it, that you may bee gaunt and fine in the wast. **1697** DRYDEN *Virg. Georg.* II. 682 Teach me.. Why flowing Tides prevail upon the Main, And in what dark Recess they shrink again. **1794** MRS. RADCLIFFE *Myst. Udolpho* i, Till I shrink into my cell again for terror of the sound. **1826** S. COOPER *First Lines Surg.* (ed. 5) 330 The eye then shrinks into the orbit. **1830** TENNYSON *Poet's Mind* 37 It [a fountain] would shrink to the earth if you came in. *fig.* **1861** READE *Cloister & H.* lxxvii, Jorian from that moment shrunk in and became impenetrable as a hedgehog.

†**b.** To fall or come away *from*. *Obs.*

**1688** HOLME *Armoury* III. 355/2 The side of a Timber House shrunk from its Mortesses.

**6. a.** To withdraw *from* a place or position, esp. in a secret or furtive manner; to turn *aside*, *away*, *back*, etc. furtively or nimbly; to slip or slink *away*. Now *rare.*

**14..** *Sir Beues* (Sutherld. MS.) 1857 Fro þe ȝates he wyl not shrynke, Tyl he haue both mete and drynke. **1530** PALSGR. 705/2 He craked afore we came hyther that he wolde do marvaylles, but nowe he is shronke asyde no man can tell whyther. **1582** *N. T.* (Rhem.) *John* v. 13 Iesvs shronke aside from the multitude. **1587** UNDERDOWNE tr. *Heliodorus* (1895) 202 When shee had thus done, shee woulde have shrunke away. **1603** KNOLLES *Hist. Turks* 1038 The Hungarians were almost all shrunk home. **1605** CHAPMAN *All Fooles* I. i, *Gost.* Who was that Shrunke at my entry here? .. *Ryn.* He shrunke not, sir, his busines call'd him hence. **1660** F. BROOKE tr. *Le Blanc's Trav.* 255 They took it, and shrunk away so in the throng, I could never hear more of it. **1825** SCOTT *Betrothed* ii, He shrunk from the hall to the seclusion of his own convent. **1837** CARLYLE *Fr. Rev.* I. VII. v, Mayor Bailly..gladly shrinks within doors. **1848** THACKERAY *Van. Fair* xlvii, After she had borne a couple of sons, [she] shrank away into a life of devout seclusion.

†**b.** ***to shrink out of the collar***: to back out, esp. of an enterprise. *Obs.*

**1636** BRATHWAIT *Rom. Emp.* 383 Some powerfull Protestant commanders..who shrunk out of the coller of obedience. **1667** PEPYS *Diary* 7 May, Sir W. Pen, like a false rogue, shrinking out of the collar,..so that the whole odium must fall on me.

†**c.** *Naut.* Of the wind: ? To blow fitfully or in gusts. *Obs.*

**1627** CAPT. SMITH *Sea Gram.* ix. 39 The wind shrinkes, that is, when you must take in the Spretsaile, and get the tacks aboord. **1698** FRYER *Acc. E. India & P.* 10 The Winds shrank upon us from off the Coast of Ginea. **1706** E. WARD *Wooden World Diss.* (1708) 21 When the Gale of Good Fortune shrinks he alters his course. **1712** E. COOKE *Voy. S. Sea* 36 The Wind shrinking, and blowing off the Island in Squals.

**7. a.** To draw *back* or give way so as to avoid physical contact or conflict; to recoil through physical weakness or lack of courage or with abhorrence *from*.

**1513** DOUGLAS *Æneis* X. viii. 115 Pallas, nocht schrynkand for the mortale dynt. *a***1548** HALL *Chron., Hen. VIII* (1550) 160 Notwithstandyng that the Romaynes shot great ordinaunces,..yet the Imperiall persones neuer shranke, but manly entered the Bulwarke. **1656** *Burton's Diary* (1828) I. 265 He put out his tongue very willingly, but shrinked a little when the iron came upon his forehead. **1670** MILTON *Hist. Eng.* v. 237 It is shamefull for a King to boast at Table, and shrink in fight. **1770** GOLDSM. *Des. Vill.* 49 Shrinking from the spoiler's hand, Far, far away, thy children leave the land. **1794** MARY WOLLSTONECR. *View Fr. Rev.* I. 133 Is it then surprising, that a very desirable woman, with a sanguine constitution, should shrink abhorrent from his embraces? **1809** W. IRVING *Knickerb.* VI. viii, Wherever he went, the enemy shrank before him. **1821** SCOTT *Kenilw.* iv, She shrunk back from his grasp. **1862** CALVERLEY *Verses & Transl.* (1894) 64 Streets, which foot of traveller shrinks from, As on hot plates shrinks the bear. **1892** GARDINER *Student's Hist. Eng.* 14 The soldiers were terrified and shrunk back.

†**b.** To give way; to collapse. *Obs.*

**1590** SPENSER *F.Q.* III. xii. 10 He..nicely trode, as thornes lay in his way, Or that the flore to shrinke he did auyse; And on a broken reed he still did stay His feeble steps, which shrunke, when hard theron he lay. **1607** SHAKS. *Cor.* v. iv. 20 The ground shrinkes before his Treading. *c***1610** *Women Saints* 194 Reason being conquered by the excesse of sorrowe shruncke. **1616** R. COCKS *Diary* (Hakl. Soc.) I. 128 Our new wall..shronk soe it was this day..puld downe.

**8. a.** To refuse or hesitate to act in the face of anything irksome, grievous, horrible, or distasteful; to recoil mentally or morally.

*c***1470** *Gol. & Gaw.* 1077 The sege that schrenkis for na schame, the schent might hym schend. **1500–20** DUNBAR *Poems* xxvii. 29 The telȝouris hairt a littill schrenkit. **1535** COVERDALE *Ps.* cxii. 8 His herte is stablished, he wil not shrencke. **1576** GASCOIGNE *Grief of Joy* Ded., I will then shrinke for no paynes untill I have..touched all the common places of mans perylous pleasures. *a***1628** PRESTON *New Covt.* (1634) 300 A man perhaps will beare many things for Religion, but if it come to death, there he shrinkes. **1784** COWPER *Task* VI. 513 Fancy shrinks..at the thought Of such a gulph as he design'd his grave. **1821** SHELLEY *Adonais* liii, Why linger, why turn back, why shrink, my Heart? **1868** J. H. BLUNT *Ref. Ch. Eng.* I. 515 There was much which might make good men shrink and hesitate.

**b.** freq. const. *from* (often governing a gerund).

**1565** J. PHILLIP *Patient Grissell* 859 No Tarquins knight, ne Appian now, shall cause mee shrinke from duetie due. *a***1578** LINDESAY (Pitscottie) *Chron. Scot.* (S.T.S.) I. 311/30 To cause him suerue or schrink fre ony pairt of his faitht in Christ Jessus. **1741–2** GRAY *Agrip.* 48 Then was the time To shrink from danger. **1813** *Sk. Char.* (ed. 2) i, I am convinced there are many, who would shrink from coming out in the manner you have described. **1818** SCOTT *Hrt. Midl.* Prol., Who hath cumbered the world with his devices, but shrunken from the responsibility thereof. **1869** FREEMAN *Norm. Conq.* (1875) III. 115 There was no sacrifice from which French policy so instinctively shrank. **1891** E. PEACOCK *N. Brendon* I. 285 Opinions, which he never shrunk from expressing. **1912** *Times* 19 Oct. 7/4 The policy of exclusion from which the Board of Agriculture has shrunk.

**c.** const. *at*.

**1576** GASCOIGNE *Droome Doomesday* Wks. 1910 II. 431 If thou perceyve any man to shrynke at death when it commeth. *a***1625** FLETCHER *Hum. Lieut.* I. i, I have seen him do such things, belief would shrink at. **1732** POPE *Ess. Man* II. 229 What happier natures shrink at with affright. **1780** *Mirror* No. 71 That delicacy which made him..shrink at the idea of asking a pecuniary favour. **1831** SCOTT *Cast. Dang.* xiv, The abbot would not shrink at inflicting upon me the death due to an apostate nun. **1839** HOOD *John Day* xiv, At last he made a vow To break his being's link; For he was so reduced in size At nothing he could shrink.

**d.** const. inf.

**1544** BETHAM *Precepts War* II. lxxiii. L viij b, For the encrease of his renowme, they wyll not shrynke: to bestowe and spende theyr lyfe. **1549** COVERDALE, etc. *Erasm. Par. 1 Cor.* 43 Nor shrynke ye to take paynes. **1602** HEYWOOD *Wom. Killed w. Kindn.* v. i, He would not shrinke to spend a thousand pound, To giue the Mountfords name so deepe a wound. **1869** F. W. NEWMAN *Misc.* 107 Novelists do not shrink to tell the form of a hero or heroine's features. **1878** BROWNING *La Saisiaz* 23 Would I shrink to learn my life-time's limit—days, weeks, months or years?

†**9.** To be a deserter or rebel; to fall *away from* duty or allegiance, or *from* a person. *Obs.*

**1553** T. WILSON *Rhet.* (1580) 62 Your Sister would not dooe her duetie, but shranke awaie. **1560** DAUS tr. *Sleidane's Comm.* 123 They can not forsake nor shrynke from the true doctrine. *Ibid.* 276 b, Whan he was gone, the fellowes of that conspiracie, shranke away immediatly. **1577** HANMER *Anc. Eccl. Hist.* 118 Such as shrinked were to be vpholden and cured. **1594** SHAKS. *Rich. III*, v. iii. 222 Ile play the Ease-dropper, To heare if any meane to shrinke from me.

**II.** Transitive (mainly causative) senses.

**10. a.** To cause to contract or be reduced in size, volume, or extent; to cause to contract by moisture, heat, or cold; to cause (a limb, sinew, plant) to wither or (the skin) to wrinkle. Also with *up*.

**1398** TREVISA *Barth. De P.R.* XV. cxxxv. (1495) 538 An herbe namyd Apium risus: that drawe and shrynke jawes of men. *a***1425** tr. *Arderne's Treat. Fistula*, etc. 62 Ellez walld þai schrenk þe stomake. *a***1530** J. HEYWOOD *Wether* 978 (Brandl), I loue no launders that shrynke my gere in wettynge. **1593** SHAKS. *3 Hen. VI*, III. ii. 156 To shrinke mine Arme vp like a wither'd Shrub. **1611** BEAUM. & FL. *Knt. Burning Pestle* III. 12 Let them..Start at a shadow, and shrink up their bloud. **1637** MILTON *Lycidas* 133 Return Alpheus, the dread voice is past, That shrunk thy streams. **1646** CRASHAW *Sospetto d' Herode* xxii, That the Great Angell-blinding light should shrinke His blaze, to shine in a poore Shepherds eye. **1679** MOXON *Mech. Exerc.* ix. 155 If the Rain wet them, instead of shrinking them, it will swell them. **1680** C. NESSE *Ch. Hist.* 172 God shrank his sinews, and makes him stand like an antick statue. **1712–14** POPE *Rape Lock* II. 132 Alum styptics with contracting pow'r Shrink his thin essence like a rivel'd flow'r. **1832** TENNYSON *Mariana in South* v, The steady glare Shrank one sick olive sere and small. **1866** REDGRAVE *Cent. Painters* II. 602 The moisture of the paste shrinks the spot of canvas to which it is applied. **1875** F. T. BUCKLAND *Log-bk.* 57 A human head which has by some process or other been shrunk to about the size of a large orange.

**b.** *spec.* To treat (a textile material) with water so that it may not shrink after it is made up.

**1856** [see SHRINKING *vbl. sb.* 1 b]. **1883** 'SYLVIA' *Lady's Guide Dressmaking* 122 Braid is the best trimming for.. frocks. It should always be 'shrunk' before being put on the dress.

**c.** *Mech.* To cause (a piece, e.g. the tyre of a wheel, the jacket of a cannon) to be fixed tightly *on* (*to*) another (which it is intended to fit) by heating it, slipping it into place when sufficiently expanded, and then rapidly cooling it. Also with *on* (adv.) and occas. *absol.*

**1839** *Civil Engin. & Arch. Jrnl.* II. 449/1 To make the wheel in the usual way and then shrink the railway tire.. upon it. **1861** RUSSELL in *Times* 26 Oct., A simple..piece of artillery, with a thick iron band shrunk on over the breach. **1889** *Pall Mall Gaz.* 25 June 2/1 Krupp began with solid guns and found himself obliged to come to the English system of building up guns by the shrinking on of hoops. At the present time France, Germany, Italy, and Russia shrink as we do.

**d.** *transf.* To reduce in number. *rare.*

**1832** GOODRIDGE *Voy. S. Seas* 65 We endeavoured to shrink them [*sc.* mice] by destroying immense quantities.

**11.** To draw (the body, the limbs, oneself) into a smaller compass.

*c* **1374** Chaucer *Boeth.* I. pr. i. (1868) 5 Sche constreynede and schronk hir seluen lyche to þe comune mesure of men. **1606** Sylvester *Du Bartas* II. iv. *Tropheis* 1081 Her Alabastrine well-shapt Limbs shee shrinks. **1649** Davenant *Love & Hon.* II. ii, The chaste Indian plant, That shrinks and curles his bashfull leaves at the Approach of man. **1705** Collier *Ess. Mor. Subj.* I. (1709) 100 A modest Man, if he was somewhat Taller than his Neighbors, would chuse to shrink himself into the Dimensions of the Company. **1712** Addison *Spect.* No. 303 ¶13 The Multitude and Rabble of Spirits immediately shrink themselves into a small Compass. **1875** Morris *Æneid* XII. 861 Her body huge she shrank.

**12.** In immaterial sense: To reduce to smaller limits or compass.

**1628** Feltham *Resolves* II. vii. 16 'Tis the sawcie seruant, that causes the Lord to shrinke his descending fauours. **1645** Milton *Tetrach.* Wks. 1851 IV. 176 That were a phrase to shrink the glorious omnipresence of God speaking, into a kind of circumscriptive absence. **1812** Cary *Dante, Purg.* IX. 44 Thy strength Shrink not, but rise dilated. **1837** Carlyle *Fr. Rev.* VIII. ii, Logical cobwebbery shrinks itself together. **1891** J. Martineau *Ess. & Addr.* IV. Pref., If to the dwarfed and altered thought I had tried to shrink the grand old language.

†**13.** To cause to withdraw or disappear; to draw *in* (the horns, the claws); also with *back*, *up*. Hence in allusive phr. signifying withdrawal from a position of prominence, from an undertaking, etc.

*c* **1374** Chaucer *Troylus* I. 300 And þough he erst hadde poured vp and doun, He was þo glad his hornes yn to shrynke. **1412–20** Lydg. *Chron. Troy* I. 2199 Cometh Schame anoon.. And causeth Loue hornys for to schrynke. **1594** Kyd *Cornelia* III. i, The cheerefull Cock.. Doth sing to see how Cynthia shrinks her horne. **1596** *Edw. III*, I. i. 138, I will make you shrinke your snailie hornes! **1608** D. T[uvill] *Ess. Pol. & Mor.* 57 b, The Lyon is a Lyon, though he shrink vp his clawes. **1629** Milton *Hymn Nativ.* xxii, The Libyc Hammon shrinks his horn. **1642** D. Rogers *Naaman* 24 My wretched.. soule may provoke thee to shrinke in thy graces. **1642–4** Vicars *God in Mount* 76 The rest (who more wisely shrunk-in their heads, and recanted their former oversight). **1681** Dryden *Span. Friar* III. ii, The Devil.. puts out his Horns to doe a mischief, and then shrinks 'em back for safety, like a Snail into her shell. **1713** Young *Last Day* II. 301 To make the Sun shrink in his beam.

**14. a.** To draw (the head, the hand, etc.) *aside*, *back*, or *away* in a furtive, ashamed, or retiring manner. Now *rare*.

*c* **1489** Caxton *Sonnes of Aymon* x. 257 Whan bayard sawe Mawgis, he began to shrynke his eeres [orig. *etreindre les oreilles*]. **1575** Gascoigne *Flowers* Wks. 1907 I. 65 To sitte a side and shrinke His harbraind head with out dame dainties dore. **1581** Pettie tr. *Guazzo's Civ. Conv.* III. (1586) 166 b, He had shrunke his head out of the coller of those insupportable paines. **1613–16** W. Browne *Brit. Past.* II. iii. ad fin,. The Riuer.. Shrunke his graue head, beneath his siluer waues. **1615** Chapman *Odyss.* xx. 455 Thus snatcht he.. a Neats foot, And threw it at Vlysses: who, his head Shrunke quietly aside. *c* **1620** Fletcher, etc. *Lover's Progr.* I. i, We made them shun us, And shrink their rugged heads. **1880** Meredith *Tragic Com.* (1881) 64 She shrank her hand back.

†**b.** *to shrink in the neck*: to flinch, recoil.

**1581** Pettie tr. *Guazzo's Civ. Conv.* III. (1586) 124 One of them asked him what she was: who poore man shrinking in his neck, said he knew her not. **1705** Collier *Ess. Mor. Subj.* III. 13 When did they refuse to lay their Throat fair, or shrink in their Neck at the dispatching blow?

†**c.** = shrug *v.* *to shrink up* (occas. *in*) *one's shoulders*: to shrug one's shoulders; *fig.* (with *at*) to regard with displeasure, aversion, or indifference.

**1605** Wotton in *Life & Lett.* (1907) I. 336 They shrink up the shoulder, as if it were a greater matter than we are aware of. *c* **1645** Howell *Lett.* (1754) 115 Among others that shrink in the Shoulders at it. **1676** *Packet Adv. Men Shaftesb.* 76 If ye talk of State-Commodities, they shrink the shoulder, and say nothing. **1719** De Foe *Crusoe* II. (Globe) 543 He shrunk up his Shoulders at it. **1720** —— *Capt. Singleton* iv. (1840) 61 They shrunk up their shoulders, as Frenchmen do.

†**15. a.** To shun, avoid. *Obs.*

**1513** Douglas *Æneis* VIII. Prol. 61 The schipman schrenkis the schour, and settis to schore. **1582** Stanyhurst *Æneis* II. 34 In this last byckring I shrunck no danger or hazard. **1609** Holland *Amm. Marcell.* 392 Gratianus.. as yet but a stripling.. shrunke not five souldiors. **1688** Holme *Armoury* III. xvii. (Roxb.) 118/2 A man resolued to abide the utmost hazard of Battle, and not to shrink his aduersary.

**b.** *to shrink collar*: = 6 b. *Obs. rare.*

**1579–80** North *Plutarch* (1595) 907 He began.. to rowse himselfe, and to lift vp his head: but he shrunke choller againe soone after.

†**16.** To quit. *Obs. rare.*

**1594** Lyly *Mother Bombie* IV. ii, Thou knowest wee are towne borne children, and wil not shrinke the citie.

**17.** *Comb.* **shrink film** = shrink-wrap *sb.*; **shrink fit** = *shrinkage fit* s.v. shrinkage 4; **shrink-ring**, a ring of metal that is shrunk on; a ring in a structure that bears the strain of expansion and shrinkage.

**1967** *Times Rev. Industry* May 76/3 *Shrink film*: as a replacement for fibre-board cartons in containing canned and bottled goods during distribution. **1969** L. S. Mounts in W. R. R. Park *Plastics Film Technol.* v. 124 Shrink films are sealed by special point sealers, hot wire.. or impulse. **1882** *Amer. Machinist* 8 Apr. 9/1 How much should be allowed in making a shrink fit of a wrought iron crank to the shaft? **1941** L. S. Marks *Mech. Engineer's Handbk.* (ed. 4) 923 Shrink fits are used in places where a force fit would be difficult to assemble, as for example, locomotive wheel tires. **1970** K. Ball *Fiat 600, 600D Autobook* i. 16/1 The starter ring is a shrink-fit on the flywheel. **1902–3** *Jrnl. Inst. Electr. Engin.* XXXII. 419 Well-made shrink-ring jointed cast-steel flywheels. *Ibid.* 410 To cast the boss in sections and have two very heavy shrink rings round the boss.

**'shrinkable**, *a.* [f. prec. + -able.] Capable of being shrunk, liable to shrink.

**1891** in *Cent. Dict.* **1969** W. R. R. Park *Plastics Film Technol.* viii. 181 Heat shrinkable polyvinyl chloride tubes in a range of diameters are becoming available.

Hence **shrinka'bility**.

**1946** A. J. Hall *Stand. Handbk. Textiles* 273 Shrinkability in washing is a feature of textile materials to which a great deal of attention has been given. **1975** I. Stewart *Concepts Mod. Math.* xiii. 189 The 'shrinkability' of a closed curve is clearly a topological property.

**shrinkage** ('ʃrɪŋkɪdʒ). [f. shrink *v.* + -age.]

**1.** The act or fact of shrinking; reduction in the size or volume of a substance or material due to contraction such as is caused by heat, cold, or wet.

**1800** Colquhoun *Comm. Thames* ii. 76 Deficiencies of goods far beyond what can arise from natural waste or shrinkage. **1852** *Nicholson's Encycl. Archit.* I. 74 All timber is liable to shrinkage by the evaporation of the moisture which is always present. **1853** Lyell *Princ. Geol.* II. xiv. (ed. 9) I. 327 The mud.. solidifies, and becomes traversed by cracks, caused by shrinkage. **1884** *Contemp. Rev.* July 62 The shrinkage of the lakes has permitted systematic excavations to be made in their former beds. **1889** Rider Haggard *Cleopatra* Introd., Notwithstanding.. the shrinkage of the flesh, I think the face was one of the most imposing and beautiful that I ever saw.

**2. a.** The amount of such contraction or loss in bulk, volume, or measurement.

**1862** *Catal. Internat. Exhib.* II. x. 27 Various specimens of clays.. made up into squares to show their relative shrinkages. **1875** Knight *Dict. Mech.* 2169/1 Brass contracts rather more [than cast iron], $\frac{3}{16}$ inch shrinkage to the foot being allowed. **1884** *Sci. Amer.* Suppl. XVIII. 7197 All substances that tend to decrease the refractory character of the basic brick increase their shrinkage.

**b.** *Gun-making.* In shrinking on hoops or tubes, the difference between the inner diameter of the outer cylinder and the outer diameter of the inner cylinder.

**1891** in *Cent. Dict.* **1894** *Times* 31 Aug. 6/1 The complicated calculations connected with the 'shrinkage' and tensions of the various parts of built-up guns.

**3. a.** Of immaterial things: Diminution or reduction in quantity, amount, or size; depreciation or decrease in value; the amount of such diminution.

**1873** 'Mark Twain' *Gilded Age* xliv. 397 They invariably allowed a half for shrinkage in his statements. **1879** H. James jun. *Hawthorne* 129 The shrinkage and extinction of a family. **1879** *Standard* 21 May 2/1 The failure is attributed to bad debts, shrinkage in the value of goods, and the withdrawal of capital. **1880** Jefferies *Hodge* II. 266 There has been proceeding a general shrinkage, as it were, of speculative investment. **1891** *Times* 9 Oct. 9/6 The total shrinkage was £40,000.

**b.** *spec.* in *Comm.*, an allowance made for the reduction in takings due to wastage, theft, etc.

**1961** *Times* 6 Jan. 6/3 An allowance of up to 1 per cent is made for pilfering, the euphemistic word for it being 'shrinkage'. **1972** *Guardian* 14 July 12/6 Around £300 is lost each year.. through.. shrinkage. Shrinkage is not just customer pilferage. It includes errors, incompetence and inexperience. **1981** *Times* 4 Mar. 16/1 For some time supermarkets and department stores have referred to shoplifting euphemistically as shrinkage on their balance sheets.

**4.** *attrib.*: *shrinkage-resistant* adj.; **shrinkage cavity**, a cavity in metal caused by shrinkage; **shrinkage crack** *Geol.*, a crack formed on the surface of a bed of rock and due to shrinkage caused by exposure to sun and air; a crack similarly formed in other materials; **shrinkage fit**, a fit made by shrinking one cylindrical piece on to another; **shrinkage rule** = *contraction rule* (see contraction 9).

**1923** Glazebrook *Dict. Appl. Physics* V. 358 (*caption*) Shrinkage cavities at surface of aluminium alloy ingot. **1973** G. J. Davies *Solidification & Casting* ix. 180 (*caption*) A large shrinkage cavity in the interior of an aluminium-bronze sand casting. **1867** Murchison *Siluria* xviii. 437 In the Gaspé sandstones casts of shrinkage-cracks are very common. **1872** *Q. Jrnl. Geol. Soc.* XXIX. 59 These nodules.. are highly mineralized; for they exhibit wide shrinkage-cracks. **1930** *New Statesman* 27 Dec. 357/2 And even as regards telegraph poles and the like a preference is given to those with long shrinkage cracks. **1895** W. Kent *Mech. Engineer's Pocket-bk.* 973 (*heading*) Shrinkage fits. **1928** F. D. Jones *Handbk. Encycl. Engin.* 977 A cylindrical part which is to be held in position by a shrinkage fit is first turned a few thousandths of an inch larger than the hole in which it is to fit; the diameter of the latter is increased by heating, and after the part is inserted, the heated outer member is cooled, causing it to grip the pin or shaft with tremendous pressure. **1946** *Nature* 14 Sept. 386/1 The greatly increased demand for shrinkage-resistant garments by the Forces.

**shrinker** ('ʃrɪŋkə(r)). [f. shrink *v.* + -er[1].]

**1.** One who shrinks or recoils from the truth, from duty, danger, or the like; in the 16th cent. one who shrinks *from* the faith of the Gospel or its obligations. (Cf. shrinking *ppl. a.* 2 a.)

**1554** Knox *Godly Let.* C viij, Too fearfull shrinkers from the truth, for feare of worldly troble. **1563–83** Foxe *A. & M.* 2103/2 Richard Denton, a shrinker from the Gospell. **1564** *Brief Exam.* ******ij, You shal not neede to terme your betters.. to be enemies or shrinkers. **1575–85** Abp. Sandys *Serm.* xiv. 239 Another is a shrinker, another halfe a papist. **1611** Cotgr., *Tergiversateur*, a flincher, shrinker, starter. *c* **1635** *Roxb. Ball.* (1887) VI. 433 We are no cowardly shrinkers, but English-men true bred. **1719** D'Urfey *Pills* V. 62 A good Ale drinker; He never was a Shrinker.

**2.** A person employed in shrinking materials in various manufacturing processes.

**1921** *Dict. Occup. Terms* (1927) §190 Tyre shrinker. *Ibid.* §384 *Crabber; cloth shrinker, potter, shrinker*,.. tends crabbing machine, which passes cloth, at a suitable tension, through weighted rollers in a succession of troughs of water, .. where it is expanded or reduced to a specified width. **1960** *Classification of Occupations* (Gen. Register Office) 99/2 Shrinker and dyer.

**'shrinking**, *vbl. sb.* [f. shrink *v.* + -ing[1].]

**1.** Contraction and reduction in size or volume through the action of heat, cold, or moisture; the drawing *up* or withering (of sinews, etc.).

**1398** Trevisa *Barth. de P.R.* v. xii. (Tollem. MS.), By reuelynge and scherenkynge.. of þe synew of felynge. *Ibid.* XVIII. xxxix. (1495) 801 Shryngynge of synewes. *c* **1440** *Promp. Parv.* 449/1 Schrynkynge, *rigiditas*. **1670** Boyle in *Phil. Trans.* V. 2046 The Bladder, whose regular Intumescencies and shrinkings sufficiently manifested, that the vessel.. did not leak. **1671** Woodhead *St. Teresa* I. xxxiii. 231 That shrinking up of all my sinnews. **1679** Alsop *Melius Inq.* Introd. 22 We must allow for shrinking in the Silk-grograin Phrase of Rhetoricians. **1707** Mortimer *Husb.* 110 Except what it [corn] loseth in the first Year's shrinking, and loss of Weight. **1816** J. Smith *Panorama Sci. & Art* II. 324 The regular shrinking of clay by heat. **1822–34** *Good's Study Med.* (ed. 4) I. 635 Coldness and shrinking of the extremities. **1860** Tyndall *Glac.* II. viii. 264 Successive shrinkings [of a glacier].. have occurred at intervals of centuries.

**b.** (See shrink *v.* 10 b.)

**1856** Miss Warner *Hills Shatemuc* xii, They [socks] wouldn't want shrinking.

**2.** Physical, mental, or moral recoiling *from* a burden, danger, etc.

**1580** Hollyband *Treas. Fr. Tong*, *Affaissement*.. a shrinking vnder a great burthen. **1611** Cotgr. *Tergiversation*,.. a flinching.. or shrinking backe. **1663** J. Spencer *Prodigies* (1665) 234 A kind of prodigious shrinking of the Eye of Heaven from the view of so black a wickedness. **1782** Cowper *Poet.* etc. 66 His censure reach'd them as he dealt it, And each by shrinking show'd he felt it. **1848** Thackeray *Van. Fair* lxv, [She] never mentioned her name but with a shrinking and terror. **1854** H. Miller *Sch. & Schm.* (1858) 509 Not without some craven shrinkings. **1882** J. H. Blunt *Ref. Ch. Eng.* II. 137 There was no shrinking here from a full declaration of the Royal Supremacy.

*attrib.* **1891** Farrar *Darkn. & Dawn* xxvii, One shrinking motion, one stifled scream.

†**3.** Shrugging (of the shoulders). *Obs.*

**1638** Junius *Paint. Ancients* 293 The shrinking up of the shoulders.. is a gesture belonging to a base, servile, and craftie knave.

**4.** Estrangement. (Cf. next 2 a.)

**1842** Manning *Serm.* i. (1848) 13 The sins of the heathen world.. began in a shrinking of the heart from God.

**'shrinking**, *ppl. a.* [-ing[2].]

**1.** That shrinks, contracts, is reduced in size or volume, or is withered or shrivelled. Also *fig.*

?*a* **1400** *Morte Arth.* 1857 Schalkes they schotte thrughe schrenkande maylez. **1583** *Burgh. Rec. Edin.* (1882) IV. 277 Yorkschyre clayth, cairsayes, and all sort of schrynking clayth. **1631** Anchoran *Comenius' Gate Tongues* 31 *Pandus Asellus*.. The shrinking or crooked little asse. **1805** Cary *Dante, Inf.* xxv. 57 Thus up the shrinking paper, ere it burns, A brown tint glides. **1883** *Daily News* 3 Oct. 2/5 Reports of shrinking prices in China.

**2.** †**a.** Rebelling (against God); backsliding.

**1535** Coverdale *Isa.* xxx. 1 Wo be to those shrenkinge children.. which seke councel, but not at me. **1535** —— *Jer.* ix. 2 They be all adouotrers and a shrenckinge sorte. *Ibid.* xxxi. 22 How longe wilt thou go astraie, o thou shrenkinge [**1560** *Geneva* rebellious] doughter? **1564** *Brief Exam.* **iiij b, The shrinking & refusing Ministers of London. [**1565** J. Hall *Crt. Vertue* 63 Adulterers because they be And eke a shrynkyng sorte.]

**b.** Recoiling physically, mentally, or morally from what is difficult or distasteful; retiring.

**1742** C. Wesley *Hymn, 'Come, O thou Traveller unknown'*, What though my shrinking flesh complain. **1810** Southey *Kehama* XIV. xiv, The flames, which.. seem'd to dart Their hungry tongues toward their shrinking prey. **1848** Thackeray *Van. Fair* lxvi, She.. made a shrinking, but amicable, salutation to Major Dobbin. **1875** Manning *Miss. Holy Ghost* x. 263 If the will be soft, shrinking, inconstant, and cowardly. **1891** Meredith *One of our Conq.* xxx, Her mother's shrinking distaste from any such hectic themes as this.

†**c.** *shrinking shrub*: the sensitive plant.

**1640** Parkinson *Theat. Bot.* 1618, *Stirpanimans seu Frutex impatiens*, The shrinking shrubbe. **1659** R. Lovell *Herbal* 524 Shrinking shrub, *Herba impatiens*.

**d.** *shrinking violet*, a shy or modest person.

**1915** N. L. McClung *In Times like These* vi. 83 Voting will not be compulsory; the shrinking violets will not be torn from their shady fence-corner; the 'home bodies' will be able to still sit in rapt contemplation of their own fireside. **1949** E. Coxhead *Wind in West* iii. 83 You believe in the shrinking-violet technique, do you? **1966** R. Severn *Desperate Rendezvous* viii. 70 'Time will convince you both how indispensable I *have* been...' Wilson scowled. 'A real shrinking violet, aren't you?' he said. **1976** *Listener* 22 July 90/1 Frayn has not forgotten the underdog... The shrinking violet (as he rightly recognizes) is the most dangerous plant in the glades of privilege.

†**3.** Shivering, shuddering. *Obs.*

**1611** SHAKS. *Cymb.* IV. iv. 30 The shrinking Slaues of Winter.

Hence **'shrinkingly** *adv.*, in a shrinking manner, with a shrinking look, in a manner expressive of unwillingness, dislike, shyness, etc.; **'shrinkingness** (*rare*).

**1817** MOORE *Lalla Rookh, Veiled Prophet* II. 235 Her left hand, as shrinkingly she stood, Held a small lute. **1835** J. P. KENNEDY *Horseshoe Robinson* liii. (1860) 549 That feminine reserve and shrinkingness which we are wont to praise. **1851** G. W. CURTIS *Nile Notes* xxxv. 176 There was no light.. except what curious daylight stole shrinkingly in at the low door. **1858** DICKENS *Lett.* (1880) II. 47 When I peep shrinkingly from my study-windows. **1884** *Liverpool Merc.* 18 Feb. 5/2 Lord Salisbury and Sir Stafford Northcote appeal shrinkingly and indirectly for the reversion of the trust.

†**'shrinkling,** *vbl. sb. Obs.* In 6 -eling. [Cf. Sw. *skrynkla* to wrinkle, shrivel.] Contraction or drawing *together* (of the body).

**1545** RAYNOLD *Byrth Mankynde* 94 Yf she be..taken among in the laboryng with conuulsyon or shrinkeling together.

**shrink-wrapping** ('ʃrɪŋk,ræpɪŋ), *vbl. sb.* [f. SHRINK *v.* + WRAPPING *vbl. sb.*] The process of packaging an article by causing a thin plastic film to contract around it so as to cling tightly to its surface.

**1959** *Packaging & Display Encycl.* (ed. 5) IV. 352 Polyvinylidene films..are still mostly connected with the shrink-wrapping of meats. **1968** *Packaging* Feb. 61/2 The.. machine..represents a major forward step in the shrink-wrapping field. **1971** *British Printer* Jan. 99/2 Müller can now produce machinery for..shrink-wrapping.

Hence **'shrink-wrap** *sb.*, the plastic film used in shrink-wrapping; also (as a back-formation) as *v. trans.*; hence **'shrink-wrapped** *ppl. a.*; **'shrink-wrapper**, a machine used for shrink-wrapping.

**1961** *Packaging Rev. Data Bk.* 283/2 Oriented film..is under development as a shrink-wrap for poultry, hams, cheese and preserve pot covers. **1968** *Packaging* Feb. 61/2 One unit..replaces the tray-erector, product-loader, and shrink-wrapper. **1969** *Ibid.* Apr. 33 (*caption*) A..principle ..of..shrinkwrapping the entire load—in one continuous sequence. **1970** *Register of Packaging* 19 Up to 30 shrink wrapped packs per minute. **1978** *Listener* 20 July 73/3 Apples that..keep well..shrink-wrapped on the super-market shelves. **1981** *Times Lit. Suppl.* 30 Jan. 108/3 *The Writers' and Poets' Yearbook*..is cased in boards coated with a shrinkwrap, transparent laminate that looks like a badly fitting condom.

†**shrip,** *sb. Obs.* Forms: 3–4 schrippe, 4 shrippe, 5 s(c)hryppe; sherpe, shyrpe. [Parallel form to SCRIP *sb.*[1]; but the existence of the two forms is difficult to account for. Cf., however, Merovingian L. *schirpa, scirpa*, and *schrippa*, beside *scrippum*, OF. *escherpe, eschirpe*.] = SCRIP *sb.*[1]

*c* **1290** *S. Eng. Leg.* 41/259 A coppe of seluer stilleliche þis luþere Man gan bringue And dude in heore schrippe softeliche. **1362** LANGL. *P. Pl.* A. VI. 26 Sauh I neuer Palmere with pyk ne with schrippe [*v.r.* scrip] Such a seint seche bote now in þis place. *c* **1384** CHAUCER *H. Fame* 2123 (Fairf.), Pilgrimes With shrippes bret ful of lesenges. *a* **1400** *Octouian* 1357 Pyk and palm, schryppe and slaueyn He dyghte hym as palmer, queynt of gyn. **1426** LYDG. *De Guil. Pilgr.* 6220 Towchyng shyrpe & bordoun. **1568** TURNER *Herbal* III. 14 A shepehardes pouch or shrippe.

**shrip** (ʃrɪp), *v.* Now *dial.* Also shirp. [App. f. root **skrep-*: see SCREPE, SCRAPE, SHRAPE *vbs.* Cf. OE. (*ȝe*)*sceorpan* str. vb., to shave, shred (whence perh. the form *shirp*); also G. *schripfen, schrepfen, schrupfen*, dial. to cut off the tips of a growing plant.] *trans.* To shave, shred; to clip, lop, prune, trim.

**1609** C. BUTLER *Fem. Mon.* K 5 b, Put a brimstone-match in the one end beeing slit, and the other end beeing shript sticke into the side of the hoale. **1664** EVELYN *Sylva* 20 Being suffered to dry in the Sun upon the Branches, and the spray shrip'd off about the decrease in August. *Ibid.* 103 Brush-wood which is shripped off from the branches of Copse-wood. *Ibid.* (1776) 155 Such as they reserve for spears in Spain, they keep shriped up close to the stem. **1881** *Isle of Wight Gloss.*, *Shrip*, to clip a hedge, or cut hair close. **1893** *Wilts. Gloss.*, *Shirp*, or *Shrip*, (1) 'to shirp off', to shred or cut off a little of anything; (2) 'to shrip up', to shroud up the lower boughs of roadside trees, to cut off the side twigs of a hedge or bush.

Hence **shripping** *vbl. sb.*

**1634** WITHER *Embl.* IV. ix, I have seene such twiggs, afford them shade, By whom they were the meanest shrippings made, Of all the Wood. **1910** *Spectator* 16 Apr. 619/1 His [*sc.* a hedger's] work in some shires is known as 'shripping'.

†**shritch,** *sb. Obs.* Forms: α. 5 shryche, schryche, 6 shrich(e, 7 schriche. β. 7 shreech, shreitch. [f. SHRITCH *v.*; cf. SCRITCH *sb.*, SCREECH *sb.*[1]]

**1.** A screech, shriek.

α. **1470–85** MALORY *Arthur* XVIII. xii. 745 Sir Lauayn.. gaf a grete shryche and a merueillous gryfely grone. *a* **1586** SIDNEY *Arcadia* (1622) 383 Giuing a pitifull but sweet shrich. **1622** MABBE tr. *Aleman's Guzman d'Alf.* I. 145 Letting the light fall out of her hand for feare, shee gaue withall a great schriche. **1650** HOWELL *Giraffi's Rev. Naples.* I. 30 With howlings and unusuall schriches.

β. **1596** SPENSER *F.Q.* VI. iv. 18 Whose eares those shrieches shrill..did thrill. **1650** S. SHEPPARD *Candido* 21 With a loud shreitch she leaped out of the bed. **1652–62** HEYLIN *Cosmogr.* III. (1673) 104/2 With their fearful shreeches affrighting Passengers.

**2.** = SHRITCH-OWL.

*c* **1475** *Pict. Voc.* in Wr.-Wülcker 763/3 *Hic strix*, a schryche.

**shritch,** *v. Obs.* or *dial.* Forms: 3 schirche, 4 schriche, schryche, 6 shryche, shri(t)ch, 6, 9 schrich. *Pa. t.* and *pa. pple.* 4 schirȝt-e, shirt, 4–5 s(c)hriȝt-e, s(c)hright-e, s(c)hriht-e, -y-, sright-e; 4 schrichid, 5 shryched. [Parallel form to SCRITCH *v.*]

**1.** *intr.* To shriek, screech.

*a* **1250** *Owl & Night.* 223 Þu schirchest & ȝollest to þine fere. **13..** *K. Alis.* 5738 By Porus conseil hogges hy took, And beten hem so they shrightte. *c* **1330** *Arth. & Merl.* 4739 Þe folk schirsten [*read* schirȝten] so heiȝe & loude þat it schilled in to þe cloude. *Ibid.* 6403 Þe paiens schirt & made dol. *c* **1374** CHAUCER *Troylus* V. 320 The owle..Hath after me shright [*v.rr.* schriht, sright, shryght] alle þis nyghtes two. *c* **1386** —— *Nun Pr. T.* 580 (Camb. MS.), And ther-with all thei schrichid & schoutid. **1470–85** MALORY *Arthur* XXI. v. 850 The quenes and ladyes wepte and shryched that hit was pyte to here. **1557** *Tottel's Misc.* (Arb.) 238 And to the Gods and to the skies they shright. *a* **1575** GASCOIGNE *Posies, Flowers* 58, I..schrich to ease my morning minde. **1590** SPENSER *F.Q.* III. viii. 32 Downe in her lap she hid her face, and loudly shright. **1841** HARTSHORNE *Salopia Antiqua* 564 Schriching as soon as ivir yo touchen him.

**2.** *trans.* To utter with shrieking.

**1534** MORE *Comf. agst. Trib.* III. Wks. 1261/1 That hideous howling that those hel houndes shold shryche.

Hence †**shritching** *vbl. sb.* and *ppl. a.*

*c* **1374** CHAUCER *Troylus* V. 382 As rauenes qualm or schrychynge of thise owlis. **1398** TREVISA *Barth. De P.R.* VII. xxxvii. (1495) 436 Ulula is a foule that hathe that name of shrichynge and cryeng. **1576** GASCOIGNE *Philomene* 22 The Throstle she, which makes the wood to ring With shryching lowde.

†**shritch-owl.** *Obs.* 6 shryche-, shritch-, shriech-, schreech-, 6–7 shriche-, 7 shreech, 8 schrich-. [f. SHRITCH *v.* + OWL *sb.* Cf. SCRITCH-OWL.] = SHRIEK-OWL.

**1538** ELYOT *Dict.*, *Striges*, shryche oules. *a* **1586** SIDNEY *Arcadia* II. (1605) 157 Casting forth as pitifull cries as any shrich-owle. **1595** SPENSER *Epithal.* 345 Let not the shriech Oule, nor the Storke be heard. **1596** SHAKS. *3 Hen. VI*, II. vi. 56 That fatall Schreechowle. **1603** DRAYTON *Bar. Wars* V. xlii. 112 Vnder his eaue th buzzing shreechowle sings. **1761** ELIZ. CARTER in *Mem.* (1808) I. 230 We wanted..to have the ground planted with yew and cypress,..and restore the schrich owls and ravens.

†**shrite.** *Obs.* Also 7 shreight. [Of obscure origin: cf. SHREITCH and SHRIKE *sb.*[2] (*dial.* = missel-thrush).] The missel-thrush.

**1668** WILKINS *Real Char.* II. v. §3. 149 Missle-Bird, Shreight. **1678** RAY *Willughby's Ornith.* 187 The Missel-bird or Shrite; Turdus viscivorus major. [**1802** MONTAGU *Ornith. Dict.* **1839** MACGILLIVRAY *Brit. Birds* II. 114.]

**shrivalty,** obs. form of SHRIEVALTY.

**shrive,** *sb. rare.* [f. next.] Used for SHRIFT *sb.* 9.

**1867** 'OUIDA' *Idalia* viii, When they met again, he swore it should be for shorter shrive and deadlier work.

**shrive** (ʃraɪv), *v. arch.* Pa. t. shrove (ʃrəʊv), Pa. pple. shriven ('ʃrɪv(ə)n). Forms: 1 scrífan, 2–6 scrive, (3 ssriwe), 3–4 ssrive, -y-, screve, sc(h)rif, 3–6 schrive, -y-, 4 shrif(e, shryf(f)e, schreve, 4–5 schryf, 4–6 shryve, (5 schrywe, shrevy, 6 schriffe, *Sc.* schryif, schirryve, 6, 8–9 *pseudo-arch.* schrieve, 7 shreeve), 4– shrive. Pa. t. 1 -scráf, 3–4 ssrof, 4– 5 schro(o)f, (4 shroof, schroff, shref (?), 5 shroff, shrofe, shroef, scherof, shrow), 4– shrove; *north.* 3–4 scraf, 4 s(c)hraf, 4–5 schrafe, 5 shraiff, shrafe, shrave, 6 schrave; *wk.* 4–5 s(c)hryved, 7–9 shrived. *Pa. pple.* 1 ȝescrifen, 2 iscrifen, 3 ischrive(n, 3–4 i-, ys(s)rive, 4–5 i-, ys(c)hryve(n; 3 shrifen, 3–4 scriven, 4 schrive(n, scryven, -wen, schrif(f)yne, schryfyne, 4–5 shrive, schreve, -yn, 4–6 s(c)hryve, -en, (5 schrifen, schryvin, shrivin, shrevyn, schrywe, screffe), 5–6 shreve(n, (6 schreven, -in, shereven, shervon, shryff); *wk.* 6 shriev'd, shriv'd, 9 shrived. [Com. Teut. (wanting in Gothic): OE. *scrífan (-scráf, scrifon, ȝe-scrifen)*, to allot, assign, decree, adjudge, impose as a sentence, impose penance, regard, care for, corresp. to OFris. *scrîva (skref, skreven)*, to write, impose penance (WFris. *skriuwe, skreau, skreaun*, NFris. *skriiw, skreew, skrewen*, EFris. *schriuwe* to write), OS. *skrîban* to write, (M)LG. *schrîven, schreev, schrêven*, MDu. *schrîven, screef, ghescrêven* to write, paint, describe (Du. *schrijven, schreef, geschreven*), OHG. *scrîban*, MHG. *scrîben, schreip, geschriben* to write, draw, paint, describe, appoint, prescribe (G. *schreiben, schrieb, geschrieben*), ON. and Icel. (weak and with short *i*) *skrifa, -aða, -aðr* to paint, write, MSw. *skriva, -adhe, -adhu*, (strong) *skref, skrivin*, Sw. *skrifva, skref, skrifven*, Da. *skrive, skrev, skreven* (locally also weak); ad. L. *scrībere* to write.]

**1.** *trans.* In OE. (const. dat.) To impose penance upon (a person); hence, to administer absolution to; to hear the confession of.

*a* **776** *Poenit. Ecgberti* II. xvi. in Thorpe *Anc. Laws* (1840) II. 188 Ne hire nan preost scrifan ne mot ær heo þone sinscipe forlæte. *a* **975** *Canons of Edgar* lxv. ibid. 258 We lærað þæt ælc preosta scrife & dædbote tæce þam þe him andette. **1027–34** *Laws Cnut* II. lxviii. §1 A man sceal þam unstrangan men..liþelicor deman & scrifon þonne þam strangan. *c* **1175** *Lamb. Hom.* 25 Ȝif ic forlete þe preost walde eskien on ester dei hwa me scriue. *c* **1200** ORMIN 15253 Þatt lærede genge, Þatt iss ȝuw sett abufenn.. To spellenn ȝuw off Crisstenndom, To shrifenn ȝuw & huslenn. *c* **1205** LAY. 18392 Ælc mon scriuen oðer swulc hit weoren his broðer. **138.** *Pol. Poems* (Rolls) I. 265 Be war that no frer ham shryfe. **1470–85** MALORY *Arth.* XXI. x. 855 He..prayed the bysshop to shryue hym and assoyle hym. **1579** HAKE *Newes out of Powles* iii. (1872) C vij, Wyse man you are no doubt..the Vicar of saint Fooles Go shriue you. **1633** FORD *'Tis Pity* II. E, Giue me leaue To shriue her; lest shee should dye vn-absolu'd. **1798** COLERIDGE *Anc. Mar.* VII. xiv, O shrieve me, shrieve me, holy man! **1808** SCOTT *Marm.* I. xxi, He shall shrieve penitent no more. **1841** JAMES *Corse de Leon* ii, 'I will go with you..to shrive the dying', said the priest. **1849** MACAULAY *Hist. Eng.* iv. I. 436 He found that none of her chaplains knew English or French enough to shrive the king. **1889** JESSOPP *Coming of Friars* v. 219 There was none to shrive them.

const. *of* (the sin).

*c* **1205** LAY. 32074 He þe scal scriuen of þine weorld lifen þat þine sunen alle scullen þe from falle. *a* **1300** *Cursor M.* 23151 Vnnethes sal man find an in lede þat wel will scriue þam o þis sake. **1525** *St. Papers Hen. VIII* (1836) IV. 419 To schriffe or absolve yaim of thaire synnys.

**b.** with extended application.

**1607** T. D[EKKER ?] & WILKINS *Jests* 18 Three waiting gentlewomen sitting vp late one euening began to shriue one another, and to know what manner of Louers each other had. **1829** POE *Tamerlane* Poems (1859) 206 Earth may shrive me of the sin Unearthly pride hath revelled in. **1881** O'SHAUGHNESSY *Songs of Worker* 17 To tell the folk of love, of love to ease The burdens of their labour and their heart, Of love to shrive them of their sin. **1912** *Engl. Rev.* Dec. 144 Europe has become for the first time a Christian civilisation, shriven at last by the unChristian materialism of Bismarckian blood and iron.

**c.** *absol.* or *intr.* To perform the office of a confessor; to exercise the ministry of absolution; to hear confessions. *rare.*

*c* **1000–50** *De Off. Episc.* xi, Ofer ealle þa scire þe he on scrife. **1377** LANGL. *P. Pl.* B. xx. 302 Conscience called a leche þat coude wel shryue. *c* **1440** *Promp. Parv.* 449/1 Schryvyn, or here schryftys, *audire confessiones.* **1579** SPENSER *Sheph. Cal.* Aug. 55 A holly eue..When holly fathers wont to shrieue. **1855** MACAULAY *Hist. Eng.* xvii. IV. 90 Priests were praying, preaching, shriving, holding up the host and the cup.

**2.** *pass.* To 'take shrift' (see SHRIFT *sb.* 1); to be confessed; to make one's confession and receive absolution and penance. Const. †*of*, *by*, †*at*, †*with*, or †*to* the confessor.

*c* **1000** ÆLFRIC *Saints' Lives* xii. 291 Eow ȝebyrað þæt ȝe beon ȝescrifene on ðissere wucan oððe huru on ðære oðre. *c* **1175** *Lamb. Hom.* 27 Ȝif he bið wel iscrifen and godfurht. *a* **1225** *Ancr. R.* 332 Ase ofte ase ich am ischriuen euer me þuncheð me unschriuen. *a* **1300** *Vox & Wolf* 176 in Hazl. *E.P.P.* I. 64 Were thou i-sriue, And sunnen heuedest al forsake. *c* **1300** *Havelok* 2489 Hwan..he was wit þe prestes shriue. *c* **1375** *Sc. Leg. Saints* iii. (*De Sancto Andrea*) 898 To na man will I schriffyne be bot anerly to ȝow. *c* **1386** CHAUCER *Sompn. T.* 387, I haue be shryuen [*v.rr.* schryue, schreue] this day at my curat. *a* **1400** *Leg. Rood* 195 Wat man ..For his sinnus sori and schereuen be. *c* **1425** *Cast. Persev.* 550 in *Macro Plays* 93 Þanne schal he deye, & not be schrywe. *c* **1440** *Pol. Rel. & L. Poems* 159 *note*, Yff thowe be screffe. **1470–85** MALORY *Arth.* Table of Contents 26 How he was shryuen to an heremyte. *c* **1530** LD. DORSET in Ellis *Orig. Lett.* Ser. III. II. 148 It were petie he shuld be hanged tyll he had ben well shereven. **1555** MACHYN *Diary* (Camden) 94 To be shryff and fast iij days in on wyke. *c* **1570** *Durham Depositions* (Surtees) 160 Elizabeth Watson..hard no preiching, nor was shervon. **1570–6** LAMBARDE *Peramb. Kent* (1826) 209 You ought first to bee shriven of one of the Monkes. **1575** *Gammer Gurton* V. ii, Since Diccon hath confession made & is so cleane shreue. **1592** SHAKS. *Rom. & Jul.* II. iv. 194 She shall at Frier Lawrence Cell Be shriu'd and married. **1596** DRAYTON *Legends* iv. 861 So he were shriev'd, what need he care a pin? **1848** LYTTON *Harold* i, He died but shriven and absolved. **1882** 'OUIDA' *Maremma* i, Straightway would he go to the church and be shriven.

const. *of*, rarely *from* (the sin).

*c* **1200** *Trin. Coll. Hom.* 59 We agen alle to ben shrifene of ure synnes her we biginnen to fasten. *a* **1300** *Cursor M.* 26401 O þaa Sinnes þou was of scriuen a. *c* **1400** *St. Alexius* (Laud 622) 338 Euery sonenday houseled he was, And shryuen also of vche trespas. **1481** CAXTON *Reynard* xii. (Arb.) 25 Yf I were shryuen of my synnes, my soule shold be the clerer. **1821** JOANNA BAILLIE *Metr. Leg.*, *Columbus* iii, Souls..from trespass shriven.

**3.** *refl.* To make one's confession, go to confession, confess.

*a* **1225** *Ancr. R.* 68 Sum uniseli, hwon heo seide þet heo schrof hire, haueð ischriuen hire al to wundre. *a* **1300** *Cursor M.* 26398 Þan behouis him screue him halli. **1390** GOWER *Conf.* I. 61 Tell forth my Sone, and schrif the clene. *c* **1400** MAUNDEV. (Roxb.) xiii. 59 Þai say Godd bad neuer þat a man schuld schryfe him till anoþer man. *a* **1450** *Knt. de la Tour* (1868) 13 And so she shroue her and was sethe of holy lyff. **1530** PALSGR. 706/1, I wyll shrive me this lente at the Augustyne fryres, for there is pardon. **1533** GAU *Richt Vay* To Rdr. 3 Quhow men and vemen sal scriue thayme and quhou thay sal rekkine al thair sinnis to thair schrift fader. **1577** VAUTROUILLIER *Luther on Ep. Gal.* 237, I was wont to shriue my selfe with great deuotion. **1641** PRYNNE *Antipathie* 40 King Iohn..was poysoned..by a Monke of that House; who went to the Abbot and shrived himselfe.

**1859** TENNYSON *Elaine* 1094 Bid call the ghostly man Hither, and let me shrive me clean, and die.

const. *of* (the sin).

*a* **1225** *Ancr. R.* 266 Schrif þe þerof to morwen. *a* **1300** *Cursor M.* 26408 Þof þou scraf þe o þi dede. *c* **1386** CHAUCER *Pars. T.* ¶ 106 Priuee synnes of whiche they shryue hem priuely. *c* **1440** *Jacob's Well* 178 Þe chanoun . . schroof hym to þe bysschop of þat synne. **1456** SIR G. HAYE *Law Arms* (S.T.S.) 16 The veniall synnis that commounly men schryvis thame of here.

†**b.** with extended application. Also const. *of* (Sc.): To renounce. *Obs.*

*c* **1374** CHAUCER *Troylus* II. 440 Here I me shryue and seye That wikkedly ye don vs boþe deye. **1500–20** DUNBAR *Poems* ix. 9 To The, my sweit Saluiour, I me schirryve. *Ibid.* 137, I schryve me of all cursit cumpany. *a* **1529** SKELTON *Bouge of Court* 215 To you oonly, me thynke, I durste shryue me For now am I . . dysposed To shewe you thynges that may not be disclosed. *a* **1568** *Bannatyne MS.* (Hunter. Club) 92 Ryse with thi ransoner fro deid, And the of all thy synnys schryfe. **1625** GILL *Sacr. Philos.* i. 4 [Zeus] that shreeves himselfe to his wife Iuno for all his slipperie pranks.

**4.** *intr.* To confess one's sins, go to confession.

*a* **1300** *Cursor M.* 26600 And for þe scam man thinc scriuand, It sal for part o penance stand. **1390** GOWER *Conf.* I. 317 We ben sett to schryve of love. *c* **1425** *Eng. Conq. Irel.* 130 The wolf spake to hym, and shroue [*c* **1440** *Rawl. MS.* confeste hyr] to þe preste. *c* **1450** *St. Cuthbert* (Surtees) 1625 He wald . . of his synnes to him schryue þat he synned in all his lyue. *c* **1532** DU WES *Introd. Fr.* in *Palsgr.* 1069 The preest [in the mass] . . fyrst shrivyng to us. **1802** SCOTT *Gray Brother* xxx, And who art thou, thou Gray Brother, That I should shrive to thee? **1832** HAWKER *Cornish Ball.* (1908) 19 'Tis not to pray—'tis not to shrive—Therefore, what does she there? **1844** MRS. BROWNING *Brown Rosary* I. x, A nun . . Who mocked at the priest when he called her to shrive.

†**b.** Rendering L. *confiteri* of the Vulgate: To ascribe praise and glory *to* God. *Obs.*

*a* **1300** *E.E. Psalter* vii. 18, I sal schrive to Laverd after his rightwisnes. *a* **1325** *Prose Psalter* xxix. 4 Syngeþ to our Lord . . and shryueþ to þe mynde of his holinesse. *a* **1340** HAMPOLE *Psalter* vi. 5 He is noght . . in hell wha sall shrife til þe. *a* **1400** *Prymer* (1891) 71, I schal schryue to thee lord in al myn herte.

†**5.** *trans.* To confess (sins). *Obs.*

*a* **1300** *Cursor M.* 27105 To preist his sinnes scriue. *c* **1380** WYCLIF *Wks.* (1880) 330 [Ps. xxxii. 6], I seide, i shulde shryue my synnes aȝens me to þee, lord. *c* **1450** *St. Cuthbert* (Surtees) 7081 And all þe case to him he shraue.

†**b.** *transf.* To reveal, disclose. *Obs.*

*c* **1374** CHAUCER *Troylus* II. 579 Now haue I plat to yow myn herte schryuen. *a* **1500** *Chaucer's Dreme* 2026 C.'s Wks. (1598) 365 b, Al my secre to you I plaine, and shriue. **1818** KEATS *Isabella* viii, I cannot live Another night, and not my passion shrive.

**6.** To forgive, pardon (a sin). *rare.*

The first quot. is doubtful.

**1303** R. BRUNNE *Handl. Synne* 588 Ȝyf þou trowyst synne shal be forȝeue withoute repentaunce & shryue [*v.r.* repente here & be clene schreuyn]. **1837** HOOD *Desert-Born* 126 'Nay then', cried I—(heav'n shrive the lie!) 'to tell the secret truth.'

†**7. a.** To question, examine (a person). *Obs.*

**1592** NASHE *P. Penilesse* G 2, Beleeue me, thou shriuest me very neere in this latter demaund. **1596** SPENSER *F.Q.* IV. xii. 26 She gan him soft to shrieue. **1610** G. FLETCHER *Christ's Vict. Earth* xxxvii, Gently our Saviour shee began to shrive, Whither he wear the Sonne of God, or no.

†**b.** ? To inquire into (a matter). *Obs.*

**1651** CLEVELAND *Poems* 37 Shrive but their Titles, and their money poize, A laird & twenty pound pronounc'd with noise, When construed, but for a plain Yeoman go, And a good sober two-pence.

**8. a.** To relieve (one) *of* a burden; †to rob.

**1604** DEKKER *Honest Wh.* Wks. 1873 II. 169, I am here for shriuing those two fooles of their sinfull packe. **1899** R. BRIDGES *Poems, Fair Brass* 21 A . . tomb: Such as to look on shrives The heart of half its care.

**b.** To remove, lift (a burden) *from. rare.*

[**1641** MILTON *Animadv.* Wks. 1851 III. 236 To shreeve the purses of unconfessing and unmortify'd sinners]. **1812** BYRON *Ch. Har.* II. lxxviii, To shrive from man his weight of mortal sin.

†**9.** *pass.* ? To be bound in an obligation. *Obs.*

**1338** R. BRUNNE *Chron.* (1725) 138 The barons & þe clergie in on wer alle schryuen, Vnto kyng Henrie ageyn William suld be gyuen.

†**10.** *trans.* To reconcile (a person) *to* a course of action. *Obs.*

**1587** FLEMING *Contn. Holinshed* III. 1325/2 To reconcile, shriue, & win hir maiesties subiects to their diuelish intent. **1594** NASHE *Terrors Nt.* D 1 Much wonder I how treason and murder dispense with the darknes of the night, how they can shriue themselues to it.

†**11.** Const. gen. in OE., *of* in ME.: To reck of, care for. *Obs.*

*c* **897** ÆLFRED *Gregory's Past. C.* xliv. 322 Ne he ne scrife ðæs hlisan buton hu he ryhtost wyrce. *Ibid.* lv, Hi ne scrifon hwæðer hit wære ðe dæȝ ðe niht ðonne ðonne hi synȝodon. *a* **1000** *Boeth. Metr.* x. 29 Deað þæs ne scrifeð. **13..** *K. Alis.* 3884 (Bodl. MS.), Alisaunder nouȝth of hym shroof [*Linc. Inn MS.* gaf] Ac perciens to fore hym droof.

**shrive**, obs. form of SHERIFF.

ˈ**shrivel**, *sb.* Also 6 **shrevel**. [f. SHRIVEL *v.*] Something shrivelled up; †*pl.* wrinkles in the skin; a shrivelled skin; a contracted word.

**1547** BOORDE *Brev. Health* II. lviii. (1557) Cj, Rvge is the latin woorde. In Englishe it is named shreuels whiche is a runninge together of the skyn in a mans face and necke. **1835** *Blackw. Mag.* XXXVIII. 153 We caught an eel, which we skinned, and wore the shrivel for many a day round our ankle. **1873** F. HALL *Mod. Engl.* 163 Nor is any regard for rule or regularity to be seen . . in our decurtate *cab, cent, chap* . . or in such shrivels as *aid, alms*.

**shrivel** (ˈʃrɪv(ə)l), *v.* Also 7 **shriule**. [Origin unknown. (Cf. Sw. dial. *skryvla* to wrinkle.)]

**1.** *intr.* To become contracted and wrinkled or curled up, as from great heat or cold. Also with *up, away*.

**1612** T. TAYLOR *Comm. Titus* ii. 13 That shortly the heauens themselues shall shriule away like a scrowle. **1706** PHILLIPS (ed. Kersey), To *Shrivel*, to Wrinkle, to run up in Wrinkles or Scrolls. **1707** MORTIMER *Husb.* (1721) II. 312 When the Stalks begin to shrivel at the part next the Branch. **1796** WITHERING *Brit. Plants* (ed. 3) IV. 171 This elegant little Agaric is seldom found in full perfection, as it soon shrivels and loses its brilliant colours. **1805** SCOTT *Last Minstr.* VI. xxxi, When, shriveling like a parched scroll, The flaming heavens together roll. **1842** LOUDON *Suburban Hort.* 585 The incipient bunches twist and shrivel up just before coming into bloom. **1843** R. J. GRAVES *Syst. Clin. Med.* 392 Two . . ulcers which speedily scabbed, shrunk and shrivelled away. **1882** VINES tr. *Sachs' Bot.* 457 It forms a papilla . . at the apex which shrivels when the spore ripens.

*pass.* **1588** GREENE *Perimedes* 11 Hir face shriueled, and parched with the Sunne. **1604** N. F. *Fruiterers Secrets* 27 When Pippins, and other long lasting fruite, begin to be shriueled. **1798** FERRIAR *Illustr. Sterne* iv. 110 That his nose might be shrivelled with cold. **1825** T. HOOK *Sayings* Ser. II. *Passion & Princ.* v, The lamb was shrivelled up to a cinder. **1885** CLODD *Myths & Dr.* I. iii. 22 So scorched was it . . that it was shrivelled to the smallest of creatures.

**b.** *transf.* and *fig.* To be reduced to an inanimate or inefficient condition; (of a person) to shrink physically or mentally.

**1680** H. MORE *Apocal. Apoc.* 60 This Pagan Hierarchy shrivelled up with all the false Deities, and Priests therein. **1818** SCOTT *Br. Lamm.* xx, I swore that my rage and revenge should pursue his enemies, until they shrivelled before me like that scorched-up symbol of annihilation. **1835** LYTTON *Rienzi* v. v, I felt his soul shrivel at my gaze. **1875** FARRAR *Silence & Voices* ii. 37 All life shrivelled into a miserable 'if' and an empty 'might have been'. **1887** JESSOPP *Arcady* iii. 70 Undeveloped faculties that shrivel for want of using.

**2.** *trans.* To cause to be contracted or shrunk into wrinkles. Often with *up*.

**1608** SHAKS. *Per.* II. iv. 9 A fire from heaven came and shrivell'd up Their bodies. **1682** GREW *Anat. Pl.* 10 Lest its new access into the Ayr, should shrivel it. **1751** SMOLLETT *Per. Pickle* cv, Crabtree shrivelling up his face like an autumn leaf. **1782** A. MONRO *Compar. Anat.* (ed. 3) 5 This . . covers the trunk, serving to shrivel the skin, in order to drive off insects. **1856** MRS. STOWE *Dred* xxxiv, That fearful collapse, which . . shrivels the most healthy countenance . . to the shrunken . . image of decrepit old age. **1877** THOMSON *Voy. Challenger* I. i. 17 In the tropics a saturated solution is much too strong, and shrivels up delicate tissues.

**b.** *transf.* and *fig.* To reduce to inanition, helplessness, or ineffectualness.

**1663** BP. PATRICK *Parab. Pilgr.* viii. (1687) 30 This is ever the fruit of hard and penurious thoughts of God, that they shrivel up mens hearts too. **1683** HOWE *Union Prot.* Wks. 1862 IV. 266 The want of such a diffusive love shuts up and shrivels the destitute parts. **1824–9** LANDOR *Imag. Conv.* Wks. 1846 I. 68 Milton . . shrivelled up the lips of his revilers by the austerity of his scorn. **1844** DICKENS *Chimes* iii, Wither me and shrivel me, and free me from the dreadful thoughts that tempt me in my youth! **1859** *Habits Gd. Society* ix. 284 How the very thought must have shrivelled her up. **1901** *Scotsman* 12 Mar. 7/4 A passage which the House listened to very closely, fully realising how it finally shrivelled up malignant gossip.

ˈ**shriveldy**, *a.* [f. SHRIVELLED + -Y.] Withered.

**1840** MRS. TROLLOPE *M. Armstrong* iii, A poor rickety, shriveldy sort of a child.

†ˈ**shriveling.** *Obs. rare.* [f. SHRIVE *v.* + -LING.] Contemptuous term for: One under spiritual direction.

**1603** HARSNET *Pop. Impost.* 104 He comforts his holy shriuelings, his ghostly good children, telling them . . [etc.].

**shrivelled** (ˈʃrɪv(ə)ld), *ppl. a.* Also 6 **shryveled**, 7–8 **shrivel'd**, 7– (now *U.S.*) **shriveled**. [f. SHRIVEL *v.* + -ED[1].] Drawn together or contracted so as to have or form wrinkles and to appear as if dried up.

**1565** STAPLETON tr. *Bede's Hist. Ch. Eng.* 173 The vayne and soyle of that grounde is not shryueled nor fleaten, but grene and full of grasse. **1633** G. HERBERT *Temple, Flower* ii, Who would have thought my shrivel'd heart Could have recover'd greenesse? **1665** SIR T. HERBERT *Trav.* (1677) 26 The Mannatee . . her face is like a shriveled Buffolo or Cow. **1697** DRYDEN *Virg. Georg.* I. 158 When . . shrivell'd Herbs on with'ring Stems decay. **1726** POPE *Odyss.* XIX. 88 These lean shrivelled limbs unnerved with age. **1770** *Phil. Trans.* LX. 304 A poor shriveled-up . . carcase of a bird. **1816** SCOTT *Old Mort.* xxxix, Pushing him back from her with her trembling hand and shrivelled arm. **1830** M. DONOVAN *Dom. Econ.* I. 91 Malt that is shrivelled is not of the best quality. **1882** W. BALLANTINE *Exper.* vi. 63, I never saw him without thinking of a shrivelled crab apple.

**b.** Of persons whose skin is wrinkled or whose limbs are withered or 'dried up'.

**1605** B. JONSON *Volpone* II. i, Your shrivell'd sallad-eating artizans. **1824** W. IRVING *T. Trav.* II. 114 A shrivelled old lady, with a face of parchment. **1846** MRS. GORE *Engl. Char.* (1852) 100 The name of French Cook conveys to the popular mind the image of a lean and shrivelled individual in a white nightcap and apron. **1877** TENNYSON *Harold* III. i, I, old shrivell'd Stigand.

**c.** *transf.* and *fig.* Contracted, reduced to small proportions.

**1628** DONNE *Serm.* (1660) III. iii. 37 That shiver'd, and shrivel'd, and ravel'd, and ruin'd soule. **1685** *Reflect. on Baxter* 11 Such a shriveled account as R. B. gives of this Chapter. **1883** S. C. HALL *Retrospect* II. 115 A repulsive countenance . . indicative of a naturally shrivelled heart and contracted soul.

**d.** *Comb.*

**1850** R. G. CUMMING *Hunter's Life S. Afr.* vii. 147 An extremely ancient and shrivelled-looking Bushman. **1859** BOYD *Recreat. Country Parson* Ser. I. viii. 303 Some utilitarian old hunks, sharp-nosed, shrivelled-faced.

**shrivelling** (ˈʃrɪv(ə)lɪŋ), *vbl. sb.* [f. SHRIVEL *v.* + -ING[1].] The action of the verb SHRIVEL.

*a* **1631** DONNE *Serm.* (1649) II. xv. 126 A shriveling of my flesh with superstitious and meritorious fastings. **1667** *Phil. Trans.* II. 454 Some shriveling of the outward skin of the Bark. **1842** LOUDON *Suburban Hort.* 441 Ventilation by continual currents of air . . acts in the same way as light, in producing shrivelling. **1883** *Sunday Mag.* July 435/2 The shrivelling of the Eastern Roman empire. **1899** *Allbutt's Syst. Med.* VIII. 600 If the sclerotic shrivelling be well-marked.

ˈ**shrivelling**, *ppl. a.* [f. SHRIVEL *v.* + -ING[2].] That shrivels; *Bot.* = MARCESCENT.

**1776** WITHERING *Bot. Arrangem. Veget.* 258 Stitchwort. . . Petals . . flat; oblong; shrivelling. **1816** A. BOSWELL *Sheldon Haughs* (1830) 167 Stealin change o' shriv'lin time Had quench'd the vigour o' his prime. **1849** DE QUINCEY *Engl. Mail Coach* Wks. 1854 IV. 345 Like a shrivelling scroll from before the wrath of fire! **1873** MISS BROUGHTON *Nancy* I. 33 Oh, spring! spring! with all your searching east winds, with your late shrivelling frost.

**shriven** (ˈʃrɪv(ə)n), *ppl. a.* [pa. pple. of SHRIVE *v.*] Confessed, absolved.

**1846** DICKENS *Pict. Italy, Ital. Dream*, I had my foot upon the spot, where . . the shriven prisoner was strangled. **1896** A. AUSTIN *England's Darling* II. iii, As every shriven soul must answer Him Whose Sceptre doth not pass.

**shriver** (ˈʃraɪvə(r)). [f. SHRIVE *v.* + -ER[1].] One who shrives, a confessor.

**1340** *Ayenb.* 140 Þe ssrifte ssel by yhol, naȝt todeld ine vele ssriveres. **1393** LANGL. *P. Pl.* C. I. 64 Holy churche & charite choppe a doun swich shryuers. **1483** *Cath. Angl.* 338/2 A schryfer, *confessor*. **1593** SHAKS. *3 Hen. VI*, III. ii. 108 When hee was made a Shriuer, 'twas for shift. **1637** N. WHITING *Albino & Bellama* 83 The shreevers to their Lords returne with smiles. **1661** K. W. *Conf. Char., Temporizer* (1860) 51 Turne shrivers in nuneries.

ˈ**shriving**, *vbl. sb.* [f. SHRIVE *v.* + -ING[1].] The action of the verb SHRIVE, shrift: **a.** Confession; **b.** the hearing of confessions.

*a* **1225** *Ancr. R.* 268 Lease swefnes, & false scheauwinges [*MS. T* schriuinges]. *a* **1300** *Cursor M.* 26101 To quam we sal vr scriuing mak. *c* **1400** *Rom. Rose* 6448 Who so hath in his felyng The consequence of such shryuyng. **1591** SPENSER *M. Hubberd* 543 Better a short tale, than a bad long shriuing. **1664** H. MORE *Myst. Iniq.* xxi. 81 Those that by this Shriving of persons know much of their Interest or disinterest. **1694** MOTTEUX *Rabelais* IV. xlix. 192 As for shriving, . . there can be no great harm in't. **1837** CARLYLE *Fr. Rev.* III. IV. i, To the Priest they send her she gives thanks; but needs not any shriving. **1875** J. C. COX *Churches Derbysh.* I. 171 After shriving had gone out of fashion the ringing of the bell [on Shrove Tuesday] was continued.

**c.** *attrib.* as ***shriving time***; †**shriving cloth**, sackcloth worn by penitents; †**shriving pew, seat, stool**, a confessional.

**1487–8** *Rec. St. Mary at Hill* (1904) 130 For naylles for þe schryvyng peawe. **1505** in H. J. Feasey *Holy Wk. Cerem.* (1897) 97 vj yernes perteynyng to the shryvyng stole for Lenton. **1534** *Engl. Ch. Furniture* (1866) 204 An altar cloth made of shryvynge clothes. **1545** *Churchw. Acc. St. Dunstan's, Canterb.* (MS.) For mendyng of ye Chyrche and makyng of ye schrewyng sett xiiijd. **1589–90** in J. C. Cox *Churchw. Acc.* (1913) 193 Payd for mendinge of a pewe called the shrivinge pewe 1s. **1602** SHAKS. *Ham.* v. ii. 47 He should the bearers put to sodaine death, Not shriuing time allowed.

**shroad**, obs. f. SHREWD.

**shrob(be**, obs. ff. SHRUB.

**shrode**, obs. f. SHREWD, SHROUD.

**shroe**, obs. f. SHREW *sb.*

**shroff** (ʃrɒf), *sb.* Also 7 **sheroff, -affe, -iffe, sharoffe, sherrafe, shraff, shrofe**, 7–8 **sheraff**. [Anglo-Indian corruption of SARAF.] A banker or money-changer in the East; in the Far East, a native expert employed to detect bad coin.

**1618** in Foster *Engl. Factories Ind.* (1906) 8 The sheraffs are poore and begerly. **1621** *Ibid.* 265 Wee cannot put of oure ryalls but as that onely sharoffe please to take them. *Ibid.* 352 Shrofes. **1625** PURCHAS *Pilgrims* II. 1431 Twelve Sheriffes that is men to buy and sell Pearles, Diamonds, and other pretious Stones, and to exchange Gold and Silver. **1698** FRYER *Acc. E. India & P.* 52 Amongst whom were Shroffs, or Money-changers. **1776** *Trial of Nundocomar* 22/2 It is the custom of Shroffs to get the body of the bond wrote by their Gomastahs, and they sign it with their own hands. **1816** 'QUIZ' *Grand Master* II. 18 The breakfast soon dispatch'd, they're off, To borrow money from a shroff. **1888** KIPLING *Departm. Ditties* (ed. 3) 81 Deeply indebted to the village shroff. **1904** *North-China Herald* 27 May 1121/3 A shroff employed by Messrs. Musterberg & Co.

*attrib.* **1882** '*Fan Kwae' at Canton* 58, I have heard of as much as fifty taels (about $70) being paid to an important Shroff-shop for such a transaction.

Hence **shroff** *v. trans.*, to examine (coin) in order to separate the genuine from the base; also *absol.*; whence **shroffing** *vbl. sb.* and *ppl. a.*; ***shroffing school***, a school in which the art of detecting false coin is taught.

**1757** CLIVE in Beveridge *Hist. India* (1862) I. 592 [In vain did Clive represent that] the money could not be divided till it was shroffed. **1860** T. L. PEACOCK *Gryll Grange* xviii, Two stock-jobbing Jews, and a shroffing Parsee. **1878** H. A. GILES *Gloss. Ref.* 129 (Yule) Shroffing schools are common in Canton, where teachers of the art keep bad dollars for the purpose of exercising their pupils. **1882** '*Fan Kwae' at Canton* 55 The process of shroffing which it [money] underwent before being deposited in the treasury. **1906** *Sat. Rev.* 14 Apr. 451/1 The potential revenues of China are immense, but they are 'shroffed'..by every hand through which they pass.

**shroffage** ('ʃrɒfɪdʒ). Also 7 **shraffage, sherofferage.** [f. prec. + -AGE. Cf. 16th cent. It. *xarafaggio*, Sp. *cerafagio*.] The commission charged for shroffing coin.

**1629** in Foster *Engl. Factories India* (1909) III. 354 Shraffage is halfe a riall per every thousand rialls. **1676** STREYNSHAM MASTER *Diaries* (1911) I. 394 The Councell doe know that there is a Sherofferage..allowed in all these parts. **1766** T. BROOKS *Coins E. Indies* 49 Brokerage 1½ per Cent. Shroffage 1 per Thousand. **1817** *By-Laws Levant Co.* 24 Commission and shroffage on cash remitted from one part of the dominions of the Grand Signior to another..1 per cent.

**shroffe**, obs. variant of SHRUFF[2].

**Shroftide, Shroft Tuesday,** obs. ff. SHROVE-TIDE, SHROVE TUESDAY.

**shrog.** *north. dial.* [Parallel to SCROG; see SCR-.] A bush; also *pl.* underwood.

*c* **1460** *Towneley Myst.* xiii. 455, I haue soght with my dogys All horbery shrogys. **15..** *Robyn Hood & Guy of Gisborne* 113 They cutt them down two summer shroggs, That grew both under a breere. **1601** MUNDAY *Downf. Earl Huntingdon* III. ii. E4b, From Barnsdale shrogs, to Notinghams red cliffes. **1703** THORESBY in Ray *Philos. Lett.* (1718) 336 *Shrogs*, a company of Bushes, of Hazel, Thorns, briers. **1824** [CARR] *Craven Gloss.*, *Shrogs*, bushes or underwood.

**shroge**, obs. form of SHRUG.

**Shropshire** ('ʃrɒpʃə(r)). The name (in OE. *Scrobscír*, *Scrobbesbyriȝscír*) of a west-midland county of England, used as the distinguishing epithet of things coming from or associated with the county, as ***Shropshire cheese, damson, pie.***

**1577** B. GOOGE *Heresbach's Husb.* III. (1586) 147b, In England, the best Cheese is the Chesshyre, and the Shropshyre, then the Banbury Cheese. **1747** MRS. GLASSE *Cookery* 73 A Shropshire Pye. **1837** *Penny Cycl.* VIII. 298/2 (*Damson*) Much the finest variety..is that called the Shropshire damson.

**b.** (*a*) An old breed of horned sheep peculiar to Shropshire; (*b*) a modern breed of black-faced hornless sheep obtained by crossing with the Southdown. Also, an old breed of long-horn cattle, and of swine.

**1768** A. YOUNG *Tour Southern Counties* (1769) 139 That fine breed of hogs which at Barnet market are called the Shropshires. **1803** PLYMLEY *Agric. Shropsh.* 241 The old Shropshire ox was remarkable for a large dewlap. *Ibid.* 260 The old Shropshire sheep..have black or mottled faces and legs. **1841** *Penny Cycl.* XXI. 358/2 Varieties of the short or middle-woolled breeds of sheep, and among them were the old Shropshires. **1886** C. SCOTT *Sheep-Farming* 12 For quality of mutton, the Shropshire, by universal opinion, comes next to the Southdown.

**shroub**, obs. form of SHRUB.

**shroud** (ʃraʊd), *sb.*[1] Forms: 1–3 **scrud,** (1 **scruud,** 3 **srud, srut**), 3–4 **schrud,** 3–6 **shrud,** 4–5 **schrowde,** 4–6 **schroud(e,** 4–7 **shroude,** (4 **ssroud, shrout(e,** 5 **shrude, shrowed,** 6 **schrowd, shrow'd, shrowdde,** 7 **sroude**), 5–7 **shrowde,** 5–9 **shrowd,** 4– **shroud.** [OE. *scrúd* str. neut. = ON. *skrúð* neut. (also *skrúðe* wk. masc.), fittings, furniture, ornament, also, some kind of textile fabric (Norw. *skrud* ornament, attire, MSw. *skruþer* masc., state clothing, ornaments, Sw. *skrud* masc., attire); f. OTeut. **skrūd-*, long-wk.-grade of **skreud-* to cut (see SHRED *sb.*).]

†**1. a.** A garment; an article of clothing; *sing.* and *pl.* (one's) clothes, clothing, habiliments. *Obs.*

*c* **1000** ÆLFRIC *Gloss.* in Wr.-Wülcker 151/6 *Habitus*, scruud. *c* **1000** —— *Gen.* xlv. 22 And [he] sealde hira ælcum twa scrud. *c* **1200** ORMIN 137 All ane shridd wiþþ haliȝ shrud Ȝede he till Godess allterr. *c* **1205** LAY. 5362 Þeos eorles heom gerden mid godliche scruden [*c* **1275** scrude]. *a* **1225** *St. Marher.* 19 Feirlec ant strencðe beoð his schrudes. **13..** *E.E. Allit. P.* B. 47 Þus schal he be schent for his schrowde feble. **1362** LANGL. *P. Pl.* A. Prol. 2, I schop me in-to a schroud [B. in shroudes] A scheep as I were. *c* **1440** *York Myst.* xxix. 364 Lo, here a shrowde for a shrewe. *c* **1470** *Gol. & Gaw.* 599 Schaip the evin to the schalk, in thi schroud schene. **1508** DUNBAR *Tua mariit wemen* 252, I wes schene in my schrowd. **1535** STEWART *Cron. Scot.* II. 34 Thair semelie schroud likeas siluer scheue. **1594** MARLOWE & NASHE *Dido* III. iii, My princely robes..are layd aside, Whose glittering pompe Dianas shrowdes supplies. **1638** G. SANDYS *Paraphr. Job* xxxviii, Swadled, as new-borne, in sable shrouds.

**b.** In generalized use: Clothing, vesture.

*a* **1122** *O.E. Chron.* (Laud MS.) an. 1070 Swa maneȝa gersumas on sceat & on scrud [etc.]. *c* **1175** *Lamb. Hom.* 63 Gif..to þe flesce scrud and clað. *c* **1250** *Gen. & Ex.* 176 Al erue..ðe sulde him her,..to fode, and srud, to helpen ðe lif. *a* **1300** *Cursor M.* 3250 Bath gold and stan for maiden scrude.

**c.** *transf.* and *fig.*, esp. the 'vesture' in which the world or the things of nature are 'clothed'; also, the 'veil' of flesh. *Obs.*

*c* **1175** *Lamb. Hom.* 79 Ho hine bireueden of þere muchele mihte þet crist him hafde iȝefen of al þer orþe scrude, of þe uisces iþe wetere and fuȝeles iþe lufte. *c* **1200** *Vices & Virtues* 95 Wel him ðe..hafð ðat faire scrud of charite all besett mid ȝimstanes of gode werkes. *c* **1200** ORMIN 17591 & tohh iss þeȝȝre baþre [*sc.* man and the world] shrud þurrh Cossmos wel bitacnedd. *a* **1225** *Leg. Kath.* 914 Þus he schrudde & hudde him,..mid ure fleschliche schrud. *a* **1300** *Cursor M.* 9380 Til alkin thing he gafe, þair kind scrud al for to haue. ? *a* **1366** CHAUCER *Rom. Rose* 64 And then bicometh the ground so proud That it wol have a newe shroud.

**d.** Plumage. *Obs.*

*a* **1400** *Pistill of Susan* 85 Þer schene briddes in schawe schewen heore schroude. *c* **1450** HOLLAND *Howlat* 914 So fair is my fetherem I haf no falowe; My schrowde and my schere weid schir to be schawin.

**2. a.** The white cloth or sheet in which a corpse is laid out for burial; a winding-sheet.

**1570** LEVINS *Manip.* 217/2 A shroude, *amiculum funerale.* **1588** SHAKS. *L.L.L.* v. ii. 479 Die when you will, a smocke shall be your shrowd. **1611** CORYAT *Crudities* 71 The shroud wherin our Sauiours blessed body was wrapped. **1649** DAVENANT *Love & Hon.* III. iii, Let her make love to a sexton, and steale shrowds. **1702** STEELE *Funeral* I. i, I carried home to your house the shroud the gentleman was buried in last night. **1790** COWPER *Stanzas for Year 1790*, 16 Soon the grave must be your home, And your only suit a shroud. **1847** PRESCOTT *Peru* (1850) II. 287 His remains, rolled in their bloody shroud. **1848** LYTTON *Harold* II. iii, If England needs defenders when I and Godwin are in our shrouds.

¶ By association with the black of mourning, *shroud* has received the epithet *sable.*

**1637** MILTON *Lycidas* 22 And as he passes turn, And bid fair peace be to my sable shrowd. **1724** D. MALLET *Will. & Marg.* ii, Clay-cold was her lilly hand, That held her sable shroud. **1805** SCOTT *Last Minstr.* VI. xxiii, Each Baron, for a sable shroud, Sheath'd in his iron panoply. **1887** W. S. GILBERT *Ruddigore* II, Inky clouds, Like funeral shrouds.

**b.** In fig., allusive, and symbolic uses.

**1742** YOUNG *Nt. Th.* IV. 809 How swift the shuttle flies, that weaves thy shroud! **1820** SHELLEY *Autumn* 4 The Year On the earth her death-bed, in a shroud of leaves dead, Is lying. *c* **1860** BRYANT *New & Old* ii. Poet. Wks. (1891) 283 These gay idlers, the butterflies, Broke, to-day, from their winter shroud. **1865** RUSKIN *Sesame* ii. §92, I do not wonder at the sensualist's life, with the shroud wrapped about his feet. **1869** J. H. NEWMAN in W. Ward *Life* (1912) II. 281 Dress me up, and you will soon have to make my shrowd.

**c.** *dial.* The charred sooty piece at the top of a burning wick which requires snuffing. (Supposed to betoken a death.)

**1877** *Manley & Corringham Gloss.* **1894** H. NISBET *Bush Girl's Rom.* 142 The guttering..candles..melted from their blackened..wicks, all unheeded and shroud-environed.

†**3.** A place or dwelling which affords shelter; a retreat; a shelter, esp. one of a slight or temporary kind, as a tent or shed. *Obs.*

*c* **1380** *Sir Ferumb.* 2416 Þe þef..fond hure þer..liggyng vnder shroute. *Ibid.* 3358 Ameral atte is soper he of-say sittynge vnder shrout. *c* **1450** LYDG. *Life Our Lady* lxvii. (1484) kiij b, [The sun] To shewe his light in euery shroude & shade. **1552** B. GILPIN *Serm. bef. Edw. VI* (1630) 33 As for turning poore men out of their holdes, they take for no offence..They turne them out of their shrouds as mice. **1576** GASCOIGNE *Philomene* xlix, Unto a selly shrowde A sheepcote closely builte Amid the wooddes. **1577–87** HARRISON *England* II. xix. 205 in *Holinshed*, Our countrie conuerted..into the walks and shrowds of wild beasts. **1616** R. C. *Times' Whistle* (1871) 151 Then shall we see Christ comming in the cloudes, When some will wish whole mountaines were their shroudes. **1634** MILTON *Comus* 147 Run to your shrouds, within these Brakes and Trees. **1656–7** *Burton's Diary* (1828) I. 364 When men pull down their houses that are ruinous, they try awhile by setting up shrowds, but finding them drop in, they build their houses again.

**4.** *pl.* (rarely *sing.*) A crypt, vault; esp. applied to the Chapel of St. Faith in St. Paul's Cathedral. (Cf. CROWD *sb.*[2]) Now *Hist.*

**1550** LEVER (*title*), A fruitfull Sermon made in Poules church at London in the Shroudes. **1552** ELYOT *Dict.*, *Apogæum*, a shrowdes or lyke buildinge vnder the grownde. **1599** HAKLUYT *Voy.* II. I. 153 A church vnder the ground, like to the shrouds in Pauls. **1601** HOLLAND *Pliny* XXVIII. ix. II. 321 Shee goeth downe into the vault or shrouds out of which she delivereth her prophesies. **1611** COTGR., *Apogée*, a shrowd, or denne under th' earth. **1790** PENNANT *London* (1793) 392 The preacher [at Paul's Cross] went, in very bad weather, to a place called the Shrowds. **1868** MILMAN *St. Paul's* vii. 164 According to some accounts the Shrouds were in the triforium of the church.

†**5. a.** Shadow, shade; *fig.* protection. *Obs.*

*a* **1586** SIDNEY *Ps.* XCI. ii, Soft hiv'd with wing and plume Thou in his shrowd shalt ly. **1588** KYD *Househ. Phil.* Wks. (1901) 248 To retyre them from the heate..vnder the shade of a Tree, or shroude of a Church. **1606** SHAKS. *Ant. & Cl.* III. xiii. 71 To heare from me you had left Anthony, And put your selfe vnder his shrowd, the vniuersal Landlord.

**b.** The branches of a tree, considered as affording shade. *Obs.* (Cf. SHROUD *sb.*[3])

**1597** DRAYTON *Heroic. Ep.* 49 Where like a mounting Cedar he should beare His plumed top, aloft into the ayre; And let these shrubs sit vnderneath his shrowdes. **1611** BIBLE *Ezek.* xxxi. 3 The Assyrian was a Cedar in Lebanon with faire branches, and with a shadowing shrowd. [So 1884 Revised.]

**6.** A thing serving as a covering or protection; a defence; a covering, screen, veil, 'cloak', disguise. Now somewhat *rhetorical.*

**1558** G. CAVENDISH *Poems* (1825) II. 171, I shall set my shrowd for my defence, Under the mantell of well wyllyng audyence. **1587** A. DAY *Daphnis & Chloe* (1890) 3 The greatest forwardness craueth a shrowd, and the meanest matter cannot be without defence. **1605** B. JONSON *Volpone* v. ii, Jove..Could not inuent, t' himselfe, a shroud more subtile, To passe Acrisivs guardes. **1621** G. SANDYS *Ovid's Metam.* v. (1632) 186 Sol, obscur'd in shrowds Of exhalations. **1651** CLEVELAND *Poems* 33 Thus Israel-like, he travells with a cloud, Both as a conduct to him, and a shroud. **1697** POTTER *Antiq. Greece* III. x. (1715) 94 Their Tops were covered with raw Hides, and other Shrowds, to preserve them from Fire-balls and missive Weapons. **1699** POMFRET *Dies Noviss.* 103 Swath'd in substantial shrowds of night, The sick'ning sun shall from the world retire. **1808** SCOTT *Marm.* VI. xxvi, At length the freshening western blast Aside the shroud of battle cast. **1814** —— *Ld. Isles* I. Introd., Beneath a shroud of russet dropp'd with gold Tweed and his tributaries mingle still. **1850** KINGSLEY *Alton Locke* xxvi, A grey shroud of rain sweeping up from the westward. **1867** 'OUIDA' *Cecil Castlemaine* 6 The thickest shroud of the ivy.

**7.** Technical senses.

†**a.** In a windmill, a protective addition to horizontal sails. **b.** Either of the two annular plates at the periphery of a water-wheel, forming the ends of the buckets. **c.** A rim or flange cast on the ends of the teeth of a gear-wheel.

**1576** *Reg. Mag. Sig. Scot.* 1580–93 (1888) 101/1 Sustentando dictum molendinum in omnibus necessariis, preter in new schrouddis to be mylne aves. **1629** ROUS *Diary* (Camden) 41 Her [*sc.* a crow's] nest was layd betweene the shrowdes in the toppe saile [of a windmill]. **1660** R. D'ACRES *Elem. Water-drawing* 9 Some of these [horizontal sails of a mill] are made to go with shrouds or shelters, others without. *Ibid.*, Though the shrouds may keep blustring winds away, yet neither it, nor any thing else can keep the Air away. **1759** *Phil. Trans.* LI. 126 This wheel was two inches in the shroud or depth of the bucket. **1797** J. CURR *Coal Viewer* 31 [Specification for] jinneys for conveying the corves..1 Shroud for the middle, 2⅜ [inches] by 1, and 1 ditto for the Brake. **1884** F. J. BRITTEN *Watch & Clockm.* 291 The space occupied by the shrouds precludes their use in watches, but in the going parts of clocks they answer well.

**d.** *Engin.* A circular band attached to the circumference of the rotor of a turbine; a flange on the tip of a turbine rotor blade (flanges on adjacent blades usu. interlocking so as to form a continuous band).

**1906** J. W. SOTHERN *Marine Steam Turbine* (ed. 2) II. 54 At the outer ends..the blades fit..into a channel-shaped brass ring, or 'shroud', as it is called. **1951** COHEN & ROGERS *Gas Turbine Theory* v. 106 Although shrouds have been used on superchargers, they have not come into general use so far on impellers for gas turbines. **1967** N. E. BORDEN *Jet-Engine Fundamentals* 93 The shrouds form a band around the perimeter of the turbine rotor which interlocks the blades at their tips and reduces vibration. **1971** P. J. MCMAHON *Aircraft Propulsion* v. 162 What may show the difference between a turbine and a compressor stage would be the fitting of shrouds on turbine blades.

**e.** A temporary covering for part of a spacecraft, esp. one which protects and streamlines the payload of a rocket during launching.

**1965** W. R. CORLISS *Space Probes & Planetary Exploration* x. 235 The shroud gives probes that customary conical appearance before deployment of the articulated sections. **1966** [see DOCK *v.*[2] 5]. **1975** K. W. GATLAND *Missiles & Rockets* viii. 184 Above that, enclosed in a shroud, were the Airlock Module, Multiple Docking Adapter and Apollo Telescope Mount.

**8.** *attrib.* and *Comb.* in sense 2, as ***shroud-cloth, -plait*** (poet.), ***-rags***; ***shroud-bound, -like*** adj. and adv., ***-maker, -manufacturer***; **shroud-brass**, a memorial brass in which the deceased is represented in his shroud; **shroud-plate** = 7 b.

**1865** NEALE *Hymns Parad.* 24 *Shroud-bound, tomb-held,..Thou canst raise me. **1890** *Daily News* 21 Oct. 5/2 Perhaps, a more truly morbid and abominable effigy never disgraced the walls of a place of worship than the *shroud brass. **1912** J. S. M. WARD *Brasses* 82 Skeletons. These are not so common as shroud brasses. *a* **1847** ELIZA COOK *To Mem. Burns* I, Thy 'magic mantle's' glowing sheen, Burst through thy *shroud-cloth ere 'twas seen. **1697** DRYDEN *Virg. Georg.* I. 25 Thou, whose Hands the *Shrowd-like Cypress rear. **1835** LYTTON *Rienzi* x. v, In her shroud-like garments and attenuated frame, she seemed..as a spectre. **1913** *Engl. Rev.* May 244 The Vicar, his surplice clinging shroudlike to his lank figure. **1892** SIMMONDS *Dict. Trade Suppl.*, **Shroud Manufacturer*, a maker of grave clothes for a corpse. *c* **1864** G. M. HOPKINS *Poems* (1967) 117, I desire They swathe and lace the *shroud-plaits o'er my face. **1844** H. STEPHENS *Bk. Farm* II. 326 On the inside of the *shroud-plates are formed the grooves for securing the ends of the buckets. *a* **1847** ELIZA COOK *Dust* iii, He sorts the *shroud-rags, he heaps gray bones.

**shroud** (ʃraʊd), *sb.*[2] Forms: 5 **shrowthe-s, shrode-s, srowde,** 5–7 **shrowde-s,** 6 **schroude-s, showed(e)-s, shrowes** (?), 6–7 **shroude-s,** 6–8 **shrowd-s,** 7 **shreed-s,** 7– **shroud-s.** [Prob. a use of SHROUD *sb.*[1]; cf. the mod. naut. phrase 'to *clothe* the mast with the shrouds'; a mast or spar without its rigging is said to be 'naked'. The sense of 'shrouds of a ship' attributed to ON. *skrúð* and to Norw. *skrud* is not authenticated.

'Remembering that in the 15th c. the headropes (or shrouds) were very numerous, the appropriateness of the term shroud seems obvious' (L. G. Carr Laughton).]

**1.** A set of ropes, usually in pairs, leading from the head of a mast and serving to relieve the latter of lateral strain; they form part of the standing rigging of a ship.

**a.** *pl.* (See also *fore-shrouds* FORE-[1] 3 d, *main-shrouds* MAIN *a.* 10, *mizen-shrouds* MIZEN 3; for an extended use see BENTINCK-, BOWSPRIT-, BUMKIN-, FUTTOCK-*shrouds.*)

**1458** in *Archæologia* XXIX. 328 The mast hathe a welle good stay, Wt shrowthes sure. *c* **1485** *Digby Myst.* (1882) III. 1720 In-to þe shrowdes I woll me hye. *c* **1500** *Cocke Lorelles B.* 12 Some one the shrowedes dyde clyme. **1531** in J. Strutt *Mann. & Cust. Eng.* (1776) III. 53 Item 9 shrowds and a backe staye on either syd. **1589** in Hakluyt *Voy.* 282 Another walkes vpon the hatches, another climbes the shrowes. **1642** D. Rogers *Naaman* 496 As in a ship each boy hath his taske, some to row..others to climb the shreeds. **1666** Dryden *Ann. Mirab.* cxlviii, To try new Shrouds one mounts into the wind, And one, below, their Ease or Stiffness notes. **1726** Shelvocke *Voy. round World* 436 They seem to have but little regard to the support of their masts, to which their stays and shrouds hold no proportion. **1840** R. H. Dana *Bef. Mast* xxiii, In an instant every one sprung into the rigging, up the shrouds, and out on the yards. **1883** *Chamb. Jrnl.* 141 A heavy sea boarded the ship, dashing us into the mizen rigging, where we grasped the shrouds, and were saved.

**b.** *collect. sing.*

**1465** *Mann. & Househ. Exp.* (Roxb.) 200 Payd be my mastyr for ropes for hyr srowde, ij.li. **1588** in *Harl. Misc.* (Malh.) II. 45 He shall shew lights, one in the poop, and another two showed high. **1691** T. H[ale] *Acc. New Invent.* 126 Fitting of the Shrowd so as to make way for the gibbing of the Yards. **1814** Scott *Ld. Isles* III. xxiii, The favouring breeze, when loud It pipes upon the galley's shroud.

**c.** *sing.* Any one of such ropes.

**1748** *Anson's Voy.* III. v. 341 The mast itself is supported ..by the shrowd..and by two stays. **1762** Falconer *Shipwr.* II. 236 Secure your lines! grasp every man a shroud! **1851** H. Melville *Whale* ix. 50 Stumbling to the deck [he] grasps a shroud to look out upon the sea. **1882** Nares *Seamanship* (ed. 6) 48 Each..bowsprit shroud [is] secured to its collar.

**d.** *fig.*

**1595** Shaks. *John* v. vii. 53 All the shrowds wherewith my life should saile, Are turned to one thred. **1602** Marston *Antonio's Rev.* II. ii, Readie to discharge Their pretious shot into the shrouds of heaven. **1667** Denham *Direct. Painter* II. 70 He quickly taught, pours in continual Clouds Of chain'd Dilemma's through our sinew'd Shrouds.

**2. a.** (See quot.)

**1875** Knight *Dict. Mech.*, *Shroud*, the chains by which the smoke-stack is braced, in steamers.

**b.** = *shroud line* below.

**1942** F. H. Colvin *Aircraft Handbk.* (ed. 5) 679 (*caption*) Drawing the shrouds into their pockets in the seat pack. **1957** L. L. Beckford *A.B.C. of Aeronaut.* 74/1 Fastened firmly between the gores are strong cords, called Shrouds, which distribute the load evenly over the Canopy. **1973** 'A. Hall' *Tango Briefing* x. 119 Watch the ground. The whisper of wind in the shrouds... He'd had to give me five seconds..so that the 'chutes wouldn't foul each other.

**3.** *attrib.* and *Comb.* **shroud-bridle** (see quot.); **shroud hawser**, a shroud-laid rope; **shroud-knot**, a knot used in repairing a parted shroud; **shroud-laid** *a.*, applied to rope composed of four (formerly sometimes three) strands laid right-handed with a heart; **shroud line**, any of the straps joining the canopy of a parachute to the harness; (usu. *pl.*); cf. *rigging lines* s.v. rigging (*vbl.*) *sb.*[2] 2 c; **shroud-plate** (see quot.); **shroud-stopper**, a rope connecting parts of a shroud below or above a damaged part (1867 Smyth *Sailor's Word-bk.*); **shroud-tackle, -truck** (see quots.).

**1875** Knight *Dict. Mech.*, **Shroud-bridle*, a kind of crow-foot fastened to the shrouds, to hold sheets, braces, etc. **1744** J. Philips *Jrnl. Exped. Anson* 150 We receiv'd..a thirteen Inch Cable and a *shroud Hawser. *c* **1860** H. Stuart *Seaman's Catech.* 30 How do you make a *shroud-knot? **1860** *All Year Round* No. 66. 382 'Which knot?' asked Toby. 'Single or double wall, single or double diamond, Matthew Walker, spritsail-sheet, stopper, or shroud?' **1800** *Naval Chron.* III. 474 Three strond *shroud-laid rope. **1825** Budge *Miner's Guide* 98 The term 'shroud-laid' is used to distinguish a rope of three strands or parts from another of nine strands, which is termed 'cable-laid'. **1875** Bedford *Sailor's Pocket Bk.* x. (ed. 2) 360 Shroud-laid rope 4 strands and a heart Right-handed. **1929** A. F. Collins *Aviation* xii. 184 The pilot chute and big parachute, together with its *shroud lines that hold it to the harness, are made so that they fold up in a very small pack. **1973** 'A. Hall' *Tango Briefing* xix. 240 The supply 'chute was draped across a spur of rock... The shroud lines were badly twisted. **1875** Knight *Dict. Mech.*, **Shroud plate*, 1. *a.* An iron plate fixed to a ship's side for the attachment of the shrouds. *b.* A ring surrounding a mast and to which the futtock-shrouds are secured. **1769** Falconer *Dict. Marine* (1789), *Couladoux*, *shroud-tackles, which are used in the gallies..in the Mediterranean, in the place of dead-eyes and laniards. **1867** Smyth *Sailor's Word-bk.*, **Shroud-trucks*. **1875** Knight *Dict. Mech.*, *Shroud-truck*,..a wooden thimble secured to the shrouds and acting as a fair-leader for the running-rigging.

**shroud** (ʃraʊd), *sb.*[3] Now *dial.* [Formally identical with shroud *sb.*[1], but with sense independently derived from the sense 'to cut' of the root. Cf. shred *sb.*] **a.** *collect. sing.* and *pl.* Loppings of a tree, branches or twigs cut off. **b.** (chiefly *pl.*) A branch or bough.

**1475-6** in Swayne *Sarum Churchw. Acc.* (1896) 361 Of William Pole for the shrowde of the same elme, viijd. **1538** Elyot *Dict.*, *Sarmenta*, twigges or shroude of trees cut of. **1555** Eden *Decades* (Arb.) 73 Shrouddes of younge vines. *c* **1640** J. Smyth *Lives Berkeleys* (1883) I. 114 Tythes for beech wood, loppes, shrowds, willowes. **1669** Worlidge *Syst. Agric.* (1681) 15 Aquatick Trees, whose shrowds shall exceed in value the Grass they injure. **1862** Lowell *Biglow P.* Ser. II. vi. 93 In ellum-shrouds the flashin' hangbird clings.

**shroud** (ʃraʊd), *v.*[1] Forms: 3-4 scrude, 4 schroude, schruden, 4-5 shrude, 4-6 shroude, 5 shrowden, schrowude, 5-6 schroude, 6-7 shrowd(e, 7 shrow'd, shreud, shrewd, 6- shroud. *Pa. t.* 6-7 shrowded, 6- shrouded; *contr.* 3-4 scrud, 4 schrud, shroude, scrowd. *Pa. pple.* 3-4 scruded, 5 schruedede, 5 i-shrowdyd, schrouded, y-shrouded, 6-7 shrowded, 7 schroudit, 4- shrouded; *contr.* 3-4 scrud, 4-6 schroud, 5 schroude, 6 schroud, shrowed, 7 shroud. [f. shroud *sb.*[1] Cf. shride *v.*[1]]

†**1.** *trans.* To clothe. *Obs.*

*a* **1300** *Cursor M.* 10448 Anna, leuedi,..scrud þe fair and mend þi chere! *Ibid.* 16346 Iesus thoght ful mikel scam quen he sua scruded was. *c* **1400** *Anturs of Arth.* 20 (Thornton MS.) Schruedede in a schorte cloke. *c* **1407** Lydg. *Reson & Sens.* 353 A mantel large hir self to shroude. *c* **1450** Holland *Howlat* 84 Myterit..Schroude in his schene weid.

†**b.** *transf.* To adorn, deck. *Obs.*

*a* **1300** *Cursor M.* 8322 It sal be precius and prude, þe werc he sal sua semele scrude. *Ibid.* 23404 He þat wroght al thing in lede And scrud þam alle in þair fairhede. ? *a* **1366** Chaucer *Rom. Rose* 55 Ther is neither busk nor hay In May, that it nil shrouded been. **1500-20** Dunbar *Poems* lxi. 3 Quhen gilletis wilbe schomd and schroud, That ridden ar baith with lord and lawd?

**2.** To give shelter or housing to; to shelter. *arch.*

Now only with admixture of 5 or 6.

*c* **1450** Lydg. *Life Our Lady* xviii. (1484) cvj, Quod gabriel within thy blessyd syde The holy ghoost shal I shrowdyd be. **1579** Spenser *Sheph. Cal.* Apr. 32 The whiles our flockes doe graze about in sight, And we close shrowded in thys shade alone. **1582** Stanyhurst *Æneis* IV. 80 Fayre fowls.. showded in hard bed Of thorny thickets. **1603** Knolles *Hist. Turks* (1621) 83 Thrust out of all they had,..not knowing where to shroud their heads. **1614** Raleigh *Hist. World* I. iv. 68 One of these trees considered with all his young ones may (indeede) shrowde foure hundred or foure thousand horsemen. **1671** Milton *P.R.* IV. 419 Ill wast thou shrouded then, O patient Son of God. **1859** C. Barker *Assoc. Princ.* i. 13 Some quiet cell, where they might shroud their grey hairs. **1860** Farrar *Orig. Lang.* i. 17 The joyous birds, shrouded in cheerful shade.

†**b.** *refl.* To take shelter. *Obs.*

**1553** T. Wilson *Rhet.* Pref. A iiij b, Having neither house to shroude them in, nor attyre to clothe their backes. **1590** Spenser *F.Q.* I. i. 6 Angry Ioue an hideous storme of raine Did poure into his Lemans lap..And this faire couple eke to shroud themselues were fain. **1620-55** I. Jones *Stone-Heng* (1725) 8 Some..made themselves places of Lome and Twigs.., to creep into, and shroud themselves in. **1642-4** Vicars *God in Mount* 193 They forced all the Musketeers.. to run in and shroud themselves within their pikes. **1653** H. Cogan tr. *Pinto's Trav.* xvii. 60 They came into the Port to shrewd themselves from the storm as others did.

**c.** *intr.* To seek shelter or retirement; to take shelter or refuge. *arch.*

**1579** Spenser *Sheph. Cal.* Feb. 122 In his small bushes vsed to shrowde The sweete Nightingale. **1610** Shaks. *Temp.* II. ii. 42, I will here shrowd till the dregges of the storme be past. **1634** Milton *Comus* 316 If your stray attendance be yet lodg'd Or shroud within these limits. **1648** J. Raymond *Il Merc. Ital.* Pref. 1 A weather beaten Traveller needs no such Umbrilla as a Patron to shroud under. *c* **1746** Collins *Ode to Fear* 48 Wilt thou shroud in haunted cell, Where gloomy Rape and Murder dwell? **1793-4** Wordsw. *Guilt & Sorrow* xx, One who, forced from storms to shroud, Felt the loose walls of this decayed Retreat Rock. **1818** Keats *Endym.* IV. 190 What enamour'd bride Cheated by shadowy wooer from the clouds, But hides and shrouds Beneath dark palm-trees by a river side?

†**d.** *intr.* and *pass.* To be huddled *up* or *together*.

**1530** Palsgr. 702/1 Se howe yonder kyne shrowde to gyther for colde. **1553** T. Wilson *Rhet.* 64 b, Beastes and birdes without reason love one another, thei shroude, and thei flocke together. **1623** J. Taylor (Water P.) *World runnes on Wheeles* Wks. (1630) II. 242 Peoples guts like to be crushed out being crowded and showded vp against stalls.

**3.** To cover so as to protect; to screen from injury or attack; to afford protection to. ? *Obs.*

*a* **1300** *Cursor M.* 9902 Þis castel..o luue and grace..wit kirnels es vm-sett ful well, scrud on ilk side wit sele. *c* **1475** *Rauf Coilyear* 459 Trewlie that tenefull was trimland than, Semelie schapin and schroud in that Scheild schene. *c* **1580** in *Archæologia* XI. 224 Vnder the protection of ye peere.. whereby thay are shrowed from the radge of the sea. *c* **1582** *Ibid.* 227 No shelues of beache haue euer growne or remayned longer then they haue byn shrowded and protected by the peer. **1587** Fleming *Contn. Holinshed* III. 1309/1 Whom he would in no wise shrowd or haue in his house and companie. **1618** Latham *Falconry* II. (1633) 84 Shee will grow so farre in loue..with you..and account her selfe safely shrowded when she hath your companie. **1674** N. Fairfax *Bulk & Selv.* 40 The main Castleward to shrowd these weaklings from blows and qualmes. **1810** Scott *Lady of L.* II. xiii, From ire Of Scotland's king who shrouds my sire.

†**b.** *refl.* To protect oneself, seek protection. *Obs.*

**14..** Lydg. *Beware of Doubleness* 72 They have no better proteccioun But shroude hem under doublenesse. **1575** tr. *Marlorat's Apoc.* 49 The sayde lawlesse libertie of whore-hunting..shrouded it selfe vnder the bond of brotherly loue. **1615** W. Lawson *Country Housew. Garden* (1626) A 2, I could..so shroud my selfe from scandall vnder your honourable fauour. **1692** T. Watson *Body Divin.* 376 The Thief that shrowds himself under Law. **1698** Fryer *Acc. E. India & P.* 2 A great many [Ships] that had shrowded themselves under our Protection..

†**4.** To conceal in a secret place or in a secret manner. Often *refl.*, to retire to a hiding-place; *pass.* to be in hiding. *Obs.*

*c* **1402** Lydg. *Compl. Bl. Knt.* 147, I..gan..Among the busshes me prively to shroude. **1560** Becon *New Catech.* Wks. (1564) 389 Shal any man be able to shroude himselfe in such a corner, that I can not espye him? **1563-70** Foxe *A. & M.* (ed. 2) 2125/2 [She] shrouded her selfe in a low ditch with nettles. **1588** Shaks. *L.L.L.* IV. iii. 137, I haue beene closely shrowded in this bush, And markt you both. **1603** —— *Ham.* (1st Qo.) 1452 [III. iv. 2] I'll shrowde my selfe behinde the Arras. **1612** Webster *White Devil* I. ii. 40 Shrowd you within this closet, good my lord. **1641-2** Chas. I *Wks.* (1662) I. 395, I am come to demand such Prisoners ..and do believe they are shrowded in the City.

†**b.** *intr.* To be concealed, lie hid. *Obs.*

*c* **1450** Lydg. *Life Our Lady* xlviii. (1484) g vi, The septer of whom..shal..neuer cese ne in couert shroude. **1576** Gascoigne *Philomene* vi, How covertly doth sorow shrowde, In trymmest worldely toys. **1649** Lovelace *Lucasta, Amyntor's Grove*, Or have you seene the Lightning shrowd, And straight breake through th'opposing cloud? **1662** R. Mathew *Unl. Alch.* 65 Many..shroud under a cloak of Religion.

**5.** To hide from view, as by a veil, darkness, cloud; to cover so as to conceal; to screen, veil.

**1426** Lydg. *De Guil. Pilgr.* 22288 The tother party, wonder myrk, Schrouded with a cloude dyrk. **1503** Hawes *Examp. Virtue* IX. 162 Lycyna eke dyd her shrowde Vnder a blacke and mysty clowde. **1607** *Merry Devil Edmonton* II. iii. 77 That disguise will hardly shrowd my woe. **1624** Capt. Smith *Virginia* II. 32 Thus shrowding his body in the skinne by stalking he approacheth the Deere. **1697** Dryden *Virg. Georg.* I. 444 The Father of the Gods his Glory shrouds, Involv'd in Tempests, and a Night of Clouds. **1797** Mrs. Radcliffe *Italian* i, A monk whose face was shrouded by his cowl. **1820** W. Irving *Sketch Bk.* II. 59 A thin transparent vapour..threatening gradually to shroud the landscape. **1827** Lytton *Pelham* vi, I was shrouded at that moment from his sight by one of the yew trees. **1902** Buchan *Watcher by Threshold* 288 The hills, shrouded in grey mist. **1912** *Stage Year Bk.* 27 They performed in evening dress, but were shrouded in sombre cloaks and masks.

**6.** In immaterial sense: To screen from observation; to envelop or wrap *up*, as in obscurity or mystery; to veil under an appearance or 'show': sometimes with implication of disguise or concealment for an evil purpose.

**1412-20** Lydg. *Chron. Troy* I. 2262 Whiche in þe ende, to her confusioun, Can vnder sugre schrowden her poysoun. **1509** Hawes *Past. Pleas.* II. (1555) 40 The poetes.. underneth the trouth doth so shroude, Both good an yll. **1579** Gosson *Sch. Abuse* Ep. Ded. (Arb.) 16 The shorteste Pamphlette may shrowde matter. *c* **1585** *Faire Em* II. ii. 91 Is this William the Conqueror, shrouded vnder the name of sir Robert of Windsor? **1634** W. Tirwhyt tr. *Balzac's Lett.* 340, I honour vertue..under what shape soever it is showded. **1642** H. More *Song of Soul* II. iii. II. xlii, Nor doth the soul that in this flesh doth croud Her self rely on that thick vapour where she's shroud. **1726** Pope *Odyss.* XIX. 343 Irresolute of soul, his state to shrowd In dark disguise. **1837** Carlyle *Fr. Rev.* II. v. v, The Queen, shrouded in deepest mystery. **1838** Prescott *Ferd. & Is.* vii. (1846) I. 328 Its proceedings were impenetrably shrouded from the public eye. **1855** —— *Philip II* II. xii. I. 288 We find her communications..frequently shrouded in cipher. **1867** Freeman *Norm. Conq.* (1877) I. 64 The whole of the short reign of Eadwig is shrouded in mystery. **1874** Green *Short Hist.* vi. §3. 286 His indolence and gaiety were mere veils beneath which Edward shrouded a profound political ability.

**b.** *refl.*

*a* **1569** Kingesmyll *Confl. Satan* (1578) 12 He shrowdeth himselfe under the robe of trueth. **1576** Gascoigne *Grief of Joy* IV. xi. Wks. 1910 II. 550, I graunt that pastyme ys the lowly porte, Wherein mans mynde, maie shrewd itself full oft. **1606** Bryskett *Civ. Life* 84 If it happen that any abuse do grow and shrowd it selfe vnder the name of a custome. **1650** Fuller *Pisgah* IV. ii. 21 The remains of that nation, which escaped that dismall overthrow, shrowded themselves under the names of some neighbouring people. **1791** Burke *App. Whigs* Wks. 1842 I. 518 Mr. Burke, instead of shrowding himself in exploded ignorance [etc.]. **1823** Scott *Quentin D.* xii, Courage occasionally shrouds itself under the show of modest timidity. **1882** W. Ballantine *Exper.* xxiv. 233 He shrouded himself with a solemn air as if he was thinking profoundly. **1889** H. F. Wood *Englishman Rue Caïn* xi, When I see some fellow shrouding himself in studied silence.

**7.** To put a shroud on (a corpse), lay in a shroud; hence, to prepare for burial, bury.

**1577** T. Kendall *Flowers of Epigr.* 77 This cuttes, his graue must cost a groate, to shrowde his carrin corse. **1604** Shaks. *Oth.* IV. iii. 24 If I do die before, prythee shrow'd me In one of these same Sheetes. **1610** *Women Saints* 24 That I may for pouertie be shrowded in a sheete of an other bodies. **1681** *Disc. Tanger* 24 The Earl commanded the two dead Bodies..to be decently washt, and shrouded. **1718** G. Sewell *Proclam. Cupid* 8 He has been shrowded—full three hundred Years. **1812** H. & J. Smith *Horace in London* 129 Chaunt, widow'd muse, my dying speech, And shroud my ashes in the abbey. **1856** Grote *Greece* II. xcvi. XII. 453 He ..caused his dead body to be honorably shrouded and transmitted into Macedonia for burial. **1858** R. S. Hawker in *Life* (1905) 307 The..place wherein I have laid out and shrouded and coffined now four and twenty dead Sailors.

†**8.** To include, embrace. *Obs. rare.*

**1593** Nashe *Christ's T.* T 4 b, Vnder Gluttony, I shrowde not onely excesse in meate, but in drinke also.

**9.** *Mech.* To furnish (the sail of a windmill, a water-wheel) with shrouds. Also in gen. use with reference to the provision of a shroud in var. technical senses. Cf. shroud *sb.*[1] 7.

**1660** L. D'acres *Elem. Water-drawing* 9 The other sort of Horizontal sailes with shrouds, move more quietly, but with no worthy strength, though the one half be shrouded never so wel. **1834-6** Barlow in *Encycl. Metrop.* (1845) VIII. 88/2 The sides [of a breast wheel] are also sometimes close shrouded, or closed in on the sides to retain the Water, and it thus becomes a sort of bucket wheel. **1869** Rankine *Machine & Hand-tools* Pl. J 3 The crank plate..being shrouded to a certain extent around the periphery. **1913** S. J. Reed *Turbines applied to Marine Propulsion* iii. 41 In both of the above systems the tips of the blades are shrouded with a steel strip, a projecting piece being left on the blade tip which passes through a hole in the shroud and which is eventually riveted over. **1948** *Chambers's Jrnl.* July 392/2 Mica is used to support the input sockets, thus preventing breakdowns owing to heat, and the sockets are also shrouded for safety and the prevention of shock. **1966** *McGraw-Hill Encycl. Sci. & Technol.* IV. 292/2 Shrouding a propeller may be used on a ship to decrease interference of propeller and hull.

**shroud** (ʃraʊd), *v.*[2] *local.* Also 6–7 **shrowd(e, shrood.** [f. SHROUD *sb.*[3] Cf. SHRIDE *v.*[2]] *trans.* To lop (a tree or its branches); also with *off*; occas. *absol.*

**1577–87** HARRISON *England* II. xxii. 212 in *Holinshed*, To shrowd, staie vpright, and cherish the same [trees] in the blustering winters weather. **1581** J. BELL *Haddon's Answ. Osor.* 493 [One] who..may pare away all rotten and vnsauory subtilties,..may shrowde of all vnprofitable and withered superfluities and reduplications. **1582** *B.N.C. Docum.* (Marston R.[2] 2), The Queen may shrood or lop anie tree or trees. **1662** HERNE in *Collect.* (O.H.S.) I. 246 All such pollards the tenants..shrowd when they make their hedges. **1764** *Museum Rust.* II. lii. 149, I..requested him either to cut down the elms, or permit me to shrowd them. **1861** HUGHES *Tom Brown at Oxf.* xxxv, By the time the tree was felled and shrouded, Tom was in a convalescent state. **1887** HARDY *Woodlanders* xiii, I'll climb up this afternoon and shroud off the lower boughs. *c* **1890** MORRIS in Mackail *Life* (1899) I. 7 The said hornbeams were all pollards, being shrouded every four or six years.

**shroud**, obs. form of SHREWD.

**shroudage** ('ʃraʊdɪdʒ). *poet.* [f. SHROUD *sb.*[2] + -AGE.] The shrouds (of a ship).

**1893** F. THOMPSON *Poems* 72 Its vaporous shroudage drenched with icy rain. **1901** H. TRENCH *Deirdre Wed*, etc. 101 He, acquainted well with every tone Of madness whining in his shroudage slender.

**'shrouded**, *ppl. a.* [f. SHROUD *v.*[1] + -ED[1].] Concealed, veiled; sheltered; enveloped in a shroud.

**1600** NASHE *Summers Last Will* G 2 Cunning shrowded rogues. **1708** *Phil. Trans.* XXVI. 79 The Pholad, or Shrouded Shell. **1821** JOANNA BAILLIE *Metr. Leg.*, *Lady Griseld Baillie* xli, Joy appears with shrouded head. **1821** LAMB *Elia* I. *Old Benchers Inner T.*, That goodly pile.. confronting..the lighter, older, more fantastically shrouded one. **1840** CARLYLE *Heroes* vi, Brave old Samuel Johnson, in his shrouded-up existence. **1870** DISRAELI *Lothair* lxi, One of them pressed her finger to her shrouded lips. **1888** MEREDITH *Hymn to Colour* v, Shall man.. learn the secret of the shrouded death, By lifting up the lid of a white eye?

**b.** *Mech.* (See quot.)

**1875** KNIGHT *Dict. Mech.*, *Shrouded gear*,..cog-gear in which the cogs are protected by a flange coming out even with the face of the wheel, so that the interdental spaces are in effect mortises in the face of the wheel.

**'shrouder.** *rare*[−1]. [f. SHROUD *v.*[1] + -ER[1].] One who shrouds or covers up.

*a* **1591** H. SMITH *Serm.* (1675) 244 Noah..is made naked with sin, to shew that sin is no shrouder, but a stripper.

**'shrouding**, *vbl. sb.*[1] [f. SHROUD *v.*[1] + -ING[1].]

**1.** †Clothing (*obs.*); covering with a shroud or screen; protection, concealment; laying in a shroud.

*a* **1300** *Cursor M.* 27930 Fole contenance and ful scruding. **1615** W. LAWSON *Country Housew. Garden* (1626) 13 Stone-wals..are the best..for fencing, lasting, and shrouding of your yong trees. *a* **1617** HIERON *Wks.* II. 260 Shelter and shrowding from such mischiefs as the life of man is subiect to. **1674** N. FAIRFAX *Bulk & Selv.* Ep. Ded., A..Cedar.. within the bosom of whose shrowdings I must be cloakt from wind and weather. **1856** LD. COCKBURN *Mem.* (1874) iii. 152 Gillespie's Hospital for the shrouding of aged indigence. **1858** R. S. HAWKER in *Life* (1905) 308 The shrouding and placing in his house of wood.

**2.** *Mech.* The shrouds of a water-wheel forming an annular rim at the ends of the buckets.

**1797** *Encycl. Brit.* (ed. 3) XVIII. 903/2 The ring of board ..making the ends of the buckets is called the shrouding.. and *QP* is called the depth of shrouding. **1834–6** BARLOW in *Encycl. Metrop.* (1845) VIII. 88/2 In some cases the shrouding is omitted, in which case great accuracy is requisite in forming the race and hanging the wheel. **1850** WEALE *Dict. Terms Archit.* 514 A water-wheel..consists of ..shaft, arms, buckets, and shrouding. **1875** J. H. COLLINS *Metal Mining* 96 The wheel..having 10 wrought-iron arms ..rivetted or bolted to the centre, and to the shrouding.

**3.** *attrib.* †**shrouding board**, ? a protecting board; †**shrouding place**, a hiding-place; so †*shrouding corner*; **shrouding-plate** = *shroud-plate* SHROUD *sb.*[1] 8; †**shrouding sheet**, a winding sheet.

**1679–80** in Swayne *Churchw. Acc. Sarum* (1896) 343 A stay and a *shrowding board, 1s. **1610** HOLLAND *Camden's Brit.* I. 224 This Isle afforded him a very fit *shrowding corner. **1571** GOLDING *Calvin on Ps.* xi. 1 For all his seeking of *showding places everywhere, yet he could nowhere fynd any courtesie. **1611** FLORIO, *Velabro*, a booth or shrouding place. **1639** H. AINSWORTH *Annot. Ps.* lxi. 4 [A safe hope] or shrowding place, where hee hoped for, and had found safe shelter. **1844** H. STEPHENS *Bk. Farm* II. 326 The *shrouding plates are bolted upon the buckets and soling. **1576** CURTEYS *Two Serm.* A vj, The rich men of this world shall..carry away with them nothing but a *shrowding sheet. **1576** NEWTON *Lemnie's Complex.* (1633) 242 Lapped in their shrowding sheets, and tyed after the manner of dead Corses. **1610** HOLLAND *Camden's Brit.* I. 569 Enwrapped in an Ox-hide for a shrouding sheet. **1699** LD. TARBUT in Pepys *Diary* (1870) 688 If they see a man with a shrouding-sheet in the apparition.

**'shrouding**, *vbl. sb.*[2] [f. SHROUD *v.*[2]] Lopping of trees; *pl.* loppings.

**1725** *Bradley's Fam. Dict.*, *Shrouding*, the Lopping of Trees. **1764** *Museum Rust.* II. lii. 150 Green showdings of trees.

**'shrouding**, *vbl. sb.*[3] [f. SHROUD *sb.*[2] + -ING[1].] The shrouds of a ship.

**1890** R. BRIDGES *Passer-by* iii, Aslant with trim tackle and shrouding.

**'shrouding**, *ppl. a.* [f. SHROUD *v.*[1] + -ING[2].] That shrouds, veils, covers, or conceals.

**1623** MARKHAM *Country Housew. Gard.* III. v. (1665) 76 They both require a strong and shrowding fence. **1826** MISS MITFORD *Village* II. 214 Madame la duchesse, in her hideous shrouding cap. **1863** I. WILLIAMS *Baptistery* xxii. (1874) 67 Here, from the terrors of the grave, The new-born Church..Issued, as from a shrouding cave. **1883** DIXON *Mano* II. iv. 77 She..Back to her horse withdrew for shrouding gown. **1888** E. GERARD *Land beyond Forest* xliii, A carved oak chair heavily wreathed in shrouding cobwebs.

**'shroudless**, *a.* [f. SHROUD *sb.*[1] + -LESS.]

**1.** Without a shroud or winding-sheet.

**1758** DODSLEY *Melpomene* xi, A mangled corse..lies shroudless, unentomb'd. **1821** SCOTT *Pirate* xvi, Tolling shroudless seamen's knell. *a* **1848** O. W. HOLMES *Lexington* 52 Shroudless and tombless they sunk to their rest.

**2.** Unshrouded, unobscured.

**1841** C. SWAIN *Mind* IV. xxxv, Above, the stars in shroudless beauty shine.

**shroudly**, obs. form of SHREWDLY.

**shroudy** ('ʃraʊdɪ), *a. rare.* [f. SHROUD *sb.*[1] + -Y.] Affording shelter.

**1634** MILTON *Comus* 315 (MS. Trin. Coll.), If yo[r] stray attendance be yet lodg'd w[th]in these shroudie limits.

**Shrove**, *sb. Obs.* exc. *dial.* [Short for SHROVE-TIDE or SHROVE TUESDAY.] Shrovetide, or the merrymaking connected therewith.

**1579** in Feuillerat *Revels Q. Eliz.* (1908) 327 During Christmas..& Shrove. **1621** BRATHWAIT *Nat. Embassie*, etc. 178 In their wakes, shroues, wassel-cups, or tides. **1913** *19th Cent.* July 133 Nora was to marry Tom Mahony next Shrove.

**b.** *Comb.*: **shrove-cake**, a small cake made to give children who go shroving (Halliwell, 1847); †**shrove-cock** = *shroving-cock* (see SHROVING *vbl. sb.* b); †**shrove-prentice**, one of 'a set of ruffianly fellows, who took upon them at Shrovetide the name of London Prentices, and in that character invaded houses of ill-fame' (Halliwell).

**1638** DAVENANT *Madagascar*, etc. 29 More cruell than Shrove-Prentices, when they (Drunk in a Brothell House) are bid to pay. **1659** *Lady Alimony* v. ii. I 4, O ye pittiful Simpletons, who spend your days in throwing Cudgels at Jack a Lents or Shrove-Cocks.

**shrove**, *v. Obs.* exc. *dial.* [f. *shrove-* in SHROVE-TIDE.] *intr.* To keep Shrove-tide; to make merry. Often in (*to go*) ***a-shroving*** (locally applied to the practice of going round singing for money on Shrove Tuesday).

**1586** J. HOOKER *Hist. Irel.* in *Holinshed* II. 99/1 He trauelled to Rome a shrouing, of set purpose to be merrie. **1596** NASHE *Saffron Walden* P 2 b, To certefie him that verie shortly hee would send him a couple of Hennes to Shroue with. **1611** FLORIO, *Berlingaccione*, one that loueth to shroue euer and make good cheere. **1620** in *Crt. & Times Jas. I* (1849) II. 198 Those ladies have invited them to a masque ..so that on Thursday next, the king, prince, and all the court go thither a shroving. *a* **1625** FLETCHER *Noble Gent.* III. ii, To see him stated thus, as though he went A shroving through the City. *c* **1645** HOWELL *Lett.* IV. vii. (1892) II. 571 Hans Boobikin, a rich Boor's Son, whom his Father had sent abroad a Fryaring, that is, shroving in our Language. [See also SHROVING *vbl. sb.*]

†**'Shroveday.** *Obs. rare*[−0]. In 5 **shrof-**. [See SHROVE-TIDE.] Shrove Tuesday.

**14..** *Voc.* in Wr.-Wülcker 571/3 *Carniprivium*, shrofday.

**Shrove Monday.** ? *Obs.* Also 6 **shroff.** [See SHROVE-TIDE.] The Monday before Shrove Tuesday.

*c* **1450** *Bale's Chron.* 195 in *Six Town Chron.* (1911) 121 The monday clept shrovemonday folewyng the xxi day of ffeverer. **1523** R. HILLES in *Songs, Carols*, etc. (1907) p. xiv, The sh[r]off monday þat was the VIII day of februari. **1589** in Hakluyt *Voy.* 231, I Departed out of London..vpon Shroue munday 1583. **1671** in *12th Rep. Hist. MSS. Comm.* App. v. 22 Here is no newes but that the grand ballett is not to be danced till Shrove-Munday. **1709** *Rider's British Merlin*, Fair on Shrovemonday at Newcastle under Line. **1837** *Penny Cycl.* VIII. 32/1 Principal fairs held in Cornwall:—..Liskeard, Shrove Monday [etc.].

**shrove-mouse**, obs. form of SHREW-MOUSE.

†**Shrove Sunday.** *Obs.* Also 5–6 **shrof(f, -ffe,** 6 **shroft, shrofe.** [See SHROVE-TIDE.] The Sunday in Shrove-tide, Quinquagesima Sunday.

**1463** *Maldon, Essex Crt. Rolls* Bundle 38 No. 2 Dominica vocata Shrofsunday. *a* **1500** *Gough Chron.* in *Six Town Chron.* (1911) 164 On Shrofe Sonday the kyng hadd purposed to have goone Northward. **1556** *Chron. Grey Friars* (Camden) 96 The xxiij. of February [1555] was Shroft sonday. **1570** in D. Digges *Complete Ambass.* (1655) 51 Mr. Norris is arrived here yesterday, being Shrove-sunday. **1612** SELDEN *Illustr. Drayton's Poly-olb.* XI. 207 That the Clergy should fast from Quinquagesima (that is, Shrove-sunday) to Easter. *a* **1662** HEYLIN *Laud* I. (1668) 66 Laud preaching on Shrove-Sunday, Anno 1614. **1843** KEITH *Treat. Globes* 183 Shrove Sunday or Quinquagesima Sunday is 7 weeks Before Easter.

†**Shrove Thursday.** *Obs. rare.* App. erron. for SHEER THURSDAY = Maundy Thursday.

**1518–19** *Rec. St. Mary at Hill* (1904) 301 Paid for watur on shrofthursday & on Estur Even for þe fount..j[d]. **1530** PALSGR. 267/2 Schrove thursday, *jevuedy absolu* [on pp. 266/2, 811/2 glossed correctly 'Sherethursday'].

**'Shrove-tide.** Also 5 **schrof-, -ffe-, shorff-,** 5–6 **shrof(f)-,** 6 *north.* **s(c)hraf-,** 6–7 **shros-** (?); 6 **shrosty** (?), **shrovety.** [Of obscure origin.

The first element is undoubtedly related to SHRIVE and refers to the custom of being shriven in preparation for Lent.

An OE. **scráf* shriving, confession, f. *scrífan* to SHRIVE, would account phonologically for *shrove-*, but, if the form actually existed, the absence of evidence for this group of words until the 15th c. is remarkable. (Other early names for the season were FASTENS-EEN, FAST-GONG, FASTINGONG.)]

The period comprising Quinquagesima Sunday and the two following days, 'Shrove' Monday and Tuesday.

*c* **1425** *Orolog. Sapient.* vii. in *Anglia* X. 386/39 þe sondaye In Quinquagesime, with þe tweyne dayes folowynge, þat is clepyd Schroftyde. *c* **1512** *Regul. Northumbld. Househ.* (1770) 377 From Alhallowtid to Shraftide. **1544** *Star Chamber Cases* (Selden Soc.) II. 250 Frome all halouday vntyll Shrostyde. **1597** SHAKS. *2 Hen. IV.* v. iii. 38 'Tis merry in Hall, when Beards wagge all; And welcome merry Shrouetide. *c* **1618** MORYSON *Itin.* IV. 488 Paying their tribute to the Pope at Shrostyde, when they are allowed to shewe publike games. **1670** LASSELS *Voy. Italy* I. 214 Having spunn out thus the time till near Carnavale or shroftide. **1795** SOUTHEY *Joan of Arc* x. 434 He could sing Carols for Shrove-tide, or for Candlemas. **1853** ROCK *Ch. Fathers* III. II. 61 Shrove-tide, or the week before Lent.

**1544** in *Sel. Cases Crt. Requests* (Selden Soc.) 96 The tenauntes..shall befor Shrosty next..pay the rerages of the same. **1573** in Feuillerat *Revels Q. Eliz.* (1908) 212 To know ..his pleasure for preparacions to be made against Shrovety.

**b.** *fig.* A time of merriment.

**1840** LONGF. *Span. Stud.* III. i, Enjoy the merry shrove-tide of thy youth!

**c.** *attrib.*, as ***Shrovetide even, -fool***; †**Shrovetide cock**, a cock tied up and pelted with sticks on Shrove Tuesday; †**Shrovetide hen**, a hen sent as a present on Shrove Tuesday.

**1598** BP. HALL *Sat.* IV. v, A Shroftide Hen, Which bought to giue, he takes to sell agen. *c* **1640** H. BELL *Luther's Colloq. Mens.* (1652) 283 The world cannot live without such Vizards and Shrovetide-Fools. **1700** DRYDEN *Fables*, *Cock & Fox* 106 Never was Shrovetide-Cock in such a Fear. **1768** TRUSLER *Hogarth Moralized* 180 Throwing at a cock, the universal shrove-tide amusement. **1789** WOLCOTT (P. Pindar) *Subj. for Painters* 7 Martyr beat like Shrovetide cocks with bats. **1820** SCOTT *Monast.* xxxiv, As surely..as ever cock fought on Shrove-tide-even.

**Shrove Tuesday.** Also 5 **chrofte-,** 5–6 **shrof-,** 6 **shroff-, shroft-, shraf-.** [See prec.] The Tuesday immediately preceding Ash Wednesday; often called *pancake day*.

*a* **1500** *Gough Chron.* in *Six Town Chron.* (1911) 159 On Chroftetewesday the Erle of Warwikk come from Caleis w[t] a faire felloshipp. **1599** NASHE *Lenten Stuffe* E 4 They would ..stand crosse-gag'd with knives in their mouthes from one Shroft-tuisday to another. **1620** J. TAYLOR (Water P.) *Wks.* (1630) I. 115/2 By the vnmanerly maners of Shroue-Tuesday Constables are baffled, Bawds are bang'd, Punckes are pillag'd. *c* **1640** [SHIRLEY] *Capt. Underwit* IV. ii. in Bullen *O. Pl.* (1883) II. 381 Tis Shrovetuesday and the prentices are pulling downe Covent Garden. **1764** *Oxf. Sausage* 22 Let glad Shrove-Tuesday bring the Pancake thin. **1817** BYRON *Beppo* i, Some weeks before Shrove Tuesday comes about, The people take their fill of recreation. **1911** MACCULLOCH *Relig. Anc. Celts* xiv, A cock or hen was ceremonially killed and eaten on Shrove Tuesday.

**b.** *allusively.* A time of merriment.

**1609** B. JONSON *Silent Wom.* III. i, Neuer a time, that the ..collegiates come to the house, but you make it a shroue-tuesday! **1621** J. TAYLOR (Water P.) *Praise Beggery* D 2, May euery day of the yeare be a Shrouetuesday.

**c.** *attrib.*, as ***Shrove Tuesday night, pancake***; †**Shrove Tuesday cock** = *Shrovetide cock*.

**1615** T. HERBERT *News Islington* (Halliw. 1848) 21 As flat as a Shrove-Tuesday pancake. *a* **1625** FLETCHER *Nice Valour* III. iii, Never was Shrove-tuesday Bird So cudgell'd. **1634** T. CAREW (*title*) Coelum Britannicum. A masque..on Shrove-Tuesday night. **1697** R. PIERCE *Bath Mem.* Pref. 6 [He] does..set up a Shrove-Tuesday Cock, for every one to throw at. **1848** WHATELY *Let.* in *Life* (1866) II. 135, I should reply, I will not set up any proposal like a Shroue-Tuesday cock for you to pelt at.

**'shroving**, *vbl. sb. Obs.* exc. *dial.* [f. *shrove-* in SHROVE-TIDE; cf. SHROVE *sb.* and *v.*] The keeping of Shrove-tide; the merrymaking characteristic of this season; festive rejoicing; carnival.

**1580** TUSSER *Husb.* (1878) 180 At Shroftide to shrouing, go thresh the fat hen. **1599** DEKKER *Shoomakers Hol.* v. v. (1610) K 4 A day of shrouing which I promist to al the mery prentises of London. **1617** MORYSON *Itin.* III. 173, I have seene Curtizans..in time of shroving, apparrelled like men, in carnation or light coloured doublets and breeches. *a* **1656** HALES *Gold. Rem.* III. (1673) 4 What else..was the whole life of this miserable man here, but in a manner a perpetual

Shroving? **1855** *N. & Q.* Ser. I. XI. 239 [In the Isle of Wight] Shroving, shroving, I am come to shroving.

**b.** *attrib.* and *Comb.*, as ***shroving day, dish, time, ware, week***; **shroving cock, hen** = *Shrovetide cock, hen.*

**1537** tr. *Latimer's Serm. bef. Convoc. Clergy* Cij, They.. liue euery day as though al their life were a shrouynge tyme. **1593** G. HARVEY *Pierce's Super.* Wks. (Grosart) II. 115 His shrouing ware [is] but lenten stuff. **1603** FLORIO *Montaigne* III. xiii. 656, I..keepe my shroving dayes vpon fish dayes; and my feasts vpon fasting-dayes. **1611** in *Songs Lond. Prentices* (Percy Soc.) 152, I will lay my lips to a fat shroving hen That none of these will 'er be had againe. **1612** in *Crt. & Times Jas. I* (1848) I. 235 The king came to town, and tarried here all that Shroving week. **1621** QUARLES *Argalus & P.* Introd., That he may stand like a Jack a Lent, or a Shroving Cock, for Everyone to spend a Cudgel at. **1625** B. JONSON *Staple of N.* Induct., His sweating put me in mind of a good Shrouing dish..a stew'd Poet! **1660** MILTON *Free Commw.* Wks. 1851 V. 421 Before so long a Lent of Servitude, they may permit us a little Shroving-time first. **1692** R. L'ESTRANGE *Fables* cccxcviii. 372 The Cudgelling of Shroving-Cocks is a Barbarous custom.

**shrow**, obs. form of SHREW.

**'shrowardly,** *adv. nonce-wd.* [? f. *shrow*, SHREW *sb.*[2] after *frowardly*.] = SHREWDLY.

**1689** ETHEREDGE *Love in Tub* I. ii, Now haue I..wounded her reputation shrowardly.

**shrowd(e,** obs. forms of SHREWD, SHROUD.

**shrub** (ʃrʌb), *sb.*[1] Forms: 2–7 **shrubbe**, 4–6 **s(c)hrobbe**, 6 **shroub, shrewb**, 6–7 **shrubb**, 7 **shrob**, 6– **shrub**. [App. repr. OE. *scrybb* fem. (occurring only once) presumed to mean 'shrubbery, underwood'. There may have been a parallel form **scrubb* without umlaut. (SCRUB *sb.*[1] is a parallel form.)

The following forms seem to be all related to the Eng. word and their meanings point to a general sense of 'rough plant or bush': NFris. *skrobb* the broom plant, underwood, brushwood, WFlem. *schrobbe* climbing wild pea or vetch, Norw. *skrubba* dwarf cornel, Da. dial. *skrub* brushwood.]

**1. a.** A woody plant smaller than a tree; *spec.* in *Bot.* a perennial plant having several woody stems growing from the same root.

**972** in Birch *Cartul. Sax.* (1893) III. 603 Of þare stan stræte andlang sorybbe [*Note*, 'or *scrybbe*, the MS. indistinct'] þæt hit cymð to Acantune. **11..** *Ibid.* I. 58 Fram Winebriȝth westriȝte to one weie þet geþ to Winchestre þat is ihoten shrubbeshedde bitwiene þe shrubbes and Winebriȝt.

**1387** TREVISA *Higden* (Rolls) II. 61 Schroysbury..hatte Schroisbury of schrobbes and fruyt þat grewe somtyme on þat hille. **1393** LANGL. *P. Pl.* C. I. 2 Y shop me into shrobbis [*v.r.* schrubbes] as y a shepherde were. **1398** TREVISA *Barth. De P.R.* XVII. ci. (1495) 666 Mirtus is a lytyll tree as it were a shrobbe. **1530** PALSGR. 267/2 Schrobbe a busshe, *arbrisseau*. **1553** EDEN *Treat. Newe Ind.* (Arb.) 18 This tree (or rather shrubbe) is deuided into many braunches. **1610** HOLLAND *Camden's Brit.* (1637) 595 A very thicket of shrobs upon an hill. *a* **1700** EVELYN *Diary* 30 Sept. 1644 Rosemary, lavender, lentiscs, and the like sweet shrubes. **1791** W. GILPIN *Forest Scenery* I. 98 The holly can hardly be called a tree, tho it is a large shrub. **1802** WORDSW. *Farewell* 11 The flowering shrubs that deck our humble door. **1870** YEATS *Nat. Hist. Comm.* 197 The cotton shrub is cultivated in India. **1870** HOOKER *Stud. Flora* 342 Salix herbacea..The smallest British shrub.

*transf.* **1653** R. SANDERS *Physiogn.* 144 On thy thighs, Though meagre, ugly shrubs of hair arise.

**b.** *fig.* and in proverbial use.

**1592** *Soliman & Pers.* V. iii, The shrub is safe when the Cedar shaketh. **1604** T. WRIGHT *Passions* IV. ii. §1. 127 These men questionlesse haue some little shrubs of pride and vanitie. **1646** G. DANIEL *Poems* Wks. (Grosart) I. 213, I was Shap't Only to flutter in the lower Shrubbs Of Earth-borne follies. **1672** SIR T. BROWNE *Let. Friend* §37 They who thus timely descend into themselves, cultivating the good seeds which nature hath set in them..become not shrubs but cedars in their generations.

†**2.** A twig, sprig, sprout. *Obs.*

*c* **1530** TINDALE *Jonas* Prol. B viij b, It greueth thyne hert for the losse of a vile shrobbe or spraye. **1585** FETHERSTONE tr. *Calvin on Acts* vii. 30 The thicker the bush is, and the more store of shrubbes it hath. *a* **1592** GREENE *Jas. IV*, (1861) 206 The rose although in thorny shrubs she spreads, Is still the rose. **1647** HEXHAM I, Full of shrubs, *vol spruyten*.

†**3.** A mean, inferior, insignificant person; = SCRUB *sb.*[1] 5. *Obs.*

**1566** DRANT *Sat.* I. x. E vj b, Suche carelesse, brainlesse, senslesse shrubbs. **1656** S. WINTER *Serm.* 93 God's..ey and his heart was towards them..though poor shrubs praying in the temple. **1683** BUNYAN *Greatn. Soul* (1691) 131 The Gyants in grace, as well as the weak and shrubs. **1690** C. NESSE *Hist. & Myst. O. & N. Test.* I. 200 The poor shrub had sped so well in prayer.

**4.** *attrib.* and *Comb.*

**1567** MAPLET *Gr. Forest* 44 Fumitorie..is a bushie or shrublike Herbe. **1582** STANYHURST *Æneis* III. 61 Aparrayld In shrub weeds thorny [*consertum tegimen spinis*]. *c* **1710** CELIA FIENNES *Diary* (1888) 220 Ye squares are full of gooseberry and Shrub-trees. **1786** ABERCROMBIE *Gard. Assist.* 317 In most of the tree and shrub kinds. **1796** WITHERING *Brit. Plants* (ed. 3) II. 448 Stems rather shrub-like. *a* **1817** T. DWIGHT *Trav. New Eng.*, etc. (1821) II. 457 Currants, gooseberries, and other kinds of shrub fruit. **1841** BROWNING *Pippa* Introd. 46 All the while thy rain Beats fiercest on her shrub-house window-pane. **1870** C. KINGSLEY *At Last* xi, The welcome shade of low shrub-fringed cliffs. **1897** MARY KINGSLEY *W. Africa* 52 A dry land shrub-belt. **1933** A. OSBORN *Shrubs & Trees* v. 38 Endeavour to visualize the shrub-border when its inmates are fully grown. **1978** R. E. HEATH *Miniature Shrubs* p. vii, A shrub border once planted needs very little after care.

**b.** *spec.* applied to shrubby plants and to other natural objects resembling shrubs, as ***shrub coral, worm***; also **shrub cotton**, a variety of the cotton plant intermediate between the herbaceous and the arborescent; †**shrub-mallow**, marsh mallow, *Althæa*; †**shrub-nightshade**, woody nightshade, *Solanum Dulcamara*; **shrub oak**, = *scrub-oak*, SCRUB *sb.*[1] 6 c; †**shrub pea**, the shrubby pea of Barbados; **shrub rose**, a rose, esp. a species or variety long in cultivation, allowed to follow its natural pattern of growth; cf. OLD ROSE a; **shrub-shilling**, a variety of the pine-tree shilling (see PINE-TREE b) of Massachusetts (*Cent. Dict.*); **shrub-snail**, a European snail, *Helix arbustorum*; **shrub trefoil, yellowroot** (see TREFOIL, YELLOWROOT).

**1640** PARKINSON *Theat. Bot.* 857 *Shrub spotted Arsmart of Virginia. **1681** GREW *Musæum* III. §1. iii. 275 The *Shrub-Coral *Corallium fruticosum*. **1858** HOMANS *Cycl. Comm.* 434/1 The pod of the *shrub cotton differs from that of the herb in being egg-shaped. **1640** PARKINSON *Theat. Bot.* 298 *Shrub Mallow with a white or purple flower. **1664** *Shrub nightshade [see NIGHTSHADE[1] 2]. **1688** HOLME *Armoury* II. iv. 75/2 The Shrub Night-shade, hath a dark brown stock and branches, the flowers like the common Night-shade, in one white, in another blew. **1753** HANWAY *Trav.* (1762) I. VII. lxxxix. 408 Passing through..several forests of *shrub oaks. **1784** J. BELKNAP *Tour White Mts.* (1876) 18 Among the brakes and wind-falls and shrub oaks on the pitch pine plain adjoining the Pond. **1868** LOSSING *Hudson* 213 Making our way..through gorges filled with shrub-oaks. **1691–6** PLUKENET *Almagestum* Wks. 1769 III. 291 Phaseolus Barbadensis fruticosus Septennii durationis. The Seven Years Pea, and The *Shrub Pea. **1948** G. S. THOMAS in *Jrnl. R. Hort. Soc.* LXXIII. 170 (*heading*) *Shrub roses for the modern garden. **1980** A. WILSON *Setting World on Fire* II. iv. 117 She runs a shrub rose nursery garden in Sussex. **1861** HULME tr. *Moquin-Tandon* II. III. 175 The Helix..Arbustorum, Linn., or *shrub snail. **1668** CHARLETON *Onomast.* 55 *Fruticarii*..*Shrub-worms.

**shrub** (ʃrʌb), *sb.*[2] [Variant of SHRAB, or metathetic ad. Arab. *shurb* drink, draught.]

**1.** A prepared drink made with the juice of orange or lemon (or other acid fruit), sugar, and rum (or other spirit).

Often ***rum-shrub***; also with other qualifying words indicating the ingredient which takes the place of the rum in drinks prepared in this way to which the name 'shrub' is extended.

**1747** *Gentl. Mag.* 468 A mixture of lemon juice and rum (shrub as they call it) may be carried in any quantity, as it will keep a long time. **1762** *Chron.* in *Ann. Reg.* 118 Three seamen dropt down with fatigue and thirst, though wine, rum, and shrub were given them alternately. **1764** ELIZA MOXON *Eng. Housew.* (ed. 9) 145 To make Orange Shrub. **1808** *Sporting Mag.* XXX. 99, 38 gallons of rum shrub. **1835** DICKENS *Sk. Boz, Miss Evans*, Miss Ivins's friend's young man would have the ladies go into the Crown, to taste some shrub. **1863** TREVELYAN *Compet. Wallah* (1866) 138 Beer-shrub, brandy-shrub, sherry-shrub, Simkin-shrub, tea-shrub. **1888** BESANT *Fifty Yrs. Ago* xi, Is there any living man who now calls for shrub?

**2.** *U.S.* A cordial or syrup made from the juice of the raspberry, with vinegar and sugar.

**1860** O. W. HOLMES *Elsie V.* vii, Mr. Peckham, would you be so polite as to pass me a glass of shrub? Silas Peckham.. took from the table a small glass cup, containing a fluid reddish in hue and subacid in taste. **1884** C. D. WARNER *Their Pilgr.* xi, Sipping their raspberry shrub in a retired corner of the bar-room.

**shrub** (ʃrʌb), *v.* [Of mixed origin: partly parallel form to SCRUB *v.*, partly f. SHRUB *sb.* With sense 4 cf. MDu. *schrobben* to scratch or root in the ground.]

†**1.** *trans.* = SCRUB *v.*[1] 1. *Obs.*

**13..** *K. Alis.* (Laud MS.) 4310 Þe knaues graiþen her hors & shrubben.

†**2.** *intr.* To rub or scratch the body; to fidget.

*c* **1460** J. RUSSELL *Bk. Nurture* 300 With youre body be not shrubbynge. **1594** NASHE *Unfort. Trav.* L 1, As how? as how? sayde Zadoch, shrugging and shrubbing.

†**3.** *trans.* To scratch. *Obs.*

**1657** W. COLES *Adam in Eden* lvii, Asses love to.. shrub their backs with its prickles [the rest-harrow].

†**4.** *trans.* To grub up (bushes); to rid (ground) of shrubs or stumps. *Obs.*

**1553** *Short Catech.* in J. Randolph *Enchir. Theol.* (1792) I. 68 The husbandemen that fyrst vse to shrubbe and roote out the thornes..oute of their ley land. **1573** BARET *Alv.* G 573 To Grub, to shrubbe, or rid from bushes or trees. **1611** COTGR., *Desfricher*, to grub, shrub, rid the ground from rootes.

†**5.** To lop (a tree, its branches); also *fig.* *Obs.*

**1573** A. ANDERSON *Expos. Benedictus* 64 The Papistes.. though they be woll shrubbed, and shred, yet they begin euen nowe before the springe, to budde. **1611** SPEED *Hist. Gt. Brit.* IX. xxiii. 81 These accusations, were rather to shrub off his faire top. **1650** FULLER *Pisgah* II. i. 56 Shroudly shrubbing their branches, God rent them up by the roots. **1682** GREW *Anat. Plants* Introd. 3 Trunks, some being more Entire, others Branched, others Shrub'd.

†**6.** To cudgel. *Obs.*

**1599** GREENE *Pinner of Wakefield* v. i, Were not for shame, I would shrub your shoulders well. **1706** PHILLIPS (ed. Kersey), To *Shrub one*, to cudgel or bang him soundly.

**7.** *pass.* To be planted with shrubs.

**1886** R. F. BURTON *Arab. Nts.* (abr. ed.) I. 140 A running stream whose banks were shrubbed with bushes of rose and jasmine. **1891** 'ANNIE THOMAS' *That Affair* II. ix. 144 A secluded spot, well treed and shrubbed in.

Hence **shrubbing** *vbl. sb.*

**1611** COTGR., *Defrichage*, the shrubbing, or grubbing vp of yong wood. **1654** GAYTON *Pleas. Notes* III. v. 92 Sancho imputes all his shrubbings to his Masters perjuries.

**shrubbage** ('ʃrʌbɪdʒ). Also 8 **shrubidge**. [f. SHRUB *sb.*[1] + -AGE.] Shrubbery.

**1713** *Rolls Crt. Attachm. Walth. For.* (1873) I. 6 To fell the two Shrubidges cont. ab[t]. 90 acres lyeing in Layton Walk. **1893** J. W. BARRY *Studies Corsica* 234 This ever-green shrubbage.

**shrubbed** (ʃrʌbd), *a.* [f. SHRUB *sb.* or *v.* + -ED.]

†**1.** Stunted; = SCRUBBED *a.* 1; also, shrubby.

**1539** *Cockersand Chartul.* (Chetham Soc.) 1204 There be ..CC shrubbed Okes & Asshes cropped & shredd. **1589** WARNER *Alb. Eng.*, *Æneidos* 150 b, Neere at hand were growing diuers shrubbed Trees. **1597** GERARDE *Herbal* II. cccxxxviii. 788 *Althæa frutex Clusii*. Shrubbed Mallowe. **1599** MINSHEU s.v. *Coral*, It groweth in the sea like a shrubbed stump. **1681** R. KNOX *Hist. Rel. Ceylon* IV. x. 165 The Woods in all these Northern Parts are short and shrubbed.

**2.** Planted with shrubs.

**1895** *Daily News* 16 Feb. 6/4 A path..with shrubbed borders on each side.

**shrubberied** ('ʃrʌbərɪd), *a.* [f. SHRUBBERY + -ED.] Planted or bordered with shrubbery.

**1856** HAWTHORNE *Engl. Note-bks.* II. 53 The shrubberied paths. **1885** *Harper's Mag.* Mar. 520/2 Miniature parks,.. flowered, shrubberied, and statued.

**shrubbery** ('ʃrʌbərɪ). [f. SHRUB *sb.*[1] + -ERY.]

**1.** A plantation of shrubs; a plot planted with shrubs.

**1748** LADY LUXBOROUGH *Let. to Shenstone* 16 Oct., Nature has been so remarkably kind this last Autumn to adorn my Shrubbery with the flowers that usually blow at Whitsuntide. **1791** NEWTE *Tour Eng. & Scot.* 139 A beautiful shrubbery of birch, oak, and alders. **1841** B. HALL *Patchwork* I. x. 158 The house and terrace were sheltered by a thick shrubbery. **1877** BLACK *Green Past.* ii, She passed through some dense shrubberies..until she came to an open space at the edge of a wood.

*attrib.* **1786** ABERCROMBIE *Gard. Assist.* 56 Grass lawns, gravel walks, shrubbery compartments. **1895** SCULLY *Kafir Stories* 58 [He] walked quickly down the shrubbery path.

**2.** Shrubs collectively or in a mass.

**1777** G. FORSTER *Voy. round World* I. 64 Several species of lizards, land-tortoises, and serpents frequent the dry shrubbery. **1837** HT. MARTINEAU *Soc. Amer.* 15 Birch and ash grew around the bases of the pillars, and shrubbery tufted the sides. **1883** *Harper's Mag.* Jan. 199 The light-toned masses of maple, alder, and small shrubbery along the water-side.

**3.** *transf.* A beard or whiskers. *joc.*

**1937** WODEHOUSE *Lord Emsworth & Others* ii. 101 Something has eaten off Sir Preston's moustache... I met him outside, and the shrubbery had completely disappeared. **1966** J. S. COX *Illustr. Dict. Hairdressing* 137/2 *Shrubbery*, a false beard; also the natural beard.

**'shrubbiness.** [f. SHRUBBY + -NESS.] The state of being like a shrub or planted with shrubs.

**1727** BAILEY vol. II, *Shrubbiness*, Fulness of Shrubs. **1851** *Beck's Florist* 122 It is evident that no advance towards shrubbiness can be attained by crossing the present Florists' varieties [of Calceolarias] amongst themselves.

**'shrubbish,** *a.* [f. SHRUB *sb.*[1] + -ISH.] Like a shrub.

**1656** W. DU GARD tr. *Comenius' Gate Lat. Unl.* 33 Those fenny ones are of a Shrubbish nature, as the Rush. **1694** WESTMACOTT *Script. Herb.* 152 The wild [pomegranates] are a shrubbish low tree.

†**'shrubble.** *Obs. rare*$^{-1}$. [f. SHRUB *sb.*[1] + -LE.] A little sprout or spray.

**1674** N. FAIRFAX *Bulk & Selv.* 128 The seed heaves up from a sprouting or shrubble to the scantling of height..that nature has cut out for it.

**shrubby** ('ʃrʌbɪ), *a.* [f. SHRUB *sb.*[1] + -Y.]

**1.** Having the habit, growth, or size of a shrub; *spec.* having perennial woody stems rising from the root. In early use freq. applied to trees of stunted growth (cf. SCRUBBY *a.*[1] 1).

**1581** MARBECK *Bk. Notes* 734 Mirrhe is a little shrubby tree. **1597** BACON *Coulers Gd. & Euill* Ess. (Arb.) 148 The shootes or vnderwood that grow neare a great..tree, is the most pyned and shrubbie wood of the field. **1630** CAPT. SMITH *Advts. Planters New Eng.* 22 Three or foure short shrubby old Cedars. **1679** EVELYN *Sylva* (ed. 3) 2 These [trees] we shall divide into the Greater and more Ceduous, Fruticant, and Shrubby. **1707** MORTIMER *Husb.* (1721) I. 66 Plants appearing Withered or Blasted, Shrubby and Curled, are the effects of immoderate Wet or Heat, and Cold interchangably. **1773** *Hist. Brit. Dom. Amer.* II. v. §2. 290 The timber is too small, shrubby, and gnarly. **1808** PIKE *Sources Mississ.* (1810) III. App. 22 On all the small streams there are shrubby cotton-trees. **1884** BOWER & SCOTT *De Bary's Phaner.* 593 The thick masses of wood of shrubby and tree-like Chenopodiaceæ.

**b.** In specific names of plants, often rendering L. *fruticosus*.

**1597** GERARDE *Herbal* III. xiv. 1129 *Polemonium siue Trifolium fruticans*. Shrubbie Trefoile. **1640** PARKINSON *Theat. Bot.* 1677 The shrubby wild Bay of Candy. **1775** *Phil. Trans.* LXVI. 15 *note*, The *brassica sylvestris*, or shrubby cabbage. **1857** THOREAU *Maine W.* ii. (1869) 98 Shrubby-willows or sallows. **1862** JOHNS *Brit. Birds* 426 The *Suæda fruticosa*, Shrubby Sea Blite, of botanists. **1884** W. MILLER *Plant-n.* 57/2 Shrubby Grass. The genus *Thamnochortus*.

†**c.** Of persons: Stunted, undersized. *Obs.*

**1603** OWEN *Pembrokeshire* v. (1891) 41 This kinde of people I finde to be..shorte of growth, broade, and shrubbye.

**2.** Of the nature of or consisting of shrubs.

**1540** *Mem. Fountains* (Surtees Soc.) 343 A close of pasture with myche shrubby wood therein. **1633** T. STAFFORD *Pac. Hib.* I. iii. (1821) 43 A lowe shrubbie boggie wood. **1681** R. KNOX *Hist. Rel. Ceylon* IV. x. 165 The Woods began to be very full of Thorns, and shrubby Bushes. **1708** J. PHILLIPS *Cyder* I. 8 The goats their shrubby brouze gnaw pendent. **1816** SCOTT *Old Mort.* xvi, Troopers..posted behind the cover of the shrubby copses of alders. **1869** A. R. WALLACE *Malay Archip.* vii. (1874) 115 The undergrowth consisting of fine herbaceous plants, tree-ferns, and shrubby vegetation.

**3.** Covered, planted, or overgrown with shrubs.

**1598** YONG *Diana* 441 The beauties of the shrubby hils. **1609** HOLLAND *Amm. Marcell.* 135 Through blind wayes in forrests and shrubbie places. **1634** MILTON *Comus* 306 Due west it rises from this shrubby point. **1717** BERKELEY *Jrnl. Tour Italy* Wks. 1871 IV. 546 A stony, rocky, shrubby tract. **1814** BRACKENRIDGE *Jrnl.* in *Views Louisiana* 227, I..wandered several miles through shrubby hills. **1865** W. G. PALGRAVE *Arabia* I. 218 We stopped near noon in a little shrubby plain.

**4.** Characteristic of a shrub or its habit.

**1776** WITHERING *Bot. Arrangem. Veget.* 804 Shrubby, somewhat woody, as the stems of the Rose. **1816** *Encycl. Perth.* V. 639/1 It rises with a shrubby stalk 8 or 9 feet high. **1870** HOOKER *Stud. Flora* 203 Tanacetum..Herbs often shrubby below. **1882** *Garden* 11 Mar. 161/1 The foliage, which is produced on a strong, round, shrubby stem, is very dark green.

**shrubless** (ˈʃrʌblɪs), *a.* [f. SHRUB *sb.*[1] + -LESS.] Without shrubs.

**1816** BYRON *Pris. Chillon* ix, Shrubless crags. **1862** MRS. SPEID *Last Yrs. India* 34 Aden—shrubless, flowerless, dusky, grim, and scorious.

ˈ**shrublet.** [-LET.] A small shrub.

**1886** *Offic. Handbk. Cape G. Hope* 303 Shrublets of 1 to 2 feet. **1897** BRYCE *Impr. S. Africa* 10 A country..covered..with grass or shrublets fit for cattle. **1900** B. D. JACKSON *Gloss. Bot. Terms, Shrublet*, an undershrub.

So ˈ**shrubling** [-LING].

**1854** *Tait's Mag.* XXI. 456 The spring..bedecks the poorest shrubling.

**shruff**[1] (ʃrʌf). *Obs.* exc. *dial.* [Parallel to SCRUFF *sb.*[1]] Refuse, esp. for burning; light refuse wood, cinders, etc. used for fuel.

**1399** LANGL. *Rich. Redeles* II. 154 Thus baterid þis bred on busshes aboute, And gaderid gomes on grene þer as þe walkyd, þat all þe schroff and schroup sondrid ffrom oþer. **1592** GREENE *Conny Catch.* 24 Store of shruff dust and small cole. **1674** N. FAIRFAX *Bulk & Selv.* 151 The shruff, moss and hair that the nest was thwackt together of. *a* **1800** PEGGE *Suppl. Glose, Shruff*, light rubbish wood, a perquisite to hedgers. Norf. and Suff. **1893** ZINCKE *Wherstead* 100 'Shruff' for the dry wood in the hedges.

**shruff.**[2] ? *Obs.* Also 6 shroffe, 7 shroof. [? ad. G. *schroff* fragment of mineral (Jacobsson in Grimm).] Old brass (or copper). Also *attrib.* in ***shruff brass, metal.***

**1541–2** *Act 33 Hen. VIII*, c. 7 §1 It was enacted, that noe person .. shoulde .. carrye .. any Brasse Copper .. Gunemettall ne Shroffe Metal into anye parte..beyonde the Sea. *a* **1618** *Rates Marchandizes* G 2, Shruffe or old Brasse. **1693** *Phil. Trans.* XVII. 736 Brass Shruff serves instead of so much Copper. **1700** *Ibid.* XXII. 475 Brass-Shruff..is a collection of pieces of old Brass, which is usually procured in small parcels. **172.** in Beawes *Lex. Mercat.* (1752) 678 Battery and Brass Shruff. **1787** *Jackson's Oxford Jrnl.* 7 Apr. 3/3 The following sorts of Copper, viz. Tile, Shruff, Shot, ..[etc.]. **1825** J. NICHOLSON *Oper. Mech.* 709, 8 oz. of shruff brass.

**shrug** (ʃrʌg), *sb.* Also 7 shrugg. [f. SHRUG *v.*]

†**1. a.** A tug, pull. **b.** A shake (of the hand).

The first quot. is obscure.

*c* **1460** *Play Sacram.* 597 Here master master ware how ye tugg The devylle I trowe w[t] in shrugge for yt gooth rebylle rable. *c* **1620** Z. BOYD *Zion's Flowers* (1855) 12 Unto this fellowe..I'le goe, And with my hand will give a shrug or two. **1742** H. WALPOLE *Let. to Mann* 7 July, All the effect this notable speech had was to frighten my uncle, and make him give two or three shrugs extraordinary to his breeches.

**2.** A raising and contraction of the shoulders to express dislike, disdain, indifference, or the like.

**1594** NASHE *Unfort. Trav.* 69 It is growen to a common prouerbe, Ile giue him the Neapolitan shrug, when one intends to play the villaine, and make no boast of it. **1596** SHAKS. *Merch. V.* I. iii. 110 Still haue I borne it with a patient shrug. **1617** MORYSON *Itin.* II. 167 To these exceptions hee answered with a Spanish shrug of the shouldier. **1619** FLETCHER *Mons. Thomas* I. ii, Sirrah, no more of your French shrugs I advise you. **1711** STEELE *Spect.* No. 75 ¶6 He contradicts with a Shrug, and confutes with a certain sufficiency. **1775** MME. D'ARBLAY *Early Diary* 3 Apr. He is a lively man, full of chat, and foreign shrugs and gestures. **1831** SCOTT *Ct. Robt.* iii, A scarce visible shrug of apology. **1860** TYNDALL *Glac.* I. xxiv. 170 The Guide Chef..met me with a polite sympathetic shrug. **1872** DARWIN *Emotions* xi. 267 He ordered a Bengalee to climb a lofty tree; but the man, with a shrug of his shoulders, and a lateral shake of his head, said he could not. **1886** T. FROST *Remin. Country Journalist* 99, I passed on, with a smile and a shrug.

†**3.** A shifting or hitching of the body, a fidgety movement (cf. SHRUG *v.* 5). *Obs.*

**1626** W. HAWKINS *Apollo Shroving* 72 There is a drowsie shrugge..This shrugge is commonly performed with displaying out the armes, and yawning with the mouth. *Ibid.* The Misers shrugge, the winter shrugge, the drowsie shrugge, the lousie shrugge.

†**4.** A shiver, shudder. *Obs. rare.*

**1713** WODROW *Corr.* (1842) I. 448 The Lord Advocate died..without any shruggs of death.

**5.** A short, close-fitting woman's jacket or shoulder stole with sleeves, orig. knitted or crocheted. Also *attrib.*, as ***shrug jacket.*** orig. *U.S.*

**1957** *Knitted Outerwear Times* 12 Aug. 23/2 Women are buying the Orlon shrug for wear over sleeveless dresses and in air conditioned rooms. **1962** *Guardian* 5 Oct. 8/5 (*caption*) This ensemble..is made up of skirt and shrug in royal blue loose weave mockknit. **1973** *Country Life* 25 Jan. 250/2 Lucca lamb shrug. **1980** *Times* 12 Feb. 7/6 Camisole top and shrug jacket takes 7 50g balls of 3 Suisses Barbara.

**shrug** (ʃrʌg), *v.* Forms: 5 schrugge, shrukke, 5–7 shrugge, 6 shroge, shruck, 8 shrugg, 6– shrug. [Of obscure origin.

Sw. dial. *skrukka, skrugge* to crouch, sit doubled up, Da. *skrukke, skrugge* to duck with the head, to walk with a stoop, are probably unconnected.]

**1.** *intr.* To shiver; to shudder for cold or fear. Now *rare* or *Obs.*

*c* **1400** [see SHRUGGING *vbl. sb.*]. *c* **1440** *Promp. Parv.* 449/1 Schruggyn [*Winch. MS.* shruggon], *frigulo.* **1549** COVERDALE, etc. *Erasm. Par. 1 Peter* iv. 11 b, As often as we loke backe at them, we shrugge for feare to remembre suche fylthynes of lyfe. **1580** BLUNDEVILE *Horsemanship, Horse's Dis.* lxxxiv. 35 He will be chill, and shrug for cold. **1609** DEKKER *Gull's Horn-bk.* v. 27 The French Lacquey, and Irish Foote-boy, shrugging at the doores. **1642** D. ROGERS *Naaman* 580 To shrugge in cold weather, and to wish a fire. *a* **1677** MANTON *Serm.* Ps. cxix. 136 He that shrugs when he sees a snake creep upon another. **1702** S. PARKER tr. *Cicero's De Finibus* II. 130 It makes me shrugg when I call to mind the Agonies which he suffer'd.

**2.** To raise (and contract) the shoulders, esp. as an expression of disdain, indifference, disclaiming responsibility, etc.; in early use also, †to cringe.

*c* **1450** in Aungier *Syon* (1840) 299 They schal not..caste oute ther armes or handes, nor schrugge withe the scholders. **1577–87** HOLINSHED *Chron.* III. 1154/2 If they did either frowne or shrug at him. **1607** SHAKS. *Cor.* I. ix. 4 Where great Patricians shall attend, and shrug, I'th'end admire. **1610** —— *Temp.* I. ii. 367 Hag-seed, hence:..shrug'st thou (Malice)? **1680** DRYDEN *Kind Kpr.* I. i. 11 Here will you take me at my word? *Wood* (*Shrugging up*) *Troppo poco, troppoco.* **1788** MME. D'ARBLAY *Diary* 10 Jan., I was quite shocked for her, and could only shrug in dismay. **1818** SCOTT *Rob Roy* xxxiii, Ewan..shrugged, as one who would express by that sign that what he was doing was none of his own choice. **1859** MEREDITH *R. Feverel* xliv, Adrian,..rose and accompanied him out of the room, shrugging. **1880** CABLE *Grandissimes* xiv, The quadroon shrugged.

**3. a.** *trans.* To raise and contract (the shoulders) in this way. Formerly often with *up.*

**1547** BOORDE *Introd. Knowl.* 187 Yf he cast hys head at the one syde, and do shroge vp hys shoulders. **1594** NASHE *Unfort. Trav.* B 2 b, The action that he vsed, of shrucking vp his shoulders,..and biting the lip. **1596** —— *Saffron Walden* G 2, If..I had not seene him shrug his shoulders, and talk of going to the Bathe. **1603** DEKKER *Wond. Yeare* Wks. (Grosart) I. 137 Shrugging his shoulders together. **1712** STEELE *Spect.* No. 264 ¶2 He..shrugs his shoulder when you talk of Securities. **1805** WORDSW. *Waggoner* I. 66 He shrugs his shoulders, shakes his head. **1835–6** *Todd's Cycl. Anat.* I. 359 The triangular space between the deltoid and pectoral may be seen even in the living person when the shoulders are shrugged up. **1876** GREEN *Stray Studies* 48 The Italian shrugs his shoulders and submits in a humorous way.

**b.** *fig.* ***to shrug*** (something) ***off*** or ***aside***: to dismiss or reject (something) in an offhand manner; to be unaffected by.

**1909** WEBSTER, Shrug off. **1932** *Now & Then* Spring 15/2 He might shrug aside or be bored or even disgusted by *Strange Interlude* or *Mourning Becomes Electra.* **1949** *Catholic Times* 4 Mar. 5/1 The disgrace of Yalta can never be shrugged off. **1963** *Observer* 17 Feb. 23/5 Some house-flies and mosquitoes can now shrug off not one but several of the most lethal poisons. **1981** *Times* 18 Apr. 21/5 The stockmarket has also shrugged aside the collapse of Hedderick Stirling Grumbar.

**4.** *nonce-uses.* **a.** To bring by shrugging (*into*..).

**1766** GOLDSM. *Vic. W.* xviii, It is not the composition of the piece, but the number of starts and attitudes that may be introduced into it that elicits applause. I have known a piece with not one jest in the whole shrugged into popularity.

**b.** To express by means of a shrug.

**1897** 'A. HOPE' *Phroso* i, He..shrugged a tolerant 'As you will', with eloquent shoulders.

†**5.** *intr.* (and *refl.*) To move the body from side to side as with uneasiness, or as a gesture of joy or self-satisfaction; to fidget about. *Obs.*

*c* **1460** [see SHRUGGING *vbl. sb.* 2]. **1567** HARMAN *Caveat* (1869) 71 The good man of the house shrodge [? *read* shrogde] hym for Ioye, thinking to hym selfe, I wyll make some pastyme with you anone. **1601** [? MARSTON] *Jack Drums Entert.* III. D 4 b, Mounsieurs Goat drunke, and he shrugges, and skrubbes, and hees it for a wench. *a* **1631** DONNE *Sat.* I. 74 He..grins, smacks, shrugs, and such an itch endures, As prentises, or schoole-boyes which doe know Of some gay sport abroad, yet dare not goe. **1628** DEKKER etc. *Witch of Edmonton* IV. ii. stage dir., Enter Dog, shrugging as it were for joy, and dances. **1651** H. MORE *Second Lash* in *Enthus. Tri.*, etc. (1656) M 2 b, That Book..I intended onely for a stumble to wake you (that you might shrugg and rub your eyes, and see in what a naked condition you are). **1652** *Roxb. Ball.* (1891) VII. 479 The Louse gave a tug, that made the Taylor shrug.

**6.** *refl.* and *intr.* To draw oneself together, 'curl' oneself up; to shrink. ? *Obs.*

**1603** FLORIO tr. *Montaigne* III. ix. 588 Let mee shrowd and shrugge my selfe into my shell, as a tortoise. **1616** B. JONSON *Devil an Ass* I. iv. 80 stage dir., Hee shrugs himselfe vp in the cloake. **1725** N. ROBINSON *Th. Physick* 39 How Plants, when they first begin to bud, will shrug and contract the little Stem. **1845** S. JUDD *Margaret* I. xvii, Robin, the bird,..shrugs and folds itself into its feathers.

†**7.** *intr.* To shrink back or away, cower; occas. const. inf., to hesitate to do something. *Obs.*

**1576** GASCOIGNE *Grief of Joy* II. lv, That from the sonne we shrug into the shade And drowping sitt. **1589** FLEMING *Virg. Georg.* I. 7 But that thou dost refuse and shrug to know such slender cares. **1642** D. ROGERS *Naaman* 385 Let us not ..shrug at the difficulty. **1675** BROOKS *Golden Key* Wks. 1867 V. 191 Will you shrug, and shrink, and faint, and fret when you are reproached for his name?

†**8.** *trans.* To contract or jerk uneasily. *Obs.*

**1678** BUTLER *Hud.* III. i. 173 He shrugg'd his sturdy Back, As if he felt his Shoulders ake.

**9.** To jerk, pull or tug *up.* *U.S.*

**1807** J. BARLOW *Columb.* III. 441 Zamor, the chieftain of the Tiger-band,..Shrugg'd up his brinded spoils above the rest. **1889** MARY E. WILKINS *Far-away Melody* etc. (1891) 29 She lay quietly, her shawl shrugged up over her face.

**10.** *intr.* To manœuvre one's arms and shoulders *into* a garment. Also *refl.*

**1930** H. ASHTON *Dr. Serocold* I. iii. 43 She shrugged herself into her stiff overcoat and began to button it all the way up to her chin. **1937** D. ALDIS *Time at her Heels* ii. 33 And shrugging into her brown suit coat she followed her sons and daughter downstairs. **1974** J. DOWELL *Look-off Bear* 6, I shrugged into my warm red-and-black-checked mackinaw jacket.

Hence **shrugged** (ʃrʌgd) *ppl. a.*; also *fig.*

**1850** ROBERTSON *Serm.* Ser. III. i. (1857) 4 An arched eyebrow, a shrugged shoulder. **1874** G. M. HOPKINS *Jrnl.* 23 May (1937) 195 Trees, clouds, and mountaintops 'seized' or 'shrugged' as in Turner.

ˈ**shrugging,** *vbl. sb.* [f. SHRUG *v.* + -ING[1].]

†**1.** Shivering. *Obs.*

*c* **1400** *Lanfranc's Cirurg.* 120 A scharp feuere falliþ, þe which arrigor [= a rigor], þat is to seie a cold schurgynge [? *read* schrugynge], goiþ tofore. *a* **1586** SIDNEY *Arcadia* II. (1912) 217 The touch of the cold water made a prettie kinde of shrugging come over her bodie. **1678** R. L'ESTRANGE *Seneca's Mor., Anger* ii. (1696) 352 A kind of Horror, and Shrugging upon the Sprinkling of Cold Water.

**2.** Raising and contracting the shoulders.

*c* **1460** RUSSELL *Bk. Nurture* 287 Nor pikynge, nor trifelynge, ne shrukkynge as þauȝ ye wold sawe. *a* **1693** *Urquhart's Rabelais* III. xvii. 141 The..shrugging of her hulchy Shoulders. **1693** EVELYN *De La Quint. Compl. Gard.* I. 136 The shrugging up of the Shoulders.

†**3.** Shrinking, hesitation. *Obs.*

**1617** HIERON *Wks.* II. 351 There is with many a kind of shrugging at this dutie.

ˈ**shrugging,** *ppl. a.* [f. SHRUG *v.* + -ING[2].]

†**1.** Shivering, shuddering. *Obs.*

*a* **1586** SIDNEY *Arcadia* II. (Sommer) 178 b, With a shrugging kinde of tremor in all her principall partes.

†**2.** ? Causing shivers, chilling. *Obs.*

**1598** DRAYTON *Heroic. Ep.* 88 The shrugging ayre about thy Temples hurles.

†**3.** Cringing. *Obs.*

**1629** EARLE *Microcosm.* (Arb.) 88 Hee begs too, onely not in the downeright for Gods sake, but with a shrugging God blesse you.

**4.** That shrugs, or is accompanied by a shrug of the shoulders.

**1814** L. HUNT *Sonn.* Poems (1860) 233 The rambler..Feels..in his shrugging neck the resolute blast. **1859** MEREDITH *R. Feverel* xxxvi. Adrian ventured a shrugging protest in her behalf. **1910** *Contemp. Rev.* Mar. 336 Her hunched and shrugging shoulder-blades.

Hence ˈ**shruggingly** *adv.*, with a shrug.

**1589** PUTTENHAM *Engl. Poesie* I. viii. (Arb.) 36 The third me thinks shruggingly saith, I kept not to sit sleeping with my Poesie till a Queene came and kissed me. **1901** *Daily Express* 18 Mar. 4/4 Students of international politics..shruggingly express the opinion that Morocco will drift along.

ˈ**shruggish,** *a.* [f. SHRUG *v.* + -ISH.] Inclined to shrug the shoulders; contemptuous.

**1877** G. MACDONALD *Marq. Lossie* lxxii, A conventional visitor was certain to feel very shruggish at first sight of the terms on which the marquis was with 'persons of that sort'.

**shrukke,** obs. form of SHRUG.

**shrunk** (ʃrʌŋk), *ppl. a.* [pa. pple. of SHRINK *v.*]

**1.** Contracted or reduced in size; drawn together into a smaller compass; †reduced in power, means, or the like. Also with *together, up, away.*

**a.** in predicative use.

**1530** PALSGR. 705/2 My leather purse is shronke. **1540** —— *Acolastus* II. I. Hij, My bely or panche is all wasted quyte vp or shronke to gether. **1592** KYD *Murther I. Brewen* Wks. (1901) 291 Vomiting till his intrailes were all shrunke and broken. **1607** SHAKS. *Timon* III. ii. 68 Timon is shrunke indeede. **1663** STAPYLTON *Slighted Maid* Prol., Men are shrunk in Brain as well as Stature. **1675** EVELYN *Terra* (1676) 68 Sedums..when to all appearance shrunk and shrivel'd up. **1823** SCOTT *Quentin D.* xxviii, My dominions ..are somewhat shrunk in compass. **1827** —— *Chron. Canongate* iii, The wood paneling was shrunk and warped. **1845** BUDD *Dis. Liver* 245 The brain..is generally somewhat shrunk.

**b.** in attributive use. Now somewhat *rare.*

**1592** SHAKS. *Rom. & Jul.* IV. i. 104 In this borrowed likenesse of shrunke death Thou shalt continue two and forty houres. **1593** —— *Lucr.* 1455 Her blew bloud chang'd to blacke in euerie vaine, Wanting the spring, that those shrunke pipes had fed. **1600** —— *A.Y.L.* II. vii. 161 His shrunke shanke. **1609** B. JONSON *Masque* Wks. (1616) 955 As low as lies Old shrunk-vp Chaos. **1631** MASSINGER *Believe as You List* IV. iv, To stretch my shruncke up sinnewes at an ore. **1675** HANNAH WOOLLEY *Gentlew. Comp.* 185 The withered or shrunk Barberries. **1784** COWPER *Task* I. 392 The flaccid, shrunk, And wither'd muscle. **1835** *Court Mag.* VI. 71/2 She was of shrunk growth, if not positively deformed. **1849** CUPPLES *Green Hand* xv. (1856) 149 Till his shrunk face was as quiet on the pillow as if he'd been really at home the first night after a voyage. **1907** G. F. SCOTT ELLIOT *Rom. Plant Life* xv. 196 The 'shrunk' or folded condition of the leaflets.

**2.** Of cloth: That has been subjected to the process of 'shrinking'.

**1895** *Stores Price List*, White Flannels... Cream Tennis, Twill (Shrunk).

**3.** Fitted *on* by the process of shrinking.

**1908** *Westm. Gaz.* 18 Aug. 4/2 Eight cylinders, arranged V-fashion, with shrunk-on brass water-jackets.

**shrunken** (ˈʃrʌŋk(ə)n), *ppl. a.* [pa. pple. of SHRINK *v.*] = SHRUNK *ppl. a.* 1.

**a.** in predicative use.

*c*950 *Lindisf. Gosp.* Luke vi. 6 Hond his ðiu suiðra ʒescruncan *manus eius dextra arida.* **1390** GOWER *Conf.* I. 98 Hire Lippes schrunken ben for age. **1398** TREVISA *Barth. De P.R.* XVII. xxiii. (1495) 617 Synewes that ben shronken wyth the Crampe. **1471** CAXTON *Recuyell* (Sommer) I. 43 This dede man of whom the skyn was scorched, the flessh rosted, the senewes shronken. **1582** BENTLEY *Mon. Matrones* iii. 290 My bones are so bruised, my sinewes are so shrunken. **1873** MISS BRADDON *Lucius Davoren* i, Very shrunken are the stores which Lucius Davoren guards. **1876** BRISTOWE *Theory & Pract. Med.* (1878) 785 The liver shrunken and indurated. **1877** BLACK *Green Past.* xxx, The mamma was shrunken and shrivelled.

**b.** in attributive use.

*c*1400 *Ragman Roll* ix. in Wright *Anecd. Lit.* 84 Your shrunkyn lyppis and your gowuldyn tethe. **1590** SPENSER *F.Q.* I. ix. 20 The.. shrunken synewes of her chosen knight. **1625** BACON *Ess., Truth* (Arb.) 500 If there were taken out of Mens Mindes, Vaine Opinions, Flattering Hopes.. it would leaue the Mindes, of a Number of Men, poore shrunken Things. *Ibid., Boldness* 519 That puts his Face, into a most Shruncken, and woodden Posture. **1795** SOUTHEY *Joan of Arc* II. 210 Pale and shrunken cheeks. **1855** DICKENS *Dorrit* I. v, The baking-dish was served up.. on a shrunken cloth at an end of the dining-table. **1860** *W. Smith's Dict. Bible* I. s.v. *Antioch*, Modern Antakia is a shrunken and miserable place. **1860** GEO. ELIOT *Mill on Fl.* II. iv, He had rather a shrunken appearance. **1879** —— *Theo. Such* xvi. 281 The shrunken meaning that popular or polite speech assigns to 'morality'.

**shryffe, shryve**, obs. ff. SHERIFF, SHRIVE.

**shshsh.** An extended SH!

Hence **shshshing** *vbl. sb.*

**1848** [see SH]. **1873** H. E. P. SPOFFORD *Pilot's Wife* in *Casquet Lit.* IV. 13/2 She and the nurse made such a racket between them, with their shshshing and trotting and patting and stirring and tipping.

**shtchee, shtchi**, varr. SHCHI.

‖**shtetl** (ˈʃtɛt(ə)l, ˈʃteɪt(ə)l). Also **shtetel**. Pl. **shtetlach, shtetlakh, shtetls.** [Yiddish, 'little town', f. G. *stadt.*] A small Jewish town or village in Eastern Europe. Now *Hist.* Also *transf.*

**1949** *Yivo Ann. Jewish Soc. Sci.* IV. 87 Swistocz.. was considered one of the larger towns (*shtetl*) in the district of Grodno. **1963** M. SAMUEL *Little did I Know* ix. 137 The *Shtetlach!* Those forlorn little settlements in a vast and hostile wilderness, isolated alike from Jewish and non-Jewish centers of civilization. **1968** L. ROSTEN *Joys of Yiddish* 370 The world of the Jews in Germany.. was vastly different from the world of *shtetl* Jews in eastern Europe. **1972** *New Society* 3 Aug. 228/1 People who, in former reincarnations, were clerks and schoolmarms in the *shtetls* of Minsk, Pinsk and Milwaukee. **1973** *Times* 3 Feb. 13/4 Jewish food is the diet of the *shtetel*—the small village. **1976** *Nat. Observer* (U.S.) 6 Mar. 19/1 In the *shtetlakh*, the small towns, they lived lives of grinding poverty amid the constant expectation of external attack. **1977** *Listener* 31 Mar. 422/4 The little Jewish townships of Russia, the *shtetlach.* **1978** *Times Lit. Suppl.* 10 Nov. 1314/2 Hitler swept away the *shtetls* of Eastern Europe.

‖**shtibl** (ˈʃtiːb(ə)l). Also **shtiebel, shtieble, stiebel.** Pl. **shtibblach.** [Yiddish; cf. Ger. dial. *stüberl* small room.] A small synagogue or Jewish house of worship.

**1929** I. GOLLER *Five Bks. Mr. Moses* I. i. 10 Reb Zalman, Rabbi of the *Shtiebel* off Commercial Street. *Ibid.* ii. 15 A single, large room the *Shtiebel*, combination of synagogue, house of study, library and club-room for the disciples of Reb Zalman. **1960** H. RABINOWICZ *Guide to Hassidism* x. 120 The *stiebel* (literally 'room').. played a vital rôle. It served both as place of worship and as house of study... In the *stiebel* the Hassidim communed with God and with themselves. **1967** C. POROK *Chosen* vii. 116 Each Hasidic sect had its own house of worship—shtibblach, they were called. **1973** *Jewish Chron.* 14 Sept. 22/1 The new cathedral synagogue of Jerusalem.. will make Herod's temple look like a shtibl. **1976** C. BERMANT *Coming Home* II. iv. 173, I belong to two synagogues, a large one.. and a gilded little bethel with about two dozen members called a *shtieble.*

‖**shtik** (ʃtɪk). *U.S. slang.* Also **schtick, schtik, shtick.** [Yiddish, f. G. *stück* piece, play.]

**1.** An act or stage routine; a joke, a 'gag'. Hence *transf.* (freq. slightly *derog.*), a patter, a 'line'; a gimmick or characteristic style. orig. *Theatr.*

**1961** A. BERKMAN *Singers' Gloss. Show Business* 78 A piece of business; a gag or joke.. *shtik.* **1962** 'E. MCBAIN' *Empty Hours* 129 The girl didn't say a word. She didn't have to. The effect was almost comic, akin to the cocktail-party scene... The word '*shtik*' crossed Meyer's mind. **1964** S. BELLOW *Herzog* 60 'Let's cut out all the *shtick*,' said Gersbach. 'Let's say you're a crumb.' **1968** P. TAMONY *Americanisms* (typescript) No. 19. 2 Consistency is not the schtick of protestors. **1973** *Times* 30 July 5/5 Emotionally controlled.. and minus the usual Streisand shtick, it [*sc.* a film] is arguably the best performance of her career. **1974** P. GZOWSKI *Bk. about this Country* 46/1 People who are professionally funny—guys who do schticks—are less funny than he is. **1977** *Time* 19 Dec. 12/2 The former Prime Minister is not at all apologetic about his Yuletide shtik, pointing out that he has chosen to write books and sell records rather than go the David Frost route.

**2.** A particular area of activity or interest, a sphere or 'scene'.

**1968** *Atlantic Monthly* Sept. 50/1 My first assignment was to a gentle middle-aged Jewish household, hardly my schtik. **1972** *New York* 1 May 13/2 This unfortunately overlong satire on the sexology schtick of our times. **1976** *Publishers Weekly* 15 Mar. 55/2 A husband trying to puzzle out his woman, women-God-bless-them in general, and the whole female *shtick.*

**Shtokavian, Shtokavski:** see ŠTOKAVIAN.

‖**shtook** (ʃtʊk). *slang.* Also **schtook, schtuck, shtuck,** etc. [Origin unknown: app. not a Yiddish word.] Trouble; esp. in phr. ***in (dead) shtook.***

**1936** G. INGRAM *Muffled Man* iv. 68, I to come to you if I'm in 'stook'. **1960** *News Chron.* 16 Feb. 6 In fact, I'm in shtook. **1970** G. F. NEWMAN *Sir, You Bastard* 280 The filth, who was supposed to be in dead shtook, was sitting there like he owned the gaff. **1971** F. NORMAN *Dodger-Greaser* vii. 136 It'd be a terrible fing if none or us could 'elp each uvva aht nar an' then wen we're in dead schtook. **1975** *Observer* 27 Apr. 33/1 The scheme went awry, landing David in shtuck with the Law and jeopardising his lucrative future. **1978** J. GARDNER *Dancing Dodo* xxxi. 246 You know I'm in schtuck with my bosses.

‖**shtoom** (ʃtʊm), *a.* and *v. slang.* Also **schtoom, shtum(m),** etc. [Yiddish, f. G. *stumm* (also used) silent, mute.] **A.** *adj.* Silent, speechless, dumb. Esp. in phr. ***to keep*** (or ***stay***) ***shtoom.*** Occas. also as *sb.*

**1958** F. NORMAN *Bang to Rights* 15, I think it's much better to keep shtoom. **1972** J. CAINE *Hamlet, my Boy* x. 141 Keep *shtumm* and you won't get plugged. **1974** L. DEIGHTON *Spy Story* iv. 41 So far, both sides have kept stumm about these operations. **1981** J. BARNETT *Firing Squad* ii. 14 Stay schtoom. If the law does come round you don't go near... It's got to be total schtoom on this. **1981** G. MARKSTEIN *Ultimate Issue* 209 Keep stumm about how you heard... You can always say you picked up a rumour.

**B.** *v. intr.* To be quiet, to shut *up.* Also *trans.*: cf. *shut it* s.v. SHUT *v.* 4 b (c).

**1958** F. NORMAN *Bang to Rights* 72 You can always shtoomup if any screws are earholeing. **1973** BOYD & PARKES *Dark Number* ii. 21 You start something, and then just when it's getting interesting you shtoom up. **1982** 'J. GASH' *Firefly Gadroon* xvii. 185 Shtum it. Sounds carry in this.

**shtshi**, var. SHCHI.

**shtuck**, var. SHTOOK.

‖**shtup** (ʃtʊp), *v. slang.* [Yiddish; cf. Ger. dial. *stupfen* to nudge, jog.]

**1.** *trans.* To push. Hence also as *sb.*

**1968** L. ROSTEN *Joys of Yiddish* 374 'Don't *shtup*', means 'Don't push'—both literally and figuratively... A man who *shtups* himself in 'di hoykhe fenster' (the high windows) is a man who is a social climber. **1977** M. T. BLOOM *13th Man* vii. 136 What the fuck hell is now holding up the works?.. Give them a *shtup. Ibid.* xi. 182 I'm trying to give fate a *shtup*, a push, to hurry up and resolve matters.

**2.** *trans.* and *intr.* To copulate (with).

**1969** P. ROTH *Portnoy's Complaint* 83 Why, *of course* he was *shtupping* her. **1974** D. WESTLAKE *Help* v. 35 He'd go on home.. shtup the wife.. then shlep on back here. **1977** *Custom Car* Nov. 67/2 Italian men can actually murder their wives if they find 'em shtupping around.

**shu**, variant of SHE, SHOO.

‖**shuba** (ˈʃuba). Also **shooba**; anglicized **shube** (6 **shoube**, 6–7 **shub**, 8 **shoobe**, 9 **schub, shoub**). [Russian *shuba.*] A fur gown or greatcoat. †Also, a piece of fur.

**1591** HORSEY *Trav.* (Hakl. Soc.) 234 Two shubs or gowns of white armmens. **1598** HAKLUYT *Voy.* I. 54 Their shoubes or gownes are hayrie on the outside, and open behinde, with tailes hanging downe to their hammes. **1656** *Act Commw.* c. 20 Rates (1658) 466 Furs called.. Calaber, Shubs of Calaber, the piece or Shub 02 00 00. **1753** HANWAY *Trav.* (1762) I. VI. lxxxiii. 380 A full great coat lined with fur [*Note*, The Russians call it a shoobe.] **1814** LADY LYTTELTON in *Corr.* (1912) 181 Dress, a quadruple shawl and fur shuba over it. **1825** VISCT. STRATFORD DE REDCLIFFE in *Life* (1888) I. 358 A panoply of bearskin, a *schub* of grand dimensions. **1849** MRS. ATKINSON *Tartar Steppes* viii. (1863) 177 During the greatest heat they wore horse-skin shubes. **1904** WHISHAW *Tiger of Muscovy* xxviii, Amy stood dressed in her fur shooba.

**Shuboth**, var. SHABBAT.

**shubrach**, variant of SHABRACQUE.

**shubunkin** (ʃuːˈbʌŋkɪn). Also **Shubunkin.** [Jap., f. *shu* vermilion + *bun* portion, division + *kin* gold.] A goldfish, *Carassius auratus*, that is multicoloured with black spots and red patches and has elongated fins and tail.

**1917** W. T. INNES *Goldfish Varieties* ii. 26 One of the more recent introductions is the Shubunkin. **1928** *Daily Express* 5 July 8/4 'I'll just bring these Shubunkins to the front for you.' And he coaxed into view a magnificent creature with a blue body covered with red, black, yellow and brown spots. **1971** *Country Life* 1 Apr. 774/3 For common goldfish and shubunkins this [depth of water] can be reduced to 9 or 12 inches. **1980** *West Lancs. Evening Gaz.* 25 Aug. 17 First in the shubunkins.. came second in the any variety of goldfish section.

**shuch:** see SHEUGH, SUCH.

**shuck**, *sb.*¹ *Obs.* exc. *dial.* Forms: 1 **scucca, sceocca,** 3 **s(c)ucke, schucke, shuke.** [OE. *scucca*, perhaps f. root *skuh-* to terrify (cf. SHY).]

†**1.** A devil, fiend. *Obs.*

*Beowulf* 939 (Gr.) þæt hie wideferhð leoda landʒeweorc laþum beweredon scuccum and scinnum. *c*888 ÆLFRED *Boeth.* xxxix. §6 Ða wyrd he þonne wyrcð.. ðurh þara scuccena mislice lotwrencas. *c*1000 *Ags. Gosp.* Matt. iv. 10 Ða cwæð se hælend to him, gang þu sceocca on-bæc. *c*1205 LAY. 6838 Swa vuele he luuede his lif þat þe scucke hine i-fenge. *a*1225 *Juliana* 56 Ant tu þat schucke art schucken [*v.r.* shuken] herien ant heien. *c*1230 *Hali Meid.* 59 þen laðe vnwiht, þe hellene schucke.

**2.** *dial.* A spectre hound.

**1850** *N. & Q.* Ser. I. I. 468 Shuck the Dog-fiend. This phantom I have heard many persons in East Norfolk.. describe as having seen as a black shaggy dog, with fiery eyes. **1893** *Daily News* 28 Sept. 4/7 Mr. F. A. Paley was not uneducated.. yet he saw Shuck!

**shuck** (ʃʌk), *sb.*² Chiefly *dial.* and *U.S.* Also **shock.** [Origin unknown.]

**1. a.** A husk, pod, or shell; *esp.* the outer covering or strippings of Indian corn, chestnuts, hickory nuts, etc. See CORN-SHUCK.

**1674** RAY *S. & E.C. Words* 77 A *Shuck*: an husk or shell; as Bean-shucks, Bean-shells, per Anagramatismum τοῦ Husk forte. **1741** *Compl. Fam.-Piece* I. i. 21 The Shucks of Almonds dried and beaten to Powder. **1811** *Mass. Spy* 12 June 4/3 The straw and the shucks, after the stacks are in, will bestow a cover on them impenetrable to drought. **1847** ALB. SMITH *Chr. Tadpole* vii, Looking about as digestible as .. a chesnut shuck. **1872** SCHELE DE VERE *Americanisms* 45 Shucks are very much prized at the South as fodder for cattle. **1892** KIPLING & BALESTIER *Naulahka* 55 Ill-fitting as the shuck on a dried cob.

**b.** A fruit skin.

**1872** BROWNING *Ring & Bk.* VII. 840 Three hundred thousand bees and wasps Found her [*sc.* a fig] out, feasted on her to the shuck.

**c.** The shell of an oyster or clam.

**1881** INGERSOLL *Oyster-Industry* 248.

**d.** The shell-like covering of some larvæ.

**1886** *Field* 23 Jan. 104/1 To secure the swiftly darting larvæ.. before emerging from the 'shuck'.

**e.** Phr. ***to light a shuck***: to leave in a hurry, to hurry away.

**1905** *Dial. Notes* III. 86 *Light a shuck*, to go in a hurry, to move on, to keep away from danger. **1938** in B. A. Botkin *Treas. S. Folklore* (1949) III. i. 459 He jumped outen the water and lit a shuck for camp. **1947** *True* Nov. 108/2 But the Espinosas lit a shuck for the mountains. **1971** J. V. ALLEN *Cowboy Lore* IV. 71 So he saddled up old Chaw one night and lit a shuck this way.

**2.** As a type of something valueless.

**a.** *gen.* **b.** in negative phr., esp. in ***not worth shucks*** = good for nothing. **c.** A mean or contemptible person. **d.** (See quot.) **e.** Nonsense, deception, sham.

**a. 1851** MAYNE REID *Scalp Hunters* III. iii. 36 They'd whip us to shucks on the parairer [= prairie]. **1859** BEECHER *Life Thoughts* Ser. II. 120 They [*sc.* infidels] shake and rend His truths until they think that they have destroyed them, but they have only cleared them of the shuck. **1890** *Nature* 20 Feb. 376 That record—a mere dry shuck, emptied of nearly all that makes natural history delightful. **1897** *Century Mag.* Aug. 591 That's the biggest shuck and the littlest nubbin I ever did see.

**b. 1847** ROBB *Squatter Life* 135 He ain't wuth shucks, and ef you don't lick him fur his onmannerly note, you ain't wuth shucks, nuther. **1868** *All Year Round* 10 Oct. 431 As for your being a furrener, it don't matter shucks. **1897** *Outing* XXX. 174/2 We couldn't parly-voo worth shucks. **1910** CHURCHILL *Mod. Chron.* III. x, It don't amount to shucks, as we used to say in Missouri.

**c. 1862** LOWELL *Biglow P.* Ser. II. iii. 206 Fer such mean shucks ez creditors are all on Lincoln's side. **1887** *Kentish Gloss.*, A regular old shuck.

**d. 1872** SCHELE DE VERE *Americanisms* 47 During the Civil War,.. the original Blue Backs of the Confederacy.. soon became known as Shucks, a name sufficiently significant of their evil repute as a circulating medium.

**e. 1958** G. LEA *Somewhere there's Music* 163, I know about double negative too, but that's a lot of shuck. **1959** *Encounter* June 43 Despite his rejection of marriage as middle-class 'shuck' (phoney), the Beatnik's Wedding is an important event. **1972** *Islander* (Victoria, B.C.) 25 June 14/4 This is a good book and as they say in.. Texas: 'I'm not putting the shuck on you' so get it and read it. **1980** A. TOFFLER *Third Wave* xix. 261 The recently graduated son.. proclaims the nine-to-five job a degrading sham and a shuck.

**3.** *pl.* as an interj. of contempt or indifference.

**1847** J. M. FIELD *Drama in Pokerville* 68 And Mr. Bagly was there... [to shoot] any gentleman who might say 'shucks!'. **1885** 'M. TWAIN' in *Century Mag.* Feb. 557/2 'We can spare it'. 'Oh, shucks, yes, we can spare it'. **1906** GUNTER *Prince in Garret* ix. 220 'Shucks, I know girls better than you do', was the ex-schoolmistress's reply.

**4.** *attrib.* and *Comb.*

**1835** J. P. KENNEDY *Horse-Shoe Robinson* xl, A shock-bed was spread for the lady. **1843** W. FRAZIER *Jrnl.* July (1930) 27 Our cargo.. was a motley pile.. from broken skillets, up to rickety bedsteads and *shuck*-mattresses. **1860** *Knickerbocker Mag.* June 613 We..enjoyed in common our shuck-mattress and scanty quilts. **1885** 'M. TWAIN' in *Century Mag.* Feb. 547/2 There's always cobs around about in a shuck tick, and they poke into you. **1887** EGGLESTON *Graysons* ix, There were some shuck-bottom chairs, and a splint-bottom rocking-chair. **1888** *Ibid.* xxxi, He drew up another shuck-bottomed chair. **1952** A. LOMAX *Mister Jelly Roll* 136 I want you shuck-sharks and crooks to get out of town.

**shuck**, *v.*[1] [Of obscure origin. Cf. the dial. *shuck*, to shiver, also to shirk (work).] *intr.* To shrink, draw back, hesitate.

**1620** JER. DYKE *Sel. Serm.* (1640) 351 It was Gods price then; and they shukt not at it. *Ibid.*, Those be the shuckings of earthly hearts. **1643** TRAPP *Comm. Gen.* xvii. 26 To shew his prompt and present obedience, without shucking and hucking, without delays and consults. **1684** BUNYAN *Seas. Counsel* To Rdr. A 6 Those bitter pills, at which we so whinch and shuck. *a* **1688** —— *Saints' Knowl.* Wks. 1853 II. 11 Usually in these [afflictions], though they make us shuck whenever they come upon us, blessing coucheth.

**shuck**, *v.*[2] orig. and chiefly *U.S.* Also **shock**. [f. SHUCK *sb.*[2]]

**1.** *trans.* To remove the shucks from (corn, etc.).

**1819** W. FAUX *Mem. Days* (1823) 211 My host had a large party..assembled to effect a corn shucking, something like an English hawkey, or harvest home. Corn shucking means plucking the ears of Indian corn from the stalk. **1881** INGERSOLL *Oyster-Industry* (Fish. Industr. U.S.) 248 *Shock*, to open or 'shuck' clams or oysters. **1887** GOODE, etc. *Fish. Industr. U.S.* v. II. 553 The average price paid for shucking raw oysters is 15 cents a gallon. **1888** EGGLESTON *Graysons* xxx, To shuck out..eight or ten ears of corn.

**2.** *transf.* and *fig.* **a.** To remove, throw or strip *off*, get rid of (also occas. used outside N. Amer.).

**1848** MAJOR JONES *Sk. Travel* 178 After shuckin out the passengers and baggage,..they tuck us down a steep hill to the steambote. **1856** *Yale Lit. Mag.* XXI. 144 The cussed fever and ague had jist shucked his meat clean off. *a* **1860** A. B. LONGSTREET *Southern Sk.* 31 (Bartlett), He'd shuck off his coat to fight. **1891** *Century Mag.* Nov. 62 They have never shucked their boyhood. **1966** *Listener* 3 Nov. 650/2, I regard it as a great fortune to have shucked off this amount of remorse about intellectual achievement. **1968** *N.Y. Times Book Rev.* 23 June VII. 1/1 That an actively practicing attorney..should ever be able to shuck them off long enough to produce a book..struck me as a most unlikely miracle. **1969** G. MACBETH *War Quartet* 28 The deflector bag Filled with loose cases, shucked out. **1969** *New Yorker* 12 Apr. 86/2 Then the astronaut shucks the box from the tube, which he discards as a doctor might throw away the protective part of a syringe. **1975** *Times Lit. Suppl.* 4 July 725/1 The work of a British historian that shucks off the weight of this ponderous tradition. **1976** *New Yorker* 19 Apr. 98/2 Odd thing: Joanne, now living in Connecticut, has hung on to her Southern accent; the two others, both New Yorkers, have shucked theirs. **1978** *Guardian Weekly* 1 Jan. 18/4 Spanish boys and girls have shucked the race for money... Marriage and children are not a goal. Neither is wealth.

**b.** *refl.* and *intr.* To slip *out of* one's clothes; to strip oneself.

**1848** MAJOR JONES *Sk. Travel* 117, I shucked out of my old clothes. **1897** R. M. JOHNSTON *Old Times in Middle Georgia* 37 Sam..shucked hisself out his workin'-clothes.

**3. a.** *trans.* and *intr.* To deceive, fool or 'kid' (someone). *slang.*

**1959** L. LIPTON *Holy Barbarians* 25, I didn't shuck the customers enough to please the crook who was running the car lot. **1966** [see sense b below]. **1969** S. GREENLEE *Spook who sat by Door* xiii. 114 He soothed them and told them to go home..and he did not shuck. You either work at a cover or forget it. **1976** C. WESTON *Rouse Demon* xviii. 88 You shucking me, man, I didn't get rid of nobody! **1979** *Maclean's Mag.* 4 June 6/3 The petulant Keith Jarrett is an example: 'He's shucking.'

**b.** ***shucking and jiving***: fooling. Cf. JIVE *v.* 1 a. *U.S. Blacks.*

[**1966** E. BULLINS *Theme is Blackness* (1973) 27 Yawhl jivin'...yawhl shuckin'.] **1969** H. R. BROWN *Die Nigger Die!* ii. 25, I told him he should think about it, but I knew I was schuckin' and jivin'. **1974** H. L. FOSTER *Ribbin', Jivin', & Playin' Dozens* v. 195 For many blacks, shuckin' and jivin' is a survival technique to avoid and stay out of trouble.

Hence **shucked** *ppl. a.*; **'shucker**, one who shucks oysters or clams; **'shucking** *vbl. sb.* (see sense 1 above).

**1872** *Golden Hours* IV. 397/1 The colored shuckers are considered the best because they will throw down a small oyster, and only open the large or medium-sized ones. **1886** *Appleton's Ann. Cycl.* 524/2 To fix the standard of measurement of shucked oysters in the State. **1887** GOODE, etc. *Fish. Industr. U.S.* v. II. 553 Estimating the average amount made by the shuckers at $6 a week.

**shuck**, dial. form of SHOCK *sb.*[1]

**shucker**, obs. form of SUCKER.

†**'shuckle**, *v. Obs.* [app. by-form of CHUCKLE *v.*] *intr.* To chuckle; also, to cluck.

**1598** FLORIO, *Colleppolarsi d'allegrezza*, to shuckle, to chuck or rouze ones selfe to gladnes and mirth. **1684** OTWAY *Atheist* v. 63 Would but my little Partridge call, methinks I could so shuckle, and run, and Bill, and clap my Wings about her. Hah!

**shud.** *Obs.* exc. *dial.* (E. Angl., Yorks., Derbs., Heref.) Also 5 **schudde**, 9 **shod**. [Late ME. *schudde*, of obscure origin.

A Teut. root **skeud-*: **skaud-*: **skud-* with the sense 'to cover' seems to be evidenced by LG. *schode*, G. *schote* pod, Eng. dial. SHOOD, ON. *skauðir* pl. (Norw. *skau*), MLG. *schôde*, horse's sheath, ON. *skjóða* bag, purse, and perh. MLG., MDu. *beskudden* to protect.]

A shed.

*c* **1440** *Promp. Parv.* 449/1 Schudde, hovel, or swyne kote, or howse of sympyl hyllynge to kepe yn beestys, *catabulum*. **1657** REEVE *God's Plea* 175 Let not..the thatched shuds be neater built then your tiled houses. **1688** *Holmesfield Crt. Rolls* in Addy *Sheff. Gloss.* s.v., A shud near to the said barn. **1787** W. H. MARSHALL *Norfolk* (1795) II. 388 *Shud*, shed. *a* **1825** FORBY *Voc. E. Anglia*, *Shod*, *Shud*, a shed.

**shud**, obs. form of SHOOD, husk of oats.

**shudder** ('ʃʌdə(r)), *sb.* [f. SHUDDER *v.*]

**1.** An act of shuddering; a convulsive tremor of the body occasioned by fear, repugnance, or chill.

Phr. *to give one the shudders*.

**1607** SHAKS. *Timon* IV. iii. 137, I know you'l sweare, terribly sweare Into strong shudders, and to heauenly Agues Th' immortall Gods that heare you.

**1824** MISS FERRIER *Inher.* vi, An aguish shudder. **1841** DALLAS *Past. Superint.* 212 [She] said..before I spoke of the Communion, that seeing it last Sunday, 'gave her the shudders'. **1851** LONGF. *Golden Leg.* iv. *Neighboring Nunnery*, Through all my limbs a shudder ran. **1872** DARWIN *Emotions* xii. 302 The first sensation of fear, or the imagination of something dreadful, commonly excites a shudder. **1908** *Sat. Rev.* 13 June 750/2 They solemnly adjure the author not to waste..talent..on giving us the shudders.

**2.** A tremulous or vibratory movement; a quiver.

**1865** SWINBURNE *Chastelard* I. i. 15 The soft and rapid shudder of her breath In talking.

**shudder** ('ʃʌdə(r)), *v.* Forms: 4 **shodder**, 5 **shodur, shuder, shoter, shadyr** (?), 5–6 **shoder**, 6– **shudder**. [ME. *shod(d)re*, cognate with MLG. *schôderen*, also *schaderen* (LG. *schuddern*, whence mod.G. *schaudern*), MDu. *schûderen*, frequentative formation (see -ER[5]) on the root *skŭd-* to shake.

To this root belong also (1) MLG., LG. *schudden* (whence app. MSw., Sw. *skudda*, and NFris. *skorre* for **skodde*), (2) OFris. *schedda* (WFris. *skodzje*, NFris. *sköddi*), OHG. *scuttan*, *scut(t)en* (MHG. *schüt(t)en*, G. *schütten*, whence mod.G. frequent. *schüttern*), (3) LG. *schuddeln*, OHG. *scutilôn* (MHG. *schüteln*, G. *schütteln*), (4) OHG. *scutisôn* to shudder, *scutisôd* 'trepidatio'.]

**1. a.** *intr.* To have a convulsive tremor of the body caused by fear, abhorrence, or cold; hence, to tremble with horror or dread.

*a* **1310** in Wright *Lyric P.* xxxix. 110 For doute leste he valle he shoddreth ant shereth. *c* **1450** *Cov. Myst.* (Shaks. Soc.) 158 We xulde shadyr for no shoure. *c* **1460** *Towneley Myst.* xxx. 98, I shoterd and shoke I herd sich a rerd. *a* **1529** SKELTON *Col. Cloute* 68 Thus eche of other blother The tone agayng the tother: Alas, they make me shoder! **1593** DRAYTON *Ecl.* x. 4 The poore Heards..Shuddred with keennes of the winters cold. **1602** MARSTON *Antonio's Rev.* II. iii, Thou wrapt in furres, beaking thy lymbs 'fore fiers Forbidst the frozen Zone to shudder. *a* **1700** DRYDEN *Theod. & Hon.* 312 With Horror shuddring, on a heap they run. **1788** MME. D'ARBLAY *Diary* 13 Feb., I shuddered, and drew involuntarily back, when..I saw Mr. Burke. **1814** SCOTT *Ld. of Isles* III. xxxi, He..mark'd him shudder at the sword. **1848** THACKERAY *Van. Fair* xxxix, Only two or three domestics shuddered in the bleak old servants' hall. **1871** L. STEPHEN *Playgr. Eur.* (1894) ii. 41 The masses of ice and snow..make him openly shudder. **1885** 'MRS. ALEXANDER' *At Bay* ii, I have seen you look surprised when I have started and shuddered at trifles.

**b.** *transf.*

**1769** *Junius Lett.* xxix. 132 There are still some facts in store at which human nature would shudder. **1833** T. HOOK *Parson's Dau.* III. ii, Her gentle heart, shuddering as it did with horror at his premeditated cruelty. **1848** THACKERAY *Van. Fair* x, My mind shudders when I think of her awful, awful situation.

**c.** With *away*, *up*: To shrink *from*.

**1668** DRYDEN *Maiden Q.* v. i, As children..First try the water with their tender feet; Then, shuddering up with cold, step back again. **1853** MRS. GASKELL *Ruth* xviii, She shuddered up from contemplating it. **1855** —— *North & S.* xxv, She shuddered away from the threat of his enduring love. **1893** MARY E. MANN *In Summer Shade* x, Mentally shuddering away from the picture he had called up.

**d.** const. inf.; esp. in colloq. phr. ***I shudder to think*** with obj. clause.

**1742** YOUNG *Nt. Th.* IV. 249 A midnight, nature shudder'd to behold. **1777** TOPLADY *Hymn*, *'Deathless Principle'* v, Shudder not to pass the stream. **1861** MEREDITH *Phantasy* xxix. Poet. Wks. (1912) 116 Already I shuddered to feel the wave, As I kept sinking slowly. **1872** GEO. ELIOT *Let.* 4 Aug. (1956) V. 297, I shudder a little to think what a long book it will be. **1952** M. LASKI *Village* iii. 53 What they're going to think of us abroad, I shudder to think. **1970** A. PRICE *Labyrinth Makers* xii. 161 What he'll make of you I shudder to think!

**2.** *nonce-uses.* **a.** To go *out* with a shudder.

**1852** THACKERAY *Esmond* III. xiii, The roses had shuddered out of her cheeks.

**b.** *trans.* To shake *off* with a shudder.

**1827** HOOD *Hero & Leander* cv, Lo! how she shudders off the beaded wave.

**3.** *intr.* To move tremulously, vibrate, quiver.

**1849** CUPPLES *Green Hand* xiv, Still catching the fierce rush of the gale..which steadied her though she shuddered to it. **1856** MRS. BROWNING *Aur. Leigh* III. 276 My pulse Would shudder along the purple-veined wrist Like a shot bird. **1869** FARRAR *Families of Speech* i. 25 The full dawn of which the earliest beams had shuddered through the darkness some years before.

**4.** *trans.* To cause to shudder. *rare.*

**1639** CHAPMAN & SHIRLY *Tragedie of Chabot Admirall of France* I. sig. B, Loud conscience has a voyce to shudder greatnesse. *c* **1801–3** W. BLAKE *Auguries Innoc.* 8 A robin redbreast in a cage Puts all Heaven in a rage. A dove-house fill'd with doves and pigeons Shudders Hell thro' all its regions. **1925** E. BLUNDEN *English Poems* 58 A drowned sheep lodged In a black holt of alders, Its poor fleece brown and vile, To shudder young beholders.

†**5.** *intr.* and *trans.* To scatter. *Obs.*

*c* **1400** *Destr. Troy* IV. 1335 All shodurt as shepe, shont of his way. *Ibid.* 3706 The shippis with shire wynd shodert in twyn. *Ibid.* 6581 He..Shent of þo shalkes, shudrit hom itwyn.

**'shudderful**, *a.* [f. SHUDDER *sb.* + -FUL.] Causing shudders. Hence **'shudderfully** *adv.*

**1872** STEVENSON *Lett.* (1911) I. 44 She cries out—O so shudderfully. **1901** *League Jrnl.* 16 July 465 A sharp and shudderful contrast.

**'shuddering**, *vbl. sb.* [f. SHUDDER *v.* + -ING[1].] The action of the verb SHUDDER.

*c* **1440** *Pallad on Husb.* I. xc, A shuddering [*v.r.* shoughturyng] a flusshing, & affray He [*sc.* the peacock] maketh thenne. **1565** GOLDING *Ovid's Met.* IV. A ij b, A shuddryng throughe her stracke. **1737** *Gentl. Mag.* VII. 630/1 With universal shudd'ring, and dismay. **1796** MORSE *Amer. Geog.* I. 288 They have intervals of shuddering, as if they were in a strong fit of the ague. **1812** MME. D'ARBLAY *Diary* (1876) IV. 205 The..event..I never even yet recollect without an inward shuddering. **1888** *Athenæum* 20 Oct. 516/1 Strong shudderings and revulsions.

**'shuddering**, *ppl. a.* [f. SHUDDER *v.* + -ING[2].]

**1.** That shudders; trembling with cold, fear, or abhorrence; quivering, vibrating.

**1596** SHAKS. *Merch. V.* III. ii. 110 And shuddring feare, and greene-eyed iealousie. **1602** MARSTON *Ant. & Mel.* III. Wks. 1856 I. 30 The shuddering morne that flakes, With silver tinctur, the east vierge of heaven. **1742** W. COLLINS *Ode Fear* 53 With shudd'ring meek submitted thought. **1764** GOLDSM. *Trav.* 65 The shudd'ring tenant of the frigid zone. **1855** TENNYSON *Maud* II. IV. vii, In the shuddering dawn. **1872** O. W. HOLMES *Poet Breakf.-t.* v, The massive turret shudders with the shuddering rocks on which it rests. **1891** FARRAR *Darkn. & Dawn* xxviii, A light laugh woke a shuddering echo along the fretted roof.

**2.** Characterized or accompanied by shuddering.

**1586** WARNER *Alb. Eng.* I. vi. (1589) 20 Saue howlings out and shuddering feare came nought to eare or sight. **1794** MRS. RADCLIFFE *Myst. Udolpho* xxvi, Pointing with a shuddering emotion to Annette. **1797** —— *Italian* ii, A shuddering presentiment. **1863** GEO. ELIOT *Romola* I. iii, I have a shuddering sense of what there is inside. **1882** *Sat. Rev.* 6 May 567/1 To leave on the hearer an impression of shuddering disgust. **1893** W. H. HUDSON *Idle Days Patag.* i. 2 Strange grating and grinding noises, and shuddering motions of the ship.

**b.** Causing one to shudder. *rare.*

**1848** LADY LYTTELTON in *Corr.* (1912) 384 The notion of his being actually put to death..is shuddering!

**'shudderingly**, *adv.* [f. prec. + -LY[2].] In a shuddering manner; with a shudder or shudders.

**1592** NASHE *Strange Newes* F 3 The..Mariner, that talks quakingly and shudderingly of a storme that hee hath newly toyld through. **1797** MRS. RADCLIFFE *Italian* vii, Vivaldi shudderingly turned to look on it again. **1823** MISS EDGEWORTH in *Scott's Fam. Lett.* (1894) II. 179 *note*, The touch of insanity in the brother's character in the last shudderingly fine scene. **1846** TRENCH *Mirac.* xxix. (1862) 414 She would most shudderingly contemplate that beloved form made a spectacle to strangers.

**'shuddersome**, *a.* [f. SHUDDER + -SOME.] Causing a shudder. Also *transf.*, inclined to shudder. Hence **'shuddersomely** *adv.*

**1893** *Strand Mag.* VI. 694 Below the nose a pale, ghastly, half-open mouth. It was shuddersome. **1893** *Pall Mall Gaz.* 23 Dec. 11/2 There is something ghastly, something shuddersome about the little piece. **1903** A. M. BINSTEAD *Pitcher in Paradise* ii. 52 One of those shuddersomely refined affairs that are supposed to be meat and drink to the giddy suburbanite. **1941** I. L. IDRIESS *Great Boomerang* xxii. 168 Eastern daggers of shuddersome shape, weapons of many nations. **1969** O. BLAKISTON *For crying out Shroud* iii. 29, I don't..really feel so shuddersome about the smallest of bald patches.

**'shuddery**, *a.* [f. SHUDDER + -Y.] Characterized by or causing shuddering; 'creepy'.

**1863** R. S. HAWKER in *Life* (1905) 450 My health is shuddery—nine-tenths mental too. **1880** *World* 9 June, Wilkie Collins grows..more spectral and shuddery.

Hence **'shudderiness**.

**1874** R. H. HUTTON *Crit. Contemp. Th.* (1894) I. 68 The dreary hopelessness and shudderiness,..if I may coin a word, of the mood depicted.

**Shuddery, Shudra**: see SUDRA, an Indian caste.

**shuddup** (ʃʌ'dʌp), vulgar corruption of imp. *shut up* (see SHUT *v.* 19 m). Cf. SHADDUP, SHURRUP.

**1940** C. MCCULLERS *Heart is Lonely Hunter* II. xii. 217 'You dumb dumb dumb—' 'Shuddup! Shuddup!' **1978** F. MULLALLY *Deadly Payoff* xiii. 180 'Shuddup,' Macdonald snorted.

**shude**: see SHOOD.

**shuder**, var. SUDDER.

**shue, shoo,** *v. Sc.* [See SHOVE *v.*¹, etym. note.] *intr.* To swing, play at see-saw. Hence **shue** *sb.*, a swing, see-saw. Cf. SHUGGIE-SHUE.
**1808** in JAMIESON. **1890**, etc. (see Eng. Dial. Dict.).

**shue**, obs. f. SHOO, SUE *v.*

**shuf**, obs. f. SHOVE *v.*¹

**shufe**, obs. pa. t. of SHAVE *v.*

**shuff** (ʃʌf), *sb.* An inferior class of brick.
**1843** *Civil Engin. & Arch. Jrnl.* VI. 349/2 The principal varieties of bricks were called 'malm paviors', 'stocks', 'grizzles', 'places', and 'shuffs'. **1843** *Mech. Mag.* XXXIX. 192 The shuffs were sold for an inferior price governed by their quality, as they were frequently quite rotten.

**shuff,** *a. dial.* (see Eng. Dial. Dict.). [dial. var. of SHY *a.*] Shy.
**1688** BUNYAN *Christ as Adv.* Wks. 1852 I. 173, I am dull and stupid that way; will not Christ be shuff and shy with me because of this?

**shuff**, obs. form of SHOVE *v.*¹

**shuffle** (ˈʃʌf(ə)l), *sb.* [f. SHUFFLE *v.*]
†**1.** A shifting from one place to another; an interchange of positions. *Obs.*
**1674** N. FAIRFAX *Bulk & Selv.* 100 The very life and soul of motion is shuffle or sawing. **1692** BENTLEY *Boyle Lect.* i. 27 The unguided agitation and rude shuffles of Matter.
**2.** A tricky exchange or alternation (of arguments, expedients, etc.).
**1641** MILTON *Animadv.* Wks. 1851 III. 185 With a slye shuffle of counterfeit principles chopping and changing till he haue glean'd all the good ones of their minds. **1860** SMILES *Self Help* viii. 215 Life becomes a mere shuffle of expedients.
**3.** An evasive trick, evasion, subterfuge.
**1628** FELTHAM *Resolves* II. ii. 4 All the vnwelcome Shuffles that the poore rude World puts on him. **1653** H. MORE *Antid. Ath.* III. iv. §5 A man that is unwilling to admit of anything supernatural would please himself with this general shuffle and put-off. **1690** C. NESSE *Hist. & Myst. O. & N. Test.* I. 46 Adam's first reason or shuffle was that he heard Gods voice. **1737** WATERLAND *Eucharist* 85 Socinus's pretended Reasons..were mere shuffle and pretence. **1842** G. S. FABER *Prov. Lett.* (1844) II. 316 So as to leave no room for shuffle or evasion. **1861** S. BROOKS *Silver Cord* xli. (1865) 225 That seems a shuffle. You can say where the documents are, if you please to do so. **1893** M. PEMBERTON *Iron Pirate* 201 You'll answer it now, yes or no, plain word and no shuffle.
**4.** Movement of the feet along the ground without lifting them; a gait characterized by such movement.
**1847** L. HUNT *Men, Women, & Bks.* I. iv. 62 The bear..dancing him from side to side in its heavy shuffle. **1849** MACAULAY *Hist. Eng.* v. I. 533 His gait distinguished from that of other men by a peculiar shuffle. **1862** *Lillywhite's Cricket Scores & Biogr.* I. 436 In delivering the ball he neither ran nor walked up to the crease, but advanced with a sort of 'shuffle'. **1886** G. R. SIMS *Ring o' Bells*, etc. 10 The shuffle of little tired feet along the passage.
**5.** A dance of a simple kind, in which the feet are shuffled along the floor. Also *spec.*, a modern popular dance to jazz or rock and roll music, evolved orig. from Negro folk-dance; the music to which this is danced. ***double shuffle***: one in which two movements of the same kind are made by each foot alternately.
**1659** H. MORE *Immort. Soul* II. xviii. 321 The rude shuffles and dancings of the Cretick Corybantes. **1821** P. EGAN *Life in London* II. v. 287 The *kidwys* and *kiddiesses* were footing the double shuffle against each other. **1837** MARRYAT *Snarleyyow* x, He would warm himself with the double-shuffle. **1840** R. H. DANA *Bef. Mast* xxiii, They all turned-to and had a regular sailor's shuffle till eight bells. **1842** DICKENS *Amer. Notes* vi, Single shuffle, double shuffle, cut and cross-cut. **1894** E. SCOTT *Dancing* 84 The hornpipe step, familiarly known as the double-shuffle. **1925** (*jazz music title*) Shanghai Shuffle. **1935** K. BURCHILL *Step Dancing* iv. 14 Swing the leg forward from the knee, so that the ball of your foot strikes the ground as it comes through... From this position swing the lower part of the leg back to its original position, striking the ground at the same time with the ball of the foot... These two movements..done in this order, constitute what is known as the 'Shuffle'. **1955** KEEPNEWS & GRAUER *Pictorial Hist. Jazz.* ix 97 Such slightly later recordings as *Riverboat Shuffle*. **1956** M. STEARNS *Story of Jazz* xvii. 203 The arrangements now sound heavy and cluttered and the rhythm was almost of the 'shuffle' variety. **1976** J. VAN DE WETERING *Corpse on Dike* (1977) xvi. 159 The combo..played a slow shuffle, very easy to get into.
**6. a.** The act of shuffling playing-cards; also *ellipt.* (a player's) turn to shuffle.
**1651** HOBBES *Leviath.* I. xi. 48 Nor any such hope to mend an ill game, as by causing a new shuffle. **1728** SWIFT *Jrnl. Mod. Lady* Wks. 1755 III. II. 195 The deal, the shuffle, and the cut. **1894** MRS. F. ELLIOT *Roman Gossip* v. 162 The next shuffle of the cards finds him leading a hermit's life. **1894** MASKELYNE *Sharps & Flats* 140 To allow a certain number of cards to remain undisturbed is a comparatively simple matter in any shuffle.
**b.** phr. ***lost in the shuffle***: overlooked or missed in the mêlée or multitude. *U.S.*
**1930** D. RUNYON in *Collier's* 22 Mar. 21/4, I find we are about lost in the shuffle of guys with little mustaches. **1955** *New Yorker* 11 June 74/3 Mr. Ewell's efforts to be quietly funny are lost in the shuffle. **1981** W. SAFIRE in *N.Y. Times Mag.* 8 Feb. 12/2 The book itself would then get lost in the shuffle.
**c.** *transf.* A redistribution of ministerial posts within a government or cabinet. Cf. RESHUFFLE *sb.*
**1941** C. MACKENZIE *Red Tapeworm* xxii. 296, I hope we shall have no more of these Cabinet shuffles for the time being! **1966** —— *Paper Lives* xiv. 184 Mr Williamson, who was hoping like Mr Upjohn to find himself in the Cabinet at the next shuffle, ceased to argue. **1976** J. I. M. STEWART *Memorial Service* xiii. 204 The government was judged likely soon to undergo one of those 'shuffles' that English political mythology declares to be periodically essential.

**shuffle** (ˈʃʌf(ə)l), *v.* Forms: 6 shoofle, shooffell, shuffil, -ell, shoffle, 6–7 shuffel, 6–8 shufle, 7 shoffel, 6– shuffle. [Early modern Eng.; 16th c. *shoofle*, *shoffle*, *shufle*, etc., ad. or cogn. w. LG. *schüffeln*, also *schuffeln* to walk clumsily or with dragging feet, mix (corn), shuffle (cards), deal dishonestly, play unfairly; frequent. f. Teut. root **skuf*- (*skub*-) to SHOVE. (Cf. SCUFFLE and SHOVEL *v.*²)]
**1. a.** *intr.* To move the feet along the ground without lifting them, so as to make a scraping noise; to walk with such a motion of the feet; to go with clumsy steps or a shambling gait; also said of the feet. Often with advs. Also (*colloq.*) *fig.* with *off* to die; (in playful allusion to *Hamlet*: see sense 5 d, quot. 1602).
**1598** MARSTON *Sco. Villanie* B 4 b, Both of them goe a good seemely pace, not stumbling, shuffling. **1627** DRAYTON *Agincourt* 59 Another, his [arms] had shackled by the feete; Who like a Cripple shuffled on the ground. **1719** DE FOE *Crusoe* I. (Globe) 300 The Bear..shuffling along at a strange Rate. **1778** MISS BURNEY *Evelina* xviii. (1791) II. 104 He came shuffling into the room with his boots on. **1810** CRABBE *Borough* xiii, An old brown pony..Who shuffled onward, and from side to side. **1818** SCOTT *Br. Lamm.* x, In making his bow, one foot shuffled forward..the other backward. **1827** —— *Jrnl.* 5 Jan., I can now shuffle about and help myself to what I want. **1852** THACKERAY *Esmond* I. Introd., Shuffling backwards out of doors in the presence of the sovereign. **1902** R. BAGOT *Donna Diana* v. 43 The electric bell..rang... The servants shuffled to their feet and went to answer it.
*transf.* **1576** R. PETERSON *Galateo* (1892) 80 If a man or woman should..shuffle backwarde vpon their taile. **1845** GOSSE *Ocean* ii. (1849) 81 [Plaice] reside wholly upon the bottom [of the sea], shuffling along by waving their flattened bodies, fringed with dorsal and anal fins. **1874** WOOD *Nat. Hist.* 7 The creature shuffles along..by help of its arms.
*fig.* **1922** A. HUXLEY *Mortal Coils* 124 One has to bring them [*sc.* obituary notices] up to date every year or so for fear of being caught napping if one of these old birds chooses to shuffle off suddenly. **1977** *N.Y. Rev. Bks.* 4 Aug. 29/3 She thought—if one had to 'shuffle off'—it would be terrific to be electrocuted while playing a bass guitar in a rock group.
**b.** To move restlessly or fidget in one's seat.
**1881** *Durham Univ. Jrnl.* 17 Dec. 133 They shuffle on their seats and become impatient. **1895** 'MERRIMAN' *Grey Lady* II. ii, Captain Bontnor shuffled in his seat and likewise in his speech.
**c.** *trans.* To move (the feet) along the ground or floor without raising them.
**1576** R. PETERSON *Galateo* (1892) 17 Some men vse to..playe the dromme with their fingers, or shoofle their feete. **1819** KEATS *Lamia* I. 356 Men, women, rich and poor..Shuffled their sandals o'er the pavement white. **1833** HT. MARTINEAU *Briery Creek* v. 114 Two or three boys and girls shuffled their feet on the matting.
**d.** To perform (a dance or a dance-step) with a shuffle. Also *absol.* or *intr.*
**1818** SCOTT *Br. Lamm.* xiii, Bruin..rose up upon his hind-legs, and instantly began to shuffle a saraband. **1833** [SEBA SMITH] *Lett. J. Downing* iii. (1835) 38 'Change partners, and shuffle the next'; and so they chang'd, and shuffled and changed. **1872** 'ALIPH CHEEM' *Lays of Ind* (1876) 5 Girls..who shuffled and beat A strange time with their feet.
**2. a.** To manipulate (the cards in a pack) so as to change their relative position, with the object of preventing the players from knowing the order in which the cards lie. Formerly freq. in allusive use, ***to shuffle the cards*** = to manipulate matters.
**1570** LEVINS *Manip.* 184/17 To shuffle cardes, *confundere*. **1577** *F. de Lisle's Legendarie* G viij b, Al was but a new practise whereby to shuffle the cardes as we say, and so to heape one discord vpon another. **1591** FLORIO *2nd Fruites* 69 Goe to, shooffell the cardes verie well. **1596** NASHE *Saffron Walden* M 3 They fell to dansing..; in a trice so they shuffled the cards of purpose..that..he must tread the measures about with the foulest..fury that might be. **1638** BURTON *Anat. Mel.* (ed. 5) III. iii. I. ii, They turned up trumpe, before the Cards were shufled. **1643** *Plain English* 17 [They] had shuffled their cards so cunningly as to be out of the reach of law. **1709** STEELE *Tatler* No. 50 ¶ 11 He is now shuffling the Cards, and dealing to Timothy. **1717** PRIOR *Alma* II. 235 We sure in vain the cards condemn: Ourselves both cut and shuffled them. **1784** COWPER *Task* I. 474 To deal and shuffle, to divide and sort, Her mingled suits and sequences. **1829** LYTTON *Devereux* I. iv, Let us see if, at sixteen, we cannot shuffle cards, and play tricks with the gamester of thirty. **1894** MASKELYNE *Sharps & Flats* 139 The cards are..in their original positions, although they appear to have been perfectly shuffled.
**b.** *absol.* or *intr.*, freq. allusively, esp. in phr. ***shuffle and cut.***
**1589** [? LYLY] *Pappe w. Hatchet* C iij (1844) 27 Weele make you deale, shuffle as well as you can we meane to cut it. **1592** MARLOWE *Mass. Paris* I. ii, Since thou hast all the Cardes within thy hands To shuffle or cut, take this as surest thing: That..thou deale thy selfe a King. **1602** HEYWOOD *Woman killed w. Kindn.* III. ii, Shuffle, Ile cut; would I had neuer dealt. **1680** COTTON *Compl. Gamester* (ed. 2) 58 The Dealer shuffles, and the other cuts. **1694** CONGREVE *Double Dealer* II. i, Since we have shuffled and cut, let's e'en turn up trump now. **1706** E. WARD *Wooden World Diss.* (1708) 93 He..shuffles and cuts with every one who has to do with him. **1748** WALPOLE *Let. to Mann* 26 Dec., A little astonished at seeing the Count shuffle with the faces of the cards upwards. **1810** CRABBE *Borough* x, They draw, they sit, they shuffle, cut and deal. **1862** 'CAVENDISH' *Whist* (1879) 6 The dealer has always the right to shuffle last. **1864** KNIGHT *Passages Work, Life* I. iii. 167 The princes..at the faro-table of Vienna shuffled and cut for the destinies of the world.
*Proverb.* **1620** SHELTON *Quix.* III. xxiii. 160 O Cousin, I say, Patience and Shuffle. *a* **1839** PRAED *Poems* (1864) II. 141 And cut the fiercest quarrels short With—'Patience, gentlemen—and shuffle!'
**c.** *trans.* To produce or put *in* (a card or a certain succession of cards) in shuffling. Chiefly *fig.*
**1583** MELBANCKE *Philotimus* F ij b, The fault..was..in her mother, which in shuffling the cards shufled in a knaue too many. **1594** ? GREENE *Selimus* Wks. (Grosart) XIV. 251 Vnlesse I shuffle out my selfe a king. **1648** *Hunting of Fox* 40 Your creatures were shuffled among all the knaves in the packe. **1654** WHITLOCK *Zootomia* 425 Shuffling and cutting ones selfe a Fortune in this scambling World. *Mod.* I will try and shuffle myself a good hand this time.
**3.** To push along, about, or together in a disorderly mass or heap, or in a manner suggesting the shuffling of feet.
**1567** HARMAN *Caveat* xxiv, He shuffels vp a quayntitye of strawe..into some pretye carner of the barne where she maye conuenientlye lye. **1577–87** HOLINSHED *Chron.* III. 1065/1 They..strewed againe the rushes that were shuffled with strugling. **1616** *Rich Cabinet* A a 2 To beginne another discourse when a man is telling a story..is as if you should shuffle stones against him which goeth [= walks]. **1695** WOODWARD *Nat. Hist. Earth* VI. (1723) 279 The Sea, by this Access and Recess, shuffling the empty Shells. **1725** P. BLAIR *Pharmaco-Bot.* III. 133 They Wash Cloaths, shufling, shifting of it. **1875** SOUTHWARD *Dict. Typogr.* 63 He then lets the further side rest upon the table, and shuffles the sheets gradually away from him.
**4. a.** To put or throw *together* in one mass indiscriminately, incongruously, or without order; to huddle or jumble together.
**1570** LEVINS *Manip.* 127/45 To Shuffil, *confundere*. **1609** HOLLAND *Amm. Marcell.* 32T The enemies rankes were broken, and for feare so shufled together, that [etc.]. **1629** H. BURTON *Babel no Bethel* I Comparing my arguments to scroles shufled together in a lottery pott. **1662** J. DAVIES tr. *Mandelslo's Trav.* 268 They..eat upon the ground, sometimes shuffling flesh, and fish, and fruits together all into the same dish. **1685** SOUTH *Serm.* Prov. xvi. 33 (1727) I. 297 When Lots are shuffled in a Lap, Urn, or Pitcher. **1806–7** J. BERESFORD *Miseries Hum. Life* (1826) xx. 260 Your shoes shuffled by a rascally servant into the general heap. **1883** V. STUART *Egypt* 66 The..granite blocks are..mingled together and piled on one another..as if shuffled by some giant. **1899** J. G. FRAZER *Orig. Totemism* ii, The various clans..do not live isolated from each other, but are shuffled up together within a narrow area.
**b.** With immaterial obj.
**1634** HEYWOOD *Lanc. Witches* III. Wks. 1874 IV. 211 Was there ever such a medley of mirth, madnesse, and drunkennesse, shuffled together? **1647** COWLEY *Mistr., Distance* iv, Hearts by Love, strangely shuffled are, That there can never meet a Pare! **1699** BENTLEY *Phal.* 272 Eusebius's Histories are so shuffled and interpolated, and so disjointed from his Tables. *a* **1732** ATTERBURY (J.), He has shuffled the two ends of the sentence together. **1823** LAMB *Elia* II. *Rejoicings New Year*, Good Days, bad Days so shuffled together. **1830** MACAULAY *Misc. Writ.* (1860) II. 20 Let us now shuffle the censuses of England and France together.
**c.** To mingle or join indiscriminately *with* or *among* others.
**1593** KYD *Let. Sir J. Puckering* Wks. (1901) p. cviii, Some fragments of a disputation..affirmd by Marlowe to be his, and shufled wth some of myne. **1648** WINYARD *Mids.-Moon* 2 Shuffle him with the rest oth' visitors. **1662** J. DAVIES tr. *Olearius' Voy. Ambass.* (1669) 282 With so little observance or order, that..the servants were shuffled in among their Masters. **1713** *Guardian* No. 108. 104, I..should not have minded them had they been still shuffled among the crowd. **1742** YOUNG *Nt. Th.* VII. 708 The pang of seeing worth..soon shuffled in the dark With ev'ry vice.
**5. a.** To bring *in* in a deceitful, tricky, or surreptitious manner; to smuggle (a thing) *in* or *into* (something else); to thrust *in* somehow or other.
**1565** JEWEL *Replie Harding* (1611) 201 Quite altering the words that hee found, and shuffling in, and interlacing other words of his owne. **1593** *Tell-Troth's N.Y. Gift* (1876) 10 The wicked..labour..to shuffle in suspition amongst those that are free from thought thereof. **1610** T. ROBINSON *Justif. Separat.* Wks. 1851 II. 490 A bundle of corn shuffled into a field of weeds..cannot make the field a corn-field. **1622** PEACHAM *Compl. Gentl.* xiii. 150 Coates [of arms] sometimes are by stealth purchased, shuffled into Records and Monuments, by Painters. **1736** WATTS *Logic* III. iv. §3 Nor ..cheat your Understanding by changing the Question, or shuffling in anything else in its Room. **1759** ROBERTSON *Hist. Scot.* II. 35 He acknowledged that he had shuffled in this letter among other papers which he laid before the king to be signed.
†**b.** To remove, put *aside* or *away* in a hurried, secret, or underhand manner. *Obs.*
**1598** SHAKS. *Merry W.* IV. vi. 29 Her Mother..hath appointed That he shall likewise shuffle her away. **1646** R. BAILLIE *Anabaptism* (1647) Ep., Then was it good time for them to come in play, and..to shuffle all others, who had managed the Game whilst it was hazardous. **1649** *Bounds & Bonds Obed.* 40 We know..how Joseph was shuffled away by his owne friends and kindred. **1666** in *10th Rep. Hist. MSS. Comm.* App. v. 18 A maid servant, who..was on a

sudden shuffled out of the said house. *a* **1754** FIELDING *Univ. Gallant* II. i, It seems, he is not proper company for me, or you would not have shuffled him away yesterday.

**c.** To bring, put, or thrust *into* or *out of* a position or condition in a haphazard, underhand, or shirking manner, or by rough-and-ready means.

**1628** SHIRLEY *Witty Fair One* V. i, A spruce Captain, newly crept out of a Gentleman Vsher, and shufled into a Buffe Iurkin with gold Lace. **1654** BRAMHALL *Just Vind.* V. (1661) 95 By Slight of hand.. to shuffle this Canon out of the Acts of the Councel. **1692** BENTLEY *Boyle Lect.* V. 4 That all the Bodies of the first Animals and Plants were shuffled into their several Forms.. fortuitously. **1729** LADY FANSHAWE *Mem.* 267 Thus was he shuffled into your father's Employment. **1810** W. WILSON *Hist. Diss. Ch.* III. 83 Nothing can shuffle out the covenant of grace, but a secret conversing with a covenant of works. **1826** SCOTT *Jrnl.* 27 Oct., Calais.. might.. have been shuffled out of our hands during the Civil wars. **1844** KINGLAKE *Eothen* viii. (1847) 92 She shuffled away the subject of poor dear Somersetshire, and bounded onward into loftier spheres of thought. **1860** TRENCH *Serm.* xxi. 247 He that shuns and shirks the task of his life, shuffles it from him. *c* **1860** M. ARNOLD *Mixed Ess., Democracy* (1879) 43 To treat them as if they had been shuffled into their places by a lucky accident.

**d.** ***to shuffle off***: to get rid of or evade (something difficult, arduous, or irksome) in a perfunctory or unsatisfactory manner; to dispose of evasively; to shirk (a duty or obligation).

In mod. use freq. in echoes of Shaks. *Ham.* III. i. 67.

**1601** SHAKS. *Twel. N.* III. iii. 16 And euer oft good turnes, Are shuffel'd off with such vncurrant pay. **1602** —— *Ham.* III. i. 67 When we have shuffel'd [*sic*] off this mortall coile. **1642** D. ROGERS *Naaman* 38 Men shuffle them [*sc.* judgements] off thus. **1653** H. MORE *Antid. Ath.* I. iv. §4 Though he would shuffle off the trouble of apprehending an Infinite Deity. **1784** SIR J. REYNOLDS *Disc.* xii. (1876) 42 To evade and shuffle off real labour. **1807-8** W. IRVING *Salmag.* 375 With the full expectation of shuffling off the remnant of existence, after the excellent fashion of that merry Grecian, who died laughing. **1861** THACKERAY *Four Georges* II. (1876) 46 [They] are obliged for propriety's sake to shuffle off the anxious inquiries of the public. **1863** LYTTON *Caxtoniana* xxii. II. 70 In reality he shuffles off duty. **1890** SAINTSBURY *Ess. Engl. Lit.* 272 A mania which some of his admirers have ..endeavoured to shuffle off.

†**e.** ***to shuffle up***: to manage in secret; to hush up. *Obs.*

**1588** LAMBARDE *Eiren.* IV. xvi. 581 If it be pronounced at the Bench openly..and not shuffled up in a chamber.. secretly. **1605-24** BRETON *I pray you be not angry* (Grosart) 6/2 The matter cleanly shuffled vp, and shee with sorrow rather to confesse it in secret. **1608** WILLET *Hexapla Exod.* 551 The Spanish Inquisition, which is shuffled vp in corners.

**6. a.** *intr.* and *refl.* To get *in*, *into* or *out of* a position or condition, by some means or other, in an underhand, shifty, or evasive manner.

**1565** HARDING *Answ. Jewel* 375 b, In regard of the Rome they haue shuffled them selues into. **1579-80** NORTH *Plutarch* (1595) 511 Sylla valiantly following on his victory, shuffled in [to the City] among them as they fled. **1780** COWPER *Lett.* 4 Mar., We were concerned at your account of Robert, and have little doubt but he will shuffle himself out of his place. **1826** MOTLEY *Corr.* (1889) I. 6, I might enter Sophomore,.. but if I should manage to shuffle in I should always be the worst in my class. **1851** HELPS *Comp. Solit.* iv. (1874) 48 He would have contrived to shuffle awkwardly out of wealth and dignities. **1887** *Westm. Rev.* June 281 He shuffles out of the consequences by vague..charges of undue influence.

**b.** ***to shuffle*** †***over***, ***through***: to perform hurriedly or perfunctorily, get through somehow.

**1656** BAXTER *Ref. Pastor* Pref. b, If there should be any found.. that will shuffle over the work. **1681** FLAVEL *Meth. Grace* xxiv. 418 Dost thou shuffle over thy duties as an interruption to thy business and pleasures? **1820** W. IRVING *Sketch Bk.* I. 219 The service..was shuffled through.. coldly and unfeelingly. **1820** J. W. CROKER in *C. Papers* 20 Dec., If we had but a spokesman or two we should shuffle through the session. **1860** GEO. ELIOT *Mill on Fl.* II. iv, Tom was gradually allowed to shuffle through his lessons with less vigour.

†**c.** To make scrambling efforts, scuffle. *Obs.*

**1609** DANIEL *Civ. Wars* VIII. xcix, Shuffling for your roomes Of ease or honor. **1611** SHAKS. *Cymb.* V. v. 105 Your life, good Master, Must shuffle for it selfe. *a* **1625** FLETCHER *Night-Walker* I, He that shall sit down frighted with that foolery Is not worth pity, let me alone to shuffle.

**7. a.** To act in a shifting or evasive manner; to shift one's ground in argument, etc.; to make use of deceitful pretences or shifty answers.

**1598** SHAKS. *Merry W.* II. ii. 25, I..am faine to shuffle: to hedge, and to lurch. **1652-62** HEYLIN *Cosmogr.* III. (1682) 5 So shuffling with the Macedonian and Syrian Kings, that betwixt both they still preserved their own estates. **1668** O. SANSOM in *Acc. Life* (1710) 60 When you should have produced it [a money-account], you shuffled, and shifted it off; pretending a Mistake. **1706** HEARNE *Collect.* (O.H.S.) I. 222 Mr. Milles did not frankly own it, but seem'd to shuffle about it. **1815** *Sporting Mag.* XLVI. 165 To him they shuffled in the same manner, and gave him the like false description of themselves. **1856** FROUDE *Hist. Eng.* I. 125 He said and unsaid, sighed, sobbed, beat his breast, shuffled, implored, threatened.

**b.** So ***to shuffle up and down***.

**1633** AMES *Fresh Suit* II. 80 Those that are devoted to the Ceremonies may shufle up and downe, first to order, and when they are beaten thence, to Decencie. *c* **1645** HOWELL *Lett.* 5 June 1635, The Bishop of Halverstadt and Count Mansfelt shuffled up and down a good while. [**1871** JOWETT *Plato* I. 96 He shuffles up and down [στρέφεται ἄνω καὶ κάτω] in order to conceal the difficulty into which he has got himself.]

†**8. a.** *trans.* To manipulate unfairly. *Obs.*

**1589** [? LYLY] *Pappe w. Hatchet* (1844) 32 With their wresting and shuffling holie Writ. **1593** BILSON *Govt. Christ's Ch.* 209 If I shuffle any writers wordes, or dazel the Readers eies. **1641** in 'Smectymnuus' *Vind. Answ.* Pref. a 2 b, This Authour is misalledged... This Councell shuffled up with little fidelitie.

**b.** ***to shuffle up***: to get or put together hastily or in a perfunctory manner; to patch up. *Obs.*

**1532** MORE *Confut. Tindale* Wks. 357/1 Yet haue I not so slightly sene vnto mine own, nor shoffled it vp so hasteli,.. but that [etc.]. **1589** NASHE *Anat. Absurd.* B 4 b, Some stitcher..hath shuffled or slubberd vp a few ragged Rimes. **1607** DEKKER *Westw. Hoe* Wks. 1873 III. 295 Like Country Atturnies, wee are to shuffle vp many matters in a forenoone. **1643** BAKER *Chron., Hen. VII*, (1653) 355 To shuffle up a Summary proceeding by examination, without tryall of Jury. **1659** *Lady Alimony* II. iii, A mad match soon shuffled up!

**c.** To treat (a matter) in an equivocal fashion.

**1637** GILLESPIE *Eng. Pop. Cerem.* III. iv. 59 He shuffleth the point deceitfully. **1726** WODROW *Corr.* (1843) III. 251 The Moderator shuffled the matter.

**9. a.** In immaterial sense: To put (a thing) *off from* one to another, or *upon* a person.

**1612** SIR J. DAVIES *Why Ireland*, etc. 168 Their possessions.. being shuffled and changed, and remoued so often from one to another. **1642** R. CARPENTER *Experience* IV. v. 144 Looke how they shuffle the matter, and give it from one hand to another amongst themselves. **1692** R. L'ESTRANGE *Fables* ccxxxiii. 203 If any thing Hits, we take it to our Selves, if it Miscarries, we shuffle it off to our Neighbours. **1745** *De Foe's Engl. Tradesm.* ii. (1841) I. 18 The warehouse-man shuffles them back upon the clothier to lie for his account. **1875** McLAREN *Serm.* Ser. II. vii. 125 Is he trying to shuffle off guilt from his own shoulders? **1879** FROUDE *Cæsar* xiii. 189 Those who most agreed in what he had done, were not ashamed to shuffle off upon him their responsibilities. **1882** *Mrs. Raven's Temptation* I. 281 I'll shuffle him off upon the governor.

†**b.** To put (a person) *off* (*with* an excuse, a makeshift). *Obs.*

**1659** D. PELL *Impr. Sea* 574 Will any Land-lord bear with his Tennant that shuffels him off from year to year? **1662** J. DAVIES tr. *Olearius' Voy. Ambass.* (1669) 287 Those whom the king had sent to him would not be shuffled off with that answer. **1690** C. NESSE *Hist. & Myst. O. & N. Test.* I. 77 It cannot consist with a gracious heart to shuffle off the great God with slight services.

†**c.** To cheat (a person) *out of* a thing. *Obs.*

**1627** in *Lismore Papers* Ser. II. (1888) III. 150 He would spend his whole estate before he should be shuffled out of his landes. **1660** PEPYS *Diary* 4 July, I..had great fears that they will shuffle me out of them [*sc.* houses].

**10. a.** *trans.* To shift from one place to another; to move *about* this way and that.

† ***shuffle the slipper***, the game of hunt-the-slipper.

**1694** *Phil. Trans.* XVIII. 92 Several Houses now standing were shuffled and moved some Yards from their places. **1697** DRYDEN *Æneid* XI. 1166 Apollo..granting half his pray'r, Shuffled in winds the rest, and toss'd in empty air. **1760-72** H. BROOKE *Fool of Qual.* (1809) I. 16 Our hero was beaten..at draw-glove and shuffle the slipper. **1781** COWPER *Truth* 320 Yon cottager, who weaves at her own door..Shuffling her threads about the live-long day.

†**b.** *intr.* To shift *about* hesitatingly. *Obs.*

*c* **1645** HOWELL *Lett.* 28 Nov. 1635, The French shuffle yet well enough upon the Frontiers of Germany and Lorrain. **1697** DAMPIER *Voy.* (1729) I. 79 The Wind would shuffle about to the Southward again, and fall flat calm.

†**c.** To pass *into* a succession of conditions. *Obs.*

**1635** SHIRLEY *Traitor* ii. D 4 b, The Elements Shuffle into innumerable changes.

**11. a.** To put (a thing) *into* a receptacle, put or take (a thing) *on*, *off*, etc. in a clumsy or fumbling manner.

**1694** tr. *Marten's Voy. Spitzbergen* in *Acc. Sev. Late Voy.* II. 161 By it stands a Boy that shuffles the Fat by degrees into a Bag. **1837** CARLYLE *Fr. Rev.* III. VI. ii, His shoulders shuffle the loose coat off them. **1839** JAMES *Louis XIV*, II. 62 The secretary shuffled the papers hastily under the table cover. **1847** DISRAELI *Tancred* III. ii, He shuffled off his slippers at the threshold. **1865** DICKENS *Mut. Fr.* III. iii, When he has shuffled his clothes on. **1869** TROLLOPE *He knew*, etc. lvii. (1878) 319 She could only shuffle her letter back into her pocket.

**b.** *intr.* To get *into* an article of clothing in a clumsy or fumbling manner.

**1865** KINGSLEY *Herew.* xli, Ailward shuffled into his harness. **1883** V. STUART *Egypt* 112 The inhabitants.. shuffled into their slippers.

**c.** To fumble. *rare.*

**1812** *Examiner* 30 Nov. 767/2 Collingbourn observed the prisoner busily shuffling about his pockets.

**12.** *Comb.*: **shuffle beat** = SHUFFLE RHYTHM; **shuffle-breeches** (meaning obscure); **shuffle-cap**, 'a play at which money is shaken in a hat' (J.); **shuffle rhythm**, a slow strongly syncopated rhythm (see quot. 1940); **shuffle-wing**, the hedge-sparrow, *Prunella modularis.*

**1955** SHAPIRO & HENTOFF *Hear me talkin' to Ya* 21 They played the *shuffle beat on the snare drum. **1977** *National Observer* (U.S.) 22 Jan. 22/4 A lot of it's the old southern shuffle beat. Music you could get up and dance to. **1822** COBBETT *Cottage Econ.* (1823) §107 The old *shuffle-breeches band of the Quarterly Review. **1712** ARBUTHNOT *John Bull* II. iii, He lost his Money at Chuck-Farthing, *Shuffle-Cap, and All-Fours. **1759** STERNE *Tr. Shandy* I. x, Even chuck-farthing and shuffle-cap themselves stood gaping till he [the village parson] had got out of sight. **1940** *Swing* June 13/3 The typifying characteristic of the Savitt band is its '*shuffle rhythm', which is distinguished..by its ..4/4 jazz time. **1967** *Boston Sunday Herald* 30 Apr. 14/4 From shuffle rhythm to rock he waxed them all. **1829** J. L. KNAPP *Jrnl. Natur.* 151 The hedge sparrow, or *shufflewing. **1909** W. H. HUDSON *Afoot in England* xxiv. 289, I also love the smaller vocalists—the modest shuffle-wing and the lesser whitethroat. **1977** *Sunday Tel.* 6 Feb. 15/7 This is a day on which to..watch truly aggressive chaffinches competing with shufflewings.

**shuffle-board**: see SHOVEL-BOARD.

**ˈshuffled**, *ppl. a.* [f. SHUFFLE *v.* + -ED[1].] Huddled up, jumbled together.

**1685** DRYDEN *Alb. & Alb.* II, In shuffled Heaps they hither tend. *a* **1683** OLDHAM *Wks.* (1686) 71 No shuffled Atoms did the well built work compose.

**shuffler** (ˈʃʌflə(r)). [f. SHUFFLE *v.* + -ER[1].]

†**1.** One who mixes up or jumbles. *Obs.*

**1611** COTGR., *Brouilleur*, a..disorderly shuffler, or mingler of things together.

**2.** One who acts in a shifty or evasive manner; a slippery, shifty person. In first quot. *transf.*

**1621** BP. MOUNTAGU *Diatribæ* 321 If it be..that this first Tithe is euery where stiled by the name of Tithes payed at Ierusalem: your second Tithe, for ought I see, may goe stand by for a shuffler, or it must bee confounded with the first. **1629** H. BURTON *Truth's Tri.* 46 See this crafty shuffler how hee can packe this close. **1723** WATERLAND *2nd Vind. Christ's Div.* 157 Unless He were the greatest Prevaricator and Shuffler imaginable. **1836** LYTTON *Athens* (1837) II. 520 Sophocles in private life was a profligate, and in public life a shuffler, and a trimmer. **1883** *Manch. Exam.* 26 Nov. 5/2 If [he] is not the meanest and most pitiful shuffler who ever stood on a platform.

†**3.** *Cant.* ? A drinker. *Obs.*

**1642** *Tom Nash his Ghost* title-p., To the three scurvy Fellowes of the upstart Family of the Snufflers, Rufflers and Shufflers. **1652** BRATHWAIT *Barnabies Summons*, For all Malaga men, called Vintners, Sack-drawers..Tub-Taysters Snuffers, Rufflers,..Shufflers,..Suck-spigots, Spewterers.

**4.** One who shuffles cards.

**1894** MASKELYNE *Sharps & Flats* 154 If the sharp is a fine shuffler.

**ˈshuffling**, *vbl. sb.* [f. SHUFFLE *v.* + -ING[1].]

**1.** The action of moving the feet along the ground without lifting them; the dragging and scraping of feet over a surface.

***double-shuffling***: the performance of a double shuffle.

**1608** DEKKER *Dead Tearme* Wks. (Grosart) IV. 51 What shuffling, what shouldering, what Justling. **1859** DICKENS *Haunted House* VIII. 48 There ensued such toe-and-heeling, and buckle-covering, and double-shuffling. **1869** 'LEWIS CARROLL' *Phantasmagoria* 99 Old shufflings on the sanded floor. **1873** MISS BROUGHTON *Nancy* ii, A noise of shuffling and scrambling to their feet on the part of the congregation.

**2.** The re-arrangement of the cards in a pack.

**1579** NORTHBROOKE *Dicing* (1843) 142 They haue such sleightes in sorting and shuffling of the cardes. **1591** FLORIO *2nd Fruites* 69 What a shooffling doo you keepe with those cardes? **1659** H. NEVILE (*title*), Shuffling, Cutting, and Dealing, in a Game at Pickquet. **1796** BURKE *Regic. Peace* iv, The cutting and shuffling of Cards. **1840** HOOD *Miss Kilmansegg* 2002 The rattling of dice and the shuffling of cards. **1856** LT. COL. B** *Whist player* (1858) 18 In shuffling, the cards must be above and free from the table.

*fig.* *c* **1652** J. SMITH *Sel. Disc.* IV. 89 That all the shuffling and cutting of atoms could produce such a divine piece of wisdom as this is.

**3.** The shifting of a thing about or from one place to another; change of the position (of things) with reference to each other; mixing or jumbling *together*.

**1602** SHAKS. *Ham.* IV. vii. 135 So that with ease, Or with a little shuffling, you may choose A Sword vnbaited. **1661** BOYLE *Scept. Chym.* II. 162 A new shuffling and Disposition of the Component Particles of a body. **1691** RAY *Creation* (1714) 37 The fortuitous shuffling together of its component Materials. **1692** R. L'ESTRANGE *Fables* xli. 43 This Shuffling of the Bat in the Paw of the Weazle. **1890** *Hardwicke's Sci. Gossip* XXVI. 143/2 After some sidling of the head and shuffling of the wings. **1891** *Athenæum* 8 Aug. 189/3 'Charybdis', the title-piece..seems as if it might have come to its pre-eminence merely by a chance shuffling of the leaves.

**b.** *Printing.* (See quot.)

**1841** SAVAGE *Dict. Printing*, *Shuffling*. This is..part of the process of Knocking-up, when the paper is laid in heaps, after having been taken down from the poles, to make it lie even at the edges.

**4.** Shifty or evasive dealing or conduct; †*occas.* evasion (*of* something).

**1579** W. WILKINSON *Confut. Fam. Love* 4 Herein you do but rayse dust with your shufflyng. **1602** SHAKS. *Ham.* III. iii. 61 There is no shuffling, there the Action lyes In his true Nature. **1646** J. HALL *Horæ Vac.* 113 There is rather a shuffling of approaching dangers, then preventing them from afarre. *a* **1716** SOUTH *Serm.* (1744) II. 112 The ambiguity and shuffling of a partial historian. **1823** LAMB *Elia* II. *Poor Relations*, The truth must out without shuffling. **1842** MIALL *Nonconf.* II. 1 That species of shuffling, which goes by the name of expediency. **1884** *Truth* 13 Mar. 375/2 All the rest is shuffling and subterfuge.

**ˈshuffling**, *ppl. a.* [f. SHUFFLE *v.* + -ING[1].]

**1.** That shuffles in walking; that drags the feet over the ground without lifting them. Hence, of a walk, pace, gait: Consisting of or characterized by a shuffle.

**1596** SHAKS. *1 Hen. IV*, III. i. 135 The forc't gate of a shuffling Nagge. **1609** *Old Meg of Herefordsh.* (1816) 1 The courts of kings for stately measures:..the country for shufling dances. **1697** COLLIER *Ess. Mor. Subj.* II. (1703) 45 The hurry of the pursuit will make but a shuffling pace.

**1727** SOMERVILE *Happy Disapp.* 57 He knew him by his shuffling pace. **1815** ELPHINSTONE *Acc. Caubul* Introd. (1842) I. 9 A kind of shuffling trot. **1848** DICKENS *Dombey* ii, He was a strong..round-shouldered, shuffling, shaggy fellow. **1889** JESSOPP *Coming of Friars* ii. 57 A ragged, shuffling tramp on the road.

**2.** Of persons: Given to shifty or evasive action or behaviour.

**1616** R. COCKS *Diary* (Hakl. Soc.) I. 94 A shuffling fello, not worthy water for his hier. **1674** *Essex Papers* (1890) I. 182, I find them very backward & shufling in all their Paym$^{ts}$. **1715** ADDISON *Tryal Count Tariff*, The Court found him a false, shuffling, prevaricating rascal. **1833** HT. MARTINEAU *Manch. Strike* i. 12 The mean-spirited, shuffling knave. **1878** LECKY *Eng. in 18th Cent.* II. viii. 439 So timid in danger, and so shuffling in difficulty.

**b.** Of action, conduct, speech: Evasive, shifty.

**1644** PRYNNE & WALKER *Fiennes' Trial* 29 Colonell Fiennes.., said in a shuffling manner, I confess he was a Governour *de facto*, but not *de jure*. **1660** H. MORE *Myst. Godl.* v. xvii. 203 They held the Creed in the plain literal sense thereof without any shuffling Allegories. **1712** ARBUTHNOT *John Bull* III. x, Though he durst not directly break his appointment, he made many a shuffling excuse. **1787** JEFFERSON *Writ.* (1859) II. 171 The shuffling conduct of Barrois. **1831** SCOTT *Ct. Robt.* xxi, The wily, ambidexter, shuffling policy of the Emperor. **1851** THACKERAY *Eng. Hum.* iii. (1876) 246 Dick made a shuffling excuse that he could not see her.

**3.** That shuffles cards.

**1777** [T. SWIFT] *Gamblers* 11 Great Father of the Shuffling Crew! [*margin* Mr. Hoyle].

**'shufflingly,** *adv.* [f. prec. + -LY$^{2}$.] With a shuffling gait; in a shuffling or evasive manner.

**1657** J. SERGEANT *Schism Dispach't* 110 How shufflingly the Doctor behaves himself. **1681** DRYDEN *Span. Friar* I. i, Perhaps I may go shufflingly at first; for I was never before walk'd in Trammels. **1865** DICKENS *Mut. Fr.* I. xvi, The honest man had shufflingly declined. **1879** MEREDITH *Egoist* xxxiii, Vernon..apologized to him shufflingly.

**shuffly** ('ʃʌflɪ), *a.* [f. SHUFFLE *v.* + -Y$^{1}$.] Characterized by shuffling; inclined to shuffle.

**1926** *Blackw. Mag.* Oct. 539/2 The step slower and, if possible, more shuffly. **1952** J. MASTERS *Deceivers* xxi. 240 That shuffly, shy old fool. **1974** N. FREELING *Dressing of Diamond* 66 He banged on the counter, brought the shuffly man out.

**shuffy** ('ʃʌfɪ), *a.* [f. SHUFF + -Y.] Of bricks: Friable from being badly burnt.

**1850** DOBSON *Bricks & Tiles* 38 Shuffs. These are unsound and shuffy—that is, full of shakes. **1873** ROBERTSON *Engin. Notes* 33 If the intensity of the heat is intermittent the bricks will be shuffy like piecrust.

**shufti, shufty** ('ʃʊftɪ, ʃʌ-), *sb. slang* (orig. *Mil.*). [f. next.]

**1.** A look or glance. Esp. in phr. ***to take*** (or ***have***) ***a shufti.***

**1943** *Gen* 16 Jan. 11/2 Take a shufti at that. That's Stephanie. **1947** D. M. DAVIN *Gorse blooms Pale* 201 She took another good shufty at us. **1965** J. PORTER *Dover Two* x. 133 Take a shufty at this lot! **1971** WHILLANS & ORMEROD *Don Whillans* x. 81 'Let's have a shufti at that description then,' said Joe, and we both examined the piece of paper covered with Snell's handwriting. **1980** R. ADAMS *Girl in Swing* xix. 245 Good idea, old boy. I'm game. Let's 'ave a crafty shufti round with that in mind, shall we?

**2.** *Comb.*, as **shufti-kite**, a reconnaissance aircraft; **shufti-scope**, a probe (see quots.).

**1944** T. H. WISDOM *Triumph over Tunisia* 172 When the Hun shufti-kites were kept away..the U.S. Second Corps moved..to the coastal stretch in the north. **1948** PARTRIDGE *Dict. Forces' Slang* 169 *Shuftiscope*, instrument used by doctors for exploring the interior of a dysentery case. A telescope or periscope. **1962** *Times* 12 Apr. 9/4 When officers were making a routine check of the vehicle with an instrument they call a 'shufti-scope' they found the watches. Mr. Eaton explained that the 'shufti-scope' is an instrument consisting of a probe with a light through which it is possible to see into cavities.

**shufti, shufty** ('ʃʊftɪ, ʃʌ-), *v. slang* (chiefly *Mil.*). Now *rare*. [f. Arab. *šufti* have you seen?, f. *šāf* to see.] *intr.* To look or watch; to glance. Freq. in *imp.*

**1943** C. H. WARD-JACKSON *It's Piece of Cake* 54 *Shufty*, look, watch. Thus, the orderly room sergeant to a Waaf clerk as he sights a squadron of Liberators through the headquarters' window, 'Shufty!' **1947** *Amer. Speech* XXII. 267 The word *shufti* was among the most commonly used, comprehending in its meaning both the noun and the verb 'look'..'to shufti around' [etc.].

†**shug,** *v. Obs. rare*$^{-1}$. [If not some error, perh. a forced use of *shug* SHOG *v.*] *intr.* ? To force one's way, shove *in*.

**1638** DEKKER, etc. *Witch of Edmonton* v. i. (1658) 56, I am for greatness now..; There I'll shug in, and get a noble countenance; Serve some Briarean Footcloth-strider.

**shug,** variant of SHOG *v.*

**'shuggie-,shue,** *sb. Sc., Ir.* and *north.* Also 7, 9 shoggie-shou, -show, 9 shuggy shoe, -shew, -shoo, -shaw. [Cf. SHOG *v.* and SHUE *sb.* and *v.*] The pastime of swinging; a swing (esp. at a fair), hence *jocularly* the gallows; also a see-saw. Hence **shuggy-shue** *v. intr.* to sway about. (See *Eng. Dial. Dict.*)

**1653** URQUHART *Rabelais* I. xxii. 96 There he played..at swaggie, waggie or shoggieshou [F. *a la brandelle*]. **1836** W. CARLETON *Fardorougha* xvi, You'd a' got a touch of the *Shuggy Shoe. Note* Gallows.

**shuggle, shugh,** var. ff. SHOGGLE, SHEUGH.

†**shugh.** *int. rare*$^{-1}$. [Cf. SHOO *int.*$^{2}$] Used as an exclamation of impatience.

**1640** BROME *Antipodes* v. v. *Joy*. Shugh, give me leave. *Byp. I* must take charge I see o' th' dagger agaìne.

‖**shugo** ('ʃugo). Also **Shugo.** [Jap.] In the Japanese feudal system: a military governor.

**1893** F. BRINKLEY tr. *Hist. Empire Japan* iv. 171 His Majesty sanctioned the appointment of High Constables (*Shugo*) in the various provinces. **1933** F. C. JONES *Japan* i. 13 As is usual under feudal conditions, the *Shugo*..made their posts hereditary. **1974** *Encycl. Brit. Macropædia* X. 64/2 It was the job of the *shugo* to recruit metropolitan guards and keep strict control over subversives and criminals.

**shuin,** obs. variant of SEWIN$^{1}$.

**1655** MOUFET & BENNET *Health's Improv.* 187 *Shuins*, seem unto me a kind of Salmon.

**shuite,** obs. form of SUIT.

‖**shuka** ('ʃuːkə). Also **Shukkah.** [Swahili.] A long piece of fabric, now commonly worn as a shawl-like garment in East Africa.

**1856** R. F. BURTON *First Footsteps E. Africa* ii. 29 As regards the word Tobe, it signifies, in Arabic, a garment generally: the Somal call it 'Maro', and the half Tobe a 'Shukkah'. **1936** F. STARK *Southern Gates Arabia* xi. 123 The visitors from outside came wrapped in their shuka, a square black shawl with two fringed sides which they wore draped over their heads and bodies, the two lower corners knotted together and the upper ones thrown over one arm. **1971** *Standard* (Dar es Salaam) 7 Apr. 6/3 (Advt.), Tasini leads the way in the latest dress print designs. Shukas, Vitenges etc.

‖**shul** (ʃuːl). Also **shool.** [Yiddish, f. G. *schule* school.] The synagogue.

[**1804** M. WILMOT *Let.* 17 July in *Russian Jrnls.* (1934) I. 114 They walked with down cast eyes and penitent countenances to the School (as the Synagogue is call'd).] **1874** HOTTEN *Slang Dict.* 288 *Shool*, Jews' term for their synagogue. **1876** GEO. ELIOT *D. Deronda* IV. xxxiii. 136/1 This evening is the Sabbath..and I go to the *Shool*. **1892** [see HESPED]. **1932** L. GOLDING *Magnolia Street* I. xiii. 235 The presentation will be at night, after *shool*. **1957** L. STERN *Midas Touch* I. i. 19 The Kosher food, the ceremonial prayers, coming here to *shul*. **1977** *New Yorker* 9 May 41/3 Her great-uncle Zindel, a former shammes in a shul that had been torn down.

‖**Shulchan Aruch** ('ʃulxən 'aːrux). Also **Shulh(h)an Arukh.** [Heb., lit. table prepared.] The name of a work on Jewish religious practice by Joseph ben Ephraim Caro (1488–1575) now accepted as the standard guide to Orthodox observance.

**1901** M. GASTER *Hist. Anc. Synagogue Spanish & Portuguese Jews* 47 It is an abstract of the *Shulhhan Arukh of Caro* containing all the laws and ceremonies of a practical utility, condensed into a very small form. **1922** *Aspects Jewish Life & Thought* 43 This popular edition of the greater work is the *Shulchan Aruch*..which was first published in the year 1565. **1957** *Encycl. Brit.* X. 18/2 The codes, especially Joseph Qaro's *Shulhan Arukh*, became the halachic authority in Jewry. **1978** I. B. SINGER *Shosha* ii. 22 He breaks every law of the Shulchan Aruch, yet at the same time he preaches Jewishness.

**shulder, -dre, -dur,** obs. forms of SHOULDER.

**shule:** see SHOOL *v.*, SHOVEL.

**shulleng(e,** obs. forms of SHILLING.

**'shullock.** *Obs.* exc. *dial.* In 7 schullock, 9 *dial.* shollock, shullok. [Of obscure origin: cf. dial. *shallock, shollock* vb., to idle about, to slouch.] Used as a term of contempt.

*a* **1603** T. CARTWRIGHT *Confut. Rhem. N.T.* (1618) 642 M. Calvins great skill..could not without blushing be lacked of such schullockes and skipjackes as you be. **1841** R. W. HAMILTON *Nugæ Lit.* 359 *Shollock*. A very dirty fellow,—bad in look as shabby in appearance.

**shulwar,** var. of SHALWAR.

**shumac, shuman:** see SUMACH, SHAMAN.

**Shumerian,** variant of SUMERIAN.

**shumsheer,** variant of SHAMSHEER.

**shun** (ʃʌn), *sb. rare*$^{-1}$. [f. the verb.] The action of shunning; in phr. ***upon the shun.***

**1822** SCOTT *Peveril* Pref. Let., Our friend is so much upon the shun..that it must be no light temptation which will withdraw him from his incognito.

**shun** (ʃʌn), *v.* Pa. t. and pa. pple. **shunned** (ʃʌnd). Forms: *α.* 1 scunian, 3 scunien, schunien, shunen(n, sconien, sonen, sunen, schunen, 3–4 schonen, schonie, 4 shonie, -ye, schonne, schwne, 4–5 shonen, shone, schone, 4–6 shonne, 4–7 shunne, 5–6 shon (6 schune, shonn), 6– shun; *irreg. pa. t.* 7 (once) shan. *β.* 1 -sceonian (in compounds), *north.* (ȝi)scynia, 3 sceonie, 4 shine, shenye, 5 *pa. t.* shynte. [OE. *scunian* (chiefly in compounds, *á-, onscunian*), a wk. verb not found in the other Teut. langs. Of obscure origin.

If the primary sense was 'to hide oneself (from)', the vb. might be a derivative from the Teut. and Indogermanic root **sku-* to cover, hide.

The *β* forms are prob. due to the effect of the palatal *sc* on the following vowel.]

†**1.** *trans.* To abhor, detest, loathe. *Obs.*

**1023** in Thorpe *Dipl. Angl. Sax.* (1865) 318 Of eallan ðan mannan ðe ðær ȝehænde beoð mid ane mode wurð he ȝescunned. *a* **1200** *Vices & Virtues* 7 þat ȝie hatien and scunien, ouer alle þing, ðes awerȝhede senne. *c* **1200** ORMIN 2550 Drihhtin shuneþþ alle þa þatt unnclænnesse follȝhenn. *c* **1205** LAY. 14869–72 Mi uader..scunede [*c* **1275** sonede] þene cristindom & þa hæðene laȝen luuede..þa we sculleð sceonien [*c* 1275 hatie]. *a* **1250** *Owl & Night.* 229 For vych þing þat schonyeþ riht, hit luuyeþ þuster & hateþ lyht. *Ibid.* 792 Vor myne crafte men me luuyeþ Vor þine strengþe men þe schunyeþ.

†**2. a.** To seek safety by concealment or flight from (an enemy, his pursuit, etc.). *Obs.*

*a* **950** *Guthlac* xix. (Gonser) 159/7 And hine Ceolred se kyning hider and þider wide aflymde, an he his ehtnysse and his hatunge fleah and scunode. **1607** SHAKS. *Cor.* I. vi. 44 The Mouse ne're shunn'd the Cat, as they did budge From Rascals worse then they. **1638** W. LISLE *Heliodorus* II. 36 A liuing Greeke from dead Ægyptian ran, And long time that, which could not hurt him, shan.

**b.** To evade, elude (a blow, missile). *Obs.*

*a* **1586** SIDNEY *Arcadia* III. (Sommer) 317 b, But Amphialus seeing the blow comming, shunned it with nimble turning his horse aside. **1590** SPENSER *F.Q.* II. v. 4 [He] lightly shunned it [the stroke]. **1667** MILTON *P.L.* II. 810, I forewarn thee, shun His deadly arrow.

**3.** To avoid (in mod. prose use always to avoid persistently or habitually) from repugnance, fear, or caution; to keep away from (a person or his society, a place, etc.); to avoid encountering or exposing oneself to (dangers, conditions), using or having to do with (a thing); to eschew, abstain carefully from (an action, an indulgence, etc.).

**a.** with obj. a person, his company, etc.

*c* **1175** *Lamb. Hom.* 79 Al se hwat se he forgulte wes al [animals] hit him ulel [? *read* uleh] and scunede. *c* **1250** *Gen. & Ex.* 1864 Ðat folkes kin god bad him sunen. **13..** *K. Alis.* 6157 (Laud MS.), Aqueyntaunce of alle men hij shoneþ. **1377** LANGL. *P. Pl.* B. XI. 427 Euery man hym shonyeth. **1393** *Ibid.* C. XIV. 245 Ech man shoneþ hus companye. *a* **1450** LOVELICH *Grail* lv. 76 The kyng was A lepre..and so Orible..that Eche Man schoned his Compenye. **1590** SHAKS. *Mids. N.* II. i. 142 If you will patiently dance in our Round,..goe with vs; If not, shun me and I will spare your haunts. **1607** ROWLANDS *Famous Hist.* 13 Society he shuns, and keeps alone. **1667** MILTON *P.L.* IV. 319 So passd they naked on, nor shund the sight Of God or Angel. **1784** COWPER *Task* III. 88 Then he that sharp'd..Was mark'd and shunn'd as odious. *Ibid.* VI. 307 The tim'rous hare.. Scarce shuns me. **1865** DICKENS *Mut. Fr.* III. viii, So.. shunning human approach, this troublesome old woman hid herself. **1880** DIXON *Windsor* III. xxiv. 238 The nobler class of Catholics shunned him.

**b.** with obj. a thing, a place, external conditions or circumstances, dangers, an enemy, etc.

*c* **1200** ORMIN 9395 ȝiff þatt tin eȝhe iss ali unnhal..Itt shuneþþ..þe sunness brihhte leome. *a* **1225** *Ancr. R.* 86 Vor ȝif heo hit [hore fulðe] stunken, ham wolde..speowen hit ut þer, and schunien hit þer efter. *a* **1250** *Owl & Night.* 590 (Jesus MS.) þar to þu draust..& oþer clene stude þu schunest. **1382** WYCLIF *Lev.* xi. 11 ȝe shulen not eete the flesh of hem, and the faln to deeth ȝe shulen shonne [1388 eschewe]. *c* **1420** *Chron. Vilod.* 1548 Bot euery mon may well knowe & wyte What he was, by-cause þat he shynte & dred þe cresse. **1577** GOOGE tr. *Heresbach's Husb.* I. 18 Yf.. you finde it sweete, it is a signe of riche grounde..yf it be saltishe, it is to be shunned. **1591** SHAKS. *Two Gent.* I. iii. 78 Thus haue I shund the fire, for feare of burning. **1611** BIBLE *Transl. Pref.* ¶9 Neither is it the true man that shunneth the light, but the malefactour. **1697** DRYDEN *Æneid* Ded. (e), I have shun'd the *Cæsura* as much as possibly I cou'd. For wherever that is us'd it gives a roughness to the Verse. **1710–11** ATTERBURY *Serm.* (1734) III. 93 It is not supposed, that we should have Power always to Resist, unless we before-hand do what is in our Power to Shun Temptation. **1717** PRIOR *Alma* I. 482 He hates the fight, and shuns the foe. **1781** COWPER *Charity* 239 Thy lips have..Taught me what path to shun and what pursue. **1847** TENNYSON *Princess* Prol. 38 O noble heart who..Nor bent, nor broke, nor shunn'd a soldier's death. **1849** MACAULAY *Hist. Eng.* v. I. 616 They rode on all day, shunning towns and villages. **1865** LIVINGSTONE *Zambesi* x. 204 A strange superstition makes them shun this sacred place.

*absol.* **1818** SHELLEY *Lines Euganean Hills* 23 The dreamer ..Longing with divided will, But no power to seek or shun.

**c.** with obj. a mode of action, expression, or behaviour, an occupation, employment, subject of conversation, a mental condition or the like (often expressed by inf. or gerund).

*c* **1175** *Lamb. Hom.* 111 þet clene wif scunað ȝitsunge. *c* **1200** ORMIN 4502 Itt niss nohht lihht To betenn hefiȝ sinne, & forrþi birrþ þe shunenn aȝȝ To fallenn ohht tærinne. *c* **1200** *Trin. Coll. Hom.* 13 þe man þe hit meðeð riht þe suneð aleð gestninge and idel wil. **1340–70** *Alex. & Dind.* 449 Wiþ us schineþ euery schalk in schippus for to saile. **1387** TREVISA *Higden* (Rolls) III. 459 We schoneþ and forsakeþ foule slewþe and leccherie. *a* **1400** *New Test.* (Paues) *Tit.* iii. 9 Bote schenye þou questyones of foly. *c* **1449** PECOCK *Repr.* II. xiii. 227 The vce of thilk thing is to be shoned, eschewid, and avoidid. **1544** BETHAM *Precepts War* I. cxl. G vij b, Commaunde your souldyours, that they shunne to spoyle and robbe temples. **1590** SPENSER *F.Q.* I. x. 60 Thenceforth the suit of earthly conquest shonne. **1617** MORYSON *Itin.* I. 16, I ever shunned to goe twice one way. **1697** DRYDEN *Virg. Past.* IX. 21 Had not Phœbus warn'd me ..To shun debate, Menalcas had been slain. **1742** BERKELEY

*Let.* Wks. 1871 IV. 282, I would say, shun late hours. **1845** M. PATTISON *Ess.* (1889) I. 19 The thorny subject which they were delicately shunning in their conversation. **1847** TENNYSON *Princess* III. 205 We touch on our dead self, nor shun to do it. **1868** NETTLESHIP *Ess. Browning* i. 40 The majority of those who are growing old..shun looking back at all.

*absol.* **1377** LANGL. *P. Pl.* B. v. 169 Amonge monkes I miȝt be ac many tyme I shonye.

**d.** *transf.* and *fig.* Said *poet.* of things.

**13..** *E.E. Allit. P.* B. 1101 So clene was his hondelyng vche ordure hit schonied. **1610** SHAKS. *Temp.* IV. i. 116 Scarcity and want shall shun you. **1701** ADDISON *Let. fr. Italy* 56 See how the golden groves around me smile, That shun the coast of Britain's stormy Isle. **1813** SHELLEY *Q. Mab* IV. 101 The meteor-happiness, that shuns his grasp.

**4. a.** To escape (a threatened evil, an unwelcome task). Now *rare* or *Obs.*

*c* **1275** *Moral Ode* 159 in *O.E. Misc.* 63 Eure he wolde..in godnesse wuyne Wiþ þat he myhte helle fur euer fleon and schonye. **1413-46** HOCCLEVE *Minor P.* i. 193 How may we two, the deeth eschue or shone? **1593** SHAKS. *3 Hen. VI*, II. iii. 13 They follow vs with Wings, And weake we are, and cannot shun pursuite. **1614** GORGES *Lucan* VII. 295 That thus repulst thou shunst the griefe To see the slaughtred heapes that lye? **1667** MILTON *P.L.* x. 1062 [He will] teach us further by what means to shun Th' inclement Seasons, Rain, Ice, Hail and Snow. **1784** JOHNSON in *Boswell* (1904) II. 537 If a man were to go by chance at the same time with Burke under a shed, to shun a shower. **1870** BRYANT *Iliad* I. VI. 207 No man of woman born Coward or brave, can shun his destiny.

†**b.** To prevent the occurrence of (an action, event), to guard against (some inconvenience). *Obs.*

**1338** R. BRUNNE *Chron.* (1725) 111 Bot Henry Dauid sonne,..Contek for to schonne, to Steuen mad feaute. **1613** LADY E. CAREW *Mariam* I. i, For hee by barring me from libertie, To shunne my ranging, taught me first to range. **1697** DRYDEN *Virg. Georg.* III. 245 To shun this Ill, the cunning Leach ordains..To feed the Females, e'er the Sun arise. **1796** JEFFERSON *Writ.* (1859) IV. 154, I devoutly wish you may be able to shun for us this war. **1798** BLOOMFIELD *Farmer's Boy, Spring* 159 Prowling Reynard..To shun whose thefts was Giles's evening care.

†**5.** *intr.* To shrink with dread; to be afraid. *Obs.*

*a* **1000** *Durham Ritual* 32/5 Giscynia, *metuere*. *a* **1300** *Cursor M.* 15173 Þe fleche was dutand for to dei,..It was ful sconand for þe sare. *a* **1325** *Maudelein* 24 in Horstm. *Altengl. Leg.* (1878) 163 For euer he schoneþ þat haþ misgilt. *c* **1375** *Sc. Leg. Saints* iv. (*Jacobus*) 164 þe bukis all he brocht..and prayt him to bryne þam sone. 'Na', said he, 'for þat I schone þe rek of þame suld noyus be'. *c* **1440** *York Myst.* x. 244 It is goddis will, it sall be myne, Agaynste his saande sall I neuer schone.

†**6. a.** To shrink back physically; to move or go aside (so as to escape or evade some person or thing); to fly (from an enemy, etc.); also with *aside*, *away*. *Obs.*

*c* **1330** R. BRUNNE *Chron. Wace* (Rolls) 14128 Þey couþe nought fighte, ne to-gydere wone, Ne at tyme stande ne schone. *a* **1375** *Joseph Arim.* 496 Betere hit were douhtilyche to diȝen on or oune, þen wiþ schendschupe to schone and vs a-bak drawe. ? *a* **1400** *Morte Arth.* 314 Ne no more schoune fore þe swape of theire scharpe suerddes. **14..** *Sir Beues* (O) 3591 Fro his stroke away they dyd shone. **1530** PALSGR. 704/1 And I had nat shonned asyde, he had hyt me in the eye. **1577** *Test. 12 Patriarchs* (1706) 152 If ye be good doers, both unclean spirits shall flee from you, and shrewd beasts shall shun for fear of you. *a* **1586** SIDNEY *Arcadia* III. (Sommer) 269 He shunned as much as he could, keeping onely his place for feare of punishment. *a* **1600** *Flodden Field* xli. in Child *Ballads* III. 357/1 Doubtlesse while your liues wold last you wold never shun beside the plaine.

*fig.* **1572** J. JONES *Bathes of Bathes Ayde* II. 18 b, The salte taste is that, which..byteth the tonge... The bitter taste is that, which seemeth to shunne away from the tongue.

**b.** To keep away, refrain *from*. *Obs.*

**1382** WYCLIF *Ecclus.* iv. 23 Sone, waite tyme, and shone awei fro euel [Vulg. *devita a malo*]. **1578** HUNNIS in *Parad. Dainty Devises* 24 To shonn, from bralls, debate and strife.

**7.** *trans.* To screen, hide. Now only *dial.*

**1627** C. MACGEOGHEGAN tr. *Ann. Clonmacnoise* 12 Fintan ..shunned himself from the violence thereof [i.e. of the flood] in a caue. *Ibid.* 13 All the foule..gathered themselves there to shunn themselves. **1890** *Glouc. Gloss.*, *Shun*, to screen, e.g., a shrub planted to hide back premises.

**8.** *dial.* To shove, push. [Perh. another word.] Cf. SHUNT *v.* 3.

**1674** RAY *S. & E.C. Words* 76 To *Shun*: to shove. Suss. **1851** *N. & Q.* Ser. I. III. 205/1 In an assault case at Reigate, I heard the complainant say of a man who had hustled him, 'He kept shunning me along: sometimes he shunt me on the road'. **1875** W. D. PARISH *Sussex Gloss.* s.v. *Shun*, He shunned me off the pavement. **1876** *Surrey Gloss.*, s.v., They havn't made the hole large enough to get a stick in to shun the dung back.

**9.** *Comb.* †**shun-field**, one who shuns the battlefield; **shun-pike** *U.S.* (see quot. 1911); hence **shunpike** *v. intr.*, to drive along minor roads, avoiding the toll on turnpikes, or for pleasure; **shunpiker**; **shun-piking** *vbl. sb.*; †**shun-thank**, one who grudges thanks.

**1675** HOBBES *Odyss.* XIV. 199 My vertue won her, I no shun-field [φυγοπτόλεμο] was. **1853** *Albany Even. Atlas* 9 Apr. 4 The Oswego Canal..has been called a 'shun pike'. Produce sent by Lake Ontario and the Oswego Canal, avoids tolls on the canals west of Syracuse. **1862** LOWELL *Biglow P.* Ser. II. ii. 22 Ef your soul Don't sneak thru shun-pikes so 's to save the toll. **1911** *Encycl. Brit.* XXVI. 1053/1 A shunpike, or road constructed to facilitate evasion of tolls on a turnpike road, may be closed by injunction. **1964** *Collier's Encycl. Yearbk.* 70 Besides making long trips at high speed, motorists could take part in sports car rallies, chug about in antiques, 'shunpike' on quiet back roads. **1967** *Sat. Rev.* (U.S.) 22 Apr. 55 (Advt.), Smooth roads, beautiful scenery —what more could a shunpiker want? **1961** M. BEADLE *These Ruins are Inhabited* iv. 41 George's reaction was to avoid all main roads—which is a good idea anyway if you're not in a hurry, the virtues of shun-piking being self-evident. **1972** *Alberta Motorist* (Edmonton) Apr. 6/3 There are, of course, many times when shunpiking is preferable for the traveller. **1593** *Passionate Morrice* 81 But were not they shonne-thanks they would speake better of Honesties sonne.

**'shun** (ʃʌn). Colloq. abbrev. of ATTENTION 5, representing the verbal distortion and stress when used as a military command.

**1888** KIPLING *Plain Tales from Hills* 242 Stan'at—*hease*, '*Shun*. **1928** *Granta* 2 Nov. 76/1 Prisoner! 'Shun. Move to the right in fours. **1955** W. FAULKNER *Fable* 108 'Bridesman,' he said but at that moment the major said ''Shun!'

†**shunch**, *v. Obs. rare.* In 3 **schunchen**. [Of obscure origin; ? related to SHUN *v.*] *trans.* To terrify, frighten (away or from the way). Cf. ASHUNCH.

*a* **1225** *Ancr. R.* 312 Auh we schuncheð [*v.rr.* schutten, schuchteð] hine ueor awei hwon we doð deadliche sunne. *a* **1225** *Juliana* 34 To drif drihtin þen deouel..þat weneð me to schrenchen and schunchen of þe weie.

**shund**, variant of SCHYND.

*a* **1688** J. WALLACE *Descr. Orkney* (1693) 93 *Shundbil*, the decreet past by the Foud.

‖**shunga** (ˈʃungaː). Also **shun-ga**. [Jap., f. *shun* spring + *ga* picture.] An example of Japanese erotic art; a painting or print of a pornographic nature.

**1964** *New Society* 17 Dec. 20/2 These paintings were *shunga*, 'Spring Pictures', which is the delicate Japanese euphemism for..erotic art. **1970** *Oxf. Compan. Art* 1172 With the exception of Sharaku almost all the 600 to 700 artists in the movement produced pornographic prints, known as *shun-ga* or 'spring pictures'. **1981** G. MACBETH *Kind of Treason* ii. 23 Quite a good collection of [Japanese] prints. A Hiroshige. Some *shunga*.

**shungite** (ˈʃʊŋgaɪt). *Min.* Also **schungite**. [ad. G. *schungit* (A. von Inostranzeff 1886, in *Neues Jahrb. für Mineral.* I. 92), f. *Schunga* (Russ. *Shunga*), name of a village in Russia close to the Finnish border: see -ITE[1].] (See quot. 1972.)

**1892** E. S. DANA *Dana's Syst. Min.* (ed. 6) 8 Schungite from the Olonets Government, Russia, is a similar amorphous form of carbon intermediate between anthracite and graphite, occurring in phyllite. **1916** *Trans. & Proc. Geol. Soc. S. Africa* XVIII. 130 Schungite and graphitoid merge into graphite, but the difference is not crystalline merely, for the latter yields graphitic acid on oxidation, while the former do not. **1941** *Compt. Rend. (Doklady) de l'Acad. des Sci. de l'URSS* XXXIII. 358 Other authors arrived at an opposite conclusion, to the effect that the crystalline phase existing in anthracite and shungite is graphite, but..in a highly dispersed state. **1946** *Mineral. Abstr.* IX. 202 Eleven analyses of shungite from Shunga, Lake Onega, and other localities in eastern Karelia show C 46–99, ash 1–46, $V_2O_5$ 0·016–0·77%, &c. **1968** *Ibid.* XIX. 102/1 The use of schungite to obtain combustible gases. **1972** *Gloss. Geol.* (Amer. Geol. Inst.) 656/2 *Shungite*, a hard, black, amorphous, coal-like material containing over 98% carbon, found interbedded among Precambrian schists. It is probably the metamorphic equivalent of bitumen, but it may represent merely impure graphite.

**shunless** (ˈʃʌnlɪs), *a.* [f. SHUN *v.* + -LESS.] That cannot be shunned or avoided.

**1607** SHAKS. *Cor.* II. ii. 116 Alone he entred The mortall Gate of th' Citie, which he painted With shunlesse destinie. **1897** F. THOMPSON *New Poems* 139 This to the shunless fardel of the world Nerves my uncurvèd back.

**shunnable** (ˈʃʌnəb(ə)l), *a.* [f. SHUN *v.* + -ABLE.] That may be shunned.

**1570** LEVINS *Manip.* 3/6 Shunnable, *deuitabilis*. **1824** C. WELLS *Joseph & Brethren* I. v. 77 You're shunable.

**shunned** (ʃʌnd), *ppl. a.* [f. SHUN *v.* + -ED[1].] Avoided.

**1591** SPENSER *Virg. Gnat* 364 Shun'd destruction doth destruction render. **1878** C. STANFORD *Symb. Christ* viii. 221 The lowly, the lost, the shunned, the shelterless.

**shunner** (ˈʃʌnə(r)). [f. SHUN *v.* + -ER[1].] One who shuns.

**1806** W. TAYLOR in *Ann. Rev.* IV. 565 The shunner of battles. **1862** LYTTON *Str. Story* I. 348 So gay and boon a companion, yet a shunner of wine.

**shunning** (ˈʃʌnɪŋ), *vbl. sb.* [f. SHUN *v.* + -ING[1].] The action of SHUN *v.*

**1546** COVERDALE, etc. *Erasm. Par. Rom.* x. 1–4 The shonnyng of dead carkasses. **1693** DRYDEN *Juvenal* Introd. 80 Juvenal..tyes himself..to the shuning of Moral Evil.

**shunning** (ˈʃʌnɪŋ), *ppl. a.* [f. SHUN *v.* + -ING[2].] That shuns.

**1583** MELBANCKE *Philotimus* D div, O Tantal, that indeuorest to drinke the shuning water.

**shunt** (ʃʌnt), *sb.* [f. SHUNT *v.*]

**1.** An act of shunting. †**a.** An act of drawing back. *Obs. rare*⁻¹.

**13..** *Gaw. & Gr. Knt.* 2268 Þat oþer schalk wyth a schunt þe schene wyth-haldez.

**b.** In Railway use and *transf.* from this: see SHUNT *v.* 4, 5.

**1862** J. SIMMONS *Railway Traveller's Handy Bk.* 12 A thin line in the middle of trains..represents a shunt. **1884** H. SMART *Post to Finish* xlvi, Damme if ever they persuade me into doing another 'shunt'. **1886** *Pall Mall Gaz.* 31 Dec. 1/1 The shunt from the German to the Austrian alliance was due to the desire..to support the Prince of Battenberg in his struggle against Russia. **1898** H. G. WELLS *Certain Pers. Matters* 132 All primitive men and most animals swear. It is an emotional shunt.

**c.** *slang.* A motor accident, a crash: esp. a nose-to-tail collision. Also **shunt-up** (on analogy with PILE-UP 1), a multiple crash.

**1959** in *Chambers's Twentieth Cent. Dict.* Add. **1967** *Economist* 11 Feb. 544/3 The characteristic American accident is a multivehicle shunt on a freeway. **1976** J. WAINWRIGHT *Bastard* vii. 91 Mist..happens on motor-ways, and is the cause of multi-car shunt-ups, where radiators kiss bumper bars. **1978** G. VAUGHAN *Belgrade Drop* vi. 41 'Another bloody shunt,' Yardley groaned. The Zagreb trunk was notorious for accidents.

**2. a.** *Electr.* A derived circuit introduced to diminish the current flowing through the main circuit; esp. a resistance coil connected in parallel with a dynamo, etc.; more fully ***shunt circuit, coil***. ***in shunt***: connected so as to form a multiple current.

**1863** R. S. CULLEY *Pract. Telegr.* 99 The 'shunt' system can be applied with advantage. The shunt is a wire connecting the two ends of the galvanometer coil. **1885** P. HIGGS *Magn. Dyn. Electr. Mech.* 101 Dynamo-machines.. with the main circuit, or 'series' electro-magnet coils wound on the same arm or limb of the electro-magnet, as contains the 'shunt' coils. *Ibid.* 225 The total resistance of a circuit from which shunt-circuits are taken is less than its own resistance. **1893** SLOANE *Electr. Dict.* s.v. *Shunt Winding*, A dynamo or motor is shunt-wound when the field magnet winding is in shunt or in parallel with the winding of the armature.

**b.** *Telegr.* A device for diverting the current from one line to another; a switch; also *attrib.*

**1878** EDISON in *N. Amer. Rev.* CXXVI. 536 To keep wires in proper repair, and give, by switch or shunt arrangement, prompt attention to subscriber No. 923 in New York.

**c.** *Med.* A natural or artificial route, esp. from a vein to an artery, whereby blood may bypass a capillary bed; the passage of blood along such a route. Also, the surgical construction of such a route.

**1923** *Medicine* II. 20 Deficient oxygenation of the arterial blood..caused..by an unaerated shunt of venous blood into arterial. *Ibid.* 33 The readiness with which cyanosis develops or increases, during exercise, in a patient with an unaerated shunt. **1937** BEST & TAYLOR *Physiol. Basis Med. Pract.* XXXV. 581 (*caption*) A portion of the blood passes through unaerated channels (shunt) from the venous to the arterial system. **1961** *Lancet* 30 Sept. 728/2 2 patients..had both undergone splenectomy some time before portocaval shunt was performed. **1980** *Amer. Speech* LV. 47 Clamps used to stop blood flow through a shunt when kidney dialysis is initiated.

**d.** *Biochem.* An alternative metabolic pathway; *spec.* (freq. as ***hexose monophosphate shunt***) the pentose phosphate cycle.

**1953** *Jrnl. Bacteriol.* LXVI. 17 It has been possible to infer..the existence of a sequence of reactions, the hexosemonophosphate shunt, which may serve in nature as a major pathway for the aerobic breakdown of carbohydrate by filamentous microorganisms. **1964** [see pentose phosphate shunt s.v. PENTOSE 2]. **1967** M. E. HALE *Biol. Lichens* viii. 118 Insoluble metabolic shunt products often serve as reserve food. **1970** [see RIBOSE].

**3.** *Railways.* A switch.

**1842** *Civil Engin. & Arch. Jrnl.* V. 85/2 The sub-contractor..had to..lay down the temporary road, including turn-outs, shunts, crossings, etc.

**4.** *Ordnance.* Short for *shunt rifled gun*, also a curve in the rifling of a shunt rifled gun (see 5 b).

**1864** *Daily Tel.* 4 May, The breech-loader had the shortest range,..the Armstrong shunt came next. **1866** *Chamb. Encycl.* VIII. 698/2 [The grooves] run together for a short distance, until a shunt narrows the whole groove.

**5.** *attrib.* and *Comb.* **a.** (in sense 2), as ***shunt terminal, winding***, etc.; **shunt box** (see quot. 1893); **shunt dynamo**, a shunt-wound (q.v.) dynamo; **shunt machine, motor**, a direct-current motor in which the field and armature windings are connected in parallel with respect to the supply; **shunt running** (see quot.); **shunt-wound** *a.*, having the shunt circuit wound in parallel with the main circuit.

**1878** *Telegr. Jrnl.* 15 Sept. 375/1 A new galvanometer *shunt box. **1893** SLOANE *Electr. Dict.*, *Shunt Box*, a resistance box designed for use as a galvanometer shunt. The box contains a series of resistance coils which can be plugged in or out as required. **1881** *Nature* XXIV. 533 A generator of electricity of the kind now known as the *shunt dynamo. **1888** *Rep. Brit. Assoc. Adv. Sci. 1887* 616 In a *shunt machine the current through the coils of the second magnet may be controlled by the addition of a resistance in series with it. **1953** E. MOLLOY *Small Motors & Transformers* ii. 17 [Differential compounding] is sometimes employed to secure further improvement of the speed characteristic of a shunt machine, in cases where the load is variable. **1883** *Jrnl. Soc. Telegr. Engineers & Electricians* XII. 310 A coiled magneto-machine.., in which we have a magneto-generator acting as a brake, and a *shunt motor. **1977** *N.Z. Herald* 5 Jan. 3/7 And once in Auckland, tied up by traffic lights and other vehicles, he switches over completely to his shunt motor for a quiet, anxiety-free tour of the town. **1911** HOBART *Dict. Electr. Engin.* s.v., In energy meters..furnished with a friction compensation for the low loads there is a tendency of the meter to work with no current in the circuit to which it is connected... This is referred to as '*shunt running'. **1895** *Pract. Electr. Engin.* I. 10 *Shunt-winding means that one branch of the circuit only encircles the cores. **1883** *Pall Mall Gaz.* 14 Sept. 4/1 The conductor is connected..to a single *shunt-wound dynamo machine.

**b. shunt line, road,** a railway siding; also **shunt-rifling,** a method of rifling cannon so that the projectile undergoes a shunt or lateral change of position in the process of loading; so ***shunt (rifled) gun, shunt shot, shunt system.***

**1864** *Daily Tel.* 18 May, It was found necessary to re-vent the *shunt gun. **1904** *Westm. Gaz.* 10 May 9/2 If the Reading line were clear it would be impossible for the No. 18 *shunt line to be clear also. **1866** *Even. Standard* 13 July 7 The 600-pounder Elswick *shunt-rifled gun. **1868** *Rep. Munitions of War* 146 The *shunt rifling was evidently devised for the better centering of the shot. **1864** *Daily Tel.* 18 May, Conditions detrimental to the proper flight of the *Shunt shot. **1866** *Chamb. Encycl.* VIII. 698/2 Sir William Armstrong devised the '*shunt' system.

**shunt** (ʃʌnt), *v.* Forms: 3-4 schunt, 4 shont, 5 s(c)hount, shontt, 5- shunt. *Pa. t.* 4 schunt, 5 shont, schounte; schontid, 6- shunted. [Of obscure origin.

The ME. senses coincide with certain senses of SHUN *v.*, to which, indeed, some of the above-cited forms of the pa. t. may in certain instances possibly belong. It seems not impossible that this vb. may be a derivative of SHUN *v.*]

†**1. a.** *intr.* To start or go aside (so as to avoid some person or thing); to shy; to shrink or steal away; to hang back. *Obs.*

*a* **1225** *Ancr. R.* 242 (MS. T) Ne beo nawt þe skerre hors iliche þæt schuntes [*v.r.* blencheð uor one scheadewe upo þe heie brugge]. **13..** *E.E. Allit. P.* B. 605 In þe hyȝe hete..He was schunt to þe schadow vnder schyre leuez. **13..** *Gaw. & Gr. Knt.* 1902 He [the fox attacked with the sword] schunt for þe scharp. *Ibid.* 2280 Quod G:, 'I schunt onez, & so wyl I no more. ? *a* **1400** *Morte Arth.* 1055 Thane he dressede one his schelde, schuntes no lengere. *a* **1400-50** *Wars Alex.* 180 Sen it is sett to be soo & slipe it ne may, Ne schewid to be na noþire schap, ne we to schount nouthire. *c* **1400** *Destr. Troy* 600, I will shunt for no shame of my shene fader. *Ibid.* 10998 Ne shamys you not shalkes to shunt of þe fild. *c* **1440** *York Myst.* xlvi. 59 þei schonte for no schoutis his schappe for to schende it, þei rasid hym on rode. **15..** *Song of John Nobody* viii. in Strype *Cranmer* (1694) II. 139 Then I drew me down into a dale, wheras the dumb deer Did shiver for a shower, but I shunted from a freyke.

**b.** To start, move suddenly. *Obs. rare.*

*a* **1400-50** *Wars Alex.* 580 In þe same tyme he seuyrd fra þi wambe, þe erd & all þe elementis so egirly schontid. **14..** *Tretyce* in *W. of Henley's Husb.* (1890) 47 Yeff your land ly in marres..& it be ereyd to depe at þe secund falowe..Your ploughe shall com to no harde grounde but go schoutyng [? *read* schonting] all in myrre. **1775** Ash, *Shunt* (*v. int. a local word*), to give a sudden start.

†**2.** *trans.* To elude (a blow, etc.); also, to turn aside (shame) from (a person). *Obs.*

*c* **1400** *Rowland & O.* 1334 Hade he nott schounte his stroke thore, For sothe he hade bene slayne. *c* **1400** *Destr. Troy* 2544 Let hym tegh to þe tempull..And let other men ..For to shunt vs of shame, shend of our foos. *c* **1460** *Towneley Myst.* xxix. 361 Mi flesh it quakys as lefe on lynde, to shontt the showres sharper then thorne.

**3.** To shove or push aside or out of the way. Also *intr.* of a thing, to move from its proper position, to give way. Chiefly *dial.*

**1706** Phillips (ed. Kersey), To *Shunt*, a Country-Word for to shove. **1775** Ash, *Shunt* (*v.t., a local word*), to shove, to push. *Shunting* (*p.a., a local word, from* shunt), giving a sudden start; shoving, pushing with a sudden motion. **1850** S. Bamford *Dial. S. Lanc.* Gloss., *Shunt*, to give way; to move from a place. **1852** *N. & Q.* Ser. I. V. 450/1 In the North of England..speaking of a thing, a wall or foundation, which has moved from its position, we should say, 'it has shunted'; or of a thing which requires moving, 'Shunt it a little that way', 'Shunt it at the other end'. **1863** Sir R. Alcock *Capital of Tycoon* I. xiii. 268 After being punted a mile over the shallows, and another mile shunted or sleighed over the mud!

**4. a.** To move (a train or some portion of it) from the main line to a side-track or from one line of rails to another; also to move *back.*

**1845** *Min. Proc. Inst. Civil Engin.* IV. 252 At intermediate stations, the waggons are now 'shunted' to their proper places, in a siding, by the engine which has propelled them along the main line. **1849** Alb. Smith *Pottleton Legacy* xxxiv. 410 As the men came up to 'shunt' it [the horse-box]. **1849-50** *Weale's Dict. Terms* s.v., When an engine, carriage, or train is moved off the main line to a siding, it is then said to be 'shunted'. **1852** F. S. Williams *Our Iron Roads* App. 384 [A] porter.., while holding the points to shunt a train, had his ankle injured. **1881** *Times* 19 Jan. 10/2 The train was accordingly shunted on to the up line and proceeded back to town. **1907** J. H. Patterson *Man-Eaters of Tsavo* i. 14 The train was shunted back to where the ostrich had fallen.

*absol.* **1852** F. S. Williams *Our Iron Roads* App. 378 Passenger train came into collision with an engine which was shunting.

**b.** *fig.* To push aside or out of the way; to side-track; also, to get rid of.

**1858** *Sat. Rev.* 13 Mar. 261/2 Practically, General Peel is not shunted, but shelved. **1869** 'Wat. Bradwood' *The O.V.H.* xix, Which [horse] had we best shunt?..one's as good as the other to win, but the price makes all the difference. **1887** Lowell *Old Eng. Dramatists* (1892) 3 Since then,..my mind has been shunted off upon the track of other duties. **1904** May Sinclair *Divine Fire* 255 That two hundred ought to be three thousand, and if it isn't paid I shall have to shunt the business.

**5. a.** *intr.* To move off the main line; to move from one line of rails to another.

**1851** *N. & Q.* Ser. I. III. 204/2 At a certain station the parliamentary 'shunts' to let the Express pass. **1883** *Harper's Mag.* Mar. 537/1 There we would wait, and back and shunt and change.

**b.** *transf.* and *fig.* To move out of the way.

The dial. (Lancs., etc.) use = 'to go away, be off' may be in part a direct development from sense 1.

**1869** 'Wat. Bradwood' *The O.V.H.* xix, It's no use at all for us two to run against each other, that's flat; our horse shall shunt for your'n, if your'n won't for ours. **1892** G. R. Lowndes *Camping Sk.* 26 Let's shunt from here.

**6. a.** *Electr.* To divert (a portion of an electric current) by means of a shunt (see SHUNT *sb.* 2); also, to divert current from (a galvanometer).

**1873** F. Jenkin *Electr. & Magn.* xvi. §3 (1881) 235 If a galvanometer with the resistance G be shunted by a shunt of the resistance *S*, the resistance of the shunted galvanometer will be [etc.]. **1878** *Telegr. Jrnl.* 15 Sept. 376/1 The necessary portion of the current is shunted off from the galvanometer. **1911** Hobart *Dict. Electr. Engin.* II. 617/1 A winding which shunts or by-passes a portion of the main supply.

**b.** *Med.* To pass (blood) through a shunt. Cf. SHUNT *sb.* 2 c.

**1923** *Medicine* II. 18 A condition..in patients with congenital perforate septum of the heart, where a fraction of the blood is shunted directly from the right heart to the left without passing through the lungs. **1950** Best & Taylor *Physiol. Basis of Med. Pract.* (ed. 5) xxxv. 435/1 Most of the blood is shunted to the arterial side through channels which normally close at, or shortly after, birth.

**7.** To turn (the shot) in a shunt rifled gun by means of a shunt or curve in the rifling (see SHUNT *sb.* 4, 5 b).

**1866** *Chamb. Encycl.* VIII. 698/2 When the groove becomes narrowed..the shot is shunted over to the left.

**8.** *Stock Exchange.* (See quot.)

**1908** *Times* 22 Jan., Forbidding them to shunt, according to the definition of shunting which seems to be generally received—namely, dealing between markets by London and provincial firms on joint account, and with a division of profits and losses.

**'shunted,** *ppl. a.* [f. SHUNT *v.* and *sb.* + -ED.]

**1.** In senses of the verb.

**1896** *Godey's Mag.* Feb. 199/2 The shunted hero was.. heir to a considerable fortune.

**2.** *Electr.* Provided with a shunt.

**1873** [see SHUNT *v.* 6]. **1911** Hobart *Dict. Electr. Engin.* II. 344/2 Shunted Meter, and electricity meter provided with a low-resistance shunt [etc.].

**shunter** ('ʃʌntə(r)). [f. SHUNT *v.* + -ER[1].]

**1.** A railwayman employed to shunt trains. Also, a mechanical device to facilitate shunting.

**1852** F. S. Williams *Our Iron Roads* App. 381 William Lear, shunter, foot crushed. **1876** *L'pool Daily Post* 3 Oct. 5/1 One of the last new things in mechanical inventions is a railway shunter. It is a wooden lever [etc.].

**2.** *Stock Exchange.* (See quot.)

**1888** *Glasgow Even. Times* 24 Aug. 3/6 A 'shunter' is..a broker who buys or sells a stock in one market in the belief that he will be able immediately to cover the transaction in another at a profit.

Hence **'shuntership.**

**1894** Blatchford *Merrie Eng.* xix. 149 Promotion to a head shuntership..should be counted as high enough ambition.

**shunting** ('ʃʌntɪŋ), *vbl. sb.* [f. SHUNT *v.* + -ING[1].] The action of the verb.

**1775** Ash, Suppl., *Shunting*, the act of giving a sudden start. **1858** Simmonds *Dict. Trade*, *Shunting*, moving a train into a siding, or on to another line of rails. **1861** *Sat. Rev.* 7 Sept. 239 At every station there is a multiplication of points, shunting, and signals. **1961** *Lancet* 23 Sept. 693/2 Arteriovenous shunting may be..applicable to more mammalian species..than has been previously considered. **1974** *Nature* 9 Aug. 489/1 Because of the incompletely divided ventricle, shunting of venous blood from the right atrium to the systemic circuit..may occur.

*attrib.* **1885** *Pall Mall Gaz.* 14 Apr. 6/1 The company intend to construct on this a shunting yard.

**shupac,** var. SHOEPACK.

**shuppare, shuppend:** see SHEPPER, -END.

**shurbet, shure, shurk, shurl:** see SHERBET, SHOWER, SHIRK, SHIRL.

†**shurn,** *v. Obs. rare.* In 4-5 schurn, 5 schorne, 6 shurne, 7 sherne. [Altered form of SCURN *v.*] *trans.* To avoid, shun.

*a* **1300-1400** *Cursor M.* 19446 (Gött.) He sau him croised þat ilke turn þat he for stani[n]g suld noght schurn. *Ibid.* 20960. *Ibid.* 23338. *c* **1440** *Promp. Parv.* 448/1 Schornyn, or a-chewyn, *vito.* **1538** Bale *Thre Lawes* II. Bij, I wyll non of the trulye, But shurne thy cumpanye, As I wolde the deuyll of helle. *Ibid.* B v b, If ye wyll shurne the head ake. **1546**—— *Eng. Votaries* I. (1560) 63 b, The strete..hathe euer sence bene shurned in al general processyons.

**shurn(e, shurral,** var. ff. SHARN, SHIRREL.

**shurrup** (ʃʌ'rʌp, ʃʊ'rʊp), vulgar corruption of imp. *shut up* (see SHUT *v.* 19 m). Also **shurr up.** Cf. SHADDUP, SHUDDUP.

**1893** S. Grand *Heavenly Twins* I. I. iv. 27 Barbara politely requested her to 'shurrup!' a word of the boys which she permitted herself to borrow. **1929** J. B. Priestley *Good Companions* III. iv. 553 'Shurr up!' the voice jeered, before anybody else could make a sound. **1960** C. Ray *Merry England* 173 You shurrup, shurrup: I've just about had enough of you. **1978** J. Wainwright *Ripple of Murders* 40 Shurrup, Richard, don't show your ignorance.

†**shurt,** *v. Obs.* Forms: 3, 6 (*Sc.*) schurt, 3 schirt, ? 5-6 shurt. [repr. OE. (*ȝe*)*scyrtan* to shorten:—prehistoric **skurtjan* f. **skurt-* SHORT *a.* For the development of sense cf. SHORT *v.* 3 and ON. *skemta* to amuse, f. *skamm-r* short.] *intr.* To amuse oneself, to pass the time. Also *refl.* Hence †**'shurting** *vbl. sb.*, amusement, pastime.

*a* **1225** *Ancr. R.* 422 Auh talkeð mid ouer meidenes and mid þeaufule talen schurteð ou to-gederes. *a* **1300** *Cursor M.* 8240 All frutes he plantede in þat place, For his schirting and his solace. **1513** Douglas *Æneis* v. Prol. 7 ȝoung folk thaim schurtis with gam, solace and play. **15..** *Turn. Tottenham* 11 (1631) B, It befell in Tottenham on a deare day, There was made a shurting by the high-way.

†**'shurvy,** *a. Obs.* [f. **shurf* (:—OE. *sceorf*: see SCURF *sb.*) + -Y.] ? Scurfy.

*a* **1529** Skelton *Agst. Garnesche* 132 Your skyn scabbyd and scuruy, Tawny, tannyd, and shuruy.

**shush** (ʃʊʃ, ʃʌʃ), *v.* [Echoic, representing a repetition of SH *int.* Cf. SHSHSH.]

**1.** *trans.* To call or reduce (someone) to silence by uttering the sounds denoted by *sh-sh.* Also const. advs.

**1925** P. Gibbs *Unchanging Quest* xvii. 127 She would ..'shush' away any intruders who came to interrupt her private conversation. **1930** E. Ferber *Cimarron* i. 6 The woman listened... They shushed their children when they moved or whimpered. **1949** 'J. Tey' *Brat Farrar* xxv. 225 'The Ashbys cleaning up as usual,' the voice said, and was instantly shushed. **1961** J. Heller *Catch 22* (1962) xxii. 223 'Stop shouting, will you?' Yossarian shushed him. **1971** Wodehouse *Much Obliged, Jeeves* xv. 152 The ancestor.. would, I think, have developed the theme had I not shushed her down with a raised hand. **1980** *Christian Sci. Monitor* (Midwestern ed.) 4 Dec. B3/2 He shushes them or storms at them or coaches them.

**2. a.** *intr.* To call for silence in this manner. Freq. *imp.* **b.** To become or remain silent.

**1924** 'O. Douglas' *Pink Sugar* v. 52, I stood patiently while Nellie 'shushed' under her breath as she brushed, directing me at intervals to 'Stand still, will ye!' **1929** J. B. Priestley *Good Companions* II. i. 273 He gets no further, being fiercely requested by several of his colleagues to 'shush'. *Ibid.* III. iv. 553 Some people laughed. The remainder indignantly shushed again and then clapped. **1969** M. Pugh *Last Place Left* xix. 140 'Shush, you bloody pig,' he said, for the collie was growing impatient. **1972** J. Wilson *Hide & Seek* v. 81 'Sh, now, there's a good girl.' 'I won't shush. I want to go home.' **1977** 'J. Bell' *Such a Nice Client* vi. 63 'That's the idea. Shush!' The manageress was back.

**shush** (ʃʊʃ, ʃʌʃ), *sb. colloq.* [f. the vb.] An utterance of the exclamation 'Sh!' Also *transf.*, quiet. Cf. HUSH *sb.*[2] 1 a.

**1954** R. Fuller *Fantasy & Fugue* v. 115, I got him out among the shushes and tut-tuts before the attendants could reach him. **1959** I. & P. Opie *Lore & Lang. Schoolch.* x. 193 Let's 'ave a bit of shush. **1971** 'A. Burgess' *MF* vi. 71 There was a response of frightened shushes. **1982** *Observer* (Colour Suppl.) 25 Apr. 11/2 Can we have a little shush please?

**shushing** ('ʃʊʃɪŋ, 'ʃʌʃɪŋ), *vbl. sb.* [f. SHUSH *v.* + -ING[1].] The action of the verb. Also *attrib.*, as ***shushing noise, sound.***

**1929** J. B. Priestley *Good Companions* III. iv. 552 It raised a loud and jeering laugh from that quarter, though the rest of the audience immediately made shushing noises. **1937** *Richmond* (Va.) *News-Leader* 9 Sept. 3/1 (*heading*) No 'shushing' at Nazi parley. **1972** *Listener* 15 June 806 The sound of a gourd rattle to make a 'shushing' sound. **1981** A. Edwards *Sonya* i. 27 There was much shushing in the front parlor if the children came in.

**shush-shush,** *a. rare.* [Reduplicated form of SHUSH *v.* or *sb.*] **a.** Echoic, designating something that makes a repeated soft sound like a shush. **b.** = HUSH-HUSH.

**1954** *New World Writing* VI. 44, I measured..his shush-shush tread in my presence. **1963** *Listener* 24 Jan. 182/1 It is his [*sc.* the defence correspondent's] job to know what is going on in the shush-shush world behind the 'D' notices.

**Shuswap** ('ʃʊswɒp), *sb.* and *a.* Also †**Shooshap, Shouswap, Shushwap.** [ad. Shuswap *səxʷepmx* Shuswap Indians.] **A.** *sb.* **a.** A North American Indian people inhabiting southern British Columbia. **b.** Their language. **B.** *adj.* Of or pertaining to this people or their language.

**1838** S. Parker *Jrnl. Exploring Tour* (1842) 313 West of these [*sc.* the Kettle Falls Indians] are the Sinpauēlish..; and below these are the Shooshaps, having a population of five hundred and seventy-five. **1845** [see CARRIER 2 b]. **1904** A. G. Morice *Hist. Northern Interior Brit. Columbia* 6 In case of death the bodies were buried among the Chilcotins and the Shushwaps. *Ibid.* iv. 51 This so-called Carrier vocabulary is made up of Shushwap words. **1927** *Internat. Jrnl. Amer. Linguistics* IV. 120 Salisham—Interior dialects: Shuswap; Lillooet. **1959** E. Tunis *Indians* 130/2 The Shushwap were a typical tribe of the interior Salish. **1965** *Canad. Jrnl. Linguistics* Spring 86 Terms found in those Salisham languages which are geographically the closest, particularly Kalispel..and Shuswap where available. **1976** *Shuswap Visitor's Guide* 10/3 According to a Shuswap Indian legend, you will find a place of perpetual summer.

**shut** (ʃʌt), *sb.* Forms: *α.* 7-8 shutt, 8 shoot, 7- shut; *β.* 5 schett. [f. SHUT *v.*]

**1.** Something which shuts off or closes up.

†**a.** A locking-bar or bolt. *Obs.*

*c* **1460** *Promp. Parv.* (Winch.) 315 On-doyng, or onpynnynge schettis or sperellys, *apparicio.* **1611** Speed *Hist. Gt. Brit.* IX. xxi. §67 With what key K. Henry opened the golden shut of the Popes Consistory for his free accesse, ..I cannot say. **1662** *Comenius' Janua Ling. Triling.* 130 As you come to the gate on both the sides are the posts; and in one of them the hinges..but in the other are the shuts (shutting bars) [L. *claustra*]. **1845** DISRAELI *Sybil* III. iv, He knocked the corner of a lock into my head twice, once with a bolt and once with a shut; you know what that is; the thing what runs into the staple.

**b.** A shutter for a window. Now *dial.* (See *Eng. Dial. Dict.*)

**1611** COTGR., *Volet*..also a shut, or wooden window to shut ouer a glasse one. **1655** tr. *Sorel's Com. Hist. Francion* III. 67 A small window, which never had a shut [orig. *volet*]. **1690** W. WALKER *Idiomat. Anglo-Lat.* 414 Open the shut.

**c.** *gen.* A hinged or sliding door or plate for closing an aperture; †a valve. Also in *Mining*: see quot. 1886.

**1651** *Life Sarpi* (1676) 18 Those inward shuts or folds that are within the Veins. **1688** HOLME *Armoury* III. xvii. (Roxb.) 105/2 A Morion..with a shut to secure the face. **1691** RAY *Creation* II. (1704) 304 Therefore were there no Shuts or Stopples made for the Ears. **1715** DESAGULIERS *Fires Improv.* 121 You may have two Shuts if you will, made..to shut up, or open both Holes. **1844** H. STEPHENS *Bk. Farm* II. 267 A small sliding shut should be made in the partition. **1886** BARROWMAN *Sc. Mining Terms* 60 *Shuts*, movable or hinged supports for the cage at a pithead.

†**2.** An enclosure; a stew for fish. *Obs.*

**1605** CAMDEN *Rem.*, *Surnames* 102 Shot or Shvt, A Keepe [Munster]. **1662** *Comenius' Janua Ling. Triling.* 85 Then part of the fish he sells, part he shuts up in his shuts.

**3.** The action, time, or place of shutting. Chiefly *poet.*, the close (of day), the closing in (of evening).

**1667** MILTON *P.L.* IX. 278 As in a shady nook I stood behind, Just then returned at shut of evening flowers. **1690** DRYDEN *Amphit.* II. i, I have been in an Ague fit, ever since shut of Evening. **1742** BLAIR *Grave* 764 At the Shut of Ev'n, the weary Bird Leaves the wide Air. **1819** KEATS *Hyperion* II. 36 When the chill rain begins at shut of eve. **1869** WHITTIER *Norembega* 19 At shut of day a Christian knight Upon his henchman leaned. **1899** MEREDITH *Cageing Ares* Poet. Wks. (1912) 522 Whereof they won, From hourly wrestlings up to shut of lids, Her ready secret.

**4.** A join, mend, splice; a weld, the line of junction of two pieces of welded metal. *cold shut*, an imperfect weld due to chill; an imperfection in a casting, caused by the flow of liquid metal on a chilled surface.

**1721** PERRY *Daggenh. Breach* 60 To joint close into the Grooves..and make an effectual Shut like one entire Sheet of Timber. **1831** J. HOLLAND *Manuf. Metal* I. 114 The entire length and shape were produced without a shut. **1877** W. RICHARDS *Manuf. Coal Gas* 217 The castings must be free from any imperfections, such as honeycombs, 'cold shuts', cracks, or flaws.

**5.** *dial.* A riddance; esp. in phr. *a good shut*. (Cf. SHUT *v.* 11 and SHUTTANCE.)

**6.** *Comb.*, as **shut-knife** *dial.*, a clasp-knife, a pocket-knife.

**1879** J. SPILLING *Johnny's Jaunt* i. 8, I took out my shet-knife and cut her a..huncheon off the loaf. **1913** D. H. LAWRENCE *Sons & Lovers* vii. 210 But they managed to procure a loaf and a currant-loaf, which they hacked into pieces with shut-knives, and ate sitting on the wall near the bridge. **1979** in R. Blythe *View in Winter* i. 63 He'd whittle away at things... He was that cliver [*sic*] with his shutknife.

**shut** (ʃʌt), *v.* Pa. t. and pa. pple. shut. Forms: *Pres. stem* α. 1 scyttan, 3–4 schutte, 4–5 s(c)hitte, 4–6 shutte, 5–6 shytt(e, shyt, (also 9 *dial.*) shit, (5 schytte, 6 schut, shute, shot), 7 shutt, 6– shut; β. 4 ssette, (3 *sing. pres. ind.* 4 sset, *imper.* 3 scete, 4 ssete), 4–5 schette, 4–6 shette, (6 *Sc.* schet), 5–6, 9 *dial.* shet; γ. 4–5 schete, 4–6 shete, 6 sheet. *Pa. t.* α. 1 -scytte, 4–5 schutte, s(c)hitte, (4 shutte, 4, 6 shytt, 5 shyt, s(c)hytte, 6 shutt), 5– shut; β. 3–6 shette, 4–5 schette, 5 schet(t, shet; β. 4 schittide, 5 shytted, 9 *dial.* shutted. *Pa. pple.* α. 2 -scutted, 4–5 shyt, 5–6 shutte, (4 schit(t, schytte, 5 -yschutte, shytte, shit(t)e, 6 shyt(t, shitt), 5–6 shutte, (also 9 *dial.*) shit, 6–7 shutt, 5– shut; β. 4–5 ischet, (4 ys(c)het, yscheot, ysset, ischette, schet(t), 4–6 shette, schet, (also 9 *dial.*) shet, 5–6 shett; γ. 6 sheet; δ. 5 schowt(?), 6 shott, 6, 9 *dial.* shot; ε. 7– (now *dial.* and *arch.*) shutten. [OE. *scyttan* (more freq. in the compound *forscyttan* FORSHUT):—prehistoric *skuttjan, f. *skut- wk. grade of the root of SHOOT *v.* Cf. OFris. *schetta* (WFris. *skette*, *sketsje*), (M)LG., (M)Du. *schutten* to shut, shut up, obstruct. (The formal coincidence of the MHG. and mod.G. *schützen* to protect is prob. accidental.)

The normal representation of OE. *scyttan* would be *shit*; down to the 16th c. this was the prevailing form, though the Kentish *shette* (used by Chaucer and Gower) was also very common. The mod. form appears to have been originally West Midland.]

**I.** The simple verb.

†**1.** *trans.* To put (a lock, bar, bolt, etc.) in position so as to fasten a door, etc. *Obs.* (Cf. SHOOT *v.* 13.)

*c* **1000** ÆLFRIC *Gram.* xxxvii. (Z.) 220 *Sero* (*seras*) ic scytte sum loc öððe hæpsiᵹe. *c* **1370** *Gregorius* (Horstm.) 669 Þe Fisschere on his feire feet þe lok schutte ful faste i wis. **1426** LYDG. *De Guil. Pilgr.* 3084 Tvnshetten & to shette ageyn Lokkys echon. **1633** RUTHERFORD *Lett.* III. (1675) 193, I have gotten now, honour to my Lord, the gate to open the store, and shut the bar of his door.

†**2.** To fasten (a door or aperture) with a lock or bar. *Obs.*

*c* **1320** *Sir Beues* 3031 A..schette þe dore wiþ þe keie. *c* **1400** *Gamelyn* 292 And thanne was it y-schet faste with a pin. **1474** CAXTON *Chesse* III. viii. (1883) 149 The cheste that was shette wyth iii lockis. **1509** in Willis & Clark *Cambridge* (1886) I. 477 A stronge Chest..having iiij lockes and iiij keyes to shete and open the same. **1686** tr. *Chardin's Trav. Persia* 74 The Door is shut with a piece of Felt. **1825** SCOTT *Betrothed* xxi, By keeping doors shut.

*absol.* **1637** MILTON *Lycidas* 111 Two massy keys he bore of metals twain (The golden opes, the iron shuts amain).

**3. a.** To bring (a door, gate, window, lid, etc.) into the position in which it closes the aperture. *to shut fast*: to shut so that it cannot easily be opened. Also (orig. *U.S.*) in pa. pple. with verbs of movement, as *draw*, *push*, etc., denoting completion of an action; equivalent to TO *adv.* 4.

As words like *door*, *gate*, etc. usually admit of being used for the aperture together with that which closes it, this sense passes into sense 7.

*c* **1200** *Vices & Virtues* 143 Ga into þine bedde..and scete ðe dure. **13..** *K. Alis.* 5821 (W.) The men of that cite.. ronnen to her gates fast, And hem shetten wel on hast. *Ibid.* 6185 In the water is heore gates;..When hit is flod, y-scheot [*Laud* yshet] they beoth. ?*a* **1366** CHAUCER *Rom. Rose* 529, I fond a wiket smal So shet that I ne mighte in goon. *c* **1369** —— *Dethe Blaunche* 335 My wyndowes were shette [*v.rr.* shet, shyt] echon. *c* **1380** WYCLIF *Wks.* (1880) 67 Þer nys noon þat shittiþ frely þe doris of þe temple. *c* **1412** HOCCLEVE *De Reg. Princ.* 1094 Thogh his dore be noght shit. *c* **1440** *Generydes* 5773 The gates ar all shett of that Citee. **1483** *Cely Papers* (Camden) 141 They schytte the gattes. **1521** *Cov. Leet-bk.* 669 The gates of the Citee shal-be shot euery nyght at viij of the clok. **1526** TINDALE *Luke* xi. 7 Nowe is the dore shett. *a* **1539** in *Archæologia* XLVII. 52 That doore.. contynually to stand shitt the tymes of dyvyne seruice. **1577** GOOGE tr. *Heresbach's Husb.* III. 119b, The windowes.. being kept shut in winter. **1629** MAXWELL tr. *Herodian* (1635) 53 The Citizens..shut their doores. **1647** TRAPP *Comm.*, *Heb.* iv. 1 When the gate is shut. **1667** MILTON *P.L.* VIII. 240 Fast we found, fast shut The dismal Gates, and barricado'd strong. **1737** *Gentl. Mag.* VII. 608/2 The Gate used to be kept shut. **1829** SCOTT *Anne of G.* xxxiv, He would not even condescend to shut his gates. **1848** THACKERAY *Van. Fair* liv, The publican shutting his shutters. **1884** *Century Mag.* Nov. 13 He..pushed the ground-glass door shut. **1895** P. HEMINGWAY *Out of Egypt* I. iii. 26 Every house had its green blinds closely shut. **1902** O. WISTER *Virginian* xiv. 163 Our wheels clucked over the main-line switch. A train-hand threw it shut after. **1911** H. S. HARRISON *Queed* ii. 23 The last boarder rising drew shut the folding-doors into the parlor. **1933** E. O'NEILL *Ah, Wilderness!* I. 18 She slams the door shut. **1957** T. SLESSOR *First Overland* 256 We slam shut the windows, as the car slides down through the rocks.

*absol.* **1388** WYCLIF *Isa.* xxii. 22 He schal opene, and noon schal be that schal schitte. **1825** T. HOOK *Sayings* Ser. II. *Sutherl.* I. 110 The servants by their pointed civilities, their zealous activity in opening and shutting,..declared the joyous moment at hand.

**b.** const. *against*, †*to* (or dative), *upon* (a person, etc., to prevent his ingress or exit, or access to him).

**1340** *Ayenb.* 210 Huanne þou sselt bidde god..ine þine herte, ssete þe dore ope þe. *c* **1450** *Knt. de la Tour* 145 They fonde the gatis shette and closed ayenst hem. **1518** *Star Chamber Cases* (Selden Soc.) II. 132 Wyllyam..shytt the doore to hym. **1633** T. ADAMS *Exp. 2 Pet.* ii. 5. 580 The Lord ..himselfe shut the doore of the Arke upon Noah. **1737** *Gentl. Mag.* VII. 467/1 He finds the Gates shut against him. **1848** THACKERAY *Van. Fair* lxvi, She walked out of the room with a most majestic air, and shut her own door briskly on herself. **1876** BESANT & RICE *Golden Butterfly* Prol. ii, Adam was not more destitute when the garden-gates were shut on him.

**c.** *transf.* and *fig.* (and in figurative context).

**1340** *Ayenb.* 189 To þe fole maydenes..god ham ssette þe gate of þe sposayles. **1534** MORE *Comf. agst. Trib.* III. Wks. 1246/2 We shal not fayle..to haue a doore shet vpon vs where we haue none shette on vs now. **1750** GRAY *Elegy* 68 And shut the gates of mercy on mankind. **1770** BURKE *Pres. Discont.* 51 Resistance to power, has shut the door of the House of Commons to one man. **1850** TENNYSON *In Mem.* xliv, Before God shut the doorways of his head. **1861** PALEY *Æschylus* (ed. 2) *Agam.* 1302 *note*, Men are never satiated with prosperity, and never shut their doors against it.

**d.** *intr.* for *refl.* Of a door, etc.: To close of its own accord, or by some unseen agency. Also, to admit of being shut, or of being shut in a specified manner.

**1470–85** MALORY *Arthur* XIII. iii. 615 Alle the dores & wyndowes of the palays shut by them self. **1648** HEXHAM II, *Een Schuyf-venster*, A Drawing-windowe that opens and shutts. **1687** LOVELL tr. *Thevenot's Trav.* I. 199 The Door.. shuts with a strong Bar behind it. **1825** SCOTT *Talism.* iv, The last chorister had no sooner crossed the threshold of the door, than it shut with a loud sound. **1871** R. ELLIS *Catullus* lxvii. 40 [Addressing the door] Hung to the beam, you shut mutely or open again.

**4.** *trans.* To close (something) by bringing together the outward covering parts.

**a.** To close (one's eyes). Also *fig.*, esp. in *to shut one's eyes to*, *against*, *on*; to ignore, refuse to recognize or consider.

*c* **1366** CHAUCER *Rom. Rose* 296 She..shette hir eien for disdeyn. **1421–5** HOCCLEVE *Lerne to Die* 872 They close & shitte the yen of hir mynde. **1575** TURBERV. *Faulconrie* 292 The hawke will sniffe often and shet her eyes towards night. **1661** BOYLE *Style Script.* (1675) 52 The plainest rustics, if they will not wilfully shut their eyes, may, by the benefit of its light, direct their steps. *a* **1711** NORRIS *Pract. Disc.* (1716) II. ii. 35, I cannot shut my Eyes against Manifest Truth. **1732** BERKELEY *Alciphr.* vii. §9 Wks. 1871 II. 303 Shut your eyes to assist your meditation. **1854** KINGSLEY *Lett.* (1878) I. 415 That man is to be pitied who can shut his eyes to facts. **1907** J. H. PATTERSON *Man-Eaters of Tsavo* x. 115 He levelled his revolver at the dead leopard, and shutting his eyes tightly, fired four shots in rapid succession.

**b.** (*a*) *to shut* (one's) *mouth*: chiefly in pregnant sense, to cease from speaking, to hold one's tongue. So in mod. slang, *to shut* (one's) *head, face* (see FACE *sb.* 2a for examples of the latter). (*b*) *to shut* (another's) *mouth*: to render unable to speak, reply, find fault, disclose secrets, etc.; occas. to prevent (an animal) from devouring. (*c*) *shut it* (in imperative): close one's mouth, hold one's tongue.

**1340** *Ayenb.* 179 Þe dyeuel þet him zet beuore þe ssame him uor to ssette þane mouþ. **1535** COVERDALE *Isa.* lii. 15, & yᵉ kinges shal shut their mouthes before him. **1535** —— *Dan.* vi. 22 My God hath sent his angel, which hath shut the lyons mouthes. **1809** MALKIN *Gil Blas* x. xi. (Rtldg.) 377 If, on his return, his father ventured to remonstrate..Gaspard shut his mouth at once, with..an impertinent answer. **1876** 'MARK TWAIN' *Tom Sawyer* xviii, Shut your heads and let Tom go on!

**1886–96** in Farmer & Henley *Slang* (1903) VI. 202/1 Oh, shut it! Close your mouth until I tell you when. **1908** G. SANGER *Seventy Years Showman* x. 33 'Shut it!' said one of the showmen roughly; 'save your breath for the next scene.' **1945** G. MILLAR *Maquis* viii. 163 'Enough,' cried Boulaya. 'Shut it, Frisé... You know nothing.'

**5. a.** To close by folding up or bringing together of parts (e.g. a book, †a letter, a clasp-knife, one's hand); to bring (†one's arms) together.

?*a* **1366** CHAUCER *Rom. Rose* 1082 Aboute hir nekke of gentil entaile Was shet the riche chevesaile. *c* **1374** —— *Troylus* II. 1226 She shette it [*viz.* a letter]. **1412–20** LYDG. *Chron. Troy* III. 58 A paunce of plate, whiche of þe silf behinde Was schet and clos. **1423** JAS. I *Kingis Q.* viii, My buke I schet. *c* **1489** CAXTON *Sonnes of Aymon* xiv. 335 Whan Rypus sawe that Rychard was confessed, he..made hym mounte vpon the ladder, & dyd shit the cheyn wherat he shold hang. **1576** GASCOIGNE *Steel Glas* Epil., I shut my glasse, before you gasde your fill. **1585** T. WASHINGTON tr. *Nicholay's Voy.* II. vii. 37b, A yeallow Cypresse wrought vpon goldfolie, which they shut and knit fast behind their coyfe. **1614** GORGES *Lucan* II. 44 And then her armes she spreads and shuts. **1815** SCOTT *Guy M.* xlix, The disappointed Dominie shut his ponderous tome. **1863** G. MACDONALD *Dav. Elginbrod* II. iii, She..shut the piano. **1886** WALSINGHAM & PAYNE-GALLWEY *Shooting* I. 175 Loaders..should be made to learn..in shutting the gun always to raise the stock to the barrels. **1894** BARING-GOULD *Kitty Alone* II. 162 He shut his knife. **1905** ELINOR GLYN *Viciss. Evangeline* 233, I can't shut the clasp of my journal.

*fig.* **1722** *Lond. Jrnl.* 23 June 3/2 On Friday last were shut the Transfer Books of the South-Sea Company. *a* **1754** [see SHUTTING *vbl. sb.* 1].

**b.** *intr.* for *refl.* Also with sense †to become optically continuous, to leave no visible gap.

**1582** WATSON *Passionate Cent.* ix. (Arb.) 45 So shuts or sprouts my ioy as doth this flow're. **1668** DRYDEN *Even. Love* IV. (1671) 56 *Stage direct.*, The Scene Shuts. **1670** NARBOROUGH *Jrnl.* in *Acc. Sev. Late Voy.* I. (1694) 72 The South-Land..shuts against the North-Land to a Man's sight. *Ibid.* 75 At Cape Quad the Lands shut one with the other, as if there were no farther passage. **1723** P. BLAIR *Pharmaco-Bot.* I. 45 It's Flower opens in the Forenoon, from eight till towards Noon, and then it shuts. **1878** JOAQUIN MILLER *Songs of Italy* 126 Earth and the sky and the sky and the sea, Seem shutting together as a book that is read.

†**c.** *fig.* (*trans.*) To close (one's life). *Obs.*

**1390** GOWER *Conf.* I. 253 The vicair general..His laste day..Hath schet as to the worldes ye.

**d.** *pass.* and *intr.* Of the day: To close in. Of winter: To set in, become settled.

**1814** SCOTT *Lord of Isles* III. xx, The shades come down —the day is shut. **1854** LOWELL *Indian-Summer Rev.* xxii, Ere Winter wholly shuts.

**6.** *trans.* To weld. (Cf. SHOOT *v.* 38, SHUT *sb.* 4.)

**1490–1555** [see SHUTTING *vbl. sb.* 1b]. **1604** *Churchw. Acc. St. Michael's Oxf.* (MS.), For shuttinge the Irons of the pumpe. **1844** *Mech. Mag.* XL. 176 The best method of shutting cast-steel. **1886** in *W. Somerset Word-bk.* **1949** K. S. WOODS *Rural Crafts England* II. ii. 33 The tyres have to be tightened by cutting out a piece and rejoining or shutting them with a smaller circumference to grip the wheel. **1964** H. HODGES *Artifacts* v. 86 For nearly all purposes the most effective way of joining iron was by welding or shutting.

**7.** To close (an aperture) by placing something upon it or by drawing something across it; to stop up (a road) with obstacles or barriers.

**1362** LANGL. *P. Pl.* A. VI. 92 To wynne vp þe wiket-ȝat þat þe wey schutte. *c* **1440** *Gesta Rom.* xciii. 423 (Add. MS.) The way to helle is shitte to hire. *c* **1450** *Cov. Myst.* (1841) 228 With this ston this grave we shytte. **1585** T. WASHINGTON tr. *Nicholay's Voy.* IV. xv. 130 Strong men..kept the postes and passages so shutte, that they kept away the corne and victuals from all Italie. **1604** E. G[RIMSTONE] *D'Acosta's Hist. Indies* IV. viii. 229 They then invented the *Soccabous*.., the which they shut with doores. **1735** JOHNSON *Lobo's Abyssinia* Descr. xv. 143 They would..for ever shut the Passage into Abyssinia. **1852** CONYBEARE & HOWSON *St. Paul* (1859) II. 459 After that time..the sea was shut; and the winter had been a stormy one. **1869** FREEMAN *Norm. Conq.* (1876) IV. xvii. 31 Not a road was shut against him. **1911** *Daily Graphic* 2 Dec. 4/3 Every exit was barred, every passage shut with a human barricade.

**8. a.** To prevent access to or egress from (a place, building, etc.) by closing the doors or apertures. Now *rare* (superseded by *shut up*: see 19e) exc. in *to shut a shop*.

**1340** *Ayenb.* 154 Þanne is þe castel ziker and ysset. **1382** WYCLIF *Acts* v. 23 We founden the prisoun schit with al diligence. **1471** CAXTON *Recuyell* (Sommer) 574 The Troians shytted her Cyte. **1526** TINDALE *Luke* iv. 25 In the dayes off Helyas, when hevyn was shet thre yeres and syxe monethes. **1592** SHAKS. *Rom. & Jul.* v. i. 56 Being holy day, the beggers shop is shut. **1837** CARLYLE *Fr. Rev.* II. v. viii, This latter [the Feuillant Club] she..has the satisfaction to see shut. **1848** DICKENS *Dombey* xxiii, Rob the Grinder made his own bed, preparatory to shutting the shop. **1886** C. E. PASCOE *Lond. To-day* xxxviii. (ed. 3) 324 Bank-Holiday with the shops of London shut.

**b.** *intr.* for *refl.*

**1801** *Med. Jrnl.* V. 160 The Post-office is just going to shut.

†**c.** fig. (*trans.*) *to shut* (a person's) ***heart***: to render him incapable of showing feeling. Also *intr.* for *refl.* of the heart. *Obs.*

*c* **1374** CHAUCER *Troylus* III. 1086 Ther-with þe sorwe so his herte shette That from his eighen fil þere not a tere. **1390** GOWER *Conf.* I. 328 Sche mihte noght o word on hih Speke oute, for hire herte schette.

**d.** *to shut one's purse*, etc. †*from, against*: to refuse help to.

*c* **1380** WYCLIF *Wks.* (1880) 272 ȝit ony man see his broþer haue nede & schitte his purs & mercy fro hym. **1576** GASCOIGNE *Droome Doomes Day* Wks. 1910 II. 380 Whose table is not shut from any poore or needy. **1780** *Mirror* No. 102 Men whose purses are shut against their friends.

**9. a.** To enclose, secure, or confine (a person or thing) *in* or *within* a place, building, or receptacle; to put *in* a place and shut the door. Also *refl.* Also occas. const. with other preps., *under, between*, etc.; rarely without const. (Cf. *shut in* 15.)

**13..** *Seuyn Sag.* (W.) 2455 Th'emperour him ladde.. Into his chaumbre..And whanne thai were therinne i-schet. **13..** *Guy Warw.* (1891) 418 Gij in to his chaumber gan to gon, & schett him þer in anon. **13..** *E.E. Allit. P.* C. 452 Al schet in a schaȝe. *c* **1374** CHAUCER *Troylus* III. 726 Whan Dane here seluen shette Vnder þe bark. **1388** WYCLIF *Luke* iii. 20 Eroude tetrark..schitte Joon in prisoun. *c* **1450** *Knt. de la Tour* xxiv. 34 Thei..shette hym in a chambre. **1471** CAXTON *Recuyell* (Sommer) 494 She had shytte hit in one of her coffres. **1483** —— *Golden Leg., St. Barbara* (Kelmscott) 1050 Hir fader took her by the heer and drewe hir doun fro the montayn and shytte her faste in pryson. **1556** *Aurelio & Isab.* (1608) A iij, There then being the lady by the ordinaunce of her father shutte. **1561** T. HOBY tr. *Castiglione's Courtyer* IV. (1577) T iv, He slept shut into a chest. **1575** GASCOIGNE *Fruites of Warre* cl. Wks. 1907 I. 171 Herewith we had..Nor meale, nor malt, nor meane..To get such geare if once we should be shut. **1697** DRYDEN *Virg., Georg.* IV. 240 The rest, in Cells apart, the liquid Nectar shut. **1729** G. ADAMS tr. *Sophocles, Antig.* III. v. II. 52 *note*, He was shut into a den, and so starved to Death. **1865** RUSKIN *Sesame* ii. §91 You shut yourselves within your park walls and garden gates. **1894** R. BRIDGES *Shorter Poems* V. xi. 19 We laughed and sang at nightfall, shut By the fireside glow. **1898** 'MERRIMAN' *Roden's Corner* viii. 87 It was Von Holzen's habit to shut himself within his cottage for days together.

**b.** *transf.* and *fig.* Of immaterial things.

*c* **1374** CHAUCER *Boeth.* V. pr. v. (1868) 170 It is raþer þe simplicite of þe souereyn science þat nis nat enclosed nor yshet wiþinne no boundes. *c* **1384** —— *H. Fame* 524 O thought that wrote al that I mette And in the tresorye hyt shette Of my brayn! *a* **1542** WYATT *Poems 'The knot which first'* 39 My deadly grief, and pains so strong Which in my heart be firmly shytt.

†**10. a.** To bar or exclude (a person) *from* some possession or enjoyment; to restrain *from* doing something. *Obs.*

*c* **1400** *Pilgr. Sowle* (Caxton) I. xxxi. (1859) 35 To exclude hym and schytte hym fro this deute. *c* **1412** HOCCLEVE *De Reg. Princ.* 2567 Leste our Lord God hym from his grace schitte. **1579** GOSSON *Sch. Abuse* (Arb.) 30 If men for good exercise, and women for theyr credite, be shut from Theaters, whom shall we suffer to goe thither? **1653** HOLCROFT *Procopius, Goth. Wars* I. 25 The Romans made use of those mills, but for want of water were shut from their Baths. **1719** YOUNG *Busiris* IV. i, We can no more than shut him from escape, Till further force arrive.

**b.** To separate (one thing) *from* another; to cut off from view. *Obs.*

**1697** DRYDEN *Virg., Ecl.* vi. 54 The tender Soil then stiffning by degrees, Shut from the bounded Earth, the bounding Seas. **1807** J. BARLOW *Columb.* I. 36 Whose hovering sheets, along the welkin driven,..shut the eye from heaven. **1831** *Society* I. 14 A turn in the road shut them from his sight.

**11. a.** †To set (a person) free *from*, relieve *of* (something troublesome). *Obs.* exc. in passive (*dial.* and *colloq.*) *to be, get shut of*, (*dial.*) *shut on, to shut one's hands of*: to be rid of, free from; also *ellipt.*

?*a* **1500** *Chester Pl.* (?47) II. 31 Though he have healed thee, Shute from us shall he not be. *Ibid.* 33 To shutte hym of his dangere. **1575–6** *Durham Depos.* (Surtees) 312 This examinate promised..that he wold marye the said Grace..so that he might be shutt of the promises he hadd maid to one Marian Raic. **1596** NASHE *Saffron Walden* To Rdr. D 3, Doo what I can, I shall not be shut of him. **1621** CADE *Serm.* 45 He cannot be quiet till hee bee shut of it [his divell]. **1692** *Scarronides* II. Pref. 2 After his Taylor and Valet have shut their hands of him. **1737** WHISTON *Josephus, Antiq.* XIV. i. §3 His own life would be in danger, unless he..got shut of Aristobulus. **1827** J. F. COOPER *Prairie* xii, Happy will it prove for the boy if he is well shut of them. **1848** MRS. GASKELL *Mary Barton* I. v. 68 As for a bad man, one's glad enough to get shut on him. **1890** 'R. BOLDREWOOD' *Col. Reformer* (1891) 223 Types which all cattleholders agree in desiring to get shut of. **1892** STEVENSON & OSBOURNE *Wrecker* xxii, Your family pays money to be shut of you. **1914** D. H. LAWRENCE *Widowing of Mrs. Holroyd* III. 84 Who dost think wor goin' ter stop when we knowed 'e on'y kep on so's to get shut on us. **1976** S. BARSTOW *Right True End* I. iv. 65 'I haven't *got* her.' 'You're well shut, from all I hear.'

**b.** *dial.* To get rid of, make away with (money).

**1797** T. WRIGHT *Autobiog.* (1864) 254 For fear I should shut it [the money]. **1824** [CARR] *Craven Gloss., Shut*, to spend. 'It'll shut a seet o' brass.' **1872** *Hartley's Yorkshire Ditties* Ser. II. 11 An' aw shan't ha' to come home and tell My old lass, ha' aw've shut all mi brass.

**II.** Combined with advs.

†**12. shut about.** *trans.* To close on all sides. *Obs. rare*$^{-1}$.

**13..** *Bonaventura's Medit.* 989 þey shette hyt [the sepulchre] a boute with a grete stone.

**13. shut down. a.** *intr.* To be closed with a lid; to come close down like a lid. Of fog, night: To come down and blot out the view.

**1807** SOUTHEY *Espriella's Lett.* I. 161 The whole shuts down a-top, and closes in front, like a cabinet. **1880** 'MARK TWAIN' *Tramp Abroad* xix. 182 We got to..Heidelberg before the night shut down. **1891** E. ROPER *By Track & Trail* i. 12 The fog shut down on us once more. **1897** 'O. RHOSCOMYL' *White Rose Arno* 140 The night shut down. **1900** *Blackw. Mag.* Mar. 385/2 The forest shuts down upon the edge of the running water.

**b.** *trans.* To close by lowering, etc.

**1794** MCPHAIL *Treat. Cucumber* 91 The lights of the cucumber bed were kept close shut down day and night. **1836** O. W. HOLMES *Music-grinders* 72 Then..shut the window down. **1842** LOUDON *Suburban Hort.* 499 The lights may be shut down.

**c.** To close (a manufactory). *absol.* To stop working.

**1877** RAYMOND *Statist. Mines & Mining* 226 The hands..forced the superintendent to shut down. **1880** *Paper & Printing Trades Jrnl.* xxx. 6 Most of the paper-mills that were shut-down..are being started anew. **1912** KEITH *Human Body* xv. 241 When men and women lead sedentary and quiet lives their lungs are partly shut down.

**d.** *Mech.* To stop or switch off (a device or machine, esp. an engine); to cause to stop working or running. Also *absol.*

**1895** G. W. LUMMIS-PATERSON *Management of Dynamos* x. 148 When shutting down a machine, the load should first be gradually reduced..by easing down the engine. **1911** MARSHALL & SANKEY *Gas Engines* vi. 175 [Filling the reservoir] is done when shutting down the engine so soon as the gas is turned off. **1948** H. CONSTANT *Gas Turbines* xi. 137 The best that can be done is to shut down as many engines as possible and operate the remainder at a power output giving reasonable efficiency. **1969** I. KEMP *Brit. G.I. in Vietnam* viii. 163 We all 'shut down'—switched off our engines and made fast the rotor blades to the tails of the helicopters. **1976** *Physics Bull.* Aug. 339/2 Two samples were taken from the low-sulphur plant: one at ambient temperatures 30 days after the boiler had been shut down. **1980** *Daily Tel.* 10 Mar. 3/2 A nagging 'oil migration' problem..could eventually have forced a pilot to shut down the engine.

**e.** *Physics.* To stop (the chain reaction) in a nuclear reactor; to stop (a nuclear reactor) from producing useful power by making the fuel assembly subcritical.

**1945** HAWLEY & LEIFSON *Atomic Energy* 157 Knowing just when to shut down the chain-reaction..would be quite a problem. **1951** *Nucleonics* Jan. 5/2 If the temperature of the uranium exceeds 60°C, the pile is automatically shut down. **1963** B. FOZARD *Instrumentation Nuclear Reactors* xiii. 164 Unless a heavy-water reactor is shut down for such a long period that there is a significant fall in the activity of the high-energy gamma emitters, it has a built-in neutron source. **1976** *Sci. Amer.* Jan. 27/2 The level of radioactivity in a standard 1,000-megawatt reactor is very high: about 10 billion curies half an hour after the reactor is shut down.

**f.** *intr.* Of a device, machine, or installation, esp. a nuclear reactor: to cease to operate.

**1945** H. D. SMYTH *Gen. Account Devel. Atomic Energy for Military Purposes 1940–45* viii. 81 The half-life of the U-239 is so short that its concentration becomes negligible soon after the pile shuts down. **1960** *Engineering Index 1959* 246/2 During power failures of up to 1·5 sec duration..synchronous motors usually shut down. **1976** *Sci. Amer.* July 36/1 After the reactor had shut down, the evidence of its activity was preserved virtually undisturbed through the succeeding ages of geological activity. **1978** *Nature* 19 Oct. 576/2 As the voltage dropped rapidly various sensors began to shut down, and within a few minutes the satellite ceased to respond to commands sent up from ground control stations. **1979** *Daily Tel.* 15 Aug. 32/3 The Sea Kings will operate throughout the night but the others do not have night capability and will have to shut down for the night.

†**14. shut forth.** *trans.* To push (a person) out, to extrude, expel. *Obs.*

**1513** DOUGLAS *Æneis* XI. xvii. 43 The sonnys furthschet [L. *exclusi*], that pety was to seyn, Befor thair wepand wofull faderis eyn. **1564** ANNE LADY BACON tr. *Jewel's Apol.* II. ii. (1859) 21 There is now no nation which may truly complain that they be shut forth [*se exclusam esse*].

**15. shut in. a.** *trans.* To prevent access to or confine (a person or thing) by shutting a door, etc. or closing a receptacle. Also *refl.*

*c* **1425** *Cursor M.* 17670 (Laud MS.) Ye shytte me in oon a friday At Euyn-tide in-to þat stede. **1471** CAXTON *Recuyell* (Sommer) 163 The fayr danes whom the kynge acrysius holdeth fast shytte in wyth oute any rayson. **1530** PALSGR. 704/1 You have shytte in the dogge. **1614** GORGES *Lucan* III. 100, I needs must scorne this double flout, To shut me in, or shut me out. *a* **1700** EVELYN *Diary* 19 Aug. 1654, These men went in with axes and hammers, and shut themselves in. *Ibid.* 18 Jan. 1671, I found him shut in. **1841** W. SPALDING *Italy & It. Isl.* III. 170 The present walls, with their eleven gates, shutting in the whole population, were built about 1557. **1842** LOUDON *Suburban Hort.* 518 A row of trusses of straw is laid side by side over the whole, to shut in the steam. **1847** C. BRONTË *Jane Eyre* xxvi, I shut myself in.

**b.** To enclose with a barrier, hem in.

**1398** TREVISA *Barth. De P.R.* V. xiv. (1495) 120 Mala (in Grewe) is the lewre and in the face lewres shyttyth in eyther side of the nose. **1816** TUCKEY *Narr. Exped. R. Zaire* vi. (1818) 212 Both ends of the reach being shut in by land. **1830** MARRYAT *King's Own* xxvi, We had shut in the battery [*i.e.* taken up a position from which it was shut in by a promontory]. **1863** 'C. BEDE' *Tour in Tartan-land* 152 The Loch is shut in by a long-withdrawing range of mountains. **1869** FREEMAN *Norm. Conq.* (1876) III. xiii. 292 Wooded hills..shut in the view on every side.

†**c.** To close (a shop, building, gate, etc.). *Obs.*

**1390** GOWER *Conf.* III. 291 The bathes and the Stwes bothe Thei schetten in be every weie. **1556** *Chron. Grey Friars* (Camden) 34 The church was shott in from monday unto thursday. **1568** GRAFTON *Chron.* II. 143 The people shut in their shops, and came out in harnesse in great multitudes. **1611** MIDDLETON & DEKKER *Roaring Girl* II. i. D 1 b, The shop will be shut in presently. **1648** GAGE *West Ind.* 71 The gates were shut in.

**d.** *Oil Industry.* To cease drawing oil or gas from (a well).

**1931** W. H. EMMONS *Geol. Petroleum* (ed. 2) xvi. 527 In 1923, during a period of overproduction, certain groups of wells were shut in while others near by were pumped. **1962** T. C. FRICK *Petroleum Production Handbk.* II. xxx. 8 Pressure readings obtained while the well is being cleaned before the well is shut in. **1971** *West Indian World* 5 Nov. 16/2 All 17 wells had encountered satisfactory oil sand sections and were at present 'shut in' and awaiting the installation of an eight-inch pipeline.

**e.** *intr.* Of the day, evening, etc.: To close in, grow dusk. Also of the days: To shorten. Now *rare.*

**1623** JOBSON *Golden Trade* 15 From 3. vntil the euening shut in. **1662** J. DAVIES tr. *Olearius' Voy. Ambass.* 399 The Ambassadors..got to the City ere day-light was shut in. **1680** COTTON *Compl. Gamester* (ed. 2) 4 The day being shut in. **1748** RICHARDSON *Clarissa* (1811) IV. 158 Observing the sun-shine begin to shut in, I yielded. **1760–72** H. BROOKE *Fool of Qual.* (1809) I. 171 As day by day began gradually to shut in. **1924** [implied in SHUTTING *vbl. sb.* 3].

†**f.** To meet together with no space between.

*c* **1710** CELIA FIENNES *Diary* (1888) 122 Flints..cut so exactly square and even to shutt in one to another that ye whole wall is made without cement.

**g.** To be closed in (to the view).

**1816** TUCKEY *Narr. Exped. R. Zaire* iv. (1818) 152 Just where the river shuts in. **1849** CUPPLES *Green Hand* xiii. (1856) 124 The opposite shore..shut in so far upon the other,..that, steering from the south'ard, one would never know there was a river there at all.

**16. shut off. a.** *trans.* To prevent the passage of; to cut off (steam, etc.) by the closing of a valve or tap. Also, to close (a dark lantern).

**1824** R. STUART *Hist. Steam Engine* 132 The motion of the piston was equalized by shutting off the steam sooner or later from the cylinder. **1904** H. B. M. WATSON *Hurricane Isl.* xx. 285, I shut off the lantern.

*fig.* **1844** W. BARNES *Poems Rur. Life* Gloss., 'To shut off work', to leave off work. **1903** F. W. H. MYERS *Hum. Pers.* 180 To shut off pain when we know it will be useless.

**b.** To cut off, separate *from.*

**1833** ARNOTT *Physics* (ed. 5) II. 102 There are inlets of the sea, occasionally shut off from the parent ocean. **1890** 'R. BOLDREWOOD' *Col. Reformer* (1891) 154 Great crags.., shutting off this bay from the other portions of the coast. **1893** BENT in *Geog. Jrnl.* II. 142 A large lake..which was shut off along one side by a very fine dyke or wall.

**c.** *intr.* To come to a halt; to cease talking or writing. *U.S.*

**1896** 'MARK TWAIN' in *Harper's Mag.* Sept. 526/1 'Now who—' He shut off sudden. **1902** J. LONDON *Let.* 12 July (1966) 136 Someone is going down town, so I'll shut off and give them a chance to mail this. **1938** V. WOOLF *Let.* 18 June (1980) VI. 241 He rang me up late on Wednesday... He said he had travelled post haste from Prague to see Leonard. I said, A misunderstanding. Then we shut off.

**17. shut out. a.** *trans.* To exclude (persons, also commodities, light, air, etc.) from a place, situation, circumstances, etc.; to deny (a person) right of entry to a place, etc.

**1382** WYCLIF I *Macc.* x. 75 He shitte [**1388** schittide] hym out fro the citee. **1390** GOWER *Conf.* II. 98 Ther is no lock mai schette him oute. **1487** *Cely Papers* (Camden) 172 Of a yͤ felles the wych the Holonders hayd schowt wt. **1526** *Pilgr. Perf.* (W. de W. 1531) 25 All pleasure of the body he shette out of his hert by yͤ vowe of chastite. **1660** F. BROOKE tr. *Le Blanc's Trav.* 397 Our former errour, and the basenesse of the Portuguese, shut us quite out of this country. **1672** DRYDEN *2nd Pt. Conq. Granada* IV. i, Make haste and draw the Curtain while you may; You but shut out the twilight of my day. **1742** BLAIR *Grave* 684 Heav'ns Portals wide expand to let him in; Nor are his Friends shut out. **1819** TAUNTON *Rep. Cases Comm. Pleas* VII. 480 The Defendant is completely shut out from taking the ground of mutual credit by his own statement. **1849** MACAULAY *Hist. Eng.* v. I. 654 An exile, shut out from public employment. **1856** *N. Brit. Rev.* XXVI. 157 When we close one eye, we shut out the quantity of light which entered that eye as reflected from a different part of the room. **1842** LOWELL *Forlorn* xvi, For, whom the heart of Man shuts out, Straightway the heart of God takes in. **1895** P. HEMINGWAY *Out of Egypt* I. i. 10 The stuffy ill-lighted rooms at the back of the houses, shut out from view of the authorities.

**b.** Phr. *to shut* (some one) ***out of doors***, † ***out of the gates.***

**1508** FISHER *7 Penit. Ps.* cxlii. Wks. (1876) 261 One that by chaunce was that nyght shette out of the gates. **1530** PALSGR. 704/1 She hath shytte me out of dores. **1818** SCOTT *Br. Lamm.* xxi, And Ravenswood's dirty usage of me—shutting me out of doors to dine with the lackeys.

**c.** To screen from view.

**1856** KANE *Arctic Expl.* I. ix. 101 A large headland..shutting out all points farther north. **1899** MRS. E. COTES *Path of Star* xv. 160 Orchids hung from above, shutting out the garden. **1906** E. V. LUCAS *Wand. Lond.* i. 11 Long white blinds that shut out the house opposite.

**d.** *Baseball.* (See quot. 1896. Cf. *shut out* sb. s.v. SHUT *ppl. a.* 2.) Also *transf.* in other games and *fig.* *N. Amer.*

**1881** *N.Y. Herald* 17 July 10/3 The Domestics were shut out in every inning up to the eighth, when by bunching their hits they scored two earned runs on a single by Mahny. **1894** *Spalding's Base Ball Guide* 40 Nichols..shut out the St. Louis team without a game to their credit out of four games played. **1896** R. G. KNOWLES & MORTON *Baseball* 88 [A pitcher] who performed the remarkable feat of shutting out (*i.e.*, disposing of a team in their whole nine innings without a run being scored) Baltimore, Cleveland [etc.]. **1952** in Wentworth & Flexner *Amer. Dict. Slang* (1960) 475/2 The last time [the Princeton football players] were shut out Penn did it on Nov. 3, 1946. **1957** *Northland News* (Uranium City, Sask.) 7 Jan. 7/2 [Ice hockey] The Flyers shut-out the blue and gold for the second time by a 2–0 count. **1976** *National Observer* (U.S.) 15 May 2/1 Reagan shut out Ford in Texas, winning all 96 delegates to the National Convention.

**18. shut to.** **a.** *trans.* To close (a door); †to shoot (a bolt).

*a* **1225** *Ancr. R.* 95 & ȝif..he worþe his hond forð touward þe þurl cloð, swiftliche anonriht schutteð al þet þurl to. *c* **1250** *Gen. & Ex.* 1078 Ðis angels two droȝen loth in And shetten to ðe dure-pin. *c* **1440** *Jacob's Well* 243 Sche..schett to þe dore. **1526** TINDALE *Acts* xxi. 30 Forthwith the dores were shut to. **1665** PEPYS *Diary* 16 July, A little pretty daughter of my Lady Wright's most innocently come out afterward, and shut the door to. **1886** STEVENSON *Kidnapped* iii, The door was cautiously opened and shut to again behind me. **1891** C. ROBERTS *Adrift Amer.* 128 A half-breed Indian that was loafing about there to shut-to the door.

**b.** *intr.* for *refl.*

**1912** M. HEWLETT in *Engl. Rev.* Apr. 9 The earth's door shuts-to again.

**19. shut up.** **a.** *trans.* To place or store away in a closed box or other receptacle; to keep from view or use; to confine within bounds. *lit.* and *fig.* †Also to withhold (one's money, kindness, etc.) *from* a person.

*c* **1400** *Pety Job* 364 in *26 Pol. Poems* 132 Tyll he..wylne to be shut vp in hys cheste. **1426** LYDG. *De Guil. Pilgr.* 17922 To shit vp gold in coffers. **1526** TINDALE *1 John* iii. 17 Whosoever..seyth his brother in necessitie, and shetteth vppe his compassion from him. **1530** PALSGR. 704/1 He hath shytte up his treasour in a wall. **1540** —— *Acolastus* I. i. D ij, He neuer perceyued my goodnesse to be shut vp towardes hym. **1544** BETHAM *Precepts War* I. xciv. E vij, Whose names are worthye to be spred immortall, in euery age, whose fame should not be shutte vp, or hydde in any posteritie. **1612** CHAPMAN *Rev. Bussy d'Ambois* V. v. 138 Our sensive spirits..can take..the same forms they had When they were shut up in this body's shade. **1691** tr. *Beddevole's Ess. Anat.* 120 Each Lobe [of the Liver] is shut up [Fr. *renfermé*] in a very delicate Membrane. **1742** YOUNG *Nt. Th.* II. 467 Thoughts shut up, want air, And spoil. **1825** T. HOOK *Sayings* Ser. II. *Passion & Princ.* xii. III. 268 Cutting long slips of muslin..and shutting them up in boxes. **1863** DANA *Man. Geol.* 27 The waters are shut up within the great basin, the Caspian and Aral being the seas which receive those waters that are not lost in the plains.

†**b.** To comprise, include; to condense in brief expressions. *Obs.*

**1622** PEACHAM *Compl. Gentl.* vi. 49 Shutting vp whole and weightie Sentences in three words. *a* **1674** TRAHERNE *Chr. Ethics* (1675) 472 There are three things which beget love, beauty, benefits, and praises: they are all three shut up in goodness.

**c.** (*a*) To confine (a person or animal) in prison or in some kind of restraint; to keep in seclusion; to hem (a person) round in order to prevent his escape. Also (chiefly *refl.*) to shut the door on (a person within a place, room, etc.) to prevent access; *pass.* to be closeted with.

*c* **1489** CAXTON *Sonnes of Aymon* xiii. 312, I shall bryng hym agen wyth me vnto you all, were he shitte vp in x prisons. **1530** TINDALE *Lev.* xiii. 4 Then let the preast shitt him vpp seuen dayes. **1534** —— *Acts* xxvi. 10 Many of the sainctes I shut vp in preson. **1573** TUSSER *Husb.* (1878) 119 A houell will..serue thee in winter..to shut vp thy porklings thou mindest to fat. **1604** E. G[RIMSTONE] *D'Acosta's Hist. Indies* V. xv. 367 These Virgines thus shut vp into these monasteries. **1645** SYMONDS *Diary* (Camden) 173 These garrisons shutt up by the rebells. *a* **1700** EVELYN *Diary* 21 Oct. 1670, Din'd with the Treassurer, and after dinner we were shut up together. **1741** MIDDLETON *Cicero* (1742) III. 222 He shut him up closely by sea, as well as land. **1798** SOPHIA LEE *Canterb. T.*, *Young Lady's T.* II. 476 Those for whom the feast should have been preparing,.. remained shut up at home. **1837** CARLYLE *Fr. Rev.* I. III. viii, Whom, however, Loménie..shuts up in the Bastille. **1855** MACAULAY *Hist. Eng.* xv. III. 613 The Jacobites..were forced to shut themselves up in their houses. **1859** JEPHSON *Brittany* i. 1, [I] shut myself up with my own thoughts. **1896** MRS. CAFFYN *Quaker Grandmother* 276 The dogs were always shut up on moonlight nights.

*fig.* **1526** TINDALE *Gal.* iii. 23 Before that fayth cam, we were kept and shut vppe vnder the lawe. **1726** SWIFT *Gulliver* III. ii. 189 The whole compass of their thoughts and mind being shut up within the two forementioned Sciences. **1875** HELPS *Soc. Press.* i. 3 How we are all shut up in our own small selves.

(*b*) In some games of skill: To surround (the pieces of an opponent) in such a manner that a move becomes impossible without capture. Also said of the player. In *Dominoes*, see quot. 1870.

**1474** CAXTON *Chesse* IV. ii. (1883) 168 For yf he be taken or ded or ellis Inclusid and shette vp [etc.]. **1870** *Routledge's Ev. Boy's Ann.* 340 Endeavouring to keep the command of the game [dominoes], so that you can block it at any moment, or, as it is technically termed, 'shut it up'. **1875** JOWETT *Plato* (ed. 2) III. 371 Unskilful players of draughts are at last shut up by their skilled adversaries.

(*c*) To compel by the exclusion of alternatives *to* some particular conclusion, course of action, etc.

**1836** *Rob Stene's Dream* (Maitland Club) Introd. 12 We are thus shut up to the conclusion, that the Poem must have been composed between 27th January, 1590–1,..and 28th February, 1591–2. **1843** H. ROGERS *Ess.* (1860) III. 44 He plies the Oxford Tractists with this argument very fairly, and shows..that they are shut up to one of two courses.

**d.** To close (an entrance, aperture, etc.); to pull (a door, window, etc.) to; †to stop up, make impassable (a road). Also *occas.* to shut permanently (the eyes, mouth). Now *rare.*

**1526** TINDALE *Matt.* xxv. 10 The gate was shett vppe. **1560** *Ovid's Narcissus* A iv b, And deth shut vp those eyes. **1570** T. WILSON tr. *Demosth. Orat.* ii. 15 All the Ports and Hauens in the Countrie are shutte vp by reason of the warres. **1608** WOTTON *Life & Lett.* (1907) I. 411 The ways being all shut up with frosts, and snows. **1631** T. POWELL *Tom of All Trades* 32 If the Merchant sit still, the most of them may shut up their Shop windowes. **1785** PALEY *Mor. Philos.* III. I. xv. (1841) 89 When a tradesman shuts up his windows, to induce his creditors to believe that he is abroad. **1802** R. BROOKES *Gazetteer* (ed. 12) s.v. *Lepanto*, The harbour is small, and may be shut up by a chain. **1826** COBBETT *Rur. Rides* (1885) II. 100 Let them answer this question, or shut up their mouths upon this subject. **1827** FARADAY *Chem. Manip.* xix. (1842) 506 Closing the extremities of tubes so as to shut up one end. **1852** MRS. STOWE *Uncle Tom's C.* xl, Well, his mouth's shut up at last. **1891** KINNS *Graven in Rock* viii. 290 The ancient Egyptians had closely shut it [the entrance] up.

*fig.* **1576** GASCOIGNE *Droome Doomes Day* Wks. 1910 II. 375 If the outward wandring be shut up, the inward accesse to God is opened.

**e.** To close, prevent access to or exit from (a place, a house, shop, room, etc.); †to screen by an enclosure *from* (obs.); *Agric.* to close (a meadow) to pasture, in preparation for a hay crop; to close (a box or other receptacle); *Naut.* to stop the leaks in (a ship). ***to shut up shop***: see SHOP *sb.* 8 b.

Also in Biblical phrases, ***to shut up the heavens***, to withhold rain; ***to shut up the womb***, to render barren.

**1530** TINDALE *Lev.* xiv. 38 Then let the preast..shett vp the housse for .vii. dayes. **1530** —— *Deut.* xi. 17 And then the wrath of the Lorde..shott vp the heauen that there be no rayne. **1535** COVERDALE *Job* iii. 10 Because it shut not vp the wombe that bare me. **1576** GASCOIGNE *Droome Doomes Day* Wks. 1910 II. 246 Gluttony dyd shut up Paradyse. **1592** *Arden of Feversham* II. ii. 52 Tis very late, I were best shute vp my stall. *a* **1700** EVELYN *Diary* 16 July 1665, Two houses were shut up in our parish. **1711** ADDISON *Spect.* No. 110 ¶ 5 His mother..had shut up half the Rooms in the House. **1733** ARBUTHNOT *Ess. Effects Air* vi. 121 Cities in Greece, shut up from Northerly Winds, were unhealthy. **1765** *Museum Rust.* IV. 275 Their food, four small pastures... Two of them I fed in the spring, rather late before I shut them up for hay. **1805** COLLINGWOOD in Nicolas *Disp. Nelson* (1846) VII. 110 *note*, The Achille wanted caulking much. I ordered a gang on board of her to shut her up before the wet weather comes. **1838** DICKENS *O. Twist* xxvii, Noah, you shut up the shop. **1840** *Jrnl. R. Agric. Soc.* I. IV. 396 The field is now shut up till the time of harvesting the crop. **1848** THACKERAY *Van. Fair* lxvii, Let us shut up the box and the puppets. **1859** GEO. ELIOT *Adam Bede* Epil., The workshops have been shut up half an hour or more.

*fig.* **1702** O. HEYWOOD *Diaries* (1885) IV. 296 Alas then my heart was shut up.

**f.** To close (something) by folding together, to fold (something) up. Also *intr.* for *refl.* Also, †to fit closely *together*.

**1611** BIBLE *Job* xli. 15 His scales are his pride, shut vp together as with a close seale. **1819–23** P. BARLOW in *Encycl. Metrop.* (1845) III. 473/1 A machine shutting up in the form of a chest, or box. **1833** T. HOOK *Parson's Dau.* III. x, Shutting up the easel itself, [she] deposited it in the corner. **1857** HUGHES *Tom Brown* I. iii, And he, shutting up the knife ..accompanied them to the cottage. **1891** *Punch* 25 Apr. 201/2 Smart new boy in cloak-room has noted gentlemen shutting up their crush hats. **1911** *Daily Graphic* 2 Dec. 4/3 Shutting up the little book he had been reading.

†**g.** To conclude, wind up (a subject, discourse, etc.); to finish up (an act, a period of time, etc.), to bring to an end *with*. *Obs.*

**1575** GASCOIGNE *Making of Verse* Wks. 1907 I. 471 The two last [lines] do combine and shut up the Sentence. **1577–87** HARRISON *England* II. vi. 171/2 in *Holinshed*, Some making their entrie with egs, and shutting vp their tables with mulberies. **1581** J. BELL *Haddon's Answ. Osorius* 158 To shutte up the matter in fewe wordes. **1585** KYD *Sp. Trag.* II. iv. 17 And heauens haue shut vp day to pleasure vs. **1601** W. LEIGH *Soules Solace* (1617) 18 Hee shut vp his blessed life, with these blessed words [etc.]. **1620** VENNER *Via Recta* viii. 182, I must aduertise them that shut vp their meale with drinke, that they doe it with a moderate draught. **1633** *Battle of Lutzen* 28, I shut up all concerning this point in this Assertion. **1638** A. READ *Chirurg.* i. 1 In the last Lecture..I shut up the doctrine of ulcers. *c* **1650** in Bromley *Collect. Roy. Lett.* (1787) 309 Thus I will shut up my long and tedious letter. **1706** E. WARD *Wooden World Diss.* (1708) 102 He constantly shuts up the Week with a Debauch. **1741** WESLEY *Wks.* 1872 I. 303, I will shut up this melancholy subject with part of a letter.

**h.** *colloq.* To be the end of (a matter).

**1857** DICKENS *Dorrit* I. xii, Now, I'll tell you what it is, and this shuts it up;..I'll let him off for another five down and a bottle of wine; and if you mean done, say done, and if you don't like it, leave it.

**i.** *intr.* Of a period of time, state of things, a discourse, an action: To come to an end. *arch.*

**1609** *Old Meg of Herefordsh.* (1816) 2 The sports growing to the end, and shutting up. **1667** PEPYS *Diary* 31 Mar., The month shuts up only with great desires of peace in all of us. **1865** SWINBURNE *Chastelard* V. ii. 180 So here my time shuts up.

**j.** Of a person: †To end one's course of action (*obs.*); to bring one's remarks to a close. Now *rare.* (Cf. m.)

**1628** BP. HALL *Contempl.* xx. *Joash & Elisha* 21 The Joash of Judah having been preserved..by Jehoiada the priest.. shuts up in the unkinde murther of his sonne. **1657** J. WATTS *Scribe, Pharisee*, etc. I. 72 And now (to shut up) I will give you a brief recapitulation. **1700** R. CROMWELL *Let.* in *Eng. Hist. Rev.* (1898) XIII. 121, I fear how farre my penn hath runn; it is but reasonable to shut up. **1868** THIRLWALL *Lett.* (1881) II. 175, I must now shut up.

**k.** Of a commercial house: To close its doors, stop payment. *rare.*

**1841** THACKERAY *Gt. Hoggarty Diam.* x, The very day when the Muff and Tippet Company shut up.

**l.** *trans.* To cause (a person) to stop talking, to reduce to silence. Also to silence (hostile artillery).

**1814** JANE AUSTEN *Mansfield Park* III. xvi. 305 Her son, who was always guided by the last speaker, by the person who could get hold of and shut him up. **1857** DICKENS *Dorrit* I. xiii, I say to them, What else are you made for? It shuts them up. They haven't a word to answer. **1860** W. H. RUSSELL *Diary in India* I. 291 Our artillery seemed to shut the hostile guns up. **1861** HUGHES *Tom Brown at Oxf.* v, When I got there I was quite shut up. **1866** *Mysteries of Isis* 7 The Captain shuts up poor Henry..and he can't say a word in return. **1887** *Poor Nellie* (1888) 16 Looks at you and shuts you up just like Snorker, my old form master.

**m.** *intr.* (*colloq.* or *slang.*) To shut one's mouth, to stop talking. (Cf. j.) Often in imperative.

**1840** *Picayune* (New Orleans) 10 Oct. 2/4 The Dutch-man got a hint to 'shut up' from one of the officers. **1853** 'C. BEDE' *Verdant Green* I. viii, Order! or-*der*! shut up, Bouncer! **1858** TROLLOPE *Dr. Thorne* v, On this occasion he seemed to be at some loss for words: he shut up, as the slang phrase goes. **1905** ELINOR GLYN *Viciss. Evangeline* 134 He nearly had a fit, and shut up at once.

**n.** Of a racehorse: To refuse to go on running in a race.

**1859** LEVER *Dav. Dunn* xxix, Some horses..drag their feet along, all weary and tired; if you push them a bit, they shut up, or they answer the whip with a kind of shrug.

**shut** (ʃʌt), *ppl. a.* [pa. pple. of SHUT *v.*]

**1. a.** In senses of the verb: Closed, fastened up, folded together, etc.

**1474** CAXTON *Chesse* II. iv. (1883) 51 Wyth a closid and shette purse shalt thou neuer haue victorye. **1528** PAYNELL *Salerne's Regim.* 24 The open aier wolde be chosen and..the shutte aier be eschewed. **1615** R. COCKS *Diary* (Hakl. Soc.) I. 89 He would cary both our open and also our shut letters. **1748** RICHARDSON *Clarissa* VI. 72 Speaking words of tenderness through his shut teeth. **1830** CARLETON *Traits* (1843) I. 27 The dog..laying his shut paw upon Jack's nose. **1894** KIPLING *Jungle Bk.* 57 His first stroke..was sent home with shut mouth in silence.

*transf.* **1817** BYRON *Manfred* I. i, By thy shut soul's hypocrisy. **1907** SIR O. LODGE *Subst. Faith* x. 63 Their shut minds and self-satisfied hearts are things to marvel at.

**b.** (See quot.)

**1809** R. LANGFORD *Introd. Trade* 52 When the word *shut* is placed after any particular stock, it denotes no transfer can be made, as the books of the Stock or company are adjusting.

**c.** *Paper-making.* (See quot.)

**1825** J. NICHOLSON *Oper. Mech.* 376 In a well-made sheet of paper the fibres are ranged in a horizontal and parallel direction, and a manufacturer describing such a sheet of paper, would say that the stuff was well shut.

†**d.** ***shut face***: ? an air of mystery. *Obs.*

**1626** B. JONSON *Staple of N.* IV. iv. 64 With all your.. lookes out of the politicks, your shut-faces, And reseru'd Questions, and Answers that you game with.

†**e.** ***shut sound, vowel*** = CLOSE *a.* 1 d. Also used to designate a short vowel of the quality used in closed syllables. *Obs.*

**1841** W. SPALDING *Italy & It. Isl.* III. 222 Those who inhabit the valley of the Po..have derived..a strong tendency to nasal sounds and shut vowels. **1849** CRAIG *Dict.*, *Key to Pronunc.*, A. Shut sound, as in man... E. Shut sound, as in men... O. Shut sound, as in hot.

**f.** ***shut couplet***: (see quot.)

**1896** G. SAINTSBURY *Hist. 19th Cent. Lit.* i. 7 What has been called the 'shut' couplet—the couplet more or less rigidly confined to itself, and not overlapping.

**2.** *Comb.*: with advs. as ***shut-away*** adj.; with adjs., as ***shut-eyed***, ***-minded*** (so ***-mindedness***), ***-mouthed***. See also SHUT-IN *a.* and *sb.*, SHUT-OUT *a.* and *sb.*, SHUT-UP *a.*

**1911** GALSWORTHY *Patrician* II. xvi. 253 Her face had a strange, brooding, *shut-away look, as though he had frightened her. **1913** 'SAKI' *When William Came* (1914) xvi. 272 He looked round again at the rolling stretches of brown hills; before he had regarded them merely as the background to this little shut-away world. **1959** *Listener* 12 Mar. 473/1 The sensitive, shut-away man. **1934** J. A. LEE *Children of Poor* (1949) III. 68 Prayer was tiring in the extreme, in an atmosphere of tense, sweaty, *shut-eyed sanctity. **1956** H. GOLD *Man who was not with It* (1965) xxx. 283, I watched Belle's shut-eyed face compose with fatigue. **1960** T. HUGHES *Lupercal* 37 And look in at the byre's Blaze of darkness: a sudden shut-eyed look Backward into the head. **1977** *Sunday Mail* (Brisbane) 20 Nov. 27/4, I don't want to get *shut-minded as I get older. **1981** *Times Lit. Suppl.* 16 Jan. 60/4 At this stage in such a review it is a common *topos* to remark that thanks are due to the editor or author for raising weighty questions. It may seem churlish or shut-minded, but for £45 one might also expect a few answers. **1933** C. C. MARTINDALE in M. Leahy *Conversions to Catholic Church* ix. 91 A priestly work of incredible *shut-mindedness, but..homage-worthiness. **1936** C. SANDBURG *People, Yes* 113 In Vermont a *shut-mouthed husband finally broke forth to his wife. **1959** W. R. BIRD *These are Maritimes* viii. 217 That made him awful mad but he wouldn't say anything. He's what you'd call 'shut-mouthed'.

**shut**, var. SHUTT.

**shut-down.** [Cf. SHUT *v.* 13.]

**1. a.** A shutting down; the closing for a time of a factory, etc. Also *attrib.*

The sense in quot. 1857 is uncertain.

**1857** *Knickerbocker* XLIX. 35 'I'll be just exactly shot if you *don't*!' he added with a patent diabolical shut-down. **1884** *Boston Jrnl.* 16 Oct. 7 The Acushnet paper-mill at New Bedford had started up after a shut-down of two months. **1888** *Pall Mall Gaz.* 8 May 12/1 The shut-down movement has thus far been successful, but every advance in prices induces the opening of new wells. **1889** *Engineering* 11 Oct. 434/3 There has really been a 'shut down' of a large number of [oil-]wells, to check a wasteful over-production. **1901** *Chambers's Jrnl.* Jan. 29/1 In the old days when we had a grievance we could talk it over with the boss; but today if there is a shut-down nobody knows anything about it except that it has been ordered from headquarters in New York. **1931** *Economist* 15 Aug. 308/2 The Ford shutdown will restrict August production. **1959** *News Chron.* 2 July 4/3 What do you propose..to prevent a shutdown of the national papers? **1967** *N.Y. Times* (Internat. Ed) 11 Feb. 2/2 Classes resumed quietly at Madrid University today after a 10-day shutdown because of campus battles between students and the police. **1972** M. JONES *Life on Dole* vi. 51 The Dowlais shut-down had several consequences. It took away the one industrial enterprise that kept going all through the week.

**b.** The cessation of broadcasting for the day on any particular channel or station; the time at which this occurs.

**1959** *Listener* 19 Mar. 499/1 The peak viewing-hours from 7.0 p.m. to shut-down. **1973** *Times* 15 Dec. 2/7 (*heading*) TV staggers shutdown.

**2. a.** The cessation of operation of a machine, device, or installation, esp. as a result of a fault.

**1911** J. F. C. SNELL *Power House Design* x. 352 The.. security against a shut-down arising from the duplicate sets of bus bars. **1916** *Standard. Rules Amer. Inst. Electr. Engin.* 35 This method consists in the measurement of the temperature of windings by their increase in resistance, corrected to the instant of shut-down when necessary. **1936** *Discovery* Apr. 113/2 In the event of a shut-down of the power unit, an alternative supply is available from the storage battery. **1953** [see INPUT *v.* 3]. **1971** *New Scientist* 7 Jan. 19/1 An abrupt shutdown is a very different affair from the computer operator pushing the computer 'off' buttons. **1976** M. MACHLIN *Pipeline* liv. 542 The breakdown at Pump Station One and Three..resulted in an automatic shutdown of the entire pipeline.

**b.** *Physics.* The stopping of the chain reaction in a nuclear reactor when the fuel assembly is made subcritical.

**1945** H. D. SMYTH *Gen. Acct. Devel. Atomic Energy for Military Purposes 1940–45* vii. 71 A shut-down for servicing could be effected. **1951** *Nucleonics* Jan. 5/1 There are two sets..of emergency shut-down rods. **1963** B. FOZARD *Instrumentation Nuclear Reactors* xiii. 162 The delay due to xenon poisoning in restarting after a shut down cannot be reduced or eliminated. **1978** N. L. FRANKIN in Foley & Van Buren *Nuclear or Not?* 120 [Boron steel control rods] drop down into the core ensuring a rapid shutdown.

†**shute**[1]. *Obs.* Forms: 1 scyte, 3 scute, ssute, schute, shute. [OE. *scyte* str. masc., corresponds to OHG. and MHG. *schuz* (mod.G. *schuss*) :—OTeut. **skuti-z*, f. **skut-*: see SHOOT *v.*

This word, with ME. *u* = *ü*, is distinct from *shute* var. of SHOOT *sb.*[1]]

**1.** A shot, a blow. (Cf. SHOOT *sb.*[1] 1.)

*c* **1000** *Ags. Gloss.* in *Haupt's Zeitschr.* (1853) IX. 478/2 *Ictibus*, scytum. *c* **1205** LAY. 1461 Corineus bleintes & þene scute bi-berh. **1297** R. GLOUC. (Rolls) 8132 So þat to þe toun walle hii come atte laste And þe oþere hadde ilore hor ssute of bowe & of arblaste Ne hii ne miȝte vor oþer ginnes stones vp hom caste.

*fig.* *a* **1225** *Ancr. R.* 60 Al riht so, mid þen ilke wepnen, þ is mid scute of eien; mid spere of wundinde word. *Ibid.* 62 Hwo se is wise & iseli, wið þe schute wite hire, þ is wel hire eien: vor al þe vuel þ euer is cumeð of þen eien arewen.

**2.** The action of shooting or sprouting. (Cf. SHOOT *sb.*[1] 2.)

*a* **1300** *Leg. Holy Rood* ii. 132 Wiþ a cercle of seluer he bond ech ȝeres scute þere So þat wiþþinne þritti ȝer þis tre wox wel heie.

**3.** A sharp twinge of pain. (Cf. SHOOT *sb.*[1] 3 c.)

*a* **1300** *Marina* 202 in Horstm. *Altengl. Leg.* (1878) 173 Such shute com in þe womones hed,..& [heo] þer after wax riht wod.

**shute**[2] (ʃuːt). *Weaving.* [An old variant of SHOOT *sb.*[1], retained in this technical sense.]

**1.** The weft. (Cf. SHOOT *sb.*[1] 4.)

**1721** C. KING *Brit. Merch.* II. 17 Our Perpets that are all worsted Chains, and only the Shute of Woollen-Yarn, don't come to the Money. **1853** PERKINS *Haberdashery* (ed. 8) 45 The black is the warp, and the white or yellow (as the colour may be) the shute or shot. **1874** H. H. COLE *Catal. Ind. Art. S. Kens. Mus.* 217 A length of the thread, which he determines to make use of for his weft or shute.

**2.** A variety of raw silk; tram silk.

**1839** URE *Dict. Arts* 1102 There are three denominations of raw silk; viz., organzine, *trame* (shute or tram), and floss. **1868** [see TRAM *sb.*[1] 1].

**shute**[3] (ʃuːt). *dial.* Also 9 shut. [app. in part a dial. form of SHOOT *sb.* and partly a variant spelling of CHUTE *sb.*[1]]

**1.** A channel or open trough for conveying water, esp. to a lower level; a gutter fixed beneath the eaves of a building. (Cf. SHOOT *sb.*[1] 5 b.)

**1790** DUNSFORD *Hist. Mem. Tiverton* 106 *note*, The stream of water..is conveyed over a deep road behind the hospital by a leaded shute. **1836** MRS. BRAY *Tamar & Tavy* II. xxx. 291 *note*, To cut off three bits of lead about the size of a half farthing; each from three different shuts (meaning spouts) for the cure of fits. **1910** W. H. DAVIES in *Engl. Rev.* June 385 When Sparrows twitter in the shutes.

**2.** A sudden flood in a river, a freshet. (Cf. SHOOT *sb.*[1] 5, CHUTE *sb.*[1] 1.)

**1839** *Heref. Gloss.*, *Land-shut*, a land-flood. **1879** MISS JACKSON *Shropsh. Word-bk.* s.v., Theer's a tremenjus shut o' waiter i' the river.

**3. a.** A steep (artificial) channel or enclosed passage, down which ore, coal, grain, etc. is 'shot' to reach a receptacle below. (Cf. CHUTE *sb.*[1] 3, SHOOT *sb.*[1] 6 a.)

**1847** *Illustr. Lond. News* 21 Aug. 125/1 Stones were also put under her with long shutes from the deck. **1869** *Routledge's Ev. Boy's Ann.* 613 Conducts the meal to the 'hoppers', and through them down 'shutes' to a horizontal cylinder. **1877** BURROUGHS *Taxation* 137 Coal shutes..are taxable.

**b.** (See quot.)

**1882** JAGO *Anc. Lang. & Dial. Cornw.* 263 *Shute*,..the watering place where the women fill their pitchers from the 'shute'. Also, a small stream of water running from a shute or channel.

**4.** (See CHUTE *sb.*[1] 5.)

**1879** JENKINSON *Guide I. of Wight* 94 The St. Lawrence or Whitwell Shute.

**5.** = CHUTE *sb.*[1] 3 b.

**1961** R. P. HOBSON *Rancher takes Wife* iii. 47 Each had a corral system with shute and squeeze, and a log horse-pasture. **1971** J. S. GUNN *Distrib. Shearing Terms N.S.W.* 10 *Shute*, the opening through which a shorn sheep is pushed. *Ibid.*, *Shute*, the ramp outside down which a shorn sheep is pushed to the counting-out pen.

'**shut-eye.** *colloq.* [f. SHUT *v.* + EYE *sb.*[1]] Sleep; sleeping.

[**1896** KIPLING *Seven Seas* 217 (*heading*) The shut-eye sentry.] **1899** *Navy & Army Illustr.* 9 Dec. 307 The remainder of the dinner hour..is spent in smoking and perhaps dozing (a little shut-eye). **1923** C. E. MONTAGUE *Fiery Particles* 174 'We'll go to-morrow,' I said. 'A bit of shut-eye for me now.' **1936** A. HUXLEY *Eyeless in Gaza* xxiv. 346 Time for your spot of shut-eye. **1942** 'M. INNES' *Daffodil Affair* II. 68 Or game of cards... After a long party nothing like a hand or two before shut-eye. **1958** 'CASTLE' & 'HAILEY' *Flight into Danger* i. 25 Goodnight... I can sure use some shut-eye. **1977** *Time* 31 Jan. 6/1 Air Force Two indeed came equipped with a place to catch up on shut-eye between stops. 'Can you sleep on a plane?' asked Ford. Said Mondale, 'I'm going to find out.'

'**shut-in**, *a.* and *sb.* *orig. U.S.* [SHUT *ppl. a.* 2: cf. SHUT *v.* 15.] **A.** *adj.* **1.** Enclosed, hemmed in; *esp.* of a person: confined by severe weather or by physical or mental disability; isolated by self-absorption; abstracted.

**1849** CUPPLES *Green Hand* xiv. (1856) 139 As for the dead shut-in appearance of it,..you'd never think it was a river. **1909** *Sunday School Times* (Philadelphia) 27 Feb. 110 She had brought a handful of flowers and a heart full of sunshine to the shut-in mother. **1912** [see AUTISM]. **1932** *Brit. Jrnl. Psychol.* Apr. 301 Subject 6 has fewer friends..because she is so 'shut in' and difficult to get to know. **1943** J. B. PRIESTLEY *Daylight on Saturday* xviii. 133 You could tell by the shut-in look on their faces as they worked that they were busy thinking about these things. **1957** [see CLAUSTROPHOBIC *a.* b]. **1975** *Budget* (Sugarcreek, Ohio) 20 Mar. 7/4 Neal C. Troyer..and Dan L. Schwartz's spent Sat. at Nappanee visiting shut-in relatives, Bis. John L. Schwartz and Mrs. Lizzie Borkholder who is blind.

**2.** *Oil Industry.* Of or pertaining to oil and gas wells that are shut in; applied *esp.* to production capacity that is available but not being utilized.

**1931** *Economist* 28 Mar. 671/2 Production from the new East Texas fields is weakening prices, and the vast amount of shut-in production is a constant menace. **1960** *Fortnightly Rev.* (Anderson & Strudwick, Richmond, Va.) 19 Aug., The long struggle to obtain markets for Canada's large shut-in natural gas reserves was finally concluded last week. **1962** *Listener* 10 May 796/2 There remains a huge quantity of shut-in oil capacity overhanging the market and depressing prices. **1974** P. L. MOORE et al. *Drilling Practices Manual* xii. 314 The shut-in drill pipe pressure is easy to obtain if there is no back-pressure valve in the drill string.

**B.** *sb.* **1.** A person who is confined by severe weather or by a physical or mental disability; a withdrawn person, one who is isolated from normal social interaction.

**1904** *Prosp. Mass.* (U.S.A.) *Blind Assoc.* 2 The lonely and the unbusy, the shut-ins in body and in mind. **1949** *Richmond* (Va.) *Times-Dispatch* 1 Feb. 9/2 (*heading*) Salad dressing diet palls on storm shut-ins. **1952** *Catholic Times* 25 July 7/4 It is the 'shut-ins' and sufferers who give the greatest of all contributions—their sufferings. **1966** *Daily Tel.* 25 May 19/5 The first Sunday in June is Shut-In's Day, a special day set aside each year to remember the sick and housebound. **1975** C. POTOK *In Beginning* ii. 118 Better a man..who is a man of the world and can also learn than a bearded shut-in with the brain of a genius and the soul of a calf. **1979** *Arizona Daily Star* 22 July J6/4 Volunteers are needed to grocery shop for elderly shut-ins.

**2.** *Oil Industry.* A state or period of being shut in.

**1962** T. C. FRICK *Petroleum Production Handbk.* II. xxx. 7 Subsurface-pressure gauges are very useful in wells where liquids accumulate in the wellbore during shut-in. **1977** R. D. LANGENKAMP *Handbk. Oil Industry Terms & Phrases* (ed. 2) 152 There is a great difference between a shut-down and a shut-in... A well is shut in when its wellhead valves are closed, shutting off production.

Hence **shut-'in-ness**, the quality of being confined, secluded, or withdrawn into oneself.

**1913** D. H. LAWRENCE *Let.* ? 10 June (1962) I. 210 The world gets a queer feeling of shut-in-ness, as if it stifled one, the horizon being too near, the sky too low. **1920** *Chambers's Jrnl.* Jan. 23/2 Leaving the bowl of the crater with its strange sense of shut-in-ness. **1952** *Jrnl. Mental Sci.* XCVIII. 310 There is evidence that shy, shut-in people are more liable to schizophrenia than outgoing folk, but this is disputed, and some psychiatrists maintain that the 'shut-inness' is just an early stage of the illness.

**shuting(e**, obs. forms of SHOOTING *vbl. sb.*

**shut-off**, *sb.* and *adj.* Also **shutoff**. [Cf. SHUT *v.* 16.] **A.** *sb.* **1.** Something which shuts off: a tap, valve. Also, something used for stopping the operation of anything. Also *attrib.*

**1869** RANKINE *Machine & Hand-tools* Pl. G 1, The shut-off valve. **1892** *Photogr. Ann.* II. Advt. p. clxii, Automatic Shut-off. **1951** *Nucleonics* Nov. 16/2 Two..plates are used in controlling the reactor; the other two act as emergency shut-offs. **1970** N. ARMSTRONG et al. *First on Moon* xiii. 313 Okay, I'm going to open up the main shutoffs. Ascent feed closed. **1973** R. LUDLUM *Matlock Paper* xxii. 188 He found the shut-off button and pressed it. **1978** *N.Y. Times* 30 Mar. B 8 (Advt.), A pocket-size recorder that's perfect for school, office or home. Has end-of-tape shut-off.

**2.** A cessation of flow, supply, or activity.

**1889** *Cent. Dict.* 5606/1 *Shut-off*, stoppage of anything. **1919** *Summary of Operations Calif. Oil Fields* (Calif. State Mining Bur.) V. 1. 8 *Collar shut-off*, an accidental 'shut-off' supposed to be occasioned by the accumulation of material between the walls of a well and the casing at, or just above, a collar. **1942** *Sun* (Baltimore) 28 Dec. 18/4 A threatened shutoff of tin containers. **1974** *Spartanburg* (S. Carolina) *Herald-Jrnl.* 21 Apr. A2 (Advt.), Easily adjusts from powerful stream to fine spray to complete water shut-off. **1977** *Nature* 6 Jan. 29/1 Neither *alt* nor *mod* mutants affect the shutoff of host protein or rRNA synthesis *in vivo*.

**B.** *adj.* [SHUT *ppl. a.* 2.] Disconnected, stopped; isolated, withdrawn.

**1913** D. H. LAWRENCE *Sons & Lovers* v. 96 That peculiar shut-off look of the poor who have to depend on the favour of others. **1933** S. SPENDER *Poems* 45 The airliner with shut-off engines Glides over suburbs. **1939** C. ISHERWOOD *Goodbye to Berlin* 91, I felt a most marvellous sort of shut-off feeling from all the rest of the world. **1982** 'J. ROSS' *Death's Head* iv. 30 She said nothing more, waiting in a shut-off silence.

**shut-'out**, *a.* and *sb.* [SHUT *ppl. a.* 2: cf. SHUT *v.* 17.] **A.** *adj.* **1.** That is shut out or excluded; isolated, remote.

**1853** KANE *Grinnell Exp.* xli. (1856) 378 A relation with the shut-out world. **1853** MRS. GASKELL *Let.* Sept. (1966) 245 He..was rather intimate with Lord Palmerston at Cambridge, a pleasant soothing reflection now, in his shut-out life. **1860** GEO. ELIOT *Let.* 5 Sept. (1954) III. 342 It is a better house than I care to have, but as it is more shut out than anything we have seen..I accept the luxury.

**2.** In Bridge, of a bid: pre-emptive or otherwise intended to discourage the opposition from bidding. Also *transf.* of a financial bid.

**1916** [see PRE-EMPTIVE *a.* 2]. **1921** A. E. M. FOSTER *Auction Bridge* 52 Pre-emptive bids are, in my opinion, a mistake, unless they are of the nature of necessary shut-out bids. **1932** [see PRE-EMPTIVE *a.* 2]. **1959** REESE & DORMER *Bridge Players' Dict.* 167 An opening bid of three or four in a suit is in nearly all systems a weak shutout bid, based on a long suit with little or no outside strength. **1969** *Observer* 12 Jan. 11/1 Joe Hyman, chairman of Viyella International, ought to be worried by Courtaulds' 15s. 6d. a share shut-out bid for English Calico. **1982** *Times* 22 Jan. 13/5 The Council for the Securities Industry moved yesterday to ban 'shut out' takeover bids. It has become popular for one company to take control of another by buying or obtaining promises which give it 50 per cent control before anyone else can make counter proposals.

**3.** In Baseball and other games: characterized by the failure of the losers to score; that prevents the opponents from scoring. Chiefly *N. Amer.*

**1949** *Minot* (North Dakota) *Daily News* 22 July 8/8 He led his Grand Forks team to a one-hit shutout victory over Duluth. **1974** *News & Press* (Darlington, S. Carolina) 25 Apr. 11/1 Riding to victory on the two hit shutout pitching of Reece Ammons and the strong bat of Darrell Lloyd, the St. John's Blue Devils blitzed the Manning Monarchs 6–0. **1978** *Monitor* (McAllen, Texas) 21 May 3B/5 The Purple team scoring a 9–0 shutout win over the White unit in a controlled scrimmage.

**B.** *sb.* **1.** In Baseball and other games: a match or innings in which one side does not score; prevention from scoring. Also *fig.* Chiefly *N. Amer.*

**1889** *Pueblo* (Colorado) *Opinion* 21 July 4/5 The Springs were 'fated' from the start, and narrowly escaped a shut out. **1897** *Encycl. Sport* I. 79/2 (Baseball) *Shut out*, an innings in which a side does not score a run. **1936** *N.Y. Herald Tribune* 2 Oct. 10/2 The national scoreboard looked pretty bad. In fact it looked so much like a shutout for the team that you voted a change of management in order to give the country a chance to win the game. **1937** *Evening Standard* 25 Feb. 31 The Swiss may fully extend Britain, and maybe even break Foster's proud run of 'shut-outs'. **1955** *Edmonton Jrnl.* 4 Jan. 10/4 A few hours later he secured that elusive shutout that had escaped him so far this season. **1972** *Newsweek* 31 July 43/3 Fischer routed Mark Taimanov..6 to 0, for the first shutout in the history of grandmaster chess. **1972** *N.Y. Times* 3 Nov. 39/1 Senator McGovern may lose every state in the Union, and..his only chance of avoiding a shut-out lies with the people..in California and the District of Columbia. **1977** *Wandsworth Borough News* 16 Sept. 10/3 Putney St. Mary's Senior 'D' and U/12 'A' teams were in good scoring form, both winning their matches after scoring 10 goals apiece. For the 'D' team it was a complete shut-out. **1978** J. IRVING *World according to Garp* xix. 426 Roberta pitched a shutout.

**2.** A shut-out bid: see sense 2 of the adj. above.

**1936** E. CULBERTSON *Contract Bridge Complete* 17 *Shut-out*, an unnecessarily high bid, designed to make it difficult for the other side to enter the auction. **1982** *Observer* 17 Jan. 17/5 The Takeover Panel's consent to the 'shut-out'.

† **'shut-purse.** *Obs. rare*⁻¹. In 4 ssette pors. [f. SHUT *v.* + PURSE *sb.*] The 'shutter of purses': the title of the demon of miserliness.

**1340** *Ayenb.* 187 Of zuiche volke is lhord a dyeuel and mayster, þet is ine helle, þet is ycleped ssette pors.

**shutt** (ʃʌt). *local.* Also **shut.** [See SHOAT[1].] = GRAYLING 1 a.

**1939, 1952** [see PINK *sb.*[2] 2 b].

**'shuttable,** *a. nonce-wd.* [f. SHUT *v.* + -ABLE.] Capable of being closed.

**1854** GREENWOOD *Haps & Mishaps* 111 An easy carriage, open, but shuttable at will.

**'shuttance.** *dial.* [f. SHUT *v.* (sense 11) + -ANCE.] Riddance.

**1826** WILBRAHAM *Chesh. Gloss.* (ed. 2). **1856** P. THOMPSON *Hist. Boston* 723 Good shuttance of bad rubbish. **1886** MABEL PEACOCK *Tales & Rhymes* 124 (E.D.D.) She's gotten good riddance an' shuttance o' him.

**shutter** ('ʃʌtə(r)), *sb.* [f. SHUT *v.* + -ER[1].]

**1. a.** *gen.* One who or something which shuts.

**1611** COTGR., *Fermeur*, a shutter, closer, fastener. **1683** SNAPE *Anat. Horse* IV. ii. (1686) 153 The two other Muscles of the Eye-lid are called Shutters. **1788** *Act 28 Geo. III*, c. 51 §18 Watermen, Lock Shutters, Pound Keepers. **1907** *Outlook* 3 Jan. 12/1 Janus in the old mythology was the porter of heaven, the 'opener' and the 'shutter'.

**b.** Also with advs. as ***shutter up, -in.***

**1542** BRINKLOW *Lament.* (1874) 110 Well ye bysshoppes, and ye chanons of the churche of Beell, ye shutters vp of Godes Worde. **1611** COTGR., *Obturateur*, a stopper or shutter vp. *c* **1633** B. JONSON *Eupheme, Elegie on my Muse* 219 That houre, The last of houres, and shutter up of all. **1869** E. J. REED *Shipbuild.* xxi. 468 If the plate were a 'shutter in' of a strake both butts would require to be fitted against plates already in place.

**2.** *spec.* **a.** A movable wooden or iron screen, applied to the outside or the inside of a window, to shut out the light or to ensure privacy or safety.

It may consist of a single board or plate (hinged like a door, sliding in a frame, or altogether detachable), of a number of boards or plates hinged together, or of a combination of laths or flat rods of wood or metal working on rollers. A window may have one shutter or several.

Phr. ***to put up the shutters***: to bring one's business to a close for the day or permanently.

[**1683** TRYON *Way to Health* 178 The close drawing of the Window-Shutters, Hangings, and Curtains.] **1720** S. SEWALL *Diary* 20 Oct. (1882) III. 270 She..clos'd the Shutters. **1792** BELKNAP *Hist. New-Hampsh.* III. 258 Another hole is made in the side of the house for a window, which is occasionally closed with a wooden shutter. **1814** WORDSW. *Excurs.* VII. 178 Yet were the windows of the low abode By shutters weather-fended. **1819** *Ann. Reg., Chron.* (1820) 42 One of the watchmen heard a noise at one of the shutters [of the shop]. **1837** DICKENS *O. Twist* (1838) I. iv. 62 The undertaker had just put up the shutters of his shop, and was making some entries in his day-book. *Ibid.* v, Take down the shutters, yer idle young ruffian! **1863** *Appleby's Handbk. Mach. & Iron Work* 95 Patent revolving iron shutters. **1877** TROLLOPE *Amer. Senator* I. iii. 27 If..you won't have any client that isn't a gentleman, you might as well put up your shutters at once. **1889** LD. LYTTON in Lady B. Balfour *Lett.* (1906) II. 389 He is only lingering now to put up the Parliamentary shutters. **1890** CONAN DOYLE *Capt. Polestar*, etc. 172 A few old-established houses..put up their shutters and confessed themselves beaten.

¶ With reference to the use as an improvised litter or stretcher for carrying a person who has been wounded or taken ill.

**1843** DICKENS *Christmas Carol* ii. 60 As if the other fiddler had been carried home, exhausted, on a shutter. **1859** LEVER *Dav. Dunn* lxxi, I made it clear that you were really married, and to the daughter of a man that would send you home on a shutter, if you threw any doubt on it.

**b.** A folding cover hinged to a picture-frame in order to protect the picture from light, dust, etc.

*a* **1700** EVELYN *Diary* 8 Feb. 1645, That admirable paynting of Raphael..preserv'd in shutters of wainscott. **1762–71** H. WALPOLE *Vertue's Anecd. Paint.* (1786) I. 224 He..painted..in St. Peter's, the shutters of an altar-piece. **1909** *Q. Rev.* July 169 An admirable altar-piece..which consisted of a magnificent centre-piece of goldsmith's work and shutters adorned with paintings.

**c.** *Photogr.* A device for opening and closing the aperture of a lens in order to regulate the duration of the exposure.

**1862** *Catal. Internat. Exhib.* II. XIII. 9 A camera and shutter of new design. **1907** J. A. HODGES *Elem. Photogr.* (ed. 6) 17 A reliable shutter..of the roller-blind..type.

**d.** *Founding.* A gate or movable partition designed to cut off the passage to a mould from the channel in which the molten metal flows.

**1856** *Illustr. Lond. News* 23 Aug. 194/1 The shutter, or gate, was then lifted, and the metal allowed to flow.

**e.** *Organ-building. pl.* The louvre-boards forming one or more sides of the swell-box, which are opened and shut by a pedal or lever, so as to regulate the volume of sound from the swell-organ.

**1881** C. A. EDWARDS *Organs* 122 The swell shutters should be left open.

**f.** (See quot.)

**1883** GRESLEY *Gloss. Coal-mining* 220 *Shutter.* 1. A movable sliding door having balance weights attached, fitted within the outer casing of the Guibal fan, for regulating the size of the opening... 2. The vibrating arm or door of the Cooke Ventilator.

**g.** *Clockmaking.* (See quot.)

**1884** F. J. BRITTEN *Watch & Clockm.* 35 Bolt and Shutter. An obsolete contrivance for keeping clocks going while winding. During the going of the clock the shutter—a plate of metal—stood in front of the winding square.

**h.** A lid or slide for obscuring the light of a lamp or lantern.

**1910** J. BUCHAN *Prester John* i. 11 An evil-smelling old tin lantern with a shutter. **1911** *Act 1 & 2 Geo. V*, c. 45 §4 (4) Every light carried on a locomotive..shall be fitted with such shutters or other contrivances as will enable the light to be temporarily screened in an effective manner.

**i.** (See quot.)

**1898** *Encycl. Sport* II. 168/2 (Punt shooting) *Shutter*, the movable portion of the wash streak, through which the punter works his punt with paddles or set pole.

**j.** A device for regulating the supply of cooling air to the radiator of an internal-combustion engine.

**1918** *Aëronaut. Jrnl.* XXII. 119 A metal ring is in position on the underside of the radiators within reach of the pilot. This is apparently intended to carry a semi-circular disc to act as a radiator shutter. **1935** *Times* 2 Oct. 6/5 The temperature of the water is controlled by thermostatically-operated radiator shutters. **1957** FRAZEE & ESHELMAN *Tractors & Crawlers* v. 173 Shutters..are used on some tractors to reduce the air flow through the radiator. **1971** M. TAK *Truck Talk* 142 *Shutters*, louvers that are located between the tractor's grill and the radiator of the engine and that open and close like venetian blinds.

**3.** *attrib.* and *Comb.*: simple attrib., as ***shutter-bar, -bolt, -hinge, -panel***; objective, as ***shutter-maker.*** Also **shutter-blind**, a blind with louvres to admit air; **shutter-case**, a box or fitting into which shutters may be put or folded when not in use; **shutter-dam**, a dam having gates which are opened and closed by hydraulic pressure obtained by water driven through pipes by means of a turbine; **shutter eye** (see quot. *a* 1884); **shutter-front, -lid**, a covering or lid constructed to roll up after the manner of a flexible shutter; **shutter-rebate**, a groove cut into a window-frame to support a shutter; **shutter-stand** = *shutter-case*; **shutter-telegraph** = SEMAPHORE; **shutter weir**, a type of movable weir consisting of one or more leaves pivoted about a horizontal axis at or towards the bottom and held nearly vertical until released.

**1737** *Salmon's Country Builder's Estimator* (ed. 2) 103 Upright Window-Bars, *Shutter-Bars. **1833** LOUDON *Encycl. Archit.* §555 In *shutter blinds..the movement is effected by a lever handle fixed on one of the luffer boards. **1737** *Salmon's Country Builder's Estimator* (ed. 2) 112 *Shutter Bolts are sold from 10*s.* 6*d.* to 18*s.* 6*d.* per Dozen. **1810** *Hull Improv. Act* 55 [To] make any..*shutter-cases or shutter-stands. **1884** KNIGHT *Dict. Mech.* Suppl., *Shutter Dam. *a* **1884** KNIGHT *Dict. Mech.* Suppl. 807/2 **Shutter eye*, an eye for hanging a shutter to, having a projecting flange or support, which is built into the wall. **1930** *Gen. Catal. Tools & Supplies* (Buck & Hickman Ltd.) 1081 (*heading*) Pointed gate and shutter hooks and eyes. **1887** *Pall Mall Gaz.* 22 Aug. 11/2 A finely wrought gilt frame with a *shutter front to conceal its contents. **1737** *Salmon's Country Builder's Estimator* (ed. 2) 107 *Shutter-Hinges are sold by the Dozen. **1901** *Lady's Realm* X. 652/2 A small secretaire in satin-wood with a *shutter lid. **1881** *Instr. Census Clerks* (1885) 54 *Shutter maker. **1903** CONRAD & HUEFFER *Romance* iii. 20 Rangsley knocked on a *shutter-panel. **1901** P. M. JOHNSTON in *Archæol. Jrnl.* 64 A shallow *shutter-rebate. **1810** *Shutter-stand [see *shutter-case*]. **1859** SALA *Tw. round Clock* (1861) 301 Some [dancers] are inclined..to ..imitate the action of the old *shutter-telegraphs with their arms. **1880** *Engineering* 30 Jan.. 102/1 The needle and *shutter weirs had been the most extensively adopted, and were the best types of movable weirs... The shutter weir was the most suitable for high weirs across rapid rivers, and where the navigation was conducted by flushing. **1928** F. JOHNSTONE-TAYLOR *River Engin.* iii. 69 The shutter weir, as a form of barrage, is not a new introduction, having been used..principally in Central Europe, for a number of years.

**b.** *Photogr.* (cf. 2 c). In ***shutter-adjustment, -speed, -work***; instrumental, ***shutter-exposure, -exposed*** adj.; objective, ***shutter-setting.*** Also **shutter-bug** *slang* (orig. *U.S.*), an enthusiastic photographer; also *attrib.*; **shutter priority**, used *attrib.* and *absol.* to designate automatic working in which the user sets the shutter speed and leaves the appropriate aperture to be set by the camera when the exposure is made; **shutter release**, the button on a camera that is pressed to cause the shutter to open; **shutter speed**, the nominal time for which a shutter is open at a given setting.

**1892** *Photogr. Ann.* II. 331 The lens and part of the *shutter adjustment are in view. **1940** *Amer. Speech* XV. 357 The amateur..is known as a clicker, a snapper,..a *shutterbug. **1972** *New Nation* (Singapore) 25 Nov. 9/8 It is unspoilt by shutter-bug tourists. **1979** *Arizona Daily Star* 8 Apr. 1. 3/6 (Advt.), 4 canyon tours... Our best for shutterbugs includes round trip transportation & lodgings plus photo stop at Casa Grande Ruins. **1891** *Anthony's Photogr. Bull.* IV. 323 A rapid *shutter exposed plate. **1889** *Ibid.* II. 317 These plates after development are compared with the negative of *shutter exposure. **1974** L. GAUNT *Canon Reflex Way* 24 The system can be converted to *shutter-priority automatic working. **1978** *SLR Camera* Aug. 31/1 (Advt.), With the new Minolta XD7 a flick of a switch allows you to change the system to suit the subject —shutter priority *or* aperture priority *or* fully manual. **1958** *Newnes Compl. Amat. Photogr.* 37 At the B setting, the shutter remains open as long as the *shutter release is kept pressed. **1979** *Amat. Photographer* 30 May 97/3 Initial pressure on the shutter release lights the viewfinder LEDs which indicate the speed to be chosen by the camera. **1892** *Photogr. Ann.* II. Advt. p. cclxxx, Plate-changing and *shutter-setting is effected by simply drawing out and pushing back the rod shown in block. **1889** *Anthony's Photogr. Bull.* II. 335 The *shutter speed was slower in comparison with the moving train. **1906** R. C. BAYLEY *Compl. Photographer* xiii. 158 In the Frena camera a method of regulating the shutter speed by regulating the size of the opening in a rotating disc was employed. **1977** J. HEDGECOE *Photographer's Handbk.* 162 Fast shutter speeds—say 1/250 sec or shorter—usually eliminate problems of camera shake. **1891** *Anthony's Photogr. Bull.* IV. 323 For rapid *shutter work..the best plan is to use a medium quantity of alkali.

**shutter** ('ʃʌtə(r)), *v.* [f. SHUTTER *sb.*]

**1.** *trans.* To close with a shutter. Also with *adv.*

**1826** B. HALL in Lockhart *Scott* (1839) VIII. 360, I found the windows shuttered up. **1856** LEVER *Martins of Cro' M.* xxix. 309 The doors were closed, the windows shuttered. **1863** DICKENS *Uncomm. Trav.* xxi, Here is Garraway's, bolted and shuttered hard and fast. **1897** *Spectator* 26 June 909/1 An appeal to the people of Kilrush to shutter their shops. **1910** J. BUCHAN *Prester John* i. 15 Tam who had seized and shuttered his lantern, coming last.

**b.** *transf.* and *fig.*

**1882** *Society* 16 Dec. 16/2 The basilisk glance..had to be shuttered down. *c* **1886** KIPLING *Other Verses* (1899) 102, I took a country twice the size of France, And shuttered up one doorway in the North. **1887** HARDY *Woodlanders* xviii, The windows of Fitzpiers's soul being at present shuttered. **1892** KIPLING *Barrack-room Ballads* 175, I barred my gates with iron, I shuttered my doors with flame.

**2.** *refl.* (with advb. complement). To close oneself *in*, shut oneself *off*, with shutters.

**1878** STEVENSON *Inland Voy.* 60 A workman or a pedlar cannot shutter himself off from his less comfortable neighbours. **1880** *Athenæum* 14 Aug. 203 The farmers.. would shutter themselves in and drink strong beer and gin for days and days on end.

**shuttered** ('ʃʌtəd), *ppl. a.* [f. SHUTTER *v.* and *sb.* + -ED.] Closed with shutters; provided with shutters. Also *fig.*

**1845** TALFOURD *Vacation Rambles* I. 155 Green-shuttered white 'Pensions'. **1885** R. L. & F. STEVENSON *Dynamiter* ii. 9 Shop after shop displayed its shuttered front. **1901** P. M. JOHNSTON in *Archæol. Jrnl.* 68 It must have had its grated and shuttered opening. **1927** J. R. THEOBALD in *Oxf. Poetry* 34 A clothèd woman all alone Beneath her shuttered sky. **1930** R. CAMPBELL *Adamastor* 76 The day burns through their blood Like a white candle through a shuttered hand. **1957** M. STEWART *Thunder on Right* i. 15 Her heart began to beat lightly and fast, but her face was shuttered, and she gave no sign.

**'shuttering,** *vbl. sb.* [f. SHUTTER *v.* and *sb.* + -ING[1].] **1. a.** The action of the vb. SHUTTER. **b.** Material for making shutters.

**1868** W. CORY *Lett. & Jrnls.* (1897) 253 This is a detestable practice, shuttering; I rebel against it. **1898** MACEY *Specif. Detail* 371 Movable sheet-iron shuttering.

**2. a.** = *formwork* s.v. FORM *sb.* 22. **b.** = FORM *sb.* 18 b.

**1895** E. DE V. BUCKINGHAM *Contractors' Price-Bk.* 371 (*heading*) Concrete building casing and shuttering (per yard super). **1902** *Min. Proc. Inst. Civil Engin.* CXLIX. 298 If the shutterings or drums are well made and kept well greased, a fairly good and even face can be obtained by mixing the concrete rather wet, and well chopping down behind the shutterings or drums. **1919** *Spectator* 25 Oct. 539/2 The soil..to be used without admixture..and to be thrown direct into the shutterings. **1939** *Archit. Rev.* LXXXVI. 35 The facing slabs..can be used, when braced, as external shuttering to a reinforced concrete wall. **1959** *Listener* 27 Aug. 316/2 Exposed concrete shows the least incidents of the shuttering, the joints of the planks, the fibres and knots of the wood. **1976** *Star* (Sheffield) 20 Nov. (Advt.), Shuttering joiners required.

**shutterless** ('ʃʌtəlɪs), *a.* [f. SHUTTER *sb.* + -LESS.] Without a shutter.

**1830** LYTTON *P. Clifford* i, A high, narrow, shutterless casement. **1885** R. BUCHANAN *Annan Water* i, The wind.. rattled the shutterless windows.

**'shutterwise,** *adv.* [f. SHUTTER *sb.* + -WISE.] After the manner of or like a shutter.

**1880** MRS. R. O'REILLY *Sussex Stor.* I. 315 He swept the boots and all his paraphernalia off the board, and fastened it shutterwise.

**shutting** ('ʃʌtɪŋ), *vbl. sb.* [f. SHUT *v.* + -ING[1].]

**1. a.** In trans. senses of the verb; closing, fastening up, drawing together, etc.

? *a* **1366** CHAUCER *Rom. Rose* 1598 For ther is noon so litel thing So hid, ne closed with shitting, That it ne is sene. *c* **1440** *Promp. Parv.* 445/2 Schetynge, or lokkynge wythe lokkys, *seracio.* **1562** *Child-Marriages* 116 The shuttinge of windowes. **1670** G. H. *Hist. Cardinals* I. III. 75 The said shutting of their mouths. *a* **1754** SIR J. STRANGE *Rep.* (1782) I. 615 The day of the shutting of the books. **1779** H. WALPOLE *Let. to Mann* 7 July, The shutting of our ports against France.

**b.** Welding, splicing.

**1490** in *Archæol. Cant.* (1886) XVI. 298 For schettyng of the..bell claper viij d. **1495** *Naval Acc. Hen. VII* (1896) 150 Shutyng & Amendyng of v boltes. **1555** *Ludlow Churchw.*

*Acc.* (Camden) 62 For shutynge on of the old hynges.. ij d. **1794** *Rigging & Seamanship* I. 78 *Shutting* is joining or welding one piece of iron to another.

**2.** Something which closes fast, a bar, shutter. Usually *pl.* Also, a junction, a place where two things come together.

*c* **1440** *Promp. Parv.* 445/2 Schetynge, or schettynge, or sperynge, *clausura.* **1450–80** tr. *Secreta Secret.* xxxv. 24 Than frote welle thyn heed, for it openyth the shettyngis of þi brayne. **1610** BARROUGH *Meth. Physick* I. xxiii. (1639) 39 You must.. fasten cupping glasses to the shutting of the joynts. *a* **1679** SIR J. MOORE *Eng. Interest* (1703) 108 The Bar or Shutting [of the door of a bee-hive] is to be made four square, of some heavy Matter, as Lead.

**3.** In intransitive senses of the verb: The close of a day, evening, etc.; nightfall.

**1598** GREENWEY *Tacitus, Ann.* I. v. (1622) 8 In the night, or in the shutting of the euening. **1699** *Relat. Sir T. Morgan's Progr.* 13 The Major-General desired his Excellency, that he would give orders to them.. to keep themselves in readiness.. for at the shutting of the Night he would fall on. **1924** C. MACKENZIE *Heavenly Ladder* xix. 247 They finished decorating the church just before the shutting in of a still and humid dusk.

**4. a.** In comb. with various advs.

*c* **1440** *Promp. Parv.* 445/2 Schettynge in, *inclusio...* Schettynge owte, *exclusio.* **1577** tr. *Bullinger's Decades* I. ix. 86 In the shuttinge vppe and ende of all ages. **1583** MELBANCKE *Philotimus* Z iv b, The setting of the Sun, and shutting in of nighte, belong to Zephyr. **1642–4** VICARS *God in Mount* 191 A little before shutting in of day-light. **1722** DE FOE *Plague* (Rtldg.) 54, I mention'd.. shutting of Houses up. **1798** in Nicolas *Disp. Nelson* (1846) VII. p. clvi, The thickness of the smoke at the shutting in of the evening. **1838** DICKENS *O. Twist* xxvii, The shop was not closed, although it was past the usual hour of shutting-up. **1875** SCRIVENER *Lect. Grk. Test.* 14 The deliberate shutting out of a large.. portion of available evidence. **1891** *Daily News* 3 Mar. 2/4 The shutting down of the mines in America. **1899** *Allbutt's Syst. Med.* VII. 677 The sudden shutting off of the blood-supply to a limited area of the brain.

**b.** Specific uses: **shutting off** (see quot.); **shutting up,** (*a*) see quot. 1852; (*b*) welding; (*c*) ***shutting-up time***: the hour for closing the shop, etc.; **shutting together** = *shutting up* (*b*).

**1884** F. J. BRITTEN *Watch & Clockm.* 240 *Shutting Off. A term used to describe the operation of throwing the winding wheels [of a fusee watch] out of action. **1852** G. W. JOHNSON *Cottage Gard. Dict.* 824 *Shutting-up is closing the lights of frames, pits, greenhouses, and stoves, which have been opened for the admission of air. **1883** CRANE *Smithy & Forge* 43 Joining two pieces of bar or rod together which the smith usually denominates 'shutting up' or '*shutting together'. **1889** 'R. BOLDREWOOD' *Robbery under Arms* xxx, It was latish.. and near shutting-up time.

**5.** *attrib.*, as **shutting joint, post,** the joint or post against which a door or gate closes; **shutting stile** (see quot. 1955).

**1823** *Practical Builder* iii. 182 (*heading*) On the formation of the shutting-joints of doors. **1929** T. CORKHILL in R. Greenhalgh *Joinery & Carpentry* I. III. 171 The hinge is on the concave and the result is an extremely awkward shutting joint. **1944** N. W. KAY *Pract. Carpenter & Joiner* vi. 140 As a curved rebate is not always possible the shutting joint is set out to a straight surface tangential to the greatest radius on the framing. *a* **1877** KNIGHT *Dict. Mech.* III. 2170/1 *Shutting post*, the post or joint against which a gate or door is closed. **1909** *Chambers's Jrnl.* Nov. 764/1 On the under side of the shutting post is a small roller which runs on to a bracket on the shutting post itself, thus taking up the whole weight of the gate when it is closed. **1909** WEBSTER, Shutting stile. **1955** N. W. KAY *Mod. Building Encycl.* 613 *Shutting stile*, door or window stile opposite the hanging stile.

**'shutting,** *ppl. a.* [-ING².] That shuts.

**1634** in *Archæologia* XXXV. 197 Fower shutting windowes. **1803** STRANGFORD *Poems of Camoens* (1810) 52 When.. night-drops bathe each shutting bell [of a flower]. **1850** T. T. LYNCH *Theoph. Trinal* v. 83 A shutting gate.. we hear. **1900** ELWORTHY *Horns of Honour* ii. 143 The grinning opening and shutting jaws.

**shuttle** (ˈʃʌt(ə)l), *sb.*¹ Forms: 1 sciutil, scytel, 4–9 (now *dial.*) **shittle, 5 shotil, shetil, schytle, schetyl(le, s(c)hutylle, 6 shetyll, shuttyll, shyttel(l, shittell, shettle, shoottle, 7 shutle, shuttel, 6– shuttle.** [OE. *scytel* ? masc.:—prehistoric **skutil* f. Teut. root **skut-*: see SHOOT *v.* Cf. ON. *skutill* harpoon; also Sw., Da. *skyttel* (of obscure history) and Da. *skytte*, Norw. *skyt, skjøt* = sense 2 below.]

†**1.** *OE.* A dart, missile, arrow. *Obs.*

*c* **875** *Erfurt Gloss.* 1177 *Jaculum*, sciutil. *c* **1000** *Ags. Ps.* (Thorpe) lxiii. 7 Syndon hyre wita scytelum cilda æȝhwæs onlicost.

**2. a.** An instrument used in weaving for passing the thread of the weft to and fro from one edge of the cloth to the other between the threads of the warp. ***fly shuttle*** (see FLY *sb.*² 8).

The normal form of the shuttle resembles that of a boat, whence its name in various langs. (L. *navicula*, F. *navette*, G. *weberschiff*). Along the middle is an axis or 'spindle', on which revolves the 'quill' or 'bobbin', a cylinder carrying the thread of the weft.

**1338** in Dugdale *Monasticon* (1819) II. 585/2 Item pro weblomes emptis xx*s*... Item pro iiij shittles pro eodem opere ij*s* vj*d*. *c* **1400** *York Memorandum Bk.* (Surtees) I. 85 Cum instrumento dicti artificii vocato *shotil.* **14..** *Nom.* in Wr.-Wülcker 728/15 *Hec navecula*, schetylle. **1483** *Cath. Angl.* 338/2 A Schutylle (*v.r.* shvtylle), *nauicula, panus.* **1510** STANBRIDGE *Vocabula* (W. de W.) C j b, *Pecten*, the shuttyll. **1570** LEVINS *Manip.* 195/40 A shuttle, *radius.* **1577** HANMER *Anc. Eccl. Hist., Evagrius* IV. vii. (1585) 473 A weauers shittell. **1585** WITHER *ABC for Laymen* 131 The sliding to and fro of the shettle in weauing. **1613** PURCHAS *Pilgrimage* (1614) 736 The Fishers Boats are made like to a Weauers Shutle. **1676** HOBBES *Iliad* XXII. 444 She trembling stood, and let her Shittle fall. **1714** GAY *Sheph. Wk.* Prol. 71 Ye Weavers, all your Shuttles throw. **1831** G. R. PORTER *Silk Manuf.* 221 The shuttle is formed from a piece of boxwood. **1908** [MISS E. FOWLER] *Betw. Trent & Ancholme* 84 John's loom and shuttle could be heard.

**b.** *fig.* and in similative use.

**1598** SHAKS. *Merry W.* v. i. 25, I fear not Goliah with a Weauers beame, because I know also, life is a Shuttle. **1742** YOUNG *Nt. Th.* iv. 809 How swift the shuttle flies, that weaves thy shroud. **1844** EMERSON *Lect., Young Amer.* Wks. (Bohn) II. 293 The locomotive and the steamboat like enormous shuttles shoot every day across the thousand various threads of national descent. **1896** KIPLING *Seven Seas* 4 Swift shuttles of an Empire's loom that weave us, main to main. **1896** A. AUSTIN *England's Darling* II. iv, When War's loud shuttle shall have woven peace.

**3.** *transf.* **a.** A thread-carrying device in the form of a weaver's shuttle, used for knotting, tatting and embroidery.

**1767** MRS. DELANY *Lett.* 4 Jan., Ser. II. (1862) I. 91 Mrs. Jeffreys has bought me a very elegant shuttle for two guineas. ? **1770** MRS. RAVAUD *Let. to Mrs. Delany* 10 Nov. *ibid.* 309, I want to know if the inclosed knotting is what you would have it... Its merit.. is entirely owing to the instrument with which it is fabricated, the nonpareille shuttle of singular service. **1882** CAULFEILD & SAWARD *Dict. Needlework* 476 [Recent improvements in Tatting.] The use of a second thread or Shuttle, which enables straight lines and scallops to be worked, as well as the original ovals.

**b.** A reciprocating thread-holder in a sewing-machine, which carries the lower thread through the loop of the upper one to make a lock-stitch.

**1846** in *Abridgm. Specif. Patents, Sewing* (1871) 10 [The] application of a shuttle, in combination with a needle. **1860** *Ure's Dict. Arts* III. 647 A small shuttle, which has a horizontal motion beneath the cloth, is now caused to pass through this loop, carrying with it its own thread. **1875** KNIGHT *Dict. Mech.* 2116/2 The [Singer sewing-] machine makes a lock-stitch by means of a straight eye-pointed needle and a longitudinally reciprocating shuttle.

**c.** In a telephone (see quot.).

**1879** PRESCOTT *Sp. Telephone* 388 One of its coils is connected.. to a V-shaped piece of metal, termed the shuttle, which, in its normal position, rests with one end against an adjustable screw.

**d.** A curved type-bar (in some typewriters) guided into position by a race.

**1911** in WEBSTER.

**4.** A shuttlecock. Also the game. Now only in *Badminton.*

*c* **1440** *Promp. Parv.* 447/1 Schytle, chyldys game, *sagitella.* *a* **1591** H. SMITH *Serm.* (1622) 252 Or like unto a Shittle, which flittereth from the hand of a child. **1895** *Official Laws Badminton* 11.

†**5.** = RADIUS *sb.* 1 c. *Obs. rare*⁻¹.

Perh. only a mistranslation of L. *radius*, one sense of which is 'weaver's shuttle'.

**1662** *Comenius' Janua Ling. Triling.* 48 One arm bone; two of the elbow, (the ell and shuttle).

**6.** †**a.** A trochoid shell (see quot. 1750). *Obs.* **b.** In full ***weaver's shuttle***, a shuttle-shell, esp. *Radius volva*; also, the shell of this gastropod.

**1750** POCOCKE *Trav.* (Camden) 46 *Trochi entrochi...* The trochi are many of them like shuttles.. some are an oblong oval, which they call shuttles: the country people call them fairy stones. **1815** BURROW *Elem. Conchol.* 199 Bulla Volva. Weaver's Shuttle. B. Birostris. Bastard Weaver's Shuttle. B. Gibbosa. Short gibbous Shuttle; the Gondola. **1861** P. P. CARPENTER in *Rep. Smithsonian Instit.* 1860, 195 The Weaver's Shuttle (*Radius volva*). *Ibid.* 196 The creature folds its foot round the *Gorgonias* on which it lives, carrying its shuttle gracefully over its head.

**7.** A book name for certain species of moths.

**1832** J. RENNIE *Butterfl. & Moths* 51 The Shuttle (*Agrotis radia*, Curtis)... Probably a variety of *A. Radiola...* The small Shuttle (*A. Radiola*, Stephens) appears in June.

**8. a.** A shuttle-train (see 9 b).

**1895** in *Funk's Stand. Dict.*

**b.** A shuttle service of aircraft; *esp.* one operated by an airline for which reservation of seats is not a requirement; an aircraft flying on such a service.

**1942** [see *shuttle route*, sense 9 a below]. **1944, 1961** [see *shuttle service*, sense 9 b below]. **1964** MRS. L. B. JOHNSON *White House Diary* 9 Apr. (1970) 104, I could have caught a much later plane if I could only have ridden the shuttle. **1971** R. THOMAS *Backup Men* x. 84, I got in line for the Eastern shuttle... It's rumored that if Eastern doesn't have a seat for you on its regular shuttle to New York, it will roll out a special plane just for you. **1973** *Daily Tel.* 11 Sept. 6/4 British Caledonian is to extend its low fare 'Moonjet Service'—Britain's first no-reservation walk-on, walk-off shuttle—to Belfast. **1977** *Time* 10 Oct. 4/1 Freddie Laker's bargain-basement transatlantic shuttle, the no-frills, no-reservations Skytrain, was finally aloft, carrying passengers between London and New York at the rock-bottom round-trip fare of $236. **1978** R. LUDLUM *Holcroft Covenant* xiii. 153 The shuttles to Paris were frequent, the customs procedures lax.

**c.** More fully, ***space shuttle***. A space rocket with wings enabling it to land like an aircraft and be used repeatedly.

Quot. 1960 is fictional.

**1960** 'J. WYNDHAM' in *New Worlds* Nov. 41 The acceleration in that shuttle would spread you all over the floor. **1969** *New Scientist* 5 June 513/2 NASA has announced the formation of task groups to look into.. a re-usable low-cost 'Space Shuttle' to relay men and materials to and from the [space] station... The space shuttle.. would be fired off vertically, shed its fuel tanks and, upon return, land horizontally at an airport. *Ibid.* 2 Oct. 7/1 Another shuttle plying on a regular basis between Cape Kennedy and this large space laboratory. **1972** *National Observer* (U.S.) 27 May 6/3 The shuttle's primary mission is to carry satellites into earth orbit and release them, at a cost below that of the expendable rockets now used to launch satellites. **1981** *Daily Tel.* 15 Apr. 1 The American space shuttle landed on a dry lake bed in California's Mojave Desert yesterday to complete the maiden flight of the first re-usable rocketship.

**d.** A series of journeys for the purpose of shuttle diplomacy (see sense 9 b below).

**1975** *Daily Tel.* 29 Aug. 24/3 (*heading*) Raid as peace shuttle nears end. *Ibid.*, Dr. Kissinger completed the last legs of his Middle East shuttle yesterday. **1977** *Time* 17 Jan. 30 It was a diplomatic shuttle, but not exactly in the Kissinger mode. *Ibid.*, Thus [Ivor] Richard's shuttle has been dubbed by some officials and journalists in southern Africa a safari of salvation.

**9.** *attrib.* and *Comb.* **a.** Obvious combs. (senses 2 and 3) as ***shuttle-driver, -maker, -quill, -winder***; (sense 6) as ***shuttle-tribe***; (sense 8) ***shuttle bus, flight, plane, raid, rocket, route, ship***; also ***shuttle-shaped*** adj., ***shuttlewise*** adv.

**1951** *Sun* (Baltimore) 18 May 3/1 The cars—some are called '*shuttle busses' because they operate from the West (executive offices) Wing to the East Wing [of the White House]—carry messengers too. **1972** *Times* 8 June 7/2 Traffic jams.. that officials hoped would be averted by the bicycles and shuttle buses. **1979** *United States 1980/81* (Penguin Travel Guides) 259 During the summer, a shuttlebus runs from the lakefront to the courthouse. **1801** *Encycl. Brit.* Suppl. II. 796/1 From its lower end there go two small cords to the *shuttle drivers. **1944** *News* (Tuscaloosa, Ala.) 25 June 1/3 Three crewmen also were lost as a result of the attack on the fields, apparently those used by Italian based and Britain-based bombers in the *shuttle flights over Axis targets. **1961** *N.Y. Times* 10 May 90/5 The shuttle flights between the two pairs of cities carried 6,147 passengers in their first week... Passengers arriving by bus, cab or car would be able to step out at the terminal door within 150 feet of the shuttle planes. **1977** *New Yorker* 19 Sept. 40/1 She had to drive home alone, while he took a shuttle flight in the opposite direction. **1412** in Riley *Mem. Lond.* (1868) 584 [William Blakeney] *shetil-maker. **1944** *Britannica Bk. Year* 770/1 *Shuttle*, combining form. Involving vehicles, especially aircraft, making repeated trips between fixed points, as.. 'shuttle raid', '*shuttle plane'. **1961** [see *shuttle flight* above]. **1976** J. CROSBY *Nightfall* xii. 68 [He] left for the shuttle plane to New York. **1661** PETTY in Birch *Hist. Roy. Soc.* (1756) I. 59 To which purpose there is somewhat considerable in the winding the yarn upon these *shuttle-quills. **1943** *Time* 18 Oct. 85/1 The.. pilot flew on his first mission eight weeks ago, joined the first *shuttle raid on Germany, flew safely to Africa, [etc.]. **1953** J. N. LEONARD *Flight into Space* 87 They say that von Braun's great *shuttle rockets—to say nothing of his space station—would surely fail. **1942** *R.A.F. Jrnl.* 30 May 22 The danger zone, which is the *shuttle route of the German Focke-Wulf Condors. **1802** BINGLEY *Anim. Biog.* (1813) II. 224 The eyes are lodged in a *shuttle-shaped band of black. **1869** E. NEWMAN *Brit. Moths* 317 The Shuttle-shaped Dart (*Agrotis puta*). **1959** *Amazing Stories* June 12/1 Hubbard visited the spaceport.. and watched the *shuttle-ships come and go. **1861** P. P. CARPENTER in *Rep. Smithsonian Instit.* 1860, 196 None of the Cowry or *Shuttle tribe have any operculum. *a* **1877** KNIGHT *Dict. Mech.* III. 2171/2 **Shuttle-winder*, a device for winding a shuttle, such as the round shuttle of the Wheeler and Wilson sewing-machine, or a tatting-shuttle. **1879** HOWELLS *Lady of Aroostook* iii. 38 The ferryboats thrust *shuttlewise back and forth between either shore made a refreshing sound.

**b.** Special comb.: † **shuttle armature** *Electr.*, an armature having a single coil wound upon an elongated iron former shaped like a shuttle (*obs.*); **shuttle-bearer,** the lay or batten of a loom; **shuttle bombing,** bombing carried out by planes taking off from one base and landing at another; so **shuttle bomber; shuttle-bone,** † (*a*) each of the bones of the forearm; (*b*) the navicular bone in the foot of a horse; **shuttle-box,** † (*a*) the cavity in the side of a shuttle to hold the spindle (*obs.*); (*b*) 'a tray or case at the end of the shuttle-race to receive the shuttle' (Knight *Dict. Mech.* 1875); **shuttle car,** a vehicle for making frequent short journeys, *spec.* one for the underground haulage of coal; **shuttle-carrier,** the arm or other device which reciprocates the shuttle in a sewing-machine; **shuttle-crab,** a paddle-crab, *Callinectes hastatus* (*Cent. Dict.* 1891); **shuttle diplomacy,** diplomatic activity involving a series of journeys to and fro, *esp.* by a mediator travelling between disputing parties; hence **shuttle diplomat; shuttle-kissing** (see quot.); † **shuttle-prick,** the spindle of a shuttle; **shuttle-race,** the ledge or track along which the shuttle passes; **shuttle service,** a service of shuttle-trains; more widely, any transport service in which vehicles or aircraft travel to and fro between fixed points at frequent intervals; **shuttle-shell,** a gastropod of the genus *Radius*; † **shuttle-spire,** ? = *shuttle-prick*; **shuttle-train,** a train running a short distance to and fro, as on a short branch line; † **shuttle-trough** = *shuttle-box* (*a*); † **shuttle-wound armature** *Electr.* = *shuttle armature* above (*obs.*).

**1890** SLINGO & BROOKER *Electr. Engin.* viii. 241 That the design of the *shuttle armature is faulty may easily be proved, for, after being rotated for a little time, the iron shuttle or core gets quite warm. **1924** S. R. ROGET *Dict. Elect. Terms* 226/2 *Shuttle armature*, a simple form of armature now rarely used, except in very small machines, with a single coil connected to a two-part commutator and lying in the two broad slots in an elongated core built up of stampings in the shape of an H with rounded sides. Also called *Siemens 'H' armature*. **1835** URE *Philos. Manuf.* 350 Exercising their arms and shoulders..by resting their hands on the lay or *shuttle-bearer. **1944** *Yank* 28 July 7 They are not *shuttle bombers, and they did not fly from Italy to Russia intentionally. **1944** *Newsweek* 10 Jan. 27 Last summer the RAF and the Eighth both tried *shuttle bombing. **1954** *Times* 10 Aug. 4/1 The city may be important for another reason—as one end of a shuttle-bombing route similar to those which worked so effectively in Europe. **1688** HOLME *Armoury* II. xvii. 417/2 The Cubitus..doth consist of two Bones; the *Shuttle Bones. **1832** PERCIVALL *Anat. Horse* 60 The Navicular or Shuttle Bone (*Os Naviculare*). **1688** *Shuttle box [see *shuttle trough* below]. **1888** *Encycl. Brit.* XXIV. 464/1 (*Weaving*), A ledge ..which forms the 'shuttle race' for carrying the shuttle in 'picking' from and to the shuttle boxes at each end of the lay. **1905** CALKINS & HOLDEN *Mod. Advertising* v. 89 They also have many *shuttle cars, or [street]cars that make short runs. **1956** ATKINSON & WHITE in D. L. Linton *Sheffield* 276 The shuttle cars transport the ore to the main-road conveyors which discharge the ironstone at the surface into wagons. **1979** *Jrnl. R. Soc. Arts* CXXVII. 89/2 Rubber tyred shuttle cars can be used from the continuous miner to the main transport system if the floor is hard enough. **1860** *Ure's Dict. Arts* III. 649 (*Sewing-machine*), At the commencement of the return of the shuttle, an inclined piece upon the *shuttle carrier bears against a lateral stud upon one end of a short rocking or oscillatory shaft. **1974** *Between Lines* (Newtown, Pa.) 15 Feb. 2/3 So beware of an over-celebration of Kissinger's *shuttle diplomacy, heroic as it's been. **1976** *Birmingham Post* 16 Dec. 2/5 Mr. Richard plans a round of 'shuttle diplomacy' in Southern Africa seeking support for more direct British involvement in the decolonisation of Rhodesia. **1979** H. KISSINGER *White House Years* p. xxi, The October 1973 Middle East war and the 'shuttle diplomacy' that followed. **1977** *Time* 13 June 80 Or consider Henry Kissinger. Understandably, Citizen K's style has changed perceptibly from that of the *shuttle diplomat. **1908** *Bath Daily Chron.* 22 Apr. 1/7 The practice known as '*shuttle-kissing'—sucking the weft through the eye of the Shuttle. **1688** *Shuttle prick [see *shuttle trough* below]. **1831** G. R. PORTER *Silk Manuf.* 216 A shelf, called the *shuttle-race, is formed by making the bottom bar broader than the side rails. **1868** MORRIS *Earthly Par.* I. II. 378 (*Cupid & Psyche*), As I drove The ivory shuttle through the shuttle-race. **1871** *Abridgm. Specif. Patents, Sewing* 14 Sewing by means of a vibrating needle and a shuttle travelling in a circular shuttle-race. **1892** *Q. Rev.* Oct. 486 The South-Eastern used, twenty years back, to run a '*shuttle' service every ten minutes between Charing Cross and Cannon St. **1905** *Westm. Gaz.* 3 July 6/3 This 'shuttle' service of electric trains. **1933** *Times* 28 Feb. 9/4 Shuttle services from the outer districts connecting with the trunk and City routes can be substituted for through services from the suburbs to the City. **1944** A. JACOB *Traveller's War* xxviii. 419 It is the same kind of non-stop bombing shuttle service with which Conyngham, the A.O.C. Western Desert, achieved such great results in Africa. **1961** *Wall St. Jrnl.* 20 Mar. 2/3 Eastern Airlines said it wants to start a low-cost air 'shuttle' service between Boston, New York and Washington. **1966** 'H. MACDIARMID' *Company I've Kept* viii. 189 About..the..date of my birthday, Biggar Post Office had to run what was virtually a shuttle-service several times a day to deliver the masses of mail. **1969** *Guardian* 18 Jan. 1/4 We can expect to see a permanent Russian space station in orbit.., probably with a shuttle service of Russian scientists from earth. **1978** *Detroit Free Press* 5 Mar. D. 16/3 It is more a commercial than a resort hotel, but it has a pool and runs a daily shuttle service to nearby public beaches for guests. **1861** P. P. CARPENTER in *Rep. Smithsonian Instit.* 1860, 195 Family *Ovulidæ*. (Egg and *Shuttle Shells.) **1744** in *Phil. Trans.* (1746) XLIII. 194 There was extracted from him..an iron *Shuttle Spire, four Inches long. **1888** A. R. DIEHL *Two Thousand Words* 190 **Shuttle-train*, one that takes short runs back and forth. **1923** *World Almanac* 503/2 A shuttle train runs between 50th Street and 59th Street on Sixth Avenue. **1942** *Sun* (Baltimore) 7 Mar. 20 When loss of tires has forced the automobile from use, shuttle trains, supplemented by busses, will be the most practical..means for the transportation of workers in this area. **1974** *Encycl. Brit. Macropædia* XV. 494/2 In 1965 the first Freightliner container..shuttle trains began running on British Railways. **1688** HOLME *Armoury* III. 289/1 The parts of a Shuttle are, the *Shuttle Trough, or Box, is the square hole on the top of it, in which the Pin or Shuttle Prick is set within two holes having Yarn..wound about it. **1893** G. KAPP *Dynamos, Alternators, & Transformers* ix. 209 The simplest example of an open-coil armature is the so-called *shuttle-wound armature. **1902** *Encycl. Brit.* XXVII. 577/1 The second or drum method was used in the original 'shuttle-wound' armatures invented by Dr. Werner von Siemens in 1856.

†**'shuttle**, *sb.*[2] *Obs.* Forms: α. 1 scyt(t)el, scetel, 4 ssettel, 5 schettel, schyt(t)yl; β. 1 scyttels, scyttyls, scytels, scettels, 2 scutles. [OE. *scyt(t)el*, *scyt(t)els*:—prehistoric **skutil*, *-isli*, f. **skut-* in *scyttan* to shut; the two OE. words have different suffixes, but their forms coalesced in ME.: see -EL, -ELS. Cf. WFris. *skoattel*, EFris. *schötel*, NFris. *sködel*.

The mod. dial. *shuttle* (*shittle*, *shettle*, *shottle*) horizontal bar of a gate (see *Eng. Dial. Dict.*), is perh. the same word.]

**1.** A bolt or bar, as of a door.

**971** *Blickl. Hom.* 87 Ealle þa isenan scyttelas helle loca wurdan tobrocene. *a* **1000** *Kent. Gloss.* 658 in *Haupt's Zeitschr.* (1877) IX. 55 Scetel, *vectis*. *c* **1000** ÆLFRIC *Hom.* I. 70 Ða scytelses [*v.r.* scittelsas] to burston. *a* **1023** WULFSTAN *Hom.* (1883) 230 Openiað þas ʒeatu and þa fæstan scytelsas. *c* **1175** *Lamb. Hom.* 127 þet is þet [loc] þeðe deofel ne con unlucan, þet is þet scutles þeðe deofel ne mei nefre to-cysan. **1340** *Ayenb.* 94 'My zoster, my lemman, þou art a gardin besset, myd tuo ssettles,' þet is þe grace of god, and of angles. *c* **1440** *Promp. Parv.* 365/1 Ondoynge, or op(y)nynge of schettellys, or sperellys. *Ibid.* 447/1 Schyttyl, or sperynge, *pessulum, vel pessellum*.

**2.** ? A shutter or a partition.

**1614** T. GODWIN *Rom. Antiq.* xviii. 15 By the drawing aside of some wainscot shuttles..a newe partition might seeme to be put vp.

**shuttle** ('ʃʌt(ə)l), *sb.*[3] Forms: 5 schetel, 6, 9 *dial.* shittle, 8– shuttle. [f. SHUT *v.* + -LE.

It is uncertain whether the word represents OE. *scyttel*, *scyttels* (see prec.) in an unrecorded sense, or was a new formation in ME.]

**1.** A flood-gate which opens to allow the flow and regulate the supply of water in a mill-stream. Also a similar gate in a drain. Also 'one of the sections of a shutter-dam' (*Cent. Dict.* 1891).

*c* **1440** *Promp. Parv.* 445/2 Schetelys, or gote, *supra, aquagium*. **1583** *Inquisition of Sewers* 7 (N.W. Linc. Gloss.), The same sewer from the foresaid fields end to the shittle shall be diked, scowred and cleansed..by Mr. William Dalyson. **1738** *Phil. Trans.* XLI. 167 The Miller..went immediately, and let down the Shuttle. **1812** NOUAILLE in *J. Nicholson's Oper. Mech.* (1825) 111 The shuttle or gate slides upon the floor of the trough, so as to..determine the quantity of water to be let out upon the wheel. **1832** *Holderness Drainage Act* 13 Stocks, shuttles and other works of drainage. **1845** *Jrnl. R. Agric. Soc.* V. II. 400 The sluices or cloughs used then being merely what now would be called shuttles. **1877** *N.W. Linc. Gloss.*, *Shittle*,..the shuttle of a drain. 'The shittle agean th' fish-pond is o' no use noo.' **1887** *Fishng Gaz.* 2 Apr. 207/2 The..field..opposite the 'shuttle' or flood gate.

**2.** A small gate or stop through which metal is allowed to pass from the trough to the mould.

**1858** SIMMONDS *Dict. Trade*. **1875** KNIGHT *Dict. Mech.*

**shuttle** ('ʃʌt(ə)l), *sb.*[4] *Sc.* and *Devonshire*. Also 7 schottlle, 7– shottle. [Of doubtful origin: perh. f. SHUT *v.* + -LE. Cf. prec.]

A small drawer, esp. one fixed in a chest, in which small articles were stored. Also 'a kind of box in the upper part of a chest, extending across; used for keeping money'; also 'a till in a shop, a money-box' (Jam.).

**1626** WEDDERBURNE *Compt Bk.* (S.H.S.) 142 Ane aikin frez pres with schottles of aik thairin. **1699** ELIZ. WEST *Mem.* (1865) 114, I thought they were like a cabinet full of shuttles and in every shuttle there was a jewel. **1719** HAMILTON *Epist. to Ramsay* I. 32 Gin that my haff-pay siller shottle Can safely spare it. **1815** SCOTT *Guy M.* xxxviii, Those eyes..were now sharply and alertly darting their glances through shuttles, and trunks, and drawers, and cabinets, and all the odd corners of an old maiden lady's repositories. **1823** —— in *Lockhart* (1839) VII. 105 Like the inside of an antique cabinet with drawers and shottles and funny little arches. **1836** MRS. BRAY *Tamar & Tavy* (1836) III. xxxiv. 80 And I thought of the old names by which the little drawers and boxes in such [old cabinets] were called, —the shuttles. **1866** R. CHAMBERS *Ess.* Ser. I. 152 A set of docketed papers, tied up with red tape, and deposited in shottle fifteen. **1870** J. K. HUNTER *Life Studies* 158, I had three white half-croons in the shuttle o' my kist.

**'shuttle**, *a.* Variant of SHITTLE *a.*, unsteady, shaky, etc., surviving *dial.* (see *Eng. Dial. Dict.*).

**1542** UDALL *Erasm. Apoph.* 307b, Metellus was so shuttle-brained that even in the middes of his tribuneship he left his office in Roome. **1553** *Respublica* v. ii. 85 (Brandl), That shuttle brained, tall, long man. **1602** R. T. 5 *Godlie Serm.* 200 To some shallow heads, shuttle braines, and simple wits, it seemeth to be [etc.]. **1617** COLLINS *Def. Bp. Ely* II. x. 497 Howsoeuer our shuttle-pated Adioynder thinke of it. *a* **1649** *MS. Poems temp. Chas. I* (Halliw.), Nor can you deeme them shuttle-headed fellowes, Who for the Lord are so exceeding zealous. *c* **1660** *Rump Songs* I. 7 Is it not strange, that in that Shuttle-head Three Kingdoms ruines should be buried? *c* **1682** J. COLLINS *Making Salt in Eng.* 15 A mixture of harsh shuttle Sand. **1886** *W. Somerset Word-bk.*, *Shuttle*, quick, lithe, active... Also applied to any dry or easily slipping matter, as grain, seeds, sand, &c. **1888** STEVENSON *Black Arrow* I. ii, See there how shuttle-witted are these girls.

Hence †**'shuttly** *adv.*, unsteadily.

**1661** PETTY in Birch *Hist. Roy. Soc.* (1756) I. 59 To which purpose the quill is too short for the axis whereon it rowls, and moves as shuttley upon it as may be.

**shuttle** ('ʃʌt(ə)l), *v.* In 6 shutle. [Partly or perh. wholly f. SHUTTLE *sb.*; but possibly in part a frequentative f. SHOOT *v.*: see -LE.]

**1. a.** *trans.* To move (a thing) briskly to and fro like a shuttle. Also, to throw swiftly. *Obs.* exc. *dial.*

**1550** COVERDALE *Spir. Perle* xxxi. 260 He yᵗ hath an heauy burthen vpon hys back, yᵉ more he shutleth and moueth yᵉ same, yᵉ more doeth it greue hym. **1823** GALT *Entail* lxiv, He would hae grippit me by the cuff o' the neck and the back o' the breeks and shuttled me through the window. **1840** CARLYLE *Let.* 17 Mar. in Froude *Life Lond.* (1884) I. 177 A face of most extreme mobility, which he shuttles about..in a very singular manner while speaking. **1857** MEREDITH *Farina* (1865) 52 Now general commotion shuttled them.

**b.** To transport in a vehicle or craft operating a shuttle service. Also *transf.*

**1930** E. FERBER *Cimarron* xxi. 334 With his geological knowledge..and his familiarity with the region, he was shuttled back and forth from one end of the state to the other. **1945** *Times* 13 Sept. 5/7 There has been no difficulty about shuttling prisoners resident in the British and American zones. **1965** *Listener* 30 Sept. 482/2 So what happens to the old patient? Does he or she get shuttled around to one hospital after another? **1971** *Nature* 27 Aug. 632/1 That malate may serve to 'shuttle' reducing equivalents from cytoplasm to mitochondria. **1975** *Daily Tel.* 1 May 1 Scores of transport aircraft shuttle Vietnamese evacuees from Guam, Wake Island, and the Philippines to America at the rate of up to 5,000 a day. **1977** *Offshore Engineer* May 49/2 Two 15,000t tankers shuttle the oil to Spanish refineries. **1978** H. WOUK *War & Remembrance* xiv. 148 Trains devoted to shuttling the Jews rolled eastward jam-packed and went back empty.

**2.** *intr.* To go or move backwards and forwards like a shuttle; to travel quickly to and fro. Also, to travel in one direction using a shuttle service. Also *transf.*

**1823** GALT *Gilhaize* lxxxiv, In the clear linn the trouts shuttled from stone and crevice. **1837** CARLYLE *Fr. Rev.* II. VI. i, Their corps go marching and shuttling, in the interior of the country. **1884** *Harper's Mag.* July 270/1 It is as though a section of roadway shuttled to and fro between the shores. **1910** *Spectator* 23 Apr. 666/2 Faster ships shuttle to and fro weaving the political web more and more rapidly. **1935** M. M. ATWATER *Murder in Midsummer* i. 6 A few automobiles, like overgrown beetles, shuttled back and forth along the concrete highways. **1966** *Aviation Week & Space Technol.* 5 Dec. 95/1 Analyses could be made automatically or by astronauts shuttling from earth to the satellite laboratory, staying one month or more and then returning to earth. **1971** 'A. BURGESS' *MF* iv. 42 He was not to be seen: perhaps he had shuttled off to Boston or somewhere. **1973** *Internat. Relations Dict.* (U.S. Dept. State Library) 38/1 Henry Kissinger personally shuttled back and forth between Jerusalem and Cairo. **1975** *Sci. Amer.* Jan. 13/3, I moved 'temporarily' to the University of Liverpool in 1965 and have shuttled between the departments of genetics and zoology ever since. **1977** *Time* 15 Aug. 19/3 Although it was not on his original schedule, Vance decided to shuttle back to Amman, Damascus and Alexandria to convey Israeli views to Sadat and Assad. **1978** R. LUDLUM *Holcroft Covenant* xiii. 157 France's domestic airline shuttled about the country with splendid irregularity. **1979** *Sci. Amer.* Jan. 29/1 (*caption*) The trains shuttle back and forth without being uncoupled, acting much like a conveyor belt.

**3.** *Sc.* To ply the shuttle, weave. (See *Eng. Dial. Dict.*)

Hence **'shuttling** *ppl. a.*

**1860** *All Year Round* No. 41. 344 The flutes began in a whirling, shuttling movement.

**shuttlecock** ('ʃʌt(ə)lkɒk), *sb.* [f. SHUTTLE *sb.*[1] (q.v. for forms) + COCK *sb.*[1] Cf. SHUTTLE-CORK.]

**1.** A small piece of cork, or similar light material, fitted with a crown or circle of feathers, used in the game of 'battledore and shuttlecock' (see 2) and also in the game of Badminton.

**1522** SKELTON *Why not to Court* 351, I trow all wyll be nought, Nat worth a shyttel cocke. **1591** SPENSER *M. Hubberd* 804 A thousand wayes he them could entertaine,.. With dice, with cards,..With shuttelcocks. **1599** NASHE *Lenten Stuffe* 74 This playing with a shettlecocke, or tossing empty bladders in the ayre. **1604** MIDDLETON *Ant & Nightingale* C 3 b, His head was drest vp in white Feathers like a Shuttle-Cock. **1626** BRETON *Fantasticks* Oct. C 4 b, The shuttel-Cocke with the Battel-doore is a pretty house-exercise. **1688** BUNYAN *Water of Life* 116 (end), They toss their Vanities about as the Boys toss their Shittle-Cocks in the Air. **1777** SHERIDAN *Trip to Scarb.* Prol., Made up, like shuttlecocks, of cork and feather. **1801** C. K. SHARPE *Let.* 12 Jan. *Corr.* 1888 I. 103 With long stiff feathers stuck round their heads like those of a shittle-cock. **1838** LYTTON *Alice* VI. i, Vast interests and solemn causes are no longer tossed about like shuttlecocks on the battledores of empty tongues. **1897** *Encycl. Sport* I. 70/2 (Badminton) *Shuttlecock*, the missile employed, which consists of a cork crowned with feathers, from 3 to 5 inches in length.

**b.** *fig.*

**1602** DEKKER *Satiromastix* F 2 b, What made these paire of Shittle-cockes heere? what doe they fumble for? **1700** T. BROWN tr. *Fresny's Amusem.*, *Westm. Hall* Wks. 1709 III. I. 49 Certain..Sollicitors and Barristers, make it their whole business to keep the Shuttle-cock [Chancery suits] in motion. **1760–72** H. BROOKE *Fool of Qual.* (1809) III. 130 The shittlecock of conversation may fall to the ground. **1858** DK. ARGYLL *Autobiog.* (1906) II. 124 This Reform question ought not to be made the shuttlecock of party. **1884** *Pall Mall Gaz.* 5 Dec. 5/1 The best American securities are periodically the shuttlecock of unscrupulous speculators.

**2.** The game (more fully ***battledore and shuttlecock***, now played only by children) in which the shuttlecock is hit with the battledore backwards and forwards between two players, or by one player into the air as many times as possible without dropping it.

**1599** B. JONSON *Cynthia's Rev.* II. iv, Shee can..play at shittle-cock. **1628** BURTON *Anat. Mel.* II. ii. IV. (ed. 3) 255 The ordinary recreations which we haue in Winter..are Cardes..shuttlecocks, balliardes [etc.]. **1711** SWIFT *Jrnl. to Stella* 20 Sept., And get somebody to play shuttlecock with you, Madam Stella. **1842** LOVER *Handy Andy* xiv, Pray Mr. F... are you fond of shuttlecock?

*fig.* **1858** SEARS *Athan.* iii. 20 They were only playing at shuttlecock with words.

**3.** A Mexican malvaceous shrub, *Periptera punica*.

**1829** LOUDON *Encycl. Plants* 588 *Periptera punica*. Shuttlecock. **1840** PAXTON *Bot. Dict.* **1866** *Treas. Bot.* s.v.

**4.** *attrib.* and *Comb.*, as ***shuttlecock-maker***.

**1628** FORD *Love's Mel.* I. ii, A shittlecock maker.

**b.** quasi-*adj.* Light, tossed hither and thither.

**1660** R. BURNEY Κέρδιστον Δῶρον Ep. Ded. II. 11 He [Cromwell] brought the Shuttlecock opprobrie upon the grave Counsell of the Land, and called them together only to kick them out. **1754** STUKELEY *Mem.* (Surtees) III. 191 Now our shittlecock heads think of nothing but France. **1826** MISS MITFORD *Village* II. 83 Or any other shuttlecock pate, giddy with happiness and vanity. **1903** J. C. SMITH in *R. Wallace: Life & Last Leaves* 137 Shuttlecock retort was a familiar game with him.

**'shuttlecock,** *v.* [f. SHUTTLECOCK *sb.*] **1.** *trans.* To throw, send backwards and forwards or to toss like a shuttlecock. Also *fig.* **1687** R. L'ESTRANGE *Brief Hist. Times* I. 14 Transubstantiation, and Idolatry, the Bug-bear of the Times, has not been more Shittle-Cock'd, then this Argument. **1853** *Tait's Mag.* XX. 365 He is shuttle-cocked between London and Edinburgh. **1859** THACKERAY *Virgin.* lxxvii, 'Yes, if the phrase is to be shuttlecocked between us,' I answered hotly. **1904** *Blackw. Mag.* Mar. 402 [Certain Companies] shuttlecocked their assets and liabilities from one to the other for balance-sheet purposes. **1955** *Times* 10 Aug. 5/2 What Rostand lightly shuttlecocks to and fro across this barrier M. Anouilh might nowadays have said more sadly.

**2.** *intr.* To move or go backwards and forwards. **1780** H. WALPOLE *Let. to Miss Berrys* 8 Nov., A letter may have shuttle-cocked about. **1960** *Times* 23 Feb. 4/5 Miss Maxine Audley..played a part shuttle-cocking between lover, son, and husband.

**†'shuttle-cork.** *Obs.* [f. SHUTTLE *sb.*[1] + CORK *sb.*] = SHUTTLECOCK *sb.* In quot. *attrib.* *a* **1627** MIDDLETON *Chaste Maid* III. (1630) 38 Their short figging little shittle-corke-heeles.

**'shuttleless,** *a.* [f. SHUTTLE *sb.*[1] + -LESS.] Adapted to work without a shuttle. **1888** *Daily News* 10 Sept. 7/3 A shuttleless lockstitch sewing machine. **1890** *B'ham Weekly Post* 1 Feb. 1/5 The shuttleless loom. **1961** *Textile World* July 30 Shuttleless looms. **1967** *Economist* 29 Apr. 459/3 Popularly known as 'the green box', the BD 200, together with the shuttleless jet loom, could revolutionise the Czech industry. **1975** *Guardian* 27 Jan. 15/1 Most loom-builders were thinking in terms of shuttleless machines.

**†'shuttle-pin.** *Obs.* [? SHUTTLE *sb.*[2]] Some kind of fastening for harness. **1587** MASCALL *Cattle, Horses* (1596) 119 Harnesses..and all things belonging thereunto, as..belly wanties with tack, or shootle pin, tide to euery hawm with a string.

**shuttler** ('ʃʌtlə(r)). *rare.* [f. SHUTTLE *v.* (sense 3) + -ER[1].] A weaver. **1870** J. K. HUNTER *Life Studies* 155 He was the prettiest shuttler I ever saw. **1897** *Ardrossan & Saltcoats Her.* 17 Sept. 5 The shuttlers in the employment of Stewart, Moir & Muir..ceased work.

**shuttler,** obs. form of SUTLER.

**shuttling** ('ʃʌtlɪŋ), *vbl. sb.* [f. SHUTTLE *v.* + -ING[1].] **1.** The action of using a shuttle (also *fig.*); the action of fixing the cop in the shuttle; *concr.* that which serves the purpose of a shuttle. **1874** H. H. COLE *Catal. Ind. Art S. Kens. Mus.* 217 He then prepares the shuttling, which is more like a long knitting needle than an ordinary English shuttle, winding on it a length of the thread. **1879** *Cassell's Techn. Educ.* IV. 399/1 To render the shuttling of the cop a matter of as little nicety as possible. **1889** *Century Mag.* Jan. 422/1 Those [olive groves] in the distance look more hoary and soft, as though a veil of light cunningly woven by the shuttling of the rays hung over them.

**2.** Travelling to and fro. **1937** R. S. MORTON *Woman Surgeon* i. 15 This periodical shuttling between Virginia and New Jersey entailed as much preparation and inconvenience as a modern voyage to the Antarctic.

**'shut-up,** *a.* [SHUT *ppl. a.*: cf. SHUT *v.* 19.] **1.** That has been shut up. **1614** GORGES *Lucan* x. 443 [He] relies Vpon the hope of shut vp wayes. *a* **1887** JEFFERIES *Field & Hedgerow* (1889) 315 Job had a lot of shut-up rooms in his house.

**2.** That can be shut up; foldable. **1799** JANE AUSTEN *Let.* 8 Jan. (1952) 50 Martha kindly made room for me in her bed, which was the shut-up one in the new nursery. **1911** R. NEVILL *Floreat Etona* x. 307 The furniture of the rooms... For the most part..consisted of a shut-up bed, a 'burry' (bureau) washstand, which also closed up, and sock cupboard.

‖**shutur sowar** ('ʃʊtə sʌ'wɑː(r)). *Anglo-Indian.* Also shuta-, shootar-. [Urdū a. Pers. *shutur suwār* (f. *shutur* camel + *suwār*: see SOWAR).] A camel rider. **1834** COL. MOUNTAIN *Mem.* (1857) 135 A couple of riding camels and an attendant Shootar Suwar. **1840** W. G. OSBORNE *Crt. & Camp Runjeet Sing* 179 Sent a Shuta surwar..off with an express to Simla. **1849** EASTWICK *Dry Leaves* 78 A body of eighty camel riders, or Shutur Sawârs, to use the Persian term, arrived.

**shuv(v)er,** var. SHOVER.

**shuyster,** variant of SHYSTER.

**shva,** var. SHEVA.

**shvartze, shvartzer,** varr. SCHVARTZE, SCHVARTZER.

**shwa,** var. SCHWA.

**shwanpan,** variant of SWANPAN.

**shwere,** obs. form of SWEAR.

**shy** (ʃaɪ), *sb.*[1] Pl. shies. [f. SHY *v.*[1]] A sudden start aside made by a horse when it sees an object that frightens it. **1791** 'G. GAMBADO' *Ann. Horsem.* ix. (1809) 106 [The horse] made a sort of a shy towards the cliff. **1857** READE *Course of True Love* 166 In the middle of a great shy which her mare made. **1908** *Edin. Rev.* Oct. 472 We pass it by with a courteous bow which has in it something of a horse's shy at the uncanny.

*fig.* **1900** MARY E. WILKINS *Parson Lord* 35 He has stepped along in his path of duty without a kick or a shy.

**shy** (ʃaɪ), *sb.*[2] *colloq.* Also *rare* shie. Pl. shies. [f. SHY *v.*[2]] **1. a.** A quick, jerking (or careless) throw, as of a stone, etc. **1791** BRAND *Pop. Antiq.* (1813) I. 67 The person who throws..has three *shys*, or throws, for two pence. **1835** DICKENS *Sk. Boz. Greenwich Fair*, Jack-in-the-box—three shies a penny. **1849** W. S. MAYO *Kaloolah* ii. (1850) 25 Swinging his cap round his head, he gave it a shie over the lee quarter. **1854** W. COLLINS *Hide & Seek* I. vii. 194, I never remember wanting to throw a rotten egg at any of my fellow-creatures before—but I feel certain that I should enjoy having a shy at Mr. Jubber! **1859** JEPHSON *Brittany* xv. 245 When he was a boy, he..used to think it good fun to have a 'shy' at these windows.

**b.** *Eton Football.* A point scored in the 'Wall' game (see quot. 1881). **1868** *Field* 28 Nov. 446/3 This match..ended in favour of the School by five shies to nothing. **1881** *Pascoe's Everyday Life Public Schools* 54 Once behind this [calx] line, the player's object is to get it [the ball] up..with his foot against the wall and touch, when he gets a 'shy'; that is, the privilege of throwing the ball at the goals, while the other side.. defend them. Of course, if he succeeds in reaching the goals, he gets a goal... More generally the game is decided by the number of 'shies' got.

**2.** *fig.* **a.** An attempt to damage by sarcasm or verbal attack; a 'fling' *at* a person or thing. **1840** DE QUINCEY *Mod. Superst.* Wks. 1862 III. 313 If Rousseau thought fit to try such tremendous appeals by taking 'a shy' at any random object, he should have governed his sortilege..with something more like equity. **1854** THACKERAY *Newcomes* xvi, 'You are always having a shy at Lady Ann and her relations', says Mr. Newcome... 'A shy! How can you use such vulgar words, Mr. Newcome?' **1859** DE QUINCEY *Pref. Memor.* Wks. 1862 X. p. xvii, The Doctor ..resolved to 'take a shy', before parting, at the most consecrated of Milton's creations. **1873** B. HARTE *Washington in N. Jersey* in *Fiddletown*, etc. 94 I'd like to get a shy at G. W. some time.

**b.** A trial, an experiment; a 'shot', a 'go'. **1824** P. EGAN *Boxiana* IV. 149 'I am sure you are too generous to let a brave man want; and I never knew an appeal made here in vain.' 'Well then, go it' echoed one of the East-enders; 'I like to have a shy for my money.' Half crowns, shillings and sixpences were instantly thrown upon the stage. **1848** THACKERAY *Let.* in *Introd. to Pendennis* Wks. 1898 II. p. xxxiv, Sometimes I have a shy myself, and I don't lose or win twenty francs. **1857** DICKENS *Dorrit* II. vi, He would be all the better for a temporary shy at an entirely new scene and climate. **1881** C. GIBBON *Heart's Probl.* vi. (1884) 86 Have a shy at putting the case plainly to me. **1887** HENLEY *Culture in Slums* iii. 7 I've had at Pater many a shy.

**3. a.** One who throws, a thrower or shyer. **1884** *Lillywhite's Cricket Ann.* 103 A good field and shy.

**b.** *coconut shy*: see COCO, COCOA 4 e.

**shy** (ʃaɪ), *a.* Forms: 1 scéoh (? *inflected* scíon), 3 scheouh, scheowe, 5 schey, 6 shey, 7–8 shie, shye, 7– shy. [OE. *scéoh* (very rare; also in comb. *scéohmód* of timid mind), corresp. to MHG. *schiech*:—OTeut. type **skeuhwo-*; an ablaut variant (OTeut. type **skuᵍwu-, -wjo-*) appears in MDu. *schuwe*, *schu* (mod.Du. *schuw*), Norw. dial. *skygg*, MSw., Da. *sky*; the synonymous mod.G. *scheu* is a new formation after the related *scheu* fem. (MHG. *schiuhe*) fear, abhorrence, *scheuen* to be shy of, fear (MHG. *schiuhen* to be shy of, avoid, also causatively to drive away, OHG. *sciuhen* to frighten); f. Teut. root **skeuhw-* to fear, to terrify, whence prob. G. *schüchtern* shy; for other derivatives of the root see SHEWEL. The affinities that have been suggested for the root are very doubtful.

The phonetic development of mod.E. *shy* (ʃaɪ) from OE. *scéoh* is parallel with that of *thigh* from *þéoh*. Divergent forms in dialects are SHUFF (:—OE. *sceōh* with rising diphthong) and SKEIGH (with unexplained initial). It is noteworthy that the pronunciation (ɔɪ) is current in many dialects in which (ɔɪ) does not ordinarily correspond to the (aɪ) of standard Eng.]

**1.** †**a.** Easily frightened or startled. *Obs.* *c* **1000** *Riming Poem* 43 (Gr.) Nu min hreþer is hreoh heowsiþum [*read* heofsiþum] sceoh nydbysgum neah. *a* **1225** *Ancr. R.* 242 Lokeð þet ȝe ne beon nout iliche þe horse þet is scheouh, & blencheð uor one scheadewe... To scheowe heo beoð mid alle þet fleoð uor ane peinture. *c* **1440** *Promp. Parv.* 444/2 Schey, or skey, as hors, or styȝtyl. **1648** HEXHAM II. s.v. *Schouw, Een Schouw paerdt*, A Shye Horse, a Fearefull Horse.

**b.** *dial.* Of a horse: Skittish, unmanageable; high-mettled. Hence (?) of persons (see quot. 1840).

Cf. the OE. gloss 'scion, *peculantis*' (read *petulantis* as in Aldhelm *De Laud. Virg.* 4705, to which the gloss refers) in *Wr.-Wülcker* 517/16.

**1787** W. H. MARSHALL *Norfolk* (1795) II. 388 *Shy*, hare-brained; high-mettled; head-strong; as wild colts, &c. **1840** SPURDENS *Suppl. to Forby*, *Shy*, wild in conduct... A *shy* boy, or a *shy* girl is wanton, unsteady, amorous. **1860** *Hotten's Slang Dict.* s.v., *Shy* has also the sense of flighty, unsteady, untrustworthy.

**2.** Easily frightened away; difficult of approach owing to timidity, caution, or distrust; timidly or cautiously averse to encountering or having to do with some specified person or thing; suspicious, distrustful. Const. *of*. **a.** of persons. **1600** HAKLUYT *Voy.* III. 391 Certaine souldiers..caried away captiue certaine of the people of the countrey, which caused the rest of them to be so shey and fearefull. **1606** WARNER *Alb. Eng.* XVI. cv. 412 This noble lustie Gentleman ..Grew thenceforth shie of Women, and a Timon vnto men. **1622** S. WARD *Life Faith Death* 48 Yet is it but our folly to be so shye of this sight, for though [etc.]. *a* **1639** WOTTON *Parallel Essex & Buckhm.* Reliq. (1651) 11 Princes ..are (by wisdome of State) somwhat shye of their Successors. **1660** INGELO *Bentiv. & Ur.* II. (1682) 24 We should not be so shie of Death, for it is the only passage to Immortal Life. **1683** CAVE *Ecclesiastici, Athanasius* 53 Men generally became more shy of his acquaintance. **1687** NORRIS *Poems* 36 But when we come to seize th'inviting prey, Like a Shy Ghost, it vanishes away. **1702** DE FOE *Shortest Way Dissenters* 27 The primitive Christians were not more shie of a Heathen-Temple, or of Meat offer'd to Idols,..than [etc.]. **1718** OCKLEY *Saracens* (1848) 446 Abdallah was still shy of him, and did not employ him in any considerable post. **1824** BYRON *Juan* XVI. xxxvi, The spectre has grown shyer. **1834** DICKENS *Sk. Boz, Boarding Ho.* ii, Since the catastrophe recorded in the last chapter, Mrs. Tibbs had been very shy of young-lady boarders. **1885** [W. H. WHITE] *M. Rutherford's Deliv.* iv. (ed. 9) 52 The women in the countryside were shy of her. **1903** C. E. OSBORNE *Father Dolling* ii. (1905) 21 He thought he could do more good as a layman, especially with young men, as so many of the latter are 'shy' of the clergy.

**b.** of an animal, bird, etc. **1674** RAY *S. & E.C. Words* 76 *Shie* or *shy*, apt to startle and flee from you, or that keeps off and will not come near. **1697** DAMPIER *Voy.* (1699) I. 70 They [flamingoes] are very shy, therefore it is hard to shoot them. **1748** *Anson's Voy.* II. iv. 157 This place..abounds with goats, who, not being accustomed to be disturbed, were no ways shy or apprehensive of danger. *Ibid.* III. ii. 309 The cattle..were not shy of us. **1772** T. SIMPSON *Vermin Killer* 20 Some have a notion that crows are shy of powder. **1816** TUCKEY *Narr. Exped. R. Zaire* i. (1818) 31 Some covies of guinea fowl were seen, but too shy to be shot at. **1863** W. C. BALDWIN *Afr. Hunting* iv. 99 They [sea-cows] were very shy, and showed poor heads. **1867** F. FRANCIS *Angling* i. (1880) 58 If the fish remain shy, leave the swim for a couple of hours. **1908** [MISS E. FOWLER] *Betw. Trent & Ancholme* 34 The robin is more shy.

**c.** *to be* or *look shy on* or *at*: to regard with distrust or suspicion. **1837** CARLYLE *Fr. Rev.* I. III. viii, The very Courtiers looked shy at it. **1848** THACKERAY *Van. Fair* xiii, Hulker & Bullock are looking shy at him. **1872** GEO. ELIOT *Middlem.* vi, How will you like going to Sessions with everybody looking shy on you?

**d.** As last element in Combs.: frightened (of), averse or reluctant (to). **1884**, etc. [see GUN-SHY *a.*]. **1928**, etc. [see *work-shy* adj. s.v. WORK *sb.* 34]. **1934**, etc. [see *book-shy* adj. s.v. BOOK *sb.* 19]. **1938** *Amer. Speech* XIII. 188/1 *Needle-shy*, a phobia.. which manifests itself in a revulsion against using the hypodermic needle or seeing it used. **1972** *Sat. Rev.* (U.S.) 28 Oct. 33/3 The extent to which rather sophisticated people remain telephone-shy is remarkable. **1972** *Guardian* 24 Nov. 32/1 Traffic shy commuters.

**3. a.** Fearful of committing oneself to a particular course of action; chary, unwilling, reluctant. Const. *of*, *in*, *about*, *at*, and *to* with infinitive. *a* **1628** PRESTON *Breastpl. Faith* (1630) 29 Be not thou shye in taking of him; for you have free liberty. **1633** G. HERBERT *Temple, Brit. Ch.* vii, She..is so shie of dressing, that her hair doth lie About her eares. **1638** SANDERSON *Serm.* (1681) II. 98 They that are guiltiest of folly, are the shiest to own it. *c* **1645** HOWELL *Lett.* (1655) I. III. xxviii. 148 His Majesty ..desir'd them..now that they had detected the Treason, to discover also the Traytors; but they were shy in that point. **1663** BUTLER *Hud.* I. i. 46 Although he had much Wit, H' was very shie of using it. **1683** MOXON *Mech. Exerc., Printing* 81, I..have as good an Opinion of these Rules, as those have that are shyest of discovering theirs. **1711** G. HICKES *Two Treat. Chr. Priesth.* (1847) II. 395 Why then are you so shy in owning their rectoral power? **1712** ARBUTHNOT *John Bull* I. viii, A stinking ulcer, which made everybody shy to come near her. **1742** BLAIR *Grave* 514 That stood aloof, as shy to meet. **1815** SCOTT *Guy M.* xxx, The local magistrates, from timidity or worse motives, have become shy of acting against them. **1817** JAS. MILL *Brit. India* v. v. II. 506 Distrust of the English power, now violently shaken, made his father shy. **1848** THACKERAY *Van. Fair* xviii, Be shy of loving frankly. **1859** DICKENS *T. Two Cities* I. ii, In those days, travellers were very shy of being confidential on a short notice. **1890** W. BOOTH *Darkest Engl.* II. v. 190 Families are naturally shy at receiving these poor unfortunates. **1913** JANE E. HARRISON *Anc. Art & Ritual* iv. 91 Some of us now-a-days are getting a little shy of deliberately cursing our neighbours on Ash Wednesday. **1940** *Ann. Reg. 1939* 362 So much money had already been lost..that investors were shy.

**b.** Averse from admitting (a principle), or from considering (a subject). Const. *of*. **1641** 'SMECTYMNUUS' *Vind. Answ.* vi. 84 That which the Remonstrant would perswade his reader we are shie of. *a* **1645** LAUD *Hist. Troubles* iii. (1695) 106, I see too, that too many Men are shye of Good Works. **1662** STILLINGFL. *Orig. Sacræ* II. vi. §16 The present Jews..are grown very shy of the argument drawn from thence. **1662** H. MORE *Philos. Writ.* (1712) Pref. Gen. p. xx, At which Timidity of mine, none can justly wonder that considers how shie the ancient Fathers were of the Globosity of the Earth. **1676** GLANVILL *Ess.* I. 26 Nor are we shy of their Informations, because they were hid from Ages. **1678** CUDWORTH *Intell. Syst.* Pref., So far from being shy of such an Hypothesis, as that they were even Fond thereof.

**c.** Phrases. †*to make shy of*: to be shy of, to be afraid of (doing). *to fight shy*: see FIGHT *v.* 9. **1638** FEATLY *Strict. Lyndom.* I. 152 They made shie of reading Scripture, for feare of being made Heretiques thereby.

† **d.** *shy of oneself*: unwilling to expose oneself.
**1722** DE FOE *Plague* (1756) 103, I was..now to thrust myself in among so many People, who for some Weeks, had been so shye of myself, that if I met any Body in the Street, I would cross the Way from them.

†**4.** Cautiously reserved; wary in speech or action. *Obs.*
**1603** SHAKS. *Meas. for M.* III. ii. 138 A shie fellow was the Duke. *Ibid.* v. i. 54 As shie, as graue..As Angelo. *a* **1691** WOOD *Life* (O.H.S.) I. 152 He..found him very shie; but..he was very free afterwards in his communications.

**5. a.** Shrinking from self-assertion; sensitively timid; retiring or reserved from diffidence; bashful.
**1672** VILLIERS (Dk. Buckhm.) *Rehearsal* III. ii (Arb.) 75 Shie Maid. **1782** MISS BURNEY *Cecilia* IV. vi, But shy, quite too shy; no drawing her out. **1845** DISRAELI *Sybil* v. vii, A little shy at first, but he only wants bringing out. **1859** *Habits Gd. Society* 29 People too shy or too stupid to talk. **1884** F. M. CRAWFORD *Rom. Singer* I. 87 Nino is not a shy boy. *transf.* **1823** WORDSW. *Sonn.*, '*Not Love, not War*' 14 The flower of sweetest smell is shy and lowly.

**b.** of a person's actions, etc.
**1713** ADDISON *Guard*, No. 100 ¶8 The Venus de Medicis ..is represented in such a shy retiring posture, and covers her bosom with one of her hands. **1722** STEELE *Consc. Lovers* III. i, All your Skittishness, shy Looks, and at best but coy Compliances. **1852** THACKERAY *Esmond* I. i, Performing a shy obeisance to the mistress of his house.

**c.** *fig.*
**1641** MILTON *Animadv.* Wks. 1851 III. 191 Such an Anatomie of the shiest and tenderest particular truths. **1874** GREEN *Short Hist.* vii. §7. 412 The shy revival of English letters during the earlier half of Elizabeth's reign. **1878** BROWNING *La Saisiaz* 27 Had but fortune favored, bidden each shy faculty advance. **1878** B. TAYLOR *Deukalion* II. v. 88 The earth, in her shy embraces, Conceals the traces Of the secret birth of the Stream.

**d.** *transf.* Of a place, etc.: Retiring, secluded.
**1822–56** DE QUINCEY *Conf.* Wks. 1862 I. 226 *note*, Shy recesses of the lake. **1841** DICKENS *Barn. Rudge* iv, It was a modest dwelling—but a shy blinking house. **1853** M. ARNOLD *Scholar Gypsy* viii, A heap of flowers Pluck'd in shy fields and distant Wychwood bowers. **1885** LOWELL *Coleridge* Writ. 1890 VI. 72 He was the first to observe some of the sky's appearances and some of the shyer revelations of outward nature. **1899** C. G. HARPER *Exeter Road* 124 These places are all shy and retiring, tucked away up bye-lanes.

**6.** In various transferred uses of sense 2. **a.** Of plants, trees, etc.: Unprolific, not bearing well. Also rarely of *birds*: Not breeding freely.
**1823** J. BADCOCK *Dom. Amusem.* 47 The golden pippin has gradually become a shy grower in this country. **1836** MRS. TRAILL *Backwoods Canada* xiv. 246 The plant..seems to be a shy blossomer. **1852** *Beck's Florist* 193 It is rather a shy bearer, though it blooms very profusely. **1869** LOWELL *Study Wind., Gard. Acquaint.* (1871) 7 A small foreign grape-vine, rather shy of bearing. **1905** P. C. MITCHELL *Offic. Guide Gard. Zool. Soc.* (ed. 3) 7 An excellent table-bird but a shy breeder. **1905** RIDER HAGGARD *Gard. Yr.* July 239 They are shy flowerers.

**b.** *U.S.* Short (*of*), lacking. Also const. *on. Betting slang* (see quot. 1895).
**1895** *Funk's Stand. Dict.* s.v., Having a less amount of money at stake than is called for by the rules of the game; short; as, to be shy a dollar in the pool. **1896** S. CRANE *Little Regiment* etc. 187 None..knew how an orderly sergeant ranked, but then it was understood to be somewhere just shy of a major-general's stars. **1897** *Columbus* (Ohio) *Dispatch* 21 Sept. 5/4 The police department is much too shy of funds already. **1903** [see *long green* s.v. LONG *a.*[1] A. 18]. *a* **1904** A. ADAMS *Log of Cowboy* ix. 132, I ordered Joe to tie his [the ox's] mate behind the trail wagon and pull out one ox shy. **1975** R. STOUT *Family Affair* (1976) iv. 46, I merely thought *some* women were a little shy on brains, present company not excepted.

**7.** *colloq.* or *slang* in uses derived from sense 5.
**a.** Of questionable character, disreputable, 'shady'.
**1849** THACKERAY *Pendennis* xxv, Rather a shy place for a sucking county member. **1860** DICKENS *Uncomm. Trav.* x, Nothing in shy neighbourhoods perplexes my mind more. **1864** H. J. BYRON *Paid in Full* v, Hadn't shy turf-transactions been more than hinted at? **1865** DICKENS *Mut. Fr.* I. xii, The two men, very shy characters. **1869** J. ROBERTS *Billiards* 254 Shell out is a 'shy' game for a public room. **1908** *Blackw. Mag.* Feb. 252/2 Gambling hells and shy saloons.

**b.** Doubtful in amount or quality.
**1821** D. HAGGART *Life* 39 Although I had not been idle during these three months, I found my blunt getting shy. **1850** THACKERAY *Contrib. Punch* Wks. 1900 VI. 165 That uncommonly shy supper of dry bread and milk-and-water. **1862** —— *Philip* xix, The dinner, I own, is shy, unless I come and dine with my friends. **1865** M. LEMON *Loved at Last* ix, Any place will do, as her geography is rather shy, and I can make her believe anything.

**8.** *dial.* Of the wind: **a.** Chill, keen, piercing. **b.** 'Not exactly fair for the ship's course' (*Whitby Gloss.*, 1876). See *Eng. Dial. Dict.*
[The origin of sense a is not clear; it may be a distinct word. Sense b seems a natural development from 2.]
**1828** [CARR] *Craven Gloss.*, *Shy*, keen, piercing. 'A shy wind'. **1891** *Century Dict. Shy* a., Scant. The wind is said to be shy when it will barely allow a vessel to sail on her course.

**9.** *Comb.* as *shy-breeding*, *-eyed*, *-footed*, *-looking*, *-making*, *-retiring*, etc. adjs.; *shy-brightly* adv.
**1842** LOUDON *Suburban Hort.* 447 The *shy-breeding black sorts. **1922** JOYCE *Ulysses* 205 Eglintoneyes..looked up *shybrightly. **1910** J. MASEFIELD *Ballads & Poems* 80 The *shy-eyed delicate deer. **1952** R. FINLAYSON *Schooner came to Atia* 118 Shy-eyed kiddies ran out to look. **1917** J. MASEFIELD *Lollingdow Downs* 86 *Shy-footed beauty dear. **1879** ALEXINA M. RUTHQUIST in *Mem.* (1893) 95 His *shy-looking wife. **1930** E. WAUGH *Vile Bodies* ii. 19, I shall just ring up every Cabinet Minister and *all* the newspapers and give them all the most *shy-making details. **1940** M. ALLINGHAM *Black Plumes* xv. 175 Great heroism, like great cowardice, is shy-making, and they were all..embarrassed. **1974** *Listener* 21 Nov. 677/1 Dr Ray rightly quotes enough of their shy-making exchanges. **1742** BLAIR *Grave* 328 From stubborn shrubs Thou wrung'st their *shy-retiring virtues out, And vex'd them in the fire.

**shy** (ʃaɪ), *v.*[1] Also 7 shie, shye. [f. SHY *a.*]
OE. had app. a vb. *scýhan, scýan* to take fright (= sense 3 below) f. the adj. = OHG. *schiuhen*. Cf. the following quot.: *c* **1000** ÆLFRIC *Lives Saints* xxxi. 971 þa scyddon [*MS. K.* scyhdon] þa mulas þe þæt cræt tuȝon, ðurh his to-cyme afyrhte.]

**1.** *intr.* To take a sudden fright or aversion; to make a difficulty, 'boggle' about doing something; to recoil, shrink. Const. *at*, *from*: rarely *to* with infinitive. Now usually felt as *transf.* from 2.
**1650** B. *Discolliminium* 40 Why [do] they shye so strangely at this new Ingagement? **1778** S. CRISP 8 Dec. in *Mme. D'Arblay's Diary* (1891) I. 93, I mean such freedoms as ladies of the strictest character..perhaps would shy at being known to be the authors of. **1783** MME. D'ARBLAY *Diary* 19 June, He was too well-bred to force himself upon me, and finding I shied, he left me alone. *a* **1814** *Word of Honor* III. i. in *New Brit. Theatre* I. 364 A man who loves another's wife, Will never shy to take a wife himself To screen his base intrigue. **1838** LYTTON *Alice* v. ii, The more publicity is given to this arrangement, the more difficult for Evelyn to shy at the leap. **1889** MAY CROMMELIN & BROWN *V. Vyvian* II. xv. 248 She is shying from the thought. **1911** BARRIE *Peter & Wendy* v. 81 The only thing he shied at was the sight of his own blood. **1912** ELINOR GLYN *Halcyone* xxvii. 245 He was not buried in that outer circle of oblivion from which the thoughts unconsciously shy.

**2.** Of a horse: To shrink or start back or aside through sudden fear. Const. *at*, rarely *from*.
**1796** J. LAWRENCE *Treat. Horse* I. 166 Thorough-bred hacks are..the least liable to shy of all others. **1823** SCOTT *Quentin D.* ix, The horse shyed from the boar. **1861** GEN. P. THOMPSON *Audi Alt.* III. 217 There is no use in being ill-humoured because a young horse shies. **1879** BEERBOHM *Patagonia* 20 [The horse] stumbled on, occasionally shying wildly at the glimmering whiteness of some heap of bleached guanaco bones. **1897** *Encycl. Sport* I. 342/1 (Driving) *Shy*, to spring suddenly either sideways or backwards from fear, or from excess of spirits.

**3.** *to shy off* (rarely *to shy out of* something, *to shy away*); To slip away in order to avoid a person or thing; *fig.* to find a means of evasion.
**1792** *Elvina* I. 38 We are obliged to shy off. **1843** MIALL in *Nonconformist* III. 209 Men who desire to get rid of the question..shy off, with wonderful dexterity from all allusions to it. **1856** MASSON *Ess.* iv. 101 The style of poetry ..as all modern readers confess by the alacrity with which they shy out of the way of reprinted specimens of it [etc.]. **1867** AUGUSTA WILSON *Vashti* xiii, His blue eyes rather shied away from mine. **1894** A. ROBERTSON *Nuggets* 111 Elsie was shying off from Alec.

**4.** *trans.* To shun or avoid (a person, thing, or immaterial thing).
**1802** BENTHAM *Mem. & Corr.* Wks. 1843 X. 399, I am inclined to suspect he shies the subject. **1806** SURR *Winter in Lond.* II. 75 He has shied me lately. **1830** FONBLANQUE *Eng. under 7 Administr.* (1837) II. 50 His Grace [Wellington] had shyed the City Feast, being frightened by a Donkey. **1834** MARRYAT *P. Simple* xxxv, Troubridge..was not a man to shy his work. **1872** A. GRAY *Lett.* II. 623, I shy or refuse such applications generally.

**b.** *Pugilism.*
**1812** *Sporting Mag.* XXXIX. 22 It struck us that the Black shyed his adversary. **1819** *Ibid.* N. S. IV. 236 He had too much of the Teddy Tay spirit about him to wince or shy it.

**5.** To render timid or shy; to frighten *off*.
**1845** YOUATT *Dog* iii. 84 A rate given at an improper time ..disgusts the honest hound, it shies and prevents from hunting the timid one. **1853** KANE *Grinnell Exp.* xxii. (1856) 173 A little projection of the main field to windward shied them off.

Hence **'shying** *vbl. sb.* and *ppl. a.*
**1796** J. LAWRENCE *Treat. Horse* I. 81 This was not the effect of starting or shying, to which she [the mare] was at no rate addicted. **1869** J. H. NEWMAN in W. Ward *Life* (1912) II. 257, I hope my shying, as I do, will not keep you from speaking out. *a* **1900** DK. ARGYLL *Autobiog.* (1906) II. 82 They seemed to go suddenly mad, like shying horses or stampeded mules.

**shy** (ʃaɪ), *v.*[2] Chiefly *colloq.* Also 8 shie. [Of obscure origin.
The earliest use suggests that it may have arisen in some way from the expression SHY COCK.]

**1.** *intr.* To throw a missile, esp. carelessly or by a jerk. Const. *at*.
**1787** BENTHAM *Def. Usury* xiii. 164 He looks upon it as a sort of cock for him..to shie at. **1790** GROSE *Prov. Gloss.* (ed. 2), *Shie*, or *Shy*. To shy at a cock, to throw at a cock with a stick. Kent. **1820** J. H. REYNOLDS *Fancy* (1906) 34 I've shy'd with stick, to win a bit The backy-box of brown japan. **1840** DE QUINCEY *Mod. Superst.* Wks. 1862 III. 313 To shy at a cow within six feet distance. **1851** THACKERAY *Stray Papers* (1901) 269 Raikes..justly prided himself upon shying at the sticks better than any man in the army. **1889** BODLEY in *19th Cent.* Nov. 801 The Anglo-Saxon race alone is capable of propelling a missile in the method known as 'shying'.

**2. a.** *trans.* To fling, throw, jerk, toss; also with *at*, etc.
**1793** W. B. STEVENS *Jrnl.* 26 Mar. (1965) I. 74 It was but the other day he thought that every man ought to *shy* Jack Dawson from their Houses and Lo now he is his *dear friend*. **1828** EGAN *Boxiana* IV. 159 The Birmingham Youth..also shied his castor with a confident air. **1831** TRELAWNY *Adv. Younger Son* vii, He then shyed his gold-laced cocked hat. **1835** MARRYAT *Jacob Faithful* xxxiii, I wish he hadn't shied the cat at her. **1853** 'C. BEDE' *Verdant Green* I. viii, When you came to shy empty bottles..he couldn't stand that sort of game. **1857** READE *Never Too Late* xv, He..shied the pieces of glass carefully over the wall. **1874** WALCH *Head over Heels* 74 We could shy up our caps for a feller. **1880** MRS. PARR *Adam & Eve* 233 Her own glass and its contents were shyed to the other end of the room. **1886** G. ALLEN *Maimie's Sake* xviii, I shied the stuff away.

**b.** *transf.* and *fig.*
**1827** SCOTT *Jrnl.* 26 Mar., I cannot keep up with the world without shying a letter now and then. **1860** SIR H. ACLAND in J. B. Atlay *Mem.* (1903) 290 Washington..has a few palaces shied down upon a rubbishy heath. **1868** HELPS *Realmah* (1876) 245 He would merely shy barbarous words, half-Latin, half-Greek at us. **1882** H. C. MERIVALE *Faucit of B.* II. ii. 161 Then you bolted from Oxford, and shied up your fellowship.

**shyche**, obs. form of SUCH.

† **shy cock, 'shy-cock.** *slang. Obs.* [f. SHY *a.* + COCK *sb.*[1]] (? A cock that refuses to fight; also, a cock that is 'shy' or not easily caught. ? Hence:) A wary or cowardly person; also, 'One who keeps within doors for fear of bailiffs' (Grose *Dict. Vulgar T.* 1785).
**1768** GOLDSM. *Goodn. Man.* III, There is not a prettier scout..after a shy-cock than he. **1771** SMOLLETT *Humph. Cl.* 6 May ii, She laid all her snares for Dr. Lewis..but the doctor being a shy cock would not be caught with chaff. **1796** F. REYNOLDS *Fortune's Fool* v. 59 The members rose, lock'd the door, and call'd me a shycock!—forced the pistol into my hand. **1804** *Naval Chron.* XII. 396 He is a *shy-cock*.

**shyer**[1] ('ʃaɪə(r)). [f. SHY *v.*[1] + -ER[1].] A horse which shies.
**1829** J. LAWRENCE *Horse* vi. 35 With affected shyers some severity may be necessary. These chaps generally fix upon some particular shying but: for example, [etc.]. **1886** *York Herald* 9 Aug. 9/3 The horse..was found to be a bad 'shier', and accordingly it was returned.

**shyer**[2] ('ʃaɪə(r)). [f. SHY *v.*[2] + -ER[1].] One who throws.
**1895** in *Funk's Stand. Dict.* **1905** *F. Sugg's Cricket Annual* 46 A good shier can save many runs.

**shyish** ('ʃaɪɪʃ), *a.* [f. SHY *a.* + -ISH.] Somewhat shy.
**1754** SHEBBEARE *Matrimony* (1766) II. 80 Which Salutation he received with but a shyish Kind of Reception. **1825** LAMB *Let. to Wordsw.* May, Do write to Sir G. B., for I am shyish of applying to him. **1858** J. BLACKWOOD in Mrs. G. Porter *Ann. Publishing Ho.* (1898) III. 31[Tennyson] is a striking-looking man, with a shyish, almost awkward, but manly and not unbecoming manner.

**shylle**, obs. form of SHELL.

**Shylock** ('ʃaɪlɒk). The name of the Jewish money-lender in Shakespeare's *Merchant of Venice*; *allusively*, an extortionate usurer. Also, a Jew, a pawnbroker; in *U.S.* (with small initial), an abusive term for a moneylender; = *loan-shark* s.v. LOAN *sb.*[1] 5. (These uses are considered offensive.) Also *attrib.*
**1786** R. CUMBERLAND *Observer* (ed. 2) III. No. 64. 30 Smoke the Jew!..Out with Shylock. **1894** GUNTER *King's Stockbroker* ii. 24 'Won't I beggar my boarders!' With this Shylock idea in his mind,..Lanty cries excitedly to a waiter. **1898** *Westm. Gaz.* 2 July 1/3 The essence of the real Shylock's business is that he extorts money from his victims on threats of various kinds. **1898** W. J. LOCKE *Idols* vi. 81 He could raise the money, cry quits with the urbane and gentle-mannered Shylock. **1901** SKRINE *Life Sir W. Hunter* xiv. 261 The peasantry must be delivered from thraldom to village Shylocks. **1930** *Sat. Even. Post* 5 Apr. 48/1 There are also guys present who are called Shylocks, because they will lend you dough when you go broke at the table, on watches or rings..at very good interest. **1935** *Sun* (Baltimore) 28 Dec. 1/3 The jury held the backbone of the 'shylock' or usury racket had been broken in the city by Dewey. **1951** TURKUS & FEDER *Murder, Inc.* v. 121 'Sometimes it's as good as 3,000 per cent,' one of the shylocks..explained. **1959** I. & P. OPIE *Lore & Lang. Schoolch.* xvi. 346 Today, children colloquially refer to a Jew as a Yid, Shylock, or Hooknose. **1972** *Report to Commissioner* 121 The Panthers are worse than the shylocks... They keep bleeding you. **1976** *Sunday Times* (Lagos) 1 Aug. 21/4 They are expected to alleviate the suffering of the common man who for long has been a victim of Shylock landlords. **1978** S. BRILL *Teamsters* iv. 150 A member who couldn't meet his shylock payments often found that the union people he 'elected', became enforcers against him.

Hence **'Shylock** *v. trans.*, to force (a person) to repay a debt, esp. at an exorbitant rate of interest; **Shy'lockian, 'Shylocky** *adjs.*, after the manner of or characteristic of Shylock; **'shylocker** *U.S.*, one who charges an exorbitant rate of interest; **'shylocking** *vbl. sb.* (*U.S.*)
*a* **1818** M. G. LEWIS *Jrnl. W. Ind.* (1834) 50 It had such a kind of Shylocky taste of raw flesh about it. **1884** *Truth* 4 Sept. 374/1 The terms paid for accommodation were so onerous that the bargain had been a Shylockian one. **1930** H. G. WELLS *Autocracy of Mr. Parham* IV. v. 308 They bullied and quarrelled when we were only too ready for acquiescent action. They Shylocked Europe. **1933** A. G. MACDONELL *England, their England* xiii. 242 One or two of them have had a bit of hard luck lately, and one can't Shylock the poor devils. **1951** TURKUS & FEDER *Murder, Inc.* v. 120 Loan-sharking. 'Shylocking,' it is called. **1961** *Brooklyn Law Rev.* XXVIII. 41 Such activities are the 'shakedown racket', 'shylocking' (where interest of 20% per week is charged...) and labor extortion. **1973** *Listener* 27 Jan. 878/3 Today's Dillinger..controls vice, dope and

shylocking (usury) throughout his State. **1973** J. Gores *Final Notice* xii. 73 He's an enforcer for a shylocker.. with lots of sweet loans to push the vigorish up.

**shyly** (ˈʃaɪlɪ), *adv.* Also **shily.** [f. SHY *a.* + -LY[2].] In a shy manner; with shyness.

**1701** C. Wolley *Jrnl. New York* (1860) 55 Two other Ministers.. who behav'd themselves one towards another so shily and uncharitably as if Luther and Calvin had bequeathed.. their virulent and bigotted Spirits upon them. **1797** T. Holcroft tr. *Stolberg's Trav.* III. lxxix. (ed. 2) 209 The buffalo cow shyly looks about her. **1848** Mill *Pol. Econ.* I. vii. §5 Nations whose commodities are looked shily upon by merchants. **1867** F. Francis *Angling* i. (1880) 58 A very killing plan when the fish are biting shyly. **1884** *Harper's Mag.* July 209/1 Tadoussac.. hides shyly behind its hills.

**shylyng,** obs. form of SCHELLING.

**shymar,** variant of CHIMER[1] *Obs.*

**1674** Blount *Glossogr.* (ed. 4) **1716** M. Davis *Athen. Brit.* III. *Diss. Author Lat. Drama* 35.

**shynd,** variant of SCHYND.

**shynde,** obs. form of SHEND *v.*[1]

**shyness** (ˈʃaɪnɪs). Also **shiness.** [f. SHY *a.* + -NESS.] The condition or quality of being shy.

**1651** Davenant *Gondibert* III. ii. 78 But when he mark'd that he did from them move With sodain shyness, he suppos'd it shame. **1662** H. More *Philos. Writ.* (1712) Pref. p. iii, Men have a shyness and jealousy against such Truths as they have not been acquainted with. **1673** Sir W. Temple *Ess. Adv. Trade Irel.* Misc. I. (1680) 132 This both checks the growth of the common breeds, and gives them an incurable shyness, which is the general vice of Irish Horses. **1710** Steele *Tatler* No. 201 ¶1 The Woman.. is treated with Shiness and Indifference. **1748** *Anson's Voy.* I. vi. 68 Vicunnas.., by reason of their shyness and swiftness, are killed with difficulty. **1818** Oxley *Jrnls. Two Exped. N.S. Wales* (1820) 328 By making them small presents of hooks, lines, &c., this shiness has soon worn off. **1825–9** Mrs. Sherwood *Lady of Manor* IV. xxvii. 285 A word, a look, the neglect of a salutation.. have often produced a shyness among the dearest friends. **1853** Kane *Grinnell Exp.* xxvi. (1856) 214 The shyness of the seal is proverbial. **1909** *Spectator* 30 Oct. 677/1 There are certain shynesses which we regard as becoming.

**shynful,** variant of SHENDFUL *a. Obs.*

**shype ax,** variant of CHIP-AXE.

*c* **1500** *Deb. Carpenters Tools* in Hazl. *E.P.P.* (1864) I. 79 The shype ax seyd unto the wryght [etc.].

**shypoo** (ˈʃaɪpuː, ʃaɪˈpuː). *Austral slang.* Also **shipoo.** [Origin unknown.] Inferior liquor; a public house that sells this. Also *attrib.*

**1901** *Bulletin Reciter* 30 We drank the shypoo deeply, till the lateness of the night. **1908** E. G. Murphy *Jarrahland Jingles* 108 The swell exclusive club, Have swept the shypoo shanty from its lair amid the scrub. **1917** [see Aussie *sb.* and *a.* 1]. **1934** *Bulletin* (Sydney) 22 Aug. 20/1 That bubbling drink and spuming We used to call shypoo? **1936** H. Drake-Brockman *Sheba Lane* 237 How about managing that shipoo for me? **1962** T. Ronan *Deep of Sky* 218 A hostelry ... restricted to the sale of beer and wine. Locally this was known as the 'Shypoo Shop'. I'm not sure of the derivation of 'Shypoo'. I think it is bastard Chinese for soft drink. To the sturdy second wave of pioneers of West Kimberley, beer and wine were soft drinks.

**shyrpe,** variant of SHERPE *Obs.*

**shyrrywyke,** obs. form of SHERIFFWICK.

**shyryf(e,** etc. obs. forms of SHERIFF.

**shyst,** obs. form of SCHIST.

**1793** [Earl Dundonald] *Descr. Culross* 6 A stratum of Feruginous Sulphurious Slate or Shyst.

**shyster** (ˈʃaɪstə(r)). Also **shuyster.** [Of obscure origin.

It might be f. SHY *a.* (sense 7, disreputable) + *-ster*; but this sense of the adj. is app. not current in the U.S.]

**1.** 'A lawyer who practises in an unprofessional or tricky manner; especially, one who haunts the prisons and lower courts to prey on petty criminals; hence, any one who conducts his business in a tricky manner' (*Funk's Stand. Dict.* 1895). Also *attrib.* or *adj.* Orig. and chiefly *U.S. slang.*

**1844** G. Wilkes *Mysteries of Tombs* 44/1 He is consulted by the magistrates on all important points of law, and the inferior shysters look upon him with a reverence approaching veneration. **1849** G. G. Foster *New York in Slices* 20 He must.. wait next day for the visits of the 'shyster' lawyers—a set of turkey-buzzards whose touch is pollution and whose breath is pestilence. **1856** *Knickerb. Mag.* Apr. XLVII. 434 (Thornton *Amer. Gloss.*) If these two 'shuysters' on the other side could get one more drink down your throat, you couldn't travel at all. **1857** *N.Y. Tribune* 13 Mar. (Bartlett 1860) The shysters, or Tombs lawyers, were on hand, and sought to intercede for their clients. *a* **1860** *N.Y. Tribune* (ibid.), When a man or woman is thrown into prison, a shyster leech gets access to him, and extorts from him his last cent under the pretence of obtaining his liberation. **1877** Black *Green Past.* xli, They ..looked on a prominent civic official as a mere shyster. **1902** Boothby *Uncle Joe's Legacy* 98 The shyster lawyer. **1943** M. H. Harris *Vegetative Eye* 15 Not to Memory, with its shyster lackey, Association. **1952** *Manch. Guardian Weekly* 19 June 3 They call Taft's 'shyster methods' so necessary. **1961** *Listener* 14 Dec. 1046/1 A solicitor's chief clerk who persuades his shyster employer to leave the country to avoid embezzlement charges. **1981** J. Wainwright *All on Summer's Day* 31 The shyster lawyers ..swear blind the client's been manhandled while in police custody.

**2.** *Austral.* Alteration of SHICER.

**1938** X. Herbert *Capricornia* (1939) xxi. 306 You lousy sweatin' old shyster you. **1941** Baker *Dict. Austral. Slang* 66 *Shyster*, a worthless mine.

Hence **'shystering** *vbl. sb.* and *ppl. a.*

**1860** *Knickerb. Mag.* Nov. LVI. 458 (Thornton *Amer. Gloss.*) A kind of twopenny shystering smartness and snap-judgment smartness. **1872** Bristed in R. G. White *Amer. View Copyright* (1880) 40 At Tuesday's session an unprepossessing person.. made a 'shystering' pettifogging speech. **1895** *Weekly Exam.* (San Francisco) 19 Sept. 2/6 Those sharp practices generally passing under the name of shystering.

**si** (siː). *Mus.* [Cf. quots. 1850 and 1875. For various accounts as to the originator, see Grove *Dict. Music* and Littré.] In solmization, the seventh note of the scale.

**1728** Chambers *Cycl.* s.v., *Si*, in Music, a Seventh Note, added within this Sixty Years, by one le Maire, to the Six ancient Notes. **1797** *Encycl. Brit.* (ed. 3) XII. 545 *note*, A note which is a tone immediately above the tonic, as *re* in the mode of *ut*, and *si* in that of *la*, is termed a sub-tonic. **1850** Helmore *Plain-Song* iv. 22 The syllable *si* for the seventh sound of our octave was in more recent times added, from the initial letters of the closing words, *Sancte Iohannes*. **1875** Stainer & Barrett *Dict. Mus. Terms* s.v. *Notation*, Here was a *sa* for the seventh note of the scale; but.. it was not employed. In later use, in order to mark another semitone by the final *i* (as in *mi*) *sa* was turned into *si*.

**si,** obs. pa. t. of SEE *v.*

**siacalle,** obs. variant of JACKAL *sb.*

**Siad,** obs. variant of SAYYID.

**siafu** (sɪˈɑːfuː). [Swahili.] = *safari ant* s.v. SAFARI 3 d. Also *attrib.*

[**1920** G. D. H. Carpenter *Naturalist on Lake Victoria* xii. 276 The ant that most obtrusively calls for notice is the well known *Dorylus* or 'Safari ant',.. in Kiswahili called 'Siafu'.] **1959** E. Huxley *Flame Trees of Thika* xv. 154 The rain brought out the *siafu*. Those fearful black rivers of implacable insects poured between their low mud banks over the garden. **1976** [see *safari ant* s.v. SAFARI 3]. **1977** Reader & Croze *Pyramids of Life* 212/1 The most effective and thorough carnivore hunter in the forest is a colony of siafu (*Dorylus*), the so-called army ant.

**siagonology** (saɪəgəˈnɒlədʒɪ). [f. Gr. σιαγόν-, σιαγών jaw-bone + -OLOGY.] (See quot.)

**1895** Raven *Hist. Suffolk* 253 Something may be discoverable by craniology,.. odontology, or siagonology, which is the science of jaw-bones.

**siagush,** variant of SYAGUSH.

**sial** (ˈsaɪəl). *Geol.* Also **Sial.** [a. G. *sial*, f. *si-licium* SILICON + *al-uminium* ALUMINIUM.

The name was altered from *sal* (see SAL[4] 2) by G. Pfeffer in order to avoid confusion with other meanings of that word (see A. Wegener *Die Entstehung der Kontinente und Ozeane* (1920) iii. 22 and quot. 1924 below).]

The discontinuous upper layer of the earth's crust represented by the continental masses, which are composed of relatively light rocks rich in silica and alumina and may be regarded as floating on a lower crustal layer of sima; the material of which these masses are composed.

**1922** [see SAL[4] 2]. **1923** *Rep. Brit. Assoc. Adv. Sci. 1922* 364 Sial masses drift through the Sima like icebergs through the sea. **1924** J. G. A. Skerl tr. *Wegener's Orig. Continents & Oceans* iii. 36 Following a short communication from Pfeffer I should like to write 'Sial' instead of 'Sal' in order that there may be no confusion with the Latin word for Salt. **1927** Peake & Fleure *Apes & Men* ii. 18 Various crises have led to the splitting of the Sial, and.. its fragments have wandered off in many directions. **1950** P. H. Kuenen *Marine Geol.* ii. 118 The isostatic equilibrium of the crust requires a considerable thickness of granitic sial in the continents and a rock of greater density in the oceanic sections. **1954** [see SAL[4] 2]. **1978** D. Bridgwater et al. in D. H. Tarling *Evol. Earth's Crust* ii. 63 In the type of Archaean craton displayed in southern Africa break up and partial destruction of earlier sial probably took place in a different tectonic regime.

Hence **si'alic** *a.*[1], of or pertaining to the continental crust or the material of which it is made.

**1924** J. G. A. Skerl tr. *Wegener's Orig. Continents & Oceans* iv. 59 Molten sialic masses (granite) from the under side of the South American block.. have emerged on its posterior edge. **1944** A. Holmes *Princ. Physical Geol.* ii. 14 There should be bulges.. where gravity is relatively low; that is to say, wherever the outer part of the crust is composed of light sialic rocks. Such places are the continents. **1955** *Sci. Amer.* Sept. 62/1 Because granite is the chief sialic rock and basalt the chief simatic one, the continents are most commonly described as granitic and the ocean basins as basaltic. **1970** *Ibid.* Feb. 32/3 Stresses in the earth's crust may crack the sialic layer, producing faults and fissures that can be as much as 20 meters wide. **1975** *Nature* 3 Apr. 397/2 Localised partial melting of ancient, sialic crust may.. occur in the zone of heating above large bodies of basic igneous magma introduced into high crustal levels.

**sialadenitis:** see s.v. SIALO-.

**siala'gogic,** *sb.* and *a. Med.* Also **sialo-.** [See next and -IC.] = next.

**1891** in *Cent. Dict.*

**sialagogue** (ˈsaɪələgɒg), *sb.* and *a. Med.* Also **sialogogue.** [a. F. *sialagogue* (1752), or ad. mod.L. *sialagogus, -um*, f. Gr. σίαλον saliva + ἀγωγός leading, drawing forth: cf. *cholagogue, emmenagogue*.]

**A.** *sb.* A medicine which has the effect of producing a flow of saliva.

α. **1794–6** E. Darwin *Zoon.* (1801) II. 461 Any acrid drug, as pyrethrum, held in the mouth acts as a sialagogue externally by stimulating the excretory ducts of the salivary glands. **1841** *Penny Cycl.* XXI. 448/1 Remote sialagogues are first received into the system by the stomach or other channels. **1855** Garrod *Materia Medica* 231 When chewed it acts as a sialagogue, and is sometimes used in relaxed states of the uvula and tonsils.

β. **1783** *Encycl. Brit.* (ed. 2) X. 8153/1 *Sialogogues*, medicines which promote the salivary discharge. **1834** *Good's Study Med.* (ed. 4) I. 662 Admitting all that can be said in favour of employing mercury as a sialogogue. **1859** J. Tomes *Dental Surg.* 490 The local remedies for toothache, ..excepting only sialogogues.

**B.** *adj.* Inducing a flow of saliva.

**1855** Garrod *Materia Medica* 54 Its sialagogue power is shown in the increase of the salivary fluid and mucous secretions of the mouth. **1876** Bartholow *Mat. Med. & Therap.* (1879) 262 It has remarkable sialagogue property.

**sialectasis** (saɪəˈlɛktəsɪs). *Path.* [f. SIALO- + Gr. ἔκτασις dilatation.] Dilatation of the ducts of the salivary glands, usu. the parotids.

**1940** *Brit. Jrnl. Surg.* XXVII. 713 The term 'sialectasis' which has been used to describe the condition is not strictly correct etymologically, translating as 'a stretching out or dilatation of the saliva'. **1953** *Brit. Med. Jrnl.* 19 Dec. 1359/2 The underlying pathology in.. sialectasis, sialangiectasis, or chronic recurrent parotitis, is obscure, but the essential feature is obstruction of the parotid ducts. **1974** J. D. Maynard in R. M. Kirk et al. *Surgery* ix. 201 The parotid architecture may be normal or reveal the curious appearance reminiscent of radiographs of bronchiectasis, called sialectasis. **1977** [see SICCA[2]].

**sialic,** *a.*[1]: see SIAL.

**sialic** (ˈsaɪəlɪk), *a.*[2] *Biochem.* [f. Gr. σίαλ-ον saliva + -IC.] *sialic acid*: any acyl or related derivative of a neuraminic acid.

Orig. applied *spec.* to a substance of this type (then of unknown structure) isolated from the salivary glands of cattle.

**1952** G. Blix et al. in *Acta Chem. Scand.* VI. 359 Besides this substance, for which we propose the provisional name sialic acid, the mucin contains small amounts of carbohydrate of the dihexose-hexosamine type. **1957** —— in *Nature* 25 May 1088/2 Sialic acid is suggested as group name for the acylated neuraminic acids. **1967** *New Scientist* 16 Feb. 414/1 Twenty years elapsed before the structure of this complex sugar was determined, and by then it was clear that it was only one of a family of sugars called sialic acids, all of which had an unusually long backbone of nine carbon atoms. **1978** *Nature* 16 Feb. 674/2 Sialic acids.. of the red blood cell (RBC) membrane are considered to play an important part in the physiology of the RBC.

**sialidase** (saɪˈælɪdeɪz). *Biochem.* [f. prec. + -ID[4] + -ASE.] = NEURAMINIDASE.

**1956** Heimer & Meyer in *Proc. Nat. Acad. Sci.* XLII. 731 The bond split must be O-glycosidic rather than N-glycosidic... The name 'sialidase' is proposed for the enzyme responsible for this action. **1963** Barka & Anderson *Histochemistry* iii. 94 Sialidase, an enzyme that selectively removes sialic acid.. from mucopolysaccharides, eliminates the metachromatic staining and Alcian blue affinity of some acid mucopolysaccharides. **1978** A. White et al. *Princ. Biochem.* (ed. 6) xxix. 916 It remains unclear how sialic acid in mammals or galactose in birds and reptiles is removed in vivo from plasma glycoproteins, although sialidase and β-galactosidases are present in many tissues.

**siallite** (ˈsaɪəlaɪt). *Geol.* [ad. G. *siallit* (H. Harrassowitz 1926, in *Fortschr. Geol. Palæont.* IV. 263), f. as SIAL: see -ITE[1].] Weathered rock that is largely composed of hydrous aluminium silicates and is highly leached of alkalis. So **sia'llitic** *a.*

**1933** H. Greene tr. *Vageler's Introd. Tropical Soils* v. 127 Where the amount of water is small and the period of action is short, as in the case of arid and semi-arid districts, siallitic and allitic bodies are formed in small amount. *Ibid.* 140 The soil becomes podsolised. The long-held opinion that this produces not merely siallites in general but a quite special kaolin and kaolinite can no longer be maintained. **1965** B. T. Bunting *Geogr. of Soil* xiv. 168 Other forms of brown earth are formed on siallitic parent materials which may overlie chalk.

**sialo-** (saɪələʊ), before a vowel also **sial-,** comb. form of Gr. σίαλον saliva, used as a formative element in *Med.*, as **ˌsial(o)ade'nitis** [Gr. ἀδήν gland], inflammation of a salivary gland; **'sialolith** [-LITH], a calculus in a salivary gland; hence **ˌsialoli'thiasis**, the presence of such a calculus; **sialorrhœa** (-ˈriːə) [-RRHŒA, -RRHEA], excessive flow of saliva.

**1859** Mayne *Expos. Lex.* (1860) 1159/2 Sialadenitis. **1925** Marshall & Piney *Textbk. Surg. Path.* vi. 123 Chronic sialo-adenitis may affect either the parotid or submaxillary and may be associated with calculi. **1977** *Arch. Virol.* LIV. 352 Sialoadenitis produced by PRCV.. was morphologically compatible with SDAV-induced lesions. [**1855** Dunglison *Dict. Med. Sci.* (ed. 12) 787/2 *Sialolithi*, calculi, salivary.] **1862** Mayne *Med. Vocab.* (ed. 2) 373/2 *Sialolithus*, a salival calculus; a sialolith. **1910** Adami & Nicholls *Princ. Path.* II. xvii. 396 Concretions composed of phosphate or carbonate of lime are not uncommonly found within the [salivary] duct (sialoliths), sometimes causing or associated with cystic dilatation of the ducts and acini. **1973** *Brit. Dental Jrnl.* CXXXV. 292/2 The sialolith was club-shaped, yellow in colour and measured 14 mm in length. **1859** MAYNE *Expos. Lex.* (1860) 1160/1 Sialolithiasis. **1916** L. F. BARKER *Monographic Med.* III. VIII. 264 Stone is sometimes palpable in a salivary duct (sialolithiasis). **1973** *Brit. Dental Jrnl.* CXXXV. 291/1 Sialolithiasis, the formation of a calculus in the duct or gland substance of a major or minor salivary gland, occurs most commonly in the middle-aged adult. **1846** *Lond. Med. Gaz.* XXXVII. 379/1 In the idiopathic sialorrhœa..the flow takes place as well in the night as in the day time. **1888** *Buck's Handbk. Med. Sci.* VI. 251/1 The term sialorrhea, while indicating an abnormal flow, does not necessarily imply abnormal secretion. **1933** *Ann. Rep. London County Council* IV. III. 135 At the same time the face may be distorted into a spasmodic grimace, accompanied by flushing, lachrymation and sialorrhœa. **1978** *Jrnl. R. Soc. Med.* LXXI. 346 Abnormal conditions, such as excessive diarrhoea, sialorrhoea or sweating.

**sialoglycoprotein** (ˌsaɪələʊglaɪkəʊˈprəʊtiːn). *Biochem.* [f. SIAL(IC *a.*[2] + -O + *glycoprotein* (s.v. GLYCO-).] Any glycoprotein in which sialic acid residues form a major constituent of the side chains.

**1963** A. GOTTSCHALK in Florkin & Stotz *Comprehensive Biochem.* VIII. i. 29 All sialo-glycoproteins have some features in common. Invariably their sialic acid residues occupy a terminal position and are linked through a neuraminidase susceptible α-ketosidic linkage to another sugar residue. **1965** *Biochimica & Biophysica Acta* CI. 166 A homogeneous 7·1 S sialoglycoprotein..composed of 5·9% neutral carbohydrates, 4·8% aminosugars and 4·4% sialic acid. **1976** *Nature* 20 May 236/2 Liposomes bearing sialoglycoproteins can participate in agglutination reactions mediated by appropriate lectins.

**sialography** (saɪəˈlɒgrəfɪ). *Med.* [f. SIALO- + -GRAPHY.] Radiography of the ducts of a salivary gland after they have been injected with a radio-opaque fluid.

**1931** *Brit. Jrnl. Surg.* XIX. 142 Sialography will demonstrate abnormalities, dilatations, and obstructions of the larger and smaller parotid ducts. **1960** *Radiology* LXXIV. 138/1 Secretory sialography has been a useful aid in determining whether tumors in the submaxillary and parotid regions are within or adjacent to the major salivary glands. **1975** *Ibid.* CXVII. 220/1 Sialography, the demonstration of ducts and parenchyma of the major salivary glands by injection of contrast material in the gland's main secretory duct, has been practiced since its first description by Arcelin in 1913. **1977** [see SICCA[2]].

Hence **ˈsialogram**, an X-ray photograph made by this technique; **sialoˈgraphic** *a.*

**1931** *Brit. Jrnl. Surg.* XIX. 144 The sialogram shows the main duct of the gland, the larger branches, and the ductules, all well filled with lipiodol. **1938** *Surg., Gynecol. & Obstetr.* LXVII. 777 A sialographic study of 23 normal parotid glands and 76 cases of neoplastic disease of the parotid. **1974** J. D. MAYNARD in R. M. Kirk et al. *Surgery* ix. 201 If symptoms are sufficiently worrying to the patient and a sialogram reveals gross dilation of the main duct, ablative..surgery is indicated. **1976** *Radiology* CXXI. 747/1 A..curved side-hole cannula for use in sialographic procedures.

**sialomucin** (saɪələʊˈmjuːsɪn). *Biochem.* [f. SIAL(IC *a.*[2] + -O + MUCIN.] Any mucin containing sialic acid residues in the molecule.

**1958** L. ODIN in Wolstenholme & O'Connor *Ciba Found. Symp. Chem. & Biol. Mucopolysaccharides* 235 The second main type of epithelial glycoprotein contains sialic acid as its characteristic carbohydrate constituent... This type of glycoprotein will for convenience be called sialomucin. **1976** *Path. Ann.* XI. 172 A recent study of the mucin.. suggests that it is a sialomucin with minor sulphomucin and neutral mucin components.

**sialon** (ˈsaɪəlɒn). *Chem.* [f. the chemical symbols for silicon (*Si*), aluminium (*Al*), oxygen (*O*), and nitrogen (*N*).] Any of a large class of refractory materials which have crystal structures similar to those of silica and the silicates but contain aluminium and nitrogen in the polymeric framework in addition to silicon and oxygen.

**1973** K. H. JACK in *Trans. & Jrnl. Brit. Ceramic Soc.* LXXII. 380/1 The structural unit of β-silicon nitride is $SiN_4$; of α it is on average $SiN_{3.9}O_{0.1}$; of oxynitride it is $SiN_3O$; and of the new 'sialons' it is (Si, Al)(O, N)$_4$. **1975** P. POPPER *Special Ceramics* VI. p. ix, Several papers deal with materials in the Si-Al-O-N or Mg-Si-Al-O-N system. Colloquially, workers in this field have become accustomed to refer to them as 'sialons'. **1981** *Economist* 11 Apr. 98/3 The new materials mentioned at last week's conference included..very strong ceramics called sialons.

†**sialoquent**, *a. Obs.*[—0] [Irreg. f. Gr. σίαλον + pres. pple. of L. *loqui* to speak.] (See quot.)

**1656** BLOUNT *Glossogr.*, *Sialoquent* (*sialoquus*), that spits much in his speech.

**siamang** (ˈsaɪəmæŋ). [Malay *si(y)āmang*, f. *āmang* black.] A species of large ape (*Hylobates syndactylus*), with long black hair, found in Sumatra and the Malay Peninsula.

**1822** SIR STAMFORD RAFFLES in *Trans. Linnæan Soc.* XIII. 242, I have recently procured a living Siamang, which is very tame and tractable. **1838** *Penny Cycl.* XII. 408/1 The Siamang of the Malays..has a peculiar formation of the hands or feet of the lower extremities. **1880** *Cassell's Nat. Hist.* I. 75 The ability to walk well was proved when a tame Siamang used to walk along a cabin table at sea, without disturbing the crockery.

**siambock**, obs. form of SJAMBOK.

†**Siamer.** *Obs. rare.* [See next and -ER.] A native of Siam.

**1697** DAMPIER *Voy.* (1729) I. 504 The Siamers were now at Wars with the English. **1727** A. HAMILTON *New Acc. E. Ind.* II. xlviii. 196 When the Siam Army and Fleet threatned Cambodia, the King knew his Inability to withstand the Siamers.

**Siamese** (saɪəˈmiːz), *a.* and *sb.* [f. the name of the country *Siam* (now Thailand) + -ESE. Cf. F. *Siamois.*]

**A.** *adj.* **1. a.** Of or pertaining to Siam or its inhabitants; also in the specific names of animals or birds.

**1693** A. P. tr. *De la Loubère's Hist. Rel. Siam* 8 The Siamese History is full of Fables. **1728** CHAMBERS *Cycl.* s.v. *Aloes*, The Siamese Embassadors. **1797** *Encycl. Brit.* (ed. 3) I. 494/1 From this Shanscrit are derived the sacred characters of Thibet,.. the Singalese, Siamese, Maharatan, ..&c. **1827** GRIFFITH tr. *Cuvier* III. 406 The Siamese Pig is small, long bodied, very low on the limbs. **1876** *Nature* XIV. 343/2 The additions to the Zoological Society's Gardens.. include..a Siamese Pheasant (*Euplocamus prælatus*). **1880** *Cassell's Nat. Hist.* IV. 265 A species..is called the Siamese Muggar, and has a close resemblance to the Marsh Crocodile of India.

**b.** ***Siamese cat***, a lightly built shorthaired cat belonging to a breed originally found in Thailand, distinguished by buff-coloured fur with points of brown, blue, or other colours, and a narrow head with large ears and slanting blue eyes; so ***Siamese kitten***.

**1871** *Illustr. London News* 22 July 63/2 It [*sc.* the variety class at the Crystal Palace cat show] contained..a singular Siamese cat, coloured precisely like a black-faced pug-dog. **1889** H. WEIR *Our Cats* 73 Siamese Cat. Among the beautiful varieties of the domestic cat brought into notice by cat shows, none deserve more attention than 'The Royal Cat of Siam'. **1942** Siamese kitten [see *pet-shop* s.v. PET *sb.*[1] 3 d]. **1958** *Listener* 18 Sept. 410/1 There are many legends and stories about the origin of Siamese cats but few facts. **1972** ING & POND *Champion Cats of World* 109 The Siamese Cat Club was founded in 1901.

**c.** ***Siamese fighter, fighting fish***, a brightly coloured, often red, tropical fish, *Betta splendens*, native to Malaysia and Thailand, and distinguished by enlarged fins and tail.

**1929** W. T. INNES *Goldfish Varieties* (ed. 11) 256 (*caption*) *Betta splendens*, Cambodia variety, or Veiltail Siamese Albino Fighting Fish. **1968** R. CLAPPERTON *No News on Monday* i. 9 Fifty bucks' worth of aquarium: two purple Siamese fighters hovering motionless, separated by glass. **1971** *Ceylon Observer* (Mag. ed.) 19 Sept. 2/6 (Advt.), Goldfish..Siamese Fighters. **1977** D. J. COFFEY *Encycl. Aquarium Fish* 67/1 Siamese Fighting-fish are aggressive.

**2. a.** ***Siamese twins***, two male natives of Siam, Chang and Eng (1811–1874), who were united by a tubular band in the region of the waist. Hence *gen.*, any pair of twins physically united by their tissues; *sing.* one of a pair of such twins. Also *attrib.* (in sing.) and *fig.*

**1829** *Times* 25 Nov. 2/6 The Siamese United Twins. *Ibid.* 26 Nov. 2/3 It is announced..in the Paris papers of Monday, that the Sardinian girl with two heads died on the preceding day. The Siamese twins will therefore have a clear field in that capital. **1835** DICKENS in *Evening Chron.* 18 June 4 They were three long graces in drapery, with.. another..the three fates with another sister—the Siamese twins multiplied by two. **1859** GEO. ELIOT *Let.* 27 Feb. (1954) III. 27 People who have been inseparable and found *all* their happiness in each other for five years are in a sort of Siamese-twin condition that other people are not likely to regard with tolerance or even with belief. **1879** *Mind* IV. 331 Should the empiricists succeed in their attempt to resolve such Siamese-twin elements into habitual juxtapositions. **1883** *Encycl. Brit.* XVI. 765/2 The most intelligible form of double monstrosity, like the Siamese twins. **1883** E. W. HAMILTON *Diary* 18 Dec. (1972) II. 526 Chamberlain also spoke briefly. He passed a high eulogy on Dilke—they are the Siamese twins of politicians. **1899** *Daily News* 15 Mar. 4/4 The death of M. Erckmann..removes the last of the Siamese twins of French fiction. **1900** H. W. SMYTH *Gk. Melic Poets* 278 Kteatos and Eurytos, the Siamese Twins of Greek mythology. **1922** JOYCE *Ulysses* 404 Heated argument..regarding the juridical and theological dilemma in the event of one Siamese twin predeceasing the other. **1926** J. S. HUXLEY *Ess. Pop. Sci.* 235 Partial constriction [of a newt embryo] produces partial doubling or 'Siamese twins'. **1937** H. H. NEWMAN et al. *Twins* xiii. 355 Conjoined twins (Siamese twins) show marked differences in height, weight, features, and intelligence. **1957** MANKOWICZ & HAGGAR *Encycl. Eng. Pott. & Porc.* 202/1 The Kentish Siamese twins, Eliza and Mary Chalkhurst (who died in 1734 at the age of 34) were apparently made in redware. **1957** E. H. SHEPARD *Drawn from Memory* ix. 172 She was a queer experiment in ship design, a sort of Siamese twin of a ship; two complete hulls joined together in the middle. She had two sets of engines and two funnels. **1961** R. B. LONG *Sentence & its Parts* iv. 106 Here *on Thursdays* is followed by two complete nucleuses, tied together in Siamese-twin fashion by joint possession of the introductory adjunct. **1965** E. GOWERS *Fowler's Mod. Eng. Usage* (ed. 2) 554/1 *Siamese twins.* This seems a suitable term for the many words which, linked in pairs by *and* or *or*, are used to convey a single meaning. *Ibid.* 554/2 Whenever a Siamese twin suggests itself to a writer, he should be on his guard; it may be just the phrase he wants, but it is more likely to be one of those clichés that are always lying in wait to fill a vacuum in the brain. **1970** G. GREER *Female Eunuch* 245 The bitter animosity..of divorce is unknown where individuals have not become Siamese twins. **1972** MILLER & KEANE *Encycl. & Dict. Med. & Nursing* 876/1 New techniques in surgery..are making it possible to separate some Siamese twins whose physical links are highly complex. **1981** *Birds* Spring 63/1 My neighbour found Siamese twin starlings caught on some old wire... They had two legs each, but only three feet. The inner leg of each bird was joined together with one foot between them. **1981** *N.Y. Times Mag.* 19 July 6/4 The Kennedy prose style was a product of him and his Siamese twin, Theodore Sorensen, writing freely with his free arm.

**b.** Twin; closely connected or similar. Also, pertaining to or characteristic of Siamese twins.

**1833** T. HOOK *Parson's Dau.* I. xii, We must leave the ladies to themselves for a short time, in order to take another glance at the Siamese willow-wearers at Ullsford. **1851** H. MELVILLE *Moby Dick* II. xxx. 206 So, then, an elongated Siamese ligature [*sc.* monkey-rope] united us. **1857** BREEN *Mod. Eng. Lit.* 72 They toss the lord and his page in the same blanket, and then they turn them adrift in the Siamese character of 'milord'. **1904** HICHENS *Woman with Fan* vi, Miss Schley's said to be like me not only in appearance but in other ways. Are we really so Siamese? **1955** E. BOWEN *World of Love* v. 87 In step, in Siamese closeness, they paced towards it. **1969** N. J. BERRILL *Person in Womb* xiii. 158 Siamese conditions meant death of mother and offspring during the agony of delivery.

**c.** ***Siamese coupling***, a form of coupling used for fire-hose. Also ***Siamese connection***.

**1891** *Scribner's Mag.* Jan. 63/2 The siamese coupling, by which the power of two or more engines may be united on one hose. **1914** J. KENLON *Fires & Firefighters* xxii. 322 A length of three-inch hose is attached to the pipe and strapped to the ladder with a siamese connection on the ground.

**B.** *sb.* **1.** A native of Siam.

**1693** A. P. tr. *De la Loubère's Hist. Rel. Siam* 6 The Name of Siam is unknown to the Siamese. **1797** *Encycl. Brit.* (ed. 3) XVII. 449/1 The Siamese prepare the land for tillage as soon as the earth is sufficiently moistened by the floods. **1808** LEYDEN in *Asiatic Res.* X. 240 The *Thay* language is that which is used by the Siamese. **1842** PRICHARD *Nat. Hist. Man* 238 The average height of the Siamese is 5 feet 3 inches.

**2.** The language of Siam.

**1759** *Universal Hist., Mod.* VII. 238 The Siamese resembles the Chinese in several respects: it consists mostly in monosyllables, and has neither declensions nor conjugations. **1808** LEYDEN in *Asiatic Res.* X. 242 The *T'hay* language, or Siamese. **1854** LATHAM in *Orr's Circle Sci., Org. Nat.* I. 315 The Khamti language..is so like the Siamese of the capital [etc.]. **1886** *Encycl. Brit.* XXI. 855/1 The foreign ingredients in Siamese are principally Sanskrit.

**3.** A Siamese cat.

**1893** J. JENNINGS *Domestic or Fancy Cats* ii. 17 A pure-bred Siamese is a valuable cat. **1939** T. S. ELIOT *Old Possum's Practical Cats* 15 It was a Siamese had mauled his missing ear. **1950** W. DE LA MARE *Inward Companion* 70 That crafty cat, a buff-black Siamese, Sniffing through wild wood. **1973** 'E. MCBAIN' *Let's hear it for Deaf Man* iii. 37 Janik himself resembled a cross-eyed Siamese, blue eyes magnified behind bifocals..a tuft of black hair behind each ear.

**4.** A Siamese coupling or connection.

**1914** J. KENLON *Fires & Firefighting* xxii. 322 Run in two lines, connect to the siamese, raise the bed ladder to the desired position and the stream is controlled from the street by guys. **1969** *Publ. Amer. Dial. Soc.* LII. 55 *Siamese*,..a connector joint used for reducing two lines into one line. 'A Siamese will allow more pressure than a single line.'

**Siamese** (saɪəˈmiːz), *v.* [f. prec. A. 2.] *trans.* To join, unite, or couple, after the manner of the Siamese twins.

**1830** *Fraser's Mag.* I. 427 They are..Siamesed by a cord which defies the knife of the most skilful surgeon. **1834** *Blackw. Mag.* XXXV. 510 We are Siamesed to France; we cannot cut asunder the link without hazarding blood. **1902** *Encycl. Brit.* XXVIII. 405 Three or four lines of 2½ inch hose are united or 'Siamesed' into one larger one.

Hence **Siaˈmesed** *ppl. a.*

**1833** T. HOOK *Parson's Dau.* I. xi, The master of the George appeared at the head of his waiters, bearing the Siamesed repast for the two disconsolate lovers. **1914** J. KENLON *Fires & Firefighting* 377 For siamesed lines, an allowance was made for the loss in the siamese connection and for 20 feet of 3½-inch lead hose. **1942** POTTS & HARRISS *Fire Pumps & Hydraulics* viii. 59 Where series pumping has to be resorted to it is desirable to employ 'Siamesed' lines, i.e. to duplicate the deliveries from the pump or pumps in the series up to the final pump. **1970** B. KNOX *Children of Mist* i. 20 The Jaguar..had twin carburetters plus a siamesed exhaust.

†**Siamit(e.** *Obs.* A native of Siam.

**1601** R. JOHNSON *Kingd. & Commonw.* (1603) 193 Although he be Lord of nine kingdomes, yet useth he no other nation in the war but the Siamits. **1613** PURCHAS *Pilgrimage* v. ii. 387 The Siamites commonly hold, that God created all things. **1699** DAMPIER *Voy.* (1729) II. I. 16 The Siamites and Chinese.

**siampan**, obs. form of SAMPAN[1].

**siatica**, obs. form of SCIATICA.

**sib** (sɪb), *sb.*[1] Now *rare.* Also 1 sibb, 4 syb; (1–3 *inflected*) 5 sibbe, 5–6 sybbe. [Common Teut.: OE. *sib(b*, = OFris. *sibbe*, OS. *sibbia*, *sibbea* (MLG. *sibbe*), OHG. *sippia*, *sippa* (MHG. and G. *sippe*), ON. **sif* (pl. *sifjar*), Goth. *sibja*, related to next.]

**1.** Kinship, relationship.

*Beowulf* 2431 Heold mec and hæfde Hreðel cyning, ȝeaf me sinc and symbel, sibbe ȝemunde. *c* **893** K. ÆLFRED *Oros.* I. ii. 30 Hio ȝesette..þæt nan forbyrd nære æt ȝeliȝere betwuh nanre sibbe. *c* **1050** *O.E. Chron.* (MS. C) an. 1049, Ða wende Beorn for þære sibbe þæt he him swican nolde. **13..** *K. Alis.* 1712 (Laud MS.), For his nexte by syb Cosyn Beep jubiter and Appolyn. *c* **1489** CAXTON *Sonnes of Aymon* i. 18 Manye of theim were of Sybbe to hym. **1491** —— *Vitas Patr.* (W. de W. 1495) II. 197/2 They hadde noo sybbe or kyndrede togydre; but oonly of that theyr husbondes were brethern germayn. **1534** MORE *Comf. agst. Trib.* II. Wks.

1186/2 The doughter of pusillanimitie, & therby so nere of sybbe vnto the nights feare. **1549** CHALONER *Erasm. on Folly* C iv, Do you not count hym next of sybbe to a fool? **1804** W. TARRAS *Poems* 14 Lat's try this income, how he stands, An' eik us sib by shakin' hands. **1858** M. PORTEOUS *Souter Johnny* 8 Tam could bauldly claim Sib wi' an auld heroic name.

†**2.** Peace, amity, concord. *Obs.*

*c* **825** *Vesp. Ps.* xxvii. 3 Ða ðe spreocað sibbe mid ðone nestan. *Ibid.* xxxvii. 4 Nis sib banum minum. *c* **900** tr. *Baeda's Hist.* III. xiv. 194 Ne meahte he hwæðere mid þone cyning..sibbe habban; ac swa micel..unsibb betweoh him aras, þætte heo heora weorod & fyrd ȝesomnodon. *c* **1154** *O.E. Chron.* an. 1140, He helde him for fader, & he him for sune, & sib & sæhte sculde ben betwyx heom. *c* **1205** LAY. 11308 Ich þe wulle luuien & halden þe for lauerd mid sæhte & mid sibbe. *c* **1275** *Duty Christians* 98 in *O.E. Misc.* 144 We schulde among vs habben ay soþe luue and sibbe.

**sib** (sɪb), *a.* and *sb.*² Forms: 1- sib, 1-4, 6, 9 sibb, 4-6 syb (5 sybb), 8 *Sc.* sub; (1-3 *inflected*) 4-7, 9 sibbe, 4, 6 sibe, 5-6 sybbe (5 cybbe). [OE. *sib(b*, = OFris. (and Fris.) *sib*, MDu. *sib(be*, *zibbe*, OHG. *sippi* (MHG. *sippe*), Goth. (*un*)*sibjis*. With the sb. uses cf. OFris. *sibba*, *sibbe*, MDu. *sibbe*, etc., OS. *sibbio* (MLG. *sibbe*), OHG. *sippo* (G. *sippe*, *sipp*) kinsman. See also I-SIB *a.*]

**1. a.** Related by blood or descent; akin. Now chiefly *Sc.* or *arch.*, but also used *spec.* of canaries (see quot. 1882).

*Beowulf* 387 Hat in gan seon sibbe ȝedriht samod ætgædere. *c* **950** *Lindisf. Gosp.* Luke xiv. 12 Nelle ðu ȝeceiȝa friondas ðina..ne sibbo *vel* cuðo menn. *c* **1200** *Trin. Coll. Hom.* 157 Alse þe man doð þe ȝifeð his almes fader oðer moder, suster oðer broðer, oðer oðre swo sibbe þat he aghte mid rihte to helpen to feden. *c* **1250** *Gen. & Ex.* 1468 Ðo wurð Rebecca childre bere,.. At on burdene ghe under-stod two ðe weren hire sibbe blod. **13..** *Cursor M.* 20068 (Gött.), Iesu crist..cald til him sant iohan þat was his sibe ner kinsman. *a* **1350** *SS. Simon & Jude* 237 in Horstm. *Altengl. Leg.* (1881) 140 þat he suld haue done licheri With ane þat was his sib woman. **1390** GOWER *Conf.* III. 332 Bot of hem tuo a man mai liere What is to be so sibb of blod. *a* **1400-50** *Alexander* 586, I of my blode haue, Ane of my sede, I supose, & sibbire of þe twa. *c* **1470** HENRY *Wallace* v. 872 Sib sister sone he wes to gud Wallace. *a* **1529** SKELTON *E. Rummyng* 100 The deuyll and she be syb. *a* **1578** LINDESAY (Pitscottie) *Chron. Scot.* (S.T.S.) I. 299 [He] intendit to marie hir gif he might haue had the popis lecence, because hir husband befoir and hie was sibe. **1816** SCOTT *Antiq.* xxxiii, By the religion of our holy Church they are ower sibb thegither. **1875** R. L. WALLACE *Canary Bk.* iii. 51 He said, very gravely, 'Weel, sib bred is sib bred, an I thocht that anybody kenned what that was.' However, I found that the meaning of the words was consanguinity. **1882** *Bazaar* 15 Feb. 175 'Sib breed'..is a word used in the North for the particular kind of canary employed for mule breeding, and really means that the birds have been bred in-and-in for a number of years. **1888** D. GRANT *Chron. Keckleton* 48 The Brodies, as the sibbest relatives,..had taen chairge. **1891** *Bazaar* 20 Feb., Grand sib hen canaries, pink eyed strain, to breed light mules. **1902** BATESON & SAUNDERS *Rep. Evolution Comm. R. Soc.* I. 4 The possibility..should not be forgotten that the prepotency of the sib-bred hens may have been an original character of their particular strain. **1961** R. B. BENNETT *Budgerigars, Canaries & Foreign Finches* xxi. 155 *Sib-bred*, the young from related birds bred in and in for many years. In-bred.

**b.** *transf.* Closely related in some way.

**1500-20** DUNBAR *Poems* vi. 55 We weir als sib as seue & riddill. **1567** DRANT *Horace, Sat.* H vij b, Pithagoras, when shall thy beanes, or colewoorte sybbe of kynde, Refreshe my hungry appetyte? *c* **1620** A. HUME *Brit. Tongue* (1865) 21 For c and k are sa sib, that the ane is a greek and the other a latin symbol of one sound. **1637** RUTHERFORD *Lett.* (1862) I. cvi. 269 Sense of death is a sib friend and of kin and blood to life. **1897** *Naturalist* 84 The singular stability and depth of his conviction, often reiterated to those mentally sib, that Matter was All.

**2. a.** Related by blood or kinship *to* (or †*with*) a person. †In early use also with dative.

*c* **1200** ORMIN 323 To streonenn streon, to wurrþenn sibb Wiþþ kingess & wiþþ preostess. *c* **1250** *Gen. & Ex.* 228 Ut of his side he toc a rib, And made a wimman him ful sib. *c* **1330** R. BRUNNE *Chron. Wace* (Rolls) 12648 A knyght þer was, hight Quyntalyn, Syb þemperour, & his cosyn. ? *a* **1366** CHAUCER *Rom. Rose* 1199 Largesse..Hilde by the honde a knyght of prys, Was sibbe to Artour of Britaigne. *c* **1440** *Gesta Rom.* lxx. 323 þou art..wele ny sybbe to my lord, for he is thyne Eem, and þou art his cosyn. **1470-85** MALORY *Arthur* III. iii. 103 This poure man..is not his fader; he is no thyng syb to hym. **1534** MORE *Comf. agst. Trib.* III. vi, Many one..that neither shall be sib to thy blood, nor any word bear of thy name. **1579** SPENSER *Sheph. Cal.* May 269 Sicker, I am very sybbe [*gloss*, of kinne] to you. **1600** *Maid's Metam.* IV. ii, That Shepheardesse so neare is Sib to me, As I ne may (for all this world) her wed. **1808** SOUTHEY *Chron. Cid* 244 You are sib to the damsels. **1848** LYTTON *Harold* I. i, She is sibbe to Githa, wife of Godwin. **1888** H. MORTEN *Hospital Life* 43 Remember, I am sib to none but yourself now, and you should be good to me.

**b.** *transf.* or *fig.* Closely related, allied, akin, or similar, *to* some other thing.

*c* **1200** *Trin. Coll. Hom.* 219 þe uuemeste bou is sib þe neþemeste rote. *c* **1380** WYCLIF *Sel. Wks.* III. 86 Witeþ wel, þis maundement is sibbe to many synnes. *c* **1430** *Hymns Virgin* (1867) p. xvi, At .xxx. yere he is named a man And syb to the bull of nature stronge. **1532** MORE *Confut. Tindale* Wks. 469/1 But there is none of those storyes any thing sybbe to saynt Johns ghospel. **1577-87** HOLINSHED *Chron.* I. 13/1 The English interiection, Fough, which is vsed in lothing a ranke or strong sauour, seemeth to be sib to the other. **1601** HOLLAND *Pliny* II. 101 It must be vsed with moderation, for otherwise it breedeth drowsinesse, sib to the lethargy. **1637** GILLESPIE *Eng. Pop. Cerem.* Ep. B, Nearer to Sycophancy then to Sincerity, and..sibber to appeaching Hostility, then fraternall Charity. **1760-74** FERGUSSON *Rising of the Session* Poems (1845) 29 Though a dram to Rob's mair sib Than is his wife. **1786** T. WALKER *Ep. to Burns* (Jam.), I'm but a ragget cout mysel', Owre sib to you. **1826** J. WILSON *Noct. Ambr.* Wks. 1855 I. 220 The seeds of an aphorism—at least if it be..sib to an apophthegm—never were in him. **1894** LATTO *Tam. Bodkin* ix. 88 A toom head an' licht heels bein' raither sib to ane anither.

†**c.** *Sc.* Having a right or claim *to* a thing. *Obs.*

**1701** *Suppl. Dict. Decis. Crt. of Session* (1826) IV. 503 Some argued..that creditors seemed to be much sibber to these annual rents than the factors. **1721** KELLY *Scot. Prov.* 197 It is something to be Sub to a good Estate.

**3.** *absol.* as *sb.* **a.** As *pl.* Kinsfolk, relatives. Also *fig.*

*a* **1000** *Soul & Body* 4 þonne se deað cymeð, asundrað þa sibbe, þa þe ær somud wæron. *a* **1200** [see FREMD *a.* 4]. *c* **1250** *Gen. & Ex.* 2503 He bad sibbe cumen him bi-foren, Or he was ut of werlde boren. **1297** R. GLOUC. (Rolls) 7086 þis child wax so wel & þeu, as iseie fremde & sibbe. *c* **1315** SHOREHAM I. 68 So drawyþ hy affinite Wyþ alle þyne sibbe, Ase þou of hire sibben draȝst. *c* **1400** MAUNDEV. (Roxb.) xxv. 115 Nowþer of fader ne broþer, sibbe ne fremmed. **1440** J. SHIRLEY *Dethe K. James* 25 His tirannye ynmeasurable, without pite or mercy to sibbe or to freme. **1755** R. FORBES *Shop Bill* xii, Gloves likewise, to hap the hand of fremt an' sib. **1882** *Mrs. Raven's Temptation* III. 350 All nice people are related to each other, and so are all nasty people—God's sib, and Satan's sib—the two!

**b.** A kinsman or kinswoman.

*a* **1023** WULFSTAN *Hom.* xxx. 146 þær ne byð sybbes lufu to oðrum. *a* **1300** *Cursor M.* 27174 Quat man he es þat did þe sin,..Sib or fremd, lok quar it es. **1393** LANGL. *P. Pl.* C. VII. 135 Dame purnele, a prestes file [*v.r.* sibbe], priouresse worth hue neuere. **1582** STANYHURST *Æneis* I. (Arb.) 29 Thee murther he whusted, His syb in her mourning with long coynd forgerye feeding. *a* **1593** MARLOWE *Edw. II*, III. ii, Tush Sib, if this be all, Valoys and I will soone be friends againe. **1625** BP. MOUNTAGU *App. Cæsar* 139 So also with our Puritans, very Sibs unto those Fathers of the Society. **1868** BROWNING *Ring & Bk.* II. 513 From goody, gossip, cater-cousin and sib. **1894** F. S. ELLIS *Reynard the Fox* 213 It is Lapreel the Coney, My old-time sib, my ancient crony.

**c.** *Anthrop.* A kinship group among Anglo-Saxon and other Germanic peoples (see quot. 1918); hence used for various other kinds of lineal or cognatic kinship groups. Also as *pl.*, the membership of such a group.

**1890** F. B. JEVONS tr. *Schrader's Prehist. Antiq. of Aryan Peoples* IV. xii. 398 The Teutonic sib.., as long as it was an agrarian and military unit, is to be conceived as having been purely agnatic. **1901** *Jrnl. R. Anthrop. Inst.* IV. 68 Two brothers, and still more, a father and son, cannot fall into two different sibs. **1918** F. S. PHILBRICK tr. *Huebner's Hist. Gmc. Private Law* I. iii. 114 The primitive Germans lived in ..sibs that based their kinship solely upon descent from a common tribal male ancestor. **1919** *Amer. Anthropologist* XXI. 28 The sib, like the family, is a kinship group... On the one hand, it excludes one half of the blood-kindred—the father's side of the family in matronymic, the mother's side in patronymic societies. On the other hand, it admits on equal terms all kindred of the favored side regardless of degree and even individuals considered blood-relatives merely through legal fiction. **1949** G. P. MURDOCK *Social Structure* iii. 47 If all persons born with the name Smith in our society regarded themselves as related, they would constitute a patri-sib. Some unilinear societies lack true sibs, possessing only lineages. The great majority, however, possess sibs... A sib normally includes several lineages. **1950** A. R. RADCLIFFE-BROWN in Radcliffe-Brown & Forde *African Systems of Kinship & Marriage* 15 The arrangement of kin by degrees of nearness or distance was based on sibship... A man's sib were all his cognates within a certain degree. *Ibid.*, It is evident that no two persons can have the same sib, though for two unmarried full brothers, *A* and *B*, every person who was sib to *A* was sib to *B*, and *A* and *B* were sib-kinsmen of one another. A person cannot be said to 'belong' to a sib or be a member of a sib in the sense in which he can be said to belong to a lineage or a clan or a village community. **1967** R. FOX *Kinship & Marriage* i. 50 There are other usages [for *clan* and *lineage*] which cause considerable confusion... American writers often use *sib* as the generic term with *patri-sib* and *matri-sib* as the sub varieties. This is quite wrong... The Anglo-Saxon *sib*..was not a descent group at all. *Ibid.* vi. 167 The kindred..was known as the sib... Amongst the Teutonic peoples, the sib was the exogamic unit. **1968** G. D. MITCHELL *Dict. Sociol.* 160 The British usage confines *sib* to an ego-centred group of cognates within a certain degree; it is thus synonymous with some meanings of kindred.

**d.** Chiefly *Genetics.* A brother or sister, another individual of the same parentage (see also quot. 1933).

**1919** *Genetics* IV. 496 The observations..show themselves to be a strictly homogeneous population, with correlation much larger than that between sibs. **1931** E. & C. PAUL tr. E. Baur et al. *Human Heredity* xi. 508 The methods ..known as the brother-and-sister method or as the sib method. [*Note*] The word 'sib' or 'sibling' is coming into use in genetics in the English-speaking world, as an equivalent of the convenient German term 'Geschwister'. **1933** *Proc. R. Soc. Edin.* LIII. 106 A comparison of the resemblance between ordinary sibs and fraternal twins may be used. [Note] Here and throughout sib is used to denote brothers and sisters of different birth-rank. **1937** *Nature* 2 Oct. 573/1 Genetical research shows that height has little value as an indicator of relationships and specific distinctness, since a plant two inches high may be a sib to a plant twenty inches high. **1958** *Times* 18 Jan. 4/3 Among other problems possibly was the danger of sibs—offspring of the same parent—marrying. **1974** *Nature* 12 Apr. 594/2 The foundation stock of the highly resistant flock had parents and sibs that did not develop scrapie.

**e.** *attrib.* as *sib bond*, *group*, *-mate*, *-mating*, *-pair*, *selection*, *system*.

**1938** *Jrnl. R. Anthrop. Inst.* LXVIII. 301 With Trobriands and Hopi the successive sib bond exists through females. **1901** *Ibid.* XXXI. 68 The size of the sib group has always been determined by economic facts. **1920** R. H. LOWIE *Primitive Society* vi. 107 Sib-mates of the same generation usually call one another siblings, and from this.. it is but a step to feeling that marriage between sib-mates would be incestuous. Hence we find as one of the most common traits of the sib the law of exogamy. **1949** G. P. MURDOCK *Social Structure* iv. 73 They are wives and clansmen of one group of disputant men, sisters and sibmates of the other. **1949** R. A. FISHER *Inbreeding* iii. 47 A mating of parent and offspring interpolated in a series of sib-matings does not advance the inbreeding process so much as a sib-mating would have done. **1971** *Brit. Med. Bull.* XXVII. 45/2 Sib-pair comparisons have also been used to separate the effects of family size..upon intelligence. **1956** *Genetics* XLI. 367 (*heading*) Isolation of preadaptive mutants in bacteria by sib selection. **1934** *Nature* 19 May 743/1 The sib system, and its attendant naming habits, is the most flourishing part of the old thought system.

**sib** (sɪb), *sb.*³ Also **Sib.** Colloq. abbrev. of SIBILANT *sb.* 2.

**1957** D. E. WALKER *Lunch with Stranger* 142 British memoirs published since the war have confirmed both the speed with which the Sibs reached the German High Command and the disruptive influence they had there. **1958** *Punch* 8 Jan. 96/1 A Sib, short for sibilant, is a story or rumour concocted to promote a set purpose, generally the sales of a particular product. **1965** B. SWEET-ESCOTT *Baker Street Irregular* iii. 98 The rumours or 'sibs', as they were called, were devised by a high-powered committee in London... Success or failure was judged by the degree to which the sibs were repeated by enemy or neutral newspapers and broadcasting transmissions. **1975** P. FUSSELL *Gt. War & Mod. Memory* ix. 328 One department [of the Special Operations Executive] did nothing but contrive 'sibs'—bizarre and hair-raising rumours to be spread over the Continent.

**Sibbald** ('sɪbəld). The name of Sir Robert Sibbald (1641-1722), Scottish naturalist, used in the possessive to designate the blue whale, *Balænoptera musculus.*

**1897** R. LYDEKKER *Conc. Knowledge Nat. Hist.* 173 The largest..of all whales, is the blue, or Sibbald's rorqual.., commonly known to the American whalers by the name of 'sulphur-bottom'. **1937** [see *blue whale* s.v. BLUE *a.* 12 a]. **1972** *Oxf. Bk. Vertebrates* 190/1 Sibbald's Rorqual..has a world-wide distribution and migrates between high and low latitudes.

**sibbed**, *a. dial.* [f. SIB *a.*] Akin.

**1674** RAY *N.C. Words* 40 *Sib'd*: a kin; *no sole sib'd*, nothing akin: No more sib'd then sieve and riddle, that grew both in a wood together. **1818** WILBRAHAM *Chesh. Gloss.*, *Sibbed*, related to, of kin.

**sibbens** (also **-ans**, **-ins**), var. of SIVVENS.

**sibbered, -ridge:** see SIBRED.

**sibber-sauce.** *Obs.* exc. *dial.* [Perh. ad. L. *cibāri-us* pertaining to food.] A sauce; a compound or concoction of this nature. Also *fig.*

**1556** OLDE *Antichrist* 132 b, To this use serue..many drinkes and sibber sawces. **1583** STUBBES *Anat. Abus.* I. (1879) 64 They would neuer go about to coulour their faces with such sibber-sawces. *a* **1603** T. CARTWRIGHT *Confut. Rhem. N.T.* (1618) 588 Which with another sibber-sawce of vain words they haue set before him here again. *c* **1613** SIR E. COKE in Amos *Gt. Oyer Poisoning* (1846) 249 The composition of his own sibber sauces. **1868-98** in Yorkshire glossaries (in the form *sipper-sauce*).

**Sibbil**, obs. f. SIBYL.

**sibbits:** see SIBRED.

'**sibboleth**, *v. rare*⁻¹. [See SHIBBOLETH.] *intr.* To speak with a special pronunciation.

**1638** SIR T. HERBERT *Trav.* (ed. 2) 154 At this day [it] is call'd *Spawhawn* (or as they Sibboleth, *Sphawhawn*) and by most writers differently spelled.

**Sibelian** (sɪ'beɪlɪən), *a.* and *sb.* [f. *Sibelius* (see below) + -AN.] **A.** *adj.* Of, pertaining to, or characteristic of the Finnish composer Jean Sibelius (1865-1957) or his music. **B.** *sb.* An admirer or adherent of Sibelius; an interpreter of his works.

**1935** C. GRAY *Sibelius* 64 The instrumental roles are reversed, with the strings constituting a background of a typically Sibelian kind. **1937** *Sunday Times* 29 Aug. 5/2 The No. 4..is of exceptional interest to the Sibelian student now in the light thrown on it by the No. 7 and 'Tapiola'. **1943** *Scrutiny* XI. 171 Some passages of characteristically Sibelian cross-rhythmed moto perpetuo. **1966** *Punch* 23 Feb. 291/2 The Sibelian atmosphere of magic, melancholy and old solitude. **1975** *Gramophone* Oct. 598/2 Shostakovich's view of the symphony is Mahlerian rather than Sibelian. **1976** *Ibid.* June 52/2 She has put all Sibelians in her debt by including the inspired Serenades on her record. *Ibid.* Oct. 608/2 Last month Decca released a version of the *Four Legends* conducted by no less a Sibelian than Jussi Jalas, the composer's son-in-law.

**Siberia** (saɪ'bɪərɪə). The name of a region of the U.S.S.R. in Asia used as a type of a cold, inhospitable place, or a place of exile, banishment, or imprisonment. Also *fig.*

**1841** GEO. ELIOT *Let.* 17 Feb. (1954) I. 81 Probably this projected transportation may be to a Cape of Good Hope instead of a Siberia. **1876** C. M. YONGE *Three Brides* I. x. 159, I used to be Camilla to all the neighbourhood, and here I find myself..banished to Siberia. **1926** C. PLUMB in *Oxf. Poetry 1925* 40 The seas shall not seem vast Siberias of Time. **1952** R. CAMPBELL tr. *Baudelaire's Poems* 80 In my Siberia a bright explosion as of tropic heat. **1972** *Listener* 21 Dec. 857/3 In 1830 Andrew Jackson..[ordered] that all the Indian tribes..be removed to the west of the Mississippi.. to the 'Siberia' of the Far West. **1974** 'J. LE CARRÉ' *Tinker*,

*Tailor, Soldier, Spy* xi. 82 Guillam departed for the siberias of Brixton.

**Siberian** (saɪˈbɪərɪən), *a.* and *sb.* Also 8 **Sibirian**. [f. the name of the country *Siberia* + -AN.]

**A.** *adj.* **1.** Of or belonging to, characteristic of, Siberia.

**1719** DE FOE *Crusoe* II. (Globe) 600 A faithful Muscovite Servant, or rather a Siberian Servant. **1789** G. WHITE *Selborne* cvi, The writer..thinks he never before or since has encountered such rugged, Siberian weather. **1802** PINKERTON *Mod. Geogr.* I. 317 Russia exchanges her precious Siberian furs for tea, silk, and nankeen. *Ibid.* II. 72 The oak, and the hazle,..cannot exist in a Siberian climate. **1890** GUNTER *Miss Nobody* xv, The draughts in the lobbies of this house are simply Siberian.

**2.** In special applications: **a.** In names of animals or birds, as ***Siberian cow, dog, husky, ibex, rabbit, tiger, weasel; Siberian crane, crow, falcon, finch, thrush***, etc.

**1774** GOLDSM. *Nat. Hist.* (1776) III. 32 The zebu, or little African cow, and the grunting, or *Siberian cow, are but different races of the bison. **1785** LATHAM *Gen. Synop. Birds* III. I. 37 *Sibirian Crane..inhabits the vast marshes and lakes in Sibiria. **1829** GRIFFITH tr. *Cuvier* VIII. 331 The Siberian Crane,..*Ardea Gigantea. Ibid.* VII. 181 *Siberian Crow, *Corvus Sibiricus.* **1800** SHAW *Gen. Zool.* I. II. 278 The *Siberian Dog (*Canis Sibiricus*)..may be sub-divided into several races, differing as to strength and size. **1781** LATHAM *Gen. Synop. Birds* I. I. 113 *Sibirian Falcon..has the bill and air of a Kestrel. **1872** COUES *N. Amer. Birds* 130 *Siberian Finch. Dusky purplish; neck above pale yellowish. **1854** MEALL *Moubray's Poultry* 177 Russian or *Siberian [Fowl]. **1783** LATHAM *Gen. Synop. Birds* II. I. 124 *Sibirian Grosbeak. **1809** SHAW *Gen. Zool.* VII. I. 207 *Siberian Hawk. *Falco Sibiricus.* **1930** *Amer. Kennel Gaz.* Jan. 26/1 The *Siberian huskies are recognized as the ideal dogs for driving. *Ibid.* Nov. 73/1 The breed of dog known as the Siberian Husky has been recognized by the Stud Book Committee. **1950** J. HAMBLETON *Abitibi Adventure* 74 In their equipment was included a two-dog team, made up of Siberian huskies, blue-eyed beauties trained for generations to pull their hearts out and to survive the utmost rigors of the north. **1972** *Even. Telegram* (St. John's, Newfoundland) 24 June 14/1 Various types of Northern dogs were used including Siberian Huskies. **1827** GRIFFITH tr. *Cuvier* V. 356 The *Siberian Ibex, *Ibex Alpium Sibiricarum.* **1881** LYELL *Pigeons* 81 The smooth-legged chequered or spangled ones are known in this country as Ural ice, while the rough-legged spangled birds are called *Siberian ice [-pigeons]. **1781** LATHAM *Gen. Synop. Birds* I. I. 391 *Sibirian Jay..inhabits Siberia; but its manners are totally unknown. **1827** GRIFFITH tr. *Cuvier* III. 90 The *Siberian Rabbit (*Lepus Tolai*). **1901** *Ibis* 417 *Siberian Thrush... The nest was found on the Yenesei River by Mr. Popham in 1895. **1954** D. A. BANNERMAN *Birds Brit. Isles* III. 166 There is some reason to suppose that the Siberian thrush..has occurred in Britain. **1895** R. LYDEKKER *Hand-bk. Carnivora* I. 150 A specimen of the *Siberian Tiger, apparently the first brought alive to Europe, was exhibited recently in Hagenbeck's menagerie in Amsterdam. **1956** M. L. TAYLOR *Tiger's Claw* vii. 59 'Can you read the Chinese ideogram on his head?' he inquired of me. 'It is *wang* meaning king. In the north it is believed that only Siberian tigers carry this mark.' **1978** *Times* 27 Oct. 32/8 (Advt.), Large Siberian tiger skin mounted on red satin, £600. **1783** LATHAM *Gen. Synop. Birds* II. II. 556 *Sibirian Titmouse, *La Mesange de Siberie.* **1884** COUES *N. Amer. Birds* 267 *Parus cinctus*, Siberian Titmouse. *Ibid.* 284 *Motacilla ocularis*, *Siberian Wagtail. **1783** LATHAM *Gen. Synop. Birds* II. I. 456 *Sibirian Warbler, *Motacilla montanella.* **1800** SHAW *Gen. Zool.* I. II. 431 *Siberian Weesel, *Viverra Sibirica.* **1827** GRIFFITH tr. *Cuvier* II. 291 The Siberian Weasel, or Chorok.., resembles the Polecat in size, form, and proportions.

**b.** In names of plants, trees, or fruits, as ***Siberian barley, cedar, crab*** (apple), ***elm, iris, larch, larkspur, oat***, etc.

**1831** LOUDON *Encycl. Agric.* (1857) §5083 The *Siberian barley..was introduced to this country in 1768, but is believed to be now lost or merged in the parent species. **1763** J. BELL *Trav. St. Petersburg* I. 250 Towards the Baykall lake, are high hills..covered with tall trees; among which are many..*Siberian cedars. **1838** J. C. LOUDON *Arboretum & Fruticetum Britannicum* IV. 2275 The Siberian Stone Pine, or Siberian Cedar..—The cones are said to be longer, and the scales larger, than in the Swiss variety. **1967** M. T. MIROV *Genus Pinus* iii. 233 Russians call *P. sibirica* 'Siberian cedar', which causes a great deal of confusion. **1974** *Nomencl. Commerc. Timbers* (*B.S.I.*) 69 'Siberian cedar' (UK)... This name is liable to be confusing and its use should be discontinued. **1767** ABERCROMBIE *Ev. Man his own Gardener* (1803) 671/2 The *Siberian Crab; the tree dwarfish and the fruit small. **1887** RUSKIN *Præterita* II. 142 Nor were all the apples..worth a single dishful of the Siberian crabs of Herne Hill. **1904** *Outing* Oct. 84/2 The English elm and the cork-bark and *Siberian elms are also desirable. **1981** *Sci. Amer.* Aug. 40/3 Many Asian species, such as the Chinese elm..and the Siberian elm.., are comparatively resistant to infection. **1823** J. BADCOCK *Dom. Amusem.* 48 Another variety that flourishes well, comes from the Foxley apple and the *Siberian harvey. **1802** PINKERTON *Mod. Geogr.* II. 72 The black and white hellebore, the *Siberian iris. **1882** *Garden* 3 June 391/3 Other upright-shaped bouquets are of..Siberian Iris. **1838** J. C. LOUDON *Arboretum & Fruticetum Britannicum* IV. 2352 The *Siberian larch was introduced into England by Messrs. Loddiges..about the end of the last century. **1969** T. H. EVERETT *Living Trees of World* iv. 41/1 The Siberian larch.., a close relative of the European larch, grows to 120 feet tall. **1882** *Garden* 25 Mar. 201/3 The *Siberian Larkspur, with its handsome foliage and tall spikes of dark ..flowers. **1805** R. W. DICKSON *Pract. Agric.* I. 578 In the *Siberian or Tartarian oat the grains are thin and small. **1856** MORTON *Cycl. Agric.* II. 489/1 Siberian Early White Oat.—This variety is originally from the north of Europe, and was sent to this country in 1839. **1832** *Planting* (L.U.K.) 34 *Pinus Siberica*, *Siberian pine. **1958** *N.Z. Timber Jrnl.* Sept. 87/1 Siberian pine: *Pinus cembra* var. *sibirica*..and *P. koraiensis*... Shipped from Vladivostok. **1802** PINKERTON *Mod. Geogr.* II. 72 The *Siberian plum, and crab,..form thickets of exquisite beauty. **1837** P. KEITH *Bot. Lex.* 204 If the *Siberian Sowthistle shuts at night the ensuing day will be fine. **1832** *Planting* (L.U.K.) 125 The *Siberian stone or Cembra pine, is a highly ornamental species in England. **1838** Siberian stone pine [see *Siberian cedar* above]. **1861** BENTLEY *Man. Bot.* 659 *Pinus Cembra*, the Siberian Stone Pine, has also edible seeds. **1923** A. REHDER in L. H. Bailey *Cultivated Evergreens* v. 303 Siberian Stone P[ine]. A form with shorter leaves and larger cones [than *Pinus cembra*]. **1967** N. T. MIROV *Genus Pinus* iii. 233 Its 'common' English name, 'Siberian stone pine', is rather inappropriate. **1763** MILLS *Pract. Husb.* I. 475 Another species of vetch, viz. the *Siberian,..bids fair to become, perhaps, the most useful of all for fodder. **1925** G. W. DEEPING *Sorrell & Son* xxxvii. 375 A half wild patch of..purple and gold tulips, and burning orange *siberian wallflowers. **1933** *Jrnl. R. Hort. Soc.* LVIII. 172 The Siberian Wallflower..probably merits that name as little as the one by which it is commonly known. **1979** C. E. L. PHILLIPS *New Small Garden* x. 137 The slightly later Siberian wallflower..is a glowing orange ball of fire. **1775** *Ann. Reg.* 150 A field of *Siberian wheat.. in..Yorkshire.

**c.** Miscellaneous, as ***Siberian oil-seed, plague***.

**1858** SIMMONDS *Dict. Trade*, *Siberian oil-seed*, a local name in Canada for the *Camelina sativa*, or Gold of pleasure. **1884** *Encycl. Brit.* XVII. 58/1 Anthrax..is epizootic..in.. Siberia, where it is known as the *Sibirskaja jaswa* (Siberian boil-plague). **1885** *Western Daily Press* 19 Jan. 7/5 The woolsorters' disease, known also as splenic fever, malignant pustule, and Siberian plague.

**B.** *sb.* **1.** A native of Siberia.

**1719** DE FOE *Crusoe* II. (Globe) 605 The Siberian, who was Servant to the young Lord, told us [etc.]. **1782** J. BROWN *Compend. View Religion* I. ii. 35 The Siberians.. cast their newly born infants into rivers. **1854** *Orr's Circle Sci., Org. Nat.* I. 324 The Arctic Ocean, which washes the sea-board of the Laps and Siberians.

**2.** *pl.* Shares in Siberian gold-mines.

**1906** *Westm. Gaz.* 21 Nov. 11/1 The catalogue of 'Siberians' will..be added to in a day or two by the registration of the Kluchi Gold Mines.

**3.** A Siberian husky.

**1928** *N.Y. Times* 29 Jan. II. 1/5 Seppala left the line without a word to his furry, sharp-eared Siberians. **1944** C. CLAY *Phantom Fur Thieves* 137 The Siberian..was originally bred and raised in Siberia, is smaller in size than a huskie, more stockily built, more heavily furred.

Hence **Siˈberianize** *v.*, to send to Siberia; to render Siberian in character.

**1864** *Daily Tel.* 9 Aug., After a century of Cossacking, bombarding, knouting, and Siberianising. **1880** MISS BIRD *Japan* I. 3 The climate of Northern Yezo is Siberianized by the cold current from the Sea of Okotsk.

†**siˈberite.** *Min. Obs.* [f. *Siber-ia* + -ITE; named by C. Lermina (1799).] = RUBELLITE.

**1802** *Phil. Trans.* XCII. 316 The tourmalin of a purplish red colour..is exactly similar to that of Siberia, to which the names of rubellite, of daourite, and of Siberite, have been successively given. **1823** W. PHILLIPS *Min.* (ed. 3) 127 Rubellite..occurs in a granite mountain in the Uralian chain in Siberia,..whence this mineral has been also called Siberite. **1868** WATTS *Dict. Chem.*

**ˈsibilance.** [See SIBILANT and -ANCE, and cf. F. *sibilance*.] The character of being sibilant; a hissing sound. Also, an undue prominence of sibilants, *esp.* in reproduced sound.

**1823** SOUTHEY *Lett.* (1856) III. 397 The word preceding ends with *s*, and would occasion too marked a sibilance to be admitted without necessity. **1892** ZANGWILL *Bow Myst.* 116 He felt like the author to whose ears is borne the ominous sibilance of the pit. **1939** A. CLARKE *Coll. Plays* (1963) 92 The words of the Chorus become a mere sibilance. **1943** A. L. ROWSE *Cornish Childhood* 87 Her voluminous skirts which made such a lovely sibillance [*sic*] whenever she moved. **1960** G. A. BRIGGS *A to Z in Audio* 183 *Sibilance*, a fault in reproduction in which consonants and, in particular, 's' sounds are given unnatural prominence. **1962** A. NISBETT *Technique Sound Studio* iv. 82 'Tilting' such a ribbon was at one time commonly used as a means of discriminating against sibilance (a voice defect which seems to be less of a nuisance than it has been in the past). **1974** —— *Use of Microphones* 24 Sometimes intelligibility is improved by using a microphone with a peak..in the 6000–8000 Hz frequency range... But this may also enhance the natural sibilance of some voices. **1979** *Amer. Poetry Rev.* Mar./Apr. 26/1 Now if we take out the first one we risk sibilance by having the *s* of 'Ignatius' run into the *s* of 'swallows'.

**ˈsibilancy.** *rare.* [See next and -ANCY.] = prec.

**1871** EARLE *Philol. Eng. Tongue* i. 88 At present the sibilancy of English is a European proverb. **1876** LOWELL *Among my Bks.* Ser. II. 288 Certainly Milton would not have avoided them for their sibilancy.

**sibilant** (ˈsɪbɪlənt), *a.* and *sb.* [a. L. *sībilant-*, *sībilans*, pres. pple. of *sībilāre* to hiss, whistle. In 1 b directly a. F. *sibilant*.]

**A.** *adj.* **1. a.** Having a hissing sound; of the nature of, characterized by, hissing.

**1669** HOLDER *Elem. Speech* 45 It were easie to add a Nasal Letter to each of the other pair of Lisping and Sibilant Letters. **1817** KIRBY & SP. *Entomol.* (1818) II. 240 A third [insect] of the same tribe..emits a small sibilant or chirping noise. **1842** BORROW *Bible in Spain* vii, The language..had become less sibilant, and more guttural. **1880** *19th Cent.* XXXIX. 829 The ghost of Shakspere..would probably join in the sibilant chorus.

**b.** *spec.* in *Pathol.* (See quots.)

**1833** *Cycl. Pract. Med.* I. 229 The dry bronchial rhonchus ..includes two varieties, the sibilant and sonorous rhonchus. **1876** BRISTOWE *Th. & Pract. Med.* (1878) 388 As a general rule, hissing and whistling sounds or sibilant rhonchi arise in the smaller tubes. **1898** *Allbutt's Syst. Med.* V. 30 The respiratory murmur..may be replaced by sibilant râles.

**2.** Making a hissing or whistling sound.

**1802** SHAW *Gen. Zool.* III. 530 Sibilant Snake. *Coluber sibilans.* *a* **1876** M. COLLINS *Pen Sketches* (1879) I. 77 Horse chestnuts and elms and sibilant poplars in front.

**B.** *sb.* **1.** A speech-sound having a hissing effect; a sound of the nature of *s*.

**1788** W. JONES in *Asiatick Researches* I. 11 Next come different classes of *dentals*, and among the first of them should be placed the *sibilants.* **1822** J. THELWALL *Poet. Recreat.* 165 There must be no clashing of consonants, no hissing of sibilants, particularly in the termination of the lines. **1844** *Proc. Philol. Soc.* I. 195 A sibilant of which the exact sound is still a matter of some doubt. **1876** S. BIRCH *Rede Lect. on Egypt* 32 The final sigma of the Greeks is represented by the Egyptian sibilant.

**2.** A rumour started and spread for propaganda or advertising purposes. Cf. WHISPER *sb.* 2.

**1957** *Observer* 27 Oct. 18/7 The sib-spreader, that fortunate extrovert with a cast-iron digestion who is employed to dash about bars and cocktail parties spreading carefully composed sibilants or selling rumours. **1958** [see SIB *sb.*[3]].

Hence **ˈsibilantly** *adv.*

**1891** *Harper's Mag.* Apr. 739/1 It echoed sibilantly.

**sibilate** (ˈsɪbɪleɪt), *v.* Also 9 **sibillate**. [f. ppl. stem of L. *sībilāre* to hiss, whistle.]

**1.** *intr.* To hiss; to utter a hissing sound.

**1656** BLOUNT *Glossogr.*, *Sibilate*, to whistle or hiss. **1823** *Examiner* 332/1 The disposition to sibilate became uncontroulable. **1863** BATES *Nat. Amazons* iv. (1864) 71 Its voice is a harsh, grating hiss: it makes the noise when alarmed, all the individuals sibilating as they fly..away.

**2.** *trans.* **a.** To announce or say with a hissing sound.

**1837** *New Monthly Mag.* XLIX. 577 The 'Goose and Gridiron' sibillates the joys of supper. **1903** K. D. WIGGIN *Rebecca of Sunnybrook Farm* xix. 199 'How about cookies?' 'Do you think it's worth while?' sibilated Miss Miranda. **1910** O. BROWNING *Mem. Sixty Yrs.* xx. 318 Two portly gentlemen..turned round towards me, hissed violently and sibilated the word 'Poet' thinking, I suppose, that I was Robert.

**b.** To assail (an actor) with hissing.

**1864** *Daily Tel.* 28 Dec. 5/1 Vociferous tragedians who would now be sibilated by a Victoria gallery.

Hence **ˈsibilating** *ppl. a.*; **ˈsibilatingly** *adv.*

**1776** BURNEY *Hist. Mus.* (1789) II. iv. 309 Why the Spanish should have so many sibillating endings. **1831** *Fraser's Mag.* III. 399 He then proceeds..in a circumlocutory sibillating whisper. **1862** SALA *Accepted Addr.* 190 The pit began to be sibilatingly cat-calling, uproarious.

**sibilation** (sɪbɪˈleɪʃən). Also 9 **sibill-**. [ad. late L. *sībilātio*, noun of action f. *sībilāre*. So F. *sibilation*.] The action of hissing or whistling; a hissing or whistling sound.

**1626** BACON *Sylva* §176 All Metals quenched in water give a Sibilation or hissing Sound. **1684** tr. *Bonet's Merc. Compit.* IX. 328 When children make a noise and sibilation as they suck the Milk. **1755** JOHNSON *Dict.*, *S*..unhappily prevails in so many of our words that it produces in the ear of a foreigner a continued sibilation. **1802** W. TAYLOR in *Monthly Mag.* XIII. 10 Its sibillations are attached to its most necessary inflections. **1847** TENNYSON *Princ.* i. 174 He with a long low sibilation, stared As blank as death in marble. **1892** W. H. HUDSON *La Plata* 8 The sharp fitful sibilations of the dry wiry grasses on the barren places.

**b.** *spec.* Hissing as a sign of disapproval.

**1822** *Examiner* 109/2 The ecstasies of..the major part.. set sibilation at defiance. **1854** *Blackw. Mag.* LXXVI. 703 The play was sent to Orcus..amidst hideous sibilation.

**sibilator** (ˈsɪbɪleɪtə(r)). *rare.* In 5 **siblatour**, 9 **sibillator**. [Agent-noun, on L. types, f. SIBILATE *v.*] One who hisses or whistles.

*c* **1440** *Gesta Rom.* xxxv. 137 (Harl. MS.), In that oþere side is an hisser or a siblatour, and he hissithe so swetlye [etc.]. **1844** J. T. HEWLETT *Parsons & W.* v, 'What's up?' replied the sibillator.

**sibilatory** (ˈsɪbɪlətərɪ), *a.* Also **sibill-**. [See SIBILATE *v.* and -ORY.] Of the nature of, marked or expressed by, hissing.

**1830** *Fraser's Mag.* I. 621 Mr. Hunt, however, notwithstanding his sibillatory reception, told the saintly squad a homely truth. **1858** *Chamb. Jrnl.* IX. 213 Emitting a long sibillatory whistle. **1881** *World* 28 Dec., A suspicion of sibilatory indignation.

**sibilous** (ˈsɪbɪləs), *a.* [f. L. *sībil-us* adj. + -OUS.] Hissing, sibilant.

**1768** G. WHITE *Selborne* xvi, The grasshopper lark began his sibilous note in my fields last Saturday. **1768** PENNANT *Brit. Zool.* II. 240 Its sibilous note is observed to cease about the latter end of July. **1822** GOOD *Study Med.* I. 537 He [Laennec] distinguishes five principal kinds of rattle:..4 The dry sibilous, or hissing. **1859** SEMPLE *Diphtheria* 68 The respiration was accelerated, was becoming sibilous. **1890** *Australian Girl* I. xiii. 192 There was a faint sibilous sound.

‖**sibilus** (ˈsɪbɪləs). [a. L. *sībilus* sb.]

†**1.** A hissing in the ears. *Obs.*

*c* **1400** *Lanfranc's Cirurg.* 254 Greet sownynge in þe eeris & sibillus, & defaute of heeringe & deefnes.

**2.** *Path.* A sibilant râle.

**1887** in *Cassell's Encycl. Dict.* **1898** *Allbutt's Syst. Med.* V. 146 When rhonchus and sibilus are present over the whole of both lungs..it is unlikely that the bronchitis is complicated with pneumonia.

**Sibiriak** (sɪˈbɪrjæk). Also Sibiryak. [Russ. *Sibiryák* Siberian.] A Siberian descended from European Russian settlers. Also *attrib.* or as *adj.*

**1903** W. GERRARE *Greater-Russia* viii. 105 The Siberiaks, as the descendants of the early settlers in the west province are called, are of average height. **1916** M. A. CZAPLICKA *My Siberian Year* xii. 243 The Sibiriak—that is, broadly speaking, the colonial whose ancestors have been settling in Siberia, voluntarily or involuntarily, since, say, the end of the Middle Ages. *Ibid.* 245 An anthology of Sibiriak songs ..would provide an illuminating document for the student of Siberian life. **1974** *Encycl. Brit. Macropædia* XVI. 726/1 There were long-established Russian peasant societies in certain parts of Siberia, in many cases the descendants of exiled religious dissidents. Such people, known as Sibiryaks or 'local Russians', have a culture and an outlook differing markedly from those of the people of European Russia.

†**sib-laȝ.** *Obs.*⁻¹ [f. SIB *sb.*¹ or *a.* + ON. *lag* community, partnership.] = SIBRED.

*c* **1205** LAY. 412 He hefde muchele strengþe..of þan Troyscen monnen, þe weren his moder isib; for þare sibe-laȝe luue hem wes bi-tweonen.

**siblatour,** obs. form of SIBILATOR.

**sibling** (ˈsɪblɪŋ). [f. SIB *a.* + -LING¹.]

†**1.** One who is of kin to another; a relative. *Obs.*

*c* **1000** ÆLFRIC *Gen.* xix. 12 Hæfst þu suna oððe dohtra on þisre byriȝ..oððe æniȝne sibling? *c* **1425** *Eng. Conq. Ireland* 102 He yaf hymself to lecherye; & nat only to many sengle wommen, bot he ne synned [= shunned] neþer spousbrych ne syblynges.

**2. a.** *Genetics* = SIB *sb.*² 3 d; hence also **b.** chiefly *Anthrop.* each of two or more children of a common parent or parents. Also *fig.*

**1903** K. PEARSON in *Biometrika* II. 369 These [calculations] will enable us..to predict the probable character in any individual from a knowledge of one or more parents or brethren ('siblings', = brothers or sisters). **1930** *Nature* 15 Nov. 766 A few were odd twins who had a brother or sister at school, and the remainder were either siblings of twins, or pairs of siblings unconnected with twins. **1933** L. SPIER *Yuman Tribes* vii. 209 She needed to know no more than the sex and relative ages of the siblings from whom the lines were traced to give..the terms used between any pair in the succeeding generations. **1941** *Jrnl. R. Anthrop. Inst.* LXXI. 7/2 A group of siblings is constituted by the sons and daughters of a man and his wife in monogamous societies, or of a man and his wives where there is polygyny, or of a woman and her husbands in polyandrous communities. **1950** M. FORTES in Radcliffe-Brown & Forde *Afr. Systems of Kinship* 273 Next to the bond between mother and child none is so strong as that between siblings by the same mother. **1957** V. W. TURNER *Schism & Continuity in Afr. Soc.* iii. 68 Thus uterine siblings and matrilineal parallel cousins remained together throughout life. **1957** *Observer* 24 Nov. 15/1 There are..echoes of 'Death of a Salesman'—the loyal, harassed wife, the two disenchanted siblings, and the salesman father with an unfulfilled dream. **1970** *Nature* 19 Dec. 1221/2 In the herring gull.., the chick hatching from this third egg suffers a much higher mortality than either of its siblings. **1972** *Daily Tel.* 20 Mar. 2/7 The line dividing the Kevin Street Sinn Fein organisation and its terrorist sibling, the Provisional IRA, is almost invisible. **1974** 'J. MELVILLE' *Nun's Castle* vii. 153 Siblings and kinsfolk did not have to be friends.

**3.** *attrib.* and *Comb.*, as ***sibling group***; **sibling rivalry**, rivalry arising from the jealousy that can exist between siblings; **sibling species** *Biol.*, one of a pair or group of reproductively isolated populations whose members are morphologically very similar; cf. *twin species*.

**1957** V. W. TURNER *Schism & Continuity in Afr. Soc.* p. xx, The headman's uterine sibling group. **1975** H. & C. GEERTZ *Kinship in Bali* ii. 57 One brother may farm the plot of land as sharecropper to the sibling group as a whole. **1930** *Smith Coll. Stud. in Social Wk.* I. 6 (*title*) Two studies in sibling rivalry. **1959** MARTIN & STENDLER *Child Behav. & Devel.* (rev. ed.) xvi. 553 The most common form of jealousy in young children is sibling rivalry. **1972** C. RAPHAEL *Feast of History* iv. 118 Moses..shows more than a hint of sibling rivalry in his attitude to his brother Aaron. **1979** WATSON & LINDGREN *Psychol. of Child* (ed. 4) iv. 125 Adler was also keenly aware of the conflicts and tensions among siblings.. the intense competition—sibling rivalry—for status, power, and parental attention. **1940** E. MAYR in *Amer. Naturalist* LXXIV. 258 Sibling species: The opposite condition exists where pairs or larger groups of related species are so similar that they are generally considered as one species. **1942** —— *Systematics & Origin of Species* vii. 151, I call.. morphologically similar and closely related, but sympatric species, sibling species. This corresponds to the 'dual species' of Pryer and of Hering (1935). **1979** *Nature* 7 June 557/2 The eastern meadowlark (*Sturnella magna*) and western meadowlark (*S. neglecta*) are sibling species of songbirds in secondary contact throughout a narrow zone of sympatry in central North America.

Hence **ˈsiblingship** = SIBSHIP 1.

**1950** M. FORTES in Radcliffe-Brown & Forde *Afr. Syst. of Kinship & Marriage* 273 The range within which the bond of siblingship is accepted as automatically binding. **1957** V. W. TURNER *Schism & Continuity Afr. Soc.* vii. 226 These are all means..of reducing the strength of uterine siblingship. **1970** [see KINSHIP 1 b].

†**sibman.** *Obs.* [f. SIB *a.* + MAN. *Sib man* or *men* also freq. occur written as separate words.] Kinsman.

*a* **1300** *Cursor M.* 20243 Til hir scho cald Hir sibmen. *Ibid.* 27943 Incest, þat es for to lij Bi þat þi sibman has line bi. **1375** BARBOUR *Bruce* III. 403 For his sibmen wonnyt thar-by, That helpyt him full wilfully. **14..** *Nom.* in Wr.-Wülcker 690 *Hic affinis*, a sybmane. *c* **1440** *Alph. Tales* 11 Sho lete hur carvur, þat was hur awn syb-man, hafe at do with hur.

**sibness** (ˈsɪbnɪs). In later use only *Sc.* Also 3, 7 sibnesse, 6–7 *Sc.* -nes; 3, 5 sybnesse, 4 subnes. [f. SIB *a.* + -NESS. Cf. Fris. *sibbens.*]

**1.** Relationship, kinship.

*a* **1240** *Wohunge* in *O.E. Hom.* I. 275 Nu, mi swete ihesu, leaued haue i for þi luue flesches sibnesse. *c* **1275** *On Serving Christ* 76 in *O.E. Misc.* 92 þureh þe sybnesse of seynt iohan ..Louerd haue mercy of vs euervychon. *c* **1300** *Harrow. Hell* 208 For þi godnese art þou min, More for þi godnesse þen for þine sibnesse. **1398** TREVISA *Barth. De P.R.* VIII. x. (Bodl. MS.), If mercurius is coniuncte þereto..he disposeþ a man..to writing and is the hous of kynrede & nyȝe subnes. **1535** STEWART *Cron. Scot.* I. 58 For sic sibnes and also sic incest For till abhor, him thocht that that wes best. *a* **1598** ROLLOCK *Serm.* Wks. 1849 I. 386 Thou will count thy sibnes with this man and that man. **1609** SKENE *Reg. Maj.* 29 Gif she be separate fra him, for parentage, and sibnes of blude. **1872** MICHIE *Deeside Tales* (1908) 9 People were wont to say of any inextricable problem, 'ye might as soon unravel the sibness o' the Gordons o' Girnock'. *c* **1892** RANKIN in Storey *Ch. of Scotl.* II. 421 The relation of godfather and godmother which had nothing to do with bodily *sibness* at all.

**b.** *transf.* or *fig.*

*a* **1658** DURHAM *Comm. Revelation* xi. (1680) 433 We would observe the sibnesse and identity of this trumpet with the seven viols. **1692** A. PITCAIRN *Assembly* IV. iii. 53 Pastoral Relations and Scriptural Sibnesses. **1744** E. ERSKINE *Serm.* Wks. 1871 III. 216 The wondrous sibness between Christ and His Church.

†**2.** *collect.* Kinsfolk, relatives. *Obs.*⁻¹

*a* **1290** *Pains of Hell* (MS. Digby 86) 109 þe wreieþ his sibnesse oþer his steleþ Abouen his heien þe flod heleþ.

**ˈsibred.** *Obs.* exc. *dial.* Forms: α. 1 sibreden, 5 -redin, sybredyn(e; 4–5 sib(be)radyn. β. 3–5 sibrede, 4–5 sybrede (5 cybrede, sybreed), 6 sybrade; 4 sibred, 5–6 syb(b)red, 6 sybberid, 7 sibbered; 7 sibrit, 9 *dial.* sibberet(s), sib(b)ret(s), -rit(s), etc. γ. *Sc.* 5 sibrend, sibrent. [See SIB *a.* and -RED, and cf. GOSSIPRED.]

**1.** Relationship, kinship, consanguinity.

α. **1127** *O.E. Chron.* an. 1127, þe ilce Willelm hæfde æror numen ðes eorles dohter of Angeow to wife, oc hi wæron siððan to-tweamde for sibreden. ? *a* **1400** *Morte Arth.* 691 For the sybredyne of me, fore-sake noghte this offyce. *c* **1400** *Destr. Troy* 10326 þurgh sibradyn first, Thou was aliet to þat lynage. **1483** *Cath. Angl.* 338/2 A Sybredyn, *consanguinitas*.

β. **1297** R. GLOUC. (Rolls) 10108 þulke ȝer þe king him let vor sibrede to dele. *a* **1300** *Cursor M.* 12674 Iesu broþer cald was he For sibred, wirschip, and bunte. **1390** GOWER *Conf.* III. 284 Every man it scholde drede, And nameliche in his Sibrede. *c* **1425** *Eng. Conq. Ireland* 42 All other,..that sybrede or other frendshypp hadden to hym,..weren I-dryue out of englond. *c* **1470** HARDING *Chron.* CXXIX, But for sibrede & consanguinitee They were departed by papall iudgement.

*transf.* **1575** LANEHAM *Lett.* (1871) 4 Ioyning these too togither, with the nighness allso of the woords, and sybred of the toongs.

γ. *c* **1425** WYNTOUN *Cron.* II. i. 75 Til sibrent [*v.r.* sibrend] haffande na knawlage And but al reuerens of maryage.

**2.** *E. Anglian dial.* The banns of marriage.

Prob. from the mention, in the banns, of 'sibred' as an impediment to the marriage.

*c* **1440** *Promp. Parv.* 455/1 Sybrede,..*banna*. *c* **1440** *Jacob's Well* 21 Alle, þat..don swyche weddynges be solemnysed, & wyth-oute syb-redes, in cherchys, in chapellys, or in oratoriis. **1513** *Will of Poly* (Somerset Ho.), If she bee maried as sone as hir sybbred bee asked. **1674** RAY *S. & E.C. Words* 76 *Sibberidge*, or *Sibbered*; the Banes of Matrimony, *Suff.* **1823** E. MOOR *Suffolk Words* 348 *Sibrit*, banns of matrimony. **1860** AGNES STRICKLAND *Old Friends* 214 After their sibright was out-asked. **1884** J. S. ORTON *Beeston Ghost* 4 T'will be a precious long awhile afore the paarson axes my sibbret.

**sibship** (ˈsɪbʃɪp). [f. SIB *sb.*² + -SHIP.]

**1.** *Anthrop.* The state of belonging to a sib, or to the same sib (SIB *a.* and *sb.*² 3 c).

**1908** *Rep. Brit. Assoc. Adv. Aci. 1907* 654 *Sib and sibship*, the old word *sib* may be used for the relationship set up by membership of the sept. **1924** W. H. R. RIVERS *Soc. Organ.* ii. 22 All the people of a village or district..believe themselves to be related to one another, and thus form a characteristic example of sibship. **1950** [see SIB *a.* and *sb.*² 3 a].

**2.** *Biol.* and *Med.* A group comprising all the individuals born to a particular pair of parents.

**1919** *Genetics* IV. 489 Fraternal resemblance is usually not far from ·54, so that 46 percent of the variance of the population occurs within the sibship. **1925** *Jrnl. Genetics* XV. 259 An acre of $F_2$ plants and an acre of $F_3$ sibships. **1939** *Nature* 18 Mar. 484/2 The fall in the birth-rate may be due to diminution in family size... Thus the average sibship in Great Britain now is said to be half of what it was fifty years ago. **1949** C. STERN *Princ. Human Genetics* 389 In sibships of 10, chance alone will give rise, on the average, to 1 sibship in 1024 of all boys. **1958** *Immunology* I. 49 Eight goldfish from the same sibship as before. **1978** *Brit. Med. Jrnl.* 14 Jan. 72/1 There is a high incidence of spontaneous abortion in sibships in which a case of anencephaly or spina bifida has occurred.

†**ˈsibsomeness.** *Obs. rare.* [f. OE. *sibsum*, f. SIB *sb.*¹] Peace, concord.

*a* **900** *O.E. Chron.* (Parker MS.) an. 860, On godre ȝeþuærnesse and on micelre sibsumnesse. *c* **1175** *Lamb. Hom.* 91 þa weren alle mid sibsumnesse, and fuleden þam apostles. *c* **1275** *Passion our Lord* 599 in *O.E. Misc.* 54 Sibsumnesse eu beo among, ne beo ye nouht of-dredde.

**Sibyl** (ˈsɪbɪl). Forms: α. 4–7 sibil (4 sibbil), 5–7 sibill (7 sibell); 4–5, 7 sibille, 4, 6 sibile (5 *Sc.* sebile), 6 sibylle; 7– sibyl, 7–8 sibyll. β. 4 sybyl, 5 -ylle, 7 -yll; 4, 6– sybil, 5–7 sybill, 6–7 sybille. [a. OF. *Sibile*, *Sebile* (F. *Sibylle*), or ad. med.L. *Sibilla*, L. *Sibylla*, *Sibulla*, a. Gr. *Σίβυλλα*; the explanation of this as Doric *Σιοβόλλα* = Attic *Θεοβούλη* is given by Jerome. In sense 1 now usually written with a capital, in sense 2 with a small letter.]

**1.** One or other of certain women of antiquity who were reputed to possess powers of prophecy and divination.

In later times the number of these was usually set down as ten, flourishing at different times and places in Asia, Africa, Greece, and Italy.

*a* **1300** *Cursor M.* 6999 þe first sibile o pers, Men findes of in al wers. *c* **1374** CHAUCER *Troylus* V. 1450 He for sibille his suster sente, That called was Cassandre al aboute. **1390** GOWER *Conf.* II. 383 That Sibille of whom ye wite, That alle men yit clepen sage. *c* **1450** *Myrr. our Ladye* 299 Hethen prophesyes, whiche spake of the comynge of Crist, & specyally one of the Sybylles. **1513** DOUGLAS *Æneid* VI. Prol. 70 Oft by Sibillis sawis he [Virgil] tonis his stevin. **1547–64** BAULDWIN *Mor. Philos.* (Palfr.) 2 Lactantius doubteth not to count him [Hermes] among the sibiles and prophets. **1591** SHAKS. *1 Hen. VI*, I. ii. 56 The spirit of deepe Prophecie she hath, Exceeding the nine Sibyls of old Rome. **1646** SIR T. BROWNE *Pseud. Ep.* v. xi. 250 The Pictures of the sybills are very common, and for their Prophecies of Christ in high esteem with Christians. **1712** ADDISON *Spect.* No. 495 ¶10 The Prophecies of the Sybils..made many Years after the Events they pretended to foretell. **1788** GIBBON *Decl. & F.* xliii. IV. 307 Their industry had scooped the Sibyll's cave into a prodigious mine. **1831–3** E. BURTON *Eccl. Hist.* xvii. (1845) 373 The verses of the Sibyls were known to the heathen from a remote antiquity. **1870** EMERSON *Soc. & Solit.* Wks. (Bohn) III. 54 The grand sibyls and prophets, painted in fresco by Michel Angelo.

*transf.* **1513** DOUGLAS *Æneid* VI. Prol. 145 Thou art our Sibill, Cristis modir deir.

**2.** A prophetess; a fortune-teller, a witch.

**1589** GREENE *Menaphon* (Arb.) 56 How now Samela, wilt thou be a Sybil of mishap to thy self? **1604** SHAKS. *Oth.* III. iv. 70 A Sybill..In her Prophetticke furie sow'd the Worke. **1632** HEYWOOD *1st Pt. Iron Age* I. i, Thou art no Sibill, but from fury speak'st, Not inspiration; we reguard thee not. **1775** SHERIDAN *Duenna* I. iii, Thou wanton sybil, thou amorous woman of Endor. *Ibid.* II. iii, Handsome! Venus de Medicis was a sibyl to her. **1811** J. B. S. MORRITT *Let.* 28 Dec. in Lockhart *Scott*, I often heard of her in my early youth, from a sibyl who lived in the park. **1856** BOKER *Francesca da Rimini* I. i, Bah! on your sibyl and her prophecy! **1871** B. TAYLOR *Faust* (1875) I. vi. 111 O sibyl excellent, enough of adjuration!

*attrib.* and *Comb.* *a* **1718** PARNELL *Fairy Tale* 181 This tale a Sybil-nurse areed. **1811** W. R. SPENCER *Poems* 115 To pow'r like thine no sybil spells pretend. **1831** CARLYLE *Sart. Res.* II. vii, Shouting question after question into the Sibyl-cave of Destiny. **1839–52** BAILEY *Festus* (1848) xix. 220 She sibyl-like Instinct with inspiration.

**3.** *Ornith.* (See quot.)

**1829** GRIFFITH tr. *Cuvier* VI. 437 Sibyl Warbler, *Sylvia Sperata*.

‖**Sibylla** (sɪˈbɪlə). Also 4 sibila, 6–7 sibilla; 4 sybila, 6–7 sybilla. [a. L. *Sibylla*: see prec.] = SIBYL 1.

*a* **1300** *Cursor M.* 7031 þan ras þe thrid sibila, þat man clepis delphica. **1513** DOUGLAS *Æneid* VI. i. 99 Gevand respons onto this Sibilla. **1596** SHAKS. *Merch. V.* I. ii. 116 If I liue to be as olde as Sibilla, I will dye as chaste as Diana. **1611** COTGR., *Sibyllin*, prophecying, of a Sybilla, or Sybilla-like. **1842** *Smith's Dict. Gr. & Rom. Antiq.* s.v. *Divinatio*, The Sibylla whose books gained so great an importance at Rome, was, according to Varro, the Erythraean. *Ibid.*, Prophecies by some Bacis or Sibylla.

†**Siˈbyllianist.** *Obs. rare.* = SIBYLLIST 1.

*a* **1641** BP. MOUNTAGU *Acts & Mon.* (1642) 209 So farre, that for their frequent testimonies from them, the Pagans commonly styled Christians, Sibyllianists.

**Sibyllic** (sɪˈbɪlɪk), *a.* Also Sybilic. [f. SIBYL + -IC.] = next.

*a* **1849** POE *Ulalume* Poems (1859) 71 Its Sybilic splendor is beaming with Hope and Beauty. **1870** *Nation* XI. 390 Sibyllic enough to be extremely puzzling to the average mind. **1894** TABLE *Poems* 19 With sibyllic omen Seeming thus to say.

**Sibylline** (ˈsɪbɪlaɪn), *a.* and *sb.* Also 8–9 Sybil(l)ine, 9 Sibyline; and with lower-case initial. [ad. L. *Sibyllīn-us*, f. *Sibylla* SIBYL. Cf. F. *sibyllin*, †*sibillin*.]

**A.** *adj.* **1.** Pertaining to, uttered or written by, one or more of the Sibyls.

In this sense usually with a capital, and qualifying *books* or *oracles*: on the nature of these see *Encycl. Brit.* XXII. 13.

**1579–80** NORTH *Plutarch, J. Cæsar* (1612) 738 That it was written in the Sybilline prophecies, how the Romaines might ouercome the Parthians. **1678** CUDWORTH *Intell. Syst.* 282 Concluding the whole business of the Sibylline Oracles..to have been a mere Cheat and Figment; and that there never was any thing in those Sibylline Books [etc.]. **1725** tr. *Dupin's Eccl. Hist. 17th C.* I. 21 The Fathers are to be excused for citing the Sybilline verses as true. **1776** GIBBON *Decl. & F.* xi. I. 361 The Sibylline books enjoined ceremonies of a more harmless nature. **1841** *Penny Cycl.* XXI. 477/1 It may be that at this time a number of Sibylline oracles were forged and circulated. **1882** FARRAR *Early Chr.* II. 219 It had probably originated from the expectations of Jews and Christians, and is found again and again in the Sibylline books.

**2.** Oracular, occult, mysterious.

**1817** COLERIDGE (*title*), Sibylline Leaves; a Collection of Poems. **1834** H. MILLER *Scenes & Leg.* i. (1857) 3 The Sybiline tomes of tradition are disappearing in this part of the country. **1852** MRS. JAMESON *Leg. Madonna* (1857) 42 Looking out, with..her slightly dilated, sybilline eyes, quite through the universe. **1888** R. GARNETT *Emerson* i. 21 Her habitual mode of expressing herself was abrupt and sibylline.

*Comb.* **1834** H. MILLER *Scenes & Leg.* x. (1857) 152 Here are a few sybilline-like leaves, the sole records, of his common everyday affairs.

**3.** Excessive, exorbitant.

In allusion to the Sibyl who sold three books to Tarquinius Superbus at the price of the original nine.

**1859** HELPS *Friends in C.* Ser. II. Introd. 11 My terms are Sybilline. **1876** LOWELL *Among my Bks.* Ser. II. 224 To set a Sibylline value on their verses in proportion as they were unsalable.

**4.** Resembling a Sibyl.

**1837** CARLYLE *Fr. Rev.* I. v. iv, See Camille Desmoulins.. rushing out, sibylline in face; his hair streaming. **1861** PEARSON *Early & Mid. Ages Eng.* ii. 14 Suetonius Paulinus penetrated to the sacred island of Mona, exterminated the priests and white-robed Sibylline women who thronged the shores.

**B.** *sb.* In *pl.*, the Sibylline oracles or books.

**1875** *Encycl. Brit.* II. 177/2 It was still the main object of the sibyllines to combat heathenism itself. **1895** SALMOND *Doctr. Immortality* IV. i. 411 These Sibyllines have come down to us only in the most confused and uncertain form.

**'Sibyllism.** [f. SYBIL + -ISM.] Prophecy, soothsaying.

**1833** CARLYLE *Misc.* III. 225 And himself, in a moment of sibylism, emitted that surprising announcement. **1875** *Encycl. Brit.* II. 177/2 Fusing the remnants of Greek sibyllism with their native prophecy.

**Sibyllist** ('sɪbɪlɪst). Also 7 **Sybillist.** [ad. late Gr. Σιβυλλιστής: see SIBYL and -IST.]

**1.** One who believes in the Sibylline prophecies; especially applied to the early Christians who accepted the Sibylline writings as genuine.

**1605** J. DOVE *Confut. Atheism* 53 The heathens called the Christians Sybillistes, because Christian religion was most of all proued out of the Sybils Oracles. **1678** CUDWORTH *Intell. Syst.* 284 Upon Celsus mentioning a Sect of Christians called Sibyllists, Origen tells us, that these.. were called so in way of disgrace, by other Christians. **1846** S. SHARPE *Hist. Egypt fr. Earliest Times* xiii. 429 Celsus charges the Christians with being sibyllists.

**2.** A writer or compiler of Sibylline oracles.

**1899** *Contemp. Rev.* Dec. 811 A favourite device on the part of a Sibyllist is to review all the kings of the period just before his own time.

**Siby'llistic,** *a. rare.* [f. SIBYL + -ISTIC.] Of or pertaining to, characteristic of, the Sibyls.

**1797** T. GREEN *Diary Lover of Lit.* (1810) 39 The sudden and violent transitions..from sibyllistic fury to colloquial familiarity. **1853** *Blackw. Mag.* LXXIV. 559 The sybilistic Latin inscription..has sometimes driven curious travellers frantic to discover its purport.

**sic** (sɪk), *a. Sc.* and *north.* α. (Chiefly *Sc.*) 5- **sic** (6 **syc**), 5-9 **sick,** 5-7, 9 **sik** (5 **syk**). β. (Chiefly *north.*) 5-7 **syke** (6 **sayk,** 7 **syik**), 5- **sike.** [Reduced form of *swik, swilk*: see SUCH *a.* The form *sike* may have arisen under the influence of SLIKE *a.* The examples from early texts are probably due to the 15th century scribes.]

= SUCH *a.*

**1.** In ordinary attributive use.

α. **1375** BARBOUR *Bruce* VIII. 180 Sloppis..left he..of sic quantite, That fyffe hundir mycht sammyn ryde. **1424** *Sc. Acts, Jas. I* (1814) II. 6/1 At þai þat sik treis pertenys to [etc.]. *c* **1450** HOLLAND *Howlat* 93 With sic courtassy as he couth, on kneis he fell. **1508** KENNEDIE *Flyting w. Dunbar* 26 Pretendand the to wryte sic skaldit skrowis. **1596** DALRYMPLE tr. *Leslie's Hist. Scot.* I. 5 The beimes of the Sone..in sik brichtnes. **1609** SKENE *Reg. Maj.* 6 In his court ..there is sick vprightnes. **1678** SIR G. MACKENZIE *Crim. Laws Scot.* II. (1699) 235 Together with sick witnesses as best knows the verity of the Premisses. **1721** RAMSAY *Prospect of Plenty* 6 That store which Heav'n In sic abundance to their hands has giv'n. **1814** A. WILSON *Loss o' the Pack*, Sic cheeks! sic een! Sic smiling looks! were never, never seen. **1858** M. PORTEOUS *Souter Johnny* 30 At sic change ye'll grow clean wud.

β. *c* **1375** *Sc. Leg. Saints* xvi. (*Magdalene*) 166 Sike lufe til hyre had Ihesu swet. *c* **1400** *26 Pol. Poems* 125 Whether thy dayes, lord, be syke As mennys dayes, that dwellen here? **1480** *Newcastle Merch. Vent.* (Surtees) I. 3 Wppon payn of syke fin as shalbe thought reasonable. **1579** SPENSER *Sheph. Cal.* Feb. 211 Sike fancies weren foolerie. **1589** PEELE *Eclogue Gratulatory* 31 Sike verse, I tell thee, ought have a great vaunt. **1604** *Urie Court-bk.* (1892) 4 Fewaill..syik as petteis, turris, or haidder. **1665** BRATHWAIT *Comment Two Tales* 82 Is it Love, a God's Name, or some sike giddy thing that girds you? **1787** GROSE *Prov. Gloss.*, *Sike*, such. **1855** ROBINSON *Whitby Gloss.*, *Sike*.., such, similar. 'Sike and sike like',..all are alike in the matter.

**b.** Used with numerals in comparisons, as ***by sic seven***, seven times (more, better, etc.).

*c* **1470** HENRY *Wallace* v. 388, I meyn fer mar the tynsell off my men, Na for my selff, mycht I suffir sic ten. **1500-20** DUNBAR *Poems* xxx. 22 In haly legendis haif I hard..Ma sanctis of bischoppis, nor freiris, be sic sevin. **1560** ROLLAND *Seven Sages* 45, I beleue to haue ane better..be sic thre Nor is the auld. **1574** *Sat. Poems Reform.* xlii. 347 Quhais number..As greiter..ȝea, be sic thre.

**2.** Followed by *a* (or †*ane*).

α. **1375** BARBOUR *Bruce* I. 77 Thir twa..Quhilk suld succeid to sic a hycht. *c* **1475** *Rauf Coilȝear* 67, I wait na worthie harberie..to serue sic ane man. **1567** *Satir. Poems Reform.* iii. 98 Think on, thairfoir, quhill ȝe haue sic ane cryme. **1596** DALRYMPLE tr. *Leslie's Hist. Scot.* II. 65 The king commandes thame..to be present at sik a day. **1609** SKENE *Reg. Maj.* 133 To answere to sic ane man, anent sic ane thing, or in sic ane cause, or to sic ane Breive. *a* **1724** in Ramsay *Tea-t. Misc.* (1733) I. 8, I think my doghter winna gloom On sick a lad as ye. **1786** BURNS *Twa Dogs* 86 Buirdly chiels, and clever hizzies, Are bred in sic a way as this is. **1814** SCOTT *Wav.* xxix, I cannot enter into ony carnal transactions on sic a day. **1816** —— *Old Mort.* xxxv, De'il tak me if they mak sic a guse o' Cuddie.

β. *a* **1400-50** *Alexander* (D.) 1968 With syke a soume for to seke a sawt vs to ȝelde. *c* **1526** SKELTON *Magnyf.* 1103 Herde ye euer syke another? **1586** FERNE *Blaz. Gentrie* 21 It would make a man mad to heare this fable-teller make syke a declaration. **1674** RAY *N.C. Words* 64 *Sike* a thing, such a thing. **1692** *Sc. Presbyt. Eloq.* (1738) 118 Do you remember how you put out sike a sweet Saint of mine? *a* **1718** PARNELL *Fairy Tale* 118 Was never wight in sike a case.

**3.** *absol.* Such person(s) or thing(s).

*c* **1375** *Sc. Leg. Saints* xxxviii. (*Adrian*) 14 For-þi folk mony fundine ware, þat for to sla sik wald nocht spare. *a* **1400-50** *Alexander* 4272 Sike as growis on þe gronde..þat we fede vs with in-fere. *c* **1470** HENRY *Wallace* II. 353 Perchance ye say, that Bruce he was none sik. **1561** WINȜET *Wks.* (S.T.S.) I. 15 Sen we reid nane callit be God onlie, except sick as schew thair power geuin to thaim be Him. **1588** A. KING tr. *Canisius' Catech.* 125 Bot sic as..willinglie sinnes agane, thay sinne aganis Christ. *a* **1724** in Ramsay *Tea-t. Misc.* (1729) 17, I hae na meikle, But sick's I hae ye's get a Pickle. **1825-1876** [see SIC-LIKE *sb.*].

‖**sic,** *adv.* (and *sb.*) [L. *sic* so, thus.] A parenthetical insertion used in printing quotations or reported utterances to call attention to something anomalous or erroneous in the original, or to guard against the supposition of misquotation. Also as *sb.*, an instance of 'sic'.

**1887** SWEET *Second Anglo-Sax. Reader* Pref., A prefixed star calls attention to an erroneous or anomalous form, being thus equivalent to 'sic'. **1910** [used s.v. SIC *v.*]. **1937** *Scrutiny* Sept. 131 As for what Miss Lynch calls 'his really serious affair with Harriet' (I feel this deserves a *sic*), it is purely theatrical. **1963** J. MITFORD *Amer. Way Death* ii. 27, I do not like repeated use of *sic*... The reader who is fastidious about usage will hereafter have to supply his own *sics*. **1973** E. TAYLOR *Serpent under It* (1974) xiv. 224 He called the librarian..and asked him to check... Hence the 'sic'.

Hence **sic** *v.*, to mark with a 'sic'. *nonce-wd.*

**1889** BAX *Ethics Socialism* (1902) 94 The modern reviewer's taste is not really shocked by half the things he *sics* or otherwise castigates.

**sic,** obs. or dial. form of SIKE.

**sic,** var. SICK *v.*[2]

**sicamor(e, sicamour,** obs. ff. SYCAMORE.

**Sican** ('sɪkən). Also **Sikan.** [ad. L. *Sicānus*, pl. *-ī*: see SICANIAN *a.*] A member of an ancient people inhabiting Sicily at the time of the coming of the Sicels (see SICEL *sb.* and *a.*).

**1887** *Encycl. Brit.* XXII. 15/1 It is possible..that..the Sikans..belonged to the earlier non-Aryan population of western Europe. **1911** *Ibid.* XXV. 24/2 They [*sc.* the Sicels] found in the island a people called Sicans. **1968** M. FINLEY *Hist. Sicily* ii. 23 The Sicans who were apparently thinner on the ground than the Sicels, seem also to have been more resistant to Hellenization. **1970** *Oxf. Classical Dict.* (ed. 2) 985/1 Thucydides..attributes an Iberian origin to the Sicans.

**Si'canian** (sɪ'keɪnɪən), *a.* and *sb.* [f. L. *Sīcani-us*, f. *Sīcanī* (usually *Sicānī*), Gr. Σικανοί, a tribe inhabiting part of Sicily.] **A.** *adj.* **a.** Sicilian. *poet.* **b.** *Archæol.* Denoting the Neolithic period in Sicily. **c.** Of or pertaining to the Sicans. **B.** *sb.* = SICAN.

**1629** T. HOBBES tr. *Thucydides' Peloponnesian War* VI. 350 After them, the first that appear to have dwelt therein, are the Sicanians. **1647** COWLEY *Mistr.*, *Coldness* iv, Alphæus found not a more secret trace, His lov'd Sicanian Fountain to embrace. **1795** LANDOR *Gebir* VI. 173 And now Sicanian Etna rose to view. **1875** MORRIS *Æneid* v. 24 The way..To brother-land of Eryx leal and safe Sicanian port. **1876** F. TOZER *Class. Geogr.* x. 117 The original inhabitants of Sicily were two tribes, the Sicanians in the west, and the Sicels in the east, both of whom belonged to the same Graeco-Italian stock as the Greeks themselves. **1909** T. E. PEET *Stone & Bronze Ages Italy & Sicily* v. 123 By Professor Orsi..the pre-Hellenic period in the island, excluding the palaeolithic, is divided into five divisions. To the first of these he gives the name Sicanian; the other four are called respectively First, Second, Third and Fourth Siculan periods. **1911** *Encycl. Brit.* XXV. 20/1 The most important of the towns to which a Sicanian origin can be with certainty assigned..are: Hyccara..; Omphakē..; and Camicus. **1957** *Ibid.* XX. 603/1 The term Sicanian is applied to that period of the Stone Age which followed the palaeolithic period exemplified in the remarkable rock engravings of the cave near Palermo.

**sicarian** (sɪ'kɛərɪən). *rare.* Also 4 **-ien, -yen.** [f. L. *sīcārius*, f. *sīca* dagger.] An assassin. Also *attrib.* or as *adj.*

*a* **1400** N.T. (Paues) *Acts* xxi. 38 [He] ledde into deserte foure powsande of men sicaryens. (Sicariens wore men þat maden fauchons or lytel swerdes.) **1654** VILVAIN *Epit. Ess.* vi. 33, 4 Sicarians..slu..Becket. **1879** FARRAR *Christ* II. lx. 362 In a nation which produced the sicarii, Pilate had given a fatal precedent of sicarian conduct.

So **si'carious** *a. rare*[−1].

**1811** W. TAYLOR in *Monthly Rev.* LXV. 236 These prejudices..may occasion Sicilian vespers, and expose to sicarious destruction every British resident.

**sicatrize,** obs. form of CICATRIZE *v.*

‖**sicca**[1] ('sɪkə). *Anglo-Indian.* Also 7 **secau, seccawe, siccau, sickaw,** 9 **sikka.** [a. Pers. (Arab.) *sikkah* a die for coining, the impression on money.]

**1.** ***sicca rupee*** (also †***rupee sicca***), originally, a newly-coined rupee, accepted at a higher value than those worn by use; latterly, a rupee coined under the Government of Bengal from 1793, and legally current till 1836, of a greater weight than the Company's rupee.

**1619** in W. Foster *Eng. Factories in India* (1906) I. 113 Wherein wee have observed your request of rupees secaus coorah. **1620** *Ibid.* 182 In the exchange of rupees secaus for hundies. **1683** in Yule & Burnell *Hobson-Jobson* 633/1 Having received 25,000 Rupees Siccas for Rajamaul. **1776** *Trial of Nundocomar* 24/1 One lack of sicca haulee Banaris rupees. **1777** RICHARDSON *Pers. Dict.* I. 1033 A sicca rupee, of full standard weight. **1806** T. MAURICE *Ind. Antiq.* 246 The gross amount of its revenue is stated at 54,47,985,13 sicca-rupees. **1859** LANG *Wand. India* 177 'You shall, in future, receive it in sicca rupees', said the Lieutenant.

**b.** *ellipt.* = prec.

**1757** in Scrafton *Indostan* (1770) 68 The Company shall be allowed..to coin siccas, both of gold and silver, of equal fineness with those of Muxadavad. **1763** *Ann. Reg.*, *St. Papers* (1764) 191, I will cause the rupees coined in Calcutta to pass respect equal to the siccas of Morshedabad. **1886** YULE & BURNELL *Hobson-Jobson* 632/2 This rupee, which is the sicca of more recent monetary history, weighed 192 grs. troy, and then contained 176·13 grs. of pure silver.

**2.** ***sicca weight***: (see quot. 1833).

**1833** *India Regulation* (Y.), The use of the sicca weight of 179·666 grains,..being in fact the weight of the Moorshedabad rupee of the old standard,..shall be discontinued. **1850** *Directions Rev. Off. N.W. Prov.* 224 The liquor..is liable to a fixed duty per gallon of 304 Sicca Weight, on being removed from the enclosure.

**sicca**[2] ('sɪkə). *Path.* [ellipt. for mod.L. *keratoconjunctivitis sicca.*] The symptom of reduced or no lachrymation, with consequent dryness and inflammation of the conjunctiva, characteristic of Sjögren's syndrome; used *attrib.* as ***sicca syndrome*** to designate the occurrence of this symptom in the absence of rheumatoid arthritis.

**1938** *Acta Ophthalmologica* XVI. 176 (*heading*) The initial stage of glandular changes in the sicca syndrome. **1949** *Ibid.* XXVII. Suppl. 33. 1 (*heading*) Kerato-conjunctivitis sicca and the sicca syndrome. *Ibid.* 9 The bulk of the sicca patients in my material are rheumatics. **1967** *Amer. Jrnl. Med.* XLIII. 50/1 Sjögren's syndrome is characterized clinically by dryness of the conjunctiva and mucous membranes (sicca syndrome), and by frequent episodes of salivary and lacrimal gland enlargement. **1977** *Proc. R. Soc. Med.* LXX. 483/2 In the 'sicca' or Sjogren syndrome, Patey & Thackray (1955) have described lymphoid tissue in and around intralobar ducts which breaches the walls and allows radiopaque dye to escape during sialography, causing 'punctate sialectasis'.

**siccan** ('sɪkən), *a. Sc.* and *north.* Forms: 6 **sikkin, sickin,** 6, 8 **sicken,** 8- **siccan,** etc. [f. SIC *a.* + KIN *sb.*[1] 6 b.] Such, such-like.

**1513** DOUGLAS *Æneid* v. xii. 69 Thus as he mvsis, stad in sikkin dowt. **1573** *Satir. Poems Reform.* xli. 58 For thow may rew by all the rest That this day thow wants sickin ane. **1589** *Marprel. Epit.* B, He hath giuen the cause sicken a wipe in his bricke. **1725** RAMSAY *Gentle Sheph.* IV. ii, My lad frae books can gather siccan sense. **1786** *Har'st Rig* xl, Minden plain, Whare siccan heaps o' French were slain. **1816** SCOTT *Antiq.* xxi, The savour of the wallflowers, and siccan shrubs as grow on thae ruined wa's. **1899** CROCKETT *Kit Kennedy* 96 There never was siccan a boy as that Kit o' yours.

**si'ccaneous,** *a. rare.* [f. L. *siccāneus* (Columella), f. *siccus* dry.] Dry, arid.

**1656** BLOUNT *Glossogr.*, *Siccaneous*, dry of nature, that hath no Rivers or Springs to water it. **1821** R. POLLOK in *Life* 77 Some of our addle-headed modern critics have certainly dug the sentiment from the siccaneous heaps of ancient criticism.

†**'siccate,** *v. Obs. rare.* Also as *pa. pple.* [f. ppl. stem of L. *siccāre.*] *trans.* To make dry.

**1570** J. DROUT *Gaulfrido & Bernardo* F viij, Whose watered plants scarse sicate were, Till he this same did close. **1623** COCKERAM I, *Siccate*, to dry vp. **1657** TOMLINSON *Renou's Disp.* 214 They are used..to roborate and siccate the brain.

†**si'ccation.** *Obs.* [ad. L. *siccātio* (Pliny), f. *siccāre* to dry.] The action or process of drying.

**1612** WOODALL *Surgeon's Mate* Wks. (1653) 274 Siccation is the drying up of excremental humidity in bodies. **1657** TOMLINSON *Renou's Disp.* 146 Seeds after siccation are reposed in glass vessels.

**siccative** ('sɪkətɪv), *a.* and *sb.* [ad. late L. *siccātīv-us*, f. *siccāre* to dry: see -ATIVE.]

**A.** *adj.* Having the property of absorbing moisture; drying.

**1547** BOORDE *Brev. Health* §377 If the wounde be depe, vse siccatiue playsters. **1615** G. SANDYS *Trav.* (1637) 134 So did they with the juyce of cedars; which by the extreame bitternesse, and siccative facultie,..subdued the cause of interior corruption. **1839** URE *Dict. Arts* 896 Such oils are said to be drying or siccative. **1847** A. SMEATON *Builder's Man.* 143 It may be rendered siccative at pleasure, by adding a little vitriol of zinc. **1869** *Eng. Mech.* 19 Mar. 575/1 Lead is siccative with reference to..linseed oil.

**B.** *sb.* A substance that dries up moisture, esp. as used in oil-painting; a dryer.

**1825** J. NICHOLSON *Operat. Mechanic* 639 To which add some powerful siccative, or dryer, as red lead. **1882** GOSSE *Gray* v. 98 The successive criticisms of a swarm of Dryas-dusts, each depositing his drop of siccative.

†**sicced**, *a. Obs.*⁻¹ [f. L. *sicc-us*: perh. intended for **siccid*.] Dry.

**1667** PRIMATT *City & C. Builder* 2 A Season that is too sicced or dry.

†'**siccicate**, *v. Obs. rare.* [irreg. f. L. *siccus* or *siccāre*.] = SICCATE *v.*

**1639** T. DE GRAY *Expert Farrier* 21 The scorching heats will so siccicate and dry the planks. *Ibid.* 238 Corrupt cholericke bloud siccicating the flesh. *Ibid.* 291 They do siccicate and dry up many bad humours.

†**si'ccific(al**, *a. Obs.*⁻⁰ [f. L. *siccific-us*, f. *siccus* dry.] (See quots.)

**1656** BLOUNT *Glossogr.*, *Siccifical*, that hath power to make dry. **1721** BAILEY, *Siccifick*, causing Siccity.

†'**siccitude.** *Obs.*⁻¹ [f. L. *siccus*.] = next.

**1599** LINCHE *Anc. Fiction* X iij, A general siccitude throughout the whole composition of our bodies.

'**siccity.** ? *Obs.* [ad. L. *siccitas*, f. *siccus* dry: see -ITY. So F. *siccité* (1425), It. *siccità*.] Dryness; absence of moisture.

**1477** NORTON *Ord. Alch.* v. in Ashm. (1652) 62 It is humor sollid constant with siccitie. *Ibid.* 76 Thick Liquor with us hath siccity. **1594** PLAT *Jewell-ho.* I. (1653) 96 The eating of much salt..breeds barrennesse to mans body by the extream siccity thereof. **1615** G. SANDYS *Trav.* 288 Those sands, which a long calme disunites by reason of their siccitie. **1646** SIR T. BROWNE *Pseud. Epid.* 172 The reason some..attempt to make out from the siccity and drines of its flesh. **1698** FRYER *Acc. E. India & P.* 328 An undeniable Argument of its Frigidity, and thence a farther concomitant of its Siccity. **1762** tr. *Busching's Syst. Geogr.* III. 186 If the blood retains its siccity, the people are struck with terror. **1782** *European Mag.* II. 350 Heat is the common property of fire and air,..siccity of earth and fire. *a* **1849** H. COLERIDGE *Ess.* (1851) II. 290 This must..express not physical siccity, but that unfruitfulness which in the desert results from want of moisture.

**siccophant**, obs. form of SYCOPHANT.

**sice** (saɪs), **size** (saɪz). Forms: α. 5 sysse, 5–6 sys, 6 syse, syis; 5 sis, 5– sise, 6– size. β. 5– sice, 6–7 syce. [a. OF. *sis*, *siis* (mod.F. *six*):—L. *sex* six. So MDu. *sijs* (infl. *sise*).]

**1.** The number six marked upon dice; a throw in which the die turns up six. Often in figurative contexts and phrases, as *to set at cinque and sice* (see CINQUE 3).

α. *c* **1386** CHAUCER *Monk's T.* 671 Thy sys fortune hath turned in-to Aas. **1474** CAXTON *Chesse* III. viii, He caste thre dyse, and on eche dyse was a sise, which made xviij poyntes. **1509** BARCLAY *Shyp of Folys* (1874) I. 295 Thoughe sys or synke them fayle, The dyse oft renneth upon the chaunce of thre. *a* **1550** *Image Hypocr.* in *Skelton's Wks.* (1843) II. 438 Seke some better chaunce Yourselves to avaunce, With sise, synke, or synnes, For he laughes that wynnes. *Ibid.* 442 With sise, sinke, and quatter. **1668** DRYDEN *Evening's Love* III. i, So, I have a good chance, two caters and a size. **1684–5** SOUTH *Serm.* (1715) I. 297 What Reason in the World can he have to presume, that he shall..throw an Ace rather than a Size? **1712** SWIFT *Jrnl. Stella* 31 May, The die is cast, and is a spinning, and till it settles, I cannot tell whether it be an ace or a sise. **1837** LOCKHART *Scott* III. x. 327 He no more knew whether he had written well or ill, than whether a die thrown out of a box was to turn up a size or an ace.

β. *c* **1430** LYDG. *Min. Poems* (Percy Soc.) 166 Whos chaunce gothe neyther on synk nor sice. **1572** *Satir. Poems Reform.* xxxiii. 124 Quhilk thing thay did sa Syce vp and Sink downe. **1576** FLEMING tr. *Caius' Dogs* (1880) 26 Our countrymen for their carelessnes of lyfe, setting all at cinque and sice, are of a contrary iudgement. **1600** W. WATSON *Decacordon* (1602) 144 Topsie turvie, vpside downe, sincke shall vp and sice shall vnder. **1688** [see 1 c (*b*)]. **1789** M. MADAN tr. *Perseus* (1795) 79 What The lucky sice would bring. **1861** PALEY *Æschylus* (ed. 2) *Agam.* 32 Each of the three dice falling with the sice uppermost.

**b.** *sice cinque*, a throw with two dice turning up six and five. Similarly *sice quatre, trey, deuce.*

In quot. *a* 1618 with pun on *cinquepace*.

*c* **1386** CHAUCER *Man of Law's Prol.* 125 Your bagges been nat fild with ambes as But with sys cynk, that renneth for your chaunce. **1552** HULOET, Number of eyghte on the dyce, as sice deux. [*a* **1618** SYLVESTER *Lacrymæ Lacrymarum* 102 Bats, Harpies, Syrens, Centaurs, Bib-all-nights, Sice-sink-ap-Asses, Hags.] **1658** J. JONES *Ovid's Ibis* 75 Deuce ace cannot pay scot and lot, and Sice Sink will not pay. **1694** MOTTEUX *Rabelais* v. x. (1737) 37 They were call'd..Sice cinque, Sice quater, Sice trey. **1748** HOYLE *Backgammon* iii. §8 Size-Deuce, a Man to be brought from the five Men placed in your Adversary's Tables. *Ibid.* iv. §6 A probability of throwing..Quatre-Trois. or Size-Cinque.

**c.** *size-ace, sice-ace.* (*a*) A throw with two dice turning up six and one; also *fig.* (*b*) A variety of backgammon (see quot. 1688).

(*a*) **1592** *Nobody & Someb.* in Simpson *Sch. Shaks.* (1878) I. 337 *Sico.* Give me some bales of dice. What are these? ..*Som.* Those bar Sizeaces. **1594** NASHE *Unfort. Trav.* Wks. (Grosart) V. 172 A number of good fellowes would giue size ace and the dice that with as little toyle they could leaue Tyburne behinde them. **1641** in Rushw. *Hist. Coll.* (1692) III. I. 217 Here Satan stays, when these Persons..will give Satan Size-ace and the Dice, at Irish, in enthralling the Lives of the Subjects. **1663** DRYDEN *Wild Gallant* I. iii, Size ace I have thrown. **1748** HOYLE *Backgammon* iii. §7 Size Ace, you are to take your Barr Point, for a Gammon, or for a Hit. **1832** *Fraser's Mag.* V. 475 Behind this size-ace of our species we think we recognise Mr. John Bowyer Nichols. (*b*) **1688** HOLME *Armoury* III. xvi. (Roxb.) 63/2 Sice-Ace. It is played with six or more men apeece where the one load the other with Aces, and sices beares onely and dubbletts throws againe, and he that hath first borne his men wins.

**2.** *size-point.* **a.** In backgammon, the sixth point from the inner end of each table.

**1552** HULOET, Sice or the nombre of sixe on the dice or yᵉ sice poynt in tables, *senio.* **1748** HOYLE *Backgammon* viii. §7 Suppose A to have 2 Men upon his Size Point in his own Tables. **1801** STRUTT *Sports & Past.* IV. ii. 282 Changing the ace point in the English game for the size point.

†**b.** The six in dice. *Obs.*

**1648** HEXHAM II, *Sesken*, the Size point on a Die.

**3.** *slang.* Sixpence.

**1660** TATHAM *Rump* IV. i. Wks. (1879) 254 He..allows me the merry sice a day to spend till better times come. **1684** *Roxb. Ball.* (1885) V. 459 He'l print for a Sice, (For that is his price) Your Name (that you may brag 'twas so done) on the Ice! **1709** *Brit. Apollo* No. 56. 3/1 For want of Sice to hire a Bed. *Ibid.* No. 71. 3/2 For two and six Pence and a Sice too. [**1830** LYTTON *Paul Clifford* iii, As Mrs. Lobkins expressed it, 'two bobs for the Latin, and a sice for the vartue'!]

**sice**, obs. form of SIZE.

**Sicel** ('sɪsəl, 'sɪkəl), *sb.* and *a.* Also **Sikel.** [ad. Gr. Σικελός.] **A.** *sb.* **a.** A member of an ancient people of Sicily. **b.** The language of this people. **B.** *adj.* **a.** Of or pertaining to the Sicels or their language. **b.** *poet.* Sicilian.

**1838** C. THIRLWALL *Hist. Greece* II. xii. 92 The Sicels and the Phœnicians gradually retreated before the Greeks. **1881** B. JOWETT tr. *Thucydides* I. 409 The Sicels were originally inhabitants of Italy,..there are Sicels still in Italy, and the country itself was so called from Italus a Sicel king. **1887** *Encycl. Brit.* XXII. 15/1 Some Sikel elements made their way into the Greek life of Sicily. **1895** L. JOHNSON *Poems* 37 Oh! Hellas lies far hence, Far the blue Sicel sea. **1911** *Encycl. Brit.* XXV. 24/2 That the Sicels spoke a tongue closely akin to Latin is plain from several Sicel words which crept into Sicilian Greek, and from the Siceliot system of weights and measures. **1939** L. H. GRAY *Foundations of Lang.* 335 Besides the Italic dialects proper, mention must also be made of *Sicel*, of which a few glosses and an inscription of three lines have been preserved, and which seems to have belonged either to this group or to Ligurian. **1948** T. J. DUNBABIN *Western Greeks* i. 40 It appears that the Sikels moved from Sicily to Italy, not vice versa. **1974** *Encycl. Brit. Micropædia* IX. 182/2 The most important Sicel gods were the Palici..; Adranus..; and the goddess Hybla. **1977** *Canad. Jrnl. Linguistics* Spring 31 Messapic and Sicel in the south take on new significance vis à vis Iberian.

**Siceliot** (sɪs-, sɪ'kɛlɪɒt), *sb.* and *a.* Also **Sikeliot, -ote.** [ad. Gr. Σικελιώτης, f. Σικελία Sicily: see -OT², -OTE.] **A.** *sb.* One of the ancient Greeks who colonized Sicily, distinguished from the Sicels who had settled in Sicily before their coming. **B.** *adj.* Of or pertaining to the Siceliots.

**1836** C. THIRLWALL *Hist. Greece* III. xxii. 263 [They were] linked together by the common name of Siceliots. **1842** *Penny Cycl.* XXIV. 407/1 The intimate knowledge which he [*sc.* Thucydides] shows respecting the history of the Italiotes and Siceliots. **1887** *Encycl. Brit.* XXII. 16/1 The ancient kingship was perhaps kept on or renewed in some of the Sikeliot and Italiot towns. **1892** *Athenæum* 7 May 597/3 In Syracuse then lay the last hopes of rescue for the Siceliot Greeks. **1931** D. MACIVER *Greek Cities in Italy & Sicily* xii. 172 Gela was chosen for the Pan-Sikeliot conference of Greek Cities in 424 B.C.

†**sicer.** *Obs.* Forms: 4 ciser, cisar, 5 cisere, cysar, cyser, cesare; 4 seser, 5 sychere, syser, 6–7 sicer, 7 sicere. [ad. late L. *sicera* (med.L. *cisera*, *cisara*): see etym. note to CIDER.] Intoxicating liquor, strong drink.

*a* **1300** *Cursor M.* 10982 Mikel for right sal he suinc, And noþer win ne ciser [*Gött.* seser] drinc. *Ibid.* 12679 He dranc neuer cisar ne wine. *c* **1375** *Sc. Leg. Saints* xxxvi. (*Baptista*) 67 Wyne & cesare he ne sal drinke. *c* **1450** *Mirour Saluacioun* (Roxb.) 116 Teres of synners certein whilk ere contrite trewely Ere wyne and Cisere to seintis. **1582** N.T. (Rhem.) *Luke* i. 15 Wine and sicer he shal not drincke. **1609** BIBLE (Douay) *Deut.* xiv. 26 Thou shalt buy..wine also and sicere. [**1623** LISLE *Ælfric on O. & N. Test.* To Rdr. p. xxx, No man hauing but the English tongue onely is able to vnderstand it. Witnesse their Parasceue of the Pasche, their Azimes, their Wine and Sicer.]

**sich(e**, obs. or dial. ff. SITCH, SUCH.

†**siche**, *sb. Obs. rare.* [Related to next: cf. SIKE *sb.*] A sigh.

*c* **1000** *Sax. Leechd.* I. 388 Ic me..on godes helde bebeode, wiþþ þane sara sice, wið þane sara sleʒe. *c* **1200** *Trin. Coll. Hom.* 83 Þeh he him bidde mid his muð, he ne fecheð noht þe sore siches onneðerward his heorte.

†**siche**, *v. Obs.* Also 3–5 syche. *Pa. t.* 3 sihte, syhte, 3–4 siʒte, 4 syʒte, siʒt, 5 syght. *Pa. pple.* 4 y-siʒt. [OE. *sícan*, whence in ME. both *sīchen* (siːtʃ-) and *sīken* SIKE *v.* In OE. a strong verb (cf. the past t. *onsāc*), but in ME. transferred to the weak class represented by *rǣcean*, *tǣcean*, etc. After *siche* became obsolete, the pa. t. *sight* was associated with SIGH *v.*, and remained in use till the 17th c.] *intr.* To sigh.

α. *c* **893** K. ÆLFRED *Oros.* II. viii. 92 Þæt wæron þa tida þe Romane nu æfter sicað. *c* **1000** *Ags. Psalter* (Thorpe) vi. 5 Ælce niht on minum bedde ic sice and wepe. *c* **1205** LAY. 12772 Þe king gon siche sare. *c* **1275** *Passion our Lord* 463 in *O.E. Misc.* 50 Louerd, he seyde, þench on me, and bi-gon to syche [*rime* kyneriche]. **13..** *St. Gregory* (Vernon MS.) 31 For þi suster i mai wel siche [*rime* riche]. **1387** TREVISA *Higden* (Rolls) V. 353 Þe kyng byhelde þe man and þe place, and siched sore. **1422** tr. *Secreta Secret.*, *Priv. Priv.* 232 Yf he syche,..that man lowyth the and dreddyth.

β. *c* **1200** *Trin. Coll. Hom.* 169 Iob..an-hefde þo his egen to heuene..and sore sihte. *c* **1250** *Owl & Night.* 1291 Þe nyhtegale sat and syhte. **13..** *Guy Warw.* 4683 Þan stode þer sir Gij vp-riʒt: Wel depe in hert he haþ y-siʒt. *c* **1350** *Will. Palerne* 2971 Sorwfuliche sche siʒt. **1387** TREVISA *Higden* (Rolls) VIII. 227 Whanne he wook and syʒte [L. *suspirante*]. *c* **1450** *St. Cuthbert* (Surtees) 3420 He ansuerd noʒt, bot sare syght.

Hence †'**siching** *vbl. sb. Obs.*

**1387** TREVISA *Higden* (Rolls) IV. 287 Herodes..was i-tormented..wiþ ofte brekynge of sore sichinges [*v.r.* sychyngs].

‖**Sicherheitsdienst** ('zɪçərhaɪtsdiːnst). [G., f. *sicherheit* security + *dienst* service.] The security branch of the Schutzstaffel (SS) of the Nazi party, set up in 1931–2. Also *attrib.*

**1947** [see *S.D.* s.v. S 4 a.]. **1958** P. KEMP *No Colours or Crest* i. 9 His murder at the hands of Gestapo or *Sicherheitsdienst.* **1966** N. FREELING *Dresden Green* I. 44 The highly successful delivery of five of the area Sicherheitsdienst group, trousers round their ankles. **1976** T. ALLBEURY *Only Good German* iv. 23 The SD, the Sicherheitsdienst, were an SS outfit under Walter Schellenberg.

†**sichet.** *Obs.* [f. ME. *siche* SITCH; recorded only in Latinized forms *sichetus*, *-a*, *-um*.] A small watercourse. Cf. SIKET.

*c* **1133** in Dugdale *Mon. Angl.* (1825) V. 323/1 Ad quendam sichetum versus austrum. **1258** in Madox *Formul. Angl.* 88 Tres [selliones] jacentes inter Terram..et Sichetam sive Sicheta. [*c* **1260–80** in Eyton *Antiq. Shropshire* (1859) IX. 187 Nine seylions.., whereof three lay beyond the sichet towards Sponleg.] **1319** *Reg. Dunfermline* (Bann. Cl.) 149 Ascendendo..per vnum Sychetum se extendentem apud Le Aly.., & sic ab illo sycheto [etc.].

**sichomure**, obs. form of SYCAMORE.

**sicht**, Sc. form of SIGHT.

**Sichuana**, obs. var. SETSWANA.

**Sicilian** (sɪ'sɪlɪən), *a.* and *sb.* [f. L. *Sicilia* Sicily + -AN.]

**A.** *adj.* **1. a.** Of or pertaining to Sicily or its inhabitants; characteristic of Sicily or the Sicilians.

**1611** SHAKS. *Wint. T.* v. i. 164 My best Traine I haue from your Sicilian Shores dismiss'd. **1649** OGILBY *Virg.*, *Bucolicks* iii. (1684) 14 *note*, Archimedes, that famous Sicilian Mathematician. **1693** DRYDEN *Persius* (1697) 451 Sicilian Tortures, &c. Some of the Sicilian Kings were so great Tyrants, that the Name is become Proverbial. **1728** CHAMBERS *Cycl.* s.v. *Silk*, Part of the Sicilian Silks are Raw. **1781** COWPER *Heroism* 24 All the charms of a Sicilian year. **1871** *Schellen's Spectrum Anal.* 259 In most of the Sicilian drawings there is a tendency to an annular form.

**b.** Of or pertaining to the Italian dialect of Sicily.

**1842** W. C. TAYLOR *Anc. Hist.* xiv. §1 (ed. 3) 381 Zancle ..deriving its first name from the old Sicilian word Zanclos signifying a reaping-hook. **1881** *Encycl. Brit.* XIII. 495/1 The Sicilian vocalism is conspicuously etymological. **1975** *Times Lit. Suppl.* 31 Oct. 1296/3 Dialect seems diminishing and parochial to the serious writer... We can meet good Sicilian or Venetian or Roman dialogue, but not good Italian dialogue.

**2. a.** In special collocations, as ***Sicilian embroidery*** (see quot. 1882); ***Sicilian defence, game, opening*** (in chess); ***Sicilian Vespers*** (see quot. 1728).

**1611** COTGR., *Vespres Siciliennes*, the Sicilian Evensong; mischiefes done, or death inflicted, in a place, and time, of imagined securitie. **1656** BLOUNT *Glossogr.* s.v. *Vespers*, *Sicilian Vesperas*, is taken proverbially [etc., copying Cotgrave]. **1728** CHAMBERS *Cycl.* s.v. *Vespers*, Sicilian Vespers,..a general Massacre of all the French in Sicily, in the Year 1282; to which the first Toll that call'd to Vespers was the Signal. **1802** PINKERTON *Mod. Geogr.* II. 638 After the Sicilian vespers, 1282, Sicily was seized by a fleet sent by the kings of Arragon. **1847** H. STAUNTON *Chess-Player's Handbk.* v. ii. 371 The Sicilian Game... In the opinion of Jaenisch..this is the best possible reply to the move of I.P. to K's 4th. **1852** —— *Chess Tournament* 29, I have before taken occasion to remark that in this position of the Sicilian Opening, the first player may gain time..by taking off the Kt. at once. **1875** G. H. D. GOSSIP *Chess-Player's Manual* IV. xxx. 799 The 'Sicilian' is now considered by most modern authorities to be a comparatively weak mode of play... We are of the opinion that the Sicilian defence is not so bad as it has been represented. **1882** CAULFEILD & SAWARD *Dict. Needlewk.* 448/2 *Sicilian Embroidery*, an effective and easy work, formed with muslin, thin cambric, and braid, and is used for trimmings to washing dresses or for tea cloths and ornamental linen. **1883** *Standard* 28 Apr. 3/1 Noa and Tchigorin drew a Sicilian opening. **1900** *Knowledge* 1 Aug. 192/1 The success attending the Sicilian defence is especially noteworthy. **1975** *Amer. Speech 1971* XLVI. 232 One can hear heated arguments on the virtues of the Maroczy Variation of the Scheveningen System in the Sicilian Defence to the King's Pawn Opening.

**b.** In names of plants, products, etc., as ***Sicilian hore-hound, radish, toad-flax; Sicilian earth, saffron; Sicilian sword-fish.***

**1731** MILLER *Gard. Dict.* s.v. *Linaria*, Sicilian Toad-Flax, with many Stalks, and a Leaf of the White Lady's Bedstraw. **1748** *Anson's Voy.* II. i. 117 A vast profusion of turnips and Sicilian radishes. **1770** PENNANT *Brit. Zool.* IV. 141 Sicilian Sword-Fish. **1822** *Hortus Anglicus* II. 98 *Marrubium Peregrinum.* Sicilian White Horehound. **1846** LINDLEY *Veg. Kingd.* 161 Sicilian saffron is obtained from Crocus odorus, according to Gussone. **1867** BRANDE & COX *Dict. Sci.*, etc. III. 440/2 *Sicilian Earth*, a name sometimes given to fossil bezoar, which appears to be of a similar character to Armenian Bole.

**B.** *sb.* **1.** A native of Sicily.

**1513** Douglas *Æneid* v. vi. 16 Of Troianis samyn and Sicilianis a rout. **1644** Milton *Areop.* (Arb.) 60 He whom an honest quæstorship had indear'd to the Sicilians. **1685** Dryden *Pref. to Sylvæ* Ess. (Ker) I. 266 Theocritus writ to Sicilians, who spoke that dialect. **1728** Chambers *Cycl.* s.v. *Silk*, The rest of Italy and Spain learned from the Sicilians and Calabrians the Management of the Silk-Worms. **1788** Lemprière *Class. Dict.* s.v. *Metelli*, A general of the Roman armies against the Sicilians and Carthaginians. **1825** Lytton *Zicci* 5 The Sicilians are all ill-bred, bad-tempered fellows. **1880** 'Ouida' *Moths* III. 10 Her Sicilian had been also on the banks of the Teple.

**2.** = Siciliana. *rare*$^{-1}$.

**1728** Chambers *Cycl.*, *Sicilian.* in Music, &c., a Kind of gay sprightly Air, or Dance; somewhat of the Nature of an English Jig.

**3.** = sicilienne.

**1908** *Daily Chron.* 11 June 11/5 Machinists.—Skirts, voiles, and Sicilians.

**4.** A language or dialect spoken in Sicily, *spec.* a dialect of modern Italian.

**1818** Keats *Let.* 3 May in R. M. Milnes *Life, Lett., &c. J. Keats* (1848) I. 135 Or may I woo thee In earlier Sicilian? **1859** B. W. Dwight *Mod. Philol.* I. 187 Italian: (Dialects, Lombard; Genoese; Florentine; Neapolitan, Sicilian, ..&c.). **1880** A. H. Sayce *Introd. Sci. Lang.* II. vii. 119 Sicilian, for instance, reads like a new language. **1933** L. Bloomfield *Language* iv. 64 *Ligurian* (round the present Riviera) and *Sicilian* in Sicily, may have been close to Italic. **1968** D. Mack Smith *Medieval Sicily* v. 63 Giacomo of Lentini, author of a Provençal-type lyric which is the first poem in true Sicilian that has survived. **1978** *Language* LIV. 184 Sicilian reflects the seven-vowel Southern Romance vocalism.

‖**Sicili'ana.** Also pl. -ane. Also Siciliano, siciliano; pl. sicilianos, siciliani. [It., fem. of *Siciliano* Sicilian.] A dance of the Sicilian peasantry, resembling a jig; the music for this. Also, a piece in $\frac{6}{8}$ or $\frac{12}{8}$ time resembling this music. Also *attrib.*

**1724** *Short Explic. For. Wds. in Mus. Bks.*, *Siciliane*, a Kind of Jig. **1782** *Ann. Reg.* II. 11 In Christmas time all quarters of Naples resound with pastorali or Siciliane, a kind of simple rural music, executed by..shepherds, upon a species of bagpipes. **1866** *Chambers's Encycl.* VIII. 704/1 *Siciliana*, in Music, a name given to a slow, soothing, pastoral description of air, in $\frac{6}{8}$ time. **1873** H. C. Banister *Music* 250 *Siciliana*, an old Sicilian dance in $\frac{6}{8}$ time, with a Satarello movement. **1883** Grove *Dict. Mus.* III. 491/2 *Siciliana, Siciliano, Sicilienne*, a dance rhythm closely allied to the Pastorale. **1947** C. Gray *Contingencies & Other Essays* v. 118 The frequent recurrence in Bellini's music of 12-8 rhythms, called in seventeenth- and eighteenth-century music *Siciliani*, seems always to have been a feature of the popular music of his countrymen. **1959** D. Cooke *Lang. of Music* ii. 100 The siciliano movement in Brahms's St. Anthony Variations. **1968** *Listener* 20 June 814/1 Their variety was astonishing, from the lyrical sicilianos which the history books praise, to vigorous virtuoso pieces. **1970** W. Apel *Harvard Dict. Music* (ed. 2) 774/2 The *siciliana* occurs as a slow movement in early sonatas..as well as in vocal music..whenever gentle pastoral scenes are to be represented musically. **1974** *Early Music* July 197/1 A delightful siciliano aria for alto to the words 'Qui sedes ad dexteram Patris'. **1979** *Ibid.* Oct. 545/2 A profusion of characteristic ideas, charming *Sicilianos*, bubbling *Allegros*, idiomatic and elegant writing for the instrument.

‖**sicilienne** (sɪsɪlɪ'ɛn). [F., fem. of *sicilien* Sicilian.] **1.** A fine poplin made of silk and wool.

**1873** *Young Englishwoman* Jan. 24/1 Sicilienne, a new kind of silk, both soft and glossy. **1881** Miss Braddon *Asphodel* II. 235, I had quite made up my mind to wear that pearl-gray sicilienne which you all so much admired. *Ibid.* III. 225 Her pale-gray cashmere gown, and flounced sicilienne petticoat. **1889** *Tablet* 16 Feb. 260 The bridesmaids' dresses were composed of white sicilienne.

**2.** *Mus.* = Siciliana.

**1883** [see Siciliana]. **1927** *Daily Tel.* 12 Feb. 5/2 The Sicilienne was quiet and restful.

**sick** (sɪk), *a.* and *sb.* Forms: α. 1–3 seoc (1 seoch, sioc), 2–3 seo(c)k; 3 sæc, seac, seak (9 *dial.*), 3, 6 seake; 1–3 sec (5 cec), 2–5 sek (5 cek), 2–6 seke (5 ceke), 5 seeke; 3 siec, 4 siek(e, 4–6 (9 *dial.*) seek, 5 seyk, 5–6 *Sc.* seik. β. 3 suc, sic, 3–6 sik (4 zik), 6–7 sicke (6 sycke), 6– sick (9 *dial.* zick). γ. 3–5 sijk (4 siik, syyk, 5 siyk), 4–5 sijke (4 siike, 5 syike); 3–5 syk, 4–6 syke (4 zyke); 3–5, 7 sike. [Common Teut.: OE. *séoc*, = OFris. *siak, sieck, sek* (WFris. *siik*, †*sjeack*), MDu. *siec, ziec* (Du. *ziek*), OS. *siok, seok, siak* (MLG. *sêk, seik, sik*, LG. *seek, siek, sük*), OHG. *siuh, sioh, seoh, siach, siech* (MHG. and G. *siech*), ON. and Icel. *sjúkr* (Norw. and Sw. *sjuk*, Da. *syg*), Goth. *siuks*. Relationship to other Teutonic roots is uncertain, and no outside cognates have been traced. The variation of vowel in some ME. forms is not easy to account for.]

**A.** *adj.* **I. 1. a.** Suffering from illness of any kind; ill, unwell, ailing. Also, *to go sick*, to become ill, to report sick.

α. *c* **888** K. Ælfred *Boeth.* xxxvi. §5 Swa swa læca ȝewuna is..ðonne hi siocne mon ȝesioð. **971** *Blickl. Hom.* 59 Eal swylce seo lange mettrumnes biþ þæs seocan mannes. *c* **1020** *O.E. Chron.* (Laud MS.) an. 1015, Þa læȝ se cyng seoc æt Cosham. *c* **1205** Lay. 6781 Swa þe king seoc [*c* 1275 seac] læi. *c* **1250** *Gen. & Ex.* 1175 Abimalech wurð sek on-on. **13** .. *K. Alis.* 6978 (Laud MS.), Now man is hool, now man is seek. **1390** Gower *Conf.* I. 65 He makth him siek, whan he is heil. *c* **1440** *Generydes* 199 Youre fader is right seke this day. **1477** Caxton *Dictes* 9 It proffiteth as a good medicine couenably yeven to them that be seke. **1549** *Compl. Scotl.* xx. 165 Quhat medycyn can help ane seik man that hurtis hym selue vilfully? **1580** Haye in *Cath. Tract.* (S.T.S.) 46 Is any seake amang you, lat him call for the preistes of the kirk. **1855** [Robinson] *Whitby Gloss.* s.v. *Seak*, 'I was nowther seak nor sair when I said it',..that is, in no way incapable of giving my evidence.

β. *c* **1200** *Moral Ode* 201 (Trin. Coll. MS.), Nare noman elles dead ne sic ne non unsele. *c* **1275** Lay. 2794 Þo iwarþ þe king sick. *c* **1330** R. Brunne *Chron. Wace* (Rolls) 3861 Elydour feyned hym sik to lye. *c* **1380** Wyclif *Wks.* (1880) 46 Þouȝ I be simpul & sik neþeles I wile euere haue a clerk þat schal do me dyuyne office. *c* **1450** Lovelich *Grail* li. 187 These herbes don me but distresse,..for I am Sykkere thanne I was before. **1526** *Pilgr. Perf.* (W. de W. 1531) 16 b, So that none of them was sycke or miscaryed by yᵉ waye. **1568** Grafton *Chron.* II. 493 In this meane while, king Henry waxed sicker and sicker. **1630** *R. Johnson's Kingd. & Commw.* 191 The one of these being very sicke, and, as was thought, in danger of death. **1674** Godfrey *Inj. & Ab. Physic* 83 Instead of growing sicker, they are far more chearfull. **1709** *Tatler* No. 86 ¶3 At whose right hand he had sat at every Quarter-Sessions this Thirty Years, unless he was Sick. *a* **1774** Goldsm. *Hist. Greece* II. 183 At Issas he barbarously put to death all the Greeks who were sick in that city. **1848** Thackeray *Van. Fair* xxxiv, If she could be spared to come down and console a poor sick lonely old woman. **1879** [see sense 1 f below]. **1891** Freeman in Stephens *Life* (1895) II. 443 She too has been sick and sent up to Ilkley in Yorkshire. **1902** W. B. Yeats *Where there is Nothing* (1903) IV. i. 77 No fear, they won't refuse a sick man. **1915** D. O. Barnett *Lett.* 53 He's lots better this morning,..and he is not 'going sick' at all. **1927** E. J. Thompson *These Men thy Friends* 12 Filthy climate. No fun. But she just carries on. Hasn't gone sick once in six months. **1936** G. B. Shaw *Millionairess* II. 164 You are my doctor: do you hear? I am a sick woman: you cannot abandon me to die. **1945** *Chambers's Jrnl.* Sept. 452/1 'And you're telling me that you've never had a few days off?.. Not even for sick-leave?' 'I was never sick, sir.' **1952** [see lead *sb.*[1] 6 b]. **1956** D. Jacobson *Dance in Sun* II. ix. 91 'Hey,' he said rudely to Fletcher, 'are you sick?' **1959** V. Watkins *Cypress & Acacia* 23, I found him feeble and sick. And cold. **1962** G. Lawton *John Wesley's English* iii. 57 When Wesley is sick he is 'laid-up.' **1976** *Evening Post* (Nottingham) 15 Dec. 24/4 Willis went sick during the opening match in Poona.

*fig.* **1593** Shaks. *Rich. II*, II. i. 96 Thy death-bed is no lesser then the Land, Wherein thou lyest in reputation sicke. **1596** —— *1 Hen. IV*, IV. iii. 56 Sicke in the Worlds regard.

γ. *c* **1290** *S. Eng. Leg.* I. 28 Þis bok he leide ope þis man, ase he so sijk þer lay. *Ibid.* 132 Þe Monenday sore syk þe bischop thomas lay. *a* **1320** *Sir Tristr.* 3126 Þai wende þe quen wald dye, So sike sche was bi siȝt. ? *a* **1366** Chaucer *Rom. Rose* 1358 That is a fruyt ful wel to lyke, Namely to folk whan they ben syke. *c* **1449** Pecock *Repr.* II. ix. 194 The feend..made the peple sijk. *c* **1489** Caxton *Sonnes of Aymon* xii. 294, I have lever dye than be longe syke. **1552** Latimer *Serm. Lincoln* v. (1571) 101 Our Sauiour was going to the house where this young mayde lay syke.

**b.** Const. *of, with* (†*in, on*).

Also in figurative contexts, cf. 3 and 4.

*c* **1380** Wyclif *Sel. Wks.* II. 23 Men þat ben siike in þe palesy. **1390** Gower *Conf.* II. 148 Be war..thou be noght sik Of thilke fievere [jealousy] as I have spoke. *a* **1533** Ld. Berners *Huon* cxi. 385 Many sondry frutys so fayre..that a syke man of any infyrmyte shuld sone recouer helth. *a* **1548** Hall *Chron., Hen. VI*, 13 b, Ihon Lilie fel sicke on the gowte. **1579** W. Fulke *Heskins' Parl.* 136 To a sicke man of the ague, all drinkes seeme bitter. *a* **1618** Sylvester *Auto-Machia* 68 Sick to my Self I run for my reliefe: So, Sicker of my Physicke than my Griefe. **1643** Trapp *Comm. Gen.* xxxvii. 11 Self-love, ignorance, &c...make the soul sick of the fret. **1731–8** Swift *Polite Conv.* i. Wks. 1751 XII. 209 You are sick of the Mulligrubs with eating chopt Hay. *a* **1774** Goldsm. tr. *Scarron's Com. Romance* (1775) I. 320 This inn-keeper..being sick of a violent fever. **1884** Quincy *Figures of Past* 199 New York had succumbed to the influenza. Everybody had been..sick with it.

**c.** Of parts of the body: Not in a sound or healthy state.

In later use usually with suggestion of sense 2.

**1340** *Ayenb.* 148 Yef þe on leme is zik oþer y-wonded. *c* **1400** *Brut.* cci. 229 Seynt Thomas come vnto him, and enoynted oueral his sike side. **1471** Caxton *Recuyell* (Sommer) I. 35 Wher the heed is seke or euyll, þe membres may not be hoole ner good. **1561** Hollybush *Hom. Apoth.* 33 b, Laye thys upon the sycke place. **1668** Culpepper & Cole *Barthol. Anat.* I. xvii. 48 The kidneys might be sick, or ..could not be nourished with good blood. **1700** *Transactioneer* 48 At last his Third Finger was sick. **1786** Mrs. A. M. Bennett *Juvenile Indiscr.* I. 169 And had a sick stomach. **1807** Southey *Espriella's Lett.* II. 115 A Sick Stomach will not digest the food that may be forced down it. **1821** Shelley *Hellas* 781 All that it inherits Are motes of a sick eye.

**d.** *sick man*, a term frequently applied, during the latter part of the 19th cent., to the Sultan of Turkey. Also *fig.*, orig. applied to Turkey and hence to other countries, regions, etc., and in extended uses.

The first quot. refers to a conversation between the Tsar Nicholas I and Sir G. Seymour at St. Petersburg on the 21 Feb. 1853.

**1853** *Ann. Register, Hist.* 252, I am not so eager about what shall be done when the sick man dies, as I am to determine with England what shall not be done upon that event taking place. **1855** J. Martineau *Essays*, etc. I. (1890) 428 It was all right not to let the 'sick man' be frightened into convulsions. **1860** Motley *Netherl.* ii. I. 30 That formidable potentate, not then the 'sick man' whose precarious condition and territorial inheritance cause so much anxiety in modern days. **1860** S. S. Cox *Eight Years in Congress* (1865) 129 'Mexico is our "sick man".' 'Yes; she is to America what Turkey is to Europe.' **1868** C. Schurz *Speeches, Corr. & Pol. Papers* (1913) I. 456 The South is our 'sick man'... The 'sick man' has been operated upon by Democratic doctors once more. **1888** S. Lane-Pool *Turkey* xvii. 343 The Powers have always acted on the principle that somebody must serve as a dyke between Russia and the Bosphorus, and that Turkey, being there, had better be maintained in her position. The 'Sick Man' of the morbid mind of Nicholas must be galvanized into sufficient vitality to sit up and pretend to be well. **1897** *Japan Times* 30 Mar. 3/4 Mr Valentine Chirol, who shortly after the war published in the London *Times* a series of remarkable articles exposing the rottenness of China..has recently been in the East again..and has commenced a second series of equally striking articles on the 'Sick Man of Asia'. **1901** *Daily Express* 18 Mar. 4/4 French dealings with the Sultan of Morocco, the Sick Man of Africa. **1918** *Times* 3 Jan. 5/1 The Sick Man of Europe has changed his doctors, and the new doctors..have prescribed participation in the European war. *Ibid.* 5/2 The Sick Man finds himself less sick than his neighbour, and Russia defenceless offers her flanks to Turkey's sharpest blades. **1929** H. M. Kallen *Frontiers of Hope* 451 Under the terms of the Peace the Jew has simply been made to replace the Turk as the Sick Man of Europe. **1959** *Listener* 30 July 168/2 It was Italy which turned the Austrian empire into a second 'sick man'. **1961** N. Smart in I. Ramsey *Prospect for Metaphysics* v. 80 Natural theology is the Sick Man of Europe. **1963** *Times* 31 Jan. 11/1 There is no imminent threat to it, but once that is passed India would be on the way to becoming in economic terms the sick man of Asia. **1967** *Listener* 26 Jan. 116/2 In December 1958 France was the sick man of Europe; it had no exchange reserves and was incapable of facing the Common Market. **1970** R. Lowell *Notebook* 205 The movie's not always the sick man of the arts. **1974** *Times* 4 May 8/4, I have been wondering who now qualifies for the title of Sick Man of Sound Broadcasting. **1979** G. St. Aubyn *Edward VII* vii. 319 China was the sick man of the Orient over whose corpse the vultures hovered.

**e.** *north. dial.* In childbed, confined, lying-in.

**1828** *Craven Gloss.* **1878** *Cumbld. Gloss.*

†**f.** Said of pigeons which have lost their young and so have no recipient for the soft food that they regurgitate. *Obs.*

**1765** *Treat. Domestic Pigeons* 21 If your Pigeons do not hatch, because their eggs are addle, or otherwise, you should give them a pair, or at least one young one, to feed off their soft meat, which would be apt to make them sick. **1854** L. A. Meall *Moubray's Poultry* viii. 455 We have never observed the old birds 'sick' (as most books assert they are) when the young have died. **1879** L. Wright *Pract. Pigeon Keeper* iii. 37 In order that another young one from some other pair..may be given the parents to feed off their soft meat, and save them from 'going sick' with it.

**g.** *slang* (orig. *U.S.*). Of a drug addict, craving for a dose of a drug, suffering from withdrawal symptoms.

**1951** *N.Y. Times* 15 June 14/6, I..would walk up and.. ask the bartender: 'Say, have you seen so-and-so yet?' I says: 'Man, I'm sick.' **1953** W. Burroughs *Junkie* vii. 69 The usual routine is to grab someone with junk on him, and let him stew in jail until he is good and sick. **1967** M. M. Glatt et al. *Drug Scene* vii. 91 Even now, more than two years after leaving hospital, I still feel sometimes sick in the morning when I am tense or upset, and I feel sick whenever I see syringes or 'addicts' in TV plays.

**2. a.** Having an inclination to vomit, or being actually in the condition of vomiting.

**1614** B. Jonson *Bart. Fair* v. vi, O lend me a bason, I am sicke, I am sicke. **1656** [? J. Sergeant] tr. *T. White's Peripat. Inst.* 130 Those who are sick with riding in a Coach. **1719** De Foe *Crusoe* II. (Globe) 341 He was very sick, and brought it up again. **1778** Mme. D'Arblay *Let.* 5 July, Precipices, that, to look at, make my head giddy and my heart sick. **1815** *Croker Papers* (1884) I. iii. 75 The men were all sick, and the women and children thought they were going to the bottom. **1900** *Allbutt's Syst. Med.* V. 628 The patient, if he is in the house, usually crouches over the fire and feels sick and giddy.

*fig.* **1855** Tennyson *Maud* I. xiii. 11 But his essences turn'd the live air sick. **1856** Bryant *Autumn Woods* vi, When the noon of summer made The valleys sick with heat.

**b.** More fully *sick at* (or *to, in*) *the stomach.*

**1653** H. More *Antid. Ath.* II. vii, The Dog, when he is sick at the Stomach, knows his Cure, falls to his Grass, vomits, and is well. **1671** H. M. tr. *Erasm. Colloq.* 489 Antronius comes..to say, that he is sick at the stomach. **1753** A. Murphy *Gray's Inn Jrnl.* No. 48, Sick in my Stomach all the Morning—Owing to their hard Food. **1796** *Grose's Dict. Vulgar T.* (ed. 3), *Sick as a horse.* Horses are said to be extremely sick at their stomachs, from being unable to relieve themselves by vomiting. **1831** T. Hope *Ess. Orig. Man* II. 320 The elephant [will] eat sugar-plums till he turns sick at the stomach. **1863** Trollope *Small House at Allington* xxxvi, in *Cornh. Mag.* Aug. 228 How well can I remember the terror created within me by..a certain fine old gentleman... I would become sick in my stomach. **1923** [see here *adv.* 5 b]. **1947** A. Huxley *Let.* 9 Apr. (1969) 570, I heard a bit of the *Parsifal* Good Friday music at Easter-time.., and it made me feel even more 'sick to my stomach', as the Americans say, than in the past. **1948** 'J. Tey' *Franchise Affair* xiii. 139 You make me sick—Cat-sick. Sick to my stomach. **1955** *Jrnl. Canad. Linguistic Assoc.* Mar. 17 Another expression which has some striking variants depending on the choice of preposition is *sick at the stomach.* In the Northern speech area of the United States the usual equivalent is *sick to the stomach*; in the Midland and Southern areas, *at* is the usual preposition... In New England..and most of the Yankee settlement areas, *to* enjoys a virtual monopoly. In northwest New York State, however, *sick at the stomach* is unusually common. **1975** *Times* 30 June 17/5 If all the factories are nationalized I shall walk out of here sick to the stomach.

**c.** In phrases *sick as a dog, horse*, etc. (Sense sometimes merging with 4). Also *sick as a parrot* (a fanciful catch-phrase, chiefly used *joc.*).

**1705** Vanbrugh *Confederacy* II. i, If..he shou'd chance to be fond, he'd make me as sick as a Dog. **1731–8** Swift *Polite Conv.* i. Wks. 1751 XII. 209 Poor Miss, she's sick as a Cushion, she wants nothing but stuffing. **1765** Sterne *Tr.*

Shandy VII. ii, I am sick as a horse, quoth I, already. a 1843 Southey Doctor (1847) VII. 79 T' Trees gang fleeing by.. an' gars yan be as seek as a peeate. 1854 Miss Baker Northampt. Gloss., Sick as a horse, a common vulgar simile, used when a person is exceedingly sick without vomiting. 1861 Hughes Tom Brown at Oxf. III. xi. 207 It turned me as sick as a dog. a 1906 'T. Collins' Rigby's Romance (1946) xli. 221 Well, by-and-by I woke up, sick as a dog, with my face all scorched, and I lay down again. 1915 J. Buchan 39 Steps vii. 161, I had a crushing headache, and felt as sick as a cat. 1947 A. Ransome Great Northern? xix. 238 'Sick as cats with himself,' said Nancy. 1979 Private Eye 16 Feb. 12/1 The Moggatollah admitted frankly that he was 'sick as a parrot' at the way events had been unfolding. 1982 Daily Star 5 Feb. 5/6 Peter the budgie was sick as a parrot until a vet diagnosed his problem yesterday. Peter.. has got gout!

**d.** In phrases to worry (oneself), be worried, sick.

1952 M. Laski Village v. 89 Edith Wilson had heard about Wendy's illness, and worried herself sick, not knowing what to do for the best. 1961 'J. le Carré' Call for Dead iv. 37 You look worried sick. 1977 R. Ludlum Chancellor Ms. xxx. 320 She hasn't been able to sleep. She's worried sick.

**II. †3.** Spiritually or morally ailing; corrupt through sin or wrong-doing. Obs.

c 960 Rule St. Benet (Schröer) ii. 11 Ʒif he.. his seocum, þæt is synfullum dædum ealle lacnunge ʒeʒearewade. a 1000 Juliana 65 Hæðne wæron beʒen, synnum seoce, sweor & aþum. a 1225 Ancr. R. 176 þet fleschs wolde.. makien sic þe soule. a 1300 Cursor M. 25329 Bot if þi saul it be sua seke þat þou þi mode mai nagat meke. 1377 Langl. P. Pl. B. xx. 303 Go salue þo þat syke ben and þorw synne ywounded. 1404-8 26 Pol. Poems vii. 5 The flesch.. Is wormes mete, and sek of synne. 1435 Misyn Fire of Love 90 To so seyk & vnclene myndis.. Aungell foyd sall not sauyr. 1596 Dalrymple tr. Leslie's Hist. Scot. I. 109 Mony was seik of ane vice; to wit, immoderat libertie of lyfe. 1613 Shaks. Hen. VIII, II. iv. 204, I meant to rectifie my Conscience, which I then did feele full sicke. 1738 Wesley Ps. VI. i, And heal my Soul diseas'd and sick.

**4. a.** Deeply affected by some strong feeling, as (a) sorrow, (b) longing, (c) envy, (d) repugnance or loathing, producing effects similar or comparable to those of physical ailments.

(a) a 1000 Fate of Apostles 2 Ic þysne sang siðgeomor fand On seocum sefan samnode wide. a 1000 Guthlac 1050 Ne beo þu on sefan to seoc! c 1374 Chaucer Boeth. III. met. xii. (1868) 107 He song.. wiþ as myche as loue.. myȝte ȝeuen hym and teche hym in his seke herte. 1581 Pettie Guazzo's Civ. Conv. II. (1586) 77 It will make you sicke at the heart to see it. 1591 Shaks. Two Gent. I. i. 69 Thou Iulia thou hast.. Made Wit with musing, weake; hart sick with thought. 1611 Bible Prov. xiii. 12 Hope deferred maketh the heart sicke. 1784 Cowper Task II. 6 My soul is sick, with ev'ry day's report Of wrong and outrage. 1820 Shelley Witch Atl. 178 Liquors.. whose healthful might Could medicine the sick soul to happy sleep. 1850 Tennyson In Mem. l. 3 When.. the heart is sick, And all the wheels of Being slow. 1886 Robinson Courting May Smith VI. i, She was ill at ease, and sick at heart.

(b) c 1388 Wyclif Song Sol. v. 8 If ȝe han founde my derlyng, that ȝe telle to hym, that Y am sijk [L. langueo] for loue. c 1460 Sir R. Ros La Belle Dame 53 These seke lovers I leve that to hem longes. 1597 Shaks. 2 Hen. IV, v. iii. 142 Boote, boote Master Shallow, I know the young King is sick for mee. 1613 —— Hen. VIII, II. ii. 83, I would not be so sicke though for his place. 1637 B. Jonson Sad Shepherd I. ii, She's sick of the young shepherd that be-kiss'd her. 1820 Shelley Prometh. Unb. II. ii. 28 When one [nightingale].., Sick with sweet love, droops dying away. 1842 Tennyson Talking Oak 71 This girl, for whom your heart is sick, Is three times worth them all. 1875 —— Harold I. i, Sick as an autumn swallow for a voyage.

(c) c 1390 Gower Conf. I. 159 If evere yit thin herte was Sek of an other mannes hele? 1606 Shaks. Tr. & Cr. I. iii. 132 So euery step Exampled by the first pace that is sicke Of his Superiour, growes to an enuious Feauer. 1613 —— Hen. VIII, I. ii. 82 What we oft doe best, By sicke Interpreters.. Is not ours, or not allow'd.

(d) 1590 Shaks. Mids. N. II. i. 212, I am sicke when I do looke on thee. 1599 —— Much Ado II. ii. 5 Any barre.. will be medicinable to me, I am sicke in displeasure to him. 1819 Shelley Cenci II. i. 122 Thy milky, meek face makes me sick with hate! 1860 Tennyson Sea Dreams 155 It makes me sick to quote him.

**b.** slang. Disgusted, mortified, chagrined.

1853 Surtees Sponge's Sp. Tour (1893) 254 Thinking.. how sick he was when the jury.. gave five hundred pounds damages against him. 1895 Westm. Gaz. 28 Mar. 7/1 Those who backed the popular fancies in the winter must be feeling, in popular parlance, pretty sick.

transf. 1896 Kipling Seven Seas, Rhyme Three Sealers, The sickest day for you.. was the day that you came here.

**c.** Phr. to make (a person) sick.

1819, 1860 [see sense 4 a(d) above]. 1911 G. B. Shaw Blanco Posnet 30 A man like you makes me sick. 1937 'G. Orwell' Road to Wigan Pier xii. 228 It makes one sick to see.. men sweating their guts out to dig a trench.., when some easily devised machine would scoop the earth out in a couple of minutes. 1944 M. Laski Love on Supertax i. 18 The Duchess lost her temper. 'You make me sick!' she shouted. 1978 T. Allbeury Lantern Network iii. 34 He talks like a schoolboy. All that 'knocking the Germans for six' stuff, it makes me sick.

**5. a.** Thoroughly tired or weary of a thing.

1597 Shaks. 2 Hen. IV, I. iii. 87 The Common-wealth is sicke of their owne Choice. 1603 Breton Dial. Pithe & Pleasure Wks. (Grosart) II. 14/1 Where the sonne is sike of the father, the sister of the brother. 1710 Tatler No. 257 ¶3, I was quickly sick of this tawdry Composition of Ribands, Silks and Jewels. 1797-1805 S. & Ht. Lee Canterb. T. I. 7 Heartily sick of his host, himself, and his travels. 1842 Miall in Nonconf. II. 281 The world is sick of such societies. 1884 Manch. Exam. 7 May 5/4 There are plenty of Tories everywhere who are sick of the old party traditions.

**b.** In phrases sick and tired of (cf. sick-tired, sense 11), sick to death of.

1783 'J. H. St. John de Crèvecœur' Sk. 18th-Cent. Amer. (1925) 298, I am quite sick and tired of these pretended conscientious non-fighting mortals. 1884 E. W. Nye Baled Hay 124 We are sick and tired of pointing out different avenues of wealth to be laughed at and ridiculed. 1890 E. Dowson Let. c 11 Sept. (1967) 166, I am sick to death of this place. 1925 F. S. Fitzgerald Great Gatsby ix. 205 'You young men think you can force your way in any time,' she scolded. 'We're getting sick in tired of it.' 1953 R. Lehmann Echoing Grove 117 He was sick to death of the sound of these three crass monosyllables which he seemed always to be reiterating. 1976 Milton Keynes Express 9 July 2/6, I believe people are sick and tired of half-truths and evasions.

**III. 6.** Mentally affected or weak. Also, morbid, enjoying sick humour (see sense 7 f below). Now rare.

Cf. OE. séocmód adj. in Napier Contrib. O.E. Lex.

c 1340 Hampole Pr. Consc. 772 þan waxes his gaste seke and sare, And his face rouncles. 1551 T. Wilson Logike (1580) 10 b, Some menne are so sicke in their braine, that thei are neuer wise. 1692 S. Patrick Answ. Touchstone 223 If they are not sick in their wits. 1817 Shelley Rev. Isl. v. xxvii. 3 It was a tone Such as sick fancies in a new-made grave Might hear. 1959, 1960 [see sense 7 f below]. 1961 Times 17 July 14/5 Mr. Sahl is disapproving of the so-called 'sick' comedians of America. 1961 Webster s.v. [1]sick, A sick personality. 1962 Listener 25 Oct. 692/3 From Korea James Mossman reported on the Panmunjom truce-line (a raree-show for tourists these days, I gather: how sick can people get?). 1964 L. Nkosi Rhythm of Violence 45 Don't mind them, honey! They're the sickest bunch of people you ever saw.

**7. a.** Of things: Out of condition in some respect; corrupted or spoiled; spec. of wine which has become turbid, or of quicksilver (see quot. 1875).

1388 Wyclif Isaiah xxiv. 7 Vyndage morenyde, the vyne is sijk [L. infirmata]. c 1440 tr. Pallad. on Husb. III. 939 Thy tre is seek, oyldregges water mynge [etc.]. c 1460 Russell Bk. Nurture 116 in Babees Bk. 125 Ʒiff swete wyne be seeke or pallid, put in a Rompney for lesynge. a 1470 Dives & Pauper (W. de W.) VII. x. 290/1 Yf a man or woman selle a seke thynge for an hole thynge wyttyngly to begyle the byer, he doth theeft. 1513 Douglas Æneid III. ii. 153 The seik ground denyis his fruite and fudis. 1697 Tryon Way to Health xv. (ed. 3) 369 A Medicine of a loathing Quality, and far Sicker in Nature than the distempered Patient. 1703 Art & Myst. Vintners 7 Renish [wine].. commonly grows sick in June, if not rack'd. 1743 Lond. & Co. Brewer III. 208 If the Wort is sick, it cannot fail of communicating its unwholesome Quality to the Blood. 1817 in Trans. Ill. State Hist. Soc. 1910 (1912) 147 Sick Milk, Sick Wheat, a plenty of Ague near the large streams. a 1821 Keats Hyperion I. 189 Instead of sweets, his ample palate took Savour of poisonous brass and metal sick. 1847 H. Howe Hist. Collect. Ohio 274 Those lands were too sick for wheat, making 'sick' wheat, so termed, because when made into bread, it had the effect of an emetic. 1868 H. C. R. Johnson Argentine Alps 103 The people very generally drink the wine new, the year after it is made—just as likely it is sick. 1875 Ure's Dict. Arts II. 696 The quicksilver constantly became 'sick',.. and lost apparently all its natural affinity for gold. 1892 Longman's Mag. Nov. 83 Should the hot and dry weather long continue, a curious phenomenon takes place. The mere is said to be 'sick'; that the eels are so there can be no doubt. 1915 Rep. Brit. Assoc. Adv. Sci. 1914 672 The fertility of this 'sick' soil can be restored by merely heating it for an hour or two to a temperature approaching that of boiling water. 1921 Brit. Mus. Return 74 in Parl. Papers XXVII. 651 The treatment and cleaning of sick and dirty coins. 1930 N. & Q. 16 Aug. 124/2 A cheese.. is sick when it has been over soured or over acidulated, and in time 'weeps', gradually becoming soft inside. 1947 I. L. Idriess Isles of Despair xvi. 106 Some roots are 'sick', eaten through and through by boring insects. 1965 Listener 2 Sept. 358/1 Soils can be said to be 'potato sick', 'rose sick', 'flax sick', etc.

fig. 1596 Shaks. Merch. V. v. i. 124 This night methinkes is but the daylight sicke. 1606 —— Tr. & Cr. I. iii. 103 O, when Degree is shak'd,.. The enterprize is sicke. 1781 Cowper Retirem. 738 A sepulchre.. Where all good qualities grow sick and die. 1822 J. Flint Lett. fr. Amer. 111 When the sick system dies, the public will see the full amount.. they have to suffer for their credulity. 1931 H. Crane Let. 13 June (1965) 371 As for Mexico.. you were right, it's a sick country. 1959 Washington Post 18 Nov. A 16/2 Some czars in the labor movement will scream over this resort to the courts to straighten out so-called internal affairs of sick unions, but for racket-harassed workers it is an event of the first importance. 1960 Wall St. Jrnl. 2 Feb. 4 He has taken other sick businesses and has done a marvelous job with them. 1973 Black Panther 14 July 6/2, I was basically looking at myself.. people of my complexion struggling for their liberation. I saw how sick conditions were. 1976 Smythies & Corbett Psychiatry iii. 29 Concepts like a 'sick' society have become commonplace.

**b.** Said of the young and ungrown feathers of a bird in moulting-time.

1589 Puttenham Eng. Poesie III. xxiii. (Arb.) 272 These fowles in their moulting time, when their feathers be sick. 1592 Greene Disput. 22, I see the fayrest Hawke hath oftentimes the sickest feathers. 1655 Fuller Ch. Hist. v. 187 If a Seraphim himself should be a Bishop, he would either finde or make some sick feathers in his wings. 1820 Keats Eve St. Agnes xxxvii, A dove.. with sick unpruned wing.

**c.** Of fish, etc.: In the spawning stage.

1728 Chambers Cycl. s.v. Herring, The shotten and sick Herrings [are sorted] by themselves. 1885 Encycl. Brit. XVIII. 107/1 The mass of ova.. is spoken of by oyster fishers as 'white spat', and an oyster containing them is said to be 'sick'.

**d.** Naut. Requiring repairs.

More common in combs. as iron-sick, nail-sick.

1854 Eliz. S. Sheppard Counterparts I. 7 And the Shelley, she lays down at X, sick of paint. 1893 Alston & Walker Seamanship (ed. 3) 55 Sick Seams.—Are those in which the stitches are worn, and give way here and there.

**e.** Stock Exchange. Slow, dull.

1870 Medbery Men. & Mysteries of Wall St. 137 A Sick market; the market is Ill. When brokers very generally hesitate to buy. 1880 Daily News 13 Dec. 7/2 The [wool] market has been somewhat sick. 1904 Daily Chron. 22 Mar. 2/5 Kaffir shares were again rather sick, and closed lower.

**f.** colloq. Of humour, a joke, etc.: macabre, providing amusement by reference to something that is thoroughly unpleasant.

1959 Punch 2 Sept. 106/1 The prototype of sick jokes is one that goes 'But apart from that, Mrs. Lincoln, how did you enjoy the play?' 1959 Guardian 16 Oct. 10/3 Feiffer.. belongs.. to the new American fashion of sick humour... Like those gifted sick comedians Mort Sahl and Lenny Bruce.. he is able to go straight to the springs of derision and aggression where so much humour begins. 1959 Washington Post 26 Nov. D 22/1 'Sick comedy,' defines Berman carefully, 'is comic material which violates what we regard as the limits of sensitivity—poking fun at a cripple.. or kidding a typhoon that killed thousands.' 1960 Guardian 7 Oct. 15/3 Jules Feiffer, regarded as one of the 'sick' school of cartoonists, is not as sick as all that... No one is sicker than Charles Addams. 1961 Harper's Bazaar Feb. 84/2 To enjoy.. the sick joke.. you have to.. swallow jokes about cancer, corruption, homosexuality, third degree, race prejudice and insanity. 1965 Times Lit. Suppl. 25 Nov. 1035/4 This has been a time of sick laughter. 1968 M. Woodhouse Rock Baby xvii. 164 How long exactly does it take to become a bomb-disposal expert? And don't tell me that you learn by your mistakes because I'm not in the mood for sick jokes. 1975 P. Fussell Gt. War & Mod. Memory vi. 228 There is extant a postwar version of such a record [of battle],.. aimed at what today might be called the Sick Nostalgia Market. 1978 D. Devine Sunk without Trace xxv. 226 'How does it feel.. to be back in the bosom of your family?' Judy said sharply: 'I'm not in the mood for sick jokes.'

**8.** Of a sickly hue; pale, wan.

1592 Shaks. Rom. & Jul. II. ii. 8 Be not her Maid since she is enuious, Her Vestal liuery is but sicke and greene. a 1822 Shelley Triumph Life 430 A light of heaven, whose half-extinguished beam Through the sick day.. Glimmers. 1845 Mangan Germ. Anthol. I. 139 Out, out, sick light! Out, flickering taper!

**9.** Accompanied by illness or sickness; denoting sickness. Cf. sick headache in sense 12. Also in fig. contexts.

1593 Shaks. Rich. II, II. ii. 84 Now comes the sicke houre that his surfet made. 1647 Trapp Comm. Rom. ii. 19 So spending thy time in a still dream, but thou shalt have sick waking. 1656 Earl Monm. Boccalini's Advts. fr. Parnass. 273, I did first exactly consider the body of the State of Rome in its sick condition. 1746 Francis tr. Horace, Ep. I. xviii. 159 They dread A sick Debauch and aching Head. 1827 Carlyle Germ. Rom. II. 176 Seventeen sick and pitiable years, before death put a period to her sufferings. 1889 Repentance of Paul Wentworth III. 297 A sick despair was at his heart.

**10.** (Chiefly from the absolute or substantival use: see B.)

**a.** Appropriated or given up to, occupied by, one or more persons in a state of illness, as sick-bay, -berth, -bungalow, -bunk, -chamber, -couch, etc. Also sick-bed, -house, -room.

Cf. older Flem. sieckkamer, -stoel (Kilian), G. siechkammer, -stube, -zimmer, Sw. sjukstuga, -säng.

1813 J. Thomson Lect. Inflam. 465 The temporary *sick-bay, in which they had been heretofore, being pulled down. 1846 A. Young Naut. Dict., Sick-bay, a place set apart in a ship for invalids or wounded men. 1919 W. Lang Sea Lawyer's Log i. 6 Then our guide, a Leading Seaman,.. conducted us to the doctor's quarters—or 'sick bay', as he expressed it. 1971 P. D. James Shroud for Nightingale iii. 60 She's in the sick bay... It's part of the private wing. 1803 Med. Jrnl. IX. 284 We offer the plan of a *Sick Berth, which is to be considered as the hospital of a ship of the line. 1863 A. Young Naut. Dict., Sick-berth attendant, formerly termed Lob-lolly Boy; in a ship of war, a person who attends the surgeon and his assistants. 1845 Stocqueler Brit. India 244 At Almorah there are five bungalows, called *sick bungalows, belonging to government. 1856 Kane Arct. Expl. I. xvii. 200 Nearly all our party.. were tossing in their *sick-bunks. 1825 Scott Betrothed xxvii, Margery, whose element was a *sick-chamber. 1886 Ruskin Præterita I. 431 The grief and anxiety of a sick chamber. 1760-72 H. Brooke Fool of Qual. (1809) IV. 4 The *sick-couch is preparing, with.. agonies and death. 1817 Shelley Rev. Islam IV. v. 5 That gentle Hermit.. By my sick couch was busy to and fro. 1856 Kane Arct. Expl. II. xviii. 187, I had carried Mr. Goodfellow to the *sick-station with my dog-sledge. 1748 Anson's Voy. II. ii. 132 We set up a.. copper-oven near the *sick tents. 1632 Sherwood, The *sick-ward of an hospitall, la maladerie. 1813 J. Thomson Lect. Inflam. 491 The efficacy of these vapours in destroying the offensive smells which occur in sick-wards.

**b.** Of or pertaining to, connected with, persons suffering from illness, as sick-allowance, -benefit, -book, -club, cookery, etc.

1863 Trevelyan Compet. Wallah (1866) 198 His first ideas.. run in the line of sick-leave and *sick-allowances. 1909 Chambers's Jrnl. 26 Dec. 56/2 Members who.. may have received *sick-benefit. 1952 Sick benefit [see approved ppl. a. 6]. 1867 Smyth Sailor's Word-bk., *Sick-book, an account of such officers and men as are on the sick list on board, or are sent to an hospital, hospital-ship, or sick-quarters. 1851 Mayhew Lond. Lab. (1864) II. 331 Among these workmen are no Trade Societies, no Benefit or *Sick-Clubs. 1871 Napheys Prev. & Cure Dis. II. iii. 489 *Sick-cookery should more than half do the work of the poor patient's weak digestion. 1731-8 Swift Polite Conv. I. 137 This is my *sick Dish; when I am well, I'll have a bigger. 1867 Smyth Sailor's Word-bk., *Sick-flag, the yellow quarantine flag. 1849 F. B. Head Stokers & Pokers v. (1851) 53 A portion of the proceeds being handed over to the *sick-fund for persons.. hurt in the service. 1899 Month May 462 To master the principles of *sick-insurance. 1840 Col. Hawker Diary (1893) II. 179 He would use all interest to get home on *sick leave. 1943 J. B. Priestley Daylight on Saturday xxix. 231 He'll be home on sick leave.., the doctor says. 1976 Times 8 Mar. 12/8 Staff are entitled to paid sick leave only if there is a reasonable prospect of their return to duty. 1867 Smyth Sailor's Word-bk., *Sick-mess, a table for those on the doctor's list. *a* **1660** in J. Morris *Troubles Cath. Foref.* (1872) vi. 277 The Cellaress and *Sick Mistress.. remained there. **1739** Bp. Herring in J. Duncombe *Lett.* (1773) II. 135 A woman, in a *sick night-cap hanging over the stairs. **1887** *Spectator* 15 Oct. 1385 A member of a Benefit Society is not allowed, when receiving *sick-pay, to put his hand to a stroke of work. **1897** *Allbutt's Syst. Med.* II. 953 A low temperature is always accompanied by a decrease in the *sick-rate. **1595** Shaks. *John* iv. i. 52 But you, at your *sicke seruice had a Prince. **1802** Mrs. E. Parsons *Myst. Visit* IV. 37 Discharged with a *sick ticket to go home. **1867** Smyth *Sailor's Word-bk.*, *Sick-ticket*, a document given to an officer, seaman, or marine, when sent to an hospital. **1846** McCulloch *Acc. Brit. Empire* (1854) II. 593 In like manner the *sick-time is augmented principally by the attacks.

**11.** *Comb.*, as *sick-brained*, *-feathered*, *-hearted*, *-thoughted*; *sick-fallen*, *-pale*, *-sweet*, *-tired*; *sick-making* ppl. adj. and vbl. sb.; also *sick-child*, *-heart* used attrib.

**1658** *2nd Narr. Parl.* in *Harl. Misc.* (1809) III. 474 Whether the protector, and the great men his confederates, be not rather to be termed fanatick, whimsical, and *sick-brained, than those who [etc.]. **1824** Miss Ferrier *Inher.* xxvii, In a soft, whining, *sick-child sort of voice. **1605** *Tryall Chevalr.* i. ii. in Bullen *Old Pl.*, Idle love, The *sick-fac't object of an amorous brayne. **1595** Shaks. *John* iv. iii. 153 And vast confusioun waites As doth a Rauen on a *sicke-falne beast. **1687** Dryden *Hind & Panther* iii. 614 The latter brood,..*Sick-feather'd, and unpractis'd in the sky. **1875** Morris *Æneid* xii. 850 *Sick-heart men. *a* **1835** Mrs. Hemans *Poems* (1875) 541 Sing to thy child, the *sick-hearted, Songs of a spirit oppress'd. **1930** E. Waugh *Vile Bodies* i. 7 Sometimes the ship pitched and sometimes she rolled... 'Too, too *sick-making,' said Miss Runcible, with one of her rare flashes of accuracy. **1938** Dylan Thomas *Let.* c 6 July (1966) 203 There will be speechmaking, drunkmaking, sickmaking and we must all dress up. **1949** N. Mitford *Love in Cold Climate* i. vi. 59 I'm in a terrible do about my [stolen] bracelet of lucky charms—no value to anybody else—really—too too sick-making. **1976** I. Illich *Limits to Medicine* 7 What has turned health care into a sick-making enterprise is the very intensity of an engineering endeavour. **1978** *Times* 5 Oct. 2/4 What is sickmaking is the IBA..trying to make the BBC out as the monster and them the viewers' guardian. **1810** Crabbe *Borough* xx. 314 She and that *sick-pale brother. **1922** Joyce *Ulysses* 444 The odour of the *sicksweet weed floats toward him. **1592** Shaks. Ven. & Ad. 5 *Sick-thoughted Venus makes amaine vnto him. **1631** Quarles *Samson* viii, From his loathed Bed, Sicke-thoughted Samson rose. **1861** J. Barr *Poems* 11 (E.D.D.), I'm *sick tired o' a bachelor life. **1896** *Harper's Mag.* Apr. 742/2 Gordon was sick-tired of journalistic chatter.

**12.** Special combs., as **sick-bag**, a bag provided in aircraft, ships, etc., as a receptacle for vomit; **sick call**, (*a*) (orig. and chiefly *Mil.*), a call sounded to summon those reporting sick to a place of treatment; an assembly for medical treatment; (*b*) a visit made to a sick person; (*c*) a summons to visit a sick person; **sick headache** = migraine; also in phrases as a type of something useless or unhelpful; **sick parade** *Mil.*, an inspection of those who are ill; the people on sick parade; **sick visiting** (see quot. 1933).

**1962** W. Schirra in *Into Orbit* 33 On the plane, John Glenn and Al Shepard took one of the brown paper 'sick-bags' and scribbled on it: 'Here is the answer to the air sickness problem.' **1976** 'D. Halliday' *Dolly & Nanny Bird* vi. 71 The accustomed routine with Kleenex and sick bags..and barley sugar. **1836** J. Hildreth *Dragoon Campaigns to Rocky Mountains* 114 Every morning..'sick call' blows. **1850** E. Price (*title*) Sick calls: from the diary of a missionary priest. **1883** Lady Herbert tr. *Life St. John Baptist de Rossi* iii. iv. 147 The servants never again dared to fail to warn him of any sick call. **1930** F. A. Pottle *Stretchers* 31 Sick call is blown before the dispensary door. **1931** P. J. Joyce *John Healy* ii. 37 That imperious, unmistakable sick-call knock. **1945** *Yank* 13 July 19/2 A punitive measure to discourage falling out for sick call. **1976** *Billings* (Montana) *Gaz.* 27 June 1-B/4 There is a daily sick call by a local doctor for the inmates. **1977** *New Yorker* 24 Oct. 106/2 A third way for an inmate to see a doctor is to go to sick call, which is held each weekday morning at Green Haven on the first floor of the Hospital-Segregation Building. **1978** J. Carroll *Mortal Friends* iv. ii. 389, I was a young priest at the time, see, and I get this sick-call. **1778** Fothergill in *Med. Observ.* (1784) VI. 103 Remarks on that Complaint commonly known under the Name of the Sick Head-ach. **1799** *Med. Jrnl.* I. 286 A dissertation on the sick head-ach,..by Dr. Nathaniel Dwight. **1857** M. O. Colt *Jrnl.* 18 May (1862) xii. 218, I..was obliged..to..stay two nights and one day, suffering with a sick headache. **1915** D. O. Barnett *Lett.* 153 Shrapnel is for defenders, to stop an advance of infantry, but no more use against prepared positions than a sick headache. **1977** 'E. Crispin' *Glimpses of Moon* xii. 252 That pair in the back, between them, are about as much use as a sick headache. **1915** 'I. Hay' *First Hundred Thousand* xi. 137 M'Splae departs, grumbling, and reappears on sick parade a few days later. **1927** R. H. Mottram *Spanish Farm Trilogy* 258 Do you know what a sick parade I've got? Eighty! Yes, I have. **1966** *Times* 9 July 9/7 Command Orders say... Sick Parade has now become 'sick list'. **1933** *O.E.D. Suppl.* s.v. sick *a.* and *sb.* 10 b, *Sick visiting*, the visiting of the sick, esp. by a minister of religion. **1960** N. Nicholson *William Cowper* 13 A most exacting life of piety, prayer-meetings, self-denial, and sick-visiting. **1977** *West Briton* 25 Aug. 11/1 He paid tribute to Mr. Clay's work, especially his sick visiting.

**B.** *absol.* or as *sb.*

**1.** *absol.* as pl. Those who, such as, are suffering from illness.

α. c **1000** *Ags. Gosp., Mark* xvi. 18 Ofer seoce hi hyra handa settað & hi beoð hale. c **1175** *Lamb. Hom.* 37 To seke gan and þa deden helpen to buriene. *a* **1225** *Ancr. R.* 330 Sume helpe..uorte lecnen mid þe seke. *a* **1300** *Cursor M.* 14078 Giueand mani seke þair hele. **1390** Gower *Conf.* I. 265 Ther is phisique for the seke. *a* **1450** Myrc 1841 When þow schalt to seke gon, Hye þe faste. **1483** Caxton *Gold. Leg.* 95 b/2 He comanded that the feble and seke shold be sette aparte by them self. **1596** Dalrymple tr. *Leslie's Hist. Scotl.* I. 90 To restore to thair health seik and waik.

β. **1526** *Pilgr. Perf.* (W. de W. 1531) 153 b, Visytynge the sycke, comfortynge y^e^ prisoner. **1592** Lyly *Gallathea* i. i, It's hard for the sicke to followe wholesome counsaile. **1639** S. Du Verger tr. *Camus' Admir. Events* 218 The sicke of the dropsie augment their thirst in drinking. **1681** Belon *New Myst. Physic* 49 Supposing that the Sick are duly prepared. **1748** *Anson's Voy.* iii. i. 293 Fresh provisions were distributed amongst the sick. **1803** *Med. Jrnl.* X. 224 The sick were so numerous that it became necessary to call in..a nurse. **1888** H. Morten *Hospital Life* 49 Her friends were the sick and suffering.

γ. *a* **1225** *Ancr. R.* 32 Gedereð in owre heorte alle sike & alle sorie. c **1250** *Kent. Serm.* in *O.E. Misc.* 28 Uisiti þe poure and to sike. *a* **1300** *Assump. Virg.* (Camb. MS.) 63 Poure and sike he dude god, And seruede hem. **1340** *Ayenb.* 267 Ich y-ȝeȝ..þe tribz..of poure, and of zyke. **1404–8** *26 Pol. Poems* vi. 39 Fede non hungry, ne cloþe no bare;..Visite no syke. c **1440** *Jacob's Well* 254 To haue compassioun on alle syke & sory.

**2.** A person suffering from illness. ? *Obs.*

c **888** K. Ælfred *Boeth.* xxxviii. §7 Swa swa se sioca ah þearfe þæt hine mon læde to þæm læce. c **1205** Lay. 17716 Ne ræche ich nane garsume.., Ah ælche seocken ich hit do For luue of mine drihtene. *a* **1300** *Cursor M.* 8060 To se þat seke a turn he made, In sekenes sar he fand him stad. c **1375** *Sc. Leg. Saints* ix. (*Bartholomew*) 90 And with þat wourd ..þe seke wes heylit of his care. **1412** Lydg. *Troy Bk.* i. 3627 A medicine Availeth nat, whan þe seke is ded. c **1450** *Merlin* 52 Plese it yow to axe of youre devynour, yef this seke shall euer be hoill of this sekenesse. **1526** Tindale *Matt.* ix. 6 Then sayd he vnto the sicke of the palsey. **1799** Underwood *Dis. Child.* (ed. 4) I. 301 In which interval the sick passes a high-coloured urine.

**3. a.** A disease or illness (*obs.*); a fit of sickness; a sickening. *rare* exc. in phr. *to give* (a person) *the sick*, to nauseate, to disgust.

It is doubtful whether even the older examples have any direct connexion with such forms as Goth. *siukei*, OHG. *siuhhî* (G. *seuche*, *sieche*), Icel. *sýki*, etc.

*a* **1300** *Cursor M.* 10407 þai..Wit-vten want has alle þair wis, Wit-vten seke, wit-vten sare. **13..** *Ibid.* 14147 (Gött), þe seke him saris fra heued to fote. **1808** Jamieson, *Sick*, sickness, a fit of sickness; as, 'The sick's na aff him'. **1849** *Sessions Paper* 26 Nov. 5 If I have many such markets as this, it will give me the sick. **1897** Maugham *'Liza of Lambeth* i, This is too bloomin' slow, it gives me the sick. **1939** 'G. Orwell' *Coming up for Air* IV. v. 257 As for the picturesqueness,..it merely gives me the sick. **1960** *Spectator* 11 Nov. 751 Rackham and all give me the sick.

**b.** Colloq. phr. *on the sick*, incapacitated by illness, receiving sickness benefit.

**1976** *News of World* 14 Mar. 11/2 My Dad used to be on the sick for a long time and couldn't work. **1976** *Par Golf* Aug. 39/3, I didn't realise this would get in the papers. It could cost me my job. I'm on the sick. **1976** L. Thomas *Dangerous Davies* vii. 68, I took it [*sc.* an allotment] on..but then I was on the sick for months..and the council..takes it off me.

**4.** Vomited matter.

**1959** I. & P. Opie *Lore & Lang. Schoolch.* ix. 162 Spread it on the butty nice and thick, Swallow it down with a bucket of sick. **1966** *Listener* 3 Nov. 651/3 Middle-aged Chelsea ladies are crawling about in each other's sick. **1977** *Ibid.* 3 Mar. 282/4 There's blood on the windscreen, sick on the trousers.

**sick**, *v.*¹ Forms: 2 seocan, 4 seke, 5 cekyn, seeke(n; 4 sijken, 5 syken, sike, syk; 6– sick (7 sicke). [f. sick *a.* Cf. Fris. *siikje*, MDu. *sieken* (Du. *zieken*), MLG. *sêken*, *sûken* (LG. *sîken*, *sûken*), OHG. *siuhhan*, *-ên*, *-ôn* (MHG. and G. *siechen*), ON. *sjúkask* (refl.), Goth. *siukan*.]

†**1.** To suffer illness; to fall ill, sicken. *Obs.*

*a* **1150** in *Archiv Stud. neu. Spr.* CXVII. 25 Languet, seocet. *a* **1300** *Cursor M.* 11816 þat caitif vn-meth and vn-meke, Nu bigines he to seke. **1382** Wyclif *2 Kings* xiii. 14 Helise forsothe sijkide in sijknesse. c **1400** *Brut* cxxviii. 303 þat he þat siked þis day, deid on þe iij. day after. c **1440** *Promp. Parv.* 65 Cekyn or wexe seke, *infirmor*. **1594** Peele *Battle of Alcazar* i. ii, To sick as Envy at Cecropia's gate, And pine with thought and terror of mishaps. **1597** Shaks. *2 Hen. IV*, iv. iv. 128 A little time before That our great Grand-sire Edward sick'd, and dy'de.

**2.** *trans.* To cause to sicken; to make ill. Now *rare.*

*a* **1300** *Cursor M.* 14147 þe sare him sekes fra hede to fote. *a* **1340** Hampole *Psalter* xxvi. 4 Myn enemys þat angirs me, þei are sekid & doun fell. *a* **1645** Heywood *Apollo & Daphne* Wks. 1874 VI. 289 His piercing beams I never shall endure, They sicke me of a fatall Calenture. **1909** J. Masefield *Tragedy of Nan* iii. 64 You talk rude to the quality... Talk as'd sick a savage.

**3.** *intr.* To act as a sick-nurse. *nonce-use.*

**1844** Dickens *M. Chuzzlewit* xxv, Whether I sicks or monthlies, ma'am, I hope I does my duty.

**4.** *trans.* and *intr.* To vomit, to spew *up*. Also *fig.*

**1924** C. Mackenzie *Old Men of Sea* xix. 333 The volcano started in sicking up red-hot pitch and all. **1930** Kipling *Thy Servant a Dog* 25, I have ate grass and sicked up. **1930** *Dial. Notes* VI. 83 [Child loq.] I sicked all over my yew dress. **1937** L. A. G. Strong *Swift Shadow* 209 But the snow do turn my stomach and I sicked in the hedge. **1948** 'N. Shute' *No Highway* 162 It can't do me any good if I sick it all up. **1954** 'N. Blake' *Whisper in Gloom* vii. 100, I can't go sicking it all up to the police. **1966** C. Sweeney *Scurrying Bush* xiii. 188 On the way the reptile sicked up another hen, and half-way it regurgitated a third hen on the floor of my vehicle. **1975** *Times* 16 Jan. 18/3 A planeload of passengers sicking their breakfast. **1980** *Sunday Tel.* (Colour Suppl.) 21 Dec. 11/3 She sings *Away in a Manger*..and drinks lots of drinks and then she sicks up.

**sick** (sɪk), *v.*² Also sic. [dial. var. of seek *v.*]

**1.** *trans.* Of a dog: To set upon, attack (an animal). Chiefly in imperative.

**1845** J. J. Hooper *Some Adv. S. Suggs* 154 Sick him Pomp,..sick, sick, si-c-k him Bull. **1890** *Golden Days* (Philadelphia) 6 Sept. (Cent.), 'Sic 'em, Andy!' screamed Granny... The growls and snarls of the fighting animals.. made a terrific din. **1908** *Westm. Gaz.* 19 Sept. 8/2 'Sick 'un then'. Now 'sicking' a hedgehog is a job which few dogs care to tackle. **1933** 'R. Crompton' *William—the Rebel* i. 14 The small white dog, evidently mistaking William's contemptuous 'Huh!' for a new form of 'Sick him!' gave a low growl and sprang forthwith upon the astonished Wotan. **1952** Wodehouse *Barmy in Wonderland* v. 53 'Sic 'em, Tulip,' he said. **1977** *Globe & Mail* (Toronto) 2 Mar. 5/2 All my dogs are attack-trained..but they won't respond to English commands... It's so little kids can't tell him to sic someone.

**2. a.** To incite or encourage (a person) to attack. Const. with *on* adv. or prep. Also, to set (a dog or other animal) *on* or *at*.

**1845** J. J. Hooper *Some Adv. S. Suggs* 151 If I was to sick them on your old hoss yonder, they'd eat him up afore you could say Jack Robinson. **1885** Mary N. Murfree *Prophet Gt. Smoky Mountains* xi, He sick-ed him on all the time. **1892** Kipling & Balestier *Naulahka* v. 50 Tarvin applauded both parties, sicking one on the other impartially for the first ten minutes. **1899** B. Tarkington *Gentl. Indiana* viii. 131 Seems some of the boys..sicked the dogs on him. **1909** J. Masefield *Tragedy of Nan* ii. 28 Hope they'll catch 'im and 'ang 'im. I'd like to sick the dogs at 'em. **1932** W. Faulkner *Light in August* xiii. 286 They couldn't run him away if they was to sick them bloodhounds on him. **1977** J. Hodgins *Invention of World* iii. 75 He threatened to turn the stones into slobbering wolves and sic them on her.

**b.** *fig.* To set (a person) to work *on*; to set (a person) to pursue, observe, accompany, etc. (const. *on* or *on to*).

**1923** E. B. White *Let.* 2 Jan. (1976) 62 The Times sicks me on feature stuff because the city editor discovered early in the game that city politics appear only in humorous light to me. **1929** R. Lardner *Round Up* xxvi. 327 All I told him was that he'd have to let me pick my own roommate after this and not sic no wild man on to me. **1939** Wodehouse *Uncle Fred in Springtime* i. 18 Why should you barge in here, gnashing your bally teeth, just because Horace sicked Claude Polt, private investigator, on to you? **1958** 'E. Dundy' *Dud Avocado* ii. iv. 221 I'll never forgive you for.. sic-ing the sort of person the Contessa is on him. **1958** R. Stout *Champagne for One* (1959) xiv. 172 He had cleared away some underbrush, for instance who had sicked the cops on Laidlaw. **1972** R. Thomas *Porkchoppers* (1974) xxviii. 240 Penry works for me. If you need something done ..then I'll sic him on it.

**sick**, obs. f. seek *v.*; var. sic *a.*, sike.

**sick-bed.** [sick *a.* Cf. MDu. *siecbedde* (Du. *ziekbed*), LG. *sükbedde*, MHG. *siechbette* (G. *-bett*), Sw. *sjukbädd*.] A bed upon which a person lies ill.

c **1425** *Cursor M.* 3632 (Trin.), Ar he deȝed in seke bed his benisoun he wolde him ȝyue. **1662** Strype in *Lett. Lit. Men* (Camden) 177 That is wont to bring you upon a sick bed. *a* **1673** Caryl in Spurgeon *Treas. David* cxvi. 2 If from a sick bed he be raised to health. **1705** Stanhope *Paraphr.* II. 297 The many fruitless Remorses, and broken Vows, of Affliction and Sick-beds. **1749** Fielding *Tom Jones* v. ii, Considered a sick-bed to be a convenient scene for lectures. **1837** Lockhart *Scott* I. ix. 301 Much exhausted with their attendance on a protracted sickbed. **1875** Jowett *Plato* (ed. 2) I. 98 Had not many a man better never get up from a sick bed?

*attrib.* **1730** Boston *Mem.* xi. 375 A design..that it might be a convenient sick-bed room. **1848** Thackeray *Van. Fair* xix, Sick-bed homilies and pious reflections are..out of place in mere story-books.

**sicken** ('sɪk(ə)n), *v.* Forms: α. 3 secnen, 4–5 (9 *dial.*) seeken (5 -enyn), 5–6 seken (5 -ene), sekyn, 9 *dial.* seaken. β. 3 sikni, 4–5 sicnen, sijknen, sikynyn, 6 sycken, 6– sicken. [f. sick *a.* + -en⁵. Cf. OIcel. *sjúkna*, MSw. *siukna* (Sw. *sjukna*).]

**1. a.** *intr.* To become affected with illness, to fall ill or sick. Also const. *of* or *with*.

α. c **1200** Ormin 4771 He warrþ all..Full hefiȝlike secnedd. **1382** Wyclif *2 Kings* viii. 29 Ochozias..came doun to visyten Joram..in Jezrael, the whiche seekened there. c **1460** Metham *Wks.* (E.E.T.S.) 148 To knowe qwat schuld be-falle off hym that sekenyth in ony day off the mone. **1470–85** Malory *Arthur* Contents xxi. xii, How syr Launcelot began to sekene & after dyed. **1509** Hawes *Past. Pleas.* xvi. (Percy Soc.) 63 My hert sekened and began to waxe sore. **1530** Palsgr. 708/2, I sekyn, I waxe sycke.

β. c **1290** *S. Eng. Leg.* I. 293/187 Anon-riȝt he bigan to sikni; and þare riȝt adoun lay. **1382** Wyclif *1 Sam.* xxx. 13, I bigan to sikynyn the thridde dai hens. —— *Isaiah* xxxviii. 1 In tho daȝes sicnede Ezechie vnto the deth. **1530** Palsgr. 708/2 My father syckened first upon saynte Bartylmewes evyn. **1568** Grafton *Chron.* II. 162 At this tyme the king sickened, and [was] forced to kepe his bed. c **1600** Shaks. *Sonn.* cxviii. 4 We sicken to shun sicknesse when we purge. **1657** *Penit. Conf.* xii. 331 Being in Normandy [he] sickned, of that disease whereof he died. **1705** J. Logan in *Pennsylv. Hist. Soc. Mem.* X. 35 The same night he sickened, as he thought of a surfeit of cherries, and in two days died. **1771** T. Hull *Sir W. Harrington* (1797) IV. 113, I was told that Lord C. had sickened much after his bleeding. **1807** *Med. Jrnl.* XVII. 249 The people who were sickening very fast with the small-pox. **1847** Prescott *Peru* (1850) II. 327 Some sickened and sank down by the way. **1868** Freeman *Norm. Conq.* (1877) II. 354 Soon after his restoration the Earl began to sicken.

*transf.* *a* **1822** Shelley *'Music, when soft voices die'* 3 Odours, when sweet violets sicken, Live within the sense they quicken. 1825 *Gentl. Mag.* XCV. I. 130 A small white insect, which caused . . the trees to sicken and to bear no fruit that year.

**b.** *fig.* or in fig. contexts.

*a* 1225 *Ancr. R.* 368 Monie ancren . . witeð so hore heale, þet þe gost unstrencðeð & secneð ine sunne. 1601 SHAKS. *Jul. C.* IV. ii. 20 When Loue begins to sicken and decay. 1629 MILTON *Hymn Nativity* xiv, Speckl'd vanity Will sicken soon and die. 1706 ESTCOURT *Fair Example* II. i, Why did she swear, unless it was to strengthen her Resolution, that began to sicken? 1770 GOLDSM. *Deserted Vill.* 262 In these . . The toiling pleasure sickens into pain. *a* 1827 WORDSW. *Somnambulist* 80 Day sickens round her, and the night Is empty of repose. 1861 ALEXANDER *Gospel of Jesus Christ* 113 The appetite has sickened and so died.

**c.** Used with complement.

1813 BYRON *Corsair* I. i, Let him . . Cling to his couch, and sicken years away.

**d.** *to sicken for*: to be in the early stages of (a disease which is not yet manifest); to be 'coming down' with.

1883 F. MONTGOMERY *Blue Veil* II. vii. 218, I was sickening for the mumps. 1977 *Sunday Times* 16 Jan. 30/5 Amiss, sickening for the flu which prevented him fielding, got his bat caught in his pads.

**2. a.** To feel faint with horror or nausea; to revolt or experience revulsion *at* something.

1601 SHAKS. *All's Well* v. iii. 207 A most perfidious slaue . . Whose nature sickens but to speak a truth. 1606 —— *Ant. & Cl.* III. x. 17 Mine eyes did sicken at the sight, and could not Indure a further view. 1703 POPE *Thebais* 136 The day beheld, and sickning at the sight, Veil'd her fair glories in the shades of night. 1784 COWPER *Tiroc.* 167 The young apostate sickens at the view. 1800 MRS. HERVEY *Mourtray Fam.* II. 157 Sickening with disgust, she rose abruptly, and pulled the bell. 1836 J. GILBERT *Atonement* vi. (1852) 165 How frightful is this portrait! the heart sickens as we contemplate it. 1868 TENNYSON *Lucretius* 196, I hate, abhor, spit, sicken at him.

**b.** To grow weary or tired *of* a thing.

1782 MISS BURNEY *Cecilia* I. v, Cecilia now began to sicken of her attempt. 1858 O. W. HOLMES *Aut. Breakf.-t.* x. 96 Men sicken of their houses until at last they quit them.

**c.** To pine with yearning; to long eagerly.

1802 SCOTT *Let.* in *Lockhart* (1837) I. xi. 351 Why is it that a Swiss sickens at hearing the famous Ranz des Vaches? 1815 SHELLEY *Alastor* 181 His strong heart sunk and sickened with excess Of love. 1897 BARTRAM *People of Clopton* 146 I'll catch the next train to Bitham, for I'm sickenin' to get back theer.

**3.** To grow pale; to fade.

1853 G. JOHNSTON *Nat. Hist. E. Borders* I. 250 The fronds sicken to a rich brown when touched by the first frosts. 1896 *Idler* Mar. 175 Expiring as a whole orb of moon sickens and disappears.

**4.** *Chem.* Of mercury: To become 'sick'.

1882 A. G. LOCKE *Gold* 21 The mercury employed for amalgamation . . sickens or 'flows' when ground up with pyritous rocks. [See also the *vbl. sb.*]

**5. a.** *trans.* To affect with illness; to make sick.

1694 CROWNE *Regulus* I, A Ghost! a damp evaporates from the word Which sickens me to death. 1714 PURCELL *Cholick* 175 To disengage those Insects from their Adherence to the Guts, to sicken, kill, and discharge them out of the Body. 1775 ROMANS *Hist. Florida* App. 53 I have heart of an instance of one of this kind [hog-fish] having sickened some people. 1843 R. J. GRAVES *Clin. Med.* xiv. 176 The first six doses seemed to sicken him a little, but he did not vomit until after the seventh dose. 1902 BUCHAN *Watcher by the Threshold* 90 His fetid breath sickened me.

**b.** *fig.* or *transf.*

1613 SHAKS. *Hen. VIII*, I. i. 82, I do know Kinsmen of mine . . that haue By this, so sicken'd their Estates, that neuer They shall abound as formerly. 1801 *Farmer's Mag.* Aug. 312 The want of variety in the rotation would sicken the crops. 1850 TENNYSON *In Mem.* lxxii. 7 Which sicken'd every living bloom. 1876 ISA CRAIG KNOX in Whittier *Songs of Three Centuries* 310 The pool was still; around its brim The alders sickened all the air.

**6. a.** To give (one) a sickener; to make (one) sick or tired *of* a thing.

1797 NELSON in Nicolas *Disp.* (1845) II. 341 The Blenheim, passing between us and the Enemy, gave us a respite, and sickened the Dons. 1809 MALKIN *Gil Blas* XII. viii. ¶5 His keeper sickened him of the project. 1824 SCOTT *St. Ronan's* xxxvi, I . . learned enough of what was going on, to give Jekyl a hint that sickened him of his commission. 1874 GREEN *Short Hist.* ii. §1. 63 The long peace sickened men of this fresh outburst of bloodshed and violence.

**b.** To affect with nausea, loathing, or disgust.

1825 T. HOOK *Sayings* Ser. II. *Sutherl.* (Colburn) 21 The familiarity with which she treated her brother-in-law . . so sickened Jane, that she ordinarily affected illness. 1842 LOVER *Handy Andy* xxi, Being already sickened by various disgusting exhibitions of the damsel's affectation.

**c.** To render faint with fear or horror.

1821 SHELLEY *Hellas* Prol. 109 The storm Of faction, which like earthquake shakes and sickens The solid heart of enterprise. 1867 AUGUSTA WILSON *Vashti* xxii, The strained, almost ferocious expression of her keen eyes sickened his soul. 1883 F. M. CRAWFORD *Dr. Claudius* xviii, If we look to the right or the left we must see that which sickens the sense of sight.

Hence **'sickened** *ppl. a.*

1814 SCOTT *Ld. Isles* II. xxvi, Was not the life of Athole shed To soothe the tyrant's sicken'd bed?

**sickener** ('sɪk(ə)nə(r)). [f. prec. + -ER¹.] Something which nauseates or disgusts; an overdose or excess of anything; a sickening experience.

1809 MALKIN *Gil Blas* v. i. ¶30 A fricassee, and . . soup, . . greasy with mutton fat, were enough to have given a sickener to the inveterate stomachs of a regiment. 1853 W. JERDAN *Autobiog.* IV. xvi. 306 This was indeed a sickener to a careful biographer. 1882 G. MACDONALD *Weighed & Wanting* II. v. 51 A vision of the kind of creature he was capable of loving . . would have been—to use a low but expressive phrase—a sickener to her.

**b.** Used of a shot or blow.

1834 COL. HAWKER *Diary* (1893) II. 54, I gave him such a sickener with the first barrel that I made him haul his wind. 1895 MEREDITH *Amazing Marriage* I. xvi. 185 Kit fetched his man an ugly stroke on the round of the waist behind . . , a sickener of a stroke, if dealt soundly.

**sickening** ('sɪk(ə)nɪŋ), *vbl. sb.* [f. the vb. + -ING¹.] The fact of becoming sick or ill; an instance of this.

Also, in dial. use, confinement, child-bed.

1382 WYCLIF *Jer.* xvi. 4 With dethes of siknyngus thei shul die. 1816 CHALMERS *Let.* in *Life* (1851) II. 53 To sustain you under all the sickenings, and faintings, and languishings of your earthly disease. 1858 *Merc. Mar. Mag.* V. 305 Not a case nor a sickening has been heard of. 1882 *Electro-Amalg. Co. Prospectus* 5 [It] prevents it from what is technically termed 'sickening' in the presence of arsenic, sulphur, oil, or any other substances . . deleterious to the action of mercury in amalgamating with gold or silver.

**sickening** ('sɪk(ə)nɪŋ), *ppl. a.* [f. as prec. + -ING².]

**1.** Falling or turning sick.

1725 POPE *Odyss.* IV. 600 The . . gentle power . . With nectared drops the sickening sense restored. 1746 HERVEY *Medit.* (1818) 272 The malignant influence gained upon her sickening orb. 1810 SCOTT *Lady of L.* III. viii, Patient the sickening victim eyed The life-blood ebb in crimson tide. 1817 SHELLEY *Rev. Islam* III. xxvi. 9 A whirlwind keen as frost Then in its sinking gulfs my sickening spirit tossed. *fig.* 1728 POPE *Dunc.* IV. 636 The sick'ning stars fade off th' æthereal plain. 1748 GRAY *Alliance* 71 Must sick'ning virtue fly the tainted ground? 1774 GOLDSM. *Nat. Hist.* I. Pref., He thus ranges, without an instructor, confused, and with sickening curiosity, from subject to subject.

**2.** That causes sickness, nausea, or faintness; that disgusts or revolts; repulsive, loathsome. Also in weakened sense.

1789 MME. D'ARBLAY *Diary* 9 Jan., As they all consisted in almost unheard-of indignities . . I will not give the sickening relation. 1800 *Med. Jrnl.* III. 123 Nocturnal sweats, . . induced by the sickening influence of digitalis. 1836 J. HALLEY in *Mem.* (1842) 58 Have had a most sickening job in shortening an article of my own for the Presbyterian Review. 1857 MILLER *Elem. Chem., Org.* xi. §1 (1862) 747 They gradually putrify and emit a sickening odour. 1886 *Athenæum* 30 Oct. 564/3 Nothing more sickening than the Indian wars of the United States is to be found in history. 1922 [see FED *pa. pple.*]. 1924 M. ARLEN *Green Hat* ii. 67 In ten years' time . . Hilary will be the only Liberal left in Parliament, looking happier and younger and more sickening than ever. 1925 D. MACKAIL *Greenery Street* viii. 179 But, Ian, Daphne's thing is a subscription dance . . . *Please* don't be so sickening. 1937 W. H. SAUMAREZ SMITH *Let.* 8 Feb. in *Young Man's Country* (1977) ii. 56 Isn't it too sickening that I shall get to Singapore just after Margaret's and Ronald's departure.

*transf.* 1877 RAYMOND *Statist. Mines & Mining* 101 All base substances . . cannot be taken up by the mercury, neither do they have any 'sickening' effect upon the mercury.

Hence **'sickeningly** *adv.*

1839 LADY LYTTON *Cheveley* (ed. 2) I. viii. 180 The duchess was sickeningly civil. 1864 *Daily Telegr.* 27 Sept., The outside is generally burnt up, and the inside sickeningly raw. 1886 *Sat. Rev.* 7 Aug. 183 A series of sickeningly inhuman outrages were committed.

**sicker** ('sɪkə(r)), *a.* and *adv.* Now *Sc.* and *north. dial.* Forms: α. 1 sicor, 2–6 sicer (5 sycher), 4–5 sicur(e, 5 sycur), 4, 6 sicir, 9 siccer, siccar; 2–9 siker (3 -err), 3–5 sikere, 4–5 sikir, sikur (5 -our, -yr, -re); 3–6 syker (6 -ar), 4–5 sykere, -ir, -yr (4 -ire, -ur); 4 zik-, zykere, 5 cykere, -yr; 5–6 sikkir (5 -yr, 6 sykkyr), 5–6 (9 *dial.*) sikker (6 -ar); 4 syckyr, 5–6 sickir, sycker, 4– sicker. β. 4 secir, 4–5 secure (5 -ur, sekur); 4–6 (9) seker (6 secker), 4–6 sekir, -yr (5 cekyr), 5–6 sekire (5 -yre). [OE. *sicor* (rare), = OFris. *sikur*, *siker* (Fris. *siker*), OS. *sikur*, *sikor* (MLG. and MDu. *seker*, Du. *zeker*), OHG. *sihhur*, *sichur*, etc. (MHG. and G. *sicher*); MDa. *seeker*, *secker* (Da. *sikker*), MSw. *siker*, *sigher* (Sw. *säker*) are from German. The word is an early Teutonic adoption of L. *sēcūrus* SECURE *a.*, with the stress shifted to the first syllable.]

In ME. both adj. and adv. were very extensively employed, and the precise sense intended is not always clear. After 1500 the word is rarely used except by Scottish writers, but also remained current in the north of England: for a fuller exhibition of the senses in which it occurs in modern dialect, see the *Eng. Dial. Dict.*

**A.** *adj.*

**I. 1.** Free from danger or harm; secure, safe.

*c* 897 K. ÆLFRED *Gregory's Past. C.* liv. 425 Ðif we ðæt ȝedone mid nanum ðingum ne betað ne ne hreowsiað, ne bio we no ðæs sicore. *c* 1200 *Trin. Coll. Hom.* 5 Þanne beð noman siker, ar he ihere þat lufliche word of ure louerd ihesu cristes swete muðe, *venite benedicti* [etc.]. 1387 TREVISA *Higden* (Rolls) II. 227 Men were first naked and vnarmed, nouȝt siker aȝenst bestes, noþer aȝenst men. 1435 MISYN *Fire of Love* 3 Þat felynge of gostely fyer . . in þe whilk þai knawe þame-self sekyr. *c* 1491 *Chast. Goddes Chyld.* 7 The thyrde cause is for man sholde not holde hymselfe siker. For grete trust of sikernes engendreth neclygence.

**b.** Associated or attended with safety or security from danger, etc.

*a* 1225 *Ancr. R.* 70 Holi olde ancren muwen don hit . . , auh hit nis nout siker þing, ne ne limpeð nout to þe ȝunge. 1387 TREVISA *Higden* (Rolls) IV. 175 And see þeeves grevede and robbede al þe see, so þat þe Romayns . . hadde no siker seillynge wiþ oute oþer socour. *c* 1450 *St. Cuthbert* (Surtees) 6764 Þar ware monkes . . [who] Thoght þai stode in sykir case. 1567 TURBERV. *Ovid's Ep.* 125 There may Leander make a safe and sicker stay. 1894 CROCKETT *Raiders* (ed. 3) 152, I'm as great on the side o' the law as it's siccar to be in thae uncertain times.

**c.** Of places or paths.

*c* 1275 *Moral Ode* 43 in *O.E. Misc.*, Heo doþ heore ayhte in siker stude þat sendeþ hit to heoue-riche. 13 . . *K. Alis.* 7065 (Laud MS.), Þise . . leden hym, by siker paas, Al to þe gates of Caspyas. *c* 1400 tr. *Secreta Secret., Gov. Lordsh.* 111 Þe stede þat þou fightys on with þy aduersers, be it semynge euer more seker, ffor þarfore shal þyn hoste peyne hem mekyll more to fight. 1508 DUNBAR *Tua Mariit Wemen* 285 A lufsummar leid . . That couth be secrete and sure . . , And sew bot at certayne tymes, & in sicir places. 1821 SCOTT *Pirate* iv, Na na, he sall walk a mair siccar path, and be a dainty curate.

**2.** That may be depended on; in which one can put reliance, confidence, or trust; certain, sure.

*c* 1100 in *Anglia* XI. 377 Swyðe sicore forȝyfonnysse se mæiȝ him biddan æt gode. 1297 R. GLOUC. (Rolls) 1268 Þo þe emperour hurde þis, he ne truste wel þer to Wiþ oute siker ostage such þing to do. 1303 R. BRUNNE *Handl. Synne* 7538 Seynt Poule techyþ vs . . A sykyr fyght þat wyl nat fayle. 1470–85 MALORY *Arthur* VII. xviii. 240 Syker assuraunce and borowes ye shal haue. 1546 *Reg. Privy Council Scot.* I. 46 In the maist stratest forme, and sikrest still of obligatioun that can be devisit and maid. 1609 SKENE *Reg. Maj.* 86 He may attach him be sicker pledges, to enter and compeir in the Kings court. 1678 SIR G. MACKENZIE *Crim. Laws Scot.* I. vi. §xix, Their Goods should be put under sicker Burrows. 1837 R. NICOLL *Poems* (1843) 90 He was a carle in his day And siccar bargains he could mak.

*Proverb.* *c* 1440 CAPGR. *Life St. Kath.* II. 250 It is more sekyr a byrd in your fest Than to haue iij. in þe sky a-boue.

**b.** Of persons.

*c* 1350 *Leg. Rood* (1871) 76 Seker men he sett to wake. 14 . . in *Q. Eliz. Acad.* 85 A goode sykere frende is yuell to fynde. 1493 *Festivall* (W. de W. 1515) 40 A more syker attorney may noo man be than god is. 1533 BELLENDEN *Livy* II. iv. (S.T.S.) I. 142 It is nocht facill to be declarit, nor ȝit Is It writtin be sekire authoris. 1658 CARSTAIRS in Durham *Comm. Rev.* Pref. p. i, The ablest, sickerest and most accomplished ministers. 1768 ROSS *Helenore* II. 84 He was a sicker boy. 1878 DICKINSON *Cumbld. Gloss.* s.v., He's a varra sicker body.

**c.** Of defensive armour.

*c* 1400 *Rowland & O.* 354 Ane hawberke . . þat sekire was of Mayle. *c* 1450 *St. Cuthbert* (Surtees) 4465, I a siker shelde sall be. *a* 1578 LINDESAY *Chron. Scot.* (S.T.S.) I. 66 To theif and reiver he was ane sicker targe.

**3.** Having a firm foundation or support; firm, unshaken, fast.

1297 R. GLOUC. (Rolls) 2493 As moche place . . þat ich þeruppe mowe a siker bold rere. *c* 1375 *Cursor M.* 2230 (Fairf.), Make we a sicure tour . . þat may reyche vn-til heyuen. *c* 1440 *Gesta Rom.* iv. 10 Þoȝ such perforacion be goode, and don for þat þe wall shuld be made moore sikir and stronger. *a* 1573 in Calderwood *Hist. Kirk Scot.* (1843) II. 272, I thinke not the ground so sicker, as that I durst build my conscience therupon. 1785 BURNS *Death & Dr. Hornbook* 28 Setting my staff wi' a' my skill, To keep me sicker. 1858 M. PORTEOUS *Souter Johnny* 10 He wad hae stood right steeve and sicker And brav'd their dudgeon. *fig.* 1787 THOM *Jock o' Knowe* 28 (E.D.D.) Resolve is sickerest when it's placed On a foundation wrought.

**b.** Not liable to be disturbed or unsettled; stable, assured, certain.

1340 *Ayenb.* 78 Þet is þe uayriste lyf an þe zykeriste þet is ine þise wordle. 1390 GOWER *Conf.* I. 22 The world stant evere upon debat, So may be seker non astat. 1500–20 DUNBAR *Poems* lxxii. 130 Grace become gyd and governour, To keip the house in sicker stait. 1591 SPENSER *M. Hubberd* 430 Being some honest Curate, or some Vicker Content with little in condition sicker. 1857 RIDDELL *Psalms* xc. 17 Sete thou siccer the wark o' our han's apon us. 1886 HALIBURTON *Horace* 41 (E.D.D.), Mak' your union siccar.

†**c.** Of number: Fixed, definite. *Obs.*⁻¹

1377 LANGL. *P. Pl.* B. xx. 254 Kynde wil ȝow teche, That in mesure god made alle manere thynges, And sette hem at a certeyne and at a syker noumbre.

**d.** Prudent, careful, especially with regard to money matters; wary, cautious.

*c* 1662 LIVINGSTONE in *Sel. Biogr.* (Wodrow Soc.) I. 208 He is a sicker man: he thinks he will only preach against Poprie, and not make with other controversies. *a* 1800 R. JAMIESON *Pop. Ball.* (1806) I. 292 There, couthie, and pensie, and sicker, Wonn'd honest young Hab o' the Heuch. 1808 JAMIESON s.v., He, who is tenacious of his own rights or property, is said to be a sicker man. 1894 HESLOP *Northumbld. Gloss.*, *Sicker*, sly, inward minded. It is frequently prefixed by 'gey'. 'He's a gey sicker yen.'

**4.** That cannot be doubted; indubitable; absolutely certain.

*c* 1375 *Cursor M.* 4134 (Fairf.), Ful secure veniaunce god wil take. 1435 MISYN *Fire of Love* 105 Deed to vs is sykyr, þe owre of deed truly vnsikyr. 1567 TURBERV. *Ovid's Ep.* 61 My handes displayde gave siker signes and tokens of my paine. 1827 SCOTT *Tales Grandfather* 1st Ser. viii, 'Do you leave such a matter to doubt?' said Kirkpatrick, 'I will make sicker'. 1881 *Good Words* 774/1 We made sicker than he was wi' you.

†**b.** Genuine, good. *Obs.*⁻¹

*a* 1400–50 *Alexander* 1042 Sexti thousand þai him send of sekire besandis.

**5.** Certain of its effect; effective, sure.

1338 R. BRUNNE *Chron.* (1810) 41, I salle ȝow say, For to saue ȝour lond wele, a fulle siker way. *c* 1400 *Rowland & O.* 1382 A sekere stroke was there sett. *c* 1470 HENRY *Wallace* II. 408 A seker straik drewe he. 1560 ROLLAND *Seven Sages* 76, I . . hes the tane into the sicker snair. 1567 *Satir. Poems Reform.* vii. 219 Thir Nobillis dois bot rycht, Gif thay the Quene keip still in sicker gaird. 1710 in Calderwood *Dying Testimonies* (1806) 152 Strive to make sicker work in time. *c* 1820 BEATTIE *John o' Arnha* (1826) 23 The charm is firm and sicker.

*transf.* **1843** J. Ballantine *Gaberlunzie* xii. (1875) 309 Time's a sicker master, an' we maun a' bend afore him.

6. Securely fastened or held.

*a* **1425** *Cursor M.* 16905 (Trin.), þe princes of prestis of þe lawe went to þat monument And made hit sikur as hem þou3t. **1560** Rolland *Seven Sages* 95 Than art thow sicker in the snair. **1891** A. Gordon *Folks o' Carglen* 139 Aundrew stretchit his length on the grun', an' they had him siccar as a nail.

II. 7. Having assured possession or prospect *of* something. ? *Obs.*

*a* **1200** *Trin. Coll. Hom.* 51 Efter þan þe hie weren wuniende in ierusalem, and weren hole and sunde, and sikere of here giue. *a* **1300** *Cursor M.* 4134 If yee do suilk an outrake Ful siker may yee be o wrake. *c* **1450** *Merlin* ii. 32 He that wende to be siker of me hath failed of his purpos. **1567** *Gude & Godlie B.* 130 Always sall he be sicker of this, That is neidful to want na thing. **1719** Ramsay *To Hamilton* iii. xi, Sicker of thae, winter and simmer, Ye're well enough.

†**b.** Having sure mastery *of* an art. *Obs.*$^{-1}$

*c* **1470** Henry *Wallace* iv. 559 Few off thaim was sekyr of archary.

8. Having confident or certain knowledge; fully assured or convinced. With various constructions, as dependent clause (usually with *that*), *to* with inf., *of* (*for, in, on, with*), or ellipt. for these.

(*a*) *c* **1200** Ormin 4844 Beo þu sikerr þatt he shall þe 3ifenn eche blisse. **1297** R. Glouc. (Rolls) 7353 Siker þou be þou ne ssalt me finde in none hurne. *a* **1320** *Sir Tristr.* 2067 Sir, siker 3e be, þi self schal se þat ri3t. *c* **1400** *Laud Troy-bk.* 10013, I am sicur be my dreme That I am lorn. **1552** Abp. Hamilton *Catech.* 31 Thow suld be sikkar that the..matter quhilk thou confermis with ane eith is trew.

(*b*) *c* **1275** *Moral Ode* 40 in *O.E. Misc.*, þe mon þat wile syker beo to habbe godes blysse, Do wel him seolf þe hwile he may. *c* **1340** Hampole *Pr. Consc.* 8559 þai salle be þare syker and certayne To have endeles ioy. *c* **1400** *Destr. Troy* 7991 Make vs sekur, on the same wise, oure soile for to leue.

(*c*) *c* **1320** *Cast. Love* 952 Ne beo þou in wonhope non, Ac ful siker þou beo þer-on. **1377** Langl. *P. Pl.* B. xvi. 234, I am ful syker in soule þer-of. ? **1404–8** *26 Pol. Poems* v. 51 Be not to sykere of þyne hele. *a* **1500** *Songs, Carols*, etc. (E.E.T.S.) 34 Ther-of thow art siker & sure. **1876** F. K. Robinson *Whitby Gloss.* s.v., I'se sikker on't.

(*d*) *c* **1330** *Arth. & Merlin* 5551 (Kölbing), Ac arst 3e schul me make siker. *c* **1470** H. Parker *Dives & Pauper* (W. de W. 1496) ii. vi. 115/1 Yf he be not syker, but only weneth to be syker, he shall not swere that it is so. **1876** C. C. Robinson *Mid-Yks. Gloss.* s.v., In idiomatic phrases, expressive of emphatic belief. 'I'm sikker and sure.'

†**9.** Assured of its object; confident, certain. *Obs.*

*a* **1225** *Leg. Kath.* 1217 þurh hwam we mahten habben sikere bileaue to arisen alle efter him. **1340** *Ayenb.* 13 Ine zikere hope þet iesu crist godes zone ssolde come. *c* **1450** *Myrr. our Ladye* 257 Lyghtne oure sowles with seker hope. **1533** Gau *Richt Vay* 29 The sekir faith..quhilk is in godis word and doctrine.

†**10.** Having a sense of security; confident. *Obs.*

*a* **1340** Hampole *Psalter* ii. 11 With quakynge, swa þat 3oure ioy be noght ouere sykire. *c* **1375** *Sc. Leg. Saints* iii. (*Andrew*) 957 Be sikyr, douchtyr, and dred nocht!

**B.** *adv.*

†**1.** With security; safely; confidently. *Obs.*

*c* **1205** Lay. 15092 Dead is Vortimer þe king, & siker þu miht hider comen. *c* **1330** R. Brunne *Chron. Wace* (Rolls) 14250 3yt Arthur hadde lenger abiden, þe sykerere myghte Moddred haue ryden. **1387** Trevisa *Higden* (Rolls) IV. 163 Forto go þe saveloker and þe sikerer to cruel bataille a3enst Marius. *c* **1440** *Pallad. on Husb.* xii. 267 Hem that remayne al sikur maystow sowe.

2. Assuredly, certainly, without doubt.

*c* **1275** *Passion our Lord* 286 in *O.E. Misc.* 45 Siker þu ert myd him a galilewis mon. **1390** Gower *Conf.* I. 154 So seker as I have a lif, Thou scholdest thanne be my wif. *c* **1450** Lovelich *Merlin* 6442 '3is, Sikyr, lady!' this womman gan seye. **1579** Spenser *Sheph. Cal.* Apr. 159 Sicker I hold him for a greater fon. **1614** J. Davies (Heref.) *Commend. Poems* Wks. (Grosart) II. 19 Now, siker (Wernocke) thou hast split the marke. *a* **1717** Parnell *Fairy Tale* Wks. (1833) 18 The board was laid, And siker such a feast was made As heart and lip desire.

**b.** With verbs of saying or affirming: As a certainty, as a fact.

*a* **1275** *Prov. of Alfred* 524 Siker ich it te saige, letet gif þe liket. **14..** *Life St. Kath.* (Halliw.) 8 Or ellys sekyr y telle the That thou schalt dedd bee! **1500–20** Dunbar *Poems* xx. 47 Sicker I 3ow asseure, He rewlis weill, that sa weill him can gyd.

3. Effectively, strongly, firmly.

*c* **1450** *Gesta Rom.* xxv. 96, I put a gret stone aboute thi necke, & yit þou Rise; I triste now I shalle pley sikir with the. **17..** *Laird of Wariston* 22 in Child *Ballads* IV. 31/2 The nurice she knet the knot, And O she knet it sicker! **1792** A. Wilson *On Men Sawing Timber*, Experience ne'er sae sicker tells us, As when she lifts her rung and fells us. **1818** Rodger *Poems* (1897) 167 Lay't into our loof, We'll haud it sicker.

4. Securely; without risk of falling or shifting.

*a* **1586** Montgomerie *Misc. Poems* v. 55 3our feet ar not so sicker sett. **1641** *Ferguson's Sc. Prov.* No. 310 He rode sicker that never fell. **17..** Ramsay *Wyfe of Auchtermuchty* iv, They sicker raid that neir did faw. *a* **1774** Fergusson *Poems* (1788) II. 20 Ye wha canna staun sae sicker. **1863** Quinn *Heather Lintie* 201 Within oor hearts..Aye siccar shalt thou reign. **1867** G. W. Donald *Poems* (1879) 54/1 There's nae man nae sicker set But he may shift his stool.

**sicker** ('sɪkə(r)), *v.*¹ Now *rare* or *Obs.* Forms: α. 3 sikeri, -ery, sykery, 4 siker(e, -ir, -ur), 4–5 sykere(n, 5 -yn), 8 sicker, 9 siccar. β. 4–5 sekere, 5 sekyr(e. [ME. *sikeri, sikeren*, etc. (f. sicker *a.*), = OFris. *sikura, sik(e)ria*, OS. *sikorôn* (MLG. and MDu. *sekeren*, Du. *zekeren*), OHG. *sihhorôn* (MHG. *sicheren*, G. *sichern*).]

1. *trans.* To assure (a person) of safety.

**1297** R. Glouc. (Rolls) 11323 In eiþer half to sikeri him freres him gonne lede. **13..** *Metr. Hom.* (Vernon MS.) in *Herrig's Archiv* LVII. 287 þou weore worþi for to dye.. Bote for I er sikerde þe Schalt þou haue no skaþe for me. *c* **1400** *Apol. Loll.* 17 Oþer wis may not boþe kirk bring a man out of synne, ne for3ef þe peyn, nor man siker.

2. To assure (a person) of one's good faith by a pledge or formal promise.

**1297** R. Glouc. (Rolls) 3155 A þousend pound..ichim wolde 3iue anon,..& þat ich im wolde mid treuþe sikery him vaste an hond. **1338** R. Brunne *Chron.* (1810) 53 Edward sikerd him wele, to mak William his heyre. *c* **1450** *Erle Tolous* 1030 Wolde ye sekyr me, wythowt fayle, For to holde trewe counsayle.

**b.** *refl.* To put one's trust *in* a person.

*a* **1300** *Cursor M.* 11868 þat we ger get vs leches tuin, In quilk we mai siker vs in.

**c.** To betroth (a woman) *to* one.

*c* **1384** Chaucer *L.G.W.* 2128 *Ariadne*, Now be we duchessis bothe I & 3e And sekerede to the regalys of Athenys.

3. To assure (one) of a fact.

*c* **1375** *Sc. Leg. Saints* xxxiii. (*George*) 932, I sal be before þame bowne in-to þis sammyne aray..I sekyre 3ou. *c* **1400** Love *Bonavent. Mirr.* xxvii. (1908) 144 Than he,..willynge that thei schulde no lenger be distourbeled and trauailled, sykerde hem of his presence.

4. To confirm by pledge or surety.

**1338** R. Brunne *Chron.* (1810) 69 þerof he mad me skrite,..& for to sikere his dede, set þer to his seale. **1350** *Will. Palerne* 1463 Sad seurte was sikered on boþe sides þanne, þat menskful mariage to make. *a* **1450** *Le Morte Arth.* 2331 A trews they sette and sekeryd thare.

5. To secure, make sure or certain of; to make fast, fix firmly.

**1708** Bruce *Good News in Evil Times* 40 Sicker what ye will, if the main Chance be not sickered, I'll not give a gray Groat for you. **1824** Mactaggart *Gallovid. Encycl.* s.v. *Sned*, The runt must be siccard in the den, so that the [scythe-] blade may have a snanging sound.

Hence **'sickering** *vbl. sb.*

*a* **1450** *Le Morte Arth.* 2322 That thay shall make me A sekeringe A trews to holde vs by-twene.

**'sicker**, *v.*² *rare.* Also 3 sikeri. [OE. *sicerian*, = LG. *sîkeren*, G. *sickern* (dial. *sikern*), app. related to OHG. *sîhan* to strain, filter: see sye *v.*] *intr.* Of water: To trickle; to ooze or leak.

*c* **897** K. Ælfred tr. *Gregory's Past. C.* lvii. 437 Swiðe lytlum siceraδ ðæt wæter & swiðe degellice on ðæt hlece scip. *c* **1290** *S. Eng. Leg.* I. 318 þare beoz ase it veynene weren onder eorþe mani on, þat sikeriez [*text* sikeniez] out of þe se. **1903** in *Eng. Dial. Dict.* (Lincolnshire).

†**'sickerhead.** *Obs.*$^{-1}$ [f. sicker *a.* Cf. Du. *zekerheid*, G. *sicherheit* (OHG. *sihhurheit*), etc.] Assurance, certainty.

*c* **1250** *Owl & Night.* 1265 Naueþ mon no sikerhede, þat he ne may wene & adrede þat sum vnhap neih him beo.

†**'sickerlaik.** *Obs.*$^{-1}$ In 3 sikerlec. [f. sicker *a.* Cf. MSw. *sik(e)rlek.*] Certainty.

*a* **1225** *St. Marher.* 14 þenne þurh þis sikerlec seche ich earst uppon ham.

**'sickerly**, *adv.* Now *Sc.* and *north. dial.* Forms: see sicker *a.* Also 1 -lice, 3–5 -liche (3 -lichen, 4 -lich), 4–5 -lyche; 3 -like, 4 -lik, -lic; *comp.* 3 -loker, 4 -laker; 3 -li3, 4–5 -li (4 -le), 5–6 -lye, 6–7 (9) -lie. [Late OE. *sicerlīce* (f. *sicer* sicker *a.*), = MDu. *sekerlike, -lijc* (Du. *zekerlijk*), MLG. *sekerliken*, OHG. *sichurlîcho*, MHG. *sicherliche* (G. *-lich*), MSw. *sikerlika*, etc.]

†**1.** With full certainty or conviction. *Obs.*

*c* **1100** in Napier *Contrib. O.E. Lexicogr.* 57 For þan þe þa apostles scolden witen sicerlice þæt he arisen wæs of deaðe. *c* **1200** Ormin 5322 þe birrþ witenn sikerrli3, Forr Goddspell-boc itt kiþeþþ. *c* **1375** Barbour *Bruce* iv. 662 That 3he trow this sekirly, My twa sonnys with 3ow sall I Send. **1390** Gower *Conf.* I. 327 As he which demeth sikerly That sche be ded. *c* **1449** Pecock *Repr.* ii. i. (Rolls) 132 If a treuthe be knowen bi doom of resoun, thanne it is knowen or sureli and sikirli; or it is knowen oonli probabili and likeli. **1552** Abp. Hamilton *Catech.* (1884) 13 To trow sickirly that God is almychty. **1586** Ferne *Blaz. Gentrie* 22 But I holde full sickerlie..that he fyndeth but few gentlefolks [etc.].

2. Without doubt; undoubtedly, certainly, decidedly, assuredly.

α. *c* **1220** *Bestiary* 106 His hope is al to gode-ward,..ðat is te sunne sikerlike. *a* **1300** *Havelok* 2301 Lokes nou, hw he is fayr; Sikerlike he is hise eyr. **1390** Gower *Conf.* I. 114 Tho wiste he..That he was sikerliche ded.

β. *c* **1200** Ormin 5754 þa shallt tu wurrþenn sikerrli3 An off Drihhtiness chilldre. *a* **1320** *Sir Tristr.* 3237 And meriadok, sikerly, In his help gan he be. *c* **1386** Chaucer *Prol.* 137 And sikurly sche was of gret disport, And ful plesant. *c* **1470** Henry *Wallace* viii. 594 Jornay thai socht, and sekyrly has found. **1548** Udall, etc. *Erasm. Par. Matt.* vi. 44 That sikerly is true praise. *c* **1580** in *Montgomerie's Poems* (S.T.S.) 279, I was applesit to pleiss 3ow sickerly. **1736** W. Thompson *Epithal.* xi. 5 Such colours, sikerly, suit Hymen best. **1825** in Brockett *N.C. Gloss.* **1876** F. K. Robinson *Whitby Gloss.* s.v., 'Ay, ay, sikkerly', yes, yes, assuredly.

**b.** Qualifying verbs of affirming: Positively.

**1340** *Ayenb.* 64 Huanne me zuereþ zikerliche of þinge þet me nis na3t ziker. *c* **1440** *Generydes* 2095 The xij$^{te}$ward the kyng of Orkenaye.., I say yow sekerly. **1533** Bellenden *Livy* i. i. (S.T.S.) I. 15 Quha may sikkerlie afferme sa remote & vncouth historie?

3. With assurance; confidently.

*c* **1205** Lay. 7883 Sikerlichen we sculden uaren & fehten wið þon kæisere. *c* **1340** Hampole *Pr. Consc.* 2469 Na man may trayste sikerly In hys gude dedys, þat he dus here. *c* **1400** *Beryn* 1542 In whom shuld the sone have trust & feith sikirly, If his Fadir faylid hym? **1551** Robinson tr. *More's Utopia* i. (1895) 102 Wherby I can not see what good they haue doone, but that men may more sickerlye be euell.

4. Without danger or harm; securely, safely.

*c* **1290** *S. Eng. Leg.* I. 142 He chaungede is name þe sikerloker forto go. *a* **1340** Hampole *Psalter* lxv. 5 þai sall pass in flode,..in meknes, for swa he passis sikirly. *c* **1412** Hoccleve *De Reg. Princ.* 1093 The poore man slepith ful sikirly On nyghtes, thogh his dore be noght shit. **1533** Bellenden *Livy* i. xv. (S.T.S.) I. 84 þe samyn thing..was possibill and mycht sikkirlie be done. *c* **1665** Livingstone in *Sel. Biogr.* (Wodrow Soc.) I. 268 How sickerly is that laid up from the reach of the roughest hands! **1897** Ld. E. Hamilton *Outlaws* 27 There's nae a man in Liddesdale can sickerly lead a party at night thro' the Foulbogshiel.

5. In a secure manner; firmly, fast.

*c* **1205** Lay. 26801 þer heo wel wisten sikerliche to halden þene riche mon of Rome. *c* **1375** *Sc. Leg. Saints* iv. (*Jacobus*) 123 His handis bundyne sekyrly behynd his bak. *Ibid.* xxxv. (*Thadee*) 125 [He] closit þe dure sekyrly, & selyt it with led. *a* **1400–50** *Alexander* 2401 þat Iowell..was full sekirly & soft all in silke falden. *a* **1810** J. Finlay in Ford *Harp of Perthshire* (1893) 419 What sorrow gars him haud it sae sickerlie? **1828** Buchan *Ball.* I. 112 Twa for keepers o' the guard, See that to keep it sickerlie.

**b.** In the manner of an obligation; bindingly.

*a* **1300** *Cursor M.* 25162 Halden sikerlik es he Vs to here in vr mister. **1340** *Ayenb.* 64 Huanne me behat zikerliche þet me na3t not yef me hit may uoluelle. ? *a* **1400** *Morte Arth.* 439, I salle hym sekyrly ensure, undyre my seele ryche, To seege þe cetee of Rome wyth-in sevene wyntyre.

6. In a stable or steady manner.

*c* **1375** *Lay Folks Mass Bk.* (MS. B) 526 þou make my loue ..sykerly sett..to loue þe wele. *c* **1430** *Pilgr. Lyf Manhode* i. civ. (1869) 56 Thilke that leneth him sikerliche ther to may not falle. **1552** Abp. Hamilton *Catech.* 142 b, That thou may be sickerly groundit in the trew faith of this sacrament. **1822** Galt *Provost* xiv, [He] had again got himself most sickerly installed in the Guildry. **1895** Crockett *Men of Moss-Hags* xlvi, To learn ye how siccarly to sit your beast.

7. With certainty of result; efficaciously.

**1340** *Ayenb.* 195 Ase þe lanterne þet me berþ beuore þe manne him let bet and more zikerlaker þanne þe ilke þet me berþ behynde þe regge. **1398** Trevisa *Barth. De P.R.* v. xxviii. (Bodl. MS.), No partie of the body toucheþ so sekerlich as þe hand. *a* **1548** Hall *Chron., Hen. V*, 72, We.. shal ordaine for the gouernaunce of our sayd father sekyrly, lovingly and honestly. *c* **1817** Hogg *Tales & Sk.* III. 71, I would have aimed as sickerly as possible.

8. Sharply, severely, smartly.

**1596** Dalrymple tr. *Leslie's Hist. Scot.* v. lxxxiv. (S.T.S.) I. 304 He first..mett sickerly with the Jnduellaris of Lochquhaber. ? **1609** in Row *Hist. Kirk* (Wodrow Soc.) 265 Whilk might make a few..conveen together..and censure sickerlie those corrupters of the Kirk. **1685** Renwick *Serm.* (1776) 177 God shall make them pay sickerly for it. **1775** *Baillie's Lett. & Jrnls.* I. 384 Who spoke against conclusions, got usually so sickerly on the fingers that they had better been silent. **1808** Jamieson, *Sickerly*,..smartly, severely; in relation to a stroke.

**'sickerness.** *Obs.* exc. *Sc.* [f. sicker *a.*]

**1.** †**a.** Certain prospect or possession *of* something; assurance; certainty. Also with inf. *Obs.*

*c* **1100** in Napier *Contrib. O.E. Lexicogr.* 57 Heo habbeð blisse for þære sicornysse Godes rices. *a* **1300** *Cursor M.* 27017 Again þe toþer hoping, þat es In werldes welth [to] hald sikernes, We finde a..sample laid. *a* **1340** Hampole *Psalter* i. 1 þe ferth is sykirnes neuer to lose þat goed. **1390** Gower *Conf.* II. 134, I not in what manere I scholde Of worldes good have sikernesse. *c* **1460** *Wisdom* in *Macro Plays* 37 He xall..dey in sekyrnes of joy perpetualle. **1523** Skelton *Garl. Laurel* 1597 Twene hope and drede My lyfe I lede, But of my spede Small sekernes.

**b.** Certainty with regard to fact.

*a* **1300** *Cursor M.* 3472 Oure lauerd..Had don hir in to sikernes..Quat suld be þaa childer vie. **1390** Gower *Conf.* I. 105 He doth al his thing be gesse, And voideth alle sikerness. *c* **1450** *Myrr. our Ladye* 162 She sayeth as yf yt were paste for syckernesse of the fulfyllynge. **1533** Bellenden *Livy* i. i. (S.T.S.) I. 7 To write þe said history with mare faith and sikkirnes. **1897** *Shetland News* 15 May (E.D.D.), Dis I sed we mair dan ordinar sikkerness.

†**2.** Sense of security; self-confidence. *Obs.*

*a* **1225** *Ancr. R.* 234 Sikernesse streoneð 3emeleaste & ouerhowe, & boðe..inobedience. *a* **1340** Hampole *Psalter* ii. 11 Dred is wirkere of vertus, and sykirnes brynges neclígence. *a* **1400** Hylton *Scala Perf.* (W. de W. 1494) ii. xi, He my3t so falle into rechelesnes & into fals sikernes. **1587** *Mirr. Magistr.* (1610) 327 In their most weale, let men beware mishap, And not to sleepe in slumbring sickernesse.

3. The state or condition of being secure; freedom from danger or harm.

*c* **1230** *Hali Meid.* 7 Se seli sikernesse as ha was in..under Godes warde. *a* **1300** *Cursor M.* 1158 Hou sal ani herthli flesche lende wit þe in sikernese. *a* **1340** Hampole *Psalter* cxlv. 1 Till crist, þare is þi rest and þi sikirnes. *c* **1412** Hoccleve *De Reg. Princ.* 26 In mene estaat eek sikernesse at all Ne saw I noon. **1464** *Rolls of Parlt.* V. 563/2 Caleis stode in grete sikernesse. **1526** Skelton *Magnyf.* 2539 A playne example of worldly vaynglory, Howe in this worlde there is no sekernesse. **1590** Spenser *F.Q.* iii. xi. 55 She..drew her selfe aside in sickernesse.

†**b.** A means or source of security. *Obs.*

**1483** Caxton *Gold. Leg.* 76 b/2 Almesse is a grete sykernesse to fore the hye god unto all them that doo it. *c* **1557** Abp. Parker *Ps.* civ. 295 The rockes, all inaccesse, To Conies bee theyr sikernesse.

†**4.** Security for the performance of a treaty, contract, etc.; an instance of this, a bond, pledge.

*a* **1225** *Ancr. R.* 342 'And haue ine wille þet tu nult nan more sunegen.' Lo! þus ne askede he non oðer sikernesse.

c 1290 *S. Eng. Leg.* I. 129 þe king him het þe panewes ȝelde oþur sikernesse him make. a 1375 *Joseph Arim.* 623 'Do me sikernesse þer-to,' seis Ioseph þenne. c 1425 *Eng. Conq. Irel.* 8 Of this was good sekernes Imaked on ether half. c 1470 [H. PARKER] *Dives & Pauper* (W. de W. 1496) II. ix. 118/2 A Jewe lente a crysten man a grete somme of golde..& toke no sykernesse of hym but his fayth.

†**5.** Sure keeping; safe custody. *Obs.*

1678 SIR G. MACKENZIE *Crim. Laws Scot.* I. ix. §ix, He shall abide in Sickerness (id est, in Prison) at the King's will.

**Sickertian** (sɪˈkɜːtɪən), *a.* [f. *Sickert* (see below) + -IAN.] Reminiscent of, or in the manner of, the works of the English painter W. R. Sickert (1860–1942).

1959 *Times* 27 May 7/3 He would seem to be an unwilling draughtsman—although a few delightful drawings in a Sickertian manner are shown. 1964 L. DEIGHTON *Funeral in Berlin* xiv. 85 The Sickertian backwaters of Camden Town. 1976 *Times* 1 May 7/1 Sylvia Gosse..became a competent artist, practising in a Sickertian style.

†ˈ**sickerty.** *Obs.* In 5 sykyrte, sikerte(e, sekurtie, sekirite. [f. SICKER *a.*, after *security.*] = SICKERNESS.

1405 in W. Fraser *The Lennox* (1874) II. 58 To the mar sykyrte and fulfilling of al thir pointis and articulis in thir Indenturis contenit. c 1440 *Alph. Tales* 428 Þou sulde be bettur provid with sekurtie of a sheperde tofall þan for to hafe a grete hall. a 1475 ASHBY *Active Policy* 185 Howe may any estate be in seurtee..Or in any wise be in sikertee, If couetous folke be in his favour?

**sicket**, variant of SIKET.

ˈ**sick-house.** Now *rare.* [f. SICK *a.* Cf. MDu. *siechuus, ziechuys,* MLG. *zeekhûs,* MHG. *siechhûs* (G. *-haus*), Sw. *sjukhus.*] A house set apart for sick persons; a hospital.

1491 *Anc. Deed* A. 7494 (P.R.O.), Roberte Bigott Sekeman Ownere of yᵉ Sekehowes of Walsyngham. 1549 *Anc. Cal. Rec. Dublin* (1889) 421 The Maior for the tyme being..shall survey the sek houssis of this cittie. 1612 *Extr. Aberd. Reg.* (1848) II. 308 Agnes Jamesoun..to hawe hir residence and ludging within the almes and seikhous betuixt the tounis. 1658 in J. Morris *Troubles Cath. Foref.* (1872) I. vi. 315 The great room of the sick-house was wholly spoiled. 1787 *Med. Comment.* II. 369 The child..had been admitted into the sick-house. 1799 W. TOOKE *View of Russian Emp.* II. 219 They were principally set against the sick-houses and quarantines. 1845 STOCQUELER *Handbk. Brit. India* (1854) 244 The sick-houses are, of course, totally unfurnished. 1899 KIPLING *Stalky* 103 When he was in the sick-house last month.

**sickie** (ˈsɪkɪ). Also sicky. [f. SICK *a.* and *sb.* + -IE.] **1.** *Austral.* and *N.Z. colloq.* A day's sick leave, usu. taken without sufficient medical reason.

1953 T. A. G. HUNGERFORD *Riverslake* 11 Now and then there would be one or more off on a sickie—they changed their jobs so frequently that they never let their sick leave accumulate. 1959 D. HEWETT *Bobbin Up* 81 She wished she could take a sickie tomorrer, but it was payday. 1969 *Telegraph* (Brisbane) 28 Oct. 8/2 If we don't feel just right we don't go up. We have a 'sickie' and everyone understands. 1974 *N.Z. Woman's Weekly* 8 July 5/3 Because of the nature of the work it was impossible to plan time off for social functions at short notice. As a result a small percentage of cabin crew staff resorted to 'sickies'. 1981 *Courier-Mail* (Brisbane) 5 Sept. 5/2 A part-time fireman's sense of duty cost him his job after he answered an emergency call when he was taking a 'sickie' from work.

**2.** *N. Amer. slang.* One who is mentally ill or perverted. Also *attrib.* or as *adj.*

1973 *Ottawa Jrnl.* 1 Aug. 34/2, I hope she gets professional help because these sickies usually get worse, not better. 1974 P. DE VRIES *Glory of Hummingbird* (1975) x. 135 'Shall I..make it clear..I'm a sickie?' 'No!..this—ailment of yours..it's an expression of some deep-seated conflict.' 1975 *Chronicle-Herald* (Halifax, N.S.) 2 Aug. 26/2 Dade County's entire homicide squad was mobilized..to search for a 'sickie' who murdered two attractive young women. 1977 *Chicago Tribune* 2 Oct. VII. 3/2 A sickie Army lieutenant who tries to run off with the reporter's daughter.

**sick-in** (ˈsɪkɪn). *U.S.* [f. SICK *a.* + -IN³.] Industrial action in which a group of workers absent themselves from work on the pretext of sickness. Cf. SICKOUT, SICK-OUT.

1974 *Spartanburg* (S. Carolina) *Herald* 25 Apr. B8/9 The 'sick-in' forced cancellation of eight of the 11 scheduled U.N. meetings Tuesday. 1976 *N.Y. Times* 7 Sept. 35/4 New Orleans police stage sick-in. 1977 *Monitor* (McAllen, Texas) 12 June 54/1 Millard Holden,..president of the Independent Produce Haulers of America, said he had heard 'sick-in' by independent truckers would be called over the July 4 holiday.

**sickinge**, obs. variant of SIKING *vbl. sb.*

ˈ**sickish**, *a.* [f. SICK *a.* + -ISH.]

**1.** Somewhat ill or sick, indisposed; disordered.

1581 MULCASTER *Positions* xxx. (1887) 110 To speake first of the weake and sickish bodie. 1601 HOLLAND *Pliny* II. 369 As Beares, when they feele themselues sickish or not well at ease, cure themselues with eating Pismires. 1663 BOYLE *Usef. Exp. Nat. Philos.* II. vi. 185 Though..[it] did make her sickish, especially, when she slept upon it. 1710 SWIFT *Jrnl. to Stella* 31 Oct., I had a fit of giddiness:..then it went off, leaving me sickish. 1773 T. PERCIVAL *Ess.* II. 95 He..was chilly, sickish, and had shooting pains in the head. 1824 GALT *Rothelan* III. 199 A sickish and peevish gentlewoman. 1882 STEVENSON *New Arab. Nts.* (1884) 32 You feel a little sickish?..take a little brandy.

*fig.* 1586 WARNER *Alb. Eng.* v. xxvii. (1612) 132 Our heires waxe sickish of our health, too long oure heere abode.

**2.** Somewhat nauseating or sickening.

1727 S. J. *Vineyard* 36 Your Grapes..must not be over Ripe, for..the Wine will be Sickish and Ropey. a 1817 T. DWIGHT *Trav. New Eng.* (1821) II. 450 In passing these receptacles, we were saluted by a sweet, sickish effluvium, oppressive to the lungs. 1856 HAWTHORNE *Eng. Note-bks.* (1879) II. 345 The atmosphere was a little faint and sickish.

Hence ˈ**sickishly** *adv.*, ˈ**sickishness.**

1727 BAILEY (II), *Queasiness*, Sickishness at the Stomach. 1733 G. CHEYNE *Eng. Malady* II. xi. §2 (1734) 228 [Not] with such frequent Vomitings, but rather a continued Sickishness. 1779 *Sylph* II. 6, I felt a sickishness and chill all over me. 1847 WEBSTER, *Sickishly*, in a sickish manner. 1880 *Literary World* (Boston, U.S.) 24 Apr. 139/1 Most writers upon him are either unpleasantly bitter or sickishly sweet.

**sickle** (ˈsɪk(ə)l), *sb.* Forms: α. 1 sicul, sicol, sicel, 3–5 sikel, 4 sikil, sikul(le, 6 sikell; 4 sykel, 5 sykelle, sykyl, sykol, 6 sykyll; 4 sekil, 5 sekelle, -ylle, zekill; 6 sick-, sikk-, sykkell; 4 sygle, 6–7 sicle; 6 syckle, 7 siccle, 6– sickle. β. 5 cykylle, 5 cikle, 6–7 cickle, 7–8 cycle. [OE. *sicol, sicel,* = MDu. *sek-, sik-, sykele, siccle, sickele* (Du. *sikkel*), MLG. *sekele* (LG. *sekel*), OHG. *sichila* (G. *sichel*; cf. Flem. *zichel*, †*sichel*); also MSw. *sikil*, MDa. *sig(h)il* (Da. *segel*). It is not certain that the word can be regarded as an early adoption of the Campanian L. *secula*, f. *secāre* to cut.]

**1. a.** An agricultural implement similar in form and use to a reaping-hook, but properly distinguished from this by having a serrated cutting-edge.

α. a 1000 in Wr.-Wülcker 234 *Falx*,..rifter, *vel* sicul. c 1000 *Ags. Gosp.* Mark iv. 29 He sent his sicol forþam þæt rip æt is. a 1100 *Gerefa* in *Anglia* IX. 263 Siðe, sicol, weodhoc. a 1225 *Leg. Kath.* 825 Þu schalt setten sikel forð. c 1290 *S. Eng. Leg.* I. 312 A luyte rondel ase a sikel Men seoth þar-on liȝt. c 1340 *Nominate* (Skeat) 527 *Sarcle, faux et faucil*, Wedehoke, sythe and sikulle. 1377 LANGL. *P. Pl.* B. III. 306 But if he do it smythye In-to sikul or to sithe, to schare or to kulter. c 1440 *Promp. Parv.* 455/2 Sykyl, *falcillus, falcicula.* 1489 CAXTON *Faytes of A.* II. xxxix. 163 A croked yron made after the facion of a zekill. 1523 FITZHERB. *Husb.* §28 A hande-rake..in the lyfte hande, and a syckle in the ryghte hande. 1542 HEN. VIII *Decl. Causes War w. Scots* C iv, As trew as the allegation of hym that is burnte in the hande, to saye he was cut with a sikell. 1600 NASHE *Summers Last Will & Test.* 871 Roome for the sithe and the siccles there. 1669 WORLIDGE *Syst. Agric.* (1681) 332 *A Sickle*, a toothed Reap-hook. 1750 GRAY *Elegy* 25 Oft did the harvest to their sickle yield. 1796 *Campaigns 1793–4* II. x. 69 The peasants were preparing to put the sickle to the grain. 1833 J. HOLLAND *Manuf. Metal* II. 50 The scythes and the sickles of the present day differ hardly at all from those in use nearly a thousand years ago. 1856 MORTON *Cycl. Agric.* II. 10/1 The saw-edged sickle, the smooth-edged hook, and the heavy sickle employed in cutting beans. 1875 KNIGHT *Dict. Mech.* 1898 The reaping-hook..has no teeth, and this distinguishes it from the sickle.

β. c 1440 *Promp. Parv.* 77/1 Cykylle, *fassilla vel fassicula.* 1497 *Naval Acc. Henry VII* (1896) 88 Cikles, vdd. di.; Sithes, vj. 1565 COOPER *Thesaurus*, *Falces messoriæ*, cickles: siethes. 1615 G. SANDYS *Trav.* 244 Messana was at the first called Zancle, of the crookednesse of the place, which signifieth a cycle. 1664 BUTLER *Hud.* II. iii. 292 Chase evil spirits away by dint Of Cickle, Horseshoo, Hollow-flint. 1791 NEWTE *Tour Eng. & Scot.* 410 The poor native..gathers the short and scanty grass with his cycle, or hook.

**b.** *fig.* or in figurative contexts.

1596 SPENSER *State Irel.* (Globe) 680/1 Godes harvest..is even readye for the sickle. 1602 DEKKER *Honest Wh.* Wks. 1873 II. 103 For all Times sickle has gone ouer you, you are Orlando still. 1658 SLINGSBY *Diary* (1836) 208 Be it your care to reserve a sickle for your own harvest. 1718 *Free-thinker* No. 23. 163 Labourers of every Kind may find Room to put in a Sickle. 1742 YOUNG *Nt. Th.* I. 194 Each Moment has its sickle, emulous Of Time's enormous scythe. 1825 MACAULAY *Ess., Milton* (1897) 6 In the vast field of criticism on which we are entering, innumerable reapers have already put their sickles. 1868 H. LAW *Beacons of Bible* (1869) 148 Wrath's sickle will do its work.

**2.** Something having the curved or crescent form of a sickle, in various special applications.

†**a.** An ornamental design in metal-work or embroidery. †**b.** An ancient military siege-implement (L. *falx*). **c.** A form of spur or gaff for a fighting-cock. **d.** A tail-feather of a cock. **e.** An instrument used in lacquering.

1459 in *Somerset Med. Wills* (1901) 188 [Two silver gilt basins] pounced [with knots of] sykols. *Ibid.* 189 [Two] Auter clothes [with one] frountell..[with divers] Compassis [of] sikels [curiously embroidered]. 1472 in *Wilts. Archæol. Mag.* XI. (1868) 337 A paire of cruettis of silver and gilte, wᵗʰ knottes of sikels. 1607 TOPSELL *Four-f. Beasts* (1658) 491 So also doth the Ram sometime put forth the sicle, and sometime pull it in, and hide it within the frame. c 1710 in Ashton *Soc. Life Q. Anne* I. 301 A single battle fought with Sickles, after the East India manner. *Ibid.*, One Cock with a Sickle, and 4 Cocks with fair Spurs. 1882 *N. Middlesex Adv.* 7 July 3/2 Against the insertion of false *sickles*..the judge of Hamburgs and bantams has..to be on his guard, a good tail..being of special importance in competition. 1884 C. G. W. LOCK *Workshop Rec.* Ser. III. 309/1 The tapper then goes round provided with the..scraping sickle.

**f.** Applied to the crescent moon, etc.

1657 W. RAND tr. *Gassendi's Life Peiresc* II. 128 That secondary and weak light, which the Moon showes, besides her silver Sickle, within her Quarter. 1847 TENNYSON *Princ.* I. 100 Ere the silver sickle of that month Became her golden shield. 1875 LONGF. *Amalfi* vii, Far away Sweeps the blue Salernian bay With its sickle of white sand.

**g.** A group of stars in the constellation Leo.

1882 in OGILVIE. 1885 SIR R. S. BALL *Story of Heavens* xviii. 383 The Sickle is specially famous..as containing the radiant point from which the periodic shooting star shower known as the Leonids diverges.

**3.** *attrib.* and *Comb.*, as *sickle-blade, -maker, -man, -manufacturer, -sweep, -teeth.*

1846–50 A. WOOD *Class-bk. Bot.* 166 Its long, drooping pods..resemble a *sickle blade, or rather a curved sword blade. 1483 *Cath. Angl.* 328/1 A *sekylle maker, *falcarius.* 1619 *Canterbury Marr. Licences* (MS.), Lancelot Symans of Horsmonden, sicklemaker. 1610 SHAKS. *Temp.* IV. i. 135 You Sun-burn'd *Sicklemen of August weary. 1821 SHELLEY *Hellas* 249 Yet the harvest to the sicklemen Is as a grain to each. 1855 SINGLETON *Virgil* I. 18 The seasons which the sickleman..should observe. 1858 SIMMONDS *Dict. Trade*, *Sickle-manufacturer, a maker of sickles. 1897 CROCKETT *Lochinvar* xxix. 261 Green flats of sparse grass, terminating in sweet *sickle-sweeps of yellow sand. 1897 R. MUNRO *Prehist. Prob.* 330 He discusses the peculiarities of the structure of *sickle-teeth.

**b.** Similative, as *sickle-billed, -houghed, -pinioned, -shaped, -winged*; *sickle-like, -wise.*

1782 LATHAM *Gen. Synop. Birds* I. II. 705 *Sickle-billed Creeper... Bill an inch and three quarters in length, curved like a sickle. 1872 COUES *N. Amer. Birds* 75 Sickle-billed Thrush. Californian Mockingbird. 1884 *Ibid.* 523 *Rostrhamus*, Sickle-billed Kites. 1607 MARKHAM *Caval.* III. (1617) 15 To bee (as some tearme it) *sickle-hought behinde, that is somwhat crooked in the cambrell ioynt, as Hares and Greyhounds are, is not amisse. 1840 *Penny Cycl.* XVIII. 64 *Sickle-like tail-feathers. 1874 WOOD *Nat. Hist.* 287 The close-set plumage of the Swallow tribe, their long sickle-like wings. 1763 *Phil. Trans.* LIII. 419 There were still remaining several of the suckers..disposed along its *sickle-shaped Pinnulæ. 1849 THACKERAY *Pendennis* vi, The sickle-shaped moon is growing every instant brighter in the heavens. 1884 BOWER & SCOTT *De Bary's Phaner.* 351 A strongly-curved..vascular plate, sickle-shaped in cross-section. 1870 GILLMORE tr. *Figuier's Reptiles & Birds* 468 Among the more remarkable species we may note..the *Sickle-winged Humming-bird. 1876 LANIER *Clover* 100 And curls it, sharp, And *sicklewise, about my poets' heads.

**4.** Special combs., as †**sickle-bear**, an epithet of the god Saturn; **sickle-bill**, *Ornith.* (see quots.); †**sickle-boon**, tenant-service rendered by reaping (see BOON *sb.*¹ 6); **sickle-feather** (see quots.); **sickle-ham, -hough** (see quot. and *sickle-houghed* in 3 b); **sickle-moon**, the crescent moon (cf. 2 b); **sickle-oyster** (see quot.); **sickle-pea**, a variety of pea having a curved pod; **sickle-pod**, an American species of rock-cress; **sickle scaler** *Dentistry*, an instrument with a curved blade for removing scale from teeth; **sickle-tedder**, a workman who cuts the teeth in a sickle.

1591 SYLVESTER *Du Bartas* I. iv. 385 Thou, rich, benign, Ill-chasing Jupiter, Art (worthy) next thy Father *sickle-bear. 1872 COUES *N. Amer. Birds* 262 *Numenius*, Long-billed Curlew. *Sickle-bill. 1880 *Cassell's Nat. Hist.* IV. 21 All of these have a long curved bill, and include..the Sickle-bills (*Drepanornis* and *Epimachus*). 1438 *Add. Roll* 41659 (MS.), Reddit per annum v. s. iiii d, iiii *sikilbons et i [hay]bone. *Ibid.*, xx d. tres ob. for hys sekylbone. 1546 *Yorks. Chantry Surv.* (Surtees) 290 To John Hunt for sicle bonez, ijᵈ. 1688 HOLME *Armoury* II. 251/1 The Cocks..tail consists all of crooked bending feathers (*Sickle Feathers as some call them). 1849 D. J. BROWNE *Amer. Poultry Yd.* (1855) 25 The sickle feathers of the tail are perhaps equally characteristic of the genus. 1799 *Sporting Mag.* XIV. 186 *Sickle-hams or *sickle-houghs, in horses, may be compared to knock or nap-knees in men. 1875 RUSKIN *Hortus Inclusus* (1887) 42 Bright morning. *Sickle moon just hiding in a red cloud. 1758 *Phil. Trans.* I. 526 Small oblong oysters, which the workmen call the *sickle-oyster, some of them being found crooked. 1731 MILLER *Gard. Dict.* s.v. *Pisum*, The *Sickle Pea is much more common in Holland than in England. 1763 MILLS *Syst. Pract. Husb.* IV. 109 The Sickle pea, or Sugar pea, which is much cultivated in several foreign countries. 1856 MORTON *Cycl. Agric.* II. 576 Varieties of Field Peas... White Sickle. 1846–50 A. WOOD *Class-bk. Bot.* 166 *Sickle Pod... A plant remarkable for its long, drooping pods. 1930 W. H. O. MCGEHEE *Text-bk. Operative Dentistry* 930/2 (Index), *Sickle scalers. 1956 H. M. GOLDMAN et al. *Periodontal Therapy* v. 94 The sickle scaler has a blade with two or four cutting edges. 1962 BLAKE & TROTT *Periodontology* x. 97 Fine sickle scalers are used for subgingival scaling. 1833 J. HOLLAND *Manuf. Metal* II. 56 There is a peculiarity in the handling of his hammer and chisel by a *sickle tedder.

†ˈ**sickle**, *a. Obs.* Forms: 3 sikel, 5 sikkil, 6 sickil, sickle; 5 seckle, sekkul, sekyl, seekle. [f. SICK *v.* + -LE 1.] Sickly.

c 1290 *S. Eng. Leg.* I. 466 Heore beire broþur lazarus was swyþe sikel a man. c 1440 *Pallad. on Husb.* Tab. 269 Olyuys, sikkil, to hele in Marche. *Ibid.* XI. 139 The tendir plaunte is take anoon,..and sekkul beth the grete ysette. c 1475 *Cath. Angl.* (MS. A) 327/2 A Sekylman, *valitudinarius.* 1570 LEVINS *Manip.* 121 Sickle, *valetudinarius.*

†ˈ**sickle**, *v.*¹ *Obs.* Forms: 1 siclian, 1–2 sæclian, 3 sæclen, secli, 4 seccle. [f. SICK *a.* + -LE 3.] *intr.* To be or fall ill, to sicken.

c 1000 *Sax. Leechd.* III. 151 *Diu egrotat*, lange he siclaþ. a 1122 *O.E. Chron.* (Laud MS.) an. 1066, Ða wæs Leofric abbot of Burh æt þæt ilca feord & sæclode þær & com ham. 1154 *Ibid.* an. 1154, þa sæclede he & ward ded. c 1205 LAY. 30549 þa iwarð þe king þere isæcled ful swiðe. a 1225 *Ancr. R.* 50 Leste..oure soule secli so sone heo is ute. c 1350 *Will. Palerne* 575 Sche..seccleled in a seknesse.

**sickle** (ˈsɪk(ə)l), *v.*² [f. SICKLE *sb.*: cf. SICKLED *ppl. a.* b, SICKLING¹.] **1.** *trans.* To cut with a sickle. Also *absol.*

1922 J. MASEFIELD *Dream* 13 All golden ripe and ready to be shorn By sickling sunburnt reapers singing staves. 1927

H. E. FOSDICK *Pilgrimage to Palestine* i. 4 The harvesters were sickling golden grain on the Shephelah hills. **1971** *Country Life* 2 Dec. 1501/1 The English labourer sickles his corn in August, the French labourer has it in by that time.

**2.** *Path.* **a.** *intr.* Of red blood cells: to become crescent- or sickle-shaped. Of blood: to exhibit sickling.

**1923** *Amer. Jrnl. Dis. Children* XXVI. 133 The blood of the father..was normal on being drawn, but 'sickled' after standing for variable periods of time at room temperature. **1946** *Lancet* 10 Aug. 204/1 Severely anæmic blood always sickles far more readily than blood which is not anæmic. **1970** R. W. MCGILVERY *Biochem.* iv. 75 Even the cells of heterozygotes will sickle if the oxygen tension is low enough. **1981** *Sci. Amer.* Mar. 117/1 After cyanate treatment and washing, the *AS* cells remained competent as hosts for *P. falciparum*, but now they did not sickle as readily.

**b.** *trans.* To cause to sickle.

**1977** *Lancet* 20 Aug. 411/1 The desickling agent..reacts with red cells which had been deoxygenated and sickled with sodium metabisulphite.

**sick-leave**: see SICK *a.* 10 b.

**sickle-bill(ed**: see SICKLE *sb.* 3 b, 4.

**sickle cell.** *Path.* [f. SICKLE *sb.* + CELL *sb.*[1]]

**1.** One of the characteristic crescent-shaped red cells found in the blood of people with sickle cell anæmia.

[**1910** *Arch. Internal Med.* VI. 517 (*heading*) Peculiar elongated and sickle-shaped red blood corpuscles in a case of severe anemia.] **1923** *Johns Hopkins Hosp. Bull.* XXXIV. 42/2 It may..be appropriate to mention here the relationships of blood grouping to another phenomenon occurring in this family, namely, the presence of the so-called 'sickle cells' or crescentic red blood corpuscles. **1946** *Lancet* 10 Aug. 204/1 As long as the diagnosis rested on the presence of sickle cells in stained films, the condition was rarely identified. **1968** *Times* 13 Nov. 16/1 The membranes of sickle cells took longer to remove than those of normal cells, a difference that could be related to the impaired ability of sickle cells to carry oxygen.

**2.** *attrib.*, as ***sickle cell count, family, individual, phenomenon***; **sickle cell anæmia, disease**, a frequently fatal form of anæmia, characterized by the presence of red blood cells that are rich in sickle cell hæmoglobin and sickle readily, and occurring in individuals homozygous for the sickle cell gene: **sickle cell gene**, an autosomal gene found in man, which when heterozygous produces the sickle cell trait and when homozygous sickle cell anæmia, and which is especially common in tropical Africa; **sickle cell hæmoglobin**, an abnormal hæmoglobin which tends to produce a characteristic crescent shape in red cells containing it; **sickle cell trait**, a relatively harmless condition, characterized by the presence of red blood cells containing some sickle cell hæmoglobin and conferring some resistance to malaria; (formerly applied to the characteristic sickling of the red cells which is seen *a fortiori* in sickle cell anæmia).

**1922** *Jrnl. Amer. Med. Assoc.* 14 Oct. 1318/2 (*heading*) Sickle cell anemia. **1924** *Ibid.* 5 July 16/1 Several new phases have been brought out since the time, fourteen years ago, when I described what for want of a better term, I [*sc.* J. B. Herrick] called sickle cell anemia. **1969** *Times* 28 Aug. 8/2 The gene for sickle cell anaemia..persists in certain African populations because it confers resistance against malaria. **1977** *Rolling Stone* 21 Apr. 8/1 He missed..the appearance of a frightening new phenomenon in the American black community: the replacement of sickle cell anemia with Potomac Fever as *the* crippling disease among blacks. **1970** P. OLIVER *Savannah Syncopators* 41 Those [tribes] on the coast include a large proportion with high counts of the sickle-cell gene making them resistant to malaria and able to withstand heat and high humidity; those in the savannah belt include large numbers of tribes with low sickle-cell counts and lower resistance to malaria. **1949** *Science* 25 Nov. 547/2 (*heading*) On the genetics of sickle cell disease. **1961** R. D. BAKER *Essent. Path.* xviii. 492 In sickle cell disease the spleen is often enlarged with intensely red cut surface. **1981** *Westindian World* 28 Aug. 13/2 Sickle cell disease is a blood disorder. It only affects African, Afro-Caribbean and Asian people. **1972** *Science* 13 Oct. 138/3 Physicians who treat sickle cell families emphasize the difference between sickle cell anaemia..and sickle cell trait. **1946** *Lancet* 10 Aug. 204/1 It seems clear that the sickle-cell gene originated in Africa and was carried by slaves to North and South America. **1961** *Times* 21 July 9/5 The population has a genetic resistance to malaria... They possess what is known as a sickle-cell gene, which results in their haemoglobin being abnormal. **1950** *Nature* 21 Oct. 677/1 Dr. F. Eirich, who had first directed our attention to this peculiar disease, gave us a sample of sickle-cell hæmoglobin solution. **1971** *New Scientist* 24 June 762/2 He found that in sickle cell haemoglobin one negatively charged glutamic acid in each of the two normal $\beta$ chains was replaced by an electrically neutral valine. **1958** *Oxf. Univ. Gaz.* 23 Apr. 892 A study of the physique, growth, and fertility of sickle cell and normal individuals in malarious and non-malarious areas of Nigeria. **1926** *Amer. Jrnl. Dis. Children* XXXII. 334 (*heading*) The sickle cell phenomenon. **1928** *Lancet* 24 Mar. 614/1 Sickle cell or drepanocytic anæmia is found only in negroes with the sickle cell trait—that is, whose red cells become distorted into sickle-shaped cells under certain conditions. **1959** *Listener* 26 Nov. 919/2 Sickle cell trait can be found in parts of Africa, in some Mediterranean countries, and in parts of India. **1978** R. B. SCOTT *Price's Textbk. Pract. of Med.* (ed. 12) XIV. 1156/1 In sickle-cell trait where there is only 30–40 per cent haemoglobin S, symptoms are rare.

'**sickled**, *ppl. a.* [f. SICKLE *sb.*]

**1. a.** Provided with a sickle. **b.** Cut by means of a sickle.

**1730–46** THOMSON *Autumn* 1321 When Autumn's yellow lustre..tempts the sickled swain into the field. **1765** *Museum Rust.* IV. 359 They..can house their mown corn as early as they could house sickled corn.

**2.** *Path.* [or f. SICKLE *v.*[2]] Of a red blood cell: sickle-shaped.

**1923** *Johns Hopkins Hosp. Bull.* XXXIV. 339/1 All the cells in the preparation kept in the dark had reversed within two days, whereas the controls remained sickled for a period of three days to one month. **1949** *Science* 25 Nov. 543/1 Under sufficiently low oxygen pressure..all the cells of both types assume the sickled form. **1971** *New Scientist* 24 June 762/1 The sickled cells tend to clog the circulation and to break up before they reach the life span of normal red cells.

**sicklemia** (sɪk(ə)l'iːmɪə). *Path.* [contraction of *sickle* (*cell anæ*)*mia*.] Sickle cell anæmia or the sickle cell trait. Hence **sickl'emic** *a.*

**1932** *Amer. Jrnl. Med. Sic.* CLXXXIII. 386 The term sicklemia has been suggested instead of sickle-cell anemia because a grave anemia is not constantly found in these patients. It is perhaps best reserved for those cases that show sickling without anemia. **1949** *Science* 25 Nov. 543/1 Less than 1 percent of those [erythrocytes] in the venous circulation of sicklemic individuals..are normally sickled. *Ibid.* 545/2 We have assumed that one of the two components of sicklemia hemoglobin is identical with sickle cell anemia hemoglobin and the other is identical with the normal compound. **1961** R. D. BAKER *Essent. Path.* xviii. 492 The hereditary trait of sickling of red corpuscles is usually found in apparently normal individuals. However, 2 to 4 per cent of Negroes with sicklemia have sickle cell anemia because of hemolysis of the abnormal red cells. **1973** B. J. WILLIAMS *Evolution & Human Origins* iv. 61/1 In thalassemia and, to a less marked extent, sicklemia, there are changes in bone marrow.

'**sickler.** [f. SICKLE *sb.*]

**1.** One who uses a sickle; a reaper.

**1638** SANDYS *Paraphr. Job* xxiv, Their Sicklers reape the Corne another sowes. **1855** SINGLETON *Virgil* I. 90 When on his golden tilths The farmer would the sickler bring. **1907** *N. & Q.* 10th Ser. VIII. 114 In the cornfields, where more hands were needed—men as sicklers.

**2.** *Path.* A person with sickle cell anæmia or the sickle cell trait.

**1932** *Amer. Jrnl. Med. Sci.* CLXXXIII. 388 Normal gall bladders have been observed in 'sicklers' at autopsy who have had attacks of severe pain and rigidity in the upper right quadrant of the abdomen. **1954** *Brit. Med. Jrnl.* 6 Feb. 291/2 In a group of 102 sicklers from the Balovale district of Northern Rhodesia only 10 (9·8%) had blood slides showing malaria parasites, whereas in a comparable group of 491 non-sicklers 75 (15·3%) had malaria parasites. **1978** *Observer* (Colour Suppl.) 26 Nov. 58/1 In the old days, 'sicklers' rarely reached adulthood.

**sicklerite** ('sɪklərait). *Min.* [f. the name *Sickler* (see quot. 1912) + -ITE[1].] A phosphate of lithium, bivalent manganese, and ferric iron, $Li(Mn,Fe)(PO_4)$, found as masses of brown orthorhombic crystals.

**1912** W. T. SCHALLER in *Jrnl. Washington Acad. Sci.* II. 145 Sicklerite. Named after the Sickler family, formerly of Pala [in San Diego county, California]. Found in cleavable masses..on Hiriart Hill near Pala... Results from the alteration of lithiophilite. **1975** *Fortschritte der Mineral.* LII. Special Issue 299 A large suite of secondary phosphates including sicklerite,..heterosite and others were derived from the primary minerals by hydrothermal alterations which leached alkali ions from the structures with concomitant oxidation of bivalent iron and manganese.

**sickless** ('sɪklɪs), *a.* [f. SICK *a.* + -LESS.] Free from sickness or ill-health.

*a* **1547** SURREY in *Tottel's Misc.* (Arb.) 6 To languish without ache, sicklesse for to consume. **1567** TURBERV. *Epit.* etc. 75 b, In happie helth when sicklesse limmes haue lyfe. **1606** MARSTON *Sophonisba* IV. i, Giue me long breath, yong beds, and sicklesse ease. **1853** J. CUMMING *Foreshadows* 126 That was an earnest..of a sickless state.

† '**sicklew**, *a. Obs. rare.* Forms: 4 siklewe, 5 sicke-, sekelew, 5–6 syklow. [f. SICK *a.* + -LEWE.] Sickly; unhealthy.

**1387** TREVISA *Higden* (Rolls) I. 257 þe south..is..vnholsom and siklewe for men to wonye ynne. *Ibid.* III. 303 þey bulde þe citee Sene fore here olde men and siklewe. **1465** *Paston Lett.* II. 185 The parson seyd he was agyd and syklow, and he wold not be trobelyd herafter. **1482** *Monk of Evesham* (Arb.) 102 His brethirne yat wer sickelew and febul. ? **1503** in *Lett. Rich. III & Hen. VII* (Rolls) I. 233 The kyngis grace is but a weke man and syklow.

† '**sicklewort.** *Obs.* [f. SICKLE *sb.*] **a.** The scarlet pimpernel. **b.** The plant self-heal (*Prunella vulgaris*).

Gerarde appears to be the source of all later references.

*c* **1450** *Alphita* (Anecd. Oxon.) 196/2 [*Ypia*] *maior*, ..*angl.* marie goldwert, *secundum quosdam, an.* sikelwert *uel* chikemete. **1597** GERARDE *Herbal* 507 Brunell is called in English Prunell, Carpenters herbe, Selfeheale, and Hookeheale, and Sicklewoort. **1611** COTGR. s.v. *Oingtereule.* **1766** *Museum Rust.* VI. 448. **1863** PRIOR *Plant-n.*, Sicklewort, from the shape of its flowers, which seen in profile resemble a sickle, *Prunella vulgaris.*

**sicklied** ('sɪklɪd), *a.* [f. SICKLY *a.*] Rendered sickly or mawkish.

**1835** LYTTON *Rienzi* VI. ii, Even in the light of heaven there seemed a sicklied and ghastly glare. **1842** MANNING *Serm.* xiv. (1848) I. 205 The poor sicklied workman in the manufactory. **1889** *Spectator* 16 Nov., The sort of sicklied sentiment which the age seems most to appreciate.

'**sicklify**, *v. rare.* [f. SICKLY *a.* + -FY.] *trans.* To make sick or sickly.

**1851** MAYHEW *Lond. Lab.* II. 76 All I felt was giddy; I wasn't to say hungry, only weak and sicklified. **1876** MISS YONGE *Womankind* viii, Sent forth as supposed good books ..to sicklify and sentimentalise good girls.

**sicklike**, obs. form of SIC-LIKE.

'**sicklily**, *adv.* [f. SICKLY *a.*] In a sickly manner.

**1727** BAILEY (vol. II.), *Peakingly*, sicklily, wearily. **1840** BROWNING *Sordello* II. 846 His will swayed sicklily from side to side. **1870** LE FANU *Willing to Die* III. 22 The first grey chill of winter's dawn hung sicklily over the landscape.

**sickliness** ('sɪklɪnɪs). [f. SICKLY *a.* + -NESS.] The state or fact of being sickly; delicacy of constitution, ill-health.

**1565** COOPER *Thesaurus, Infirma valetudo*, sickelinesse. **1593** SHAKS. *Rich. II*, II. i. 142, I do beseech your Maiestie impute his words To wayward sicklinesse, and age in him. **1633** G. HERBERT *Priest to the Temple* x, Not only sickness breaks these obligations of fasting, but sickliness also. **1697** DRYDEN *Virg. Life* (1721) I. 60 His Sickliness, Studies, and the Troubles he met with, turn'd his Hair gray before the usual time. **1777** WATSON *Philip II* (1839) 471 The inclemency of the season, the sickliness of his army,..and a scarcity of provisions. **1822–34** *Good's Study Med.* (ed. 4) IV. 85 Manifesting a considerable degree of sickliness in all their functions. **1896** A. J. C. HARE *Story of my Life* I. 109 [It] had much to do with accounting for my after sickliness.

**b.** *transf.* and *fig.*

**1656** EARL MONM. tr. *Boccalini's Advts. fr. Parnass.* II. lxx. (1674) 223 That action..proceeding..from sickliness of mind, as a lover of novelties. **1818** HAZLITT *Eng. Poets* viii. (1870) 201 His Irish melodies are not free from affectation and a certain sickliness of pretention. **1882** 'OUIDA' *Maremma* I. 90 The sickliness of the shore, seems little to affect children.

'**sickling**[1]. [f. SICKLE *sb.*]

**1.** The action of cutting with a sickle. Also *attrib.*

**1598** FLORIO, *Segatura*, a sawing, a mowing, a sickling. **1765** *Museum Rust.* IV. 358 The adoption of our method of sickling. *Ibid.*, The wages..on the sickling scheme.

**2.** *Path.* The adoption of a crescent shape by red blood cells.

**1923** *Johns Hopkins Hosp. Bull.* XXXIV. 339/1 From these experiments it may be concluded that the sickling is an inherent property of the red blood cells and that the patients' sera are without effect on normal erythrocytes. **1961** R. D. BAKER *Essent. Path.* xviii. 491 In the absence of oxygen the hemoglobin S forms crystals which cause the erythrocytes to assume peculiar sickled or oat forms. The sickling can be demonstrated in Negroes with sicklemia by allowing moist preparations of blood to stand, thus using up the oxygen. **1977** *Time* 28 Nov. 56/3 The Rockefeller scientists realized that any treatment for this genetic disease ..had to be directed at stopping the characteristic sickling, or distortion, of the red blood cells that occurs after they unload their cargo of oxygen.

'**sickling**[2]. [f. SICK *a.* + -LING. Cf. G. *siechling.*] A sickly or delicate person.

**1834** *New Monthly Mag.* XLI. 215 That they wear the red and white of health,..these sicklings cannot deny. *a* **1849** MANGAN *Poems* (1859) 297 Why should a man, like a girl or a sickling, Suffer his lamp to be quenched in the tomb?

'**sick-list.** [SICK *a.* 10 b.] An official list of sick persons, esp. soldiers or sailors.

**1748** SMOLLETT *R. Random* I. xxvii. 246 After the captain came on board, our first mate..went to wait on him with a sick list. **1794** NELSON 10 Oct. in Nicolas *Disp.* (1845) I. 495 Our Sick-list is now seventy-seven, almost all objects for the Hospital. **1834** MARRYAT *P. Simple* (1863) 211 As I could not appear on the quarter-deck, I was put down on the sick-list. **1841** HAWTHORNE *Amer. Note-bks.* (1883) 233, I intend to keep myself on the sick-list this one day longer. **1883** 'MARK TWAIN' *Life on Miss.* 309 Which one numbered the biggest sick-list? **1951** *Sport* 27 Jan.–2 Feb. 4/2 With Flewin, Thompson and Spence all cluttering up the Fratton sick-list, Jack volunteered his services in the pivotal position.

Hence **sick-listed** *a.*, placed on the sick-list.

**1891** in *Cent. Dict.*

**sickly** ('sɪklɪ), *a.* Forms: 4 sek-, 5 seke-, seekly, 6 *Sc.* seiklie; 4 sykliche, 6 syck(e)ly, 6–7 sickely, sicklie, 6– sickly (7 -ley). [f. SICK *a.* + -LY[1]. Cf. MDu. *siekelic* (Du. *ziekelijk*), MHG. (and G.) *siechlich*, OIcel. *sjúkligr*, Norw. *sjukleg*, Sw. *sjuklig*, Da. *sygelig.*]

**1. a.** Ailing or indisposed; in a poor state of health; not robust or strong.

*c* **1350** *Will. Palerne* 1505 Whan þemperour..seie him so sekly þat he ded semed,..sorwe sank to his hert. *c* **1374** CHAUCER *Troylus* II. 1528 Thou nedelees Counseylest me, that sykliche I me feyne! *c* **1440** *Promp. Parv.* 451/2 Seekly, or ofte seke, *valitudinarius.* **1483** *Cath. Angl.* 327/2 A Sekely man, *valitudinarius.* **1540** *Act 32 Hen. VIII*, c. 44 The impotent syckely and aged people, which be not able to travaile to the said Churches. **1598** SHAKS. *Merry W.* III. iv. 61, I am not such a sickely creature, I giue Heauen praise. **1623** R. CARPENTER *Consc. Christian* 99 When you shall lie on your beds sickly, or in health conferre with your souls secretly. **1691** HARTCLIFFE *Virtues* 55 Another of this way of Life, being sickly, expressed much Courage in.. adventuring upon any hard Enterprize. **1748** *Anson's Voy.* I. iv. 50 The Captains of the squadrons represented to the Commodore, that their ships companies were very sickly. **1779** HAMILTON *Wks.* (1886) VII. 575 The troops and seamen arrived in a very sickly condition. **1833** HT. MARTINEAU *Manch. Strike* ii. 20 Being in the air so much.. prevents my being sickly, as I used to be. **1894** H.

DRUMMOND *Ascent Man* 339 A mother who did not care for her children would have feeble and sickly children.

*absol.* **1837** T. HOOK *Jack Brag* xi, Jack made an attempt at popularity amongst the sicklies at Cheltenham.

*fig.* **1561** T. NORTON *Calvin's Inst.* II. 98 Leuing the pretence of necessitie, wherein they haue but a weake and sickly defence. **1613** PURCHAS *Pilgrimage* (1614) 17 In this sickely and elder age of the world. **1674** *Essex Papers* (Camden) I. 164 As in Sick bodies, so in Sickly governments, Change is desired. **1757** BURKE *Abridgm. Eng. Hist.* I. iv. Wks. X. 243 Armorica..was then, like many other parts of the sickly empire, become a mere desert.

**b.** Of plants, etc.: Characterized by a feeble or unhealthy growth.

**1697** DRYDEN *Virg. Past.* v. 55 No fruitful Crop the sickly Fields return. **1713** YOUNG *Last Day* I. 63 Yet all must drop, as autumn's sickliest grain. **1748** GRAY *Alliance* 1 As sickly Plants betray a niggard Earth. **1837** LYTTON *E. Maltrav.* 3 The herbage grew up in sickly patches. **1880** C. R. MARKHAM *Peruv. Bark* 79 He found..the seeds of *C. lancifolia* represented by three sickly plants.

**c.** Of the mind: Weak, disordered.

**1741-2** GRAY *Agrippina* 72 How oft in weak and sickly minds The sweets of kindness lavishly indulg'd Rankle to gall. **1781** CRABBE *Library* 60 Here alt'ratives by slow degrees control The chronic habits of the sickly soul.

**d.** Of things: (cf. SICK *a.* 7).

**1826** *Art of Brewing* (ed. 2) 32 The beer..cannot recover itself, but remains sickly, and becomes sour.

**2.** Of conditions, etc.: Connected with, arising from, characterized by, ill-health.

**1406** HOCCLEVE *La Male Regle* 15 My body empty is,..and ful of seekly heuynesse. *c* **1412** —— *De Reg. Princ.* 124 My seekly distresse For-bad myn eres vsen hire office. **1567** *Gude & Godlie B.* (S.T.S.) 40 To satisfie his seiklie appetyte. **1689** EVELYN *Diary* 29 Mar., Things far from settled.., by reason of the slothfull, sickly temper of the new King. **1704** F. FULLER *Med. Gymn.* (1711) 140 A sickly Complaining Life they lead, because they will not take Courage. **1783** M. CUTLER in *Life*, etc. (1888) II. 213 The sickly state of several families..in this place. **1831** D. E. WILLIAMS *Life & Corr. Lawrence* II. 490 It represented the youth..with a pensive and rather a sickly countenance. **1887** MISS BRADDON *Like & Unlike* i, Of all the evils that can befall a man, I think a sickly youth must be the worst.

*transf.* **1885** *L'pool Daily Post* 30 June 4/6 Faded twigs keeping up a sickly struggle for existence.

†**3.** Pertaining to sickness or the sick. *Obs.*

**1601** SHAKS. *All's Well* II. iii. 118 Thou know'st shee ha's rais'd me from my sickly bed. **1640** BROME *Sparagus Garden* IV. vi, Give me my Gowne and Cap though, and set mee charily in my sickly chaire. **1726** SWIFT *Stella's Birthday* 77 Wks. 1751 VII. 127 She at your sickly Couch will wait. *a* **1814** *Apollo's Choice* II. iii. in *New Brit. Theatre* IV., The sweet delight of tending on a sickly couch.

**4.** Marked by the occurrence or prevalence of sickness; unhealthy.

**1602** SHAKS. *Ham.* III. iii. 96 This Physicke but prolongs thy sickly dayes. **1697** DAMPIER *Voy.* (1699) 223 This is a very sickly place and I believe hath need enough of an Hospital. **1744** BERKELEY *Siris* §77 In the late sickly season of the year. *a* **1774** GOLDSM. *Surv. Exp. Philos.* (1776) II. 39 The island..became sickly and unhealthful to an extreme degree. **1822-34** *Good's Study Med.* (ed. 4) I. 645 The ship lay out in the open bay; no vessel near her was sickly. **1849** MACAULAY *Hist. Eng.* iii. I. 424 The year 1685 was not accounted sickly.

**5.** Causing sickness or ill-health; producing discomfort or nausea.

**1604** E. G[RIMSTONE] tr. *D'Acosta's Hist. Indies* II. xiv. 114 To live vnder a heaven or aire that is contrarie, troublesome or sicklie. **1697** DRYDEN *Virg. Georg.* III. 721 From the vicious Air, and sickly Skies, A Plague did on the dumb Creation rise. **1754** GRAY *Progr. Poesy* 49 Night, and all her sickly dews. **1781** GIBBON *Decl. & F.* xxx. III. 159 The sickly, and almost pestilential, exhalations of low and marshy grounds. **1855** BAIN *Senses & Int.* II. iv. §20 We have sweet odours that are sickly, in other words, depressing. **1882** DE WINDT *Equator* 113 Dense grey mists ..enshrouding the pretty village in their sickly vapours.

**6.** Of light, colour, etc.: Faint, feeble.

**1695** PRIOR *Taking of Namur* xiii, In vain France hopes, the sickly Light Shou'd shine near William's fuller Day. **1813** SHELLEY *Q. Mab* IX. 124 The broad beam of day, which feebly once Lighted the cheek of lean Captivity, With a pale and sickly glare, then freely [etc.]. **1862** MISS BRADDON *Lady Audley* iii, The pale lavender muslin faded into a sickly grey. **1888** 'J. S. WINTER' *Bootle's Childr.* x, When the sickly winter sun was feebly trying to shine through the grey clouds.

*fig.* **1825** MACAULAY *Ess., Milton* (1897) 5 A far-fetched, costly, sickly, imitation.

**7.** Of feelings, etc.: Weak, mawkish.

**1766** GOLDSM. *Vic. W.* iii, His soul laboured under a sickly sensibility of the miseries of others. **1805** FOSTER *Ess.* IV. ii. 138 The fastidiousness of sickly taste. **1869** J. MARTINEAU *Ess.* II. 42 The sure mark of a sickly unreality in morals.

**8.** *Comb.*, as ***sickly-born, -coloured, -looking, -scented, -sweet.***

**1818** SCOTT *Hrt. Midl.* i, This was the elderly and sickly-looking person, who had been precipitated into the river along with the two young lawyers. **1851** MAYHEW *Lond. Lab.* I. 358 He was sickly-looking, seemed dispirited at first. **1864** TENNYSON *En. Ard.* 260 Now the third child was sickly-born and grew Yet sicklier. **1882** *Garden* 18 Mar. 186/1 A sickly coloured sward throughout the summer. **1912** R. A. FREEMAN *Singing Bone* 136 The same idea having occurred to me, I applied the handle of the knife to my nose and instantly detected the sickly-sweet odour of musk. **1932** D. GASCOYNE *Roman Balcony* 85 The courtesan in the sickly-scented secrecy of her thick-curtained chamber. **1951** S. SPENDER *World within World* 267 We had to distinguish between those which smelt like pear-drops, carnations and sickly-scented hay. **1965** G. MCINNES *Road to Gundagai* xiii. 222 The room was..sickly-sweet.

†**'sickly**, *adv. Obs. rare.* [f. SICK *a.* + -LY².] In a sick manner; with sickness.

**1572** J. JONES *Bathes of Bathes Ayde* Ep. Ded. 2 When the state of the body is sicklie affected. **1605** SHAKS. *Macb.* III. i. 107 Whose execution..Grapples you to the heart and loue of vs, Who weare our Health but sickly in his Life.

**sickly** ('sɪklɪ), *v.* [f. SICKLY *a.*]

**1.** *trans.* **a.** To cover *over* (or *o'er*) with a sickly hue. Chiefly *fig.*

Usually in direct echoes of the Shakspere passage.

**1602** SHAKS. *Ham.* III. i. 85 Thus the Natiue hew of Resolution Is sicklied o're, with the pale cast of Thought. **1637** SUCKLING *Aglaura* III. i, Hope..has so sicklied o're Their resolutions that we must not trust them. **1760** C. JOHNSTON *Chrysal* (1822) III. 227 Her features regular; but want had sicklied over their beauty. **1784** *Universal Mag.* I. 204 But there too, Superstition's hand Had sicklied every feature o'er. **1847** *Proc. Berw. Nat. Club* II. v. 225, I have seen the china-rose..sicklied all over with the myriads that thronged its leaves. **1876** W. PAGE-ROBERTS *Law & God* (ed. 4) 122 A man's virtues begin..to get an unhealthy cast and to be sicklied o'er.

**b.** To render sickly or pale. Also *fig.*

**1763** CHURCHILL *Ep. to Hogarth* Poems 1767 I. 111 Thy Drudge..Sicklies our hopes with the pale hue of Fear. **1807** FENTON *Epistles* 52 Sicklied with age, and sour'd with self-disgrace. **1879** MEREDITH *Egoist* xxiii, The silver lustre of the maid sicklied the poor widow.

**2.** *intr.* To assume a sickly appearance.

**1882** 'OUIDA' *Maremma* I. 186 The broad oak foliage sicklied and looked parched.

†**'sickman.** *Obs.* [f. SICK *a.* + MAN *sb.* Now only as two words, and so freq. in ME.] A man who is ill.

*c* **1340** *Nominale* (Skeat) 216 *Homme malade gist en liter*, Sikeman lith in hors-bere. **1422** tr. *Secreta Secret., Priv. Priv.* 202 The Prayer of feyth shall hele the sekeman. *c* **1460** *Play Sacr.* 556 By what deuyll dyleth hym so long to tare, A seekman myght soone myscary. *c* **1520** NISBET *John* xi. 1 Thar was a seekman, Lazarus of Bethanie. **1607** SHAKS. *Cor.* I. i. 182 Your Affections are A sickmans Appetite. **1626** BACON *Sylva* §953 As if you should tell a Servant of a Sickeman, that his Master shall recover [etc.].

**sickness** ('sɪknɪs). Forms: see SICK *a.* Also 1 -nysse, 4-5 -nys, -nis; 3-6 -nesse, 3-7 -nes, 5 *Sc.* -nace. [f. SICK *a.* + -NESS. Cf. obs. Flem. *siecktenisse* (Kilian).]

**1. a.** The state of being sick or ill; the condition of suffering from some malady; illness, ill-health.

*α.* *c* **967** *Canons Edgar* §36 We læraδ þæt æniȝ unfæstende man husles ne abiriȝe, buton hit for ofer-seocnesse sy. *a* **1023** WULFSTAN *Hom.* xliii. (1883) 209 þæt god wolde..heo mid mislicre seocnesse æt mannum ȝenyman. *c* **1205** LAY. 19303 Octa iherde suggen of seocnesse þas kinges. *c* **1250** *Gen. & Ex.* 775 God sente on him sekenesse & care. *a* **1300** *Cursor M.* 1025 Sekenes suld he neuer drei. **1390** GOWER *Conf.* I. 128 Sche hath seknesse feigned. *c* **1460** METHAM *Wks.* (E.E.T.S.) 155 Yff man or woman take sekenes that day, thei schuld sone recouer. **1540** *Act 32 Hen. VIII*, c. 42 §1 To provide..for the helth of man's body whan infirmities and secknes shalhappen. **1565** *Reg. Privy Council Scot.* I. 357 Personis that..takis seiknes in thair Hienessis army. **1894** HESLOP *Northumbld. Gloss.* 614 *Seekness*, sickness.

*β.* *a* **1225** *Ancr. R.* 188 Al ower wo, sicnesse, & oðerhwat. **13..** *Sir Beues* 3918 While Saber lai in is siknesse. **1340** *Ayenb.* 95 Wyþoute steruinge and wyþoute zyknesse and wyþ-oute ealdinge. **1412** 26 *Pol. Poems* xi. 90 Myn enemys y shal..ȝeue syknes and drede. **1526** *Pilgr. Perf.* (W. de W. 1531) 5 b, Whiche..whan we be in sycknes is our medycyne and helth. **1560** DAUS tr. *Sleidane's Comm.* 230 b, He is troubled with syckenes. **1606** SHAKS. *Ant. & Cl.* II. ii. 173 Noble Anthony, not sicknesse should detaine me. **1651** HOBBES *Leviath.* II. xxviii. 162 When he falleth into sicknesse by the doing of some unlawfull act. **1712** POPE *To Miss Blount* 60 Those Age or Sickness soon or late disarms. **1772** PRIESTLEY *Inst. Relig.* (1782) I. 25 Pangs..occasioned by lingering sickness. **1804** COLERIDGE *Lett.* (1895) 451 To whom I owe that my bed of sickness has not been in a house of want. **1864** TENNYSON *En. Ard.* 825 A languor came Upon him, gentle sickness.

*γ.* **13..** *Sir Beues* 3900 In grete Grese..Saber gret sikenesse tok. **1377** LANGL. *P. Pl.* B. XII. 2 Idel was I neuere ..in sikenesse ne in helthe. *c* **1450** *Godstow Reg.* 404 To which-so-ever she wold..assigne hit in helth or in sikenesse. *c* **1511** *1st Eng. Bk. Amer.* (Arb.) Introd. 27 With sykenesse they dye nat. **1542** WRIOTHESLEY *Chron.* (Camden) I. 140 Toke such a thought and sykenes that he dyed thereof.

**b.** *transf.* and *fig.*

*a* **1340** HAMPOLE *Psalter* 494 Adam þat broght me in seknes of ded. *c* **1380** WYCLIF *Sel. Wks.* II. 23 Disciplis of Anti-crist agreggen þe siiknesse of þer folk. **1422** tr. *Secreta Secret., Priv. Priv.* 202 Wyth fastynge is sawid the Sekenys of body, and wyth Prayere the Sekenesse of Sowle. **1491** *Chast. Goddes Chyld.* 20 They..deye by longe contynuaunce of ghostli siknesse. **1633** FORD *Broken Ht.* v. ii, Look upon my steadiness, and scorn not The sickness of my fortune. **1695** LD. PRESTON *Boeth.* IV. 185 For if a depraved Temper be, as it were, the Sickness of the Soul. **1721** YOUNG *Revenge* II. i, I urg'd him to it, Knowing the deadly sickness of his heart.

**2. a.** A particular disease or malady.

Also freq. with defining terms, as *falling-, green-, horse-, joint-, sea-sickness* (q.v.).

*α.* *c* **1000** *Sax. Leechd.* III. 126 þanne ys god þæt mann fore-sceawie hwanne seo seocnysse siȝ. **1338** R. BRUNNE *Chron.* (1810) 103 þe þrid day of Aduent..þe kyng a seknes hent. *c* **1400** MAUNDEV. (Roxb.) xi. 44 He was made hale, what sekenes so he had. **1486** *Bk. St. Albans* a ij, To vnderstonde theyr sekenesses and enfirmitees. **1526** *Grete Herball* cxxiii. (1529) H ij b, Agaynst sekenesses of the mylt as Plinius sayth. **1596** DALRYMPLE tr. *Leslie's Hist. Scot.* (S.T.S.) I. 5 That sair seiknes, named the sueit of Britannie, cam nevir till ws.

*β.* *c* **1290** *S. Eng. Leg.* I. 132 þe bischop thomas lay, In þe syknesse of maldeflanke. **1382** WYCLIF *John* v. 4 He..was maad hool of what euere siknesse he was holdun. **1489** CAXTON *Faytes of A.* II. xxxv. 149 There is noo syknes but that som socours is gyuen therunto. *a* **1548** HALL *Chron., Hen. V*, 82 Every man judged as he thought, and named a sickenes that he knew. **1563** T. GALE *Antidot.* II. 52 It is then good for Sciaticus and other colde sickennesses of the ioyntes. **1649** BP. REYNOLDS *Hosea* iv. 75 The healing of a sicnesse by a Physician. **1697** DRYDEN *Virg. Georg.* III. 671 The Causes..Of ev'ry Sickness that infects the Fold. **1725** N. ROBINSON *Th. Physick* 199 The Nature of the Sickness will scarce suffer the Patient to remove for the Benefit of the Air. **1849** JAMES *Woodman* xii, One of those sicknesses of childhood which come and pass away.

*γ.* *c* **1330** *Arth. & Merl.* 64 (Kölbing), Sone after,..A gret sikenes þe king him toke. **1382** WYCLIF *Matt.* viii. 17 He toke oure infirmytees, and bere oure sykenessis. *c* **1425** tr. *Arderne's Treat. Fistula*, etc. 35 þan owe þe leche..bisily biholde wiþin, and considere if þe sikenes be mortified. **1529** MORE *Dyaloge* II. Wks. 194/2 Saint Roke we sette to se to the great sykenes, bycause he had a sore. **1556** *Chron. Grey Friars* (Camden) 24 The ix. day of the same monyth [July, 1551] beganne the gret sykenes callyd the swetth.

**b.** *fig.*

**1340** *Ayenb.* 16 þanne is hit [pride] þe meste periluse zyknesse. *c* **1400** *Rom. Rose* 2644 If evere thou knewe of love distresse, Thou shalt mowe lerne in that siiknesse. **1435** MISYN *Fire of Love* 65 þe venemus seyknes of lust. **1500-20** DUNBAR *Poems* lxv. 8 Ane paralous seiknes is vaine prosperite. **1607** SHAKS. *Timon* v. i. 31 A kinde of Will or Testament Which argues a great sicknesse in his iudgement That makes it. **1719** YOUNG *Busiris* III. i, I feel a deadly sickness at my heart. **1872** MORLEY *Voltaire* (1886) 11 His was one of the robust and incisive constitutions, to which doubt figures as a sickness.

**c.** A defect in wines. (Cf. SICK *a.* 7.)

**1674** W. CHARLETON (*title*), Mysterie of Vintners, or a brief Discourse concerning the various Sicknesses of Wines.

**d.** A disease in sheep; braxy.

**1794** *Stat. Acc. Scotl.* XII. 4 Of these, what is called the *sickness*, is generally the most common and the most fatal. **1822** [see BRAXY 1]. **1831** *Sutherland Farm Rep.* 78 in *Husb.* III. (L.U.K.), An inflammatory disease of the stomach, called 'sickness', or 'braxy'.

**3.** A disturbance of the stomach manifesting itself in retching and vomiting.

**1604** E. G[RIMSTONE] *D'Acosta's Hist. Indies* III. ix. 145 The sicknes of the sea, wherewith such are troubled as first begin to go to sea, is a matter very ordinarie. **1732** ARBUTHNOT *Rules of Diet* in *Aliments*, etc. 306 Sickness is one of the most troublesome symptoms attending a Fever. **1771** SMOLLETT *Humph. Cl.* (1857) 183, I was too much engrossed by the Sickness at my stomach to think of anything else. **1821** MOORE *Mem.* (1853) III. 209 Bessy had been obliged to go to bed from sickness of stomach and head. **1889** D. J. MATTHEWS *Dis. Women* (ed. 4) xviii. 149 You have here then..sickness, or sickness and vomiting if the pain is severe.

**4.** *fig.* Utter disgust or weariness.

**1779** MME. D'ARBLAY *Diary* 13 June, His sickness of the world..grows more and more obvious every day. **1821** LAMB *Elia* Ser. I. *Quaker's Meeting*, When the spirit is sore fretted, even tired to sickness of the janglings..of the world.

**5.** Sickly hue.

**1849** RUSKIN *Sev. Lamps* ii. §16. 45 The green and yellow sickness of the false marble.

**6.** *attrib.*, as ***sickness allowance, benefit, insurance, repentance, summer, year.***

**1673** KIRKMAN *Unlucky Citizen* A iij b, The late great sickness year 1665. **1674** J. B[RIAN] *Harvest-Home* iii. 12 Sickness-repentance will not be enough. **1690** CHILD *Disc. Trade* (1698) 28 The foregoing discourse I wrote in the Sickness-summer at my country habitation. **1891** *Daily News* 28 Jan. 7/1 The altered term of sickness allowance. *Ibid.*, The plaintiff's sickness benefit was liable to immediate cessation. **1911** *Q. Rev.* July 209 Sickness-insurance. *a* **1974** R. CROSSMAN *Diaries* (1976) II. 745 This sickness insurance provides that if you are sick for ten days or more you are paid at the end of the tenth day and the three waiting days at the beginning are included.

**sicknik** ('sɪknɪk). *U.S. slang.* Also **sicknic.** [f. SICK *a.* + -NIK.]

**a.** One who is mentally ill. **b.** One who indulges in sick humour.

**1959** R. BLOCH *Blood Runs Cold* (1963) 161 This is a real sicknik. A masochist, like. **1961-2** *Amer. Scholar* XXXI. 108/1 Then all at once (seemingly), in 1959, the sicknics were at hand. **1966** *New Statesman* 19 Aug. 261/1 The silliest definition of the art of Lenny Bruce is that of a 'sick' comedian (or 'sicknik', according to *Time* magazine), since it is so manifestly the sicknesses of society he was getting at. **1968** [see -NIK].

**'sick-nurse**, *sb.* [SICK *a.* 10.] A nurse who attends upon the sick.

**1816** SCOTT *Antiquary* III. xiii. 284 He has had an infernal tumble..and..I have sent your friend, Sweep-clean..to act as his sick-nurse. **1821** —— *Kenilw.* vii, I could not be expected to watch him like a sick-nurse. **1837** HT. MARTINEAU *Soc. Amer.* II. 155 She was a sick-nurse, when my friend knew her. **1890** 'L. FALCONER' *Mlle. Ixe* v. (1891) 133 At one time I was a sick nurse.

Hence **'sick-nurse** *v.*, to act as a sick-nurse. **sick-nursish** *a.*, appropriate to a sick-nurse.

**1844** KINGLAKE *Eothen* xix, This homely, sick-nursish illustration of the effect produced upon one's mind by the mere vastness of the great Pyramid. **1897** VOYNICH *Gadfly* (1904) 2/1 You were tired out with sick-nursing and being up at night.

**sicko** ('sɪkəʊ). *U.S. slang.* [f. SICK *a.* + -O².] = SICKIE 2.

**1977** J. WAMBAUGH *Black Marble* (1978) xi. 245 But, Clarence, listen! She's a sicko. Some kinda fruitcake or somethin. **1982** *Chicago Sun-Times* 25 Nov. 7/2 Is it asking too much for these sickos to stop bothering decent women?

**sickout, sick-out** (ˈsɪkaʊt). orig. and chiefly *U.S.* [f. SICK *a.* + OUT *adv.*, on the analogy of 'walk-out'.] = SICK-IN. Also *attrib.*

**1970** *Wall St. Jrnl.* 13 Apr. 1/3 The air controllers' 'sickout' is showing 'continuing improvement', the Government reported yesterday. On Saturday a Federal district judge ordered leaders of the Professional Air Traffic Controllers Organization to tell their members to go back to work or produce medical certificates of illness. **1974** *Trinidad Guardian* (Port-of-Spain) 16 Oct. 4/1 (Advt.), After all these strikes, sickouts, go-slows, and not a penny increase yet, now these merciless taxis up by 25% plus. **1977** *N.Y. Post* 18 June 1 The Yonkers police sickout crisis. **1978** *Telegraph* (Brisbane) 30 Oct. 12/1 Flights worldwide were delayed by a 'sick-out' of [Pan-American] flight attendants who had voted against a strike at the weekend.

†**ˈsickrel.** *Cant. Obs.*$^{-0}$ [f. SICK *a.* + -REL.] 'A puny, sickly creature.'

*a* **1700** B. E. *Dict. Cant. Crew.*

**ˈsick-room.** [SICK *a.* 10.] A room occupied by, or set apart for, the sick. Also *attrib.*

**1749** FIELDING *Tom Jones* v. ii, Seldom out of the sick-room. **1826** SCOTT *Jrnl.* 4 May, On visiting Lady Scott's sick-room this morning I found her suffering. **1871** NAPHEYS *Prev. & Cure Dis.* II. ii. 421 A room especially designed for the sick-room. **1897** VOYNICH *Gadfly* (1904) 10/2 All the unhealthy fancies born of loneliness and sickroom watching had passed away.

**sicky**, var. SICKIE.

**siclato(u)n**, variants of CICLATOUN *Obs.*

†**sicle.** *Obs.* Forms: α. 3–8 sicle, 5–6 sycle, 6–7 sickle. β. 4–6 cicle, 6 cycle. [a. OF. *sicle, cicle* (mod.F. *sicle*), ad. late L. *siclus*, a. Gr. σίκλος, σίγλος, ad. Heb. *sheqel*: see SHEKEL. Cf. MDu. *sicle, cicle, cikel*, Du. *sikkel*, G. †*sickel, sikel.*]

**1.** A shekel.

α. *a* **1225** *Ancr. R.* 398 Me solde his euesunge..uor two hundred sicles of seolure. **1382** WYCLIF *Ezek.* xlv. 12 Forsothe a sicle shal haue twenti halpenns; forsothe twenti syclis, and fyue and twenti syclis maken a besaunt. *c* **1400** LOVE *Bonavent. Mirr.* xxxvi. (1908) 188 Tweyne mytes, the ferthe parte of a sicle. **1535** COVERDALE *2 Kings* vii. 16 A buszshel of fyne meell was solde for a Sycle, and two buszshels of barlye for a Sycle also. **1565** JEWEL *Reply Harding* (1611) 436 With the holy Sicle, we must buy Christ, that may put away our Sinnes. The holy Sicle beareth the forme of our Faith. **1602** L. LLOYD *Briefe Conf.* 77 The Elders of that citie should..mearce him in an hundred sickles of siluer. **1649** JER. TAYLOR *Gt. Exemp.* III. xiv. 45 The accustomed imposition a Sicle or didrachme, the fourth part of an ounce of silver.

β. **1387** TREVISA *Higden* (Rolls) IV. 135 Mina is a manere weiȝte oþer a maner money, and weieþ sixty cicles. *c* **1400** LOVE *Bonavent. Mirr.* ix. (1908) 62 The child..was bouȝt aȝen as a seruaunt for v. penyes, that weren cleped cicles. **1548** UDALL, etc. *Erasm. Par. Acts* 28 b, A sepulchre whiche Abraham bought for an hundreth siluer cicles. *a* **1591** H. SMITH *Serm.* (1866) I. 405 A cycle or a homer, or an ephah.

**2.** An ancient Persian coin, worth half of a silver stater. *rare*$^{-1}$.

**1725** tr. *Dupin's Eccl. Hist. 17th C.* v. I. 184 He begs Aleander to send him the figur'd Inscription of the Sicles, of which he had spoke to him.

**3.** The value of two silver pennies. *rare*$^{-1}$.

**1720** J. JOHNSON *Canons Eng. Ch.* DCCXXXIV. viii, We will that the Adulterers pay thirty Sicles, or sixty Pieces of Silver to the Church.

**sic-like** (ˈsɪklaɪk), *a.*, *sb.*, and *adv. Sc.* and *north.* Forms: see SIC *a.* and LIKE *a.*

**A.** *adj.* Similar; such-like; of such a kind.

**1442** *Extr. Aberd. Reg.* (1844) I. 7 Giff ony man dois sik like case in tyme to cum,..he sal pay sik like payne vnforgiffin. **1474** *Acc. Ld. High Treas. Scot.* I. 52 To Keire curour passand with sic like lettres, iijs. **1549** *Compl. Scot.* x. 84 There is ane syklik exempil of pirrus kyng of eporite. **1588** A. KING tr. *Canisius' Catech.* 2 The holie sacrament off the alter, and siclyk secreit mysteris of our religione. [**1614** J. DAVIES (Heref.) *Commend. Poems, Ecl.* 51 Wks. (Grosart) II. 21/2 To gab of sikliche notes of misery.] **1786** BURNS *Twa Dogs* 63 Ev'n the ha' folk fill their peghan Wi' sauce, ragouts, an' sic like trashtrie. **1818** SCOTT *Rob Roy* xxv, Constables, and sic-like black cattle. **1829**– in northern glossaries. **1867** W. ANDERSON *Rhymes* 9 (E.D.D.), Flingin' crackers at ither, or some siclike wark.

**B.** *sb.* Such kind of thing(s) or person(s).

**1500–20** DUNBAR *Poems* xx. 36 Be nocht in countenance ane skornar,..Bot dowt siclyk sall stryk the in the neck. **1596** DALRYMPLE tr. *Leslie's Hist. Scot.* I. 93 This was thair maner, and this day the hilande men..weiris even siklyke. *c* **1620** A. HUME *Brit. Tongue* I. iii, In this diphthong we commit a grosse errour,..spelling how, now, and siklyk with w. **1786** BURNS *Twa Dogs* 74 A Cotter howkan in a sheugh,..Bairan a quarry, an' sic like. **1825** JAMIESON *Suppl.* s.v., 'What sort of fowk are the rest of them?' ..'They're just sic and sicklike.' **1876** F. K. ROBINSON *Whitby Gloss.* 170/2 'Sike an Sike-like were there.'

**C.** *adv.* Similarly; in like manner; in such wise.

**1513** DOUGLAS *Æneid* III. x. 45 Sic lyke as quhar that, with thair hie toppis, The big akis [etc.]. **1597** SKENE *De Verb. Sign.* s.v. *Annexation*, And sik-like..with consent of the three Estaites, it was statute [etc.]. **1640–1** *Kirkcudbr. War-Comm. Min. Bk.* (1855) 50 And sicklyke, it is appoyntit that everie heritor and tennant [etc.]. *a* **1670** SPALDING *Troub. Chas. I* (1850) I. 134 And siclike thair wes aucht gentilmen appointed to watche his lodging. **1708** *Lond. Gaz.* No. 4456/1 And sicklyke We..Command all..the said Dukes..to give all due Respect to Our Commissioners. **1752** LOUTHIAN *Form of Process* 133 And sicklike upon the..Day ..foresaid, I passed to the Market-cross. **1888** *Scot. Serm.* in *Brit. Workman* May, An' siclyke it is wi' the Heavenly Word.

**sicomancy**: see SYCOMANCY.

**sicomer, -our**, obs. forms of SYCAMORE.

**siconye**, variant of CICON(I)E *Obs.*

**sicory**, obs. form of CHICORY.

**sicsac**, variant of ZICZAC.

‖**sic transit** (siːk ˈtrænzɪt). Also erron. **transitur.** [L.] A catch-phrase expressing the impermanence of things, in full ***sic transit gloria mundi***, 'thus passes the glory of the world'.

The phrase is possibly an adaptation of a passage of Thomas à Kempis (see quot. *a* 1471). For the use of these words in papal coronations see *King's Classical & Foreign Quotations* (ed. 3, 1904) 319.

[*a* **1471** T. À KEMPIS *Imitatio Christi* (1827) I. iii. 7 O quam cito transit gloria mundi.] **1601** JONSON *Every Man in his Humour* v. i. sig. Mv, See, see, how our Poets glory shines brighter and brighter, still, still it increaseth, oh now its at the highest, and now it declines as fast: you may see gallants, *sic transit gloria mundi.* **1777** H. WALPOLE *Let.* 5 Dec. (1904) X. 163 General Howe must probably return to defend New York. *Sic transit gloria mundi!* **1833** LORD LYTTON *Godolph.* III. xxiii. 250 His breathing..died away as insensibly as an infant. *Sic transit gloria mundi!* **1851** GEO. ELIOT *Let.* 4 Oct. (1954) I. 364 Sic transitur—i.e. the money from my pocket. **1915** D. H. LAWRENCE *Crown* in *Reflections on Death of Porcupine* (1925) 92 Despair comes over us when it [*sc.* the body] passes away. '*Sic transit*', we say, in agony. **1951** 'J. WYNDHAM' *Day of Triffids* v. 104 'Never—never again now will you see a sight like that,' I told myself. '*Sic transit*—.' **1965** A. NICOL *Truly Married Woman* 16 They looked at it [*sc.* a Roman ruin] silently... 'Sic transit,' he'd said as they drove away. **1971** S. JEPSON *Let. to Dead Girl* v. 50 What was once my dressing room is dismantled..(*Sic transit gloria mundi*, and so on).

**sictuate**, obs. form of SITUATE.

**sicula** (ˈsɪkjʊlə). *Palæont.* [a. L. *sīcula*, dim. of *sīca* curved dagger.] The small conical or dagger-shaped structure secreted by and containing the initial member of a colony of graptolites.

**1893** *Lunds Univ. Årsskrift* XXIX. XII. 3 The sicula is seen to project from the right side obliquely upwards towards the median groove, thus separating the rounded bases of the two moieties of the rhabdosoma. **1910** [see *rhabdosome* s.v. RHABDO.]. **1970** R. M. BLACK *Elements Palaeont.* xiv. 211 The sicula was secreted by the first members (a zooid) of the colony and the thecae were formed by the subsequent zooids by a process of budding.

**Siculan** (ˈsɪkjuːlən), *a.* and *sb.* [f. L. *Sicul-us*, ad. Gr. Σικελ-ός (see SICEL *sb.* and *a.*) + -AN.]

**A.** *adj.* **a.** *Archæol.* Denoting the Chalcolithic, Bronze, and Iron Ages in Sicily. **b.** *poet.* Sicilian. **B.** *sb. Archæol.* A member of a people of Siculan culture. Also **Siculian, Siculic.**

**1896** *Jrnl. Hellenic Studies* XVI. 134 Orsi's investigations during the last seven years have included nearly every period, from the pure stone age with its pre-Siculic indigenous population, to the time of the Christian catacombs... Orsi has been able to follow down to the fifth century B.C. traces of this strange Siculian civilization. **1901** G. SEIGI *Mediterranean Race* xiv. 283 The presence.. of objects of Mycenean character in the first Siculic period. **1909** [see SICANIAN *a.*]. **1928** *Antiquity* II. 145 The veil has been half lifted from the romantic history of the Siculans who lived near Locri Epizephyrii. **1948** T. J. DUNBABIN *Western Greeks* i. 40 The Siculan culture of prehellenic Lokroi and kindred sites in Bruttium is not older than the tenth century. **1957** *Encycl. Brit.* XX. 603/2 A few rock-hewn tombs of the first Siculan period have been discovered near Palermo. **1975** G. EWART *Be my Guest!* II. 45 Not Siculan feastings sweet will bring forth smell.

**Siculo-** (ˈsɪkjuːləʊ), used as combining form of L. *Siculus* Sicilian, as in ***Siculo-American, -Arabian, -Arabic, -Moresque, -Phœnician, -Punic.***

**1764** *Phil. Trans.* LIV. 405 This character on one of the Siculo-Punic medals. **1770** *Ibid.* LXI. 96 The ancient Siculo-Punic, and Siculo-Phœnician, characters. **1884** *Encycl. Brit.* XVII. 639 The true Siculo-Punic coins, that is, those actually struck by the Carthaginians in Sicily. **1939** *Burlington Mag.* Oct. 171/1 Twelfth-century Siculo-Arabic combs and croziers. **1966** *Economist* 2 July 51/1 It [*sc.* the Mafia] revived with the help of the Siculo-American gangsters employed to ease the Allied landings in Sicily. **1974** K. CLARK *Another Part of Wood* iii. 115 Leigh Ashton ..had a good eye for art of all kinds, but what he really loved was a small fragment of Sassanian silk, a Persian pot or a Siculo-Arabic ivory.

**Sicyonian** (sɪkɪˈəʊnɪən), *sb.* and *a.* Also 7 Sicionian; Sikyonian. [f. L. *Sicyōnius*, f. *Sicyōn*, a. Gr. Σικυών: see -IAN.] **A.** *sb.* A native or inhabitant of Sicyon, an ancient Greek city in the northern Peloponnese. **B.** *adj.* Of or pertaining to Sicyon.

**1642** J. HOWELL *Forraine Travell* xvi. 206 Among the Sicionians there were admitted..[no] Physitians. **1841** *Penny Cycl.* XXI. 126/2 They [*sc.* Dipœnus and Scyllis] were employed by the Sicyonians to make for them certain statues of their gods. **1887** *Encycl. Brit.* XXII. 32/2 Clisthenes was the most powerful and famous of the Sicyonian despots. **1958** R. LIDDELL *Morea* II. i. 41 There is also a small sanctuary of the nymphs: here Sicyonian brides made offerings. **1976** R. J. HOPPER *Early Greeks* viii. 214 His victorious chariot was later preserved at Delphi under a form of *baldacchino*, the 'Sikyonian *monopteros*' decorated with archaic sculpture.

**sid.** *Sc.* [app. a var. of SEED *sb.*, but the pron. (sɪd) is not used in Sc. in the usual senses of that word.] An inner husk of grain detached from the kernel in grinding. Usu. in *pl.*

**1673** *Justiciary Rec.* (S.H.S.) II. 166 [He] called for a lippie of Sidds to his Dogs. **1801** *Farmer's Mag.* Apr. 215 After grinding the sharps, I..sifted them with a common meal sieve; they produced 7 pecks of meal and 1 peck of sids. **1865** *Blue Bk., Dock & Victualling Yard Expend.* 59 Offal Stores. These consist..of sids, husks, and dust, arising from the conversion of oats into oatmeal.

‖**Sida** (ˈsaɪdə). *Bot.* [mod.L., ad. Gr. σίδη some water-plant.] A genus of malvaceous plants of a woolly or downy character, indigenous to warm climates; a plant of this genus, esp. *Sida rhombifolia* or Queensland hemp. Also ***Sida-weed.***

**1753** *Chambers' Cycl.* Suppl., *Sida*, in botany, the name of a genus of plants, constituted by Linnæus [etc.]. **1797** *Encycl. Brit.* (ed. 3) XVII. 461/1 This description belongs chiefly to the sida; but it will also apply to the malva crispa. **1819** *Pantologia* X. s.v., The following species are propagated... Rhomb-leaved sida... Great bindweed-leaved sida [etc.]. **1887** MOLONEY *Forestry W. Afr.* 192 While belonging with Jute to the lower grade of textile fibres, *Sida* is much to be preferred. **1889** MAIDEN *Useful Plants* 139 *Sida rhombifolia*,..'Common Sida Weed,' 'Queensland Hemp'.

**sidalcea** (sɪˈdælsɪə). [mod.L. (A. Gray in G. Bentham *Plantas Hartwegianas* (1848) 300), f. SIDA + *Alcea*, the names of related genera.] An annual or perennial herb of the genus so called, belonging to the family Malvaceæ, native to western North America, and bearing racemes of white, pink, or purple flowers.

**1882** *Gardener's Chron.* XVIII. 439 The remark applies with full force to the Sidalcea. **1922** A. J. MACSELF *Hardy Perennials* II. 190 The Sidalceas grow erect with spikes of bloom resembling small Hollyhocks. **1962** R. PAGE *Educ. Gardener* vii. 213 One of the sidalceas..has spikes of soft rose-pink flowers and rather dull green foliage. **1976** *Country Life* 11 Mar. 619/1 Gardeners are..dividing treasured perennials..sidalceas, ligularias and chelone among them.

**Sidamo** (sɪˈdɑːməʊ). Also **Sidama, Sydama.** [Native name.] A group of Cushitic-speaking peoples in southwestern Ethiopia; a member of one of these peoples. Also, the language of these peoples. Also *attrib.* or as *adj.*

**1834** S. GOBAT *Jrnl. Three Years' Residence in Abyssinia* ii. 166 A month's journey to the w.s.w. of Shoa he had found a little Christian empire, who have a particular language, called Sidama, and books. *Ibid.* iv. 305 Kidam Mariam had with him a slave..of Sidama... He said that the Sidamas are Christians. **1868** J. C. HOTTEN *Abyssinia & its People* II. v. 200 Kaffa is a wealthy and fertile kingdom; the inhabitants are proud and handsome... They still retain a recollection and traces of the Christian faith... The Gallas, with whom they are incessantly at war, call them, in derision, 'Sydama', originally signifying Christian. **1910** *Encycl. Brit.* XII. 894/1 Similar dialects are those of the Sid(d)àma tribes, south of Abyssinia. **1939** L. H. GRAY *Foundations of Language* 366 Mixed with Ethiopic-speakers are the Agaw dialects..; and in the south-west are the Sidama (Gudella, Kaffa, Kullo-Walamo, Bambala, etc.). **1972** *Bk. of Thousand Tongues* (ed. 2) 392/2 Sidamo is spoken by an estimated 100,000 people in highland areas north and east of Lake Abaya, southwestern Ethiopia. **1974** *Encycl. Brit. Macropædia* VI. 1013/1 Those Galla and Sidamo who retain their traditional cosmologies..are more firmly anchored in the present.

**sidar**, obs. variant of CIDER.

**Sidcot** (ˈsɪdkət). Also **sidcot**, (*erron.*) **Sidcott.** [f. the name of the Australian-born aviator *Sid*ney *Cot*ton (1894–1969), who designed it.] In full ***Sidcot (flying) suit.*** A warm one-piece suit worn by aviators or the like (see quot. 1969). Hence **ˈSidcotted** *a.*, dressed in a Sidcot.

**1921** *Flight* XIII. 635/2 When Mr. Courtney was testing the 'D.H.6' fuselage fitted with the experimental 'Alula' wing at Brough..the weather was rather cold, and he was wearing his 'Sidcot' suit. **1927** T. E. LAWRENCE *Let.* 30 Dec. (1938) 563, I often think of you, and always as a rather shapeless Sidcotted bundle, peering over the rim..of a Virgin in mid air. **1928** *Motor-Cycling* 11 Jan. 240/1 An objection frequently raised against it, is that the Sidcot leaves the ankles entirely unprotected. **1940** *War Illustr.* 26 Jan. 19 Here are the two pilots of the Meteorological Flight, wearing warm Sidcot flying suits and oxygen masks, before taking to the air. **1942** R. HILLARY *Last Enemy* ii 45, I pulled on my sidcot and gloves and slipped my feet into the comforting warmth of my fur-lined boots. **1954** W. FAULKNER *Fable* 113 He took the pistol from the Sidcott's knee-pocket. **1964** G. LYALL *Most Dangerous Game* xxii. 186 Climbing into the Sidcot suit and slinging a Sten gun round my neck. **1969** BARKER & COTTON *Aviator Extraordinary* iii. 33 The suit had a warm lining of thin fur, then a layer of airproof silk, then an outside layer of light Burberry material, the whole being made in one piece just like a set of overalls... For a name I took the first three letters of my Christian and surnames—'Sidcot'.

†**sidder**, *v. Sc. Obs.*$^{-1}$ (Meaning obscure.)

*c* **1560** A. SCOTT *Poems* (S.T.S.) ii. 62 Strangmen of armes and of micht Wer sett thame for to sidder.

**sidder**, variant of SIDDOW.

‖**siddha** ('sɪdə). Also **Siddha**. [Skr., f. *sidh-* to be fulfilled.] In Indian religions, one who has attained perfection, a saint, a semi-divine being; *spec.* in Jainism, a perfected, bodyless being, freed from the cycle of rebirths.

**1846** [see GANDHARVA]. **1883** M. M. WILLIAMS *Relig. Thought & Life in India* vii. 191 All who are uninitiated into this system [*sc.* Sāktism] are styled 'beasts' (pasu), the initiated being called Siddha, 'the perfect ones'. **1971** *Illustr. Weekly India* 11 Apr. 11/3 At the end of a period of thirty years, the venerable ascetic Mahavir became a *siddha*, freed from the cycle of birth.

‖**siddhi** ('sɪdi). Also **Siddhi**. [Skr., lit. 'fulfilment', f. as prec.] In Indian and Tibetan religion, a collective name for supernatural or magical powers acquired by meditation or other practices. Also in *pl.* in same sense.

[**1863** E. SCHLAGINTWEIT *Buddhism in Tibet* vi. 56 The reciting of Dhāranīs, if combined with the practise of magical rites and supported by morality and contemplation, leads to superhuman faculties (in Sanskrit Siddhi).] **1882** [see MANDALA]. **1921** C. ELIOT *Hinduism & Buddhism* II. xxxii. 282 The religious life prescribed in the Tantras commences with the initiation and requires the supervision of the Guru. The object of it is *Siddhi* or success, the highest form of which is spiritual perfection. **1941** A. HUXLEY *Grey Eminence* ix. 218 He was deeply impressed by any manifestation of the *siddhis*, as the Indians call them, the psychic powers which may be aroused by meditation and to which the wiser mystics pay as little attention as possible. **1960** [see MUDRA]. **1970** *Man, Myth & Magic* v. 146/3 The idea of an astral body is very old. Ancient Indian writings describe the eight *siddhis* or supernormal powers which can be acquired through a type of yoga called *Pranayama*. **1977** *Time* 8 Aug. 44/2 The teachers have now brought those wares to the American market: lessons that will lead trainees to the Siddhis, or supernatural powers.

'**siddle**, *sb. north. dial.* [Of obscure origin.] Downward slope; dip (of a coal-seam).

**1851** GREENWELL *Coal-trade Terms, Northumb. & Durh.* 47 *Siddle*, the inclination of a seam of coal. **1894** HESLOP *Northumb. Gloss.* s.v., The general direction of the strips in open-field tillage lands was regulated by the siddle of the ground.

Hence '**siddle** *v.*, to slope downward, to dip.

**1894** HESLOP *Northumb. Gloss.* s.v., Just ayont, the seam o' coal begins to siddle.

**Siddonian** (sɪ'dəʊnɪən), *a.* [f. *Siddon(s* (see below) + -IAN.] In the style of, or typical of, the acting of the English tragic actress Mrs. S. Siddons (1755–1831).

**1795** T. WILKINSON *Wandering Patentee* III. 120, I have not observed the audience ever thought of heat in the Dog-days, when the Siddonian queen was followed. **1894** W. ARCHER *Theatrical World of 1893* 192 She is an imposing artist of the Siddonian school. **1931** C. ST. JOHN *Ellen Terry & Bernard Shaw* 64 The concealment of her ears, and her Siddonian deportment, made an indelible impression on him [*sc.* Shaw]. **1946** G. B. SHAW in *Drama* Winter 8 [She] burst in on me and demanded a Siddonian part.

'**siddow**, '**sidder**, *a.* Now *dial.* Forms: α. 7 sydowe, siddowe, 8– siddow (9 seedow), 8–9 sidda. β. 8 sidore, 9 sidder (cidder). [Of obscure origin.] Soft, tender, mellow.

Current in W. Midland counties, chiefly of peas, grain, or other vegetables. It is doubtful whether Grose is right in giving the word as a sb. and vb.

**1602** MARSTON *Antonio's Rev.* IV. iii, Finde they a chinke, they'l wriggle in and in, And eat like salt sea in his siddowe ribs. **1622** W. BURTON *Descr. Leicest.* 174 Long agoe it [Lindley] hath had the praise for good sydowe pease (as they tearm them). **1721** MORTIMER *Husb.* I. 66 Sandy Land marled will bear good Sidore, or white or blue Pease, and also Turneps. **1787** GROSE *Prov. Gloss.*, *Sidda*, pease or vegetables that boil soft. These pease will sidda. **1789** W. H. MARSHALL *Glouc.* I. 331 Peas, which become soft by boiling, are said to be 'siddow', a well sounding term, which is much wanting in other districts. **1854** MISS BAKER *Northampt. Gloss.*, *Sidder*, a term applied to malting barley. A shower of rain on barley, after it is cut, is said..to make it sidder, i.e. promote its growth in the cistern and make it work better. **1881** *Leicestersh. Gloss.*, *Sidder*, light; loose; friable; mealy: applied to soil that breaks up readily, peas that boil to a flour, yeast dumplings that are properly swelled, &c.

**siddown** (sɪ'daʊn), repr. a colloq. pronunc. of the imperative *sit down!* (see SIT *v.* 23).

**1936** J. CURTIS *Gilt Kid* iv. 44 'Siddown,' he retorted waving an imperious hand. **1953** K. TENNANT *Joyful Condemned* iii. 22 'Siddown,' he advised Jake Fletcher, who took the straight-backed chair. **1967** G. GREENE *May we borrow your Husband?* 110 'Siddown,' he said, 'make yourself comfortable.' **1975** D. BEATY *Electric Train* 165 What do you know about it, sonny?.. Siddown! Siddown!

**Siddur** ('sɪdʊə(r)). Also **Sidoor, Sidur**, and with small initial. Pl. **Siddurim**. [Heb. *siddūr*, lit. 'order'.] A Jewish prayer book containing prayers and other information relevant to the daily liturgy. Cf. MACHZOR.

**1864** *Chambers's Encycl.* VI. 155/1 These early collections of prayers generally contained also compositions from the hand of the compiler, and minor additions, such as ethical tracts, almanacs, &c., and were called *Siddurim* (Orders, Rituals), embracing the whole calendar year, week-days and new moons, fast and festivals. **1905** *Jewish Encycl.* X. 171/1 The collection, in one book, of the year's prayers for week-days, Sabbaths, holy days and fast-days is generally known as the 'Seder Tefillot', or simply the 'Siddur'. **1911** Z. HODES (*title*) Studies in Sidoor. **1925** W. O. E. OESTERLEY *Jewish Background of Christian Liturgy* i. 35 The next [extant collection of prayers] in date is the Siddur ('Order' of prayers..) of Sa 'adya (A.D. 892–942). **1949** S. GAON *Devel. Jewish Prayer* 6 Collections of prayers..called..*sidur* ..from the noun 'seder', which..originally..meant 'collection'. **1976** H. KEMELMAN *Wednesday Rabbi got Wet* li. 297 He had forgotten to take the prayerbook with him... She picked up the *siddur* and followed him.

**side** (saɪd), *sb.*[1] Forms: 1– side (1 siide, 3 siðe, 4 sijde, zide), 4–5 sid (4 said); 2–6 syde (4 syide, zyde, 5 syede, cyyde, 9 *dial.* seyde), 5–7 syd (5 syyd). [Common Teut.: OE. *síde*, = OFris. (and mod.Fris.) *side*, MDu. *side*, *zide* (Du. *zijde*) and *sië*, *syë* (Du. *zij*), OS. *sîde* (MLG. *side*), OHG. *sîta* (MHG. *sîte*, G. *seite*), ON. and Icel. *síða* (MSw. *siþa*, *sidha*, Sw. and Norw. *sida*, Da. *side*); not recorded in Gothic. Perhaps connected with SIDE *a.*, and originally denoting the long part or aspect of a thing.

The form *siðe* in *Gen. & Ex.* 1295 is prob. ad. ON. *síða*.]

**I. 1. a.** Either of the two lateral surfaces or parts of the trunk in persons or animals, extending between the shoulders and the hips; the corresponding part in fishes, reptiles, etc.

*c* **725** *Corpus Gloss.* L 328 *Lumbus*, side. *c* **900** tr. *Baeda's Hist.* III. vii. [ix.] (1890) 178 His hors..ongon wealwian, & on æȝhwæðre siidan hit ȝelomlice oferwearp. *c* **950** *Lindisf. Gosp.* John xix. 34 An ðara cempa mið spere sidu his untynde. *c* **1000** ÆLFRIC *Gen.* ii. 21 þa ȝenam he an ribb of his sidan. *c* **1175** *Lamb. Hom.* 147 Weren his side mid speres orde iopened. *c* **1200** ORMIN 4777 Shulldre, & bacc, & side, & halls, & hæfedd. *c* **1275** *Sinners Beware* 266 in *O.E. Misc.*, þer cumeþ god myd his rode, His honde and his syde al a blode. *a* **1300** *Cursor M.* 627 Vte of his side..Wit-oten sare a rib he tok. **1390** GOWER *Conf.* I. 40 Whan the sharpnesse of the spore The horse side smit to sore. *c* **1420** LYDG. *Assembly of Gods* 349 She weryd ii bokelers, oon by her syde. **1486** *Bk. St. Albans* e iij b, With the hede, With the shulderis and the sides. *c* **1530** LD. BERNERS *Arth. Lyt. Bryt.* 339 Syr, there is two ribbes broken in sir Rowlandes syde. **1592** SHAKS. *Ven. & Ad.* 625 His brawny sides, with hairy bristles arm'd. **1646** SIR T. BROWNE *Pseud. Ep.* 342 Were this true, it would autoptically silence that dispute out of which side Eve was framed. **1697** DRYDEN *Virg. Georg.* III. 344 Their Dewlaps and their Sides are bath'd in Gore. **1743** BULKELEY & CUMMINS *Voy. S. Seas* 145 Down his Sides, and all the Belly Part, is white Wool. **1782** MISS BURNEY *Cecilia* v. xii, With a look that implied 'I'll fit you for this!' [he] put his hands to his sides. **1824** MRS. CAMERON *Pink Tippet* I. 7 Esther Jones was now come out at the door, her arms were on her side. **1879** BROWNING *Halbert & Hob* 30 At once did [he]..Drop chin to breast, drop hands to sides.

*fig.* **1605** SHAKS. *Macb.* I. vii. 26, I haue no Spurre To pricke the sides of my intent. **1620** T. PEYTON *Glasse of Time* 62 The earth henceforth shall now no more endure Vnlesse thou till, and much her sides manure. **1738** tr. *Guazzo's Art Convers.* 159 Evil Princes have evil sides; that is, bad Counsellors.

†**b.** Used with reference to generation or birth. (Cf. LOIN *sb.* 2 b.) *Obs.*

*a* **900** *O.E. Martyrol.* 26 June 106 Hiȝ wæron acennede of Constantines sidan,..þæt ys of ȝestreonde. *a* **1400–50** *Alexander* 348 Now has þou, woman,..with-in þi twa sydis Consayued him. *c* **1485** *Digby Myst.* (1882) III. 1758 þe chyld þat be-twyx my sydes lay. **1500–20** DUNBAR *Poems* lxxxvi. 25 Thy blyssit sydis bair the campioun. **1634** MILTON *Comus* 1009 From her fair unspotted side Two blissful twins are to be born. **1817** SHELLEY *Rev. Islam* Ded. ix, From thy side two gentle babes are born.

**c.** In phrases denoting the effect of exertion in speaking (after L. *latera*), or boisterous mirth.

(*a*) **1604** HIERON *Wks.* I. 485 O master preacher!..Spare your sides. I am well enough. **1621** SANDERSON *Serm.* I. 215 Having thus dispatched my message, it is now time I should spare both your ears, and my own sides. *a* **1626** BP. ANDREWES 96 *Serm.* xix. (1661) 394 It confirmed them: it gave them sides, and strength.

(*b*) **1611** SHAKS. *Cymb.* I. vi. 69 The iolly Britaine.. laughes from 's free lungs: cries, oh, Can my sides hold, to think [etc.]. **1632** MILTON *L'Allegro* 32 Sport that wrincled Care derides, And Laughter holding both his sides. **1687** T. BROWN *Saints in Uproar* Wks. 1730 I. 80 You'd break a man's sides with laughing. **1781** COWPER *Expost.* 548 It shakes the sides of splenetic disdain. **1840** DICKENS *Old C. Shop* li, Tom Scott..bade fair to split his sides with laughing.

**d.** In phr. ***through the sides of***, denoting an indirect attack on a person or thing.

**1684** BUNYAN *Holy Life* Wks. 1855 II. 527 There are many that..watch for an opportunity to speak against him, even through the sides of those that profess him. **1699** M. HENRY *Life P. Henry* in Wordsw. *Eccl. Biogr.* (1818) VI. 268 That the name of God..be not blasphemed, nor religion wounded through their sides. **1791** BOSWELL *Johnson* an. 1768, About this time Dr. Kenrick attacked him, through my sides, in a pamphlet. **1801** STRUTT *Sports & Past.* Introd. §33 The other party, who..were not sparing in their severity, but wounded the ordinance itself through the sides of its defender.

**2. a.** In phrases denoting close proximity to a person (properly to one hand or the other), as ***by one's side***.

*a* **825** *Vesp. Psalter* xc. 7 Fallað from sidan ðire ðusend & ten ðusend. **971** *Blickl. Hom.* 43 Naht feor from þæs mæsse-preostes sidan. *c* **1205** LAY. 25756 Arður eode abute, & his cnihtes bi his siden. *c* **1300** *Havelok* 371 Knictes an sweynes bi here siden. **1593** SHAKS. *Rich. II*, III. ii. 80 All Soules that will be safe, flye from my side. **1667** MILTON *P.L.* XI. 176 Let us forth, I never from thy side henceforth to stray. **1697** DRYDEN *Virg. Georg.* IV. 680 Th' Infernal Troops.. list'ning, crowd the sweet Musician's side. **1749** GRAY *Installat. Ode* 34 With Freedom by my side, and soft-eyed Melancholy. **1784** COWPER *Task* VI. 40 Allur'd By ev'ry gilded folly, we renounc'd His shelt'ring side. **1848** THACKERAY *Van. Fair* xxxii, She passed five hours by her friend's side. **1859** TENNYSON *Geraint & Enid* 14 Not at my side. I charge thee ride before.

**b.** *side by side*, (*a*) (also *side †for*, *† to side*), close together and abreast of each other; in later use also of things, and freq. const. *with*; also (hyphened) as *attrib. phr.* Hence ***side-by-sideness***.

*c* **1205** LAY. 19824 þa duȝeðe..hine þer bureden bi leofen his broðer; side bi side beiene heo þer liggeð. **13..** *Cursor M.* 1786 (Gött.), Thinc no man ferli þat þar suam Side bi side, bath wolf and man. *c* **1450** in Aungier *Syon* (1840) 347 So that the syngers sytte togyder syde to syde. **1529** in *Proc. Berw. Nat. Club* II. 63 *note*, Their plouche is drawen be foure beastis going syde for syde. **1614** J. KING *Vitis Palatina* 30 They that walk side to side, and cheeke to cheeke, walke as companions. **1637** RUTHERFORD *Lett.* (1862) I. clxxxviii. 463 That proud thing, myself, will not play, except it ride up side for side with Christ. **1686** tr. *Chardin's Trav. Persia* 88 They rank themselves, either in a circle, or side by side. **1749** FIELDING *Tom Jones* IV. viii, The sculls lay side by side. **1810** SCOTT *Lady of L.* I. xii, Fox-glove and night-shade, side by side. **1850** TENNYSON *In Mem.* cxiv, A higher hand must..guide Her footsteps, moving side by side With wisdom. **1908** *Daily Chron.* 29 Nov. 9/5 The side-car..has the advantages of ready convertibility, low cost, and high speed..together with the far greater sociability afforded by the side-by-side accommodation. **1930** *Times Educ. Suppl.* 27 Dec. p. i/3 Side-by-side valves instead of the overhead valves. **1956** R. REDFIELD *Peasant Society & Culture* i. 20 Those early comparisons were side-by-side comparisons of societies unaffected by cities and civilization. **1970** *Gloss. Aeronaut. & Astronaut. Terms* (*B.S.I.*) VIII. 9 *Side-by-side assembly*, an assembly of connecting rods in which a number of similar plain connecting rods are arranged successively side-by-side with narrow big-ends usually carrying roller bearings.

*Comb.* **1865** J. GROTE *Explor. Philos.* I. 166, I suppose co-existence in space means proximity, side-by-sideness—equally exclusive of occupation of the same space or of a remote one.

(*b*) Designating a double-barrelled shotgun with barrels set side by side (cf. OVER-AND-UNDER *a.*). Also *absol.* and *ellipt.* as *sb.*

**1950** R. SHAUGHNESSY *Skeet & Trapshooting* iii. 30 Double-barreled guns are manufactured in two styles, one known as the *over-and-under*, the other as the *side-by-side*. **1961** Side-by-side sb. in WEBSTER. **1964** H. L. PETERSON *Encycl. Firearms* 139/1 Henry Nock's patent breech of 1787. .. It was possible to shorten barrels..for a sporting gun... Shortening the barrels made the guns still lighter, and this in turn made the side-by-side double-barreled fowling piece practical. **1979** G. HAMMOND *Dead Game* ii. 32, I saw all the guns... Two..were over-and-unders, the rest side-by-sides. **1980** *Outdoor Life* (U.S.) (Northeast ed.) Oct. 53/1, I had this double-barreled side-by-side 20-gauge Savage-Fox, the ugliest thing ever made.

**3.** One of the lateral halves of the body of an animal, or the part about the ribs, used for cooking. Now chiefly in ***side of bacon***.

In the first quot. the reference is to a child.

**13..** *Cursor M.* 8715 (Gött.), Wid suord it sal be delt in tua, And ether sal haue a side in hand. *c* **1430** *Two Cookery-bks.* 25 Loke þat þow haue fayre sydys of Pyggys, & fayre smal Chykenys wyl & clene skladdyd & drawe. *c* **1480** HENRYSON *Fables, Fox, Wolf, & Cadger* xxvi, It is ane syde of Salmond, as it wer. **1599** in *Antiquary* XXXII. 242 One side of baconn. **1665** PEPYS *Diary* 4 April, A great dish of side of lamb. **1727** GAY *Fables* I. xxi, They undermined whole sides of bacon. **1766** GOLDSM. *Vic. W.* v, The 'squire ..sent us a side of venison. **1820** SCOTT *Monast.* xiii, The haggis and the side of mutton, with which her table was set forth. **1844** H. STEPHENS *Bk. Farm* II. 167 After the carcass has hung 24 hours, it should be cut down by the back-bone, or chine, into two sides. **1897** *Daily News* 28 Sept. 8/3 The small carcases from which come the Wiltshire sides most popular with the Canadian consumer.

**II. 4. a.** One or other of the two longer (usually vertical) surfaces or aspects of an object, in contrast to the ends, or of the two receding surfaces or aspects, in contrast to the front and back.

The precise application depends to some extent on the form of the object and its position in relation to the observer.

*c* **825** *Vesp. Psalter* cxxvii. 3 Swe swe wintreow ȝenyht-sumiende in sidum huses ðines. *c* **897** K. ÆLFRED *Gregory's Past. C.* xxii. 169 Tweȝan stengas..sting ut ðurh ða hringas bi ðære earce sidan. *c* **1340** *Nominale* (Skeat) 878 *A coustes, claies, et roulous*, Be sydes, hirdeles, and cartesoulis. **1375** BARBOUR *Bruce* XV. 28 Cum we than on thame at a syde. **1382** WYCLIF *Exod.* xxxvii. 5 The whiche he putte into the rynges that weren in the sides of the arke. **1542** UDALL *Erasm. Apoph.* 132 b, When menne dooe mocke any bodye thei wagge their handes up & down by their eares at the sydes of their hedde. **1581** in Feuillerat *Revels Q. Eliz.* (1908) 345 Castell with yᵉ falling sydes. Tree with shyldes. **1628** P. SMART *Vanitie Popish Cerem.* 33, I trow there are but two sides of a long table, and two ends. **1654–66** EARL ORRERY *Parthen.* (1676) 520 The credulous Nymph..concealed a Lamp, by her Beds side. **1726** LEONI *Alberti's Archit.* I. 71/2 He..fastened these Beams..each with two braces..bound round and fastened of opposite sides. **1794** T. DAVIS *Agric. Wilts.* 69 They seldom use any overlays or outriggers, either at the ends or sides [of a waggon]. **1847** W. C. L. MARTIN *The Ox* 138/1 The sides of the tongue become gangrenous. **1857** T. MOORE *Handbk. Brit. Ferns* (ed. 3) 18 A harder layer,..with thick dotted sides. **1886** BARING-GOULD *Court Royal* I. iii. 37 My boots are scat at the sides.

**b.** One or other of the bounding lines or surfaces of any right-lined figure or object.

*a* **1400–50** *Alexander* 2215 All þe sidis of þe cite þat sechus had biggid. **1495** *Trevisa's Barth. De P.R.* (W. de W.) III. xvii, A rounde shape hathe noo sydes wᵗ corners. **1551** ROBINSON tr. *More's Utopia* II. (1895) 120 Neuer a one of them all hath of anye syde lesse then xx. myles of grounde, and of some sydes also muche more. **1570** BILLINGSLEY *Euclid* I. prop. 21. 31 Not euery figure hauing three angles hath also onely three sides. **1628** P. SMART *Vanitie Popish Cerem.* 33 Make it [the table] square, and then it will haue foure sides, and no end, or foure ends and no side. **1715** tr. *Gregory's*

*Astron.* (1726) I. 353 Again, in the Triangle *M P N*, the Sides *P M*, *P N* being given, .. the base *M N* is found. **1774** M. Mackenzie *Maritime Surv.* 2 Having two Sides and an Angle opposite to one of them, to find another Angle. **1830** Herschel *Study Nat. Phil.* 254 A ray of light after its emergence from such a crystal acquires sides. **1848** Thackeray *Van. Fair* lxvi, A large window, with three sides of glass. **1863** E. V. Neale *Anal. Th. & Nat.* 135 The relations of the sides of each triangle to each other .. are the effects of its triangular form.

*fig.* **1857** Geo. Eliot *Ess.* (1884) 69 On its theoretic and perceptive side, Morality touches Science; on its emotional side, poetic Art.

**c.** In a rounded, cylindrical, or spherical object, a part of the surface having a particular aspect.

*c* **1055** *Byrhtferth's Handboc* in *Anglia* VIII. 319 Æfre byð on sumere sidan þære eorðan dæȝ. **1602** Shaks. *Ham.* I. i. 85 Our Valiant Hamlet (For so this side of our knowne world esteem'd him). **1667** Milton *P.L.* III. 722 Look downward on that Globe whose hither side With light from hence, though but reflected, shines. **1747** Gray *Cat* 1 'Twas on a lofty vase's side. **1788** Cowper *Mischievous Bull* 7 Woodpeckers explore the sides Of rugged oaks for worms. **1826** *Art of Brewing* (ed. 2) 141 [Apples] with a tinge of red streaks on the sunny side. **1868** Lockyer *Elem. Astron.* §214 Hence we only see one side of our satellite [the moon].

**d.** *Math.* (See quots.)

(*a*) **1660–1706** [see ROOT *sb.*[1] 14 a]. **1728** Chambers *Cycl.* s.v., Side of a Power, is what we otherwise call the Root, or Radix. **1841** *Penny Cycl.* XXI. 490/2 The same geometrical analogies by which a number multiplied by itself was called a *square*, procured for the number itself the name of *side*.

(*b*) **1728** Chambers *Cycl.*, *Side of a Polygonal Number*, is the Number of the Terms of the Arithmetical Progression, that are summed up. **1795** Hutton *Math. Dict.* s.v. *Polygonal Numbers*, The *Side* of a Polygonal number is the number of points in each side of the Polygonal figure when the points in the number are ranged in that form.

**e.** *Mining.* (See quots.)

**1839** Ure *Dict. Arts* 981 A compartment, or pannel, formed in working the coal, is called a side of work. **1867** W. W. Smyth *Coal & Coal-mining* 136 From this latter the main workings, called *sides of work*, are opened in the form of a square or parallelogram.

**5.** That part of the framework of a ship or boat extending from stem to stern between the gunwale and the main-wale or the water-line.

*c* **1000** Ælfric *Gen.* vi. 16 Duru þu setst be þære sidan wið neoðan and þu macast þreo fleringa binnan þam arce. *a* **1300** *Cursor M.* 1670 Quen þi timber es festend wele þou wind þe sides ilk dele. **1530** Palsgr. 270/1 Syde of a bote, *bort*. **1596** Shaks. *Merch. V.* I. i. 32 Dangerous rocks, Which touching but my gentle Vessels side Would scatter all her spices on the streame. *c* **1614** Sir W. Mure *Dido & Æneas* I. 273 The tumbling billowes fast her syddes assaill. **1705** *Lond. Gaz.* No. 4093/1 A French Man of War .. came within Musket-shot along her side. **1795** Nelson 7 Feb. in Nicolas *Disp.* (1845) II. 5 The Ships built at Toulon have their sides, beams, decks, and straight timbers from this Island. **1839** R. S. Robinson *Naut. Steam Eng.* 61 Great care is taken in fitting the pipes through the ship's sides. **1889** Welch *Text Bk. Naval Archit.* 104 On the stronger sides of recent first-class battle ships .. the combined thickness of this plating is $2\frac{1}{4}$ inches.

**6. a.** The slope of a hill or bank, especially one extending for a considerable distance. (Cf. BANK-, HILL-, MOUNTAIN-SIDE.)

*c* **1250** *Gen. & Ex.* 1295 Men seið ðat dune-is siðen on Was mad temple salamon. **1382** Wyclif *2 Sam.* xiii. 34 Myche puple cam bi the out weye fro the side of the hil. *c* **1400** *Destr. Troy* 5863 Hym list for to rest, And bowet fro the batell to þe bonke side. **1553** T. Wilson *Rhet.* (1580) 176 The side of a bancke. **1634** Milton *Comus* 295 Under a green mantling vine That crawls along the side of yon small hill. **1667** —— *P.L.* I. 232 A Hill Torn from Pelorus, or the shatter'd side Of thundring Ætna. **1757** Gray *Bard* 11 Down the steep of Snowdon's shaggy side. **1774** Goldsm. *Nat. Hist.* (1776) I. 150 It is still overlooked by tremendous mountains; their sides covered with snow. **1811** Pinkerton *Mod. Geogr.* (ed. 3) 303 The eruptions rarely attain the summit [of Etna], but more usually break out at the sides.

**b.** The outskirts of a wood, town, etc. ? *Obs.*

*a* **1300** *Cursor M.* 5734 Þe flok he fedd opon a tid, Bi a wildrin wod side. *c* **1386** Chaucer *Wife's T.* 133 In his way, it hapnyd him to ride .. under a forest side. *c* **1430** Lydg. *Min. Poems* (Percy Soc.) 228 By a wylde wodes syde As I walked myself alone. *a* **1548** Hall *Chron., Edw. IV*, 12 Vnder a woddes side, thei couertly espied them passe forward. **1592** Shaks. *Rom. & Jul.* I. i. 129 Vnderneath the groue of Sycamour, That West-ward rooteth from this City side. **1640** Habington *Edw. IV*, 83 The Earle labouring to escape, at a Woods side where was no passage. **1706** Hearne *Collect.* (O.H.S.) I. 242 Next Bray-Wood side. **1750** Gray *Elegy* 101 Him have we seen the Greenwood side along.

**7. a.** The bank or shore of a river or water; also, the land or district bordering on a river. (Cf. *burn-*, RIVER-, SEA-, WATER-SIDE.)

**1320–30** *Horn Ch.* 54 In clifland bi tese side. *c* **1400** *Destr. Troy* 5799 All backward [they] hom bere to þe buerne side, Þat fer from þe flode might no freke wyn. **1432–50** tr. *Higden* (Rolls) I. 65 There be monye deipe places of waters nye to the sydes of the sees. **1513** Douglas *Æneid* IX. xiii. 28 Towartis the ryveris syde alaw. **1588** Parke tr. *Mendoza's Hist. China* 313 If they chance to finde a man in the waters side he wil eate him all. **1697** Dryden *Virg. Georg.* III. 230 Let 'em .. Range the Forrest, by the Silver side Of some cool Stream. **1774** Goldsm. *Nat. Hist.* (1776) IV. 160 The place of meeting .. is always by the side of some lake or river. **1810** Scott *Lady of Lake* I. xxiii, As her light skiff approach'd the side. **1836** *Penny Cycl.* VI. 317/1 Carrickfergus .. situated on the W. shore or Antrim side of Belfast Loch.

**b.** A surface serving to enclose or bound a space or hollow.

**1474** *Coventry Leet Bk.* 389 Þat the dryver of the Bochours Carre .. throwe his intrelles and oþer stuffe .. in myddes of þe pitte & not be þe sides. **1577** B. Googe *Heresbach's Husb.* IV. (1586) 173 In the bankes and sides of these Ponds, you must have Bushes and Creeke holes. **1611** Bible *1 Sam.* xxiv. 3 Dauid and his men remained in the sides of the caue. **1702** *Milit. & Sea Dict.* s.v., Sides of Horn-works .. and such-like Out-works .. are the Ramparts and Parapets that enclose them on the Right and Left from the Gorge to the Head. **1797** Mrs. Radcliffe *Italian* vi, Three sides of this were enclosed by lofty buildings lined with ranges of cloisters. **1857** Miller *Elem. Chem., Org.* vi. §2 (1862) 475 A mirror-like coating of reduced silver is formed on the sides of the vessel. **1868** Tennyson *Lucretius* 253 The very sides of the grave itself shall pass. **1878** T. Hardy *Ret. Native* v. ix, The sides of the pool were of masonry, to prevent the water from washing away the bank.

**8. a.** One or other of the two surfaces of a thing having little or no appreciable thickness; also, the outer or inner surface or aspect of a thing.

See also *right* and *wrong side* under these adjs., and cf. the combs. INSIDE, OUTSIDE.

**1382** Wyclif *Exod.* xxxii. 15 Berynge in hoond two tablis of testymonye wrytun on eithir side. **1562** J. Heywood *Prov. & Epigr.* (1867) 71, I know on which syde my bread is buttred. **1588** Shaks. *L.L.L.* v. ii. 8 A sheet of paper Writ on both sides the leafe. **1604** —— *Oth.* IV. ii. 146 Some such Squire he was That turn'd your wit, the seamy-side without. **1711** Swift *Jrnl. to Stella* 22 Nov., I'll say no more on this side the paper. **1826** Kirby & Spence *Entom.* III. 529 *note*, They are gratified to see that M. Latreille has adopted this term in the work quoted on the other side. **1895** *Bookman* Oct. 12/1 A small volume of some forty-seven pages, printed on one side only. **1899** Raymond *No Soul above Money* iii, He knew both sides of a penny, for all he looked so daft.

**b.** *spec.* (See quot.)

**1875** Knight *Dict. Mech.* 2172/1 *Side*, .. the surface on the right or dressed side of cloth.

**c.** In prov. phr. ***the other side of the coin*** (***penny***, etc.) = ***the reverse of the medal*** s.v. MEDAL *sb.* 3 b; ***the other side of the shield***: see SHIELD *sb.* 1 d.

**1904** Yeats *Let.* ? 20 Jan. (1954) III. 425 *The Shadowy Waters* .. is more of a ritual than a human story... *Cuchullain* or *The King's Threshold* are the other side of the halfpenny. *Ibid.* Apr. 433, I am reckless in mere speech that is not written. You are the other side of the penny, for you are admirably careful in speech. **1966** *Listener* 19 May 713/1 The social and psychological pressures are not different things but often just different sides of the same penny. **1975** M. Russell *Murder by Mile* ix. 92 Angus Hamilton's .. to address members and answer questions. He thought it might present an opportunity to put across the other side of the coin.

**d.** Each of the two grooved faces of a gramophone record. Also *slang*, a recording made on this; a record. In extended use, of tape recording. Cf. *flip side* s.v. FLIP *sb.*[2] 7.

**1936** *Rhythm* Apr. 28/1 American Brunswick, Columbia and Vocalion have a blanket contract with Irving Mills for so many sides a year. **1948** *N.Y. Age* 18 Dec. 2/6 We expect 'Skiffle Blues' to be one of our big sides in the coming weeks. **1950** *Down Beat* 14 July 11 (*heading*) Will the Louis sides on cylinder ever turn up? **1960** J. Baldwin *Another Country* (1962) II. iii. 310 'How about some sides?' .. Lorenzo put on something .. by the Modern Jazz Quartet. **1971** D. E. Westlake *I gave at Office* 133 There was some tape left. Tape three, side two, the one just before this. **1979** *Guardian* 9 June 12/7, I had to wait until side two for any bloom of Schubertian joy.

**9. a.** A page of a book or writing. *Obs.* or *arch.*

**1530** Palsgr. 270/1 Syde of a boke that is written, *pagee*. **1579** W. Fulke *Heskins's Parl.* 241 He rehearseth halfe a side of M. Iewels wordes. **1634** Sir T. Herbert *Trav.* 141, I will adde one side concerning Paradice, and then will goe on without digression. **1676** Marvell *Mr. Smirke* 14 One of his sides in *Quarto*, for Falshood, Insolence, and Absurdity contains a Book in *Folio*. **1742** Richardson *Pamela* III. 104 We thought you should have written a side upon that Subject at least. **1826** Lamb *Pop. Fallacies* ix, A man might blur ten sides of paper in attempting a defence of it.

**b.** *Tanning.* (See quot. 1885.)

**1763** *Ann. Reg.* 92 Georgia .. exports: 1602 sides of tanned leather. **1852** C. Morfit *Tanning & Currying* (1853) 23 The number of sides of sole leather inspected during the last five years. **1885** *Harper's Mag.* Jan. 274/2 After soaking, the hides are .. cut through the middle of the back to separate them into 'sides'.

**c.** *Theatr.* A page of typescript containing an actor's part and cue words (usu. *pl.*).

**1933** P. Godfrey *Back-Stage* iii. 37 An experienced actor, being offered a part, is unimpressed by the number of 'sides' it contains, a 'side' being a half-quarto sheet of typescript. **1963** 'E. McBain' *Ten plus One* (1964) vii. 73 'She had memorized all of her sides—' Richardson paused here to see whether or not anyone had caught his use of the professional term 'sides' .. —'in the first two nights of rehearsal.' **1976** R. James *House is Dark* xiii. 135 'Don't see why actors ever gave up sides... They're so much easier.' .. 'Haidee, it wasn't for the sake of the actors that they used sides. It was supposed to prevent actors from duplicating a hit script and going off with it on their own.'

**10.** An aspect or view of something immaterial. ***to look on*** (or *to*) ***the bright*** (or ***worst***, etc.) ***side***: see LOOK *v.* 18 d.

*c* **1449** Pecock *Repr.* v. vi. 514 If thilk gouernaunce be .. profitable to him in othere goostli sidis. **1657** Owen *Saints' Persev.* xv. Wks. 1851 XI. 539 It being the will of God to give us, as to his [David's] fall, his dark side and his sin to the full. **1840** Thirlwall *Greece* lvii. VII. 263 The future was not without its bright side. **1858** Carlyle *Fredk. Gt.* VIII. v. (1872) III. 44 His first aim is to find-out the ridiculous side of everyone. **1891** E. Peacock *N. Brendon* I. 139 The better side of his vulgar nature came out.

**III. 11. a.** Place or direction with reference to some central point; a point of the compass. (Cf. NORTH-, SOUTH-SIDE.) Also *fig.* (quot. 1838).

*c* **825** *Vesp. Psalter* xlvii. 3 On sidan norðdaeles [is] cestre cyninges ðes miclan. *c* **1205** Lay. 21774 Þer walleð of þan mæren a moniare siden .. sixti wateres. *c* **1290** *S. Eng. Leg.* I. 124 So þat respit was þar-of I-nome, and ech wende in his side. *a* **1400–50** *Alexander* 5021 Bot þi sire soile in na side see sall þou neuire. *c* **1420** *Sir Amadace* (Camden) xxxix, On summe side wille hit falle. Sum curtas mon ȝette may he fynde. **1648** Milton *Ps.* lxxx. 45 Her branches on the western side Down to the Sea she sent. **1697** Dampier *Voy.* 467 A Fire, with a few Boughs before it, set up on that side the wind was of. **1777** Watson *Philip II* (1839) 497 He found it necessary to approach the town on that side, on which there lay a wood or forest. **1784** Cowper *Task* v. 150 Lamps gracefully dispos'd, and of all hues, Illumin'd ev'ry side. **1838** Macaulay in Trevelyan (1876) II. vii. 9 On that side he multiplied his precautions, and set double watch.

**b.** In phrases ***on*** (†***of***) ***each*** or ***every side, on all sides***.

*c* **1205** Lay. 621 His ferde he sette on ælchere siden. **1382** Wyclif *Luke* xix. 43 Thei schulen make thee streyt on alle sydis. **1390** Gower *Conf.* I. 16 Tobroke is Cristes folde, Wherof the flock .. Devoured is on every side. **1440** *Promp. Parv.* 365/1 On evyrysyde, *undique, circumquaque*. **1513** Bradshaw *St. Werburge* II. 1060 Counnyng surgeans were sought vpon euery syde. **1582** Stanyhurst *Æneis* II. (Arb.) 53 Troytowne is fired of al sydes. **1617** Moryson *Itin.* I. 178 A most pleasant valley, compassed on all sides with mountaines. **1681** Dryden *Abs. & Achit.* 689 On each side bowing popularly low. **1686** tr. *Chardin's Coronat. Solyman* 38 Thus the Apartment is open of all sides. **1711** Addison *Spect.* No. 110 ¶2 The Ruins of the Abby are scattered up and down on every Side. **1831** Scott *Ct. Rob.* viii, Thanks to Heaven were returned on all sides.

**12. a.** One or other direction to either hand of an object, space, or imaginary line; the position, space, or area implied in this. † ***of a side***, on each side. ***the other side***: see OTHER *a.* 2 d (*a*).

*c* **1000** Ælfric *Hom.* I. 454 Ðeos ðridde India hæfð on anre sidan þeostru, and on oðere ðone grimlican garsecȝ. *a* **1340–** [see RIGHT *a.* 20]. **1382** Wyclif *Ezek.* xli. 19 A face of man .. of this syde, and a face of lyoun .. on the tother syde. *c* **1450** *Contin. Brut* II. 571 They stode on þe lifte syde; and al þat abode within the toun stode on þe right syde. **1500–20** Dunbar *Poems* xlvi. 12 Vndir this brench ran doun a revir bricht .. Quhair did, vpone the tothair syd, persew A nychtingall. **1613** Purchas *Pilgrimage* (1614) 51 Taurus divideth it in the middest: On the North side is that which is called Asia interior. **1644** Digby *Nat. Bodies* xxxi. §1, The strength .. of the two lights .. on this side, and on that side the point of concurse. **1678** Bunyan *Pilgr.* I. (1900) 144 Upon the bank of the River, on the other Side, they saw the two shining men again. **1701** Farquhar *Sir H. Wildair* I. i, The pinners are double ruffled with twelve plaits of a side. **1746** Francis tr. *Horace, Epist.* i. xvii. 73 He, who hears him, chaunts on t'other Side, With me your Bounty, ah! with me divide. **1781** Cowper *Hope* 374 Suppose the beam should dip on the wrong side. **1875** Knight *Dict. Mech.* 458/1 The American car has a gangway lengthwise of the car, the seats on each side reversible.

*fig.* **1641** in *Buccleuch MSS.* (Hist. MSS. Comm.) I. 288, I know he is fast riveted on that side, if the Commons give him not a jostle. **1722** De Foe *Plague* (1754) 16 But I had a farther Obligation laid on me on the same Side. **1819** Shelley *Peter Bell 3rd* Prol. 25 He who has O'er the grave been forced to pass To the other side.

**b.** In phrases ***on*** (†***of***) ***either*** or ***each side, on both sides***.

*c* **1205** Lay. 27242 Þa sænde heo a ba siden al þa men auoten. *a* **1300** *Cursor M.* 6263 Þe see on aiþer side þam stod Als walles tua, quils þai for yod. *a* **1400–50** *Alexander* 1520 He .. sammes þaim on aithire side with silken rapis. *c* **1480** *Little Child. Bk.* 66 in *Babees Bk.* 20 Whan þou etyst, gape not to wyde That þi mouth be sene on yche a syde. **1633** P. Fletcher *Purple Isl.* II. xxx, At that cave's mouth, twice sixteen porters stand, .. Of each side foure [etc.]. **1667** Milton *P.L.* II. 649 Before the Gates there sat On either side a formidable shape. **1823** Southey *Penins. War* I. 415 The altars on either side had their respective relics. **1867** W. L. Newman in *Quest. Reformed Parl.* 79 The mountain backbone, .. from which the streams flow down on either side.

**c.** *fig.* ***on the*** (adjective) ***side***, tending towards the condition or aspect described. Cf. *on the safe side* s.v. SAFE *a.* 9 c.

**1713** [see RIGHT *a.* 10 c]. *c* **1805** G. Colman in M. R. Booth *Eng. Plays of 19th Cent.* (1973) III. 69 It's prophesying on the sure side, to foretell a thing when it has happened. **1864** Trollope *Can You forgive Her?* I. xi. 90 He is just a shade too good... But it's a fault on the right side. **1923** A. J. Anderson *Soul Sifters* xxiv. 252 'Michelmore was always on the rough side!' he remarked aloud. **1952** A. J. Cronin *Adventures in Two Worlds* xii. 97 She was on the thin side .. and her liquid, brownish eyes were too large. **1974** A. Morice *Killing with Kindness* ii. 14 He was a bit on the tired side, but .. he's accustomed to long hours.

**d.** ***on this*** (or ***the other***) ***side***: with reference to the Atlantic Ocean. Cf. *this* (etc.) *side of the puddle* s.v. PUDDLE *sb.* 1 c. *colloq.* (chiefly *U.S.*).

**1884** *Naturalist's World* Sept. 155/2 Canadian Postal Science College .. is a society which has grown up very rapidly 'on the other side'. **1928** Wodehouse *Money for Nothing* vii. 129 There's dozens of people on the other side who'll buy it.

**13. a.** The space lying to either hand *of*, or in any direction from, a specified place, point, etc.

For fig. uses see also RIGHT *a.* 10 d and WRONG *a.*

**1382** Wyclif *Rev.* xxii. 2 In the mydle of the street of it, and on ech sijde of the flood [was] the tree of lijf. *c* **1400** Maundev. (1839) xxii. 234 And at o syde of the Emperours Table, sitten many Philosofres. **1462** *Cal. Anc. Rec. Dublin* (1889) 314 The gardeyn that ys on the north syd of the yat. *a* **1548** Hall *Chron., Hen. VIII*, 73 On the other hand or syde of the gate was set a pyller. **1593** Shaks. *2 Hen. VI*, II. i. 43 On the East side of the Groue. **1606** —— *Ant. & Cl.* III. ix. 1 Set we our Squadrons on yond side o' th' Hill. **1671** Milton *P.R.* IV. 33 A river, of whose banks On each side an Imperial City stood. **1782** Cowper *Gilpin* 138 And there he threw the wash about On both sides of the way. **1857** Miller *Elem. Chem., Org.* i. §3 (1862) 59 Oxidizing actions are in constant operation unperceived on every side of us. **1871** Freeman *Norm. Conq.* (1876) IV. 74 Of him we have heard in two widely different characters on different sides of the sea.

*fig.* **1599** SHAKS. *Much Ado* II. i. 327 [My heart] keepes on the windy side of Care. **1818** SCOTT *Hrt. Midl.* ix, She's not to be forgotten on this side of time. **1891** E. PEACOCK *N. Brendon* I. 8 She was on the less enviable side of fifty.

**b.** Const. without *of*, in such phrases as ***on this, that, the other, side*** (a place).

**1340** HAMPOLE *Pr. Consc.* 5415 þe devels on ilk syde þam sal stande. *a* **1400–50** *Alexander* 1200 All þe bestaill.. þat he mi3t se on any syde þe cite of Gadirs. **1432** *Rolls of Parlt.* IV. 410 No place elles where on þat syde þe See. **1523** LD. BERNERS *Froiss.* I. lxxxvi. 110 Than sir Aymery drewe his people alonge on the dykes within the barryers, and the archers redy on bothe sydes the way. **1560** DAUS tr. *Sleidane's Comm.* 188 b, Thre dayes Jorney on this syde Venise. **1651** R. CHILD in *Hartlib's Legacy* (1655) 23 Vines grow threescore miles on this side Paris. **1673** *Essex Papers* (Camden) I. 53 Since you are on that side y^e water. **1749** FIELDING *Tom Jones* VIII. xiii, On the other side the willows. **1771** GOLDSM. *Hist. Eng.* I. 339 The provinces were laid waste on each side his passage. **1827** SOUTHEY in *Corr. w. C. Bowles* (1881) 117 Had you been as much on this side London as you are beyond it, you might easily have met us there! **1887** LOWELL *Democracy* 46 This outburst of feeling on both sides the sea.

*fig.* **1676** WALTON *Angler* (ed. 5) xxi, There be as many miseries beyond riches, as on this side them. **1710** R. WARD *Life H. More* 234 There is nothing absolutely or completely Perfect on this side Heaven. **1711** ADDISON *Spect.* No. 40 ¶1 Good and Evil happen alike to all Men on this side the Grave. **1868** BROWNING *Ring & Bk.* VI. 143 That's all we may expect of man, this side The grave.

**c.** ***on this side*** (*of*), before (a specified date).

**1436** HEN. VI in *Hist. MSS. Comm., Var. Coll.* IV. 198 He that calleth hym Duc of Burgeyne disposyth hym.. on this side Estre nyxt to lay assege to oure toun of Caleys. **1472–3** *Rolls of Parlt.* VI. 4/2 The seid x^th part to be assessed .. a this syde the morn of the fest of the Purification. **1530–1** *Act 22 Hen. VIII*, c. 12 The seales aboue rehersed, shall bee made.. on this syde the feast of the Natiuitie of sayncte John Baptist nexte commynge. **1771** T. HULL *Sir W. Harrington* (1797) IV. 235 But all, I fear, wont be completed on this side Christmas. **1874** T. HARDY *Far fr. Mad. Crowd* lvii, He's not at hand, and won't be this side of eleven o'clock.

**d.** ***on this side*** (*of*), short of.

*c* **1449** PECOCK *Repr.* I. xiv. 78 The other is openest in suerte of likelihode or of probabilite a this side suerte. **1647** H. MORE *Poems* Pref., [He] hath attempted bravely, but yet methinks on this side of Mathematicall evidence. **1667** MILTON *P.L.* II. 101 We are at worst On this side nothing.

**e.** In *fig.* phr. ***the other side of the hill***, those aspects of a situation which are unknown at present. Also *transf.*, the latter part of life, and in *Mil.* contexts, the enemy position or activities.

**1852** DUKE OF WELLINGTON in *Croker Papers* (1884) III. xxviii. 275 We amused ourselves by guessing what sort of a country we should find at the other side of the hills we drove up... When I expressed surprise at some extraordinary good guesses he [*sc.* Croker] had made, he said, 'Why, I have spent all my life in trying *to guess what was at the other side of the hill*.' **1926** C. B. WATERLOW in H. Golding *Wonder Bk. of Motors* 12 It is not only what is on the other side of the hill that matters, but everything along the road. **1948** B. H. L. HART (*title*) The other side of the hill. **1957** C. SMITH *Case of Torches* i. 5, I had to go through a lot of badinage.. about .. how old I was getting and what it was like on the other side of the hill. **1960** G. MARTELLI *Agent Extraordinary* 15, I.. wish.. to express my gratitude.. to [the].. technical director of the flying bomb sites.. for allowing me a glimpse of the 'other side of the hill'. **1978** *Times* 30 Jan. 13/2 Mr Peyton.. began to argue for a revalued green pound... He .. correctly read what was on the other side of the hill (that is, the Government itself would soon have to revalue).

**14.** †**a.** ***on side***, to one side, aside. *Obs.*

**1375** BARBOUR *Bruce* XI. 344 On athir hand The tothir battalis suld be gangand Behynd, on syde a litell space. **1377** LANGL. *P. Pl.* B. XVII. 57 Feith had first si3te of hym, ac he flegh on syde. *c* **1400** *Laud Troy Bk.* 5848 Ector wiste him hurt he feled, He rod on-syde and him keled. *c* **1475** HENRYSON *Abbay Walk* 5 On caiss I kest on syd myne e, and saw þis writtin vpoun a wall. *a* **1548** HALL *Chron., Hen. VI*, 101 This battayl was sore foughten, for hope of life was set on side on euery parte. **1579** TOMSON *Calvin's Serm. Tim.* 350/2 What shall it auaile vs to start on side from the rule which hee hath giuen vs?

**b.** In various phrases denoting position, movement, or inclination away from a central line or point. Also *fig.*

**1586** A. DAY *Eng. Secretary* I. (1625) 23 Stately trees (some tops whereof the wind seemeth to wreath and turne at one side). **1588** *Marprel. Epist.* (Arb.) 43 Put your corner cap a litle nere a toe side. **1611** SHAKS. *Wint. T.* III. iii. 20 To me comes a creature, Sometimes her head on one side, some another. *a* **1688** BUNYAN *Israel's Hope Encouraged* Wks. 1855 I. 600 It would be too great a step to a side to treat of all those mercies. **1712** J. JAMES tr. *Le Blond's Gardening* 169 The middle Shoot.. is found.. to lean of one Side a little. **1782** *A. Monro's Compar. Anat.* (ed. 3) 126 From each side .. a bony bridge is produced backwards, and to a side. **1820** SHELLEY *Œd. Tyr.* II. ii. 76 Your Majesty In such a filthy business had better Stand on one side. **1827** CARLYLE *Germ. Rom.* II. 162 Happening sometime after to be standing with him by a side at the window. **1887** *Contemp. Rev.* Jan. 64 It must.. be understood that I place his private character entirely to one side.

**c.** *ellipt.* A side-dish, entrée.

**1848** THACKERAY *Van. Fair* xlii, If those sides, or *ontrys*, as she calls 'em, were'nt served yesterday, I'm d—d.

**d.** *Billiards.* Direction given to a ball by striking it at a point not directly in the middle.

**1873** BENNETT & CAVENDISH *Billiards* 125 In putting on side, all that has to be done is to strike the ball on the side instead of in the middle. **1901** *Q. Rev.* Apr. 483 The mysteries of 'side' began to perplex players.

**e.** ***on the side*** (orig. *U.S.*). (*a*) Served separately from the main dish.

**1884** *Bad Lands Cow Boy* (Little Missouri, Dakota Terr.) 7 Feb. 1/5 'Gimme that snake rare—milk gravy on the side,' was hallooed to the cook. **1916** *Literary Digest* 18 Mar. 766/3 'Beef stew and a cup of tea for me,' the new arrival said. 'Bossy in a bowl—boiled leaves on the side,' sang the waiter. **1975** D. LODGE *Changing Places* ii. 95 A club sandwich with french fries on the side.

(*b*) In addition; surreptitiously, without acknowledgement. (Freq. with connotation of dishonesty: illicitly; outside wedlock.)

**1893** *Congress. Rec.* 18 Dec. 360/1 He will have no pension attorney, for a silent partner, no relative doing business 'on the side' with that bureau. **1904** *N.Y. Times* 22 June 3 To attend the big fair and receive the entertainment of St. Louis on the side. **1927** *Daily News* 11 Mar. 2/2 Y' see, Bill's in the rag-and-bone trade and he does a bit [of receiving] on the side. Just anythink he can pick up. **1937** D. L. SAYERS *Zeal of thy House* II. 44 Pocketing commissions and that sort of thing? Doing little deals on the side? **1953** R. LEHMANN *Echoing Grove* IV. 226 An independent career-woman with a successful love life on the side. **1968** R. L. HUDSON *Grace is not Blue-eyed Blond* xi. 145 What would some of you say if I told you that I, as a married man, have had three women on the side? **1977** *Gay News* 24 Mar. 14/4 They may.. gear their expectations to include sexual contacts on the side.

(*c*) *spec.* in addition to one's regular or ordinary occupation; as a subsidiary source of income (also with occas. implication of irregularity).

**1898** *N.Y. Jrnl.* 26 Aug. 9/3 Samuel.. started an ice cream parlor, with cigars, tobacco and delicatessen on the side. **1915** WODEHOUSE *Something Fresh* iv. 107 'I'm not asking you to be a valet and nothing else.' 'You would want me to do some cooking and plain sewing on the side, perhaps?' **1928** S. LEWIS *Man who knew Coolidge* I. 13 I'd never made a peep about how maybe it'd be a good stunt for him to go out and maybe earn a little money on the side. **1945** *Reader's Digest* July 22/1 There is a good job teaching music theory .. lined up for him. And he is composing on the side. **1960** N. MARSH *False Scent* I. 29 I'm trying, on the side, to break out in a rash of serious writing. **1977** *Navy News* Dec. 1/3 We do not have information about how many people do jobs on the side, but I suspect that that practice is not confined to the Armed Forces.

**15. a.** A part *of* a place or thing lying in one or other direction from a centre or median line. Also without *of*.

**1428** *E. E. Wills* 81 To the wherk of the Ill of the toon side of the Cloistere in the Chirchehawe. *c* **1450** *St. Cuthbert* (Surtees) 883 To þe este syde in england, Of þis prouynce þou ert ordaynd. **1537** LAYTON in *Lett. Suppress. Monasteries* (Camden) 156 To ryde downe one syde [of the country] and to cum up the other. **1607** SHAKS. *Cor.* I. i. 48 The other side a'th City is risen: why stay we prating heere? **1686** BURNET *Trav.* III. (1750) 160 There are whole Sides of Streets without Inhabitants. **1706** E. WARD *Wooden World Diss.* (1708) 43 To keep his Grinders from mouldering.. he supplies both Sides with Grists at once. **1707** CHAMBERLAYNE *Pres. St. Gt. Brit.* III. xi. 386 One Side of it [a school] stands upon great Stone Pillars, in a large Court. **1834** K. H. DIGBY *Mores Cath.* V. v. 134 It was the custom .. for the men to be placed on one side of the church and the women on the other. **1886** PASCOE *Lond. of To-day* xl. (ed. 3) 342 This side, on an afternoon in the season, is a place where fashionable ladies meet half their fashionable acquaintance.

*fig.* **1562** J. HEYWOOD *Prov. & Epigr.* (1867) 74 Than were ye deafe, ye could not here on that syde. **1780** COWPER *Progr. Err.* 549 He has no hearing on the prudent side.

**b.** A region, district, or the inhabitants of this. Cf. COUNTRY-SIDE. Also succeeding or suffixed to the names of places or regions to form adj. or advb. phrases in the sense 'in (or on, towards) the area specified', esp. as STATESIDE *a.* and *adv.*

*a* **1400–50** *Alexander* 2115 All þe citis of þa sidis he sesis þam clene. *Ibid.* 3867. *c* **1410** *Sir Cleges* 87 He dwellyd be Kardyfe syde. *a* **1548** HALL *Chron., Hen. VIII*, 35 The next daye.. the forward passed a bridge.. into Flaunders syde & there lay. *a* **1623** BUCK *Rich. III*, I. (1646) 8 In Cumberland .., where he much resided,.. all that Northerne side generally honouring.. his Deportment. **1664** in Dircks *Life Marq. Worc.* (1865) xviii. 329 Not only at Gloucester Side, but all the way to the west. **1726** [see SOUTH-SIDE b]. **1743** W. STUKELEY *Palæogr. Sacra* 8 Rejoicing especially was the practice.. at public sacrifice, which they call *Panegyres*; a meeting of a side of a county, a province. **1810** SCOTT *Lady of L.* II. xxviii, The King's vindictive pride Boasts to have tamed the Border-side. **1898** N. MUNRO *J. Splendid* xxxii, He had been set on the slip by a wherry that had approached from Cowal side. **1924** E. M. FORSTER *Passage to India* xxxvii. 323 Jolly good poems, I'm getting published Bombay side. **1966** K. GILES *Provenance of Death* ii. 58 An Italian industrialist who does a lot of business Moscow-side.

**c.** A portion of a building set apart for particular persons or purposes. Also *fig.*

**1340** *Ayenb.* 151 þes yerþe is priour ine þe cloystre of þe zaule... Verst ine þe herte þet heþ tuo zides. **1482** in *Eng. Hist. Rev.* XXV. 121 The Chaunters of the Queres of the Bretherne and Systerne Sydes of Syone aforeseid. *c* **1529** in *Archaeol.* (1884) XLVII. 52 All the sayd ladyes bothe off the abbesse side and of the misericorde. **1904** GRIFFITHS *50 Yrs. Public Service* xiv. 205 The female 'side' of a prison gives more trouble to the authorities than the male.

**d.** ***side of bone***: (see quots.).

**1820** SCORESBY *Acc. Arctic Regions* I. 456 Each series, or 'side of bone', as the whalefishers term it, consists of upwards of 300 laminæ. **1836** *Uncle Philip's Convers. Whale Fish.* 23 There are in the mouth two 'sides of bone', as the whale fishers call them.

**e.** ***side-of-the-mouth*** adj. phr., spoken aside or (as) from the side of the mouth; delivered in a rough drawling manner; pungently demotic. Also, of the style of such utterances.

**1958** *Listener* 7 Aug. 203/1 Hoarse, side-of-the-mouth cracks of quite shattering pessimism. **1960** G. COULTER in M. T. Williams *Art of Jazz* 170 A racy, side-of-the-mouth idiom. **1974** *Publishers Weekly* 25 Mar. 52/3 Describes in blunt, side-of-the-mouth prose how he was given the 'contract' [to kill someone].

**f.** Also ***to laugh on the other, wrong side*** (***of one's face, mouth***): see LAUGH *v.* 1 b.

**16. a.** The line or limit, on either side, up to which something extends.

**1340** HAMPOLE *Pr. Consc.* 4280 His lawes sal pas and his powere Fra þe est syde til þe west, thurgh þe world here. *a* **1548** HALL *Chron., Edw. IV*, 233 b, The grate, which extended from the one syde of the bridge, even directly to the other. *c* **1655** MILTON *Sonn.* xxii. 12 My noble task, Of which all Europe talks from side to side. **1833** TENNYSON *Lady of Shalott* III. 43 The mirror crack'd from side to side. **1860** TYNDALL *Glac.* I. vii. 54, I followed the veins several times from side to side.

**b.** ***side-to-side*** adj. phr., characterized by movement from one side to the other.

**1934** in WEBSTER. **1950** J. DEMPSEY *Championship Fighting* xxii. 157 Motions that made my head an elusive side-to-side target. **1955** W. W. DENLINGER *Compl. Boston* I. 132 This formation [*sc.* bandy legs] results in a side-to-side gait. **1962** 'K. ORVIS' *Damned & Destroyed* ix. 59 Her head began a loose, disjointed, side-to-side swaying.

**IV. 17. a.** Used to denote the action, attitude, etc., of one person, or a set of persons, in relation to another or others.

*c* **1250** *Owl & Night.* 429 Euerich blisse him is vnwille.. Al so þu dost on þire syde. **1297** R. GLOUC. (Rolls) 3167 þe king ek in is syde is herte up on him caste. *c* **1350** *Will. Palerne* 1463 Sad seurte was sikered on boþe sides þanne, þat menskful mariage to make. **1362** LANGL. *P. Pl.* A. II. 36 Alle þis Riche Retenaunce.. Weoren bede to þe Bruytale on Bo two þe sydes. **1423** in *Hist. MSS. Comm., Var. Coll.* IV. 83 This endenture y made.. be thyxte the Dene & the Chapetre of Exter yn the on syde & the Mayer & the Comynce of Exeter.. yn the other syde. **1590** *Plain Perc.* 23, I am sure I shall not be pinchd on the parsons side. **1605** SHAKS. *Lear* V. i. 61 Hardly shall I carry out my side, Her husband being aliue. **1768** STERNE *Sent. Journ.*, *The Riddle*, I was sorry on my side for the occasion I had given him. **1822** SCOTT *Nigel* xiv, In declaring your trust in me, you have done what is honourable to yourself,.. and in no way undeserved on my side. **1848** THACKERAY *Van. Fair* lxvi, He was, on his side too, very anxious to see Mrs. Osborne. **1876** J. PARKER *Paracl.* I. x. 154 From the divine side there can be nothing sudden.

**b.** In phrases denoting a contrast between different views, considerations, facts, etc. (Cf. HAND *sb.* 32 i.)

*c* **1250** *Owl & Night.* 299 Alured seyde an oþer syde A word þat is isprunge wide. *a* **1300** *Cursor M.* 13038 On oþer side was hir ful wa, If sco suld part king herod fra. **1390** GOWER *Conf.* I. 122, I.. preie yow That ye wole axe on other side If [etc.]. **1538** STARKEY *England* I. iii. 70 We may.. a the one syde to stretly juge.. the hole mater,.. or els, of the other syde [etc.]. **1581** PETTIE *Guazzo's Civ. Conv.* II. (1586) 61 But on the other side, he must not use superfluous words. **1626** BACON *Sylva* §902 Men are to be Admonished, on the other side, that [etc.]. **1725** tr. *Dupin's Eccl. Hist. 17th C.* II. 67 As on the one side, Reason discovers it to be fit, that Man should be Immortal; so on the other side [etc.]. **1732** BERKELEY *Alciphr.* III. § 1 After a nice inquiry, and balancing on both sides.

†**c.** ***in other sides***, in other respects. ***upon the side of***, with regard to. *Obs.*

*c* **1340** HAMPOLE *Prose Tr.* 41 Or ells we er noghte disposede by clennes of lyffynge in oþer sydis for to ressayue his grace. **1390** GOWER *Conf.* I. 330 Mi fader, upon loves side Mi conscience I woll noght hyde.

**d.** One of the two alternative views which may be taken of a question, problem, argument, etc. Also *transf.* in collective sense (quot. 1812).

**1597** SHAKS. *Lover's Compl.* 113 But quickly on this side the verdict went. **1711** SHAFTSB. *Charac.* II. iv. (1714) II. 305 One of those timorous Arguers.. so intent in upholding their own side of the Argument. **1782** PRIESTLEY *Corrupt. Chr.* I. III. 305 Much was written on both sides of the question. **1812** L. HUNT in *Examiner* 31 Aug. 547/2 Public dinners given by any side of a question. **1884** *Times* (weekly ed.) 19 Sept. 7/3, I am sure that there are two sides to the question.

**e.** A division of a school devoted to a particular class of studies. (Cf. MODERN *a.* 2 e.)

**1884** *Jrnl. Educ.* 1 Sept. 348/2 Modern sides have grown and flourished. *Ibid.*, Latin and Greek on the Classical side. **1890** *Spectator* 13 Dec. 860/2 Efforts to expand the 'modern side', as they call it in English public schools.

**18. a.** The position or interests of one person, party, etc., in contrast to that of an opposing one. Chiefly in phr. *on (one's) side*. Prov. phr. ***on the side of the angels***: in favour of a spiritual interpretation (of human nature); more loosely, on the side of right despite the risk of unpopularity.

*a* **1300** *Cursor M.* 7547 Godd es euer on rightwis side, Werraiand again wrangwis pride. *c* **1380** WYCLIF *Sel. Wks.* I. 124 He þat is on Goddis syde, he heeriþ Goddis wordis. **1445** in *Anglia* XXVIII. 256 The parlement pierys.. Seyen the duke of yorke hath god vpon his side. *c* **1500** *Melusine* 29 Your enemys ben not here, and knowe you, fayre sire, that I am of your party or syde? **1560** DAUS tr. *Sleidane's Comm.* 442 b, Therefore thought they now, or els never, y^t God was on theyr side. **1617** MORYSON *Itin.* II. 141 To the end that the Spaniards might see the meere Irish served on our side. **1668** LADY CHAWORTH in *12th Rep. Hist. MSS. Comm.* App. V. 10 Mr. Ho.. deserves a better fate than to be ever of the loosing side. **1714** R. FIDDES *Pract. Disc.* II. 194 The multitude.. will always declare on the side of fortune. **1778** MISS BURNEY *Evelina* xxxii, He's the most impertinentest person in the world, and isn't never of my side. **1849** MACAULAY *Hist. Eng.* vi. II. 51 All the influence of Barillon was employed on the other side. **1864** DISRAELI *Church Policy* 26 Is man an ape or an angel?.. I am on the side of the angels. **1894** H. DRUMMOND *Ascent Man* 434 All Nature is on the side of the man who tries to rise. **1926** *Punch* 22 Dec. 700/1 Miss Marguerite Williams.. is so firmly posted on the side of the angels that I can forgive her if she occasionally seems rather to force the note. **1941** A. L. ROWSE *Tudor Cornwall* ii. 52 Mr. Tawney tells us..that 'their silence was the taciturnity of men, not the speechlessness of dumb beasts'. Though that may a little be questioned, no doubt he is on the side of the angels. **1956** G. H. VALLINS *Pattern of Eng.* vii. 171 'Different from' reminds the reader that whatever other men have done.., Fowler himself is on the side of the angels. **1979** 'C. AIRD' *Some die Eloquent* vii. 99 He had always in any case been on the side of the angels anyway. Apes were less appealing.

**b.** In phr. ***to take a*** (or ***one's***) ***side, take sides.*** Also † ***to hold side*** (with one).

*c* **1489** CAXTON *Sonnes of Aymon* ix. 238 Nevertheles he came, and helde syde wyth his broder. **1700** DRYDEN *Pal. & Arc.* III. 570 The nicest eye could no distinction make, Where lay the advantage, or what side to take. **1719** DE FOE *Crusoe* I. (Globe) 249 He would take my Side to the last drop of his Blood. **1823** KEBLE *Serm.* ii. (1848) 38 Careful always to take the safe side in practice. **1877** SPURGEON *Serm.* XXIII. 398 Weak-minded people who cannot take sides with a persecuted truth. **1888** BURGON *Lives 12 Gd. Men* II. xi. 317 Every resident of mark found himself in a measure compelled to take a side.

**19.** Kinship or descent through father or mother.

*c* **1400** MAUNDEV. (Roxb.) xxv. 120 Half sisters of þer fader syde wedd þai, bot noȝt of þer moder syde. **1442** *Rolls of Parlt.* V. 45/1 Englissh of his Moder side,..and aparte Englissh on his Fader side. *a* **1547** SURREY *Æneid* IV. 331 From his graundfather by the mothers side Cillenes child so came. **1653** H. COGAN tr. *Pinto's Trav.* xxix. 113 Peradventure a kinswoman to one of you, by his side that begot me in this miserable exile. **1710** STEELE *Tatler* No. 132 ¶8 He traced up his Descent on both Sides for several Generations. **1837** LOCKHART *Scott* I. ii. 61 As far as they could be followed, either on the paternal or maternal side. **1847** C. BRONTË *J. Eyre* xi, To be sure I am distantly related to the Rochesters by the mother's side.

**20. a.** One of the parties in a transaction, battle, or debate; a political party; a faction.

In phrases with *on* (as ***on either side***) the sense may approach that of 12b and 17.

**1375** BARBOUR *Bruce* II. 346 On athir syd thus war thai yhar, And till assemble all redy war. *c* **1400** *Destr. Troy* 9680 Aither syde, after sun, soght to þere holde. **1473** *Rental Bk. Cupar-Angus* (1879) I. 175 The pairtyng of the Grange forsade with the consent of bath the sydis wes made at Martymes. **1560** DAUS tr. *Sleidane's Comm.* 100b, How obstinate the Romishe syde was in the convocation at Auspurge. **1591** SAVILE *Tacitus, Hist.* II. xciii. 108 In trueth by his comming the side was reuiued. *a* **1639** W. WHATELEY *Prototypes* I. xx. (1640) 207 The Conquering side is often more miserable by sinning than the conquered by slaughter or captivity. **1676** LADY CHAWORTH in *12th Rep. Hist. MSS. Comm.* App. V. 34, 5000 of each side killed on the place. **1726** *Wodrow's Corr.* (1843) III. 249 A certain side are highly disappointed. **1823** SOUTHEY *Hist. Penins. War* I. 464 The loss on either side, in this pursuit, appears not to have been great. **1888** BRYCE *Amer. Commw.* II. li. 284 A general battle, in which each side feels that it cannot allow any odds to the other.

**b.** One of the parties in an athletic or sporting contest or game of skill.

**1698** LASSELS *Italy* I. 140 That side which throws the ballon over the rails of the other side wins the day. **1716** *Lond. Gaz.* No. 5536/4 There will..be 31 Cocks shewed of a side. **1737** in Waghorn *Cricket Scores* (1899) 17 Kent side went in first and got 99 notches, then Surrey side went in and got 31. **1837** HOOD *Agric. Distr.* i, Which side had won the cricket match. **1862** *Cornhill Mag.* Sept. 378 'We'll play sides, of course', said Lily. **1898** J. A. GIBBS *Cotswold Village* xi. 230 The rest of our team included the jovial miller;..the village curate, who captained the side..; one or two farmers; [etc.]. **1947** N. CARDUS *Autobiogr.* II. ii. 194 A boy fixes figures painted on square bits of tin—just the total of the batting side, the fall of the wickets, and the score of the last man out. **1977** C. MARTIN-JENKINS *Jubilee Tests* II. iv. 87 England's only difference from their Centenary Test side was the replacement of Fletcher by Barlow.

**c.** (so many)-***a-side***, indicating the number of players that may compose a team on the field of play. Usu. *attrib.* of a sport or match, as ***five-a-side football***, etc. Cf. SEVEN *a.* 2g.

**1900** [see SEVEN *a.* 2g]. **1926** *Times* 12 Apr. 6/5 The following are the results of yesterday's matches in the Seven-a-side Tournament. **1932** *Times Lit. Suppl.* 30 June 484/2 It is now over a century since it [*sc.* shinty] was played, seventy-five or so a-side. **1951** *Sport* 27 Apr.–3 May 4/3 A five-a-side football match is being played between Glasgow's Celtic and Rangers. **1973** J. M. WHITE *Garden Game* 104 We do sanction two-a-side encounters from time to time, or even three-a-side. **1978** *Cornish Guardian* 27 Apr. 13 At a Cub Scout's six-a-side football competition.. Mrs. M. Dean..presented the winners' shield.

**d.** ***to let the side down***: see LET *v.*[1] 32b.

**21.** † **a.** One of the two divisions of a choir. ***side for side, on sides***, alternately. *Obs.*

**1519** HORMAN *Vulg.* 11b, The quere syngeth syde for syde. **1583** FOXE *A. & M.* 1405/2 The Psalmes should be sung on sides, the one side of the quier singing one verse, the other another.

**b.** In Cambridge University, the body of students under the supervision of a particular tutor in a college.

**1852** BRISTED *Five Yrs. Eng. Univ.* 11 A large college has usually two Tutors,..and the students are equally divided among them—on their sides the phrase is. **1859** FARRAR *J. Home* v, Mr. Grayson, the tutor on whose 'side' he was entered. **1882** J. W. CLARK in *Old Friends at Cambr.* (1900) 40 Tutor of one of the three *sides*, as they were called, into which Trinity College was then divided.

**V.** *attrib.* and *Comb.*

**22.** Attrib. in sense 1, as ***side-cover, -fellow, -mate, -sore, -stitch.***

**1611** SHAKS. *Temp.* I. ii. 326 Thou shalt haue cramps, Side-stitches, that shall pen thy breath vp. **1636** BRATHWAIT *Rom. Emp.* 49 Envy (which is alwayes the side-mate of vertue) repined. **1690** C. NESSE *Hist. O. & N. Test.* I. 34 A collateral companion or side-fellow, or yoke-fellow. **1826** KIRBY & SP. *Entomol.* III. xxxv. 598 The *epipleura* or side-cover..that covers the sides of the body. **1898** *Allbutt's Syst. Med.* V. 346 The name Pleurisy.., side-sore of Early English.

**23. a.** Attrib., denoting 'situated or lying towards or at the side', as ***side-aisle, -altar, -bench, -chancel, -channel, -cut, -drain, -entrance, -gate, outlet, -path, turning, ward, -window, -yard***, etc.

**1711** G. HICKES *Two Treat. Chr. Priesth.* (1847) I. 322 Such tables may be set up in any *side aisle on either side of the chancel. **1858** HAWTHORNE *Fr. & It. Jrnls.* (1872) I. 6 Here in the recess of every arch of the side-aisles..there was a chapel. **1542** in Legg *Clerk's-bk.* (1903) App. VIII. 92 Except the Curatt say masse at a *side awter. **1859** JEPHSON *Brittany* x. 166 Among the side-altars I observed one dedicated to Saint Anne. *c* **1350** *Will. Palerne* 4565 þe real rinkes..at þe heiȝe dese, & alle oþer afterward on þe *side benches. *c* **1440** *Promp. Parv.* 455/1 Sydebynche.., *subsellium*. **1535** COVERD. *Ezek.* xli. 9 The foundacion of the *syde chambres was a meterodde (that is sixe cubites) brode. **1571** in Legg *Clerk's-bk.* (1903) App. IV. 73 The parishe shall have for breakinge the grownd for a pyt, in the *side chanselles x s. **1838** *Civil Eng. & Arch. Jrnl.* I. 97/2 The sides [of the roadway], where the water is received into the gutters, or *side channels. **1679–88** *Secr. Serv. Money Chas. & Jas.* (Camden) 155 The carving work of the tabernacle and the degrees in the *side chappell at Whitehall. **1866** GEO. ELIOT *F. Holt* (1868) 40 The space of a large side-chapel was taken up by the tombs of the Debarrys. **1805** ALLNUTT *Navig. Thames* 24 The Number of *Side-cuts, Pound-locks, and Weirs, that may be required. **1838** *Civil Eng. & Arch. Jrnl.* I. 97 Ditches termed open *side drains, are made parallel to the axis of the road. **1907** *Daily Mail Year Bk.* 74/2 In turn the prevailing form of body has been the..*side-entrance phaeton, and the landaulet and limousine. **1926** W. W. JACOBS *Sea Whispers* v. 113 To leave by the side-entrance was the best way of avoiding trouble. **1976** *Northumberland Gaz.* 26 Nov. 18/1 (Advt.), Hall, sitting room,..side entrance, porch. **1814** *Selby & M. Weighton Road Act* ii. 5 When any new *side gate or side gates shall be erected. **1601** HOLLAND *Pliny* II. 482 In his time..men began at Rome to bestow siluer vpon their cupboords and *side liuery tables. **1967** *Gloss. Sanitation Terms* (*B.S.I.*) 10 **Side outlet tee*, a tee which incorporates an additional branch at 90° both to the main pipe and to the leg of the tee. **1972** L. M. HARRIS *Introd. Deepwater Floating Drilling Operations* x. 98 The subsea blowout-preventer stack..should have two side outlets for the choke and kill-line connections. **1831** SCOTT *Ct. Rob.* iii, *Side passages opened into it. **1854** DICKENS *Hard Times* II. xii. 250 Indifferent to the rain,..she struck into a *side-path parallel with the ride. **1897** *Cath. Mag.* Oct. 246 A side-path which opened out into a sun-baked space. **1924** R. S. HICHENS *After Verdict* II. vii. 181 She's always in the wholesome centre... No false steps into side-paths for her. **1859** *Habits of Gd. Society* Pref., Two *side-pavements and a very bad road. **1535** COVERD. *Judges* xvi. 3 But Samson..toke holde on both yᵉ *syde portes of yᵉ gate of the cite. **1575** *Appius & Virginia* in Hazl. *Dodsley* IV. 136 And at Simkin's *side-ridge my lord stood talking. **1844** H. STEPHENS *Bk. Farm* II. 404 The dung-hill should be placed on a head-ridge or side-ridge of the field. **1842** BORROW *Bible in Spain* ii, Our repast ..we ate in a little *side room with a mud floor. **1711** STEELE *Spect.* No. 14 ¶15 At the Hay-Market the Undertakers forgetting to change their *Side-scenes. **1850** THACKERAY *Pendennis* iv, He watched her at the side-scene—where she stood waiting to come on the stage. **1617** MORYSON *Itin.* I. 273 The rest of the *side streetes and allies being of poore building. **1894** HALL CAINE *Manxman* V. xxii, Philip turned into a side street. **1775** *Ann. Reg.* I. 117, 13 culverts, 8 *side trunks, and 4 weirs. **1946** *Law Rep.* 5 Oct. 334 She was executing a manoeuvre of turning from the near side into a *side turning on her off-side. **1965** M. SPARK *Mandelbaum Gate* iii. 54 He dodged down a side-turning into the shop of an Arab dealer. **1869** TOZER *Highl. Turkey* I. 299 At last we struck up a *side valley. **1968** M. ALLINGHAM *Cargo of Eagles* iii. 42 She shared a *side ward..with two other old ladies. **1535** COVERDALE *Ezek.* xl. 16 The chambers and their pilers within, rounde aboute vnto yᵉ dore, had *syde wyndowes. **1851** MANTELL *Petrifactions* i. 7 The rooms are lighted by side-windows, instead of by sky-lights. **1959** M. SUMMERTON *Small Wilderness* x. 131, I rolled down the side window. Instantly the car was hazed with incoming fog. **1976** *Derbyshire Times* (Peak ed.) 3 Sept. 6/2 The youth admitted kicking the side window of the car twice. **1879** W. WHITMAN *Daybooks, & Notebooks* (1978) I. 139 The window where I sit..opens on a spacious *side-yard. **1979** *Kingston* (Ontario) *Whig-Standard* 29 Mar. 21/2 Narrow side yards could block fire trucks.

**b.** Denoting 'situated, placed, or fixed at or on the side of something', as ***side armour, -band, -beam, -bolt, -chest, -crust***, etc.

A number of technical combs. of this kind are fully explained in Knight *Dict. Mech.* (1875 and 1884).

**1883** *Whitaker's Alm.* 445/2 One iron-clad.., 9-in. *side armour. **1889** WELCH *Naval Archit.* 141 Ships provided with thick side armour are known as armoured vessels. **1805** DICKSON *Pract. Agric.* I. Pl. xxix, This is put across the ends of them lengthways, so as to form a *side band. **1611** COTGR., *Iumelles*, the cheekes, or *side-beames of a presse. **1688** HOLME *Armoury* III. 306 The several parts of a Bit... The *Side Bolts. **1850** R. G. CUMMING *Hunter's Life S. Afr.* (ed. 2) I. 23 Along the sides of the waggon, and outside it, are two longer and narrower chests called *side-chests... The side-chests are very convenient for holding tools. **1780** *Mirror* No. 17 It had..battlements like the *side-crust of a Christmas goose-pye. **1814** SCOTT *Wav.* xxxv, The well-powdered ears which appeared beneath his neat military *side-curls. **1821** —— *Kenilw.* vi, The cushions, *side-curtains, and the very foot-cloth. **1912** *Motor Manual* (ed. 14) iv. 161 The only car for such weather conditions is a covered one, either one with a Cape cart hood with side curtains well down,..or the more complete enclosure of limousine or landaulet. **1980** L. LEWIS *Private Life of Country House* iii. 35 We bought a secondhand T model Ford... It..had a hood and talc side-curtains. *c* **1475** *Pict. Voc.* in Wr.-Wülcker 777 *Hoc calatrale*, a *sydedocer. **1862** *Chambers's Encycl.* IV. 349/1 *Side-fishes are long pieces of timber dove-tailed on the opposite sides of a made mast. **1742** MRS. DELANY *Life & Corr.* (1861) II. 185 Order him to send me down a very good coach and four horses with *side-glasses. **1861** DICKENS *Gt. Expect.* xxx, He pulled up his shirt-collar, twined his *side-hair. **1591** PERCIVALL *Sp. Dict.*, *Azicates de espuelas*, the *side irons of spurs, *Calcarium costæ*. **1889** GRETTON *Memory's Harkback* 116 The pace..was..quite enough to bid a nervous traveller hold hard by the side-iron. **1863** A. YOUNG *Naut. Dict.* 217 *Side-Keelsons, are additional keelsons laid on the floors, one on each side of the main keelson, to afford additional strength and stability. **1728** R. MORRIS *Ess. Anc. Archit.* 78 If the Key[stone] be double, the *Side-Key is ½ of the Width. **1942** *Side parting [see PIPE *sb.*[1] 1c]. **1982** D. PHILLIPS *Coconut Kiss* v. 43 Grace asked if she could do her hair with a side parting and a slide. **1881** GREENER *Gun* 262 With a strong hand turn-screw turn out the *side-pins, and remove the locks and hammers together. **1768–74** TUCKER *Lt. Nat.* (1834) I. 513 To take care that this stone lies firm upon solid ground, and..do not indeed take its support from some *side-props. **1856** 'STONEHENGE' *Brit. Rural Sports* 347/1 He [a colt] is led about by the cavesson,..without any *side-reins being attached. **1846** A. YOUNG *Naut. Dict.* 306 The Feed-Pump..is also worked by *side-rods. *c* **1860** H. STUART *Seaman's Catech.* 12 Who attends the *side scale? The right rear-man. **1867** SMYTH *Sailor's Word-bk.* 625 *Side-scale*, a simple graduation..for the quick elevation or depression of the guns. **1513** DOUGLAS *Æneid* I. iii. 49 The storme ourset, raif ruvis and *syde semis. **1844** *Regul. & Ord. Army* 154 Top of Front, from Side-Seam to Side-Seam (when Buttoned), 13 Inches. **1876** *Clin. Soc. Trans.* IX. 73, I then applied a well-padded *side-splint with foot-piece to the inner side of the leg. **1805** R. W. DICKSON *Pract. Agric.* I. 36 The *side standards, by being brought nearer to the perpendicular situation, are enabled to sustain considerably more weight. **1827** SIR H. STEUART *Planter's G.* (1828) 260 The two *Side-Stays..are made as short as possible, in order to prevent interference with the branches. **1846** HOLTZAPFFEL *Turning* II. 703 The sawpit..has two stout timbers running the whole length, called *side strakes. **1754** BARTLET *Farriery* 356 A is a pad, to which is fastened a circingle B. CC two *side straps, one on each side the horse. **1802** JAMES *Milit. Dict.*, *Side-straps*, in a field carriage, are flat iron bands which go round the side-pieces. **1445–6** *Durh. Acc. Rolls* (Surtees) 630 Pro..x paribus de *Sydtrace ad viij *d.* **1794** *Rigging & Seamanship* 10 **Side-trees*, the lower main pieces of a made-mast. *c* **1860** H. STUART *Seaman's Catech.* 73 Two side trees, one on each side, and dowelled and bolted to the spindle. **1523** FITZHERB. *Husb.* §4 The dryuinge of his *syde-wedges, forewedge, and hele-wedge. **1867** *Amer. Naturalist* Aug. 287 Their ears are often tufted, and one species, at least, has '*side-whiskers' formed by the true fur, in addition to the labial bristles which ordinarily receive this name. **1888** FERGUS HUME *Mme. Midas* I. ii, Heavy side whiskers and moustache.

**c.** Denoting 'growing out to the side', as ***side-bough, -branch, -growth, -spray***, etc. See also SIDE-SHOOT.

**1707** MORTIMER *Husb.* (1721) II. 29, I am rather for cutting only of the *Side-boughs, than heading of them. *Ibid.* 73 If you would not have a Tree put forth *side-Branches, prune them up in February. **1880** C. R. MARKHAM *Peruv. Bark* 80 A rapidly rising, slender, tall stem, devoid of side branches. **1868** *Rep. U.S. Comm. Agric.* (1869) 256 Trimming off such straggling *side growth as may be in the way of the workmen. **1864** HIBBERD *Rose Bk.* 89 They will be likely to throw out a good deal of *side-spray that will soon cause the trees to be as crowded as before. **1796** W. H. MARSHALL *Midl. Co.* (ed. 2) II. 387 *Toes* or **sidespurns*, the spreading roots of trees.

**24. a.** 'Directed or tending sideways, exerted or taking effect laterally, indirect,' etc., as ***side-beam, -blow, -course, -drawing, -eye, -flash, -glimpse, -jump***, etc.

**1935** *Discovery* Nov. 341 (*caption*) The advantages of a *side-beam:..the beam can be followed as it strikes the objects bordering a country road. **1978** R. V. JONES *Most Secret War* xx. 169 If another aircraft flew down one of the side beams, the result should be a second line intersecting with the first at the exact location of the station. **1692** BENTLEY *Boyle Serm.* 230 What natural agent could..impell them so strongly with a transverse *side-blow. **1893** F. ADAMS *New Egypt* 88 The natural trend of the *side-course of the river is from the east to the west. **1884** W. S. B. MCLAREN *Spinning* 220 The sliver is drawn off by *side-drawing. **1922** JOYCE *Ulysses* 48 A *side-eye at my Hamlet hat. **1958** J. KEROUAC *On Road* 189 Looking at me with the same wary insolent side-eye. **1889** RUSKIN *Præterita* III. 96 It was impossible for him to speak to any one he cared for, without some *side-flash of witty compliment. **1890** 'MARK TWAIN' *Let.* 11 Feb. in J. Brown *Lett.* (1912) 452 The charm of the painter is so strong that one can't keep his entire attention on the developing portrait, but must steal *side-glimpses of the artist. **1869** *Routledge's Ev. Boy's Ann.* 386 As a breaker approaches, meet it by a *side jump. **1828** *Life Planter Jamaica* 345 Wishing..to procure, by *side means, information of who he was. *a* **1704** LOCKE (J.), The parts of water..will, by a *side motion, be easily removed. **1768–74** TUCKER *Lt. Nat.* (1834) I. 42 While we work, or study, or converse, we often change our posture, turn our eyes, and make many side motions having no connexion with the purpose we are about. **1856** 'STONEHENGE' *Brit. Rur. Sports* 363/2 The saddle..being small and light will not bear much *side-pull. **1863** HAWTHORNE *Our Old Home* (1879) 119 Illuminated by some *side-ray from himself. **1820** SCOTT *Abbot* xxix, The Lady of Lochleven, at whom this *side-shaft was lanched. **1859** G. MEREDITH *R. Feverel* xvi, With another *side shot at the confidential clerk. **1863** W. C. BALDWIN *Afr. Hunting* iii. 80, I determined on firing at his knee, if I could not get a side-shot between the ear and the eye. **1760–72** H. BROOKE *Fool of Qual.* (1809) III. 116 He made a *side-stroke at me. **1873** BENNETT & CAVENDISH *Billiards* 9 The tip being once added to the cue, side-stroke soon followed as a matter of course. **1781** COWPER *Retirement* 690 To..stab religion with a sly *side-thrust. **1821** LOCKHART *Valerino* I. xii. 254 Your side-thrust is the only one I would lay an as upon. **1855** *Ecclesiologist* XVI. 338 The lofty and unstable outer walls of the wide nave would be forced apart by the side-thrust of the vaulting. **1894** H. SPEIGHT *Nidderdale* 381 A protective wall, preventing a destructive *side-wash, has been built. **1597** J. KING *On Jonas* (1599) 257 It is his will by obliquity, a *side-will, vnproper, vndirect.

**b.** 'Seen from, looking towards, the side,' as ***side-elevation, -front***. Also SIDE-VIEW.

**1775** SHERIDAN *Rivals* IV. ii, I wish the lady would favour us with something more than a side-front. **1853** URE *Dict. Arts* (ed. 4) II. 509 Fig. 1193. represents this twin furnace in a side elevation.

**c.** 'Spoken aside or in an undertone,' as ***side-remark, soliloquy, speech, -talk***.

*a* **1910** 'MARK TWAIN' *What is Man?* in *Harper's Mag.* Oct. 673/1 He was treated to many side remarks by his fellows. **1968** *Economist* 3 Feb. 13/1 Formal statistical tables .., so that everybody can tell what each Wilsonian side-remark is meant to mean. **1842** LOVER *Handy Andy* xxxiv, In a side soliloquy. **1809** MALKIN *Gil Blas* XII. iii. ¶7 This side speech explained to me the plot. **1917** G. S. GORDON *Let.* 14 Feb. (1943) 70 This is all side-talk compared with the great thing that has happened to you. **1931** B. BROWN *Talking Pictures* x. 250 The need for silence in the studio is increased, since side talk, coughs, etc., are liable to be picked up.

**d.** 'Apart from the main point or course of anything, subsidiary,' as ***side-conflict, -result***. See also SIDE-EFFECT, -ISSUE.

**1878** BOSW. SMITH *Carthage* 291 Throughout these first six years..a side conflict was raging in Spain. **1894** *Westm. Gaz.* 15 Nov. 2/1 Such mere side-results as an influx of berry-pickers from London and Liverpool into the holly-growing districts.

**25.** Objective and parasynthetic, as ***side-convulsing, -piercing, -shaking; side-mouthed, -sighted, -spotted, -striped***.

**1605** SHAKS. *Lear* IV. vi. 85 O thou side-piercing sight! **1751** SMOLLETT *Per. Pic.* xciii, Various distortions and side-shakings. **1818** SHELLEY *Rosalind* 1065 Forcing the point of a barbed dart Into its side-convulsing heart. **1861** SWINBURNE *Queen Mother* III. i, Cunning little heads And side-mouthed puppets quaintly cut on it. **1879** *Man. Artill. Exerc.* 201 The 80-pr. is side-sighted, and has drop trunnion sights. **1899** W. T. GREENE *Cage-Birds* 60 The Diamond Sparrow..is a pretty bird, and is also called the Side-spotted Finch. **1899** F. V. KIRBY *Sport E.C. Africa* 324 Side-striped Jackal (*Canis adustus*).

**26.** Forming combs. used attributively, as ***side-spring boot***, etc. (See also *side-wheel* in 27.)

**1832** J. RENNIE *Consp. Butterfl. & Moths* 178 The Side Spot Triangle. **1862** *Illustr. Catal. Internat. Exhib., Brit.* II. No. 4962, The ordinary side-spring boots. **1884** W. S. B. MCLAREN *Spinning* (ed. 2) 218 The side-drawing method secures a very large amount of doubling. **1892** GREENER *Breech Loader* 17 The side-lever snap-action gun. **1898** *Daily News* 10 May 6/2 A big thousand ton side-paddle frigate. **1907** *Yesterday's Shopping* (1969) 629/2 Plain quality side-lock hammerless guns. **1955** R. CHURCHILL *Game Shooting* IV. ii. 193 Apart from the action of fully-automatic guns, all game guns are built either with what is called the sidelock action or the box lock.

**27.** Special combs., as **side action** *Pharm.* = SIDE EFFECT 2; **side-axe**, an axe with a handle slightly bent to one side; **side band** *Telecommunication*, a band of frequencies above or below a carrier frequency, within which lie the frequencies produced by modulation of the carrier; **side-basset** (see quot. 1860); **side-bet**, a bet of one side against another; **side-bit**, a part of a shirt; **side boy** (see quot. 1846); **side-burn** [alteration of BURNSIDE, after *side-hair*, etc.], orig. *U.S.*, a short side-whisker; usu. *pl.*; hence **side-burned** *a.*; **side-burthen** (see quot.); **side chair**, an upright wooden chair without arms; **side circuit** *Teleph.* (see quot. 1916); **side counter-timber**, *Naut.* (see quot.); **side-cousin**, ? one not quite a cousin; **side cut** *Oil Industry* = *side stream* (*b*) below; **side-cutting** (see quot.); **side-drawn** *a.*, sketched from the side; **side drift** *Mining*, etc., a horizontal tunnel leading off the main passage (cf. DRIFT *sb.* 15); **side-drum**, a drum which is slung at the side of the performer; also in *Jazz*, etc.: a drum (usu. part of a set) placed on a stand beside the performer; **side-entry**, (*a*) a side-entrance; an area outside the side-door of a house; (*b*) *Bridge*, a card providing access to a hand in a suit other than trumps (cf. ENTRY 1 f); **side-file** (see quot.); **side-filister**, a form of plane; **side-forming** (see quots.); **side frequency** *Telecommunication*, a particular frequency in a side band, equal, in the case of amplitude modulation, to the carrier frequency plus or minus a particular modulating frequency; **side gallery**, either of the two galleries along the side of the debating chamber of the House of Commons, divided to seat Members and others; †**side-glass** *v.*, ? to ogle through the side-glass of a coach; **side-grafting** (see quot.); †**side-half**: *on side-half*, apart; *a side-half*, about; †**side-hand**, on one side *of* (see also SIDENHAND); **side-handed** *a.*, indirect; †**side-hankle** *v.*, to hobble (a horse) on one side; †**side-haying**, hedging at the sides of land; **side-head(ing)** *Journalism* (see quot. 1889); †**side-hinge**, a butt-hinge; **side-hold** *Mountaineering*, a hold in which the rock is gripped from the side; **side-hook** (see quot. 1825); **side-ill**, *Sc.*, some disease in sheep; **side-ladder** (see quots.); **side lamp**, a lamp placed at the side (see also quot. 1885); *spec.* of a motor vehicle = SIDE-LIGHT 3 c; **side-land**, a strip of land lying along the side of a ploughed field; also *attrib.*, sloping (cf. *Eng. Dial. Dict.*); **side-laning, -lay** (see quots.); **side lever** *Mech.*, each of two beams located on the sides of some forms of steam engine, which transmit motion from the cross-head of the pistons to the connecting rods; **side-loader**, a fork-lift truck in which the fork is located at the side of the vehicle; **side lobe**, any lobe in the response or radiation pattern of a radio aerial other than the central, or main, lobe; **side-lock**, † (*a*) *pl.* that part of a wig that covers the ears and neck; (*b*) a lock of hair worn at the side of the head (also *fig.*); **side-mark** (see quots.); **side mill** *Engin.*, a circular milling cutter with teeth on its face, so that it cuts in the direction of its axis of rotation; also, a cylindrical cutter used with its axis parallel to the surface of the workpiece, so that the cutting action occurs along its length; hence **side milling** *vbl. sb.*; **side-nippers** (see quot.); **side-note**, a note made or placed at the side of a page; **side-partner** *U.S. colloq.*, a close associate at work; hence, a colleague or 'side kick'; **side-piece**, a piece fixed or attached at one side (see also quots.); **side-plane**, a plane which cuts at the side (Knight, 1875); **side-plate** (see quots.); **side play** *Mech.*, freedom of movement from side to side; **side reaction** *Chem.*, a subsidiary reaction taking place in a chemical system at the same time as a more important reaction; **side rebate-** or **rebating-plane** (see quots.); **side-rest** (see quot.); **side-rib** (see quots.); **side road**, (*a*) a minor or subsidiary road; a road leading from or to a main road; (*b*) *spec.* (*Canad.*) in Ontario, a road which passes along the side boundary of a concession; **side salad**, a salad served as a side dish; †**side-school**, *Sc.*, a small school in an out-of-the-way district; **side scraper** *Archæol.*, a broad flint implement with a scraping edge on one of the longer sides of the flake (cf. RACLOIR); **side-screen**, †(*a*) in landscape, a secondary feature set on both sides of the principal to show perspective; (*b*) one of the side-curtains of a open motor vehicle (in quot. 1970, of the cab of a railway locomotive); †**side-scription**, a former Scottish method of subscribing documents (cf. *side-sign*); **side-seat**, (*a*) the mode of sitting on horseback which accompanies a side-saddle; (*b*) a seat facing or placed at the side in any form of transport; †**side-sele** (?); †**side-sign** *v.*, to sign (a document) by writing the name at the side, where the sheets are pasted together; †**side-span** *v.* (see quot.); **side-split** *Canad.*, a split-level house with fewer storeys on one side than the other; **side-splitter**, a very funny story, farce, etc.; **side-splitting** *a.*, that convulses with merriment, extremely funny; also as *vbl. sb.*; hence **side-splittingly** *adv.*; **side-stream**, (*a*) a tributary stream or subsidiary current; also *fig.*; (*b*) *Oil Industry*, a fraction drawn off at an intermediate tray in a distillation column; **side-stroke** *Swimming*, a stroke employed in swimming on the side; also as advb.; **side suit**, in *Cards*, a suit other than trumps, esp. (in *Bridge*) a long suit; **side-sway**, (*a*) a rolling motion from side to side in a moving vehicle; (*b*) a sideways movement or displacement of the upper part of a building or structure as a result of wind pressure; **side-tackle**, *U.S.* in football, one or other of two players stationed at each end of the rush-line; **side-taking**, taking one side or other in a dispute, etc.; **side tone**, *Teleph.*, the reproduction of the user's voice in a telephone receiver; a sound so heard; **side-tool**, a tool cutting on the side, used in wood-turning; **side-trawler**, a trawler in which the nets are set and hauled over the sides; **side trip**, a detour or deviation (also *fig.*); a voyage or excursion aside from the main journey, esp. for sightseeing; **side valve** *Mech.*, a valve that is mounted alongside the cylinder in an internal-combustion engine and opens into a sideways extension of the combustion chamber; freq. *attrib.*; **side-wheel**, *attrib.*, of steamers, having paddle-wheels at the sides; **side wheeler**, (*a*) a side-wheel steamer; (*b*) *U.S. Baseball*, a side-arm or left-handed pitcher; (*c*) *U.S.*, a pacing horse with a rolling gait (see quots.); **side-wing** *Theatr.* = WING *sb.* 9 c; also *transf.* in *pl.*, side-whiskers (*slang*); **side-work**, (*a*) in fortification, a lateral work; (*b*) the action of bounding sidewards, on the part of a horse.

**1933** M. B. MUSE *Pharmacol. & Therapeutics* i. 42 Morphine sulphate..when administered as an analgesic has numerous *side actions some of which are harmless. **1875** *Carpentry & Join.* 8 The *side axe.., with one bevel, is free from this drawback, as it is held with the blade vertical. **1922** *Proc. I.R.E.* X. 363 A modulated radio telephone wave consists of two components, one, the carrier frequency itself and the other, the so-called *side bands, which are the actual modulated components. **1943** *Electronic Engin.* XV. 339/2 If only one side-band is received, a local oscillator must supply the suppressed carrier frequency..before the detector stage. **1974** *Physics Bull.* Mar. 91/2 Attention was drawn to..the use of side bands generated in the visible region by laser mixing techniques as an alternative to direct comparison of infrared and visible wavelengths. **1686** *Side-basset [see BASSET *sb.*[3]]. **1860** *Eng. & For. Mining Gloss.* (ed. 2) 78 *Side-bassett*, a transverse direction, or at right angles with the line of dip. **1894** H. GARDENER *Unoff. Pat.* 277 The *side bet, as they called it, must be won. **1897** *Westm. Gaz.* 6 Feb. 6/1 If Mr. Ives wishes to challenge me for the championship I shall be pleased to accept and make a side-bet of any amount he wishes. **1840** BARHAM *Ingol. Leg.* Ser. II. *Aunt Fanny* v, One of those queer little three-corner'd straps, Which.. ladies call '*Side-bits', that sever the 'Flaps'. **1823** J. F. COOPER *Pilot* I. iii. 31 The shrill whistle of the boat-swains mate, as he recalled the *side-boys. **1846** A. YOUNG *Naut. Dict.* 283 *Side-boys*, in a ship of war, are boys employed to take charge of the man-ropes, and attend on any officers or other individuals coming on board from or going off in a boat. **1916** 'TAFFRAIL' *Pincher Martin* i. 2 Eyed critically by the grinning side-boy and the messenger. **1977** *Navy News* Sept. 25/2 Shipmate Fred Talbot was nominated 'side boy' for the evening and he piped the Mayor aboard. **1887** *Chicago Jrnl.* 1 Aug., McGarigle has his mustache and small *sideburns still on. **1936** G. GREENE *Journey without Maps* II. iv. 197 He was..handsome in his native robe and his sideburns. **1977** 'J. LE CARRÉ' *Hon. Schoolboy* xii. 264 Cy.. had sideburns and..looked like a Mormon missionary. **1941** B. SCHULBERG *What makes Sammy Run?* iv. 75 A swarthy, *sideburned Latin. **1976** *Listener* 29 July 103/1 The headmaster, the richly sideburned Mr Terry Ellis. **1857** P. COLQUHOUN *Compl. Oarsman's G.* 31 *Side burthens are extra thwarts laid in provisionally to carry sitters. **1905** *Side chair [see ROCKER[1] 4 b]. **1968** *Canadian Antiques Collector* July 32 (Advt.), Sheraton side chairs in mahogany with red damask upholstery. Circa 1810. **1916** *Standard. Rules Amer. Inst. Electr. Engineers* 95 A *side circuit is a two-wire circuit forming one side of a phantom circuit. **1957** W. FRASER *Telecommunications* v. 122 It is possible to transmit speech on the phantom circuit without interference to either side-circuit. *c* **1850** *Rudim. Navig.* (Weale) 147 **Side counter timber*, the stern-timber which partakes of the shape of the topside, and heels upon the end of the wing transom. **1875** TENNYSON *Q. Mary* II. iii, And little Jenny—though she's but a *side-cousin. **1949** *Our Industry* (Anglo-Iranian Oil Co. Ltd.) (ed. 2) iii. 95 Reverting now to the question of drawing off '*side-cuts', the product on any one tray must always be contaminated by some traces of lighter components. **1970** W. G. ROBERTS *Quest for Oil* viii. 85 At the point where we wish to draw off side-cuts or intermediate fractions, special trays are put in. **1842** *Civil Eng. & Arch. Jrnl.* V. 84/2 The cutting..was in the line of railway, or what is called back-cutting, in contradistinction to earth got out of the line, which is called *side-cutting. **1649** G. DANIEL *Trinarch.* To Rdr. 166 To run vneuen as a Roman Face *Side-drawne. **1872** 'MARK TWAIN' *Roughing It* 279 He disappeared in the gloom of a '*side drift' just as a head appeared in the mouth of the shaft. **1940** *Chambers's Techn. Dict.* 768/1 *Side drift*, an adit. *c* **1800** BUSBY *Dict. Mus.*, **Side-drum*, the common military Drum. **1856** BERLIOZ *Instrument.* 231 The side-drum is only a drum longer than the preceding one. **1875** STAINER & BARRETT *Dict. Mus. Terms*, *Side-drum*, a small military drum frequently used in the orchestra. **1926–7** [see *gong-drum* s.v. GONG[2] 1 c]. **1956** Side-drum [see BOOMY *a.*]. **1885** S. O. JEWETT *Marsh Island* 195 The old farmer and his crony moved their chairs into the square *side-entry. **1901** W. CHURCHILL *Crisis* 13 He did not discuss his ambitions at dinner with the other clerks in the side entry. **1958** *Listener* 23 Oct. 669/2 North is unlikely to have the heart suit and a side entry. **1977** *Homes & Gardens* Feb. 14 The hand with the long suit has few side-entries. **1884** KNIGHT *Dict. Mech.* Suppl. 808/1 **Side File*, for trimming up the outside edges of the cutting points of saws after setting, to prevent setting. **1875** *Carpentry & Join.* 28 The *side filister is a rebate plane of more complicated..construction, being fitted with shifting guides or fences regulating the depth and width of cut. **1838** *Civil Eng. & Arch. Jrnl.* I. 97/1 To make what is termed a *side forming, which is done by raising the whole embankment at once. **1842** FRANCIS *Dict. Arts*, *Side Forming*, a road-way formed by paring down part of a hill or other steep, so as to form a road upon the side of it. **1925** *Proc. I.R.E.* XIII. 295 In the case of the *side frequencies produced by the modulator tube and delivered through the circuit.. there will be no emfs. to balance them out and they will be impressed upon the amplifer. **1978** P. H. SMALE *Telecommunication Systems* ii. 18 The sum of carrier and modulating signal frequencies is called the upper sidefrequency. **1883** T. E. MAY *Treat. on Law, Privileges, Proc. & Usage of Parliament* (ed. 9) xi. 341 A member may speak from the *side galleries, appropriated to members, but not from below the bar. **1930** B. FELL *Palace of Westminster* 41 The seating on the floor of the House accommodates 368 members and there is room in the side galleries for another 82. *a* **1974** R. CROSSMAN *Diaries* (1976) II. 402 During the all-night sitting on the Abortion Bill the side galleries would have to be closed because otherwise there would be no door-keepers. **1689** SHADWELL *Bury F.* III, Then will I..to the Park. *Wildish.* So will I; where I will *Side-glass you. **1693** —— *Volunteers* IV. i, My side-glassing you at the park. **1704** *Dict. Rust.* (1726) s.v. *Graft*, *Side Grafting;..take off from a smooth part in the West side, as much Bark as [etc.]. *c* **1400** LOVE *Bonavent. Mirr.* I. (1908) 263 Oure lorde Jesu came and aperede to hir.., gretynge hir on *side half in thise wordes. *c* **1400** *Found. St. Barth.* vii, Herry the first xxx$^{ty}$ yere, and a sidehalfe [L. *circiter*] the thirde yeare of his reigne. **1577–87** HARRISON *Descr. Brit.* xiii. in *Holinshed* 71 The Avon riseth at Navesbie in the borders of Northhamptonshire, a little *side hand of Gillesborow. **1579–80** NORTH *Plutarch* (1612) 603 He turned his horse head vpon a sudden, and leauing his enemies side-hand of him that had him in chase, he closely stole by them. **1845** THACKERAY *Legend Rhine* xiii, She made some *side-handed enquiries regarding Otto. **1621** SANDERSON *Serm.* I. 189 A third sort [are]..like an unruly colt... These would be well fettered and *side-hanckled for leaping. **1610** W. FOLKINGHAM *Art Surv.* II. ii. 49 Compound Contiguall Boundage is more significant, as *side-haying, head-shawing. **1889** *Cent. Dict.*, **Side-head*... In *printing*, a heading or a sub-head run in at the beginning of a paragraph, instead of being made a separate line. **1964** *New Statesman* 21 Feb. 303/3 We shall present these pieces in a way which makes their character as editorial opinion less equivocal, by prefixing a generic side-head. **1971** D. AYERST *Guardian* xxiv. 347 The *Guardian* gave Churchill only those two or three lines towards the end of the story below a modest side-head: 'The Home Secretary'. **1968** *Heidelberg News* Sept. 4/1 Send him a picture and supply a caption as a *side heading. **1679** MOXON *Mech. Exerc.* ix. 160 In a Battend-door,..they use Cross-Garnets. If a Fram'd Door, *Side Hinges. **1920** G. W. YOUNG *Mountain Craft* iv. 162 '*Side'-holds, where the edge or point of rock projects and is grasped sideways. **1977** D. LAW *Starting Mountaineering & Rock Climbing* vi. 68 Most of the holds for jamming are side holds, but some can be used for a vertical pull-up. **1823** P. NICHOLSON *Pract. Builder* 252 Every joiner should have, at least, two *side-hooks of equal size. **1825** J. NICHOLSON *Operat. Mechanic* 585 A flat piece of wood, which has two projectiing knobs, on opposite sides, one at each end, called a *side-hook*, is used, to keep the piece which has to undergo the operation of the saw steady. **17..** *Patie's Wedding* in Herd *Coll.* (1776) II. 190 I'se cut the craig o' the ewe That had amaist died of the *Side-ill. **1798** MIDDLETON *View Agric. M'sex.* 87 These carts, with the addition of movable head, tail, and *side ladders or copps, carry hay, corn, and straw. **1867** SMYTH *Sailor's Word-bk.* 624 *Side ladder*, or *Accommodation-ladder*, a complete staircase structure used in harbour by most large ships. **1891** C. ROBERTS *Adrift Amer.* 232 There was a side ladder over, which I got hold of, and..climbed on board. **1826** J. O'KEEFE *Recoll. Life* I. x. 376 His shaggy dress took fire from the *side-lamps. **1885** E. B. IVATTS *Railway Management at Stations* 550 *Lamp* (*side*), lamps for showing red lights at the two sides of guards' vans at the end of a train, as signals to an approaching train..and white lights towards the engine driver to enable him looking back to see that no portion of his train has broken away. **1912** *Motor Manual* (ed. 14) iii. 124 It is possible..to adapt electric lighting very successfully to any car, both for interior lighting of limousines and landaulets, and for head, side and rear lamps. **1963** *Times* 30 Apr. 13/4 The many heavy lorries which..only have one pin-head size nearside sidelamp in the town. **1763** *Museum Rust.* (ed. 2) I. 101 This practice of carrying the upper bed of earth from the head and *side lands on to the field, is very common among the Essex farmers. **1828** *Sporting Mag.* XXIII. 104 The sideland, uneven parts of ground such as small mole-hills. **1838** HOLLOWAY *Prov. Dict.*, *Sidelands*, the outside parts of a ploughed field, adjoining the hedges, running parallel with the lands or warps. **1860** *Eng. & For. Mining Gloss.* (ed. 2) 78 **Side-laning*, making the gate-road (when abandoned for that purpose)..part of the new side of work. **1576** TURBERV. *Venerie* 246 You may deuide your Greyhounds into three sundry parts, viz. Teasers, *Sidelayes, and Backsets, or Receytes. *Ibid.* 247 The sidelayes are to be let slippe at y$^{e}$ side of a Deare or after him. **1888** JACOBI *Printer's Vocab.* 125 *Side lay*, the margin of a given measurement on one side of a sheet in printing. **1946** A. MONKMAN in H. Whetton *Pract. Printing & Binding* v. 64/2 Assuming the ordinary half-sheet of sixteens is on the machine, and the side-lay for printing the first side is at the foot of page 1, there would be a regular and accurate margin from page 1. **1839** *Side lever [see *sway-beam* s.v. SWAY-]. **1846** A. YOUNG *Naut. Dict.* 305 The curved sweep which the ends of the side-levers describe. **1882** SENNETT & ORAM *Marine Steam Engine* I. i. 3 The side-lever type of engine, though very heavy and occupying a large space for the power developed, was safe and reliable. **1939** H. W. DICKINSON *Short Hist. Steam Engine* vi. 108 This type was taken up by other makers under the name of the side-lever engine, and remained for about forty years the established type for marine-engine practice. **1960** *Times* 16 Mar. (Canberra Suppl.) p. iv/6 The forward bulkhead..must move one frame aft to accommodate the mechanism of the *side-loader. **1973** *Scotsman* 19 Feb. 3/1 (Advt.), We produce the largest and most versatile range of frontlift and sideloader trucks in the UK. **1946** *Proc. I.R.E.* XXXIV. 335/2 After either the *side-lobe level or the position of the first null is specified, the position of the other nulls and of the side lobes can be found by simple calculation. **1975** D. G. FINK *Electronics Engineers' Handbk.* xxv. 25 In angle, the response function $\chi(\theta,\phi)$ is simply the antenna pattern... It has a main lobe in the direction to which it is matched, and side lobes extending over all visible space. **1688** R. HOLME *Academy of Armory* II. xviii. 463/2 The **side Locks*, are those as cover and keep warm the ears and neck, being a degree shorter than the former [*sc.* 'The *Bottom Locks*']. **1848** THACKERAY *Van. Fair* xxxii, Always giving his side-locks a twirl. **1889** *Century Mag.* Sept. 710/1 The monuments represent him as a prince and nothing more, still wearing the side-lock of juniority. **1944** S. BELLOW *Dangling Man* 23 The street..presented itself in one of its winter aspects, creased and with thin sidelocks of snow. **1978** I. B. SINGER *Shosha* xi. 196 Old women in bonnets of beads and ribbons, men with white beards and sidelocks. **1818** HAZLITT *Eng. Poets* vii. (1870) 164 The *side-mark of the age at which they were done, wears out in works destined for immortality. **1888** JACOBI *Printers' Vocab.* 125 *Side mark*, the fixed mark on the side which a sheet is laid to in printing on a machine. **1898** H. S. WILSON *Practical Tool-Maker & Designer* i. 15 Select some good-sized straddle or *side mills. **1954** H. W. PORTER et al. *Machine Shop Operations & Setups* ix. 312 This makes it possible to finish two or more parallel surfaces at the same time by using two or more side mills. **1910** D. DE VRIES *Milling Machines* xv. 449 The sharpening of the left side teeth of a *side milling cutter with a cup wheel. **1954** H. W. PORTER et al. *Machine Shop Operations & Setups* ix. 312 Straddle milling requires two side-milling cutters. **1973** J. G. TWEEDDALE *Materials Technol.* II. vi. 146 Side-milling uses a cylindrical multifluted cutter (usually spirally fluted) which rotates on an axis parallel to the workpiece and is traversed across it to cut, progressively, tangentially into it. **1846** HOLTZAPFFEL *Turning* II. 906 Other cutting pliers called *side-nippers are oblique. **1776** W. ROBERTSON *Let.* 8 Apr. in *Corr. Adam Smith* (1977) 193, I should wish that in the 2d Edition you would give..what the Book-sellers call *Side-notes. **1858** FROUDE *Hist. England* IV. 537 Persons.. who have observed the traces of his pen in sidenotes and corrections. **1890** *N.Y. Even. Post* 23 May 8/2 The arrest was made by the witness's *side partner, it being his night off. **1921** R. D. PAINE *Comrades Rolling Ocean* ix. 159 We shall have to consult my side-partner, Briscoe. **1802** JAMES *Milit. Dict.* s.v. *Rider*, The axle-tree, upon which the *side-pieces rest, in a four-wheel carriage. **1849** Side-piece [see MOB-CAP]. **1854** MISS BAKER *Northampt. Gloss.*, *Side-pieces*, the longitudinal pieces of timber lying under the rafters between the ridge and wall-plates. **1867** SMYTH *Sailor's Word-bk.* 625 *Side-pieces*, parts of a made mast. **1928** *Daily Express* 16 Aug. 5/2 A car (with a left-hand drive and a hood but no side-pieces). **1680** *Lond. Gaz.* No. 1532/4 A Pair of French Pistols,..the Stocks of Maple, Silver *side-plates, and Silver Caps. **1756** C. SMART tr. *Horace, Sat.* II. iv, I am found to be the first that served up this grape with apples in neat little side-plates. **1879** tr. *Haeckel's Evol. Man* I. 303 The two lateral portions of the mesoderm..are usually called side-plates. **1861** J. BOURNE *Treat. Steam-Engine* (ed. 5) viii. 352/1 The guide blocks are of brass, and in wearing down they maintain their position in the groove. This mode of construction prevents *side play. **1905** E. C. C. BALY *Spectroscopy* iii. 50 It is..necessary that the jaws move smoothly in their grooves without any trace of side play. **1934** WEBSTER, *Side reaction. **1936** *Jrnl. Amer. Chem. Soc.* LVIII. 2210/2 The small deviations observed..may be due to the fact that the side reactions..are more prominent in one case than in the other. **1973** *Sci. Amer.* Oct. 60/3 High-energy intermediates are frequently formed in chemical syntheses, but if they are not isolated from water or other reactive substances, they decompose in side reactions that lower the yield of the reaction. **1846** HOLTZAPFFEL *Turning* II. 489 When..the rebate plane is meant to cut at the side, it is called the *side-rebate plane. **1825** J. NICHOLSON *Operat. Mechanic* 582 The former are used to smooth the side of a rebate, and therefore are called *side rebating-planes. **1680** MOXON *Mech. Exerc.* x. 181 Turnners have another Rest, called the *Side-Rest. This they use when they Turn the flat sides of Boards. **1582** STANYHURST *Æneis* IV. (Arb.) 103 Thee top wyth *sideryb of Atlas He sees. **1844** *Regul. & Ord. Army* 106 New side rib for carbine, with ring fitted. **1852** SEIDEL *Organ* 37 Between the upper and under-board there are six boards,..four longer ones, two on each side of the bellows, called side-ribs. **1854** T. C. KEEFER *Ottawa* 72 The municipalities have taxed themselves too heavily for the main road..to be able to build also the *side roads. **1873** *Woodstock* (Ontario) *Sentinel* 5 Dec. 3/4 To Joseph Whaley for pine timber for culvert on first side road, $1.00. **1958** R. LIDDELL *Morea* II. viii. 190 South of Argos, a side-road, off the main road to Tripolis, leads to Kefalári. **1968** *Globe & Mail* (Toronto) 13 Feb. 3/6 The partly frozen body..was found Sunday beside the Nixon Side-road. **1976** *Western Mail* (Cardiff) 22 Nov. 1/2 The other man was seen standing..near a vehicle on a little-used side road. [**1951** F. BROBECK *Good Salad Bk.* 9 A small salad served with the main course, or after it, on a decorative plate is the old-fashioned side dish salad.] **1972** D. SALE *Love Bite* II. xvii. 212 She..helped herself to a *side salad of avocado in French dressing. **1980** P. ABLEMAN *Shoestring's Finest Hour* iv. 73, I queued for a hefty portion of shepherd's pie and a side salad. **1863** *Good Words* 727 In the more distant valleys where even the small *side-schools could not penetrate. **1872** J. EVANS *Anc. Stone Implements* xiii. 272 When the instrument is broader than it is long, it has been termed a *side scraper. **1921** R. A. S. MACALISTER *Text-Bk. European Archaeol.* I. vii. 321 The side-scraper.., a flake with secondary chipping along one edge, making it fit to scrape the interior of hides in preparing garments. **1977** *Sci. Amer.* Nov. 126/2 Among the Upper Industry tools at Hoxne were a small number of the flake implements that are traditionally called 'side scrapers' and are presumed to have played a role in the dressing of hides. **1782** W. GILPIN *Observ. on River Wye* ii. 8 Every view on a river, thus circumstanced [with steep banks], is composed of four grand parts; the area, which is the river itself; the two *side-screens, which are the opposite banks, and mark the perspective; and the front-screen, which points out the winding of the river. *a* **1817** JANE AUSTEN *Northanger Abbey* (1818) I. xiv. 263 He talked of fore-grounds, distances, and second distances—side-screens and perspectives. **1932** *News Chron.* 6 Aug. 3/5 The assailant thrust a six-chambered revolver through a side-screen and fired. **1958** L. DURRELL *Mountolive* xv. 276 He drove up..in his pennoned car, rejoicing in..the whickering of wind at the side-screens. **1970** N. FLEMING *Czech Point* xiv. 191 The canvas sidescreens to the cab flapped in the wind. **1978** A. PRICE *'44 Vintage* xiii. 160 The staff car..with a closed canvas hood and side-screens. **1838** W. BELL *Dict. Law Scotland* 916 **Side-scription*. **1856** 'STONEHENGE' *Brit. Rural Sports* 538 In spite of her *side-seat, the body should be square to the front. **1889** *Cent. Dict.*, *Side-seat*,..in a vehicle of any kind, a seat with the back against the side of the vehicle, as usually in a horse-car or omnibus. **1901** *Daily News* 5 July 4 In the stern with the side-seats out there is room for 3 or 4 drift-nets. **1922** JOYCE *Ulysses* 591 The car and horse..turn. Corny Kelleher on the sideseat sways his head to and fro in sign of mirth at Bloom's plight. **1395** in *East Anglian* Ser. II. IV. 85, j *sydsele, & j londplate & j rast. **1708** J. CHAMBERLAYNE *Pres. St. Gt. Brit.* (1710) 418 If there be more Sheets than one in the *Decreit*, the Principal Clerk *side-signs the joyning of every Two Sheets. **1750** ELLIS *Mod. Husb.* VI. II. 97 **Side-span* [sheep], as we call it, by tying a fore-leg to a hind-leg, with an allowance for length of string. **1968** *Globe & Mail* (Toronto) 15 Jan. 23/1 (Advt.), Why not see this spacious *side-split..in Etobicoke? **1864** *Harper's Mag.* Feb. 422/1, I send you three samples [of letters].., hoping thereby to reciprocate some of your *side-splitters. **1903** A. M. BINSTEAD *Pitcher in Paradise* v. 133 As regards poetry I have already had a sidesplitter entitled 'Don't chalk your cue before a lady' accepted by Mr Arthur Roberts. **1860** S. MORDECAI *Virginia* xiv. 188 These among other *side-splitting tales, which he told and acted with the skill of a Matthews. **1881** *Daily Telegr.* 27 Dec., This..past master of the art of side-splitting. **1881** *Harper's Monthly* LXIII. 266 No matter how side-splitting the story might be. **1907** A. BENNETT *Grim Smile Five Towns* 7 Something *side-splittingly funny—one of the best jokes that ever occurred. **1970** *Daily Tel.* 6 Aug. 6/2 The reader is..given an at times side-splittingly funny account of the eccentricities of Frazer and his wife. **1900** *Knowledge* 1 Dec. 273/1 The rotten condition of the surface is seen when one of the larger *side-streams cuts its way down to the Durance. **1935** *Petroleum* (Inst. Petroleum Technologists) 84 The provision made for taking side-streams has greatly extended the usefulness of the fractionating tower. **1939** *John o' London's Weekly* (Suppl.) 9 June p. ii/2 The cliffs of Norfolk and Suffolk are menaced by the sidestream of a tidal current that flows westwards into the Wash. **1960** *Times* 29 Sept. 15/7 His writings are in the stimulating side-stream of scholarly diaries. **1973** D. ANDERSEN *Ways Harsh & Wild* i. 42 You'll see the waves splashing up the sides of the canyon and falling back to form a hogsback in midstream that's a yard higher than the sidestreams. **1973** R. PRIESTLEY in G. D. Hobson *Mod. Petroleum Technol.* (ed. 4) viii. 271 Products of a volatility intermediate between the overhead and bottoms products are withdrawn as sidestreams. **1867** C. STEEDMAN *Man. Swimming* 105 The five movements—three for the legs and two for the arms—required for the performance of the *side stroke. *a* **1936** KIPLING *Something of Myself* (1937) ii. 34 One set of verses which exactly set the time for my side-stroke when I bathed in the big rollers. **1962** A. SEXTON *All my Pretty Ones* 55 The old-fashioned side stroke. **1976** J. MCCLURE *Rogue Eagle* xi. 185 Buchanan..waded in and swam sidestroke downstream of the gelding. **1952** I. MACLEOD *Bridge is Easy Game* xiv. 181 The commonest case is when dummy has a long solid *side suit. **1960** C. H. GOREN *New Contract Bridge in Nutshell* 13 In a side suit, the fourth card is considered a long card. **1974** *National Skat & Sheepshead Q.* Mar./Apr. 29 This decision is based upon the official rule of calling a side suit ace. **1930** *Sidesway [see ROLLING *vbl. sb.*$^{2}$ 6 b.]. **1932** CROSS & MORGAN *Continuous Frames of Reinforced Concrete* iv. 108 In many problems in the analysis of rigid frames..a solution assuming no movement of the joints does not satisfy statistics because the shear in all columns of any one story is not equal to the known shear in that story. This indicates sidesway..of the frame sufficient to make $\Sigma H = O$. **1961** E. LIGHTFOOT *Moment Distribution* v. 123 After moments have been apportioned to the frame,..a single or double cycle of joint balance and carry-over is performed (with the frame restrained against sidesway). **1980** *Daily Tel.* 11 June 14/5 [In the Princess] fast cornering producing rather a lot of side-sway. **1891** *N.Y. Tribune* 20 Oct. 5/4 (Funk), He was ..*side-tackle on his college foot-ball team. **1640** BP. HALL *Episc.* II. 140 Emulation and *side-takings amongst, and against their teachers. **1898** B. GREGORY *Side Lights* 504 Side-taking does not become party. **1917** G. D. SHEPARDSON *Telephone Apparatus* xiv. 234 Some arrangements seem to give more trouble than others from '*side-tones', whereby the speaker hears his own words too strongly. *a* **1944** K. DOUGLAS *Alamein to Zem Zem* (1946) 38 The operator..breathed and hummed into the microphone, listening for sidetone. **1978** *Sci. Amer.* Mar. 59/1 Too little side tone gives the telephone an unnatural 'dead' sound and tends to cause the user to talk too loudly. **1846** HOLTZAPFFEL *Turning* II. 516 For the insides of cylinders, the *side-tool.. is sometimes used. **1962** J. TUNSTALL *Fishermen* ii. 46 The whole-freezer *side-trawler is a..compromise solution in which conventional side-trawling is retained. *a* **1911** D. G. PHILLIPS *Susan Lenox* (1917) II. viii. 212 He's got a nasty streak in him... He put me on the Island once for a little *side trip I made. **1929** L. F. CARR *Amer. Challenged* 3 He was forced to borrow money for a little side trip to New York. **1966** *Guardian* 24 Dec. 4/3 Another family..spent three weeks in Jutland, with a side trip of a couple of days in Copenhagen. **1979** N. & I. LYONS *Champagne Blues* 78, I.. make arrangements for special side trips, room supplements, extended tour packages. **1928** *Daily Mail Year Bk.* p. lxiv, 3·49 H.P. *side valve 'sports' model. **1946** [see L 3]. **1973** J. LEASOR *Host of Extras* ix. 179 My heart was pounding like an old side-valve engine on a long hill when the ignition's too retarded. **1857** M. F. MAURY in Corbin *Life* (1888) 135 She was a *side-wheel steamer. **1884** *Harper's Mag.* Mar. 514/1 Such boats as they are!—*side-wheelers and stern-wheelers. **1911** *Spalding's Official Base Ball Guide* 277 Redfern, side-wheeler, with Flowers, McFarlin and Reis with the other end up, made the pitching department a clever one. **1926** *Amer. Speech* I. 369/2 [Baseball] They are 'south-paws' or 'port-siders' or 'side-wheelers' when they are left-handed. **1936** *Literary Digest* 1 Aug. 35/2 Pacers have a rolling, lunging movement that has earned them the nickname of 'wigglers' or 'side-wheelers'. Left front and left rear legs come up together, followed by a counterbalancing lunge to the right. **1948** *Times Digest* (Richmond, Va.) 15 Mar. 17/4 The lanky Cincinnati Reds' sidewheeler has added a new pitch to his repertoire. **1953** *Sun* (Baltimore) 10 Aug. B15/2 Mac Hayman [will]..handle the speedy sidewheeler in her three stake engagements at the Ocean Downs Raceway. **1707** E. SETTLE *Siege of Troy* III. 23 The Scene opens and discovers a Grove..over a Tarras Walk, is seen a Beautiful Garden of six *side Wings. **1811** L. SUMBEL *Mem. Life* III. 220 And a fourth, with locks *bushed* out on his temples, burlesquing the side-wings of your noble head. **1814** JANE AUSTEN *Mansfield Park* I. xiii. 257 Just a side wing or two run up..and three or four scenes to be let down. **1881** *Atlantic Monthly* Sept. 402/1 It seems as if certain actors in some preceding comedy of his were standing at the side-wings, and critically watching the progress of the after-piece. **1748** SMOLLETT *Rod. Random* I. 302 A *sidework composed of earth gabions or fascines. **1890** 'R. BOLDREWOOD' *Col. Reformer* (1891) 102, I [never] saw a new arrival that could sit a buck-jumper, even if he only propped straight forward, and didn't do any side-work.

**side** (saɪd), *sb.*$^{2}$ *slang.* [Of doubtful origin; perhaps identical with prec. (? in sense 14 d), but cf. SIDE *a.* 4.] Pretentiousness, swagger, conceit. Freq. in phr. ***to put on side***, to give oneself airs.

**1878** HATTON *Cruel London* VIII. ii, Cool, downy cove, who puts side on. **1880** PAYN *Confid. Agent* xi, The Captain sauntered up the Mews, with a good deal of 'side on', which became a positive swagger as he emerged into the more fashionable street. **1882** *Standard* 29 Sept. 5/2 With..all our 'offishness', or 'side', as they call it, we and our cousins in the Far South get along amazingly well. **1896** J. HOCKING

*Fields of Fair Renown* xii. 128 They seem to have no side; they are all as jolly as may be.

**side**, Sc. f. SCYTHE; obs. f. SEED *sb.*; var. SITHE (time).

**side** (saɪd), *a.* Now *Sc.* and *north. dial.* Forms: 1–3, 5 **sid**, 4–6 **syd**, 4–9 **syde**, 5 **syyd**, **cyyd(e**, 4– **side**. [OE. *síd*, = ON. *síðr*, MSw. *siþer*, *sidher* (Norw., Sw., Da. *sid*); also MDu. *side*, *zide* low, MFlem. *sijt* (rare) extensive.

ON. *síðr* is recorded only in sense 3, but MSw. *siþer* and Norw. *sid* have also the MDu. sense of 'low, low-lying'.]

†**1.** Large, ample, spacious, extensive. *Obs.*

*Beowulf* 437 þæt ic sweord bere oþðe sidne scyld. *a* **1000** *Andreas* 762 Æfter þyssum wordum weorud hlosnode ȝeond þæt side sel. **1340–70** *Alex. & Dind.* 481 þe side se we mow sen set vp-on erþe. *c* **1400** *Destr. Troy* 7570 Oure pepull to sle, Oure Citie to sese and oure side londes. *Ibid.* 7670 Saght þai the sure prinse thurgh the syde batell.

†**b.** Far-off, distant; going far. *Obs. rare.*

**1399** LANGL. *Rich. Redeles* IV. 28 [They] lete write writtis all in wex closid, .. And sente side sondis to schreuys aboute. *c* **1400** *Destr. Troy* 1513 His towne was takon ..; His Suster sesyd and soght into syde londis.

**2.** Extending lengthways; long. Chiefly in phr. ***wide and side*** (cf. SIDE *adv.*[1] 1).

*a* **1000** *Cædmon's Gen.* 1655 Ꝺesetton þa Sennar sidne & widne leoda ræswan leofum mannum. *c* **1200** ORMIN 9174 And ta wass Romess kinedom Full wid & sid onn eorþe. **13..** *Sir Beues* 818 þe bor so loude cride, Out of þe forest wide and side. *c* **1330** R. BRUNNE *Chron. Wace* (Rolls) 7503 Namore lond, wyd ne syd, þan y may sprede a boles hyd. *c* **1440** *Pallad. on Husb.* III. 1052 Chese a boor Gret bodied, side & wide, ek rather rounde Then longe. **1583** [see SIDENESS]. **1591** SYLVESTER *Du Bartas* I. ii. 175 Their forms do vanish, but their bodies bide; Now thick, now thin, now round, now short, now side. **1876** WHITEHEAD *Daft Davie* 190 A street so 'syde-and-wyde' that there was elbow-room for everyone in Boulder in it. **1894** HESLOP *Northumbld. Gloss.* s.v., Aa'll tyek some o' this check; say, a yard side.

*transf.* **1399** LANGL. *Rich. Redeles* III. 170 If I sothe shall saie, and shonne side tales.

†**b.** Of a house-roof: High or steep. *Obs.*

*c* **1440** [implied in SIDENESS]. **1674** RAY *N.C. Words* 41. **1788** W. H. MARSHALL *Yorksh.* II. 351 *Side*, long, deep; spoken of a roof.

**3.** Reaching or hanging far down on the person; long: **a.** Of garments, sleeves, etc. †***side-robe*** (1658), = LONG ROBE. (See also SIDE-COAT.)

*Beowulf* 1444 Scolde here-byrne, hondum ȝebroden, sid ond searo-fah, sund cunnian. *c* **1000** ÆLFRIC in Thorpe *Laws* II. 370 Iohannes .. ȝeseah urne Drihten mid alban ȝescridne, and seo wæs sid niðer oð ða andcleowa. *a* **1310** in Wright *Lyric P.* x. 37 Betere is were thunne boute laste, then syde robes ant synke into synne. **1382** WYCLIF *Gen.* xxxvii. 23 As he cam to his britheren, thei nakiden hym the side coote to the hele. *a* **1400–50** *Alexander* 1925 þat I may .. A side slauyn him sewe & send him to his modire. **1459** *Paston Lett.* I. 475 First, a goune of clothe of golde, with side slevis, sirples wise. **1523** FITZHERB. *Husb.* §151 Theyr cotes be so syde, that they be fayne to tucke them vp whan they ryde. **1545** BALE *Image Both Ch.* I. C v b, I sawe hym clothed wyth a syde lynnen garment doune to the grounde. **1615** G. SANDYS *Trav.* 109 Some of the yonger sort .. weare side coates of linnen .. girt to their wasts. **1658** F. OSBORNE *Tradit., Mem. Q. Eliz.* 25 It abated the price of his opposers, the most of whom belonged to the side-robe. **1753** *Stewart's Trial* App. 20 Allan was .. dressed in a blue side coat, a red vest, and feathered hat. **1781** J. HUTTON *Tour to Caves* (ed. 2) Gloss. 95 *Side*, long, as garments are when too big. *a* **1878** AINSLIE *Land of Burns* (1892) 339 My gude grey plaid, baith syde an' wide, I airtit to the wun'. **1886** *S.W. Lincs. Gloss.*, *Side*, long: usually applied to a coat, as 'Side coat', for Great coat.

*absol.* *a* **1272** *Luue Ron* 47 in *O.E. Misc.* 94 An ende, ne werie mon so syde, he schal to-dreosen so lef on bouh. *c* **1340** HAMPOLE *Pr. Consc.* 1534 Now wers men short and now syde.

**b.** Of the beard, hair, etc.

*c* **1290** *S. Eng. Leg.* I. 368 His berd is long and sid i-nouȝ. *a* **1300** *Cursor M.* 8079 Lang and side þair brues wern, And hinged all a-bout þair hern. *c* **1375** *Sc. Leg. Saints* ix. (*Bartholomew*) 218 þare-with a syd berd it had. *c* **1400** MAUNDEV. (Roxb.) xxii. 100 In anoþer ile er folk whas eres er so syde þat þai hing doune to þe kneesse. *c* **1500** MEDWALL *Nature* 756 (Brandl), I loue yt well to haue syde here. **1596** DALRYMPLE tr. *Leslie's Hist. Scot.* I. 29 Oxne and bules snawquhyte with a mane thick and syde. **1600** HOLLAND *Livy* XLIV. xix. 1182 The haire of their head long, their beards side and overgrowne. **1616** SURFL. & MARKH. *Country Farme* VII. xxii. 679 He hath a round thicke head, a short nose, .. broad and sydelips.

**c.** Narrow, strait, clinging.

*a* **1825** FORBY *Voc. E. Anglia* 300 In modern usage .. we .. use the word in the sense of strait. 'This sleeve is too side, it must be let out.'

**4. a.** Haughty, proud.

**1508** [implied in SIDE *adv.*[1] 3]. **1674** RAY *N.C. Words* 41. **1695** KENNETT *Par. Antiq.* s.v. *Sidelinge*, A side woman. **1888** *Sheffield Gloss.* s.v., I met Mrs. —— in the town, and she was very side.

**b.** *Sc.* Severe or hard *on* or *upon* one.

**1825** in JAMIESON. **1895** ROY *Horseman's Word* iii, Hout, tout, Tam! .. you're just some syde on Geordie.

**5.** *Comb.*, as ***side-bellied***, †***-fathomed***, †***-faxed***, ***-haired***, ***-lipped***, ***-tailed***, ***-waisted***.

*Beowulf* 302 Sidfæþmed scip, on ancre fæst. *c* **1000** ÆLFRIC *Saints' Lives* xix. 221 þa ȝefeng hine an treow be ðam fexe sona, forðan þe he wæs sidfæxede. **14..** *Tundale's Vis.* 869 His mouthe was wyde, he was syde lyppud. **1523** FITZHERB. *Husb.* §77 The fourthe [property of a fox is] to be syde-tayled. **1576** TURBERV. *Venerie* 18 When the bytches are lyned, and that they beginne to be sydebellyed. *Ibid.* 50 Of the browne Hartes there be some great, long, and side haired. **1599** NASHE *Lenten Stuff* Wks. (Grosart) V. 227 Of a bounzing side-wasted parish in Lancashire, we haue a flying voyce dispersed. **1631** WEEVER *Anc. Funeral Mon.* 180 Like our side-wasted Parishes in Lancashire, whose extensure is so large [etc.]. **1822** AINSLIE *Land of Burns* 190 He wore an old light blue, side-tailed coat.

†**side**, *adv.*[1] *Obs.* Also 3 **sid**, 4 **syd**, 6 **syde**. [OE. *síde* (f. *síd* SIDE *a.*), = MDu. *side* (Du. *zijd*, Fris. *syd*), MLG. *sîde*.

The usual Eng. phrase *wide and side* corresponds to MDu. *wide en side* (Du. *wijd en zijd*, Fris. *wiid en syd*), MLG. *wîde unde sîde*, *wît unde sît*; also MSw. *siit oc wiit*.]

**1.** To a great distance or length; far. Chiefly in ***wide and side***, far and wide.

*a* **900** CYNEWULF *Elene* 277 Heht ða ȝebeodan .. side & wide ȝeond Iudeas [etc.]. *a* **1121** *O.E. Chron.* (Laud MS.) an. 959, He .. Godes lof rærde, wide & side. *c* **1200** ORMIN 10258 Sannt Johaness word Sprang wide & side o lande. *c* **1275** LAY. 4961 Wide and side he somnede ferde. **13..** *Cursor M.* 1646 (Gött.), Couaytise, lechuri, and pride, Has spred þis world lang and side. *c* **1330** *Arth. & Merl.* 200 (Kölbing), Y .. wered ȝou wiþ mi power, Wide & side, fer & ner. **1621** BP. MOUNTAGU *Diatribæ* 490 For the Grecian Colonies were diffused farre and neere, wide and side.

**2.** Low down; towards or on the ground.

**1297** R. GLOUC. (Rolls) 2513 þis maide out of chambre com .., side drou hire tail. **1377** LANGL. *P. Pl.* B. v. 193 As a letheren purs lolled his chekes, Wel sydder þan his chyn þei chiueled for elde. **14..** in *Tundale's Vis.*, etc. (1843) 152 Her tongis honged owt full syde. *c* **1538** LYNDESAY *Minor Poems* 575, I think it is ane verray scorne That euery Lady of the land Suld haue hir taill so syde trailland!

**3.** Proudly, boastfully. (Cf. SIDE *a.* 4 a.)

**1508** DUNBAR *Twa Mariit Wemen* 196 God wait quhat I think quhen he so thra spekis: And how it settis him so syde to sege of sic materis.

**side**, *adv.*[2] [f. SIDE *sb.*[1], by ellipse of prep.]

†**1.** To one side *of* a place. *Obs.*$^{-1}$

**1650** FULLER *Pisgah* II. xiii, A good way side of Jerusalem lies a melancholy Bay.

**2.** *Comb.* with pres. or past pples., denoting 'by, from, or to the side', as ***side-flowing***, ***-hanging***, ***-lying***; ***side-bended***, ***-cast***, ***-seen***.

**1382** WYCLIF *Isaiah* xliv. 4 Buriowne thei shuln among erbes .. bisyde the syde flowende watris [L. *præterfluentes aquas*]. **1592** R. D. *Hypnerotomachia* (1890) 5 b, A rare Obelisk .. the heigth whereof .. did exceed the toppes of the sidelying mountaynes. **1601–2** DANIEL *Civ. Wars* VII. xliv, The cast of her side-bended eye, did showe Both sorrow and reproofe. **1608** SYLVESTER *Du Bartas* II. iv. IV. *Decay* 639 Even as a Winde .. Bears down the Trees in a side-hanging Wood. **1807** J. BARLOW *Columb.* v. 275 As on a side-seen storm .. The flames fork round the semivault of heaven. **1891** MEREDITH *One of our Conq.* II. i. 1 The head deferentially sidecast.

**side** (saɪd), *v.*[1] [f. SIDE *sb.*[1] Cf. MDu. *siden*, *ziden* to set aside, go aside, obs. G. *seiten* (*syten*), to stand aside.]

**I.** *trans.* †**1.** To cut or carve (a pig or haddock) into sides. *Obs.*

*c* **1470** *Hors, Shepe & G.* (Roxb.) 33 A Pigge heded & syded, a lambe & kyde shuldred. **1486** *Bk. St. Albans* F vij b, An Haddoke sided. **1508** *Bk. Keruynge* in *Babees Bk.* 267 Syde that haddocke. [**1854** BADHAM *Prose Halieut.* 343 The reader will remember, when he puts the slice into a fish, that he gobbets trout .. and sides haddocks.]

**2. a.** To have (one) on that side. *rare*$^{-1}$.

**1590** SPENSER *F.Q.* III. ix. 27 His blind eye, that syded Paridell, All his demeasnure from his sight did hyde.

**b.** To come by the side of. *rare*$^{-1}$.

**1600** FAIRFAX *Tasso* XIX. lxxvii, He sided there a lustie louely las, And with some courtly tearmes the wench he bords.

**c.** To walk or stand by the side of; to be side by side with (a person, etc.).

**1613** CHAPMAN *Masque Middle Temple & Lincoln's Inn* A 2 b, Euery one of these horse, had two Moores, .. that for state sided them. **1631** MASSINGER *Emperor East* IV. iii, Do you hold it, now, As a disparagement, that I side you, lady? **1821** LAMB *Elia* I. *Old Benchers Inner T.*, The terrace is, indeed, left... The old benchers had it almost sacred to themselves... They might not be sided or jostled. **1896** *Archæol. Jrnl.* LIII. 41 The monoliths siding this shrine were pulled down.

**d.** *fig.* To rival, equal, match.

**1603** B. JONSON *Sejanus* IV. v, Whom he .. Hath rais'd from excrement to side the gods. **1668** CLARENDON *Life* (1759) I. 53 He had sure read more .. than any Man I ever knew, my Lord Falkland only excepted, who I think sided him.

**3.** To support or countenance (one). *Obs.*

**1591** LAMBARDE *Archeion* (1635) 172 The Offenders .. were belike so brested, sided, and backed with a many friends, tenants, and followers. **1607** SHAKS. *Cor.* I. i. 197 [They] side factions, & giue out Coniecturall Marriages, making parties strong [etc.]. **1618** FLETCHER *Chances* I. ii, Let it raise wild-fires, .. Yet I must through, if ye dare side me.

**4.** *refl.* To take a side or party. (Cf. 11.)

**1591** SAVILE *Tacitus, Hist.* II. xiv. 60 The prouince of Narbon, which had sided itselfe and sworne to Vitellius. **1625** BACON *Ess.*, *On Faction* (Arb.) 83 Kings had need beware, how they Side themselues, and make themselues as of a Faction or Partie. **1901** *Univ. & Ludg. Mag.* July 296 They side themselves with the light blue or the dark blue, just as their friends belong to a particular university.

**5.** To assign to one of two sides or parties.

*c* **1600** SHAKS. *Sonn.* xlvi, To side this title is impannelled A quest of thoughts, all tennants to the heart.

**6.** *dial.* To put in order, arrange; to clear or tidy up. Freq. ***to side up***.

**1825–** in northern dialect glossaries. **1847** MRS. CARLYLE *Lett.* I. 394, I have plenty to employ me, in siding drawers. **1874** WAUGH *Chimney Corner* (1879) 36 Here, Sally; help me to side this table.

*absol.* **1842** R. OASTLER *Fleet Papers* II. 410 It will be left for me to clean, and 'side', and 'make all right again'.

**b.** To put aside, remove; to clear *away*.

**1848** MRS. GASKELL *Mary Barton* x, Mrs. Wilson was 'siding' the dinner things. **1853** —— *Ruth* ii, Whenever things are mislaid, I know it has been Miss Hilton's evening for siding away! **1894** HALL CAINE *Manxman* VI. xiv, Now side everything away. The medicines too, put them in the cupboard.

**7.** *Naut.* To draw (a rope) *over* or *out*.

**1834** MARRYAT *P. Simple* (1863) 41 'Ease off the larboard hawser, Mr. Jenkins, if you please.'—'Side her over, gentlemen, side her over.' **1867** SMYTH *Sailor's Word-bk.* 624 *Side out for a bend*, .. to draw the bight of a hempen cable towards the opposite side.

**8.** To make of certain dimensions on the side; to square the sides of (timber).

**1794** *Rigging & Seamanship* 15 *Heel-Pieces* are sided to the same size as the side-trees. **1797** *Encycl. Brit.* (ed. 3) XVII. 402/2 The breast hook should also be .. sided ninetenths of the beams of the lower deck. **1826** HAWKINS *The Oak* 15 The operation of 'siding' or squaring the tree. *c* **1850** *Rudim. Navig.* (Weale) 95 They are sided larger than the rest.

**9.** To furnish (a structure) with sides.

**1868** *Rep. U.S. Comm. Agric.* (1869) 366 Not a doubt exists of the economy of siding and roofing wooden bridges.

**II.** *intr.* †**10.** With *it*. To enter into rivalry.

*a* **1635** NAUNTON *Fragm. Reg.* (Arb.) 27 He soon got honour, and no sooner there, but he began to side it with the best, even with the Protector.

**11.** To take a side; to join or form sides or parties. (Cf. 4.)

**1607** SHAKS. *Cor.* IV. ii. 2 The Nobility are vexed, whom we see haue sided In his behalfe. *a* **1658** CLEVELAND *Rustick Rampant* (1687) 450 Many of these unhappy Men were awed to side, without either Malice to his Person or Power. **1712–14** POPE *Rape Lock* v. 39 All side in parties, and begin th' attack. *a* **1738** SWIFT (J.), The equitable part of those who now side against the court, will probably be more temperate. **1887** *Pall Mall G.* 31 Oct. 2/1 Children .. differ so much from one another, and 'side' so unexpectedly, that [etc.].

**b.** Const. *with*. (The more frequent use.)

**1600** HOLLAND *Livy* XXIX. vi. 713 The citie of Locri, .. in the generall revolt of all Italie, had sided also with the Carthaginians. **1647** N. BACON *Disc. Govt. Eng.* I. lxv. (1739) 138 In case the King would not concur, the people generally sided with the Lords. **1712** HEARNE *Collect.* (O.H.S.) III. 368, I was afraid otherwise that Dr. H. would have accidentally .. sided with Mr. Oddy. **1766** FORDYCE *Serm. Yng. Wom.* (1767) I. i. 32 The partial world is ready to side with them. **1849** MACAULAY *Hist. Eng.* v. I. 556 Again he encountered a pertinacious opposition. The seamen sided with Hume and Cochrane. **1875** JOWETT *Plato* (ed. 2) IV. 231 There are few modern readers who do not side with Protagoras, rather than with Socrates.

*transf.* **1667** MILTON *P.L.* II. 905 Levied to side with warring Winds, and poise Thir lighter wings.

**12.** To move or turn sideways. Also *fig.*

**1668** ETHEREDGE *She wou'd if she cou'd* v. i, We'll foot it, and side, my pretty little miss. **1841** CATLIN *N. Amer. Ind.* (1844) I. xiv. 106 Gradually siding up to the lodge. **1879** *Expositor* IX. 117 In living English there is a tendency to let the word 'holy' side off and appropriate itself to the designation of right moral character.

**b.** *Mining.* (See quot.)

**1851** GREENWELL *Coal-trade Terms, Northumb. & Durh.* 47 *Side over*, to drive headways course across a pillar of coal, in working the broken.

**13.** To keep alongside; to abut *on* at one side.

*a* **1641** FINETT *For. Ambass.* (1656) 16 The Savoyard getting the start and siding allwayes close to the Spanish Ambassador. *a* **1647** HABINGTON *Surv. Worc.* (Worcs. Hist. Soc.) II. 201 A plentifull vale .. sydinge on Bredon hyll.

**14.** To measure (so much) on the side.

**1891** *Cent. Dict.* s.v., It sides 14 inches.

**side**, *v.*[2] *slang* (now *rare*). [f. SIDE *sb.*[2]] *intr.* To be conceited or boastful; to 'put on side'. Also with *about*.

**1906** R. BROOKE *Let.* 4 June (1968) 54 This school-life .. calls to me... I play my part with zest, alternately 'siding' and ragging. **1909** WODEHOUSE *Mike* v. 26 There's just a chance you might try to side about a bit soon.

**'side**, aphetic Sc. f. ASIDE *prep.*

**1810–** in *Eng. Dial. Dict.*

**sideage** ('saɪdɪdʒ). Also **sidage**. [f. SIDE *sb.*[1] + -AGE.] **a.** A charge made for keeping trucks on a railway siding. **b.** The lateral portions of a building or the like collectively.

**1896** *Times* 18 Dec. 13/5 The action was .. in respect of sidage or standage rent charged upon trucks .. which remained more than four days upon their sidings. **1899** *Westm. Gaz.* 18 Aug. 6/1 They are utilising the frontage, or sideage, of the theatre in Drury-lane for shops with flats above.

**'side-arm**, *a.* (and *adv.*) [SIDE *sb.*[1] 26.]

**1.** Performed or delivered with a swing of the arm extended sideways, esp. in *Baseball*. Cf. ROUND-ARM *a.* and *adv.*

**1908** *Baseball Mag.* June 32/1 The spit ball .. when pitched with a side arm movement will go out. **1909** *Amer. Mag.* Aug. 402/2 He pitched .. two fast side arm balls, high and outside. **1939** 'N. BLAKE' *Smiler with Knife* xii. 188 The unerring side-arm flick .. had surprised many confident run-stealers before now. **1948** *Sun* (Baltimore) 15 Mar. 17/8 Blackwell said his best pitch was a fast sidearm ball. **1978** *Detroit Free Press* 5 Mar. c8/3 'He struck me out three times one day,' said Williams. 'He threw the sidearm slider and it would come into your face and explode.'

**2.** as *adv.* With a sweep of the arm extended sideways; in a side-arm manner.

**1958** I. Cross *God Boy* vii. 55 She swam sidearm alongside me. **1973** C. Sagan *Cosmic Connection* (1975) xv. 112 As pitcher, he could throw the ball sidearm—at the horizon at between twenty and thirty miles per hour.

**'side-arms.** [side *sb.*[1]]

**1.** *Mil.* Weapons worn at the side, such as sword, dagger, or bayonet.

**1760** *Cautions & Advices to Officers of Army* 21 No Man shall appear in the Streets without his Side-arms [etc.]. **1779** A. St. Clair in Sparks *Corr. Amer. Rev.* (1853) II. 303 The garrison are prisoners of war, and the officers have liberty to wear their side-arms. **1821** *John Bull* 7 Jan. 32/1 The soldiers drew their side-arms and wounded several persons severely. **1844** *Queen's Regul. & Ord. Army* 158 The practice of wearing Side-Arms, when not on duty, being forbidden by General Order, is not to be resorted to except on special occasions. **1893** Selous *Trav. S.E. Africa* 390 All armed with rifles and side arms.

**2.** *Artill.* (See quot. 1879.)

**1812** Mesurier in Napier *Penins. War* App. (Rtldg.) II. 480 We have the guns posted with their proper side-arms and shot piles. **1879** *Man. Artill. Exerc.* 179 'Side arms' means sponge, rammer, wad hook, and shell-extractor.

**side-bar.** [side *sb.*[1]]

**1.** *Law.* **a.** A former bar in the Outer Parliament House in Edinburgh (see quot. 1838). Also *attrib.*

**1708** J. Chamberlayne *Pres. St. Gt. Brit.* ii. (1710) 418 The Ordinary is to make a Report of their Interloquitor, which he Reports in the Outer House the next day ordinarily, or at the side Bar the next Week. **1819** *Blackw. Mag.* IV. 564 He should have stuck to side-bar quirks. **1838** W. Bell *Dict. Law Scotl.* 916 *Side-bar*, the name given to the bar in the Outer Parliament House, at which the Lords Ordinary were in use to call their hand-rolls.

**b.** A former bar in Westminster Hall. Hence ***side-bar rule*** (see quot. 1825).

**1795** Burke *Regic. Peace* iv. (C.P.S.) 349 The criminal will climb from the dock to the side-bar, and take his place.. with the counsel. **1825** Hone *Every-day Bk.* I. 156 Formerly, attorneys stood within this bar every morning during term, and moved the judges for the common rules, called side-bar rules, as they passed to their courts... The rules are [now] obtained at the rule-office; but each rule still expresses that it has been granted upon a 'side-bar' motion. **1883** *Law Times* LXXVI. 58/1, I do not now decide whether a view can still be obtained without a motion by a side-bar rule under rule 48 of R.G., H.T. 1853.

**2.** A toll-bar on a side-road.

**1861** *The Star & Dial* 28 Oct., The relief of the parish from the turnpikes and side-bars now existing in the several roads of the parish.

**3.** ***side-bar keel***, a form of iron keel for ships.

**1869** Reed *Ship-building* ii. 25 This is the arrangement known as the 'side-bar keel', and a very excellent arrangement it is for external iron keels. **1874** Thearle *Nav. Archit.* 269 The next kind of keel in order of frequency of adoption is the centre plate or side bar keel.

**4.** A lateral bar or longitudinal side-piece, as in a saddle, carriage, etc. Also *attrib.*

**1875** Knight *Dict. Mech.* 2172/2. **1884** *Ibid.* Suppl. 808/1. **1886** *Pall Mall G.* 7 Sept. 14/1 It has wheels of oak, with springs of the finest steel, arranged like a side-bar buggy.

**5.** ***side-bar whiskers*** *U.S. local*, side-whiskers, side-burns.

**1882** G. W. Peck *Peck's Sunshine* 55 He was a red-faced man, with these side-bar whiskers. **1975** *Amer. Speech 1972* XLVII. 155 Some of my earliest memories of childhood in the Up Country of South Carolina.. center upon the hearing of the lively and colorful word *tea-hounds*... Invariably the expression was employed humorously.. when a person referred to side-bar whiskers, rather bushy projections extending from the hairline to below the ears and worn with an unbearded chin.

**6.** A secondary newspaper article featuring some aspect of a main story in the same publication. *U.S. Journalism.*

**1948** C. D. MacDougall *Interpretive Reporting* (rev. ed.) 695 *Sidebar*, a complete article on one phrase of a longer story, run separately. **1967** R. J. Serling *President's Plane is Missing* iv. 70 Bat us out a good sidebar on anything that's ever happened to a presidential plane. **1977** *Time* 17 Jan. 5/2 The cover story was written by Morrison, with a sidebar on Felker by Michael Demarest.

**sideboard** ('saɪdbɔəd). [side *sb.*[1]]

**1. a.** A table (*esp.* for taking meals at) placed towards the side of a room, hall, etc.

**13..** *E.E. Allit. P.* B. 1398 þenne was alle þe halle flor hiled with knyȝtes, & barounes at þe side-bordes bounet ay-where. **1377** Langl. *P. Pl.* B. xiii. 36 Pacience and I were put to be macches, And seten by owre selue at a syde-borde. **1470–85** Malory *Arth.* vii. v. 220 The knyght.. took hym vp and sette hym at a syde bord, and sette hym self afore hym. **1531** *Test. Ebor.* (Surtees) VI. 26 The side borde in the haull with the tristillis sett in the ground. **1575** Gascoigne *Flowers* Wks. (1587) 40 Side Boords be laid aside, the tables end is gone. **1616** Middleton *Civitatis Amor* Wks. 1885 VII. 288 They.. dined that day in his [the Prince's] presence, at a sideboard. **1690** *Lond. Gaz.* No. 2533/3 A Table raised 3 Steps under a Canopy for the Emperor and King, at each end of which was a Side-board. **1726** Pope *Odyss.* xx. 348 The rich banquet in the dome prepar'd, (An humble side-board set) Ulysses shar'd.

**b.** A piece of dining-room furniture for holding side-dishes, wine, plate, etc., and often having cupboards and drawers.

**1671** Milton *P.R.* ii. 350 At a stately side-board by the wine.. in order stood Tall stripling youths rich clad. **1693** Congreve in Dryden *Juvenal* xi. (1697) 288 No Side-boards then, with gilded Plate were dress'd. **1710** *Tatler* No. 205 ¶ 1 The sumptuous Sideboard to an ingenuous Eye has often more the Air of an Altar than a Table. **1791** Boswell *Johnson* 13 April 1781, It would not be amiss to have some cold meat, and a bottle of wine upon a side-board. **1845** Disraeli *Sybil* (1863) 198 An immense unwieldy side-board, garnished with a few wine-glasses of a deep blue colour. **1882** Miss Braddon *Mt. Royal* III. i. 4 The butler ..had been carving at the side-board during the conversation.

**c.** The contents of a sideboard. *rare*$^{-1}$.

**1782** Miss Burney *Cecilia* vi. x, 'I would as soon,' answered Cecilia, 'take with me the side-board of plate.'

**d.** *attrib.*, as ***sideboard cloth, ornament,*** †***table.***

**1679** *Hist. of Jetzer* Pref. A b, They saw him every day.. Dine at a Side-board Table by himself. *c* **1716** in J. O. Payne *Rec. Eng. Catholics of 1715* (1889) 105 Sideboard cloaths 6. **1785** Cowper *Let. to J. Newton* 19 Mar., The sideboard-table.. was equally unfit for my purpose. **1815** W. Taylor in *Monthly Mag.* XXXVIII. 42 Montague mentions the sideboard-man of Cardinal Caraffi. **1865** Ruskin *Sesame* ii. §80 You bring up your girls as if they were meant for sideboard ornaments.

**2. a.** A board forming the side, or a part of the side, of any structure.

**1611** Cotgr., *Tessons d'un pressouër*, the side-boords of a presse. **1772–84** *Cook's Voy.* (1790) I. 175 The grander canoes.. are ornamented with open work..; the side-boards ..are embellished with tufts of white feathers. **1852** Seidel *Organ* 130 The side-board of a groove may be cracked. **1861–2** *Ulster Jrnl. Arch.* IX. 145 On the wheel-cars or carts were subsequently put 'side-boards', to rest the feet on. **1875** Knight *Dict. Mech.* 2173/1 *Sideboard*,.. a vertical board at the side of a work-bench,.. for supporting one end of a piece of work.

**b.** An additional and removable board placed on the side of a cart or wagon to increase its carrying capacity.

**1832** *Stamford Mercury* 27 Jan. 2/5, 2 narrow wheeled waggons.. with raves and sideboards. **1833** *Ridgemont Farm Rep.* 131 in *Husb.* (L.U.K.) III, The waggons.. are well formed, with side-boards fixed on the top of the body. **1867–** in *Eng. Dial. Dict.*

**3.** *slang.* in *pl.* **a.** A stand-up collar.

**1857** *Slang Dict.* 18. **1874** 'Uncle Bob' *Lett. to Children* (1875) xiv. 87 Starting with our standing collars on, we managed to get to the church... Some mischievous boy would cry out, 'Come out of those sideboards.'

**b.** Side-whiskers (*Cent. Dict.* 1891).

**1907** *Daily Chron.* 7 Dec. 5/7 You have described the duke as having small whiskers?—Yes, they were sideboards. Where did you get that name?—I have been in America... You call them sideboards?—Yes, or sideburns. **1956** D. M. Davin *Sullen Bell* ii. iv. 136 He was a miserable little sod, with sideboards and an American tie. **1961** H. S. Turner *Something Extraordinary* i. 9 The boys are dressed in the Teddy style, with tight trousers and sideboards. **1975** M. Bradbury *History Man* vi. 97 He takes his razor.. clipping at the line of the sideboards.

**side-bone.** [side *sb.*[1]]

**1.** That part of the pelvis on either side of a bird or fowl which is easily separated from the backbone in carving; also sometimes, the scapula or shoulder-blade.

**1819** Syd. Smith *Wks.* (1859) I. 261 A bird of such monstrous dimensions, that a side-bone of it will dine three real carnivorous Englishmen. **1842** Lover *Handy Andy* v, After giving away both wings, and all the breast, two side-bones, and the short legs. **1883** *Harper's Mag.* Aug. 456/1 The sweet morsel of the oyster out of a side bone.

**2.** A rib.

**1848** C. C. Clifford *Aristoph. Frogs* 38 A fat paunchy fellow:.. his buttocks they strike And his side-bones they poke.

**3.** Ossification of the side cartilages in a horse's foot.

**1886** A. B. Allen in *Amer. Agriculturist* (Cent.), Heaves, curb, spavin, sidebone, and ringbone are the most ordinary ailments in horses.

**'side-box,** *sb.* [side *sb.*[1]] A box or enclosed seat at the side of a theatre.

**1678** Otway *Friendship in Fasion* v. i, The Side-Box at the Play-house. **1703** Steele *Tender Husb.* i. i, You are only (when my wife goes to the play) to sit in a side box with pretty fellows. **1788** H. Mackenzie in *Trans. Soc. Edinb.* (1790) II. 174 It is only the mob in the side-boxes who.. can hear unmoved the sentiments of compassion, of generosity, or of virtue. **1842** *Penny Cycl.* XXIV. 297/1 No less preposterous is the practice of continuing the side-boxes up to the proscenium.

*attrib.* **1695** Congreve *Love for L.* v. ii, Hang your side-box beaux! **1703** Farquhar *Inconstant* i. ii, You have a good side-box face, a pretty impudent face. **1784** Cowper *Task* ii. 624 Soon enough.. T' ensure a side-box station at half price.

**b.** The occupants of a side-box.

**1712–4** Pope *Rape Lock* v. 14 Why bows the side-box from its inmost rows? *a* **1732** Gay *Toilette* Poems 1737 II. 80 Nor shall side-boxes watch my restless eye.

Hence **side-box** *v.*, to gaze at from a side-box.

**1689** Shadwell *Bury F.* iii. i, [I will] never have my Eyes off you, while I Side-box you in the Play-house.

**'sidecar.** Also **side-car, side car.** [side *sb.*[1]]

**1. a.** A conveyance in which the seats face to the sides, a jaunting-car. Now *Hist.*

**1881** *Macm. Mag.* XLIV. 388 Mrs. Roche wore a silk dress on Sunday and drove to mass on her 'side car'. **1963** 'A. Bridge' *Dangerous Islands* ix. 140 The Irish side-car, now almost extinct, is one of the least comfortable vehicles imaginable. The driver sits easily foursquare behind the horse, but the passengers perch on two long seats with a high back between them, parallel with the direction of the vehicle —and since side-cars are now never used except on very rough roads, they are jerked about, clinging to the back between the seats. **1974** *Encycl. Brit. Micropædia* V. 529/2 *Jaunting car*, also called *jaunty car* or *side-car*, two-wheeled, open vehicle, popular in Ireland from the 19th century, was unusual in having lengthwise passenger seats, either facing each other (inside the car) or back to back (outside).

**b.** A vehicle designed to be attached to the (near-)side of a motor-cycle to accommodate one or more passengers. Occas. attached to a bicycle.

**1903** *Hardwareman* 13 June 520/1 The side car is.. the most sociable attachment for a motor bicycle. **1927** Kipling *Limits & Renewals* (1932) 177 'What did he do afterwards?' "Bought a side-car to his bike, to hold more vegetables.' **1935** H. Moore *Compl. Cyclist* v. 44 Until recently the cycling of a married couple was seriously restricted by the birth of a child... Now, the tandem-cum-sidecar, bearing a family of three (or more), is a fairly common sight. **1951** T. Sterling *House without Door* ii. 12 He sat on a bicycle which had a large white sidecar. **1978** J. Irving *World according to Garp* i. 17 The pilot hurried to have Garp transferred to the sidecar of a medic's motorcycle.

**2.** A cocktail made of brandy and lemon juice with a dash of an orange liqueur.

**1928** S. Lewis *Man who knew Coolidge* i. 61 Mame took a Bronx, and Delmerine took a side-car. **1930** Auden *Poems* 12 I'll have a sidecar, thanks. **1952** S. Kauffmann *Philanderer* (1953) v. 77 They ordered sidecars and Suzy said.., 'Not too strong... I've got a lot of drinking to do to-night.' **1978** M. Dickens *Open Book* vi. 49 Once or twice at cocktail parties, I saw someone I knew and had to.. keep my head down as I cruised the crowd with my tray of sidecars and white ladies.

Hence as *v. intr.*, to drive a motor-cycle with a side-car attached; to travel in a side-car; also **'side-car(r)ing** *vbl. sb.*; **'sidecarist**, one who drives or travels in a motor-cycle combination. Now *rare.*

**1911** *Motor Cycle* 19 Jan. 21 (Advt.), Best after tests for sidecaring,.. for economy. **1914** *Motor Cycling* 12 May 8, 3½ h.p. is insufficient for sidecarring at a satisfactory speed. **1920** *Motor Cycle* 29 Apr. 487/2, I make this request because of its importance to sidecarists. **1923** *Ibid.* 25 Oct. 665/2 No doubt she would feel small and lonely when sidecarring by herself in one of these ample-looking bodies.

**side chain.** [side *sb.*[1]] †**1.** A chain mounted at the side of a vehicle for any purpose (see quots.). *Obs.*

**1849–50** J. Weale *Dict. Terms, Side Chains*, chains and hooks fixed to the sides of the tender and engine for safety, should the central drag-bar give way. **1883** W. S. Gresley *Gloss. Coal-Mining* 221 *Side chain*, a chain hooked on to the sides of tubs when running upon an engine-plane or jig, to keep all the tubs together in case a coupling breaks. **1886** *Encycl. Brit.* XX. 247/2 Some [railway] companies have gone further and placed the guard or side chains upon springs.

**2. a.** *Chem.* A chain of atoms attached to the principal part of a molecule.

**1886** Roscoe & Schorlemmer *Treat. Chem.* III. iii. 7 If two atoms of hydrogen [in benzene] be replaced by elements or radicals, termed 'side chains', three isomeric compounds may be formed whether the entering element or side chain be identical or different. **1927** Haldane & Huxley *Animal Biol.* ii. 73 The whole [chromosome] is like a gigantic single organic chemical compound, since the molecules of such a chemical compound are all made up of smaller parts—the side-chain and radicals and single atoms. **1974** *Sci. Amer.* June 59/3 They [*sc.* the catecholamines] have in common a chemical structure that consists of a benzene ring on which there are two adjacent hydroxyl groups and an ethylamine side chain.

**b.** *Physiol.* A structure postulated to project from the surface of a cell and to constitute a receptor (receptor 3 a) in Ehrlich's theory of immunological action; so ***side-chain theory.***

**1900** tr. P. Ehrlich in *Proc. R. Soc.* LXVI. 433 We may assume that the protoplasm consists of a special executive centre.. in connection with which are nutritive side-chains, which possess a certain degree of independence, and which may differ from one another according to the requirements of the different cells. *Ibid.* 440, I have now laid before you the fundamental facts which up to the present constitute our knowledge in the field pertaining to immunity, and which can be most easily and successfully explained through the agency of 'side-chain theory'. **1911** *Rep. Brit. Assoc. Adv. Sci. 1910* 635 Ehrlich has given a graphic representation of this process in his side-chain theory. **1935** N. P. Sherwood *Immunol.* vi. 121 In Ehrlich's theory these free chemical entities or cast-off side chains constitute the antibodies found in the circulation. **1974** *Encycl. Brit. Macropædia* VI. 510/1 Only if the haptophore group of a toxic molecule combines with the side chain of the cell can a bacterial toxin act upon a cell. The affected organism then produces great quantities of the side chains, all of them 'gauged' to the disease-producing agent. These immune bodies prevent a renewed infection.

**'side-coat.** Now *dial.* [side *a.* 3.]

**1.** A long coat, a greatcoat.

For unhyphened examples, some of which may strictly belong here, see side *a.* 3 a.

**1598** Bp. Hall *Sat.* iv. ii. 19 Lolioes side-cote is rough Pampilian. **1609** *Ev. Woman in Hum.* ii. ii. in Bullen *O. Pl.* IV, I grieve to see this double garded age, all side-coates, all foole. *a* **1653** Gouge *Comm. Heb.* xii. 1 If a man be to run a race,.. he will not run in a long side-coat, which may dangle about his feet, and hinder him. **1695** Kennett *Par. Antiq.* s.v. *Sidelinge*, In the North, wastcoats are call'd Side-coats. **1856** P. Thompson *Hist. Boston* 723 You've got a side-coat on.

†**2.** *pl.* Long clothes worn by children. *Obs.* Cf. long coat.

**1607** *Lingua* iii. ii, How he played at blow-point with Jupiter, when he was in his side-coats. **1663** S. Patrick *Parab. Pilgr.* iii. 8 That truth was but a stripling, or rather went in side-coats till it came to their schools.

**'side-comb.** orig. *U.S.* [SIDE *sb.*[1] 23 b.] A comb used to secure a woman's hair, esp. at the side of the head.

**1824** *Missouri* (Columbia) *Intelligencer* 8 May 3/3 (Advt.), Tortoise shell, tuck and side combs. **1851** H. MAYHEW *London Labour* I. 346/1 A few earrings and ear-drops, and sometimes a few side-combs. **1897** *Globe* 18 Feb. 6/3 Diamond side-combs in her hair. *c* **1909** D. H. LAWRENCE *Collier's Friday Night* (1934) II. 28 She finishes stroking her hair up with her side-combs. **1966** *Olney Amsden & Sons Ltd. Price List* 35 *Side comb*.. boxed 3 dozen singles 10/- per box.

**sided** ('saɪdɪd), *ppl. a.* [f. SIDE *sb.*[1] and *v.*[1]]

**1. a.** Having sides; furnished with sides.

**1486** *Bk. St. Albans* f iv b, A Grehounde shulde be.. Syded lyke a Teme. **1570** BILLINGSLEY *Euclid* XII. prop. 7. 367 Sided Columnes (sometime called prismes) are triple to pyramids, hauing one base and equall heith with them. **1602** J. DAVIES (Heref.) *Mirum in Modum* Wks. (Grosart) I. 7 The Head is like a House.. Vaulted with Bone, and with Bone likewise sided. **1668–9** COSIN in Willis & Clark *Cambridge* (1886) III. 38 A large square area.. surrounded or sided with walkes and arched columnes. **1904** *N.Y. Sun* 7 Aug. 20 The yard is sided with cabins. **1952** DYLAN THOMAS *Coll. Poems* 21 The boy she dropped from darkness at her side Into the sided lap of light grew strong.

**b.** With qualifying adj. (or adv.) prefixed.

**14..** in *Harrow. Hell* Introd. 25 After the fox, [the horse is] prik-eryd, fayr-sided, schorte trottyng. **14..** [see LONG-SIDED *a.*]. **1577** [see DEEP *a.* IV. b]. **1660–** [see MANY-SIDED *a.*]. **1669** [see FOUR, C. 1 b]. **1674** N. FAIRFAX *Bulk & Selv.* 91 Take we a square body in the world unevenly sided. **1731** W. HALFPENNY *Perspective* 9 To find the Perspective Plan of a Pentagon, or five-sided Figure. **1804** *Naval Chron.* XII. 161 A French black-sided Cutter. **1871** B. STEWART *Heat* (ed. 2) §54 The hot water box below was made of zinc, double sided and encased in wood. **1889** WELCH *Text Bk. Naval Archit.* i. 15 It.. varies.. to more than 100 per cent. in high sided vessels.

**2.** *Naut.* Having a (specified) dimension in the direction contrary to that of the moulding.

**1794** *Rigging & Seamanship* 10 *Sided*, the dimensions of any piece contrary to which it is moulded. **1797** *Encycl. Brit.* (ed. 3) XVII. 398/2 Draw a line in the body plan parallel to the middle line, at a distance equal to the half of what the stem is sided. **1867** SMYTH *Sailor's Word-bk.*, *Siding* or *Sided*, the dimensions or size of timber, the contrary way to which the mould side is placed.

**3.** Of timber: Dressed upon one or more sides.

**1865** *Navy Dockyard Acc.* (Blue Book) 8 The average loss on rough timber is found by experience to be about 50 per cent. and on sided and square timber about 30 per cent. **1880** *Lumberman's Gaz.* 7 Jan. 28 A floor is made of 'sided pieces', or boards smoothed only on one side.

†**4.** Allied to one side or another. *Obs. rare.*

**1613** in Birch *Crt. & Times Jas. I* (1848) I. 287, I do not readily remember all their names, nor how they were sided. **1620** E. BLOUNT *Horæ Subs.* 142 To take heed, that when factions be sided, his Greatnesse vphold not one faction, to the decay and ruine of the other.

Hence **'sidedness**, (*a*) in combs., as ***many-***, ***one-***, ***two-sidedness*** (q.v.); (*b*) one-sidedness; lack of symmetry in a superficially symmetrical structure or system.

**1906** [see POLARIZATION 1]. **1970** A. L. LEYNINGER *Biochem.* xxvii. 617 (*heading*) Sidedness of the transport process. **1972** *Sci. Amer.* Feb. 32/2 Such proteins are evidently located exclusively on only one side of the membrane. This information lends credence to the concept of sidedness in membranes. **1976** *Word 1971* XXVII. 240 The above contention finds support from another aspect of human evolution, that is, the sidedness or dominancy in either of the two hemispheres of our brain.

**'side-dish.** [SIDE *sb.*[1]] A dish which is accessory or additional to the principal one in a course; a dish of the kind commonly used for this purpose.

**1725** *Fam. Dict.* s.v. *Leg of Mutton*, A Side-dish of a farced Leg of Mutton. **1747–96** MRS. GLASSE *Cookery* v. 75 The kidneys make a pretty side-dish of themselves. **1820** BYRON *Juan* v. xxxii, A roast and a ragout, And fish, and soup, by some side dishes back'd. **1853** SOYER *Pantropheon* 383 [It] would have been then a little *entre-met*, or a cold side-dish (*hors-d'œuvre*). **1881** 'RITA' *My Lady Coquette* ii, Cook suggests various side-dishes for the dinner.

*fig.* **1819** LOCKHART *Peter's Lett.* lxxi. III. 241 Some practised punster, who has been invited chiefly with an eye to this sort of exhibition (from which circumstance he derives his own nickname of a side-dish).

**'side-door.** [SIDE *sb.*[1] Cf. Fris. *syddoar*, MDu. *zijtdore* (Du. *zijdeur*), G. *seitentür*.]

**1. a.** A door in the side of a building, garden, or the like; a door on one side of, or subsidiary to, the main door.

**1535** COVERDALE *1 Kings* vi. 34 Ether dore had two syde dores one hanginge to another. **1611** BIBLE *Susanna* 18 They ..went out themselues at priuie doors [*marg.* Or, side doores] to fetch the things. **1820** SCOTT *Monast.* xxiv, Christie of the Clinthill.. emerged at that instant from the side-door under the archway. **1855** MRS. CARLYLE *Lett.* II. 265 The clerk, opening a small side-door. **1894** *Outing* XXIV. 230/2 In a.. fruitless search for some side-door entrance to a shop or restaurant.

**b.** *fig.*

**1930** *Times* 21 Mar. 15/5 We maintain that these 'side door' credits are endangering our chances of securing recognition of our bonds. **1965** *New Statesman* 30 Apr. 676/1 The proposed conference on Cambodia—an attempt to settle Vietnam through a side-door—may prove abortive.

**2. side-door Pullman** *N. Amer. slang* (chiefly *Tramps*'), a railway goods wagon with sliding doors in the sides, a box-car; a freight car.

**1887** M. ROBERTS *Western Avernus* xvii. 237 When the engine.. started out, I lighted a match and took a look at my .. travelling carriage, or 'side-door Pullman', as the 'tramps' .. facetiously call them. **1918** R. W. LARDNER *Treat 'em Rough* 10 If they didn't have all the luck in the world they would be rideing [*sic*] around the country in a side door Pullman with all their baggage on. **1927** L. F. RANLETT *Let's Go* 34 A train of 'side-door Pullmans'.. drew up at the railway station.

**'side-effect.** [SIDE *sb.*[1] 24 d.] **1.** *gen.* A subsidiary consequence of an action, occurrence, or state of affairs; an unintended secondary result.

**1884** tr. *Lotze's Metaph.* 435 The view that all psychical life is a side-effect of the physical process of formation. **1933** E. BLUNDEN *Mind's Eye* (1934) I. 59 Here the side-effects of the quarrels south of the Canal.. were felt and paid for in some casualties. **1959** B. WOOTTON *Social Sci. & Social Pathol.* xi. 336 The problem is, moreover, made more difficult still by the second of the potentially unfortunate side-effects of reformative penal treatment. **1974** 'D. CRAIG' *Whose Little Girl are You?* ii. 23 A side effect of sobriety he had found to be deadly fatigue.

**2.** *Med.* An effect (usu. for the worse) of a drug or other chemical other than that for which it is administered; usu. *pl.*

**1939** WRIGHT & MONTAG *Textbk. Materia Med. Pharmacol. & Therapeutics* x. 112 The effects which are not desired in any particular case are referred to as 'side effects' or 'side actions' and, in some instances, these may be so powerful as to limit seriously the therapeutic usefulness of the drug. **1952** *Chambers's Jrnl.* June 384 A new alkaloid, built to the same molecular pattern, but with slight modifications, has been synthesised; it is equally anti-malarial but its side-effects are less toxic. **1961** *Lancet* 19 Aug. 390/1 The commonest complication of anticoagulant therapy is hæmorrhage. Numerous reports describe the frequency and nature of this side-effect. **1978** E. HARTMANN *Sleeping Pill* ii. 16 In the usual doses, paraldehyde does not produce severe side effects.

**'side-face.** [SIDE *sb.*[1]] The human face in profile; a view or representation of this.

**1696** VANBRUGH *Relapse* I. iii, Your honour's side-face is reduced to the tip of your nose! **1712** STEELE *Spect.* No. 485 ¶3 It was pleasant to see him diversify his Loveliness, sometimes obliging the Passengers only with a Side-face, with a Book in his Hand. **1752** SIR H. BEAUMONT *Crito* 24 Artists usually chuse to give a Side-face, rather than a Full one. **1889** GRETTON *Memory's Harkback* 306 It is said that no picture is extant of Cardinal Wolsey showing more than the side-face.

**'side-fly.** ? *Obs.* [SIDE *sb.*[1]] A species of horse-fly.

**1658** ROWLAND tr. *Moufet's Theat. Ins.* 935 The English call it a side-fly or a Horse-fly. **1713** DERHAM *Phys.-Theol.* VIII. vi. *note*, A rough whitish Maggot.. within the *intestinum Rectum* of Horses; I suspect the Side-Fly proceeds from it. **1773** G. WHITE *Selborne* liii, Familiar to horsemen in the south of England, under the name of forest-fly, and, to some, of side-fly, from its running sideways like a crab.

**'side-foot,** *v. Association Football.* [SIDE *sb.*[1]] *trans.* To strike (the ball) with the (in)side of the foot.

**1950** *Sport* 22–28 Sept. 10/2, I like to see the player who .. sidefoots the ball to a nearby colleague and starts a quick-passing movement. **1960** *Times* 19 Sept. 17/4 Robson side-footing the ball into the net. **1977** *Irish Press* 29 Sept. 18/5 He sent a cross to Jovanovic, who side-footed the ball into the net.

Hence as *adv.*, with the side of the foot; **'side-footed** *ppl. a.*

**1968** *Listener* 23 May 682/3 It's the way I kick, side-foot. **1974** *Observer* 1 Sept. 18/5 Latchford.. steered a side-footed volley to Rimmer's left.

**'side-glance,** *sb.* [SIDE *sb.*[1]] A glance directed sideways.

**1611** COTGR. s.v. *Queue*, To cast a side-glaunce at. **1709** STEELE *Tatler* No. 13 ¶1 When a well-made Man appeared, he was sure to have a Side-glance of Observation. **1752** SIR H. BEAUMONT *Crito* 24 The Fascination, or stroke of Love, is most usually, I believe, conveyed, at first, in a Side-glance. **1888** J. PAYN *Myst. Mirbridge* xxiii, 'My lads,' said he with a side-glance at the girls, 'I have got news for you.'

**b.** *fig.* An indirect or slight reference.

**1831** BLAKEY *Free-Will* 4 Some writers pass by the doctrine of free-will with a side glance. **1860** FREEMAN *Hist. Ess.* Ser. I. (1871) iv. 82 Yet it has been with at least a side-glance to questions of this sort.

So **'side-glance** *v.*

**1737** *Gentl. Mag.* VII. 182/1 But from th' effulgence of a distant eye, Or by the side-glanc'd light'ning pierc'd we die. **1901** G. DOUGLAS *Ho. w. Green Shutters* 35 A big.. man, whose little side-glancing eyes seemed always alert for scandal.

**'side-hill.** Now *U.S.* [SIDE *sb.*[1]] A hill-side, an acclivity.

**1708** [see below]. **1807** VANCOUVER *Agric. Devon* (1813) 44 The steep side-hills, which form the small but handsome vale of Ashcombe. **1857** THOREAU *Maine W.* (1894) 82, I arrived upon a side-hill, or rather side-mountain. **1893** K. SANBORN *S. California* 85 As to the safety of the ascent, no one need hesitate who is free from settled prejudice against a side-hill.

*attrib.* **1708** *Lond. Gaz.* No. 4489/3 The Fee-simple and Inheritance of the Manor of Park-Manston,.. containing.. 46 Acres of Uplands, or Side-hill-Lands,.. are to be sold. **1861** STEPHENS & BURN *Farm-buildings* § 1762 Plan of second storey of American side-hill barn. **1875** KNIGHT *Dict. Mech.* 2173/1 *Side-hill Plow*, a plow whose cutting apparatus is reversible, so as to throw its furrow-slice to the right or left, as may be desired. **1897** HOWELLS *Landlord at Lion's Head* 219 They walked down the side-hill street.

**'side-issue.** [SIDE *sb.*[1] 24 d.] A subsidiary issue.

**1873** M. ARNOLD *Lit. & Dogma* (1876) p. xxi, To judge the Creed by that method was a side-issue. **1928** *Sat. Rev.* 20 Oct. 515/2 The secret is well kept and the various side issues are interesting and bewildering. **1938** [see CREATIVE *a.* 1 b]. **1958** *Times* 29 Sept. 11/2 The floor will go down fighting on the side-issue of the platform's acceptance of the *status quo* for the public schools. **1982** F. DAVIES *Death of Hit-Man* ix. 151 Zio must be here for something far more important. Not just to kill Denton. That must have been a side-issue.

**'side-kick.** *slang* (orig. *U.S.*). [Back-formation from next.] **1.** A companion or close associate; *spec.* an accomplice or partner in crime; a subordinate member of a pair or group. More *loosely*, a friend, a colleague.

**1906** H. GREEN *At Actors' Boarding House* 85 The Red Swede.. sat over a pint of champagne with Dopey Polly.. and his side kick, the Runt. *a* **1911** D. G. PHILLIPS *Susan Lenox* (1917) II. xvii. 394 'Now, what d'ye think of that?' said Black Mustache to his 'side-kick.'.. 'Guess we'd better run her in, Pete.' **1927** J. M. SAUNDERS *Wings* iv. 173 'I want two of you,' the Major said, 'who is your side-kick?' 'Armstrong,' Johnny admitted unwillingly. **1934** *Bulletin* (Sydney) 25 July 47/1 Snowy was good at soft things; as a rule, you could trust him as a sidekick to help you to a clear getaway. **1956** M. PROCTER *Pub Crawler* viii. 102 He's Frank McGeen's sidekick. They team up together in jobs of this sort. **1960** *Times* 14 Oct. 18/7 Miss Moira Redmond, as an ex-wife.., made a takingly crisp and sub-acid side-kick. **1976** *New Yorker* 23 Feb. 82/3 Christopher Lloyd was funny as a drug-ridden sidekick of the defunct singer. **1981** 'J. MCVEAN' *Seabird Nine* xiii. 154 It was the White House. .. And not just some little cotton-tail sidekick either, but counsel to the President.

**2.** *Criminals' slang.* = SIDE-POCKET 1. *U.S.*

**1916** *Lit. Digest* 19 Aug. 424/2 Pockets range from 'side kicks' to 'double insiders'. **1935** *Amer. Speech* X. 20/2 *Side-kick* [formerly] one's pal. In modern argot a side pocket in the coat; it is doubtful if there is any connection. **1955** D. W. MAURER in *Publ. Amer. Dial. Soc.* XXIV. 125 The outside pockets in an overcoat are called *side kicks* (from which we get a venerable American idiom).

**3.** An incidental criticism; a passing or indirect attack, a 'side-swipe'.

**1958** *Economist* 1 Feb. 384/2 Two intriguing passages in Mr. Thorneycroft's speech were, first, what could be taken as a sidekick at the Government's insistence on Britain having the H-bomb. **1971** *Scotsman* 20 May 10/1 Parents came in for a good many side-kicks these days, he said. 'Blame the parents' was a recurring cry.

**'side-kicker.** *slang* (orig. *U.S.*). Now *rare.* [SIDE *sb.*[1]] = SIDE-KICK 1.

**1903** 'O. HENRY' in *McClure's Mag.* Feb. 432 Billy was my side-kicker in New York. **1926** J. BLACK *You can't Win* xiv. 189, I cast about for a 'sidekicker'. **1929** *Papers Mich. Acad. Sci., Arts & Lett.* X. 322/1 *Side-kicker*, sleeping companion; bosom chum. **1933** *Bulletin* (Sydney) 6 Sept. 41/2 'One's known as Yargus,' George says, 'and his sidekicker as the Snake.'

**'sidelang(le,** *v. north.* and *Sc.* [f. SIDE *sb.*[1] + LANGLE *v.* An example of *side lanyel* as a sb. occurs in the *Yorksh. Dial.* (1684) 171.] (See quots. and cf. SIDE-LINE *v.*)

α. **1641** BEST *Farm. Bks.* (Surtees) 28 Those that have theire ewes tupped betimes will usually hopple or sidelange their tuppes. **1788** W. H. MARSHALL *Yorksh.* II. 351 To *Sidelong*, to fetter, as a preventive from straying, or breaking pasture, by chaining a fore and a hind foot of the same side together. **1868–** in Yorkshire glossaries. **1869** KENNEDY *Evenings Duffrey* 190 Sidelanged, spancelled, and fettered, they [Irish Papists] must draw a trace [etc.].

β. **1825** JAMIESON *Suppl.*, *Side-langel*, to tie the fore and hind foot of a horse together on one side. **1838** HOGG *Tales, Katie Cheyne* ii, I am settled, tied up, tethered, side-langled.

**'sideless,** *a.* [f. SIDE *sb.*[1]] Without sides; open at the sides.

**1817** COLERIDGE *Biogr. Lit.* xii. I. 267 No less a contradiction than an infinite circle or a sideless triangle. **1834** PLANCHÉ *Brit. Costume* xi. 163 The sideless garment faced with fur, and terminating in long full skirts. **1877** *Athenæum* 3 Nov. 571/3 The ladies.. wear the sideless cotehardies which were so common in their day.

**'side-light.** Also side light, sidelight. [SIDE *sb.*[1] Cf. Fris. *sydljacht*, *-ljocht* (in sense 2), G. *seitenlicht* (in sense 1).]

**1. a.** Light coming from the side.

**1610** HOLLAND *Camden's Brit.* (1637) 818 The side light that the sunne beames cast all night long. **1891** *Cent. Dict.* s.v., To take a photograph by side-light.

**b.** *fig.* Incidental light or information upon a subject.

**1862** J. BROWN *Let.* 4 Feb. (1912) 193, I like so much your saying that about the breeding of my mind, and all the side-lights and sub-suggestions. **1871** B. TAYLOR *Faust* (1875) I. 221 The reader needs all the side-lights which can be thrown upon its translated forms. **1886** SYMONDS *Renaiss. It., Cath. React.* (1898) VII. x. 120 Side light may be thrown upon Sarpi's judgment.. by considering [etc.].

**2. a.** A window, or opening for light, in the side of a building, ship, lamp, etc.

**1827** FARADAY *Chem. Manip.* i. 14 One side light should however in all cases be provided [in a laboratory]. **1875** KNIGHT *Dict. Mech.* 2174/1 *Side-light*,.. a plate of glass in a frame fitted to an air-port in a ship's side. **1898** *Cycling* 61 Sliding side-lights should be fitted,.. and lamps with weak springs are to be avoided.

**b.** A side-portion of a large window; a window by the side of a door or other window.

**1851** HAWTHORNE *Ho. Seven Gables* iv, She..gazed through the dusty side-lights of the portal. **1860** G. E. STREET in *Archæol. Cant.* III. 117 The tracery has quatrefoiled circles over the side-lights.

**3.** *Naut.* **a.** A light carried on either side of a ship under way in the night.

**1887** in *Cassell's Encycl. Dict.*

**b.** A night-lantern in the gangway of a warship.

**1891** in *Cent. Dict.*

**4.** One of the small warning lights on either side of the front (or rear) of a motor vehicle, which when lit show the position and width of the vehicle, esp. at night; a sidelamp.

**1912** *Motor Manual* (ed. 14) iii. 120 Much better side lights have been provided than ever existed before. **1955** *Times* 16 Aug. 2/7 British motorists are singularly reluctant to use the lights of their cars—motorists abroad invariably switch on their sidelights much earlier. **1973** A. BEHREND *Samarai Affair* xi. 108 One headlamp and both sidelights had been broken.

**'side-line,** *sb.* [SIDE *sb.*[1]]

**1. a.** A line extending along or towards one side of a thing or space; *spec.* in *Football* and other sports: a line marking the edge of the playing area at the side; a touch-line. Also, the area immediately outside this. Also *fig.* with allusion to the position of a spectator observing but removed from the action of a game, esp. in phr. ***on*** or ***from the sidelines.***

**1768** PENNANT *Brit. Zool.* (1776) III. 226 In young fish the space above the side line is marked with small black spots. **1862** *Chambers's Encycl.* IV. 413/2 Two side-lines, called goal-lines, are drawn from each of the goals. **1886** J. DWIGHT *Lawn-Tennis* II. i. 41 He may play down the side-line or he may lob. **1899** H. A. QUINN *Pennsylvania Stories* 24 The coaches on the side lines were not so jubilant. **1962** [see BYE *sb.* 1 c]. **1977** *Cleethorpes News* 27 May 15/2 It was a close game, with plenty of support on the sidelines.

*fig.* **1934** WEBSTER, *Side-line*... The standpoint of those not immediately participating. **1939** *Times* 2 Nov. 8/3 The Russian Government were well satisfied with the policy announced by the Supreme Soviet two months ago—standing on the sidelines and watching Germany, England, and France fight out the war. **1954** T. S. ELIOT *Confidential Clerk* I. 18 But as you're here, Eggers, I can just relax. I'm going to enjoy the game from the side-lines. **1974** J. MANN *Sticking Place* x. 151, I can't sit on the sidelines all my life, producing academic dissertations.

*attrib.* **1908** *Westm. Gaz.* 15 June 9/1 (Tennis), Barrett scored many aces by clean side-line drives.

**b.** A railway or tramway line extending away from the main line.

**1890** KIPLING *From Sea to Sea* (1899) II. xxix. 62 Livingstone is..the junction for the little side-line that takes you to the Yellowstone National Park. **1898** *Westm. Gaz.* 4 Oct. 10/1 There remain the South London and the Southwark and Deptford Companies' systems. These, however, are but sidelines west and east.

**c.** *Canad.* = *side road* (*b*) s.v. SIDE *sb.*[1] 27.

**1834** in W. A. Langton *Early Days in Upper Canada* (1926) 91 The concession lines run N.17 1/2W. and the side lines I am told are not exactly perpendicular. **1896** J. L. GOURLAY *Hist. Ottawa Valley* 34 The concessions and sidelines in these townships were 66 feet wide.

**2.** A line used for securing an animal by tying together the fore and hind leg on one side.

**1831** YOUATT *Horse* xviii. 320 The side-line is a very simple and useful method of confining the horse. *Ibid.* 321 When both legs are included in the hobble or rope (as in another way of using the side line).

**3.** An auxiliary line of goods, trade, or occupation.

**1890** *New York Tribune* 9 Mar. (Cent.), Wanted..Salesman to carry as a side-line a new line of advertisement specialty. **1898** *Westm. Gaz.* 31 Dec. 5/3 In the cycling trade the agents..are exercised in their minds over the question of 'side lines'. They want something to do in the dull season. **1937** 'G. ORWELL' *Road to Wigan Pier* i. 8 Brooker..was a miner by trade, but he and his wife had been keeping shops of various kinds as a side-line all their lives. **1966** *Listener* 13 Jan. 67/3 Few of them managed to make a good living out of their art alone, without running a side-line such as a brewery or an insurance office. **1977** *New Yorker* 29 Aug. 47/2 His sideline computer-service business thrived. **1979** D. GAGEBY in J. J. Lee *Ireland 1945–70* 130 It caused suspicion among journalists whose sideline earnings on correspondence for English or American papers seemed to be threatened.

**'side-line,** *v.* [f. the *sb.*]

**I.** *trans.* **1.** To secure (cattle or horses) with a side-line.

**1837** W. IRVING *Rocky Mountains* I. ii. 36 The horses were 'side lined', as it is termed: that is to say, the fore and hind foot on the same side of the animal were tied together, so as to be within eighteen inches of each other. **1863** *Pilgr. over Prairies* I. 154 After unharnessing and sidelining our cattle ('sidelining' is tying the fore and hind legs on the same side within eighteen or twenty inches of each other). *a* **1904** A. ADAMS *Log Cowboy* x. 151 We hobbled every horse and side-lined certain leaders.

**2.** *pass.* (or as *ppl. a.*) Of a sportsman: to be forced to remain out of competition on the side-lines, esp. through injury. Also *fig.* Occas. *actively*, of an injury, etc. orig. and chiefly *U.S.*

**1945** *Sun* (Baltimore) 30 June 8/2 Snead is once more sidelined with his back ailment. **1947** *News-Age-Herald* (Birmingham, Alabama) 20 July 1B/7 Charley Keller..is recovering..from an operation to relieve the back ailment that has sidelined him for several weeks. **1949** *Cavalier Daily* (Univ. of Virginia) 22 Oct. 1/5 Gene Schroeder, still side-lined with a shoulder injury. **1966** *N.Y. Times* (Internat. ed.) 22 Apr. 12/8 Buckpasser..is sidelined with a hoof injury. **1970** [see *defenceman* s.v. DEFENCE *sb.* 9]. **1975** *Amer. Speech 1972* XLVII. 143 Although polio cruelly limited her for many years to the use of one arm, Betty Adler was never sidelined. **1977** *Daily Express* 29 Jan. 38/4 Ian Wallace and Mick Ferguson, their first-choice front men who have been side-lined for the last six weeks.

**3.** To mark (a passage of text) for special attention by a line or lines drawn in the margin; *spec.* (of confidential matter) to indicate that it should not be printed or published.

**1968** *Guardian* 24 July 8/1 The..witnesses had been encouraged to speak freely with the assurance that they would be allowed to 'sideline' those parts of the evidence that they did not wish to see published. **1978** *Observer* 10 Dec. 1/7 The all-party committee..is expected to exercise traditional discretion in 'sidelining' or censoring Cabinet minutes.

**4.** *fig.* To remove from the centre of activity or attention; to place in an inferior position.

**1973** H. GRUPPE *Truxton Cipher* (1974) xx. 218 He even persuaded the brass to put him in charge of the special project... The Navy was glad to do it. Sideline him for a bit. **1976** *National Observer* (U.S.) 22 May 10/2 President Nixon vetoed the legislation in 1971, and since then, a lack of congressional and Administration support has sidelined the Mondale approach.

**II. 5.** *intr.* To engage *in* as a subsidiary occupation or sport.

**1944** *College Topics* (Univ. of Virginia) 30 Mar. 3 Captain Nat Boyd is specializing in the hurdles and broad jumping and sidelining in the high jump. **1975** B. GARFIELD *Hopscotch* xv. 147 The kingpin in town was a back-porch country lawyer who..sidelined in real estate.

**sideling** ('saɪdlɪŋ), *sb.* Forms: 4 **sydelynge,** 5 **sydlyng,** 6 **syd(e)ling;** 4 **sidelyng,** 8– **sideling** (9 *Sc.* **-lin**); 9 **sidling,** *dial.* **siddlin,** etc. [f. SIDE *sb.*[1] + -LING[1].]

†**1.** A strip or piece of land lying by the side of a larger portion or by a stream. *Obs.*

**1399** in Kennett *Par. Ant.* (1695) 531 Fons de Goldwell.. cujus aqua manat..præter dictas buttes, et ideo vocantur Sydelynges. *Ibid.* 532 Ab hoc furlong procedunt le Sidelyngs de quibus patet superius. *c* **1450** *Godstow Reg.* 369 The tythis of ix. buttis I-called Sydlyngis, liyng at the lowsy thorn, bitwene j. acre of lond..and j. pece of lond. **1576** in W. H. Turner *Select. Rec. Oxford* (1880) 387 A bracke betwixte two sydelings called the greate and little sydlings to be dammed uppe. **1726** in W. Wing *Ann. Steeple Aston* (1875) 54 One sideling of Pasture ground of about an acre. *Ibid.* 55 One small sideling of ground and Comon of Pasture for one Cow and one Horse.

**2.** A slope or declivity, *esp.* one along the side of which a track or road runs.

**1808** JAMIESON s.v., *The sidelins* (*sidlings*) of a hill, i.e. the declivity. **1852** MUNDY *Antipodes* v. (1855) 127 We..got upon a 'sidling' on the slope of the hill. **1881** MRS. C. PRAED *Policy & P.* I. xi. 230 A sideling that afforded no footing for his horse would necessitate a descent into the bed of the creek. **1886** ELWORTHY *W. Som. Word-bk.*

**3.** *U.S.* = SIDING *vbl. sb.* 7.

**1859** BARTLETT *Dict. Amer.* (ed. 2), *Sidling*, a place at which to turn off on a railroad to wait for a passing engine. The English term is siding.

**sideling** ('saɪdlɪŋ), *adv.* and *a.* Forms: 4 **sidlyng,** 5 **sydlyng,** 6 **-ling;** 5–6 **sydelyng(e,** 6– **sideling** (7 **-line;** *Sc.* 8 **-lin,** 9 **-lan**); 6–7, 9 **sidling** (*Sc.* **-lin'**). [f. SIDE *sb.*[1] + -LING[2]. Cf. MDu. *side-*, *zidelinge*, MLG. *syd-*, *zydeling(e*. An OE. comb. *sidlingweȝ* occurs in Kemble *Cod. Dipl.* III. 446.]

**A.** *adv.*

**1.** With a sideward movement; in a sidelong direction; sideways; obliquely.

*c* **1330** R. BRUNNE *Chron. Wace* (Rolls) 10348 Ȝyf any connyng man of þo Standeþ stille, or sidlyng can go. *c* **1400** *Destr. Troy* 7320 Prothenor..Set hym a sad dynt Sydlyng by-hynd. **1470–85** MALORY *Arthur* x. lxiv. 524 Thenne they lasshed to gyder many sad strokes & tracyd and traueryd now bakward now sydelyng. **1506** *Mem. Hen. VII* (Rolls) 290 So the King of Castile went sidling into the closet and drew the King in by the arm. **1589** PUTTENHAM *Eng. Poesie* III. (Arb.) 300 Such as retire from the Princes presence..go backward or sideling for a reasonable space. **1609** W. M. *Man in Moone* (1849) 30 Hee hath the witte yet to enter sideling, like a gentlewoman with an huge farthingall. **1646** SIR T. BROWNE *Pseud. Ep.* 142 Crabs move sideling, Lobsters will swim swiftly backward. **1702** S. PARKER tr. *Cicero's De Finibus* I. 14 If all his Atoms must descend Sideling, they'll never join one another. **1789** D. DAVIDSON *Seasons* 45 Sidelin to the fight They both come on. **1830** W. PHILLIPS *Mt. Sinai* I. 392 Or east, or west, or sideling to the north, Or south careering, it is follow'd still.

†**2. a.** To or on one side (*of* a thing). *Obs. rare.*

**1543** RECORDE *Arithm.* 132 b, Farthynges..must be set in a voyde space sydelynge beneth the pennes. **1657** HOWELL *Londinop.* 349 Worcester House lies sideling of it. **1786** BURNS *Lord Daer* v, I sidling shelter'd in a nook, An' at his lordship steal't a look.

†**b.** With an inclination to one side. *Obs.*

**1603** FLORIO *Montaigne* (1634) 518 All Alexanders followers bare their heads sideling, as he did. **1612** SHELTON *Quix.* I. I. viii, I pray you sit right in your saddle, for you ride sideling, which proceeds, as I suppose, of the bruising you got by your fall. **1718** MOTTEUX *Quix.* (1733) I. 62 Sit a little more upright in your Saddle; you ride sideling methinks.

†**3.** With the side *toward* something. *Obs.*[−1]

**1548** PATTEN *Exped. Scotl.* G vj, The enemies were in a fallowe felde, wherof the furrowes lay sydelyng towarde our men.

†**4.** On a side-saddle; facing to the side. *Obs.*

**1603** FLORIO *Montaigne* I. xlviii. (1632) 158 To ride up and downe.., ever sitting sideling, as women use. **1619** MIDDLETON *Love & Antiq.* Wks. 1885 VII. 326 Queen Anne ..being the first that taught women to ride sideling on horseback. **1698** J. CRULL *Muscovy* 299 This Horse..upon which the Patriarch rides sideling.

†**5.** So that the top and bottom are turned to the sides. *Obs. rare.*

**1611** FLORIO, *Catagráphi*, images or pictures standing biase or sideline. **1712** SWIFT *Public Sp. Whigs* Wks. 1751 VIII. 9 A Fellow nailed up Maps in a Gentleman's Closet, some sideling, others upside down.

**B.** *adj.*

†**1.** Situated towards or at the side(s). *Obs.*

**1548** VICARY *Anat.* iii. (1888) 27 [The] Parietales..be the bones of the sideling parts of the head. **1552** UDALL tr. *Germinus' Anat.* B iij b/2 The Chekes are the sydelynge parts of the face.

**2.** Directed or moving sideways; oblique.

**1611** COTGR., *Oblique*,..sideling, bowed, winding. **1665** MANLEY *Grotius' Low C. Wars* 18 Sideling and oblique Accusations were admitted. **1678** DRYDEN *Kind Keeper* II. i. The peaking Creature,..with a sideling Look, as if one Cheek carry'd more byass than the other. **1763** DODSLEY *Leasowes* in *Shenstone's Wks.* (1777) II. 304 The eye is carried by a sideling view down a length of lawn. **1771** FOOTE *Penseroso* v. 237 The sideling glance Of bigot malice. **1828** SCOTT *Fair M. Perth* xxiii, Henry struck him a sideling blow on the steel head-piece. **1845** G. OLIVER *Coll. Biogr. Soc. Jesus* p. iii, They cast no sideling glance to interest. **1890** HALL CAINE *Bondman* II. v, 'We know you are watching him,' he added, with a sideling motion of the head towards Government House.

**b.** *fig.* Of speech, etc.: Indirect.

**1789** ROSS *Helenore* (ed. 3) 105 For Nory's sake, this sideling hint he gae.

**3.** Having an inclination; sloping, steep.

**1611** COTGR., *Callate*,..a sideling, or sloping peece of ground. **1808** in JAMIESON. **1821** CLARE *Vill. Minstr.* II. 44 The green hill's sideling slope. **1854** *Jrnl. R. Agric. Soc.* XV. II. 246 It is a good plan to plough sidling ground in a circle. **1894** *Harper's Mag.* Feb. 356/2 Never have I seen hills as sideling as these.

Hence †**'sidelingwise** *adv. Obs.*[−1]

**1587** HOLINSHED *Chron., Hist. Scotl.* 102/2 Two Pictish horssemen running at Colgerme sidelingwise, bare him quite through.

**sidelings** ('saɪdlɪŋz), *adv.* Now *dial.* Forms: 4–6 **sydlynges** (5 **-lyngs,** 6 **-lyngis,** 9 **-lins**); 4–5 **sidelynges** (6 **sedelinges,** *Sc.* **sidelingis**), 6– **sidelings,** 8–9 **sidelins** (**-lans, -lens**); 5 (9 *dial.*) **sidlings,** 6 **-lingis,** 9 **-lins.** [f. SIDE *sb.*[1] + -LINGS. Cf. Fris. *sydlings*, Du. *zijdelings*, G. *seitlings*. In Sc. dial. also used as an adj.]

**1.** = SIDELING *adv.* 1; also, indirectly, with indirect speech; with a side-look.

*c* **1330** R. BRUNNE *Chron. Wace* (Rolls) 10869 Frolle vp stirte, & sydlynges glent. *a* **1400–50** *Alexander* 2057 þe pouwere of Persy..Seȝes sidlings doun slayn of þaire blonkis. *c* **1430** *Syr Gener.* (Roxb.) 4206 Right befor the king of kinges Manassen fel deid doun sidelinges. **1562** TURNER *Herbal* II. (1568) 93 Theophrast maketh orobum to grow sydlynges. **1593** NASHE *Foure Lett. Conf.* Wks. (Grosart) II. 263 In a verse, when a worde of three sillables cannot thrust in but sidelings. **1613** M. RIDLEY *Magn. Bodies* 16 That she wave not sidelings or turne about. **1675** V. ALSOP *Anti-sozzo* 407 Why should others be forced to crowd in and wedge themselves through a narrow wicket sidelings? **1785** BURNS *To Wm. Simpson* ii, Ironic satire, sidelins sklented, On my poor Musie. **1807–10** TANNAHILL *Poems* (1846) 70 I'll sidelins hint—na, bauldly tell, I whyles think something o' mysel'. **1856** J. SMITH *Merry Bridal* 66 Sidelins he meets the cauld averted gaze O'them that kent him in his better days.

†**2.** = SIDELING *adv.* 2 a. *Obs.*

?*a* **1400** *Morte Arth.* 1039 Bot thow moste seke more southe, sydlynges a lyttille. *c* **1450** in Aungier *Syon* (1840) 309 Se that the deske..be set atte sowth ende of that awter ..sidelynges a fowre fote. **1533** BELLENDEN *Livy* II. xxi. (S.T.S.) I. 216 Ane weyng of horss men come sidlingis þe batall of Veanis. **1579** J. JONES *Preserv. Bodie & Soul* I. xxvi. 49 In what sorte the light in the Chamber is to be placed... If sidelings, it may cause the Infant to proue squint. **1613** M. RIDLEY *Magn. Bodies* 16 If ankors by layd out, either forward, or backward, or sidelings.

†**3.** = SIDELING *adv.* 3. *Obs.*

**1561** HOLLYBUSH *Hom. Apoth.* 10 Take a greate basin, set it sedelinges to a wall, so that it do leane holy vpon the wall.

**4.** Side by side; abreast.

**1552** LYNDESAY *Monarche* 2730 Sick breid, abufe the wallis, there was, Thre cartis mycht sydlingis on thame pas. **1805–** in *Eng. Dial. Dict.*

**5.** = SIDELING *adv.* 4.

*a* **1825** FORBY *Voc. E. Anglia* 300 Women sit on horseback sidlings, and men stradlings. **1898** in *Eng. Dial. Dict.*

**'sidelong,** *adv.*[1] and *a.*[1] Also **side-long.** [f. SIDE *sb.*[1] + -LONG. Cf. MDa. *sidelangs*, MSw. *sidholangs* adv.] **A.** *adv.*

**1.** Towards the side; sideways, obliquely.

**1580** BARET *Alvearie*, Sidelong or sidewise, *ex obliquo.* **1589** NASHE *M. Marprelate* Wks. (Grosart) I. 121 A crooked generation, that loues to swym side-long with the Crabbe. **1602** R. CAREW *Cornwall* 10 b, Their maner of working in the Loadmines, is to follow the Load as it lieth, either sidelong, or downe-right. **1667** MILTON *P.L.* VI. 197 As if.. waters forcing way Sidelong, had push't a Mountain from his seat. **1718** *Freethinker* No. 17 Taking her Hoop in one Hand in a great Fury, she squeezes side-long through a Passage two Yards wide. **1816** SCOTT *Antiq.* xl, With these words she sunk back on the settle, and from thence sideling to the floor. **1867** RUSKIN *Time & Tide* x. §58 That blue-lipped serpent—working its way sidelong in the sand.

**2.** Along the sides. *rare*$^{-1}$.

**1592** R. D. *Hypnerotomachia* 19 b, Which aulter (as I may tearme it) sidelong about, wrought with leaves.

**3.** So as to show the side. *rare*$^{-1}$.

**1610** GUILLIM *Heraldry* VI. v. (1611) 264 This forme of Helmet placed sidelong and close doth Ger. Leigh attribute to the dignity of Knight.

**4.** To the side *of*; side by side; presenting the side *to* something.

**1643** *True Informer* 40 The Parliaments Forces were within six miles side-long of him. **1803** *Edwin* III. iii. 49 When..our bands were engaged in war, sidelong we fought. **1846** HAWTHORNE *Mosses* II. xii, Seated within the shop, sidelong to the window. **1895** KIPLING *2nd Jungle Bk.* 203 Each [dog] was fastened sidelong to his neighbour's neck.

**5.** On the side; with the side to the ground.

**1667** MILTON *P.L.* IV. 333 Side-long as they sat recline On the soft downie Bank damaskt with flours. **1748** THOMSON *Cast. Indol.* I. xl, Behoves no more, But sidelong, to the gently-waving wind, To lay the well-tun'd instrument reclin'd. **1757** W. WILKIE *Epigoniad* IV. 95 He..sidelong on the beach the galley laid. **1870** MORRIS *Earthly Par.* II. III. 334 Side-long the plough beside the field-gate lay.

**b.** Inclining to one side in moving along a slope.

**1879** JEFFERIES *Wild Life* vi. 119 On the hills where the waggons have to run 'sidelong' to pick up the crops one side higher than the other.

**6.** As *prep.* By or along the side of.

**1523** FITZHERB. *Husb.* §38 If she wyl not stande syde longe all the lambe, than gyue her a lytell hey. **1822** SCOTT *Halidon Hill* I. ii, We'll..descend Sidelong the hill; some winding path there must be.

**B.** *adj.*

**1.** In a slanting direction; in a sloping position; inclining to one side; lying on the side.

**1597** A. M. *Guillemeau's Fr. Chirurg.* 28/4 We must make the apertione sydelonge or contradictorye, when we purpose to iterate the phlebotomye. **1718** ROWE tr. *Lucan* v. 928 This [wave] lays the sidelong Alder on the Main, And that restores the leaning Bark again. **1748** GRAY *Alliance* 91 With side-long plough to quell the flinty ground. *c* **1830** LONGF. *Spirit of Poetry* 30 The..upland where the sidelong sun.., at evening, goes. **1871** PALGRAVE *Lyr. Poems* 36 As he who whilst the side-long vase ran clear Dream'd down whole years in fancy.

**b.** *spec.* Of ground: Sloping.

**1792** BELKNAP *Hist. New-Hampshire* III. 105 In side long ground, the stick by its rolling would overset the sled. **1802** E. DARWIN *Orig. Society* IV. 165 Green sloping lawns construct the sidelong scene. **1838** SIMMS *Public Wks. Grt. Brit.* 36 The area of any cross section in sidelong ground. **1873** ROBERTSON *Engineering Notes* 48 Sidelong ground must be cut into steps before embanking over it.

**2.** Directed to one side or sideways.

**1608** BP. J. KING *Serm.* 24 Mar. 2 The comming so neare togither, of two..so great festiuities.., giueth mee so iust an occasion, togither with my principal aime at the one, to haue a collateral, sidelong aspect at the other. **1635** SWAN *Spec. M.* v. §2 (1643) 169 Their motion is a laterall or side-long motion. **1737** *Gentl. Mag.* VII. 570 With a side-long look, Poor William thro' the heart was struck. **1791** COWPER *Iliad* XXI. 319 With a sidelong sweep Assailing him. **1818** BYRON *Juan* I. clxxiii, Regarding both with slow and sidelong view. **1861** THACKERAY *Round. P., Ogres*, He gives a dreadful sidelong glance of suspicion. **1887** HALL CAINE *Son of Hagar* III. i, Indicating with a sidelong nod the room to the left.

*transf.* **1743** FRANCIS tr. *Hor., Odes* III. xxii. 10 Yearly shall bleed a festal Swine, That meditates the side-long Wound.

**b.** Glancing, moving, or extending sideways.

**1818** SHELLEY *Rev. Islam* III. xxxiv. 8 Past the pebbly beach the boat did flee On sidelong wing, into a silent cove. **1864** SWINBURNE *Atalanta* 1305 But the sidelong arrow slid. **1877** TENNYSON *Harold* III. i. 87 [It] shot out sidelong boughs across the deep.

**3.** Indirect; not straightforward or open.

**1654** Z. COKE *Logick* 25 We have seen the direct degrees; now follow the Collateral, or sidelong, which is called Difference. **1697** C. LESLIE *Snake in Grass* (ed. 2) 380 Their side-long Answers, and silly Excuses will not do. **1832** HT. MARTINEAU *Homes Abroad* vi. 82 They did not see the winks, and the side-long smiles. **1853** R. S. SURTEES *Sponge's Sp. Tour* (1893) 148 Hazarding promiscuous sidelong sort of observations, that might be taken up by anybody. **1883** *Longman's Mag.* Nov. 97 A sinister look, which even the Captain could not help noting in a sidelong fashion.

† **'sidelong,** *adv.*[2] and *a.*[2] *Obs. rare.* [f. SIDE *adv.*[1] and *a.* + LONG *a.*] = SIDE *a.* and *adv.*[1]

**1576** GASCOIGNE *Steele Gl.* Epil. (Arb.) 82 They be no boyes, which weare such side long gowns. **1591** SPENSER *M. Hubberd* 354 And now the Foxe had gotten him a gowne, And th' Ape a cassocke sidelong hanging downe. —— *Vision Bellay* ix, An hideous bodie big and strong I sawe, With side-long beard.

**'side-look.** [SIDE *sb.*[1]] An oblique look; a side-glance. Also *fig.*

**1705** STEELE *Tender Husb.* IV. i, That Side-look hides the Mole on the left Cheek. **1820** SYD. SMITH *Wks.* (1859) I. 316 In that straight line he went on for fifty years, without one side-look. **1880** BLACKMORE *Mary Anerley* xli, With a side-look he let her know that he did not wish to hurt her feelings.

So **'side-looker, -looking.**

**13..** *MS. Digby 86* fol. 168 b, þe hare..þe westlokere, The waldeneie, the sid-lokere. *c* **1435** *Torr. Portugal* 1650 As he caste a side lokyng, He saw a lady in her bed syttyng.

**'side-looking,** *a.* [SIDE *sb.*[1]]

**1.** Characterized by looking sideways.

**1829** J. F. COOPER *Wept of Wish-ton-Wish* I. iii. 37 A demure, side-looking young woman kept her great wheel in motion. **1956** H. GOLD *Man who was not with It* (1965) iv. 36 Those others turned me back..to the side-looking cast in Phyl's eyes, her black hair short-cropped with a calculating wildness.

**2.** Producing or being a radar or sonar beam transmitted sideways and downwards, usu. from an aircraft for the mapping of relief.

**1961** B. L. CORDRY et al. in G. Merrill *Airborne Radar* xiv. 777 In side-looking systems..the orientation of the antenna may not be changed easily. **1964** *Jrnl. Geophysics Res.* LXIX. 3824/1 Narrow-beam lateral echo sounders are similar to standard echo sounders except that the transducer is mounted to give a side-looking beam that is a few degrees below horizontal. **1971** P. O'DONNELL *Impossible Virgin* i. 6 From film taken by side-looking radar he could penetrate.. the earth's skin, to..the bed-rock below. **1977** *Sci. Amer.* Oct. 93/2 The acute grazing angle of the microwave illumination of side-looking radar emphasizes the form of the land, and the large areas that can be surveyed under constant conditions favor the recognition of extensive features.

† **'sidely,** *adv. Obs.*$^{-1}$ [f. SIDE *sb.*[1]] In an indirect manner; indirectly.

*c* **1380** WYCLIF *Sel. Wks.* I. 324 ȝif a man aȝenstondiþ God and doiþ aȝens his wille, ȝit Goddis wille is fillid asideli [*v.r.* sydely] by punishinge of þis man.

**'sideman.** [f. SIDE *sb.*[1]]

† **1.** = SIDESMAN 1. *Obs.*

**1570** FOXE *A. & M.* (ed. 2) 2098/1 He beyng one of the Church Wardens or side men. **1577** HARRISON *England* II. v. (1877) I. 134 In villages they are commonlie made churchwardens, sidemen, aleconners, constables. **1602** CAREW *Cornwall* 82 Besides this Incumbent, euery parish had certaine officers, as Churchwardens, Sidemen. **1636** DAVENANT *Wits* III. i, It is worth all the Bells in your Church Steeple, Though your Sexton and Side-men hung there too, To better the peal. **1682** in *Picture of Liverpool* (1834) 108 Thomas Mathews elected sideman for the remainder of the Year.

† **2.** A partisan. *rare*$^{-1}$. *Obs.*

**1600** W. WATSON *Decacordon* (1602) 93 The partie that brought it was a sideman of the Iesuits.

† **3.** (See quot.) *rare*$^{-1}$. *Obs.*

*c* **1600** EDMONDS *Obser. Cæsars Comm.* 130 The first, second and third, and so forward in each file, are called Side-men in respect of the same numbes in the next file.

† **4.** = OYSTER *sb.* 3. *Obs.*

**1632** SHERWOOD, The sidemen of a pullet, *les huistres d'une poulle.*

**5.** A supporting musician in a jazz or dance band. Cf. *front man* (ii) s.v. FRONT *sb.* 14. orig. *U.S.*

**1936** *Amer. Mercury* XXXVIII. p. x/2 *Side man*, any musician in the band except the leader. **1943** P. E. MILLER *Yearbk. Pop. Music* 7/2 He began playing in bands just a few years later, and was soon accepted as a desirable sideman. **1961** *Radio Times* 21 Dec. 53/4 *Jazz Club.* Humphrey Lyttelton..welcomes as his guests two former Lyttelton sidemen Jimmy Skidmore on tenor sax and Johnny Picard on trombone. **1977** J. WAINWRIGHT *Do Nothin' till You hear from Me* v. 67 Goodman and Dorsey..had tight section work, when needed—but they let their sidemen cut loose, and weave their own patterns.

**side meat.** *N. Amer.* (chiefly *Southern* and *Western U.S.*). [SIDE *sb.*[1]] Salt pork or bacon, usu. cut from the side of the pig.

**1868** *Overland Monthly* Nov. 468/1 But they do not thrive after transplanting any better than do the corn pone of Virginia..and the 'side-meat' of Missouri. **1873** J. H. BEADLE *Undevel. West* xxiv. 482 Two bright-eyed, graceful, copper-colored *señoritas* bring me a supper of coffee, side meat, eggs, and *tortillas de mais.* **1939** J. STEINBECK *Grapes of Wrath* v. 43 But—you see, a bank or a company can't do that, because those creatures don't breathe air, don't eat side-meat. **1957** M. SHULMAN *Rally round Flag, Boys!* (1958) xiv. 158 Accents that recalled hominy grits and sidemeat. **1975** G. V. HIGGINS *City on Hill* viii. 208 None of these intellectual-emotional phenomena is an adequate substitute for side meat and greens.

† **'siden,** *adv. Obs.* [OE. *sídan*, f. *síd* SIDE *a.*] = SIDE *adv.*[1] 1.

**932** in Birch *Cartul. Sax.* II. 389 Of ȝehwilcum stowum wydan and sydan ȝegaderod. *c* **1205** LAY. 139 Muche lond he him ȝef..siden & widen. *Ibid.* 15405 He lette his men riden widen & siden.

† **'sideness.** *Obs.* [f. SIDE *a.*]

**a.** Length. **b.** Height (of a roof).

*c* **1375** *Sc. Leg. Saints* xli. (*Agnes*) 158 God send sic sydnes in hyre hare þat scho wes cled mare ewinely with hare þane with hire clathis in hy. *c* **1380** WYCLIF *Sel. Wks.* II. 62 þei maken þer abitis myche, boþe in widnesse and sidnesse. *c* **1440** *Promp. Parv.* 474 Stepnesse, or sydenesse of a roof, *elevacio.* **1530** PALSGR. 270/1 Sydenesse, *longevr.* **1583** P. STUBBES *Anat. Abuses* E ij, The other contayneth neither length, breadth or sidenes (beeing not past a quarter of a yarde side) wherof some be paved. **1607** MARKHAM *Caval.* II. (1617) 258 When you..haue made both the bitt cheekes of an euen sidenesse.

† **sidenhand,** *adv. Obs.* Also 5 sydnandys. [f. OE. *sídan*, gen. sing. of *síde* SIDE *sb.*[1] + HAND *sb.*] Aside; on one side *of.*

*c* **1330** R. BRUNNE *Chron. Wace* (Rolls) 5019 Cesar conseilled wiþ Androche, þat he wolde come out of þe cite, And turne a sidenhand o valeye. *c* **1440** *Promp. Parv.* 455/1 Sydnandys, or a-syde, *oblique.* **1538** LELAND *Itin.* (1907) I. 9 The hedde of Avon Ryver risethe a litle sidenhand [*printed* -ham] of Gilesborow village, and cummith by it there first receyving a botom. [Cf. *side-hand* under SIDE *sb.*[1] 27.]

**side-on,** *adv.* and *a.* [SIDE *sb.*[1] + ON *adv.* 7 b; cf. HEAD-ON *adv.* and *a.*] **A.** *adv.* ('*side-'on*). With one side directed towards the point of reference; from the side. **B.** *adj.* ('*side-on*). Directed from or towards one side; indirect. Of a collision: involving the meeting of one side of a vehicle with an object.

**1909** L. M. MONTGOMERY *Anne of Avonlea* xiv. 154 His farm is side-on to the Newbridge road. **1928** *Daily Mail* 16 Aug. 13/7 Side-on collisions frequently occur owing to blurred side curtains. **1960** *Times* 10 June 19/1 He may have been a little more side-on at the moment of delivery. **1976** LD. HOME *Way Wind Blows* xi. 156 One of our delegation was sitting with a side-on view of the rostrum. **1977** J. CLEARY *Vortex* viii. 204 Wind was hitting the car side-on.

**'side-pocket.** [SIDE *sb.*[1]]

**1.** A pocket in the side-portion of a garment (esp. a coat or jacket).

**1760–72** H. BROOKE *Fool of Qual.* (1809) III. 116 Pulling out his butcher's knife from a sheath in his side-pocket. **1796** *Grose's Dict. Vulgar T.* (ed. 3) s.v., He has as much need of a wife as a dog of a side pocket; said of a weak old debilitated man. **1824** SCOTT *St. Ronan's* xxx, Buttoning his coat over the arms, which were concealed in a side-pocket ingeniously contrived for that purpose. **1862** WHYTE MELVILLE *Inside the Bar* iii. 265 He's no more use for a hunter now, than a cow has for a side-pocket. **1901** *Macm. Mag.* Apr. 465/2 He brought an old coat one day, and amused himself firing through the side-pockets.

*attrib.* **1898** *Westm. Gaz.* 13 Jan. 4/2 He wore a..side-pocket jacket which fitted him like a glove.

**2.** (See quot.)

**1850** R. G. CUMMING *Hunter's Life S. Afr.* (ed. 2) I. 23 Along the sides of the tent are suspended rows of square-cut canvas bags, called side-pockets.

**'side-post.** [SIDE *sb.*[1]]

**1.** One of the posts at either side of a doorway; a door-post. (Chiefly in Biblical echoes.)

**1535** COVERD. *Exod.* xii. 22 Stryke it vpon the vpper poste and vpon the two syde postes. [Similarly 1572 and 1611.] **1697** C. LESLIE *Snake in Grass* (ed. 2) 140 The striking of its Blood upon the Side-posts of their Houses. **1738** WARBURTON *Div. Legat.* II. 635 Striking the blood on the side-posts. **1865** J. H. INGRAHAM *Pillar of Fire* (1872) 562 To sprinkle its blood on the side-posts and on the lintel. **1874** RUSKIN *Val D'Arno* 217, I intended..to have insisted, at some length, on the decoration of the lintel and side-posts.

**2.** A post supporting a roof at or towards one side of it.

**1625** in Willis & Clark *Cambridge* (1886) I. 197 The syde-postes of yᵉ roofe. **1850** PARKER *Gloss. Arch.* (ed. 5) 427 *Side-posts* in a roof-truss, are posts placed in pairs at an equal distance from the middle. **1862** —— *Richman's Gothic Archit.* 200 The vaulting-shafts or half pillars..carrying either the ribs of the vault, or the side posts of the open timber roof.

**'sider**[1]. [f. SIDE *v.*[1] 11.] One who sides *with* a person or cause; a partisan, adherent.

**1616** J. LANE *Contn. Sqr.'s T.* III. 211 False dice and carders, with all cheatinge crewes, siders that feede, nay blo self-gaine-made faction. **1656** S. H. *Gold. Law* 4 What then can nocent Charls Stuart, or his siders with, say for themselves? **1665** WINSTANLEY *Loy. Martyrol.* 171 A desparate Enemy to the Old King all along,..a greater Sider with Cromwel.

Hence † **'sidership.** *Obs.*

**1594** NASHE *Unfortunate Trav.* Wks. (Grosart) V. 21 The world is well amended, thought I, with your Sidership.

**'sider**[2], forming the second element in a comb. or collocation, as ***near sider***, a horse standing on the near side; ***hillsider***, one living on a hillside, etc. See also INSIDER and OUTSIDER.

**1841** LEVER *C. O'Malley* cxii, I like that near sider with the white fetlock. **1865** H. KINGSLEY *Hillyars & Burtons* xii, Those who think they know something of them might fancy that 'Old', 'Vandemonian', or even 'Sydney Sider', were not particularly offensive. **1891** S. C. SCRIVENER *Our Fields & Cities* 11 The Trentsiders have a manner peculiarly their own. **1898** [see HILLSIDER].

**sider,** obs. form of CIDER.

**'side-rail.** [SIDE *sb.*[1] 23 b.] A rail placed or fixed at the side of something.

**1754** J. BARTLET *Gentl. Farriery* (ed. 2) 354 Let an assistant, standing on the side rail of a brake,..raise the horse's tail very gently. **1790** W. H. MARSHALL *Rur. Econ. Midl.* II. 437 *Geering*, the ladders and side rails of a waggon. **1805** R. W. DICKSON *Pract. Agric.* I. 34 By means of a crooked side-rail, bending archwise over the hind wheel, the bodies..are kept low. **1852** WIGGINS *Embanking* 132 Placing gates and side-rails to those marshes. **1903** *Cornhill Mag.* Oct. 571, I leaned against the side-rail [of the yacht] beside her.

**sideral** (ˈsaɪdərəl, ˈsɪdərəl), *a.* Also 6 syderall, 7–8 -al; 7 siderall. [ad. L. *sīderālis*, f. *sīder-*, *sīdus* constellation, star. Cf. F. *sidéral*, †*syderal* (16th cent.).]

**1.** Of or pertaining to the stars; sidereal, starry.

**1594** BLUNDEVIL *Exerc.* II. I. xxxviii. (1597) 170 b, The Astronomicall yeare is either Tropicall or Syderall. **1653** GATAKER *Vind. Annot. Jer.* 48 He sends for those of his Egyptian Wizards, whome he deemed most skilful in the Sideral Science. **1683** MOXON *Mech. Exerc., Printing* 38 The Syderal Observations set forth in Tycho's name. **1807** J. BARLOW *Columb.* x. 7 So shone the earth, as if the sideral train, Broad as full suns, had sail'd the ethereal plain. **1870** EMERSON *Soc. & Solit.* Wks. (Bohn) III. 2, I who am only waiting..to..put diameters of the..sideral orbits between me and all souls.

**2.** Coming from, caused by, the stars. Chiefly of malign influences.

**1611** SPEED *Hist. Gt. Brit.* IX. xiii. §27 As if it had beene a syderall infection or generall Lunacy. **1667** MILTON *P.L.*

x. 693 These changes in the Heav'ns..produc'd..sideral blast, Vapour, and Mist, and Exhalation hot. **1708** J. PHILIPS *Cyder* I. 31 The vernal nippings and cold syderal blasts. **1799** *Monthly Rev.* XXX. 570 The virgin mud, fecundated..by the sideral influence. **1805** *Poet. Reg.* 175 Worse than mildew hoar Or Sideral blast is he.

**siderant** ('sɪdərənt), *a. Path.* [a. F. *sidérant.*] Striking and paralyzing suddenly.

**1896** *Allbutt's Syst. Med.* I. 664 The 'type foudroyante' of French authors, which may also be called the fulminant, siderant, apoplectic, or malignant type.

**side'raphthite.** [f. Gr. σίδηρος iron + ἄφθιτ-ος undecaying.] (See quot.)

**1884** C. G. W. LOCK *Workshop Rec.* Ser. III. 39/1 A new alloy, which resembles silver, and is very ductile and malleable, is composed of 65 parts iron, 23 of nickel, 4 of tungsten, 5 of aluminium, and 5 of copper... The metal is called 'sideraphthite'.

†**'siderate,** *v. Obs.* [f. ppl. stem of L. *sīderārī* to be planet-struck, f. *sīder-*, *sīdus* constellation, star.] *trans.* To strike with malign (sidereal) influence, to blast. Chiefly in passive: To be blasted, struck with lightning; also *fig.*, to be thunder-struck.

**1623** COCKERAM I, *Siderate*, to blast. **1646** SIR T. BROWNE *Pseud. Ep.* 335 Parts cauterized, gangrenated, siderated and mortified, become black. **1654** VILVAIN *Epit. Ess.* v. xxxiii. 102 The 2 Persons that were suddenly siderated or slain and scorched in bed together with Lightning. **1679** V. ALSOP *Melius Inq.* II. v. 307 This is Demonstration that puts the Controversie beyond all exception, and the poor Nonconformists are siderated with the violence of it!

**side'ration.** Now *rare.* Also 7–8 **syd-**. [ad. L. *sīderātio* blast, blight, palsy, f. *sīderārī*: see prec. So F. *sidération*, †*syderation* (16th cent.).]

**1.** Blasting of trees or plants.

**1623** COCKERAM II. A iv b, A Blasting thereof, *Stellation, Syderation.* **1656** BLOUNT *Glossogr.*, *Syderation*, Blasting of Trees with great heat and drought, Tree-plague. **1686** GOAD *Celest. Bodies* III. i. 383 If God hath ordained Sideration of Plants, or blasting of Fruits, must we accuse the Creation? **1691** RAY *Creation* (1714) 304 Producing a Mortification or Syderation in the parts of Plants. **1721** BAILEY, *Sideration*, the Blasting of Trees or Plants, with an Eastern Wind or with excessive Heat and Drought. [Hence in Miller *Gard. Dict.* (1731).]

**2.** Sudden paralysis; complete mortification of any part of the body.

**1612** COTTA *Disc. Dang. Pract. Phys.* I. vii. 59 The sicke are also sodainly taken..with a senseless trance and generall astonishment or sideration. **1638** A. READ *Chirurg.* iv. 27 An absolute coldnesse..causeth the sideration or death of the part. **1638** DRUMM. OF HAWTH. *Irene* Wks. (1711) 172 This hath been in them a Sideration, the Blasting of some unhappy Influence. **1702** C. MATHER *Magn. Chr.* VII. vi. (1852) 575 Rabid animals, which, by a most unaccountable syderation from Heaven, had now neither strength nor sense left 'em to do anything for their own defence.

**3.** *Path.* (See quots.)

[**1788** *Med. Comm.* II. 182 *Sideratio*, or Erysipelas of the head and face. **1809** PARR *Med. Dict.* II. 583 *Sideratio*,..a sphacelus or a species of erysipelas, vulgarly called a *blast.*] **1828–32** in WEBSTER (citing Parr). **1849** CRAIG, *Sideration*, in Pathology, a name given to erysipelas of the face or scalp, from an idea of its being produced by the influence of the planets.

**sidere,** obs. form of CIDER.

**sidereal** (saɪ'dɪərɪəl), *a.* Also 7–9 **siderial** (7 **syd-**); 7–8 **sydereal** (7 **-all**). [f. L. *sīdere-us*, f. *sīder-*, *sīdus* constellation, star + -AL[1].]

**1.** Of or pertaining to the stars.

**1647** H. MORE *Pref. to Antipsychopannychia*, Upon which pure bright sydereal phantasms unprejudiced reason may safely work. **1651** —— *Enthus. Tri.* (1712) 32 That a Man has a sydereal body besides this terrestrial which is joined with the Stars. **1692** J. SALTER *Triumphs of Jesus* 24 Display your Glories ye Syderial States. **1739** H. COVENTRY *Philemon to Hydaspes* III. 76 [A] most expressive, as well as permanent Symbol of the Sidereal Splendors. **1792** *Phil. Trans.* LXXXII. 26 Among the changes that happen in the sidereal heavens we enumerate the loss of stars. **1831** CARLYLE *Sart. Res.* I. iii, What thinks Boötes of them, as he leads his Hunting-Dogs over the Zenith in their leash of sidereal fire? **1868** SPENCER *Princ. Psychol.* (1872) I. I. vii. 137 That general Astronomy which includes our whole sidereal system. **1874** FARRAR *Christ* I. iii. 29 That any strange sidereal phenomenon should be interpreted as the signal of a coming king, was in strict accordance with the belief of their age.

**2.** Star-like, lustrous, bright. *rare.*

**1634** BP. HALL *Contempl.*, *N.T.* IV. xiv. 201 With what a blushing astonishment doth she behold his sydereall countenance cast upon her. **1649** J. H. *Motion to Parl.* 30 Provoking some sydereall and flaming soules to display themselves in their full..lustre.

**3.** Of periods of time: Determined or measured by means of the stars. In ***sidereal day, month, year, time*** (see quots.).

**1681** WHARTON *Disc. Yrs. & Months* Wks. (1683) 71 The Sydereal year is the space of time, in which the Sun returns to the same star from whence he departed. **1715** tr. *Gregory's Astron.* (1726) I. 242 The Astronomic Year is also twofold, ..namely, the Sydereal and Tropical. The Sydereal Year.. is 365 Days, 6 Hours, and 10 Minutes nearly. **1794** G. ADAMS *Nat. & Exper. Phil.* IV. xlii. 127 There must be one more siderial day in a year than there are solar days. **1812** WOODHOUSE *Astron.* viii. 50 A clock regulated by the transit of fixed stars, or adapted to sidereal time. **1846** A. YOUNG *Naut. Dict.* 95 The interval between the departure and return of a meridian to the sun is called a solar day; in the case..of a star, a sidereal day. **1868** LOCKYER *Elem. Astron.* §434 The sidereal month is the interval between two successive conjunctions of the moon with the same fixed star.

**b.** Of a clock: Showing sidereal time.

**1812** WOODHOUSE *Astron.* Pref., An observation expressed by..the seconds of a sidereal clock.

**4.** Of planetary or lunar motion: Relative to the stars.

**1815** J. SMITH *Panorama Sci. & Art* I. 554 Its annual sidereal revolution is calculated, by Laplace, to be performed in 1681 days, 17 hours, 57 seconds. **1833** HERSCHEL *Astron.* viii. 252 The sidereal periods of the planets may be obtained..by observing their passages through the nodes of their orbits. **1868** LOCKYER *Guillemin's Heavens* (ed. 3) 66 *note*, This revolution is called a sidereal revolution in contradistinction to the 'synodic revolution', because, relatively to the Sun, the planet again occupies the same portion of the heavens.

**5.** Concerned with the stars.

**1833** HERSCHEL *Astron.* 372 Chap. xii. Of Sidereal Astronomy. **1853** —— *Pop. Lect. Sci.* v. §28 (1873) 204 Thus opening another chapter in the history of sidereal mensuration. **1870** tr. *Pouchet's Universe* (1871) 519 The nebulæ mark the limits of sidereal investigation.

Hence **si'derealize** *v.*; **si'dereally** *adv.*

**1816** G. S. FABER *Orig. Pagan Idol.* I. 34 That very goddess, whose peculiar symbol was a ship.., is yet asserted to be sidereally the moon. **1873** PATER *Renaissance* viii. 150 German literature transformed, siderealised, as we see it in Goethe, reckons Winckelmann among its imitators.

**si'derean,** *a. rare.* [f. as prec. + -AN.] Sidereal, starry.

**1656** BLOUNT *Glossogr.*, *Siderean*, of, or like stars, shining, bright; heavenly. **1857** B. W. PROCTER *Dram. Sc.* 342 They brought me down..Siderean music from the Pleiades.

**si'dereous,** *a. rare*[−1]. [f. Gr. σίδηρος iron.] Composed of iron.

**1830** *Fraser's Mag.* I. 503 Did the God of Hell, therefore, weep only from one eye, which rained the sidereous torrent of woe—the iron sleet of teary shower?

**si'deric,** *a. rare*[−1]. Pertaining to iron.

**1876** *Encycl. Brit.* V. 459/2 These elements he asserted were composed of the three principles sideric salt and sulphur and mercury.

**'siderism[1].** [f. L. *sīder-*, *sīdus* star.] The doctrine of a sidereal influence upon terrestrial things or events.

**1891** in *Cent. Dict.*

**'siderism[2].** [f. Gr. σίδηρος iron.] The supposed effects of magnetic influence upon the human body.

[**1850** OGILVIE, *Siderismus.*] **1891** in *Cent. Dict.* **1898** LANG *Making of Religion* ii. 32 Ritter thought he had detected a new force, 'Siderism.'

**siderite[1]** ('sɪdəraɪt, saɪ'dɪəraɪt). *Min.* [In early use a. F. *siderite* (16th c.), or ad. L. *sīderītes* m., *sīderītis* f., a. Gr. σιδηρίτης, -ῖτις, f. σίδηρος iron. In later use directly f. Gr. σιδηρ-ος + -ITE[1] 2 b.]

†**1.** Loadstone. *Obs.*

**1579** PUTTENHAM *Eng. Poesie, Partheniades* (1811) vii. 50 Not flint, I trowe, I am a lyer; But syderite that feeles noe fier. **1607** ? BREWER *Lingua* IV. i, Hee fastens a post, vpon which he hangs me in a corde a Siderite, of Herculian stone. **1694** MOTTEUX *Rabelais* IV. lxii, He hang'd on a Gibbet by a Rope a very large Siderite or iron-like Stone,..commonly call'd Load-stone.

**2.** (See quot. 1623 and SIDERITES.)

**1623** COCKERAM III, *Siderite*, a stone like iron, hauing power to set variance amongst men. **1656** in BLOUNT *Glossogr.* **1861** KING *Antique Gems* (1866) 67 The Siderites, of a steel colour and very heavy, were doubtless Sapphires, for they could be drilled by means of another Diamond.

†**3.** A phosphate of iron; pharmacosiderite, cube-ore. *Obs.*

So named by Bergmann (1790) under the impression that it was a new metal.

**1795** *Phil. Trans.* LXXXV. 335 The white matter I supposed was the siderite of Bergman; which is now believed to be phosphate of iron. **1796** KIRWAN *Elem. Min.* (ed. 2) II. 179 Iron in a Reguline state united to Phosphorus is called Siderite. **1805** *Phil. Trans.* XCV. 325 The error which subsisted for a few years, respecting the compound formerly called siderite.

†**4.** Hornblende. *Obs.*

**1811** PINKERTON *Petral.* I. 4 Siderite sometimes composes entire mountains... This important substance..is the horn-blende of the German miners. *Ibid.* 9 In general.. when the substance has a crystallised and silky appearance, it must be classed among the siderites.

**5.** A blue variety of quartz.

Named by Moll (1797).

**1823** W. PHILLIPS *Min.* (ed. 3) 210 Siderite..is compact, of a greyish or greenish blue colour, is nearly as hard as quartz, and possesses a resinous or waxy lustre. **1841** *Penny Cycl.* XIX. 200/1 Blue Quartz, Siderite, occurs crystallized and massive. **1860** PIESSE *Lab. Chem. Wonders* 72 The beautiful amethyst, the blue siderite, the yellow Cairngorm.

**6.** Rhombohedral carbonate of iron, native ferrous carbonate, spathic iron-ore.

Named by Haidinger (1844); also called SIDEROSE.

**1850** ANSTED *Elem. Geol. Min.*, etc. 206 There is a strong tendency in these crystalline carbonates to assume a spherical form; and hence the name Siderite and Sphærosiderite. **1879** *Encycl. Brit.* X. 228/2 Siderite, Chalybite, or Spathic Iron (carbonate of iron) occurs both crystallized and massive. **1894** *Harper's Mag.* Jan. 410 Siderite, or spathic ore, so called from its sparry or glassy crystals, is a combination of iron with carbonic acid (Fe $OCO_2$).

**7.** A meteorite consisting mainly of iron.

**1875** *Nature* XII. 521/1 The great division of meteorites into iron masses or siderites, mixed masses or siderolites.., and aërolites or stony meteorites,..seems to be a sufficiently logical division. **1881** *Ibid.* XXIV. 508 The detection of carbon, while it agrees with the element's occurrence in siderites and carbonaceous aërolites, reminds us [etc.].

**siderite[2].** *Bot.* [ad. L. *sīderītis*, Gr. σιδηρῖτις, f. σίδηρος iron: cf. prec.] A plant of the genus *Sideritis*; see IRON-WORT.

**1753** *Chambers's Cycl.* Suppl. s.v. *Sideritis*, In all the siderites the flowers grow in circles round the stalks. **1828–32** in WEBSTER (citing Coxe and Parr).

†**side'rites.** *Obs.* = SIDERITE[1] (senses 1–3).

**1553** EDEN *Treat. New Ind.* (Arb.) 14 That whiche is of the colour of yron is called siderites. **1601** HOLLAND *Pliny* II. 629 Siderites is much like to yron: and supposed it is, That ..it will breed discord and maintain dissention still. Of this Siderites is made another stone,..called Sideropœcilos, for the sundry spots therein. **1611** COTGR., *Siderite*, the yron-like stone Siderites, which, as some imagine, hath power to set men at oddes. **1750** *Leonardus' Mirr. Stones* 233 *Siderites*, is a Stone in Colour not much unlike Iron. **1794** SULLIVAN *View Nat.* I. 469 Regulus of manganese, siderites, and regulus of molybdena.

**side'ritic,** *a. rare.* [f. SIDERITE[1] + -IC.] Of the nature of siderite (in senses 3 and 4).

**1796** KIRWAN *Elem. Min.* (ed. 2) II. 180 Sideritic Calx. This consists of Calx of Iron united to Phosphoric acid. **1811** PINKERTON *Petral.* I. 8 As the stones, confessedly called basalts by the ancients, often present marks of crystallisation, being sideritic rocks or primitive traps.

**sidero-[1]** ('sɪdərəʊ, saɪ'dɪərəʊ), combining form of Gr. σίδηρος iron.

**1.** In various names of minerals, as ***sidero-calcite, -clepte, -graphite, -schisolite***; also ***sideromagnesian*** adj.; **sidero'natrite** [ad. Sp. *sideronatrita* (A. Raimondi *Minerales del Perú* (1878) 209)], an orthorhombic hydrated basic sulphate of ferric iron and sodium, $Na_2Fe(OH)(SO_4)_2.3H_2O$, which is a secondary mineral found in very arid regions as yellow masses or crusts, and can be prepared artificially as needle-shaped crystals; **sidero'phyllite** [Gr. φύλλον leaf], a variety of biotite containing a high proportion of ferrous iron and aluminium but little ferric iron and little or no magnesium; **'siderotil** (-tɪl, -taɪl) [a. G. *siderotil* (A. Schrauf 1891, in *Jahrb. d. k.-k. geol. Reichanstalt* XLI. 381), f. Gr. τίλ-ος anything plucked (f. τίλλειν to pluck)], a hydrated ferrous sulphate, $FeSO_4.5H_2O$, found as triclinic fibrous crusts and needles of a white or pale yellow or green colour (see also quot. 1964).

A considerable number of other compounds, which have had little or no currency in English, may be found in Watts' *Dict. Chem.* and Chester's *Dict. Min.*

**1794** KIRWAN *Elem. Min.* I. 109 It may be inferred that *braun spar*, or *sidero-calcite, exhibits in its composition various gradations to or from the sparry iron ore. **1811** PINKERTON *Petral.* I. 127 The sidero-calcite and ferri-calcite of Kirwan have little connection with the present subject. **1823** W. PHILLIPS *Min.* (ed. 3) 210 *Sideroclepte..is massive, translucent, of a yellowish green colour. **1820** J. TORREY in *Amer. Jrnl. Sci.* II. 176, I have just discovered a new mineral, or one which I cannot find described. It is a compound of metallic iron and plumbago... I have called it *Sidero-graphite. **1896** CHESTER *Dict. Min.*, *Siderographite*, ..considered a native compound of iron and graphite, but probably a furnace product. **1811** PINKERTON *Petral.* I. 131 It is so much impregnated with iron, that it belongs to the *sideromagnesian rocks. **1890** *Amer. Jrnl. Sci.* CXL. 202 Associated with the *sideronatrite..is a grayish white laminated mineral, ferronatrite, which is also often intermixed through the whole mass of the sideronatrite. **1935** J. W. MELLOR *Comprehensive Treat. Inorg. & Theoret. Chem.* XIV. 345 Sideronatrite occurs in orange-yellow or straw-yellow, crystalline masses of fine, fibrous structure which separate into thin splinters. **1975** *Nature* 5 June 472/1 Alteration has produced haematite and goethite on the outer parts of the concretions, whereas the inner parts contain jarosite, gypsum, baryte, celestine and sideronatrite. **1880** H. C. LEWIS in *Proc. Acad. Nat. Sci. Philadelphia* XXXII. 255 The name of **Siderophyllite*..has been given in allusion to the large percentage of iron which it contains. **1967** *Mineral. Abstr.* XVIII. 142/1 High temperature metasomatically altered granites of Jurassic and Cretaceous age [in Upper Kolyma, Russian S.F.S.R.] locally include fayalite and siderophyllite greisens in association with Sn deposits. **1825** *Brewster's Edin. Jrnl. Sci.* II. 372 He [Dr. Wernekingk] described *Sideroschisolite as occurring in small simple three-sided and six-sided pyramids. **1868** WATTS *Dict. Chem.* V. 240 *Sideroschisolite*, a ferroso-ferrous silicate, occurring..in Brazil, in hexagonal crystals. **1897** *Mineral. Mag.* XI. 335 *Siderotil... $FeSO_4 + 5H_2O$. Idria, Carniola. **1920** *Amer. Jrnl. Sci.* CCL. 229 Melanterite, either natural or artificial, is commonly coated with a white powder of siderotil and the fine powder [of the former] will dehydrate after standing for some months to the pentahydrate. **1964** *Amer. Mineralogist* XLIX. 820 From a study of natural and synthetic iron sulfates, it is concluded that the name siderotil should be applied to $(Fe,X)SO_4.5H_2O$, where X is any cation or group of cations individually less abundant than Fe. The pure compound probably does not exist in nature, but several examples of the cuprian variety are known.

**2.** In miscellaneous combs., as **sideroa,chrestic** (-ə'krɛstɪk) *a. Path.* [ad. mod.L. *sideroachrestica* (coined in Ger. by L. Heilmeyer et al. 1957, in *Schweiz. med. Wochenschr.* LXXXVII. 1237/2), f. Gr. ἄχρηστ-

*os* useless (f. ἀ- A- 14 + χρῆσθαι to use)], designating a form of hypochromic anæmia in which impaired synthesis of hæmoglobin renders treatment with iron of no avail; **'siderochrome** *Biochem.* [ad. G. *siderochrom* (H. Bickel et al. 1960, in *Experientia* XVI. 131/2), f. Gr. χρῶμα colour], any of various compounds concerned with the transport of iron in bacteria; **'siderograph**, an engraving produced by siderography; **sidero'graphic** *a.*, pertaining to siderography; so **sidero'graphical** *a.* (Webster, 1828–32); **side'rographist** (see quot.); **side'rography**, a method of engraving on steel, introduced by Perkins and Fairman and employed especially for bank-notes; **sidero'lithic** *a.*, of the nature of a siderolite; **sidero'penia** *Med.* [-PENIA], an abnormally low concentration of iron in the blood; hence **sidero'penic** *a.*; **'siderophage** *Med.* [Gr. φαγεῖν to eat, devour] (see quot. 1970); **'siderophil(e**, **sidero'philic** *adjs.* *Geol.* and *Chem.* [ad. G. *siderophil* (V. M. Goldschmidt 1923, in *Skrifter utgit av Videnskapsselsk. I: Mat.-nat. Kl.* III. 5); see -PHIL, -PHILE], applied to elements which are commonly found in metallic phases (sometimes *spec.* in association with iron) rather than combined as silicates or sulphides, and are supposed to have become concentrated in the earth's core; **sidero'philin** *Biochem.* [-PHIL, -PHILE + -IN[1]] = TRANSFERRIN; **'sideroscope**, an instrument used to detect minute quantities of iron by means of a combination of magnetic needles; **'siderosome** *Med.* [-SOME[4]], a particle of non-hæmoglobin iron in a cell; **sidero'techny**, 'the metallurgy of iron' (*Cent. Dict.*).

**1961** *Amer. Jrnl. Clinical Path.* XXXV. 338/1 The patients suffered from an anemia which was resistant to all forms of therapy except blood transfusion and had an erythroid hyperplasia of the bone marrow with a conspicuous accumulation of iron-staining granules in the developing erythrocytes. Similar instances have been described.. under the term '*sideroachrestic anemia'. **1970** A. E. LEWIS *Princ. Hematol.* xiii. 205 Sideroachrestic anemia is a very rare, hereditary anemia, refractory to treatment with iron, vitamins, or folic acid. **1961** *Chem. Abstr.* LV. 23684 Sideromycins, sideramines, and other unidentified Fe-contg. biol. active substances are taken together as a group called *siderochromes. **1976** *Nature* 19 Aug. 722/2 Microbial iron-transport compounds, or siderochromes are of two general structural types, the phenolates and the hydroxamates. **1875** KNIGHT *Dict. Mech.* 2174/2 *Siderograph. **1819** (*title*), Specimens and Description of Perkins and Fairman's Patent *Siderographic Plan to prevent Forgery [of bank-notes]. **1820** J. PERKINS in *Trans. Soc. Arts* XXXVIII. 47 We, the proprietors of the Siderographic art. **1847** WEBSTER, **Siderographist*, one who engraves steel plates, or performs work by means of such plates. **1820** *Gentl. Mag.* XC. I. 349 *Siderography. **1899** *Edin. Rev.* Oct. 326 Intermediate or *siderolithic varieties consist of an amalgam of metal and stone. **1938** J. WALDENSTRÖM in *Acta Med. Scand.* Suppl. XC. 395 All these factors may lead to the same result, most suitably called *sideropenia. **1946** M. M. WINTROBE *Clinical Hematol.* (ed. 2) xii. 533 Anemia was not present in all of his cases but low plasma iron (sideropenia) was consistently found. **1971** J. H. DAGG et al. in Goldberg & Brain *Rec. Adv. Haematol.* ii. 107 Sideropenia causes well-defined chemical and biochemical changes, and may be associated with the clinical tissue signs found in iron deficiency states. **1939** *Acta Radiol.* XX. (*heading*) 618 The roentgenological diagnosis of *sideropenic dysphagia. **1971** J. H. DAGG et al. in Goldberg & Brain *Rec. Adv. Haematol.* ii. 105 An erythrocyte protoporphyrin level above 40·0 μg per 100 ml. erythrocytes and a transferrin saturation of less than 16 per cent taken together, allow a firm diagnosis of the sideropenic state without the necessity for marrow biopsy. **1970** PASSMORE & ROBSON *Compan. Med. Stud.* II. xxi. 11/1 In lesions where there has been much haemorrhage, phagocytosis of iron pigment results in a pigmented stippling of the cytoplasm [of macrophages], and such cells are termed *siderophages. **1977** *Lancet* 30 July 244/1 No siderophages were found in the cerebrospinal fluid on the 10th day. **1923** *Siderophil [see *lithophil(e* adj. s.v. LITHO-]. **1950** RANKAMA & SAHAMA *Geochem.* iv. 93 It may be assumed that the typically siderophile elements.. are enriched in the nickel-iron core of the Earth. **1954** A. MUIR *Goldschmidt's Geochem.* 680 The scarcity of all the platinum metals in the lithosphere is due to their extremely siderophil nature. **1977** *Nature* 20 Jan. 197/3 The siderophile and volatile elements on the Moon are depleted relative to the Earth and meteorites. **1971** C. B. MOORE in B. Mason *Handbk. Elemental Abundances in Meteorites* xiv. 127 Although by definition silicon is a lithophilic element, evidence also shows that under highly reducing conditions in meteorites it may also be *siderophilic. **1949** A. L. SCHADE et al. in *Arch. Biochem.* XX. 170 (*heading*) Carbon dioxide in complex formation with iron and *siderophilin, the iron-binding component of human plasma. **1971** *Nature* 28 May 250/1 Transferrin (siderophilin) is a beta-globulin found universally in vertebrate serum. **1828–32** WEBSTER s.v., *Sideroscope. **1837** BREWSTER *Magnet.* 352 This apparatus, which he calls a sideroscope, is shewn in the annexed figure. **1970** *Haematologia* IV. 301 In spite of the active rhopheocytosis, ferritin aggregates (*siderosomes) were found in the erythroblasts only exceptionally. **1972** W. J. WILLIAMS et al. *Hematology* viii. 80/2 Cells containing siderosomes or 'iron bodies' are usually reticulocytes. **1979** *Experientia* XXXV. 256/1 The hepatic increase of ferric deposits (ferritin, siderosomes and lipofuscin aggregates) more or less overloaded in iron in relatives of idiopathic hemochromatosis is well-known.

**sidero-**[2] ('saɪdərəʊ, 'sɪdərəʊ), irregular combining form of L. *sīder-*, *sīdus* star, in **'siderolith** = SIDEROLITE[2] (*Cent. Dict.*); **'sideropore** [ad. mod.L. *sideropora*, Blainville], one of a genus of zoophytes.

**1846** J. D. DANA *Zooph.* (1848) 519 They [the Seriatopores] graduate into the Sideropores on one side, and into the slender Pocillopores on the other.

**sideroblast** ('sɪdərəʊblɑːst, -æ-). *Med.* [f. SIDERO-[1] + -BLAST.] A normoblast containing one or more granules of ferritin.

**1954** E. KAPLAN et al. in *Blood* IX. 204 For the purpose of this report these cells were designated as 'sideroblasts' in analogy to the term siderocyte already generally accepted for erythrocytes with iron-staining inclusions. *Ibid.* 212 The term sideroblast was proposed for normoblasts with nonstaining inclusions. **1962** BOTHWELL & FINCH *Iron Metabolism* 289 Sideroblasts are absent in iron-deficiency anemia. **1972** PASSMORE & ROBSON *Compan. Med. Stud.* III. xxi. 29/2 Ring sideroblasts were first observed in 1949 in guinea-pigs suffering from lead poisoning. They were first described in man in 1953. **1976** *Lancet* 18 Dec. 1364/1 The patient's bone-marrow exhibited a variable number of normal sideroblasts ranging from 20 to 70%.

Hence **sidero'blastic** *a.*, of, pertaining to, or characterized by the presence of sideroblasts; *esp.* in ***sideroblastic anæmia***.

**1956** *Blood* XI. 250 (*heading*) Chronic refractory anemia with sideroblastic bone marrow. **1972** *Nature* 10 Mar. 73/1 A similar although lesser degree of defective synthesis is seen in two other conditions due to haem deficiency, namely sideroblastic anaemia, and iron deficiency anaemia. **1977** *Blood* L. 165/2 Sideroblastic anemia.. is a heterogeneous group of disorders with different basic biochemical abnormalities.

**siderocyte** ('sɪdərəʊsaɪt). *Med.* [f. SIDERO-[1] + -CYTE.] An erythrocyte containing one or more granules of non-hæmoglobin iron.

**1941** H. GRÜNEBERG in *Nature* 26 July 114/2 The 'iron cells' or 'siderocytes' do not stain diffusely, but show blue granules which vary in number from one to a dozen or more and in size from fairly large blobs down to the finest dust-like stipples. **1944** WHITBY & BRITTON *Disorders of Blood* (ed. 4) ii. 36 In some conditions, especially after splenectomy, iron granules may be found in red cells by the prussian blue reaction. The significance of these so-called siderocytes.. is unknown. **1966** [see PAPPENHEIMER]. **1977** *Blood* L. 165 The excessive non-heme iron accumulated in *f/f* fetal siderocytes is located within mitochondria.

Hence **sidero'cytic** *a.*, of, pertaining to, or characterized by the presence of siderocytes.

**1957** *Blood* XII. 168 Neither red cells nor inclusion bodies were lost when siderocytic blood was transfused into a recipient without a spleen.

**siderolite**[1] ('sɪdərəʊlaɪt, saɪ'dɪərəʊlaɪt). [f. SIDERO-[1] + -LITE.] A meteorite composed of a mixed mass of iron and stone.

**1863** *Phil. Mag.* XXV. 49, I propose calling.. the intermediate varieties (including the Pallasites of Rose), in which the iron is continuous and associated with silicate, by the term Aërosiderolites or Siderolites. **1875** *Nature* XII. 522/1 The existence of great masses of siderolites like those of Pallas and from Atacama. **1883** *Science* I. 129/1 The iron has the associations usual in siderolite.

**siderolite**[2]. [ad. F. *sidérolithe*: see SIDERO-[2].] (See quot.)

**1849** CRAIG, *Siderolites*, a name given by Lamarck to those Nummulites which have a stellated appearance, from the margin being bristled with points.

**sidero'mancy**[1]. [f. SIDERO-[1].] (See quot.)

**1823** CRABB *Technol. Dict.*, *Sideromancy* (Ant.), a species of divination performed by burning straws, &c., on red-hot iron, in which operation conjectures were formed from the manner of their burning, &c.

**sidero'mancy**[2]. [f. SIDERO-[2].] Forecasting the future by means of the stars.

**1859** *Sat. Rev.* VII. 179 What most likely the prophet would in conversation mention as a general scrimmage, but in sideromancy describes as, 'nations bristling with bayonets, &c.'

**'side-rope.** Also 6 sithe-. [SIDE *sb.*[1]]

†**1.** A trace for a horse. *Obs.*

**1483** *Cath. Angl.* 339/1 A Syde rape, *retinaculum.* **c 1520** *Mem. Ripon* (Surtees) III. 206, ij lytyll lynys callyd syde ropes. **1556** *Lanc. Wills* (Chetham Soc. N.S.) I. 15 In wheles, ploowes, Iron sydropes, ij shode wheles, w[th] suche nessesaryes, xxv s. **1599** *Ibid.* (1861) III. 9, ix draught oxen w[th] duble furniture of yokes, waynes, and sitheropes.

**2.** A guy attached to a mast or pole.

**1726** LEONI *Alberti's Archit.* II. 13/1 The head of the mast .. we may guide.. by means of the two side Ropes, as with two Reins.

**3.** A rope for clambering up a ship's side.

**1839** MARRYAT *Phant. Ship* xli, You might.. have let me had a side-rope, my hearties.

**siderose,** *a.* and *sb. rare.* [f. Gr. σίδηρ-ος iron + -OSE[1]. Cf. SIDEROUS *a.*[2]]

**A.** *adj.* Similar to (that of) iron.

**1811** PINKERTON *Petral.* I. 4 Weight, siderose: sometimes approaching the barytose.

**B.** *sb.* = SIDERITE 6.

Named by Beudant (1832).

**1856** DANA *Min.* (ed. 3) 85 Carbonate of Iron (Ironspar; Spathic iron; Siderose).

‖**siderosis** (sɪdə'rəʊsɪs). *Path.* [mod.L. (F. A. Zenker 1866, in *Deutsch. Arch. f. klin. Med.* II. 70), f. Gr. σίδηρος iron; see -OSIS.]

**1.** Accumulation of oxide of iron in the lungs.

**1880** FLINT *Princ. Med.* 186 The changes are similar to those of anthracosis and of siderosis. **1898** *Allbutt's Syst. Med.* V. 248 Thus authors have described the results of inhaling.. metallic particles as siderosis.

**2.** The accumulation in the tissues of siderotic material.

**1890** G. M. GOULD *New Med. Dict.* 401/1 *Siderosis*, the pigmentation of the lymphatic glands, liver and kidneys, so called from the presence of iron in the pigment. **1906** J. L. SALINGER tr. Ehrlich & Lazarus in R. C. Cabot *Dis. of Metabolism of Blood, Animal Parasites, Toxicology* 314 Siderosis is *always* found [in progressive pernicious anemia], that is, an abnormally increased amount of iron in the internal organs, especially in the liver, in the spleen, in the bone marrow, and in the lymph-glands. **1966** WRIGHT & SYMMERS *Systemic Path.* I. xxi. 661/1 The Bantu people of South Africa show a very high incidence of cirrhosis of the Laënnec type in association with extensive siderosis.

**3.** The condition in which the lens of the eye is stained with rust derived from an embedded particle of iron. [f. mod.L. *siderosis bulbi* (G. von Bunge 1891, in *Verhandl. des X. Internat. Med. Congr., 1900* IV. x. 151).]

**1895** H. R. SWANZY *Handbk. Dis. of Eye* (ed. 5) vi. 190 A discoloration occurs in cases where particles of iron have been imbedded in the eye. Siderosis.. is the name given to this.. condition. **1926** *Trans.. Ophthalm. Soc.* XLV. 281 Particles [of iron] embedded deeply in the sclera do not give rise to siderosis. **1962** D. G. COGAN in A. Pirie *Lens Metabolism Rel. Cataract* 292 One curious property of the epithelium is its capacity to bind and accumulate iron. The entity, called siderosis lentis, may result.. from an intraocular foreign body of iron.

Hence **side'rotic** *a*, formed from or rich in insoluble iron compounds derived from the breakdown of hæmoglobin; of or pertaining to siderosis.

**1932** W. BOYD *Text-Bk. Path.* xxviii. 719 All the cases of splenic anemia do not show siderotic nodules, nor are the nodules confined to this disease. **1941** *Nature* 18 Oct. 470/1 The amount of siderotic material per siderocyte is generally small. **1978** J. BATTEN in R. B. Scott *Price's Textbk. Pract. Med.* ix. 909/2 Siderotic lung disease.

†**side'rosous,** *a. Obs.*$^{-0}$ [ad. late L. *sīderōsus*, f. *sīder-*, *sīdus* star.] (See quot.)

**1656** BLOUNT *Glossogr.*, *Syderosous*, Planet strucken; also full of Stars.

**siderostat** ('sɪdərəʊstæt). *Astr.* [f. SIDERO-[2], after *heliostat*.] An astronomical instrument by which a star under observation may be kept within the same part of the field of a telescope.

**1877** G. F. CHAMBERS *Astron.* (ed. 3) *Vocab.* 916 A form of the instrument [heliostat] specially used for astronomical purposes is called a siderostat. **1878** LOCKYER *Stargazing* 343 One of the most recent additions to astronomical tools is the Siderostat. **1881** ABNEY *Photogr.* 289 Before the introduction of Foucault's siderostat a telescope would have had to be mounted equatorially, and a clock motion would probably have been necessary.

Hence **sidero'static** *a.*

**1879** *Proc. Roy. Soc. Dublin* II. 361 The Siderostatic Telescope.. is principally intended for solar spectroscopic investigation. **1885** AGNES CLERKE *Hist. Astron.* 450 An instrument with 'siderostatic' mounting.

†**'siderous,** *a.*[1] *Obs.*$^{-1}$ [f. L. *sīder-*, *sīdus* star.] Star-like, sidereal.

**1646** SIR T. BROWNE *Pseud. Ep.* III. xi. (1686) 104 The mystical conjunction of Hawk and Lion, implying the genial or the syderous Sun.

**siderous,** *a.*[2] *rare.* [f. Gr. σίδηρος iron.] Having the qualities of iron; ferreous.

**1811** PINKERTON *Petral.* Introd. p. xxxviii, The siliceous, the argillaceous, the magnesian [earths]; contemporary with which two last, was that of the ferruginous, or.. siderous. *Ibid.* I. I. Domain I. Siderous.

**siderurgical** (sɪdə'rɜːdʒɪkəl), *a.* [f. next + -ICAL.] Pertaining to siderurgy.

**1870** tr. *Figuier's Primitive Man* 302 A model.. of a siderurgical establishment belonging to the earliest iron epoch. **1878** *Ure's Dict. Arts* (ed. 7) IV. Suppl. 470 At present siderurgical industry yields two series of products.

**siderurgy** (sɪdə'rɜːdʒɪ). [a. Gr. σιδηρουργία working in iron, f. σιδηρουργός an iron-worker, f. σίδηρος iron + ἔργον work.] The metallurgy of iron and steel.

**1891** in *Cent. Dict.* **1897** *Durh. Univ. Jrnl.* 20 Mar. 297 The art of siderurgy must have made considerable advances before it was possible to manufacture a flint and steel.

**'sides** (saɪdz), *prep.* and *adv.* Now *dial.* and *colloq.* [aphetic f. BESIDES.] Besides; moreover.

**1579** E. HAKE *News out of Powles Churchyd.* D iij, All this theyle haue, and else much more, sydes Marchpane and greene Cheese. **1839–** in *Eng. Dial. Dict.* **1901** F. HUME *Golden Wang-ho* i, 'Sides, they'll want to——. **1918** C. MACKENZIE *Sylvia Scarlett* II. iv. 331, I didn't seem to want them no more. 'Sides, I've got seven already. **1936** M. MITCHELL *Gone with Wind* v. 79 It's too late den. Dey's already mahied [*sc.* married]. 'Sides, gempmums specs dey wives ter have sense. **1968** J. WHEELER SMITH in W. King *Black Short Story Anthol.* (1972) 37 'He didn't hurt you none, did he?' 'No, he didn't bother me, sides looking mean.' **1975** 'J. LYMINGTON' *Spider in Bath* i. 11 It's not like that. Sides, the job helps his pension.

**ˈside-ˌsaddle**, *sb.* (and *adv.*). [SIDE *sb.*[1]]

**1.** A saddle so contrived as to enable a woman to sit with both feet on one (usually the left or near) side of a horse; in mod. use *spec.* one with horns or crutches to support and give a hold to the knees of the rider, who sits facing forward with the right knee raised.

**1493** *Mem. Ripon* (Surtees) III. 164 Imprimis sol. Willelmo Burton pro emendacione unius syd saddyl quæ fuit dominæ Markyndfeld, 5*d.* *a* **1548** HALL *Chron., Hen. VIII*, 214 Wylliam Coffin Master of the Horses leadyng a spare horse with a syde saddle. **1598** STOW *Surv.* 65 King Richard tooke to wife Anne, daughter to the King of Boheme, that first brought hither the riding upon side saddles. **1630** HAKEWILL *Apol.* (ed. 2) 273 The vse of hoppes in our drinke, of riding in coaches, and of side-saddles, but since the time of Richard the 2 here with vs. **1661** PEPYS *Diary* 17 Sept., So I went..to take leave, and of Mr. Townsend did borrow a very fine side-saddle for my wife. **1716–8** LADY M. W. MONTAGU *Lett.* I. xxxvi. 134 My side-saddle is the first that was ever seen in this part of the world. **1758** JOHNSON *Idler* No. 13 ¶8 She has twenty covers for side-saddles. **1823** LADY GRANVILLE *Lett.* (1894) I. 228 Nobody has hinted at a side-saddle or wheeled vehicle for me. **1865** W. G. PALGRAVE *Arabia* II. 176 We remounted our side-saddles and galloped homewards. **1880** in Mrs. P. O'Donoghue *Ladies on Horseback* 266 Being able to sit square and ride straight on a side-saddle.

**b.** Used as *adv.* On a side-saddle; sideways.

**1885** *Globe* 5 Nov. (Cassell), Anne of Bohemia exhibited the new fashion of riding side-saddle which she had introduced into England. **1905** SLADEN *Playing the Game* x. 101 The same bench does for natives and foreigners; the natives squat on it or sit on it side-saddle.

**2.** *attrib.*, as ***side-saddle fashion, rider, riding, shoulders.***

**1575** R. B. *Appius & Virg.* B 3 With bobbing and bum, Our side saddle shoulders shal sheilde that doth come. **1788** COWPER *Let. to Rev. J. Newton* 19 April, He thenceforth rode behind, in the side-saddle fashion, with both legs on a side, and thus they proceeded till they came near to Oxford. **1893** MRS. A. M. HAYES (*title*), The Horsewoman: a Practical Guide to Side-Saddle Riding. **1897** *Westm. Gaz.* 23 Aug. 8/2, I started in the Haute Ecole, as a side-saddle rider.

**3. side-saddle flower** (or **plant**). **a.** An American swamp-plant of the genus *Sarracenia*, the leaves of which retain a considerable quantity of water.

For various explanations of the name see the earlier quots.

**1738** *Phil. Trans.* XL. 347 From the Shape of the Flower, they are in Virginia called the Side-saddle-flower. **1822** *Hortus Anglicus* II. 19 *Sarracenia Flava.* Yellow Side-saddle Flower... *S. Purpurea.* Purple Side-saddle Flower. .. The name is derived from the fancied resemblance of the stigma to a pillion. **1845–50** MRS. LINCOLN *Lect. Bot.* xxxi. 169 This plant is found in swamps; its common name, Side-saddle flower, is given in reference to the form of its leaf. **1861** BENTLEY *Man. Bot.* 182 They may be seen in the Pitcher plants,..in the Side-saddle plant.., and in many others. **1884** *Harper's Mag.* Nov. 840/2 The small plants called the American 'side-saddle flowers' (*Sarracenia*).

**b.** The plant *Darlingtonia californica.*

**1866** *Treas. Bot.* 384/1 The only species,..known as the Californian Side-saddle flower or Pitcher-plant, is a perennial herb growing in marshy places.

Hence **ˈside-saddle** *v.*

**1778** TICKELL *Prol. to Camp*, Side-saddle my horse! ah, lace my stays! **1892** A. E. LEE *Hist. Columbus* I. 371 So numerous were the animals, saddled, and 'sidesaddled',.. that they were commonly spoken of as 'the cavalry'.

**ˈside-scan,** *a.* Also **side scan, sidescan.** [SIDE *sb.*[1] 24.] Applied to side-looking sonar (and radar), esp. on a ship.

**1967** *Undersea Technol.* Apr. 24/2 The most important feature of side scan sonar..is its ability to produce a permanent, continuous, graphic record of what it 'sees'. **1969** *New Scientist* 20 Feb. 393/2 A range of sidescan sonars is now available. **1978** *Nature* 5 Jan. 49/2 Side-scan sonar has been used previously to profile icebergs, by lowering a sonar transducer vertically, at a known rate, from the side of a boat. **1979** *Ibid.* 29 Mar. 399/1 These surfaces were revealed by side-scan radar from aircraft in surveys made by the Brazilian government.

So **ˈside-scanner; ˈsidescanning** *a.*

**1960** *Guardian* 20 July 2/6 In view of the development of side-scanning photography these flights were provocative while not violating international air-space. **1968** *Observer* 4 Feb. 3/3 A standard sonar device is used to sweep a large area and echoes of all possible wrecks are picked up and charted. The side-scanner then moves in to check each echo in detail. **1968** *Proc. 5th Symp. Remote Sensing of Environment* 534 The resolution of a side-scanning sonar instrument depends primarily on the width of the beam in the horizontal plane..and on the duration of the pulses. **1978** *Navy News* Oct. 5/1 She is equipped with echo sounders to measure the depth of water as well as side-scanning sonar which gives a view of the sea bed when locating wrecks.

**ˈside-shoot.** [SIDE *sb.*[1] 23 c.] A shoot growing out from the side of a stem. Also *fig.*

**1721** MORTIMER *Husb.* II. 222 The strongest Side-shoots having Joints sufficient for laying, are to be chosen. **1786** ABERCROMBIE *Gard. Assist.* 110 Plant, and propagate by slips and cuttings of the side-shoots, and rooted off-sets. **1825** *Greenhouse Comp.* I. 129 At no time should more than one flower-bud be allowed to come forward on each side-shoot. **1868** *Rep. U.S. Comm. Agric.* (1869) 256 The first step is to trim away the straggling side-shoots. **1890** CHILD *Ballads* IV. 40 This broil was no sooner settled than another sprouted, a side-shoot from the same stem.

**ˈside-show.** [SIDE *sb.*[1] 24 d.] A 'show' which is subsidiary to a larger one; a minor attraction in an exhibition or entertainment; hence, a minor incident or issue, a subordinate matter or affair. Also *fig.*, esp. in *Mil.* contexts: cf. SHOW *sb.*[1] 15 b.

**1855** BARNUM *Life* xii. 316 In attending to what might be termed my 'side shows', or temporary enterprises, I have never neglected the American Museum. **1866** C. H. SMITH (*title*) Bill Arp, so called. A side show of the Southern side of the War. **1869** 'MARK TWAIN' *Innoc. Abr.* liii. 573 And so I close my chapter on the Church of the Holy Sepulchre... With all its clap-trap side-shows and unseemly impostures of every kind. **1884** *Dicken's Dict. Lond.* 24/3 The price of admission is one shilling, besides 'side shows'. **1884** *Times* (weekly ed.) 17 Oct. 17/2 General Butler is conducting his Speech-making 'side-show' through New York. **1893** *Daily News* 11 Jan. 2/3 A charity bazaar, and..the entertainments which are given at those places in what are called the side shows. **1900** *Westm. Gaz.* 11 Sept. 2/1 The 'side shows', as the various sectional meetings are termed, were all well attended. **1915** D. H. LAWRENCE *Rainbow* xiii. 381 But Ursula never told about Winifred Inger. That was a sort of secret side-show to her life. **1919** *Daily Express* (Dublin) 18 Mar. 3/6 (*heading*) Side shows. Sir Chas. Monro's despatch. Important minor operations. **1931** T. E. LAWRENCE *Let.* 13 Apr. (1938) 718 Your war-history has become one of my constant reference books, for the main war; and that its chapters on the side-shows are so crisply black-and-white as to make exciting stories of them. **1959** *Listener* 12 Mar. 444/1 Not even sideshows in the Yemen or police operations by the army in a riotous colony will save them. **1977** P. MOYES *To kill Coconut* xiii. 178 'What in hell is going on up in the forest.'.. 'I told you, that's a side-show.'

*attrib.* **1894** *Daily News* 28 June 6/5 With so little side-show attraction.

**ˈside-slip,** *sb.* [f. SIDE *sb.*[1] + SLIP *sb.* and *v.*]

†**1.** ? A slope or rise. *Obs.*[−1]

In mod. Linc. dial. *on the side-slip of* means 'somewhat to the side of'.

**1649** in *Archaeol.* (1792) X. 434 The scite of this manor house being placed on the side slipp of a rising ground.

**2.** An illegitimate child. Cf. BY-SLIP 2.

**1872** GEO. ELIOT *Middlem.* xl, The old man..left it to this side-slip of a son that he kept in the dark.

**3.** 'A division at the side of the stage of a theatre, where the scenery is slipped off and on.'

**1882** in *Imperial Dict.* (Annandale) Suppl.

**4.** A slip taken from the side of a plant.

**1891** in *Cent. Dict.*

**5. a.** The action or fact of slipping sideways, *esp.* on the part of a cycle or motor-car.

**1896** *Daily News* 16 Nov. 4/2 Cyclists..came ignominiously to earth by reason of the demon 'side-slip'. **1898** *Westm. Gaz.* 5 Dec. 5/1 A lady cyclist met with a serious accident from side-slip near Leytonstone.

**b.** *Aeronaut.* = SLIP *sb.*[3] 9 j; also, a manœuvre in which this is deliberately produced.

**1910** *Flight* 25 June 493/1 Is the banking..sufficient to overcome centrifugal movement (which is of course a sort of side-slip) or not? **1915** [see OVERBANK *v.* 2 a]. **1928** *Observer* 1 July 17/3 With the greatest of ease they performed side-slips, vertical dives, and loops. **1969** K. MUNSON *Pioneer Aircraft 1903–14* 108/1 He eventually made a safe landing after the machine was put into a side-slip—a manoeuvre which, as Dallas Brett later recorded, was then 'popularly regarded as being in the nature of a preliminary funeral rite'. **1978** *Sci. Amer.* Nov. 137/1 The fixed rear fin had tended to correct this condition by causing the machine to turn in the direction of the sideslip.

**c.** *Skiing* and *Surfing.* The action of descending (a slope or wave).

**1913** [see SIDE-SLIP *v.* c]. **1959** P. MOYES *Dead Men don't Ski* iv. 51 Now they were tackling the sideslip—skidding sideways down icy slopes, their skis flat against the mountain-side. **1968** *Surfer Mag.* Jan. 24/3 Sliding sideways in a controlled sideslip until you reach the bottom of the wave. **1970** N. FLEMING *Czech Point* i. 10, I..went into a twenty foot long sideslip and stopped.

**d.** *fig.*

**1916** H. BARBER *Aeroplane Speaks* p. v, The dreadful haltings, the many side-slips, the irregular speed, and, in short, the altogether disconcerting ways of a pen. **1921** GALSWORTHY *To Let* II. p. vi, He therefore confined himself to discussing with Dumetrius whether Monticellis would come again..and the future of Johns, with a side-slip into Buxton Knights.

**ˈside-slip,** *v.* [f. the *sb.*]

**a.** *intr.* To slip sideways.

**1887** *Cycling* (Badm. Libr.) 359 Side-slipping.—Most riders of dwarf bicycles have experienced this when riding on greasy roads. **1902** in *Cassell's Dict.* Suppl. **1904** *Blackw. Mag.* Oct. 534/1 They will prance and curvet, sideslip [etc.].

**b.** *Aeronaut.* Of an aeroplane: to move sideways, *esp.* towards the centre of curvature while turning (cf. SKID *v.*[1] 3 c). Also *trans.*, to cause to do this. Cf. SLIP *v.*[1] 9 c.

**1911** *Flight* 23 Sept. 830/2 He turned sharply to the left, permitting the machine to bank up too much, whereupon it side-slipped to the ground. **1928** *Rep. & Mem. Aeronaut. Res. Comm.* No. 1187. 6 The aeroplane is side-slipped with the rudder bar central. **1935** C. DAY LEWIS *Time to Dance* 36 From three thousand feet they tilted Over, side-slipped away. **1941** POPE & OTIS *Elem. Aeronaut.* ix. 84 It is possible ..to sideslip the plane even during a turn of the 'S'. **1966** M. WOODHOUSE *Tree Frog* xxv. 183 The whole plane felt dead and we sideslipped fast. **1978** *Sci. Amer.* Nov. 139/1 Every so often the machine would lose control and simply sideslip into the ground.

**c.** *Skiing.* To descend sideways. Cf. sense 5 c of the *sb.*

**1913** A. LUNN *Ski-ing* iii. 79 The expert makes great use of the side-slip for getting down difficult ground... Run with your ski in the normal position for traversing a slope... Flatten them against the slope and slip sideways. Then run a little way in the normal position and again side-slip. **1952** ISELIN & SPECTORSKY *Invitation to Skiing* vi. 101 When you can side slip and stop at will, you are ready for the next exercise. **1972** 'M. YORKE' *Silent Witness* II. 13 Knees flexed ..he had side-slipped down the sheer drop from the shoulder of the mountain.

**d.** *transf.* and *fig.* Also occas. *trans.*

**1917** 'CONTACT' *Airman's Outings* v. 139 Snatches of familiar flying-talk..side-slipped away from Archie. **1921** GALSWORTHY *To Let* I. iii. 36 His heart moved in a disconcerting manner, as if it had side-slipped within his chest. **1930** *London Mercury* Feb. 319 Here he was suddenly realising that they controlled another mode of clutching. Better to side-slip that too—if he could. **1931** *Technol. Rev.* Nov. 67/1, I was cruising along 43d Street when along came Bill, Sam, and Charlie in formation, and we all side-slipped into a speakeasy and did a lot of barroom flying. **1960** T. MCLEAN *Kings of Rugby* xi. 120 He offered dummy passes, sidestepped, sideslipped. **1964** D. MACARTHUR *Reminiscences* v. 125 The problem was to sideslip my troops westward..before their path would be cut off from the north.

So **side-slipping** *vbl. sb.* and *ppl. a.*

**1887** [see sense a above]. **1904** *Motor Cycle* 18 Apr. 361/3 Side-slipping is a great bugbear to motor cyclists. **1916** 'BOYD CABLE' *Action Front* 1 A wet night, a greasy road, and a side-slipping motor-bike. **1930** [see NOSE-DIVE *v.* 1 a]. **1949** A. FAWCUS *Skiing Simplified* ii. 49 Sideslipping is the easiest way to get down a steep slope without having to turn. **1950** *Gloss. Aeronaut. Terms (B.S.I.)* I. 10 *Side-slipping*, motion of an aircraft relative to the air such that the air flow has a component along the lateral axis. **1975** *Oxf. Compan. Sports & Games* 957/1 The secret of giant slalom is good control of the ski edges to prevent wasteful sideslipping.

†**sideslips,** *adv. Obs.*[−1] In 4 sideslepis. [Cf. SIDE-SLIP *sb.*] ? Sideways, aslant.

*c* **1330** R. BRUNNE *Chron. Wace* (Rolls) 13162 On Borel & Cador þat formest went, þe Romayns a-side [*v.r.* sideslepis] on hem glent.

**sidesman** (ˈsaɪdzmən). [f. SIDE *sb.*[1] Cf. SIDEMAN.]

**1.** One of the persons elected as assistants to the churchwardens of a parish.

There is no foundation for the statement, which is as old as the 17th cent., that *sidesman* in this sense is a corruption of *synodsman*. In the 17th cent. *assistant* is sometimes used interchangeably with *sidesman*.

**1632** D. LUPTON *Lond. & Co. Carbonadoed, Apparators*, They have much businesse with the Churchwardens and Sides-men. **1667** *Answ. Quest. out of North* 12 There are in all, Threescore and fourteen thousand Churchwardens and Sides-men in England. **1726** AYLIFFE *Parergon* 171 A Gift of such Goods, made by them without the Consent of the Sides-men or Vestry, is void. **1766** ENTICK *London* IV. 45 Two church-wardens, and two sidesmen. **1857** TOULMIN SMITH *Parish* 70 A part of what has, more lately, been reckoned as one duty of the churchwardens,—the making of presentments—was formerly that of the Sidesmen only. **1898** *Westm. Gaz.* 2 Feb. 5/1 General Moberly was for some twenty years a sidesman at this church.

*fig.* or *transf.* **1644** BULWER *Chiron.* 7 But have likewise punctually set downe the office of these sides-men the Hands. **1716** M. DAVIES *Athen. Brit.* II. 210 Those Preaching sides-men of Prophesying Congregations. **1886** J. CORBETT *Fall of Asgard* II. 195 On either side, the men of understanding, whom the young king had taken for his sidesmen, had their place.

**b.** An assistant to a municipal or civil officer. *local.*

**1835** *Municipal Corpor. Rep.* 2585 The Sides-men [of Beaumaris] are assistants merely to the town stewards, and similarly appointed. **1885** *Law Times* LXXIX. 156/1 The cutting of the wood in Wedholme fell into the hands of sixteen sidesmen elected by the tenants.

†**2.** A partisan; = SIDEMAN 2. *Obs.*

**1648** MILTON *Tenure of Kings* 41 How little leasure would they find to be the most pragmatical Sidesmen of every popular tumult and Sedition? **1651** CLEVELAND *Poems* 22 He, with his little sides-man Lazarus.

**3.** A player in the game of bowls.

**1843** *Proc. Berw. Nat. Club* II. 54 One of the sidesmen runs before, and lays himself down at the spot most suitable for the ball striking, in order that his marrow may direct his aim thither.

**4.** One who supports another from the side.

**1863** *Pilgr. Prairies* I. 271 Placing Wahtogachto on the quietest [horse], supported..by two able sidesmen, [they] took their way across the prairie.

**ˈside-step,** *sb.* [SIDE *sb.*[1] or *adv.*[2]]

**1.** A step to one side; *spec.* in *Rugby Football*, a step to the side, as to avoid a tackle, made while running with the ball. Also *Sc.*, a false step wrenching the limb (Jam. 1882). Also *fig.*

**1789** *Rules & Reg. Field Exercises Army in Ireland* I. 8 The *Side-step*, or march, is very necessary on many occasions when halted. **1847** *Infantry Man.* (1854) 48 The side or closing step must..be frequently practised. **1859** F. A. GRIFFITHS *Artil. Man.* (1862) 6 The length of the side step, which is always taken in quick time, is 10 inches. **1927** [see JINK *v.*[1]]. **1940** 'GUN BUSTER' *Return via Dunkirk* II. viii. 148 We've got to make a side-step, giving up part of the ridge we're now holding. **1960** V. JENKINS *Lions down Under* xi. 161 Risman did the rest with two perfect side-steps.

**2.** A step fixed to the side of a ship, vehicle, etc.

**1867** SMYTH *Sailor's Word-bk.* 625 *Side-steps*, pieces of wood bolted to the side of a ship for the convenience of ascending.

**ˈside-step,** *v.* [f. prec.] **1. a.** *intr.* To step to one side. Also *transf.*, to go aside from the direct route; to make a side-trip.

**1901** *Scribner's Mag.* Apr. 422/1 Skipper..raised his head, and side-stepped stiffly. **1927** *Ladies' Home Jrnl.* Jan. 62, I was glad I side stepped, for the journey..was worth a deviation. **1951** *Sport* 6–12 Apr. 15/2 He twists, turns, side-steps and swerves beautifully. **1973** 'D. HALLIDAY' *Dolly &*

*Starry Bird* xv. 230 Sophia sidestepped and walked sharply past Charles.

**b.** *fig.* To practise evasion; to avoid an issue or prevaricate.

*a* **1911** D. G. PHILLIPS *Susan Lenox* (1917) II. xi. 276 What do you think of that, Terry? I offered her a twenty and she sidestepped. **1930** P. MACDONALD *Link* vii. 114 I've even asked Dinwater that flat out on two occasions. But he's always side-stepped.

**c.** *Skiing.* (See quots.)

**1924** *Ski Terms* in *Tourist* Winter Sports No. 12/2 *Side stepping*, climbing by lifting the skis horizontally. **1976** *Webster's Sports Dict.* 390/2 *Sidestep*, to climb a slope by employing a sidestep.

**2. a.** *trans.* To avoid by stepping to the side; *spec.* in *Football.*

**1905** 'O. HENRY' in *N.Y. World* (Mag. section) 12 Mar. 5/4 I've lost two inches of my tail trying to sidestep those swinging doors. **1920** W. CAMP *Football without Coach* 93 The man who catches the ball will not be able to sidestep him or pass him. **1931** *Times* 16 Feb. 5/1 Once, Arigho.. managed to side-step Reeve. **1976** *Sunday Mail* (Glasgow) 28 Nov. 46/6 The striker took his time, sidestepped a tackle and neatly shot low past Rennie.

**b.** *fig.*

**1900** ADE *Fables in Slang* 56 The Parents decided to give Clarence a large Measure of Liberty, that he might become Acquainted with the Snares and Temptations of the World when he was Young, and thus be Prepared to side-step the Pitfalls when he was Older. **1906** *Springfield* (Mass.) *Weekly Republ.* 27 Sept. 8 The Idaho republicans are deftly side-stepping the anti-Mormon issue. **1915** WODEHOUSE *Psmith Journalist* xxiii. 173 If I can put him away, it gets me into line with Jimmy, and he can't side-step me. **1932** E. WALLACE *When Gangs came to London* xxviii. 287 One of the best gunmen that ever sidestepped the chair. **1947** E. O. SCHLUNKE in *Coast to Coast 1946* 51 But to make sure he wasn't 'side-stepped', Krantz turned up at the railway station. **1964** *English Studies* XLV. 21 Many people side-step the recognition of a plurality of Englishes by such judgments as: 'Oh, that's not English, that's American.' **1977** *Time* 8 Aug. 25/1 If the British government continues on the line it appears to be following, we will be able to sidestep them and arrive at an internal settlement.

**3.** *trans.* To cause (a person or thing) to move sideways; to transfer to the side.

**1969** A. GLYN *Dragon Variation* viii. 245 Jeff's Queen was *en prise*, and he side-stepped her one square where she would still be able to defend the Rook's Pawn. **1974** *Daily Tel.* 26 Mar. 16 Peter Dimmock, general manager of BBC Enterprises... Mr Dimmock, formerly general manager of BBC Outside Broadcasts, was sidestepped to his present job.

Hence **'side-stepper**, one who steps sideways or avoids a direct course or issue; **'side-stepping** *vbl. sb.*, stepping sideways, evasiveness, avoidance; also as *ppl. a.*

**1901** G. V. HOBART *Down Line with John Henry* 100, I was the likeliest side-stepper that ever did a grass-chopping speciality. **1909** *N.Y. Even. Post* (semi-weekly ed.) 1 Mar. 1 Had not Mr. Fairbanks been a really wonderful side-stepper, their essential differences might have long ago become public property. **1912** J. SANDILANDS *Western Canad. Dict. & Phrase-Bk.*, *Sidestepping*, wandering from the argument, evading the question. **1932** *Blue Valley Farmer* (Oklahoma City) 17 Mar. 6/5 When America is grappling with things fundamental, tired and disgusted with side-stepping, buck-passing and plain lying.. the country must content itself with a stone when it asked for bread. **1949** 'J. TEY' *Brat Farrar* xii. 100 The conversational ground he moved on was firm. There was need for neither side-stepping nor manoeuvre. **1960** *Times* 16 June 16/2 'Autumn' with its evocative side-stepping harmonies, was delightfully sung. **1970** *Times* 28 Sept. 12/7 The sidestepping at blinding speed of Gerald Davies on the right wing. **1980** N. FREELING *Castang's City* xvi. 105 A dodgy rapid sidestepper, a clever elusive runner.

**'side-stick.** *Printing.* [SIDE *sb.*[1] 23 b.] One of a pair of sticks, usually of wood, with one side slanting, used in locking up a form.

**1683** MOXON *Mech. Exerc.*, *Printing* p. viii, By Furniture is meant the Head-sticks, Foot-sticks, Side-sticks,.. and Quoyns. **1728** CHAMBERS *Cycl.* s.v. *Printing*, Some of these are placed at the Top of the Pages, call'd *Head-sticks*;.. others at the Sides, call'd *Side sticks*. **1808** STOWER *Printer's Grammar* 203 Having dressed the inside of our pages, we proceed to do the same to their outsides, by putting side sticks and foot sticks to them. **1879** *Print. Trades Jrnl.* XXVIII. 12 The inventor claims for them that they are a perfect system of locking-up without side-sticks.

**sides to 'middle**, *adv.* (and *adj.*) *phr.* Also -into-, side to middle. [SIDE *sb.*[1]] Of a sheet of bed-linen: with the sides and middle changing places, as a worn sheet cut down the centre and resewn thus to prolong its useful life. Also (hyphened) as *adj. phr.*

**1861** MRS. BEETON *Bk. Househ. Managem.* ii. 24 Sheets should be turned 'sides to middle' before they are allowed to get very thin. **1884** E. NESBIT *Let.* in D. Langley Moore *E. Nesbit* (1933) v. 71, I have done 2 sheets 'sides into middle'. **1949** H. ASHTON *Parson Austen's Daughter* viii. 309 She.. had to sleep on sheets which had been turned side to middle. **1950** B. PYM *Some Tame Gazelle* xv. 161 Although the Archdeacon had not personally made the bed, he knew that there were sides-to-middle sheets on it. **1963** 'J. M. BERRISFORD' *Gardening in Lime* ii. 24 After six to eight weeks the whole [compost] heap may be turned, sides to middle, with the top material becoming the bottom. **1972** 'S. WOODS' *They love not Poison* viii. 112 Jenny [was] diligently hemming a sheet that Mrs. Dibb wanted turned 'sides to middle'.

**'side-swipe**, *sb.* [f. the vb.; cf. also SIDE-WIPE.]

**1.** A glancing blow from or on the side (esp. of a motor vehicle). Chiefly *U.S.*

**1917** *Dialect Notes* IV. 400 He struck it with a *side-swipe*. **1935** *Evening Sun* (Baltimore) 7 Mar. 25/3 A few days ago we said there is no such word as *sideswipe* in the dictionary... *Side-wiping* puts the shine on the car—*side-swiping* takes it off. **1964** D. SOLOMON *Accidents on Main Rural Highways* 1. 2 Nearly half of all accident involvements were either rear-end collisions or same-direction sideswipes. **1968** *Autocar* 14 Mar. 24/3 With adjustable front seats there is weakness in sideswipe. **1977** *Time* 24 Jan. 2/3 (Advt.), The ESV's have proved their life-saving value in head-on and rear-end collisions, side-swipes and roll-overs.

**2.** A passing jibe or verbal attack; an indirect rebuke or criticism.

**1924** KIPLING *Prophet & Country* in *Debits & Credits* (1926) 193 A side-swipe at the practically non-existent birth-rate. **1959** *Sunday Times* 29 Nov. 25/6 Wolf Mankowitz has reshaped his satire on show business... A few side-swipes are allowed. **1964** *Ann. Reg. 1963* 26 He allowed himself one side-swipe at the security services, declaring that 'the £60 million spent on these services under the right hon. gentleman's premiership have been less productive.. than the security services of the *News of the World*.' **1977** M. WALKER *National Front* vii. 179 Martin Webster.. again warned of the enemy within in an article.. which included a series of side-swipes against 'the trimmers, the popularity-seekers and moderates'.

**'side-swipe**, *v.* Chiefly *U.S.* [SIDE *sb.*[1]] *trans.* To strike (something) a glancing blow on or with the side (esp. of a motor vehicle).

**1904** *Philadelphia Even. Tel.* 12 Nov. 16 The west-bound St. Louis Express, while pulling on to a siding, was sideswiped by the east-bound Pittsburg Limited. **1916** *Daily Colonist* (Victoria, B.C.) 15 July 2/4 Five persons were injured.. when a motor car.. overturned on the boulevard, after sideswiping a stalled car. **1938** D. BAKER *Young Man with Horn* I. v. 41 No sidewalks there, and one out of ten cars doing its best to sideswipe them. **1960** I. CROSS *Backward Sex* iii. 66 The cup slid from one end of the tray to the other, sideswiping the teapot on the way. **1973** K. GILES *File on Death* ii. 29 A grey car.. came up fast... It side-swiped her and drove on.

**'side-table.** [SIDE *sb.*[1] 23.] A table placed beside the wall of a room (*esp.* a dining-room), or to the side of a main or high table.

**1377** LANGL. *P. Pl.* B. XII. 200 þo þat seten atte syde table or with þe soueregines of þe halle. **1393** —— C. XVI. 42 Pacience and ich.. seten by ous selue at a syd-table. *c* **1450** in Aungier *Syon* (1840) 377 Other sustres schal sytte at the syde tables in ther order as they be professyd. **1483** *Cely Papers* (Camden) 135 We schuld paye noo more for owre burdd but iij s. iiij d. fl. a weke at the hye tabull and ij s. viij d. at the syde tabull. *c* **1500** *For to serve a Lord* in *Babees Bk.* (1868) 368 After the high principall tabill sette with brede & salte, thenne salte-selers shall be sette uppon the syde-tablys. **1617** MORYSON *Itin.* III. 135 Towards the confines of Flanders, the Hoasts onely cover the table, and a side table, upon which everie passenger hath his glasse. **1665** PEPYS *Diary* 13 Sept., The wind, blowing into the room.., flung down a great blow-pott that stood upon the side-table. **1710** ADDISON *Tatler* No. 148 ¶ 10, I saw a noble Sirloin on the Side-Table. **1760–72** H. BROOKE *Fool of Qual.* (1809) IV. 58 Harry ordered a side-table to be covered for him and them. **1848** DICKENS *Dombey* xxvi, Besides which, the Native had private zests and flavours on a side-table, with which the Major daily scorched himself. **1888** 'J. S. WINTER' *Bootle's Childr.* xiii, The pantry-boy and the two kitchen-maids.. took their own meals at a side-table in the same room.

**'side-track**, *sb.* Orig. *U.S.* [SIDE *sb.*[1] 23.]

**a.** A railway siding.

**1835** *Maine Farmer* 24 July 198/1 One of the principle [*sic*] dealers here has offered to lay a side track from the road to his own storehouse. **1876** G. A. CROFUTT *Trans-Continental Tourist* 41 Waterloo is a small side-track station. **1881** *Chicago Times* 14 May, The side-tracks of all the roads along nearly their entire lengths were filled with cars loaded with freight. **1894** *Times* 5 May 9/4 The stolen train was eventually run on a side track at Palmer, in Washington State.

**b.** A side-path.

**1892** [see MIDDLE-OF-THE-ROAD]. **1966** 'J. HACKSTON' *Father clears Out* 113 Trooper Caldecott riding along the soft, silent side-tracks that led to the Sunday trading.

**c.** *transf.* and *fig.*

**1901** *Congress. Rec.* XXXIV. III. 2476/1, I do not propose to be side tracked by any Senator from the other side of the Chamber. I myself will decide when I will go on the side track. **1935** B. MALINOWSKI *Coral Gardens & their Magic* II. VI. v. 239 Man never runs on the sidetrack of magical verbiage. **1972** J. PHILIPS *Vanishing Senator* (1973) III. ii. 136 Couldn't you try rental agencies? It wouldn't be a side track for you, Inspector.

**'side-track**, *v.* Orig. *U.S.* [f. prec.]

**1.** *trans.* To run or shunt (a train, etc.) into a siding. Also *fig.*, to push or set aside; *spec.* to divert or lead (a person) from the main course; to turn (something) aside from prominence.

**1880** *News & Press* (Cimarron, New Mexico) 19 Feb. 4/3 Short skirts are now worn for dancing dresses, and the gentlemen are no longer obliged to wait for the ladies to side-track their trains before they can pass. **1881** *Chicago Times* 14 May, It [the corn] has been side-tracked and kept in the sun and rain somewhere along the road. **1886** *Pall Mall G.* 19 June 14/1, I saw several new locomotives which had been side-tracked and allowed to go to ruin. **1887** *Scribner's Mag.* in Farmer *Americanisms* (1889) 487/1 Mebbe them thar lieyers side-tracked him with their everlastin' quashtuns, an' ef so, he warn't so pow'ful much ter blame. **1889** *Voice* (N. York) 4 Apr., In the end, that course will side-track and defeat the reform. **1891** F. H. SMITH *Col. Carter* 139 Yancey broke away again, but Fitz side-tracked him with a gesture, and asked the colonel to repeat Klutchem's exact words. **1897** *Pop. Sci. Monthly* Nov. 56 Such a project was, in fact, sidetracked in favor of the census of school children. **1918** W. S. CHURCHILL *Let.* 12 Jan. in M. Gilbert *Winston S. Churchill* (1977) IV. Compan. I. 231 Munitions are everywhere being side-tracked to the claims of food, of civil imports, of Allies, and of dollars. **1929** C. CONNOLLY *Let.* in *Romantic Friendship* (1975) 325 Delicious people not so young are all somehow sidetracked. **1931** L. A. G. STRONG *Garden* xxxv. 324 He'd be all the worse to deal with, if he saw he'd been sidetracked. **1970** C. JAMES in Rubinstein & Stoneman *Education for Democracy* 157 Acknowledgement of special interests is vitally important in adolescence and should not be side-tracked into extra-curricular events. **1978** T. ALLBEURY *Lantern Network* xi. 160 Bailey disliked the fruity voice.. and.. the attempt to side-track him.

**2.** *intr.* To run into a siding. Also *fig.*, to diverge from the main road or course.

**1888** *Harper's Mag.* Mar. 650 One train had side-tracked to await the train from the opposite direction. **1893** *Advance* (Chicago) 8 June, The business of the minister is to preach the gospel, not.. to side-track on great moral issues.

Hence **'side-tracked** *ppl. a.*, **'side-tracking** *vbl. sb.*

**1892** *46th Ann. Report Amer. Miss.* 140 These side-tracked brothers and sisters of our own Protestant lineage. **1892** A. E. LEE *Hist. Columbus* II. 209 Sidetracking amply sufficient for the great mass of sojourning special trains was provided. **1947** *Mind* LVI. 291 The abnormal violence of the reaction against Idealism must, I think, be held primarily responsible for the side-tracking of its doctrine of judgment. **1981** A. PRICE *I'll soldier no More* 54 Through all the verbiage and side-tracking he held to his primary objectives.

**'side-view.** [SIDE *sb.*[1] 24 b.] A view of anything obtained or taken from the side. Also *fig.*, a side-reference *to* something.

**1715** POPE *Iliad* Pref. C 3, He not only gives us the full Prospects of Things, but several unexpected Peculiarities and Side-Views, unobserv'd by any Painter but Homer. **1748** RICHARDSON *Clarissa* (1768) II. 75 Only, that I know, she has a side-view to her daughter. **1793** HOLCROFT tr. *Lavater's Physiog.* i. 14 Passion.. will snatch off the mask and give.. us a side-view of their true form. **1819** *Pantologia* s.v. *Shipbuilding*, The whole length of the ship is represented according to a side-view, perpendicular to the keel. **1839–52** BAILEY *Festus* 105 When both are side-views only of one thing. **1877** *Encycl. Brit.* VII. 170/2 On the side view, by which the valve is presented to the eye of the observer.

**'sidewalk.** Also side-walk, side walk. [SIDE *sb.*[1] 23.]

**1.** A walk or path running parallel to a main or central one. *rare*$^{-1}$.

**1667** DAVENANT & DRYDEN *Tempest* I. ii, 'Tis composed of three walks of cypress-trees; each side-walk leads to a cave... The middle-walk is of great depth.

**2.** A (raised) path for foot-passengers along the side of a street, road, etc.; a footway or pavement. Now chiefly *U.S.*

**1739** LABELYE *Piers Westm. Bridge* 69 The Side-walks for the Foot-passengers are.. raised about a Foot above the Carriage-way. **1815** J. ADAMS *Wks.* (1856) X. 125 Walking in the streets of Philadelphia, I met, on the opposite side-walk, Colonel Joseph Lyman. **1824** F. BURNEY in *Jrnls. & Lett.* (1980) VIII. 525 The streets [of Trier] were dreadfully ill paved, without any side Walk. **1826** *United Empire Loyalist* (Toronto) 1 July 39/4 Some regulation with respect to the improvement of the sidewalks, may be considered as necessary. **1837** HAWTHORNE *Twice-told T.* ii, The side walks of the street.. are immediately thronged with two long lines of people. **1883** *Harper's Mag.* Apr. 724/1 On the outside of the sidewalk were planted American elms. **1891** G. MEREDITH *Let.* 27 May (1970) II. 1030 The way to propitiate them [*sc.* reviewers] is to keep along the side-walks, out of the sun. **1936** D. GASCOYNE *Man's Life is this Meat* 29 On the sidewalks houses eat the afternoon. **1951** R. CAMPBELL *Light on Dark Horse* ii. 27 The sidewalk.. was still unpaved in those days. **1966** G. W. TURNER *Eng. Lang. in Austral. & N.Z.* viii. 172 Cities have footpaths, though pavement is also used and Aucklanders seem to be able to use side-walk as well. **1971** *Rand Daily Mail* 27 Mar. 6/4 Wait on the sidewalk after getting off a bus. **1977** 'J. D. WHITE' *Salzburg Affair* xiii. 111 The sidewalks with their cheerful.. tourists, street musicians, girls.

**3.** Comb., as ***sidewalk cafe, skate, song, tree***; **sidewalk superintendent** *joc.* (chiefly *U.S.*), an idler who watches and gives unsolicited advice at construction works, road repairs, etc.; **sidewalk surfing** *slang* (orig. *U.S.*) = SKATEBOARDING *vbl. sb.*; hence **sidewalk surfer**.

**1940** R. CHANDLER *Farewell, my Lovely* viii. 54 The sidewalk café.. was bright and cheerful inside, but the.. tables outside under the striped awning were empty. **1979** P. HARCOURT *Sleep of Spies* I. vii. 96 The week in Paris passed very quickly... We spent a lot of time.. idling in sidewalk cafés. **1925** *Sears Catal.* (ed. 150) 751 Improved extension sidewalk skates. **1977** *Montgomery Ward Catal.* Spring-Summer 509/1 Junior rink-style sidewalk skates. **1883** *Century Mag.* Oct. 929/2 Little sermons in rhyme that are sure to catch the ear and to become hackneyed as a sidewalk song. **1940** *Sun* (Baltimore) 30 Mar. 20/7 The walk.. is covered so that the sidewalk superintendents can meet in rainy weather. **1970** R. P. WARREN *Incarnations* 46 Sidewalk superintendents turn now From their duties and at you stare. **1976** A. CASSORLA *Skateboarder's Bible* 9 Weird-wheeling sidewalk surfers can be seen whipping over the blacktop from Reno to Rio de Janeiro. **1965** *National Observer* (U.S.) 5 Apr. 12/1 Remember the hula hoop? The popularity attained by that hip-swinging fad in the late 1950s is fast being dwarfed by a new teen-age craze known as sidewalk surfing or skateboarding. **1899** *Scribner's Mag.* XXV. 58/2, I followed the shadows of the sidewalk-trees down to the next corner.

Hence '**sidewalked** *a.* or *pa. pple.*, having, or provided with, sidewalks or foot-pavements.

**1884** *Harper's Mag.* Mar. 516/2 There is..no sidewalked street. **1893** *Home Mission N. York* LXV. 593 Miles of streets have been opened, graded, planked, and sidewalked.

'**sidewall.** [SIDE *sb.*[1] 23.]

**1.** A wall forming the side of a structure, room, or enclosure.

**1381** *Durham Halm. Rolls* (Surtees) 171 Et quod le sid-wall sit in altitudine vij pedes. *c* **1470** *Gol. & Gaw.* 249 Apone that riche river..The side-wallis war set. **1535** COVERDALE *Ezek.* xli. 9 The thicknesse of the syde wall without. **1642** FULLER *Holy & Prof. St.* IV. xxi. 352 Which two Proverbs speak no more contradiction, then he that saith that the two opposite side-walls of an house hold up the same roof. **1690** W. WALKER *Idiomat. Anglo-Lat.* 238 It was almost side-wall high. **1726** LEONI *Alberti's Archit.* II. 62/2 The rail or side-wall of the Bridge... The height of this side-wall..must be four foot. **1815** SCOTT *Guy M.* xxvii, The side-walls had long since given way to time. **1844** H. STEPHENS *Bk. Farm* II. 420 Upon this the side-walls are to be founded. **1884** W. C. SMITH *Kildrostan* 43 One sidewall long had in ruins lain.

*transf.* **1868** *Rep. U.S. Comm. Agric.* (1869) 258 The stakes are the means of adding side-walls, as it were, to the hedge. **1882** BENTLEY *Man. Bot.* (ed. 4) 52 Sieve-plate on the side-wall.

**2.** *Sport* (esp. *Squash Rackets*). A wall forming one side of a court.

**1902** [see BOAST *v.*[3], *sb.*[2]]. **1935** *Encycl. Sports* 582/2 [Squash] If..the server makes his ball hit the side wall or roof or floor before it hits the front wall,..he loses his innings. **1963** *Times* 4 Feb. 4/3 This service was nothing more than an astutely placed lob, but which, when hit with reverse spin, clung to the sidewall. **1975** *Oxf. Compan. Sports & Games* 823/1 [Real tennis] The side walls are in play up to a height of about 18 ft. (5·5 m.), where the windows begin.

**3. a.** The side of a vehicle's tyre (TYRE *sb.*[5] 2), usu. untreaded and freq. marked or coloured distinctively. Freq. *attrib.*, as ***sidewall tyre*** (also *absol.* as sb.).

**1922** *Encycl. Brit.* XXXII. 729/2 The outside of the [tyre's] carcass is entirely covered with rubber; the sides with a 'sidewall' layer. *c* **1949** in M. McLuhan *Mech. Bride* (1967) 83 White sidewall tires..available at extra cost. **1972** *Daily Tel.* (Colour Suppl.) 20 Oct. 10/4 Hans Galli, their chief test-pilot, was..convinced that radial-ply tyres were unsuitable for aircraft because of their flexible sidewalls. **1976** J. LEE *Ninth Man* 70 The car... White sidewalls. Radio and heater.

**b.** A surface at either side of a hovercraft that projects downwards underneath it and helps to contain the air-cushion. Freq. *attrib.*

**1960** *Aeroplane* XCIX. 149/1 This is a type of Hovercraft with side walls which are partially immersed in water. **1960** *Economist* 6 Aug. 585/3 William Denny..is to enter a new field for British companies and develop what are called side-wall craft. **1968** *Economist* 18 May 76/3 The car ferry versions of the sidewall hovercraft now being planned.. should provide direct competition with the biggest hydrofoil..now building. **1975** *Nature* 6 Feb. 391/1 The development of a 200-passenger sidewall hover-ferry.

**sideward** ('saɪdwəd), *adv.* and *a.* [f. SIDE *sb.*[1] Cf. MDu. *sijtwert*, *zijdwaert*.]

**A.** *adv.* Towards one side or the other.

*c* **1430** *Art Nombryng* 3 We writene in this art to the lift side-warde, as arabiene writene, that weren fynders of this science. *a* **1513** FABYAN *Chron.* (1516) v. cxxvii. 64/1 Euyn soo became of hym,..he myghte goo or Ryde frowarde or sydewarde, but towarde the Chapell myght he in no wyse atteygne. *a* **1586** SIDNEY *Arcadia* III. (1605) 278 He fell side-ward downe. **1621** QUARLES *Argalus & P.* (1678) 117 With that blow Amphialus last made, his arm had so O'er-struck it self; that sideward to the ground He fell. **1663** MARQ. WORC. *Cent. Inv.* §95 Whether the Deer run forward, sideward, or start backward. **1831** *Blackw. Mag.* XXX. 972 Stones far outshooting, or sideward leaving the tee. **1851** TRENCH *Study Words* ii. §36 The leaps and springs, now forward, now sideward, now upward. **1888** *Harper's Mag.* Apr. 740 Frenzied blasts came to buffet the steamer forward, sideward.

**B.** *adj.* **1.** Directed, moving, or tending towards one side.

**1831** LARDNER *Hydrost.* vii. 131 In sailing vessels this sideward inclination is a matter of comparatively slight importance. **1878** BESANT & RICE *Celia's Arb.* I. xi. 152 A few weeks before, and they were..striding with a sideward lurch after cows. **1899** *Westm. Gaz.* 9 Aug. 2/1 The sun.. then rises with a slight sideward movement.

**2.** Situated on one side; lateral.

**1866** AITKEN *Pract. Med.* II. 59 Sharp collision among the blood-discs, passing from sideward veins into a large vessel.

'**sidewards,** *adv.* [f. SIDE *sb.*[1] Cf. Du. *zijwaarts*, G. *seitwärts*.]

*Syduardys* in the *Promp. Parv.* (E.E.T.S.) 410 is app. an error for *sydnandys* SIDENHAND.

**1.** To one side. Cf. SIDEWARD *adv.*

*a* **1648** LD. HERBERT *Life* (1886) 73 When it is requisite only to make a horse go sidewards, it will be enough to keep the reins equal in his hands. **1694** *Martens' Voy. Spitzbergen* in *Acc. Sev. Late Voy.* II. 114 He doth not look downwards, but streight before, and sidewards. **1807** W. TAYLOR in *Monthly Mag.* XXIII. 13 The rash fling sidewards. **1912** J. STEPHENS *Crock of Gold* vi. 57 He was not looking at her but far away sidewards across the spreading hill.

**2.** In a position on one side; aside. Also const. *of* or *from*.

**1723** *Pres. State Russia* II. 410 Docks for building of Ships are now Sidewards of the Citadel. **1827** CARLYLE *Germ. Rom.* II. 139 Sidewards from the farm-house lay some offices for the storing of produce and implements. **1871** B. TAYLOR *Faust* (1875) I. xiv. 153 And side-wards she, with young unwakened senses, Her simple, homely life commences.

'**side-waver.** *dial.* Also 7 -wiver, 9 -wafer, -wefer. [f. SIDE *sb.*[1] with obscure second element.

With sense 1 cf. the Northumb. *inwaver*, *inwiver* a bar of wood inside a boat, on which the seats rest. Sense 2 seems to be derived from the verbs *wave* or *waver*.]

**1.** A purlin.

**1611** COTGR., *Filiere*,..a side-wauer. **1641** *Louth Rec.* (1891) 110 To Carter for two fyne Poules for sidewivers for the schole, vs. vj d. **1671** in Holmes *Pontefract Bk. Entries* (1882) 103 Item, for syde wavers, 2. o. o. **1703** THORESBY *Let. to Ray*, *Bawks*, the large timber beams that support the roof by sign-trees, under the side-wavers. **1788** W. H. MARSHALL *Yorksh.* II. 351 *Sidewaver*, the purline of a roof. **1850** PARKER *Gloss. Arch.* (ed. 5) 377 In some districts purlins are called ribs,..in Lincolnshire side-wavers.

**2.** *Coal-mining.* (See quot. 1851.)

**1851** GREENWELL *Coal-trade Terms, Northumb. & Durh.*, *Side-wavers*, the loose sides of a drift or open-cast, which would, if unsupported, soon fall. **1868** SCOTT *Ventilat. Coal-mines* 28 (E.D.D.), A side-wafer, or a frame of stone, most dangerous to look at, as it appeared ready to drop. *Ibid.* 31 The sides of the shaft..had given way; large side-wefers had slidden off.

'**sideway,** *sb.* Also side-way. [SIDE *sb.*[1] 23. Cf. MDu. *sijt-*, *zijdwech* (Du. *zijweg*), G. *seitenweg*, Da. *sidevej*, Sw. *sidoväg*.]

**1.** A path or way diverging from, or lying to the side of, a main road; a byway; also *fig.*

**1552** HULOET, Bypathes, byway, or sydewaye, out of the hyghe waye. **1660** F. BROOKE tr. *Le Blanc's Trav.* 220 We took a side-way towards the towns. **1832** BREWSTER *Nat. Magic* ii. 17 In a path or road where there was no side-way by which the figure could escape. **1874** LISLE CARR *J. Gwynne* I. iii. 69 From this her mind would slant off into a sideway.

**2.** A (raised) path along the side of a road; a footway. Now *U.S.* Cf. SIDEWALK 2.

**1738** RICHARDSON *De Foe's Tour Gt. Brit.* (ed. 2) III. 319 A Causeway or Walk, well pav'd with flat Freestone, such as the Side-ways in Cheapside and Cornhil. **1852** D. G. MITCHELL *Reveries Bachelor* IV. I. vii, Below, dim figures are gathering on the narrow sideways to look at the solemn spectacle. **1886** *Philadelphia Times* 9 Apr. (Cent.), Every inch of roadway,..and every inch of sideway,..was covered by people.

*attrib.* **1804** J. GRAHAME *Sabbath* (1808) 24 Mark the father 'mid the sideway throng.

'**sideway,** *adv.* and *a.* [SIDE *sb.*[1]]

**A.** *adv.* = SIDEWAYS *adv.*

**1612** PEACHAM *Gentl. Exerc.* (1634) 33 The beames of the Sunne comming oblikely or sideway. **1715** LEONI *Palladio's Archit.* (1742) I. 8 The first course being laid the lesser part out-side; the second the length laid side-way. **1776** *Trial of Nundocomar* 21/2 Maha Rajah then looked at me sideway angrily. **1793** SMEATON *Edystone L.* §174 At the distance of a foot sideway it might have got through by piercing the wall alone. *c* **1850** LOWELL *Extreme Unction* vi, My snake-turned nature, sunk in slime, Starts sideway with defiant hiss. **1851** HAWTHORNE *Ho. Seven Gables* vi, The faint gleam..showed the blanched paleness of her cheek, turned sideway towards a corner.

**B.** *adj.* Directed or moving towards or from one side; indirect; sidelong.

*c* **1800** R. CUMBERLAND *J. de Lancaster* (1809) I. 274 Paying a side-way compliment to his daughter. **1810** CRABBE *Borough* iii. 322 But there is hope that from these founts may flow A side-way stream, and equal good bestow. **1863** GEO. ELIOT *Romola* iv, [He] turned a slow sideway gaze on the stranger. **1883** *Nonconf. & Independent* 20 Dec. 1146/3 A stolen sideway peep into other men's bosoms.

**sideways** ('saɪdweɪz), *adv.* and *a.* [f. SIDE *sb.*[1] + -WAYS.]

**1.** From one side.

**1577** B. GOOGE *Heresbach's Husb.* III. (1586) 128 Let him that keepes them, offer them a little meate, not sidewaies, or behinde, but before coying them al the while. **1712** *Spect.* No. 524 ¶6 Where they lost the full Prospect of the Radiant Pillar, and saw it but side-ways. **1725** *Fam. Dict.* s.v. *Rabbet*, If the Wind be side-ways, it may do well enough.

**2. a.** Presenting the side instead of the face, front, or end; with the side foremost; in the direction of the side; facing to the side, etc.

**1598** W. PHILLIP tr. *Linschoten* 5 But it is a side-wind, and we must alway lie sidewaies in the wind almost untill wee come to the cape de Bona Speranza. **1612** PEACHAM *Gentl. Exerc.* III. ix. (1634) 157 A Lion is given sometimes but halfe,..sometime but his head only, which is never borne but sideways, and with one eye. **1713** DERHAM *Phys. Theol.* Pref. (1720) 6 The Beards..are not to be seen, unless they are laid in a due posture in the Microscope, viz. side-ways. **1771** LUCKOMBE *Hist. Print.* 344 Taking..five quires off his Heap in both his hands.., he shakes them long-ways and side-ways, to and fro. **1818** COBBETT *Polit. Reg.* XXXIII. 596 Their great Quack..would have pushed them along, either long-ways or side-ways, head-foremost or heels-foremost, through all their difficulties. **1840** DICKENS *Old C. Shop* v, Some side-ways, some head first, some stern first. **1866** G. MACDONALD *Ann. Q. Neighb.* ix. (1878) 140 A.. narrow stair, upon which two people could not pass without turning sideways and squeezing.

**b.** Const. *to* or *towards*.

**1795** SOUTHEY *Lett. fr. Spain* (1799) 104 The course of the Ezla..has altered much since the bridge was built. It now stands sideways to the current. **1825** J. NEAL *Bro. Jonathan* I. 79 Lucy Armstrong..sat..sideways towards Peters.

**c.** Const. *on* (ON *adv.* 7 b): = SIDE-ON *adv.*; also (hyphened) as *adj.*

**1972** *Guardian* 28 Jan. 6/1 Methods of reducing injuries when a car is hit sideways-on by another car. **1973** W. BARLOW *Alexander Principle* ix. 141 We need to look once more at our spines and our stance sideways on. **1976** J. SNOW *Cricket Rebel* 37 By the time I returned to Sussex.. I was very much more a 'sideways-on' bowler.

**3. a.** In a lateral or sideward direction; towards one side; obliquely.

**1611** COTGR., *A costiere*, aside, sideling, sidewayes. *c* **1618** MORYSON *Itin.* IV. viii. (Roxb.) 142 And two [guns] of like greatnes..were turned towards the Gallye to shoote syde-wayes. **1692** BENTLEY *Boyle Lect.* vii. 236 The Atoms may not only fly side-ways, but over likewise and under each other. *a* **1774** GOLDSM. *Surv. Exp. Philos.* (1776) I. 408 Thus far as to water spouting horizontally, or as we usually say sideways from a vessel. **1798** COLERIDGE *Anc. Mar.* III. xiv, We listened and looked sideways up! **1838** WHEWELL in *Life* (1881) 191 The horse slipped down side-ways on a hard-frozen slope, and I fell on my shoulder. **1868** LOCKYER *Elem. Astron.* §176 He will find that the axis is not then inclined either to or from the Sun, but sideways. **1892** A. RITCHIE *Rec. Tennyson* I. viii. 48 He told me to look..if the field-lark did not come down sideways upon its wing.

**b.** ***to look sideways***: to look with a scornful side-glance; askance; to regard something in a furtive or improper manner; *spec.* to glance amorously or suspiciously *at*.

**1844** 'J. SLICK' *High Life in N.Y.* I. xiv. 217 If he dared looked sideways at his [i.e. another's] wife or sister. **1860** MISS KAVANAGH *Seven Years* III. 142 If any one should look sideways at you for what has passed, let that person expect to settle it with me. **1895** CONRAD *Almayer's Folly* 160 This thought caused him to pluck up heart and look at Nina sideways. **1921** B. GILBERT *Old England* 70 But he was known to be paying to three different women for a child each, And his housekeeper beginning to look sideways. **1974** N. MARSH *Black as he's Painted* vi. 162 It wouldn't..be anything out of the way if they got round to looking sideways at each other.

**c.** In colloq. phr. ***to knock sideways***: to astound, as with pleasure or shock; to dumbfound, to amaze.

**1925** B. TRAVERS *Mischief* iv. 60 She could have engaged in a viva voce competition with the editor of *The Dog World* and knocked him sideways. **1942** J. B. PRIESTLEY *Black-Out in Gretley* vii. 169 When anybody..does something or has something that suddenly knocks me sideways, I feel I ought to mention it... It's like paying a debt. **1957** R. MASON *World of Suzie Wong* II. iv. 149 Their attitude is basically commercial... But my guess is that this stuff will knock them sideways. **1960** M. STEWART *My Brother Michael* xvi. 203, I can't seem to think straight... I feel knocked kind of sideways.

**d.** *Comb.*, as ***sideways-looking*** adj. = SIDE-LOOKING *a.*

**1962** *Daily Tel.* 29 Oct. 22/3 A new method of obtaining aerial pictures is by 'sideways looking' radar. **1966** *Geo-Marine Technol.* Oct. 18 Sideways-looking sonars produce acoustic pictures of the surface of the sea-bed. **1979** 'M. M. KAYE' *Shadow of Moon* (ed. 2) xxxiv. 408 The dark, secretive, sideways-looking eyes.

**4.** So as to incline to one side.

**1631** MILTON *Epit. March'ess Winchester* 42 But the fair blossom hangs the head Side-ways. **1870** SWINBURNE *Ess. & Stud.* (1875) 333 A beautiful head of a youth bent sideways.

**5.** At one side (*of* a place).

**17..** in *Chambers' Cycl.* (1753) s.v. *Coursing*, No horseman or footman is to go before or sideways, but all strait behind. **1805** EUGENIA DE ACTON *Nuns of Desert* II. 2 We proceeded..till we reached a cottage, about a mile sideways of Marston.

**6.** By an indirect way or route; indirectly.

**1723** *Pres. St. Russia* II. 277 Whatever Provisions were with the greatest difficulty bought up Sideways in the Country and carried to them, were to be paid for double and treble the value. **1877** TENNYSON *Harold* I. i. 260 Side not with Tostig in any violence, Lest thou be sideways guilty of the violence.

**7.** As *adj.* = SIDEWAY *a.*

**1868** *Rep. U.S. Comm. Agric.* (1869) 253 There will be no sagging, nor any side-ways deflection of the setting guide or the row. **1899** *Daily News* 6 Dec. 5/1 The present Press seats at Lord's are in the grand stand with a sideways view of the game.

'**side-wind.** Also side wind, sidewind. [SIDE *sb.*[1]]

**1.** A wind blowing from one side, or on the side of a vessel, etc.

**1398** TREVISA *Barth. De P.R.* XI. iii. (Bodl. MS.), Wyndes beþ twelue, foure þerof beþ icleped cardinales, chief windes, and .viii. collaterales, syde windes. *c* **1410** *Master of Game* (MS. Digby 182) ii, þer kynde is for þe moste parte to flee euer in þe wynde, till he be nere ouercome; or at the leste syde wynde so þat it be euer in his nosethrille. **1598** [see SIDEWAYS *adv.* 2]. **1604** E. G[RIMSTONE] *D'Acosta's Hist. Indies* III. xi. 155 The force of the winde continuing still, being a side wind, the Admiralles shippe discovered an opening. **1666** DRYDEN *Ann. Mirab.* ccxxxvi, One mighty squadron, with a sidewind sped, Through narrow lanes his cumbered fire does haste. **1776** GIBBON *Decl. & F.* xiii. I. 434 Orators have celebrated the daring courage of the Romans, who ventured to set sail with a side-wind, and on a stormy day. **1801** STRUTT *Sports & Past.* II. i. 56 He ought also to know how to take the advantage of a side wind. **1858** GREENER *Gunnery* 133 A strong side wind was blowing at the time.

**b.** In figurative contexts.

**1611** MIDDLETON & DEKKER *Roaring Girl* I. i, With a side winde Must I now saile, else I no hauen can finde. **1642** FULLER *Holy & Prof. St.* III. iii. 157 Some sail to the port of their own praise by a side-wind. **1697** DRYDEN *Ded. Æneis* Ess. (ed. Ker) II. 164 All this while I have been sailing with some side-wind or other toward the point I proposed in the beginning.

**2.** *fig.* An indirect means, method, or manner. Chiefly in phr. ***by a side-wind***.

**1648** C. WALKER *Hist. Independency* I. 119 What they could not carry with a fore-wind, they now brought in againe with a side-wind. **1658–9** *Burton's Diary* (1828) IV. 9 Let us come to a question by a side-wind, rather than by no wind. **1726** SWIFT *Gulliver* I. v, Others..could not forbear some Expressions, which by a Side-wind reflected on me. **1766** BLACKSTONE *Comm.* II. 117 Acts of parliament have by a sidewind countenanced and established them. **1812** *Ann. Reg., Gen. Hist.* 18 The fact of which excess only came out by a side wind when the bill was brought forward. **1841** J. W. CROKER in *C. Papers* 12 Feb., Let the House.. pass a distinct law against the practice, but not attempt to do it by a sidewind. **1888** BRYCE *Amer. Commw.* I. x. 132 This is an attempt to evade and by a sidewind defeat the provision of the Federal Constitution.

**3.** *attrib.* as *adj.* Indirect, oblique; illegitimate.

**1680** OWEN *Union among Protestants* Wks. 1851 XIV. 521 This jurisdiction, exercised with a side-wind power distinct from the public justice of the nation, is a great cause of weakening. **1702** *Eng. Theophrastus* Pref. 2 Others, by the nipping strokes of a side-wind Satyr, have endeavoured to tickle men out of their Follies. **1812** *Examiner* May 293/1 The sort of side-wind defence which some of his Majesty's Ministers had set up. **1863** COWDEN CLARKE *Shaks. Char.* xiii. 339 One of those sly, side-wind girds at the French. **1897** *Trans. Devon Assoc.* XXIX. 455 Reginald.., side-wind son of Henry I.

Hence **'side-winded** *a.*, = sense 3; also as *adv.*, by a side-wind, indirectly. *rare.*

**1710** *New Map Trav. High-Ch. Apostle* 4 [He] had written side-winded for the Pagan Pretender's Title. **1825** T. HOOK *Sayings* Ser. II. *Sutherl.* (Colburn) 19, I discovered..by a side-winded inquiry, that he is..worth more than two hundred thousand pounds. **1833** —— *Parson's Dau.* II. ii, Emma received these side-winded lectures as her father wished.

**'side-winder**[1]. *U.S.* and *dial.* [f. SIDE *sb.*[1] + *winder* a blow.] A heavy blow with the fist delivered from or on the side. Also *fig.*

**1840** *Daily Pennant* (St. Louis) 14 May (Th. s.v. Sockdologer), Tim gives him a sockdologer and two side-winders, and leaves him for dead on the spot. **1846** J. CODMAN *Sailor's Life & Sailor's Yarns* 31 'Take that then, for want of a shillaleh!' said the lumper, giving him a side-winder with his fist. *a* **1859** in Bartlett *Dict. Amer.* s.v., To seize..the opportunity of dealing Recorder Smith what the boys call a side-winder. **1860** O. W. HOLMES *Professor* ii, The boys of my time used to call a hit like this a 'side-winder'.

**'side-winder**[2]. *U.S.* [f. SIDE *sb.*[1] + WIND *v.*]

**1.** Any of several small rattlesnakes, esp. *Crotalus cerastes.*

**1875** H. C. YARROW in *Rep. U.S. Geogr. Surveys West of 100th Meridian* V. 535 They were also seen in Arizona, and are called 'side-winders' by the settlers, owing to their peculiar lateral progressive motion. **1888** *Riverside Nat. Hist.* III. 402 The New Mexicans have named this animal the 'side-winder', because of the slightly lateral motion which they have in passing forwards. **1906** *Out West* Feb. 136 It is..a land of the side-winder, the Gila monster, the scorpion and the centipede. **1949** *Nat. Hist.* May 212/2 Among other interesting tracks are the slanting 'ladder-rung' trails of the sidewinder rattlesnakes. **1971** 'D. SHANNON' *Ringer* ix. 149 Royce shied back at the sight of him as if he'd been a sidewinder.

**2.** *transf.* and *fig.*

**1906** *McClure's Mag.* XXVI. 414 You never could tell where Texas Pete was goin' to jump next. He was a sidewinder and a diamond-back and a little black rattlesnake all rolled into one. **1936** G. ROUNDS *Ol' Paul* 21 It was known as the orneriest river... It was an old 'side winder' for fair. **1940** W. FAULKNER *Hamlet* IV. i. 244 Hup, you broom-tailed hay-burning sidewinders. **1964** R. MURPHY *Pond* ix. 129 'They grew up with her and knew what a sidewinder she was.' 'What's a sidewinder?' Joey asked. 'It's a rattlesnake, but I meant it as a sort of troublemaker.'

Hence as a back-formation, **'side-winding** *ppl. a.*, moving like a side-winder (also *fig.*); also as *vbl. sb.*; **'side-wind** *v. intr.*

**1902** H. DAY *Pine Tree Ballads* 150 That was a side-windin' answer for him. **1954** J. A. PRINGLE *Common Snakes* p. vi, Some of the adders have a peculiar side-winding movement for crawling over loose sand. **1969** A. BELLAIRS *Life of Reptiles* I. iii. 105 It is generally believed that sidewinding is the most efficient type of locomotion which a snake can use over a smooth sandy surface... *Crotalus cerastes* can sidewind at about 2 mph. **1972** *World of Wild Wheels* (Custom Car) 65/1. His side-winding Anglia symbolises everything that Hot Rod racing is all about. **1977** 'J. LE CARRÉ' *Hon. Schoolboy* xvii. 403 Occasionally a yellow bus came sidewinding down the hill toward them.

**'side-wipe.** *dial.* and *U.S.* [f. SIDE *sb.*[1] + WIPE *sb.*]

**1.** An indirect rebuke, censure, or hint. *dial.*

**1757** in Mrs. Barbauld *Life Richardson* (1804) VI. 279 Your third paragraph..is such a mixture of kindness and crossness, of spite and good nature, of side-wipes plain and friendly intimations. **1828**- in dialect glossaries (Sc., Yks., Linc., Northampton).

**2.** = SIDE-WINDER[1].

*c* **1850** *Southern Sketches* 31 (Bartlett, 1859), Arch would fetch him a side wipe on the head, and knock him into the middle of next week. **1893** HESLOP *Northumbld. Gloss.*

**'side-wiper.** *dial.* and *U.S.* [f. as prec. + WIPER.]

**1.** = prec.

**1888** J. C. HARRIS *Free Joe* 58 Write him a note,..and fling in a kind of side-wiper about New Jersey. **1893** COZENS-HARDY *Broad Norf.* 94 *Sidewiper*, a blow on the side of anything with a stick.

**2.** *U.S.* The massasauga, or other rattlesnake of a similar type. Cf. SIDE-WINDER[2].

**1889** in *Cent. Dict.* s.v. *Crotalophorus.*

**sidewise** ('saɪdwaɪz), *adv.* and *a.* [f. SIDE *sb.*[1] + -WISE.]

**1.** In a lateral direction; to one side; sidewards.

**1571** DIGGES *Pantom.* I. xviii. Fb, Go sidewise from thence as afore in a right angle. **1594** T. B. *La Primaud. Fr. Acad.* II. 75 Because man, as also all other creatures goe forward, and not backward or sidewise. **1616** J. LANE *Contn. Sqr.'s T.* VIII. 222 Whole troopes, and shockes of pikes, sidewise, and foreright, vibrant thrustes in strikes. **1661** LOVELL *Hist. Anim. & Min.* Isagoge b7b, These only amongst crustates swimme not, but goe, and that side-wise. **1728** CHAMBERS *Cycl.* s.v. *Terra*, A Series of very low.. Leaps, which a Horse makes forward, bearing sidewise. **1809** A. HENRY *Trav.* 296 The men..each moved sidewise, first up, and then down the room. **1854** GREENWOOD *Haps & Mishaps* 83 Joltings, backwards, forwards, and sidewise. **1880** H. JAMES *Portrait Lady* ii, 'It's a dear old place,' said the young man, looking sidewise at his neighbour.

**2.** = SIDEWAYS 2.

**1608** TOPSELL *Serpents* (1658) 811 They are not folded round about one another like unto Serpents, but are straightly closed together side-wise. **1646** SIR T. BROWNE *Pseud. Ep.* 151 Some couple laterally or sidewise as wormes. **1702** *Eng. Theophrastus* 102 They gall us front and side-wise like Rams. **1877** A. B. EDWARDS *Up Nile* v. 109 A native boat meets us, floating down side-wise with the current. *Ibid.* vi. 150 An old disused water-wheel lying up sidewise against the bank like a huge teetotum. **1880** H. JAMES *Portrait Lady* iii, On the other side..was an old house..standing sidewise to the street.

**3.** On or from the side.

**1613** PURCHAS *Pilgrimage* II. xviii. (1614) 207 If they beate spice, the morter must lie side-wise. **1723** CHAMBERS tr. *Le Clerc's Archit.* I. 116 They must needs have a woful Effect, when view'd sidewise.

**4.** In an indirect manner; indirectly.

**1654** Z. COKE *Logick* 18 A reasonable soul..is placed in the Predicament of Substance, but side-wise, not directly.

**5.** = SIDEWAYS 4.

**1828–32** WEBSTER s.v., To hold the head sidewise.

**6.** As *adj.* Directed towards one side; sideward. Also *fig.*

**1853** DICKENS *Bleak Ho.* xii, An enjoyment expressed.. by an additional tightness of face, thin elongation of compressed lips, and sidewise look. **1894** *Outing* XXIII. 392/1 As they passed Nan-mogie, each man gave a sidewise bow. *a* **1914** JOYCE *Stephen Hero* (1944) 48 You're a 'cute fellow, said Stephen in a sidewise fashion.

**sidey:** see SIDY *a.*[2]

**sideyns,** variant of SITHENCE *Obs.*

**Sidhe** (ʃiː), *sb. pl. Ir. Mythol.* Also **sidhe** and (*sing.*) **Sidh.** [Ellipsis (not found in Irish) of Ir. (*aos*) *sídhe* people of the fairy mound: cf. *folk of peace* s.v. FOLK 3 c and BANSHEE.] The hills of the fairies; fairyland, faerie. Hence (esp. in the writings of W. B. Yeats), the fairy folk, fairies, freq. regarded as the mythical gods of ancient Ireland. Cf. SHEOGUE.

**1793** I. HELY tr. *O'Flaherty's Ogygia* II. III. xxii. 55 When the princesses saw these venerable gentlemen..they looked upon them to be the people of the Sidhe. The Irish call these Sidhe, aërial spirits or phantoms; because they are seen to come out of pleasant hills, where the common people imagine they reside: which fictitious habitations are called by us Sidhe or Siodha. **1880** S. FERGUSON *Conary* in *Poems* 95 These wicked sprites,..men of the *Sidhs*..Who played their pipes before us, led us on Into..the night. **1899** W. B. YEATS *Wind among Reeds* 1 (*title*) The hosting of the Sidhe. **1899** —— *Let.* 21 June (1954) 321, I myself try to avoid the word 'fairy'.. *Sidhe* or 'gentry' or 'the others' is better. **1906** S. GWYNN *Fair Hills Irel.* ii. 34 The heroes of the mysterious Tuatha de Danann who after their defeat by the Milesians withdrew from daylight into the recesses of the earth—and who are still there, fairy folk, the people of the *Sidhe.* **1919** W. B. YEATS *Only Jealousy of Emer* in *Two Plays for Dancers* 25 What one among the Sidhe has dared to lie Upon Cuchulain's bed and take his image? **1941** L. MACNEICE *Poetry of W. B. Yeats* iv. 79 Yeats's world of the Sidhe and curlews. **1977** N. ARROWSMITH *Field Guide to Little People* 20 The Sidhe live a very domestic life if undisturbed, caring for their animals, drinking whisky, borrowing milk and meal. *Ibid.* 21 The Sidhe are thin, up to six feet in height, handsome and young-looking despite their great age.

‖**sidi** ('siːdiː). Forms: 7 seedi, syddy, 7–8 siddy, 8 siddee, 9 siddhee, seddee, sidi, sídí, seedy, seide. [a. Urdū *sīdī*, Marāthī *siddhī*, ad. Arab. *sayyidī* 'my lord': see SAYYID.] Originally, a title of honour given in Western India to African Muslims holding high positions under the kings of the Deccan; in later use, an African, a Negro. Now chiefly in comb. *sidi-boy.*

**1615** W. BEDWELL *Arab. Trudgman*, Seedi, a name or title of honour, yet attributed vnto meane persons. **1698** FRYER *Acc. E. India & Persia* 147 An Hobsy, or Arabian Coffery (they being preferred here to Chief Employments, which they enter on by the name of Siddies). *Ibid.* 168 Syddies. **1757** GROSE *Voy. E. Indies* 91 These [islands] were in the hands formerly of Angria, and the Siddies, or Moors. **1761** CAMBRIDGE *War in India* 216 The Mogul appointed the Siddee, who was chief of a colony of Coffrees, to be his Admiral. **1813** J. FORBES *Oriental Mem.* III. 167 Among the attendants of the Cambay nabob..are several Abyssinian and Caffree slaves, called by way of courtesy Seddees, or Master. **1849** EASTWICK *Dry Leaves* 197 A long narrow dirty street, crowded with spectators, among whom might be noticed a great number of Sidis or blacks.

*Comb.* **1867** G. E. CLARK *Seven Years of Sailor's Life* viii. 86, I wandered off alone to the 'Seide' boys village of fishermen. **1890** *Pall Mall G.* 21 Aug. 3/1 Where Malay jostles Chinaman..and Arab elbows seedy-boy. **1898** P. MANSON *Trop. Diseases* xiv. 233 This form of the disease.. among the Lascars and sidi-boys of steamers trading to India.

**siding** ('saɪdɪŋ), *vbl. sb.* Also 7, 9 **sideing.** [f. SIDE *v.*[1] or *sb.*[1] + -ING[1].]

**I. 1. a.** The action of taking sides in a conflict or debate; party spirit, partisanship, factiousness.

Common in the first half of the 17th cent.

**1604** HIERON *Wks.* I. 497 When as..men fall to haue great reasoning among themselues, there cannot but follow a kind of division and siding. *a* **1653** G. DANIEL *Idyll.* iv. 57 For Sideing is a madnes, where the Hand Acts to a Somewhat we but vnderstand In the Relations. **1661** BAXTER *Last Work Believer* Wks. (1846) 255 She was seriously religious without any taint of siding or faction.

*attrib.* **1605** SANDYS *Europæ Spec.* (1632) 183 Having found that siding course..to be a false ground and ruinous to them that take it. **1647** TRAPP *Comm. Heb.* x. 25 It was then, it was afterwards, and is still in these siding and separating times.

**b.** An instance of taking or forming sides.

Common in 17th cent., sometimes in quasi-concrete use.

**1603** HOLLAND *Plutarch's Mor.* Ded. p. i, The turbulent tempests and bloudy broiles of factious sidings. **1640** BP. REYNOLDS *Passions* xxxviii. 491 Nor indeed is there any thing which had bred more Distempers in the Body of Learning, than Factions and Sidings. **1717** WODROW *Corr.* (1843) II. 323 What gatherings there have been, and sidings of great men mixing themselves in every case almost.

**c.** Const. *with.*

**1654** WHITLOCK *Zootomia* 226 It shadeth the minde from the inconveniences of Quarrells, Disputes, Sidings with Opinions. **1662** J. DAVIES tr. *Olearius' Voy. Amb.* 421 By reason of his siding with the Muscovian Merchants. **1680** BAXTER *Cath. Commun.* (1684) 10 All Christians must earnestly oppose Divisions, and Sects, and sidings with Strife and Envy. **1887** *Pall Mall G.* 15 Jan. 6/1 The clear-headed parish priest, whose siding heart and soul with his people is to my mind proof conclusive that they have right on their side.

**2.** The action of tending or moving to a side.

**1646** SIR T. BROWNE *Pseud. Ep.* 62 The variation of the compasse is..a deflexion and siding East and West from the true meridian. **1894** *Daily News* 7 July 6/6 When the bell rings to clear the course, there is again the 'siding' of the little boats to watch.

**3.** The action of laying out the sides of a field.

**1610** FOLKINGHAM *Art of Survey* II. ii. 49 Collateratge Actiue, as siding, furrowing,..impayling, immuring [etc.].

**4.** *U.S.* The action of dressing or trimming the sides of timber.

**1875** KNIGHT *Dict. Mech.* 2175/1 *Siding*,..that part of the operation of forming or trimming ship's timbers, etc., which consists in giving them their correct breadths. **1879** *Lumberman's Gaz.* 15 Oct., Mulays were used in siding down for the gang [saw].

*attrib.* **1875** KNIGHT *Dict. Mech.* 2175/1 *Siding-machine*, a machine for sawing timbers. **1879** *Lumberman's Gaz.* 5 Nov., The machinery first put in included a mulay and a siding mill.

**II. 5.** †**a.** A side of anything. *Obs.*[−1]

**1627** SPEED *England* xlii. §2 The forme thereof is Triangle, and differs not much in the Sidings.

**b.** orig. and chiefly *U.S.* The boarding (usu. timber) forming the sides of a building; weather-boarding. Also (with *a* and pl.), a piece of this.

**1829** J. F. COOPER *Wept of Wish-ton-wish* I. xvii. 246 [Dwellings] constructed of a firm frame-work, neatly covered with sidings of boards. **1858** SIMMONDS *Dict. Trade, Sidings*, a name in America for long wedge-shaped boards, used for the sides or roofs of houses. **1866** *Morning Star* 31 Dec., The necessities of heat in the tropical department enforce the use of large quantities of wood for flooring, sidings [etc.]. **1874** J. W. LONG *Amer. Wild-fowl* iv. 89 Strips of weather-boarding, or 'siding', as it is called out West, may be made to take their place. **1946** E. HODGINS *Mr Blandings builds his Dream House* xiii. 191 The mason subcontractor was stalled in his tracks since..no finished siding could even begin to be nailed to the sheathing. **1958** *N.Z. Timber Jrnl.* Sept. 87/1 *Sidings*, weatherboards for vertical surfaces. Varieties incude: feather-edge, novelty, rebated, ship-lap. **1968** *Globe & Mail* (Toronto) 17 Feb. 1/2 Outside the house, a black hole in the white siding showed where one bullet had driven through the living room wall. **1970** *Washington Post* 30 Sept. B. 13/7 (Advt.), A sparkling white home is yours with Reynolds aluminum siding installed by Hechinger.

*attrib.* **1875** KNIGHT *Dict. Mech.* 2568/2 Siding-tiles are used as a substitute for weather boarding. *Ibid.* 2749/2 *Weather-board*, lapping siding-boards for houses.

**c.** = SIDELING *sb.* 2. *Austral.* and *N.Z.*

**1891** G. CHAMIER *Philosopher Dick* I. xiii. 360 He told him to mind the siding by the shoot. **1902** H. LAWSON *Joe Wilson* in *Prose Works* (1946) 350 The dark box-scrub-covered ridges ended in steep 'sidings' coming down to the creek-bank. **1904** G. B. LANCASTER *Sons o' Men* 28 Must have gone over the siding. **1931** F. D. DAVISON *Man-Shy* (1934) xii. 165 The scrubbers were grazing along an ironbark siding. **1975** *N.Z. Jrnl. Agric.* Sept. 27/2 The animal which grazes mostly on non-treated areas—such as gullies or sidings—.. will not be fully protected.

**6.** *Naut.* (See quot. *c* 1850.)

**1797** *Encycl. Brit.* (ed. 3) XVII. 399/2 Set off in the half-breadth plan the siding of the middle and after fashion-piece. *c* **1850** *Rudim. Navig.* (Weale) 147 *Siding*,..the size or dimensions of timber the contrary way to the moulding, or moulded side. **1869** SIR E. REED *Shipbuild.* iv. 72 The body post, while retaining a very large siding, has a comparatively small moulding. **1874** THEARLE *Nav. Arch.* 10 The logs should be about 14 or 16 inches siding.

*attrib.* **1846** A. YOUNG *Naut. Dict.* 283 Siding dimension, in ship-building, implies the breadth of a piece of timber.

**7. a.** A short piece of additional track parallel to the main line of a railway or tramway, and

connected with it by switches, for enabling trains, trucks, etc., to pass each other or to lie by.
**1825** Wood *Pract. Treat. Railroads* 299 BB[1] is a siding or passing for the carriages going in opposite directions. **1849** Sir F. B. Head *Stokers & Pokers* iv. (1851) 50 The carriages, after being unhooked,..are rapidly carried off into the sidings. **1881** Froude *Short Stud.* (1883) IV. vi. 377 Our journey was brought unexpectedly to an end by the train running into a siding.
*attrib.* **1850** *Mechanic's Mag.* Nov. 370 Beckers' self-acting siding-stop. **1897** *Daily News* 14 June 7/2 To reduce the accounts of traders for siding rents by 50 per cent.

**b.** A passing-place in a canal.
**1852** *Mechanic's Mag.* July 4 Passing-places or sidings, to enable trains of boats going in opposite direction to meet and pass each other. **1883** Dillwyn *Sp. Parl.* 19 July, To increase the carrying capacity of the Canal..in deepening the channel, or by adding sidings.

**siding** (ˈsaɪdɪŋ), *ppl. a.* [f. side *v.*[1] + -ing[2].]
**1.** Taking the side or part of a person or cause.
**1634** Milton *Comus* 212 The vertuous mind, that ever walks attended By a strong siding champion, Conscience. **1645** —— *Tetrach.* Wks. 1851 IV. 243 There is yet to this our exposition, a stronger siding freind, then any can be an adversary. **1833** Mrs. Browning *Prometh. Bound* Wks. (1904) 145 The antique Chronos and his siding hosts.
**b.** Taking a side; factious, partisan. *rare*[−1].
**1661** Baxter *Moral Prognost.* i. xciv. 22 An Opinionative, Modal, and Siding Religiousness, hath ever more Followers ..than true Holiness.
**2.** Forming a side or border; bordering. *rare*[−1].
**1833** Mrs. Browning *Prometh. Bound* Wks. (1904) 150 Along the sands of the siding deep..he follows me.

**sidle,** *sb.* [f. the vb.] An act of sidling; a sidelong or oblique movement.
**1853** R. S. Surtees *Sponge's Sp. Tour* xxi. 108 Turning the sidle into a stately sail, with a haughty sort of sneer. **1883** *Harper's Mag.* Feb. 394/1 The final sidle up to dock was a very inglorious effort of poling. **1900** *Longman's Mag.* Apr. 533 Susan coming forward with a coquettish sidle.

**sidle** (ˈsaɪd(ə)l), *v.* Also 9 *dial.* **siddle.** [Prob. a back-formation from sideling *adv.*, on the analogy of verbs in -le 3.]
**1. a.** *intr.* To move or go sideways or obliquely; to edge along, esp. in a furtive or unobtrusive manner, or while looking in another direction; to make advances in this manner.
**1697** Vanbrugh *Æsop* iii, A crab-fish once her daughter told..She could not bear to see her go, Sidle, sidle, to and fro. **1708** Swift *Abol. Chr.* Wks. 1751 IV. 114 No more than one can get in at a time, and that not without stooping, and sideling, and squeezing his Body. **1753-4** Richardson *Grandison* (1781) IV. iv. 24 Sir Harry..sidled to the door,.. and then slipped out. **1780** Cowper *Progr. Error* 562 Halting on crutches of unequal size;..They sidle to the goal with awkward pace. **1822** Lamb *Elia* ii. *On Books & Reading*, I used to admire how he sidled along, keeping clear of secular contacts. **1851** D. Jerrold *St. Giles* vii. 63 He sidled into a corner of the room. **1886** Ruskin *Præterita* I. v. 158, I was put on big horses that jumped, and reared, and circled, and sidled.
*transf.* and *fig.* **1765** Sterne *Tr. Shandy* viii. i, Ever and anon straddling out, or sidling into some..digression. **1821** Clare *Vill. Minstr.* II. 92 Ye know the foot-path sidles down the hill. **1841** L. Hunt *Seer* (1864) ii. 72 Till 'Smith's Terrace', or some such interloper, came sidling in front of it with forty new tenements. **1866** R. Chambers *Ess. Fam. & Hum.* Ser. i. 151 He sidles into conversation with some overseer of the workmen.
**b.** To make one's way in a horizontal or transverse direction about an incline; *spec.* in *Mountaineering* = traverse *v.* 21. *N.Z.*
**1950** *N.Z. Jrnl. Agric.* Oct. 295/1 Sowing was done following the contours and from higher to lower altitudes, as a man tends to climb when sidling. **1958** *Tararua* XII. 29 To *sidle*, to go around the side or across the face of a hill, is a characteristic New Zealand expression, strange to the Englishman or Australian. **1971** *N.Z. Listener* 19 Apr. 56/5 They got up the lower scree, sidled across the first face into a couloir, but they were getting bombed so they cramponed up to just below a gendarme.
**2.** *dial.* **a.** To saunter, lounge about.
**1781** J. Hutton *Tour to Caves* (ed. 2) 95 *Sidle*, to saunter. **1828** Carr *Craven Gloss.* s.v. 'To sidle about a place,' to lurk or skulk about. **1841** Foster in *Life & Corr.* (1846) II. 402 Just sidling about to see sights. **1866** Brogden *Prov. Lincs.*, *Sidle*, to lounge about for some ulterior purpose.
**b.** (See quot.)
**1828** Carr *Craven Gloss.* s.v., 'To sidle about a person,' to attend him obsequiously. **1855** [see sidling *ppl. a.*].
**3.** *trans.* To move, turn, or direct sideways.
**1779** T. Twining in *Recreat. & Stud.* (1882) 62 Let us at least..give it a little gloss of novelty, by spelling it Tuineing, ..or something that shall sidle us away a little from those vulgar tribes of Western Twinings and Twynings. **1846** Mrs. Gore *Eng. Char.* (1852) 138 Shoving, sidling, and swerving the said ill-fitting drawer into its original position. **1855** Browning *Old Pictures in Florence* x. 7 Not sidling a glance at the coin of their neighbour. **1887** Jessopp *Arcady* iii. 90 He sidled his horse towards the fence and picked a rosy apple from the bough.

**sidling** (ˈsaɪdlɪŋ), *vbl. sb.* Also 8 **sideling.** [f. sidle *v.* + -ing[1].] The action of the vb. sidle; an instance of this.
**1759** *Compl. Lett. Writer* (ed. 6) 225 Her sidling, and swaddling, and foolish unalterable simper. **1792** *Elvina* I. 139 It was not 'till after many sidlings and swimmings that she was prevailed on to sit down. **1852** Mundy *Our Antipodes* v. (1855) 127 To start off at full speed, and thus to get the wheels to 'bite' again, is the only way to redeem an incipient sidling.

**sidling** (ˈsaɪdlɪŋ), *ppl. a.* [f. sidle *v.* + -ing[2].] That sidles, in the senses of the vb.
**1855** [Robinson] *Whitby Gloss.*, *Sideling*, insinuating by word or action. 'A sideling, wheedling sort of a body.' **1864** *Realm* 27 Apr. 1 An apparently quiet, inoffensive, purring, gliding, sidling animal. **1898** Mrs. H. Ward *Sir G. Tressady* 414 [He] walked with rather sidling steps to the door.
Hence **ˈsidlingly** *adv.*
**1873** Browning *Red Cott. Nt.-Cap* 805 Hand in hand, —Or side by side,..On every good work sidlingly they went.

**sidling,** variant of sideling.

**Sidneian** (ˈsɪdnɪən, sɪdˈniːən), *a.* Also 7 **Sydnæan, Sydnian; Sidneyan.** [f. the name of Sir Philip *Sidney* (1554-86), English statesman and man of letters, + -an.] Of, pertaining to, or characteristic of the life and works of Sidney.
*c* **1610** Chapman *Sonnet* [to the Earl of Montgomery] in *Homer Prince of Poets* sig. Ee3[v], There runs a blood, faire Earle, through your cleare vains,..Which still the liuing Sydnian soule maintaines. **1646** Crashaw *Steps to Temple* 137 Sydnæan showers Of sweet discourse, whose powers Can Crowne old Winters head with flowers.
**1931** E. Blunden in *Mind's Eye* (1934) i. 53 It was Sidneian virtue in our colonel to invite even F. into the log cabin for a drink and a tune. **1952** D. Davie *Purity of Diction in Eng. Verse* App. B. 199 The 'sprezzatura' of Castiglione and the Sidneyan ideal. **1965** K. Graham *Eng. Criticism of Novel* ii. 39 Hardy's..eventual abandonment of the novel for poetry can perhaps be foreseen in the high, Sidneyan aims he set for it.

**Sidonian** (saɪˈdəʊnɪən), *sb.* and *a.* Also 7 **Syd-, Zid-.** [f. L. *Sidōni-us*, a. Gr. Σιδώνιος, f. Σιδών (Phœn. and Heb. *Tsīdōn*), the Phœnician city of that name.]
**A.** *sb.* A native or inhabitant of Sidon.
The Wycliffite versions of the Bible use *Sidonees* (*-eis*), *Sidonyes* (*-yis*), etc. In *Deut.* iii. 9 Coverdale has *Sidons*. The usual spelling (*Zidonian*) in the 1611 version is due to the Hebrew form.
**1535** Coverdale *Judges* x. 12 Did not..the Sidonians, the Amalechites and Maonites oppresse you? **1611** Bible *Deut.* iii. 9 Which Hermon the Sidonians call Syrion. *Ibid.*, *Judges* xviii. 7 They were farre from the Zidonians. *a* **1701** Maundrell *Journ. Jerus.* (1721) 31 The second [city was the seat] of the Sidonians. **1788** Lemprière *Class. Dict.* (1792), *Tyrus*, a very antient city of Phœnicia, built by the Sidonians. **1857** Wilkinson *Egypt. Pharaohs* 102 The Greeks were indebted to the Sidonians for many secrets in the working of metals.
**B.** *adj.* Of or pertaining to Sidon.
**1594** Marlowe & Nashe *Dido* i. i. 213 The kingly seate of Southerne Libia, Whereas Sidonian Dido rules as Queene. **1620** T. Granger *Div. Logike* 71 By her..habite, or attire, *id est*, her Sidonian cloake. **1667** Milton *P.L.* i. 441 Astoreth,..To whose bright Image nightly by the Moon Sidonian Virgins paid their Vows and Songs. **1746** Francis tr. *Horace, Ep.* ii. ii. 274 Garments tinctur'd with Sidonian Dye. **1842** Prichard *Nat. Hist. Man* 142 This language.. was the idiom of the Sidonian and Tyrian states. **1886** *Guide Exhib. Galleries Brit. Mus.* 193 To a later period of the Sidonian workshops may probably be referred a number of small bottles of various forms.

**Sidoor,** var. Siddur.

**Sidra(h,** varr. Sedra.

**sidre, -ur,** obs. froms of cider.

**sidth.** *dial. rare.* Also **sith.** [f. side *a.* + -th[1].] Length; depth.
**1855** *Norfolk Wds.* in *Trans. Philol. Soc.* 36 As we say, 'the width and the sith,' or the sidth. **1879** Miss Jackson *Shropsh. Word-bk.*, *Sidth*, the measurement of the side of an object,—'lenth, width, and sidth'. **1882** in *Lancs. Gloss.* **1891** Jessie Fothergill *Kith & Kin* 93 A gown should be.. walking width and striding sidth.

**Sidur,** var. Siddur.

**†ˈsidy,** *a.*[1] *dial. Obs.* (See quot.)
**1674** Ray *S. & E. Co. Wds.* 77 *Sidy*: surly, moody. Suss. [Hence in later glossaries.]

**sidy** (ˈsaɪdɪ), *a.*[2] *colloq.* [f. side *sb.*[2]] Inclined to 'put on side'; conceited.
**1898** *Woman at Home* Oct. 57/1 Tommy wasn't half a bad fellow once... I never counted him sidey. **1899** *Daily News* 22 June 7/3 A 'sidy chap' is universally detested, and every chance is seized to 'take him down a peg'. **1913** C. Mackenzie *Sinister St.* I. ii. iii. 179 The porter was frightfully sick at having to give me a telegram. He is a sidy swine. **1935** 'N. Blake' *Question of Proof* viii. 154 'It is possible that he could have thought he had a chance of being elected?' 'Oh, I should think so; he was sidey enough.' **1946** B. Marshall *George Brown's Schooldays* xxviii. 115 He couldn't very well put himself in first because people might think it rather sidey.

**sie,** *sb.* and *v.*: see sye.

**Siebel** (ˈsiːb(ə)l), the name of *Siebel* Flugzeugwerke K.G., a German aircraft manufacturing company, used *attrib.* in *Siebel ferry*, a power-driven troop and freight landing-craft developed by them during the war of 1939–45. Also *absol.*
**1942** *R.A.F. Jrnl.* 18 Apr. 4 (*caption*) This is the largest scale photograph yet taken of..a Siebel Ferry. Gun positions are visible at the four extremities. **1946** R. Capell *Simiomata* i. 36 A Siebel ferry was moving out of the harbour. *Ibid.*, The Siebel..made things unpleasant with air-bursts. These ferries, accommodating about 150 troops, carry two 88 mm. guns. **1973** D. Hamilton-Hill *SOE Assignment* vii. 100 Siebel Ferries—the special invention of the German Kriegsmarine—double (in parallel) enlarged canoe-type gun boats.

**siec,** obs. f. sick.

**†siecle.** *Obs.* Forms: 5 **sekil, sekyll, syecle,** 6 **seicle, siecle, secle.** [a. OF. *secle, siecle* (mod.F. *siècle*), ad. L. *sæculum*: see secular. The mod.F. form is occasionally used as a foreign word, esp. in the phrase *fin de siècle* (q.v.).]
**1.** The world (in the religious sense).
*c* **1400** *Rule St. Benet* 37 When any wymmen of þe sekil.. cummis at aske þordir [= the order], man salle noght light-like gif it tam. *Ibid.* 39 When any riche man of þe sekil.. offirs his doȝtir til god and til haly kirke. *c* **1450** *St. Cuthbert* (Surtees) 2500 Of his leuyng þai suld noȝt wondir, Na halde it haly all þof it ware Solitary fra þe sekyll fare.
**2.** An age or period.
**1483** Caxton *Gold. Leg.* 429/1 The whyche god creatour ..be thanked..by all the syecle and syecles. **1549** *Compl. Scot.* 3 The verteouse verkis dune be ȝour antecessours in oure dais ar euident til vs in this present seicle. **1589** Puttenham *Eng. Poesie* ii. xi. (Arb.) 125 Yet those trifles are come from many former siecles vnto our times.
**3.** A century.
*c* **1532** Du Wes *Introd. Fr.* in *Palsgr.* 1079 The Romayns [reckoned] by lustres, whiche ben fyve yeres:..a secle is an hundred yere.

**†siede,** *v. Obs.*[−1] [a. MDu. *sieden* (Du. *zieden*): see seethe *v.*] *trans.* To boil.
**1481** Caxton *Reynard* (Arb.) 30 Ye may doo what ye wille,..ye may siede me, or roste, hange, or make me blynde.

**siedge,** obs. form of siege.

**†sief.** *Obs. rare.* Also **sieff, seif.** [ad. Arab. *shiyāf*, f. *shwf* to see, to adorn oneself.] (See quots.)
*c* **1550** H. Lloyd *Treas. Health* F iij, Sief is a confectyon made after the fashion of a suger lofe & most be dyssoluyd in licour before it be receiuid. **1656** Ridgley *Pract. Physick* 128 The Collirium or Sieff that follows, is useful. [**1704** J. Harris *Lex. Techn.* I, *Collyrium*, is an oblong or round Tablet or Trochisk, used formerly in Distempers of the Eyes; and was then called by the Arabian Name of *Seif* or *Sief*.]

**siege** (siːdʒ), *sb.* Forms: 3-7 **sege** (5 **cege, seche**), 4-5 **segh(e**; 4 **seeg,** 6-7 **seege, seage,** 6 **saige**; 4-5 **sige,** 5- **siege,** 5-6 **syege,** 5-8 **seige**; 5 **sedche,** 6 **sedge, syedge,** 7 **seidg(e, si(e)dge, segge.** [a. OF. *sege, seige, siege* (mod.F. *siège*):—pop. L. **sēdicum*, f. **sēdem* (L. *sēdem, sēdes*) seat. Hence also MDu. *siege, siegye, siedse* seat, siege.]
**I. 1. † a.** A seat, *esp.* one used by a person of rank or distinction. *Obs.*
*a* **1225** *Ancr. R.* 238 þeos sege & teos seoue crunen haueð þi diciple þeos ilke niht of earned. *c* **1290** *S. Eng. Leg.* I. 228 Seue taperes weren in þe queor..And foure-and-twenti segene;..And þe Abbodes sege was a-midde þe queor. **13..** *E.E. Allit. P.* C. 93 'Oure syre syttes,' he says, 'on sege so hyȝe'. **1387** Trevisa *Higden* (Rolls) I. 221 þerynne is.. dyuers oute goynges, benches, and seges [*L. sedilia*] all aboute. *c* **1412** Hoccleve *De Reg. Princ.* 3259 He..ledde hym to his tente,..And in his real seege and his chaiere As blyue hym sette. **1470-85** Malory *Arthur* iii. ii. 101 The Bisshop..blessid the syeges with grete Royalte..and there sette the viij and xx knyghtes in her syeges. **1509** Barclay *Shyp of Folys* (1570) 153 The scribe in writing..Sitting in his siege acloyde with couetise. **1590** Spenser *F.Q.* ii. ii. 39 Guyon..From lofty siege began these words aloud to sound. **1614** Lodge *Seneca* 148 The sieges in a Theater ordained for Knights, appertaine to all Knights of Rome. *a* **1616** B. Jonson *Masque Oberon* 213 *note*, The Knights masquers sitting in their severall sieges.
*fig.* **1604** Shaks. *Oth.* i. ii. 22, I fetch my life and being, From Men of Royall Seige.
**† b.** An ecclesiastical see. *Obs.*
**1297** R. Glouc. (Rolls) 2813 Change worþ of bissopriches & þe digne sege iwis Worþ ybroȝt to kaunterbury, þat at londone nou is. *c* **1330** R. Brunne *Chron. Wace* (Rolls) 7760 He sente to Rome, to seint Romeyn,..He kepte þe sege of the apostoylle. *c* **1375** *Sc. Leg. Saints* ii. (*Paul*) 398 Quhen pape cornel þe sege of rowme gouernyt wele. *c* **1400** *Apol. Loll.* 50 So þat ani þing be askid for bischoppis, abbots, or oþer personis, to be putt in þer segis. **1456** Sir G. Haye *Law Arms* (S.T.S.) 21 The kirk of Alexandrye..said that sanct Petir maid his sege thare and his charter. **1547** *Bk. of Marchauntes* c vj, A woman which held and possessed the pontifical syedge two yeres. **1579** Fenton *Guicciard.* ix. (1599) 367 A day wherein..are offered the tributes which are due to the seege Apostolike.
**† c.** *Sc.* A bench or form; a class. *Obs.*
**1560** *Bk. Discipline* in Knox *Hist. Ref.* (Wodrow) II. 213 In the first Colledge..of the Vniversitie thair be four classes or saigeis. *a* **1614** J. Melvill *Diary* (Wodrow) 69 Upon this premonition he continowes halff a yeir as guid a bern as was in the seage.
**† d.** A class or category. *Obs.*[−1]
**1630** Brathwait *Eng. Gentlem.* (1641) 109 Wee shall first proceed with such as follow, being ranked in the same siedge, because recreations of the same nature.
**e.** *Siege Perilous*: the vacant seat at King Arthur's Round Table which could be occupied without peril only by the Knight destined to achieve the Grail. Also *fig.*
[*c* **1230** *La Queste del Saint Graal* (1967) 4 Et einsi alerent tant qu'il vindrent au grant siege que len apeloit le Siege Perilleux. *Ibid.* 7 Tuit li compaignon de la Table Reonde

furent venu et li siege aempli, fors seulement cil que len apeloit le Siege Perilleus.] *c* **1470** MALORY *Works* (1967) I. 102 But in the Sege Perelous there shall nevir man sitte but one, and yf there be ony so hardy to do hit he shall be destroyed, and he that shall sitte therein shall have no felowe. **1870** TENNYSON *Holy Grail & Other Poems* 43 There stood a vacant chair... And Merlin call'd it 'The Siege perilous', Perilous for good and ill. **1922** J. BUCHAN *Huntingtower* xiii. 256 There in a coign of the old battlements he would prove an ugly customer to the pursuit. Only one at a time could reach that siege perilous. **1959** P. LE GENTIL in R. S. Loomis *Arthurian Lit. in Middle Ages* xix. 261 Three scenes, the fateful occupation of the Siege Perilous and the two visits to the Grail castle, constitute the main pattern.

**2.** †**a.** A place in which one has his seat or residence; a seat of rule, empire, etc. *Obs.*

*c* **1374** CHAUCER *Boeth.* I. pr. iv. (1868) 13 Is þis þe librarie wyche þat þou haddest chosen for a ryȝt certeyne sege to þe in myne house. *c* **1400** MAUNDEV. (1839) xix. 211 In that Cytee was the firste Sege of the Kyng of Mancy. **1483** CAXTON *Gold. Leg.* 194/2 He ordeyned and Instytuted Parys to be the chyef syege of the royame. **1592** WARNER *Alb. Eng.* VIII. xliii. 206 He [Constantine] made his siege Bizantium, that retaines his name ere since. **1630** BRATHWAIT *Eng. Gentlem.* (1641) 138 They may be fitly compared to the Hedge-hogge, who hath two holes in his siedge: one towards the South, another towards the North.

*fig.* **1566** PAINTER *Pal. Pleas.* I. 56 He fixed her so fast in the siege of his remembraunce, as if he had been a yonge man. **1591** LODGE *Catharos* vi. 56 The braine, which according to some Philosophers is the siege of humane seed.

†**b.** The place in which a thing is set, or on which a ship lies. *Obs. rare.*

*c* **1380** *Sir Ferumb.* 2183 Þe dore.. fleȝ Out of þe Hokes & fram hir sege x. vet y-mete wel neȝ. **15..** *Ship Laws* in *Balfour's Pract.* (1774) 622 (Jam.), Gif the ship be on ane hard saige, the master sould gar the shipman amend it incontinent, that the ship tak na skaith.

**c.** The station of a heron on the watch for prey. Hence, a group or flock of herons.

A *siege of herons* is included in most of the old lists of 'companies of beasts and fowls'.

*c* **1452** in *Trans. Philol. Soc.* (1909) III. 51 Sege of Betowrys. Sege of hayrynnys. Sege vnto a Castelle. **1575** TURBERV. *Faulconrie* 113 Having found the Hearon at siege you must get you with your Falcon up into some high place. **1633** MASSINGER *Guardian* I. i, A hearn put from her siege.. shall mount So high [etc.]. **1674** N. COX *Gentl. Recreat.* (1677) 205 If you finde a wild Hern at Siege. **1801** J. STRUTT *Sports & Pastimes* I. ii. 28 A *sege* of herons, and of bitterns. **1937** J. W. DAY *Sporting Adventure* 106 They [*sc.* herons] are about in pairs instead of the 'sieges' of half a dozen or more which one met only a month ago fishing on the tide line. **1977** *Islander* (Victoria, B.C.) 5 June 3/2 A siege of herons flying home against a sunset sky.

†**3. a.** A privy. Also *to go to siege*, to go to stool, to ease oneself. *Obs.*

*c* **1400** *Lanfranc's Cirurg.* 12 (Add. MS.), Ȝif he may noȝt go to sege onys a day, helpe hym þereto oþere wit clysterye, oþere with suppositorye. *c* **1440** *Alph. Tales* 122 Þis clerk.. slew þaim bothe, & cut þaim in pecis & keste þaim in a sege. **1544** PHAER *Pestilence* (1553) O j b, He ought euery day to goe to siege once. **1555** BP. BONNER *Prof. & Necess. Doctrine* U j, Dooe they passe into the seage from us as other meates doe?

**b.** Evacuation. *Obs.*

*c* **1460** J. RUSSELL *Bk. Nurture* 954 in *Babees Bk.*, Aftur slepe and sege, honeste will not hit denay. **1539** ELYOT *Cast. Helthe* (1541) 55 b, If he which oftentymes unconstrayned hath had great sieges, be sodeynly stopped. **1578** LYTE *Dodoens* 574 The juyce of the wilde Letuce.. scoureth by siege the waterie humours. **1605** TIMME *Quersit.* I. v. 19 The philosophicall salt is of greatest virtue and force to purge:.. whether it bee the belly, by siege;.. or the body, by sweate. **1669** W. SIMPSON *Hydrol. Chym.* 244 Clogging medicines.. are.. carryed off by seidge. **1700** T. BROWN tr. *Fresney's Amusem.* 97 The Patient should swallow as much *Aqua Fortis*, as would dissolve the Knife.., and bring it away by Seige.

**c.** Excrement, ordure. *Obs.*

**1515** BARCLAY *Egloges* ii. Wks. (1570) B iv, The lordes siege & rurall mens ordure Be like of Sauour. **1561** HOLLYBUSH *Hom. Apoth.* 3 Make pillets thereof.. and put that into the bodye; the same retayneth the sege. *a* **1610** HEALEY *Theophrastus* (1636) 72 Then he tels you that his Sieges were blacker then broth. **1662** J. CHANDLER *Van Helmont's Oriat.* 183 Less is discussed out of us, with a small and more hard siege or excrement.

**d.** *Comb.*, as *siege-hole*, *-house*. *Obs.*

**1440** *Coventry Leet Bk.* 194 The sege houses in þe West-orcherd were graunte to hym. **1477–9** *Rec. St. Mary at Hill* (1905) 87 For clensyng of the Sege holis, xviij d. **1519** HORMAN *Vulg.* 170 b, A segehouse wold be vnder the open aire betwene two wallis. **1647** LILLY *Chr. Astrol.* l. 353 It is hid in a.. Siege-house or Jakes, where people Seldome come.

†**4.** The anus or rectum. *Obs.*

**1561** HOLLYBUSH *Hom. Apoth.* 5 The same refrayne the vp braythinge into the head and driue downward to the siege. **1578** LYTE *Dodoens* 37 It helpeth.. the inflammation of the eyes, and fundament or siege. **1646** SIR T. BROWNE *Pseud. Ep.* 144, I beheld them excluded by the passage of generation, near the orifice of the seidge. **1670** MILTON *Hist. Eng.* v. Wks. 1851 III. 213 His body was diseas'd in his youth with a great soreness in the Siege.

**5.** *techn.* **a.** The floor of a glass-furnace.

**1839** URE *Dict. Arts* 577 The central space is occupied by the grate-bars; and on either side is the platform or fire-brick siege. **1890** W. J. GORDON *Foundry* 136 The rocky crust of clay left by the old pot on the furnace siege.

**b.** A hewer's table or bench.

**1854** H. MILLER *Sch. & Schm.* (1858) 329 To roll up a large stone to the sort of block-bench, or *siege*, as it is technically termed, on which the mass had to be hewn.

**II. 6. a.** The action, on the part of an army, of investing a town, castle, etc., in order to cut off all outside communication and in the end to reduce or take it; an investment, beleaguering. Also const. *of*. Also *transf.* and *fig.*

In early use sometimes approaching the concrete sense of 'investing force'. For the phrases *to lay* and *to raise a siege* see LAY *v.*[1] 19 and RAISE *v.*[1] 29.

*a* **1300** *Cursor M.* 7070 Her-of thar naman be in were, For-qui þe sege lasted ten yeire. *c* **1385** CHAUCER *L.G.W.* 1909 *Ariadne*, Nysus doughtyr stod vp-on the wal, And of the sege saw the maner al. **1415** HOCCLEVE *Min. Poems* ii. 197 Rede the storie of Lancelot de Lake,.. The seege of Troie or Thebes. *c* **1489** CAXTON *Blanchardyn* lii. 200 He was not seen of theym that were atte the syege. **1515** *Scot. Field* 48 in *Chetham Misc.* II, Now leve we our king lying at the sedge. **1560** DAUS tr. *Sleidane's Comm.* 42 After many battels and sundry sieges, he subdueth them. **1609** DEKKER *Peace is Broken* Wks. (Grosart) IV. 165 So many troubles.. following both the armies (by meanes of the tedious Siege). **1653** HOLCROFT *Procopius, Goth. Wars* I. 12 Why fear you this seige.., secured by these walls and souldiers? *a* **1738** SWIFT *Hen. I*, Wks. 1768 IV. 275 In hopes to draw the enemy from the siege of so important a place. **1770** LANGHORNE *Plutarch* (1851) I. 237/1 He returned to the siege of Chalcedon. **1814** SCOTT *Ld. of Isles* III. x, We must .. instant pray our Sovereign Liege, To shun the perils of a siege. **1876** VOYLE & STEVENSON *Milit. Dict.* (ed. 3) 383/2 The penetrating power of the arms which would now be used at a siege is far greater than it used to be. **1911** *Times* 5 Jan. 6/2 (*heading*) Foreign opinion on the Stepney siege. **1980** *Daily Tel.* 5 June 8/6 Police forced their way into a flat .. after a man had barricaded himself in... During the two-hour siege the man's wife sustained a broken nose.

*fig.* *c* **1600** SHAKS. *Sonn.* lxv, O how shall summers hunny breath hold out Against the wrackfull siedge of battring dayes. **1611** MIDDLETON & DEKKER *Roaring Girl* D j b, Ile lay hard siege to her. **1644** DIGBY *Nat. Bodies* iv. §4. 29 So that noe part of the body.. be free from the siege of the dense body that presseth it. *c* **1700** DRYDEN *Theo. & Hon.* 33 Love stood the siege, and would not yield his breast. **1751** JOHNSON *Rambler* No. 93 ¶3 Interest and passion will hold out long against the closest siege of diagrams and syllogisms.

**b.** Without article. *to lay siege to*: see LAY *v.*[1] 19.

*c* **1375** *Sc. Leg. Saints* vii. (*Jacob*) 443 To Ierusaleme .. [he] com.. & gret sege gert till It lay. *a* **1400** *Minor Poems fr. Vernon MS.* xxix. 38 Sone Sire Rollo wiþ his Route Bi-sette þat Citee wiþ sege a-boute. **1436** HEN. VI in *Rep. Hist. MSS. Comm., Var. Coll.* IV. 199 Kyng Edward.. lay at sege at the seid towne. **1513** WRIOTHESLEY *Chron.* (Camden) I. 9 The King of England that tyme lyenge at seege before Turney in France. **1590** SPENSER *F.Q.* II. xi. 5 That castle to assaile.. And lay strong siege about it. **1673** TEMPLE *United Prov.* Wks. 1720 I. 26 He took the Place, after three Years Siege. **1814** SCOTT *Ld. of Isles* v. xvi, If my Liege May win yon walls by storm or siege. **1848** W. H. KELLY tr. *L. Blanc's Hist. Ten Y.* II. 415 Since the king declared Paris in a state of siege. **1873** MRS. H. KING *Disciples, Ugo Bassi* vii. (1877) 258 Though choleric at times, Still a good ruler for a state of siege.

**c.** A period of illness, struggle, or difficulty. *U.S.*

**1840** R. H. DANA *Bef. Mast* xxvi, From this [work] we escaped, having had a pretty good siege with the wooding. **1898** E. C. HALL *Aunt Jane* 9 She was as pale and peaked as if she had been through a siege of typhoid. **1929** *Randolph* (W.Va.) *Enterprise* 11 Apr. 1/1 The.. Literary Society had another heavy siege Tuesday night of this week. **1952** R. CHANDLER *Let.* 31 July (1966) 27 She is weakened by a long siege of bronchitis. **1975** *Publishers Weekly* 11 Aug. 113/1 After her own siege with breast cancer, the author consulted with other victims.

**7.** *attrib.* and *Comb.*, chiefly designating apparatus, etc., used in carrying out a siege, as ***siege-artillery***, ***-carriage***, ***-gun***, ***-machine***, ***-park***, etc.; also ***siege-craft***, ***-day***, †***-garland***, ***-operations***, ***-ward***; (in *transf.* senses) ***siege action***, ***tactics***.

**1977** *Evening Post* (Nottingham) 24 Jan. 5/8 The threat to car jobs in the Midlands grew today as delivery drivers began another week of '*siege action' at three big Leyland factories. **1837** CARLYLE *Fr. Rev.* I. IV. iv, Fire and thunder of *siege and field artillery. **1867** SMYTH *Sailor's Word-bk.* 625 *Siege-artillery*, the ordnance.. used for overpowering the fire and destroying the defences of a fortified place. **1875** KNIGHT *Dict. Mech.* 2175/1 It is mounted on a *siege-carriage, and forms part of the train of an army. **1898** *Athenæum* 29 Oct. 603/1 There is.. a treatise on *siegecraft in the Vatican Library. **1884** *Mil. Engin.* I. II. 17 Separate intermediate depôts.. containing the necessary supplies for a '*siege day'. **1601** HOLLAND *Pliny* I. 116 The same was called also an Obsidionall coronet or *siege-garland. **1858** SIMMONDS *Dict. Trade*, ***Siege-gun**, a heavy gun.. used to batter down or effect a breach in an enemy's wall. **1875** KNIGHT *Dict. Mech.* 2175/2 Siege-gun carriages differ from those of ordinary field-pieces in being stronger and heavier. **1852** GROTE *Greece* II. lxxxii. X. 621 Having provided himself with fresh *siege-machines. **1862** CARLYLE *Fredk. Gt.* XII. ii. III. 194 There ensured a ringing frost;—not favourable for *Siege-operations. **1870** *Pall Mall G.* 13 Oct. 11 If.. the German *siege-park is composed of some four or five hundred guns. **1876** VOYLE & STEVENSON *Milit. Dict.* (ed. 3) s.v. *Park*, A siege park comprises the guns collected together at the commencement of the investment of a fortress. **1977** P. HILL *Fanatics* 109 Those two have been trained in *siege tactics. **1859** GLEIG *Life Wellington* xviii, He had no *siege-train at hand, nor any other means wherewith to approach the place in regular form. **1876** VOYLE & STEVENSON *Milit. Dict.* (ed. 3) 384 *Siege Train*, the men, guns, and material collected together for the conduct of a siege. *Ibid.*, **Siege Wagon*, a general service wagon fitted with movable trays for shot and shell. *c* **1450** LOVELICH *Grail* xiii. 353 They.. sien there Tholome.. That Comeng was tho to the *segeward. **1879** *Man. Artill. Exerc.* 135 Five-feet *siege wheels with metal naves. **1888** *Century Mag.* Sept. 660/1 Pope.. surrounded the place by *siege-works in which he could protect his men.

**b. siege economy**, an economic situation in which the availability of imported goods is severely restricted by import controls and the export of capital is curtailed; **siege mentality**, a defensive or paranoid attitude of mind based on an assumption of hostility in others.

**1962** S. E. FINER *Man on Horseback* vii. 92 By 1940 the parties had been dissolved, the zaibitsu harnessed to a siege economy. **1979** H. S. KENT *In on Act* xii. 131 The phrase 'siege economy' is sometimes used today to conjure up a last desperate plight in which, under the protection of high tariff walls, we would try to grow our own food, labour grimly in our mines and make the things we needed most; and so control our foreign trade as to bring in the additional supplies that we could not do without. **1969** J. L. MCKENZIE *Roman Catholic Church* III. iv. 222 This revival could not have come about without relaxation of the 'siege mentality'. **1976** *Deb. Senate Canada* 8 Mar. 11590/2 With the growing siege mentality in the suburbs of our major urban areas, the people know that crime is not under control.

**siege** (si:dʒ), *v.* Forms: 4–5 (6 *Sc.*) sege, 5 seyge, 5 (6–7 *Sc.*) seige, 6 *Sc.* saige, 4– siege; 6 sedge, 6–7 siedge. [f. prec., or aphetic f. ASSIEGE *v.*]

**1.** *trans.* To besiege, beleaguer, lay siege to.

**13..** *K. Alis.* 2667 (Laud MS.), Quyklich to Tebe toun Hij wenten & seged it environ. **1390** GOWER *Conf.* I. 348 Anon this Cite was withoute Belein and sieged al aboute. *c* **1440** *Alph. Tales* 226 Þer was.. neuer cetie þat he segid bod he wan it. *c* **1470** HENRY *Wallace* IX. 1662 The cuntre rais, quhen thai herd off sic thing, To sege Dowglace. **1515** *Scot. Field* 23 in *Chetham Misc.* II, Then our king.. Saith 'I will sedge it aboute, within this seaven daies'. **1549** *Compl. Scot.* 89 The kyng of France vas past ouer the alpes to siege paue. **1615** BRATHWAIT *Strappado* (1878) 165 There plant thy Cannon, siedge her round about, Be sure (my Boy) she cannot long hold out. **1637** HEYWOOD *Dial.* iii. Wks. 1874 VI. 141 Great Babylon, Mighty in walls, I sieg'd, and seised on. **1762** *Gentl. Mag.* XXXIII. 333/1 'Tis not for me our arduous toils to shew; Nor tell 'midst dangers how we sieg'd the foe. **1805** SCOTT *Last Minstrel* IV. iv, They sieg'd him a whole summer night. **1893** *Nat. Obs.* 7 Jan. 184/2 He lived in the Castle when the French sieged it.

†**2.** To place; to seat (oneself). *Obs. rare.*

*c* **1425** WYNTOUN *Orig. Cron.* III. ix. 1086 Qwhar euir þat stane ȝe segit se, Þar sal þe Scottis be regnande. **1594** R. C[AREW] *Godfr. Bulloigne* (1881) 74 Part on the right, part on the left this band Siedgeth it selfe, their wreakfull king before. Pluto sits in the mids.

Hence **sieged** (si:dʒd) *ppl. a.*

**1567** GOLDING *Ovid's Met.* v. (1593) 125 A chil-cold swet my sieged limmes opprest. **1592** WYRLEY *Armorie* 140 These two could not agree, which he should part To sucker sieged frends. *c* **1611** CHAPMAN *Iliad* v. 205 Since in a sieged towne, I thought our horse-meate would be scant. **1612** DRAYTON *Poly-olb.* xviii. 415 Who, to remove the foe from sieged Harflew, sent, Affrighted them like death. **1831** CARLYLE *Sart. Res.* II. vii, In sea-storms and sieged cities and other death-scenes.

†**'siegeable**, *a. Obs.*[−1] [f. SIEGE *v.* + -ABLE.] Capable of being besieged.

**1569** STOCKER tr. *Diod. Sic.* II. xxxvi. 84 He entrenched it on that side it was siegeable.

**Siegenian** (si:'gɛnɪən), *a. Geol.* [f. *Siegen*, name of a town and region in North Rhine-Westphalia, W. Germany, + -IAN.] Pertaining to our designating a stage of the Lower Devonian in N.W. Europe, immediately above the Gedinnian, or the epoch or age during which it was deposited. Also *absol.*

**1922** *Proc. Geologists' Assoc.* XXXIII. 12 The higher horizon also includes many Siegenian species. **1928** E. NEAVERSON *Stratigraphical Palaeont.* xi. 255 In Britain.. the Siegenian stage is best represented by the Meadfoot beds of South Devon. **1931** [see FAMENNIAN *a.*] **1967** M. R. HOUSE in W. B. Harland et al. *Fossil Record* I. 47 The goniatites appear in the mid-Siegenian as simple primitive types which soon diversify rapidly. **1979** R. ANDERTON et al. *Dynamic Stratigr. Brit. Isles* x. 130/2 Non-marine faunas of ostracoderm and placoderm fish fragments and plant remains.. indicate a lower Devonian (Siegenian) age for the group.

**siegenite** ('si:gənaɪt). *Min.* [f. *Siegen* (see prec.).] A nickeliferous variety of linnæite.

**1854** DANA *Syst. Min.* (ed. 4) II. 68 Siegenite.. is a Nickel-Linnæite. **1866** WATTS *Dict. Chem.* IV. 44 Nickel-Linnæite. Siegenite. Linnæite.. in which a considerable proportion of the cobalt is replaced by nickel.

**'siege-piece.** [SIEGE *sb.* 6.]

**1.** A coin or piece of money, characterized by unusual shape and imperfect workmanship, struck and issued during a time of siege.

**1736** FOLKES *Gold Coins* 7, I have among the Siege-Pieces seen a Twenty-Shilling Piece of Gold, struck at Pontefract. **1798** H. WALPOLE *Reminis.* in *Lett.* (1857) I. p. xcii, My narrative will probably resemble siege-pieces, which are struck of any promiscuous metals. **1853** HUMPHREY *Coin-coll. Man.* i. 5 The rude 'siege pieces' struck without coining apparatus in different parts of the kingdom. **1879** H. PHILLIPS *Notes Coins* 12 There are various siege pieces of Charles I, who never in all his extremities resorted to the expedient of a debased coinage.

**2.** A piece of ordnance employed in sieges.

**1799** *Hist. Europe* in *Ann. Reg.* 25/1 The French found in the towers of Joppa ten pieces of cannon and about twenty indifferent siege-pieces.

**sieger** ('si:dʒə(r)). Now *rare.* Also 6 *Sc.* segear, 6–7 seiger. [f. SIEGE *v.* + -ER.] A besieger.

**1533** BELLENDEN *Livy* v. ix. (S.T.S.) II. 179 It had done during all þe said tyme mare dammage to þe segearis þan It gat. **1556** *Aurelio & Isab.* (1608) B v, He ordeyned that the house shoulde be sette aboute with his siegers. **1611** SPEED *Hist. Gt. Brit.* IX. viii. (1623) 555 He gaue commaund to his Seneschalle.. to withdraw the Seigers. **1774** *Poetry* in *Ann.*

*Reg.* 215 The more delay the siegers found, .. More fierce they mount the breach. **1825** SCOTT *Betrothed* xxix, Then let us make a fair sally upon the siegers. **1842** I. WILLIAMS *Baptistery* I. iv. (1874) 41 To .. take his part With siegers or besieged.

**Siegfried Line** (ˈsiːgfriːd laɪn). [tr. G. *Siegfriedlinie*, f. the name of the hero *Siegfried* of Wagner's *Ring* cycle (and of the MHG epic poem the *Nibelungenlied*).] The line of fortifications occupied by the Germans in France during the war of 1914–18. Similarly, the line of defence constructed along Germany's western frontier before the war of 1939–45.

[**1923** KIPLING *Irish Guards in Great War* I. 204 The Hindenburg line, known to the Germans as 'Siegfried'.] **1936** H. A. L. FISHER *Hist. Europe* III. xxxiii. 1144 A position which had been fortified with elaborate care, and was known by the Germans as the Siegfried and by the English as the Hindenburg line. **1938** *Times* 25 Oct. 14/4 The evening newspapers [in Berlin] published to-day the first photographs of the so-called 'Siegfried Line', the massive fortifications which are being erected on the western frontiers of the Reich. **1939** *Times* 22 Sept. 6/7 What song is to be the 'Tipperary' of this war? The first candidate would seem to be 'The Washing on the Siegfried Line'. Its chorus is sufficiently simple and singable:—We're gonna hang out the washing on the Siegfried Line. Have you any dirty washing, mother dear? We're gonna hang out the washing on the Siegfried Line... If the Siegfried Line's still there. **1946** *R.A.F. Jrnl.* May 157, I rode straight through the Siegfried Line with dug-outs and then a line of anti-tank traps strung out across the countryside. **1978** E. MALPASS *Wind brings up Rain* xxiv. 221 Cholera .. had broken out .. in the Siegfried Line.

‖**Sieg Heil** (ziːg haɪl), *int.* Also **Sieg-heil, sieg heil**, etc. [Ger., lit. 'Hail victory'.] The victory salute used by the Germans during the Nazi regime, esp. at political rallies, etc. Also as *sb.* and *v. intr.* Hence **sieg-'heiling** *ppl. a.* Cf. HEIL *int.*

**1940** 'N. BLAKE' *Malice in Wonderland* ii. 31 The hysterical pitch of the Sieg Heils at a Nazi congress. **1944** V. G. GARVIN tr. *R. Gary's Forest of Anger* xxii. 89 He has only done his duty. Nothing else. Sieg-heil! **1967** R. M. STERN *Kessler Legacy* iii. 29 Your newspaper character probably .. marched and *Sieg Heiled* with the rest of the boys. **1968** *Guardian* 25 Apr. 1/1, 200 dockers arrived .. to shout 'Enoch! Enoch! Enoch!' in 'Sieg heil' tempo. **1968** *Listener* 26 Sept. 403/3 Thus, by 1935, her pictorial records of militarised youngsters, marching young men and sieg-heiling fathers of families were worth uncountable battalions to the Fuehrer. **1976** *Scotsman* 20 Nov. (Weekend Suppl.) 2/6 The film, with its 'Sieg Heils' and hysterical atmosphere, is still trotted out in documentaries about the 1930s. **1978** A. NEAVE *Nuremberg* xxii. 257, I half expected them to rise, salute and cry '*Sieg Heil*'!

**sieging** (ˈsiːdʒɪŋ), *vbl. sb.* [f. SIEGE *v.*] The action of besieging; a siege.

**13..** *Cursor M.* 7070 (Gött.), Here-of thar na man be in were, For qui þe seging lastid ten ȝere. **1382** WYCLIF *Isaiah* xxix. 3, I shal kaste aȝen thee an hep, and the strengthis I shal sette in to thi seging. *c* **1440** *Gesta Rom.* lxi. 255 Thenne the duke besegid long this castelle. And as thei wer thus in segeing [etc.]. *c* **1470** HENRY *Wallace* XI. 855 Wallace .. At Sanct Jhonstoun was at the segeyng still. **1504** *Acc. Ld. High Treas. Scot.* II. 431 To Hannis, gunnar, .. for to pas in the Ilis to the segeing of Carneburgh. **1596** DALRYMPLE tr. *Leslie's Hist. Scot.* II. 18 S. Jhones toun, efter lang segeing, is tane. **1858** CARLYLE *Fredk. Gt.* IV. v. (1872) I. 435 Stralsund has been taken, since that, by Prussian sieging.
*attrib.* **1809** CAMPBELL *Gert. Wyom.* I. iv, On plains [which] no sieging mine's volcano shook. **1837** CARLYLE *Fr. Rev.* I. VII. x, Well for them, that Insurrection has only pikes and axes; no right sieging-tools! **1858** —— *Fredk. Gt.* XVIII. xii. (1872) VIII. 21 Friedrich is not thought to shine in the sieging line as he does in the fighting.

**siegnior**, obs. f. SIGNOR.

**siek(e**, obs. ff. SICK.

**siel**, obs. f. CEIL *v.*, SEEL *v.*; var. SILE *v.*

**sieling**, obs. f. CEILING.

**siely**, obs. f. SEELY.

**Siemens** (ˈsiːmənz, ‖ˈziːməns). The name of four German-born brothers, Ernst Werner (1816–92), Karl Wilhelm or Charles William (1823–83), Friedrich (1826–1904), and Karl (1829–1906) (von) *Siemens*, used *attrib.* and in the possessive: **1.** To denote processes or devices discovered, invented, or developed by one or more of the brothers.

The brothers were closely associated in invention and manufacturing, and it is frequently not possible to attribute a given invention or process to any one of them. Their name is often combined with that of another inventor.

**a.** *Steel-making.* Sometimes in Comb. with the name of Pierre Blaise Emile *Martin* (1824–1915), French engineer, as ***Siemens pyrometer, regenerator***; **Siemens('s) furnace**, an open-hearth furnace; **Siemens-Martin furnace** = *Siemens furnace*; **Siemens-Martin process**, the process, invented by Martin, of melting pig iron and scrap steel together in a Siemens furnace, usu. in alkaline conditions; **Siemens process**, a process similar to the Siemens-Martin process, but usu. carried out in acidic conditions; **Siemens producer**, a form of gas producer developed by the Siemens brothers (see PRODUCER 3).

**1866** *Chambers's Jrnl.* 25 Aug. 543/2 For .. any .. process in which an intense heat is required, the Siemens furnace is eminently suitable. **1875** *Ure's Dict. Arts* (ed. 7) III. 909 Another modification of the Siemens process consists in the use of finely-divided iron in the spongy state .. instead of bars or other manufactured forms of malleable iron. *Ibid.* 910 Two processes are employed at the Landore works: the Siemens-Martin process, which consists .. in dissolving scrap-metal or steel in a bath of pig-metal, to which spiegeleisen is finally added; and the ore-reducing process. *a* **1877** KNIGHT *Dict. Mech.* III. 2365/2 In the Martin-Siemens reverberatory furnace the decarbonization of the pig-iron is effected by the reactions, upon the molten bath, of wrought-iron or ore and of the furnace-flame. **1877** Siemens producer [see REGENERATOR 2 a]. **1879** *Encycl. Brit.* IX. 846/1 The most perfect method of utilizing the waste heat hitherto applied is that of the Siemens regenerator, in which the spent gases are made to travel through chambers, known as regenerators or recuperators of heat. **1881** *Ibid.* XIII. 294/2 The calorific value of a unit of weight of gas from a Siemens producer is about 650. *Ibid.* 304/1 The other Siemens pyrometer depends on the alteration of the electrical resistance of a platinum wire when heated. *Ibid.* 305/1 The ball of a Siemens pyrometer can be introduced into the tuyere through the orifice. *Ibid.* 348/2 The Pernot furnace .. is substantially a Siemens-Martin furnace with a rotating bed. **1923** GLAZEBROOK *Dict. Appl. Physics* V. 515/1 The development of the mass production of steel by the Bessemer, Siemens, and subsequent processes rendered modern engineering possible on the present scale. **1973** R. D. PEHLKE *Unit Processes Extractive Metallurgy* iv. 88 The Siemens-Martin process, commonly referred to as the open hearth process, was developed at about the same time as the Thomas process. **1974** *Encycl. Brit. Macropædia* XVII. 640/1 The Siemens furnace used a grate for burning solid fuel, .. and the duct-work necessary to convey the gases from one end of the furnace to the regenerator chamber and the hot air to the grate at the other end was complex and inefficient. *Ibid.*, Pierre and Emile Martin in France in 1864 built a furnace that was fired by gas and placed a set of two Siemens regenerator chambers at each end of the furnace. *Ibid.*, This furnace became known as the Siemens-Martin furnace, or, more commonly, as the open-hearth furnace.

**b.** In similar technical applications, as ***Siemens('s) direction finder, dynamo, (electro-)-dynamometer, relay, wattmeter***, and in the names of various forms of lamp.

**1867** R. S. CULLEY *Handbk. Pract. Telegr.* (ed. 2) IX. 184 Siemens' relay consists of an electromagnet of the usual horse-shoe form. **1879** *Telegr. Jrnl.* VII. 318/2 (*heading*) Siemens' electric lamp. *Ibid.* 412/2 (*heading*) Siemens' differential electric lamp. **1882** *Encycl. Brit.* XIV. 633/1 In the Siemens differential lamp, .. a potential or shunt coil and a current coil oppose each other; as the arc lengthens the current becomes less, and the potential greater, each acting to cause the carbons to approach. **1884** H. R. KEMPE *Handbk. Electr. Testing* (ed. 3) xii. 284 Like galvanometers, the Siemens electro-dynamometer is not susceptible of great accuracy when readings are very low. **1886** J. MAIER *Arc & Blow Lamps* v. 40 A large Siemens' dynamo at 450 revolutions after two hours' work became so hot that the electro-magnets began to fire. **1892** W. P. MAYCOCK *Electr. Lighting & Power Distribution* I. v. 122 Siemens' wattmeter is very similar in appearance to the electro-dynamometer. **1912** *Motor Manual* (ed. 14) iii. 125 The Siemens metallic tungsten lamps are practically unaffected by shock. **1922** GLAZEBROOK *Dict. Appl. Physics* II. 4/1 If the current measured passes through both coils the scale division will approximately follow a 'square law', as in the case of the Siemens dynamometer. **1927** S. H. LONG *Navigational Wireless* v. 86 (*heading*) Instructions for operating the Siemens direction finder. **1930** T. E. HERBERT *Telegraphy* (ed. 5) viii. 258 Siemens-Halske Relay. This relay is developed from the original Siemen's [*sic*] relay. **1966** *McGraw-Hill Encyl. Sci. & Technol.* IV. 476/2 If the same current flows through all coils in series, as in the early Siemen's [*sic*] electrodynamometer .., the instrument can be calibrated as an ammeter.

**2.** *Electr.* †**a.** A unit of resistance, used esp. in Germany, slightly smaller than the ohm. Usu. in the possessive, as ***Siemens'(s) unit***. *Obs.*

**1867** R. S. CULLEY *Handbk. Pract. Telegr.* (ed. 2) II. 30 'Siemens' Unit' is one metre of pure mercury, of one square millimetre section, at a temperature of 32°. Thus the Ohm and the Siemens are really alike. **1899** J. E. YOUNG *Electr. Testing for Telegraph Engineers* iv. 48 A third standard, Siemens's unit, equals 0·954 B.A. ohm.

**b.** (Usu. written **siemens.**) [Named after Charles William *Siemens*.] A unit of conductance, equivalent to the mho.

**1935** *Proc. Nat. Acad. Sci.* XXI. 579 (*table*) Siemens. **1936** *Jrnl. Inst. Electr. Engineers* LXXVIII. 238/2 The names 'hertz' and 'siemens' likewise were voted for the names of the practical units of frequency and conductance respectively. **1963** JERRARD & MCNEILL *Dict. Sci. Units* 128 The siemens is the practical unit of conductance and is equivalent to the mho... The unit, although approved by the I.E.C. in 1933 has not yet replaced the mho. **1972** [see PASCAL 2]. **1978** *Nature* 27 July 379/1 Unit ion conductances of a few picosiemens or greater have been reported.

**sien(ce**, obs. ff. SCION.

**Siena, Sienna** (sɪˈɛnə). Also †**Syenna.** [The name of a city and province in the Tuscany region of central Italy. In sense 1, *ellipt.* for TERRA SIENNA.]

**1.** (Usu. written *Sienna.*) **a.** A ferruginous earth used as a pigment in oil and water-colour painting (called *burnt sienna* when it has been exposed to a red heat). **b.** The colour of this pigment, a rich reddish brown. Also *attrib.* or *Comb.*, as ***sienna-brown, -red***.

[**1760** SHENSTONE *Wks. & Lett.* III. 309 A terra-sienna or very rich reddish brown. *Ibid.* 314 Terra-sienna is a delightful colour.] **1787** W. WILLIAMS *Mech. Oil Colours* 44 Siena earth .. is a fine colour, but comes little into use. [**1825** J. NICHOLSON *Operat. Mechanic* 642 Fawn-colour with burnt terra de sienna, or burnt umber and white.] **1853** *Zoologist* II. 4059 Minute granules of a rich sienna-brown hue. **1874** COUES *Birds N.W.* 150 They are of a light-green color, .. speckled with sienna and other rich shades of brown. **1876** *Pall Mall G.* 18 Oct. 4/1 Satchels of seeds, deep purple, sienna red, russet gold, and green.

**2.** ***Siena marble***, a reddish mottled stone obtained from the neighbourhood of Siena.

**1774** *Builder's Magazine* 129 The body of the work may be of statuary, and the columns of Syenna marble. **1802** MRS. EDGEWORTH *Let.* 6 Dec. in C. Colvin *Maria Edgeworth in France & Switzerland* (1979) 46 The Salle for public Lectures is .. 30 feet high supported by 4 pillars of Sienna Marble. **1848** E. RUSKIN *Let.* 20 July in M. Lutyens *Ruskins & Grays* (1972) xiv. 126 The pillars of polished Sienna marble... John said .. it made him quite sick. **1894** A. HEATON *Record of Work* Pl. 8 (*caption*) Grate with brass mouldings, Sienna marble slips, and plain .. tiles. **1947** J. C. RICH *Materials & Methods of Sculpture* viii. 228 Most of the Siena marbles are veined. Siena Unie, a bright yellow variety, appears to be the only one with little or no marking. **1975** *Country Life* May (*Suppl.*) 35 George III painted console table, with .. fine Siena marble tops.

**sienc(e**, obs. ff. SCIENCE.

**Sienese** (siːəˈniːz, saɪəˈniːz), *sb.* and *a.* Also **Siennese.** [f. *Siena, Sienna* (see def.) + -ESE.]

**A.** *sb.* **1.** An inhabitant or native of Siena, a city in Tuscany.

**1756–7** tr. *Keysler's Trav.* (1760) II. 86 The Siennese produce this inscription to invalidate the boast of the Florentines. *c* **1830** *Encycl. Metrop.* (1845) XII. 479/1 For a while the Siennese flattered themselves that their liberty would be recoverable. **1887** *Encycl. Brit.* XXII. 43 The Sienese took possession of their fortress.

**2.** An artist belonging to the Italian school of painting developed at Siena during the 14th and 15th centuries. Also *transf.*, a painting produced by such an artist.

**1888** H. ATTWELL *Italian Masters* 6 The Sienese lack the robust simplicity of Giotto, and were little influenced by the austere spirit of Dante. **1921** A. HUXLEY *Crome Yellow* ii. 12 Henry Wimbush was forced to sell some of his Primitives .. four or five nameless Sienese—to the Americans. **1959** *Listener* 26 Nov. 940/2 Minor Sienese are thick on the ground and so are lesser painters of the Dutch school. **1977** 'R. WEST' *Celebration* 541 Oh, your Florentines, your Sienese, your Umbrians!

**B.** *adj.* Of or pertaining to Siena.

**1814** J. MAYNE *Jrnl.* 20 Oct. (1909) ix. 154 We walked through the principal parts of the town .. and enjoyed the pure Siennese tongue. *c* **1830** *Encycl. Metrop.* (1845) XII. 499/2 They obtained possession of many of the Siennese ports. **1850** MRS. JAMESON *Leg. Monast. Ord.* (1863) 392 In a rare Sienese print of the fifteenth century. **1882** 'OUIDA' *Maremma* I. 73 The winged boys of the Siennese Masters.

**sienite, sienitic**, var. SYENITE, SYENITIC.

**Sienna**: see SIENA.

**Siennese**, var. SIENESE.

**siens, sienz**, obs. ff. SCIENCE.

**siens, sient**, obs. ff. SCION.

**sier, sierce, sierge**, obs. ff. SIRE, SEARCE, CIERGE.

**sierozem** (ˈsɪərəʊzɛm). *Soil Sci.* Also **serozem.** [ad. Russ. *serozém*, f. *séryĭ* grey + *zemlyá* earth, soil.] A type of soil, usu. calcareous and poor in organic material, that is characterized by a brownish-grey surface horizon grading into harder, carbonate-rich lower layers, and is developed typically under mixed shrub vegetation in arid climates.

**1934** *Soil Sci.* XXXVIII. 485 On the steeper, and consequently drier, slopes sierozems (gray soils) are developed. **1965** B. T. BUNTING *Geogr. Soil* xii. 142 The cooler Russian and Argentine deserts have light grey serozem. **1976** H. E. DREGNE *Soil of Arid Regions* 79 A typical Serozem .. from near Isfahan in Iran .. had a 1 cm. thick desert pavement of fairly angular volcanic rocks overlying a loose, light brownish-gray, coarse sandy loam 4 cm. thick. **1977** J. C. F. TEDROW *Soils of Polar Landscapes* viii. 138 Traditionally, pedologists have focused their taxonomic investigations on the mature terrestric soils—Podzol, Chernozem, Sierozem, and so forth.

‖**sierra** (sɪˈɛrə). Also 7 **ser(r)a.** [Sp. *sierra*:—L. *serra* saw.]

**1. a.** In Spain and parts of Latin America: A range of hills or mountains, rising in peaks which suggest the teeth of a saw.

**1613** PURCHAS *Pilgrimage* (1614) 873 Peru is diuided into three parts, which they call Llanos, Sierras, and Andes. **1632** LITHGOW *Trav.* x. 445 Spaine generally, is a masse of mountaines, .. the Rockie Seraes or Alpes so innumerable. **1691** EVELYN *Corr.* (1879) III. 469 There are vast ones [caves] under those Alps & Sierras from whence our rivers derive their plentifull streames. **1745** P. THOMAS *Jrnl. Anson's Voy.* 68 The Andes and Scirras [*sic*] are two Ridges of Mountains that run from North to South. **1812** BYRON *Ch. Har.* I. xxxii, Doth Tayo interpose his mighty tide? Or dark Sierras rise in craggy pride? **1843** PRESCOTT *Mexico* III. v, Although the bleak winds of the sierra gave an austerity to the climate. **1885** *Encycl. Brit.* XVIII. 673/1 The sierra of Peru may be .. divided into four sections.

*attrib.* **1884** Coues *N. Amer. Birds* 422 *Cyanocitta stelleri frontalis*,.. Sierra Jay.

**b.** In general use: A mountain-range of this description.

**1807** R. Southey *Lett. from England* II. xxxiv. 95 A range of mountains standing in the three provinces of Worcester, Gloucester, and Hereford... This sierra is justly admired for the beauty of its form. **1850** W. Irving *Mahomet* xxxii. (1853) 141 Their rocky sierras on the east separated Azerbîjân from.. the shores of the Caspian. **1865** W. G. Palgrave *Arabia* I. 96 The main range of Djebel Shomer, a long purple sierra of most picturesque outline.

**2.** *Astr.* = chromosphere.

**1851** G. B. Airy in *Mem. R. Astron. Soc.* XXI. 7, I saw that the sierra, or rugged line of projections,.. had arisen. **1871** Proctor *Light Sci.* 97 The objectionable word *chromosphere* (for *chromatosphere*) should be replaced by *sierra*. **1883** —— in *19th Cent.* Nov. 876 In the sierra or chromatosphere the presence and nature of many other vapours are noted.

**3.** = cero.

**1889** in *Cent. Dict.* **1905** D. S. Jordan *Guide Study of Fishes* II. xvi. 266 Almost exactly like it [*sc.* the Spanish mackerel] in appearance is the pintado, or sierra. **1965** A. J. McClane *Stand. Fishing Encycl.* 793/2 Sierra are found along the Pacific coast of America from San Diego to Peru.

Hence **si'erran** *a.*

**1873** B. Harte *Fiddletown*, etc. 92 It was in a Sierran solitude, where I had encamped. **1885** *Encycl. Brit.* XVIII. 673/1 Sierran flora.

**Sierra Leone** (sɪ'ɛrə lɪ'əʊn), the name of a republic of West Africa, used *attrib.* in **Sierra Leone peach**, a shrub or small tree, *Nauclea latifolia* (formerly *Sarcocephalus esculentus*) of the family Rubiaceæ, native to tropical Africa, or its edible reddish fruit; = *Guinea peach* s.v. Guinea 1.

**1866** Lindley & Moore *Treas. Bot.* II. 1020/1 *S[arcocephalus] esculentus* has pink flowers and an edible fruit, of the size of a peach, whence it has been called the Sierra Leone Peach. **1965** M. S. Nielsen *Introd. Flowering Plants W. Afr.* xi. 173 Sierra Leone or Guinea Peach.. is a bush or small tree in savanna with dark red, juicy fruit balls.

Hence **Sierra Le'onean, -ian**, an inhabitant or native of Sierra Leone; also as *adj.*, of or pertaining to Sierra Leone.

**1791** A. M. Falconbridge *Let.* 8 June in *Narr. Two Voyages to River Sierra Leone* (1802) iv. 83 The people appear more inclined to industry than the Sierra Leonians. **1897** M. H. Kingsley *Travels W. Afr.* 680 Bishop Ingram would have been able to write a more cheerful and hopeful book.. if the Sierra Leonians had had a thorough grounding in technical culture. **1910** T. J. Alldridge *Transformed Colony* ix. 75 The Sierra Leonean trader feels all this pretty badly, especially as every Sierra Leonean wants to trade. **1926** *Chambers's Jrnl.* Nov. 660/1 Sierra-Leonean solicitors were hurrying to final interviews with retained advocates. **1957** M. Banton *W. Afr. City* vi. 104 At the [1931] census the term 'Sierra Leonian' was adopted for persons previously classified as 'Liberated Africans and their descendants'. **1974** *Times* 4 May (Sierra Leone Suppl.) p. i/1 Rhythm plays a particularly important role in the way of life of all Sierra Leoneans. **1976** *Sunday Times* (Lagos) 31 Oct. 5/4 The Sierra Leonian repatriates.. played a much greater role.

**sierse**, obs. form of searce *v.*

**sies**, var. sis *int.*

**si'est**, *v.* [f. next.] *intr.* To take a siesta.

**1839** Chalmers in Hanna *Mem.* (1852) IV. vi. 76, I addressed a full church and siested as usual.

**siesta**[1] (sɪ'ɛstə). [Sp. *siesta* (Pg. *sesta*):—L. *sexta* sixth (hour); hence, in Sp. and Pg., the hottest part of the day, rest or sleep taken at this time.] An afternoon rest or nap; *esp.* that commonly taken during the hottest hours of the day in tropical countries. Also *transf.*

**1655** Howell *Lett.* IV. i, When he slept his *Siesta* (as the Spaniard calls it) or afternoon sleep. **1667** Earl Bristol *Elvira* I. in Dodsley *O. Pl.* (1780) XII. 147 What, sister, at your Siesta already? if so, You must have patience to be wak'd out of it. **1788** Burke *Corr.* (1844) III. 76 We have just risen from our *siesta*, and have no news. **1816** Keatinge *Trav.* (1817) I. 156 Without his siesta and segar,.. he would think his lot a hard one in this world. **1840** R. H. Dana *Bef. Mast* xix, After dinner we usually took a short siesta, to make up for our early rising. **1882** Miss Braddon *Mt. Royal* I. viii. 243, I must go and get my siesta, or I shall be as stupid as an owl all the evening. **1946** D. C. Peattie *Road of Naturalist* i. 19 Its crepuscular flowers are large as those of a wild rose when they open.. great mothlike petals languidly expanding, as if still oppressed with the long siesta of the day. **1947** J. Stevenson-Hamilton *Wild Life S. Afr.* iii. 27 The rhinoceros, startled suddenly from his midday siesta, rushes blindly at the intruder.

*fig.* **1856** R. A. Vaughan *Mystics* (1860) II. 29 Most men prefer a sleeping conscience to a tender one; and for such the Romish Church offers a perpetual siesta. **1884** Sime *To & Fro* 8 On duty which knows no siesta.

**b.** Without article.

**1834** Marryat *P. Simple* (1863) 123, I called with my handkerchief full of segars for the father, but he was at siesta, as they called it. **1869** Mrs. S. Hawthorne *Notes Eng. & Italy* III. ii. 322 It was the hour of siesta, and the monks were.. fast asleep. **1892** E. Reeves *Homeward Bound* 318 Deep recesses on either side for cushioned luxurious siesta. **1899** C. J. C. Hyne *Further Adventures Capt. Kettle* ii. 30 'Right,' said Kettle. 'I'll siesta too.' **1956** G. Durrell *My Family & Other Animals* xv. 201 The rest of the family, finding they could not siesta with the argument going on, assembled to find out the trouble. **1976** L. Deighton *Twinkle, twinkle Little Spy* i. 7 The staff have noisy arguments about who should siesta on the cold stone floor.

**Siesta**[2] (sɪ'ɛstə). *Chess.* The name of a town in Italy, used *attrib.* in ***Siesta gambit, variation***, a continuation of the Ruy Lopez opening popularized in a tournament held there (see quot. 1965).

**1935** Smith & Dash tr. *Znosko-Borovsky's How to play Chess Openings* 54 This line is known as the Siesta Gambit and has been much played in recent years. **1948** G. Abrahams *Teach yourself Chess* III. v. 195 P to $KB_4$ gives the Siesta variation which is playable. **1965** *Listener* 29 Apr. 651/3, 1 P-$K_4$ P-$K_4$ 2 N-$KB_3$ N-$QB_3$ 3 B-$N_5$ P-$QR_3$ 4 B-$R_4$ P-$Q_3$ 5 P-$B_3$ P-$B_4$: the so-called 'Siesta' variation, which, despite its name, leads to lively play and provides an early counter to White's positional grip on the centre.

†**siester**, Anglicized form of sistrum. *Obs.*

**1595** Duncan *App. Etym.* (E.D.S.), *Plectron*, a fiddle-stick, or a siester pen.

**si'estose**, *a.* *rare*$^{-1}$. [f. siesta.] Reposeful, indolent.

**1845** Ford *Handbk. Spain* VII. 516 They prefer to enjoy a siestose negation not merely of comforts but of necessaries rather than to labour.

**sieth**, variant of sithe *v.*, to strain.

**siethe**, obs. form of scythe.

**siethes**, variant of sithes, chives.

‖**sieur**[1] (sjø(r)). Now *arch.* [Fr.: cf. monsieur.] Used as a courtesy title or form of address.

**1772** in D. Arundell *Sadler's Wells* (1965) iii. 28 Principal dancers. Sieur Daiguevill*e* and his pupils. **1893** S. Weyman *Gentleman of France* I. iii. 66 You have not told me yet, sieur, where we stay to-night. **1901** G. B. Shaw *Admirable Bashville* III. 124 Bumpkin Fitz Algernon de Courcy Cashel Byron, sieur of Park Lane and overlord of Dorset. **1981** P. Vansittart *Death of Robin Hood* II. ii. 40 John's dwarf, Sieur Marc,.. now discarded winter as he might a cloak.

‖**sieur**[2] (sjœ:(r)). *S. Afr.* [ad. Afrikaans *seur*, f. Du. *sinjeur* lord, master: ultimately related and assimilated to prec.] A respectful form of address or reference to a superior; master, 'sir'.

**1812** A. Plumptre tr. *Lichtenstein's Trav. S. Afr.* I. 118 The former [*sc.* the Hottentots] only address their master by the title of *Baas* (Master), while the slaves address him as *Sieur* (lord). **1886** G. A. Farini *Through Kalahari Desert* 312 You ought not to have stayed here last night; the klein Sieur was very anxious. **1942** 'B. Knight' *Sun climbs Slowly* xviii. 154 'Missis, *Sieur*,' she shrilled excitedly. 'The veld is on fire.' **1968** K. McMagh *Dinner of Herbs* 56 The maid who took the early morning coffee reported this to the sieur.

**sieva** ('si:və). [Origin unknown.] A kidney bean belonging to an American variety of *Phaseolus lunatus*, or its edible seed.

**1888** G. D. Merrill *Hist. Coös County* v. 42 The Indians had.. a kind of bean called now 'seiva [*sic*] bean'. **1949** *Nat. Geogr. Mag.* Aug. 159/1 The lima beans grown by the various Indian tribes.. varied from the present small types used by the Hopi Indians in the Southwest to the Sieva type found in the East. **1972** Y. Lovelock *Veg. Bk.* I. 55 The scimitar-podded kidney bean.., also known as Hibbert, sieva or sugar bean, grows wild in tropical America and is also cultivated.

**sieve** (sɪv), *sb.* Forms: α. 1 sibi, 1–2 sife, 1–2, 5–6 **syfe (syfa)**, 4 **syfue**, 4, 6 **syffe**, 5 **syff**, 6–7 **siff**; 4 **seyf**, 5 **seyfe, sefe**, 6 **seiffe**. β. 4–7 **sive (siue)**, 6 **cive**; 4–6 **syve (syue)**, **cyve (cyue)**, 6 **scyve**. γ. 4–6 **seve (seue**, 5 **sewe, ceve)**, 6 **seeue, ceeue**, 7 **seeve**, 6–7 **seave**. δ. 7 **seive, scieve**, 6– **sieve**. [OE. *sife*, = MDu. *seve* (Du. *zeef*), MLG. *seve* (LG. *seve*, *sefe*, etc.), OHG. *sib*, *sip* (G. *sieb*, also dial. *sib*, *sip*, *siff*, etc.). The stem, which may be ultimately related to that of sye, to strain, is the base of sift *v.*]

**1. a.** A utensil consisting of a circular frame with a finely meshed or perforated bottom, used to separate the coarser from the finer particles of any loose material, or as a strainer for liquids.

In agricultural and similar work a *sieve* is usually distinguished from a *riddle* by having finer meshes.

α. *c* **725** *Corpus Gloss.* C 873 *Crebrum*, sibi. **9..** *Ags. Gloss.* in Wr.-Wülcker 215 *Crebrum*, *cribellum*, sife. *c* **1000** *Sax. Leechd.* II. 94 Asift þurh sife, meng wiþ hunige. **1396–7** *Durh. Acc. Rolls* (Surtees) 214, 1 syffe. *c* **1430** *Two Cookery-bks.* 20 Take Appelys an sethe hem, an Serge hem þorwe a Sefe in-to a potte. **1483** *Cath. Angl.* 339/1 A Syfe, *crybrum*. **1508** *Acc. Ld. High Treas. Scot.* IV. 110 For ane siff to sift gunpowdir, ij s. **1530** Palsgr. 270/1 Syfe to cyfte corne in, *crible*. **1595** Duncan *App. Etym.* (E.D.S.), *Excerniculum*, a sife or boulteclaith.

β. *c* **1320** *Sir Tristr.* 1946 A siue he fond tite, And bond vnder his fete. *c* **1340** *Nominale* (Skeat) 529 Fan, berelep, and syue. **1382** Wyclif *Eccl.* xxvii. 5 As in the smyting of a cyue shal abide stille pouder. *c* **1440** *Promp. Parv.* 78/2 Cyve for corne clansynge, *cribrum*, *cribellum*. Cyve, for mele, *furfuraculum*. **1530** Palsgr. 205 Cyve to syfte with, *crible*. **1577** B. Googe *Heresbach's Husb.* IV. (1586) 184 You must strain the waxe through a siue, or such like thing. **1642** Fuller *Holy & Prof. St.* II. xxi. 136 Here they had great plenty of rain, poured (not as in other places, as it were out of sives, but) as out of spouts. **1687** A. Lovell tr. *Thevenot's Trav.* I. 95 The dust.. sticks to the faces of those that handle the Sive.

γ. *c* **1340** *Nominale* (Skeat) 138 W[oman] weruth seue and riddell. **1357–8** *Ely Sacr. Rolls* II. 181 In ij seves et j redel emptis. *c* **1400** *Lanfranc's Cirurg.* 219 Boile it longe in watir, & þanne cole it þoruȝ a seue. *c* **1430** *Two Cookery-bks.* 32 Take a seve or a whete-rydoun. **1577** *Wills & Inv. N.C.* (Surtees, 1835) 422 Five ryddells and seaves to wynnowe corne, x$^{d}$. **1594** Plat *Jewell-ho.* II. 33 If you would keep your rose cakes without worms, you must.. set them in ceeues. *c* **1620** Boyd *Zion's Flowers* (1855) 136 Our memory is like a seave. **1683** Pettus *Fleta Min.* I. 19 Take Ashes burnt from any light Wood.. and put them into a Seeve.

δ. *a* **1591** H. Smith *Serm.* (1592) 665 Like sieues which hold water no longer than they are in the Riuer. **1703** Moxon *Mech. Exerc.* 251 Sieves.. to sift the Lime and Sand withal. **1769** Mrs. Raffald *Eng. Housekpr.* (1778) 197 When it boils strain it through a fine sieve. **1846** Greener *Sci. Gunnery* 30 The discs.. striking against the sides of the sieves, force it through the apertures. **1869** Phillips *Vesuv.* iv. 113 The upper part of the cone was perforated like a sieve.

**b.** In phrases denoting something that cannot be done, or that is waste of labour.

**1390** Gower *Conf.* I. 294 For as a Sive kepeth Ale, Riht so can Cheste kepe a tale. **1477** Norton *Ord. Alch.* I. in Ashm. (1652) 17 As he that fetcheth Water in a Sive. **1515** Barclay *Egloges* I. (1570) A vj/1 Such thinges.. To thee be as sure as water in a siue. **1589** Greene *Menaphon* (Arb.) 48 Suppose she were a Vestall,.. shee might carrie water with Amulia in a siue. **1616** Hieron *Wks.* I. 586 That which is said in the prouerb, where one doth milke a goate, another holds vnder a siue. **1686** Horneck *Crucif. Jesus* xxii. 741 That's no better, than taking up water in a sieve, which runs out as fast as it is put in. **1813** Picken *Poems* II. 135 That wad been milkin' his cow in a sieve.

**c.** *fig.* Of things.

*c* **1611** Chapman *Iliad* V. 511 Then stirring th' idle siue of newe, did all their forces aske. **1643** Caryl *Sacr. Cov.* 4 The Articles passe them through a finer Sieve. **1647** May *Hist. Parl.* I. vii. 73 Those inventions were but sives, made of purpose to winnow the best men. **1889** Gretton *Memory's Harkback* 218 All that, as they thought, was past and gone with their ordination..; they had passed through the Bishop's sieve. **1896** *Allbutt's Syst. Med.* I. 927 The infection was, so to speak, caught on the sieve—that is to say, the infected ships gave rise to cases of plague within the quarantine station.

**d.** *fig.* Of persons; *esp.* one who cannot keep a secret.

**1601** Shaks. *All's Well* I. iii. 208 Yet in this captious, and intenible Siue I still poure in the waters of my loue. **1646** Quarles *Sheph. Oracles* vi, Here's none but wee, I am no Sive? I prithee, Swain, be free. **1668** Dryden *Even. Love* I. i, As you are a waiting-woman; as you are the sieve of all your lady's secrets, tell it me. **1704** Swift *T. Tub* vii, Those judicious Collectors.., by some called the Sieves and Boulters of Learning. **1811** Byron *Hints fr. Hor.* 734 *note*, The sieve of a patron let it out.

**2. a.** As used by witches for sailing in.

*a* **1585** Montgomerie *Flyting* 461 Nicneuen.. to teach it gart take it To saill sure in a seiffe, but compass or cart. **1605** Shaks. *Macb.* I. iii. 8 But in a Syue Ile thither sayle. *a* **1613** Overbury *A Wife*, etc. (1638) 158 Like a witch in a scive. **1820** Keats *Eve St. Agnes* XIV, Thou must hold water in a witch's sieve. **1830** Scott *Demonol.* ix. 312 Another frolic they had, when, like the weird sisters in Macbeth, they embarked in sieves.

**b.** As used for purposes of divination. Commonly ***sieve and shears***. Cf. riddle *sb.*[2] 1 b.

**1596** Lodge *Wits Miserie* 18 If he loose any thing, he hath readie a siue and a key. **1602** in Goudie *Diary J. Mill* 185 To quite hir selff.. for the turning of ane siff and riddill for ane pair scheiris. *a* **1635** Randolph *Jealous Lovers* I. x, A man cannot find out their Meaning without the 'Sieve and Sheers'. **1692** E. Walker tr. *Epictetus' Mor.* xxxviii, Questions which by Sieve and Sheers are try'd. **1843** Lytton *Last Bar.* I. v, Thinkest thou.. I can read thee all riddles without my sieve and my shears?

**3.** Used as a measure, or for holding anything. Also, a kind of basket used chiefly for market produce.

*a* **1440** *Found. St. Bartholomew's* (E.E.T.S.) 26 Sche answerd that she hadde but oonly .vii. Ceves ful of malte. **1464** *Mann. & Househ. Exp.* (Roxb.) 272 Payd for di. a tymbre and iij. scyvys of letuse, iiij. s. **1556** *Richmond Wills* (Surtees) 92 Item xx mettes of barle sawne oppon the ground... Item xxvj seves of ottes sowin. **1636** Davenant *Wits* I. i, Apple-Wives That wrangle for a Sieve. **1793** Steevens *Notes Shaks. Tr. & Cr.* II. ii, Sieves and half-sieves are baskets to be met with in every quarter of Covent-garden market. **1805** R. W. Dickson *Pract. Agric.* II. 587 In other parts the early gatherings are.. sent to the markets in half-bushel sieves. **1887** Parish & Shaw *Kentish Gloss.* 149 In West Kent, sieve and half-sieve are equivalent to bushel and half-bushel.

**4.** In calico-printing: (see quots.).

**1839** Ure *Dict. Arts* 215 The colouring matter.. is spread .. upon fine woollen cloth, stretched in a frame over the wax cloth head of a wooden drum or sieve. **1879** *Cassell's Techn. Educ.* I. 197/2 The mordant.. is applied to the block by pressing the latter upon what is termed a 'sieve' (a box covered with woollen cloth).

**5.** *Math.* **a.** In full ***sieve of Eratosthenes*** [tr. Gr. κόσκινον Ἐρατοσθένους, f. the name of the Greek scientific writer of the 3rd c. B.C. who devised it]. A method of finding the prime numbers in a (usu. consecutive) list of numbers by deleting in turn all the multiples of all possible prime factors.

**1803** tr. *Bossut's Gen. Hist. Math.* 18 The famous sieve of Eratosthenes.. affords an easy and commodious method of finding prime numbers. **1857** *Proc. Ashmolean Soc.* III. 128 To Eratosthenes of Alexandria.. is attributed the invention of the method by which the primes may successively be determined in order of magnitude. It is termed.. 'the sieve of Eratosthenes'. **1945** E. T. Bell *Development of Math.* (ed. 2) iv. 89 Boethius reproduced the sieve of Eratosthenes and offered some amusing trifles on figurate numbers. **1966** Ogilvy & Anderson *Excurs. Number Theory* viii. 97 There is no known formula that turns out the prime numbers. Essentially the only way to find them is by the use of the 'sieve' devised by Eratosthenes.

**b.** A method of estimating or finding upper and lower limits for the number of primes, or of numbers not having factors within a stated set, that fall within a stated interval.

**1897** *Nature* 6 May 10/2 (*heading*) Sieve for primes. **1952** *Proc. Internat. Congr. Mathematicians* I. 286 Ever since Viggo Brun introduced his ingenious sieve-method, it has been a very important tool in connection with problems in the theory of primes. **1972** M. N. Huxley (*title*) The distribution of prime numbers: large sieves and zero-density theorems.

**6.** *attrib.* and *Comb.*, as ***sieve-basket, -bottom, -cloth, -drum, -fashion, -frame; sieve-witted*** adj.

**1598** Chapman *Seven Bks. Iliad* Ded. A 4 b, Our siue-witted censors, through whose braines all thinges exact and refinde, run to the earth in heapes. **1609** N. F. *Fruiterers Secrets* 4 They poure them out gently into their siues, or broad baskets made siue-fashion. **1839** Ure *Dict. Arts* 215 The inverted sieve drum should fit the paste tub pretty closely. *Ibid.* 216 The printer seizes the block.. and daubs it twice.. upon the sieve cloth. **1844** H. Stephens *Bk. Farm* II. 332 The sieve-frame.. is 28 inches in length and 5 inches in depth. **1858** Simmonds *Dict. Trade, Sieve-bottoms*, attachments for the frame of a sieve made of horse-hair or wire, etc. **1893** K. Sanborn *S. California* 140 They.. placed acorns in a sieve basket.

**7. a.** Special combs.: †**sieve-alphabet** (see quot.); **sieve analysis**, a particle-size analysis of a powdered or granular material made by passing it through sieves of increasing fineness; †**sieve-bone** (see quot.); **sieve lackey**, a species of moth; **sieve map**, a map upon which the distribution of a number of features is depicted by means of transparent overlays; †**sieve prophet** (see 2 b); **sieve-raggings** (see Ragging *vbl. sb.*[3] 2); †**sieve-stone**, a species of tufa.

**1663** Marquis of Worcester *Cent. Inv.* Index p. iv, A *Sieve-alphabet [§34 To write.. by holes in the bottom of a Sieve]. **1928** C. C. Wiley *Princ. Highway Engin.* ii. 25 Gravel should be well graded from fine to coarse. This is determined by a *sieve analysis. The sieve analysis curve for a high-grade gravel should approximate a straight line. **1971** R. Hardbottle tr. *Grassmann's Physical Princ. Chem. Engin.* v. 302 Sieve analysis, in which the grains are passed in succession through sieves of various finenesses, gives directly a cumulative curve, in which.. the masses or weights of the different fractions are given. **1594** T. B. *La Primaud. Fr. Acad.* II. 123 A little bone in the top of the nose, which is pierced through like to a little sieue. Hereupon it is called by the Phisicions the *siue-bone. **1832** J. Rennie *Butterfl. & Moths* 46 The *Sieve Lackey (*Eulepia Cribrum*) appears in June. [**1938** E. G. R. Taylor in *Geogr. Jrnl.* XCII. 25 The last map.. is constructed on what I have termed the sieve method.] **1952** Monkhouse & Wilkinson *Maps & Diagrams* iv. 190 E. G. R. Taylor produced a map upon which all areas in Great Britain unsuitable for industrial location were indicated in solid black. These areas were determined by superimposing isopleths representing certain specific factors... This process was termed 'sieving out' and the resultant maps are sometimes referred to as '*sieve-maps'. **1965** *Listener* 27 May 774/2 When to these were added those areas of real natural beauty within the conurbation.. and areas of the highest agricultural value.. the result (which we called the regional sieve map) was an exceedingly complex jig-saw puzzle. **1638** Mayne *Lucian* (1664) 131 If but a *Sive-prophet appear among them,.. they presently flock together, and gape at him. **1681** Grew *Musæum* III. i. v. 305 The *Seive-Stone. *Lapis Cribriformis.*

**b.** In botanical terms having reference to sieve-like openings in the walls or ends of plant-cells, as **sieve-cell, disk, -pore, -tissue, -tube, -vessel**; also Sieve-plate 1.

**1875** Bennett & Dyer tr. *Sachs' Bot.* 23 The Sieve-structure which occurs in the sieve-cells of the fibro-vascular bundles of vascular plants. *Ibid.* 24 The opening of the sieve-pores has not yet begun. *Ibid.* 101 The latticed cells or sieve-tubes frequently have sieve- or latticed discs in their longitudinal walls. **1887** Bentley *Man. Bot.* (ed. 5) 55 What are commonly known as sieve-tubes or sieve-vessels.

**sieve**, obs. form of Seave, a rush.

**sieve** (sɪv), *v.* Also 5 cyue, 6 sy(e)ue, syve. [f. Sieve *sb.* Cf. MDu. and MLG. *seven, zeven* (LG. *seven, sefen*, etc.), MHG. *siben* (G. *sieben*), *siffen*.]

**1.** *trans.* To pass through a sieve; to sift or strain.

**1499** [see the *vbl. sb.*]. **1530** Palsgr. 719/2 You can never make so fyne floure whan you do but syve your meale, as you shall do whan you boulte it. **1552** Huloet, Bult, raunge, or syeue meale, *succerno*. **1824** Mactaggart *Gallovid. Encycl.* 442 Sieving milk through a syle. **1844** H. Stephens *Bk. Farm* III. 909 A strong brine of salt and boiling-water.. is made and sieved through a cloth. **1885** *Encycl. Brit.* XVIII. 225/2 The fibres of wood.. are then sieved according to fineness, collected, and pressed into pulp.

**b.** To take *out* by sifting. In quots. *fig.*

**1860** Gen. P. Thompson *Audi Alt.* cxxiii. III. 74 They will find no lack of reasons why they and their representatives should not be sieved out of parliament. **1885** *Eng. Mech.* 235 The blue or short wave-lengths of the spectrum are sieved out first.

**2. a.** To perforate with holes like a sieve.

**1853** *Whistle-Binkie* Ser. II. 29 Tak care o' your breeks that they dinna get sieved.

**b.** To bore in the manner of a sieve.

**1875** Lanier *Symphony* 32 We sieve mine-meshes under the hills.

**3.** *intr.* To pass as through a sieve.

**1863** H. Melville *Moby Dick* cxxv, Oh God! that man should be a thing for immortal souls to sieve through!

Hence **'sieving** *vbl. sb.*

**1499** *Promp. Parv.* (Pynson), Cyuynge or clensinge, *colatura*. **1592** Nashe *P. Penilesse* (ed. 2) 8 Greediness.. busies himselfe.. in syuing of Muckhills and shop dust, whereof he will boult a whole cartload to gaine a bowd Pinne. **1824** Landor *Imag. Conv.* Wks. 1853 I. 79/1 After this sieving, after this pounding and trituration of the coarser particles [etc.].

**sieved** (sɪvd), *ppl. a.* [f. Sieve *v.* + -ed[1].] Passed through a sieve.

**1949** *Nat. Geogr. Mag.* Aug. 172/2 [Kale and collards].. in a finely chopped or 'sieved' form as food for babies. **1971** *Nature* 30 Apr. 559/2 Sanidines were extracted by elutriation of crushed and sieved pumice breccia.

**'sieveful.** [See -ful 2.] The fill of a sieve. Also *fig.*

*a* **1440** *Found. St. Bartholomew's* (E.E.T.S.) 26 She mesurid one cevefull And yaue it to the mynystris. *a* **1658** Cleveland *Char. of Diurn. Maker* (1677) 102 A Sieveful of Ballads and Godly Books. **1693** Dryden *Let.* Wks. 1893 XVIII. 111 For feare the few damsins shou'd be all gone, desire her to buy me a sieve-full. **1725** *Fam. Dict.* s.v. *Hop Garden*, When it is thus fastned, cast in two or three Sieve-fulls of Hops. **1856** Morton *Cycl. Agric.* I. 193/2 A skilful workman takes a sieveful from the unfinished heap. **1895** Saintsbury *Corrected Impressions* x. 89 A very sieve-ful of holes.

**sieve-like**, *a.* [f. Sieve *sb.*] Resembling a sieve; perforated like a sieve.

**1591** Sylvester *Du Bartas* I. i. 369 Thence is't that Garden-pots, the mouth kept close, Let fall no liquor at their sive-like nose. **1639** W. Sclater *Worthy Commun.* 3 So sieve-like are our memories, that they doe.. let slip.. what should better be retained. *a* **1650** May *Old Couple* III, So dying aldermen Pour out at once upon their sieve-like heirs Whole gusts of envi'd wealth. **1766** *Compl. Farmer* s.v. *Glanders*, The os ethmoides, or sieve-like bone, through which the olfactory nerves pass. **1837** P. Keith *Bot. Lex.* 257 When the juice of the sugar-cane has been boiled down to a syrup, it is put to cool into sieve-like vessels. **1887** Bentley *Man. Bot.* (ed. 5) 56 The partition walls.. are.. only thickened in a sieve-like manner.

**'sieve-maker.** [Sieve *sb.*] One who makes sieves.

**14..** *Nom.* in Wr.-Wülcker 686 *Hic cribrarius*, syfmaker [*printed* fys-]. *c* **1470** *Promp. Parv.* (K.) 457/2 Seve makere, ..*cribrarius*. **1572** in *Essex Rev.* (1906) XV. 212 Hugh Humfrey, the syvemakers son. **1601**–*a* **1661** [see sievier]. **1723** *Lond. Gaz.* No. 6159/3 John Griffin,.. a Sieve-maker by Trade. **1858** Simmonds *Dict. Trade, Sieve-maker*, a manufacturer of screening machines and sieves. **1892** *Daily News* 9 Nov. 5/4 A peasant on foot and a sievemaker driving a single horse tarantass.

**sieve-plate.** [Sieve *sb.*]

**1.** *Bot.* A sieve-like plate on the wall of a plant-cell. (Cf. Sieve *sb.* 7 b.)

**1875** Bennett & Dyer tr. *Sachs' Bot.* 24 The sieve-plates do not at present show anything of the subsequent more complicated structure. **1882** Vines *ibid.* 89 In this condition the septum, perforated by a number of pores, is termed a *Sieve-plate*; it is usually broader than the diameter of the tube, which therefore appears dilated at.. the sieve-plates.

**2.** *Zool.* (See quot.)

**1888** Rolleston & Jackson *Anim. Life* 566 A calcareous plate placed at the base of the arm interradially, and called in the latter case a sieve-plate.

**3.** In paper-making, a plate through which pulp is strained.

**1891** in *Cent. Dict.*

**'siever.** Now *rare* or *Obs.* Also 5 cyver, 7 seaver. [f. Sieve *sb.*]

**1.** A sieve-maker.

*c* **1440** *Promp. Parv.* 78/2 Cyver, or maker of sevys.., *cribrarius*. **1616** *Mem. St. Giles, Durham* (Surtees) 46 Rec[d] of Rychard Robeson, Seaver. *c* **1800** in H. Speight *Nidderdale* (1894) 384 Sievers, fellmongers, tanners, weavers, bleachers.

**2.** A sifter.

**1835** Carrick *Laird of Logan* (1854) 189 Robin's associates were three of the 'Sievers' of Sessantilly, the rival mill to Goodie.

**Sievers** ('siːvəz, ‖'ziːfərs), the name of Eduard *Sievers* (1850–1932), German philologist, used *attrib.* of the rule formulated by him, (*Beitr. z. Gesch. d. deutschen Sprache u. Lit.* (1878) V. 129) that in Indo-European, (post-consonantal) unaccented *i* and *u* before a vowel were consonantal after a short syllable and vocalic after a long syllable; also, this rule as modified by later scholars, or as applied by them to particular early Indo-European languages.

F. Edgerton (*Language* X (1934) 235 f. and elsewhere) played an important part in developing and modifying the rule, which is now sometimes called 'Sievers-Edgerton's Law'.

**1934** *Language* X. 235 (*title*) Sievers's law and IE. weak-grade vocalism. **1939** E. Prokosch *Compar. Gmc. Gram.* 92 The difference in treatment according to the character of the preceding syllable.. may have been Indo-European; this view was first expressed by Sievers... It is frequently referred to as 'Sievers' Law'. **1953** *Jrnl. Eng. & Gmc. Philol.* LII. 149 The essential characteristic of the P[roto-]I[ndo-]E[uropean] resonants was their three-fold function as vowel, e.g. [i], consonant, [y], or vowel plus consonant [iy], as conditioned by the preceding phonemes; the description of this variation is generally known as Sievers' Law. It is most clearly apparent in our Vedic Sanskrit documents. **1959** A. Campbell *Old Eng. Gram.* 164 This interchange of *į* and *ij* is called Sievers' law. **1966** M. B. Emeneau in Birnbaum & Puhvel *Anc. Indo-Europ. Dialects* 126 While Sievers-Edgerton's law was in full working order, something other than *pūrva-* must have been the phonemic form. **1975** Lass & Anderson *Old Eng. Phonol.* 273 The earliest instance in Germanic.. of an important role being played by the long/short syllable dichotomy, is the set of phenomena associated with the *vokalischen Auslautsgesetz* ('law of vocalic finals'), now usually called 'Sievers's Law', or the 'Sievers-Edgerton Law'.

**Sievert** ('siːvət). The name of R. M. *Sievert*, 20th-c. Swedish radiologist, used to denote either of two units of dose of ionizing radiation. †**a.** ***Sievert unit*** (see quot. 1955). *Obs.* **b.** (Written *sievert*.) (See quot. 1977.)

**1945** C. W. Wilson *Radium Therapy* iii. 70 For the practical determination of the Sievert unit dose by this method, the measurement is made.. with a chamber having walls of a finite thickness. **1955** *Gloss. Terms Radiology* (*B.S.I.*) 19 *Sievert unit*, a unit of gamma-ray dose, being the dose of radiation delivered in one hour at a distance of 1 cm from a point source of 1 mg of radium element enclosed in platinum 0·5 mm thick. It is numerically equal to about 8·4 röntgens. **1977** *Ann. ICRP* I. III. 4/1 The special name for the unit of dose equivalent is the sievert (Sv): 1 Sv = 1 Jkg[−1] (= 100 rem). **1982** *Sci. Amer.* Feb. 34/2 The data come from fairly high doses of radiation (·5 sievert to two sieverts).

†**'sievier.** *Obs.* Forms: (see quots.). [f. Sieve *sb.* + -ier.] = Siever.

*c* **1440** *Promp. Parv.* 457/1 Syvyȝere, or maker of syvys (*K.* siveyer,.. *P.* syuyer), *cribrarius*. *c* **1460** *Ibid.* (Winch.) 84 Cyueȝere. **1601** F. Godwin *Bps. of Eng.* 529 The son of a poore man there, a Syueyer or Syve-maker by his occupation. *a* **1661** Fuller *Worthies* I. *Durham* (1662) 297 William Siveyer was born at Shinkley.., where his Father was a Siveyer or Sive-maker. [**1894** Wylie *Hist. Eng., Hen. IV*, II. 481 His father is said to have been a sievier or bolter-maker.]

†**sievy**, *a.* *Obs.*[−1] [f. Sieve *sb.* + -y.] Like a sieve, unable to retain.

**1724** tr. *Castelnau's Mem.* 47 When affairs of this kind come to be imparted to women, a sex so generally sievey that they can keep no secrets.

**siew, siex**, obs. forms of Sue *v.*, Six.

**sif**, var. Seif.

**sifaka** (sɪ'fækə). Also **sifac**. [Malagasy.] A small arboreal primate belonging to the genus *Propithecus* of the family Indriidæ, native to Madagascar and distinguished by whitish silky fur with darker patches on the head and limbs, a hairless black face, and a long tail.

**1845** *Encycl. Metrop.* XVI. 429/1 It [sc. *Cercopithecus Memæus* Cuv.] is a native of Cochin China and Madagascar, where it is called *Sifac*. **1901** W. Rice *Animals* 37 A smaller indri with a long tail is the sifaka, the native name of a pretty animal which.. goes about by day in bands of six or eight. **1930** *Times Educ. Suppl.* 1 Mar. (Home & Classroom Suppl.) p. ix/2 The monkey-lemurs, or sifakas, are purely arboreal. **1961** *Listener* 2 Nov. 709/1 A sifaka lemur seen in David Attenborough's 'Zoo Quest to Madagascar'. **1978** *Nature* 19 Oct. 587/1 White sifaka and ringtailed lemur populations have remained stable since 1963 in the privately protected 100-hectare reserve at Berenty.

**siff**, obs. form of Sieve *sb.*, Sift *v.*

**siff**, var. Syph.

**'siffilate**, *v.* *rare*[−1]. [irreg. f. F. *siffler*: see next.] *trans.* To whisper.

**1837** Marryat *Dog Fiend* ix, 'He's gone,' was siffilated above and below.

**siffle** ('sɪf(ə)l), *v.* Also 4–5 **syfle**, 5 **sifle**. [ad. F. *siffler*, †*sifler*:—L. *sīfilāre*, var. of *sībilāre*: see Sibilate *v.*] *intr.* To blow with a sibilant sound; to whistle, hiss.

**13..** *E.E. Allit. P.* C. 470 Syþen he.. sayez vnte Zeferus þat he syfle warme. **13..** *Gaw. & Gr. Knt.* 517 Quen Zeferus syflez hym-self on sedez & erbez. **1480** Caxton *Ovid's Met.* xv. viii, The gode in forme of a serpent.. syfled after his avenement. **1491** —— *Vitas Patr.* (W. de W. 1495) I. viii. 13 b/1 Incontynent that the dragon aperceyued hym he came to hym siflinge.

**1862** D. Richmond *Through Life & For Life* xviii. 231 The damp, raw morning air, which siffled in from the open door. **1876** Mrs. Whitney *Sights & Ins.* xxv, The air siffled gently through the low grass.

Hence **'siffling** *vbl. sb.* and *ppl. a.* Also **'siffle** *sb.*, a sibilant râle (*Cent. Dict.* 1891).

**1603** Holland *Plutarch's Mor.* 1221 Neither doe ordinary hounds understand the signes that huntsmen use, nor every horse the siffling and chirring of the escuirry. **1866** *Cornh. Mag.* Mar. 313 What joy when Angus drew a long siffling breath.

†**'sifflement.** *Obs.*[−1] [a. F. *sifflement*, f. *siffler*: see prec.] A whistling noise.

**1607** ? Brewer *Lingua* I. i, Like to the winged chanters of the wood, Uttering nought else but idle sifflements, Tunes without sense, words inarticulate.

**siffleur** (siflœr). Also †*erron. pl.* **siffleux**. [Fr., lit. a whistler.] **1.** *Canad.* One of several animals that make a whistling noise, esp. the hoary marmot, *Marmota caligata*, or its flesh used as food. Cf. Whistler 2 b.

**1703** tr. *La Hontan's New Voy. N. Amer.* I. 62 Certain little Beasts, call'd Siffleurs, or Whistlers. **1808** S. Fraser *Jrnl.* 18 June (1960) 86 They gave us a *siffleur* (marmot) which is the first fresh meat we tasted since our departure. 1858 J. PALLISER *Jrnl.* 22 Aug. in *Palliser Papers* (1968) 274 The only animal which we have seen is the siffleur, whose shrill whistle we heard for the first time close to our encampment. 1898 F. RUSSELL *Expl. Far North* 249 Ground squirrels or 'siffleux' as they are known to the Company's people, are a characteristic feature of the barren portions of Arctic America. 1949 *Canad. Alpine Jrnl.* May 32 They dined on 'delicious siffleur' which tasted on the tongue like 'very delicate mutton or the fat of sucking pig'. 1968 R. M. PATTERSON *Finlay's River* 209 La Guarde shot a couple of siffleurs—marmots or whistlers—lean, miserable things at that season.

2. (with fem. *-euse*). One who entertains professionally by whistling.

1827 T. DIBDIN *Reminiscences* II. vi. 122 The following is from a celebrated *siffleur*: .. 'I Take the Liberty of Inclosing a few Lines, to Inform you that I am a Beautyfull Whistler If you Please to Give Me one Trial on the Stage.' 1912 *Music Hall & Theatre Review* 11 Jan. 31/1 'Who is He', a clever siffleur, charms everyone with his mimicry of birds. 1981 *Times* 26 Feb. 13/1 Melba's friend Adeline Murrelli was not a singer but that almost forgotten artist, a siffleuse, or whistler.

**sift**, *sb. rare.* [In sense 1 = MDu. *sifte, zifte* (Du. *zift*), also MDu. and MLG. *sichte*. In other senses f. SIFT *v.*]

†1. A sieve. *Obs.*

1499 *Promp. Parv.* (Pynson), Cyue or cifte, *cribrum, cribellum.* 1648 HEXHAM II. s.v. *Zijgen*, To Runne through a Sift, or a Strainer.

2. The act of sifting (in quot. *fig.*); the fact of falling as from a sieve.

1814 MME. D'ARBLAY *Wanderer* I. 60, I don't say this by way of a sift. 1866 B. TAYLOR *Poet's Jrnl.* Dec., The rustling sift of falling snow.

3. 'Something that falls or passes as if from the meshes of a sieve; sifting or sifted material' (*Cent. Dict.* 1891).

1876 G. M. HOPKINS *Wr. Deutschland* iv, in *Poems* (1967) 52, I am soft sift In an hourglass. 1962 M. E. MURIE *Far North* II. ix. 192 The little sift of snow on the ice was marked only by tracks of ox.

**sift** (sɪft), *v.* Forms: 1 siftan, 4 siften (5 -yn), 6–7 sifte (6 siffte), 4– sift (7 siff); 1 syftan, 4–6 syfte, 5 cyftyn, 6 cyfte; 1 seftan, 5, 7 seft; also *pa. pple.* 5 syfte, 6 sefte. [OE. *siftan, syftan*, = MDu. *siften, suften* (Du. *ziften*), MLG. *siften*; also MDu. and MLG. (and hence G.) *sichten*, Du. and WFlem. *zichten*. The stem is that of SIEVE *sb.*]

1. *trans.* To pass (something) through a sieve, in order to separate the coarse from the fine particles, or to strain.

*c* 725 *Corpus Gloss.* C 873 *Crebrat*, siftið. *c* 888 K. ÆLFRED *Boeth.* xxxiv. §11 Swa swa mon meolo seft [*v.r.* sift]; ðæt meolo ðurȝcrypð ælc ðyrel. *c* 1000 ÆLFRIC *Gram.* (Z.) 137 *Cribro*, ic syfte. *c* 1386 CHAUCER *Can. Yeom. T.* 388 Al this mullok in a sive y-throwe, And sifted, and y-piked many a throwe. 1398 TREVISA *Barth. De P.R.* XVII. lxvii. (Tollem. MS.), Mele is grounde at mylle, and sefted with a seue. *c* 1415 *Rec. St. Mary at Hill* (1905) p. xcvi, A dyssh full of aysshes fayre syfte. *c* 1430 *Two Cookery Bks.* 38 þan bray hem smal y-now; & þerow a crees bunte syfte hem. *c* 1440 *Promp. Parv.* 77/1 Cyftyn, *cribro.* 1530 PALSGR. 718/2, I wyll nat syft my meale thorowe this syve, it is to course. 1555 EDEN *Decades* IV. (Arb.) 82 The myners .. in dyuers places syfted the same on the drye lande. 1603 in Gage *Hist. & Antiq. Hengrave* (1822) 23 Item, one fier sholve made like a grate to seft the seacole wth. 1687 A. LOVELL tr. *Thevenot's Trav.* II. 85 They sweep a place very clean to sift the lime in, and when it is sifted they make it up in a heap. 1709 STEELE *Tatler* No. 69 ¶11 Two of the Fair Sex, who are usually employed in sifting Cinders. 1769 MRS. RAFFALD *Eng. Housekpr.* (1778) 171 Pound and sift three quarters of a pound of loaf sugar. 1832 G. R. PORTER *Porcelain & Glass* 303 The same powdered whiting .. may be used again .. upon being ground and sifted. 1865 DICKENS *Mut. Fr.* I. viii, A country contract which was to be sifted before carted.

b. In *fig.* or *transf.* uses.

1535 COVERDALE *Amos* ix. 9 Though I siffte yᵉ house of Israel amonge all nacions. 1589 ? LYLY *Pappe w. Hatchet* L.'s Wks. 1902 III. 408 They haue sifted the holie Bible, and left vs nothing as they say, but branne. 1611 BIBLE *Isaiah* xxx. 28 To sift the nations with the sieue of vanitie. 1653 H. COGAN tr. *Pinto's Trav.* iv. 8 The things of God .. lose their value and force, when they are sifted through so many hands. 1822 W. TENNANT *Thane of Fife* I. lxxv, When the North [wind] should burst his bleak confines, And in his icy boulter sift the snow. 1871 TYNDALL *Fragm. Sci.* (1879) I. iv. 129 The solar light is sifted by the landscape.

2. *fig.* a. To make trial of (a person).

In early quots. after Luke xxii. 31.

*a* 1300 *Cursor M.* 15523 He wil þe sift nu if he mai, as man dos corn or bran. 1535 COVERDALE *Luke* xxii. 31 Satan hath desyred after you, that he might siffte you euen as wheate. *c* 1590 MARLOWE *Faustus* xiii, Sathan begins to sift me with his pride. 1624 T. SCOTT *Vox Dei* 76 Is it not a great and dangerous temptation, (o all yee that know what temptation is, what it is to be siffed, what it is to resist) that young men meet in the world? 1642 FULLER *Holy & Prof. St.* IV. xv. 315 For these reasons Lady Elizabeth was closely kept and narrowly sifted all her Sisters reigne. 1718 *Free-thinker* No. 74. 140 The more .. the Sincere Man .. is sifted, the more he is intrusted.

b. To subject (one) to close questioning.

*a* 1566 R. EDWARDS *Damon & Pithias* (E.E.D.S.) 47 The knave beginneth to sift me. 1588 GREENE *Pandosto* (1843) 37 He therefore began to sifte her more narrowly on this manner. 1617 MORYSON *Itin.* III. 30 Being curiously sifted by the guard at the City-gate, and being asked many questions. 1694 GIBSON in *Lett. Lit. Men* (Camden) 235 For fear it should be some you have employ'd, I have got one to sift him. 1726 SWIFT *Gulliver* II. vi, He multiplied his Questions, and sifted me thoroughly upon every Part of this Head. 1756 H. WALPOLE *Let. to Mann* 16 May, I sifted Dr. Pringle himself, but he would not give me a positive answer. 1818 SCOTT *Hrt. Midl.* xvii, You must speak with this wench, .. you must sift her a wee bit. 1861 READE *Cloister & H.* lv, Blind Hans's boy .. was sifted narrowly by my master, and stammered and faltered.

3. *fig.* To examine closely into, to scrutinize narrowly, so as to find out the truth.

1573 G. HARVEY *Letter-bk.* (Camden) 11 Thes men .. whos opinions I have desirid to be thurrouly siftid. 1592 TIMME *Ten Eng. Lepers* L 4, Let no man take upon him to scan and sift Gods workes. 1646 SIR T. BROWNE *Pseud. Ep.* I. viii. (1686) 23 We may explore and sift their verities. 1735 BERKELEY *Free-think. in Mathemat.* §15 Others who are not afraid to sift the principles of human science. 1774 J. BRYANT *Mythol.* II. 189, I have endeavoured with great pains to sift the history to the bottom. 1821 SCOTT *Kenilw.* xxxiv, We will sift this matter to the uttermost. 1849 ROBERTSON *Serm.* Ser. I. xxi. (1866) 350 It is .. very hard to sift a slander. 1884 L. J. JENNINGS *Croker Papers* I. i. 14 The art with which he sifted the evidence of the witnesses.

b. Similarly with *out.*

1577 HANMER *Anc. Eccl. Hist.* (1619) 85 When as Tatianus promised to sift out the darke speeches and hidden mysteries of Holy Scripture. 1594 T. B. *La Primaud. Fr. Acad.* II. 578 This word .. ought to teach us not to sift out the life of our soveraigne prince. 1642 FULLER *Holy & Prof. St.* IV. vii. 272 If the cause be difficult, his diligence is the greater to sift it out. 1662 J. DAVIES tr. *Olearius' Voy. Amb.* 70 They were lodg'd in my house for some dayes, which I spent in sifting out their humour and manner of life. 1737 WHISTON *Josephus, Hist.* II. ii. §2 He tried to sift out the accounts of the money. 1827 POLLOK *Course T.* I, Severely sifting out The whole idea.

†c. To search; to try. *Obs.*

1611 MIDDLETON & DEKKER *Roaring Girl* D.'s Wks. 1874 IV. 148, I will sift all the tauernes ith citty, .. Ile find her out. 1627 E. F. *Hist. Edw. II* (1680) 18 They sift each way might break this fond inchantment.

4. To separate, to take or get *out*, by the use of a sieve. Also *transf.* and in fig. contexts.

1428 *Eng. Misc.* (Surtees) 6 He syfted oute of yt half a bushell of plaster and lyme. 1502 ARNOLDE *Chron.* (1811) 87 The marchauntis straungers nowe use .. to sarse, syfte & trye out the best greyne. 1554–9 *Songs & Ball., Phil. & Mary* (Roxb.) 4 And eke the fyne flowr from the bran nerly syfft. 1602 *Narcissus* (1893) App. I. 7, I have sifted out .. the flower of my fancye. 1631 GOUGE *God's Arrows* I. §15. 21 Yet can the Lord .. as a few precious jewels in .. a great heap of rubbish sift them out. 1758 REID tr. *Macquer's Chym.* I. 262 Having sifted out and thrown away all the finest particles. 1843 CARLYLE *Past & Pr.* I. v. 39 That it will be got sifted, like wheat out of chaff, from the Twenty-seven Million British subjects. 1872 W. K. CLIFFORD *Lect.* (1879) I. 176 The lightest gas comes out quickest, and is as it were sifted from the other.

*refl.* 1874 L. STEPHEN *Hours Libr.* (1892) I. iii. 109 In Pope .. the grain has sifted itself from the chaff.

b. *fig.* To find *out*, get to know, by a process of elimination or close inquiry.

1586 A. DAY *Eng. Secretary* II. 87 When by interrogation we sift out any thing. 1651 HOBBES *Leviath.* III. xxxii. 195 To labour in sifting out a Philosophicall truth. 1726 *Adv. Capt. R. Boyle* (1768) 240, I endeavour'd to sift the Secret from him. 1805 G. ELLIS *Let.* in Lockhart *Scott* (1837) II. ii. 75, I should think Ritson himself .. would be puzzled to sift out a single additional anecdote of the poet's life. 1833 T. HOOK *Parson's Dau.* II. vii, Then, perhaps, you may sift out some farther particulars. 1851 HELPS *Comp. Solit.* x. (1874) 170 It will be investigated, and what is true in it be sifted out.

5. To clear or clean *from* impurities, etc., by means of a sieve; also *fig.*, to clean (one) *out of* money.

1591 GREENE *Conny Catch.* II. Wks. (Grosart) X. 95 He .. little suspected that his Countreyman the Setter had sifted him out of his money. *c* 1632 DRUMM. OF HAWTH. *Elegy Gustavus Adolphus*, You are at best but honourable Earth; .. how e're sifted from that courser Bran Which doth compound, and knead the common Man. 1660 SHARROCK *Vegetables* 17 Sift it from stones and rubbish.

6. a. To cover *over*, by letting something fall through a sieve.

1563 HYLL *Arte Garden.* (1593) 14 The which allies and walkes you shall sift ouer with the finest sand.

b. To let fall through, scatter from or by means of, a sieve. Also *fig.*

1664 EVELYN *Kal. Hort.* (1729) 204 If this [soil] be too stiff, sift a little Lime discreetly with it. 1674 FLAVEL *Husb. Spiritualized* (ed. 2) 264 The finest and richest mould must be sifted about the roots. 1747–96 MRS. GLASSE *Cookery* xx. 316 You must sift some fine sugar upon your cake when it goes into the oven. 1772 T. SIMPSON *Vermin-Killer* 26 Cover it lightly over with earth, .. sift it over the trap. 1821 CLARE *Vill. Minstr.* I. 85 Along the floor some sand I'll sift. 1855 DELAMER *Kitchen Garden* (1861) 37 After sowing, .. sift over the top a thin layer of cinder-ashes or lime-rubbish. 1869 B. HARTE *Luck Roaring Camp* 31 Again from leaden skies the snow-flakes were sifted over the land.

7. *intr.* To use a sieve; to do sifting. Chiefly *fig.*, esp. to pry *into*, make inquiry.

1535 COVERDALE *Amos* ix. 9 Like as they vse to sifte in a syue. 1590 GREENE *Never too Late* Wks. (Grosart) VIII. 153, I hope this proffer is but a tryall .. to sift at my secret intent. *a* 1625 FLETCHER *Noble Gent.* v. iii, Although he puts his nobles in disguise .. to sift into my words. 1641 MILTON *Animadv.* Wks. 1851 III. 205 You sifted not so clean before, but you shuffle as foulely now. 1699 BENTLEY *Phal.* 287, I will not sift into them too minutely. 1779 MME. D'ARBLAY *Let.* Dec., He has desired me to sift for what room you have, and to sound as to convenience. 1874 *Slang Dict.* 290 *Sift*, to embezzle small coins, those which might pass through a sieve—as threepennies and fourpennies—and which are, therefore, not likely to be missed.

8. To pass or fall as through a sieve.

1599 A. M. tr. *Gabelhouer's Bk. Physicke* 2/2 Madefye it with Rosewater least that it fal on a heap and sift throughe. 1855 LONGF. *Hiaw.* ii. 137 He it was who sent the snow-flakes Sifting, hissing through the forest. 1867 AUGUSTA WILSON *Vashti* xxxiv, Golden leaves were sifting down on the marble floor. 1893 *Scribner's Mag.* Sept. 305/1 The April sunshine sifts in through an open window.

Hence **'siftage**, sifted matter. *rare*⁻¹.

1881 BLACKMORE *Christowell* vii, At this he worked hard, .. pulling asunder the fibrous clods, but not reducing them to siftage.

**sifted** ('sɪftɪd), *ppl. a.* [f. SIFT *v.*] That has been passed through a sieve.

1485 *Nottingham Rec.* III. 243, vij stryke of syfted lyme. 1563 HYLL *Arte Garden.* (1593) 154 Put fine sifted earth, either into an old basket, or deepe earthen pan. 1605 WILLET *Hexapla Gen.* 353 The plowed, tilled, or sifted feilds. 1707 MORTIMER *Husb.* (1721) I. 298 A Composition made of slacked sifted Lime and Linseed Oil. 1819 SHELLEY *Peter Bell* VII. viii. 3 A genteel drive up to his door, With sifted gravel neatly laid. 1888 RUTLEY *Rock-Forming Min.* 8 A sifted sample .. of such fineness that each particle consists of one mineral species only.

*fig.* 1589 NASHE *Martin Marprelate* Wks. (Grosart) I. 95 The sifted Greeke witte of Father Augustine. 1878 *Masque Poets* 75 The sifted silver of the night Rained down a strange delight.

**sifter** ('sɪftə(r)). [f. as prec. + -ER¹.]

1. One who sifts, in lit. or fig. senses.

1579 LYLY *Euphues* Epist. Dedicatory, Though the stile nothing delight the dayntie eare of the curious sifter. 1587 GOLDING *De Mornay* xxxiv. (1592) 547 Some searchers and sifters of words. 1611 COTGR., *Cribleur*, a sifter. 1720 T. BOSTON *Fourfold State* (1797) 311 Such is the exactness of the sieve and care of the sifter. 1752 FIELDING *Covent Gard. Jrnl.* No. 23, They elude the enquiries of the most diligent sifters of antiquity. 1851 MAYHEW *Lond. Lab.* II. 172/2 A medium-sized dust-yard will employ .. six sifters. 1871 R. B. VAUGHAN *S. Thomas of Aquin* II. 646 He did not take for granted like the Sophist... He was a winnower and a sifter.

b. *Ornith.* (See quot.)

1872 DARWIN *Orig. Species* (ed. 6) vii. 183 Ducks .. subsist by sifting the mud and water; and the family has sometimes been called *Criblatores*, or sifters.

2. A utensil or apparatus for sifting; a sieve; also *dial.*, a fire-shovel, kitchen shovel.

1611 COTGR., *Crible*, a siue, or sifter; raunging siue. 1840 *Penny Cycl.* XVII. 209/1 The pulp is first made to flow from the vat upon a wire frame, or sifter. 1875 KNIGHT *Dict. Mech.* 2175/2 Sifters are used for sifting ashes from cinders; flour from lumps, etc. 1881 *Porcelain Wks., Worcester* 7 The number of pumps, sifters, and presses which are employed.

**'sifting**, *vbl. sb.* [f. as prec. + -ING¹.]

1. The action of the verb, in various senses.

*c* 1440 *Promp. Parv.* 77/1 Cyftynge, *cribracio.* *c* 1460 *Ibid.* (Winch.) 410 Syftynge [*P.* siffinge] or clensynge, *collacio, collatura.* 1473 *Rental Bk. Cupar-Angus* (1879) I. 171 Tha sal do thar diligens .. with wedyng, renouyng and syftyng of seid. 1555 EDEN *Decades* (Arb.) 212 They moue them rownde aboute after the maner of syftynge. 1579 FULKE *Heskins' Parl.* 222 He scoffeth .. at our spirituall sifting of the sacrament. 1607 HIERON *Wks.* I. 262 To intend the sifting and scanning of euery pretended way of saluation. 1615 CHAPMAN *Odyss.* XVI. 432 Time will aske much, to the sifting out Of each mans disposition, by his deeds. 1736 HERVEY *Mem.* I. 138 Examinations and siftings seldom turning to the account of those who have the reins of power. 1841 MYERS *Cath. Th.* III. §19. 70 The weighing and sifting of traditional testimony. 1884 *Athenæum* 24 May 660/1 The heap has undergone a certain sifting and classification.

*attrib.* 1844 H. STEPHENS *Bk. Farm* II. 283 Sifting-machines have been contrived for the purpose. 1861 STEPHENS & BURNS *Farm-buildings* §1773 In Mr. Downing's work, a plan of what is there termed a 'sifting-shed' [for separating pigs] is given.

2. *pl.* That which is removed or separated by means of a sieve.

1600 SURFLET *Countrie Farme* I. xxii. 131 The sheaues of wheate and rie are good for them: and sometimes bran mixed with siftings. 1611 COTGR., *Cribleure*, .. siftings. 1763 MILLS *Pract. Husb.* II. 280 *note*, The siftings would otherwise have been more considerable in so many years. 1845 *Beck's Florist Jrnl.* 30, I would recommend to add to it .. either sand, lime rubbish, or lime siftings. 1886 *Daily News* 15 Sept. 2/4 Tea .. ; black leaf, 8*d.* to 1*s.* 1*d.*; siftings, 5½*d.*

**'sifting**, *ppl. a.* [-ING².] That sifts or separates; searching.

1642 H. MORE *Song of Soul* I. ii. cviii, How had she admired Thy sifting wit, thy speech and person lov'd. 1762 *Crazy Tales* 24 He was in such a sifting cue, Till she discover'd all she knew. 1850 MᶜCOSH *Div. Govt.* I. ii. (1874) 51 Its superstitions could not stand the sifting light of modern science. 1895 *Tablet* 9 Nov. 739 The sifting power of water in motion is very great.

**sig**, *sb. dial.* and *U.S.* Also seg, sigg, zig(g. [Of obscure origin; the form does not correspond to older Flem. *seycke* (Kilian), G. *seiche*, in the same sense.] 1. Urine.

1691 RAY *S. & E. Co. Wds.* 113 *Sig*, Urine, Chamber-lie. 1746 *Gentl. Mag.* XVI. 408/2 [Exmoor Vocab.], *Zigg*, urine. 1825 JENNINGS *Observ. Dial. W. Eng.* 67. 1886 ELWORTHY *W. Somerset Word-bk.* 670 The woollen factories used to supply to any householder who would .. undertake to 'save' the 'sig', a tub or vat for the purpose.

2. A solution applied to the grain side of leather before it is stained black. ? *Obs.*

1897 C. T. DAVIS *Manuf. Leather* (ed. 2) 623 In the making of 'sig' stains, blacks and pastes for leather, borax is the currier's friend. 1900 H. C. STANDAGE *Leather Worker's Manual* iv. 69 *Seasoning for Oil-Grain Leathers*—This is sometimes called 'sig'. It is a fluid which is put onto the skin, so as to dye or stain it, or otherwise prepare it for being blackened on the grain side. 1903 L. A. FLEMMING *Pract. Tanning* 51 A good 'sig' is made of forty gallons of water, twelve pounds of salts of tartar, five pounds of bichromate of potash and one quart of ammonia.

†**sig**, *v.* *Obs.*$^{-1}$ [Cf. prec.] *trans.* To steep in, or sprinkle with, urine.

**1581** in *Southern Times* 27 Oct. (1883) 3/4 That no tuckers do sig or wash any cloths upon the Sabbath Day.

**sig.**, in printing, abbreviation of SIGNATURE.

**1866** G. SIMPSON *Let.* 30 May in *Geo. Eliot Lett.* (1956) IV. 263 Vol. II. is on the Machines up to Sig. K. 9 and the whole of it will be on to morrow. **1959** *N. & Q.* Dec. 461/1 In the Preface to the Lay-Reader of Richard Baxter's *Gildas Salvianus: The Reformed Pastor* (1656), sig. C. 8, the following passage occurs. **1972** P. GASKELL *New Introd. Bibliogr.* 99 (*caption*) Sheet of duodecimo..with two signatures..(12° in 8s and 4s, 2 sigs.).

†**sigalder**, *sb.* *Obs. rare.* [f. OE. *sige* victory + GALDER.] A charm or incantation.

*c* **1000** *Saxon Leechd.* I. 388 Syge-gealdor ic begale, sige-gyrd ic me wege. *a* **1225** *Ancr. R.* 208 Sigaldren [*v.r.* sigaldrie], & false teolunges, leuunge on ore & of swefnes, & alle wichchecreftes.

Hence †**sigalder** *v.*, to enchant, bewitch. *Obs.*

**1303** R. BRUNNE *Handl. Synne* 503 þere was a wycche, and made a bagge, A bely of leþyr,.. She sygaldryd so þys bagge bely þat hyt ȝede and soke mennys ky.

†**sigaldry**. *Obs. rare.* Also 3 **-rie**, 4 **sygaldrye**. [f. prec. + -Y.] Enchantment, sorcery.

*a* **1225** [see SIGALDER *sb.*]. **13..** *K. Alis.* 7015 (W.), Quede and harme he wil me spye,.. Gef he wot of this sygaldrye [*Laud* trigoldrye] That this trowes [= trees] kan lye. ? *a* **1500** *Chester Pl., Crucifixion* (Shaks. Soc.) II. 69 Burye hym wher thy wil be, But look thou make no sigaldry To raise him up agayne.

**Sigatoka** (sɪŋgə'təʊkə). Also **Sing-**. [Name of the district of Fiji where the disease was first observed.] Used *attrib.* and *absol.* to designate a disease of banana plants caused by the fungus *Cercospora musæ*, characterized by the appearance on the leaves of elongated spots, followed by rotting of the entire leaves.

**1925** *Agric. Circular Dept. Agric. Fiji* V. 68 Sigatoka Disease—This is by far the most important of the banana diseases of Fiji. **1958** *New Scientist* 26 June 258/1 Sigatoka has spread to virtually all the banana growing areas since it was discovered in 1903. **1963** A. BURNS *Fiji* II. iii. 197 Leaf-spot disease, which affects bananas in various parts of the world, is often referred to as Singatoka Disease, because it was first identified in the Singatoka area of Viti Levu. **1972** C. W. WARDLAW *Banana Dis.* xi. 314 In Fiji, it became notorious in 1913 in the Sigatoka valley—hence the name 'Sigatoka Disease' or simply 'Sigatoka'.

**sig(g)e**, obs. forms of SIEGE *sb.*

**sigge(n**, obs. forms of SAY *v.*[1]

**sigh** (saɪ, *Sc.* sɪx), *sb.* Forms: *α.* 5 **syhe**, 5–6 **syghe**, 6 **sygh**; 4–7 **sighe**, 4– **sigh**. *β.* *Sc.* 6 **sych(e**, 6, 8–9 **sich**, 6, 9 *arch.* **siche**, 9 **sicgh**; *north.* 9 **seegh**. [f. the vb.]

**1.** A sudden, prolonged, deep and more or less audible respiration, following on a deep-drawn breath, and esp. indicating or expressing dejection, weariness, longing, pain, or relief.

*α.* **13..** *Cursor M.* 15169 (Gött.), Ful mani sari sigh, i-wis, þar sank tille his herte. *c* **1381** CHAUCER *Parl. Foules* 248 Withyn the temple of syghes [*v.r.* syhes] hote as fyre.., Whyche syghes engendryd were with desyre [etc.]. *c* **1400** *Pilgr. Sowle* (Caxton, 1483) IV. xxxi. 80 He draweth a depe sighe fro the herte rote. *c* **1489** CAXTON *Sonnes of Aymon* xvi. 372 Rowland..sawe not durandall his swerd, wherof he dyde caste a grete syghe. **1500–20** DUNBAR *Poems* viii. 2 Thou may complain with sighis lamentable The death of Bernard Stewart. **1595** DANIEL *Civ. Wars* I. lxxxvii, Wringing her hands (as one that griev'd and prayd) With sighes commixt with words. **1611** SHAKS. *Wint. T.* I. ii. 287 Stopping the Cariere Of Laughter, with a sigh. **1642** FULLER *Holy & Prof. St.* V. xix. 440 In their sighes they breathed many a prosperous gale to Nassau's party. **1711** ADDISON *Spect.* No. 7 ⁋1 The Lady..said to her Husband with a Sigh, My Dear, Misfortunes never come Single. **1757** GRAY *Clerke* 14 A sigh; an unavailing tear. **1822** HAZLITT *Table-t.* II. ii. 19 A sigh uttered from the fulness of the heart, an involuntary aspiration born and dying in the same moment. **1878** M. A. BROWN tr. *Runeberg's Nadeschda* 38 A sigh of admiration is His full heart's only language now.

*transf.* **1817** KEATS *I stood tip-toe* 12 There crept A.. noiseless noise among the leaves, Born of the very sigh that silence heaves.

*β.* **1513** DOUGLAS *Æneid* XIII. v. 115 Drawand the sobbis hard and sychis smart. **1567** *Satir. Poems Reform.* xi. 116 With sobbing sych I to ȝou send This my complaint. **1593** A. HUME *Treat. Consc.* vi, [He] will vtter his passions..with sichis, and with sobbes. **17..** RAMSAY *Some of the Contents* ix, His eisy sangs..Sall be esteimd quhyle sichs saft lufe betray. **1802** R. ANDERSON *Cumbld. Ball.* (*c* 1850) 32 Now, hey for seeghs and sugar words. **1879** G. MACDONALD *Sir Gibbie* xlvi, She gae a gret sich, an' a sab.

**2.** *transf.* A sound made by the wind, suggestive of a sigh.

**1810** SCOTT *Lady of L.* I. xi, Creeping shrubs, of thousand dyes, Waved in the west-wind's summer sighs. **1815** SHELLEY *Alastor* 8 Autumn's hollow sighs in the sere wood. **1848** L. HUNT *Jar of Honey* v. 64 Like the sigh that answers a wind over a churchyard.

**3.** *Comb.*, as ***sigh-blown***, ***-born***, ***-broken***, ***-clogged***, ***-like***, ***-swollen***, etc.

*a* **1586** SIDNEY *Arcadia* (1622) 396 At length he ended His oft sigh-broken dittie. **1601** MARKHAM *Mary Magd. 3rd Lament* 15, I will suppresse my sigh-swolne sadnesse. **1611** COTGR., *Han*, the..sigh-like voyce, wherewith woodcleauers, &c., keepe time to their stroakes. **1633** G. HERBERT *Temple, The Collar* 19 Recover all thy sigh-blown age On double pleasures. **1648** J. BEAUMONT *Psyche* XVII. lxiii, With such potent passion did she breath That sigh-clogg'd Word. *a* **1847** ELIZA COOK *Under the Moon* ix. 1 We may breathe a farewell in a sigh-deepened tone. **1849** DE QUINCEY *Eng. Mail Coach* Wks. 1862 IV. 331 Suggesting solemn and sigh-born thoughts. **1873** BRENNAN *Witch of Nemi* 12 Bathed in the streams of sigh-fermented tears. **1911** J. A. THOMSON *Biol. of Seasons* II. 193 When the young bird appears to be contented and very comfortable, it utters a plaintive, almost sigh-like cheep. **1964** J. C. CATFORD in D. Abercrombie et al. *Daniel Jones* 32 Auditory effect, 'sigh-like' mixture of breath and voice: one form of voiced [h].

**sigh** (saɪ, *Sc.* sɪx), *v.* Forms: *α.* 4 **sihe(n**, 4–5 **syhe(n**, 5 **syh(gh)yn**; 4–5 **siȝ(h)e**, **siȝȝe** (4 **six-**), **syȝ(h)e**, 5 **sye**. *β.* 4–5 **sighen**, 4–7 **sighe** (5 **sighye?**), 5–6 **syghe**, 6– **sigh**. *γ.* *Sc.* 5–6 **sych**, 5–6, 9 **sich**. *δ.* 4–6 **seigh**, 5 **seye** (?), 6 **segh**; *Sc.* 5 **seych**, 9 **seich**, **sech**. *ε.* *Pa. t.* 6–7 (9 *dial.*) **sight** (7 **sigh't**), 6 **seight**. [ME. *sihen*, *siȝen*, *sighen*, etc., prob. a back-formation on *sihte*, *siȝte*, pa. t. of SICHE *v.*, through the guttural having more phonetic appropriateness than the palatal sound. The old pa. t., however, survived in literary use down to the 17th cent.; it may also have been the source of the variant SIGHT *v.*[2] Further variations are SITHE *v.* and the dialect *sife*, *siff*.]

**1. a.** *intr.* To emit, give, or heave a sigh.

In ME. freq. in phrase ***to sigh sore***.

*α.* **13..** *Cursor M.* 2959 (Gött.), Abraham syhid in his hert ful sare. **1382** WYCLIF *Joshua* xv. 18 She siȝide [1388 siȝȝide], as she sat in the asse. —— *Job* iii. 24 Er I shul ete, I siȝhe. *c* **1420** *Prymer* (1895) 34 To þee we siȝen, gronynge in þis valey of teeris. *c* **1440** *Promp. Parv.* 455/2 Syhghyn, for mornynge (*K.* syhyn..), *suspiro*.

*β.* *a* **1300** *Cursor M.* 14221 Quen thomas..Hard þat ded was lazarus,..He sighed sar. **1390** GOWER *Conf.* II. 319 Sche fond non amendement To syghen. *a* **1400–50** *Alexander* 5584 þe berne..Sighis selcuthly sare & sadli he wepis. **1434** MISYN *Mending Life* 130 It is no meruell þof it say syghand: 'Qwho sall gif me þe, my broþer?' **1530** PALSGR. 718/1 He syghed tyll his herte dyd nerehande bruste. **1560** DAUS tr. *Sleidane's Comm.* 342 To sigh, and to wincke as thoughe he were a slepe. **1669** DRYDEN *Tyrannic Love* III. i, And when his strength is wanting to his mind, Looks back, and sighs on what he left behind. **1697** —— *Virg. Georg.* IV. 673 On thee,..in Desarts all alone, He call'd, sigh'd, sung. **1727–46** THOMSON *Summer* 1188 They ..talk'd the flowing heart, Or sigh'd and look'd unutterable things. **1781** COWPER *Expost.* 722 My soul shall sigh in secret, and lament A nation scourg'd. **1819** SCOTT *Ivanhoe* xli, The young knight sighed, therefore, and held his peace. **1854** TENNYSON *Marriage Geraint* 307 Then sigh'd and smiled the hoary-headed Earl.

*γ.* **1375** BARBOUR *Bruce* III. 350 Men mycht haiff sene.. knychtis, for thar luffis sak, Baith sich, and wep. *c* **1470** HENRY *Wallace* IX. 972 Wallace tharfor sichit with hart full sar. **1508** DUNBAR *Twa Mariit Wemen* 446, I sich, without sair hert, or seiknes in body. **1583** *Leg. Bp. St. Androis* 459 The vther gaid hame..Sichand, and durst say no mair. **1791** LEARMONT *Poems* 113 She sicht sair i' her bed. **1884** D. GRANT *Lays & Leg. North* 92 The Cooper didna sich an' grain.

*δ.* **1377** LANGL. *P. Pl.* B. XVIII. 89 He seighed & sayde, 'sore it me athynketh'. *c* **1400** *St. Alexius* 122 (Laud MS. 108), His fader at hom seyetȝ sore, & seyþ 'allas! allas!' *c* **1440** *Generydes* 1416 Ye seigh gretly, I prae yow telle me why. **1529** MORE *Dyaloge* I. Wks. 130/2 Some sely woman seking saint Sythe when she seghyth for miscasting of her kayes. **1877** NEILSON *Poems* 57 (E.D.D.), They sech loud an' lang. **1883** CURRIE *Poems* 44 (E.D.D.), Nae langer noo I seich and mane.

*ε.* ? *c* **1550** *Sir Andrew Barton* in *Surtees Misc.* (1890) 65 The merchauntes answered, soore they sight. **1592** BRETON *Pilgr. Paradise* Wks. (Grosart) I. 14/2 Shrinking downe, it sight, and spake no more. **1633** COWLEY *Poet. Blossoms, Constantia & Philetus* 329 With that..He sight, as if they'd coole his torment's ire. **1689** CARLILE *Fortune-Hunters* I. i, He lookt indeed and sight, and set his Cravat-string, and sight agen. **1828** CARR *Craven Gloss.*, *Sight*, sighed.

**b.** *fig.* and *transf.*

**1667** MILTON *P.L.* IX. 783 Nature from her seat Sighing through all her Works gave signs of woe. **1708** *Brit. Apollo* No. 83. 3/1 To hear her after, *Sigh in Welsh*, (Which ill-bred Clowns will call a Belch). **1775** SHERIDAN *Duenna* I. i, Tell me, my lute, can thy soft strain..So softly sing, so humbly sigh, That [etc.]?

**c.** Of the wind, trees, etc.: To make or give out a sound suggestive of a sigh.

**1757** GRAY *Bard* 24 Hark, how each giant-oak, and desert cave, Sighs to the torrent's aweful voice beneath! **1764** GOLDSM. *Trav.* 104 Like yon neglected shrub..That.. sighs at every blast. **1820** SCOTT *Monast.* ix, A chill easterly wind was sighing among the withered leaves. **1830** TENNYSON *Claribel* 4 The solemn oaktree sigheth. **1855** —— *Maud* I. XXII. vii, Whenever a March-wind sighs He sets the jewel-print of your feet In violets.

**2. a.** To express desire or longing by the utterance of sighs; hence, to wish or long ardently. Const. *for* (†*after*), or *to* with inf.

**1549** COVERDALE, etc. *Erasm. Par. Phil.* 8 Yet in soule our conuersacion is in heauen, sighing continuallye thither. **1565** COOPER *Thesaurus*, *In aliquam suspirare*, to sigh after one, or for one. **1596** SPENSER *F.Q.* VI. viii. 20, I was belou'd of many a gentle Knight,.. Full many a one for me deepe groand and sight. **1604** E. G[RIMSTONE] tr. *D'Acosta's Hist. Indies* I. vi. 18 Many Spaniards..sigh for Spaine, having no discourse, but of their countrie. **1711** ADDISON *Spect.* No. 205 ⁋3 The Foreigner sighs after some British Beauty, whom he only knows by Fame. **1746** FRANCIS tr. *Horace, Ep.* I. xx. 5 You..fondly praise The public World, even sighing to be read,—Unhappy Book! **1847** MARRYAT *Childr. N. Forest* iv, He sighed for the time when the King's cause should be again triumphant. **1855** TENNYSON *Maud* I. 11, Long have I sigh'd for a calm.

**b.** To be sorry, feel sorrow. Const. *that*, *to*.

**1642** H. MORE *Song of Soul* I. iii. 39 Fair semblances these Apterites Do make of good, and sighen very sore, That God no stronger is. **1670** DRYDEN *Conq. Granada* I. III. i, May your Heroick Act so prosperous be, That Almahide may sigh you set her free. **1734** POPE *Ess. Man* IV. 148 And which more blest? who chain'd his country, say, Or he whose Virtue sigh'd to lose a day?

**3.** *trans.* **a.** To speak or utter (words, etc.) with a sigh. Chiefly with advs., as *forth* and *out*.

**1553** T. WILSON *Rhet.* 117 b, Some sighes out their woordes. Some synges their sentences. **1588** SHAKS. *L.L.L.* III. i. 13 To..sigh a note and sing a note. **1607** —— *Cor.* I. i. 209 They..sigh'd forth Prouerbes. **1624** QUARLES *Job Militant* §8 Bvt wretched Iob, sigh't forth these words, and said, Ah me! **1797** JANE AUSTEN *Sense & Sens.* xxxvii, Marianne sighed out her similar apprehension. **1825** T. HOOK *Sayings* Ser. II. *Man of Many Fr.* (Colburn) 120 It is rather too late..for you and I to sit up sighing out romances in real life. **1859** TENNYSON *Elaine* 1341 The Queen..sigh'd in passing, 'Lancelot, Forgive me'. **1879** MISS BRADDON *Cloven Foot* xxxviii, 'Yes,' sighed Celia, 'He went early on Tuesday morning'.

**b.** To emit, give out, impart, etc., by sighing. Freq. with advs., as *away*, *forth*, *out*. Also *transf.*

**1593** SHAKS. *Rich. II*, III. i. 20 [I] Haue..sigh'd my English breath in forraine Clouds. **1607** —— *Cor.* IV. v. 121 Neuer man Sigh'd truer breath. **1638** SIR T. HERBERT *Trav.* (ed. 2) 273 Sapores..sighed out his affrighted ghost, at the age..of seventy one. **1725** POPE *Odyss.* XIV. 51 Far from his country roams my hapless lord! Or sigh'd in exile forth his latest breath. *a* **1796** BURNS *On a Bank of Flowers* iii, He gaz'd, he wish'd, he fear'd, he blush'd, And sigh'd his very soul. **1850** TENNYSON *In Mem.* LXXXV[I]. iii, Sweet after showers, ambrosial air,..sigh The full new life that feeds thy breath Throughout my frame. **1875** FARRAR *Silence & Voices* i. 5 Hundreds of martyrs sighed away their souls amid the flames.

**c.** With cognate obj.

**1789** BLAKE *Songs Innoc.* f. 6, Think not, thou canst sigh a sigh, And thy maker is not by. **1847** C. BRONTE *J. Eyre* II. ii. 37 She sighed a sigh of ineffable satisfaction, as if her cup of happiness were now full. **1888** MRS. H. WARD *R. Elsmere* III. xli. 225 Robert sighed a long sigh.

**4. a.** To spend, consume, or while away (time) by sighing. Also with *away* and *out*.

**1599** SHAKS. *Much Ado* I. i. 204 Thou wilt needes thrust thy necke into a yoke,..and sigh away sundaies. **1653** MILTON *Ps.* vi. 11 Wearied I am with sighing out my dayes. **1700** PRIOR *Carmen Sec.* 229 Sighing the Moments that defer Our Ease.

**b.** To bring into a certain state or condition by sighing. Also *transf.* and *refl.*

**1603** SHAKS. *Meas. for M.* I. ii. 178 Thy head stands so tickle on thy shoulders, that a milke-maid, if she be in loue, may sigh it off. **1813** SCOTT *Rokeby* II. i, The gale had sigh'd itself to rest. **1850** MRS. BROWNING *Sonn.*, *Prospect*, As fretful children do, Leaning their faces on the window-pane To sigh the glass dim.

**5. a.** To lament (an event, circumstance, etc.) with sighing.

*c* **1600** SHAKS. *Sonn.* xxx, I sigh the lacke of many a thing I sought. **1602** MARSTON *Ant. & Mel.* 111, No..kinsman left To weepe my fate, or sigh my funerall. **1695** PRIOR *Ode Queen's Death*, Ages to come..Shall bless her Name, and sigh her Fate.

†**b.** To desire or long for (something). *Obs.*

**1650** EARL MONM. tr. *Senault's Man bec. Guilty* 224 God's beauty is then..that, that we ought to sigh, all other desires are unjust.

**sigh**, erron. var. of SITH, since; obs. var. SYE.

†**siȝe**. *Obs.* Also 3 **syȝe**, **sy**, **si**. [OE. *sige*, = OFris. *si*, OS. *sigi* (MLG. and MDu. *sege*, Du. *zege*), OHG. *sigi*, *sigo*, *sigu* (MHG. *sige*, G. *sieg*), Goth. *sigis*. OE. had also *sigor*, = ON. *sigi* (Sw. *seger*, Da. *sejr*).]

**1.** Victory in battle or conflict.

*c* **893** K. ÆLFRED *Oros.* I. ix. 42 þa Cretense hæfdon þone grimlecan sige. *a* **1122** *O.E. Chron.* (Laud MS.) an. 1066, Se Norrena cyng ahte siges geweald. *c* **1175** *Lamb. Hom.* 13 Ah ic eou ȝife siȝe and streinþe þet ȝe maȝen ower feond ouer cumen. *c* **1200** ORMIN 11421 To winnenn siȝe & oferrhannd Off himm þurrh Cristess hellpe. *c* **1205** LAY. 16199 þa heo iseȝen þat heo siȝen næfden. *Ibid.* 17409 Heo swunken ful swiðe ah næfden heo syȝe.

**2.** A position of victory or triumph.

*a* **1200** *St. Marher.* 123 Ther ha schineth seoueuald schenre then the sunne i si ant i selhthe. *a* **1225** *Juliana* 11 (Bodl. MS.), Sei me hwi þu forsakest þy sy & ti selhðe.

**3.** *Comb.*, as ***siȝe-craft***; ***siȝe-fast*** adj.

See also SIGALDER and SIGALDRY. A large number of combs. occur in OE. texts.

*c* **900** tr. *Baeda's Hist.* II. ix. 124 He sigefæst swa eft ham ferde. **971** *Blickl. Hom.* 167 Eallum Godes halgum he is sigefæstra & gecorenra. *c* **1200** ORMIN 16958 þatt lede þatt iss siȝȝefasst. *c* **1205** LAY. 15501 þe king..bad heom.. fondien þat soðe mid heore siȝe-craften, whær on hit weore ilong [etc.].

**sigher** ('saɪə(r)). [f. SIGH *v.*] One who sighs.

**1602** MARSTON *Antonio's Rev.* IV. iii, When my daughters exequies approach, Let's all turne sighers. **1612** *Two Noble K.* II. i, I could wish my selfe a Sigh to be so chid, or at least a Sigher to be comforted. **1703** STEELE *Tender Husb.* IV. i, Never was there such a sigher..as that unfortunate youth, during the absence of her he loved. **1740** CIBBER *Apol.* (1756) I. 225 Their lovers are generally constant simple sighers, both of a mind. **1826** SCOTT *Jrnl.* 16 June, I have been no sigher in shades—no writer of 'Songs and sonnets [etc.]'. **1879** BLACK *Macleod of Dare* xxx, Is she likely..to prove a sigher?.. A woman who goes about the house all day sighing.

**sighful** ('saɪfʊl), *a. rare.* [f. SIGH *sb.* + -FUL.] Sorrowful; sad.

**1606** SYLVESTER *Du Bartas* II. iv. I. *Tropheis* 1285 In a cave hard by he roareth out A sigh-full Song. *a* **1618** —— *Hymn of Alms* 276 A sighfull Air (though Soule-less) to respire. **1893** F. THOMPSON *Poems* 53 The dank thoughts that shiver Upon the sighful branches of my mind.

Hence '**sighfully** *adv. rare.*

**1900** *Academy* 27 Oct. 375/2 Cromwell..'sought the Lord'..sighfully and tearfully, beating his breast. **1905** W. J. LOCKE *Morals Marcus Ordeyne* x. 213 My aunt sighfully acquiesced, and for a while we discussed the depravity of human nature. **1925** T. DREISER *Amer. Trag.* (1926) II. III. xxv. 321 And here he wearily and sighfully drew forth his large white handkerchief once more.

**sighing** ('saɪɪŋ), *vbl. sb.* [f. SIGH *v.*]

**1.** The action of the verb; sorrow, grief.

*α. a* **1300** *E.E. Psalter* xxxvii. 9 Lauerd,..fra þe noght hid es mi sighinge. *a* **1400** *Hymns Virgin* (1867) 27 My loue is euere in siȝinge While y dwelle in þis way. **1412-20** LYDG. *Chron. Troy* I. 2295 Whan þat þei were to-gidre sette, þis Medea with syȝing first abreyde. **1535** COVERDALE *Isaiah* lxi. 2, I might geue vnto them..ioyful oyntment for sighinge. **1596** SHAKS. *1 Hen. IV*, II. iv. 365 A plague of sighing and griefe, it blowes a man vp like a Bladder. **1629** MILTON *Hymn Nativ.* xx, From haunted spring..The parting Genius is with sighing sent. **1703** ROWE *Ulysses* IV. i, Your Breasts that heave with sighing. *a* **1827** GOOD *Study Med.* (1829) I. 510 Often accompanied, in sighing, with deep and long drawn intonations, which we call groans. **1877** M. FOSTER *Physiol.* II. ii. (1879) 356 Sighing is a deep and long-drawn inspiration chiefly through the nose followed by a somewhat shorter, but correspondingly large expiration.

*attrib. a* **1300** *E.E. Psalter* vi. 6 (Vesp. MS.), I swanke in mi sighinge-stede. **1603** PETOWE *Eliza's Funerall* A iv, Your sighing weedes put off. **1615** CHAPMAN *Odyss.* XXI. 15 In the quiver were Arrows a number, sharp and sighing gear. **1746** FRANCIS tr. *Horace, Ep.* I. vii. 37 And o'er the flowing Bowl, in sighing Strain, [give me] To talk of wanton Cinera's Disdain.

*β. c* **1375** *Sc. Leg. Saints* i. (*Peter*) 666 Cristne men þat saw þis thinge, faste cuth gret with ser sichinge. **1528** LYNDESAY *Dreme* 333 Dolour Infinyte,..With sobbyng, syching, sorrow, and with syte. *a* **1586** MONTGOMERIE *Misc. Poems* lii, Oursett with inwart siching sair. **1819** W. TENNANT *Papistry Storm'd* (1827) 224 Was nocht but grief..And sichan' 'mang the monkish bands.

**b.** With *a* and pl. An instance of this; a sigh.

*a* **1300** *Cursor M.* 1088 Quen he eie a-pon him kest, A sighing of his hert brest. *c* **1380** *Sir Ferumb.* 1040 Fyrumbras ..made a grete syȝyng. *a* **1400-50** *Alexander* 5052 With sare sighingis & sadd for sake of his wirdis. *c* **1440** *Gesta Rom.* ii. 6 As he lay in a certeyne tyme by the fire, in siȝyngis and gryntingis. **1526** *Pilgr. Perf.* (W. de W. 1531) 59 b, Shewynge the same with swete teares and often syghynges. *a* **1568** A. SCOTT *Poems* (S.T.S.) x. 53 Thair is nocht wie Can estimie My sorrow and my sichingis sair. **1651** WITTIE tr. *Primrose's Pop. Err.* III. 158 Broth made of an old cock..is good for long feavers, sighings [etc.]. **1877** M. ARNOLD *New Sirens* 70 Round our hearts with long caresses, With low sighings, [1849 sighs hath] Silence stole.

**2.** *transf.* Of the wind, etc.

**1653** JER. TAYLOR *Serm. for Year* v. 60 The poor bird was beaten back with the loud sighings of an easterne winde. **1794** MRS. RADCLIFFE *Myst. Udolpho* xxx, No sound was heard, except the sighing of the wind among the battlements. **1817** SHELLEY *Pr. Athanase* II. ii. 43 The far sighings of yon piny dale Made vocal by some wind. **1842** LOVER *Handy Andy* xxi, The gentle sighing of a broken pane of glass. **1869** TOZER *Highl. Turkey* II. 258 The sighing of the wind in the trees.

**sighing** ('saɪɪŋ), *ppl. a.* [f. SIGH *v.*]

**1.** Accompanied by, uttered with, a sigh. Also *transf.*

*c* **1440** *Found. St. Bartholomew's* (E.E.T.S.) 22 This man, cummynge a-forne the Auter.., with sighynge terys his mercy mekely besowght. **1509** HAWES *Past. Pleas.* XVI. (Percy Soc.) 68 And than to hym..I did complayne, wyth syghing teres depe. **1633** P. FLETCHER *Elisa* II. l, Sleep sighing words; stop all your discontenting; Sleep beaten breast [etc.]. **1821** SHELLEY *Adonais* xvi, Wan they stand and sere.., With dew all turned to tears; odour, to sighing ruth. **1863** I. WILLIAMS *Baptistery* II. xxix. (1874) 155 Happy he, when..earth's sighing gladness Wrings the heart no more.

**2.** Of persons, etc.: That sigh(s). Also *transf.*

**1593** SHAKS. *3 Hen. VI*, II. v. 117 My sighing brest, shall be thy Funerall bell. **1753-4** RICHARDSON *Grandison* VI. xxxix. 255 In our happiest prospects, the sighing heart will confess imperfection. **1781** COWPER *Expost.* 309 Successive loads succeeding broils impose, And sighing millions prophesy the close. **1810** JANE PORTER *Scottish Chiefs* xliii, I am no gloomy, no sighing recluse. **1850** MRS. BROWNING *Sonn. fr. Portug.* IX, To let thee..hear the sighing years Re-sighing on my lips renunciative.

**b.** *transf.* Of the wind, trees, etc.

**1746** HERVEY *Medit.* (1818) 192 Let sighing Gales breathe ..in harmonious consonance to Him. **1821** SHELLEY *Hellas* 178 A wind Will rush out of the sighing pine-forest. **1860** KINGSLEY *Misc.* II. 139 Between the high banks of sighing reed. **1890** 'R. BOLDREWOOD' *Col. Reformer* (1891) 302 The sighing, whispering, sad-voiced water-oaks.

'**sighingly,** *adv.* [f. prec. + -LY².] In a sighing manner; with or accompanied by sighing.

**1402** HOCCLEVE *Lett. of Cupid* 22 Her wordes spoken ben so syghyngly. **1491** CAXTON *Vitas Patr.* (W. de W. 1495) II. 307 She answered syghynly; alas, holy fader [etc.]. **1621** LADY M. WROTH *Urania* 253 Then turnd she sighingly within her bed. **1678** BUNYAN *Pilgr. Progr.* (1900) 40 Christian..had no more talk but with himself, and that sometimes sighingly. **1760-72** H. BROOKE *Fool of Qual.* (1809) I. 137 The populace, sighingly, gave my Arabella for lost. **1791** MME. D'ARBLAY *Diary* 5 Aug., The statues, busts, and pictures, which again I sighingly quitted, with a longing wish [etc.]. **1833** MRS. JAMESON *Crt. Beauties Chas. II* (1872) 170 He was for this time seriously and sighingly in love. **1842** MRS. BROWNING *Gk. Chr. Poets* ii. ¶3 To go back sighingly to the tragedy, where we shall have to sigh again.

†'**sighingness.** *Obs.*⁻¹ [f. as prec. + -NESS.] The condition of uttering sighs.

*a* **1300** *E.E. Psalter* ci. 6 Fra steuen of mi sighingnesse [*v.r.* sikingnesse] Kliued mi mouth to mi flessche.

**sighless** ('saɪlɪs), *a. rare.* [f. SIGH *sb.* + -LESS.] Giving or sending forth no sigh.

*c* **1835** MRS. BROWNING *Felicia Hemans* i, O'er the sighless songless lips, the wail and music wedding. **1838** —— *Seraphim* Epil. iii, So soon to lie Sighless, because then breathless, in the tomb.

**sight** (saɪt), *sb.*¹ Forms: *α.* 1 **sihð,** 2-3 **sihðe** (3 sihh-), 4 **siþe,** 4-5 **sith, syth,** 5 **syththe;** 1 **sighð,** 3 **sig(ð)he, sihȝeðe,** 4 **ziȝþe, zyȝþe,** 5 **syȝth,** 6 **sygth.** *β.* 2-3 **syhte,** 2-4 **siht(e,** 3 **seht(e, sichte,** 4-6 *Sc.* **sicht, sycht,** 7 *Sc.* **seicht;** 3-4 **seȝt** (4 **seiȝt**), 3-5 **siȝt(e,** 4 **-tte), siȝhte, syȝt(e;** 3 **sigt(e, sygte,** 5 **sygt;** 4-6 **syght** (5 **seght**), 4-7 **syghte, sighte,** 3- **sight;** 4-7 **site,** 9 *north.* **seet.** [OE. *sihð* (rare, usually *ȝesihð, ȝesiht,* I-SIGHT), = MDu. *sicht, zicht* (Du. *zicht,* Fris. *sicht*), MLG. *sichte* (hence Da. and Sw. *sigt*), OHG. *siht* (G. *sicht*), f. *sih-* the stem of SEE *v.* + -TH¹.]

**I. 1. a.** A thing seen, esp. of a striking or remarkable nature; a spectacle.

In early use chiefly of something strange or supernatural.

*c* **950** *Lindisf. Gosp.* Mark ix. 9 [He] bebead ðæm þætte ne ænigum..ða sihðo ȝesæȝdon. *c* **1160** *Hatton Gosp.* Mark xvi. 8 Hyo..wæren aferde for þare sihðe þe hyo ȝeseaȝen. *a* **1225** *Leg. Kath.* 1607 Ha awundreden ham swiðe of þat sihðe. *c* **1275** LAY. 3897 þreo daiȝes hit reinede blod... þat was a wel wonder siht. *c* **1340** HAMPOLE *Pr. Consc.* II. 911 Swa grysly a sight saw he never nane. **1390** GOWER *Conf.* I. 115 Wherof the Cite sore afflyhte, Of hem that sihen thilke syhte. *c* **1450** *Merlin* ii. 37 Vnder that water be two dragons that see no sight. *c* **1470** HENRY *Wallace* vii. 441 The sycht with out was awfull for to se. **1526** *Pilgr. Perf.* (W. de W. 1531) 306 b, My hert bresteth to se this syght. **1561** T. HOBY tr. *Castiglione's Courtyer* I. (1577) F ij, White teeth is a good sight in a woman. **1632** LITHGOW *Trav.* x. 433, I saw in Irelands North-parts, two remarkable sights:..The other as goodly sight I saw. **1700** DRYDEN *Ovid's Met.* XIII. *Acis, Polyphemus, & Galatea* 157 What fouler sight can be, Than the bald branches of a leafless tree? **1742** YOUNG *Nt. Th.* I. 306 How sad a sight is human happiness To those whose thought can pierce beyond an hour! **1803-6** WORDSW. *Ode Intim. Immort.* i, The earth, and every common sight. **1854** BREWSTER *More Worlds* ii. 17 There is, perhaps, no sight in the material world more magnificent than that of the starry firmament. **1889** MIVART *Orig. Human Reason* 53 A name can only be a certain sound, or, if written, a certain sight.

†**b.** A vision. ***Book of sights,*** the Apocalypse.

*c* **950** *Lindisf. Gosp.* John, Int. 1 Iohannes..in pathma ealond þæt boc ðæra sighðana [L. *apocalipsen*] eac awrat. *c* **1290** *S. Eng. Leg.* I. 32 Him-sulf he cam bi niȝhte, And schewede heom ȝware is heued lay ase it were in a siȝhte. *a* **1300** *Cursor M.* 18984 Yur yongmen [sal] sightes se. Yur eldrin men sal dremes dreme. **1340** *Ayenb.* 133 þou miȝt.. ete of þe trawe of liue, ase god zayþ ine þe boc of ziȝþe. **1530** PALSGR. 270/1 Sight that disceyveth ones jugement, *illusion*. **1581** A. ANDERSON *Shield of Safetie* (title-p.), Vpon Symeons sight, in hys Nunc dimittis. **1611** COTGR., *Vision*, a vision, sight, apparition, fantasie. **1825** LAMB *Mem. Liston* in *Eliana* (1867) 64 He was subject to sights, and had visions.

**c.** *pl.* Those features or objects in a particular place or town which are considered to be specially worth seeing.

**1632** LITHGOW *Trav.* IX. 400 We tooke a Guide, and so proceeded in our sights. *a* **1700** EVELYN *Diary* Apr. 1646, We came this evening to Brescia, which next morning we traverst..in search of antiquities and new sights. **1760-2** GOLDSM. *Cit. W.* lxv, You may go and see sights the whole day. **1835** MRS. CARLYLE *Lett.* I. 44 Other sights we have seen none, except the British Museum and the King and Queen. **1886** RUSKIN *Præterita* I. vi. 183 A high class courier, well acquainted with the proper sights to be seen in each town.

**d.** In colloq. phr. ***a sight for sore eyes:*** a person or thing one is glad to see, esp. a welcome visitor.

[**1738** SWIFT *Polite Conv.* I. 7 The Sight of you is good for sore Eyes.] **1826** HAZLITT in *New Monthly Mag.* XVI. 38 Garrick's name was..proposed..on condition he should act in tragedy and comedy... What a *sight for sore eyes* that would be! **1871** *Monthly Pkt.* Christmas 108 You're a sight for sair ee'n the now! I'm just aboot in the awfuest swither ever a body was. **1897** R. MARSH *Crime & Criminal* xxiii. 192 He was a sight for sore eyes... I like to see a man that is a man. **1931** E. O'NEILL *Mourning becomes Electra* (1932) 125 You certainly are a sight for sore eyes, Vinnie! **1973** *People's Jrnl.* (Inverness) 28 July 4/5 Elizabeth..and Sheena had done wonders,..and the buffet was a sight for sore eyes.

**e.** Something which calls forth contemptuous, horrified, or amused glances; a shocking, repulsive, or ridiculous spectacle. *colloq.*

[**1694** W. PENN *Rise of Quakers* ii. 53 It was not very easie to our Primitive Friends, to make themselves Sights and Spectacles, and the Scorn and Derision of the World.] **1862** F. W. ROBINSON *Owen* II. v. iv. 288 I'm getting better now, ..I was a sight last week. **1911** M. BEERBOHM *Zuleika Dobson* xx. 296 Clarence curbed the brotherly intention of telling her she looked 'a sight' in them. **1940** W. FAULKNER *Hamlet* III. i. 229 'Ain't he a sight now,' Snopes cackled.

**f.** ***sight unseen:*** without previous inspection, without seeing the object to be acquired. orig. *U.S.*

**1892** *Dialect Notes* I. 231 To trade knives *sight unseen* is to swap without seeing each other's knife. **1898** *Yearbk. U.S. Dept. Agric. 1897* 427 The intelligent farmer of today has got beyond trading 'sight unseen' or 'buying a cat in a bag' when it comes to fertilizers. **1940** F. D. DAVISON *Woman at Mill* 94, I learned that he had selected sight-unseen, that he had now come to look over his property for the first time. **1962** V. NABOKOV *Pale Fire* 82, I have had occasion to say something about the amenities of my habitation. The charming, charmingly vague lady..who secured it for me, sight unseen, meant well, no doubt. **1968** *Listener* 7 Mar. 303, I said you were mad to advertise our modest needs—sight unseen—in the New Statesman. **1979** *Daily Tel.* 3 Feb. 34/2, I am recommending this [TV film], sight unseen, because the first offering in the series..was so good.

**2. a.** A show or display *of* something; hence, a great number or quantity; a multitude; a 'deal' or 'lot'. Now *colloq.* or *slang.*

**1390** GOWER *Conf.* I. 121 Out of his sepulture Ther sprong..Of floures such a wonder syhte [etc.]. **1432-50** tr. *Higden* (Rolls) VI. 239 He..brouȝhte to Yorke also a noble siȝhte of bookes. **1449** *Paston Lett.* I. 85 Ye sawe never suche a syght of schyppys take in to Englond thys c. wynter. **1538** LELAND *Itin.* (1769) V. 91 A great redy Poole, whither an innumerable sight of Stares resort at night. **1577-82** BRETON *Flourish upon Fancie* Wks. (Grosart) I. 10/1 A sight of Asses then, there stoode in Battell ray. **1621** BURTON *Anat. Mel.* II. iii. III, O ye Gods, what a sight of things do I want? **1752** STUKELEY *Mem.* (1882) I. 83 An infinite sight of rare flowers. **1778** SHERIDAN & TICKELL *Camp* I. ii, They wear..a large hat and feather, and a mortal sight of hair. **1800** JANE AUSTEN *Lett.* (1884) I. 231 She expresses herself more warmly than the rest, for she sends him a 'sight of thanks'. **1871** M. COLLINS *Marq. & Merch.* III. viii. 216 A sight of gentlemen goes over to see that old lady.

**b.** Used adverbially. *colloq.* or *slang.*

**1836** T. HOOK *G. Gurney* II. 49 One..eats and drinks a considerable sight more than one does at home. **1854** HAWTHORNE in Bridge *Pers. Recoll.* (1893) 144 It is a devilish sight harder to write to a President..than to a private man. **1860** GEO. ELIOT *Mill on Floss* I. ii, He's had a fine sight more schoolin' nor I ever got. **1889** G. ALLEN *Tents of Shem* II. 122 You're a sight too clever for me to talk to. **1931** R. CAMPBELL *Georgiad* i. 12 He could be.. heterosexual with either, too—A damn sight more than you or I could do! **1958** *Times* 16 Oct. 17/1 Surrey..will have to do a sight better than they did yesterday if they are to make their presence fittingly felt in the current Rugby Union county championship. **1977** 'E. CRISPIN' *Glimpses of Moon* xii. 241 Be a sight cooler there than it is here, I reckon. **1979** C. P. SNOW *Coat of Varnish* xvi. 133 Money might be fun, but if I had to choose I'd a damn sight rather try for the top jobs.

**c.** Phr. ***by a long, damn,*** etc., ***sight,*** by a long way, by a good deal (usu. in negative contexts). *U.S. colloq.*

**1834** C. A. DAVIS *Lett. J. Downing* 41 'Gineral, do you want another report?' 'Not by a darn'd sight.' **1840** *Niles' Register* 9 May 149/2 He asked him if he was not going for Harrison and the whigs. 'No,' said he, 'not by a d——d sight.' **1844** *Republican Sentinel* (Richmond, Va.) 22 June 1/2 These animals begin to venture out a little of nights, since the Baltimore Convention, but are slyer by a long sight than foxes. **1884** 'MARK TWAIN' *Huck. Finn* i. 5, I asked her if she reckoned Tom Sawyer would go there, and she said not by a considerable sight. **1894** —— in *Century Mag.* Mar. 779/2 It ain't on'y jist Essex blood dat's in you, not by a long sight. **1931** E. O'NEILL *Mourning becomes Electra* (1932) 248 But I don't wish to convey that he approves of all I've set down—not by a damned sight! **1959** E. POUND *Thrones* ciii. 88 But not his fault by a damn sight. **1976** M. MACHLIN *Pipeline* xxii. 272 The excitement ain't through here by a damn sight.

†**3.** Aspect, appearance, look. *Obs.*

*c* **1205** LAY. 25586 Com an wunderlic deor æst in þan leofte ladlic an sehte. **1297** R. GLOUC. (Rolls) 147 Ely of fairest place, of fairest siȝt roucestre. **1362** LANGL. *P. Pl.* A. I. 57 þat dungun in þat deope dale þat dredful is of siht. **1382** WYCLIF *Ecclus.* xi. 2 Preise thou not a man in his fairnesse; ne dispise thou a man in his siȝt [L. *visu*]. *c* **1440** *Promp. Parv.* 452/1 Semely, yn syghte, *decens*. **1486** *Bk. St. Albans* c vj, Neuer the lees this engraylyng is no propur langage aftir the sight of thys cros. **1535** COVERDALE *Ezek.* xliii. 2 His sight to loke vpon was like the first. **1581** MARBECK *Bk. Notes* 280 His bearde, which was now growne and did chaunge the sight of his face verie much. **1609** BIBLE (Douay) *Ezek.* i. 22 *comm.*, A similitude over the heades of the living creatures of the firmament, as it were the sight of christal dreadful. *c* **1680** BEVERIDGE *Serm.* (1729) I. 532 All that by false weights, false measures, or false sights have imposed upon their customers.

**II. 4. a.** The perception or apprehension *of* something by means of the eyes; the presentation *of* a thing to the sense of vision.

*a* **1225** *Ancr. R.* 94 Ȝe schulen hebben..þe brihte sihðe of Godes nebscheft. *a* **1300** *Cursor M.* 10841 þis leuedi duted noght þe sight O þis angel þat was sa bright. *c* **1386** CHAUCER *Knt's T.* 1239 Wel hath Fortune y-turned thee the dys, That hast the sighte of hire, and I thabsence. **1491** CAXTON *Vitas Patr.* (1895) 75 The sonne of a heerd man, the whyche was as deed only by the syghte of the sayde dragon. *a* **1533** LD. BERNERS *Huon* xxxiii. 68 They loste yᵉ syght of yᵉ castell, it was clene vanysshyd a way. **1585** T. WASHINGTON tr. *Nicholay's Voy.* II. i. 31 Wee had on our left hande the sight of the Ilandes. **1635** J. HAYWARD tr. *Biondi's Banish'd Virg.* 30 But no sooner lost shee once the sight of him [etc.]. **1640** BP. REYNOLDS *Passions* Ep. Ded., So far hath your Highness vouchsafed (having happened on the sight of this Tractate) to express favour thereunto. **1743** BULKELEY & CUMMINS *Voy. S. Seas* 15 Therefore he never inform'd the Captain of the Sight of Land. **1818** SCOTT *Hrt. Midl.* xxxii, I did think the sight on her would but vex your Reverence. **1845** PATTISON *Ess.* (1889) I. 27 Unable any longer to bear the sight of one who had pleaded guilty to so great a crime. **1885** E. GARRETT *At Any Cost* v. 85 He had had a preconceived idea which the sight of Mr. Sandison shattered for ever.

**b.** With possessive pron. or genitive case.

*c* **1175** *Lamb. Hom.* 79 Ierusalem bitacneð griþes sihþe. *c* **1200** ORMIN 674 Ȝiff he seþ þatt mann iss ohht Forrfæredd off hiss sihhþe. *c* **1275** *Moral Ode* 361 in *O.E. Misc.*, Nis þer no Murehþe so muchel so is godes syhte. *c* **1386** CHAUCER *Can. Yeom. T.* 866 If þat youre eyen kan nat seen aright,

Looke þat youre mynde lakke noght his sight. **1594** Daniel *Cleopatra* IV. 1074 Although they need such actors of deceit, Yet still our sight seemes to vpbraid their wrong. **1607** Shaks. *Timon* I. i. 255 You must needs dine with me... I am ioyfull of your sights. **1697** Dryden *Virg. Past.* x. 70 You, (alas, that I shou'd find it so!) To shun my sight, your Native Soil forego. **1702** Rowe *Tamerl.* I. i, When thy lov'd Sight shall bless my Eyes again. **1873** Browning *Red Cott. Nt.-cap* 263 Sully yourselves no longer by my sight!

**c.** Without article, chiefly in phrases as ***to catch, have, lose sight of.***

*a* **1225** *Ancr. R.* 106 To ȝiuen þe ancre brihte sihðe of heouene. *a* **1300** *Cursor M.* 23330 Þe seli sal o þaim ha sight, Bot þof þai se þam [etc.]. **1377** Langl. *P. Pl.* B. xvii. 57 Feith had first siȝte of hym, ac he flegh on syde. *c* **1425** *Eng. Conq. Ireland* (1896) 6 Mych hit gladet his hert..þat he myght in fayr weder haue somdell syght of his lond. *c* **1595** Capt. Wyatt *R. Dudley's Voy. W. Ind.* (Hakl. Soc.) 49 Our Generall sent Captain Jobson and the master to take sight of such commodities as they weare ladend withall. **1674** Boyle *Excell. Theol.* II. iii. 155 That he was able at first sight of them to give each of the beasts a name expressive of its nature. **1697** Dryden *Virg. Georg.* III. 289 With Sight of Arms and Sounds of Trumpets nurst. **1748** *Anson's Voy.* II. xii. 263 Our people ran after him.., but as he had the advantage of being on horseback, he soon lost sight of them. **1820** Keats *Isabella* xlviii, Wondering, Until her heart felt pity to the core At sight of such a dismal labouring. **1837–** [see catch *v.* 46]. **1898** Flor. Montgomery *Tony* 13 As if he dreaded losing sight of her.

*fig.* **1737** *Gentl. Mag.* VII. 73/1 It would not be much Matter what I began upon, for I would presently lose Sight of that. **1837** P. Keith *Bot. Lex.* 296 The conjecture was not lost sight of by contemporary or succeeding botanists. **1875** Jowett *Plato* (ed. 2) IV. 42 The higher the view which men take of life, the more they lose sight of their own pleasure or interest.

**d.** The first perception or view *of* something. Usually in phr. ***at*** or ***upon (the) sight of.***

**1471** *Little Red Bk. Bristol* (1900) II. 130 That incontinent vpon the sighte of thies ye schew [etc.]. **1565** *Reg. Privy Council Scot.* I. 341 The thrid day nixt efter the resset and sycht heirof. **1582** N. Lichefield tr. *Castanheda's Conq. E. Ind.* I. ii. 7 At sight of which the Captaine generall went to lande. **1625** in Rymer *Fœdera* (1726) XVIII. 60 Upon Sight of theis our Letters Pattents. **1670–98** Lassels *Voy. Italy* II. 9 The servant upon sight of the paper, presently threw her fifty crowns. **1734** tr. *Rollin's Anc. Hist.* (1827) I. 361 On sight of them drew up their forces. **1771** *Encycl. Brit.* III. 351/1 At sight of the sharps or flats prefixed to the tune to be sung,..you have of course the places of the semitones. **1810** Scott *Lady of Lake* II. xxvii, Sir Roderick..Redden'd at sight of Malcolm Græme.

**e.** A position or point commanding or giving a view *of* something. Chiefly ***in*** or ***within (†the) sight of.*** Also *transf.*

*a* **1533** Ld. Berners *Huon* lxxxi. 241 He came within the syght of Burdeux. **1585** T. Washington tr. *Nicholay's Voy.* I. xii. 14 Passing further towards the sight of the yles De la Galite, & des Symboles. **1610** Holland *Camden's Brit.* (1637) 700 Fountaines, built within the sight of it [Ripon]. **1662** J. Davies tr. *Mandelslo's Trav.* (1669) 279 The 16. About 10. in the morning we passed in sight of Dover-Castle. **1807** W. Irving *Salmag.* (1824) 321 When that the army of the Hoppingtots did peregrinate within sight of Gotham. **1822** Shelley tr. *Calderon's Mag. Prodig.* I. 71 Even within the sight of the high towers of Antioch. **1890** *Spectator* 29 Nov. 764/1 We are not yet in possession of ritual peace, but for the first time we are fairly in sight of it.

**5. a.** A view, look, or glimpse *of* something.

*c* **1205** Lay. 20929 Nænne siht of londe iseon heo ne mahten. **1297** R. Glouc. (Rolls) 1623 He nolde þe gywes leue ȝiue..þat hii moste of þe boru enes abbe an siȝte. **1393** Langl. *P. Pl.* C. xx. 57 Faith on hym hadde furst a sight ac he fleih a-syde. *c* **1420** *Sir Amadace* (Camden) lii, Quen aythir of othir hade a siȝte, Suche a lufue be-tuene hom liȝte. *c* **1470** Henry *Wallace* v. 240 Schyr Jhone Butler..Out fra his men of Wallace had a sicht. **1560** Daus tr. *Sleidane's Comm.* 204 b, Whan the Pristes not without monye let them have a syght therof. **1632** Lithgow *Trav.* IX. 397 [His] presence to me after so long a sight of Hethnike strangers was exceeding comfortable. **1692** Ray in *Lett. Lit. Men* (Camden) 198 You should have had a sight of the Copy. **1766** Goldsm. *Vic. W.* xxviii, He had some difficulty, he said, to get a sight of his landlord. **1832** Ht. Martineau *Homes Abroad* vii. 99 One sight of a savage in a life-time was as much as most settlers had. **1857** Trollope *Barchester T.* xii, A sight of you, Mr. Harding, is good for sore eyes.

**†b.** ***at one sight***, in a single look, from one point of view. *Obs.*

*c* **1470** *Gol. & Gaw.* 483 Seuyne score of scheildis thai schew at ane sicht. **1632** Lithgow *Trav.* VI. 283 The City ..can not be seene all at one sight; saue on this Mountaine.

**c.** *fig.* A look *into* a matter. Cf. insight *sb.*[1] 2 b.

**1592** Greene *Ned Browne* Wks. (Grosart) XI. 27 There is no Art but he will haue a superficiall sight into. **1760–72** H. Brooke *Fool of Qual.* (1809) II. 131, I joined myself to a house-painter..on condition of his giving me a sight into his business.

**d.** *Sc.* A station on the bank of a river, etc., from which the movements of salmon are observed.

**1805** *State Leslie of Powis*, etc. 56 (Jam.), That the fishers used sights, during the fishing season, upon Fraserfield's grounds..; that the westmost sight was above the Fluicky-shot [etc.].

**e.** *Poker.* A show of hands; *spec.* one called for by a player who has insufficient chips or money to equal another's bet, but bets as much as he can. *U.S.*

**1821** G. Long *Hoyle's Games Improved* 162 The youngest hand..may *call a sight*... If he *calls a sight* the cards must be shown in rotation, the player who calls showing last, and the best hand shown wins the pool. **1850** H. G. Bohn *Bohn's New Hand-bk. Games* 381 Should one of the party over-reach the amount that is in possession of an adversary, a '*sight*' may be demanded. **1887** *Courier-Jrnl.* (Louisville, Kentucky) 23 Jan. 15/7 Then a rule sprang up that a man should be allowed a sight for his money. **1940** O. Jacoby *On Poker* 150 Even though a player's hand is beaten in sight, he should make no move to fold it except in his proper turn. **1964** E. Sinclair *Poker* v. 142 If a player who is beaten in sight bets against the cinch hand, he will be allowed to withdraw his bet from the pot after his attention had been drawn to the fact that he is beaten in sight.

**f.** A sale of packets of uncut diamonds.

**1940** *Economist* 2 Mar. 385/1 A significant hint on the likely evolution of the British exchange control technique was provided last week on the occasion of the latest diamond 'sights' held in London. **1966** J. Wainwright *Crystallised Carbon Pig* xv. 74 The Diamond Corporation hold monthly 'sights'—auctions, I suppose you could call them. They sell anything between three million and five million pounds' worth of stones at each 'sight'. **1978** *Times* 9 Mar. 23/6 The rough gems are sold by the CSO at 10 'sights' (sales) a year. .. London holds the most important sights.

**6.** With omission of the dependent genitive, in phrases related to 4 d:

**a.** ***at (†the, as to the) first sight.***

(*a*) *a* **1300** *Cursor M.* 8029 He kneu þam at þe first sight. *c* **1400** Maundev. (1839) v. 40 At the firste sight..Men knele to him. **1456** Sir G. Haye *Law Arms* (S.T.S.) 160 As to the first sicht, it semys that [etc.]. *a* **1548** Hall *Chron., Hen. VIII*, 43 b, Hys serjante porter, which knewe hym at the fyrste sighte. **1579, 1702** [see first *a.* 1 e]. **1730** Bailey (fol.), *Axiom*,..a Proposition whose Truth every Person perceives at the first Sight.

(*b*) *a* **1593, 1611** [see first *a.* 1 e]. **1651** Hobbes *Leviath.* II. xxvi. 137 In which definition, there is nothing that is not at first sight evident. **1710** Steele *Tatler* No. 166 ¶3 You may see them at first Sight grow acquainted by Sympathy. **1773** *Life N. Frowde* 29 I'm glad to see him, however, he has pleased me at first Sight. **1846** Mill *Logic* I. vi. §1 Propositions which at first sight present themselves as verbal. **1875** [see first *a.* 1 e].

**b.** ***at*** (formerly also ***on*** or ***upon***) ***sight***, used spec. with reference to the payment of bills. Also, in this connexion, ***after sight*** (see quot. 1835).

(*a*) **1617** Moryson *Itin.* I. 277 Let it be expressed in your bill that the money be paid upon sight. **1682** Scarlett *Exchanges* 63 He that receives a Bill payable at sight, or some dayes after sight, &c. **1708** Mrs. Centlivre *Busy Body* II. i, The frugal hand can bills at sight defray. **1767** Franklin *Wks.* (1887) IV. 86 Being payable in cash, upon sight, by the drawer. **1835** *Penny Cycl.* IV. 399/1 At first, no doubt, the order was to pay..'on sight'. *Ibid.*, In modern times, the more frequent practice has been to make them payable at so many days after sight. **1861** Goschen *For. Exch.* 53 We have..considered all bills as drawn payable at sight.

(*b*) **1673** *Humours Town* 60 One that will play at sight, tilt at sight (that is without Thought or Consideration), and whore at sight. **1721** Ramsay *Ode to the Ph——* vi, If they command the storms to blaw, Then upo' sight the hailstanes thud. **1773** *Phil. Trans.* LXIII. 270 Those who are not able to sing at sight. **1890** 'R. Boldrewood' *Col. Reformer* (1891) 205, I swore to shoot the old warrigal at sight. **1892** *Speaker* 3 Sept. 277/1 The cowboy who lives in constant apprehension of being shot at sight.

**c.** ***at*** (so many) ***days'*** (etc.) ***sight***, of bills.

**1701** *Lond. Gaz.* No. 3730/4 A Bill drawn..at 6 days sight. **1716** *Ibid.* No. 5472/4 A Bill..payable..at 15 Days Sight. **1818** Scott *Rob Roy* xv, A goldsmith's bill at six days' sight. **1866** Crump *Banking* v. 100 Inland bills of exchange are drawn on demand, at so many days', or weeks', or months', sight or date, as the case may require.

**7. a.** A look or glance (at something or in a certain direction). Now *rare* except in slang phr. ***to take sights***, to observe, to watch.

*c* **1275** *Moral Ode* 280 in *O.E. Misc.*, Þer schule þe wrecche soulen iseon þat sunegeden bi sihtes. **13..** *Cursor M.* 7886 (Gött.), Þe king kast anis on hir a sight. *a* **1400** *Minor Poems fr. Vernon MS.* xxix. iii. 119 Þe damysele caste on hire a siht. **1559** *Mirr. Mag., Dk. Suffolk* v, Fortune euer since I was a lad, Did smile vpon mee with a chearefull sight. *a* **1568** A. Scott *Poems* (S.T.S.) iii. 18 Be sicht or smyle lat non knaw ȝour intentis. **1611** Cotgr., *Oeil*, the eye;..a sight, a looke. **1700** Moxon *Math. Dict.*, *Compass*, an Instrument..much more easy to be understood by a Sight, than the best description. **1844** Mrs. Browning *Drama of Exile* 141, I fell..struck blind By the sight within your eyes. **1894** Hall Caine *Manxman* III. xx, When you are coming down the alley give a sight up, sir, and you'll see me. **1934** P. Allingham *Cheapjack* xiv. 175 He pointed out a Rolls-Royce which stopped at the entrance of the fair... 'Take sights at that Rolls,' he said. 'There'll be some right mugs turn up in a minute.' **1950** R. M. Howe *Gross's Criminal Investigation* (ed. 4) viii. 163/1 *Take sights*, looking out (especially for suitable house to break into). **1962** *New Statesman* 21 Dec. 897/3 Once we have all this information, we start 'taking sights', and this means watching the house, from the grounds, for the best part of a week.

**b.** An observation with a surveying or other similar instrument; an aim with a gun, etc.

**1834** *Reg. Deb. Congr. U.S.* 25 Feb. 691, I supposed for once in my life I saw gentlemen in the open field, and might be able to draw a fine sight upon them. **1835** Sir J. Ross *Narr. 2nd Voy.* viii. 121 Some sights obtained for the chronometer gave the longitude 94° 40'. **1849** H. Miller *Footpr. Creator* Pref. (1874) p. lxvi, Across which he may safely take his sights and lay down his angles. **1882** Floyer *Unexpl. Baluchistan* 151 All the way down I was either taking sights or working them out, and soon got pretty handy with my sextant.

**c.** *slang.* (See quots.)

**1836** T. Hook *G. Gurney* II. 77 She proceeded to place her two hands extended in a right line from the tip of her nose.., after the fashion of what is called taking a double sight. **1860** *Slang Dict.* 214 'To take a sight at a person,' a vulgar action employed by street boys to denote incredulity, or contempt for authority, by placing the thumb against the nose and closing all the fingers except the little one, which is agitated in token of derision. **1872** *Routledge's Ev. Boy's Ann.* 186/1 Playfully 'taking a sight' with extended finger and thumb.

**d.** *U.S.* 'A straight stretch of road, as one along which a sight may be taken in surveying; a line uninterrupted by a bend or an elevation' (*Cent. Dict.*).

**1848** Bartlett *Dict. Amer.* 303 In North Carolina the distance that can be seen on a road is called a *sight*.

**III. 8. a.** The faculty or power of seeing, as naturally inherent in the eye; eyesight.

*c* **1200** *Trin. Coll. Hom.* 61 Ȝif he binimeð us ure sihte,.. oðer us crokeð on fote oðer on honde. *c* **1290** *S. Eng. Leg.* I. 27 Ore swete louerd..smot him and bi-nam him is siȝt. **13..** *Sir Beues* 3108 Þow hauest so swonke.., þow hauest neȝ for-lore þe siȝt. *c* **1380** Wyclif *Sel. Wks.* II. 308 Þre siȝtis fallen to man; þe first is bodili siȝt, þat fallip to mannis eien, þe while he wakiþ. **1460** Capgr. *Chron.* (Rolls) 8 He began first graving in metallis, to plesauns of the sith. **1484** Caxton *Fables of Alfonce* xii, I praye to the goddes that they vouchesauf to send me my syght ageyne. **1530** Palsgr. 270/1 Sight, *ueve, uision.* **1599** Davies *Immort. Soul* xxx. 13 Most Eyes have perfect Sight, tho' some be blind. **1637** Heywood *Lond. Spec.* Wks. 1874 IV. 315 Sight is the most soveraigne sence, the first of five. **1664** Power *Exp. Philos.* Pref. 15 The knowledge of Man..hath hitherto been determin'd by the view or sight. **1743** Bulkeley & Cummins *Voy. S. Seas* 145 They are exceeding nimble, of an exquisite quick Sight. **1832** Ht. Martineau *Ella of Gar.* iii. 35 He has a keener sight into the place of storms than we. **1833** Mrs. Browning *Prometh. Bd.* 77 A spectacle that turns The sight o' the eyes to pity. **1872** Morley *Voltaire* (1886) 7 His sight was exquisitely keen and clear.

**b.** *fig.* Mental or spiritual vision. With definite article, *spec.* = second sight. Chiefly *Sc.*

*c* **1200** Ormin 5799 Fowwre der..þatt Godess þeww Ezechyel Sahh þurrh gastlike sihhþe. *a* **1225** *Ancr. R.* 94 Þis ..cnowunge kumeð of gostliche sihðe. *c* **1350** *S. Ambrosius* 43 in Horstm. *Altengl. Leg.* (1878) 8/2 Þat inward siht þat Ambrose hedde in God Almiht. *c* **1380** Wyclif *Sel. Wks.* II. 308 Þe þridde..is siȝt of mynde of mannis soule. **1412–20** Lydg. *Chron. Troy* II. 2848 Ȝif þat euery wiȝt Aduerten schuld & castyn in his siȝt Of future þing [etc.]. *a* **1586** Sidney *Ps.* xxv. i, To thee, O Lord most just, I lift my inward sight. **1664** H. More *Myst. Iniq.* I. xiv. §7 The sight of their Mind more directly penetrative into the Divine presence. **1735** Bolingbroke *On Parties* 135 The Sight of the Mind differs very much from the Sight of the Body. **1781** Cowper *Charity* 395 The soul, whose sight all-quick'ning grace renews. **1924** W. Holtby *Crowded Street* xxix. 195 They say she's got the 'sight'—you know, second sight. **1925** W. Duke *Scotland's Heir* x. 223 At the last the Sight came upon him, and he reared upright, crying with outflung arms that he saw bloody claymores. **1959** E. H. Clements *High Tension* v. 80 The factor stared at him. 'Why, Kilmorrin, you have the sight!' **1977** C. McCarry *Secret Lovers* x. 129, I do believe you see me in everything I do. If you haven't the sight, then what is the explanation?

**c.** Contrasted with *faith*.

*c* **1382** Bible (Wyclif) *2 Cor.* v. 7 For we walken bi feith, and not bi cleer siȝt. **1611** *Ibid.* (A.V.), For we walke by faith, not by sight. **1834** J. H. Newman *Parochial Sermons* I. xvii. 258 And all these inducements to live by sight and not by faith are greatly increased, when men are engaged in any pursuit which properly *belongs* to the intellect. **1858** W. Brock *Sir H. Havelock* xiii. 216 He might well have doubted of success had he walked by sight. **1871** H. Alford in *Hymns Anc. & Mod.* (1875) 285/1 Forward, marching eastward Where the heaven is bright, Till the veil be lifted, Till our faith be sight. **1981** M. Green *I believe in Satan's Downfall* vii. 201 To walk by sight would be the very antithesis of the trusting walk of faith to which God's Messiah, along with all men, was called.

**9. a.** The sense or power of vision in relation to the individual possessing or exercising it; freq. approaching to a concrete use, = eye or eyes. †Formerly also in *pl.* of a number of persons, etc.

*c* **1200** Ormin 5495 Wiþþ þatt itt iss inn heoffness ærd Biforenn Godess sihhþe. *a* **1225** *Leg. Kath.* 904 He is to ure sihðe unsehelich in his ahne cunde. *a* **1300** *Cursor M.* 7886 Þe king kest ans on hir his sight. **1340** *Ayenb.* 267 Ich wente myne ziȝþe uor to yzi þe ilke holy ordres of þe gostes. *c* **1380** Wyclif *Wks.* (1880) 206 To make his soule fair..to goddis siȝtte as he makiþ him bisi..for þe siȝtte of men. *c* **1450** in Aungier *Syon* (1840) 307 Kepyng ther sy3th, and ther countynaunce saddly and religiously. **1484** Caxton *Fables of Æsop* III. x, Thow arte now moche playsaunt and fayr to the syghte of me. **1561** Hollybush *Hom. Apoth.* 35 The same are pale under their syghte and leane. **1592** Greene *Disput. Conny Catch.* Wks. (Grosart) X. 257 He..would present his hart as a Tragick sacrifice to the sight of his cruel mistresse. **1697** Dryden *Virg. Georg.* IV. 587 The slipp'ry God will..various Forms assume, to cheat thy sight. **1700** —— *Sigism. & Guisc.* 715 Nor farther word she spoke, but closed her sight. *a* **1771** Gray *Tophet* 5 Our mother-church with half-averted sight. **1827** Keble *Chr. Y.* 7 A fouler vision yet; an age of light, Light without love, glares on the aching sight.

*pl.* **1509** Hawes *Past. Pleas.* IX. (Percy Soc.) 33 O all ye cursed and such evyll fooes, Whose syghtes be blynded over all wyth foly. **1589** Greene *Tullie's Love* Wks. (Grosart) VII. 112 Beautiful Ladies tickled with an earnest desire to satisfie their sightes with his Personage. **1638** Sir T. Herbert *Trav.* (ed. 2) 125 From the hill tops wee dazell our sights in view of that sandy, stony, sterill desert.

**b.** ***in one's sight***, before one's eyes.

*c* **1205** Lay. 25597 Me þuhte a mire sihȝeðe [*c* **1275** in mine sihte] þat þa sæ gon to berne. *a* **1300** *Cursor M.* 622 Fiss on sund, and fouxl on flight, Was broght all fort in his sight. **1382** Wyclif *Rev.* xiii. 13 It made fijr for to come doun fro heuen in to erthe, in the siȝt of alle men. *c* **1450** Holland *Howlat* 62 Be I seyne in thar sicht,..Sum will me dulfully dicht. **1509** Hawes *Past. Pleas.* XLIV. (Percy Soc.) 214 All thyng was visible In Goddes syght. **1560** Daus tr. *Sleidane's Comm.* 5 b, He was advised by his frendes not to come in the Cardinalles syght. **1617** Moryson *Itin.* I. 232 In the sight of the World, so as none should be able to denie it. **1812** Crabbe *Tales* ii. 370 His wife, his children, weeping in his sight.

**c.** ***to sight***, to the eye; so as to be seen.

*a* **1300** *Cursor M.* 23968 þai had him bath for-driuen and draun, Als sceud es us to sight. *a* **1400–50** *Alexander* 1252 It was semand to siȝt as all þe soyle trymblid. **1582** STANYHURST *Æneis* I. (Arb.) 28 We hard of no showting, too sight no sister apered. **1746** FRANCIS tr. *Hor., Art Poet.* 208 He breaks to Light, And pours his specious Miracles to Sight. **1784** COWPER *Task* I. 602 Not rude and surly, .. And terrible to sight.

**10. a.** The range or field of one's vision; chiefly in phr. *out of one's sight*. Also *spec.* (quot. *c* 1865).

*c* **1200** ORMIN 3387 þeȝȝ wenndenn fra þa wakemenn All ut off þeȝȝre sihhþe. *c* **1350** *Will. Palerne* 420 [He told] how sone of his seiȝt þe bestes seþþen ware. **1390** GOWER *Conf.* III. 377 Or be me lief or be me loth, Out of my sighte forth he goth. *c* **1470** HENRY *Wallace* IV. 19 For he na tyme suld be fra hys sicht. **1595** DUNCAN *App. Etym.* (E.D.S.), *Horizon*, the circle bounding our sicht. **1638** JUNIUS *Paint. Ancients* 18 The visible things are gone out of our sight. **1697** DRYDEN *Virg. Georg.* I. 500 Watchful Herons.. Gain on the Skies, and soar above the Sight. **1761** HUME *Hist. Eng.* (1812) I. vi. 321 The two armies lay in sight of each other. **1772–84** *Cook's Voy.* (1790) V. 1787 The ridge of mountains is interrupted by a plain of several leagues in extent, beyond which the sight was unbounded. **1819** SHELLEY *Cenci* I. iii. 168 Now get thee from my sight. *c* **1865** WYLDE in *Circ. Sc.* I. 76/1 The difficulty experienced by all persons.., is to find what is called their 'sight'; that is, the focal distance of the lens.

**b.** Without article, in the phrases ***in sight***, ***out of sight***. See also OUT-OF-SIGHT *adj. phr.* (*sb.*).

(*a*) *a* **1300** *Cursor M.* 15884 Petre he folud him on ferr, For durst he noght in sight. **1377** LANGL. *P. Pl.* B. XIX. 175 Blessed mote þei alle be.. That neuere shal se me in siȝte as þow doste nouthe. *c* **1420** *Sir Amadace* (Camden) xxxvii, He wende that no mon hade him herd, For he seȝhe non in siȝte. **1550** CROWLEY *Last Trumpet* 1330 Kepe Gods feare in syght. **1656** EARL MONM. tr. *Boccalini's Advts. fr. Parnass.* II. lxxix. (1674) 231 For fear of their Creditors, they have all played least-in-sight. **1717** POPE *Iliad* x. 222 And hostile Troy was ever full in Sight. **1816** SCOTT *Old Mort.* xxxvii, Bothwell Bridge was at a little distance, and also in sight. **1887** BOWEN *Æneid* III. 220 Goats in the meadows feeding without one watchman in sight.

(*b*) ? *a* **1400** *Arthur* 342 þey sayleþ faste: Arthour owt of syȝt ys paste. *c* **1450** tr. *De Imitatione* I. xxiii. 30 Whan man is oute of siȝt, sone he passiþ oute of mynde. *c* **1530** H. RHODES *Bk. Nurture* in *Babees Bk.* 79 If thou must spit, or blow thy nose, keepe thou it out of sight. **1562** J. HEYWOOD *Prov. & Epigr.* (1867) 133 Out of sight out of minde. **1617** MORYSON *Itin.* I. 171 As soone as I was out of sight, I walked further towards the East. **1711** BUDGELL *Spect.* No. 77 ¶6 Remembering the old Proverb, Out of Sight out of Mind, I left the Room. **1797–1805** S. & H. LEE *Cant. T.* I. 350 He perceived [them] driven down the coast, and nearly out of sight. **1840** R. H. DANA *Bef. Mast* xxiii, When the sea breeze died away she was nearly out of sight. **1885** *Law Rep.* 14 *Q.B.D.* 874 He remained, as he alleged, out of sight of anyone entering the shop.

**c.** ***out of*** (***all***) ***sight***, immeasurably, beyond all comparison.

**1821** in *Byron's Wks.* (1846) 586/1, I consider Don Juan as out of all sight the best of your works. **1835** MRS. CARLYLE *Lett.* I. 26 In most respects my situation is out of sight more suitable than it was at Craigenputtock. **1880** *Ch. Times* 22 Oct. 684 Under the old management, it was out of sight the most comic journal in England.

**11. a.** The exercise of the faculty of vision; the act of seeing or looking; esp. ***by sight***, freq. denoting merely visual, as contrasted with more intimate, knowledge.

**1297** R. GLOUC. (Rolls) 183 Me knoweþ hem in eche lond bi siȝte þar me hem seþ. *c* **1330** *Assump. Virg.* 628 (Brit. Mus.), Oure mayne þee knewe þat ilke nyȝt, Bothe bi speche and by syȝt. **1377** LANGL. *P. Pl.* B. XIV. 13, I.. soiled it with syȝte or sum ydel speche. **1509** HAWES *Past. Pleas.* XX. (Percy Soc.) 98 On whome my hole delyght Dayly was sette, upon her to have sight. *a* **1568** A. SCOTT *Poems* (S.T.S.) xiv. 5 The kocatrice keilis wᵗ hir sicht. **1604** E. G[RIMSTONE] tr. *D'Acosta's Hist. Indies* III. xvi. 172 A thousand sortes of hearbes and flowers, .. in such sort, as a man cannot well conceive them without sight. **1680** EVELYN *Diary* 30 Aug., He told us that the things most worthy of our sight would be [etc.]. **1700** ASTRY tr. *Saavedra-Faxardo* I. 334 Then came flocking to him.. those too who knew him not but by sight. **1831** *Society* I. 292, I assure you I mistook the person; Lord Conway is barely known to me by sight.

**b.** Examination, inspection, scrutiny. ***bill of sight***: (see quot. 1821).

In quots. 1452 and 1655 sense 12a is possible.

**1452–3** *Cal. Rec. Dublin* (1889) 278 To gywe in the names of the tenantis.. by the sighte of R. Dowdall. **1619** in W. Foster *Eng. Factories in India* (1906) 79 Pretending itt to reserve them only for his first sight. **1655** in Picton *L'pool Munic. Rec.* (1883) I. 188 Repaired and amended.. at yᵉ sight and discression of Mr. Maior. **1662** *Order Ho. Comm. as to Customs* (1663) 1 For a Bill of sight, Bill of Sufferance, or any other imperfect Warrant. **1821** J. SMYTH *Pract. of Customs* 327 A Merchant, .. ignorant of the real quantities and qualities of his Goods, .. may apply to the Collector and Comptroller for a Bill of Sight or View, in order that they may be brought on shore and examined. **1833** *Act 3 & 4 Will. IV*, c. 52 §24 An entry by Bill of Sight.

**c.** ***line of sight***: (cf. LINE *sb.*² 11). Also *transf.* with reference to the transmission of radio waves, etc.; freq. *attrib.* (with hyphens); ***line-of-sight velocity*** = ***radial velocity***.

**1559** [see LINE *sb.*² 11]. **1893** BALL *Story of Sun* 184 The amount of their movements along the line of sight. **1920** A. S. EDDINGTON *Space, Time & Gravitation* viii. 135 In the case of the sun we know by other evidence exactly what the line-of-sight velocity should be; but we have not this knowledge for other stars. **1955** *Times* 18 July 8/2 The others [*sc.* ways of transmitting radio waves], employing in one case 'very high', and in the other 'ultra high' frequencies, are extremely reliable but until now they have been limited to line-of-sight transmission. **1956** H. S. JONES in A. Pryce-Jones *New Outl. Mod. Knowledge* 129 When the first measurements of the line-of-sight velocities of some of these objects [*sc.* spiral nebulae] were made, they were found to be surprisingly large. **1963** G. TROUP *Masers & Lasers* (ed. 2) ix. 158 Infra-red masers might be applied to line-of-sight terrestrial communications. **1972** *Sci. Amer.* Feb. 76/1 Microwave radio links are limited to line-of-sight operation.

**12. a.** Opinion, estimate, judgement; respect, regard, view. Now *rare*.

*a* **1300** *Cursor M.* 11853 'Godd men,' he said, 'quat es your sight O mi fader þat þus es dight?' **1362** LANGL. *P. Pl.* A. Prol. 32 Summe chosen Chaffare to cheeuen þe bettre, As hit semeþ to vre siht þat suche men scholden. ? *a* **1400** *Morte Arth.* 3289 The secunde sir.. þat sewede thame aftyre Was sekerare to my sighte, and saddare in armes. **1536** BELLENDEN *Cron. Scot.* IX. xix. (1541) B b iv, He had nothir reuerence to god, nor sicht to the commoun weil. *a* **1572** KNOX *Hist. Ref.* Wks. 1846 I. 419 At youre awin sychtis sche will sett fordwart that caus at hir power. **1607** in *Antiquary* XXXII. 242 To be disposed at the sight of [supervisors of will]. **1674** *Playford's Skill Mus.* III. 2, I assume that the true sight and judgment of the upper three must proceed from the lowest. **1851** WESTCOTT *Introd. Study Gospels* viii. (ed. 5) 396 The first step to a right understanding of the Gospels must be the abandonment of this point of sight.

†**b.** Knowledge, skill, insight. Const. *in*. *Obs.* (Very common in the 16th cent.)

**1530** PALSGR. 270/1 Sight, knowledge, *perspicasité*. **1535** CRANMER *Misc. Writ.* (Parker Soc.) II. 303 Surely I do much marvel of them both.. having such sight in scriptures and doctors. **1581** in *Confer.* II. (1584) M iij, His sight in Greke was very litle or none at all. **1600** *Dr. Dodypoll* I. ii. in Bullen *O. Pl.* IV. 108 His sweete discourse, His sight in Musick and in heavenlie Arts.

**IV. 13. a.** The pupil of the eye. Now *dial.*

*c* **1400** *Lanfranc's Cirurg.* 247 Macula is a wem in a mannys iȝe, & summe be white þerof & sittiþ vpon þe siȝt of þe iȝe, & summe bisidis þe siȝt. **1530** PALSGR. 270/1 Sight of the eye, *le noyre de loyil*. **1601** HOLLAND *Pliny* I. 155 In either eie they haue two sights or apples. **1683** SNAPE *Anat. Horse* III. viii. (1686) 123 The horney Tunicle or Coat of the Eye, with the pupilla or sight. **1736** BRACKEN *Farriery Impr.* (1757) II. 14 What they mean by the Ground of the Eye, is the Pupil or Hole thro' the Iris and Uvea, which the common People call the Sight of the Eye. **1751** R. PALTOCK *P. Wilkins* xiv. (1883) 43/1 His eyes were small and blue, with a large black sight in the middle. **1808** JAMIESON, *Sicht* of the ee. **1889** in *Eng. Dial. Dict.* (Yorksh.).

†**b.** A visor. *Obs.*

**1508** *Acc. Ld. High Treas. Scot.* IV. 122 For the grathing of the gilt ermyt [*sic*] my Lord of Owbigne gaif the King and for making of ane new sicht to it. *a* **1548** HALL *Chron., Edw. IV*, 197 b, The point of the axe of the lord Scales happened to enter into the sight of the healme of the bastard. **1597** SHAKS. *2 Hen. IV*, IV. i. 121 Their eyes of fire, sparkling through sights of Steele. **1654–66** EARL ORRERY *Parthen.* (1676) 647 He pull'd down the sight of his Helmet.

**c.** *pl.* Spectacles. Now *dial.*

**1619** H. HUTTON *Follies Anat.* (Percy Soc.) 39 An aged man, which spectacles did use Having them filcht.., Fearing the thiefe would not his sights restore [etc.]. **1667** PEPYS *Diary* 18 Oct., I bought me two new pair of spectacles of Purlington..; and his daughter.. do advise me two very young sights. **1823** E. MOOR *Suffolk Words* 350 *Sights*, spectacles, glasses. **1899** in *Eng. Dial. Dict.*

†**d.** (See quot.) *Obs.*⁻¹

**1640** in Entick *London* (1766) II. 165 Glass-plates, or sights for looking-glasses.

**14. a.** An appendage to a surveying or observing instrument, serving to guide the eye.

**1559** W. CUNNINGHAM *Cosmogr. Glasse* 137 A ruler with two sightes, which we moue to and fro. **1571** DIGGES *Pantom.* I. vii. D j b, Forget not to haue two equall fine plates of brasse persed in the middes (for your sightes). **1669** STURMY *Mariner's Mag.* II. xvi. 93 Take the Quadrant and look through the Sight at E. **1676** PHILLIPS *Purch. Pattern* 131 If a man have but a Ruler with sights.. he may draw the foresaid lines to the several angles of the field. **1715** tr. *Gregory's Astron.* (1726) I. 282 A Quadrant.. and an Index moving upon its Center, furnished with Telescopic Sights. **1790** BURKE *Fr. Revol.* Wks. V. 312 An accurate land-surveyor, with his chain, sight, and theodolite. **1833** HERSCHEL *Astron.* ii. 83 The tube or sight, fastened on the circle, works in the solid metallic centring. **1879** *Cassell's Techn. Educ.* IV. 93/1 This prism.. has, when so placed, a notched 'sight' on its upper surface.

**b.** A device, of the nature of a projection or notch, on a fire-arm or piece of ordnance, etc., to assist in taking aim; a telescopic device or other optical aid designed for this purpose; ***in one's sights***, visible through the sights of one's gun; also *fig.*, esp. in phr. ***to raise one's sights***, to adopt a more ambitious objective.

In fire-arms and ordnance the sights are usually two in number, one at or near the muzzle and the other near the breech, the latter being adjustable so as to vary with the distance. In large guns the forms are often very complex.

**1588** LUCAR tr. *Tartaglia's Colloq. Shooting* 18 When the levell sight which is set uppon the mouth of the peece is precisely so high as the levell sight which is set uppon the taile of the peece. **1591** SIR J. SMYTH *Instr. Milit.* 191 All their mosquets should be of one heigth or caliver of bullets with open sights. **1647** HEXHAM I, The sight of a crosse-bow, *het gesight*. **1681** W. ROBERTSON *Phraseol. Gen.* (1693) 1128 The sight in a gun or cross-bow, *scutula*. **1847** *Infantry Man.* (1854) 34 The foresight is aligned through the back sight with the object. **1890** *Times* 6 Dec. 15/3 Thousands of rounds were fired so rapidly.. that in some cases the sights were actually melted. **1942** T. RATTIGAN *Flare Path* I. 20 I've got 'im in my sights, and 'e's getting bigger all the time. **1950** *Economist* 9 Dec. 1002/2 The United States must now raise its sights, in terms of both manpower and production. **1956** A. H. COMPTON *Atomic Quest* 151 Colonel Marshall.. had helped greatly in raising our sights as to the magnitude of the production task. *Ibid.* 339 It is in part the competition between societies that is forcing us to readjust our educational sights. **1959** *N.Z. Listener* 10 July 4/2, I did, for many months, seeing apprehensively that the Army would be raising its sights on compulsory marshalling of our manpower little by little. **1962** *Times* 26 Apr. 7/3 Set your sights a little higher than the kitchen and try to trim your appearance to the job. *Ibid.* 5 Dec. 4/3 Lawry setting his sights on a century. **1967** MRS. L. B. JOHNSON *White House Diary* 5 Dec. (1970) 596 First, he said, we have raised our sights. We have set our national goals to have a clean country. **1971** *Nature* 31 Dec. 499/2 Two years ago, the Government Actuary was estimating that the population would have grown from 56 million at present to.. 68 million by the turn of the century, but he has since been forced by more recent trends to lower his sights. **1976** J. SNOW *Cricket Rebel* 35 They were not Gloucestershire batsmen at the other end of my sights that day but the England selectors.

**c.** Any of a number of nails in the sides and ends of a billiard table, used in marking out the table for some forms of carom billiards.

**1864** W. B. DICK *Amer. Hoyle* 419 A line is drawn down the centre of the table, from the centre nails or sights in the *head* and *lower* cushions. **1890** CHAMPLIN & BOSTWICK *Cycl. Games & Sports* 81/1 Each carom table has on it two spots, along an imaginary line drawn lengthways through the centre from the middle rails or 'sights' in the head and lower cushions: the first, opposite the second 'sight', is sometimes called the light red spot, the second, opposite the sixth 'sight', the dark red spot. **1910** *Encycl. Brit.* III. 939/1 In the case of the Triangular Baulk-line, lines are drawn at the four corners from the second 'sight' on the side-rails to the first sight on the end-rails, forming four triangles within which only a limited number of caroms may be made.

**15.** The opening in a picture-frame; that part of the picture which shows in this.

**1850** [see *sight-measure* in 17].

**V. 16.** *attrib.* and *Comb.* (chiefly objective), as ***sight-aching***, ***-fitting***, ***-hungry***, ***-hunter***, etc.

**1593** NASHE *Christ's Tears* Wks. (Grosart) IV. 224 The ..*sight-acking botches of theyr vnsatiate intemperance, they will vnblushingly lay foorth. **1611** COTGR., *Advenant*, handsome, .. well beseeming, .. *sight-fitting. **1880** L. WALLACE *Ben-Hur* V. xii. 349 There the close of the exercises found them, patient and *sight-hungry as at the beginning. **1848** *Blackw. Mag.* Aug. 185 That professional *sight-hunters should go *sight-hunting. **1743** BLAIR *Grave* 288 The Star-surveying Sage close to his Eye Applies the *Sight-invigorating Tube. **1593** NASHE *Christ's Tears* Wks. (Grosart) IV. 194 *Sight-killingly with his.. frownes, he shall teache him, both that he is, and what he is. **1605** SYLVESTER *Du Bartas* II. iii. I. *Vocation* 1008 What can the Sight of the *Sight-maker dim? **1610** SHAKS. *Temp.* I. ii. 203 Ioues Lightning, the precursers O'th dreadfull Thunder-claps more momentarie And *sight out-running were not. **1870** LOWELL *Study Wind.* I. 12 Their enemies were hidden in their own *sight-proof bush. **1784** COWPER *Task* IV. 759 That *sight-refreshing green Is still the liv'ry she [Nature] delights to wear. **1814** F. BURNEY *Let.* 24 Aug. (1978) VII. 438 But for Heaven's sake send him no more *sight-seekers, who expect 'The Hero' to give dinners, & shew Lyons! **1844** ALB. SMITH *Adv. Mr. Ledbury* vi, The majority of sight-seekers.. know.. little about the venerable edifice. **1895** E. OWEN in *Wks. G. Edwards* p. ix, There were then no fashionable inns to give accommodation to sight-seekers. **1896** *Cath. Mag.* June 350 It would be happiness to add its name to our list of *sight-seen countries. **1596** FITZ-GEFFREY *Sir F. Drake* (1881) 31 Monsters of nature, Nile-bred Crocodiles, *Sight-slaying Basilisks. **1676** MARVELL *Mr. Smirke* 44 The King of Virginia, that had two Squires .. to lift up his Eye-lids.. I am not bound to be any of his *Sight-supporters. **1899** *Allbutt's Syst. Med.* VI. 613 There was a slight attack of left hemiplegia with headache, vertigo, and *sight-troubles.

**b.** In terms relating to the taking of surveys or observations, or denoting appliances used for this purpose, as ***sight-alidade***, ***-aligner***, ***-angle***, ***-beam***, etc.

**1900** H. M. WILSON *Topogr. Surveying* vii. 161 A small *sight-alidade was devised by the author both for sighting directions, and for determining elevations by vertical angulation. **1892** GREENER *Breech-Loader* 97 The *sight-aligner and adjustable gun, invented in 1882. **1571** DIGGES *Pantom.* I. xxxiv. K ij b, From the Centre thereof, extend right lines.., wryting as before vppon euery of them the names of their places or markes, whereof they are the *sight Angles. *a* **1400** in Halliw. *Rara Mathem.* (1841) 63 Go toward it and froward it til þi *sight beme passe by þe heght of þe ȝerde and of þat thyng. **1669** STURMY *Mariner's Mag.* II. xiii. 82 The Sight-beams over the ends of the Crosses. **1859** RUSKIN *Perspective* i. 99 The *Sight-magnitude of a line is the magnitude which bears, to the real line, the same proportion that the distance of the picture bears to the distance of the object. **1835** C. F. HOFFMAN *Winter in West* II. 171 The long western rifle has three *sight-pieces on the barrel. **1874** J. W. LONG *Amer. Wild-fowl* i. 24 Sight-piece small and close to the muzzle. **1859** RUSKIN *Perspective* Introd. 9 The point S is to represent the point opposite which you wish the observer of your picture to place his eye in looking at it. Call this point the *Sight-point. **1883** R. G. WHITE *W. Adams* 121 He threw up his left arm, and took a *sight rest on it [with his revolver]. **1731** W. HALFPENNY *Perspective* p. iv, The Groove E, wherein the *Sight-Staff slides to and fro. **1669** STURMY *Mariner's Mag.* II. xiv. 85 If you see all Skie and no Water, then draw your *Sight-Vane a little lower. **1863** A. YOUNG *Naut. Dict.* (ed. 2) 297 The sight vanes are pieces of brass standing perpendicularly to the plane of the instrument.

**c.** In terms relating to the practice of watching the keys of a typewriter while typing, as ***sight method***, ***system***, ***technique***, ***typing***, ***typist***, ***writer***, ***writing***. Cf. *touch-typing*, etc. s.v. TOUCH-.

**1904** A. E. MORTON *Mod. Typewriting* (ed. 2) 12 There are two methods of manipulation, one the 'touch', and the other the 'sight' system. **1918** M. B. OWEN *Typewriting Speed* 145 The constant shifting of the eyes in sight writing. *Ibid.* 147 The sight typist writes spasmodically. *Ibid.* 153 Many sight writers use all the fingers. **1928** M. CROOKS *Touch Typewriting for Teachers* ii. 10 A typist writing by the Sight method expends about six times as much.. energy.. as that expended by the Touch typist. *Ibid.* 11 The properly trained Touch typist is capable of greater speed than the

Sight typist. **1935** A. C. Marshall *Princ. Teaching Typewriting* i. 1 It is.. hardly necessary now to advocate the 'touch' system as against 'sight-typing'. *Ibid.* 2 The maximum speed ever attained by a sight-typist has never exceeded 60 per cent of that of equivalent touch experts. **1969** L. J. West *Acquisition of Typewriting Skills* viii. 183 Will not early sight typists form a habit of sight typing?.. How does one wean learners away from sight techniques?

**17.** Special combs.: **sight bar**, a metal bar forming part of the breech-sight of a gun; **sight bill** *U.S.*, a bill of exchange payable on presentation; **sight-board** = *sight-screen* below; **sight-chase**, a chase in which the dogs hunt by sight; **sight cheque**, *U.S.*, a cheque or draft payable on presentation; †**sight-court**, a place for public shows; **sight draft** = *sight cheque*; **sight edge** *Naut.*, (see quot. 1948); **sight feed**, a device through which the feeding of lubricant or fuel may be seen; also (with hypen) *attrib.*; **sight gag**, a joke which achieves its effect visually; †**sight-glasses**, spectacles; **sight-holder**, a diamond merchant entitled to buy diamonds at a sight (see sense 5 f above); **sight liability**, an obligation to pay money on presentation of a cheque or bill of exchange; **sight-line**, (*a*) (see quot. 1859); (*b*) a straight line extending from the eye of a spectator to an object or area being watched; *spec.* a line from the eye of a spectator in a theatre to the edge of the part of the stage which that spectator can see; **sight-measure** (see sense 15); **sight-player**, one who is able to play music at sight; so **sight-playing**; **sight-read** *v. intr.* and *trans.*, to read (a piece of music) at sight; **sight-reader**, one who is able to read music at sight; so ***sight-reading***; **sight record** *Ornith.*, a record of the sighting (not the capture) of a bird; **sight-screen** = screen *sb.*[1] 1 g; **sight-setter**, on a warship, a member of a gun-crew whose duty is to keep the gun-sight at the correct elevation as shown by the range indicator (see also quot. 1973); †**sight-shot**, the range of vision; **sight-singing**, the practice or art of singing at sight; **sight tube**, (*a*) a tube through which observations are made; (*b*) a transparent tube connected to a tank or cistern so as to display the level of the liquid inside it.

**1884** *Naval Encycl.* 751/2 **Sight-bar*, a metal bar on which the range in yards, or in degrees, is marked. It is a part of the breech-sight, and, by raising or lowering it, different ranges are obtained. **1920** Carter & Arnold *Field Artillery Instruction* iii. 47 The rocking bar sight consists of a rocking bar.. and a sight bar. **1853** *Southern Literary Messenger* XIX. 89/2 Mr. Thompson agreed to accommodate him with a *sight bill on his correspondent in Raleigh. **1887** *Courier-Jrnl.* (Louisville, Kentucky) 5 May 7/3 Eastern exchange was firm, and there were more buyers than sellers of New York sight bills at 80c per $1,000 premium. **1898** K. S. Ranjitsinhji *With Stoddart's Team* (ed. 4) iii. 49 [At Adelaide] the *sight-boards behind the bowler's arm appeared to be but reminders of the existence of such things for a better purpose in England. **1955** Miller & Whittington *Cricket Typhoon* I. i. 13 Tiny white pavilion and tinier white sight-boards. **1975** N. Nicholson *Wednesday Early Closing* vi. 129 Every.. excuse for hindrance and delay was.. tried—asking for the sight-boards to be moved,.. looking round at the fielders, testing the bat. **1897** *Outing* XXX. 127/1 Just in time to witness a short but pretty '*sight chase'. The dogs have seen the fox. **1863** 'E. Kirke' *My Southern Friends* xxii. 232, I enclose you *sight check of Branch Bank of Cape Fear on Bank of Republic, for $10,820. **1553** Grimalde *Cicero's Offices* (1556) 87 *Sightcourts, galereywalkes, and new churches, the more reuerentlie I fynde fault with for Pompeyus sake. **1850** G. N. Jones *Florida Plantation Rec.* (1927) 60 Your favor of the 22nd ult. enclosing *sight draft on Messrs Habersham for $200. **1904** 'O. Henry' *Cabbages & Kings* xiv. 254 It's a gold mine. It's a sight-draft on your president man for twenty thousand dollars. **1979** O. Sela *Petrograd Consignment* 34 At the bank.. letters of authority were presented, mandates altered and instructions given for the preparation of sight drafts. **1911** *Encycl. Brit.* XXIV. 971/1 The projections of the plate and longitudinal *sight edges are drawn in the body plan on the floor. **1948** R. de Kerchove *Internat. Maritime Dict.* 676/2 *Sight edge*, the edges of the plates, in clinker-built plating, which are visible on the outside of the shell, on the top of decks and tank top, and on the opposite side from the stiffeners on bulkheads. **1888** *Lockwood's Dict. Mech. Engin.* 319 **Sight feed lubricator*, a lubricator.. in which the flowing or non-flowing of the oil is always apparent at sight, being enclosed in, or having to pass through a glass vessel. **1902** A. C. Harmsworth et al. *Motors* ix. 172 If a Dubrulle mechanical lubricator is used, examine the ball valves sometimes, and do not trust entirely to the sight feed. **1928** *Daily Tel.* 16 Oct. 7 Non-crushable back-lamps and sight-feed fuel gauges on the dashboard are in demand for the new cars. **1957** *N.Y. Herald Tribune* 7 Nov. 24/4 The line gags are like the *sight gags: they're not quite sturdy enough to be up and around yet. **1977** *Time* 2 May 49/3 *I Love My Wife*.. is dotted with paralyzingly funny sight gags. **1605** tr. *P. de Loyes' Treat. Spect.* 59 It is well knowne that ordinarily the spectacles or *sight-glasses do make letters to seeme more great than they are indeede. **1973** *Times* 19 June (Bombay Suppl.) p. xii/3 Bombay has at least 2,000 diamond businesses, of which about 1,400 are members of the Diamond Merchants' Association. Of these 43 are '*sight-holders' of the Diamond Trading Company of London, which means that they are notified of the 10 'sightings' which the DTC holds every year. The sight-holders are the only people in India to whom the DTC will sell. **1930** *Economist* 27 Sept. 556/2 It may be desirable to modify present standards as regards the ratio of gold cover to notes and *sight liabilities. **1958** *Spectator* 24 Jan. 97/2 The proportion of sight-liabilities covered by reserves is no better than in 1945. **1859** Ruskin *Perspective* Introd. 9 Through the Sight-point, S, draw a horizontal line GH, right across your paper from side to side, and call this line the *Sight-line. **1917** E. B. Kinsila *Mod. Theatre Construction* iv. 60 One of the most important requisites in designing an auditorium is the establishment of correct sight lines. **1957** J. Osborne *Entertainer* 11 The sight-lines are preserved by swagging. **1958** *Archit. Rev.* CXXIII. 352/2 The second case [for the substitution of wire fence for hedgerow] is to provide sightlines at corners. **1971** P. Gresswell *Environment* 264 Sight lines have to be kept open at bends and corners. **1975** I. Melchior *Sleeper Agent* (1976) ii. 65 He positioned himself so that he had optimum sight lines down the side street. **1977** *Time Out* 28 Jan.–3 Feb. 43/2 Check seating plan before buying tickets as many seats have restricted sight lines. **1850** *Jrnl. of Design* IV. 58 *Sight measure $4\frac{1}{8} \times 3\frac{1}{4}$. **1909** *Chambers's Jrnl.* May 334/2 Ask an accomplished *sight-player how he is able to translate so readily the symbols he reads with the eye into their relative notes. *Ibid.* 334/1 He maintains that s*ight-playing does not depend upon an accurate knowledge of the relationship between notes and keys. **1944** W. Apel *Harvard Dict. Music* 680/1 The greatest enemy of sight-playing is playing by heart. **1903** A. W. Patterson *Schumann* 181 We want more than a facility to '*sight read' in order to fully comprehend. **1959** 'F. Newton' *Jazz Scene* ii. 30 Jazz cannot at present be adequately noted down on paper, and if it could, would almost certainly be far too complex for players to sight-read. **1974** *Guardian* 22 Mar. 14/4 Paul Beard, the [orchestra] leader, asked him whether he would like to stay on, making him sight-read part of Vaughan Williams's Fourth Symphony as an audition. **1866** *Athenæum* No. 2000. 277/2 The best *sight-readers in Europe. **1874** Ouseley *Mus. Form* 5 A man may be a thoroughly accomplished musician,.. a perfect sight-reader [etc.]. **1864** *Reader* 30 Apr. 551/2 The singer's power of independent '*sight-reading'. **1934** *Brit. Birds* XXVIII. 31 All but one of these are '*sight-records', but in some cases the writer had already made the acquaintance of the species in other lands. **1959** D. A. Bannerman *Birds Brit. Isles* VIII. 35 A sight-record of a frigate bird observed off the south-west coast of Ireland on 25th May 1953 by W. K. Richmond, was published in the *Fair Isle Bulletin*. **1956** N. Cardus *Close of Play* 20 The sixth ball.. was fielded on the boundary's edge at the *sight-screen behind MacDonald's arm. **1977** T. Heald *Just Desserts* v. 92 At either end of the ground were white sightscreens on wheels. **1909** *Cent. Dict. Suppl.*, *Sight-setter. **1916** 'Taffrail' *Pincher Martin* xvi. 307 Some order came through a voice-pipe to the gun; whereupon the sight-setter twiddled a small wheel and peered anxiously at a graduated dial. **1920** *Blackw. Mag.* Mar. 332/2 Dully from the concealed gun positions echoed the calls of the sight-setters. **1973** J. Quick *Dict. Weapons & Military Terms* 400/1 *Sight setter*, the gun-crew member who sets the range and deflection data ordered by the officer controlling the fire. **1663** Cowley *Ess., Obscurity*, It only makes me run faster from the place, till I get, as it were, out of *sight-shot. **1801** Busby *Dict. Mus.* s.v. *Solmization*, This preparatory exercise, so necessary to *sight-singing. **1898** *Westm. Gaz.* 29 Oct. 5/2 Sight-singing in elementary schools. **1851** H. Melville *Moby Dick* III. xxxviii. 221 The crushed copper *sight-tubes of the quadrant. **1859** *Times* 7 Jan. 8/4 He can enter an enemy's harbour under water and make surveys, only showing above the surface a sight tube, no more than one half inch in diameter, and retire still under water. **1900** W. M. Stine *Photometrical Measurements* iii. 77 Adjust the telescopic sight tube until the different portions of the field are sharply outlined. **1905** *Motor Manual* (ed. 7) iv. 78 The oil.. enters a series of sight tubes. **1951** *Proc. Physical Soc.* B. LXIV. 49 The level of the liquid in the annular gap can be deduced from observations of its level in a vertical sight-tube attached to the filling apparatus.

†**sight**, *sb.*[2] *Obs.* Forms: 4 siȝt(e, 4–6 sight, 6 syght. [Cf. sight *v.*[2] Not related to Du. *zucht*, which is for earlier **suft*.] A sigh.

*a* **1300** *Cursor M.* 15169 Mani sari sight [*v.r.* sigh, sikyng] .. þar sanc vn-til his hert. *c* **1350** *Will. Palerne* 924 My seknes wiþ my siȝtes sumtime slakes. **1584** Lodge *Forbonius & Prisceria* 30 Not waying of her many louing sightes, Her watrie eyes, her secret moane by nights. **1584** *Pleas. Com. Two Ital. Gentl.* D j, By the smoake of loouers scalding sightes [*rime* flightes].

†**sight**, *sb.*[3] *Obs. rare.* [? ad. LG. *sichte*: see sift *sb.*] A sieve or strainer.

**1559** Morwyng *Evonym.* 376 Pres it out strongly and put the decoction prest out through a wullen sight, and pres it out, that the substance may remain in the sight.

**sight** (saɪt), *v.*[1] Also 6 *Sc.* sycht, sicht. [f. sight *sb.*[1] Cf. MDu. *sichten*, *zichten* (rare), G. *sichten* (naut.), Da. *sigte*, Sw. *sigta*.]

**1.** *trans.* †**a.** *Sc.* To look at, view, inspect, examine, scrutinize. *Obs.*

**1556** *Peebles Burgh Rec.* (1872) 234 To.. pas done with ane of the baillies to sycht the saidis stanis. **1578** *Supplication General Assembly* in *Misc. Wodrow Soc.* (1844) 402 Quhen as zour Grace hes sichtit thir our laboris. **1632** Lithgow *Trav.* vii. 303 None of us all knowing what was in the Clogbags till they were sighted. **1678** Sir G. Mackenzie *Crim. Laws Scot.* i. viii. § 1 The Body must in this case be sighted by Physitians. **1706** in J. Watson *Jedburgh Abbey* (1894) 42 That necessar it is workmen be imployed to sight and repair the samyn.

**b.** To examine by taking a sight.

**1884** *Truth* 13 Mar. 372/1 He reports.. that the rails, sighted crosswise, are not as true as they should be.

**2. a.** To get or catch sight of, to see, to get or go within sight of (anything).

**1602** Warner *Alb. Eng.* xiii. lxxvi. 315 Nor doth our Eie-sight see it selfe, nor Soule that sighteth it. **1632** Lithgow *Trav.* viii. 375 Wilde beasts, whose hollow cryes, as we heard in the night, so we too often sighted their bodies in the day. **1819** O'Meara *Trans. St. Helena* 36 The remarks which he asserts to have been made relative to sighting Napoleon. **1853** Kane *Grinnell Exped.* iv. (1856) 33 On the same day.. we sighted the mountainous coast of Greenland. **1887** Besant *World Went* vii, We sighted her one morning at daybreak.

**b.** *spec.* Of bills: (see quot.).

**1866** Crump *Banking* v. 103 A bill drawn at so many days' sight, must be computed exclusively of the day on which it is sighted, and inclusively of the day it falls due.

**c.** To take aim at (an object); to level or aim (a fire-arm, etc.) at a target.

**1871** *Harper's Mag.* Dec. 48/2 No sooner, however, did he 'sight', or try to sight, the horseman in question,.. than the thumping against the ribs again began. **1901** F. Norris *Octopus* ii. vi. 521 With the words, he dropped to one knee, and sighting his rifle carefully, fired into the group of armed men. **1976** D. Storey *Saville* i. iv. 36 Take out the bullets, and sight it at various objects outside the window.

**3. a.** *intr.* To take a sight, *esp.* in shooting.

**1787** in *Maryland Hist. Mag.* (1924) XIX. 265 The mother of the complainants wife sighted with a compass from the tree. **1842** J. F. Cooper *Jack o' Lantern* xxviii, Together they sighted, and together they fired. **1883** *Harper's Mag.* Jan. 201/1 Then stooping and sighting along it, he moves the outer end of the lath. **1896** *Daily News* 27 July 9/3 He took matters very coolly, and sighted several times before he was satisfied.

**b.** With *in.* To correct the sights of (a fire-arm, etc.) by testing and adjustment. *N. Amer.*

**1958** *Washington Post* 31 Oct. d6/3 The Berwyn Rod & Gun Club invites deer hunters to sight-in their rifles during all-day open house sessions on Nov. 2 and Nov. 9. **1971** W. Hillen *Blackwater River* x. 91, I started him off right by sighting-in his new rifle, and soon he was hitting the apple box every time. **1972** *Islander* (Victoria, B.C.) 24 Sept. 13/1 Heading into the woods with a rifle that hasn't been sighted-in makes no more sense than driving an automobile without a gasoline gauge. **1980** *Outdoor Life* (U.S.) (Northeast ed.) Oct. 94/3 A Leupold 4X compact scope (made specially for the Kimber rifle) mounted and sighted in at the factory.

†**sight**, *v.*[2] *Obs.* Also 5 *Sc.* sicht-, 6 syght. [? f. *sight(e*, pa. t. of siche *v.*] *intr.* To sigh.

*c* **1375** *Sc. Leg. Saints* xxvi. (*Nicholas*) 1138 In his hart he mad mayne & sichtit sare. *c* **1450** *Abce* in *Q. Eliz. Acad.* 67 Be not to sadde, to sorry, ne sight not to deep. *c* **1475** in *Rel. Antiq.* I. 71 Whan other men doyth sleype, Thene do I syght and weype.

'**sightable**, *a.* [f. sight *v.*[1]] Comparatively clear.

**1888** *Times* 18 Aug. 5/1 At 3 o'clock the chief officer reported that the weather was 'sightable', with occasional rain.

**sighted** ('saɪtɪd), *ppl. a.* [f. sight *sb.*[1] + -ed.]

**1.** Having sight of a specified kind.

See also *dim-*, *far-*, *long-*, *sharp-*, *short-*, *weak-sighted*.

**1552–** [see quick-sighted]. **1586–** [see clear-sighted]. **1594** Nashe *Unfort. Trav.* Wks. (Grosart) V. 159 Of an ill tree I hope you are not so ill sighted in graffing to expect good frute. **1596** Spenser *Hymn Beauty* 235 Louers eyes more sharply sighted bee Then other mens. **1615** Chapman *Odyss.* vi. 162 That he might see this lovely-sighted maid. *a* **1680** Butler *Rem.* (1759) II. 6 By which both senses being united Does render them much better sighted. **1791–3** in *Spirit Publ. Jrnls.* (1799) I. 17 Who guide the helm of Britain half-seas over, Yet double-sighted keep an eye on Port. **1846** Ruskin *Mod. Paint.* II. iii. xii. § 1 Any of us whose heart is rightly tuned, or whose mind is clearly and surely sighted. **1866** S. B. James *Duty & Doctr.* (1871) 153 Uncivilized, imperfect-sighted heathen men.

**b.** Having sight *like* something specified.

**1602** Dolman *La Primaud. Fr. Acad.* (1618) iii. 643 Those are sighted like the bat, who see not the things most manifest in nature. **1611** Shaks. *Wint. T.* i. ii. 388 Make me not sighted like the Basilisque.

**2.** Endowed with sight; able to see. Also *absol.*

**1836** Landor *Minor Prose Pieces* Wks. 1853 II. 467/2 Above all others, blind or sighted, he is so ready to take advantage of the slightest word, that [etc.]. **1860** *Macm. Mag.* III. 56 If the sighted would help the blind. **1888** *Pall Mall G.* 31 July 2/2 Two pretty boats manned each by six blind little lads and one sighted person.

*transf.* **1887** *Athenæum* 17 Dec. 818/3 Without sighted supervision the industrial competition [of the blind] with seeing workmen is too unequal to be maintained.

**3.** Furnished or fitted with a sight or sights.

**1859** *Musketry Instr.* 28 It may sometimes occur that the rifle is not accurately sighted as to elevation. **1879** *Man. Artill. Exerc.* 142 The gun is sighted centrally. **1893** Selous *Trav. S.E. Africa* 432 One's rifle ought to be carefully sighted up to at least four hundred yards.

**4.** (See quot.)

**1873** Maxwell *Electr. & Magn.* I. 306 If the hair as seen through the lens appears straight and bisects the interval between the black dots it is said to be in its sighted position.

'**sightening.** [f. sight *sb.*[1]] In calico-printing, a fugitive colour used to test the quality of the work.

**1875** Knight *Dict. Mech.* 2176/2.

**sighter** ('saɪtə(r)). [f. sight *v.*[1]]

†**1.** *Sc.* An inspector. *Obs.*

**1708** in *Hist. Regality of Musselburgh* (1857) 22 The two present magistrates and sighters to be present at the cutting and selling.

**2.** In card-sharping: (see quot.).

**1894** Maskelyne *Sharps & Flats* 196 'Sighters'.. are simply minute dots upon the faces of the cards.

**3.** A sighting shot in rifle or artillery shooting. Also *transf.* and *fig.*

**1897** *Times* 23 July 8/1 Black, a sighter for tie shots, made 11 [bulls] in succession. **1899** *Westm. Gaz.* 24 July 4/3 They had.. to fire three tie-shots off with a sighter allowed. **1920** G. S. Gordon *Let.* 17 Sept. (1943) 139 You were charming about my article... Richmond, in a brief post-card, called the thing a 'bull's-eye'. I call it a sighter; and some day I shall have the second shot. **1960** *Times* 11 Apr. 3/7 An early sighter by Albaladejo gave some inkling of what was in store in the matter of dropped goals.

†**'sightful,** *a. Obs.* [f. SIGHT *sb.*[1]]

**1.** Visible.

*c* **1375** *Sc. Leg. Saints* l. (*Catherine*) 369 [He] is a god,.. wnsichtfull and sichtfull bedene. **1387-8** T. USK *Test. Love* Prol. (Skeat) l. 58 The unsene privitees of god, made to us sightful..in our contemplacion and understonding. *Ibid.* III. ix. 98 How was it, that sightful manna in deserte to children of Israel was spirtuel mete? **1545** RAYNOLD *Byrth Mankynde* Hh vij, These vaynes appering..immediatly vnder the skyn, very conspicuous and syghtful.

**2.** Endowed with sight; seeing. Also *fig.*

**1594** CAREW *Huarte's Exam. Wits* (1596) 59 The vnderstanding groweth more sharpe and sightfull. *Ibid.* 97, I cannot forgoe to thinke, that the reasonable soule seuered from the body..hath a power sightfull. **1613** CHAPMAN *Masque Inns of Crt.* Plays 1873 III. 106 Tis passing miraculous that your dul and blind worship should so sodainly turne both sightful and witful.

**3.** Sightly, pleasant to the eye.

**1565** STAPLETON tr. *Bede's Hist. Ch. Eng.* 180 His priest.. set forth the buildings with divers comely and sightfull workes. **1571** GOLDING *Calvin on Ps.* xvi. 11 The fulnesse of joye is matched ageinste the syghtfull entycements of the worlde.

Hence †**'sightfulness**, the power of seeing. *Obs.*

*a* **1586** SIDNEY *Arcadia* II. (1605) 149 Let vs not winke though void of purest sightfullnesse. *Ibid.* 219 My praier is Thou maist loue her, that I may see thy sightfullnesse.

**sighth,** obs. form of SITHE, to sigh.

**'sight-hole.** [SIGHT *sb.*[1]] A hole to see through, *esp.* in a surveying or other instrument.

**1559** W. CUNNINGHAM *Cosmogr. Glasse* 29 Then rayse up and downe the ruler (having two sight holes made in it) unto the sonne. **1596** SHAKS. *1 Hen. IV*, IV. i. 71 Wee of the offring side Must..stop all sight-holes. **1646** EARL MONM. tr. *Biondi's Civil Wars* VI. 72 Slain by the splinter of a Lance which wounded him thorow the sight-hole of his Helmet. **1692** *Capt. Smith's Seaman's Gram.* II. xxiv. 130 Which will shew at what height the Sight-hole standeth. **1769** *Phil. Trans.* LIX. 296 A small sight-hole, made through a piece of brass. **1823** J. BADCOCK *Dom. Amusem.* 50 The sight-hole.. is still unfurnished with a glass of any sort. **1898** *Engineering Mag.* XVI. 110/2 The sight-holes provided in the smoke-boxes of certain stationary boilers of the locomotive type.

†**b.** The pupil of the eye. *Obs.*

**1670** *Phil. Trans.* V. 1027 They contract much their pupilla or sight-hole of the Eye.

**sighting** ('saɪtɪŋ), *vbl. sb.*[1] [f. SIGHT *v.*[1]]

†**1.** A method of cheating at dice. *Obs.*

*c* **1752** *Art & Myst. Gaming* Title-p., The Art and Manner of working with a Great-Box; Eclipsing, Sighting, Waxing and Popping, &c.

**2.** The action of looking, catching sight *of*, inspecting or examining, etc. Also, an instance of catching sight (esp. of something rare or unusual).

**1853** KANE *Grinnell Exp.* xxv. (1856) 203 The mere sighting of a distant coast. **1896** *Daily News* 21 Dec. 2/1 Thus enabling the docking, sighting, cleaning, painting and undocking of vessels to be accomplished in one tide. **1955** W. GIRVAN *Flying Saucers & Common Sense* i. 13 It was not long before sightings were being reported elsewhere than in Scandinavia. **1968** *Listener* 4 July 18/2 Our objection is against the extraterrestrial origin of the phenomena, and most of us base our disbelief on the very large number of 'sightings' that have been reported. **1976** *Scotsman* 15 Dec. 9/4 The experiment to reintroduce the white-tailed eagle to the Isle of Rhum National Nature Reserve is reported to be going well, with sightings of the released birds.

**3. a.** The action of giving to a gun the proper elevation and direction to hit the object aimed at.

**1884** *Times* (weekly ed.) 8 Feb. 1/3 The gunners were ignorant of the process of sighting. **1893** F. ADAMS *New Egypt* 235 The British Admiral bore ungrudging witness.. to the excellent sighting of the guns.

**b.** *sighting-in*, the action of correcting the sights of a fire-arm, etc. Cf. SIGHT *v.*[1] 3 b. *N. Amer.*

**1958** *Washington Post* 31 Oct. D6/3 (*heading*) 2 Days are Set for Sighting-In. **1962** *Wildlife Rev.* Dec. 9 The opening of a sighting-in range at Maiden Creek some 12 miles north of Cache Creek has been welcomed with enthusiasm by sportsmen. **1970** R. A. STEINDLER *Firearms Dict.* 229/1 *Sighting-in*, process of adjusting the sights, usually the rear one, or the elevation..& windage..adjustments of a scope, so that the bullet will hit a predetermined point of aim on the target at a specific distance. Much of the trial & error method of sighting-in a rifle can be eliminated by the use of a collimator.

**4.** *attrib.*, esp. *sighting-shot*, a preliminary shot allowed to each competitor in a shooting-match.

**1909** *Cent. Dict.* Suppl. 1217/1 Modern turrets usually have three sighting-hoods, one in the center line for the turret training-pointer and one on each side for the two gun-pointers. **1973** J. QUICK *Dict. Weapons & Military Terms* 400/1 *Sighting hood*, an armored hood with viewing slits in the sides, as on the top of a turret, a submarine, etc. **1895** *Outing* XXVI. 397/2 The disk of the sighting rod is turned up to coincide with the sight. **1897** *Westm. Gaz.* 30 Nov. 5/1 The sighting-room of the Royal Gun Factories. **1872** *Daily News* 15 July, He..fired his two sighting-shot bull's-eyes straight from the shoulder. **1861** *Times* 12 July, They had sold..8,000 tickets for the sighting targets. **1946** *Nature* 12 Oct. 518/2 Radiation from a 5 sq. mm. area of tyre falls on to the cell via an arrangement which comprises a water-cooled copper sighting-tube and a rotating slotted disk which serves as the radiation chopper. **1958** J. NEEDHAM in *Aspects of Translation* 86 And there are holes which take the place of the sighting-tube for looking up (at the heavenly bodies).

†**'sighting,** *vbl. sb.*[2] [f. SIGHT *v.*[2]] Sighing.

**13..** *Cursor M.* 10496 (Gött.), To-quilys scho mened þus hir care, wid weping and wid sihting sare. **1520** *Calisto & Melib.* A iij, Craft in them renewyng that neuer decays, Theyre seyenges, sightynges, prouokynges, theyr plays.

†**'sighting,** *vbl. sb.*[3] [? ad. LG. *sichting* (G. *sichtung*), vbl. sb. f. *sichten* to sift: cf. SIGHT *sb.*[3]] The result of straining; strained matter.

**1559** MORWYNG *Evonym.* 376 Sieth this sighting to the thiknes of hony.

**sightless** ('saɪtlɪs), *a.* [f. SIGHT *sb.*[1] + -LESS.]

**1.** Unable to see; destitute of the power of sight; blind.

*c* **1250** *Gen. & Ex.* 1528 Ysaac Wurðede sighteles and elde swac. **1387-8** T. USK *Test. Love* I. i. (Skeat) 15 Thus witless thoughtful, sightles lokinge, I endure my penaunce in this derke prison. **1435** MISYN *Fire of Love* 54 And for he þis vtward Ioys onely desirs, in in-wardly & vnsene blyndyd als wer sytheles to fyre gois. *a* **1585** MONTGOMERIE *Cherrie & Slae* 305 Baith sichtles, and michtles, I grew almaist at ainis. *c* **1600** SHAKS. *Sonn.* xliii, When in dead night thy faire imperfect shade..on sightlesse eyes doth stay. **1674** N. FAIRFAX *Bulk & Selv.* 47 Were all seeing things sightless, there would be no colours. **1725** POPE *Odyss.* VIII. 221 He who sightless wants his visual ray. **1791** COWPER *Iliad* v. 824 Sightless, of all thought bereft, He sank. **1842** LONGF. *Warning* ii, A cruel mockery of his [Samson's] sightless woe. **1879** G. ALLEN *Colour-Sense* iii. 27 The eye of the bee, of the cuttlefish, and of the eagle, have each apparently been separately developed from unlike remote sightless ancestors.

*fig.* **1781** COWPER *Charity* 416 The truth she loves a sightless world blaspheme. **1881** H. JAMES *Portr. Lady* liii, She performed this journey with sightless eyes, and took little pleasure in the countries she traversed.

**b.** Deprived of the sight *of* something. *rare*[−1].

**1632** LITHGOW *Trav.* x. 470 Being sightlesse of company, and humane faces.

**2.** Invisible, unseen, dark; impenetrable by vision.

**1589** WARNER *Alb. Eng.* II. xi. 44 The scouring windes that sightlesse in the sounding aire doe flie. **1603** HARINGTON in *Nugæ Ant.* (1804) I. 343, I have been well nighe driven heretofore into narrowe straits, amongste state rocks and sightless dangers. **1613** HEYWOOD *Braz. Age* Wks. 1874 III. 249 Hath any sightlesse and infernall fire Laid hold vpon my flesh? **1740** [S. BOYSE] *Deity* (1749) 11 He shuns the view of Sense, Lost in the blaze of sightless excellence. **1789** MRS. PIOZZI *Journ. France* I. 45 Following a soaring falcon through the half-sightless regions of the air. **1812** J. HENRY *Camp. agst. Quebec* 115 They were even sightless to us, we could see nothing but the blaze from the muzzles of their muskets. **1850** TENNYSON *In Mem.* cxv, Drown'd in yonder living blue The lark becomes a sightless song. **1888** B. W. RICHARDSON *Son of a Star* I. xii. 184 Touchless with human hands, Sightless with human eyes.

†**3.** Unsightly. *Obs.*

**1595** SHAKS. *John* III. i. 45 Full of vnpleasing blots, and sightlesse staines. **1632** LITHGOW *Trav.* VIII. 375 Ah! sightlesse desarts! fil'd with barren Sands!

**4.** Out of sight.

**1632** LITHGOW *Trav.* IX. 381 Tvnneis beene sightlesse left, I sought the Ile Of little Malta. **1816** SCOTT *Antiq.* xxxi. (motto), Their tears..as they fall, sink sightless.

Hence **'sightlessly** *adv.*, without having the faculty of sight.

**1847** in WEBSTER. **1883** E. ARNOLD *Indian Idylls* 241 He lay,..with fierce eyes Roving the wood, and seeing sightlessly. **1892** ZANGWILL *Bow Myst.* 159 His eyes ranged sightlessly after the boy.

**'sightlessness.** [f. prec.] Lack of sight.

**1847** in WEBSTER. **1853** RUSKIN *Stones Ven.* III. iv. §13 It is one instance only out of the myriads which might be given of sightlessness in modern art. **1854** GREENWOOD *Haps & Mishaps* 90 There was a full assortment of the halt..and the crippled—all degrees of sightlessness and unsightliness. **1893** R. JEFFREY *Visits to Calvary* 227 Your sightlessness is a sad deprivation.

**sightliness** ('saɪtlɪnɪs). [f. next.] Comeliness, handsomeness, beauty.

**1561** T. HOBY tr. *Castiglione's Courtyer* I. A 2 b, A Citye in fourme of a palaice, and that not onelye with ordinarie matters,..but also for sightlynesse. **1598** BARKCLEY *Felic. Man* (1631) 658 The delectible shew and sightliness of the tree. **1642** FULLER *Holy & Prof. St.* IV. 303 Thus glasse-eyes may be used, though not for seeing but for sightlinesse. **1740-1** RICHARDSON *Pamela* (1824) I. xv. 253, I, a poor girl, who..had only a kind of imputed sightliness of person. **1767** T. BOSTON *Crook in Lot* (1805) 11 Faith will discover a hidden sightliness in it, under a very unsightly outward appearance. **1846** TRENCH *Mirac.* xviii. (1862) 313 Much that for its little sightliness was nothing accounted of, shall prove true metal. *a* **1878** SIR G. SCOTT *Lect. Archit.* (1879) II. 170 Another mode of giving sightliness to the squared dome.

**sightly** ('saɪtlɪ), *a.* and *adv.* [f. SIGHT *sb.*[1] Cf. MDu. *sichtelijc* (Du. dial. *zichtelijk*), MHG. *sihtlich* (G. *sichtlich*), visible, etc.]

†**1.** Visible; conspicuous. *Obs.*

**1532** MORE *Confut. Barnes* VIII. Wks. 775/1 The wel knowen church [is] so builded..that it shal alway be syghtlye, and can not be hyd. **1571** GOLDING *Calvin on Ps.* lxxiv. 12 Many manifest deliverances had bin exhibited too the elect people as it were uppon a syghtly stage. **1579** TOMSON *Calvin's Serm. Tim.* 2/1 [God] doeth not come downe from heauen, in sightly shape to speake vnto us.

**b.** *U.S.* Of places: Open to the view; that may be seen from a distance; commanding a wide prospect.

**1828-32** WEBSTER, We say, a house stands in a sightly place. **1892** ALICE M. EARLE *Sabbath in New Engl.* i. 5 Our Puritan ancestors dearly loved a 'sightly location'; and were willing to climb uphill cheerfully..for the sake of having a meeting-house which showed off well.

**2.** Pleasing to the sight; fair to look at; handsome, beautiful.

**1562** J. HEYWOOD *Prov. & Epigr.* (1867) 148 In a Iuggler, that lightnes is sightly. **1592** GREENE *Conny Catch.* III. 11 In such sightlie roumes it may easily bee thought, Citizens vse not to haue anie thing meane. **1611** BIBLE *Transl. Pref.* ¶12 They did not..proportion the houses in such comely fashion, as had bene most sightly and conuenient. *a* **1652** BROME *Covent Garden* I. i, Here's Architecture exprest indeed! It is a most sightly scituation, and fit for Gentry and Nobility. **1748** *Anson's Voy.* II. xii. 264 They were mounted on very sightly horses. **1790** BURKE *Fr. Rev.* (ed. 2) 265 If their schemes were perfectly consistent in all their parts, it would make only a more fair and sightly vision. **1850** W. SCORESBY *Cheever's Whalem. Adv.* viii. (1858) 107 The sightly constellation of the southern cross. **1887** BALL *Nat. S. Amer.* 322 The absence of sightly buildings is not felt.

**b.** As *adv.* Handsomely, finely.

**1591** HORSEY *Trav.* (Hakluyt Soc.) 224 This ambassador was..sightly enterteyned. **1592** WYRLEY *Armorie, Ld. Chandos* 42 They forward came bedect right sightly. **1610** HOLLAND *Camden's Brit.* I. 290 Nor Rhodes, with Alcal and Elba, regard the robes with crosse Sightly beset. **1784** COWPER *Task* III. 649 He, therefore, who would see his flow'rs dispos'd Sightly and in just order,..Forecasts the future whole.

**'sightman.** *Sc.* [f. SIGHT *sb.*[1]] One who is stationed to watch the movements of salmon.

**1794** *Statist. Acc. Scot.* XI. 93 They are..called sightmen, because..they become wonderfully quick-sighted in discerning the motion and approach of..salmon.

**'sight-see,** *v.* [Back-formation from *sight-seeing* (cf. first quots.), f. SIGHT *sb.*[1] 1 c.]

**1.** *intr.* To see sights, visit objects or places of interest.

**1824** R. HEBER *Narr. Journey Upper Provinces India* (1828) I. xii. 302, I had been sight-seeing from five till nearly ten o'clock. **1835** *Court Mag.* VI. 146 The ruins of Tintern, ..Alas! now profaned by a sight-seeing crew. **1843** LADY GRANVILLE *Lett.* (1894) II. 345 She sight-sees from the dawn of day. **1887** *World* 23 Feb. 15 Who..sight-see all day, and return to their gilded cars to dine and sleep. **1913** E. WHARTON *Custom of Country* xxx. 412 'I suppose you've been to that old church over there?'.. 'Oh, of course; when I used to sightsee. Have you never been to Paris before?' **1925** C. CONNOLLY *Let.* 28 Feb. in *Romantic Friendship* (1975) 61 Nor is there anywhere near to tempt one to sightsee. **1976** *Church Times* 30 July 7/3 It seems to me infinitely more absurd—if art and architecture mean anything to you at all, and if you can sight-see in reasonably unhurried and uncongested comfort—*not* to want to see the best in this line that civilisation has to offer. **1979** R. JAFFE *Class Reunion* II. v. 168 'And then I thought I'd just sightsee.' Dutifully she told him everything she had seen.

**2.** *trans.* To visit the principal sights of (a place).

**1968** J. WAINWRIGHT *Web of Silence* 109, I spent the day sight-seeing Berlin. **1976** *New Yorker* 29 Mar. 95/2 (Advt.), Meet the chefs, inspect kitchens, plus sightsee the highlights from Cortina to Rome. **1977** *Daily Colonist* (Victoria, B.C.) 19 June 25/3 Macao is only 2½ miles long. Has 300,000 people. You sightsee it in an hour.

**'sight-seeing,** *vbl. sb.* [f. SIGHT *sb.*[1] 1 c.] The action or occupation of seeing sights.

**1824** R. HEBER *Narr. Journey Upper Provinces India* (1828) I. xv. 380 Morning rides, evening sight-seeing. **1847** FR. A. KEMBLE *Later Life* III. 250 It involves what I have no taste for—i.e., sightseeing. **1883** F. M. PEARD *Contrad.* xiv, The duke escaped the sight-seeing which bored him.

*attrib.* **1827** MRS. B. HALL *Let.* 13 Dec. in *Aristocratic Journey* (1931) 146 This has been another regular sight-seeing day. **1863** J. C. JEAFFRESON *Sir Everard's Dau.* 87 Amongst the country folk..who paid Sharsted a sight-seeing visit. **1892** GUNTER *Miss Dividends* (1893) 109 Mrs. Livingston proposes a sight-seeing drive about the city. **1916** *Daily Colonist* (Victoria, B.C.) 9 July 6/3 The picnic party left the Gorge terminus during the early forenoon in the special sight-seeing car of the B.C. Electric Railway. **1925** C. MORLEY *Thunder on Left* xiii. 170 People were always driving up in crowds to visit his secrets. Like sight-seeing busses loaded with excursionists. **1976** *National Observer* (U.S.) 30 Oct. 5/1, I spotted an empty sightseeing bus moving slowly up Collins Avenue.

**'sight-seer.** [f. as prec.] One who goes about to see the sights of a place or places.

**1834** G. CRABBE JUN. in *Poet. Wks. G. Crabbe* I. viii. 207 A friend in town procured us those very eligible rooms for sight-seers, in Osborne's Hotel, Adelphi. **1849** CURZON *Monast. Levant* xv. 204 Nothing better or worse than Englishmen and sightseers. **1860** THACKERAY *Round. Papers, Week's Holiday*, Humour and grotesqueness, which gives the sight-seer the most singular zest and pleasure. **1884** SALA *Journ. South* I. xx, The..society-loving patrons of the Roman season are a very different class from the sightseer.

**sightsman** ('saɪtsmən). [f. SIGHT *sb.*[1] Cf. SIGHTMAN.]

**1.** One who points out sights or objects of interest; a local guide, a cicerone.

*a* **1700** EVELYN *Diary* 6 Nov. 1644 Our Sights-man (for so they name certain persons here who get their living by leading strangers about to see the City).

**2.** One who reads or performs music at sight.

**1776** BURNEY *Hist. Music* (1789) IV. vi. 263 This musician, who was..of considerable eminence..both as a sights-man and voluntary player. **1801** BUSBY *Dict. Mus.*, *Sightsman*, the appellation given to him who reads, or sings, music readily at first sight: hence we say, 'such a one is a good Sightsman'.

**3.** ? One who takes sight with a pistol.

**1790** *Bystander* 169 How serious a thing it is to call all the duellists that ever lived, from the Roman Gladiators to the sightsmen of the present day, rascals.

**sight-worthy** ('saɪtwɜːðɪ), *a.* [f. SIGHT *sb.*$^1$ + WORTHY *a.*] Worth seeing or visiting.

**1605** DANIEL *Queen's Arcadia* Ded., For maiestry, and power, can nothing see Without it selfe, that can sight-worthy be. **1642** FULLER *Holy & Prof. St.* III. iv. 159 Cambridge..and Oxford,..where the worst Colledge is more sight-worthy then the best Dutch Gymnasium. **1791** BENTHAM *Mem. & Corr.* Wks. 1843 X. 263 For sight-worthy persons at Plymouth, More mentioned Mudge, whom you know of old. **1894** C. H. COOK *Thames Rights* 111 Objects not so sight-worthy as broadcloth.

Hence **'sight-worthiness**.

**1849** J. FORBES *Physician's Holiday* ii. (1850) 13 A temporary halt may be called, according to the nature or sight-worthiness of the locality.

**'sighty,** *a. Obs.* exc. *dial.* [f. SIGHT *sb.*$^1$ + -Y. Cf. obs. Flem. *sightigh* (Kilian), MLG. *sichtich*, OHG. *(ge)sihtig*, MHG. *sihtig* (older G. *sichtig*), visible (in G. also 'seeing').]

†**1.** Sightly, fair, handsome. *Obs.*

**1387** TREVISA *Higden* (Rolls) V. 269 A wonder faire mayde,..and wonder siȝty for men to byholde. **1533** BELLENDEN *Livy* I. iv. (S.T.S.) I. 28 The romanis dressit furth þis play In the maist solempne maner þai culd or mycht, to mak It þe more sichty and glorius to the pepill.

†**2.** Visible, conspicuous. (See also quot. *c* 1440.)

**1398** TREVISA *Barth. De P.R.* XIX. i. (Bodl. MS.), The reson of siȝty þinge is roted and ischape in liȝt. *c* **1440** *Promp. Parv.* 455 Syghty, *visibilis*. *Ibid.*, Syghty, or glarynge, ..*rutilans*. *c* **1475** *Partenay* 1229 Antony..in hys iaw bare A hurt ful of pain Off a lyon, which al hys life bare ful sighty. **1533** BELLENDEN *Livy* V. xvi. (S.T.S.) II. 203/2 þare souerane manhede & vertew was sa notabill and sichty. **1536** —— *Cron. Scot., Cosmogr.* v. Biij, The peple thairof ar.. maist sychty in craft of cheualrie. **1570** LEVINS *Manip.* 111 Sighty, *visibilis*.

**3.** Keen-sighted; clever. Now *dial.*

*a* **1425** *Cursor M.* 13448 (Trin.), Is noon so siȝty foule of eȝe [as the eagle], Ny so fer to fle may dreȝe. **1579** TOMSON *Calvin's Serm. Tim.* 453/1 We are sighty inough to our owne profite. **1869** *Lonsdale Gloss.*, *Sighty*, quick at seeing how a thing ought to be done.

**sigil** ('sɪdʒɪl). Also 7 sigill. [ad. late L. *sigillum* (in class. L. *sigilla* neut. pl.), dim. of *signum*: see SIGN *sb.*]

**1.** A seal or signet. Also *attrib.*, as *sigil-mark*.

*a* **1610** PARSONS *Leicester's Ghost* (1641) 14 Giges went invisible By turning of the sigill of his Ring Toward his palme. **1657** TOMLINSON *Renou's Disp.* 132 Another figure ..imprinted by some sigil. **1814** CARY *Dante, Par.* XXVII. 48 Sigil-mark Set upon sold and lying privileges. **1880** WEBB *Goethe's Faust* I. i. 41 A book with sevenfold sigil is the Past! **1883** A. DOBSON *Old World Idylls* 243 Touched by the awful sigil of his right.

**2.** *Astrol.* An occult sign or device supposed to have mysterious powers.

**1659** T. PECKE *Parnassi Puerp.* 153 Love scorns, that any Remora should be: That's the true Sigil, moving Gallantrie. **1672** SIR T. BROWNE *Let. Friend* §13 Amulets, spells, sigils, and incantations, practised in other diseases, are seldom pretended in this. **1711** POPE *Temple of Fame* 105 Of Talismans and Sigils [they] knew the pow'r, And careful watch'd the Planetary hour. **1813** SCOTT *Trierm.* I. vi. Sign and sigil well doth he know. **1842** BARHAM *Ingold. Leg.* Ser. II. *Raising the Devil*, He drew the mystic circle's bound,.. He traced full many a sigil there.

**3.** *Rom. Antiq.* A small image.

**1738** CHAMBERS *Cycl.* s.v. *Sigillaria*, Some derive the origin of sigils and figures, in this solemnity, from the argei [etc.].

**sigilism** ('sɪdʒɪlɪz(ə)m). [ad. mod.L. *sigilism-us*, f. Sp. *sigilo* seal (of confession).] (See quot.)

**1865** *Englishman's Mag.* Feb. 114 The following appear to be the principal crimes against which the edicts of the Inquisition were fulminated..: immorality in the confessional, sigilism (or revealing the secrets of the confessional).

**sigilla,** pl. of SIGILLUM.

†**'sigillar,** *a. Obs.*$^{-0}$ = SIGILLARY *a.* 1.

**1656** BLOUNT *Glossogr.*, *Sigillar*, of or belonging to a Seal or Mark. **1658** PHILLIPS, *Sigillar*, belonging to a seal or sealing.

‖**sigillaria** (sɪdʒɪ'lɛərɪə). *Geol.* [mod.L., f. *sigillum* seal: see SIGIL. Named by Brongniart (1822).] A fossil tree, the leaf-scars of which resemble the impressions of a seal, found chiefly in coal deposits.

**1831-3** LINDLEY & HUTTON *Fossil Flora* I. 155 It is extremely probable..that Sigillaria was a Dicotyledonous plant. **1836** BUCKLAND *Geol. & Min.* I. 473 The longitudinal flutings of the trunks of Sigillariæ. **1849** J. H. BALFOUR *Man. Bot.* §1183 Some suppose Sigillarias to be allied to Tree-ferns, others to Coniferæ. **1876** PAGE *Adv. Text-bk. Geol.* xiv. 255 We may notice the sigillaria, so called from the seal-like impressions on its fluted trunk.

Hence **sigi'llarian** *a.* and *sb.*; **sigi'llarid**; **sigi'llar(i)oid** *a.*

**1870** *Geol. Mag.* VII. 293 The fossil *sigillarian forests of Nova Scotia. **1883** *Science* I. 523/2 A number of animals entombed in stumps of sigillarians in the coal-measures of Nova Scotia. **1877** LE CONTE *Elem. Geol.* (1879) 316 The Lycopods [were represented] by gigantic Lepidodendrids and *Sigillarids. **1870** *Geol. Mag.* VII. 293 These specimens ..probably represented other types of *Sigillarioid trees. **1872** NICHOLSON *Palæont.* 474 The Sigillarioid plants, regarded by different authorities as being Coniferous, or Lycopodiaceous. **1879** GEIKIE in *Encycl. Brit.* X. 345/2 Lepidodendroid and *sigillaroid plants abound, as well as calamites.

**'sigillarist.** *rare*$^{-1}$. [irreg. f. L. *sigill-um* SIGIL: cf. next.] A sigillographer.

**1898** *Berks., Bucks., & Oxon Archaeol. Jrnl.* Jan. 110 Mr. A. P. Ready, the well known sigillarist.

**sigillary** ('sɪdʒɪlərɪ), *a.* [f. (late) L. *sigill-um* SIGIL: see -ARY. Cf. F. *sigillaire* and med.L. *sigillarius*, *-aris* sb.]

**1.** Of or pertaining to a seal or signet; connected with the use or making of seals, etc.

**1652** EVELYN *Corr.* (1827) IV. 4 All those sigillary formalities of a perfect instrument. **1895** *Athenæum* 13 July 57/2 Several of their seals are given, which are striking examples of the sigillary art.

**2.** Subject to, or characterized by, the influence of a sigil or charm.

*a* **1834** SURTEES in G. Taylor *Mem.* (Surtees) 233 That maiden kiss hath holy power O'er planet and sigillary hour.

‖**sigillata** (sɪdʒɪ'leɪtə, sɪgɪ'lɑːtə). Also Sigillata. [L., = sealed: see TERRA SIGILLATA.] = TERRA SIGILLATA 3. Also *attrib.*

**1903** *Amer. Jrnl. Archaeol.* VII. 485 This study of the origin of the Gallo-Roman *sigillata* is preliminary to a complete publication. **1936** J. H. ILIFFE (*title*) Sigillata wares in the Near East. **1938** *Burlington Mag.* Jan. p. xiv/2 Southern Spain has already been known as one of the chief pottery centres of the Roman Empire... But that 'sigillata-ware' was actually made there is not so clear. **1948** *Proc. Prehistoric Soc.* XIV. 79 Sea-borne trade with the Province is shown by a sherd of Sigillata. **1966** G. SIMPSON in Oswald & Pryce *Introd. Study of Terra Sigillata* (ed. 2) p. iii, No attempt was made originally to give an exhaustive description of varieties of Sigillata which had no definite chronological value.

**sigillate** ('sɪdʒɪlət), *ppl. a.* [ad. late L. *sigillatus*, pa. pple. of *sigillāre*: see next.]

**1.** *Bot.* Marked with impressions resembling those made by a seal.

[**1856** HENSLOW *Dict. Bot. Terms* 173 *Sigillatus*, when a rhizoma is marked by scars left by the fall of branches successively developed upon it.] **1858** in MAYNE.

**2.** Of pottery: Decorated with impressed patterns.

**1891** in *Cent. Dict.*

**sigillate** ('sɪdʒɪleɪt), *v.* Also 5 *pa. pple.* sygylate. [f. *sigillāt-*, ppl. stem of late L. *sigillāre* to seal, f. *sigillum* SIGIL.] *trans.* To seal; to seal up. Also *transf.*

**1471** RIPLEY *Comp. Alch.* X. vii. in Ashm. (1652) 180 And in one Glas do all thys surely sygylate. **1612** WOODALL *Surg. Mate* Wks. (1653) 229 Mercurie..To sigillate thou do'st not fail. **1620** VENNER *Via Recta* vii. 111 By sigillating the mouth of the stomacke..they represse..the hot fumes that vaporate to the head. **1652** S. S. *Secretaries Studie* 200 To fasten, and, as it were, to sigillate, and affix to us the unmercifulness of men. **1833** *Fraser's Mag.* VII. 269 In one moment the passport was sigillated.

**'sigillated,** *ppl. a.* [f. prec. + -ED$^1$.]

**1.** Impressed with a seal; esp. ***sigillated earth***, Lemnian earth, sphragide (after med.L. *terra sigillata*).

Cf. Lithgow *Trav.* (1632) III. 97, 'The latter [name] is in force, because the earth being made up in little pellets, is sealed with a Turkish signet.'

**1657** TOMLINSON *Renou's Disp.* 396* The best of medicinal earths..is that the shop-men call Lemnian Earth, and sometimes Sigillated Earth. **1697** EVELYN *Numismata* i. 11 Baked and sigillated Earth..used for money. **1852** TH. ROSS tr. *Humboldt's Trav.* II. xxiv. 502 It is known that great use is still made in the East of the bolar and sigillated earths of Lemnos, which are clay mingled with oxide of iron.

**2.** = SIGILLATE *ppl. a.* 2. (*Cent. Dict.*)

**sigillation** (sɪdʒɪ'leɪʃən). [See SIGILLATE *v.* and -ATION.] The action of sealing; the fact of being sealed; the impression of a seal.

**1642** R. C. *Union Christ & Ch.* 4 That which..receiveth the Sigillation here below is like to the Shape and Forme of those things above. **1657** TOMLINSON *Renou's Disp.* 132 This..impressed form or sigillation is of little moment. **1802-12** BENTHAM *Ration. Judic. Evid.* (1827) II. 462 Since the art of writing has become comparatively common, sigillation, in the character of a source of real evidence, has gone completely out of use. **1840** G. S. FABER *Prim. Doctr. Regen.* 70 Its outward sigillation or official ratification is the ordinance of Baptism.

†**'sigillative,** *a.* and *sb. Med. Obs.* [ad. med.L. *sigillātīv-us*: see SIGILLATE *v.* and -IVE. So obs. F. *sigillatif*.]

**a.** *adj.* Serving to seal or close up. **b.** *sb.* An application serving to close a wound.

*c* **1400** *Lanfranc's Cirurg.* 342 Sigillatiuis, & cicatrizatiuis, & consolidatiuis ben al oon. **1541** COPLAND *Guydon's Form.* Tij b, The helpes conglutynatyues, consolydatyues, and sigillatyues be of .xvj. fourmes. **1612** WOODALL *Surg. Mate* Wks. (1653) 171 Quicksilver..is..so incarnative and so sigillative or siccatrizing. *a* **1693** *Urquhart's Rabelais* III. xxvi. 215 Sigillative cod.

**sigilled** ('sɪdʒɪld), *a.* [f. SIGIL + -ED$^2$.] Wearing a seal or signet-ring.

**1864** R. S. HAWKER *Quest Sangraal* 17 Beneath, came up a gloved and sigill'd Hand.

**sigillistic** (sɪdʒɪ'lɪstɪk), *a.* [See SIGIL and -ISTIC.] Pertaining to seals.

**1867** *Herald & Genealogist* IV. 14 The study of our sigillistic antiquities.

**sigillographer** (sɪdʒɪ'lɒgrəfə(r)). [f. L. *sigillum* SIGIL: see -GRAPHER.] One who pursues, or is skilled in, the study of seals.

**1882** *Proc. Soc. Antiq.* IX. 53 Of the foreign heraldic seals ..I have little to say..; their importance for the English sigillographer is but slight. *Ibid.* 181 This eminent palæographer and sigillographer.

**sigillography** (sɪdʒɪ'lɒgrəfɪ). [f. as prec.: see -GRAPHY.] The science or study of seals.

**1879** *Athenæum* 27 Dec. 827 The splendid volume devoted by M. Demay to sigillography. **1886** *Ibid.* 11 Sept. 341/3 It is only of late years that much attention has been paid to Byzantine sigillography.

‖**si'gillum.** [See SIGIL.]

**1.** A small figure of a person. *rare*$^{-1}$.

**1637** B. JONSON *Sad Shepherd* II. ii, Binding characters, through which she wounds Her puppets, the sigilla of her witchcraft.

**2.** *R.C. Ch.* The seal of confession. Cf. SEAL *sb.*$^2$ 2 b.

**1927** F. A. MARKS tr. *Kurtscheid's Hist. Seal of Confession* 1 Since the Middle Ages we have for this obligation the technical term Seal of Confession (*sigillum, signaculum confessionis*). **1937** S. O'FAOLÁIN *Purse of Coppers* 49 To add to his difficulty—for it was no help to know what, under the *sigillum*, he must pretend not to know—he had just been told in the sacristy by her employer that a pair of her best boots was missing.

**3.** A sign or symbol; an abbreviation; an identifying character.

**1966** B. MALAMUD *Fixer* iii. 83 Please note, if you will, the sigillum on my coat lapel. **1978** *Language* LIV. 5 The true picture of dialect classification, either regionally or socially, is not known; nor is it implied by the sigilla of *DED*.

**SIGINT, Sigint** ('sɪgɪnt), abbrev. of *signal(s) intelligence* s.v. SIGNAL *sb.* 5 e.

**1969** THOMAS & CROWLEY *New Acronyms & Initialisms 1969* 376 SIGINT, Signal Intelligence (Military). **1972** *New Scientist* 2 Mar. 467 Generally speaking the larger part of the staff of all Sigint headquarters consists of scientists and engineers. Apart from actual cryptanalysis, there is a continuing need to improve intercept equipment. **1976** *Time Out* 21 May 8/2 Each country's signals intelligence (SIGINT) agency has authority to monitor communications in one area. **1979** J. BARNETT *Backfire is Hostile!* ii. 29 She was in charge of Sigint... Signals intelligence. **1980** J. MCNEIL *Spy Game* xviii. 182 What do you know about SIGINT?.. Signals Intelligence?.. You know that's the Agency's main role over here?

‖**'sigla.** [L. *sigla* neut. pl., perh. a contracted form of *sigilla*, pl. of *sigillum* SIGIL.]

**a.** Letters (esp. initials) or other characters used to denote words; abbreviations or marks of abbreviation. Also *transf.* and *fig.*

**1706** in PHILLIPS (ed. Kersey). **1801** *Gentl. Mag.* LXXI. II. 1097 The characters..belong not to any alphabet, but are probably *Sigla*. **1832** GELL *Pompeiana* II. 122 The sigla which are supposed to be the private marks of the scribes. **1869** TOZER *Highl. Turkey* II. 358 The small mark after the T is one of the sigla which it was customary in inscriptions ..to put..before and after numeral letters. **1963** V. NABOKOV *Gift* ii. 86 On the soft red sand one could make out the sigla of a summer day: the imprints of a dog's paws, the beaded tracks of a wagtail. **1973** D. OSMOND-SMITH tr. *Bettetini's Lang. & Technique of Film* i. 61 If this image comes to be interpreted as the *sigla* of the preconceptual schema..it will only be of value for its semantic content.

**b.** Editorial designations of versions of an early literary text, esp. those used in the preparation of an edition. Also *sing.* siglum.

**1939** R. B. MCKERROW *Prolegomena for Oxf. Shakespeare* iii. 83 Round brackets enclosing a siglum are also used as a warning that the edition thus indicated has a reading which differs. **1950** *Classica et Medievalia* XI. 7, I prefer to use the same *siglum* for the New Testament and the Patrick section [of a manuscript]. **1962** E. J. DOBSON in Davis & Wrenn *Eng. & Medieval Studies* 128, I use the following sigla: A = MS. C.C.C.C. 402 (ed. J. R. R. Tolkien, E.E.T.S. 249, 1962); C = MS. Cotton Cleopatra C VI; [etc.]. *Ibid.*, References to any text other than A are preceded by the siglum of that text. **1975** *N. & Q.* Feb. 53/2 Twenty texts of the *Epistola Cuthberti* are not recorded by Dobbie. We give them below; for each of those that Brotanek enumerates we give his siglum..; we also give some versions not listed by Brotanek, with our sigla.

Hence **si'glarian** *a.*, pertaining to sigla.

**1818** BURNEY in *Parr's Wks.* (1828) VIII. 643 Garrard is the only book on the Siglarian subject which I possess.

†**'sigle.** *Obs. rare.* [ad. L. *sigla*.] (See quots. and SIGLA.)

**1614** SELDEN *Titles Honor* 21 Their supposed Coat also, of later time, being foure *Betaes*... The *Betaes* are interpreted as the sigles of *Βασιλεὺς Βασιλέων, Βασιλεύων Βασιλεῦσι*. *Ibid.* 162 About those times χ alone was a known sigle for our Sauiour. **1656** BLOUNT *Glossogr.*, *Sigles*, notes, breviatures, initial Letters set for words.

**sigleton,** late variant of CICLATOUN *Obs.*

‖**siglos** ('sɪglɒs). Pl. sigli, sigloi. [Gr.] **a.** A unit of weight (see quot. 1911). Also *attrib.* **b.** A silver coin of ancient Persia.

**1911** *Encycl. Brit.* XIX. 871/2 The unit of weight in the East was the shekel (*siglos*)... Starting from the siglos as unit, they [*sc.* the Greeks] invented a money-mina of 50 sigli... The siglos-units.. chiefly employed in Asia Minor were the following [etc.]. *Ibid.* 903/2 Darius chose two weights, the gold shekel of 8·4 grammes and the silver drachm of 5·58 grammes... The gold coin was called the daric, the silver the siglos. *Ibid.* The regal coinage is of darics.. and subdivisions in gold and of sigli and subdivisions in silver. **1962** R. A. G. CARSON *Coins* 82 Both the gold darics and the silver sigloi are bean-shaped pieces with a type on obverse only and an oblong incuse on the reverse. **1962** D. HARDEN *Phoenicians* xii. 166 The Persians themselves.. minted their *darics* and *sigloi* primarily for use in their Greek dominions in Asia Minor. **1972** *Oxf. Univ. Gaz.* CII. Suppl. No. 3. 46 Perhaps the most important aspect of this hoard is the inclusion of a number of worn (and countermarked) Persian sigloi.

**siglum**: see SIGLA b.

**sigma** ('sɪgmə). [L. *sigma*, Gr. σίγμα, the 18th letter of the Greek alphabet.]

**1.** The name of the Greek letter Σ, σ, ς the equivalent of the English S, s, in its uncial form having the shape of **C**.

**1607** TOPSELL *Four-f. Beasts* 290 Written with *Iota* and simple *Sigma*. **1736** AINSWORTH *Lat. Dict.* s.v. S, Which opinion is made more probable by the small form of the Greek *sigma*. **1833** *Penny Cycl.* I. 385/2 The difference between the *shin*.., and the Greek *sigma*.. depends solely upon the altered position. **1859** MILLARD tr. *Kühner's Gr. Gram.* 4 The Sigma (σ), at the end of a word, takes the form ς. **1876** S. BIRCH *Rede Lect. on Egypt* 32 The final sigma of the Greeks is represented by the Egyptian sibilant.

**2.** Something having the form of **S** or **C**.

**1788** GIBBON *Decl. & F.* liii. V. 481 The square before the sigma [= semicircular portico] was decorated with a fountain. **1877** COUES & ALLEN *N. Amer. Rod.* 32 The loops of enamel.. do form a sort of sigma [etc.; see SIGMODONT].

**3.** *Physics* and *Chem.* **a.** [After S 5.] Used to designate electrons, orbitals, molecular states, etc., possessing zero angular momentum about an internuclear axis; ***sigma-*** (or σ-) ***bond***, a bond formed by a σ-orbital.

Usu. written σ when it refers to one electron and Σ when it refers to a molecule as a whole.

**1929**, etc. [see PI *sb.* 3]. **1939** J. W. T. SPINKS tr. *Herzberg's Diatomic Molecules* v. 260 For multiplet Σ states the character positive-negative depends on whether *K*.. is even or odd. **1952** L. N. FERGUSON *Electron Structures of Org. Molecules* ii. 21 In butadiene, each carbon atom forms three σ bonds. **1963** W. J. MOORE *Physical Chem.* (ed. 4) xiv. 600 In the electronic excitation an electron is removed from a π orbital and placed in a σ orbital. **1964** R. G. PARR *Quantum Theory of Molec. Electronic Structure* iii. 41 It is supposed that somehow the effect of the others, the sigma electrons, can be lumped into the Hamiltonian for the pi electrons. **1966** PHILLIPS & WILLIAMS *Inorg. Chem.* II. xxviii. 341 The vinyl anion, $C_2H_3^-$, binds directly to cobalt (III) of vitamin $B_{12}$ as a simple σ-bonded ligand. **1972** DEPUY & CHAPMAN *Molec. Reactions & Photochem.* vi. 103 The numbers refer to the atoms at either end of the sigma bond which is thought of as moving. **1978** P. W. ATKINS *Physical Chem.* xv. 471 Thus an oxygen molecule, which.. has two π*-electrons, could be in either a Σ state (the electrons orbiting in opposite directions) or in a Δ state (the electrons orbiting in the same sense around the bond).

**b.** *Particle Physics.* Used, usu. *attrib.*, to denote any of a triplet of hyperons (and their antiparticles) having an average mass of approximately 1190 MeV (2340 times that of the electron), a spin of ½, zero hypercharge, and unit isospin, and which on decaying usu. produce a nucleon and a pion (if charged) or a lambda particle and a photon (if neutral). Freq. written as Σ.

**1954** GELL-MANN & PAIS in *Proc. Glasgow Conf. Nuclear & Pleson Physics* (1955) 347 The.. apparent existence of both a positive and a negative hyperon which we shall call $\Sigma^{\pm}$ with the decay schemes $\Sigma\pm \rightarrow N + \pi\pm + (\sim 115$ MeV), $\Sigma\pm \rightarrow P + \pi^0 + (\sim 115$ MeV). **1955** *Nuovo Cimento* II. 824 An event, interpreted as the disappearance of a charged Σ-hyperon in flight, has been observed.. in the Brookhaven cosmotron. **1961** W. S. C. WILLIAMS *Introd. Elementary Particles* xii. 298 Any subsequent Σ decays in flight. **1963** K. W. FORD *World of Elementary Particles* vi. 179 (*caption*) A negative pion.. collides with a proton and produces two strange particles, a neutral sigma and a neutral kaon... The sigma particle lives too short a time to move a measurable distance.., decaying almost at once into a lambda and a photon. **1976** *Sci. Amer.* Jan. 46/2 The baryons with the lowest mass are those with a spin of 1/2. There are eight of them: two nucleons (*N*).., a lambda particle (Λ).., three sigma particles (Σ).. and two cascade particles (Ξ).

**4.** Biochem. *ellipt.* for *sigma factor*, sense 6 below.

**1970** *New Scientist* 23 July 176/1 Soon after infection.. the phage makes its *own* sigma, which redirects the host core enzyme to start making a different set of phage proteins.

**5.** *Statistics.* A standard deviation: used in the singular as if the name of a unit.

**1978** N. R. ULLMAN *Elem. Statistics* iii. 68 The difference is 0·5 inches, or, since σ = 0·29.. 1·72 standard deviations apart or 1·72 σ (1·72 sigma) apart. *Ibid.* 69 You can express values in terms of sigma or in terms of 'so many sigma units from the mean'. **1979** *Nature* 29 Mar. 411/1 On each radiocarbon analysis, one sigma counting errors are given.

**6.** *Comb.*, as **sigma factor** *Biochem.*, a component of RNA polymerase which determines where transcription begins.

[**1969** R. R. BURGESS et al. in *Nature* 4 Jan. 44/2 GG enzyme contains, in addition, two extra bands which we shall designate σ and τ. *Ibid.* 46/1 The presence of the stimulating factor, σ, greatly enhances the amount of RNA synthesis. *Ibid.* 46/2 σ and similar factors could.. act as positive control elements regulating the amount of synthesis of different classes of RNA.] **1969** *Times* 9 May 12/6 The sigma factor helps to specify which genes are expressed. **1970** *Nature* 29 Aug. 886/1 Today sigma factor proteins.. are central to all attempts to explain the positive control of gene expression. **1976** *Proc. Nat. Acad. Sci.* LXXIII. 3961 (*heading*) Purification and characterization of a putative sigma factor from *Chlamydomonas reinhardi*. *Ibid.* 4405 (*heading*) Induction of sigma factor synthesis in *Escherichia coli* by the N gene product of bacteriophage lambda.

Hence **'sigmaspire** (see quot.). **'sigmate** *a.*, having the form of a sigma. **'sigmate** *v. trans.*, to add a sigma or *s* to (a word, stem, etc.); hence ***sigmated*** ppl. a. **sigmatic** (sɪg'mætɪk) *a.*, characterized by the addition of sigma or *s* to the stem. **sig'mation**, the addition of *s* to a word, etc. **'sigmatism**, ‖**sigma'tismus**, (*a*) the marked use or repetition of *s*; an instance of this; (*b*) defective articulation of sibilants. **'sigmatize** [cf. late Gr. σιγματίζειν] *v. trans.*, to mark with the letter *s*.

**1887** *Encycl. Brit.* XXII. 417/2 (Sponges), One of the simplest forms [of microscleres] is the *sigmaspire..; it looks like the letter C or S, according to the direction in which it is viewed, its actual form being that of a single turn of a cylindrical spiral. **1887** *Amer. Naturalist* XXI. 937 [Sponges] with *sigmate flesh-spicules. **1849** T. K. ARNOLD *First Gr. Bk.* 5 The root of the future is got from the root of the present (or infinitive) by *sigmating it. *Ibid.* 22 The first Aorist of the Active is formed by adding ᾰ to the *sigmated root.. and prefixing the augment. **1889** *N. & Q.* 7th Ser. VIII. 216/2 The question of the plural treatment, or otherwise, of some sigmated words is fair matter for discussion. **1888** KING & COOKSON *Sounds & Infl. Gr. & Lat.* xv. 444 The inflexions of the *sigmatic aorist. **1897** *Trans. Philol. Soc.* 233 We have also a subjunctive of the sigmatic aorist. **1889** *N. & Q.* 7th Ser. VII. 142/1 This fondness for pluralizing.. is constantly showing itself both in a purely senseless *sigmation and in a duplication of the plural ending. **1888** A. H. BUCK *Reference Handbk. Med. Sci.* VI. 617/1 Lisping, or *Sigmatism, is the most common form of stammering. It consists of giving *s* a wrong sound, usually that of *th*, by carrying the tip of the tongue too far forward, so as to touch the upper teeth. **1889** *Classical Rev.* III. 270 The sigmatism is quite Ovidian. **1891** *Athenæum* 21 Feb. 246/2 Sophocles, 'O.T.' 425, should have been quoted as the most remarkable, and at the same time effective, example of sigmatism in Greek tragedy. **1933** S. M. STINCHFIELD *Speech Disorders* iv. 76 The boys led in the number of cases of sigmatism, stuttering.., deafness and speech defects as a whole. **1957** *Dental Practitioner* VII. 220/2 Speech may be 'thick', which I tend to associate with the large tongue and the lateral sigmatism which suggests tongue behaviour. **1965** W. R. BRAIN *Speech Disorders* 154 Various disorders of the production of s (sigmatism) have been recognized. **1887** *Q. Rev.* Oct. 369 There are three inseparable necessities which may be remembered by a *sigmatismus—site, soil, and sympathy. **1654** H. L'ESTRANGE *Chas. I* (1655) 145 Mr. Prynne.. was.. to be stigmatized, or if you will *sigmatized, on both Cheeks with the letter S for a Schismatick.

**sigmatropic** (sɪgmə'trɒpɪk), *a. Chem.* [f. SIGMA + -TROPIC.] Involving the movement of a sigma bond to a new pair of atoms within a molecule.

**1965** WOODWARD & HOFFMANN in *Jrnl. Amer. Chem. Soc.* LXXXVII. 2511/2 We define as a sigmatropic change of order [*i*, *j*] the migration of a σ-bond, flanked by one or more π-electron systems, to a new position whose termini are *i* − 1 and *j* − 1 atoms removed from the original bonded loci, in an uncatalyzed intramolecular process. **1974** GILL & WILLIS *Pericyclic Reactions* iii. 84 The transition state of a sigmatropic change is.. reminiscent of the transition state of a cyclo-addition reaction.

**sigmodont** ('sɪgmədɒnt), *a.* and *sb. Zool.* [f. Gr. σίγμα SIGMA + ὀδοντ-, ὀδούς tooth.] **a.** *adj.* Belonging to the *Sigmodontes*, a class of murine animals in which the molars exhibit sigmoid patterns. **b.** *sb.* An animal belonging to this class.

**1877** COUES & ALLEN *N. Amer. Rod.* 32 The loops of enamel.. do form a sort of sigma, but it is usually a broken and always a distorted one, never more evident than in some other sigmodont forms. **1884** *Encycl. Brit.* XVII. 5/1 A represents the upper molars of a Mus, and B the corresponding teeth of a Sigmodont. *Ibid.* 6/2 Other groups,.. probably descendants of Sigmodont Muridæ.

**'sigmoid**, *a.* and *sb.* Chiefly *Anat.* [ad. Gr. σιγμοειδής: see SIGMA and -OID.]

**A.** *adj.* **1.** Having the shape of the uncial sigma **C**; crescent-shaped, semicircular.

Chiefly in ***sigmoid cavity, notch, valve***.

**1670** *Phil. Trans.* V. 2097 We did also observe two Ventricles with the tricuspid or sigmoid-valves. **1741** A. MONRO *Anat. Nerves* (ed. 3) 252 A large semicircular or sigmoid Concavity is left. **1798** HINDERWELL *Hist. Scarborough* II. I. 213 Nautilites, or Ammonites,.. with sigmoid or curved ridges. **1831** KNOX *Cloquet's Anat.* 74 The condyle is separated from the coronoid process by the sigmoid notch. *Ibid.* 206 It is the inner side.. of the head of the radius that is received into the small sigmoid cavity of the ulna. **1898** *Allbutt's Syst. Med.* V. 922 Relative insufficiency of the sigmoid valves due to dilatation of the aortic ring.

**2.** Having a double curve like the letter S.

Esp. ***sigmoid colon, flexure***, the last curving portion of the colon before terminating in the rectum.

**1786** *Phil. Trans.* LXXVI. 306 The sigmoid flexure of the colon immediately presented itself to view. **1797** M. BAILLIE *Morbid Anat.* (1807) 174 The gut.. is narrower at the sigmoid flexure than at any other part. **1848** *Proc. Berw. Nat. Club* II. 267 The flower stalk is.. round,.. gracefully bent in a sigmoid flexure. **1873** MIVART *Elem. Anat.* ii. 61 The beautiful sigmoid curvature of the vertebral column. **1896** *Quain's Elem. Anat.* (ed. 10) III. IV. 113 The sigmoid colon may be defined as that part of the colon which is attached to the left iliac fossa from the iliac crest to the brim of the true pelvis. **1962** *Lancet* 5 May 951/2 Anterior resection of the rectum with primary sigmoid-rectal anastomosis for neoplasm of the rectosigmoid region and sigmoid colon.

**B.** *sb.* **a.** The sigmoid flexure of the colon.

**1891** in *Cent. Dict.* **1897** *Allbutt's Syst. Med.* III. 967 The sigmoid may be so distended as to reach quite over to the right side of the abdomen.

**b.** A sigmoid curve (*Cent. Dict.*).

Hence **sigmoi'dectomy** [-ECTOMY], surgical excision of the sigmoid flexure; **sigmoi'dicity**, the extent to which a curve is sigmoid (S-shaped); **sigmoi'ditis**, inflammation of the sigmoid flexure; **'sigmoidscope** (see quot.); cf SIGMOIDOSCOPE.

**1904** *Brit. Med. Jrnl.* 3 Dec. 1503 By means of the electric sigmoidscope.. a clear view of every portion of the inside of the bowel may be obtained, even as high as the top of the sigmoid flexure. **1906** P. L. MUMMERY *Sigmoidoscope* 55 In the cases of acute proctitis or sigmoiditis an examination with the sigmoidoscope may afford useful information. **1915** B. G. A. MOYNIHAN *Abdominal Operations* (ed. 3) II. 490/1 (Index), Sigmoidectomy. **1938** H. E. BACON *Anus, Rectum, Sigmoid Colon* xix. 695 (*heading*) Abdominal resection (sigmoidectomy)—one-stage procedure. **1968** A. WHITE et al. *Princ. Biochem.* (ed. 4) xi. 243 For hemoglobin, a similar plot yields a sigmoidal curve.. which obeys the relationship known as the Hill equation $y = Kx^n/(1 + Kx^n)$ where.. the exponent n gives a measure of the sigmoidicity of the curve. **1977** *Arch. Biochem. & Biophys.* CLXXXIV. 300/1 With the enzyme from *Am[aranthus] edulis*, the response to increasing malate was qualitatively similar to that recorded for the *At[riplex] spongiosa* enzyme but sigmoidicity was more pronounced.

**sigmoidal** (sɪg'mɔɪdəl), *a.* [See prec. and -AL[1].] = SIGMOID *a.*

**1666** J. SMITH *Solomon's Portrait. Old Age* 233 The sigmoidal Portals hindering its return, it [the blood] must pass through the Streiner of the Lungs. **1753** *Chambers's Cycl. Suppl.* s.v. *Sigmoides*, The semicircular cavity of the cubit.. is sometimes also called the sigmoidal-cavity. **1826** KIRBY & SP. *Entomol.* IV. xxxviii. 55 The pupa.. has likewise a pair of long sigmoidal ones [respiratory organs] on the back of the trunk. **1833-4** *Encycl. Metrop.* (1845) VI. 598/2 The beds of coal and accompanying strata are bent into a sigmoidal flexure. **1879** RUTLEY *Study of Rocks* xi. 187 At times they have a somewhat sigmoidal flexure.

Hence **sig'moidally** *adv.*, in a sigmoidal manner.

**1854** *Orr's Circ. Sci., Org. Nat.* I. 218 The femur.. is sigmoidally bent. **1886** *Geol. Mag.* (N.S.) III. 150 The sigmoidally curved folds of the ganoine.

**sigmoidoscope** (sɪg'mɔɪdəskəʊp). *Med.* [f. SIGMOID *a.* and *sb.* + -O + -SCOPE.] A speculum for examining the lower bowel and for assisting in minor operations therein. Cf. SIGMOIDSCOPE s.v. SIGMOID.

**1900** in DORLAND *Med. Dict.* 599/2. **1906** P. L. MUMMERY *Sigmoidoscope* 7 The introduction of the electric pneumatic sigmoidoscope represents a great advance in our powers of accurate diagnosis. **1974** R. M. KIRK et al. *Surgery* vi. 123 Polyps can be removed through a sigmoidoscope using a snare.

Hence as *v. trans.*; also **sigmoido'scopic** *a.*, performed or ascertained by means of a sigmoidoscope; **sigmoido'scopically** *adv.*; **sigmoi'doscopist**, one who uses a sigmoidoscope; **sigmoi'doscopy**, examination by means of a sigmoidoscope.

**1900** DORLAND *Med. Dict.* 599/2 Sigmoidoscopy. **1906** P. L. MUMMERY *Sigmoidoscope* 37 A sigmoidoscopic examination will give valuable information if there is any question of being able to remove the growth. **1961** L. MARTIN *Clinical Endocrinol.* (ed. 3) vi. 163 Intestinal symptoms and sigmoidoscopy or barium enema appearances will be diagnostic. **1962** *Lancet* 26 May 1095/1 Of the 20 patients receiving control treatment only 7 improved symptomatically and 8 sigmoidoscopically. **1966** *Ibid.* 25 June 1420/2 Heaven forbid that some future 'Chief of Service' should licence me to sigmoidoscope my cases of earache in this surgery. **1976** *Path. Ann.* XI. 28 Rectal examination may reveal blood, as may sigmoidoscopy, when the blood can often be seen coming from higher in the bowel. **1977** *Proc. R. Soc. Med.* LXX. 273/2 Sigmoidoscopic biopsy of the stricture at 14 cm showed chronically inflamed mucosa with no tumour tissue. **1977** *Lancet* 29 Oct. 893/2 The sigmoidoscopist was not able to recognise the type of enema a patient was receiving by the sigmoidoscopic appearances on the morning after an overnight retention enema.

**sign** (saɪn), *sb.* Forms: *α.* 3–6 sygne, 3–7 signe (4 sigine?), 5–6 sygn (5 sygyn?), 4– sign; 4–5 singne, 4–5 syngne (5 synn-); 4, 6–7 *Sc.* sing(e, 5–6 *Sc.* syng(e, 5 senge). *β.* 4–7 sine, 4–6 syne (4 synne, 5 syn, cyne, scien, 6 *Sc.* synd). [a. F. *signe*, †*sine*, ad. L. *signum* mark, token, etc.]

**I. 1. a.** A gesture or motion of the hand, head, etc., serving to convey an intimation or to communicate some idea. Freq. in the phrases ***to make a sign*** or ***signs***, and ***by signs***.

*a* **1225** *Ancr. R.* 70 Heo schal habben leaue to.. makien signes touward hire of one glede chere. *c* **1350** *Will. Palerne* 2740 To þe hert & þe hinde he turned him a-ȝeine, & bi certeyn signes sone he hem tauȝt. c 1385 CHAUCER *L.G.W.* 2367 *Philomene*, She..preyede hym with signys to gon Vn-to the queen..And be signys swor hym manye an oth [etc.]. c 1400 MAUNDEV. (Roxb.) xxii. 100 þai speke noȝt, bot..makez signes as mounkes duse. 1508 DUNBAR *Tua Mariit Wemen* 467, I have ane secrete serwand,..That me supportis of sic nedis, quhen I a syne mak. 1530 PALSGR. 702/2 I spake nothyng to him, but I shewed hym of it by signe otherwise. 1595 SHAKS. *John* IV. ii. 237 Thou didst vnderstand me by my signes, And didst in signes againe parley with sinne. 1626 BACON *New Atl.* 4 Warning us off by signes that they made. 1664 BUTLER *Hud.* II. ii. 758 Then Hudibras, with face and hand, Made signs for Silence. 1712 STEELE *Spect.* No. 454 ¶4 The Coachmen make Signs with their Fingers..to intimate how much they have got that Day. 1791 MRS. RADCLIFFE *Rom. Forest* x, The moment Peter saw her he made a sign of silence. 1839 FR. A. KEMBLE *Resid. in Georgia* (1863) 37 More by signs and dumb show than words. 1873 DIXON *Two Queens* XVI. ii. III. 193 Scores of starving men were ready on a sign to hunt him down.

†**b.** A show or pretence *of* something. *Obs.*

c 1400 MAUNDEV. (Roxb.) iii. 10 He made signe of etyng and feyned as he had etyn. 1485 CAXTON *Chas. Gt.* 230 The whyche..made to hym synge of loue and of subgectyon..vnder the shadowe of decepcyon. a 1548 HALL *Chron., Hen. VI*, 91 b, Then he and all his companye made a signe of retraite.

**c.** A signal.

1601 SHAKS. *Jul. C.* v. i. 23 Mark Antony, shall we giue signe of Battaile?.. No Cæsar. 1615 G. SANDYS *Trav.* 298 The Charioteers started their horses upon a signe given. 1678 *Life Black Prince* in *Harleian Misc.* (1809) III. 144 The sign of battle, being given by King Philip, was entertained with clamours and shouts. 1708 CHAMBERLAYNE *Pres. St. Gt. Brit.* (1710) 349 From the top..they made a Sign by Fire, when they apprehended any imminent Danger. 1817 SHELLEY *Rev. Islam* x. vii, With secret signs from many a mountain-tower, With smoke by day, and fire by night.

**2. a.** A mark or device having some special meaning or import attached to it, or serving to distinguish the thing on which it is put.

Freq. in *sign of the cross* (cf. CROSS *sb.* 3 b).

c 1290 *S. Eng. Leg.* I. 84 Heo made þe signe of þe croiz. 13.. *Cursor M.* 6078 (Gött.), On ilk a post..A sine of tau *T* make ȝe þer. 1393 LANGL. *P. Pl.* C. xv. 40 Crist cam and confermede and holy kirke made, And in sond a sygne wrot. c 1420 LYDG. *Assembly of Gods* 1040 Vertew commaundyd euery wyght To pauyse hym vndyr the sygne of the roode. c 1440 *Pallad. on Husb.* XI. 22 Now nede is sette a signe on euery vyne That fertile is, scıouns of hit to take For settyng. 1526 *Pilgr. Perf.* (W. de W. 1531) 26 b, Marked..not onely with the sygne of the crosse in our garmentis,..but also (I trust) with the sygne of tau in our soules. 1560 DAUS tr. *Sleidane's Comm.* 334 With his crosiers staffe [he] maketh the signe of the crosse upon the highest walles. 1653 H. MORE *Antid. Ath.* II. vi, Observing that several Herbs are marked with some Mark or Sign that intimates their virtue. 1733 BERKELEY *Th. Vision Vind.* §40 A great number of arbitrary signs, various and opposite, do constitute a Language. 1769 ROBERTSON *Chas. V, State Europe* Note x, It was usual for persons who could not write, to make the sign of the cross in confirmation of a charter. 1833 N. ARNOTT *Physics* (ed. 5) II. 236 The common visual signs on the retina..are of all signs the most readily learned or understood. 1884 *Cath. Dict.* (1897) 258/1 The Church, accustomed to bless everything with the sign of the cross.

†**b.** A bookmark; = REGISTER *sb.*[1] 7 a. *Obs.*[−0]

1483 *Cath. Angl.* 340/1 A Syne of a buke, *registrum*.

**c.** A conventional mark, device, or symbol, used technically (as in music, algebra, botany, etc.) in place of words or names written in ordinary letters.

1557 RECORDE *Whetst.* S j b, Nombers Cossike, are soche as bee contracte vnto a denomination of some Cossike signe. *Ibid.* S ij b, There be other .2. signes in often vse, of whiche the firste is made thus + and betokeneth more: the other is made – and betokeneth lesse. 1597 MORLEY *Introd. Mus.* 104 The note whereupon the following part must begin, is marked with this signe .?. 1609 DOWLAND *Ornith. Microl.* 87 A signe is the successiue distribution of one and the same Close, in..a Song. 1662 PLAYFORD *Skill Mus.* I. x. (1674) 32 The Perfect of the Less..; its Sign or Mark is made thus. 1728 CHAMBERS *Cycl.* s.v. *Character*, Ordinarily..in Algebra, the Sign [of multiplication] is omitted, and the two Quantities put together. 1832 LINDLEY *Introd. Bot.* 422 In botany a variety of marks, or signs, are employed to express particular qualities or properties of plants. 1875 JOWETT *Plato* (ed. 2) IV. 150 Two minus signs in arithmetic or algebra make a plus.

†**d.** *Math.* A point. *Obs. rare.*

1570 BILLINGSLEY *Euclid* I. def. 1, A signe or point is that which hath no part. *Ibid.*, Vnity..is lesse materiall then a signe or poynt.

**e.** *Math.* That aspect of a quantity which may be either positive or negative.

1820 G. PEACOCK *Differential & Integral Calculus* 112 The sign of $d^2u$ may be easily determined. 1836 A. DE MORGAN *Differential & Integral Calculus* xiv. 369 When there is a change of sign, $y$ is a maximum (M), or a minimum ($m$), according as the change is from + to – or from – to + ($x$ increasing). 1924 G. F. SWAIN *Structural Engin.* xiii. 350 It is obvious that $n_1$ will have the same sign as $ft$, and $n_2$ the opposite sign. 1957 G. E. HUTCHINSON *Treat. Limnol.* I. ix. 597 Where biochemical oxygen uptake or production occurs, no general rule as to the sign of the divergence from saturation will be possible. 1978 C. P. MCKEAGUE *Elem. Algebra* i. 23 To multiply any two real numbers simply multiply their absolute values, the sign of the answer is 1. positive if both numbers had the same sign..2. negative if the numbers had opposite signs.

†**3.** A mark of attestation (or ownership), written or stamped upon a document, seal, etc. *Obs.*

1362 LANGL. *P. Pl.* A. II. 82 Þe Deede was a-selet, Be siht of sir Symoni and Notaries signes. 1377 *Ibid.* B. xx. 270, I wolde..þat ȝe were in þe Registre, And ȝowre noumbre vndre notaries sygne. c 1460 *Oseney Reg.* 133 The forsaide x. acris..lien in the Northefelde of the foresaide towne with owre syne woonyd i-seeled. 1474 CAXTON *Chesse* II. i. (1883) 22 Not only her promises but their othes her sealis and wrytynges & signes of their propre handes. 1558 in *10th Rep. Hist. MSS. Comm.* App. V. 388 In wittnes hereof we have..set hereunto our signes and common sealle. 1609 BIBLE (Douay) *Jer.* xxxii. 44 The fieldes..shal be written in a booke, and the signe shal be stamped on, and a witnes shal be taken.

†**4.** A figure or image; a statue or effigy; an imprint. *Obs.*

1362 LANGL. *P. Pl.* A. IV. 112 Bere no seluer ouer see þat bereþ signe of þe kyng. 1387 TREVISA *Higden* (Rolls) I. 229 Þere is anoþere signe and tokene to fore þe popes paleys; an hors of bras and a man sittynge þeron. c 1440 *Pol., Rel., & L. Poems* (1903) 152 Ther ys ȝette a syne of his fote On a marbull stone þer as he stode. 1589 WARNER *Alb. Eng.* VI. xxix. (1602) 143 For often Vprores did ensue for him, as vndeceast, Howbeit solemnely inter'd, himselfe, or Signe at least.

†**5. a.** A device borne on a banner, shield, etc.; a cognizance or badge. *Obs.*

c 1290 *S. Eng. Leg.* I. 158 Ane Croiz, þat Man fer isaiȝ,..þat was signe of is baner. c 1350 *Will. Palerne* 3213 Swete sire, ȝe me saye what signe is þe leuest to haue schape in þi scheld to schene armes? 1399 *Rolls of Parlt.* III. 452 That thei..gyf no Liverees of Sygnes, no make no Retenue of men. c 1420 LYDG. *Assembly of Gods* 355 A garland of yuy he [Bacchus] chase for hys sygne. 1461 *Coventry Leet-bk.* II. 319 [That they] neyther were ne vse oure most honnorable signe, nor any other lordes or gentilles signe, tokyn or lyuere. 1562 LEGH *Armorie* 47, I will therfore shewe you of signes yt are borne, and do occupie the same Escocheon.

**b.** Something displayed as an emblem or token; *esp.* an ensign, banner, standard. *Obs.*

c 1400 *Song Roland* 503 An C thoussand of good men..with proud synes of silk lifte on loft. c 1440 *York Myst.* xvii. 222 Vn-to þat Prince I rede we praye, That till vs sente his syngne [*sc.* the star] vnsoght. 1483 CAXTON *Gold. Leg.* 305/1 He is had among the companye of Angels as banerer and berynge the signe of oure lord. 1500–20 DUNBAR *Poems* xxxviii. 4 The signe trivmphall rasit is of the croce. 1596 DALRYMPLE tr. *Leslie's Hist. Scotl.* II. 300 Monie standarts and syngis..left be the Jnglismen, be the Scotis ar tane. 1667 MILTON *P.L.* VI. 776 The great Ensign of Messiah blaz'd Aloft by Angels born, his Sign in Heav'n.

**c.** *spec.* A pilgrim's token. *Obs.*

1362 LANGL. *P. Pl.* A. VI. 12 An hundred of ampolles on his hat seeten, Signes of Synay and Schelles of Galys. c 1400 *Beryn* 171 Then, as manere & custom is, signes þere þey bouȝte. *Ibid.* 175, 191.

**d.** *pl.* Insignia. *Obs. rare.*

1591 SPENSER *M. Hubberd* 1016 Yet at the last..He all those royall signes had stolne away.

**6. a.** A characteristic device attached to, or placed in front of, an inn (†house) or shop, as a means of distinguishing it from others or directing attention to it; in later use commonly a board bearing a name or other inscription, with or without some ornament or picture. Also, a board giving information, directions, etc.

1467 in *Eng. Gilds* (1870) 405 That no person sille none ale out of his place, but he haue a signe at his dorre. c 1470 *Promp. Parv.* (K.) 456/1 Syne of an in. 1539 TAVERNER *Erasm. Prov.* (1552) 42 The Englysh prouerbe is this. Good wyne nedeth no signe. 1593 SHAKS. *2 Hen. VI*, v. ii. 67 Vnderneath an Ale-house paltry signe, The Castle in S. Albons. 1617 MORYSON *Itin.* III. 156, I did never see nor heare that they have any publike Innes with signes hanging out. 1667 PRIMATT *City & C. Build.* 69 Note, That they weigh with the Balconie, the Bars that are to fasten the sign thereunto. 1727 SWIFT *Imit. Horace* II. vi. 72 To read the Lines Writ underneath the Country Signs. 1780 *Mirror* No. 82 Putting up their pictures as signs for their taverns and ale-houses. 1816 J. SCOTT *Vis. Paris* (ed. 5) 91 The signs of the shops are very elegant;—that is to say, they are elegant for signs. 1859 JEPHSON *Brittany* ix. 134 The first thing that met my eye..was a sign over a public-house. 1904, etc. [see *road sign* s.v. ROAD *sb.* 9 b].

*fig.* 1642 FULLER *Holy & Prof. St.* I. viii. 20 Fools! who to perswade men that Angels lodged in their hearts, hung out a devil for a signe in their faces. a 1684 LEIGHTON *Wks.* (1816) 429 Fantastic garb in apparel, which is the very bush or sign hanging out, that tells a vain mind lodges within. 1825 SCOTT *Talism.* iv, I am but the vile and despised sign, which points out to the wearied traveller a harbour of rest and security, but must itself remain for ever without doors.

**b.** In phr. ***at the sign of*** (*the Bell*, *Sun*, etc.).

1501 *Alcock's Mons Perfect.* Colophon, Enprynted at London in flete strete at the sygne of ye sonne by Wynkin de worde. 1542–3 *Act 34 & 35 Hen. VIII*, c. 12 One little lane stretching from the said way, to the signe of the bell at Drewry lane ende. 1672 *Heath's Flagellum* Title-p., Sold at his Shop at the Signe of the Crown. 1722 DE FOE *Col. Jack* (1840) 94 We baited at an inn, at the sign of the Falcon. 1749 FIELDING *Tom Jones* VIII. viii, Chose for their house of entertainment the sign of the Bell. 1828 SCOTT *F.M. Perth* xx, An appointment to meet with the others of his company at the sign of the Griffin.

†**c.** ***at the sign of the moon***, in the open air by night. (After Fr. *à l'enseigne de la lune.*) *Obs.*

1613 PURCHAS *Pilgrimage* III. x. (1614) 294 They often lodge (saith Willamont) at the signe of the Moone; and the like moderation they vse in diet and apparel. 1679 G. R. tr. *Boaistuau's Theat. World* II. 107 The Souldier is for the most part alwayes waking, having his Quarters at the Sign of the Moon.

**II. 7. a.** A token or indication (visible or otherwise) *of* some fact, quality, etc. Also ***the signs of the times***, indications of current trends; now freq. as *sing.* phr. with leading indef. article.

1297 R. GLOUC. (Rolls) 3744 Þer nas nour aboute kniȝt..bot hii of sute were Of king arthures hous, oþer som signe þer of bere, Of robes oþer of armes. 13.. *E.E. Allit. P.* B. 489 Þat was þe syngne of sauyte þat sende hem oure lorde. c 1386 CHAUCER *Melib.* §53 It is signe of gentil herte whan a man..desireth to han a good name. c 1400 *Lanfranc's Cirurg.* 181 If þe place be whijt & neische..it is a signe of fleume. 1484 CAXTON *Fables of Avian* viii, [He] hath shewed to the grete sygne or token of loue. 1525 BIBLE (Tyndale) (1526) *Matt.* xvi. 3 Can ye not discerne the sygnes of the tymes? a 1533 LD. BERNERS *Gold. Bk. M. Aurel.* (1546) C iii b, He bare in his hande the signe or token of the office, wherby he lyued. 1594 in *Cath. Rec. Soc. Publ.* V. 285 All with black hoods, which with us is a signe of gentlewomen. 1638 JUNIUS *Paint. Ancients* 228 Though it be no signe of a more polished, yet is it a marke of a greater wit. 1697 DRYDEN *Virg. Georg.* III. 670 The Causes and the Signs..Of ev'ry Sickness that infects the Fold. 1750 GRAY *Long Story* 89 [It was] no sign of grace, For folks in fear are apt to pray. 1829 T. L. PEACOCK *Misfort. Elphin* x, They here found..materials of spinning and embroidering, and other signs of female inhabitancy. 1833 *Daily Nat. Intelligencer* 17 July 3/3 We have stood upon our '*reserved rights*' of neutrality, to watch the signs of the times. 1863 GEO. ELIOT *Romola* xxii, Working people..bearing on their dress or persons the signs of their daily labour. 1874 GREEN *Short Hist.* iv. §5. 202 The exile of Gaveston was the sign of the Barons' triumph. 1907 *Nature* 14 Mar. 459/1 This book is an interesting sign of the times. 1921 J. GALSWORTHY *To Let* II. xi. 214 '*He's* a sign of the times,' muttered Soames, 'if you like.' 1953 A. J. TOYNBEE *World & West* vi. 93 The people who have read the signs of the times and have taken action in the light of these indications are the obscure missionaries of half-a-dozen Oriental religions. 1977 *Gay News* 24 Mar. 19/3 Last year, perhaps as a sign of the times, Take Six notched up over 80 mentions in everything from the *Daily Mirror* to the Italian glossioso *L'Uomo*.

**b.** Used without const., or with clause following.

c 1380 WYCLIF *Sel. Wks.* II. 258 Signes of þe olde lawe weren toknes of oure signes now, as þei ben tokenes of þe blisse of hevene. 1422 tr. *Secreta Secret., Priv. Priv.* 232 They haue many tokenys or syngnes by wych a man may deme the Physnomye. 1483 CAXTON *Cato* 5 Of the foure Sygnes or tokens by whiche is knowen trewe loue. 1560 DAUS tr. *Sleidane's Comm.* 55 b, To axe of God a sygne wherby he maye testifie, that he careth for us. a 1656 BP. HALL *Rem. Wks.* (1660) 192 The thing signed is usually put for the sign itself. 1690 LOCKE *Hum. Und.* III. x. (1695) 277 The using of Words, without clear and distinct Ideas; or, which is worse, signs without any thing signified. 1766 GRAY *Impromptus* 12 A sign you have eat just enough and no more. 1833 TENNYSON *Two Voices* 270 Know I not Death? the outward signs? 1885 S. O. JEWETT *Marsh Island* xii, She never had given a single sign that she loved or meant to marry him. 1890 W. JAMES *Princ. Psychol.* II. xxii. 356 Language is a system of signs, different from the things signified, but able to suggest them. c 1902 C. S. PEIRCE *Coll. Papers* (1932) II. §92 Genuine mediation is the character of a *Sign.* 1922 tr. *Wittgenstein's Tractatus* 53 The sign is the part of the symbol perceptible by the senses. 1938 C. W. MORRIS (*title*) Foundations of the theory of signs. 1947, 1949 [see SIGNIFIANT]. 1954 [see SIGNIFIER b]. 1964 GOULD & KOLB *Dict. Soc. Sci.* 641/2 Sign denotes any stimulus which, because of association with another stimulus, elicits a response appropriate to but in the absence of the original stimulus. 1978 *Incorporated Linguist* Summer 60/3 Modern society's haste to read inadvertently into signs (in the Barthesian sense) rather than decipher the simple message. 1979 S. G. J. HERVEY *Axiomatic Semantics* vii. 61 By the law of excluded middle, any given sign is either simple or complex, but not both.

**c.** Without article, in phr. ***in sign of*** (or ***that***).

1297 R. GLOUC. (Rolls) 3986 Branches hii bere Of oliue, as in signe þat hii aȝen pays nere. a 1300 *Cursor M.* 5121 He kist þam all in signe o saght. 1362 LANGL. *P. Pl.* A. XI. 98 In signe þat I schulde bi-sechen hire of grace. 1474 CAXTON *Chesse* II. iv. (1883) 44 The kynge..gyrdeth a boute them a swerde in signe that they shold abyde and kepe hym. 1546 *Reg. Privy Council Scot.* I. 30 In signe and takin herof my Lord Governour hes takyn baith thair handis. 1593 SHAKS. *3 Hen. VI*, IV. viii. 26 In signe of truth, I kisse your Highnesse Hand. 1611 SIR W. MURE *Mes Amours* 39 Receaue, in sing that thou hes won the field, The bow. 1718 POPE *Iliad* x. 321 In sign she favour'd their intent, A long-wing'd heron great Minerva sent. 1865 MILL *Exam. Hamilton* 381 An animal is called a bull, in sign of its possessing certain attributes.

**d.** *Theol.* Phr. ***outward visible sign*** and varr., in sacramental ordinances, the outward and visible aspect which symbolizes the inward and spiritual aspect. Also *transf.*

1553 J. BRADFORD in Coverdale *Lett. Martyrs* (1564) 293 There is Idolatry in worshipping the outwarde signe of breade and wyne. 1604 *Bk. Com. Prayer, Catechism*, Q. How many partes be there in a Sacrament? *A.* Two: the Outward visible signe, and the Inward spirituall Grace. c 1816 J. MARRIOTT *Hymn*, Grant to this child the inward grace, While we the outward sign impart. 1861 tr. *O Food that Weary Pilgrims Love!* in *Hymns, Anc. & Mod.* (Introits & Anthems) p. xvii, O Jesu, Whom, by power divine Now hidden 'neath the outward sign, We worship and adore. 1898 A. G. MORTIMER *Cath. Faith & Practice* I. 124 The matter [of a sacrament] is the outward sign; the form that which determines the matter to its special use or purpose. 1921 J. GALSWORTHY *To Let* III. x. 288 In the union of the great-granddaughter..with the heir of a ninth baronet was the outward and visible sign of that merger of class in class which buttresses the political stability of a realm. 1931 V. DIXON *Sebastian Wile* II. ii. §1 Her governess had said farewell, outward and visible sign that Martha's days of childish servitude were over. 1938 *Doctrine in Church of England* II. 127 The ordinary scholastic use is to employ the word [*sc.* sacrament] as meaning the outward and visible sign. 1951 A. POWELL *Question of Upbringing* iii. 157 Monsieur Dubuisson accepted the brandy as the outward and visible sign of reconciliation. 1962 WILSON & TEMPLETON *Anglican Teaching* ix. 180 The Catechism..defines a Sacrament as 'an outward and visible sign of an inward and spiritual grace..ordained by Christ Himself'.

**e.** *U.S.* The trail or trace of wild animals, etc.

Sometimes in pl., but the sing. is the technical use.

1692 *Cal. Virginia St. Papers* (1875) I. 44 We Ranged about to see if we could find ye tract of any Indians, but we could not see any fresh signe. 1746 *New Hampsh. Hist. Soc. Coll.* (1834) IV. 208 By the sign of this ambush, and by the sign of their going off, in a single file, it was supposed there could not be less than 50 or 60 Indians. **1821** J. Fowler *Jrnl.* 3 Nov. (1898) 33 Heare We find the first fresh Sign of bever. *Ibid.* 7 Nov. 36 We see old sign of Indeans... We again See the Sign of White men a Head of us. **1847** Ruxton *Mexico & Rocky Mts.* xxi. 170 On the banks of the river I saw some fresh beaver 'sign'. *Ibid.*, We saw Indian sign on the banks of the river. **1851** Mayne Reid *Scalp Hunt.* xxxii. 243 Buffalo 'signs' appeared as we rode into them. **1890** L. C. D'Oyle *Notches* 68 We had noticed bear 'sign' in a thick patch of rose-bushes. *Ibid.*, Lots of fresh 'sign', but no bear.

**f.** *Med.* An objective evidence or indication of disease (as opposed to a subjective one, or *symptom*); often used with the name of one who associated an indication with a disease characterized by it, to designate the former.

**1842** W. A. Guy *Hooper's Physician's Vademecum* (new ed.) I. iii. 16 The word sign has not precisely the same meaning as the term symptom, though the two terms are sometimes used without much discrimination... Cough, expectoration, dyspnœa, hectic fever, night sweats, and emaciation, are *symptoms* of pulmonary consumption, but they are not *signs*, for each of them may occur in other diseases; but cavernous respiration and pectoriloquy are signs. *Ibid.*, The term *physical* sign is in common use among medical men: it means a sign which is an object of sense. Thus heat, redness, and swelling are physical signs of inflammation, pectoriloquy of phthisis, coagulable urine of disease of the kidney. **1851** R. P. Cotton *Phthisis & Stethoscope* i. 12 Physical signs by themselves, as a general rule, determine nothing more than physical conditions..; hence it is, that we require the use of other rules, as well as a knowledge of the patient's history and general symptoms. *Ibid.* ii. 24 Diminished resonance is one of the earliest and most characteristic signs of phthisis. **1872** W. Williams *Princ. & Pract. Vet. Surg.* xiii. 244 The diagnostic signs of elbow-joint lameness are, first, the semi-flexed position of the limb.. whilst standing still; and the dropping of the head and anterior parts of the body during action. **1886** J. Finlayson *Clin. Manual for Study Med. Cases* (ed. 2) ii. 51 A pain is a 'Symptom' (subjective); a bulging chest, to which it may be due, is a 'Sign' (objective): giddiness is a 'Symptom' (subjective); the staggering resulting from it is a 'Sign' (objective). **1908** *Practitioner* Jan. 10 We do not obtain ankle clonus, or Babinsky's, or Oppenheim's sign. **1927** G. W. Deeping *Kitty* xv. 193 Mr. St. George had an undoubted paraplegia. There was definite spasticity of the lower limbs... Babinski's sign was present. **1956** A. I. Littlejohn tr. *D. Wirth's Vet. Clin. Diagnosis* 1 Symptoms in the medical sense are not available to the veterinary diagnostician, but the substitution of the term 'symptom' for 'sign' in veterinary usage is widespread. **1971** S. Magalini *Dict. Med. Syndromes* 148/1 Dercum's [syndrome]... *Symptoms.* Prevalent in women 40 to 60 years of age. Pain in part of body where localized accumulation of fat occurs. Asthenia, headache... *Signs.* Subcutaneous accumulation of fat elevated, dry, reddish, or bluish, anesthesia and diminished cutaneous sensibility. **1974** T. McGinnis *Well Dog Bk.* (1979) 95 Because your dogs cannot describe their feelings in words, they technically have no symptoms, only *signs* which are any objective evidence of disease or injury you can detect.

**8. a.** A trace or indication *of* something; a vestige. Chiefly in negative phrases.

**13..** *Seuyn Sag.* 2934 (W.), So he traueld monethes thre, And no signe of hyr kowth he se. **1390** Gower *Conf.* III. 315 With the craftes whiche he couthe, He soghte and fond a signe of lif. *c* **1440** *York Myst.* xi. 100, I se ȝondyr a ful selcouth syght, Wher-of be-for no synge was seene. **1567** Allen *Def. Priesthood* 228 Wherof yet in most Churches ther remaineth a smal signe, by disciplin geuen [etc.]. *c* **1586** C'tess Pembroke *Ps.* cxv. iii, [No] signe of sound their throates can show. **1715** Leoni *Palladio's Archit.* (1742) II. 66 The Aqueducts.. whose Ruins and Signs are to be seen on the Road. **1726** Swift *Gulliver* I. i, I.. could not discover any Sign of Houses or Inhabitants. **1795** *Ann. Reg., Hist.* 109 No signs of such an intention were perceivable. **1872** Black *Adv. Phaeton* xxx. 407 There is no sign of life in this wild place.

†**b.** A mere semblance *of* something. *Obs.*

**1607** Breton *A Murmurer* Wks. (Grosart) II. 8/2 Oh fine foole, how thou wouldest haue the signe of a man stand for a man? **1673** Dryden *Marr. à-la-Mode* II. i, If it be but to punish that sign of a Husband there; that lazy Matrimony. **1693** Congreve *Old Bach.* III. iii, I would not have you draw yourself into a premunire, by trusting to that sign of a man there.

**9.** An indication of some coming event; *spec.* an omen or portent.

**13..** *Cursor M.* 22430 (Gött.), Forn domes-dai þai sal be sene, wid sorful sines ful fijf-tene. **1387** Trevisa *Higden* (Rolls) II. 165 Soche þey declareþ certeynliche by schewynge of tokenes and of synnes [*v.r.* synes] þat beeþ in suche a schulder boon. **1513** Douglas *Æneid* IV. viii, How Dido send hir sistir Enee to pray, And of the grisly singis did hir affray. **1542** Boorde *Dyetary* xl. (1870) 302 That there is lykle [*sic*] hope of amendment, but sygnes of deth. **1593** Shaks. *3 Hen. VI*, v. vi. 44 The Owle shriek'd at thy birth, an euill signe. **1621** T. Williamson tr. *Goulart's Wise Vieillard* 94 The auncient Iewes had this saying, that it is *bonum omen*, a good signe to see an old man in a house. **1725** *Fam. Dict.* s.v. *Clouds*, When.. waterish Clouds appear on the Tops of Hills, it is a Sign of Rain to follow. **1793** Cowper *Tale* 61 Seamen much believe in signs. **1817** Shelley *Rev. Islam* x. xvi, These signs the coming mischief did foretell. **1833** Tennyson *May Queen* III. x, If it come three times, I thought, I take it for a sign.

**10. a.** An act of a miraculous nature, serving to demonstrate divine power or authority.

In Biblical use, after L. *signum*, Gr. σημεῖον.

*a* **1300** *Cursor M.* 13420 Þis was þe formast sign he did. *Ibid.* 13438 Sli signe did crist at þis bridall. **1382** Wyclif *Acts* iv. 22 The man was more than of fourty ȝeeris, in the which this sygne of heelthe was maad. **1611** Bible *Acts* ii. 43 Many wonders and signes were done by the Apostles. **1665** J. Spencer *Vulg. Proph.* 59 But every Sign is not (if we speak accurately) a Miracle. **1727** De Foe *Syst. Magic* I. iii. (1840) 73 Pharaoh, in contempt of Moses and Aaron, and the sign or miracle they had shown. **1876** Mellor *Priesth.* iv. 179 His hearers no sooner caught the word 'faith', than they demanded a sign which might warrant it.

†**b.** A marvel or wonder. *Obs.*$^{-1}$

*a* **1400–50** *Alexander* 4934 Sire, þou sall see with þi siȝt slike signes, or þou passe, As neuire segge vndire son saȝe bot þine ane.

**11.** *Astr.* **a.** One or other of the twelve equal divisions of the Zodiac, each distinguished by the name of a constellation and frequently denoted by a special symbol.

*c* **1340** Hampole *Pr. Consc.* 4803 Þe twelfte day aftir, þe sternes alle And þe signes fra þe heven sal falle. **1390** Gower *Conf.* III. 108 Ther ben signes tuelve, Whiche have her cercles be hemselve Compassed in the zodiaque. *c* **1430** Lydg. *Min. Poems* (Percy Soc.) 2 Whan Phebus whas.. yronne Out of the signe, wiche callyd is aquary. **1483** Caxton *Cato* e v b, The man whych is borne in a good planette or sygne. **1509** Hawes *Past. Pleas.* XXII. (Percy Soc.) 105 He sette.. The bodies above to have their moving, In the xii. signes them selfe to domify. **1555** Eden *Decades* (Arb.) 279 At that tyme the soonne was in the north signes. **1610** Holland *Camden's Brit.* (1637) 182 Vnder what Signe in heaven Britaine lieth. *a* **1646** J. Gregory *Posthuma* (1650) 299 Now look what Sign of the twelv shall bee found to rise up in the Horoscope or Angle of the East, that is the Sign-Regent of that Hous or Citie. **1709** Steele *Tatler* No. 100 § 3, I was looking.. on that Sign in the Heavens which is called by the Name of the Ballance. **1812** Woodhouse *Astron.* xxix. 289 The motions of Jupiter's satellites are according to the order of the signs. **1868** Lockyer *Elem. Astron.* § 37 These are called the zodiacal constellations (very carefully to be distinguished.. from the signs of the zodiac bearing the same name).

†**b.** A constellation. *Obs. rare.*

**1398** Trevisa *Barth. De P.R.* VIII. xxiii. (Bodl. MS), Arcturus is a signe ymade of vij. sterres. *Ibid.*, Orioun is a signe that ariseth in wintere. **1490** Caxton *Eneydos* xii. 46 The sygne of Oryon. **1565** Cooper *Thesaurus*, *Orion*.. was .. translated among the sterres, & there is the signe called in latine *Jugula.* **1611** Cotgr. s.v. *Orion.*

**III. 12.** *attrib.* and *Comb.*, as (sense 1) ***sign-language*** (also *fig.*), ***-maker***, ***-speech***, ***-talk***; (sense 2 c) ***sign-symbol***; (sense 5) ***sign-mark***; (sense 6) ***sign-iron***, ***-painter***, ***-writer*** (writer 1 b), ***-writing***; (sense 7) ***sign-situation***, ***-system***, ***-using*** vbl. sb. and ppl. adj., ***-word***; (sense 11) † ***sign-carrier***.

**1653** R. Sanders *Physiogn.* 1 A Zodiack..; the Latins call it *Signifer*, that is to say, *Sign-carrier. **1778** *Phil. Trans.* LXIX. 44 On passing through the streets of London in his walks, before the *sign-irons were taken down. **1836** in *Hist. Chesterfield* (1839) 45 Having a sign, sign-iron, sign-post, or shew-board suspended from or in front of such house. **1847** T. H. Gallandet in *Amer. Ann. Deaf & Dumb* I. 59 They originate from elements of this *sign-language which nature furnishes to man wherever he is found, whether barbarous or civilized. **1865** Tylor *Early Hist. Man.* ii. 25 The teacher remarked that I did not seem to be quite a beginner in the sign-language. **1960** S. Plath *Colossus* 39 These.. sheets.. Speak in sign language of a lost other-world. **1981** *Amer. Speech* LVI. 130 Sign language is as adequate for the deaf as any vocal-auditory language is for a hearing person. **1889** Mivart *Orig. Hum. Reason* 66 Such a movement is a true 'sign', being a movement made depicting a fact with the intention of conveying to other minds the ideas of the *sign-maker. **1840** Browning *Sordello* IV. 387 The Kaiser's ominous *sign-mark had first place, The crowned grim twy-necked eagle. **1725** *New-Eng. Courant* 15 Feb. 1/2, I would oblige every *Sign-Painter to serve seven Years at College, before he presum'd to handle Pencil or Paint-Box. **1776** Burney *Hist. Mus.* I. 221 The painter should have had about the same degree of merit with a good sign-painter in Europe. **1814** Sir R. Wilson *Priv. Diary* (1862) II. 346 For fear the head should not be recognised as the saint's, a brown cap is put upon it by the sign-painter. **1942** *Burlington Mag.* Jan. 9/1 Ireland takes this sketch as a proof that Hogarth contemplated setting up as a sign-painter. **1923** Ogden & Richards *Meaning of Meaning* i. 15 There may be a very long chain of *sign-situations intervening between the act and its referent. **1977** *Dædalus* Fall 105 Literature.. though it is.. a form of communication.. is cut off from the immediate pragmatic purposes which simplify other sign situations. **1873** Cayley in *Messenger Math.* II. 17 Theorems in Relation to Certain *Sign-Symbols. **1924** R. H. Bell *Mystery of Words* 101 A study of the general principles of language has brought out the nature of the linguistic *sign-system. **1977** R. H. Brown in Douglas & Johnson *Existential Sociol.* ii. 90 These norms and rules form a sign system that is itself subject to the feedback of experience. **1897** Kipling *Capt. Cour.* 133 How was it my French didn't go, and your *sign-talk did? **1890** W. James *Princ. Psychol.* II. xxii. 357 In the human child.. these ruptures of contiguous association are very soon made; far off cases of *sign-using arise when we make a sign now; and soon language is launched. **1938** C. W. Morris *Found. of Theory of Signs* i. 1 Men are the dominant sign-using animals. **1957** C. E. Osgood et al. *Measurement of Meaning* i. 3 The behavior of the sign-using organism. **1894** *N. & Q.* 8th Ser. V. 6/1 It is a *sign-word only, not a term of affinity. **1871** J. Callingham *Sign Writing* i. 1 It is curious that the term '*sign-writer' is not to be found in any encyclopædia or dictionary, ancient or modern... Even Kelly's ponderous 'Post Office London Directory' does not deem the sign-writer worthy of separate enumeration in its list of trades. **1977** J. McClure *Sunday Hangman* xiii. 151 A family of losers trying to find the right words for the signwriter. **1871** J. Callingham (*title*) *Sign writing. **1954** 'J. Wyndham' *Jizzle* 49 Elmer was a house-painter who doubled in the less spacious art of sign-writing. **1978** *Dumfries & Galloway Standard* 21 Oct. 21/2 (Advt.), All types of signwriting undertaken.

**b.** Special combs., as **sign-behaviour**, behaviour that is dependent on a sign (sense 7); **sign bit** *Computers*, a sign digit located in a sequence of binary digits; **sign-design** (see quot. 1942); **sign digit** *Computers*, a digit, located in a sequence of digits, whose value depends on the algebraic sign of the number represented; **sign-event**, a particular occurrence of the use of a sign (sense 7); **sign-process**, the process whereby a token or indication becomes operative or functions as a sign; **sign stimulus** *Biol.*, the component or characteristic of an external stimulus which is effective in initiating a particular innate behavioural response in an animal perceiving it, regardless of the presence or absence of the remainder of the stimulus; **sign-vehicle**, the token or indication that acts as a sign.

**1946** C. W. Morris *Signs, Lang. & Behav.* i. 7 And goal-seeking behavior in which signs exercise control may be called sign-behavior. **1964** Gould & Kolb *Dict. Soc. Sci.* 641/2 Sigh-behaviour is found in all levels of animal life. **1962** *Gloss. Terms Automatic Data Proc. (B.S.I.)* 19 Where the sign digit is a binary digit it is often known as a sign bit. **1975** T. Bartee *Introd. Computer Sci.* ii. 47 The sign bit is set apart from the magnitude bits by a . in each word... An alternate technique uses a box for the sign bit. **1942** R. Carnap *Introd. Semantics* § 3.5 The word 'sign' is ambiguous. It means sometimes a single object or event, sometimes a kind to which many objects belong. Whenever necessary, we shall use 'sign-*event*' in the first case, 'sign-*design*' in the second. **1944** *Mind* LIII. 36 The sign-design is what is usually meant when we use such words as 'symbol', 'word', 'sentence'. It is the form or structure common to a set of actual occurrences (sounds, marks, gestures) whereby they function symbolically. **1974** M. Taylor tr. *Metz's Film Lang.* iii. 90 Between words—pure 'sign events' as they are called in American semiotics, events that never occur twice.. and language.. there is room for the study of 'sign designs', sentence patterns. **1947** A. W. Burks et al. in J. von Neumann *Coll. Wks.* (1963) V. 46 Our numbers are 40 digit aggregates, the left-most digit being the sign digit. **1950** *Proc. R. Soc.* A. CCII. 574 The first digit is regarded as a sign digit and a 'binary point' supposed to exist before the second digit. **1969** J. J. Sparkes *Transistor Switching* viii. 194 The sign digit is normally 'o' for positive numbers. **1942** Sign-event [see *sign-design* above]. **1973** *Screen* Spring/Summer 164 *Spoken words*.. are pure 'sign-events' incapable of being reproduced twice over and therefore impossible to study scientifically. **1946** C. W. Morris *Signs, Lang. & Behav.* i. 3 Terms which are commonly used in describing sign-processes. **1957** C. E. Osgood et al. *Measurement of Meaning* i. 5 A first step toward a behavioral interpretation of the sign-process. **1934** E. S. Russell *Behaviour of Animals* ii. 33 The principle of representative stimuli, or sign stimuli as we may call them for short, is illustrated not only in the flight reactions of animals.. but even more clearly in.. food-finding behaviour. **1967** A. Manning *Introd. Animal Behaviour* iii. 39 There are many examples of auditory and chemical sign-stimuli too. Turkey hens which are breeding for the first time will accept as chicks any object which makes the typical cheeping call. On the other hand.. deaf turkey hens kill most of their chicks because they never receive the auditory sign-stimulus for parental behaviour. **1975**, **1980** Sign stimulus [see releaser c]. **1938** C. W. Morris *Found. of Theory of Signs* i. 4 In such cases *S* is the sign vehicle.., *D* the designatum, and *I* the interpretant of the interpreter. **1955** T. H. Pear *Eng. Soc. Differences* i. 33 Status symbols are sign-vehicles, cues which determine the status to be imputed to a person.

**sign** (saɪn), *v.*[1] Also 4–7 **signe**, 5–6 **sygne**, 6 **syne**, 7 **sine**, *Sc.* **singe**. [ad. F. *signer* (†*siner*) or L. *signāre*, f. *signum* sign *sb.*]

**I. 1. a.** *trans.* To mark, protect, consecrate, etc., *with* the sign of the cross.

*c* **1305** *St. Edmund* 66 in *E.E.P.* (1862) 72 In mie foreheuede iwrite mie name þu schalt iseo; Signe þerwiþ þi foreheued & þi breost also. *c* **1315** Shoreham I. 15, Ich signi þe wiþ signe of croys. **1552** *Bk. Com. Prayer, Bapt. Inf.*, We receyue this childe into the congregacion of Christes flocke and doe sygne hym wyth the signe of the crosse. **1634** Canne *Necess. Separ.* (1849) 248 They are to wear surplices, sign children in baptism with the sign of the cross. **1753** Challoner *Cath. Chr. Instr.* 3 The Use of signing ourselves with the Sign of the Cross. **1834** K. H. Digby *Mores Cath.* v. vii. 193 St. Gregory the Great says, that it was the custom to sign the penitential bread with a cross. **1878** Gairdner *Rich. III*, vi. 269 He kissed the ground and signed himself with the cross.

**b.** To cross (*esp.* oneself).

*c* **1400** Love *Bonavent. Mirr.* xlvii. (1908) 252 Than sche wipeth his face and kisseth it,.. and so signede and blessed hym. **1530** Palsgr. 718/1, I shall syne me on the forheed from the dyvell and all his angels. **1648** J. Beaumont *Psyche* XVII. cxxvii, How know I but thou art some fair-dress'd Feind To make me foul? and here himself he sign'd. **1855** Browning *Fra Lippo Lippi* 155 Shaking a fist at him with one fierce arm, Signing himself with the other because of Christ. **1861** Lytton & Fane *Tannhäuser* 100 Then, sign thyself, and peaceful go thy ways.

**c.** To make the sign of (the cross) by a movement of the hand.

**1810** Scott *Lady of Lake* III. iv, He pray'd, and sign'd the cross between. **1872** A. de Vere *Leg. St. Patrick, Baptism* ii, With that small hand.. He signed the Cross. **1896** A. Austin *England's Darling* I. i, Nay, sign the cross upon your brow and sleep.

**d.** To figure (the cross) *in* some material.

**1825** Scott *Betrothed* x, Pointing to the cross signed in white cloth upon his left shoulder.

**2. a.** To place some distinguishing mark upon (a thing or person); to mark with a sign.

**1398** Trevisa *Barth. De P.R.* XVI. viii. (Bodl. MS.), Grauers vse the peces þerof [i.e. adamant] to signe and to þirle precious stones. **1601** Shaks. *Jul. C.* III. i. 206 Heere thy Hunters stand Sign'd in thy Spoyle, and Crimson'd in thy Lethee. **1615** G. Sandys *Trav.* 228 They.. wore garments of black, signed with a white crosse. **1697** Dryden *Æneid* IX. 130 There sprung A Light that sign'd the Heav'ns, and shot along. **1726** Pope *Odyss.* XIX. 456 The scar, with which his manly knee was sign'd. **1843** RUSKIN *Mod. Paint.* I. II. vii. §20. 94 The reversed imagery of their darkness signed across by the soft lines of faintly touching winds.

*fig.* **1582** N. T. (Rhem.) *John* vi. 27 For him the Father, God, hath signed. —— *Eph.* iv. 30 The holy Spirit of God: in which you are signed vnto the day of redemption. *a* **1652** J. SMITH *Sel. Disc.* vii. 329 Since the Israelites are signed with the holy seal in the flesh, they are thereby acknowledged for the sons of God. **1697** DRYDEN *Virg. Georg.* I. 634 Earth, Air, and Seas, with Prodigies were sign'd. **1862** F. T. PALGRAVE in *Bk. of Praise* (1866) 242 Saviour pure and holy, Sign us with thy sign.

**b.** To stamp as a sign *upon* something. *rare.*

**1605** BACON *Adv. Learn.* I. vi. §16 The omnipotency of God, which is chiefly signed and engraven upon his works.

**c.** In *pass.* To have as signatures.

**1706** HEARNE *Collect.* 4 Feb., The leaves signed, a i. a iij.

†**3.** To put a seal upon (something). Also *intr.*, to use seals. *Obs.*

**1382** WYCLIF *Rev.* xxii. 10 Signe, or seele, thou not the wordes of prophecie of this book. **1581** MARBECK *Bk. Notes* 969 He.. put him in the bottomles dungeon, & shut him vp, & signed him with his seale. **1638** JUNIUS *Paint. Ancients* 178 The Easterne Countries or Ægypt doe not yet signe, sayth he, being contented with bare letters.

**4. a.** To attest or confirm by adding one's signature; to affix one's name to (a document, etc.).

**1477** EARL RIVERS (Caxton) *Dictes* 11 Signe nor seale them not til thou haue ouerseen them. **1513-4** *Act 5 Hen. VIII*, c. 1 Preamble, Every writting obligatorie.. signed and sealed in fourme above rehersed. **1596** SHAKS. *Merch. V.* IV. i. 397, I am not well, send the deed after me, And I will signe it. **1617** MORYSON *Itin.* II. 52 The Lord Deputies entertainement to be paid according to the List after following, which List was to be signed by the Lords. **1686** tr. *Chardin's Trav. Persia* 63 The Caimacan was ready to sign the Pass. **1713** SWIFT *Jrnl. to Stella* 16 Mar., They have had some expresses, by which they count that the peace may be signed by that time. **1776** *Trial of Nundocomar* 22/2 It is the custom of Shroffs to get the body of the bond wrote by their Gomastahs, and they sign it with their own hands. **1818** CRUISE *Digest* (ed. 2) II. 199 Where an account is regularly settled between the parties, and signed by them, it will carry interest. **1874** T. TAYLOR *Leic. Square* iii. 64 His commission was not signed till April, owing to delays.

*fig.* **1613** R. HILL *Pathw. Piety* (1615) M4 As the preaching of the Gospell is Gods powerfull instrument to sign our saluation. **1659** MILTON *Rupt. Comm.* Wks. 1851 V. 401, I perswade me, that God was pleas'd with this Restitution, signing it as he did, with such a signal Victory. **1878** RUSKIN *Notes* 50 Turner always signs a locality with some given incident.

**b.** To fix *down*, make *over*, give *away*, by signing.

**1589** GREENE *Menaphon* (Arb.) 75 We would with our blood signe downe such spels on the Plaines [etc.]. **1712** HEARNE *Collect.* 21 June, This Tenement he signed over to his Sons. **1846** DICKENS *Battle of Life* I, Signing away vague and enormous sums of money. **1858** TROLLOPE *Dr. Thorne* I. xiv. 284 A man signs away a moiety of his substance.

**c.** With *in.* To secure the admittance of (a person) to a hotel, club, etc., by signing a register; to record the entrance of (a person) into a building, etc.

**1930** A. P. HERBERT *Water Gipsies* xxv. 368 Isn't he sleeping in the hotel himself?.. Didn't want to sign you in as his wife, I shouldn't wonder. **1957** C. MACINNES *City of Spades* I. xi. 79, I shall sign you in till Johnny come, and check with him later. **1971** R. HILL *Advancement of Learning* xvi. 222 'Have you been signed in?'.. Of course, it was a club. 'Then you can't buy a drink, can you?' **1977** J. P. ANDERSON in Douglas & Johnson *Existential Sociol.* vi. 191 His face fell a foot when the social worker told him that Viejas Rehabilitation Center was the only place he could get in, that he would have to sign himself in for from three to six months. **1978** M. Z. LEWIN *Silent Salesman* xviii. 107, I know of at least one person who was in Research [Laboratory] Three on the twenty-seventh who isn't signed in or out.

**d.** With *out.* To secure the release of (a person or thing) by signing; to record the removal of (a thing) or the departure of (a person) from a building, etc.

**1963** V. NABOKOV *Gift* iii. 187 He signed out the complete works of Chernyshevski from the state library. **1968** *Globe & Mail* (Toronto) 13 Feb. 11/6 The nurse replied that he had been signed out by the doctor. **1972** D. E. WESTLAKE *Cops & Robbers* (1973) x. 137 Why don't you shlep on back to the [police] station and sign us both out? **1978** [see sense 4 c above].

**5. a.** *intr.* To affix one's signature; also const. *to.* Also, to make a written contract *with*, and const. *for*, as authorization or acknowledgement of receipt. ***to sign on the dotted line***: see DOTTED *ppl. a.* 1 c.

**1617** MORYSON *Itin.* II. 150 Another letter.. signed below, not above (as she usually signed). **1655** tr. *Sorel's Com. Hist. Francion* XII. 27 It was therefore better.. to cause him.. to sign to whatsoever he had confessed. **1726** SHELVOCKE *Voy. round World* (1757) 32 The articles we signed to at Plymouth, were never read in our hearing. **1766** BLACKSTONE *Comm.* II. 377 Though the witnesses must all see the testator sign,.. yet they may do it at different times. **1818** LADY MORGAN *Autobiog.* (1859) 27 Having signed and sealed for the future 'Italy', he will not let me allude to it now. **1858** LD. ST. LEONARDS *Handy-Bk. Prop. Law* xviii. 137 They must both sign in your presence. **1879** O. W. HOLMES *Archbishop & Gil Blas* 24 That is why my hand looks shaky when I sign for dividends. **1938** L. BEMELMANS *Life Class* II. iv. 160, I won't pay for anything that isn't properly ordered... I pay only for things I sign for. **1956** B. HOLIDAY *Lady sings Blues* (1973) xxii. 181 The only royalties I get are on my records made after I signed with Decca. **1957** C. SMITH *Case of Torches* i. 10 'Some of the boys in the laboratory.. think they compromise their independence if they sign for something.' 'All the other boxes have been signed for.' **1966** J. B. PRIESTLEY *Salt is Leaving* v. 61 If a Miss Tiller asks for me, tell her we've gone in. I've already signed for her. **1967** E. S. GARDNER *Case of Queenly Contestant* xvi. 206 He said he would take care of all my expenses... I.. sign for meals in the hotel restaurant. **1974** *Times* 5 Feb. 11/7 John Alderton and Pauline Collins.. have signed with London Weekend Television to appear as husband and wife in a new comedy series. **1977** P. D. JAMES *Death of Expert Witness* II. 100 We let them borrow the key and they sign for it in a book in the office.

*fig.* *a* **1704** T. BROWN *Lett. to Gent. & Ladies* Wks. 1709 III. II. 91 Thou hast the daintiest smacking Lips in the Universe, that would invite a Hermit to sign and seal upon them.

**b.** (*a*) With *off. gen.*, to record that one is bringing something to an end, to stop doing something; *spec.* (i) *Broadcasting*, to cease broadcasting, to announce the end of a broadcast; (ii) to fall silent, to withdraw one's attention; (iii) to record leaving one's work, to stop work; (iv) *Bridge*, to indicate by a conventional bid that one is ending the bidding.

**1838** EMERSON *Addr. Cambr.* Wks. (Bohn) II. 200 In the country neighbourhoods, half parishes are signing off, to use the local term. **1859** BARTLETT *Dict. Amer.* (ed. 2), *To sign off*, to release a debtor by agreeing to accept whatever he offers to pay. **1878** MRS. STOWE *Poganuc P.* iii. 18 The revolution.. which broke up the State Church and gave to every man the liberty of 'signing off', as it was called, to any denomination that pleased him. **1923** *Sci. Amer.* Nov. 310/3 The local broadcasting stations have 'signed off' for the night. **1929** WODEHOUSE *Mr. Mulliner Speaking* vi. 206 If you're trying to propose to me, sign off. There is nothing doing. **1933** A. MCCABE *Contract without Tears* 165 Had North wished to sign-off at this point he would have bid five diamonds. **1937** *Speculum* Apr. 268 Tired copyists expressed their relief at signing off from their labors. **1948** *Times* 2 Sept. 2/7 Reluctance to sign off with no additional values has led to many [Contract Bridge] players getting out of their depth. **1953** W. R. BURNETT *Vanity Row* xxi. 188 Lynch was.. listening to a comedy programme... 'Be with you in a minute... They're just about to sign off.' **1954** M. PROCTER *Hell is City* I. v. 30 What time did you sign off?.. Since then you've been in some pub... You've been working on that murder, I suppose. **1957** F. HOYLE *Black Cloud* xi. 210 If the politicians started.. arguing.. the Cloud would sign off altogether. It's not going to waste its time talking to gibbering idiots. **1962** *Listener* 1 Mar. 394/3 He bid 5 N.T., which by convention asked his partner to bid Six Diamonds if he held the King of the agreed suit, hearts, and otherwise to sign off in Six Hearts. **1965** 'J. LE CARRÉ' *Looking-Glass War* xxiii. 241 'The transmission's stopped.'.. 'Did he sign off?' **1971** H. TREVELYAN *Worlds Apart* xvii. 193 By the summer of 1964 Khrushchev had decided to have nothing to do with Vietnam either and virtually signed off. **1974** R. M. PIRSIG *Zen & Art of Motorcycle Maintenance* i. 23 John signs off every time the subject of cycle repair comes up. **1976** *Times* 1 May 12/7 North can hardly be blamed for seeking a slam when his partner could have 'signed off' by responding Five Diamonds to Five Clubs. **1976** *Milton Keynes Express* 30 July 13/1 In a statement Hawkins said he did not sign off because the Works job was only temporary and he was afraid he would not be able to sign on again. **1979** *Irish Times* 28 Sept. 3/1 A decision will be made later as to whether this progressive three-year-old will sign off for the season in the St Simon Stakes or the Champion Stakes.

(*b*) With *on. spec.* (i) to record one's arrival at work, to begin work; (ii) to sign a contract to join an organization, etc.; (iii) to register at the Department of Employment (formerly Labour or Employment Exchange) in order to obtain unemployment benefit. (Cf. 6 c.)

**1862** *Railway Traveller's Handy Bk.* 8 In most Government offices the *employés* are compelled to 'sign on', as it is called, when they arrive in the morning. **1885** *St. James's Gaz.* 23 Sept. (Cassell), One set of men signed on after having only seven hours' absence from work. **1930** E. POUND *XXX Cantos* ix. 37 Until he signed on with Siena. **1936** N. MITCHISON *Fourth Pig* 29 If I didn't keep it up, there'd be a dozen knocking themselves over to get my job. And then it would be signing on again at the Labour. **1941** *Illustrated* 6 Sept. 21 She hands him the emergency slip. It says that he must sign on at 8 a.m. for the 9.30 special. **1955** *Times* 18 Aug. 5/1 Some of our men there had signed on for three or five years because they had been told they would learn a trade, but they were just batmen and doing no training at all. **1960** C. MACINNES *Mr. Love & Justice* 45 Frankie had paid his last visit to the Labour because.. he wasn't going through the comedy of 'signing on' any more. **1974** P. WRIGHT *Lang. Brit. Industry* ii. 31 Bus drivers and conductors have instead to *sign on*... They may have to make a personal appearance before the traffic inspector to show that they are not drunk or otherwise unfit. **1976** *Yorkshire Evening Press* 9 Dec. 3/4 If you gave up work voluntarily then you could be disqualified from receipt of unemployment benefit for up to six weeks, and you would have to 'sign on' and hold yourself available for employment every week. **1981** B. HINES *Looks & Smiles* 18 You take this [card] up to the Social Security office and sign on at the time it says here. *Ibid.* 44 Miserable bunch of bastards, the sergeant said... Anybody'd think they'd been forced to sign on.

**c.** With *up.* To enrol, to enlist; to give support *to.*

**1903** A. H. LEWIS *Boss* 186 You can tell by th'way they go to bat, whether th' Blackberry has signed up to them to kill our franchise. **1926** *Ladies' Home Jrnl.* Apr. 25 So she signed up for evening classes. **1942** E. PAUL *Narrow St.* xxxiv. 306 It was generally accepted in our street after that that France was eager to sign up with Russia against Hitler. **1942** E. WAUGH *Put out More Flags* i. 69 What I thought of doing was to sign up with you... It's a great help to start in a decent regiment. **1951** *Listener* 31 Jan. 172/2 Inducing other governments to sign up to professions of high moral and legal principles. **1975** M. BRADBURY *History Man* vi. 99 I've signed up for an evening class. **1977** T. HEALD *Just Desserts* i. 11 Collingdale had had to sign up as a novice friar.

**d.** With *out, in.* To record one's departure from, arrival at, a hotel, club, etc., by signing a register; also *fig.*

**1951** G. GREENE *End of Affair* II. ii. 65 It was.. as though I had signed out of the war. **1966** G. BURNETT *Dead Account* xii. 97 And my name's Brook. Where do we sign in? **1968** 'G. BAGBY' *Another Day—Another Death* vii. 142 It seemed impossible that.. all the police who'd been poring over the book could have missed someone who signed in and hadn't signed out. **1978** M. Z. LEWIN *Silent Salesman* xviii. 108 I'd like a list of all the people who signed in or out of Research Three.

**6. a.** *trans.* To write or inscribe (one's name) as a signature.

**1817** SCOTT *Lett.* I. 407, I am about to sign my name three hundred times. **1858** LD. ST. LEONARDS *Handy-Bk. Prop. Law* xviii. 137 Then you should sign your name in their presence. **1888** BESANT *Fifty Yrs. Ago* 78 Forty per cent. of the men.. could not sign their own names.

**b.** *refl.* To denominate or designate (oneself) in a signature or signatures.

**1885** *Manch. Exam.* 28 Sept. 5/2 A correspondent of last week's *Spectator*, who signs himself a 'Liberal Solicitor'.

**c.** To engage by the signing of an agreement. Also with *on, up*; also *fig.*

**1889** in *Cent. Dict.*, The Athletics have signed a new player. **1894** *Times* 25 Sept. 10/6 When crews are not signed on board, a large proportion of them are missing when the boat is ready to sail. **1894** *Westm. Gaz.* 27 Sept. 1/3 The men can only be 'signed on' in the presence of the Board of Trade officer. **1927** WODEHOUSE *Meet Mr Mulliner* i. 29 If George had been a member of the Olympic Games Selection Committee, he would have signed this woman up immediately. **1932** *Radio Times* 1 Apr. 5/2 Seversky immediately signed the violinist up for his broadcast. **1956** B. HOLIDAY *Lady sings Blues* (1973) iii. 35 Joe Glaser, the big agent and manager.. signed me up on the spot. **1963** WODEHOUSE *Stiff Upper Lip, Jeeves* iii. 26 While I personally.. would run a mile in tight shoes to avoid marrying Stiffy, I knew him to be strongly in favour of signing her up. **1980** G. M. FRASER *Mr American* xxiii. 442 Your friend Pip is to be one of the top turns in the cabaret—I suppose they signed her up as soon as they saw the early editions.

**II. 7. a.** *trans.* To indicate, signify, betoken.

*a* **1375** *Joseph of Aramathie* 185 þat signede Ihesu crist.. was nout out-wiþ so cler bote wiþ-inne he was clene. *a* **1585** POLWART *Flyting w. Montgomerie* 633 His asse eares.. signe in short space, The franticke foole sall grow madde like Mahowne. **1628** GAULE *Pract. The.* 36 That he hath lost it, doth but signe he had it not. **1652** —— *Magastrom.* 184 A broad forehead signes or marks a man stupid. **1845** BAILEY *Festus* (ed. 2) 135 This branch, Which waveth high o'er all, oh, let it sign Thine own Eternal Son's humanity. **1884** R. H. NEWTON *Bk. Beginnings* 127 The Asherah, the original of the Maypole, signs the productivity of nature.

†**b.** *intr.* To prognosticate, bode. *Obs.*

**1601** WEEVER *Mirr. Mart.* C viij, To prophesie from Comets, or deuine, Tis foolerie; they neither cause nor signe. **1606** SHAKS. *Ant. & Cl.* IV. iii. 15 Musicke i' th' Ayre.. It signes well, do's it not?

†**8.** *trans.* To designate. *Obs.*$^{-1}$

**1669** STURMY *Mariner's Mag.* I. ii. 23 An Angle is most commonly signed by three Letters, the middlemost whereof sheweth the Angular Point.

**9. a.** *intr.* To make a sign or signs by some movement of the hand, etc.; *spec.* to use a sign language.

**1700** DRYDEN *Pal. & Arc.* III. 494 Then signing to their heralds with his hand, They gave his orders from their lofty stand. **1819** SCOTT *Ivanhoe* viii, Prince John with his truncheon signed to the trumpets to sound the onset. **1869** TENNYSON *Coming Arthur* 317 She.. sign'd To those two sons to pass, and let them be. **1909** WEBSTER, *Sign*, To communicate or converse in a sign language. **1977** *Rolling Stone* 16 June 46/1 Washoe used to sign to the others quite a bit, but of course the chimps she was signing to didn't respond. **1978** *Detroit Free Press* 5 Mar. 10/4 Strangely, many educators of deaf students don't sign (use sign language). **1980** *Nat. Geographic* June 849 Bin was picking up sign language... He didn't talk to Princess; he signed to her as he also did with other non-signing orangutans.

**b.** *trans.* To intimate, convey, by a sign; *spec.* to communicate or express (something) in a sign language.

**1719** DE FOE *Crusoe* I. (Globe) 208 Upon this he sign'd to me, that he should bury them with Sand. **1820** SCOTT *Monast.* xix, He.. held up his finger to him as he signed farewell. **1821** —— *Kenilw.* xii, He, too, signed a mournful greeting to Tressilian. **1896** *Harper's Mag.* Apr. 724 [He] signed me next morning that we should camp here. **1909** WEBSTER, *Sign*, To signify by, or express in a sign language. **1975** J. GOULET *Oh's Profit* i. 4 Liedlich and his wife, Nancy, had signed the month, the hand-dance that was the month April. **1975** *Church Times* 15 Aug. 2/2 The lessons will be signed by deaf readers and the Lord's Prayer by one who is also blind. **1978** *Oxford Times* 16 June 2 The British Deaf Association Choir.. 'signed' the hymns.

**III. 10.** Comb., as **sign-in**, the action of signing in (see senses 4 c and 5 d); also used *attrib.* and *absol.* of a register in which people sign in; **sign-off**, the action of signing off (see sense 5 b (*a*)); *Broadcasting*, the end of transmission, an announcement of this; also *attrib.*; **sign-on**, the action of signing on (see senses 5 b (*b*) and 6 c); *Broadcasting*, the start of transmission; **sign-out**, the action of signing out (see senses 4 d and 5 d); the signature of one who has signed out; **sign-up**, the action of signing up or the state of having signed up (see senses 5 c and 6 c); also, a person who has signed up; also *attrib.*

**1968** 'G. Bagby' *Another Day—Another Death* vii. 142 He showed me the porter's sign-in. The man had come in quite early. **1972** 'J. Lange' *Binary* 8 A guard with a sign-in book stood in front of the elevator. Graves..took the pen and wrote his name, his authorization, and the time. **1978** S. Brill *Teamsters* iii. 115 Their names were the first entered every morning in the sign-in register at the Fund's reception desk. **1942** E. Culbertson *Official Bk. Contract Bridge* xv. 187 Finally, there is the sign-off bid... The sign-off may be made even if the responder hold one Ace. **1949** *Cavalier Daily* (Univ. Virginia) 23 Sept. 1/3 A non-affiliated station ..will be on the air only during the daylight hours. Sign-on and sign-off times will vary from month to month. **1958** *Listener* 30 Oct. 709/2 The sign-off for his partner would clearly be Five Hearts. **1960** *News Chron.* 27 June 3/1 One [question]..was used by the producer as a rather abrupt sign-off. **1961** [see *sign-on* below]. **1962** H. T. Moore *Coll. Lett. D. H. Lawrence* I. p. xxi, Lawrence's sign-off line was often a foreign phrase. **1971** H. Trevelyan *Worlds Apart* xvii. 194 So now they could no longer stay silent and issued the expected 'sign-off' statement on Vietnam, evidence that they were powerless to take any diplomatic initiative. **1976** *Time* 20 Dec. 47/2 Remember his sign-off as he was being expelled from a Democratic Convention: 'This is John Chancellor, somewhere in custody.' **1948** *Seafarers' Log* 9 Jan. 5/2 One thing about the pay-offs and sign-ons we had: All the beefs were settled aboard ship to everybody's satisfaction. **1949** [see *sign-off* above]. **1961** *Time* 19 May 53/1 The toughest TV critic..dared the station and network operators and owners to sit down in front of their sets from sign-on to sign-off. **1968** 'G. Bagby' *Another Day — Another Death* vii. 142, I looked at the later sign-outs. Those covered the mob of cleaning women. **1940** *Sun* (Baltimore) 17 Sept. 9/7 Talbot, with a 'sign up' of 391,.. led all the counties. **1941** *Ibid.* 14 Feb. 7/1 'There is a direct need for immediate sign-up' of nurses for army duty. **1945** *National Legionnaire* (U.S.) Sept. 1 (*heading*) Legion speeds sign-up of 12,000,000 War II victors. **1951** *Daily Progress* (Charlottesville, Va.) 5 Mar. 3/2 Sign-ups through the end of last month totaled 1,033. **1972** *Jrnl. Social Psychol.* LXXXVII. 118 A sign-up sheet was then distributed and students were asked to indicate whether..they would be willing to volunteer for the experiment. **1974** *News & Reporter* (Chester, S. Carolina) 22 Apr. 10-A/1 This will be a singles tournament and sign up will start Saturday morning at 10 a.m. **1980** *Dirt Bike* Oct. 5/1 The little gray-haired lady at the sign-up booth is your wife, or your girlfriend.

†**sign**, *v.*$^{2}$ *Obs.* Forms: 4–6 signe, 5 segne, 5–6 sygne; 4 syngne, 5–6 syne. [Aphetic f. assign *v.*] *trans.* To assign, appoint.

**1338** R. Brunne *Chron.* (1810) 163 Tent & pauillon tille Isaac did he signe. **1389** in *Eng. Gilds* (1870) 35 þat alle the bretheren..shullen ben redy at that day..in wat stede that he syngnyt hem. *c* **1430** Lydg. *Paternoster* 284 in *Min. Poems* (E.E.T.S.), Cause his lord was ageyn hym ffell He was fetryd and signed to prysoun. **1467–8** *Rolls of Parlt.* V. 621/1 Many arraunt Theves..become Provers, and desire a Coroner to be signed unto theym to make their appelles of dyvers Felonyes. *c* **1510** Barclay *Mirr. Gd. Manners* (1570) E iij, Like as a wise warriour signeth a souldiour For enemies aproching to watche and to espie. *a* **1533** Ld. Berners *Huon* cxxix. 473 So euery man londyd excepte suche as were sygned to kepe the shyppes. **1582** Stanyhurst *Æneis* I. (Arb.) 19 The Emperor heaunlye..too thee the auctoritye signed Too swage seas surging.

**sign**, obs. form of sine *sb.* and sing *v.*

**signable** ('saɪnəb(ə)l), *a.* [f. sign *v.*$^{1}$ + -able.]
**1.** That may be signed (Ogilvie *Suppl.* 1855).
**2.** Capable of signing.

**1802** Canning *Let.* in *Diaries & Corr. Ld. Malmesbury* IV. 96, I commit the paper to your discretion. If signable people should fall in your way, or if unsignable,..use it.

†**signacle.** *Obs.* Also 4–5 sygn-, 5 synacle; *Sc.* 6 signakle, 8 sinacle. [a. OF. *signacle*, *sinacle*, etc., ad. late L. *signāculum*, dim. from *signum* sign *sb.*]

**1.** A sign, seal, mark, figure.

**1382** Wyclif *1 Cor.* ix. 2 ȝe ben the sygnacle, or litil signe, of myn apostilhed in the Lord. ? *c* **1400** Lydg. *Æsop's Fab.* iii. 171 The name of god..Is the signacle of the celestial seale. *c* **1450** tr. *De Imitatione* III. lix. 140 This grace is..a propre signacle of þe chosen children of god. **1483** Caxton *Gold. Leg.* 431 b/1 He had the Sygnacle or fygure of the holy crosse in soo right grete reuerence that he eschewed to trede on hit. **1500–20** Dunbar *Poems* lxxxv. 18 All thing maling we dovne thring, Be sicht of his signakle. *a* **1555** Bradford *Medit.* (1607) 96 The sacrament of circumcision, which as the Apostle calleth the seale or signacle of righteousnes. **1656** in Blount *Glossogr.*

**2.** A sign or gesture.

*c* **1450** Lovelich *Grail* xxxviii. 62 Whanne Nasciens knew that he hol was Be the signacle of [= made by] þe Man In that plas. **1490** Caxton *Eneydos* v. 21 The sayd wymmen were alle dyssheuelled,..makynge merueylous synacles, as theyr custume was in that tyme.

**3.** *Sc.* A slight token or trace.

**1768** Ross *Helenore* I. 8 Never a sinacle of life was there. **1790** Shirrefs *Poems* Gl. 32 *Sinacle*, a grain, a small quantity.

**signage** ('saɪnɪdʒ). Chiefly *N. Amer.* [f. sign *sb.* + -age.] Signs collectively, esp. public signs on facia boards, signposts, etc.; the design and arrangement of these.

**1976** *Federal Suppl.* (U.S.) CDXIV. 1168/1 All signage, stationery, forms, calling cards and other symbols are identical with no distinction between the main bank and the drive-in facility. **1976** *National Observer* (U.S.) 21 Aug. 8/2 They are being a lot tougher on signage and landscaping and buildings. **1979** *Amer. Banker* 28 Feb. 4 The overall appearance of your bank, the building, the grounds, the signage. **1981** *Beautiful Brit. Columbia* Fall 16/2 Many British Columbians..have traced Lewis and Clark's travels through the Pacific northwest, following rustic highway signage and visiting the many historic stopping places. **1983** *N.Y. Times* 23 Oct. VIII. 7/1 The cacophony of visual accents in the Times Square area—the graphics and the signage. **1986** *Your Business* Mar. 32/1 Every aspect of a company's personality is reviewed..to the design of invoices and signage.

**signal** ('sɪgnəl), *sb.* [a. F. *signal* (OF. also *seignal*, *seignau*, etc.), = Pg. *sinal*, Sp. *señal*, It. *segnale*, med.L. *signāl(e*, a Romanic formation on L. *signum* sign: see -al$^{1}$ 4. Used by Chaucer and Gower, but otherwise evidenced only from the end of the 16th century.]

†**1. a.** A visible sign; a badge or symbol. *Obs.*

*c* **1384** Chaucer *Ho. Fame* I. 459 Tho saugh I.. alle the mervelouse signals Of the goddys celestials. **1390** Gower *Conf.* III. 57 In his hond He bar the signal of his lond With fisshes thre. **1601** Sir W. Cornwallis *Disc. Seneca* (1631) 7 His other signals of authority, the deckings of a corrupt minde.

**b.** A mark of distinction or honour. *Obs.*

**1655** M. Carter *Honor Rediv.* (1660) 3 Vertue being still admired, and honored, and some signall put upon it. **1685** Bunyan *Seventh-day Sabbath* v, Now what another signal was here [i.e. at the day of Pentecost] put upon the first day of the week.

**2.** A sign, token, or indication (*of* something). In later use not clearly separable from sense 4.

**1591** Shaks. *1 Hen. VI*, II. iv. 121 In signall of my loue to thee. **1594** —— *Rich. III*, v. iii. 21 (Qtos.), The wearie sonne ..Giues signall of a goodlie day to-morrow. **1646** Sir T. Browne *Pseud. Ep.* I. iv, The bread and wine which were but the signalls or visible signes..were made the things signified. **1715** De Foe *Fam. Instruct.* I. i. (1841) I. 12 'Tis a signal that he has no thought of mercy in store for them. **1725** —— *Voy. round World* (1840) 320 All this while we saw no people, nor any signals of any. **1782** V. Knox *Ess.* xcv. (1819) II. 190 To whom we wish to display some signal of our love. **1820** Shelley *Ode to Naples* 113 The signal and the seal..Art thou of all these hopes. **1848** Thackeray *Van. Fair* xviii, The arrival of the piano, which, as she conjectured, must have come from George, and was a signal of amity on his part.

**3.** A sign agreed upon or understood as the occasion of concerted action, *esp.* one ordering the movement of troops or ships; also *fig.*, an exciting cause.

**1593** Shaks. *Rich. II*, I. iii. 116 Attending but the signall to begin. **1611** Coryat *Crudities* 16 Presently they gaue the Signall to Hernand Teillo, that lay vnder the towne with his ambuscado. **1667** Milton *P.L.* v. 702 All obey'd The wonted signal. **1724** De Foe *Mem. Cavalier* (1840) 176 The signal of battle being given with two cannon shot we marched in order of battalia. **1770** Langhorne *Plutarch* (1851) I. 60/2 The pæan..was the signal to advance. **1816** J. Wilson *City of Plague* III. iii, Go on deck, and tell me if thou seest The signal flying for close line of battle. **1860** Tyndall *Glac.* I. xix. 134 This was the signal for a grasp all round. **1874** Green *Short Hist.* vi. §5. 318 The meeting of the Emperor [Charles] with Henry at Southampton gave the signal for a renewal of the war.

**4. a.** A sign or notice, perceptible by sight or hearing, given especially for the purpose of conveying warning, direction, or information.

**1598** Drayton *Heroical Ep.* Poems (1619) 212, I..being ship'd, gave signall with my Hand Vp to the Cliffe where I did see thee stand. **1667** Milton *P.L.* XI. 72 The Son gave signal high To the bright Minister that watch'd, hee blew His Trumpet. **1698** T. Froger *Voy.* 8 We likewise made signals to the other ships. **1719** De Foe *Crusoe* I. 12 The Master..order'd to fire a Gun as a Signal of Distress. **1732** Lediard *Sethos* II. IX. 281 The garrison beat..a signal of surrender. **1797** Mrs. Radcliffe *Italian* xii, And, as she drew nearer to Olivia, gave a signal and passed on to her cell. **1814** Scott *Ld. of Isles* III. xxiii, It was a keen and warning look, And well the Chief the signal took. **1896** *Law Times Rep.* LXXIII. 615/1 A bell rang which was a signal..that a train was coming.

**b.** An object serving to convey an intimation.

**1687** A. Lovell tr. *Thevenot's Trav.* I. 94 There is a small Church in the Sea,..which serves for a Light-house and Signal. **1774** Mackenzie *Mar. Surv.* II. 84 When the Surveyor is at a proper Station, the Assistant must set up the black Signal. **1838** Railway signal [see railway 3]. **1859** Geo. Eliot *A. Bede* xlvii, He has something in his hand —he is holding it up as if it were a signal. **1878** Gurney *Crystallogr.* 105 Let these signals..be so placed that the same horizontal plane will pass through each of them.

**c.** A modulation of an electric current, electromagnetic wave, or the like by means of which information is conveyed from one place to another; the current or wave itself; also, a current or wave whose presence is regarded as conveying information about the source from which it comes. Also = *signal strength*, sense 5 e below.

**1855** D. Lardner *Electric Telegraph* v. §121 The signals transmitted appear upon the telegraphic instrument informing the agent whence the dispatch will come. **1873** *Trans. Inst. Engineers & Shipbuilders in Scotland* XVI. 119 If several thousand Leyden Jars were distributed along an aerial line of telegraph..the signals through the line would exhibit exactly the same inductive retardation as those sent through the actual submarine line. **1902** *Proc. R. Soc.* LXX. 256 For transmitting signals, an aerial wire or wires were attached to one of two spark balls fitted to an induction coil, the other ball being earthed. **1923** *Radio Times* 28 Sept. 2/2 After sunset signals may increase very considerably. **1958** *Times* 18 Jan. 7/3 The problem of how to reach Iraq and the Persian Gulf area with an adequate signal has yet to be solved. **1961** *New Scientist* 26 Jan. 199/3 The picture signal which indicates by amplitude modulation of a carrier wave how bright each point on a line should be, is interrupted at the ends of each line by synchronizing pulses. **1961** G. Millerson *Technique Telev. Production* ii. 19 The current, known as the video or picture signal, is subsequently amplified and passed to the video switching console. **1965** *New Statesman* 30 Apr. 674/2 The signals received from it [*sc.* Early Bird satellite] on the ground are extremely weak —about one-millionth of a normal TV signal in a fringe area. **1970** J. Earl *Tuners & Amplifiers* iv. 78 Signal delivered by the control section..is just right for feeding into the power amplifier section. **1978** Pasachoff & Kutner *University Astron.* xi. 302 Various objects in space emit electromagnetic signals in the radio part of the spectrum.

**5.** *attrib.* and *Comb.* **a.** Attrib. with sbs. denoting something employed as, or used in giving, a signal or signals, as ***signal apparatus***, ***arm*** (arm *sb.*$^{1}$ 6 c), ***beacon***, ***bell***, ***code***, ***fire***, ***flag***, ***strip***, etc.; also, denoting something used in receiving a signal or signals, as ***signal pad*** (pad *sb.*$^{3}$ 4). Also objective, as ***signal-processing***.

**1841** *Penny Cycl.* XIX. 258/1 It is usual to affix a *signal apparatus to them. **1901** *Railway Mag.* May 463/2 A neighbouring *signal-arm falls. **1949** M. Taylor *Railway Signalling* i. 6 Near the top of the post is the signal arm which is always on the left of the post when the viewer is facing the signal. **1962** A. Lurie *Love & Friendship* xv. 293 Coarse grass grew along the track, and the signal arm was rusted at all clear. **1856** Kane *Arct. Expl.* I. xxvi. 345 A large *signal-beacon or cairn. **1897** D. Butler *Ch. & Par. Abernethy* 180 The mere use of the *signal-bell of the hand-bell-ringer. **1832** Marryat *N. Forster* xli, Captain Drawlock..had the *signal-book in his hand. **1865** Alex. Smith *Summer in Skye* I. 266 The sailor in possession of the signal-book reads the signal. **1877** J. Habberton *Jericho Road* 94 Between the societies of neighboring counties there often existed *signal-codes, and unwritten extradition and reciprocity treaties. **1952** M. K. Wilson tr. *Lorenz's King Solomon's Ring* viii. 82 The whole complicated 'signal code' of the jackdaw. **1849** Macaulay *Hist. Eng.* iii. I. 290 The *signal fires were blazing fifty miles off. **1802** James *Milit. Dict.* s.v., Although *signal flags, in modern engagements, have been generally laid aside [etc.]. **1814** Scott *Ld. of Isles* IV. xxx, Might not my father's beadsman hoar..Kindle a *signal-flame? **1758** in J. S. McLennan *Louisbourg* (1918) 414 Light gales and fair weather, later thick fog. Fired *signal gun. **1797** *Encycl. Brit.* (ed. 3) XVIII. 336/2 A signal-gun to be fired. **1842** Lever *J. Hinton* vi, When the signal-gun announced the commencement of the action. **1930** R. Campbell *Adamastor* 74 The rocks, spray-clouded, are your signal guns. **1837** *Civil Eng. & Arch. Jrnl.* I. 13/2 The..height of the lower or *signal lamp. **1902** *Chambers's Jrnl.* July 479/2 The apparatus is simply a new glass for the signal-lamp, facing along the same way and throwing a powerful beam of light over the whole length of the arm. **1932** G. Greene *Stamboul Train* I. i. 5 A signal lamp turned from red to green. **1804** Nelson 23 Feb. in Nicolas *Disp.* (1846) VII. p. ccxix, It is recommended..to be careful that the *Signal-lights for knowing each other are clear. **1844** *Civil Eng. & Arch. Jrnl.* VII. 237 Igniting the composition forming the signal light. **1881** *Signal-light [see *running light* s.v. running *vbl. sb.* 17 a]. **1936** *Discovery* Sept. 289/2 Motor-car headlights, signal lights and searchlights. **1976** *Billings* (Montana) *Gaz.* 5 July 8-A/6 The Utah Highway Patrol requested drivers to stay off the roads as signal lights were off through much of the state. **1873** M. Arnold *Lit. & Dogma* (1876) 270 These three texts..may well stand as the great *signal-marks pointing to it. *a* **1873** Lytton *Pausanias* 36 From several of the vessels the trumpets woke a sonorous *signal-note. **1958** P. Kemp *No Colours or Crest* iv. 54 By the operator's stool..were some *signal pads. **1975** T. Allbeury *Palomino Blonde* x. 63 The Morse came and he was getting it down on his signal pad. **1964** R. F. Ficchi *Electr. Interference* vi. 99 Another way to reduce susceptibility to unwanted signals in cables is to use various *signal-processing methods to improve the signal-to-noise ratio. **1766** R. Jones *Fireworks* IV. 135 *Signal-rockets..are headed with stars, serpents, &c. **1887** *Spectator* 30 July 1019/2 A signal-rocket sent up from the flag-ship. **1802** James *Milit. Dict.* s.v., A continual discharge of these *signal shells. **1812** S. Rogers *Columbus* Poems (1839) 43 When hark, a *signal shot! **1850** R. G. Cumming *Hunter's Life S. Africa* (1902) 101/1 Their comrades..requested me to fire signal-shots at intervals. **1917** 'Contact' *Airman's Outings* 261 The whole party circles round the aerodrome until the *signal strips for 'Carry on' are laid out on the ground. **1954** W. Faulkner *Fable* 87 He reached the aerodrome and saw the ground signal-strip laid out on it;..not until he saw the other aeroplanes on the ground or landing or coming into land did he recognise it to be the peremptory emergency signal to all aircraft to come down. **1828** *Lights & Shades* II. 259 The distant *signal-whistle of a gang of robbers. **1895** *Mod. Steam Engine* 51 The signal whistle is shown at *g*. **1814** Scott *Ld. of Isles* VI. xxx, When mute Amadine they heard Give to their zeal his *signal-word. **1831** —— *Ct. Rob.* xxii, Thou wilt not forget that the signal word of the insurrection is Ursel.

**b.** With sbs. denoting a place or thing from which signals are given or worked, as ***signal box***, ***bridge***, ***cabin***, ***gantry***, ***house***, etc.

**1829** Marryat *F. Mildmay* vi, I was..intent on looking for the telegraphic *signal-box. **1884** *Encycl. Brit.* XX. 238/2 Distant signals..worked by wire communication from the signal box, were, it is believed, first introduced.. in 1846. **1899** F. T. Bullen *Way Navy* 75 As I write comes a messenger from the *signal-bridge..with a copy of signal just made from the flagship. **1889** Findlay *Eng. Railway* 69 The *signal cabin contains a most complicated piece of mechanism, called the 'locking frame'. **1927** A. Mee *Children's Treasure House* III. 1819/1 A *signal gantry (one of those large bridges covered with signals which stand near important junctions or great termini). **1939** [see gantry 2 b]. **1976** *Physics Bull.* Dec. 556/1 A total of 15 signal gantries span the roadway for a distance of about 8 km. **1796** *Gentl. Mag.* LXVI. I. 369 In the first distance is seen the *signal-house, with Bogner..beyond. **1892** E. Reeves *Homewd. Bound.* 160 Most of the signal-house keepers and dredge men along the canal seem French. **1811** Sir W. Scott *Dodson's Rep.* I. 19 Notice was given from the Spanish *signal-post that an enemy was hovering on the coast. **1848** K. H. Digby *Compitum* I. 15 The notices, the signal-posts as it were, in life's forest. **1802** James *Milit. Dict.* s.v., It is usual to fix a red flag..to point out the spot where the general or officer commanding takes his station in front of a line. This is called the *signal staff. **1898** Sir G.

PARKER *Battle of Strong* xxxv, Not far from her was the signal-staff which telegraphed to another signal-staff inland. Upon the staff now was hoisted a red flag. **1816** KIRBY & SP. *Entomol.* xvii. (1818) II. 43 The soldiers at these *signal-stations sat quite still during the intervals of silence. **1867** AUGUSTA WILSON *Vashti* xxv, Under his steady gaze the blood rose slowly to its old signal-station on her cheeks. **1766** SMOLLETT *Trav.* I. x. 159 It seems to have been intended, at first, as a watch, or *signal-tower.

**c.** With sbs. denoting persons connected with signalling, as ***signal boy***, ***corps***, ***lieutenant***, etc. Also objective, as ***signal fitter***.

**1888** *Daily News* 18 Dec. 6/4 The dead body of..the *signal boy at Spa-road Station..was found..on the line. *a* **1885** G. B. MCCLELLAN *Own Story* (1887) 135 The weak point in the *signal corps..was that its officers were not trained soldiers. **1895** *Outing* XXVI. 396/1 The Signal Corps is a body of highly trained soldiers whose duty it is to provide the methods of communication between the different forces of an army. **1898** *Westm. Gaz.* 15 July 5/3 Two *signal fitters were standing in the four-foot way. **1858** SIMMONDS *Dict. Trade*, **Signal lieutenant*, an officer in the Royal Navy having the charge of signals on board a flag-ship. **1867** SMYTH *Sailor's Word-bk.* 626 *Signal-officer*, in a repeating frigate, a *signal-midshipman; in a flag-ship, a flag-lieutenant. **1829** MARRYAT *F. Mildmay* iii, The *signal officers..had to make out the number of the flag. **1898** *Westm. Gaz.* 23 Apr. 8/2 Accompanied by a signal officer and a small prize crew. **1895** *Outing* XXVI. 399 A new equipment for the *Signal Service, the captive balloon. **1871** *Fair France* ii. 66 Female officials, down to *signalwomen and pointswomen, who at country stations stood, flag in hand, solemnly attentive to duty.

**d.** With other parts of speech, as ***signal-like*** adj.

**1935** *Amer. Speech* X. 250/1 The result obtained..are functionally independent groups of sounds, each of the groups reflecting one of the basic, signal-like values in the given language. **1961** *Brno Studies in English* III. 51 Its survival may be satisfactorily explained by the signal-like character of *oi* in foreign and emotionally coloured words.

**e.** Special combs., as **signal anxiety** *Psychol.*, anxiety which, according to the theory put forward by Freud in 1926, acts as a signal of danger to the ego; **signal-caller** *N. Amer. Football*, a player who signals to other members of his team what the next move and formation should be; **signal detection** *Psychol.*, the detection of signals, esp. with regard to the observer's vigilance and sensitivity; also *attrib.*; **signal generator** *Electronics*, an instrument that can generate modulated or unmodulated electrical waveforms of known amplitude and frequency, used in adjusting and testing electronic apparatus; **signal intelligence**: see *signals intelligence* below; **signal-noise ratio** = *signal-to-noise ratio* below; **signal plate** *Television*, in some types of camera tube, a plate electrode whose capacitance relative to the adjacent photo-electric surface is used to provide the picture signal; **signal reaction** (see quot. 1976); **signal red**, a vermilion colour; **signal(s) intelligence**, intelligence derived from the monitoring, interception, and interpretation of radio signals and similar transmissions (cf. SIGINT, SIGINT); **signal strength**, the amplitude or power of a signal, esp. of a broadcast signal as it reaches a given location or is received by a given aerial; **signal-to-noise ratio** *Radio* and *Electronics*, the ratio of the strength of a desired signal to that of unwanted noise interference, usu. expressed in decibels; also *transf.* to non-electrical systems.

[**1928** J. RICKMAN in *Internat. Jrnl. Psychoanal.* (Suppl. 2) 63 The situation which conditions the anticipation is the danger situation which gives, so to speak, the 'Anxiety Signal' of impending helplessness.] **1948** E. JONES *Papers on Psycho-Anal.* (ed. 5) xiv. 315 Primary anxiety, no less than the later 'signal' anxiety, belongs essentially to these defensive measures. **1968** C. RYCROFT *Crit. Dict. Psychoanal.* 154 Signal anxiety..in Freud's formulation is the response of the ego to internal danger and the stimulus to the formation and use of defence-mechanisms. **1975** in S. Arieti *Amer. Handbk. Psychiatry* (ed. 2) IV. xxi. 485/1 The finely modulated, discrete and homeostatically balanced responses of the adult, such as 'signal anxiety'. **1971** L. KOPPETT *Guide to Spectator Sports* ii. 48 The quarterback now handles the ball on every play... He must be the signal-caller, too, because the attack is now concentrated in his hands. **1979** *Arizona Daily Star* 5 Aug. c 9/1 John Banaszak jarred the ball loose from Bills signal caller David Mays. **1954** TANNER & SWETS in *Psychol. Rev.* LXI. 409/2 The mathematical model of signal detection is applicable to problems of visual detection. **1971** D. E. BROADBENT *Decision & Stress* iii. 75 We cannot..take the success of signal detection theory in psychophysics as if it guaranteed its adequacy in the case of vigilance. **1979** in Hamilton & Warburton *Hum. Stress & Cognition* v. 148 Signal detection methodology is now the more widely used approach in the study of vigilance. **1929** K. HENNEY *Princ. Radio* xv. 376 The circuit diagram is that of the General Radio Signal Generator, a device which consists of a radio-frequency oscillator, a means of measuring and controlling its output, and a means of using any desired part of this output for purposes of measuring receivers. **1950** J. H. REYNER *Encycl. Radio & Television* 564/1 For the testing and alignment of receivers, signal generators giving modulated waves are available. **1972** *Jrnl. Social Psychol.* LXXXVII. 119 These tapes were made by recording square wave pulses produced by a Hewlet-Packard low-frequency signal generator. **1958** *Guardian* 22 May 3/1 Thompson and Miller trained for 'a specialised and secret duty in Signal Intelligence', Mr Jones continued. **1969** Signal intelligence [see SIGINT, SIGINT]. **1972** *New Scientist* 2 Mar. 466/1 The generic term for the business today is Signal Intelligence (Sigint). **1934** A. L. ALBERT *Elec. Communication* xv. 412 Just as in transmission over wires, it is necessary that the signal-noise ratio is high, and that fading is not excessive. **1962** *Daily Tel.* 6 July 21/7 However efficient the detectors and however good the signal-noise ratio, there will always be the possibility of doubt. **1934** V. K. ZWORYKIN in *Jrnl. Franklin Inst.* CCXVII. 10 Consider the circuit of a single photo-electric element in the mosaic... Here *P* represents such an element, and *C* its capacity to a plate common to all the elements, which hereafter will be called the 'signal plate'. **1975** K. WICKS *Television* 19 After striking the signal plate, the electron beam returns along the tube, attracted by the positive charge on a series of five electrodes called dynodes. **1946** F. P. CHISHOLM in W. S. Knickerbocker *Twentieth Century English* 183 Signal-reactions..and other neuro-semantic disorders are often combined with brilliant verbal facility. **1976** N. POSTMAN *Crazy Talk* 195 A signal reaction is what happens when words have lost their referential or symbolic aspect and instead assume the character of religious icons. **1936** *Times Educ. Suppl.* 21 Nov. p. iv/1 Gules..is not included in the range, but signal-red, similar but not quite so yellow, takes its place. **1977** *Western Morning News* 30 Aug. 2/7 Jaguar XJS; brand new;..signal red; beige trim. **1976**, etc. Signals intelligence [see SIGINT, SIGINT]. **1912** *Marconigraph* II. 269/2 Observations..showed that during totality the signal strength was increased. **1935** *Discovery* Sept. 278/1 The successive signal strengths are proportioned to the corresponding light and shade areas of the image focused by the lens upon the mosaic. **1968** M. WOODHOUSE *Rock Baby* xiii. 130 He..showed me..the tiny signal-strength meter on the side. **1978** *Broadcast* 20 Nov. 16/1 The report of the meeting..referred only to discussion of [Radio] Hallam's signal strength. **1935** *Proc. IRE* XXIII. 713 A single tone was used to modulate the transmitter when measuring signal-to-noise ratios. **1966** D. G. BRANDON *Mod. Techniques Metallogr.* 239 The overall quantum efficiency for high-energy electrons can be of the order of 0·2 and is only limited by the necessity to achieve a reasonable signal-to-noise ratio in the emulsion. **1974** HARVEY & BOHLMAN *Stereo F.M. Radio Handbk.* ii. 32 A reduction in carrier deviation means that a smaller signal is available at the output of the receiver demodulator and consequently the signal-to-noise ratio is lowered.

**signal** ('sɪgnəl), *a.* [irreg. ad. F. *signalé*, pa. pple. of *signaler* to distinguish. In senses 2 and 3 the meaning has been influenced by the sb.]

**1.** Striking, remarkable, notable, conspicuous: **a.** Of persons.

**1641** J. JACKSON *True Evang. T.* I. 23 Two great and signall Historians give in evidence against him [etc.]. **1670** CLARENDON *Hist. Reb.* xv. §57 He then betook himself wholly to the sea, and quickly made himself signal there. **1702** *Eng. Theophrastus* 16 It is very easie to decide which of these impertinents is the most signal. *c* **1780** H. WALPOLE *Last Jrnls.* (1910) II. 36 The signal criminal [Dr. Dodd] suffered decently. **1805** FOSTER *Ess.* II. v. I. 178 Signal villains of every class.

**b.** Of things or events.

**1647** CLARENDON *Hist. Reb.* I. §100 He died in a season most opportune,..and which in truth crowned his other signal prosperity in this world. **1662** STILLINGFL. *Orig. Sacræ* II. iv. §8 The extraordinary Prophets whom God did call out on some more signal occasions. **1705** ADDISON *Italy* (1733) 46 Those that are in any signal Danger. **1760–2** GOLDSM. *Cit. W.* lxxx, All now thought that he would take the most signal revenge. **1772** PRIESTLEY *Inst. Relig.* (1782) II. 195 The Israelites gained a most signal victory. **1839** JAMES *Louis XIV*, IV. 393 But the same French general suffered a signal reverse..in the following year. **1849** MACAULAY *Hist. Eng.* vi. II. 30 The ministers were told that the nation expected, and should have, signal redress. **1878** LECKY *Eng. in 18th C.* II. 1 It was a signal proof of the wisdom of the English legislators.

†**2.** Distinctive, significative. *Obs.*

**1652** NEEDHAM tr. *Selden's Mare Cl.* 84 Badges or signal Ornaments of the Proconsul of Asia. *a* **1663** SANDERSON *Cases Consc.* (1678) 190 The signal note of the Godly party.

**3.** Constituting or serving as a sign.

**1655** FULLER *Ch. Hist.* I. 2 The signall Oak which the Druides made choice of, was such a one, on which Misletoe did grow; by which privie token, they conceived, God marked it out, as of soveraigne vertue, for his service. **1873** M. ARNOLD *Lit. & Dogma* 244 Long before his signal Crucifixion Jesus had died, by taking up daily that cross which his disciples..were to take up also.

**signal** ('sɪgnəl), *v.* [f. the sb.]

**1.** *trans.* To make signals to (a person, ship, etc.); to summon, direct, or invite by signal.

**1805** in Nicolas *Disp. Nelson* (1846) VI. 463 The Captain of the Ship was signalled on board the Victory. **1892** STEVENSON *Across Plains* I It was..five o'clock when we were all signalled to be present at the Ferry Depôt. **1897** WATTS-DUNTON *Aylwin* XII. iii, The girl came out, and signalling me to enter, went leisurely down-stairs.

**2. a.** To communicate or make known by signalling; to notify or announce by signal(s).

**1871** R. ELLIS *Catullus* lxiv. 233 Soon as on home's fair hills thine eyes shall signal a welcome. **1885** *Manch. Exam.* 17 June 5/2 Even when storms are signalled off the Irish coast, they often take a totally new..course. **1889** G. FINDLAY *Eng. Railway* 65 In 1830 the only arrangement made for signalling the trains was a flag by day or a lamp by night.

**b.** To mark out clearly; to signalize. Also, to indicate, esp. unofficially or indirectly. Cf. SIGNALIZE *v.* 5.

**1869** SWINBURNE *Ess. & Stud.* (1875) 308 The noble dirge which signals with its majesty of music the consummation of Calantha's agony. **1873** M. ARNOLD *Lit. & Dogma* (1876) 280 Signalling and extolling that character in Christianity into which fineness of perception enters most. **1962** *Amer. Speech* XXXVII. 214 Since one member of the pair [of pronominal forms] is functionally redundant, the usage in different dialects may be expected to vary far more than for forms which signal significant differences. **1963** *Ibid.* XXXVIII. 52 The slots, or, more accurately, the units that can fill the slots, signal their meanings by their positions relative to each other... Some units signal their meaning without regard to position. **1978** *Times* 24 Apr. 2/1 The government seemed yesterday to be signalling its willingness to concede a reduction in the highest rates of income tax. **1979** *Tucson* (Arizona) *Citizen* 20 Sept. 1A/5 U.S. economic indicators signal the dollar should be lower than current rates. **1981** *Times* 25 Sept. 19/1 Sterling is now lower than when the Bank of England signalled higher interest rates a week last Monday.

**3.** To work (a railway) in respect of signals; to furnish with signalling apparatus.

**1888** *Pall Mall G.* 21 Jan. 2/1 This line was a part of the London and Greenwich Railway, and was..maintained and signalled by us. **1904** *Westm. Gaz.* 19 June 10/2 Some portions of the principal railroads are fully signalled, but on many others hardly any signals are used.

**4.** *intr.* To give notice, warning, or information, or make any other communication, by signal.

**1864** HOSMER *Color-Guard* 76 They are signalling night and day..by flag and fire. **1877** J. D. CHAMBERS *Divine Worship* 199 The Officiator,..signalling to the Penitents, should begin the Antiphon.

**signaletic** (sɪgnə'lɛtɪk), *a. Math.* [irreg. f. SIGN *sb.* or SIGNAL *sb.* Cf. F. *signalétique* (in a different sense), f. *signaler* vb.] Relating to the algebraic signs plus and minus.

**1853** SYLVESTER in *Phil. Trans.* CXLIII. 546 A signaletic or Semaphoretic series is a sequence of disjunctive terms, considered solely with reference to the algebraical signs of plus and minus which they respectively carry. **1889** CAYLEY in *Nature* XXXIX. 218/1 They are signaletic functions, indicating in what manner..the roots of the one equation are intercalated among those of the other.

**signalist** ('sɪgnəlɪst). [f. SIGNAL *sb.* + -IST.] One who makes signals; one specially employed in signalling; a signaller.

**1836** *Fraser's Mag.* XIV. 39 For the cause of my coming, you know that, my charming little signalist. **1881** *Appleton's Ann. Cycl.* 548 He was enabled to furnish each army corps ..with a competent force of skilled signalists.

**sig'nality.** Now *rare.* [f. SIGNAL *sb.* or *a.*]

†**1.** The quality of a sign or indication. *Obs.*

**1646** SIR T. BROWNE *Pseud. Ep.* 224 Had they conceived any more then a bare signality in this Star,..they would not have computed from its Heliacall ascent which was of inferiour efficacy.

†**2.** Signification; significance. *Obs.*

**1646** SIR T. BROWNE *Pseud. Ep.* I. xi. (1650) 33 That the same should fall out at a remarkable time..may admit a Christian apprehension in the signality. **1658** —— *Garden Cyrus* Wks. (Bohn) II. 502 Though he that considereth the plain cross [etc.]..will hardly decline all thought of Christian signality in them. **1693** J. BEAUMONT *On Burnet's Th. Earth* II. 111 Blew and red, denoting the two great destructions of the World..; so that the Rainbow carries a mixt signality.

**3.** Notability, distinction.

**1650** BULWER *Anthropomet.* Ep. Ded., Had I had a Signality of Spirit to summon Democriticall Atomes to conglobate into an intellectuall Forme. **1665** GLANVILL *Scepsis Sci.* Address p. xi, Now it seems to me a Signality in Providence in erecting your most Honourable Society in such a juncture of dangerous Humours. **1899** *Contemp. Rev.* Sept. 442 The battle of Azincourt reproduced the astonishing facts of Crècy and Poictiers with, if possible, even greater signality.

**signalization** (sɪgnəlaɪ'zeɪʃən). *Psychol.* [f. SIGNALIZ(E *v.* 4 + -ATION.] A term derived from the work of I. P. Pavlov (1849–1936) for the process whereby a signal comes to elicit the same response as the original stimulus.

**1927** G. V. ANREP tr. *Pavlov's Conditioned Reflexes* ii. 22 The underlying principle of this activity is signalization. The sound of the metronome is the signal for food, and the animal reacts to the signal in the same way as if it were food. **1969** in K. H. Pribram *Memory Mechanisms* 137 The conditioned reflex..enables the animal to adjust itself to the essential factors of the external and internal world on the basis of the principle of signalization.

**signalize** ('sɪgnəlaɪz), *v.* [f. SIGNAL *a.* + -IZE.]

**1. a.** *trans.* To make signal; to distinguish; to render conspicuous, remarkable, or note-worthy.

**1654** FLECKNOE *Ten Years Trav.* 102 Let none ever hope the like advantages, that are not signaliz'd by some remarkable qualities. **1686** PLOT *Staffordsh.* 21 The death of Germanicus was signaliz'd by another [meteor]. **1704** HEARNE *Duct. Hist.* (1714) I. 244 When..his Glory [was] sufficiently signalized, then he discarded those Instruments. **1761** HUME *Hist. Eng.* II. xli. 425 She named Whitgift.., who had already signalised his pen in controversy. **1861** MAY *Constit. Hist. Eng.* (1863) I. i. 45 This debate was signalised by the opposition speech of Sir Fletcher Norton, the Speaker. **1883** *Contemp. Rev.* XLIV. 7 Leo the Tenth.. desired to signalize his reign by building the grandest church in the world.

**b.** To make known or display in a striking manner.

**1702** FARQUHAR *Twin Rivals* III. i, Has he ever signalised his courage? *a* **1716** SOUTH *Serm.* (1744) X. 146 The final issue of God's dealing with such as have signalized their patience. **1748** *Anson's Voy.* II. x. 322 He was very desirous of signalizing his talents by some enterprize. *a* **1806** C. J. FOX *Reign Jas. II* (1808) 125 The parliament opened..with an enthusiastick zeal, to signalize their loyalty.

**c.** *refl.* To distinguish (oneself) by some notable action or qualities. †Also const. *from*.
**1654** EARL MONM. tr. *Bentivoglio's Wars Flanders* 289 There were two Captains of Launces with the Prince who had particular occasion to signalize themselves. **1689** LUTTRELL *Brief Rel.* (1857) I. 577 A list of the officers in Derry that signalized themselves against the enemy. **1709** STEELE *Tatler* No. 77 ⁋5 A thousand extravagancies, by which they would signalize themselves from others. **1763** J. BROWN *Poetry & Music* iv. 37 Among the savage Tribes, the Chiefs are they who most signalize themselves by Dance and Song. **1813** T. CHALMERS in Hanna *Mem.* (1849) I. xii. 324 Let me make a point of bringing forward nothing in conversation for the purpose of signalising myself. **1869** TYNDALL *Notes Lect. Light* §462 Gypsum possesses three planes of cleavage,..one of which particularly signalizes itself by its perfection.

**2.** To characterize or mark conspicuously.
**1698** FRYER *Acc. E. India & P.* 95 Their Habit is the main thing that signalizes them more than their Virtue. **1776** ADAM SMITH *W.N.* v. I. (1904) II. 316 The inhabitants.. have been frequently united..and the havoc and devastation of Asia have always signalised their union. **1817** KIRBY & SP. *Entomol.* (1818) II. 241 The symbol of death which signalizes its thorax. **1861** LD. BROUGHAM *Brit. Const.* xi. 160 Such tyrannous acts as we thus find to have signalized the Anglo-Norman reigns. **1882** PEBODY *Eng. Jrnlism.* x. 74 He awoke in time to hear the cheers which signalised the success of the Minister's speech.

**3.** To point out, note or mention specially, draw attention to.
*a* **1711** KEN *Hymns Evang.* Poet. Wks. 1721 I. 131 Our Lord..At John's request the Traytor signaliz'd. **1833** I. TAYLOR *Fanat.* vi. 196 Some of the most portentous exhibitions of ungovernable violence that..have been signalized in history. **1835** SIR W. HAMILTON *Disc.* (1853) 543 Not a single voice was raised in either House to signalize the mis-statement. **1885** FFOULKES *Prim. Consecration* viii. 379 The Gallican spirit breathing throughout his works has been already signalised.

**4. a.** To make signals to; to communicate with by means of a signal.
**1824** BYRON *Let. to Muir* 2 Jan., They were signalising their consort with lights. **1857** R. TOMES *Amer. in Japan* vii. 153 Two guns were fired..for the purpose probably of signalizing the authorities at the Capital. **1874** HOLLAND *Mistr. Manse* xix. 75 She saw a stalwart man arise..And pause a breath, to signalize Some one beyond her stinted view.

**b.** *intr.* To make or send signals.
**1853** FELTON *Fam. Lett.* i. (1865) 8 We have signalized to Liverpool by way of Holyhead. **1857** *Chamb. Jrnl.* VII. 78 Developing a theory of signalising by pulsations.

**5.** To announce by a signal or signals. Also, to indicate.
**1875** BEDFORD *Sailor's Pocket-bk.* vi. (ed. 2) 216 Who would then signalize to them where they might safest attempt to land. **1961** *Texas Stud. Lit. & Lang.* III. 283 Pip's abject leave-taking of Miss Haversham..signalizes his homage to a supposed patroness. **1964** W. H. DRAY *Philos. Hist.* 53 The willingness of the revisionists to apportion blame, however, does not signalize a return to the sectional type of partisanship. **1966** R. S. RUDNER *Philos. Social Sci.* 15 A definition signalizes the redundancy or eliminability of a term. **1976** *Network* (Brit. Social. Assoc.) No. 6. 2/1 When people are trying to change their status..they seek to change their name, both to signalize the change that has taken place and to give form to the identity they are trying to shape.

**6.** [SIGNAL *sb.*] *U.S.* and *Austral.* To provide (an intersection, etc.) with traffic signals.
**1961** in WEBSTER. **1977** *Sunday Mail* (Brisbane) 29 June 2/2 We had 158 signalised intersections at June 30 last year, 65 signalised pedestrian crossings..and 281 floodlit ones.

Hence **'signalized** *ppl. a.*
**1652** EARL MONM. tr. *Bentivoglio's Hist. Relat.* 53 One of the gallantest and most signalized Princesses that ever lived. **1819** T. CHALMERS *Serm.* (1836) I. 214 The special and signalised object of his kindness. **1870** W. ARNOT in *Life* x. (1877) 439 This is a signalised and monumental spot of the continent.

**signallee** (sɪgnəˈliː). Also **signalee**. [f. SIGNAL *v.* + -EE¹.] One to whom a signal is made or transmitted.
**1898** KIPLING *Fleet in Being* iii. 31 Presently we saw a signal, but end on, as flags are apt to be when the signaller is dead up wind and the signallee down.

**signaller** (ˈsɪgnələ(r)). Also *U.S.* **signaler**. [f. SIGNAL *v.* + -ER¹.]
**1.** One who signals; *esp.* one specially employed to transmit signals.
**1863** LITTLEDALE *Offices East. Ch.* 209 About the hour of Dawn all the signallers sound. **1869** *Pall Mall G.* 21 Aug. 12 A large force..without signallers or telegraphists. **1887** *Times* 25 Aug. 4/4 The signallers with the column were very busy.

**b.** One who uses signals in card-playing.
**1885** PROCTOR *Whist* ix. 98 An original signal..should mean..that the signaller is..very strong in trumps.

**2.** A thing or apparatus used for signalling.
**1872** SHIPLEY *Gloss. Eccl. Terms* 108 A hand-clapper or signaller used as a bell. **1894** *Westm. Gaz.* 15 Oct. 7/2 An automatic signaller, which will..save fogmen's lives and be always ready.

**signalling** (ˈsɪgnəlɪŋ), *vbl. sb.* Also *U.S.* **signaling**. [f. SIGNAL *v.*] The action of making or transmitting signals.
**1860** TYNDALL *Glac.* II. x. 276 By rough signalling he first stood near the place where the first stake was to be driven in. **1876** VOYLE & STEVENSON *Milit. Dict.* 424/1 Visual signalling was formerly carried on by semaphores, but it has been superseded by army signalling and sun telegraphy. **1886** *Pall Mall G.* 21 May 4/1 Any new system of signalling which may be arranged between two or more players.

*attrib.* **1876** *Daily News* 30 Nov. 5/3 The loss of the Vanguard..was in the main due to imperfect signalling arrangements. **1889** G. FINDLAY *Eng. Railway* p. vi, My obligations to..the Signalling Superintendent.

**signally** (ˈsɪgnəlɪ), *adv.* Also 7 **signaly**. [f. SIGNAL *a.* Cf. obs. F. *signalement* in the same sense.] In a signal or striking manner.
**1641** in *Archaeologia* I. 99 The Lord of hosts did signally appear for us. *a* **1676** HALE *Prim. Orig. Man.* II. viii. (1677) 205 But if we follow the Account of the Septuagint,..the advantage of the Increase would be signally greater. **1748** *Anson's Voy.* II. iii. 139 The same cruelty which they had so often and so signally exerted against their Spanish neighbours. *c* **1800** FOSTER *Life & Corr.* (1846) I. 230 A being signally marked from her co-evals. **1856** STANLEY *Sinai & Pal.* i. (1858) 55 It is hard to recall another institution, with such opportunities so signally wasted. **1868** FREEMAN *Norm. Conq.* (1877) II. 433 All attempts to limit the choice of the electors beforehand had always signally failed.

**'signalman**. [f. SIGNAL *sb.* 3 and 4.]
**1.** A man employed to make, convey, display, or give signals. (Chiefly in *Naval* use.)
**1737** *Chamberlayne's St. Gt. Brit.* II. 115 Mr. John Dominick Grana, Signal-man. **1834** CAPT. MARRYAT *P. Simple* (1863) 117 Our captain was determined not to see it, and ordered the signal-man not to look that way. **1867** SMYTH *Sailor's Word-bk.* 626 *Signal-man*, the yeoman of the signals; a first-class petty officer in the navy. **1898** KIPLING *Fleet in Being* 16 A signalman pattered by to relieve his mate on the bridge.

**2.** A railway employee who attends to the signals which show whether the line is clear or not.
**1840** *B'ham Jrnl.* 28 Nov. 4/2 At every station there shall be an officer or officers under the name of 'signal men'. **1866** *Chamb. Jrnl.* III. 271 A very simple and complete method of communication between the signalman and switchman.

**signalment** (ˈsɪgnəlmənt). *rare.* [ad. F. *signalement*, f. *signaler* to mark out.] A description of a person wanted by the police; a distinguishing mark.
**1778** *Ann. Reg.* 196 A French signalment, or hue and cry, was received at..Bow Street..of a most horrid murder. **1804** BENTHAM *Mem. & Corr.* Wks. 1843 X. 414 Were a signalment of this kind once established in the character of a mark of infamy is it not to be apprehended that the above-mentioned custom of self-marking would cease? **1856** MRS. BROWNING *Aur. Leigh* VI. 399 The foiled police Renounced me. 'Could they find a girl and child, No other signalment but girl and child?'

†**'signance**. *Obs. rare.* Also 5 **sygn-**. [See SIGN *v.*¹ and -ANCE.] Signification, indication.
*c* **1400** *Rowland & O.* 1074 A glofe to his pensalle he hase, In Sygnance of his were. **1610** W. FOLKINGHAM *Art of Survey* II. vi. 57 The Kalender or Index serues for a Directory to expedite the intimation of particulars with signance of due Characters.

**signans** (ˈsɪgnænz). *Linguistics* and *Semiotics.* [L., pr. pple. of *signāre* to signify.] = SIGNIFIANT. Opp. SIGNATUM.
**1953** C. E. BAZELL *Linguistic Form* 29 Multiple oppositions, rare or unknown in the signans, are normal in the signatum. **1954** *Litera* (Istanbul) I. 31 In a code, each discrete signans has a discrete signatum; for instance in the Morse code a certain combination of dots and dashes signifies a certain combination of strokes and points. **1956** JAKOBSON & HALLE *Fundamentals of Lang.* I. ii. 15 The 'expression plane' of language, as he christened the aspect named *signans* in Stoic and Scholastic tradition,..is to be studied without any recourse to phonetic premises. **1959** *Jrnl. Individual Psychol.* XV. 62 The *signans* is perceptible, the *signatum* intelligible... Thus we perceive the sound-shape of the word *tree* and, on the other hand, we may translate this word by other verbal signs with more or less equivalent *signata* but each with a different *signans*.

‖**sig'nanter**, *adv. rare.* [Late L.] Expressly, distinctly, definitely.
**1614** JACKSON *Creed* III. 58 He might signanter say to the one [etc.]. **1656** HEYLIN *Extraneus Vapulans* 172 The Doctrine being confessed on all sides to be signanter, and expressly pointed at.

†**'signantly**, *adv. Obs.*⁻¹ [f. L. *signant-*, ppl. stem of *signāre* to mark, etc.] ? = prec.
*a* **1656** VINES *Lord's Supper* (1677) 394 Chrysostom takes this word [οὖν] signantly.

**signary** (ˈsɪgnərɪ). [f. L. *signum* sign + -ARY¹, after *syllabary*.] An arrangement of signs; the signs which constitute the syllabic or alphabetic symbols of a language.
**1902** *Encycl. Brit.* XXVII. 730/2 Probably all the signs in the hieroglyphic signary can be employed in their primary sense. **1909** A. J. EVANS *Scripta Minoa* I. p. v, I have endeavoured to supply a preliminary apparatus criticus in the form of tables and explanatory catalogues of the different signaries. **1924** L. ECKENSTEIN *Tutankhaten* v. 42 There were other scribes of other signaries and languages who inscribed soft clay tablets with a copper stilus. **1932** *Antiquity* VI. 375 Nearly all the Phoenician signs were already in use in Egypt as far back as the 1st dynasty, part of the larger series of the Mediterranean signary.

**signatary** (ˈsɪgnətərɪ). [ad. F. *signataire.*] = SIGNATORY *sb.*
**1858** *Times* 13 Aug. 7/1 The signataries of these two remarkable petitions. **1867** *Queen's Speech* in *Hansard* CLXXXV. 4 All the Powers, Signataries of the Treaty of 1856. **1884** SYMONDS *Shaks. Predec.* viii. 269 Within the jurisdiction of the signataries.

**signate** (ˈsɪgnət), *a.* and *sb.* [ad. L. *signāt-us*, pa. pple. of *signāre* to mark, etc.]
**A.** *adj.* Marked or distinguished in some way.
**1649** J. ELLISTONE tr. *Behmen's Epist.* xxxii. §14 The Signate-star above your pole shall help you. **1710** tr. *Werenfels' Disc. Logom.* 101 Then follow..the States, Amplications,..Signate Matter,..and whole Cart-loads of Qualitys. **1826** KIRBY & SPENCE *Entomol.* xlvi. IV. 286 *Signate*.., marked with signatures. **1888** ROLLESTON & JACKSON *Anim. Life* 152 The second form of quiescent pupa, known as obtected, larvate, or signate, is characteristic of *Lepidoptera*.

†**B.** *sb.* A distinguishing mark or quality. *Obs.*
**1662** J. CHANDLER *Van Helmont's Oriat.* 116 The power of the Species or particular kinde being unfolded, it assumeth divers Colours and Signates.

†**'signate**, *v. Obs.*⁻¹ [f. ppl. stem of L. *signāre*: see prec.] *trans.* To stamp, mark.
**1653** R. SANDERS *Physiogn.* b j b, All plants..which have their stalks signated with cuts and slits (as it were) are sanative to scars and wounds.

**signate**, variant of SENNET *Obs.*

**signation** (sɪgˈneɪʃən). Now *rare.* [ad. late L. *signātiōn-em*, noun of action f. *signāre* to SIGN.]
**1.** The action of signing with the cross, or of marking with a seal.
**1607** *Schol. Disc. agst. Antichr.* I. ii. 76 Whence is the Vnction called signation, consignation, obsignation (with the like) but from the Crosse? **1637** C. DOW *Answ. H. Burton* 207 The blessed Eucharist wherein they acknowledge..no other exhibition than by way of signation or obsignation. **1679** C. NESSE *Antichrist* 13 John makes no mention of him in the signation of the tribes. **1883** *Ch. Times* XXI. 953/1 The Greek signation with the Cross is made from right to left.

†**b.** The action of marking in a particular way, or the fact of being so marked. *Obs.*
**1659** H. MORE *Immort. Soul* III. iii. 7 Those other Examples of the Signation of the Fœtus from the Mothers' Fancy, which Fienus rejecteth.

†**2.** A distinctive mark. = SIGNATURE *sb.* 4. *Obs.*
**1646** SIR T. BROWNE *Pseud. Ep.* 100 It somewhat resembles an horseshooe, which..Baptista Porta hath thought too low a signation, and raised the same unto a Lunarie representation. **1653** R. SANDERS *Physiogn.* b j, The shels of Sea-snails having the signation of long ears.

†**'signator**¹. *Sc. Law. Obs.* Also 5–7 **signatour**. [App. ad. L. *signātōr-ius*: see SIGNATORY.] = SIGNATURE *sb.* 1.
**1473–4** *Acc. Ld. High Treas. Scot.* I. 2 A remissione be the King to certane personis..grantit be a signatour subscriuit with the Kingis hand. **1510** *Exch. Rolls Scot.* XIII. 649 That all the tennentis and forestaris..that has tane thair stedingis that thai cum and raise thair signatouris. **1580–1** *Reg. Privy Council Scot.* III. 349 Sindrie his subjectis..ceissis not to present thair signatouris, letters, and petitiounes, unto his Majesties self. **1626** CHAS. I in *3rd Rep. Hist. MSS. Comm.* 423/1 He did passe a signator of the said honour in your name. **1678** SIR G. MACKENZIE *Crim. Laws Scot.* II. xi. §i, The *habilis modus* of granting which Rights is by Signator.

**signator**² (sɪgˈneɪtə(r)). *rare.* [a. L. *signātor*, agent-noun from *signāre* to SIGN.] A signatory.
**1650** J. FRENCH tr. *Paracelsus' Nat. Things* IX. 100 It is convenient for us..to declare by whom things are signed, and who the Signator is. **1893** *Westm. Gaz.* 29 Dec. 6/1 The signators to the above letter are members of high standing on the Stock Exchange.

**signatory** (ˈsɪgnətərɪ), *a.* and *sb.* [ad. L. *signātōrius* of or belonging to sealing, f. ppl. stem of *signāre* to SIGN.]
**A.** *adj.* †**1.** Used in sealing. *Obs.*
**1647** TORSHELL *Design to Harmonize the Bible* 24 Georg. Longus of Milain, concerning signatory Rings. **1656** BLOUNT *Glossogr.*, *Signatory*, that is used or serves to seal withal; As *Annulus signatorius*, a Seal-Ring, a Signet.

**2.** Forming one of those (persons or states) whose signatures are attached to a document.
**1870** *Standard* 16 Nov., The Emperor is ready to come to an understanding with the signatory Powers. **1892** A. E. LEE in *Hist. of Columbus* I. 116 The signatory chiefs agreed to deliver up all captives, and to keep the peace forever.

**B.** *sb.* One of those whose signatures are attached to a document of any kind. (Cf. SIGNATARY.)
**1866** *Contemp. Rev.* I. 261 That the twenty signatories were..the majority of the members present in the Lower House. **1893** LIDDON *Life Pusey* I. xi. 268 An address to the Archbishop of Canterbury, assuring him of the adherence of the signatories to the doctrine..of the Church.

**signatum** (sɪgˈnɑːtəm). *Linguistics* and *Semiotics.* [L., neut. sing. pa. pple. of *signāre* to signify.] = SIGNIFIÉ. Opp. SIGNANS.
**1953**, etc. [see SIGNANS]. **1962** R. JAKOBSON *Sel. Writings* I. 658 This criticism has been repeatedly mistaken for an attempt to withdraw the *signatum* from the scope of any phonemic analysis.

**'signatural**, *a. rare*⁻¹. [f. SIGNATURE *sb.* 6.] According to signatures.
**1683** MOXON *Mech. Exerc., Printing* xxv. ⁋2 Laying the Heaps is to place them..in an orderly Signatural Succession.

**signature** ('sɪgnətjʊə(r)), *sb.* [ad. med.L. *signātūra*, f. *signāre* to sign, mark, etc., or a. F. *signature* (16th c.).]

**1.** *Sc. Law.* A writing prepared and presented to the Baron of Exchequer by a writer to the signet, as the ground of a royal grant to the person in whose name it is presented. (Bell.) Cf. SIGNATOR[1].

**1534** *Acc. Ld. High Treas. Scot.* VI. 219 To pas with writingis and signaturis to be subscrivit be the Kingis grace. **1574** *Reg. Privy Council Scot.* II. 383 Ane signature anent the confirmatioun of ane charter grantit to hir. *c* **1630** SIR T. HOPE *Minor Practicks* (1726) 85 All Signatures of Prelacies, and great Benefices; and also all Signatures of the Officers of State, pass under the Great Seal only. **1690** *Scot. Acts Parl.* (1822) IX. 200/1 The signatures and Charters of all vassalls of Kirklands. **1765–8** ERSKINE *Inst. Law Scot.* II. v. §82 Before the union of the two crowns in 1603, all signatures passed under the King's own hand. **1838** W. BELL *Dict. Law Scot.* s.v., Every Crown charter is preceded by a signature containing the principal clauses of the charter, and specifying the seal or seals through which it is to pass.

**2. a.** The name (†or special mark) of a person written with his or her own hand as an authentication of some document or writing.

**1580** HOLLYBAND *Treas. Fr. Tong, La signature d'vn Notoire*, the signature or marke of a Notarie. *a* **1633** COKE *On Litt.* (1642) II. 556 A bill superscribed with the signature or signe manuall, or royall hand of the King. **1771** *Junius Lett.* liv. (1780) 294 He asserts that he has traced me through a variety of signatures. **1794** MRS. RADCLIFFE *Myst. Udolpho* xxix, To make a last effort to procure that signature which would transfer her estates in Languedoc. **1829** SOUTHEY *All for Love* IX. xv, The fatal signature appear'd To all the multitude, Distinct as when the accursed pen Had traced it with fresh blood. **1848** THACKERAY *Van. Fair* ix, I wish I had Miss MacWhirter's signature to a cheque for five thousand pounds. **1875** JOWETT *Plato* (ed. 2) V. 424 On so much of what has been said..they shall put the seals of all the judges with their signatures in writing.

**b.** The action of signing one's name, or of authenticating a document by doing so.

**1621** LD. KPR. WILLIAMS in *Fortescue P.* (Camden) 162 Some things wee must offer to the kings signature when the clarkes are not to bee found. **1803** J. MARSHALL *Const. Opin.* (1839) 5 The last act to be done by the president is the signature of the commission. **1818** CRUISE *Digest* (ed. 2) VI. 63 He therefore did not mean the signature of the two first sheets as a signature of the whole will: there never was a signing of the whole.

†**3.** The action of impressing or stamping. *Obs.*

**1605** BACON *Adv. Learn.* II. xxi. §2 There is impressed upon all things..a third [desire] of Multiplying and extending their fourme upon other things: whereof the multiplying or signature of it upon other things, is that which we handled by the name of Active good.

**4. a.** A distinctive mark, a peculiarity in form or colouring, etc., on a plant or other natural object, formerly supposed to be an indication of its qualities, esp. for medicinal purposes. Now only *Hist.*

**1613** PURCHAS *Pilgrimage* (1614) 505 Some also pretending themselues Natures Principall Secretaries, haue found out in these..not onely Temperatures.., but Signatures of Natures owne impression. **1638** MEDE *Wks.* (1672) p. v, He would take occasion to speak of the Beauty, Signatures, useful Vertues and Properties of the Plants then in view. **1697** COLLIER *Ess. Mor. Subj.* II. (1703) 127 Whether men, as they say of plants, have signatures to discover their nature by, is hard to determine. **1748** tr. *Werenfels' Diss. Superst.* 21 There are some that think those Herbs the fittest for curing those Parts of a Man's Body, to which they bear some Sort of Resemblance, commonly called a Signature. **1806** A. HUNTER *Culina* (ed. 3) 240 It is probable that the golden colour of the fish..induced the ignorant to suppose, that it was given by Providence as a signature to point out its medicinal quality. **1858** CARPENTER *Veg. Phys.* §756 In former times such resemblances were greatly attended to by physicians, who termed them 'signatures'. **1898** *Westm. Gaz.* 3 June 5/1 According to this law, the best way of obtaining the 'signatures' of drugs is by healthy persons testing them on themselves.

**b.** A distinguishing mark of any kind.

*a* **1626** ANDREWES *Serm.* (1856) I. 12 The Saviour..taking on Him 'Abraham's seed' must withal take on Him the signature of Abraham's seed, and be..circumcised. **1659** *Gentl. Calling* 33 It is become..the badge and signature of a modern Wit, thus to be one of David's fools, in saying there is no God. **1750** G. HUGHES *Barbados* Pref. p. iv, There is not the smallest part of this Globe left without evident signatures of God's goodness. **1775** J. HARRIS *Philos. Arrangem.* Wks. (1841) 298 It is a kind of universal signature, by which nature makes known to us the several species of her productions. **1850** ROBERTSON *Serm.* Ser. II. (1856) 89 The capacity of ennui is one of the signatures of man's immortality. **1940** R. MORRISH *Police & Crime-Detection* xii. 114 All these marks, however minute in themselves, form the specific 'signature' or identity of any fire-arm. **1952** M. ALLINGHAM *Tiger in Smoke* xi. 185 You knifed three people..and..you went and left your signature all over the shop. **1960** T. HUGHES *Lupercal* 27 No Signature but this threshold-held hollow Remained of some vigorous souls That had Englished for Elizabeth. **1966** *Listener* 17 Nov. 746/1 An obvious pointer..is the prevalence of Shostakovich's musical 'signature'—D-S-C-H (D-E flat-C-B)—and its derivatives. **1971** *Daily Tel.* 22 Jan. 13/2 Signature of his collection: the V-necked pullover on every outfit. **1979** F. KERMODE *Genesis of Secrecy* iii. 56 The episode..is a sort of reticent signature, like Alfred Hitchcock's appearances in his own films. **1979** *Studies in Eng. Lit.: Eng. Number* (Tokyo) 109 Indeed, this prosodic 'signature' is written on page after page of the *Pisan Cantos.*

**c.** A stamp, impression. Also *fig.*

**1649** JER. TAYLOR *Gt. Exemp.* Disc. iii. §9 So does meditation produce those impresses and signatures which are the proper effects of the mystery. **1697** BURGHOPE *Disc. Relig. Assemb.* 71 It wou'd..dissolve the..foot-steps and signatures of the Deity on our souls. **1725** POPE *Odyss.* IV. 76 Vulgar parents cannot stamp their race With signatures of such majestic grace. **1781** COWPER *Retirement* 54 To trace, in nature's most minute design, The signature and stamp of pow'r divine. **1814** CARY *Dante, Par.* VII. 105 Goodness celestial, whose broad signature Is on the universe. **1849** RUSKIN *Seven Lamps* iii. §8. 71 See by how many artifices.. time and storm will set their wild signatures upon it. **1871** J. R. MACDUFF *Mem. Patmos* 142 The martyrs of the Roman catacombs, who have left the significant signature of their sufferings on vases and monumental tablets.

**d.** *spec.* = *signature tune*, sense 9 below.

**1932** [see *signature tune*, sense 9 below]. **1937** *Printers' Ink Monthly* May 42/2 *Signature*, the musical number or sound effect which regularly identifies a program. **1962** A. NISBETT *Technique Sound Studio* ix. 160 It is not so common for the start of a record to provide a good crisp opening signature.

**e.** Any pattern or characteristic in the physical properties or behaviour of a particular object, substance, etc., by which it can be identified; freq. a characteristic response which it gives to a test.

**1960** *Jrnl. Histochem. & Cytochem.* VIII. 288/1 Failure to demonstrate striking differences in 'pH signature' between analogous components of normal and carcinoma cells did not particularly surprise us. **1967** *Electronics* 6 Mar. 50/3 The new radar will gather 'signatures' of orbital vehicles as well as reentering missiles. **1969** *New Scientist* 2 Oct. 21/2 The Concorde's signature from a given height will be less ponderous than that of the Boeing. **1971** *Sci. Amer.* July 77/3 The characteristic signature of a supernova remnant is the emission of radio waves whose distribution of energy with wavelength is nonthermal. **1973** D. KYLE *Raft of Swords* (1974) iii. 21 Super-sensitive acoustic receivers.. which can instantly identify a vessel's 'signature'; in other words, indentify the distinctive sounds made by a particular vessel. **1977** A. HALLAM *Planet Earth* 41/3 Its magnetic signature allowed an age to be assigned to each piece of ocean floor. **1980** *Globe & Mail* (Toronto) 23 Aug. 2/5 The concept includes means of reducing the infra-red 'signature' given off by engine heat, thus defeating the ability of sensors to 'see' aircraft or vehicles even in darkness.

**5. a.** An image; a figure; an imitative mark. Now *rare* or *Obs.*

**1658** SIR T. BROWNE *Garden of Cyrus* iii, The Bryar.. maintains its pentagonall figure, and the unobserved signature of a handsome porch within it. **1673** RAY *Journ. Low C.* 237 Sir Thomas Brown..sent me the picture of one [a hen's egg]..having the perfect signature of a Duck swimming upon it. **1681** GREW *Musæum* III. i. i. 259 A Stone with the Signature of a Button-Fish upon it. **1782** PRIESTLEY *Corrupt. Chr.* II. VIII. 108 They added the signature of the cross. **1826** KIRBY & SP. *Entomol.* xlvi. IV. 286 *Signatures*, ..markings upon a surface resembling in some degree letters and characters.

†**b.** A nævus, a birth-mark. *Obs.*

**1682** GLANVILL *Saddducismus* I. 15 The fancy of the Mother can [form] the stubborn matter of the Fœtus in the womb, as we see it frequently doth in the instances that occur of Signatures and monstrous Singularities.

**6.** *Printing.* **a.** A letter or figure, a set or combination of letters or figures, etc., placed by the printer at the foot of the first page (and frequently on one or more of the succeeding pages) of every sheet in a book, for the purpose of showing the order in which these are to be placed or bound. Abbrev. *sig.*

**1656** BLOUNT *Glossogr.* s.v., Among Printers the mark or letter they set at the bottom of every sheet printed, as A, B, C, &c. to tell their Quires by, and distinguish one sheet from another, is called the Signature. **1683** MOXON *Mech. Exerc.*, *Printing* xxii. ¶4 If it be the First Page of the first Sheet of a Book the Signature is A. **1707** HEARNE *Collect.* (O.H.S.) I. 339 The Signatures (there being no pages) are towards the top of the Leaf. **1710** *Ibid.* III. 47 The Signatures shew it to be 8vo. **1775** WARTON *Hist. Eng. Poet.* II. 15 *note*, It is in quarto, with signatures to Kk. **1824** J. JOHNSON *Typogr.* II. 135 It is customary to begin the first sheet of every work with signature B, leaving A for the title sheet. **1864** *N. & Q.* 3rd Ser. VI. 266 Detached Sheet: 4to; signature, Dddddddd. **1895** *Trans. Bibliogr. Soc.* II. II. 112 It is usually said that the earliest instance in which printed signatures were employed was the *Praeceptorium Divinae Legis* of Johannes Nider, printed by Koelhoff at Cologne, in 1472.

*attrib.* **1888** JACOBI *Printers' Vocab.* 125 *Signature line*, the line of quadrats at the bottom of a page in which the signature letter or figure is placed. *Ibid.*, *Signature page*, the first page of a sheet, on which the signature appears. **1896** *Moxon's Mech. Exerc., Printing* p. xviii, The old signature marks that would confuse the bookbinder.

**b.** A sheet, as distinguished by its signature.

**1712** HEARNE *Collect.* (O.H.S.) IV. 37, I shall send you.. the Signatures F, G, H, I, of Mr. Dodwell's Dissertation. **1785** W. TOOKE in *Lett. Lit. Men* (Camden) 430 As soon as such a number of books are perfected, the surplus of the various signatures are thrown aside for wrappers. **1901** D. COCKERELL *Bookbinding* i. 34 The sheets of a newly printed book are arranged in piles in the printer's warehouse, each pile being made up of the same sheet or 'signature'. **1965** *Times Lit. Suppl.* 14 Oct. 928/3 This word 'signature' is.. often used when the user appears to mean either 'leaf' or 'quire'. **1981** *Printing World* 28 Jan. 13/3 Signatures can be perforated down the back for 'slotted' (also known as 'notched' or 'burst') binding.

**7.** *Mus.* A sign, or set of signs, placed at the beginning of a piece of music, immediately after the clef, to indicate its key or time.

**1806** CALLCOTT *Mus. Gram.* II. iv. 126 All the Signatures beyond six may be expressed by a smaller number by changing the name of the Tonic. **1839** *Penny Cycl.* XIII. 206/2 There are in name thirty different keys, and as many signatures are in actual use. **1875** STAINER & BARRETT *Dict. Mus. Terms* s.v., There are two kinds of signature, the time-signature and the key-signature.

**8.** *Pharm.* (See quot. 1951.)

**1856** E. PARRISH *Introd. Pract. Pharmacy* V. ii. 418 The prescription may be divided, for the purpose of study, into the following parts..: 1. The superscription. 2. The inscription. 3. The subscription. 4. The signature. **1901** T. SOLLMANN *Textbk. Pharmacol.* vi. 105 The directions to the patient (signature) are always written in English, so that the patient can read them. **1951** A. GROLLMAN *Pharmacol. & Therapeutics* 753 A prescription traditionally includes the following parts: 1. The superscription... 2. The inscription or body of the prescription... 3. The subscription... 4. The signature.., which includes the directions for the patient.

**9.** Special Comb.: **signature tune**, a piece of music that always precedes or follows a particular programme or a performance by a particular entertainer or band; also *transf.* and *fig.*

**1932** *Daily Mail* 4 Mar. 11/4 B.B.C. Band's 'Signature'. 'Just the Time for Dancing' and 'Till Next Time' are the titles of the 'signature' tunes selected by Mr. Henry Hall for his new B.B.C. Dance Band, to be used every time the band begins or concludes a broadcast. **1934** *Punch* 8 Aug. 164/2 My dearest memory of the place [*sc.* Bilgesea] is that there was never a moment at which wailing could not be heard. It is..the 'signature-tune'..of English holiday-makers throughout the country. **1938** O. SITWELL *Those were Days* IV. iii. 462 Diminutive moonstones and giant chrysanthemums were her signature-tune, her speciality almost, you might say, what she lived for. **1950** E. PARTRIDGE *Here, There & Everywhere* 181 With Lewis Carroll the verse-form often serves the same purpose as a signature-tune. **1958** P. GAMMOND *Duke Ellington* II. 72 The Duke and Bubber wrote *East St Louis toodle-oo*..and this became..the band's signature tune. **1962** A. NISBETT *Technique Sound Studio* ix. 161 Vocal music is not usually suitable for prefading, and is therefore rarely used for a closing signature tune. **1972** T. LILLEY *'K' Section* xl. 192 The six o'clock news signature tune. The familiar introductory pictures. **1977** *N.Y. Rev. Bks.* 26 May 3/3 'And trod so sweetly proud' and 'In this blind bitter land' come from Yeats's well-recognized signature tune rather than from an imagination strenuously engaged with its experience.

Hence '**signatureless** *a.*, having no signature, unsigned; without signatures.

**1830** LYTTON *P. Clifford* xxiii, Thus (abrupt and signatureless) ended the expected letter. **1892** *Athenæum* 18 June 790/2 In the volume called 'Love's Looking Glass' the poems are ranged signatureless.

**signature** ('sɪgnətjʊə(r)), *v.* [f. the sb.]

†**1.** *trans.* To indicate symbolically; to mark out, designate. *Obs.*

**1653** R. SANDERS *Physiogn.* b j, Plants which signature the Secrets, have a secret specifique vertue against sterility. **1740** CHEYNE *Ess. Regimen* p. xxx, Those who..have been signatur'd to intellectual Professions. *Ibid.* liv, Water being signatur'd, by its greatest Fluidity and Insipidity, for carrying alimentary particles..through all the strait meanders of animal Life.

**2.** *Printing.* To put a signature on (a sheet).

**1889** T. MACKELLAR *Amer. Printer* (ed. 17) 135.

**3.** To put one's signature to; to authenticate or confirm by one's signature.

**1900** *Westm. Gaz.* 2 June 2/3 Then followed the signatured address of a substantial householder of Courbevoie. **1909** *Eng. Rev.* Mar. 636 The meaning..was that he should 'signature' the ugly thing.

'**signaturist.** *rare.* [f. SIGNATURE *sb.* 4 + -IST.] One who maintains the theory or doctrine of signatures in plants, etc.

**1646** SIR T. BROWNE *Pseud. Ep.* 96 Signaturists have somewhat advanced it, who..have made men suspect there was more therein, then ordinary practice allowed. [Hence in Blount *Glossogr.* (1656), but wrongly explained.] **1786** FERRIAR in *Manch. Mem.* (1790) III. 50 Baptista Porta was not only a demonologist, but a signaturist, that is, a believer in the conformity of the virtues of plants to certain external appearances, supposed to be impressed by guardian angels.

†'**signaturize**, *v. Obs.*$^{-1}$ [f. as prec. + -IZE.] *trans.* To symbolize, signify.

**1669** W. SIMPSON *Hydrol. Chym.* 224 Making the character to signaturize the thing represented.

**sign-board** ('saɪnbɔəd). [SIGN *sb.* 6.]

**1.** A board on which the sign of a shop, inn, or other place of business is painted or otherwise displayed. Also *fig.*

**1632** in E. B. Jupp *Carpenters' Co.* (1887) 297 All signe boards of Wainscott or carved. **1688** HOLME *Armoury* III. 102/1 A Chandler..Dipping of a Staff or Rod of Candles in Tallow..I have seen often times Painted on Sign-boards, to signifie the dwelling-house of a Chandler. **1793–4** WORDSW. *Guilt & Sorrow* xvi, No swinging sign-board creaked from cottage elm. **1817** COLERIDGE *Biogr. Lit.* (Bohn) 89 Our very sign-boards..give evidence that there has been a Titian in the world. **1844** EMERSON *Misc.* (1855) 308 Let him in the county-town..put up his sign-board, Mr. Smith, Governor. **1872** YEATS *Techn. Hist. Comm.* 90 Some of the sign-boards of these ancient Roman inns have been disclosed amongst the ruins of Herculaneum and Pompeii. **1934** V. WOOLF *Oliver Goldsmith* in *Captain's Death Bed* (1950) 15 Bodies and hearts are attached to these sign-board faces.

**2.** Chiefly *U.S.* A board on a guide-post to direct travellers, etc.

**1829** A. ROYALL *Mrs. Royall's Pennsylvania* II. 38 You scarcely go a mile in Pennsylvania but you see a *Preacher* —as signboards are called. They point out the road but never travel it. **1883** *Wheelman* I. 298 They found a sign-board pointing to Swampscott and Lynn. **1972** *Straits Times* 25 Nov. 18/4 Although there are sign boards on either side of the estate indicating that it is closed to lorry traffic, these lorries continue to rumble through the estate.

**signe**, obs. f. SIGN *sb.* and *v.*, SING *v.*, SINE *sb.*

**signed** (saɪnd), *ppl. a.*$^{1}$ [f. SIGN *v.*]
†**1.** Sealed. *Obs.*$^{-0}$
**1647** HEXHAM I, A signed letter, *een gezegelden brief*.
**2.** Provided with a signature or signatures. Also *fig.*
**1648** HEXHAM II, *Geteeckende artijckelen*, signed articles. **1752** J. LOUTHIAN *Form Process* (ed. 2) 76 Upon an signed Information given in against the said C.D. **1772** *Ann. Reg.* II. 202/1 A protest was entered against a signed list, pretending to be sent by Lord Forbes. *c* **1893** H. G. WELLS *Let.* in *Experiment in Autobiog.* (1934) I. vi. 392 They have let me sign an article in the *Pall Mall Gazette*,.. and signed articles in dailies is a distinct advance for a poor wretch like me. **1930** G. B. SHAW *Apple Cart* I. 30 The ultimatum is here..and I shall not leave this room until I have His Majesty's signed pledge that its conditions will be observed. **1942** *World Rev.* Apr. 38/1 Key features of the newspaper contents were signed articles, and dramatic and literary *critiques* contributed by the greatest writers. **1959** *Times Lit. Suppl.* 5 June 334/2 It is a signed portrait. It is also a highly appealing, fair and convincing one. **1973** *Times* 28 Apr. 11/3 Both recordings contain versions of the 'signed' motet *Illibata Dei*, so called because the composer's name is spelled out in the text as an acrostic.
**3.** *Mus.* Placed as a signature. *rare.*
**1662** PLAYFORD *Skill Music* (1674) 8 These three Cliffs are called the three signed Cliffs, because they are always set at the beginning of the Lines on which is prickt the Song or Lesson. **1728** CHAMBERS *Cycl.* s.v. *Character*, Characters of Sign'd Clefs.

† **signed** *ppl. a.*$^{2}$ Aphetic f. ASSIGNED *ppl. a. Obs.*
**1898** MORRIS *Austral Eng.* 418 *Signed Servant*, obsolete contraction for *Assigned Servant*.

**signed** (saɪnd), *a. Arith.* [f. SIGN *sb.* + -ED$^{2}$.] Having a (plus or minus) sign; esp. as ***signed number***, a positive or negative integer.
**1873** *Proc. Lond. Math. Soc.* IV. 111 A signed magnitude. **1905** *Proc. R. Soc. Edin.* XXV. 372 The sum of the signed primary minors of a determinant. **1950** *Math. Tables & Other Aids to Computation* IV. 103 A word may represent a signed-binary number lying somewhere between $-2^{40}$ and $+2^{40}$. **1966** J. H. CADWELL *Topics in Recreational Math.* xiv. 160 We shall prove that all derivatives at these points are signed integers or zero. **1969** J. J. SPARKES *Transistor Switching* viii. 193 When writing 'signed' numbers the sign digit is identified with a bar over it.

**signed**, obs. form of SINGED.

**signee** (saɪˈniː). [f. SIGN *v.*$^{1}$ + -EE$^{1}$.] One who has signed a contract or register.
**1953** *Sun* (Baltimore) 24 Apr. B20/2 Ken Jackson.. became the thirty-third Colt signee yesterday. **1970** G. F. NEWMAN *Sir, You Bastard* i. 13 Generally the officials were never so subtle, nor the signees so sensitive, as to be influenced by surroundings. **1977** *Times of Zambia* 12 Sept. 8/7 Montgomery, a recent signee from Celtic of the Scottish Premier League in UK.

**signer** (ˈsaɪnə(r)). [f. SIGN *v.*$^{1}$ + -ER$^{1}$.]
**1. a.** One who signs; a signatory.
**1611** COTGR., *Signeur*, a signer, subscriber; marker. **1718** WODROW *Corr.* (1843) II. 404, I am flattered with a hundred signers at Glasgow. **1771** LUCKOMBE *Hist. Print.* 121 This was laid open in the said petition: the signers of it were, John Harrison [etc.]. **1854** E. G. HOLLAND *Mem. J. Badger* x. 172 He secured more than a hundred signers to the pledge. **1884** MRS. F. MILLER *Life Ht. Martineau* 199 Her name headed the list of signers.
**b.** *U.S.* (Usu. with capital initial.) *spec.* One of the signatories to the Declaration of Independence.
**1865** M. B. CHESNUT *Diary* 29 Mar. in C. V. Woodward *M. Chesnut's Civil War* (1981) xxxiii. 772 What is the use of being the grandson of a signer if one is not a loyal gentleman? **1913** E. WHARTON *Custom of Country* vii. 90 The high dark dining-room with..dim portraits of 'Signers' and their females. **1928** W. A. WHITE *Masks in Pageant* 67 The grandson of a President and the great-grandson of a Signer. **1973** A. POWELL *Temporary Kings* i. 48 He is descended.. from what is known as a 'Signer', one Bulton Gwinnett, who set his name to the Declaration of Independence.
**2.** One who communicates by signs.
**1893** *World's Congress Instruct. Deaf* 89 These associations produce the best and most graceful signers.

**signet** (ˈsɪgnɪt), *sb.* Forms: 4- signet, 4-7 signett (6 -eth), 4, 6 signete, 5-6 -ette; 5 sygnet, -at, 5-6 sygnette, 6 -ete; 4 syngnette, 5 *Sc.* singnet. [a. OF. *signet* (also *sinet* SINET), or ad. med.L. *signētum*, dim. of OF. *signe*, L. *signum* seal, SIGN *sb.* Hence also MDu. and MLG. *signet* (Du. *signet*, dial. *singenet*).]
**1.** A small seal, usually one fixed in a finger-ring.
*c* **1374** CHAUCER *Troylus* II. 1087 With his salte teres gan he bathe The ruby in his signet, and hit sette Upon the wex. **1390** GOWER *Conf.* II. 320 Sche..lappede it togedre tho And sette hir signet therupon. **1450** *Rolls of Parlt.* V. 212/2 Robbed hym of..his Signet, and other dyvers Juelx. **1463** *Bury Wills* (Camden) 38 My signet of gold, with a pellican and my armys grave ther in. **1535** COVERDALE *Jer.* xxii. 24 Though Iechonias..were the signet off my right honde, yet will I plucke him of. **1580** LYLY *Euphues* (Arb.) 449 All hys victoryes and vertues were not for to bee drawne in the Compasse of a Sygnette. **1638** JUNIUS *Paint. Ancients* 177 They wrought onyx stones enclosed in ouches of gold, graven as signets are graven. **1726** AYLIFFE *Parergon* 483 A Bishop's private Seal or Signet bearing his own Coat-Armour. **1770** LANGHORNE *Plutarch* (1851) I. 353/2 Taking his signet from his finger. **1825** SCOTT *Talism.* ii, That diamond signet, which thou wearest on thy finger, thou holdest it, doubtless, as of inestimable value? **1889** J. DICKIE *Words of Faith*, etc. (1893) 254 Your name is graven on the signet on his hand.
**2.** A small seal of this kind in formal or official use, esp. as employed to give authentication or authority to a document.
*c* **1400** MAUNDEV. viii. (1839) 82, I hadde Lettres of the Soudan, with his grete Seel; and comounly other Men han but his Signett. **1428** *E.E. Wills* (1882) 83 þerto I point my signet and my syne manuell. **1459** *Paston Lett.* I. 455 Doutyng that summe of the forseyd sealys of armys or sygnettes remayne stille amonges myn officeres. **1535** COVERDALE *1 Kings* xxi. 8 She wrote a letter vnder Achabs name, and sealed it with his signet. **1561** *Maitland Club Misc.* III. 283 Gewyn vnder ye Superintendentis signet and subscripsion at Sanctandrois. **1634** SIR T. HERBERT *Trav.* 46 Euery house of Quality, Magazen and Monastery were sealed vp, with the Signets of the Duke and Merchants. **1726** SWIFT *Gulliver* I. i, His Excellency..producing his Credentials under the Signet Royal [etc.]. **1754** ERSKINE *Princ. Scot. Law* (1809) 34 All our supreme courts have seals or signets, proper to their several jurisdictions. The Courts of Session and Justiciary used formerly the same signet, which was called the King's. **1821** BYRON *Sardanap.* I. ii, Empower me with thy signet To quell the machinations. **1839** THIRLWALL *Hist. Greece* VII. 61 In packages sealed with his own signet.
*fig.* **1742** YOUNG *Nt. Th.* VII. 254 In man the more we dive, the more we see Heav'n's signet stamping an immortal make.
†**b.** In phr. *clerk of one's signet. Obs.*
**1546** *Supplic. Poore Commons* (E.E.T.S.) 78 The clerke of his signet no doubte it was, for he vsed to cary his masters ryng in his mouth. **1577-87** HOLINSHED *Chron.* III. 920/2 A clearke of his closet..and two clearks of his signet.
**3.** *spec.* The smaller seal originally used by the sovereigns of England and Scotland for private purposes and for certain documents of an official character; in later Scottish use serving as the seal of the Court of Session. Also called ***privy*** or ***King's*** (***Queen's***) ***signet***. Hence ***Clerk of*** (or ***to***), ***Keeper of, the signet***, and Sc. ***writer to the signet*** (see WRITER).
(*a*) **1417** in Déprez *Dipl. Angl.* (1908) 100 Yeven under owr signet atte owr castel of Touque ye xii day of aoust. **1578** in Feuillerat *Revels Q. Eliz.* (1908) 300 For the privie seale and the signet for the Revells money. **1607** COWELL *Interpr.*, *Clerk of the Signet*, is an officer attendant continually upon his maiesties Principal Secretary, who alwaies hath the custody of the priuie signet. *a* **1633** COKE *On Litt.* (1642) II. 556 The duty of the Clerk of the Signet is to write out such grants or letters patents as passe by bill signed..to the Privy Seal. **1663** GERBIER *Counsel* f 3, One of the Clarkes of the Signet.
(*b*) **1489** *Acc. Ld. High Treas. Scot.* I. 108 Item, to the clerkis of the singnet for the writin of letteris, be a precep, ij vnicornis, xxxvj *s.* **1561** *Reg. Privy Council Scot.* I. 186 And ordanis the signet to ansuer lettres upoun his deliverance. **1592** *Sc. Acts Parl.* (1814) III. 569 The kepair of the signet sall write on the bak of þe signatur the speciall day that he affixit the signet. **1638** *Reg. Privy Counc. Scot.* VII. 101 Wee ..command..all keepers of the signet, from signeting thairof. **1695** *Sc. Acts Parl.* (1822) IX. 462 All Writs passing under the Signet, called the Signet of the Lords of Session, be subscribed by a Writer as Clerk to the said Signet. **1708** J. CHAMBERLAYNE *St. Gt. Brit.* (1710) 667 The Keepers and other Officers of the Queens Signet. **1765-8** ERSKINE *Inst. Law Scot.* I. iii. §39 When the signet is mentioned indefinitely, that of the session is commonly understood; which is also called the King's signet. **1838** W. BELL *Dict. Law Scot.* 168 The clerks or writers to the signet. *Ibid.*, The society is now under the keeper of the signet. **1851** MACAULAY *Hist. Eng.* xiii. III. 350 The Parliament.. assumed the power of stopping the signet, in other words, of suspending the whole administration of justice.
†**b.** A document given under this signet. *Obs.*
**1477** in *Antiquary* (1891) 105/1 The foresaid Mayor resceyved a prive signet by the hande of a servante of the Kyngs, the tenour whereof herafter ensueth. **1490** *Coventry Leet Bk.* 538 Ther was delyuered fro the Kynges grace a priue signet vnto Master R. Colman, Mair of þis Cite; the tenour wherof hereaftur ensueth.
**4.** An impressed seal or stamp; *esp.* the stamp or impression of a signet.
**13..** *E.E. Allit. P.* A. 837 Lesande þe boke with leuez sware, þere seuen syngnettez wern sette in-seme. **1382** WYCLIF *Rev.* v. 2 Who is worthi for to opene the boke, and for to vnbynde the signetes of it? **1559** *Rec. Monast. Kinloss* (1872) 150 To thir our Literis of Bailziaries..our signet is affixed. **1603** SHAKS. *Meas. for M.* IV. ii. 209 Heere is the hand and Seale of the Duke: you know the Charracter I doubt not, and the Signet is not strange to you? **1701** STANHOPE *Medit. S. Aug.* 249 Let me bear thee upon my heart as a signet. **1746** FRANCIS tr. *Horace, Epist.* II. ii. 202 Although the Felon's Fork Defac'd the Signet of a Bottle-Cork. **1821** SCOTT *Kenilw.* xli, See, here is his signet, in token of his instant and pressing commands. 'It is false!' said the Countess; 'thou hast stolen the warrant.'
**b.** *fig.* A mark, sign, stamp.
**1662** OWEN *Animad. Fiat Lux* xx. Wks. 1851 XIV. 162 The time will come when this Platonical Signet [the theory of purgatory]..shall be utterly exterminated out of the confines of the church of God. **1814** CARY *Dante, Parad* XI. 100 [St. Francis] from Christ Took the last signet, which his limbs two years Did carry. **1852** HAWTHORNE *Blithedale Rom.* xviii, I fancied that this smile..was the Devil's signet on the Professor.
†**5.** A signal. *Obs. rare.*
**1590** *Pasquil's Apol.* I. D iiij b, The signet shall be giuen, and the fielde fought. **1687** TAUBMAN *London's Triumph* 8 The Boatswain having given his signet by his Whistle.
**6.** *attrib.* and *Comb.*, as *signet-cylinder, letter, -office, seal, -wise.*
**1626** in Rushw. *Hist. Coll.* (1659) I. 223 That your Committees have..sent a general Warrant to his Signet-Office. *a* **1722** FOUNTAINHALL *Decis.* (1759) I. 5 The Lords declined to meddle, pretending they would not annul the King's signet letters. **1762-71** H. WALPOLE *Vertue's Anecd. Paint.* (1786) III. 158 Lewis Payne engraved two signet seals for Charles II. **1838** W. BELL *Dict. Law Scot.* 889 It is more than probable that, when the..forms of the old law came to be disused, Signet Letters, as they are termed, succeeded them. **1871** P. SMITH *Anc. Hist. East* x. §9 (1881) 205 The delicately striped and fringed dresses shewn on the most ancient signet-cylinders. **1877** W. JONES *Finger-ring* 466 The bezel is an irregular octagon, in the centre there is cut, signet-wise, a device. **1908** SCARGILL-BIRD *Guide Doc. P. Rec. O.* 81 The Signet Letter differed from the Writ of Privy Seal by omitting from the face of the document both the name and titles of the King and of the person to whom it was addressed.

**signet**, obs. variant of CYGNET.

ˈ**signet**, *v. Sc.* Also 6 **signat.** [f. the sb.] *trans.* To stamp with a signet. Also *fig.*
**1496** *Acc. Ld. High Treas. Scot.* I. 321 Giffin to a boy, to ryn fra Edinburgh to Linlithquho to Watte Chepman to signet tua letteris to pas to woddis, xij *d.* *a* **1578** LINDESAY (Pitscottie) *Chron. Scot.* (S.T.S.) I. 90 This wreittand [= writing] beand subscryuit and signatit with the kingis signit was..delyuerit to Schir Patrick Gray. **1609** SKENE *Reg. Maj., Forme of Proces* 111 Stewards, or Baillies, sall haue ane signet..with the quhilk they sall signet all letters, and precepts execut be them. **1638** *Reg. Privy Counc. Scot.* VII. 101 Wee..command..all keepers of the signet, from signeting thairof. **1685** SIR G. MACKENZIE *Religious Stoic* i. 6 With whose image it is signeted. **1752** J. LOUTHIAN *Form Process* (ed. 2) 71 These Letters are signet with the Seal of Court. **1858** CARLYLE *Fredk. Gt.* II. iii. (1872) IV. 48 Friedrich..soon manufactured the necessary Pass-port, signeted in due form. **1868** *Act 31 & 32 Vict.* c. 100 §13 Summonses passing the signet shall continue to be signeted as at present.
*transf.* **1829** SCOTT *Anne of G.* xxxv, The citation was.. written, as was the form, upon parchment, signeted with three crosses, and stuck to the table with a knife.
Hence ˈ**signeting** *vbl. sb.*
**1687** A. HAIG in J. Russell *Haigs* (1881) xi. 332 It cost 1 lib. 10 sh. for signeting. **1875** *Sc. Acts* XII. Index s.v. *Signet*, Ratification of an act of sederunt regarding the signeting of summonses.

**signet-ring.** [SIGNET *sb.*]
**1.** A finger-ring containing a signet.
**1681** GREW *Musæum* III. i. iv. 290 All the smaller Gems were used especially for Signets and Signet-Rings. **1726** AYLIFFE *Parergon* 132 Such are sealed on Wax only,..that is to say, with the Impression of a Signet-Ring. **1813** SCOTT *Let.* in *Lockhart* (1837) III. ii. 101 A Sultan who consulted Solomon on the proper inscription for a signet-ring. **1861** KING *Antiq. Gems* (1866) p. xxxviii, Signet-rings must have attained universal popularity in Greece before 600 B.C. **1878** J. MILLER *Songs of Italy* 82, I would be the richest King That ever wore a signet-ring.
**2.** *Path.* Used, usu. *attrib.*, to describe cells and organisms that resemble signet rings in appearance.
**1901** J. EWING in *Jrnl. Exper. Med.* V. 446 At a very early period of its development the æstivo-autumnal parasite in the present cases assumed a very characteristic ring shape. Many of these rings early developed a thickening of one segment, and to these bodies of various sizes the term 'signet-ring' very aptly applies. *Ibid.* 448 In six cases taking quinine typical signet-ring forms were seen in the peripheral blood 60 to 72 hours after the beginning of the paroxysm. **1928** L. E. H. WHITBY *Med. Bacteriol.* xxi. 209 The most characteristic form of the trophozoite is the so-called 'signet-ring' form, in which the chromatin granule or 'dot' is at one side. **1961** [see KRUKENBERG]. **1966** WRIGHT & SYMMERS *Systemic Path.* I. xv. 511/1 When the mucus-secreting cells are anaplastic they appear as rounded cells, with the nucleus displaced to one side by a globule of mucus in the cytoplasm ('signet-ring cells'); 'signet-ring cell' carcinomas are highly malignant.

†ˈ**signeur**, obs. variant of SENIOR *sb.*
**1588** SHAKS. *L.L.L.* I. ii. 10 *Boy.* By a familiar demonstration of the working, my tough signeur. *Brag.* Why tough signeur? Why tough signeur?
So †ˈ**signeury**, seniority. *Obs.*
**1594** SHAKS. *Rich. III*, IV. iv. 36 If ancient sorrow be most reuerent, Giue mine the benefit of signeurie.

**signeury**, obs. form of SEIGNEURY.

**signifer** (ˈsɪgnɪfə(r)). Now *rare.* [a. L. *signifer*, f. *signum* SIGN *sb.* + *-fer* bearing. So obs. F. *signifer* (in sense 2).]
†**1.** The Zodiac. *Obs.*
*c* **1374** CHAUCER *Troylus* V. 1020 Cynthea hir char-hors over-raughte..And Signifer his kandles sheweth brighte. *c* **1425** WYNTOUN *Cron.* I. xvi. 1582 His coursse haldande be hym selff..Sex monethe and twa ȝher Fra he entre in þe Signifere. **1535** STEWART *Cron. Scot.* I. 89 He knew..Of signifer the greit obliquitie Fra Aries to Cancer. **1601** HOLLAND *Pliny* II. iv, The circle called Signifer, or the Zodiake.
**2.** A standard-bearer, leader.
*c* **1450** HOLLAND *Howlat* 359 The Empriour Almane the armes he weris, As signifer souerane. **1596** WARNER *Alb. Eng.* x. lix. (1602) 257 Now to the Tribes was Dauid as the Zodiacke in the Signes, Euen Signifer to euery Prince that circled his Confines. **1902** *Speaker* 14 June 305/2 Quiet are Clan and Chief, and quiet Centurion and Signifer.
So **sigˈniferent** [cf. OF. *signiferant*], **sigˈniferous** *adjs.*, bearing a standard.
**1656** BLOUNT *Glossogr.*, *Signiferous*,..that bears a sign, Standard or Image. **1819** *Blackw. Mag.* V. 548 Let the present work..be lauded in the tuneful periods of his signiferent admirer.

**signi'fiable,** *a. rare.* [f. SIGNIFY *v.*] Capable of being signified.

**1857** *Encycl. Brit.* XIII. 610/2 It might then be determinable, and signifiable through the form of expression. **1885** *Ibid.* XVIII 766/2 Now what is it that is directly signifiable in the world about us?

**† sig'nifiance.** *Obs.* Also 3-4 signefia(u)nce, 4-5 signifiaunce (5 -yfi-, -yffy-); 4 syngnefi-, 5- fyaunce, etc. [a. OF. *signe-, signifiance*, etc.: see SIGNIFY *v.* and -ANCE.] = SIGNIFICANCE.

*c* **1250** *Kent. Serm.* in *O.E. Misc.* 28 Nu ye habbet i-herd þo signefiance of þo offringes þet maden þo þrie kinges of heþenesse to gode. *c* **1330** R. BRUNNE *Chron. Wace* (Rolls) 8243 þe white dragon ys syngnefiaunce þat þey schul take of þe vengaunce. *c* **1374** CHAUCER *Troylus* v. 362 A straw for alle swevenes signifiaunce! **1422** tr. *Secreta Secret., Priv. Priv.* 135 A signyfiance and a tokyne of connynge and vndyrstondynge. **1483** CAXTON *G. de la Tour* e b, Here may the sinnar take faire signyffyaunce or ensample. *c* **1570** *Pride & Lowl.* (1841) 3 Of his woords and speach who did misdeeme, Or sought not rather their signifiance.

‖**signifiant** (siɲifjɑ̃). *Linguistics* and *Semiotics.* [Fr., pres. pple. of *signifier* to signify.] A sound, symbol, or image, or a sequence of sounds, etc., as opposed to the meaning expressed; the physical element of a sign. Opp. SIGNIFIÉ.

[**1916** F. DE SAUSSURE *Cours de Linguistique Générale* I. i. 101 Nous appelons *signe* la combinaison du concept et de l'image acoustique; mais dans l'usage courant ce terme désigne généralement l'image acoustique seule... Nous proposons de conserver le mot *signe* pour désigner le total, et de remplacer *concept* et *image acoustique* respectivement par *signifié* et *signifiant*; ces derniers termes ont l'avantage de marquer l'opposition qui les sépare soit entre eux, soit du total dont ils font partie.] **1939** [see SAUSSUREAN *a.*] **1947** *Word* III. 8 Signs are the primary objects of linguistic study. Words, word-groups, and sentences are all signs—signifiants linked with signifiés. **1949** *Archivum Linguisticum* I. 1 But the morpheme is a sign in the sense of de Saussure, an association of a *signifiant* and a *signifié* upon equal terms. **1964** *Language* XL. 307 He [*sc.* Firth] rejected all distinction between langue and parole, and signifiant and signifié. **1973** [see MENTALISM 2]. **1973** *Screen* Spring/Summer 220 A *signifiant* (the pattern of alternating images) and a *signifié* (the indication of a simultaneity between the corresponding actions).

**signific** (sɪg'nɪfɪk). *Linguistics.* [f. SIGNIFIC(ANT *sb.*] = RADICAL *sb.* 1 c. Also *attrib.* Cf. PHONETIC *sb.*

**1923** B. KARLGREN *Analytic Dict. Chinese & Sino-Japanese* 1, I never use the term 'radical', as it wrongly conveys the idea of 'radix, racine, root' which is quite a different notion in general philology from that of signific: the meaning indicating part in the Chinese character. *Ibid.* 4 Nine tenths of all Chinese characters consist of one 'signific' and one 'phonetic'. **1948** R. A. D. FORREST *Chinese Lang.* ii. 38 The signific element in each case [*sc.* a character] denotes, or, more commonly, merely suggests, an order of ideas to which the meaning of the whole belongs. **1951** SHAU WING CHAN *Elementary Chinese* p. xvi, The last category is known as Chuañchù... It includes characters having identical significs and somewhat similar meanings but different phonetics. **1964** *Language* XL. 104 What sometimes appeared..to be a graphic element totally unrelated to the phonemic shape of the morph in question and hence by default a semantic 'key' or 'signific' was often in reality a phonetic element in the script. **1973** *Sci. Amer.* Feb. 54/2 When the 'horse' phonetic is combined with the signific for 'jade', we have *mă*, which means 'agate'.

‖**significacio** (sɪgnɪfɪ'kɑːsɪəʊ). Also significatio. [med.L.:—L. *significātio* significance.] An allegorical meaning; an innuendo.

**1933** R. TUVE *Seasons & Months* iii. 85 The commonplace *significatio* of Phoebus is to be explained..as a literary inheritance rather than the last faint rumbling of wheels in a pagan festival of the Sun. **1936** C. S. LEWIS *Allegory of Love* i. 1 It is essential to this form that the literal narrative and the *significacio* should be separable. **1968** J. A. W. BENNETT *Chaucer's Book of Fame* iii. 104 The emphatic negative is not a mere trope; it underlines the double *significacio.* **1969** R. A. LANHAM *Handlist Rhetorical Terms* 92 *Significatio,*..an innuendo.

**significance** (sɪg'nɪfɪkəns). [a. OF. *significance*, or ad. L. *significantia*, f. L. *significāre* to SIGNIFY: cf. SIGNIFIANCE. Not frequent before the 19th cent., but cf. next.]

**1. a.** The meaning or import *of* something.

*c* **1450** *Merlin* ii. 39 Often axed Vortiger of Merlyn the significance of the two dragons. [*Ibid.* 40 significaunce.] **1649** MILTON *Eikon.* viii. 73 Empty sentences, that have the sound of gravity, but the significance of nothing pertinent. *a* **1699** STILLINGFL. (J.), If he declares he intends it for the honour of another, he takes away by his words the significance of his action. **1825** COLERIDGE *Rem.* (1836) II. 349 What the several significances of each must or may be according to the philosophic conception. **1851** D. WILSON *Preh. Ann.* (1863) II. iv. ii. 225 The special significance of the symbols. **1871** RUSKIN *Fors Clav.* iii. 11 One great species of the British squire, under all the three significances of the name.

**b.** Without const.: Meaning; suggestiveness.

**1814** SCOTT *Wav.* xxxvii, She gave Waverley a parting smile and nod of significance. **1863** GEO. ELIOT *Romola* III. xxiv, To one who is anxiously in search of a certain object the faintest suggestions have a peculiar significance. **1866** G. MACDONALD *Ann. Q. Neighb.* xxix. (1878) 501 She had looked at me strangely—that is, with some significance in her face.

**2.** Importance, consequence.

**1725** DE FOE *Voy. round World* (1840) 15 Of such significance, that, for many years, it was counted a great exploit to pass this Strait. **1733** P. SHAW tr. *Bacon's De Sap. Vet.* (1803) 77 All their endeavours, either of persuasion or force, are of little significance. **1841** MYERS *Cath. Th.* III. §4. 12 Many of the statutes and ordinances..derive their chief significance from their reference to Egyptian rites and institutions. **1867** SPENCER *First Princ.* I. i. §4 (1875) 17 In the existence of a religious sentiment..we have a second evidence of great significance. **1875** JOWETT *Plato* (ed. 2) III. 155 The omission is not of any real significance.

**3.** *Statistics.* The level at or extent to which a result is statistically significant; freq. *attrib.*, as ***significance level; significance test***, a method used to calculate the significance of a result; hence ***significance testing*** vbl. sb.

**1888** J. VENN *Logic of Chance* (ed. 3) xix. 486 As before, common sense would feel little doubt that such a difference was significant, but it could give no numerical estimate of the significance. **1907** *Biometrika* V. 183 Let it be reasonable to suppose a quantity significant when it is $\beta$ times its standard deviation, or $\beta/\cdot 67449$ times its probable error, then we have for significance test: $m - M >$ [etc.]. Several other cases of probable error tests of significance deserve reconsideration. **1947** *Ibid.* XLVII. 139 The problem of testing the significance of difference between two proportions..receives early attention in textbooks on mathematical statistics. *Ibid.*, Such a difference in levels of significance in the solution of an everyday problem is obviously puzzling. **1960** *Amer. Sociol. Rev.* XXV. 202/2 In the test of this hypothesis a Chi-square of 34·34 was obtained, considerably lower than Chi-square at the ten per cent significance level for 34 degrees of freedom. **1970** *Nature* 25 July 384/2 Calculations of significance are based on the significance of the difference between paired observations using Student's *t* test. **1972** A. W. F. EDWARDS *Likelihood* i. 2 The rejection of the theory led to the flowering of alternative methods of inference, particularly significance-testing and estimation, to which we are heirs today. **1977** P. JOHNSON *Enemies of Society* xi. 157 In psychology, for example, it is notorious that 'results' used to confirm hypotheses are often no better than random data because significance tests would validate almost anything.

**significancy** (sɪg'nɪfɪkənsɪ). [See prec. and -ANCY.]

**1.** The quality of being highly significant or expressive; expressiveness.

*c* **1595** CAREW *Excell. Eng. Tongue* in G. G. Smith *Eliz. Crit. Ess.* II. 286 What soeuer tongue will gaine the race of perfection must runn on those fower wheeles, Significancye, Easynes, Copiousnes, & Sweetnes. *Ibid.* 288 Neither maye I omitt the significancy of our prouerbes, concise in wordes but plentifull in number. **1641** J. JACKSON *True Evang. T.* II. 142 It is of brave significancy to expresse the..cleansing quality of Christs blood. **1697** DRYDEN *Virg.* Postscr. to Rdr., Antiquated words..are never to be reviv'd, but when Sound or Significancy is wanting in the present Language. **1709** BERKELEY *Th. Vision* §125 By the clearness and significancy of what he says. **1712** SWIFT *Let. Eng. Tongue* Wks. 1751 IV. 241 Dunces of Figure, who had Credit enough to give rise to some New Word,..tho' it had neither Humour nor Significancy. **1824** COLERIDGE *Aids Refl.* (1848) I. 301 Though its own beauty, simplicity, and natural significancy had pleaded less strongly in its behalf. **1847** C. BRONTE *J. Eyre* xvii, 'I will tell you in your private ear,' replied she, wagging her turban three times with portentous significancy. **1871** J. R. MACDUFF *Mem. Patmos* xii. 162 This interpretation is brought out with greater force and significancy in the verse which follows.

**2.** The quality of being significant, of having a meaning or import.

**1631** J. BURGES *Answ. Rejoined, Lawfuln. Kneeling* 53 Significancy maketh a Ceremony to bee evill. **1672** MARVELL *Reh. Transp.* I. 247 The imposing of a significant Ceremony, is no more than to impose significancy upon a word. **1707** NORRIS *Treat. Humility* vii. 273 As there is significancy in motion, so there are some passions which motion only can speak. **1754** EDWARDS *Freed. Will* II. x. (1762) 96 Again (if Language is of any Significancy at all) if Motives excite Volition, then they are the Cause of its being excited. **1816** J. GILCHRIST *Philos. Etym.* 23 As there is a relation between these two methods of significancy, the one may be employed to explain the other. **1850** BLACKIE *Æschylus* II. 296 The significancy of a name affords of itself no presumption against its historical reality.

**b.** The meaning or import (*of* something).

**1641** J. JACKSON *True Evang. T.* I. 50 If we withall take the word Martyr in the fullest importance and significancy of the word. **1668** HOWE *Blessedness Righteous* (1825) 6 The word..hath the significancy we here give it. **1774** *Chesterfield's Lett.* (1792) I. Advt. p. xi, They are so varied and their significancy thrown into..so many different lights, that they could not be altered. **1786–1805** H. TOOKE *Purley* (1829) I. 40 The right use, significancy, and force of all words except the names of Ideas. **1840** *Blackw. Mag.* XLVII. 153 These symbols had lost their significancy to the mob. **1866** CANDLISH *1st Ep. St. John* xv. 167 Such is the import and significancy of the proposition that Jesus is the Christ.

**† c.** A significant thing. *Obs.*

**1635–56** COWLEY *Davideis* IV. Note 28 That Oyl mixt with any other liquor, still gets uppermost, is perhaps one of the chiefest Significancies in the Ceremony of Anointing Kings and Priests.

**3.** Importance, consequence.

**1679** in *Somers' Tracts* I. 75 Of what little Significancy the Resolves of the Council..are to the imposing a Supreme Ruler upon the Nation. **1712** ADDISON *Spect.* No. 317 ¶2 They are neither missed in the Commonwealth, nor lamented by private Persons. Their Actions are of no Significancy to Mankind. **1753** HANWAY *Trav.* (1762) I. Ded. p. viii, This opinion of our own significancy will however be corrected by the judgment of the public. **1847** S. AUSTIN *Ranke's Hist. Ref.* III. 71 Zwingli..kept mainly in view the practical significancy of scripture as a whole. **1864** J. H. NEWMAN *Apol.* ii. (1904) 39/1 Men on either side..attached no significancy to the fact.

**significans** (sɪg'nɪfɪkænz). *Linguistics* and *Semiotics.* [L., pres. pple. of *significāre* to signify.] = SIGNIFIANT. Opp. SIGNIFICATUM.

**1964** E. PALMER tr. *Martinet's Elem. General Linguistics* i. 24 Every linguistic sign comprises a significatum, its meaning or value..and a significans through which the sign is made manifest. **1972** HARTMANN & STORK *Dict. Lang. & Linguistics* 209/1 *Signifier*... Alternative term: significans, ..signifiant.

**significant** (sɪg'nɪfɪkənt), *a.* and *sb.* [ad. L. *significant-*, stem of *significans*, pres. pple. of *significāre* to SIGNIFY.]

**A.** *adj.* **1.** Full of meaning or import; highly expressive or suggestive: **a.** Of words, etc.

**1579** E. K. *Ded. Spenser's Sheph. Cal.*, Other some.., if they happen to here an olde word, albeit very naturall and significant, crye out streightway [etc.]. **1596** BACON *Max. & Use Com. Law* Pref., Because it is most familiar to the Students and..most significant to expresse conceits of law. **1620** SHELTON *Quix.* To Rdr. A 2 b, Endeuour to deliuer with significant, plaine, honest, and wel-orded words thy Iouiall and cheerefull discourse. **1668** *Publisher's Pref. to Rolle's Abridgment* 2 His Arguments were fitted to prove and evince,..his words few, but significant and weighty. **1769** E. BANCROFT *Guiana* 328 They are mutually entertained..with a variety of fables, which are merry, significant, and replete. **1781** J. RIPLEY *Sel. Orig. Lett.* 41 Let the words English and Scotch be obliterated and lost in that more ancient and significant word Britons. **1849** MACAULAY *Hist. Eng.* vi. II. 117 He lived and died, in the significant phrase of one of his countrymen, a bad Christian, but a good Protestant. **1875** JOWETT *Plato* (ed. 2) I. 262 [He] breaks off with a significant hint.

**b.** Of things, gestures, actions, etc.

**1643** TRAPP *Comm. Gen.* xli. 11 That is, no vain dreame, but significant, and deserving an interpreter. **1710** SHAFTESB. *Charac.* (1737) II. III. ii. 393, I saw so significant a Smile on Theocles's Face, that it stopt me. **1778** MISS BURNEY *Evelina* lxxii, She looked at me with a significant archness that made me colour. **1831** LAMB *Elia* II. *Ellistoniana*, Gathering up his features into one significant mass of wonder, pity, and expostulatory indignation. **1858** FROUDE *Hist. Eng.* III. 87 The upper house had been treated in disputes which had arisen with significant disrespect. **1874** GREEN *Short Hist.* iv. §5. 204 A significant act followed these emphatic words.

**c.** Important, notable.

*a* **1761** LAW *Comf. Weary Pilgr.* (1809) 19 Whoever he is ..that seems..to have made himself significant in any kind of religious distinction. **1857** MAURICE *Mor. & Met. Philos.* IV. vi. §6. 209 A little man may be a very significant man. **1890** *Amer. Jrnl. Sci.* Ser. III. XL. 66 Arsenic acid can be evaporated..without danger of significant volatilization.

**2. a.** Having or conveying a meaning; signifying something.

**1597** HOOKER *Eccl. Pol.* v. lxv. §5 A special dislike they have to hear that ceremonies now in use should be thought significant. **1608** TOPSELL *Serpents* (1658) 626 Their voyce was not a significant voyce, but a kinde of scrietching. **1693** J. EDWARDS *Author. O. & N. Test.* 103 Adam gave..proper and significant names to all creatures. **1751** HARRIS *Hermes* Wks. (1841) 124 For all words are significant, or else they would not be words. **1843** MILL *Logic* I. vii. §1 A general, which is as much as to say a significant name. **1871** C. DAVIES *Metric Syst.* III. 157 The names of the months were to be significant.

**b.** Conveying information about the value of a quantity; esp. in ***significant digit, figure***, a digit which has its precise numerical meaning in the number containing it, and is not a zero used simply to fill a vacant place at the beginning or end.

Earlier terms are *significative* and *signifying figure.*

**1690** LEYBOURN *Curs. Math.* 148 To have 6 Cyphers before the significant figure of each of them. **1706** W. JONES *Syn. Palmar. Matheseos* 22 Multiply the Significant Figures by the former Rules, and annex to the Product as many Cyphers. **1798** HUTTON *Course Math.* (1799) I. 4 The first nine are called Significant Figures, as distinguished from the cipher, which is quite insignificant of itself. **1879** THOMSON & TAIT *Nat. Phil.* I. I. §431 Few measurements of any kind are correct to more than six significant figures. **1938** A. E. WAUGH *Elem. Statistical Method* ii. 8 If we are told that the distance is 1000·00 miles, there are six significant figures, since it was not necessary to put in the zeros to locate the decimal point. **1957** R. A. BUCKINGHAM *Numerical Methods* i. 6 The numbers 0·000101 and 0·000999, both of which have the same absolute accuracy afforded by 6 decimals, and 3 significant figures, may yet have relative errors differing by an order of magnitude. **1962** C. BELL et al. *Fund. Arith. for Teachers* xi. 192 The value 3·1416 is said to be accurate to five significant figures. *Ibid.* xv. 231 If a measurement is expressed as a natural number, it is not always possible to determine the number of significant digits. **1965** I. ADLER *New Look at Arith.* iv. 228 Zeros which are not significant can always be replaced by words which serve the same function. *Ibid.* 231 When two approximate numbers are multiplied, the product has at most as many significant digits as there are in that one of the two numbers that has the fewer significant digits. **1968** *Brit. Med. Bull.* XXIV. 216/2 This [*sc.* a mathematical value] is not 'significant' but is printed out routinely. **1971** *Physics Bull.* Oct. 597/3 Does any analyst doing routine tests have the right to quote his result to four figures, and pretend that the fourth is also significant?

**c.** *Significant Form, significant form Aesthetics*, a hypothetical quality, thought to be common to all great works of art, that evokes an aesthetic response and is considered to be more significant than the subject-matter.

**1914** C. BELL *Art* II. i. 8 What quality is shared by all objects that provoke our aesthetic emotions?.. In each, lines and colours combined in a particular way, certain forms and relations of forms, stir our aesthetic emotions. These relations and combinations..I call 'Significant Form'; and

'Significant Form' is the one quality common to all works of visual art. **1914** R. FRY in *Nation* 7 Mar. 938/2 Why must the potter who is to make a superbly beautiful pot not think only of its significant form, but think first and most passionately about its functions as a pot? **1929** D. H. LAWRENCE *Paintings* 20 The critics stepped forth and abstracted his good apple into Significant Form, and henceforth Cézanne was Saved. **1959** H. B. ALLSOPP *Future of Arts* xiv. 120 Some abstractionists persist in seeking what Clive Bell called 'significant form' which is significant without being significant of anything. I suspect that this idea is nonsense. **1965** *Brit. Jrnl. Aesthetics* V. 113 Significant form cannot be attributed primarily to works of art on the ground that aesthetic emotion obtained from works of art is more intense than that felt in the contemplation of natural objects and pure forms.

**3.** Expressive or indicative *of* something.

**1793** HOLCROFT tr. *Lavater's Physiog.* viii. 48 Blue eyes are generally more significant of weakness.. than brown or black. **1827** G. HIGGINS *Celtic Druids* Pref. p. i, Thus words are sounds significant of ideas. **1841** HELPS *Ess.*, *Judgm. Other Men* (1842) 37 The most important of his actions may be anything but the most significant of the man. **1867** SMILES *Huguenots Eng.* ix. (1880) 143 One of the first acts of Louis XIV.. was significant of his future policy with regard to the Huguenots.

**4.** quasi-*adv.* = SIGNIFICANTLY.

**1861** LYTTON & FANE *Tannhäuser* 14 The sullen barons on each other stared Significant.

**5.** *Statistics.* Of an observed or calculated result, such as the difference between the means of two samples: having a low probability of occurrence if the null hypothesis is true; ***statistically significant***, significant at some conventionally chosen level, freq. five per cent.

A result is said to be significant at a specified level of probability if it will be obtained or exceeded with not more than that probability when the null hypothesis is true.

**1885** *Jrnl. R. Statistical Soc.* (Jubilee Vol.) 187 In order to determine whether the observed difference between the mean stature of 2,315 criminals and the mean stature of 8,585 British adult males belonging to the general population is significant [etc.]. **1907** *Biometrika* V. 318 Relative local differences falling beyond + 2 and − 2 may be regarded as probably significant since the number of asylums is small (22). **1925** R. A. FISHER *Stat. Methods Res. Workers* iii. 47 Deviations exceeding twice the standard deviation are thus formally regarded as significant. **1931** L. H. C. TIPPETT *Methods Statistics* iii. 48 It is conventional to regard all deviations greater than those with probabilities of 0·05 as real, or statistically significant. **1969** *Sci. Jrnl.* Nov. 57/1 The attitude scores differed only slightly and the differences were not statistically significant. **1970** *Nature* 25 July 376/2 Analysis of variance gave highly significant population and fertilizer effects. **1971** *Daily Tel.* (Colour Suppl.) 29 Oct. 35/4 The result, although occurring more often than other conjunctions, did not occur often enough to be statistically significant; i.e. a statistician would have said it was a chance occurrence. **1971** *Nature* 26 Nov. 231/2 If.. fifteen experiments are performed to detect a relationship which is not present, the probability that one or more experiments will give a result significant at the 0·05 level is 0·54.

**B.** *sb.* Something which expresses or conveys a meaning; a sign, symbol, indication.

**1588** SHAKS. *L.L.L.* III. i. 131 Beare this significant to the countrey Maide Iaquenetta. **1591** —— *1 Hen. VI*, II. iv. 26 Since you are tongue-ty'd, and so loth to speake, In dumbe significants proclayme your thoughts. **1628** FELTHAM *Resolves* II. xx. 64, I see not, but that Diuinity, put into apt significants, might rauish as well as Poetry. **1655** STANLEY *Hist. Philos.* (1687) 435/2 The second Question concerning Words, is of their Power, περὶ σημαινόντων, of Significants. **1825** COLERIDGE *Aids Refl.* (1848) I. 273 The contradictory admission, that Regeneration is the *significatum*, of which Baptism is the significant. **1830** WORDSW. *Egyptian Maid* 251 In my glass significants there are Of things that may to gladness turn this weeping.

Hence **sig'nificantness**, 'significancy' (Bailey, vol. II, 1727).

**significantly** (sɪgˈnɪfɪkəntlɪ), *adv.* [f. prec. + -LY².] In a significant manner; so as to convey some meaning; expressively, meaningly.

**1577** tr. *Bullinger's Decades* (1592) 445 He doth more significantly expres his meaning in that which followeth. **1607** TOPSELL *Four-f. Beasts* (1658) 75 Therefore Terence did significantly describe a good servant by the name of Dromo. **1663** MARQ. WORC. *Cent. Inv.* §33 To write with a Needle and Thred.. so that one stitch shall significantly shew any letter. **1738** tr. *Guazzo's Art Convers.* 107 There are many who have a good Invention, yet want to express themselves significantly. **1794** SULLIVAN *View Nat.* I. 321 There are those [waters].. that are significantly called mineral and medicinal. **1801** CHARLOTTE SMITH *Lett. Solit. Wand.* I. 307 They looked significantly at each other. **1877** FROUDE *Short Stud.* (1883) IV. I. vi. 69 An embassy was despatched to Rome, John of Oxford.. being significantly one of its members.

**significate** (sɪgˈnɪfɪkət), *sb.* Also 5, 7 -at. [ad. L. *significāt-um*, pa. pple. neut. of *significāre* to SIGNIFY. So obs. F. *significat*.] That which is signified or symbolized.

*c* **1449** PECOCK *Repr.* II. v. 163 The likenes of a signe to his significat (that is to seie, to the thing signified bi him). **1569** J. SANFORD tr. *Agrippa's Van. Artes* 7 Wyse men haue taken in hand to make rules of speaking, that is, the constructions of the Regimente, and of the Significates. **1655** STANLEY *Hist. Philos.* (1687) 435/2 Chrysippus divided Dialectick into two parts,.. of Significants, and Significats. **1827** WHATELY *Logic* II. i. §3 A common term stands for several individuals. *Note.* These individuals are called its *significates*. **1874** *Contemp. Rev.* XXIV. 692 In a symbol there is always something more to be understood than the symbol itself—namely, the significates.

†**significate**, *pa. pple. Obs. rare.* [ad. pa. pple. of L. *significāre*: see prec.] Signified, indicated.

**1432-50** tr. *Higden* (Rolls) II. 373 Thauȝhe fables be not trewe, neuertheles thei cause trawthe in the thynge significate by theyme. **1533** BELLENDEN *Livy* (S.T.S.) II. 272 Thus war sex centuris of horsmen ekit.. vnder the auld Names as war significate afore be augurys.

**significatio**, var. SIGNIFICACIO.

**signification** (sɪgnɪfɪˈkeɪʃən). Forms: 4- signific- (5 singn-), 5 signe-, 6 signifyc-; 4-5 signyfyc-; 4 sygnyfic-, 5-6 sygnifyc-, sygnyfyc- (5 -ffyc-), 6 sygnific-; also 4 -acioun, 5 -acyoun, -aciown, 4-6 -acion, -acyon (5 -asion). [a. OF. *signification, -aciun*, etc., or ad. L. *significātio*, noun of action f. *significāre* to SIGNIFY.]

**1. a.** The fact or property of being significant or expressive of something.

*a* **1300** *Cursor M.* 3380 Bot þai it did for sum reson, And thoru significacion. *c* **1400** MAUNDEV. (Roxb.) xxi. 96 It es noȝt done withouten a grete significacion and a grete cause. *c* **1450** *Merlin* ii. 38 Send after alle the gode men of thi londe to se the bataile, for it hath grete singnificacion. **1532** MORE *Confut. Tindale* Wks. 471/2 He sayth that so it might in dede, yf yᵗ the wycked Pope had not taken away the significacions of our sacramentes from vs. **1597** HOOKER *Eccl. Pol.* v. lxv. §5 Ceremonies destitute of signification are no better than the idle gestures of men whose broken wits are not masters of that they do. **1643** TRAPP *Comm. Gen.* ix. 14 The Rainbow hath in it two contrary significations, *viz.* of rain, and fair-weather. **1788** *Encycl. Brit.* (ed. 3) II. 290/2 An additional character.. is necessary, which has no signification when placed by itself.

**b.** Importance, consequence, significance. Now *rare* or *dial.*

**1670** CLARENDON *Hist. Reb.* xv. §42 Who, as soon as they were removed,.. were found to be of no signification, or to have influence upon any men. **1725** DE FOE *Voy. round World* (1840) 276 A station of life where.. gold.. would be of no value.., nay, not of signification enough to make a present of. **1760** *Impostors Detected* I. Advt. 7, I met with the following MSS. which at that time I thought of little signification. **1794** GODWIN *Caleb Williams* 84 It is no signification putting your questions to us. We only do as we are directed. **1839** SIR G. C. LEWIS *Gloss. Heref.* s.v., *Of no signification*, of no importance. **1854** MISS BAKER *Northampt. Gloss.* s.v., It's of no signification.

**c.** *Semiotics.* The process of signifying; the production of signs.

**1946** C. MORRIS *Signs, Language & Behavior* iv. 111 Since a sign can denote without its interpreter knowing whether or not it denotes.. it is evident that signification and knowledge are not limited to that portion of the world which acts as a direct stimulus to an interpreter's behavior. **1957** J. MARITAIN in R. N. Anshen *Language* I. v. 88 Animals make use of signs without perceiving the relation of signification. To perceive the relation of signification is to have an *idea*, i.e., a spiritual sign. **1973** *Screen* Spring/Summer 94 Each of them is in other contexts the signifying substance of one or more signification systems other than the cinema. *Ibid.* 109 In cinema signification (the process of the production of signs) is described by Metz as always more or less motivated, that is non-arbitrary.

**2.** That which is signified by something; meaning, import, implication. Freq. const. *of*.

**a.** Of words, etc. *spec.* in *Semiotics* (see quots. 1964 and 1976).

**1398** TREVISA *Barth. De P.R.* XVII. clxii. (Bodl. MS.), Tabula.. is in one significacioun a mete borde. **1432-50** tr. *Higden* (Rolls) III. 155 Cresus askede then cownsaile of his Goddes, whiche deceyuede hym by a worde equiuocate,.. hauenge diuerse significaciones. *c* **1465** *Pol., Rel., & L. Poems* (1866) 37 This worde Anima hath many significacions. **1532** MORE *Confut. Tindale* Wks. 417/1, I sayde.. that this is trewe of the vsuall significacion of these wordes themselfe in the English tounge. **1588** FRAUNCE *Lawiers Log.* I. ii. 10 b, Which are Greeke woordes of like signification. **1611** BIBLE *Transl. Pref.* ¶15 Diuersitie of signification and sense in the margine.. must needes doe good. **1651** HOBBES *Leviath.* I. iv. 13 The Name *Body* is of larger signification than the word *Man.* **1718** *Free-thinker* No. 62. 47 Care was taken, that the Children.. should have such Names as were of an agreeable Signification. **1769** E. BANCROFT *Guiana* 206 The Fire Snake, as it is called, from the signification of its Indian name. **1844** *Proc. Philol. Soc.* II. 1 The form of the word, its sound and spelling, and the signification. **1881** *Nature* XXIV. 443 As one conversant with geography in any extended signification of the word. **1964** C. MORRIS *Signification & Significance* i. 3 'Significations'.. are not 'entities' in any objectionable sense, but certain describable aspects of complex behavioral processes in the natural world. **1976** T. EAGLETON *Crit. & Ideology* iii. 72 The text takes as its object, not the real, but certain significations by which the real lives itself—significations which are themselves the product of its partial abolition.

**b.** Of things, events, etc.

*c* **1450** LOVELICH *Merlin* 2929 Thou behyhgtest forto tellen me here the signefycaciown of the dragowns tweyne. *c* **1489** CAXTON *Sonnes of Aymon* vi. 152, I shall expowne and declare vnto you the signyfycasion of this dreme. **1535** COVERDALE *Daniel* ii. 6 Shewe me the dreame and the significacion of it. *a* **1610** HEALEY *Cebes* (1636) 106 Much talke had wee about the signification of this portraiture, but none could conceive truly what it should intend. *a* **1720** SEWEL *Hist. Quakers* To the King, To dig up Antiquities from the dark, by searching out the Signification of Statues and Inscriptions. **1794** T. TAYLOR *Pausanias' Descr. Greece* III. 104 The signification, too, of the entrails gave them the highest reason to hope that the gods would be propitious to them. **1855** PUSEY *Doctr. Real. Pres.* Note A. 21 The natural signification is not changed on account of a signification annexed by the institution.

**3. a.** A thing, event, action, etc., which is significant or expressive of something.

**13..** *Coer de L.* 339 The tayle henge to the grounde: That was sygnyfycaciou[n] The hethene folke to brynge doun. *c* **1386** CHAUCER *Nun's Pr. T.* 159 That dremes ben significaciouns As wel of ioye as tribulaciouns. **1470-85** MALORY *Arthur* x. lxiii. 523 The whiche was a ful wonderful beest and a grete sygnyfycacyon, for Merlyn profecyed moche of that beest. **1525** LD. BERNERS *Froiss.* II. clxxxvii. [clxxxiv.] 572 As he rode forwarde in the forest of Mans, a great sygnifycacyon fell to hym. **1579** FULKE *Heskins' Parl.* 233 Saint Luke, & S. Paule, vse manifest tropes, figures, and significations. **1612** T. TAYLOR *Comm. Titus* ii. 14 Other Papists teach us, that in the masse is not the very same true and reall oblation, but onely a commemoration and signification of it. **1683** *Perswasive to Communion* 26 Are not Kneeling, and lifting up the Eyes, significations of the Reverence we owe? **1849** LYTTON *Caxtons* 16 In all these fables, certain philosophers could easily discover symbolic significations of the highest morality.

**b.** ***in signification of***, in token of. *rare.*

*c* **1391** CHAUCER *Astrol.* II. §31 Now is thin Orisonte departed in 24 parties.., in significacion of 24 partiez of the world. **1586** A. DAY *Eng. Secretary* I. (1625) A 2 In signification of the will I have to doe unto your Lordship any acceptable service.

†**c.** A sign, mark, indication, trace. *Obs.*

**1576** FLEMING tr. *Caius' Eng. Dogges* (1880) 5 (So that there be some signification of bloud shed) these Dogges.. can disclose & bewray the same by smelling. **1607** TOPSELL *Four-f. Beasts* (1658) 98 They have nothing but small bunches—as it were, significations of their horns to-come. *Ibid.* 395 A great floud of waters.. swept them all away, leaving no more behinde then naked and bare significations of former buildings.

†**d.** A sign, gesture, cry, etc., serving to indicate desire or feeling. *Obs.*

**1607** TOPSELL *Four-f. Beasts* (1658) 112 By his gestures and movings they conjecture his meaning..; giving.. ready obedience to his significations. **1691** RAY *Creation* I. 43 No Cruelty could be exercised towards them, which is contrary to the doleful Significations they make when beaten or tormented.

**4. a.** An indication or intimation of something.

**1426** LYDG. *De. Guil. Pilgr.* 22234, I.. Prayed hir.. That sche wolde anoon devyse There-off by exposicyoun, A cleer sygnyffycacyoun. **1432-50** tr. *Higden* (Rolls) II. 209 The creaciones of wondres be causede otherwhile to the significacion of thynges to comme. **1542** HEN. VIII *Decl. agst. Scottes* B iij, All these.. gyue suche signification of theyr arrogancy, as it is necessary for vs to oppresse it in the begynning. **1586** BURGHLEY in *Leicester Corr.* (Camden) 306 Comming to me with signification that he was to depart erly in the next morning. **1638** JUNIUS *Paint. Ancients* A 3 Feeling myself inspired with courage by the signification of your noble desire.., I stoutly fell to my taske. **1674** *Essex Papers* (Camden) I. 238 You gave me an intimation of a.. Letter coming..., I returne you many thanks for this signification. **1719** *Col. Rec. Pennsylvania* III. 73 Until further Signification of his Majestys or their Excellencys Pleasure. **1741** MIDDLETON *Cicero* III. IX. (ed. 3) 15 Caesar .. could never draw from the people any public signification of their favour.

**b.** *spec.* Notification in proper legal form.

**1533-4** *Act 25 Hen. VIII*, c. 20 §5 Letters patentes.. commaundyng such archebishop, to whom any such significacion shalbe made, to confirme the said election. **1586** T. B. *La Primaud. Fr. Acad.* (1589) 299 Patents and commandements should be held in suspence and deferred, thirtie daies after signification and knowledge of them. **1728** CHAMBERS *Cycl.* s.v., Some Significations are to be made to the Person himself; or, at least, at his House. **1881** *Daily News* 17 Jan. 5/1 It was contended that the statutory deprivation.. displaced the old proceeding by signification to the Court of Chancery.

Hence **signifi'cational** *a.*

**1953** H. H. PRICE *Thinking & Exper.* iv. 117 Our question concerning the 'tied' (as opposed to 'free') character of significational thinking.

†**sig'nificatist.** *Obs. rare.* [Cf. next and -IST.] (See quots.)

**1585-7** T. ROGERS *39 Art.* (1607) 289 The Symbolists, Figurists, and Significatists, who are of opinion that the faithful at the Lord's supper do receive nothing but naked and bare signs. **1625** BP. MOUNTAGU *App. Cæsar* 297 The Figurists, Significatists, Symbolists, taught you this Doctrine, who acknowledge nothing.. but naked and bare signes.

**significative** (sɪgˈnɪfɪkətɪv), *a.* and *sb.* Also 5 significatyf, 6 -tyue, 6-7 -tiue, 7 -tyve. [a. OF. *significatif, -ive*, or ad. late L. *significātīv-us*: see SIGNIFY *v.* and -ATIVE.]

**A.** *adj.* **1.** Serving to signify something; having a signification or meaning.

*a* **1400** in Halliw. *Rara Mathem.* (1841) 29 A cifre tokeneth nothinge but he maketh other the more significatyf that comith after hym. *c* **1425** *Crafte Nombrynge* (1897) 13 þou most borow on of þe next figure significatyf in þat rewe. **1541** COVERDALE *Old Faith* x. (1547) H j b, Wherby Christ testified.. that all thinges significatyue in the tabernacle.. were now fulfilled and abrogate. **1589** PUTTENHAM *Eng. Poesie* III. iv. (Arb.) 159 Which surplussage to auoide, we are allowed to draw in other words single, and asmuch significatiue. **1607** *Schol. Disc. agst. Antichr.* I. i. 32 You shall finde the Crosses of the Lordes Supper to be significatiue alone. **1639** ROBARTS *God's House & Service* x. 81 It must be taken in that significative sence, which we give thereof. *a* **1734** NORTH *Lives* (1826) I. 33 To say truth, barbarous as it [law French] is thought to be, it is concise, aptly abbreviated, and significative. **1756** J. WITHERSPOON *Treat. Regeneration* (1804) 146 Multitudes cannot be described in juster or more significative terms. **1816** KIRBY & SP. *Entomol.* xvii. (1818) II. 65 It does not appear that, like the bees, they emit any significative sounds. **1861** MAX MÜLLER *Sci. Lang.* Ser. I. (1864) 338 In these sesquipedalian compounds the significative root remains distinct.

**b.** Serving as a sign or indication *of* something.

1637–50 in Row *Hist. Kirk* (Wodrow Soc.) 264, I have receaved your short but right significative letter of your sound and ardent affection.. toward the cause. 1651 HOBBES *Leviath.* II. xxxi. 192 Those Attributes are to be held significative of Honour, that men intend shall so be. 1664 H. MORE *Myst. Iniq.* 240 So plain is it that an Hail-storm is significative of the incursion and assault of an enemie. 1713 *Guardian* No. 170, The use of letters, as significative of these sounds. 1859 RUSKIN *Two Paths* v. §164 Your close-set wooden paling.. is significative of pleasant parks. 1875 *Good Words* II. 130 On various minds it [Niagara] leaves various impressions; and perhaps this is significative of its real power.

**2.** Highly significant or suggestive.

1677 MARVELL *Corr.* Wks. (Grosart) II. 540 After this weighty and significative message, the Secretary added [etc]. 1678 R. BARCLAY *Apol. Quakers* v. §20. 157 A familiar Example, yet very significative in this case. 1855 MOTLEY *Dutch Rep.* II. 122 On the night of the 8th September, Egmont received another most significative and mysterious warning. 1860 RUSKIN *Mod. Paint.* V. IX. xi. §31 How strangely significative, thus understood, those last Venetian dreams of his become.

**B.** *sb.* A thing or word serving to signify or indicate something.

1641 'SMECTYMNUUS' *Vind. Answ.* ii. 36 The Surplice is a significative of divine alacritie and integritie. 1765 in *Ann. Reg., Charact.* (1767) 135 Attacah, Deliverance, Pihahiroth, whether an appellative or significative. 1788 tr. *Swedenborg's White Horse* 16 Scarce any one knows.. that those Significatives were derived from the Ancient Representative Churches to the Gentiles. 1893 *N. Y. New-Church Messenger* 19 Apr. 243 Our entire written language is a system of significatives pure and simple.

Hence **sig'nificativeness**.

1665 J. SERGEANT *Sure Footing* 31 You hold that any particular Text you alledge is truly a part of the Scriptures Letter, and not foisted in, or some way altered in its significativeness. 1697 —— *Solid Philos.* 276 From the Nature of the Words, as Words; that is, from their Significativeness. 1860 WORCESTER (citing *Westm. Rev.*).

**significatively** (sɪg'nɪfɪkətɪvlɪ), *adv.* [f. prec. + -LY².] In a significative manner; by signification; suggestively; expressively.

1564 RASTELL *Confut. Jewel's Serm.* 140 The body of Christ is, onlye.. sacramentallie, significatiuelye,.. imaginatiuelie, in the Sacrament. 1579 FULKE *Heskins' Parl.* 203 The same is eaten in the sacrament as in a mysterie, significatiuely. 1624 GATAKER *Transubst.* 13 That the Bread be Christs body significatively (that is, by signification onely). *a* 1661 FULLER *Worthies* I. vi. (1662) 18 *Amiral* (thus compounded) was significatively comprehensive of his Jurisdiction.

**significator** ('sɪgnɪfɪkeɪtə(r)). [a. med.L. *significātor*, agent-noun f. L. *significāre* to SIGNIFY. Cf. F. *significateur*.]

**1.** *Astrol.* **a.** The planet by which the querent or the quesited is specially signified (see quot. 1647).

1584 R. SCOT *Discov. Witchcr.* XI. xxi. (1886) 169 They seeke to find out the meaning of the significators, attributing to them the ends of all things. 1647 LILLY *Chr. Astrol.* 48 When we name the Lord of the Ascendant, or Significator of the Querent, or thing quesited; we meane no other thing then that Planet who is Lord of that Signe which ascends, or Lord of that Signe from which house the thing demanded is required. 1671 BLAGRAVE *Astrol. Pract. Phys.* Pref. 4 Who is strongest in the Heavens by essential dignities, shall afflict the Principal significator of the sick. 1815 SCOTT *Guy M.* iv, There was one significator, which pressed remarkably upon our astrologer's attention. 1895 *Mod. Astrol.* I. 21 The position of the Significator, or lord of the Ascendant, in the fixed sign Taurus.

**b.** (See quot.)

1728 CHAMBERS *Cycl.* s.v. *Ascendent*, The Degree of the Equator which rises upon the Horizon, at the Time of the Birth of any one,.. is also called the First House, the Oriental Angle, and the Significator of Life.

**2.** That which signifies or indicates. *rare.*

1649 HEYLIN *Relat. & Observ.* II. 252 To leavy warre against the Parliament, shall stand alone, be the onely significator, and take up the whole roome in the Endictment. 1669 WORLIDGE *Syst. Agric.* (1681) 292 The most principal significator of the varieties of weather, the Countryman esteems the Moon to be.

**significatory** (sɪg'nɪfɪkətərɪ), *a.* and *sb.* [ad. late L. *significātōri-us*.]

**A.** *adj.* Serving to signify or intimate.

1579 FENTON *Guicciard.* VII. (1599) 288 Cæsar caused to be publikely read the Popes writ, with many other letters significatorie from diuerse places. 1641 WILKINS *Mercury* xx. (1707) 82 These Informations by significatory Fires, have been of Ancient Use. 1663 OWEN *Vind. Animadv.* Wks. 1851 XIV. 430 Hadrian.. refused to receive him into the society of patriarchs upon his sending of his significatory epistle. 1831 KEIGHTLEY *Mythol.* 68 His name appears to denote invisibility, significatory of the nature of the realm over which he ruled. 1880 *19th Cent.* Sept. 430 The significatory relation between a substantive and its.. verb.

**B.** *sb.* A thing significative. *rare.*

1660 JER. TAYLOR *Worthy Communicant* i. 42 Here being (as in baptisme) a double significatory of the spirit, a word and a signe.., it is certain he will joyn in this ministration.

**signifi'catrix.** *Astrol.* [L. fem. form corresponding to *significator*.] = SIGNIFICATOR 1 a.

1647 LILLY *Chr. Astrol.* lxxiii. 421 The ☽ her Significatrix [being] neer the ☉. 1653 R. SANDERS *Physiogn.* 152 The Moon is.. commonly significatrix in Flegmatick nativities.

**significatum** (sɪgnɪfɪ'kɑːtəm). *Linguistics* and *Semiotics.* [L., neut. sing. pa. pple. of *significāre* to signify.] That which is signified or denoted; *spec.* = SIGNIFIÉ. Opp. SIGNIFICANS.

1865 S. HODGSON *Time & Space* ii. 44 It is of the utmost importance in reasoning to distinguish which kind of object or significatum it is which is expressed, or concealed, by a word or set of words. 1946 C. MORRIS *Signs, Lang. & Behavior* 17 Those conditions which are such that whatever fulfills them is a denotatum will be called the significatum of the sign. 1964 [see SIGNIFICANS]. 1974 G. LEECH *Semantics* v. 73 The set of conditions (e.g. the qualities of being edible, tasty, nourishing) which make the bone a denotatum of $S_1$ [*sc.* a buzzer sound] constitute the *significatum* of the sign.

**sig'nificature.** *rare*⁻¹. = SIGNIFICANCE 1.

1855 McCOSH *Div. Govt.* II. i. (ed. 4) 124 The morphological significature of the limbs of vertebrate animals has likewise been determined by Professor Owen.

‖**significavit** (sɪgnɪfɪ'keɪvɪt). *Eccles. law.* [L., 3rd sing. perf. indic. of *significāre* to SIGNIFY. Cf. OF. *significavit* (Godef.).] A form of writ employed in ecclesiastical cases; *spec.* one formerly issued by Chancery for the arrest of an excommunicated person; also, the bishop's certificate on which such a writ is based.

*c* 1386 CHAUCER *Prol.* 664 Of cursing oghte ech gilty man him drede.. And also war him of a significavit. 1559 *Boke Presidentes* 14 b, The fourme of a Sygnyficauit to the Metropolytane of the prouins vpon a newe foundacyon of a byshopriche. 1562–3 *Act 5 Eliz.* c. 23 §6 After any Significavit being of Recorde in the sayd Courte of Chancerie, the tenour of suche Significavit by Mittimus shalbee sent [etc.]. 1607 MIDDLETON *Phœnix* II. iii, No, No I say; if it bee for defect of Apparance, take me out a speciall Significauit. *a* 1683 J. OWEN *True Nat. Gosp. Ch.* x. (1689) 216 Of what use a Significavit and Capias may be in this case I know not. 1714 BURNET *Hist. Ref.* III. III. v. 261 He sent a Significavit of some Heretics to be delivered to the Secular Arm. 1767 BURN *Eccl. Law* II. 206 At the common law, a certificate of the bishop, whereupon a significavit was to be granted, ought to express the cause. 1881 *Daily News* 17 Jan. 5/1 The first point taken.. was that the Judge.. had no power to enforce obedience to an inhibition issued under the Act by the process of significavit.

**sig'nifics.** [f. SIGNIFIC-ANCE, on the analogy of forms in *-ics* (see -IC 2). Introduced by Lady Welby in 1896.] A proposed science and educational method based upon the importance of realizing the exact significance of terms and conceptions, and their influence on thought and life.

The terms *signific(al* adjs., *significally* adv., and *significian* sb., have also been employed.

1896 LADY WELBY in *Mind* (Jan.) 32 Taking advantage of the child's endless store of interest and curiosity, it ought to be easy to make 'Significs' or 'Sensifics' the most attractive of studies. 1903 —— *Ibid.* 161 Significs, then, will bring us the philosophy of Significance, i.e. a raising of our whole conception of meaning to a higher and more efficient level.

‖**signifié** (siɲifje). *Linguistics* and *Semiotics.* [Fr., pa. pple. of *signifier* to signify.] A concept or meaning as opposed to its expression in a physical medium (phonetic, graphic, etc.); the semantic element of a sign. Opp. SIGNIFIANT.

[1916: see SIGNIFIANT.] 1939 [see SAUSSUREAN *a.*]. 1947, etc. [see SIGNIFIANT]. 1963 J. LYONS *Structural Semantics* iii. 41 Here it may be noted that there is no need whatsoever to posit a common conceptual 'signifié', or 'meaning', to account for identity of application between different languages.

**'signified,** *ppl. a.* (*sb.*) [f. SIGNIFY *v.*]

**A.** *ppl. a.* Indicated.

1638 W. MOUNTAGU in *Buccleuch MSS.* (Hist. MSS. Comm.) I. 277 God fit us for the signified time. 1644 MILTON *Areop.* (Arb.) 33 More gently.. then other Courts.. would have endur'd the least signifi'd dislike. 1786 A. GIB *Sacr. Contempl.* I. 33 A signified and sealed promise of eternal life.

**B.** *absol.* as *sb.* That which is indicated; *Linguistics* and *Semiotics* = SIGNIFIÉ (opp. SIGNIFIER b).

1939 L. H. GRAY *Foundations of Lang.* 16 In the speaker's mind a concept arises... This concept is termed the *signified*. 1954, etc. [see SIGNIFIER b].

**'signifier.** [f. as prec. + -ER¹.] **a.** One who or that which signifies; a significator.

1532 MORE *Confut. Tindale* Wks. 383/2 He meaneth yᵗ.. yᵉ sacrament.. is no cause thereof.. but only a bare signyfier & a shewer therof. 1586 LUPTON *1000 Notable Things* §59 Whosoeuer falles sicke in that yere wherein there is an Eclipse, and the Signifiers of the sayd Eclipse be in the Ascendent [etc.]. 1607 *Schol. Disc. agst. Antichr.* 97 It is God who is the signifier vnto vs of things spirituall. 1624 [see SIGNIFYING *ppl. a.*]. 1668 CULPEPPER & COLE *Barthol. Anat.* III. vii. 143 It hath Muscles, which Platenis terms the signifiers of the Affections of the Mind.

**b.** *Linguistics* and *Semiotics.* = SIGNIFIANT. Opp. SIGNIFIED *sb.*

1954 U. WEINREICH *Languages in Contact* ii. 9 It becomes possible for the bilingual to interpret two signs whose semantemes, or signifieds, he has identified as a compound sign with a single signified and two signifiers, one in each language. 1960 W. BASKIN tr. *de Saussure's Course in Gen. Linguistics* I. i. 67 The bond between the signifier and the signified is arbitrary. 1967 LAVERS & SMITH tr. *Barthes's Elements of Semiology* III. 65 The commutation test consists of artificially introducing a change in the plane of expression (signifiers) and in observing whether this change brings about a correlative modification on the plane of content (signifieds). 1973 *Screen* Spring/Summer 89 In a great many cases the term 'form' designates the film *signifier*.. and the term 'content' its *signified*. 1976 T. EAGLETON *Crit. & Ideology* iii. 72 History, one might say, is the *ultimate* signifier of literature, as it is the ultimate signified. 1977 A. SHERIDAN tr. *Lacan's Écrits* iii. 69 The symptom is here the signifier of a signified repressed from the consciousness of the subject. 1979 *Dædalus* Summer 72 He has only to offer the Signifier, 'Lie'—which could mean 'tell an untruth'—for Othello to snatch the Signified, 'lie with'.

**c.** *U.S. slang* (chiefly *Blacks'*). One who boasts or makes insulting remarks or insinuations, esp. in an attempt to exceed others in exaggeration.

1962 *Jrnl. Amer. Folklore* July–Sept. 212 The monkey is a 'signifier', and one of the methods he uses for inflaming the lion is to indicate that the elephant has been 'sounding' on the lion. 1965 H. GOLD *Man who was not with It* xxii. 204 When he bragged like any carnie signifier, then I wondered where and why I was going. 1972 J. MARYLAND in T. Kochman *Rappin' & Stylin' Out* 209 The following verbal play is indicative of the type that might be found in any of a number of shine parlors.. or street corners where the signifiers can be found congregating each day.

†**signifure.** *Obs. rare.* [app. a. OF. *signifeure, f. *signifier* to SIGNIFY.] Signification, sign.

*c* 1450 *Coventry Myst.* (Shaks. Soc.) 200 My baptyme is but signifure Of his baptyme. *Ibid.* 367 Have not prophetys.. Spoke be tokenys in signifure That Cryste xuld deye for ȝour valure?

**signify** ('sɪgnɪfaɪ), *v.* Also 3–5 signe- (3, 5 singne-), 4–6 signy-; 4–6 sygni- (5 sygne-, syni-), 5–6 sygny- (5 syngny-); and 4 -fi, 3–5 -fie, 4–6 -fye. [ad. F. *signifier* (12th c., = Prov. *signifiar, -ficar*, Sp. and Pg. *significar*, It. *significare*), ad. L. *significāre*, f. *signum* SIGN *sb.*]

**1. a.** *trans.* To be a sign or symbol of; to represent, betoken, mean.

*c* 1250 *Kent. Serm.* in *O.E. Misc.* 27 þet Gold þet is bricht.. signefieth þe gode beleaue þet is bricht ine þe gode cristenemannes herte. *a* 1340 HAMPOLE *Psalter* Prol., þis boke is distyngid in thris fyfty psalmes, in þe whilk thre statis of cristin mannys religion is sygnifyd. 1402 *Pol. Poems* (Rolls) II. 56 Foure angels singnefien foure general synnes. 1470–85 MALORY *Arthur* XIII. xiv. 631 The two knyghtes sygnefyen the two dedely synnes. 1560 DAUS tr. *Sleidane's Comm.* 65 b, This signifieth my body. 1597 HOOKER *Eccl. Pol.* v. lviii. §2 The secret grace which they [the sacraments] signifie and exhibit. 1611 BEAUM. & FL. *Philaster* I. i, Then took he up his Garland and did shew, What every flower as Country people hold, Did signifie. 1687 DRYDEN *Hind & P.* I. 424 For what is signify'd and understood, Is, by her own confession, flesh and blood. 1729 BUTLER *Serm.* Wks. 1874 II. 56 These words are intended to signify certain forms of civility. 1753 HOGARTH *Anal. Beauty* xi, The arrows [of Apollo] may be allowed to signify the sun's rays. 1869 RUSKIN *Q. Air* §8 It may be easy to prove that the ascent of Apollo in his chariot signifies nothing but the rising of the sun.

*absol.* 1533 FRITH *Answ. More* (1829) 331 Now, if they be signs, then they do signify, and are not the very thing itself. 1652 GAULE *Magastrom.* 228 Every voyce, therefore, that is significative, first of all signifies by the influence of the cœlestial harmony.

**b.** To betoken, foreshow, indicate as something that is to take place. Also *absol.*

13.. *K. Alis.* 596 (Laud MS.), þe eye rounde shal signifie þat he shal habbe seignorye Of þis rounde myddell erd. 1390 GOWER *Conf.* I. 306 A Raven, be whom yit men mai Take evidence, whan he crieth, That som mishapp it signefieth. *c* 1440 *York Myst.* xv. 15 Or he be borne in burgh hereby,.. A sterne shulde schyne and signifie, With lightfull lemes. *a* 1450 *Knt. de la Tour* (1868) 11, Y wille shewe you what youre auision signifiethe. *c* 1475 *Brut* (1908) 603 þere aperyd in þe ffirmament a gret sterre,.. which synified gret sorw, & myschef þat fylle aftyrward. 1530 PALSGR. 718/1, I sawe a marvaylouse thyng in the ayre yesterday what so ever it dothe signifye. 1665 COWLEY in Johnson *L.P.* (1868) 8 What this signifies, or may come to in time, God knows; if it be ominous it can end in nothing less than hanging.

**2.** Of words, etc.: To have the import or meaning of; to mean, denote.

*a* 1300 *Cursor M.* 22988 Ierom sais.. þat Iosaphat mai signifi Vr lauerd dome. *a* 1400 *Pistill of Susan* 287 What signefyes, gode sone, þese sawes þat þou seis? 1432–50 tr. *Higden* (Rolls) II. 151 For *dal* in the langage of theyme signifiethe parte. *c* 1510 MORE *Picus* Wks. 18/1 This name Jesus signifieth a sauioure. 1610 HOLLAND *Camden's Brit.* (1637) 204, I have heard likewise, that *Caer* in the Syriack tongue, signified, *a Citie*. 1696 WHISTON *Th. Earth* II. (1722) 173 The very Name of Typhon.. signifies a Deluge or Inundation. 1770 J. CLUBBE *Misc. Tracts* II. 141 Which is expressed by a word in the Hebrew, that signifies *to initiate*. 1837 P. KEITH *Bot. Lex.* 40 The autumn is designated by a term signifying the fall of the leaf. 1876 TAIT *Rec. Adv. Phys. Sci.* (ed. 3) 365 We now employ the term *Energy* to signify the power of doing work.

*absol.* 1668 H. MORE *Div. Dial.* IV. xiii. (1713) 315 You are to understand.. that the Kingdom of God in the New Testament signifies variously. 1681 T. FLATMAN *Heraclitus Ridens* No. 66 (1713) II. 161 Conscience and Honesty are general Words, and signify, according to the mind of the Speaker.

**3. a.** To make known, intimate, announce, declare.

1297 R. GLOUC. (Rolls) 3233 Me cluped him Vter pendragon.. & þat was to singnefie þat merlin him clupede dragon in is prophecye. 1382 WYCLIF *Acts* xi. 28 Oon of hem.. signyfiede bi the spirit a greet hungir to comynge in al the roundnesse of erthis. *c* 1400 *Rom. Rose* 7165 Thus myche wole our book signifie, That while Petre hath maistrie May never Johan shewe welle his myght. 1513 DOUGLAS *Æneid* VII. v. 141 The self stranger, quham fatale destane Signifyit to cum furth of ane wncouth stede To be his son in law. 1560 DAUS tr. *Sleidane's Comm.* 228 It is reported not onlie in Germany, but also sygnyfyed oute of Italye, and other places. 1604 E. G[RIMSTONE] *D'Acosta's Hist. Indies* VI. v. 442 A man of iudgement may aske, how they could signifie their conceptions by figures. 1663 GERBIER *Counsel* d 5,

When no living creature was come from Europe into that part of America to signifie that newes. **1749** FIELDING *Tom Jones* (1775) III. 69 The 'squire and the parson..were smoaking their pipes together, when the arrival of the lady was first signified. **1781** GIBBON *Decl. & F.* xix. (1787) II. 132 His first step was to signify a concise and haughty mandate. **1837** LOCKHART *Scott* III. x. 324 In compliance with Scott's wish as signified in the letter last quoted. **1884** *Graphic* 16 Aug. 162/3 Her Majesty has signified her intention of subscribing 200*l.* to the Building Fund.

**b.** Const. *to* (†*unto*).

*c* **1430** LYDG. *Min. Poems* (Percy Soc.) 127 To signefie to pope and to prelate, How this world is a thurghfare ful of woo. **1490** CAXTON *Eneydos* xvii. 65 He..stroof wyth hymself by what wayes he myghte signyfie it vnto her..for to gyue her lesse sorowe. **1560** DAUS tr. *Sleidane's Comm.* 226 b, The Duke of Saxon and the Lantzgrave immediately signifye to themperour by letters the whole matter. **1597** MORLEY *Introd. Mus.* Ded., To publish these labors of mine vnder your name..to signifie unto the world my thankfull mind. **1605** CAMDEN *Rem., Allusions* (1623) 140 It was also signified vnto him, they were borne in..Northumberland. **1689** *Col. Rec. Pennsylv.* I. 300 He thought they were obliged to yᵉ Govr. for signifying these things to them. **1776** ADAM SMITH *W.N.* I. ii. (1904) I. 15 Nobody ever saw one animal, by its gestures and natural cries, signify to another, this is mine, that yours. **1855** MACAULAY *Hist. Eng.* xviii. IV. 162 A prince who obstinately refused to comply with the general wish of his people signified to him by his Parliament.

†**4.** To compare, liken *to* something. *Obs.*

**1456** SIR G. HAYE *Law Arms* (S.T.S.) 284 The quhyte colour..is signyfyit to the vertu of puritee. **1470–85** MALORY *Arthur* XVII. ix. 703 Wel oughte oure lord be sygnefyed to an herte.

†**5.** To hint at. *Obs. rare.*

**1513** MORE *Rich. III* (1883) 70 Other thinges, which the said worshipful doctor rather signified then fully explaned.

†**6.** To notify or inform (a person). *Obs.*

**1523** LD. BERNERS *Froiss.* I. lxxxvi. 108 Sir Gaultier of Manny sent certayne messangers to the kyng of Englande, signyfieng hym howe [etc.]. **1566** in Marsden *Court Adm.* (Selden) II. 135 Plezeth your..Lordshipp to be signyfied that I have receivid your..writ of supersedeas to me dyrectid. **1610** HEYWOOD *Gold. Age* III. i, Messengers dispatch'd to signifie My sonne of our distresse. [**1690** LOCKE *Hum. Und.* II. xiv. §23 Without some regular periodical Returns, we could not..signify others the Length of any Duration.]

**7.** *intr.* To be of importance or consequence; to have significance; to avail or matter: **a.** With advs., as *much*, *little*, *nothing*, or in questions with *what*.

**1661** MARVELL *Corr.* Wks. (Grosart) II. 58 The House left Liddall to prosecute him at law, but I believe it will not signify much. **1686** tr. *Chardin's Trav. Persia* 33 But it signify'd little. *a* **1715** BURNET *Own Time* (1724) II. 38 His speech signified nothing towards the saving of himself. **1757** FOOTE *Author* I, Lord! what signifies carrying such a lumb'ring thing about? **1818** SCOTT *Hrt. Midl.* iii, 'It signifies little,' replied Captain Porteous; 'your pain will be soon at an end'. **1845** M. PATTISON *Ess.* (1889) I. 27 Condemned Praetextatus must be, and what did it signify by what semblance of law or justice? **1878** BROWNING *La Saisiaz* 30 What signifies repugnance? Truth is truth howe'er it strike.

**b.** Without qualifying word.

**1677** W. HUGHES *Man of Sin* II. iii. 48 Is he not made to stand by as a Cypher, when she alone must signifie in all these Devotions? **1743** BULKELEY & CUMMINS *Voy. S. Seas* 14 The Captain's Answer was, It does not signify. **1762–71** H. WALPOLE *Vertue's Anecd. Paint.* (1786) III. 113 The anecdotes of Cooper's life are few; nor does it signify; his works are his history. **1817** LADY GRANVILLE *Lett.* (1894) I. 91 His eye is still bloodshot, but nothing to signify. **1894** BARING-GOULD *Kitty Alone* II. 156 There was no metal to signify at the butt-end. **1903** SOMERVILLE & 'ROSS' *All on Irish Shore* iii. 75 'Did many people say it?' asked Mr Gunning... 'Oh, no one whose opinion signified!' retorted Fanny Fitz. **1930** A. P. HERBERT *Water Gipsies* ii. 16 Don't worry, Fred. It don't signify.

**8.** *intr. U.S. slang* (chiefly *Blacks'*). To boast or brag; to make insulting remarks or insinuations.

**1932** *Evening Sun* (Baltimore) 9 Dec. 31/5 *Signify*, to pretend to have knowledge of a matter or subject in which one is poorly informed. **1935** Z. N. HURSTON *Mules & Men* I. vii. 161 'Aw, woman, quit tryin' to signify.' 'Ah kin signify all Ah please, Mr. Nappy-chin.' **1948** *Common Ground* Summer 42/2 He was signifying and getting his revenge through songs. **1968** *Down Beat* 7 Mar. 38/3 One night Billie brought the personal element into focus by 'signifying', which in Harlemese means making a series of pointed but oblique remarks apparently addressed to no one in particular, but unmistakable in intention in such a close-knit circle. **1969** C. MITCHELL *Lang. Behavior in Black Urban Community* iii. 96, I wasn't signifying at her, but..if the shoe fits, wear it. **1973** A. DUNDES *Mother Wit* 141/2 A sample of some of the special techniques and forms of extended word play should convince even the most adamant sceptic that no black child who can signify or play the dozens can rightly be called lacking in verbal skills.

**'signifying,** *vbl. sb.* [f. prec. + -ING¹.]

**a.** Signification, intimation, indication.

**13..** *K. Alis.* 587 (Laud MS.), þe kyng..had þerof dotaunce,..And bad hem telle of whiche þing It mi3th be signifieyng? **1382** WYCLIF *1 Mac.* vii. 45 Thei sungen in trumpis after hem with signyfiyngus. *c* **1450** LOVELICH *Merlin* 2868 Thanne of merlyne often axede þe kyng what of the dragouns was þe signefyeng. **1535** COVERDALE *Isaiah* xx. 3 It is a token and signifienge of the thinge, that after thre yeare shal come vpon Egipte and Ethiopia. **1580** HOLLYBAND *Treas. Fr. Tong*, *Denoncement*, a signifying, a declaring. **1664** H. MORE *Myst. Iniq.* 33 Signes appropriated to the signifying of that honour we owe to God.

**b.** *U.S. slang* (chiefly *Blacks'*). The act of boasting, baiting, insulting, or making insinuations. Also *attrib.*

**1959** A. ANDERSON *Lover Man* 21 'Y'all hush your signifying,' I said. 'That there's a *lady*, and I won't have y'all signifying 'bout her like that.' **1964** *Amer. Folk Music Occasional* I. 75 'Signifying' is a children's device, and is severely 'put down' by adults. **1970** [see JONING *vbl. sb.*]. **1974** H. L. FOSTER *Ribbin', Jivin', & Playin' Dozens* v. 206 Mezzrow describes a signifying scene in Big John's bar in Harlem. **1977** *Maledicta* Summer 15 Young blacks have verbal contests like this in anti-family insults, called *sounding* or *signifying*.

**'signifying,** *ppl. a.* [-ING².] **a.** That signifies or denotes; significant. †***signifying figure, number***: (see SIGNIFICANT *a.* 2 b).

**1542** RECORDE *Gr. Artes* (1575) 43 Of those ten one doth signifie nothing... The other nyne are called Signifying figures. **1579** FULKE *Heskins' Parl.* 69 The same offering.. is called the passion..of Christ,..in a signifying mysterie. **1624** BEDELL *Lett.* xii. 161 If..you finde you haue taken manie nullities for signifying numbers, manie smaller signifiers for greater; correct the totall. **1644** BULWER *Chirol.* 2 There is a signifying voyce in the naturall signes of the Hand.

**b.** *U.S. slang* (chiefly *Blacks'*). That boasts, insults, or makes insinuations.

**1956** M. STEARNS *Story of Jazz* (1957) i. 11 The language is Creole French and the New Orleans Creoles call it a 'signifying song'. In spite of its gaiety and rhumba-like rhythms, this song cuts two ways and the *sali dame* (dirty lady) to which it is addressed is about to have her reputation shredded. **1969** *Negro Digest* Sept. 14 *Signifying* poetry holds a special fascination for me. **1974** H. L. FOSTER *Ribbin', Jivin', & Playin' Dozens* v. 207 Deep down in the jungle where the coconuts grow/Lived the signifyingest motherfucker that the world ever know.

**signing** ('saɪnɪŋ), *vbl. sb.* [f. SIGN *v.*¹ + -ING¹.]

**1. a.** The action of making or appending one's signature; confirmation by signature.

**1611** COTGR., *Signature*, a signature, signing, subscribing. **1655** *Nicholas Papers* (Camden) II. 329 Since the signeing of my letter I received yours of Jun. 1st. **1711** STEELE *Spect.* No. 82 ¶1 My Steward brings his Receipt ready for my Signing. **1771** LUCKOMBE *Hist. Print.* 102 A patent ready drawn for queen Elizabeth's signing. **1809** R. LANGFORD *Introd. Trade* 20 The signing and endorsement must be attested by one witness. **1855** MACAULAY *Hist. Eng.* xvii. IV. 104 The signing of the treaty was deferred till the Lords Justices..should arrive.

**b.** With adverbs, as ***signing-in, -off, -on, -out, -up.*** Also *attrib.*

**1925** PATERSON & WEBSTER *Man. Locomotive Running Shed Management* viii. 103 The signing-on times of cleaners are arranged with due regard to the finishing times of the engines they are required to clean. **1948** H. INNES *Blue Ice* iii. 77 He gave the signing-off whistle..then our attention was called back to the radio. **1950** *Sport* 7–11 Apr. 14/3 He is Allenby Chilton,..to whom Liverpool gave a trial before the United engaged him, for a £10 signing-on fee, in 1938. **1965** 'T. HINDE' *Games of Chance* II. iv. 203 The purpose of the signing-in book..is to ascertain that all staff are arriving punctually. **1968** *Brit. Med. Bull.* XXIV. 222/1 The computer equivalent of the signing out inspection of the report by the laboratory staff. **1973** *Guardian* 23 May 6/8 There is no signing-on at the new job centre. **1974** HAWKEY & BINGHAM *Wild Card* xiv. 124 A laxness among certain members of staff regarding signing-out procedures for items drawn from stock. **1976** E. DUNPHY *Only a Game?* v. 159 The signing-on fee is crucial in football these days. **1981** J. SCOTT *Distant View of Death* xii. 162 Signing in and signing out meant nothing to Rosher... He simply worked.

**2.** *Eccl.* The action of making the sign of the cross.

**1782** PRIESTLEY *Corrupt. Chr.* II. VII. 84 They made several signings with the cross. **1877** J. D. CHAMBERS *Divine Worship* 362 The number and time of these Signings certainly varied.

**3.** *transf.* One who has signed a contract.

**1974** *Motor Cycle* 23 Mar. 10/6 (*caption*) Hackney's new signing, Norwegian Dag Lovaas (left) chats with Kings Lynn international Malcolm Simmons. **1977** *Times* 4 Aug. 6/6 Macdonald, a £330,000 buy from Newcastle..and Hudson, a £200,000 signing from Stoke..were sent home.. because of alleged misconduct on the tour.

**'signing,** *ppl. a.* [-ING².] That signs; entitled to sign; esp. ***signing officer*** (see quot. 1867).

**1805** COLLINGWOOD 28 Oct. in Nicolas *Disp. Nelson* (1846) VII. 219 Signed by yourself, First Lieutenant and signing Officers. **1867** SMYTH *Sailor's Word Bk.* 624 A document..certified by the signing officer and the surgeon. *Ibid.* 626 *Signing officers*, the captain, senior lieutenant, master and purser (now paymaster).

**signior,** etc.: see SIGNOR.

**signioresse,** variant of SEIGNORESS.

**signless** ('saɪnlɪs), *a.* [f. SIGN *sb.* + -LESS.]

**1.** Destitute of a sign, sign-board, or sign-post.

**1684** S. G. *Angl. Spec.* 482 Their Signless Houses are a Sign of Rich and Eminent inhabitants. **1887** HISSEY *Holiday on Road* 190 The modern hotel, of course, is signless. **1903** *Smart Set* IX. 110 That signless, dusty road.

**2.** *Math.* Of quantities: Having no sign of direction; having no distinction of positive or negative.

**1875** STEWART & TAIT *Unseen Universe* iii. §97 We now deal with quantities which cannot possess direction,..and are therefore all to be treated..as signless quantities... Now mass is of course a signless quantity.

**3.** Making no sign; motionless.

**1856** MRS. BROWNING *Aur. Leigh* VIII. 595 Poems.. Which moved me in secret, as the sap is moved In still March-branches, signless as a stone.

**sign-manual.** [SIGN *sb.* + MANUAL *a.* 1.]

**1.** An autograph signature (*esp.* that of the sovereign) serving to authenticate a document.

**1428** *E.E. Wills* 83 And þerto I point my signet and my syne manuell. **1459** *Rolls Parlt.* V. 351/2 All the Lordes.. and every of theym..settyng therto his Seale and Signe manuell, as here under apperith. **1536** *Wardr. Acc. Hen. VIII* in *Archæologia* IX. 252 Geven under oure signe manuelle, at oure castille of Wyndesore. **1560** in Feuillerat *Revels Q. Eliz.* (1908) 112 Thiese our Lettres signed with our signemanuell shalbe your sufficient warraunt. **1648** CHAS. I *Let.* in Thoms *Notes on Combe Martin* (1902) 37 Giuen under our Sign Manuel At Court at Newport. **1688** *Pennsylv. Arch.* I. 103 Untill Wee shall send you New Orders under Our sign manual. **1724** SWIFT *Drapier's Lett.* iii. Wks. 1751 VIII. 325 Orders, and Directions,..have been issued under the Royal Sign Manual. **1764** T. HUTCHINSON *Hist. Mass.* (1765) 344 They were distinguished by King James.., by a letter under his sign manual. **1818** SCOTT *Let.* in *Lockhart* (1837) IV. iv. 113 The Crown-room..was opened by certain Commissioners, under authority of a sign-manual. **1863** H. COX *Instit.* III. vi. 671 The Royal sign-manual, or signature of the Sovereign, is usually written on the upper-left-hand corner of the instrument. **1898** BODLEY *France* III. iii. II. 142 A personage..who, by his sign-manual, can soften the severity of the revenue officials.

*fig.* **1894** MRS. DYAN *Man's Keeping* (1899) 58 The handshake, sign-manual of fealty.., did not pass between them.

**2.** A sign made with the hand or hands.

**1841** CATLIN *N. Amer. Ind.* (1844) I. xvi. 116 Commands which were uniformly given by signs manual.

†**'signment**¹. *Obs.* In 5 si(g)ne-, 6 sygnement. [Aphetic form of ASSIGNMENT: cf. SIGN *v.*²] Assignment, appointment.

**1429** *Pol. Poems* (Rolls) II. 147 He is redy to delyvir hym, and not abasshe, By signement of the kyng, tyme and place. **1479–81** *Rec. St. Mary at Hill* (1905) 106 Item, payd to Nevell the iremonger at the synement of the parysshe for diuerse stuffe boght of hym. **1525** LD. BERNERS *Froiss.* II. xxxix. 121 They were payde of theyr wages, or had suffycyent sygnement, so yᵗ they were pleased.

†**'signment**². *Obs.*⁻¹ [f. SIGN *v.*¹] A body of persons who have signed a document or agreement.

*a* **1660** *Contemp. Hist. Irel.* (Ir. Archæol. Soc.) I. 223 They name the former signment the Assembly of Ireland both Nobles and Comons;..all the nobilitie of the faction did signe to this Henritian oathe.

‖**signor** ('siːnjɔː(r)), *sb.* Also 6–9 signior (7 -iour, -ier). [It. *signor*, reduced form of *signore* SIGNORE, = Sp. *señor*, Pg. *senhor*, F. *seigneur*:—L. *seniōr-em*, acc. of *senior* SENIOR *a.* and *sb.* See also SEIGNEUR and SEIGNIOR.]

**1.** In Italian use, or with reference to Italians: A term of respect placed before the name of a man in addressing him or speaking of him, now equivalent to the English 'Mr.'

**1584–7** GREENE *Tritameron of Loue* II. Wks. (Grosart) III. 140 By my faith (Signior Aretino) you haue found such a knot in a Rysh as will bee so hard to vntye as Gordias was. **1596** SHAKS. *Tam. Shr.* II. i. 85 A thousand thankes signior Gremio. **1605** B. JONSON *Volpone* I. i, Signior Coruino, come most wisht for! **1736** *Gentl. Mag.* VI. 648/1 These are the Thoughts of Signior Muffei. **1756–7** tr. *Keysler's Trav.* (1760) III. 350 The houses of..the signiors Verzi, Pompeii, and Pellegrini. **1818** SHELLEY *Tasso* 3 Did you inform his Grace that Signor Pigna Waits with state papers for his signature? *Ibid.* 13 O trust to me, Signor Malpiglio, Those nods [etc.]. **1863** *Chambers's Encycl.* V. 657/1 Ratazzi..was succeeded in office by Signor Farini.

*fig.* **1630** J. TAYLOR (Water P.) *Wks.* D dd i, Mounsieur Claret, and sweet Signior Sacke.

**b.** Used without the name, as a form of address, equivalent to 'sir' in English.

**1590** SHAKS. *Com. Err.* IV. i. 36 Good Signior take the stranger to my house. **1599** B. JONSON *Ev. Man out of Humour* IV. iii, O but Signior, had you such a wife as mine is. **1797** MRS. RADCLIFFE *The Italian* i, The stranger..said, 'Signor, your steps are watched'. **1842** LOVER *Handy Andy* iv, 'Isn't one fight a day enough for you, signor?' said the doctor. **1863** 'OUIDA' *Held in Bondage* (1870) 68 Thank you, signor, a thousand thanks.

**c.** An Italian gentleman, *esp.* a singer.

**1779** SHERIDAN *Critic* I. i, Haven't we the Signors and Signoras calling here, sliding their smooth semibreves? **1782** V. KNOX *Ess.* (1819) II. cxvi. 290 The door is always open to player signiors and signioras.

**2.** A person of note or distinction; one having rank or authority; a gentleman or nobleman; an overlord. See also GRAND SIGNIOR.

*a* **1577** SIR T. SMITH *Commw. Eng.* (1609) 12 Amonge whom there is no right Lawe nor Commonwealth compact but onely the will of the Lord and Signior. **1630** MASSINGER *Picture* II. ii, You *Signiers* Haue no businesse with the soldier. **1632** LITHGOW *Trav.* II. 63 The commodity of which redounds yearely to the Venetians, for they are Signiors thereof. **1668** R. L'ESTRANGE *Vis. Quevedo* (1708) 50 You know they are Cavaliers and Signiors already, and now (forsooth) they have an Itch upon them to be Princes. **1748** SMOLLETT *Roderick Random* lxvi, [He] promised to procure for us the company of an English signior. **1803** SYD. SMITH *Wks.* (1859) I. 56/2 The great mass of territorial proprietors in Denmark are the signiors, possessing fiefs with very extensive privileges. **1885** J. PAYN *Talk of Town* I. 47 Wise and reverend signors may well have learnt by experience to take trifling annoyances with equanimity.

†**signor**, *v. Obs.*⁻¹ In 6 signour. [a. OF. *signourer*, *seignorer*, etc., f. *seignor* SEIGNEUR.] *intr.* To have lordship.

**1559** *Kal. Shepherds* xxxviii. (Wally) k v b, Leo hath the great trees, that is to say he signoureth ouer them.

‖**signora** (si'ɲora). Also 7–8 signiora. [It. *signora*, = Sp. *señora*, Pg. *senhora*, a fem. formed on *signore*, etc.: see SIGNOR *sb.*] A term of respect applied to Italian ladies, corresponding to 'Mrs.' and 'Madam' in English; hence (with *a*, *the*, etc.), a lady of Italian nationality.

α. **1636** MASSINGER *Gt. Dk. Florence* IV. i, I am in private to conferre a while With this Signiora. **1654** GAYTON *Pleas. Notes* I. vi. 19 The acts [of] Chivalry of the twenty four Signiora's. **1766** [ANSTEY] *Bath Guide* x, But talks of the Op'ras and his Signiora, Cries bravo, benissimo, bravo, Encora. **1775** *Ann. Reg.* II. 63 Anecdotes of Signiora Gabrieli, the celebrated Opera Singer.

β. **1766** SMOLLETT *Trav.* v. I. 64 An Italian *signora* makes no scruple of telling you [etc.]. **1806** SURR *Winter in London* III. 39 'This is Francis's writing beyond all question,' said the signora. **1821** BYRON in Moore *Life* (1832) V. 262 Got off my horse to walk in an avenue with a Signora for an hour. **1847** C. BRONTË *J. Eyre* xxvii, I sought my ideal of a woman amongst English ladies, French countesses, Italian signoras, and German Gräfinnen. I could not find her.

‖**signore** (si'ɲore). [It., the fuller form of *signor*.] = SIGNOR.

**1594** [see SIGNORY 3]. **1622** PEACHAM *Compl. Gent.* i. 15 In Naples..euery base groome..must be termed Signore. **1641** MILTON *Ch. Govt.* II. i, I know Bilson hath decipher'd us all the galanteries of Signore and Monsignore. **1820** T. S. HUGHES *Trav.* I. ix. 267 That worthy signore was enjoying his siesta. **1856** BOKER *Betrothal* III. iii, I have an airy weapon that can..make our satin signore Grovel for life.

‖**signoria** (siɲo'ria). [It., = Sp. *señoria*, Pg. *senhoria*, F. *seigneurie*: cf. SIGNORY.] The governing body of some of the Old Italian republics, *esp.* that of Venice.

**1549** THOMAS *Hist. Italie* 79 b, All offices of preeminence, as of the Signoria. **1622** in *Crt. & Times Jas. I* (1848) II. 334 The Venetian ambassador gave notice of such a thing.., by order, as he said, from the signoria. **1686** AGLIONBY *Painting Illustr.* 362 When a Fisherman presents the Signoria of Venice with Saint Mary's Ring. **1763** *Brit. Mag.* IV. 327 His Excellency then made his speech to the Doge, and Signoria, in the English language. **1841** W. SPALDING *Italy & It. Isl.* II. 276 Few towns appear to have fared so ill as Siena, in which..for the signoria he also nominated the first set of members.

**signorial** (siː'njɔərɪəl), *a.* [f. SIGNORY + -AL¹. Cf. SEIGNORIAL.] Pertaining to a signory.

**1875** MAINE *Hist. Inst.* v. 123 The legacy from tribal sovereignty to signorial privilege. **1883** SYMONDS *Ital. Byways* iv. 69 They regarded knighthood as a part of their signorial parade.

‖**signorina** (siɲo'rina). [It., dim. of *signora* SIGNORA.] The Italian term of respect applicable to a young unmarried lady.

**1820** T. S. HUGHES *Trav.* I. ii. 42 A long story about a beautiful signorina of ancient times. **1884** F. M. CRAWFORD *Roman Singer* I. 31 The signorina was born here. *Ibid.* 72 My time is yours, signorina.

†**si'gnority.** *Obs. rare.* In 5 sygnyoryte, 6 signioritie, 8 -ty. [Cf. OF. *seignourité* (Godef.), med.L. *senioritas*. See also SEIGN(I)ORITY.] Lordship, government.

*a* **1529** SKELTON *Col. Cloute* 927 They shewe them polytyke, Pretendyng grauyte And sygnyoryte, With all solempnyte. **1547** BALDWIN *Mor. Philos.* 29 The Athenians and Megarenes had made great warre..to haue had the signioritie of his [Solon's] country Salamina. **1792** SIBLY *Occult Sci.* I. 26 Besides these signiorities of the sun, moon and planets, the fixed stars have also their principalities in the heavens.

†'**signorize**, *v. Obs.* Also signiorize. [f. SIGNOR + -IZE, or ad. obs. F. *signoris(s)-*, *signoriz-*, lengthened stem of *sign-*, *se(i)gnorir*, f. *seigneur* SEIGNEUR. See also SEIGNORIZE *v.*]

**1.** *intr.* To rule, reign, have or exercise dominion. Usually const. *in* or *over*.

α. **1594** KYD *Cornelia* III. iii. 212 Now Caesar..Sits signiorizing in her seate. **1612** J. DAVIES (Heref.) *Muse's Sacr.* Wks. (Grosart) II. 49/1 Let that which thou mad'st not, neuer signiorize O'er me that thou hast made. *a* **1658** HEWYT *Serm.* 171 (Todd), At the time that He was to come, Judah must lose the scepter; not then to rule or signiorize in Judah.

β. **1594** KYD *Cornelia* I. 55 So many Nations..Ore whom (saue heauen) nought could signorize. **1613** tr. *Mexia's Treas. Anc. & Mod. Times* 26/2 To the perdition of him [Adam] who had bin Created to Signorize and beare Maistry over all Beastes in the World. **1651** HOWELL *Venice* 24 Upon the Continent of Italie She [Venice] doth Signorize over three entire Provinces.

**b.** With *it*: To play the master. *rare.*

**1611** COTGR., *Faire le dessus*, to domineere, to signorize it.

**2.** *trans.* To govern, control, exercise dominion or rule over (anything).

**1594** KYD *Cornelia* III. ii. 8 Rome, thou are tam'd, and th' earth..Doth laugh to see how thou art signiorizd. **1600** FAIRFAX *Tasso* IV. xlvi, As proud as he, that signoriseth hell. **1602** J. DAVIES (Heref.) *Mirum in Modum* Wks. (Grosart) I. 8/2 There doth shee sit..And by hir might doth signiorize the Minde. *Ibid.* 26/2 Alphons, the tenth that Spaine did signiorize.

Hence †'**signorizing** *vbl. sb.* and *ppl. a. Obs.*

**1588** KYD *Househ. Phil.* Wks. (1901) 261 Admonition.. vttered with more austeritie and signiorising termes. **1593** NASHE *Christ's T.* Wks. (Grosart) IV. 89 Eleazer..was the first that seminarizd thys hope of signiorizing and freedome amongst them. **1609** J. DAVIES (Heref.) *Holy Rood* Wks. (Grosart) I. 26/1 Fraile-Fleshes signiorizing Tyrant, fell.

†'**signorship.** *Obs. rare.* In 7 signior-. [f. SIGNOR *sb.*] The rank or condition of a signor. Used as a form of address.

**1636** MASSINGER *Gt. Dk. Florence* IV. i, 'Tis a device..as shal make your Signiorship know I have not beene your Butlar for nothing. **1637** —— *Guardian* I. i, Make choice Of either title, which your signiorship please.

**signory** ('siːnjərɪ). Forms: α. 5 *Sc.* sigeniery (!), 6 sygneoury, 6–7 signiorie, 6–9 signory. β. 5 *Sc.* signery, 6–7 sygnory (6 syng-), signorie (6 sygn-), 5– signory. [Originally a. OF. *signerie*, *signorie*, etc., var. of *seignorie* (see SEIGNIORY), subsequently influenced by It. *signoria* (see SIGNORIA).]

**1.** Lordship, domination, rule.

α. *c* **1375** *Sc. Leg. Saints* xxxvii. (*Vincent*) 106 Othir til our goddis sacrify & haf riches & sigeniery [*sic*]. **1509** HAWES *Past. Pleas.* XI. (Percy Soc.) 44 Makyng them lese theyr worthy sygneoury. **1594** KYD *Cornelia* III. iii. 107 Th' inextinguible thyrst of signiorie. **1604** T. WRIGHT *Passions* v. §2. 216 His Lord and Maister will give him signiorie and authority over all he possesseth. **1632** W. LITHGOW *Trav.* II. 64 The Signiory thereof belongeth to Venice. **1790** BURKE *Fr. Rev.* 146 This our recognition of a signiory paramount. **1818** HALLAM *Mid. Ages* (1872) I. 423 The same sanction was given to those temporary delegations of the signiory to a prince. *a* **1850** ROSSETTI *Dante & Circle* I. (1874) 232 My heart, my mind, and all my life, Are given in bondage to her signiory.

β. *c* **1375** *Sc. Leg. Saints* xxviii. (*Margaret*) 330 And sa thru his ded mychtely of deid [he] oure-come þe signery. *c* **1440** *Generydes* 6980 He was a man of grete renown, Sowdon of perce with all his signory. **1523** LD. BERNERS *Froiss.* I. xxvii. 41 The ysle of Creth, the which was vnder their sygnorie. **1533** BELLENDEN *Livy* III. xvii. (S.T.S.) II. 17 Quhat signorie, quhat wikkit empire is this..þat ȝe pretend? **1600** HOLLAND *Livy* XXVI. i. 582 To..returne unto their old alleagence and obedience to their wonted signorie of Rome. *a* **1660** *Contemp. Hist. Irel.* (Ir. Archæol. Soc.) II. 166 His.. designe is noe other thinge then the temporall signorie of this distracted kingdome. **1875** MAINE *Hist. Inst.* v. 123 Eldest son after eldest son succeeded to the signory.

**b.** Authority or supremacy expressed in looks or bearing. *rare.*

**1598** YONG *Diana* 243 They sawe two louely Shepherdesses (though by their coye lookes shewing a kinde of signorie and statelinesse aboue any other). **1856** MRS. BROWNING *Aur. Leigh* IV. 300 Among the gallery portraits of our Leighs, We shall not find a sweeter signory Than this pure forehead's.

**2.** A lordship, domain, territory.

α. **1555** EDEN *Decades* (Arb.) 211 The kyngedomes and signiories whiche confine with the sayde sea. **1605** VERSTEGAN *Dec. Intell.* vi. (1628) 181 Their proper Signiories, Lordships or places which they possessed. **1698** FRYER *Acc. E. India & P.* 51 This region of Malabar..is divided into several Petit Signiories. **1796** H. HUNTER tr. *St.-Pierre's Stud. Nat.* (1799) III. 673 They were empowered to receive gifts and bequests of money, houses, lands, signiories, nay even of slaves.

*transf.* **1607** J. DAVIES (Heref.) *Summa Totalis* Wks. (Grosart) I. 11/1 These thrust out Reason of her Signiorie (The Braines) where erst she sate in Siluer Throne.

β. *a* **1533** LD. BERNERS *Huon* cxiv. 404 To conquere agayne your herytage, londys, and sygnoryes. **1598** STOW *Surv.* i. (1603) 3 The state, comunalty or Signory of the Trinobantes. **1613** PURCHAS *Pilgrimage* v. viii. 412 To divide the soile into many Signories and Kingdomes. **1670** MILTON *Hist. Eng.* I. Wks. 1851 III. 15 His Sons..won them Lands and Signories in Germany. **1753** RICHARDSON *Grandison* (1781) V. xxix. 202, I shall take a view of the works projecting by the Duke of Modena, in order to render his little Signory considerable.

†**3.** = SIGNORSHIP. *Obs. rare*⁻¹.

**1594** CAREW *Huarte's Exam. Wits* 225 Signore, your signory shall vnderstand, that souldiers who haue enioyed the libertie of Italy, cannot content themselues to make abode in Spain.

**4.** A governing body, *esp.* that of Venice or other mediæval Italian republic. Cf. SIGNORIA.

**1604** T. WRIGHT *Passions* v. 159 The Arcadian signorie consider..the inhabitants..barbarous, sauage, and wild. **1612** W. SHUTE tr. *Fougasses's Venice* II. 481 A goodly Church..whither the Signory and Clergy doe yeerely goe in procession. **1652** M. NEEDHAM tr. *Selden's Mare Cl.* 99 The Venetians and their Signiory for very many ages have been and are in possession of the aforesaid Gulf. **1756** NUGENT *Gr. Tour, Italy* III. 138 The legislative authority is lodged in the great senate, consisting of the signory, and 400 noblemen. The signory consists of the Doge and twelve other members. **1820** BYRON *Mar. Faliero* I. i. 3 But still the Signory is deep in council. **1837** HALLAM *Hist. Lit.* I. iii. §59 The Palazzo Vecchio, in which the signiory of Florence held their councils. **1873** DIXON *Two Queens* IV. xx. viii. 108, 'I hear on good authority,' said Fisher to the Signory, 'that Cardinal Wolsey is not now in favour of a divorce'.

**sign-post**, *sb.* [SIGN *sb.*]

**1. a.** A post supporting a sign, usually that of an inn or shop.

**1620** FLETCHER *Chances* III. i, If this geer hold, Best hang a sign-post up, to tell the Signiors, Here ye may have lewdness at Liverie. **1642** MILTON *Apol. Smect.* Wks. 1851 III. 258 Hung out like a toling signe-post to call passengers. **1670** *Moral St. Eng.* 92 A good Inn hath very seldome a bad Sign-post. **1711** ADDISON *Spect.* No. 28 ¶3 When did the Lamb and Dolphin ever meet, except upon a Sign-Post? **1784** COWPER *Task* IV. 483 Fell Discord,..Perch'd on the sign-post, holds with even hand Her undecisive scales. **1818** BYRON *Juan* I. ii, [They] fill'd their sign-posts then, like Wellesley now. **1849** MACAULAY *Hist. Eng.* v. I. 634 The signpost of the White Hart Inn served for a gallows. **1876** BANCROFT *Hist. U.S.* III. xix. 521 He..was menaced with being hanged, like Porteus of Edinburgh, upon a sign-post, if he did so.

*fig.* **1889** DOYLE *Micah Clarke* 107 We..were gazing in silence at this sign-post of death, when..a bundle of rags.. at the foot of the gallows began suddenly to move.

**b.** *attrib.* and *Comb.*, as ***sign-post dauber***, ***painter***, ***painting***, ***picture***.

**1677** DRYDEN *To Lee* 51 But how should any sign-post dauber know The worth of Titian or of Angelo? **1682** —— *Medal* Ep., But Sign-post painting will serve the turn to remember a Friend by. **1751** EARL ORRERY *Rem. Swift* (1752) 83 While there remained a sign-post painter in the world. **1779** *Mirror* No. 9 Those same Latin scraps,..which you sometimes hang out by way of sign-post inscription at the top of your paper. **1815** L. SIMOND *Tour Gt. Brit.* II. 216, I never saw such a collection of miserable sign-post pictures any where before.

**2.** A guide- or direction-post, set up to indicate the proper road to a place; a finger-post. Also *fig.* and *attrib.*

**1863** LD. LYTTON *King of Amasis* I. II. iii, The stretched forefinger of a common sign-post. **1889** GRETTON *Memory's Harkback* 149, I came to a signpost directing me to the left. **1961** *Atlanta Constitution* 17 Aug. 5 In the..breathless state of being in love the usual signposts that guide you to lasting and satisfying relationships are sometimes obscured. **1962** *Listener* 6 Dec. 958/2 He therefore studies talk more closely and discovers that..by selecting signpost phrases, he can convey what is being felt by what is unsaid. **1969** I. & P. OPIE *Children's Games* p. viii, Full use has been made of the signposts, clearly marked for those willing to look for them, that are provided by *The Oxford English Dictionary* and *The English Dialect Dictionary*.

So '**signpostless** *a.*, not equipped with or marked by sign-posts.

**1962** *Times* 22 Feb. 14/4 The signpost-less lanes of Surrey. **1968** *Economist* 16 Mar. 12/2 A preposterous, unanalysable, ignorant, signpostless, meandering mess.

'**signpost**, *v.* Also sign-post. [f. prec.] *trans.* To direct or indicate by means of or in the manner of a sign-post; to equip or provide with sign-posts. Also *fig.* Hence '**signposted** *ppl. a.*, '**signposting** *ppl. a.* and *vbl. sb.*

**1895** A. A. GRACE *Maoriland Stories* 105, I shall just sign-post 'em up to the station when they come. **1922** W. J. LOCKE *Tale of Triona* xxiii. 265 The road undulated..with a steeply sloping drop of thirty feet to the valley. Such spots were grimly sign-posted for motorists. **1923** *Daily Mail* 19 May 5 Where the road is not so good and badly needs proper signposting. *Ibid.* 21 May 4 Dartmoor is moderately well signposted. **1930** *Aberdeen Press & Jrnl.* 8 May 5 The R.A.C. propose only to signpost the main arteries. **1938** *Sun* (Baltimore) 16 May 8/1 Even more marked improvements have been made. There are what are called 'sign-posted' reviews. **1946** E. LINKLATER *Private Angelo* viii. 81 They had reconnoitred, by routes that camel-ribs signposted, the farthest Libyan oases. **1953** X. FIELDING *Stronghold* 57 A forbidden area metaphorically signposted 'noli me tangere'. **1955** *Times* 6 Jan. 6/1 They were also signposting a ring road for through traffic avoiding the central London area. **1961** *N. & Q.* Nov. 440/1 There are textual notes at the foot of each page, ludicrously signposted by a system of expanding alphabetical cycles. **1971** P. GRESSWELL *Environment* 104 Some councils are prepared to spend money on signposting. **1975** J. B. HARLEY *O.S. Maps* p. xiii, A principal objective is to indicate what the map user is likely to find on a particular map series and..to signpost what is omitted. **1976** *Howard Jrnl.* XV. I. 39 The different themes and possible groupings of the essays could perhaps have been signposted better to make the reader's task easier. **1978** A. & G. RITCHIE *Anc. Monuments Orkney* 22 This cairn is approached by a signposted path on the N side of the Trumland to Westness road. **1981** *Times* 2 Sept. 21/1 It was as recently as June that the board [of Trusthouse Forte] reported on the six months to last April. This signposted a dreadful year for hotels.

‖**signum** ('sɪgnəm). Pl. signa. [L., see SIGN *sb.*] A mark or sign.

**1848** *Scottish Jrnl. Topogr.* I. 296/2 The sword hilts [are] filagreed over with peculiar signa, probably cabalistic charms for the prevention of witchcraft. **1862** *Chambers's Encycl.* III. 638/2 In addition to his subscription, the notary was formerly in use in Scotland to add his *signum*, which was a flourish of the pen. **1875** STAINER & BARRETT *Dict. Mus. Terms*, *Signa*, characters and signs in mediæval music.

‖**sigri** ('sɪgriː). [Gujarati *sagḍī*.] A fire or stove used for cooking.

**1949** J. R. LAWRENCE *Indian Embers* 56 All day our bedding is spread over wicker cages enclosing a charcoal sigri. **1954** J. MASTERS *Bhowani Junction* 127 The invisible charcoal fumes from the sigri tingled in my nostrils. **1964** M. MALGONKAR *Bend in Ganges* xxxiv. 334 Sundari was bending over the sigri..turning the toast. **1970** 'B. MATHER' *Break in Line* xx. 245 Out here, away from the charcoal *sigri*, the cold was intense.

†**sigrim** (also sigrums), obs. var. ISEGRIM.

*a* **1300** *Vox & Wolf* in Hazl. *E.P.P.* I. 62 Quod the vox: 'Wo is now there? Iche wene hit is Sigrim that ich here'. *c* **1430** LYDG. *Min. Poems* (Percy Soc.) 169 The sleyghti fox ..And sigrums chief wardeyn of the folde.

**sih**, obs. pa. t. of SEE *v.*

**siht(e, sihþe**, obs. ff. SIGHT.

**sihte**, pa. t. of SICHE *v.* to sigh.

**siik, sijk**, obs. ff. SICK *a.*

**sijken**, var. SICK *v.*

‖**sijo** (ˈsiːdʒəʊ). [Korean.] **a.** A type of Korean vocal music. **b.** A Korean lyric poem usu. consisting of twenty-four syllables divided into three lines. Also *attrib.*

**1898** I. L. BIRD *Korea & her Neighbours* xii. 191 There are three classes of Korean vocal music, the first being the *Si-jo* or 'classical' style, *andante tremuloso*, and 'punctuated with drums'. **1954** W. STEVENS *Let.* 9 July (1967) 840 Here are your sijos... The poems are charming, at least to me. But Korean poetry..is a delicacy, like bees' knees and apple hips. **1960** P. HYUN *Voices of Dawn* 28 The metaphysical *sijo* poets. **1971** *Korean Folklore & Classics* III. 86 The satto read sijo silently shaking himself..to forget his tediousness. **1972** *Korea Past & Present* xiv. 319 Kagok is a five-stanza form which is accompanied by an orchestra, whereas Sijo is a three-stanza form without orchestra. But they are similar in the sense that both use Sijo poems as words. **1977** *Korea* (Korean Overseas Information Service, Seoul) 57/3 The most popular Korean poetic form, the *Sijo*.

**sijt**, obs. f. SITE.

**sik**, obs. form of SIC *a.*, SICK, SIKE, SIKH.

**sika**[1] (ˈsiːkə). [ad. Japanese *sika* deer.] A small red deer, *Sika nippon*, native to Japan and eastern China and widely naturalized elsewhere. Also *attrib.*

**1891** in *Cent. Dict.* **1898** *Westm. Gaz.* 25 Feb. 4/3 The elk, the Virginian deer, and the Japanese and Manchurian sikas. **1900** *Q. Rev.* July 202 The Japanese sika, Chinese swamp deer and hybrids live wild in the state forests. **1909** E. PROTHEROE *Handy Nat. Hist.: Mammals* x. 365 The Sika.. is a beautiful brilliant chestnut, thickly spotted with white. **1957** O. BRELAND *Animal Friends & Foes* i. 38 Important deer..include..the sika deer of eastern Asia. **1966** *Punch* 19 Oct. 596/2 The sika-deer of Brownsea Island left its restricted space some years ago for the Dorset mainland. **1978** *Lancashire Life* Nov. 70/1 The last Lord Ribblesdale.. also introduced the Sika deer which roam the district to this day. **1981-2** *Deer Farmer* (N.Z.) Summer 3 But we have farmed other breeds, such as fallow and sika.

‖**sika**[2] (ˈsika). [Bengali, ad. Skr. *śikyà* sling.] A rope hanger for suspending baskets, etc.

**1974** *Observer* (Colour Suppl.) 15 Sept. 40 (Advt.), Sikas are traditionally used in Bangladesh village homes instead of kitchen cupboards. **1979** *Church Times* 26 Oct. 13/3 Jute *sikas* (basket hangers), bags and place-mats from Bangladesh form an attractive part of Traidcraft's range.

**Sikan**, var. SICAN.

**sike, syke** (saɪk), *sb.*[1] *north.* and *Sc.* Forms: α. 4- syke, 6 sy(c)k, 9 seyke. β. 7- sike, 8-9 sick (9 saik). [The northern form repr. OE. *sīc* SITCH. Cf. ON. *sík*, Icel. *síki*, Norw. *sik*, *sike*, Da. *sig* (MDa. *siig*, *sige*), in the same sense.]

**1.** A small stream of water, a rill or streamlet, esp. one flowing through flat or marshy ground, and often dry in summer; a ditch or channel through which a tiny stream flows.

In former times freq. used as a boundary between lands, fields, etc. (cf. sense 2).

[*c* **1169** in Dugdale *Monast. Angl.* (1830) VI. 236 Ex alia parte nigræ quercus, usque ad sicam Polterkeved, quæ cadit in Ring. *a* **1214** *Liber de Melros* I. 78 Usque ad primum sicum ex aquilonali parte de Lilisyhates.]

α. *c* **1330** R. BRUNNE *Chron. Wace* (Rolls) 8165 Sykes do ȝe graue & groupe, þe water þer-inne men schal scoupe. **1375** BARBOUR *Bruce* XI. 300 The sykis alswa thair doune Sall put thame to confusioune. *c* **1425** *Cast. Persev.* 427 in *Macro Plays*, Myth I ryde be sompe & syke,..certis þanne schulde I be fryke. *c* **1480** HENRYSON *Fables*, *Trial Fox* xxxvi, To fetche water this fraudfull foxe furth fure, Sydelingis abak he socht vnto ane syke. **1573** *Nott. Rec.* IV. 152 Stakyng of serteyne plankes in the medowes ouer serteyne syckes. **1596** DALRYMPLE tr. *Leslie's Hist. Scotl.* I. 145 Ouir dykes and dubis, sykes and seuches thay sould spang and leip. **1664-5** *Act 16-17 Chas. II*, c. 11 §1 Forty Acres..in..Thurlby Fenn..are to be left for Lakes and Sykes for the receipt of Waters. **1726** THRELKELD *Stirp. Hibern.* 138 Marsh Marygold..in the small Sykes or watery Plashes of moist Meadows..copiously. **1818** SCOTT *Lett.* II. 4 My lake is but a millpond, my brooks but sykes. *a* **1849** H. COLERIDGE *Poems* (1850) II. 192 He prized the stream that turned the wealthiest mills Less than the syke that trickles down the fell. **1889** RAINE *Hist. Hemingborough* 165 Fenny ground traversed by sykes and ditches.

*attrib.* **1719** *Min. Baron Crt. Stitchill* (S.H.S.) 180 Ground carrying grass tho' never so coarse, such as that called Syke grass.

β. **1611** *N. Riding Rec.* (1884) I. 219 The passage at Noletbridge sike..is decayed and many times very dangerous. **1674** RAY *N.C. Words* 41 A *Sike*: a little Rivulet. **1787** GROSE *Prov. Gloss.*, *Sick*, a small stream or rill. **1811** WILLAN in *Archaeologia* XVII. 157 *Bor-sike*, the name of a place, signifies the cottage by the sike. **1831** HODGSON in Raine *Mem.* (1858) II. 221 The bed of a sike that runs in the direction of the road. **1896** BLASHILL *Sutton-in-Holderness* 13 Certain low marshy channels called 'sikes'.

**b.** A gully; a dip or hollow.

**1859** W. WHITE *Northumbld. & Border* 363 On one of the slopes, a syke—that is a gully—was pointed out to me. **1884** *N. & Q.* 6th Ser. X. 455/1 In Yorkshire *syke* is understood to be a dip in the ground.

†**2.** A stretch of meadow; a field. *Obs. rare.*

**1479** *Priory of Hexham* (Surtees) II. 6 Idem t[enet] ij sykes prati,..Adam del Hyll t[enet] j syk, et r. p. a. ij d. **1641** BEST *Farm. Bks.* (Surtees) 38 The Mount-Sikes is 5 dayworkes, and had in it..seaven score and two grasse cockes..; the waine-way into this close is att the gate a little within the gate of the Greate-Sikes. **1669** WORLIDGE *Syst. Agric.* (1681) 331 A *Sike*, a Quillet or Furrow.

**sike**, *sb.*[2] Now *dial.* Forms: 3 sic, 3-4 sik, 3-5, 9 sike; 4-5 syk(e, 9 *dial.* soik. [var. of SICHE *sb.* Cf. Fris. *sike* a breath.] A sigh.

*a* **1225** *Ancr. R.* 284 Ȝif eni is þet naueð nout þe heorte þus afeited, mid seoruhfule sikes..grede on ure Louerd. *c* **1310** in Wright *Lyric P.* xxxii. 92 Ich have siked moni sik, lemmon, for thin ore. *c* **1374** CHAUCER *Troylus* III. 801 With a sik she sorwfully answerde. *c* **1386** —— *Frankl. T.* 136 Thanne wolde she sitte adoun..And seyn right thus, with sorweful sikes colde. **14..** HOCCLEVE *Minor P.* xxii. 364 Vp he threew an heuy syk, And hire awook. **1878** *N. & Q.* 5th Ser. IX. 396 Her give a great sike, and then died. **1885** BRIERLEY *Ab-o'th-Yate Yankeeland* ii. (E.D.D.), A good soik of relief.

†**b.** Without article: Sighing. *Obs.*

*c* **1250** *Gen. & Ex.* 1239 Ðor sat his moder in sik and sor. *c* **1310** in Wright *Lyric P.* xi. 40 Me thuncheth min herte wol breke a two, for sorewe ant syke. *a* **1400** *Minor Poems fr. Vernon MS.* xxix. 61 Wiþ syk and serwe..Heo souhte wher heo mihte wiþ him mete.

**sike** (saɪk), *v.* Now *dial.* Forms: α. 3-4 siken, 4-5 sikyn; 3- sike (5 siȝke), 9 *dial.* soik; 5-9 sick (9 *dial.* sic). β. 3 syken, 4- syke (4 zyke). [var. of SICHE *v.* Cf. MDu. *versiken* to sigh, Fris. *sykje* to draw breath.]

**1.** *intr.* To sigh.

α. *c* **1175** *Lamb. Hom.* 43 Summe of þan monne sare wepeð... Summe þer graninde sikeð. *a* **1225** *Ancr. R.* 32 Alle monne sores setteð in ower þouhte, & sikeð to vre Louerd. *c* **1290** *S. Eng. Leg.* I. 122 Seint Thomas wep In is heorte, and sore bi-gan to sike. *a* **1320** *Sir Tristr.* 2621 Tristrem..sikeþ, for soþe to sain, Wiþ sorwe and michel pain. *c* **1385** CHAUCER *L.G.W.* 1165 *Dido*, She siketh soore, and gan hire selfe turmente. **1423** JAS. I *Kingis Q.* xliv, Gif ȝe be warldly wight, that dooth me sike. *c* **1450** *Pride of Life* 163 (Brandl), Þou nast no nede to sike sore. **1864** RAMSBOTTOM *Lanc. Rhymes* 17 His mother, eh, Lord! heaw hoo soikt. **1889** T. PINNOCK *Black Country Ann.* 67 (E.D.D.), We chaps cast..eyes on the ground an' we siked.

β. *c* **1250** *Owl & Night.* (J.) 1352 Þat heo vor summe sottes lore þe yorne bit and sykeþ sore. *a* **1310** in Wright *Lyric P.* xxix. 85, I syke when y singe, for sorewe that y se. **1393** LANGL. *P. Pl.* C. XIX. 16 'Now, certes,' ich seide and sykede for ioye. *c* **1430** *Syr. Gener.* 1046 Priuelie than he gan to syke. **1482** *Monk of Evesham* (Arb.) 23 He was seyn often.. sykyng alow in his breste as a manne slepyng had wepte. **1515** *Scottish Field* 388 in *Chetham Misc.* (1856), His servauntes they maie syke, and sorowe for his sake.

**b.** *dial.* To sob or cry.

**1841** HARTSHORNE *Salop. Antiq.* Gloss., *Sike*, to cry, lament, sob. **1851** STERNBERG *Northampt. Dial.*, *Sike*, to cry, sob, or violently bewail.

†**2.** *trans.* To emit or give (a sigh). *Obs.*$^{-1}$

*c* **1310** in Wright *Lyric P.* xxxii. 92 Ich have siked moni syk, lemmon, for thin ore.

**sike**, var. SIC *a.*, SICK *a.* and *v.*

**sikel(l**, obs. forms of SICKLE *sb.*

**Sikel**, var. SICEL *sb.* and *a.*

**sikelatoun**, var. CICLATOUN *Obs.*

**Sikeliot(e**, varr. SICELIOT *sb.* and *a.*

**sikenes(se**, obs. ff. SICKNESS.

**siker**, obs. f. SICKER.

**siket.** Now *dial.* Forms: 3-5, 9 siket (4 syket), 5-6, 9 sicket, 9 secket. [f. SIKE *sb.*[1] + -ET[1]: cf. SICHET. Recorded chiefly in the Latinized forms *sikettus*, *-etus*.] A small watercourse or sike.

**1300** in *Archaeologia* (1857) XXXVII. 435 Per quendam sikettum qui vocatur Cavereswellebrok. *Ibid.*, Inde per eundem sikettum usque ad..Kavereshull. **1318-9** in Dugdale *Monast. Angl.* (1830) VI. 1. 558/1 In longitudine inter duos sikettos, quorum unus cadit inter Northwayt et Waytwra. **1479** *Priory of Hexham* (Surtees) II. 16 A fonte praedicto versus austrum per j sikettum usque Sewynscheles moss. *Ibid.*, Per dictum bogg usque quoddam siketum. **1550** *Survey Borders* in Hodgson *Northumb.* (1828) II. III. 184 From thence till a place over a letche or litle sicket called the stepping stones. **1894** HESLOP *Northumbld. Gloss.*, *Sicket, siket, secket*, a small syke, a small brook, a rivulet.

**Sikh** (sɪk, siːk), *sb.* (and *a.*) Forms: α. 8-9 Seek, Seik, 8 Seekh, 9 Seikh. β. 8 Syke, Syc, Sicque, 8-9 Sik (9 Sík), 9- Sikh (Sik'h, Síkh). [Hindī *sikh* (Skr. *śishya*), disciple. The spellings *seek(h*, *sík(h*, and the pron. (siːk), may have been due to association with Hindī *sīkh* learning, *sīkhna* to learn.]

**1.** A member of a monotheistic religious group, originally established in India (chiefly in the Punjab) by Guru Nanak in the early part of the 16th century.

The majority of Sikhs are still located in the Punjab in northern India, but many are now living in other parts of India, and in Africa, Europe, the United States, and elsewhere. Sikhs became famous for their military prowess in the 19th century during the period of British imperialism. The Sikh religion requires its members, among other institutionalized customs, to wear a turban, and this has brought Sikhs into conflict with authorities in some countries outside India in the second half of the present century, mainly because of local regulations about the wearing of crash helmets on motor cycles.

α. **1781** WILKINS in *Asiatic Res.* (1799) I. 288 That sect of people who are distinguished from the worshippers of Brahm, and the followers of Mahommed, by the appellation Seek. **1784** in Seton-Karr *Select. fr. Calcutta Gaz.* (1864) I. 13 The Seekhs..have plundered all that quarter. **1800** *Asiatic Ann. Reg.* III. 51/1 It is imagined he has taken refuge in the country of the Seiks. **1830** *Encycl. Metrop.* (1845) XXI. 283/2 *marg.*, Seiks.

β. **1785** *European Mag.* IX. 453 For ease the slow Mahratta spoils, And hardier Sik erratic toils. **1815** ELPHINSTONE *Acc. Caubul* (1842) I. 109 All that is desirable to know respecting the Siks, the most remarkable part of the population. **1838** *Penny Cycl.* XII. 233/2 The Sikhs.. consider the profession of arms the religious duty of every individual. **1896** YOUNGSON *40 Yrs. Punjab Mission* v. 39 A Sikh must possess five things—a dagger, an iron bracelet, short breeches, long hair, and a comb.

**2.** *attrib.* or as *adj.* Of or pertaining to the Sikhs.

**1845** *Encycl. Metrop.* XXV. 1348/1 The principal alphabets formed from the Nāgarī, are the Bengalī..and Sikh or Punjābī. **1853** STOCQUELER *Mil. Encycl.* 257/1 A proclamation was issued, declaring the Sikh states.. attached to the British dominions. **1866** *Chambers's Encycl.* VIII. 718/2 The second volume of the Sikh scriptures. **1896** YOUNGSON *40 Yrs. Punjab Mission* v. 39 Gobind Singh.. renewed an old Sikh rite.

Hence **ˈSikhism**, the tenets or principles of the Sikhs.

**1849** J. D. CUNNINGHAM *Hist. Sikhs* iii. 96/1 There are also elements of change within Sikhism itself. **1866** *Chambers's Encycl.* VIII. 719/2 The numerous divisions into which Sikhism, as a system of belief and practice, has ramified. **1880** SIR R. TEMPLE *India in 1880* 120 Sikhism.. is one of those inflammable things which a spark might kindle into a flame. **1896** YOUNGSON *40 Yrs. Punjab Mission* i. 4 Sikhism is like Buddhism a revolt from priestcraft and ritual.

**sikhara**, var. SHIKHARA.

**sikil**, obs. f. SICKLE *sb.*; var. of SWIKEL *a. Obs.*

**ˈsiking**, *vbl. sb.* Now *dial.* [f. SIKE *v.* + -ING[1].] = SIGHING *vbl. sb.* 1.

*a* **1300** *Havelok* 234 Þer was sobbing, siking, and sor. **1340** *Ayenb.* 171 Vorþenchinge acseþ grat zorȝe and greate zykinges of herte. *c* **1400** *Laud. Troy Bk.* 662 Loue.. trauayles here wondir strong With thought and sykyng euere among. *c* **1420** *Chron. Vilod.* 1865 He with sore sykyng and snobbyng bothe Vnswered þe monke. **1482** *Monk of Evesham* (Arb.) 24 Amonge his lamentacions and sykynges ..he asayde..to opene his yes. **1886** BRIERLEY *Cast upon World* xviii, I hate to yer [= hear] that soikin' an' meeonin'.

*attrib.* **13..** *E.E. Psalter* vi. 6 (Egerton MS.), I swank in mi sikinge-stede.

**siking**, *ppl. a. rare*$^{-1}$. [f. SIKE *v.* + -ING[2].] That sighs; sighing. Hence †**ˈsikingness**.

**13..** [see SIGHINGNESS]. *c* **1616** FLETCHER *Thierry & Theod.* v. i, Thou hast a bonny countenance and a blithe, promising mickle good to a siking wemb.

**sikkell**, obs. f. SICKLE *sb.*

**Sikkimese** (sɪkɪˈmiːz), *a.* and *sb.* [f. *Sikkim* (see below) + -ESE.] **A.** *adj.* Of or pertaining to Sikkim, a country in the eastern Himalayas. **B.** *sb.* A native or inhabitant of Sikkim; *collect.* the people of Sikkim.

**1861** J. C. GAWLER *Dispatch* 15 Feb. in H. St. G. M. Mcrea *Regimental Hist. 45th Rattray's Sikhs* (1933) I. 149 Captain Impey's column surprised the Sikkimese camp at Temi. **1938** G. GORER *Himalayan Village* i. 36 During the eighteenth and early nineteenth centuries the Lepchas fought with the Sikkimese against the continued invasions of the Nepali and Bhutanese. **1955** *Times* 3 June 7/3 The devout Sikkimese who asked that no human foot should profane the final high places that their faith holds sacred. **1960** 'S. HARVESTER' *Chinese Hammer* i. 10 Sikkimese metalwork and Kashmiri brocades. **1973** *Times* 12 Apr. 8/7 The Bhutia-Lepchas and the Sikkimese Nepalis have, however, parity in the State Council. **1978** C. HUMPHREYS *Both Sides Circle* xx. 212 The inhabitants were a blend of Lepcha, Bhutia and other races besides the native Sikkimese.

**siklatoun**, variant of CICLATOUN *Obs.*

**siknesse**, obs. f. SICKNESS.

**sikni**, obs. f. SICKEN *v.*

**sikonye**, var. CICON(I)E, stork, *Obs.*

**sikr(a**, varr. SHIKHARA.

**Siksika** (ˈsɪksɪkə). Also †Seksikai, Siksikai. [Blackfoot, f. *siksi-* black + *-ka* foot.] The Blackfoot Indians, *esp.* those of the northernmost of the three peoples which comprise the Blackfoot.

**1843** tr. *Wied-Neuwied's Trav. Interior N. Amer.* xix. 245 The Blackfeet form a numerous nation, which is divided into three tribes, speaking one and the same language. These tribes are—1. The Siksekai or Seksekai, the Blackfeet properly so called. *Ibid.*, The Siksekai signifies, in their language, Blackfoot. **1902** *Encycl. Brit.* XXIX. 466/1 Blackfeet (Siksika). **1910** in F. Hodge *Handbk. Amer. Indians* II. 570/1 A band of the Kainah division of the Siksika. **1923** M. BARBEAU *Indian Days in Canadian Rockies* Addenda, 197 The Blackfoot..were the Bedouins of the Plains... Their three subdivisions, consisting of the Blackfoot proper (or Siksika), the Blood, and the Piegan.. considered themselves as of one family. **1942** O. LEWIS *Effects of White Contact upon Blackfoot Culture* ii. 7 The Blackfoot, Blood and Piegan tribes are at present time located on four reserves, of which three are in Alberta, Canada, and one in Montana... To avoid confusion we shall use the Blackfoot term 'Siksika' to refer to the Northern Blackfoot, and the term Blackfoot to refer to all three tribes. **1952** J. R. SWANTON *Indian Tribes N. Amer.* 396 The Siksika are divided into the following subtribes: The Siksika or Blackfeet proper, [etc.].

**sikul(le,** obs. ff. SICKLE *sb.*

**sikynyn,** obs. f. SICKEN *v.*

**Sikyonian,** var. SICYONIAN *sb.* and *a.*

†**sil.** *Obs. rare.* [a. L. or Fr. *sil* ochre.] Some kind of ochre.

**1601** HOLLAND *Pliny* XXXIII. xiii. II. 485 As touching Ochre or Sil, it is exceeding hard to be reduced into pouder. **1610** W. FOLKINGHAM *Art of Survey* I. iii. 5 Colours amongst the Minerall Oare of Gold and Siluer, as Sil, Azure.

**silage** (ˈsaɪlɪdʒ), *sb.* [Alteration of ENSILAGE, after SILO.] **1.** Green fodder preserved by pressure in a silo or stack; = ENSILAGE 2. Also *attrib.*

**1884** *Pall Mall G.* 25 Nov. 5/2 The testimony of all who have tried ensilage is that a given quantity of grass converted into silage [etc.]. **1894** J. K. FOWLER *Recoll. Old Co. Life* xii. 136 The silo was opened and the silage proved excellent.

**2.** *attrib.* and *Comb.*, as ***silage clamp*** (CLAMP *sb.*[3]), ***loader***, ***-maker***, ***stack***; ***silage-feeding***, ***-making*** vbl. sbs.; ***silage-fed*** ppl. adj.; **silage cutter**, a stationary machine for chopping a crop into short lengths for silage and elevating it into a silo; also, a silage harvester; **silage harvester**, a machine for cutting a standing crop as it travels, chopping it into short lengths for silage, and elevating it into another vehicle.

**1961** *Farmers' Weekly* 6 Oct. 117/1 The loose housing and the self-feed silage clamps. **1978** *Cornish Guardian* 27 Apr. 15/7 (Advt.), 131 acre accredited dairy farm..milking parlour, silage clamp. **1962** *Trans. Amer. Soc. Agric. Engin.* XIX. 117 (*heading*) Code for testing silage cutters. **1967** MARTIN & LEONARD *Princ. Field Crop Production* (ed. 2) viii. 208 Corn and sorghum row crops for silage are harvested with a field silage cutter or a forage harvester. **1972** *Country Life* 15 June 1580/1 Silage feeding to the flock..usually begins just before Christmas. *Ibid.* 1580/3 It is usually the practice in silage-fed flocks to introduce a cereal supplement just before lambing. **1931** J. B. DAVIDSON *Agric. Machinery* xxv. 266 To reduce the labor of handling green fodder and to dispense with the use of binding twine, the operations of cutting and harvesting silage are combined in the silage harvester, and the cut silage is delivered to a wagon as it is drawn beside the harvester through the field. **1977** *Cork Examiner* 8 June 15/5 (Advt.), Used Kidd silage harvester, good working condition, £525. **1971** *Power Farming* Mar. 8/3 The operation of the American silage loader..is explained in the captions to the accompanying photographs. **1924** W. J. MALDEN *Grassland Farming* xi. 152 The silage-maker has two points to consider. **1960** *Farmer & Stockbreeder* 2 Feb. 55/2 Most of the people I have talked to have been experienced silage-makers. **1924** W. J. MALDEN *Grassland Farming* xi. 149 Heating is really an aid in silage-making, because under the moist heat the stiffest stems yield, and compression becomes easy. **1960** *Farmer & Stockbreeder* 16 Feb. 73/2 In spite of the great progress in silage-making in the last few years, the amount of permanent grass and temporary leys made into hay in Britain still far exceeded the amount conserved by all the other processes put together. **1888** *Times* 24 July 13/1 In a season like the present a good silage stack is about the only means of securing and preserving grass.

Hence **ˈsilage** *v. trans.*, to preserve by ensilage.

**1885** *Field* 19 Dec. (Cassell), Any grass in excess of the requirements of the stock could be silaged.

**silajit** (ˈsɪlədʒɪt). Also **shilajatu**, **sillajeet**, etc. [a. Hind. *shila-jit*, Skr. *śilājit*, *śilājatu* bitumen, f. Skr. *śilā* rock + *jit* conquering or *jatu* essence.] A name given to various solid or viscous substances found on rock in India and Nepal (see quot. 1903), esp. a usu. dark-brown odoriferous substance which is used in traditional Indian medicine and probably consists principally of dried animal urine.

**1811–12** F. BUCHANAN *Acct. Bihar & Patna* (1936) II. III. iii. 467 About three miles farther in the same direction..a very peculiar substance called silajit exudes. **1833** G. PLAYFAIR tr. *Taleef Shereef* 96 Sillajeet is the urine of the hill wild goat, which when the animal is rutting, is discharged on the stones and evaporated by the sun's heat. **1903** *Jrnl. R. Asiatic Soc. Bengal* LXII. II. 98 One of the most peculiar medicinal substances of the East is that called Silajit or Shilajatu. It is known by the former name in Hindi and Persian, and by the latter in Bengali and Sanskrit. **1964** *New Statesman* 3 Apr. 517/2 He was extolling the miraculous properties of his ointment, guaranteed to contain the purest silajit brought from Tibet.

**silane** (ˈsaɪleɪn). *Chem.* [ad. G. *silan* (A. Stock 1916, in *Ber. d. Deut. Chem. Ges.* XLIX. 108): see SILICON and -ANE.] Any of the large class of hydrides of silicon analogous to the alkanes; *spec.* silicon tetrahydride, $SiH_4$, a colourless gas which has strong reducing properties and is spontaneously flammable in air.

**1916** *Jrnl. Chem. Soc.* CX. II. 319 The suggestion is made that the term 'silanes' be accepted generally for the saturated compounds of silicon and hydrogen, the various members being distinguished thus: $SiH_4$, monosilane; $Si_2H_6$, disilane; [etc.]. **1935** *Nature* 9 Mar. 397/2 The oxidation of silane resembles very closely that of phosphine rather than that of methane. **1958** *Times Rev. Industry* June 26/3 The gaseous compound silane, $SiH_4$, is produced by reacting silicon tetrachloride with lithium aluminium hydride. **1977** *Whitaker's Almanack 1978* 1034/1 Work has now begun on cleaning and repairing these figures [on Wells Cathedral] and..it is hoped that the use of lime and silanes will prevent further decay of the stone surfaces.

**silanize** (ˈsaɪlənaɪz), *v.* [f. SILAN(E + -IZE.] *trans.* To treat (silica-based material, esp. support material for chromatography) with reagents which render the surface more inert by converting reactive groups to organosilicon groups. Hence **ˈsilanized** *ppl. a.*, **ˈsilanizing** *vbl. sb.* Also **silaniˈzation**, treatment of this kind.

**1962** *Analytical Chem.* XXXIV. 891/3 To eliminate possible adsorption effects, the material was silanized with Siliclad. *Ibid.*, Silanizing reduced the specific surface to about 2 sq. meters per gram. *Ibid.* 892/1 A weighed amount of silanized Chromosorb-R. **1968** *Jrnl. Chromatogr.* XXXIV. 305 By silanizing the support surface we obtained changes in the chemical character of the surface. *Ibid.* 308 The effect of surface silanization on the structure of the internal support pores is obvious. **1973** *Nature* 30 Mar. 339/1 A 5·75 inch disposable pipette plugged with silanized glass-wool. **1975** WILLIAMS & WILSON *Biologist's Guide to Princ. & Techniques Pract. Biochem.* iii. 70 This is normally achieved by silanization of the support with such compounds as hexamethyldisilazane.

**Silastic** (sɪˈlæstɪk). *Chem.* Also **silastic**. [f. SI(LICON + E)LASTIC *a.* and *sb.*] A proprietary name for silicone rubber. Freq. *attrib.*

**1946** *Rubber Age* Feb. 580/1 Silastic is an almost entirely inorganic synthetic elastomer. **1947** *Official Gaz.* (U.S. Patent Office) 2 Dec. 26/1 Dow Corning Corporation... *Silastic.* For compositions..comparable to..rubber prior to vulcanization but containing organosilicon polymers... Claims use since July, 1945. **1953** *Electronic Engin.* XXV. 309/1 Also recently introduced is a range of tropical suppressor filter units which are hermetically sealed in a metal container with silastic terminals. **1965** *Trade Marks Jrnl.* 12 May 632/1 Silastic. **1980** *Recent Advances Surg.* X. 66 A silastic strain gauge.

‖**silat** (sɪˈlæt). Also **Silat**. [Mal.] The Malay art of self-defence, practised in a series of exercises as a martial art or accompanied by drums as a ceremonial display or dance.

[**1900** W. W. SKEAT *Malay Magic* vi. 381 Those who have any skill amuse the company with exhibitions of Malay fencing (*main silat*).] **1910** R. J. WILKINSON *Papers on Malay Subjects: Life & Customs* III. 27 Even if it does drag on..as a game for Malay boys, the *main silat* will never preserve in its new form the curious wealth of technicalities associated with the national weapon of the country. **1972** M. SHEPPARD *Taman Indera* vi. 85 The first henna dance..took place in the palace garden... The only accompaniment to this dance was supplied by *Silat* drums—double-headed barrel drums. *Ibid.* x. 142 There are a great many varieties of Silat and different teachers specialize in different types. **1978** T. WILLIAMSON *Technicians of Death* xiii. 112 Silat, the Malayan martial art where the hands and arms are used for defence and the knees and feet for attack.

‖**silbador** (sɪlbəˈdɔə(r)). Pl. **silbadores**, **silbadors**. [Sp., = whistler.] One who uses the whistled language *silbo* (see next).

**1957** *Archivum Linguisticum* IX. I. 44 The melodies whistled to silbadores proved completely unintelligible. **1965** *Sun* 24 July 5/5 A top silbador can be heard up to nine miles away... The silbadors have a voice range of two octaves.

‖**silbo** (ˈsɪlbəʊ). Also **Silbo**. [Sp., = a whistle, whistling.] A form of whistled Spanish used by the inhabitants of Gomera in the Canary Islands, in order to communicate across long distances. Also known as ***Silbo Gomero***.

**1957** *Archivum Linguisticum* IX. I. 44 There are abundant references to the silbo and at least two full-length studies. **1964** A. CLASSE in D. Abercrombie et al. *Daniel Jones* 43 The investigation of a whistled form of Spanish (Silbo Gomero). .. We tested one group of consonants which are invariably confused in the Silbo. **1977** *Sci. Amer.* May 141/2 In the Spanish Civil War military signals were on occasion cast in Silbo, but there were Gomerans on both sides and so the measure-countermeasure drama soon ran its course. **1978** *Verbatim* Sept. 13/1 A phonetic analysis of the Silbo Gomero of Canarian Spanish is extended feature by feature to the articulated whistle.

**silc(k,** obs. ff. SILK.

**silcott** (ˈsɪlkɒt). ? *Obs.* Also **silcot**, **Sillcott**. [f. SIL(K *sb.* + COTT(ON *sb.*[1]] A material made of cotton finished to resemble silk, chiefly used for underskirts. Cf. SILKETTE.

**1894** J. E. DAVIS *Elem. Mod. Dressmaking* (1895) 93 Varieties of silkette or silcot (cotton finished to look and feel like silk). **1923** *Daily Mail* 17 Feb. 10 (Advt.), Petticoat of Silcott edged with pleated and hemstitched flounce. *Ibid.* 28 Feb. 5 Silcott Petticoat with small crystal frill.

**silcrete** (ˈsɪlkriːt). *Geol.* [f. SIL(ICA + CON)CRETE *sb.*] A quartzite formed of sand grains or pebbles cemented together by silica; a siliceous duricrust.

**1902** G. W. LAMPLUGH in *Geol. Mag.* IX. 575, I have the hardihood to suggest that the term might be complemented by equivalents,—'silcrete', for sporadic masses in loose material of the 'greywether' type, indurated by a siliceous cement. **1950** *Antiquity* XXIV. 209 More than 90 per cent of these implements are of 'ferricrete sandstone', the others being of 'silcrete sandstone'. **1977** A. HALLAM *Planet Earth* 85 Bedrock became deeply weathered to give striking weathering crusts (duricrusts) composed of iron and aluminum oxides (in the case of ferricretes) or silica (in the case of silcretes).

**sild** (sɪlt). [a. Da., Norw. *sild* herring: cf. SILE *sb.*[3]] A small immature herring, *Clupea harengus*, esp. one caught in northern European seas.

**1921** *Handbk. Norway & Sweden* (Admiralty) viii. 157 The true sardine..does not occur in northern waters. Norwegian 'sardines' are now known in commerce as 'sild'. **1962** E. M. CRUICKSHANK in G. Borgstrom *Fish as Food* II. iv. 195 With small fish like the sild, the entire fish is processed.

**sild(e,** var. SELD *adv.*

**silde,** obs. f. SELD *sb.* (shed, building).

**silden,** obs. f. SHIELD *v.*

**sildom,** obs. f. SELDOM.

**sile** (saɪl), *sb.*[1] *north.* and *Sc.* Also 4–5, 9 **syle**, 6 **syelle**, 8–9 *dial.* **soil**. [Of doubtful origin; perh. repr. OE. *sýl* pillar, column.] A large roofing-timber or rafter, usually one of a pair. Also ***sile-tree***.

**1338–40** *Durham Acc. Rolls* (Surtees) 377, vij copule de syles longitudinis xvj pedum, et iiij[or] copule de syles longitudinis xxviij[to] pedum. **1371** *Durham Halm. Rolls* (Surtees) 111 Reparabit unam grangiam de uno pare de siles et duobus gauil forks. **1582** *Wills & Inv. N.C.* (Surtees, 1860) 46 In the hay barne. Certaine sawen baulkes, viz., ix dormonds, and j sile. **1762** *Phil. Trans.* LII. 513 A round hole..was pierced through the carved oak,..and a piece of the main soil..struck off. **1770** *Ibid.* LXI. 75 Upon this pillar rested a large oak soil. **1811** AITON *Agric. Surv. Ayrsh.* 114 The roof was formed of strong cupples termed Syles, set up 8 or 10 feet distant from each other. **1825** BROCKETT *N.C. Gloss.*, *Syles*, the principal rafters of a house. **1842** GWILT *Archit.* Gloss. 1033 *Soils*, a provincial term, chiefly..used in the north, signifying the principal rafters of a roof. **1878** DICKINSON *Gloss. Cumbld.*, *Sile trees*, the timber roof-blades of a thatched clay house.

**sile** (saɪl), *sb.*[2] *north.* (and *Sc.*). Also 5–7, 9 **syle**, 6 **syell**. [a. ON. **síl* (Norw. and Sw. *sil*): cf. SILE *v.*[2]] A strainer or sieve, esp. one for milk.

**1459–60** *Durham Acc. Rolls* (Surtees) 89, j pelvis cum foraminibus vocata j Syle. **1483** *Cath. Angl.* 339/2 A mylke Syle, *colatorium*. **1563** *Wills & Inv. N.C.* (Surtees, 1835) 207, ij great bowells, iij wodd skailles, one syle. *Ibid.* 208 One syell, j vergeus barrell, vj mylk bowlls. **1570** LEVINS *Manip.* 130 A Sile, *colum*. **1615** MARKHAM *Eng. Housew.* II. vi. (1668) 144 The bottom of this Syle through which the milk must pass, must be covered with a very clean-washt fine linnen-cloth. **1684** *Yorkshire Dial.* 35 Now let us hame and late for Bowls and Sile. **1788** W. H. MARSHALL *Yorksh.* II. 352 *Sile*, a milk-strainer. **1825–** in dial. gloss. (Yks., Northumbld., Lancs., Nott., Linc., etc.).

**sile** (saɪl), *sb.*[3] *north.* and *Sc.* Also 9 **syle** (*dial.* **soil**); **sill**. [Of Scand. origin: cf. ON. and Icel. *síld*, MSw. *sildh*, *silþ* (Sw. *sill*), Norw. and Da. *sild* herring; also Icel. *síli* (older *síl*) a herring.] Young herring.

α. **1769** PENNANT *Brit. Zool.* III. 288 The young herrings ..are then from half an inch to two inches long: those in Yorkshire are called Herring Sile. **1847** HALLIW., *Soil*, the fry of the coal-fish. *Cumb.* **1863** JEAN INGELOW *Poems* 186 Our folk call them syle and nought but syle, And when they're grown, why then we call them herring. **1881** DAY *Fishes Gt. Brit.* I. 295 The fry are called..soil, poodler, billets or billiards up to one year of age. **1883** DAY *Fishes Gt. Brit. & Irel.* II. 210 Small ones [herring] not larger than a sprat are termed sills, or sile.

β. **1847** HALLIW., *Sill*, the young of a herring. *North.* **1863** *Rep. Commiss. Herring-trawling Scotl.* §51. 26 The herring is found under four different conditions: 1st, Fry or Sill. **1883** [see α].

**sile,** dial. variant of SOIL *sb.*

**sile,** *v.*[1] *Obs.* exc. *north. dial.* Also 4–5, 9 **syle**. [Prob. of Scand. origin: cf. Norw. and Sw. dial. *sila* to flow gently, to pour with rain; but these senses have something in common with SILE *v.*[2], and are usually associated with that word.]

**1.** *intr.* To go, pass, move; to glide. Usu. with preps. or advs.

**13..** *E.E. Allit. P.* B. 131 He..Solased hem with semblaunt & syled fyrre; Tron fro table to table & talkede ay myrþe. *c* **1400** *Rowland & O.* 401 Til a chambire gan pay syle, And gayly gan hym dighte. *c* **1400** *Destr. Troy* 1973 Sile furth of my sight in a sad haste. *c* **1420** LYDG. *Lyfe Our Ladye* (Caxton) d ij, And fysshe eke with fynnes silid fayre. **1821** CLARE *Vill. Minstr.* I. 14 As sober evening sweetly siles along. **1876** F. K. ROBINSON *Whitby Gloss.*, *Sile past*, to glide by.

**2.** To fall or sink (*down*). Also *dial.*, to subside.

*a* **1400–50** *Alexander* 3043 (Ashm.), Siles doun on aithire side selcuth kniȝtis, Sum darid, sum dede, sum depe wondid. *c* **1420** *Avow. Arth.* xvi, With sit siles he a-downe, To brittun him the king was bowne. *c* **1470** *Gol. & Gaw.* 524 He hard ane bugill blast..As the seymly sone silit to the rest. **1674** RAY *N.C. Words* 41 To *Sile* down: *Lincoln*, to fall to the bottom, or subside. **1827** CLARE *Sheph. Cal.* 180 The white sand..Now swimming up in silver threads, and then Slow siling down to bubble up again.

**b.** *dial.* To fall down in a swoon; to faint *away*.

**1790** GROSE *Prov. Gloss.*, *To sile away*, to faint away. **1820** CLARE *Rural Life* (ed. 3) 152 'Your Nelly's beguiled!' She said, and she siled on the floor. **1854** MISS BAKER *Northampt. Gloss.*, *Sile*, to faint, to sink, or subside gradually.

**3.** †**a.** Of tears, etc.: To flow. *Obs.*

*c* **1400** *Destr. Troy* 9210 Terys on his chekes Ronen full rifely..þen he driet vp the dropes, & [? *read* þat] dreghly can syle. **1790** GROSE *Prov. Gloss.*, *To sile o'er*, to boil over.

*a* **1800** *Lord Derwentwater* iii. in Bell *Rhymes N. Bards* (1812) 225 When he read the three next lines The tears began to sile. **1807** [see the *ppl. a.* below]. **1829** BROCKETT *N.C. Gloss.* (ed. 2), *Sile*, to percolate, to flow. **1878** DICKINSON *Cumbld. Gloss.* s.v. *Syle*, 'It syl't and bled,' after the manner of a syle.

**b.** *dial.* Of rain: To pour (*down*).

**1703** THORESBY *Let. Ray* (E.D.S.), *It Siles*, i.e. rains fast. **1828** CARR *Craven Gloss.*, *Sile*,..to pour down with rain. **1865** *Cornh. Mag.* July 33 Rain in the Northern counties, when it falls perpendicularly, is said to 'sile down', as if in allusion to its passing through a sieve. **1870** E. PEACOCK *Ralf Skirl.* III. 171 'It'll sile down till night,'..replied the groom.

Hence †'**siling** *vbl. sb.* and *ppl. a. Obs.*

*c* **1400** *Destr. Troy* 1307 þe kyng..siket full sore with sylyng of teris. ? *a* **1400** *Morte Arth.* 3794 Thane syghande he saide, with sylande terys. **1807** STAGG *Poems* 65 Rashly they scale the scattran swathe,..An' seylin sweats their haffets bathe.

**sile**, *v.*$^{2}$ Now *dial.* Also 5–7, 9 **syle**, 8–9 *Sc.* **seil**, 8 **soil**. [Of Scand. origin: cf MSw. *siila*, *sila*, Sw. and Norw. *sila* in the same sense, perh. related to Fris. *silje* to sift.]

**1.** *trans.* To strain; *esp.* to pass (milk) through a sieve or strainer.

**14..** *MS. Lincoln A. i. 17* fol. 281 in *Halliw.* s.v., Temper it with hate ale, and sythene syle it thorowe a hate clathe. *c* **1450** *Bk. Curtasye* in *Babees Bk.* 322 þo euwere thurgh towelle syles clene His water into þo bassynges shene. **1570** LEVINS *Manip.* 131 To syle milke, *colare lac.* **1615** MARKHAM *Eng. Housew.* (1660) 150 You shall take your milk ..as it comes from the Cow, and syle it into a clean Tub. **1674** RAY *N.C. Words* 44 To *Soil* milk, to cleanse it. **1721** KELLY *Sc. Prov.* 274 Our Sowins are ill sowr'd, ill seil'd, ill-salted,..and few o' them. **1788** W. H. MARSHALL *Yorksh.* II. 352 *To Sile*, to strain, as fresh milk from the cow. **1818** SCOTT *Hrt. Midl.* xiv, The brown four-year-auld's milk is not seiled yet. **1825-** in dial. glossaries (E. Anglia, Northamp., Linc., etc.). **1892** J. LUCAS *Kalm's Eng.* 173 That which was over was siled in the above-named manner and made into butter.

*transf.* **1820** *Blackw. Mag.* May 159 The..gentle Nith canna call a single fin its ain,—they syle its current through the herling nets 'tween yule and yule. **1847** J HALLIDAY *Rustic Bard* 264 The purest o' water is siel'd through the rock.

†**2.** *dial.* To pour. *Obs.*

**1787** GROSE *Prov. Gloss.* s.v. *Syle*, He siled a gallon of ale down his throat.

Hence **siled** *ppl. a.*; '**siling** *vbl. sb.* Also '**siler**, a milk-strainer (cf. SILING-DISH).

**1615** MARKHAM *Eng. Housew.* II. iv. 109 *marg.*, Silling of milke. *a* **1800** PEGGE *Suppl. Grose*, *Sil'd Milk*, skimmed milk. **1856** HENDERSON *Pop. Rhymes* 82 He handed her the milk-strainer, the milsey, or seiler.

†**sile**, *v.*$^{3}$ *Obs.* Chiefly *Sc.* Also 6–7 **syle**. [ad. OF. *ciller* (*siller*), f. *cil* eyelash, or med.L. *ciliare* (Du Cange). The usual English form is SEEL.]

**1.** *trans.* To sew up (the eyes of a hawk). *rare*$^{-1}$.

**1398** TREVISA *Barth. De P.R.* XII. ii. (Tollemache MS.), Ofte þe yȝen of suche briddes [hawks] beþ þere siled, closid oþer hid.

**2.** To cover (the eyes or sight). Also with *up*.

*c* **1500** KENNEDIE *Passion of Christ* 448 Sum..filit his cristall eyne, And silit his sicht, as he a fule had bene. **1575** *Reg. Privy Counc. Scotl.* II. 479 Tuke thame nakit furth of thair beddis, and sylit thair eyis unto the tyme thay had distroyit the saidis houssis. **1629** SIR W. MURE *True Crucifix* 649 Now, siling vp his eyes, Hee streight must show Who him did most with causelesse strips infest.

**b.** *fig.* To deceive (the sight).

**1584** HUDSON *Du Bartas' Judith* II. 155 Thus siling humain sight, it changed form: One while a Rod, one while a creeping worm. *c* **1614** SIR W. MURE *Dido & Æneas* III. 422 Wast for this thow sought by slight To syle my sight, thy curst designes to cloake?

**c.** To deceive, beguile, or mislead (a person). A common Scottish use in the 16th century.

**1508** DUNBAR *Gold. Targe* 217 Dissymulance was besy me to sile. *c* **1550** LYNDESAY *Trag. Abp. St. Andrews* 205 With sweit and subtell wordis I did hym syle. **1585** JAS. I *Ess. Poesie* (Arb.) 33 With doubtsum talk she craftely begylde, Not only Grece, but Spaine and Indes she sylde.

**3.** To cover, hide, conceal.

*c* **1480** HENRYSON *Test. of Cresseid* 10 Quhen Titan had his bemis bricht Withdrawin doun, and sylit vnder cure. *c* **1500** KENNEDIE *Passion of Christ* 92 Silit he wes vnder schaddew of syn. **1513** DOUGLAS *Æneid* XIII. Prol. 42 Baith man and beste..Involuit in tha schaddois warrin sild. **1551** ABP. HAMILTON *Catech.* 70 Thai offend the Juge, fra quhom thai syle and hyde the veritie.

Hence †**siled** *ppl. a. Obs.*

**1567** *Satir. Poems Reform.* iv. 129 Quhair Venus anis gettis in hir gouernance Sic sylit subiectis felterit in hir snair. **1612** J. DAVIES (Heref.) *Muse's Sacr.* Wks. (Grosart) II. 48/2 While like a siled Doue, we (Lord) aspire.

†**sile**, *v.*$^{4}$ *Obs.* Also 5–6 **syle**. [Sc. and northern var. of CEIL *v.*] = CEIL *v.* 2.

*c* **1450** HOLLAND *Howlat* 671 [A palace] Pantit and apparalit proudly in pane, Sylit semely with silk. *c* **1532** DU WES *Introd. Fr.* in *Palsgr.* 949 To sile a wale, *lambroisser.* **1535** COVERDALE *1 Kings* vi. 20 He syled the altare with Ceder.

Hence †**siled** *ppl. a.*, ceiled.

**1535** COVERDALE *Judges* iii. 20 He sat in a syled Sommer perler. —— *Haggai* i. 4 Ye youre selues can fynde tyme to dwell in syled houses.

**sile-clout, -dish.** [f. SILE *sb.*$^{2}$ or *v.*$^{2}$] (See quots.)

**1668** *Markham's Eng. Housew.* II. vi. 144 After your Milk is come home, you shall..strain it from all unclean things through a neat and sweet kept Syledish. **1691** RAY *N.C. Words* 67 A *Sile-dish*, a straining or cleansing Dish. **1876** F. K. ROBINSON *Whitby Gloss.*, *Sile-clout*, the cloth stretched over the hole of the milk-strainer.

**silen** ('saɪlən). Also 6, 7 **sylen(e**. [ad. L. *Sīlēn-us*, ad. Gr. *Σειληνός*: see SILENUS.]

**1.** (Usu. with capital initial.) *Gr. Mythol.* One of the *Sileni* or wood-gods; a species of satyr.

**1584** R. SCOT *Discov. Witchcr.* VII. xv. (1886) 155 In our childhood our mother's maids have so terrified us with.. satyrs, pans, faunes, sylens,..that we are afraid of our own shadowes. **1601** HOLLAND *Pliny* XXXV. x. II. 544 Lascivious wantonnesse, which he pourtraied by three drunken Sylenes making merrie and banketting togither. **1842** *Penny Cycl.* XXII. 184/2 His [i.e. Socrates] appearance was not unlike that of the Silens and Satyrs. **1854** KEIGHTLEY *Mythol.* (ed. 3) 206 Hermés and the Silens 'mingle in love' with the nymphs in pleasing caverns.

**2.** *Zool.* A species of macaque.

**1848** tr. *Hoffmeister's Trav. Ceylon*, etc. 147 They were Silens, (*Inuus Silenus*) a species of short-tailed monkey.

**sile'naceous**, *a. Bot.* [f. SILEN-E + -ACEOUS.] Belonging to the *Sileneæ*, a division of the order *Caryophyllaceæ*. Also **si'lenal** *a.* and *sb.*, typified by the genus *Silene*; a plant of this kind.

**1836** LINDLEY *Veget. Kingd.* (1846) 495 The Silenal Alliance. *Ibid.*, Natural Orders of Silenals. **1838** *Penny Cycl.* VIII. 475/2 *Dianthus*, a beautiful genus of Silenaceous Dicotyledonous plants.

**silence** ('saɪləns), *sb.* Forms: 3–6 **scilence**, 4–6 **scylence**, 6 **scylens**; 4–5 **cilence**; 5 **sylens(e**, 6 *Sc.* **silens**, 5–6 **sylence**, 3– **silence**. [a. OF. *silence*, *scilence*, ad. L. *silentium*, f. *silēre* to be silent: cf. Prov. *silenci*, Sp. and Pg. *silencio*, It. *silenzio*.]

**1. a.** The fact of abstaining or forbearing from speech or utterance (sometimes with reference to a particular matter); the state or condition resulting from this; muteness, reticence, taciturnity. Occas. with *a* or in pl.

*a* **1225** *Ancr. R.* 78 Ine silence & ine hope schal beon ower strencðe. *Ibid.*, Heo mei ec hopien þet heo schal ec singen þurh hire scilence sweteliche ine heouene. *c* **1375** *Sc. Leg. Saints* xxxiii. (*George*) 637 [He] gert scilence be mad, til he had sad þat wes in his gule. **1388** WYCLIF *Acts* xix. 33 And Alisaundre axide with his hoond silence, and wolde ȝelde a resoun to the puple. *c* **1420** LYDG. *Assembly of Gods* 44 In Plutoys name [there was] commaundyd silence. **1474** CAXTON *Chesse* II. iii. (1883) 38 And oftetymes they selle as welle theyr scilence as theyr vtterance. **1535** COVERDALE *Job* xxix. 21 Vnto me men gaue eare,..& with sylence they taried for my councell. **1597** SHAKS. *2 Hen. IV*, II. ii. 178 No word to your Master that I am yet in Towne. There's for your silence. **1601** CAMPION *Wks.* (1909) 24 Doe not demaund why I am mute: Loues silence doth all speech confute. *a* **1668** DAVENANT *News fr. Plymouth* I. i, Silence becomes Men best, when Women talk. **1720** OZELL *Vertot's Rom. Rep.* I. III. 157 The People intimidated, kept in a profound Silence for some Time. **1781** COWPER *Retirement* 414 The tongue..Shall own itself a stamm'rer in that cause, Or plead its silence as its best applause. **1818** SHELLEY *Julian* 363 Nor dream that I will join the vulgar cry; Or with my silence sanction tyranny. **1847** EMERSON *Poems* Wks. (Bohn) I. 471 Ye taught my lips a single speech, And a thousand silences. **1875** FARRAR *Silence & Voices* ii. 29 What is called the silence of ignorance may sometimes be the silence of repudiation, sometimes even the reticence of scorn. **1967** G. STEINER *Lang. & Silence* 415 Dickens, Hopkins, Kipling are examples of modern writers whose root sensibility was oral, and who tried to adapt essentially oral means to the silences of print.

*personif.* **1607** SHAKS. *Cor.* II. i. 192 My gracious silence, hayle: Would'st thou haue laugh'd, had I come Coffin'd home? **1667** MILTON *P.L.* IV. 604 The wakeful Nightingale ..all night long her amorous descant sung; Silence was pleas'd. **1815** SHELLEY *Alastor* 65 And Silence, too enamoured of that voice, Locks its mute music in her rugged cell. *a* **1875** G. M. HOPKINS *Poems* (1967) 31 Elected Silence, sing to me.

**b.** In the phrases ***to keep*** (or †***hold***) ***silence, to break silence, in silence***.

(*a*) *a* **1225** *Ancr. R.* 22 Vrom þet, efter Preciosa, holdeð silence. *c* **1290** *S. Eng. Leg.* I. 228/324 Hov holde ȝe so silence þat neuer on ne spekez with oþur? *c* **1375** *Sc. Leg. Saints* xl. (*Ninian*) 336 As þai come til his presence, he gert þe puple kepe scilence. *c* **1450** *Rule Syon Monast.* liii. in *Collect. Topogr.* I. (1834) 31 Alle schal there kepe hyghe silence. **1471** CAXTON *Recuyell* (Sommer) I. 122 With this Iupiter helde his pees and kept scilence. **1560** DAUS tr. *Sleidane's Comm.* 18 He required him that his adversaries might kepe silence. **1782** PRIESTLEY *Corrupt. Chr.* II. IX. 211 They kept a strict silence all the week. **1819** SHELLEY *Cenci* IV. iv. 88 He keeps firm silence; but these lines found on him May speak. **1841** LANE *Arab. Nts.* I. 102 This is an event respecting which it is impossible to keep silence.

(*b*) **1390** GOWER *Conf.* I. 86 Thus fulofte my silence I breke. *c* **1400** *Destr. Troy* 2525 Than Troilus..brake Sylense belyue, and abrode saide. **1590** SPENSER *F.Q.* I. i. 42 He [Morpheus] mumbled soft, but would not all his silence breake. **1667** MILTON *P.L.* IX. 895 At length First to himself he inward silence broke. **1718** POPE *Iliad* XIX. 461 He broke Eternal silence, and portentous spoke. **1783** BURNS *Poor Mailie* 12 At length poor Mailie silence brak. **1842** BROWNING *Pied Piper* iv, An hour they sate in council, At length the Mayor broke silence.

(*c*) *c* **1380** WYCLIF *Sel. Wks.* I. 93 We shulden be tymes reste, and preye to God in scilence. *c* **1430** LYDG. *Min. Poems* (Percy Soc.) 41 He kept the nyhte in peas and silence. *c* **1450** *St. Cuthbert* (Surtees) 993 þan sole in silence sall he sitt, And rays him self abouen his witt. **1610** HOLLAND *Camden's Brit.* (1637) 566 In speech will I ever render thankes, and in silence acknowledge my selfe most deepely endebted. **1746** FRANCIS tr. *Horace, Epist.* I. xvii. 75 But had the Crow his Food in Silence eat, Less had his Quarrels been. **1757** W. WILKIE *Epigoniad* VII. 192 Amaz'd we stood; in silence, each his mind To fear and hope alternately resign'd. **1827** in Scott *Chron. Canongate* Introd. App., The next toast..he wished to be drunk in solemn silence. **1889** *Sat. Rev.* 9 Feb. 145/2 A brave man suffers in silence.

**c.** ***to put to silence***, to silence by argument or prohibition; †to put to death; also †***to put silence (un)to***, to reduce to silence.

(*a*) **1382** WYCLIF *Matt.* xxii. 34 Pharisees, heerynge that he hadde put silence to Saducees. **1508** KENNEDIE *Flyting w. Dunbar* 41 Heir I put sylence to the in all partis. **1677** YARRANTON *Eng. Improv.* 155, I know writing Books of Trade..puts a silence unto the whole History, be it never so good.

(*b*) **1502** ARNOLDE *Chron.* (1811) p. xxxvii, The ii. sonnys of Kinge Edward were put to silence. **1529** MORE *Dyaloge* I. Wks. 127/1 Ye haue put me to sylence, that I dare not nowe bee bolde to tell you that I haue sene it my selfe. **1579** W. WILKINSON *Confut. Fam. Love* Brief Descr. iiij b, Which wordes so often he repeated, that thereby he put Barry to silence. **1601** SHAKS. *Jul. C.* I. ii. 290 Murrellus and Flauius, for pulling scarffes off Cæsars Images, are put to silence. *c* **1680** BEVERIDGE *Serm.* (1729) I. 499 So as to put them to silence. **1846** TRENCH *Mirac.* xix. (1862) 326 He had put them to silence and to shame before all the people. **1879** M. J. GUEST *Lect. Hist. Eng.* xlii. 424 Tyndale..would.. sometimes put all the dignitaries to silence by his arguments.

*fig.* **1581** J. BELL *Haddon's Answ. Osor.* 254 Such force and dexterity, as may be able to putte your overthwart obstinacy to scilence. **1590** J. SMYTH in *Lett. Lit. Men* (Camden) 60 My little Booke..shall be put to silence and abolished.

**d.** Used imperatively, = Be silent; make no noise.

**1590** SHAKS. *Mids. N.* V. i. 266 But silence, heere comes Thisby. **1667** MILTON *P.L.* VII. 216 Silence, ye troubl'd waves, and thou Deep, peace. **1728** POPE *Dunc.* III. 165 Silence, ye Wolves! while Ralph to Cynthia howls. **1819** SHELLEY *Cyclops* 475 Silence now! Ye know the close device. **1873** SYMONDS *Grk. Poets* vii. 225 Silence! Hush! what noise was this?

**e.** The renunciation of speech chosen or vowed by certain religious or monastic orders, *esp.* the Trappists; a period during which the members of a community or retreat renounce speech. Freq. in phr. ***the rule of silence***.

**1387**, *c* **1450** [see sense 7]. *a* **1631** DONNE *Poems* (1633) 69 Harmelesse fish monastique silence keepe. **1884** ADDIS & ARNOLD *Cath. Dict.* 804/1 Probably the most trying part of all the discipline is the silence, no monk being allowed to speak to his brother on any occasion. **1921** G. O'DONOVAN *Vocations* xxii. 305 Hush, Sister. The rule of silence is no joke. **1957** P. L. FERMOR *Time to keep Silence* 67 There is a special dispensation from the rule of silence for the monks who deal with the abbey livestock when they are actually addressing their dumb charges. **1978** *Oxford Diocesan Mag.* Dec. 17/1 Then there was the two days' retreat... At no time..was the sense of fellowship more apparent than during the silence.

**f.** Proverbial phr. ***silence is golden. silence gives consent***: see CONSENT *sb.* 1 c.

**1834** CARLYLE *Sart. Res.* III. iii, in *Fraser's Mag.* June 668/1 As the Swiss Inscription says: *Sprechen ist silbern, Schweigen ist golden* (Speech is silvern, Silence is golden). **1865** W. WHITE *Eastern England* II. ix. 129 Silence is golden, says the proverb. We apprehended the full significance thereof when far away from busy thoroughfares. **1935** M. V. HUGHES *Vivians* vii. 138 'Did you tell him about that?' 'No, and I'm wondering whether I ought to?' 'I shouldn't if I were you. Silence is golden.' **1980** J. O'NEILL *Spy Game* xxv. 239 'I'll tell you the rest..on the way back.' He sealed her lips with a finger. 'Meanwhile, silence is golden.'

**2. a.** The state or condition when nothing is audible; absence of all sound or noise; complete quietness or stillness; noiselessness. Sometimes personified. Also const. *of* (the night, etc.).

**1382** WYCLIF *Isaiah* viii. 6 The watris of Siloe, that gon with cilence. **1398** TREVISA *Barth. De P.R.* X. ii. (1495) 27 b, Derknesse is seen yf noo thynge is seen, & scylence is knowen yf noo thynge is herde. **1500-20** DUNBAR *Poems* xxxv. 1 Lucina schynnyng in silence of the nicht. **1590** SPENSER *F.Q.* III. i. 59 Whenas all the world in silence deepe Yshrowded was. **1602** SHAKS. *Ham.* II. ii. 506 But as we often see against some storme, A silence in the Heauens. *c* **1630** MILTON *Upon the Circumcision* 5 Through the soft silence of the list'ning night. **1738** WESLEY *Hymns*, '*Regent of all the Worlds above*' iii, Fair Queen of Silence, Silver Moon. **1784** COWPER *Task* VI. 84 Stillness, accompanied with sounds so soft, Charms more than silence. **1832** MACAULAY *Armada* 49 Then bugle's note and cannon's roar the deathlike silence broke. **1850** TENNYSON *In Mem.* xix, There twice a day the Severn fills;..And makes a silence in the hills. **1878** BROWNING *La Saisiaz* 25 Can I..sharpen ear to recognize Sound o'er league and league of silence?

**b.** Used allusively to denote the state beyond this life. Chiefly in pl. and with initial capital.

**1803-6** WORDSW. *Ode Intimat. Immortality* ix, Power to make Our noisy years seem moments in the being Of the eternal Silence. **1851** CARLYLE *Sterling* I. i, To return silently, with his small, sorely foiled bit of work, to the Supreme Silences. **1908** E. MILLER *Martyrs of the Moors* 55 In fear and darkness his soul floated out to the great Silence.

**c.** ***Tower of Silence***, one of a number of small towers upon the summit of which the Parsees place their dead (see quot. 1865).

**1865** *Chambers's Encycl.* VII. 300 Their dead are not buried, but exposed on an iron grating in the Dokhma, or tower of Silence, to the fowls of the air. *c* **1880** GRANT *Hist. India* I. lxix. 359/1 The exposure of their dead in the Towers of Silence, to be eaten by the birds.

**d.** Phr. ***the rest is silence*** and varr., in allusion to the last words of the dying Hamlet (SHAKES. *Ham.* V. ii. 368).

**1910** GALSWORTHY *Justice* II. 49 Once this cheque was altered and presented, the work of four minutes—four mad minutes—the rest has been silence. **1939** A. HUXLEY *After Many a Summer* II. i. 187 If only the rest were silence!.. What joy if the rest of Wordsworth had been silence, the rest of Coleridge, the rest of Shelley! **1982** *Daily Tel.* 2 June 16/4 In most of the countries involved the eternal tug-of-war between Government and news media has long since ended. The curtain has fallen. The rest is silence.

**e.** A period of silence observed in memory of the dead, *esp.* the two minutes' silence kept on the anniversary of Armistice Day (11 Nov. 1918) or, since 1946, on Remembrance Sunday.

**1919** *Times* 12 Nov. 15/6 The Great Silence... At 11 o'clock yesterday morning the nation, in response to the King's invitation, paid homage to the Glorious Dead by keeping a two minutes' silence for prayer and remembrance. *Ibid.* 16/1 On the Stock Exchange, after the silence, a gong was sounded. **1926** A. TOPHAM *Chron. Prussian Court* xx. 245 We discussed among other things the *Titanic* disaster [1912] which had recently happened, and I remember referring to 'the silence' of two minutes by which the Canadian railways and churches had honoured the memory of the Canadians who had perished. **1929** *B.B.C. Year-bk. 1930* 78 Broadcasting the Silence November 11th, 1928. **1972** 'E. LATHEN' *Murder without Icing* (1973) xxii. 188 The game was preceded by a two-minute silence in memory of Billy Sicagusa. **1982** D. PHILLIPS *Coconut Kiss* vi. 52 You march once round the playground and salute the flag... Then you go in for the two minutes' silence.

**3. a.** Omission of mention, remark, or notice in narration. Chiefly in phrases ***to pass with, pass over in, silence.***

**1513** BRADSHAW *St. Werburge* Prol. 114 It were no reason her name be had in scylence, But to the people her name be magnyfyed. **1585** T. WASHINGTON tr. *Nicholay's Voy.* IV. xxxiii. 156 Ordinances, which I passe with silence. **1600** J. PORY tr. *Leo's Africa* III. 131, I would much rather haue smothered such matters in silence. **1667** MILTON *P.L.* VI. 385 Eternal silence be thir doome. **1711** ADDISON *Spect.* No. 1 ¶3 As for the rest of my Infancy, there being nothing in it remarkable, I shall pass it over in Silence.

**b.** Neglect or omission to write (about something); failure to communicate or reply.

**1617** MORYSON *Itin.* II. 206 By Don Jeans silence from Spaine, this overture.. tooke no effect as long as the Queene lived. **1698** FROGER *Voy.* Aj, The silence of all those who made the voyage with me, constrained me to expose it to publick view. **1771** *Junius Lett.* liv. (1788) 292, I understand that the public are not satisfied with my silence;—that an answer is expected of me. **1790** PALEY *Horæ Paul.* II. i. 9 The silence of the historian.. concerning any contribution, might lead us to look out for some different journey.

†**4.** A small hammer used to command silence or order. *Obs.*⁻¹

**1556** in Jupp *Acc. Carpenters' Comp.* (1887) 139 He helde not his peess before the master hade knockyd with the sylence iij tymes.

**5.** *Mus.* A rest.

**1752** tr. *Rameau's Treat. Music* 171 This Silence or Rest can be made but upon a Concord or consonant Note. **1856** MRS. BROWNING *Aur. Leigh* v. 342 The soul.. With all its grand orchestral silences To keep the pauses of its rhythmic sounds.

**6.** *Distill.* Want of flavour in distilled spirit. (Cf. SILENT *a.* 5 c.)

**1879** *Spon's Encycl. Manuf.* I. 229 Owing to its 'silence', there is no possibility of detecting afterwards from what source it has been obtained.

**7.** *attrib.* and *Comb.*, as ***silence time***, and in recent use ***silence-box, command, room, rule***, etc.; ***silence-loving*** adj.; **silence cabinet**, (*a*) = *silence-box*; (*b*) (see quot. 1929).

**1889** *Telephone* I. 471/1 The public is also admitted to a silence-box at the Nottingham Post Office. **1894** *Daily News* 28 Mar. 3/1 These particulars are telephoned into a silence-box at the Central Savings Bank. **1893** PREECE & STUBBS *Man. Teleph.* 227 At most telephone exchanges a 'silence cabinet' is provided in the public office. **1929** *B.B.C. Year-bk. 1930* 309 In Savoy Hill there are nine studios, six of which are equipped with silence cabinets (these are small rooms adjacent to the studios from which the announcer can speak before switching over to the studio itself). **1855** F. W. FABER *Growth in Holiness* ix. 147 It wrung a cry even from the silence-loving Heart of our ever-blessed Saviour. **1912** W. OWEN *Let.* 23 June (1967) 142 The firm Superintendent of their Sunday School, the silence-loving, and the melancholy-voiced, on that day capered about the lawn among them. **1958** S. HYLAND *Who goes Hang?* xviii. 77 They were in the Silence Room of the Library, a room in which conversation.. is.. a tabu. **1959** T. S. ELIOT *Elder Statesman* II. 47 And remember, when you want to be *very* quiet There's the Silence Room. With a television set. **1894** *Daily News* 14 May 5/1 He promised the modification and virtually the abolition of the silence rule. **1387** TREVISA *Higden* (Rolls) V. 19 Speke wolde he nevere, as it is i-write in þe questiouns þat he wroot in his scilence tyme. *c* **1450** in Aungier *Syon* (1840) 268 Eche suster.. shalle answer thus aȝene in lyke voyce thof it be sylence tyme.

**silence** (ˈsaɪləns), *v.* Also 6 silense. [f. prec.]

**1.** *trans.* To cause or compel (one) to cease speaking on a particular occasion; also, to overcome in argument.

**1603** SHAKS. *Meas. for M.* v. i. 181 Silence that fellow: I would he had some cause to prattle for himselfe. **1683** D. A. *Art of Converse* 18 If they happen to be silenc'd by another they become on a sudden ill humour'd. **1733** *Present State of Popery* 21 This learned priest has silenc'd the parson. **1797** MRS. RADCLIFFE *Italian* xiii, Paulo was silenced for a while by a significant look from his master. **1825** SCOTT *Betrothed* xvii, Silenced by this hint, the chirurgeon betook himself to his proper duty. **1877** FROUDE *Short Stud.* (1883) IV. I. iv. 47 The Archbishop of York peculiarly irritated Becket, and was silenced by a violent answer.

*refl.* **1604** SHAKS. *Ham.* III. iv. 4 Ile silence me e'ene heere: Pray you be round with him.

*fig.* **1736** BUTLER *Anal.* I. i. Wks. 1874 I. 18 How difficult it is to silence imagination enough to make the voice of reason even distinctly heard. **1791** MRS. RADCLIFFE *Rom. Forest* i, And, for a time, silenced his conscience.

**b.** To cause (an animal or thing) to cease from giving out its natural sound; to still, quieten.

**1604** SHAKS. *Oth.* II. iii. 175 Silence that dreadfull Bell, it frights the Isle, From her propriety. **1735** SHERIDAN in *Swift's Lett.* (1768) IV. 99 Upon desiring him to silence our dog. **1789** COWPER *Mrs. Throckmorton's Bulfinch* 59 That beak.. Might have repaid him well, I wote, For silencing so sweet a throat. **1810** SCOTT *Lady of Lake* III. iii, The mountain eagle.. spread her dark sails on the wind, And.. Silenced the warblers of the brake. **1859** TENNYSON *Merlin & V.* 391 It is the little rift within the lute That by and by will make the music mute, And ever widening slowly silence all.

**c.** To stop, suppress (a noise or sound).

**1818** SCOTT *Hrt. Midl.* xvii, Silence her cursed noise, if you should throttle her. **1819** —— *Ivanhoe* xxxi, An awful pause of horror silenced each murmur of the armed spectators.

**2.** To reduce (a person, etc.) to silence by restraint or prohibition, esp. in order to prevent the free expression of opinions.

**1597** SHAKS. *2 Hen. IV*, v. ii. 97 Imagine me, taking your part, And in your power, soft silencing your Sonne. **1607** —— *Cor.* II. i. 263 He would Haue.. silenc'd their Pleaders, And dispropertied their Freedomes. **1644** MILTON *Areop.* (Arb.) 38 We may not marvell, if not so often bad, as good Books were silenc't. **1691** WOOD *Ath. Oxon.* I. 157 He saw that the R. Cath. Religion would be silenced in England. **1727** BOYER *Dict. Royal* II, To silence the Play-house, *interdire la Comedie*. **1861** HOOK *Lives Abps.* I. i. 2 Oppression was legalised and Parliaments were silenced. **1879** B. TAYLOR *Germ. Lit.* 165 If arms silence laws, they silence letters all the more speedily.

**b.** To put down, repress (any expression of feeling, etc.).

**1647** SANDERSON *Serm.* II. 207 To silence all tumultuous thoughts and secret murmurings of our evil hearts. **1651** HOBBES *Leviath.* IV. xlvi. 380 Let them [*sc.* opinions] be silenced by the Laws of those, to whom the Teachers of them are subject. **1788** GIBBON *Decl. & Fall* xlv. IV. 434 The complaints of the people could no longer be silenced by the splendid names of a legislator and a conqueror. **1833** HT. MARTINEAU *Tale of Tyne* vii. 124 She vehemently silenced poor Tim's suggestions. **1874** GREEN *Short Hist.* iii. §5. 139 A threat of excommunication silenced the murmurs of the clergy.

**3. a.** *Mil.* and *Naval.* To compel (a gun, battery, or ship) to cease firing; to disable by superior fire; to stop (the fire of a gun).

**1748** SMOLLETT *Rod. Rand.* xxxiii, The enemy's fire.. slackened, and towards evening was quite silenced. **1755** in *Naval Chron.* (1799) I. 9 We silenced three of her lower deck guns. **1844** H. H. WILSON *Brit. India* I. 345 The batteries.. opened on the town and fort, and soon silenced their fire. **1893** FORBES-MITCHELL *Gt. Mutiny* 96 A number of the best shots.. were selected to try and silence the fire from the battery.

**b.** *slang.* (See quot.)

**1785** GROSE *Dict. Vulgar T.*, *To silence a man*, to knock him down, or stun him.

†**4.** To leave unmentioned or unnoticed; to pass over in silence, to omit. *Obs.*

**1602** WARNER *Alb. Eng.* Epitome 381 The Surname Tuder: wherein.. that of Plantagenet is inclusiuely silenced. **1627** W. SCLATER *Exp. 2 Thess.* (1629) 133 The.. coniectures of the late Interpreter.. I willingly silence. **1660** HOLMWOOD in J. Bland *Trade Revived* Pref., I was.. injoyned.. to silence his name, and have accordingly delivered sundry books to divers worthy Persons under a Nonemus.

†**5.** To get rid of (a thing) by maintaining silence. Const. *away*. *Obs.*⁻¹

**1788** MME. D'ARBLAY *Diary* IV. IV. 197 The subject.. being always embarrassing to me,.. I silenced it away.

**6.** *intr.* To cease speaking; to become silent or still. *rare.*

**1560** ROLLAND *Seven Sages* 30 The Heralds bad sone silence all and ceis. **1594** R. CAREW *Tasso* (1881) 13 The olde man silenst here. *Ibid.* 91 There silenc'd she, and seemed a disdaine Royall and noble flamed in her face. **1886** RANDOLPH *Mostly Fools* III. i. 25 The busy bustling room silenced and sobered instantly.

**silenced** (ˈsaɪlənst), *ppl. a.* [f. prec.]

**a.** That has been reduced or put to silence; *spec.* forbidden to preach or hold services on account of refusal to comply with some order.

**1606** (*title*), A Christian.. Offer of a most indifferent Conference.. abovt the maine and principall Controversies betwixt the Prelats, and the late silenced and deprived Ministers. **1644** in Wilkins *Polit. Ball.* (1860) I. 15 The silenc'd clergy.. In your damnation will bear share. **1681** BAXTER *Apol. Nonconf. Min.* 1 Apology for the Silenced ministers. **1731** CALAMY *Life* (1830) I. i. 77, I went afterwards to Mr. Tatnal's, who was the silenced minister of St. John Evangelist. **1737** POPE *Horace, Ep.* II. i. 237 The silenc'd Preacher yields to potent strain. **1818** BYRON *Ch. Har.* IV. cxii, In yon field below, A thousand years of silenced factions sleep. **1825** LD. COCKBURN *Mem.* (1856) 352 Its old and long silenced claims.. were now revived. **1836** H. ROGERS *Life Howe* iv. 150 Though Howe was an ejected minister, he could not consent to be a silenced one.

**b.** Of a gun: fitted with a silencer.

**1965** [see GUNSEL 2]. **1974** 'I. DRUMMOND' *Power of Bug* vii. 106 Why *did* the chap poke a silenced pistol through the window? **1980** *Daily Tel.* 15 Oct. 3 He would not shoot Henry MacKenny with a silenced firearm.

**silencer** (ˈsaɪlənsə(r)). [f. SILENCE *v.* + -ER¹.]

**1.** One who, or that which, silences; a conclusive argument or retort.

**1635** STRAFFORD *Lett.* (1739) I. 419 Death (the great Silencer of all our Words and Thoughts). **1684** BAXTER *Twelve Argt.* Post. N 3, Both Extreams.. are silencers of all that would undeceive them. **1817** KEATS *To Georgiana A. Wylie* 64 Bane of every wicked spell; Silencer of dragon's yell. **1871** G. MEREDITH *Harry Richmond* xv, But my retort .. was a silencer.

**2.** A piece of mechanism attached to a motor vehicle and used to silence or reduce the sound naturally caused by its working; also, a similar contrivance attached to a maxim gun, rifle, etc.

**1898** *Autocar* 5 Feb. 93/2 A more satisfactory silencer than the average run of silencers on Bollées. **1905** *Engineering* 20 Oct. 529/3 This form of silencer is not necessarily confined to marine motors. **1926** G. HUNTING *Vicarion* vi. 98 He must have had a silencer on his gun. **1950** G. BRENAN *Face of Spain* vii. 149 Nine hours in a bus without a silencer.. over mountain roads full of pot-holes. **1958** *Economist* 25 Oct. 349/3 Silencers on the engines reduce their efficiency by 4 to 5 per cent, and the total weight of silencing equipment is 1,600 lb, equivalent to 8 passengers. **1978** R. LUDLUM *Holcroft Covenant* iii. 44 He opened the door, pulled out his revolver and fired, the gunshot muted by a silencer.

Hence ˈ**silencered** *a.*, of guns: fitted with a silencer (cf. SILENCED *ppl. a.* b).

**1967** J. WAINWRIGHT *Worms must Wait* lxxxii. 214 They heard the tiny crack of the silencered Luger.

ˈ**silencing**, *vbl. sb.* [f. SILENCE *v.* + -ING¹.] The action of the verb in various senses.

**1596** NASHE *Saffron Walden* Wks. (Grosart) III. 123 Neuer exceeding a penny a quart, day nor night; and this deare yeare, together with the silencing of his loombes, scarce that. **1635** STRAFFORD *Lett.* (1739) I. 406 This only.. hath been my motive for the silencing this Business thus long. **1651** BAXTER *Saints' Rest* II. vi. §4 *marg.*, About the time of the silencing of Ministers. **1691** WOOD *Ath. Oxon.* II. 607 From that time to his silencing, he was a very zealous person for promoting the cause. **1751** J. BROWN *Ess. Shaftesb. Charac.* 62 So much for the silencing, which is the only conviction, of obstinacy and ignorance. **1895** *Athenæum* 31 Aug. 281/2 Very probably there was some partial silencing of the archery on one flank of the English host.

ˈ**silencing**, *ppl. a.* [-ING².] That reduces to silence; conclusive.

**1800** SWANSTON *Serm. & Lect.* I. 224 This was a silencing question. **1870** *Daily Telegr.* 6 Oct., It is impossible to give any silencing answer to those pestilent querists.

†ˈ**silency.** *Obs. rare.* [See SILENCE *sb.* and -Y.] Silence.

**1634** LENTON *Inns of Crt. Anagrammatist* B iv, And, in Love's silency, Whisperd each other, Lord, what a back hath he! **1642** H. MORE *Song of Soul* I. ii. 20 The Moon in silency Doth passe by night. *Ibid.* iii. 65 In solem silency this vapour rose.

**Silene** (saɪˈliːnɪ). *Bot.* [mod.L. (Linnæus), f. L. *Sīlēnus* SILENUS.] A genus of caryophyllaceous plants typifying the tribe *Sileneæ*. Also (with lower-case initial) a plant belonging to this genus; catchfly.

**1785** MARTYN *Rousseau's Bot.* xix. (1794) 274 In *Cucubalus* it [the calyx] is much inflated, and in *Silene* it is swelling. **1796** WITHERING *Brit. Pl.* (ed. 3) II. 414 It is evident from Ray's description that the Dover plant is a Silene, and not a Cucubalus. **1846** LINDLEY *Veget. Kingd.* 497 Some Silenes are scattered in many different parts of the globe. **1882** *Good Words* Mar. 184 Overgrown by masses of pink silene or tall graceful asphodels.

**Silenic** (saɪˈliːnɪk), *a.* [f. SILEN-US + -IC.] Resembling Silenus or one of the Sileni.

In both passages the reference is to Socrates.

**1822** SHELLEY *Prose Wks.* (1888) II. 108 Appearances in themselves excessively Silenic. **1850** GROTE *Greece* II. lxviii. VIII. 605 Its effect was enhanced.. by the very eccentricity of his Silenic physiognomy.

**silenite**, obs. form of SELENITE.

**silent** (ˈsaɪlənt), *a.* and *sb.* [ad. L. *silent-em*, pres. pple. of *silēre* to be silent.]

**A.** *adj.* **1. a.** Keeping or maintaining silence; refraining from speech or utterance; speechless, mute, dumb. Also, taciturn, reticent, reserved. Phr. ***strong silent man*** (or ***person, type***, etc.): a man who conceals and controls his feelings.

**1565** COOPER *Thesaurus*, *Taciturnulus*, somwhat silente. **1580** FULKE *Dang. Rock* 164 He is as silent as a Stone. **1588** GREENE *Perimedes* Wks. (Grosart) VII. 22 Delia by being silent, seemed to consent. **1611** SHAKS. *Wint. T.* IV. iv. 178 *Pol.* She dances featly. *Shep.* So she do's anything, though I report it That should be silent. **1664** MARVELL *Corr.* Wks. (Grosart) II. 167 Upon so extraordinary occasions.. had I an hundred tongues I should be struck silent. **1715** POPE *Iliad* I. 430 At awful Distance long they silent stand, Loth to advance, or speak their hard Command. **1797** MRS. RADCLIFFE *Italian* i, Which kept him silent, notwithstanding his wish to speak. **1821** SCOTT *Kenilw.* vi, If I could think myself the cause of Tressilian's ruin,.. I might be brought to be silent. **1840** CARLYLE *Chartism* iv. 30 With this strong silent people have the noisy vehement Irish now at length got common cause made. **1848** DICKENS *Dombey* i, They were both silent for a time, she weeping. **1875** JOWETT *Plato* (ed. 2) IV. 374 Throughout the two dialogues Socrates continues a silent auditor. **1905** M. BEERBOHM in *Sat. Rev.* 23 Sept. 401/1 He is going to cry? No, the hero is one of those strong, silent men. **1913** C. MACKENZIE *Sinister Street* I. II. xv. 407 She said I must be careful not to grow up into a strong silent Englishman, because their day was done. **1919** A. A. MILNE *Not that it Matters* 142 It is useless to model ourselves now on the strong, silent man of the novel whose face is a shutter to hide his emotions. **1936** W. S. MAUGHAM *Cosmopolitans* 260 These for the most part are strong silent men who waste no words. **1978** L. CHARTERIS *Saint & Templar Treasure* (1979) i. 25 I've always fancied myself as the strong silent type.

*absol.* **1778** MISS BURNEY *Evelina* lxiv, She has neither leisure nor thought to attend to the silent.

**b.** *transf.* and *fig.* of things.

**1605** SHAKS. *Lear* I. iv. 70 My duty cannot be silent, when I thinke your Highnesse wrong'd. **1659** *Gentl. Calling* (1696) 160 Idleness though a Crying sin..hath been the silentest of my guilts. **1757** GRAY *Epitaph Mrs. Clarke* I Where this silent marble weeps, A friend, a wife, a mother, sleeps. **1779** *Mirror* No. 61, There is a silent chronicle of past hours in the inanimate things amidst which they have been spent. **1824** BYRON *Juan* XVI. viii, The song was silent, and the dance expired. **1838** LYTTON *Alice* 16 Respect the silent heart of your mother. **1862** TENNYSON *Ded. Idylls* 16 All narrow jealousies Are silent; and we see him as he moved.

**c.** Of animals, birds, etc.

**1801** LATHAM *Gen. Synop. Birds* Suppl. II. 204 Silent Tanager... Inhabits the thick woods of Guiana... A solitary bird. **1809** SHAW *Gen. Zool.* VII. II. 330 Silent shrike... Native of the interior of Africa and the Cape of Good Hope. **1832** TENNYSON *Œnone* 25 The grasshopper is silent in the grass.

*phrase.* **1828** LYTTON *Pelham* lx, The silent sow sups all the broth. **1855** HALIBURTON *Nature & Hum. Nature* I. vii. 201 The silent pig is the best feeder.

**d.** ***as silent as the grave***: of a place, hushed, containing no natural noise; of a person, secretive, discreet.

**1823** J. F. COOPER *Pilot* I. vi. 78 'Does he keep silent?' 'As the grave.' **1829** W. SCOTT *Jrnl.* 1 July (1946) 89 The house ..became silent as the grave. **1889** R. L. STEVENSON *Master of Ball.* iii. 62 We..lowered ourselves softly into a skiff, and left that ship behind us as silent as the grave. **1936** W. S. MAUGHAM *Cosmopolitans* 269, I will be as silent as the grave, but honestly I don't understand. What does it all mean?

**2.** Of writers, books, etc.: Omitting mention of or reference to, passing over or disregarding, something in narration; containing no account or record. Const. † *in*, *of*, *as to*, † *to*.

**1601** R. JOHNSON *Kingd. & Commw.* (1603) 171 For (to be silent in matters of more auncient memory) about the yeare of our lorde 1300 [etc.]. **1629** PEMBLE *On Zachary* 92 Why were they silent of the other fasts, and touch onely vpon this? **1686** PLOT *Staffordsh.* 398 Our Historians..would not certainly have been silent of so considerable a structure, had they been the Authors of it. **1762** FOOTE *Orators* I. Wks. 1780 II. 25 The Court-Register has been silent to the members of common-council. **1774** GOLDSM. *Nat. Hist.* (1776) I. 280 Although history be silent as to many other inundations of the like kind. **1858** *Nat. Rev.* Oct. 505 The men of letters are so silent of them as to indicate [etc.]. **1871** FREEMAN *Norm. Conq.* (1876) IV. xviii. 224 As to the other shire.. history is equally silent.

**3. a.** Characterized or marked by silence or absence of speech; performed, made, suffered, etc., in silence or without speaking.

***the silent system***, a method of discipline enforced in a prison, penitentiary, etc., which imposes complete silence on all occasions.

**1592** DANIEL *Compl. Rosamond* 128 Sweet silent Rhetorique of perswading eyes. **1597** HOOKER *Eccl. Pol.* v. lxv. §5 Religion hauing likewise her silent rites. **1655** FULLER *Ch. Hist.* IX. 204 Princes politickly understanding their mutual secret language (not to say silent signs). **1691** HARTCLIFFE *Virtues* 319 His Religion was to be placed in a sober and silent Piety. **1746** FRANCIS tr. *Horace, Epist.* I. xiv. 20 A Country-Life was then your silent Prayer. **1779** *Mirror* No. 27, That silent and majestic sorrow which commands our reverence and our admiration. **1819** SCOTT *Ivanhoe* xxxviii, The younger knights told each other with their eyes, in silent correspondence [etc.]. **1836-7** DICKENS *Sk. Boz, Scenes* xvii, We went over the House of Correction..to witness the operation of the silent system. **1866** GEO. ELIOT *F. Holt* (1868) 14 She took care that they should be silent tears. **1891** *Fishing Gaz.* 14 Feb. 85/3 Then he drank a silent whiskey and left.

**b.** Of letters: Not sounded or pronounced; mute. See also quot. 1662.

**1605** CAMDEN *Rem.* (1623) 27 The adding..of our silent E, in the end of some words. **1662** PLAYFORD *Skill Mus.* I. viii. (1674) 26 Pauses or Rests are silent Characters, or an artificial omission of the Voyce or Sound. **1711** J. GREENWOOD *Eng. Gram.* 301 Other Letters..are quiescent or silent. **1869** ELLIS *E.E. Pronunc.* I. 570 The final *e* seems to have become silent even in 14. or 13. in the northern parts of the country. **1881** TYLOR *Anthrop.* vii. 179 The now silent letters are relics of sounds which used to be really heard in Anglo-Saxon.

**c.** Unmentioned, unrecorded; marked by the absence of any record. *rare.*

**1616** in *Cath. Rec. Soc. Publ.* III. 46, I cannot keep silent the singular pietie & bouldnesse of a certaine woeman. **1868** MILMAN *St. Paul's* ii. 28 He was bishop..for ten silent years. **1981** MACNIVEN & MOORE *Literary Lifelines* p. v, Silent corrections have been limited to restoring transposed letters.

**d.** (See quot.)

**1888** HERON *Church Sub-Apostolic Age* 90 His quotations are what have been called 'Silent', without any mention of the source.

**e.** Of a cinema film: unaccompanied by sound recording. Also in extended use to designate that which is related to or concerned with the silent film industry.

**1914** [see FILMDOM]. **1918** *N.Y. Times* 25 Nov. 11/3 (*heading*) Two opera stars in silent films. **1927** *Melody Maker* Sept. 933/3, I can see very little difference between the music appropriate to the spoken drama and that for the silent screen. **1941** B. SCHULBERG *What makes Sammy Run?* iv. 59 He was married to one of the big silent stars. **1967** *Listener* 30 Nov. 712/2 Rooming houses full of stars of silent pictures whom nobody remembers. **1977** R. BARNARD *Death on High C's* ii. 19 In Owen's production..you will be the silent-film heroine, and I will be the silent-film handsome seducer.

**4. a.** Characterized by the absence of sound or noise; quiet, noiseless, still.

**1588** SHAKS. *L.L.L.* II. i. 22 Till painefull studie shall outweare three yeares, No woman may approach his silent Court. **1594** —— *Rich. III*, v. iii. 85 The silent houres steale on, And flakie darkenesse breakes within the East. **1638** JUNIUS *Paint. Ancients* 14 The nights..whose length is abundantly able..to stirre up our phantasie by a silent quietnesse. **1667** MILTON *P.L.* II. 547 Others more milde, Retreated in a silent valley. *a* **1770** JORTIN *Serm.* (1771) V. 42 The Providence of God acts in a silent and mysterious manner. **1794** COLERIDGE *Tears in Solitude* 1 A green and silent spot, amid the hills, A small and silent dell! **1833** TENNYSON *Lotos Eaters* 16 Three mountain-tops, Three silent pinnacles of aged snow. **1887** L. OLIPHANT *Episodes* iv. 67 It involved..bark-canoeing on distant and silent lakes.

**b.** Making, or giving out, no noise or sound.

**1753** CHALLONER *Cath. Chr. Instr.* 220 From..this Day.. our Bells are silent throughout the Catholic Church. **1798** in Nicolas *Disp. Nelson* (1846) VII. p. clvi, The Guerrier and Conquérant..continued for a considerable time to fire..a gun or two, and about 8 o'clock..were totally silent. **1827** POLLOK *Course Time* IX, He went abroad, With foot as silent as the starry dews. **1859** TENNYSON *Marriage of Geraint* 321 A piece of turret stair Worn by the feet that now were silent. **1890** *R. Academy Catal.* 52 North Sea fishermen call screw steamers 'Silent Deaths', from their noiseless approach.

**c.** Of machinery, etc.: operating with or causing a minimum of noise.

**1887** *Encycl. Brit.* XXII. 524/1 Dr. Otto's 'silent' engine, introduced in 1876, was the first successful motor of the modern type. **1904** A. B. F. YOUNG *Compl. Motorist* (ed. 2) iv. 103 The silent working of the Lanchester car makes it also an extremely useful carriage for town use. *a* **1943** H. A. WHITCOMBE in J. Joyce *Trams of Past* (1979) 25 The citizens of Birmingham were proud of their steam trams and acclaimed them before all others for their..smooth and silent running.

**5.** † **a.** Of the moon: Not shining. *Obs.*

*a* **1646** J. GREGORY *Posthuma* (1650) 202 The most easie deliverie..is alwaies in the increas, toward and in the full of the Moon, and the hardest labors in the new and silent Moon. *a* **1727** NEWTON *Daniel* I. xi. (1733) 160 The Jews referred all the time of the silent moon, as they phrased it, that is, of the moon's disappearing, to the old moon.

**b.** Inactive, quiescent, not operative.

**1745** tr. *Columella's Husb.* IV. xxx, The proper time for setting them is before they bud, while the rods are silent [L. *dum silent virgæ*]. **1828-32** [see *silent partner*, sense 7 below]. **1867** ARGYLL *Reign of Law* I. 34 In many animal frames there are what have been called 'silent members', members which have no reference to the life or use of the animal. **1878** HUXLEY *Physiogr.* 203 A volcano, after being silent for ages, may suddenly start forth into fresh life. **1899** *Allbutt's Syst. Med.* VII. 643 One of the so-called 'silent' areas of the brain; for lesions in this situation are not infrequently latent, that is unattended with definite localising symptoms. **1974** *Nature* 1 Feb. 295/2 Enhancing serum as used in series *b* was then absorbed to remove Ag-B antibodies but possibly not antibodies against (? serologically silent) products of other genes in the MHC, if such exist. **1979** *Ibid.* 5 July 12/3 The recessive scrapie allele is likely to be widespread but clinically 'silent' in these breeds.

**c.** Of distilled spirit: Possessing no flavour.

**1839** URE *Dict. Arts* 405 Well purified or clean spirits, such as the distillers call silent whiskey. *Ibid.* 1255 A little silent spirit of wine being poured in. **1879** *Spon's Encycl. Manuf.* I. 228 The Irish distillers..assert further that the Scotch produce or 'silent spirit' as they agree to term it.. possesses no flavour.

**d.** *Med.* Not giving rise to or showing readily apparent signs or symptoms.

**1928** W. OVEREND *Radiogr. of Chest* II. iv. 49 There are two forms of silent pneumonia: a hilar which does not reach the pleura; and a cortical which does not reach the hilum. **1951** [see LATENT *a.* d]. **1979** *Jrnl. R. Soc. Arts* CXXVII. 171/2 We have had no great disease problem associated with them as yet but I have a feeling that the natural host is often a silent carrier.

**6.** *Comb.* **a.** With adverbial force, as ***silent-blessing, -falling, -gliding, -marking, -speaking***, etc.

*c* **1611** CHAPMAN *Iliad* xv. 35 Thou Flood, whose silent-gliding waues, the vnder ground doth beare. **1728-46** THOMSON *Spring* 882 Like silent-working Heaven, surprising oft The lonely heart with unexpected good. **1786** BURNS *Lament* ix, Oft has thy silent-marking glance Observ'd us. **1820** KEATS *Lamia* II. 148 Wherefore flout The silent-blessing fate, warm cloister'd hours? **1850** TENNYSON *In Mem.* xcv. 26 On the silence broke The silent-speaking words. **1868** J. H. NEWMAN *Verses Var. Occas.* 157, I will.. view Each shrivelling stalk and silent-falling leaf.

**b.** Parasynthetic, as ***silent-footed, -lighted***.

**1845** J. R. LOWELL *To Future* in *Graham's Mag.* XXVIII. 52 And he can see the grim-eyed Doom From out the trembling gloom Its silent-footed steeds toward his palace goading. **1850** TENNYSON *In Mem.* Concl. 112 The silent-lighted town. **1895** CLIVE HOLLAND *My Japanese Wife* 11 A white cat flits ghost-like and silent-footed across the path.

**7.** Special collocations: ***silent band*** = *silent majority* (*b*) below; ***silent cop*** (*Austral.*) (see quot. 1934); ***silent*** (***dog***) ***whistle***, a high-frequency whistle producing a note audible to a dog but scarcely audible to a human being; ***silent heat*** (*Vet.*), ovulation occurring without the signs of œstrus; † ***silent highway***, a river or canal (*obs.*); ***Silent Land***, used allusively to denote the state beyond this life; ***silent majority***, (*a*) the dead; (*b*) the mass of people whose views remain unexpressed, esp. in political contexts; those who are usu. overlooked because of their moderation; ***silent partner*** (*U.S.*) = *sleeping partner* s.v. SLEEPING *ppl. a.* 5 a; ***silent policeman*** (*N.Z.*) = *silent cop* above; ***silent service*** (see quot. 1929); ***silent spring***, in allusion to the title of the work by R. Carson (see quot. 1962), which drew attention to the danger to the natural environment inherent in the use of toxic chemicals; ***silent vote*** (*U.S.*), the vote of those whose political leanings are not known in advance of their vote being cast; so ***silent voter***.

**1866** G. MEREDITH *Let.* 15 Jan. (1970) I. 326 Will bawlings in the street avail?.. They irritate the slumbering dominant party, without strengthening the insurgent. What is being done in the *Fortnightly*, for instance..does strengthen, while it increases the silent band. **1934** T. WOOD *Cobbers* x. 122 A circle in the middle of cross-roads, for example, round which all traffic changing direction must swing; a round yellow blob, known here [*sc.* in Adelaide] as the Silent Cop, or the Poached Egg. **1959** D. HEWITT *Bobbin Up* 2 This was the corner, by the silent cop, where she and Roy had come to grief. **1961** C. WILLOCK *Death in Covert* iv. 64 Attached..to the lapel of Gumbe-Howard's coat was a silent dog whistle, and attached..to his heels was a silent dog. **1965** D. FRANCIS *For Kicks* xiii. 173 That's a silent whistle... For dogs... You can't hear it very well..but of course a dog can. **1980** J. W. HILL *Intermediate Physics* xvi. 150 The 'silent' dog whistle produces a note too high for the human ear but heard by a dog. **1950** N. BARRON *Dairy Farmer's Vet. Bk.* vi. 65 Cows sometimes have short and possibly 'silent' heats that pass unnoticed, when the ovary produces the egg but the cow does not show any outward sign of being in season. **1970** W. H. PARKER *Health & Dis. Farm Animals* vi. 58 The cow tends to be more generous with her signs of oestrus unless she is on a low plane of nutrition, when she may have a 'silent heat' like the ewe. **1848** *Punch* XV. 158/1 New towns have lately sprung up.. on each side of the Thames. If the population manages to keep pace with the mania for building, the 'silent highway' will soon become as noisy as the New Cut. **1875** *Birmingham Daily Mail* 5 Mar. 2/5, I speculate on the incalculable good that a 'Home' would do in rescuing girl-babies of the silent highway from the unwomanly scenes of their wasted young lives. **1935** *Times* 28 Feb. 14/2 This Cinderella of the bridges that span London's silent highway. **1853** *Working Man's Way in World* xiv. 320 (*heading*) Parents and friends in the Silent Land. **1939** L. M. MONTGOMERY *Anne of Ingleside* xxvii. 186 Ah well, Anne dearie, they've both passed long since into the Silent Land. **1874** *Harper's New Monthly Mag.* Sept. 468 (*heading*) The silent majority. **1910** *Motor World* 31 Mar. 851/1 (*heading*) Two join the 'silent majority'. Death calls at Detroit and Buffalo and claims well known men. **1955** C. V. WEDGWOOD *Great Rebellion* I. II. iv. 256 The King in his natural optimism still believed that a silent majority in Scotland were in his favour. **1970** *Guardian* 11 May 10/2 The Midwest..is 'silent majority' country. **1976** *National Observer* (U.S.) 1 May B4/4 Two-thirds of all marriages in the United States still succeed. So often silent majorities of this kind are too readily forgotten. **1828-32** WEBSTER s.v., A silent partner in a commercial house. **1894** S. LEAVITT *Our Money Wars* 221 His Wall St. concern..came to grief in 1890; also a concern in Buffalo in which he was a silent partner. **1974** R. L. SIMON *Wild Turkey* xii. 82 They're only the directors. There's someone behind them. Another investor... It's a silent partner. **1965** F. SARGESON *Memoirs of Peon* iv. 88 A silent policeman had been prised from its street-moorings. **1929** *Papers Mich. Acad. Sci., Arts & Lett.* X. 323/2 *Silent Service*, the Navy. This is a reference to the long silent vigil of the British Fleet. **1937** T. RATTIGAN *French without Tears* I. 40 You naval people never talk about yourselves, do you? *Rogers.* Well, you know, silent service and all that. **1982** *Daily Tel.* 2 June 16/3 The Army learned certain lessons in Northern Ireland. The silent service did not share that experience. **1962** R. CARSON (*title*) Silent spring. **1970** *N.Y. Times* 12 June 38 The Caspian Sea is probably the most dramatic battle-ground of Soviet Russia's looming silent spring and to date this battle is being lost to oil, petroleum products, industrial and city sewage, ballast and waste from ships. *Ibid.* 27 June 28 If we don't develop suitable pesticides—and use them —we really will have Silent Spring because there won't be any trees left for the birds to sing in. **1981** J. SUTHERLAND *Bestsellers* x. 112 Guilt about man's depredation of his and other species' environment, at the 'silent spring' which he has brought. **1936** *Durant* (Okla.) *Daily Democrat* 2 Nov. 2/4 The regents and police pensions amendments have the best chances of carrying, but even they are endangered by the 'silent vote'. **1952** *Economist* 6 Sept. 556/1 It is believed that there will be a substantial 'silent' vote against Mr. McCarthy by other citizens unwilling or unable to take a public stand against him. **1884** *Judge* 12 Nov. 140/2 To the Silent Voter, who was to make himself Felt for Cleveland: Tell me where you are and all will be forgiven.

**B.** *sb.* † **1.** The time of silence. *Obs.*[−1]

**1593** SHAKS. *2 Hen. VI*, I. iv. 19 Deepe Night, darke Night, the silent of the Night.

**2.** A device by which a clock or alarm may be prevented from striking or acting.

**1834-6** *Encycl. Metrop.* (1845) VIII. 634/1 The three-armed piece *s t u*, which is called the strike or silent. **1871** R. S. CULLEY *Pract. Telegr.* (ed. 5) 228 A switch of this kind attached to an alarum is called a 'silent'.

**3.** A silent film (see sense 3 e of the adj.).

**1929** *Morning Post* 24 May 12/7 Every recognised tradition of the 'silents' seems to have gone by the board. **1977** 'J. LE CARRÉ' *Hon. Schoolboy* xvii. 404 Even the latest films up here are silents.

**si'lential**, *a.* *rare.* [Cf. next and -AL[1].] Accompanied by, connected with, silence.

**1709** S. SEWALL *Diary* 6 Nov., Mr. Pemberton..read her Confession immediately, and by the silential vote restored her. **1712** *Ibid.* 2 Apr., What the Church had done in their Nomination, was by a Silential Vote Approved. **1859** J.

WILSON *Mem.* ix. 390 From some unknown silential principle..he had declined to reveal the secrets.

**silentiary** (saɪˈlɛnʃərɪ). [ad. late L. *silentiari-us*, f. L. *silentium* silence: see -ARY. So F. *silenciaire.*]

**1.** One who observes or recommends silence, *esp.* from religious motives.

**1611** COTGR., *Silentiaire*, a silenciarie, a patron or patterne of silence. **1657** TRAPP *Comm. Ps.* v. 4 The word signifieth Be dumb; and hereupon all our Silentiaries have founded their superstitious opinions and practices. **1844** *N. British Rev.* I. 141 A few solitaries, silentiaries, stylites,..from their caves and pillars, pleaded this interposition. **1883** SWINBURNE in *Fortn. Rev.* XXXIV. 513 The Gospel according to St. Coprostom the Silentiary [i.e. Carlyle].

**2.** An officer of the Byzantine court, whose duty originally was to obtain silence, but who frequently acted as a confidential adviser or agent. Now *Hist.*

Blount *Glossogr.* (1656) has: '*Silentiary*, a Gentleman Usher, who sees good rule and quietness kept'.

*a* **1677** BARROW *Pope's Supremacy* VI. xvi. (1680) 400 That notable passage in the Synod of Chalcedon; where Bassianus ..saith, Our..Emperor..afterwards sent his rescript by Eustathius the Silentiary. **1788** GIBBON *Decl. & F.* xlii. IV. 263 He had served ten years a silentiary of the Byzantine palace. **1833** *Blackw. Mag.* XXXIV. 117 Agathias' friend, Paul the Silentiary.., who at the court of Justinian held an ..office corresponding to that of Gentleman Usher. **1895** *Edin. Rev.* Apr. 479 The contemplation of the spectacle raises the Silentiary to his highest key.

**b.** An official whose duty it is to command silence.

**1838** *Fraser's Mag.* XVIII. 180 The silentiary, standing by the main pillar of the hall, smote lustily upon it with his rod, to command silence. **1883** SEEBOHM *Eng. Village Comm.* 240 The columns..are sometimes cased in metal, and the silentiary, to call attention, strikes one of them with his staff.

**silentious** (saɪˈlɛnʃəs), *a.* [Cf. late L. *silentiōsus*, It. *silenzioso*, Sp. and Pg. *silencioso*, F. *silencieux.*] Given to silence.

**1879** WEBSTER *Suppl.*, *Silentious*, habitually silent; taciturn; reticent. **1895** HOWELLS in *Century Mag.* June 184/1 Those silentious minstrels who grind small, mute organs at the corners of the pavement.

**ˈsilentish**, *a. rare.* [f. SILENT *a.*] Somewhat silent.

**1737** OZELL *Rabelais* IV. 175 A small, still, silent (or, if you will, Silentish) Sound. **1948** E. BLUNDEN *Shakespeare to Hardy* (1956) xii. 168 Among those who were present..at Dickens's public readings, a 'silentish young man'.

**ˈsilently**, *adv.* [f. SILENT *a.* + -LY[2].]

**1.** In a silent manner; without speaking, in silence; without noise or commotion, noiselessly, quietly; without mention or notice.

**1570–6** LAMBARDE *Peramb. Kent* (1826) 157, I could not silently slip over such impieties. **1590** SHAKS. *Mids. N.* III. i. 206 Tye vp my louers tongue, bring him silently. **1617** MORYSON *Itin.* I. 246 The Turkey company in London was at this time..silently enjoying the safety and profit of this trafficke. **1667** MILTON *P.L.* v. 130 She..silently a gentle tear let fall. **1730** WATERLAND *Rem. Clarke's Exp. Ch. Catech.* ii, What the compilers recommended chiefly to our faith, he silently passes over. **1784** COWPER *Task* IV. 419 These ask with painful shyness, and, refus'd Because deserving, silently retire! **1832** LYTTON *E. Aram* I. xi, Ellinor silently made room for her cousin beside herself. **1878** LECKY *Eng. in 18th C.* I. 313 Most of the.. congregations had silently discarded the old doctrine of the Trinity.

†**2.** Gradually, imperceptibly. *Obs.*[−1]

**1668** CULPEPPER & COLE *Barthol. Anat.* I. xiii. 30 It goes by little and little straight forward, and is silently terminated towards the spleen.

**ˈsilentness.** [f. SILENT *a.* + -NESS.]

**1.** Maintenance of silence; avoidance of speech or utterance; reticence; speechlessness.

*a* **1623** AINSWORTH *Annot. Ps.* xl. 3 [= xxxix. 2] With stillnesse, or, silentnesse. **1727** BAILEY (vol. II.), *Silentness*, silence. **1817** BYRON *Lament of Tasso* v, And if my eyes reveal'd it, they, alas! Were punish'd by the silentness of thine. **1836** MRS. BROWNING *Poet's Vow* v. iv, I charge thee, by the living's prayer, And the dead's silentness. **1882** MRS. CRAIK *Little Mother* II. 39 Dorcas with her silentness and careworn face.

*transf.* **1860** FABER *Bethlehem* iii. (1865) 153 There was something in the silentness of His look, which compelled worship.

**2.** The condition of being silent or still; absence of sound or noise; silence, stillness, noiselessness, quietness. Chiefly *poet.*

**1795** COLERIDGE *Anc. Mar.* VI. xvii, The moonlight steeped in silentness The steady weathercock. **1813** SHELLEY *Q. Mab* VIII. 74 Where the shrill chirp of the green lizard's love Broke on the sultry silentness alone. **1849** *Tait's Mag.* XVI. 105 The tingling silentness of solemn midnight ..lulled the spirit. **1886** RUSKIN *Præterita* I. vi. 201 The smooth pavement under the wheels adding with its silentness to the sense of dream wonder in it all.

**b.** With *a.*

**1819** WIFFEN *Aonian Hours* 88 A sound beneath—a silentness above. **1865** *Cornh. Mag.* XI. 360 In the keen cold air There was a hush, a sleepless silentness.

‖**Silenus** (saɪˈliːnəs). Pl. Sileni (saɪˈliːnaɪ). [L. *Sīlēnus*, ad. Gr. Σειληνός: cf. SILEN.]

**1.** *Gr. Mythol.* The foster-father of Bacchus, and leader of the satyrs; also, a wood-god, a satyr.

**1710** W. KING *Heathen Gods & Heroes* xxvii. (1722) 134 Several cruel Dæmons, Satyrs, Sileni and Tityri. *a* **1734** NORTH *Lives* (1826) II. 44 He was a very Silenus to the boys, ..the students of the law, to make them merry whenever they had a mind to it. **1738** CHAMBERS *Cycl.* s.v. *Satyr*, The poets usually confound the Satyrs, Sylvans, Sileni, Fauns, and Panes. **1820** SHELLEY *Hymn of Pan* 18 The Sileni, and Sylvans, and Fauns, And the Nymphs of the woods and the waves. **1831** KEIGHTLEY *Mythol.* 204 The Satyrs..when old were called Sileni.

**2.** *Zool.* A species of macaque. Also *attrib.*

**1871** *Cassell's Nat. Hist.* I. 117 The Silenus Ape, usually miscalled Wanderoo, is so baboonish that, although it has a long tail, it cannot be placed with the Common Macaque.

†**ˈsiler.** *Bot. Obs.* [a. L. *sīler.*]

**1.** With the epithet *mountain*: An umbelliferous plant of the genus *Seseli.*

Given without the distinguishing epithet in Crabb *Technol. Dict.* (1823) and *Treas. Bot.* (1866).

**1548** TURNER *Names Herbes* (E.D.S.) 73 Seseli massiliense is called in the Poticaries shoppes, siler montanum, it may be called in englishe, siler montayne. **1551** —— *Herbal* I. (1568) 4 Dronken with syler mountayne and Frenche spykenarde. **1605** SYLVESTER *Du Bartas* II. i. III. 621 The Mountain-Siler helpeth Goats to yean. **1607** TOPSELL *Four-f. Beasts* (1658) 236 Some use Siler of the Mountains to procure conception in Mares and Cowes. **1656** RIDGLEY *Pract. Physick* 344 Take ..Siler mountain, one dram.

**2.** A species of willow or osier.

The orig. sense of L. *siler*; app. never current in English.

**1607** TOPSELL *Four-f. Beasts* (1658) 201 The root of the greater Siler decocted in Goats milk. [**1753** *Chambers' Cycl. Suppl.* s.v.]

† **siler**, obs. form of CELLAR. Cf. SILLER.

**1525** *Test. Ebor.* (Surtees) V. 212 My tenementes in the Hye Strete with a grete siler bowndyng next to Cristofer Lurte.

**silery**, obs. variant of CILERY.

**Silesia** (saɪˈliːʃ(ɪ)ə). Also 7–8 **Slesia**, 7 **Sleasia.** [The Latinized form of the name of a province in the east of Germany (G. *Schlesien*). See also SLEAZY *a.*]

**1.** Used *attrib.* with *cloth, lawn*, etc. = next.

**1674** BLOUNT *Glossogr.* (ed. 4) s.v. *Sleasie Holland*, That onely is properly Slesia, or Silesia linnen cloth, which is made in, and comes from the Countrey Silesia in Germany. [**1696** J. F. *Merch. Wareho. laid open* 28 Being called Sleasie-Lawns, the name Sleasia it takes from a town called Sleasia in Germany.] **1710** WHITWORTH *Acc. Russia* (1758) 82 The Hollanders..bring wines, paper,..brocades, Silesia cloth, and all sorts of gallanteries. **1712** E. COOKE *Voy. S. Sea* 363, 3 of Silesia Linnen.

**b.** A fine linen or cotton fabric originally manufactured in Silesia.

**1727** W. MATHER *Young Man's Comp.* 411 The Commodities..exported..are Iron, Copper, Slesias, Sheets, Sayes [etc.]. **1764** *Ann. Reg.* 107 Fine printed linens of all sorts, cambricks, Britannias, Silesias, hats, etc. **1769** *Public Advertiser* 14 Nov. 3/3 Buckrams, glazed Linens,.. and Quadruple Silesias. **1800** *Hull Advertiser* 3 May 2/2, 10 pieces containing 1223 ells of 7-eights fine white Silesia. **1807** J. HALL *Trav. Scot.* I. 213 The principal manufacture of Newburgh is that of Silesias. **1893** *Outing* XXII. 122/2 Some dull-tinted light cloth, as lawn, cambric or silesia.

**2.** The distinctive name of a variety of lettuce.

In Mills (1763) and Loudon (1824) the form is *Cilicia.*

**1731** MILLER *Gard. Dict.* s.v. *Lactuca*, The most valuable of all the Sorts of Lettuces in England are the Versailles, the Silesia and Cos. **1796** C. MARSHALL *Gardening* xv. (1813) 241 The Silesia lettuce is much admired by some, though at present but little cultivated.

**Silesian** (saɪˈliːʃ(ɪ)ən), *a.* and *sb.* [f. prec. + -AN.]

**A.** *adj.* **a.** Of or pertaining to Silesia. Also in special applications, as ***Silesian beet, bole, cloth***, etc.

*c* **1645** HOWELL *Lett.* (1650) II. 81 In a different character from the Dalmatian, Croatian,..Silesian, and other nations towards the West. **1681** GREW *Musæum* III. III. iii. 348 Silesian Bole..feels as smooth as Castile-Soap. **1707** ADDISON *Pres. St. War* Wks. 1766 III. 271 The Silesian fund..enabled that Prince [Eugene] to make a conquest of Italy. **1753** *Chambers' Cycl.* Suppl. s.v. *Terra*, Silesian Earth, in the materia medica, a fine astringent bole. **1839** *Penny Cycl.* XIII. 243/2 Lettuce (Hardy Hammersmith,.. Large White Malta, or White Silesian). **1851–4** *Tomlinson's Cycl. Useful Arts* (1866) II. 687/2 The second group is represented by the white Silesian beet. **1876** BANCROFT *Hist. U.S.* VI. xxxii. 120 A plan for a direct commerce with America, so as to open a sale for Silesian cloths. **1881** LYELL *Pigeons* 86 The Silesian swallow pigeon..is marked on the head with only a frontal spot.

**b.** ***Silesian stem***, a shouldered stem of a goblet or candlestick, supposed to have been so named in honour of George I for whom a goblet with such a stem was first made. Hence ***Silesian-stemmed*** adj.

[**1925** F. BUCKLEY *Hist. Old Eng. Glass* ix. 72 The waisted bowl,..and the pediment, or Silesian-shouldered stem, were both novelties at this time.] **1929** W. A. THORPE *Hist. Eng. & Irish Glass* I. v. 171 The shouldered stem is commonly known as 'Silesian', but it is certainly not exclusive to that part of Germany. *Ibid.* vi. 204 For about twenty years..the Silesian stem remained constant and English stem growth was at a standstill. **1961** E. M. ELVILLE *Collector's Dict. Glass* 166 (*caption*) Silesian-stemmed glass moulded on the four shoulders with GR in relief. **1978** *Country Life* 19 Oct. 1170/2 It is a very pretty glass (I always fall for the high-shouldered, so-called Silesian stem which is apparently not Silesian at all). **1979** 'J. GASH' *Grail Tree* ii. 22 An engraved lead-glass cordial glass..among some Silesian-stemmed glasses.

**B.** *sb.* A native of Silesia.

**1669** J. OWEN *Truth & Innocence Vind.* Wks. 1852 XIII. 418 A Silesian who gave the ensuing account of his faith. **1797** *Encycl. Brit.* (ed. 3) XIV. 565/1 The Silesians and Bohemians have corrupted their dialects in the very same manner. **1862** CARLYLE *Fredk. Gt.* XII. ii. III. 177 Printed.. Proclamation, briefly assuring all Silesians, of whatever rank, condition or religion [etc.].

**silex**[1] (ˈsaɪlɛks). [L. *silex* flint. So F. *silex.*] Flint, silica.

*a* **1592** GREENE *Orpharion* Wks. (Grosart) XII. 68 The precious stone Silex is full of secret vertue.

**1753** *Chambers' Cycl.* Suppl., *Silex*, flint, in natural history, the name of a genus of semi-pellucid stones [etc.]. **1794** SULLIVAN *View Nat.* I. 433 Most of the ambiguous stones..contain, besides portions of calcareous and argillaceous earths, certain portions of the silex also. **1805** *Phil. Trans.* XCV. 231 If the stone contain silex, this earth will be separated in the process of solution and evaporation. **1840** J. BUEL *Farmer's Companion* 35 Silex is apparent in the epidermis of Indian corn, wheat, oats, and the hollow grasses. **1878** HUXLEY *Physiogr.* xvi. 271 It would..be a highly fossiliferous limestone with more or less silex.

*attrib.* **1887** *Daily News* 20 June 2/6 Valuable seams of hematite ore and silex pottery clay. **1895** *Outing* XXVI. 36/1 The collection of silex grains that for courtesy we called the road.

**Silex**[2] (ˈsaɪlɛks). The proprietary name of a coffee-making machine in which boiling water is drawn through ground coffee in a filter by the creation of a vacuum.

**1914** *Official Gaz.* (U.S. Patent Office) 31 Mar. 1370/2 Silex. Particular description of goods.—Coffee-percolators. **1934** *Trade Marks Jrnl.* 12 Sept. 1187/2 *Silex...* Coffee making appliances, kettles and kettle stands, milk heating and pasteurizing utensils, urns and urn stands, coffee sets [etc.]... The Silex Company.., State of Connecticut, United States of America; manufacturers. **1949** H. MACLENNAN *Precipice* iv. 267 The coffee had bubbled into the top of the Silex. **1971** J. HENDERSON *Copperhead* xv. 191 A girl appeared with a Silex of coffee and the usual paper cups.

**silf(e**, obs. forms of SELF.

**silgreen**, dial. variant of SENGREEN.

**silhouette** (sɪluːˈɛt), *sb.* [From the name of Étienne de *Silhouette* (1709–67), a French author and politician.

According to the usual account, which is that given by Mercier *Tableau de Paris* 147, the name was intended to ridicule the petty economies introduced by Silhouette while holding the office of Controller-general in 1759, but Hatzfeld & Darmesteter take it to refer to his brief tenure of that office. Littré, however, also quotes a statement that Silhouette himself made outline portraits with which he decorated the walls of his château at Bry-sur-Marne.]

**1. a.** A portrait obtained by tracing the outline of a profile, head, or figure by means of its shadow or in some other way, and filling in the whole with black; an outline portrait cut out of black paper; a figure or picture drawn or printed in solid black.

Details within the outline are sometimes indicated by white or gold lines. For an account of various methods employed in obtaining such portraits or pictures, see the *Penny Cycl.* XXII. 8.

**1798** W. TAYLOR in *Monthly Rev.* XXVII. 388 At best but the shadow of a shade,..the silhouette of a bust. **1801** FUSELI *Lect. Art* i. 9 Skiagrams, simple outlines of a shade, similar to those which have been introduced to vulgar use by the students and parasites of Physiognomy, under the name of Silhouettes. **1806** J. BERESFORD *Miseries Hum. Life* XII. xxix, Whenever they send me their silhouettes, or what do they call them, I chuck them out of the window. **1860** THACKERAY *Lovel* ii, She had..silhouettes of her father and mother..hung up in the lodgings. **1880** *Print. Trades Jrnl.* xxx. 40 The beauty of silhouettes (pictures printed in solid black) depends upon two things—artistic ability and careful printing.

*attrib.* **1835** [see SILHOUETTIST]. **1841** BARHAM *Ingol. Leg.* Ser. II. *Auto-da-fé* ii, A garment..stuck thick With multiplied silhouette profiles of Nick. **1895** *Daily News* 1 May 6/4 The archaic, dry, and silhouette style of the picture.

**b.** *fig.* A slight verbal sketch or description in outline of a person, etc.

**1819** LADY MORGAN *Autobiog.* (1859) 313 The baron's *silhouette* of the Lady of Copet..was certainly very amusing. **1857** C. BRONTE *Professor* iii, The silhouette I have just thrown off. **1894** J. KNIGHT *Garrick* xvii. 311 Actors..of whom Pepys has given us silhouettes, and Colley Cibber portraits.

**2. a.** A dark outline, a shadow in profile, thrown up against a lighter background.

**1843** THACKERAY *Irish Sketch-Bk.* II. xiii. 233 Ghostly looking *silhouettes.* **1847** C. BRONTE *J. Eyre* xxviii, Entering the gate and passing the shrubs, the silhouette of a house rose to view; black, low, and rather long. **1866** WHITTIER *Snow-Bound* 167 The cat's dark silhouette on the wall. **1887** RIDER HAGGARD *A. Quatermain* 186, I saw the black silhouette of the old Zulu raise its arm in mute salute.

**b.** The contour or outline of a garment.

**1920** *Glasgow Herald* 27 Nov. 4 The silhouette of this season is..much more attractive than that last year approved by Dame Fashion. *Ibid.* 4 Dec. 4 See that you preserve the silhouette of the gown. **1978** *Country Life* 17 Aug. 472/1 The new silhouette..is straight, narrow and short, with well defined, padded shoulders.

**3.** ***en*** (or ***in***) ***silhouette***, in outline, in profile.

**1832** J. P. KENNEDY *Swallow B.* (1860) 18 At that hour nature draws her pictures *en silhouette.* **1886** *Illustr. Lond. News* 6 Feb. 142/2, I shall be presented to you *en silhouette*, all black, and you will be required to recognise the portrait.

**1889** *Harper's Weekly* XXXIII. Suppl. 60 This framing of trees, which stand out in silhouette against a bright blue sky.

**silhou'ette,** *v.* [f. prec.]

**1.** *trans.* To represent in silhouette, to throw up the outline of. Chiefly used in past participle, and const. *against* or *upon.*

**1876** R. F. BURTON *Gorilla L.* I. 137 We guided ourselves ..towards a ghostly point, whose deeper blackness silhouetted it against the shades. **1882** BRET HARTE *Flip* i, A spur of the coast range, which had been sharply silhouetted against the cloudless western sky. **1897** MARY KINGSLEY *W. Africa* 48, I have seen it silhouetted hard against tornado-clouds.

*refl.* **1890** S. J. DUNCAN *Social Departure* 311 The great ships silhouetted themselves upon a sky..gloriously blue.

**2.** *intr.* To show like a silhouette.

**1884** *Harper's Mag.* June 110/2 Their huge crowns silhouetting in clear-cut outlines against the eastern sky.

Hence **silhou'etted** *ppl. a.*, **silhou'etting** *vbl. sb.* Also **silhou'ettist**, a maker of silhouettes.

**1835** (*title*), Treatise on Silhouette Likenesses, by Monsieur Edouart, Silhouettist to the French Royal Family. **1888** W. D. LIGHTHALL *Young Seigneur* 97 The delicate silhouetting of the trees along the shore. **1890** *Eng. Illustr. Mag.* July 748 The photographer..has focussed the silhouettist out of existence. *Ibid.* 752 If silhouetting be allowed to possess an artistic side. **1894** MAX PEMBERTON *Sea Wolves* iv. (1901) 23 The black hulls of innumerable barges and the silhouetted shapes of great steamers.

**silica** ('sɪlɪkə). [f. L. *silic-, silex* SILEX[1]. Cf. F. *silice.*] **a.** An important mineral substance (the dioxide of silicon), which in the form of quartz enters into the composition of many rocks, and is contained in sponges and certain plants.

**1801** *Encycl. Brit.* (ed. 3) Suppl. I. 254/1 Silica, when dried, is a soft white powder, without either taste or smell. **1851** RICHARDSON *Geol.* (1855) 81 Silica and alumina besides being present in almost all vegetable and animal substances. **1878** HUXLEY *Physiogr.* 202 The water generally holds silica in solution.

**b.** *attrib.* and *Comb.* ***silica-borate, dust, skeleton***; ***silica-plated*** *adj.*; **silica glass** = *quartz glass* s.v. QUARTZ 2 a; **silica gel**, hydrated silica in a hard granular form which is very hygroscopic and is used as a desiccant; **silica wool** = *slag wool* s.v. SLAG *sb.* 6.

**1859** R. HUNT *Guide Mus. Pract. Geol.* (ed. 2) 114 A silica-borate of lead, prepared by Professor Faraday. **1918** *Act 8 & 9 Geo. V.* c. 14 § 1 (3) Any industry..involving exposure to silica dust. **1920** *Jrnl. Amer. Chem. Soc.* XLII. 971 The mere fact that a chemically inert substance like silica gel is found exhibiting such marked absorptive properties is sufficient in itself to indicate that the cause of adsorption does not lie in the interaction of adsorbent and adsorbed substance. **1956** *Nature* 18 Feb. 329/1 The acid mixture was separated on a silica gel column into acetic and propionic acids. **1977** J. HEDGECOE *Photographer's Handbk.* 36 If you are storing a camera in an unfavorable climate put it in a plastic bag with the packet of silica gel which is supplied with most new cameras. **1916** *Chem. Abstr.* X. 103 (*heading*) Silica glass. **1919** *Nature* 23 Oct. 153/1, I have recently observed that 'silica glass' possesses a remarkable crystalline or quasi-crystalline structure when examined in the polariscope. **1965** B. J. MOODY *Compar. Inorg. Chem.* xviii. 268/2 Silica may be fused in the oxy-hydrogen blowpipe flame, softening at 1500–1600° C and fusing above 1700° C. .. The amorphous vitreous product is a supercooled liquid, silica glass, quartz glass, fused quartz or just silica. **1870** tr. *Pouchet's Universe* 26 Ehrenberg, on analyzing a shower of fine dust.., found eighteen species of silica-plated animalcules. **1882** VINES tr. *Sachs' Bot.* 36 Silica-skeletons are obtained most abundantly from epidermal cells and from Diatoms. **1906** *Chambers's Jrnl.* Aug. 599/1 Slag-wool, or silica-wool, is in appearance and properties similar to asbestos.

**silicate** ('sɪlɪkeɪt, -kət). [f. prec. + -ATE[4]. So F. *silicate.*] **a.** Any salt, ester, or anion of a silicic acid; any substance (e.g. very many minerals and rocks) which is regarded as being formed from silica together with other oxides, and has an extended polymeric anionic structure built up from linked ($SiO_4$) tetrahedra. Cf. SILICIATE.

**1811** *Phil. Trans.* CI. 176 A compound salt, consisting of silicate of alumina, and fluate of alumina. **1846** J. BAXTER *Libr. Pract. Agric.* (ed. 4) I. 36 The cereals require the alkalies and silicates liberated by the lime. **1872** W. S. SYMONDS *Rec. Rocks* i. 12 Amongst the other volcanic minerals the most important are the silicates of alumina, lime, magnesia, potash, and soda. **1891** *Jrnl. Chem. Soc.* LX. II. 814 (*heading*) Action of phosphorus oxychloride on ethereal silicates and their chloro-derivatives. **1937** W. L. BRAGG *Atomic Structure of Minerals* ix. 146 The classification of the silicates by their silicon-oxygen structures..corresponds to a large extent to the usual mineralogical classification. The structure is so rigid in the pyroxenes and amphiboles, micas, felspars and zeolites that it decides the crystal form. **1959** BERRY & MASON *Mineralogy* xv. 462 Silicate classification is based on the types of linkages, which are as follows: 1. Independent tetrahedral groups... 2. Double tetrahedra structures [etc.]. **1962** P. J. & B. DURRANT *Introd. Adv. Inorg. Chem.* xviii. 605 In most silicates the $SiO_4$ tetrahedra are not discrete, but are parts of larger systems in which certain oxygen atoms are held in common by two tetrahedra.

**b.** *Comb.*, as **silicate board**, a board made fireproof by being saturated with silicate; **silicate cotton**, slag-wool; **silicate paint**, 'natural silica, when dried and forming an almost impalpable powder, mixed with colours and oil' (Annandale *Imperial Dict.* 1882).

**1881** *Daily News* 24 Dec. 3/4 Some incombustible, non-conducting material—preferably silicate cotton, which is manufactured from blast furnace slag. **1884** KNIGHT *Dict. Mech.* Suppl. 810/1 *Silicate-Board*, an incombustible board for roofing.

**silicated** ('sɪlɪkeɪtɪd), *a.* [f. L. *silic-, silex*: cf. prec. and F. *silicaté.*] Coated or impregnated with silex or silica.

**1800** HENRY *Epit. Chem.* (1808) 100 With a larger proportion of alkali,..this earth affords a compound called silicated alkali. **1819** J. G. CHILDREN *Chem. Anal.* 427 A concentrated solution of silicated potassa. **1849** MURCHISON *Siluria* xiv. 356 The silicated moulds of shells. **1879** RUTLEY *Stud. Rocks* xi. 177 Liparites, trachytes, andesites and other highly-silicated eruptive rocks.

**silication** (sɪlɪ'keɪʃən). [Cf. prec. and -ATION.] Combination with silica; silification.

**1869** PHILLIPS *Vesuv.* xi. 311 According to the nature of the particular current, its order of silication, [etc.]..changes in the mineral constituents are more or less easy. **1904** *Monogr. U.S. Geol. Survey* XLVII. viii. 667 Silication of carbonates, forming silicates and releasing carbon dioxide, is one of the chief reactions of the zone of anamorphism. **1923** *Jrnl. Geol.* XXXI. 176 Magnetic end-stage emanations ..produce a bewildering series of silication..silicification, gametization and metallic-mineralization effects.

So **silicati'zation**, 'the process of combining with silica, so as to change to a silicate'.

**1864** WEBSTER, citing DANA. [Cf. F. *silicatisation.*]

[**silice**, an error for SILICLE.

Webster (1828–32), citing Martyn. The word is misprinted in the second edition (1796) of the *Language of Botany*.]

**si'liceo-**, combining form of SILICEOUS, as in ***siliceo-calcareous, -felspathic, -fluoric.***

**1816** *Edin. Rev.* XXVI. 163 Silceo-calcareous sand. **1822** IMISON *Sci. & Art* II. 78 A permanent acid gas, called the Siliceo-fluoric acid. **1839** DE LA BECHE *Rep. Geol. Cornwall*, etc. vii. 203 A hard siliceo-felspathic compound.

**siliceous** (sɪ'lɪʃəs), *a.* [ad. L. *siliceus*, f. *silic-, silex* flint: cf. F. *siliceux* and SILICIOUS *a.*] Containing or consisting of silica; of the nature of silica: **a.** Of mineral substances.

**1656** BLOUNT *Glossogr.*, *Siliceous*,..of or pertaining to flint, flinty. **1783** WITHERING tr. *Bergman's Mineral.* 59 Siliceous Earth. **1794** SULLIVAN *View of Nature* I. 430 What some call vitrescent earths, others denominate siliceous. **1813** SIR H. DAVY *Agric. Chem.* (1814) 194 Siliceous sandstone, which is composed of fine quartz or sand, united by a siliceous cement. **1851** RICHARDSON *Geol.* xii. 380 The upper greensand, in some localities,..consists of a sharp siliceous sand. **1879** D. M. WALLACE *Australasia* iv. 71 They consist of..sandy ironstone, or even hard siliceous rock enclosing quartz pebbles.

**b.** Of plant or animal structures.

**1813** SIR H. DAVY *Agric. Chem.* (1814) 57 The siliceous epidermis..protects the bark from the action of insects. **1845** DARWIN *Voy. Nat.* i. 5 This dust consists..of infusoria with siliceous shields, and of the siliceous tissue of plants. **1868** CARPENTER in *Sci. Opin.* 174/2 Imbedded in this mud there came up an extraordinary collection of siliceous sponges.

**silici-** ('sɪlɪsaɪ), combining form of SILEX or SILICA, as in ***silicicalcareous, -fluoric; silicicalce, -murite***; **silici'clastic** *a. Petrol.*, applied to clastic rocks and deposits that are not carbonates; **'silicicole, sili'cicolous** *adjs. Bot.* [L. *colĕre* to inhabit], growing best in siliceous soil.

**1796** KIRWAN *Elem. Min.* (ed. 2) I. 102 Silicicalcareous freestones, which are often porous, and serve for filtering stones. **1811** PINKERTON *Petral.* II. 202 Contiguous, on the one side to the white chalky stone, and on the other to the silicicalce. **1961** J. BRAUNSTEIN in *Bull. Amer. Assoc. Petroleum Geologists* XLV. 2017/2, I dare to submit two new terms... These are, 'calciclastic'.., referring to clastic carbonate rocks, and, 'siliciclastic'.., referring to clastic non-carbonate rocks (which are almost exclusively silicon-bearing, either as forms of quartz or as silicates). **1976** *Nature* 3 June 440/1 Two major subdivisions are considered —the siliciclastic and carbonate tidal deposits. Recent siliciclastic examples include the classic tidal flats of the North Sea, [etc.]. **1965** BELL & COOMBE tr. *Strasburger's Textbk. Bot.* 753 Species characteristic of particular soils have long been known,..e.g. halophytes.., or calcicole or silicicole (calcifuge) plants. **1901** *Jrnl. R. Microsc. Soc.* 53 J. A. Cl. Roux has grown a number of silicicolous (arenaceous) plants in calcareous soils, and finds that..the seedling plants develop tardily and imperfectly. **1932** FULLER & CONARD tr. *Braun-Blanquet's Plant Sociol.* vi. 187 In humid regions the leaching of carbonates sets in upon dolomite.., and acidophilous plants follow in the train of the progressive acidification of the dolomite soil. This occurrence of silicicolous plants on dolomite substrata was first noticed by Sendtner. **1826** HENRY *Elem. Chem.* I. 646 The effects of heating potassium in silici-fluoric gas. **1855** SCOFFERN in *Orr's Circ. Sci., Chem.* 168 Silici-fluoric acid. **1796** KIRWAN *Elem. Min.* (ed. 2) I. 144 Magnesia mixed with Silex. Silicimurite.

†**si'liciate**, obs. var. SILICATE.

**1814** J. BLACK tr. *Berzelius' Syst. Mineral.* 29 Silica considered as an acid possesses the property of giving siliciates of many different degrees of saturation... These we shall hereafter call siliciates. **1854** RONALDS & RICHARDSON *Chem. Technol.* (ed. 2) I. 107 The oxide of iron which remains in the coke forms with the siliciate a slag or scar when the carbon is consumed.

**silicic** (sɪ'lɪsɪk), *a. Chem.* [f. SILIC-A (or L. *silic-* SILEX[1]) + -IC. Cf. F. *silicique.*] Pertaining to, consisting of, or formed from silica. Chiefly in ***silicic acid***, a very weakly acidic substance obtained esp. by the action of acids on solutions of silicates and usu. existing in the form of colloidal solutions which contain $H_4SiO_4$ (*orthosilicic acid*) but consist mainly of polymeric oxyacids derived from this; any of these constituent acids.

**1817** T. THOMSON *Syst. Chem.* (ed. 5) II. 92 It might therefore be distinguished by the name of silicic acid, which would be more systematic than the term silica. **1857** MILLER *Elem. Chem., Org.* iii. § 3 (1862) 188 Every acid forms at least one ether, and some, such as the silicic and boracic, furnish more than one. **1883** *Science* I. 490/1 The silica was prepared by decomposing silicic flouride with water. **1898** [see *lactonitrile* s.v. LACTO- 2]. **1913** E. HATSCHEK *Physics & Chem. of Colloids* v. 41 If a solution of sodium silicate..is decomposed by a slight excess of hydrochloric acid, and the mixture is dialysed until the free acid and the sodium chloride have been removed, there remains in the dialyser a perfectly clear colourless sol of silicic acid. **1955** *Sci. Amer.* Sept. 65/3 The more volatile or acidic or silicic constituents of the fluid rock beneath the surface may have concentrated in the original uplifts. **1973** E. G. ROCHOW in J. C. Bailar et al. *Comprehensive Inorg. Chem.* I. xv. 1409 The relations between silicon dioxide and water are so close..that it often is difficult to distinguish between solutions of silica, solutions of distinct molecular silicic acids, colloidal dispersions of silica, the definite hydrates of $SiO_2$, hydrated silica in general, and silica gel.

**silicide** ('sɪlɪsaɪd). *Chem.* [f. SILIC-A + -IDE.] A compound of silicon with one other element.

**1868** WATTS *Dict. Chem.* s.v., Silicide of calcium has a lead-grey colour, metallic lustre, and scaly crystalline structure. **1880** *Encycl. Brit.* XIII. 352/1 Silicious spiegeleisen (or manganese silicide..) is prepared by the ordinary blast furnace methods.

**silici'faction.** *rare.* = SILICIFICATION.

**1881** *Jrnl. Bot.* X. 27 He distinguishes between silicifaction and petrifaction.

**siliciferous** (sɪlɪ'sɪfərəs), *a.* [f. L. *silici-, silex* SILEX[1] + -FEROUS. So F. *silicifère.*] Yielding or producing silex or silica.

**1796** KIRWAN *Elem. Min.* (ed. 2) I. 101 Siliciferous Marlites.—Of these there are many varieties. **1799** —— *Geol. Ess.* 184 It is so much the more siliciferous as it approaches more to granitic mountains. **1839** DE LA BECHE *Rep. Geol. Cornwall*, etc. xii. 372 The siliciferous and calciferous hydrates of iron. **1853** TH. ROSS tr. *Humboldt's Trav.* III. xxvi. 118 It is a siliciferous subsulphate of alumina and potash.

**silicification** (sɪˌlɪsɪfɪ'keɪʃən). [f. as prec. + -FICATION. So F. *silicification.*] The process of becoming silicified; conversion into silica.

**1830** LYELL *Princ. Geol.* I. 214 In some places where silicification is in progress, the sources from whence the mineral matter is derived are as yet unknown. **1844** *Civil Eng. & Arch. Jrnl.* VI. 444/1 The act of petrification being the act of silicification and consequent change of the organic body. **1884** BOWER & SCOTT *De Bary's Phaner.* 510 The old wood of plants which are characterised by extensive silicification of almost all their parts.

**silicified** (sɪ'lɪsɪfaɪd), *ppl. a.* [f. next + -ED[1]. Cf. F. *silicifié.*] Converted into silica. Chiefly in ***silicified wood.***

**1822** J. PARKINSON *Outl. Oryctol.* 49 The nodules of chalk flint frequently contain the silicified remains of sponge. **1844** *Civil Eng. & Arch. Jrnl.* VI. 442/1 The silicified and other mineralized bodies. **1876** PAGE *Adv. Text-bk. Geol.* xv. 279 The silicified trunks of tree-ferns.

**silicify** (sɪ'lɪsɪfaɪ), *v.* [Cf. prec. and -FY.]

**1.** *trans.* To convert into, impregnate with, silica.

**1830** LYELL *Princ. Geol.* I. 120 The wood and fruit of the cocoa-nut tree..silicified by the waters of some mineral spring. **1849** DANA *Geol.* ix. (1850) 526 Ejections of basalt.. buried the mud,..silicifying the shells, and hardening the rock. **1872** NICHOLSON *Palæont.* 4 Fossil wood which has been 'silicified' or converted into flint.

**2.** *intr.* To undergo silicification.

**1828–32** in WEBSTER. **1844** *Civil Eng. & Arch. Jrnl.* VI. 442/1 The term petrification being an absurdity as applied to bodies in the act of silicifying.

Hence **si'licifying** *vbl. sb.*

**1863** DANA *Man. Geol.* 70 All the fossils of a rock..are changed to silica (quartz) by a silicifying process.

**silicious** (sɪ'lɪʃəs), *a.* [f. L. *silic-, silex* SILEX[1] + -IOUS.] = SILICEOUS *a.*

(*a*) **1721** BAILEY, *Silicious*, Flinty, belonging to Flint. **1801** *Farmer's Magazine* Nov. 389 Argile or pure clay, silicious or sandy earth, and calx, or calcareous substances. **1850** DAUBENY *Atom. The.* xii. (ed. 2) 395 By far the greater number of silicious minerals are examples of the kind last alluded to. **1876** PAGE *Adv. Text-bk. Geol.* iii. 60 The silicious sinter of the Iceland geysers.

(*b*) **1851** RICHARDSON *Geology* iv. 72 Many deposits..are composed of the silicious shields of fossil infusoria. **1859** T. MOORE *Brit. Ferns* (1864) 107 The jointed tubular silicious stems, and terminal cones of fructification. **1896** DK. ARGYLL *Philos. Belief* 104 The silicious sponges, whose skeletons are composed of glass.

†**silicite.** *Obs.* [f. L. *silic-* SILEX[1] + -ITE[1] 2 b.] Labradorite, or a variety of this.

**1843** T. THOMSON in *Philos. Mag.* Ser. III. XXII. 190 The fourth mineral..I have distinguished by the name of Silicite, from the great resemblance which it has to quartz in its external aspect. **1850** ANSTED *Elem. Geol., Min.* etc. 193 Glaucolite and Silicite are other varieties [of Labradorite].

†**'silicited,** *a. Obs.* [irreg. f. L. *silic-* SILEX[1].] = SILICATED.

**1796** KIRWAN *Elem. Min.* (ed. 2) I. 499 Precipitated from *liquor silicum* (silicited alkali). **1799** —— *Geol. Ess.* 283 Hence those that are most silicited, as they contract less, discover less verticality.

†**silicium** (sɪ'lɪʃ(ɪ)əm). Also silicum. *Obs.* [mod.L., f. *silic-* SILEX[1] + -IUM. Named by Sir H. Davy.] = SILICON.

**1808** SIR H. DAVY in *Phil. Trans.* XCVIII. 353 Had I been so fortunate as..to have procured the metallic substances I was in search of, I should have proposed for them the names of silicium, alumium, zirconium, and glucium. **1812** —— *Chem. Philos.* 364 No compound of silicum and chlorine is known. **1822** IMISON *Sci. & Art* II. 91 It is imagined, however, that Silicium forms an alloy with iron. **1861** SIR W. FAIRBAIRN *Iron* 156 The silicium is first attacked, neither the iron nor carbon being operated upon to any extent while any silicium remains. **1868** JOYNSON *Metals* 57 A portion of the carbon, and almost the whole of the silicum, is removed from it. **1871** TYNDALL *Fragm. Sci.* (1879) I. i. 9 The flints within the chalk we know to be a compound of oxygen and silicium, called silica.

**si'liciuret.** *Chem.* [f. prec. Cf. F. *siliciure.*] = SILICIDE.

**1827** F. LUNN in *Encycl. Metrop.* IV. 662/1 A siliciuret of potassium is obtained, which cannot exist in water. **1842** *Penny Cycl.* XXII. 9/2 Some of the metals may be combined with silicon: these compounds, which are not important, are termed Siliciurets.

**si'liciu,retted,** *a.* [f. prec. + -ED[1].] Combined or impregnated with silicon.

**1857** GRAHAM *Elem. Chem.* (ed. 2) II. 675 Siliciuretted hydrogen, a remarkable gaseous compound of silicon and hydrogen, is produced when a bar of aluminium containing silicon is connected with the positive pole of a Bunsen's battery. **1869** ROSCOE *Chem.* 149 Siliciuretted Hydrogen is a colourless gas formed by the action of hydrochloric acid upon a compound of magnesium and silicon.

**silicle** ('sɪlɪk(ə)l). *Bot.* [ad. F. *silicule* or L. *silicula.*] A small short seed-pod.

**1785** MARTYN *Rousseau's Bot.* ii. (1794) 31 The second [order] contains those [flowers] whose seed-vessel is a silicle, that is, a small and very short pod. **1812** *New Botanic Gard.* I. 46 The silicle is entire, oval, and full of brown seeds. **1846** J. BAXTER *Libr. Pract. Agric.* II. 257 It will flower and produce abundance of seed, which, when the silicles or pouches become ripe, may be gathered. **1861** MRS. LANKESTER *Wild Flowers* 29 The fruit is a pod... When long, it is called a silique, and, when short, a silicle.

**silico-** ('sɪlɪkəʊ), combining form of SILICA or SILICON: **a.** With adjs., as ***silico-alkaline, -ferruginous, -fluoric, -magnesian, -skeletal, -talcose.***

**1851-4** *Tomlinson's Cycl. Useful Arts* (1866) I. 783/1 Charcoal in excess in a mixture of *silico-alkaline glass, gives a yellow colour. **1875** FORTNUM *Maiolica* i. 4 The vitreous silico-alcaline or glass glazed wares. **1849** DANA *Geol.* viii. (1850) 439 They owe their appearance..to a *silico-ferruginous solution. **1827** F. LUNN in *Encycl. Metrop.* IV. 656/1 The compounds of silicon and boron, being also Acids, [should] be called *silico-fluoric and boro-fluoric Acids. **1868** *Fownes' Chem.* (ed. 10) 368 Silicofluoric acid gives a white precipitate with barium salts. **1842** J. B. FRASER *Mesopot. & Assyria* xv. 344 Gray or blueish sandstone, containing red nodules of a *silico-magnesian substance. **1885** *Encycl. Brit.* XIX. 849/2 *Silico-skeletal Radiolaria in which the central capsule is uniformly perforated all over by fine pore-canals. **1849** DANA *Geol.* xvii. (1850) 622 The *silico-talcose rocks..project in jagged points.

**b.** With nouns, as ***silico-aluminate, -borate, -borocalcite, -fluate, -fluoride, -titanate;*** **silico'carnotite** [cf. CARNOTITE, an unrelated mineral named after the same person], a silicate and phosphate of calcium, $Ca_5(PO_4)_2SiO_4$, found as orthorhombic crystals (coloured blue by impurities) in basic slag from steelmaking processes; **silico-'manganese**, a ferro-alloy containing relatively high proportions of manganese and silicon, *spec.* one containing 65 to 70 per cent manganese and 12 to 25 per cent silicon which is used in steel-making as a manganese-containing additive and as a deoxidizer; **,silicomo'lybdic acid**, any of a class of polyanionic oxyacids obtained when mixed solutions containing a molybdate and a silicate are acidified; *esp.* a yellow crystalline solid of this kind whose formation is the basis of a colorimetric determination of silicon; so **silico'molybdate**, an anion or a salt of such an acid; **silico'phosphate** = *phosphosilicate* s.v. PHOSPHO-.

**1868** WATTS *Dict. Chem.* V. 266 *Silico-aluminates, -borates. **1868** *Philos. Mag.* Ser. IV. XXXV. 40 The exclusive occurrence of the hard nodules of *silicoborocalcite in anhydrite. **1911** V. A. KROLL in *Jrnl. Iron & Steel Inst.* LXXXIV. 126 These crystals, which are of a beautiful dichroic-blue colour, will be distinguished in the present paper by the name *Silico-Carnotite. **1949** *Mineral. Mag.* XXVIII. 496 Silicocarnotite is found in basic slags rich in phosphorus. **1971** *Tschermaks Mineral. und Petrogr. Mitteilungen* XVI. 19 The nature of the $PO_4/SiO_4$ substitution in silicocarnotite should be resolved by collecting X-ray intensity data from a crystal known to be free from impurities. **1827** F. LUNN in *Encycl. Metrop.* IV. 656/1 The *silico-fluates of potash, soda, lime, and barytes are formed [etc.]. **1836-41** BRANDE *Chem.* (ed. 5) 1031 A total condensation ensues, and a dry silico-fluate of ammonia results. *Ibid.* 1032 *Silico-fluoride of barium is gradually precipitated when silico-fluoric acid is mixed with chloride of barium. **1869** ROSCOE *Chem.* 147 A compound of this substance with..potassium silico-fluoride. **1895** E. L. RHEAD *Metallurgy* ix. 112 Siliconeisen and *silico-manganese are irons containing silicon, or silicon and manganese... They are employed in steel manufacture. **1941** *Trans. Amer. Soc. Mech. Engineers* LXIII. 367/2 Both high-manganese and silicomanganese steels equal the chrome-vanadium steel tested and may have commercial advantages. **1956** W. D. HARGREAVES in D. L. Linton *Sheffield* 280 The city therefore uses quite large tonnages of pig-iron and of alloying metals..such as..silico-manganese. **1881** *Jrnl. Chem. Soc.* XL. 880 Ammonium *silico-molybdate is obtained in small yellow octahedrons, by mixing nitric acid solutions of ammonium molybdate and an alkaline silicate. **1928** J. H. YOE *Photometric Chem. Analysis* I. xxxi. 366 Silicates and phosphates form yellow silico- and phosphomolybdates with ammonium molybdate in acid solution. On treatment with sodium sulfite the silico- and phosphomolybdates give a blue reduction product. **1973** E. G. ROCHOW in J. C. Bailar et al. *Comprehensive Inorg. Chem.* I. xv. 1466 Silicon is one of 36 elements which have been reported as central atoms of heteropoly acid aggregates (borotungstates, phosphovanadates, silicomolybdates, etc.). **1871** *Jrnl. Chem. Soc.* XXIV. 157 (*heading*) A few remarks on the yellow precipitate containing *silico-molybdic acid. **1956** *Nature* 3 Mar. 435/1 Analysis was carried out by measuring absorptiometrically the colour produced by the reduction of the silico-molybdic acid complex with ascorbic acid. **1927** *Jrnl. Agric. Sci.* XVII. 143 Stead..concluded that the most soluble phosphate was a *silico-phosphate represented by $5CaO.P_2O_5.SiO_2$. **1963** C. R. COWELL et al. *Inlays, Crowns, & Bridges* vii. 77 A fine-grain silicophosphate cement of the appropriate shade is most suitable for cementation because it possesses some degree of translucency. **1868** WATTS *Dict. Chem.* V. 263 Mosandrite is a hydrated *silicotitanate.

**silicoflagellate** (,sɪlɪkəʊ'flædʒəleɪt). [f. SILICO- + FLAGELLATE *sb.*] A marine flagellate of the family Silicoflagellidæ, distinguished by a siliceous skeleton and radiating spines.

**1906** M. HARTOG in Harmer & Shipley *Cambr. Nat. Hist.* I. iii. 86 The Silicoflagellate family Dictyochidae..have a skeleton of a similar nature. **1961** R. D. MANWELL *Introd. Protozool.* iii. 29 Living silicoflagellates are almost exclusively marine and pelagic in habit. **1978** *Nature* 16 Mar. 244/2 Apart from being an important structural component of diatoms and silicoflagellates..it [*sc.* silicon] is necessary for DNA polymerase activity in diatoms.

**silicon** ('sɪlɪkən). [f. L. *silic-* SILEX[1]. Named by T. Thomson, in place of Sir H. Davy's SILICIUM.] **1.** A non-metallic element, which in respect of its abundance in the ground ranks next to oxygen, and is usually found combined with this as *silica*; it may be obtained in the form of powder, scales, or crystals. Chemical symbol Si.

**1817** T. THOMSON *Syst. Chem.* (ed. 5) I. 252 The base of silica has been usually considered as a metal, and called silicium. But..as it bears a close resemblance to boron and carbon, it is better to class it along with these bodies, and to give it the name of silicon. **1857** MILLER *Elem. Chem., Org.* iii. §3 (1862) 197 When absolute alcohol is gradually added to chloride of silicon, a powerful reaction occurs. **1876** ROUTLEDGE *Disc.* 32 The silicon, most of the carbon, and some of the iron itself are oxidized in this process.

*attrib.* **1869** ROSCOE *Chem.* 342 Silicon ethyl..is obtained by the action of zinc ethyl on silicon tetrachloride. **1884** KNIGHT *Dict. Mech.* Suppl. 810/1 *Silicon Steel*, a steel in which silicon replaces a part of the usual carbon.

**2.** Special comb.: **silicon carbide**, a hard refractory compound of silicon and carbon SiC: see CARBORUNDUM; **silicon chip**, a chip (CHIP *sb.*[1] 2 f) of silicon; **silicon ester**, any ester of silicic acid, *spec.* tetraethyl orthosilicate, $Si(OC_2H_5)_4$, a colourless flammable liquid which is readily hydrolysed to silica and is used in paints, weatherproof coatings for masonry, etc., and as a binding agent for moulds; **silicon iron, steel**, cast iron, or steel (respectively) containing a relatively high proportion of silicon, added to increase the magnetic permeability and/or the resistance to corrosion and heat; **Silicon Valley** orig. *U.S.* [from the use made of silicon chips], the Santa Clara valley, S.E. of San Francisco, where many leading U.S. microelectronic firms are located; **silicon wafer**, a wafer of silicon from which individual silicon chips can be separated (cf. WAFER *sb.*).

**1893** *Chem. News* LXVIII. 3A/2 (*heading*) The analysis of silicon carbide. **1982** JACKSON & DAY *Better than New* 138/2 Silicon carbide abrasives are used extensively for furniture renovation. **1965** *Sci. Amer.* Nov. 66/3 Engineers..saw the possibility of producing complete circuits within a silicon chip by forming all the circuit elements by diffusion. **1979** *Daily Tel.* 3 Oct. 14/4 Perhaps..the biggest gains will be possible from the sophisticated electronic 'engine management' control systems now being developed with the aid of the silicon chip and mini computer **1923** A. P. LAURIE *Brit. Pat. 221, 342* 1/1 According to my earlier application silicon esters are applied to the stone and allowed gradually to hydrolise in position. **1969** *Kirk-Othmer Encycl. Chem. Technol.* (ed. 2) XVIII. 217 The silicon esters of organic acids, or silicon carboxylates, are also known and are prepared by the reaction of the acid with silicon halides. **1878** *Chem. News* 27 Dec. 299/2 This metallic mass is a silicon iron, remarkably rich in silicon, and evidently the product of a blast-furnace. **1970** *Materials & Technol.* III. x 769 These principles have been incorporated in the manufacture of conventional materials such as silicon-iron for electrical transformers. **1882** *Jrnl. Iron & Steel Inst.* 376 Peculiarities of silicon steel are: the adhesive scale which covers it; a low degree of weldability; and a very fine grain. **1975** D. G. FINK *Electronics Engineers' Handbk.* VI. 80 Silicon steels, known as electrical steels, are very widely used for low- and intermediate-frequency applications. **1974** *Fortune* June 135/2 They have turned part of Santa Clara County into 'Silicon Valley', the world capital of semiconductor technology. **1980** *N.Y. Times* 22 June IV. 8E In more recent years 'Silicon Valley' has grown up along the peninsula from San Francisco through Stanford University to San Jose. **1956** *Bell Syst. Technical Jrnl.* XXXV. 3 After diffusion the entire surface of the silicon wafer is covered with the diffused n- and p-type layers. **1977** *Sci. Amer.* Sept. 111/3 The pure, single-crystal silicon wafers that bear the circuits are much larger: currently three or four inches in diameter.

**silicone** ('sɪlɪkəʊn). *Chem.* [f. SILIC(O- + -ONE.]

†**1.** Also -on. [ad. G. *silicon* (F. Wöhler 1863, in *Ann. d. Chem. u. Pharm.* CXXVII. 263).] A yellow solid obtained by the action of concentrated hydrochloric acid on calcium silicide and said to be a compound of silicon, hydrogen, and oxygen. *Obs.*

**1863** F. WOHLER in *Chem. News* 10 Oct. 172 The relative proportions of the combined silicium and calcium are in general those necessary to form the compound $CaSi_2$... It is only by means of this compound that we can..explain the composition and mode of formation of the yellow body which is obtained by the action [on it] of hydrochloric acid, and which I shall now describe under the name of *Silicon.* **1909** *Jrnl. Chem. Soc.* XCVI. II. 806 The colourless substance, leucone, which is produced by exposing silicone to light and air, represents an intermediate step in the oxidation of silicone to silicon dioxide. **1946** J. R. PARTINGTON *Gen. & Inorg. Chem.* xviii. 506 By the action of concentrated hydrochloric acid on calcium silicide Wöhler (1863) obtained a yellow solid which he called silicone and formulated $Si_4H_4O_3$.

**2. a.** Formerly, the name given to any supposed compound of silicon analogous to the ketones, having a formula RR'SiO (R, R' being organic radicals); in mod. use, any of a large group of synthetic organosilicon polymers (siloxanes) based on chains or networks of alternating silicon and oxygen atoms, many of these being good electrical insulators with high durability, and finding uses as liquids, greases, rubbers (notably in cosmetic surgery), or resins.

[**1906** *Jrnl. Chem. Soc.* XC. I. 128 The gelatinous diphenylsilicone (diphenyl silicoketone).] *Ibid.* 563 The silicones present in the residues..are mixtures, in variable proportions, of silicoformic anhydride and silico-oxalic acid. **1912** *Ibid.* CI. II. 2106 The term *silicone* has already been used to denote the analogues of the ketones, and may be advantageously retained for this purpose. **1948** *Q. Rev. Chem. Soc.* II. 26 The word 'silicone' was originally used by Kipping to denote the silicon analogues of ketones (RR'Si:O, cf. RR'C:O) but he soon recognised that monomeric silicones are incapable of existence; in fact, no compound containing the group Si:O is yet known. **1957** *Listener* 31 Oct. 719/2 The manufacturers use silicones partly because they give some resistance to spilled liquids and because dust does not readily adhere to the film of polish. **1979** [see SHOOT *v.* 23 h].

**b.** *attrib.*, as ***silicone polish, resin, rubber***, etc.

**1944** *Chem. & Engin. News* 10 July 1134/3 Silicone resins, used as insulating varnishes and bonds, definitely fill the void between organic and inorganic insulating materials. *Ibid.* 25 Nov. 2016/1 Silicone rubber..has been developed by the General Electric Co., Schenectady, and was demonstrated at the Engineers' Club in New York on November 14. **1955** *Radio Times* 22 Apr. 52/1 (Advt.), New Goddard's Silicone Wax has revolutionized polishing. It's put wonder-working silicones into hard wax. **1958** *Times Rev. Industry* May 26/3 The core is clamped with steel clamps, and while still under pressure is bound with silicone varnish. **1960** *Farmer & Stockbreeder* 22 Mar. (Suppl.) 10/2 First, put the pointing in good repair, then treat the wall with a silicone waterproofing liquid. **1969** T. C. THORSTENSEN *Pract. Leather Technol.* xiv. 235 As a result of silicone treatment, shoes can be made that are for all practical purposes completely water-repellent. **1971** A. DIMENT *Think Inc.* vii. 129 Her breasts were..very firm... Maybe a few silicone injections I thought cynically. **1973** *Materials & Technol.* VI. viii. 602 Silicone resins, being thermally stable, are used as impregnating varnishes, moulding compounds, encapsulants, and in laminates. **1974** *Sci. Amer.* Mar. 71/1 Artificial heart valves and experimental heart-bypass pumps are often fabricated from silicone rubber because the polymer has a lower tendency than most organic polymers to trigger the clotting of blood. **1976** *Gramophone* Nov. 755/3, I recommend the use..of silicone polish, applied thinly and evenly with a soft cloth, starting from the label to take up the surplus, and working outwards.

**c.** *Comb.*, as ***silicone-impregnated, -proofed, -treated*** adjs.; ***silicone-treat*** vb. trans.

**1956** *Nature* 25 Feb. 365/2 Reversed-phase chromatography using silicone-impregnated kieselguhr columns. **1976** *Shooting Times & Country Mag.* 9–15 Dec. 7/1 (Advt.), The GARCIA gun and reel silicone impregnated cloth. Protects and cleans all metal. **1956** *Good Housek. Home Encycl.* (ed. 4) 251/2 Silicone-proofed rainwear and ski-clothes. **1958** *Times* 20 Jan. 11/5 Where traditional upholstery material is used on chairs..they should be silicone-treated. **1946** *Canad. Med. Assoc. Jrnl.* LV. 29/1 The difference between clotting times in untreated ..and silicone-treated..tubes is equally marked with plasma. **1956** *Good Housek. Home Encycl.* (ed. 4) 99/2 Silicone-treated furnishing fabrics.

Hence **'siliconed** *ppl. a.*, coated, impregnated, or otherwise treated with a silicone or silicone-based material; **'siliconing** *vbl. sb.* Also (as a back-formation) **'silicone** *v. trans.*

**1950** *Jrnl. Appl. Physiol.* III. 366 Venous blood was collected in a 10-ml. siliconed syringe. *Ibid.* 375 Siliconing of the syringe appears a worth-while precaution. **1959** *Listener* 1 Jan. 43/1 Siliconing really does prevent the food from sticking [to the frying pan]. **1973** 'E. McBain' *Let's hear it for Deaf Man* viii. 124 A woman..with bleached blond hair and siliconed breasts. **1977** *Listener* 10 Nov. 611/2 The motel on the dunes, its beams shiny and siliconed in the clear light. **1978** *Morecambe Guardian* 14 Mar. 29/1 (Advt.), Sandblasting and siliconing. **1980** 'D. Kavanagh' *Duffy* iv. 68 She was naked, thinnish, with..breasts which had probably been siliconed.

**'siliconize**, *v.* [f. silicon + -ize.]

**1.** *trans.* To cause to combine with silicon or its compounds; esp. to subject (a metal) to a process in which the surface is impregnated with silicon so as to form a protective coating.
**1880** [implied in siliconizing below]. **1948** N. E. Woldman *Metal Process Engin.* viii. 222 The iron or steel to be siliconized is subjected to the action of silicon carbide or ferrosilicon, or a mixture of the two and chlorine at temperatures of 1700 to 1850° F. **1977** R. B. Ross *Handbk. Metal Treatments & Testing* 349 It is generally more economical to produce components in high-silicon cast iron rather than cast irons which are subsequently Siliconized.

**2.** [f. silicone.] To impregnate, coat, or otherwise treat with silicones or silicone-based material. Usu. in ppl. adj. (see below).
**1957** [implied in siliconized below]. **1963** *Obstetr. & Gynecol.* XXI. 47/1 The glassware was siliconized to prevent adsorption of the isotopes.

So **'siliconized** *ppl. a.*, **'siliconizing** *vbl. sb.*; also **,siliconi'zation**, treatment or combination with silicon or a silicone.
**1880** *Encycl. Brit.* XIII. 351/2 The presence of alkaline silicates in the furnace promotes the siliconizing of the iron. **1920** Webster, Siliconized. **1924** *Industr. & Engin. Chem.* Nov. 1112/1 An oxidizing atmosphere would tend to oxidize both the silicon and the iron simultaneously and prevent true siliconization. **1946** *Iron Age* 4 Apr. 75/2 These siliconized shafts replaced shafts made of stainless and nitrided steel. **1947** Kirk & Othmer *Encycl. Chem. Technol.* I. 579 Other diffusion treatments for mild and other steels are calorizing, chromizing, and siliconizing. **1950** *Chem. Abstr.* XLIV. 4856 This method of siliconization permits a further increase of corrosion resistance of 18Cr-8Ni stainless steel, of Monel metal, and of pure Ni. **1957** *Archit. Rev.* CXXII. 354/2 T. & W. Farmiloe will demonstrate the qualities of their siliconized paints, put on the market since the last exhibition. **1977** *Hot Car* Oct. 97/3 (Advt.), Tough, resilient, siliconised enamel cuts out labour. **1978** *Nature* 28 Sept. 322/2 A double-barrelled glass micro-pipette, pretreated with a siliconising agent.

**silicosis** (sɪlɪ'kəʊsɪs). *Path.* [ad. It. *silicosi* (A. Visconti: see C. L. Rovida in *Annali di Chim. applicata alla Med.* (1871) LIII. 103), ult. f. L. *silic-* silex[1] + -osis.] A lung disease induced by inhaling flinty or siliceous particles.
**1881** *Jrnl. Anat. & Physiol.* XV. 395 According to the nature and character of the irritant, certain forms [of pneumokoniosis] are distinguished, the chief of which are anthracosis, chalicosis or silicosis, and siderosis. **1898** *Allbutt's Syst. Med.* V. 248 Thus authors have described the results of inhaling siliceous particles as chalicosis or silicosis. **1903** *Nature* 1 Oct. 527/2 The malady is silicosis pure and simple, a dust disease.

Hence **sili'cotic** *a.*, affected by silicosis. Also as *sb.*
**1913** *Mem. S. Afr. Inst. Med. Res.* No. 3. 120 The amount of silica in the ash is greater in that from the silicotic lung than in that from the normal lung. **1938** *Jrnl. Amer. Med. Assoc.* 19 Nov. 1928/1 Clinicians, who see only the disabled silicotic patient with advanced lesions, often complicated by tuberculosis, are insisting that only such conditions represent the true picture of silicosis. **1948** [see *pneumoconiotic* s.v. pneumo-]. **1980** D. Pownall *Between Ribble & Lune* i. 20 Aaron's disease, a form of silicotic lung infection caused by the dust.

‖**silicula** (sɪ'lɪkjʊlə). *Bot.* [L., dim. of siliqua.] A short pod containing seed; a silicle.
**1760** J. Lee *Introd. Bot.* II. iii. (1765) 79 In the first order *Siliculosa*, the Pericarpium is a *Silicula*, little *Siliqua*. **1793** Martyn *Lang. Bot.* s.v. *Siliqua*, The *Silicula* does not differ from this essentially, but only in form and size. **1830** Lindley *Nat. Syst. Bot.* 14 Fruit a siliqua or silicula. **1847** W. E. Steele *Field Bot.* 109 Silicula roundish or oblong, entire or notched. **1872** Oliver *Elem. Bot.* II. 138 Compare the long capsule of Wallflower (a siliqua); the short capsule of Shepherd's-purse Capsell (a silicula).

Hence **si'licular** *a.*, 'having the shape or appearance of a silicula' (*Cent. Dict.* 1891).

**'silicule**. *Bot. rare.* [a. F. *silicule*, ad. L. *silicula*.] = silicula.
**1793** Martyn *Lang. Bot.*, *Silicula*, a Silicule, Silicle, little Pod or Pouch. **1857** J. G. Wood *Comm. Obj. Seashore* 33 Its specific title 'siliculosus' is given to it on account of the silicules, or little pod-like bodies, that are found on the branches.

**siliculose** (sɪlɪkjʊ'ləʊs), *a. Bot.* [ad. mod.L. *siliculōs-us*, f. *silicula*: cf. F. *siliculeux*.] Bearing small short pods.
**1731** Bailey vol. II. (ed. 2), *Siliculose*, husky or full of husks. **1759** B. Stillingfleet *Misc. Tracts* (1762) 357 Horses are nicer in choosing than any of our cattle; siliquose and siliculose plants particularly are not relished by them. **1785** Martyn *Rousseau's Bot.* xxiii. (1794) 320 The *Siliculose* or short-podded order leads the way. **1857** A. Gray *First Less. Bot.* (1866) 230 *Siliculose*, bearing a silicle, or a fruit resembling it.

So **si'liculous** *a.*, 'having silicles or little pods, or pertaining to them' (Webster, 1828-32).

**silicum**, variant of silicium.

†**silicuret**, obs. variant of siliciuret.
**1842** Parnell *Chem. Anal.* (1845) 12 The platinum combining with the silicon in the ashes to form a silicuret of platinum.

**siligineous**, *a. rare*⁻⁰. [ad. L. *silīgineus*, f. *silīgin-*, *silīgo* winter wheat.] 'Belonging to, or made of fine flour' (Blount, ed. 4, 1674). Also **siliginose** *a.*, 'made of fine Wheat' (Bailey, vol. II, 1727); **si'liginous** *a.* (Craig, 1848).

†**'siling**, *vbl. sb. Obs.* Also 5 cyl-, 5–6 sylyng(e; 6 sylinge, *Sc.* syiling, 6–7 syling. [f. sile *v.*[4] + -ing[1].] = ceiling *vbl. sb.*
**1483** *Tintinhull Churchw. Acc.* (Som. Rec. Soc.) 195 It. pro le sylyng ecclesie, ijs. ixd. It. pro factura le cylyng, xvs. **1497** *Acc. Ld. High Treas. Scotl.* I. 357 To the kervour that tuk in task the siling of the chapel. **1543** in *Essex Rev.* XV. 42 The chancell is in decay in tymber, tyling and sylynge. **1589** *Lanc. Wills* (Chetham Soc.) II. 207 All the sylinge and wainescott in the hall and parlor. **1629** Z. Boyd *Last Battell* 612 The olde syling that was once fast joyned together with nailes will begin to cling. *Ibid.*, The stars which are like golden nailes into the syling of the world.
*attrib.* **1535** Coverdale *Ps.* lxxiii. 6 They cutt downe all the sylinge worke of ye Sanctuary. **1565** *Richmond Wills* (Surtees) 179 Plew tymbre and sylinge bourds, with other hustlements.

**'siling-dish.** *dial. rare.* [f. *siling* sile *v.*[2]] A strainer for milk.
**1573** Baret *Alvearie*, A Siling dish, *vide* Colander and Strainer. **1578** in *Linc. N. & Q.* (1889) I. 232 In the Mylke House:..Item a sileing dishe. **1828** Carr *Craven Gloss.*, *Siling dish*, a dish for the purpose of straining milk.

‖**siliqua** ('sɪlɪkwə). Pl. siliquae. [L., a pod.]

†**1.** The carob-tree. (Cf. silique 1.) *Obs.*
*c* **1440** *Pallad. on Husb.* III. 978 Now..is to renewe The siliqua in plaunte & seedes trewe.

**2.** *Bot.* A long pod-like seed-vessel.
**1704** J. Harris *Lex. Techn.* I, *Siliqua*, in Botany, is the Seed-vessel, Husk, Cod, or Pod, of such Plants as are of the Leguminous kind. **1760** J. Lee *Introd. Bot.* I. vi. (1765) 13 *Siliqua*, a Pod, is a Pericarpium of two Valves, wherein the Seeds are fastened along both the Sutures or Joinings of the Valves. **1793** Martyn *Lang. Bot.* s.v., The proper *Siliqua* is two-celled, having a partition running the whole length of it. **1861** S. Thomson *Wild Fl.* III. (ed. 4) 268 The wallflower seed-vessel is a Siliqua. **1872** Oliver *Elem. Bot.* II. 138 Compare the long capsule of Wallflower (a siliqua);..the siliqua of Radish.

**3.** *Anat.* A formation suggesting a husk or pod.
**1891** in *Cent. Dict.*

**4.** A Roman silver coin of the 4th and 5th centuries A.D., of the value of $\frac{1}{24}$th of a solidus.
**1889** *Jrnl. Hellenic Stud.* X. 95 All the mediaeval standards were based upon the gold solidus of Constantine the Great..divided into 24 *siliquae* or κεράτια (from whence comes *carat*). **1927** A. R. Burns *Money & Monetary Policy Early Times* x. 243 From about the middle of the 4th century A.D. the *siliqua*, the half of the *miliarense*, became increasingly important. **1940** [see aureus]. **1962** R. A. G. Carson *Coins* 185 Siliquae were struck mainly by Italian mints for Arcadius and Honorius and by the Gallic mints for the usurpers in control there.

Hence **sili'quaceous** *a.*, of the nature of, suggestive of, a siliqua.
**1744** *Phil. Trans.* XLIII. 97 A siliquaceous Aperture, with a Row of Seeds ready to fall through it.

**siliquæform**: see siliquiform.

†**siliquastre.** *Obs. rare.* [ad. mod.L. *siliquastrum* (which in class.L. means pepperwort), f. L. *siliqua* pod.] (See quots.)
**1708** in *Phil. Trans.* XXVI. 79 *Punctularia*, the Punctulary, Sope stone, or Porous Marble Siliquastre. *Ibid.*, *Siliquastrum*, the Shale, or Siliquastre: An Ichthyodont, resembling leguminous Husks.

**silique** (sɪ'liːk). *Bot.* Also 5 selyque. [a. F. *silique*, or ad. L. *siliqua* pod.]

†**1.** = siliqua 1. *Obs.*
*c* **1440** *Pallad. on Husb.* XII. 312 The serue and medlar & selyque [*v.r.* Silique] tre.

**2.** = siliqua 2.
**1785** Martyn *Rousseau's Bot.* ii. (1794) 30 When it is ripe, it becomes a kind of flat pod, called *silique*. **1806** J. Galpine *Brit. Bot.* 242 Silique covered with roughish tubercles. **1864** *Reader* 30 Apr. 559 Iodanthus..and Thelypodium..have terete and torulose siliques. **1872** Darwin *Orig. Spec.* (ed. 6) vii. 174 The flowers..in the upper part of the spike [bear] lanceolate, two-valved, and two-seeded siliques.

**sili'quiferous**, *a. Bot.* [f. L. *siliqua*: see -ferous.] Pod-bearing.
**1693** *Phil. Trans.* XVII. 619 A siliquiferous Tree, with the Leaves of Beech. **1725** Sloane *Jamaica* II. 32, I told him that this tree of Jamaica had a papilionaceous flower, and was siliquiferous.

**si'liquiform**, *a. Bot.* [f. as prec.: see -form. So F. *siliquiforme*.] Having the form of a silique.
**1847** in Webster, citing Smith. **1861** Bentley *Man. Bot.* 320 When a fruit possesses the general structure of the siliqua,..it has been named a *Ceratium* or a siliquiform [**1887** siliquæform] capsule.

**siliquose** (sɪlɪ'kwəʊs), *a.* [ad. mod.L. *siliquōsus*, f. L. *siliqua*: cf. F. *siliqueux* (1549).]

**1.** *Bot.* Bearing pods or siliques.
**1693** *Phil. Trans.* XVII. 687 In this Sixth Volume we have describ'd and figur'd 61 Trees and Shrubs, the greatest part whereof are Siliquose. **1712** *Ibid.* XXVII. 425 This is not a Siliquose Tree. **1759** [see siliculose]. **1822** Good *Study Med.* III. 247 A free use of the siliquose and coniferous plants as a part of the common diet. **1839** Hallam *Hist. Lit.* III. iii. §13 This is manifest in siliquose plants and in palms. **1857** A. Gray *First Less. Bot.* (1866) 231 *Siliquose*, bearing siliques or pods which resemble siliques.

**2.** Having the form of a silique. **a.** *Bot.*
**1821** W. P. C. Barton *Flora N. Amer.* I. 83 Capsule siliquose, stipitate. **1830** Lindley *Nat. Syst. Bot.* 235 Fruit capsular or succulent; the former siliquose and 2-valved. **1866** *Treas. Bot.* 255 The fertile..[fronds are] divided into linear somewhat siliquose segments.
*Comb.* **1830** Lindley *Nat. Syst. Bot.* 9 The siliquose-fruited genera, such as Glaucium and Eschscholtzia.

**b.** *Path.* (See quots.)
**1825** Good *Study Med.* (ed. 2) III. 85 Under this variety [of small-pox] was reckoned by the best writers the siliquose, or that which consists of soft and empty vesicles. *a* **1827** *Ibid.* (1829) IV. 234 Schmidt supposed that, in infants, the siliquose cataract might be caused by convulsions.

**'siliquous**, *a. Bot.* Now *rare.* = siliquose 1.
**1668** Wilkins *Real Char.* II. iv. §5. 96 Herbs..considered according to their Seed-vessels, may be distinguished into..Siliquous; containing their seeds in long pods. *Ibid.* 100 Siliquous Herbs not Papilionaceous. **1688** Holme *Armoury* II. 117/2 Siliquous seed [are] such as are born in husks, cods, or shells. **1731** Miller *Gard. Dict.*, *Siliquous*, having Seed-Vessels, Husk, Pod, or Shell. **1895** H. Callan *From Clyde to Jordan* xviii. 188 Siliquous vegetables like double peas.

**silk** (sɪlk), *sb.* and *a.* Forms: α. 1 sioloc, seoloc, seoluc, seolc, 3 seolk (solk), 4 seolke; 3 selc, 4–5 selk(e. β. 4 silc, 4– silk (6 silck), 4–7 silke; 4–5 sylk(e, 5 cylk(e, 6 sylcke. [OE. *sioloc*, *seoloc*, etc. (for earlier **siluc*) masc., varying in form and gender from ON. and Icel. *silki* neut. (Norw., Sw., and Da. *silke*); not found in the other Germanic languages, but represented also by OSlav. *shelkŭ* (Russ. *shelk'*). The ultimate source is commonly supposed to be L. *sēricus* or Gr. σηρικός silken, f. L. *Sēres*, Gr. Σῆρες, the oriental people (perhaps the Chinese) from whom silk was first obtained. The change of *r* to *l* may have taken place in some language through which the word passed into Slavonic use and thence into the early Baltic trade.]

**I. 1. a.** The strong, soft, lustrous fibre produced by the larvæ of certain bombycine moths which feed upon mulberry leaves, etc., and by certain spiders; silken thread or filament.
*Virginian silk* (a plant-name): see Virginian.
*c* **888** [implied in silken *a.* 1]. *a* **1000** *Boeth. Metr.* viii. 24 Næs þa scealca nan þe..cuðe..heora wæda..sioloce siowian. *c* **1000** *Sax. Leechd.* II. 56 Seowa mid seolce fæste. **13..** *E.E. Allit. P.* B. 790 Royl rollande fax to raw sylk lyke. **1387** Trevisa *Higden* (Rolls) III. 33 Arbaces fond hym spynnynge reed selk at þe distaf. **1463–4** [see raw *a.* 2a]. *c* **1511** *1st Eng. Bk. Amer.* (Arb.) Introd. 35/1 They spynne lyke the wormes yat the sylke spynneth. **1535** Coverdale *Isaiah* xix. 9 Soch as laboure vpon flax & sylcke. **1601** Holland *Pliny* I. 124 The Seres, famous for the fine silk that their woods do yeeld. **1634** Milton *Comus* 716 Spinning Worms, That in their green shops weave the smooth-hair'd silk. **1712** *Lond. Gaz.* No. 5010/4 China Raw and Thrown Silk and Sleeve Silk. **1774** Goldsm. *Nat. Hist.* (1776) VIII. 52 After some months feeding, they lay, upon every leaf, small bundles, or cones of silk. **1835** Ure *Philos. Manuf.* 234 The matter of the silk is liquid in the body of the worm, but it hardens in the air. *Ibid.* 235 The silk of a cocoon weighs two and a half grains. **1882** Caulfeild & Saward *Dict. Needlewk.* 459/1 That part of ravelled silk thrown on one side in the filature of the cocoons.
*transf.* **1608** Topsell *Serpents* 694 They bowel them, and fill their bodies with sugar, and silk of wooll.

**b.** In the phr. *of silk*, denoting the substance of which a garment, etc., is composed; freq. passing into sense 2.
*c* **1205** Lay. 22764 Claðes soften al of white seolke. *c* **1275** *Ibid.* 4549 Of solke was þat seil-cloþ. *c* **1340** *Nominale* (Skeat) 551 Bauderik of sylke. **1362** Langl. *P. Pl.* A. Prol. 84 þer houeþ an Hundret In Houues of selk. *c* **1400** Maundev. (Roxb.) xix. 87 Wele arraid with clathez of gold and of silke. **1451** Capgr. *Life St. Gilbert* xxxviii. 117 þe seide relikes were wounde..in a cloth of silk precious I-now. **1535** Coverdale *1 Sam.* ii. 19 His mother also made him a litle cote of sylke. **1576** Gascoigne *Steele Gl.* (Arb.) 60 Our sutes of Silke. **1611** Shaks. *Cymb.* II. iv. 69 Her Bed-chamber..was hang'd With Tapistry of Silke. **1640** in Entick *London* (1766) II. 169 Boradoes of silk. **1842** Tennyson *Launcelot & Guinevere* 24 A gown of grass-green silk she wore.

**c.** In comparisons, esp. *soft as silk*.
*a* **1310** in Wright *Lyric P.* ix. 36 Body ant brest wel mad al, ..Eyther side soft ase sylk. *c* **1386** Chaucer *Sqr.'s T.* 605 Theigh thou..straw her cage faire and soft as silk. *c* **1400** *Destr. Troy* 3993 Cassandra..was a Clene Maydon, Semely of a Sise, as the silke white. *c* **1400** *26 Pol. Poems* 126 My bloode ys nessher than ys sylke. **1508** Dunbar *Tua Mariit Wemen* 96 Soft and soupill as the silk. *a* **1732** Gay *New Song of New Similies* v, Plump as a Partridge was I known, And Soft as Silk my Skin.

**d.** A silken thread.
**1684** R. Waller *Nat. Exper.* 67 We took..the bladder out of another Fish, and tyed the two Ends with a Silk. **1891** *Penny Postage Jubilee* iv. 69 Three red and two blue silk threads run parallel across the Mulready cover, the two 'silks' appearing under the design.

**e.** Silk sold in the form of thread or twist for sewing; freq. with defining word, as ***embroidery***, ***sewing silk***, etc.

**1480-1826** Sewing silk [see SEWING *vbl. sb.*[1] 4]. **1851** *Illustr. Catal. Gt. Exhib.* III. III. 506/1 Veil, vest, and shawl embroidering silk. **1920** A. K. ARTHUR *Embroidery Bk.* ii. 10 Silks of different makes, embroidery or knitting, filosel,.. and..'Tyrian', are all good for various purposes. **1951** L. TOWN *Bookbinding by Hand* xiv. 175 This is necessary to prevent fraying of the sewing silk as it passes round the headband. **1973** C. GAVIN *Snow Mountain* xxiii. 392 The drawn-thread work they were doing, on coarse linen with silks brought from their home.

**f.** ***artificial silk*** [cf. F. *soie artificielle* (de Chardonnet 1884, in *French Pat. 165,349*)] = RAYON[1] 3. Also shortened to ***art silk*** (also ***artsilk***).

**1885** *Jrnl. Soc. Chem. Industry* 29 Jan. 34 Mr. J. B. Payne exhibited..some samples of 'artificial silk', a new filament produced by pressure through a die, from pyroxylin, the invention of Mr. J. W. Swan. **1922** *Daily Mail* 2 Dec. 1 (Advt.), Three charming designs in silcot, cotton, satin and art silk stockinette. **1924** [see RAYON[1] 3 a]. **1928** *Lancet* 24 Mar. 631/2 Mr. Kelly asked the Home Secretary whether the Home Office had received any reports as to the conditions of health of workpeople employed in artificial silk factories. **1928** *Daily Mail* 3 Aug. 18/2 Snias and British Enkas were firmer among Artsilks. **1935** *Economist* 2 Nov. 854/1 Swedish exports to Italy consist to a large extent of chemical pulp..most of it rayon cellulose for artificial silk. **1944** A. L. BOWLEY *Stud. Nat. Income 1924-1938* 170 The excise on Artificial Silk has been charged since July 1925. **1957** H. CROOME *Forgotten Place* 15 A brilliant orange artsilk coverlet on a double bed..artsilk curtains of a different shade framing the windows.

**2. a.** The cloth or textile fabric woven or made from this.

*c* **1000** *Sax. Leechd.* III. 174 ðyf man mæte ðæt he seoluc oððe godweb hæbbe. *c* **1275** *On Serving Christ* 23 in *O.E. Misc.* 91 For seolk, ne for cendal, ne for deore wedes. *c* **1290** *S. Eng. Leg.* I. 392 With clene linnene cloth..And noþer in pal ne in seolke. **1362** LANGL. *P. Pl.* A. VII. 19 And ȝe, loueli Ladies.., þat habbeþ selk, and sendel souweþ..Chesybles for Chapeleyns. *a* **1400-50** *Alexander* 2401 þat Iowell..was full sekirly & soft all in silke falden. **1534** MORE *Comf. agst. Trib.* III. Wks. 1220/1 It maketh vs..gooe much more gay and glorious in sight, garnyshed in sylke. **1579** W. WILKINSON *Confut. Fam. Love* 75 They..affirmed, it was vnlawfull to weare silke. **1650** HOWELL *Lett.* III. 33 Cloth is the more substantiall..; But silk is more smooth and slik. **1654** tr. *Martini's Conq. China* 35 Their Boots, which they make either of Silk, or of Horse-skin. **1708** *Lond. Gaz.* No. 4472/4 At the Marine Coffee-house..will be expos'd to Sale ..92 Chests China Silk,..3 Bales of super-fine Piedmont Silk. **1760** GOLDSM. *Cit. World* lxxvii, I was this morning to buy silk for a night-cap. **1834** MCCULLOCH *Dict. Commerce* (ed. 2) 1029 Silk had..been used by persons of distinction two centuries previously. **1908** *Betw. Trent & Ancholme* 276 This lady wore grey silk.

*fig.* *c* **1315** SHOREHAM I. 33 Ne wynd þou naut þy senne ine silke. **1796** H. HUNTER tr. *St.-Pierre's Stud. Nat.* (1799) II. 90 The beauty of that [goat] which Nature clothes with silk on the rocks of Angora. **1843** LYTTON *Last Bar.* I. iii, He who has little silver in his pouch must have the more silk on his tongue.

**b.** Used allusively to indicate the rank of a King's (or Queen's) Counsel, marked by the right to wear a silk gown, esp. in the phrases to ***receive***, ***obtain***, or ***take silk***; also (*rare*), ***to have silk***. Collectively, denoting the persons wearing such gowns. (Cf. 3 d.)

**1810** BENTHAM *Art of Packing* (1821) 49 Our solicitor has heard with due attention the speeches delivered from learned silk. **1866** A. J. MUNBY *Diary* 2 Nov. (1972) 229 Dined in Hall..the talk was of who is to have silk presently and make way for us rising juniors. **1875** TROLLOPE *Prime Minister* (1876) I. iii. 36 He had..worked in a stuff gown till he was nearly sixty... He would take his silk as an honour for his declining years. **1882** *Daily News* 25 May 2/5 He received silk in 1868. **1882** *Society* 4 Nov. 20/1 Ere long he 'spoiled silk' (as the saying is), and was made a Serjeant. **1897** *Standard* 16 Oct. 3/4 [He] soon obtained great distinction.., which increased on his taking silk. **1925** W. S. MAUGHAM *Painted Veil* vii. 25 He was still a junior and many younger men than he had already taken silk. **1979** G. WAGNER *Barnardo* viii. 130 Thesiger..had become a QC... He had two juniors..who later took silk.

**c.** As the material of a jockey's jacket. Esp. in phr. ***to sport***, ***don***, or ***wear silk***: to ride (in a race).

**1884** H. SMART *From Post to Finish* I. xv. 243 Next week Gerald would 'don silk'..and be embarked on the career she had marked out... Had she done right?.. And yet, with his aptitude for riding..what better path..was open to him? **1891** *Daily News* 10 Dec. 2/5 A capital start was made with the Snow Steeplechase for which seven sported silk. **1898** A. E. T. WATSON *Turf* x. 189 A gentleman, when this misfortune happens to him..can cease to wear silk, or at any rate need not ride over hurdles or fences.

**d.** A parachute; chiefly in phr. ***to take to*** or ***hit the silk***, to bale out of an aircraft by parachute. *U.S. Air Force slang.*

**1933** *Jrnl. R. Aeronaut. Soc.* XXXVII. 828 The American pilot..remarked that if he had engine trouble over England he would 'take to the silk', in other words abandon his machine and come down by parachute. **1943** R. WHELAN *Flying Tigers* 100 After gaining altitude Mott's plane burst into flames and he 'hit the silk'. **1956** N. MARSH *Off with his Head* (1957) viii. 177 Over Germany..we got clobbered and I hit the silk.

**3. a.** With *a* and *pl.* A particular make of silk cloth or fabric.

**1538** STARKEY *England* I. iii. 94 Fyne clothys, says and sylkys. **1568** GRAFTON *Chron.* II. 672 Sondry riche merchaundises, as cloth of Gold, Siluer, Veluet, Satten, and other silkes. **1613** PURCHAS *Pilgrimage* (1614) 399 Our silkes haue the name of this Region, where it is made of a most fine wooll. **1748** *Anson's Voy.* II. x. 238 Chinese silks coming almost directly to Acapulco. **1797** MRS. RADCLIFFE *Italian* i, She passed whole days in embroidering silks. **1859** TENNYSON *Geraint & Enid* 693 One among his gentlewomen Display'd a splendid silk of foreign loom. **1897** WATTS-DUNTON *Aylwin* VIII. ii, An eccentric dress of Japanese silks.

**b.** *pl.* Garments made of silk; silk stockings. *spec.* a jockey's cap and jacket carrying the horse-owner's colours. Cf. sense 2 c above.

**1508** DUNBAR *Tua Mariit Wemen* 68 My self suld be full semlie with silkis arrayit. **1602** *How to Choose a Good Wife from a Bad* IV. iii, A huffing wench..whose ruffling silks Make with their motion music unto love. **1691-** [see RUSTLE *v.* 2 b]. *a* **1704** T. BROWN *Sat. French King* Wks. 1730 I. 60 My spouse, alas! must flaunt in silks no more. **1784** COWPER *Task* VI. 941 As she sweeps him with her whistling silks. **1837** DICKENS *Pickw.* xxi, A very dusty skeleton in a blue coat, black knee-shorts, and silks. **1946** *Sun* (Baltimore) 31 May 15/1 Lovely Imp, carrying the Maryland silks of R. Bruce Livie's..Stable, won on a disqualification. **1955** *Radio Times* 22 Apr. 9/3 The jockeys..in gaudy silks. **1977** *New Yorker* 4 July 71/1 Last Thursday, in his first appearance in silks since the accident, he won with his first mount..by a length and a quarter.

**c.** A lady's silk dress.

**1793** F. BURNEY *Let.* 4 Feb. (1972) II. 12 My love & thanks to my dear Sarah; though she ought to send my black silk. **1819** M. EDGEWORTH *Let.* ? 10 Mar. (1971) 181 Fanny wore her green silk and it looked beautiful. **1861** TROLLOPE *Tales Countries* 211 The black silk was not long,..nor wide in its skirts. **1897** SARAH GRAND *Beth Bk.* xxxix, She had never worn her white silk trimmed with myrtle.

**d.** A King's (or Queen's) Counsel; a 'silk gown'. (Cf. 2 b.)

**1884** *St. James's Gaz.* 8 Feb. 5/1 The retainer of some eighteen 'silks' and at least as many junior counsel. **1889** GRETTON *Memory's Harkback* 120 Jervis, afterwards Justice of Chester, was the senior silk.

**e.** A silk hat.

**1906** JOYCE *Let.* 12 Aug. (1966) II. 148, I am curious to know how he looked in a tall silk. **1930** D. H. LAWRENCE *Love among Haystacks* 87, I assured her her hat was adorable, and, much to my relief, I got rid of my silk and into a dressing gown.

**4. a.** orig. and chiefly *U.S.* The silk-like filiform styles of the female flower of unripe maize. Phr. ***in silk***, at that stage when the silk is prominent.

[*c* **1662** in *New England Q.* (1937) X. 126 There groweth within the Huske upon the Corne a matter like small threads which appeare out of the top of the Eare like a tuft of haire or Silke.] **1770** G. WASHINGTON *Diary* 25 Aug. (1925) I. 395 Many Stalks were putting out entire new Shoots with young and tender Silk. **1774** P. V. FITHIAN *Jrnl.* 19 July (1900) 212 The Corn is beginning pretty generally to tassel, & I saw one hill in Silk, and in Blossom. *a* **1817** T. DWIGHT *Trav. New Eng.*, etc. (1821) II. 403 Their favourite food is clover and maize. Of the latter they devour the part which is called the silk, the immediate means of fecundating the ear. **1847** D. DRAKE *Pioneer Life Kentucky* (1870) 52 By the month of August the corn is in silk. **1894** *Century Mag.* Apr. 850 The pistillate flower of the maize..was appropriately called the 'silk'. **1914** J. BURDETT-DAVY *Maize* v. 233 In some cases, and in the same breed, the silks appear before the tassels. **1950** *New Biol.* VIII. 46 Pollen from each plant is then poured on to the silks of the same plant. **1980** *Sci. Amer.* Jan. 101 Primitive corn and teosinte, with their tiny ears, have small pollen grains that cannot fertilize the kernels of large modern ears with their long silks.

**b.** A silky lustre in some rubies and sapphires, due to microscopic crystals, and considered a defect.

**1886** *Jrnl. Franklin Inst.* CXXII. 380 In many genuine rubies we find a silky structure (called *silk* by jewellers). **1903** W. R. CATTELLE *Precious Stones* 47 Rubies generally contain clusters of light or dark-colored spots... White, glistening streaks in the grain of the stone, called silk, are of frequent occurrence... If silk shows plainly when the stone is faced up, it is one of the most serious defects. **1929** M. WEINSTEIN *Precious & Semi-Precious Stones* i. 6 The peculiar optical effect shown by many natural rubies and sapphires, known as 'silk', is never seen in synthetic stones. **1976** B. W. ANDERSON *Gemstones for Everyman* xii. 152 The Burma rubies..usually..show small patches of 'silk' consisting of fine needles of rutile intersecting at 60°. These have a silky appearance by reflected light.

**5.** *ellipt.* **a.** A silk snapper. (See sense 10 and cf. SILT *sb.* 3 and 4.)

*a* **1818** M. G. LEWIS *Jrnl. W. Ind.* (1834) 104 Of the Sea Fish which I have hitherto met with, the Deep-water Silk appears to me the best.

**b.** A silk-covered cylinder in a flour-dressing machine.

**1879** *Encycl. Brit.* IX. 345/1 These [cylinders] are mounted horizontally on a spindle for revolving, and externally they are covered with silk of different degrees of fineness, whence they are called 'silks' or silk dressers.

**II.** *attrib.* and *Comb.*

**6.** Attrib., passing into *adj.* **a.** Made of silk or silken material; silken.

*a* **1350** *Will. Palerne* 4430 þat riche ring..with a red silk þrede þe quen bond..a-boute þe wolwes necke. **1362** LANGL. *P. Pl.* A. III. 276 Schal no seriaunt for þat seruise were a selk houue. **1546-7** *Test. Ebor.* (Surtees) VI. 252 My best silke hat. **1551** in Strype *Mem. Ref.* (1721) III. 116 No man under the degree of a gentleman to wear any silk points. **1632** LITHGOW *Trav.* VI. 272 [They] pay no Custome..for any silke ware. *a* **1653** GOUGE *Comm. Heb.* ix. 1 The roomes within it were divided by Silk curtains. **1730** A. GORDON *Maffei's Amphith.* 350 Pure Silk-Stuff was valued at the like Weight of Gold. **1741** *Corr. betw. C'tess Hartford & C'tess Pomfret* (1805) III. 216 With a black silk snail-string about their necks. **1825** J. NICHOLSON *Operat. Mechanic* 395 The silk-yarn employed by the weavers. **1866** *Cornhill Mag.* May 558 Cecilia sits down to the jangling instrument, with the worn silk flutings. **1893** 'J. O. HOBBES' *Study in Temptations* 138 She had also designed a black silk dolman for her Aunt Caroline.

*Prov.* (also used *allusively*). *a* **1700** B. E. *Dict. Cant. Crew* s.v. *Luggs*, Ye can ne make a Silk-Purse of a Sowe's Luggs, a Scotch Proverb. **1764** FOOTE *Mayor of G.* I. Wks. 1799 I. 174 Who can make a silk purse of a sow's ear? **1812** SCOTT 16 July in *Lockhart* (1869) III. xxiv. 401, I am labouring here to contradict an old proverb, and make a silk purse out of a sow's ear. **1907** E. GOSSE *Father & Son* ix. 239 'Even the Lord can't make a silk purse out of a sow's ear,' said Miss Marks. **1929** D. H. LAWRENCE *Pansies* 129 Women..want to change the man himself And turn the poor silk glove into a lusty sow's ear. **1932** R. ALDINGTON *Soft Answers* 47 Too late Julia realised that the best and most self-sacrificing of wives cannot make a silk purse out of a sow's ear, an Arnold Bennett out of an Oswald. **1959** M. BRADBURY *Eating People is Wrong* ii. 55 For the mass of men there is not too much to be said or done; you can't make a silk purse out of a sow's ear. **1978** *Jrnl. R. Soc. Arts* CXXVI. 339/2 She and her colleagues in the teaching profession are expected to turn children like that into silk purses, able to count, to spell, to read, to write, to understand, and so on.

*Comb.* **1648** HEXHAM II, *Een Zijde-laecken-verkooper*, a Silke-cloath-seller. **1833** *Penny Cycl.* I. 60/2 *Acacia Julibrissin*, silk-tassel acacia. **1846** LINDLEY *Veg. Kingd.* 31 Silk button galls. **1868** *Rep. U.S. Comm. Agric.* (1869) 287 Products of the silk-ribbon loom were exhibited. **1895** *Baily's Mag.* May 336/2 A regular silk jacket affair, with 'open' races, and an 'open' ditch.

**b.** With names of special fabrics, as ***silk camlet***, ***canvas***, ***chiffon***, ***damask***, ***drugget***, ***gauze***, ***jersey***, ***velvet***, etc.

**1530** PALSGR. 270/1 Sylke chamlet, *camelot de soye*. **1548** in Strype *Mem. Ref.* (1721) II. 208 A counterpoint of silk-say. **1611** COTGR., *Burat*, silke-rash; or any kind of stuffe thats halfe silke, and halfe worsted. *a* **1618** SYLVESTER *Monodia* Wks. (Grosart) II. 330/1 Embroidered gowns Of grass-green silk-shag. **1722** DE FOE *Col. Jack* xix, Fine English broad-cloths, silk, silk-druggets. **1779** *Phil. Trans.* LXIX. 673, I have also excited a very considerable electrical force on strong silk velvet. **1858** SIMMONDS *Dict. Trade*, *Silk-plush*, a material used for articles of ladies' dress; also very extensively for covering the stuff bodies of men's hats. **1880** L. TROUBRIDGE *Life amongst Troubridges* (1966) xi. 156 It was silk velvet and ten shillings a yard. **1882** CAULFEILD & SAWARD *Dict. Needlewk.* 449/2 Silk Canvas or Berlin..is of a very even and delicate make. *Ibid.*, Silk Damask is now superseded as a dress material. **1925** *Eaton's News Weekly* 26 Sept. 17 Very new, the Gossard Dancelette girdle of silk jersey. **1965** *Which?* Mar. 95/1 *Silk chiffon*, a light, open mesh fabric, soft and smooth. For scarves, lingerie, evening dresses, millinery. **1965** T. R. TREGEAR *Geogr. China* ii. 81 It was not the finely woven Chinese brocades and damasks that were wanted in Rome, for when they arrived they were unravelled and re-woven into lighter, flimsier silk gauzes.

*Comb.* **1594** *Canterbury Marriage Licences* (MS.), Jacobus Denewe.., Canterbury, silkrashweaver. **1597** *Lanc. Wills* (Chetham Soc.) II. 229 My silke rash gowne. **1601** HOLLAND *Pliny* I. 410 The silk-russet grape Ravuscula, the asse-hued grape Asinisca, please not the eie. **1825** J. NICHOLSON *Operat. Mechanic* 457 This thick liquid is passed..through fine hair and silk lawn sieves. **1858** SIMMONDS *Dict. Trade*, *Silk-gauze manufacturer*, a gauze-weaver. **1897** *Sears, Roebuck Catal.* 231/1 Ladies' black pure silk jersey mitts. **1966** P. O'DONNELL *Sabre-Tooth* vi. 91 Ilse..put on a white silk-velvet dressing gown. **1976** *Times* 9 Mar. 9 (Advt.), Hand made silk chiffon blouse. **1980** D. CREED *Scarab* xviii. 173 Her camel-coloured silk-jersey dress.

**c.** Of persons: Clad in silk. *rare.*

**1603** DEKKER & CHETTLE *Grissil* (Shaks. Soc.) 19 Those changeable silk gallants, who..read no books but a looking-glass. **1624** PURCHAS *Verses in Capt. Smith's Virginia*, Fetters are forged for Silke-sotts, Milk-sops.

**d.** Resembling silk in lustre; silky.

**1600** SHAKS. *A.Y.L.* III. v. 46 'Tis not..your blacke silke haire..That can entame my spirits. **1879** G. M. HOPKINS *Poems* (1967) 84 The vault and scope and schooling..In silk-ash kept from cooling. **1888** in *Ibid.* 198 Silk-beech, scrolled ash.

**7.** Attrib. **a.** With terms referring to the structure, operations, or produce of the silkworms, as ***silk-bag***, †***-bottom***, ***-cavity***, ***-cod***, ***-gland***, etc.

**1817** KIRBY & SP. *Entomol.* xxvii. (1818) II. 467 A superabundance of the gum which fills its *silk-bags. **1622** BONOEIL *Art of Making Silke* 72 [They] are bigger bodied, and make larger *silke-bottomes. **1881** TYNDALL *Floating Matter of Air* 11 They..fill the *silk cavities. **1620** *Observ. Silkwormes* D j, *Silke coddes, two shillings sixe-pence the pound. **1870** ROLLESTON *Anim. Life* 81 The disappearance of the *silk-glands during the pupa stage. **1881** TYNDALL *Floating Matter of Air* 14 The *silk organ itself was charged with corpuscles. **1759** *Phil. Trans.* LI. 54 This new species of *silk-pod. **1826** KIRBY & SP. *Entomol.* IV. xl. 112 There are a pair of *silk reservoirs (*sericteria*). *Ibid.* xli. 122 In general, the outlet of the *silk-secretors is at the mouth. **1622** BONOEIL *Art of Making Silke* 70 They make of one ounce of Spanish *silke-seede, eight, nine and tenne pound of silke. **1836-9** *Todd's Cycl. Anat.* II. 973/2 In the larva they [the salivary glands] constitute the *silk vessels.

**b.** With terms relating to the production, manufacture, or commercial handling of silk, as ***silk-commodity***, ***country***, ***culture***, ***district***, etc.

**1622** BONOEIL *Art of Making Silke* 71 Their clymate is nothing so proper for this *silke-commodity as Virginia is. **1728** CHAMBERS *Cycl.* s.v. *Silks*, Ardebil, another City of Persia, not far distant from these *Silk Countries. **1858** *Homans' Cycl. Commerce* 1721/2 The *silk culture was introduced into Louisiana in 1718. **1835** URE *Philos. Manuf.* 262 Throughout the *silk district of France. **1777** *Phil. Trans.* LXVII. 462 The smaller end of that part of a *silk engine called a star. **1835** URE *Philos. Manuf.* 269 Bobbin Mechanism of the Silk Engine. *Ibid.* 474 The *silk factories throughout the kingdom make little or no demand on muscular effort. **1797** *Encycl. Brit.* (ed. 3) XVII. 487/1 The *silk-loom has been much improved lately. **1868** *Rep. U.S.*

*Comm. Agric.* (1869) 300 A company was formed..and some silk-looms were imported. **1835** URE *Philos. Manuf.* 276 The portion of the *silk-machinery which contains the swifts. **1703** *Sc. Acts, Anne* (1824) XI. 50/1 The managers of the woollen and *silk manufactories. **1701** in *Cath. Rec. Soc. Publ.* VII. 98 Then we saw their *Silk Manufacture. **1825** J. NICHOLSON *Operat. Mechanic* 399 The silk manufacture now may be compared with what the cotton manufacture was about thirty years ago. **1728** CHAMBERS *Cycl.* s.v. *Mill*, There are also *Silk-Mills, for spinning, throwing, and twisting Silks. **1835** URE *Philos. Manuf.* 266 When these mechanicians took the silk-mill in hand. **1825** J. NICHOLSON *Operat. Mechanic* 393 In Piedmont..the manufacture is carried on by aid of the *silk reel. **1703** *Lond. Gaz.* No. 3918/4 Enquire..of Mr. Kimpson at the Castle, a *Silk-shop. **1728** CHAMBERS *Cycl.* s.v., The *Silk Trade is the Principal in China. **1835** URE *Philos. Manuf.* 246 The silk trade of Great Britain..may be valued at 7,000,000 *l.* sterling.

**8.** Objective: **a.** With agent-nouns, as ***silk-breeder, -carder, -doubler, -dresser, -maker, manufacturer, -mercer***, etc.

**1865** *Pall Mall G.* 26 June 10 The *silk-breeders of France are..in a position of the greatest distress. **1728** CHAMBERS *Cycl.* s.v., Carding, which was perform'd by the common *Silk-Carders. **1662** *Act 14 Chas. II* c. 15 §6 Every such Silk-winder and *Doubler. **1723** *Lond. Gaz.* No. 6187/4 Ann Brown, late of Wapping Stepney, Silk-Doubler. **1771** *Burrow's Rep.* III. 1346 In their said Trade and Business of *Silk-Dressers. **1858** SIMMONDS *Dict. Trade, Silk-dresser*, a stiffener and smoother of silk. **1842** in *Proc. Vermont Hist. Soc.* (1940) VIII. 156 Called on Mr. Dexter the *silk grower. **1858** *Homans' Cycl. Commerce* 1719/2 This filament the silk growers..unwind by various ingenious means. **1636** DAVENANT *Wits* Wks. (1673) 212 'Twill make 'em sing, like *Silk-Knitters of Cocklane. **1712** BLACKMORE *Creation* II. 66 They..ripen Food For the *Silk-Labourers of the Mulberry Wood. **14..** *Nom.* in Wr.-Wülcker 692 *Hec sereatrix*, a *sylkmaker. **1834–6** *Encycl. Metrop.* (1845) VIII. 717/2 The various plans which..our *silk manufacturers have introduced into their mills. **1779** JOHNSON *L.P., Gay*, [Gay] was sent to London..and placed apprentice with a *silk-mercer. **1823** SCOTT *Quentin Durw.* vi, The house of..Maître Pierre, the great *silk-merchant. **1858** SIMMONDS *Dict. Trade, *Silk printer*, a stamper of silk. **1844** G. DODD *Textile Manuf.* vi. 186 The *silk-reelers of Italy transfer the silk to a..reel, as they draw it from the cocoons. **1720** STRYPE *Stow's Surv.* II. 233/2 There were several..*Silk-Twisters, Foreigners,..living [c 1560] in St. Marten's Liberty. **1800** *Asiatic Ann. Reg.* 54/2 The Pundraca and Pattasutracára, or feeder of silk-worms and silk-twisters, deserve notice. **1858** SIMMONDS *Dict. Trade, *Silk-waterer*, one who clouds, waves, or waters silk, by passing two pieces..between metallic rollers.

**b.** With vbl. sbs. and ppl. adjs., as ***silk-bearing, -emitting, -growing, -reeling***, etc.

Also in names of machines, as *silk-doubling, -sizing, -softening, -sorting machine*: see Knight *Dict. Mech.* (1875) and Suppl. (1884) s.v.

**1872** DUNCAN tr. *Figuier's Insect World* iv. 221 The double *silk-bearing gland. **1729** SAVAGE *Wanderer* v. 217 The leaf the *silk-emitting reptile feeds. **1887** *Encycl. Brit.* XXII. 60/2 The ailanthus silkworm..now spread through many *silk-growing regions. **1579** *Sc. Acts, Jas. VI* (1814) III. 152/2 The offer and contracting anent the art of *silk-making. **1858** *Homans' Cycl. Commerce* 1719/2 These being the chief *silk-producing countries. **1868** *Rep. U.S. Comm. Agric.* (1869) 314 The *Bombycidæ*, or spinners, including the silk-producing moths. **1888** *Harper's Mag.* June 47 *Silk reeling is one of the industries [of Kansas]. **1844** G. DODD *Textile Manuf.* vi. 173 A subdivision is sometimes made between a 'silk-throwing mill' and a '*silk-spinning mill'; the former being for the manufacture from..perfect raw silk, and the latter from..inferior silk. **1677** MARVELL *Corr.* Wks. (Grosart) II. 354 Yesterday a Committee was appointed to consider how to encourage the *Silk-weaving in England. **1835** URE *Philos. Manuf.* 264 There has been a constant depreciation of the wages of silk weaving in France, from the year 1810. **1611** FLORIO, *Indouanadura*, a *silke-winding. **1841** BROWNING *Pippa* Introd. 71 The next twelve-month's toil At wearisome silk-winding, coil on coil!

**9.** Instrumental, etc., as ***silk-broidered, -covered, -hatted, -hosed***, etc.

**1753** WEST *Odes Pindar*, etc. I. 234 And to thy Tomb, as Off'rings, shall be brought *Silk-broider'd Mantles. **1849** NOAD *Electricity* (ed. 3) 367 They are all coated with coils of *silk-covered wire. **1903** W. LE QUEUX *Seven Secrets* (ed. 2) xxii. 219 The *silk-hatted, frock-coated existence of the fashionable physician. **1976** L. ST. CLAIR *Fortune in Death* iii. 27 A bank messenger, very properly silk-hatted and frock-coated. **1820** SCOTT *Monast.* xxvii, No *silk-hosed reveller of the presence-chamber. **1947** AUDEN *Age of Anxiety* (1948) ii. 35 And mother wrote Swift and sure in the *silk-hung saloon Her large round letters. **1876** 'OUIDA' *Winter City* xii. 369 Postillions, *silk-jacketted.., and with ribboned straw hats. **1901** *Westm. Gaz.* 29 Nov. 7/2 A romantic American,..after living as a hermit for fifteen years in consequence of an unhappy love affair, has been buried in a *silk-lined grave. **1979** *Country Life* 1 Feb. 309/1 (Advt.), Silk-lined mohair coats. **1820** KEATS *Lamia* II. 220 Each..*silk-pillow'd at his ease. **1857** G. W. THORNBURY *Songs Cavaliers & Roundheads* 306 The *silk-robed men with peacock plumes. **1918** G. FRANKAU *One of Them* in *Poet. Wks.* (1923) II. xix. 123 *Silk-socked; bright monocled; gallant. **1922** JOYCE *Ulysses* 517 Bella..lifts..a plump buskined hoof and a full pastern, silk-socked. **1884** BROWNING *Ferishtah Fancies* (1885) 8 Inside—gold-roofed *silk-walled silence round about! **1639** G. DANIEL *Vervic* 679 Noe *silke-wrapt wantons here..Shall graspe Luxurious Edward.

**10.** Special combs.: **silk-coal**, a variety of coal found in Shropshire; **silk embroidery**, embroidery worked with silk threads; **silk-glue**, sericin; **silk gown**, = sense 3 d; **silk green**, a colour-substance used in paper making; **silk-gut**, the gut in the silkworm from which the silk is produced; **silk hat**, a cylindrical hat having a light stiff body covered with silk plush or shag; †**silk-maid**, a maid employed to make silk articles of dress; **silk paper**, a kind of tissue-paper; **silk road, route** (freq. with initial capitals), a trade route from China through India to the West, used in ancient times by traders in silk; **silk-shag**, (see quot.); **silk snapper**, a Bermudan fish (see quot. and sense 5 a, and cf. *silt-snapper*); †**silk snatcher**, (see quot.); **silk waste**, the fibres which remain after the reeling of silk yarn, or those obtained from damaged cocoons; †**silk wool**, a mixed yarn made of wool and either silk or staple fibre (*obs.*).

**1803** PLYMLEY *Agric. Shropsh.* 55 Coal, called the *silk-coal. **1837** *Penny Cycl.* VII. 77/1 A piece of *silk embroidery. **1889** J. J. REIN *Industries of Japan* III. iv. 389 Oftentimes this silk embroidery is connected very skilfully with the painting or printing of the material. **1982** E. NORTH *Ancient Enemies* iii. 32 I've never yet told her about the private [American] college..where you can major in any subject... I met a girl who'd been there majoring in something like silk embroidery. **1886** tr. *Benedikt's Chem. Coal-tar Colours* 39 Both fibroine and sericine (*silk-glue) consist of carbon, nitrogen, hydrogen and oxygen. **1836–7** DICKENS *Sk. Boz, Tales* v, 'I presume you have studied for the bar?'..'No..'. 'But you have been much among the *silk gowns?' **1880** J. DUNBAR *Pract. Papermaker* 58 *Silk green is a chemically pure colouring matter, producing beautiful shades of green. **1839** URE *Dict. Arts* 1115 The rest of the entrails resembles boiled spinage, and therefore can occasion no mistake as to the *silk-gut. **1834–6** *Encycl. Metrop.* (1845) VIII. 760/2 The *silk hat, with a body of felt and a nap of silk plush. **1893** GEORGIANA HILL *Hist. Eng. Dress* II. 253 The tall silk hat, introduced from France about 1840. **1474** *Paston Lett.* III. 118 My *sylkemayde whyche makyth perte off suche as she shall weer. **1796** WITHERING *Brit. Pl.* (ed. 3) IV. 345 Thin as *silk paper. **1841** *Penny Cycl.* XX. 375 There were formerly manufactures of silk-paper in this town [Samarcand]. **1931** J. W. GREGORY *Story of Road* I. iii. 43 The northern *silk road in Asia crossed Persia and Kashgar to the Tarim Basin in Chinese Turkestan. **1936** P. FLEMING *News from Tartary* I. iv. 29 The Silk Road takes..you through Sinkiang to Kashgar and the Himalayan passes by one of two alternative routes. **1982** *Times* 25 Feb. 10/5 A community of some 200 Chinese-Jewish descendants of Silk Road traders in the ancient capital of Kaifeng, who no longer identify with Judaism. **1913** J. BUCHAN *Divus Johnson* in *Runagates Club* (1928) vi. 152 Russian geographers were interesting themselves in the line of the old *silk route to Cathay. **1949** D. CARRUTHERS *Beyond Caspian* iv. 95 The Silk Route was not a disjointed affair, built up in sections, linking likely markets. **1981** *Daily Tel.* 30 Mar. 18/5 Tartar hats..recall the Silk Route of Marco Polo. **1883** DAY *Fishes Gt. Brit.* II. 210 Young herring in Northumberland..are likewise termed *silk-shag. **1876** GOODE *Fishes of Bermudas* 55 The Schoolmaster Snapper and *Silk Snapper of the fishermen probably belong to this genus [*Lutjanus aya*, family *Pristipomatidæ*]. **1884** *Proc. U.S. Nat. Mus.* VII. (1885) 454 Some young 'Silk Snappers' brought by Mr. Gilbert from Aspinwall. **1785** GROSE *Dict. Vulgar T.*, **Silk snatchers*, thieves who snatch hoods or bonnets from persons walking in the streets. **1842** *Encycl. Brit.* (ed. 7) XX. 350/2 To introduce such alterations in the spinning of *silk waste as will supersede the cutting, carding, and scutching processes... The art of silk waste spinning..is still in its infancy. **1965** A. BREARLEY *Woollen Industry* v. 27 Silk wastes are used in woollen blends for their own distinctive merits. **1859** L. OLIPHANT *Narr. Earl of Elgin's Mission China & Japan* (1860) II. 255 The Japanese wear in winter garments thickly padded either with cotton or *silk wool. **1908** *Practitioner* Nov. 760 Silcool is a form of vegetable silk-wool. **1928** F. M. ROWE tr. *Reinthaler's Artificial Silk* vii. 128 Staple fibre yarn..cannot belie its cellulose nature; it lacks..the tenacity of wool. This can be remedied..by spinning staple fibre in admixture with wool or recovered wool... Such mixed yarns (carded or combed) termed 'silk-wool',..are still used for needlework and machine knitting.

**b.** *Bot.* In the names of trees, shrubs, or plants, as **silk-bark**, a small evergreen tree, *Maytenus acuminata*, belonging to the family Celastraceæ and native to southern Africa; **silk-maudlin, -oak**, (see quots.); **silk-tassel (bush, tree)** = GARRYA; **silk-tree** (see quots.); **silk wood**, (*a*) (see quot. 1775); (*b*) = CALABUR TREE; (*c*) = *Queensland maple* s.v. QUEENSLAND; **silk wort** (see quot.).

**1894** T. R. SIM *Flora of Kaffraria* 28 (*heading*) *Silkbark. **1907** —— *Forests & Forest Flora Cape of Good Hope* xiv. 184 Silk-bark... A small branched unarmed tree. **1912** *Cape Times* 12 Oct. 9/8 In the gorge beneath the fall an indigenous thicket, yellow-wood, Hottentot cherry, silk-bark, has been allowed to remain. **1972** PALMER & PITMAN *Trees S. Afr.* II. 1285 The silkbark or sybas has a wide distribution, occurring from eastern tropical Africa to the Cape. **1712** *Phil. Trans.* XXVII. 419 Stoll's Cape *Silk-Maudlin [is]..an ever-green Shrub, with deep dented Leaves. **1866** *Treas. Bot.* 551/2 Lofty trees..with a girth of eight feet, as in *Grevillea robusta*, the *Silk Oak of the colonists. [*Ibid.* 798/2 Silky, or Silkbark Oak.] **1897** M. E. PARSONS *Wild Flowers of California* 370 (*heading*) *Silk-tassel tree. Quinine-bush. **1949** J. T. HOWELL *Marin Flora* 211 The graceful catkins of the staminate plants make the silk tassel bush one of the most beautiful shrubs in the chaparral. **1976** *Hortus Third* (L. H. Bailey Hortorium) 495/2 *Garrya* Dougl[as]. Silk-tassel, silk-tassel bush... The garryas are ornamentals flowering in late winter and early spring. **1852** JOHNSON *Cottage Gard. Dict.* 5/1 *Acacia julibrissia* (*silk-tree). **1868** *Rep. U.S. Comm. Agric.* (1869) 201 The silk tree (*Albizzia julibrissin*) is a low-headed spreading-tree, possessed of the most graceful foliage. **1880** BESSEY *Botany* 547 Some East and West Indian trees of the genus *Bombax*..are known as Silk Trees. **1775** G. WHITE *Selborne* lxviii, Stalks of the *polytrichum commune*, or great golden maiden-hair, which they [*sc.* foresters] call *silk-wood. **1888** Silk wood: used in def. of *Calabur tree*. **1891** *Cent. Dict.*, *Silkwood*, a shrub, *Muntingia Calabura*. **1909** F. M. BAILEY *Comprehensive Catal. Queensland Plants* 91 *Flindersia..Brayleyana*.. Wood has been cut under the name of 'Silkwood'. **1948** A. L. HOWARD *Man. Timbers World* (ed. 3) 354 Maple silk-wood is moderately elastic. **1897** *Jrnl. R. Agric. Soc.* Dec. 617 One [water-weed] known locally as network or *silkwort, on account of its thread-like stems.

**c.** *Ent.* In the names of various silk-producing insects: †**silk-fly**, the silkworm moth; **silk insect, moth** (see quots.); **silk-spider**, one or other of various species of silk-spinning spiders; **silk-spinner**, a spider or a silk-moth.

**1599** T. M[OUFET] *Silkwormes* 26 *Silke-flies I meane, which not on breast alone But all throughout.. Besides pure white, else colour carry none. **1798** CRUTTWELL *Univ. Gazetteer* (1808) s.v. *China*, The *silk insects, which are different from silk-worms, resemble caterpillars. **1826** KIRBY & SP. *Entomol.* III. xxx. 220 *Attacus Paphia*, a giant *silk-moth. **1871** DARWIN *Desc. Man* II. x. (1890) 278 The male and female cocoons of the silk-moth (*Bombyx mori*). **1728** CHAMBERS *Cycl.* s.v. *Silk*, The *Silk-Spider make[s] a Silk, every whit as beautiful..as the Silk-worm. **1866** *Athenæum* No. 2019. 26/1 A species of silk-spider. **1868** C. M. YONGE *Chaplet of Pearls* II. xlii. 246 A colony of *silk-spinners, attracted by the mulberry-leaves of the old abbey garden. **1869** 'MARK TWAIN' *Innoc. Abr.* xxxiii. 365 This old dried-up reservoir is occupied by a few ghostly silk-spinners now. **1896** R. LYDEKKER *Royal Nat. Hist.* VI. iii. 95 (*heading*) The silk-spinners,—Family *Bombycidæ*.

**d.** *Ornith.* In the names of birds or fowls: **silk-bunting**, *U.S.*, one or other of the buntings of the genus *Spiza*, esp. *S. americana*; **silk cock**, a species of domestic fowl, esp. *Phasianus gallus* or *Gallus lanatus*, native to eastern Asia; **silk fowl**, a silk-cock or -hen; (see also quot. 1835–6); **silk-hen**, the female of the silk-cock; †**silk stare**, = next; **silk starling**, a species of starling (*Sturnus sericeus*), native to China.

**1884** COUES *N. Amer. Birds* 387 *Spiza*, *Silk Buntings. **1783** LATHAM *Gen. Synop. Birds* II. II. 708 *Silk Cock, *Phasianus gallus*. **1829** GRIFFITH tr. *Cuvier* VIII. 222 The Silk Cock..is of a pure white. **1835–6** *Todd's Cycl. Anat.* I. 270/1 The *Silk or Negro-fowl of the Cape de Verd Islands (*Gallus Morio*, Temminck). **1885** *Encycl. Brit.* XIX. 645/2 The silk fowl best known is that in which the plumage is perfectly white. **1868** DARWIN *Variation Anim. & Pl.* xiv, I reared a large number of mongrels from a *silk-hen by a Spanish cock. **1884** *St. James's Gaz.* 27 Nov. 5/2 In Germany the silk hen is frequently remarkable for the length of her spurs. **1783** LATHAM *Gen. Synop. Birds* II. I. 10 *Silk Stare. Size of a Starling... The plumage in general glossy and silky. **1817** STEPHENS in Shaw *Gen. Zool.* X. II. 497 *Silk starling.

**silk**, *v. U.S.* [f. the sb.] **a.** *trans.* To remove the silk from (maize).

**1847** D. DRAKE *Pioneer Life Kentucky* (1870) 52 My first business in the morning was to pull, and husk and silk enough [corn] for breakfast. **1892** *Hist. Rev. Industr. & Commercial Growth York County* (Pa., U.S.) 59 [They] make a specialty of..'silkers' for silking corn. **1972** E. WIGGINTON *Foxfire Bk.* 177 Shuck and silk corn that is in roasting ear.

**b.** *intr.* Of maize: to produce the silk.

**1878** J. H. BEADLE *Western Wilds* xv. 245 The summers are short and the nights cool. Corn will not silk. **1939** *Sun* (Baltimore) 21 July 13/4 The corn in the county is later..as the farmers have planted it so it will silk after August 10 when the danger from beetles is over. **1948** *Clarke County Democrat* (Grove Hill, Alabama) 3 June 1/3 This worm usually waits until corn bunches for tasseling or begins to silk before they attack.

**silk**, var. *swilk*, obs. form of SUCH.

**silk-cotton.** [f. SILK *sb.* + COTTON *sb.*[1]]

**1.** The silky, elastic down or fibre obtained from various bombaceous and other tropical trees, and chiefly used for packing, stuffing pillows and cushions, making paper, etc.

**1697** DAMPIER *Voy.* (1698) I. vii. 164 They [white cotton-trees] bear a very fine sort of Cotton, called Silk Cotton,..like the Down of Thistles. **1703** *Ibid.* III. i. 21 The Silk-Cotton grows on tender Shrubs, 3 or 4 Foot high, in Cods as big as an Apple. **1785** MARTYN *Rousseau's Bot.* xxiv. (1794) 340 You have here Silk-Cotton, the True Cotton, so much used in our manufactures [etc.]. **1866** *Treas. Bot.* 1009/2 The silk-cotton of the Simool..is, like other silk-cottons, not adapted for spinning. **1882** CAULFEILD & SAWARD *Dict. Needlewk.* 449/2 The Silk Cotton is enclosed within the capsules containing the seed, which is embedded in it.

*attrib.* **1857** HENFREY *Bot.* 246 *Sterculiaceæ*. The Silk-Cotton Order. **1866** *Treas. Bot.* 155/1 *Bombaceæ*, the Silk-cotton family, a group..belonging to Lindley's Malval alliance.

**2.** ***silk-cotton tree***, one or other of various species of tropical trees belonging to the genera *Bombax*, *Eriodendron*, *Ochroma*, and *Pachira*, which produce silk-cotton, esp. *B. malabaricum*, *Munguba*, or *Ceiba*, and *E. anfractuosum* or *orientale*. Cf. COTTON-TREE 1.

**1712** E. COOKE *Voy. S. Sea* 117 We found here some Guinea Pepper, and silk Cotton-Trees. **1781** *Phil. Trans.* LXXI. 168 This insect is most probably to be found in all countries where the silk-cotton-tree (*Bombax*) is indigenous. **1852** TH. ROSS tr. *Humboldt's Trav.* I. iv. 148 A silk-cotton tree.., the trunk of which, in its fourth year, had reached nearly two feet and a half in diameter. **1885** LADY BRASSEY *The Trades* 99 Herds of cattle grazed beneath the shade of huge silk-cotton trees.

**silk-dyer.** One who dyes silks.

*c* **1515** *Cocke Lorell's B.* 10 Table makers, sylke dyers, and shepsters. **1621** ELSING *Debates Ho. Lords* (Camden) 33 The Wardens of the Company of sylke dyers to sende hether 4 sylke dyers. **1709** *Lond. Gaz.* No. 4535/4 Mr. James Taylor, a Silk Dyer. **1839** URE *Dict. Arts* 125 The silk-dyers keep a black vat, and its very complex composition varies in different dye-houses.

**silke**, var. *swilk*, obs. form of SUCH.

**silked** (sɪlkt), *a.* [-ED[1].] **1.** Coated with silk; clothed in or covered with silk.

**1837** *Annals Electricity, Magnetism & Chem.* I. 112 The bar is covered with several coils of silked copper wire. **1844** NOAD *Electricity* (ed. 2) 246 Twenty-two feet of silked wire wound on a quill. **1858** J. P. JOULE *Sci. Papers* (1884) 405, 2798 yards of no. 40 silked copper wire. **1864** C. ROSSETTI *Farm Walk* in *Prince's Progress* (1866) 152 I've seen grand ladies plumed and silked. **1909** M. B. SAUNDERS *Litany Lane* iii. 33 Gorgeously furred and laced and scented and silked.

**2.** Of (the pages of) a book, etc.: having been strengthened by silking (sense 2).

**1943** *Amer. Archivist* VI. 153 Upon subjection to accelerated aging tests.. it was found that the silked papers had lost 52 per cent of their folding endurance. **1971** *Catal. Mildred C. Esty Coll. MSS Rob. Burns* (Christie's) 7, 1 p., 4to., with conjoint address leaf (considerably repaired, silked, a few words rubbed along fold).

**silken** ('sɪlk(ə)n), *a.* Forms: α. 1 seolocen (2 -ken), seolcen (siolcen), 3 seolken(e; 2 seleken, 4 selkyn, 5 selken. β. 3 sulkene, 4 silkine, 5 -in, -yn, 6 sylken, -yn, 4 silken. [f. SILK *sb.* + -EN[4].]

**I. 1.** Made or consisting of silk.

α. *c*888 K. ÆLFRED *Boeth.* xv, Seolocenra hræȝla mid mistlicum bleowum hi ne ȝimdon. **9..** *Ags. Gloss.* in Wr.-Wülcker 195 *Bombicinum*, seolcen ȝeȝerla. *c*1160 *Hatton Gosp.* Matt. xxvii. 28 Hyo.. scrydden hine mid selekene reade sicchele [*read* scyccelse]. *c*1275 *Sinners Beware* 164 in *O.E. Misc.* 77 Heo draweþ heore wede Mid seolkene þrede. **13..** [see β]. *a*1400 *Pistill of Susan* 197 Nou is Susan.. sengeliche arayed, In a selken schert. **1475-6** *Sarum Churchw. Acc.* (Swayne, 1896) 362, iiij vnce j quarter of selken frenge, v s. ij d.

β. *c*1205 LAY. 4549 Sulkene wes þat seil-clæð. **13..** *K. Alis.* 278 (Laud MS.), Yhiled myd a silken [*W.* selkyn] webbe. *a*1400-50 *Alexander* 1520 He.. sammes þaim on aithire side with silken rapis. **1474** CAXTON *Chesse* III. vii. (1883) 142 A silken threde so small that no man myght see hit. **1553** EDEN *Treat. New Ind.* (Arb.) 18 A silken fyllet of scarlet colour tied about their heddes. **1594** SPENSER *F.Q.* IV. i. 13 Like a silken veile in compasse round About her backe. **1645** PAGITT *Heresiogr.* (1661) 13 They would not suffer a man to were a Ring, or a woman a silken gown. **1725** POPE *Odyss.* VI. 95 The silken reins Shine in her hand. **1781** GIBSON *Decl. & F.* xxii. (1787) II. 343 Their silken robes were embroidered with gold. **1815** KIRBY & SP. *Entomol.* iii. (1818) I. 63 The caterpillar attached itself to a leaf by a silken girth. **1852** MRS. STOWE *Uncle Tom's C.* xix, Merry laughs were heard through the silken curtains.

*fig.* **1673** DRYDEN *Mar. à la Mode* II. i, Tho' nature gives you power To bind his duty, 'tis with silken bonds. **1746** HERVEY *Medit.* (1818) 32 How silken the yoke to such a pair, and what blessings were twisted with such bands! **1799** SICKELMORE *Agnes & Leonora* II. 68 He became firmly attached, in the silken bond of friendship, to a youth.

**2.** Worked in silk. *rare.*

**1587** FLEMING *Cont. Holinshed* III. 1346/2 Those silken pictures hallowed by the pope. **1597** SHAKS. *Lover's Compl.* 17 Oft did she heaue her Napkin to her eyne, Which on it had conceited charecters: Laundring the silken figures in the brine [etc.].

**3.** Producing silk; characterized by the prevalence of silk.

**1601** HOLLAND *Pliny* II. 407 Insomuch as we need not wonder any more at the Seres or Indians for their cotton and silken trees. **1820** KEATS *Eve of St. Agnes* xxi, The maiden's chamber, silken, hush'd and chaste. *Ibid.* xxx, Spiced dainties, every one, From silken Samarcand.

**4.** Clad in silk. (See also 8.)

**1640** CHILMEAD *Ferrand's Love Melanch.* 51 Every silken coxcombe that has but a Page at his heels. **1648** J. BEAUMONT *Psyche* VII. cxxxv, All Inns by Silken and by Purple Things Were taken up. **1738** JOHNSON *London* 164 With brisker air the silken courtiers gaze. **1806** MANT *Poems* I. 17 And distant in the glittering sunshine ride The silken sons of luxury and pride. **1820** SCOTT *Abbot* xx, Her four noble Marys and all their silken train. **1896** *Daily News* 2 July 9/2 One would look instinctively for a vision of silken ankles and the red drugget on the pavement.

**5.** Of or pertaining to silk stuffs or goods.

**1719** W. WOOD *Surv. Trade* 219 The Encouragement of our Woollen Manufacture; the Consequence of which, is the Encouragement of the Silken.

**II. 6. a.** Silky, silk-like; soft; glossy, shining, lustrous.

**1513** DOUGLAS *Æneid* XII. Prol. 129 The balmy vapour from thar sylkyn croppis Distylland hailsum.. hunny droppis. **1591** SPENSER *M. Hubberd* 591 Now blessed be the day, That I see.. your silken hyde Fil'd with round flesh. **1597** SHAKS. *Lover's Compl.* 87 His browny locks did hang in crooked curles, And euery.. wind Vpon his lippes their silken parcels hurles. **1607** ROWLANDS *Guy Warw.* (Hunterian Club) 8 Pleasing, smooth, and silken skin. **1625** MILTON *Death Fair Infant* 2 O fairest flower.., Soft silken Primrose fading timelesslie. **1697** DRYDEN *Virg. Georg.* I. 468 Sleeps are sweeter on the silken Ground. **1820** SHELLEY *Œd. Tyr.* II. i. 64 The milk-white Bulls.. in fresh dews.. Sleeking their silken hair. **1857** MILLER *Elem. Chem., Org.* v. §3 (1862) 362 It crystallizes in anhydrous silken needles. **1871** PALGRAVE *Lyr. Poems* 76 All day between them in silence The silken butterflies glide.

*fig.* **1854** MISS BAKER *Northampt. Gloss., Silken skin*, in good humour. 'He has a fine silken skin to-day.'

**b.** *spec.* in scientific names (see quots.).

**1611** COTGR., *Cotine*, Venice Sumach, silken Sumach, red Sumach. **1804** SHAW *Gen. Zool.* V. I. 221 Silken Carp, *Cyprinus Sericeus*... Brilliant violet-silvery Carp... Native of slowly-running streams in many parts of Dauria. **1832** J. RENNIE *Consp. Butterfl. & Moths* 111 The Silken Carpet (*Alcis sericearia*, Curtis) appears in July. Wings.. silky-brown, or brick-red.

**7. a.** Of words, etc.: Elegant; ingratiating, soft, flattering.

**1588** SHAKS. *L.L.L.* v. ii. 406 Taffata phrases, silken tearmes precise. **1644** JESSOP *Angel of Ephesus* 62 A late Patron of Episcopacie, who seemeth to be very neere of kinne to the Remonstrant in confidence and silken language. **1672** OWEN *Christian Love* iii, Love may work as regularly by sharp rebukes as by the most silken and compliant expressions. **1703** ROWE *Ulysses* I. i. 307, I cannot court you with a silken Tale. **1741** WATTS *Improv. Mind* (1801) 90 To be restrained by such mild and silken language. **1955** E. POUND *Classic Anthol.* I. 20 Lady of silken word.

**b.** Similarly of persons, their looks, voice, etc.

**1594** SHAKS. *Rich. III*, I. iii. 53 His simple truth must be abus'd, With silken, slye, insinuating Iackes. **1598** MARSTON *Pygmal., Sat.* ii, Then with a silken face [he] Smiles on the holy crue. *c*1765 CHURCHILL *Proph. Famine* Poems 1767 I. 88 Thus speak a form, by silken smile, and tone Dull and unvaried, for the Laureat known. **1885** *Manch. Exam.* 27 Apr. 5/4 Mr. Russell's voice, usually so soft and silken, was absolutely husky with passion.

**8.** Effeminate, luxurious.

In some examples sense 4 may be intended.

**1599** SHAKS. *John* v. i. 70 Shall a beardlesse boy, A cockred-silken wanton braue our fields? —— *Hen. V*, II. Prol. 2 Now all the Youth of England are on fire, And silken Dalliance in the Wardrobe lyes. **1648** J. BEAUMONT *Psyche* XVI. clx, Whilst fooled Thou.. Lin'st thy Commands with silken downy Ease. **1652** C. B. STAPYLTON *Herodian* 65 These Silken Syrians are no Souldiers Martiall. **1703** ROWE *Ulysses* II. i. 433 The silken Minions of the Samian Court. **1741-2** GRAY *Agrippa* 98 The silken son of dalliance, nurs'd in ease. **1821** BYRON *Sardanap.* III. i. 314 Baal himself Ne'er fought more fiercely to win empire, than His silken son to save it. **1877** L. MORRIS *Epic of Hades* II. 135 Their silken ease And royal luxury changed for blood and tears.

**9. a.** Soft, sweet, balmy; gentle.

**1599** B. JONSON *Cynthia's Rev.* III. v. 215 Silken thoughts attend this deare beautie. **1601** —— *Ev. Man in Hum.* (Qto.) III. iii. 17 In smoothe silken peace. *a*1635 BP. CORBET *Poems* (1807) 224 Those deeds.. which ne'er affright The silken slumbers in the night. **1894** G. EGERTON *Discords* 178 It is so good to sit thus bathed in silken air. **1895** W. WRIGHT *Palmyra & Zenobia* iii. 23 A splendid charger, whose neck.. swayed hither and thither to her silken touch.

**b.** Of Sounds: Soft, low.

**1784** COWPER *Task* IV. 212 Time.. has a dove's wing, Unsoil'd, and swift, and of a silken sound. *c*1800 H. K. WHITE *Clift Gr.* 81 The gray owl's silken flight. **1844** MRS. BROWNING *Lady Geraldine's Courtship* v, In her lovely silken murmur.

**c.** Of wine: Mellow, silky.

*a*1704 T. BROWN *To J. Haines* in Coll. Poems (1705) 117 'Tis all Sincerity, a Silken Wine; It Charms the Taste, and Gratifies the Nose.

**10.** *Comb.*, as ***silken-coated, -fastened, -folded, -sailed, -sandalled, -threaded, -winged***, etc. Also ***silken-shining, -soft, -stapler***.

**1593** SHAKS. *2 Hen. VI*, IV. ii. 136 As for these *silken-coated slaues I passe not. **1868** MORRIS *Earthly Par.* (1890) 61/2 A *silken-fastened book. **1847** TENNYSON *Princ.* iv. 49 Francis hatch'd In *silken-folded idleness. *a*1835 MOTHERWELL *Poet. Wks.* (1847) 64 'Tis softer than down, or This *silken-leafed flower. **1833** TENNYSON *Lady of Shalott* I. iii, Unhail'd The shallop flitteth *silken-sail'd. **1847** —— *Princ.* Prol. 149 Her tiny *silken-sandal'd foot. **1887** MEREDITH *Ball. & Poems* 157 O'er the *silken-shining pastures of the continents and the isles. **1859** LD. LYTTON *Wanderer* (ed. 2) 199 Your young feet there, *Silken-soft in each quaint slipper. **1599** T. M[OUFET] *Silkwormes* 74 Go we, let vs learne the *silken-staplers trade. **1766** *Phil. Trans.* LVI. 58 A Newtonian telescope.. furnished with a *silken-threaded micrometer. **1868** MORRIS *Earthly Par.* (1870) I. I. 338 In her lap her open hand did lie, The silken-threaded needle close thereby. **1820** SHELLEY *Witch Atlas* Ded. 9 What hand would crush the *silken-winged fly.

Hence **'silken** *v. trans.*, to invest with a silky lustre; **'silkened** *a.*, dressed in silk.

**1757** DYER *Fleece* I. 494 Nightly to house them [*sc.* sheep] dry on fern or straw, Silk'ning their Fleeces. **1841** CATLIN *N. Amer. Ind.* (1844) I. xxx. 244 The cheering smiles and graces of silkened beauty.

**'silkenly**, *adv.* [f. SILKEN *a.* + -LY[2].] In a silken manner; also in *nonce-use* (quot. 1846).

**1846** LANDOR *Exam. Shaks.* Wks. 1853 II. 286 This is not the doctrine.. of the silkenly and lawnly religious. **1861** *Temple Bar* II. 178 He makes his thoughts flow silkenly to the purring of the cat. **1865** MEREDITH *Rhoda Fleming* xxi, She was.. as silkenly insipid every evening of her life.

**silker** ('sɪlkə(r)). [f. SILK *sb.* + -ER[1].] One who works in or with silk; in various technical uses.

**1881** *Instr. Census Clerks* (1885) 50 Piano Manufacturing... Silker. *Ibid.* 69 Cotton.. Silker. **1903** *Sci. Amer. Suppl.* 24 Jan. 22629/3 From the cutters' room the leather, which has assumed the shape of the glove, is sent to the 'silkers', who embroider the back. **1921** *Dict. Occup. Terms* (1927) 200/1 *Taper*,.. *silker*; stitches tape by machine, down seam, in closing upper of a boot or shoe. *Ibid.* 203/1 *Silker*; (i) finishes cloth piece.. by stitching folds together, by hand, with a silk thread to hold them in position; (ii) sews selvedges of cloth pieces with different coloured threads of silk or of mercerised cotton.

**silkette** (sɪl'kɛt). [f. SILK *sb.* + -ETTE.] A fabric made of silk and cotton, chiefly used for lining dresses.

**1895** *Daily News* 5 Feb. 6/6 The skirt reveals itself to be lined throughout with rose-coloured 'silkette'. **1922** JOYCE *Ulysses* 735 The second pair of silkette stockings is laddered.

**silk grass.** *Bot.* Also **silk-grass**. [f. SILK *sb.* + GRASS *sb.*[1]]

**1. a.** One or other of various species of lustrous grasses native to America and the West Indies, esp. *Bromelia* or *Nidularium Karatas*; also, the fibrous leaves produced by these.

**1620** *Observ. Silkwormes* Dj, Silke grasse to be vsed for Cordage, sixe-pence the pound. **1699** WAFER *Voy.* 94 They have a Plant also which is of good use to them, call'd by us Silk-grass, tho' 'tis indeed a kind of Flag. **1703** *Lond. Gaz.* No. 3898/3 Goods out of the Mary Man of War from Vigo, consisting of.. Coppras, Silk Grass, &c. **1771** SMOLLETT *Humph. Cl.* 13 July, He.. made her a present of a purse of silk-grass. **1807** P. GASS *Jrnl.* 184 A number of the Chinook Indians came to the fort with hats.. made of the cedar bark and silk grass. **1827** ROBERTS *Voy. Centr. Amer.* 56 Large bags made of silk grass. **1864** GRISEBACH *Flora Brit. W. Ind.* 787/2.

*attrib.* **1699** WAFER *Voy.* 95 The Spanish Women make Stockins of it, which are call'd Silk-grass Stockins.

**b.** The name of various species of aloe, agave, or yucca, or of the fibre derived from these.

**1753** *Chambers' Cycl.* Suppl. *App.*, *Silk-grass*, a name used for two very different genuses of plants, the aloe and dog's bane. **1847** WEBSTER (citing *Farm. Encycl.*), *Silk-grass*, a filamentous plant of the genus Yucca. **1858** SIMMONDS *Dict. Trade*, *Silk-grass*, a name for the fine fibres of the *Agave vivipara*, and of *A. zuccæfolia*. **1859** BARTLETT *Dict. Amer.* (ed. 2) s.v. *Bear-grass*, Bear-Grass (*Yucca-filamentosa*). Sometimes called Silk Grass, from the fibres which appear on the edges of the leaves. It is not a grass.

*attrib.* **1769** E. BANCROFT *Nat. Hist. Guiana* 48 The Silk Grass Plant nearly resembles the American Aloes.

†**2. a.** Dog's-bane (*Apocynum*). *Obs. rare.*

**1670** *Phil. Trans.* V. 1152 In the same Box are Pods of a Vegetable, we call Silk-grass, which are full of a kind of most fine down-like Cotton-wool. **1753** *Chambers' Cycl.* Suppl. *App.*

†**b.** Cotton-grass. *Obs.*$^{-1}$

**1727** in *Gentl. Mag.* (1747) XVII. 23/2 A plant named silk or cotton grass from its white tuff on the top resembling the finest cotton wool.

**3.** The grass *Oryzopsis cuspidata* of the western United States, the glumes of which bear long silky hairs; also *Stipa comata* of the same region.

**1891** in *Cent. Dict.*

**silkie** ('sɪlkɪ). Also **Silkie**. [f. SILK *sb.* + -IE.] A small chicken of a variety distinguished by long, soft plumage.

**1885** *Daily News* 14 July 2/3 The little Japanese silkies are valuable for sitting on pheasants' or partridges' eggs on account of their light weight. **1937** W. W. BROOMHEAD *Poultry Breeding & Management* ix. 325/1 Silkies are quaint little fowls. *Ibid.* 326/1 (*caption*) A White Silkie Cock. **1978** *Country Life* 11 May 1285/1, I have a clutch of pure-bred Silkies being incubated now... I am not sure where the Silkie stands in bantam genealogy.

**silkie**, var. SEALCHIE, -KIE.

**silkily** ('sɪlkɪlɪ), *adv.* [f. SILKY *a.* + -LY[2].]

**a.** In a silky manner.

**1815** *Sporting Mag.* XLVI. 53 The favourite animal is silkily painted. **1859** MEREDITH *R. Feverel* xv, His hair.. fell away slanting silkily to the temples. **1870** HOOKER *Stud. Flora* 428 Glumes silkily ciliate. **1947** A. P. GASKELL *Big Game* 91 Flash young things with lipstick, long-legged in high-heeled shoes, stood silkily, smoking tailormades. **1980** K. FOLLETT *Key to Rebecca* iii. 37 'Thank heaven you're back,' he said silkily.

**b.** Smoothly, quietly; used esp. of the running of an engine or machine.

**1923** *Daily Mail* 7 Aug. 3 (Advt.), I was much impressed with the vehicle.. beautifully suspended and runs very silkily. **1962** I. MURDOCH *Unofficial Rose* xxix. 280 He drew it [*sc.* the dagger] silkily out of its sheath. **1978** *Lancashire Life* Apr. 141/1 The 132-2000.. would slip silkily into top at anything from 25 m.p.h. upwards.

**silkiness** ('sɪlkɪnɪs). [f. SILKY *a.* + -NESS.] The quality of being silky, in various senses of the adj.

**1752** SIR H. BEAUMONT *Crito* 11 That appearing Softness or Silkiness of some Skins. *a*1773 CHESTERFIELD (T.), The claret had no silkiness. **1832** *Examiner* 19/1 Sycophancy, pliancy,.. silkiness on one side, and a rasping roughness on the other. *a*1864 HAWTHORNE *Dr. Grimshawe* vi. (1891) 60 A dose of his famous preparation.. causing a delightful silkiness of sensation. **1870** HOOKER *Stud. Flora* 339 Ovary similarly variable in silkiness.

**'silking**, (*vbl.*) *sb.* [f. SILK *sb.* and *v.* + -ING.]

**1.** Silken rustling.

**1871** G. MACDONALD *W. Combermede* I. xiii. 131 The silking of her frock aroused me.

**2.** The attachment of a piece of silk or other fine material to one or both sides of a sheet of paper in order to strengthen or preserve it.

**1943** *Amer. Archivist* VI. 152 The two principal methods of restoration employed at the present time, silking and lamination with cellulose acetate foil, are described below. **1980** S. G. SWARTZBURG *Preserving Library Materials* vii. 74 The sheets can be strengthened by a covering of a thin sheet of japan tissue, pasted over the original page... This process is often called 'silking' because originally a fine chiffon fabric was used.

**1976** R. W. JUGENHEIMER *Corn* xiii. 206 The most desirable strains of corn over a period of years often have been those in which the individual plants varied considerably in date of silking and tasseling. **1977** *N.Z. Jrnl. Agric.* Jan. 13/4 The optimum time for spraying is a fortnight either side of silking.

**'silk-like**, *a.* [f. SILK *sb.* + -LIKE.] Resembling silk; glossy, lustrous.

**1672** JOSSELYN *New Eng. Rarities* 7 They breed in little Nests made up like a bottom of soft Silk-like matter. **1776**

Da Costa *Elem. Conch.* 63 They have beards..of fine, long, glossy silk-like brown fibres. 1860 *Chambers's Encycl.* I. 468/1 The silk-like down of the seeds. 1866 *Treas. Bot.* 99/2 A number of seeds provided with a tuft of glossy silk-like hairs.

**silkman** ('sɪlkmən). [f. silk *sb.* + man *sb.*[1]] One who makes or deals in silks.

1553 in *Archaeologia* XII. 394 Laurence Ball, sylkeman. 1576 in Feuillerat *Revels Q. Eliz.* (1908) 413 John Weaver.. in London silkman. 1597 Shaks. *2 Hen. IV*, ii. i. 31 Hee is indited to dinner..to M. Smoothes the Silkman. 1621 Elsing *Debates Ho. Lords* (Camden) 32 Four sylkemen and four dyers to be chosen by the Master and Wardens. 1720 Strype *Stow's Surv.* II. 246/1 The Silkmen were incorporated by King Charles I..; now they are not so. 1841 *Penny Cycl.* XIX. 491/2 The silk is bought through the London brokers or the Coventry silkmen, at a credit of five months.

**'silkness.** *rare*$^{-1}$. (App. a mock title, but the text may be corrupt.)

1601 B. Jonson *Poetaster* iii. i, Sir, your silkenesse Cleerely mistakes Mecœnas, and his house.

**silkoline** ('sɪlkəʊliːn). Also **silkaline, silkolene, S-**. [f. silk *sb.*, after crinoline.] A soft cotton fabric with a smooth finish resembling that of silk.

1896 *Proc. Internat. Typogr. Union* 64/1, 12 yds. silkaline, $1.80. 1907 *Yesterday's Shopping* (1969) 742/2 Dress Linings..Silkoline, black..yd. 0/10. 1911 *Everybody's Mag.* XXV. 795/2 The last wrinkle and darn of their blue silkolene cotton tights had vanished from the stage. 1918 *Sears Catal.* 1164/1 A beautiful rose design in a border Silkoline. 1921 *Daily Colonist* (Victoria, B.C.) 8 Apr. 20/3 (Advt.), Silkolene, 36 inches wide, in a full selection of colorings and designs. 1950 *'Mercury' Dict. of Textile Terms* 465/1 Silkaline, a very light printed, plain weave, glossy cotton fabric, made in the grey and calendered. 1970 *Kay & Co.* (Worcester) *Catal.* 1970–71 Autumn/Winter 448/2 Bonsoir 'Silkaline' Pyjamas are fashionably styled in 100% cotton.

**silk screen,** *sb.* [f. silk *sb.* + screen *sb.*[1]]

1. A screen (screen *sb.*[1] 6 b) made of silk for use in screen printing. Usu. *attrib.*, esp. in ***silk screen printing, process*** (also *absol.*).

1930 B. Zahn *Silk Screen Methods of Reproduction* 9 There is no other phase of the graphic arts which presents so many possibilities as the Silk Screen Process. *Ibid.* 10 A silk screen has the advantage of making a perfect imprint at low cost. 1934 F. A. Baker *Silk Screen Practice* i. 13 The Silk Screen Process has become a necessity to all businesses that deal in colour reproduction work. 1950 *Atomics* Jan. 22/2 The silk screen press consists simply of a piece of silk stretched wet on a frame which taughtens on drying. 1952 *Print* (U.S.) July 1/1 André Girard..has been the first to apply silk screen to the art of making books. Silk screen has gone far in the scant thirty years of its existence. 1959 *Daily Mail* 14 Aug. 1/3 Robert, a silk screen printer, and Rosemary, a typist, first met about eighteen months ago. 1967 M. Chandler *Ceramics in Mod. World* iii. 111 The ceramist may make use of silk-screen printing. 1981 *West Lancs. Even. Gaz.* 20 Feb. 21 (Advt.), Wanted: Silk screen printer with artistic and modelling abilities.

2. A print made by the silk screen process.

1977 J. Didion *Bk. Common Prayer* ii. ii. 59 The thin FBI man gazed over Charlotte's head at the 10' by 16' silk screen of Mao Tse-tung. 1979 *Farmington* (New Mexico) *Daily Times* 27 May (Entertainment Suppl.) 22/5 'Mural-sized graphics', which will be reproduced as signed, limited-edition silk-screens.

Hence **silk-screen** *v. trans.*, to print, decorate, or reproduce by the silk screen process; **silk-screened** *ppl. a.*, **silk-screening** *vbl. sb.*; also **silk-screener**, a silk-screen printer.

1961 M. Jones *Potbank* xxv. 110 Joan..was silk-screening coffee-pots. 1967 *Listener* 21 Dec. 829/3 Andy Warhol's carrier bag beautifully silk-screened with a Campbell's soup can. 1976 Woodward & Bernstein *Final Days* xi. 138 As the sheer mechanics of preparing the transcripts for public consumption intensified, David Hoopes..summoned the State Department silk-screener from a baseball game. 1976 *National Observer* (U.S.) 28 Aug. 9/2 She worked in the farm's silk-screening shop, helping to print Christmas cards. 1978 *Detroit Free Press* 16 Apr. (Detroit Suppl.) 34 (Advt.), Each is silk-screened several times to produce the most subtle of shading on multi-colored cotton prints.

**'silk-soft,** *a.* [f. silk *sb.* + soft *a.*] Having the characteristic softness of silk.

1570 T. Preston *Cambyses* D j b, Thy mother yet wil kisse thy lips silk soft and pleasant white. 1648 Herrick *Hesperides, To Sir L. Pemberton* 121 To anoint the silke-soft-skin, or bath in Asses' milke. 17.. in Herd *Sc. Songs* (1776) II. 4 Oh, there,..I'd feast on beauty a' the night, Seal'd on her silk-saft falds to rest. 1833 Tennyson *Eleanore* ii, A glorious child, dreaming alone, In silk-soft folds, upon yielding down. 1879 E. Arnold *Light Asia* 29 Her dark and silk-soft waist.

**silk stocking.** Also **silk-stocking.**

1. A stocking made of silk; usu. in *pl.*

1597 Shaks. *2 Hen. IV*, ii. ii. 17 To take note how many paire of Silk stockings thou haste. 1611 Middleton & Dekker *Roaring Girl* H iv b, Why, haue not many handsome legges in silke stockins villainous splay feete for all their great roses? 1710 *Tatler* No. 245 ¶2 Four pair of silk-stockings curiously darned. 1791 Boswell *Johnson* (Oxf. ed.) I. 135 The silk stockings and white bosoms of your actresses. 1834–6 *Encycl. Metrop.* (1845) VIII. 709/1 Henry VIII. wore the first pair of silk stockings in England.

*attrib.* and *Comb.* 1812 Jefferson *Let. to Gerry* 11 June, [They] will find their levees crowded with silk stocking gentry, but no yeomanry. 1842 Aiton *Domest. Econ.* (1857) 93 One-third of them..are sure to catch a cold..from every silk-stocking affair in the winter season. 1858 Simmonds *Dict. Trade* s.v. *Silk-throwing*, Preparing hard silk..for yarn for the silk-stocking maker.

2. a. A wearer of silk stockings. Hence in extended sense, a member of the wealthy or upper class. *U.S.*

1891 in *Cent. Dict.* 1896 *Century Mag.* Nov. 6/2 Another class rejoice in this holiday as an opportunity to sit at home ..reading in slippered ease.., or fondling the pet hobby. The 'people' call them 'silk-stockings'. 1903 *Independent* 12 Nov. 2663/1 The mass of voters look upon him as a 'silk stocking'—as one who neither understands nor sympathizes with their life.

b. *U.S. Politics.* (See quots. 1895 and 1896.)

1840 *Niles' Nat. Reg.* (Baltimore) 14 Mar. 22/1 They cried out in derision of locofoco slang—'Here go the silk stockings.' 1894 Stead *If Christ came to Chicago* 36 Hopkins was elected by the silkstockings on the one hand and the short-hairs on the other. 1895 *Funk's Stand. Dict.*, *Silk-stocking*, a member of a branch of the Whig party in the earlier part of the 19th century.

3. *attrib.* and *Comb.* a. Simple *attrib.*, as (sense 2 a) ***silk-stocking company, gentry***, etc. *U.S.*

1798 *Deb. Congress U.S.* 15 June (1851) 1948 If they wished to place them in a ridiculous point of view, or to produce for them the name of the *Silk Stocking Company*, or any other term of derision, they could not take a more effectual course to obtain it. 1812 T. Jefferson *Writings* (1904) XIII. 163, I trust..the Gores and Pickerings will find their levees crowded with silk stocking gentry, but no yeomanry. 1836 *Col. Crockett's Exploits & Adventures Texas* iv. 58 You may be called a drunken dog by some of the clean shirt and silk stocking gentry. 1874 'H. Churton' *Toinette* xiii. 154 She had managed to pick up..'a tolerable English education',..[possibly] through the charity of some teacher at the 'Silk-Stocking Academy', on 'Gentleman Ridge'. 1903 *N.Y. Sun* 28 Nov. 4 He is the representative of the wealthy intellectual, the cultured, the 'silk stocking' element, for which the people in general have no abiding affection. 1980 *Verbatim* Autumn 1/2 Next after *hill* the commonest generic is *row* (several examples already given). The most frequent response of this type was *Silk Stocking Row*.

b. Special combs.: **silk-stocking district** (or **quarter**), a district inhabited mainly by supporters of the (Whig or) Republican party.

1893 *World's Fair Puck* 18 Sept. 231/2 Mr. Astorbilt (*of the silk-stocking district*)—No; I thought I was a thousand miles away from Tammany! 1903 *N.Y. Even. Post* 30 Oct. 2 Political conditions change even in the 'silk-stocking' quarter—the middle reaches of Manhattan, between 14th Street and 96th Street. 1964 *Economist* 2 May 486/2 Mr Wallace may do well, both in the silk stocking districts, and on the waterfront.

Hence **silk-stockinged** *a.*

1850 Thackeray *Pendennis* xxxvii, John..was leaning against the door-pillar, with..his legs crossed: beautiful, silk-stockinged. 1861 Whyte Melville *Mkt. Harb.* 34 The languid man's silk-stockinged foot having been re-shod.

**'silkstone.** [See def.] A variety of coal obtained at Silkstone near Barnsley in Yorkshire.

1867 W. W. Smyth *Coal & Coal-mining* 57 The Arley mine or seam, which occupies the place of the Black Shale or Silkstone. 1891 *Times* 5 Oct. 4/4 Silkstones are still to be purchased..for moderate quantities up to 12*s.* 9*d.*

**'silk-tail.** [tr. G. *seidenschwanz*, f. G. *seide* silk + *schwanz* tail.] The waxwing or Bohemian chatterer, *Ampelis garrulus* or *G. Bohemicus*.

1685 *Phil. Trans.* XV. 1161 Ad lanios ea Avicula referenda est, quam a Germanis Silk-tail vulgo appellari audio. 1703 Ray in *Thoresby's Lett. Eminent Men* (1832) II. 23 The Silk-tail is to me a bird altogether new. 1767 G. White *Selborne* xii, I pronounced it the male *garrulus bohemicus*, or German silk-tail. 1864 Hibberd in *Intell. Obs.* V. 24 The silktail, the grosbeak, the snowflake..may occasionally be seen [in England]. 1899 *Daily News* 14 Jan. 5/1 The eggs of the common fly-catcher..acquire a blueish-green shining colour, and are then sold..as the eggs of the silk-tail.

**silk-thrower.** [f. silk *sb.* + thrower.] = silk-throwster.

1670 R. Coke *Disc. Trade* 45 The discouragement put upon the Silk-throwers by the Corporation and Company of London. 1720 Strype *Stow's Surv.* II. 233/2 This Company of Silk-Throwers..having gained their Trade.. from the Strangers since Anno quinto of Queen Elisabeth. 1731 Bailey (vol. II) s.v., Their arms are Argent, three bundles of silk Sable, on a chief a silk thrower's mill. 1858 Simmonds *Dict. Trade*, *Silk-throwers-company*, one of the minor livery companies of London, which has no hall.

**silk-throwing.** [f. silk *sb.*] The process of converting raw silk into silk yarn or thread.

1621 in Strype *Stow's Surv.* (1720) II. 234/1 Sundry Strangers that use the Trade of Silk-throwing. 1668 *Lond. Gaz.* No. 259/4 An Act to regulate the Trade of Silk-throwing. 1768 *Ann. Reg., Chron.* 70/2 The proposal for setting up the business of silk-throwing was read. 1887 *Encycl. Brit.* XXII. 62/1 Numerous attempts have been made to simplify the silk-throwing.

*attrib.* 1834–6 *Encycl. Metrop.* (1845) VIII. 709/1 In 1719, a silk-throwing mill was erected at Derby. 1880 *Encycl. Brit.* XIII. 453/1 The raw material for these silk-throwing factories.

**silk-throwster.** [f. silk *sb.* + throwster.] One who converts raw silk into silk thread.

1621 in Strype *Stow's Surv.* (1720) II. 234/1 The Silk-Throwsters humbly desire to be made a Fellowship. 1648 C. Walker *Hist. Independency* 86 One of the new Captains of the Hamlets, a Silk-Throster, and a Tub-Preacher. 1755 *Gentl. Mag.* XXV. 185 A paper..signed by forty eminent silk-throwsters and weavers. 1835 Ure *Philos. Manuf.* 239 There may..be a great increase of..Turkey raw silks without much increase in the silk-throwster's business. 1866 *Chambers's Encycl.* VIII. 726/1 This is a special trade, the silk throwster usually conducting it in large mills with extensive machinery.

**silk-weaver.** [f. silk *sb.* + weaver.] One who weaves silk stuffs; a weaver of silk fabrics.

1572 in Feuillerat *Revels Q. Eliz.* (1908) 156 The silk-weaver and her parcells. 1645 *Knaresb. Wills* (Surtees) II. 184 John Turpine of Rippon, silkweaver. 1676 Dryden *Aurengz.* Epil. 21 True English hate your Monsieur's Paultry Arts; For you are all Silk-Weavers, in your hearts. 1803 *Med. Jrnl.* IX. 140 A silk weaver, thirty-four years of age. 1835 Ure *Philos. Manuf.* 260 By this disposition, the minds of the silk-weavers in France become elevated and refined.

**'silkweed.** *Bot.* Also **silk-weed.** [f. silk *sb.* + weed *sb.*]

1. *U.S.* = milkweed 2.

1784 *Mem. Amer. Acad.* I. 424 The seeds are contained in large pods, and are crowned with white down,..resembling silk, which has occasioned the name of Silk-weed. 1814 [see milkweed 2]. 1846–50 A. Wood *Class-bk. Bot.* 458 *Asclepias cornuti.* Decaisne (*A. Syriaca*, Linn...). Common Silkweed. *Ibid.* 459 *A. phytolaccöides*, Poke-leaved Silkweed. 1857 A. Gray *First Lessons Bot.* (1866) 135 A coma, or tuft of long and soft hairs, such as we find in the Milkweed or Silkweed. 1940 J. Stuart *Trees of Heaven* 48 There is the musty smell of ironweeds, milkweeds, silkweeds,..and bull grass on the lazy wind.

2. A plant of the genus *Conferva*.

1857 Henfrey *Bot.* 450 *Confervoideæ*, Silk-weeds... Plants..of bright green, or more rarely (often temporarily) red colour. 1875 *Encycl. Brit.* I. 508/2 This is seen in Confervæ, such as the green matter often seen in ponds, and called *silk-weed*.

**silk-winder.** [f. silk *sb.* + winder.]

1. One who winds or coils silk filament or thread preparatory to weaving.

1611 Florio, *Indouanadore*, a silke-winder. 1662 *Act 14 Chas. II*, c. 15 §6 Every such Silk-winder and Doubler. 1786 *Phil. Trans.* LXXVII. 103 Since it came out of the hands of the silk-winder.

2. a. A silk-reel. b. A machine by which silk thread in the hank is transferred to the bobbin before spinning.

1858 in Simmonds *Dict. Trade.* 1875 Knight *Dict. Mech.* 2182/1 Fanshaw's silk-winder, English patent, 1827, was designed to avoid the breakage of the filament in winding the skein silk on to bobbins.

So †**silk-windress, -windster.** *Obs.*

1598 Florio, *Diuidatrice*, a silke winderesse. 1723 *Lond. Gaz.* No. 6187/4 Eleanor Brown, late of Milk-yard Shadwell, Silk-windster.

**'silk-woman.** Now *Hist.* [f. silk *sb.* + woman *sb.*] A woman engaged in the manufacture, use, or sale of silk.

*c*1440 *Promp. Parv.* 77/2 Cylke woman, *devacuatrix* (P. *auri*s*ceca*). 1455 *Rolls of Parlt.* V. 325 The Silkewymmen and Throwestres of the Craftes and occupation of Silke-werk. *c*1515 *Cocke Lorell's B.* 10 Sylke women, pursers, and garnysshers. 1567–9 Jewel *Def. Apol.* (1611) 59 The same Spirit prepared and opened the Silke-womans heart. 1834–6 *Encycl. Metrop.* (1845) VIII. 709/1 Henry [VI] having silk women, who were..probably only employed in needlework of silk. 1841 *Penny Cycl.* XIX. 488/2 In the reign of Edward III., an act was passed to prevent artificers from using more than one trade.., the silk-women..being exempted from its operation.

**'silk-work.** [f. silk *sb.* + work *sb.*]

1. Silk embroidery.

*a*1375 *Joseph Arim.* 427 Fourti knihtes douȝtres he wolde haue..forte souwe selk-werk. 1661 Tatham *London's Tryumphs* 5 The Pentioners bearing the severall sort of Silk-works. *a*1700 Evelyn *Diary* 31 Oct. 1645, The Nunns of St. Catherine's sent me flowers of silk-work.

2. The manufacture or production of silk.

1455 [see silk-woman]. 1728 Chambers *Cycl.* s.v. *Silk*, To make a further Enquiry into this New Silk-work.

3. *pl.* An establishment where silk is wrought.

1622 Bonoeil *Art of Making Silke* 76 To certifie you from the English Factory in Persia, of the art and order that they use..in the Silke-workes there. 1728 Chambers *Cycl.* s.v. *Silk*, In the French Silk-works, the greatest Part of this Silk passes for little better than a Kind of very fine Fleuret.

**silkworm** ('sɪlkwɜːm). Also 1 **sioluc-, seolcwyrm,** 5 **sylke-wyrme;** 5 **selke-, sylk(e)-, cylke-,** 5–7 **silkeworme,** etc. [f. silk *sb.* + worm *sb.* In older use freq. written as two words, and from *c* 1600 often with hyphen.]

1. The caterpillar of the mulberry-feeding moth *Bombyx* (or *Sericaria*) *mori*, orig. a native of northern China, which on changing into the pupa state spins a cocoon made of silken filament; also, the caterpillar of any bombycid or other moth which thus yields silken cocoons of commercial value.

*c*1000 Ælfric *Gloss.* in Wr.-Wülcker 151 *Bombix*, seolcwyrm. *c*1050 *Voc.* ibid. 360 *Bombix*, siolucwyrm, oððe sidwyrm. 1398 Trevisa *Barth. De P.R.* xvii. xcix, Leues of hyze beri tren ben grete and brode,..and gladly wormes eten þerof: and so silke wormes ben beste fed and norischid. *c*1425 *Voc.* in Wr.-Wülcker 643 *Hic bombex*, sylkworme. *a*1450 *Fysshynge w. Angle* (1883) 26 A bayte that bredyth on an oke leyf & a sylke worme and a cod worme togyder. 1559 W. Cunningham *Cosmogr. Glasse* 196 We call them in Englishe Silke Wormes, of which at this day the Spaniardes have greate plentye. 1599 T. M[oufet] (*title*), Silkewormes and their Flies, lively described in verse. 1622 Bonoeil *Art of Making Silke* 1 This discourse is therefore touching the feeding and intertainement of your Silke wormes. 1677 Horneck *Gt. Law Consid.* i. (1704) 8 Their prophets,..like silkworms, spun out their own bowels. **1728** CHAMBERS *Cycl.* s.v. *Silk*, The Work of 12 Spiders..only equals that of one Silk Worm. **1788** GIBBON *Decl. & F.* xl. IV. 71 Till the reign of Justinian, the silk-worms who feed on the leaves of the white mulberry-tree, were confined to China. **1836** *Penny Cycl.* V. 109/1 During the time of spinning the cocoon the silkworm decreases in length very considerably. **1871** TYNDALL *Fragm. Sci.* (1879) I. v. 139 A plague had raged among the silkworms of France.

*transf.* **1838** *Civil Eng. & Arch. Jrnl.* I. 266/1 An Improved Machine called the Silkworm, for the purpose of Spinning, Twisting, and Doubling Silk. **1856** EMERSON *Eng. Traits* x. *Wealth*, A man should not be a silk-worm; nor a nation a tent of caterpillars.

**b.** One who wears a silken gown or dress. Used contemptuously. *rare.*

**1613** BEAUM. & FL. *Honest Man's Fortune* v. iii, Thou silk-worm. What has thou in thee to deserve this woman? *a* **1704** T. BROWN *Cont. Quaker's Serm.* Wks. 1709 III. II. 3 Root out of them [*sc.* thy churches] all Anti-Christian Tiranny of most abominable Bishops; let not those Silk-worms and Magpies have Dominion over us. **1820** BYRON *Mar. Fal.* II. ii. 115 Better..call A Tartar lord, than these swoln silkworms masters! **1820** SCOTT *Monast.* xvii, Shall that English silkworm presume to beard me in my father's house?

†**c.** A woman given to frequenting drapers' shops and examining goods without buying. *Obs.*

**1712** STEELE *Spect.* No. 454 ¶5 The Silk-worms are, it seems, indulged by the Tradesmen; for tho' they never buy, they are ever talking of new Silks, Laces, and Ribbands, and serve the Owners in getting them Customers.

**2.** *attrib.* and *Comb.*, as ***silkworm breeder, disease, egg, -like*** adj., ***shed***; also **silkworm gut**, a fine, strong, light gut, made of the drawn-out glands of the silkworm (see GUT *sb.* 4d); **silkworm moth**, one or other of various bombycid moths, whose larvæ produce cocoons; **silkworm rot** (see quot.).

**1876** *Encycl. Brit.* IV. 596/2 The *silkworm breeder allows a few of the pupæ to develop into moths. **1887** *Cassell's Encycl. Dict.* s.v., *Silkworm disease. **1835** URE *Philos. Manuf.* 251 An ounce of *silk-worm eggs in France is worth two francs and a half. **1833** J. RENNIE *Alph. Angling* 66 Hook-lines..are usually made of *silk-worm gut. **1897** *Allbutt's Syst. Med.* IV. 349 The sutures may be silk, kangaroo tendon, or silkworm gut. **1672** DRYDEN *Conq. Granada* II. I. ii, I.., *silkworm-like, so long within have wrought, That I am lost in my own web of thought. **1815** KIRBY & SP. *Entomol.* x. (1818) I. 335 About the year 550.. two monks..procured in India the eggs of the *silk-worm moth. **1899** *Allbutt's Syst. Med.* VIII. 946 The transmission ..of the sporozoa of pebrine from the silkworm moth to its eggs and caterpillar. **1855** OGILVIE *Suppl.* 362/1 **Silk-worm rot*, a fungous plant, the *Botrytis bassiana*, which kills silk-worms in great numbers. **1898** *Folk-Lore* IX. 8 The same formula must be used on entering a *silkworm-shed.

**silky** (ˈsɪlkɪ), *a.* (*sb.*) [f. SILK *sb.* + -Y.]

**1. a.** Silken; made or consisting of silk.

**1611** COTGR., *Soyeux*, silky; bristlie (full of silke or of bristles). **1724** RAMSAY *Health* 20 Cosmellius may on silky twilts repose. **1743–6** SHENSTONE *Eleg.* xviii. 51 But Albion's youth..In silky folds each nervous limb disguise. **1868** *Rep. U.S. Comm. Agric.* (1869) 288 The regeneration and spinning of silky waste of all kinds.

**b.** As *sb.* (See quot. 1976.)

**1822** T. BEWICK *Memoir* (1975) ii. 16, I..was only to walk along the dark passage to the back Door and to repeat something (rather ominous indeed) about 'Silkey & Hedley Kow'. **1866** W. HENDERSON *Folk Lore Northern Counties* vii. 230 Black Heddon..was greatly disturbed by a supernatural being, popularly called Silky, from the nature of her robes. **1912** in R. Tongue *Forgotten Folk-Tales English Counties* (1970) III. v. 202 Gilsland's lord had a silky who cleaned the house-place, devilled and punched lazy serving-wenches and kept all shining clean. **1967** *Tablet* 16 Dec. 1307/2 Nearly all peoples, the world over, have believed in beings they called elves, silkies, trolls, elementals or fairies. **1976** K. M. BRIGGS *Dict. Fairies* 365 The Northumbrian and Border silky..is always female... She is a spirit dressed in rustling silk, who does domestic chores about the house and is a terror to idle servants.

**2. a.** Having the delicate softness of silk.

**1666** J. SMITH *Old Age* 144 The several graces..of Musick, the soft and silky touches, the quick and pleasant relishes. **1710** CONGREVE *An Impossible Thing* 79 His eyes a silky slumber seiz'd. **1820** PRAED *Changing Quarters* 71 Are hearts of stone So small, and soft, and silky grown? **1870** *Eng. Mech.* 11 Feb. 534 A true Cremona..may be known by the..silky quality of its tone. **1897** WATTS-DUNTON *Aylwin* II. ix, The touch of Winnie's clasping fingers, silky and soft.

**b.** Of liquor: Having a soft delicate taste.

**1743** *London & Country Brewer* IV. (ed. 2) 291 If they do not brew and sell a clear, pleasant, silky Beer. **1834** MCCULLOCH *Dict. Comm.* (ed. 2) s.v. *Wine*, The first mentioned [variety of claret]..is characterised by its silky softness on the palate. **1894** *Outing* XXIV. 473/1 Copious draughts of soft and silky claret.

*absol.* **1852** BRISTED *Five Yrs. Eng. Univ.* 50 A very enticing mixture appropriately called *silky*,..made of rum and madeira.

**3. a.** Of speech, manners, etc.: Smooth, pleasing, ingratiating, insinuating.

**1778** EARL MALMESBURY *Diaries & Corr* I. 197 Whilst they permitted themselves to be amused with silky speeches ..they were only allowing their ill-wishers to gain time. **1794** MATHIAS *Purs. Lit.* (1798) 73 Better preach With silky voice, and sacred flow'rs of speech. **1836** HOOD *Poetry, Prose, & Worse* xxiv, No documents tender and silky Are writ such as poets would pen. **1866** MRS. GASKELL *Wives & Daughters* xxix, Mrs Gibson..petted him in her sweetest, silkiest manner. **1885** *Manch. Exam.* 11 Mar. 5/5 He stated his case in his silkiest and most persuasive accents.

**b.** Of persons: Quiet or smooth of manner.

**1826** MISS MITFORD *Village* Ser. II. (1863) 325 Her smooth silky husband crept behind me with the stealthy pace of a cat. **1880** MEREDITH *Tragic Com.* (1881) 279 Imagine a quiet little advocate, very precise and silky. **1890** 'R. BOLDREWOOD' *Col. Reformer* (1891) 427 The silky, graceful *serviteur des dames.*

**c.** Of a machine, mechanism, etc., or its motion: smooth.

**1935** *Times* 23 Apr. 17/6 The engine is silky and quiet throughout its range. **1977** *Gramophone* Nov. 960/2 To provide a silky movement of the tuning control, and gearing down of the knob, the Tandberg engineers have made use of a two-gang variable capacitor with its inbuilt gearing.

**4. a.** Having the gloss of silk; resembling silk in lustre.

**1730** *Phil. Trans.* XXXVI. 344 His Tongue not hard,.. but of its natural Colour, with a silky Driness. **1797** *Encycl. Brit.* (ed. 3) XI. 446/1 Such are the minerals called silky copper ores, and several white and green earths. **1838** T. THOMSON *Chem. Org. Bodies* 764 The crystals are either silky needles or short prisms. **1857** MILLER *Elem. Chem., Org.* iii. §2 (1862) 171 White silky crystals of ethionic anhydride.

**b.** Having a texture like that of silk.

**1757** DYER *Fleece* II. 137 To spread upon its fields the dews of heav'n, And feed the silky Fleece. **1796** WITHERING *Brit. Pl.* (ed. 3) II. 50 Leaves thick,..clothed on both sides with a silvery white silky down. **1828** STARK *Elem. Nat. Hist.* I. 80 Fur dark brown, very soft, and silky, shaded with chestnut. **1840** *Penny Cycl.* XVIII. 65/1 The webs of the white feathers..are silky to the sight and touch. **1856** LEVER *Martins of Cro' M.* 121 The young girl..wrung out the rain from her long and silky hair.

**5.** *Bot.* **a.** Covered with fine, soft, close-set hairs having a silk-like gloss; sericeous.

**1776** J. LEE *Introd. Bot.* 385 *Sericeum*, silky, covered with soft silky Hairs. **1796** WITHERING *Brit. Pl.* (ed. 3) IV. 192 Stem cylindrical, silky, pinky. **1850** *Beck's Florist* Jan. 15 The leaves are narrow, lanceolate, and densely silky on both sides. **1870** HOOKER *Stud. Flora* 116 *Potentilla anserina*.. softly silky, especially on the leaves.

**b.** In the specific names of trees and shrubs: ***silky gum, willow***; **silky cornel** = next; **silky dogwood**, a large shrub, *Cornus amomum*, native to eastern North America, whose leaves have silky hairs on their lower sides; **silky oak**, one of several Australian trees of the family Proteaceæ, esp. *Grevillea robusta* or *Cardwellia sublimis*, or the oak-like timber produced by them.

**1848** A. GRAY *Man. Botany Northern U.S.* 168 (*heading*) Silky cornel. **1891** J. M. COULTER *Bot. W. Texas* I. 150 Silky cornel... Common in the Atlantic States and extending into eastern and northern Texas. **1900** B. B. SMYTH *Plants & Flowers Kansas* ii. 25 It is the Silky Dogwood; grows in clumps; and had blue berries when ripe, in broad cymose clusters. **1957** W. C. GRIMM *Bk. Shrubs* 351 The Silky Dogwood is sometimes called the Silky Cornel, Swamp Dogwood, or Kinnikinnick. **1889** MAIDEN *Useful Plants* 514 *Eucalyptus saligna*... Other New South Wales names for it are 'Grey Box' and 'Silky Gum'. **1866** *Treas. Bot.* 789/2 Silky, or Silkbark Oak, *Grevillea robusta*. **1888** F. M. BAILEY *Queensland Woods* 104 S[*tenocarpus*] *salignus*... One of the woods called Silky Oak. **1889** MAIDEN *Useful Plants* 581 *Orites excelsa*,..'Red Ash'. 'Silky Oak'. **1965** *Austral. Encycl.* II. 180/2 The northern silky oak, *Cardwellia sublimis* of Queensland, is also sometimes known as bull oak. **1891** *Ardrossan Herald* 30 Oct. 2 The little Silky Willow, *Salix fusca*, commands attention from the peculiarity of its growth.

**6.** *Nat. Hist.* Having silk-like hair, plumage, etc. **a.** In names of monkeys.

**1781** PENNANT *Hist. Quadrup.* I. 210 Silkey Monkey. **1827** GRIFFITH tr. *Cuvier* V. 42 *Simia Midas rosalia* (the Silky Tamarin). **1876** *Nature* XIV. 121/2 A Silky Marmoset (*Midas rosalia*). *Ibid.* 538/1 Two Silky Marmosets (*Hapale chrysoleucus*) from S.E. Brazil.

**b.** In names of birds; also as *sb.*, a silk-fowl.

**1783** LATHAM *Gen. Synop. Birds* II. I. 96 Silky Chatterer ..inhabits the province of Maynas, in South America. **1823** —— *Gen. Hist. Birds* VII. 9 Silky Warbler (*Sylvia sericea*). .. Inhabits the Southern parts of Spain. **1829** GRIFFITH tr. *Cuvier* VIII. 82 Silky Pigeon, *Columba Holosericea*. **1849** D. J. BROWNE *Amer. Poultry Yd.* (1855) 81 The 'silky' and 'negro' fowls,..with skin, combs, and bones which are black.

**c.** In names of moths; also as *sb.*

**1832** J. RENNIE *Consp. Butterfl. & Moths* 186 The Silky (*Orthotelia sericea*). *Ibid.* 211 Dale's Silky (*Melia ? sericea*, Stephens). **1887** *Cassell's Encycl. Dict.*, *Silky-wainscot*, a British night-moth, *Senta maritima*. *Ibid.*, *Silky-wave*, a British geometer-moth, *Acidalia holosericata*.

**7.** *Comb.*, as ***silky-black, -leaved, -looking, -soft, -textured, -voiced.***

**1742** YOUNG *Nt. Th.* II. 241 Silky-soft Favonius breathe still softer, or be chid. **1817** STEPHENS in Shaw *Gen. Zool.* X. I. 95 Silky-black Swallow, beneath white, with the forehead and throat rusty yellow. **1855** MISS PRATT *Fl. Pl.* V. 94 Silky-leaved Osier, or Smith's Willow. Leaves..white and glossy beneath. **1857** MILLER *Elem. Chem., Org.* (1862) 781 Sericin is a white silky-looking substance. **1895** CLIVE HOLLAND *Jap. Wife* 124 Wrapping up our presents in soft, silky textured rice-paper.

**silky**, var. SEALCHIE, -KIE.

**sill** (sɪl), *sb.*[1] Forms: α. 1 syl, 1, 5–6 syll(e, 2, 4 sulle, 4, 7 sille; 6 *Sc.* schyll, 7, 9 sil, 7– sill, 9 cill. β. 5 selle, 7–9 sell; 5 celle, 8–9 cell. [OE. *syll* and *sylle*, = MDu. *sulle*, MLG. *sulle*, *sul* (LG. *süll*), related to MDu. *sille*, *zille* (Fris. *sille*), MLG. *sille* (LG. *sill*), and to ON. and Norw. *svill*, *syll* (mod.Icel. *sylla*), MSw. and Sw. *syll* (dial. *svill*), Da. *syld*, also OHG. *swelli*, *swella* (MHG. *swelle*, G. *schwelle*). The precise relationship of these types to each other, and to Goth. *gasuljan* to found, or to L. *solea* the foundation of a wattled wall (Festus), is not clear.]

**1. a.** A strong horizontal timber (occas. a stone or iron substitute for this) serving as the foundation of a wall (esp. in the building of framed houses) or other structure, = GROUNDSEL *sb.*[2] 1; hence, †a large beam or piece of squared timber. Also *fig.*

In ME. poetry sometimes used in the sense of 'floor'.

*Beowulf* 775 þær fram sylle abeaȝ medu-benc moniȝ. *c* **897** K. ÆLFRED *Gregory's Past. C.* i. 27 Ðonne hi ne beoð mid nanre sylle underscotene ðæs godcundlican mæȝenes. *c* **1000** ÆLFRIC *Hom.* II. 144 Ða bæd he hi anre sylle, þæt he mihte þæt hus on ða sæ healfe mid þære underlecgan. **13..** *Gaw. & Gr. Knt.* 55 For al was þis fayre folk in her first age, on sille. *c* **1386** CHAUCER *Miller's T.* 636 He fond nowthir to selle, Ne breed ne ale, til he com to the selle, Upon the floor. *c* **1400** *Rowland & O.* 9 Of doghety men I schall ȝow telle, þat were full..Semely appon Sille. *c* **1440** *Promp. Parv.* 456/1 Sylle, of an howse, *silla, soliva*. *c* **1470** HENRY *Wallace* IX. 830 Off hewyn temyr in haist he gert thaim tak Syllys off ayk, and a stark barres mak. **1513** DOUGLAS *Æneid* XI. ix. 70 Sum to the ȝettis weltis wechty stanis, And sum gret geistis and sillys for the nanis. **1536** BELLENDEN *Cron. Scot.* VIII. xix. 58 Ambrose..brocht mony huge sillis & treis out of the nixt wod. **1651** BAXTER *Inf. Baptism* 11 Every stone under the Sill supports not the house. **1710** J. HARRIS *Lex. Techn.* II, *Sell*, in Architecture, is the Term..for the lowest piece of Timber in a Timber-building. **1725** *Fam. Dict.* s.v. *Bay*, A cross Cell to hold in the side Cells from flying out. **1793** SMEATON *Edystone L.* §100 Three-inch planks..spiked down upon the ridge-tree and upon the sills on each side. **1838** *Civil Eng. & Arch. Jrnl.* I. 387/1 The sills upon the pier-piling of the Selby bridge are fixed as opportunities are presented at low water. **1861** STEPHENS & BURN *Bk. Farm-buildings* 375 The lining..should be carried over the sill and nailed to it; the sill being wider than the studding [etc.]. **1877** E. PEACOCK *N.W. Linc. Gloss.*, *Sill*,..the bottom of a fixed bench, pew, or other like wooden erection.

*attrib.* *c* **1340** *Nominale* (Skeat) 449 *Traches et trenchons*, Sulle-trees and splentes. **1886** WILLIS & CLARK *Cambridge* I. 330 The floor and sill wall of the upper study. *Ibid.* II. 14 The arches are fenced below by a low sill-wall.

**b.** *dial.* and *U.S.* One of the lower framing-timbers of a cart or railway-car.

**1875** KNIGHT *Dict. Mech.* 457/2 The bodies consisting of sills, to which the journal-boxes were bolted. **1879** MISS JACKSON *Shropsh. Word-bk.*, *Sills*, the bottom and side pieces which form the skeleton-frame of the body of a cart or waggon—the foundation of its superstructure.

**c.** The lower horizontal members of the frame of a motor vehicle.

**1959** *Motor Man.* (ed. 36) i. 17 In the case of the Austin, a normal pressed-steel body was used, the channel-section sills of which were joined to the open faces of the channel section side-members to form substantial box sections. **1976** *Drive* Sept.–Oct. 75/1 The high boxed sills were a necessary structural link between the front and rear of the car. **1980** *Daily Tel.* 11 Sept. 7 (Advt.), Full underbody sealing and wax injection of sills and cross-members.

**2. a.** The piece of wood- or stone-work forming the lower horizontal part of a window-opening. Cf. WINDOW-SILL.

**1428** in Heath *Grocers' Comp.* (1869) 6 Unwroughte Stapylton stoone; reidy hewe for the saame for wyndowes, wyndow Iambes and sills. **1663** GERBIER *Counsel* 29 The head of the Windowes, as well as the..James, and Sils. **1815** J. SMITH *Panorama Sci. & Art* I. 252 The sills of windows have been mostly made from three feet to three feet six inches distant from the level of the floor. **1851** TURNER *Dom. Archit* I. ii. 37 A recess in the sill with a seat in each side, the usual characteristic of a domestic window. **1873** W. BLACK *Pr. Thule* xviii. 297 She..placed the plate outside the open window, on the sill.

*fig.* **1858** KINGSLEY *Longbeard's Saga* 80 High in Valhalla A window stands open; Its sill is the snow-peaks.

*Comb.* **1885** C. M. YONGE *Nuttie's Father* I. i. 6 Lovely sill boxes full of flowers in the windows. **1895** *Funk's Stand. Dict.*, *Sill-course*, a course of masonry in line with a window-sill. **1955** *Archit. Rev.* CXVIII. 126/1 Panels of woven cane hanging from the sillboards cover the radiators.

**b.** *Naut.* A port-sill (see quots. and PORT *sb.*[3] 6).

**1815** BURNEY *Falconer's Mar. Dict.*, *Sills of the Ports*, or *Port-sills*.., pieces of oak timber, let in horizontally between the frames to form the upper and lower sides of the ports. **1841** DANA *Seaman's Man.* 123 *Sills*, pieces of timber put in horizontally between the frames to form and secure any opening; as, for ports. **1867** SMYTH *Sailor's Word-bk.* 626.

**c.** *Fortif.* (See quots.)

**1859** F. A. GRIFFITHS *Artil. Man.* (1862) 248 *The sill* is the front of the sole. **1875** KNIGHT *Dict. Mech.* 2182/2 *Sill*.., the inner edge of the bottom or sole of an embrasure.

**3. a.** The threshold of a door or gateway; the lower horizontal part of a door-case. Cf. DOOR-SILL and GROUNDSEL *sb.*[2] 2. Also *Comb.*

**1591** SYLVESTER *Du Bartas* I. i. 845 Travailers..Make haste enough, if only the First Day From their owne Sill they set but on their way. **1600** HOLLAND *Livy* 1359 The lintell, cheekes and sill of the Capitoll dore, were made all of brasse. **1621** BURTON *Anat. Mel.* III. ii. I. ii. (1651) 445 When he can scarce lift his leg over a sill. **1716** SWIFT *Progr. Poetry* Wks. 1751 VII. 170 The Farmer's Goose..Grown fat with Corn..Can scarce get o'er the Barn-Door Sill. **1787** GROSE *Prov. Gloss.*, *Sill* (of a door), threshold. **1823** P. NICHOLSON *Pract. Builder* 310 Cills—These belong to the apertures of the doors and windows, at the bottom of which they are fixed. *a* **1850** ROSSETTI *Dante & Circle* I. (1874) 173 O Poverty!..he who on thy naked sill has stood [etc.]. **1906** *Expositor* Aug. 131 He laid bare an ancient gateway with four sills, one above the other.

*Comb.* **1870** *Jrnl. Ethnological Soc.* II. 417 At each end of this passage, and at right angles to it, are two square or somewhat oblong chambers. The first..was about 3 feet in width. Where it joined the central passage was a sillstone.

**1981** *Glasgow Archaeol. Jrnl.* VIII. 52/2 The main uprights were set in newly dug postholes, linked by sillbeam trenches.

*transf.* **1611** COTGR., *Sursueil*, the vpper sill, or head-peece of a doore; the peece of timber that lyes ouer a doore.

**b.** *Mining.* (See quots.)

**1747** HOOSON *Miner's Dict.* S iv, When Doorsteds are used, and the Sole of the Drift so soft, that it will not bear the Forks,..then we clap a Sill under them, which is a piece of Wood lay'd across the Drift. **1881** RAYMOND *Mining Gloss.*, *Sill*,..a piece of wood laid across a drift to constitute a frame with the posts and to carry the track of the tramway.

**c.** A horizontal timber (or structure) at the bottom of the entrance to a dock or canal-lock, against which the gates close.

**1789** *Trans. Soc. Arts* 55 To raise the sill or threshold of the flood-gates..twenty inches. **1838** SIMMS *Publ. Wks. Gt. Brit.* II. 6 The gates clap against a sill of oak. **1861** SMILES *Engineers* II. 161 The bottom of 'the Deeps'..was only two feet, six inches above the cill of Maud Foster Sluice. **1892** *Law Times Rep.* LXV. 590/1 The lock had been lengthened since its original construction, but an old sill had been left.

**d.** A horizontal timber, etc., rising above the level of a roadway.

**1853** SIR H. DOUGLAS *Milit. Bridges* 318 The whole is easily moved forward to the edge of the gap, where a high sill should be laid, to prevent the wheels from approaching too near.

**e.** A high ridge on the sea bed that effectively separates the bodies of water on either side.

**1933** *Geogr. Jrnl.* LXXXI. 571 Hamish island, situated on the shallow sill of the Red Sea. **1942** O. VON ENGELN *Geomorphol.* xix. 468 They [*sc.* fiords] are closed at the seaward end by a distinct rock sill at shallow depth, beyond which the descent to the deeper ocean waters begins. **1978** *Nature* 14 Dec. 680/2 Outflowing Mediterranean subsurface waters... They spill over the sill at Gibraltar (330 m).

**4. a.** A kind of clay found in coal-measures. Also *attrib.*, as ***sill-coal, -pencil.***

**1774** *Phil. Trans.* LXIV. 491 A shining kind of stony clay, called by the miners *sill*, lying in large beds in coal grounds. **1841** HARTSHORNE *Salop. Ant.* Gloss., *Sill-coal*, coal which my informant describes as being found 'in the clunches'. **1899** DICKINSON & PREVOST *Cumbld. Gloss.*, *Sill*, the soft clay of the coal measures, used for slate pencils, which are called sill pencils.

**b.** A bed, layer, or stratum of rock, esp. of an intrusive igneous rock. In mod. use, a tabular igneous intrusion lying parallel to the surrounding strata.

**1794** HUTCHINSON *Hist. Cumb.* I. [49]/1 Great sill red, near the bottom is alabaster, *gypsum alabastrum*. **1821** W. FORSTER *Strata* 95 Slate Sills. These Strata are of a Siliceous kind, and frequently contain small particles of mica. **1880** *Geol. Mag.* 433 The 'Slate Sills' and the 'Coal Sills' are particular beds of sandstone in the Yoredale Series. **1894** *Naturalist* 222 Intrusive igneous rocks in sills and dykes in all the Silurians. **1914** J. P. IDDINGS *Problem of Volcanism* vii. 222 Intrusions along bedding planes of stratified rocks are commonly called sills at whatever angle they may be tilted, and intrusions in fractures that transgress stratified beds are usually classed as dikes. **1977** A. HALLAM *Planet Earth* 68 Fine examples of sills are the Carboniferous dolerite sill that forms Salisbury Crags in Edinburgh, Scotland, and the Palisades sill, up to 350m (1000ft) thick, along the west bank of the Hudson River near New York.

*attrib.* **1877** RAYMOND *Statist. Mines & Mining* 159 The east drift, same level, on the sill-floor, has attained a length of 92 feet.

**5. a.** The foot or lower part *of* a title-page or title.

**1834** LOWNDES *Bibliogr. Man.* I. 426 On the sell of the compartment of the title-page is the date of 1534. **1881** BRADSHAW in *Bibliographer* Dec. 10/2 The sill of the text-title contains the device of Martin de Keyser, while the sill of the general title contains a blank shield.

**b.** (See quots.)

**1877** E. PEACOCK *N.W. Linc. Gloss.*, *Sill*.., the bottom part of a plough which slips along the ground in ploughing. **1895** W. RYE *E. Angl. Gloss.*, *Sill Iron*, the iron which connects the plough with the standards, jigs, or carriage, of a Norfolk plough.

**c.** The bottom *of* a hedge.

**1883** *Daily News* 1 Sept. 4/7 Although the hen prefers the sill of a hedgerow for her rough nest, she not unfrequently makes it in a cornfield.

**sill**, *sb.*[2] Dial. var. of THILL. Also *attrib.*

**1787** GROSE *Prov. Gloss.*, *Sills* (of a waggon), the shafts, the same as thills. **1788-** in northern dial. glossaries. **1828** CARR *Craven Gloss.*, *Sill-horse*, the shaft horse. **1877** E. PEACOCK *N.W. Linc. Gloss.*, *Sill-hank*, the hooks in the shafts of a cart or waggon for the shaft-horse to pull by.

**sill**, *v. rare.* [f. SILL *sb.*[1]] *trans.* To furnish with a sill. Also *fig.*

**1552-3** *Inv. Ch. Goods Stafford* 48 Ther was one bucket of brasse solde by the wardens, Thomas Yate & Thomas Yomans, to sylle ther church gate. **1908** *Academy* 11 July 29/2 Beneath your windows, deeply silled In red, red roses.

**sill**, obs. f. SEAL *sb.*; obs. var. *sel*, northern f. SELF; obs. f. SELL *v.*; var. SILE (herring-fry).

**sillab, sillabary, sillable:** see SYLLAB, etc.

**sillabub, syllabub** ('sɪləbʌb). Forms: α. 6 solybubbe, 7 sullabub, sullibib, 7-8 sullibub. β. 6 selybube, 6-7 seli-, 7 sellibub, sallibube. γ. 6 sillye-, 6-7 syllibub, 7 sillie bube, cilli-, 7-8 sillibub, 9 *Sc.* sillybob. δ. 6 sillabubbe, 6- silla-, 7- syllabub. [Of obscure origin: cf. SILLIBOUK and SILLUB. The most frequent spelling from *c* 1700 has been *syllabub*, under the influence of *syllable*.]

**1. a.** A drink or dish made of milk (freq. as drawn from the cow) or cream, curdled by the admixture of wine, cider, or other acid, and often sweetened and flavoured.

In common use from the 16th cent. to about the middle of the 19th cent., and revived in the 20th.

α. *c* **1537** *Thersytes* (1848) 79 You and I..Muste walke to him and eate a solybubbe. **1628** WITHER *Brit. Rememb.* IV. 1186 Some, Sulli-bibs among the Milk-maids, making. **1668** SEDLEY *Mulberry Gard.* IV. Wks. 1778 II. 52 Then they must..have the Sullabubs and Tarts brought into the Coach to 'em. **1748** MRS. S. HARRISON *House-kpr.'s Pkt.-Bk.* vii. (ed. 4) 17 Sullibubs.

β. **1570** in J. J. Cartwright *Chapters Hist. Yks.* (1872) 55 They brough this examynent a selybube to drynk. **1584** COGAN *Haven Health* cc. (1636) 190 A posset or Selibub made of Verjuice, is good to coole a cholerick stomacke. **1601** HOLLAND *Pliny* I. 348 They vsed to thicken their milk into a kind of pleasant soure curd in manner of a Sellibub.

γ. **1591-2** NASHE *Prognostication* Wks. (Grosart) II. 165 Maides this quarter shall make sillyebubbes for their Louers. **1602** in *Lyly's Wks.* (1902) I. 492 First you shall haue a dayntie sillibub; next a messe of clowted creame. *c* **1645** HOWELL *Lett.* I. IV. v, Leaue the smutty Ayr of London, and com hither.., wher you may pluck a Rose, and drink a Cillibub. **1737** *Ochtertyre House-bks.* (1907) 104 Sillibubs and cold beefe. **1822** GALT *Provost* xxx, Instead of the light tarts, and nice jellies and sillybobs that were expected.

δ. **1598** MARSTON *Pygmal.* 60 Ye Granta's white Nymphs, come & with you bring Some sillabub. **1631** BRATHWAIT *Whimzies, Pedlar* 138 This purchaseth him, upon better acquaintance, a posset or a sillabub. *a* **1668** DAVENANT *Vacation in London* Wks. (1673) 289 Her Elbow small she oft does rub; Tickled with hope of Sillabub! **1704** W. KING *Mully of Mountown* 18 Thy White-Wine, Sugar, Milk, together Club To make that gentle Viand Syllabub. **1758** JOHNSON *Idler* No. 15 ¶6 Besides what it costs me in tea and hot rolls, and syllabubs. **1817** MME. D'ARBLAY *Let.* 5 July, Some other ingredient that, when it is poured into a pan, bubbles up like a syllabub. **1853** SURTEES *Sponge's Sp. Tour* lxii. 352 How nice it would be to have..a sillabub, under those cedars. **1861** HUGHES *Tom Brown at Oxf.* xxiii. (1889) 220 We retire to tea or syllabub beneath the shade of some great oak. **1911** M. A. FAIRCLOUGH *Ideal Cookery Book* 722 Syllabubs... Fill some custard glasses rather more than half full with the mixture. **1976** *Sat. Even. Post All-American Cookbk.* 259/2 A syllabub is a ladylike version of eggnog.

**b.** *attrib.*, as ***sillabub glass, jug, pot.***

**1677** in S. Young *Hist. Worshipful Company Glass Sellers of London* (1913) App. 68 All covers for drinking or 'Sullibub' glasses ribbed and plain shall be delivered at 3s. per lb. **1723** J. NOTT *Cook's & Confectioner's Dict.* sig. Ll[1], Scum off the Froth, and put it into Syllabub Glasses. **1897** A. HARTSHORNE *Old Eng. Glasses* xix. 308 In Mr. Cuming's collection is an open-mouthed glass tumbler, a family relic, 3½ inches high, said to be of the first part of the last century, and called from time immemorial 'a syllabub or whip glass'. **1970** G. SAVAGE *Dict. Antiques* 418/2 In the 1770s the old syllabub glass, which was always on a stem and a foot, became unfashionable and was replaced by a stemless glass. **1975** *Country Life* 2 Jan. 11/3 A Syllabub Jug in Ravenscroft Glass. *a* **1648** DIGBY *Closet Opened* (1677) 230 A large syllabub-pot. **1688** HOLME *Armoury* III. xiv. (Roxb.) 9/2 He beareth sable, a possett pott, or a wassell cup, or a sallibube pott. **1723** J. NOTT *Cook's & Confectioner's Dict.* No. 188 S, Fill your Syllabub-Pot with Cyder..Sugar..Cream. **1910** *Queen* 9 July 65/1 This syllabub or posset pot is very interesting and..the date of it has been fixed at about 1700.

**2.** *fig.* **a.** Something unsubstantial and frothy; *esp.* floridly vapid discourse or writing.

**1706** PHILLIPS (ed. 6), *Sillabub*, or *Sillibub*,..is figuratively taken for a florid, but frothy and empty Discourse. **1768** WESLEY *Wks.* (1872) XII. 410 Latin and Greek books (compared with which most of the English are whipped Syllabub). **1847** SEDGWICK in Clark & Hughes *Life & Lett.* (1890) II. 113, I shall never again endure the rounded periods and syllabub of Robertson. **1852** HAWTHORNE *Blithedale Rom.* xvii, I resolved to pause, and enjoy the moral sillabub until quite dissolved away. **1889** *Daily News* 11 May 2/1 The new bonnets are the veriest trifles; mere syllabubs of frothed-up lace.

*attrib.* **1849** C. BRONTË *Shirley* xxxvi, When did I whip up syllabub sonnets, or string stanzas fragile as fragments of glass?

**b.** A mixture, combination.

**1859** THACKERAY *Virginians* lxxvii, Aunt Lambert..was one great syllabub of human kindness.

**sillack**, variant of SILLOCK.

**silladar** ('sɪlədɑː(r)). *Anglo-Ind.* Also silladari, sillahdari, silledar, sillahdar. [a. Urdū (Pers.) *silāhdār* armour-bearer, squire, f. Arab. *silāh* arms, armour.] An irregular cavalryman who provides his own horse and arms; often used *attrib.*

**1802** WELLINGTON in Gurw. *Disp.* (1844) I. 312 The horse are 2000 good,..and 1500 [of these are] silledar. **1803** *Ibid.* 323 A body of silladar horse. **1813** J. FORBES *Oriental Mem.* III. 349 A silledar, or soldier of fortune. **1842** W. MILES tr. *Hist. Hydur Naik* 173 With only six thousand stable horse, nine thousand Sillahdars,..and six guns. **1931** E. HOWELL *Mizh* i. 9 The men were on a sillahdari basis. **1960** LD. ISMAY *Memoirs* i. 7 The 21st Cavalry, like nearly all other Indian Cavalry regiments, was organised on what was known as the *silladar* system. **1974** P. MASON *Matter of Honour* i. 26 Until 1914 many regiments of cavalry were still *silladāri*—that is to say, the regiment was a kind of joint-stock company in which the trooper paid for his horse and equipment when he joined and sold them back when he left.

**sillag**, variant of SILLOCK.

**sillapak** ('siːləpæk). [ad. Eskimo *silapak*.] Also sealapack, seelapak. A white outer garment worn as camouflage by Eskimo hunters of Labrador.

[**1916** E. W. HAWKES *Labrador Eskimo* 39 Over the fur or duffle dicky a cotton slip (ci'l·apaq) is drawn.] **1942** *Beaver* (Winnipeg) Dec. 37/2 The cold pierced through his thin sillapak so that all night he jumped about to prevent the fatal drowsiness which precedes death from creeping upon him. **1952** *Ibid.* Dec. 10/2 Sometimes the hunter dons a white 'seelapak' to make himself even less conspicuous. **1959** *Weekend Mag.* (Montreal) 22 Aug. 9 A tightly-woven poplin of cotton and nylon takes the place of the wind-blocking fabric Eskimos first used for the outer garment known as sealapack.

**sillar** (siː'ljɑː(r)). *Geol.* [Sp.] An ignimbrite or volcanic tuff that has not become indurated by welding.

**1948** C. N. FENNER in *Bull. Geol. Soc. Amer.* LIX. 883 There has been a tendency to call all such deposits 'welded tuffs'... For those in which induration is primarily the result of recrystallization, and for those in which the fragments have little cohesion, another term is desirable. The local term 'sillar'.., commonly used in the Arequipa region [in Peru], has been applied in the present paper. *Ibid.* 887 These occurrences of both white and salmon sillar contain scattered inclusions of white pumice. **1965** F. H. HATCH et al. *Petrol. Sedimentary Rocks* (ed. 4) xv. 322 Both sillars and welded tuffs frequently exhibit columnar jointing, somewhat akin to that in lava flows proper. **1978** *Nature* 24 Aug. 750/1 In the outcrops visited, two distinct flow units, each up to 30 m thick, were consistently present, both exhibiting the properties of classic sillar.

†**siller**, obs. form of CELLAR *sb.*

**1422** tr. *Secreta Secret., Priv. Priv.* 142 In Suche a tyme thow shalt thy graunges and thy gerners opyn, thy Sillers disclose. **1543** *Cal. Anc. Rec. Dublin* (1889) 414 Every siller and shope within the wallis.

**siller**, variant of SILOUR; obs. f. SELLER; Sc. variant of SILVER.

**Sillery** ('sɪlərɪ). Also 7 Cel(l)ery. [f. *Sillery*, a village in the department of Marne, Champagne.] A high-class wine produced in and around the village of Sillery in Champagne.

The name usually denotes a still wine known as ***Sillery sec*** or ***dry Sillery***, formerly made from the produce of the Sillery vineyards, but now mainly obtained from the neighbouring ones of Verzenay and Mailly.

**1680** SHADWELL *Woman Captain* I. i, The richer Wines of Greece and Sicely, And Celery, Champaign and Burgundy. *a* **1688** VILLIERS (Dk. Buckhm.) *Works* (1752) 116 As for French kickshaws, cellery and champain,..in troth we 'ave none. **1819** *Metropolis* III. 182, I am sure we can muster a sandwich, and I rather think that we may get a glass of sillery with it. **1845** *Encycl. Metrop.* XXV. 1279 Of these [Champagne wines] the still is considered the choicest, under the name of Sillery, much drank in England. **1859** H. KINGSLEY *G. Hamlyn* (1900) 80/2 His Majesty's right honourable ministers in the ante-room, drinking dry Sillery in honour of the event.

*attrib.* **1844** THACKERAY in *Colburn's Mag.* May 28 Sillery Champagne (4 bottles), £2.

**sillgreen**, dial. variant of SENGREEN.

**sillibouk.** *dial.* Forms: 6 sillibucke, 8 -buck; 7 sillibouke, 9 sylibewk; 8 silli-, 9 sillybauk. [var. of SILLABUB; for the ending cf. MERRIBOWK.] A sillabub. Also *attrib.*

**1573** BARET *Alvearie*, A Sillibucke, *Lac in ceruisia suffocatum vel ingulatum.* **1632** SHERWOOD, Sillibouke, or sillibub, *laict aigre.* **1701** W. BAXTER *Note Horace's Art Poet.* 239 Unde et nostrum *Sillabub*, quod rectius ab agrestibus *Sillibuck* profertur. **1721** BAILEY, *Sillibauk*, a Sillabub. *Lincolnsh.* **1819** PAUL BOBBIN *Sequel* 40 (E.D.D.), Th'.. black two bule'd sylibewk pot. **1866** BROGDEN *Prov. Lincs.*, *Silly-bauk*, a corruption of sillabub.

**sillibub**, obs. f. SILLABUB.

**sillik**, var. SILLOCK.

'**sillikin.** *slang.* [f. SILLY *a.* + -KIN.] A simpleton.

**1860** G. A. SALA *Lady Chesterfield* 32 Poor sillikin! he knows nothing of the secret clause in the treaty. **1882** F. W. ROBINSON *Women are strange* xxiii, A self-satisfied sillikin.

**sillily** ('sɪlɪlɪ), *adv.* [f. SILLY *a.* + -LY[2].]

†**1.** Poorly, badly. *Obs. rare.*

**1581** MULCASTER *Positions* xxxv. (1887) 126 The soule it selfe is but sillyly looked to, while the bodie is in price. **1611** COTGR., s.v. *Manger*, He that makes himselfe simple shall be sillily vsed.

**2.** In a foolish, absurd, or senseless manner.

**1627** W. SCLATER *Exp. 2 Thess.* (1629) 256 How doe wee sillily call all Idolatrous, that is in vse amongst Idolaters? **1658** A. FOX *Würtz' Surg.* III. xi. 248 Such Wounds which were very deep, and were silily and ignorantly stitched. **1712** STEELE *Spect.* No. 466 ¶6 [She] affects to please so sillily, that..you see the Simpleton from Head to Foot. **1740-1** RICHARDSON *Pamela* I. xxiv. 67 He sat down, and look'd at me, and..as sillily as such a poor Girl as I. **1805** *Spirit Publ. Jrnls.* IX. 4 They sillily interested themselves in the event of a new experiment. **1843** MRS. CARLYLE *Lett.* I. 254 Neither have I sillily paid four or five pounds away for it. **1864** BROWNING *Dram. Pers.* Wks. 1896 I. 573/2, I took your arm And sillily smiled.

**sillimanite** ('sɪlɪmənaɪt). *Min.* [f. the name of Benjamin *Silliman*, an American chemist (1779-1864); named by G. T. Bowen in 1824.]

A silicate of alumina, occurring in slender rhombic prisms or in fibrous masses.

**1830** *Encycl. Metrop.* (1845) VI. 476/2 Sillimanite. **1837** DANA *Min.* 321 Sillimanite occurs in slender prisms, thickly traversing quartz, in a vein of gneiss. **1888** RUTLEY *Rock-Forming Min.* 167 Sillimannite is a mineral of frequent occurrence in gneiss and other crystalline schists.

**sillinder**, obs. form of CYLINDER *sb.*

**silliness** ('sɪlɪnɪs). [f. SILLY *a.* + -NESS.]

**1.** The quality of being silly; foolishness, senselessness.

**1604** SHAKS. *Oth.* I. iii. 309 It is sillynesse to liue, when to liue is torment. **1634** CANNE *Necess. Separ.* 220 He sayth, that the Prelates may well laugh at Mr. Iohnsons simplicity and sillinesse of wit, that thinkes to fright them with such a bugbeare as this. **1705** BERKELEY *Commonpl. Bk.* Wks. 1871 IV. 427 The sillyness of the current doctrine makes much for me. **1779** *Mirror* No. 35, If all this..proceed from silliness, we must pity the man, and there's an end on't. **1865** LIVINGSTONE *Zambesi* viii. 179 It is a combination of silliness with absurdity quite odious. **1875** JOWETT *Plato* (ed. 2) IV. 410 The silliness of the so-called laws of thought ..has been well exposed by Hegel himself.

**b.** An instance of this; a silly thing, act, etc.

**1740–1** RICHARDSON *Pamela* I. 62, I shall write on,..tho' I should have nothing but Sillinesses to write. **1854** J. S. C. ABBOTT *Napoleon* (1855) I. xxxii. 491 Behold a silliness fit for a medical student, but not for me. **1882** STEVENSON *Fam. Stud.* ii. 104 If he had said 'the love of healthy men for the female form', he would have said almost a silliness.

**2.** Mental weakness.

**1822–7** GOOD *Study Med.* (1829) IV. 194 *Moria demens stultitia.* This, which is what we ordinarily denominate silliness, is generally a natural infirmity. **1899** *Allbutt's Syst. Med.* VII. 695 Melancholia, or mere silliness, may be the earliest feature of the disease.

**sillion**, obs. form of SELION.

**sillock** ('sɪlək). *Sc.* Forms: 7 sellak, 8 -ok, 9 -ock; 8 silak, 9 sillack, -ag; 8–9 sillik, -uck (9 -uk), 8– sillock. [Orkney and Shetland dial.] A young coal-fish (saithe), at a certain stage of its first year.

**1654** BLAEU *Atlas Scotia* 138 Piscium variorum, præcipue silurorum minimorum majorum et maximorum (vulgo Sellaks, Kuythes, Colmouses) captura felix. **1793** *Statist. Acc. Scotl., Orkney & Zetland* VII. 589 Sillocks set in, in great quantities, to the bays or voes in winter. **1822** HIBBERT *Desc. Shetl. Isl.* 434 Throwing his line among the throng of sillocks with which the inlet was filled. **1854** H. MILLER *Sch. & Schoolm.* xxv. (1857) 558 A flock of sea-gulls that had been sporting in the sunshine over a shoal of sillocks. **1881** DAY *Fishes Gt. Brit.* I. 295 At this period they are from six to ten inches in length, and much esteemed as sillucks.

*attrib.* **1822** HIBBERT *Desc. Shetl. Isl.* 122 It is to the sinewless arm of youth..that the light task is resigned of wielding the sillock-rod. **1888** SAXBY *Lads of Lunda* 34 A long, tapering, sturdy wand known as a 'sillack rod'.

**sillogism(e**, obs. forms of SYLLOGISM.

**'sillograph.** *rare.* [ad. L. *sillograph-us*, ad. Gr. σιλλογράφος, f. σίλλος a satirical poem.] A writer of satires or lampoons; *spec.* applied to Timon of Phlius (*c* 268 B.C.).

**1845** LEWES *Hist. Philos.* I. 77 His state of mind is finely described by Timon the sillograph. **1849** GROTE *Hist. Greece* II. xxxvii. IV. 526 The sillograph Timon of the third century B.C.

So **si'llographer, si'llographist.**

**1656** BLOUNT *Glossogr., Sillographer*, a writer of scoffs, taunts and revilings; such was Timon. **1775** ASH, Sillographist. **1845** *Encycl. Metrop.* X. 393/1 Menippus indeed, in common with the Sillographers, seems to have introduced much more parody than even the earliest Roman Satirists.

**si'llometer.** [ad. F. *sillomètre*, irreg. f. *siller* to make way, of a ship.] An instrument intended to serve the same purpose as a log-line.

**1842** *Mechanic's Mag.* XXXVII. 141 The speed, as shown by the Sillometer, was gradually reduced from 8 miles per hour to 4.

**Sillonist** ('sɪlənɪst). *Ch. Hist.* Also ‖**Silloniste.** [ad. F. *silloniste*, f. the name of the review *Le Sillon*, founded in 1894 by Paul Renaudin.] A member of a French Catholic movement for social reform led from *c* 1902 to 1910 by Marc Sangnier. Hence **'Sillonism**, the principles and policies of the Sillonists.

**1910** *Amer. Cath. Q. Rev.* XXXV. 707 The result..can only be a democracy which will be neither Catholic nor Protestant, nor Jewish; a religion (for Sillonism, its chief state, is a religion) more universal than the Catholic Church. **1910** *Daily News* 2 Sept. 5 The Sillonists believed in certain forms of private property. **1957** *Church Hist.* XXVI. 229 Certain theologians..pretended to find errors in *Silloniste* doctrine. *Ibid.* 241 The *Sillonistes* appeared to contravene in their actions the two basic principles of the papal policy in France. **1978** J. SONDHEIMER tr. *Aubert's Church in Secularised Soc.* I. iii. 49 This was an aspect..in which Sillonism marked itself out as being the best tradition of the liberal Catholicism of the nineteenth century. *Ibid.* 50 The Sillonists had envisaged forming a spiritual polity.

**sillour(e**: see SILOUR.

**sillow**: see SULL *sb.*, plough.

†**sillub**, obs. Sc. variant of SILLABUB.

**1583** *Leg. Bp. St. Androis* 386 For ony herb scho lykis to luike: It will instruct hir how to tak it; In sawis and sillubs how to mak it.

**sillu(c)k**, variants of SILLOCK.

**silly** ('sɪlɪ), *a.*, *sb.*, and *adv.* Forms: 5 syly, 6 sylie, silie, 7 sily; 6 cillie, 6–7 sillie (6 -ye), 5– silly; 6–7 sylly (6 -ye). [Later form of ME. *sely* SEELY *a.*]

From *c* 1550 to *c* 1675 *silly* was very extensively used in senses 1–3, and in a number of examples it is difficult to decide which shade of meaning was intended by the writer.

**A.** *adj.* **1. a.** Deserving of pity, compassion, or sympathy. Now *north.* and *Sc.* Cf. POOR *a.* 6.

*c* **1425** *Seven Sages* (Percy Soc.) 1361 The sylyman lay and herde, And hys wyf answerd. *c* **1489** CAXTON *Blanchardyn* liv. 213 With these or the like exclaimes, this silly aged King ..lay still a while. **1513** DOUGLAS *Æneid* I. vi. 69 Ane husband, quhilk Sicheus hecht, had sche,..And stranglie luvit of the silly Dido. **1556** in W. H. Turner *Select Rec. Oxford* 246 The fire raging upon the silly Carcase. **1641** J. JACKSON *True Evang. Temper* III. 187 What is poore, and silly man alone, but a very scrich-owle, and satyre. **1680** OTWAY *Orphan* II. v. 685, I might have trusted him with all the secret, Open'd my silly heart, and shewn it bare. **1724** RAMSAY *Tea-t. Misc.* (1733) I. 84 Good wife, for your courtesie, Will ye lodge a silly poor man? **1764** REID *Inquiry* i. §6. 103 Is this thy pastime, O Nature, to put such tricks upon a silly creature? **1808** JAMIESON, *Silly*..in the same sense as E. *poor* is often used, denoting a state which excites compassion. **1894** HESLOP *Northumbld. Gloss.* s.v., The bit bairn's asleep noo, silly thing.

†**b.** Helpless, defenceless; *esp.* of women and children. *Obs.*

**1587** TURBERV. *Trag. Tales* (1837) 31 Making him repine, To see a sillie dame so sore distreste. **1591** SHAKS. *Two Gentl.* IV. i. 72 Prouided that you do no outrages On silly women, or poore passengers. **1610** GUILLIM *Heraldry* III. xxvi. (1660) 260 Not unlike those devillish Witches, that do work the destruction of Silly Infants. **1647** CLARENDON *Hist. Reb.* VII. §171 Who behaved themselves with such inhumanity, that they Charged among the silly Women. **1665** MANLEY *Grotius' Low-C. Wars* 938 There remained fresh Examples of their Barbarism against weak Sea-men, and silly Fisher-men.

*absol.* *c* **1580** SIDNEY *Ps.* x. 7 Lift up Thy heavnly hand, And by the sylly stand.

**c.** Of animals, *esp.* as a conventional (poetic) epithet of sheep.

**1500–20** DUNBAR *Poems* xxxii. 59 In the silly lambis skin, He crap als far as he micht win. **1564–78** BULLEIN *Dial. agst. Pest.* (1888) 63 The poor cillie Mouse crept out of her small caue.., thinkyng no harme. **1577–82** BRETON *Toyes Idle Head* Wks. (Grosart) I. 38/2 This Lady.. To hunt this silly harmlesse Harte dooth take a great delight. **1620–6** QUARLES *Feast for Wormes* Introd. 46 The Woolfe shall fawne vpon the silly Sheepe. **1646** —— *Judgem. & Mercy* Wks. (Grosart) I. 120/1 The silly Sheep reposed in their warm fleeces. **1780** COWPER *Progr. Error* 119 His silly sheep, what wonder if they stray? **1866** M. ARNOLD *Thyrsis* v, He could not keep..Here with the shepherds and the silly sheep.

**2.** Weak, feeble, frail; insignificant, trifling:

†**a.** Of persons or animals. *Obs.*

**1567** MAPLET *Gr. Forest* 71 b, Here we see that a smal sillie Bird knoweth how to match with so great a Beast. **1577** *St. Augustine's Man.* T viij b, Why raungest thou then through so many thynges O sillie man? **1611** SPEED *Hist. Gt. Brit.* IX. iii. (1632) 465 A Colliers Cart..drawn with one silly leane Beast. **1633** HERBERT *Temple, Sighs & Grones* i, Thou onely art The mightie God, but I a sillie worm. **1665** SIR T. HERBERT *Trav.* (1677) 339 They are..so innocent as not to take away the life of the silliest vermin.

**b.** Of inanimate things. Now *Sc.*

**1587** GOLDING *De Mornay* xxxii. (1617) 558 He [Christ] leaueth neither children nor kinsfolk behind him to vphold his silly kingdome. **1598** BP. HALL *Sat.* v. i. 59 Of one bayes breadth, God wot, a silly cote. **1621** BURTON *Anat. Mel.* II. iii. III. (1651) 329 When as the lofty oke is blown down, the silly reed may stand. **1660** F. BROOKE tr. *Le Blanc's Trav.* 144 Many times 'tis but a scarf or silly taffeta ribbon. **1794** G. ADAMS *Nat. & Exp. Philos.* I. xi. 35 By dissection you discover this Worker of Miracles to be nothing but a poor silly contemptible Knob or Protuberency. **1889** BARRIE *Window in Thrums* 209, I was sawin'.., an' little Rob was haudin' the booards, for they were silly but things.

**c.** Weakly, feeble, sickly, ailing. *Sc.* and *north.*

*a* **1585** MONTGOMERIE *Cherrie & Slae* 1512 To do the thing we can To pleise..This silly sickly man. **1777** *Ferguson's Scot. Prov.* I A silly bairn is eith to lear. **1818** SCOTT *Hrt. Midl.* xvii, Is there onything you would particularly fancy, as your health seems but silly? **1821** GALT *Ann. Parish* i, She was but of a silly constitution. **1889** BARRIE *Window in Thrums* vi. 49 There's Leeby 'at I couldna hae done withoot, me bein' sae silly.

†**d.** Scanty, sorry, meagre, poor. *Obs.*

**1593** SHAKS. *3 Hen. VI*, III. iii. 93 A Pedigree Of three-score and two yeeres, a silly time To make prescription for a Kingdomes worth. **1613** JACKSON *Creed* I. 187 Where they found but silly shelter. **1767** SIR R. COLVILLE in Dossie *Mem. Agric.* (1768) I. 412 Marsh land, of a light, silly, hungry soil.

**3. a.** Unlearned, unsophisticated, simple, rustic, ignorant. *Obs.* or *arch.*

*a* **1547** SURREY *Æneid* II. 392 The silly herdman all astonnied stands. **1597** HOOKER *Eccl. Pol.* v. lxxx. §5 To make the sillie people believe that the contrarie is maintained by the Bishops. **1632** HERBERT *Priest to Temple* xxi, Socrates..found Philosophy in silly Tradesmen. **1687** LOVELL tr. *Thevenot's Trav.* I. 2 From Hell (of which the silly people of the Country think the top of this hill to be the mouth). **1739** *Better Regulation Free-Thinking* 2 The glaring Absurdities of Priest-craft..daily become the Scorn and Contempt of the sillyest Part of the People. **1795** SOUTHEY *Joan of Arc* I. 41 If, as I believe, this is of Heaven, My silly speech doth wrong it.

†**b.** Of humble rank or state; lowly. *Obs.*

*a* **1568** A. SCOTT *Poems* (S.T.S.) vi. 26 So luvaris lair no leid suld lak, A lord to lufe a silly lass. **1577–87** HOLINSHED *Chron.* II. 96 He was shot thorough with an arrow amongst his men by a sillie footman. **1607** HIERON *Wks.* I. 258 Little thought shee that that silly man that sate there..was the Sauiour of the world. **1632** LITHGOW *Trav.* IX. 388 This Duke, before whose face the silly ones did shine, and the proud stiffe-necked oppressours did tremble. **1647** FULLER *Gd. Th. in Worse T.* (1841) 108 The silliest and simplest, being wronged, may justly speak in their own defence.

**c.** Of things: Plain, simple, rustic, homely.

**1570** FOXE *A. & M.* (ed. 2) 926/1 Dauid had no more but a sylie slynge, and a few stones. **1587** GOLDING *De Mornay* Ep. Ded. p. iv, Consider how the silie netts of those Fishermen drew the pride of the world..to beleeve. **1610** GUILLIM *Heraldry* IV. v. (1660) 281 Before the invention of Printing, the onely means of preserving good Arts..was by this silly instrument the Pen. **1629** MILTON *Hymn Nativity* viii, Perhaps their loves, or els their sheep, Was all that did their silly thoughts so busie keep. **1753** FOOTE *Englishm. in Paris* II. Wks. 1799 I. 46, I am quite enchanted with this new instrument; 'tis so languishing and so portable, and so soft and so silly. **1798** COLERIDGE *Anc. Mar.* v. ii, The silly buckets on the deck.., I dreamt that they were filled with dew.

**4.** Weak or deficient in intellect; feeble-minded, imbecile. In early use *Sc.*

**15..** *Christ's Kirk* 24 in *Bann. MS.* 283 Fow yellow yellow wes hir heid, But scho of lufe wes sillie. **1721** WODROW *Hist. Suff. Ch. Scotl.* (1722) II. 318 He did not recover the Exercise of his Reason fully, but was silly, and next to an Idiot. **1814** SCOTT *Wav.* lxiv, Davie's no just like other folk..; but he's no sae silly as folk tak him for. **1881** GOLDW. SMITH *Lect. & Ess.* 193 The King's uncle, being rather weak in intellect, was called Silly Billy. **1889** H. O'REILLY *50 Yrs. on Trail* 9 A girl..who was a trifle silly. She could remember nothing, and was a great trouble.

**5. a.** Lacking in judgement or common sense; foolish, senseless, empty-headed.

**1576** FLEMING *Panopl. Epist.* 24 Wee sillie soules, take the matter too too heauily. **1598** FLORIO s.v. *Zane*, A sillie Iohn, a gull, a noddie. **1611** BIBLE *2 Tim.* iii. 6 Of this sort are they which creep into houses, and leade captiue silly women. **1691** HARTCLIFFE *Virtues* 3 A wise and good Man..will neither be so stupid, as to be surpriz'd with any Disaster, nor so silly, as to encrease it by a fruitless Anxiety. **1728** YOUNG *Love of Fame* v. 212 Her soul is silly, but her body's wise. **1766** C. O'CONOR *Dissert. Hist. Scotl.* 64 Silly Man! The Ridicule recoils doubly on his own Head. **1833** HT. MARTINEAU *Fr. Wines & Pol.* v. 77, I should be very silly to pay when I might have them without. **1840** DICKENS *Barn. Rudge* iii, 'Heaven help this silly fellow,' murmured the perplexed locksmith. **1889** GRETTON *Memory's Harkback* 312 The gentlemen often came into the drawing-room with glassy eyes, and silly of speech.

**b.** Of words, actions, etc.: Evincing or associated with foolishness.

**1588** SHAKS. *L.L.L.* III. i. 77 By vertue thou inforcest laughter, thy sillie thought, my spleene. **1590** —— *Mids. N.* v. i. 212 This is the silliest stuffe that ere I heard. **1639** FULLER *Holy War* I. viii, His silly looks carried in them a despair of any worth. **1669** R. MONTAGU in *Buccleuch MSS.* (Hist. MSS. Comm.) I. 461 He writes every week the silliest, foolishest stories in the world. **1764** GRAY *J.T.* 10 At our time of life 'twould be silly, my dear. **1780** COWPER *Progr. Err.* 380 With awkward gait, stretch'd neck, and silly stare. **1835** URE *Philos. Manuf.* p. x, The silly blunder of estimating their own intrinsic resources above those of all the world beside. **1871** R. ELLIS tr. *Catullus* xxxix. 16 For silly laughter, it's a silly thing indeed.

**c.** *silly season*, the months of August and September, when newspapers supply the lack of real news by articles or discussions on trivial topics; also *transf.* and *attrib.* Hence *silly-seasoner, -seasoning.*

**1861** *Sat. Rev.* 13 July 37/2 We have, however, observed this year very strong symptoms of the Silly Season of 1861 setting in a month or two before its time. **1871** *Punch* 9 Sept. 102/2 The present time of the year has been named 'the silly season'. **1884** *Illustr. Lond. News* 23 Aug. 171/1 The 'silly season' having begun in real earnest, the newspapers are, as a necessary consequence, full of instructive and amusing matter. **1893** *Westm. Gaz.* 18 Aug. 2/2 The *Chronicle's* suicide 'silly-seasoner' promises well. **1897** *Ibid.* 20 Aug. 7/3 Various questions of bathing..form the *Telegraph's* 'silly seasoning' this year. **1910** H. G. WELLS in *Eng. Rev.* Sept. 308, I got..Burkett of the *Dial* to try over a silly-season discussion of State Help for Mothers. **1930** *Forum* Dec. 375/2 The silly season was formally launched and the Big Parade began. **1952** M. TRIPP *Faith is Windsock* i. 20 Fat daily newspapers, silly-season follies, cries of 'Give Chamberlain a peerage!' after Munich. **1971** *Jrnl. Gen. Psychol.* Jan. 151 (*heading*) The psychobiological silly season —or—what happens when neurophysiological data become psychological theories. **1976** T. HEALD *Let Sleeping Dogs Die* vii. 129 The reporters were..embarrassed at having to attend such a..silly-season event.

**d.** *Cricket.* (See quot. 1897.)

**1888** R. H. LYTTELTON in Steel & Lyttelton *Cricket* vi. 287 The English captain acceded to W. G. Grace's wish and allowed him to go forward point, or, as it is familiarly called, 'silly' point. **1897** *Encycl. Sport* I. 246 *Silly*—Applied to point, mid-on and mid-off, when they stand dangerously near the striker. **1904** *Westm. Gaz.* 11 June 3/1 Strudwick.. jumped from silly-point and caught it almost on the leg side of the wicket.

**e.** *to play silly buggers* (also *bleeders, b-s*), to fool about, to mess around. Cf. *to play buggery* s.v. BUGGERY c. *slang.*

**1961** PARTRIDGE *Dict. Slang* Suppl. 1274/1 *Silly buggers, play*, to indulge in provocative horse-play; hence, to feign stupidity: low: since ca. 1920. **1968** M. WOODHOUSE *Rock Baby* ix. 95 If they want to play silly bleeders, let them. We're technicians. **1969** M. PUGH *Last Place Left* ii. 13 You know that whatever it is, it doesn't affect humans? Don't play silly bugger, Rab. **1972** J. MCCLURE *Caterpillar Cop* iii. 43 It was too easy..and too like what happened when the gods played silly buggers. 1972 'K. ROYCE' *Miniatures Frame* iv. 50, I have to pin something on him to stop him playing silly b's. 1976 K. WATERHOUSE *Mondays, Thursdays* 45 I'm sure none of this had anything to do with the supposed threat to our privacy. It was our God-given right to play silly buggers that was threatened, and the nation responded magnificently. 1979 *Guardian* 9 Aug. 22/8 We don't want people jeopardising our position by playing silly bs.

**f.** Proverbial phr. ***ask a silly question (and you get a silly answer)***.

1969 'A. GILBERT' *Missing from her Home* v. 73 No, don't bother to answer that. Ask a silly question and you get a silly answer. 1970 M. PEREIRA *Pigeon's Blood* xi. 122 'John? Tell me straight: do you or don't you?' John Raze looked at his friend. 'Ask a silly question...' he said. Then after a pause: 'No.' 1974 *Guardian* 26 Mar. 24/6 Questionnaires..coming under the heading of 'Ask a silly question, and you get a silly answer' get their just deserts.

**g.** *Comb.*, often with quasi-adverbial force, as ***silly-bold, -clever, -looking, -mad, -mild; silly-faced, -titled; silly-like*** adv.

1592 SHAKS. *Ven. & Ad.* 1151 It [love] shall be raging mad or sillie milde. 1760 R. JAMES *Treat. Canine Madness* 186 The reason of which was owing to his [i.e. a sheep-dog's] being what we vulgarly call silly mad. 1807 ANNA SEWARD *Lett.* (1811) VI. 388 A few extracts from the silly-titled poem Epics of the Ton. 1818 SCOTT *Hrt. Midl.* viii, A tall gawky silly-looking boy of fourteen or fifteen. *a*1825 FORBY *Voc. E. Anglia* 301 *Silly-bold*, impertinently and unbecomingly free; assuming unseemly airs. 1896 G. B. SHAW in *Sat. Rev.* 11 July 36/2 Greene was really amusing, Marston spirited and silly-clever. 1903 LD. R. GOWER *Rec. & Rem.* 258 Silly-faced Charles X in the same apparel. 1946 'G. ORWELL' in *Polemic* Sept.–Oct. 8 Innumerable silly-clever Conservatives..like Sir Alan Herbert, Professor G. M. Young, Lord Elton. 1963 *Economist* 11 May 538/1 Mr Khrushchev's silly-clever forward pass in Cuba.

**6.** Stunned, stupefied, dazed, as by a blow.

1886 COLE *S.W. Linc. Gloss.* s.v., It made me quiet silly for a time. 1889 RIDER HAGGARD *King Solomon's Mines* 217, I charged with them, and got knocked silly for my pains. 1892 BESANT *Ivory Gate* II. i. 9 We're knocked a bit silly just at first.

**7.** Special collocations: **silly ass**, a foolish or stupid person (cf. ASS *sb.*[1] 2); *spec.* an amiable upper-class idiot; freq. *attrib.*; **silly billy**, a foolish or feeble-minded person; used *spec.* as a nickname of William Frederick, Duke of Gloucester (1776–1834), and of William IV (1765–1837); **silly house** *slang*, a mental hospital (cf. *funny farm* s.v. FUNNY *a.* 4); †**sillypop** *slang*, a foolish or light-headed woman (cf. POP *sb.*[2]); also *attrib.* (*obs.*); **Silly Putty** orig. *U.S.*, the proprietary name of an elastic putty-like substance with the remarkable properties of stretching, shattering, and bouncing sharply when appropriately handled, sold chiefly as a plaything; also *fig.* and with small initials; **Silly Symphony**, any of a series of animated cartoons (see quot. 1976) designed by the American cartoonist Walter Elias ('Walt') Disney (1901–66).

1901 G. B. SHAW *Captain Brassbound's Conversion* III. 290 You silly ass, you. 1905 *Punch* 22 Mar. 214/2 He inquired if Phyllis 'had done the Academy yet'? Which, as it didn't open for some days, was a silly-ass thing to say. 1945 'G. ORWELL' in *Windmill* No. 2. 18 The silly-ass Englishman with his spats and his monocle. 1973 [see KNUT]. 1978 R. V. JONES *Most Secret War* vii. 60 In the best manner of the silly-ass Englishman he blundered into one door after another in an apparent search for the lavatory. 1834 J. ROMILLY *Diary* 13 Apr. (1967) 55 He was in a towering passion for a minute but soon got into a good humour by laughing at the D. of Gloster. 'Did you see silly Billy squirted on last night? it was worth 5£.' 1872 B. JERROLD *London* xv. 124 The silly-Billy of the neighbourhood—on whom the neighbourhood is merciless. 1908 L. H. DAWSON *Nicknames & Pseudonyms* 269 *Silly Billy*, a nickname of William Frederick (1776–1834), Duke of Gloucester; also of William IV (1765–1837). 1934 R. NICHOLS *Fisbo* 48 Come, come, don't be a silly-billy. 1958 N. MARSH *Singing in Shrouds* 173 You'll think me a frightful silly-billy. 1969 A. CHRISTIE *Hallowe'en Party* xvi. 173 The King what had a head like a pear was on the throne—Silly Billy, wasn't it, William IVth. 1977 in Lewis & Baker *Wordpower* II. vi. 15 Mr Healey is a Silly Billy to have waited so long before doing so little of what everyone knew was necessary. 1969 K. GILES *Death cracks Bottle* x. 116 They used to allow me my *News of the World* in the silly house. 1894 M. BEERBOHM *Defence of Cosmetics* in *Yellow Bk.* Apr. 70 She is the veriest little sillypop. 1895 *Punch* 18 May 230/3 On styge or on cinder-path, sillypop things As want to play Man and *be* Woman are trying to fly without wings. 1950 *New Yorker* 26 Aug. 20 After absorbing the elementary facts about Silly Putty..we sought out Mr. Lee Weber, the manager of the bookshop... He told us that Silly Putty is the most terrific item the Doubleday shops have been privileged to handle since 'Forever Amber'. 1952 *Official Gaz.* (U.S. Patent Office) 341 Peter Hodgson, New Haven, Conn... Silly Putty... For the Plastic Known as Organo Silicone Designed and Sold for Use as a Modeling Clay and Amusement..by Children. Claims used since July 1949. 1954 'E. Box' *Death in Fifth Position* v. 111 Silly putty is a pink substance which, if rolled in a ball, will bounce better than rubber, which will shatter if you hit it with a hammer and which will stretch to an unbelievable length. 1963 *Punch* 2 Oct. 495/1 What children today call 'silly putty', which can be pinched and stretched into any shape or length, like toffee. 1964 *Trade Marks Jrnl.* 19 Aug. 1364/2 *Silly Putty*... Play-things made of mouldable plastics. Peter Hodgson,..New Haven, State of Connecticut, United States of America; manufacturer. 1974 P. DE VRIES *Glory of Hummingbird* (1975) v. 79 It's only your hands I'm putty in. .. Silly putty I'm afraid. 1929 *Exhibitors Herald World* 16 Nov. 53/3 Booked into the Tivoli at Toronto for a week's run, 'The Skeleton Dance', one of the Disney Silly Symphonies which are being released by Columbia Pictures, has already made three weeks there. 1936 G. GREENE *Journey without Maps* I. iii. 67 Natives..looked like grasshoppers in a Silly Symphony. 1976 *Oxf. Compan. Film* 22/1 He [*sc.* Disney] pioneered the precise integration of the animated image with sound—particularly music—in the Silly Symphony series which began in 1928.

**B.** *sb.* A silly or foolish person. *colloq.*

1858 K. H. DIGBY *Children's Bower* I. 68 While your regular critics, like great sillies, are mistaking jewels or fruits for dirt. 1889 W. S. GILBERT *Gondoliers* II, She is what is called a silly. 1896 *Punch* 14 Mar. 124 You are not to be a silly.

**C.** *adv.* = SILLILY *adv.* 2. Now *dial.* or *colloq.*

1704 CIBBER *Careless Husband* I. i, If you did but see how silly a man fumbles for an excuse, when he is a little ashamed of being in love. *a*1774 GOLDSM. tr. *Scarron's Com. Romance* (1775) II. 268, I certainly behaved very silly, and she had a right to be angry with me. 1881 W. B. EVANS *Leicestersh. Gloss.* s.v., How can you talk so silly?

**silly** ('sɪlɪ), *v.* Chiefly *dial.* [f. the adj.]

**1.** *trans.* **a.** *refl.* To render (oneself) foolish.

1866 W. GREGOR *Banffsh. Gloss.*

**b.** To render silly; to stupefy, stun.

1859 *Sessions Papers Central Criminal Court* 10 May 17, I felt great pain from the blows... It half *sillied* me at the time. 1886 COLE *S.W. Linc. Gloss.* s.v., It didn't kill it, it only sillied it a bit.

**2.** *intr.* To act foolishly; to fool *about*.

1877 E. PEACOCK *N.W. Linc. Gloss.*, *Sillying about*, acting foolishly. 1891 KIPLING *Naulahka* vi, When a man sillies about like that, promising to meet a man..and not showing up.

**sillybob, sillyebub**, obs. ff. SILLABUB.

**silly-hood.** *dial.* = next.

1836 FURNESS *Medicus-Magus* 61 Three weeks ago his silly-hood was lost. 1877 E. PEACOCK *N.W. Linc. Gloss.*

**silly-how.** Now *Sc.* and *north.* Forms: 6, 8–9 *Sc.* sely how, 9 *Sc.* seely-, seeliehoo'; 7 syllie-hoe, 7– silly-how (7 sillie), 9 *Sc.* silly-hoo, *north.* -hue, -hew. [f. *sely* SEELY *a.* and SILLY *a.* + *how* HOUVE. Cf. the equivalent Sc. *happy how* and G. *glückshaube.*] A child's caul.

1574 J. JONES *Nat. Beg. Growing & Living Things* 26 Termed in Greeke..Chorion, Secundina of the Latines, of most in English, the Sely how. 1616 A. ROBERTS *Treat. Witchcraft* 66 That naturall couer where with some children are borne, and is called by our women, the sillie how. 1648 G. DANIEL *Eclog* ii. 25 May wee not pull The Syllie-Hoe.. Away? but tarrie Infants, in the wombe Of Ignorance. 1710 RUDDIMAN *Gloss. to Douglas* s.v. *How*, In Scotland the women call a haly or sely How..a film or membrane stretched over the heads of Children new born. 1808 JAMIESON s.v. *How*. 1867 W. ANDERSON *Rhymes* 67 *note* (E.D.D.), Anyone possessing a seelyhoo' legally is always progressing in fortune. 1894 HESLOP *Northumbld. Gloss.* s.v., The silly-hue is usually preserved, and is believed to sympathise with the person whose face it covered.

**'sillyish**, *a.* *rare.* [f. SILLY *a.* + -ISH.] Somewhat foolish.

1761 MRS. SHERIDAN *S. Bidulph* IV. 175 We were all infinitely good humoured, but rather sillyish.

**'sillyism.** [f. SILLY *a.* + -ISM.] A silly expression or utterance.

1706 BAYNARD *Cold Baths* II. 268 They fled with a blushless face to their old Sillyism, 'Ha! Lord! who would have thought it?' 1840 *Blackw. Mag.* XLVII. 714 Let any contemporary sumph give vent to a sillyism respecting a great man and it is sure to be transmitted to the latest posterity.

**sillyon**, obs. forms of SELION.

†**'sillyton.** *Obs.*[−1] A simpleton.

1725 BAILEY *Erasm. Colloq.* (1878) II. 351 Sillyton [L. *inepta*], forbear railing, and hear what's said to you.

**silo** ('saɪləʊ), *sb.* [a. Sp. *silo* (hence also F. *silo*):—L. *sīrum*, acc. of *sīrus*, a. Gr. σιρός a pit to keep corn in.]

**1.** A pit or underground chamber used for the storage of grain, roots, etc.

1835 *Partington's Brit. Cycl. Arts* II. 692/2 The grain put in his *silos*, in 1819, was sound and fresh in 1824. 1852 MUNDY *Antipodes* (1857) 31 The great curiosity of Cockatoo Island is the Siloes—excavations in the solid rock, shaped like a huge bottle, 15 or 20 feet deep, by 10 wide, with a narrow neck, closed with a stone capsule luted with plaster. 1860 DOMENECH *Deserts of N. Amer.* II. 278 Winter family provisions are also placed in silos like those of the Arabs. 1894 BARING-GOULD *Deserts S. France* I. 245 There are receptacles for the manure cut in the floor, also silos for grain.

**2.** *spec.* A pit, or an air- and water-tight chamber, in which green food is preserved for fodder by ensilage (cf. SILAGE); also, a cylindrical tower or other structure erected above ground for storing grain, fodder, etc. Cf. *pit silo* s.v. PIT *sb.*[1] 15.

1881 *Leeds Mercury* 6 June 7 Storing green maize or rye in air and water-tight concreted pits or 'silos'. 1885 *Spectator* 21 Feb. 249 Tares are very difficult to deal with in the silo. 1886 STALLMAIER & FUX tr. *Luther's Constr. & Equipment of Grain Magazines* 11 A silo is erected with outside walls, and sometimes covered with slates. 1893 *Times* 11 July 4/1 Coarse hop bines may be chopped while green and put into the silo. 1904 WILCOX & SMITH *Farmer's Cycl. Agric.* 377/1 The first silos were simply pits dug in the ground... Since about 1875 silos of stone, brick and wood have come into use. 1948 *Coast to Coast 1947* 240 The silos stood up tall and straight, grey against the dazzling sky. A line of wheat-laden vehicles moved slowly up towards the hopper. 1950 *Amer. Speech* XXV. 165 Wherever it is possible to find ground that will be dry all seasons of the year, farmers build 'pit silos' and 'trench silos' rather than the cylindrical silos entirely aboveground. 1977 *Daily Tel.* 18 Mar. 8/3 The Norfolk agricultural engineering firm, Rowlands Engineers,..has started a three-shift system..to cope with export orders of more than £400,000 for grain, coffee and cocoa storage silos.

**3.** = SILAGE. *rare.*

1889 M. S. VAN DE VELDE *Cosmopolitan Recoll.* II. ii. 44 Near the spot where Mademoiselle de Montpensier, the daughter of Gaston d'Orléans, held her little court, rise the new constructions for the storage of silo. 1898 F. P. DUNNE *Mr. Dooley in Peace & War* 17 If they'd put blinders on th' mules, they wuddn't be scared back be wan iv thim Spanish fleets that a jackass sees whin he's been up all night, secretly stuffing himsilf with silo.

**4.** *transf.* A large bin used for the storage of loose materials, as cement, etc.

1920 *Glasgow Herald* 2 Sept. 3/8 The coal silos are of sufficient capacity to maintain the supply for about 20 hours in the event of the stoppage of the conveyors. 1958 *Times Rev. Industry* May 64/3 Sulphur will be imported at wharves nearby and stored in a concrete silo with a capacity of 5,000 tons. 1961 *Engineering* 9 June 794 Cement now comes in tankers and is stored in silos. 1973 *Daily Tel.* 25 July 2/3 Another [boy]..was trapped up to his waist in a cement silo for nearly three hours.

**5. a.** An underground structure in which a guided missile is stored and from which it may be fired. Also *attrib.* Cf. HARD *a.* 14 f, SOFT *a.* 19 d.

1958 *N.Y. Times* 15 June 24/4 The system will be protected against neutralization in an enemy attack because the missiles will be installed in concrete-lined underground silos. 1960 *Aeroplane* XLIX. 18/1 For these 'silo' squadrons each missile will be emplaced vertically in a reinforced concrete-lined hole, 52 ft. in diameter and about 175 ft. deep. An elevator raises the missile to the surface a few minutes before launching. 1962 *Engineering* 5 Jan. 13 The Atlas-F [rocket] variant is to be housed within a 'silo' 174 feet deep and 52 feet in diameter... The first silos for Atlas-F are already under construction. 1968 *Economist* 31 Aug. 14/1 On present plans Minuteman III is scheduled gradually to replace Minuteman I and Minuteman II in the silos that dot the prairies and mountains of the western United States. 1975 'A. HALL' *Mandarin Cypher* xiii. 196 The Chinese Republic had silos all over the mainland for reaction-take-off missiles. 1978 *Daily Tel.* 27 July 1/2 Loading the Revenge's 16 ballistic missiles from their hillside silos at Coulport started..yesterday.

**b.** *Comb.* **silo buster** *slang*, a missile which can destroy an enemy missile in its silo; so **silo-busting** *ppl. a.*

1970 *Nature* 3 Oct. 11/1 The smaller but more accurate multiple warheads..are, like the SS-9, silo-busting weapons. 1977 *Time* 3 Oct. 22/3 The U.S. has also become increasingly concerned..about existing rockets that may become 'silo busters', with the explosive force and pin-point accuracy to destroy U.S. missiles in their underground launchers.

Hence **'silo** *v. trans.*, to put (green food) into a silo; to turn into ensilage.

1883 *Standard* 5 Dec. 2/3 The cost of siloing grass..was eleven shillings. 1884 *Pall Mall G.* 17 Sept. 3/2 His crop, which was siloed yesterday in Cheshire, only yielded 18 tons per acre.

†**silour.** *Obs.* Also 5 silloure (siller), 6 siloure, siler; 5 sylour, cylour, cyllowre; sylure, cylere, 6 syler, *Sc.* sylar. [var. of CELURE: cf. SILE *v.*[4]]

**1.** A canopy. Also *attrib.*

1394 *Durh. Acc. Rolls* (Surtees) 598 In uno Silour empt. pro d'no Priore, cum tinctura de Canevas et Ridell. *a*1400–50 *Alexander* 4915 Þe silloure full of Seraphens & othire sere halows, With curtyns all of clene silke. 1418–*c*1450 [see CELURE]. 1465 *Durh. Acc. Rolls* (Surtees) 243 Lectus blodius..cum tapeta ejusdem coloris. Item j silour ejusdem coloris. 1523 in *Archaeologia* (1860) XXXVIII. 364 In the..Knyghton chamber,..syler and tester of whyte..and the conterpoynte of the same. 1548 *Will of Colman* (Somerset Ho.), One coverlett of siloure worke.

**2.** A ceiling. Also *attrib.*

1424–5 *Durh. Acc. Rolls* (Surtees) 272 Pro emendacione de sylour in aula, cum clavis empt., vj *d.* 1497 *Acc. Ld. High Treas. Scot.* I. 357 To Dauid, wricht,..in part of payment of v lib. for the sylour completing. 1513 *Ibid.* IV. 524 To James Carvour, ij[c] sylour naile, xij *d.* 1535 STEWART *Cron. Scot.* II. 56 The sylar alss wes of the sypar tre,..Richt curious carvit with money ane knot.

So †**siloured** *ppl. a.*; †**silouring** *vbl. sb.*

*c*1440 *Promp. Parv.* 77/2 Cyluerde (*H.* cyluryd, *P.* cylered), *celatus. Ibid.* 456/1 Syluryd, *celatus.* 1450–1 *Durh. Acc. Rolls* (Surtees) 276 Pro le sylorynge ejusdem camere. 1452–3 *Ibid.* 277 Pro le sylorynge domus rasture. 1494 *Acc. Ld. High Treas. Scot.* I. 238 Bocht j[c] estland burdis for the silouring of the chapell in Striueling. 1558 *Wills & Inv. N.C.* (1835) I. 184 Y[e] sillering in the parler.

**siloxane** (sɪ'lɒkseɪn). *Chem.* [ad. G. *siloxan* (A. Stock 1917, in *Ber. d. Deut. Chem. Ges.* L. 170): see SILICON, OXYGEN, and -ANE.] Any compound having a molecular structure consisting of a chain of alternate silicon and oxygen atoms, the silicon atoms being bonded to hydrogen atoms or to organic radicals. Cf. SILICONE 2 a. Freq. *attrib.*

1917 *Jrnl. Chem. Soc.* CXII. II. 204 Perhaps the greatest confusion in the nomenclature of silicon compounds is to be found in the case of substances containing the –Si–O–Si– system. It is proposed to call the parent hydrogen compounds of this type 'siloxanes', and to specify the number of silicon and oxygen atoms in such terms as 'disiloxane', 'disildioxane', etc. **1941** *Jrnl. Amer. Chem. Soc.* LXIII. 800/2 A cross-linked structure of siloxane chains. **1948** *Electronic Engin.* XX. 82/3 The silicone oils are semi-inorganic polymers in which carbon atoms of organic radicals are linked to the silicon atoms of the so-called siloxane chain. **1960** *New Scientist* 12 May 1205/2 Silicone rubber..is built up from purified siloxanes. **1974** *Encycl. Brit. Macropædia* IV. 104/2 The most useful of man-made inorganic polymers are the siloxanes (also known as silicones).

‖**silphium** ('sɪlfɪəm). [L., ad. Gr. σίλφιον.]

**1.** A plant of the Mediterranean region, yielding a gum-resin or juice much valued by the ancients as a condiment or medicine; the juice obtained from this plant, also called LASER[1].

The plant has been variously identified as *Thapsia garganica* or *silphion*, and *Narthex silphium*. It was largely cultivated for export at Cyrene on the north coast of Africa.

[**1706** PHILLIPS (ed. 6), *Silphium*, the Herb Laserwort.] **1753** *Chambers' Cycl.* Suppl. s.v. *Laser*, When Cyrene no longer afforded the *silphium*, it was sought for in other places. **1781** PENNANT *Hist. Quadr.* II. 432 These, with the plant Silphium, were used to denote the country of Cyrene, where both were found. **1820** MITCHELL *Aristoph.* I. 239 The silphium, or herb Benjamin, was much used by the ancients in medicine. **1858** BIRCH *Anc. Pottery* I. 268 The subject of Arcesilaus..attended by the different officers of his stores, and watching the weighing of the silphium. **1869** RAWLINSON *Anc. Hist.* 81 A trade by which Carthage obtained the commodities that she needed, wine, oil, dates, salt fish, silphium.

**b.** *attrib.*, as ***silphium land, plant, -spice***.

**1820** MITCHELL *Aristoph.* I. 239 Do you remember, sir, when silphium-spice was sold so cheap? **1886** *Guide Exhib. Galleries Brit. Mus.* 189 Representations of what is thought to be the silphium plant—an early source of commerce in Cyrene. **1899** MACNAGHTEN tr. *Catullus* vii. in *Story of Catullus* 28 As many grains as are of Libyan sand By rich Cyrene in the silphium land.

**2.** A genus of N. American composite plants including the rosin-weed or compass plant and the prairie dock; a plant of this genus.

**1771** *Encycl. Brit.* III. 602/1. **1800** *Abercrombie's Ev. Man own Gard.* 689/2 *Silphium*, bastard chrysanthemum. **1819** *Pantologia* X. s.v., Jagged-leaved silphium... Broad-leaved silphium. **1846–50** A. WOOD *Class-bk. Bot.* 336 *Silphium Trifoliatum*, Ternate-leaved Silphium.

**Silsbee** ('sɪlzbiː). *Physics.* The name of Francis Briggs *Silsbee* (1889–1967), American physicist, used *attrib.* and in the possessive with reference to the phenomenon (discovered by Kamerlingh Onnes and explained by Silsbee) of the destruction of the superconducting properties of a superconductor when a current exceeding a certain critical value (the ***Silsbee current***) is passed through it.

**1926** *Jrnl. Franklin Inst.* CCI. 407 As is demanded for the correctness of Silsbee's hypothesis the supra-conductivity, which was disturbed by exceeding the threshold current, was restored by applying an external magnetic field. **1932** *Proc. R. Soc.* A. CXXXVI. 65 There remained the possibility..that the effect was a manifestation of the Silsbee effect, in which the current through the superconductor produces, by its own magnetic field, a depression of the critical temperature. **1968** C. G. KUPER *Introd. Theory Superconductivity* v. 89 If a current *I* in excess of the Silsbee current..is passed through a cylindrical wire.., some destruction of superconductivity must occur. **1975** M. TINKHAM *Introd. Superconductivity* iii. 99 Silsbee's rule that the critical current cannot exceed that which produces a critical magnetic field at the superconductor.

**silt** (sɪlt), *sb.* Also 5 cylt(e, 6 sylt, 9 silth. [Of doubtful origin, but app. denoting a salty deposit: cf. Da. and Norw. *sylt*, Norw. and Sw. dial. *sylta* salt-marsh, sea beach; OLG. *sulta* (MLG. and LG. *sulte, sülte*, older Flem. *sulte*, Du. *zult*), OHG. *sulza* (MHG. *sulze*, G. *sülze*) salt-marsh, salt-pan, brine, all f. *sult-*, ablaut-variant of *salt-*: see SALT *sb.*[1] and *v.*[1] One or other grade of the same stem is also represented by OE. *un(ȝe)sylt* unsalted, Du. *zilt* adj. salt.]

**1. a.** Fine sand, clay, or other soil, carried by moving or running water and deposited as a sediment on the bottom or beach; sometimes occurring as a stratum in soil.

α. *c* **1440** *Promp. Parv.* 77 Cylte, soonde, *glarea.* **1523** SKELTON *Garland Laurel* 23 Thus stode I in the frytthy forest of Galtres, Ensowkid with sylt of the myry mose. **1610** HOLLAND *Camden's Brit.* I. 529 This Country which the Ocean hath laied to the land, by seas heaped and cast together, they it terme Silt. *a* **1676** HALE *Prim. Orig. Man.* (1677) 191 The great Changes that have been between the Sea and Lands..by casting up Silt and Sand. **1692** RAY *Disc.* 45 The interjacent Fretum having been filled up by the Silt brought down by the River Nilus. *a* **1707** PATRICK *On Deut.* xi. 11 Many times there followed, after the water was gone off, great sicknesses and diseases, by the smell of the silt which it had left behind. **1799** *View Agric. Lincoln* 265 The stratum of *silt* in this neighbourhood is every where impregnated with *salt.* **1823** BUCKLAND *Reliq. Diluv.* 190 On the east coast of England there is also a considerable addition of silt and mud on some parts. **1863** KINGSLEY *Water-Bab.* viii, Before Tom had stood there five minutes, he was buried in silt up to his ankles. **1878** HUXLEY *Physiogr.* xvii. 280 When the Thames has overflowed its banks it has deposited silt on the neighbouring land.

*fig.* **1870** LOWELL *Among my Bks.* Ser. I. (1873) 223 The perpetual silt of some one weakness. **1890** HALL CAINE *Bondman* iv, Such was the grey silt that came up to him that night from the deposits of his memory.

β. **1813** PRIEST *View Agric. Bucks.* 23 These streams..are suffered to be filled with silth, rubbish, and all sorts of aquatic plants. **1839** *Civil Eng. & Arch. Jrnl.* II. 99/1 There will be water undoubtedly, as the ground is sand and gravel, with silth below.

**b.** A bed or layer of this matter.

**1881** *Rep. Geol. Expl. N.Z.* 34 A dyke occurring close to the silts, which stretch from Tokatoka south past the Dwaroa river.

**c.** *Soil. Sci.* Applied *spec.* to particles whose sizes fall within a specified size range between those of sand and clay and to soils having a specified proportion of such particles (see quots.). Hence ***silt-grade***; ***silt-size*** sb. (adj.).

**1873** *Amer. Jrnl. Sci.* CVI. 288 It makes a material difference whether the grains of sand contained in a soil or clay are prevalently half a millimeter in diameter, or the tenth or twentieth part of that amount. Sand (or more properly silt) of the latter size is by no means impalpable. **1909** A. G. MCCALL *Physical Properties of Soils* 88 Stir up the soil remaining in the centrifugal tube and allow to stand for about one minute, or until all particles larger than silt (0·05 [mm.]) have settled. **1920** Silt grade [see SILTSTONE]. **1958** I. W. CORNWALL *Soils for Archaeologist* xi. 125 Once the silt-grade is reached (below 0·06 mm.) a moderate wind is able to transport the grains..for long distances. **1967** *Gloss. Highway Engin. Terms* (B.S.I.) 23 *Silt.* (1) A natural sediment of grading finer than sand consisting of granular products of rock weathering: it is gritty to the touch. (2) In soil analysis it comprises the fraction between 0·06 mm and 0·002 mm. **1968** R. W. FAIRBRIDGE *Encycl. Geomorphol.* 675/1 Primary forms of lime include minute grains, incrustations on silt-size grain aggregates and snail shells. **1971** *Gloss. Soil Sci. Terms* (Soil Sci. Soc. Amer.) 15/1 *Silt*, a soil separate consisting of particles between 0·05 and 0·002 mm in equivalent diameter. **1972** [see SAND *sb.*[2] 1 h]. **1976** L. F. CURTIS et al. *Soils in Brit. Isles* i. 3 The mineral matter [of soil] includes particles of clay (less than 2 μm diameter), silt (2–50 μm diameter) and sand (50 μm–2 mm diameter).

†**2.** *pl.* Dregs, refuse, scum. *Obs.*[−1]

**1635** HEYLIN *Sabbath* II. (1636) 107 The common prostitutes, such as received the silts of all the towne.

**3.** A silt-snapper (see 4).

App. an alteration of the earlier *silk(-snapper)*.

**1863** *Jamaica Notes* in *Intellect. Obs.* III. 194 The mode of fishing for deep-water Silts is very effective. **1883** *Fish. Exhib. Catal.* (ed. 4) 170 The principal salt-water fishes are ..Silts,..King-fish, Barracouta and many others.

**4.** *attrib.* and *Comb.*, as ***silt-land, -trap; silt-bearing*** adj.; **silt-bucket, grass, -ground** (see quots.); **silt loam**, a soil composed at least half of silt; **silt-snapper**, a Jamaican fish (cf. 3); **siltstone** *Petrol.* (see quot. 1920).

**1884** *Manch. Exam.* 3 May 4/7 A silt-bearing river like the Mersey. **1884** *Health Exhib. Catal.* 57/1 Silt-buckets for preventing the choking of drains. **1889** MAIDEN *Useful Plants* 104 *Paspalum distichum*,..'Sea-side Millet', 'Water Couch', 'Silt Grass'. **1863** *Jamaica Notes* in *Intellect. Obs.* III. 194 [A canoe] on its way to the Silt-ground at two hundred fathoms depth. **1927** *Daily Express* 11 July 11/3 Both fenland and silt-land in these counties boast rich alluvial soil. **1963** *Times* 1 Feb. 13/6 Being essentially a study of the silt lands that border the Wash, it did not attempt to deal in detail with the equally interesting Roman occupation of the southern part of the region. **1917** MOSIER & GUSTAFSON *Soil Physics & Management* x. 138 The silt loam soils cover extensive areas in the middle west of the United States and owe their origin to loess. **1957** H. B. VANDERFORD *Managing Southern Soils* iv. 93 Surface soils which have medium to coarse textures (sandy loams, silt loams, and clay loams) are suitable for cultivation and relatively easy to keep in good tilth. **1863** *Jamaica Notes* in *Intellect. Obs.* III. 194 The deep-water Silt-Snappers include some five different species, all similar in colour. **1920** A. HOLMES *Nomencl. Petrol.* 211 *Siltstone*, a very fine-grained sandstone, the particles of which are predominantly of silt grade. **1946** L. D. STAMP *Britain's Struct. & Scenery* xii. 116 The lower Carboniferous deposits in the Central Lowlands of Scotland are sandstones, shales, cementstones and siltstones with only occasional bands of limestones. **1977** A. HALLAM *Planet Earth* 264 The graptolites..are often common in offshore black shales and siltstones. **1946** F. D. DAVISON *Dusty* viii. 84 They..were going to clear out the silt-trap of one of the tanks. **1966** E. PALMER *Plains of Camdeboo* xviii. 301 Dams, water-troughs, silt traps.

**silt**, *v.* [f. the sb.]

**1. a.** *intr.* Of a channel, river-bed, etc.: To become filled or choked *up* with silt or sediment. Also *fig.*

**1799** *View Agric. Lincoln* 16 [The well] runs equally every year, and in all seasons,..but it is apt to silt up. **1830** LYELL *Princ. Geol.* I. 304 There is naturally a tendency in all estuaries to silt up partially. **1840** *Evid. Hull Docks Com.* 79 The harbour is silting up at the east point. **1873** G. C. DAVIES *Mountain & Mere* v. 28 As the years rolled on, the water subsided, the hollows silted up. **1955** *Times* 10 June 7/3 [The] streets of London silt up with the swelling torrent of motor traffic.

**b.** To flow or drift *in* after the manner of silt. Also *transf.* to pass gradually *away.*

**1863** H. KINGSLEY *A. Elliott* I. 33 If the wreck of the Mary Anne was moved, the sand would silt in again. **1892** CLARK RUSSELL *List, ye Landsmen* iii, It seemed to me that the electric mass was silting away north, and that there would come a clear sky in the south presently.

**2.** *trans.* **a.** Of silt: To fill, block, or choke *up* (a channel, the bed of a river or the sea, etc.) by gradual accumulation. Also rarely without *up.* Chiefly in *pa. pple.*

*a* **1825** FORBY *Voc. E. Anglia* 301 *Silt-up*, to obstruct..by a large accumulation of sand. **1832** LYELL *Princ. Geol.* II. 275 The deposits which within the historical period have silted up some of our estuaries. **1865** ESQUIROS *Cornwall* 158 The sands with which the mouth of the Exe is silted. **1875** CROLL *Climate & T.* xxix. 469 That the tendency of the sea filling this valley is to silt it up rather than to deepen it.

*transf. a* **1853** ROBERTSON *Lect.* i. (1858) 43 The sand of the desert daily silting up the temples. **1860** MAURY *Phys. Geog. Sea* x. §481 The whole Atlantic ocean would..be finally silted up with salt.

*fig.* **1855** BAILEY *Mystic* 59 While Time's last sands silt up the streams of soul.

**b.** To cover *up* or *over* with silt.

**1830** HERSCHEL *Study Nat. Phil.* II. vi. (1851) 145 To leave his shell in the mud where it becomes silted over and imbedded. **1878** HUXLEY *Physiogr.* 224 If, by the overflow of a river, the plant should become silted up in mud.

Hence **'silted** *ppl. a.*: also with *up.*

**1890** *Clacton News* 25 Jan. 2/4 The silted matter from the ditch is generally required to make up the bank. **1960** *Archaeologia Cambrensis* CIX. 56 The excavations.. revealed a massive stone platform built partly on the peat filling of a silted-up cistern.

**siltage** ('sɪltɪdʒ). *rare.* [f. SILT *sb.* + -AGE.] Silt, silted matter.

**1876** *Daily News* 30 Oct. 6/4 Siltage was brought into the canal to the extent of nearly three million cubic yards. **1902** *Monthly Rev.* Sept. 113 Internally the siltage of centuries had preserved the colouring.

**siltation** (sɪl'teɪʃən). [f. SILT *v.* + -ATION.] The action or result of silting. Freq. *attrib.*

**1932** *Min. Proc. Inst. Civil Engin.* CCXXXII. 70 Siltation Records.—As there is a considerable quantity of silt in circulation in Bombay harbour, a detailed investigation was carried out. **1949** *Radio Times* 15 July 7/3 On the foreshore the cunning Dutch made 'siltation fields'... The incoming tides deposit mud in these fields which gradually rise until they are above sea level. Then a dyke is built. **1967** L. E. CRONIN in G. H. Lauff *Estuaries* 671/1 The Potomac is a very flashy river... Droughts, floods, heavy siltation,..all present problems in its control. **1977** *Offshore Engineer* Aug. 48/4 The Port needed accurate and quick surveying to assess the siltation characteristics.

**'silting**, *vbl. sb.* [f. SILT *sb.* or *v.* + -ING[1].]

†**1.** Siltage. *Obs. rare.*

**1739** LABELYE *Piers Westm. Bridge* 5 A Shoal..made up of Sand and of the Washing or Silting of the River. *Ibid.* 64 The Silting of the River, which must accumulate in a long Course of Years.

**2.** The action of the verb; an instance of this. Usually with *up.*

**1840** *Evid. Hull Docks Com.* 230 There will be a most rapid silting up of the timber pond. **1860** *Merc. Mar. Mag.* VII. 308 The slight silting of a few inches at Holyhead.. Harbour. **1894** JESSOPP *Rand. Roam.* ii. 71 That causeway would..help..to bring about a gradual silting up of the little river.

*attrib.* **1876** PAGE *Adv. Text-bk. Geol.* xx. 416 Many of these sandy tracts are no doubt the result of ordinary silting operations.

**silty** ('sɪltɪ), *a.* [f. SILT *sb.* + -Y.] Of the nature of, or resembling, silt; composed of, or containing, silt.

**1658** FRANCK *North. Mem.* (1694) 84 Should I silently pass by and imprint no Remarks on their Silty Sands, and Silver Streams. **1838** *Civil Eng. & Arch. Jrnl.* I. 290/2 The ground towards the Middlesex side being of a looser and more sandy and silty nature. **1847** *Jrnl. R. Agric. Soc.* VIII. I. 115 The land..consists of a good thick loam upon a porous silty subsoil. **1883** E. P. RAMSEY *Food Fishes N.S. Wales* 42 Depth of water from 6 to 9 feet, with oyster-shells and silty bottom.

**siluan(e**, obs. forms of SYLVAN.

**silumin** ('sɪljʊmɪn). *Metallurgy.* [a. G. *silumin*: see SILICON and ALUMINIUM.] Any of a series of casting alloys of aluminium containing about 9 to 13 per cent silicon.

**1922** *Chem. Abstr.* XVI. 3861 Silumin... A new Al-Si alloy has been prepd. at the Metallbank in Frankfurt. **1930** *Engineering* 18 Apr. 508/1 This difficulty was partly overcome by resting the tent on slabs of Silumin. **1967** *Chem. Abstr.* LXVI. 21573 Effect of 0·0016–0·00072% Na on the kinetics of gas absorption under a steam-satd. atm. was investigated on silumins differing only in the initial Na content.

**silure** (sɪ'ljʊə(r)). *Ichth.* [a. F. *silure*, ad. L. *silūrus* SILURUS.] A siluroid fish, esp. the sheat-fish (*Silurus glanis*).

In Shaw's *Gen. Zool.* (1804) V. I. 9–27 several species are enumerated.

**1802–3** *Pallas' Trav.* (1812) I. 21 The silures and sterlets, a smaller species of sturgeon, are caught only in the spring. **1804** SHAW *Gen. Zool.* V. I. 10 European Silure. *Silurus Glanis*... The great or common Silure may perhaps be considered as the largest of all European river fishes. *Ibid.* 20 Rufous Silure... Native of South America.

**Silurian** (sɪ'ljʊərɪən, saɪ-), *a.* and *sb.*[1] [f. L. *Silur-es*, an ancient British tribe which inhabited the south-eastern part of Wales.]

**1.** Of or belonging to the ancient Silures, or to the district inhabited by them.

**1708** J. PHILIPS *Cyder* II. 89 To the utmost Bounds of this Wide Universe, Silurian Cyder borne shall please all Tasts. **1740** SOMERVILLE *Hobbinol* III. 97 Others apart, in the cool Shade retir'd, Silurian Cyder quaff. **1757** DYER *Fleece* I. 492 If your sheep are of Silurian breed. **1839** MURCHISON *Silurian Syst.* p. xxxi, We have no precise definition of the geographical limits of the Silurian kingdom. **1908** *Outlook* 14 Nov. 656/1 The hero who is sometimes called a 'British', and sometimes a 'Silurian' chief.

**2. a.** *Geol.* Orig., the name given to the system or series of Palæozoic rocks lying immediately below the Devonian or Old Red Sandstone; of or belonging to this formation, or to the period when it was deposited. Now, the name is restricted to a system of Lower Palæozoic rocks underlying the Devonian and overlying the Ordovician, so corresponding to the Upper Silurian as originally defined.

As orig. defined by Murchison the Silurian included what was subsequently called the Ordovician, and this use continued for a time after the introduction of the Ordovician in 1879.

**1835** MURCHISON in *Philos. Mag.* July 48, I venture to suggest that..the term 'Silurian System' should be adopted as expressive of the deposits which lie between the old red sandstone and the slaty rocks of Wales. **1842** MILLER *O.R. Sandst.* xiii. (ed. 2) 275 The animal organisms of the newer Silurian strata form essentially different groups from those of the Lower Old Red Sandstone. **1851** RICHARDSON *Geol.* viii. (1855) 208 The seas of the silurian and oolitic periods. **1876** *Nature* XIV. 557/2 The classification of the Silurian, Devonian, and Permo-Triassic (Poikilitic) formations. **1879** C. LAPWORTH in *Geol. Mag.* VI. 3 The Lyell-Hicks division of *Cambrian* and *Lower Silurian* are as rightly entitled to the rank of separate systems as the true or *Upper Silurian* itself. *Ibid.* 9 The general restriction of the title Silurian to the strata that are comprehended between the line marking the base of the Lower Llandovery, and that denoting the commencement of the brackish or fresh-water conditions of the typical Old Red Sandstone, appears..inevitable. *Ibid.* 15 The ideas of the extreme party which claims all the Lower Palæozoics for the Silurian are fated soon to become wholly extinct. **1902** A. J. JUKES-BROWNE *Student's Handbk. Stratigr. Geol.* vii. 64 Murchison supposed that Sedgwick's Cambrian lay entirely below his Silurian, but when the fossils were collected and described, it was found that the Upper Cambrian was equivalent to the Lower Silurian... Group after group of Sedgwick's Cambrian was gradually absorbed into it [*sc.* the Lower Silurian], till the Lower Silurian came to include the whole of the rocks (below the Upper Silurian) in which any fossils had been found. **1903** A. GEIKIE *Text-Bk. Geol.* (ed. 4) II. 934 Murchison's 'Lower Silurian' has by many writers been replaced by 'Ordovician', and his 'Upper Silurian' is in a similar manner being ousted by some other term... I shall continue to employ Murchison's terminology. **1912** *Q. Jrnl. Geol. Soc.* LXVIII. 332 In fixing the boundary between the Ordovician and the Silurian the peculiar characters and mode of weathering of the Lower Birkhill rocks have been found useful. **1931** GREGORY & BARRETT *Gen. Stratigr.* v. 77 The Silurian is now usually restricted to the strata between the Ordovician and Devonian. **1955** [see GOTLANDIAN, GOTHLANDIAN *a.*]. **1964** *Rep. Internat. Geol. Congr. XXI Sess., 1960* XXVIII. 254 The Commission transmits to the Congress the following proposals on the terminology of the Silurian and Ordovician... 1) Two systems are to be recognized between the Cambrian and Devonian systems. 2) The name of the lower shall be Ordovician. 3) The name of the upper shall be Silurian. **1971** *Jrnl. Geol. Soc.* CXXVII. 106 When the standard classification of the correlation charts is considered in relationship to local successions the Silurian of the British Isles is found to be something of a monument to stratigraphical chaos.

**b.** As *sb.* in *pl.* Silurian strata.

**1842** *Penny Cycl.* XXII. 13/2 Upper Silurians,..Lower Silurians. **1855** J. PHILLIPS *Man. Geol.* 89 It [*sc.* gneiss] may be regarded as older than the silurians of that region. **1862** *Chambers's Encycl.* III. 541/1 The clay-slates of the Lower Silurians.

**c.** *transf.*, loosely designating a primitive age or period in the remote past.

**1875** 'MARK TWAIN' in *Atlantic Monthly* Aug. 193/2 In the Old Oölitic Silurian Period, just a million years ago next November. **1962** E. SNOW *Red China Today* (1963) xvi. 116 When I last saw Mao..China was weak, disunited and bankrupt. Since then China's Silurian age had ended. 'China has stood up,' as Mao proclaimed.

**3.** Also with lower-case initial. **a.** Of, pertaining to, or designating a paper showing two or more contrasting colours on its surface; usu. applied to stationery of a blue-grey appearance. Also, of the colour itself.

**1892** J. HEYWOOD *Wholesale Catal. Stationery & Stationers' Sundries* 22 Scotch Tinted Writings... Silurian —5 8. **1930** W. DE LA MARE *On the Edge* 28 The drawer beneath contained only envelopes and letter paper—*Montrésor*, in large pale-blue letters on a 'Silurian' background. **1937** E. J. LABARRE *Dict. Paper* 153/1 *Granite* paper, also termed French grey, Ingres, Silurian grey, Mottled, Ingrain, is paper which clearly shows two or more contrasting colours of pulp on its surface. **1964** M. CLIVE *Day of Reckoning* viii. 73 Their correspondents wrote on double sheets of grey 'silurian' paper which looked hairy but was slippery.

**b.** As *sb.*, paper or stationery of this type.

**1942** H. A. MADDOX *Dict. Stationery* (ed. 2) 100 *Silurian*, a tinted writing paper formerly much in favour for note and envelopes. Characterised by a blue-grey mottled colour which gave rise to the occasional term, French Granite. **1954** *Paper Terminol.* (Spalding & Hodge) 54 *Silurian*, coloured paper, usually a writing or cover, produced by introducing into the coloured pulp, fibres dyed a deeper shade. **1960** D. HOLMAN-HUNT *My Grandmothers & I* ii. 24, I..sucked the pen and began to scratch at the grey silurian.

**si'lurian**, *sb.*[2] *Ichth.* [f. SILUR-US + -IAN.] A siluroid fish. Also **si'lurid, si'luridan, si'luride, si'lurine,** *adjs.* and *sbs.*, = SILUROID.

**1842** *Penny Cycl.* XXII. 16 A small *Silurian from Cayenne, in which there is no adipose fin. *Ibid.* 17 The head ..is flat and broader than in the other Silurians. **1891** *Cent. Dict.*, *Silurid. **1896** tr. *Boas' Text-bk. Zool.* 388 The electric Silurid (*Malapterurus electricus*). **1835** KIRBY *Hab. & Inst. Anim.* I. ii. 121 A species of fish..belonging to a genus of the family of the *Siluridans. *Ibid.* 123 The serrated bone, or first ray of the pectoral fin,..is found in other Siluridans. **1863** BATES *Nat. Amazons* ix. (1864) 247 A good supply of Jandia, a handsome, spotted *Siluride fish. **1891** *Cent. Dict.*, *Silurine.

**'Silurist.** [f. L. *Silur-es* (see SILURIAN *a.*) + -IST.] A native of the district anciently inhabited by the Silures.

Commonly used as the distinguishing epithet of H. Vaughan, who was born in Brecknockshire.

**1650** (*title*), Silex Scintillans: or, Sacred Poems and Priuate Eiaculations by Henry Vaughan Silurist.

**Siluro-** (sɪˈljʊərəʊ), used as combining form of SILURIAN *a.*, as ***Siluro-Cambrian*** adj.

**1855** J. PHILLIPS *Man. Geol.* 118 The Siluro-Cambrian series of Ireland is not yet certainly known to be anywhere complete in one district. **1873** DAWSON *Earth & Man* iv. 56 The Lower Silurian, is the Upper Cambrian of Sedgwick, and may properly be called the Siluro-Cambrian.

**siluroid** (sɪˈljʊərɔɪd), *a.* and *sb. Ichth.* [f. SILUR-US + -OID.]

**A.** *adj.* Of fishes: Belonging to the family *Siluridæ*, of the order *Physostomi*, characterized by the want of true scales, having only a naked skin or large bony plates.

**1849** MURCHISON *Siluria* x. 242 A lower position in the scale than existing Ganoid or possibly Siluroid fishes. **1871** DARWIN *Desc. Man* II. xii. 10 A siluroid fish, inhabiting the fresh waters of South America. **1884** *Athenæum* 13 Dec. 775/1 Certain marine forms—for example,..the siluroid family Ariinæ.

**B.** *sb.* A fish belonging to this family.

**1851** MANTELL *Petrifactions* 439 The Siluroids are related to the Silurus. **1876** *Beneden's Anim. Parasites* 7 A siluroid of Brazil of the genus Platystoma. **1883** *Fish. Exhib. Catal.* (ed. 4) 98 The males of some tropical sheat fishes or Siluroids also perform maternal duties.

**Silurus** (sɪˈljʊərəs). *Ichth.* Pl. Siluri. [a. L. *silurus*, a. Gr. σίλουρος. Cf. SILURE.] A genus of fish typical of the family *Siluridæ*; (also with lower-case initial) a fish belonging to this genus, esp. the sly silurus (*S. glanis*) or sheat-fish, one of the largest fresh-water fishes of Europe.

**1601** HOLLAND *Pliny* I. 243 As for the Silurus, a cut-throat he is wheresoeuer he goeth, a great deuourer. **1774** GOLDSM. *Nat. Hist.* III. i. (1862) II. 299 The Silurus or Sheath-fish. **1836** YARRELL *Brit. Fishes* I. 403 The Sly Silurus, *Silurus glanis.* **1840** tr. *Cuvier's Anim. Kingdom* 317 Their flesh is less disagreeable than that of the other Siluri. **1865** *Spectator* 14 Jan. 50 It is said that the silurus, when the prey is plentiful, will attain over 56 lb. in four years.

**Silva** (ˈsɪlvə). The name of José *Silva* (b. 1914), American electrician, used *attrib.* to denote the theory or methods devised by him to improve the functioning of one's mind.

**1971** *Nat. Observer* (U.S.) 23 Aug. 16/1 Dr. Green faults the Silva method. **1976** *New Yorker* 15 Mar. 140/3 This book traces the frantic pilgrimage he undertook to pull himself together, running through EST, gestalt therapy,.. Esalen, hypnotism, modern dance, meditation, Silva Mind Control, Arica, [etc.]. **1978** SILVA & MIELE *Silva Mind Control Method* 12 The city planner had been trained in Silva Mind Control.

**silva:** see SELVA, SYLVA.

**silvage,** obs. f. SALVAGE, SELVAGE.

**silvagee,** obs. f. SELVAGEE.

**silvan, -ite, -ity,** varr. SYLVAN, -ITE, -ITY.

**silver** (ˈsɪlvə(r)), *sb.* and *a.* Forms: α. 1 siolfor (siolofr-, siolufr-), seolfor, -fur, -fer (seolfr-, seulfr-), 2–3 seoluer (seolur-, 2 seolure), 3 soluer, solure. β. 2, 5 selfer (2 selfr-), 4 selfur; 3–5 seluer (3 selur-, 4 zeluer), 4–5 selver. γ. 1 sylofr, sylfor, -fur, 2 syluer, sylure; 1 sulfer (suulfr-), 3 suelfer, 3–4 suluer. δ. 1 silofr, 3 sillferr; 2–7 siluer (2 silur-, 5 siluere, 6–7 *Sc.* silwer), 4– silver; 4–6 siluir, -vir (5 -uire, -uyre); 4–5 syluere (5 cyl-), 4–7 syluer (5 cyl-), 5–7 sylver (5 -fer, 6 -var); 4 syluyre, 5 -uir, 5–6 -vir; 5 sylure, -wor, 6 -uur. ε. *Sc.* 6 syller, 6– siller. [Common Teut.: OE. *siolfor, seolfor*, etc., = OFris. *selover, selver* (later *selvir, silver*; WFris. *sulver*, dial. *selver*), OLFrank. *silver* (MDu. *silver, selver, sulver*, Du. *zilver*), OS. *silubar, silobar* (MLG. and LG. *silver, sülver, sulver*, etc.), OHG. *sil(a)bar, silbir*, etc. (MHG. and G. *silber*), ON. *silfr* (Icel. *silfur*, Sw. *silfver*; MSw. *silf, self, sylf*, Norw. *sylv*, Da. *sølv*), Goth. *silubr*. Related forms are found in the Balto-Slavic languages, as OSlav. *sĭrebro*, Russ. *serebro*, Pol. *śrebro*, etc., Lith. *sidabras*, Lett. *sudrabs*; as to the relationship of these and the ultimate origin of the word no definite conclusions have been established.]

**I. 1.** One of the precious metals (in general use ranking next to gold), characterized in a pure state by its lustrous white colour and great malleability and ductility. Chemical symbol Ag.

Various forms of the metal, pure or mixed with other substances, are distinguished by defining terms, as *antimonial, bromic, horn, native, red, ruby silver; capillary, shell silver*, etc. The name is also given to several natural or artificial substances resembling or imitating the real metal, as *cat, German, inflammable, mock silver.*

α. β. *c* **825** *Vesp. Psalter* lxv. 10 Swe mid fyre bið amearad seolfur. *c* **897** K. ÆLFRED *Gregory's Past. C.* xxxvii. 268 Ðonne bið hit swiðe leaslice on siolofres [*v.r.* siolufres] hiewe. **971** *Blickl. Hom.* 127 Nu hit is mid golde & mid seolfre ȝefrætwod. *a* **1175** *Cott. Hom.* 227 Hi worhtan ham anlicnessen, sum of golde, sum of selfre. *a* **1225** *Leg. Kath.* 493 þeos maumez beoð imaket of gold, & of seoluer. *c* **1290** *S. Eng. Leg.* I. 4/115 Of seluer and of gold one riche schrine heo wrouȝte. *a* **1400** N. T. (Paues) *1 Cor.* iii. 12 Gold, oþer selfer, oþer precyous stones. **1418** in *E.E. Wills* 32, vj disshes & vj Sawcers of seluer.

γ. δ. *c* **950** *Lindisf. Gosp.* John p. 188 Mid suulfre ofergylded. *a* **1000** *Riddles* xv. 2 Nu mec wlonc þeceð ȝeong haȝostealdmon golde & sylfore. *a* **1300** *E.E. Psalter* lxv. 9 þou fraisted vs, als siluer fraisted isse. *a* **1340** HAMPOLE *Psalter* xi. 7 Imange all metalles nan is þat swetterly chymes þan syluere. *c* **1440** *Promp. Parv.* 77 Cyluer, *argentum.* **1463** *Bury Wills* (Camden) 42 A peyre of bedys of sylvir. **1526** *Pilgr. Perf.* (W. de W. 1531) 3 Saynt Gregory..sayth that electrum is a myxture of syluer & golde myngled togyder. **1591** SYLVESTER *Du Bartas* I. iii. 902 Deck't with Coperass, With Gold and Silver, Lead, and Mercury. **1613** DEKKER *Strange Horse Race* Wks. (Grosart) III. 327 There likewise should you behold a Mine of Siluer, ambitiously aspiring to bee as glorious Gold. **1697** DAMPIER *Voy.* I. 269 The Silver here, and all over the Kingdom of Mexico, is said to be finer and richer in proportion than that of Potosi or Peru. **1738** GRAY *Tasso* 59 Sulphurous veins and liveing silver shine. **1779** *Mirror* No. 17, A crooked piece of silver, which he, at first, mistook for a shilling. **1813** SIR H. DAVY *Agric. Chem.* (1814) 47 Silver..burns more readily than platinum or gold. **1870** YEATS *Nat. Hist. Comm.* 359 Silver is obtained from its ores chiefly by roasting, crushing, and amalgamation with mercury.

*fig. a* **1628** PRESTON *Breastpl. Love* (1631) 187 The goodman..there is silver and golde in his speeches and actions, that is, they are likewise precious. **1897** RHOSCOMYL *White Rose Arno* 45 His tongue was silver and his heart was fire.

ε. **1575** *Gammer Gurton* II. i, As bright as any syller,..& straight as any pyller. **1725** RAMSAY *Gentle Sheph.* I. i, With sprainqs like gowd, and siller cross'd with black.

†**b.** *transf.* Quicksilver. *Obs.*

**1607** J. DAVIES (Heref.) *Summa Totalis* Wks. (Grosart) I. 13/1 Siluer selfe-mouing, we call Siluer-quick.

**c.** With *a* and pl. A piece or strip of silver.

**1856** *Orr's Circle Sci.*, *Pract. Chem.* 80 They are connected, all the zincs by one wire, and all the silvers by another wire.

**d.** *ellipt.* for *silver medal* (see sense 21 a below).

**1960** [see GOLD[1] 8 d]. **1968** *Guardian* 22 Oct. 1/1 Major Alhusen, aged 55, won the silver in the individual event, and was only two points off taking the gold. **1979** 'D. GRANT' *Moscow 5000* i. 19 Notes that would help him to win an Olympic medal. Because he would have the Silver, he told himself.

**2.** The metal regarded as a valuable possession or medium of exchange; hence, silver coin; also (chiefly *Sc.*), money in general.

α. *c* **825** *Vesp. Psalter* civ. 37 Dryhten..utalædde hie in seolfre & golde. *c* **950** *Lindisf. Gosp.* John p. 188 Æhtu ora seulfres. *a* **1122** *O.E. Chron.* (Laud MS.) an. 1102, þeofas ..þær inne naman mycel to gode on golde & on seolfre. *c* **1205** LAY. 15050 Ʒe.. senden after cnihtes, & ȝeuen heom soluer & gold. *c* **1275** in *O.E. Misc.* 89 Habbe he þe yeftes of seoluer and of golde.

β. *a* **1200** *Vices & Virtues* 33 Ne haue ðu hope te golde ne to seluer. *c* **1250** *Serm.* in *O.E. Misc.* 188 Euer of þe purse þat seluer heo tulleþ. **1340** *Ayenb.* 6 Aye þise heste zeneȝeþ þo þet to moche louieþ hire guod gold oþer zeluer. *c* **1450** *Bk. Curtasye* 745 in *Babees Bk.*, Seluer he [the almoner] deles rydand by way. **1472** *Presentmts. Juries* in *Surtees Misc.* (1890) 24 Yf it cane be prewyd þat he his bed [= is bid] no selver tharfor.

γ. *c* **897** K. ÆLFRED *Gregory's Past. C.* xlviii. 368 Gold & sylofr ic him sealde ȝenoh. *c* **950** *Lindisf. Gosp.* Matt. x. 9 Nallas ȝe aȝneȝe gold ne sulfer [*Rushw.* sylfur] ne feh on gyrdilsum iurum. **1154** *O.E. Chron.* (Laud MS.) an. 1135, Wua sua bare his byrthen gold & sylure. *c* **1205** LAY. 3570 Wenne þu wult more suluer sæche hit at me suluen. **1297** R. GLOUC. (Rolls) 7779 þe king in such manere suluer wan ynou. **1393** LANGL. *P. Pl.* C. IV. 116 þe meyre hue by-souhte Of alle suche sellers suluer to take.

δ. *c* **897** K. ÆLFRED *Gregory's Past. C.* xlviii. 368 Ðonne he doð..ðæt silofr to diofolȝieldum. **1128** *O.E. Chron.* (Laud MS.) an. 1128, Se kyng..micele ȝersumes him ȝeaf on gold & on silure. *c* **1200** *Trin. Coll. Hom.* 228 [They] waren al to gradi of siluer and of golde. *c* **1340** HAMPOLE *Pr. Consc.* 4434 He sal gyf þam..Of gold and silver gret plente. **1411** *E.E. Wills* (1882) 20 þe siluer þat schal be reseyvyd for þe londes. **1484** *Coventry Leet Bk.* 517 To gedur syluer for th' Reparacion of the same. **1583** *Leg. Bp. St. Androis* 971 The vther..Concludit schortlie for to slea him, For vyling of his syluer fra him. **1604** E. G[RIMSTONE] *D'Acosta's Hist. Indies* IV. xxxii. 295, I meane by profitable plants, those, which.. bring silver to theyr maisters. **1620** T. GRANGER *Div. Logike* 201 He hath bequeathed all his siluer to me: *ergo*, his ready money. **1800** *Asiatic Ann. Reg.* 67/2 He afterwards distributed silver, to the amount of one lack of rupees. **1845** BROWNING *Lost Leader* 1 Just for a handful of silver he left us.

ε. *c* **1720** RAMSAY *Last Speech Miser* i, Am I forc'd to die, And nae mair my dear siller see? **1790** BURNS *Tam o' Shanter* 24 Ilka melder, wi' the miller, Thou sat as lang as thou had siller. **1818** SCOTT *Rob Roy* xx, She'll hae a hantle siller. **1843** BETHUNE *Sc. Fireside Stor.* 48 Nobody will lend him siller. **1896** W. HARVEY *Kennethcrook* 52 (E.D.D.), It was seldom the weaver would come to any terms other than 'siller doon'.

†**b.** The price in silver *of* something. *Obs.*[−1]

**1411** *E.E. Wills* (1882) 19 þat alle þe londes be sold, and þe Siluer þere-of spendyd to þe avauncement of lucie, my dowter.

**3.** Articles made of silver or an alloy of silver; silverware, silver-plate.

**13..** *K. Alis.* (Laud MS.) 1156 He dude seruen Olympias In golde, in siluer [*W.* seolver], in bras, in glas. *c* **1420** *Anturs of Arth.* xxxvi, In siluer sa semly þai serue þame of the beste. *c* **1480** *Paston Lett.* III. 271, ij. lynen bagges..

with broke silver and j. old harneis gilt. **1665** SIR T. HERBERT *Trav.* (1677) 313 The Persians for the most part eat in Porcellane or earth, not valuing Silver. **1794** MRS. RADCLIFFE *Myst. Udolpho* xliv, The profusion of gold and silver that glittered on the sideboards. **1842** TENNYSON *Will Waterproof* 127 [He] Sipt wine from silver. **1864** —— *Enoch Arden* 742 For cups and silver on the burnish'd board Sparkled and shone.

*pl.* **1830** TENNYSON *Recoll. Arab. Nts.* 125 A million tapers flaring bright From twisted silvers.

**4.** The metal as used for the ornamentation of textile fabrics; silver thread. ***cloth of silver***: see CLOTH *sb.* 9 c.

**1423** *Rolls of Parlt.* IV. 255/1 Brauderie..wrought with Gold or Silver of Cipre. **1566** in Hay Fleming *Mary Q. of Scots* (1897) 499 Ten hankis off gold and ten hankis of silver the fynest that can be gottin. **1599** SHAKS. *Much Ado* III. iv. 20 Cloth a gold and cuts, and lac'd with siluer. **1611** —— *Cymb.* II. iv. 69 Her Bed-chamber..was hang'd With Tapistry of Silke, and Siluer. **1805** SCOTT *Last Minstrel* v. xvi, His cloak was all of Poland fur, His hose with silver twin'd.

**5.** As a tincture in heraldry, more commonly called ARGENT, but cf. quot. 1868.

*c* **1450** HOLLAND *Howlat* 415 A lyoun..Of siluir ȝe se shold To ramp in array. **1478** in W. G. D. Fletcher *Shropsh. Grants of Arms* (1909) 12 A cross engrayled gold or bythwen foure rosses silver, and to his tymbre a gauntelet sillver sette in a wrethe gold. **1562** LEGH *Armory* (1597) 4 Called Siluer, and blased by the name of Argent. **1728** CHAMBERS *Cycl.* s.v. *Metal*, In Engraving [arms], Gold is expressed by dotting the Coat, &c. all over; Silver, by leaving it quite blank. **1814** SCOTT *Lord of Isles* v. xxxii, Saint Andrew's cross, in blazonry Of silver, waving wide! **1868** CUSSANS *Her.* (1893) 50 In blazoning a Charge..supposed to be actually composed of metal..the terms *gold* and *silver* should be employed.

**6.** A silvery colour or lustre.

**1481** CAXTON *Reynard* xxxii. (Arb.) 85 Wherin stode somme strange hystoryes whiche were of gold, of sable, of siluer. **1592** SHAKS. *Rom. & Jul.* II. ii. 108 By yonder Moone I vow, That tips with siluer all these Fruite tree tops. **1784** COWPER *Task* I. 310 The willow such, And poplar, that with silver lines his leaf. **1820** SHELLEY *Prometh. Unb.* III. iii. 71 See the pale azure fading into silver. **1848** THACKERAY *Van. Fair* lviii, There were scarce three lines of silver in her soft brown hair. **1896** BLACK *Briseis* xvii, A swan came breasting along,..leaving behind it two flashing divergent lines of silver.

**7. a.** A variety of insect, fish, bird, etc., having silvery colouring or markings.

**1832** J. RENNIE *Butterfl. & M.* 76 The Tawny Silver. **1875** *Spectator* (Melbourne) 19 June 81/1 Common fish, such as..garfish, strangers, silvers, and others. **1879** L. WRIGHT *Pigeon Keeper* 96 Silvers are divided into what is called brown barred and black-barred. **1903** F. SIMPSON *Bk. Cat* xii. 138 At present our silvers are too full of tabby markings. **1934** *Nat. Geogr. Mag.* Feb. 211 There are four distinct species of salmon which run up the Columbia: the chinook, silver, sockeye, and chum. **1955** [see CHINOOK b].

**b.** *Photogr.* A salt of silver, *esp.* nitrate of silver.

**1891** in *Cent. Dict.* **1892** *Photogr. Ann.* II. 61 In the dark room add the silver to the collodion.

**II.** *attrib.* passing into *adj.*

**8. a.** Made or consisting of silver.

These collocations may be employed as the base of formations like *silver medallist* (see 21 a), *silver trumpeter*, etc.

**1032** in *Anglia* XI. 8 Do hi ealle to gædere þæt þritig seolfor sticca. *a* **1300** *Cursor M.* 4858 He..did a siluer cupe at hide In a sek. *Ibid.* 8242 A siluer cercle. ? **1366** CHAUCER *Rom. Rose* 97 A sylvre nedle forth I drough Out of an aguiler. **1424** *E.E. Wills* (1882) 58 One of my siluere girdeles. **1457–8** *Cal. Anc. Rec. Dublin* (1889) 297 To ber ii. sylver masys befor the Baylyfys. **1486** *Bk. St. Albans* c vij, Clense theym clene with a syluer spone. **1530** PALSGR. 270/1 Sylver vessell, *uessaile dargent.* **1563** WINȜET *Wks.* (S.T.S.) I. 114 Quhy iuge ȝe the goldin and siluir chalissis? **1621** ELSING *Debates Ho. Lords* (Camden) 33 The manufacture of gold and sylver thrydd. **1669** R. MONTAGU in *Buccleuch MSS.* (Hist. MSS. Comm.) I. 440, I am sure without this my Lord St. Alban's would not have left a silver spoon in the house. **1685** BOYLE *Eff. Motion* v. 55, I caused a Watch to be suspended by a little Silver-chain. **1725** *Portland Papers* VI. (Hist. MSS. Comm.) 83 Plenty of silver tumblers. **1764** *Ann. Reg.* 79 The size of the watch is something less than a silver two-pence. **1808** SCOTT in *Lockhart* (1869) III. xviii. 159, I..have only hopes that he may be shot with a silver bullet. **1858** SIMMONDS *Dict. Trade* s.v., The British silver coinage consists of crowns, half-crowns [etc.]. **1889** GRETTON *Memory's Harkback* 84 You will value the old silver inkstand.

**b.** In fig. contexts. (See also SPOON *sb.*)

**1602** *2nd Pt. Return fr. Parnass.* II. v. 764 We schollers fish for a liuing in these shallow foardes without a siluer hoock. **1605** BRETON *Honour Valour* viii, To fish for honour with a siluer hooke. **1611** COTGR. s.v. *Combattre*, Those that with siluer weapons fight are sure to ouercome. **1679, 1798** [see KEY *sb.*[1] 3 b]. **1805** SCOTT *Last Minstrel* v. xiii, True love..is the secret sympathy, The silver link, the silken tie [etc.]. **1843** LE FEVRE *Life Trav. Phys.* II. I. xiii. 22 They may be bribed, as we proved..when our cavalcade passed the barriers with a silver key.

**c.** Containing threads of silver, or some imitation of this.

**1728** CHAMBERS *Cycl.* s.v., Threads of pure Silver, interwove like a Silver Galoon, that has been burnt to get out the Silk. **1799** G. SMITH *Laboratory* II. 298 Silver-twist-hackle. Dub with the herl of an ostrich feather. **1858** SIMMONDS *Dict. Trade, Silver-lace*, wire coated with silver, and woven into lace. **1882** CAULFEILD & SAWARD *Dict. Needlewk.* 225/1 The Gold and Silver Laces of the present day consist of warp threads of silk, or silk and cotton combined.

**d.** Mounted or plated with silver; wrapped in silvered paper.

**1898** *Daily News* 6 Apr. 5/3 The prizes include silver handglasses and scent-bottles. **1904** *Windsor Mag.* Jan. 238/2 Tiny silver comfits wedged into every available little space.

**9.** Producing or yielding silver.

*c* **1475** *Pict. Voc.* in Wr.-Wülcker 798 *Hec argentifodina*, a sylverquarelle. *a* **1490** BOTONER *Itin.* (Nasmith, 1778) 105 Beereferrys ubi les sylver mynes fodiuntur. **1548** ELYOT, *Argentaria fodina*, a..syluer myne. *c* **1610** *Women Saints* 1 The precious earth of golde and siluer mines. **1648** HEXHAM II, *Een Zilver-ader*, a Silver-veine. **1701** DE FOE *True-born Eng.* I. 6 With all the Silver Mountains of Peru. **1789** J. WILLIAMS *Min. Kingd.* I. 257 They have for a long time been working it as a rich silver mine. **1839** DE LA BECHE *Rep. Geol. Cornwall* x. 284 As true silver-lodes are found in it, it may also be termed argentiferous. **1877** RAYMOND *Statist. Mines & Mining* 344 Some promising silver-lodes have lately been taken up. **1892** GUNTER *Miss Dividends* (1893) 9 A promising market for various silver properties.

**b.** *U.S.* (See quot.)

**1896** *Westm. Gaz.* 10 July 2/1 The 'Silver Senators'—that is, the representatives of silver-producing States.

**10.** Of or pertaining to, connected with, characteristic of, silver.

**1610** HEALEY *St. Aug. Citie of God* 262 The gold-smith in the silver-streete. *a* **1618** J. DAVIES (Heref.) *Witte's Pilgr.* Wks. (Grosart) II. 47/1 Riuers of Nectar ran on golden Sand (With siluer-cleerenesse) through that Paradice. **1670** PETTUS *Fodinæ Reg.* 33 Near to which are conveniently placed the Smelting and Refining Mills, which therefore are called the Silver Mills. **1681** GREW *Musæum* III. ii. i. 324 White Silver Ore, or of a silver-colour, from Cremnitz in Hungary. **1813** *Edin. Rev.* XXII. 148 Von Buch engaged a place in the silver-waggon. **1860** *Chambers's Encycl.* I. 158/1 Our gold and silver standards similarly stated would be 917 and 925 respectively. **1887** *Encycl. Brit.* XXII. 73/2 This alleged fall, its causes, consequences, and remedies, constitute the 'Silver Question'.

**b.** Denoting compounds of which silver forms a part.

**1797** *Encycl. Brit.* (ed. 3) XI. 442/1 Some silver amalgama is pressed upon it through a chamois skin. **1849** D. CAMPBELL *Inorg. Chem.* 8 Silver-salts exposed to light become black by the absorption of oxygen. **1868** *Fownes' Chem.* (ed. 10) 354 When chlorine gas is passed over fused silver fluoride, silver chlorine is formed. **1879** *Cassell's Techn. Educ.* II. 123/1 Gold of 20 carats with 4 carats of silver alloy.

**c.** Of or pertaining to silver articles or silverware.

**1648** HEXHAM II, *Een Zilver-schappraeye*, a Silver-cupboord. **1686, 1725** [see SCULLERY 1 b]. **1883** *Pall Mall G.* 17 April 5/1 Finding that the silver trade has rejected..what he proposed as a boon.

**d.** Advocating, relating to, etc., the adoption of silver as a currency or standard.

**1879** *Bradstreet's* 22 Oct. 5/1 The silver men are as violent and rampant as ever. **1890** *Daily News* 10 Feb. 2/4 Why should we not have stored bullion instead? Silver men will probably answer [etc.]. **1893** *Nation* 29 June 467/1 The very little game which our silver-bugs..are trying to play on us. **1901** *N. Amer. Rev.* Feb. 271 The silver cabal won at every point.

**11. a.** Used for holding (silver) money. *rare.*

**1526** *Galway Arch.* in *10th Rep. Hist. MSS. Comm.* App. V. 402 Every man or woman which makith aquavitie, honied alle [or] singill alle to be ratiffied and sold, to paye the accostomid ratte to the silver boxe. **1773** FERGUSSON *Sitting of Session* vii, Gin ony..has na lous'd his siller pocks. *a* **1837** R. NICOLL *Poems* (1842) 110 Misers make Their heaven o' a siller bag.

†**b.** *Sc.* Of payments, etc.: Made or levied in (silver) money. *Obs.*

**1579** *Reg. Privy Council Scot.* III. 143 To pay to thame the ..sylvir prices and maillis of the samyn. **1596** MELVILL *Autobiog.* (Wodrow Soc.) 332 Setting..lyff-rents successive for peyment of small siluer-dewtie. **1597** SKENE *De Verb. Sign.* s.v. *Firmarius*, Quhidder it be siluer-maill, victuall, or vther deutie. *a* **1688** DALLAS *Stiles* 279 Which Lands..amount in yearly free Rent..to [so much] Silver-Rent. **1754** ERSKINE *Princ. Law Scot.* IV. ii. (1870) 587 Even intromission with the silver rent.

**c.** Played for stakes in silver coin.

**1748** H. WALPOLE *Lett.* (1846) II. 223 There were silver pharaoh and whist for the ladies.

**12.** Having the whiteness or lustre of silver; silvery. Chiefly *poet.*

***silver lining***: see LINING *vbl. sb.*[1] 2 b.

*c* **1386** CHAUCER *Knt.'s T.* 636 And firy Phebus..dryeth in the greues The siluer dropes hangynge on the leues. *c* **1407** LYDG. *Reson & Sens.* 937 The freshnes of the clere wellys..Made the colde siluer stremes To shyne ageyn the sonne bemes. *c* **1450** —— *Secrees* 1316 The lusty Silvir dewh in the grene meedys. *c* **1450** HOLLAND *Howlat* 410 Ane..bure in till asure..Siluer sternis so fair. **1593** SHAKS. *Rich. II*, II. i. 46 This precious stone, set in the siluer sea. **1605** —— *Macb.* II. iii. 118 Here lay Duncan, His Siluer skinne lac'd with his Golden Blood. **1697** DRYDEN *Virg. Past.* VII. 52 Fair Galatea, with thy silver Feet, O, whiter than the Swan. **1738** GRAY *Propertius* iii. 21 Yonder Star..with silver light Relumes her crescent Orb to cheer the dreary Night. **1792** S. ROGERS *Pleas. Mem.* II. 202 In gentler climes their silver currents flow. **1855** KINGSLEY *Westw. Ho!* xii, A lodging..which looked out upon the silver Thames (for Thames was silver then). **1879** FARRAR *St. Paul* I. 257 Brightening more and more with the silver dawn.

**b.** Of the hair, beard, or head, when white with age. Also in fig. context.

**1590** NASHE *Pasquil's Apol.* Wks. (Grosart) I. 253 Auncient men, vpon whose siluer heads the Almond-tree hath blossomde. **1592** LYLY *Midas* II. i, If one be olde, & haue siluer haires on his beard. **1606** *Sir Gyles Goosecappe* v. i, This speech hath silver haires, and reverence askes. **1633** P. FLETCHER *Purple Isl.* VII. xl, Her silver heads adorning, (Her dotage index). **1810** JANE PORTER *Sc. Chiefs* xxviii, The long silver beard..hung over his hands. **1833** TENNYSON *May Queen* III. iv, O blessings on his kindly heart and on his silver head! **1850** —— *In Mem.* lxxxiv, To reverence and the silver hair.

*transf.* **1597** SHAKS. *2 Hen. IV*, IV. i. 43 You, Lord Arch-bishop,..Whose Beard, the Siluer Hand of Peace hath touch'd. **1635–56** COWLEY *Davideis* II. 706 No Silver Rev'rence guards the stooping Age.

**13.** Of sounds: Having a clear gentle resonance like that of silver; soft-toned, melodious.

**1526** *Pilgr. Perf.* (W. de W. 1531) 142 We shal yelde a benigne & gentyll answere, & gyue a swete syluer sounde as yᵉ tryed syluer. **1592** BRETON *C'tess Pembroke's Love* vii, Some brought in musicke of most siluer sounde. **1613** W. BROWNE *Brit. Past.* I. v. 93 A Swaine (with Lawrell crown'd) Marrying his sweet Noates with their siluer sound. **1629** MILTON *Hymn Nat.* xiii, Let your silver chime Move in melodious time. **1725** POPE *Odyss.* I. 426 The vaulted roof ..Reflecting to the queen the silver sounds. **1801** BUSBY *Dict. Mus.* s.v. *Viol d'amour*, A kind of silver sound, at once ..soft, sweet, and tender. **1839** MARRYAT *Phant. Ship* iii, He recalled..her silver voice. **1857** LD. DUFFERIN *Lett. High Lat.* 160 A mingled stream of music, light, and silver laughter.

**b.** Eloquent, persuasive, sweet-spoken.

**1594** in Ingelby *Shaks. Cent. Praise* 12 As worthie subjects of your silver pen. **1713** ARBUTHNOT *John Bull* II. viii, Serjeant such-a-one has a Silver Tongue at the Bar. **1833** HT. MARTINEAU *Briery Creek* iv, It must be such a silver tongue as never yet spoke that could persuade any nation [etc.]. **1851** D. JERROLD *St. Giles* xv. 150 Mr...Crawley; to whose silver tongue the world owed the liberty of many a ruffian. **1896** MRS. CAFFYN *Quaker Grandmother* 198, I..would give my eyes for..the silver tongues of them.

**14.** *poet.* **a.** Soft, gentle.

**1596** SPENSER *F.Q.* VI. ix. 22 All the night in siluer sleepe I spend.

**b.** Prosperous, happy. Cf. SILVER AGE 1.

**1659–60** *Ph. Skippon's Petit. to Citie of London* 1 Alas, those Silver daies are done, and this iron Age hath overtaken your poor Petitioner.

**15.** Of or pertaining to the silver age of Latin (see SILVER AGE 1 b).

**1889** JACOBS *Æsop* 14 Some of the fables..were products of Silver Latinity. **1896** *N. & Q.* 8th Ser. IX. 487 In any given passage in a silver Latin author. *Ibid.*, One of the best-known authors of the silver period, Juvenal.

**III.** *Comb.*

**16.** Objective or obj. genitive: **a.** With agent-nouns, as ***silver-chaser, -lover, -miner***, etc.

*a* **1400** N. T. (Paues) *Acts* xix. 24 For one, whos name was Demetrye, þat was a siluer-maker,..he gafe [etc.]. **1483** *Cath. Angl.* 340/1 A Syluer maker or keper, *argentarius.* **1680** C. NESS *Ch. Hist.* 242 Those sordid silver-lovers..being courtiers had a fair opportunity. **1692** *Lond. Gaz.* No. 2770/4 A Silver-spinner in Bunhill-fields. **1718** W. PENN *Wks.* (1726) I. 713, I being a Silver-Spinster. **1772** *Ann. Reg.* 153 Mr. Mansel, silver polisher, in Corbet-court. **1815** *Niles' Register* VIII. 141/2 There are..2 silver platers; 3 trunk makers [etc.]. **1819** *Pantologia* X, *Silver-beater*, one that foliates silver. **1846** HOLTZAPFFEL *Turning* II. 731 The silver-piercer sits at the silversmiths' and jewellers' ordinary work-bench. **1848** DICKENS *Dombey* viii, She is alive,..and is married to a silver-chaser. **1858** SIMMONDS *Dict. Trade, Silver-plater*, an electrotyper. **1869** 'MARK TWAIN' *Innoc. Abroad* vi. 57 To speak after the fashion of the silver-miners. **1875** KNIGHT *Dict. Mech.* 1195/2 The bane of the gold and silver miner.

**b.** With pres. pples., as ***silver-bearing, -producing, -shaming***, etc.

**1591** SHAKS. *Two Gentl.* III. i. 230 Sad sighes, deepe grones, nor siluer-shedding teares. **1648** HERRICK *Hesper., Vision*, Sitting alone..Close by a Silver-shedding Brook. *a* **1699** J. BEAUMONT *Minor Poems, Whiteness*, The Silver-shaming Grace Of the Moon's unclouded Face. *c* **1710** YALDEN *To Sir H. Mackworth* xiv, The Silver-shedding Beams of Orient Light. **1877** RAYMOND *Statist. Mines & Mining* 251, 2 to 3 feet of silver-bearing quartz. **1888** *Daily News* 5 Apr. 5/2 If Lancashire depends for custom upon silver-using countries to this extent. **1891** *Ibid.* 23 Feb. 5/7 The popular reaction against free coinage continues, extending even to the silver-producing States.

**c.** With vbl. sbs. or nouns of action, as ***silver-mining, -plating, -reduction.***

**1842** *Penny Cycl.* XXII. 25/1 The art of silver-plating was introduced at Sheffield about the middle of the last century. **1856** *Orr's Circ. Sci., Pract. Chem.* 47 The vats used for ordinary silver-plating are about twenty-four or thirty inches deep. **1872** 'MARK TWAIN' *Roughing It* p. iv, The silver-mining fever in Nevada. **1877** RAYMOND *Statist. Mines & Mining* p. ix, In all silver-reduction works. *Ibid.* 245 The silver-mining of Beaver Head County.

**17.** Parasynthetic and instrumental, of the types ***silver-armed, -axled, -bearded, -bowed, -breasted***, etc.; ***silver-bound, -mounted***, etc.

Such combinations have been very extensively used, esp. in poetry, and the number which might be formed is very great. In addition to those illustrated here, see SILVER-COLOURED, -FOOTED, -HAIRED, etc.

**a.** Denoting the use of the metal itself.

**1598** MARSTON *Sco. Villanie* I. iii, A hoode, and siluer-handled fan. **1634** MILTON *Comus* 442 Fair silver-shafted Queen for ever chaste. *c* **1640** —— *Arcades* 33 Fair silver-buskind Nymphs. **1680** *Lond. Gaz.* No. 1495/4 A Case of Silver-hafted Knives. **1748** SMOLLETT *R. Random* II. xliv. 79 A pair of silver mounted pistols. **1753** HANWAY *Trav.* (1762) II. I. ix. 49 The serjeants of the guards have silver-laced regimentals. **1813** SCOTT *Let.* in *Lockhart* (1837) III. ii. 99, I..delight in collecting silver-mounted pistols and ataghans. **1819** —— *Ivanhoe* xlv, Rowena opened the small silver-chased casket. **1843** DICKENS *Mart. Chuz.* (1844) xix. 237 To provide silver-plated handles of the very best description. **1848** THACKERAY *Van. Fair* xxxvii, There was the jewel-case, silver-clasped. **1869** TOZER *Highl. Turkey* II. 259 [He] bids [his horse]..to dig for him a grave..with his silver-plated hoofs. **1881** O. WILDE *Poems* 67 Sweeter far if silver-sandalled foot Of some long-hidden God should ever tread The Nuneham meadows. **1889** P. H. EMERSON *Eng. Idyls* 18 The grandmother looked..over her silver-rimmed spectacles. **1894** 'MARK TWAIN' *Those Twins* v. 393 The Judge..laid aside his silver-bowed spectacles. **1916** JOYCE

*Portrait of Artist* (1969) v. 176 He would think of the cloistral silverveined prose of Newman. **1916** BLUNDEN *Harbingers* 63 So silver-sandalled down those golden ways He triumphs. **1922** JOYCE *Ulysses* 506 He carries a silverstringed inlaid dulcimer... He wears dark velvet hose and silverbuckled pumps. **1928** 'BRENT OF BIN BIN' *Up Country* xv. 258 He was filling a bolster with articles of jewellery, silver-backed brushes, hand mirrors, candlesticks, silver-topped bottles, &c. **1944** W. FORTESCUE *Mountain Madness* i. 22 A wide silver-studded black leather belt. **1939** D. CECIL *Young Melbourne* vi. 155 She also created scandal by appearing..imperfectly disguised as a page, in a plumed hat, silver-laced jacket and tight scarlet pantaloons. **1976** 'D. HALLIDAY' *Dolly & Nanny Bird* xiii. 170 There's a white leather gift box in every cabin, fitted out with..silver-topped crystal bottles.

**b.** With allusion to the sound of silver.

**1593** T. WATSON *Poems* (Arb.) 191 Ioyfull birds..Whose siluer tuned songs might well haue moued her. **1608** SHAKS. *Per.* v. i. 111 My dearest wife was like this maid,..As silver-voiced. **1642** H. MORE *Song of Soul* To Rdr., I strike my silver-sounded lyre. **1844** MRS. BROWNING *Lady Geraldine's Courtship* xxii, Though sometimes she would bind me with her silver-corded speeches. **1884** *Cassell's Fam. Mag.* Apr. 271/2 The beautiful note of the silver-voiced bell-bird.

**c.** With reference to the colour or lustre of silver.

**1591** SYLVESTER *Du Bartas* I. iii. 214 The silver-fronted Star, That swells and shrinks the Seas. **1596** FITZ-GEFFRAY *Sir F. Drake* (1881) 25 Her silver-feathered turtle-doves. **1606** DEKKER *Seven Deadly Sins* Wks. (Grosart) II. 69 Euen the siluer-bearded..citizens haue giuen him welcomes. **1645** G. DANIEL *Poems* Wks. (Grosart) II. 76 When silver-winged Peace againe shall Shine. **1791** COWPER *Iliad* II. 924 The silver-eddied Peneus. **1820** SHELLEY *Witch Atlas* lvii, Like a calm flock of silver-fleeced sheep. **1830** MISS MITFORD *Village* Ser. III. (1863) 82 A silver-barked beech, or a lime tree in full blossom. **1851** J. G. WHITTIER in *National Era* 3 Jan. 106/4 Whose small waves on a silver-sanded shore Whisper of peace. **1852** TENNYSON *Ode Wellington* 136 A saviour of the silver-coasted isle. **1881** O. WILDE *Poems* 24 Lure the silver-breasted Helena Back from the lotus meadows of the dead. **1884** BROWNING *Ferishtah* 112 And where's the gloom now?—silver-smitten straight, One glow and variegation! **1903** KIPLING *Five Nations* 2 The inrolling walls of the fog and the silver-winged breeze that disperses. **1926** *Spectator* 11 Sept. 370/1 Wide silver-breasted rivers flowing to a sunlit sea. **1937** *Burlington Mag.* May 252/2 Two bowls of *Chien yao*... One is of the silver-flecked variety. **1957** R. CAMPBELL *Coll. Poems* II. 121 On the silver-sanded shores. **1962** *Daily Tel.* 5 Oct. 22/2 The silver-suited astronaut. **1967** *Coast to Coast 1965–6* 32 All manner of fabulous creatures of the deep surged and surfaced amid the molten silver-flecked arrowing lines of foaming waves.

**d.** In specific names of animals, birds, fishes, plants, etc.

**1688** HOLME *Armoury* III. 55/2 The Spanish *Silver-cupped Moly. **1752** HILL *Hist. Anim.* 252 The *silver-eyed Sparus. **1802** SHAW *Gen. Zool.* III. II. 431 Silver-eyed Snake... A Siberian species. **1809** *Ibid.* VII. II. 366 Silver-eyed crow... Native of South America. **1902** *Encycl. Brit.* XXXI. 876/1 Another useful race of compact form.., called the *silver-laced Wyandotte. **1887** BELDON in Wright *Illustr. Bk. Poultry* 382 These and all other names are gradually giving way to that of *Silver-pencilled Hamburghs. **1849** D. J. BROWNE *Amer. Poultry Yd.* (1855) 59 In the '*silver-spangled' variety, the only perceptible difference is, that the ground color is a silvery white. **1871** DARWIN *Desc. Man* II. xiv. (1890) 426 The Golden and Silver-spangled Polish..breeds. **1803** SHAW *Gen. Zool.* IV. II. 540 *Silver-spotted Sciæna... Native of the Arabian seas. **1884** GOODE *Nat. Hist. Aquat. Anim.* 320 The Silver-spotted Tunny, *Orcynus argentivittatus*. **1804** SHAW *Gen. Zool.* V. I. 174 *Silver-striped Herring... Native of the Indian and American seas. **1833** *Penny Cycl.* I. 78/2 The sycamore maple,..Silver-striped. **1882** *Cassell's Nat. Hist.* VI. 45 The *Silver-studded Blue (*Polymmatus ægon*) is common on heaths. **1819** G. SAMOUELLE *Entomol. Compend.*, *Argynnis Paphia*, the *silver-washed Fritillary. **1859** W. S. COLEMAN *Woodlands* (1866) 147 One of our handsomest butterflies—The Silver-washed Fritillary.

**18.** With pres. pples., in the sense of 'like, or with, silver', as ***silver-eddying***, ***-flashing***, ***-flowing***, etc.

**1590** SPENSER *F.Q.* II. xii. 71 The siluer sounding instruments. **1593** SHAKS. *Lucrece* 24 The morning's silver-melting dew. **1594** GREENE & LODGE *Looking Gl. G.*'s Wks. (Rtldg.) 117 Rounded with Lycus' silver-flowing streams. **1634** SIR T. HERBERT *Trav.* 46 The Siluer-shining Sand expresseth Sulpher. **1648** J. BEAUMONT *Psyche* x. cclxxiv, When Eloquence's tributary streams After the Silver-thrilling Current run. **1725** POPE *Odyssey* I. 464 Pallas..In slumber clos'd her silver-streaming eyes. **1742** GRAY *Eton* 10 Wanders the hoary Thames along His silver-winding way. **1830** TENNYSON *Recoll. Arab. Nts.* 51 The central fountain's flow Fall'n silver-chiming. **1845** HIRST *Poems* 77 Whence arise..his silver-swelling strains? **1871** PALGRAVE *Lyr. Poems* 46 The steel..Hung silver-glittering on high. **1932** D. GASCOYNE *Roman Balcony* 33 And through their long-nailed fingers Glide the silver-shining minnows. **1944** W. DE LA MARE *Coll. Rhymes & Verses* 99 There silver-shining Hesper Smiles at Mars.

**19.** Qualifying other adjectives, as ***silver-blue***, ***bright***, ***-clear***, ***-golden***, etc.

**1592** SHAKS. *Rom. & Jul.* II. ii. 166 How siluer sweet, sound Louers tongues by night. **1595** —— *John* II. i. 315 Their Armours that march'd hence so siluer bright. **1603** J. DAVIES (Heref.) *Microcosmos* Wks. (Grosart) I. 91/1 Many a glitt'ring siluer-golden spang. **1749** GRAY *Installat. Ode* 32 Oft woo'd the gleam of Cynthia silver-bright. **1830** TENNYSON *Lilian* 24 Silver-treble laughter trilleth. **1833** —— *Two Voices* 428 A little whisper silver-clear. **1871** BROWNING *Pr. Hohenstiel* 308 Where some segment silver-true Stays clear. **1914** L. WOOLF *Wise Virgins* iv. 110 The silver-green water glided by him. **1922** JOYCE *Ulysses* 537 Through silver-silent summer air the dummy of Bloom, rolled in a mummy, rolls rotatingly. **1923** D. H. LAWRENCE *Birds, Beasts & Flowers* 19 Silver-pink peach, venetian green glass of medlars and sorb-apples. **1959** W. THESIGER *Arabian Sands* xii. 242 We came to a succession of dune-chains, each of which..showed up in turn as a wavy silver-blue wall. **1959** R. GRAVES *Coll. Poems* 315 And next the silver-bright Hyperborean Queendom. **1973** J. SEABROOK *Loneliness* 117 A quiet, rather subdued woman; smart, with silver-blue hair. **1976** 'D. HALLIDAY' *Dolly & Nanny Bird* xiii. 165 The pearly capped teeth and silver-pink mouth.

**20.** With sbs., forming an attributive comb.

**1675** HOBBES *Odyssey* (1677) 38 Then by Alcandre t' Helena divine A silver brim guilt basket given was. **1677** *Lond. Gaz.* No. 1238/4 A bright silver-hair bay Gelding. **1678** PHILLIPS (ed. 4), *Silver-spoon-head*, in Archery, is the Head of some sort of Arrows, so called from the resemblance they have to the knobs of some sorts of Silver-spoons. **1799** [A. YOUNG] *Agric. Lincoln.* 385, 2000 couple of silver hair [rabbits]. **1804** SHAW *Gen. Zool.* V. I. 108 Silver-stripe Pike, *Esox Hepsetus*.

**IV. 21.** Special combs.: **silver-balli** (see quot.); **silver band**, a brass band with silver-coloured instruments; **silver bar** (see quot.); **silver bath**, a solution, esp. of silver nitrate, used for sensitizing photographic plates and printing paper; a dish to contain this; **silver-beggar**, **-black** (see quots.); **silver blond(e)** *a.*, of hair: of a very light, silvery colour, esp. as the result of bleaching (cf. *platinum blond(e)* s.v. PLATINUM 2 c); † **silver bridal** = *silver marriage*; **silver bronze** (see quot.); † **silver caustic**, lunar caustic; **silver collection**, a collection of 'silver' coins (or of money of no denomination lower than these) made at a meeting, etc.; **silver cord**, (*a*) used in phr. ***the silver cord is loosed*** and varr. (in allusion to Eccl. xii. 6) to signify the dissolution of life at death; (*b*) a symbol of excessive devotion between mother and child; **silver doctor**, an artificial fishing fly having a body of tinsel; † **silver-eyed** *a.*, wall-eyed; **silver-feast** = *silver wedding* below; **silver-fizz**, an effervescing drink based on gin and egg-white (cf. FIZZ, FIZ *sb.* 3); † **silver-foam**, litharge; **silver-fork**, used *attrib.* to designate a school of novelists about 1830 distinguished by an affectation of gentility; also applied to later novelists displaying similar characteristics; **silver glass** (see quots.); † **silver-glet**, litharge; **silver handshake**, a gratuity given on retirement or as compensation for dismissal from one's occupation (of less value than a golden handshake); † **silver hell** *slang*, a low-class gambling saloon (cf. HELL *sb.* 8) (*obs.*); † **silver-hider**, a miser; **silver jubilee**: see JUBILEE *sb.* 3 a; **Silver Lady**, an epithet applied to Miss Elizabeth Baxter (d. 1972), philanthropist, from her custom of giving silver coins to the down-and-outs of the Embankment in London, used *attrib.* to describe a charitable organization (and its appurtenances) which distributes food and hot drinks to vagrants; **silver lustre**, a composition used for silvering potter's ware; † **silver-marriage** (in Sc. form *siller*), a marriage at which each guest contributed a money-offering; **silver medal**, a medal made of or resembling silver, awarded as the second prize in a contest, esp. in the Olympic Games; hence **silver medallist**; **silver oar** (see quot. 1867); **Silver Office**, an office formerly attached to the Court of Common Pleas; **silver piece** (see the quotation for *silver bar*); † **silver-pill** (see quot.); **silver-point**, (*a*) the process of making a drawing with a silver pencil on specially prepared paper; a drawing made in this way; (*b*) the freezing point of silver under normal atmospheric pressure (about 962°C), as a thermometric fixed point; **silver-pointed** *a.*, coloured or tinged in the manner of a silver-point drawing; hence, as a back-formation, **silver-point** *v. trans.*, to cause to appear so; **silver polish**, a polish used for cleaning and brightening silver; **silver-powder**, a preparation of bismuth, tin, and mercury, used by japanners, etc. (Knight, 1875); **silver print**, a photograph produced by silver-printing; **silver-printing**, (*a*) the process of producing a photograph on paper sensitized with a silver salt; (*b*) printing in which the letters, etc., have a silver colour; † **silver quinsy**, = *silver sickness*; **silver rain** (see RAIN *sb.*[1] 4 c); **silver ring** *Racing* (see quot. 1921) (cf. TATTERSALL 1 b); also *attrib.*; **silver sand**, a fine white sand used in horticulture, etc.; **silver screen**, a cinematographic projection screen covered with metallic paint to produce a highly reflective silver-coloured surface; usu. *transf.*, the cinema generically, considered as a medium for such film projection; **silver service** (see quot. 1970); **Silver Shirts** *U.S.*, the name applied to the Silver Legion, an American fascist, anti-Semitic paramilitary group founded in 1933 and disbanded in 1940 (cf. BLACKSHIRT); † **silver-sick** *a.*, avaricious; † **silver sickness** (see quot. 1706 and cf. *silver quinsy* above); **silver-side**, the upper and choicer part of a round of beef; **silver-skin**, (*a*) a variety of potato; (*b*) an inner skin on coffee-beans; **silver solder**, a solder partly composed of silver; hence *v.* and *vbl. sb.*; † **silver-spat**, a silver-bearing rock; **silver-spoonism** (see quot.); † **silver squinsy**, = *silver sickness* above; **Silver Star**, a decoration for gallantry awarded to members of the U.S. Army and Navy (see quot. 1941); also ***Silver Star medal***; **silver state** *U.S.*, a state producing silver, or advocating free coinage of silver; *spec.* (with initial capitals) Nevada or, less freq., Colorado; **silver steel**, a fine steel containing a small amount of silver; **silver-stick** (see quot.); † **silver stone**, a variety of granite; **silver streak**, the English Channel; also *attrib.*; **silver string** (see quot.); **silver table**, (*a*) a table made of or plated with silver; (*b*) a table used for the display of silverware, freq. with raised edges (and a glass lid); **silver-tail**, **-tailed** *a.* (see quots.); **silver tea** *N. Amer.*, a tea-party at which the guests make contributions (typically, of 'silver' coin) to charity; **silver thaw**, the phenomenon of rain freezing as it falls and forming a glassy coating on the ground, trees, etc.; (see also quot. 1867); **silver thread**, used *attrib.* to denote a variety of ironstone; **silver top**, *U.S.*, a disease in grasses which whitens the upper part of the stalk; † **silver web**, a kind of confection in sugar; **silver wedding**, the twenty-fifth anniversary of a wedding (cf. *silver-feast* above); (see also WEDDING *vbl. sb.* 2 b); **silver weight**, (*a*) the weight used for silver; (*b*) the equivalent weight in silver; † **silver-worm**, a glow-worm; **silver wreck**, a wrecked silver-ship.

**1858** SIMMONDS *Dict. Trade*, **Silver-balli*, a wood obtained in Demerara from a species of Nectandra. **1933** *Radio Times* 14 Apr. 126/5 The Tullis Russell *Silver Band. **1949** 'J. TEY' *Brat Farrar* xxv. 228 'Thump! Thump! Thump!' said the drum of the Bures Silver Band. **1976** *Times* 3 May 12/4 The Eastbourne silver band, in bright red jackets, played *California Here I Come*. **1884** F. J. BRITTEN *Watch & Clockm.* 241 [The] *Silver Bar [or] Silver Piece [is] the graduated arc at the extremity of a watch regulator when it is made of silver. **1878** ABNEY *Photogr.* (1881) 61 The following formula for the *silver-bath solution is a standard one. **1889** *Anthony's Photogr. Bulletin* II. 38 The silver bath ..standing in the sun,..that it may do its dark work the better. *c* **1842** *Exposure of Impositions practised by Vagrants* 4, I shall begin with those vagrants who, generally, obtain the most, and are considered of the first class, and by some termed '*Silver Beggars', but by travellers they are called 'Lurkers'. **1864** *Slang Dict.* 230 *Silver-beggar* or *Lurker*, a vagabond who travels through the country with 'briefs' containing false statements of losses by fire, shipwrecks, accidents, &c. **1805** R. JAMESON *Min.* II. 152 *Silver-black. .. Colour bluish-black, which inclines a little to dark lead-grey. **1867** BRANDE & COX *Dict. Sci.* III. 457/2 *Silver Black*, an earthy form of Silver Glance..found in several Saxon and Hungarian mines. **1951** J. C. FENNESSY *Sonnet in Bottle* I. 29 *Silver-blond hair, silver-grey eyes. **1959** M. SUMMERTON *Small Wilderness* i. 8 The silver-blonde hair that curved..to her shoulders. **1974** D. FRANCIS *Knock Down* iii. 37 She had silver shoes and silver-blonde hair. **1624** *Rec. Presbytery of Fordyce* (MS.), Abuses at *Sylver brydells. **1888** JACOBI *Printers' Vocab.* 125 **Silver bronze*, a metallic powder used for silver printing. **1753** *Chambers' Cycl.* Suppl. s.v. *Silver*, This powder applied to ulcers, acts in the manner of the lapis infernalis, or *silver-caustic. **1957** B. & S. G. HULME BEAMAN *Ernest the Brave* 8 'I was referring to the pence expected as a result of this disgraceful exhibition!' 'Oh, Mr. Growser, sir,' Larry interrupted. 'This is supposed to be a *silver collection.' **1972** H. KEMELMAN *Monday Rabbi took Off* xxii. 145 Imagine, Katz, no charge. Not even a silver collection. **1911** J. A. THOMSON *Introd. Sci.* vi. 177 If we can use such a word, the *silver cord of the bundle of life is loosed, and earth returns to earth. The microbes of decay break down the dead, and there is a return to air and water and salts. **1934** F. S. FITZGERALD *Tender is Night* I. xiii. 76 'The silver cord is cut and the golden bowl is broken and all that, but an old romantic like me can't do anything about it.' 'I'm romantic too.' They came out of the neat restored trench, and faced a memorial to the Newfoundland dead. **1942** P. WYLIE *Generation of Vipers* xi. 185 Our land, subjectively mapped, would have more silver cords and apron strings crisscrossing it than railroads and telephone wires. **1959** J. BRAINE *Vodi* xxi. 232 Her mother, as usual, had won. And, what was hardest to forgive, had won fairly; she wasn't the Silver Cord type, she'd never been possessive. **1973** G. MACKAY BROWN *Magnus* vii. 156 Magnus Erlendson would live out his life, until such time as the silver cord was loosed, and the golden bowl broken, and the pitcher broken at the fountain. **1875** *Encycl. Brit.* II. 40/2 *The *silver doctor*, also a very great favourite. Tag, silver tinsel; tail, a topping; but, a turn of red crewel; body of silver tinsel entirely; [etc.]. **1931** *Hardy's Anglers' Guide* 31 Your fairy shrimp, just as pretty..as any Jock Scott or Silver Doctor. **1695** *Lond. Gaz.* No. 3086/4 A dark Iron grey Mare,..*Silver Eyed. **1702** *Ibid.* No. 3857/4 A small black Gelding about 13 hands... Wall or Silver-Ey'd. **1796** STEDMAN *Surinam* II. 216 The celebration of what he called his *Silver-feast, being the twenty-fifth anniversary of his marriage. **1806** MRS. BARBAULD *Wks.* (1825) II. 125 We should have great pleasure in keeping with you your silver feast, as the Germans call it when a couple have lived happily a quarter of a century together. **1901** O. WISTER *Philos. 4* in *Stories of Colleges* 68 It must have been that extra *silver-fizz you took before dinner.

1977 E. Ambler *Send no More Roses* vi. 121 He was drinking a silver-fizz, a long drink made of gin and egg-whites. 1565 Cooper *Thes.*, *Argyritis*, *siluer fome. 1611 Cotgr., *Litharge d'argent*, siluer foame. [1827 *Examiner* 18 Nov. 722/2 A writer of this accomplished stamp..also informs you that the quality eat fish with silver forks.] 1831 *Times* 15 Dec. 5/3 A single chapter of any one of them is worth more than the whole bundle of those contemptible productions of the *silver-fork school, which are called 'fashionable novels'. 1834 *Tait's Mag.* I. 59/1 A man who would die a martyr to his faith in the silver-fork school of manners and morals. 1884 J. Payn *Lit. Recollect.* 154 It had the culture of the silver-fork school without their affectation. 1974 *Times Lit. Suppl.* 4 Oct. 1092/5 The suspicion grows that this is a new-style 'silver fork' novel, with merchant bankers taking the place of noble dukes. 1797 *Encycl. Brit.* (ed. 3) XII. 62/2 Some of the rich silver ores are easily tried: for instance, *minera argenti vitrea*,..*silver-glass, which consists only of silver and sulphur. 1884 Knight *Dict. Mech.* Suppl. 813/1 *Silver Glass*, an ornamental ground and cut glass. This glass can be used in the place of plaster, marble floors, or wood inlaid work. 1668 Charleton *Onomast.* 306 *Lithargyros*, Litharge, or *Silver-glet. 1958 M. Pugh *Wilderness of Monkeys* 84 Flash Willy is just about to go back to London, pick up his *silver handshake, his sacking money, and get himself a corner in the 'I will photograph your child in your home' lark. 1979 C. Dexter *Service of All Dead* ii. 17 A little silver handshake, a little farewell party. 1835 T. Power *Jrnl.* 13 Jan. in *Impressions of Amer.* (1836) II. 196 With here and there a couple of the same sort of gemman to be met with about the *silver hells of London. 1843 'W. I. Moncrieff' *Scamps of London* I. i. 5 in *Sel. Dramatic Wks.* (1851) I, He's the principal partner in all the silver hells at the west end. 1611 Cotgr., *Serargent*,..a scrape-good, penny-father, *siluer-hider, money-hoorder. 1961 *Ann. Charities Reg. & Digest* 208/2 **Silver Lady Fund.* Mobile café out on Embankment serving hot tea and food free to the needy. Miss Betty Baxter.., E.C.4. 1978 C. A. Berry *Gentleman of Road* xv. 171 The Silver Lady van arrived and mugs of tea and meat pies were distributed. 1834–6 *Encycl. Metrop.* (1845) VIII. 468/2 The *silver lustre is differently prepared. 1825 Jamieson *Suppl.*, **Siller-Marriage*, the same with *Penny-Brydal*. 1851 W. Anderson *Rhymes* (1867) 181 (E.D.D.), Siller marriages fifty years syne war in vogue. 1908 *Silver medal [see gold[1] 8 d]. 1958 [see baton *sb.* 2 b]. 1976 *All about the Games* (Com. Org. des Jeux Olympiques) 24 Canada's 74 athletes won one silver medal. 1911 *N.E.D.* s.v. Silver *sb.* and *a.* 8, *Silver medallist. 1976 *Daily Tel.* 20 July 1/7 The cheating by Boris Onischenko, silver medallist at the Mexico City and Munich Olympics. 1771 *Ann. Reg.* I. 66 Captain Ferguson..was carried from Newgate, the Marshal of the Admiralty, the officer carrying the *silver oar, &c., attending. 1867 Smyth *Sailor's Word-bk.* 626 *Silver-oar*, one of the badges of the civil court afloat, conferring the power to arrest for debt if not less than £20. 1708 J. Chamberlayne *St. Gt. Brit.* (1710) 573 Clerk of the Queen's *Silver-Office. 1886 *Encycl. Brit.* XX. 312/1 The king's Silver Office books are the chief indexes to the fines. 1753 *Chambers' Cycl.* Suppl. s.v., **Silver-pill*, a chemical preparation of silver, formerly highly commended. 1882 Hamerton *Graphic Arts* xii. 97 *Silver-point, as practised by the best masters. 1893 McCarthy *Red Diamonds* I. 219 Marvellously artistic etchings and 'silver-points'. 1928 *Bureau of Standards Jrnl. Res.* (U.S.) I. 637 The constants *a*, *b*, and *c* are to be determined by calibration at the freezing point of antimony, and at the silver and gold points. 1967 Condon & Odishaw *Handbk. Physics* (ed. 2) v. iii. 41/1 In the neighbourhood of 1000°C new determinants of the silver point and gold point have been made in recent years. 1976 I. Murdoch *Henry & Cato* i. 46 A bright half moon was ..*silverpointing the slates and making pendant shadows beneath the..eaves. 1913 C. Mackenzie *Sinister St.* I. ii. xx. 483 They moved to Geneva, whose *silverpointed beauty for a while deceived them. 1930 R. Campbell *Poems* 1 Two sisters... Whose fingers glint with silver-pointed nails. 1895 *Montgomery Ward Catal.* Spring & Summer 193 Thorn's *Silver Polish, Liquid Form, 15c. per Bottle. 1974 'D. Fletcher' *Lovable Man* i. 37 He memorised the exact position of the silver polish and..began to polish the lighter. 1878 Abney *Photogr.* (1881) 138 The colour of the *silver print when appearing through this other metal may give a pleasing tint. 1901 *Athenæum* 12 Oct. 497/1 The views here given..cannot compare in sharpness with the unfortunately perishable silver prints. 1878 Abney *Photogr.* (1881) 28 In determining the fixing agent to employ in *silver printing, this point has to be taken into consideration. 1888 Silver printing [see *silver bronze* above]. 1706 Phillips (ed. 6), *Argentangia*, the *Silver-Quinsey. 1843 Liddell & Scott, Ἀργυράγχη, the silver-quinsy, which Demosthenes was said to have [etc.]. 1921 E. Wallace *Law Four Just Men* ix. 261, I found a poor little bookmaker in the *silver ring—the silver ring is the enclosure where smaller bets are made in Tattersall's reservation. 1926 J. Masefield *Odtaa* xv. 257 A vile, taunting, silver-ring tick. 1939 Wodehouse *Uncle Fred in Springtime* xx. 306 She is the daughter of a retired Silver Ring bookie. 1973 'I. Drummond' *Jaws of Watchdog* xvii. 227 Sandro was in Tatt's... He could also go down the social and financial scale into the Silver Ring and the cheapest enclosures. 1851 *B'ham & Midl. Gardeners' Mag.* Aug. 135, I put them [*sc.* seeds] into a wood or paper box,.. with a little dry *silver sand. 1856 Delamer *Fl. Garden* (1861) 164 How are you off for silver-sand, pasture-loam? [1921 'M. Pickford' *Let.* in V. Burnett *Romantick Lady* (1927) xxxii. 398 It is not always easy to take a classic like 'Little Lord Fauntleroy' and place it on the cold, silver screen.] 1924 *Amer. Hebrew* 22 Feb. 439 (*heading*) 'Shooting' news for the *silver screen; Pathe film editor who brings home to millions timely pictures of world events. 1931 B. Brown *Talking Pictures* i. 19 Somehow there had crept into this new field of endeavour the romance of the silver screen. 1959 *Times Lit. Suppl.* 6 Nov. 636/4 Not a night passes without one aspect or another of the far western frontier holding children from play and old men from the chimney corner on the silver screen or on 'the Telly'. 1979 A. Hailey *Overload* III. xii. 256 Cameron Clarke objected to Tunipah and the god of the silver screen had spoken. 1970 *Drive* Spring 43/1 *Silver service means that your plate is put before you empty and the various parts of your dish are served separately from silver. 1976 *Evening Standard* 14 June 25/3 (Advt.), Commis de rang for our high class Prince's Room Restaurant—must have silver service experience. 1934 *Sun* (Baltimore) 6 Aug. 6/2 A California newspaper has published the exciting news that the *Silver Shirts of America plan to put down the Communists and then take over control of the American Government. 1959 W. Faulkner *Mansion* 303 When the Silver Shirts appeared, Clarence was one of the first in Mississippi to join it. *c* 1480 Henryson *Fables, Wolf & Fox* xiii, Ye are *siluer-seik, I wait richt weill. 1548 Elyot *Lat. Dict.*, *Argentagina*, the *syluer sycknesse. 1706 Phillips (ed. 6), *Silver-sickness*, or *Silver-squincy*, is when an Advocate or pleading Lawyer, being brib'd by the other Party, feigns himself sick, or not able to speak. [1845 E. Acton *Mod. Cookery* viii. 206 The natural division of the meat will show where the silver-side of the round is to be separated from the upper, or tongue side.] 1861 Mrs. Beeton *Bk. Househ. Managem.* 283 As a whole round of beef..is too large for small families..we here give the recipes for dressing a portion of the *silver side of the round. 1876 Besant & Rice *Son of Vulc.* I. vi, Such a beautiful bit of beef too, silverside. 1881 Blackmore *Cristowell* iii, I can milk a cow, and pot a vine, and bed down a pony, and salt a silver-side. 1797 Billingsley *View Agric. Somerset* 116 The sorts [of potato] cultivated are the kidney ..and *silver skin. 1883 *Cassell's Fam. Mag.* Aug. 528/1 The beans [of coffee are] put through a winnower, which takes off a delicate skin still remaining, called the 'silver-skin'. 1682 Boyle *Contin. New Exper.* II. 18 And therefore *silver-solder could not be used in cementing the parts, but onely lead-solder. 1843 Holtzapffel *Turning* I. 434 The hard solders most commonly used are the spelter solders, and silver solders. 1900 Hasluck *Mod. Eng. Handy-bk.* 87 The flanges can be made separately, and either brazed or *silver-soldered on ends of tube. 1843 Holtzapffel *Turning* I. 443 The practice of *silver-soldering is essentially the same as brazing. 1668 Charleton *Onomast.* 301 *Saxa Metallaria*, *Silver-Spat. 1859 *Habits of Gd. Society* 50 *Silver-spoonism is, after all, vulgarity; it is an assumption of delicacy superior to the majority. 1611 Cotgr., *Argentangine*, the *siluer Squinzie, a disease wherwith many besides Demosthenes..haue beene troubled. 1681 W. Robertson *Phraseol. Gen.* (1693) 1278 The silver-squincy, when a pleader being bribed by the other side, feigns himself sick, and not able to speak. 1932 *U.S. Army Regulations* 8 Aug. No. 600–45 p. 1 The authorized decorations awarded by the United States are: *a. Awarded by the War Department*... (4) *Silver Star. 1932 *N.Y. Times* 18 Dec. II. 2/5 Captain Herbert G. Rosboro.. received the Silver Star medal today from the War Department for gallantry in action in October, 1918. 1941 J. McDowell Morgan *Military Medals & Insignia of U.S.* 76 The Silver Star was established..on July 9, 1918. This originally was a unique badge of honor, being a small silver star, 3/16-inch in diameter, designed to be worn on the ribbon of a campaign medal to indicate..'a citation for gallantry in action'... On August 8, 1932, a distinct medal, known as the Silver Star Decoration, was established as a reward to those persons previously cited in orders for gallantry in action. 1948 E. E. Cummings *Let.* 27 Aug. (1969) 185 The hyperscientific climax of this hero (a prominent killer, holder of Silver Stars & Clusters & Purple Hearts galore)'s experience. 1969 I. Kemp *Brit. G.I. in Vietnam* vii. 153 You've been awarded the Silver Star for your action at Dak To. 1982 H. Lieberman *Late Call* lxiii. 308 I'm a veteran with a silver star and a purple heart. 1866 *Eastern Slope* (Washoe, Nevada) 15 Sept. 4/1 The *Silver State struck it rich when they elected H. G. Blasdel to the Gubernatorial chair. 1871 *Harper's Mag.* Oct. 799/1 In our early days in the Silver State females were rarely to be seen in the frontier mining camps. 1885 *Weekly New Mexican Rev.* 8 Jan. 4/2 All the silver states and territories [should] organize to resist the effort which the single standard advocates are making in congress to suspend the coinage of silver. 1946 *Trail & Timberline* May 74/1 Colorado miners had been looking for gold but silver became of such importance that when the Territory became a state in 1876, it was known as the Silver State and Georgetown was called the Silver Queen. 1976 *Billings* (Montana) *Gaz.* 20 June 10-C/2 It was a bluish-gray ore—silver—and Nevada is now appropriately nicknamed 'The Silver State'. 1831 J. Holland *Manuf. Metal* I. 248 *Silver steel, having the advantage of euphony.., becomes a popular denomination in the market. 1882 Ogilvie (Annandale), **Silver-stick*, the name given to a field-officer of the Life Guards when on palace duty. 1758 Borlase *Nat. Hist. Cornw.* 100 The *Silver Stone..is of great lustre in the microscope, every other granite placed by its side looking flat and tame. 1879 *Even. Standard* 11 Nov., The answer of the citizens of London to the '*silver-streak' politicians. 1888 J. Payn *Myst. Mirbridge* v, The silver streak, on the other side of which is dear England. 1875 Stainer & Barrett *Dict. Mus. Terms*, **Silver strings*, the covered strings used on violins, tenors, violoncellos, guitars, etc. *c* 1792 C. Fiennes *Journeys* (1947) III. xii. 279 Here's a *silver table and stands and glass frame. 1897 *Westm. Gaz.* 4 Jan. 1/3, I should probably catch hold of..the things off my silver-table. 1926 A. Christie *Murder of R. Ackroyd* iv. 33 What..is called a silver table, the lid of which lifts, and through the glass of which you can see the contents. 1975 *Country Life* 10 Apr. Suppl. 48 j/1 (*caption*) A really fine Chippendale period silver table of superb quality. 1898 Morris *Austral Eng.* 419 **Silver-tail*, a bush term for a 'swell'; a man who goes to the manager's house, not to the men's hut. 1908 E. G. Murphy *Jarrahland Jingles* 116 And when they're playing billiards in their flannel tennis suits, We feel like heaving something at these silvertail galoots. 1947 G. Casey *Wits are Out* ix. 125 'Mr Fleming doesn't build for basic-wage earners,' Bill said nastily. 'He hangs around waiting his chance to build for the silvertails.' 1978 *Listener* 9 Feb. 163/3 Mr Whitlam's enemies in his own Labor Party have called him a 'silvertail', meaning a social climber. 1979 *Sunday Mail Mag.* (Brisbane) 11 Feb. 16/1 The Governor-General was, in the Premier's opinion, a super silvertail. 1890 Vogan *Black Police* 116 Those upper circles..termed in Australian parlance '*silver-tailed', in distinction to the 'copper-tailed' democratic classes. 1902 *Bladud* 19 Feb. 14/2 During the Peninsular War the 61st were the 'Silvertailed Dandies', owing to the unusual amount of silver on the tails of the officers' coatees. 1921 *Daily Colonist* (Victoria) 18 Mar. 9/4 A *silver tea will be held at the home of Mrs. H. Lloyd-Young..on Friday afternoon. 1770 G. Cartwright *Jrnl.* 22 Dec. (1792) I. 73 There was a *silver thaw in the morning, and it rained freely: very mild weather all the rest of the day. 1860 P. H. Gosse *Rom. Nat. Hist.* 3 A phenomenon I have often seen in the woods of the transatlantic countries named above, where it is familiarly called silver-thaw. 1867 Smyth *Sailor's Word-bk.* 626 *Silver-thaw*, the term for ice falling in large flakes from the sails and rigging, consequent on a frost followed suddenly by a thaw. 1891 *Standard* 26 Dec. 3/3 A 'silver thaw' is the result of rain falling from a warmer current of air at some little distance above the earth. 1855 J. Phillips *Man. Geol.* 193 Blue flats, *silver thread, and diamond ironstone. 1890 *American Naturalist* 970 It is probable that these leaf-hoppers are responsible for much of the *silver-top. 1769 Mrs. Raffald *Eng. Housekeeper* (1778) 191 Observe you don't put too much sugar down at a time for a *silver web. 1845 A. H. Clough in *Ambarvalia* (1849) 28 The *Silver Wedding! on some pensive ear..A silvery faint memorial music swells. 1861 Queen Victoria *Let.* 13 Feb. in R. Fulford *Dearest Child* (1964) 307 You must promise to be with us for our silver wedding D.V. which will be in four years. 1862 H. Marryat *Year in Sweden* II. 417 *note*, 'Silver' and 'Golden' weddings are generally kept in the North. 1889 Gretton *Memory's Harkback* 134 An old man on the verge of the silver-wedding he might have kept as Chancellor. *c* 1000 *Sax. Leechd.* III. 92 Se sester sceal weȝan twa pund be *sylfyr ȝewyht. 13.. *Sir Beues* 1725 For him a ȝaf seluer wiȝt, Er he þat hors haue miȝt. *c* 1475 *Pict. Voc.* in Wr.-Wülcker 766 *Hic auriglus*, a *sylverwurme. 1700 Wallace *Acc. New Caledonia* in *Misc. Curiosa* (1708) III. 421 He pretends it was to search for a *Silver Wreck.

**b.** In names of animals, insects, etc.; **silverback**, a mature male mountain gorilla, *Gorilla gorilla beringei*, distinguished by one or more patches of white or silvery hair just below the back of the neck; **silver buckie** (see quot. 1866); †**silver fly** (?); **silver fox**, (*a*) a North American variety of the red fox with black silver-tipped hairs, the black fox; also *transf.*, the fur of this animal, esp. as a fashion item; (*b*) a fennec, *Vulpes chama*, found in southern Africa; **silver gibbon**, the silvery gibbon (*Hylobates leuciscus*); **silver lady** (see silver-fish 2); **silver-line(s)**, a species of moth; **silver-marmoset**, **-sprig** (see quots.); **silver-tip**, a grizzly bear with white-tipped hairs; **silver y (moth)**, the gamma moth.

Various other names of moths, as *silver bar*, *cloud*, *fringe*, *ground*, etc., are given by Rennie (1832).

1963 G. B. Schaller *Year of Gorilla* viii. 221 He was a *silverback in the prime of life. 1975 J. Goulet *Human Ape* (1977) i. 5 The old silverback was having trouble breathing. 1841 *Proc. Berw. Nat. Club* I. 264 Our children call the shell **Silver-buckies* or *Silver-Willies*. 1866 Gregor *Banffsh. Gloss.*, *Siller-buckie*, the Grey purple-streaked pyramid shell (*Trochus cinerareus*). 1668 Charleton *Onomast.* 42 *Herbivora Erinopteros*,..the *Silver-fly. 1770 G. Cartwright *Jrnl.* 30 Dec. (1792) I. 76 On Niger Sound we saw a good *silver fox. 1827 Griffith tr. *Cuvier* V. 148 *Canis Argentatus* (Silver Fox). 1889 *John Bull* 2 Mar. 150/1 Bordered..with silver-fox fur and lined with cream-coloured velvet. 1892 *T. Eaton & Co. Catal.* Fall & Winter 11/2 Three-quarter capes, quilted lined, trimmed silver fox, $4. 1893 Lydekker *Roy. Nat. Hist.* I. 559 The beautiful silver, or black fox,..is usually nearly or entirely black, with the exception of the tip of the tail, which is generally white. 1912 J. Stevenson-Hamilton *Anim. Life Afr.* xv. 231 The Silver Fox (*Vulpes chama*)..is silvery-grey, the underneath parts being tawny in hue. 1936 A. Christie *ABC Murders* xix. 143 [She] wears very lovely clothes. That crêpe marocain and the silver fox collar—*dernier cri!* 1940 [see *battle bowler* s.v. battle *sb.* 14]. 1972 *Stand. Encycl. S. Afr.* VI. 170/2 The Cape or silver fox is found throughout the drier regions of South Africa. 1893 Lydekker *Roy. Nat. Hist.* I. 65 The grey or *silver gibbon, or wou-wou,..comes from the island of Java. 1832 J. Rennie *Butterfl. & M.* 155 The Green *Silver Lines. 1876 Smiles *Sc. Nat.* vi. 102 The Cream-spot Tiger moth,..the Green Silver-line. 1893 Lydekker *Roy. Nat. Hist.* I. 192 The *silver marmoset of Brazil (*Hapale chrysoleucus*). 1799 [A. Young] *View Agric. Linc.* 385 The sort [is] *silver sprig, which will not do well in other counties. 1800 Miss Edgeworth *Moral T.*, *The Will* i, The true silver grey rabbits—silver sprigs, they call them—do you know that the skins of those silver sprigs are worth any money? 1886 *Turf, Field & Farm* 26 Mar. 238/1 A *silver tip is bad enough when he's wounded, and about as active a bear as there is. 1890 L. C. D'Oyle *Notches* 70 The bear..was an old 'silver-tip', and a big one. 1832 J. Rennie *Butterfl. & M.* Index, *Silver Y. 1848 *Proc. Berw. Nat. Club* II. 329 The caterpillars of..*Plusia Gamma* (Silver Y Moth)..are of this description. 1882 *Cassell's Nat. Hist.* VI. 65 The well-known Gamma Moth, or Silver Y.

**c.** In names of birds, as **silver-bill**, (*a*) any of several birds of the genus *Munia*; (*b*) a South American tyrant bird of the genus *Lichenops*; †**silver bird**, some East Indian bird; **silver-dun**, a particular breed of domestic pigeon; **silver-eye**, one of several birds of the genus *Zosterops*, distinguished by white rings round the eyes; **silver-mealy**, a breed of pigeon; **silver pheasant** (see quots. and pheasant 2); **silver plover** (see quots. and plover 2); **silver-tongue**, *U.S.*, the song-sparrow.

1883 *List Anim. Zool. Gardens* 239 *Munia malabarica*, Indian *Silver-bill. Hab. India. *Ibid.*, *Munia cantans*, African Silver-bill. Hab. North-east Africa. 1892 W. H. Hudson *La Plata* 202, I have also seen gaucho boys catch the Silver-bill (*Lichenops perspicillata*) by hurling a stick or stone at the bird, then rushing at it. 1775 *Phil. Trans.* LXVIII. 401 Some *silver birds. 1879 L. Wright *Pigeon Keeper* 187 The *silver-duns are the aristocrats of the family. 1875 *Silver-eye [see makomako]. 1888 Newton in *Encycl. Brit.* XXIV. 824/1 By most English-speaking people in various parts of the world the prevalent species of *Zosterops* is commonly called 'White-eye' or 'Silver-eye'. 1911 A. E. Mack *Bush Days* 2 You will hear a whole chorus of bird notes..calling all together—thrushes, thickheads, silvereyes and peewees. 1965 [see *blight-bird* s.v. blight *sb.*]. 1977 *Kuwait Times* 23 Nov. 6/8 Three fell to Man, including a pigeon and a parrakeet. The rats have been responsible for at least five more (a thrush, a warbler, a fantail, a silvereye and a starling). **1879** L. WRIGHT *Pigeon Keeper* 149 Such kite-barred birds are termed '*silver-mealies' by Scotch breeders. **1829** GRIFFITH tr. *Cuvier* VIII. 23 The *Silver Pheasants (*Phasianus Nycthemerus*). **1861** C. P. HODGSON *Resid. Japan* 324 Silver pheasants come from Nambu, partridges from Sataki. **1876** *Nature* XIV. 121/2 The additions to the Zoological Society's Gardens..include a Silver Pheasant (*Euplocamus nycthemerus*). **1887** BELDON in Wright *Illustr. Bk. of Poultry* 366 The Silver-spangled Hamburgh, or Silver Pheasant as it is commonly called in Yorkshire. **1899** DEWAR *Hampsh. Highl.* v. 130 The *silver plovers or lapwings..are to be seen and heard in every direction. **1899** DICKINSON & PREVOST *Cumbld. Gloss.*, *Silver plover*, the gray plover, *Squatarola helvetica*. **1884** COUES *N. Amer. Birds* 371 *Melospiza fasciata*,..Song Sparrow. *Silver-Tongue.

**d.** In names of fishes, as **silver-belly, bream, char, -eyes, garfish, king, lamprey, pike, salmon, -side(s), sole, -spot** (see quots.); **silver eel** (see quots.); also, a young eel before the adult coloration is developed; **silver trout** *N. Amer.*, any of several silvery trout, esp. *Salmo gairdneri kamloops*; also, = KOKANEE.

A number of other American, and some Australian, fishes are also designated in this way, as *silver bass, cero, chub, hake*, etc.: see Jordan & Gilbert *Fishes N. Amer.* (1882), Goode *Nat. Hist. Aquat. Anim.* (1884) and *Amer. Fishes* (1888), Morris *Austral English* (1898).

**1882** TENISON-WOODS *Fishes N.S. Wales* 43 It is necessary to cook the *silver-belly, as it is often called, perfectly fresh. *Ibid.*, Mr. Hill..speaks of a *silver-bream or white-bream. It is probable he refers to *Gerres ovatus*, a common fish of very compressed form. **1883** E. P. RAMSAY *Food Fishes N.S. Wales* 10 *Gerres ovatus*, a small but delicious fish, known to the fishermen as 'silver bream', 'silver bellies', &c. **1769** PENNANT *Brit. Zool.* III. 269 The two others were inscribed, the Red Charr, the *Silver or Gilt Charr. **1735** SWIFT & SHERIDAN *Let.* 28 Nov. in *Wks. J. Swift* (1768) XIII. 143 For the rest, we are forced to take up with..*silver eels, and such trash. **1838** *Proc. Berw. Nat. Club* I. 175 *Anguilla latirostris*,..the Broad-nosed Eel... In the Tweed..it is distinguished from the others by the name of Silver-Eel. **1882** JORDAN & GILBERT *Syn. Fishes N. Amer.* 910 *note*, This species [*Trichiurus lepturus*] is known as 'Sabre-fish' and 'Silver Eel', on the coast of Texas. **1952** *New Biol.* XIII. 76 At the silver-eel stage..it is ready to descend the river again. **1880** DAY *Fishes Gt. Brit.* I. 35 These fishes are commonly known as sea-breams. One form termed *silver eyes is said to pursue small fishes in Cardigan Bay. **1859** BARTLETT *Dict. Amer.* (ed. 2), Bill-Fish (*Belone truncata*), a small sea-fish fond of running up into fresh water during the summer... Also called Sea-pike, *Silver Gar-fish. **1889** *Scribner's Mag.* Aug. 164/1 No one..had fared any better than I as regards tarpon... No one could boast of having even hooked a '*Silver King'. **1894** *Cosmopolitan* XVII. 31 You never have seen the equal of the silver-king—the grande coy—the tarpon. **1865** COUCH *Brit. Fishes* IV. 400 The *Silver Lamprey is always of less size than the ordinary dimensions of the Lampern. **1883** DAY *Fishes Gt. Brit.* II. 359 *Petromyzon fluviatilis*,..Lampern and silver lamprey. **1804** SHAW *Gen. Zool.* V. I. 109 *Silver Pike, *Esox argenteus*... Native of New Zealand and other islands in the Southern Ocean. **1878** J. G. BRADY *Let.* May in S. Jackson *Alaska* (1880) vii. 209 A *silver salmon, weighing thirty-eight to forty pounds, is sold for fifteen or twenty cents. **1882** JORDAN & GILBERT *Syn. Fishes N. Amer.* 307 *Oncorhynchus kisutch*, Silver Salmon. **1901** *Scotsman* 26 Mar. 5/1 The silver salmon or coho..are freely taken by means of spinning. **1820** C. S. RAFINESQUE in *Western Rev.* II. 240 *Silverside Fallfish... Vulgar names, Silverside, Shiner, [etc.]. **1851** R. GLISAN *Jrnl. Army Life* (1874) viii. 88 The purer streams from the hills abound in..silver-sides. **1873** T. GILL *Catal. Fishes East N. Amer.* 26 *Cynoscion carolinensis*.., spotted sea-trout..; spotted silver-sides. **1881** DAY *Fishes Gt. Brit.* I. 225 Smelt or sand smelt... A local name is silver-sides, from its colour. **1891** *Cent. Dict.* s.v., The brook-silversides is a graceful little fresh-water fish, *Labidesthes sicculus*. **1911** *Rep. Fisheries 1908* (U.S.) 316/2 Some of the silversides (*Atherinidæ*) are wrongly called 'smelts'. **1962** K. F. LAGLER et al. *Ichthyology* x. 284 In the brook silverside..there is a single elongate filament that serves first for temporary flotation. *Ibid.* xi. 373 Refractive errors change by several diopters during such measurements on schooling fishes, such as the silver-side (*Menidia*). **1803** SHAW *Gen. Zool.* IV. II. 308 *Silver Sole, *Pleuronectes Argenteus*..; native of the Indian seas. **1865** COUCH *Brit. Fishes* IV. 300 The fishes of the family [*Maurolicus*] which we have denominated *Silver-Spots. **1873** C. HALLOCK *Fishing Tourist* I. v. 30 To the above should be added the..brook-trout, the *silver-trout, and the..salmon-trout. **1907** T. W. LAMBERT *Fishing in Brit. Columbia* 43 Every local fisherman speaks of having caught a red side or a silver trout, and firmly believes they are distinct species. **1937**, **1970** Silver trout [see KOKANEE].

**e.** In names of plants or trees, as **silver bell (tree), bennet, berry, birch, chain, chickweed, fern, -head, herb, knapweed, oak, pine (tree), thistle, wattle** (see quots. and the various sbs.); also **silver beech**, an evergreen tree, *Nothofagus menziesii*, native to New Zealand (cf. NOTHOFAGUS); also, the timber of this tree; **silver beet** *Austral.* and *N.Z.*, the seakale beet, *Beta vulgaris*; = CHARD[2]; **silver poplar** *U.S.* = *white poplar* s.v. POPLAR 1 b; **silversword**, a perennial herb, *Argyroxiphium sandwicense*, of the family Compositæ, native to Hawaii and bearing linear leaves with silvery hairs and clusters of purplish flowers; **silver willow**, a variety of the white willow, *Salix alba* var. *sericea*, distinguished by silvery foliage.

Some other names of this type, as *silver feather, grass, hair-grass, lavender*, are current in dialect or local use.

**1889** T. KIRK *Forest Flora N.Z.* 175 The *silver-beech.. is known as 'tawhai' or 'tawai' by the Natives. **1950** *N.Z. Jrnl. Agric.* July 8/3 Durability of..less than five years.. Silver beech. **1966** *Encycl. N.Z.* I. 177/2 Silver beech.., a tree with small, thick, double-toothed leaves and a cherry-like bark on the branches and young trees, reaches heights of about 100 ft. **1882** *Garden* 15 Apr. 256/1 The *Silver or Seakale Beet is grown for the sake of the midribs of the leaves. **1915** *N.Z. Jrnl. Agric.* 20 Jan. 75 Early in February is a good time to sow silver-beet. **1951** J. FRAME *Lagoon* 98 For dinner I had semolina and silver beet. **1973** *Islander* (Victoria, B.C.) 18 Feb. 2/4 Their hulls loaded down with taro, yams, chinese cabbage (rather like silver beet) and bananas. **1977** *N.Z. Herald* 5 Jan. 2-2/1 The novelty value of spaghetti bolognaise can often get over the hurdle of the silverbeet hidden in the sauce. **1785** H. MARSHALL *Arbustrum Americanum* 57 *Silver-Bell Tree... The Corolla is of one petal, bell'd and bellied. **1831** AUDUBON *Ornith. Biog.* I. 123 The Snow-Drop Tree, Silver-Bell Tree, or Wild Olive. **1847** DARLINGTON *Amer. Weeds* (1860) 218 The *Halesia*, or Silver Bell, two species of which..are common in cultivation. **1880** BESSEY *Bot.* 505 *Halesia tetraptera*, the Silver-Bell or Snow-Drop Tree of the Southern United States. **1750** W. ELLIS *Mod. Husbandm.* I. II. 79 Black and *Silver Bennets. **1856** A. GRAY *Man. Bot.* (1860) 381 *Elæagnus argentea*,..the *Silver-Berry, may perhaps be found within our northwestern limits. **1884** *Contemp. Rev.* Aug. 334 It is here that the finest specimens of *silver birch are to be found. **1847** HALLIW., **Silver-chain*, the white laburnum. **1856** A. GRAY *Man. Bot.* (1860) 62 *Paronychia argyrocoma*. *Silver Chickweed. **1858** A. IRVINE *Brit. Plants* 176 *Gymnogramma*. This genus is..distinguished by a yellow or white powdery substance, [and] hence called Gold and *Silver Ferns. **1889** *Chambers's Encycl.* IV. 590/2 Gymnogramme,..of which *G. chrysophylla* and *G. tartarea*, both West Indian, are cultivated as the Golden Fern and Silver Fern. **1890** *Cent. Dict.* s.v. *Paronychia*, *P. argyrocoma*, the silver chickweed, or, as recently named, *silverhead. **1611** COTGR., *Tanaisie sauvage*, Wild Tansie, *Siluer hearbe. **1597** GERARDE *Herbal* 591 The great *siluer knapweed hath at his first comming vp diuers leaues spred vpon the grounde, of a deepe greene colour. **1889** MAIDEN *Useful Pl.* 220 *Stenocarpus salignus*,..'*Silver Oak'. **1694** *Phil. Trans.* XVII. 664 [The tree] brought from the Cape of Good-hope, where it is called the *Silver Pine. *Ibid.* 665 The Silver Pine-Tree. **1847** W. DARLINGTON *Agric. Bot.* 332 *Silver Poplar... Some of the grass-plats in the public squares of New York have been quite over-run by the wide-spreading suckers of this tree. **1880** BESSEY *Bot.* 173 A branch of the Silver Poplar. **1888** W. HILLEBRAND *Flora of Hawaiian Islands* 219 The 'Ahinahina' of the natives and '*Silversword' of the foreigners. **1937** *Discovery* Mar. 83 Not the least puzzling of the specialised animal and plant species of the Hawaiian Islands is the six-foot Silver-sword flower. **1965** P. WYLIE *They Both were Naked* II. vi. 302 A silver-sword plant..grows only on a few high places on two islands [of Hawaii]. **1578** LYTE *Dodoens* 526 *Silver Thistel. This Thistel is called in..Englishe..Wilde white Thistell, and Argentine. **1859** D. BUNCE *Trav. Dr. Leichhardt* iii. 19 We camped among the butts of the *Acacia affinis*, or *silver wattle. **1874** *Treas. Bot.* 1229/1 *Silver Wattle, *Acacia mollissima*. Silver Wattle of Tasmania, *Acacia dealbata*. **1884** *Cassell's Fam. Mag.* Apr. 271/1 The beautiful cool grey-green of the silver wattle. **1914** W. J. BEAN *Trees & Shrubs Hardy in Brit. Isles* II. 475 *Silver Willow.—This is the most striking of all the forms of *S[alix] alba* in the intense silvery hue of its leaves. **1976** *Country Life* 18 Mar. 682/3 A group of silver willows..are annually pollarded.

**silver** ('sɪlvə(r)), *v.* Forms: 5 cilueryn, sylveryn, 6 sylver, 6–7 siluer, 7– silver; also 9 *Sc.* siller. [f. the sb. Cf. G. *silbern*, *versilbern*, Du. *verzilveren*.]

**1.** *trans.* To cover or plate with silver; to coat with silver-leaf. Freq. with *over*.

*c* **1440** *Promp. Parv.* 456/1 Sylveryn, *argento*. **1530** PALSGR. 718/1, I wyll sylver the hafte of my dagger thorowe out. *a* **1540** BARNES *Wks.* (1573) 343/2 Their stockes be polished of the carpenter, and they bee gilded & siluered. **1601** HOLLAND *Pliny* II. 517 They haue taken vp of late another custome, to siluer the trappings especially and caparisons of their horses of seruice. **1611** COTGR., *Argenter*, to siluer ouer; to gild, or couer with siluer. **1669** PEPYS *Diary* 30 Apr., My coach..is silvered over, but no varnish yet laid on. **1753** *Chambers' Cycl.* Suppl. *App.* s.v. *Silvering*, Rub with this mixture the metal you want to silver. **1842** FRANCIS *Dict. Arts* s.v., Copper may be silvered over by rubbing it with the following powder. **1892** GUNTER *Miss Dividends* (1893) 191 There ain't enough in this vein to silver a tea-pot.

*absol.* **1728** CHAMBERS *Cycl.* s.v., Metal-Gilders silver by the Fire: Painter-Gilders, all the other Ways.

*fig.* **1839–52** BAILEY *Festus* 433 Stay thy pretty little tuneful tongue, Nor silver o'er thy syllables. They will not Pass.

**b.** To coat (glass) at the back with a mixture of tinfoil and quicksilver, esp. for use as a mirror.

**1635** [GLAPTHORNE] *Lady Mother* I. ii, This glasse Is falsly silverd, maks me look as gray As if I were four score. **1753** FRANKLIN *Lett.* Wks. 1887 II. 287 Leaf tin, such as they use in silvering looking-glasses, is best to coat them with. *c* **1790** IMISON *Sch. Arts* II. 7 After this method common window glass, &c. may be silvered. **1833** *Penny Cycl.* I. 412/1 The amalgam of tin is largely used in what is termed silvering mirrors. **1879** NEWCOMB & HOLDEN *Astron.* 93 The horizon-glass is divided into two parts, of which the lower one is silvered.

**2.** To invest or suffuse with a silvery hue or lustre.

**1594–9** GREENE *Orlando Furioso* 1178 Is not..Her face siluer'd like to the milke white shape That Ioue came dauncing in to Semele? **1633** P. FLETCHER *Purple Isl.* IX. viii, In azure arms, Silver'd with starres, and gilt with sunnie rayes. **1648** J. BEAUMONT *Psyche* XXII. ccxv, Venus whose pure lustre silvers Night. **1725** POPE *Odyss.* x. 108 Smiling calmness silver'd o'er the deep. **1797–1805** S. & HT. LEE *Canterb. T.* I. 362 The moon in full splendour silvered the wood on one side. **1822** BYRON *Juan* VII. vii, While she still silvers o'er your gloomy path. **1853** KANE *Grinnell Exp.* xxviii. (1856) 230 It silvered the hummocks and frozen leads, and gave a softened lustre to the snow. **1900** *Westm. Gaz.* 21 Mar. 10/1 A few kelts, silvered by a short trip to the sea, have been taken.

**b.** To turn (the hair, beard, etc.) white or silvery.

**1602** SHAKS. *Ham.* I. ii. 242 His Beard was..A Sable Siluer'd. **1725** POPE *Odyss.* XI. 429 Sage Echeneus, whose grave, rev'rend brow The hand of time had silver'd o'er with snow. **1784** COWPER *Task* II. 703 His head Not yet by time completely silver'd o'er. **1825** SCOTT *Betrothed* xv, She who mocks the gray hairs of a parent, never shall one of her own locks be silvered with age! **1870** DISRAELI *Lothair* xxxii, Thought, not time, had partially silvered the clustering of his raven hair.

**c.** In *pa. pple.* Shaded *off* with silver.

**1902** *Fur & Feather* 19 Sept. 229/1 Feet, ears, and face, nicely silvered off;..grand undercolour, well silvered off.

**3.** *intr.* **a.** To flow with a silvery gleam.

**1807** J. BARLOW *Columb.* I. 652 And bason'd high..The bright Superior silvers down the day. **1821** CLARE *Vill. Minstr.* I. 75 While underneath their mingling grains, The river silver'd down the plains.

**b.** To take on a silvery lustre; to fade *away* in this manner.

**1878** W. H. MALLOCK *New Republic* iv, The moon was rising over the sea, and the sea was slowly silvering under it. **1890** R. BRIDGES *Shorter Poems* III. 15 The darkness silvers away, the morn doth break.

**silver age.**

**1.** The second age of the world, according to the Greek and Roman poets, inferior in simplicity and happiness to the first or golden age.

**1565** GOLDING *Ovid's Met.* I. 131 When..the siluer age came in more somewhat base than golde. **1621** G. SANDYS *Ovid's Met.* I. (1632) 3 After Saturne was throwne downe to Hell, Ioue rul'd; and then the Siluer Age befell. **1710** W. KING *Heathen Gods & Heroes* x. (1722) 30 In Comparison of the next succeeding and the present Age,..this of Jupiter had no lower Character than that of the Silver Age. **1797** *Encycl. Brit.* (ed. 3) I. 234/2 The silver age commenced when men began to deviate from the paths of virtue. **1860** *Chambers's Encycl.* I. 76/1 Hesiod mentions five Ages—the golden, simple and patriarchal; the silver, voluptuous and godless.

**b.** The period of Latin literature from the death of Augustus to that of Hadrian.

**1736** AINSWORTH *Lat.-Eng. Dict.* p. xxx, Tacitus, Pliny the historian, Suetonius, and some other prose writers, flourished in the silver age. **1826** BUTLER *Grotius* 31 The language of the Pandects is of the silver age. **1859** TRENCH *Sel. Gloss.* 6 While 'animosus' belongs to the best period of Latin literature, 'animositas' is of quite the later silver age.

**c.** A period of Russian literature and art at the beginning of the twentieth century, considered in comparison with the golden era of the mid-nineteenth century.

**1965** P. BENNO in Hayward & Crawley *Soviet Lit. in Sixties* 179 The works of the generation of Russia's 'Silver Age' in the first three decades of the present century. **1974** T. P. WHITNEY tr. *Solzhenitsyn's Gulag Archipelago* I. I. ix. 336 Even though the Silver Age of art, four State Dumas, three wars, and three revolutions had come and gone, all Moscow drank Oldenborger's water. **1976** *Times Lit. Suppl.* 16 Apr. 450/3 The poet's life in pre-war St Petersburg... She grew up in the capital at a time when its artistic life was at its most febrile and brilliant, the height of the 'Silver Age', not only in poetry but in painting, ballet, music.

**2.** An age marked by the extensive production or use of silver.

**1740** tr. *Barba's Metals & Min.* 111 There was very little use or consumption of Quicksilver before the beginning of this new Silver Age of the World.

**Silverblu** ('sɪlvəblu:). Also Silver Blu(e. [f. SILVER *a.* + BLU(E *a.*] A mink belonging to a mutated form distinguished by silvery fur; also, the fur of an animal of this kind. Also *attrib.*

**1941** *Amer. Fur Breeder* June 8/3 Miss Esther Wyman of Harper's Bazaar magazine was shown a couple of these Platinum pelts... She..suggested that a better fur name be given them such as Silver Blue. **1942** *Ibid.* Oct. 8/3 Of the mutations the platinum or Silver Blu mink are the most prominent. **1944** *Fur Trade Jrnl. Canada* XXI. 10/1 The first offering of 'Silverblu' mink..brought a top price. **1945**, **1956** [see *mutation mink* s.v. MUTATION 7]. **1966** A. LEONARD *Mod. Mink Management* 202 (*caption*) The late William Whittingham developed the Silver Blu mink, the granddaddy of all mutations. **1968** J. IRONSIDE *Fashion Alphabet* vii. 159 Silverblu (also called Platinum): The original mutation mink, introduced in 1942.

**silver-bush.** Also silver bush.

**1.** The plant Jupiter's beard.

**1640** PARKINSON *Theatr. Bot.* 1459 *Iovis barba frutex*, the Silver Bush. **1668** WILKINS *Real Char.* 112 Winged hoary shining leaves, bearing yellow flowers in clusters... Silver Bush. **1678** PHILLIPS (ed. 4), *Silverbush*, a Plant called in Latin *Barba Jovis*, kept as a great rarity by divers Herbalists. **1731** MILLER *Gard. Dict.* s.v. *Colutea*, Ethiopian Bladder-Sena, with Scarlet Flowers, and Leaves like the Silver Bush. **1785** MARTYN *Rousseau's Bot.* xxv. (1794) 353 That which is generally called Jupiter's beard or Silver bush, from the splendid whiteness of the leaves. **1866** *Treas. Bot.* 1059/1.

**2.** *local.* Traveller's joy.

**1886** BRITTEN & HOLLAND *Plant-n.*, Silver Bush, *Clematis Vitalba*,—Jersey.

**silver-coloured,** *a.* [SILVER *sb.* 17.] Having the colour of silver; of a greyish white hue with a metallic lustre.

**1594** ? GREENE *Selimus* 154 Aged winter hath besprent my head With a hoarfrost of silver-coloured hairs. **1611** COTGR., *Ravel*,..a little sea-fish, that hath..a siluer-coloured bellie. **1679** RUSDEN *Further Disc. Bees* 5 Having three partitions in his belly, with silver-coloured lines going cross. **1707** MORTIMER *Husb.* (1721) II. 163 The Silver [Rosemary] denominated from its Silver-colour'd Leaves. **1774** GOLDSM. *Nat. Hist.* (1824) III. 228 It has also four expansive silver-coloured wings. **1831** *A. Wilson's Amer. Ornith.* IV. 358 Silver coloured tern. *Sterna argentacea.* **1871** DARWIN *Desc. Man* II. xv. (1890) 446 Dragons not rarely produce silver-coloured birds.

†**silver-cooper.** *Obs.*⁻¹ [Alteration of Du. *ziel-verkooper* 'soul-seller'.] A kidnapper.

**1796** [see CRIMP *sb.*[1] 2].

**silvered** ('sɪlvəd), *ppl. a.* [f. SILVER *v.* + -ED[2].]

**1.** Coated with silver or silver-foil; also of mirrors, glass, etc., backed with an amalgam of tin and quicksilver.

*c* **1481** CAXTON *Dialogues* 21 Thinges silverid. **1582** BENTLEY *Mon. Matrones* ii. 183 The siluered scepter of peace is offered vnto us. **1674** MOXON *Tutor Astron.* (ed. 3) 206 Place the Golden Ball representing the Sun, and the Silvered ☾ representing the ☾ in two opposite points of the Ecliptick. **1694** MOTTEUX *Rabelais* V. xxv. (1737) 109 The Silver'd Knight took the Golden Warden. **1774** C. J. PHIPPS *Voy. N. Pole* 157 In the middle..is fixed a piece of silvered-glass. **1794** W. FELTON *Carriages* (1801) I. 185 The common reflector is only a silvered back burnished. **1840** ARNOLD *Hist. Rome* II. xxxi. 255 There were a number of gilded and silvered shields. **1881** *Trans. Obstet. Soc.* XXII. 125 It was ..secured by a stout silvered-copper wire.

**b.** *Photogr.* Treated with a silver solution.

**1890** *Anthony's Phot. Bulletin* III. 407 Not permanent prints,..but on silvered paper, which were tedious to get in dull weather.

**2.** Suffused with silver lustre; silver-coloured; whitened with age; silver-haired.

*c* **1600** *Ballad Spanish Trag.* I. 15 in *Kyd's Wks.* (1901) 343 Vntill that age with siluered haires My aged head had ouerspred. **1620** T. PEYTON *Glass of Time* I. 50 The dores thereof of siluer'd Pearle most white. **1622** DRAYTON *Polyolb.* xxvi. 260 Not Ancum's silvered Eel exceedeth that of Trent. *c* **1743** FRANCIS tr. *Horace, Sec. Poem* 169 Indulge the waning Days Of silver'd Age with placid Ease. **1792** A. YOUNG *Trav. in France* 20 The amazing frame of the Pyrenees, rearing their silvered head far above the clouds. **1853** M. ARNOLD *Scholar Gypsy* xxii, Brushing through, By night, the silver'd branches of the glade. **1861** W. F. COLLIER *Hist. Eng. Lit.* 41 The thinly silvered scalp of weak old age. **1897** WATTS-DUNTON *Aylwin* II. v, That love-dream on the dear silvered sands.

†**3.** Of sounds: Sweet- or silver-toned. *Obs.*⁻¹

**1642** H. MORE *Song of Soul* II. App. 66 If an Harper harped in the Moon, His silvered sound would touch our tickled ear.

**silveren(e,** obs. forms of SILVERN.

'**silverer.** [f. SILVER *v.* + -ER[1].] One who silvers, *esp.* one who practises silvering or silver-plating as a trade.

**1598** FLORIO, *Inargentatore*, a siluerer of any thing. **1706** J. STEVENS *Eng.-Sp. Dict.*, A silverer, *argentadór.* **1839** URE *Dict. Arts* 1138 Among the metals, copper or brass are those on which the silverer most commonly operates. **1897** *Allbutt's Syst. Med.* II. 931 The silverers used to suffer considerably from mercurialism.

**silve'rette.** [f. SILVER *sb.*] A fancy breed of domestic pigeon; a bird belonging to this breed.

**1879** L. WRIGHT *Pigeon Keeper* 174 Silverettes have silver shoulders, with white bars edged with black only, tail grey, with the usual spots.

**silver-eye(s):** see SILVER *sb.* 21 c, d.

**silver fir.** [SILVER *sb.*]

**1.** A tall species of fir (*Abies* or *Picea pectinata*), native to southern and central Europe and some parts of Asia, introduced into Britain in the 17th century and extensively used for planting.

The bark of the young tree is of a silvery grey, and the leaves have two broad white lines on the under-surface.

**1707** MORTIMER *Husb.* 365 Firs are of several sorts,..but the best sort both for Beauty and Timber, is that which they call the Silver-Fir. **1789** EMMERICH *Forests* xx. 78 There are three species of Needle Wood or Firs: the Norway Fir, the Scotch Fir, and the Silver Fir. **1832** *Planting* (L.U.K.) 89 The specimens of the silver fir (*Pinus picea*) at Blair Adam.. are remarkable for size and symmetry. **1882** *Garden* 23 Dec. 548/2 The Silver Fir is a majestic tree either singly or in clump.

*attrib.* **1871** KINGSLEY *At Last* vii, Among the high Silver-fir forests of the Pyrenees.

**b.** A tree belonging to this species.

**1789** *Trans. Soc. Arts* I. 72 The greatest number of Silver Firs. **1892** *Gardener's Chron.* 27 Aug. 251/1 Some fine Silver Firs are here, one over 100 feet in height.

**2.** Applied to various other species of fir, usually with distinctive epithets (see quots.).

The 'silver firs' are sometimes classed under the genus *Picea*, and the 'spruce firs' under *Abies*.

**1834** AUDUBON *Ornith.* II. 426 The Balsam or Silver Fir.. is abundant in the State of Maine. **1874** STEWART & BRANDIS *Flora N. West India* 528 *Abies Webbiana*,..Himalayan Silver Fir. **1879** *Encycl. Brit.* IX. 225/1 The Silver Fir of Canada (*P. balsamea*)..furnishes the 'Canada balsam' used in medicine. **1880** BESSEY *Botany* 412 The Giant Silver Fir, *A. grandis*, of Oregon and California.

**silver-fish.** Also silver fish. [Cf. Du. *zilvervisch*, G. *silberfisch.*]

**1.** One of various silver-coloured fishes found in different parts of the world.

**1703** DAMPIER *Voy.* III. I. 26 Mullets, Snappers, Silver-fish, Garfish. **1712** E. COOKE *Voy. S. Sea* 342 The Silver Fish is smooth, broad, and thin, of a shining Pearl, or Silver Colour. **1731** MEDLEY *Kolben's Cape G. Hope* II. 203 The fish at the Cape call'd Silver-Fish is of the shape of a carp. **1745** P. THOMAS *Jrnl. Anson's Voy.* 195 The Fish they call the golden and silver Fish, that are found in divers Provinces [of China]. **1748** *Anson's Voy.* II. i. 125 We caught..maids, silver fish, congers. **1852** GORDON in *Zoologist* X. 3458 Common Sea Bream... In 1849 many were caught by the fishermen, who gave them the name of 'Siller-fish'. **1884** GOODE *Nat. Hist. Aquat. Anim.* 611 The Tarpum..is the 'Silver-Fish' of Pensacola. **1888** STEARNS in Goode *Amer. Fishes* 407 The Silver fish or Grande Ecaille, is common everywhere on the Gulf coast.

**2.** An insect of the genus *Lepisma*, esp. *L. saccharina* or *domestica*; a bristletail or springtail.

**1855** *Lardner's Museum Sci. & Art* VI. 62 A little insect, vulgarly called the *silver-fish*, or the *silver-lady*,..usually found in damp and mouldy cupboards, and in old wood-work. **1879** JEFFERIES *Wild Life* 96 Some tall volume which he..bent over with such delight, heedless of dust and silver-fish and the gathered odour of years. **1893** *Academy* 7 Oct. 292/1 The pest of all book lovers, the 'silver-fish' or 'silver coloured book-worm'.

**silver-foil.** Also silver foil. [SILVER *sb.* 8.]

**1.** Silver beaten out thin; silver-leaf.

**1439–40** *Norwich Sacrist's Roll* (MS.), Pro thurificacione ..cum sylverfoile circumsparso. **1499** in T. Sharp *Dissert. Cov. Myst.* (1825) 35 For colours and gold foyle & sylver foyle for iiij capps. **1565** COOPER *Thesaurus* s.v. *Argenteus, Argenteum folium*, siluerfoile. **1685** COLE in *Ray's Lett.* (1718) 197 Some..covered with a superficies as thin, and exactly of the Colour of silver Foil. **1835** *Partington's Brit. Cycl. Arts* II. 695/1 While the artist draws the paper from between the silver foil and the glass. **1883** HARDWICH *Photogr. Chem.* 103 To illustrate its action in that particular, ..place pieces of silver-foil in two test-tubes.

**2.** = SILVER PAPER 2. Cf. FOIL *sb.*[1] 4 d.

**1944** N. MAILER in E. Seaver *Cross-Section* 338 The captain took out a chocolate bar... He separated a piece of silver foil from his teeth. **1974** N. BENTLEY *Inside Information* i. 8 He slid the outside wrapping off his bar of Whole Nut... Hidden between the wrapping and the silver foil underneath was a small piece of paper.

**silver-footed,** *a. poet.* [f. SILVER *sb.* 17, after the Homeric ἀργυρόπεζα as an epithet of Thetis.] Having silvery feet; white-footed. Often *fig.*

**1620** MIDDLETON & ROWLEY *World Tost at Tennis* Induct. 34 By her side The silver-footed Thamesis doth slide. **1646** G. DANIEL *Poems* Wks. (Grosart) I. 94 Yet Silver-footed Peace may blesse our feilds. **1685** DRYDEN *Sylvæ* II. 50 By silver footed Thetis thou wert won For fierce Achilles. **1718** POPE *Iliad* XVI. 702 Who, chas'd for Murder thence, a Suppliant came To Peleus, and the silver-footed Dame. **1747** MALLET *Amyntor & Theodora* Wks. 1759 I. 124 The silver-footed dews. **1818** KEATS *Endym.* III. 51 The ministring stars..Waiting for silver-footed messages. **1870** BRYANT *Iliad* I. I. 30 The silver-footed Thetis has contrived To o'erpersuade thee.

**silver gilt.** Also silver-gilt.

**1.** Gilt silver or silverware.

**1422** in *E.E. Wills* (1882) 50 Also I bequeth to Ionet Knolles a stondyng cuppe of siluer gilte couered. **1487** *Paston Lett.* III. 463 A playn standing cupp of silver gilt. **1533** *Act 24 Hen. VIII*, c. 13 No man shall weare..any maner aglettes, buttons, broches of golde or silver gilte. **1583** STUBBES *Anat. Abus.* II. (1882) 25 Some will not sticke to sell you siluer gilt for gold. **1684** EVELYN *Diary* 17 Dec., Cover'd with chaines of silver gilt. **1844** A. P. DE LISLE in E. Purcell *Life* (1900) I. vii. 123 In the sacristy is the shrine of St. Engelbert made of silver gilt. **1886** *Guide Exhib. Galleries Brit. Mus.* 180 A group of horsemen and prostrate figure, beaten out in silver gilt. Found at Perugia.

*fig.* **1871** M. COLLINS *Marq. & Merch.* I. iv. 133 Amy.. was pure gold: Angelina..was only silver-gilt.

**b.** *attrib.* or as *adj.* Made of silver gilt.

**1705** *Lond. Gaz.* No. 4099/1 The Envoy was served in Silver-Gilt Plate. **1842** LOVER *Handy Andy* xlvii, He sported a silver-gilt snuff-box which was presented to him. **1895** JEWITT & HOPE *Corporation Plate* I. 240 The earliest pieces in point of date are the magnificent silver-gilt rose-water dish and ewer.

**2.** An imitation of gilding, consisting of silver-foil varnished with a yellow lacquer.

**1891** in *Cent. Dict.*

So †**silver-gilted** *a. Obs.*⁻¹

**1560–1** *Will of M. Bisset* (Somerset Ho.), My silver gilted caul with chains.

**silver-glance.** Also silver glance. [ad. G. *silberglanz*: see GLANCE *sb.*[2]] A variety of silver ore; argentite.

**1805** R. JAMESON *Min.* II. 155 Silver-glance... Colour dark blackish lead-grey. **1808** *Ibid.* III. 267 Silver-glance.. is one of the most common and abundant of the silver-ores. **1856** DANA *Min.* (ed. 3) 94 Silver Glance.., when pure, consists of 86·5 parts of silver, and 13·5 parts of sulphur. **1877** RAYMOND *Statist. Mines & Mining* 214 The metallic contents are..ruby silver, brittle silver, and sulphide of silver or silver-glance.

**silver grain.** Also silver-grain. [SILVER *sb.* and GRAIN *sb.*[1] 15.] (See quot. 1882.)

**1801** [see GRAIN *sb.*[1] 15]. **1832** *Planting* 8 in *Lib. Usef. Kn., Husb.* III, The wood of the elm..is distinguished by having the medullary rays, or silver grain, equal, and not crowded. **1858** CARPENTER *Veg. Phys.* §99 The thin plates which they form..are known to carpenters and cabinet-makers as the silver grain. **1882** VINES tr. *Sachs' Bot.* 131 If a thick stem is split longitudinally, the rays have the appearance, in many close woods, of glistening bands (the 'Silver-grain'), traversing the prosenchymatous woody tissue in a radial direction.

**silver grass.** Also silver-grass. [cf. G. *silbergras.*] One or other of various species of grass, *esp.*: **a.** The striped or ribbon-grass. **b.** The Australasian grasses *Danthonia pallida*, and *Poa cæspitosa*. Also **c.** *dial.* The silverweed.

**1600** R. SURFLET *Countrie Farme* II. xlii. 261 Siluer-grasse (so called, because the leaues doe resemble siluer on the backe side) doth delight in a moist and grassie ground. **1633** T. JOHNSON *Gerarde's Herbal* 18 Round headed Siluer-grasse. At the top of the stalks..there grow two or three round heads consisting of soft and white downie threds. *Ibid.*, The heade of this (which I haue thought good to call Siluer-grasse). **1854** MISS BAKER *Northampt. Gloss.*, *Silver-grass*, striped grass; common in gardens. **1889** MAIDEN *Useful Plants* 82 *Danthonia pallida*,..Silver Grass. **1893** *Wiltsh. Gloss.* 144 Silver-fern or Silver-grass, *Potentilla Anserina.*

**silver-grey,** *a.* and *sb.* [SILVER *sb.* 19.]

**A.** *adj.* Of a silvery or silver-flecked grey colour; also, having silvery grey hair.

**1607** BARKSTED *Mirrha* (1876) 22 You blushing girles, and parents siluer-gray. **1686** *Lond. Gaz.* No. 2121/4 Lost a fine large silver grey Mare. **1785** SMELLIE *Buffon's Nat. Hist.* (1791) VII. 272 The silver-gray fox of North America..is the isatis. **1810** *Sporting Mag.* XXXVI. 102 A silver-grey cock belonging to Mr. John Angood. **1857** DUFFERIN *Lett. High Lat.* (ed. 3) 268 The silver-grey ridges of gneiss and mica slate that hem in the Nordland shore. **1897** MARY KINGSLEY *W. Africa* 177 Wreaths and clouds of silver-gray mist.

**B.** *sb.* **a.** A silvery grey colour.

**1712** tr. *Pomet's Hist. Drugs* I. 16 These little Insects..are of a Silver Grey. **1792** BURNS *The Posie* v, The hawthorn.. wi' it's locks o' siller grey. **1864** TENNYSON *The Ringlet* 6 Never chilling touch of Time Will turn it silver-gray. **1907** MABEL PEACOCK *Lincolnshire Rhymes* 43 Because his hair has caught A touch of silver-gray.

**b.** *U.S. Politics.* (See quot. 1859.)

**1850** *N.Y. Tribune* 18 Oct. 5/2, I shall gladly fight on in this cause so long as I shall live, and ask no higher post than the proud one of a private in the Silver Grays. **1856** *Household Wds.* 9 Aug. 86 Silver-gray..politically means a worshipper of the past,—a hoary-headed conservative. **1859** BARTLETT *Dict. Amer.* (ed. 2), *Silver Grays.* This term originated in the State of New York, and was applied to the conservative portion of the Whig party... It was observed that many were men whose locks were silvered by age, which drew forth the remark from some one present, 'There go the silver grays!'

**c.** A variety of Dorking fowl having silvery grey plumage.

**1889** E. BROWN *Poultry* 45 Silver Greys.—This is perhaps the most beautiful of all the Dorking tribe.

**silver-haired,** *a.* [SILVER *sb.* 17.]

**1.** Having hair silvered with age. Also *fig.*

**1665** SIR T. HERBERT *Trav.* (1677) 148 Such..as have a due esteem of Silver-hair'd Antiquity. **1818** SCOTT *Hrt. Midl.* xiii, The same tall, thin, silver-haired turnkey, whom he had seen on the preceding evening. **1890** 'R. BOLDREWOOD' *Col. Reformer* (1891) 147 He made the acquaintance of more than one silver-haired pioneer.

**2.** Having hair naturally of a silvery colour.

**1678** *Lond. Gaz.* No. 1301/4 Mounted upon a brown silver-haired Gelding. **1766** *Compl. Farmer* s.v. *Rabbit*, The skins of the silver-haired ones [rabbits] sell better than any other. **1827** GRIFFITH tr. *Cuvier* V. 26 *Simia Lagothrix Canus* (Silver-haired Monkey). **1836** SIR G. HEAD *Home Tour* 248 Rabbits..of a description called by the poulterers 'silver-haired', that is to say black with a sprinkling of white hairs, more or less. **1893** LYDEKKER *Roy. Nat. Hist.* I. 279 The silver-haired bat has the most northern range of any American species.

**silver-headed,** *a.* [SILVER *a.* 17.]

**1.** = SILVER-HAIRED *a.* 1.

**1643** A. ROSS *Mel Helic.* 128 Silver-headed age, which bows The back. **1797–1805** S. & HT. LEE *Canterb. T.* I. 378 A silver-headed domestic..stood near. **1848** DICKENS *Dombey* xxx, The silver-headed butler had withdrawn.

**2.** Headed with silver.

**1759** STERNE *Tr. Shandy* I. x, Garnished with a double row of silver-headed studs. **1981** M. MCMULLEN *Other Shoe* (1982) ii. 14 She got about slowly..with the help of a silver-headed ebony cane.

**silver-hilted,** *a.* [SILVER *sb.* 17.] Of a sword: Having the hilt of silver.

**1002** in Thorpe *Dipl. Angl. Sax.* (1865) 544 Twa seolfor-hilted sweord. **1596** J. DAVIES *Epigr.* ii, A silver-hilted rapier by his side. **1690** LUTTRELL *Brief Rel.* (1857) II. 111 Our men..found among them 50 silver hilted swords. **1842** BORROW *Bible in Spain* xl, The famous Sheppard..when he appeared in public generally wore a silver-hilted sword at his side. **1887** MORRIS *Odyssey* x. 262 My war-sword silver-hilted.

**silverily** ('sɪlvərɪlɪ), *adv. rare.* [f. SILVERY *a.* + -LY[2].] = SILVERLY *adv.* 1, 2.

**1929** D. H. LAWRENCE *Pansies* 44 This wet white gleam Twitches, and ebbs hitting, washing inwardly, silverily against his ribs. *a* **1930** —— *Phoenix* (1936) 40 You hear the nightingale silverily shouting.

'**silveriness.** [f. SILVERY *a.* + -NESS.] Silvery quality or character.

Cf. Sc. '*Sillerieness*, richness in regard to money' in Jamieson *Suppl.* (1825).

**1856** MEREDITH *Shav. Shagpat* 352 None of earth were like to them in silveriness. *c* **1875** *Cassell's Nat. Hist.* III. 103 A fourth excels in the silveriness of his voice. **1885** *Westmorl. Gaz.* 17 Oct. 2/1 Salmon, whose silveriness had vanished by a month or two's living in the fresh water.

'**silvering,** *vbl. sb.* [f. SILVER *v.* + -ING[1].]

**1.** The action of the vb. in various senses.

**1738** CHAMBERS *Cycl.* s.v. *Paper*, Silvering of paper, as it is called, is another secret among the Chinese, practised [etc.]. **1753** *Chambers' Cycl.* Suppl. *App.* s.v., Silvering..is a species of gilding. **1825** J. NICHOLSON *Operat. Mechanic* 728 To plate Looking-Glasses.—This art is erroneously termed silvering. **1839** URE *Dict. Arts* 592 The silvering of plane mirrors consists in applying a layer of tin-foil alloyed with mercury to their posterior surface. **1883** *Science* II. 60/2 On some occasions the silvering has been done at night.

**b.** *attrib.*, as *silvering bath, process, room.*

**1855** *Orr's Circle Sci., Pract. Chem.* 13 Any of the well-known silvering compositions. *Ibid.* 41 Iron boilers..in close proximity to the silvering-room. **1872** E. SPON *Workshop Rec.* Ser. I. 171/2 If the pieces..are plunged into a gilding or silvering bath.

**2.** *concr.* Silver plating; a coating of silver, silver nitrate, or quicksilver.

**1710** *Tatler* No. 245 ¶2 A silver cheese-toaster with three tongues, an ebony handle, and silvering at the end. **1753** *Chambers' Cycl.* Suppl. *App.* s.v., The quick-silver thus laid on..will make a fine silvering. **1832** BABBAGE *Econ. Manuf.* xvi. (ed. 3) 149 If the silvering is injured, it can..be re-silvered. **1873** E. SPON *Workshop Rec.* Ser. I. 209/1 Should a first silvering not be found sufficiently durable,..apply a second or third coat.

**'silvering,** *ppl. a.* [f. SILVER *v.* + -ING².] That silvers; making or becoming silvery.

**1801** SOUTHEY *Thalaba* VI. xxiv, The very light came cool'd through silvering panes Of pearly shell. **1818** MILMAN *Samor* 264 Eamont..Went laughing down its sunny silvering course. **1873** G. C. DAVIES *Mount. & Mere* iv. 24 Beneath the silvering willows.

**'silverish,** *a. rare.* [f. SILVER *sb.* + -ISH.] Silver-hued, silvery; †containing silver.

**1530** PALSGR. 324/1 Sylverysshe, *argentin.* **1648** HEXHAM II, *Zilverachtigh*,..Silverish, or full of Silver. **1747** *Phil. Trans.* XLIV. 503 The Crystal or Oriental Pebble..is of a silverish Hue. **1890** *Harper's Mag.* Oct. 739/1 His eyes were a bright silverish blue.

**'silverism.** [f. SILVER *sb.* + -ISM.] The policy of adopting a silver standard for coinage.

**1895** *Forum* Feb. 674 The panic of 1893 was due to two social crazes—silverism and protectionism. **1896** *Westm. Gaz.* 14 July 9/2 The Chicago Convention has..carried Silverism to a reckless extreme.

**silverist.** *rare.* = next.

**1879** *Madras Mail* 5 Dec. 3 The..Yankee, who thought he had converted the great Chancellor from the evil of his golden ways, and made him a silverist.

**'silverite.** Chiefly *U.S.* [f. SILVER *sb.* + -ITE.] An advocate of a silver monetary standard.

**1886** *Science* VII. 267 The attempt is made to cast a slur upon the 'silverites' by calling them inflationists. **1892** *Nation* 28 Apr. 313/2 The silverites contribute to the gayety of nations from time to time.

**'silverize,** *v. rare.* [f. SILVER *sb.* + -IZE.] *trans.* To silver; to treat with a preparation of silver; to render silvery in colour.

*a* **1618** SYLVESTER *Quadrains of Pibrac* cxix. Wks. (Grosart) II. 34 When like age shall silverize thy Tresse. **1808** JAMIESON, *Silverize*, to cover with silver-leaf. **1832** H. SMITH *Poet. Misc.* 29 He had glaz'd the streamlet o'er,.. And silveris'd the bow'r. **1864** WEBSTER s.v. *Silverize*, This word and its derivatives are much used by photographers in reference to daguerreotype plates; as, a silverized plate.

**silver lead.** Also silver-lead.

†**1.** A composition of lead and tin. *Obs.*

**1601** HOLLAND *Pliny* II. 517 There is another deuise to sophisticate tin, to wit, by mixing white and blacke lead one with another.., and this maslen some call at this day, siluer lead or argentine.

**2.** Silver in combination with lead, esp. in the form of ore. Chiefly *attrib.*

**1860** PIESSE *Lab. Chem. Wonders* 80 Small portions are also obtained from the silver-lead mines of 'Old England'. **1877** RAYMOND *Statist. Mines & Min.* 227 The mines.. possess as much..value as those of any other silver-lead camp on the coast. **1879** *Cassell's Techn. Educ.* IV. 111/2 A button of silver lead is the result. *Ibid.*, The assay of silver lead ores.

**silver-leaf.** Also silver leaf. [SILVER *sb.*]

**1. a.** Silver beaten out thin; silver-foil.

**1728** CHAMBERS *Cycl.*, *Silver-Leaf*, is that the Gold-beaters have reduced into fine, thin Leaves, to be used by Gilders, &c. **1780** *Encycl. Brit.* (ed. 2) V. 3300/1 In this manner silver-leaf is fixed and burnished upon brass in the making of what is called *French plate.* **1843** HOLTZAPFFEL *Turning* I. 376 In the instances of tin-foil, gold and silver leaf, and some others, the hammer is again resorted to after the metals have been rolled. **1875** KNIGHT *Dict. Mech.* 995/2 A yellow, transparent varnish spread over silver-leaf to give it the appearance of gold.

**b.** A single piece of this.

**1728** CHAMBERS *Cycl.* s.v. *Couch*, The Gilders use Couch for the Quantity of Gold or Silver Leaves applied on the Metals in gilding or silvering. **1799** G. SMITH *Laboratory* I. 195 You may lay on the gold or silver leaves with brandy. **1875** KNIGHT *Dict. Mech.* 1240 A silver leaf is sometimes laid over the knots in superior work.

**2.** A tree or plant having silvery leaves, as the white poplar. Also *attrib.*, having silvery leaves.

**1846–50** A. WOOD *Class-bk. Bot.* 507 Abele or Silver-leaf Poplar. **1881** *Gentl. Mag.* Jan. 66 Silver-leaf iron-bark country is always in high repute for grazing. **1889** MAIDEN *Useful Pl.* 363 *Acacia pendula*,..Boree, or Silver-leaf Boree.

**3.** A disease of *Prunus* and other woody plants caused by the fungus *Stereum purpureum*, which is frequently associated with a silvery sheen of the leaves and often fatal to affected branches.

**1890** BLACKMORE *Kit & Kitty* III. ii. 27 Blister in a peach, or silver-leaf, or shanking in grapes. **1902** *Jrnl. Linn. Soc. Bot.* XXXV. 390 The disease known as 'Silver-leaf' is, so far as I am aware, confined to the *Pruneæ*, and has been the subject of observation and investigation for more than a quarter of a century. **1929** *Trans. Brit. Mycol. Soc.* XIV. 163 Silver leaf, *Stereum purpureum* Pers. **1946** H. WORMALD *Diseases of Fruit & Hops* iii. 57 The Silver Leaf Order of 1923 requires growers to cut off and burn all dead wood of plum and apple trees before 15th of July each year. **1969** P. THROWER *Every Day Gardening* xiii. 292/2 (*caption*) Branches and even complete trees can be killed by Silver Leaf disease, and fungal outgrowths form on the dead wood. First, however, the leaves take on a silvery sheen. **1977** *Field* 13 Jan. 66/1 Pruning [of plum trees] should be carried out in late spring..and preferably in dry weather. This is to avoid infection by the silver leaf fungus.

**silver-leaved,** *a.* Also -leafed. [SILVER *sb.* 17.] Having silvery leaves.

**1731** MILLER *Gard. Dict.* s.v. *Coronilla*, Silver-leav'd.. Colutea of Candia. **1822** *Hortus Anglicus* II. 231 *A. Barba Jovis.* Silver-leaved Anthyllis, or Jupiter's Beard. **1831** TENNYSON in *Gem* 131 With..drooping daffodilly, And silver-leaved lily,..I wove a crown. **1881** *Gentl. Mag.* Jan. 66 The silver-leafed variety [of iron-bark trees] is more ornamental than useful. **1889** MAIDEN *Useful Plants* 492 *Eucalyptus melanophloia*,..Silver-leaved Ironbark.

**'silverless,** *a.* Also 8–9 *Sc.* siller-. [f. SILVER *sb.* + -LESS.] Without money; having no money.

*c* **1325** *Pol. Songs* (Camden) 324 Voiz of clerk is sielde i-herd at the Court of Rome,..silverles if he come. **1393** LANGL. *P. Pl.* C. x. 119 He sente hem forth seluerles in a somer garnement. **1737** RAMSAY *Sc. Prov.* (1750) 14 A sillerless man gangs fast thro' the market. **1818** SCOTT *Hrt. Midl.* xxvi, Ye maunna gang this wilfu' gate sillerless, come o't what like. *a* **1837** NICOLL *Poems* (1842) 96 Folk sillerless may ca' us,—We ha'e unco little gear.

**silver-like,** *a.* [f. SILVER *sb.* + -LIKE.] Resembling silver in colour or substance.

**1611** COTGR., *Argentin*, argentine, siluerie, of siluer, siluerlike. **1674** N. FAIRFAX *Bulk & Selv.* 131 A roping, tough, silver-like thread of seed. **1684** LISTER in *Phil. Trans.* XIV. 745 Sand..with Mica of..Silver like, Gold like [particles]. **1849** D. CAMPBELL *Inorg. Chem.* 133 Calcium is a white silver-like metal. **1900** *Academy* 30 June 556/1 Silver-like his naked limbs.

**'silverling.** Now *arch.* [ad. G. *silberling* (OHG. *silabarling*), Du. *zilverling.*] A shekel.

**1526** TINDALE *Acts* xix. 19 They counted the price of them and founde it fifty thousande silverlynges. **1535** COVERDALE *Isaiah* vii. 23 Though there be a thousand vynes in one, and were solde for a thousand siluerlinges. *c* **1592** MARLOWE *Jew of Malta* I, Here haue I purst their paltry siluerlings. **1641** J. TRAPPE *Theol. Theol.* Ep. Ded. A 4, Every of them for the fruits thereof, was to bring a thousand silverlings. **1740** POCOCKE *Theol. Wks.* II. 120/1 These are called *Cesaphim*, pieces of silver, or Silverlings. **1873** KINGSBURY in *Speaker's Comment.* IV. 698/2 At least two hundred silverlings should be theirs.

**'silverly,** *adv.* [f. SILVER *sb.* + -LY².]

**1.** With a silvery appearance or colour.

**1595** SHAKS. *John* V. ii. 46 Let me wipe off this honourable dewe, That siluerly doth progresse on thy cheekes. **1818** KEATS *Endym.* I. 541 This river..begins to progress silverly Around the western border of the wood. **1844** MRS. BROWNING *Drama Exile* 1397 Ask, if I caught not fair and silverly His blessing. **1871** R. BROWNING *Pr. Hohenstiel* 1144 On you glide Silverly till you reach the summit edge, Then over.

**2.** With a silvery sound.

**1752** C. SMART *Omniscience of Supreme Being* 7 Cherubic Gratitude, whose voice To pious ears sounds silverly so sweet. **1820** KEATS *Hyperion* II. 128 When other harmonies, stopt short, Leave the dinn'd air vibrating silverly. **1888** MRS. H. WARD *R. Elsmere* 368 Midnight! the sounds rolled silverly out.

**silver mine:** see SILVER *sb.* 9.

**silvern** ('sɪlvən), *a.* Now *poet.* and *arch.* Forms: *α.* 1 seol(o)fren, seolfryn, selfren, 3 selvren; 1 seolfern, 3 seoluern, 4 seluern. *β.* 1 syl(o)fren, silfren, 5 sylvryn; 4–5 syl-, silueren(e, 5 cil-, silueryn, siluern(e, 6–7 silverne, 6– silvern. [OE. *seolfren, silfren*, etc., = OFris. *selvirn*, MDu. *sil-, selverijn, sulveren* (Du. *zilveren*, dial. *zulveren*), OS. *silu-, silobrin* (MLG. *sulveren*, LG. *sülvern, silvern*), OHG. *silbarîn, silberîn* (G. *silbern*), Goth. *silubreins*: see SILVER *sb.* and -EN⁴.]

**1.** Made of silver; consisting of silver.

*α. c* **888** K. ÆLFRED *Boeth.* xxxiv. §8 þa gyldenan stanas, & þa seolfrenan. *a* **900** *O.E. Martyrol.* 29 Aug., Hi pleȝodon mid gyldenum applum on selfrenum disce. *a* **1122** *O.E. Chron.* (Laud MS.) an. 1070, Hi namen þære twa gildene scrines & ix seolferne. *c* **1205** LAY. 22783 þa bollen seoluerne mid wine iuulled. *c* **1285** in *Anglia* IV. 194 Mid selvrene stikke me shal gold graven. *c* **1350** *Leg. Rood* 29 þat he wuste bi þe seluerne byȝe.

*β. a* **1000** *Boeth. Metr.* xxi. 21 Gylden maðm, sylofren sincstan. *a* **1300** *Cursor M.* 6145 þe folk of israel to boru Asked silueren vessel sere. **1382** WYCLIF *Gen.* xlv. 22 To Beniamyn he ȝaf thre hundryd silueren pens. **1420** *E.E. Wills* (1882) 42 My Sylvryn Gyrdyll to Thomas Pertnale. **1597** A. M. tr. *Guillemeau's Fr. Chirurg.* 26/3 In the which wound, we must impose a silvern or goulden pipe. **1616** J. LANE *Contn. Sqr.'s T.* VII. 227 White silverne swoord, and in his hand a pike. **1863** GROSART *Small Sins* (ed. 2) 37 Not a bell, silvern or golden, but was 'holy'. **1897** F. THOMPSON *New Poems* 70 Make me chainlets, silvern, golden.

*fig.* **1831** CARLYLE *Sart. Res.* III. iii, As the Swiss Inscription says: *Sprechen ist silbern, Schweigen ist golden* (Speech is silvern, Silence is golden). **1868** *Silent Hour* i. 4 Speech is, after all, not the silvern but the golden thing, when rightly used.

**b.** *silvern wedding*, = silver wedding (SILVER *sb.* 21).

**1880** *Daily Telegr.* 29 Dec. 5/4 Silvern Weddings are celebrations of tolerably frequent occurrence nowadays.

**2.** Silver-coloured. *rare.*

**1885** *Harper's Mag.* Apr. 815/2 Silvern as a silver bream. **1885** O. CRAWFURD *Woman's Reputation* i, The little Ringwood brook.., a silvern thread amid the green meadow-land.

**'silverness.** *nonce-wd.* [f. SILVER *sb.* + -NESS.] The essential quality of silver.

**1862** F. HALL *Hindu Philos. Syst.* 168 Instead of perceiving nacreness, he transfers the silverness..to the nacre lying in his sight.

**silver ore.** Also silver-ore. [SILVER *sb.*] An ore containing silver. ***dark red silver ore***, pyrargyrite. ***light red silver ore***, proustite.

**1297** R. GLOUC. (Rolls) 16 Engelonde is vol inoȝ..Of seluer or & of gold. *c* **1325** *Pol. Songs* (Camden) 338 He fareth in a while as thouh he hadde silver ore. *c* **1350** in Horstm. *Altengl. Leg.* (1881) 150 Men þat soght for siluer ore, Within þe erth so gun þai crepe. *Ibid.*, Oþer mynours þeder fore For to seke þam syluer ure. **14..** *Voc.* in Wr.-Wülcker 596 *Mineria*, a myne *vel* Ore.., as..syluer ore, etc. **1454** *Rolls of Parlt.* V. 272 Many mynes of silver oures. **1670** PETTUS *Fodinæ Reg.* 2 The Metal which is digged from those Veins is called Oar, as Silver oar. **1789** J. WILLIAMS *Min. Kingd.* I. 257 The cobalt was last of all cut out below by silver ore. **1796** KIRWAN *Elem. Min.* (ed. 2) II. 122 Red Silver Ore.—This species is denominated *Red* chiefly from the colour of its streak. **1805** R. JAMESON *Min.* II. 177 Black Silver-Ore... Colour iron-black. **1834–6** *Encycl. Metrop.* (1845) VIII. 414/1 Silver ores, properly so called, are very rare in England. **1837** DANA *Min.* 417 Brittle Silver Ore, *Lunites rhombicus. Ibid.* 425 Flexible Silver Ore, *Elasmites rhomboidens.* **1877** RAYMOND *Statist. Mines & Min.* 443, I have roasted nearly four thousand tons of silver-ore during the past year.

**silver paper.** Also silver-paper.

**1.** A fine white tissue-paper.

**1800** M. EDGEWORTH *Birth-Day Present* in *Parent's Assistant* (ed. 3) II. 14 She was obliged to go down with her basket but half wrapped up in silver paper. **1817** BYRON *Beppo* lvii, The..frontispiece of a new Magazine,.. Colour'd, and silver paper leaved between That and the title-page. **1851** MAYHEW *London Lab.* I. 374/1 Those gown-pieces..are almost as thin as silver-paper. **1873** MISS BROUGHTON *Nancy* II. 246 As if I had just emerged from the manifold silver papers of a bandbox.

*attrib.* **1854** MRS. GASKELL *North & South* iii, The pear, which he had delicately peeled in one long strip of silver-paper thinness.

**2.** Paper covered with silver-foil. Also, thin metal foil, used chiefly as a damp-proof wrapping for tobacco and confectionery.

**1875** KNIGHT *Dict. Mech.* 2186/1. **1905** *Strand Mag.* XXIX. 274/1 He has been sorting out the pieces of 'silver paper', as he calls them, in which packets of tobacco are wrapped. **1929** *B.B.C. Year-bk. 1930* 404 The balance of the subscriptions..is paid into the local Radio Circle Funds, which are further increased in various ways such as by the sale of 'silver paper'. **1976** W. TREVOR *Children of Dynmouth* iii. 65 The one he'd taken had green silver paper on it, a chocolate-covered toffee.

**3.** *Phot.* Paper sensitized with a silver solution.

**1898** H. MACLEAN *Photogr. Print. Process* xvi. 139 Those known as silver papers, such as gelatino-chloride, collodio-chloride, albumenised, and bromide papers.

**silver plate.** Also silver-plate.

**1. a.** A thin flat piece of silver.

**1526** TINDALE *Matt.* xxvii. 5 And he cast doune the sylver plates in the temple and departed. **1563** *Homilies* II. *Agst. Idolatry* I. F fj, Shall the goldsmyth couer hym with golde and caste hym into a fourme of syluer plates? **1728** CHAMBERS *Cycl.* s.v. *Silver*, A Tincture of Silver [made] by dissolving thin Silver Plates..in Spirit of Nitre. **1797** *Encycl. Brit.* (ed. 3) XV. 37/2 The ring..is first tinned, and then the silver-plate is gently hammered upon it. **1845** *Athenæum* 203 The delicately sensitive film which is formed on the silver plate in the Daguerréotype process. **1865** *Chambers's Encycl.* VII. 509/1 The sensibility of the silver plate was still further increased by Mr. Goddard.

**b.** A silver dish in the form of a plate.

**1710** *Tatler* No. 245 ¶2 A broad brimmed flat silver plate for sugar with Rhenish wine.

**2.** *collect.* Vessels or utensils made of silver or an alloy of silver.

**1610** HOLLAND *Camden's Brit.* (1637) 184 Pewter vessels ..compared with silver plate. *a* **1653** GOUGE *Comm. Heb.* xiii. 1 As silver-plate cleared is counted new, so this Commandment. **1717** RAMSAY *Elegy on Lucky Wood* iv, Her peuther glanc'd..Like siller plate. **1851–4** *Tomlinson's Cycl. Useful Arts* (1867) II. 531/1 The alloy of silver and copper used..for the manufacture of silver-plate. **1861** PATTISON *Ess.* (1889) I. 45 Round the apartment..was displayed in close array the silver and pewter plate.

*Comb.* **1632** LITHGOW *Trav.* x. 469 Areta, his siluer plate keeper.

**3.** Used as a jocular representation of Fr. *s'il vous plaît* please. *slang.*

**1919** *Yank Talk* 4/1 (*caption*) Silver plate! Loan me a coupla francs! **1920** *Dialect Notes* V. 79 *Silver plate*, s'il vous plaît. 'More of the mutton, Mr. Brown, silver plate.'

**silver-scaled,** *a.* [f. SILVER *sb.* 17.] Having silvery scales.

**1430–40** LYDG. *Bochas* VIII. xxv. (1558) 18 Bryght siluer scaled domageth the dragon. *c* **1450** —— *Secrees* 674 Whysperyng tounges of taast moost serpentyn, Silvir scalyd whoos mouth is ful of blood. **1513** DOUGLAS *Æneid* XII. Prol. 55 The syluer scalyt fyschis on the greit. **1653** WALTON *Angler* i. 37 The silver-scaled fish that softly swim Within the sweet brooks chrystal, watry stream. **1827** SCOTT *Highl. Widow* v, Will the ocean afford you the silver-scaled salmon of the Awe? **1861** W. F. COLLIER *Hist. Eng. Lit.* 403 A silver-scaled twenty-pounder.

**silversmith** ('sɪlvəsmɪθ). [f. SILVER *sb.* Cf. MDu. *silver-, selver-, sulversmit* (Du. *zilversmid*), OHG. *silbir-, silbersmit* (G. *silberschmied*), Sw. *silfversmed*; ON. *silfrsmiðr*, MSw. *silfsmiþer*.] A worker in silver; one who makes silverware.

*a* **1000** *Colloq. Ælfric* in Wr.-Wülcker 99 Ic hæbbe.. isenesmiþas, goldsmiþ, seolforsmiþ. **1382** WYCLIF *Wisd.* xv. 9 That me spute with gold smythis, and siluer smythis. **1534** TINDALE *Acts* xix. 24 Demetrius, a silversmyth [1526 goldsmyth], which made silver schrynes for Diana. **1706** PHILLIPS (ed. 6), *Silver-smith*, one that makes all sorts of Silver and Gold-Plate. **1794** LD. AUCKLAND *Corr.* (1862) III. 250, I wrote to you on the 9th of this month a sort of silversmith's letter. **1827** SOUTHEY *Hist. Penins. War* II. 476 Silversmiths were forbidden to purchase any articles in silver. **1879** *Cassell's Techn. Educ.* IV. 146 The productions of the silversmith are principally the result of hammering.

Hence **'silver,smithing**.

**1931** E. WENHAM *Domestic Silver* ii. 8 No period in the history of British silversmithing manifests more varying foreign influences than that of the sixteenth century. **1969** T. LLOYD in R. Blythe *Akenfield* xiv. 222 There is something else I do—silversmithing. I learnt it at evening classes. **1981** *Times. Lit. Suppl.* 20 Feb. 194/5 Ashbee'n emerges as a many-sided creativity, embracing architecture, silversmithing and printing.

**silver-tongued**, *a.* [f. SILVER *sb.* 17.] Having a pleasant or melodious utterance; sweet-spoken; eloquent.

**1592** NASHE *P. Penilesse* Wks. (Grosart) II. 61 Siluer-tongu'd Smith, whose well tun'd stile hath made thy death the generall teares of the Muses. **1618** VICARS *Commend. Verses* in *Sylvester's Wks.* (Grosart) I. 10/2 Admired Silver-Tongued Sylvester. **1713** WARDER *True Amazons* 17 Relying too much upon the silver-tongued Virgil. **1827** POLLOK *Course of Time* VII. (1860) 178 Silver-tongued Hope Promised another harvest. **1851** D. JERROLD *St. Giles* xv. 150 He—good, silver-tongued man—heeded not the miserable jest.

**silver-tree**. Also silver tree.

**1.** A tree with silvery lanceolate leaves (*Leucadendron argenteum*), native to Cape Province, South Africa.

**1731** MEDLEY *Kolben's Cape G. Hope* II. 224 The Silver Tree... These trees..are, particularly, much seen about Constantia. **1785** G. FORSTER tr. *Sparrman's Voy. Cape G. Hope* (1786) I. 32 The silver-tree, as it is called, exhibited the whole year throughout its glossy white, or silver gray leaves. **1845–50** MRS. LINCOLN *Lect. Bot.* 145 The Silver-tree (*Protea argentea*) has soft leaves resembling satin, of a silver colour. **1893** K. SANBORN *S. California* 159 To S. Africa they are indebted for the silver tree.

**2.** A West Indian tree or shrub belonging to the genus *Eugenia*.

**1756** P. BROWNE *Jamaica* (1789) 240 The shrubby Philadelphus, with Myrtle leaves; or the Silver Tree... This little tree is frequent in the red hills.

**3.** An Australian forest-tree.

**1889** MAIDEN *Useful Pl.* 604 *Tarrietia argyrodendron*,.. Silver Tree.

**'silverware.** [SILVER *sb.*] Articles, esp. tableware, made of silver or an alloy of silver.

**1860** RUSKIN *Unto this Last* iv. §57, I very seriously inquire why ironware is produce, and silverware is not? **1892** GUNTER *Miss Dividends* (1893) 17 The supper table with its fruit, flowers, crystal, silverware and decorated china.

**'silverweed.** Also silver-weed, silver weed. [SILVER *sb.* Cf. Du. *zilverkruid*, G. *silberkraut*.]

**1.** A common wayside plant of the genus *Potentilla* (*P. anserina*) with prostrate rooting stems and silvery leaves; goose-grass or wild tansy.

**1578** LYTE *Dodoens* 86 This herbe is now called..in English Wilde Tansie or Siluer weede. **1605** TIMME *Quersit.* III. 181 Let them be steeped or infused in water of siluer weed, called wilde tansey, and of parietory of the wall. **1671** PHILLIPS (ed. 3), *Silverweed*, an herb called in Latin *Argentina*. **1712** J. JAMES tr. *Le Blond's Gardening* 187 Silver-Weed, Bull-Rushes, and other aquatick Herbs. **1782** J. SCOTT *Poet. Wks.* 12 Comfry white, and hoary silver-weed. **1832** *Veg. Subst. Food of Man* 182 Silver-weed.. growing in some parts of Scotland..in times of scarcity made a substitute for bread. **1863** *Gardener's Chron.* 23 May 493 The Silver Weed is a great pest in the arable field, and especially where some damp spots remain. **1880** JEFFERIES *Gt. Estate* 129 Underfoot..the silverweed opened its yellow petals.

**2.** (See quots.)

**1796** WITHERING *Brit. Pl.* II. 326 *Sibbaldia procumbens*.., Procumbent Silver-weed. **1848** CRAIG, *Argyreia*, Silver-weed. An East Indian genus of plants, so named from the silvery appearance of their leaves.

**silver-white**, *a.* and *sb.* [SILVER *sb.*]

**A.** *adj.* Of a silvery whiteness.

**1588** SHAKS. *L.L.L.* v. ii. 905 Ladie-smockes all siluer white. **1715** ROWE *Lady Jane Grey* IV. i, Say thou, whose Head is grown thus Silver White. **1810** CRABBE *Borough* xiii. 31 His hair all silver-white, Shaking and shining. **1864** SKEAT tr. *Uhland's Poems* 2 Buoyed on clouds all silver-white.

**B.** *sb.* **1.** *local.* The white trout or finnoc.

**1834** *Proc. Berw. Nat. Club* I. 51 This fish I consider to be ..the Silver White of the Tweed tacksmen. **1882** DAY *Fishes Gt. Brit.* II. 85 White-salmon..is locally known as.. whiting, phinock, moudie-trout, silverwhite.

**2.** A pure white lead used by artists; Chinese white.

**1875** KNIGHT *Dict. Mech.* 2772/1 Kremnitz white, krems white, and silver white are synonyms of white-lead.

**silver wire.** Also silver-wire. [SILVER *sb.*] Wire made from silver. Also with *a* and pl.

**14..** *Lat.-Eng. Voc.* in Wr.-Wülcker 565 *Argentifilum*, sylver wyre. **1728** CHAMBERS *Cycl.*, *Silver-Wire*, is Silver drawn thro' the Holes of a Wire-drawing-Iron, and by this Means reduced to the Fineness of a Thread or Hair. **1842** *Penny Cycl.* XXII. 21/2 When leaf-silver or fine silver-wire is heated by voltaic electricity, it burns with a fine green flame. **1879** *Encycl. Brit.* X. 754/1 The..silver wire being, of course, composed of pure silver. **1884** KNIGHT *Dict. Mech.* Suppl. 728/2 A porous jar..surrounded by a silver wire.

*attrib.* **1849** NOAD *Electricity* 203 Chloride of silver.. decomposed by silver-wire poles. **1879** *St. George's Hosp. Rep.* IX. 617 A portion was then removed from the middle line, and the edges united again by silver-wire sutures.

Hence **silver-wiry** *a.*

**1891** HARDY *Tess* (1900) 9/2 Elderly women.., their silver-wiry hair and wrinkled faces.

**silver-wood.** [SILVER *sb.*] One or other of several West Indian trees and shrubs (see quot. 1864).

**1693** in *Phil. Trans.* XVII. 620 The Silver-wood or White-wood, called by our Author *Leucoxylum*, is by him supposed the same with the white Brasil. **1725** SLOANE *Jamaica* II. 78 Silver-Wood. This tree..has an almost smooth grey bark, with some very white spots on it. **1864** GRISEBACH *Flora Brit. W. Ind.* 787/2 Silver-wood, *Guettarda argentea*, *Zuelania lætioides*, and *Mouriria myrtilloides*.

**silver-work.** [SILVER *sb.* Cf. MDu. *silver-, sulverwerc* (Du. *zilverwerk*), MLG. *sulverwerk, -wark*, MHG. and G. *silberwerk*.]

**1.** Articles made of silver; silver vessels or ornaments; silverware. †Also *pl.*

**1535** COVERDALE *Isaiah* xxx. 22 Yf ye destroye the syluer workes of youre Idols. **1538** *Acc. Ld. High Treas. Scot.* VII. 87 All furnist chaip and ruvell witht silver werk. **1648** HEXHAM II. s.v. *Zilver-werck*, Plate or Silver-worke to serve at a table. **1753** *Chambers' Cycl.* Suppl. s.v. *Silver*, Silver works, as spurs, wrought hilts, &c. are boiled in salt, alum and argol, to give it a whiteness and clearness. **1820** SCOTT *Monast.* xvi, Every bit of..silver work have we been spoiled of since Pinkie Cleuch. **1899** *Daily News* 16 May 8/4 The artificer may be seen at work in the room in which Messrs. Liberty show the silverwork.

**2.** A place where silver is smelted.

**1674** RAY *Collect. Wds.*, *Smelting Silver* 119 The History of these Silver-works may be seen in Dr. Fullers *Worthies of Wales*, General, p. 3.

†**silverwort.** *Obs.*⁻⁰ = SILVERWEED I.

**1611** FLORIO, *Atanási*, tansie or siluerwort.

†**silvery**, *sb. nonce-wd.* [f. SILVER *sb.*] = Silver sickness (SILVER *sb.* 21).

**1387** TREVISA *Higden* (Rolls) III. 335 þanne oon of þe peple cride and seide, 'It is no squynacie but silverie [*v.r.* selvery] that it ailleþ'.

**silvery** ('sɪlvərɪ), *a.* [f. SILVER *sb.* + -Y. Cf. Du. *sulverich, zilverich*, G. *silberig*.]

**1. a.** Having the hue or lustre of silver.

**1611** COTGR., *Argentin*, argentine, silverie. **1704** PETIVER *Gazophyl.* iii. §26 This is a flat edible Fish,..Silvery above and brown below. **1742** POPE *Dunciad* IV. 421 Of all th' enamell'd race, whose silv'ry wing Waves to the tepid Zephyrs of the spring, Or swims along the fluid atmosphere. **1796** TWINING *Trav. India*, etc. (1892) 2 His thin silvery locks curled round the collar of his old-fashioned..coat. **1812** J. WILSON *Isle of Palms* I. 86 While yet the silvery glory lies, Above the sparkling foam. **1857** LIVINGSTONE *Trav. S. Africa* viii. 167 This bush has fine silvery leaves. **1886** RUSKIN *Præterita* I. 290 One small bright silvery likeness of a cloud.

**b.** *silvery iron*, an inferior kind of pig-iron, more commonly called *white iron*.

**1861** SIR W. FAIRBAIRN *Iron* 67 Under these conditions, it makes what is called white or silvery iron.

**2. a.** In names of animals, birds, and fishes, as *silvery fox, gibbon, gull, shrew mole*; *silvery gade, hair-tail* (see quots.); *silvery pout*, a small marine fish, *Gadiculus argenteus thori*, belonging to the cod family and found in north-western Europe and the Mediterranean; *silvery salmon* (see quot.).

Also in some names of moths, as *silvery arches, broad bar, hawk* (Rennie, 1832).

**1781** PENNANT *Hist. Quadrup.* I. 241 The *Silvery Fox.. abound in the wooded eminences in Louisiana. **1827** GRIFFITH tr. *Cuvier* II. 44 The Silvery or Black Fox. *Ibid.* 368 The Silvery Fox (*Canis Argentatus*) is a species which has been known for a long time. **1836** YARRELL *Brit. Fishes* II. 195 The *Silvery Gade, *Motella argenteola*. **1881** *Cassell's Nat. Hist.* V. 64 The second species (*Couchia argentata*) is commonly known as the Silvery Gade. **1827** GRIFFITH tr. *Cuvier* I. 209 The Ash-coloured or *Silvery Gibbon, also called the Wou Wou. **1871** *Cassell's Nat. Hist.* I. 81 A species which is called the Wow-wow, or Silvery Gibbon (*Hylobates leuciscus*). **1785** PENNANT *Arctic Zool.* II. 533 *Silvery Gull, *Larus argentatus*, Gull with a white head and neck. *c* **1875** *Cassell's Nat. Hist.* IV. 207 The last-named species..from its lighter colour is often called the Silvery Gull. **1836** YARRELL *Brit. Fishes* I. 182 The *Silvery hairtail, *trichiurus lepturus*. **1871** DAY *Fishes Gt. Brit.* I. 154 The hair-tail or silvery hair-tail, blade-fish. **1925** J. T. JENKINS *Fishes Brit. Isles* 155 The *Silvery Pout is not often met with close inshore. **1959** A. C. HARDY *Open Sea* II. ii. 229 The little silvery pout..is an even more deep-water species. **1804** SHAW *Gen. Zool.* V. I. 63 *Silvery Salmon, *Salmo Argentinus*. **1871** *Cassell's Nat. Hist.* I. 374 The Prairie Mole, or the *Silvery Shrew Mole (*Scalops argentatus*).

**b.** In names of trees or plants, as *silvery acacia, hair-grass, honeysuckle, oak*.

**1859** MISS PRATT *Brit. Grasses* 75 *Aira caryophyllea* ..(Silvery Hair-grass)... Its panicle is of a silvery grey colour. **1889** MAIDEN *Useful Pl.* 293 *Acacia subcærulea*,.. Silvery, or Blue-leaved Acacia. *Ibid.* 552 *Grevillea striata*,.. Silvery Honeysuckle. *Ibid.* 599 *Stenocarpus salignus*,..Silky Oak. Silvery Oak.

**3. a.** Having a clear gentle metallic resonance; silver-toned, melodious.

**1600** *Dr. Dodypoll* III. v. in Bullen *Old Pl.* III, Hanging on every leafe an orient pearle Which strooke together with the silver winde Of their loose mantels, made a silvery chime. **1824** BYRON *Juan* XV. lxi, The silvery bell rang. **1853** KINGSLEY *Hypatia* ix, In his ears one silvery voice was ringing. **1884** *St. James's Gaz.* 21 June 5/1 A peculiar soft silvery tone which contrasts very strikingly with the English bands.

**b.** Silver-voiced.

**1821** BYRON *Diary* Wks. (1846) 531/2 Burdett is sweet and silvery.

**4.** Producing silver; containing silver.

**1870** J. ORTON *Andes & Amazon* vii. (1876) 120 At one end of the valley, perched above the clouds, is silvery Potosi. **1875** JEVONS *Money* (1878) 154 It is only requisite to melt the silvery gold.

**5.** *Comb.* **a.** Qualifying other adjs., as *silvery-green, -silken, -white*, etc.

**1796** WITHERING *Brit. Pl.* (ed. 3) IV. 242 Stem hollow, silvery grey. **1802** SHAW *Gen. Zool.* III. II. 588 Silvery-brownish Slow-Worm. **1831** POE *To Helen* Poems (1859) 62 Through heaven There fell a silvery-silken veil of light. **1836–9** *Todd's Cycl. Anat.* II. 174/1 The brilliant silvery-white appearance so characteristic of the fibrous membranes. **1882** *Garden* 25 Nov. 469/3 Silvery pink, becoming darker with age.

**b.** Parasynthetic or instrumental, as *silvery-eyed, -leaved, -lined, -sided, -tongued*, etc.

**1752** HILL *Hist. Anim.* 252 The silvery-eyed, red Sparus ..is also a very beautiful fish. **1797** *Encycl. Brit.* (ed. 3) XVII. 461/2 Silvery-leaved iron-wood, a native of Carolina. **1822** *Hortus Anglicus* II. 196 *Geranium Argenteum*. Silvery-leaved Crane's Bill. **1864** TENNYSON *Islet* 20 Over-stream'd and silvery-streak'd With many a rivulet. **1872** JENKINSON *Guide to Lakes* (1879) 211 The storm was succeeded by masses of silvery-lined clouds. **1885** E. W. HAMILTON *Diary* 29 Jan. (1972) II. 783 The German Ambassador whom Bismarck suspects of being too silvery-tongued over here.

**silvester, -trial**, varr. SYLVESTER, -TRIAL.

**silvex** ('sɪlvɛks). [f. L. *silv-a* wood, woodland + Eng. *-ex*.] A hormone weedkiller that is also effective against some woody plants; 2-(2,4,5-trichlorophenoxy)propionic acid.

**1954** *Proc. Southern Weed Conf.* VII. 268 Silver was active in causing cell elongation and adventitious root formation but not active in causing formative effects. **1973** ASHTON & CRAFTS *Mode of Action of Herbicides* ix. 131 These growth regulators enhance the herbicidal effect of silvex on poison ivy. **1976** *Columbus* (Montana) *News* 3 June (Joliet Suppl.) 4/5 Dandelions are more difficult to control after they flower. Spraying with 2, 4-D, silvex or dicamba (Banvel) is recommended... Silvex also gives excellent control of chickweed.

**silvi-** ('sɪlvɪ), comb. form of L. *silva* wood, woodland. Cf. also SYLVICULTURE, SILVI-.

**silvical** ('sɪlvɪkəl), *a.* [f. as SILVICS + -ICAL.] Of or pertaining to silvics.

**1909** in WEBSTER. **1919** *Jrnl. Forestry* XVII. 276 The Commission of Conservation of Canada has during several seasons conducted silvical investigations... Studies of natural regeneration, with special reference to the effects of repeated fires, have been carried out. **1931** *Ecology* XII. 568 Müller was probably the first to look upon the humus layer in the forest as a natural biological unit, and..he was able to characterize two main types of humus layer and their biological and silvical properties. **1977** *Jrnl. Arnold Arboretum Harvard Univ.* LVIII. 307 (*heading*) Silvical characteristics of sugar maple..in northern Cape Breton Island.

**silvichemical** (sɪlvɪ'kɛmɪkəl). [f. SILVI- + CHEMICAL *a.*] Any chemical obtained from part of a tree.

**1963** L. C. BRATT in *Abstr. Papers 144th Meeting Amer. Chem. Soc.* 11D The name 'silvichemicals' is used in this paper to define chemicals and special products made from tree components, primarily wood, bark, and oleoresins as well as from pulp mill by-products. **1965** *Jrnl. Forestry* LXIII. 163/1 The silvichemicals may be divided into the two broad classifications of complex polymers or mixtures and pure organic chemicals. **1974** *Finnish Chem. Lett.* VII. 262 There are clear opportunities for the creation of a profitable enterprise producing silvichemicals from technical foliage.

**silvicide** ('sɪlvɪsaɪd). [f. SILVI- + -CIDE[1].] A substance that kills trees.

**1950** in *Forestry Terminol.* (Soc. Amer. Foresters) (ed. 2) 75/1. **1960** *Jrnl. Forestry* LVIII. 403/2 Thinning white pine stands with silvicides might be expected to result in serious backflash damage. **1976** *Amer. Industr. Hygiene Assoc. Jrnl.* XXXVII. 418/1 The increasing use of organic arsenicals.. as silvicides in forestry has raised questions concerning the health and safety of exposed workers.

**silvics** ('sɪlvɪks). [f. L. *silva*, SYLVA + *-ics*: see -IC 2.] The scientific study of the growth and life of forest trees, as a department of forestry. orig. and chiefly *U.S.* Cf. SILVICAL *a.*

**1907** (April 17) *U.S. Dept. Agric., Forest Service* Order No. 132 Silvics. [The title has been changed (April 17, 1913) to the 'Office of Forest Investigations'.] **1946** *Jrnl. Forestry* XLIV. 965/1 The forester's knowledge of the silvics of the species was pretty thin. **1948** H. J. OOSTING *Study of Plant Communities* (ed. 2) xii. 317 An important part of a forester's training is forest ecology, or silvics, in which he learns the scientific background upon which silvicultural practices are based. **1975** *Agriculture Handbk.* (U.S. Dept. Agric.) No. 486 (*title*) Quaking aspen: silvics and management in the Lake States.

**silyl** ('saɪlaɪl, -lɪl). *Chem.* [f. SIL(ANE + -YL.] The univalent group or radical $-SiH_3$; any substituted derivative of this, esp. one in which alkyl groups replace the hydrogen atoms. Usu. *attrib.*

**1916** *Jrnl. Chem. Soc.* CX. II. 319 The radicles $\cdot SiH_3$, $\cdot Si_2H_5$, and $\cdot Si_2H_3$ would be respectively designated silyl, disilyl, and disilenyl. **1939** *Ibid.* 1030 Some of the other possible reactions of the silyl radicals are more favoured than that with ethylene. **1970** *Nature* 25 July 335/2 The preparation of silylated ylides of phosphorus, arsenic and sulphur, in which the silyl group is both a stabilizing and an efficient leaving group.

Hence **sily'lation**, a reaction or process in which a substance is converted into a form having silyl substituents; also **'silylate** *v. trans.*, to subject to silylation; **'silylated** *ppl. a.*; **'silylating** *vbl. sb.*

**1938** *Nature* 3 Dec. 997/1 Trimethylsilylammonium chloride is a convenient silylating agent. **1949** *Chem. Abstr. Subject Index 1937–1946* 8856/2 Silylation. **1966** *Jrnl. Amer. Chem. Soc.* LXXXVIII. 3390/1 Bis(trimethylsilyl)-acetamide..is a silylating agent superior, in many respects, to the presently used methods. *Ibid.* 3390/2 Silylations of 'good' acceptors—alcohols, amines, carboxylic acids—can be carried out with monosilylamides since the rapidly established equilibria lie far on the product side. *Ibid.* 3391/1 The vapor pressure of the silylated product. **1969** *Kirk-Othmer Encycl. Chem. Technol.* (ed. 2) XVIII. 262 A method of silylating biologically active compounds. **1972** *Science* 12 May 683/3 Silylation was effected in pyridine with a mixture of hexamethyldisilazane and trimethylchlorosilane. **1978** *Experientia* XXXIV. 1380/1 The material..was silylated with 200μl of trimethylsilylimidazole at 65°C for 12–15h.

**Sim**[1]. [abbrev. of the personal name *Simon.*] † ***Sim subtle***, a subtle or crafty person. *Obs.*

**1581** J. BELL *Haddon's Answ. Osorius* 170b, Whereupon Simme Suttle argueth from destruction of the consequent on this wise. **1599** HAKLUYT *Voyages* II. II. 84 In his latter yeeres this Sim suttle buried himselfe in a fouresquare graue,..seuerely forbidding it to be opened.

**Sim**[2]. Now *Hist.* [abbrev. of SIMEONITE.] A Simeonite; *esp.* at Cambridge, an evangelical, religious, or quiet man.

**1851** BRISTED *Five Yrs. Eng. Univ.* 40 Passing for a terribly hard-reading man, and a 'Sim' of the straightest kind. **1860** *Slang Dict.* 214 *Sim*, one of a Methodistical turn in religion; a low-churchman; originally a follower of the late Rev. Charles Simeon. **1883** *Times* 22 Oct. 9/5 To be a Simeonite at Cambridge—the undergraduates abbreviated it into 'Sim',..—was to wear a badge of reproach.

**sim**, var. of SUM *adv.* and *conj.*; dial. f. SEEM *v.*

**sima** ('saɪmə). *Geol.* Also **Sima**. [a. G. *sima* (E. Suess *Das Antlitz der Erde* (1909) III. II. xxiv. 626), f. L. *si-licium* SILICON + *magnesium* MAGNESIUM.] The continuous basal layer of the earth's crust, composed of relatively heavy, basic rocks rich in silica and magnesia, that underlies the sialic continental masses and forms the crust under the oceans; the material of which it is composed.

The lower limit of the sima is generally taken to be the Mohorovičić discontinuity.

**1909** [see NIFE]. **1925** *Glasgow Herald* 29 Sept. 9 In continental regions it [*sc.* sial] both rises higher to form the land surface, and extends downwards into or displaces somewhat the sima, just as a ship floats on and displaces the water. **1944** A. HOLMES *Princ. Physical Geol.* iv. 41 Certain rocks of the kinds grouped together as sima (*e.g.* basalt) contain calcic plagioclase, but others are free from felspar. All of the sima rocks, however, are characterized by the abundance or predominance of heavy, greenish silicate minerals. **1950** P. H. KUENEN *Marine Geol.* ii. 127 If America were plowing through the sima westwards..one would expect a raising of the sima in front of the continent. **1970** L. KNOPOFF in Johnson & Smith *Megatectonics of Continents & Oceans* vi. 120 It seemed plausible to assert that the top of the mantle was a chemically homogeneous material. In many of the older geology texts, this material was simply called sima to describe a dense, basic rock from which the less dense, more acidic sialic crust could be derived by some process of differentiation.

Hence **si'matic** *a.*, of or pertaining to the basal crust or the material of which it is made.

**1942** R. A. DALY *Floor of Ocean* ii. 59 The oceanic sectors of the earth are characteristically simatic... Also simatic is any vitreous basalt which may form 'pockets' in the crust. **1955** [see SIALIC *a.*[1]]. **1971** *Proc. 2nd Symposium Upper Mantle Project* (Council of Sci. & Industr. Res., New Delhi) p. xix, Resting on the simatic crust, the continental blocks move, as if riding on the conveyor belt.

**sima**, obs. variant of CYMA.

‖**simagre.** *Obs. rare.* [ad. F. *simagrée*, of unknown origin.] An affected air or look.

**1678** DRYDEN *Kind Keeper* III. i, By these languishing Eyes, and those Simagres of yours, we are given to understand, Sir, you have a Mistress in this Company. **1700** —— *Ovid's Met.* XIII. *Acis, Polyphemus & Galatea* 31 Now in the Crystal Stream he looks, to try His Simagres, and rowls his glaring eye.

**simandro, simantron**, varr. SEMANTRON.

**simar** (sɪ'mɑː(r)). Forms: 7- **simarre, simar** (7 **-arr**); 8- **symar** (9 **seymar**). [ad. F. *simarre*, ad. It. *cimarra, zimarra*: cf. CYMAR and CHIMER[1].]

**1.** = CYMAR 1. Also *fig.*

α. **1641** *Ariana* 201 A Persian simarre, or mantle. **1671** tr. *Palafox's Conq. China* xxxii. 581 Their Habit is either a certain Vest, or Simar. **1720** POPE *Iliad* XVIII. 685 The maids in soft simars of linen drest. **1784** tr. *Beckford's Vathek* (1883) 128 They were wrapped in simars whiter than alabaster. **1819** SCOTT *Ivanhoe* vii, A simarre of the richest Persian silk. **1828** tr. *Manzoni's Betrothed Lovers* I. iv. 119 Trailing simars, broidered with work of Arabia. **1893** *Cent. Mag.* Aug. 640/2 The dancing girl in soft simar.

β. **1700** DRYDEN *Flower & Leaf* 341 The ladies, dress'd in rich symars were seen Of Florence satten. **1796** MRS. J. WEST *Gossip's Story* II. 78 A white frock altered into a Grecian symar for the occasion. **1813** BYRON *Giaour* 1273, I saw her..shining in her white symar, As through yon pale gray cloud the star. **1831** J. WILSON *Noctes Ambr.* Wks. III. 328 The winter..in green symar changin afore the gratefu' gaze intil the..spring. **1886** W. ALEXANDER *S. Augustine's Holiday* 217 Dark sultanas dress'd in white symars.

**2.** = CYMAR 2, CHIMER[1].

**1840** H. AINSWORTH *Tower of London* (1864) 5 They were attired in the scarlet simar, and surplice with its snowy lawn sleeves, proper to their order. **1886** tr. *Hugo's Notre Dame* VIII. ii, The simar had the worst of it in its collision with the cassock.

**simaruba** (sɪmə'ruːbə). *Bot.* and *Med.* Also 8–9 **simarouba**. [Native name in Guyana, known in Europe from *c* 1713, at first in the French form *simarouba*; the ending *-ba* is characteristic of Carib tree-names.]

**1.** A tree of the genus *Simaruba*, esp. *S. amara* or *officinalis* (formerly called *Quassia Simaruba*), a native of northern Brazil, Guyana, and some West Indian islands. Also *attrib.*, as ***simaruba bark*** (see 2), ***family, tree***.

**1753** *Chambers' Cycl.* Suppl., *Simarouba*. The bark of this plant is very successful in the cure of dysenteries. **1756** BROWNE *Nat. Hist. Jamaica* 345 The bark of the root of this tree [Terebinthus] is thought to be the Sima-rouba of the shops. **1769** E. BANCROFT *Nat. Hist. Guiana* 84 The Simaruba tree is peculiar to Guiana. **1812** J. SMYTH *Pract. Customs* (1821) 40 Simarouba Bark, is the Bark of the root of a species of Birch-tree, not yet sufficiently described. **1849** J. H. BALFOUR *Man. Bot.* §831 *Simarubaceæ*, the Quassia and Simaruba Family. **1866** *Treas. Bot.* 1060/1 *S. amara*.. yields the drug known as Simaruba-bark, which is, strictly speaking, the rind of the root.

**2.** The bark of the root of *Simaruba amara*, which contains quassine and is employed medicinally as a tonic or astringent.

**1778** WRIGHT in *Edin. Trans.* (1790) II. 79 The disorder was happily cured by the simaruba. **1789** CULLEN *Mat. Med.* II. 75 My account of the effect of bitters in the dysentery will perhaps explain the virtues ascribed to simaruba. **1822–34** *Good's Study Med.* (ed. 4) IV. 376 Decoction of bark with simarouba. **1876** CURLING *Dis. Rectum* 115 Vegetable astringents, such as simaruba and krameria. **1898** P. MANSON *Trop. Dis.* xviii. 312 Boil half an ounce of simaruba in a pint and a half of water.

**simarubaceous** (sɪməruː'beɪʃəs), *a. Bot.* [f. mod.L. *Simarubaceæ* (Richard, 1808), f. prec.] Belonging to the order of tropical trees and shrubs which includes *Simaruba* and *Quassia*.

**1841** *Penny Cycl.* XIX. 200/2 A genus of plants belonging to the Simarubaceous order. **1852** TH. ROSS tr. *Humboldt's Trav.* I. vi. 213 Among simarubaceous plants, the Quassia amara, celebrated in the feverish plains of Surinam.

**simazine** ('sɪm-, 'saɪməziːn). Formerly also **-in** (-ɪn). Also with capital initial. [f. *sim-* (ad. SYM(METRIC *a.*) + TRI)AZINE.] A colourless crystalline compound, 2-chloro-4,6-bis-(ethylamino)-1,3,5-triazine, $C_7H_{12}N_5Cl$, which is a selective weedkiller applied as an emulsion or wettable powder.

**1956** *Proc. 13th Meeting N. Central Weed Control Conf.* 57/1 During 1956, an experimental herbicide..designated as Simazin, was released to experiment stations for test purposes. **1957** *Chem. Abstr.* LI. 9995 The herbicides CMU ..and Simazine..are used..to prevent weed growth in grafting vineyards after the spring weeding. **1958** *Times* 10 Nov. 19/2 Another chemical on which interest is focused is Simazin..which kills a wide range of weeds. **1971** *Ideal Home* Apr. 120 Keep it weed free with an annual application of a simazine weedkiller like Weedex *before* weeds appear. **1978** *Financial Times* 2 Dec. 13/3 Rose beds kept clear of weeds by small annual applications of simazine.

**simba** ('sɪmbə). Also **Simba**. [Swahili.] A lion. Also *fig.*, a warrior; a leader.

**1918** E. R. BURROUGHS *Tarzan & Jewels* iii. 30 The strange white man must certainly succumb to terrible Simba. **1935** E. HEMINGWAY *Green Hills of Africa* ii. 42 A stream of..words in Wakamba ending in the word '*Simba*'. **1966** *Transition* (Uganda) XXVI. 39/1 In battle, the simbas had to walk straight forward, and keep their eyes to the front to avoid loss of invulnerability. **1975** T. DINESEN *My Sister, Isak Dinesen* v. 56 A large simba had been lying at the river-crossing and hadn't moved as he went by, only stared menacingly at him. **1976** *Drum* (E. Afr. ed.) Sept. 3/1 Has Amin now recognised his weakness? What does he now think and say? Does he still claim to be the *simba* of Africa?

**simbal(l**, obs. forms of CYMBAL.

**'simball.** *U.S.* [Cf. CYMBAL 4.] A doughnut.

**1865** MRS. WHITNEY *Gayworthys* iii, They had popped corn, and roasted apples, and eaten simballs. **1892** MARIA L. POOL *Roweny in Boston* xvii. 263 Mrs. Tuttle was frying doughnuts... Mrs. Tuttle called these fried cakes 'simballs'.

**simber**, obs. form of SIMMER *v.*

**simber salt**, obs. form of SOMERSAULT.

†**'simblic**, *a. Obs.* [f. Gr. σίμβλιος or σιμβλήϊος, f. σίμβλος beehive.] (See quot.)

**1658** ROWLAND tr. *Moufet's Theat. Ins.* 1004 Mingled with liquid Pitch and Simblick Honey; Dioscorides saith Sicilian Honey is called Simblick.

**simblin**, variant of SIMLIN.

**simchah** ('sɪmxə). Also **simcha, Simchah**. [a. Heb. *śimḥā* rejoicing.] A Jewish private party or celebration.

**1932** L. GOLDING *Magnolia Street* II. ii. 295 Perhaps, after all, it'll be a good match. There will be a *simchah*. **1959** H. PINTER *Birthday Party* II. 35 Mazoltov! And may we only meet at Simchahs! **1973** *Jewish Chron.* 19 Jan. 42/2 (Advt.), Arkay caterers. Specialists in home, hall and marquee catering for all simchas.

**Simchat Torah** ('sɪmxət 'tɔərə). Also **Simchas, Simchath, Simhat**, and hyphened. [a. Heb. *śimḥat tōrā*, f. *śimḥat*, construct case of *śimḥa* SIMCHAH, + TORAH.] The final day of the festival of Succoth, on which the annual cycle of the reading of the Torah reaches its completion.

**1891** M. FRIEDLÄNDER *Jewish Relig.* II. 480 Twice a year we have special occasion for fulfilment of this duty, viz., on *Simchath-torah* and on the *Seder*-evening. **1905** *Jewish Encycl.* XI. 365/1 The name 'Simhat Torah' came into use after the introduction of the one-year cycle for the reading of the Law. **1907** OESTERLEY & BOX *Relig. & Worship Synagogue* III. xx. 374 In some places it has..been customary for the children to tear down the 'booths' (*sukkoth*), and burn them on *Simchath Torah*. **1927** A. FELDMAN *Sabbath Spice & Festival Fare* 30 On Simchas Torah..there is a 'procession' of the Scrolls. **1960** *Jewish Chron.* 8 Apr. 35/3 To dance on *Simchat Torah*, Is there a greater pleasure? **1973** *Synagogue Light* Sept. 56 (*caption*) Israeli Hassidim celebrating Simhat Torah at the Western Wall. **1975** C. POTOK *In Beginning* iv. 213, I thought of the way my father..had danced with the Torah on Simchat Torah. **1978** I. B. SINGER *Shosha* v. 98 Only on Simchas Torah were girls allowed inside a house of worship.

**sime.** *north. dial.* Also **syme, seyme.** [a. ON. *síma* neut. (Norw., older Sw. and Da. *sime*, Sw. dial. *simme*), = OS. *sîmo* masc. (hence OE. *síma*), OFris. *sîm* rope, cord. See also SIMMON *sb.*[2]] **a.** A straw rope. **b.** (See quot. 1781.)

**1781** J. HUTTON *Tour to Caves* (ed. 2) Gloss. 97 *Syme*, a frame of straw to set pans on. **1825** J. BRIGGS *Rem.* 223 (E.D.D.), He could twist the syme, but could not wash it in the Cocker. **1899** DICKINSON & PREVOST *Cumbld. Gloss.*, *Syme, seyme*, a straw rope used for holding down the thatch of stacks.

**simenel(l**, obs. forms of SIMNEL.

**Simeonite** ('sɪmɪənaɪt). [f. the name of the Rev. Charles *Simeon* (1759–1836) + -ITE[1] 1 b.]

**a.** A follower or adherent of Simeon or a supporter of his theological doctrines; a Low Churchman or Evangelical. Also abbrev. SIM[2].

**1823** EGAN *Grose's Dict. Vulgar T.*, *Simeonites* (at Cambridge), the followers of the Rev. Charles Simeon..; they are, in fact, rank methodists. **1837** WILBERFORCE in Ashwell *Life* (1880) I. iv. 112 The Simeonites are not likely to invite us. **1884** *World* 3 Dec. 16/2 Dr. Law attracted a vast number of Low Church people to Weston, and at one time the town was as full of 'Simeonites' and their disciples as Bath or Cheltenham.

**b.** *attrib.* or as *adj.*

**1837** WILBERFORCE in Ashwell *Life* (1880) I. iv. 112 The good people there tell him one of us is to be the new (Simeonite) Rector. **1850** MACAULAY in Trevelyan *Life* (1876) II. 254, I found the stairs, the passages, and the very street..full of parsons, Puseyite and Simeonite. **1893** 'MARK RUTHERFORD' *Catharine Furze* vi, The patronage was in the hands of the Simeonite trustees.

Hence **'Simeonism**, adherence to the doctrines of Simeon.

*a* **1902** S. BUTLER *Way of All Flesh* (1903) xlvii. 213 These poor fellows formed a class apart..and it was among them that Simeonism chiefly flourished.

**simetite** ('sɪm-, 'siːmətaɪt). *Min.* Also **Simetite**. [a. It. *simetite* (O. Helm 1887, in *Malpighia* I. 54), f. *Simeto*, name of a river in Sicily: see -ITE[1].] A variety of amber, usu. reddish, found in Sicily.

**1892** E. S. DANA *Dana's Syst. Mineral.* (ed. 6) 1005 Simetite... A resin near amber from near Mt. Etna, Sicily. Remarkable for its deep red color and often showing a beautiful fluorescence. **1915** R. LANKESTER *Diversions of Naturalist* ix. 71 The Sicilian amber (called 'Simetite') was not known to the ancients. **1932** G. C. WILLIAMSON *Bk. of Amber* 209 Some of the very clearest pieces of golden Simetite possess bloom and flashes of blue. **1969** *Beaver*

Summer 29/2 Reddish amber from Sicily, called simetite, is also a succinite.

**Simhat Torah**, var. SIMCHAT TORAH.

**simi** ('sɪmɪ). [ad. Swahili *sime*.] In East Africa: a large knife; a short two-edged sword (see also quot. 1980).

**1955** *Times* 7 June 6/6 Small boys in feathers, with cowbells at their ankles and brandishing tiny *simis* (swords), stamp and dance in circles. **1961** *Encounter* Jan. 24/2 He had killed two of the Masai morans.. cutting the throat of the other with his simi. **1977** D. BEATY *Excellency* ix. 108 An African was.. holding up a thin-bladed simi knife. **1980** *Times* 3 Apr. 8/1 Mrs Joy Adamson, the naturalist and authoress of *Born Free*, was murdered with a simi (a two-edged farming implement like a sword), and an iron bar, a police witness said.

‖**Simia** ('sɪmɪə). Pl. simiæ ('sɪmɪiː). [L. *sīmia*, perh. f. *sīmus*, Gr. σιμός snub-nosed, flat-nosed.] The class of animals consisting of the apes and monkeys, and more specifically of the tailless apes only, or of certain kinds of these, as the orang-utan; also (with lower-case initial), an animal of this kind.

**1753** *Chambers' Cycl.* Suppl. s.v., More regularly, the word *simia* is the name of that kind only which has no tail. **1783** *Encycl. Brit.* (ed. 2) X. 8166/2 The simiæ being more numerous in their species than any other animals [etc.]. **1800** SHAW *Gen. Zool.* I. I. 70 It should seem rather to belong to the genus Lemur than that of Simia. **1840** *Cuvier's Anim. Kingd.* 56 The developement of brain, in all the *Simiæ*,.. is arrested at a particular stage of advancement. **1872** DARWIN in *Life & Lett.* III. 162, I cannot at present give up my belief in the close relationship of man to the higher Simiæ.

**'simiad**, *a. rare*⁻¹. [f. prec. + -AD.] Simian.

**1874** R. F. BURTON tr. *Camoens' Lusiad* v. (1880) I. 183 The simiad Negro swaying Africk strand.

**simial** ('sɪmɪəl), *a.* Now *rare*. [f. SIMIA + -AL¹.]

**1.** Of or pertaining to, consisting of, apes.

**1827** FONBLANQUE in *Life* (1874) 414 Had a Monkey Reviewer.. admonished the tribe of the aggregate of loss to the simial stomach. **1828** —— *Eng. under 7 Administr.* (1837) I. 150 Somewhere they worship a blue ape, and somewhere they incense another variety of the simial species. **1849** H. MILLER *Footpr. Creat.* viii. (1874) 136 The sea-inhabiting progenitors of the simial family. **1864** *Q. Jrnl. Sci.* I. 91 It is quite a Simial characteristic and rarely if ever occurs in Man.

**2.** Characteristic of apes; ape-like.

**1830** MARRYAT *King's Own* xiii, The builder.. skipping with all the simial ecstasy of a Frenchman. **1851** D. JERROLD *St. Giles* xxiv, Vulgar souls who, judging from their simial selves, may doubt the continence of Scipio.

**simian** ('sɪmɪən), *a.* and *sb.* [f. as prec. + -AN. Cf. F. *simien*, *-enne*.]

**A.** *adj.* **1.** Characteristic of apes; resembling that of apes; ape-like, apish.

**1607** T. WALKINGTON *Opt. Glass* vii. 82 Ther is a Simian or apish wit. **1862** MRS. SPEID *Last Yrs. India* 209 The poor little puny Tamul race of Southern India, whose general effect.. is unequivocally simian. **1883** BARING-GOULD *J. Herring* II. xxxi. 162 His face was simian in its ugliness and malignity. **1884** M. MACKENZIE *Dis. Throat & Nose* II. 428 Giving the whole face a markedly simian expression.

**2.** Of or belonging to, comprising or consisting of, the apes or *Simiæ*.

**1863** LYELL *Antiq. Man* v. 90 Those [differences] which separate the human from the simian brain. **1871** DARWIN *Desc. Man* I. vi. 199 The early progenitors of the whole Simian stock including man. **1889** *Edin. Rev.* CLXX. 375 The developement of man's intellect from simian ancestry.

**B.** *sb.* An ape or monkey.

**1880** L. WALLACE *Ben-Hur* VII. iv. 455 She.. saw Indra passing with an army of simians. **1890** STANLEY *Darkest Africa* I. xvii. 423, I should never have credited that any of the Simians understood the art of making fire.

†**similable**, *a. Obs. rare.* [ad. med.L. type **similābilis*: cf. Pg. *semelhavel*, Sp. *semejable*, It. *simiglievole*.] = SIMILAR *a.* 2.

**1493** *Acta Dom. Conc.* 17 Oct. 305/1 A ȝeris proffitis.. takin vp.. be þe said erle, as with similable wise previt before the lordis. **1494** *Ibid.* 7 July 361/1 Lik as he tuk apone him to preif in similable wise.

**similacioun**, obs. form of SIMULATION.

**similacre**, variant of SIMULACRE *Obs.*

**similar** ('sɪmɪlə(r)), *a.* and *sb.* Also 7 similare. [ad. F. *similaire* (= Sp. and Pg. *similar*), or med.L. **similāris*, f. L. *similis* like: see -AR¹, and cf. the earlier SIMILARY.]

**A.** *adj.* †**1.** Of the same substance or structure throughout; homogeneous; esp. *similar parts* (see quot. 1704). Also *transf.* (quot. 1728). *Obs.*

(*a*) **1626** BACON *Sylva* §16 Simple Bodies, which consist of severall similare Parts. **1651** HOBBES *Leviath.* II. xxii. 123 Which may be compared.. to the Similar parts of mans Body. **1678** CUDWORTH *Intell. Syst.* I. i. 32 The same kind of Nourishment taken in by animals, is turned into Blood, Milk, Flesh, Bones, Nerves, and all the other Similar Parts. **1704** J. HARRIS *Lex. Techn.* I, *Similar, or simple Parts*, by Anatomists are called such as are throughout of the same nature and texture, as all the Parts of a Bone are Bony, &c. **1728** CHAMBERS *Cycl.* s.v. *Disease*, Diseases of the Solids, he [Boerhaave] considers, either as of the simple, and Similar Parts; Or of the Organical. Similar Diseases are [etc.].

(*b*) **1669** BOYLE *Physiol. Ess.* (ed. 2) 50 Minerals appearing to the eye either to be perfectly similar, as Metals, or at least to consist but of two or three distinct ingredients, as Cinnabar. **1704** NEWTON *Optics* (1721) 4 The Light whose Rays are all alike Refrangible I call Simple, Homogeneal and Similar.

**2. a.** Having a marked resemblance or likeness; of a like nature or kind.

**1611** COTGR. s.v. *Similaire*, Similar; like, resembling. **1665** HOOKE *Microgr.* 198 The Carter Spider.. has, for two particularities, very few similar creatures that I have met with. **1750** JOHNSON *Rambler* No. 78 ¶3 Something similar, or analogous, may be observed. **1790** BURKE *Fr. Rev.* Wks. 1898 II. 124 At home we behold similar beginnings. We are on our guard against similar conclusions. **1819** SHELLEY *Peter Bell 3rd* III. iv, A set Of thieves who by themselves are sent Similar thieves to represent. **1860** TYNDALL *Glac.* II. i. 229 Dr. Wollaston pointed out a similar fact as regards hearing. **1897** TROTTER *Life J. Nicholson* iii. (1908) 51 The rest of the party were threatened with similar tortures.

**b.** Const. *to*; also formerly *with*.

*a* **1740** WATERLAND *Serm.* Wks. 1823 IX. 23 The commandment to love our neighbour, which is a duty second and similar to that of the love of God. **1749** FIELDING *Tom Jones* VIII. xiii, They.. produce similar effects with Exercise. **1832** THIRLWALL in *Rem.* (1878) III. 86 A legend of similar import with that of the death of Hercules. **1868** LOCKYER *Elem. Astron.* §357 The effect of the Earth's daily movement upon the Sun is precisely similar to its effect upon the stars. **1896** [see B. 2 below].

**3.** *spec.* **a.** *Math.*, etc. (See quots.)

**1704** J. HARRIS *Lex. Techn.* I, *Similar Segments* of a Circle are such as contain equal Angles. *Ibid.*, *Similar Triangles* are such as have all their three Angles respectively equal to one another. **1706** W. JONES *Syn. Palmar. Matheseos* 72 Similar Products are those whose Corresponding Factors are Proportional. **1798** HUTTON *Course Math.* I. 322 Equiangular triangles are similar, and are proportional to the squares of their like sides. **1823** BROOKE *Crystallog.* 57 If all the planes of any primary form be similar, as those are of the cube, rhomboid, and some other forms. **1840** LARDNER *Geom.* 111 Two geometrical figures which have the same shape or form, but are constructed on a different scale, are said to be similar figures. **1878** GURNEY *Crystallog.* 30 The edges.. which are equally inclined to each other are said to be similar.

**b.** *Mus.* Of motion: (see quots.).

**1861** J. S. ADAMS *5000 Mus. Terms* 91 *Similar Motion*, that in which two or more parts always ascend or descend at the same time. **1875** STAINER & BARRETT *Dict. Mus. Terms* s.v. *Motion*, Similar or direct motion is when parts move in the same direction either by single degrees or by skips.

**c.** *Math.* Of two square matrices: such that one of them is equal to the other premultiplied by some matrix whose determinant is not zero and postmultiplied by the inverse of the same matrix.

**1907** M. BÔCHER *Introd. Higher Algebra* xxi. 283 Two matrices connected by a relation of the form (13) are sometimes called similar matrices. **1937** A. A. ALBERT *Mod. Higher Algebra* iv. 78 Every square matrix is similar to its transpose. **1979** S. H. FRIEDBERG et al. *Linear Algebra* v. 232 Prove that similar matrices have the same trace.

**4.** *Comb.*, as ***similar-looking***, ***-sided***, ***-sized***.

**1776** DA COSTA *Elem. Conchol.* 87 Equal or similar-sided Bivalves, or whose cardo is central. **1849** D. CAMPBELL *Inorg. Chem.* 20 A similar-sized tube.. at the opposite extremity. **1874** *Treas. Bot.* 285/1 Similar-looking barks may be produced by very different species.

**B.** *sb.* **1.** A thing or person similar to or resembling another; a counterpart. Also const. *of*.

**1654** Z. COKE *Logick* 202 Let it be considered whether the Integral part be Similar or dissimilar, for Similars come rarely under consideration. **1719** SAMBER tr. *Boerhaave's Meth. Physick* 143 Therefore the Corpuscula of all firm Parts are Similars the most minute. **1763** CHURCHILL *Duellist* I, Thou Similar of Lust! **1778** *Learning at a Loss* II. 110 Admiring the horizontal Verdure of her Father's clipt Hedges; with fifty pretty little Similars full as indolently entertaining. **1831** D. E. WILLIAMS *Life Sir T. Lawrence* I. 7 In manner and conversation, he was one whose similar you seldom met with. **1885** J. MARTINEAU *Types Eth. Th.* I. I. i. §3. 161 If representative ideas, or similars, are for ever flowing off from all things in heaven and earth. **1894** *Cent. Mag.* Apr. 872/1 When had the similar of this preacher led the service in that.. house of worship?

**2.** *Med.* (See quot.)

**1896** *Allbutt's Syst. Med.* I. 222 Hippocrates pointed out the occasional value of similars, that is of drugs which produce symptoms similar to those observed in the disease for which they are given.

†**'similariness.** *Obs.*⁻¹ [f. SIMILARY *a.*] Similarity, homogeneity.

**1669** W. SIMPSON *Hydrol. Chym.* 44 It makes no alteration in the water, because of similariness of parts.

**similarity** (sɪmɪ'lærɪtɪ). [f. SIMILAR *a.* + -ITY, or ad. F. *similarité*.]

**1.** The state or fact of being similar; likeness, resemblance. (Common from *c* 1780.)

**1664** POWER *Exp. Philos.* I. 56 Both which experiments do prove an homogeneity and similarity of their substance. **1721** in BAILEY. **1771** *Junius Lett.* lxvii. (1788) 340 It arose from a fortunate similarity of principles. **1794** SULLIVAN *View Nat.* II. 280 There is a strong similarity between the Hebrew and the Scythiac languages. **1843** BETHUNE *Sc. Fireside Stor.* 91 Nothing has a greater tendency to unlock the heart.. than a similarity of misfortunes. **1879** LUBBOCK *Sci. Lect.* ii. 41 Certain insects escape danger by their similarity to plants.

**2.** *pl.* Points of resemblance.

**1838** *Murray's N. Germ.* 142 Those who are acquainted with the French metropolis will find here many similarities. **1865** LUBBOCK *Preh. Times* xv. (1878) 570 Presenting many remarkable similarities. **1897** *Sat. Rev.* 17 Apr. 418/1 There are many curious similarities between the inhabitants of Europe and North America.

**3.** *attrib.*, as ***similarity continuum***, ***set***; (cf. SIMILAR *a.* 3c) ***similarity class***, ***group***, ***transformation***.

**1952** R. R. STOLL *Linear Algebra & Matrix Theory* vii. 176 The similarity classes of transformations are in one-one correspondence with the similarity classes of $n \times n$ matrices. **1975** S. KOH et al. tr. *Satake's Linear Algebra* iii. 141 The set of all matrices which are similar to a given matrix is called the 'similarity class' of this matrix. **1960** M. ROKEACH *Open & Closed Mind* ii. 46 Recall again that we conceive of the disbelief system as a similarity continuum. **1937** A. A. ALBERT *Mod. Higher Algebra* iv. 76 We are studying the invariants of matrices $A$ under a group of transformations $A \leftrightarrow PAP^{-1}$ called the similarity group. **1977** R. HOLLAND *Self & Social Context* viii. 232 Objects normally grouped together in similarity sets may change their relationships following a revolution in science. **1961** G. HADLEY *Linear Algebra* vii. 239 Either $PAP^{-1}$ or $P^{-1}AP$ represents a similarity transformation on A. **1968** FOX & MAYERS *Computing Methods for Scientists & Engineers* v. 113 A final important iterative method.. succeeds in reducing the matrix by similarity transformation to triangular form. **1976** G. STRANG *Linear Algebra & its Applications* v. 222 Similarity transformations leave the eigenvalues unchanged.

**'similarize**, *v. rare*⁻¹. [f. SIMILAR *a.*] *trans.* To compare, liken.

**1806** ANNA SEWARD *Lett.* (1811) VI. 304 The twenty-fourth canto opens with a description of hoar-frost similarized to snow.

**similarly** ('sɪmɪlərlɪ), *adv.* [f. SIMILAR *a.* + -LY².] In a similar or like manner.

**1764** REID *Inquiry* vi. §13. 324 The point which is situate similarly to that on which the picture is made on the other eye. **1801** FOSTER in *Life & Corr.* (1846) I. 141, I have been .. just the same kind of being I was before, and just similarly employed. **1859** *Christian Remembr.* XXXVIII. 223 In that case, all other rivers.. ought to overflow similarly. **1886** *Law Rep. 32 Chanc. Div.* 28 The same observations are true of all other contracts similarly circumstanced.

*Comb.* **1862** SPENCER *First Princ.* II. x. §84 (1875) 258 The similarly-caused general currents in the air. **1874** CARPENTER *Ment. Phys.* II. xix. (1879) 680 An example of the similarly-fatal influence of undue emotion. **1878** ABNEY *Photogr.* i. 4 When such a reversed facsimile was placed over similarly-prepared paper.

†**'similarness.** *Obs. rare.* Similarity.

**1670** W. SIMPSON *Hydrol. Ess.* 104 The main Objection.. against the identity or similarness of this Artificial, with the Natural Sulphur Water. **1731** in BAILEY (vol. II.).

†**'similary**, *a. Obs.* Also 7 -iary. [See SIMILAR *a.* and -ARY². Common in the 17th cent.]

**1.** = SIMILAR *a.* 1.

(*a*) **1564** P. MOORE *Hope Health* I. iv. 7 Soche members are compounded and doe consiste of the saied similarie and like partes. **1594** T. B. *La Primaud. Fr. Acad.* II. 29 The partes then of the body are diuided into two sortes or kindes: the first is, the simple or similary parts, the other the compound parts. **1654** Z. COKE *Logick* 196 Similary parts, as blood and other Humors, Flesh, Bones, Sinews, Arteries. **1671** GREW *Anat. Pl.* I. (1682) 4 Having thus taken a view of the Organical Parts of the Bean, and other Seeds; let us next examine the Similary, *sc.* those whereof the Organical are compos'd.

(*b*) **1635** HEYWOOD *Hierarchy* III. Comm. 157 Anaxagoras .. conferred the first generation upon small and Similarie particles. **1646** SIR T. BROWNE *Pseud. Ep.* (1650) 40 Ice is a similary body, and homogeneous concretion, whose materiall is properly water. **1668** CULPEPPER & COLE *Barthol. Anat.* I. iii. 4 Fat is a similary Body void of Life.

**2.** = SIMILAR *a.* 2.

**1628** FELTHAM *Resolves* II. lxix, Hence growes the height of friendship, when two similiary Soules shall blend.. in their commixions. **1641** H. L'ESTRANGE *God's Sabbath* 125 As Augustine saith in a similarie case [etc.]. **1692** SOUTH *Serm.* (1718) IV. 46 Rhyming cadencies of similary words.

**similat(e**, obs. ff. SIMULATE *ppl. a.* and *v.*

**similation**, obs. form of SIMULATION.

**similative** ('sɪmɪlətɪv), *a.* and *sb. Gram.* [f. L. *similis* like + -ATIVE.] **A.** *adj.* Denoting or expressing similarity or likeness. **B.** *sb.* A similative word, case, verbal element, or compound. Cf. SIMILITIVE *a.*

**1884** in *N.E.D.* s.v. AIR *sb.* B. 3. **1903** *Amer. Anthropologist* Jan.–Mar. 13 Besides these, comitatives, similatives, partitives, and suffixes expressing similar ideas, are found. **1911** H. BRADLEY in *Encycl. Brit.* XXV. 209/1 The many jocularly similative uses of ordinary words, such as 'tin' for money. **1930** F. R. BLAKE in J. T. Hatfield et al. *Curme Vol. Ling. Stud.* 37 The immaterial adnominal cases are.. similative—an animal *like a pig*. **1954** PEI & GAYNOR *Dict. Linguistics* 197 *Similative*, a declensional case in certain non-Indo-European languages, denoting resemblance. (Also termed *conformative*.)

**simile** ('sɪmɪlɪ), *sb.* Also β. 7 similie, 7–9 simily. [L. *simile*, neut. of *similis* like. With the form *simily* (pl. *-ies*), cf. *query* for *quere*, *quære*.]

**1.** A comparison of one thing with another, esp. as an ornament in poetry or rhetoric.

α. **1393** LANGL. *P. Pl.* C. xx. 160 By this *simile*.. ich seo an euidence, That ho so synegeþ in þe *seynt espirit* asoilled worth he neuere. **1589** GREENE *Menaphon* (Arb.) 51 Samela had learnd.. to anatomize wit, and speake none but Similes. *Ibid.* 88 Stufft with prettie Similes and farre fetcht Metaphores. **1602** MARSTON *Ant. & Mel.* I, No simile Is pretious, choyce, or elegant enough. **1646** SIR T. BROWNE *Pseud. Ep.* I. ix. (1686) 26 Playing much upon the simile or illustrative argumentation. **1712** ADDISON *Spect.* No 303 ¶20 Milton.. never quits his Simile till it rises to some very great Idea, which [etc.]. **1779** JOHNSON *L.P.*, *Pope*, A simile, to be perfect, must both illustrate and ennoble the subject. **1825** LYTTON *Falkland* 8, I could wish..that this simile were in all things correct. **1858** DORAN *Court Fools* 167 Some of his similes are drawn from his profession. **1873** C. M. DAVIES *Unorth. Lond.* (ed. 2) 72, That was aptly illustrated by the simile of the infant that can only cry.

*β*. **1600** SHAKS. *A.Y.L.* II. i. 45 Did he not moralize this spectacle?.. O yes, into a thousand similies. **1636** DAVENANT *Platonic Lovers* Wks. (1673) 390 An excellent Similie for a Painter, That would draw a good face. **1695** J. EDWARDS *Perfect. Script.* 386 The same simily is made use of in Terence. **1728** POPE *Dunc.* I. 64 There motley Images her fancy strike, Figures ill-paired, and Similies unlike. **1759** STERNE *Tr. Shandy* II. ii, Even my similies,..my illustrations, my metaphors, are erudite. **1824** LANDOR *Imag. Conv., Delille & Landor*, The simily is imperfect, because the fact is untrue. **1846** WRIGHT *Ess. Mid. Ages* I. i. 13 [In] Anglo-Saxon poetry..Similies..are rare.

**b.** Without article.

**1682** SHEFFIELD (Dk. Buckhm.) *Ess. Poetry*, They sigh in simile and die in Rhyme. *c* **1700** PRIOR *Dial. Dead, Locke & Montaigne*, Simile is the very Algebra of Discourse. **1707** —— *A Simile* 4 'Tis but by way of Simile. **1864** LOWELL *Fireside Trav.* 165 How would he have run him up and down the gamut of simile!

**c.** *Comb.*, as ***simile-maker***, ***-monger***.

**1676** WYCHERLEY *Pl. Dealer* II. i, I cou'd not..sit to a vain young Simile-maker, tho' he flatter'd me. **1868** HELPS *Realmah* viii. (1876) 178 That sort of confusion is indulged in by all simile-mongers.

†**2.** Likeness, resemblance; similarity. *Obs.*

**1604** R. CAWDREY *Table Alph.*, *Similie*,..likenes, or resemblance. **1613** J. DAVIES (Heref.) *Muses Teares* Wks. (Grosart) I. 5/1 The Simile twixt God and Man is such, That God is said to be immortall Man. **1692** TRYON *Good Housew. made Doctor* xiv. 103 What likeness or correspondence is there between Cloves, Mace,..and..Herbs or Flesh? Verily there is no simile between them.

†**b.** The likeness of a thing. *Obs.*⁻¹

**1742** *Lond. & Country Brew.* II. (ed. 2) 151 Everything delighteth to produce its own Simile.

Hence **'simile** *v. trans.*, to express by a simile.

**1727** *Philip Quarll* 219 Having similed every different Part, he proceeds in the Representation thereof. **1972** G. JONES *Kings, Beasts, & Heroes* II. i. 75 We are told the colour of her hair and hands, her flesh and bosom, but she stays cool to view as..a wax doll. A clean doll, admittedly... And one most nobly similied.

**simili-**, comb. form of L. *similis* like, used in the sense of 'imitation', as ***simili-diamond***, ***-gold***, etc. Also *ellipt.*

**1886** GRENVILLE-MURRAY *Young Widows* 33 Gold often runs to gold, or to simili-gold, like steel to the magnet. **1892** *Harper's Mag.* Sept. 500/2 He provides the French middle classes with the finest simili-literature that there is in the market. **1898** E. P. EVANS *Evol. Ethics* v. 175 Rubies, spinels, and simili distinguishable from real diamonds only by experts.

†**si'miliancy.** *Obs. rare.* [ad. Sp. *semejanza*: cf. Pg. *semelhança*, *similhança*, It. *simiglianza*.] Similarity, likeness.

**1622** MABBE tr. *Aleman's Guzman d'Alf.* I. 21 Some long Treaty or Communication, Similiancie in condition, or some other pledges of loue. **1631** —— *Celestina* I. 26 The great similiancy and suteablenesse which both of you have in vertue.

**si'militive**, *a. rare*⁻¹. [irreg. f. L. *similis* like.] Expressing likeness.

**1678** R. BARCLAY *Apol. Quakers* v. §25. 183 This similitive Particle [*As*] makes the [*All*] which goes before, and comes after, to be of one and the same extent.

**similitude** (sɪˈmɪlɪtjuːd). Also 4–5 **symyli-**, 5 **simyli-**, 5–6 **symyly-**, **simyly-**, **symili-**, 6 **symily-**, **similytud(e**; 5 **semeli-**, 6 **semylytude**; 6 **similitewd**. [a. OF. *similitude* (= Sp. *similitud*, It. *similitudine*), ad. L. *similitūdo*, f. *similis* like.]

**1.** A person or thing resembling, or having the likeness *of*, some other person or thing; a counterpart or equal; †a similarity.

*c* **1386** CHAUCER *Miller's T.* 42 He knew nat Catoun,..That bad man sholde wedde his similitude. —— *Sqr.'s T.* 480 Pitee renneth soone in gentil herte, Feelynge his similitude in peynes smerte. *c* **1430** LYDG. *Minor Poems* (Percy Soc.) 97 This gostly manna..To us figurithe..A symilitude of the sacrament. *c* **1480** HENRYSON *Poems* (S.T.S.) III. 167 Haif rewth, lord, of thyne awin symilitude. **1526** *Pilgr. Perf.* (W. de W. 1531) 272 b, The similitude of an hande sent downe, toke me by the heer of my heed. **1632** LITHGOW *Trav.* I. 19 Romanists will worship their counterfeit similitude, in stone or tree. **1667** MILTON *P.L.* III. 384 Begotten Son, Divine Similitude, In whose conspicuous count'nance..th' Almighty Father shines. **1714** STEELE *Poet. Misc.* Ded., Men of your Talents oblige the World, when they are studious to produce in others the Similitude of their Excellencies. **1764** GOLDSM. *Hist. Eng. in Lett.* (1772) II. 174 Accustomed to cruelty,..they expected a similitude of treatment. **1791** COWPER *Iliad* II. 23 The shadow stood, similitude exact Of Nestor. *a* **1822** SHELLEY *Triumph Life* 117 Nor wanted here the just similitude Of a triumphal pageant. **1876** MOZLEY *Univ. Serm.* vi. 130 Nature..bearing a relation to something moral of which it is the similitude and type.

**2.** The form, likeness, or image *of* some person or thing.

*a* **1400–50** *Alexander* 1627 Slike a segg in my slepe me sodanly aperid, Euyn in slike a similitude & þis same wedis. *c* **1440** *Gesta Rom.* (1879) 62 By the lady..we shall vndirstond the soule formed to the symylitude of god. **1484** CAXTON *Fables of Poge* v, He hadde from the nauylle vpward the symylytude or lykenesse of a man. *a* **1513** FABYAN *Chron.* VII. (1811) 421 He had a feende in his house in the symylytude of a catte. **1594** T. B. *La Primaud. Fr. Acad.* II. 191 The first degree of this image and similitude that is in man. **1612** T. TAYLOR *Comm. Titus* ii. 13 He that waiteth for Christ..conformeth himselfe daily vnto his similitude. **1667** MILTON *P.L.* VII. 520 Let us make now Man in our image, Man In our similitude. **1871** B. TAYLOR *Faust* (1875) II. 147 Behold this flame in man's similitude.

**3.** †**a.** A sign or symbol; the symbolic representation of something. *Obs.*

*c* **1374** CHAUCER *Boeth.* III. pr. v. (1868) 75 A tyraunt..shewide by similitude þe dredes of realmes by gastnesse of a swerde þat heng ouer þe heued of his familier. *c* **1440** *Astron. Cal.* (MS. Ashm. 391), Wᵗ yn it is an hoole which shewᵗ by similitude how þe moone wexeþ and wanȝeþ. *c* **1440** LYDG. *Hors, Shepe & G.* 17, I fond to purpos A similitude Ful craftily depeyntid vpon a wall. **1558** BP. WATSON *Sev. Sacram.* vii. 39 In this Sacrament is a sygne or a figure, or a similitude of Christes body.

**b.** A comparison drawn between two things or facts; the expression of such comparison; †a simile.

*c* **1386** CHAUCER *Sec. Nun's T.* 431 Almache answerde vnto that similitude, 'Of whennes comth thyn answeryng so rude?' *c* **1400** LANGL. *P. Pl.* C. xx. 160 'By this simile [*v.r.* similitude],' he seide, 'ich seo an euidence' [etc.]. **1477** EARL RIVERS (Caxton) *Dictes* iij b, By similitude ryght so is the kyng..with his people as the saule with the body. **1522** MORE *De quat. Noviss.* Wks. 84/1, I shal put then a more ernest ymage of our condicion & that not a fained similitude but a very true fassion & fygure of oure worshipful estate. **1553** WILSON *Rhet.* 100 b, A similitude is a likenesse when two thynges, or mo then two, are so compared and resembled together, that thei bothe in some one propertie seme like. **1635** SWAN *Spec. M.* v. §2 (1643) 116 A similitude may be taken from a chest-nut..breaking in the fire. **1699** BENTLEY *Phal.* 266 To sneak away like a Cock, seems to be a very improper Similitude. **1712** ADDISON *Spect.* No. 303 ¶20 Those who are acquainted with Homer's and Virgil's way of Writing, cannot but be pleased with this kind of Structure in Milton's Similitudes. **1791** BOSWELL *Johnson* 11 April 1776, Nor could I think of a similitude to illustrate it. **1854** EMERSON *Lett. & Soc. Aims, Poet. & Imag.*, We cannot utter a sentence in sprightly conversation without a similitude. **1875** HELPS *Soc. Press.* iii. 44 London is often likened to Babylon; but the similitude is a very unjust one.

*attrib.* **1670** EACHARD *Cont. Clergy* 52 As for our metaphorical and similitude-men of the pulpit, these things to them are too still and languid.

**c.** A parable; an allegory.

Chiefly in Biblical use, after L. *similitudo*, used to render Gr. παραβολή.

*c* **1380** WYCLIF *Sel. Wks.* II. 207 Luc telliþ how Jesus seide to his disciplis þis similitude: þer was a man þat hadde a fige tree. **1388** —— *Luke* viii. 4 He seide bi a symylitude, He that sowith, ȝede out to sowe his seed. *c* **1440** *Gesta Rom.* xcvi. 426, I shall say to the an Ensawmple and a semelitude of a woman, that was a paynym. **1484** CAXTON *Fables of Æsop* I. iii, This fable made Esope for a symylytude whiche is prouffitable to many folkes. **1535** COVERDALE *Ecclus.* xlvii. 15 He couered and fylled the whole londe with similitudes and wyse prudent sentences. **1582** N. T. (Rhem.) *Luke* viii. 4 He said by a similitude. **1684** BUNYAN *Pilgr.* II. Introd. 138 A dark Similitude Will on the Fancie more it self intrude,..Then things from Similies not borrowed.

**d.** In proverbial use.

**1674** HICKMAN *Quinquart. Hist.* (ed. 2) 15 Similitudes do not run on all four, as the Proverb is. **1695** in *Misc. Curiosa* (1708) III. 89 If..this very Place was a Temple of Jupiter Belus, the Similitude will run upon all Four. **1699** BENTLEY *Phal.* Pref. p. lxxvi, Similitudes, even when they are taken from Asses, do not walk upon All Four.

**4.** The quality or state of being like; resemblance, similarity, likeness. Now somewhat *rare*.

**1387–8** T. USK *Test. Love* III. iv. (Skeat) l. 186 So than in that, it is more similitude to the everlasting presence. **1447** BOKENHAM *Seyntys* (Roxb.) 10 Be congruite Of symylytude. **1484** CAXTON *Chivalry* 1 Kynges owen to haue puyssaunce and seygnorye upon the knyghtes, and the knyghtes by symylytude oughten to haue power..ouer the moyen peple. *c* **1532** DU WES *Introd. Fr.* in *Palsgr.* 923 Specially havyng symylytude of maners togyder. **1594** T. B. *La Primaud. Fr. Acad.* II. 279 Similitude and likenesse is a great cause of loue,..because similitude maketh many things to be as one and the same thing. **1651** HOBBES *Leviath.* Introd. 2 The similitude of Passions, which are the same in all men. **1699** BENTLEY *Phal.* 287 Casaubon writ a whole Book on purpose, to shew they had no Similitude nor Affinity with one another. **1750** JOHNSON *Rambler* No. 143 ¶14 As not every instance of similitude can be considered as a proof of imitation. **1794** GODWIN *Caleb Williams* 25 A young man whom similitude of manners had rendered one of his principal confidants. **1837** P. KEITH *Bot. Lex.* 405 Such deviations..as will efface all traces of similitude of structure. *a* **1854** H. REED *Lect. Eng. Lit.* i. (1878) 42 The law which reconciles similitude and dissimilitude, the harmony of contrast. **1878** MISS J. J. YOUNG *Ceramic Art* 43 No better examples can be given of similitude.

†**b.** Likelihood, probability. In phr. *by* or *of (all, any, some) similitude*. *Obs.*

*c* **1460** METHAM *Wks.* (E.E.T.S.) 154 Qwat that a man dremyth schuld turne to trwthe be sum symylytude. **1509** HAWES *Past. Pleas.* I. (Percy Soc.) 5 To knowe whether and unto what place It woulde me bryng by any similitude. **1513** HEN. VIII in Strype *Ann. Ref.* (1824) V. 317 In caas the said retardation had not been, our said ship of al similitude had not happened into the said daungier. **1538** LELAND *Itin.* (1769) VII. 31 This castel..cam to them be similitude by Maryage. *a* **1548** HALL *Chron., Hen. IV*, D vj b, The Frenchemen whiche by all symilitude had knowledge of the kynges passage entered amongest the kynges nauie.

Hence †**si'militudeness**, = SIMILITUDE 2. *Obs.* **si'militudinq** *vbl. sb.*, a drawing of comparisons. **simili'tudinize** *v.*, to make comparisons.

**1547** BOORDE *Brev. Health* §182 Man is made to the similitudenes of God. **1681** COLVIL *Whigs Supplic.* (1751) 147 Thy own and other souls deluding, By such prophane similituding. **1837** *Fraser's Mag.* XV. 316 Melodiously similitudinising in Sapphics languid or Alcaics terse.

†**simili'tudinarily**, *adv. Obs.* [f. next + -LY².] In the manner of a similitude or simile.

**1624** GATAKER *Transubst.* 48 A man, (for example) as Christ was, cannot but similitudinarily be a Vine, a Lyon, a Rocke, &c. **1641** 'SMECTYMNUUS' *Vind. Answ.* xiii, They (labouring to do it in a familiar way) did similitudinarily call them Bishops.

†**simili'tudinary**, *a.*, *adv.*, and *sb. Obs.* [ad. med.L. *similitūdinārius* (also *-āriē* adv.), f. *similitūdo*: cf. Sp. and Pg. *similitudinario*.]

**A.** *adv.* In figurative language. **B.** *sb.* A thing resembling another. **C.** *adj.* Of the nature of a similitude or figure; expressing comparison or likeness; symbolic.

**1432–50** tr. *Higden* (Rolls) IV. 33 Kepenge silence or spekenge similitudinary [L. *ænigmatice*] where eny thynge of the Trinite was in theire werke. **1541** R. COPLAND *Guydon's Quest. Chirurg.* F iij b, There be...iij. in the rumpe which be nat very spondyles, but symylytudynaries, & as vycares. **1581** MULCASTER *Positions* xli. (1887) 242 In their similitudinarie applications. **1607** *Schol. Disc. agst. Antichr.* I. ii. 107 Sacramentall signes are similitudinary. **1642** T. GOODWIN *Heart of Christ* 111 This..is not wholly to be understood in a metaphoricall or a similitudinary sense. **1680** DR. POTTER *Christophalg.* 44 (T.), Our Saviour chose this similitudinary way to express our union with himself.

†**si'mility.** *Obs. rare.* [irreg. f. L. *similis*.] Similarity.

*c* **1470** HARDING *Chron.* I. x, As he herde in all similitee Howe Ioseph had his graund-ser enformed. **1651** BIGGS *New Disp.* ¶291 Contrariety and simility. *Ibid.* ¶295 Although simility doth proximely include familiarity.

**similize** (ˈsɪmɪlaɪz), *v.* Now *rare*. [f. L. *similis* or SIMILE: see -IZE.]

†**1.** *trans.* To imitate, copy. *Obs.*

**1605** SYLVESTER *Du Bartas* II. iii. IV. *Captaines* 454 Ile similize These Gebeonites: I will my selfe disguise To gull thee. **1616** J. LANE *Contn. Sqr.'s T.* III. 202 Sithe the castinge, how his formes and faces viewe mote similize his father, yet vntrewe.

†**2.** To compare, liken. Const. *to*, *with*. *Obs.*

**1620** E. BLOUNT *Horæ Subs.* 16 Some haue similized these kind of men with the Camelion. **1653** DUCHESS OF NEWCASTLE *Poems & Fancies* 136 Similizing the Braine to a Garden. *a* **1670** HACKET *Abp. Williams* i. (1692) 53 The best to whom he may be similized herein, is Frier Paul the Servite.

**3. a.** To symbolize; to express or describe in similes.

*a* **1668** DAVENANT *Poems* Wks. (1673) 296 We need not bring So many Flowers..To shew or similize you more. **1864** LOWELL *Fireside Trav.* 165 How Calderon would have similized this pretty creature, had he ever seen it!

**b.** *intr.* To use a simile or comparison.

**1686** DRYDEN *Duchess of York's Paper Defended* Misc. Wks. 1800 II. 496 If I may similize in my turn, a dull fellow might ask the meaning [etc.]. **1925** V. WOOLF *Common Reader* 106 She similised..eternally; the sea became a meadow, the sailors shepherds, the mast a maypole. **1976** *N.Y. Times Mag.* 10 Oct. 111/3 Have a story or anecdote for every point you wish to make. Similize. Exaggerate, euphemize, elide.

**simillimum** (sɪˈmɪlɪməm). *Homœopathy.* [L., neut. of *simillimus*, superl. of *similis*, like, similar.] The remedy indicated in a particular case, as producing in a healthy person symptoms most like those of the person to be treated.

**1849** R. E. DUDGEON tr. *Hahnemann's Organon Med.* 157 But even granting this could be done..the cure is effected only by opposing a *simillimum* to a *simillimum*. **1891** J. C. BURNETT *Greater Dis. Liver* 42 With me it is an axiom to relieve uncomfortable or dangerous organ-states with simple organ-remedies, leaving the more remote and deeper-going to be..treated, if possible, with its pathological simillimum. **1938** [see POTENTIZATION]. **1972** D. V. TANSLEY *Radionics* viii. 84 This may be dispersed radionically or with the appropriate homoeopathic similimum [*sic*].

**similor** (ˈsɪmɪlɔː(r)). [a. F. *similor* (1742), f. L. *simil-is* like + F. *or* gold.] A very yellow kind of brass used in making cheap jewellery.

**1783** *Encycl. Brit.* (ed. 2) X. 8172/1 *Similor*, a name given to an alloy of red copper and zinc, made in the best proportions, to imitate silver and gold. **1839** URE *Dict. Arts* 30 This alloy may exist in many different proportions, under which it has different names, as tombac, similor, pinchbeck, &c.

Hence **'similored** *a.*, faced with similor.

**1838** *Penny Cycl.* XI. 220/1 Yellow similored goods must only have the mercury fairly removed from them.

**simily**, obs. variant of SIMILE.

**'simioid**, *a.* [f. SIMIA + -OID.] Resembling the apes; simian.

**1895** *Pop. Sci. Monthly* Jan. 371 Man's ancestors, therefore,..were simial or simioid, 'monkeylike'.

**simious** (ˈsɪmɪəs), *a.* [f. SIMIA + -OUS.]

**1.** Belonging to the race of apes; having apish characteristics.

**1804–6** SYD. SMITH *Sk. Mor. Philos.* (1850) 190 A model of perfect conformation to the whole simious tribe. **1807** —— *P. Plymley's Lett.* iii. (ed. 3) 5 *note*, That simious parasite who is always grinning at his heels. **1864** *Sat. Rev.* 21 May, Neither woman nor man, but some simious interloper from Equatorial Africa. **1887** G. SALMON *Non-miraculous Christ.* (ed. 2) 141 Tribes of simious men gradually groping their way..from savage ignorance to.. limited knowledge.

**2.** Typical or characteristic of apes.

c**1835** SYD. SMITH *Ballot* Wks. 1859 II. 307/1 That strange simious schoolboy passion of giving pain to others. **1839** C. A. MURRAY *Trav. N. Amer.* I. 320 A low receding fore-head, a nose somewhat *simious*. [*Note.*] I believe I can justly claim the invention or anglicising of this word. **1882** TRAILL *Sterne* iv. 35 A novel in which he might give full play to his simious humour.

Hence **'simiousness**.

**1878** *Fraser's Mag.* XVII. 59 The obtrusive simiousness of the Mongolian features.

**simitar**, obs. or U.S. form of SCIMITAR.

†**'simity.** *Obs. rare.* [f. L. *sīmus* snub-nosed, flat-nosed.] The fact of being flat-nosed.

**1650** BULWER *Anthropomet.* vii. 83 Midwives..are wont to compresse the lateral parts of the Nose, that this simity of children may be the sooner abolished. *Ibid.* 127 Simity therefore is the cause, not the disease.

**'simkin¹.** *rare.* Also 9 Simpkin. [Diminutive form of the personal name *Sim* Simon: see -KIN.] A fool; a simpleton.

a**1700** B. E. *Dict. Cant. Crew, Simkin*, a Fool. **1785** GROSE *Dict. Vulg. T., Simkin*, a foolish fellow. **1861** MAYHEW *Lond. Lab.* III. 145/1 This Pierrot is the Simpkin of the ballet, and he's dressed in white, with long sleeves, and a white face.

**'simkin².** *Anglo-Indian.* Also simpkin. [Urdū corruption of *champagne*.] Champagne.

**1853** W. D. ARNOLD *Oakfield* II. iv. 127 The dinner was good, and the iced simkin, Sir, delicious. **1863** TREVELYAN *Compet. Wallah* (1866) 164 We agreed to drink our last two bottles of Simkin in honour of our signal victory. **1886** *Illustr. Lond. News* 24 July 90/3 There is a good deal of 'Simpkin' or champagne consumed in the three Presidencies.

**simlin** ('sɪmlɪn). Also 8 cimbeline, cymblin, 8– cymling, 9 cymbling, simblin; cymlin. [Alteration of SIMNEL.]

**1.** *U.S.* A species of squash having a scalloped edge. Cf. SIMNEL 2.

**1775** N. CRESSWELL *Jrnl.* 5 July (1925) 95 The rest plundered about the plantation and got some young cabbages, squashes and Cimbelines. **1785** T. JEFFERSON *Notes Virginia* vi. 68 Cymlings. *Cucurbita verrucosa.* **1794** MORSE *Amer. Geogr.* 148 Cymlings (*Cucurbita verrucosa*). **1796** B. HAWKINS *Let.* 2 Dec. (1916) 21 They made beans, ground peas, cymblins. **1813** J. TAYLOR *Arator* 138 Cimblins or pumpkins. **1814** BRACKENRIDGE *Views Louisiana* 63 Hunters tell of some curious plants on the Arkansas, amongst which are the common sun-flower, the bean, and the simblin. **1832** J. P. KENNEDY *Swallow Barn* IV. vi. 100 Little garden-patches..where cymblings.. flourished. **1847** DARLINGTON *Amer. Weeds & Usef. Pl.* (1860) 142 *Cucurbita melopepo*.., Round Squash. Cymling. a**1883** G. W. BAGBY *Sel. Misc. Writings* (1885) II. 17 A true Virginian..must have..old hare, butter-beans, new potatoes, squirrel, cymlings, snaps. **1896** *Columbus Dispatch* 24 July 9 Peel and slice tender young simlins. **1981** *Farmstead Mag.* Winter 41/1 Common pumpkins are actually a form of the same plant from which has also been developed vegetable marrows, cymlings, or cymlins (also spelled simlins), summer crookneck squashes, and yellow-flowered gourds.

**2.** *dial.* = SIMNEL 1 b.

**1847-** in dialect texts and glossaries (*Eng. Dial. Dict.*); also in combs., as *simlin-cake, -Sunday*.

**simment**, obs. form of CEMENT *v.*

**Simmental** ('sɪməntɑːl). Also Simmenthal, Zimmenthal. [a. Ger. name of the Simme valley in the canton of Berne, Switzerland.] A bull or cow of a breed of cattle, first developed in Switzerland, distinguished by their large size and red and white coats, and used for both milk and meat production. Also *attrib.*

**1959** R. B. KELLEY *Native & Adapted Cattle* iv. 62 Red Danes, Simmental, and Friesians..were seen..outside Rome. **1970** *Times* 6 Apr. 10/6 The shorthorn men are also interested in the Simmental, a big dual-purpose animal which is to be found over much of central and eastern Europe. **1973** [see LIMOUSIN 2]. **1973** *Country Life* 12 July 80/2 Of the exotic breeds, the Simmenthal are second in popularity only to the Charolais. **1980** H. M. & D. M. BRIGGS *Mod. Breeds Livestock* (ed. 4) vii. 156 The first purebred Simmental bull came to the United States in 1971. *Ibid.* 157 Simmentals are large, long, and very muscular cattle.

**simmer** ('sɪmə(r)), *sb.* [f. the vb.] The state or condition of simmering. Chiefly in phr. ***on the*** (or ***at a***) ***simmer***. Also *fig.*

**1809** MALKIN *Gil Blas* II. v. ⁋4 The kettle was kept on the simmer. **1825** LAMB *Refl. in Pillory* in *Eliana* (1867) 141 This nubbling might have helped the pot boil, when your dirty cuttings from the shambles..shall stand at a cold simmer. **1896** MRS. CAFFYN *Quaker Grandmother* xii, In a constant simmer of trying to be good.

**simmer**, Sc. form of SUMMER.

**simmer** ('sɪmə(r)), *v.*¹ Also 7 simber. [Later form of SIMPER *v.*¹, the change being probably due to a feeling of phonetic appropriateness.]

*Simming* in Beaum. & Fl. *Coxcomb* IV. vi. ("Tis still simming in her blood') may be an error for *simmering*.

**1. a.** *intr.* Of liquids: To make a subdued murmuring sound under the influence of continued heat; to be at a heat just below boiling-point. Also *transf.* of the containing vessel, etc.

**1653** MORE *Antid. Atheism* II. xii. §12 That their vital heat and moisture may not always only simber in one sluggish tenour, but some times boil up higher and seeth over. **1684** tr. *Bonet's Merc. Compit.* IV. 135 Let it simmer on a gentle Fire, then let it cool. **1750** JOHNSON *Rambler* No. 51 ⁋7 To watch the skillet on the fire, to see it simmer with a due degree of heat. **1791** COWPER *Iliad* XVIII. 432 The water in the singing brass Simmer'd. **1840** DICKENS *Old C. Shop* xviii, A large iron cauldron, bubbling and simmering in the heat. **1862** MISS BRADDON *Lady Audley* xxxix, Over the handful of fire, upon which the broth..still bubbled and simmered. **1882** 'OUIDA' *Maremma* I. 37 While her frugal supper was simmering.

*transf.* and *fig.* **1817** BYRON *Beppo* xliii, That sort of farthing candlelight which glimmers Where reeking London's smoky caldron simmers. **1841** B. HALL *Patchwork* I. ix. 150 The patient..keeps simmering [in the bath] eight or ten hours.

*refl.* **1882** G. H. HOLLISTER *Kinley Hollow* xv, Green wood will at last simmer itself into a blaze.

**b.** Of feelings, tendencies, etc.: To be in a state of gentle activity; to be on the verge of becoming active or breaking out.

a**1764** R. LLOYD *Author's Apol.* Poet. Wks. 1774 I. 2 Whose friendship serves the talking turn, Just simmers to a kind concern. **1850** MERIVALE *Hist. Rom. Emp.* liv. (1865) VI. 457 A spirit of reform..still simmered with genial warmth on the surface of society. **1860** FROUDE *Hist. Eng.* VI. 145 The disaffection was already simmering in Devonshire. **1883** *19th Cent.* May 811 This mean business had simmered on, and was at last at boiling point.

**c.** Of persons, etc.: To be in a state of suppressed excitement or agitation.

**1840** CARLYLE *Heroes* (1858) 235 This great fiery heart, seething, simmering like a great furnace of thoughts. **1876** GLADSTONE *Glean.* II. 320 When they had left him boiling, or, at least simmering, in unanimity of wrath. **1884** *Spectator* 4 Oct. 1322/1 The tribes of Afghanistan were simmering to revolt.

**d.** ***to simmer down***: to calm down from an angry or excited state. orig. *U.S.*

**1871** 'MARK TWAIN' *Lett. to Publishers* (1967) 58, I must and will keep shady and quiet till Bret Harte simmers down a little. **1897** W. BEATTY *Secretar* xiii. 102 In a while..he simmered down. **1902** C. J. C. HYNE *Mr. Horrocks, Purser* 42 First Class passengers..don't handicap matters by interference—once they have simmered down. **1972** *Times Lit. Suppl.* 22 Dec. 1561/5 There they simmer down for a space, forget their mundane cares.

**2.** *trans.* To keep in a heated condition just below boiling-point.

**1823** J. BADCOCK *Dom. Amusem.* 147 Boil and simmer it until the water having evaporated leaves the kali behind. **1850** HOLTZAPFFEL *Turning* III. 1377 It is then skimmed and simmered for about three hours. **1883** 'ANNIE THOMAS' *Mod. Housewife* 62 Simmer the whole for two hours, and strain.

†**'simmer**, *v.*² *Obs.*⁻¹ [app. a var. of SIMMON *v.*] *trans.* To cement.

**1725** W. HALFPENNY *Sound Building* 49 You must add to the under Side by a Closier..; which, if simmer'd to the Brick, will add much to the Strength..of the Work.

**'simmering**, *vbl. sb.* [f. SIMMER *v.*¹ + -ING¹.] The action of the vb.; the state of being near boiling-point; the gentle murmuring of a liquid under the influence of heat. Also *fig.*

**1707** MORTIMER *Husb.* (1721) II. 323 Experience shews it wastes less, and ferments better after so long boiling than simmering. **1753** *Chambers' Cycl.* Suppl. s.v. *Wine*, Any considerable heat, or even a degree of simmering, or tepidity. **1822** SCOTT *Peveril* xxxv, The simmering of a small pot which he had placed on the flame. **1869** BLACKMORE *Lorna D.* ii, A simmering buzzed in my heavy brain. **1898** L. STEPHEN *Stud. Biogr.* II. 56 The fact illustrates the vague simmering of an interest in German speculation.

**'simmering**, *ppl. a.* [f. SIMMER *v.*¹ + -ING².] That simmers; murmuring with a subdued sound.

**1791** E. DARWIN *Bot. Gard.* I. 26 Nymphs! you erewhile on simmering cauldrons play'd. **1843** CARLYLE *Past & Pres.* II. vii, Such is the buzz and frothy simmering ferment of the general mind. **1859** TENNENT *Ceylon* VII. ii. 255 The woods resounding with the simmering hum of insects. **1872** GEO. ELIOT *Middlemarch* v. 36 The simmering dislike of the other medical men.

Hence **'simmeringly** *adv.*

**1681** CHETHAM *Angler's Vade-m.* xxxix. §24 (1689) 276 Let the Liquour boil very leisurely and simmeringly only.

**Simmerstat** ('sɪməstæt). Also simmerstat. [f. SIMMER *v.*¹ + THERMO)STAT.] A proprietary name for a thermostatic control which regulates the temperature of the hot-plates or grill of an electric cooker or similar heating appliance.

**1938** *Trade Marks Jrnl.* 7 Sept. 1097/1 *Simmerstat*... All goods included in Class 8. Sun-Vic Controls Limited.., London W.C. 2; manufacturers. **1951** *Good Housek. Home Encycl.* 76/1 A radiant hot-plate operated by a 'simmerstat'. **1954** *Archit. Rev.* CXVI. 270 (*caption*) Polished stainless steel and plate glass; fitted with three 60-watt lamps between the heaters and simmerstat control. **1962** *Listener* 13 Sept. 411/2 The middle-priced model is distinguished by simmerstat-controlled radiant plates. **1979** *Nature* 19 Apr. p. xiv/3 The temperature of the hotplate is controlled by a Simmerstat which regulates it between 50° and 325°C.

**simmetrian, -triated, -trie**, obs. forms of SYMMETRIAN, -TRIATED, -TRY.

**'simmon**, *sb.*¹ Now *dial.* Forms: 5 symonde, 6 semonde, 7 sim(m)ond, symond; 7- simmon (8 simon). [var. of CEMENT *sb.*] Cement. (Cf. quots. 1706 and 1890.) Also *attrib.*

c**1440** *York Myst.* viii. 102 þus sall I iune it..And sadly sette it with symonde fyne. **1575** TURBERV. *Faulconrie* 98 Glewe it in with Semonde or Rosen and waxe molten togither. *Ibid.* 275 The gummie fatte of a fygge, the yolcke of an egge, or some kinde of Semonde made of purpose. **1641** *Churchw. Acc. Pittington*, etc. (Surtees) 191 Wax, rossel, and stone pitch to make symond for mending the fount stone broken by the Scotts. **1688** HOLME *Armoury* III. 382/2 A Simmon Stick..is an handle with a round head.. which hath a certain Simond clapt upon it [etc.]. *Ibid.* (Roxb.) 231/1 These vessells are..stopped close together by a certaine morter, clay or simmond. **1706** PHILLIPS (ed. Kersey), *Cement*, commonly pronounced *Simmon*, a Compound made of Pitch, Brick-dust, Plaister of Paris, &c. us'd by Chacers, Repairers, and other Artificers. **1828** CARR *Craven Gloss., Simmon*, cement. **1890** J. NICHOLSON *Folk-Lore E. Yks.* 80 When bricklayers wish to give a reddish colour to the mortar, they used pounded bricks or tiles to mix with it. This powder is called simmon, and simmon pounding was formerly the hard labour punishment in Beverley Gaol.

**'simmon**, *sb.*² *Sc.* (chiefly *Shetland*). Also 9 simmin, -an, symmon; simmond, -ind. [f. ON. *síma* SIME. Cf. Gael. *sioman*.] A rope or band made of straw or heath, esp. one used in thatching; rope of this material. Also *attrib.*

α. c**1690** in *Macfarlane's Geogr. Collect.* (S.H.S.) III. 252 The common..thacking is of a kind of Divet,..and Straw and Simmons above the same. **1812** J. HENDERSON *Agric. Surv. Caithness* 27 These [divots] are secured on the houses with ropes made of heath, or straw (provincially simmons). **1871** COWIE *Shetland* 92 The roof consists of..thin divots of dried turf, spread on wood, and covered with straw placed in a vertical direction, and held in its place by simmins or straw ropes.

β. **1808** JAMIESON, *Simmonds*, ropes made of heath and of Empetrum nigrum. **1822** HIBBERT *Desc. Shetl. Isl.* 115 Over these they lay the straw, and afterwards secure the whole with simmonds or bands formed also of straw. **1888** EDMONSTON & SAXBY *Home Naturalist* 145 A bit of simmond was woven. **1899** SPENCE *Shetland Folk-Lore* 195 Making numerous articles for domestic use from straw, such as..simmond-chairs [etc.].

**'simmon** ('sɪmən), *sb.*³ *U.S.* Colloq. abbrev. of PERSIMMON. Freq. *attrib.*, esp. as ***'simmon beer***.

a**1775** J. BOUCHER *Gloss. Archaic & Provincial Words* (1832) p. l, Brown linen shirts, and cotton jackets wear, Or only *wring-jaw* drink, and *'simmon beer*. **1839** *Southern Lit. Messenger* V. 378/2, I ask you no odds—the longest pole, you know, takes the simmon. **1883** P. M. HALE *Woods & Timbers N. Carolina* 117 The basis of a beverage, by no means despicable, called 'Simmon Beer. **1909** 'O. HENRY' *Roads of Destiny* xxi. 350 That's why you see me cake-walking with the ex-rebs to the illegitimate tune about 'simmon-seeds and cotton. **1945** B. A. BOTKIN *Lay my Burden Down* 66 'Simmon beer was good in the cold freezing weather too. **1949** [see *possum hunt* s.v. POSSUM *sb.*¹ 1 f].

**'simmon**, *v.* Now *dial.* Also 6 symon, 6-7 simon. [f. SIMMON *sb.*¹] *trans.* To cement.

**1568-9** *Sarum Churchw. Accs.* (Swayne, 1896) 283 Wex and Rosen and a fagot to symon the Stones. **1583** in Hutton *St. John Bapt. Coll.* (1898) 63 Item to Jhon Herberte simoninge certaine loose stones in the newe gate. **1663** GERBIER *Counsel* 83 French Glasse wrought with good lead, well simmoned, is worth sixteen pence a foot. **1688** HOLME *Armoury* III. 385/1 The Second thing in this quarter is the Oyle, or Simoning Brush. *Ibid.*, The Leading of the glasse is..oyled and Simoned to keep out foule weather. **1828** CARR *Craven Gloss., Simmon'd*, cemented. 'It's fearful weel simmon'd.'

**Simmonds** ('sɪməndz). *Path.* [The name of Morris *Simmonds* (1855-1925), German pathologist, who described the disease in 1914 (*Deutsch. med. Wochenschr.* 12 Feb. 322).] ***Simmonds'*** (also ***Simmonds's***, ***¶Simmond's***) ***disease***: pituitary insufficiency caused by destruction of the gland, characterized by weakness, loss of body hair, and progressive gonadal, adrenocortical, and thyroidal failure, and occurring chiefly in women; *esp.* the chronic form (cf. *Sheehan's syndrome*).

**1928** *Q. Cumulative Index Medicus* II. 993/2 Pituitary cachexia (Simmonds' disease). **1937** *Jrnl. Path. & Bacteriol.* XLV. 189 The significance of necrosis of the anterior pituitary chiefly concerns its relationship to the series of disorders of pituitary function which culminate in Simmonds's disease. **1970** PASSMORE & ROBSON *Compan. Med. Stud.* II. xxv. 6/2 The necrosis of anterior pituitary cells is followed by pituitary hypofunction (Simmond's disease).

**simnel** ('sɪmnəl). Now *arch.* or *local.* Forms: 3-4 simenel(l, 5 syme-, symynel; 5-6 symnelle (5 -nylle), 5-7 -nell, 5-9 -nel; 6-7 simnell, 6- simnel; 5 cymnel, 7 -nell, 7-8 cimnel(l. [a. OF. *simenel*, *seminel*, etc. (mod.F. dial. *simnel*), app. related in some way to L. *simila* or Gr. σεμίδαλις fine flour.

Med.L. *simen-*, *siminellus*, is merely an adaptation of the OF. or ME. word. L. *simila* is the direct source of OHG. *simela*, *semala*, etc. (MHG. *simele*, *semele*, G. *semmel*, with corresponding forms in LG., Du., Da., and Sw).]

**1.** A kind of bread or bun made of fine flour and prepared by boiling, sometimes with subsequent baking. Now chiefly *Hist.*

**12..** *Liber de situ Ecclesiæ Belli* in Dugdale *Monast.* (1821) III. 242 Constituens..panem regiæ mensæ aptum, qui simenel vulgo vocatur, habere pondere lx solidorum. c**1290** *Fleta* II. ix. §1 Panis..de Symenel [ponderabit] minus Wastello de ij s[olidis], quia bis coctus erit. c**1300** *Munim.*

*Gildhallæ* (Rolls) III. 411 Item, panis artocopi (*i.* simenel) ponderabit minus wastello per duos solidos.
c **1300** *Havelok* 779 For hom he brouthe fele siþe Wastels, simenels with þe horn. **14..** *Lat.-Eng. Voc.* in Wr.-Wülcker 565 *Artocopus*, a symynel. c **1440** *Promp. Parv.* 77 Cymnel, brede, *artocopus*. **1464** in Anstey *Munim. Acad.* (Rolls) II. 710 Panes vulgariter nuncupatos 'Wygges' et 'Symnelles'. **1535** COVERDALE *Ezek.* xvi. 19 Thou didest eate nothinge but symnels, honny & oyle. **1584** COGAN *Haven Health* (1636) 26 Cakes of all formes, Simnels, Cracknels, Buns, Wafers, and other things made of wheat flowre. **1608** WILLET *Hexapla Exod.* 663 Cakes tempered with oyle in the frying pan, and wafers boyled in water..like vnto our simnels. **1655** MOUFET & BENNET *Health's Improv.* (1746) 237 Others sod it [bread] in seam like fritters; others boild it in water like cimnels. **1725** *Fam. Dict.* s.v., Having provided Simnels made of Water according to the size of your Dish, cut 'em in Halves as it were an Orange. **1783** *Gentl. Mag.* LIII. II. 578 Some things customary probably refer simply ..to the idea of feasting... Of these, perhaps, are..cross-buns, saffron cakes, or symnels, in Passion week.., these being formerly at least unleavened. **1854** *N. & Q.* 1st Ser. X. 393 *Simnel*. In the island of Jersey the name is still applied to a kind of thin biscuit made of the finest wheaten flour and water.

**b.** A rich currant cake, usually eaten on Mid-Lent Sunday in certain districts.

**1648** HERRICK *Hesper.*, *To Dianeme*, Ile to thee a Simnell bring, 'Gainst thou go'st a mothering. **1688** HOLME *Armoury* III. 293/2 A Simnell, is a thick copped Cake, or Loaf made of white Bread, Knodden up with Saffron and Currans. **1841** HARTSHORNE *Salop. Ant.* Gloss., *Simnel*, a plumb-cake having a raised crust for the exterior. **1851** *N. & Q.* 1st Ser. III. 506 A rich sort of cake, consisting of a thick crust of saffron-bread filled with currants, citron, and all the usual ingredients of wedding-cake, which is called a simnel. **1872** HARDWICK *Trad. Lanc.* 76 The 'simnels' eaten on Mid-Lent, or 'Mothering' Sunday.

**c.** *attrib.*, as ***simnel bread***, ***-cake***; **Simnel-Sunday**, Mid-Lent, or Mothering Sunday. Also ***simnel-wise*** adj.

**1674** BLOUNT, *Simnel-bread*,..bread made of fine meal of corn. **1711** HEARNE *Collect.* (O.H.S.) III. 134 A Noble Cake, made Simnel-wise. **1766** *Compl. Farmer* s.v. *Bread*, We also meet with symnel bread manchet or roll bread, and French bread. **1819** SCOTT *Ivanhoe* xiv, A quantity of rich pastry, as well as of the simnel-bread and wastle cakes. **1837** HOWITT *Rur. Life* VI. xvi. (1862) 590 In Lancashire and Cheshire they still eat Simnel-cake on Mid-lent Sunday. **1863** CHAMBERS *Bk. of Days* I. 336/1 A sort of rich and expensive cakes, which are called Simnel-cakes.

**2.** *U.S.* A variety of squash. Cf. SIMLIN 1.

**1648** B. PLANTAGENET *Descr. New Albion* 25 Strawberries, Mulberries, Symnels, Maycocks and Horns like Cucumbers. **1705** R. BEVERLEY *Virginia* II. §19 (1722) 124 The Clypeatæ are sometimes call'd Cymnels (as are some others also), from the Lenten Cake of that Name, which many of them very much resemble.

**simo** ('saɪməʊ). [Abbrev. of *si*multaneous *mo*tion-cycle.] ***simo chart***: a chart in which the bodily movements of a worker are represented in relation to a time scale. Hence ***simo-charting*** vbl. sb.

**1928** L. M. GILBRETH in *Bull. Taylor Soc.* June 127/2 The simo charts and the synthesis work demand both time and effort. **1937** R. M. BARNES *Motion & Time Study* ix. 77 The time for each therblig recorded on the analysis sheet may be shown to scale by means of a simultaneous motion-cycle chart, commonly called a 'simo chart'. **1961** *Engineering* 15 Sept. 353/1 Fig. 2 shows the simo-charts produced by a member of a recent course; they promise particularly high savings and provide a very good example of simo-charting. **1969** P. E. RANDALL *Introd. Work Study & Organization Methods* iv. 27 A simo chart breaks hand movements down into eighteen categories.

**simoleon** (sɪ'məʊlɪɒn). *U.S. slang.* Also **samoleon.** [Origin obscure: perh. modelled on NAPOLEON 1.] A dollar.

**1896** G. ADE *Artie* vii. 63 He said I could have it for four hundred samoleons. **1913** C. E. MULFORD *Coming of Cassidy* vii. 112 Sixty-two bucks, three score an' two simoleons; all I've got, every cent. **1952** A. LOMAX *Mister Jelly Roll* 194 By the late twenties the golden simoleons began rolling in. **1977** D. ANTHONY *Stud Game* i. 8, I bet the limit, five thousand simoleons.

†**simon.** *slang.* [Prob. a fanciful use of the personal name.] A sixpence.

a **1700** B. E. *Dict. Cant. Crew*, *Simon*, Six-pence. [Hence in later slang Dicts.]

**simon(d**, obs. forms of SIMMON, cement.

†**'simoner.** *Obs. rare.* In 5 **Sym-**. [var. of SIMONIER.] A simonist, simoniac.

?a **1407** W. THORPE *Exam. & Test.* in Foxe *A. & M.* (1563) 171/1 Proude obstinate heritikes, couetous Symoners. *Ibid.*, These Symoners sell synne, suffering men and women..to lie and continue from yeare to yeare in diuers vices.

**simoniac** (sɪ'məʊnɪæk), *sb.* and *a.* Forms: α. 4 **symoniak**, 5–6 **-yake**, 6 **-iake**, 7 **-iack**; 6–7 **simoniak(e**, 6–8 **-iack(e**, 6– **simoniac**. β. 7 **simonaick.** [a. OF. *symoniake*, *simoniaque* (= Sp., Pg., and It. *simoniaco*), or ad. med.L. *simoniac-us*, f. *simonia* SIMONY.]

**A.** *sb.* One who practises simony; a buyer or seller of benefices, ecclesiastical preferments, or other spiritual things. Freq. with initial capital.

α. **1340** *Ayenb.* 41 Þeruore hi byeþ y-cleped Symoniaks alle þo þet wylleþ zelle oþer begge þe gostliche þinges. c **1420** LYDG. *Assembly of Gods* 680 Pryuy symonyakes, with false vsurers. a **1548** HALL *Chron.*, *Hen. VIII*, 246 He saied that the Pope was a Simoniack, euer sellyng gyftes. **1592** TIMME *Ten Eng. Lepers* D 3, Both the seller and the buier of spirituall things are Simoniacks. **1636** PRYNNE *Unbish. Tim.* (1661) 84 A Bishop.., although he be a Simoniack, Heretick, excommunicate Person,..may yet firmly ordain others. **1681** BAXTER *Answ. Dodwell* iii. 22 Such as divers General Councils judged Hereticks, Infidels, Simoniaks, &c. **1726** AYLIFFE *Parergon* 234 If the Bishop appears, and alledges..that the Person presented is a Simoniac, unlearned, and the like, then they are to proceed to Tryal. **1854** MILMAN *Lat. Chr.* VI. iii. (1864) III. 476 Peter Bishop of Florence was accused as a Simoniac. **1881** *Church Times* Apr. 211 We should say that simoniacs seldom disturb congregations.

β. **1637–50** Row *Hist. Kirk* (Wodrow Soc.) 50 The contraveeners to be punished with all severitie and rigour as simonaicks. **1678** JONES *Heart & Right Soveraign* 349 There was but one bishop in all the isle of Britain then, and he afterwards a Simonaick.

**B.** *adj.* = next.

**1632** D. LUPTON *Lond. & Co. Carbonadoed* (1857) 306 Like a false Canoniere, that came by his place by Simoniacke meanes. **1681** COLVIL *Whigs Supplic.* (1751) 157 [To] part the simoniac pelf, And take the one half to himself. **1688** *Act 1 Will. & Mary* c. 16 Preamble, Persons simoniack or simoniacally promoted to benefices. **1900** *Speaker* 3 Mar. 588 The Simoniac baseness of the Universities.

**simoniacal** (sɪmə'naɪəkəl), *a.* Also 7 **simonaicall.** [f. prec. + -AL[1].]

**1.** Of the nature of, pertaining to, or involving simony.

α. **1567** JEWEL *Def. Apol.* v. 562 These thinges are Simoniacal..that are forebidden in the Olde and Newe Testamente. a **1600** HOOKER *Eccl. Pol.* VII. xxiv. §8 Simoniacal corruption I may not.. suspect to be amongst men of so great place. **1642** ROGERS *Naaman* 145, I may say of this Selfe, as we say of Simoniacall contracts for Benefices, that such Simony creates a lapse. **1740** RICHARDSON *Pamela* (1824) I. lxxxiii. 443 Mr. Williams.. declined the stipulated eighty pounds.., as he thought it would have a Simoniacal appearance. **1765** BLACKSTONE *Comm.* I. 60 When the common law censures simoniacal contracts. **1827** *Bentham's Ration. Judic. Evid.* V. 582 To dispute his lessor's title, by proving that his presentation was simoniacal. **1876** FREEMAN *Norm. Conq.* V. 380 The exaction of such a price..was both oppressive and simoniacal.

β. **1648** GAGE *West Ind.* 2 If he would deliver at once all those his Purgatory Prisoners without the Simonaicall receipt of money.

**2.** Of persons: Guilty of or practising simony.

α. **1569** in Strype *Ann. Ref.* (1709) I. lv. 563 Yea, and in simoniacal heeps cathedral churches are stuffed with them, as dens of thieves. **1621** BURTON *Anat. Mel.* To Rdr. (1651) 44 What shall we expect that have such multitudes of Achans, church robbers, simoniacal patrons. **1641** MILTON *Animadv.* Wks. 1851 III. 233 Away with such young mercenary striplings and their Simoniacall fathers. **1712** STEELE *Spect.* No. 298 ¶8 The Simoniacal Ladies, who seduce the sacred Order into the Difficulty [etc.]. **1759** ROBERTSON *Hist. Scot.* VI. Wks. 1813 I. 427 Declaimed loudly against the simoniacal faction. **1848** *Q. Rev.* Mar. 122 One piece..is a song levelled at Simoniacal prelates. **1897** MRS. OLIPHANT *Makers Rome* 236 They condemned the simoniacal clergy in every rank.

β. **1631** *High Commission Cases* (Camden) 249 It is but to punish him as simonaicall. **1632** LITHGOW *Trav.* I. 20 The bribing hands of the Simonaicall Minions.

**3.** Tainted or marked by simony.

**1575–85** ABP. SANDYS *Serm.* xx. 346 We haue happely forsaken..that polluted Church, that simoniacall temple. **1641** MILTON *Ch. Govt.* II. iii, Would he preferre those proud simoniacall Courts?

Hence **simo'niacalness**, 'the being of a Simoniacal Nature' (Bailey, vol. II, 1727).

**simoniacally** (sɪmə'naɪəkəlɪ), *adv.* [f. prec.] In a simoniacal manner; with the guilt of simony.

**1600** O. E. (M. SUTCLIFFE) *Repl. Libel* II. iv. 85 They are ordeined simoniacally, and by excommunicate persons. **1688** [see SIMONIAC B]. **1695** KENNETT *Par. Antiq.* ix. 619 After his decease, a certain Clerk was simoniacally presented by those Regular Patrons. **1767** BURN *Eccles. Law* III. 325 Canons..whereby a person simoniacally promoted is punished by deprivation. **1778** JOHNSON in *Boswell* 12 May, He had purchased a living in the country, but not simoniacally. **1877** MRS. OLIPHANT *Makers Flor.* xii. 297 A bad pope, a simoniacally-appointed pope.

†**si'moniacle.** *Obs.*$^{-1}$ [a. OF. *simoniacle*, var. of *simoniaque*: cf. next.] A simoniac.

**1502** *Ord. Crysten Men* (W. de W. 1506) IV. viii. R ij, He yt well shall practyse an hondreth thyrty & foure cases of excomunycacyon..& then conforme with symonyacles and other excomunycacyons.

†**si'moniacre,** *a. Obs. rare.* In 6 **symonakre.** [a. OF. *simoniacre*, var. of *simoniaque*: cf. prec.] Simoniacal.

**1533** *State Papers Hen. VIII*, VII. 534 They sayd that we call the Pope Byshop of Rome, bastard, and symonakre. *Ibid.*, As touchyng whyddyr He be bastard or symonakre, or bothe.

†**si'monial.** *Obs. rare.* In 4 **symonyal.** [a. OF. *simonial*, f. *simonie* SIMONY.] = SIMONIAC *sb.*

c **1386** CHAUCER *Pars. T.* ¶784 Both he þat selleth and he þat byeth thynges espirituels ben cleped Symonyales.

**si'monian**[1], *sb.* and *a. rare.* Also 4 **symonyan, -yen.** [f. SIMONY + -AN, or ad. OF. **simonien*.]

†**A.** *sb.* A simoniac, simonist. *Obs.*

c **1380** WYCLIF *Serm.* Sel. Wks. II. 148 Hise ȝiftis ben not mesurid bi man, alȝif symonyens mesuren þer grace, & ȝyven pleyner absolucion..for more money. c **1380** —— *Last Age Ch.* (1840) 25 Chaffare walkynge in derkenessis is þe pryui heresie of symonyans. **1567–8** ABP. PARKER *Corr.* (Parker Soc.) 311, I sent my visitors into Norwich,.. whereof I heard..that *Quid vultis mihi dare*? had so much prevailed there among the Simonians.

**B.** *adj.* Simoniacal.

**1854** MILMAN *Lat. Chr.* VIII. i. III. 271 The clergy of Saxony resolved to expel all the intruding and Simonian bishops (those who had received investiture from the Emperor).

**Simonian**[2] (saɪ'məʊnɪən), *sb.* and *a.* [ad. med.L. **Simonianus*, f. *Simon* (see def.).]

**A.** *sb.* A member of an early Christian sect named after Simon Magus and regarded as heretical. (Cf. SIMONIST[2].)

**1585–7** T. ROGERS *39 Art.* (1625) 57 Some thinke, that to attend vpon vertue, and to practise good workes, is a yoke too heauy, and intollerable; as the Simonians. **1655** BAXTER *Quaker's Catech.* Pref. B ij, He followed the first Hereticks, the Simonians and their followers, with the same kinde of judgements. **1677** GILPIN *Demonol.* (1867) 129 There were no less than ten sorts of heretical Antichrists in the apostle John's days, the Simonians, Menandrians, Saturnalians, &c. **1728** CHAMBERS *Cycl.*, *Simonians*, a Sect of ancient Hereticks, the first that ever disturb'd Christianity. **1831–3** E. BURTON *Eccl. Hist.* (1845) 235 We are assured, that this convenient doctrine was a characteristic of the Simonians and other Gnostics. **1887** *Encycl. Brit.* XXII. 79/1 Even the Tübingen critics themselves could not deny the existence of a sect of Simonians.

**B.** *adj.* Pertaining to, characteristic of, the sect of the Simonians.

**1883** SCHAFF *Encycl. Relig. Knowl.* III. 2184 The Simonian teachings gradually take on the form of an elaborate gnostic system. **1887** *Encycl. Brit.* XXII. 79/1 *note*, Hippolytus..gives extracts from a Simonian book.

Hence **Si'monianism**, the doctrine of the Simonians.

**1887** *Encycl. Brit.* XXII. 80/2 We have therefore in Simonianism a rival system to Christianity. **1902** *Expositor* Sept. 227 There had been a revival of Simonianism in Samaria.

†**si'monical,** *a. Obs.* Also **symonical(l.** [f. SIMON-Y + -ICAL.] = SIMONIACAL.

**1570** FOXE *A. & M.* (ed. 2) 221/1 Where is Peters spirite, by whose power couetousnes is destroyed, and simonicall heresie is condempned? **1588** *Marprel. Epist.* (1843) 22 Since you were a Symonical Deane. **1626** L. OWEN *Running Register* 54 Paulus Quintus that great Symonicall Pope. **1649** MILTON *Eikon.* xiv. Wks. 1851 III. 449 Compiler of that unsalted and Simonical praier. **1686** J. S. *Hist. Monast. Conuent.* 157 His Office is to enquire whether there be any Simonical Practices..in the resignation of Benefices.

Hence †**si'monically** *adv. Obs.*

**1660** R. COKE *Power & Subj.* 268 That patron who should simonically promote any Clerk.

†**si'monient,** *sb.* and *a. Obs. rare.* Also 4–5 **symonient, -yent.** [Cf. SIMONIAN[1] and -ENT.]

**A.** *sb.* = SIMONIAC *sb.*

c **1380** WYCLIF *Wks.* (1880) 26 And siþ þei sillen treuþe ..þei ben cursed symonyentis & so heretikis. **1395** PURVEY *Remonstr.* (1851) 9 Symonientis ben sovereyne eretikis. a **1470** H. PARKER *Dives & Pauper* (W. de W. 1496) VII. 303/1 [They] that bye ony thyng spirytuel..ben called proprely symonientes.

**B.** *adj.* = SIMONIACAL *a.* 1.

**1395** PURVEY *Remonstr.* (1851) 11 Such appropringe..is theefli, fals, and symonient. a **1470** H. PARKER *Dives & Pauper* (W. de W. 1496) VII. 302/2 Some thynges be forboden for they be symonyent, as byenge and sellynge of the sacramentes of holy chirche.

Hence †**si'moniently** *adv. Obs.*

c **1400** *Apol. Loll.* 51 No man presume..symonyently, þat is to sey, for coueytise, for his labour tak ani þing.

†**si'monier.** *Obs.* Also 4 **symoniour, -ier,** 5–6 **-yer.** [Cf. prec. and -ER[1].] = SIMONIAC *sb.*

c **1380** WYCLIF *Sel. Wks.* III. 103 Þes proude clerkes, symoniours, silleres of pardoun and indulgences. *Ibid.* 211 Þer ben two maner of heretikis of whiche Englond schuld be purgid, and symonieris ben þe first. c **1440** *Alph. Tales* 480 Þus þies symonyers war confusid, & belife þe abbay was wele rewlid and clere oute of dett. **1502** *Ord. Crysten Men* (W. de W. 1506) II. i, Be in no wyse..a symonyer, or a rauenour. **1520** *Caxton's Chron. Eng.* VII. 76 b, Gregorius the 7.. proceded sharply agaynst prelates and preestes that were symonyers.

**si'monious,** *a.* Now *rare* or *Obs.* Also 7 **symonious.** [f. SIMONY + -OUS.]

**1.** = SIMONIACAL 1 and 3.

**1612** DEKKER *If it be not good* Wks. 1873 II. 276 None shall hold Three or four Church-liuings (got by Symonious gold). **1648** MILTON *Tenure Kings* 54 Gorging themselves on the simonious places of their outed predecessors. **1839** LADY LYTTON *Cheveley* (ed. 2) I. ix. 192 A simonious suit decided against her in the Ecclesiastical Court had been the result.

**2.** = SIMONIACAL 2.

**1653** MILTON *Hirelings* Preface, The oppressions of a Simonious decimating clergie. **1670** —— *Hist. Eng.* VI. Wks. 1851 III. 292 At this relation..Stigand the Simonious Archbishop..is said to have laugh't.

**'simonism.** *rare*$^{-1}$. [Cf. next and -ISM.] The practice or advocacy of simony.

**1895** *Sat. Rev.* 23 Mar. 370 For simonism and lack of manly straightforwardness, this letter has not often been paralleled.

**simonist**[1] ('sɪmənɪst). Also 7 **symonist.** [f. SIMON-Y + -IST.] One who practises or upholds simony.

**1567** JEWEL *Def. Apol.* v. 564 The Heresie of Macedonius ..is more tolerable, then is the Heresie of these simonistes.

**1583** BABINGTON *Commandm.* (1590) 5b, No excommunicate person or Simonist shall bee a patron to present. **1621** BP. MOUNTAGU *Diatribæ* 102 The Sacrilegist, and Symonist, the two Prophaners of holy things. **1670** MILTON *Hist. Eng.* IV. Wks. 1851 III. 163 Wulfer..selling the Bishoprick of London, to Wini the first Simonist we read of in this story. **1705** HICKERINGILL *Priest-cr.* II. v. 49 An Adulterer, Simonist,..Arrian. **1767** BURN *Eccles. Law* III. 336 The ecclesiastical court may proceed against a simonist. **1864** *Athenæum* 9 Apr. 502/3 A Turk might say,..if you are a Christian, you are a simonist and a persecutor.

*attrib.* **1681** HICKERINGILL *Vind. Naked Truth* II. 11 The Symonist Arch-bishop.

**Simonist**[2] ('saımənıst). *rare.* [f. *Simon* + -IST.] = SIMONIAN *sb.*[2]

**1880** *Encycl. Brit.* XI. 854/2 The various heresies..are taken up in chronological order and arranged in five main groups, the Ophite, Simonist,..and Noetian.

† **'simonite**[1]. *Obs.* = SIMONIST[1].

**1508** KENNEDIE *Flyting w. Dunbar* 525 Sarazene, symonyte, provit Pagane pronunciate. **1555** W. WATREMAN *Fardle Facions* II. x. 235 Thei ware all busie vsurers, and Simonites: bothe spirituall and Temporall. **1588** in *Liturg. Serv. Q. Eliz.* (1847) 617 All Simonites, w$^{ch}$ bye and sell, or unfytlie bestow livinges and offices.

**Simonite**[2] ('saımənaıt). [f. the name of Sir John Allsebrook *Simon* (1873–1954), Liberal politician + -ITE[1].] A supporter of Sir John Simon; used *spec.* to designate a member of the Liberal National Party which seceded in 1931 from the official Liberal Party led by Sir Herbert Samuel. Freq. *attrib.* Cf. SAMUELITE.

**1931** [see SAMUELITE]. **1932** [see MOSLEYITE]. **1957** J. BOWLE *Viscount Samuel* xvii. 287 The Liberals had to accept a measure of Protection... But the rift with the Simonites continued. **1966** T. WILSON *Downfall of Liberal Party 1914–1935* xix. 352 The dismissed employee was to appear in Parliament in 1931 as a Simonite (anti-Lloyd George) M.P. **1977** D. MARQUAND *Ramsay Macdonald* xxvii. 677 On the fiscal question..he sided with the Conservatives and Simonite Liberals against Snowden and the Samuelite Liberals. **1979** G. POTTINGER *Secretaries of State for Scotland 1926–76* vi. 54 It was natural for him to take the Simonites' side when the split with the Samuel faction came in 1931.

**simonize** ('saımənaız), *v.* Also **Simonize.** [f. *Simoniz* proprietary name of a type of car polish.] *trans.* To polish by the application of Simoniz. Also *transf.* and *fig.* So **'simonizing** *vbl. sb.*; hence **'simonized** *ppl. a.*

**1934** *Amer. Speech* IX. 114/1 The work on the car may include..vulcanizing tire cuts, and simonizing. **1942** BERREY & VAN DEN BARK *Amer. Thes. Slang* §125/6 *Simonize*, to brilliantine the hair. *Ibid.* §291/4 Curry favour; toady... *simonize the apple* or *orange.* **1949** A. MILLER *Death of Salesman* I. 17 Remember those days? The way Biff used to simonize that car? **1953** *Economist* 25 July 258/1, I have heard it said that Harvard University humanises the scientist and simonises the humanist. **1968** R. H. R. SMITHIES *Shoplifter* (1969) ix. 189 The lovingly simonized fenders, hubcaps, and bumpers. **1975** *New Yorker* 19 May 116/2 He writes of someone's being 'Nixonized', which is apparently like having a car Simonized. **1977** *Chicago Tribune* 2 Oct. XII. 73/3 (Advt.), Will do Blue Coral waxing, Simonizing & interiors.

**Simon Pure.** *colloq.* Also **Simon-Pure, Simon-pure, simon-pure.** [The name of a Quaker in Mrs. Centlivre's comedy *A bold stroke for a wife* (1717), who is impersonated by another character during part of the play.] **a.** ***the*** (***real***) ***Simon Pure***, the real, genuine, or authentic person or thing.

[**1785** 'P. PINDAR' *Lyric Odes* ix. 28 Flattery's a Mountebank so *spruce*—get riches; Truth, a plain Simon Pure, a Quaker Preacher.] **1795** T. WILKINSON *Wandering Patentee* III. 34 She in her rage denounced vengeance heartily, and said that she would advertise my production as a flimsy disgraceful imposture: But she was mistaken—for mine was the true *Simon Pure.* **1815** SCOTT *Guy M.* lvi, 'Here,' proceeded the counsellor, 'is the real Simon Pure—here's Godfrey Bertram Hewit'. *a* **1832** —— *Monast.* Introduction *note*, Each insisting that his Jedediah Cleishbotham was the real Simon Pure. **1860** W. C. PRIME *Boat Life Egypt* xxxiii. 357 If we would come with him the other way he would show us the real mummy, the Simon Pure. **1882** FLOYER *Unexpl. Baluchistan* 381, I believe the real Simon pure had been in the crowd all the time.

**b.** *attrib.* or as *adj.* Real, genuine, authentic. Also, pure, unadulterated; honest, upright.

**1869** 'MARK TWAIN' *Innoc. Abr.* xli. 436 Soon the bell—a genuine, simon-pure bell—rang. **1889** *Cent. Mag.* Jan. 337 The home of the Simon-pure wild horse is on the southern plains. **1894** HOWELLS *Trav. fr. Altruria* 125 If you want to see American individuality, the real, simon-pure article. **1913** *Jrnl. Industr. & Engin. Chem.* June 504/1 Willard Gibbs..was simon pure—in his best days he did not soil his hands even with the grime of a laboratory. **1945** R. HARGREAVES *Enemy at Gate* 282 The unsullied, Simon-Pure principles of proletarian ideology. **1951** *Manch. Guardian Weekly* 28 June 2/3 The [drug] peddlers have gone underground and the specified retailers have turned Simon-pure. **1974** *Jrnl. Ecumenical Stud.* Winter 119 The simon-pure neutrality of church leaders, paralyzed by their own myth of 'even-handedness', has embarrassed in a new way the relations between individual Christians and Jews.

† **simont, symont,** obs. ff. CEMENT *sb.* and *v.*

**1501** DOUGLAS *Pal. Hon.* III. lxvii, The purifyit siluer.. Insteid of symont was ouir all that wone. **1505–6** *Acc. Ld. High Treas. Scot.* III. 46 Item.., to set on the simont riall quhilk wes deliverit to Quinta Essencia. **1598** in Willis & Clark *Cambridge* (1886) II. 252 The windoes..shalbe well glazed and simonted.

**simony** ('sımənı). Forms: 3–6 **symonye, -ie,** (4 **-i**), 4–9 **symony;** 3–7 **simonie** (4 **-ye**), 6 **simoni,** 6– **simony.** [a. OF. *symonie, simonie* (= Sp., Pg., It. *simonia*), ad. med.L. *simonia*, f. the name of *Simon* Magus, in allusion to his offer of money to the Apostles, Acts viii. 18–19.]

**1.** The act or practice of buying or selling ecclesiastical preferments, benefices, or emoluments; traffic in sacred things. Freq. with initial capital.

*a* **1225** *Ancr. R.* 202 Simonie, Gauel, Oker. *c* **1290** *S. Eng. Leg.* I. 435 Wel vnneþe he it fond with-oute symonie. Simonie so is i-cleoped foreward for-to make To bugge liflode of holie churche. **1303** R. BRUNNE *Handl. Synne* 5511 Symonye ys, as men telle, When ȝyftys of holy cherche men selle. *a* **1340** HAMPOLE *Psalter* lxxviii. 1 Ill men..come in.. till dignytes of halykirke, þorgh maystry and symony. *c* **1380** WYCLIF *Sel. Wks.* III. 328 Siche curatis..comen not into here benefices bi þe dore,..but symonye, pride and coveitise. *c* **1449** PECOCK *Repr.* III. viii. 321 The fruyt of the chirchis riche endewing is synne of..symonye. **1482** *Monk of Evesham* xlvi. (Arb.) 93 He tolde me that for the synne of symony that he dyd..he sofred ful greuys peynys. **1534** MORE *Comf. agst. Trib.* II. Wks. 1200/2 If he came therto by simony, or some such other euyll mene. **1580** LUPTON *Sivqila* 11 Then I thinke none is admitted into that function with you, that intrude themselves into it by giftes or Simonie. **1616** R. C. *Times' Whistle* (1871) 45 But Simonie is now soe common growne, That 'tis account noe sinne, if kept vnknowne. **1664** H. MORE *Myst. Iniq.* 434 Those Revenues and Preferments which Simony..had made mere Merchandise. **1704** NELSON *Fest. & Fasts* x. (1739) 603 The Christian Church..proceeded with great Severity against such as were found guilty of Simony. **1766** BLACKSTONE *Comm.* II. 278 By simony, the right of presentation to a living is forfeited, and vested *pro hac vice* in the crown. **1823** LINGARD *Hist. Eng.* VI. 223 A pontiff unfit for his station through ignorance, incapable of holding it through simony. **1876** FREEMAN *Norm. Conq.* V. 315 In his ecclesiastical patronage Stephen stands vaguely charged with Simony.

*fig.* **1600** W. WATSON *Decacordon* 83 Which foule abuse is nothing else but a meere mentall Simonie, vsurie, sacriledge and most impious hypocrisie. **1656** EARL MONM. tr. *Boccalini's Advts. fr. Parnass.* I. lxxvii. 103 The prevarications of Advocates, the Symony used of Judges.

*attrib.* **1859** SALA *Tw. round Clock* (1861) 120 If you have a fancy to see Simony sales by auction, and advowsons.. knocked down for so many pounds sterling.

† **b.** Personified. *Obs.*

*c* **1325** *Poem time Edw. II* (Percy) iv, Trewth..dare not come..for ferde, if symonye may meet hym, he wil smyte of his berde. **1362** LANGL. *P. Pl.* A. II. 37 Sir Simonye is of-sent to asseale þe Chartres. *c* **1400** MAUNDEV. (1839) iii. 19 For now is Symonye Kyng crouned in Holy Chirche. **1588** *Marprel. Epist.* (1843) 25, I thinke Simonie be the bishops lacky. *a* **1640** J. DAY *Peregr. Schol.* (1881) 72, I haue but a poore vicaridge which one Mr. Symon-Monye, or more familiarlie sym-monie, helpt me to.

† **2.** The money paid in simony. Also *transf.*, a tip (to a verger). *Obs. rare.*

**1598** MARSTON *Sco. Villanie* II. v. 196 What though pale Maurus paid huge Symonies For his halfe-dozen gelded vicaries. **1706–7** FARQUHAR *Beaux' Strat.* II. ii, Then I, Sir, tips me the Verger with half a Crown; he pockets the Simony and Inducts me into the best Pue in the Church.

‖ **simool.** Also **semal, semul.** [Bengālī, Hindī, etc. *simul* (also *semul, sêmul, sêmal*).] The (red) silk-cotton tree of India (*Bombax ceiba*).

**1835** *Penny Cycl.* IV. 2/2 The Semul, or cotton-tree. **1855** ROYLE *Fibrous Plants India* 265 A report from the Society of Arts on two pieces of cloth made from the Simool or Silk Cotton tree. **1866** *Treas. Bot.* 1009/2 The silk-cotton of the Simool..is..not adapted for spinning. **1889** *Dict. Econ. Prod. India* I. 489 The semul cotton supplied them was better known as kapok. **1902** T. W. WEBBER *Forests Upper India* xviii. 232 The semal or cotton tree. **1932** PEARSON & BROWN *Comm. Timbers India* 138 The primary use of semul is for tea and rubber boxes.

‖ **simoom** (sı'mu:m), *sb.* Also *α.* **sam-oom, samum, semoom, simúm.** *β.* **samoon, samun, semoun, simoon, -oun.** [a. Arab. *semūm*, f. the root *samm* to poison. With the form *simoon* cf. F. *semoun, simoun.*] **a.** A hot, dry, suffocating sand-wind which sweeps across the African and Asiatic deserts at intervals during the spring and summer.

*α.* **1790** BRUCE *Trav.* IV. 559 The simoom..still continued to blow, so as to exhaust us entirely. **1799** W. TAYLOR in *Monthly Mag.* VII. 139, I should have caught an ague on these sands, Did not a simoom cheer me now and then. **1817** BYRON *Manfred* III. i. 128 The red-hot breath of the most lone simoom, Which dwells but in the desert. **1832** Semoum [see SAMIEL]. **1849** EASTWICK *Dry Leaves* 131 This place is sometimes visited with a furious tornado, or simúm, from the desert. **1865** *Fortn. Rev.* I. 461 The samoom, which is so rare a phenomenon in the Egyptian desert. **1865** W. G. PALGRAVE *Arabia* I. 18 The semoom was fairly upon us. **1870** EMERSON *Soc. & Sol., Courage*, Wks. (Bohn) III. 108 The hunter is not alarmed by bears..nor an Arab by the simoom. **1947** M. A. GARBELL *Tropical & Equatorial Meteorol.* xiii. 200/2 Algerian and Syrian samum.

*attrib.* **1854** J. S. C. ABBOTT *Napoleon* (1855) I. xiv. 239 Every passion..had swept with simoom blast over the cities and villages of France.

*β.* **1847** WEBSTER, Simoon. **1860** MRS. HARVEY *Cruise Claymore* vi. 129 Two days after their departure an unusually violent simoon came on, and every soul was buried in the sand. **1878** H. S. WILSON *Alpine Ascents* ii. 58 A simoon of impalpable fine cloud dust sweeps by. **1926** W. N. SHAW *Man. Metereol.* I. ii. 28 The principal of these are ..the bora of the Adriatic, the scirocco of Southern Italy, the samun of Algeria which is also called scirocco. **1931** A. A. MILLER *Climatol.* xiv. 253 Similar winds to the foehn occur in all mountain districts, where cyclonic storms occur. .. The Chinook..is exactly similar, so are the Samun of Persia, descending from the mountains of Kurdistan,..and many others. **1968** G. R. RUMNEY *Climatol.* xiii. 254/1 The sirocco is known as the khamsin in Egypt, leveche in southeastern Spain, where it is usually quite dry, garbi in the Aegean, samoon in Algeria, sahat in Morocco, and ghibli in Libya.

**b.** *transf.* and *fig.*

**1839** CARLYLE *Chartism* v, Force itself..has doubtless a composing effect;—against inanimate Simooms. **1847** BUSHNELL *Chr. Nurture* II. ii. (1861) 264 It is as if there were a simoon of piety blowing through the house. **1885** *Pall Mall G.* 25 Feb. 1/1 All the force and fury of Mr. Gladstone's oratorical simoom.

Hence **si'moom** *v.*, to exterminate as by a simoom.

**1821** *Blackw. Mag.* VIII. 532 They are simoom'd—blasted—annihilated.

**simorg(h,** variants of SIMURGH.

**'simosaur.** *Palæont.* [See next.] An animal belonging to the fossil genus *Simosaurus.* So **simo'saurian.**

**1880** *Libr. Univ. Knowl.* V. 410 They comprise two groups, the ichthyosaurians and simosaurians. **1896** LYDEKKER *Roy. Natural Hist.* V. 103 In the allied nothosaurs and simosaurs the limbs were better adapted for walking.

**Simosaurus** (saıməʊ'sɔ:rəs). *Palæont.* [mod.L., f. Gr. *σῑμός* snub-nosed + *σαῦρος* lizard.] A genus of Plesiosaurians belonging to the Triassic period.

**1870** NICHOLSON *Man. Zool.* (1875) 492 Of the other genera.., *Simosaurus* and *Nothosaurus* are from the Trias. **1881** *Nature* XXIV. 472 Prof. H. G. Seeley gave a detailed description of the skeleton of Simosaurus recently discovered in the Trias near Stuttgart.

**si'mosity.** *rare*$^{-0}$. [f. L. *sīmus* snub-nosed.] 'A being crooked nosed' (Bailey, 1721).

**simoun,** variant of SIMOOM.

**simous** ('saıməs), *a.* [f. L. *sīmus*, Gr. *σῑμός*: see -OUS.]

† **1.** Bending or curving inward; concave. Also of the nose: Snub, flat. *Obs.*

**1634** T. JOHNSON *Parey's Chirurg.* III. xx. (1678) 73 This Gate-vein coming out of the simous part of the Liver, is divided into six branches. **1666** J. SMITH *Old Age* (ed. 2) 71 It is on the external or forepart, gibbous or bunching outward; on the internal or hind part, simous or bending inwards. **1688** HOLME *Armoury* II. 295/2 A Swallow tailed Shelldrake. This Fowl hath a short Bill, and simous. **1697** EVELYN *Numismata* ix. 297 The nose..long, short, simous.

**2.** Having a flat nose; snub-nosed. *rare.*

**1656** BLOUNT *Glossogr.*, *Simous*, flat nosed. **1803** SHAW *Gen. Zool.* IV. I. 172 Simous Blenny, *Blennius Simus.*

**simp** (sımp). Colloq. abbrev. of SIMPLE *sb.* 2b or SIMPLETON 1: a fool, a simpleton.

**1903** W. C. THOMPSON *On Road with Circus* i. 23 In circus dialect 'yap' and 'simp' indicate a credulous rustic who is easy prey for sharpers. **1924** WODEHOUSE *Bill the Conqueror* vi. 133 You poor simp, you've got about as much chance of havin' me sneak those books for you as—well, I don't know what. **1937** N. MARSH *Vintage Murder* xv. 165 You looked a big simp, Cass. **1973** *Sat. Rev. Society* (U.S.) Mar. 72/3 Wonder Woman almost (but never quite) loses her head and heart to a weak simp, a U.S. Army Intelligence pilot. **1976** *Publishers Weekly* 19 Apr. 82/3 The book's assumption is that single men are simps who don't know the difference between a pepper mill and a can opener.

**simpai.** [Malay.] (See quots.)

**1840** *Cuvier's Anim. Kingd.* 58 The Simpai..is of a very lively red; beneath white: its face is blue; and a crest of black hairs reaches from one ear to the other. **1871** *Cassell's Nat. Hist.* I. 87 The Black-crested Monkey, or the Simpai, ..*Semnopithecus Melalophus.*

**simpathy,** obs. form of SYMPATHY.

**simpatico** (sım'pætıkəʊ), *a.* Also (fem.) **simpatica.** [It. or Sp.: see SYMPATHIC *a.*] Pleasing, likeable; congenial, understanding; sensitive, sympathetic.

**1864** H. SIDGWICK *Let.* 21 Oct. in *Memoir* (1906) ii. 119 The Frau Professorin was less 'simpatica'. **1905** E. M. FORSTER *Where Angels fear to Tread* iii. 86 The person who understands us at first sight, who never irritates us, who never bores..that is what I mean by *simpatico.* **1908** W. JAMES *Let.* 4 Oct. (1920) II. 314, I find him [*sc.* Boutroux] very *simpatico.* **1936** E. AMBLER *Dark Frontier* 80 She was infinitely—as those appreciative Italians put it—infinitely *simpatica.* **1952** A. HUXLEY *Let.* 20 May (1969) 644 There is something *simpatico* about Pascal—he is a kind of Central European Baron Munchausen. **1964** MRS. L. B. JOHNSON *White House Diary* 19 Mar. (1970) 96 Although he is very attached to the Kennedys, I thought we had established a certain simpatico relationship with him. **1976** *Observer* 22 Feb. 26/7 Sylvia reluctantly committed Ralph into the care of a blunt but *simpatico* medico who didn't talk down either to her or to us.

**simper** ('sımpə(r)), *sb.* [f. SIMPER *v.*[2]] An affected and self-conscious smile; a silly smiling look; a smirk.

**1599** B. JONSON *Cynthia's Rev.* v. iv, You become the simper, well, ladie. **1711** ADDISON *Spectator* No. 179 ¶7 The Whistler relaxed his Fibres into a kind of Simper. **1728** POPE *Dunc.* II. 6 The proud Parnassian sneer, The conscious simper, and the jealous leer, Mix on his look. **1779** G. KEATE *Sketches fr. Nat.* (ed. 2) I. 23, I suppose, by your simper,.. that but few people come now to Becket's shrine for a kiss. **1831** CARLYLE *Sart. Res.* I. iv, Some men wear an everlasting barren simper. **1872** BLACK *Adv. Phaeton* xxii, With an idiotic simper on his face.

*Comb.* **1817** *Lintoun Green* II. 22 The Boar was round as any clue, Was smooth and simper fac'd.

**b.** An affectation; a pose.

**1828** *Life Planter Jamaica* I Few would believe him, if he fell into the common simper of whining about the comfort of convicted felons.

**ˈsimper**, *v.*[1] *Obs.* exc. *dial.* Also 6 **symper.** [Prob. imitative; connexion with next appears unlikely.]

**1.** *intr.* To simmer.

**1477** NORTON *Ordin. Alch.* iv. in Ashm. (1652) 47 Remember that Water will buble and boyle, But Butter must simper and also Oyle. **1530** PALSGR. 718/1, I symper, as lycour dothe on the fyre byfore it begynneth to boyle. *a* **1608** DEE *Relat. Spirits* I. (1659) 214 It seemeth to be a great Lake of pitch: and it playeth or simpreth, as water doth, when it beginneth to seethe. *a* **1691** BOYLE *Medicin. Exp.* v. (1693) 41 Let the Vessel stand in a moderate heat, that the Liquor may simper for many hours. **1725** *Fam. Dict.* s.v. *Verjuice*, The Verjuice must not be boil'd, but let it simper only. **1736** in *Ochtertyre Ho. Bk.* (S.H.S.) Introd. p. xxxix, Letting the berries Simper in a pan. *a* **1825** FORBY *Voc. E. Anglia* 301. **1881** *Antrim & Down Gloss.* 90. **1888** *Sheffield Gloss.* 215.

**2.** *trans.* To cause to simmer. *rare*$^{-1}$.

**1694** W. SALMON *Bate's Dispens.* (1713) 686/2 You are then to add the Balsam de Tolu..and Rose-water, simpering it till the Rose-water is evaporated.

**simper** (ˈsɪmpə(r)), *v.*[2] [Of obscure origin. In sense 1 perh. related to a continental *semper* or *simper*, which is represented by Da., Norw., and Sw. dial. *semper*, *simper*, Swiss dial. *semper*, G. *zimper*, *zimpfer* (also MDu. *simper-*, *zimperlijc*, G. *zimpf-*, *zimperlich*), elegant, delicate, nice, dainty, affected, etc., and G. *zimpf-*, *zimpern*, *-eln* to be coy, etc. Mod.WFris. has *simperje* in sense 3, with adj. *simperich* peevish.]

**1.** *intr.* To smile in a silly, self-conscious, or affected manner; to smirk.

Perh. implied earlier in SIMPER-DE-COCKET.

*c* **1563** *Jack Juggler* (Roxb.) 9 She simperith, she prankith and getteth with out faylle, As a pecocke that hath spred, and sheweth hir gaye taile. **1576** FLEMING *Panopl. Ep.* 277 Simpering and smiling, he began somwhat leisurely to write. **1611** BEAUM. & FL. *Philaster* I, She is one that may.. simper when she is Courted by her Friend. **1652** OLEY *Life G. Herbert* (1836) p. cv, His birth and spirit prompted him to martial achievements,..and not to sit simpering over a book. **1770** MME. D'ARBLAY *Early Diary* 20 Apr., She.. lisps affectedly, simpers designedly, and looks conceitedly. **1832** R. & J. LANDER *Exped. Niger* III. xx. 215 Addigetta.. smiles or simpers most engagingly whenever she is more than ordinarily pleased. **1891** M. WILLIAMS *Later Leaves* v. 61 She smiled and simpered and tried to avoid the question.

†**b.** So *to simper it*. *Obs.*

**1575** NORTH tr. *Philibert's Philosopher at Crt.* 16 Counterfaite Courtiers which simper it in outwarde shewe, making pretie mouthes [etc.]. **1602** ROWLANDS *Greenes Ghost* (Hunterian Club) 27 She simpered it, and made curtesie,..as if she had neuer seene them before. **1626** MIDDLETON *Women Beware Women* III. ii, See how she simpers it, as if marmalade Would not melt in her mouth!

†**c.** With allusion to SIMPER *v.*[1] *Obs.*

**1594** NASHE *Unfort. Trav.* Wks. (Grosart) V. 37, I simpered with my countenance lyke a porredge pot on the fire when it first begins to seeth. **1731-8** SWIFT *Polite Conv.* 45 And yet she simpers like a Firmity-Kettle.

†**2.** To glimmer, twinkle. *Obs. rare.*

*c* **1620** BEAUM. & FL. *Lover's Progress* III. i, The Candles are all out. *Lanc.* But one i' th' Parlour. I see it simper hither, pray come this way. **1633** G. HERBERT *Temple, Search* iv, Yet can I mark how starres above Simper and shine.

**3.** *dial.* To whimper.

**1865** SLEIGH *Derbyshire Gloss.* **1888** *Sheffield Gloss.* 215 *Simper*, to cry, to begin to cry as a spoiled child does.

**4.** *trans.* To say or utter with a simper.

**1801** MAR. EDGEWORTH *Angelina* x, 'He, he, he,' simpered Nat. 'I am Orlando, of whom you have heard so much.' **1856** MERIVALE *Rom. Emp.* I. (1865) VI. 208 'Friends everywhere!' simpered the fool; 'pray how came you all here?'

**b.** With advs., as *away*, *forth*, *out*.

**1838** D. JERROLD *Men of Char.* III. v, He simpered away nothing of its reality into conventual no-meaning. **1843** LYTTON *Last of Barons* II. iii, Must I go bonnet in hand and simper forth the sleek personals of the choice of her kith and house? **1873** C. M. DAVIES *Unorth. Lond.* (1876) 429 Drawing-rooms, where Browning and Tennyson were simpered out to coteries.

†**simper-de-cocket.** *Obs.* Forms: (see the quots.). [app. a fanciful formation on SIMPER *v.*[2] and COCKET *a.*] An affected coquettish air; a woman characterized by this; a flirt.

In quot. 1562 used as an adj. or adv.

α. *a* **1529** SKELTON *E. Rummyng* 55 She wyll iet.. In her furred flocket, And gray russet rocket, With simper the cocket. **1621** B. JONSON *Gipsies Metam.* Wks. (Rtldg.) 619/2 Lay by..using your nimbles, In diving the pockets, And sounding the sockets Of simper-the-cockets.

β. *a* **1530** J. HEYWOOD *Weather* 877 (Brandl), I saw you dally with your symper de cokket. **1562** —— *Prov. & Epigr.* (1867) 43 Vpright as a candle standth in a socket, Stoode she that daie, so simpre de cocket. **1607** R. C[AREW] tr. *Estienne's World of Wonders* 238 Another sort of simper-de-cockets, who counterfet puppets, in speaking so finely that they wil scarce open their mouthes. **1611** COTGR., *Coquine*, a begger-woman; also, a cockney, simperde-cockit, nice thing. **1707** tr. *Wks. C'tess D'Anois* (1715) 384, I have here in my Custody, said she, a little Simper de cockit that will not let me be at quiet.

**ˈsimperer.** [f. SIMPER *v.*[2] + -ER[1].] One who simpers or smiles affectedly.

**1769** NEVILE *Imit. Juvenal* II A simp'rer, that a court affords. **1810** SCOTT *Lady of Lake* V. xxi, Well the simperer might be vain. **1816** GILCHRIST *Philos. Etym.* 216, I know what courtly simperers will think and say..of this..style of writing. **1863** MRS. OLIPHANT *Salem Chapel* vii, Those self-engrossed simperers should yet be startled out of their follies.

**ˈsimpering**, *vbl. sb.*[1] [f. SIMPER *v.*[1] + -ING[1].] Simmering.

**1477** NORTON *Ordin. Alch.* iv. in Ashm. (1652) 46 To know of the simperinge of our Stone. **1598** FLORIO, *Cremore*,..the creame or simpring of milke when it seethes.

**ˈsimpering**, *vbl. sb.*[2] [f. SIMPER *v.*[2] + -ING[1].] The action of the verb; an instance of this.

**1582** STANYHURST *Æneis*, etc. (Arb.) 141 Her look's, her simpring, her woords with curtesye sweetning. **1596** NASHE *Saffron Walden* Wks. (Grosart) III. 103 Some little coy bridling of the chin, and nice simpring and wrything his face 30. waies. **1633** G. HERBERT *Temple, Church-Porch* xxi, Simpring is but a lay-hypocrisie. **1675** TRAHERNE *Chr. Ethics* 314 Without which humility is but baseness,.. modesty but simpering, devotion but hypocrisie. **1748** RICHARDSON *Clarissa* (1811) II. xx. 140 My mother's hand was kindly put into his, with a simpering altogether bridal. **1780** MME. D'ARBLAY *Diary* May, We were now not content with simpering, for we could not forbear downright laughing. **1894** *Forum* July 584 [Co-education] takes the simpering out of the girls—the roughness out of the men.

**ˈsimpering**, *ppl. a.* [f. SIMPER *v.*[2] + -ING[2].]

**1.** That simpers or smiles affectedly. Said of persons or their features. Also *transf.*

**1586** A. DAY *Eng. Secretary* I. (1595) 70 Then is she..a simpring puppet to wonder on. **1602** DEKKER *Satirom.* Wks. 1873 I. 185 These pretty, simpering, setting things, call'd brides. **1648** HERRICK *Hesper., To Anthea lying in bed*, Like to a Twi-light, or that simpring Dawn, That Roses shew, when misted o're with Lawn. **1768** GOLDSM. *Good-n. Man* Epil., His simpering friends, with pleasure in their eyes, Sink as he sinks. **1782** MISS BURNEY *Cecilia* I. v, Young ladies dwindle into mere listeners, simpering listeners, I confess. **1826** POLWHELE *Trad. & Recoll.* I. ii. 29 A pretty silly simpering girl..was dazzled by his wit. **1877** BRYANT *Wind & Stream* iii, The simpering stream, The fond, delighted, silly stream.

**2.** Accompanied by or associated with simpering; mincing, affected.

**1595** T. P. GOODWIN *Blanchardine* II. (1890) 216 Pacing toward the Queene with a simpering smile, neither presaging mirth nor mourning. **1626** MIDDLETON *Women Beware Women* III. ii, I had rather hear one ballad sung.. Than all these simpering tunes. **1653** R. SANDERS *Physiogn.* 156 The man walks with a proud and simpring pace. **1712** W. KING *Little Mouths* 20 Betty, with bridled chin, extends her face, And then contracts her lips with simpering grace. **1862** THACKERAY *Round. P., Notch on Axe* 253, I went on meanly conversing with him, and affecting a simpering confidence. **1865** LIVINGSTONE *Zambesi* 503 It is no simpering smile.

†**ˈsimperingly**, *adv.*[1] *Obs.*$^{-1}$ [f. *simpering* SIMPER *v.*[1]] Simmeringly.

*a* **1648** DIGBY *Closet Opened* (1677) 110 When you see the milk begin to boil simp'ringly.

**ˈsimperingly**, *adv.*[2] [f. SIMPERING *ppl. a.* + -LY[2].] With a simper; in a simpering manner.

**1592** NASHE *P. Penilesse* Wks. (Grosart) II. 32 Mistris Minx, a Marchants wife,..that lookes as simperingly as if she were besmeared. **1598** MARSTON *Sco. Villanie* III. ix. 220 Why lookes neat Curus all so simpringly? **1612** *Benvenuto's Passenger* II. ii. 533 She affably and simpringly answered. **1862** SALA *Seven Sons* III. 12 He..made use of some simperingly good-hearted expressions.

**simpiesometer**: see SYMPIESOMETER.

†**ˈsimplar**, *a. Obs.*$^{-1}$ [ad. late L. *simplār-is*, f. *simplus* SIMPLE *a.*] Single.

**1610** [see DUPLAR *a.*].

**simple** (ˈsɪmp(ə)l), *a.* and *sb.* Also α. 4 **simpil, -ul,** 5 **simpel, -ill, -ulle;** 4-5 **sympile,** 5-6 **-ill,** 5 **sympel(l,** 5-6 **sympyll** (5 **-yl, -ylle, cympylle**), **sympul** (5 **-ull**), 4-6 **symple.** β. 4-6, *Sc.* 8-9 **semple,** 5-6 **sempill** (6 **-yll**). [a. OF. *simple* (12th cent., = Prov., Sp., and Pg. *simple*), ad. L. *simplus* or *simplex*. Hence also Du., Fris., G., Da., and Sw. *simpel* (MDu. also *sempel*).

L. *simplus* (in class. L. only in neut. *simplum*) is cognate with Gr. ἁπλόος, ἁπλοῦς, the first element in both being **sem-* 'one'. In *simplex* the second element is related to L. *plicāre*, Gr. πλέκειν 'to fold': cf. AFALD *a.*]

**A.** *adj.*

In early examples it is often difficult to decide in which of several possible senses the word is to be taken.

**I. 1.** Free from duplicity, dissimulation, or guile; innocent and harmless; undesigning, honest, open, straightforward.

*c* **1220** *Bestiary* 790 Simple [as the dove] and softe be we alle. *a* **1225** *Ancr. R.* 128 [False ancres] habbeð efter þe uoxe a simple semblaunt sume cherre, & beoð þauh ful of gile. **13..** *E.E. Allit. P.* B. 746 Now sayned be þou sauiour, so symple in þy wrath! **1382** WYCLIF *Matt.* x. 16 Be ȝe war as serpentis, and symple as dowues. *Ibid., Luke* xi. 34 If thin yȝe schal be symple, al thi body schal be liȝtful. *a* **1400-50** *Alexander* 4404 To sawe emang þir simpill men sedis of debate. **1485** CAXTON *St. Wenefryde* 14 A man of good lyf and symple courage. **1508** DUNBAR *Tua Mariit Wemen* 255, I semyt sober, and sueit, & sempill without fraud, Bot I couth sexty dissaif that suttillar wer haldin. **1565** JEWEL *Repl. Harding* (1611) 411 Wherein also appeareth some suspition of no simple dealing. **1614** RALEIGH *Hist. World* V. iii. 404 Bostar, the Gouernour of Saguntum, a simple man. **1669** *Relat. Raleigh's Troubles* in *Harl. Misc.* IV. 60 The Lord Cobham, a simple passionate man, but of very noble birth and great possessions. **1781** GIBBON *Decl. & F.* xxxi. (1787) III. 191 The edict which the fanaticism of Olympius dictated to the simple and devout emperor. **1781** CRABBE *Library* 243 Here wily Jesuits simple Quakers meet. **1822** SHELLEY *Fragm. Unf. Drama* 85 He was a simple innocent boy. I loved him well. **1842** LYTTON *Zanoni* 27 A simple heart may be its own best guide. **1859** TENNYSON *Guinevere* 367 The simple, fearful child meant nothing, but my own too-fearful guilt..betrays itself.

**2.** Free from, devoid of, pride, ostentation, or display; humble, unpretentious.

*c* **1290** *S. Eng. Leg.* I. 140 His oste nam wel gode ȝeme.. hov luytel he et him-selue, with wel simple mode. **13..** *E.E. Allit. P.* A. 1134 His lokez symple, hym self so gent. **1390** GOWER *Conf.* II. 41, I am so simple of port, That forto feigne som desport I pleie with hire litel hound. *a* **1400-50** *Alexander* 4664 All be we suggets in oure-selfe & simpill oure latis. *a* **1450** *Knt. de la Tour* lxiii. (1868) 84 She deigned not to do reuerence and worshippe unto the kinge..for because he was symple and debonaire. **1508** DUNBAR *Gold. Targe* 272 Be ewir obedient, Humble, subiect, and symple of entent. **1535** COVERDALE *Zech.* ix. 9 Lowly and symple is he, he rydeth vpon an asse. **1630** WADSWORTH *Pilgr.* iii. 30 A third sort of Iesuites there are, not vnfitly termed simple ones; these are wonderfull austere in their life. **1738** WESLEY *Ps.* XXXII. ii, Harmless, and pure, and undefil'd, A simple Follower of the Lamb. **1855** TENNYSON *Maud* I. x. v, A man with heart, head, hand, Like some of the simple great ones gone For ever and ever by.

**3. a.** Free from elaboration or artificiality; artless, unaffected; plain, unadorned.

Usually implying that the simplicity is a merit, but sometimes (as in quot. 1827) with suggestion of sense 7.

*c* **1330** R. BRUNNE *Chron. Wace* Prol. (Rolls) 73 Als þai haf wryten & sayd, haf I alle in myn Inglis layd, In symple speche as I couthe, þat is lightest in mannes mouthe. **1377** LANGL. *P. Pl.* B. XIII. 217 Sobrete, and symple speche, and sothfaste byleue. *c* **1450** in Aungier *Syon* (1840) 320 Ther songe schal be sadde, sober, ande symple withe out brekyng of notes. **1530** PALSGR. 324/1 Symple styll, *simple*. **1601** SHAKS. *Jul. C.* IV. ii. 22 There are no tricks, in plaine and simple Faith. **1696** PHILLIPS (ed. 5) s.v., Simple Style, an easie plain Stile. **1726** SWIFT *Gulliver* IV. xii, I rather chose to relate plain Matter of Fact, in the simplest Manner and Style. **1750** GRAY *Elegy* 32 The short and simple annals of the poor. **1752** HUME *Ess. & Treat.* (1777) I. 209 Sophocles and Terence..are more simple than Lucretius. **1827** SCOTT *Chron. Canongate* vii, It is, however, but a very simple tale, and may have no interest for persons beyond Janet's rank of life or understanding. **1860** WARTER *Sea-Board* II. 446 The simplest sermons, conveyed in the simplest language, usually do most good. **1881** FREEMAN *Subj. Venice* 249 The arcades themselves, though very good and simple, do not carry out the wonderful boldness..of the outer range.

**b.** Of persons: Free from over-refinement, unsophisticated, unspoiled.

**1794** MRS. RADCLIFFE *Myst. Udolpho* iii, The inhabitants of these mountains are a simple people. **1821** SHELLEY *Epipsych.* 429 Pastoral people.., Simple and spirited; innocent and bold.

**II. 4. a.** Of persons, or their origin: Poor or humble in condition; of low rank or position; undistinguished, mean, common.

*c* **1290** *S. Eng. Leg.* I. 49 Among lowe Men and simple deol þere was i-nouȝ. *a* **1300** *Cursor M.* 15007 Þe simple folk al o þe tun þai went him for to mete. *c* **1350** *Will. Palerne* 714 Þer nys lord in no lond..þat soþli nere simple i-nouȝ þat semly to haue. *c* **1400** *Destr. Troy* 2631 A! nobill kyng,..suffers me to say, Symple þof I be. **1441** *Pol. Poems* (Rolls) II. 206 Alas! what was myne adventure, So sodenly down for to falle,.. Now am I made sympulest of alle. **1474** CAXTON *Chesse* III. i. (1883) 78 Kynge Dauid that was first symple & one of the comyn peple. **1535** STEWART *Cron. Scot.* I. 423 All sic like.. That cuming ar of sic sempill degrie. **1570** FOXE *A. & M.* 1346/1 Thomas Cromwell,..borne of a simple parentage & house obscure. **1647** FULLER *Good Th. in Worse T.* (1841) 108 The silliest and simplest being wronged may justly speak in their own defence. **1667** MILTON *P.L.* XII. 365 His place of birth a solemn Angel tells To simple Shepherds. **1746** FRANCIS tr. *Horace, Sat.* II. vi. 112 How you joke, And love to sneer at simple Folk! **1794** BURNS *Gane is the day* ii, There's wealth and ease for gentlemen, And semple folk maun fecht and fen'. **1864** *Spectator* 537 It is sometimes objected to Mr. A. Fripp's peasant children that they are more gentle than simple.

**b.** In modest or apologetic use.

In some examples sense 9 may be intended.

*c* **1440** *York Myst.* xiv. 3, I praye þe, lord, for thy grete myght Vnto thy symple seruand see. **1481** CAXTON *Godfr.* ccxii. 311 Reduced out of Frensshe in to englysshe by me symple persone Wylliam Caxton. **1539** *Test. Ebor.* (Surtees) VI. 88 My simple bodie to be buried at Ratclif. *c* **1560** A. SCOTT *Poems* (S.T.S.) i. 223 Send be thy sempill servand Sanderris Scott. **1571** R. EDWARDS *Damon & Pithias* in Hazl. *Dodsley* IV. 94 When I am dead, my simple ghost.. Shall hover about the place.

†**c.** In phr. ***as simple as***, or ***simple though, I stand here***. *Obs.*

**1598** SHAKS. *Merry W.* I. i. 228 *Slender.* He's a Iustice of Peace in his Countrie, simple though I stand here. **1598** B. JONSON *Ev. Man in Hum.* I. i, I am his next heire at the common law, Master Stephen, as simple as I stand here. **1728** SWIFT *Mullinix & Timothy* Wks. 1751 VII. 213 And simple as I now stand here, Expect in Time to be a P——.

**5.** With designations or titles: Ordinary; not further distinguished in office or rank.

*a* **1300** *Cursor M.* 26226 Es na simple preist þat mai Sli scrift on man bot biscop lai. **1389** in *Eng. Gilds* (1870) 8 ȝif it so bifalle þat a symple brother dye. **1474** CAXTON *Chesse*

II. iv. (1883) 50 Alexander of Macedone cam on a tyme lyke a symple knyght vnto the court of Porus kynge of Inde. **1500–20** DUNBAR *Poems* xxii. 64 Ane semple vicar I can nocht be. **1593** SHAKS. *2 Hen. VI*, I. iii. 77 Salisbury and Warwick are no simple Peeres. **1657** *Narr. Late Parl.* in *Harl. Misc.* (1809) III. 456 One of the simple and new-made knights. **1855** MACAULAY *Hist. Eng.* xiv. III. 456 Perhaps no simple presbyter of the Church of England has ever possessed a greater authority over his brethren. **1875** STUBBS *Const. Hist.* II. xv. 201 This change affected however only the simple barons.

**6. a.** Of persons or their attire: Not marked by any elegance or grandeur; very plain or homely.

**1362** LANGL. *P. Pl.* A. IX. 110 He was long and lene, to loken on ful symple, Was no pride on his apparail, ne no pouert noþer. *c* **1400** *Rom. Rose* 6822, I, that were my simple cloth, Robbe bothe robbed and robbours. *c* **1450** *Merlin* xxvi. 478 The kynge..and his knyghtes..hadde don of theire helmes from theire heedes and valed theire coiffes of mayle vpon theire sholderes and com full symple. **1560** DAUS tr. *Sleidane's Comm.* 55 The body must be chastened and made leane with fasting and simple apparel. **1567** *Gude & Godlie B.* 49 3e sall him find, but mark or wying, Full sempill in ane Cribe lying. **1633** T. STAFFORD *Pac. Hib.* II. xviii. 191 Cloathed in a simple mantle, and torne trowsers.

**b.** Similarly of living, diet, abode, etc.

***the simple life***, a mode of life in which anything of the nature of luxury is intentionally avoided; also *attrib.* Hence ***simple-lifer***, a follower or proponent of the simple life. Also ***simple-liver***; ***simple-living*** vbl. sb. and ppl. adj.

**13..** *Cursor M.* 13272 (Gött.), Chese him felaus will he bigin,..mene men of simpil lijf. **13..** *Gaw. & Gr. Knt.* 503 Þe crabbed lentoun, þat fraystez flesch wyth þe fysche & fode more symple. *c* **1380** WYCLIF *Wks.* (1880) 149 What euere þing curatis holden of þe auterage ouer a sympule liflode,..it nys not here but oþere mennus. *c* **1400** LOVE *Bonavent. Mirr.* (1908) 64 Mekenesse, pouerte, and buxumnesse, that weren openly schewed in her symple dwellynge. **1474** CAXTON *Chesse* III. v. (1883) 120 But they ought to make good and symple colacion to geder. **1568** GRAFTON *Chron.* II. 88 Leopold..did take the king captiue at Dena in a village nere therevnto, in a simple house. **1579** LYLY *Euphues* (Arb.) 96 In that my welcome is so colde, and my cheere so simple. **1596** SPENSER *F.Q.* VI. ix. 16 His simple home; Which though it were a cottage clad with lome [etc.]. *c* **1610** *Women Saints* 80 Her bodie she allowed but such like short and simple foode, stanching hir hunger with herbes and barlie bredd. **1697** DRYDEN *Virg. Georg.* III. 790 Simple his Bev'rage, homely was his Food. **1736** J. THOMSON *Liberty* IV. 30 That simple Life, the quiet-whispering Grove. **1764** GOLDSM. *Trav.* 17 Blest be those feasts, with simple plenty crown'd. **1820** SHELLEY *Prometh. Unb.* III. iii. 22 There is a cave [etc.],..A simple dwelling, which shall be our own. **1862** A. J. SYMONDS *Let.* 7 Aug. (1967) I. 355, I read through..Scotch Bothie, lured on by its intense savour of nature & love of simple life. **1889** R. BUCHANAN *Heir of Linne* vii, The meal consisted of the very simplest fare, and was soon over. **1901** tr. *Wagner's The Simple Life* p. vii, What is the simple life?.. It is a form of life, described by the pastoral poets, or the New Testament, but not livable to-day [etc.]. **1909** H. G. WELLS *Ann Veronica* vii. 138 The Goopes were..following a fruitarian career..and they had reduced simple living to the finest of fine arts. *Ibid.* viii. 165 The chatter of the studios and the..discussions of the simple-life homes. **1927** W. E. COLLINSON *Contemp. Eng.* 38 During my school-days..I remember first hearing the term simple-lifers. **1933** M. ALLINGHAM *Sweet Danger* xvii. 211 If it weren't for the simple-livers on the heath..the affair would be almost plain sailing. **1956** 'J. WYNDHAM' *Seeds of Time* 231 It's mostly Janet's economies and simple-living that's built up the savings. **1978** *Listener* 14 Sept. 324/1 Members may be 'arty-crafty' and 'simple-lifers'—rather like the sort of people who nowadays promote *Vole* magazine. **1979** *Ibid.* 11 Jan. 63/3 In Cornwall..simple-living James and earth-mother Anna are variously threatened by authority, rural squalor and true terror.

†**c.** Ordinary, not festival. *Obs.*$^{-1}$

**1480** CAXTON *Myrr.* III. x. 155 In worshippyng our lord on hye dayes and simple.

**7. a.** Small, insignificant, slight; of little account or value; also, weak or feeble.

**1375** BARBOUR *Bruce* v. 258 That ves a sympill stuff to ta, A land or castell for to vyn! ?*a* **1400** *Morte Arth.* 967 Siche sex ware to symple to semble with hyme one. *c* **1450** *Merlin* vii. 116 Thei were so astoned with the hete of the fier that theire deffence was but symple. **1486** *Bk. St. Albans, Hawking* d iij b, The symplest of theis .iij. will slee an Hynde calfe. **1509** BARCLAY *Shyp of Folys* (1874) II. 80 They spoyle this pore man, so that sympyll is his porcion. **1597** DANIEL *Civ. Wars* VI. ii, Supposing some small powre would have restrained Disordred rage, sends with a simple crew Sir Humfrey Stafford. **1613** SHAKS. *Hen. VIII*, II. iv. 106 *Queen.* I am a simple woman, much too weake T'oppose your cunning. **1662** J. DAVIES tr. *Mandelslo's Trav.* 62 It lies almost in the midst of the Kingdome, and till of late was but a simple Village. **1839** SIR G. C. LEWIS *Gloss. Heref.*, *Simple*, sickly, feeble, helpless. **1875** TENNYSON *Holy Grail* 668 Their wise men..scoff'd at him, And this high Quest as at a simple thing.

†**b.** Of price or sale: Low, poor. *Obs.*

**1436** *Rolls of Parlt.* IV. 499/1 If it seme come to, that utterance and sale of the seid Wolle..be so escarse and symple as likly is to be. **1439** *Ibid.* V. 24/1 Of so sympyl prys that it may not goodly bere the costes of Staple. *c* **1480** *Pol. Poems* (Rolls) II. 284 The pryce ys sympylle, the cost ys never the lesse.

†**8.** Poor, wretched, pitiful, dismal. *Obs.*

**13..** *Sir Beues* 4050 Be þe sweuene ful wel I wat, þat Beues is in semple stat. *c* **1400** *Destr. Troy* 8247 His worshipful wife,..With his Suster beside,..þat were sory for þe sight, Semple of chere. *c* **1420** *Sir Amadace* (Camden) xxxviii, Quat mon is this, That alle this mowrnyng makes thus, With so simpulle chere? *c* **1477** CAXTON *Jason* 48 b, Jason..hering the fayr Myrro so ordeyne..of theyr sodayn departing began to make simple chere.

**9.** Deficient in knowledge or learning; characterized by a certain lack of acuteness or quick apprehension: **a.** Of persons (and animals).

**1340** *Ayenb.* 137 He is ase þet simple ssep ine huam al hit is guod and profitable..and ne wenþ and ne kan naȝt ne naȝt ne þengþ. *a* **1400** *Wycliffite Bible* Prol. (1850) I. 58 No doute to a symple man..men miȝten expoune..shortliere the bible in English [etc.]. *c* **1460** J. RUSSELL *Bk. Nurture* 1247 Symple as y had insight somwhat þe ryme y correcte. *a* **1548** HALL *Chron., Hen. V*, 29 b, Thynke you..that I am so ignorant..? Judge you me so simple, that I know not wherin the glory of a conquerour consisteth? **1596** SPENSER *State Irel.* Wks. (Globe) 609/1 A vayne conceit of simple men, which judge thinges by theyre effectes, and not by theyre causes. **1612** BRINSLEY *Lud. Lit.* xix. (1627) 220 If there be one simple in a fourme, or harder of learning then the rest, they will make him a right *Asinus.* **1640** WILKINS *New Planet* III. (1707) 169 It is a Book for the simpler and ignorant People. *a* **1718** W. PENN *Life* Wks. 1726 I. 38 Why should you render yourself unhappy, by associating with such a Simple People? **1768** WALPOLE *Hist. Doubts* 16, I say not this from any partiality or to decry the simple man as crossing my opinion. **1780** COWPER *Progr. Err.* 506 Women, ..With all the simple and unletter'd poor, Admire his learning. **1822** SCOTT *Peveril* v, Thou art as simple, I see, in this world's knowledge as ever. **1865** MOZLEY *Mirac.* i. 22 The religion too of the intelligent as well as of the simpler portion of society.

**b.** Of mental powers, etc.

**1340** HAMPOLE *Pr. Consc.* 4435 Men of symple connyng He sal turne thurgh miracles and prechyng. **1390** GOWER *Conf.* VIII. 3052* This povere bok heer I presente,..Write of my simple besinesse. *c* **1430** LYDG. *Min. Poems* (Percy Soc.) 108 Sympylle ys there consayet, when yt ys forthe broughte. *c* **1460** J. RUSSELL *Bk. Nurture* 277 Symple Condicyons of a persone þat is not taught, y wille ye eschew. **1523** LD. BERNERS *Froiss.* I. ciii. 123 They had sene parte of the demeanour of the frenchemen, the which they thoght to be but symple. **1591** SHAKS. *Two Gentl.* I. ii. 8 Ile shew my minde, According to my shallow simple skill. **1812** CRABBE *Tales* v. 257 Leave admonition,..Nor take that simple fancy to thy brain, That thou canst cure the wicked and the vain.

**c.** Of compositions, etc., esp. in apologetic use.

*c* **1430** LYDG. *Min. Poems* (Percy Soc.) 22 On my rudnesse ..to have pitee, My simple makyng for to take at gree. **1474** CAXTON *Chesse* IV. viii. (1883) 187 Praynge your good grace to resseyue this lityll and symple book. **1560** DAUS tr. *Sleidane's Comm.* Pref. 3 Humbly beseching your honour to accept this simple translation. **1590** SPENSER *F.Q.* II. x. 28 Whose simple answere, wanting colours faire To paint it forth, him to displeasance moou'd. **1595** T. P. GOODWIN *Blanchardine* (1890) 233 To larum foorth my simple musicke.

**10. a.** Lacking in ordinary sense or intelligence; more or less foolish, silly, or stupid; also, mentally deficient, half-witted (now *dial.*).

**1604** E. GRIMSTONE *Hist. Siege Ostend* 63 A Germaine.. was lame of halfe his body, and simple. **1653** J. TAYLOR *Serm. for Year* I. xxiii. 290 Unwary fools and defenselesse people were called simple. **1713** ARBUTHNOT *John Bull* II. ix, The good old Gentlewoman was not so simple, as to go into his project; she began to smell a Rat. **1778** MISS BURNEY *Evelina* lxxvi, I was extremely disconcerted..and I am sure I must look very simple. **1798** JANE AUSTEN *Northang. Abb.* (1833) II. xv. 201 You are fretting about General Tilney, and that is very simple of you! **1814** SCOTT *Ld. of Isles* v. xxi, Nay, weep not so, thou simple boy! But sleep in peace, and wake in joy. **1883** *Hampshire Gloss.* s.v., He be quite simple, poor chap.

**b.** ***Simple Simon.*** (*a*) (See quots. 1785, 1865.)

'Simple Simon' is the subject of various nursery rhymes, which may have given rise to the general use.

**1785** GROSE *Dict. Vulgar T.*, *Simple Simon*, a natural, a silly fellow. **1865** *Slang Dict.* 230 *Simon*, or *Simple Simon*, a credulous gullible person. **1899** *Westm. Gaz.* 12 June 5/1 A tall, ungainly Simple Simon of a peasant.

(*b*) *U.S. Rhyming slang.* A diamond.

**1928** M. C. SHARPE *Chicago May* 287/2 *Simple simon*, diamond. **1929** D. RUNYON in *Cosmopolitan* July 58/1, I do not see any Simple Simon on your lean and linger.

**c.** In bird-names, as ***simple tern*** (or ***viralve***), ***warbler***.

**1783** LATHAM *Gen. Synop. Birds* II. II. 500 Simple Warbler, *Motacilla campestris.* **1785** *Ibid.* III. II. 355 Simple Tern. Size of the Noddy. **1826** STEPHENS in Shaw *Gen. Zool.* XIII. I. 172 Simple Viralve (*Viralva simplex*)... Inhabits Cayenne.

**III. 11. a.** With nothing added; considered or taken by itself; mere, pure, bare; †single.

**1340** *Ayenb.* 134 Þet me ylefþ god oþe his simple worde þet al is zoþ þet he zayþ. **1483** CAXTON *Gold. Leg.* 201/2 Wicked spirites went out of the bodyes of creatures by his symple regarde and syghte. **1578** *Sc. Acts, James VI* (1814) III. 113 The haill Iniureis and attemptatis committit of befoir..suld be reparit to the sempill availl. **1590** SHAKS. *Com. Err.* v. i. 211 Nere may I looke on day,..But she tels to your Highnesse simple truth. **1600** E. BLOUNT tr. *Conestaggio* 74 It was not probable they shoulde yeelde vpon a simple Letter. **1601** SHAKS. *All's Well* II. i. 78 A medicine ..whose simple touch Is powerfull to arayse King Pippen. **1617** MORYSON *Itin.* III. 207 They who are hanged for simple theft. **1732** POPE *Ess. Man* I. 103 Yet simple Nature to his hope has giv'n..an humbler heav'n. **1797–1805** S. & HT. LEE *Cant. T.* I. 84 What need of invention? We have only to tell the simple truth. **1849** MACAULAY *Hist. Eng.* vi. II. 38 A simple majority, provided that it consisted of twelve, was sufficient to convict. **1857** MILLER *Elem. Chem.*, *Org.* iii. §4 (1862) 219 Many of the compounds..have an affinity for oxygen so powerful that they take fire by simple contact with it. **1870** MAX MÜLLER *Sci. Relig.* (1873) 321 What M. Jacolliot calls a simple translation..is, as far as I can judge, a simple invention of some slightly mischievous Brahman.

**b.** In phr. ***pure and simple.*** Cf. PURE *a.* 3.

**1875** JOWETT *Plato* (ed. 2) I. 29 That of which we are speaking is knowledge pure and simple. **1895** *Bookman* Oct. 16/2 The matter, both literary and pictorial,..has been garbage pure and simple.

**12. a.** *Med.* Of wounds, diseases, etc.: Unaccompanied by complications.

**1398** TREVISA *Barth. De P.R.* VII. lxix. (Bodl. MS.), Also semple euel schal be heeled with medicyns þat beþ semple. **1541** COPLAND *Guydon's Form.* S iv b, Al symple woundes.. ben new woundes in the partyes of ye flesshe, that onely requyreth consolydacyons. **1580** BLUNDEVIL *Horsemanship* IV. ii, For, as they [causes] be simple or compound, so doe they ingender simple or compound diseases. **1597** A. M. tr. *Guillemeau's Fr. Chirurg.* 45/4 As touchinge the simple fractures, in thre dayes once we dresse them. **1758** J. S. tr. *Le Dran's Observ. Surg.* (1771) 250 The Suppuration proceeding kindly, the Wound became a simple Wound. **1826** S. COOPER *First Lines Surg.* (ed. 5) 94 A wound is called *simple* when it occurs in a healthy subject; has been produced by a clean, sharp-edged instrument; is unattended with any serious symptoms; and the only indication is to re-unite the fresh-cut surfaces. **1877** BURNETT *Ear* 223 Simple Erythema is usually caused by local irritation from bites of insects.

**b.** *Law.* Unattended by any strengthening circumstance; not specially confirmed.

***simple contract***, one made by word of mouth or not under seal; also *attrib.*

**1546** *Reg. Privy Council Scot.* I. 37 Quhatsumevir clame, sempill supplicatioun, bill or summondis. **1765–8** ERSKINE *Inst. Law Scot.* IV. i. §24 Simple reductions, where improbation is not also libelled, are now seldom made use of. **1798** DALLAS *Amer. Law Rep.* I. 244 In the case of an intestacy, simple contract debts..must be paid out of the personal estate. **1818** CRUISE *Digest* (ed. 2) I. 468 The plaintiffs had no lien on the estates purchased by Lockyer; being creditors by simple contract only. *Ibid.* III. 41 A general resignation bond, simple and unattended with any other fact or circumstance.

**13.** Consisting or composed of one substance, ingredient, or element; uncompounded, unmixed (or nearly so): **a.** Of bodies or substances, esp. natural or organic.

**1398** TREVISA *Barth. De P.R.* x. iii. (Bodl. MS.), An element is semple and leste perticle of a bodie þat is compowned. **1471** RIPLEY *Comp. Alch.* v. viii. in Ashm. (1652) 150 The Compound corporall..Uprysyth agayne Regenerat, Sympill, and Spyrytuall. **1594** T. B. *La Primaud. Fr. Acad.* II. 29 The partes then of the body are diuided into two sortes or kindes: the first is, the simple or similary parts. **1626** BACON *Sylva* §16 Simple Bodies, which consist of severall similare Parts. **1632** LITHGOW *Trav.* VII. 319 The Sunne, beating continually vpon [the Nile water], ..maketh it become more Lighter, Purer, and Simple. **1704** NEWTON *Optics* (1721) 4 The Light whose Rays are all alike Refrangible, I call Simple, Homogeneal and Similar. **1724** WATTS *Logic* I. ii. (1736) 15 A Needle is a simple Body, being made only of Steel; but a Sword or a Knife is a Compound. **1796** KIRWAN *Elem. Min.* (ed. 2) I. 4 Simple earths are those which are incapable of being converted or analyzed.., either with each other, or into any other substance. **1811** A. T. THOMSON *Lond. Disp.* (1818) p. xlii, *Sulphur*... I have.. followed Dr. Thomson in regarding it as a simple solid. **1843** J. A. SMITH *Product. Farming* (ed. 2) 11 The number of simple, or elementary substances, at present known..is fifty-four. *a* **1862** BUCKLE *Civiliz.* III. 420 Simple solids retain after death the properties which they possessed during life.

**b.** Of medical or other preparations. ***simple colours*** (see quot. 1771).

**1398** TREVISA *Barth. De P.R.* VII. lxix. (Bodl. MS.), If he know what medicyne is semple, what compowned, what colde, what hote. *c* **1400** *Lanfranc's Cirurg.* 92 Medicyns boþe þe symple & þe compound. **1558** WARDE tr. *Alexis' Secr.* 32 b, Let the fyrste glyster be symple: that is to saye, made with water wherin ye haue boyled or sodden wheat bran, common oyle and salt. **1598** SHAKS. *Merry W.* III. v. 32 *Fal.* Go, brew me a pottle of Sacke finely. *Bard.* With Egges, Sir? *Fal.* Simple of it selfe. **1617** MORYSON *Itin.* III. 178 In the time of Queene Elizabeth the Courtiers delighted much in darke colours, both simple and mixt. **1669** W. SIMPSON *Hydrol. Chym.* 372 Volatile saline Spirit, either simple or aromatiz'd with Essences. **1738** tr. *Guazzo's Art of Conversation* 7 Not Esculapius himself, can, by the Means of Medicine, either Simple or Compound,..give you the least Help. **1771** *Encycl. Brit.* II. 223/2 Painters also distinguish colours into simple and mineral. Under simple colours they rank all those which are extracted from vegetables, and which will not bear the fire. **1825** E. HEWLETT *Cottage Comforts* xi. 145 A tablespoon full of simple peppermint water. **1859** *Habits of Gd. Society* i. 104 In Paris I learned to abjure *café au lait*, and to drink my tea simple. **1899** *Allbutt's Syst. Med.* VII. 550 A simple aperient, and a stomachic or febrifuge mixture.

**c.** In general use.

**1586** W. WEBBE *Eng. Poetrie* (Arb.) 69 A foote of two sillables, is eyther simple or mixt, that is, of like time or of diuers. *a* **1619** FOTHERBY *Atheom.* II. iv. §4 (1622) 231 This *mens*..was the first Beginning of all things, being it selfe most simple, and without any mixture. **1655–60** STANLEY *Hist. Philos.* (1687) 195/2 If desire and fear are not principal passions, it will doubtless follow, that none of the other affections are simple. *a* **1676** HALE *Prim. Orig. Man.* 11 Though he is but one, and one most simple uncompounded Being.

**14. a.** Not composite or complex in respect of parts or structure.

*a* **1425** tr. *Arderne's Treat. Fistula*, etc. 33 It was oonly symple by itself in þe flesshe, hauyng no passyng to þe tother hole. *c* **1450** *Myrr. our Lady* 107 To the souerayne Trynyte, one symple God, fader and sonne and holy gooste. *a* **1475** ASHBY *Dicta Philos.* 1142 Thre thinges be in a right simpul knot. **1530** PALSGR. 68 Dyvers substantyves be symple, that is to saye, be nat compounde with any other wordes. **1636** B. JONSON *Eng. Gram.* I. xviii, The change of vowels is, either of simple vowels, or of diphthongs. **1656** BLOUNT *Glossogr.*, *Un*, is an English Privative, which may be added at pleasure to simple words. **1731** *Phil. Trans.* XXXVII. 107 Then they fasten Potlarts to the several simple Chords, that draw up the Rings. **1779** *Mirror* No. 24, Take the simplest blossom that blows. **1824** L. MURRAY *Eng. Gram.* (ed. 5) I. 149 Those tenses are called simple tenses, which are formed of the principal, without an auxiliary verb. **1843** *Proc. Philol.*

*Soc.* I. 63 Thousands of compound words or characters which the Chinese ingeniously formed by the combinations of the simple roots. **1857** MILLER *Elem. Chem., Org.* iii. §4 (1862) 238 Both the simple and the double radicles are formed upon a similar molecular plan.

**b.** *spec.* in scientific use.

(*a*) *Bot.* (See quots.)

**1727** BAILEY (vol. II.), *Simple Leaf* (with Botanists) is that which is not divided to the middle in several Parts, each resembling a Leaf it self, as in a Dock. **1753** *Chambers' Cycl.* Suppl. s.v. *Leaf, Simple leaf* is otherwise defined, that of which the petiole carries only one. **1793** MARTYN *Lang. Bot.* s.v. *Simplex*, A Simple root... A Simple stem... A Simple fructification. **1796** WITHERING *Brit. Pl.* (ed. 3) I. 82 *Simple Cup*, one that consists of a single series of segments. *Ibid.*, *Simple Stem*, one that is undivided; or, only sending out small branches. **1855** MISS PRATT *Flower Pl.* I. 10 A flower-stalk bearing one flower only, is termed simple, as the Daisy. **1872** OLIVER *Elem. Bot.* I. vii. 73 Leaves..which are not divided into separate leaflets are termed simple. **1879** A. GRAY *Struct. Bot.* vii. (1880) 291 Simple fruits, those which result from the ripening of a single pistil. **1880** BESSEY *Botany* 433 The simple pistil is synonymous with carpel.

(*b*) (See quot. 1728.)

**1728** CHAMBERS *Cycl.* s.v. *Microscope*, The Simple [microscopes] are those which consist of a single Lens, or a single Spherule. **1867** J. HOGG *Microsc.* I. ii. 31 The simple microscope may consist of one..or of two or three lenses; but these latter are so arranged as to have the effect only of a single lens.

(*c*) (See quots.)

**1799** *Med. Jrnl.* I. 306 He distinguishes..between simple and compound muscles: in the former, the fibres lie only in one direction. **1826** KIRBY & SP. *Entomol.* IV. xlvi. 287 *Simple Ocellus*, when the ocellus consists only of iris and pupil. **1863** BATES *Nat. Amazons* I. 31 A twin ocellus, or simple eye, of quite different structure from the ordinary compound eyes. **1867** J. HOGG *Microsc.* II. i. 324 Simple hairs are merely single epidermal cells produced in a tubular filament. **1875** HUXLEY in *Encycl. Brit.* I. 130/1 Simple organisms,..that is, in which the primitive actinozoon attains its adult condition without budding or fission.

(*d*) † ***simple tone*** = ***pure tone*** s.v. PURE *a.* 1 e. *Obs.*

**1875** A. J. ELLIS tr. *H. L. F. von Helmholtz's Sensations of Tone* vii. 235 Whenever the vibrations of the air or of other elastic bodies which are set in motion at the same time by two generating simple tones, are so powerful that they can no longer be considered infinitely small, mathematical theory shows that vibrations of the air must arise which have the same vibrational numbers as the combination tones. **1878** *Proc. R. Soc. Edin.* IX. 602 According to a usage which has been adopted from the German of Helmholtz by the best English scientific writers on sound, a sound is called a 'simple tone', or without qualification a 'tone', when the variation of pressure of the air..is according to a simple harmonic function of the time. **1910** H. LAMB *Dynamical Theory of Sound* 3 The sensation corresponding to a simple-harmonic vibration is called a 'simple tone',..or merely a 'tone'.

**c.** *Eccl.* (See quots.)

**1850** *Vesper Book* Pref. p. xii, The Office as regards Vespers is said to be..Simple, when the Antiphons being sung as on Semi-doubles, the Psalms of the Feria are substituted for the Psalms proper to Feasts. **1874** *Breviary Offices* Pref. p. x, On Simple Feasts the Antiphons and Psalms at First Vespers are of the feria, and the Proper Office begins at the Chapter. **1883** *Catholic Dict.* (1897) 375 On lesser feasts the office was simple—*i.e.* the feast was merely commemorated. *Ibid.* 376 The office for simple feasts differed little from that of the feria.

**d.** *Math.* (*a*) Applied to a group that has no proper normal subgroup; and hence to an algebra or ring that has no proper ideal.

**1888** G. G. MORRICE tr. *Klein's Lectures on Ikosahedron* I. i. 7 If a group contains, apart from these improper cases, no self-conjugate sub-groups, it is called simple, otherwise it is called composite. **1900** *Ann. Math.* I. 151 We have here.. an example of two simple abstract groups of the same order which are not identical. **1939** H. WEYL *Classical Groups* iii. 85 A simple algebra..is one capable of a faithful irreducible representation. **1965** PATTERSON & RUTHERFORD *Elem. Abstract Algebra* iii. 100 The above theorem shows that a field is simple. There exist simple rings which are not fields. **1971** E. C. DADE in Powell & Higman *Finite Simple Groups* viii. 255 An algebra $A$ is simple if $A \neq \{0\}$ and if $A$ and $\{0\}$ are the only two-sided ideals of $A$. **1980** *Sci. Amer.* May 68/1 The building blocks of group theory, analogous to the elementary particles of matter or the prime factors of integers, are called simple groups.

(*b*) Used variously (see quots.). (See also sense 15 b (*b*).)

**1889** *Proc. London Math. Soc.* XX. 70 It may happen that $G_p$ consists of powers of one of its elements $a$, and has no other elements... In this case $G_p$ is called a simple group. **1965** PATTERSON & RUTHERFORD *Elem. Abstract Algebra* iv. 135 Let $p \in P(F)$ be an irreducible polynomial. Then the field $P_p(F)$ contains a sub-field isomorphic with $F$... We call the field $P_p(F)$ a simple algebraic extension of the field $F$. **1972** R. J. WILSON *Introd. Graph Theory* ii. 9 There can never be more than one edge joining a given pair of vertices of a simple graph. **1975** *Sci. Amer.* May 102/2 A simple polyhedron is one that is topologically equivalent to a sphere and whose faces are all simple polygons: polygons topologically equivalent to a disk.

**e.** ***simple structure*** (*Statistics*): a model in which numerous variables, showing various degrees of correlation, have their variances assigned to a smaller number of factors in such a way that no factor affects all of the variables.

**1935** L. L. THURSTONE *Vectors of Mind* p. viii, One of the principal problems of factor analysis is to find a unique set of co-ordinate axes, either orthogonal or oblique, which shall represent scientifically meaningful categories in terms of which the tests may be comprehended. This problem has been solved in terms of what I have called 'simple structure' of a trait configuration. *Ibid.* vi. 154 If a set of r hyperplanes of dimensionality (r − 1) exists such that each trait vector is in one or more of the hyperplanes, then the combined configuration of the trait vectors and the reference vectors will be called a simple structure or an oblique simple structure. **1972** [see ROTATION 1 d]. **1972** *Jrnl. Social Psychol.* LXXXVI. 188 There is no good scientific reason to expect agreement from analyses on..orthogonal pseudo-simple structure and oblique maximized simple structure.

**15. a.** Not complicated or involved; presenting little or no complexity or difficulty.

*c* **1555** HARPSFIELD *Divorce Hen. VIII* (Camden) 30 The knowledge of all Christendom should be so simple and grosse. **1601** SHAKS. *Twel. N.* I. v. 55 If that this simple Sillogisme will serue, so: if it will not, what remedy? **1668** CULPEPPER & COLE tr. *Barthol. Anat.* II. vi. 106 The motion of the Elements is simple, never circular. **1670** BAXTER *Cure Ch. Div.* I. ii. Pref., The simple terms of Christian Unity left us by Christ and his Apostles. **1704** NORRIS *Ideal World* II. xii. 446 God never does that by difficult ways, which may be done by ways that are simple and easie. **1797–1805** S. & HT. LEE *Canterb. T.* II. 177 A most simple train of circumstances had produced this romantic meeting. **1833** HERSCHEL *Astron.* viii. 248 All that apparent irregularity.. resolves itself into one simple and general law. **1860** TYNDALL *Glac.* II. x. 277 A simple calculation determined the daily motion of the stake. **1884** tr. *Lotze's Logic* 356 We must prefer the simpler hypothesis to the more complicated.

**b.** In various technical uses, as in *Mus.*, *Math.*, *Logic*, etc.

In some of these there is connexion with sense 14.

(*a*) *Mus.*

*c* **1475** HENRYSON *Orpheus & Eurydice* 117 First dyatesseron,..And dyapason, symple and duplycate. **1728** CHAMBERS *Cycl.* s.v. *Concord*, A simple, or original Concord. *Ibid.* s.v. *Counter-point*, Simple Counter-point, or the Harmony of Concords. **1801** BUSBY *Dict. Mus.* s.v., *Simple fugue*, or *Simple imitation*, is that style of composition in which a single subject is adopted, or some partial echo preserved among the several parts. **1867** MACFARREN *Harmony* ii. 34 In this form of note against note it is called Plain or simple Counterpoint. **1871** STAINER *Harmony* iii. §41 Intervals not exceeding the compass of an octave are termed Simple. **1873** H. C. BANISTER *Music* 10 When the beats are of the value of an aliquot part of a Semibreve..the time is termed Simple.

(*b*) *Math.*

**1594** BLUNDEVIL *Exerc.* I. xxix. (1636) 78 The Fractions wherewith you have to deale, are either simple or compound. **1704** J. HARRIS *Lex. Techn.* I, *Simple Quantities* in Algebra, are such as have but one Sign, whether Positive or Negative. **1798** HUTTON *Course Math.* I. 221 A Simple Equation, is that which contains only one power of the unknown quantity, without including different powers. *Ibid.* 110 Simple Interest is that which is allowed for the principal lent or forborn only, for the whole time of forbearance. **1859** B. SMITH *Arith. & Alg.* (ed. 6) 194 A quantity consisting of one term, as a, bx, 3abx, is called a Simple quantity, and also a Monomial. **1894** CAYLEY *Math. Papers* (1897) XIII. 533 A group,...when it cannot be thus expressed as a permutable product of two factors,..is prime or simple.

(*c*) *Logic.*

**1620** T. GRANGER *Div. Logike* 12 Artificiall Argument is either..simple, or comparate. The simple is considered simply, and absolutely without comparison. **1689** LOCKE *Hum. Und.* II. ii. §2 The simple ideas, the materials of all our knowledge, are suggested..only by..sensation and reflection. **1697** tr. *Burgersdicius' Logic* I. i. 2 Themes simple are those which are understood without a composition or complexion of notions. *Ibid.* xxvii. 109 Simple enunciation is that which cannot be resolved into more. **1704** NORRIS *Ideal World* II. iii. 139 That apprehension or perception, which is rightly said to be *simple*, because it rests in the pure view of things as they are. **1724** WATTS *Logic* 36 That idea, which represents one particular determinate thing to me, is called a singular idea, whether it be simple, or complex, or compound. **1846** MILL *Logic* I. iv. §3. 108 A simple proposition is that in which one predicate is affirmed or denied of one subject. **1864** BOWEN *Logic* v. 127 In respect to the Relation of the Predicate to the Subject, Judgments are divided into simple or absolute, and conditional.

(*d*) (see quot.)

**1730** BAILEY (fol.) s.v. *Benefices, Simple Benefices*, are such where the Parsons are only obliged to read prayers, &c.

(*e*) Applied to those vows which are taken by members of a religious order in the early stage of their profession and from which they may be dispensed; opp. to *solemn* (SOLEMN *a.* 5 a).

**1759** A. BUTLER *Lives Saints* IV. 86/2 In some houses these Gray Sisters make solemn vows, but in most they content themselves with simple vows of poverty, obedience, and chastity. **1823** C. BUTLER *Continuation A. Butler's Lives Saints* 191 He entered into the society of Jesus, and made his simple vows. **1884** ADDIS & ARNOLD *Cath. Dict.* 848/1 Whereas a simple vow makes marriage unlawful and deprives the person who has made it of the right to use his property, a solemn vow makes marriage invalid and takes away all dominion over property. **1957** *Oxf. Dict. Christian Ch.* 1451/1 Since *c.* the 13th cent. canon law has also distinguished between 'simple' and 'solemn' vows. The exact scope of the distinction is disputed, but acc. to a common view the solemnity of vows is determined by their irrevocable acceptance.

(*f*) *Anthropol.*

**1929** *N. & Q. Anthropol.* (ed. 5) 63 We might expect the simple patrilineal family to resemble our own, but this is not necessarily so. **1951** *Ibid.* (ed. 6) 70 The elementary or simple family is a group consisting of a father and a mother and their children, whether they are living together or not. **1977** P. LASLETT *Family Life* i. 13 The shape and membership of the familial group. In the West this has been confined for the most part to the parents and children themselves, what is called the nuclear family form or simple family household.

**c.** In adj. phrs., as ***simple-to-follow***, ***simple-to-operate***, etc.

**1960** *Times* 18 Jan. 15/7 A simple-to-fit filter removes dust. **1960** *Farmer & Stockbreeder* 15 Mar. (Suppl.) 13 A robust motor with a completely reliable and simple-to-operate starting unit. **1971** *Woman's Own* 27 Mar. 52/1 We have combined simple-to-build shelves with..sliding transparent drawers. **1976** *BSI News* May 11/2 The BS 4264 range is set out in a simple-to-follow table giving 26 sizes.

**IV.** †**16.** In advb. phr. ***in simple***, simply; by itself; without any other fact or circumstance. *Obs.*

**1548** GESTE *Pr. Masse* 96 Thee wordes also of thee masse canon, y[t] importe ye same ought so in simple to be taken without any far fetched glosse. *Ibid.* 102 It standeth wythe catholique doctryne y[t] in symple the..naked utterance of the consecration wordes enforce not the sacrament. *a* **1633** AUSTIN *Medit.* (1635) 103 Hee delights to have Man in simple; (alone, by himselfe) unmixt.

**17.** quasi-*adv.* Simply.

**1598** GRENEWEY *Tacitus, Germania* I. (1622) 259 Those which dwell further in the land, go more simple to worke, and..haue no buying and selling, but by exchange of commodities. **1816** BYRON *Ch. Har.* III. xvii, The moral's truth tells simpler so. **1844** LADY FULLERTON *Ellen Middleton* (1854) II. x. 30 She was dressed perfectly simple in a brown silk gown.

**18.** *Comb.* Chiefly in parasynthetic adjs., as ***simple-answered***, ***-headed***, ***-lettered***, ***-mannered***, etc.; also ***simple-seeming***.

*c* **1425** *Saints' Lives* Apol. in *Anglia* VIII. 107/7 Þe wryter, þat is but symple-letterd, neiþer can ne purposis to folowe þe wordes. **14..** in *Tundale's Vis.* (1843) 115 Ye schuld have pete To se a lady of soo hee degre So symple tyred. **1600** BRETON *Pasquil's Fooles Cap* lxi, A poore silly simple witted Asse. **1605** SHAKS. *Lear* III. vii. 43 Be simple answer'd, for we know the truth. *a* **1618** SYLVESTER *Panaretus* 332 Wks. (Grosart) II. 127 Royall Eumenia..And simple-manner'd Pistia. **1818** COLERIDGE *Friend* (1865) 177 Mere incendiary declamation for the simple-headed multitude! **1849** MURCHISON *Siluria* viii. 147 The same species of simple-plaited Orthidæ. **1859** TENNYSON *Guinevere* 307 Our simple-seeming Abbess and her nuns. **1875** 'MARK TWAIN' in *Atlantic Monthly* Aug. 195/1 Good-hearted, simple-natured young Yates. **1880** *Cassell's Nat. Hist.* III. 145 The long series of simple-toothed Rodents. **1930** E. BLUNDEN *De Bello Germanico* 16 The simple-sounding matter of pushing a truck along a French tramway is rather complex on a dark..night.

**B.** *absol.* or as *sb.*

**1. a.** As *pl.* Persons in a humble or ordinary condition of life.

*c* **1350** *Will. Palerne* 338 Be..euer of faire speche, & seruisabul to þe simple so as to þe riche. **1500–20** DUNBAR *Poems* xxii. 32 Gentill and semple of euery clan. **1535** COVERDALE *Job* xxiv. 14 Tymely in the mornynge do they aryse, to murthur the symple and poore. *c* **1560** A. SCOTT *Poems* (S.T.S.) vi. 2 Luve preysis but comparesone Both gentill, sempill, generall. **1816** SCOTT *Antiq.* xxxii, Gentle or semple shall not darken my doors the day my bairn's been carried out a corpse. **1848** KINGSLEY *Saint's Trag.* II. viii, To hear no cause, of gentle or of simple.

**b.** As *sing.* A person of this class. †Also, one of modest unassuming manners.

*a* **1400** *Relig. Pieces fr. Thornton MS.* 55 Ouer grete symplesse may make of þe symple a sott. *c* **1440** *York Myst.* xxx. 288 She beseches you as hir souerayne þat symple to saue. **1824** SCOTT *Redgauntlet* let. xi, A shilling makes a' the difference that Maggie kens between a gentle and a semple. **1882** *Mrs. Raven's Tempt.* III. 8 The simples are not bound to pick up what the gentles throw away.

**2. a.** As *pl.* Those who are unlearned, ignorant, easily misled, unsuspecting, etc.

**1560** DAUS tr. *Sleidane's Comm.* 23 The Heresyes of Wiclife and Husse.., whiche by the false enterpretation of Scripture giueth to the simple an occasion to sinne. **1579** W. WILKINSON *Confut. Fam. Love* Ep. Ded., Whisperyng peruerse thynges to seduce and beguile the simple. **1611** BIBLE *Ps.* cxix. 130 The entrance of thy wordes..giueth vnderstanding vnto the simple. **1754** SHERLOCK *Disc.* (1759) I. iii. 97 His Doctrine was framed to give Wisdom to the Simple. **1807** CRABBE *Par. Reg.* I. 182 Seeking their fate, to her the simple run. **1853** CDL. WISEMAN *Ess.* II. 338 A snare to the simple of heart.

**b.** As *sing.* An ignorant or foolish person.

**1643** TRAPP *Comm. Gen.* xxxix. 12 The harlot caught the silly simple, and kissed him. **1654** WHITLOCK *Zootomia* 440 With such like Judges..Simples passe for Physitians, and modest Physitians for Simples. **1894** H. D. LLOYD *Wealth agst. Commw.* 319 This action the paper described as 'a scheme for gulling simples'.

**3. a.** *pl.* Foolish or silly behaviour or conduct; foolishness, folly. *Obs.* exc. *dial.*

**1648** GAGE *West Ind.* 114 A little troubled with the simples, but a good hearted man. **1690** W. WALKER *Idiomat. Anglo-Lat.* 415 'To be sick of the simples,' to Act the fool. **1706** E. WARD *Wooden World Diss.* (1708) 44 His bare Shadow has cur'd many a poor Creature of the Simples. **1785** GROSE *Dict. Vulgar T.*, *Simples*,..also follies. **1894** NORTHALL *Folk Phr.* (E.D.S.) 26 To be sick of the simples, i.e. silly.

**b.** ***to be cut for*** (†***of***) ***the simples*** (see quots. *a* 1700, 1828). Orig. *cant* or *slang*, and now *dial.*

*a* **1700** B. E. *Dict. Cant. Crew* s.v., *He must be cut of the Simples*, Care must be taken to cure him of his Folly. **1731–8** SWIFT *Polite Conv.* i. 17 You should be cut for the Simples this morning. **1828** CARR *Craven Gloss.* s.v., 'Want's cutting for 't simples,' is a ludicrous expression applied to one who has been guilty of some foolish act. **1834** SOUTHEY *Doctor* cxxxvi, What evils might be averted..by clearing away bile, evacuating ill humours, and occasionally by cutting for the simples. **1880** MRS. PARR *Adam & Eve* vi. 28 'Tis time her was cut for the simples.

†**4.** A single thing. *Obs.*[−1]

**1483** CAXTON *Gold. Leg.* 379/1 God rewardeth for one Symple an hondred folde.

**5.** A simple word; a verb in its simple form or without prefix. (Cf. COMPOUND *sb.*[1] 2 c.)

**1530** PALSGR. Introd. p. xxxi, In maner ever of one syllable, except he be a compounde, and than his symple is but of one syllable. **1530** *Ibid.* 395 *Je prens* is a symple whiche hath for his compoundes *je reprens* [etc.]. **1659** [O. WALKER] *Instruct. Oratory* 25 Monosyllables..making the language dull and slow. Hence compounds more elegantly used, than their simples. **1848** VEITCH *Irreg. Grk. Verbs* Pref., The frequent absence of *simples* in whole or in part.

**6.** A medicine or medicament composed or concocted of only one constituent, *esp.* of one herb or plant (*obs.*); hence, a plant or herb employed for medical purposes. Now *arch.*

In common use from *c* 1580 to 1750, chiefly in *pl.*

*pl.* **1539** ELYOT *Cast. Helthe* (1541) 43 Where a sycknesse may be cured with symples, that is to saye, with one onely thinge that is medicinable. **1563** T. GALE *Antidot.* Pref. 2 There are an infinite number of simples which want Englyshe names. **1588** GREENE *Perimedes* Wks. (Grosart) VII. 15 Their stomacks bee made a verie Apotecaries shoppe, by receiuing a multitude of simples and drugges. **1603** DRAYTON *Bar. Wars* III. viii, The mixed Juices, from those Simples wrung, To make the Med'cine wonderfully strong. **1646** SIR T. BROWNE *Pseud. Ep.* I. vi, From the knowledge of Simples she had a Receipt to make white hair black. **1698** M. LISTER *Journ. Paris* (1699) 183 Houses well stored with tender Exoticks, and the Parterrs with Simples. **1725** POPE *Odyss.* IV. 318 Where prolific Nile With various simples cloaths the fat'ned soil. **1785** MARTYN *Rousseau's Bot.* Introd. (1794) 2 It was simples, not vegetables that they looked after. **1843** R. J. GRAVES *Syst. Med.* xxix. 368 An Irish Father, or Priest, whose knowledge is all comprehended in the virtues of two or three simples. **1889** JESSOPP *Coming of Friars* ii. 93 Cordials..were kept by the lady of the house among her simples.

*sing.* **1587** GREENE *Penelope's Web* Wks. (Grosart) V. 155 The Phisition..knoweth the nature of the Simple as well as the Gardiner that planteth it. **1598** J. DICKENSON *Greene in Conc.* (1878) 108 There is for euery sore prouided a salue, yet no simple for hartes sorrow. **1637** EARL MONM. tr. *Malvezzi's Romulus & Tarquin* 225 Men walking in the fields,..cast their eyes suddenly upon such a flower or simple. *a* **1654** SELDEN *Table-T.* (Arb.) 39 Suppose a Planet were a Simple, or an Herb. **1807** CRABBE *Par. Reg.* II. 95 From many a fragrant simple, Catharine's skill Drew oil and essence from the boiling still.

*attrib.* **1598** SHAKS. *Merry W.* III. iii. 79 These lisping-hauthorne buds, that..smell like Bucklers-berry in simple time. **1726** *Adv. Capt. R. Boyle* (1768) 50, I am only distilling some simple Waters for your Closet.

**7. a.** A single uncompounded or unmixed thing; a substance free from foreign elements, *esp.* one serving as an ingredient in a composition or mixture.

**1560** WHITEHORNE *Ord. Souldiours* (1588) 27 b, Gunpouder, is made of three simples only, that is salt peter, brimstone and coles. **1593** *Bacchus Bountie* in *Harl. Misc.* (1809) II. 273 A dainty deuised compound, of sundry simples pastiewise, as the trimming of tripes [etc.]. **1621** BURTON *Anat. Mel.* 141 To these noxious simples we may reduce an infinite number of compound, artificial, made dishes. **1648** GAGE *West Ind.* 106 Cacao..as every simple..contains the quality of the four elements. **1655** MOUFET & BENNET *Health's Improv.* (1746) 90 Their chiefest Perfume ..was made of sixteen Simples; namely, Wine, Honey [etc.].

*transf.* **1612** BRINSLEY *Lud. Lit.* p. xvi, Letters (which are the simples of this Art). **1622** MALYNES *Anc. Law-Merchant* 251 The three Simples or Essentiall parts of Trafficke, namely Commodities, Money, and Exchange of Moneys. *c* **1750** FIELDING *On Conversation* Wks. 1784 IX. 380 But besides pride, folly, arrogance, and insolence, there is another simple which vice never willingly leaves out of any composition.

**b.** A simple proposition, quantity, idea, etc.

**1654** Z. COKE *Logick* 119 As much as may be, this proposition is to be reduced to a meer simple. **1690** C. NESS *Hist. O. & N.T.* I. 29 Adam wisely understood all simples, singulars and universals. **1798** HUTTON *Course Math.* (1799) I. 114 Alligation teaches how to compound or mix together several simples of different qualities. **1879** BAIN *Educ. as Sci.* iii. 57 To strengthen an energy we must know what it is: if it is a simple, we must define it in its simplicity; if..a compound, we must assign its elements.

**c.** A simple need or requirement; a necessity.

**1859** CAPERN *Ball. & Songs* 123 My wishes and wants down to simples will sink.

**8.** *Weaving.* **a.** One of a number of lines or cords attached to the warp in a draw-loom (cf. quots.).

**1731** *Phil. Trans.* XXXVII. 107 From each of these Packthreads, just by the side of the Loom, are fastned other Packthreads called Simples, which descend to the Ground. **1825** J. NICHOLSON *Operat. Mechanic* 415 Below the warp these lines, which are called the simples, are kept in a state of tension by weights,..and in order to keep them distinctly apart, are made to pass through a board perforated with holes. **1890** *Scot. N. & Q.* III. 158 M. Simblot..connected to the neck a separate series of cords called the 'simple'..so that the draw boy could work when standing at the side of the loom.

**b.** 'A draw-loom employed in fancy weaving' (Knight *Dict. Mech.* 1875).

† **'simple,** *v.*[1] *Obs. rare.* [f. SIMPLE *a.*]

**1.** *trans.* To render (one) simple; to humble in respect of knowledge.

*c* **1425** *St. Mary of Oignies* II. iv. in *Anglia* VIII. 163/7, I, herynge þis,..and countynge my resoune noon, was sympled in myne owne sighte.

**2.** *intr.* With *at*: ? To make light of.

*a* **1652** BROME *Queen & Concubine* I. ii, That did your Champion, Madam, The Queens old Soldier, and your Father, Lady: D'ye simple at it? such a Souldier breaths not.

**simple** ('sɪmp(ə)l), *v.*[2] Now *arch.* [f. SIMPLE B. 6.] *intr.* To seek for, or gather, simples or medicinal herbs. Chiefly in phr. *to go (a) simpling* (cf. SIMPLING *vbl. sb.*). Also *fig.*

(*a*) **1643** SIR T. BROWNE *Relig. Med.* II. §8. 160 When I did but know an hundred [plants], and had scarcely ever Simpled further than Cheap-side. **1664** BUTLER *Hud.* II. iii. 823 Witches Simpling, and on Gibbets Cutting from Malefactors snippets. **1706–7** FARQUHAR *Beaux' Strat.* Prol., Simpling our author goes from field to field, And culls such fools as may diversion yield. **1718** OZELL tr. *Tournefort's Voy.* I. 172 We simpled in the Marshes. **1791** *Pop. Tales Germans* II. 88 Never did the poor physician venture to simple on the mountain again.

(*b*) **1648** ASHMOLE *Diary* (1774) 307 This day..was the first time I went a simpling. **1658** ROWLAND tr. *Moufet's Theat. Ins.* 924 As by chance I carelesly wandered here and there a simpling. **1725** DE FOE *Voy. round World* (1840) 182 Our doctors never went a simpling. **1772** GOLDSM. *Prol. to 'Zobeide'*, While botanists..Forsake the fair, and patiently —go simpling. **1791** *Pop. Tales Germans* II. 85 A doctor.. who used to go a simpling on the mountain. **1851** *Monthly Jrnl. Med. Sci.* XII. 344 In former days the Scottish herbalists used to go a-simpling after Roman medical plants.

† **simplehead.** *Obs.*[−1] [f. SIMPLE *a.* + -HEAD. Cf. MDu. and G. *simpelheit* (Du. *-heid*).] Simpleness, ignorance.

*c* **1470** HARDING *Chron.* CCXXVI. iv. 5 Of his symplehead He coulde litle within his brest conceyue.

**simple-hearted,** *a.* [f. SIMPLE *a.* + HEART *sb.*] Possessed of, or characterized by, a simple heart or spirit; ingenuous, sincere, unsophisticated; †ignorant, simple-minded (*obs.*). Also *absol.*

*c* **1400** *Pilgr. Sowle* (Caxton, 1483) IV. xxx. 80 Oftyme copre is coloured wondre lyke to gold by crafte done therto, soo that symple herted folke wene that it be fyn gold. *c* **1412** HOCCLEVE *De Reg. Princ.* 1889 Assay! þou simple-hertid goost! What grace is shapen þe, þou naght ne woost. **1711** SHAFTESB. *Charac.* (1737) II. 387 How he, with dire hypocrisy and false tears, beguiles the simple-hearted. **1775** *Hist. Voy. C. Evans & S. Cheevers Malta* 149 A brief discovery of God's Eternal Truth and a way opened to the simple hearted. **1814** SCOTT *Wav.* lx, The distress of his situation, among this honest and simple-hearted race, being considered as no reason for increasing their demand. **1848** THACKERAY *Van. Fair* lxvi, He made the most astounding revelations to the simple-hearted Major. **1897** WATTS-DUNTON *Aylwin* III. vii, It was a comfort to me to..hear the simple-hearted Cymric folk talking.

Hence **simple-'heartedness.**

**1837** LOCKHART *Scott* II. x. 343 Where..the old Statesman entered with such simple-heartedness into all the ways of the happy circle. **1877** RUSKIN *St. Mark's Rest* x. §204 Exquisite in its purity, simple-heartedness, and joyful wonder.

**simple-minded,** *a.* [f. SIMPLE *a.* + MIND *sb.*]

**a.** Having a simple mind; possessing little or no subtlety of intellect; also, feeble- or weak-minded.

**1744** AKENSIDE *Pleas. Imag.* III. 112 How sublime they move, And bending oft their sanctimonious eyes, Take homage of the simple-minded throng. **1768** BLACKSTONE *Comm.* III. 145 The weak and simpleminded part of mankind (which is by far the most numerous division). **1848** THACKERAY *Van. Fair* xxxiii, My Lord Southdown,..an epileptic and simple-minded nobleman. **1878** J. P. HOPPS *Jesus* iv. 16 These were mostly simple-minded, honest, and earnest men.

**b.** Belonging to, proceeding from, a simple mind.

**1866** *N. & Q.* 3rd Ser. IX. 458/1 Characteristic..of the.. simple-minded tenderness, and the silly superstition of the period. **1876** MOZLEY *Univ. Serm.* iv. 101 Action upon a theatre may doubtless be as simple-minded action as any other.

Hence **simple-'mindedness**; also **simple-'mindedly** *adv.*

**1847** WEBSTER, *Simple-mindedness*, artlessness. **1881** BRIGHT in *Standard* 17 Nov. 3/3 These men..call in question the Free-trade policy, and they have the courage or the simple-mindedness to believe [etc.]. **1934** A. HUXLEY *Beyond Mexique Bay* 255 An Indian who has given up his *Fiestas* would not be the simple-mindedly happy peasant beloved of Mr. Chase. **1981** *Christian Order* XXII. 264 Abandoned simple-mindedly and irresponsibly.

**simpleness** ('sɪmp(ə)lnɪs). [f. SIMPLE *a.* + -NESS. Cf. Fris. *simpelens.*]

The indefinite character of the early uses of the adj. *simple* is naturally reflected in this noun, making it often difficult to assign the examples to a specific sense.

**1.** Absence of pride, ostentation, or pretentiousness; plain or unassuming disposition or manners.

**13..** *E.E. Allit. P.* A. 909 Now hynde þat sympelnesse conez enclose, I wolde þe aske a þynge expresse. *c* **1380** WYCLIF *Sel. Wks.* (1880) 383 He þat is gratter of ȝow, loke þat he be made as ȝongar in sympilnes. *c* **1400** LOVE *Bonavent. Mirr.* (1908) 59 The mayster of mekenes and louer of sympilnesse. *c* **1450** *Mirk's Festial* 12 All his lyfe-dayes, he huld þat name of a chyld, and..mekenes, and sympulnes, and wythout maleys. **1509** BARCLAY *Shyp of Folys* (1570) 158 So muche were they geuen to simplenes And other vertues chiefe and principall. **1590** SHAKS. *Mids. N.* v. i. 83 Neuer any thing Can be amisse, when simplenesse and duty tender it. **1609** DANIEL *Civil Wars* VI. xxxv, Inlarge this vninquisitiue Beliefe: Call vp mens spirits, that simplenes retaine. **1866** JEAN INGELOW *Poems* 194 In his reverend face There was a simpleness we could not sound. **1869** MRS. WHITNEY *Hitherto* ix, So rich and beautiful that it made me afraid; but for Allard's kindness and Mrs. Cope's simpleness.

**2.** Absence of duplicity or guile; innocence, integrity, guilelessness.

**1382** WYCLIF *Gen.* xx. 5 In symplenes of myn herte, and clennes of myn hondis I dide this. —— *1 Macc.* ii. 37 Dye we alle in oure symplenesse. *c* **1400** MAUNDEV. (Roxb.) xviii. 85 Þe folk..wirschepez þe ox, in steed of Godd, for þe sympilnes and þe gudeness þat commez of him. **1401** *Pol. Poems* (Rolls) II. 71 To shewe the colour that signefieth symplenesse, and withinne..ȝe ben ravenous wolves. **1526** *Pilgr. Perf.* (W. de W. 1531) 83 b, The nexte vertue in order is simplicite or simplenes, the contrary to doublenes. **1572** BOSSEWELL *Armorie* II. 71 This byrde is the messenger of peace, ensample of simplenesse. **1616** W. BROWNE *Brit. Past.* II. iii, You ever did possesse No wisedome, but was mixt with simplenesse; So wanting malice. *a* **1850** ROSSETTI *Dante & Circle* I. (1874) 82 So much truth and simpleness entered into his heart.

**3.** Deficiency in knowledge or learning, ignorance; also, lack of mental acuteness, intellectual weakness, foolishness.

**1387** TREVISA *Higden* (Rolls) VII. 369 Aldredus, þat hopede to blende his robborie by þe sympilnesse of Wolston. *c* **1400** MAUNDEV. (1839) xv. 167 It is no marvaylle thanne, that the Paynemes..beleeven more largely, for here symplenesse. **1479** in *Eng. Gilds* (1870) 416 Such thinges as I of my sympilnesse haue not duely ne formably executed. **1482** *Monk of Evesham* (Arb.) 90 By processe of tyme owther they be ouercumme by onstabulnes or els ben dysceyuyd by sympylnes. **1535** COVERDALE *Eccl.* xiii. 8 Bewarre, that thou be not disceaued and brought downe in thy symplenesse. **1555** EDEN *Decades* (Arb.) 150 Their sympelnes is suche that they nother feared the multitude or poure of owre men. *c* **1620** Z. BOYD *Zion's Flowers* (1855) 72 That by her promises..she gull not my simplenesse. **1668** M. CASAUBON *Credulity* (1670) 185 Our Author doth declaim against the simpleness, and credulity of ordinary people. **1873** BROWNING *Red Cott. Nt.-cap* 557 'Heaven,' saith the sage, 'is with us, here inside Each man.' 'Hell also,' simpleness subjoins. **1894** *The Voice* (N.Y.) 29 Nov. 7/3 Such were the men who, in vapid simpleness, caught at the impertinent refrain of some doggerel song.

†**b.** Foolish conduct or behaviour; a foolish act or thing. *Obs.*

*c* **1450** tr. *Higden, Harl. Contin.* (Rolls) VIII. 451 He wolde avoide from his servyce his cownsellours whiche movede hym unto that symplenesse. *c* **1500** *Melusine* 194 My lordes, grete symplenes it is to you thus to traueylle your peuple for nought. **1523** CROMWELL in Merriman *Life & Lett.* (1902) I. 43 Hyt ys but a Symplenesse for us to thyncke to kepe possessions in Fraunce. **1592** SHAKS. *Rom. & Jul.* III. iii. 77 Run to my study:..Gods will, What simplenesse is this!

**4.** Poor or lowly condition; also, lack of elegance or refinement; plainness of dress, etc.

*a* **1400–50** *Alexander* 4051 Quen he þaire simpilnes sees he soroȝes in his hert, Pleynes of þaire pouerte. *c* **1440** *York Myst.* xviii. 16 Thow myghtfull maker, haue mynde on me, And se vnto my sympplenes. **1538** BALE *John Baptist* in *Harl. Misc.* (1808) I. 113 Soch autoryte As thy grace hath geuen to my poore symplenesse. **1648** J. BEAUMONT *Psyche* XX. clxxviii, Reverend John array'd in Simpleness, Did proudlyest-decked Mortals so excel. **1651** HOBBES *Gov. & Soc.* Ep. Ded., Whatsoever things they are in which this present Age doth differ from the rude simplenesse of Antiquity. **1873** MORRIS *Love is Enough* 86 He is poor, and shall scorn not our simpleness surely.

†**b.** Insignificance; trifling character or value.

*c* **1440** *Promp. Parv.* 456/1 Sympylnesse, or lytylle of valew, *exilitas.* **1530** PALSGR. Ep. to King p. iv, The symplenesse of my poore labours in that behalfe. **1570** GOOGE *Pop. Kingd.* Pref., Most humblie beseeching you to beare with the simplenesse thereof.

**5.** Absence of complexity; freedom from complications; simple character.

**1398** TREVISA *Barth. De P.R.* IV. i. (1494) e iij b, For the symplynes [*sic*] of a boystous thynge is subtylnes. *Ibid.* VII. lxix. (Bodl. MS.), Hym nedeþ to knowe þe duyring, contrarynes, semplenes, qualite and quantite of þe pacient. **1502** *Ord. Crysten Men* (W. de W. 1506) Prol. 5 Prechoures of the symplenes of the gospell. **1609** J. DOULAND *Ornith. Microl.* 83 The Ancient simplenesse of Musicke. **1618** BOLTON *Florus* III. xii. (1636) 210 The simplenesse and purity of that shepherdish originall continued. **1823** LAMB *Elia* II. *Child Angel*, O the inexplicable simpleness of dreams! **1882** *Nature* XXVII. 51 From a simpleness in structure to a wonderful differentiation thereof.

**simpler**[1] ('sɪmplə(r)). Now *arch.* [f. SIMPLE B. 6 + -ER.] One who collects or studies simples; a herbalist, a simplist.

**1591** GREENE *Farewell to Folly* Wks. (Grosart) IX. 289 Menecas the Macedonian was a very good simpler. **1601** HOLLAND *Pliny* XXI. xx. II. 105, I canot but detect the knauery of these Harbarists and simplers. **1656** W. COLE *Art of Simpling* Pref. p. i, What a rare happiness was it for Matthiolus that famous Simpler, to live in those dayes. **1720** DE FOE *Serious Refl.* ii. 33 Your Simplers have had some disputes about the sorts of it. **1774** *Westm. Mag.* II. 137 This Simpler..might..stand the foremost amongst his own vegetative tribes. **1830** JAMES *Darnley* xxxvii, Bradford had gone to seek remedies from a simpler at Boulogne. **1866** *Treas. Bot.* 35/1 Its properties are..slightly tonic; hence it comes within the province of the 'simpler'.

**b. simpler's joy,** the plant vervain.

**1760** J. LEE *Introd. Bot.* App. 327 Simpler's Joy, *Verbena.* **1863** PRIOR *Plant-n.*, *Simpler's joy*, from the good sale they had for so highly esteemed a plant, *Verbena officinalis.*

†**simpler**[2]. *Cant. Obs.* [f. SIMPLE *a.*] (See quot. 1592.)

**1592** GREENE *Conny Catch.* Wks. (Grosart) X. 39 They haue sundry praies that they cal simplers which are men fondly and wantonly geuen, whom for a penaltie of their lust, they fleece of al that euer they haue. **1602** ROWLANDS *Greenes Ghost* (1860) 43 She returneth with two or three fleshly minded Rabbets or Simplers.

**'simplesse.** *Obs.* exc. *arch.* Also 4 simplesce, 4–6 symplesse (5 -ess), 7 simpl'esse. [a. OF. *simplesse*, *-esce*, *-ece*, etc., = Prov., Sp., and Pg. *simpleza*:

see SIMPLE *a.* and -ESS². In ME. usually stressed *sim'plesse*, but cf. GOWER *Conf.* I. 62 and III. 213.]

**1.** = SIMPLENESS 1.

**1340** *Ayenb.* 140 Vor one of þe guode doȝtren þet mildenesse heþ is holy simplesse. **1390** GOWER *Conf.* I. 112 Whan he.. to so vil a povere wrecche Him deigneth schewe such simplesce. *a* **1400** *Relig. Pieces fr. Thornton MS.* 55 Ouer grete symplesse may make of þe symple a sott. **1483** CAXTON *Gold. Leg.* 195 b/1 There ben twelue vertues vyrgynal,.. that is to wete feythe,.. symplesse, Innocence, concorde.

**2.** = SIMPLENESS 2.

**1390** GOWER *Conf.* I. 70 These Prestes.. with a contrefet simplesse, Which hid was in a fals corage, Feignende an hevenely message. *a* **1470** HARDING *Chron.* CCXXVIII. iii. 2 Therle Richard of Warwike then conceyued Of the symplesse and great innocense Of Kyng Henry. **1613** W. BROWNE *Brit. Past.* I. iii, Had Nature unto man such simpl'esse given He would like Birds be farre more neere to heaven.

**3.** = SIMPLENESS 3.

*c* **1400** *Rom. Rose* 6381, I lede right a Ioly lyf, Thurgh simplesse of the prelacye; They know not al my tregetrye. **1456** SIR G. HAYE *Law Arms* (S.T.S.) 182 He throu ignoraunce and sympless gafe the sauf condyt. **1471** CAXTON *Recuyell* (Sommer) I. 107 Beholde than what symplesse shall hit be to the to hold me thus enfermed. **1537** in Ellis *Orig. Lett.* Ser. II. II. 93 Suplying your Lordship to admytte my symplesse for I have don in hit the moost of my power. **1889** LOWELL in *Atlantic Monthly* Aug. 148 Property's dividing line No hint of dispossession drew On any map my simplesse knew.

**4.** = SIMPLENESS 4.

**1390** GOWER *Conf.* I. 62 He clotheth richesse, as men sein, Under the simplesce of poverte. *c* **1440** *Gesta Rom.* xxxvi. 272 (Add. MS.), Therfore I had me in all thynges as a Religious man in symplesse. **1579** SPENSER *Sheph. Cal.* July 172 Their weedes bene not so nighly wore; Such simplesse mought them shend. *a* **1637** B. JONSON *Underwoods, Epithalamion* vi, Darting forth a dazling light On all that come her Simplesse to rebuke.

**5.** = SIMPLENESS 5.

*c* **1374** CHAUCER *Boeth.* IV. pr. vi. (1868) 136 þilke cercle þat is inrest or moost wiþynne ioineþ to þe symplesse of þe myddel.

**simpleton** ('sɪmp(ə)ltən). [A fanciful formation on SIMPLE *a.* Cf. *idleton* in the *Eng. Dial. Dict.*]

**1.** One who is deficient in sense or intelligence; a silly or foolish person; a fool.

Characterized by Johnson (1755) as 'a low word'.

**1650** B. *Discollim.* 28 If a solemn Synod may erre, what may a single Simpleton doe? **1672** *Rosemary & Bayes* 16 It was a wish of St. Austin.., but I see now that the Father was a simpleton. **1716** HEARNE *Collect.* (O.H.S.) V. 281 This Morning preached at Sᵗ. Marie's Mʳ. Poynter (that Dull Simpleton) of Merton Coll. **1769** *Junius Lett.* xxv. (1788) 139 The silly invectives of every simpleton who writes in a newspaper. **1801** MAR. EDGEWORTH *Angelina* iv. (1832) 82 A simpleton of sixteen is more an object of mercy than a simpleton of sixty. **1878** C. GIBBON *For the King* xvii, He is something of a simpleton, and did not recognise you.

*attrib.* **1859** HELPS *Friends in C.* Ser. II. II. viii. 158 The simpleton hero of one novel has no connexion with the simpleton hero of another.

**2.** *U.S.* The American dunlin or sandpiper, *Tringa* (*Pelidna*) *pacifica*.

**1891** in *Cent. Dict.*

Hence (chiefly as nonce-words) **simple'tonian, simple'tonic, 'simpletonish** *adjs.*, characteristic of or resembling (that of) a simpleton; **simple'tonianism, 'simpletonism**, character or quality characteristic of a simpleton.

**1847** LADY EASTLAKE *Jrnls. & Corr.* (1895) I. 212 Simple and childlike, and *simpletonish* in his manner. **1848** *Blackw. Mag.* LXIV. 467 The eccentricity of the baronet, the overtrust and the mistrust of mankind,.. are of the simpletonian school. **1860** MAYHEW *Upper Rhine* 331 That childish or simpletonic quality which.. young gentlemen.. denominate as 'verdant'. **1863** COWDEN CLARKE *Shaks. Char.* xvi. 394 His imagination was beguiling him with some image of captivating simpletonism; frequently and oddly confounded with simplicity. **1869** *Pall Mall G.* 13 Oct. 11 It is a pity to mark the decay of simpletonianism, even in the fashion of dolls.

†**'simplety.** *Obs. rare.* Forms: 3 simplete, 4 simplite, symplete, 5 symplyte. [a. OF. *simpleté* (Godef.): see SIMPLE *a.*] Simplicity.

*c* **1230** *Hali Meid.* 41 Simplete of semblaunt, & buhsumnesse & stilðe. **1377** LANGL. *P. Pl.* B. x. 165 þanne shaltow se sobrete and symplete-of-speche. **1382** WYCLIF *Job* ii. 9 ȝit forsothe thou abidist stille in thi symplete. *c* **1400** *Launfal* 225 Thus sat the knyght yn symplyte, In the schadowe unther a tre.

**simplex** ('sɪmplɛks), *a.* and *sb.* Also *pl.* simplicia. [a. L. *simplex* single: see SIMPLE *a.*]

**A.** *adj.* **1.** Consisting or composed of, characterized by, a single part, structure, etc.

**1594** BLUNDEVIL *Exerc.* I. xx. (1636) 43 Simplex [proportion], is when the Antecedent.. contayneth the Consequent. **1866** CAYLEY *Math. Papers* (1892) V. 402 The cone may consist of a single sheet; it is then of the simplex kind. **1895** *Funk's Standard Dict., Simplex telegraph*, a single-needle dial telegraph. **1897** *Westm. Gaz.* 10 Apr. 7/2 The new form of traction called the 'simplex traction'... The conduit is laid, not between the two rails but beneath one of the rails.

**2.** *Telegr.*, *Teleph.*, and *Computing.* Designating a system in which signals can be sent along a line in only one direction at a time; also applied to a circuit along which commands can flow in only one direction, usu. from the central processor to a peripheral. Also *absol.*

**1891** C. LANGDON-DAVIES *Explanation of Phonopore* vii. 28/1 The ordinary simplex telegraph is the one most in general use (except, possibly, in Great Britain). **1929** *Amer. Speech* IV. 290 One type of printer, which records the message on tape after the manner of a stock ticker, is known as the 'simplex'. **1967** DAVIDSON & KOENIG *Computers* xv. 525 These data communication lines are generally simplex, that is, they carry data in one direction only. **1975** *Sci. Amer.* Jan. 55 (Advt.), We have a range of modems, from 50 to 2400 bits per second, both for simplex and duplex traffic. **1977** J. R. L. ANDERSON *Death in City* xi. 170 The Radio Officer handed me a telephone... 'It's simplex, remember.. you have to take it in turns to speak and listen.'

**3.** *Biol.* Of an eye: having pigment on the posterior surface of the iris only, not on the anterior surface, and so appearing blue.

**1908** C. C. HURST in *Proc. R. Soc.* B. LXXX. 86 The eyes in which the posterior pigment alone is present in the iris, the anterior pigment being absent. Such eyes may be called simplex. **1946** [see DUPLEX *a.* 1 d].

**4.** *Genetics.* Of a polyploid individual: having the dominant allele at any particular locus represented once.

**1921** [see NULLIPLEX *a.*]. **1931** *Genetics* XVI. 178 When *R* is simplex (*Rrr*) the expected gametic ratio is 1*R*:2*Rr*:1*rr*:2*r*. *Ibid.* 183 A simplex plant (*Rrr*). **1932**, **1963** [see QUADRUPLEX *a.*].

**B.** *sb.* **1. a.** A simple uncompounded word.

**1892** *Classical Rev.* Feb. 58/2 When.. a complex was formed from any two of the above *simplicia*. **1904** *Expositor* Nov. 361 In the New Testament.. the simplex ἰδεῖν is exceedingly common.

**b.** *Linguistics.* In transformational grammar, a sentence analysed as having a single kernel structure. Cf. KERNEL *sb.*¹ 8 b (ii).

**1960** R. B. LEES *Gram. Eng. Nominalizations* iii. 101 Within the *matrix*-sentence, or any other simplex, the subject governs *-self*. **1963** *Language* XXXIX. 20 Since the second occurrence of the noun *John* repeats a noun within the same simplex, it is pronominalized to the corresponding *-self* pronoun. **1965** *Ibid.* XLI. 269 These differences in the treatment of repeated and nonrepeated material are evident in both simplexes (single-kernel sentences) and complexes (multikernel sentences).

**2.** *Geom.* The figure, in any given number of dimensions, that is bounded by the least possible number of hyperplanes: the two-dimensional simplex is the triangle, the three-dimensional simplex is the tetrahedron, and the four-dimensional simplex is bounded by five tetrahedra.

**1914** H. P. MANNING *Geom. Four Dimensions* viii. 317 In the space of five dimensions there are only three possible types of regular (convex) figures: the simplex, corresponding to the tetrahedron and pentahedroid, the orthogonal, corresponding to the cube and hypercube, and the figure reciprocal to the latter, constructed on a set of mutually perpendicular diagonals and corresponding to the octahedron and the 16-hedroid. **1929** D. M. Y. SOMMERVILLE *Introd. Geom. Four Dimensions* vii. 96 The simplest polytope in $S_n$ is the simplex $S(n + 1)$, which is bounded by $n + 1$ hyperplanes. **1975** *Sci. Amer.* May 102/2 The graph is isomorphic with the skeleton of a six-dimensional simplex, the 6-space analogue of the tetrahedron.

**3.** *Comb.*, as **simplex method**, a method of maximizing a linear function of several variables under several constraints on other linear functions; **simplex tableau**, a table displaying the constraints in problems of the type soluble by the simplex method.

[**1951** G. B. DANTZIG in T. C. Koopmans *Activity Analysis of Production & Allocation* xxi. 339 The general nature of the 'simplex' approach (as the method discussed here is known).] **1951** R. DORFMAN in *Ibid.* xxii. 351 The simplex method makes use of the fact that any point in an *n*-dimensional space can be expressed as a sum of *n* linearly independent points. **1966** S. BEER *Decision & Control* viii. 149 There are also variants of the original set of rules for finding the answer (to which the name algorithm is applied); Dantzig's own algorithm is called the Simplex Method. **1980** A. J. JONES *Game Theory* iii. 155 The relationship with our earlier notation is simply that we have replaced *A'* by *A* because this is the natural and universally accepted thing to do in setting up the simplex method. **1953** A. CHARNES in W. W. Cooper et al. *Introd. Linear Programming* II. vi. 66 As far as computations are concerned it is most convenient to arrange the data at each stage in a 'simplex tableau' as shown in Table I. **1966** A. BATTERSBY *Math. in Management* v. 125 A more usual form of presentation is the Simplex tableau in which all the variables have columns allocated to them.

**sim'plexity.** *nonce-wd.* [f. L. *simplex*, or f. SIMPLE *a.*, after *complexity*.] Simplicity.

**1849** *Tait's Mag.* XVI. 380/1 Its absolute simplexity and universality demonstrate the oneness and ubiquity of its author.

**simplex munditiis** ('sɪmplɛks mʊn'dɪtiːs). *Lat. phr.* [L., lit. 'simple in your adornments' (Horace *Odes* I. v. 5).] Unostentatiously beautiful; elegantly simple. Also used substantively.

**1766** H. BROOKE *Fool of Quality* II. xii. 274 Even the *simplex Mundities* [sic], that ornament of a clean simplicity, recommended by Horace, can operate only by intimation of deeper purity. **1803** *Edin. Rev.* III. 8 Indeed, the *simplex munditiis* stamped every thing that he did. **1874** A. J. MUNBY *Diary* 4 May (1972) 367 Wearing a rich silk dress.., and simplex munditiis as to her beautiful hair. **1933** E. BLUNDEN *Charles Lamb* 42 The same grace, the *simplex munditiis*, haunted all through his sonnets. **1949** E. POUND *Pisan Cantos* lxxx. 84 To go far and come to an end Simplex munditiis, as the hair of Circe; perhaps without the munditiis.

**simplicial** (sɪm'plɪʃəl), *a.* [f. L. *simplic-*, *simplex* single (see SIMPLEX *a.* and *sb.*) + -IAL.] Of, being, or pertaining to simplexes (SIMPLEX B. 2).

**1926** [see HOMŒOMORPH c]. **1959** E. M. PATTERSON *Topology* (ed. 2) v. 95 A geometrical simplicial complex *K* consists of a finite set of simplexes. **1976** *European Econ. Rev.* VIII. 305 The simplicial sub-division methods modelled by Scarf (1973) can be replaced by quicker Newton methods.

†**sim'plician.** *Obs.* Also simplitian, -sian. [f. SIMPLE *a.* or L. *simplic-*, *simplex*: see -ICIAN.] A simple or ignorant fellow; a simpleton. (Common *c* 1600–1650.)

**1600–9** ROWLANDS *Knaue of Clubbes* (Hunterian Club) 37 My aprehension did Ingenious-scan, That he was meerely a Simplitian. **1616** R. C. *Time's Whistle* (1871) 148 Be he a foole in the esteeme of man, In worldly thinges a meer simplician. **1662** HIBBERT *Body of Divinity* I. 152 These simplicians are much better than scorners.

**'simplicist,** *sb.* and *a.* [f. L. *simplic-*, *simplex* (see SIMPLE B. 6) + -IST. So older G. *simplicist.*]

**A.** *sb.* †**1.** One who has a knowledge of medicinal simples; a simplist. *Obs. rare.*

**1594** CAREW *Huarte's Exam. Wits* (1596) 176 We behold many Phisitions,.. great anotomists and Simplicists. *a* **1615** DONNE *Ess.* (1651) 201 As Simplicists which know the venom and peccant quality of every herbe but cannot fit them to Medicin.

**2.** One who simplifies. *rare.*

**1924** *Glasgow Herald* 24 Mar. 8 Can we ever simplify things again? Can we ever produce that statement of scientific method which will.. give us an idea of how to conduct our conduct? I believe the day of the great simplicist is beginning to dawn again.

**B.** *adj.* That simplifies; characterized by simplicity, uncomplicated.

**1934** in WEBSTER. **1949** *Sun* (Baltimore) 19 July 12/2 In the best manner of the simplicist versions of Keynesism, Mr. Nathan insists that the recession through which we are moving is due to the heavy capital formation of the last two years. **1951** S. SPENDER *World within World* 63 He had a simplicist view of things which did me good. **1979** *Church Times* 5 Oct. 13/3 Even the somewhat simplicist approach is justified by the need and desire to make the argument intelligible.

Hence **simpli'cistic** *a.*, characterized by over-simplicity.

**1950** *Archivum Linguisticum* II. 142 Streitberg's and Buck's explanations.. are both of this simplicistic.. type. **1970** *Nature* 7 Nov. 589/2 Attempts to relate simplicistic finite set theory and automata to faculties of mind and the mechanisms of the brain inevitably leads [*sic*] to such difficulties.

**simplici'tarian.** *nonce-wd.* [f. SIMPLICIT-Y + *-arian.*] One who aims at simplicity of life.

**1837** LOFFT *Self-form.* I. 71 A man of letters.. was in hardly better repute.. with those noble simplicitarians.

‖**simpliciter** (sɪm'plɪsɪtə(r)), *adv.* Orig. chiefly in *Sc. Law.* [L., adv. from *simplic-*, *simplex* simple.] Simply, absolutely, unconditionally; without any condition or consideration.

**1545** *Reg. Privy Council Scot.* I. 8 The keping of the said place sall cease simpliciter. **1570** FOXE *A. & M.* 1243/1, I sayd, yᵗ seing they had ben *simpliciter* giuen to me, I would neuer thanke him for them. **1603** *Reg. Privy Council Scot.* VI. 547 To.. ressave him to his Majesteis peax, and gif to him or ony in his name the wand thairof simpliciter in tyme cuming. **1664** BUTLER *Hud.* II. i. 185 This thing call'd Pain, Is.. Not bad *simpliciter*, nor good, But merely as 'tis understood. **1765–8** ERSKINE *Inst. Law Scot.* IV. iii. §22 Suspending the letters of diligence on which the charge was given, *simpliciter*. **1884** *Law Rep.* 27 *Chanc. Div.* 210 The outlay upon Cardiff Docks is not *simpliciter* a question between tenant for life and remainderman. **1929** A. N. WHITEHEAD *Process & Reality* 69 The Aristotelian phrase suggests the crude notion that one actual entity is added to another *simpliciter*. **1936** C. S. LEWIS *Allegory of Love* v. 222 He [*sc.* Gower] says too much, not at this point or that, but too much *simpliciter*. **1963** *Times* 28 May 9/2 Substantial damages were not awarded.. for physical injury *simpliciter*, but only for the pain and suffering and general loss of happiness which it occasioned. **1970** *N. & Q.* Dec. 453/1, I know of no evidence that 'shambles' *simpliciter* was ever used for 'brothel'. **1977** G. W. H. LAMPE *God as Spirit* vii. 178 It may suggest that the community which the Spirit creates is to be identified *simpliciter* with the institutional Church.

**simplicity** (sɪm'plɪsɪtɪ). Also 4 symplicite, 5–6 symplycyte, 6–7 simplicitie, 6 -tye. [a. OF. *simplicité* (12th c.), or ad. L. *simplicitāt-em*, f. *simplic-*, *simplex* simple: see -ITY.]

**1. a.** The state or quality of being simple in form, structure, etc.; absence of compositeness, complexity, or intricacy.

**1374** CHAUCER *Boeth.* IV. pr. vi. (1868) 136 In so mochel as it is forþest fro þe mydel symplicite of þe poynt. **1398** TREVISA *Barth. De P.R.* I. xvi. (Add. MS. 27944), He is alwey impartabil & turneþ & ioyneþ creation to his symplicite. *Ibid.* XIX. cxvi. (1495) 920 One in nombre and one in symplycyte. **1587** GOLDING *De Mornay* iii. 32 Then is it this first simplicitie which is the King. *a* **1619** FOTHERBY *Atheom.* II. x. §3 (1622) 304 His vncompounded simplicitie, is the true matter of his Vnitie. **1646** SIR T. BROWNE *Pseud. Ep.* 191 There being in them no diversitie or difference, but a simplicity of parts, and equiformity in motion. **1684** T.

Burnet *Theory Earth* I. 36 We are led.. to conceive this great machine of the World.. to have been once in a state of greater simplicity than now it is. **1743** EMERSON *Fluxions* p. xii, The Easiness and Simplicity of this Method of Demonstration. **1815** J. SMITH *Panorama Sci. & Art* I. 324 In contriving machines, simplicity of parts should always be studied. **1861** J. R. GREENE *Man. Anim. Kingd., Cœlent.* 73 It was once an ovum, whose extreme simplicity of structure might almost be said to verge upon homogeneity. **1871** T. R. JONES *Anim. Kingd.* (ed. 4) 443 The simplicity which the organ of hearing presents in this its earliest appearance.

**b.** A simple or easy task or duty.

**1875** BEDFORD *Sailor's Pkt. Bk.* v. (ed. 2) 167 A.. ready knowledge of the many important simplicities of his calling.

**c.** *spec.* in *Linguistics*, used *attrib.* with reference to the use of simplicity or economy as a criterion for evaluating a grammatical theory or description, as ***simplicity criterion, metric***, etc.

**1953** F. J. WHITFIELD tr. *Hjelmslev's Prolegom. Theory Lang.* 11 If.. linguistic theory ends by constructing several possible methods of procedure.., that one shall be chosen that results in the simplest possible description... This principle, which is deduced from our so-called empirical principle, we call the *simplicity principle*. **1962** M. HALLE in *Word* XVIII. 55, I shall.. exhibit the manner in which, by mechanical application of the proposed simplicity measure, certain formulations are chosen from among several alternatives. The plausibility and intrinsic appeal of the descriptions so selected will provide the primary justification not only for the proposed simplicity criterion, but also for the theory of generative grammar, of which the criterion is an integral part. **1968** *Glossa* II. 128 (*title*) Two proposals concerning the simplicity metric in phonology. **1976** J. S. GRUBER *Lexical Structures in Syntax & Semantics* II. ii. 330 The simplicity criterion will be useful in determining which of the two alternate forms of a definition is to be chosen for the lexical entry. **1977** *Canad. Jrnl. Linguistics* Spring 2 Such constraints.. entail a fundamental reassessment of current formulations of the simplicity metric.

**2. a.** Want of acuteness or sagacity; lack of ordinary knowledge or judgement; ignorance; rusticity.

**1514** BARCLAY *Cyt. & Uplondyshm.* (Percy Soc.) 25 Seest thou not playnly how they of the cyte Dayly dysceyveth our poore symplycyte. **1579** NORTHBROOKE *Dicing* (1843) 66 If he had done it of ignorance, necessitie, and simplicitie, then shoulde not he have died. **1613** PURCHAS *Pilgrimage* v. xvii. (1614) 537 Columbus vsed the like simplicitie of the Jamaicans to his preseruation. **1665** MANLEY *Grotius' Low C. Wars* 138 By these Subtilties.. he deluded the simplicity of such as were not very circumspect. **1719** DE FOE *Crusoe* I. 198 This was really a whimsical Thought, and I reprov'd my self often for the Simplicity of it. **1771** SMOLLETT *Humph. Cl.* (1815) 223 By the help of Humphry Clinker, who is a surprising compound of genius and simplicity. **1836** THIRLWALL *Greece* III. 1 His grandfather.. had incurred a nickname expressive of extreme simplicity. **1842** LOVER *Handy Andy* i, The postmaster, laughing at his simplicity, told him he could not tell what letter to give him unless he told him the direction. **1875** JOWETT *Plato* (ed. 2) III. 276 That other simplicity which is only a euphemism for folly.

**b.** An instance of this. *rare.*

**1592** G. HARVEY *Four Lett.* Wks. (Grosart) I. 205 Let it be.. one of our simplicities to suffer that iniury. **1610** A. COOKE *Pope Joan* 46 There are so many incongruities, simplicities, absurdities.. in his verie narration of it.

**c.** A simple person; a simpleton. *rare.*

**1633** FORD *'Tis Pity* II. vi, How do you know that, Simplicity? **1860** GEN. P. THOMPSON *Audi Alt.* civ. III. 11 Undergraduate Oxford exhorts the grown simplicities to persevere, till hopeful youth can come to their relief.

**3. a.** Freedom from artifice, deceit, or duplicity; sincerity, straightforwardness; also, absence of affectation or artificiality; plainness, artlessness, naturalness.

**1526** *Pilgr. Perf.* (W. de W. 1531) 54b, Excepte.. our mynde be subdued to simplicite and mekenes, surely our vyne wyll waxe wylde. **1587** A. DAY *Daphnis & Chloe* Title-p., Excellently describing the weight of affection, the Simplicitie of loue. **1610** HOLLAND *Camden's Brit.* 742 A man of the ancient Christian simplicity. **1649** JER. TAYLOR *Gt. Exemp.* II. x. 2 Nathanael was.. full of holy simplicity, a true Israelite without guile. **1702** *Eng. Theophrastus* 112 Plain-dealing and simplicity are the best game a man can play. **1771** WESLEY *Wks.* (1872) V. 139 Simplicity regards the intention itself, sincerity the execution of it. **1833** HT. MARTINEAU *Brooke Farm* iv. 40 Everybody.. looked up to him with respect for the simplicity of his character. **1856** KINGSLEY *Misc.* (1859) II. 18 A charming simplicity, quietly enjoying life in poverty and ignorance.

*personif.* **1597** MORLEY *Introd. Mus.* 183 To decke a lowlie matter with loftie and swelling speech, will be to put simplicitie in plumes of feathers. **1609** DEKKER *Gull's Hornbk.* Wks. (Grosart) II. 204 That excellent country Lady, Innocent Simplicity. **1773** HAN. MORE *Search after Happiness* II. 144 Hail, artless Simplicity, beautiful maid.

**b.** *transf.* A simple or ingenuous child.

**1887** RUSKIN *Præterita* II. 228 His little blue-eyed twelve-years-old simplicity of a goat-herd sister.

**c.** Simple, unsophisticated ways or manners; absence of or freedom from luxury; plainness of life. Also (in *pl.*), an instance of this.

**1585** T. WASHINGTON tr. *Nicholay's Voy.* IV. xxxvi. 159b, These Patriarches.. liue in all simplicitie & modestie. **1726** SHELVOCKE *Voy. r. World* 404 Such is the original simplicity prevailing amongst them, that the men go quite naked. **1794** MRS. RADCLIFFE *Myst. Udolpho* i, He had known life in other forms than those of pastoral simplicity. **1849–50** ALISON *Hist. Europe* VII. xliii. §82. 256 The simplicity of all surprised the conqueror, who was accustomed to the magnificence of St. Cloud. **1874** GREEN *Short Hist.* viii. §10. 583 There was a grand simplicity in the life of his [Milton's] later years.

*pl.* **1805** WORDSW. *Prelude* VI. 2 When to Esthwaite's banks And the simplicities of cottage life I bade farewell. **1878** C. STANFORD *Symb. Christ* v. 123 He still loved the simplicities of a shepherd's life.

**4.** Of language or style: Absence or lack of elegance or polish; in later use, freedom from ornateness or over-elaboration; plainness or directness of an attractive kind.

**1553** EDEN *Treat. New Ind.* (Arb.) 10 Goddes woorde, (whyche they contemned for the simplicitie of the same). **1592** G. HARVEY *Four Lett.* iii. Wks. (Grosart) I. 178 If anie haue charged mee, or do charge mee.. with simplicity, I yeeld. *a* **1625** SIR H. FINCH *Law* (1636) 386 By his gesture, countenance, or simplicity of speech, it may be discouered; which the artificiall speech of his Councell learned would hide and colour. **1697** DRYDEN *Virgil, Ess. Georg.*, The Precepts of Husbandry are not to be deliver'd with the Simplicity of a Plow-man, but with the Address of a Poet. **1783** COWPER *Lett.* 24 Nov., Wks. (1876) 149 Simplicity is become a very rare quality in a writer. **1840** H. ROGERS *Ess.* (1874) II. v. 259 True simplicity.. as it regards the expression.. means, that thoughts worth hearing are expressed in language that every one can understand. **1879** B. TAYLOR *Germ. Lit.* 73 Tennyson has endeavored to imitate the old epic simplicity.

*pl.* **1875** LOWELL *Among my Bks.* Ser. II. *Wordsworth*, The grand simplicities of the Bible.

**5.** Absence of ornament or decoration; freedom from useless accessories.

**1609** B. JONSON *Sil. Wom.* I. i, Give me a look, give me a face, That makes simplicity a grace. **1774** PENNANT *Tour Scotl. 1772*, 57 That [window] in the East end has a magnificient simplicity. **1781** COWPER *Truth* 27 It stands like the cerulean arch we see, Majestic in its own simplicity. **1828** LANDOR *Imag. Conv., Epictetus & Seneca* III. 497 What is decorated is simplicity no longer. **1856** EMERSON *Eng. Traits* vi. *Manners*, Even Brummel their fop was marked by the severest simplicity in dress. **1893** MORRIS *Gothic Archit.* 31 The cant of the beauty of simplicity (i.e. bareness and ugliness) did not afflict it.

*pl.* **1854** RUSKIN *Lect. Archit. & Paint.* i. 7 Your decorations are just as monotonous as your simplicities.

†**6.** *U.S.* = HUMILITY 3. *Obs.*

**1634** W. WOOD *New Eng. Prosp.* I. viii. (1865) 34 The Humilities or Simplicities (as I may rather call them) bee of two sorts, the biggest being as big as a greene Plover, the other as big as birds we call knots in England.

**ˈsimplicize**, *v. nonce-word.* [f. L. *simplic-*, *simplex* simple: see -IZE.] *trans.* To make simple.

**1814** L. HUNT *Feast Poets* 94 In like manner, he [Wordsworth] would clear up and simplicize our thoughts.

**simplification** (sɪmplɪfɪˈkeɪʃən). [a. F. *simplification*, f. *simplifier* to SIMPLIFY.] **1.** The action or process of simplifying or rendering less complex or elaborate; the result of this.

**1688** NORRIS *Love* I. iv. 39 Men eminently good who.. have attained to the highest degree of Mortification and Simplification of Desire.

**1802** JAMES *Milit. Dict.* s.v., The simplification of army accounts is perhaps one of the most desirable objects in finance. **1834** HT. MARTINEAU *Moral* II. 60 Nothing being wanted to its efficacy but the simplification which time and practice were sure to bring. **1884** *Law Times* LXXVII. 43/1 Military law.. appears to us to be more complicated than it need be in these days of simplification of the statutes.

**2.** *Logic.* One of the principles of inference used esp. in the calculus of propositions (see quot. 1903).

**1903** B. RUSSELL *Princ. Math.* ii. 16 We can now state the six main principles of inference, to each of which.. a name is to be given... If *p* implies *p* and *q* implies *q*, then *pq* implies *p*. This is called *simplification*, and asserts merely that the joint assertion of two propositions implies the assertion of the first of the two. **1934** COHEN & NAGEL *Introd. Logic & Scientific Method* vi. 124 In order to get the calculus [of classes] started, we must state a number of fundamental principles... The following.. are those which are usually assumed.. Principle of simplification, [etc.]. **1954** I. M. COPI *Symbolic Logic* iii. 43 Simplification (Simp.): *p.q* ∴ *p*. **1969** F. I. DRETSKE *Seeing & Knowing* ii. 57 The logical equivalence which goes under the name of simplification (P is logically equivalent to P and P).

**ˈsimplifiˌcator.** [f. SIMPLIFY *v.*, after Latin types.] One who simplifies.

**1829** I. TAYLOR *Enthusiasm* iv. (1867) 83 This is the supposition of simplificators, who.. must needs disbelieve, because theology would otherwise afford them no intellectual exercise.

**ˌsimplifiˈcatory**, *a.* [f. SIMPLIFICAT(ION + -ORY[2].] That simplifies.

**1936** W. F. R. HARDIE *Study in Plato* xi. 141 Aristotle.. makes use of the misleading simplificatory language according to which the rational soul commands the irrational soul. **1972** *N. & Q.* Dec. 446/2 Simplificatory changes like the loss of unstressed syllables.

**ˈsimplified**, *ppl. a.* [f. SIMPLIFY *v* + -ED[1].] Made or become more simple. ***simplified spelling***: a system of writing English with greater phonetic consistency than in conventional spelling; any of various schemes for such a spelling reform; hence ***simplified speller*** (*nonce-word*): an advocate or practitioner of simplified spelling.

*a* **1681** PORDAGE *Mystic Div.* (1683) 75 They are all pure simplified Spirits, not like the Angels,.. but they are pure abstracted Spirits, proceeding from the supreme Unity. **1721** R. KEITH tr. *T. à Kempis, Valley of Lilies* 48 He that is simplified and innocent, and humbly obedient. **1789** MORSE *Amer. Geogr.* Pref., It furnishes a simplified account of other countries. **1879** J. H. GLADSTONE *Spelling Reform* (ed. 2) p. v, Other advantages of a simplified spelling. **1899** 'MARK TWAIN' *What is Man?* (1917) 256, I have had a kindly feeling toward Simplified Spelling from the beginning of the movement three years ago. *Ibid.* 262, I myself am a Simplified Speller. **1907** W. JAMES *Pragmatism* vii. 260 Now the idea of this loose universe affects your typical rationalists in much the same way.. as 'simplified spelling' might affect an elderly schoolmistress. **1908** W. W. SKEAT *Presidential Address delivered at first Meeting of Simplified Spelling Society* 3 The object of the Simplified Spelling Society is to consider carefully the whole subject of our modern English spelling, with a view to the initiation of.. a moderate system of reforms. **1955** AUDEN in *Encounter* Feb. 11 In my Eden our only source of political news is gossip: In his New Jerusalem there will be a special daily in simplified spelling for non-verbal types. **1977** K. M. E. MURRAY *Caught in Web of Words* vi. 102 In 1905.. he [*sc.* James Murray] joined the American Simplified Spelling Board. **1979** *Guardian* 7 Aug. 3/1 September 30 has been nominated by the Simplified Spelling Society as an international day of Speling [*sic*] Watching.

Hence **ˈsimplifiedly** *adv.*

**1683** E. HOOKER *Mystic Div.* 67 Where.. uncompoundedly, abstractly and simplifiedly Hee stood.

†**ˈsimplifier**[1]. *Obs.*[−1] [f. SIMPLE B. 6.] A maker of simples.

**1594** PLAT *Jewell-ho.* III. 33 This skil is verie requisite for a good simplifier, because he may drie the leafe of any hearb in this maner.

**simplifier**[2] (ˈsɪmplɪfaɪə(r)). [f. SIMPLIFY *v.* + -ER[1].] One who or that which simplifies.

**1824** MOORE *Mem.* (1853) IV. 260 A chastener and simplifier of style, it being the very reverse of ambition or ornament. **1896** *Cent. Mag.* Feb. 601 He is a great simplifier of details.

**simplify** (ˈsɪmplɪfaɪ), *v.* [ad. F. *simplifier* (15th c.), ad. med.L. *simplificāre*, f. L. *simplus* simple: see -FY.]

†**1.** *trans.* (See quots.) *Obs. rare.*

**1653** H. MORE *Conject. Cabbala* IV. i, That Precept of the Pythagoreans,.. Simplifie your self, Reduce your self to One. **1692** NORRIS *Pract. Disc.* (1711) III. 132 This will recollect and simplify our souls and free us of that.. dispersion of Thought which is so great an hindrance to us.

**2. a.** To make simple; to render less complex, elaborate, or involved; to reduce to a clearer or more intelligible form; to make easy.

**1759** CHESTERF. *Lett.* ccclv. (1792) IV. 169 Let us simplify it and see what it [a disappointment] amounts to. *c* **1782** JEFFERSON *Autobiog.* Wks. 1859 I. 168 It will simplify the system of our mint to alloy both metals in the same degree. **1788** GIBBON *Decl. & F.* xliv. IV. 362 Their philosophic spirit had.. simplified the forms of proceeding. **1803** SYD. SMITH *Wks.* (1859) I. 57/2 The laws of commerce.. are simplified and expanded. **1841** LANE *Arab. Nts.* I. 73 Early in this age, they began to simplify their spoken language. **1853** J. H. NEWMAN *Hist. Sk.* (1873) II. I. iv. 163 In a state of nature man.. does not simplify and fix his motives.

*absol.* **1878** LOCKYER *Spectrum Anal.* 166 That is a wonderful simplification, and science always simplifies.

**b.** *intr.* To become (more) simple; to admit of simplification.

**1955** G. GREENE *Quiet American* IV. ii. 230 When we are young we are a jungle of complications. We simplify as we get older. **1964** K. G. LOCKYER *Introd. Critical Path Analysis* ii. 21 Thus the diagram will simplify to the following [etc.].

Hence **ˈsimplifying** *vbl. sb.*

†**ˈsimpling**, *vbl. sb. Obs.* [f. SIMPLE B. 6 or *v.*[2] + -ING[1].] The gathering or study of simples or medicinal plants.

**1597** *Gerarde's Herbal, Ded. Verses*, In commendation of Mr. John Gerard for his diligence in simpling. **1656** W. COLE *Art of Simpling* Pref. p. i, In our times, the Art of Simpling is so farre from being rewarded, that it is grown contemptible. **1718** OZELL tr. *Tournefort's Voy.* I. 14 As for us, whose prevailing Passion was Simpling, we were perpetually on the hunt all round the City. **1774** *Westm. Mag.* II. 137 Upon reading a little further, I found the Hero was a Botanist, and his toils Simpling.

**b.** *attrib.* in ***simpling voyage***.

**1597** GERARDE *Herbal* I. xxii, The Journall that I wrot of this simpling voyage. **1671** RAY *Corr.* 87, I intend.. to begin a simpling voyage into the north. **1699** *Phil. Trans.* XXI. 62 An Account of a Simpling Voyage of John Baptista Triumphetti, Botanick Lecturer.

So †**ˈsimpling** *ppl. a. Obs.*

*a* **1643** W. CARTWRIGHT *Poems* (1651) 230 'Twas.. approv'd by the simpling brotherhood.

**ˈsimplism.** [f. SIMPLE *a.* + -ISM.]

**1.** Affected or overdone simplicity of literary style. *nonce-word.*

*a* **1882** EMERSON in *Century Mag.* (1890) Feb. 624 Other writers have to affect what to him [Wordsworth] is natural. So they have what Arnold calls *simplism*, he, simplicity.

**2.** Also ‖**simplisme**. [Cf. F. *simplisme*.] A tendency to over-simplify; an over-simplification.

**1955** M. REIFER *Dict. New Words* 189/1 *Simplism, n.*, oversimplification of any matter and elimination of all complicating aspects; usually aimed at promoting uncritical conformity. **1969** C. LEECH *Tragedy* iii. 42 Wilbur Sanders.. has declared that 'Necessity neither requires nor invites cooperation'.., but this appears to be simplism. **1974** *New Society* 13 June 623/1 A fair number of marxist academics have been alarmed at this anti-fascist *simplisme* coming home to roost. **1976** P. ALEXANDER *Death Thin-Skinned Animal* x. 104 It was impossible to argue against that sort of simplism. **1977** *Times Lit. Suppl.* 11 Feb. 150/2 Gladstone's complaint in 1874 that the opposition fomented by the *Daily*

*News* had been 'one main cause' of the weakness of his late government was, of course, a simplism.

**simplist** ('sɪmplɪst). Also 6 **symplist**. [f. SIMPLE B. 6 + -IST.] One who studies simples or medicinal plants; a herbalist. Now *rare*.

**1597** GERARDE *Herbal* I. lxviii. 95 The which controuersie ..may be decided by the least and simplest Symplist in these our daies. **1601** HOLLAND *Pliny* II. 214 The Grecian Simplists describe this Moly with a yellow floure. **1646** SIR T. BROWNE *Pseud. Ep.* II. vi. 100 It hath been mistaken by some good Simplist for Amomum. **1672** JOSSELYN *New Eng. Rarities* 84 This Plant is taken by our Simplists to be a kind of Golden Rod. **1816** KEITH *Phys. Bot.* I. 39 This is a phenomenon that seems to have puzzled the simplists of antiquity not a little. **1837** —— *Bot. Lex.* 94 The simplists of earlier times were content [etc.].

‖**simpliste** (sɛ̃plist, 'sɪmplɪst), *sb.* and *a.* Also **simplist**. [Fr.] **A.** *sb.* One who adopts an over-simplified or one-sided view of something.

**1918** W. O'BRIEN *Downfall of Parliamentarianism* i. 5 The simplest of simplists will now own..that the choice of Ireland in 1890 was not that..choice between vice and virtue..which would make human judgments in great affairs an enviably easy process. **1924** *Amer. Mercury* Apr. 465/2 But Nature and History, alas! are not *simplistes*. **1967** A. COMFORT *Anxiety Makers* vi. 197 These are *simplistes*, anxious about ritual obligations, unanxious about phenomena which genuinely threaten us with death and racial extinction. **1970** *Guardian* 12 Nov. 9/1 Robert Ardrey ..is..a natural and disabling *simpliste*.

**B.** *adj.* That over-simplifies, one-sided; plain or uncomplicated in style.

**1926** L. A. CLARE tr. *Lévy-Bruhl's How Natives Think* 15 Mental processes are infinitely more elastic, complex, and subtle, and they comprise more elements of the psychic life than a too 'simplist' intellectualism would allow. **1930** *N. & Q.* CLIX. 272/2 Rather a *simpliste*, facile doctrine perhaps. **1950** T. H. MARSHALL *Citizenship & Social Class* 84 The policy, in fact, may not be *simpliste* at all. **1960** *Encounter* Jan. 86/1 He accepts a wholly *simpliste* leftist view. **1966** N. FREELING *Dresden Green* I. 38 The *Golden Age of Landscape Gardening*, simplist, giving you the idea you could do it yourself. **1973** *Times* 25 Apr. 14/6 The familiar story of the parting of the seas is told directly in Williamson's most *simplist* vein. **1977** *Church Times* 13 May 10/2 Shouldn't some kind of theology, even though it's a bit simpliste, come in here.

**sim'plistic**, *a.* [f. SIMPLE B. 6 or SIMPLE *a.*]

**1.** Of or pertaining to a simplist or to simples. **1860** in WORCESTER (citing Wilkinson).

**2.** Of the nature of, or characterized by, (extreme) simplicity. Now usu. with the connotation of excessive or misleading simplification.

*a* **1881** J. F. CLARKE (Worc.), The facts of nature and of life are more apt to be complex than simple. Simplistic theories are generally one-sided and partial. **1934** *Eng. Studies* XVI. 77 Some of the attempts at elucidating the origin of slang phrases do not seem very successful... It hardly admits of such a simplistic explanation. **1954** *Encounter* July 21/1 The Pluralists oppose the simplistic interpretations which we..inherit..from Walter Millis' accounts of war as the product of war-mongering. **1967** *Guardian* 3 July 6/1 To see the issue as an attack on middle-class values..is so much simplistic and dangerous nonsense. **1976** T. STOPPARD *Dirty Linen* 40 She's quite right... It is simplistic to speak of malice. **1980** *Jrnl. R. Soc. Arts* Mar. 215/2 It was quite evident that these rather simplistic models were inadequate.

Hence **sim'plistically** *adv.*

**1963** F. W. FREY in L. W. Pye *Communications & Political Devel.* xvii. 307 Changes which we simplistically call Westernization. **1974** *Times Lit. Suppl.* 25 Jan. 65/1 The German Democratic Republic from the first made Heine one of its classics, though sometimes reading his politics simplistically in the process. **1978** *Nature* 23 Mar. 306/1 Their basic chain mechanisms can be written simplistically as [etc.].

**simply** ('sɪmplɪ), *adv.* Forms: α. 3–4 **simpleliche** (4 **-lyche**), 5 **semplelyche**; 4 **sympel-**, 4–5 **sympliliche**; 3 **simpliche**, 4 **symplich(e**. β. 4–5 **symplely** (6 **-lily**), 4–6 **simplely** (4 **-li**), 7 **simplyly**; 4–5 **sympylly**, **-illy** (6 *Sc.* **-illie**), 5 **-el(l)y**, 5–6 **simpely** (6 *Sc.* **-illie**); 4–6 **symply** (6 **-li**), 6–7 **simplie**, 6– **simply**. [f. SIMPLE *a.* + -LY².], with later contraction as in *gently*, *nobly*. Cf. MDu. *sem-*, *simpelike* (Du. *simpellijk*).]

**1.** With simplicity (of mind) or sincerity; in an honest or straightforward manner; also, in later use, unaffectedly, artlessly.

**1297** R. GLOUC. (Rolls) 2663 þo hii come In eiþer side to Ambresbury..& þe brutons al simpleliche In god pays hii vnderstode. **1340** *Ayenb.* 134 He him lefþ simpleliche of al þet he zayþ, ase deþ þe litel child his mayster. **1382** WYCLIF *Prov.* ii. 7 He shal kepen the helthe of riȝt men, and defende the goende symplely. *c* **1440** *Jacob's Well* 181 Ne telle noȝt in þi schryfte flateryng iapys..; but symplely late þin herte & þi tunge acorde in one. *c* **1450** *Merlin* x. 140 The kynge he receyved [their homage] with gode herte and sympilliche with wepynge. **1603** SIR R. WESTON in *Lismore Papers* Ser. II. (1887) I. 80, I..protest that att my deliuery of his obligacon I delt singlyly and simplyly with you. **1667** MILTON *P.L.* XII. 569 By things deemd weak Subverting worldly strong, and worldly wise By simply meek. **1770** GOLDSM. *Des. Village* 25 The dancing pair that simply sought renown, By holding out, to tire each other down. **1867** RUSKIN *Time & Tide* v. §24 She did it beautifully and simply, as a child ought to dance. **1867** FREEMAN in W. R. W. Stephens *Life* (1895) I. 382, I was rather amused at Huxley asking me very simply whether I had read Thierry.

**2. a.** In a plain, homely, or frugal manner.

**1375** BARBOUR *Bruce* I. 331 Sone to Paryss can he ga, And levyt thar full sympylly. **1395** PURVEY *Remonstr.* (1851) 94 Freris owen to lyue sympliere and streitliere than othere religiouse. *c* **1450** *St. Cuthbert* (Surtees) 7654 þare in hungir and calde full pure þai leuyd, and sympely þai fure.

**b.** Humbly in respect of dress or surroundings.

*c* **1400** LOVE *Bonavent. Mirr.* (1908) 56 Suche a litell childe so sympilly clothed. **1568** GRAFTON *Chron.* II. 255 She went as simply as she might, to thentent that the king should not phansie her. **1570** FOXE *A. & M.* 2075/2 As he was but a Deacon, so was hee but simply or at least not priestly apparelled. **1596** DRAYTON *Legends* iv. 42 Whose meanest Cottage simply Me did shrowd.

**3. a.** In simple language, with simplicity of speech, with no attempt at style; also, so as to be readily understood, plainly, clearly.

*c* **1380** WYCLIF *Sel. Wks.* (1880) 46, I in fewe wordis & sympliche maade to write it. *c* **1384** CHAUCER *H. Fame* 854 Haue y not preved thus symply, With-outen any subtilite Of speche? *c* **1400** *Pilgr. Sowle* (Caxton, 1483) II. xli. 46 Somwhat as I can sympelly reporten I shall it now rehercen. **1474** CAXTON *Chesse* II. v. (1883) 64 Whan he spekth to hem swetly and conuerseth with hem symply. *a* **1591** H. SMITH *Serm.* (1637) 143 To preach simply, is not to preach rudely, nor unlearnedly, nor confusedly, but to preach plainly. **1638** SIR T. HERBERT *Trav.* (ed. 2) 12 As if a stupid sense made her carelesse of danger, which to sympathize I have as simply for your sport depicted. **1648** HEXHAM II, *Slechtelick seggen*, to speake Simply, or in Briefe.

**b.** *Logic.* In the simple mode of conversion applicable to propositions; opp. *per accidens* s.v. PER *prep.* 1 b. Cf. CONVERSION 4.

**1599** T. BLUNDEVILLE *Art of Logike* III. 69 They say that the disiunct being like to an absolute or simple Proposition, may be converted both simplie and per accidens. **1677** T. GOOD *Brief Eng. Tract of Logick* 31 That is *S.* denotes the Proposition designed by the preceeding vowel, to be converted simply. **1864** BOWEN *Logic* vii. 202 That it is to be converted simply. **1884** J. N. KEYNES *Formal Logic* II. iii. 74 This, being an E proposition, may be converted simply, giving, No one deserving of the fair is not brave. **1955** A. N. PRIOR *Formal Logic* II. i. 109 *Oba* and *Oab* do not convert either *per accidens* or simply.

**c.** Without unnecessary elaboration or superfluous ornament; plainly and pleasingly.

**1746** FRANCIS tr. *Horace, Art Poet.* 293 Few were its [the flute's] notes, its form was simply plain. **1816** J. SCOTT *Vis. Paris* (ed. 5) 61 This is a fine massive piece of architecture, simply grand. **1850** *Beck's Florist* Apr. 101 We found the gardens..very pretty, simply laid out, and well kept up. *Comb.* **1821** SCOTT *Kenilw.* v, A simply-attired pretty maiden.

**d.** Without complication or intricacy.

**1867** SPENCER *First Princ.* (ed. 2) §108. 308 Evolution..is illustrated most simply and clearly by this [etc.]. **1874** LOWELL *Agassiz* I. 144 A mortal..taking life as simply as a tree!

†**4.** Poorly, badly, indifferently; meanly, inadequately; weakly, feebly. *Obs.*

**1375** BARBOUR *Bruce* XVII. 134 Quhan thai the baner saw sympilly Swa standand, stuffit with sa quhoyn. **1387** TREVISA *Higden* (Rolls) VI. 355 He kouþe his gramer but sympilliche, for þat tyme was nouȝt oon techer of gramer in al his kyngdom. *Ibid.* VIII. 59 He..restored sympelliche [*L. exiliter*] þe Chartre Hous at Witham besides Salisbury. **1432–50** tr. *Higden* (Rolls) III. 85 This Anchus Marcius.. made hym tutor of his childere, but this Tarquinius remembrede that luffe symplely [L. *male*]. **1465** *Paston Lett.* II. 207 In good feyth I have ben symply intretid among them. **1489** CAXTON *Faytes of A.* II. v. 99 Other that he knewe sholde doo lytel good and that were symply armed. **1523** LD. BERNERS *Froiss.* I. lxxxix. 112 The Scottes helde but simply the trewse concludedde the yere before. **1597** MORLEY *Introd. Mus.* 182 Being inioyned to make a song [he] wil do it so simplie as one would thinke a scholler of one yeares practise might easelie compose a better. **1753–4** RICHARDSON *Grandison* I. xv. 89 Had he once gained entrance, perhaps I might have come off but simply.

**5.** In a foolish, silly, or stupid manner; without common sense or sagacity; †ignorantly. Also ***simply disposed***, of a simple disposition.

**1466** *Paston Lett.* II. 263 She hathe demenyd her ful symply bothe for youre worship and also for her awne. **1535** COVERDALE *2 Sam.* xv. 11 But they wente on symply, and knewe not of the matter. **1601** HOLLAND *Pliny* I. 195 If an elephant chance to meet with a man wandering simply out of his way in the wildernesse. **1662–3** PEPYS *Diary* 2 Jan., Sir W. Batten was paying off tickets, but so simply and arbitrarily..that I was weary of it. **1789** MRS. PIOZZI *Journ. France* I. 362 Omitting, simply enough, to carry a thermometer, one can measure the heat of nothing. **1848** THACKERAY *Van. Fair* li, People declared that she got money from various simply disposed persons, under pretence of getting them confidential appointments under Government.

**6. a.** Without addition or qualification.

**1398** TREVISA *Barth. De P.R.* XIX. cxvi. (1495) 920 One symply is one that may not be departyd in dede though he may be departyd atweyne. *a* **1425** tr. *Arderne's Treat. Fistula*, etc. 25 Eueriche of þise medicynes symply by hymself..stauncheþ wele blode. *c* **1440** *Gesta Rom.* lii. 231 (Harl. MS.), Yf eny thinge be yevin to two simplely, and that on be take or dede, al is in the powr of him or hir that is present. **1559** MORWYNG *Evonym.* 188 Smellinge waters as we call them simplely. **1598** SHAKS. *Merry W.* III. ii. 78 If he take her, let him take her simply: the wealth I haue waits on my consent. **1610** HEALEY *St. Aug. Citie of God* XVI. xxviii. (1620) 569 His body was not simply dead, but respectiuely. **1616** T. ADAMS *Pract. Wks.* (1862) III. 11 Abstractively and simply understood, it is an exceeding excellent member. **1695** LD. PRESTON *Boeth.* IV. 168 But that they have any Being, purely and simply, I deny.

**b.** Merely, only. Freq. in phr. ***simply and solely***. †Also ***all simply***.

*c* **1400** MAUNDEV. (Roxb.) xxxii. 144 þai..sweres nane athes for nathing, bot symply saise it es or it es noȝt. *c* **1430** *Pilgr. Lyf Manhode* I. xcix. (1869) 53 In the time that j made the scrippe, it sufficed al sympilliche to leeue in god perfytliche. **1561** DAUS tr. *Bullinger on Apoc.* (1573) 134 b, Therfore sayth he not simplely that there shall be no more tyme: but addeth [etc.]. **1650** T. HOBBES *De Corpore Pol.* 190 Now in those Laws which are simply Laws, the Commandement is addressed to every man. **1682** NORRIS *Hierocles* 57 For the Law does not punish Man simply, as Man, but as Evil. **1762** HUME *Hist. Eng.* (1806) IV. lxiv. 768 He ordered that such of the prisoners as should simply promise to obey the laws for the future should be set at liberty. **1787** BENTHAM *Def. Usury* ii. 9 The penal law must depend upon the simply prohibitive. **1836** J. GILBERT *Chr. Atonem.* iii. (1852) 66 It is simply a question of degrees. **1855** MACAULAY *Hist. Eng.* xx. IV. 387 The highest praise due to the royalist..was simply that he was not a traitor. **1872** C. S. CALVERLEY *Fly Leaves* 111 All least furlable things got 'furled'..simply and solely to rhyme with 'world'. **1879** MᶜCARTHY *Own Times* II. xix. 53 These men simply followed their judgment and their conscience. **1920** *Act 10 & 11 Geo. V* c. 48 Sched. II. 314 Any loss or damage due simply and solely to the existence of a state of war. **1940** *Daily Tel.* 15 Feb. 6/1 What has been done is simply and solely to adjust our domestic legislation to the pressing requirements of a particular occasion.

†**c.** Unconditionally. *Obs. rare.*

**1523** LD. BERNERS *Froiss.* I. xxvi. 38 They of the cite wolde nat yelde them vp symply, for alwaies they thought to be rescued. *a* **1548** HALL *Chron., Hen. VI*, 104 The Frenchmen fled into the Castle and there continued five daies, at the ende wherof thei rendered themselfes symply.

**d.** Without exception; absolutely.

Common in recent use as an intensive.

**1590** SHAKS. *Mids. N.* IV. ii. 9 Hee hath simply the best wit of any handycraft man in Athens. **1600** HOLLAND *Livy* XXIX. xxxiv. 735 b, Hee levied..the Numidians especially, the best horsemen simplie in all Affricke. **1621** BURTON *Anat. Mel.* I. ii. II. iv, Other Retentions and Evacuations there are, not simply necessary, but at some times. **1856** KINGSLEY *Lett.* (1878) I. 475 Your general political economy is simply undeniable. **1888** STOKES *Celtic Ch.* 176 The plates are simply magnificent. **1893** EARL DUNMORE *Pamirs* I. 247 The spot where we camped was simply too lovely for words.

**7.** *Math.* ***simply connected***: (of a surface or other continuous set of points) connected in such a way that every closed curve lying within it forms the boundary of some surface lying within it.

**1893** A. R. FORSYTH *Theory of Functions* xiv. 316 A simply connected surface is resolved by n cross-cuts into n + 1 distinct pieces, each simply connected [etc.]. **1939** M. H. A. NEWMAN *Elem. Topology Plane Sets of Points* vi. 135 The complement of a simply connected domain in the open plane may have any number of components. **1976** *Physics Bull.* Sept. 388/2 The torus is not simply connected but is otherwise a uniformly structured 2-manifold.

**'simpson**, *sb. slang.* [From the surname *Simpson*.] (See quot. 1874.) Hence **'simpson** *v.* and **'simpsonize** *v.*

**1871** *Echo* 13 Dec., It was found that the tank from which was drawn the water used in washing the cans, and, it may be, in 'Simpsonising' the milk, was in communication with a drain. **1874** *Slang Dict.* 291 *Simpson*, water used in the dilution of milk. Term in use among cowkeepers. From this the parish pump has been called Mrs. Simpson. **1901** *N. & Q.* 9th Ser. VII. 263 *To simpson*, to adulterate milk by adding water thereto, from a dairyman of this name who in the sixties was prosecuted on this account.

**simpsonite** ('sɪmpsənaɪt). *Min.* [f. the name of E. S. *Simpson* (1875–1939), Australian mineralogist + -ITE¹.] An oxide essentially of aluminium and tantalum, approximately $Al_4Ta_3O_{13}(F,OH)$, found as colourless hexagonal crystals externally altered to a dull cream.

**1939** H. BOWLEY in *Jrnl. R. Soc. W. Australia* XXV. 89 This was sufficient to indicate that it was a mineral not previously recorded so it was decided to give it the name Simpsonite in honour of Dr. E. S. Simpson.., who..has made many outstanding contributions to our knowledge of Western Australian minerals, particularly..tantalum-bearing minerals. **1959** *Mineral. Abstr.* XIV. 274/1 Simpsonite is found in a pegmatite vein near Leshai in the northern part of Kola peninsula. **1964** *Doklady Acad. Sci. U.S.S.R.: Earth Sci. Sect.* CXLVII. 147 The crystal structure of simpsonite is close-packed and has seven octahedra as its repeat distance.

**Simpson's rule** ('sɪmpsən). *Math.* [Named after Thomas *Simpson* (1710–61), English mathematician, who proposed the rule in 1743 (*Math. Dissertations* 109).] An arithmetical rule for estimating the area under a curve where the values of an odd number of ordinates, including those at the limits, are known: the approximate area is given by the sum of the first and last ordinates, double all the other odd ordinates, and quadruple all the even ordinates, multiplied by one third of the distance between adjacent ordinates. Also applied to other analogous rules (see quot. 1909).

**1875** B. WILLIAMSON *Integral Calculus* vii. 196 This and the preceding are commonly called 'Simpson's rules' for calculating areas; they were however previously noticed by Newton. **1909** *Cent. Dict.* Suppl. 1158/2 *Simpson's rules*... In *Simpson's first rule* the number of ordinates is odd... *Simpson's second rule*. In this rule the area is divided into groups of three intervals... *Simpson's 5-8 rule* is used for obtaining the area of a curve between the first pair of three equally-spaced ordinates. **1930** [see RUNGE-KUTTA]. **1933** L. M. MILNE-THOMSON *Calculus of Finite Differences* vii. 197 Show that Simpson's rule is tantamount to considering the curve between two consecutive odd ordinates as parabolic. **1980** [see RUNGE-KUTTA].

**simptom(e**, obs. forms of SYMPTOM.

‖**simpulum** (ˈsɪmpjʊləm). Pl. simpula (ˈsɪmpjʊlə). [L.] *Rom. Antiq.* A small ladle, used for dipping out wine for libations.

**1745** POCOCKE *Descr. East* II. ii. 249 An altar, with two reliefs on it, one being a person holding a simpulum. **1756** J. KENNEDY *Curiosities of Wilton Ho.* (1786) 116 She holds in her Right-Hand a Simpulum. **1858** BIRCH *Anc. Pottery* II. 315 The vases used in sacrifices were principally of earthenware, and comprised the simpulum [etc.].

**simpy** (ˈsɪmpɪ), *a. U.S. colloq.* [Perh. f. SIMP + -Y[1].] Foolish, dull-witted, simple-minded.

**1942** BERREY & VAN DEN BARK *Amer. Thes. Slang* §151/9 Foolish; silly;..*simpy*. **1946** MEZZROW & WOLFE *Really Blues* ix. 139 Some hammy clowning up on the bandstand to tickle the simpy customers. **1976** *Washington Post* 24 Oct. B7/1 The usual questions—Who is your favorite author? Who in the world would you most like to dine with?—seem out of place at the presidential level. They are, in a word, too simpy.

**sim-sim** (ˈsɪmsɪm). Also simsin. [Arab.: see SESAME.] = SESAME. Also *attrib.*

**1917** *Chambers's Jrnl.* May 294/1 Sesamum-seed, also known as..sim-sim,..is the product of an annual plant. **1930** C. G. SELIGMAN *Races Afr.* vii. 170 He smears the rain-stone with simsin oil. **1960** *Guardian* 25 Apr. 4/4 Meat and vegetables are fried in groundnut or sim-sim oil. **1972** Y. LOVELOCK *Veg. Bk.* III. 352 Sesame, also known variously as simsim, gingelly, beniseed and til, is grown in Africa, Asia, South and Central America, for the sake of its seeds, which are used to express an oil used on salads and in cooking.

**simson** (ˈsɪmsən). *dial.* Also 7 simpson. [Alteration of *sinchon, sinsion* SENCION.] The plant groundsel.

**1674** RAY *S. & E. Co. Words* 77 *Simpson*, Groundsell, *senecio*, Ess. Suff. **1777** JACOB *Catal. Plants* 105 *Senecio vulgaris*, Common Groundsel, or Simson. **1823** E. MOOR *Suffolk Words* 350 *Simson*, the common name of the groundsel—the *senesio vulgaris*. *a* **1825** FORBY *Voc. E. Anglia* s.v. *Sencion*.

**sim subtle, suttle**: see SIM[1].

**simul** (ˈsɪməl). *Chess.* [f. SIMUL(TANEOUS *a.* 1 c.] A display in which one player plays simultaneously against a number of opponents at a number of games of chess.

**1969** A. GLYN *Dragon Variation* iv. 89 He's playing twenty-four of us at once. It's a simul, simultaneous display. **1973** *Daily Tel.* 27 Jan. 11/4 Up to quite recently 'simuls' were considered very small beer by some players. **1974** SAIDY & LESSING *World of Chess* i. 26/1 (*caption*) Senior Master Edman Mednis conducts a 'simul' exhibition.

**simulacral** (sɪmjʊˈleɪkrəl), *a. rare.* [f. SIMULACRE + -AL[1].] Resembling an image.

**1875** DRAPER *Confl. Relig. & Sci.* (1876) v. 123 Their anthropomorphic notions of the nature of God and the simulachral form of the spirit of man. **1957** *Psychol. Rev.* LXIV. 126/1 We have long since given up simulacral theories of representation.

**simulacre** (ˈsɪmjʊleɪkə(r)). Forms: 4–5 **symyl-, similacre** (5 **-achre, semylacre**); 4–5, 7 **symulacre** (5 **semulacre, symolachre**), 6–7, 9 **simulachre** (6 **-acher**), 4, 7– **simulacre**. [a. OF. *simulacre* (= Catal. *simulacre*, Prov. *simulacra*, Sp., Pg., It. *simulacro*), ad. L. *simulacrum*: see SIMULACRUM.]

**1.** An image (of a god, etc.) to which honour or worship is rendered.

*c* **1375** *Sc. Leg. Saints* vi. (*Thomas*) 653, I þe commawnd, ful fend, þat þare-In is dwelland, þat þu þat semulacre brake. **1382** WYCLIF *1 John* v. 21 Litil sones, kepe ȝe fro simulacris. *c* **1400** MAUNDEV. (Roxb.) xviii. 82 Simulacres er ymages made to þe liknes of sum thing þat es kyndely; and ydoles er ymages made to þe liknes of what thing a man will þat es noȝt kyndely. **1485** CAXTON *Chas. Gt.* 206 Alle thydolles and other symylacres that he fonde, he dyd do destroye. **1531** ELYOT *Gov.* I. viii, Phidias..made of yuory the simulachre or image of Jupiter, honoured by the gentiles. **1577** HELLOWES *Gueuara's Chron.* 300 Albinius did sweare by the simulachre of Diana, not once, but thrice. **1613** *Treas. Anc. Mod. Times* I. 765/2 Infamous Dæmons possessed themselues of these Statues and Symulacres. **1800** W. TAYLOR in *Monthly Mag.* VIII. 598 Distributions have been made..of engraved and waxen simulacres of saints, with the view..of introducing..a taste for image-worship, and a love of holy idolatry. **1851** MADDEN *Shrines & Sepulchres* I. 45 As temples had their origin in tombs, so idols had theirs in the simulacres of deceased men.

**2.** An image, a material or mental representation, *of* a person or thing.

**1483** CAXTON *Gold. Leg.* 66 b/1 Whan the messagers cam they fonde a symylacre or an ymage in his bedde. **1590** FENNE *Frutes* 12 When Perdicas had espied the sumptuous simulachre of dead Alexander. **1658** *Bergerac's Satirical Charac.* xvii. 71 In fine, Simulacre of envy, leave your biting. **1830** JAMES *Darnley* (1846) 160 A knight, in whom Sir Osborne might easily distinguish the simulacre of himself. **1863** HAWTHORNE *Our Old Home* (1883) I. 306 Give the emotions that cluster about it,..and you get something like a simulachre of the object in the midst of them. **1871** FREEMAN in W. R. W. Stephens *Life* (1895) II. 17, I..sang 'Salve mundi Domine' before the simulacre of Fred. B.

Hence **ˈsimulacrize** *v. intr.*, to pretend.

**1845** S. JUDD *Margaret* II. ii, 'Are you sincere?' she asked. 'Are you not simulacrizing?'

‖**simulacrum** (sɪmjʊˈleɪkrəm). Pl. simulacra (7 -achra), and -acrums. [L., f. *simulāre* to make like, to SIMULATE. See also SIMULACRE.]

**1.** A material image, made as a representation of some deity, person, or thing.

**1599** SANDYS *Europæ Spec.* (1632) 229 The Heathen them-selves call them every where the *Effigies* and *Simulachra* of other. **1833** LYTTON *Godolphin* xxvi. 52 The far-famed simulacrum (the image of Cybele) which fell from Heaven. **1869** *Pall Mall G.* 13 Oct. 11 The dead-alive gape, stare, and hue of the lumpish simulacrums of a wax show. **1887** B. V. HEAD *Hist. Numorum* 634 The mountain is flanked by two tall conical simulacra, with radiate summits.

**2.** Something having merely the form or appearance of a certain thing, without possessing its substance or proper qualities.

**1805** *Edin. Rev.* VII. 183 Does he mean..films, shadows, or *simulacra* proceeding from real external existences. **1840** CARLYLE *Heroes* (1858) 268 An ambitious charlatan, perversity and simulacrum. *Ibid.* 280 It behoved men to quit simulacra and return to fact. **1861** THACKERAY *Four Georges* iv. (1862) 184 Nothing but a coat, and a wig, and a mask smiling below it—nothing but a great simulacrum. **1881** *Contemp. Rev.* Feb. 235 The true succession lies with those who carry the principles of the master to a more fruitful development, and not with those who embalm them as..sacred but sterile simulacra.

**b.** A mere image, a specious imitation or likeness, *of* something.

**1833** *Edin. Rev.* LVII. 334 Some spirit of life breathed into their simulacrum of a faith. **1856** RUSKIN *Mod. Painters* IV. v. xix. §6 Nightly we lay down our gold, to fashion forth simulacra of peasants, in gay ribands and white bodices. **1858** CARLYLE *Fredk. Gt.* VII. vi. (1872) II. 302 He is become a mere enchanted simulacrum of a Duke. **1877** BLACK *Green Past.* xli, A vehicle..that appeared to be the mere simulacrum of a vehicle.

**ˈsimulance.** *rare*[−1]. [Cf. SIMULANT *a.* and -ANCE.] = SIMULATION 2.

**1885** D. WILSON *Anthropology* 7 (Stand.), Man embodies an..immortal spiritual principle..which makes the resemblance of the apes to him but a mocking simulance.

**simuland** (ˈsɪmjʊlænd). [f. L. *simuland-um*, gerundive of *simulāre* SIMULATE *v.*: cf. -AND[2].] That which is simulated by a (mathematical or computer) model.

**1968** R. D. BRENNAN in J. McLeod *Simulation* i. 6/2 There should be a one-to-one correspondence between the mathematical equations and the functions of the elements of the simuland on the one hand, and between the equations and the components or algorithms of the computer on the other. **1972** G. A. MIHRAM *Simulation* v. 222 The goal is to structure entities and events that are as nearly isomorphic as possible to the elements and transformations which exist in the simuland.

**simulant** (ˈsɪmjʊlənt), *a.* and *sb.* [ad. L. *simulant-em*, pres. pple. of *simulāre* to SIMULATE.]

**A.** *adj.* Simulating; presenting the appearance *of* something else.

**1826** KIRBY & SP. *Entomol.* IV. xlvi. 348 *Simulant*,.. when the mesothorax is covered by the prothorax, and the Metathorax only is visible, under the form of an elongated or enlarged scutellum. **1891** *Cent. Dict.* s.v., A good many parts and organs..are thus simulant of others from which they are morphologically different.

**B.** *sb.* One who, or that which, simulates something else.

**1860** W. H. RUSSELL *Diary India* I. 103 These are, indeed, solemn processions, which not even youth and beauty, or their simulants, can make gay. **1979** MILLS & MANSFIELD *Genuine Article* vii. 110 The studio audience were challenged to tell the difference between a genuine diamond and an imitation. A tray of simulants containing a genuine diamond..was produced. **1979** *Nature* 6 Dec. 655/3 Yttrium aluminium garnet (YAG) and cubic zirconia are both used as diamond simulants.

**simular** (ˈsɪmjʊlə(r)), *sb.* and *a.* [irreg. f. L. *simul-āre* to simulate + -AR, perh. suggested by SIMILAR *a.*]

Some examples (in the 17th and 18th cents.) of *simular*, *simularity*, *simularly*, in the sense of *similar*, etc., are app. mere misprints or individual errors.

**A.** *sb.* One who, or that which, simulates, or puts on a false appearance (*of* something).

**1526** TINDALE *Prol. Romans* a ij b, Christ..rebuketh the Phareses.., and calleth them ypocrites, that is to saye Simulars. **1605** SHAKS. *Lear* III. ii. 54 Hide thee, thou Bloudy hand; Thou Periur'd, and thou Simular [*Qq.* simular man] of Vertue: That art Incestuous. **1791** COWPER *Odyss.* XIII. 95 His eye-lids, soon, sleep, falling as a dew, Closed fast, death's simular, in sight the same. **1809** MALKIN *Gil Blas* VI. i. ¶13 Telling us how this simular of a Catholic is more than ever wedded to his Jewish customs and ceremonies.

**B.** *adj.* Simulated, pretended, counterfeited. Also, simulative *of* something.

**1611** SHAKS. *Cymb.* V. v. 200, I return'd with simular proofe enough, To make the Noble Leonatus mad. **1847** EMERSON *Poems* Wks. (Bohn) I. 439 As in the old poetic fame The gods are blind and lame, And the simular despite Betrays the more abounding might. *a* **1859** DE QUINCEY *Posth. Wks.* (1893) II. 247 That auburn wig which was presumed by its wearer to be simular of native curls.

**simulate** (ˈsɪmjʊlət), *ppl. a.* Also 5 **similate**, 6 **symulate**; 5 **similat**, 6–7 *Sc.* **simulat**. [ad. L. *simulāt-us*, pa. pple. of *simulāre*: see next.] = SIMULATED *ppl. a.*

**1435** MISYN *Fire of Love* 4 Deuocion not holy bot similate. **1447** BOKENHAM *Seyntys* (Roxb.) 29, I wyl not tellyn..what accyoun he feynyd,..and how and be what similat facyoun Meche peple to hys favour he dreu. **1550** BALE *English Votaries* II. Pref., The sodometrouse vowe of their symulate chastyte. **1581** MARBECK *Bk. of Notes* 450 By their fained simplicitie and simulate holinesse. **1671** [? R. MACWARD] *Case Accomod. Exam.* 75 He can not prevail by his simulat condescendencies. *a* **1676** BP. GUTHRIE *Mem.* (1702) 102 The simulat division betwixt the two Marquesses of Hamilton and Argile. **1804** J. GRAHAME *Sabbath* 622 'Tis war alone that never violates The hallow'd day by simulate respect. **1845** JANE ROBINSON *Whitehall* xix. 133 Imprisoned in all that simulate magnificence.

**simulate** (ˈsɪmjʊleɪt), *v.* Also 7 **similate**. [f. L. *simulāt-*, ppl. stem of *simulāre* to make like, imitate, counterfeit, etc., f. *similis* like.]

**1. a.** *trans.* To assume falsely the appearance or signs of (anything); to feign, pretend, counterfeit, imitate; to profess or suggest (anything) falsely.

**1652** GAULE *Magastrom.* 267 This magicall sorcerer simulated the Christian faith, and was baptized. *a* **1661** FULLER *Worthies, Berkshire* I. (1662) 112 The Royalists were at night fain to hang lighted matches on the Hedges, (so to similate their aboad thereabouts) whilst they drew of. **1735** THOMSON *Liberty* III. 485 What tho' the first smooth Cæsars arts caress'd, Merit, and virtue, simulating Me? **1791** BOSWELL *Johnson* an. 1752, To suppose that Johnson's fondness for her was *dissembled* (meaning simulated or assumed). **1835** ARNOLD in *Life & Corr.* (1844) I. 407 A government..in word and action simulating reform. **1849** MACAULAY *Hist. Eng.* x. II. 610 He did not think it worth his while to simulate regret for his past errors. **1874** L. STEPHEN *Hours Libr.* (1892) I. i. 9 These..show the pleasure which he took in simulating truth.

**b.** To have the external features of, to present a strong resemblance to (something).

*a* **1661** FULLER *Worthies* (1840) III. 204 If it [a vault] be merely natural, it doth curiously imitate art; if purely artificial it doth most lively simulate nature. **1853** E. K. KANE *Grinnell Exped.* xlv. (1856) 413 We passed the hills of Disco in review, with their terraced summits, simulating the Ghauts of Hindostan. **1874** M. COOKE *Fungi* 2 Yet there are some flowering plants, which, at first sight,..simulate cryptogams.

**c.** *Zool.* = MIMIC *v.* 5.

**1876** SPENCER *Princ. Sociol.* I. I. viii. 126 Many caterpillars, beetles, moths, butterflies, simulate the objects by which they are commonly surrounded.

**d.** To imitate the conditions or behaviour of (a situation or process) by means of a model, esp. for the purpose of study or of training; *spec.* to produce a computer model of (a process).

**1947** WILLIAMS & RITSON in *Jrnl. Inst. Electr. Engineers* XCIV. IIA. 123/2 If the control system contains discontinuous devices such as relays, these must be simulated by purely electronic means. **1958** GOTLIEB & HUME *High-Speed Data Processing* xiii. 258 A computer can simulate a warehouse, a factory, an oil refinery, or a river system, and if due regard is paid to detail the imitation can be very exact. **1966** *Guardian* 16 May 3/7 Games in which the situation before the 1914–18 war or the American Mexican war is simulated repeat the original situation with up to 70 per cent reliability. **1972** *Nature* 28 Apr. 462/1 Future population changes were simulated by computer.

†**2.** To convert *into* by simulation. *Obs.*[−1]

*a* **1658** HEWYTT *Serm.* 176 We must not similate good into evil, nor truth into falshood, by wicked words or works.

†**3.** To put forward deceptively. *Obs. rare*[−1].

**1652** GAULE *Magastrom.* 366 Whereupon Hilarion..was simulated for a witch or wizard, by the paganish party.

**4.** *intr.* To pretend or feign.

**1823** ROSCOE tr. *Sismondi's Lit. Eur.* (1846) II. xxxvi. 470 Doomed to suffer and smile and simulate.

Hence **ˈsimulating** *ppl. a.*

**1875** POSTE *Gaius* (ed. 2) Add. 669 The simulating disposition..was free from the supervening rules of the simulated disposition.

**ˈsimulated**, *ppl. a.* [f. prec. + -ED[1].]

**1. a.** Pretended, feigned, assumed.

**1622** MABBE tr. *Aleman's Guzman d'Alf.* II. 318 The simulated sanctitie of a wicked and counterfeit Rogue. **1664** H. MORE *Myst. Iniq.* 358 The Horns are simulated Vertues. **1810** BENTHAM *Packing* (1821) 171 The carelessness, real or simulated, of the Judge. **1849** MACAULAY *Hist. Eng.* i. I. 62 The Puritans..prayed, and with no simulated fervour, that she might be kept from the dagger of the assassin. **1878** BROWNING *Poets Croisic* 64 Our simulated thunder-claps which tell us counterfeited truths.

**b.** Imitative of particular conditions or circumstances, usu. for purposes of experiment or training.

**1966** *Word Study* Dec. 3/1 Three-year training in simulated space flight. **1971** *Sci. Amer.* Oct. 44/2 For the purposes of the test four specially trained subjects..spent 25 consecutive days in one of the Institute's high-pressure chambers being exposed to simulated extreme depths. **1978** *Times* 4 Feb. 12/6, I was strapped into a rocket for a simulated flight through space..a ride..not so exhilarating as the old rollercoaster.

**2.** Of materials, artefacts, etc.: manufactured in imitation of other (usu. more expensive) materials or goods.

**1942** *Amer. Speech* XVII. 120 In the trade it is practically impossible to find plain words for *small*, *artificial*, and *second grade*... *Artificial* and *imitation* appear as *simulated*. **1948** H. LAWRENCE *Death of Doll* ii. 40 'A double strand of pink pearls—' 'Simulated,' said Poke. 'Phony,' agreed Moke. **1960** *Harper's Bazaar* July 67/1 Eyelash curlers in simulated gold. **1973** *Country Life* 17 May (Suppl.) 80b, A set of 8 Regency Period Simulated Rosewood Dining Chairs.

† **'simulately**, *adv. Obs.* In 6–7 simulatlie, 7 -ly. [f. SIMULATE *ppl. a.* + -LY².] Deceitfully, by or with pretence.

**1592** *Sc. Acts, Jas. VI* (1814) III. 575/1 Vnder pretens and cullour of..giftis of þair escheattis simulatlie purchest. **1629** *Reg. Privy Counc. Scot.* Ser. II. III. 197 Of the whilks arreistments the most pairt ar simulatlie and fraudulentlie made. **1654** VILVAIN *Epit. Ess.* ii. 83 Job..seriously (not simulatly) wished he had never been born. *a* **1657** SIR J. BALFOUR *Ann. Scot.* (1825) II. 29 He confessed (simulatly..) to liberat the King of suche grossnes.

**simulation** (sɪmjʊ'leɪʃən). Forms: 4–5 simil-, symylacioun (5 -acioune, -acion), 7 similation; 5–6 symulacion, -acyon (5 -acioun), 4–6 simulacion, 6– simulation. [a. OF. *simulacion*, *-ation* (= Prov. and Sp. *simulacion*, It. *simulazione*), ad. L. *simulātiōn-em*, noun of action f. *simulāre* to SIMULATE.]

**1. a.** The action or practice of simulating, with intent to deceive; false pretence, deceitful profession.

**1340** *Ayenb.* 23 And þerof wexeþ uele zennes, ase ariȝthalf; þet is to wytene: lozengerie, simulacion. *c* **1400** *Rom. Rose* 7230 He nys no full good champioun That dredith such similacioun. **1412–20** LYDG. *Chron. Troy* IV. 4504 Amonge hem silfe to bringe in tresoun, Feyned troupe and symulacioun. **1542** UDALL *Erasm. Apoph.* 170 He..did with mutual simulacion on his partie cover & kepe secrete the colorable dooyng of the saied feloe. **1577** tr. *Bullinger's Decades* (1592) 319 This precept doth commaunde vs..that ..wee doe our neighbor harme..neither by simulation nor dissimulation. **1611** SPEED *Hist. Gt. Brit.* VI. (1632) 114 His nature relishing too much of the Punick craft and simulation. **1692** SOUTH *Serm.* (1697) I. 525 A Deceiving by Actions, Gestures, or Behaviour, is called Simulation, or Hypocrisie. **1711** STEELE *Tatler* No. 213 ¶1 Simulation is a Pretence of what is not, and Dissimulation a Concealment of what is. **1788** WESLEY *Wks.* (1872) VII. 43 Simulation is the seeming to be what we are not; dissimulation, the seeming not to be what we are. **1836** LANDOR *Pericles & Aspasia* Wks. 1846 II. 379, I wish he were as pious as you are: occasionally he appears so. I attacked him on his simulation. **1872** SHIPLEY *Gloss. Eccl. Terms* 71 Fraud.., whether it consists in simulation or dissimulation.

**b.** Tendency to assume a form resembling that of something else; unconscious imitation.

**1870** MARCH *Anglo-Saxon Gram.* 28 *Simulation.* The feigning a connection with words of similar sound is an important fact in English and other modern languages: asparagus > sparrow-grass.

**2.** A false assumption or display, a surface resemblance or imitation, *of* something.

*c* **1380** WYCLIF *Wks.* (1880) 392 For als miche as it is done by symylacion of holynes, þe whiche is double wickidnes. **1471** CAXTON *Recuyell* (Sommer) II. 650 How Anthenor and Eneas..dyde hit vnder symylacion of peas. **1532** MORE *Confut. Tindale* Wks. 357/2 Woulde God they would ones rather folow him truely in faith & good workes, then in simulacion of like santytie. *a* **1667** COWLEY *Ess., Liberty*, So by the artificial simulation of some virtues, he made a shift to ensnare some honest..persons. **1873** MIVART *Elem. Anat.* 12 A solid partition or simulation of a notochord. **1876** MISS BRADDON *J. Haggard's Dau.* I. 74 Miserly as the arrangements of the household were, it was kept up with a faint simulation of a gentleman's establishment.

**3.** The technique of imitating the behaviour of some situation or process (whether economic, military, mechanical, etc.) by means of a suitably analogous situation or apparatus, esp. for the purpose of study or personnel training. Freq. *attrib.*

**1947** *Jrnl. Inst. Electr. Engineers* XCIV. IIA. 117/1 The ensuing sections will..describe the simulations of the separate [servo] units. **1958** *Business Week* 29 Nov. 76/3 Men began to raise questions..about their models of the real world. They did this by inventing games such as chess and checkers to simulate battle, games like back-gammon and Parcheesi to simulate racing. H. J. R. Murray, in his History of Board Games (Oxford, 1952), finds that such simulation games go back to the beginning of recorded history and are found in every culture. **1966** A. BATTERSBY *Math. in Managem.* vii. 159 Simulation enables a manager to study the system which he controls by imitating or 'simulating' its behaviour. **1972** *Computers & Humanities* VII. 38 The application of computer simulation techniques to the modeling of archaeological situations is one of the newest developments in computer use in archaeology. **1978** *Nature* 28 Sept. 305/1 Simulation studies on the towing of unprotected icebergs to southern continents suggest that the towing distance, ocean currents and the iceberg deterioration rate are of major importance.

**simulative** ('sɪmjʊlətɪv), *a.* Also 5 -tyue. [f. L. stem *simulāt-*: see SIMULATE *v.* and -IVE. Cf. med.L. *simulātīvē* adv.] Characterized by simulation or pretence.

**1490** CAXTON *Eneydos* xxi. 77, I do not somone hym for taccomplysshe his promyse simulatyue of the mariage of vs two. **1840** G. S. FABER *Prim. Doctr. Regen.* 296 If the Adult ..returned an insincere and simulative Answer: then..he would fail of being inwardly regenerated. **1851** —— *Many Mansions* 248 The simulative phantom of the particular individuals. **1875** POSTE *Gaius* (ed. 2) 666 The formal dispositions of Roman jurisprudence were frequently simulative.

Hence **'simulatively** *adv.*

**1816** G. S. FABER *Orig. Pagan Idol.* III. 396 Truly beginning with Nimrod, though simulatively..with Noah. **1851** —— *Many Mansions* 201 Evil will be mingled with good, the simulatively holy with the truly holy.

**simulator** ('sɪmjʊleɪtə(r)). [ad. L. *simulātor* a copier, a feigner, agent-noun from *simulāre* to SIMULATE. Cf. F. *simulateur*, Sp. and Pg. *simulador*, It. *simulatore*.]

**1.** One who practises simulation.

**1835** *Fraser's Mag.* XI. 343 Churchmen and women are of necessity simulators. **1843** GAVIN *Feigned & Fictitious Dis.* 30 That severe pain of the body will not influence some simulators to return to their duty, may be still farther evidenced. **1862** F. HALL *Hindu Philos. Syst.* 147 If a simulator..is outwardly courteous to his friends, but inwardly bears them malice, can he..be a doer of proper works?

**2. a.** A thing which simulates another.

**1899** *Allbutt's Syst. Med.* VIII. 687 Myoma and fibromyoma are also possible simulators [of keloid].

**b.** An apparatus designed to simulate the behaviour of a more complicated system; *esp.* one for training purposes that simulates the response of a vehicle, craft, or the like, having a similar set of controls and giving the illusion to the operator of responding like the real thing.

**1947** WILLIAMS & RITSON in *Jrnl. Inst. Electr. Engineers* XCIV. IIA. 112 The paper presents an outline of a method which will allow automatic control systems to be studied experimentally by means of an electronic apparatus called a 'simulator', which is constructed so as to have the same characteristic equation as the control system. **1950**, etc. [see *flight simulator* s.v. FLIGHT *sb.*¹ 15]. **1958** *Engineering* 21 Mar. 374/1 A colour print simulator will be demonstrated... The basis of the new equipment is a closed-circuit colour-television system, whose characteristics can be adjusted to match those of a desired printing system. **1967** *Guardian* 6 Mar. 12/2 The world's first locomotive simulator for driver training at the Willesden electric depot. **1970** *Daily Tel.* 16 Feb. 3/3 For the make-believe flight, Prince Philip and Young had climbed into a lunar-landing craft simulator. **1972** *Sci. Amer.* Apr. 106/3 Both mathematical and experimental demonstrations have established that the behavior of ethyl alcohol in the simulator closely approximates the behavior of propellants such as liquid hydrogen in full-scale, three-dimensional tanks that are subjected to comparable gravitational fields. **1980** P. ABLEMAN *Shoe-string's Finest Hour* i. 13 Motorways have never appealed to me. It's like driving in a simulator.

**c.** *Computers.* Also ***simulator program***. A program enabling a computer to execute programs written for a different computer.

**1960** GREGORY & VAN HORN *Automatic Data-Processing Systems* viii. 272 A simulator program is essentially a group of subroutines. *Ibid.*, A simulator is useful when changing from one computer to another. **1977** *Sci. Amer.* Sept. 153/1 Thus users of large computer systems and time-sharing services have access to cross-software assemblers, compilers and simulators (programs that enable a computer of one make or model to duplicate the actions of another). **1978** J. C. CLULEY *Programming for Mini-computers* ix. 216 In order to help tracing errors, the simulator program has many of the features of a minicomputer debugging program.

† **'simulatory**, *a. Obs. rare.* [See SIMULATE *v.* and -ORY.] Simulative.

**1618** *Hist. Perkin Warbeck* 35 These words were vttered.. with simulatory maiesty. **1623** BP. HALL *Contempl., O.T.* XIX. x, Jehoram wisely suspects this flight of the Syrians to be but simulatory and politick.

**simulcast** ('sɪməlkɑːst, -æ-), *v.* orig. *U.S.* [f. SIMUL(TANEOUS *a.* + BROADCAST *v.* 3.] *trans.* To broadcast (a programme) simultaneously on radio and television. Also, to transmit (a television programme) on two or more channels or networks at the same time. Also *absol.*

**1948** *Amer. N. & Q.* May 26/2 *To simulcast*, to broadcast by radio and television simultaneously. **1948** *N.Y. Herald Tribune* 15 June 16/6 A press agent at WCAU-TV in Philadelphia has rather timorously launched the verb 'simulcast' into the uneasy seas of the English language. **1951** *Time* 16 July 58/2 Allen alone of the top announcers 'simulcasts'—broadcasts games simultaneously for both radio and TV. **1977** *Globe & Mail* (Toronto) 8 Jan. 34/3 It used to be they'd play at different times than on the U.S. stations, but not any more. Today the Canadian stations simulcast them as much as possible.

Hence as *sb.*, a programme transmitted simultaneously by radio and television; **'simulcasting** *vbl. sb.*

**1949** *Richmond* (Va.) *News Leader* 30 Aug. 12/1 NBC has announced that it will go in for simulcasting in a big way starting this Fall. **1964** M. MCLUHAN *Understanding Media* xxxi. 311 In a group of simulcasts of several media done in Toronto a few years back, TV did a strange flip. **1976** *Broadcast* 29 Nov. 6/2 A performance of Benjamin Britten's Cantata for St Nicholas..will be networked..by both the ITV companies and ILR, making it the first nationwide stereo simulcast link-up. **1977** *Ibid.* 28 Mar. 15/3 No simulcasting of PPBs (except during elections).

† **simule**, *v. Obs. rare.* Also 6 symule, simyll. [ad. F. *simuler* (14th cent.), or L. *simulāre* to SIMULATE.] *intr.* and *trans.* To simulate or feign.

*c* **1480** HENRYSON *Fables, Cock & Fox* vi, Dissimuland in to countenance and cheir, On kneis fell, and simuland thus he said. **1528** TINDALE *Obed. Chr. Man* 159 They..simyll discorde amonge them selves when they are most agreed. **1534** WHITINTON *Tullyes Offices* III. (1540) 140 An honest man shal neyther symule nor dissymule any thyng for thentent to bye better or to sell better.

Hence † **'simuled** *ppl. a.*, simulated. *Obs.*

**1526** *Pilgr. Perf.* (W. de W. 1531) 81 Than let us despyse this symuled & false obedyence. **1585** T. WASHINGTON tr. *Nicholay's Voy.* III. xviii. 104 b, His simuled holinesse.

† **'simuler.** *Obs.*⁻¹ [f. prec. + -ER¹.] A simulator, feigner.

**1534** WHITINTON *Tullyes Offices* I. (1540) 48 We haue herde say that Socrates was swete and ornate of speche in all comunycacion a symuler whome the grekes call irona.

**simulfix** ('sɪməlfɪks). *Gram.* [f. L. *simul* at the same time + *-fix* as in AFFIX *sb.*, PREFIX *sb.*, etc.] A formative element occurring as a modification of an element in the basic word or root (i.e. an intonation sequence or a stress pattern). So **ˌsimulfi'xation**, the action of affixing a simulfix; **'simulfixed** *a.*, of an element, employed as a simulfix.

**1954** *Word* X. 212 The term 'superfix' is no more apt than 'subfix', and (the bad Latin) 'simulfix' might be even better. **1956** *Language* XXXII. 454 The process of simulfixation may be represented by a pseudo-fractional formula.. + X/Y – (= simulfixed aspect marker/underlying root-initial). **1964** [see INCOMPLETIVE *a.* (*sb.*)]. **1965** *Language* XLI. 74 Chord structures may occur—tagmemes occurring simultaneously (tone replacives, simulfixes).

**simulium** (sɪ'mjʊlɪəm). [mod.L. (P. A. Latreille *Hist. Nat. Crustacés & Insectes* (1802) III. 426), f. L. *simul-āre* to imitate + *-ium*.] A small dark-coloured blood-sucking fly of the genus *Simulium*, which may be the vector of certain diseases. Also *collect.* Cf. *buffalo fly* s.v. BUFFALO *sb.* 5.

**1902** L. O. HOWARD *Insect Bk.* 120 Simulium larvae frequent well aerated and frequently swiftly running streams. **1914** G. D. H. CARPENTER *Jrnl.* 26 July in *Naturalist on Lake Victoria* (1920) iv. 80, I went down to the rocky shore before breakfast, and was set upon by a swarm of viciously biting *Simulium*. **1932** RILEY & JOHANNSEN *Med. Entom.* xviii. 292 The Simulium flies abound in hilly regions of swift-flowing, well-aerated water. **1955** *Times* 8 July 9/7 The disease [*sc.* river blindness]..is caused by the bite of the simulium fly. **1977** *Observer* (Colour Suppl.) 6 Mar. 47/1 The agile simulium can fly twice as far as was previously thought possible.

† **simultal**, *a. Obs.*⁻¹ [irreg. f. L. *simul* + -AL¹.] Simultaneous.

**1654** VILVAIN *Chronogr.* 16 Such a sudden simultal surreption of 10 or 12 dais, wil..beget much confusion.

**simultanagnosia** (ˌsɪməltənæg'nəʊsɪə). *Psychol.* [ad. G. *simultanagnosie* (I. Wolpert 1924, in *Zentralbl. f. d. Gesamte Neurol. u. Psychiatrie* XXXV. 445), f. G. *simultan* simultaneous + Gr. ἀγνωσία ignorance (cf. AGNOSIA).] The loss or absence of the ability to experience perceived elements, such as the details of a picture, as components of a whole.

The form *simultagnosia* appears to have arisen as a misprint (see quot. 1961); and afterwards to have been taken, on the basis of its supposed etymology, to be a term for the ability that is absent in simultanagnosia (see quot. 1970).

**1936** J. M. NIELSEN *Agnosia, Apraxia, Aphasia* vii. 84 Another term for miscellaneous classification is Simultanagnosia of Wolpert. This is not an agnosia but a psychological loss on a high plane. **1959** *Brain* LXXXII. 437 There may be gross incapacity to combine the elements of the perceptual display into a coherent and integrated whole. To this type of deficit the term 'simultanagnosia' is commonly applied. **1961** W. R. BRAIN *Speech Disorders* 173 The term simultagnosia [*ed.* 2, 1965: simultanagnosia] was coined by Wolpert to describe a condition in which the patient, looking at pictures which exhibited action, failed to recognize the meaning of the whole, while the details were correctly appreciated. **1964** M. CRITCHLEY *Developmental Dyslexia* ix. 58 He observed a veritable simultagnosia, that is, an inability to grasp a meaning of a picture as a whole. **1970** HINSIE & CAMPBELL *Psychiatric Dict.* (ed. 4) 701/2 *Simultagnosia*, inability to describe the action represented in a picture. *Ibid.* 702/1 Simultanagnosia is the lack of, or any disability in, such simultaneous form perception, and is suggestive of a lesion in the anterior part of the left occipital lobe.

**simultane** (sɪməl'teɪn), *v.* orig. *U.S.* [f. SIMULTANE(OUS *a.*] **a.** *trans.* and *intr.* To do (something) simultaneously with something else. **b.** *intr.* To occur or take place at the same time.

Used only by or with reference to 'Mark Twain'.

**1880** 'MARK TWAIN' *Lett. to Publishers* (1967) 127, I mean to have the 'Atlantic' people delay my articles here-after, so that I can 'simultane' with you. **1881** *Ibid.* 142 If they don't want it, *then* we'll go to the Century... I want to 'simultane' it with some grave enough London magazine. **1897** —— *Following Equator* lxvii. 668 They..did do them all, but only in turn, not simultaneously. In the nature of things they could not be made to simultane. **1979** *UCT Studies in English* (Univ. Cape Town) Sept. 77 The failure of Bliss to simultane and the pirating of the book by the Canadian, Belford, put a great deal of stress on the young relationship, which nevertheless withstood it.

**Simultaneism** (sɪməl'teɪnɪɪz(ə)m, -'eɪnɪz(ə)m). Also ‖Simultanéisme, Simultanism. [ad. F. *Simultanéisme*.] **1.** A name given to ORPHISM 2, because of its use of the principle of simultaneous contrast (SIMULTANEOUS *a.* 1 b) (see also quot. 1959).

**1915** [see ORPHISM 2]. **1940** R. H. WILENSKI *Mod. French Painters* 238 Delaunay produced a series of Flat-pattern pictures with brightly coloured fragments of revolving discs —a type of Futurist-Dynamism which he called *Simultanéisme* and which Apollinaire christened '*Orphism*'.

**1959** H. READ *Conc. Hist. Mod. Painting* iii. 94 [Delaunay] strove in particular to combine different aspects of figures and objects in the same painting. He himself gave the name of *Simultanéisme* to this kind of painting and was later to characterize it in these words: 'Nothing horizontal or vertical—light deforms everything, breaks everything up.' **1969** R. MAYER *Dict. Art Terms & Techniques* 273/1 The chief exponent of the style [*sc.* Orphism], Robert Delaunay (1885-1941), preferred the name Simultaneism.

**2.** A movement in modern French poetry, led by Henri-Martin Barzun (b. 1881), which aimed at the effect of simultaneity of both images and sounds.

**1959** *Oxf. Compan. French Lit.* 676/2 *Simultanéisme*, one of the more ephemeral movements in modern poetry, an exaggerated mixture of *Cubisme* and *Unanimisme*. **1964** *Listener* 27 Aug. 315/3 Simultanism..has so far defeated its exponents..because we are not willing to appraise words other than intellectually, which means in logical succession. **1970** C. CAMPOS in J. Cruickshank *French Lit. & its Background* xi. 153 'Simultanéisme' was to be more influential as a technique for gathering impressions about reality than as a means of expressing a broader experience.

Hence **simul'taneist**, a practitioner of Simultaneism; also as *adj.*, in the manner of Simultaneism. Also ‖ **simultanéiste, simultanist** *adjs.*

**1923** J. GORDON *Mod. French Painters* viii. 87 It is safer to throw most recent 'isms' out of the window... The..crop of Orphists, Futurists, Synchromists, Purists, Simultaneists, Dada-ists and so on, are as a rule irritating adjectives with no real meaning. **1930** *Times Educ. Suppl.* 3 May 197/2 A short introductory chapter on 'French Poetry after 1870' briefly describes the schools or coteries of the last few decades—the symbolists,..simultaneists, cubists, unanimists, and so forth. **1959** *Oxf. Compan. French Lit.* 219/2 His [*sc.* Divoire's] collections of *simultanéiste* verse include: La Malediction des enfants (1910). **1975** T. STOPPARD *Travesties* I. 59 Herr Tristan Tzara was the initiator of a performance..of simultanist verse.

**simultaneity** (sɪməltəˈniːɪtɪ). [f. next: see -ITY, and cf. F. *simultanéité* (1754), Sp. *-eidad*, Pg. *-eidade*.]

**1.** The quality or fact of being simultaneous; occurrence at the same time. Also *spec.* in *Art*, the simultaneous representation of several views of the same object.

**1652** N. CULVERWEL *Light of Nature* 118 There's no succession in God,..there's a compleat simultaneity in all his knowledge. **1798** A. F. M. WILLICH *Elem. Crit. Philos.* 46 All the predicates of time, simultaneity, succession, &c. ..belong to it [*sc.* a sensible object]. **1802–12** BENTHAM *Ration. Judic. Evid.* (1827) II. 546 By the supposition, this asserted simultaneity is false. **1855** GROVE *Corr. Phys. Forces* (ed. 3) 13 The actual priority of cause to effect has been doubted, and their simultaneity argued with much ability. **1893** BALL *Story of Sun* 35 We may..suppose that they [*sc.* observations] have been made with absolute simultaneity. **1957** *Encycl. Brit.* XVII. 64/2 Both the Cubists and the Italian Futurists used a device known as simultaneity—the practice of combining various parts of an object, or profiles of face and figure within a design concept. **1980** *Illustr. London News* Mar. 58/3 The Italian Futurists took up the notion of simultaneity in a relatively simple-minded way.

**2.** A simultaneous attack. *rare*$^{-1}$.

**1858** CARLYLE *Fredk. Gt.* XIX. vii. (1872) VIII. 230 He stands now elaborately divided into Three groups against those Three simultaneities.

**simultaneous** (sɪməlˈteɪnɪəs), *a.* [ad. L. type **simultāneus*, formed (prob. after *mōmentāneus*) on L. *simul* at the same time: cf. F. *simultané* (1740), Sp., Pg., and It. *simultaneo*.

Med.L. *simultāneus* is given by Du Cange only in the sense of 'simulated'. Blount (*Glossogr.* 1656), citing *simultaneous* from L'Estrange, wrongly associates it with L. *simultas*, and explains it as 'that is privily displeased or hates with dissembling countenance'. Phillips (1658), as usual, repeats the mistake in different words. Marvell in his *Def. Howe* (1678) refers to the word as 'an elegant term of *The Discourse*'s own production' (*Wks.*, ed. Grosart, IV. 199).]

**1. a.** Existing, happening, occurring, operating, etc., at the same time; coincident in time.

*a* **1660** HAMMOND *Wks.* (1683) IV. 570 All that we have need of..is only Gods concurrence, whether previous or simultaneous. **1677** OWEN *Justific.* ix. Wks. 1852 III. 213 There are they [faith and repentance] so frequently conjoined in the Scripture as one simultaneous duty. **1701** NORRIS *Ideal World* I. ii. 45 He [God]..compares both means and ends together in one simple simultaneous view. **1815** KIRBY & SP. *Entom.* (1818) I. 498 They are not moved to it by a simultaneous but by a successive impulse. **1849** MACAULAY *Hist. Eng.* ii. I. 267 It was proposed that there should be simultaneous insurrections in London..and at Newcastle. **1879** HARLAN *Eyesight* iii. 42 The simultaneous use of both eyes is called 'binocular vision'.

*transf.* **1896** HOWELLS *Impress. & Exper.* 39 The railroad and the telegraph have made the little place simultaneous with New York and London.

**b.** *simultaneous contrast*: the effect of mutual modification of two contiguous areas of colour.

**1848** M. CHEVREUL in T. Graham *Chem. Rep. & Mem.* v. 187, I will designate by the term *simultaneous contrast* the modification of colour and height of tone experienced by two differently coloured objects when seen simultaneously. **1890** [see BORDER-LINE 1]. **1961** G. MILLERSON *Technique Television Production* iii. 45 The final values of any surface will vary with..simultaneous contrast. **1977** *Jrnl. R. Soc. Arts* CXXV. 616/2 Equally clear from the painting in the Fitzwilliam is Titian's awareness of what has since become known as the law of simultaneous contrast: the interaction of forms at the edges, so that the tone and colour of each is intensified by reaction with the other.

**c.** In *Chess*, denoting a number of games played against a number of opponents simultaneously by one player. Also *absol.*

**1883** G. A. MACDONNELL *Chess Life-Pictures* II. 109 One of his strongest opponents in a simultaneous *sans voir* performance lost his game. **1938** P. W. SERGEANT *Championship Chess* ii. 34 Steinitz..gave a simultaneous display against twenty-two opponents at the New Vienna Chess Club. **1964** NABOKOV & SCAMMELL tr. *Nabokov's Defence* v. 77 An onlooker knowing nothing about simultaneous chess would be utterly baffled at the sight of these elderly men in black sitting gloomily behind boards that bristle thickly with curiously cut manikins, while a nimble..lad..walks lightly from table to table. **1974** SAIDY & LESSING *World of Chess* i. 24/1 The simultaneous exhibition places a premium on quick recognition of tactical threats, strong legs, and sheer physical endurance.

**d.** *Broadcasting.* (See quots.) Cf. S.B. s.v. S 4 a.

**1923** *Radio Times* 28 Sept. 2/3 Simultaneous broadcasting is a combination of ordinary and wireless telephony, whereby it becomes possible to broadcast at one or more stations a performance given at any other station in the country. **1971** *Gloss. Electrotechnical, Power Terms* (*B.S.I.*) III. iv. 6 *Simultaneous broadcast*, broadcast by a number of transmitters of the same programme at the same time.

**e.** Denoting a running oral translation of the spoken word or one skilled in this art, as ***simultaneous interpreter, translation, translator***, etc.

**1958** R. GLÉMET in A. H. Smith *Aspects of Translation* 120 With simultaneous interpretation..your 'intellection' of the speech need not be so thorough, but your response to words must be still quicker than before—the speaker speaks, and you are speaking too. **1965** M. SPARK *Mandelbaum Gate* vi. 187 Barbara turned the switch of her earphones to other simultaneous translations—French, Italian, then back to English. **1968** 'D. TORR' *Treason Line* 40 The simultaneous interpreters in their sound-proof boxes adjusting their earphones. **1971** *Guardian* 24 Mar. 3/5 The theatre, which only performs in Yiddish, has to have earphones with simultaneous translations for the audience. **1974** *Spartanburg* (S. Carolina) *Herald* 25 Apr. B 8/9 Simultaneous interpreters returned to their glass booths at the United Nations on Wednesday. **1977** M. T. BLOOM *13th Man* (1978) ii. 18 She's a simultaneous translator... Does a lot of work for the UN and international conferences.

**2.** *spec.* in *Math.*, as ***simultaneous equation, function, root***, etc. (see quots.).

**1816** BABBAGE in *Phil. Trans.* 183 There may be another second function of $\psi$ $(x, y)$, which..may for the sake of distinction be called the second simultaneous function relative to $x$ and $y$. **1842** COLENSO *Elem. Algebra* (ed. 3) §72 Simultaneous Equations of one Dimension... Equations of this kind,..to be satisfied by the same pair or pairs of values of $x$ and $y$, are called simultaneous equations. **1842** G. PEACOCK *Treat. Algebra* I. 232 Such pairs or sets of equations in which the same unknown symbols appear, which are assumed to possess the same values throughout, are called simultaneous equations. **1882** CAYLEY *Math. Papers* XII. (1897) 124 The summation extends to all the simultaneous roots $x'$, $y'$ of the equations $U = 0$, $V = 0$.

**simultaneously** (sɪməlˈteɪnɪəslɪ), *adv.* [f. prec. + -LY[2].]

**1.** At the same time; coincidently.

**1675** BAXTER *Cath. Theol.* I. I. 28 To make the same numerical act which is a Volition simultaneously to be no Volition. **1762** KAMES *Elem. Crit.* (1764) I. 127 Dissimilar emotions may succeed each other with rapidity, but they can-not exist simultaneously. *a* **1763** SHENSTONE *Ess., Writing & Bks.* lix, He introduces the deities of both acting simultaneously. **1816** BABBAGE in *Phil. Trans.* 192 If in the function $\psi(x, y)$ we put simultaneously $\alpha(x, y)$ for $x$, and $\beta(x, y)$ for $y$. **1860** TYNDALL *Glac.* I. ii. 22 An exclamation of surprise burst simultaneously from my companion and myself. **1880** HAUGHTON *Phys. Geogr.* v. 242 The actual banks are rarely, if ever, simultaneously visible.

**2.** By means of simultaneous equations.

**1816** PLAYFAIR *Nat. Phil.* II. 225 In this way all the elements of any of the planetary orbits may be determined simultaneously.

**simultaneousness** (sɪməlˈteɪnɪəsnɪs). [f. as prec. + -NESS.] The fact, state, or quality of being simultaneous.

**1784** tr. *Beckford's Vathek* 165 The ideas..flashing before his imagination, with the simultaneousness of lightning. **1817** COLERIDGE *Biogr. Lit.* xv. (1907) II. 18 The poet gives us the liveliest image of succession with the feeling of simultaneousness! **1861** LAMONT *Seasons w. Seahorses* v. 75 The simultaneousness with which they dive and reappear again is remarkable. **1890** *Spectator* 6 Sept., It is..the simultaneousness of the desire to migrate which makes the migration so gregarious.

†**simultation.** *Obs.* *rare*$^{-1}$. [irreg. f. L. *simultas*: see next.] Quarrelling.

**1605** G. POWEL *Refut. Epist. Puritan Papist* 43 They can hardly liue peaceably among themselues without simultation.

†**simulty**[1]. *Obs. rare.* [ad. L. *simultas*, f. *simul* together, at the same time. Cf. OF. *simulté*.] A quarrel or contention.

*a* **1637** B. JONSON *Timber* (1641) 113 Imbarking himselfe in the Factions of the Family: to inquire after domesticke simulties. **1679** F. P. CRESSY *Gen. Disc.* 131 Thus we see.. in what inveterate..simulties, dissensions, and Book-warres the Protestants of all kinds and sorts doe liue.

†**simulty**[2]. *Obs.*$^{-1}$ [irreg. f. L. *simul* + -TY.] Simultaneity.

**1677** GALE *Crt. Gentiles* III. I. 16 Some scholemen say, that in free wil there is a simultie of power to opposites but not a power of simultie, i.e. a power of embracing opposites at one and the same time.

**simum**, variant of SIMOOM.

‖**simurgh** (sɪˈmɜːg). Also simurg, simorg(h. [Pers. *simurgh*, f. Pahlavi *sin* (Av. *saēna*, Skr. *çyena*) eagle + *murgh* bird.] A monstrous bird of Persian legend, imagined as rational, having the power of speech, and of great age.

*α.* **1786** tr. *Beckford's Vathek* 89 Is the Simurgh coming to pluck out my eyes? *a* **1843** SOUTHEY *Comm.-pl. Bk.* Ser. II. (1849) 459 In the Bahar Danush the Simurgh is mentioned as a genus, not an individual. This is heresy, the unity of the Simurgh being expressed in all the books of canonical romance. **1886** P. ROBINSON *Teetotum Trees* 152 Some Brobdingnagian condor like the Simurg, with feathers that were large enough for oars—or the Roc itself.

*β.* **1801** SOUTHEY *Thalaba* VIII. xix, In Kaf the Simorg hath his dwelling place The all-knowing Bird of Ages. **1864** BAILEY *Festus* (ed. 7) 305 Simorgh, and rokh, and phœnix, comet-like, Which nested in the sun. *a* **1871** DE MORGAN *Budget Parad.* (1872) 329, I am an 'old bird',..a Simorg, an 'all-knowing Bird of Ages' in matters of cyclometry.

**sin** (sɪn), *sb.* Forms: *α.* 1 syn(n, 1–2 synne, 2–5 sunne (3 sune). *β.* 1–4 senne (4 zenne, 5 senn), 3 seonne (4 sene). *γ.* 2–7 sinne (3–4 sine), 4–6 synne (5 cynne, 5–6 syne), syn (6 synn), 4– sin (4 sinn). [OE. *syn(n*, for original **sunjō*, related to continental forms with extended stem, viz. OFris. *sende*, MDu. *sonde* (Du. *zonde*), OS. *sundea*, *sundia*, OHG. *sunt(e)a*, *sund(e)a* (G. *sünde*), ON. *synð*, *synd* (Icel., Norw., Sw., Da. *synd*). The stem may be related to that of L. *sons, sont-is* guilty. In OE. there are examples of the original general sense, 'offence, wrong-doing, misdeed'.]

**1. a.** An act which is regarded as a transgression of the divine law and an offence against God; a violation (esp. wilful or deliberate) of some religious or moral principle.

The expression *for my sins* (see quot. 1842) is freq. employed in a trivial or jocular way. For *the seven deadly sins* see DEADLY *a.* 5.

*α.* *c* **825** *Vesp. Psalter* cviii. 14 Syn modur his ne sie adilʒad. *c* **888** K. ÆLFRED *Boeth.* xxxiv. §3 þæt is swiðe dyslic & swiðe micel syn þæt mon þæs wenan scyle be Gode. **971** *Blickl. Hom.* 25 Ure dæghwamlican synna þe we wið Godes willan ʒeworht habbaþ. *Ibid.* 63 Maniʒe men wenaþ þæt morþor sy seo mæste synne. *c* **1100** *O.E. Chron.* (MS. D) an. 1066, þa Frencyscan ahton wælstowe ʒeweald, eall swa heom God uðe for folces synnon. *a* **1122** *Ibid.* (Laud MS.) an. 1086, Se ælmihtiʒa God..do him his synna forʒifenesse. *c* **1175** *Lamb. Hom.* 35 Vfel is þet mon..nule him biþenchen þet his sunnen waxað. **12..** *Prayer our Lady* 31 in *O.E. Misc.* 193 Ich habbe..wel feole sunne ido þe me ofþincheð nuðe. *a* **1250** *Owl & Night.* 1395 Ne beoþ noht ones alle sunne, Vor þan hi beoþ tweire ikunne. *c* **1300** *Harrow. Hell* 12 (Digby MS.), In helle was..Dauit þe prophete and abraham, For þe sunnes of adam. **1362** LANGL. *P. Pl.* A. XI. 69 Heore seed for þat sunne þe same wo drien.

*β.* **971** *Blickl. Hom.* 43 Hie wenaþ þæt he heora senna alysan mæʒe. *c* **1200** *Trin. Coll. Hom.* 11 Ðe werc of þesternesse, þat ben alle heuie sennen. **12..** *Prayer our Lady* 5 in *O.E. Misc.* 192 Ich eom i-bunde sore mid wel feole seonne. *c* **1315** SHOREHAM III. 268 þe dede ydo in lechery Hys ryȝt a dedleche senne. **1340** *Ayenb.* 15 þe zeue heauedes of þe beste of helle byeþ þe zeuen hauedliche zennes. **1390** GOWER *Conf.* III. 224 The comun poeple..hath the kinges Senne aboght, Al thogh the poeple agulte noght.

*γ.* **1154** *O.E. Chron.* (Laud MS.) an. 1137, Suilc & mare.. we þolenden xix wintre for ure sinnes. *c* **1200** *Trin. Coll. Hom.* 7 Sainte Powel..sagh..þat hem likede here loðliche sinnes. *c* **1250** *Gen. & Ex.* 553 So cam on werlde wreche and wrake for to blissen swilc sinnes same. *a* **1300** *Cursor M.* 14010 Sco wepe hir sinnes sare. *c* **1380** WYCLIF *Sel. Wks.* III. 108 þes two beþ synnus of þe flesche. **1471** CAXTON *Recuyell* (Sommer) II. 480 All thy dayes [thou] hast lyuyd in multeplyyng of synnes & vices. **1524** WRIOTHESLEY *Chron.* (Camden) I. 14 Plenary remission of their synnes. **1594** GREENE & LODGE *Looking Gl.* F j b, And sir I pray you, what greater sinne is then iealousie? **1628** J. DOUGHTY *Serm. Church-schismes* (1628) 4 Austin..chargith them with no lesse a sinne, then with that of the holy ghost. **1676** OWEN *Serm.* Wks. 1851 IX. 325 As some men's sins grow very high, other men's graces grow very low. **1727** DE FOE *Syst. Magic* I. iv. (1840) 111 Making her dream..of the sin which he resolved to allure her to commit. **1797** MRS. RADCLIFFE *Italian* xiv, 'My mistress has committed some great sin, truly,' said the servant. **1808** LADY LYTTELTON *Let.* 9 May (1912) 11 Now, would not you have thought he was a partisan of boxing? I did for my sins. **1842** BORROW *Bible in Spain* xi, At present, for my sins, I live in a village of the plain. **1874** HARDY *Far fr. Mad. Crowd* xxviii, She felt like one who has 'Sinned a great Sin'. **1906** R. BROOKE *Let.* 1 Apr. (1968) 47 About a year ago I got, for my sins, into the top form of the school. **1961** I. MURDOCH *Severed Head* v. 44 Rosemary..is for her sins a Mrs Michelis, having got married young.., to a dislikeable stockbroker called Bill Michelis, who subsequently left her. **1973** *Times* 2 Nov. 23/3 Take the BSA case in which, for my sins and much against my will, I was concerned.

**b.** *transf.* A violation of some standard of taste or propriety.

**1780** *Mirror* No. 92 All those sins against nature and simplicity, which artists of inferior merit are glad to practise. **1907** PHYLLIS DARE *From School to Stage* viii. 146 The many literary sins I know I must have committed.

**2. a.** Without article or pl. Violation of divine law; action or conduct characterized by this; a state of transgression against God or His commands.

*original sin*: see ORIGINAL *a.* 1 b.

*c* **825** *Vesp. Psalter* cviii. 7 Ʒebed his sie in synne. *c* **950** *Lindisf. Gosp.* John viii. 34 Eʒhuelc seðe wyrcas synn, ðræl is synnes. *a* **1050** *Liber Scintill.* (1889) 230 Mæniʒe lif butan leahtre habban maʒon, butan synne hi na maʒon. *a* **1175**

*Cott. Hom.* 227 Heo was buton senne acenned and his lif was all buton synne. *a* **1225** *Leg. Kath.* 91 Ha wes offearet of scheome & of sunne. *c* **1250** *Kent. Serm.* in *O.E. Misc.* 28 So us defendet þo ilke þinges fram senne. **1303** R. Brunne *Handl. Synne* 3485 More pryde, no more synne, þan skorne god, mayst þou falle ynne. *c* **1340** Hampole *Pr. Consc.* 2357 Here may men se.. How foul es syn and how fylande. *c* **1400** *Rom. Rose* 5078 Trowe not that I wolde hem twynne, Whanne in her love ther is no synne. *c* **1470** Henry *Wallace* III. 323 Bot thou do so, forsuth thou dois gret syne. **1553** T. Wilson *Rhet.* 60 This lesson must not so curiously bee kept, as though it were sinne to make the deuision of fower, or fiue partes. **1588** Shaks. *L.L.L.* IV. iii. 177, I that am honest, I that hold it sinne To breake the vow I am ingaged in. **1631** *High Commission Cases* (Camden) 210 Such as will lye in sinne and goe on without repentance. **1681** Dryden *Abs. & Achit.* 613 Because 'tis sin to misemploy an hour. **1758** S. Hayward *Serm.* i. 4 We are all under the guilt of Sin. **1773** Mrs. Chapone *Improv. Mind* (1774) II. 14 It is your part to retire from such an occasion of sin. **1807–8** Wordsw. *Eccl. Sonn.* II. xxv, Mother! whose virgin bosom was uncrost With the least shade of thought to sin allied. **1842** Tennyson *St. Simeon Stylites* 120 A sinful man, conceived and born in sin. **1876** Mozley *Univ. Serm.* ii. 32 Old Jewish sin was heathen sin—it was open.

**b.** Personified.

**1593** Shaks. *Lucr.* 882 In thy shady cell.. Sits Sin, to seize the souls that wander by him. **1632** R. Bernard *Isle of Man* 5 Thus we see what an ungrateful Villaine Sin is to his best friends. **1667** Milton *P.L.* x. 230 Meanwhile.., Within the Gates of Hell sate Sin and Death. **1818** Shelley *Eugan. Hills* 249 Sin smiled so as Sin only can. **1842** Tennyson *Love & Duty* 8 Shall.. Sin itself be found The cloudy porch oft opening on the Sun?

**c.** In phrases ***child,*** or ***man, of sin***; ***as black,*** or ***ugly, as sin***. Also ***like*** (or ***worse than***) ***sin***: vehemently, intensely, vigorously. Cf. *like the devil* s.v. DEVIL *sb.* 16.

**1610** Shaks. *Temp.* III. iii. 53 You are three men of sinne. **1821** Scott *Kenilw.* x, Though I am as ugly as sin, I would not have you think me an ass. **1827** —— *Chron. Canongate* iv, They.. bowed civilly if folk took aff their bannets as they gaed by, and lookit as black as sin at them that keepit them on. **1840** T. C. Haliburton *Clockmaker* 3rd Ser. viii. 102 Who the plague can live on sugar-candy? I am sure I couldn't. Nothin' does for me like honey; arter a while I get to hate it like sin. **1842** Tennyson *Vision Sin* 5 From the palace came a child of sin. **1868** 'Mark Twain' *Let.* 8 Jan. (1917) I. 143, I have been working like sin all night to get a lecture written. **1929** W. Scott *Mask* i. 16 By the way, Father, dear—*who* is it that Peter Marlin hates worse than sin?

**d.** ***to live in sin***: to cohabit outside marriage.

**1838** *Ann. Rep. Bath City Mission* in G. R. Taylor *Angel-Makers* (1958) 67 Front attic, two aged people living in sin. **1855** C. Kingsley *Westw. Ho!* II. vii. 213 Why, not.. to know whether.. she's married to him or not.. and I not to know whether she's living in sin or not, Mr. William. **1925** A. P. Herbert *Laughing Ann* 92 Don't tell my mother I'm living in sin. **1974** R. B. Parker *Godwulf Manuscript* vii. 56 A couple of freaky kids living in what my aunt used to call sin.

**3. a.** A pity; a shame.

Still in colloquial use, esp. in Sc. See also *Sc. Nat. Dict.*

*c* **1300** *Havelok* 1976 It is hof him mikel sinne; He maden him swilke woundes þrinne. *c* **1470** Henry *Wallace* v. 501 'To dede in Forth he may for vs be brocht.' Lord Persye said, 'Now suthlye that war syne'. **1831** C. Darwin *Let.* 6 Sept. in F. Darwin *Life* (1887) I. v. 207 He takes out twenty chronometers, and it will be a 'sin' not to settle the longitude.

†**b.** A fear of doing wrong. *Obs. rare.*

*c* **1300** *Havelok* 2375 þat he ne sholde neuere blinne, Ne for loue, ne for sinne, Til þat he haueden Godard funde. *c* **1470** Henry *Wallace* VIII. 518 To byrn and sla off thaim he had na syne.

**4.** *Comb.* **a.** With pa. pples., chiefly in instrumental use, but sometimes denoting 'in sin' or 'from sin', as ***sin-absolved***, ***-born***, ***-burthened***, ***-clouded***, ***-crushed***, ***-drowned***, etc.

Combs. of this type are extremely common from about 1590 to 1670, and again from about 1850.

**1563** B. Googe *Eglogs* viii. (Arb.) 68 With gredy mouth he alwayes feeds vpon the Syndrownd soule. **1591** Sylvester *Du Bartas* I. v. 832 Christ, who, sin-thrall'd man to free, Became a captive. **1594** Nashe *Unfort. Trav.* Wks. (Grosart) V. 137 Farewell sinne sowed flesh. *Ibid.* 161 This triple headed Pope with all his sin-absolued whoores. **1648** J. Beaumont *Psyche* XIII. ccxv, The Curse which Heav'n injoin'd to grow On Sin-condemned Earth. **1667** Milton *P.L.* x. 596 Whom thus the Sin-born Monster answerd soon. **1681** Flavel *Meth. Grace* ix. 188 What joy must it be to a sin-burthened soul to hear the voice of pardon. **1792** R. Cumberland *Calvary* (1803) II. 49 That sacred flesh, whose bleeding stripes Heal'd our sin-wounded souls. **1843** J. G. Whittier *Hum. Sacrifice* in *Lays of my Home* 475 Oh! Never yet upon the scroll Of the sin-stained, but priceless soul, Hath Heaven inscribed '*Despair!*' **1849** J. C. Hare *Par. Serm.* II. 98 The inmost Desire of his own sin-crusht soul. **1868** J. H. Newman *Verses Var. Occas.* 253 While song is hushed.. In the sin-laden air. **1882** H. S. Holland *Logic & Life* (1885) 187 The borders.. of this sin-clouded sky. **1896** E. Dowson *Let.* May (1967) 363 Except that I want to see your classically sin-stained countenance, I should not even think of a week in Paris.

**b.** With pres. pples. and vbl. sbs. in objective use, as ***sin-afflicting***, †***-beeting***, ***-chastising***, ***concealing***, ***-doing***, etc. Also instrumental, as ***sin-soiling*** (see 4 e).

This type is common in the 17th and 19th centuries.

*c* **1200** *Trin. Coll. Hom.* 121 Ich com to.. understonden þo sinbetende on rihtwisnesse. *c* **1440** *Alph. Tales* 3 Not alonelie for hur syn-doyng.. sho was sparred in a cloce cell iij yere. **1493** *Festivall* (W. de W. 1515) 148 They be in greete peryll that breke the feest.. in synnedoynge. **1592** Nashe *P. Penilesse* Wks. (Grosart) II. 44 Wise was that sin-washing Poet that made the Ballet of Blue starch and poaking stick. **1593** Shaks. *Lucr.* 767 O comfort-killing Night,.. Vast sin-concealing chaos! **1611** J. Davies (Heref.) *Sco. Folly* ccxviii, Thy scourge of Vice, thy sinne-afflicting Muse. **1681** J. Flavel *Meth. Grace* xxviii. 492 Earnest desires of our souls to God in prayer.. for sin-mortifying grace. **1738** Wesley *Ps.* lxxx. 20 The Sin-consuming Virtue. **1774** J. Edwards *Hist. Redemption* (1793) I. iv. 85 If they came to such a dreadful sin-revenging God immediately they should die. **1819** Shelley *Cenci* IV. ii. 32 His death will be But as a change of sin-chastising dreams. **1860** Pusey *Min. Proph.* 18 Very beautiful to devils must be the sin-loving soul.

**c.** With agent-nouns, in objective use, as ***sin-absolver***, ***-discerner***, ***-forgiver***, etc.

**1592** Shaks. *Rom. & Jul.* III. iii. 50 Being a Diuine, a Ghostly Confessor, A Sin-Absoluer. *a* **1716** Blackall *Wks.* (1723) I. 88 One that makes Sin, We might render it a Sin-maker. **1839** J. Rogers *Antipapopr.* xv. §1. 312 A huge, disciplined, active army:.. not of sinopposers, but of slave-makers. **1849** J. A. Carlyle *Dante's Inf.* 48 That sin-discerner sees what place in Hell is for it. **1870** W. Graham *Lect. Ephesians* vi. 137 The character of the sin-forgiver should not degenerate into the sin-indulger.

**d.** With adjs., as ***sin-black***, ***-dark***, ***-guilty***, ***-like***, ***-proud***.

**1594** Nashe *Terrors of Night* Wks. (Grosart) III. 220 The diuell keepeth his audit in our sin-guilty consciences. **1614** Sylvester *Bethulia's Rescue* 197 Thou couldst not cleanse These Sin-proud shining Halls. **1617** A. Newman *Pleas. Vis.* 22 The stately Court,.. whose sin-like hew Dazles the Eyes of euery Wight. **1812** Shelley *Devil's Walk* xxii, Cormorants are sin-like lean, Although they eat from night to morn. **1855** Bailey *Mystic* 29 With sin-black hills engirthed. *a* **1915** Joyce *Giacomo Joyce* (1968) 10 She stands beside me, pale and chill, clothed with the shadows of the sindark nave.

**e.** With vbs., in the sense 'by sin', as ***sin-eclipse***, ***-merit***.

**1593** Nashe *Christ's T.* Wks. (Grosart) IV. 214 Our soules they keepe not from sinne-soyling, but are the onely instruments, so to soile and sinne-eclipse them. *Ibid.* 257 To make vs more wary of sinne-meriting it.

**5.** *attrib.*, as ***sin-bane***, ***custom-house***, ***-entanglement***, ***-gluttony***, ***-guilt***, ***-guiltiness***, etc.

**1605** Sylvester *Du Bartas* II. iii. I. *Vocation* 100 Sucking the *Sin-bane of Assyrian ayre. **1673** Egane (*title*), The Book of Rates now used in the *Sin Custom-House of the Church of Rome. **1668** J. Owen *Expos. Ps.* cxxx. Wks. 1851 VI. 381, I who am in the depths of *sin-entanglements. **1593** Nashe *Christ's T.* Wks. (Grosart) IV. 79 [To] kill the body & the soule both of her vnbounded *sinne-gluttonie. **1645** Rutherford *Tryal & Tri. Faith* (1845) 227 He.., by a *sin-guilt, hath transgressed a law. **1650** Trapp *Comm. Exod.* xx. 17 That the people might.. bee admonished of their *sin-guiltiness. **1861** Reade *Cloister & H.* lxvii, The pair were driving a bargain in the *Sin market. **1850** Lynch *Theoph. Trinal* x. 201 The *sin-miasma from the evil will of a man. **1650** Hubbert *Pill Formality* 14 A form of godliness without the power of it, may well be called the devils *Sin-Mould. **1535** Coverdale *Zech.* xiv. 18 This shalbe the *synneplage of Egipte and the synneplage of all people. **1624** Gataker *Transubst.* 202 Nor was there ever any *sinne-sacrifice without blood-shead. **1824** Southey *Sir T. More* (1831) I. 327 The *sin-score was settled with St. Kentigern in the regular way. **1598** Sylvester *Du Bartas* II. i. II. *Imposture* 562 The farther this foule *sin-spring flowes, It still more muddy and more filthy growes. **1615** Brathwait *Strappado* (1878) 154 True, I was blind, when thy *sin-Syren voice Made me despise my selfe.

**6.** Special combs.: **sin-bin** *slang* (chiefly *N. Amer.*) = *penalty box* (*a*) s.v. PENALTY *sb.* 5; also *transf.*; †**sin-boot**, repentance, penance; **sin bosun** *Naval slang*, a ship's chaplain; **sin-buster** *U.S. slang*, an evangelist; a clergyman; **sin city** *slang*, a title applied jocularly or otherwise to a city considered to be a place of vice; **sin-eater**, one hired to take upon himself the sins of a deceased person by means of food eaten beside the dead body; so *sin-eating*; **sin-flood** [after G. *sündflut*, an alteration of OHG. *sin-vluot* general flood], the Deluge; †**sin-money** money brought as an offering in expiation of sin; **sin-rent**, a payment made to obtain absolution for sins; **sin-shifter** *slang*, a clergyman; †**sin-wood**, mad with sin.

**1950** *Amer. Speech* XXV. 104/2 **Sin bin*, the penalty box where hockey players are sent for a few moments for infraction of rules, etc. **1958** *Herald Tribune* (Grand Prairie, Alberta) 11 Mar. 5/3 [The] game saw 37 minutes spent in the sin-bin. **1973** *Times* 10 Dec. 8/2 This game showed that it would be worth while trying the ice-hockey system of on-the-spot discipline with a 'sin-bin' to allow players to cool down. **1982** *Daily Tel.* 25 Feb. 19/5 It often took several months for an infant who has created chaos to be removed to a special school or a 'sin bin'. *c* **1175** *Lamb. Hom.* 135 Alle weldede beoð freomfulle to *sun-bote. *c* **1200** *Trin. Coll. Hom.* 137 Ure drihten him bed fulcnen on watere to synbote. **1948** Partridge *Dict. Forces' Slang* 170 **Sin boson* [sic], *the*, the Chaplain, R.N. (Lower-deck.) **1964** *Navy News* Dec. (*H.M.S. Royal Arthur* Suppl.) 1/2 Well, at least the Sin Bosun doesn't seem too old, and did you see him get all punchy during deck-hockey yesterday? **1931** L. Cochran *Flood Tides* vi. 56 'The Reverend Billy Swinnerton is to conduct a revival here.'.. 'Not that ole *sin-buster?' **1973** *Guardian* 17 Oct. 15/3 Leicester people .. saw Nottingham as a sort of *sin city because people there went to the pub at night. **1975** 'A. Thackeray' *One Way Ticket* II. 95 What's going to happen in Chicago?.. All you want to do is run amok in 'Sin City'. **1686–7** Aubrey *Gentilisme*, etc. (1881) 35 A Loafe of bread was brought out, and delivered to the *Sinne-eater over the corps. **1860** *Murray's Handbk. S. Wales* Introd. 26 The superstition of the Sin-Eater is said to linger even now in the secluded vale of Cwm Amman. **1832** Hone *Year Bk.* 19 July 858 An usage called *sin-eating undoubtedly arose in catholic times. **1550** Coverdale *Spir. Perle* xxiv. (1560) 232 When as the whole worlde beside were destroyed with the *sinne flood. **1892** J. Lucas tr. *Kalm's England* 408 Whether all these strata came into their present shape at the sin-flood.. I leave others to divine. **1611** Bible *2 Kings* xii. 16 The trespasse money, and *sinne-money was not brought into the house of the Lord. **1899** Trevelyan *Age Wycliffe* 142 Wycliffe's position about pardons, *sin-rents, and the abuse of the confessional. *a* **1912** 'T. Collins' *Rigby's Romance* (1946) 187 'Not a proper *sin shifter,' objected Dixon. 'You can't chris'n a kid, nor yet say the (adj.) words over people.' **1919** W. H. Downing *Digger Dialects* 45 *Sin-shifter*, an army chaplain. **1966** 'L. Lane' *ABZ of Scouse* II. 98 *Sin-shifter*, a parson, priest, or rabbi. *c* **1250** *Gen. & Ex.* 1073 Ðat folc vnseli, *sinne wod,.. wulden him ðor gret strengðe don.

**sin** (sɪn), *v.* Forms: α. 1 **syngian** (**synngiᵹa, -eᵹa**), 3–4 **sungen**; 1 **singian**, 3 **singen**, 4 **syngen**. β. 2–3 **sunegen** (2 **-eghen**, 3 **-egi**), 3 **sinegen, sinigen, synegen**, 4 **synegy, senegen**. γ. 3 **suneȝen, sineȝen** (**sinnȝhen**), 4 **sen(ne)ȝen, zeneȝi, synewi, sinie**. δ. 3, 5 **sunne**, 5 **senne**; 4–7 **sinne**, 4– **sin**; 4–6 **synne** (5 **synnyn, cynnyn**), 5 **syn(e**. [OE. *syngian* :—**sunigôjan*, f. **sunjō*, OE. *syn(n* SIN *sb.*; cf. Du. *zondigen*, G. *sündigen*, ON. *syndgask* refl. (Icel. *syndga*). This is normally represented in ME. by *süngen, singen* (cf. MING *v.*), but in early ME. the types *sünigen* and *süniȝen* also appear. The shorter *sünnen, sinnen* are probably due to the influence of the sb., with which the vb. finally became identical in form.]

**1.** *intr.* To commit sin; to do a sinful act.

α. *c* **825** *Vesp. Ps.* iv. 5 Eorsiað & nyllað syngian. *c* **897** K. Ælfred *Gregory's Past. C.* xvii. 109 Is ðearf ðæt hie ᵹedon .. ðæt hie ne durren syngian. *c* **1000** Ælfric *Numbers* xxii. 34 Balaam cwæð, Ic singie nitende. *a* **1200** *Moral Ode* 258 þer inne boð.. þo þe sungede muchel a drunke and an ete. *a* **1225** *Ancr. R.* 420 *note*, Ancren, sume sungið in hare wim[p]lunge na lesse þene lefdi. *c* **1250** *Gen. & Ex.* 172 God saȝ bi-fore quat after cam, ðat singen sulde firme adam. *c* **1320** *Cast. Love* 1381 þorw Adam we sungeden furst vchon. **1362** Langl. *P. Pl.* A. VIII. 165 þat.. preyers don sauen Soules þat han sunget seuen siþes dedlich. **1393** *Ibid.* C. I. 109 Hure syre sauh hem syngen and soffrede hem don ille.

β. *c* **1175** *Lamb. Hom.* 19 Ȝif we suneged, we hit sculen beote. *c* **1250** *Owl & Night.* 928 Ich wisse men myd myne songe, þat hi ne sunegi nowiht longe. *c* **1290** *S. Eng. Leg.* I. 44/336 þe menbre þov most keruen of ȝware-withþ þou i-sunegut hast. *c* **1340** *Nominale* (Skeat) 384 *Homme suette et pecche*, M[an] wischith and senegith. **1393** Langl. *P. Pl.* C. xv. 112 He þat knoweþ cleregie can sonnere a-ryse Out of synne, and be saf þow he synegy ofte.

γ. *c* **1200** Ormin 3970 þatt illke mann ne sinnȝheþþ nohht. **12..** *Prayer our Lady* 29 in *O.E. Misc.* 193 Ifurn ich habbe isuneȝet mid wurken & midd muðe. *c* **1310** *St. Edmund* 450 in *E.E.P.* (1862) 83 If y ne wende synewi dedliche, y nolde neuere hit do. **1315** Shoreham VII. 874 þo man senneȝed in paradys, Al chaungede þat flesch a-mys. **1340** *Ayenb.* 20 Ine þri maneris me may zeneȝi be þise zenne. **1393** Langl. *P. Pl.* C. XXIII. 15 Soþeliche he syneweþ nat þat so wynneþ hus fode.

δ. *a* **1300** *Cursor M.* 7955 'Sinned i haf,' coth dauid þan. **1338** R. Brunne *Chron.* (1810) 339 Adam first gan synne, did þat God forbede. **1422** tr. *Secreta Secret., Priv. Priv.* 194 He syneth not, but whoso asketh I-styrryd with concupiscens.. senneth venialy. **1426** Audelay *XI Pains of Hell* 21 Hengyng.. Sum be þe membirs of here body, þat þai han sunnyd with in herthe leuand. **1530** Palsgr. 718/2, I have synned in glotonny to night, I have stolne a horse. **1569** Rogers *Glasse Godly Love* 186 Wee dailie and hourely continually sinne. **1603** Shaks. *Meas. for M.* II. ii. 163 The Tempter, or the Tempted, who sins most? **1688** Dryden *Brit. Red.* 285 Thus Israel sinned, impenitently hard. **1714** R. Fiddes *Pract. Disc.* II. 237 A man may.. deceive him-self, and sin on with the hopes of an after-repentance. **1825** Lytton *Falkland* 119 Do not tell me that I sin, when I.. nurse the delirium [etc.]. **1859** Tennyson *Merlin & V.* 610 That he sinn'd is not believable.

**b.** Const. *against* (†*in*, *to*, *with*, etc.).

*c* **825** *Vesp. Psalter* cxviii. 11 In heortan minre ic ahydde ᵹespreocu ðin, ðæt ic ne syngie ðe [L. *tibi*]. *c* **893** K. Ælfred *Oros.* VI. x. 264 þa sæde him hiora an.. þæt he.. miclum on þæm syngade. *c* **1000** *Ags. Gosp.* Matt. xviii. 15 Ᵹyf þin broþor syngað wið þe. **13..** *Cursor M.* 2986 (Gött.), Fra touche of hir i saued þe, þat þu suld noght sinne in me. *c* **1380** Wyclif *Wks.* (1880) 313 Ȝif þin brother synneþ in þee, þou shalt snybbe hym. **1414** Brampton *Penit. Ps.* (Percy Soc.) 22, I have synned to the alone, And forfetyd ofte before thi syȝt. **1535** Coverdale *Gen.* xxxix. 9 How shulde I then do so greate euell, and synne agaynst God? **1605** Shaks. *Lear* III. ii. 59, I am a man, More sinn'd against, then sinning. **1651** Hobbes *Leviath.* II. xxix. 169 He that is subject to no Civill Law, sinneth in all he does against his Conscience. **1732** Pope *Ess. Man* I. 130 Who but wishes to invert the laws Of Order, sins against th' Eternal Cause. **1772** *Junius Lett.* lxviii. (1788) 343 Your conscience already tells you, that you have sinned against knowledge. **1841** Trench *Parables* (1877) 408 Strictly speaking, we can sin only against God. **1876** Geo. Eliot *Dan. Der.* xxxii, I think I have never sinned against her.

**c.** *spec.* To commit fornication or adultery *with* (or †*on*) one.

*a* **1225** *Ancr. R.* 56 Bersabee.. makede him sunegen on hire, so holi king ase he was. *c* **1290** *S. Eng. Leg.* I. 262/46 To alle þat with hire sunegy wolde euere redi heo was. **1375** *Cursor M.* 26261 (Fairf.), þou prest take kepe þou synne noȝt wiþ þine awen shepe. **1387** Trevisa *Higden* (Rolls) V. 143 Ȝif I seie eny of ȝoure ordre synne wiþ a womman, I wolde helye hym wiþ myn mantel. *c* **1440** *Gesta Rom.* 140 (Add. MS.), Whan he hadde synned with her, he had her more in hate than he before loved her. **1530** Palsgr. 719/1 All sortes of lecherye be naught, but specially to synne with a wedded woman. **1859** Tennyson *Elaine* 248 Another sinning on such heights with one, The flower of all the west and all the world, Had been the sleeker for it.

**d.** To offend *against* some principle, standard, etc.; to be faulty or wrong.

*a* **1704** T. BROWN *Wks.* (1711) IV. 99 This Government.. sins against the Spirit of the Revolution. **1822** BYRON *Juan* VI. lii, The most regulated charms of feature, Which painters cannot catch like faces sinning Against proportion. **1861** LD. BROUGHAM *Brit. Const.* v. 74 Our English system sins against all these canons, and sins grievously. **1888** *Nation* (N.Y.) 6 Dec. 464/2 Quite cleverly painted, and sinning chiefly by excessive prettiness.

**2.** *trans.* **a.** To do, perform, or perpetrate sinfully; to commit (a sin).

*c* **1315** SHOREHAM I. 136 Al þat he heþ iseneged her.. Eliinge brengeþ hit to nouȝte. **1682** SOUTHERNE *Loyal Brother* IV. ii, Gifted rogues, That ..Sin or unsin rebellion to the crowd. **1823** PRAED *Troubadour* I. 80 He sinned few crimes, loved many times. **1859** HAWTHORNE *Marb. Faun* xi, While there remains so much to be sinned and suffered in the world. **1879** J. HAWTHORNE *Laughing Mill*, etc. 81 In the end the sin was sinned.

**b.** *to sin one's mercies*, to be ungrateful for one's blessings or good fortune.

**1824** SCOTT *Redgauntlet* let. i, I know your good father would term this *sinning my mercies*. **1849** MRS. OLIPHANT *Marg. Maitland* I. viii. 244 Surely, Mr. Allan,..it would be sinning your mercies. **1891** *Sat. Rev.* 14 Mar. 328/1 Without wishing in any way to sin our mercies.

**c.** *to sin one's soul*, to incur the guilt of sin. *dial.*

**1894-** in *Eng. Dial. Dict.*

**3.** With preps. and advs. **a.** To bring (oneself) *into* a state, or *beyond* something, by sinning.

**1665** WALTON *Life Hooker* 37 These had sinned themselves into a belief that there was no God. **1680** C. NESSE *Ch. Hist.* 191 They had sinned themselves beyond the reach of all remedies. *a* **1716** SOUTH *Serm.* (1823) I. 170 Few consider what a degree of sottishness and confirmed ignorance men may sin themselves into.

**b.** To drive or force *away* (also *hence*) by sinning.

**1684** BUNYAN *Pilgr.* II. (1900) 164, I have sinned away your Father, and he is gone. **1688** DRYDEN *Brit. Rediv.* 292 For we have sinned him hence. **1694** *Providences of God* 84 The Lord grant we may not sin away our Mercies. **1860** PUSEY *Min. Proph.* 207 Souls which have sinned away the grace of God and are beyond its reach.

**c.** (See quots.)

**1652** LOVEDAY tr. *Calprenède's Cleopatra* Ded. A 2, At such times as your silent Authority gave me leave to want better imployment, this trifle was Sinn'd into English [from French]. **1777** FLETCHER *Bible Calvinism* Wks. 1795 IV. 241 The basest and vilest of men who have not yet sinned out their day of salvation.

**sin**, Sc. variant of SUN.

**sin** (sɪn), *adv.*, *prep.*, and *conj.* Now *Sc.* and *north. dial.* Also 4-6 (9) **syn**, 8-9 **sin'**, 8 **sun**; 4 **sine**, 6 **syne**; 5-6 **synne**, 6-7 **sinne**. [Contracted form of SITHEN: cf. SEN, SYNE, and SINCE. In later use freq. written *sin'*, as if an abbreviation of *since*.

The common early spelling *syn*, and the rare *sine*, *syne*, do not indicate a long vowel.]

**A.** *adv.* **1.** Then, thereupon; thereafter, afterwards, subsequently.

Frequent in Caxton.

*c* **1330** R. BRUNNE *Chron. Wace* (Rolls) 290 Alwey on dragon hem kepte; Syn were þey stolen þe while he slepte. **13..** *E.E. Allit. P.* C. 218 Haþeles hyȝed in haste with ores ful longe, Syn her sayl was hem aslypped on sydez to rowe. **1471** CAXTON *Recuyell* (Sommer) I. 92 He hath putte hym self in armes wyth oute my knowleche And syn sendeth for me. *c* **1489** —— *Sonnes of Aymon* ii. 64 Theyr moder..ranne for to kysse theym..and sin asked what thei had doon of theyr fader. *c* **1500** *Melusine* 245 He toke by force of armes the Erle of Fyerbourgh and syn passed in Austeryche.

**2.** From that time onwards.

**1405** *Mann. & Househ. Exp.* (Roxb.) 178 He hathe ocupyde the lond evyr syn. **1484** CAXTON *Fables of Æsop* v. x, Yf euylle is syn happed to me it is wel bestowed. **1485** *Rolls of Parlt.* VI. 339/1 The first day of this present Parlement or at any tyme syn. **1828** CARR *Craven Gloss.* s.v., I sa him last Jamsmas and I hennot sin him sin. **1886** *S.W. Linc. Gloss.* 131 He's never addled owt sin.

**3.** Ago; before now. Also *long sin*, for a long time before (quot. 1596).

**1490** CAXTON *Eneydos* xii. 44 The bodyes longe syn destroyed & conuerted in-to poulder. **1530** *Hickscorner* in Hazl. *Dodsley* I. 175 Devotion is gone many days sin. **1596** SPENSER *F.Q.* VI. xi. 44 Knowing his voice although not heard long sin, She sudden was reuiued therewithall. **1796** R. WALKER *Plebian Pol.* (1801) 32 Boh this war ov eawars wud hah bin ore monyoah yeor sun. **1869** *Lonsdale Gloss.* 74/2 It's a gud lang time sin. **1886** *S.W. Linc. Gloss.* 78, I heard the bell knoll a piece sin.

**B.** *prep.* From, after; subsequent to.

*a* **1300** *Cursor M.* 5670 Sin quen was þou vr dempster? *Ibid.* 13651 Ne it i-wiss was neuer herd Sin þe biginning o þe werld. **1455** in Scoones *Four Cent. Eng. Lett.* (1880) 5 The King is wel amended,..and hath ben syn Cristemes-day. *c* **1489** CAXTON *Sonnes of Aymon* ix. 225 Never sin that tyme was no kyng crowned in gascoyn. *c* **1500** *Melusine* 102 My lady syn your departyng hath doo made..this toun. **1788** W. H. MARSHALL *Yorksh.* II. 352, I have not seen him sin Tuesday. **1818** SCOTT *Rob Roy* xix, Things were strangely changed..sin' the sad and sorrowfu' Union. **1886** in *Cheshire Gloss.*

**C.** *conj.* **1.** From or since the time that. †Also rarely with *that*.

*a* **1300** *Cursor M.* 9323 For sin þat we war born in werld Sua selcut sagh we neuer herd. **13..** *Ibid.* 22192 (Edinb.), A soru suilc was neuir are, Sin man was made..And sine þe werde it firste bigan. *c* **1385** CHAUCER *L.G.W.* Prol. 229 (Fairf.), The fresshest syn the worlde was first bygonne. **1405** *Mann. & Househ. Exp.* (Roxb.) 178 He owyth my mastyr ffor the londe that the sayd Roper had syn he deyde ffor hys wyffe. *a* **1533** LD. BERNERS *Huon* lxi. 212 Shew me where ye haue ben syn I saw you. **1534** MORE *Comf. agst. Trib.* II. Wks. 1192/2 It neuer hath had any sample lyke, sinne the world began vnto now. *a* **1536** *Songs, Carols*, etc. (E.E.T.S.) 52 Owr kynde ys frayle,..& ever hath bene syne we knew vs. **1785** BURNS *Death & Dr. Hornbook* xii, It's e'en a lang, lang time indeed Sin' I began to nick the thread. **1859** GEO. ELIOT *A. Bede* iv, Adam's niver touched a bit o' victual sin' home he's come.

**2.** Seeing or considering that.

*a* **1300** *Cursor M.* 11212 Sin godd wald þat it sua suld be. *c* **1340** HAMPOLE *Pr. Consc.* 946 God war worthy mare to be lufed þan any creature,..Syn he es maker of althynge. *c* **1400** *Apol. Loll.* 28 Syn al power is of God,..man may do no þing, but if he ȝeue him þe miȝt. **1484** CAXTON *Fables of Auian* xvi, Syn I hold the now, thou shalt not scape fro me. *a* **1533** LD. BERNERS *Huon* lxi. 211, I care not whether I lyue or dye syn I haue founde you. **1724** RAMSAY *Tea-t. Misc.* (1733) I. 8 Now, woer, sin ye are lighted down Where do ye win. **1818** HOGG *Brownie of Bodsbeck* iii, I wish ye had suffered under ony hand but mine, sin' it be your lot. **1877** *Holderness Gloss.* 126/1.

†**b.** So *sin that*. *Obs.*

*c* **1375** *Cursor M.* 3167 (Fairf.), Quar sal we take a beste þis sacrifise to make, syn þat we haue broȝt nane. *c* **1391** CHAUCER *Astrol.* II. §4 Me semeth conuenient, sin þat I speke of the assendent, to make of it special declaracioun. **1474** CAXTON *Chesse* II. iv. (1883) 44 Syn that a knyght is capitayn of a batayll the lyf of them..lyeth in his hand.

**sinabar**, obs. form of CINNABAR.

**Sinæan** (saɪˈniːən), *a. rare.* [irreg. f. late L. *Sīnæ*, ad. Gr. Σῖναι (Ptolemy), prob. ad. Arab. *Ṣīn*, the empire of China.] Chinese.

**1667** MILTON *P.L.* XI. 390 From the destind Walls Of Cambalu..To Paquin of Sinæan Kings. **1893** R. WILSON tr. *Figuier's Human Race* iii. 292 The nations belonging to the Sinæan branch..have not the features of the Yellow Race so well defined as those belonging to the Mongolian branch.

‖**sinagot** (sinago). [Fr., f. *Séné*, a fishing village on the Gulf of Morbihan, on the west coast of France.] A two-masted Breton fishing-boat.

**1927** L. RICHARDSON *Brittany & Loire* 213 Very red are the sails of the *sinagots*. **1975** *Mariner's Mirror* LXI. 93 The name for this type, which, like a Chinese junk, sets its two yards at almost right angles to their respective masts, is *sinagot*.

**Sinaic** (seɪˈneɪɪk), *a.*[1] *rare*[−1]. [irreg. f. late L. *Sīnæ* (see SINÆAN *a.*) + -IC.] = SINÆAN *a.*

**1872** tr. *Figuier's Human Race* 205 We will separate it [the Yellow Race] into three branches—the Hyperborean, the Mongolian, and the Sinaic branches.

**Sinaic** (saɪˈneɪɪk), *a.*[2] [f. *Sinai* + -IC.] = next.

*a* **1769** RICCALTOUN *Wks.* (1772) III. 117 Neither of these were inforced with that terrible sanction..as the Sinaic law was. **1803** A. KIRKWOOD in *Mem.* (1856) 22 This first gave me a proper view of the Sinaic covenant. **1848** HAMILTON *Sabbath* i. 18 The Sabbath..was antecedent to the Sinaic code. **1863** J. G. MURPHY *Comm., Exod.* xix. 1-2 Cosmas regards Horeb as a part of the Sinaic cluster of hills.

**Sinaitic** (saɪneɪˈɪtɪk), *a.* [f. *Sinai* (a. Heb. *Sīnai*) + -ITIC.] Of, or pertaining to, Mount Sinai or the peninsula in which it is situated; given or promulgated at Mount Sinai.

**1786** A. GIB *Sacr. Contempl.* II. II. v. 106 Many things pertaining to the Sinaitic dispensation..are not necessary for being considered in this place. **1853** HORNER tr. *Lepsius' Lett. fr. Egypt*, etc. xxxiii. 294 The Sinaitic inscriptions on the sides of the valley become more frequent. **1856** STANLEY *Sinai & Pal.* I. 20 One such oasis in the Sinaitic desert seems to be the palm-grove of El-Wâdy. **1883** *Century Mag.* XXVII. 309 The actual subdivision of the pages of the Sinaitic manuscript.

**siˈnalbin.** *Chem.* [f. L. *sin-āpis* mustard + *alb-a* white: cf. SINIGRIN.] (See quots.)

**1875** WATTS *Dict. Chem.* 2nd Suppl. 832 White mustard seed contains a glucoside sinalbin, which is soluble in alcohol, and..decomposes in contact with aqueous extract of mustard. **1876** HARLEY *Royle's Mat. Med.* 735 The characteristic constituent..of white mustard [is] sinalbin. **1887** BENTLEY *Man. Bot.* (ed. 5) 451 A crystalline principle ..called sinalbin or sulpho-sinapisin.

**sinalogue**, variant of SINOLOGUE.

†**sinamer (synamer)**, ? obs. var. of SINOPER.

**1486** *Bk. St. Albans, Her.* a iij, A loys is calde sinamer or sanguine in armys. **1586** FERNE *Blaz. Gentrie* 146 Sanguine was blazonned by the name of Synamer.

**sinamine** (ˈsɪnəmaɪn). *Chem.* Also **sinnamine.** [f. L. *sin-āpis* mustard + AMINE.] A basic compound obtained from thiosinamine (see quots.).

**1850** *Fownes' Chem.* (ed. 3) 510 Sinnamine..has a powerful bitter taste, is strongly alkaline to test-paper, and decomposes ammoniacal salts. **1858** *Ibid.* (ed. 10) 853 Sinamine..crystallizes very slowly from a concentrated aqueous solution. **1868** WATTS *Dict. Chem.* V. 307 Sinamine forms a resinous precipitate with nitrate of silver.

**sinamome, -mon(d)**, obs. ff. CINNAMON.

**Sinanthropus** (sɪˈnænθrəʊpəs). [mod.L. (D. Black 1927, in *Palæontologica Sinica* D. VII. I. 21), f. SIN(O- + Gr. ἄνθρωπος man.] = *Peking man* s.v. PEKING 3. Hence **Sinanˈthropic** *a.*, of or pertaining to a fossil hominid of this kind; **Siˈnanthropoid** *a.* [-OID], resembling Sinanthropus.

**1928** *Daily Tel.* 17 Apr. 9/3 A human tooth as old as the Java ape man..has been named Sinanthropus, or 'the Peking man'. **1931** A. KEITH *New Discoveries Antiquity of Man* xvii. 260 The Sinanthropic mandibular fragment is broken short at the socket for the second incisor. **1937** *Ann. Reg. 1936* 52 Parts of three skulls of Palaeoanthropus showing Sinanthropoid features..were found in the Upper Pleistocene in Tanganyika. **1965** B. E. FREEMAN tr. *Vandel's Biospeleology* iii. 22 *Sinanthropus* used caves for shelter. **1978** *Nagel's Encycl.-Guide: China* 298 Great pride was taken in the discovery of remains of 'sinanthropus' which were older still than those found at Zhou Kou dian by Teilhard de Chardin.

**sinapate** (ˈsɪnəpeɪt). *Chem.* [f. SINAP-IC + -ATE[1] c.] A salt formed by the action of sinapic acid on an alkali.

**1857** MILLER *Elem. Chem., Org.* vii. §1. 498 *note*, An insoluble sinapate of baryta. **1868** WATTS *Dict. Chem.* V. 308 All the sinapates, excepting the barium-salt, decompose with great facility.

**sinaper**, variant of SINOPER.

**sinapic** (sɪˈnæpɪk), *a.* *Chem.* [See next and -IC.] Of, pertaining to, or derived from sinapine.

*sinapic acid*, an acid obtained from sinapine by the action of potash and soda.

**1857** MILLER *Elem. Chem., Org.* vii. §1. 497 *note*, This base, when acted upon by potash or soda, is decomposed into sinapic acid, and a new alkali, termed sinkaline. **1868** WATTS *Dict. Chem.* V. 308 Sinapic acid crystallises in small prisms.

**sinapine** (ˈsɪnəpɪn). *Chem.* Also **-in.** [f. L. *sināp-is* mustard + -INE[5].] 'An organic base, existing as a sulphocyanate in white mustard-seed' (Watts).

**1838** THOMSON *Chem. Org. Bodies* 903 There exists in it [mustard] a peculiar crystallizable body, to which they gave the name of *sulphosinapisin*; but which has been shortened by Berzelius into *sinapin*. **1857** MILLER *Elem. Chem., Org.* vii. §1. 497 *note*, An aqueous solution of sinapine has an intense yellow colour. **1878** KINGZETT *Anim. Chem.* 277 Von Babo and Huschbrunn discovered a base named sinkaline as a decomposition product of sinapine.

**siˈnapisin(e.** *Chem.* [irreg. f. L. *sināpis* + -INE[5].] (See quots.)

**1840** PEREIRA *Elem. Mat. Med.* II. 1267 We learn that black mustard seed contains myronate of potash, myrosyne, ..sinapisin, free acid,..and some salts. **1868** WATTS *Dict. Chem.* V. 310 *Sinapisine*, the name given by E. Simon..to a white, scaly, crystalline substance, which he obtained from black mustard-seed by extraction with alcohol and ether. **1875** *Ibid.* 2nd Suppl. 832 Sinapisine sulphate is insoluble in ether.

**sinapism** (ˈsɪnəpɪz(ə)m). *Med.* Also 7 **-isme.** [a. F. *sinapisme*, or ad. L. *sināpismus*, Gr. σινάπισμα mustard plaster, σιναπισμός the use of this, f. σίνᾱπι (σίνᾱπυ, etc.) mustard.] A plaster or poultice consisting wholly or partly of mustard flour; a mustard plaster.

**1601** HOLLAND *Pliny* XXIX. vi. II. 364 The places ought.. to be well prepared with the razour, and a sinapisme or rubificative made of mustard-seed. **1684** tr. *Bonet's Merc. Compit.* I. 33 To reckon up all Causticks..from a Sinapism to a Burning-Iron. **1710** T. FULLER *Pharm. Extemp.* 359 It is a Sinapism..which the Antients used much. **1783** MARTYN *Geogr. Mag.* I. 269 The sinapisms and warm cataplasms of European practise. **1834** J. FORBES *Laennec's Dis. Chest* 181 Blisters and sinapisms are of less frequent benefit. **1877** F. T. ROBERTS *Hdbk. Med.* (ed. 3) I. 29 To draw blood away from the seat of congestion by means of sinapisms, heat, or other irritants applied to the skin.

*fig.* **1895** *Contemp. Rev.* Aug. 226 So far as the writer is aware this species of military sinapism is not known in foreign armies.

**sinaˈpistic**, *a.* *rare*[−1]. [f. L. *sināpis* mustard: see -ISTIC.] Consisting of mustard.

**1879** SALA *Paris Herself Again* (1880) I. xviii. 318 In the majority of [French] places of public entertainment the sinapistic condiment is simply vile.

†**ˈsinapite.** *Obs. rare.* Also 7 **sinepites.** [f. L. *sināp-is* mustard + -ITE.] A concretionary stone composed of small granules resembling mustard-seed; a species of oolite.

**1681** GREW *Musæum* III. i. v. 295 The Sinepites, as it may be called. Being a Cluster of small hard Globules, like Mustard-seeds. **1811** PINKERTON *Petral.* I. 456 The analogy between pisolite and sinapite is also preferable, both being derived from the vegetable kingdom. *Ibid.* 457 Sinapite from Iceland.

†**ˈsinapize**, *v.* *Obs.* *rare*[−1]. [ad. F. *sinapizer* (Rabelais), ad. L. *sināpīzāre*, Gr. σιναπίζειν, f. σίνᾱπι mustard.] *trans.* To sprinkle after the manner of mustard powder.

**1653** URQUHART *Rabelais* II. xxx, He..took his head and into it synapised some powder of diamerdis.

**siˈnapoline.** *Chem.* [f. L. *sināp-is* mustard + -OL + -INE[5].] (See quots.)

**1850** *Fownes' Chem.* (ed. 3) 511 When mustard-oil is treated with oxide of lead,..carbonic acid and another basic substance [is] produced, which, when pure, crystallizes in colourless plates... Sinapoline, the body so formed [etc.]. **1857** MILLER *Elem. Chem., Org.* vii. §1. 499 Sinapoline is a feeble base which crystallizes in brilliant greasy flakes from its solution in water. **1868** WATTS *Dict. Chem.* V. 310 Sinapoline. Diallyl-carbamide... An organic base discovered by Simon..formed from cyanate of allyl, by addition of water and elimination of carbonic anhydride.

‖**Sinarquista** (siːnɑːˈkiːsta). Also (anglicized) **Sinarquist** and with small initial. [Amer.-Sp., after Sp. *anarquista* ANARCHIST; cf. SYNARCHY.] A member or adherent of the right-wing authoritarian Unión Nacional Sinarquista in Mexico, which was active between 1938 and 1960 (esp. in rural areas) and sought to restore the old order of the Catholic church and Spanish tradition, and opposed Communism, liberalism, and the policies imposed after the Revolution of 1911. Also *attrib.* or as *adj.*

**1941** *N.Y. Times* 27 Dec. 8/8 An organized campaign to combat the Sinarquista Movement in Mexico will be launched next month... The Sinarquistas, often charged with favoring totalitarian nations, have begun large-scale agrarian colonization of Lower California. **1943** *Free World* May 413/1 These are reactionary leaders among the clergy who would go much farther with the Sinarquists. **1946** M. LOWRY *Let.* 2 Jan. (1967) 88 You can even see the German submarine officers taking revenge on the Consul in the form of the *sinarquistas*. **1970** G. HUIZER in I. L. Horowitz *Masses in Lat. Amer.* xiii. 474 The danger from extremely conservative and fascist forces, such as the Sinarquist movement, was alarmingly strong. **1973** P. CALVERT *Mexico* xxii. 284 The Sinarquistas were only the tip of the iceberg.

Hence ‖**Sinarˈquismo** (anglicized **-ism**), the political doctrine of the Sinarquistas.

**1943** *Free World* May 410/2 The enigma of Sinarquism is created by the character of Mexican politics. **1953** H. F. CLINE *U.S. & Mexico* xiv. 293 *Sinarquismo*—Sinarchism—is the opposite of anarchism; the word means 'with order'. Sinarquistas are believers in 'order'. **1963** D. JAMES *Mexico & Americans* xiii. 346 Sinarquismo was essentially a rural movement arising out of peasant discontent. **1971** R. MARETT *Mexico* x. 162 The fascist phenomenon of Sinarquismo, which came to a head in the late 1930's in opposition to the radical policies of Cárdenas.

†**sinˈcanter.** *Obs.* Forms: α. 6 **cenkanter**, 6–7 **sinckanter**, 7 **sinkanter**, **sincaunter**. β. 6–7 **singcantor**, 7 **sincantor**. [Of obscure origin; the β-forms have been assimilated to *sing* and *cantor*. The variants *cinque-cater*, *cincater*, etc. (see examples under CINQUANTER), are no doubt due to association with the dicing terms *cinque* and *quatre*.] A contemptuous or depreciatory term applied to men, usually with the epithet *old*. Also *attrib.* (quot. *c* 1540).

α. *c* **1540** *Pilgrim's Tale* 708 in *Thynne's Animadv.* App. (1865) 97 The good yo[u]th..leuis the slechy podell, full of frogis, to the old cenkanter phariziecall dogis. **1596** NASHE *Saffron Walden* Epistle Ded. C 2, Being sent for to some tall old sinckanter, or stigmaticall bearded Master of Arte. **1597** G. HARVEY *Trimming of T. Nashe* Wks. (Grosart) III. 41 Then thou callest them sinckanters, which is a proper Epithite vnto thy-selfe, for Sinckanter commeth of sincke and *antrum* a hole. **1601** MUNDAY *Downfall Earl of Huntingdon* v. i. K j, A plague on ye for a blinde sinksanker [*sic*]. **1611** COTGR., *Rocard*, a hoarse mouldichaps, an ouerworne sincaunter, one that can neither whinnie, nor wag the taile. **1617** COLLINS *Def. Bp. Ely* II. x. 410 He would conjure you into a boote, or into a bench-hole for your labour, like a sawcy Sinckanter. *a* **1640** JACKSON *Creed* x. xix, One Volanerius an old Sinkanter or Gamester and Scurrilous Companion by profession.

β. **1581** HANMER *Jesuites Banner* E j b, It should appeare M. Censurer, that yee are but a nouice: you were best confer with the old singcantors, and learn further of their order. **1656** BLOUNT *Glossogr.*, *Succentor*, he that singeth the Base. .. Our phrase, *an old Sincantor*, is either a corruption from this word; or if it be written with a *C*, then tis from the Fr. *Cinquante*,..and so may be taken for one that is fifty years of age or above. **1672** R. WILD *Lett.* 8 And now I talk of the old Singcantor [the Pope], our Gracious King is worth all the Clements in Christendom.

**sincar**, obs. Sc. f. SINKER *sb.*[1]

**since** (sɪns), *adv.*, *prep.*, and *conj.* (also *a.* and *sb.*). Forms: α. 5 **synnes**, 5–6 **syns**, 6 **sins**, **synz**, **synce**, **cynce**; 5– **since**. β. 5 **sennes**, 6 **sennys**, **sens**, **senz**, 6, 9 **sence**, 7 **cence**. [Reduced form of SITHENCE, or f. SIN *adv.* + -s[1]. Cf. Du. *sinds*.]

**A.** *adv.*

**1. a.** Then, thereupon; immediately afterwards.

*c* **1450** *Langland's P. Pl.* C. v. 15 Conscience..seide hym as þe kyng saide and sitthe [*Ilchester MS.* synnes] tok hus leue. *Ibid.* XII. 171 In a myrour..hue made me to loke, And sutthe [*v.r.* sennes] seide to me [etc.]. **1483** *Cely Papers* (Camden) 139 They were..browght upp theyr and syns sworne unto the jurdyccyon of the towne. **1568** SPENSER *Visions Bellay* v. Wks. (Globe) 700/2, I hearde the tronke to grone... And since I saw the roote..Sende forth againe a twinne of forked trees.

†**b.** *since..since* (or *sith*): Now..then. *Obs.*

**1530** PALSGR. 841/2 Synce on the one syde, synce on the other, *puis dung cousté, puis de laultre*. *Ibid.* 884/1 Syns on the one syde and sythe on the other.

†**c.** Now, already. *Obs. rare.*

*a* **1553** UDALL *Royster D.* I. iii. (Arb.) 23 Haue we done singyng since? then will I in againe. *Ibid.* III. v. 55 But lo and Merygreeke haue not brought him sens?

**2.** From that time till now. In positive clauses implying continuity of action, etc., and commonly strengthened by *ever*.

**1470–85** MALORY *Arthur* IX. xli. 407 Euer syns he hath kepte me at his owne will. **1590** SHAKS. *Com. Err.* IV. i. 2 You know since Pentecost the sum is due, And since I haue not much importun'd you. **1623** LISLE *Ælfric on O. & N. Test.* Introd., Where they..have lived in sorrow and painestaking ever since. **1658** J. JONES *Ovid's Ibis* 36 He [Midas] washed himself in this river and was restored; Since the streams are feigned to be golden. **1731** *Gentl. Mag.* I. 391/1 Bluster..quitted the Surgery in a Pet, and has liv'd in the Country ever since. **1824** SOUTHEY in *Corr. w. Caroline Bowles* 62 The first of these inverterate catarrhs, which I never failed to have every year since. **1885** *Law Times* LXXX. 118/1 In 1879 he went abroad, and had ever since remained abroad.

**3. a.** Within the period, at some or any time, between then and now; subsequently, later.

**1549** LATIMER *4th Serm. bef. Edw. VI* (Arb.) 119, I hearde once a tale of a thinge yat was done at Oxforde xx. yeres a go, and the lyke hath bene sence in thys realme. **1590** SHAKS. *Com. Err.* IV. iv. 81 My bones beare witnesse, That since haue felt the vigor of his rage. **1613** PURCHAS *Pilgrimage* (1614) 36 It was written and since is lost. **1629** WADSWORTH *Pilgr.* i. 4 Her foure children, Hugh the eldest, since dead in Madrid [etc.]. **1766** GOLDSM. *Vic. W.* ix, I am since informed that swearing is perfectly unfashionable. **1798** O'KEEFFE *Wild Oats* I. i, That rogue's trick you play'd poor Miss Amelia, by..leaving her..and since marrying another lady. **1833** T. HOOK *Parson's Dau.* III. xi, More like Noah's Ark than any thing that has been since seen floating upon the face of the waters. **1885** *Spectator* 8 Aug. 1041/1 This was dimly felt at the time and has been more distinctly recognised since.

*Comb.* **1598** SYLVESTER *Du Bartas* II. ii. I. *Ark* 418 A vast multitude Of since-born mongrels. **1876** GLADSTONE in *Westm. Gaz.* 31 Dec. (1894) 1/3 The since-promoted agents of the Turkish Government.

**b.** As *adj.* That has been since. *rare.*

**1598** SYLVESTER *Du Bartas* II. i. I. *Eden* 317 That first travell had no sympathy With our since-travel's wretched cruelty. *a* **1700** EVELYN *Diary* 28 July 1641, Eldest sonne of the since Earle of Norwich. **1849** FROUDE *Nemesis Faith* 116 My since experience of Sunday evenings.

**4.** Ago; before now. With time specified, or preceded by *long*.

α. *c* **1489** CAXTON *Blanchardyn* liv. 213 Long time since.. shee fell sicke and died. **1560** DAUS tr. *Sleidane's Comm.* 94 The cause..of that sedition was declared also foure yeares synce in the assembly. **1624** *Cosin's Corr.* (Surtees) I. 32 Though his minde had ben that way 20 yeares since. **1662** J. DAVIES tr. *Mandelslo's Trav.* 226 It is certain..the Chineses have some Books printed above seven hundred years since. **1721** in J. J. Babson *Hist. Glouc., Mass.* (W.), Captain Robinson..built the first of that sort about eight years since. *a* **1774** GOLDSM. tr. *Scarron's Com. Romance* (1775) I. 33 A merchant from Lower-Maine bespoke it not half an hour since. **1823** DE QUINCEY *Lett. Educ.* iii. (1860) 58 The mere rubbishy sweepings from the works of literati long since defunct. **1862** T. L. PEACOCK *The Deceived* Wks. 1875 III. 309 He went out a little while since.

β. **1555** W. WATREMAN *Fardle Facions* I. vi. 94 That nacion had long sence bene vttrely destroied.., excepte [etc.]. **1597** in Feuillerat *Revels Q. Eliz.* (1908) 417 Beinge longe sence signed by her Majeste.

**B.** *prep.*

**1.** Ever or continuously from (a specified time, etc.) till now.

α. **1530** PALSGR. 812/2 Syns that daye, *puis ce jour la*. **1562** *Child Marriages* 49 The said John Starkie is xiiij yeres of age, and as muche as sins Whitsonday-Monday last past. **1611** BIBLE *Gen.* xxx. 30 The Lord hath blessed thee since my comming. **1734** tr. *Rollin's Anc. Hist.* II. ii. (1827) II. 6 It was five months and a half since his first setting out. **1780** *Mirror* No. 103, I inherited a law-suit, kept alive by various means, ever since the year thirty-three. **1802** WORDSW. *The Small Celandine* 14 I'm as great as they,..Since the day I found thee out. **1861** THACKERAY *Four Georges* iv. (1862) 184 He sleeps since thirty years.

β. **1535** COVERDALE *1 John* iii. 8 The deuell synneth sence yᵉ begynnynge. **1565** STAPLETON tr. *Staphylus' Apol.* 168 b, For sence the time of S. Gregory only,..we englishmen haue had the faith of Christ. **1879** MISS JACKSON *Shropshire Word-bk.* 369.

**2.** During the period between (a specified time) and now; at some time subsequent to or after.

α. **1544** in Leadam *Sel. Cas. Crt. Requests* (Selden Soc.) 70 The seid sir John..synz his entre in to the seid lordshipe.. haith gotten..dyuerse of the seid copiez of courte roll. **1582** in *Cath. Rec. Soc. Publ.* V. 27 Hee hathe said vj or vij Masses cynce his cuminge over. *c* **1645** HOWELL *Lett.* v. xxxi. (1655) I. 226 My last was of the first current, since which I received one from your Lordship. **1676** GLANVILL *Ess. Philos. & Relig.* III. 9 Diophantus, who lived long since the times of Aristotle. **1794** MRS. RADCLIFFE *Udolpho* xxxiv, Sounds which, since that period, have there sunk into silence. **1808** SCOTT *Marm.* I. xxi, Even our good chaplain..Since our last siege we have not seen. **1837** KEITH *Bot. Lex.* 115 Many advances have been made in carpological investigation since the time of Gærtner. **1880** CHURCH *Spenser* i. 25 They seem to have changed since Spenser's time.

β. **1515** A. WILLIAMSON in *Douglas's Wks.* (1874) I. Introd. p. xxi, The Kyng..has sent now sens Cristmes an vysse clerk off his Consell. *a* **1533** FRITH *Answ. More* (1548) C 6 v, I receiued a letter from him, which was written sens Chrystmas. **1552** *W. Powell's Chron. Yeres* Title-p., The noble Actes done in and sens the reigne of Kyng Henry the fourthe. **1637** HOBART in *Verney P.* (1853) 190 There has bine nothing don cence the taking in of the hornworke.

**C.** *conj.* **I.** From the time that.

**1.** Denoting a point of time to which the action or event mentioned is subsequent.

α. *a.* **14..** *Langland's P. Pl.* B. x. 224 (MS. Rawl.), Was neuer gome vpoun þis grounde, synnes god made þe worlde, Fairer vnderfonge, ne frendloker at ese, þanne me self. **1511** *Guylforde's Pilgr.* (Camden) 70 We sayled further that nyght thanne we dyde in anye daye syns we departed from Jaffe. **1588** KYD *Househ. Philos.* Wks. (1901) 252 A small patrimonie,..twice as much encreased since my father left it. **1611** BIBLE *Exod.* ix. 24 There was none like it in..Egypt, since it became a nation. **1756** BURKE *Subl. & B.* v. v, Since I wrote these papers, I found two very striking instances [etc.]. **1776** *Trial of Nundocomar* 23/1 Has he ever been out since he was last at the court house? **1825** SCOTT *Betrothed* xxvii, Since you went hence, we have received certain notice, that [etc.]. **1875** TENNYSON *Harold* I. i, Albeit no rolling stone,..Thou hast rounded since we met.

β. **1526** TINDALE *Acts* xix. 2 Have ye receaved the holy gost sence ye beleved? **1549** LATIMER *Ploughers* (Arb.) 24 Sence lording and loytrying hath come vp, preaching hath come downe.

**2. a.** Following upon a statement (or inquiry) as to the duration of the period in question.

α. **1557** N. T. (Geneva) *Acts* xxiv. 11 There are yet but twelue dayes since I went vp to Ierusalem. **1601** SHAKS. *All's Well* I. ii. 70 How long is't, Count, Since the Physitian at your fathers died? **1661** WALTON *Compl. Angler* (ed. 3) v. 124 It is so long since I learnt it, that I have forgot a part of it. **1711** STEELE *Spect.* No. 32 ¶2 Nor is it so very long since Richard the Third set up half the Backs of the Nation. **1753** FOOTE *Eng. in Paris* II. Wks. 1799 I. 49 'Tis an age since I saw you. **1780** *Mirror* No. 95 It is now above four years since I became the wife of a gentleman. **1825** SCOTT *Betrothed* v, It is long since the kites have had such a banquet. **1883** *Daily News* 22 Sept. 4/5 It is just a fortnight since Mr. Gladstone embarked.

β. **1535** COVERDALE *Joshua* xiv. 10 It is now fyue and fortie yeare sence ye Lorde spake this vnto Moses. **1565** COOPER *Thesaurus* s.v. *Cum*, It is two yere, sens he came to me first.

**b.** Used in place of 'that'.

**1647** W. BROWNE tr. *Polexander* II. ii. 194 It is..five moneths now, since these honor'd personages have suffer'd ..indignities in these Dungeons. *a* **1774** GOLDSM. tr. *Scarron's Com. Romance* (1775) I. 313 Though it is now four-score years since he has plagued all those who have any dependence on him, yet he is so well in health [etc.]. **1804** CHARLOTTE SMITH *Conversations*, etc. I. 162 It is near four months since Ella has been away.

**c.** As quasi-*sb. rare.*

**1654** WHITLOCK *Zootomia* 157 My Friend..knoweth no History but some ten or twelve Sinces in his Almanack: How long since the World was created. *Ibid.* 298 The most famous of thy Exploits will not be eminent enough to make an Almanacks Since.

**3. a.** In sentences implying continuity of action or fact during the period indicated. Also with *ever*, and (rarely) with *that*.

α. **1594** SHAKS. *Rich. III*, I. i. 82 The iealous..Widdow, and her selfe, Since that our Brother dub'd them Gentlewomen, Are mighty Gossips. **1647** W. BROWNE tr. *Polexander* II. ii. 194 Ever since I have been able to carry Armes, I have try'd divers wayes to [etc.]. **1653** WALTON *Compl. Angler* ii, We were here an hour before Sun-rise, and have given her no rest since we came. **1697** VANBRUGH *Relapse* I. iii, Here you have stood ever since you came in. **1779** *Mirror* No. 25, My gardener has tied his hair behind.. ever since he saw Mr. Papillot. **1816** J. WILSON *City of Plague* I. i. 122 Thus have I been since first the Plague burst forth. **1863** MRS. CARLYLE *Lett.* III. 155 She has lived in England since she was ten years old. **1877** MRS. FORRESTER *Mignon* I. 253, I have known him ever since he was in petticoats.

β. **1535** COVERDALE *2 Pet.* iii. 4 For sence the fathers fell on slepe, euery thinge contynueth as it was from the begynnynge. **1565** COOPER *Thesaurus* s.v. *A*, Euer sens thou waste a yonge man.

†**b.** With verbs of recollection: When; the time when. *Obs.*

**1590** SHAKS. *Mids. N.* II. i. 149 Thou remembrest Since once I sat vpon a promontory [etc.]. **1611** —— *Wint. T.* v. i. 219 Remember, since you ow'd no more to Time Then I doe now. **1690** CHILD *Disc. Trade* (1698) 73 He can remember since we had not above three merchants ships of 300 tons.

**c.** In various, chiefly jocular, comparisons, as ***since Christ was a corporal***, etc. *colloq.* (chiefly *U.S.* and *Mil.*).

**1601** SHAKES. *Twel. N.* III. ii. 18 And they haue beene grande Iurie men, since before Noah was a Saylor. **1816** KEATS *Endymion* II. 443 Never, I aver, Since Ariadne was a vintager, So cool a purple. **1900** I. L. REEVES *Bamboo Tales* 20 Private McCoy..had been in the service since George Washington was a 'lance jack'. **1921** J. DOS PASSOS *Three Soldiers* II. ii. 75 Ain't had any pay since Christ was a corporal. I've forgotten what it looks like. **1961** PARTRIDGE *Dict. Slang* Suppl. 1274/2 *Since Pontius was a pilot*, as in 'He's been in that mob since..' R.A.F. c[atch] p[hrase], testifying to long service: since ca. 1944. **1970** *N.Y. Post* 7 Apr. 5 Dana Stone had been in Vietnam since Christ was a corporal, as the grunts in the field would say.

**d.** *since when?*: used *ellipt.* as an inquiry into the duration of a state of affairs mentioned in a previous statement (freq. expressing doubt or incredulity); also, with full interrogative clause. *colloq.*

**1907** G. B. SHAW *John Bull's Other Island* IV. 84 *Broadbent (very solemnly)*: No: I am a teetotaller. *Aunt Judy (incredulously)*: Arra since when? **1966** 'G. BLACK' *You want to die, Johnny?* v. 105 'Lil's disappeared.'..'Since when?' **1977** C. WATSON *One Man's Meat* vii. 64 'Since when has Digger's father been a V.C.?' 'Since when has Digger had a father?'

**II. 4. a.** Because that; seeing that; inasmuch as.

α. *c* **1450** *Old Treat.* in *Roy's Rede me*, etc. (Arb.) 174 Syns Christ bought vs as he did other. *c* **1489** CAXTON *Blanchardyn* liv. 213 But since all humane flesh is mortall,.. what auailes my sorowful grones and passions? **1540** PALSGR. *Acolastus* II. i. I iij, Go to, let it be,..syns it lyketh so. **1577** B. GOOGE *Heresbach's Husb.* i. (1586) 7 b, Sins it is not yet dinner tyme, let vs walke about. **1611** A. STAFFORD *Niobe* 152 Whereunto I giue credit, since his succeeders do the same. **1664** BUTLER *Hud.* II. ii. 483 But since no reason can confute ye, I'll try to force you to your Duty. **1711** ADDISON *Spect.* No. 215 ¶4 Since I am engaged on this Subject, I cannot forbear mentioning a Story [etc.]. **1766** GOLDSM. *Vic. W.* xxvi, What signifies..courting his friendship, since you find how scurvily he uses you? **1833** HT. MARTINEAU *Briery Creek* iii. 59 You shall have them cheap, since there is but a poor demand for them to-day. **1895** *Manch. Guardian* 14 Oct. 5/6 All the tunnelling has to be done..by the pick, since boring machines cannot be used.

*β.* *a* **1533** Ld. Berners *Huon* xxiv. 71 Sennys he spekyth of god, me thynke we ought to speke to hym. *a* **1553** *Respublica* 1565 But sens Respublica hathe putt me to exile, where maye I goo?

**b.** So *since that.*

**1540–1** Elyot *Image Gov.* 6 The saied proverbe seemeth by hym, whiche lacked learnyng, to bee devised, sens that he preferreth ignoraunce before cunnyng. **1588** Shaks. *Com. Err.* II. i. 114 Since that my beautie cannot please his eie, Ile weepe what's left away. **1639** Gentilis *Servita's Inquis.* (1676) 878 Since that by the Princes Ministers, such a disorder is put in practice. **1682** Creech *Lucret.* 55 For since that men born blind..Know things by touch [etc.].

**sincere** (sɪn'sɪə(r)), *a.* Also 6 **sincer**, *Sc.* **-ceir**, 6–7 **syncere**, 7 **sinceare**, **senseare**. [ad. L. *sincēr-us* clean, pure, sound, etc. Cf. F. *sincère* (1549), Sp., Pg., and It. *sincero*.

The first syllable may be the same as *sim-*, in *simplex*: see simple *a.* There is no probability in the old explanation from *sine cērā* 'without wax'.]

**1.** Not falsified or perverted in any way:

**a.** Of doctrine, etc.: Genuine, pure.

**1536** *Act 27 Hen. VIII*, c. 42 §1 The syncere and pure doctrine of Goddes worde. **1597** Beard *Theatre God's Judgem.* (1612) 189 A Popish priest that was once a professor of the sincere religion. **1653** ? Hale *Brevis Disq.* in *Phenix* (1708) II. 340 Many think..that these are the true and genuine Doctrines.., which nevertheless have nothing at all common with the sincere Gospel of Christ. **1679** Burnet *Hist. Ref.* (Pocock) I. 583 It was necessary to establish a form of sincere doctrine. **1827** G. S. Faber *Sacr. Calend. Prophecy* (1844) III. 209 When sincere Christianity was propounded in all its native lustre.

**b.** True, veracious; correct, exact.

**1555** (*title*) [Lydgate's] The Avncient Historie and onely trewe and syncere Cronicle of the warres betwixte the Grecians and the Troyans. **1583** Fulke (*title*), A Defense of the sincere and true Translations of the holie Scriptures into the English tong. **1665** G. Havers *P. della Valle's Trav. E. India* 26 Those great Expeditions..: Of which nevertheless, little sincere fame arrives to us; there being no Europæan who hath written truly thereof. **1693** J. Edwards *Auth. O. & N. Test.* 74 If some few..copies had been corrupted.., the sincere number would have detected the corrupt. **1698** Hearne *Duct. Hist.* (1714) I. 161 Things worthy of our Knowledge; collected out of the most sincere and uncorrupted Monuments of Antiquity. **1861–2** R. Williams *Notes to Counsel* 16 Some sincere editions of the Bible no longer contain those warrants. **1876** Lowell *Among my Bks.* Ser. II. 19 That is the only sincere glimpse we get of the living, breathing, word-compelling Dante.

**c.** Morally uncorrupted, uncontaminated.

**1649** Roberts *Clavis Bibl.* 513 Keeping them pure and sincere against all temptations.

**2.** Pure, unmixed; free from any foreign element or ingredient: **a.** Of immaterial things.

**1538** Starkey *England* II. ii. 181 The lawys, wyche be syncere and pure reson, wythout any spot or blot of affectyon. *c* **1555** Harpsfield *Divorce Hen. VIII* (Camden) 214 For the lack of pure and sincere demonstration of the fact. **1610** Guillim *Heraldry* III. ii. (1660) 100 The motion of the Heavens is the most sincere and unlaboured of all motions. *a* **1676** Hale *Prim. Orig. Man.* (1677) 375 By this means their enjoyments are sincere, unallayed with fears or suspitions. **1722** Wollaston *Relig. Nat.* ix. 217 His present pleasures (if not so many) are more sincere and natural.

**b.** Of colours or substances.

**1546** Langley tr. *Pol. Verg. de Invent.* VI. vii. 123 b, The white coloure was thought fittest for the ded bicause it is clere, pure, and sincer, and leaste defiled. **1595** B. Barnes *Div. Cent. Sonn.* xlviii, All angels might..out bring Victorious palmes, arraide in sincere white. **1601** Holland *Pliny* XXXIII. vii. II. 476 If a man would know the true and syncere Vermillion indeed, it ought to have the rich and fresh colour of skarlet. **1615** Crooke *Body of Man* 412 Milke ..is not mingled with the bloud, but passeth out by vrine pure and sincere. **1662** J. Chandler *Van Helmont's Oriat.* 244 Surely the drink should under the first narrow examination of digestion, put off every stone, and that which is most exceeding hard and sincere. **1744** tr. *Boerhaave's Instit.* III. 254 About the Tendons the Fat in this Membrane is rather watery and mucous than sincere Fat. **1763** *Phil. Trans.* LIII. 233 Scarce any sincere gall issued forth on incision. **1802** Paley *Nat. Theol.* xxi. ii, [Water] having no taste of its own, it becomes the sincere vehicle of every other.

**c.** *spec.* Unadulterated; genuine.

**1557** N. T. (Geneva) *1 Pet.* ii. 2 As newe borne babes desire the syncere [Gr. ἄδολον] mylke of the worde. **1576** Baker *Jewell Health* 230 It is a noate or token that the spirit of the wyne was not syncere and pure. **1648** J. Beaumont *Psyche* III. cxxiv, Those courteous Trees, to mend his fare, Into his Mouth sincerest honey shed. **1679** *Hist. of Jetzer* 4 Down he kicks his Cruet of Holy-Water, adding,..they had none sincere and pure these eleven years, the Church-warden always dashing it with common water. **1868** Browning *Ring & Bk.* VII. 238 And wood is cheap And wine sincere outside the city gate. **1888** H. James *Partial Portraits* 368 There has not been as yet an American Renascence, in spite of the taste for 'sincere' sideboards and fragments of crockery.

†**d.** Free from hurt; uninjured. *Obs.*

**1700** Dryden *Ovid's Met.* XII. 133 He tried..a tough well chosen spear; The inviolable body stood sincere.

**e.** Devoid *of* something. *rare.*

*a* **1754** W. Hamilton *To Lady Mary Montgomery*, The pleasing look, sincere of art. **1874** Lowell *Agassiz* IV. ii, Our air, sincere of ceremonious haze Forcing hard outlines mercilessly close.

**3.** Containing no element of dissimulation or deception; not feigned or pretended; real, true.

**1539** *Act 31 Hen. VIII*, c. 14 Almightie god, the very author and fountaine of al true vnitie and sincer concorde. **1595** in *Cath. Rec. Soc. Publ.* V. 346 At length stirred up with the instinct of the Holy Ghost & zeale of syncere pietie. **1667** Milton *P.L.* x. 915 Witness Heav'n What love sincere, and reverence in my heart I beare thee. *a* **1699** Lady Halkett *Autobiog.* (Camden) 13 Nothing that could exprese a sinceare affection. *a* **1703** Burkitt *On N.T.*, Rev. iii. 9 Weak grace, if sincere, shall always find acceptance with Christ. **1771** *Junius Lett.* lv. (1788) 302, I am satisfied that he is a Christian upon the most sincere conviction. **1810** Miss Mitford in L'Estrange *Life* (1870) I. iv. 106 You are quite right in believing my fondness for rural scenery to be sincere. **1849** Macaulay *Hist. Eng.* vi. II. 151 A sincere anxiety for the prosperity and dignity of his excellent friend the treasurer.

**4.** Characterized by the absence of all dissimulation or pretence; honest, straightforward:

**a.** Of life, actions, etc.

**1533** Frith *Answ. More* (1829) 344 Master Wickliffe was noted..to be a man..of a very sincere life. **1603** Knolles *Hist. Turks* (1621) 1300 Such as pervert the good and sincere life of Commonweales. **1641** Hinde *J. Bruen* vi. 23 By the sincere simplicity and plainnesse of the truth of God..he mightily confuted them. **1700** Rowe *Amb. Step-Mother* II. i, Thy function Which like the Gods thou Serv'st, should be sincere. **1746** Hervey *Medit.* (1818) 112 My..sincerest acts of religion must not presume to challenge a reward. **1839** De Quincey *Recoll. Lakes* Wks. 1862 II. 176 Entering upon the dignity and the sincere thinking of mature manhood. **1841** Emerson *Ess.*, *Friendship*, Three cannot take part in a conversation of the most sincere and searching sort.

**b.** Of persons, their character, etc.

**1539** Bible (Cranmer) *2 Pet.* iii. 1, I stere vp your syncere mynde. **1570** *Satir. Poems Reform.* xxiii. 10 The worthie deids done be that Prince sinceir. **1651** Hobbes *Leviath.* III. xlii. 300 So they doe it out of a sincere conscience. **1686** tr. *Chardin's Coronat. Solyman* 25 Not having altogether the Reputation of a sincere man. **1711** Addison *Spect.* No. 57 ⁋6 A Woman is too sincere to mitigate [etc.]. **1750** Gray *Elegy* 121 Large was his bounty, and his soul sincere. **1775** Sheridan *Rivals* I. ii, If he is as..sincere as you have represented him to me. **1824** Byron *Juan* XVI. xcvii, For surely they're sincerest Who are strongly acted on by what is nearest. **1837** Thirlwall *Greece* xxxv. IV. 393 She had not one sincere friend left. **1878** Morley *Carlyle* 175 He had the unspeakable advantage..of being ruggedly sincere.

*absol.* **1611** Bible *Ps.* cxix. 1 Blessed are the vndefiled [*marg.* Or, perfect, or sincere] in the way. **1780** Cowper *Progr. Err.* 578 That prize belongs to none but the sincere. **1813** Shelley *Queen Mab* I. 124 The envied boon, That waits the good and the sincere.

**sincerely** (sɪn'sɪəlɪ), *adv.* Also 6 **syncerlye**, **syncerely**, *Sc.* **sinceirlie**, **-ly**, 7 **sincerelie**, **sincerily**. [f. prec. + -ly$^{2}$.] In a sincere manner.

†**1.** Without falsification or perversion; in a proper or correct manner. *Obs.*

**1535** Wriothesley *Chron.* (Camden) I. 30 All bishops and curates should preach the gospell of Christe syncerlye and truly. **1597** Hooker *Eccl. Pol.* v. lxii. §14 The sacrament ..is administered but not sincerely. **1613** Purchas *Pilgrimage* (1614) 107 Strabo, Iustine, and others, haue written of this people, but not sincerely.

†**b.** In good faith. *Obs.*

**1607** Topsell *Four-f. Beasts* (1658) 23, I have been sincerely informed, that there was a Horse conceived of a Bull and a Mare.

**2.** Without dissimulation or pretence; honestly, straightforwardly.

**1560** Daus tr. *Sleidane's Comm.* 229 That..they wolde not followe their affections, but treate syncerely. *Ibid.* 231 b, Therfore must they worke syncerely. **1596** Dalrymple tr. *Leslie's Hist. Scot.* I. Prol. 1 Returneng sinceirlie to the catholik concorde. *c* **1605** Rowley *Birth of Merlin* v. ii, Sincerely, Gloster, I have told you all. **1641** J. Jackson *True Evang. T.* II. 102 The doctrine of the Gospell, sincerely obeyed, first Christianizeth men, and then civilizeth them. **1711** Addison *Spect.* No. 166 ⁋8 He was so very sensible of his Fault, and so sincerely repented of it. **1802** H. Martin *Helen of Glenross* III. 286 But I envied him too much, I fear, when he won her to sincerely love him. **1856** Froude *Hist. Eng.* (1858) I. ii. 125 The nation at that time was sincerely attached to Spain. **1872** M. Collins *Princess Clarice* II. ix. 130, I most sincerely..and heartily declare that I love the Thames next to my wife.

*Comb.* **1872** *Routledge's Ev. Boy's Ann.* 5/1 Many kind and sincerely-meant words.

**b.** Used in the subscription of letters.

**1702** Charlett *Let. to Pepys* 3 Sept., Excuse all..defects in, Sir, your most sincerely obedient Servant. **1735** Mrs. Pratt in *Swift's Lett.* (1768) IV. 87, I long to have the pleasure of assuring you in person, how sincerely I am, Sir, your ever obliged and most faithful humble servant. **1817** Scott *Let.* in *Lockhart* (1837) IV. ii. 75, I beg my kindest respects to Mrs. Southey, and am always sincerely and affectionately yours, Walter Scott. **1818** Moore *Fudge Fam. Paris* vi. 228 Good-bye—my paper's out so nearly, I've only room for Yours sincerely.

†**3.** In a pure or innocent manner. *Obs.*$^{-1}$

**1578** Timme *Calvin on Gen.* 91 She [Eve] might have sincerely beheld the tree, that no lust of eating might first have assailed her mind.

†**4.** In a pure, absolute, or perfect manner or degree. *Obs.*

*a* **1577** Sir T. Smith *Commw. Eng.* (1633) 10 Seldom or never shall you find governments which are absolutely and sincerely made of any of them above named, but always mixed with another. **1605** Bacon *Adv. Learn.* II. i. §4 Narrations which are meerly and sincerely naturall. **1610** Healey *St. Aug. Citie of God* 381 His..ministers heard not with eares, but more sincerely, with intellects. **1655–60** Stanley *Hist. Philos.* (1687) 185/2 The Gods being void of corporeal mixtion understand purely and sincerely.

**b.** Completely, thoroughly, wholly.

**1576** Newton *Lemnie's Complex.* (1633) 221 When the blood is sincerely purified,..the spirits consequently are made pure. ? **1630** Milton *On Time* 14 Every thing that is sincerely good And perfectly divine. **1681** Dryden *Abs. & Achit.* 43 But life can never be sincerely blest.

†**5.** Carefully; without injury. *Obs. rare*$^{-1}$.

**1607** Topsell *Four-f. Beasts* (1658) 483 There was a monument erected in writing in the publick place at Ardea, which untill his time was there sincerely preserved.

**sincereness** (sɪn'sɪənɪs). Also 6 **syncerenes(se**, 6–7 **sincerenes(se**. [f. as prec. + -ness.] The state or quality of being sincere, in various senses of the adj.; sincerity.

**1537** Cromwell in Merriman *Life & Lett.* (1902) II. 67 Preparing in the meane tyme with suche pure syncerenes, trewly to open the worde of god. **1561** T. Norton *Calvin's Instit.* I. 5 b, Whereas they ought to haue serued him with holinesse of life and syncerenesse of hart. **1605** Bacon *Adv. Learn.* II. xxi. §3 The good of fruition or contentment, is placed eyther in the Sincerenesse of the fruition, or in the quicknesse and vigor of it. *a* **1668** Davenant *Albovine* Wks. (1673) 429 Things do differ much from the sincereness Of their first creation. **1695** Temple *Introd. Hist. Eng.* 224 Conditions..observed with great Faith and Sincereness. **1844** Browning *Colombe's Birthday* IV, The doubts yourself, in after-time, May call up of your heart's sincereness now. **1879** Arnold in *Macm. Mag.* July 203 The profound sincereness with which Wordsworth feels his subject.

**sincerity** (sɪn'sɛrɪtɪ). [ad. L. *sincēritas*, f. *sincērus* sincere: see -ity. Cf. F. *sincérité* (1519), Sp. *sinceridad*, Pg. *sinceridade*, It. *sincerità*.] The character, quality, or state of being sincere.

†**1.** Freedom from falsification, adulteration, or alloy; purity, correctness. *Obs.*

**1546** Udall in Strype *Ann. Ref.* (1824) I. 651 That England might the better attain to the sincerity of Christ's doctrine. **1579** W. Wilkinson *Confut. Fam. Love* Brief Descr. ij b, Such dayly danger honge over their heades that professed the sinceritie of the Gospel. *a* **1623** Ainsworth *Pentateuch* I. Advt., Some objections made against the sinceritie of the Hebrew Text. **1653** Baxter *Saints' R.* I. vii, Our Rest..will be absolutely Perfect and Compleat; and this both in the Sincerity and Universality of it.

†**b.** Genuineness (*of* a passage). *Obs.*$^{-1}$

**1678** Cudworth *Intell. Syst.* I. iv. §19. 363 Though this [passage]..be no where now to be found in those extant Tragedies of this Poet.., yet the sincerity thereof cannot reasonably be at all suspected by us.

**2.** Freedom from dissimulation or duplicity; honesty, straightforwardness.

**1557** N. T. (Geneva) *2 Cor.* ii. 17 But as of synceritie.. speake we in Christ. **1611** Bible *Josh.* xxiv. 14 Feare the Lord, and serue him in sinceritie, and in trueth. **1691** J. Norris *Pract. Disc.* 281 When we Contemplate his Sincerity, which consists in his candid, open and ingenuous dealing with the Sons of Men. *a* **1718** W. Penn in *Life* Wks. 1726 I. 137 Sincerity goes farther than Capacity. **1789** Belsham *Ess.* II. xxxii. 212 Martyrdom..is a very satisfactory proof of the sincerity of those who voluntarily submit to it. **1839** Keightley *Hist. Eng.* II. 27 Who can question the sincerity of these men? **1856** Froude *Hist. Eng.* (1858) II. ix. 337 Henry..felt no confidence either in the sincerity of the pope, or in the sincerity of the French King. **1870** Lowell *Study Windows* 158 There is nothing so pitilessly and unconsciously cruel as sincerity formulated into dogma.

**b.** Of feelings: Genuineness.

**1611** Bible *2 Cor.* viii. 8 To prooue the sinceritie of your loue. **1726** Pope *Odyss.* XI. 550 For thee she feels sincerity of woe. **1781** Gibbon *Decl. & F.* xviii. (1787) II. 75 The sincerity of his friendship has been suspected. **1904** Butcher *Harvard Lectures* 191 At the root of all good writing lies sincerity of conviction.

**c.** *pl.* Sincere feelings or actions.

**1840** Carlyle *Heroes* (1858) 279 Loyalty and Sovereignty ..are grounded not on garnitures and semblances, but on realities and sincerities. **1843** —— *Past & Pres.* (1858) 90 Exchange our dilettantisms for sincerities. **1877** Stubbs *Lect. Med. & Mod. Hist.* (1886) 101 Men of flesh and blood, with beliefs, sincerities and virtues.

**sincesyne:** see sinsyne.

**sinch**, variant of cinch *sb.* and *v.*

**sincipital** (sɪn'sɪpɪtəl), *a.* *Anat.* [ad. L. type **sincipitāl-is*, f. *sinciput*: see next. So F. *sincipital* (1812).] Of or pertaining to the sinciput.

**1653** Urquhart *Rabelais* I. xliv, The two triangularie bones called sincipital. **1835–6** *Todd's Cycl. Anat.* I. 745/2 He found the entire syncipital region very irregular. **1843** Wilkinson tr. *Swedenborg's Anim. Kingd.* I. ii. 62 The frontal, sincipital, temporal, and sphenoid bones. **1863** *Battlefields of South* II. 315 *note*, The occipital and sincipital regions are both large and well-balanced.

**sinciput** ('sɪnsɪpʌt). Chiefly *Anat.* Also 7 **syncipput**. [L. *sinciput*, for early **senciput*, f. *sēmi* half + *caput* head. So F. *sinciput* (1586).] The front part of the head or skull.

**1578** Banister *Hist. Man* 8 The fore part [of the head], called Sinciput, or Bregma. **1650** Bulwer *Anthropomet.* 11 When the Temples are eminent, the occiput and synciput depressed. **1689** Moyle *Abstr. Sea Chirurg.* II. vii, Mind that you apply not your Traphine on the temporal Bones, Sutures, or Sinciput. **1711** Addison *Spectator* No. 275 ⁋5 We observed a large Antrum or Cavity in the Sinciput. **1767** Gooch *Treat. Wounds* I. 279 A girl, who..was struck with the hand upon the sinciput, and became immediately blind. **1809** Byron *Bards & Rev.* Argt., Wks. 1898 I. 305 Incorporation of the bullets with his sinciput and occiput. *a* **1848** Holmes *Nux Postcœnatica* 46 All the longest heads That ever knocked their sinciputs in stretching on their beds. **1873** Mivart *Elem. Anat.* iii. 77 We have the base or basilar region, and opposite to it the vertex, sinciput, or sincipital region.

*fig.* *c* **1638** *Strafford Papers* II. 158, I..judge the other [to be]..the very sinciput, the vertical point of the whole faction.

**sinck**, obs. var. of SINK *sb.* and *v.*

**sinckanter:** see SINCANTER.

†**sincke**, obs. variant of CINQUE.

**1577–82** BRETON *Toyes Idle Head* Wks. (Grosart) I. 28/1 Setting all at sincke and syce. **1600** W. WATSON *Decacordon* (1602) 144 Sincke shal vp and sice shall vnder.

**sinckfoile**, obs. variant of CINQUEFOIL.

**sincopacion, sincope**, obs. varr. SYNCOPATION, SYNCOPE.

**sind** (saɪnd), *sb.* In 8 **synd**, 9 **syne**. [f. the vb.] A rinsing; a draught, a potation.

*a* **1774** FERGUSSON *Farmer's Ingle* iii, A heartsome meltith, and refreshing synd O' nappy liquor. **1899** CROCKETT *Kit Kennedy* 57 'Thae Shire-folk are no content wi' giein' a pot a bit syne wi' a jaw o' water,' said Heather Jock.

**sind** (saɪnd), *v. north.* and *Sc.* Also 5 **synde**, 8– **synd**; 9 **syne, sine**. [Of obscure origin. The Sc. pron. also has a diphthong (seɪnd), in contrast to the short vowel of *bind* (bɪnd), *find*, etc.] *trans.* To rinse, to wash out or *down*.

*α.* *a* **1350** *St. Nicholas* 202 in Horstm. *Altengl. Leg.* (1881) 13 Als þe childe stouped þam bihind, To tak water, þe coup to sind. **1483** *Cath. Angl.* 340/1 To Synde, *vbi* to wesche. **1752** *Scotland's Glory* 70 A cup of beer goes round at first their thirsty throats for synding. **1790** D. MORISON *Poems* 148 A lass.. There sinding out her duds. *Ibid.* 185 Wi' nimble hand she sinds her milking-pail. **1825** BROCKETT *N.C. Gloss.* s.v., To sind it down, being to take a drink after meat. **1841** W. AITKEN *Poet. Wks.* 55 A waught o' ale to sind their gab. **1860** F. FARQUHARSON in Ford *Harp of Perthshire* (1893) 216 Katie and Lizzie come in frae the kye, An' synd their milk coggies an' lay them a' by.

*β.* **1807–10** R. TANNAHILL *Poems* (1846) 13 Now Mirren's to the burn to sine her kirn. **1853** *Whistle-Binkie* Ser. II. 78 They syned doun the sappy, substantial food, Wi' a capfu' o' yill.

Hence '**sindings**, rinsings.

**1824** SCOTT *St. Ronan's* ii, A' the bits of vinegar cruets.., and ilk ane wi' the bit dribbles of syndings in it. **1868** JANET HAMILTON *Poems* 221 The milky syn'ins o' the kirn. **1876** ROBINSON *Whitby Gloss.* 171 *Sindings*, watery dregs; washings.

‖**sindaco** ('sindako). [It.: see SYNDIC *sb.*] In Italy: a mayor.

[**1881** *Encycl. Brit.* XIII. 464/1 The syndic (*sindaco*) or chief magistrate of the commune is appointed by the king for three years.] **1902** H. BELLOC *Path to Rome* 342 We came to the house of the Sindaco or Mayor. **1969** M. GILBERT *Etruscan Net* I. v. 64 Broke had been looking at the Sindaco. **1975** S. JOHNSON *Urbane Guerilla* II. 81 He would seek the permission of the Sindaco and Commune of Siena for the staging of a special or *straordinario* Palio.

**sindal(l**, obs. forms of SENDAL.

**sindar**, obs. form of CINDER.

†**sindaw**. *Obs. rare.* Also 6 **syndow, -daw**. [ad. G. *sindau* (also *sinnau, sinau*), f. *sin-* always (cf. SENGREEN) + *dau* dew.] The plant *Alchemilla vulgaris*, common Lady's mantle.

In Lyte (1578) and Parkinson (1640) as a German name only. In quot. 1621 the plant sundew may be intended.

**1548** TURNER *Names Herbes* (E.D.S.) 82 Alchimilla, other wyse called Pes leonis, is called in english our Ladies Mantel or syndow. **1562** —— *Herbal* III. (1568) 24 Alchimilla is named in English syndaw, and oure ladies mantil. **1621** BURTON *Anat. Mel.* II. iv. I. iii. (1651) 369 Bernardus Penottus prefers his Herba solis, or Dutch-Sindaw, before all the rest in this disease.

**Sindebele:** see NDEBELE.

**sindel**, obs. form of SENDAL.

**sinder**, obs. f. CINDER; Sc. var. of SUNDER.

**sinderesis**, obs. form of SYNDERESIS.

**Sindhi** ('sɪndiː), *sb.* and *a.* Also †**Sindee; Sindi**. [a. Hind. *Sindhi*, ult. f. Skr. *sindhu* river, *spec.* the Indus or the surrounding area.] **A.** *sb.* **1.** A native or inhabitant of Sind, now a province in the south-east of Pakistan, through which the Indus passes to the Arabian Sea.

**1815** M. ELPHINSTONE *Acct. Kingdom of Caubul* IV. v. 500 The Sindees with whom I have conversed. **1836** in *Corresp. relative to Sinde 1836–1838* 20 in *Parl. Papers 1843* XXXIX. 9 The notions of the most enlightened (if I may apply the term) Sindees are.. at utter variance with our customs. **1887** *Encycl. Brit.* XXII. 91/2 The Mohammedans [in Sind] may be divided into two great bodies— the Sindis proper and the naturalized Sindis. The Sindi proper is a descendant of the original Hindu. **1927** *Chambers's Jrnl.* Jan. 11/1 The little Sindi could distinguish every hoofprint and point out the goat which had made it. **1978** F. OLBRICH *Desouza pays Price* xxi. 131 Most of the Sindhis..had gathered their wealth together.. by Independence Day and descended on Bombay.

**2.** The name of a language consisting of several dialects spoken principally in Sind, but also in adjacent districts of north-west India.

**1838** *Penny Cycl.* XII. 227/2 *Sindhî*, spoken in Sinde as far as the mouths of the Indus. **1908** [see NEPALESE *a.* and *sb.*]. **1948** D. DIRINGER *Alphabet* II. vi. 376 Sindhi, spoken by three and a half million people in Sind. **1968** *Guardian* 14 Nov. 3/3 'Jiye Sind' (Long live Sind) has become among many Sindhis a form of salutation and there are demands for the elevation of Sindhi to the status of national language. **1981** V. POWELL *Flora Annie Steel* vii. 52 The strictly local dialect, a variety of Sindhi, made the setting up of female schools impracticable.

**B.** *adj.* Of or pertaining to this people or their language.

**1836** W. H. WATHEN *Gram. Sindhi Lang.* 1 There are several different alphabets used in writing the Sindhi language. **1899** *Folk-Lore* X. 413 The far renowned.. Sindhi story of Sassi and Punnun. **1946** *Civil & Mil. Gaz.* 31 Aug. 8/3 Three Sindhi merchants. **1979** V. S. NAIPAUL *Bend in River* xiv. 244 There was this Sindhi girl who had studied in England.

Also '**Sind(h)ian** *a.* and *sb.*

**1849** J. D. CUNNINGHAM *Hist. Sikhs* i. 19 The occupation, by the Sindhian Daoodpotras of the Lower Sutlej, took place within the last hundred years. **1911** D. S. MARGOLIOUTH *Mohammedanism* i. 26 An outrage committed by a Sindian on a noble Moslem. **1964** in *Panjab Past & Present* (1978) XII. 412 The Sindhian Amirs were of course alarmed to learn that Ranjit Singh positively entertained the intention of attacking Shikarpur.

**sindic(k**, obs. ff. SYNDIC.

‖**sindicato** (sindi'kato). [Sp., Pg.; cf. SYNDICATE *sb.*] In Spain, Portugal, Latin America, etc.: a trade union. *spec.* (usu. in *pl.*) a Spanish trade union of a type originally established during the regime of General Franco, and subject to close government control. Cf. SYNDICAL *a.*

**1936** *Times* 21 Aug. 9/1 The newly created *sindicatos*, or labour unions. **1957** LD. HAILEY *Afr. Survey 1956* XX. 1451 The *sindicatos* have powers of investigating grievances or disputes, and provision is made for arbitration; they also try to find employment for members who are out of work. **1964** *Ann. Reg. 1963* 285 During the year it became evident that the Catholic Workers' Brotherhoods had become trade unions in all but name..but legally the government-controlled *sindicatos* maintained their monopoly. **1965** *New Statesman* 16 Apr. 599/1 Before his death Rodolfo Romero was the secretary-general of the peasant *sindicato* at Tapatapa. **1976** *National Observer* (U.S.) 28 Feb. 16/3 Underground leaders of the workers' commissions were widely elected to the above-ground negotiating committees of sindicatos.

**sindle**, var. of SENDLE *adv.* seldom.

**sindon** ('sɪndən). Now only *Hist.* Also 5–6 **syndone**, 5–7 **sindone**; 5–7 **syndon** (5 **-oun**). [a. OF. *syndone, sindone*, or a. L. *sindon* (*-ŏnis*), a. Gr. σινδών (*-όνος*), prob. of Oriental origin.]

**1.** A fine thin fabric of linen; a kind of cambric or muslin.

*c* **1450** *Mirour Saluacioun* (Roxb.) 95 The body bewrapped in Syndone. **1582** N. T. (Rhem.) *Matt.* xxvii. 59 Ioseph taking the body, wrapt it in cleane sindon. *Ibid.*, *Mark* xiv. 51 A certaine yong man folowed him clothed with sindon vpon the bare. **1601** R. JOHNSON *Kingd. & Commw.* (1603) 163 The countrey of Media, whether the Russie merchants trauell for raw silkes, sindon, saffron and other commodities. **1631** WEEVER *Funeral Mon.* 16 They.. inuested the defunct, with..perfumed sereclothes, fine Aromaticke Sindon, and the like. **1679** BLOUNT *Anc. Tenures* 64 A Head-peece, lin'd with Syndon or fine Linen. [**1860** *Our English Home* 29 A square piece of this fabric, lined with silk or scarlet sindon.]

**2.** A piece of this fabric used for various purposes: **a.** As a shroud, *spec.* that in which the body of Christ was wrapped. Also in It. form ‖**sindone**.

*c* **1500** KENNEDIE *Passion of Christ* 1219 Ane pretius claith, quhilk we ane syndon call, That kingly corps to couer he coft syne. **1526** *Pilgr. Perf.* (W. de W. 1531) 259 The corporas [signifyeth] the syndone or sudary wherin his blessed body was.. wrapped. **1610** A. COOKE *Pope Joan* 40 Many Papists are perswaded they haue that Syndon wherein Christs body was lapped. **1650** FULLER *Pisgah* IV. vi. 117 Afterwards they were wrapped up in a Sindon, bound hand and foot with grave cloaths. **1670** LASSELS *Voy. Italy* (1698) I. 54 The Holy Syndon, wherein they say our Saviour's body was wound up and buried. **1902** tr. *P. Vignon's Shroud of Christ* ii. 50 If 'the napkin' of St. John *were* the face-kerchief, where would have been the Shroud (*sindon*)? **1912** H. THURSTON in *Month* Nov. 539 One could well imagine that when the body had been laid out and covered back and front with the long impregnated sindon, strips of linen were used to secure the feet.. keeping the sindon in its place. **1933** *Dublin Rev.* Jan. 36 St. Nino, a Georgian princess.. was told that the Sindon was formerly in the possession of St. Peter. **1963** *Guardian* 31 May 12/3 The famous Holy Shroud, or Sindone, of Turin.

**b.** As a corporas.

**1553** *Respublica* 873 Thei had thalter clothes,..with the sindons in which wer wrapte the chalices. **1885** J. H. NEWMAN *Callista* (1890) 340 The deacon received from the acolyte the *sindon*, or corporal,..and spread it upon the sacred table.

**c.** As a garment or wrapper.

**1577** HANMER *Anc. Eccl. Hist.* (1619) 32 He vsed no woollen vesture, but wore a Sindone. **1582** N. T. (Rhem.) *Mark* xiv. 52 But he casting of the sindon, fled from them naked. **1609** BIBLE (Douay) *Judges* xiv. 12, I wil geve you thirtie sindones, and as many coates. **1626** BACON *New Atl.* (1650) 10 There were found in it a Book, and a Letter; Both ..wrapped in Sindons of Linnen. *a* **1700** EVELYN *Diary* 23 Apr. 1661, Then was a coyfe put on [the King], and the cobbium, syndon, or dalmatic.

**d.** As a surgical appliance, being made up into a small roll or pledget, usually with some medicament, and used to fill up an open wound.

**1657** TOMLINSON *Renou's Disp.* 199 Pulverated and sowed in a double syndon or pure cloth. **1684** tr. *Bonet's Merc. Compit.* III. 76 A Syndon (that is a piece of fine cloth,.. having a thread fastened to the middle to draw it forth by). **1736** *Phil. Trans.* XLI. 497 A large and thick Sindon dipt in a warm detergent Lotion. **1758** J. S. *Le Dran's Observ. Surg.* (1771) 78 We placed Linen Sindons upon the *Dura Mater.*

**3.** *attrib.* Made or consisting of sindon.

*c* **1500** KENNEDIE *Passion of Christ* 1298 Thir twa knychtis ..In syndoun claith him wand with reuerence. **1573** L. LLOYD *Marrow of Hist.* (1653) 168 They [the Egyptians] sow up the body, which being done, they did put it in fine sindon cloth. **1688** HOLME *Armoury* I. 11 That Auriflamb, that was so much admired by the French, was but of one color, a square red Syndon Banner. *Ibid.* III. xviii. (Roxb.) 122/1 Holy-oke termes it a church Banner, flag or streamer, others a Syndon Banner.

Hence '**sindonless** *a.* (in sense 2 c).

*c* **1595** SOUTHWELL *St. Peter's Complaint* 25 With easie losse sharpe wrecks did he eschew, That Sindonlesse aside did naked slip.

**sindonology** (sɪndə'nɒlɒdʒɪ). [f. SINDON + -OLOGY.] The study of the Holy Shroud of Turin, in which the body of Christ was reputedly wrapped. So ˌ**sindono'logical** *a.*

**1950** *Catholic Digest* May 77/1 Dr Wuenschel.. will give an address on 'The Shroud of Turin and the Burial of Christ' this May in Rome at the International Syndonological convention. **1953** E. WUENSCHEL *Holy Shroud of Turin* (rev. ed.) 4 In 1950, he was invited to read a paper at the First Sindonological Congress at Rome—a meeting of internationally recognized authorities on the Holy Shroud of Turin. **1964** J. WALSH *Shroud* xii. 117 By the start of the Second World War the Shroud had been studied more closely than in all its previous history... The investigation..assumed the stature of a separate discipline and was given a name, *sindonology*. **1978** *Church Times* 6 Oct. 6/4 This book..alarms by an account of a visit to a Sindonological Library in New York. **1979** *Radio Times* 7–13 Apr. 86/2 Don Pietro Borga is the general secretary of the International Centre for Sindonology (study of the shroud).

Hence ˌ**sindo'nologist**, a student of the Shroud.

**1953** E. WUENSCHEL *Holy Shroud of Turin* (rev. ed.) 4 He collaborated with Dr. Paul Vignon, the greatest of all sindonologists. **1980** *Observer* 28 Dec. 3/1 It has been a disappointment to sindonologists (the name for shroud students) that the Roman Catholic authorities have refused to allow this [*sc.* carbon dating].

†'**sindony**. *Obs.* Also 6 **sendony**. = SINDON.

*c* **1450** *Cov. Myst.* (Shaks. Soc.) 336, I gyf the this sindony that I have bowth, To wynde the in whyl it is new. *c* **1502** *Joseph Arim.* 22 So Ioseph layde Ihesu to rest in his sepulture, And wrapped his body in a clothe called sendony.

**sindri, -dry**, obs. or Sc. ff. SUNDRY.

†**sine**[1]. *Obs.* Forms: *α.* 1 **sionu, sinu, sino** (*obl.* **sine**, *pl.* **sina**), 3, 5 **syne**, 4, 6 **sine**, 5 **zyne**, *Sc.* **seyne**. *β.* 4–5 **syn**; *pl.* 5 **synnes**. [OE. *sionu*, etc. (originally a *wō*-stem: see SINEW), = OFris. *sini, sine, sin* (Fris. *sine*), MDu. *sene, zene* (Du. *zeen*), MLG. and LG. *sene*, MHG. *sene, senne* (G. *sehne*, †*senne*), ON. and Icel. *sin* (Norw. *sin, sēn*), MSw. *sina, sena* (Sw. *sena*), MDa. *sinæ, senæ* (Da. *sene*). The *β*-forms may be due to Scand. influence. Cf. also HUXEN and HOCKSHIN.] A sinew.

*α.* *c* **725** *Corpus Gloss.* N 97 *Neruus*, sionu. *c* **1000** *Sax. Leechd.* II. 6 Læcedomas ʒif sin [*sic*] scrince..& ʒif sino clæppette & cwaciʒe. *c* **1000** ÆLFRIC *Gen.* xxxii. 25 Þa æthran he his sine on his þeo, and heo þær-rihte forscranc. *c* **1300** *Beket* 2429 That ther nas no flesch ileved bote synes and bar bon. *c* **1375** *Cursor M.* 3944 (Fairfax MS.), For þis enchesoun..of sine of bestes etes nane of ʒou. *c* **1430** *Two Cookery-bks.* 37 Also choppe a-mong þe zynes of þe fete clene y-pikyd. *Ibid.*, Choppe þe syneys in-to þe same milk rythte smal. *c* **1470** HENRY *Wallace* II. 401 Wallace.. Throw brayne and seyne in sondyr straik the bayne. **1544** *Extr. Reg. Aberdeen* (1844) I. 207 Selling of tauch, sine, flesche, fische.

*β.* *c* **1400** *Beryn* 588 For þe egge of þe panne met with his shyn, And karff a too a veyn, & þe nexte syn. **14..** *Towneley Myst.* xxiii. 165 Let now se and lefe youre dyn, And draw we ilka syn from syn. *c* **1450** *St. Cuthbert* (Surtees) 1073 So þat þe synnes in his ham Be þat bolnyng was drawen samen.

**sine**[2] (saɪn). Also 6–7 **sign(e**. [ad. L. *sinus* a bend, bay, etc.; also, the hanging fold of the upper part of a toga, the bosom of a garment, and hence used to render the synonymous Arab. *jaib*, applied in geometry as in sense 2. Cf. F. *sinus*, Sp. and It. *seno*.]

†**1.** A gulf or bay. *Obs. rare.* (Cf. SINUS 5.)

**1591** SYLVESTER *Du Bartas* I. iii. 98 Such is the German Sea, such Persian Sine, Such th' Indian Gulf. **1598** *Ibid.* II. ii. III. *Colonies* 94 Between the Erythrean Sea, and Persian Sine.

**2.** *Trig.* One of the three fundamental trigonometrical functions (cf. TANGENT, SECANT): Originally, the length of a straight line drawn from one end of a circular arc parallel to the tangent at the other end, and terminated by the radius; in mod. use, the ratio of this line to the radius, or (equivalently, as a function of an angle) the ratio of the side of a right-angled triangle opposite the given angle to the hypotenuse (the sine of an obtuse angle being numerically equal to that of its supplement). Abbrev. *sin.*

For *coversed, logarithmic, natural, subversed*, and *versed sines*, see the adjs.

**1593** FALE *Art of Dialling* 60 This Table of Sines may seeme obscure and hard to them who are not acquainted with Sinicall computation. **1662** HOBBES *Seven Prob.* Wks.

1845 VII. 62 You take BR,..which is the Sine of forty-five degrees. **1663** BUTLER *Hud.* I. i. 123 [He could] Resolve by Signs and Tangents streight, If Bread or Butter wanted weight. **1710** J. HARRIS *Lex. Techn.* II. s.v., Sines on the Plain Scale, Gunter's Scale, and almost all Scales have a Line, called the *Line of Sines*. **1738** *Gentl. Mag.* VIII. 10/1 The Sine of the visible Semidiameter of the Earth. **1774** M. MACKENZIE *Maritime Surv.* 63 The Sines of the Complement of the Altitude. **1833** HERSCHEL *Astron.* v. 185 The sines or tangents of such small arcs being proportional to the arcs themselves. **1847** TENNYSON *Princ.* vi. 239 Of sine and arc, spheroid and azimuth. **1880** HAUGHTON *Phys. Geogr.* III. 155 *note*, This will convert all the periodic terms ..into the sums of sines and cosines of arcs.

**b.** Const. *of* an angle.

**1728** PEMBERTON *Newton's Philos.* 361 The sine of the angle of incidence bears to the sine of the refracted angle a given proportion. **1823** BROOKE *Crystallogr.* 296 The analogy between the sines of the angles of triangles, and the sides subtending those angles. **1859** SABINE in *Man. Sci. Enq.* 91 The intensity of the Earth's magnetic force in different localities is inversely as the sines of the angles of deflection. **1864** BOWEN *Logic* xii. 407 The ratio of the sines of the angles of incidence and those of refraction is constant for the same medium.

†**3.** ***right sine***, = prec. *Obs.*

**1594** BLUNDEVIL *Exerc.* II. (1636) 103 *Sinus complementi*, is the right Sine of that Arch which is the complement of the given Arke. **1596** W. BURROUGH *Variation Compass* B v b, Which is the seconde right signe of the semidiurnall arke. **1715** tr. *Gregory's Astron.* (1726) II. 797 The Ratio between ..the Radius and the Right Sine of the Angle *ASD*. **1795** HUTTON *Math. Dict.* II. 456/1.

**4.** *attrib.*, as ***sine compass, complement, galvanometer, -inductor, -integral, rhumb, -wave***; **sine bar** *Mech.*, a device used to set out or measure angles accurately, in which one end of a bar of known length is raised on gauge blocks; **sine tone** = *pure tone* s.v. PURE *a.* 1 e; **sine wave**, a periodic oscillation of pure and simple form in which the displacement at any point is proportional to the sine of the phase angle at that point; a wave or curve resembling (a segment of) this in form.

**1915** *Engineering* 8 Jan. 42/3 A sine-bar is a flat strip of steel, planed true all over, upon which are fixed two hardened and ground plugs, 1 in. in diameter, 10 in. apart. **1975** BRAM & DOWNS *Manuf. Technol.* i. 19 The sine bar is commonly used for marking off and checking the angle of a workpiece. **1879** *Encycl. Brit.* X. 52/1 The earliest forms of standard galvanometer were the tangent and sine compasses invented by Pouillet. **1706** PHILLIPS (ed. 6) s.v., Sine Complement of an Arch or Angle, is what that Arch or Angle wants of 90 Degrees [etc.]. **1873** F. JENKIN *Electr. & Magn.* xiii. §8 Sine galvanometers can be easily made much more sensitive than tangent galvanometers. **1879** *Encycl. Brit.* VIII. 49/2 A is the fixed and B the suspended coil of the electrodynamo-meter, and S the sine-inductor. **1880** *Ibid.* XIII. 39/2 These functions..were styled the sine-integral and the cosine-integral. **1797** *Ibid.* (ed. 3) XII. 693/1 The extent from 8 points to 3¼ points, the complement of the course on sine rhumbs. **1828** MOORE *Pract. Navig.* 15 Sine rhumbs, marked (SR), is a line which contains the logarithms of the natural sine of every point and quarter point of the Mariner's Compass, figured from the left hand towards the right [etc.]. **1962** Sine tone [see LINE *v.*² 8 a]. **1976** *Times Lit. Suppl.* 3 Dec. 1522/5 Stockhausen's recent memoirs of his early years, which are sometimes strangely at odds with his correspondence of the period (particularly vis-à-vis the whole question of sine-tone synthesis). **1893** D. E. JONES tr. *H. Hertz's Electric Waves* 17 The vibration of the primary conductor is, at any rate to a first approximation, a uniformly damped sine-wave of determinate period. **1916** *Electrician* LXXVI. 800/1 The alternating current produced in the telephones is almost a pure sine wave. **1965** *Wireless World* Sept. 455/1 To verify the rated output of an amplifier a 1 kc/s sinewave is fed through it at a level sufficient to produce the rated output power. **1972** *Islander* (Victoria, B.C.) 21 May 15/2 Some of the flat fishes, such as flounders and rays, move by undulating their bodies in a flattened sine wave. Visualize this movement as a flag held horizontally in a stiff wind.

**sine**³ (ˈsaɪniː). *Eton College slang.* [a. fanciful mod.L. *sine* (*coloribus*), without (colours).] At Eton College: a House team, which excludes those awarded colours; the members of this considered *collect.*

**1922** S. LESLIE *Oppidan* xxii. 276 The *sine* was made to forego the sweetness of a long lie in order to run..before breakfast. *Ibid.* 277 As match after match was lost by the *sine*, Mouler put up a notice to say that in future *sine* were expected to do a training walk as well as their morning run. **1940** M. MARPLES *Public School Slang* 112 Idioms such as these are probably not of great age... [e.g.] *sine* (Eton): used to describe a House team excluding colours, from the dog Latin *sine coloribus*, without colours: hence *2nd sine* wrongly used = 2nd XI.

**sine**, obs. f. SIGN *sb.* and *v.*; var. of SIND *v.*

**sinecal**, obs. variant of SINICAL *a.*

ˈ**sinecural**, *a. rare.* [f. next + -AL¹.] 'Relating to a sinecure.'

**1860** WORCESTER (citing *Ecl. Rev.*). Hence in later Dicts.

**sinecure** (ˈsaɪnɪkjʊə(r), ˈsɪn-), *sb.* and *a.* Also 7 sine cura, 7–8 sine-cura, sine cure, sine-cure. [ad. L. *sine cūrā* in the phrase *beneficium sine cūrā* (see def.), from *sine* without, *cūrā* abl. sing. of *cūra* care. F. *sinécure* is from Eng. In Scotland and America, and hence generally, the first vowel is freq. pronounced short.]

**1.** An ecclesiastical benefice without cure of souls.

α. **1662** BAGSHAW in *Acc. Baxter's Suspension* 45, I hope the Bishop will be so Charitable as to provide a *Sine-Cura* for him. **1676** DEGGE *Parson's Counsellor* (1681) 197 Parsonages, Vicarages and *Sine Cura's*. **1706** PHILLIPS (ed. 6), *Sine-Cura*, or *Sine-cure*, a Benefice without Cure of Souls.

β. **1672** MARVELL *Reh. Transp.* I. 8 He can not have deserved less than a Prebend for his first Book, a Sine-cure for his second. **1700** DRYDEN *Fables, Charac. Good Parson* 71 The publick fair..Where bishopricks and sine cures are sold. **1748** LIND *Lett. Rel. Navy* (1757) III. 131 The Island has..a chaplain; but for some years past it has been made a Sine Cure. **1765** BLACKSTONE *Comm.* I. 386 When the clerk so presented is distinct from the vicar, the rectory thus vested in him becomes what is called a *sine cure*; because he hath no cure of souls. **1850** HT. MARTINEAU *Hist. Peace* v. iv. (1877) III. 241 This act abolished many ecclesiastical sinecures. **1862** GOULBURN *Pers. Relig.* IV. iv. (1873) 278 The spirit of the age is to..hate and abolish sinecures.

†**b.** An income derived from such a benefice.

**1700** T. BROWN tr. *Fresny's Amusem.* iii. Wks. 1709 III. I. 22 The Residentiary's Stalls, whose Owners made a *Sine Cure* of 400 *l. per Annum*.

**2.** Any office or position which has no work or duties attached to it, esp. one which yields some stipend or emolument.

**1676** WYCHERLEY *Pl. Dealer* v. i, Well, a Widow, I see, is a kind of a sine cure. **1705** HEARNE *Collect.* 26 Nov., He.. makes yᵉ Place in a manner a *sine-cure*; as most other Publick Readers do. **1766** ENTICK *London* IV. 368 The magistracy of the city of London have adopted this ward only as a *sine cure* for the senior alderman. **1800** COLQUHOUN *Comm. Thames* viii. 272 Many of the best institutions moulder into Sinecures. **1841** MIALL in *Nonconf.* I. 553 If all men were under the influence of religion government would be a sinecure. **1885** 'E. GARRETT' *At Any Cost* vi, Grace's duties were never oppressive, but on Sunday they were a sinecure.

**3.** *attrib.* or as *adj.* **a.** Of the nature of a sinecure; involving no duties or work.

**1761** LD. BARRINGTON in Ellis *Orig. Lett.* Ser. II. IV. 432, I never could myself understand the difference between a Pension and a Sinecure Place. **1791** NEWTE *Tour Eng. & Scot.* 360 It was not Mr. Pultney's intention to erect a sine-cure place. **1810** BENTHAM *Packing* (1821) 61 By means of sine-cures in general, and judicial sine-cure offices in particular. **1861** BERESF. HOPE *Eng. Cathedr. 19th C.* 277, I must strongly plead for the simultaneous creation of a chapter however sinecure for the present. **1868** J. H. BLUNT *Ref. Ch. Eng.* I. 22 Royal blood seems to have been thought ample excuse for a complete sinecure life. **1889** GRETTON *Memory's Harkback* 158 Martinsthorpe, a sinecure living, which consists of one ancient house and some half dozen occupants.

**b.** Holding or enjoying a sinecure.

**1812** L. HUNT in *Examiner* 12 Oct. 643/1 The Courtiers, the Sinecure-men,..who grow rich from what empties our pockets. **1844** STEPHEN *Comm. Laws Eng.* II. i. III. 76 A sinecure rector, or rector without cure of souls. **1871** M. COLLINS *Marq. & Merch.* II. v. 128 The little sinecure governess came face to face with her master.

Hence ˈ**sinecure** *v. trans.*, to appoint to, place in, a sinecure (Ogilvie *Suppl.* 1855); also ˈ**sinecured** *ppl. a.*

**1832** *Lincoln Herald* 20 Nov. 4/3 Mr. Brougham, the Lord Chancellor's sinecured brother.

ˈ**sinecureship.** *rare.* [f. SINECURE *sb.*] A position or post of the nature of a sinecure.

**1828** P. CUNNINGHAM *N.S. Wales* (ed. 3) II. 310 The culprit is merely sent back to a sinecureship in a government gang.

ˈ**sinecurism.** [f. SINECURE *sb.* + -ISM. Cf. F. *sinécurisme.*] The practice of holding or permitting sinecures; the prevalence of sinecures in the church or any other sphere of work.

**1817** BENTHAM *Parl. Reform* Introd. 233 In one point of view more flagrant is this abuse [non-attendance], even than sinecurism. **1858** GOLDW. SMITH in *Oxford Ess.* 280 Such sinecurism would..be accompanied by an undue depression and starvation of the working staff. **1878** *N. Amer. Rev.* CXXVI. 224 The English universities have suffered deeply from..clericism, celibacy, and sinecurism.

ˈ**sinecurist.** [f. as prec. + -IST. Cf. F. *sinécuriste.*] One who has or seeks a sinecure.

**1817** W. HONE (*title*), The Sinecurist's Creed. Whosoever will be a Sinecurist [etc.]. **1845** LD. CAMPBELL *Lives Chancellors* xvii. (1857) I. 266 The Masters in Chancery were considered overgrown and oppressive sinecurists. **1884** *Law Times* LXXVIII. 9/1 What else is a ground landlord but a sinecurist quartered on the land.

*attrib.* **1818** BENTHAM *Ch. Eng., Catech. Exam.* 306 The parsonages deserted by Sinecurist Incumbents. *Ibid.* 325.

‖**sine die** (ˈsaɪnɪ ˈdaɪiː, ˈsɪneɪ ˈdiːeɪ). [L., *sine* without + *diē*, abl. sing. of *diēs* day.] Without any day being specified (for reassembling, resumption of business, trial of a person or cause, etc.); indefinitely.

**1631** in Birch *Crt. & Times Chas. I* (1848) II. 125 My Lord of Salisbury's cause is put off *sine die*. **1641** SIR E. DERING *Sp. on Relig.* 9 Among all these I observe one, a very main one, to sleep *sine die*. *a* **1734** NORTH *Examen* I. iii. §146 (1740) 217 They seemed to lie there, without Bail or Trial *sine Die*. **1771** GIBBON *Lett.* 18 Nov., If I hear that your journey to Denham is put off *sine die*, or to a long day, I shall on Monday set off for London. **1803** CUTLER in *Life*, etc. (1888) II. 118 At fifteen minutes after twelve at night, the House adjourned *sine die*. **1842** BARHAM *Ingol. Leg.* Ser. II. *St. Cuthbert* vi, The *fête* was postponed *sine die*. **1892** *Nation* 22 Dec. 466/1 The reasons given for taking a recess instead of adjourning *sine die* are extremely puerile.

**sinegen**, obs. form of SIN *v.*

**Sinemurian** (sɪnəˈmjuːrɪən), *a. Geol.* [ad. F. *Sinémurien* (A. d'Orbigny *Paléont. Française. Mollusques et Rayonnés Fossiles. Terrains Jurassiques* (1842–9) I. 604), f. L. *Sinemurum*, ancient name of Sémur-en-Auxois, a town in Côte d'Or department, France + *-ien* -IAN.] Of, pertaining to, or designating a stage of the Lower Jurassic in Europe which in the modern division is next below the Pliensbachian. Freq. *absol.*

**1863** J. D. DANA *Man. Geol.* III. iii. 449 The Sinemurian (Lower Lias, named from the locality at Sémur). **1888** J. PRESTWICH *Geol.* II. xvi. 242 M. Gosselet includes the Lower- and Infra-Lias in one division—the Sinemurian, which he divides into two subdivisions—the Upper Sinemurian and the Lower Sinemurian or Hettangian. **1928** E. NEAVERSON *Stratigraphical Palaeont.* xv. 331 The most familiar Sinemurian brachiopod is the broad-plaited *Spiriferina walcotti*. **1969** BENNISON & WRIGHT *Geol. Hist. Brit. Isles* xiii. 289 A cyclic sequence of thin lime-stones and clays of Blue Lias type comprise the Hettangian followed by clays chiefly, although locally limestones may occur as high as the top of the Sinemurian.

‖**sine qua non** (ˈsaɪnɪ kweɪ nɒn, ˌsɪneɪ kwɑː ˈnəʊn). Also 8- quâ. [L., *sine* without + *quā*, abl. sing. fem. of *quī* which (agreeing with *causa*) + *nōn* not.

The Latin phrase, which is common in scholastic use, occurs in Boëthius, and had its source in Aristotelian expressions. The corresponding plural *sine quibus non* has occasionally been employed.]

**1.** With adjectival force: Indispensable, absolutely necessary or essential. **a.** Following upon a noun (orig. *cause*).

[**1588** GREENE *Perimedes* Wks. (Grosart) VII. 44 They proceede not of necessitie, as *causa sine qua non*, but as infections that flowe from the abuse.] **1615** in Birch *Crt. & Times Jas. I* (1848) I. 378 He..was in some sort as a cause *sine qua non* of their blood that were dead for the fact before him. **1678** CUDWORTH *Intell. Syst.* I. iv. 382 Which kind of Philosophers (saith he) do not seem to me, to distinguish betwixt the True and Proper Cause of things, and the Cause *Sine qua non*. *a* **1734** NORTH *Examen* III. vii. §64 (1740) 550 The Preliminary Article *sine quâ non*, was that..he should surrender his Place of Recorder. [**1811** J. ADAMS *Wks.* (1856) I. 673 They would not insist upon the fisheries or western lands as conditions *sine quibus non* of peace.]

**b.** Used attributively.

**1798** M. G. LEWIS in Lockhart *Scott* (1837) I. ix. 291 A ghost or a witch is a *sine qua non* ingredient in all the dishes of which I mean to compose my hobgoblin repast. **1840** DE QUINCEY *Style* IV. (1860) 312 Publication..is a *sine qua non* condition for the generation of literature. **1870** J. H. NEWMAN *Gram. Assent* I. iv. 39 Though acts of assent require previous acts of inference, they require them, not as adequate causes, but as *sine quâ non* conditions.

**2.** Somebody or something indispensable.

**1602** CECIL *Let.* in Moryson *Itin.* (1617) II. 221 You are not the efficient cause or *sine qua non*. **1622** MABBE tr. *Aleman's Guzman d'Alf.* I. I. ii, My mother agreed with her marriage-maker, her *Sine qua, non*,..to come one day thither to make merry. **1774** H. WALPOLE *Lett.* (1857) VI. 111 Remember, a brother is the *sine quâ non* of my reconciliation. **1786** LD. KENYON in *Brown's Chanc. Cases* II. 46 Certainty of the property, though one of the *sine quâ nons*, was wanting. **1814** *Amer. St. Papers, For. Relat.* (1832) III. 709 It was a *sine qua non* that the Indians should be included in the pacification. **1853** 'C. BEDE' *Verdant Green* I. xviii, It seemed a sine quâ non with the gentlemen who superintended the training. **1885** *Law Rep. 29 Chanc. Div.* 285 Every finding of fact that was a *sine quâ non* of the judgment.

**b.** *pl.* Breeches. (Cf. INDISPENSABLE *sb.* c.)

**1850** SMEDLEY *Frank Fairlegh* xvii, Your..negotiation with that raw-boned giant in the blue plush *sine qua nons*.

Hence **sine-qua-ˈnonical** *a.*, indispensable; **sine-qua-ˈnonniness**, indispensability.

**1816** MOORE *Mem.* (1853) II. 95 The shabbiness with which they are daily surrendering so many wise, indispensable, and sine-quâ-nonical measures to the bullies of Opposition. **1834** SOUTHEY *Doctor* iii. (A. 1) I. 20 Nature herself shows us the utility, the importance,..the sinequanonniness of pockets.

**Sineque**, var. SENECA.

‖**sine quo non.** Chiefly *Sc. Law.* [f. as SINE QUA NON, with the masc. *quō* (also pl. *quibus*) in place of the fem. *quā*.] Indispensable; also *absol.*, an indispensable person, *spec.* a curator, trustee, etc., appointed under this designation.

**1693** STAIR *Institutes* (ed. 2) IV. xx. §31 By a *Quorum*, or *sine quibus non*, in which case though the *Sine quibus non* accept not,..the Interdiction remains. **1765–8** ERSKINE *Inst. Law Scot.* I. vii. §15 The concurrence of the number fixed for the quorum, of which he who is *sine quo non* must be always one. **1819** SCOTT *Let.* in *Lockhart* (1837) IV. x. 331 Harper is a *sine quo non*. **1838** W. BELL *Dict. Law Scot.* 245 A curator *sine quo non* cannot act by himself. *Ibid.* 918 By the death or non-acceptance of the *sine quo non* the nomination fails.

†**sines.** *Obs. rare.* In 5 synys, 6 sinnes. [a. OF. *sines*, also *senes*, ad. L. *sēnī*, the distrib. answering to *sex* six.] Two sixes in dicing.

*c* **1450** *Book of Brome* 16 Synys and Catyr that ȝe haue cast. *Ibid.*, That ȝe haue cast synys and trey. **1589** NASHE *Marprelate* Wks. (Grosart) I. 161 Their Dice are so cunninglie coggd: as though they cast Sinnes for the moste parte, yet they maie in the end with a tripsie Tray, carrie all awaie smoothe.

**sine'salary.** *nonce-word.* [f. L. *sine* (as in *sinecure*) + SALARY *sb.*] An office without pay.

*a* **1843** SOUTHEY *Life A. Bell* (1844) I. 110 Some of these offices may have been Sinecures; but..none of them were Sinesalaries.

**sine'scriptual,** *a. nonce-word.* [Cf. prec. and SCRIPTURAL *a.*] Not possessing the Scriptures.

**1840** G. S. FABER *Christ's Disc. Capernaum* 101 He places Ireneus and the contemporary sinescriptual nations an entire century later than that in which he was writing.

**Sinesian** (saɪ'niːʃ(ɪ)ən), *a.* [f. late L. *Sin-æ* (see SINÆAN) + -ESE + -IAN.] Of or pertaining to the Chinese and kindred races or to those parts of Asia inhabited by them.

**1899** *Eng. Hist. Rev.* Apr. 226 A remarkable fact in the history of Sinesian civilisation. **1905** *Athenæum* 16 Sept. 361/2 Now, through Japan, the West has made a definite breach in Sinesian exclusiveness.

**sinester,** obs. form of SINISTER *a.*

†**sinet.** *Obs.* Also 6 synat, synet, senett. [a. OF. *sinet*, var. of *signet* SIGNET *sb.*] A signet.

*c* **1440** *Gesta Rom.* xlviii. 213 (Harl. MS.), He openid hit, & sawe þerein letters selid withe the sinet of þe Emperoure. **1502** *Croscombe Churchw. Acc.* (Somerset Rec. Soc.) 25 A ryng of sylver and gylt and a synat of sylver. **1530** PALSGR. 187 *Signet*, a synet. **1554** MACHYN *Diary* (Camden) 51 Ther was a man..hangyd, dran, and quartered, for conterffeyting the quen senett.

†**sineth,** *adv.*, *prep.*, and *conj. Obs.* In 5 senith, sinneth. [app. an alteration of *sethen* SITHEN.] = SINCE *adv.*, *prep.*, and *conj.*

**1542** HARVEL in *St. Papers Hen. VIII* (1849) VIII. 706, I wrote to the same the first of thinstant; and senith her is arivid..the Turkes Ambassadour. —— *Ibid.* IX. 38 Senith my last letters..the comming owt of Barbarossa hath ben her divulgid. **1556** *Aurelio & Isab.* (1608) B ij, Sinneth that what soever loveth well, is never lefte of the unluckie.

**Sinetic** (sɪ'nɛtɪk), *a.* [var. of SINITIC *a.*] Chinese.

**1893** R. WILSON tr. *Figuier's Human Race* 235 We shall separate it into three branches—the Hyperborean, the Mongolian, and the Sinetic branches. **1898** *Blackwood's Mag.* Jan. 144 Their low foreheads, leering Sinetic eyes, the lewd lips and heavy hair.

†**sine'titular,** *a. Obs.* [f. L. *sine* without + *titul-us* title.] Without a title (for ordination).

**1642** JER. TAYLOR *Episc.* (1647) 183 That decree of Chalcedon against Sinetitular ordinations.

**sinew** ('sɪnjuː), *sb.* Forms: α. 1 *pl.* seonuwa, seon(o)we, 2 seonewe, 3 sen(u)we, 3-4 senue, 3-7 senewe, 4-5 zenew, 5-6 senew; 4-6 senow, -owe, 5-6 senou; 6 senaw. β. 1 sionwe, sinwe, sinu(w)-, 4-7 sinewe (6 sinn-), 5- sinew, 6-7 sinue (6 sinnue); 1, 4-7 synewe (7 synn-), 4-6 synew (5 cynew, 6 syneu); 4 synue, 4-5 syn(u)we (5 cynwe), 5 synu, cynu. γ. 4 synoghe, 4, 6 synou, 5 synnou, 5-7 synnow (5 cynow-); 4 sinou, 5-7 sinow-, 6-8 sinnow. δ. *Sc.* (and *north.*) 5 (9) senon, 6 sennon, 9 sennen; 5-6 senown (5 sennoun, -own); 6 synnoun, 9 sinnon, sinnen (sinner). [OE. *seon(o)we*, *sionwe*, etc., oblique forms from the nom. *sionu*, *sinu*: see SINE *sb.*[1] The *w* of the stem also appears in OHG. *senewa*, *senuwa*, *senwe*, etc., and in MDu. *zenewe*, *zenuwe* (Du. *zenuw*). With the Sc. and northern forms in *-n* cf. *minnon* for MINNOW and *talloun* for TALLOW.]

**1.** *Anat.* A strong fibrous cord serving to connect a muscle with a bone or other part; a tendon. Also in fig. context (quot. 1560).

α. *Beowulf* 817 Seonowe onsprungon, burston ban-locan. *c* **1000** *Saxon Leechd.* III. 48 Seonuwa [synd] fortogene & ða tan scrinceð up. *a* **1200** *St. Marher.* 7 Ant þenne ichulle tellen, hwen þu al to torren art,..alle þine seonewen. *c* **1205** LAY. 6498 þat deor..forbat him þa breste, ban and þa senuwen. *c* **1290** *S. Eng. Leg.* I. 175 þere nas no flesch bileued bote senue and bare bon. *c* **1380** WYCLIF *Sel. Wks.* II. 23 Paralitikes..mai not riȝtli move þer partis for feblenesse of þer senewis. *c* **1400** *Destr. Troy* 8794 The bavme..Bret thurgh the bones and the big senowis. **14..** *Metr. Voc.* in Wr.-Wülcker 627 *Neruus*, zenew. *c* **1450** *Merlin* xx. 339 Grete and lene and full of veynes and of senewes. *a* **1529** SKELTON *P. Sparowe* 46 Wherewith my handes I wrange, That my senaws cracked. **1547** BOORDE *Brev. Health* x. 10 b, A senowe the whyche doth growe out of the myddle of the spondyls. **1560** DAUS tr. *Sleidane's Comm.* 101 To sende their ayde against the Turke..were to unarme them selves and to cut their owne senewes.

β. *a* **1000** *Andreas* 1425 Nu sint sionwe toslowen. *c* **1000** *Saxon Leechd.* II. 282 On þa saran sinua & aswollenan.. bind on gate tyrdelu. *Ibid.* 328 ðif sinwe syn forcorfene, nim renwyrmas [etc.]. *a* **1300** *Cursor M.* 3941 þe maister sinu of his the. *Ibid.* 3944 O sinnu etes neuer juu. *c* **1305** *St. Christopher* 194 in *E.E.P.* (1862) 65 Hire lymes burste.. Necke & synuen & oþer ek. **1382** WYCLIF *Gen.* xxxii. 25 He towchide the synwe of his hip. *a* **1400-50** *Stockh. Med. MS.* 97 To stawnche blod of weyne or of synuwe. *c* **1430** *Two Cookery Bks.* 53 Take fayre Buttes of Porke..& clene pyke a-way þe bonys & þe Synewes. *c* **1440** *Promp. Parv.* 78/1 Cynew,..of armys, or leggys, *nervus*. **1584** R. SCOT *Discov. Witchcr.* III. vi. 37 A spirit hath no flesh, bones, nor sinewes. **1601** HOLLAND *Pliny* II. 162 The oil or ointment..is comfortable to the sinues. **1658** A. FOX *Würtz' Surg.* I. iii. 11 It happeneth..that through this needless stitching of the sinews, is caused the running of sinews. **1727-46** THOMSON *Summer* 507 While his big sinews full of spirits swell. **1771** SMOLLETT *Humph. Cl.* (1815) 215 You cannot conceive.. how it braces every sinew of the human frame. **1810** SCOTT *Lady of L.* III. xiii, Such cause of haste Thine active sinews never braced. **1865** SEELEY *Ecce Homo* iii. (ed. 8) 23 No one questioned the stoutness of Samson's sinews.

γ. *c* **1340** HAMPOLE *Pr. Consc.* 1917 Ilka vayn and ilka synoghe and lith. *c* **1425** tr. *Arderne's Treat. Fistula*, etc. 39 þe mouþe of þe lure wiþ þe lacertes and þe synowes..was vtterly gnawen away. **1483** *Cath. Angl.* 341/1 With owtyn Synows, *eneruus*. **1535** COVERDALE *Ezek.* xxxvii. 6, I wil geue you synowes, & make flesh growe vpon you. **1577** B. GOOGE *Heresbach's Husb.* III. (1586) 126 His thighes full of synowes, and his legs well knitte. **1604** BRETON *Passionate Sheph.* Wks. (Grosart) I. 7/2 Each Sinow, Limme and ioynt, Perfect shape in euery point. **1611** COTGR., *Nerf*, a Synnow.

δ. *c* **1375** *Sc. Leg. Saints* vii. (*James the Less*) 631 His senownys þat drawyn ware to-gyddyre, lousyt rycht þare. **1470** HENRY *Wallace* v. 297 His houch sennownnis he cuttyt all atanys. *c* **1500** KENNEDIE *Passion of Christ* 450 All his body þai fret, Saris his senonis. **1552** LYNDESAY *Monarche* 4921 Quhen that cald humour dounwart dois proceid, In Senownis it causis Arthetica. **1596** DALRYMPLE tr. *Leslie's Hist. Scot.* I. v. 287 Vanes, synnounis, banes. **1829** BROCKETT *N.C. Gloss.* (ed. 2), *Sinnon*, for sinew. **1894** HESLOP *Northumbld. Gloss.* 616 He cut yen o' the senons o' his leg wi' the adge.

**b.** A tendon taken out of an animal body and used for some purpose, esp. for binding or tying with; hence, †a snare; a string in a musical instrument.

*a* **1300** *Cursor M.* 7195 Wit seuen sinous wa sa me band, I tint my strenth. *c* **1388** WYCLIF *Judges* xvi. 7 Seuene coordis of senewis. *a* **1400** *Prymer* (1891) 82 Thou settest my foot in a synewe [L. *in nervo*]. **1535** COVERDALE *Judges* xvi. 7 Samson sayde vnto her: Yf I were bounde with seuen roapes of fresh senowes, which are not yet dryed vp, I shulde be weake, and as another man. **1555** EDEN *Decades* (Arb.) 95 They thrust the synew within the sheethe therof. **1591** SYLVESTER *Du Bartas* I. v. 513 Th' inchanting sinnewes of his Instrument. **1855** LONGF. *Hiawatha* iii. 77 His linden cradle,..Safely bound with reindeer sinews. **1875** BANCROFT *Native Races Pacific St.* I. 56 A sling or net made of woven sinews.

†**c.** *transf.* A rib in a leaf. *Obs. rare.*

**1551** TURNER *Herbal* I. Bj, Whose leues are..more depe cut in, towarde the synowe that goeth thorow the myd lefe. **1578** LYTE *Dodoens* 251 The stemmes whereof, with the synewes of the leaves.., are all redde. **1585** [see NERVE *sb.* 6 a].

**d.** In sing., as a substance or material.

**1825** J. NEAL *Bro. Jonathan* I. 268 He appeared powerful enough to crush the boy—sinew and bone. **1845** DARWIN *Voy. Nat.* vi. (1879) 118 The tassels had been fastened by split sinew.

†**2.** A nerve. *Obs.*

**1398** TREVISA *Barth. De P.R.* III. xvii. (1495) 62 The synewe that hyghte *neruus obticus*, an holow sinew, is hidde in the vtter partye of the brayne. *c* **1400** *Lanfranc's Cirurg.* 24 From þe brayn comen .vij. peire cordes, & þei ben clepid sensible senewis. **1545** RAYNOLD *Byrth Mankynde* I. x, The brayne, of whom all the sinewes take their originall. **1578** BANISTER *Hist. Man* I No portion of sinewes, which are the immediate organs of sence, is in their [bones] substaunce disseminated. **1612** WOODALL *Surg. Mate* Wks. (1653) 86 When..the Marrow of the back bone is hurt, there followeth the resolution of the sinewes (which hindereth the function of the sense and motion). **1621** BURTON *Anat. Mel.* I. i. II. iii, Nerves or Sinews, are Membranes without, and full of Marrow within.

**3.** Chiefly *pl.* Strength, energy, force.

**1560** DAUS tr. *Sleidane's Comm.* 393 b, For this intent.., y^t ther should no sinewes nor force at all be lefte in all Germany. *c* **1595** CAREW in G. G. Smith *Eliz. Crit. Ess.* (1904) II. 292 The Italyan is pleasante but without synewes, as to stillye fleeting water. **1617** MORYSON *Itin.* III. 194 His authoritie hath no sinews. **1722** WOLLASTON *Relig. Nat.* iii. 49 That they may not be ignorant..what it is that gives sinews to an inference, and makes it just. **1856** FROUDE *Hist. Eng.* III. 61 He should find..that their arms had not wholly lost their ancient sinew. **1878** MORLEY *Carlyle* 175 It [Carlylism] is Byronism with thew and sinew.

**4.** The main strength, mainstay, or chief supporting force, *of* something.

The plural has been more freq. employed than the sing.

*sing.* **1579** NORTH *Plutarch*, *Cleomenes* (1896) V. 223 He that sayed first, that Money was the sinewe of all things, spoke it chiefly in my opinion, in respect of the warres. **1589** *Pasquil's Return* B, Bursting the sinew of peoples obedience. **1606** SHAKS. *Tr. & Cr.* I. iii. 143 The great Achilles, whom Opinion crownes, The sinew, and the forehand of our Hoste. **1684** BP. BURNET tr. *Utopia* 151 There must follow upon it a dissolution of all Justice, which is the chief Sinew of Society. **1721** RAMSAY *Prospect of Plenty* 210 Thou nervous sinnow of baith war and law! **1880** *Christian World* 137 The advanced Liberals..supply the bone, the sinew, the muscle, and the fighting power of the party.

*plur.* **1587** FLEMING *Contin. Holinshed* III. 343/2 A man may well saie, that chiualrie is the fundation and sinewes of a commonweale. **1600** HOLLAND *Livy* VII. xxxix. 277 The principall authors of the mutinie, who were the sinewes and strength thereof. **1624** BEDELL *Lett.* vi. 104 Take away these words, and the sinewes of the sentence are cut. **1691** HARTCLIFFE *Virtues* p. xiv, The Principles of Irreligion do unjoynt the Sinews of all Government. **1760** JOHNSON *Idler* No. 96 ¶ 4 Indolence and effeminacy..relaxed the sinews of his resolution. **1791** MRS. RADCLIFFE *Rom. Forest* i, The time may come..when death shall dissolve the sinews of Avarice. **1818** HALLAM *Mid. Ages* (1872) I. 252 Whenever he thought fit to exert the sinews of his prerogative. **1857** RUSKIN *Pol. Econ. Art* 23 The discipline of the masses has hitherto knit the sinews of battle. **1870** J. BRUCE *Life Gideon* xi. 197 It is pre-eminently practical as touching the very soul and sinews of our faith.

**b.** In phr. *the sinews of war*, i.e. money. †Also in sing. (quot. 1598).

After L. *nervi belli pecunia* (Cicero *Phil.* v. ii. 5).

*c* **1550** *Disc. Common Weal Eng.* (1893) 87 These coins and treasures be not with out cause called of wise men..The senowes of warre. **1560** DAUS tr. *Sleidane's Comm.* 272 The Duke of Saxon, although he wanted the Senewes of warre, yet he battred Gemund. **1598** BARRET *Theor. Warres* 120 His Indian fleet bringing the sinew of his warres. **1621** BRATHWAIT *Nat. Embassie* (1877) 139 We surpasse their state, In power, in riches, sinewes of sharpe warre. **1668** DRYDEN *Even. Love* III. i, If you had the sinews of war, I am sure you would be flying out. **1751** *Narr. H.M.S. Wager* 5 That part of the World, from whence their immense Wealth, the Sinews of War, is chiefly derived. **1827** HALLAM *Const. Hist.* (1876) II. viii. 87 There was one possible.. method of obtaining the sinews of war—the convocation of parliament. **1874** BURNAND *My Time* v. 39 As to the sinews of war, had he not already provided for the improbable adversities of the future?

**5.** *Comb.* **a.** In terms denoting contraction or strain of the sinews, as ***sinew-bound***, ***-grown***, ***-shrunk(en)***, ***-strained***.

**1603** FLORIO *Montaigne* II. viii. (1632) 214 An old, crazed, sinnow shronken, and nigh dead father. **1645** DANIEL *Poems* Wks. (Grosart) II. 23 My Sober Muse can say how it did wound My Sinnew-bound Vnusefull Members. **1654** H. L'ESTRANGE *Chas. I* (1655) 105 The King..was sinew-shrunk, and wanted money the sinews of war. **1686** *Lond. Gaz.* No. 2163/4 A brown bay Mare.., Sinew-strain'd on the near Leg before. **1705** *Ibid.* No. 4125/4 He is a little Sinew-strain'd of the inside of the off Foot before. **1828** CARR *Craven Gloss.*, *Sinner-grown*, having a contraction in the sinews, of which sinner is a corruption.

**b.** Miscellaneous, as ***sinew-backing***, ***-bruise***, ***-corded***, ***-shrinking***, ***-singer***; **sinew-water**, synovia, joint-oil.

**1598** SYLVESTER *Du Bartas* II. i. III. *Furies* 173 The sinew-shrinking Dead-laughing Apium. *Ibid.* II. ii. IV. *Columnes* 717 The Guide of supplest fingers On (living-dumb, dead-speaking) sinnew-singers. **1599** A. M. tr. *Gabelhouers' Bk. Phys.* 312/1 These Playsteres cure all woundes, whether they do thruste, or cut, yea and althoughe the very sinnuewater did issue therout. **1658** A. FOX *Würtz' Surg.* I. vi. 26 That corrosive..resisteth forcibly the sinew-water, called the joynt-water. **1725** *Fam. Dict.* s.v. *Horse-feeder*, Strains, Over-Reaches, Sinew-Bruises, and the like. **1847** TENNYSON *Princ.* v. 524 Supple, sinew-corded, apt at arms. **1896** GRINNELL *Story Indian* 151 The nocks were cut, and the sinew backing applied.

**sinew** ('sɪnjuː), *v.* [f. prec.]

**1.** *trans.* To run through, tie together, cover over with, or as with, sinews. *rare.*

**1592** NASHE *P. Penilesse* 13 Her gray breast, and her speckled side sayles, all sinnowed with siluer quilles. **1596** SHAKS. *3 Hen. VI*, II. vi. 91 So shalt thou sinow both these Lands together. **1607** MARKHAM *Caval.* VI. (1617) 55 After the tree is sinewed, you shall then glew strong canuase all ouer the wood also.

**2.** To supply with sinews; to strengthen as by sinews; to nerve, harden. Chiefly *fig.*

*a* **1614** DONNE *Βιαθανατος* (1648) 86 Out of a duty to Sinew and strengthen..the Doctrine of our Blessed Saviour. **1625** —— *Serm. 3 Apr.* 6 Thy Almightie Arme, sinewed euen with thine owne indignation. **1643** SPINKES *Serm. Oxford 19 Apr.* C 3 b, The kingdome being sinewed and flesht with the addition of so much new strength and force, flourisheth. **1718** D'URFEY *Grecian Heroine* v. i, My Clindor's, and Clorona's Wrongs,..sinew my old Flesh. **1766** GOLDSM. *Vic. W.* xxvii, We should then find that creatures, now stuck up for long tortures,..might, if properly treated, serve to sinew the state in times of danger. **1852** CULROSS *Lazarus Revived* 34 Christianity needs something to nerve and sinew it. **1879** TODHUNTER *Alcestis* 14 Sinew thy heart to hear; for death is dreadful. **1891** F. TENNYSON *Poems* 480 Such might Sinews old custom.

**sinewed** ('sɪnjuːd), *ppl. a.* Also 8 sinnewed. [f. SINEW *sb.* or *v.*]

**1.** Having sinews of a specified kind.

**1588** KYD *Househ. Phil.* Wks. (1901) 239 A youth..well proportioned, tough sinewed, and of a strong constitution. *a* **1700** DRYDEN (J.), Strong sinew'd was the youth, and big of bone.

**2.** Strengthened with sinews; strong, firm, vigorous, powerful, sinewy.

**1604** DRAYTON *Owle* 1450 The great Eagle..Whose sinewed wings..Beat the thin air. **1644** BULWER *Chiron.* 5 This strengthens Speech with nerves and the sinewed cords of twisted Reason. *c* **1720** TICKELL *Ode to Earl of Sunderland* iii, The flower of chivalry, who drew With sinew'd arm the stubborn yew. **1894** WHITBY *Mary Fenwick's Daughter* III. 82 Five feet eight of sinewed stature.

†**3.** Seated in the sinews. *Obs.*$^{-1}$

**1601** CHESTER *Love's Martyr*, etc. (1878) 85 Tis good for sinewed aches.

**'sinewer.** *rare.* [f. SINEW *v.*] A strengthener.

**1810** A. WILSON *Poems & Lit. Prose* (1876) II. 352 Toil, blest sinewer of the poor.

**'sinewiness.** *rare*$^{-1}$. [f. SINEWY *a.* + -NESS.] The character, state, or quality of being sinewy.

**1727** BAILEY (vol. II.), *Nervousness*, fulness of Nerves, sinewiness, Strength, &c.

†**'sinewish,** *a. Obs. rare.* Also 6 synowysshe, sinuishe. [f. SINEW *sb.* + -ISH[1].] Pertaining to the sinews; having sinews; sinewy.

**1530** PALSGR. 324/1 Synowysshe, belongynge to ones synouse, *arterique*. **1586** HOOKER *Hist. Irel.* II. xxiv. in *Holinshed*, His [Hugh de Lacy's] neck was short, and his bodie..sinewish. **1597** A. M. tr. *Guillemeau's Fr. Chirurg.* 2 b/1 The sinuishe partes of the boddye.

†**'sinewize**, *v.* *Obs.*$^{-1}$ [f. SINEW *v.* + -IZE.] *trans.* To furnish with sinews.

**1599** B. JONSON *Ev. Man out of Hum.* III. i[ii], Such an Anotomie of Witte, so Sinewiz'd and Arteriz'd, that 'tis the goodliest Modell of pleasure that euer was, to beholde.

**'sinewless**, *a.* Also 6 sinewe-, 7 sin(n)ewlesse. [f. SINEW *sb.* + -LESS.]

**1.** Destitute of sinews.

**1552** HULOET, Sinewelesse, or hauing no sinewes. **1767** S. PATERSON *Another Trav.* I. 245 That were to make headless trunks, and sinewless arms. **1798** W. TAYLOR in *Monthly Rev.* XXV. 515 The Farnesian Hercules, so muscular before, so sinewless behind. **1815** BYRON *Hebrew Melodies, Saul* i, His foot, in bony whiteness, glitter'd there, Shrunken and sinewless.

**2.** Lacking vigour; feeble, weak, powerless.

**1644** [H. PARKER] *Jus Populi* 44 Regiment in the first ages was rather too milde and sinewlesse than too violent and rigorous. **1656** *Artif. Handsom.* 193 All that ever was said against these Helps of beauty, seems to many wise women.. weak and sinnewlesse. **1829** K. H. DIGBY *Broadstone of Honour* I. *Godefridus* 294 The arms which once slew the Nemæan lion may become sinewless. **1869** J. KER *Serm.* (1874) I. 63 A weak sinewless Christianity. **1872** S. MOSTYN *Perplexity* I. viii. 145 Look at those hands; they are white, thin, sinewless.

**sinewous** ('sɪnjuːəs), *a.* Also 5 synew-, 7 sinnew-, 8 sineuous. [f. SINEW *sb.* + -OUS.] Sinewy; also *fig.*, strenuous, vigorous.

In quot. 1745 perh. intended for *synovial*.

**1495** *Trevisa's De P.R.* v. xxv. 134 The necke is synewous to make wylfull meuynge. **1586** HOOKER *Hist. Irel.* II. x. in *Holinshed*, His armes and other lims more sinewous than fleshie. **1663** in Kendall *Travels* (1809) I. xii. 143 Errors corrupt, by sinnewous dispute, He did oppugne and clearly them confute. **1745** ELIZA HEYWOOD *Female Spect.* III. 298 They [*sc.* snails] are..furnished with a sineuous juice, which, distilling from their pores, becomes a hard consistence. **1861** LYTTON & FANE *Tannhäuser* 13 Men, who ..scann'd His sinewous frame, compact of pliant power.

**sinewy** ('sɪnjuːɪ), *a.* Also α. 4 senewy; 5 synnevy, 7 synewy, -ie; 6 sinnewie, sinewye, 6–7 sinewie, 7 -ewey. *β.* 5 senowy; synnowy, 5, 7 synowy (6 -owie); 6 sinnowy, 7 -ie, 6–7 sinowie, -owy (6 -owye). [f. SINEW *sb.* + -Y. Cf. Du. *zenuwig*, G. *sehnig* (†*zenich, synnig*).]

†**1.** Made of sinews. *Obs. rare*$^{-1}$.

**1382** WYCLIF *Judges* xvi. 7 If with seuen senewy [L. *nerviceis*] coordis.. Y were boundun, Y shal be feble as other men.

**2.** Furnished with, full of, sinews.

**1398** TREVISA *Barth. De P.R.* v. xxv. (Bodl. MS.), The nekke..[is] senewy to make wilfull meuyng. *a* **1425** tr. *Arderne's Treat. Fistula*, etc. 85 þe face and þe leggez, and synowy placez and bony. **1563** T. GALE *Antidot.* II. 32 It.. helpeth the sinowye partes. **1576** TURBERV. *Venerie* 233 The sides of the dogges bulke, or vpon his thighes, or suche sinewye places. **1603** J. DAVIES (Heref.) *Microcos.* Wks. (Grosart) I. 24/1 For in the sinewes.. This pow'r is plac'd, or in the Synewy skin. **1633** P. FLETCHER *Purple Island* II. xx. *note*, The fleshie pannicle is a membrane very thick, sinewy, woven in with little veins. **1725** *Fam. Dict.* s.v. *Embrocation*, Nothing is more powerful to remove obstinate Swellings in the sinewy Parts. **1885** *Where Chineses Drive* 186 The only meat he could find to operate on was part of an awfully sinewy leg of beef.

*Comb.* **1844** H. STEPHENS *Bk. Farm* II. 246 The usual price received for lean, stringy-fleshed, sinewy-legged fowls, is far from remunerative.

**3.** Having strong, well-developed, or prominent sinews.

Usually implying strength, but sometimes leanness.

**1422** tr. *Secreta Secret., Priv. Priv.* 226 Who-so hath the fete well shappyn, grete toes and synnowy, sholde bene stronge and hardy. *c* **1440** *Pallad. on Husb.* IV. 704 The thies sadde and senowy, not to side. **1586** MARLOWE *1st Pt. Tamburl.* II. i, His armes and fingers long and sinowy. **1606** SHAKS. *Tr. & Cr.* II. iii. 259 [Let] Bull-bearing Milo his addition yeelde To sinnowie Aiax. **1667** *Phil. Trans.* II. 567 Those [whales] have great teeth.. and are very sinewy. **1725** POPE *Odyss.* v. 581 Fainting as he touch'd the shore, He dropt his sinewy arms. **1817** SHELLEY *Rev. Islam* I. xiii. 7 The vast bird would,.. with his sinewy neck, Dissolve in sudden shock those linked rings. **1855** MOTLEY *Dutch Rep.* VI. vii, In person, Orange was above the middle height, perfectly well made and sinewy. **1882** SERGT. BALLANTINE *Exper.* xxiii. 227 He was a sinewy little fellow.

*transf.* **1656** HEYLIN *Surv. France* 171 The Gates are very large and strong, as well in the sinewie composition of themselves, as in the addition of the Drawbridge.

**b.** *transf.* Of qualities, attributes, etc.: Derived from the possession of (strong) sinews; having the strength characteristic of sinews.

**1588** SHAKS. *L.L.L.* IV. iii. 308 As motion and long during action tyres The sinnowy vigour of the trauailer. **1602** MARSTON *Ant. & Mel.* Prol., Oh! that our Muse Had those abstruse and synowy faculties. **1641** MILTON *Animadv.* Wks. 1851 III. 186 Even this veine of laughing.. hath ofttimes a strong and sinewy force in teaching and confuting. **1784** COWPER *Task* v. 288 When at length mankind Had reach'd the sinewy firmness of their youth. **1810** SCOTT *Lady of Lake* I. xxviii, Few were the arms whose sinewy strength Sufficed to stretch it forth at length. **1873** 'OUIDA' *Pascarel* I. 7 Men were glad with the same sinewy force.. as made them in other times laborious.

**c.** Of language, writings, arguments, etc. (Cf. NERVOUS *a.* 3.)

**1600** E. BLOUNT tr. *Conestaggio* A 2 A faithfull, elegant, sinewie, and well digested historie. **1641** J. JACKSON *True Evang. T.* iii. 194 Nervous and sinewy Arguments. **1718** *Free-thinker* No. 18 The Latin Tongue has something Masculine, and Sinewy. **1863** *Sat. Rev.* 284 An out-of-door life encourages and produces a straightforward, intelligible, sinewy style. **1885** *Manch. Exam.* 18 Mar. 3/3 His nervous sinewy literary style will not be thrown away.

**d.** Similarly of speakers and writers.

**1598** SYLVESTER *Du Bartas* II. ii. II. *Babylon* 605 Cæsar, who knowes as well to write, as war: The Sinnewie Salust. **1644** BULWER *Chirol.* 162 Thus the sinewie Epigrammatist.

**4.** Of the nature of sinews; tough, stringy.

**1578** BANISTER *Hist. Man* 52 They [the muscles] are sinewie and broad in their begynning. **1594** T. B. *La Primaud. Fr. Acad.* II. Ep. to Rdr., Being dispersed into the muscles and skinne by meanes of certaine sinowie threedes concurring in manner of a net. **1612** WOODALL *Surg. Mate* Wks. (1653) 95 Sinowie Ligaments bruised and broken. *a* **1631** DONNE *Poems* (1650) 49 For if sinewie thred my braine lets fall Through every part. **1909** PATTERSON *Grip of the Nyika* 247 Tied up with bands of sinewy tree-bark.

†**5.** Strung with sinews. *Obs. rare.*

?*a* **1593** MARLOWE *Hero & Leander* I. 371 All deepe enrag'd, his sinowie bow he bent. **1624** QUARLES *Job Militant* xv, The sinowy Bow, and deadly-headed Launce, Shall breake in shiuers. **1659** LOVELACE *Poems* (1864) 242 So by the sinewy lyre now strook we see Into soft calms all storm of poesie.

**sinewy**, obs. variant of SENVY.

† **siney**, obs. form of *sené* SENNA.

**1580** HOLLYBAND *Treas. Fr. Tong*, *Vn petit arbre dict Baguenaudier*, a tree called Siney.

‖**sinfonia** (sinfo'nia, sɪn'fəʊniːə). *Mus.* Pl. **sinfonie, -ias.** [It., = SYMPHONY.] **a.** In early Italian opera: the overture. **b.** A symphony. **c.** (Used in the title of) a small symphony orchestra or chamber orchestra.

**1773** C. BURNEY *Present State of Music in France & Italy* 382, I heard a *sinfonia* or overture and a chorus.. which were excellent. **1818** W. GARDNER tr. *Bombet's Lives of Haydn & Mozart* 256 The sinfonia in *The Creation*, which represents the rising of the sun, is an exemplification of this theory. **1828** E. HOLMES *Ramble among Musicians of Germany* 180 The composition given this afternoon was Mozart's Jupiter sinfonia. **1884** *Encycl. Brit.* XVII. 87/1 The sinfonia or overture which is often associated with his [*sc.* Scarlatti's] name. **1924** A. HAM *Outl. Mus. Form* xix. 82 An Overture.. is an expansion of the Sinfonia or Symphony. **1946** DAVID & MENDEL *Bach Reader* I. 39 Neither the Inventions and the Sinfonias nor the two books of the *Well-Tempered Clavier*.. were printed during Bach's lifetime. **1967** I. SPINK *Hist. Approach to Mus. Form* iii. 98 These operas were not in recitative throughout. They also included choruses, dances and instrumental pieces or *sinfonie*. **1976** *Leicester Mercury* 16 July, He had recently contacted about 60 top class instrumentalists.. with the intention of forming an orchestra which.. would be called the Rutland Sinfonia.

Also **sinfonia concertante** (kontʃer'tante) [CONCERTANTE], a symphonic work exhibiting characteristics of the concerto.

**1903** R. HUGHES *Mus. Guide* I. 266/2 *S. concertan'te, concerta'ta, concertate*... concerto for many instrs., a concerto symphony. **1928** *Musical Times* 1 Feb. 165/1 M. Ansermet.. conducted William Walton's new 'Sinfonia Concertante' for orchestra and pianoforte. **1946** MENDEL & BRODER tr. *Einstein's Mozart* xvi. 274 Mozart cultivated this form less and less as the years went on. He abandoned the *sinfonia concertante*, and separated its ingredients. **1950** R. HUGHES *Haydn* vii. 80 At the fourth concert on 9th March [1792] the endearing *Sinfonia concertante* for violin, cello, oboe and bassoon was performed for the first time. **1959** [see ARGUABLY *adv.*]. **1979** *Early Music* July 415/2 Clarinettists will find in the E flat Symphony by the Earl of Kelly.. what amounts to a *sinfonia concertante*.

‖**sinfonietta** (sinfoni'etta, sɪnfəʊ'njɛtə). *Mus.* [It., dim. of prec.] **a.** A short, simple form of symphony. **b.** = SINFONIA c.

**1907** T. S. WOTTON *Dict. Mus. Terms* 180 *Sinfonietta*, a little Symphony, e.g. Raff's sinfonietta for 10 wind instruments. **1923** *Daily Mail* 20 Feb. 7 Mr. Eugene Goossens.. introduced.. his first symphony (shyly entitled a 'Sinfonietta'). **1947** A. EINSTEIN *Music in Romantic Era* xi. 131 But does not the lack of a slow movement make even a sinfonietta into a suite, a more or less disconnected succession of movements? **1970** *Music & Musicians* June 53 Playing at the Elizabeth Hall on March 25 before a miserably small audience, the Bournemouth Sinfonietta, ably directed by Nicholas Braithwaite. **1973** D. EWEN *Orchestral Music* xii. 207 His [*sc.* Hindemith's] major works ..included.. two compositions with humorous overtones: the Concerto for Woodwinds, Harp and Orchestra (1949) and Sinfonietta in E (1950). **1982** *Times* 29 Nov. 11/1 The London Sinfonietta settled down last night to become a string orchestra in a stabler sort of programme.

**sinful** ('sɪnfʊl), *a.* and *sb.* Forms: 1 synn-, 1–6 syn- (5 cyn-), 4–6 synne-; 2–3 sun-, 3 sune-; 2–3 sen-, 4 zen-; 3– sin- (3 sinn-, 6 sinne-); also 1–6 -full, 3 -uull, 3–4 -fol, -uol. [f. SIN *sb.* + -FUL. Cf. ON. and Icel. *syndafullr* (Norw. and Sw. *syndfull*, Da. *syndefuld*).]

**1. a.** Of persons, etc.: Full of sin; wicked, corrupt.

*c* **825**- [see b and c]. *c* **950** *Lindisf. Gosp.* Luke v. 8 ðeong from me, forðon monn synnfull Am. **971** *Blickl. Hom.* 43 þa lareowas sceolan synnfullum mannum eadmodlice tæcan. *c* **1175** *Lamb. Hom.* 149 þis is alle sunfulle monne leddre. *c* **1200** ORMIN 12048 Nohht ne wære he þanne Godd Acc sinnfull mann & wrecche. *c* **1250** *Kent. Serm.* 31 in *O.E. Misc.*, Se leprus signefieþ þo senuulle men. *a* **1300** *Cursor M.* 9050 Es nan sinfuller þan i. **1399** GOWER *Praise of Peace* 45 This sinful world was al paiene tho. *c* **1400** MAUNDEV. (Roxb.) xv. 70 þai call vs synfull and wikked. *c* **1440** *Promp. Parv.* 78/1 Cynfulle,.. *peccosus*. **1500–20** DUNBAR *Poems* xc. 7 We synfull folk sulde be more deligent. **1526** TINDALE *Romans* viii. 3 In the similitude of synfull flesshe. *a* **1586** SIDNEY *Ps.* I. iv, They that sinne in sinfull breast do cherish. **1662** STILLINGFL. *Orig. Sacræ* III. iv. 5 To execute his justice upon the sinful World. **1671** MILTON *P.R.* I. 162 His weakness shall o'ercome Satanic strength.., and mass of sinful flesh. **1781** COWPER *Truth* 383 What is man? Sinful and weak, in ev'ry sense a wretch. **1849** JAMES *Woodman* ii, You will not find it in this sinful world.

**b.** *absol.* in *pl.* (with or without *the*).

*c* **825** *Vesp. Psalter* ix. 18 Bioð ȝecerde ða synfullan in helle. *c* **950** *Lindisf. Gosp.* Mark ii. 16 He æt.. mið synnfullum & bærsynnigum. *c* **1175** *Lamb. Hom.* 95 He nalde mid his to-cume þa sunfullen fordemen. *a* **1240** *Lofsong* in *O.E. Hom.* I. 209 þuruh al þet ðu tawhtest and þoledest for sunfule in eorðe. **13..** *Cursor M.* 104 (Gött), Scho.. rayses þe sinful quen þai fall. **1377** LANGL. *P. Pl.* B. XIX. 22 Synful aren solaced & saued bi þat name. **1624** FLETCHER *Wife for a Month* IV. v, Shame attend the sinful, I know my innocence.

**c.** *absol.* in *sing.* †Also with *a*, a sinful person.

*c* **825** *Vesp. Psalter* cxxxix. 4 Hald mec, dryhten, of honda synfulles. **971** *Blickl. Hom.* 61 þonne se synnfulla.. his lif ȝeendaþ. *c* **1175** *Lamb. Hom.* 85 þe prost þet scal among cristene monkun þene sunfulle of sunne clensen. *c* **1275** *On Serving Christ* 25 in *O.E. Misc.*, þer is þe sunfulle vnsofte to beon Hwer he not no wey fyr for to fleon. *a* **1300** *Cursor M.* 13978 A seli sinful was sco þis. **1340** *Ayenb.* 90 To wende þane zenuolle and connynge an speches. *c* **1400** *Pol. Poems* (Rolls) I. 317 Christ suffered a sinful to kisse his fete.

**2. a.** Of acts, etc.: Involving sin; characterized or marked by sin.

*c* **1200** ORMIN 4182 Fra sinnfull word & werrc, Fra sinnful þohht & wille. **1297** R. GLOUC. (Rolls) 8357 Help hom & vorȝif hom þulke sunuol dede. *a* **1340** HAMPOLE *Psalter* xvii. 49 þai ere eldid, þat is in þaire ald synful lyf. **1390** GOWER *Conf.* I. 365 For certein Somme of gold [they] acorden That thilke horrible sinfull dede Assoiled was. **1535** COVERDALE *Wisd.* iii. 13 Blessed is.. yᵉ baren & vndefyled, which hath not knowne the synfull bedd. **1552** ABP. HAMILTON *Catech.* (1884) 4 It is.. ane synfull and ane damnabil thing. *c* **1600** SHAKS. *Sonn.* ciii, Were it not sinfull then striuing to mend, To marre the subiect that before was well? **1649** ROBERTS *Clavis Bibl.* 160 Notwithstanding all Davids Piety and integrity he was overtaken with many sinfull failings. **1742** C. WESLEY '*God of all power*' iv, Purge me from every sinful blot,.. Cleanse me from every sinful thought. **1835** J. H. NEWMAN *Par. Serm.* (1837) I. iii. 42 Like that bad prophet at Bethel.. while he sat at his sinful meat. **1866** GEO. ELIOT *F. Holt* (1868) 25 But many sinful things were highly agreeable to her.

**b.** Highly reprehensible. Also, as a strong intensive: excessive in manner or extent; 'dreadful', 'wicked'. *colloq.*

**1863** T. G. SHAW *Wine* 33 He considered it 'sinful' to expend 10/6 on a bottle of any wine. **1880** J. C. HARRIS *Uncle Remus* xxviii. 122 De way he stir up dem bees wuz sinful. **1920** WODEHOUSE *Damsel in Distress* ii. 35 The money that boy makes is sinful.

Hence † **sinfulhead**, sinfulness. *Obs.*

*c* **1250** *Gen. & Ex.* 180 Wilde der.. pine man wið sorwe and dred, And don hem monen his sinfulhed. *a* **1400** *St. Bernard* 541 in Horstm. *Altengl. Leg.* (1878) 50 For I knowe my sunfolhede Boþe in word, þouȝt and dede.

**sinfully** ('sɪnfʊlɪ), *adv.* Forms: (see quots.). [f. SINFUL *a.* + -LY².]

**1.** In a sinful manner; wickedly, iniquitously.

α. *c* **1200** ORMIN 16155 Follc.. þatt tær wass inne unnlaȝheliȝ & sinnfullike sammnedd. **1297** R. GLOUC. (Rolls) 9147 þe erchebissop of kanterbury.. Sacred him.. wel sunuolliche [*v.r.* synoulyche] alas. *c* **1330** R. BRUNNE *Chron. Wace* (Rolls) 14055 Moddred.. synfullyke had reysed stryf. *c* **1450** *Merlin* xxvi. 497 Sir,.. ye sey euill and synfulliche.

*β.* *a* **1300** *Cursor M.* 28431 In tendes haue i lett don in Sinfully in tent to wyn. *c* **1385** CHAUCER *L.G.W.* 2550 *Phyllis*, Syn thus synfully ȝe me be-gile. *c* **1440** *Promp. Parv.* 78 Cynfully, *criminose*. **1526** *Pilgr. Perf.* (W. de W. 1531) 239 b, Neuer inordynatly couet thy neyghbours wyfe, to vse her synfully. **1594** SHAKS. *Rich. III*, II. i. 119 All this from my Remembrance, brutish wrath Sinfully pluckt. **1685** BAXTER *Paraphr. N.T.* Matt. xiii. 13 They have.. sinfully shut their own eyes. **1879** R. T. SMITH *Basil the Great* ix. 108 Adam by eating sinfully transmitted sin.

**2.** Very reprehensibly. Also in weakened use: excessively.

**1869** 'MARK TWAIN' *Innoc. Abroad* xlv. 475 So sinfully ugly that she couldn't smile after ten o'clock Saturday night without breaking the Sabbath. **1888** D. C. MURRAY *Weaker Vessel* xiii, We were a sinfully indiscreet and curious young couple to talk of the affairs of others as we did. **1898** KIPLING *Fleet in Being* i, Affable young gentlemen prepared, even sinfully delighted, to take chances not set down in books. **1912** [see JUMP *sb.*¹ 7]. **1976** *New Yorker* 24 May 113/3 It's also guaranteed to be *sinfully* comfortable with its built-in headrest and body-conforming mattress.

**sinfulness** ('sɪnfʊlnɪs). Also 5 synfullnes, 5–6 -fulnesse. [f. SINFUL *a.* + -NESS.] The state or character of being sinful; wickedness, iniquity.

**14..** in *Tundale's Vis.* (1843) 148 Of my wreched synfullnes To gyff me grace. *c* **1440** *Promp. Parv.* 456/1 Synfulnesse, *peccabilitas, viciositas*. **1530** PALSGR. 270/2 Synfulnesse, *maluatie*. **1653** H. MORE *Antid. Ath.* I. i. §2 By reason of the Sinfulness and Corruption of their Natures. **1675** BURTHOGGE *Causa Dei* 43 The Sinfulness therein is only against God. **1761** WESLEY '*Jesus, if still*' vi, The sinfulness of sin. **1838** DICKENS *Nickleby* xvi, Mr. Gallanbile dines late on the day of rest, in order to prevent the sinfulness of the cook's dressing herself. **1878** LECKY *Eng. in 18th C.* II. 192 The absolute sinfulness of resistance.

**sing** (sɪŋ), *sb.* [f. SING *v.*¹]

**1.** The sound made by a bullet or other projectile in its flight.

**1871** *Daily News* 1 Mar., I distinctly heard the sing of the bullet overhead. **1897** C. BIGHAM *With Turkish Army in Thessaly* vi. 43 Here the first bullets began to pass over our heads; but from the sing we judged them to be spent. **1917** E. C. MIDDLETON *Way of Air* 70 The familiar 'sing' of an approaching shell. **1930** *Carmina* Oct. 45 The sing Of a stone from the sling.

**2. a.** An act of singing; the power of singing. Also, a hearty sing-song or round of collective singing (chiefly *U.S.*).

**1850** N. Kingsley *Diary* 1 Sept. (1914) 140 We had a fine sing in the Evening which put me in mind of home. **1875** I. L. Bird *Six Months in Sandwich Islands* xii. 175 There have been pleasant little gatherings for sewing..and on Sunday evenings what is colloquially termed, 'a sing'. **1884** *Congregationalist* Febr. 103 An English audience..enjoy a good, hearty, congregational 'sing'. **1907** *Cassell's Mag.* Feb. 324/2 Why don't you sing..? You have heaps of 'sing' in you. **1932** A. Huxley *Brave New World* iv. 73 In the Ealing stadium a Delta gymnastic display and community sing was in progress. **1964** 'J. H. Roberts' *'Q' Document* (1965) ix. 211 Skiers were gathered around in an alcoholic community sing. **1972** *Village Voice* (N.Y.) 1 June 96/4 Open sing, Verdi's Requiem. **1981** *Libr. Congr. Inf. Bull.* 16 Jan. (Staff News), Staff members and their families gather in the Great Hall for the annual carol sing.

**b.** ***on the sing***: (of a kettle) singing. Cf. sing *v.*[1] 6 a.

**1927** W. Deeping *Kitty* xxx. 384 'All the kettles—.' ..'Two are boiling, miss; the other's on the sing.'

**sing** (sɪŋ), *v.*[1] Pa. t. **sang, sung.** Pa. pple. **sung.** Forms: *Inf.* 1 **singan**, 3–4 **singen** (3 **sinken**, 4 **singyn**), 3–4 **singe** (4 **zinge**), 4– **sing**; 1 **syngan**, 3–5 (6) **syngen** (4–5 **syngyn**, 5 **cyngyn**), 4–5 **synge** (4 **seynge, zynge**), 5–6 **syng** (6 **synng**). *Pa. t. sing.* 1– **sang** (4 **zang**), 4–6 **sange**; 1, 4–7 **song**, 4–6 **songe, soong**, 6 **soung**, 6– **sung** (6 **sunge**); also *2nd pers.* and *subj.* 3 **sunge, songe.** *Pa. t. pl.* 1 **sungon, -an**, 1, 4–5 **sungun**, 2–4 **sungen** (3 **sunggen**), 4 **songen, so(u)nguen**, 3–4 **sunge, songe.** *Pa. pple.* 1 **ʒesungen**, 3 **i-sunge(n**; 1, 4–6 **sungen** (4 **sungun**), 4–6 **sunge**, 6 **soung, sownge, soong(e**, 6– **sung**; 3–4 **i-songe**, 4–6 **songen** (4 **-yne**, 6 **-in**, 5–6 **-on**), 5–6 **songe**, 5–7 **song.** [Common Teut.: OE. *singan*, = OFris. *sionga* (WFris. *sjonge*, dial. *soenge*), MDu. *singen* (Du. *zingen*), OS. and OHG. *singan* (G. *singen*), ON. *syngva* (Icel. and Norw. *syngja*, Sw. *sjunga*, Da. *synge*), Goth. *siggwan* (= *singwan*). No related forms have been traced in other languages.

*Sung* was the usual form of the pa. t. in the 17th and 18th cents., and is given by Smart in 1836 with the remark 'Sang ..is less in use'. Recent usage, however, has mainly been in favour of *sang*.]

**I.** *intr.* **1. a.** To articulate or utter words or sounds in succession with musical inflections or modulations of the voice, so as to produce an effect entirely different from that of ordinary speech; *spec.* to do this in a skilled manner, as the result of training and practice.

*to sing dumb, small*: see dumb *a.* 3 c, and small *adv.*

*c* **825** *Vesp. Ps.* cxxxvii. 5 Alle cyningas..singen in songum dryhtnes. *c* **888** K. Ælfred *Boeth.* i, He..ongan wepan & þus singend cwæð. *c* **950** *Lindisf. Gosp.* Matt. xi. 17 We sungun iuh & ne plægdeʒe. **971** *Blickl. Hom.* 149 Hwæt is..þis folc þe her þus hlude singeþ? *c* **1250** *Gen. & Ex.* 34 Ðu giue me seli timinge..Queðer so hic rede or singe! **1297** R. Glouc. (Rolls) 2349 Ech mon..songe al day bi þe stret ase vor is onour. *c* **1330** R. Brunne *Chron. Wace* (Rolls) 15085 To þe cite þey come singand. **1362** Langl. *P. Pl.* A. xi. 190 Þus bed þe do-bet,..Sike with þe sory, singe with þe glade. *c* **1400** *Pilgr. Sowle* (Caxton, 1483) iv. xx. 65, I songe to rathe, for I sange by the morowe And now at eue I wepe. *c* **1420** *Chron. Vilod.* 3073 Angels, þat weron bothe bryȝt & shene,..song lowde with myelde steuene. **1517** Torkington *Diary* (1884) 63 On of the Jewys began to syng, and than all the women daunsed. **1614** J. Davies (Heref.) *Eclogue* 74 Enaunter they..songen lowdly for so deere desart. **1667** Milton *P.L.* ii. 553 The harmony (What could it less when Spirits immortal sing?) Suspended Hell. **1750** Gray *Long Story* 58 They flirt, they sing, they laugh, they tattle. **1769** Sir W. Jones *Palace Fortune* Poems (1777) 27 No shepherd sung beneath the rosy bowers. **1803–5** Wordsw. *Solitary Reaper* 27, I saw her singing at her work. **1852** Mrs. Stowe *Uncle Tom's C.* xvi. 157 I've been up in Tom's room, hearing him sing. **1884** F. M. Crawford *Rom. Singer* I. 10 He never sang except in Church.

*fig.* *c* **825** *Vesp. Psalter* xxix. 13 Ðæt singe ðe wuldur min. **1382** Wyclif *Isaiah* lv. 12 Mounteynes and hilles shul singe bifor ȝou preising. **1611** Bible *Job* xxxviii. 7 The morning starres sang together. **1757** Gray *Bard* 123 Bright Rapture calls, and soaring, as she sings, Waves [etc.]. **1775** Sheridan *Duenna* i. i, Tell me, my lute, can thy soft strain..So softly sing, so humbly sigh. **1871** Lowell *Study Windows, Pope*, I do not think that Pope's verse anywhere sings.

**b.** Const. *to* (†*by, in*) an instrument of music.

*c* **825** *Vesp. Psalter* lxx. 22 Ic singu ðe in citran. *c* **1000** *Ags. Ps.* (Thorpe) lxx. 20 And [ic] þe on sealm-fatum, singe be hearpan. **1382** Wyclif *1 Chron.* xvi. 5 Asaph forsothe schuld syngyn in cymbalis. **1565** Cooper *Thesaurus, Canere ad tibiam*, to singe to the shalme. **1608** Shaks. *Per.* iv. Prol. 26 When to the lute She sung. *a* **1700** Evelyn *Diary* 10 Oct. 1645, Who had a daughter..that played and sung to nine severall instruments. **1792** A. Young *Trav. France* 132 Mademoiselle Le Blanc singing to her systrum.

**c.** *fig.* To cry out with pain; to make a noise, to boast, *about* something. ***to sing different*** (cf. 10 a).

*c* **1386** Chaucer *Friar's T.* 13 But certes, lechours dide he grettest wo; They sholde singen, if that they were hent. **1897** *Westm. Gaz.* 22 Dec. 4/1 Matters are looking up. Still there is nothing much to sing about on our part even now. **1897** E. Phillpotts *Lying Prophets* i. ix, If you comed to be a bride, you'd sing different.

**d.** ***to sing for one's supper*** (also †***dinner***): for lack of money. Usu. *fig.*, to provide entertainment or a service in return for a benefit received (often, a meal).

*c* **1744** *Little Tommy Tucker* in *Tommy Thumb's Pretty Little Song Bk.* 10 Little Tom Tucker Sings for his Supper What shall he Eat White bread and Butter. **1803** J. Kenney *Raising the Wind* i. i. 4 As you sometimes sing for your dinner, now you may whistle for your breakfast. **1949** N. Mitford *Love in Cold Climate* i. iii. 30 [At] the various house parties..I had been to..I knew that I was expected..to sing for my supper by being, if possible, amusing. **1972** T. P. McMahon *Issue of Bishop's Blood* (1973) ix. 134 Thanks for the dinner.. Is it too bad a pun to say I'm ready to sing for it?

**e.** ***to sing along***: to sing in accompaniment to a song or piece of music. Also const. *with* the performer. Cf. sing-along *sb.* and *a.*

**1959** *Time* 17 Aug. 60/3 Whether anyone actually sings along with the sing-along albums probably does not bother ..Miller. **1973** *Observer* (Colour Suppl.) 29 Apr. 41/3 They all stand on the tables and sing along and stamp their feet. **1977** R. L. Duncan *Temple Dogs* (1978) i. ii. 46 He was singing along with the piano player, his voice shrill.

**2. a.** To tell *of* (†*by*) in song or in verse.

*c* **900** tr. *Baeda's Hist.* iv. xxiv. 346 Song he ærest be middanȝeardes ȝesceape & bi fruman moncynnes. *c* **1205** Lay. 24211 Sone heo gunnen singe of Arðure þan kinge. **13..** *K. Alis.* 7613 (Laud MS.), Þe lefdy wandreþ in a plas, And syngeþ of Dido & Eneas. **1390** Gower *Conf.* I. 290 Ha, who herde evere singe or rede Of such a thing as that was do? *a* **1529** Skelton *Maner of World* 169 Sometime we song of myrth and play. **1565** Cooper *Thesaurus, Cantatus*, songe of: praysed. **1605** Camden *Rem.* (1623) 8 Most truely our Lucan singeth of this our countrey. **1697** Dryden *Virg. Georg.* iv. 807 Thus have I sung of Fields, and Flocks, and Trees, And of the waxen Work of lab'ring Bees. **1788** Cowper *Gratitude* 56 The poets will swear that I dream, When I sing of the splendour of mine. **1821** Scott *Kenilw.* xxxvii, Marshalled by two Minstrels, who sung of war and ladies love. **1864** Dasent *Jest & Earnest* (1873) II. 233 So he began his song, and first he sung of the Orkney Earls across the western main.

*fig.* **1887** *Illustr. Lond. News* Summer No. 2/1 His gait and carriage Sang..of ploughed fields.

**b.** To compose in verse; to make poetry.

**1637** Milton *Lycidas* 10 Who would not sing for Lycidas? he knew Himself to sing, and build the lofty rhyme. **1709** Pope *Ess. Crit.* 659 He..judg'd with coolness, tho' he sung with fire. **1784** Cowper *Task* ii. 312 Studious of song, And yet ambitious not to sing in vain. **1827** Pollok *Course T.* x, Thus have I sung beyond thy first request. **1871** Smiles *Charac.* x. (1876) 267 Horace, Virgil, and Dante still sing as when they lived.

†**3.** To chant or intone, in the performance of divine service; to say mass. *Obs.*

**1297** R. Glouc. (Rolls) 3932 Clerkes songe as riȝt was, þat ioye it was to hure. **1362** Langl. *P. Pl.* A. Prol. 83 Persones and parisch prestes..askeþ leue and lycence at londun to dwelle, To singe þer for Simonye. *c* **1400** Maundev. (1839) iii. 19 Thei suffre not the Latynes to syngen at here Awteres. **1432–50** tr. *Higden* (Rolls) V. 9 [The pope] ordeynede that brede ordeynede to synge with scholde be pure brede and clene. **1538** *Lett. Suppress. Monast.* (Camden) 222 He songe in thys chapell, and hadde the offeringes for hys lyving. **1599** Shaks. *Hen. V*, iv. i. 319, I haue built two Chauntries, Where the sad and solemne Priests sing still For Richards Soule.

**4. a.** Of birds: To produce tuneful or musical sounds; to warble.

*a* **1000** *Phœnix* 124 Se haswa fuȝel..swinsað & singeð sweȝle toȝeanes. *c* **1250** *Owl & Night.* 1663 Foweles boþe grete & smale..sungen al so uale wise. **13..** *Cursor M.* 1031 (Gött.), Soun of foulis þat þar singes. **1390** Gower *Conf.* I. 53 He herde among the leves singe The Throstel with the nyhtingale. *c* **1440** *Jacob's Well* 149 Þei fare as þe cuc-cuke, þat syngyth but of him-self. **1515** *Scottish Field* 435 in *Chetham Misc.* (1856), Birdes brayden to the bowes, And boldlie they songen. **1588** Shaks. *Titus A.* iii. i. 158 Did euer Rauen sing so like a Larke? **1611** —— *Cymb.* ii. iii. 22 Hearke, hearke, the Larke at Heauens gate sings. **1667** Milton *P.L.* v. 198 Ye Birds, That singing up to Heaven Gate ascend. **1766** Gray *Kingsgate* 10 No tree is heard to whisper, bird to sing. **1774** G. White *Selborne* lx, Wrens sing all the winter through, frost excepted. **1822** Coleridge *Lett.*, etc. II. 116 Like a gleam of sunshine..setting all the birds a-singing. **1908** *Betw. Trent & Ancholme* 27 The birds singing in the old apple-trees.

**b.** Of cocks: To crow. Also with *out.*

In early use after L. *cantare* in the Vulgate.

*c* **950** *Lindisf. Gosp.* Matt. xxvi. 34 On ðisser næht ær ðon hona singe *vel* crawe. *c* **1000** Ælfric *Hom.* II. 248 Se hana sona hlud-sweȝe sang. **1382** Wyclif *Mark* xiv. 72 Bifore the cok synge twyes, thries thou schalt denye me. *c* **1386** Chaucer *Reeve's T.* 313 This joly lyf han thise two clerkes lad, Til that the thridde cok bigan to synge. **1602** Shaks. *Ham.* i. i. 160 The Bird of Dawning singeth all night long. **1830** Tennyson *Mariana* 27 The cock sung out an hour ere light.

**c.** Said of the raven, sea-mew, toad, etc., and (in later use) of the cricket.

*a* **1000** *Cædmon's Genesis* 1983 Sang se wanna fuȝel under deoreðsceaftum. *a* **1000** *Seafarer* 22 Dyde ic me to gomene ..mæw singende fore medodrince. **1340** *Ayenb.* 156 Þe asse ..beginþ to lheape and yernþ to-yens him..and beginþ zinge grat-liche. **1555** Eden *Decades* (Arb.) 220 These toades synge after three or foure sortes. **1608** Shaks. *Per.* iii. Prol. 7 And crickets sing at the oven's mouth. *a* **1668** Davenant *Man's the Master* iii. ii, When crickets sing, why should not we? **1789** G. White *Selborne* lxxxviii, The new inhabitants [i.e. crickets] stayed some time, and fed and sung. **1846** Dickens *Cricket on Hearth* iii, A Cricket sings upon the Hearth.

**d.** *Criminals' slang* (now chiefly *U.S.*). = *sing out* (sense 5 c). Also ***to sing like a canary.*** Orig. in proverbial phr. † ***he that sings once, weeps all his life after*** and varr.

**1612** T. Shelton tr. *Cervantes' Don-Quixote* i. iii. viii. 193 Here it is quite contrary, quoth the slave, for He that sings once, weepes all his life after. **1710** S. Palmer *Moral Essays on Proverbs* lxxii. 197 He that Sings in Disaster, shall Weep all his Life-time After. 'Tis generally suppos'd, that this Proverb was born in a Jail. *Sing*..is, when one of the Gang Tattles, Confesses, and Accuses the Rest.

**1929** Hostetter & Beesley *It's a Racket!* 238 *Sing*, to confess. **1937** [implied at singing *vbl. sb.* 1 c]. **1946** *Sun* (Baltimore) 10 Dec. 1/3 A former army colonel 'sang' about the operation of military government there. **1950** R. Himmel *I'll find You* (1958) xvii. 117 She's singing like a canary. She turned up at headquarters..and said she had some information on a killing. **1964** L. Nkosi *Rhythm of Violence* 65 Who knows, maybe he's even goin' to sing to the police! **1981** P. Niesewand *Word of Gentleman* xix. 126 You don't think they'd sing like canaries?.. They'll sing, Claud. .. If they thought it would help them, they'd tell on their mothers.

**5. a.** With *out.* Also *spec.* in nautical use.

**1530** Palsgr. 718/1, I synge out, or I synge a loude, *je chante a playne voix.* **1840** R. H. Dana *Before Mast* ii, The sailors 'singing out' at the ropes in their hoarse and peculiar strains. *Ibid.* xvii, Sailors, when heaving at a windlass.., always have one to sing out.

**b.** To call or cry *out.*

**1813** *Sporting Mag.* XLI. 43 Sing out, and we shall come. **1850** W. Scoresby *Cheever's Whalem. Adv.* iii. (1858) 34 Sing out when we head right! **1889** Jerome *Three Men in Boat* 93 They all got crazy at last, and sang out for the keeper. **1901** Mrs. C. Bagot *Links with Past* 44 A marine made it a point of honour to take a flogging in silence—a sailor thought it no disgrace to 'sing out'.

†**c.** *Cant.* To peach, turn informer. *Obs.*

**1815** Scott *Guy M.* xxviii. *note*, To sing out or whistle in the cage, is when a rogue, being apprehended, peaches against his comrades. **1816** —— *Old Mort.* xliii, The thing will never keep two days longer, and the first bird that sings out will get the reward.

**6. a.** Of things: To give out a ringing, murmuring, or other sound having the quality of a musical note.

*Beowulf* 323 Hringiren scir song in searwum. *c* **897** K. Ælfred *Gregory's Past. C.* xxiii. 174 Se hearpere..ȝedeð ðæt hie [the strings] noht unȝelice ðæm sone ne singað þe he wilnað. *a* **1023** Wulfstan *Hom.* xl. (1883) 183 In þam dæȝe singað þa byman. **1523** Fitzherb. *Husb.* §10 Go vppon the lande, that is plowed, and if it synge or crye, or make any noyse vnder thy fete, than it is to wete to sowe. **1596** Shaks. *Merch. V.* iv. i. 49 When the bag-pipe sings i' the nose. **1642** Fuller *Holy & Prof. St.* i. viii. 20 One said, He loved to heare his carter though not his cart to sing. **1797** *Encycl. Brit.* (ed. 3) XVIII. 872/2 When the liquor in the barrel has done singing, stop the vessel close. **1839** Ure *Dict. Arts* 1271 They hear these stoppings begin to sing or call, as they say, whenever an interruption takes place in any point. **1850** S. Dobell *Roman* vi. Poet. Wks. (1875) 85, I do forget..that the music of her shores is singing Still in your ears. **1887** Besant *The World went* i, On the other hob stood a kettle, singing comfortably.

**b.** Of missiles, etc.: To sound in this way by reason of rapid motion through the air; to move with a singing sound.

**1565** Cooper *Thesaurus* Introd. 2 An arrowe that singeth as hee goeth. **1633** Bp. Hall *Hard Texts, N.T.* 213 The plagues of God shall be sent as so many arrowes singing into thy bosom. **1676** Hobbes *Iliad* (1677) 235 So many spears went singing by his head. **1716** Pope *Odyss.* viii. 138 The discus flies, And sings with unmatch'd force along the skies. **1761** Gray *Fatal Sisters* 22 Pikes must shiver, javelins sing. **1813** Byron *Br. Abydos* ii. xxv, Whose bullet through the night-air sang? **1883** Stevenson *Treas. Isl.* xviii, It did all our hearts good to see him..make the blade sing through the air.

**7.** Of the ears: To ring, tingle, be filled with a humming sound.

**1621** Burton *Anat. Mel.* i. iii. ii. ii, Their eares sing now and then. **1819** Scott *Ivanhoe* xl, I had forgotten the buffet, though mine ear sung after it for a whole day. **1849** Eastwick *Dry Leaves* 112 The eye grows dizzy, and the ear sings with heat.

**8.** To admit of being sung; to be usually sung.

**1728** Chambers *Cycl.* s.v. *Melody*, Yet so far as the Bass may be made airy, and to sing well, it may be also properly said to be Melodious. **1821** Mrs. Hemans *Lett.* in. H. F. Chorley *Mem.* (1837) I. 83, I am anxious that the words should both sing well and read well. **1873** O'Curry *Lect. Anc. Irish* III. 391 Those verses..which sing to the air of *Ar Eire*, etc.

**II.** *trans.* **9. a.** To utter (songs, etc.) with musical modulations of the voice; also (quot. 1553), to articulate (words) in a singing tone.

Said of birds, etc., as well as of persons. Sometimes used *fig.* (cf. sense 2) to denote the composition of verse.

*c* **825** *Vesp. Psalter* cxxxvi. 4 Hu singað we song dryhtnes in eorðan fremðre? *c* **888** K. Ælfred *Boeth.* ii, Ða lioð þe ic wrecca ȝeo lustbærlice song, ic sceal nu heofiende singan. *c* **1000** *Sax. Leechd.* II. 352 Þas galdor mon mæȝ singan on wunde. *c* **1175** *Lamb. Hom.* 7 Ebreisce folc sungen heore leof song ure helende to wurðinge. *a* **1250** *Prov. of Alfred* 355 Ne ilef þu neuer..alle þe þinge þat þu iherest singe. **1297** R. Glouc. (Rolls) 3940 So murye & so gret was þat song þat me song þerinne wyde. **13..** *K. Alis.* 5195 (Laud MS.), Mery tyme it is in maij, þe foules syngeþ her lay. **1340** *Ayenb.* 268 Hy zonge þane zang þet non oþer ne may zynge. *a* **1400–50** *Alexander* 3698 Þai made as mery melody & musik þai sanng As in þe moneth of Mai. **1470–85** Malory *Arthur* x. xxxi. 464 The harper had songe his songe to the ende. **1530** Palsgr. 718/1, I synge him..a balade. **1553** T. Wilson *Rhet.* 117 b, Some sighes out their woordes. Some synges their sentences. **1601** [Bp. W. Barlow] *Serm. Paules Crosse* Pref. 14 How the late Earle..song eyther the 54. or the 94. Psalme. **1660** Ingelo *Bentiv. & Ur.* i. (1682) 149 If they have not the words, which are sung, by heart, they have Copies of them given to them. **1710** Pope *Windsor For.* 434 To the list'ning swains First in these fields I sung the sylvan strains. **1798** Coleridge *Fears in Solitude* 18 The singing-lark (that sings unseen The minstrelsy that solitude loves best). **1827** D. Johnson *Ind. Field Sports* 202 A hundred dancing-girls sung their sprightly airs. **1846** Dickens

*Cricket on Hearth* I, It's a dark night, sang the Kettle. **1848** THACKERAY *Van. Fair* lxi, Suppose, on the other hand, your swan sings quite a different sort of dirge.

**b.** With object denoting the key, voice, note, etc. Also *fig.* (quot. 1600).

*c* **1386** CHAUCER *Miller's T.* 146 Ther to he song som tyme a loud quynyble. **1423** JAS. I *Kingis Q.* liv, Quhare are thy notis smale, That thou of loue has song this morowe-tyde? ?*a* **1450** [see BASS *sb.*[5] 1]. **1500–20** DUNBAR *Poems* xxii. 17 The pyet..Fenȝeis to sing the nychtingalis not. **1552** HULOET, Tenor, or he that singeth a tenor, *succentor*. **1600** HOLLAND *Livy* XLV. xxxi. 1222 The third [statesman] betweene, sung a meane, and was crosse to the one and the other. **1611** COTGR. s.v. *Chanter*, Who doth sing so merrie a note as he that cannot change a groat? *a* **1700** EVELYN *Diary* 25 July 1684, A Frenchman who sung an admirable basse. *a* **1791** WESLEY *Wks.* (1872) VIII. 319 They must sing only the tenor. **1888** *Encycl. Brit.* XXIV. 275/1 So that an adult male can still sing the soprano parts.

**c.** With advs., as *forth*, *out*, *over*.

**1390** GOWER *Conf.* I. 134 Thus I sang hem forth fulofte In halle. *a* **1400** *Minor Poems fr. Vernon MS.* xxix. ii. 42 Þe child..neuer-þe-latere song forþ his song. **1611** BIBLE *Wisd.* xviii. 9 The fathers now singing out the songs of praise. **1675** BROOKS *Gold. Key* Wks. 1867 V. 303 How can he sing out the high praises of God? **1813** SCOTT *Rokeby* II. xvi, While linnet, lark, and blackbird gay, Sing forth her nuptial roundelay. **1848** THACKERAY *Van. Fair* xxvi, She sate down at the piano.., and sang over all her father's favourite old songs.

**10.** In phrases: **a.** ***to sing another song*** or ***a different tune***, to speak or act in a very different manner.

**1390** GOWER *Conf.* I. 260 O thou, which hast desesed The Court of France be thi wrong, Now schalt thou singe an other song. **1588** J. UDALL *Diotrephes* (Arb.) 18 If they had euen my experience, they would sing another song. **1600** HEYWOOD *If you know not me* Wks. 1874 I. 207 The Queene must heare you sing another song Before you part with vs. **1711** W. KING tr. *Naude's Ref. Politics* iii. 91 The Jesuits begin to play their part, and sing another song. **1828** SCOTT *F.M. Perth* xxxiii, If it was not within two days of Palm Sunday, herself would make you sing another song. **1890** HENTY *With Lee in Virginia* 124, I imagine he would sing a different tune if the blue coats ever get to Richmond.

**b.** ***to sing the same*** (or ***one***) ***song***, to tell the same tale, to harp on the same strain.

**1550** BALE *Eng. Votaries* II. Oj, In all their counsels they songe styll one song. **1583** STUBBES *Anat. Abus.* II. 39, I haue hard prisoners (and not any almost but they sing the same song)..crie out against brookers. **1646** BP. MAXWELL *Burd. Issach.* 14 This is so much obeyed, that the Ministers of the Kings Family, or Parish, must sing the same song. **1863** tr. *Ruffini's Vincenzo* II. xi. 183 After you have been here twelve months..you will sing the same song as I do now. **1898** LD. E. HAMILTON *Mawkin* viii, He was singing the same song himself just, no later than yestreen.

**c.** ***to sing sol-fa, sorrow, woe***, to lament.

**1566** GASCOIGNE *Supposes* IV. ii, If I come neere you, hemp-string, I will teache you to sing sol fa. **1748** JARVIS *Quix.* I. III. iv, It would be of service and use only to those who are dubbed knights..; as for the poor squires, they may sing sorrow. **1818** SCOTT *Rob Roy* xxxii, I will take such ample vengeance, that the very stones of their glens shall sing woe for it this hundred years to come!

**d.** ***to hear a bird sing***, etc., denoting the receipt of private information. (Cf. BIRD *sb.* 4.)

**1597** SHAKS. *2 Hen. IV*, V. v. 113, I heare a Bird so sing, Whose Musicke (to my thinking) pleas'd the King. **1618** FLETCHER *Loyal Subj.* IV. ii, I heard a Bird sing, they mean him no good office. **1672** VILLIERS (Dk. Buckhm.) *Rehearsal* II. ii. (Arb.) 53, I..heard besides a grave Bird sing That they intend, sweet-heart, to play us pranks. **1845** DISRAELI *Sybil* 285, I have had a bird too singing something in my ear these two days past.

**11. a.** To chant or intone (a lesson, mass, etc.).

Sometimes used in much the same sense as SAY *v.*[1] 9.

*a* **850** *Lorica Prayer* 9 in *O.E. Texts* 174 Sing ðonne pater noster. *c* **960** *Rule St. Benet* (Schröer) xi. 35 Singe man ærest sex sealmas & þonne on ende fers. *c* **1030** *Ibid.* (Logeman) 39 Si an [ræding] of ðære ealdan ȝecyðnysse..ȝeræd oððe sungen. *c* **1122** *O.E. Chron.* (Laud MS.) an. 1122, þa hwile þe þa munecas sungen þære messe. *c* **1175** *Lamb. Hom.* 51 Þe halie ureisuns þe me singeð in halie chirche. *a* **1225** *Ancr. R.* 424 Bi þe weie ase heo geð go singinde hire beoden. **1297** R. GLOUC. (Rolls) 9348 Þe bissop of lincolne is masse song þo. **1310** *St. Brendan* (Bälz) 315 Þe wile we singeþ evesong, hi schulleþ sitte and ete. **1338** R. BRUNNE *Chron.* (1810) 172 Better him wer..messe [to have] songen, & serued God alle myght. **1431** *Rec. St. Mary at Hill* (1905) 14 An honest Preest sufficiantly lerned in dyvynete to syng & sey dyuyne seruice. **1483** in *Lett. Rich. III & Hen. VII* (Rolls) I. 9 The masse of requiem..was songon by the archbishop of Yorke. **1503** *Ibid.* 201 The Pater Noster was songen. **1593** NASHE *Christ's T.* (1613) 172 Because we may not build Monasteries, or haue Masses, Dirges, or Trentals sung for our soules [etc.]. **1699** J. JACKSON *Let. to Pepys* 25 Dec., The Cardinals, &c., entering afterwards to sing vespers. **1700** T. BROWN tr. *Fresny's Amusem.* iii. Wks. 1709 III. I. 22 Those Ladies that look thro' their Fingers while the Service is Singing. **1753** CHALLONER *Cath. Chr. Instr.* 93 In the high or solemn Mass the Gospel is sung by the Deacon. **1808** SCOTT *Marm.* VI. Introd. 31 On Christmas eve the mass was sung.

*fig.* **1827** POLLOK *Course T.* VII, Whom fierce Winter seized,..And sang the requiem of his shivering ghost.

†**b.** With *out*: To exhaust the value of (a sum of money) in the celebration of masses. *Obs.*

*c* **1530** *Plumpton Corr.* (Camden) 228 When your prest at Boynton had song out all your ten pound, he kepes him still at his cost.

**12. a.** To declare, relate, recount, or celebrate, in song or verse.

*c* **825** *Vesp. Psalter* xx. 14 Hefe up, dryhten, in meȝne ðinum; we singað..meȝen ðin. *c* **888** K. ÆLFRED *Boeth.* vii. §3 Hwæt singað þa leoðwyrhtan oðres be ðisse woruld buton mislica hwearfunga? **971** *Blickl. Hom.* 231 He þa..wæs Drihtnes lof singende on þæm carcerne. *c* **1205** LAY. 22976 Ne [is] al so[t]h ne al les, þat leod-scopes singeð. *a* **1325** *Prose Psalter* xx. 13 We shul syngen & psalmen þy vertuz. **1390** GOWER *Conf.* I. 203 Thurgh tresoun of hire false tunge, Which thurgh the lond was after sunge. *c* **1400** *Beryn* 786 Philippus Augustinus, as songen is in layis,..Was Emperour I-chose. **1531** ELYOT *Gov.* I. vii, After he..had songen the gestes and actes marcial of the ancient princis of Greece. **1557** *Tottel's Misc.* (Arb.) 150, I haue not songen, how This mischiefe came: but I intend With wofull voice to sing it now. **1636** HEYWOOD *Challenge Beauty* II. i, I shall be Ballated, Sung up and downe by Minstrills. **1697** DRYDEN *Virg. Georg.* IV. 3 Mecænas, read this other part, that sings Embattel'd Squadrons and advent'rous Kings. **1738** GRAY *Propertius* iii. 15 Sing with what a careless Grace she flings Her artful hand. **1762** SIR W. JONES *Arcadia* Poems (1777) 122 He sung the woes of artless swains. **1820** BYRON *Juan* III. lxxix, He sung the Sultan and the Pacha. **1850** MRS. JAMIESON *Leg. Monast. Ord.* (1863) 61 He sang the creation of the world, and the origin of man.

*transf.* **1749** FIELDING *Tom Jones* XII. xii, Jones afterwards proceeded very gravely to sing forth the happiness of those subjects who live under such a magistrate.

**b.** ***to sing one's praises***, to be loud in laudation of (a person, etc.).

**1565** COOPER *Thesaurus* s.v. *Cantus*, To synge ones greate prayse. **1610** B. JONSON *Alch.* II. i, I'll Be bound the players shall sing your praises, then, Without their poets. **1778** MME. D'ARBLAY *Diary* 26 Aug., Dr. Johnson..was so caught by it..that he has sung its praises ever since. **1858** THACKERAY *Virgin.* xxxi, May we modest Œnophilists not sing the praises of our favourite plant?

**c.** To proclaim in a musical or resonant manner; to announce clearly or distinctly. Also *fig.*

**1605** *First Part of Ieronimo* I. i, My knee sings thanks vnto your highnes bountie. *c* **1616** FLETCHER *Thierry & Theod.* I. ii, I hear a tempest coming, That sings mine and my kingdom's ruin. *a* **1668** DAVENANT *Man's the Master* III. ii, They sung us thanks ere we made them a fire. **1837** A. TENNENT *Vis. Glencoe* 5 Hark how the pibroch shrilly sings The deeds of other years. **1848** THACKERAY *Van. Fair* xviii, Before whose door the watchman sang the hours when she was asleep. **1897** *Pall Mall Mag.* Nov. 356 Put my eyes out, and I'll sing you the soundings foot by foot.

**d.** To call *out*. Also *transf.*

**1833** M. SCOTT *Tom Cringle* i, 'Port your helm,' sung out the boatswain. **1837** DISRAELI *Venetia* I. xvii, Suddenly a scout sang out that a party was in sight. **1848** THACKERAY *Van. Fair* lvii, Moon and stars shining overhead, and the bell singing out the watch. **1850** —— *Pendennis* iv, Clavering clock sang out one. **1901** *Daily Express* 28 Feb. 6/5 As the baskets go down they sing out the number where the money is to be placed.

**13. a.** To bring into a certain state, or to a certain place, by or with singing. Const. with preps. and advs. Also, †to lull by singing.

*a* **1500–34** *Coventry Corpus Christi Plays* (1902) 29 Here the wemen cum in wythe there chyldur, syngyng them. **1530** PALSGR. 718/1, I have songe thy brother aslepe. **1595** SHAKS. *John* V. vii. 23 This pale faint Swan, Who..sings His soule and body to their lasting rest. **1600** —— *A.Y.L.* IV. ii. 13 Then sing him home, the rest shall beare this burthen. **1730–46** THOMSON *Autumn* 190 Like the gay birds that sung them to repose. **1778** MISS BURNEY *Evelina* xxi, If ever they do again, I'll give them leave to sing me to Bedlam for my pains. **1821** CLARE *Vill. Minstr.* II. 3 The blackbird sang the sun to bed. **1868** MORRIS *Earthly Par.* (1870) I. I. 306 The garden birds sang down the setting sun. **1877** MRS. OLIPHANT *Makers Flor.* i. 21 All Florence danced and sung the sweet May in.

**b.** To take, drive, force, etc., by or with singing. Const. *away*, *forth*, *off*, *out of*, etc.

**1604** SHAKS. *Oth.* IV. i. 200 Oh she will sing the Sauagenesse out of a Beare. **1650** A. B. *Mutat. Polemo* 15 To be chirpingly drunk, and sing away sorrow. **1788** COWPER *Mischievous Bull* 23 The angry Muse thus sings thee forth, And claps the gate behind thee. **1810** CRABBE *Borough* xxiii. 154, I put on the man, Sing off my sighs, and trifle as I can. **1830** PRAED *Palinodia* vii, When Laura sings young hearts away. **1875** MCLAREN *Serm.* Ser. II. vi. 102 A truth which syren voices are constantly trying to sing us out of believing.

**c.** To spend or pass *away* (life) in singing.

**1816** SHELLEY *Dæmon of World* II. 163 The winged habitants, That in the woods their sweet lives sing away.

**d.** To make (one's way) with singing.

**1890** HALL CAINE *Bondman* II. iii, There is a full stream that tumbles into the sea..after singing its way down from the heights of Barrule.

**e.** Of the Aboriginal inhabitants of Australia: to endow (an object) with magical properties by singing; to bring a magical influence to bear on (a person or thing) by singing.

**1899** SPENCER & GILLEN *Native Tribes Central Austral.* xvi. 537 The wound was not serious..but he persisted in saying that the spear had been sung, and that..he was going to die, which accordingly he did. **1914** B. SPENCER *Native Tribes N. Territory* iii. 140 As soon as the ground was cleared ..all the men retired to one side and, to the accompaniment of trumpets..and clapping of hands, it was 'sung'. This 'singing' was supposed to make the ground..in good order so that the performers could dance well. **1959** A. UPFIELD *Bony & Black Virgin* xvii. 158 The aborigines..dug up their rainstones and rubbed them with their magic stones, and 'sang' them in a secret camp. And then it rained. **1975** *Times* 8 Nov. 5/1 The Premier of Queensland was put under a death spell by Aborigines last night... An Aboriginal.. said 'These people have sung him and he should start dying from now on.'

**III. 14.** In combs., as † **sing-alone** *nonce-wd.*, a solo singer; **sing-in** [IN[3]], a musical performance in which the audience participates in the singing; † **sing-man** *nonce-wd.*, a singing man.

**1691** tr. *Emillianne's Frauds Rom. Monks* 208 Besides these there were in a little Box near the Altar, four Musicians, called Sing-alones. *Ibid.* 221 The Abbot sung the first Verse of Even-song, which was continued by the Music and Sing-men. **1968** *Lebende Sprachen* XIII. 67/1 Neologismen mit *in* im Englischen und Deutschen... sing-in, sit-in, [etc.]. **1970** *New Yorker* 19 Dec. 16 Sing-in at Philharmonic Hall—Handel's 'Messiah' directed (seriatim fortunately) by nineteen directors. **1976** *Flintshire Leader* 10 Dec. 13/2 (*heading*) Penyffordd 'sing-in'.

**sing** (sɪŋ), *v.*[2] *Sc.* (and *north.*). Also 6 **signe**. *Pa. t.* **singed, singet, -it**; also **sang, sung**. [Northern form of SINGE *v.*, perh. based on the early pa. t. and pa. pple. *sengde*, *sengd*. Frequently conjugated after SING *v.*[1]] *trans.* To singe.

**1543–5** *Aberdeen Register* XVIII. (Jam.), Sche causand sing the said houiss with ane turf of hedder. **1596** DALRYMPLE tr. *Leslie's Hist. Scot.* I. 95 Thay thresche na stuf, bot with fyre thay signe it into the pile vpon the ground. *Ibid.*, Quhen thay haue signet it, thay winnow it. **1633** *Orkney Witch Trial* in Dalyell *Darker Superst. of Scot.* (1834) 193 Fyre ane piece of linying cleath, and sing ane hair of the beast. *a* **1689** W. CLELAND *Poems* (1697) 19 Rebellious Books, Whose paper well might serve the Cooks, To sing their Poultrie. **1725** RAMSAY *Gentl. Sheph.* II. i, Fat are the puddings,—heads and feet well sung. **1828** BUCHAN *Ballads* (1875) I. 122 [It] sang the points o' her yellow hair. **1884** GRANT *Lays & Leg. North* 29 He steed until the flames hed sung The whiskers on his cheek.

**sing**, obs. Sc. form of SIGN *sb.*

**sing**, var. SHENG.

**singable** ('sɪŋəb(ə)l), *a.* Also 4 **syngabil**. [f. SING *v.*] That can be sung; suitable for singing.

In common use only from about 1865.

*a* **1340** HAMPOLE *Psalter* cxviii. 54 Syngabil [L. *cantabiles*] was til me þi rightwisyngis. **1597** MORLEY *Introd. Mus.* Annot., The Minime they esteemed the least or shortest note singable, and therefore indiuisible. **1681** MORELLI *Let. to Pepys* 11 Apr., All Baptist's bases are singable, where many of Pedro's are not so. *a* **1861** MRS. BROWNING *Lett. R. H. Horne* (1877) I. 268 You probably know his ballads, which have a certain singable beauty in them. **1880** HAWEIS *Poets Pulpit* 178 He knew that the singable parts were generally imbedded in a portion which was not singable.

Hence '**singableness**; also **singa'bility**.

**1869** *Pall Mall G.* 2 Dec. 12 That consummate simplicity and *singableness* which make Heine's lyrics so dear to his countrymen. **1888** *Alliance News* 5 May 352 Lyric character (singability).

**Singalese**, variant of SINHALESE.

**singalie**, obs. Sc. form of SINGLY *adv.*

'**sing-along**, *sb.* and *a.* Also **sing-a-long** and as one word. [f. the vbl. phr. *to sing along*: see SING *v.*[1] 1 e.] **A.** *sb.* **1.** A song or recording to which one can sing along in accompaniment (esp. a light popular song with an easy rhythm).

**1959** *Time* 17 Aug. 60/3 The nation's mature citizens are merely striking back at rock'n'roll, buying the sing-alongs. **1968** *Globe & Mail* (Toronto) 3 Feb. 23/1 A Gay Nineties room with sing-alongs, familiar tunes of that era. **1971** *Ink* 31 July 16/2 Those ringing certainties which made 'Woodstock' and 'Big Yellow Taxi' into such cosy sing-alongs. **1981** J. WAINWRIGHT *Urge for Justice* I. xii. 84 He could tickle the old ivories..could hammer out a singalong with the best.

**2.** A sing-song to the accompaniment of a song-leader or tune.

**1973** B. BROADFOOT *Ten Lost Years* xxii. 256 There would be a sing-along, or the manager maybe would just pull a lucky number from a hat. **1975** *Daily Mail* 9 June 18/1 Someone in the next room's having a sing-along! **1979** *Guardian* 27 June 11/8 The insulting..notion that working-class audiences want only a beery community sing-along on their night out.

**B.** *adj.* Of a song, recording, etc.: to which one can sing along in accompaniment. Of or characterized by this unsophisticated but cheerful style.

**1959** [see SING *v.*[1] 1 e]. **1967** *Melody Maker* 1 Apr. 9 How can the Beatles' best..single yet be ousted by so many sing-along melodies and slush-ridden lyrics? **1974** *Financ. Times* 24 Apr. 2/3 Happy music in singalong style. **1977** P. HILL *Liars* ii. 9 A group of relatives were following the words of a sing-along record.

**Singapore** (sɪŋə'pɔər, sɪŋg-). The name of a city and island-republic (formerly, British Crown Colony) in South-East Asia, used *attrib.*, usu. as ***Singapore (gin) sling***, to designate a cocktail with a base of gin and cherry brandy.

**1930** *Savoy Cocktail Book* I. 190 Singapore Sling. The Juice of $\frac{1}{4}$ Lemon. $\frac{1}{4}$ Dry Gin. $\frac{1}{2}$ Cherry Brandy. Shake well and strain into medium size glass, and fill with soda water. Add 1 lump of ice. **1948** D. S. EMBURY *Fine Art of mixing Drinks* xi. 299 Singapore Gin Sling. Of all the recipes published for this drink I have never seen any two that were alike. Essentially it is simply a Gin Sling with the addition of cherry brandy. **1960** J. J. ROWLANDS *Spindrift from House by Sea* i. 28 Building your own house, he told us after his third Singapore gimlet, is an experience akin to a spiritual awakening. **1969** R. THOMAS *Singapore Wink* xi. 118 I'm going to have a Singapore Sling in the bar of the Raffles Hotel. **1976** *Times* (Singapore Suppl.) 19 July p. iv/4 In 1915 a barman, Mr Ngian Tong Dron, tried mixing two measures of gin with one of cherry brandy and one of orange, pineapple and lime juice..the Singapore gin sling was born.

**Singaporean** (sɪŋəˈpɔːrɪən, sɪŋg-), *a.* and *sb.* Also (occas.) **-ian.** [f. prec. + -AN.] **A.** *adj.* Of or pertaining to Singapore.

**1880** [see *moth orchid* s.v. MOTH *sb.* 3]. **1927** *Malaya Tribune* 27 Dec. 7/6 Feckless Singaporean Scots. **1972** *Times* (Singapore Suppl.) 4 July p. ii/3 The Government has been alleged..to have sacrificed important aspects of Chinese culture and language in order to create its image of the Singaporian nation. **1977** *Hongkong Standard* 12 Apr. 16/5 He spoke to 360 striking Singaporean metal workers earlier in the day.

**B.** *sb.* A native or inhabitant of Singapore.

**1927** *Malaya Tribune* 5 Jan. 9/2 (*heading*) World's motor record by Singaporeans. **1956** D. DAVIES *More Old Singapore* 40 A working day in the life of a Singaporean. **1965** *Times* 12 Aug. 8/1 Speaking to Malay journalists, Mr. Lee begged the Malays not to worry. He..insisted that 'Singapore is not a Chinese country nor a Malay country nor an Indian country... It belongs to the Singaporeans.' **1975** P. THEROUX *Great Railway Bazaar* xxiii. 238 Singaporeans are great assemblers of appliances.

**singara**, variant of SINGHARA.

**Singatoka**, var. SIGATOKA.

**singcantor**, variant of SINCANTER *Obs.*

**singe** (sɪndʒ), *sb.* Also 7 **sindge.** [f. the vb.] The act or effect of singeing; a slight surface burn, a scorch. Also *fig.*

**1658** SIR T. BROWNE *Hydriot.* iii. 34 Other incinerable substances were found so fresh, that they could feel no sindge from fire. **1760–72** H. BROOKE *Fool of Qual.* (1809) III. 80, I could not be cast into the furnace, and come forth without a singe. **1850** HT. MARTINEAU *Hist. Peace* IV. xiii. (1877) III. 123 Lafayette traversed a purgatory of human passions without a singe from any flame. **1855** BROWNING *Bp. Blougram* 722 Break fire's law.., although the penalty Be just a singe? **1888** SHORTHOUSE *Countess Eve* xi, An appalling mystic light—the singe and glow of the flame of the pit!

**singe** (sɪndʒ), *v.* Forms: 1 **sæn(c)gan, sen(c)gan,** 4 **zeng,** 4–6 **senge** (5 **seenge**), 7 **sendge;** 5–6 **synge,** 6 **syndge,** 6–8 **sindge,** 7 **sindg,** 6– **singe.** See also SING *v.*[2] [OE. *sencgan*, = OFris. *senga, singa* (WFris. *singe*, dial. *sinzje*), MDu. and Du. *zengen*, MLG. and MHG. *sengen* (G. *sengen*, †*sängen*), related to Icel. *sangr* singed, *sengja* singed taste, Norw. *sengra, sengla* to smell of burning. The stem **sang-* may be related to SING *v.*[1] and have reference to the sound produced by violent singeing.]

**1.** *trans.* **a.** Of persons, etc.: To burn (something) superficially or lightly, to burn the ends or edges of (hair, wings, etc.); *esp.* to subject (the carcase of a pig, fowl, or other animal) to flame or fire in order to remove the bristles or hair.

*c* **1000** in Thorpe *Laws* I. 436 Ðyme eac swan ðæt he æfter sticunge his slyht-swyn wel behweorfe, sæncge. *c* **1386** CHAUCER *Wife's Prol.* 349 For who so wolde senge a Cattes skyn, Thanne wolde the Cat wel dwellen in his In. *a* **1420** *Wycliffite Bible* Lev. xxiii. 11 *marg.*, The eeris of corn weren sengid in fier, and the cornes..weren schakun out. **1474** CAXTON *Chesse* III. ii. 74 He wold not that they shold vse ony yron but to brenne and senge his heeris. **1530** PALSGR. 718/1 Take away this candell, I have synged my heare. **1577** B. GOOGE *Heresbach's Husb.* III. (1586) 152 b, With a flame made with strawe, or stickes, syndge him. **1626** T. H[AWKINS] tr. *Caussin's Holy Crt.* 42 No man blameth the candle..though butter flyes sindge theyr winges in it. **1675** HOBBES *Odyssey* (1677) 167 He..fetcht in two young pigs: not long he staid, But kill'd, sindg'd, jointed, roasted. **1710** STEELE *Tatler* No. 112 ⁋2 [He] either clipped the Wings, or singed the Tails, of his innocent Captives. **1769** MRS. RAFFALD *Eng. Housekpr.* (1778) 57 Take your goose ready dressed, singe it and pour over it a quart of boiling milk. **1836** W. IRVING *Astoria* II. 103 The hunters..will venture so near as sometimes to singe his hair with the flash of the rifle. **1886** PASCOE *London of To-day* xl. (ed. 3) 345 If the hair is..to be dressed, singed, shampooed.

*fig.* **1583** GREENE *Mamillia* II. Wks. (Grosart) II. 259 They are singed at the sight of her faire face. **1771** SMOLLETT *Humph. Cl.* (1815) 71 She had gone such lengths in the way of flirting with a recruiting officer, that her reputation was a little singed. **1855** KINGSLEY *Westw. Ho!* xxix, I go forthwith..down the coast, to singe the King of Spain's beard. **1869** BROWNING *Ring & Bk.* VII. 1640 'Twas truth singed the lies And saved me.

†**b.** To burn, consume with fire; to cauterize (a sore). *Obs.*

*a* **1400–50** *Alexander* 5206 We sall his cite & him-selfe synge in-to poudire. **1615** G. SANDYS *Trav.* 242 Who will forget Catania? of high fame For pietie of brothers sindg'd in flame. **1621** SANDERSON *Serm.* I. 171 It must needs be some grief..to the patient to have an old festered sore searched and singed.

**c.** *techn.* To pass (a woven fabric) over a heated plate or roller, or through gas flame, in order to remove superfluous fibres, or to dress the nap.

**1728**, **1800** [see SINGEING *vbl. sb.*]. **1839** URE *Dict. Arts* 1139 In some shops, semi-cylinders of copper..have been substituted for those of iron, in singeing goods prior to bleaching them. **1875** *Ure's Dict. Arts* (ed. 7) I. 369 For goods to be finely printed both sides are singed.

**2.** Of fire or flame: To burn (something) slightly or superficially. Also *techn.* (cf. 1 c).

**1340** *Ayenb.* 229 Þet uer þet zengþ and bernþ ofte þe huyte robe of chastete and of maydenhod. **1494** *Act 11 Hen. VII*, c. 27 They..take a light candell..which sengieth and brenneth away the cotton of the same fustyan. **1560** DAUS tr. *Sleidane's Comm.* 255 b, It singed trees and turned them up by the rootes. **1596** SHAKS. *Merch. V.* II. ix. 79 Thus hath the candle sing'd the moath. **1659** LOVELACE *Poems* (1864) 191 The fire Might sindge thy upper down attire. *a* **1700** EVELYN *Diary* 7 Sept. 1666, The..smoake and fiery vapour, continu'd so intense that my haire was almost sing'd. **1782** J. BROWN *Nat. & Rev. Relig.* II. iii. 202 It did not singe their clothes or hair. **1871** L. STEPHEN *Playgr. Eur.* (1894) vii. 159 A bright flash of lightning seemed to singe our beards. **1884** KNIGHT *Dict. Mech.* Suppl. 813/2 The flame applied directly under the roller singes the cloth thoroughly.

*transf.* **1612** DRAYTON *Poly-olb.* v. 312 The scorching sky Doth singe the sandy wilds of spiceful Barbary.

†**b.** Used to describe the effect produced by intense cold. (Cf. BURN *v.*[1] 13 d.) *Obs.*

**1600** HOLLAND *Livy* XXI. xxxii. 411 The cattell, sheepe, oxen, and horses, singed with cold. **1601** —— *Pliny* II. 319 Hogs grease..healeth burns and scaldings, yea, though one were scortched and sendged with snow.

**3.** To take *off*, remove, by superficial burning.

**1590** SHAKS. *Com. Err.* V. i. 171 The Doctor, Whose beard they haue sing'd off with brands of fire. **1651** HOBBES *Leviath.* IV. xliv. 348 Depose their erroneous Doctrines, and Traditions, and have them as it were sindged off. **1748** *Anson's Voy.* III. viii. (ed. 4) 503 The galeon's colours being singed off the ensign-staff in the beginning of the engagement. **1825** J. NICHOLSON *Operat. Mech.* 415 These operations consist generally of singing the superfluous fibres from the surface of the cloth, by drawing it over hot irons. **1844** G. DODD *Textile Manuf.* ii. 48 *Singeing-furnace*, a heated surface of copper, over which the strip of cotton is drawn rapidly.., by which the light airy filaments are singed from the surface of the cloth.

**singe**, obs. f. SIGN *sb.* and *v.*[1], SING *v.*

**singed** (sɪndʒd), *ppl. a.*[1] Forms: 4 **seynd,** 5 **seynt;** 4 **senged,** 6 **singde,** 6–7 **sindg'd,** 7–8 **sing'd,** 7– **singed.** [f. SINGE *v.* + -ED[1].] **a.** That has been subjected to the process of singeing; scorched or slightly burnt, or presenting the appearance of this; parched.

*c* **1386** CHAUCER *Nun's T.* 25 Milk and broun breed.. Seynd Bacon and somtyme an Ey or tweye. *c* **1395** *Plowman's Tale* 19 (Thynne), He knew wel by hys senged snoute, He was a man wonte to walke about. **1426** LYDG. *De Guil. Pilgr.* 13703, I sawh a wekke..Pyled and seynt as any kaat. **1594** *1st Pt. Contention* I. iv, Where Pluto in his firie Waggon sits, Ryding amidst the singde and parched smoakes. **1634** MILTON *Comus* 928 Summer drouth, or singed air Never scorch thy tresses fair. **1693** DRYDEN *Persius* vi. 497 Shall I be fed With sodden Nettles, and a sing'd Sow's Head? **1700** —— *Fables, Cock & Fox* 34 Rashers of sindg'd bacon on the coals. **1725** POPE *Odyss.* XIV. 475 Then the sing'd members they with skill divide. **1820** SCOTT *Monast.* xvi, Flesh, which, in its sable and singed shape, seemed [etc.]. **1829** GRIFFITH tr. *Cuvier* VIII. 42 Singed Grous, *Pterocles Exustus*. **1884** W. S. B. MCLAREN *Spinning* (ed. 2) 27 A yellow singed appearance is given by using soap with much resin, or much alkali.

**b.** ***singed cat***, in allusive use (see quots.). *U.S.* (Parallel Sc. allusive uses incorporate the related form SINGED *ppl. a.*[2] (cf. quot. 1737).)

**1836** *Spirit of Times* 9 Apr. 61/1 Without our Jersey friends bring on a 'singed cat', or some nag, now outside the fence, turns up a trump, the above comprise the entries for the 4 mile day. **1837** J. C. NEAL *Charcoal Sketches* 48 His new friend, however, proved..to be like a singed cat, much better than he looked. **1847** HALIBURTON *Old Judge* I. ii. 44 It don't do to hang a feller for his looks, after all, that's a fact; for that crittur is like a singed cat, better nor he seems. **1858** in Bartlett *Dict. Amer.* (1859), We reckon there'll be fun; as a Cincinnati paper says Pryne is a perfect singed cat. **1859** *Ibid.*, *Singed cat*, an epithet applied to a person whose appearance does him injustice.

**singed** (ˈsɪŋɪt, sɪŋd), *ppl. a.*[2] *Sc.* (and *north.*). Also 8–9 **singet,** 9 **singit.** [f. SING *v.*[2] + -ED[1].] = prec. Also *fig.* and *Comb.*

*a* **1682** SEMPILL *Blythsome Wedding* 64 A sing'd sheep's head and a haggize. **1737** RAMSAY *Sc. Prov.* (1750) 40 He's like the singed cat, better than he's likely. **1789** BURNS *Kirk's Alarm* vii, Singet Sawney! Singet Sawney! Are ye huirdin' the penny? **1808** JAMIESON, *Singit-like*, puny, shrivelled. **1857** J. STEWART *Sk. Scot. Character* 64 (E.D.D.), Your singit shargie o' a laddie.

**singeing** (ˈsɪndʒɪŋ), *vbl. sb.* Also 7 **cingeing,** etc. [f. SINGE *v.* + -ING[1].] The action of the vb., in various senses. Also *fig.*

*c* **1440** *Promp. Parv.* 453/1 Seengynge,..*ustillacio*. **1591** PERCIVALL *Sp. Dict.*, *Chamusquina*, singeing with fire. *c* **1626** BACON *Advt. touching Holy War* (1629) 40, I remember Drake, in the vaunting stile of a Souldier, would call this Enterprise: The Cingeing of the King of Spaines Beard. **1728** CHAMBERS *Cycl.* s.v. *Sheering*, Some use the Phrase Sheering of Hats, for the passing of Hats made of Wooll over the Flame of a clear Fire...Others call this Flaming and others Sindging. **1764** HARMER *Observ.* iv. §23. 183, I do not remember an account of any things being prepared for food by singeing. **1800** *Patent Specif.*, *Bleaching, Dyeing*, etc. (1859) 78 All kinds of woollen cloth ..may be finished..by singeing instead of cropping or shearing. **1820** BYRON *Juan* v. cli, The singeing of a single inky whisker. **1859** CORNWALLIS *New World* I. 177 The forest, instead of being burnt up, merely showed signs of singeing. **1895** J. L. MAXWELL *Life W. B. Thomson* x. 101 My attention was drawn to an intolerable smell of singeing.

**b.** *Comb.*, as ***singeing-furnace, -lamp, plate, -machine, stove***, etc.

**1800** *Patent Specif.*, *Bleaching, Dyeing*, etc. (1859) 78 Drawing the cloth..over the singeing plate. **1805** LUCCOCK *Nature of Wool* 158 For this purpose he employs the shears, the singing stoves and the press with its heated plates. **1844** G. DODD *Textile Manuf.* ii. 48 Singeing-furnace. **1872** GEO. ELIOT *Middlem.* xxvii, Flirtation, after all, was not necessarily a singeing process. **1875** KNIGHT *Dict. Mech.* 2186/2. **1884** *Ibid.* Suppl. 813/2 A gas singeing machine intended for removing or dressing the nap on woven goods.

ˈ**singeing**, *ppl. a.* [-ING[2].] That singes; burning, scorching.

**1598** YONG *Diana* 286 Then thornes More sharpe and pricking with thy singing scornes. **1602** MARSTON *Antonio's Rev.* III. ii, May I be numd with horror, and my vaines Pucker with sing'ing torture. **1891** MISS DOWIE *Girl in Karp.* 229 In the singeing heat of..ten o'clock.

Hence ˈ**singeingly** *adv.*

**1655–87** H. MORE *App. Antid.* (1712) 220, I confess that the Bodies of Devils may be not only warm, but sindgingly hot. *Ibid.* 221.

**singel**, obs. form of SHINGLE *sb.*[1]

**singer**[1] (ˈsɪŋə(r)). Also 4 **syngere,** 5–6 **synger;** 5 **synggare,** 6 **syngar, singar(e.** [f. SING *v.*[1] + -ER[1]. Cf. Fris. *sjonger*, MDu. *singer*, MHG. *singære*, G. *singer.*]

**1. a.** One who sings; a trained vocalist; also *spec.* in eccl. use (quot. 1843).

*c* **1330** R. BRUNNE *Chron. Wace* (Rolls) 4024 After Sysilly com Glegabret, A syngere of þe beste get. *c* **1386** CHAUCER *Pard. T.* 17 And right anon thanne comen Tombesteres,.. Syngeres with harpes. *c* **1440** *Promp. Parv.* 456/1 Synggare, *cantor*. **1486** *Rec. St. Mary at Hill* (1905) 5 Namely, that he ..help the Syngers after his cunnyng in the honour of our blessed lady. **1538** STARKEY *England* II. i. 154 Marchauntys therof [pleasures] and craftys men, syngarys and playarys apon instrumentys. **1598** SHAKS. *Merry W.* I. iii. 29 His filching was like an vnskilfull Singer, he kept not time. *a* **1652** BROME *City Wit* III. ii, He has been..one of the sweet singers to the city Funerals. **1756–7** tr. *Keysler's Trav.* (1760) IV. 393 The vocal musicians, or singers,..perform even in private houses for money. **1781** GIBBON *Decl. & F.* xxxi. III. 216 Three thousand singers, with the masters of the respective chorusses. **1828** SCOTT *F.M. Perth.* x, My judgment is not deep, my lord; but the singer may dispense with my approbation. **1843** HAMMOND *Def. Faith Œcumen. Councils* 183 If a Sub-deacon, Reader, or Singer commits the same things. **1880** 'VERNON LEE' *Italy* III. ii. 113 Farinelli..was proud of being a singer and afraid of being a political agent.

**b.** Of song-birds. (More frequently *songster.*)

**1626** BACON *Sylva* §239 We see also, that Cock-birds, among Singing-birds, are ever the better singers. **1849** CRAIG s.v., The canary is a fine singer. **1896** tr. *Boas' Text-bk. Zool.* 462 Singers (*Sylviadæ*)... Some of them noted singers.

**c.** An informer. Cf. SING *v.*[1] 4 d. *Criminals' slang.*

**1935** *Amer. Speech* X. 20/2 *Singer*, a stool pigeon or trusty who carries tales to the administration. (Obs.) **1961** *John o' London's* 30 Nov. 610/3 An informer, then a *squealer*, is now more often referred to..as a *singer*.

**2.** A composer of poetry or verse; a poet.

**1560** BIBLE (Geneva) *2 Sam.* xxiii. 1 Dauid.., the swete singer of Israel. **1652** (*title*), Herbert's Remains, or, sundry Pieces of that sweet Singer of the Temple. *a* **1704** T. BROWN *Presbyt. Proposals* Wks. 1711 IV. 126 Quakers, Muggletonians and Sweet-Singers of Israel. **1874** GREEN *Short Hist.* vii. §7. 423 Amidst the throng in Elizabeth's antechamber the noblest form is that of the singer who lays the 'Faerie Queen' at her feet. **1880** LANIER *Sci. Eng. Verse* Pref., Wyatt, Surrey, Sackville, and a host of less known or unknown singers.

*attrib.* *c* **1843** CARLYLE *Hist. Sk.* (1898) 74 A sterling man, a true Singer-heart. **1906** *Month* July 90 Some prayer that has come through the centuries from a singer-saint.

**3.** Special Combinations with *singer's*: **singer's node, nodule** *Path.*, a small pale swelling on a vocal cord; **singer's seat** *U.S.*, a choir-seat or bench (cf. *singing-seat* s.v. SINGING *vbl. sb.* 4 b).

**1953** C. WAKELY *Faber Med. Dict.* 389/2 *Singers' nodes*, or *nodules*... Syn. *chorditis tuberosa*. **1961** R. D. BAKER *Essent. Path.* xv. 360 Overuse of the voice can cause traumatic laryngitis and 'singer's nodes', and a biopsy will demonstrate minute hematomas in various stages of scarring. **1967** *Punch* 29 Mar. 458 Singer's Nodule, the name for a minute warty excrescence on overworked vocal apparatus. **1974** PASSMORE & ROBSON *Compan. Med. Stud.* III. xxxii. 22/2 Vocal nodules. These are called singer's nodes because they are seen in singers, particularly sopranos and tenors, but they also occur in others who use their voices excessively, with faulty voice production. **1777** Singer's seat [see CHORISTER 1 a]. **1861** MRS. STOWE *Pearl of Orr's Island* (1862) ix. 84 Aunt Ruey..had in her youth been one of the foremost leaders in the 'singers' seats'.

**singer**[2] (ˈsɪndʒə(r)). [f. SINGE *v.* + -ER[1].] One who or that which singes.

**1875** KNIGHT *Dict. Mech.* 2187/1 *Singer*, an apparatus through which cotton or woolen goods are passed to relieve them of their fluff, preparing them for the dyer. **1891** in *Cent. Dict.*

†ˈ**singeress.** *Obs. rare.* [f. SINGER[1] + -ESS.] A female singer.

**1382** WYCLIF *Ezra* ii. 65 In hem singeres and singeressis, two hundrid. —— *Ecclus.* ii. 8, I made to me singeris and singeresses.

‖**singerie** (sɛ̃ʒri). [Fr., apish behaviour or trick, a collection of monkeys; cf. CHINOISERIE.] A piece of porcelain, painting, etc., in which monkeys are represented in anthropomorphic (often quasi-Chinese) attitude; work done in this style (esp. popular in the eighteenth cent.). Also *transf.* Cf. *monkey band, orchestra* s.v. MONKEY *sb.* 18 a.

[**1820** M. EDGEWORTH *Let.* 4 June (1979) 142 The white wainscot..is painted with grey imitation of Indian ink pictures of monkeys in mens and womens clothes... I have some notion of having somewhere read of this cabinet of monkeys.] **1920** A. STRATTON *Eng. Interior* 61 So many influences were tending to shape the arts in that century, that it is not surprising to find reflections of the French 'Chinoiserie' and 'Singerie' styles in English houses. The French painters Jean François Clermont..and Jean Pillement..both worked in this country, and their fanciful 'Singeries', in which monkeys play the rôle of horsemen and sportsmen, have a certain charm. **1920** E. SITWELL *Wooden Pegasus* 13 (*title*) Singerie. **1957** *Economist* 9 Nov. (Suppl.) 15/2 This style..gives excessive weight to the rest of their lives, which is that of the characters in Miss Mitford's novels: one-tenth genuine emotion (a bit more for Voltaire) and nine-tenths *singerie*. **1963** N. PEVSNER *Wiltshire* 520 Ceiling with *singeries* by *Andieu de Clermont*,..far too finicky for Inigo's architecture. **1977** FLEMING & HONOUR *Penguin Dict. Decorative Arts* 742/1 The vogue for *singeries* did not begin much before the end of the c17 and reached its height of popularity in the c18 when it became associated with *chinoiserie*... *Singeries* were painted on walls, in porcelain and faience, worked in piqué and in marquetry, embroidered and printed in textiles.

**Singh** (sɪŋ). Also †Sing(e. [a. Hind. *siṅgh* lion, f. Skr. *siṁha* lion, 'the powerful one'.]

**1.** A great warrior: a cognomen or title of respect borne by several of the warrior castes of northern India, or a surname adopted by male Sikhs.

**1623** N. BANGHAM et al. *Let.* 5 Apr. in W. Foster *Eng. Factories in India* (1908) 218 Beinge soe hotly persued by Abdala Chan and Rajae Sursinge. **1797** *Encycl. Brit.* IX. 213/2 In 1770 the rajah died, and was succeeded by his son Cheit Sing. **1841** *Penny Cycl.* XIX. 276/2 The bravery and talents of the regent Zalim Singh. **1888** KIPLING *Departmental Ditties* (1890) 18 Chimbu Singh from Bikaneer..Jowar Singh the Sikh. **1955** *Times* 5 July 13/3 Maharana Sir Fateh Singh Bahadur, the head of the Sessodia Rajputs..had personal as well as dynastic claims to veneration.

**2.** As a simple noun.

**1851** J. THACKWELL *Narr. Second Sikh War* 227 The British guns were so overwhelming..and their fire so rapid and precise, that the enemy declared there was a ball for every Sing. **1914** J. J. H. GORDON *Sikhs* iv. 39 They were then hailed as 'Singhs' or lions of their race, and declared to be the Khalsa—the select... All the rest of the disciples present were similarly baptised and declared Singhs. **1930** G. B. SCOTT *Relig. & Short Hist. Sikhs* iii. 30 After receiving the Pahal, the novice is no longer a Sikh or scholar only, he is *Singh*, a lion, and is entitled to affix that word to his name. **1973** 'S. HARVESTER' *Corner of Playground* II. viii. 150 He thought about his grand-father Swaran,..first Singh of the family in Africa, a coolie who came..to build the railway from Mombasa to Victoria Nyanza.

**Singha'lee.** *rare*$^{-1}$. = SINHALESE 2.

**1847** *Simmons' Col. Mag.* May 14 We've been a studying Singhalee.

**Singhalese**, variant of SINHALESE.

‖**singhara** (sɪŋ'hɑːrə). Also singara. [Hindī *siṅghārā*.] The water-chestnut (*Trapa bispinosa*) of India, or the edible nut produced by this. Usually *attrib.* with *nut*.

**1834** *Penny Cycl.* II. 478/2 The Singhara nut..forms an object of general cultivation in the lakes which surround the city of Cashmere. **1859** *All Year Round* No. 32. 126 The seeds of the araucarian pine,..and the singhara, or water-nut, are all highly recommended..as substitutes for potatoes. **1885** *Encycl. Brit.* XVIII. 71/2 The jhils supply the villages with wild rice..and the singhara water-nut.

**singilly**, obs. form of SINGLY *adv.*

**singing** ('sɪŋɪŋ), *vbl. sb.* Also 4-6 syngyng(e, 5 cyngynge, etc. [f. SING *v.*¹ + -ING¹.]

**1. a.** The action of the verb; chanting; also, matter suitable for singing.

*a* **1300** *Cursor M.* 20587 Omang þat singing and þat gleu Our leuedi hir sun ihesu knew. **1377** LANGL. *P. Pl.* B. XI. 145, I [was] saued, as ȝe may se, with-oute syngyng of masses. *c* **1400** *Rule St. Benet* 1162 In ayn oþer plase sais he þat angels sal our synging se. *c* **1440** *Promp. Parv.* 78 Cyngynge of songe, *cantus*. *Ibid.*, Cyngynge of masse, *celebracio*. **1484** *Paston Lett.* III. 314 Sche seyd that ther wer non dysgysyngs, ner harpyng, ner lutyng, ner syngyn. **1535** COVERDALE *1 Chron.* vii. 31 They mynistred before the habitacion of the Tabernacle of witnes with syngynge. **1579** SPENSER *Sheph. Cal.* May 21 With singing, and shouting, and iolly chere. **1611** BIBLE *Song Sol.* ii. 12 The time of the singing of birds is come, and the voice of the turtle is heard in our land. **1632** LITHGOW *Trav.* III. 90 They are naturally inclined to singing. **1700** TYRRELL *Hist. Eng.* II. 763 Yet was he received by the Clergy with a Solemn Procession and Singing. **1772** WESLEY *Jrnl.* 21 Apr., Every one stood up at the singing. **1817** SHELLEY *Fragm.*, *To one Singing* 2 Upon the liquid waves of thy sweet singing. **1863** W. C. BALDWIN *Afr. Hunting* 72 The horrid noise which the Kaffirs made, and call singing. **1872** T. HARDY *Under Greenw. Tree* Pref., Some of these compositions which now lie before me..are good singing still.

**b.** With *a* and pl. An instance of this. Now *N. Amer.* (chiefly *Southern*), a gathering joined for collective singing, esp. at a church; a hearty sing-song.

*c* **1374** CHAUCER *Troylus* III. 1716 In blisse, and in syngynges, This Troylus gan all his lyf to lede. *c* **1440** *Jacob's Well* 164 Leccherous maners, as kyssynges, felynges, dern syngynges. **1591** SPENSER *M. Hubberd* 454 Their Diriges, their Trentals, and their shrifts, Their memories, their singings, and their gifts. **1661** *Papers Alter. Prayer-bk.* 80 They use not the same prayers, singings or readings. **1684** *Foxe's A. & M.* III. 390 Neither their singings, nor their sayings, shall bring us out of Hell. **1860** O. L. JACKSON *Colonel's Diary* (1922) 17, I was at a singing at Woodward Church. **1934** C. CARMER *Stars fell on Alabama* II. ii. 49 Ain't seen him since the singin' down at Samanthy. **1949** B. A. BOTKIN *Treas. S. Folklore* I. iv. 93 All through the South, of course, the church is an important social and cultural force, its sociability running the gamut of church-going.. bush-arbor revivals, all-day singings with dinner on the grounds, church suppers, singing schools, [etc.]. **1962** E. LUCIA *Klondike Kate* viii. 172 Families got together for 'singings' around the parlor piano and to play games. **1975** *Budget* (Sugarcreek, Ohio) 20 Mar. 3/5 They all had supper at the Lehman home and a singing was held later in the evening.

**c.** The action of turning informer or laying information against someone. Cf. sense 4 d of the vb. *Criminals' slang.*

**1937** *Sat. Even. Post* 18 Dec. 85/1 One actually preferred a three-year penitentiary term to singing. **1940** *Daily Progress* (Charlottesville, Va.) 21 Mar. 3 (*heading*) 'Singing' at murder syndicate's hunting ground. **1973** *Times* 12 Apr. 7/4 The terrified 'singing' of the Sicilian 'Valachi' to delighted magistrates in Palermo has landed 36 Mafia suspects in jail.

**2. a.** The emission of a clear musical note by fermenting or heated liquids.

*c* **1460** J. RUSSELL *Bk. Nurture* 113 ȝiff þe wyne reboyle, þow shalle know by hys syngynge. **1854** MISS BAKER *Northampt. Gloss.* s.v., The sound made by damp wood when burning is also called singing.

**b.** *Teleph.* A continuous self-excited oscillation of audible frequency in a telephone circuit, normally resulting from excessive positive feedback.

**1923** T. E. HERBERT *Telephony* xxvi. 829 If two repeaters are in circuit, spaced so closely that the line loss between them is less than the gain given by each 'singing' or 'howling' will persist continuously. **1962** C. F. BOYCE *Open-Wire Carrier Telephone Transmission* xi. 231 Singing affects not only the channel which is unstable but may also cause crosstalk into another system or overloading of line amplifiers. **1975** R. L. FREEMAN *Telecommunication Transmission Handbk.* vi. 48 To control singing all four-wire paths must have some loss.

**3.** A sound of a musical character having its origin *in* the ears or head.

**1605** CHAPMAN *All Fools* v. i, I'll swear I had A singing in my head a whole week after. **1614** W. B. *Philosopher's Banquet* (ed. 2) 78 The iuyce..allayes the singing in the Eares. **1656** HARRINGTON *Oceana* (1700) 163, I have a singing in my head like that of a Cartwheel. **1766** *Phil. Trans.* LVII. 70 The giddiness in my head, singing in my ears,..were now considerably abated. **1889** *Jrnl. Anthropol. Instit.* XIX. 119 Singings in the ear, gurglings in the throat.

**4.** *attrib.* and *Comb.*, as ***singing commercial***, ***face***, ***gear***, ***-master***, ***matter***, ***robes***, ***-school***, ***skill***, ***-voice***; **singing-bone**, *dial.*, the funny-bone; **singing book**, a book to sing from; **singing-e'en**, *Sc.*, New Year's eve; **singing game**, a traditional children's game in which singing accompanies associated actions; †**singing gift** (see quot.); †**singing loaf**, = SINGING BREAD; **singing-muscle**, one of the syringeal muscles of a singing-bird (*Cent. Dict.*); **singing point** *Teleph.*, the maximum gain that a telephone repeater can have without being liable to self-oscillation in the circuit; †**singing psalms**, the metrical version of the psalms used for singing in church; †**singing wine**, ? wine used in celebrating mass.

**1854** MISS BAKER *Northampt. Gloss.*, *Singing-bone, the sharp bone at the edge of the elbow. **1580** ALLEN in J. Gillow *Haydock Papers* (1888) 17 To employ the same summe.. upon a payre of organs, one table, and certayne *singing bookes. **1607** [? BREWER] *Lingua* I. ix, When shall wee heare a new set of singing-books, or th' viols, or the consort of Instruments. **1793** in *Essex Inst. Hist. Coll.* (1885) XXII. 148 Voted to obtain 6 Psalm Books and 6 Singing Books for the use of the Parish. **1872** MRS. STOWE *Oldtown Fireside Stories* 130 They tore out all the leaves of the hymn-books, and the singin'-books besides. **1948** B. ROSE *Wine, Women & Words* 11, I wrote the first *singing commercial. **1955** *New Yorker* 23 Apr. 74/1, I approached Mr. Chayefsky's film with no great hope that the thing would prove to be much more interesting than a singing commercial. **1806** A. DOUGLAS *Poems* 24 *Singin'-e'en she's owre aft seen, She's shakin' hands wi' fifty. **1846** DICKENS *Cricket on Hearth* II, He hadn't what is generally termed a *singing face. **1881** *Folk-Lore Rec.* III. II. 169 The following '*Singing Games' are still played and sung by the children of Bocking, in Essex ..I. Mary's gone a-milking..II. Thread the Tailor's needle ..III. Nuts in May [etc.]. **1905** G. ADE *Let.* 7 Nov. (1973) 33 One or two of the old-fashioned singing games which went as well in the *Sho-Gun*. **1975** B. MEYRICK *Behind Light* xiv. 183 Playing the singing games 'Jenny is a-weeping', 'In and out the stalky bluebells'. **1530** *Knaresb. Wills* (Surtees) I. 26 That he shall have his tytle and *singynge geyr boughte at the coste of my sayd wyeffe. *c* **1440** *Promp. Parv.* 456/2 *Syngynge ȝyfte, or reward for syngynge, *syparium*. **1530** TINDALE *Pract. Prelates* f viij, A great deale of flower wolde not make so manye hostes, as they call them, or *syngynge loues. **1546** PHAER *Bk. Childr.* (1553) T viij b, Make a fewe pylles of aloes,..wynde them in a piece of a singing lofe,.. and let them be swalowed. **1711** ADDISON *Spect.* No. 112 ⁋2 He..employed an itinerant *Singing-Master..to instruct them rightly in the Tunes of the Psalms. **1754** *N.Y. Mercury* 11 Mar. 3/2 William Tuckey, Singing-Master, Desires to inform all lovers of Psalmody, that..all persons may be taught by him on very reasonable terms. **1891** *Harper's Mag.* Oct. 813/1 The precentor, or singing-master, as he was called, was a tall young man in a black suit with white ruffles. **1928** W. B. YEATS *Tower* 2 And to be the singing masters of my soul. **1976** J. DRUMMOND *Funeral Urn* xvii. 89 He was planning to make a concert singer of her. He'd engaged a singing-master—ostensibly to train the Amber choir, but in fact for Bess. **1818** SCOTT *Rob Roy* xxxvii, If there is any truth in your news, is it a *singing matter, you scoundrel? **1924** K. S. JOHNSON *Transmission Circuits for Telephonic Communications* xiv. 166 The *singing point or the limiting condition beyond which satisfactory operation of the repeater cannot be maintained. **1934** *Post Office Electr. Engineers Jrnl.* XXVII. 231/2 The vertical scale gives the singing point of a repeater in decibels. **1679** BUNYAN *Fear of God* Wks. 1852 I. 473, I will set it before thee both as it is in the reading and in the *singing psalms. **1710** W. BEVERIDGE *Wks.* (1846) VIII. 615 Great endeavours..have been made..to cast out the Old, and bring in a New Version of the Singing-Psalms. **1841** DE QUINCEY *Homer & Homeridæ* Wks. 1857 VI. 362 When his *singing robes were on,..the *rhapsodos* held his stick in his right hand. **1736** AINSWORTH, A *singing school, *ludus musicus*. **1838** G. F. GRAHAM *Mus. Comp.* Introd. p. x, In the sixth century Pope Gregory I established a singing-school at Rome. *c* **1600** F. DAVISON in Farr *S.P. Eliz.* (1845) II. 331 Let my tongue lose *singing skill. **1880** LANIER *Sci. Eng. Verse* i. 28 These are the limits for the human *singing-voice. **1558** *Fraternity Holy Ghost, Basingstoke* (1882) 9 Item payed for *singinge wyne, ij d.

**b.** Of places used for singing in, as ***singing-gallery***, ***-house***, ***loft***, ***-pew***, ***-place***, ***-room***, ***-seat***, ***theatre***.

**1688** MIÈGE *Grt. Fr. Dict.* I, *Jubé*,..a singing Place. *a* **1700** EVELYN *Diary* 14 Sept. 1644, At the end of it is a Cupola or singing theatre. **1750** *Phil. Trans.* XLVI. 708 The Reading-Desk stands just by the Singing-Pew. **1770** *Ibid.* LXI. 74 The lightning entered..through two places in the roof, one near the singing loft. **1774** in *Essex Inst. Hist. Coll.* (1884) XXI. 271 Voted Liberty to beuld a singing Seat in the front of the Gallearry Pues. *c* **1820** S. ROGERS *Italy, Como* (1839) 211 That shady nook, a singing place for birds. **1842** F. WITTS *Diary* 22 Oct. (1978) 167 The remains were to be deposited at the west end of Upton St. Leonards church, under the singing gallery, near the font. **1850** THACKERAY *Pendennis* xx, The theatres and singing-houses which these roaring young blades frequented. **1851** J. W. HUDSON *Hist. Adult Educ.* 157 Singing-rooms are numerous, prosperous and constantly well-attended. **1864** WHITTIER *Wreck of Rivermouth* 109 In the singing-seats young eyes were dim. **1883** C. C. PERKINS *Ital. Sculp.* 139 A singing-gallery (cantoria) in the Cathedral. **1902** A. BENNETT *Anna of Five Towns* ii. 34 Mynors..should have been in his place in the 'orchestra' (or, as some term it, the 'singing-seat') of the [Methodist] chapel. **1976** *S. Wales Echo* 27 Nov. 12/6 (Advt.), Sing along with Mike and Charles at the newly decorated singing-room upstairs.

**'singing**, *ppl. a.* Also 4-5 syngynge. [-ING².]

**I. 1. a.** That sings; giving forth song.

*c* **1340** *Nominale* (Skeat) 128 Syngynge man silden weputh. *c* **1586** C'TESS PEMBROKE *Ps.* LXVI. ii, All earth, I say, and all earth dwellers, Be of his worth the singing tellers. **1599** SHAKS. *Hen. V*, I. ii. 198 The singing Masons building roofes of Gold. **1779** *Mirror* No. 24, We have the whistling plow-man, the singing milk-maid. **1798** COLERIDGE *Fears in Solitude* 3 O'er stiller place No singing skylark ever poised himself. **1820** SHELLEY *Prometh. Unb.* IV. 515 The bright visions, Wherein the singing spirits rode and shone. **1882** J. PARKER *Apostolic Life* I. 12 Like a singing angel newly sent from the glad heavens.

**b.** In names of birds, etc.

**1864-5** WOOD *Homes without H.* xii. (1868) 218 A most beautiful pensile nest is made by the Singing Honey-Eater (*Ptilotus sonorus*). **1884** GOODE *Nat. Hist. Aquat. Anim.* 253 The *Batrachidæ* are represented on the Pacific coast by the 'Singing-fish', or 'Toad-fish', *Porichthys porosissimus*.

**2.** Specially or professionally employed in singing; engaged or hired to sing: **a.** ***singing man***, a man engaged to sing in an ecclesiastical choir.

**1527-8** *Rec. St. Mary at Hill* (1905) 346 Paide to a singing-man of Sent Anthis..for keping of our lady mas. **1597** MORLEY *Introd. Mus.* 156 To haue plaide it on the Organes with a quier of singing men. **1602** CAMPION *Art Eng. Poesie* ii. 6 Sir Thomas Moore..makes two sundry Epitaphs vpon the death of a singing man at Westminster. **1655** FULLER *Ch. Hist.* II. xvii. 179 He heavily aggravated the debauchednesse of Singingmen. **1725** *Portland Papers* VI. (Hist. MSS. Comm.) 100 Mr. Bierly..married a daughter of Dan. Williams the Singing-man of Westminster. **1789** BURNEY *Hist. Mus.* III. i. 22 He procured a singing-man's place in the cathedral of Norwich. **1801** BUSBY *Dict. Mus.*, *Singing-Man*, the appellation formerly given by the common people to the gentlemen of cathedral choirs. **1905** E. CANDLER *Unveiling of Lhasa* xiv. 269 The Abbot begins the chant, and the monks, facing each other like singing-men in a choir, repeat the litany.

*fig.* **1594** NASHE *Unfort. Trav.* Wks. (Grosart) V. 120 As many sortes of shrill breasted birdes, as the Summer hath allowed for singing men in her siluane chapels.

**b.** Similarly ***singing boy***, ***clerk***. Also, in other than ecclesiastical use, ***singing girl***, ***woman***.

**1535** COVERDALE *2 Chron.* xxxv. 25 All the syngynge men and wemen [**1611** the singing women]. **1548** ELYOT *Dict.*, *Cantrix*,..a syngyng woman. **1666** PEPYS *Diary* 26 Feb., And hither come cushions to us, and a young singing-boy to bring us a copy of the anthem to be sung. **1682** N. O. *Boileau's Lutrin* IV. 25 Let Singing-boyes Whose Pension's pay for 't, do those Drudgeries! **1709** STEELE *Tatler* No. 41 ⁋6 Mr. John Taplash..desires your Vote for Singing-Clerk of this Parish. **1776** *Addit. Wks. Pope* I. 35 With wives I never sin, But singing girls and mimicks draw me in. **1820** T. MITCHELL *Aristoph.* II. 302 The dicast..enters with a torch in one hand, and leads a singing-girl in the other. **1880** BROWNING *Muléykeh* 59 For a couple of singing-girls his robe has he torn in two.

**3.** ***singing bird***, a bird that sings; a songster. Usually applied to cage-birds; the pl. is also sometimes used as a rendering of OSCINES 2.

**1565** COOPER *Thesaurus*, *Cantrices aues*, syngyng byrdes. **1593** SHAKS. *Rich. II*, I. iii. 288 (Q.¹), Suppose the singing birds musitions. **1626** [see SINGER¹ 1 b]. **1711** ADDISON *Spect.* No. 5 ⁋7 The next time it is Acted, the Singing Birds will be Personated by Tom-Tits. **1774** GOLDSM. *Nat. Hist.* (1776) V. 339 Of the Canary-bird, and other hard billed Singing-birds. **1818** SCOTT *Rob Roy* v, They are like imprisoned singing-birds. **1871** T. R. JONES *Anim. Kingd.* (ed. 4) 772 It is owing to the capacity of the air-cells that the Singing Birds are enabled to prolong their notes.

*transf.* **1848** KINGSLEY *Saint's Trag.* III. iv, Mealy-mouthed inquisitors, and shaven singing-birds.

**4. a.** That makes or gives out a sound of a musical character (cf. SING *v.*[1] 6).

**1565** COOPER *Thes., Sagitta stridens*, a syngyng arow. **1629** QUARLES *Argalus & P.* III. Wks. (Grosart) III. 274/1 His winged messenger..did hide His singing feathers in his wounded side. **1642** FULLER *Holy & Prof. St.* v. xvi. 423 Malice, which,..like hollow singing bullets, flies but halfway to the mark. **1716** POPE *Iliad* v. 214 Through the thick storm of singing spears he flies. **1791** COWPER *Iliad* XVIII. 432 The water in the singing brass Simmer'd. **1820** SHELLEY *Prometh. Unb.* IV. 235 Sounds Sweet as a singing rain of silver dew. **1855** LONGF. *Hiaw.* Introd. 48 Beyond them..Stood the groves of singing pine-trees.

**b.** ***singing arc***, a direct current arc across which is connected a tuned circuit, causing the arc to oscillate and emit a sound at the frequency of the tuned circuit. ***singing-buoy***, a buoy having something attached which gives out a singing sound. ***singing coal*** (see quot. 1883). ***singing glass*** (see quot. 1875). ***singing hinny*** (north. dial.), a kind of cake which emits a hissing sound while cooking on a girdle. ***singing sand***, desert or beach sand that emits a singing, whistling, humming, or other continuous sound when disturbed. ***singing tree***, a West Indian tree, the pods of which make a singing sound when stirred by the wind.

**1903** *Sci. Abstr.* VI. 30 The author suggests replacing the ordinary high-capacity condensers necessary to produce Duddell's '*singing arc' by the much less costly aluminium condenser. **1906** *Electrician* 21 Dec. 375/1 Limitations as to frequency..beset the use of the singing arc as a transformer of the direct mains current into uninterrupted high-frequency alternating current. **1950** STARLING & WOODALL *Physics* xxxvi. 874 The singing arc..where electrical and thermal factors are involved in the maintenance of oscillations. **1894** *Outing* XXIV. 460/2 A *singing-buoy had been torn from its moorings. **1855** J. PHILLIPS *Man. Geol.* 193 Strata, including *singeing [*sic*] coal. **1883** GRESLEY *Gloss. Coalm.* 223 *Singing Coal*, a bed of coal from which gas is ordinarily issuing from the partly-exposed face in the mine, producing a hissing sound. **1669** PEPYS *Diary* 23 Feb., I had one or two *singing-glasses made, which make an echo to the voice, the first that ever I saw. **1792** G. GALLOWAY *Poems* 34 To see..Mr. Cartwright's singing glasses. **1875** KNIGHT *Dict. Mech.* 2187/1 *Singing-glass*, a thin, sonorous glass vessel, which yields an echo when vibrated by a sound. **1825** BROCKETT *N.C. Gloss.*, *Singin* or **Singing-hinny*, a kneaded spice cake baked on the girdle; indispensable in a pitman's family. **1863** MRS. GASKELL *Sylvia's Lovers* iv, Neither cream nor finest wheaten flour was wanting for 'turf-cakes' and 'singing-hinnies'. [**1884** *Proc. Amer. Assoc. Adv. Sci. 1883* 251 (*heading*) The singing beach of Manchester, Mass.] **1897** MARY KINGSLEY *W. Africa* 175 A patch of *singing sand under my feet. **1941** R. A. BAGNOLD *Physics of Blown Sand & Desert Dunes* xvii. 251, I have found singing sand on the slip-faces of both seif and barchan dunes and of drifts formed under the shelter of cliffs. **1970** R. JOHNSTON *Black Camels of Qashran* viii. 133 The night-long background music of the dunes was silenced. They were through the singing sands. **1885** LADY BRASSEY *The Trades* 340 The *flamboyant*..is very abundant here [the Bahamas]; as is also the '*singing' tree, which we first saw in Jamaica.

**II. 5.** Of the nature of singing; having the musical qualities of song.

*a* **1425** *Cursor M.* 11244 (Trin.), Aungels..brouȝt word with syngynge steuen. *a* **1586** SIDNEY *Ps.* XXXIII. ii, O now accord Violls with singing voice. *c* **1586** C'TESS PEMBROKE *Ps.* LXVIII. xi, On the Lord your singing gladnes spend. **1697** C. LESLIE *Snake in Grass* (ed. 2) 115 A She-Preacher..with a Trembling Voice, and Singing Tone. **1725** RAMSAY *Gentl. Sheph.* I. ii, The water fa's, and makes a singand din. **1762** *Ann. Reg.* II. 37, I have acquired by habit that singing tone of voice which is common in our mountains. **1860** TYNDALL *Glac.* II. xvii. 317 The intervals between the louder reports being filled by a low singing noise.

†**singing bread.** *Obs.* [Cf. SING *v.*[1] 3 and 11.] The wafer used in the celebration of the mass.

**1432-3** *Will of E. Strete* (Comm. Crt. London), Duo par de bakyngirnes, unum pro shosynlyngbred [?] & aliud pro singyngbred. **1453** *Test. Ebor.* (Surtees) II. 190 Item j box of silver covered, for syngyngbrede. **1527** in Lewis *Life Fisher* (1855) I. 314 These prestis makith us to beleve, that the synginge brede they holde ouer their hedes is god, and it is but a cake. **1570** B. GOOGE *Pop. Kingd.* IV. 51 b, And least in grave he shoulde remaine, without some companie, The singing bread is layde with him. **1616** SURFL. & MARKHAM *Country Farme* v. xxii. 585 Singing breads are made after the manner of Oublies, saue only that the meale whereof they are kneaden is not mingled with Honey, Sugar, or any manner of Leaven whatsoever.

**singing cake.**

† **1.** = SINGING BREAD. *Obs.*

**1553** BECON *Reliques of Rome* (1563) 258 A patten with the hoste or singing cake. **1560** DAUS tr. *Sleidane's Comm.* 43 He hath..delivered into his handes a chalice with wine and water, also the gilt Patent with a singing Cake. **1577-87** HOLINSHED *Chron.* III. 1102/2 A cat.., with hir fore feet tied togither, and a round peece of paper like a singing cake betwixt them. **1607** R. C[AREW] tr. *Estienne's World Wond.* 342 Vnconsecrated singing cakes (as they terme them).

† **b.** Used as a wafer for sealing with. *Obs.*

**1582** MUNDAY *Eng. Rom. Life* 5 These Letters finished, and sealed vp with singing Cake, he delyuered vnto vs.

**2.** *Sc.* A cake given to singers on Hogmanay.

**1894** 'H. HALIBURTON' (J. L. ROBERTSON) *Furth in Field* 28 Money was sometimes added to the ordinary gift of 'singing' cakes and cheese. **1894** MELDRUM *Margrédel* I. 6, I remember that dining at the Oliphant's crowned the joy of singing-cakes and other delights.

'**singingly**, *adv.* [f. SINGING *ppl. a.*] In a singing manner or tone.

**1575** G. NORTH tr. *Philibert's Philosopher at Court* 16 Counterfaite Courtiers..speaking lispingly, and answering singingly. **1856** DORAN *Knight's & their Days* viii. 122 He..takes the half dozen damsels..and swings singingly along with them in search of the roving Scot.

**single** ('sɪŋg(ə)l), *sb.* Also 5 sengle, 6 syngle, *Sc.* singill. [Substantival use of SINGLE *a.*]

**1. a.** *Falconry.* The middle or outer claw on the foot of a hawk or falcon. Now only *arch.*

Chiefly in *pl.*, the middle claws being called the ***long singles***, and the outer the ***petty singles***. In early use the singles were distinguished from the pounce and talon; later writers sometimes use the word vaguely to denote all the claws.

**1486** *Bk. St. Albans* a iiij, The clees that are upon the myddil stretchers ye shall call the longe sengles. And the uttermost clees ye shall call the pety sengles. **1575** TURBERV. *Falconrie* 123 If a falcon trusse..you muste cope his tallantes, his powlse, and his petie single. **1607** HEYWOOD *Wom. killed w. Kindn.* Wks. 1874 II. 99 Both her petty singles And her long singles griped her more than other. **1614** LATHAM *Falconry* (1633) 134 When you do perceiue that your Hawke hath caught a straine..in any of the lesser ioynts of the singles. **1688** HOLME *Armoury* II. 237/2 The Singles, or Petty Singles, are the Toes of the Hawk. **1820** SCOTT *Monast.* xxiv, What! struggling, fluttering, aiming at me with beak and single? **1860** H. AINSWORTH *Ovingdean Grange* 61 Like the Barbary falcon, armed with strong singles and pounces. **1882** *Blackw. Mag.* Sept. 368 Like the muirfowl quivering in the singles of a falcon.

**b.** *Hunting.* The tail of a deer.

**1576** TURBERV. *Venerie* 243 The tayle of Harte, Bucke, Rowe, or any other Deare, is to be called the Syngle. **1590** COCKAINE *Hunting* D j, He will close vp his mouth as though he had not been..hunted that day, making a bragge and setting vp his single. **1634** SIR T. HERBERT *Trav.* 14 Such as want that treasure, make use of singles of Deere, beaks of Birds [etc.]. **1675** COTTON *Burlesque upon B.* 175 That single wagging at thy Butt, Those Gambrils, and that cloven foot. **1711** PUCKLE *Club* 90 His next discourse was of the tail or single of a deer. **1854** MISS BAKER *Northampt. Gloss.*, *Single*, the tail of a deer. Used on the north-eastern side of the county. **1865** G. F. BERKELEY *Life & Recoll.* II. 280 We found a doe... I killed her myself, and cutting off the single ..I presented it to D'Anchald.

*transf.* **1592** LYLY *Midas* IV. iii, There was a boy leasht on the single... *Licio.* Whats that? *Pet.* Why, a boy was beaten on the taile with a leathern thong.

†**c.** *pl.* Entrails, intestines. *Obs.*[−1]

**1567** GOLDING *Ovid's Met.* VII. 353 She put thereto the..flesh and feathers of a Witch.., The Singles [L. *prosecta*] also of a Wolfe.

**2.** *Sc.* and *north. dial.* A handful or small bundle of gleanings.

The form current in the west midlands is SONGLE.

**1508** DUNBAR *Flyting* 116 Thow lay full prydles in the peise this somer, And fane at evin for to bring hame a single. **1615** in Ritchie *Churches of St. Baldred* 150 He did thresh but a verie short space— twa or thre Singles—in his necessitie. **1786** *Har'st Rig* xxvi, They're great thieves. For which they're ordered far behind, To mak such singles as they find. **1806** A. DOUGLAS *Poems* 123 They're fu' glad To gather singles on the shade. **1894** HESLOP *Northumbld. Gloss.* 643 Gleaning is often described as 'gatherin singles' or as singlin... Singles are bundled and carried home on the 'gatherer' and afterwards 'bittled'.

**3.** In various specific or technical senses.

†**a.** A particular step in dancing. *Obs.*

**1531** ELYOT *Gov.* I. xxiii, The thirde motion, called singles, is of two unities seperate in pasinge forwarde. **1611** COTGR., *Simple*,..a single in dauncing.

**b.** A simple uncompounded word.

**1589** PUTTENHAM *Eng. Poesie* II. xvi. (Arb.) 145 The sillable *prooue*..is long in all his singles and compoundes *reproòue, approòue, disproòue.*

†**c.** *Sc.* One half of a doubled amount. *Obs.*

**1592** *Exch. Rolls Scotl.* XXII. 574 He sall mak payment.. for the singill of the dowbill of the few-ferme of the landis of Catslak.

**d.** A form of change in bell-ringing.

**1684** R. H. *School Recreat.* 93 Another Way of Ringing Twenty Four Changes, Doubles and Singles on Four Bells.

**e.** A single (as opposed to a double) flower.

**1796** C. MARSHALL *Gardening* v. (1813) 62 The farina of the singles transported by bee or wind will spoil the seed of the doubles.

**f.** A silk thread consisting of a single strand.

**1831** G. R. PORTER *Silk Manuf.* 197 Raw silk, before it can be used in weaving, is made to take one of three forms, being converted into either singles, tram, or organzine. **1844** G. DODD *Textile Manuf.* vi. 184 There is a kind called dumb singles, which consists of silk merely wound and cleaned... Another manufactured variety, called thrown singles, is silk which has been wound, cleaned, and thrown. **1879** *Cassell's Techn. Educ.* II. 154/2 By *singles* is signified one of the reeled threads twisted.

**g.** *Cards.* (See quots.)

**1850** *Bohn's Hand-bk. Games* 162 *Single*, (at long whist) scoring the game after your adversary has scored five or more; at short whist, after he has scored four. **1876** CAMPBELL-WALKER *Correct Card* (1880) Gloss., *Single, a*, —making game after your adversary has scored three or four up.

**h.** *Cricket*, etc. A hit for which one run is scored; a single point. Also in *Baseball*, *spec.* = *one-base hit* s.v. ONE *numeral a.* 35.

**1851** J. PYCROFT *Cricket Field* ii. 24 Ever and anon a single or a double are safely played away. **1858** *New York Tribune* 25 Aug. 5/6 Smith made three by singles. **1867** *N.Y. Mercury* 2 Aug. 6/5 The sharp fielding of the Athletics caused the retirement of their opponents for a single. **1880** *Chicago Inter-Ocean* 29 June 8/3 Force's winning run came off a wild throw by Ward, a sacrifice and single. **1883** *Daily Telegr.* 15 May 2/7 Mr. Hawke added another single off that bowler. **1948** *Herald-Press* (St. Joseph, Mich.) 14 Aug. 7/2 Green also bashed out a triple and single during the game. **1974** *Anderson* (S. Carolina) *Independent* 23 Apr. 6A/2 The Astros broke a scoreless tie in the fourth on Bob Watson's single, a wild pitch, and Doug Rader's double.

**i.** *Tennis, Golf*, etc. A game or match in which only one person on each side plays at one time.

**1884** *Daily News* 3 Sept. 3/5 The first rounds of the Gentlemen's Singles..were decided as follows. **1896** *Westm. Gaz.* 26 Nov. 4/1 J. H. Taylor won the singles competition with a score of 76.

**j.** A locomotive engine having a single pair of driving-wheels. Now only *Hist.*

**1901** *Railway Mag.* Jan. 31/2 The engine hauling the 9.45 a.m. was No. 22, one of the rebuilt 8 ft. singles. **1931** *Times Educ. Suppl.* 27 June p. iii/3 A famous locomotive,..one of the original 9 ft. singles built for the Bristol and Exeter Railway.

**k.** *pl.* Single-screened coal.

**1921** *Glasgow Herald* 7 Dec. 9 Coals used in smithwork say 'pearls' and 'singles', varied from 15*s.* to 18*s.* per ton f.o.b. **1931** [see DOUBLE *sb.* 3 r].

**l.** *U.S. Theatr.* (See quot. 1923.) Cf. *single act* s.v. SINGLE *a.* 17 a.

**1923** *N.Y. Times* 7 Oct. IX. 2/1 *Single*, an artist working alone as an act. **1955** L. FEATHER *Encycl. Jazz* (1956) 118/2 After Keaton broke up temporarily in 1949, she worked as a single, but rejoined Keaton for several tours. **1962** J. MCCABE *Mr. Laurel & Mr. Hardy* i. 26 Following the *Sleeping Beauty* season, he went on as a single again..for a few odd engagements. **1976** *National Observer* (U.S.) 24 Jan. 18/5 For the past 18 years George Burns has practiced his profession as a single. He has worked..in night clubs and concert halls; he has appeared..on television talk shows.

**m.** A one-dollar bill (*U.S.*). Also *occas.*, a one-pound note. Cf. ONCER 2. *slang.*

**1936** J. WEIDMAN in *Amer. Mercury* May 86/2, I took out my wallet... I pulled out two singles. **1961** 'J. LE CARRÉ' *Call for Dead* vii. 78 There he was..showering old singles on me like used tote tickets. **1964** L. DEIGHTON *Funeral in Berlin* xlii. 258 'Do you have a pistol or a knife or a persuader?' 'I have a persuader... Two hundred dollars in singles.' **1977** H. FAST *Immigrants* I. 35 He..took out a wad of bills, peeling off two fives and two singles.

**n.** A gramophone record having only one item (typically, of popular music) on each side; an item of music on such a record.

**1949** [see *pop single* s.v. POP *a.* 1 c]. **1958** *Gramophone* Dec. 328/1 There is a single by Nino Rico and his Orchestra. **1965** G. MELLY *Owning Up* xi. 135 His version of 'Rock Island Line', originally part of a Chris Barber in Concert LP, was requested so often on the radio that it was put out as a single and rose to be top of the Hit Parade. **1981** *Listener* 1 Jan. 31/2 A track released as a single..topped the singles chart.

**o.** An engine with only one cylinder; a motor-cycle or car having such an engine.

**1951** B. OSBORNE *Mod. Motorcycles* iii. 19 The designer of hot-stuff singles will scornfully mention Italy's Monza,.. where riders of high-revving Italian 'fours' have been.. completely licked by one of the finest single-cylinder racers ever turned out of a Birmingham factory. **1955** D. SCOTT-MONCRIEFF *Veteran & Edwardian Motor-Cars* vi. 111 The old long-stroke singles and twins were no longer allowed [in 1911]; only four- and six-cylinder cars. **1963** BIRD & HUTTON-STOTT *Veteran Motor Car Pocketbk.* 189 It was soon apparent that the small 4-cylinder engine was destined to supplant the big singles and twins which had served so long for light car work. **1976** *New Motorcycling Monthly* Oct. 24/3 It is every inch a purpose-built motorcycle, and must have been a welcome addition to a scene that still reveres our own BSA 'Gold Star' and Matchless singles.

**4.** A single thing, person, etc. ***in singles***, each one separately, singly.

**1646** SIR T. BROWNE *Pseud. Ep.* II. vi, If..any [trees] be so strongly constituted,..they may..perform that in some singles which is observable in whole kinds. **1826** J. WILSON *Noct. Ambr.* Wks. 1855 I. 133 Houndin the wolves in singles or pairs or flocks. **1838** HOOD *Clubs* v, Friends dropping in at close of day To singles, doubles, rubs. **1895** *Scottish Antiq.* X. 79 In singles or in pairs men began to put in an appearance.

**5.** *ellipt.* in general application. **a.** = *single ticket* s.v. SINGLE *a.* 17 a.

**1889** E. DOWSON *Let.* 1-2 Apr. (1967) 59 If I could see things..as he does I would take a first class single for La Trappe to-morrow. **1903** L. MERRICK *Quaint Companions* iv. 49 She congratulated herself on having taken only a 'third single' at Brighton. **1936** *Punch* 5 Feb. 141/1 'Single to Liverpool Street,' I said with easy hauteur. **1972** 'R. CRAWFORD' *Whip Hand* I. ix. 55 He..booked a single on the next flight to London.

**b.** A single bedroom, esp. in a hotel. Cf. SINGLE *a.* 11 d.

**1963** [see DOUBLE *sb.* 3 n]. **1967** A. HUNTER *Gently Continental* ii. 12 He goes up to Clooney's room... Number 7 is a small single at the end of the landing. **1973** E. PACE *Any War* I. 5 Yes, sir, the hotel could provide two singles with bath. **1977** B. ALDISS in *Winter's Tales 23* 12 She opened a door to a narrow room... 'It's a bit noisy, but it's the only single I've got.'

**c.** An unmarried or unaccompanied man or woman; a person living alone. Freq. *pl.*

**1964** W. & J. BREEDLOVE *Swap Clubs* ii. 57 A *single* is a man or woman who swings alone, without someone to swap. **1967** D. FRANCIS *Blood Sport* viii. 97 Family groups, mostly, and three married couples. No singles except me. **1972** P. A. WHITNEY *Snowfire* (1973) iv. 52, I had met most of the guests... Some were married, but there were a few young singles too. **1980** R. L. DUNCAN *Brimstone* iii. 59 We have a club rule against singles.

**6.** Special combination, in *pl.*: **singles bar** *U.S.*, a bar which caters esp. for young unmarried people in search of social companions.

**1969** S. M. Coy *Single Girl's Bk.* vii. 34 Singles bars..are generally frequented by those under thirty... The good singles bars are crowded, which provides protective covering for the girl who is timid. **1971** D. E. Westlake *I gave at Office* 141, I looked around to find myself in a sort of New York singles' bar without people. **1974** R. M. Strozier in *Atlantic Monthly* Mar. 44 When I visit the East Side singles bars, some of these upper-class snooty girls look down on you. **1979** *United States 1980/81* (Penguin Travel Guides) 228 Like the Rangoon, the Saloon draws a healthy singles-bar crowd.

†**single**, obs. var. of (or error for) singlo.

**1721** *Lond. Gaz.* No. 5934/3, 35 Tubs Single Tea per Hertford. **1730** Capt. W. Wriglesworth *MS. Log-bk. of the 'Lyell'* 12 Oct., 50 Chests of Bohea and 50 Chests of Single.

**single**, obs. or dial. f. cingle (horse-girth, etc.).

**single** ('sɪŋg(ə)l), *a.* Forms: 4–5 sengle (4 seyngle), 5 sengil(l, sengell(e, cengylle, 6 sengyll; 5–6 syngle, singill (5 syngil, 6 syngyll), 5– single. [a. OF. *single*, *sengle* (also *saingle*, *sangle*, etc.; mod.Picard dial. *single*, Norman *sangle*):—L. *singulum* (in class. L. only pl. *singulī*, etc.) one, individual, separate; the first syllable is identical with the *sim-* of *simplus* simple *a.*

Some of the senses placed under branch II, though less original than those of branch I, are slightly earlier and more common in Middle English.]

**I. 1.** In predicative use: Unaccompanied or unsupported by others; alone, solitary. **a.** With the substantive verb, or in constructions implying this.

**1340–70** *Alex. & Dind.* 33 We ben sengle of us silf, & semen ful bare, Nouht welde we now [etc.]. *c* **1407** Lydg. *Reson & Sens.* 3225 And my partye is but in veyn, So sengle that I stonde in doute; For Venus hath so gret a route Ageynes me [etc.]. *a* **1548** Hall *Chron., Hen. VII*, 60 b, Hys eyes graye, hys teethe syngle and heare thynne. *a* **1593** Marlowe *Edw. II*, iv. v, Edmund away,..be not found single for suspect: Proud Mortimer pries neare into thy walkes. **1648** J. Beaumont *Psyche* xvi. xxv, Still I'm alone, yea singler than alone; In Absent Him I from my self am gone. **1678** Butler *Hud.* iii. i. 796 Our Noblest Senses act by Pairs,..But those that serve the Body alone, Are single and confin'd to one. **1741** Middleton *Cicero* I. v. 392 They left Clodius single in the opposition. **1780** *Mirror* No. 90, He is left alone, single and unsupported, like a leafless trunk. **1803–5** Wordsw. *Solitary Reaper* i, Behold her, single in the field. **1860** Mill *Repr. Govt.* (1865) 115/2 In the first place, each executive officer should be single, and singly responsible for the whole of the duty.

**b.** With other verbs, in quasi-advb. use.

**13..** *Gaw. & Gr. Knt.* 1531, I com hider sengel, & sitte. *a* **1648** Ld. Herbert *Hen. VIII* (1683) 342 His Birth being otherwise so obscure and mean, as no man had ever stood so single. **1673** Dryden *Amboyna* iv. i, I desir'd that he would leave the Company and meet me single here. **1711** Addison *Spect.* No. 7 ¶1 My Dear, Misfortunes never come Single. **1798** Webbe in Owen *Wellesley's Desp.* (1877) 6 All our former..exertions were made against Tippoo single, and unsupported by the French. **1841** Dana *Seaman's Man.* 16 The royal braces go single. **1855** M. Arnold *Balder Dead* iii. 6 See, here is Hermod, who comes single back From Hell.

†**c.** Unsupported by other evidence. *Obs.*$^{-1}$

*c* **1449** Pecock *Repr.* iii. xii. 356 Wherfore this that Girald writith of this voice is ful sengil to be beleued.

**2. a.** Individual, as contrasted with larger bodies or numbers of persons or things.

*c* **1400** *Destr. Troy* 7867 For þere-as men are so mony,..All put in a purpos with a plain wille; þof the syngle mon say, & it sothe be, Hit is demyt for dulle. **1641** 'Smectymnuus' *Vind. Answ.* iv. 56 Though these were but single men yet they were martyrs. **1697** Dryden *Virg. Georg.* iii. 713 Nor do those Ills on single Bodies prey; But oft'ner bring the Nation to decay. **1717** Pope *Iliad* x. 196 Each single Greek..Stands on the sharpest edge of death or life. **1741** Middleton *Cicero* I. vi. 409 Laws to inflict penalties on single persons by name. **1856** Froude *Hist. Eng.* (1858) I. i. 68 No single mind in single contact with the facts of nature could have created out of itself a Pallas..or a Lear. **1876** Mozley *Univ. Serm.* iv. 93 We hear sometimes of single remarkable acts of virtue, which spring from minds in which there is not the habit of virtue.

*absol.* **1865** Neale *Hymns Paradise* 48 There the gifts of each and single All in common right possess.

**b.** Of, pertaining to, or connected with, one person only. Freq. with possessive pronoun.

**1592** Kyd *Sol. & Pers.* ii. ii, With my single fist Ile combat thee. **1616** R. C. *Times' Whistle* (1871) 58 Although he had noe other company But his sole single selfe to satisfie. **1672** Marvell *Corr.* Wks. (Grosart) II. 397 So that I must adventure to give you my single opinion, submitting to better judgements. *c* **1710** Celia Fiennes *Diary* (1888) 74, I observ'd their prayers were all made on the first person and single, though before the body of people. **1781** Gibbon *Decl. & F.* xix. II. 139 Constantius..acknowledged, that his single strength was unequal to such an extent of care. **1818** Scott *Hrt. Midl.* xxxvii, He had, almost by his single and unassisted talents, stopped the irruption of the banded force of all the Highland chiefs. **1842** Tennyson '*You ask me, why*' v, Should banded unions..induce a time When single thought is civil crime. **1878** B. Taylor *Deukalion* ii. ii. 60 What hinders me to make my single will The world's whole law?

†**c.** *at single hand*, single-handed, unaided. *Obs.*

**1607** Topsell *Four-f. Beasts* (1658) 575 There is hardly any Dog so couragious, as to adventure upon a Wolf at single hand.

**3.** Separate; distinct from each other or from others; not combined or taken together.

In the first quot. used distributively, after the Latin.

**1432–50** tr. *Higden* (Rolls) II. 309 Iacob..blessenge his childer with single benedicciones. **1573** L. Lloyd *Marrow of Hist.* (1653) 11 The poor Greek..opened his purse and gave unto the Emperour four single halfpence. **1599** B. Jonson *Ev. Man out of Hum.* ii. i, He might have altered the shape of his argument, and explicated them better in single scenes. **1658** Sir T. Browne *Hydriot.* ii. (1736) 22 All Urns contained not single Ashes. *a* **1693** *Urquhart's Rabelais* iii. xvii, A Rams Cod stored with Single Pence. **1711** Addison *Spect.* No. 124 ¶1 A Man..who communicates his Writings to the World in loose Tracts and single Pieces. **1779** *Mirror* No. 24, It will readily be admitted, that the preference, in every single object, is due to the former. **1826** *Art of Brewing* (ed. 2) 89 Dropped by single pieces into the copper while in full boil. **1864** Bowen *Logic* x. 316 The beginning of all Knowledge is in single acts of the Perceptive or Acquisitive Faculty. **1884** tr. *Lotze's Metaph.* 486 Each single fibre, at the spot where it receives the stimulus, can attach to it the extra-impression described.

**4.** Undivided, unbroken, absolute. *rare.*

**1590** Spenser *F.Q.* ii. x. 21 Being consorted with Manild, For thirst of single kingdome him he kild. **1634** Milton *Comus* 204 Yet nought but single darknes do I find. **1701** Swift *Contests Nobles & Commons* iii, The madness of the people, who..were now wholly bent upon single and despotick slavery.

**5. a.** One only; one and no more. Sometimes strengthened by *one.*

**1538** Elyot, *Simplus*, sengle in numbre, one only. **1590** Shaks. *Mids. N.* ii. ii. 50 Two bosomes interchanged with an oath, So then two bosomes, and a single troth. *c* **1600** —— *Sonn.* xxxix, For this, let vs deuided liue, And our deare loue loose name of single one. **1687** A. Lovell tr. *Thevenot's Trav.* i. 34 He'll order the Master to take no money from them, and that with a single word. **1728** Young *Love Fame* iii. 59 Thus all will judge, and with one single aim. **1790** Paley *Horæ Paul.* vi. §5 Wks. 1825 III. 169 The prisoner was bound to the soldier by a single chain. **1821** Scott *Kenilw.* xiii, He observed that Wayland purchased in each [shop] only one single drug. **1856** Sir B. Brodie *Psychol. Inq.* I. iii. 92 In one case, the mind may be occupied with a single object, or a single idea. **1875** Jowett *Plato* (ed. 2) IV. 495 We have observed the tendency of Plato to combine two or more subjects..in a single dialogue.

*absol.* **1833** Mrs. Browning *Prometh. Bound* 94 Why how could they Draw off from thee one single of thy griefs?

**b.** In emphatic use after a negative, or an adv. denoting scarcity.

**1709** Steele *Tatler* No. 50 ¶11, I will not write one single Word about any such Matters. **1743** Bulkeley & Cummins *Voy. S. Seas* 188 What must become of the rest who have not a single Penny? **1780** *Mirror* No. 94, Hardly a single house did I find inhabited by the same persons I left in it. **1849** Macaulay *Hist. Eng.* vi. II. 123 During a whole week, not a single private letter from beyond the Tweed was delivered in London. **1857** Buckle *Civiliz.* I. xii. 664 France had not possessed a single man who dared to think for himself.

**c.** With *even*, or implying this.

**1774** Goldsm. *Nat. Hist.* (1776) V. 351 Sometimes they find a difficulty in rearing even a single nest. **1816** J. Wilson *City of Plague* ii. iii. 25, I don't expect this Plague Will change its quarters, long as it has left A single man alive. **1879** L. Stephen *Hours Libr.* Ser. iii. 183 From a single phrase, as from a single gesture, we can often go far to divining the character of a man's thoughts.

**6. a.** Sole, only, one. Also used for emphasis with a superlative. **b.** Mere.

**1639** Ld. Digby *Lett. conc. Relig.* (1651) 61 By the easy abuse, if not by the single use of Images. **1728** R. Morris *Ess. Anc. Archit.* xviii, These are not the single Enemies I have to encounter with. **1748** Melmoth *Fitzosborne Lett.* xlviii. (1749) II. 30 That he should not leave so important a creature as man, to the single guidance of his own precarious faculties. **1827** Southey *Hist. Penins. War* II. 672 Heroes who carry victory with their single presence. **1849** Macaulay *Hist. Eng.* iii. I. 287 The single bed of a poor family had sometimes been carried away and sold. **1862** Stanley *Jew. Ch.* (1877) I. v. 87 To the outer world the earlier period of the race, with the single exception of Abraham, was an entire blank. **1969** [see loop *v.*[1] 7]. **1972** *New Yorker* 8 July 1 (Advt.), The single biggest travel buy to anywhere, ever. **1978** *Church Times* 15 Dec. 11/2 Sir Ronald has also, since last September, been chairman of the Central Board of Finance in Church House, and is thus the single most powerful figure in Church finance.

**7.** Standing alone in comparison with other persons or things; unique, singular.

**1633** Ford *'Tis Pity* iv. i, That you may know my single charity, Freely I here remit all interest I e'er could claim. **1658** *Whole Duty Man* vi. §13 He will be sure to commit them [sins], rather than run the disgrace of being too single and precise. **1728** R. Morris *Ess. Anc. Archit.* 22 Some there are who appear single in Opinion, only to be continually opposite to the common Judgment of Mankind. **1750** H. Walpole *Lett.* (1848) II. 347, I..am almost single in not having been to see him. **1786** J. Jay in Sparks *Corr. Amer. Rev.* (1853) IV. 131 Favor your country with your counsels on such an important and single occasion. **1815** Mackintosh *Sp. Ho. Comm.* 27 April, Wks. 1846 III. 358 Single among representative assemblies, this House is now in the seventh century of its recorded existence. **1817** H. T. Colebrooke *Algebra*, etc. Notes & Illustr. p. xlvii, The Rómaca and Paulisa are single of the names.

**II. 8. a.** Unmarried, celibate. (See also quot. 1847.) Also *absol.* as pl.

*single man*, a bachelor. *single woman*, a spinster; †a prostitute (quots. 1530 and 1657).

**1303** R. Brunne *Handl. Synne* 7361 Ȝyf weddyd man sengle woman takeþ. *c* **1380** Wyclif *Wks.* (1880) 73 And sugetis taken ensaumple at here curatis, boþe weddid men & sengle. *c* **1449** Pecock *Repr.* ii. iv. 155 A syngil man and a syngil womman. **1509** Hawes *Past. Pleas.* xxxii. (Percy Soc.) 156 Who that is single and wyll have a wyfe, Right out of joy he shall be brought in stryfe. **1530** Palsgr. 270/2 Syngle woman, a harlot, *putayn*. **1620** T. Granger *Div. Logike* 28 The Single man committing fornication sinneth lesse than the Adulterer. **1657** Howell *Londinop.* 337 No Stew-holder, or his Wife, should let or stay any single Woman to go and come freely at all times. **1685** Baxter *Paraphr. N.T.* 1 Cor. vii. 26 No doubt but it is much more for their..quiet to be single, than to have a Wife or Husband. **1747** *Gentl. Mag.* 485 A lady..thinking Mr. C. single and disengaged. **1782** Miss Burney *Cecilia* x. x, A single woman is a thousand times more shackled than a wife. **1817** Byron *Beppo* xxxviii, The fair *single* part of the creation. **1847** Lipscomb *Buckingham* I. 582 The inmates,..being..single persons, whether having been married or not. **1888** Bryce *Amer. Commw.* xciii. III. 298 No one dreams of drawing any distinction between the single and the married.

*fig.* **1613** Shaks. *Hen. VIII*, i. i. 15 Men might say Till this time Pompe was single, but now married.

**b.** Of, pertaining to, or involving celibacy, *esp.* in *single life.*

For the phrase *single blessedness*, see blessedness b.

**1549** Coverdale, etc. *Erasm. Par. 2 Cor.* 55 As in my other letters I required you not to leade a syngle lyfe. **1557** N.T. (Geneva) *1 Cor.* Argt., He answereth to certeine pointes..touching single life. **1610** Holland *Camden's Brit.* 596 Lawes were enacted touching the single lives of Priests. **1612** Bacon *Ess., Marr. & Single Life* (Arb.) 266 A single life is proper for Churchmen. **1751** Johnson *Rambler* No. 112 ¶6 They that have grown old in a single state. **1773** Foote *Bankrupt* i. Wks. 1799 II. 100 A single service is best suited to me. **1812** Crabbe *Tales* viii. 251 But shall his Bride your single state reproach? **1836** T. Hook *G. Gurney* I. iv. (1850) 62 Without having changed her state of single-unblessedness.

*Comb.* **1597** Beard *Theat. God's Judgem.* (1631) 410 These are the godly fruits of those single life-louers, to whom the vse of marriage is counted vnlawful.

**c.** Designating a person who is bringing up a child or children without the assistance of a marital partner. Chiefly in phr. *single parent (family).*

**1969** J. Sprey in B. Schlesinger *One-Parent Family* 16 Stigmatization of the single-parent family, and especially of single parents, does occur. **1976** *Women's Report* Sept./Oct. 7/1 This, coupled with the fact that more women are voluntarily becoming single mothers by refusing to have their babies adopted has caused the government to set up a Cabinet Committee on Family Affairs. **1977** C. Fremlin *Spider-Orchid* vii. 55 Peggy Summers was having teenage troubles at last, and wasn't managing so marvellously as a single parent after all. **1980** *Times* 24 Jan. 9/8 Gingerbread caters for all categories of single parents; the divorced, separated, widowed, unmarried, or those whose partners may be in hospital or prison.

†**9.** In slight raiment; without cloak or armour; marked by scantiness or simplicity *of* clothing. *Obs.*

**13..** *K. Alis.* 204 (Laud MS.), Dame olympias, amonge þis pres, Sengle rood, al mantel les. **13..** *Coer de L.* 1067 And seyngle in a kertyl he stood, Abood the lyon fers and wood. **1380** *Sir Ferumb.* 1071 [They] ounarmede him þo anon, & wan he was sengle amoung hem þer, hy auysed is schap echon. **1387** Trevisa *Higden* (Rolls) I. 353 Men of þis lond..beeþ sengle of cloþinge, scarse of mete, cruel of herte. *a* **1450** *Knt. de la Tour* (1868) 168 He was not so gay aourned, ne so sengle of clothes, but he had on hym good and warme gownes.

†**10.** Of cloth, garments, etc.: Of one thickness of material; unlined. *Obs.*

*c* **1375** *Sc. Leg. Saints* v. (*John*) 152 Skantly had Ilkane of þa a singill clath, fore-owtine ma. *a* **1450** *Knt. de la Tour* (1868) 168 A hood of scarlatte sengle & wythoute furrynge. *Ibid.* 169 A shorte and sengle gown withoute lynynge. **1459** *Paston Lett.* I. 475 Item, j. gowne of blewe felwett.., slevys sengle. **1530** Palsgr. 270/2 Syngle gowne, *robe sengle. Ibid.*, Syngle kyrtell, *corset simple.* **1552** *Inv. Ch. Goods* (Surtees) 24 One vestment of blewe single sattene. **1670** Eachard *Cont. Clergy* 90 A much more sparing dyet is fitter; and a single-coat, though it be never so ancient and thin, is fully sufficient.

**11. a.** Composed or consisting of only one part, feature, etc.; not double, compound, or complex; also, of the ordinary or small size, as distinguished from double *a.* 4.

For various special uses, see 17.

**1387** Trevisa *Higden* (Rolls) I. 347 Many depe diches and castelles sengle, double, and treble, and many wardes strongliche i-walled. **1449** in *Cal. Proc. Chanc. Q. Eliz.* (1830) II. Pref. 55 þe sengell gistes of þe same flore at þe fronte shullen be in brede..ix inches. **1466** *Mann. & Househ. Exp.* (Roxb.) 347, v. doble polyves and a sengelle. **1521** Fisher *Serm. agst. Luther* Wks. (1876) 324 A sengell threde is nothynge so stronge as is a double. **1540** in Greene *Hist. Worcester* II. App. p. ii, Item ij masers, one with a dowbilbond, the other with a sengylbond. **1592** West *1st Pt. Symbol.* i. §26 b, When a thing is purchased or gotten..by gift or legacie, or some other such single title. **1663** Gerbier *Counsel* 45 Single Rafters six and three Inches. *Ibid.* 96 Nor do provident builders rivet locks only at the one side, for that a thief within doores..makes that single riveting of no use as to security. **1688** Holme *Armoury* iii. xix. (Roxb.) 154/2 The maner of which beatings is performed by single and double..blows. **1711** *Milit. & Sea Dict.* s.v. *Tenaille*, The Single Tenaille, a Work, the Head whereof is form'd by two Faces, making one Angle Rentrant. **1827** Steuart *Planter's G.* (1828) 192, I mean single carts, or carts drawn by one horse. **1845** *Proc. Philol. Soc.* II. 89 The vowels generally, whether single or diphthongal, are sounded as they are in Italian. **1862** Smiles *Engineers* III. 89 A single line furnished with sidings to enable the laden waggons to pass the empty ones. **1875** Knight *Dict. Mech.* 2480 A single whip..is the simplest tackle. It consists of one single block and a fall.

†**b.** Of artillery. *Obs.*

**1546** *Reg. Privy Council Scot.* I. 54 Small artailyery sik as double falcoun, single falcoun. *a* **1578** Lindesay (Pitscottie) *Chron. Scot.* (S.T.S.) I. 367 Collveringis, myans and doubill falcouns, singill falcouns and hagbuttis of fund.

**c.** Of flowers: Having only one whorl or set of petals; also, of plants: Bearing such flowers; opposed to DOUBLE *a.* 1 d.

**1551** TURNER *Herbal* (1568) 30 Ther groweth a flour like a syngle rose in the tope of thys herbe. **1594** PLAT *Jewel-ho.* III. 33 You may also drie Paunsies, Stock-gilliflowers, and other single flowers. **1615** W. LAWSON *Country Housew. Gard.* (1626) 54 The sweet muske Rose double and single. **1664** EVELYN *Kal. Hort.* (1729) 198 Single and double Hepatica. **1731** MILLER *Gard. Dict.* s.v. *Hyacinthus Tuberosus*, The Single sort is by far the fairer Flower. **1796** C. MARSHALL *Gardening* v. (1813) 62 No single flowers should be suffered to grow in a garden where there are double ones. **1812** *New Botanic Garden* I. 29 With single blue flowers, with double blue flowers. **1852** G. W. JOHNSON *Cottage Gard. Dict.* 339 In double flowers..the corolla is much more durable than in single ones.

**d.** Intended for or accommodating one person.

*a* **1859** MACAULAY *Hist. Eng.* xxiii. V. 73 A single bedroom. **1867** AUGUSTA WILSON *Vashti* xxxiii, A strip of faded carpet stretched in front of a small single bedstead. **1886** PASCOE *London of To-day* i. (ed. 3) 34 Single bedrooms cost from 4*s.* to 15*s.* per day.

**†12. a.** Simple; plain; without further qualification or addition. *Obs.*

*c* **1421** *26 Political Poems* 105 While obley in yrnes or boyst ys stoken, Hit nys but bred, and sengyl bake. *c* **1450** LOVELICH *Grail* lii. 705 Whanne Piers vndirstood that he A kyng was Of so hy degre, and wende he hadde ben A single knyht [etc.]. **1453** *Rolls of Parlt.* V. 271/1 Bynde hem..by obligation or obligations, aswell sengell as conditionell. **1600** SURFLET *Countrie Farme* III. liv. 556 Some doe make this oile after the simplest and singlest sort. **1678** SIR G. MACKENZIE *Crim. Laws Scot.* I. xix. §vi, God Almighty intended not that single Theft should be punished by death. **1736** BUTLER *Anal.* I. ii. 47 Perhaps divine goodness..may not be a bare single disposition to produce happiness.

**†b.** Slight, poor, trivial. *Obs.*

*c* **1449** PECOCK *Repr.* II. viii. 184 Ymagis of God..forto make bi hem sengil and leuke remembrauncis. **1585** DANIEL *Notable Deuises* Wks. (Grosart) V. 302 Hauing..maried a wife of singulare beautie, but (according to the common rumour) of single honestie. **1597** SHAKS. *2 Hen. IV*, I. ii. 207 Is not your voice broken? your winde short? your wit single? *a* **1616** BEAUM. & FL. *Queen of Corinth* III. i, He utters such single matter in so infantly a voice. **1638** RAWLEY tr. *Bacon's Life & Death* (1650) 19 The Sect of the Essenes among the Jews..used a single or Abstemious Diet.

**13. a.** Of beer, ale, etc.: Weak, poor, or inferior in quality; small. Now *arch.* Also *transf.*

**1485** in *9th Rep. Hist. MSS. Comm.* I. 177/2 A vessell of single bere to the gonners, xii d. **1505** in *10th Rep.* ibid. App. V. 392 That there be no sale bread, singill ale, nor honyed alle..mad in towne, but by ffre men. **1594** *Knack to Know a Knave* in Collier *Five Old Plays* (Roxb.) 386 Your drinke is too strong... Single beere is better far both for your profit and your seruants health. *a* **1635** BP. CORBET *Poems* (1647) 30 Although I thinke Poets were nee'r infus'd with single drinke. *Ibid.*, Let your Channels flow with single tiffe. **1704** *Lond. Gaz.* No. 4032/4, 11 Pieces of single French Brandy. **1820** SCOTT *Monast.* xviii, An hogshead of ale at Martlemas, of the double strike, and single ale at pleasure.

**b.** Of whisky: pure, not mixed or blended.

**1920** *Glasgow Herald* 22 July 4 No man who knows whisky when he tastes it would prefer them [*sc.* advertised blends] to a 'single' whisky. **1958** *Spectator* 27 June 838/1 It would have been before the days of proprietary whiskies; it would be interesting to know which 'single' or 'self' whisky he used and its strength. **1968** I. C. TAYLOR *Highland Whisky* (An Comunn Gaidhealach) 5 It is an excellent dry single malt. **1977** C. MCCULLOUGH *Thorn Birds* vii. 136 Twelve-year-old single-malt Scotch.

**14. a.** Simple, honest, sincere, single-minded; free from duplicity or deceit.

**1519** HORMAN *Vulg.* 55 He is a good sengyll soule, and can no harme. **1595** SPENSER *Col. Clout* 727 Single Truth and simple Honestie Do wander up and downe despys'd of all. **1613** SHAKS. *Hen. VIII*, v. iii. 38, I speake it with a single heart, my Lords. **1633** FORD *Broken H.* IV. i, Sure, he's an honest, very honest gentleman; A man of single meaning. **1682** SIR T. BROWNE *Chr. Mor.* III. §20 To single Hearts doubling is discruciating. **1809** JEFFERSON *Writ.* (1830) IV. 134 To those whose views are single and direct, it is a great comfort to have to do business with frank and honorable minds. **1848** DICKENS *Dombey* xxxiii, [Such as] nothing but a pure and single heart [could have] expressed. **1873** WHITNEY *Oriental & Ling. Stud.* 83 The single devotion of the Brahman student.

**b.** Of the eye, after Biblical use.

**1526** TINDALE *Luke* xi. 34 When thine eye is single; then is all thy body full of light. **1577** *F. de Lisle's Legendarie* I iv, Considering with a single eye the parties in this cause, ye shall finde that [etc.]. **1669** N. MORTON *New Eng. Mem.* A 2, I onely crave of thee to reade this following Discourse with a single eye. *c* **1680** BEVERIDGE *Serm.* (1729) I. 63 He that looks upon these words with a single eye. **1863** KINGSLEY *Water-Bab.* 343 Keep your eye single, and your hands clean. **1884** *Century Mag.* Mar. 925 All readers of his know..how absolutely single his eye is.

**15.** Of a combat or fight: Between two persons; man to man. (See also COMBAT *sb.* 1 b.)

[**1590** SIR J. SMYTH *Disc. Weapons* 46 b, If it be enemie to enemie single, they then are not to discharge their peeces.] **1592** KYD *Sp. Trag.* I. iii, I saw him, hand to hand, In single fight with their Lord Generall. **1610** HOLLAND *Camden's Brit.* 360 Who in this Iland by a single combate tried it out. **1639** FULLER *Holy War* II. i. (1840) 48 He..killed Rodulphus, the duke of Saxony, in single fight. **1711** ADDISON *Spect.* No. 9 ¶7 The President..was said to have killed half a dozen in single Combat. *Ibid.* No. 70 ¶5 Let you and I end our Quarrel in single Fight. **1820** SCOTT *Monast.* xxxvii, Reserving my right to defy my Lord of Murray and my Lord of Morton to single duel. **1838** ARNOLD *Hist. Rome* I. 4 At last Ascanius met him man to man and slew him in single fight. **1867** FREEMAN *Norm. Conq.* (1877) I. App. 706 That the two kings shall decide the matter by single combat.

**16.** In quasi-advb. use.

*a* **1450** *Le Morte Arth.* 1795 Non Armore he dyde hym vppon Bot A Robe All sengle wrought. *a* **1483** *Liber Niger* in *Househ. Ord.* (1790) 58 [The] Controller..is thirde in estate..aftyr the Steward, but at no tyme..within thys courte covered in servyse, and but single served. **1681** *Lond. Gaz.* No. 1663/4 They lye Unmored, and ride single, and intend to Sail this Afternoon. **1707** MORTIMER *Husb.* (1721) I. 83 They commonly lay twelve or fourteen loads of Chalk upon an Acre, where they lay it single. **1837** LOCKHART *Scott* III. x. 343 My venerated friend, who was—unlike, perhaps, some others of the company at that hour—able to hear accurately, and content to *see single*.

**III. 17. a.** Special collocations; ***single act*** (*Theatr.*), a performance (orig. in vaudeville) by one entertainer; also, an entertainer who performs unaccompanied; ***single anchor*** (see quot. 1867) also *fig.*; † ***single billet***, single-stick; ***single bond*** (*Chem.*), a chemical bond in which the two atoms share one pair of electrons only; ***single care*** (see quot.); ***single change*** (see quot. 1688); ***single chant*** (see CHANT *sb.* 2); ***single cream***, cream with a low fat content; ***single crown*** (*Naut.*), a single crowning given to a knot (see CROWN *v.*[1] 14, CROWNING *vbl. sb.* 4); ***single end*** (*Sc.*, chiefly Glasgow), a one-roomed flat; ***single entry***, (*a*) (see ENTRY 9 b); (*b*) listing of a title at only one place in a catalogue, bibliography, or index, without cross-references; an entry so created; ***single fare***, the charge for conveyance on an outward journey (but not back); ***single file***, a line of men one behind the other; ***single Gloucester*** (see GLOUCESTER); ***single house*** (see quot. 1818); ***single-jack*** (*N. Amer.*), a short hammer used in percussive hand-drilling by one person alone; ***single line*** (see quot.); † ***single officer*** (see quot.); ***single premium***, a sum which covers the entire cost of insurance in a single payment; † ***single rapier***, the rapier only (without dagger); ***single reed*** (*Mus.*), a reed or blade of other material that serves as the sounding apparatus of certain wind instruments; † ***single sentinel*** or ***soldier***, a private soldier (*Sc.*); ***single shot***, used, usu. *attrib.*, with reference to a facility for producing a single event where repeated action is normal, as on an automatic weapon; ***single side band*** (*Telecommunication*), either of the two side bands normally associated with the carrier of a broadcast transmission; freq. *attrib.* with reference to a method of transmission in which only one side band is transmitted, the other being suppressed along with the carrier; also short for *single side band transmission*; † ***single sword***, ? singlestick; ***single ten***, the ten of a card-suit; (see also quot. *a* 1700); ***single ticket***, a ticket entitling a traveller to a single journey outward, as opp. to a return ticket (cf. RETURN *sb.* 1 e).

**1952** GRANVILLE *Dict. Theatrical Terms* 163 **Single act*, a solo performance in vaudeville, e.g. a ballad singer, a juggler, an acrobat, an impersonator, or a *raconteur*. **1960** B. KEATON *My Wonderful World of Slapstick* v. 89, I went to New York to see if I could get work there on my own. As a single act. That's what vaudeville people called it. **1822** C. ARBUTHNOT *Let.* 2 Sept. (1941) 31, I wish you to keep yrself at *single anchor, for shd. the Govt. be broken up, you must hurry to me. **1839** MARRYAT *Phant. Ship* viii, The *Ter Schilling*..lay at single anchor. **1867** SMYTH *Sailor's Word-bk.* 627 *Single anchor*, a ship unmoored, having hove up one bower, rides by the other. **1613** BEAUM. & FL. *Captain* II. i, No more Than..Fighting at *single Billet with a Barge-man. [**1889** G. M'GOWAN tr. *Bernthsen's Text-bk Org. Chem.* i. 50 A double bond between two carbon atoms is looser, and therefore more easily broken than a single one.] **1903** WALKER & MOTT tr. *Holleman's Text-bk. Org. Chem.* I. 150 When a *single bond between two carbon atoms is converted into a double one, the directions of the affinities of each of the two carbon atoms must undergo an appreciable alteration. **1966** WILLIAMS & FLEMING *Spectrosc. Methods in Org. Chem.* iii. 45 The stretching vibrations of single bonds to hydrogen give rise to the absorption at the high frequency end of the spectrum. **1898** *Allbutt's Syst. Med.* VIII. 429 The law which enables a person of unsound mind..to be placed..under what is technically designated '*Single Care'—that is, under certificates in the house of a medical man or other person. **1688** HOLME *Armoury* III. 462/2 The *Single Change, is when all the Bells ring, and one is changed only from Round Ringing. **1872** ELLACOMBE *Bells of Ch.* in *Ch. Bells Devon* iii. 39 About the year 1642..single changes were first attempted. **1861** J. S. ADAMS *5000 Mus. Terms* 91 **Single Chant*, a simple harmonized melody extending only to one verse [etc.]. **1875** STAINER & BARRETT *Dict. Mus. Terms* s.v. *Chant*, A single chant is in two strains, the first of three, and the second of four bars in length. **1955** J. G. DAVIS *Dict. Dairying* 320 The manufacture of cream was prohibited during the war but in 1951 sale was permitted for a few weeks. The standards laid down were: *single cream 18 per cent. (usually homogenised), double cream 48 per cent. **1962** *Listener* 26 July 155/1, ½ pint of real single cream. **1979** A. PARKER *Country Recipe Notebk.* viii. 108 Single cream is thin cream for pouring. It will not whip. **1808** *Single crown [see DOUBLE WALL]. **1883** *Man. Seamanship Boys' Training Ships* (Admiralty) (1886) 121 Form a double-wall, single-crowned, then lay the strands by the sides of those in the single-crown. **1897** J. WRIGHT *Scenes Sc. Life* 27 'A *single en', or one apartment. **1935** MCARTHUR & LONG *No Mean City* i. 1 Cavity beds are..a feature of the Glasgow slums... The ordinary 'room-and-kitchen' apartment, and even the one-roomed 'single-end', always include a cavity bed or beds. **1981** P. TURNBULL *Deep & Crisp & Even* iv. 60 He took a single end in Maryhill and sent for his wife. **1826** *Encycl. Metrop.* (1845) I. 462/2 The more obvious method .., which is called Book-keeping by *Single Entry. **1849** FREESE *Comm. Class-Bk.* 103 If my books were kept by single entry, I should simply credit Smart & Co. for the coffee. **1963** *Guide to Universal Decimal Classification* (B.S.I.) i. 7 Generally speaking, each document gets only one entry in the classified file, and this method of 'single entry' is assumed for the time being. Many UDC users, however, favour a method of 'multiple entry', whereby a document on Harvesting of cereals, for instance, would get an entry under both Cereals and Harvesting. **1976** B. BUCHANAN *Gloss. Indexing Terms* 123 Single entry systems fail to correct completely the separations caused by the application of a citation order..; for this, multiple entry systems are necessary. **1777** P. THICKNESSE *Year's Journey* I. vii. 52, I could not refrain from giving her a double fee, for a *single fare. **1841** C. DICKENS *Let.* 14 Sept. (1969) II. 383, I wish you'd take an opportunity..of asking all about the Fares—what a single fare is—what a double fare—what a cabin with child-stowage. **1972** C. FREMLIN *Appointment with Yesterday* i. 11 A small oblong of card-board... 'Single fare, £1.40' is what it said. **1670** COTTON *Espernon* II. 394 He therefore commanded some Foot Companies to steal over silently, and by *single Files. **1853** SIR H. DOUGLAS *Milit. Bridges* 255 Sufficient only to support infantry marching in single file. **1865** TYLOR *Early Hist. Man.* v. 83 To place the different elements of a sentence in succession, in single file so to speak. *a* **1700** EVELYN *Diary* 16 July 1654, The humourous old Knight has built a long *single house of 2 low stories. **1818** SCOTT *Hrt. Midl.* xxvi, Dumbiedikes was what is called in Scotland a *single* house; that is, having only one room occupying its whole depth from back to front. **1961** *Press* (Vancouver) 1 Sept. 11 The mechanization of mines in 1890—the replacing of hand-steel, *single-jack and double-jack, by drilling machines—had created new problems. **1875** KNIGHT *Dict. Mech.* 2187/2 **Single-line*, a single rein leading from the hand of the driver to a strap forked a little behind the hames, and proceeding thence to the bit-rings. **1759** in *Eng. Historical Rev.* (1897) XII. 763 We are *Single Officers, that is, only one Livetenant to a Company. **1877** *Cassell's Family Mag.* Jan. 83/2 Net *Single and Annual Premiums. **1880** *Encycl. Brit.* XIII. 171/2 We conclude..that the single premium at age 20 for a whole-term assurance of £1 according to the H[m] mortality table, reckoning interest at 3 per cent., is £·32886 or 6*s.* 7*d.* **1975** R. L. CARTER *Handbk. Insurance* II. §i.2.8 The single premium bond is essentially an investment contract in which a lump sum is paid to the insurance company at the inception of the policy, and..invested in units. **1709** STEELE *Tatler* No. 31 ¶3 The historian mentions, when he attack'd Thalestris, it was only at *single Rapier. **1883** GROVE *Dict. Mus.* III. 90/1 It is possible to replace it [*sc.* the Double reed] in both these instruments by a *single reed of clarinet shape, beating against a small wooden mouthpiece. **1920** U. DAUBENY *Orchestral Wind Instruments* vi. 55 There are no instances of the single reed in Egyptian sculpture, but cylindrical pipes of great age fitted with single-beating reeds have been found in Greece. **1964** S. MARCUSE *Musical Instr.* 478/1 Single reeds are idioglott or heteroglott... The beating reed is the most common among Western single reeds (the clarinet reed, for example). **1721** WODROW *Hist. Suff. Ch. Scot.* II. v. (1830) II. 168 A person of quality,.. standing before an ensign, lieutenant, or *single sentinel. **1942** *R.A.F. Jrnl.* 3 Oct. 29 We fired three rounds with the Tommy gun from the hip (with the *single-shot mechanism). **1971** J. M. SMITH *Digital Logic* iv. 67 The one-shot or single-shot generator is a device for producing a pulse output from a trigger signal input. **1977** 'J. MCVEAN' *Bloodspoor* xx. 263 Hanson switched the Schmeisser regulator to single-shot and started to fire back. **1923** *Proc. IRE* XI. 40 It is of particular importance for long wave radio telephone transmission where the width of a *single side-band is so large a fraction of the total frequency range available that the number of independent channels is at best very limited. *Ibid.* 41 The use of single side-band transmission has probably progressed farthest in connection with carrier telephony over wires. **1959** K. HENNEY *Radio Engin. Handbk.* (ed. 5) xviii. 8 In most commercial single-side-band transmitters the SSB signal is generated in an SSB generator at a frequency in the range of 100 to 500 kc. **1976** *Electronics Today Internat.* July 10/3 In areas around cities, these channels are congested and so many stations have changed over to Single Sideband, which gives higher communications efficiency and an extra 48 channels. **1816** SCOTT *Antiq.* xxvii, Not knowing..how far the manners of a *single soldier might have been corrupted by service in a great house. **1688** HOLME *Armoury* III. xix. (Roxb.) 159/1 Two Fencers,..makeing triall of their skill, with back-sword or *single sword, sword and buckler and the like. **1593** SHAKS. *3 Hen. VI*, v. i. 43 Whiles he thought to steale the *single Ten, The King was slyly finger'd from the Deck. *a* **1700** B. E. *Dict. Cant. Crew*, *Single-ten*, a very foolish, silly Fellow; also Nails of that size. **1829** HUNTER *Hallamshire Gloss.*, *Single-ten*, A person playing at Whist may be heard to say: I have neither ace, face, nor single-ten. **1859** *A.B.C. or Alphabetical Railway Guide* Aug. 121 London, Paris, and the Continent... Fares throughout (*Single Tickets, available for four days), First Class, 28/0; Second Class, 20/0. **1979** 'J. LE CARRÉ' *Smiley's People* (1980) xvii. 212 He bought a second-class single ticket to Hamburg.

**b.** With sbs. in *-er*, as ***single-driver***, ***-hander***, ***-loader***, ***-peeper***, ***-roomer***, ***-seater*** (see also attrib. uses at 18), ***-sticker***, ***-striker***, etc.; ***single-boater*** (see quot. 1933); ***single-decker***, †(*a*) *U.S.* (see quot. 1896); (*b*) an aircraft, tramcar, etc., having only one deck; now usu. a single-decked bus; freq. *attrib.*; ***single-hander***, (*a*) an action performed single-handedly or without assistance (in quot. 1877, a chase) (*rare*); (*b*) one who sails a boat single-handed; a single-handed yachtsman.

**1933** S. BRADFORD *Shell-backs* 70 A *single boater is a trawler not fishing with a fleet but on its own. **1934** W. WOOD *Fleeters* iv. 59 The single-boaters..far outnumbered the fleeters. **1896** C. H. HASWELL *Reminisc. Octogenarian in N.Y.* xv. 332 James P. Allaire had constructed..a four-story house designed for many tenants... It is what is now termed a '*single-decker', that is, but one suite of rooms on a floor. **1910** *Sphere* 20 Aug. 176/1 The first aeroplane illustrated is the Santos Dumont aeroplane or single-decker. **1930** *Aberdeen Press & Jrnl.* 12 Feb. 6/3, I see that the L.C.C. has been selling off old single-decker tramcars at £5 apiece. **1935** S. BECKETT *Echo's Bones*, The little single-decker. **1935** *Discovery* Feb. 58/2 In these vehicles the main entrance is in front, beside the driver as in many single-decker coaches already on the road. **1954** M. PROCTER *Hell is City* I. i. 11 A red-and-white bus..was approaching... It was a..single decker. **1962** L. DEIGHTON *Ipcress File* xxx. 196 At the bottom of the street was a single-decker bus. **1976** P. R. WHITE *Planning for Public Transport* iii. 56 The rear-engine layout was also adopted for single-deckers. **1897** *Pall Mall Mag.* Mar. 347 The '*single driver' is the familiar name applied to locomotives propelled by one pair of driving-wheels. **1877** *Coursing Calendar Autumn 1876* 217 War Note never seeing the hare, Adventurer fell in for a *single-hander of great length, the first-named being drawn ultimately. **1893** *Outing* XXII. 145/2 The cost of a single-hander depends on the size of the boat. **1954** H. INNES *Strange Land* I. 18 'There should be two men on board her.' 'Well, this bloke was single-handed.'..'He was a single-hander all right.' **1976** P. HEATON *Single-handers* i. 26 Alain Colas..is a racing singlehander, a competitor. **1887** *Daily News* 6 Oct. 6/2 The rifle can then be used as a *single-loader. **1785** GROSE *Dict. Vulgar T.*, **Single peeper*, a person having but one eye. **1889** GRETTON *Memory's Harkback* 305 They are recorded as 'single peepers',..having lost an eye. **1916** H. BARBER *Aeroplane Speaks* Pl. xxvi, A 50 h.p. Gnome *single-seater. **1972** 'M. YORKE' *Silent Witness* II. ii. 19 Twin chairs were not so bad... But this chair-lift was a single-seater and you rode alone. **1887** *Daily Telegr.* 10 Sept. 2/5 None of the big *single-stickers..showed any signs. **1898** *Cycling* 62 Repeating bells are preferable to *single-strikers. **1889** *20th Cent.* (N.Y.) Apr. 6 He says that is a fair question which no *Single-taxer ever answers, but that if it is evaded the whole single-tax theory vanishes.

**18.** With sbs., forming combs. used attributively, as ***single-action, -bar, -beat, -cell, -channel, -coil, -colour, cylinder***, etc.; ***single-cell protein***, protein derived from a culture of single-celled organisms; ***single-electrode*** (*Chem.*), with reference to a half-cell considered in isolation; ***single-lens reflex (camera)*** (*Photogr.*), a reflex camera in which the lens that forms the image on the film is also used to provide the image in the viewfinder (by means of a mirror behind the lens that is automatically moved out of the way when the shutter release is operated) (cf. *SLR* s.v. S 4 a); ***single-plate clutch*** (see quot. 1940); ***single-start*** (*Engin.*), designating a screw-thread or worm gear that has one continuous thread along its entire length; ***single-vision*** (*Ophthalm.*), (of spectacles) of which each lens is a single optical element; not bifocal, etc.; ***single-wire***, designating an electrical wiring system in which current is carried by one wire, the return being provided by the chassis or frame of the apparatus or installation or the earth.

Combs. of this type have been very frequent in recent use. For a number of technical examples, see Knight *Dict. Mech.* (1875) and *Suppl.* (1884).

**1852** SEIDEL *Organ* 36 *Single-action bellows..is generally very small. **1863** A. YOUNG *Naut. Dict.* 20 Atmospheric, or Single Action, Engine. **1964** *Amer. Speech* XXXIX. 104 There is a break—in speech, a *single-bar juncture; in writing, a comma or dash—between the noun and its juncture. **1966** 'M. HALLIDAY' *Wicked as Devil* iv. 36 Helen switched on a single-bar electric fire. **1688** HOLME *Armoury* III. 398 A *Single Beak Pellican with a screw, of some..called a Screw'd tooth Forcer. **1884** F. J. BRITTEN *Watch & Clockm.* 241 The chronometer and duplex are the best known examples of *single-beat escapements. **1838** BELL *Dict. Law Scot.* 867 In the *Single Bill roll is inserted all petitions..and other notes or applications to either Division of the Court. **1977** P. JOHNSON *Enemies of Society* ix. 127 Marx, by contrast, has a *single-cause theory: all the evils of society arise from private property; abolish that, and they will disappear. **1849** NOAD *Electricity* (ed. 3) 228, Fig. 152 represents the *single-cell apparatus. **1968** MATELES & TANNENBAUM *Single-Cell Protein* i. 7 Some may wonder where the name '*Single-Cell Protein' came from and why it was adopted. It was invented at M.I.T. in May 1966, as a result of the insistent prodding of Professor Carroll Wilson. **1970** *Daily Tel.* (Colour Suppl.) 19 June 14 Single cell protein is one of the most 'exotic' of various new food sources. **1977** Single cell protein [see *single-celled*, sense 19 below]. **1962** A. NISBETT *Technique Sound Studio* ii. 33 *Single-channel 'monophonic' recordings. **1977** *Proc. R. Soc. Med.* LXX. 382/1 Single-channel extracochlear stimulation will only provide low frequency information. **1967** *N.Y. Herald Tribune* (Internat. ed.) 11–12 Feb. 3/7 (Advt.), Walk on or drive on to one of these fine ultra-modern *single-class ships for an overnight crossing in absolute comfort. **1977** *Listener* 17 Mar. 347/3 They built ..for the propagation of middle-class values..a vast process of specialised, single-class development. **1962** SIMPSON & RICHARDS *Physical Princ. Junction Transistors* iii. 38 One pass of the specimen is then equivalent to several passes in a *single-coil apparatus and the removal of impurities is accelerated. **1935** B. RACKHAM in *Chinese Art* (Burlington Mag. Monographs) 20 The beauty of celadon, turquoise, crackled white and other *single-colour glazes. **1964** *Gloss. Letterpress Rotary Printing Terms* (*B.S.I.*) 19 *Single colour unit*, a section of the press embodying one printing couple to print one side of the web in one colour. **1960** *Guardian* 9 Nov. 8/3 The 'News Chronicle'..charged for display advertising at the rate of £13 per *single column inch. **1976** J. BINGHAM *God's Defector* iv. 43 A single-column picture of himself at the church door. **1955** *Notes on Science in USA 1954* (Brit. Commonwealth Scientific Office, N. Amer.) 29 The large number of experiments that are now being performed on *single crystal specimens. **1956** *Nature* 14 Jan. 77/2 In fundamental research, much work is being done on single-crystal specimens, whereby grain-boundary effects and some other variables are eliminated. **1888** JACOBI *Printers' Vocab.* 125 **Single cylinder machines*, machines for printing one side at a time only. **1929** *Times* 2 Nov. 4/7 The chassis, with rather lighter driving axles and springs is sold for *single-deck and coach operation. **1967** M. CHANDLER *Ceramics in Mod. World* ii. 84 Single-deck tunnel kilns. **1860** *All Year Round* No. 66. 382 'Which knot?' asked Toby. 'Single or double wall, *single or double diamond?' **1913** *Jrnl. Amer. Chem. Soc.* XXXV. 24 No satisfactory method has been found for determining the absolute magnitude of any *single electrode potential. **1965** PHILLIPS & WILLIAMS *Inorg. Chem.* I. ix. 312 It has proved very difficult, some believe impossible, to measure absolute single-electrode potentials. **1944** STEWART & WILSON *Rec. Adv. Physical & Inorg. Chem.* (ed. 7) 384 It is probable that *single electron bonds..enter into the *average* final structure for diborane. **1968** M. S. LIVINGSTON *Particle Physics* iii. 39 The spectra of single-electron atoms such as $He^+$ and $Li^{+2}$. **1942** *R.A.F. Jrnl.* 27 June 1 A service between London and Paris with *single-engine modified Service aircraft. **1978** R. LUDLUM *Holcroft Covenant* xxxvii. 423 A small single-engine plane circled in the night sky above the flat pasture in Chambéry. **1868** *Rep. U.S. Comm. Agric.* (1869) 238 One and three-quarters pound of *single-eye pieces produced ten pounds. **1967** R. ARDREY *Territorial Imperative* iii. 93 Unlike any other ape and like few monkeys, the gibbon lives in a *single-family group, paired on a territory usually for life. **1980** *Washington Post* 4 Dec. DC1, 49 buildings containing about 600 units are being transfered from rental status or private single-family ownership to condominiums. **1899** MORROW *Bohem. Paris* 138 A *single-file march round the room is started. **1857** MILLER *Elem. Chem., Org.* i. §1 (1862) 15 An additional screen of *single iron plate. **1892** GREENER *Breech Loader* 6 The cheaper quality laminated steel,..known in the trade as single-iron Damascus. **1977** *Time* 19 Dec. 29/3 The right-to-lifers are *single-issue individuals... They vote on what he or she says about abortion. **1946** H. JACOB *On Choice of Common Lang.* 39 Four *single-language frequency lists. **1978** *Language* LIV. 8 Table 2 shows the number of entries which fulfill the structural conditions for apical displacement, after we eliminate single-language entries and the disqualified ones. **1940** *Chambers's Techn. Dict.* 772/1 **Single-layer winding*, a type of armature winding in which there is only one coil-side per slot. **1946** *Nature* 21 Sept. 422/1 The reflectors consist of single-layer and multiple-layer films. **1936** *Discovery* Aug. 237/1 The camera..has 4½ times the stereoscopic parallax of the *single-lens and five-lens cameras. **1940** A. L. M. SOWERBY *Wall's Dict. Photogr.* (ed. 15) 547 In a single-lens reflex, pressure on the release first lifts the mirror.., and then releases the focal-plane shutter. **1955** T. A. LONGMORE *Med. Photogr.* (ed. 5) III. 374 Being a single lens reflex camera there is a complete absence of parallax, so that the image seen on the focusing screen is exactly the same as that which will be recorded on the film. **1957** *Encycl. Brit.* XVII. 825/2 A single-lens camera may be provided with a beam splitter.., giving two adjacent photographs on the normal picture area. **1962** L. S. SASIENI *Optical Dispensing* xiii. 334 Apart from the single-lens magnifiers..there are a number of telescopic units. **1977** L. GAUNT *Olympus Bk.* 8 The final part of the 35 mm single-lens reflex viewing system is the eye-piece lens, focused on the viewfinder screen via the reflecting surfaces of the prism. **1771** LUCKOMBE *Hist. Print.* 271 Neat Workmen prevent a division of a *single-letter syllable at the end of lines. **1878** H. MACCOLL in *Proc. Lond. Math. Soc.* X. 26 The monomial (or single-letter) statements. **1964** D. WARD in D. Abercrombie et al. *Daniel Jones* 393 For the convenience of readers not familiar with Cyrillic a single-letter transliteration system is given. **1876** VOYLE & STEVENSON *Milit. Dict.*, **Single lever bridge*, composed of two frames locking into each other, and not meeting at a greater angle than 120°. **1886** WILLIS & CLARK *Cambridge* I. 330 Each chamber had a lofty narrow *single-light window. **1846** HOLTZAPFFEL *Turning* II. 543 The shaft of..the *single-lip auger. **1880** GROVE *Dict. Mus.* II. 591/2 Soon after the Restoration, Ralph Dallam built an organ for St. George's Chapel, Windsor... It was a *single-manual organ only. **1978** *Early Music* Oct. 585/1 An Italian single-manual harpsichord bearing a spurious inscription dated 1740 but actually of earlier date. **1884** E. W. HAMILTON *Diary* 2 Dec. (1972) II. 746 Lord Hampden..likes the system of *single-member Districts, for which he has long been an advocate. **1889** *Pall Mall G.* 29 Oct. 2/1 In 1885, the country was practically divided into single-member electoral districts. **1956** J. LOTZ in L. White *Frontiers of Knowl.* xiv. 221 The single-word, or better, *single-morpheme sentences of the young child..cannot be analyzed into phonemes nor combined into sentences. **1860** G. PRESCOTT *Elect. Telegr.* 108 The double-needle telegraph may easily be arranged so that it shall act as a *single-needle telegraph only. **1949** L. FEATHER *Inside Be-bop* i. 6 The *single-note solo style was a complete departure from the pattern of solos in chords established by..conventional jazz guitarists. **1922** JOYCE *Ulysses* 698 Water closet..with opaque *singlepane oblong window. **1892** A. M. WORTHINGTON *Dynamics of Rotation* ii. 20 Any rigid body may be regarded as made up of such ideal *single-particle systems. **1970** G. K. WOODGATE *Elem. Atomic Struct.* v. 87 For *N* non-interacting electrons with no spin-orbit interaction we find it convenient to go back to the single-particle representation. **1941** *Pacific Affairs* XIV. 76 The emergence of a fully totalitarian '*single-party State'. **1979** E. NORMAN *Christianity & World Order* v. 66 Tanzania—a country with a rigidly enforced socialist collectivization and a single-party constitution. **1964** S. CRAWFORD *Basic Engin. Processes* iii. 93 The vertical plate is tack-welded in position ..and then finally welded by either the *single-pass or the multiple-pass techniques. **1969** *Computers & Humanities* IV. 43 Clearly, there should be much less occasion for careless errors and omissions in a multiple-pass system like Regener's than in a single-pass system like IML. **1957** *Loneliness* (Women's Group on Public Welfare) iii. 41 The number of *single-person households..increased by 104 per cent between 1931 and 1951. **1900** *Jrnl. Brit. Inst. Electr. Engin.* XXIX. 246 The motor is being supplied with *single-phase currents. **1946** *Nature* 31 Aug. 307/2 The electrolytic polishing of multi-phase metals is usually more difficult than that of single-phase metals owing to differing properties..of the different phases. **1979** *Dictionaries* I. 31 Editors are not restricted to *single-phrase descriptions. **1843** HOLTZAPFFEL *Turning* I. 31 The '*single-piece bow' is made of one rod of hickory, lancewood, or yew-tree. **1926** *Motor Man.* (ed. 26) iii. 49 (*caption*) *Single-plate clutch, showing internal details. **1940** *Chambers's Techn. Dict.* 772/2 *Single-plate clutch*, a friction clutch..in which the disc-shaped or annular driven member, fabric-faced, is pressed against a similar face on the driving member by springs. **1970** K. BALL *Fiat 600, 600D Autobk.* v. 45/1 The clutch, common to both the 600 and 600D series engines, is a conventional dry, single plate type with a spring cushioned hub as part of the driven plate. **1957** SIMPSON & WEIR *Weaver's Craft* iii. 25 A tightly packed weft of thick hand-spun or *single-ply rug wool. **1967** *Jane's Surface Skimmer Systems 1967–68* 13/2 A segmented skirt of single-ply neoprene-nylon fabric. **1935**, **1959** *Single-point [see INSTANTANEOUS *a.* 1 d]. **1979** *North Sea Progress* (Shell Internat. Petroleum Co.) 6 The field will be served by tankers at single-point mooring buoys to take the oil production. **1931** *Illustr. London News* 29 Aug. 342/3 The electrical system is 12 volts, with *single-pole wiring. **1975** G. J. KING *Audio Handbk.* x. 223 The slope of a single pole RC network always ultimately assumes a rate close to 6 dB/octave. **1832** BABBAGE *Econ. Manuf.* xv. (ed. 3) 138 A kind of lace, called '*single-press', was manufactured. **1919** *Daily Mail Year Bk.* 112/2 Many thousands of these are in service; to which the term '*single-purpose machines' is applied. **1943** J. S. HUXLEY *TVA* v. 27 The single-purpose costs which can be directly allocated to one or other of the functions. **1971** *Fremdsprachen* XV. 46 Each single-purpose use may be justified on its own, but the complete effect of piecemeal development can be chaos. **1931** G. JACOB *Orchestral Technique* iii. 23 *The Clarinet* (*single-reed instrument). **1976** D. MUNROW *Instr. Middle Ages & Renaissance* vi. 39/4 The French word *chalumeau* has been applied to the shawm as well as a detached double-reed bagpipe chanter..and the single-reed precursor of the clarinet. **1856** 'STONEHENGE' *Brit. Rur. Sports* II. II. xi. 363/2 One pound is the usual allowance for *single-rein bridles. **1868** *Rep. U.S. Comm. Agric.* (1869) 251 Neither neat nor efficient *single-row hedge can be made without the aid of stakes. **1946** *Nature* 5 Oct. 469/1 The aircraft rocket enabling a *single-seat fighter to deliver a salvo equal in hitting power to the broadside from a small cruiser. **1967** *Jane's Surface Skimmer Systems 1967–68* 8/1 It has built a single-seat vehicle designated Naviplane N 101. **1910** R. LORAINE *Diary* 10 Apr. in W. Loraine *Robert Loraine* (1938) vi. 104 A small *single-seater monoplane. **1930** *Engineering* 7 Mar. 316/1 Following upon a recent order for five Bristol Bulldog all-steel single-seater fighter aeroplanes, the Latvian Government has placed a further order..for seven additional Bulldog machines. **1973** J. LEASOR *Host of Extras* i. 21 In 1911..with a single-seater body..a Rolls-Royce covered a quarter-mile stretch at Brooklands at 101 miles an hour. **1845–50** MRS. LINCOLN *Lect. Bot.* v. 166/2 *Sicyos angulata*, *single-seed cucumber. **1961** *Guardian* 11 Dec. 7/7 Higher salaries..have made a *single-set drama..cost more nearly $100,000. **1971** J. ELSOM *Theatre outside London* x. 181 Low-cast, single-set comedies, with the occasional mystery play or classic revival. **1939** A. H. WHIPPLE *Educ. up to Fifteen Years* 36 Experiments should be conducted in *single-sex schools to ascertain.. whether or not the education of girls should differ in important respects from that of boys. **1980** *Times* 19 Feb. 2 Applications to Oriel, the only remaining men's single-sex college, are down again. **1892** BRIGHTON *Sir P. Wallis* 278 One of the finest *single-ship actions ever fought. **1841** *Penny Cycl.* XXI. 410/2 *Single-sole shoes or 'pumps'. **1577** STANYHURST *Descr. Irel.* in *Holinshed* I. 23/2 A meaner tower might serue such *single soule kings as were at those daies in Ireland. **1622** MABBE tr. *Aleman's Guzman d' Alf.* I. 105 To see what a single-sole Gentleman I was, and how like a naked cottage I lookt. **1872** *Dublin Rev.* Apr. 444 What can be done in the way of *single-span Gothic churches. **1958** M. L. HALL *Newnes Compl. Amat. Photogr.* ii. 32 *Single-speed rotary or single-leaf shutters, placed either in front of or behind the lens. **1975** *Language for Life* (Dept. Educ. & Sci.) vi. 95 Unfortunately, if most of their reading is of the single-speed kind, children will be habituated to becoming single-speed readers. **1922** GLAZEBROOK *Dict. Appl. Physics* II. 891/2 *Single-stage amplifiers. **1945** H. D. SMYTH *Gen. Acct. Devel. Atomic Energy Mil. Purposes* iv. 40 Single-stage separators had effected the enrichment of the U-235 on a laboratory scale to about the degree predicted theoretically. **1956** *Spaceflight* I. 24/1 The first stage resembles the Viking rocket which attained a record altitude (for single-stage rockets) of 158·4 miles in 1954. **1964** S. CRAWFORD *Basic Engin. Processes* xiv. 301 On a *single-start thread the lead and the pitch are identical. **1975** BRAM & DOWNS *Manuf. Technol.* iv. 120 The depth of a single-start thread stands in a definite relationship to its pitch. **1947** A. WARING *Approach to Better Housing* ii. 33 While not advocating the provision of *single-storey dwellings for large families..nevertheless these can be planned for small families and aged people..quite as successfully as the two-storey dwelling. **1970** D. GOLDRICH et al. in I. L. Horowitz *Masses in Lat. Amer.* v. 183 They are housed predominantly in single-story dwellings on individual plots. **1964** C. BARBER *Linguistic Change in Present-Day Eng.* iv. 86 The word *greatcoat* is a modern example of a transitional state between a double-stress and a *single-stress form. **1825** J. NICHOLSON *Operat. Mechanic* 47 When a *single-stroke steam-engine is made to turn a mill. **1959** WIMSATT & BEARDSLEY in *Publ. Mod. Lang. Assoc. Amer.* LXXIV. 595 The *single-syllable foot occurs in lines that sound like this: 'Weave, weave, the sunlight in your hair'. **1959** *Daily Tel.* 6 Mar. 21/3 The Ministry has suggested that *single-tier highway authorities with less than 200,000 people in their areas should be set up in Greater London. **1977** *Whitaker's Almanack 1978* 624 For the purpose of local government Northern Ireland has a system of 26 single-tier district councils. **1688** HOLME *Armoury* III. 398 The second [instrument]..is termed a *Single tooth Pincer, of some a Forcer. *c***1860** H. STUART *Seaman's Catech.* 74 The top-masts are made in one spar, and are called *single tree. **1865** LUBBOCK *Preh. Times* 345 They have single-tree canoes. **1904** A. B. F. YOUNG *Compl. Motorist* xi. 247 There are some *single-tube pneumatic tyres in which the whole of the fabric is constructed in one piece. **1935** *Discovery* Feb. 44/1 (*caption*) Guide-cradle for launching single-tube rockets. **1963** *Gloss. Mining Terms* (*B.S.I.*) III. 13 *Single-tube core barrel*, the simplest core barrel, having only a single cylindrical tube. **1940** *Chambers's Techn. Dict.* 772/2 **Single-turn coil*, an armature coil consisting of a single turn of copper bar. **1962** CORSON & LORRAIN *Introd. Electromagn. Fields* vi. 236 We consider single-turn coils for simplicity. **1883** *Whitaker's Alm.* 445/1 The *Huascar* is an iron low freeboard *single-turret ram. **1860** *Single wall knot [see *single diamond knot*]. **1936** *Discovery* Aug. 237/1 The world's largest *single unit multi-lens aerial mapping camera. **1973** *Tucson* (Ariz.) *Daily Citizen* 22 Aug. 27/2 We have passed the time when we can afford the luxury of building single-unit homes. **1959** *Gloss. Terms Packaging (B.S.I.)* 43 **Single-use tube*, a tube with sufficient contents for one use only. **1969** *Computers & Humanities* III. 138 The heavy-duty Selectric typewriter also requires frequent adjustments for uniform impressions, plus a single-use ribbon for publication output. **1962** L. S. Sasieni *Optical Dispensing* vii. 174 Logically a *single-vision lens prescribed for reading would be the most comfortable. **1971** *Optometry Today* 24 This team is capable of examining, prescribing, fabricating and dispensing single-vision lenses, mounted in frames, on the spot. **1707** Mortimer *Husb.* (1721) I. 48 In Sussex they use much the *single Wheel-plough. **1902** *Encycl. Brit.* XXXIII. 228/2 In 1892..he established communication between Lavernock Point and an island called Flat Holme..by placing at these positions insulated *single-wire circuits, earthed at both ends. **1913** V. B. Lewes *Oil Fuel* iv. 108 The single-wire system must not be adopted for any part of the electric lighting installation in vessels carrying petroleum. **1907** W. James *Pragmatism* vii. 239 All the great *single-word answers to the world's riddle, such as God, the One, Reason, Law, [etc.]. **1964** R. H. Robins *Gen. Linguistics* 284 Compound verbal expressions ..fulfil some of the semantic functions of the single-word tense forms of other languages. **1825** J. Nicholson *Operat. Mechanic* 497, B, the *single worm screw.

**19.** Parasynthetic, as ***single-banked, -barrelled, -bedded, -blossomed, -celled, -coloured, -decked, -edged, -ended, -engined***, etc. Also ***single-seatedness*** sb.; ***single-stranded*** (*Biochem.*), (of a nucleic acid) consisting of only one sequence of nucleotides; hence ***single-strandedness***.

Many examples of this type occur in recent use.

**1861** *Illustr. Lond. News* 13 July 35 One of its best *single-banked life-boats. **1821** E. Baker *Remarks on Rifle Guns* (ed. 8) 114 The average weight of a *single-barrelled gun should be from 6lbs to 6lbs 4oz. **1850** R. G. Cumming *Hunter's Life S. Afr.* (1902) 83/1, I took my heavy single-barrelled rifle. **1880** 'Mark Twain' *Speeches* (1923) 83 He possessed a single-barrelled fame before; he will possess a double-barrelled fame now. **1788** J. Woodforde *Diary* 20 May (1927) III. 27, I had a very good *single bedded Room to night. **1892** I. Zangwill *Childr. Ghetto* III. 188 Here single-bedded cabins could be had as low as fourpence a night. **1972** 'G. North' *Sergeant Cluff rings True* xix. 146 The single-bedded ward had its memories... A constable.. watched the bed in which the Sergeant had once lain wounded. **1762** *Phil. Trans.* LII. 660 Some *single blossomed plants..of the Gardenia. **1899** W. James *Talks to Teachers* xiv. 163 In biology, we used to have interminable discussion as to whether certain *single-celled organisms were animals or vegetables, until Haeckel introduced the new apperceptive name of Protista, which ended the disputes. **1977** G. Scott *Hot Pursuit* xii. 105 Single cell protein is produced by single-celled animals: bacteria, yeasts, fungi, that sort of thing. **1703** tr. H. van Oosten *Dutch Gardener* II. iv. 60, I think the *single colour'd to be the best..because the tulip that is already changed and striped, doth easily mix her colours together; and this is the reason why the single colours that come from them, have not so strong a colour as those from the single coloured ones. **1940** W. Stevens in *Accent* Autumn 12 The single-colored, colorless, primitive. **1869** *Single-decked [see double-deck]. **1972** 'G. North' *Sergeant Cluff rings True* xiv. 112 The single-decked bus..laboured up the hill. **1598** Hakluyt *Voy.* I. 62 The richer sort haue *single edged swords with sharpe points. **1817** Miller *Bampt. Lect.* 40 The single-edged sword of temporal visitation fell blunted from the hearts of stone. **1952** *Proc. IRE* XL. 11/1 Since the output is *single ended, the feedback can be made directly from the midpoint of the output stage to a preceding single-ended stage. **1975** *Official Transcript Techn. Papers Ann. Nat. Cable Television Assoc. Convention* (New Orleans) 24 Investigations were conducted on an operating cable television system to explore methods of increasing the channel capacity of broadband single-ended amplifiers. **1964** *Oceanogr. & Marine Biol.* II. 47 Transportation was by means of *single-engined aircraft. **1978** R. V. Jones *Most Secret War* xxxiv. 301 It happened that a unit of single-engined fighters had been formed in the preceding weeks by Major Hajo Herrmann. **1803** Shaw *Gen. Zool.* IV. II. 265 *Single-finned Bullhead... The gill-covers consist of a single lamina. **1707** Mortimer *Husb.* (1721) II. 209 Of both which sorts there are great Variety of Colours, some being double, and others *single Flowered. **1756** Hill *Brit. Herbal* 440 Great single-flowered Mountain Hawkweed. **1840** Hodgson *Hist. Northumb.* III. II. 361/2 *Orthotrichum cupulatum*, *Single-fringed sessile fruited Bristle-moss. **1846** Grote *Greece* I. xxi. II. 261 The case..against *single-headed authorship of the Odyssey. **1847** Ld. Lindsay *Chr. Art* I. 130 A black single-headed, hoary-haired giant. **1889** G. Findlay *Eng. Railway* 48 The steel rails..are of the single-headed section. **1721** R. Bradley *Philos. Acc. Wks. Nature* 91 Some of the Pigs will be Cloven-footed, and others *single-hoof'd. **1777** Pennant *Brit. Zool.* IV. 16 Claws with a *single-hooked moveable fang. **1800** Shaw *Gen. Zool.* I. I. 198 *Single-horned Rhinoceros. **1721** *Lond. Gaz.* No. 6012/6 A Man and a Woman in a Lane, *single Hors'd. **1899** *Westm. Gaz.* 8 Sept. 5/3 He was driven in a single-horsed brougham. **1725** *Fam. Dict.* s.v. *Colchicum*, A yellow, *single-leav'd Flower. **1829** Marryat *F. Mildmay* v, They were *single-masted. **1884** Bower & Scott *De Bary's Phaner.* 300 Many have certainly a reticulum of bundles, even when they are '*single-nerved'. **1840** J. W. Bowden *Life Gregory VII.* I. 60 The long *single-pointed mitre. **1905** J. London *Let.* 4 Apr. (1966) 169 You and I are both fighters, and *single-purposed fighters too. **1933** 'R. Crompton' *William—the Rebel* viii. 164 They were all large, single-purposed, unsmiling men. **1920** U. Daubeny *Orchestral Wind Instruments* vi. 55 Somewhat similar rude *single-reeded pipes are still used by Italian shepherds and Roman pifferari. **1911** G. B. Shaw *Getting Married* 129 Very few couples can live in a *single-roomed tenement without exchanging blows quite frequently. **1808** Bentham *Sc. Reform* 36 The many-seated has given place to *single-seated judicature. **1830** —— *Corr.* Wks. 1843 XI. 40 In this sub-department..you find..many-seatedness established —by you, *single-seatedness, I see, is preferred. **1753** *Chambers' Cycl.* Suppl. s.v. *Sicyoides*, The *single-seeded Canada cucumber. **1870** Garrod *Mat. Med.* (ed. 3) 272 The olive fruit..is a smooth, elliptical, single-seeded drupe. *a* **1834** Coleridge in *Lit. Rem.* (1839) IV. 165 This is not quite so perspicuous and *single-sensed as Archbishop Leighton's sentences in general are. **1903** G. B. Shaw *Man & Superman* III. 112 She [*sc.* Nature] created him in order to produce something better than the *single-sexed process can produce. **1934** L. B. Pekin *Progressive Schools* iv. 62, I cannot imagine any teacher who has given co-education a fair trial..ever returning to a single-sexed school. **1851** H. Melville *Whale* lxxviii. A whip..travelling through a *single-sheaved block. **1679** *Lond. Gaz.* No. 1403/4 A Silver hilted *single sheld Sword. **1937** *Discovery* Sept. 284/1 *Single-sided, long-playing, unbreakable durium-type records so popular a few years ago. **1977** *Gramophone* Aug. 262/3 Frank Andrews (London, NW10) points out that Zonophones were single-sided until June 1911. **1956** *Nature* 18 Feb. 334/2 A number of strains [of lucerne] planted as *single-spaced plants in the field. **1959** J. Thurber *Years with Ross* xi. 191 Ross sat down at his typewriter..and wrote..a remarkable five-page single-spaced letter. **1975** T. Allbeury *Special Collection* xv. 99 A foolscap sheet in single-spaced typing. **1803** Shaw *Gen. Zool.* IV. II. 335 *Single-spotted Chætodon. **1835** J. E. Alexander *Sk. in Portugal* v. 113 By the side of the road to Santarem was the quarter of Colonel Shaw, a long *single-storied peasant's house in a vineyard. **1967** *Antiquaries Jrnl.* XLVII. 275 The hall probably rose clear above this east room, which may have been roofed as a single-storeyed lean-to. **1954** *Proc. R. Soc.* A. CCXXIII. 94 Most of these earlier formulations..have involved *single stranded structures and must be rejected. **1964** G. H. Haggis et al. *Introd. Molecular Biol.* iv. 79 The RNA component of the virus is a long single-stranded nucleic acid chain. **1978** *BioSystems* X. 102/1 Double stranded DNA would be unsuitable because, unlike single-stranded RNA it cannot fold up on its own to form specific and complex 3D structures. **1974** *Nature* 5 Apr. 507/1 They..exhibit greater buoyant densities due to the presence of RNA sequences and/or some degree of *single strandedness. **1890** W. James *Princ. Psychol.* I. xiv. 558 The 'cue' was given by *single-syllabled words called out by an assistant. **1948** E. Sitwell *Notebk. on Shakespeare* vi. 72 In such lines [from *King Lear*]..the single-syllabled words take on the hugeness of those new-made stones that Deucalion and Pyrrha, the Deluge being over, found and cast behind their backs. **1856** Meredith *Shav. Shagpat* (1909) 245 The Queen..being now the mistress of the *single-thoughted. **1603** J. Davies (Heref.) *Sonn., To Univ. of Oxford*, With double lines of *single-twisted Rime. **1702** *Lond. Gaz.* No. 3840/4 A black Hat with a single-twisted white Hatband. **1796** W. H. Marshall *W. England* II. 211 *Single-wheeled plows. *a* **1832** J. Bentham *Logic* vii, in *Wks.* (1843) VIII. 252/1 Finding a more appropriate *single-worded denomination for the species. **1893** W. Minto *Logic* I. ii. 68 Whether this is single-worded or many-worded is..a grammatical question.

**20. a.** With pa. pples. and ppl. adjs., as ***single-cut*** (of files), ***-dyed, -filed, -grown, -hung, -lanted, -reefed, -refined, -riveted***; ***single-tuned*** (*Electronics*), having a single tuned circuit between two active devices.

**1831** J. Holland *Manuf. Metal* I. 302 In this state the file is what is called a *single-cut. **1846** Holtzapffel *Turning* II. 819 When the file is spoken of, a double-cut file is always implied, unless a single-cut file, or a rasp, is specifically named. **1875** Knight *Dict. Mech.* 2187/1 *Single-cut File*, a file having but a single rank of teeth. **1696** J. F. *Merch. Wareho. laid open* 9 Pillow Fustians,..some of them *single dyed. **1853** G. Johnston *Nat. Hist. E. Bord.* I. 107 Let us walk on, *single-filed. **1833** Tennyson *Palace of Art* I, Muskscented blooms.., In bunch or *singlegrown. **1823** P. Nicholson *Pract. Build.* 593 **Single-hung*; in window-sashes, when one only is moveable. **1630** *Tincker of Turvey* Ep. Ded., I have drunke double-lanted ale, and *single-lanted. **1860** *Merc. Mar. Mag.* VII. 173 The topsails were *single reefed. **1718** Mrs. M. Eales *Receipts* 28 A Pound of *single-refin'd Sugar. **1869** Rankine *Machine & Hand-tools* App. 44 In *single-rivetted joints there is but one row of rivets. **1947** F. E. Terman *Radio Engin.* (ed. 3) vii. 346 The band width in the case of an amplifier system employing double-tuned circuits is defined in the same manner as for a system employing *single-tuned circuits. **1975** D. G. Fink *Electronics Engineers' Handbk.* XIII. 43 The two common types [of tuned interstage] are the single- and double-tuned interstage.

**b.** With pres. pples., as ***single-cutting, -driving, -living, -shooting***. Also with vbl. sbs., as ***single-boating, -manning, -spacing***.

**1563** in Strype *Ann. Ref.* (1709) I. xxxv. 349 Single-living men, that is to say, unmaried, and especially unmaried priests. **1846** Holtzapffel *Turning* II. 549 The cone countersink may be viewed as a multiplication of the common single-cutting drill. **1888** *Encycl. Brit.* XXIII. 559 Single-driving rear-steerers were at this time [1877] very common. **1891** *Daily News* 4 Feb. 3/3 All magazine rifles must be more costly than single-shooting rifles. **1934** W. Wood *Fleeters* iv. 59 Men who are only used to Iceland and single-boatin' aren't any good at this fleetin' job. **1956** F. C. Avis *Bookman's Conc. Dict.* 273/1 *Single spacing*, the style of typewriting in which the lines of characters follow immediately after each other without any interlinear spacing, equivalent to 'Solid' typesetting. **1958** E. Newby *Short Walk in Hindu Kush* ii. 21 A great spate of letters.. neatly typed in single spacing. **1965** *Times* 22 Oct. 8/7 The proposal that single manning of locomotives should be introduced within a year or two. **1973** *Guardian* 31 Dec. 13/8 London Transport..has launched..single-manning. .. But the single-manned buses..take up to five times as long at stops. **1978** *Church Times* 21 July 5/4 A letter of more than two pages in single-spacing.

**c.** With vbs., as ***single-knock, -plate, -rivet, -space***.

**1834** *Tait's Mag.* I. 735/1 The original plotter.., who has single-knocked at so many mansions in Grosvenor Square [etc.]. **1839** Ure *Dict. Arts* 998 The ingot is now dressed carefully with the file on one or two faces, according as it is to be single or double plated. **1874** Thearle *Naval Archit.* 103 The edges of the plating above this height..may be single riveted. **1961** *Guardian* 6 Feb. 9/5 Press releases would be single-spaced to save paper. **1963** D. Heyes *12th of Never* (1964) i. 8 He..continued typing..and..single-spaced the final line to squeeze it in.

**single** ('sɪŋg(ə)l), *v.*[1] [f. the adj.]

**1.** *trans.* To separate or part from each other; to take asunder. Now *rare.*

**1570–6** Lambarde *Peramb. Kent* (1826) 114 For as much as the office[s]..of later daies have been united inseparably, I wil not lose the labour in going about to single them againe. **1584** D. Fenner *Def. Ministers* (1587) 11 Wee will..single them a little, and deale with them seuerallie. *a* **1600** Hooker *Eccl. Pol.* VII. i. §2 Not..to offer the edge of the axe unto all three boughs at once, but rather to single them, and strike at the weakest first. **1828** *Trial W. Dyon & his Son at York* 20 The reports were so near together, that I could scarcely single them.

*refl.* **1596** Danett tr. *Comines* 144 Whensoeuer his men scattered & singled themselues, some of them came short home. **1600** Breton *Strange Fort. Two Princes* Wks. (Grosart) II. 11/2 Spying certaine Ladies..comming into the garden, they singled themselues one from another. **1623** Bingham *Xenophon* 115 That the Army should more easily passe singling themselues..than if they clustred and thronged at a Bridge.

**2.** *Hunting.* To separate (one deer, etc.) from the herd; to pick out and chase separately. Also with *forth* or *out.*

**1575** Gascoigne *Flowers* Wks. 1907 I. 109 The meanes to single forth The stricken Deare which doth in heard remaine. **1590** Cokaine *Treat. Hunting* Dj, Then the Huntsmans part is to applie the hounds well vntill they haue singled the wearie Deere againe. **1674** N. Cox *Gentl. Recreat.* (1677) 60 Follow the largest Head of the whole Herd, which you must endeavour to single out for the Chase. **1735** Somerville *Chase* III. 324 The grisly Boar is singled from his Herd As large as that in Erimanthian Woods. **1841** Lane *Arab. Nts.* I. 127 From the moment he singles out an Antelope the whole body are in motion. **1873** Black *Pr. Thule* xiii. 202 The hound had at length singled out a particular deer.

*fig.* **1579** Lyly *Euphues* (Arb.) 35 He behaued himselfe so warily, that hee singled his game wiselye. **1588** Shaks. *Titus A.* II. i. 117 Single you thither then this dainty Doe, And strike her home by force, if not by words. **1593** —— *3 Hen. VI*, II. iv. 12 Nay Warwicke, single out some other Chace, For I my selfe will hunt this Wolfe to death. **1711** Addison *Spect.* No. 125 ¶8 We should then single every Criminal out of the Herd, and hunt him down.

**3. a.** To separate (one person or thing) from others; to draw or take aside or apart.

**1593** Shaks. *3 Hen. VI*, II. iv. 1 Now Clifford, I haue singled thee alone. **1632** Heywood *Four Prentises* I. Wks. 1874 II. 216 Why have you singled me alone? *a* **1658** Rowley, Tourneur, etc. *Witch Edmonton* III, I have not shewn this cheek in company, Pardon me now: thus singled with your self [etc.]. *a* **1672** Sterry *Freed. Will* (1675) 25 Singling every thought, setting it naked in its own proper form.

*refl.* **1588–9** Greene *Metam.* Wks. (Grosart) IX. 73 When wee were in the greene meades, Meribates and my daughter had singled themselues. **1602** Breton *Wonders Worth Hearing* Wks. (Grosart) II. 9/1 A couple..for serious cause of conference had singled themselues together.

**b.** Const. *from.*

**1582** Stanyhurst *Æneis* II. (Arb.) 58 Theare stood an od corner from vulgar companye singled. **1587** Fleming *Contn. Holinshed* III. 401/2 Sir Richard Greenefield being singled from his fleet, all alone arriued in the Iland of Hispaniola. **1697** Dryden *Æneid* XI. 901 Him soon she singled from the flying Train, And slew with ease.

*refl.* *a* **1639** Spottiswood *Hist. Ch. Scot.* VI. (1677) 320 He singled himself from his company. **1698** Fryer *Acc. E. India & P.* 2 That our Ships might have the Liberty that Night to single themselves from the Crowd of other Ships.

†**c.** With *forth* (cf. 5). *Obs.*

**1593** Shaks. *3 Hen. VI*, II. i. 12, I..watcht him how he singled Clifford forth. **1599** B. Jonson *Ev. Man out of Hum.* V. i, If wee can, [let us] single her forth to some place. **1636** tr. *Florus' Hist.* 10 Horatius..faynes himselfe to flie, so to single forth the enemie.

**4.** To pick out or distinguish from others.

In quot. 1671 with allusion to a challenge.

**1588** Shaks. *L.L.L.* II. i. 28 In that behalfe..we single you, As our best mouing faire soliciter. **1604** T. Wright *Passions* VI. 304 How, when we would remember, can we single a Flye from the vniversity of beastes, foules and fish. **1671** Milton *Samson* 1092 Dost thou already single me? I thought Gives and the Mill had tam'd thee. **1701** Stanhope *St. Aug. Medit.* II. vii. (1720) 129 He singled thee from the rest. **1749** Smollett *Regicide* IV. ii, He, whom my jealousy ..Hath singled for destruction! **1805** Southey *Madoc* I. v, Up the side he sprang, And look'd among the crew, and singling me Fell at my feet. **1822** Shelley '*We meet not as we parted*' iii, That moment from time was singled As the first of a life of pain.

*refl.* **1812** Coleridge in *Lit. Rem.* (1836) I. 383 The instinct..in each man of declaring his particular existence, and thus of singling or singularizing himself.

**5. a.** With *out.* To choose or select from a number of persons or things, *esp.* (in later use) in order to distinguish by particular notice or attention; to pick or mark out, to destine.

**1629** Baker in Ellis *Orig. Lett.* Ser. II. III. 258 This bearer will convey hether such bookes as it shall please you to single out and deliver to him. **1697** Dryden *Virg. Past.* IV. 74 Begin, auspicious Boy,..and with a smile thy Mother single out. **1710** Addison *Tatler* No. 120 ¶ 2 Every Man singled out some Woman to whom he offered his Addresses. **1782** Miss Burney *Cecilia* V. i, Having singled her out, he was regarding her. **1846** Trench *Mirac.* XXX. (1862) 434 The man..now singles out the blessing which he craves. **1888**

BURGON *Lives 12 Gd. Men* II. v. 18 Singling out.. from the entire body of the Clergy a man under suspicion of heresy.

**b.** Const. *as*, *for*, or with inf.

**1633** BP. HALL *Occas. Medit.* (1851) 88 The want whereof dejects us beyond measure, as men singled out for patterns of misery. **1662** PEPYS *Diary* 10 May, I find that he do single me out to join with me apart from the rest. **1692** BENTLEY *Boyle Lect.* vi. 186 This is the Passage which Lucilio Vanino singled out for his Text. **1726** DE FOE *Hist. Devil* I. xi. (1840) 159 Satan saw God had evidently singled out the Israelites.. to favour them. **1780** *Mirror* No. 88, I doubted not that they would single me out as a prodigy of learning and genius. **1833** HT. MARTINEAU *Manch. Strike* viii. 85 This woman having been singled out as an example. **1856** BOND *Russia at Close of 16th c.* (Hakl. Soc.) Introd. 61 The Protector.. had singled him out for the execution of a secret commission. **1869** TROLLOPE *He knew*, etc. xxxi, The one she has singled out as the recipient of her kindness.

**c.** To select for special mention or comment.

**1628** PRYNNE *Cens. Cozens* 66, I will onely single out some three or four of his chiefe absurdities. **1672** SIR G. MACKENZIE *Pleadings* Pref. A iij b, Pointed and short pleading, wherein the Speaker singles out a point, and presses it. **1711** ADDISON *Spect.* No. 35 ¶11, I shall not scruple.. to single out any of the small Wits, that infest the World with such Compositions. **1872** BLACK *Adv. Phaeton* xxx. 404 America and not Germany had been singled out by the poet. **1891** *Spectator* 5 Dec. 809 It is time to single out one or two works by members.

**d.** *refl.* To separate (oneself) from a number of others.

**1885** PASCOE *London of To-day* xiii. 120 Two or three horses at last emerge again, and single themselves out.

**6.** To bestow singly. *rare*$^{-1}$.

**1652** FULLER *Holy & Prof. St.* (ed. 3) 498 Wishing that.. whatsoever good was singl'd on them, may joyntly be heaped upon you.

**7.** To thin (seedling plants), so as to leave each plant separate; to pick *off* (shoots). Also const. *out*.

**1731** MILLER *Gard. Dict.* s.v. *Dipsacus*, Singling out the Plants to about six or eight Inches Distance. **1801** *Farmer's Mag.* Jan. 51 The turnip being singled by the hand-hoe. **1846** J. BAXTER *Libr. Pract. Agric.* (ed. 4) II. 196 As they grow up in the spring the young shoots should be singled off to one. **1884** F. J. LLOYD *Sci. Agric.* 255 When the turnip plants are tolerably advanced, or rough leaved, they are singled.

*transf.* **1858–61** J. BROWN *Horæ Subs.* ii. 42 He has not the art of 'singling' his thoughts, an art.. as necessary for young fancies as young turnips.

*absol.* **1886** [see SINGLER *sb.*]. **1896** P. A. GRAHAM *Red Scaur* xii. 175 This'll never do, singlin' wi' your best things on.

**8. a.** To render single, to reduce to one; to concentrate. Also *refl.*

**1824** *Blackw. Mag.* XVI. 29 The acquisition of knowledge.. is best.. made, by limiting, almost by singling to the mind, the objects of attainment. **1836** LANDOR *Pericles & Aspasia* Wks. 1846 II. 371 This reproof.. singled his aim.

**b.** *Naut.* (See quot.)

**1867** SMYTH *Sailor's Word-bk.* 627 *To Single*, to unreeve the running part of topsail sheets, &c., to let them run freely, or for harbour duty.

**c.** *Naut.* With *up*: to cast off all turns of rope except one. Also *intr.*

**1900** J. C. CANTWELL *Diary* 17 May in *Rep. Operations U.S. Revenue Steamer Nunivak* (1904) iv. 57 The lines by which the *Nunivak* was held to the shore were singled up. **1925** R. CLEMENTS *Gipsy of Horn* vi. 103 Our moorings had been singled up. **1959** C. S. FORESTER *Hunting Bismarck* 8 Already sailors at the lines were singling up and then casting off. **1966** T. PYNCHON *Crying of Lot 49* ii. 31 The little submarine.. was at the quai, singling up all lines.

**9.** *intr.* **a.** To go singly; to separate from others. Also with *out* and *off*.

**1616** J. LANE *Contn. Sqr.'s T.* v. 338, Theare them he findes in martial discipline well ordred,.. taught.. to double ranckes, and singel backe in place. **1676** HOBBES *Iliad* IV. 292 Let.. all go on At once. To single is to weaken you. **1759** GOLDSM. *Pres. State Pol. Learn.* viii. Wks. (Globe) 435/1 A reflection somewhat mortifying to the author who breaks his ranks, and singles out for public favour. **1769** —— *Hist. Rome* (1786) I. 204 Titus Manlius.., burning with shame to see the whole body of the Romans intimidated, boldly singled out against Metius. **1904** in *Eng. Dial. Dict.* s.v., Single off, as cattle do when they are sick, or going to calve, &c.

**b.** *U.S.* (See quot. and cf. SINGLE-FOOT.)

*a* **1864** W. S. CLARKE (Webster), Many very fleet horses, when overdriven, adopt a disagreeable gait,.. in which the two legs of one side are raised almost.. simultaneously. Such horses are said to single, or to be single-footed.

**c.** Of a railway track: To become single.

**1899** *Daily News* 19 Sept. 6/7 Just before Penybont the track singles for a short tunnel.

**d.** *Baseball.* Of a batter: to hit a single (sense 3 h); to make a one-base hit. Also *trans.*, by singling to enable (another player) to reach home base.

**1916** *Chicago Tribune* 7 Oct. 13/1 In the ninth, the first man up singled. **1949** *Clarke County Democrat* (Grove Hill, Alabama) 22 Sept. 2/5 The first St. Michael batter singled. **1966** *N.Y. Times* (Internat. ed.) 22 Apr. 12/1 Felipe Alou singled in the first inning off Ray Culp. **1970** *Globe & Mail* (Toronto) 28 Sept. 19/3 Adolfo Phillips singled home Ron Brand in the 11th inning. **1978** *N.Y. Times* 30 Mar. D 19/4 In the third, Ken Henderson doubled, John Stearns singled and it was 4–0.

Hence **'singled** *ppl. a.*, selected.

**1870** SWINBURNE *Ess. & Stud.* (1875) 108, I take to witness four singled poems.

†**'single**, *v.*² *Obs. rare.* [ad. F. *singler* (now *cingler*), nasalized form of OF. *sigler*, ad. ON. *sigla* to sail.] *intr.* To sail. Also †**'singling** *ppl. a.*

**1584** HUDSON *Du Bartas' Judith* IV. 122 The perfite pylot.. with singling sheet doth shunne Cyanes straits. **1587** GREENE *Euphues his Censure* Wks. (Grosart) VI. 189 The Maryners ready with a Cockboate to set them aboorde hoysed sayles, and singling into the mayne, bad farewell to Ithaca.

**single-acting**, *ppl. a.* [f. SINGLE *a.* 20 b.] Acting in one direction or by one method, *spec.* of a steam-engine (see quot. 1875). Opposed to DOUBLE-ACTING.

**1825** J. NICHOLSON *Operat. Mechanic* 174 The double-acting engine.. exerting twice the power of the single-acting engine. **1869** RANKINE *Machine & Hand-tools* Pl. F 3, Single-acting hammers are those which are raised by the pressure of steam, and fall by gravity alone. **1875** KNIGHT *Dict. Mech.* 2187/1 *Single-acting Engine*, an engine in which steam is admitted to one side only of the piston.

**single-'blind**, *a.* [f. SINGLE *a.*, after DOUBLE(-)BLIND *a.*] Applied to a test or experiment conducted by one person on another in which information about the test that may lead to bias in the results is concealed from one of the parties.

**1963** *Amer. Jrnl. Psychiatry* CXX. 67/1 The single-blind study showed relief of symptoms with mephenoxalone in 3 of 9 patients. **1976** *Sci. Amer.* Jan. 8/3 The test was not even single-blind. **1978** *Nature* 20 Apr. 729/1 The studies were performed open or single-blind, in most cases with randomised placebo controls. **1981** *Brit. Med. Jrnl.* 11 July 22/2 If the identity of the treatment is concealed only from the assessor then the trial is single-masked or single-blind... The term 'single-blind' has also been applied to trials in which only the patient is in the dark, although this is not nearly so important as the assessor being in the dark.

**'single-breasted**, *a.* [f. SINGLE *a.* 19.] Of a coat, waistcoat, etc.: Having only one thickness over the breast; not doubled by overlapping. Opposed to DOUBLE-BREASTED.

**1796** TWINING *Trav. India*, etc. (1894) 2 His thin silvery locks curled round the collar of his old-fashioned single-breasted coat. **1828** *Lights & Shades* I. 296 Next in favour to the frock is the short single-breasted jacket. **1862** BURTON *Bk. Hunter* 31 Had chance thrown to him a court single-breasted coat [etc.]. **1885** PASCOE *London of To-day* xii. 112 The coat altered its form, and became a dress coat, single-breasted.

**single-eyed**, *a.* [f. SINGLE *a.* 19.]

**1.** *fig.* Having the eye single or sound; sincere, honest, straightforward. (Cf. SINGLE *a.* 14 b.)

**1705** HICKERINGILL *Priest-cr.* (1721) I. 32 The.. general Council.. was at Ariminum, who were all (but one single-ey'd Man) Arians. **1857** KINGSLEY *Two Y. Ago* xx, You are.. too noble, single-eyed, self-sacrificing to endure my vanity. **1890** *Spectator* 19 July 74/1 Those who best understand what may be done by single-eyed, eager, and resolute clergymen.

**2.** *lit.* Having one eye or eye-like mark; one-eyed, monoculous.

**1839** *Penny Cycl.* XV. 348/1 None of these single-eyed monsters [*Cyclopia*].. live for more than an hour or two after birth. **1872** *Routledge's Ev. Boy's Ann.* June 420/1 Its single-eyed spot near the tip of the fore-wings.

†**single-fold**, *a. Obs.*$^{-1}$ Simple.

**1651** BIGGS *New Disp.* ¶82 The single-fold doctrine of simples hath stood deserted, and forlorn.

**single-foot**, *sb. U.S.* [Cf. SINGLE *v.*¹ 9 b.] A particular gait of a horse, variously identified with the amble and the rack; see also quot. 1882.

**1882** STILLMAN *Horse in Motion* 117 Single-foot is an irregular pace,.. distinguished by the posterior extremities, moving in the order of a fast walk and the anterior ones in that of a slow trot. **1893** MUYBRIDGE *Descr. Zoopraxogr.* 31 The amble has various local names, such as the 'single foot', the 'fox trot', etc. **1897** HOWELLS *Landl. at Lion's Head* 154 This mare can walk like a Kentucky horse,.. I believe I could teach her single-foot.

So **single-foot** *v.*, **single-footed** *a.*, **single-footer**, **single-footing** *ppl. a.*

*a* **1864** Single-footed [see SINGLE *v.*¹ 9 b]. **1890** *Harper's Mag.* Jan. 246 The horse often single-foots faster than he trots. *Ibid.*, It is often said that a single-footing horse never trots well. *Ibid.* 247 My best single-footer is my fastest trotter.

**single grave.** *Archæol.* [f. SINGLE *a.* 17, 18: tr. Du. *enkelgraf* single grave.] A barrow-grave containing the remains of only one person. Freq. *attrib.*, *spec.* (esp. with initial capitals) designating a culture characterized by individual burial which first flourished in northern Germany and Scandinavia during the later Neolithic Age, or representatives of this.

[**1898** S. MÜLLER in *Aarb. f. nord Oldk.* 157 (*heading*) De jydske Enkeltgraver fra Stenalderen.] **1936** J. G. D. CLARK *Mesolithic Settlement of Northern Europe* ii. 73 The triangular-sectioned flake arrowhead.. is abundant in passage-graves and occurs in single-graves. **1937** E. V. GORDON tr. *Shetelig & Falk's Scand. Arch.* v. 66 It can be shown that the single-grave people, with their characteristic battle-axes and their own pottery, came from.. central Europe. **1954** S. PIGGOTT *Neolithic Cultures* xii. 378 In Denmark the Single-grave invasion takes place after the LG IV marine transgression. **1955** *Univ. Lond. Inst. Archaeol. Ann. Rep.* XI. 39 The discovery at Ohlenburg,.. of a devolved Single-Grave beaker. **1957** V. G. CHILDE *Dawn Europ. Civilization* (ed. 6) ix. 160 Archaeologically these graziers are known only by little cemeteries of barrows, and so they are termed the Single Grave folk. **1963** S. PIGGOTT in Foster & Alcock *Culture & Environment* iv. 60 Glasbergen and Van der Waals have shown the Single Grave element to be represented by their Footed Beakers, with an absolute date of *c.* 2200 B.C. **1970** BRAY & TRUMP *Dict. Archaeol.* 212/2 This [burial] rite.. links the Single-Grave cultures with the great Corded Ware-Battleaxe complex.

**single-hand**, *a.* [f. SINGLE *a.* 18 + HAND *sb.*]

**1.** Performed, worked, managed, played, by one 'hand' or person. † ***single-hand cricket***, = SINGLE-WICKET.

**1761** in Waghorn *Cricket Scores* (1899) 54 A great match at single-hand cricket. **1835** URE *Philos. Manuf.* 245 In our single-hand ribbon-loom, the weaver can make but a piece and a half a week. **1872** RAYMOND *Statist. Mines & Mining* 3 The gradual extension of 'single-hand drilling'. **1893** *Outing* XXII. 143 A single-hand cruiser is a sail-boat.. capable of being managed by one man.

**2.** ***single-hand weaver***, one who works his loom without assistance. So ***single-hand trade***.

**1768** *Ann. Reg.* I. 58 Several of the journeymen single-hand weavers were seized by their antagonists. **1841** *Penny Cycl.* XIX. 491/1 The undertaking system applies now only to the single-hand trade in the country districts. *Ibid.*, Three-fourths of the single-hand weavers are women.

**single-handed**, *a.* [f. SINGLE *a.* 19.]

**1. a.** Of actions: Carried on or performed by one person, ship, etc., alone or unaided, or by one person on each side.

**1709** *Brit. Apollo* No 18. 2/2 Q. D. and T. play at single handed whisk. **1818** SCOTT *Rob Roy* xxxix, Rashleigh.. maintained a desperate and single-handed conflict with the leader of the band. **1824** MISS MITFORD *Village* Ser. I. (1863) 129, I shall never forget one single-handed course of our good friend's favourite little bitch Helen. **1840** MARRYAT *Poor Jack* xlvii, They had two single-handed encounters. **1881** *Encycl. Brit.* XII. 808/2 Despite the single-handed exertions of Lieutenant.. Edwardes.

**b.** Adapted for using with one hand.

**1834** MEDWIN *Angler in Wales* I. 172 Do you use a single or double-handed rod?

**c.** = SINGLE-HAND *a.* 1.

**1886** *Field* 30 Jan. 140/1, I should not advise any topmast for a single-handed sailing boat.

**2. a.** Working alone or unassisted; without the aid, help, or support of others; by one's self; unaided, unsupported. Also passing into *adv.*

**1768** *Ann. Reg.* I. 57 Many journeymen weavers, distinguished by the names of single-handed weavers. **1815** JEFFERSON *Writ.* (1830) IV. 249 We have beaten them single-handed at sea. **1840** THIRLWALL *Greece* lv. VII. 100 Rome, single-handed, could not long have withstood such an army. **1877** CREIGHTON *Age of Elizabeth* v. i, He was surrounded by an atmosphere of suspicion, and.. stood single-handed. **1900** J. SLOCUM *Sailing Alone around World* xxi. 272 On the 4th of June, 1898, the *Spray* cleared from the United States consulate, and her license to sail single-handed, even round the world, was returned to her for the last time. **1939** G. B. SHAW *Geneva* I. 4, I have to do it singlehanded too: I havnt even an office boy to help me. **1970** G. M. FRASER *General danced at Dawn* 144 Lance-Corporal Michael O'Leary, who took on crowds of Germans singlehanded.

**b.** Using one hand only.

**1844** H. STEPHENS *Bk. Farm* II. 511 A single-handed sower makes a bout to sow a ridge.

**c.** Having only one hand or workman.

**1847** in WEBSTER. [Hence in recent Dicts.]

Hence **single-'handedly** *adv.*, **-'handedness**.

**1882** EBSWORTH *Roxb. Ball.* IV. Introd. p. x, He hopes to press on vigorously and single-handedly, to the speedy completion of the entire work. **1899** *Westm. Gaz.* 18 May 2/1 Singlehandedness among menservants is the last resource of the incompetent. **1964** *Duckett's Reg.* Mar. 41/2 America's most famous Franciscan, who almost singlehandedly Christianised America's Pacific Coast. **1979** *N.Y. Rev. Bks.* 25 Oct. 10/1 Barbara Underwood.. boasts that she single-handedly made *one quarter of a million dollars* for the cult.

**single-hearted**, *a.* [f. SINGLE *a.* 19.]

**1.** Possessed of a single or sincere heart; straightforward, honest, sincere; simple-hearted.

**1577** *Test. 12 Patriarchs* (1604) 83 The single-hearted man coveteth not gold,.. but only hath an eye to God's will. **1644** CROMWELL *Lett.* 6 Sept., In this Cause I hope to approve myself an honest man and single-hearted. **1658–9** in *Burton's Diary* (1828) III. 593, I can say I am plain hearted and single-hearted. **1812** SCOTT *Let.* in *Lockhart* (1837) II. xii. 392 The Duke's mind was moulded upon the kindliest and most single-hearted model. **1838** DICKENS *Nickleby* xxx, He is the most grateful, single-hearted, affectionate creature, that ever breathed. **1899** *Edinb. Rev.* Oct. 508 Life at Court was distasteful to the single-hearted priest.

**2.** Of actions, etc.: Proceeding from or characterized by sincerity of heart or purpose.

**1804** MATILDA BETHAM *Biog. Dict. Women* 736 Her eloquent, and, as it were, single-hearted appeal to impartial posterity. **1874** SYMONDS *Sk. Italy & Greece* (1898) I. ix. 185 [He] had hitherto acted with a single-hearted view to his own interests. **1893** *The Advance* (Chicago) 22 June, The single-hearted earnestness of the Templars is impressive.

Hence **single-'heartedly** *adv.*, **-'heartedness**.

**1642** H. MORE *Song of Soul* Notes 163/1 *Monocordia*,.. Single-heartednesse. **1837** T. HOOK *Jack Brag* i, The sincerity and single-heartedness of one of the purest, gentlest Nora Creenas that ever walked. **1857** RUSKIN *Elem. Drawing* ii. 192 The more quietly and single-heartedly you take each step in the art, the quicker.. will your progress be.

**1881** HOWELLS *Foregone Conclusion* x, I would fain have lived single-heartedly.

**'singlehood.** [f. SINGLE *a.* + -HOOD.] The state of being single or unmarried; spinsterhood.

**1840** LADY C. BURY *Hist. of Flirt* xx, My mother.. would not see me the last day of my singlehood. **1881** MRS. A. R. ELLIS *Sylvestra* II. 166 Betty was satisfied with her singlehood so long as [etc.].

**single-horse,** *a.* [f. SINGLE *a.* 18.]

**1.** Of vehicles: Made to be drawn by a single horse; one-horse.

**1764** *Ann. Reg., Chron.* 96/1 He regularly attended unkennelling the fox in his single-horse chair. **1780** *New Newgate Cal.* V. 105 They stopped a single-horse chaise, in which were a Mrs. Constable.. and her servant-maid. **1805** R. W. DICKSON *Pract. Agric.* I. 35 They are.. thought inferior to the single-horse cart. **1851** *Official Catal. Gt. Exhib.* 366 Light single-horse cart, for farming purposes. **1860** W. G. CLARK *Vac. Tour* 49 We engaged a large-wheeled single-horse vehicle.

**2.** Used with or for one horse.

**1798** R. DOUGLAS *Agric. Surv. Roxb.* 50 A smaller hook coming from the middle of two lesser stretchers, or single-horse trees.

**single-line,** *a.* [f. SINGLE *a.* 18.]

**1.** Consisting of or having only a single line of plants, rails, etc. Also, of or pertaining to things ranged in a single line; *spec.* ***single-line traffic*** (see quot. 1954).

**1868** *Rep. U.S. Comm. Agric.* (1869) 256 In single-line hedge the saplings are so wound between as to press against the stakes. **1889** GRETTON *Memory's Harkback* 322 Some few years since a single line railway was made between the two towns. **1897** *Daily News* 1 Sept. 3/1 Between Malvern and Hereford there are two long single-line tunnels. **1924** *Beaver* (Winnipeg) Aug. 410 In the extreme north, single-line hitching [of dogs to sleds], and fan hitching is in general use. **1937** *Burlington Mag.* Feb. 93/2 The National Gallery led the way.. towards the open, single- or double-line hanging which is now the rule. **1954** *Gloss. Highway Engin. Terms (B.S.I.)* 54 *Single-line traffic*, traffic constrained to movement in one direction in a single traffic lane. **1967** G. F. FIENNES *I tried to run Railway* i. 3, I had learned by heart the Block Regulations for double and single lines, the Guard's Rules and the Rules of Single Line Working. **1967** E. LEMARCHAND *Death of Old Girl* xx. 226 There was a bad smash and a big pile-up... It was an hour before they got even single-line traffic going again. **1970** O. JOHN *Diamond Dress* iii. 39 Part of the autostrada is down to single line traffic... Road repairs.

**2.** Taking up, or making, one line in writing or printing.

**1892** A. OLDFIELD *Man. Typogr.* iv, A single-line motto in pearl caps. **1892** PLUMMER *Two Saxon Chron.* I. 132 *n.*, After [the year] 1001 several single-line annals had been marked out.

**single-minded,** *a.* [f. SINGLE *a.* 19.]

**1.** Sincere in mind or spirit; honest, straightforward; simple-minded, ingenuous; single-hearted.

**1577** HARRISON *England* II. i. (1877) I. 34 Or else the single minded bishops shall see the living bestowed upon such as doo deserve it. **1668** H. MORE *Div. Dial.* I. iv. (1713) 10 Such a single-minded Soul as Philopolis will.. prove a glorious Citizen of Heaven. **1815** JANE AUSTEN *Emma* xxxviii, An unpretending, single-minded, artless girl. **1859** MILL *Liberty* ii. 50 Single-minded in his devotion. **1869** LECKY *Europ. Morals* I. 42 The single-minded religious enthusiast, incapable of dissimulation or procrastination.

**2.** Proceeding from or characterized by sincerity or honesty of mind.

**1836** H. ROGERS *J. Howe* iii. (1863) 67 The letters.. serve to show, with what single-minded purpose, these great men laboured. **1864** BURTON *Scot Abr.* I. i. 50 The single-minded fidelity that had been nourished within them.

**3.** Having but one aim or purpose.

**1860** *All Year Round* No. 44. 413 He was a more single-minded and one-idea'd man than even his patron and master.

Hence **single-'mindedly** *adv.*, sincerely, frankly; with singleness of aim or purpose; **single-'mindedness.**

**1579** W. WILKINSON *Confut. Fam. Love* 39 We might.. stand *single myndedly obedient vnto his documentable Sentences. **1876** MEREDITH *Beauch. Career* III. viii. 136 Single-mindedly selfish men may be seen through and through. **1876** F. E. TROLLOPE *Charming Fellow* x, Such force of character as consists in pursuing one's own way single-mindedly. **1833** T. HOOK *Parson's Dau.* II. ii, If *single-mindedness, straightforward policy, and a resolution to do good, are characteristic of simplicity. **1865** *Sat. Rev.* 4 Feb. 148/2 The seriousness and singlemindedness which made him an influence on all who came in contact with him.

**†single money.** *Obs.* [SINGLE *a.* 3.] Small money, small change.

**1591** GREENE *Conny Catch.* II. Wks. (Grosart) X. 117 There came an other and bought a knife and should haue single money againe. **1593** NASHE *Christ's T.* Wks. (Grosart) IV. 96 If there were euer a good fellow.. would sweare and forsweare for single-money. **1625** in Rymer *Fœdera* (1726) XVIII. 143/1 They are growne.. of very necessary and daily Use instead of single Money. **1641** BROME *Joviall Crew* v. i, Tell fortunes, and cozen our poor country-people of their single money. *a* **1693** *Urquhart's Rabelais* III. iv, Gold, Silver, single Money.

**'singleness.** [f. SINGLE *a.* + -NESS.]

**1.** Sincerity, straightforwardness, honesty, integrity; freedom from deceit, duplicity, or guile.

**1526** TINDALE *2 Cor.* ix. 11 That.. ye maye be made ryche in all Synglenes. **1549** COVERDALE, etc. *Erasm. Par. 2 Cor.* 54 The poorer they became.. throughe theyr godly liberalitie, the rycher are they growen in gentle heartes and singlenes. **1796** MME. D'ARBLAY *Camilla* III. 392 Ashamed to have heeded.. advice so contrary to the singleness of the doctrines of her father. *a* **1822** SHELLEY *Assassins* i. Prose Wks. 1888 II. 148 A character superior in singleness and sincere self-apprehension to the slavery of pagan customs. **1845** DISRAELI *Sybil* (1863) 108 With artlessness.. and a degree of earnest singleness. **1874** CREIGHTON *Hist. Ess.* i. (1902) 13 The purity and singleness of his first motive was gone.

**b.** Const. *of* heart, mind, eye, etc.

**1535** COVERDALE *Wisd.* i. 1 Haue a good opinion of the Lorde, & seke him in the synglenesse of hert. **1575–85** ABP. SANDYS *Serm.* xx. 357 The thirde [virtue] is singlenesse of heart. **1660** JER. TAYLOR *Worthy Comm.* i. v. 94 We must speak of his power.. with joyfulness and singleness or simplicitie of heart. **1798** V. KNOX *Chr. Phil.* (ed. 3) Pref. p. x, A consciousness of having, with singleness of heart, espoused a cause beneficial to mankind. **1828** MACAULAY *Hallam* Ess. (1897) 57 Unsparing devotion, boldness of speech, and singleness of eye. **1842** MISS MITFORD in L'Estrange *Life* (1870) III. ix. 154 Miss Martineau is a person of great singleness of mind, sincere and truthful. **1846** J. BAXTER *Libr. Pract. Agric.* (ed. 4) II. p. xxxiii, Respected for his integrity, industry, and singleness of character. **1885** *North Star* 18 May 3/2 Doing what he held to be his life-work with singleness of soul.

**2.** The state or condition of being unmarried, or of not marrying again (quot. *a* 1817); celibacy.

**1560** BIBLE (Geneva) *1 Cor.* vii. 28 *note*, He doth not preferre singlenes as a thing more holy than mariage. **1560** DAUS tr. *Sleidane's Comm.* 437 Whether becometh better the ministers of the church, mariage or singlenesse. **1788** MME. D'ARBLAY *Diary* 24 July, Whether he is happy or not in marrying, I am sure he will be wretched in singleness. **1800** WORDSW. *Michael* 78 His days had not been passed in singleness. His Helpmate was a comely matron. *a* **1817** JANE AUSTEN *Persuasion* i, Sir Walter's continuing in singleness requires explanation. **1881** H. JAMES *Portrait of Lady* xliv, She appeared to have accepted the idea of eternal singleness.

**b.** A single or unmarried person. *rare*$^{-1}$.

**1818** BYRON *Let. to Rogers* 3 March, They are marrying the remaining singleness of the royal family.

**3.** The quality of being single; the fact of consisting of one in number or kind; oneness.

In the Shaks. quotation used punningly for 'simplicity'.

**1592** SHAKS. *Rom. & Jul.* II. iv. 70 O single sol'd ieast, Soly singular for the singlenesse. **1608** ARMIN *Nest Ninn.* (1842) 4 Since all is one, and one all that's car'd for, singlenesse hath such regard [etc.]. **1620** VENNER *Via Recta* viii. 176 Neither alwaies.. ought variety, or singlenes of meats to be exhibited. **1839** MURCHISON *Silur. Syst.* I. xlii. 574 The mind becomes impressed with the singleness of nature's laws. **1841** D'ISRAELI *Amen. Lit.* (1867) 130 The first writers, combining in a singleness of taste, may construct a particular style. **1870** ROLLESTON *Anim. Life* p. xcv, The singleness of the larval velum.

**†b.** Unmixed nature or quality. *Obs.*$^{-1}$

**1695** LD. PRESTON *Boeth.* IV. 194 That pure Simplicity or Singleness, dwelling in the Divine Nature.

**†c.** Singularity. *Obs. rare.*

**1728** R. MORRIS *Ess. Anc. Archit.* 21 Novelty and Singleness were as destroying.. to Art, as all the Barbarism.. of the Enemies of the Romans. *Ibid.* 22 To appear single for the sake of Singleness.

**4.** The fact of standing alone; solitude, solitariness, isolation.

**1805** WORDSW. *Prelude* XIV. 211 Here keepest thou in singleness thy state: No other can divide with thee this work. **1816** BYRON *Chillon* xiii. *note*, From its singleness and diminutive size [it] has a peculiar effect upon the view.

**5.** The quality or fact of having one single aim or purpose; concentration of the faculties upon one object. Const. *of* (purpose, aim, etc.).

**1806** WORDSW. *Happy Warrior* 40 Who comprehends his trust, and to the same Keeps faithful with a singleness of aim. **1833–5** J. H. NEWMAN *Hist. Sk.* (1873) II. II. ii. 234 His unrivalled charm.. lies in his singleness of purpose. **1873** HAMERTON *Intell. Life* x. ii. 344 He lived in it with an unhesitating singleness of purpose. **1886** *Athenæum* 30 Oct. 560/3 His failure seems.. due to a want of singleness of aim.

**single-o,** *sb.*, *a.*, and *adv. U.S. slang* (chiefly *Criminals'*). [f. SINGLE *a.* 1; cf. O *int.* 3.]

**A.** *sb.* **a.** In gaming: ? the number one. **b.** A crime perpetrated without an assistant. Also, a solitary or single person, a loner; *spec.* a criminal who works alone.

**1916** H. L. WILSON *Somewhere in Red Gap* vi. 262 She exposed some very distressing facts about his [*sc.* her husband's] nature the time she put five apiece on the three numbers and the single-o come up. **1930** R. CHADWICK in *Liberty* 5 July 20/2, I have my first experience in single-o jobs... The first single-o is a street heist. **1931** G. IRWIN *Amer. Tramp & Underworld Slang* 170 *Single O*, one working a lone 'game' or 'racket'. One travelling alone for preference. **1942** BERREY & VAN DEN BARK *Amer. Thes. Slang* §461/3 *Single O*, one who works without a confederate.

**B.** *adj.* Solitary, lone; unaccompanied; *spec.* of (one who engages in) criminal activity without an accomplice.

**1930** [see the sb. above]. **1950** *Harper's Mag.* Feb. 71/2 There are 'single-o' heist-men, such as the one known in the papers as Slick Willie, who has robbed large and well-protected banks single-handed, but the vast majority of the brotherhood work in mobs. **1955** D. W. MAURER in *Publ. Amer. Dial. Soc.* XXIV. 83 He [*sc.* a lone pickpocket] is usually referred to as a *single o tool*, a *single handed tool*, or a *single o cannon*.

**C.** *adv.* Alone; independently; without an accomplice.

**1948** *Even. Bull.* (Philadelphia) 7 Apr. 39/7 Instead of working single-o as was his custom. Ernie used an accomplice to drive the getaway car. **1955** D. W. MAURER in *Publ. Amer. Dial. Soc.* XXIV. 100 He's a guy that will muzzle around single o. **1962** 'K. ORVIS' *Damned & Destroyed* xii. 83 Little Faysy wants to go dream-streeting single-o.

**'singler,** *sb. local.* [f. SINGLE *v.*$^1$ 7 + -ER$^1$.] One who singles or thins out plants.

**1878** 'SAXON' *Gall. Gossip* 333 (E.D.D.), Singlers, my boy, singlers;.. they're always grumbling. **1886** *S.W. Lincs. Gloss.* 131 She's gone singling, they can't get singlers enew. **1899** *Dundee Advt.* 21 Nov. 4/2 The singler has more at his control in the making or unmaking of the crop than average observers imagine.

**singler,** variant of SANGLIER, wild boar.

**†'singler,** *a. Obs.* Forms: α. 5 sengler, 5–6 syngler (5 -e), 4–6 singler. β. 5–6 synglar (6 -e). [ad. OF. *sengler*, *seingler*:—L. *singulār-is* SINGULAR *a.*] = SINGULAR, in various senses.

α. *c* **1374** CHAUCER *Boeth.* II. pr. vii. (1868) 57 Nat only þe names of singler men ne may nat strecchen, but eke þe fame of Citees. **1469** *Cal. Rec. Dublin* (1889) 336 If any of the portoures goo owt with cariage into the contry, for ther sengler avayle. **1486** *Bk. St. Albans, Hawking* b iij b, Iff ye haue a chastised hounde,.. vncouple him.. and goo to a sengler partrich. **1514** in *Eng. Gilds* (1870) 146 To alle and syngler covenantes and grauntes. **1579** FENTON *Guicciard.* VII. (1599) 295 Maximilian retaining still a singler ambition in this iorney, would admit no companion.

β. *c* **1470** HENRY *Wallace* XI. 241 Bot for a dog,.. I will haiff nayn, bot synglar as I ga. *c* **1500** *Sc. Poem on Heraldry* 190 in *Q. Eliz. Acad.* 100 The quhiche stanis.. ar so precyus singlare. **1542** UDALL in *Lett. Lit. Men* (Camden) 2 My singlar good Maister.

So **†'singlerly** *adv.*, singularly; **†'singlerty**, singleness. *Obs.*

**13..** *E.E. Allit. P.* A. 429 Now for synglerty o hyr dousour, We calle hyr fenyx of Arraby. *c* **1400** *Apol. Loll.* 8 It longiþ to þe gretnes of God to graunt singlerly þeis priuilegs. *c* **1450** *St. Cuthbert* (Surtees) 714 þe singlerte [L. *solitudo*] of þi lyfis ende. **1487** HEN. VII in *Epist. Acad. Oxon.* (1898) II. 524 Wherby ye shall singlerly please us.

**single-soled,** *a.* [f. SINGLE *a.* 19. Cf. *single-sole* in attrib. use, s.v. SINGLE *a.* 18.]

**1.** Of boots or shoes: Having a single thickness of material in the sole.

**1541** *Extr. Reg. Aberdeen* (1844) I. 453 The best dowbill solit schoine.. and the best singill solit schoine thai can mak. **1596** NASHE *Saffron Walden* F 4, In the single-soald pumpes of his aduersitie. **1640–1** *Kirkcudbr. War-Comm. Min. Bk.* (1855) 149 The inch of single-solled schoes, of the best sort, at xvjd. the inch... The secund sort of single-solled schoes, at xiiijd. the inch. **17..** *Souters of Selkirk* in Scott *Border Minstr.* (1802) I. 249 And up wi' a' the braw lads, That sew the single soaled shoon. **1820** SCOTT *Monast.* xiii, Commendations of her fair guest, from the snood, as they say, to the single-soled shoe. **1862** *Catal. Internat. Exhib., Brit.* II. No. 4977, The fastening can be used with single-soled or light boots.

**†2.** *fig.* Of persons: Poor, mean, of little account or worth. *Obs.*

**1588** FRAUNCE *Lawiers Log.* I. xvii. 62 Singlesowld Lawyers and golden Asses. **1593** P. STUBBES *Motive to Good Wks.* 93 Then should not our land have beene pestered with so many up-start single-soled Gentlemen. **1607** R. C[AREW] tr. *Estienne's World of Wonders* 189 Those silly soules, the singlesoled priests. **1611** COTGR., *Gentilhommeau*, a small, or single-soled, Gentleman; a Gentleman of low degree. **1640** BASTWICK *Ld. Bishops* iv. D 3 b, Excommunication is a Solemne businesse, not to be.. done in a blind Court, and by a single soled Priest.

**single-stick,** *sb.* Also singlestick. [f. SINGLE *a.* + STICK *sb.*] Fighting, fencing, or exercise with a stick provided with a guard or basket and requiring only one hand.

**1771** SMOLLETT *Humph. Cl.* (1815) 200 An exciseman, whom he challenged to a bout at single-stick. **1806** *Sporting Mag.* XXVII. 5 A grand match at single-stick was played at.. Botley. **1848** THACKERAY *Van. Fair* lvii, He larked with the midshipmen, played single-stick with the mates. **1895** SNAITH *Mistress Dorothy Marvin* xxxii, To fence and play singlestick or quarterstaff.

*attrib.* **1881** *Times* 2 Feb. 10/5 The single-stick play.. was remarkable for its ambidexterity. **1885** PASCOE *London of To-day* xiii. 139 The main features of the tournament are single-stick combats, sword and bayonet contests [etc.].

**b.** A stick used for this.

**1837** LOCKHART *Scott* III. i. 8 Tall, vigorous, athletic, a dauntless horseman, and expert at the singlestick. **1850** THACKERAY *Pendennis* xxxi, A man who.. has his opponent's singlestick before him.

**c.** 'A wooden sword used on board ship for teaching the use of the cutlas' (*Cent. Dict.*).

Hence **single-stick** *v. intr.*, to fight or fence with a single-stick.

**1900** G. SWIFT *Somerley* 39, I was Laertes because I could singlestick rather well.

**singlet** ('sɪŋglɪt). Also *dial.* senglet, cinglet. [f. SINGLE *a.* + -ET$^1$, after DOUBLET.]

**1.** An unlined woollen garment (knitted or woven), now usually close-fitting and worn as an undershirt or jersey. Also *attrib.*

*c* **1746** J. COLLIER (Tim Bobbin) *View Lanc. Dial.* (1806) 31 When I.. come to grope in my Singlet pocket for my sawt. **1790** GROSE *Prov. Gloss.*, *Singlet*, a waistcoat not lined, as opposed to a doublet. **1828** CARR *Craven Gloss.*, *Singlet*, an under waistcoat. *c* **1861** J. T. STATON *Rays fro' th' Loominary* 40 Ben Brattles had as good a hert in him.. as ever beat below a senglet. **1885** *Longman's Mag.* V. 493 He desired his dresser to strip off his singlet. **1899** F. T. BULLEN

*Log Sea-waif* 67 My only garments were a flannel singlet and a pair of canvas trousers.

†**2.** A single sheaf (of grain). *Obs. rare.*

**1778** [W. H. MARSHALL] *Minutes Agric.* 18 Aug. 1776, For, in case of rain, it [i.e. wheat] is much safer in singlets, than even in shock. **1796** —— *W. Eng.* I. 175 Setting up mown corn in singlets..would..be the most eligible practice.

**3. a.** *Physics* and *Chem.* A single line in a spectrum, not part of a multiplet; an atomic or molecular energy level or state possessing (in the case of fine structure) zero electronic spin and orbital angular momenta giving only one value of the quantum number *J*, or (in the case of hyperfine structure) zero electronic and nuclear angular momenta, giving only one value of the quantum number *F*; a molecular state in which all electron spins are paired. Freq. *attrib.*

**1920** *Astrophysical Jrnl.* LII. 2 An investigation of the Doppler effect led Stark to the conclusion that the parhelium (singlet) series are due to electronic disturbances in helium atoms which have lost two electrons. **1922** *Phil. Trans. R. Soc.* A. CCXXIII. 137 In the arc spectra of the alkaline-earth elements, in addition to triplet series, there are series of singlets and also certain 'intercombination' lines. **1928** *Proc. R. Soc.* A. CXVII. 147 The general equations of type (18) apply to ortho-helium (considered as a singlet system) as well as par-helium. **1934**, **1937** [see INTERCOMBINATION]. **1972** DEPUY & CHAPMAN *Molec. Reactions & Photochem.* iii. 33 Molecular states with all electrons paired are called singlet states. **1977** *Nature* 3 Nov. 15/3 A number of papers dealt with experimental techniques, especially interesting were those on the use of dye lasers for excitation of singlet oxygen.

**b.** *Particle Physics.* A multiplet (sense b) of one sub-atomic particle.

**1937** *Physical Rev.* LI. 119/2 For an element of the mass [*formula follows*] certain states in which the neutrons are in the doublet, the protons in the triplet state, exactly coincides [*sic*] in approximation (1) with a state in which the neutrons are in the quartet, the protons in the singlet state. **1961**, **1962** [see OCTET, OCTETTE 3 c]. **1977** *Nature* 21 July 202/1 Before the advent of charm in 1976 all known mesons were found to come in multiplets of 9 (nonets) and all known baryons in groups of 1, 8 or 10 (singlets, octets or decuplets).

**single tax.** *Econ.* [f. SINGLE *a.*: tr. Fr. *impôt unique.*] **a.** A tax on that part of land value known as unearned profit (*produit net*), proposed by François Quesnay (1694–1774) and favoured by the Physiocrats. (See esp. quot. 1931.)

**1853** J. R. MCCULLOCH *Sketch Life & Writings F. Quesnay* in *Treat. & Ess. Econ. Policy* 436 It is needless to make any remarks on the exploded notion of Quesnay with respect to agriculture being the only source of wealth, or on his project for consolidating all taxes into a single tax (*l'impôt unique*), to be laid direct on land! **1880** *Nation* 12 Aug. 118/2 All this is accomplished by adopting the *impôt unique* of the physiocrats—the single tax on land—provided the tax be high enough to leave the cultivator nothing but wages [etc.]. **1931** *Amer. Econ. Rev.* XXI. 607 The peculiar characteristic of the Physiocrats' single tax is to be found in the idea of *produit net*. It was not essentially a single tax on land at all. It was a single tax on surplus agricultural products. **1966** A. GILPIN *Dict. Econ. Terms* 185 The Physiocrats..favoured a single tax—an 'impôt unique'—on land, arguing that the cultivation of land was the only work really productive of wealth.

**b.** A tax on land value as the sole source of public revenue, proposed by Henry George (1839–97). Freq. *attrib.*

**1879** H. GEORGE *Progress & Poverty* VIII. iv. 383 The effect of substituting for the manifold taxes now imposed a single tax on the value of land would hardly lessen the number of conscious taxpayers, for the division of land now held on speculation would much increase the number of tax payers. **1891** *Century Mag.* Sept. 795/1 Here we have the core and essence of the single-tax philosophy—confiscation. **1917** *Amer. City* Apr. 384/1 May I..call serious attention to land value taxation—the single tax—which I believe should be regarded as..a satisfactory and just system of revenue. **1926** *Daily Colonist* (Victoria, B.C.) 14 July 2/5 The single tax method of taxation was praised enthusiastically. **1933** H. G. WELLS *Shape of Things to Come* II. 244 Utah had become a practically autonomous Single-Tax State. **1944** G. B. SHAW *Everybody's Political What's What?* xxxvii. 322 If he proves that he knows as much about economic rent as Thomas De Quincey and Henry George did..he must not be asked whether his conclusions are the Conservative ones of De Quincey, the Single Tax of George, or the revolutionary ones of Marx. **1950** *World-Herald Mag.* (Omaha) 26 Mar. 9/2 The once prominent single tax movement, no longer a red hot political issue, is one which has continued on unobtrusively. **1979** *Vole* 8 Nov. 25/1 His [*sc.* George's] Single Tax would confiscate, not the land, but the rents presently paid to owners.

**c.** ***Single Tax Party***, the English name for a Danish political party inspired by the economic principles of Henry George (see sense b above).

**1950** *Manch. Guardian* 15 Sept. 6/2 The most remarkable feature, however, was the rise of the Danish single-tax party (disciples of Henry George who call themselves the Union of Justice). **1961** *Denmark* 91/2 Of new parties the Communist Party and the Single-Tax Party proved to be durable. **1970** W. G. JONES *Denmark* vi. 134 A new part called Danmarks Retsforbund—normally known in English as the Single Tax Party..has had parliamentary representation and is still in existence.

Hence **single-taxer** (also with initial capitals), a believer in the advantages of a single tax; a member of the Single Tax Party.

**1889** *20th Cent.* (N.Y.) 6 Apr. 102/1 He says that is a fair question which no Single-taxer ever answers, but that if it is evaded the whole single-tax theory vanishes. **1934** B. RUSSELL *Freedom & Organization 1814–1914* xi. 124 Both Socialists and Single-Taxers derived their proposals from him [*sc.* Ricardo]. **1941** [see JEHOVAH 2]. **1968** *Times Lit. Suppl.* 25 Apr. 436/5 A front-parlour discussion group that included communists, spiritualists, psychic researchers and single taxers.

†**'singleton**[1]. *Obs.* [a. OF. *singleton*, var. of *sigleton*, etc.: see CICLATOUN.] A coverlet of cloth of gold used in creating a Knight of the Bath.

The quot. is translated from a French account of the ceremonies at the creation of Knights of the Bath, printed in N. Upton *De Studio Milit.*, etc. (ed. Bysshe, 1654) 22.

**1656** DUGDALE *Warwickshire* 533 The Chandler shall take for his Fees..the Bed wherein he first lay, after his Bathing, together with the Singleton and other necessaries. [Hence in Holme (1688) III. 56/1.]

**singleton**[2] ('sɪŋg(ə)ltən). [f. SINGLE *a.* Cf. SIMPLETON.]

**1.** *Card-playing.* In whist or bridge: The only card of a suit in a hand. Also *attrib.*

**1876** CAMPBELL-WALKER *Correct Card* vi. (1880) 41 If..the lead is a singleton..it may be right to put on the ace. **1885** PROCTOR *Whist* Pref., The absolute rejection of the Singleton lead. *Ibid.* viii. 91 While doubt remains as to the position of trump strength, avoid..discarding a singleton.

**2. a.** A single thing, as distinct from a pair.

**1892** *Athenæum* 6 Aug. 191/1 The Duke de Broglie has usually issued the volumes of his elaborate history..in pairs. He now appears with a singleton.

**b.** *Bibliogr.* (See quot. 1952.)

**1952** J. CARTER *ABC for Book-Collectors* 166 *Singleton*, a jargon word (of recent origin in this sense), meaning a single leaf, where a conjugate pair would be expected... A singleton will either be the surviving leaf where the other has been severed for insertion elsewhere, or the severed half in its inset position, or an extra leaf. **1957** [see BIFOLIUM]. **1975** *Anglo-Saxon Eng.* IV. 116 Leaves 5 and 8 in quire 43 are singletons.

**3.** A single entry in a competition. Also *attrib.*

**1898** *Field* 27 Aug. 368 Two instances of singleton entries, and of consequent walks over for the leading prize.

**4. a.** A child resulting from a single rather than a multiple birth.

**1931** A. GESELL in C. Murchison *Handbk. Child Psychol.* vi. 158 Twins have always captured much attention from singletons! **1942** E. B. HURLOCK *Child Devel.* vii. 186 In the size of vocabulary, mean length of sentence, and articulation, twins were retarded as contrasted with singletons of the same age. **1980** *Daily Tel.* 5 Nov. 3/2 Identical twins tend to marry less often than singletons.

**b.** One who is alone or unaccompanied, as an only child or unmarried person. Also *spec.* an undercover agent who operates alone.

**1937** E. M. CHANNON *Son of his Parents* iii. 63 I'm a singleton. But we had an Anglo-Indian kid here for a couple of years, and he and I did our lessons together. **1969** *Daily Tel.* 9 Apr. 14/7 Two wealthy singletons with £5,000 a year apiece would each pay £2,400 10s od and their combined net income would be £5,199; married they would pay £6,083 10s od in tax. **1977** C. MCCARRY *Secret Lovers* iii. 32 He was alone, a singleton in the jargon, living under deep cover, with an ordinary passport and no protection from his government.

**c.** The only one of its kind or class; a set having only one member. Also *attrib.*

**1966** [see INJECTIVE *a.*]. **1975** *Language* LI. 648 A singleton like *perdition* (or *conflagration*)..has no relatives like **perdite* **perditive*. **1977** *Canad. Jrnl. Linguistics* 1976 XXI. 144 The speaker uses the definite description as a characterization of a (singleton) set, whose members he wants to say something about.

**single track,** *sb.* and *a.* [SINGLE *a.*] **A.** *sb.* **1.** A single pair of railway lines (occas. of tramlines). Also (with hyphen) *attrib.*

**1832** *Amer. Rail Road Jrnl.* I. 245/1 The entire length of single track [is] yet to be laid. **1837** H. MARTINEAU *Society in Amer.* II. II. ii. 192 On the 26th of November, 1833, the first car traversed the whole length of the single track. **1869** *Bradshaw's Railway Man.* XXI. 422 There are..190 miles of double track, and 130 miles of sidings.., making the entire length of track equal to 1,137 miles of single track. **1898** *McClure's Mag.* Mar. 390/1 Running a first-class train on a single-track branch. **1942** 'N. SHUTE' *Pied Piper* i. 18 The little engine puffed along its single track, pulling its two old coaches through a country dripping with thawing snow. **1955** A. ROSS *Australia 55* ix. 108 A river runs through it, also a single-track railway line. **1976** P. R. WHITE *Planning for Public Transport* viii. 164 A number of single-track control systems exist, in which the overriding principle is that only one train has authority to occupy a section at any one time.

**2.** A recorded strip on magnetic tape that does not have another strip alongside it, usu. occupying almost the full width of the tape. Also *attrib.* and as *adv.*

**1959** W. S. SHARPS *Dict. Cinemat.* 129/1 *Single-track recorder*, a magnetic tape recorder using a single track, usually the full width of the tape. **1962** A. NISBETT *Technique Sound Studio* vi. 116 It is best to do all original recording single track, and to use other tracks only when copying. **1975** G. N. PATCHETT *F.M. Reception* III. xvi. 162 The whole tape is normally used for professional recording. It is known as single track.

**B.** *adj.* Concentrated on or capable of only one line of thought or action, obsessional, esp. in phr. ***single-track mind*** (chiefly *U.S.*) (cf. *one-track* adj. s.v. ONE *numeral a.* 35); affording no choice or opportunity of divergence.

**1919** *Ladies' Home Jrnl.* Feb. 35/1 The average girl no longer has a single-track mind. **1924** A. J. SMALL *Frozen Gold* iv. 108 Sitka Charley's was a single-track mind; dour and grim and devilishly dogged, but still, single-track. **1933** *Times Educ. Suppl.* 21 Oct. 349/3 In every school, no matter whether it be 'single-track' or 'multi-bias', there will always be a certain number who fail to come up to the standard set by the school. *c* **1942** L. MUMFORD *City Devel.* (1946) 152 To make up for a single-track concentration, there must be range of vision and comprehensiveness of understanding. **1964** *Listener* 26 Mar. 508/1 Under the Criminal Justice Act 1948, the double-track system of preventive detention was replaced by a single-track system. **1978** S. SHELDON *Bloodline* xxxi. 302 Max Hornung had a single-track mind.

**single-tree.** *U.S.* and *Austr.* = SWINGLE-TREE.

**1847** WEBSTER s.v., A single-tree is fixed upon each end of the double-tree when two horses draw abreast. **1858** SIMMONDS *Dict. Trade, Single-tree*, a crosspiece for fastening harness. **1890** 'R. BOLDREWOOD' *Miner's Right* iii. 24 The old mare..moved herself square to a singletree by which her trace-chains were fastened.

**single-valued,** *a. Math.* [SINGLE *a.*] Having a unique value for each value of its argument(s); that maps to one and only one point, number, etc. Hence **single-valuedness**, the property of being single-valued.

**1879** MAXWELL *Electr. & Magn.* (1881) II. 252 The potential of the magnetic system is single valued at every point of space. **1882** [see REVERSE *sb.* I a]. **1946** *Nature* 27 July 128/2 In Indian longitudes..the base of the stratosphere is always sharp and clear-cut and single-valued in summer, but is just one of several inversions in winter. **1968** C. G. KUPER *Introd. Theory Superconductivity* iii. 52 To guarantee single-valuedness, we must impose the flux quantization condition. **1970** G. K. WOODGATE *Elem. Atomic Struct.* ii. 17 Thus $\Phi$, like $\Theta$, is a single-valued function of its argument. This single-valuedness is not a necessary postulate of wave mechanics, but a result derived from the condition that we are working in a central field in $(r, \theta, \phi)$ space.

**single-wicket.** [f. SINGLE *a.* 5.] A form of cricket in which there is only one wicket and consequently only one batsman at a time.

**1736** in Waghorn *Cricket Scores* (1899) 13 Whom they beat before at single-wicket. **1770** J. LOVE *Cricket* 16 Scarce any youth wou'd dare At single Wicket, try the doubtful War. **1833** NYREN *Yng. Cricketer's Tutor* 49 The parties in a match at single wicket vary in number from one to six on a side. **1887** J. ASHBY STERRY *Lazy Minstrel* (1892) 55 She'll vanquish any boy her size At games of single-wicket!

*attrib.* **1736** in Waghorn *Cricket Scores* (1899) 16 A great single-wicket match was played between the three countymen and the three Londoners. **1803** *Laws of Cricket* 9 In single-wicket matches, if the striker moves out of his ground to strike the ball, he shall be allowed no notch.

**'singling,** *vbl. sb.* [f. SINGLE *v.*[1] + -ING[1].]

**1.** The action of the verb; selection from a number; separation from others. Chiefly with *out.*

**1625** BACON *Ess., Dispatch* (Arb.) 249 Order, and Distribution, and Singling out of Parts, is the life of Dispatch. **1660** *Trial Regic.* 79 It is not the singling out of a few persons that makes a Parliament. **1667** *Termes de la Ley* 560 Severance is the singling of two or more that are joyned in a writ. **1911** M. BEERBOHM *Let.* 3 Nov. (1964) 210 Your singling-out of that phrase..is a proof that Rothenstein and Ruskin are right about reverence for nature. **1964** F. BOWERS *Bibliogr. & Textual Crit.* VI. iv. 200 Sir Walter Greg's singling-out of this as the clinching evidence.

**2.** The action of singling or thinning out plants. Also *attrib.*

**1844** H. STEPHENS *Bk. Farm* II. 16 Whether the great deficiency is occasioned by the death of plants after the singling process has been completed?..or the distance left by the singling is greater than we desire? **1899** *Dundee Advt.* 21 Nov. 14 Much of the success in root-growing depends on the singling process.

**3.** *Distill.* (See quots.)

**1830** M. DONOVAN *Dom. Econ.* I. 226 The distillation may proceed as rapidly as [it] can run without coming foul or muddy, until 2400 gallons have been drawn off: these constitute what are called singlings. **1884** KNIGHT *Dict. Mech.* Suppl. 816/1 *Singlings*, the first to come over, the crude spirit of distillation.

**'singling,** *ppl. a. rare.* [f. as prec. + -ING[2].] That renders single or separates.

**1598** MARLOWE *Hero & Leander* I. 258 Wilt thou liue single still? one shalt thou bee, Though neuer-singling Hymen couple thee. **1621** QUARLES *Esther* iii, Till singling Death this sacred knot vndoe, And part this new-made One, once more in two.

**singlo** ('sɪŋləʊ). Also 9 sunglo. [See def.] A kind of green China tea, orig. obtained from the Sung-lo range of hills in the southern part of the province of Gan-hwuy (or Anhui). Also *singlo tea.*

The form SINGLE, occurring in the 18th cent., is prob. a mere error of printing or transcribing.

**1699** OVINGTON *Ess. Tea* 11 The second sort is Singlo, or Soumlo with the Chinese. **1701** *Phil. Trans.* XXIII. 1206 The Bing Tea is the second growth in April: and Singlo the last in May and June. **1760** *Ann. Reg.* 132 The East-India ships..have brought..1,533,200 [lb.] of singlo. **1832** *Veg. Subst. Food of Man* 379 The kind of green tea..most abundant is called Singlo,..the name of a mountain on which it grows. **1852** FORTUNE *Tea Countrys China* 86 Travellers who seek Sunglo tea may now search in vain, that which is sold in the markets is a mere counterfeit.

†**singlure.** *Obs.*$^{-1}$ In 4 synglure. [f. SINGLE *a.*] Singleness, uniqueness.

**13..** *E.E. Allit. P.* A. 8 Quere-so-euer I Iugged gemmez gaye, I sette hyr [the pearl] sengeley in synglure.

**singly** ('sɪŋglɪ), *adv.* Forms: 4 senglely, 5 syngnlelie, 6 singlely; 4 sengeley, -ly, -(l)lic, 5 sengeliche; 4 singelli, 6 singilly, *Sc.* singalie; 4 sengli, 5 senglyche, 6- singly. [f. SINGLE *a.* + -LY², with later contraction as in *simply*, etc.]

**1. a.** As a single thing or person; apart from others or a number; by its (her, him, one) self; separately.

*a* **1300** *E.E. Psalter* cxl[i]. 11 Sengli I am til I forthfare. *c* **1330** R. BRUNNE *Chron. Wace* (Rolls) 6081 Let vs senglely a-wey fare. *c* **1374** CHAUCER *Boeth.* III. pr. ix. (1868) 85 þei ne mowe ȝeuen but o þing senglely of alle þat men seken. *c* **1440** *Alph. Tales* 463 þe same iij hostis at sho had had away syngnlelie, ilkone be þer one, sho broght þaim agayn in hur byll. *a* **1555** LATIMER *Serm. & Rem.* (Parker Soc.) 353 Fearing..lest while singly I have to answer to so many [etc.]. **1597** J. KING *On Jonas* (1618) 70 If there be more Gods, than one, then singlely and apart they must needs haue lesse strength. **1649** DAVENANT *Love & Hon.* v. iii, And wish some man that boasts your masters bloud Were singly here to undergoe their fate. **1673** [R. LEIGH] *Transp. Reh.* 98 He is greater then his subjects singly and apart. **1717** PRIOR *Alma* III. 118 Mingl'd with the neighb'ring Herd, She slights what erst She singly fear'd. **1748** *Anson's Voy.* III. ii. 310 The fruit..grows singly and not in clusters. **1826** LAMB *Pop. Fallacies* xiii, The good things of life are not to be had singly, but come to us with a mixture. **1871** R. ELLIS *Catullus* lxxxvi. 2 Each point singly 'tis easy to grant.

**b.** Without the aid or support of others; unaided, unassisted, single-handed.

**1608** SHAKS. *Tr. & Cr.* III. iii. 247 Hee must fight singly to morrow with Hector. **1633** HEYWOOD *Eng. Trav.* IV. Wks. 1874 IV. 73 Singlie of my selfe I will oppose all danger. **1698** FRYER *Acc. E. India & P.* 173 He was not able to cope with him singly. **1725** POPE *Odyss.* III. 268 Great Ulysses shall suppress these harms, Ulysses singly, or all Greece in arms. **1849** MACAULAY *Hist. Eng.* ii. I. 199 Such was her strength .., that no enemy could singly withstand her.

**2.** †**a.** Simply; without any more. *Obs.*

*a* **1400** *Pistill of Susan* 196 Nou is Susan in sale, sengeliche arayed, In a selken schert, with scholdres wel schene. **1579** *Reg. Privy Council Scot.* III. 127 The said Capitane being in the menetyme singalie accumpanyit with ane servand.

†**b.** Slightly, poorly, ineffectively. *Obs.*⁻¹

**1548** PATTEN *Exped. Scotl.* L v b, Their crosses wear so narrowe and so singly set on, that a puff of wynde might haue blowen them from their brestes.

**c.** Solely, only; merely. Now *rare* or *Obs.*

**1654-66** EARL ORRERY *Parthen.* (1676) 263 Neither was it singly Canitius's treachery, which gave the Roman General this confidence. **1686** BURNET *Trav.* IV. (1750) 177 For if the Pope derives anything from St. Peter, all that is singly in himself. **1740** CHESTERF. *Lett.* c. (1792) I. 279 People do not improve, singly, by travelling, but by the observations they make. **1762-71** H. WALPOLE *Vertue's Anecd. Paint.* (1786) II. 222 Sir Toby Matthew's title to a place in this work depends singly upon a letter from the Duchess of Buckingham to the Duke. **1795** HORSLEY *Serm.* (ed. 2) 235 St. Peter upon this occasion spoke singly for himself.

†**3.** Sincerely, truly, honestly. *Obs.*

**1526** TINDALE *N.T.* To Rdr., My Conscience beareth me recorde, that of a pure entent, singilly and fayethfully I have interpreted itt. **1637** RUTHERFORD *Lett.* (1862) I. lxxxiii. 212 If your Lordship and others with you..set yourselves singly to seek the Lord and His face.

**4.** *Comb.*, as *singly-charged*, *-read*, *-refractive*, *-seated*.

**1711** SHAFTESB. *Charac.* (1737) III. 320 Inquiring.. whether it were the apocryphal scripture, or the more canonical?.. The singly-read, or that of various readings? **1829** BENTHAM *Justice & Cod. Petit., Abr. Petit. Justice* 86 Sufficient..should be the power of the singly-seated absolutist. **1879** RUTLEY *Stud. Rocks* x. 115 A singly-refractive substance containing fixed bubbles also occurs in some sodalite. **1924** *Phil. Mag.* XLVII. 282 The number of particles due to doubly-charged, singly-charged, and neutral helium atoms..varied in number over..a wide range. **1965** PHILLIPS & WILLIAMS *Inorg. Chem.* I. v. 176, *hv* may be taken as the ionization potential of an ion (i.e. for a singly-charged positive ion, the second ionization potential of the element, and for a singly-charged negative ion, the electron affinity of the element).

**singnet**, obs. form of CYGNET, SIGNET.

**singrene**, obs. form of SENGREEN.

**sing-sing**¹. *nonce-word.* [Imitative.] A singing or ringing sound.

**1659** TORRIANO, *Tintínno*, any shrill ting.., gurgling, sing-sing, or sharp sounding of bells or bazons.

**sing-sing**². [Native name.] An African antelope, *Kobus sing sing* or *defassa*. Also *attrib.*

**1854** *Eng. Cycl., Nat. Hist.* I. 254 This animal is called Sing-Sing by all the negroes..The English on the Gambia call it a Jackass-Deer from its appearance. *c* **1875** *Cassell's Nat. Hist.* III. 19 The Nagor,..the Sing-sing, and the Water-buck are closely allied African Antelopes. *Ibid.* 20 The Sing-sing Antelope. **1894** LYDEKKER *Roy. Nat. Hist.* II. 304 The sing-sing (*Cobus defassa*), from Western and Central Africa,..differs from the water-buck by its fine and soft hair.

**sing-sing**³. [Reduplicative pidgin formation f. SING *v.*¹] In Papua New Guinea: an occasion of feasting and musical celebration.

**1899** C. M. E. DAVID *Funafuti* v. 58 Opataia..came to say that there was to be a sing-sing that night in the schoolroom, in honour of the expedition. **1924** E. RAFF *Let.* 10 Jan. in F. E. Williams *Orokaiva Magic* (1928) I. 100 At one of the 'sing sings' (dances) a follower who fell down 'dead' was promptly revived. **1943** S. W. REED *Making of Mod. New Guinea* vii. 211 In the native villages the initiation ceremonies, tribal dances, and *singsing* will continue to express a mode of life utterly foreign to the European. **1968** *Telegraph* (Brisbane) 3 Sept. 18/6 Cattle given to New Guinean farmers for breeding are being killed and eaten at 'sing sings' (festivals).

**sing-song**, *sb.* [f. SING *v.*¹ + SONG *sb.*]

**1.** A ballad, a piece of verse, having musical rather than poetical qualities, esp. one of a monotonous or jingling character.

**1609** *Ev. Woman in Hum.* IV. i. in Bullen *O. Pl.*, My posts shall not be garded with a little sing song. *a* **1661** FULLER *Worthies, Berks.* I. (1662) 86 This sing-song was made on the English by the Scots. **1709** *Brit. Apollo* No. 70. 3/2 Her Sing-Songs..sound as well as Country Ding-Dongs. *a* **1734** NORTH *Examen* I. ii. §130 (1740) 101 There was a Magazine provided of..Pictures and Sing-songs for the Service at Oxford. **1851** D. JERROLD *St. Giles* xxx. 315 A beautiful legend; a nice sing-song to send men to sleep.

*transf.* **1854** MISS BAKER *Northampt. Gloss.*, *Sing-song*, a wearisome repetition of any tale or grievance. 'Don't make such a sing-song about it.'

**2. a.** Verse or rhyme of the above type.

**1693** T. RYMER *Short View Trag.* 34 Campanella tells us, that the German and Gallican Heresie began with Sing-Song, and is carried on by Comedy and Tragedies. **1735** POPE *Prol. Sat.* 226, I ne'er..daggled thro' the town, To fetch and carry sing-song up and down. **1775** MME. D'ARBLAY *Diary, Let. to Crisp* 19 Nov., I would recommend to such worthy judges, the sing-song and prettiness of Waller and Cowley. **1833** *Westm. Rev.* Jan. XVIII. 35 Its place is taken by the despised melodrame, the sing-song of opera. **1856** MERIVALE *Rom. Emp.* I. (1865) VI. 207 His actions are celebrated in most grandiloquent sing-song.

**b.** Tone of voice marked by a monotonous rise and fall, with a kind of singing effect.

**1822** C. B. BROWN *Carwin*, etc. II. 115 Their tone was an insipid sing-song, or a monotonous uniformity. **1835** WILLIS *Pencillings* II. xliii. 43 Crying out the invitation to prayer in a long drawling sing-song. **1887** JESSOPP *Arcady* ii. 50 The fine old Norfolk words, and twang, and squeaky sing-song have gone.

†**3.** A singer, minstrel. *Obs.*⁻¹

**1694** MOTTEUX *Rabelais* v. xviii, Rhimers, Poets,..Sing-songs, Musitianers.

**4. a.** An amateur concert of an informal nature; a convivial meeting where each person is expected to contribute a song. Now more usu. a gathering for, or session of, community singing.

**1769** *Trinculo's Trip* 19 The dinner o'er, the sing-song done. **1857** RITCHIE *Night Side London* 192 The wealthy [have] their 'ancient concerts'—the costermongers what they term their sing-song. **1865** *Slang Dict.* 231 *Sing-Song*, a choral meeting at a pot-house. **1869** J. GREENWOOD *Seven Curses of London* ii. 19 The London factory-bred girl..has her 'young man', and accompanies him of evenings to 'sing-songs' and raffles. **1885** *Times* 11 Feb. 8/1 On Christmas night the whole camp was *en fête*, a capital sing-song having been got up. **1899** KIPLING *Stalky & Co.* II. 252 'Had some rippin' sing-songs in camp, too,' said Tertius. **1914** D. O. BARNETT *Let.* 18 Dec. (1915) 28 We've got some sing-songs and smokers on for Christmas. **1933** *Sun* (Baltimore) 21 Oct. 14/6 Harvard students will..learn old German drinking songs at the German Sing-Song conducted by James W. Hawkes. **1968** 'J. LE CARRÉ' *Small Town in Germany* ix. 147 Wednesday was welfare. Ping pong night. Sing song night. **1974** J. AIKEN *Midnight is Place* i. 30 Ey, David! Coom to t'sing-song at t'Mason's Arms tonight?

**b.** The style of singing usual at a concert or gathering of this description.

**1893** MILLIKEN *'Arry Ballads* 3 A sand-parlour'd shanty devoted to sing-song and swipes.

**5.** *attrib.* **a.** Of persons: Making mere jingling rhyme or monotonous verse; delighting in trivial or simple singing.

*a* **1687** VILLIERS (Dk. Buckhm.) *Poems* (1775) 141 And sing-song Durfey..Lives by his impudence, and not the muses. **1700** T. BROWN tr. *Fresny's Amusem.* 51 The poets ..from Huffing Dryden, to Sing-Song Durfey. **1760** MRS. DELANEY *Life & Corr.* (1861) III. 620 A good-humoured sing-song man. **1794** W. COMBE *Boydell's Thames* I. 282 The severity of the sing-song satirist. **1872** *Punch* 16 Nov. 200/1 You know that the sing-song lot mostly dislike good music.

**b.** Of the nature of sing-song; characterized by a jingling triviality or a monotonous rise and fall.

**1734** *Prompter* 24 Dec. 1/1 Are the Opera's any more than Sing-song Concerts? **1739** WHITEHEAD *Manners* 8 What sing-song Riot, and what Eunuch-squawling. **1810** SCOTT 24 Oct. in *Fam. Lett.* (1894) I. vi. 196, I have other four little tales, or sing-song kind of verses. **1812** *Baker's Biogr. Dram.* II. 313/2 A satire on the sing-song and raree-show insignificance of modern operas. **1832** MACAULAY *Let.* 21 July in *Trevelyan*, Shall I tell you the news in rhyme? I think I will send you a regular sing-song gazette.

**c.** Monotonous in cadence.

**1825** J. NEAL *Bro. Jonathan* I. 89 A regular sing-song intonation. **1857** HUGHES *Tom Brown* i, Repeating in true sing-song vernacular the legend of St. George. **1874** BURNAND *My Time* xxii. 198 He addressed him in an unctuous tone, and in a sing-song style.

**6.** Special Comb.: **sing-song girl**, a Chinese girl who entertains men by singing and dancing (*euphem.* one of easy virtue); **sing-song theory**, the theory (propounded by Jespersen) that language evolved from primitive singing.

**1934** 'A. BRIDGE' *Ginger Griffin* 326 So there will be more war in China because of a foreigner's idle love-letter to a sing-song girl. **1939** AUDEN & ISHERWOOD *Journey to War* 157 Even the singsong girls have changed their style. **1965** J. VON STERNBERG *Fun in Chinese Laundry* iv. 82 On the first floor were gambling tables, singsong girls. **1978** *China Now* Mar./Apr. 19/2 The shocking thing was that in the cities —where officials danced or played with sing song girls— there were grain and food. **1939** L. H. GRAY *Foundations of Lang.* 40 Language has been traced by some to primitive rhythmic chants and to singing (the sing-song theory). **1973** *Current Anthropol.* XIV. 27/3 He makes no reference to Jespersen's classic 'sing-song' theory of language origin (1922). Though this label was applied to Jespersen's hypothesis..by his critics, there seems little doubt that he believed language to have been chanted before it was spoken.

Hence **'sing-,songy** *a.*

**1892** E. LYTTON *Let.* 20 July in E. Lutyens *Blessed Girl* (1953) viii. 155 Vic is made to read poetry aloud to us. He has a very sing-songy voice. **1900** *Pall Mall Mag.* Sept. 107 Reading in deep guttural tones, and in a sing-songy way.

**sing-song**, *v.* [f. prec.]

**1.** *trans.* **a.** To force by means of singing.

**1726** WELSTED *Dissembled Wanton* I. i, In Short, we are Sing-Songed at once out of our Senses and our Money.

**b.** To utter or express in a monotonous chant. Also, with direct speech as obj.

**1867** *Our Young Folks* March (Stand.), Some singsonged the multiplication table. **1882** 'EDNA LYALL' *Donovan* vi, Now they sing-song all the things so, and I can't seem to pick myself up. **1884** *Graphic* 15 Nov. 519/3 One sing-songing the alphabet. **1931** [see CALLER *sb.* 1 e]. **1963** R. WOLFF *I, Keturah* II. iv. 171 'You can't catch me. You can't catch me,' he singsonged. **1976** P. A. LAKE *Leffert's Disease* 173 'I'm sorry, he's not here,' she sing-songed with her nasal twang.

**2.** *intr.* To sing, make verses, utter words, etc., in a sing-song manner.

**1830** W. TAYLOR *Hist. Surv. Germ. Poetry* I. 131 On the linden, birds were thronging, All chirping, warbling, singing songing. **1875** TENNYSON *Q. Mary* II. i, There's no glory Like his who saves his country: and you sit Sing-songing here. **1901** G. DOUGLAS *Ho. w. Green Shutters* 267 He sing-songed, always saying '*this* fine bullock' in exactly the same tone of voice.

‖**singspiel** ('zɪŋʃpiːl). *Mus.* Also **Singspiel**. [Ger., f. *singen* to sing + *spiel* play.] A semi-dramatic performance in which song and dialogue alternate, popular in Germany in the latter part of the eighteenth century.

**1876** F. L. RITTER *Hist. Mus.* 266 The 'Singspiel' or 'operette' as constructed by Hiller, makes use of the spoken dialogue, as does the French comic opera. **1880** *Grove's Dict. Mus.* II. 519/1 That best and truest form of German Opera, the 'Singspiel'. **1911** E. J. DENT *Mozart's Opera 'The Magic Flute'* 4 [Schikaneder] gave a season of German 'Singspiel' (comic opera) at Vienna in the winter of 1784-5. **1930** *Observer* 23 Mar. 25 Many [operettas] of the German 'singspiel' type could be done. **1942** E. BLOM *Music in Eng.* ii. 24 English ballad opera crept into Germany by the back door and served as the direct model for the German *Singspiel*. **1962** *Guardian* 7 Feb. 9/1 Cherubini..evolved a style of *opéra comique*..not unlike the *singspiel* of Mozart ('Seraglio'). **1977** *Times Lit. Suppl.* 10 June 710/5 A more general discussion of *opera seria*, *Singspiel*, etc.

†**singster.** *Obs. rare.* [f. SING *sb.* + -STER.] A singer.

**1388** WYCLIF *2 Sam.* xix. 35 May Y here more the vois of syngeris ether of syngsters? **1553** BECON *Reliques of Rome* (1563) 120* All the worshippyng of God semeth to be set in these singsters. **1606** S. GARDINER *Bk. Angling* 103 The singster of Israel hath taught vs our Lesson.

**singstress.** *rare.* = SONGSTRESS.

**1873** LELAND *Egypt. Sketch-Bk.* 127 When they call a singstress a Ghawâzi, it is as if you were to call Nillson a *corps de ballet*.

**singular** ('sɪŋgjʊlə(r)), *a.*, *adv.*, and *sb.* Forms: α. 4-6 **synguler**, 4-5 **-ere**; 4-7 **singuler**, 4-5 **-ere**, 4-6 **-ier**, 5 **-eer**; 5 **senguler(e**. β. 4-6 **syngular**, 6 (chiefly *Sc.*) **singulair**, 6-7 **-are**; 5- **singular**. [a. OF. *singuler*, *-eir*, *-ier*, and *singulaire*, or ad. L. *singulāris*, f. *singulī* SINGLE *a.* The form with *-er* from OF. continued in use till the 17th cent.]

A. *adj.*

**I. 1.** †**a.** Living alone or apart from the herd.

Only as an inaccurate rendering of L. *singularis ferus* in Ps. lxx[i]x. 14, where *singularis* is the sb. (see SANGLIER).

*c* **1340** HAMPOLE *Ps.* lxxix. 14 þe bare of þe wod outtermyd it; and þe syngulere wildbest has etyn it. **1382** WYCLIF *Ps.* lxxix. 14 The bor of the wode outlawide it; and the singuler wilde beste destroȝide it. *a* **1400** *Minor Poems fr. Vernon MS.* xxiii. 942 Hegge þou a-boute vr vyn-ȝard,..þat woodnes us hurte ne make aferd Of þe wylde best singulere. **1609** BIBLE (Douay) *Ps.* lxxix. 14 The singular wilde beest hath eaten it.

**b.** Alone; away from others; solitary. *rare.*

**1382** WYCLIF *Mark* iv. 10 And whenne he was singuler, or by hym silf, the twelue..axiden hym for to expowne the parable. **1728** VENEER *Sincere Penitent* Pref. p. xi, His way of living was singular and retired. **1787** W. H. MARSHALL *E. Norfolk* (1795) II. 388 *Singular*, lone or single, as a singular house, or farm.

**2. a.** One only; one and no more; single.

In quot. 1377 prob. with allusion to sense 3 a.

**1377** LANGL. *P. Pl.* B. IX. 35 He was synguler hym-self and seyde *faciamus*. *c* **1386** CHAUCER *Pars. T.* ¶ 14 þe repentaunce of a singuler synne & nouȝt repente of alle his oper synnes..may nouȝt auaile. **1485** CAXTON *Chas. Gt.* 221 This geaunte yssued oute of the towne, and demaunded synguler persone ayenst a persone. *a* **1500-20** in *Dunbar's Poems* (1893) App. iv. 8 Thocht sevin ȝeir I war avysit..Ane singulare thing to put in dyte; It suld with sum men be dispysit. **1576** NEWTON *Lemnie's Complex.* (1633) 22 Thus the soule, although it be singular,..yet bringeth forth sundry and manifold actions. **1625** BP. MOUNTAGU *App. Cæsar* 147 Some of the antient Fathers..apply it unto one singular individuall man onely, and no otherwise. **1648** J. BEAUMONT *Psyche* XXI. lvi, Knit up in a most mysterious Knot Of simple singular Triplicity. **1765-8** ERSKINE *Inst. Law Scot.* II. vii. §1 He succeeds to that subject by a singular title.

†**b.** Exclusive; sole. *Obs.*

*c* **1380** WYCLIF *Sel. Wks.* III. 342 Oon mai seie þat he aloone is Cristis viker here in erþe, and he haþ power singuler to taxe gracis as him likiþ. **1395** PURVEY *Remonstr.* (1851) 68 What auctorite is to the bisshop of Rome to approppre to hymsilf principal power, eithir singuler, of byndinge and assoilinge. **1528** ROY *Rede me* (Arb.) 34 The masse was only oure singuler suffrage To delivre the people from their synne. **1592** HARVEY *Foure Lett.* iv. Wks. (Grosart) I. 228 The singular marke, whereat euery Arte & euery vertue is to leuell.

**c.** Forming the only one of the kind; unique, solitary, single. Also (with *the*), sole, only.

*a* **1555** LATIMER *Serm. & Rem.* (Parker Soc.) 101 Now I will shew you what man is..; but I will not speak of that singular Son of man, which was Christ. *a* **1641** BP. MOUNTAGU *Acts & Mon.* (1642) 215 The Copy being singular, and none extant any where else. **1687** A. LOVELL tr. *Thevenot's Trav.* I. 21 The arch whereof is..almost singular in its kind and architecture. *a* **1715** BURNET *Own Time* (1766) I. 2 He was the singular instance in Scotland. **1756** WASHINGTON *Lett.* Writ. 1889 I. 241 A laudable example this, and I hope not singular one. **1788** FRANKLIN *Autobiog.* Wks. 1840 I. 156 This is perhaps a singular instance in the history of mankind. **1881** WESTCOTT & HORT *Grk. N.T.* Introd. §308 Singular readings, as they are usually called, which have no other direct attestation whatever. **1897** *Daily News* 28 Aug. 4/5 But the Reign of Terror is a singular event, and the Commune of 1871..is no parallel whatever.

†**d.** Of practice: Confined to one object. *Obs.*[−1]

**1592** G. HARVEY *Four Lett.* iv. 55 Singular practise the only singuler, and admirable woorkeman of the world.

**3. a.** *Gram.* Denoting or expressing one person or thing. Chiefly in ***singular number*** (also used *fig.*). Opposed to PLURAL *a.* 1.

L. *singularis* appears in this sense from the time of Varro onwards.

**1387** TREVISA *Higden* (Rolls) IV. 17 Evericheh in þe singuler nombre was i-cleped Anthiochus. **14..** *Crowned King* (Skeat) 46 To shewe you my sentence in singuler noumbre; To peynte it with pluralitee my prose wolde faile. **1530** PALSGR. Introd. p. xxvi, Theyr synguler nombre hath a great meyny of dyvers terminations. **1561** T. NORTON *Calvin's Inst.* I. 21 b, They simply vsed the singular name of God as if they were contented with one God alone. **1591** PERCIVALL *Sp. Dict.* B 3, There are two numbers, the singular speaking of one, the plurall of moe. **1611** COTGR. s.v. *Que*, An interrogatiue of the Singular Number. *a* **1708** BEVERIDGE *Thes. Theol.* (1711) I. 258 Why, *I believe*, in the singular number? **1818** STODDART *Gram.* in *Encycl. Metrop.* I. 64/1 (1845) We call 'I love' singular, and 'we love' plural. **1872** MORRIS *Eng. Accidence* 99 *Alms, eaves, riches*, though treated as plurals, are singular in form. *Ibid.* 100 *Summons* is a singular form..and is usually treated as such, making the pl. *summonses*.

**b.** *Logic.* (See quots.)

After various uses of L. *singularis* in scholastic logic: cf. the note to B. 1 d.

**1654** Z. COKE *Logick* 200 A singular accident is [that] which cleaves to a singular substance. **1697** tr. *Burgersdicius' Logic* II. viii. 32 Singular syllogisms depend upon this maxim, whatever things agree in one single third, those also agree amongst themselves. **1724** WATTS *Logic* I. iii. §3 That idea which represents one particular determinate thing to me, is called a singular idea. **1846** MILL *Logic* I. ii. §3 An individual or singular name is a name which is only capable of being truly affirmed, in the same sense, of one thing. *Ibid.* iv. §4 The proposition is singular when the subject is an individual name. **1855** ABP. THOMSON *Laws Th.* §74 A judgment about an intuition, as 'Northumberland House is near Charing Cross', is a Singular judgment. **1870** JEVONS *Elem. Logic* iii. (1875) 18 A singular term is one which can denote only a single object.

**c.** *Math.* (See quots.) ***singular matrix*** (see quots. 1964, 1972); ***singular solution***, a solution of a differential equation that cannot be obtained directly from the complete primitive; *esp.* a solution whose graph is the envelope of the graphs of the complete primitive.

**1836** A. DE MORGAN *Differential & Integral Calculus* xi. 191 If there be a singular solution it is $y = a$.. We have only found the singular solution from the primitive itself. **1845** —— in *Encycl. Metrop.* II. 370/1 There is..what we may call a *singular* solution for every particular form of $\theta$, which deserves the attention of mathematicians. **1859** G. SALMON *Less. Introd. Higher Algebra* 45 We shall call those values which make all the differentials vanish, the *singular roots* of the quantic. **1867** BRANDE & COX *Dict. Sci.*, etc. III. 461/2 A singular solution of a differential equation..is a function of $x$ and $y$ [etc.]. *Ibid.* 462/1 The discovery of such solutions depends upon that of singular integrals of the differential equation under consideration. **1869** CAYLEY *Math. Papers* VII. 244 Certain forms of the singular curve. **1873** —— in *Messenger of Math.* II. 12, I consider the singular solution to be that given by the equation which belongs to the envelope-locus (viz. I do not recognise any singular solution which is not of the envelope species). **1886** —— *Math. Papers* XII. 395 The point $x = a$ is in this case said to be a singular point in regard to the differential equation. **1957** L. FOX *Two-Point Boundary Probl.* i. 2 The most general solution of an ordinary differential equation of order $n$ contains $n$ arbitrary constants. This general solution is called the Complete Primitive, and a Particular Integral is obtained by giving specific values to these arbitrary constants. Non-linear equations may also have singular solutions, not obtainable from the complete primitive. **1964** N. N. HANCOCK *Matrix Anal. Electr. Machinery* ii. 18 A 'singular' matrix is one for which the determinant formed by the same array is of zero value. **1972** A. G. HOWSON *Handbk. Terms Algebra & Anal.* viii. 43 If there is no matrix $B$..such that $AB = BA = I$, then $A$ is said to be singular.

**4.** Of persons: †**a.** Holding no office; having no special position; private. *Obs.*

*c* **1386** CHAUCER *Melib.* ¶40 (Cambr. MS.), Ryȝt as a senguler persone synnyth in takynge vengeaunce of a-nothir man, righ[t] so synnyth the Iuge ȝif he do no vengeaunce. *c* **1400** *Brut* ccx. 242 þat fro þis day afterward ȝe shulle nouȝt be cleymede Kyng,..but..shul bene holde a singuler man of all þe peple. **1526** *Pilgr. Perf.* (W. de W. 1531) 8 b, As moche as is in me, I forbede all synguler persones from the studyenge of this treatyse. **1583** STUBBES *Anat. Abus.* II. 79 You would not haue anie priuate or singuler man of what degree soeuer, to haue the patronage..of anie ecclesiastical liuing.

**b.** ***singular successor***, in Scots Law, one who acquires feudal property by a single title (usually that of purchase) as distinguished from an heir, who succeeds by a general or universal title.

*c* **1630** SIR T. HOPE *Minor Practicks* (1726) 138 The Assignation will not be valid against a singular Successor who acquires a real..Right with the Liferent. **1747** *Act 20 Geo. II*, c. 50 §12 The Methods of procuring Entry by Heirs, or Singular Successors, or Purchasers of lands in Scotland. **1797** HOME & KAMES *Decis. Crt. Session* IV. 69 It was a fixed point, that general burdens are ineffectual against creditors and singular successors. **1838** W. BELL *Dict. Law Scot.* 957 He holds them as his inherent right,..of which he cannot be deprived..by the right of the vassal's heir or singular successor. **1887** *Pall Mall Gaz.* 9 Aug. 4/1 It is a quibble of the worst kind..first to tax them as singular successors and then to tax the heir when he succeeds to the family property.

†**5.** Of a fight or combat: = SINGLE *a.* 15. *Obs.*

From the 16th cent. chiefly in Sc. use.

**1382** WYCLIF *1 Sam.* xvii. 8 Chesith of ȝou a man, and come he doun to a synguler strijf. **1432-50** tr. *Higden* (Rolls) III. 331 Lucius Mallius callede a Frensche man to a singuler bataile. **1483** CAXTON *Gold. Leg.* 65 b/2 They shold chese a man to fight a synguler batail ayenst golyas. **1567** *Reg. Privy Council Scot.* I. 525 He had cowartlie refusit singular combat bayth of a Barroun and Gentilman undefamit. **1606** BRYSKETT *Civ. Life* 66 The singular fights or combats.. happened evermore betweene enemies of contrary nations. **1678** SIR G. MACKENZIE *Crim. Laws Scot.* I. xii. §2 Wherein singular Combats are discharged, there is an exception made of such as are fought with His Highness licence. **1752** J. LOUTHIAN *Form of Process* (ed. 2) 22 Of old, the Party accused had his Election, whether to vindicate himself, by singular Combat, or be tried by an Inquest. **1826** SCOTT *Woodst.* xiv, Those in his high place fight no singular combats.

†**6.** Single in form or dimensions. *Obs.*[−1]

**1452** in Willis & Clark *Cambridge* (1886) I. 282, iij sengulere Principalls..in Scantlyon accordyng to the Principalls.

**II.** †**7. a.** Separate, individual, single. *Obs.*

*c* **1340** HAMPOLE *Pr. Consc.* 7457 þan bihoves þam,.. For ilka syn þat þai dyd here, Have certayne payne singulere. **1387-8** T. USK *Test. Love* III. vi. (Skeat) l. 59 Right as everich hath thus singuler instrumentes by hemselfe, they han as wel dyvers aptes and dyvers maner usinges. **1414** *Rolls of Parlt.* IV. 58/2 To be bounde to hem, and to othere persones,..in singuler obligacions. *c* **1430** LYDG. *Minor Poems* (Percy Soc.) 63 In whiche psalmes..in synguler lettris fyve, This blessid name Maria, there may he see. **1578** BANISTER *Hist. Man* I. 5 It is tyme we approche to the singular description of Bones. **1592** tr. *Junius on Rev.* i. 4 This is the particular or singular inscription. **1614** RALEIGH *Hist. World* III. (1634) 127 He equalled all others in the seuerall vertues, which in each of them were singular. **1668** CULPEPPER & COLE *Barthol. Anat.* I. xxviii. 68 The confusion and rupture as it were, of the singular determinate parts. **1701** SWIFT *Contests Nobles & Commons* v, That because Clodius and Curio happen to agree with me in a few singular notions, I must therefore blindly follow them in all. **1719** LONDON & WISE *Compl. Gard.* 135 Common Remarks for certain singular Cases relating to the Pruning of all manner of Trees.

†**b.** Esp. in ***singular man*** or ***person***. *Obs.*

*c* **1380** WYCLIF *Sel. Wks.* III. 442 þe generalte of þis preyere lettes not oure Lord God to here syngulere personys, aftur þei ben worþi. *c* **1450** PECOCK *Bk. Faith* I. vii. (1909) 89 Every singuler persoone of the same chirche. *a* **1513** FABYAN *Chron.* VII. (1811) 244 Lyke as one man is kynde of all synguler men, and in euery synguler man is yᵉ kynde of all mankynde. **1523** LD. BERNERS *Froiss.* I. ccxii. 260 Our subiectes, comons, colleges, vniuersities, or syngular personnes, what someuer they be. **1615** CROOKE *Body of Man* 243 Not..for conseruation of the life of the *indiuiduum* or singular man, but for propagation of the whole species. **1642** JER. TAYLOR *Episc.* (1647) 93 The succession therefore..was made by singular persons, not by a Colledge. *a* **1677** BARROW *Serm.* Wks. 1716 II. 85 Thus doth humane nature, being in each singular man, shew the existence of..its original author and pattern.

**c.** In phr. ***all and singular***, every one. Also rarely ***each and singular***. Now *arch.*

(*a*) **1472** *Rec. St. Mary at Hill* (1905) 17 To..fulfille all & singuler my willes & ordenaunces herevnder wreten. **1546-7** *Test. Ebor.* (Surtees) VI. 248 All and singuler thos my landes. **1583** in Feuillerat *Revels Q. Eliz.* (1908) 360-1 Summa Totallis of..all & singuler the paimentes. **1656** SANDERSON *Serm.* (1689) 20 All and singular the 39 Articles. **1739** *Col. Rec. Pennsylvania* IV. 346 Inviolably observed in all and singular the parts thereof. **1781** *Articles of Confederation U.S.* §13 Each and every of the said Articles .., and all and singular the matters..therein contained. **1838** in W. Bell *Dict. Law Scot.* 558 All and singular the felonies,..and all and singular other the premises.

(*b*) **1535-6** *Act 27 Hen. VIII*, c. 42 §1 The tenthe of all and singuler dignyties. **1552** *Bk. Com. Prayer, Ordering of Deacons*, All and synguler actes and Statutes. **1838** in W. Bell *Dict. Law Scot.* 558 The truth..of all and singular articles and circumstances.

(*c*) **1667** DRYDEN *Maiden Q.* I. i, With both of 'em; with each and singular of 'em. **1843** GEO. ELIOT in Cross *Life* (1885) I. 123 To say to all and singular, 'Swallow my opinions and you shall be whole'. **1875** STUBBS *Const. Hist.* II. xiv. 152 The common concordant and unanimous consent of all and singular.

†**8. a.** Of or pertaining to, connected with or affecting, the individual, in contrast to what is common or general; personal, private, one's own.

*c* **1340** HAMPOLE *Prose Tr.* 5 When I had takene my syngulere purpos and lefte þe seculere habyte. *c* **1380** WYCLIF *Sel. Wks.* III. 509 Alle persones of what kynne privat sectis, or singuler religioun. *c* **1380** —— *Wks.* (1880) 82 To seie þe pater noster þat crist made hym self, & not.. singuler preieres made of vs self. *c* **1400** LOVE *Bonavent. Mirr.* (1908) 60 And for they wolde no singuler prerogatif thei kepten the comoun lawe as othere. **1475** *Bk. Noblesse* 7 The duc off Burgoyn..slow many thowsands..to revenge a synguler querel. **1514** BARCLAY *Cyt. & Uplondyshm.* (Percy Soc.) 33 Of lyberte, wyll, & synguler pleasure,..poore people they devour. **1581** J. BELL *Haddon's Answ. Osor.* 92 b, Not accordyng to the proportion of that singular righteousnesse whiche is of ourselves, and peculiar to every of us. **1651** BIGGS *New Disp.* 18 Many truths, now of reverend esteem and credit, had their birth and beginning once from singular and private thoughts. **1692** R. L'ESTRANGE *Josephus, Antiq.* IV. vi. (1733) 87 Yours is a singular God, that's only to your selves.

†**b.** *esp.* Of profit, advantage, gain, etc. *Obs.*

*c* **1384** CHAUCER *Ho. Fame* I. 310 That shal be take for delyte, Loo, or for synguler profite. **1390** GOWER *Conf.* III. 152 Anon for singulier beyete Drouh every man to his partie. **1422** tr. *Secreta Secret., Priv. Priv.* 132 Sum Pryncis ther bene, that for thar owyn Synguler auauntage..takyn atte har talent trew men goodis. **1474** CAXTON *Chesse* III. iii. (1883) 95 For they entende to theyr synguler wele and prouffyt and not to the comyn. **1542** UDALL *Erasm. Apoph.* 257 b, One that preferred the dignitee..of the commenweale, before his owne singulare avauntage. **1581** W. STAFFORD *Exam. Compl.* ii. (1876) 61 For a time they gat much, and so abased the credite of theyr Predecessors to theyr singuler Luker. **1656** EARL MONM. tr. *Boccalini's Pol. Touchstone* (1674) 280 The Spaniards (whose proper nature it is, to reap singular profit from the fear in which they.. have put..neighbouring Princes).

†**c.** Special; peculiar *to* one. *Obs. rare.*

**1500-20** DUNBAR *Poems* lxxxiii. 31 And to ȝour schervand singulair, Welcum, my awin Lord Thesaurair. **1590** SIR J. SMYTH *Disc. Weapons* 2 The excellent effects of our peculiar and singular weapon the Long Bowe. *c* **1710** CELIA FIENNES *Diary* (1888) 266 Common Law which is singular to our nation.

**III.** †**9. a.** Separate from others by reason of superiority or pre-eminence. *Obs.*

**1377** LANGL. *P. Pl.* B. XIII. 283 So syngulere by hym-self as to syȝte of þe poeple, Was none suche as hym-self. ?*a* **1400** *Morte Arth.* 172 Twa knyghtes hym servede, Singulere sothely, as Arthure hym selvyne. **1613** DAY *Dyall* ix. (1614) 234 Are we not bound to keep it [the Sabbath] singular and inviolable. **1635** PAGITT *Christianogr.* II. v. (1636) 31 Lucifer, that would have beene singular, and alone above all his fellow Angels.

†**b.** Of persons: Eminent, distinguished, notable.

**1497** BP. ALCOK *Mons Perfect.* i. 1 A suppreme & a synguler mayster to teche you al thynge. **1554** in Strype *Eccl. Mem.* (1822) III. App. xx. 58 If..ye neglect so singular a pilot in such a tempest of affairs. **1581** MARBECK *Bk. of Notes* 1 Common places..gathered out of the workes of diuers singular Writers. **1606** CHAPMAN *Mons. D'Olive* I. i, Her behaviour to it Is like a singular musitian To a sweete instrument. **1647** LILLY *Chr. Astrol.* clxvi. 710 A late Minister of the Church of England, and a Singular Astrologian. **1691** WOOD *Ath. Oxon.* I. 817 A great Linguist, a singular Grecian, and an exact Philologer.

†**c.** Used in forms of address, esp. to a person of title. *Obs.* (Common in the 16th c.)

In later use only with *good*: cf. 14.

*c* **1450** HOLLAND *Howlat* 483 My singuler souerane, of Saxonis the wand! **1485** CAXTON *Chas. Gt.* 3 To satysfye.. my good synguler lordes..I haue enprysed..to reduce this ..book in to our englysshe. *a* **1555** LATIMER *Serm. & Rem.* (Parker Soc.) 367 To the right honourable master, secretary to the king's grace, his singular good master. **1586** A. DAY *Eng. Secretary* I. (1625) 19 To the right Worshipfull and my singular good Lady Mother. **1616** W. HAIG *Let.* in J. Russell *Haigs* (1881) vii. 155 To the Right Honourable my singular good Lords, the Earl of Dunfermline [etc.]. **1638** JUNIUS *Paint. Ancients* Ded. A 2, The Countesse of Arundell and Surrey, my singular good Ladie and Mistresse.

†**d.** Specially active *in*, or good *at*, something.

**1606** in *Lismore Papers* Ser. II. (1887) I. 98 The humble affection we have to be singulare in your service. **1654** GAYTON *Pleas. Notes* IV. ii. 183 With Pathetick expressions, which he was singular at, the Manchegan could not choose but melt into pity.

**10.** Above the ordinary in amount, extent, worth, or value; especially good or great; special, particular. Common from *c* 1500 to *c* 1650; now *rare.*

**a.** Of immaterial things, qualities, etc.

*α.* *a* **1340** HAMPOLE *Psalter* lxxix. 14 þe deuel..is þe wild best þat is of syngulere creulte. *Ibid.* p. 523 This blessid mayden..in syngulere ioy..was glad in cryst. **1424** HEN. VI in Ellis *Orig. Lett.* Ser. II. I. 99 The singulier diligence and the ful notable service that ye doon unto us. **1477** EARL RIVERS (Caxton) *Dictes* 1 To gyue therfore synguler louynges and thankes. **1566** *Pasquine in Traunce* 110 The same is a singuler token and most plaine demonstration of his worde. **1585** T. WASHINGTON tr. *Nicholay's Voy.* I. ii. 1 b, My Lady of Aramount of most feruent desire and singuler affection was attending her husbande.

*β.* *c* **1460** FORTESCUE *Abs. & Lim. Mon.* xvii. (1885) 152 And so þe kynge shall lese the offices, as ffor any syngular service he shall haue ffor hem. **1509** FISHER *Funeral Serm. C'tess Richmond* Wks. (1876) 291 She was also of singular easynes to be spoken vnto. **1579** W. WILKINSON *Confut. Fam. Love* A ij b, An euident declaration of the singular good will..of God towardes his creatures. **1612** BRINSLEY *Pos. Parts* (1669) p. v, I find a singular benefit hereby in causing all my lowest to stand or sit together. **1651** HOBBES *Leviath.* II. xxviii. 164 Offices, or any other singular marke of the Soveraigns favour. **1725** DE FOE *Voy. round World* (1840) 277 To our singular satisfaction we found the water..ran.. eastward. **1769** ROBERTSON *Chas. V*, x. III. 219 For this, too, he found an expedient with singular art and felicity. **1841** MYERS *Cath. Th.* III. §28. 104 The instance..is of singular significance in this matter. **1847** HELPS *Friends in*

*C.* I. iv. 56 A theory that has done singular mischief to the cause of recreation.

†**b.** Of remedies, medicines, etc.: Excellent; highly efficacious or beneficial. In predicative use freq. const. *against* or *for*. *Obs.*

(*a*) *a* **1340** HAMPOLE *Psalter* xvii. 7 My lord; þat is remedy syngulere amange anguysses of þis warld. **1398** TREVISA *Barth. De P.R.* XIX. lxxiii. (1495) 904 Butter taken in to the body is a synguler helpe ayenst venym. **1538** STARKEY *England* II. i. 152 A syngular remedy for the sklendurnes of our polytyke body. **1615** MARKHAM *Country Contentm.* I. xvii, Cast out all the mud and filth, which is a singular compost for Land, upon the bank. **1657** W. COLES *Adam in Eden* lvii, It is a singular drink for the falling sickenesse. **1694** SALMON *Bate's Dispens.* (1713) 245/1 It is a singular Thing against a Gonorrhæa.

(*b*) **1578** LYTE *Dodoens* 55 Pimpernell.. is singuler against the bytings of venemouse beasts. **1600** SURFLET *Countrie Farme* I. xii. 70 In the paine of the hemorrhoides there is nothing more singular then the perfume made of shauings of iuorie. **1657** S. PURCHAS *Pol. Flying-Ins.* 174 It [i.e. honey] is singular for gout and for the cure of all wounds. **1712** tr. *Pomet's Hist. Drugs* I. 4 It is singular for the Stone.

†**c.** Of persons. (Cf. 9 b.) *Obs.*

**1485** CAXTON *Paris & V.* (1868) 54 Dere and specyal brother and synguler frende. **1605** BACON *Adv. Learn.* I. vii. §4 Six princes, all learned, or singular favourers and advancers of learning. **1654** tr. *Martini's Conq. China* 132 One only City.., whose President was.. my very singular friend. **1738** tr. *Guazzo's Art of Convers.* 6 A most able Physician and singular Friend.

**11.** Remarkable; extraordinary, unusual, uncommon. Hence, rare, precious.

A common sense of *singularis* in classical Latin.

*c* **1400** *Pilgr. Sowle* (Caxton) v. v. (1859) 76 There I sawe a merueylous cerkle, of syngulere gretnesse. **1474** CAXTON *Chesse* III. vi. (1883) 133 Boece whiche was.. tresor of rychesses, singuler house of sapience. **1526** *Pilgr. Perf.* (W. de W. 1531) 1 b, I sholde haue a synguler iewell to bere in my bosom. **1585** T. WASHINGTON *Nicholay's Voy.* IV. vi. 117 [They] are much giuen to.. vsing singular perfumes. **1643** SIR T. BROWNE *Relig. Med.* 54, I could not chuse but say, it was the singularest, and superlative piece that hath been extant since the Creation. *a* **1680** BUTLER *Rem.* (1759) II. 5 A great Philosopher,.. famous far and near, As one of singular Invention. **1766** PORNY *Elem. Heraldry* v. (1777) 140 Had it not been for the singular conduct of this brave person, the King had then remained a prisoner. **1779** *Mirror* No. 62, This was a proof of his good-nature, as well as of his singular presence of mind in critical situations. **1812** WOODHOUSE *Astron.* xiii. 135 One or two theorems of singular geometrical elegance and beauty. **1853** J. H. NEWMAN *Hist. Sk.* (1873) II. I. i. 30 The Romans.. admired the singular quality and workmanship of the wooden columns. **1862** STANLEY *Jew. Ch.* (1877) I. i. 9 To refuse to do so would be to decline the use of.. a singular gift of Providence.

†**12.** Differing *from* others in opinion; standing alone; peculiar in this respect. *Obs.*

**1621** BP. MOUNTAGU *Diatribæ* 152 Iarhi, you confesse, was of another minde; and thinke you, that Iarhi was therein singular from all the old Iewes? **1653** WALTON *Angler* I. v, Lest you will think him singular in this opinion, I will tell you, this seems to be believed by our learned Doctor Hakewill. **1709** POPE *Ess. Crit.* 425 The Vulgar thus through Imitation err; As oft the Learn'd by being singular. **1754** FRANKLIN *Lett.* Wks. 1887 II. 343, I find the author has been led.. to the same strange conclusion.. in which I feared I should for some time have been singular. **1791** BOSWELL *Johnson* Feb. 1766, Sir, he must be very singular in his opinion, if he thinks himself one of the best of men.

**13.** Different from or not complying with that which is customary, usual, or general; strange, odd, peculiar.

*a* **1684** LEIGHTON *Wks.* (1835) I. 119 It is no Wonder that the Godly are by some called Singular and Precise. *a* **1700** EVELYN *Diary* 27 Apr. 1667, Suitable to her extravagant humour and dresse, which was very singular. **1774** GOLDSM. *Nat. Hist.* (1776) IV. 341 Its manner of procuring its prey, is one of the most singular in all natural history. **1794** MRS. RADCLIFFE *Myst. Udolpho* xxxiv, In one of my excursions.. I overheard a singular conversation. **1824** LANDOR *Imag. Conv.* Wks. 1846 II. 155 He was called strange and singular long before he was acknowledged to be great. **1860** TYNDALL *Glac.* I. vii. 55, I clambered up among these singular terraces. **1875** MANNING *Mission Holy Ghost* vii. 189 Those who make themselves singular in their dress and manners are seldom free from vanity.

†**14.** Quasi-*adv.* Singularly, especially, particularly. *Obs.* (Cf. 9 c.)

**1530** PALSGR. 270/2 Synguler pure thyng, *chose deslite*. **1548–9** *Bk. Com. Prayer, Offices* (Mar.) 23 That shall be to hym a singuler great coumforte. **1581** W. STAFFORD *Exam. Compl.* iii. (1876) 90 When a singuler good workeman in any mistery comes. *a* **1604** HANMER *Chron. Irel.* (1809) 123 Hee proved a singular learned man. *Ibid.* 318 The Realme of Ireland at this time was singular well governed. **1693** CONGREVE *Old Bach.* I. iv, A singular good principle.

**15.** *Comb.*, as ***singular-looking***, ***-minded***, ***-witted*** adjs.

**1610** HEALEY *St. Aug. Citie of God* VIII. xii. 302 He was an admirable, singular witted man, inferior to none. **1815** SCOTT *Guy Mann.* xxiii, This wild and singular-looking woman. **1831** —— *Ct. Robert* vii, The survivors of these singular-minded men. **1878** SMILES *Robt. Dick* iii, [He] took up a singular-looking nut.

**B.** *sb.*

**1. a.** A single person; an individual. Now *rare*.

**1420** in Rymer *Foedera* (1710) IX. 917 Tounes, Comunaltees and Singulers. **1549** COVERDALE, etc. *Erasm. Par. Thess.* 14 So deare a singular, and so necessarie a companion. **1619** W. SCLATER *Exp. 1 Thess.* (1630) 15 Of Singulars, all we haue, is a probable conjecture. *a* **1637** B. JONSON *Timber* Wks. (Rtldg.) 756/1 Eloquence would be but a poor thing, if we should only converse with singulars; speak with man and man together. **1854** S. DOBELL *Balder* xxiv. 158 This.. I give To thee, and am no poorer; no, nor thou.., nor a singular of all Who ever shall possess it.

**b.** A single thing; a single point or detail.

**1615** CROOKE *Body of Man* 700 All compound thinges are of greater force then Singulares. **1620** E. BLOUNT *Horæ Subs.* 204 As for *Epitomes*.. for one that meanes to goe through all the singulars; they seeme quite vnnecessary. *a* **1711** KEN *Hymnarium* Poet. Wks. 1721 II. 121 The whole Creation heedfully survey, Each Singular minutely weigh.

**c.** Contrasted with a class or species.

**1640** *Canterburians Self-Conviction* Postscr. 1 To make them but two singulars under one spece. **1642** H. MORE *Song of Soul* II. II. III. xxvi, She.. Calls kinds immortall, though their singulars do waste. **1661** GLANVILL *Van. Dogm.* 124 Every man.. owns something, wherein none are like him: and these are as many, as humane nature hath singulars. **1832** AUSTIN *Jurispr.* (1879) II. 1037 A species; that is to say, a class consisting exclusively of mere individuals or singulars.

**d.** *pl.* Contrasted with universals.

The use of L. *singulare*, *-aria*, in contrast to *universale*, *-alia*, goes back to Boëthius.

**1643** DIGGES *Unl. Taking Arms* ii. 46 This notion of universall speculatively distinguished from singulars. **1669** GALE *Crt. Gentiles* I. I. i. 4 His Universal Ideas.. he makes to be the.. great Exemplar and image of al singulars. **1690** C. NESS *Hist. O. & N.T.* I. 29 Adam wisely understood all simples, singulars and universals. **1737** *Gentl. Mag.* VII. 15 Think you, that God's Providence is.. employ'd about Universals?.. But if God takes care of Singulars [etc.]. **1864** BOWEN *Logic* vii. 180 Their Knowledge being confined, as we have seen, to Intuitions,—to Singulars.

**2.** *Gram.* The singular number; a word in its singular form.

**1398** TREVISA *Barth. De P.R.* XVII. cxxxiii. (Bodl. MS.), *Porrum* is *hoc Porrum* in þe singuler & *hii porri* in þe plurel. **1530** PALSGR. 127 Howe all maner participles forme theyr.. plurel nombres out of theyr singulars. *a* **1637** B. JONSON *Eng. Gram.* I. xiii, The first [declension] maketh the plural of the singular, by adding thereunto *s*. **1751** HARRIS *Hermes* Wks. (1841) 162 The.. imperative has no first person of the singular. **1799** *Asiatic Researches* II. 211 Their Feminine Singulars are used in the Persian as Participles. **1839** *Penny Cycl.* XIII. 313/1 The aspirate has taken the place of the τ or σ in the nominative singular. **1872** MORRIS *Eng. Accidence* 99 The plurals of some substantives differ in meaning from the singulars.

†**3.** Personal or private profit or gain. *Obs.*$^{-1}$

**1419** in *26 Polit. Poems* 71 For defaute of Iustice, and singulere to wynne, þey were rebell.

†**4.** A single or ordinary rafter. *Obs.*

Cf. the mod. Somerset *singler* (Elworthy *Word-bk.* 671). **1452** in Willis & Clark *Cambridge* (1886) I. 282 Atte euery joynt of the Crest tre atte the Principalls and sengulers shalbe halff Angells. Also atte.. euery end of the sengulers atte the Jowpye shalbe an Angel.

†**5.** = SANGLIER. *Obs. rare.*

**1486** *Bk. St. Albans* e iij, A Synguler is he so: for a lone he will goo. **1688** [see SANGLIER].

‖**singulare tantum** (sɪŋgjʊˈlɑːreɪ ˈtæntəm). *Gram.* Also **singularis tantum**. Pl. **singularia tantum**. [L. neut. phr., 'singular only'.] A word which has only a singular form: usu. applied to mass (or uncountable) nouns. Cf. PLURALE TANTUM.

**1940** A. H. GARDINER *Theory of Proper Names* 27 A *singulare tantum* has developed a plural by cutting the designated entity, like a worm, into two parts. **1962** H. M. HOENIGSWALD in Householder & Saporta *Probl. Lexicogr.* 109 The ordinary coverage of singularia tantum, is mostly limited to mass nouns. **1979** *Trans. Philol. Soc.* 160 This is why the plural of *dahyu-* in the sense of 'nations' would have been *translatable* into Elamite only by *taššup*, a word which at xwāning was doomed to come out as the singularis tantum *kāra-*.

**singularism** (ˈsɪŋgjʊlərɪz(ə)m). [See -ISM.] A philosophy which explains the phenomena of the universe from a single principle: opp. to PLURALISM. Cf. MONISM.

**1897** PILLSBURY & TITCHENER tr. *Külpe's Introd. Philos.* iii. 107 It is customary to distinguish the various views that can be held upon this question by the terms *monism, dualism* and *pluralism*. But as the difference expressed by the first two is.. predominantly qualitative, it seems better to make a.. quantitative antithesis, and to speak only of *singularism* and *pluralism*. The former explains or deduces all the phenomena of the universe from one single principle. **1911** J. WARD *Realm of Ends* 24 If the difficulties of Pluralism point the way to Singularism they will at least serve to make the character of the One clearer than any 'cheap and easy monism'.. can ever do. **1931** A. WOLF in W. Rose *Outl. Mod. Knowl.* xiii. 576 The philosophy of James is perhaps best understood as a reaction against the excessive intellectualism, and the monism or singularism of absolute idealism.

ˈ**singularist.** [f. SINGULAR *a.* + -IST.]

†**1.** One who differs from others, or from what is generally accepted; one who affects singularity.

**1593** G. HARVEY *Pierce's Super.* II. 101 One vnlearned Singularist hath more in him, then ten learned Precisians. **1596** NASHE *Saffron Walden* Wks. (Grosart) III. 66 Some smirking singularists, brag Reformists, and glicking Remembrancers.. seeke to be masons of infinite contradiction. *a* **1641** BP. MOUNTAGU *Acts & Mon.* (1642) 45 The private faults, opinions, conceits of Factionists, Singularists, or so, bee Fathered upon the Church. *a* **1677** BARROW *Serm.* xxxiv. (1686) III. 378 Men not enduring to be termed.. a clownish singularist, or non-conformist to ordinary usage, a stiff opiniatre.

**2.** *Eccl.* One who holds a single benefice, as contrasted with a PLURALIST. *rare.*

**1799** MORNINGTON in Stanhope *Life Pitt* III. 192 To make my brother Gerald a fat pluralist: he is at present a meagre singularist. **1832** *Fraser's Mag.* V. 550 The effect.. will be.. to make the rich and influential clergyman a pluralist, and keep the poorer class singularists probably for life.

†**singuˈlaritan.** *Obs. rare.* [Cf. next and -AN.] = SINGULARIST 1.

**1647** TRAPP *Marrow Gd. Authors* in *Comm. Ep.* 697 *Patres sic judicant, ego vero sic*, saith another Singularitan. **1653** BP. WEBBE *Pract. Quiet.* (1657) 237 Such Singularitans there were among the Corinthians, who standing upon their own proud conceit contemned others.

**singularity** (sɪŋgjʊˈlærɪtɪ). Also 4 **syngularyte**, 5–6 **-ite**; 5–6 **singularite(e**, 5 **-yte(e**, 6–7 **-itie**, 6 **-itye**. See also SINGLERTY and SINGULERTY. [ad. F. *singularité* (12th c.), or late L. *singulāritas*, f. *singulāris* SINGULAR: see -ITY.]

**I.** †**1.** Singleness of aim or purpose. *Obs. rare.*

*a* **1340** HAMPOLE *Psalter* iv. 10 þai perisch þat sekis many thyngs, and syngularite is halden in halymen, for þai sett all þaire hert to luf anly a god. **1640** in Rushw. *Hist. Coll.* III. (1692) I. 130 Is there in us that which God requires, Unity, Purity, and singularity of heart?

†**2.** A single or separate thing or entity; a unit.

*c* **1374** CHAUCER *Boeth.* v. met. iii. (1868) 160 Whan þe soule.. seeþ.. god, þan knoweþ it to-gidre þe somme and þe singularites, þat is to seyn, þe principles and eueryche by hym self. **1548** GESTE *Pr. Masse* 139 'Wee' importeth a multitude and not a singularitee. **1606** BRYSKETT *Civil Life* 162 (As Aristotle sayth) the knowledge of vniuersalities springeth from singularities. **1682** SIR T. BROWNE *Chr. Mor.* (1756) 120 Persons of short times.. know not singularities enough to raise axioms of this world. **1708** *Brit. Apollo* No. 40. 1/2 Tho it be an Usual thing in the Hebrew.. for a Plural Word to denote a Singularity.

**3.** The quality or fact of being one in number or kind; singleness, oneness. Now *rare*.

**1583** STUBBES *Anat. Abus.* II. (1882) 80 The singularitie of one man may easilie be abused. **1593** BILSON *Govt. Christ's Ch.* 245 The singularitie of one Pastour over each flocke is commanded. **1608** HEYWOOD *Lucrece* II. ii, Barren Princes Breed danger in their singularitie. **1671** FLAVEL *Fount of Life* viii. 20 He is described by the Singularity of his Mediation, One Mediator, and but one. **1711** G. HICKES *Two Treat. Chr. Priesth.* (1847) II. 390 The unity of each Church resteth on the singularity of the pastor. **1713** ARBUTHNOT *John Bull* II. xx, Why may not John Bull be *Us*..? I hope John Bull is no more confined to Singularity than Nic. Frog. **1806** *Phil. Trans.* XCVI. 225 The projectile motions of the planets.. are all decidedly in favour of a marked singularity of direction. **1850** ROBERTSON *Serm.* Ser. III. xi. (1853) 132 Not merely the singularity in the number of God's Being.

**II. 4.** †**a.** The fact or condition of being alone or apart from others; solitariness. *Obs. rare.*

**1398** TREVISA *Barth. De P.R.* VI. xxiii. (1495) 212 Men vsyd to ete togyders in open place, leest syngularite [*Bodl. MS.* singulerite] schuld brede lechery. **1607** TOPSELL *Four-f. Beasts* (1658) 189 Goats love singularity, and may well be called Schismaticks among Cattel, and therefore they thrive best lying together in small numbers.

**b.** A solitary instance.

**1814** J. ADAMS *Wks.* (1856) X. 106 A friendship of forty years, I have found a rarity, though not a singularity.

†**5. a.** Private or personal profit or gain. *Obs.*

**1426** LYDG. *De Guil. Pilgr.* 23661 Wherfore the Spon that thou hast seyn ys called 'Syngularyte', thyng to possede in propurte. **1436** *Pol. Poems* (Rolls) II. 190 But covetyse and singularite Of one [*v.r.* owne] profite.. Hathe done us harme. *c* **1450** BURGH *Secrees* 2223 Comende that Officeer.. As hym that loueth moore prosperite, vnyversal of thy Regioun Than pryvat avayl to his singularyte.

†**b.** Desire to be specially favoured. *Obs.*$^{-1}$

*c* **1491** *Chast. Goddes Chyld.* x. 26 Some of thyse men by a grete singularytee desire of god some specyalle yefte.

†**6.** Distinction due to, or involving, some superior quality; special excellence or goodness. *Obs.*

*c* **1450** in Aungier *Syon* (1840) 378 No singularite of metes and drynkes be had in the freytour. **1538** STARKEY *England* II. i. 153 Dylygently to attayne in al artys and crafte gret syngularyte. **1558** WARDE tr. *Alexis' Secr.* (1568) 62 b, In lyke maner may you dresse and trymme Peches and other fruites: a thing of great singularitie. **1620** E. BLOUNT *Horæ Subs.* 358 There were conioyned all singularities together, best workmen, best wits,.. and so in euery kinde Superlatiue. **1632** LITHGOW *Trav.* x. 482 The kindnesses of whom.. argued in them a greater singularitie of kindnesse and compassion.

**7. a.** The fact or quality of differing or dissenting from others or from what is generally accepted, esp. in thought or religion; personal, individual, or independent action, judgement, etc., esp. in order to render one's self conspicuous or to attract attention or notice. (Common from 1590 to 1700.)

**1502** *Ord. Crysten Men* (W. de W. 1506) IV. xxx, Syngularyte, as not to vouchesaufe to do as done other. *a* **1568** ASCHAM *Scholem.* II. (Arb.) 147 This mislikyng of Ryming beginneth not now of any newfangle singularitie. **1593** G. HARVEY *New Letter* B, Excellency hath in all ages affected singularity. **1601** CORNWALLIS *Ess.* II. i, It comes too neere singularitie, and a desire to be noted. **1665** BOYLE *Occas. Refl.* (1848) 359 The Day will come, when those that despise his Singularity, will envy his Happiness. **1715** BENTLEY *Serm.* x. 369 He that zealously vends his Novelties, what is he but a Trader for the fame of Singularity? **1753–4** RICHARDSON *Grandison* VI. xxix. 181 Singularity is usually the indication of something wrong in judgment. **1814** CARY *Dante, Par.* XXIX. 92 So much the restless eagerness to shine, And love of singularity, prevail. **1887** LOWELL *Democracy* 10 That conceit of singularity which is the natural recoil from our uneasy consciousness of being commonplace.

**b.** Const. *of* (opinion, etc.).

**1617** MORYSON *Itin.* II. 114 Doctor Latwar,..affecting some singularitie of forwardnesse, more then his place required,..was mortally wounded. **1622** in *Fortescue Papers* (Camden) 184, I neaver affected singularity of opinion either in myself or any other man. **1771** *Ann. Reg.* II. 166 Tacitus's only aim seems to have been singularity of expression. **1779** *Mirror* No. 19, That singularity of opinion, which is the natural consequence of his want of opportunities of comparing his own ideas with those of others. **1822** HAZLITT *Table-T.* Ser. II. xvi. (1869) 327 Avoid singularity of opinion as well as of every thing else.

†**c.** Dissent or separation *from* (something). *Obs.*

**1680** BAXTER *Answ. Stillingfl.* vi. 15 Is our Consent with the Universal Church, or your Singularity from it, liker to Schism or Separation? **1681** *Whole Duty Nations* 12 These Holy Men['s]..Singularity from Sin and False Worship.

**8. a.** Individual character or property; individuality; distinctiveness.

**1583** STUBBES *Anat. Abus.* II. (1882) 11 There is a certaine singularitie, interest, and proprietie in euerie thing. **1613** PURCHAS *Pilgrimage* (1614) 491 Some particulars..may be said touching some of them in other places, according to the singularitie of each Nation in this so manifolde a profession. **1648** J. BEAUMONT *Psyche* XXI. lii, That Singularity which seemeth so Close girt to every Individual Creature. **1778** MISS BURNEY *Evelina* I, This room..is without ornament, elegance, or any sort of singularity, and merely to be marked by its length. **1836-7** SIR W. HAMILTON *Metaph.* xxviii. (1859) II. 169 All the special determinations which give it [a triangle]..singularity or individuality.

**b.** The fact or condition of departing or deviating from what is customary, usual, or normal; peculiarity, eccentricity, oddity, strangeness.

**1768** STERNE *Sent. Journ., Passport,* The Count smiled at the singularity of the introduction. **1794** S. WILLIAMS *Vermont* 150 The manners and customs of the Indians are marked with a singularity peculiar to the savage. **1815** W. H. IRELAND *Scribbleomania* 122 *note,* The following anecdote, which, for its singularity, surpasses even the attempts of Chatterton. **1821** CRAIG *Lect. Drawing,* etc. v. 303 There is another species of rock which I shall mention, on account of its singularity. **1830** D'ISRAELI *Chas. I.* III. iv. 56 The singularity of his manners had attracted as much notice as his eminence at the bar.

†**c.** A special or particular kind *of* (something).

**1776** ADAM SMITH *W.N.* I. vii. (1869) I. 63 Some natural productions require such a singularity of soil and situation, that [etc.].

**9.** With *a* and *pl.* **a.** An instance of individual departure from common ideas or practice.

**1570** GRINDAL *Let.* in *Rem.* (Parker Soc.) 305 He hath a busy head, stuffed full of Singularities. **1613** PURCHAS *Pilgrimage* II. ix. (1614) 154 When afterwards in a singularitie he had gone aside into a Caue, and there mewed vp himselfe. **1692** DRYDEN *St. Euremont's Ess.* 98 He fear'd the singularities which came from a false Spirit. *Ibid.* 336, I pardon our religious Men the sad Singularity of eating nothing but Herbs. **1710** STEELE *Tatler* No. 166 ¶1 The World is so overgrown with Singularities in Behaviour, and Method of Living. **1790** PALEY *Horæ Paul.* i. 7 Numerous expressions and singularities of style. **1849** MISS MULOCK *Ogilvies* 14 Even slight singularities of dress—usually puerile and contemptible affectations. **1884** *L'pool Mercury* 22 Oct. 5/4 The singularities of his character and the misfortunes of his life.

**b.** A distinctive, noteworthy, or curious thing; esp. *pl.*, notable features or objects; †the sights (*of* a place).

**1570-6** LAMBARDE *Peramb. Kent* (1826) 131 Since Douer is not far off let us make unto it and unfold the singularities of the same. **1593** MUNDAY *Def. Contraries* 15 Countrey houses..beset with cleere fountaines, Vineyardes, Meadowes,..and other singularities. **1632** LITHGOW *Trav.* I. 15 Many haue wrote of the singularities of old Rome. **1653** H. COGAN tr. *Pinto's Voy.* lvii. 225 When we had well observed the singularities of this Temple. **1760** *Ann. Reg., Chron.* 78 Numbers are daily crouding from this city..to view these singularities [petrified human bodies]. **1801** STRUTT *Sports & Past.* IV. ii. 275 One of them [chess-boards], a perfect singularity, is of circular form. **1808** BENTHAM *Scotch Reform* 2 But as Africa of old was noted for physical, so have the British islands been in modern times for psychological singularities.

*transf.* **1599** B. JONSON *Cynthia's Rev.* IV. v, Al the choisest singularities of the court were vp in pantofles.

**c.** A peculiar, exceptional, or unusual feature or characteristic.

**1663** J. SPENCER *Prodigies* (1665) 382 There is a singularity therein in regard of the nature of it. **1796** WITHERING *Brit. Pl.* (ed. 3) I. 121 From these singularities of structure, it is probable that the generation of these plants is effected in some mode not yet understood. **1817** MILL *Brit. India* II. iv. I. 167 The trials by ordeal..have been thought a mighty singularity in the institutions of our Gothic ancestors. **1822-7** GOOD *Study Med.* (1829) III. 227, I have..seen several of these singularities, and especially the renewal of the sight and hearing. **1852** CAYLEY *Math. Papers* II. 28 On the singularities of curves. **1883** WALLEM *Fish Supply Norway* 22 It is a singularity of the export..of cured fish that [etc.].

**d.** *Math.* A point at which a function takes an infinite value.

**1893** A. R. FORSYTH *Theory of Functions* xxi. 606 All the essential singularities of a discontinuous group lie on the axis of *a* when the group is real. **1939** [see SCHWARZSCHILD 2]. **1959** *Listener* 27 Aug. 320/1 At the start of the expansion certain quantities in our differential equations become infinite. This frequently happens with differential equations, and when it does the equation is said to contain a mathematical singularity. **1977** *Sci. Amer.* July 126/3 Gauss did much more with complex numbers. In 1811 he discovered what is now called Cauchy's theorem: The integral of a complex analytical function around a closed curve that encloses no singularities is zero.

**e.** *Astr.* A region in space-time at which matter is infinitely dense.

**1965** *Physical Rev. Lett.* XIV. 58/1 An exterior observer will always see matter outside $r = 2m$, the collapse through $r = 2m$ to the singularity at $r = 0$ being invisible to him. **1972** *Nature* 21 Apr. 378/2 In the physical world..we may take the phrase 'space-time singularity' to mean a region in which space and time have become so locally distorted that the present laws of physics are no longer applicable. **1979** *Jrnl. R. Soc. Arts* CXXVII. 579/1 A central 'singularity' where tidal forces (the difference between the gravitational acceleration of his head and his feet) would become infinite, and he would be crushed out of existence.

**singularize** ('sɪŋgjʊləraɪz), *v.* [f. SINGULAR *a.* + -IZE. Cf. F. *singulariser.*]

**1.** *trans.* To mark conspicuously; to make distinct or conspicuous; to distinguish, signalize.

**1589** G. HARVEY *Pierce's Super.* I. Wks. (Grosart) II. 111 If any thing miraculously singularizeth witt, it is Impudence. **1644** J. GOODWIN *Innoc. Triumph.* (1645) 35 Separated from all its fellows by this parenthesis of preferment,..and one other of them..singularized with this parenthesis. **1657** J. SERGEANT *Schism Dispach't* 402 There is not a word there expressing any distinction..to any other Apostle, much lesse singularizing each of them distinctly. **1704** *Collect. Voy.* (Churchill) III. 2/2 It has some Properties which do..singularize it. **1735** J. HUGHES tr. *Fontenelle's Dial.* III. iv. (ed. 3) 145 True Wisdom wou'd too much distinguish and singularize its Possessors. **1894** *The Voice* (N.Y.) 20 Dec. 6/3 He was a Capet, a family name singularized by the recurrence of these warrior prelates.

*refl.* **1685** *Gracian's Courtier's Oracle* 202 They affect..to singularize themselves by an extraordinary air. **1771** SMOLLETT *Humph. Cl.* 30 Apr., The two Amazons who singularised themselves most in action. **1785** C'TESS OF R. *Ess.* II. 16 Resolving to do..something good, in order to singularize themselves. **1812** COLERIDGE in *Lit. Rem.* (1836) I. 383 The instinct..in each man of declaring his particular existence, and thus of singling or singularizing himself.

**2.** To make singular or one; to individualize; to convert into the singular number. *rare.*

**1663** SPARKE *Prim. Devotion* 337 What is the meaning of this hymn so trebled, so singularized, but three distinct Persons, yet one onely Lord God? **1694** R. BURTHOGGE *Reason* 154 The Great Work..of the Body is to Singularize and Individuate the General Vital Principle of the Universe. **1828** [J. R. BEST] *Italy as it is* 404 The situation of Baia, the moderns have singularized the name, is preferable to that of Naples.

Hence **'singularized, 'singularizing** *ppl. adjs.* Also **singulari'zation.**

**1614** JACKSON *Creed* III. 247 Thus we..speake of the Church indefinitely taken,..not appropriated to any indiuiduall, or singularized person. **1657** J. SERGEANT *Schism Dispach't* 415 Where no such distinction or singularizing expression was found. **1889** *N. & Q.* 7th Ser. VII. 310/2 Your correspondent asks for examples of ignorant singularization.

**singularly** ('sɪŋgjʊləlɪ), *adv.* Forms: α. 4 syngulerlyche, 5 singuleerliche; 4-6 syng-, singulerly (4 -li, 6 -lie, -lye). β. 5-6 syngularly, 6- singularly (6 -lie). [f. SINGULAR *a.* + -LY[2].]

**1.** Singly; apart from, unaccompanied or unaided by, any or all others; by oneself or itself; one by one, separately, individually. Now *rare.*

*a* **1340** HAMPOLE *Psalter* xxi. 21 All proude men, þat raises þaim vp syngulerly, and suffers na felaghis. **1387-8** T. USK *Test. Love* III. v. (Skeat) I. 94 Ye, and yet other-whyle with wil assenteth, singulerly by him-selfe. *a* **1400** *Pilgr. Sowle* (Caxton, 1483) IV. xx. 65 On the wylle I oute throwe my salt teres, for syngulerly on the my look is set. *a* **1470** HARDING *Chron.* CCVI. iii, [He] faught full worthely With George Turnaile in lyestes syngulerly. **1526** *Pilgr. Perf.* (W. de W. 1531) 29 Therefore by theyr parcelles syngularly they be to be declared. **1541** *Act 33 Hen. VIII,* c. 28 §2 Euery of them ..maie retaine singulerlie to euery one of them in his house ..one chaplein. **1653** BAXTER *Christian Concord* 109 That man..who will do all alone, singularly or on his own head. **1690** LEYBOURN *Curs. Math.* 345 In truth there are 4 Roots, but every one singularly equal to *b.* **1839-48** BAILEY *Festus* 70/1 He..Would solemnly and singularly curse Each minute [etc.].

**b.** With special application or reference to one person or thing.

**1456** *Paston Lett.* I. 390 Yf I have rehersed wyttyngly the text of the Gospell syngularly unto your maistership, I beseche you to be had excused. **1592** G. HARVEY *Four Lett.* iii. 49, I speake generally to euery springing wit: but more specially to a few: and at this instante singularly to one. **1644** JESSOP *Angel of Ephesus* 11 The denomination is not to be taken..Singularly or Personally, but..collectively. **1679** MOXON *Mech. Exerc.* viii. 138 Though I have spoken singularly of one Principal Post, yet as you work this, you must work all four Principal Posts.

**c.** After one's own fashion; independently.

**1669** GURNALL *Chr. in Arm.* Introd. i. 3/2 The Christian is to walk singularly, not after the World's guise. **1671** MILTON *P.R.* III. 57 His lot who dares be singularly good. [**1806** S. ROGERS *Written in Westminster Abbey* 16 Round Him, who dared be singularly good.]

**2.** In the singular number; so as to denote one.

*c* **1380** WYCLIF *Sel. Wks.* II. 345 He seid not pluraliche, þat he shulde ȝyve it to his seedis, but singulerly, to his seed. *a* **1522** LILY *Grammar* in *Shaks. Jahrbuch* (1908) 89 How verbes..varye in ther modes,..and in theyr persones, bothe syngularly and plurally. **1575** FENTON *Gold. Epist.* (1577) 74 Christ pardoning this theefe, sayd not, *Amen dico vobis,* but speaking singularly, he sayd, *Amen dico tibi.* **1607** TOPSELL *Four-f. Beasts* (1658) 181 The Hebrews call them [goats] singularly *Ez,* and plurally *Izim.* **1678** CUDWORTH *Intell. Syst.* 246 Though that Poet speak more than once of God Singularly.

**3.** In a special manner; to an unusual degree or extent; specially, particularly, unusually.

*c* **1430** *Pilgr. Lyf Manhode* II. cv. (1869) 115 Youre wit is singuleerliche to alowe and to preyse. **1447** BOKENHAM *Seyntys* (Roxb.) 8 Most singulerly Verteuous be hyr excellent cheryte. **1509** FISHER *Funeral Serm. C'tess Richmond* Wks. (1878) 290 In which .iiii. [things] the noble woman Martha.. was syngulerly to be commended and praysed. **1549** COVERDALE, etc. *Erasm. Par. Rom.* 44 Salute Persis, whome I syngulerlye loue. **1620** E. BLOUNT *Horæ Subs.* 344 You shall see the ouercomming of the Citie, liuely set forth, and the holy things..singularly expressed. **1664** H. MORE *Myst. Iniq.* xiv. 47 They were singularly well accomplished therein. **1725** DE FOE *Voy. round World* (1840) 122 They had something singularly honest and sincere in their faces. **1797-1805** S. & HT. LEE *Canterb. Tales* I. 81 A forgetfulness of himself, that was singularly charming. **1825** W. COBBETT *Rur. Rides* (1885) II. 1 The afternoon was singularly beautiful. **1855** MACAULAY *Hist. Eng.* xxii. IV. 718 A man of singularly clear judgment and singularly lofty spirit. **1884** R. W. CHURCH *Bacon* ix. 223 His Latin..is singularly forcible and expressive.

†**4.** Excellently, admirably, particularly well. *Obs.*

**1576** FLEMING *Panopl. Epist.* 76 Caesar, the proper youth, is singularly disposed. **1599** B. JONSON *Cynthia's Rev.* IV. i, That rebatu becomes thee singularly. **1617** MORYSON *Itin.* II. 72 Master Secretary..spake singularly for the justifying of her Majesties speciall care.

**5.** Oddly, strangely, peculiarly. *rare.*

**1752** J. HILL *Hist. Anim.* 292 *Cyclopterus,* the lump-fish: This is a very singularly-shaped fish..and of a remarkably clumsy figure. **1820** SCOTT *Monast.* Introd. Ep., The quires of paper thus singularly conferred on me. *a* **1864** HAWTHORNE *Amer. Note-bks.* (1879) I. 39 Here I am, settled since night before last,..and living very singularly.

**singularness** ('sɪŋgjʊlənɪs). Now *rare.* [f. SINGULAR *a.* + -NESS.] The quality or state of being singular; singularity, † singleness.

**1530** PALSGR. 270/2 Syngulernesse, *singvlarité.* **1549** COVERDALE, etc. *Erasm. Par. 2 Cor.* 58 Nor by anye other waye proue [they] theyr owne syngularnesse, but by deprauynge other mennes actes. **1571** GOLDING *Calvin on Ps.* lxv. 12 That the frutefull yeeres excell in singularnesse of beauty. **1650** WEEKES *Truth's Conflict* Pref. A 2 They do require a singularnesse of intention, and raisednesse of mind. **1657** *Deuine Louer* 17 The greatnesse or singularnesse of our Priuiledges. **1727** BAILEY (vol. II.), *Singularness,*.. also, a particular way of behaviour, &c., affectedness. **1900** P. C. SIMPSON *Fact of Christ* ii. 32 A singularness by which He is not only separate from sinners, but is also distinct from saints.

**singulary** ('sɪŋgjʊlərɪ), *a. Logic.* [f. L. *singulāris* SINGULAR *a.*: see -ARY[2].] Involving just one element.

**1940** W. V. O. QUINE *Math. Logic* i. 13 Conjunction and alternation are binary, in that they combine statements two at a time. But denial..is singulary. [*Note*] The series of adjectives 'binary', 'ternary', 'quaternary', 'quinary',.. leaves mathematicians in a quandary when $n = 1$. It is customary to stammer out some such makeshift as 'unary' or 'uninary' or 'unitary'. But the proper word is apparent if we reflect that the series of Latin distributives 'bini', 'terni', 'quaterni', 'quini',..begins with 'singuli'. **1954** *Word* X. 227 There are singulary operations, but no singulary relations... An example of a singulary operation in mathematics is 'reciprocal of'. **1965** N. CHOMSKY *Aspects of Theory of Syntax* iii. 132 Many of the optional singulary transformations of Chomsky..must be reformulated as obligatory transformations.

**singulative** ('sɪŋgjʊlətɪv). *Gram.* [ad. F. *singulatif*: cf. SINGULAR *a.* and -ATIVE.] (See quot. 1966); also, a singular form.

[**1952** MEILLET & COHEN *Langues du Monde* (ed. 2) 1279 *Singulatif,* morphème ayant pour fonction de donner à un mot une valeur de singulier, généralement par opposition à un collectif.] **1966** M. PEI *Gloss. Linguistic Terminol.* 250 *Singulative,* a morpheme having for its function to give a word the force of a singular, usually by way of opposition to a collective (*rice, rice-grain*). **1970** J. McN. DODGSON *Pl.-Names Cheshire* I. 151 The *-inn, -enn* suffix is not diminutive but a singulative... The singulative effect would indicate some particularised aspect of a location—e.g. a particular piece of moorland in a general area of moors. **1977** *Word* *1972* XXVIII. 194 *Clocs*: plural *clocsiau*...; doubly characterized plural, with a new 'singulative' *clocsen.*

**singuler(e,** obs. forms of SINGULAR.

† **'singulerty.** *Obs.* In 5 sin-, syngulerte. [a. OF. *singulerté*: see SINGULAR *a.* and -TY.] = SINGULARITY.

**1414** in *26 Polit. Poems* 58 Syngulerte is sotyle þefte. þey calle hit custom, froupe to blende. *c* **1440** *Jacob's Well* 70 Syngulerte..is whan a man folwyth his owyn wyll for pompe, & wyll noȝt do as wysere don. *a* **1470** HARDING *Chron.* LXXXVI. vii. (MS. Ashm. 34), The publyke cause afore þe singulerte, [He] Preferred ay as it of ryght shuld be.

**'singulo-,** comb. form of L. *singulus* single, in **singulo-silicate,** a unisilicate.

**1883** *Encycl. Brit.* XVI. 62/2 Of cuprous..silicates,..the singulo-silicate is red, dense, and rather refractory. *Ibid.,* The singulo-silicate and bi-silicate combinations.

**'singult.** Now *arch.* [ad. L. *singultus* a sob, a speech broken by sobs.]

**1.** A sob.

In the two quotations from Spenser, as well as in *Tears Muses* 232 and *Colin Clout* 168, the word is misprinted *singulf* in the original editions.

**1590** SPENSER *F.Q.* III. xi. 12 There an huge heape of singultes did oppresse His strugling soule. **1596** *Ibid.* v. vi. 13 With deepe sighes, and singults few. **1616** BROWNE *Brit. Past.* II. i, When her teares were stopt from eyther eye, Her singults, blubbrings, seem'd to make them flye Out at her oyster-mouth. **1621** QUARLES *Esther* xv, Thus her plain'full mone, Commixt with bitter singults, she exprest. **1748** MELMOTH *Fitzosborne Lett.* (1763) 291 Whiles frequent singults check'd his faltring tale. *a* **1756** G. WEST *Educ.* in *Dodsley's Coll. Poems* (1782) IV. 30 Heart-thrilling cries, with sobs and singults sore. **1820** SCOTT *Monast.* xxix, Had he foreseen it was to cost you these tears and singults.

†**2.** = SINGULTUS 1. *Obs.*⁻¹

**1661** LOVELL *Hist. Anim. & Min.* 366 The singult, or hicket, which is a convulsive motion of the stomach.

**sin'gultient**, *ppl. a. rare.* [ad. ppl. stem of L. *singultīre* to sob: see prec.] Sobbing.

**1660** HOWELL *Parly of Beasts* 23 Som of ripe age will screech, cry, and howle in so many disordered notes and singultient accents. **1879** L. MORRIS *Ode of Life* (1880) 4 The great Universe wakes with a deep-drawn singultient breath.

**sin'gultous**, *a. rare*⁻⁰. [f. SINGULT: cf. next.] 'Relating to, or affected with, hiccough.'

**1851** DUNGLISON *Med. Lex.*

†**sin'gultuous**, *a. Obs.*⁻¹ [ad. obs. F. *singultueux*, f. L. *singultus*.] Characterized by or attended with hiccuping.

**1575** BANISTER *Chyrurg.* I. (1585) 190 There hath followed singultuous feuers and death itself at the length.

†**singulture.** *Obs.* [f. L. *singult-us*.] = next.

**1657** TOMLINSON *Renou's Disp.* 235 Its faculty is..to abate singulture.

‖**singultus** (sɪŋ'gʌltəs). [L. Cf. SINGULT.]

**1.** *Path.* Hiccups, hiccuping.

Given in the *Physical Dict.* (1657) and in Blancard, Harris, etc., but without evidence of actual use in English.

**1754-64** SMELLIE *Midwifery* III. 180 A fever intervened ..attended with singultus. **1767** GOOCH *Treat. Wounds* I. 395 Sickness, vomiting, singultus, languor, anxiety. **1818-20** E. THOMPSON *Cullen's Nosologia* 197 Dry cough, vomiting, singultus. **1880** FLINT *Princ. Med.* 313 Singultus may be produced by pressure on the phrenic or branches of the pneumogastric nerve.

**2.** A sob. *rare.*

**1824** BYRON *Juan* xv. ii, But, more or less, the whole's a syncope Or a singultus—emblems of emotion.

**sinh** (ʃaɪn, sɪn(t)ʃ, saɪn'eɪtʃ). *Math.* Abbrev. of *hyperbolic sine* s.v. HYPERBOLIC *a.* 2 b.

**1873** *Messenger of Math.* II. 190 Sinh *x* and cosh *x* are of course the hyperbolic sine and cosine of *x*, viz. $\frac{1}{2}(e^x - e^{-x})$ and $\frac{1}{2}(e^x + e^{-x})$. **1891** [see COSH]. **1972** A. G. HOWSON *Handbk. Terms Algebra & Anal.* xxxiii. 164 Sinh and cosh both have domain R; the image of sinh is R.

**Sinhala** (sɪn'hɑːlə), *sb.* and *a.* [a. Skr. (see SINHALESE).] **A.** *sb.* = SINHALESE *sb.* and *a.* 2.

**1954** PEI & GAYNOR *Dict. Linguistics* 198 *Sinhala*, modern vernacular Sinhalese, mixed with foreign words. **1961** *Times* 27 June 13 The Official Language Act of 1958 came into effect at the beginnng of this year, and without reference to Tamil prescribes Sinhala as the sole official language of Ceylon. **1977** *Economist* 3 Sept. 62/1 Mrs Bandaranaike fought an election on a platform of 'Sinhala only' as Sri Lanka's state language.

**B.** *adj.* = SINHALESE *sb.* and *a.* 3.

**1926** M. C. RASANAYAGAM *Anc. Jaffna* vi. 231 The Pallava king..says in one of his inscriptions that he vanquished 'the Sinhala king who was proud of the strength of his arms'. **1962** *Housewife* (Ceylon) Feb. 9 Local hand-made clay tiles based on traditional Sinhala designs. **1963** *Guardian* 2 May 10/3 An Act of 1956 prescribed the Sinhala language as the one official language of Ceylon.

**Sinhalese** (sɪnhə'liːz), *sb.* and *a.* Also **Singhalese, Singalese.** [f. Skr. *Sinhala* Sri Lanka (Ceylon) + -ESE. Cf. CINGALESE.

The plural *Singales* used by Purchas (1613) and Herbert (1634) does not appear to be of this formation: it may represent the Skr. pl. *Sinhalās*.]

**1.** As *pl.*, the native inhabitants of Sri Lanka (formerly Ceylon). Also *sing.*, a Sinhalese native of Sri Lanka. The Sinhalese are properly members of an Aryan people deriving from N. India and now forming the majority of the population of Sri Lanka.

**1801** *Asiatick Researches* VII. 32 The *Singhalais* assert, from record, the total destruction and regeneration of the universe, many other times. **1802** PINKERTON *Mod. Geogr.* II. 313 The natives of Ceylon, called Singalese,..are not so black as those of Malabar. **1842** PRICHARD *Nat. Hist. Man* 242 The Kandians and the Singhalese resemble each other in manners, language, and religion. **1887** *Encycl. Brit.* XXII. 198/2 The 'tic-polonga' of the Singalese. **1913** L. WOOLF *Village in Jungle* iii. 45 He was tall for a Sinhalese, broad-shouldered, and big-boned. **1948** [see CEYLONESE *a.* and *sb.*].

**2.** The language spoken in Sri Lanka.

**1801** *Asiatick Researches* VII. 401 The end of the soul is called, in Singalese, *Nivani.* **1802** PINKERTON *Mod. Geogr.* II. 318 The language is Singalese; and there are some Mahometans. **1861** *Chambers's Encycl.* II. 738/2 Their [*sc.* the Veddahs] language..is a dialect of the Singhalese.

**3.** As *adj.* Belonging or pertaining to Sri Lanka or to the native inhabitants of that island.

**1797** *Encycl. Brit.* (ed. 3) I. 494/1 From this Shanscrit are derived the sacred characters of Thibet, the Cashmirian,.. and Tamoul; the Singalese, Siamese, Maharattan [etc.]. **1802** PINKERTON *Mod. Geogr.* II. 311 In the reign of Claudius, embassadors were sent to Rome by a Singalese rajia. *Ibid.* 314 Religious books in the Tamulic..and Singalese languages. **1890** *Contemp. Rev.* LVII. 257 Sixty years ago the Sinhalese priesthood were intensely illiterate. *Ibid.* 270 According to the Sinhalese narrative.

**sinhalite** ('sɪnhəlaɪt). *Min.* [f. as SINHAL(ESE *sb.* and *a.* + -ITE¹.] A borate of aluminium and magnesium, $MgAlBO_4$ (usu. also containing iron), which forms pale yellow to deep brown orthorhombic crystals resembling olivine and frequently of gem quality.

**1952** CLARINGBULL & HEY in *Mineral. Mag.* XXIX. 843 For this new mineral the name *sinhalite* is proposed, from Sinhala the Sanskrit name for Ceylon. **1952** *Times* 4 Dec. 3/3 Sinhalite..was previously thought to be an olivine rich in iron. **1965** *Amer. Mineralogist* L. 1979 The sinhalite from Ceylon had a density of 3·494, corresponding to a composition $(Al,Mg)_{1.95}Fe_{0.05}BO_4$. Judging from the absorption data, most of the iron in sinhalite is divalent. **1971** *Jrnl. Gemmology* XII. 154 One of the few sinhalites we have officially tested..was an attractive golden brown specimen.

**Sinic** ('sɪnɪk), *a.* Also 7 **Sinick.** [ad. med.L. *Sinic-us* (med.Gr. Σινικός), f. late L. *Sīnæ*: cf. SINÆAN *a.*] Chinese.

**1662** STILLINGFL. *Orig. Sacræ* III. iv. §8 Martinius tells us ..that the antient writers of the Sinick history speak much of the Flood. **1861** HULME tr. *Moquin-Tandon* I. iv. 27 Bory de St. Vincent..admits fifteen species of Men. These are, 1st, the Japetic;..5th, the Sinic.

**sinical** ('sɪnɪkəl), *a. Math.* Also 6 **sinicall**, 8 **sinecal** (?). [f. SINE² + -ICAL.] Of or relating to a sine or sines; employing or founded upon sines.

**1593** FALE *Art of Dialling* 60 This Table of Sines may seeme obscure and hard to them who are not acquainted with Sinicall computation. **1673** FLAMSTEED in Rigaud *Corr. Sci. Men* (1841) II. 171 By this sinical projection..I can find the hour of the day to a minute. **1762** FALCONER *Shipwr.* I. 751 In chiliads next the analogy is sought: And on the sinical triangle wrought.

†**b.** ***sinical quadrant***, a former nautical instrument having intersecting sines drawn from each side.

**1669** STURMY *Mariner's Mag.* II. i. 47 Instruments in esteem amongst Navigators..are chiefly..the Plain Scale, the Sinical Quadrant, the Plain Sea-Chard, and the True Sea-Chard. **1695** ALINGHAM *Geom. Epit.* 69 Several Mathematical Instruments, as sinical Quadrant, Forestaff [etc.]. **1701** MOXON *Math. Instr.* 18 [Description given, copied by Harris, Kersey, etc.]. **1728** CHAMBERS *Cycl.* s.v. *Quadrant.* **1781** J. ADAMS (*title*), The Description and Use of a new much-improved Sinical Quadrant. **1788** *Trans. Soc. Arts* VI. 185 The plain Triangle..[is] better than the sinecal Quadrant.

**Sinicism** ('sɪnɪsɪz(ə)m). [f. SINIC *a.* + -ISM.] Chinese manners, customs, or principles; affectation or adoption of what is Chinese.

**1891** in *Cent. Dict.* **1899** *Eng. Hist. Rev.* Apr. 228 The reference is a mere sinicism. Even cowry shells, commonly used in early China as currency, were never so employed in Japan.

**sinicization** (ˌsɪnɪsaɪ'zeɪʃən). [f. next + -ATION.] The action or process of sinicizing.

**1898** *Athenæum* 26 Nov. 747/3 Shinto might have become a religious and ethical system, but its development was arrested by Sinicization and Buddhism. **1899** *Eng. Hist. Rev.* Apr. 209 It is of primitive Japan, of its birth and final sinicisation, that the story..is attempted in the following pages.

**sinicize** ('sɪnɪsaɪz), *v.* [f. SINIC *a.* + -IZE.] *trans.* To invest with a Chinese character.

**1889** *Athenæum* 28 Sept. 414/2 While the civilization of Japan becomes every year more and more Westernized, her language..becomes more and more Sinicized. **1904** *Ibid.* 22 Oct. 547/3 Japan was never really sinicized, and what was best in China never became hers.

Hence **'sinicized** *ppl. a.*

**1899** *Eng. Hist. Rev.* Apr. 218 A thoroughly sinicised and variously manipulated version. **1905** *Athenæum* 16 Sept. 361/2 Even the Buddhism which rules the minds of men.. from the Himalayas to Sagalin is of a sinicized character.

**Sinico-** ('sɪnɪkəʊ), combining form of med.L. *Sinicus* SINIC *a.*, as in ***Sinico-Annamitic***; **Sinico-Japanese** *sb.* and *a.* = *Sino-Japanese* s.v. SINO-¹ 2, 3. Now *rare.*

**1838** P. S. DU PONCEAU *Diss. Nature & Char. Chinese Syst. Writing* p. xxix, Those Sinico-anamitic words, if they are really in use, do not belong to the original language. **1866** F. V. DICKINS tr. *Teika's Hyak Nin Is'shiu* p. vii, Such ill-sounding Sinico-Japanese syllables as rets', bats' mats', teats', shuts', and the like. **1884** tr. *J. J. Rein's Japan* 396 The Japanese Language.. Yamoto- and Sinico-Japanese. **1902** *Encycl. Brit.* XXIX. 729/1 Like all fine specimens of the Sinico-Japanese school, the prices are too high to attract wide custom.

**sinification** (ˌsɪnɪfɪ'keɪʃən). [See SINIFY *v.* and -FICATION.] Sinicization.

**1900** *Athenæum* 4 Aug. 145/3 The Japanese have introduced the whole Chinese system of ideographs, one result of which..is a peculiar sinification..of the vocabulary. **1966** D. WILSON *Quarter of Mankind* xxi. 206 There is no separate Hongkong nationality. Sinification of public life proceeds very slowly. **1977** *Daily Tel.* 12 Feb. 16 The aim is 'sinification' of Tibet.

**sinify** ('sɪnɪfaɪ), *v.* [f. *Sini-*, comb. form of L. *Sīnæ* (see SINÆAN *a.*) + -FY.] *trans.* To sinicize.

**1900** *Spectator* 15 Sept. 330 The European who becomes Sinified is a degraded being. **1942** A. J. GRAJDANZEV *Formosa Today* iii. 35 Only 95,400 of them are classified as 'savages'..the remaining 60,500 being 'civilized', that is, they are 'sinified'. **1966** *Economist* 1 Oct. 58/1 But he [*sc.* Mao] did not sinify the basic philosophical principles of Marxism. **1977** *Times* 12 Oct. (China Suppl.) p. vii/7 The central Government has often been accused of 'sinifying' the minority nationality areas of China.

**'sinigrin.** *Chem.* Also **sinnigrine.** [irreg. f. L. *si-nāpis* mustard + *nigra* black + -IN¹ or -INE⁵.] Myronate of potassium.

**1876** HARLEY *Royle's Mat. Med.* 735 The characteristic constituent of black mustard is myronate of potassium, or sinigrin. **1887** BENTLEY *Man. Bot.* (ed. 5) 451 The elements of this oil exist in the seed [of Black Mustard], in the forms of myronate of potash or sinigrin and myrosin.

**sinister** ('sɪnɪstə(r)), *a.* Forms: α. 5-6 **synystre, synistre,** 5-7 **sinistre;** 6 **syne-,** 7-8 **sinester;** 5-6 **syny-,** 5-7 **syni-,** 5- **sinister.** β. 5 **senestre,** 5-6 **sene-,** 5 **seni-,** 6 **senyster.** [a. OF. *senestre, sinistre* (mod.F. *sinistre*, = Pg. and It. *sinistro*, Sp. *siniestro*), or L. *sinister* left, left-hand. The more original senses of the word are in English later and less common than the transferred.

The stressing shown by examples in verse down to the time of Pope is *si'nister*. Johnson (ed. 4, 1773) gives '*sinister*, but adds 'it seems to be used with the accent on the second syllable, at least in the primitive, and on the first in the figurative sense', and this distinction is retained by Smart (1836), though previously rejected by Walker.]

**I.** †**1. a.** Of information: Given with intent to deceive or mislead, esp. so as to create a prejudice against some person; prompted by malice or ill-will. *Obs.*

**1411** *Rolls of Parlt.* III. 650/2 And of all that by sinistre information, I havyng doute of harme of my body,..dyd assemble thise persones. **1485** *Exch. Rolls Scotl.* IX. 646 *note*, Gif..Johne informit the kingis heines that the said acris pertenit nocht to the said tennandis, that it was wrang and senister informacion. **1534** MORE in Ellis *Orig. Lett.* Ser. I. II. 49 That..no synistre information move your noble Grace to have eny more distrust of my trowth. **1566** *Reg. Privy Council Scot.* I. 416 Upoun sinister informatioun maid to thair Lordships,..the said Robert wes lattin to libertie; albeit the saidis Lordis perfytelie now undirstandis the contrarie.

†**b.** Similarly of suggestions, advice, etc. *Obs.*

**1450** *Rolls of Parlt.* V. 179/2 By sotill meanes and sinistre suggestions. **1480** *Coventry Leet Bk.* 433 þe hasty, sinistre and seducious suggestion & labour made be Laurens Saunders. *a* **1548** HALL *Chron., Hen. IV*, 8 b, The evell & sinister councell of perverse and flatteryng persons. **1559** *Mirr. Mag., R. Tresilian* xvi, Kynge Richarde, By synister aduyse, had tourned all vpsodowne. **1569** in Ellis *Orig. Lett.* Ser. I. II. 257 Doubting what synister complainte may be now againste me. **1601** B. JONSON *Poetaster* v. iii, The sinister application Of the malicious, ignorant, and base Interpreter.

†**2.** Of opinions, etc.: Prejudicial, adverse, unfavourable, darkly suspicious. *Obs.*

**1432** *Paston Lett.* I. 35 That the said Erle may have knowleche therof, to th' entent that he may..not dwelle in hevy or synistre conceit or opinion. **1533** MORE *Apol.* xxxvii. Wks. 904/1 It wyl be hard to bring anye suche sinister opinion of him in any good honest mans head. **1589** G. HARVEY *Pierce's Super.* I. 17 Let me not bee mistaken by sinister construction. **1604** T. WRIGHT *Passions* VI. 313 We passe into the corners of other mens soules..by rash judgements and sinister suspitions. **1648** BOYLE *Seraph. Love* xxiv. (1700) 146 We are apt to harbor sinister thoughts of the Contriver of a Plot. *a* **1713** ELLWOOD *Autobiog.* (1765) 67 Some evil Suspicion or sinister Thoughts concerning me. **1795** *Sewel's Hist. Quakers* I. Pref. p. xv, This is a very sinister and preposterous conceit.

**3.** Of actions, practices, etc.: Dishonest, unfair; not straightforward, underhand; dark.

Common *c* 1470 to 1650, esp. with *arts, courses, labours, means, ways.*

**1455** *Paston Lett.* I. 326 The sinistrez, maliciouse, and fraudulent laboures and rapportes of our sayd ennemyes. **1483** *Plumpton Corr.* (Camden) 43, I am right sory & any synister wayes of my adversaryes be shewed unto you. **1502** ATKYNSON tr. *De Imitatione* III. li, Thou..sekest for thy defence derke & synyster excuses. **1549** *Compl. Scotl.* xix. 160 The sinister ministratione of thy office, is the special cause of the scisma. **1612** BACON *Ess., Of Judicature* (Arb.) 456 Persons that are full of nimble and sinister tricks and shiftes. **1655** FULLER *Ch. Hist.* v. 165 Such who consult with covetousness in matters of conscience, embracing sinister courses to save charges. **1759** DILWORTH *Pope* 84 Private letters..which were obtained in a sinister manner by him. **1800** COLQUHOUN *Comm. Thames* xv, Cheap Fish..might be sold all the year if no sinister arts were used to prevent it. **1829** I. TAYLOR *Enthus.* i. (1867) 18 We ought not to heed the injudicious, and perhaps sinister, delicacy of some persons who had rather that truth should remain for ever sullied [etc.].

**4. a.** Corrupt, evil, bad, base.

**1474** *Rolls of Parlt.* VI. 110/1 Contynuyn in habundaunce of goodes and havour, to their sinister pleasure. **1477** EARL RIVERS (Caxton) *Dictes* 7 Leste ye be let or withdrawen therfro by eny sinistre or euil temptacion. **1549** *Compl. Scotl.* Ep. Ded. 2 Ane sinister inuentit false titil contrar our realme. **1574** WHITGIFT *Def. Aunsw.* iii. Wks. 1851 I. 302 When do partial and sinister affections more utter themselves, than when an election is committed to many? **1612** T. TAYLOR *Comm. Titus* ii. 12 Many in some blind and sinister respect or other, can come to heare Ieremie speaking from the Lord. **1656** BRAMHALL *Replic.* 16 He speaks of bad manners and vitious humors and sinister affections,..as envy, contention, contumacy, incontinency. **1780** BURKE *Sp. Econ. Reform* Wks. 1842 I. 254 To see us pervert our skill into a sinister and servile dexterity, for the purpose of evading our duty. **1823** BYRON *Juan* XIII. xxi, These were advantages:..he thought—It was his foible, but by no means sinister—That [etc.]. **1827** HOOD *Craniology* 79 Till one gets mastery good or sinister, And comes in like a new prime-minister. **1860** W. COLLINS *Wom. in White* xi, To the same hidden source and the same sinister influence.

b. Of motives, aims, etc.

Common from *c* 1590, esp. with *designs, ends, motives, views. sinister interest*, esp. in the works of the Utilitarian philosophers (see quot. 1827).

*a* **1533** LD. BERNERS *Gold. Bk. M. Aurel.* (1546) Q viij, Ye suppose my good desyres be sinister. **1594** HOOKER *Eccl. Pol.* IV. ix. §3 Is it so strange a matter to find a good thing furthered by ill men of a sinister intent and purpose? **1628** PRYNNE *Love-locks* 14 Men in our dayes doe nourish their Haire and Loue-lockes out of Vaine-glory, Pride,..and such like Sinister and sinfull ends. **1656** BRAMHALL *Replic.* viii. 324 If Henry the eighth had any other private sinistre grounds known only to himself, they doe not render the Reformation one jod the worse in it self. **1710** PRIDEAUX *Orig. Tithes* ii. 45 They may out of sinister and corrupt designs give false Judgments. **1771** *Junius Lett.* lxv. (1788) 337, I do not mean to enter into an examination of the partial, sinister motives of your conduct. **1804** WELLINGTON in Gurw. *Desp.* (1837) III. 133 The Marhatta Chiefs..have frequently applied to him to exert the influence..to carry their sinister objects. **1817** J. BENTHAM *Plan Parl. Reform* iii. p. xi, Here we have one partial, one separate, one sinister interest..with which the universal..interest has to antagonise. **1824** J. S. MILL in *Westm. Rev.* II. 347 When romance assumes the garb of history,..it infallibly allies itself with the sinister interests of the few. **1827** J. BENTHAM *Rationale Evid.* V. IX. i. 6 Interest when acting in such a direction and with such effect as to give birth to falsehood may be termed sinister interest. **1856** FROUDE *Hist. Eng.* (1858) I. ii. 133 Wolsey..soon satisfied the king that he had no sinister intentions. **1861** J. S. MILL *Repr. Govt.* vi. 118 The evils arising from the prevalence of modes of action in the representative body dictated by sinister interests (to employ the useful phrase introduced by Bentham), that is, interests conflicting more or less with the general good of the community. **1871** MORLEY *Condorcet* in *Crit. Misc.* Ser. I. (1878) 43 All the evils came from the sinister interests of the nobles.

†c. Erring; erroneous; astray *from* the right path. *Obs. rare.*

**1526** *Pilgr. Perf.* (W. de W. 1531) 63 b, Despyse suche synystre feares and shames, for they comme of the ennemy. **1549** COVERDALE *Erasm. Par. Gal.* 18 The sinistre rooted persuasion of the Jewes. **1632** LITHGOW *Trav.* IV. 157 They haue also this sinister opinion, that at the day of Iudgement..Mahomet shall appeare. **1634** HABINGTON *Castara* I. (Arb.) 12, I never felt a wanton heate, nor was my invention ever sinister from the straite way of chastity.

†5. Of persons: Acting or advising to one's detriment. *Obs. rare.*

*c* **1500** *Melusine* 258 Yf some of his synester frendes haue informed geffray. *a* **1548** HALL *Chron., Hen. VI,* 91 The displeasures to hym doen by the quene and her sinister counsailors.

6. a. Of omens, etc.: Portending or indicating misfortune or disaster; full of dark or gloomy suggestiveness; inauspicious, unfavourable.

Orig. denoting omens seen on the left hand, which was regarded as the unlucky side: cf. 9 c and DEXTER *a.* 1 c.

**1579** NORTH tr. *Plutarch, Marcellus* (1895) II. 370 To withdraw the evill from them these sinister tokens did threaten. **1600** E. BLOUNT tr. *Conestaggio* 29 Guided by some sinister starre. **1611** JONSON *Catiline Consp.* I. i, All the several ills that visit earth, Brought forth by night with a sinister birth, Plagues, famine, fire. **1700** MOXON *Math. Dict.* s.v., [When] Saturn [is] in *Aries*, and Mars in the same Degrees of *Gemini*,..Saturn is said to cast a Sinister Aspect to Mars. **1792** GOUVR. MORRIS in Sparks *Life & Writ.* (1832) II. 180 From such facts it is impossible not to draw the most sinister presages. **1828** SCOTT *F.M. Perth* xix, Dorothy..had that strong appetite for collecting and retailing sinister intelligence, which is often to be marked in the lower classes. **1855** MACAULAY *Hist. Eng.* xviii. IV. 230 Many said that those words, when examined, would be found full of sinister meaning. **1873** HORNER *Florence* (1884) I. xv. 226 The death of a lion [in Florence] was deplored as a sinister omen.

b. Of looks, etc.: Suggestive of evil or mischief.

**1797–1805** S. & HT. LEE *Canterb. T.* I. 374 In the countenance of St. Auber he thought he discerned something watchful and sinister. **1824** W. IRVING *T. Trav.* II. 112 The sinister expression with which she regarded the travellers. **1853** LYTTON *My Novel* III. ii, Such a smile!—so disagreeable and sinister! **1864** BURTON *Scot Abr.* II. i. 9 The typical Irish immigrant, with his sinister animal features.

*fig.* **1838** THIRLWALL *Greece* xxxviii. V. 68 This article, of so sinister an aspect, seems to have been inserted chiefly with a view to Thebes. **1838** PRESCOTT *Ferd. & Is.* (1846) I. vii. 318 It gives a sinister expression to her otherwise unblemished character.

*Comb.* **1838** DICKENS *O. Twist* xxxi, A rather ill-favoured countenance, and a turned-up, sinister-looking nose. **1884** COLBORNE *With Hicks Pasha* 131 Their only visible tenants being sinister-looking vultures.

c. Of natural objects, places, etc.

**1844** HOOD *Forge* 31 As wild a night As ever was known on that sinister height. **1856** KANE *Arctic Expl.* I. vii. 69 The sky looks sinister; a sort of scowl overhangs the blink. **1894** P. PINKERTON *Adriatica, Venice in Autumn*, I hear the madmen scream From sinister San Servolo.

7. Attended with mishap, misfortune, or disaster; unlucky, unfortunate; adverse.

Common *c* 1580 to 1670, esp. with *accident, chance, fate, fortune.*

**1576** FLEMING *Panopl. Epist.* 115 If I be intercepted with some sinister chaunce. **1580** LYLY *Euphues* (Arb.) 242 A trauailer that hath sustained harm by sinister fortune. **1642** ROGERS *Naaman* 8 Promising but a Sinister successe. **1670** MILTON *Hist. Eng.* III. Wks. 1851 III. 112 Thir Countrie, whose sinister fate had now blinded them for distruction. **1761** HUME *Hist. Eng.* I. xii. 287 Leicester himself, in case of any sinister accident, could easily take shelter in the city. **1792** COWPER *Lett.* 16 Sept., With no sinister accident to retard or terrify us. **1860** MOTLEY *Netherl.* xliv. IV. 243 A sinister event..had opened the series of transactions in the East, and had cast a gloom over the public sentiment at home.

8. Unfavourable, harmful, or prejudicial *to* a person, his interests, etc.

**1725** POPE *Odyss.* xx. 304 The bird of Jove Truss'd..a trembling dove: Sinister to their hope! **1771** BURKE *Corr.* (1844) I. 285 By some accident very sinister to me, you absolutely forget the defence. **1805** *Brathwait's Barnabees Jrnl.* Introd. (1818) 40 A place very sinister to English princes. **1851** HAWTHORNE *Twice-told T.* Ser. II. *Main Street*, Such a life was sinister to the intellect, and sinister to the heart.

II. 9. a. Situated on the left side of the body.

*c* **1475** *Partenay* 3049 The sinistre Arme smote he vppon. *c* **1500** *Melusine* 84 Raymondyn..putte..the hand senester at hys nek. **1597** A. M. tr. *Guillemeau's Fr. Chirurg.* 54/1 My Lord of Gyuri receaved a terrible shot in his sinistre shoulder. **1606** SHAKS. *Tr. & Cr.* IV. v. 128 My Mothers bloud Runs on the dexter cheeke, and this sinister Bounds in my fathers. **1682** DRYDEN *Mac-Fl.* 120 In his sinister hand ..He placed a mighty mug of potent ale. **1842** LOVER *Handy Andy* xxxix, The old lady substituted a black silk shade to obfuscate her sinister luminary.

*Comb.* *a* **1658** LOVELACE *Poems* (1864) 158 That which still makes her mirth to flow, Is our sinister-handed woe.

*absol.* **1861** in A. E. Lee *Hist. Columb.* (1892) II. 437 All the infinite variety of shakes..was executed upon the devoted sinister and dexter of the President.

b. Lying on or towards the left hand.

**1483** CAXTON *Gold. Leg.* 436 b/2 The preest translateth his book to the synyster parte of the aulter. **1600** DYMMOK *Ireland* (1843) 39 The sinister winge of the vantguard. *c* **1611** CHAPMAN *Iliad* XIII. 310 In the Greeks' left wing, The Trojans saw the Cretan king..And his attendant..Both cheering the sinister troops. **1650** FULLER *Pisgah* 67 We have placed the name of Amorites on the sinister front of this our description. **1830** GLEIG *Country Curate* I. iii. 48 Of the doors,..that behind is fastened to the sinister lintel by..five latches. **1871** M. COLLINS *Marq. & Merch.* III. iii. 74 A card with the name of the journal..engraved in the sinister corner.

c. With reference to omens. (Cf. 6.)

**1675** HOBBES *Odyss.* xx. 24 Then o'er their heads an Eagle flew on high Sinister. **1717** POPE *Iliad* XII. 257 The victor eagle, whose sinister flight Retards our host. **1734** tr. *Rollin's Anc. Hist.* (1827) I. Pref. 50 By the sinister flight of birds.

10. *Her.* Forming, or situated on, the left half of a shield (regarded from the bearer's point of view; cf. DEXTER). Also *absol.*

Cf. also BAR-, BATON-, BEND-SINISTER.

**1562** LEIGH *Armorie* 41 The sinister point..is in the left side of the same escocheon. **1637** HEYWOOD *Royal Ship* 43 Shee pointeth to Hercules on the sinister side, with his club in his hand. **1709** STRYPE *Ann. Ref.* I. Introd. 8 The sinister half [of the escutcheon] being as it were obscured or cut off. **1730** BAILEY (fol.), *Tenne*..is expressed in Engraving by Lines diagonal, from the Sinister Chief and Traverse. **1797** *Encycl. Brit.* (ed. 3) VIII. 447/2 The Bend is an ordinary formed by two diagonal lines, drawn from the dexter-chief to the sinister-base. **1864** BOUTELL *Her. Hist. & Pop.* xiv. 169 The sinister half of the impaled shield. **1868** CUSSANS *Heraldry* (1893) 53 *Purpure*, diagonal lines drawn from sinister to dexter.

b. *sinister bend*, = *bend-sinister*, BEND *sb.*[2] 3.

**1612** J. DAVIES (Heref.) *Muse's Sacr.* Wks. (Grosart) II. 83/2 A Sanguine-field, that beareth Harts, in chiefe, crost with sinister-bends. **1820** LAMB *Elia* I. *South-Sea Ho.*, His lineal pretensions, like his personal, favoured a little of the sinister bend.

11. Directed to the left; characterized by moving or turning towards the left. *rare.*

**1615** G. SANDYS *Trav.* 84 A hundred Knights Circling the sad pile with sinister rites [L. *ex more sinistro Orbe*]. **1644** BULWER *Chiron.* 102 To draw sinister circles, or rashly to fling the Hand up and downe. **1822** J. PARKINSON *Outl. Oryctol.* 224 *Ostrea serra*: suborbicular, sinister, gigantic.

12. Relating to the use of the left hand. *rare*$^{-1}$.

**1818** W. TAYLOR in *Monthly Rev.* LXXXVI. 7 It became practicable to keep the left hand habitually clean,..and there was no longer any occasion to persist in those sinister forbearances, which are..commanded.

**sinisterity** (sɪnɪˈstɛrɪtɪ). Now *rare.* [ad. late L. *sinisteritas*: see prec. and -ITY.]

†1. Sinister character; perversity; dishonesty. *Obs.*

**1647** TRAPP *Comm. 1 Thess.* i. 5 Sinisterity of ends is here opposed to sincerity in Gods work. **1659** FULLER *App. Inj. Innoc.* II. 101 The activity of the Romish Priests to gain Proselites: their dexterous sinisterity in seducing Souls. **1758** JORTIN *Life Erasmus* I. 113 On this point they judged not amiss, nor with their accustomed sinisterity, if we may be permitted to use that word.

†2. Lack of skill or dexterity; clumsiness, awkwardness. *Obs.*$^{-0}$

**1623** COCKERAM I, *Sinisteritie*, vnhandsomnesse. **1656** BLOUNT *Glossogr.*, *Sinisterity*,..lack of grace in doing a thing.

3. Use of the left hand; skill in this.

**1877** SHILLETO in *Cambr. Jrnl. Philol.* VII. 155 The Latin thief's *sinisterity* of hand became proverbial.

**sinisterly** (ˈsɪnɪstəlɪ), *adv.* Forms: see SINISTER *a.*; also 6 -lye, 6–7 -lie. [f. SINISTER *a.* + -LY[2]. Cf. L. *sinistrē*, F. *sinistrement.*]

1. In an inauspicious or unlucky manner; unfortunately; ominously.

**1465** *Paston Lett.* II. 174 Yff onye thyng falle sinistrely only yn theyr deffaut, as God defend. **1586** WARNER *Alb. Eng.* II. vii. (1602) 30 Beholding how sinisterly the double fight hath past. **1611** COTGR., *Malheureusement*,..vnluckily, vnfortunately, sinisterly, disastrously. **1624** HEYWOOD *Gunaik.* I. 37 If any thing sinisterlie happen unto him through his owne temeritie. **1930** D. H. LAWRENCE *A Propos of Lady Chatterley's Lover* 6 The effect is peculiarly depressing, sinisterly high-brow. **1946** G. MILLAR *Horned Pigeon* xxi. 346 The ducks looked happy and healthy, perhaps sinisterly so. **1969** [see RENTIER]. **1974** E. JONES *Barlow comes to Judgement* 48 There is nothing sinisterly secret about the WHY Club.

†2. In a derogatory manner; with malicious depreciation. *Obs.*

**1491** CAXTON *Vitas Patr.* (W. de W. 1495) II. 260 b/1 They asked what man..had so euyll and synystryly spoken of the sayd abbot. **1506** *Eng. Misc.* (Surtees, 1890) 52 Oon Bartrame Dawson..is senysterly defamed that he shulde be a Scottysshman borne. **1579** *Reg. Privy Council Scot.* III. 158 Heiring that his just and necessarie intentioun..to be sinisterlie reportit of. **1606** J. CARPENTER *Solomon's Solace* vii. 26 He hath not opened..both [his ears] vnto him which hath sinistrelie..slaundered me. **1608** D. T. *Ess. Pol. & Mor.* 128 b, Hee ouerthrewe Marcellus, by accusing him to haue spoken somewhat sinisterly of Caesar.

†3. In an unfavourable sense; with a bias towards the worst view. *Obs.*

Very common down to *c* 1650, esp. with *conceive, interpret,* and *judge.*

**1529** MORE *Supplic. Souls* Wks. 297 Such as would be glad sinisterly to misseconster euery thyng towarde the clergy. **1538** WRIOTHESLY in Ellis *Orig. Lett.* Ser. II. II. 110, I write this unto You bicause you may peraventur here sumwhat hereof, and the thing percase sinisterly interpreted. **1581** G. PETTIE tr. *Guazzo's Civ. Conv.* (1586) I. 13 b, The mallice of men is so greate, that they..thinke sinisterlie and preposterouslie of all the good deedes which are wrought. **1600** HEYWOOD *1st Pt. Edw. IV*, Wks. 1874 I. 77 If now some giddy fancy in your braine Make you conceiue sinisterly of her. **1653** GAUDEN *Hierasp.* 274, I would have nothing in Him, that is justly to be blamed, or sinisterly suspected.

†4. a. With evil intent or purpose; maliciously, malevolently. *Obs.*

**1549** *Compl. Scot.* Ep. Ded. 2 Quhen thai & mordocheus var sinisterly accusit, and alse persecutit, be amman. **1586** A. DAY *Eng. Secretary* I. (1625) 88 A matter sinisterly suggested unto you against mee without any maintainable reason. **1642** *Consid. Duties Prince & People* 20 As there are those that are sinisterly officious to the one, so are there toward the other. *a* **1691** A. WOOD *Hist. & Antiq. Univ. Oxf.* (1796) II. 444 The scholars' arms..were not borrowed of them, as some had sinisterly suggested.

†b. Unfavourably; adversely. *Obs.*

*a* **1600** HOOKER *Answ. Travers' Supplic.* §6 That I am.. one which refuse to be at peace with such as embrace the truth, and side my selfe with men sinisterly affected thereunto. **1618** *Barnevelt's Apol.* B 3, The Gouernours of the free cities were sinisterly affected towards the State.

†5. In a wrongful or wicked manner. *Obs.*

**1532** MORE *Confut. Tindale* Wks. 615/2 Nowe is not the tytle of hys Chapter so sinistrelye written and wryed awaye from the poynte. **1581** *Reg. Privy Council Scot.* III. 394 Sinisterlie purchest upoun wrang narratioun maid to oure Soverane Lord. **1617** COLLINS *Def. Bp. Ely* II. ix. 381 Dissembling our sinnefulnesse, and reioycing sinisterly in our supposed perfection. **1625** B. JONSON *Staple of N.* v. ii, You told me you had got a growen estate, By griping meanes, sinisterly.

†6. Clumsily; awkwardly. *Obs. rare.*

**1628** EARLE *Microcosm.* (Arb.) 41 Hee [the scholar] ascends a horse somwhat sinisterly, though not on the left side. **1633** BP. HALL *Hard T.*, *N.T.* 258 The fooles heart and hand goes sinisterly to work. **1650** B. *Discollim.* 14 Some of our new Architectors have read some Authors..with their left eyes, which makes them work with their left hands, so sinisterly.

**ˈsinisterness.** *rare.* [f. as prec. + -NESS.] The quality of being sinister, in various senses.

**1659** GAUDEN *Tears Ch.* 62 The ignorance,..precipitancy and sinisternesse of their silly censures. **1727** BAILEY (vol. II. ed. 2), *Sinisterness*, Unfairness, Self-Interestedness [**1730** (fol.) *adds* Aukwardness].

**ˈsinistrad,** *adv. rare.* [f. L. *sinistra* left hand + *-ad* (see DEXTRAD).] To or towards the left side; sinistrally. Also with *of.*

**1803** J. BARCLAY *New Anat. Nomencl.* 166 In the head and trunk,..Sinistrad will signify towards the sinistral [aspect]. **1808** —— *Muscular Motions* 331 All muscles..must..be situated either dextrad or sinistrad of the mesial plane. **1885** *Buck's Hand-bk. Med. Sci.* VIII. 109 The section-plane.. passed just sinistrad of the meson.

**sinistral** (ˈsɪnɪstrəl), *a.* Also 5 **sinistralle**, 6 **synys-**, **synis-**, **sinistrall**. [a. OF. *sinistral* (*senestral*), or ad. med.L. **sinistrālis*: see SINISTER and -AL[1].]

I. †1. Adverse; unlucky. *Obs. rare.*

*c* **1475** *Harl. Contin. Higden* (Rolls) VIII. 445 Dredynge not sinistralle fortune in batells.

†2. Likely, or designed, to cause mischief. *Obs.*

**1534** in Ellis *Orig. Lett.* Ser. III. II. 298 To geue to yow notycyon of certyn synystrall matters, contrary to o[r] realme of Ynglond. **1536** BOORDE *Let.* in *Introd. Knowl.* (1870) 52 Stultycyusly thorow synystrall words, I dyd as many of þat order doth. **1561** F. COX *Retraction* (title-p.), Certain sinistral and devilish acts.

†3. Darkly suspicious; very unfavourable. *Obs.*

**1560** DAUS tr. *Sleidane's Comm.* 365 Neither will they therefore conceive any sinistrall suspicion of so great a king. *Ibid.* 392 b, Divers men have had a sinistrall opinion of him. **1572** KETHE *Serm. Blandford* Pref. A 2, Their sinistral reportes of my Sermon.

†4. Heterodox; unsound. *Obs.*

**1545** COVERDALE *Abridgem. Erasm. Enchirid.* Prol., But what so euer is spoken..that same is..iudged of them to be of a wrong and synistrall oppinion. **1547** BOORDE *Introd. Knowl.* xvi. (1870) 165 Synistrall opinions, as concernynge prestes to haue wyues, wyth such like matters.

II. 5. a. Situated on the left side of the body; of or pertaining to the left hand or side.

**1803** J. Barclay *New Anat. Nomencl.* 121 As for the lateral parts of the trunk, *Right* and *Left* might still denote these; although..*Dextral* and *Sinistral* might perhaps be preferable. **1828** *Harrovian* 185 A letter of goodly dimensions in the digits of our sinistral hand. **1894** *Nation* 30 Aug. 163/3 Because so few people are left-handed, a very good clue is afforded when a sinistral sign is discovered.

**b.** *spec.* (See quot. 1866.)

**1839** *Penny Cycl.* XIII. 498/1 Shell thin..; internal lip dilated, the aperture ovate or ovato-lanceolate, sinistral. **1866** R. Tate *Brit. Mollusks* iii. 45 When the aperture is on the left hand side it is said to be sinistral.

**c.** *fig.* Illegitimate. (Cf. LEFT-HANDED *a.* 5.)

**1897** Hazlitt *Four Generations* II. 172 To the country which paid him so well, he proved himself grateful by distributing his sinistral representatives of both sexes pretty freely, when there was a berth at his disposal.

**6.** *Conch.* Characterized by turning spirally from right to left; reversed, left-handed.

**1833** *Penny Cycl.* I. 510/2 The *Syphonariæ*..are the only shells they can be confounded with, by their being sinistral. **1839** *Ibid.* XIII. 499 [They] explain how..appearances place a sinistral animal in a dextral shell. **1881** Bock *Head-Hunters Borneo* xxiii. 242 They also brought me a sinistral Helix of a dark, reddish brown colour. **1888** Rolleston & Jackson *Anim. Life* 474 It is rare for a left-handed or sinistral twist to be normal in a given genus or species.

**7.** Of flat-fishes: Having what is properly the left side converted into the upper or coloured one.

**1882** Day *Fishes Gt. Brit.* II. 1 When referring to the pleuronectoids the terms right (dextral) or left (sinistral) are employed with reference to the position of the upper or coloured side.

**8.** Of persons: Left-handed. Also as *sb.*, a left-handed person.

**1904** *Westm. Gaz.* 6 Aug. 11/3 Two per cent. of mankind are naturally sinistral. **1927** [see DEXTRAL *a.* 1 c]. **1964** M. Critchley *Developmental Dyslexia* xiv. 84 The patient declared herself to be right-handed, but she wore her wrist-watch on the right arm like many sinistrals do.

**9.** *Geol.* Being or pertaining to a strike-slip fault in which the motion of the block on the farther side of the fault from an observer is towards the left. Opp. *dextral*.

**1942** E. M. Anderson *Dynamics of Faulting* v. 55 E. E. L. Dixon has distinguished the types of displacement as right-hand and left-hand heaves... The two classes of fault-planes may well be termed 'dextral' and 'sinistral'. *Ibid.* 71 The Bala fault-zone..is undoubtedly sinistral. **1964** A. Holmes *Princ. Physical Geol.* (ed. 2) ix. 219 In strike-slip faults the relative displacement of the block on the far side of the fault, as viewed from the ground, may have been either to the right (giving a right-lateral or dextral fault) or to the left (giving a left-lateral or sinistral fault). **1978** *Nature* 5 Jan. 50/2 The Bathurst and McDonald faults.., which form the boundaries of the Slave wedge are major sinistral and dextral strike-slip fault systems that extend for hundreds of kilometres.

**sinistrality** (sɪnɪˈstrælɪtɪ). [f. prec. + -ITY.] The state or quality of being sinistral.

**1852** Roget *Thesaurus* p. xxii. *note*, I have..framed from the adjectives..*sinistral*, and *gaseous*, the abstract nouns ..*sinistrality*, and *gaseity*. **1888** *Proc. U.S. Nat. Mus.* XI. 604 A certain coincidence between conditions of temperature and dextrality or sinistrality of the species [*Synaptura*]. **1904** *Sat. Rev.* 10 Sept. 326 The meaning which the disputants attach to what they call sinistrality.

**sinistrally** (ˈsɪnɪstrəlɪ), *adv.* [f. as prec.]

†**1.** In a sinister manner; perversely, wrongly.

**1548** Udall, etc. *Erasm. Par. Matt.* vii. 49 Sinistrally expounding thynges that be doutfull. **1560** Daus tr. *Sleidane's Comm.* 467 He..had heard how sinistrally.. many euill men spake and thought of him.

**2.** Towards the left.

**1847** in Webster. **1881** Le Conte *Sight* 19 To rotate it on its axis outward, i.e. dextrally..for the right and sinistrally for the left.

**3.** *Conch.* and *Bot.* With the whorl, spathe, or the like turning towards the left.

**1854** Woodward *Mollusca* II. 202 Operculum sinistrally sub-spiral. **1881** *Jrnl. Linnean Soc.* XV. 273 Sinistrally inclined ribs. **1883** *Jrnl. Bot. Brit. & For.* 237 The spathes ..are rolled up indifferently either way—either dextrally or sinistrally.

**siniˈstration.** *rare.* [f. L. *sinistr-*, stem of *sinister* + -ATION. Cf. med.L. *sinistrāre* to go on the left hand, to be adverse.] **a.** A moving or turning leftwards. **b.** The state or condition of being sinistral.

**1891** in *Cent. Dict.*

**siˈnistrine**, *a.* [f. as prec. + -INE[1].] Left.

**1792** *Baron Munchausen* xxix. 133 Either [champion] stamped his foot sinistrine.

**sinistro-** (ˈsɪnɪstrəʊ), used as combining form of SINISTER, in the sense 'on, situated in, directed or turning towards the left', as *sinistro-cerebral*, *-gyrate*, *-gyric* adjs.; *sinistro-sacrad* adv.

**1803** J. Barclay *New Anat. Nomencl.* 174 The position of the heart in the thorax;..we may say its direction from the mesial plane is sinistrad and sacral, or sinistro-sacrad. **1885** *Proc. Soc. Psychol. Research* III. 43 The replacement of some sinistro-cerebral by some dextro-cerebral centre of sight or speech. **1887** *Amer. Jrnl. Psychol.* I. 194 All movements of the hand..from right to left are sinistrogyric. **1898** *Daily Graphic* 16 Feb. 9/4 The writing..was sinistrogyrate, or centrifugal.

**sinistrorsal** (sɪnɪˈstrɔːsəl), *a.* [f. next + -AL[1].] **a.** (See first quot.) **b.** = SINISTRAL *a.* 6.

**1828–32** Webster (citing Henry), *Sinistrorsal*, rising from left to right, as a spiral line or helix. **1840** *Cuvier's Anim. Kingd.* 345 The whorls turn obliquely to the right side in nearly all the species, but in a small number to the left; and the latter are named *reversed*, (or *sinistrorsal*). **1842** *Penny Cycl.* XXII. 51/2 Shell sinistrorsal, pyriform, very ventricose. **1868** *Nat. Encycl.* I. 697 *Ancylus*, a genus of little fresh-water snails..; the animal being, as Rang considers, sinistrorsal.

Hence **siniˈstrorsally** *adv.*

**1884** *Proc. Zool. Soc.* May 364 The heterostrophe or sinistrorsally spiral apex.

**sinistrorse** (ˈsɪnɪstrɔːs), *a.* [ad. L. *sinistrorsus*, contracted f. **sinistrōvorsus*, f. *sinister* left + *vertĕre* to turn.]

**1.** *Bot.* Twining or turning spirally from right to left.

The word has been used in two opposite senses, owing to a difference in the supposed position of the observer: see quot. 1870 and cf. note on DEXTRORSE.

**1856** Henslow *Dict. Bot. Terms* 174 *Sinistrorse*,..towards the left hand. **1870** *Henfrey's Bot.* (ed. 2) 100 In determining the direction of spirals,..it is usual to suppose one's self standing in the axis of the organ; but many authors suppose themselves standing in front of it;..hence great confusion in the application of the terms *dextrorse* and *sinistrorse*. **1879** A. Gray *Struct. Bot.* (ed. 6) iv. §3. 140 Direction of Overlapping..may be either to the right (dextrorse) or to the left (sinistrorse).

**2.** Moving or going towards the left.

**1891** in *Cent. Dict.*

**sinistrous** (ˈsɪnɪstrəs), *a.* Also 6 sinistrus, -terous, sinystrous. [f. the stem of L. *sinister* SINISTER *a.* + -OUS.

The stressing *siˈnistrous* appears occasionally in verse, and is given by Smart (1836) as proper to sense 5.]

**I.** †**1.** Erroneous, perverse, heretical. *Obs.*

**1560** Whitehorne tr. *Machiavelli's Arte Warre* 1 b, There hath growen these sinisterous opinions, which maketh men to hate the warlike seruice. **1581** J. Hamilton in *Cath. Tract.* (S.T.S.) 76 Euerie curious heid..mycht..apply thame to ane peruerse and sinistrous sense. **1632** Lithgow *Trav.* v. 194 They approue the apprehension of such a sinistrous opinion with these arguments.

†**2.** Malicious, unfair, prejudiced. *Obs.*

**1593** in Spottiswood *Hist. Ch. Scot.* vi. (1677) 400 The sinistrous informations of ill-disposed people. **1632** Lithgow *Trav.* I. 2 Concerning sinistrous censures. **1693** R. Fleming *Disc. Earthquakes* 14 How sad a Token is it, when such are not only rejected, but have a sinistrous and false Application made of the same. **1751** Johnson *Rambler* No. 176 ⁋8 The sinistrous interpretations or absurd remarks of haste and ignorance.

†**3.** Underhand; dishonest; corrupt. *Obs.*

**1600** W. Clarke in *Archpr. Controv.* (Camden) I. 168 These moste indirecte and sinisterous procedinges. **1637** Gillespie *Eng. Pop. Cerem.* Ep. A 2, A pitty it is to see the crooked and sinistrous courses of the greattest part. **1689** *Trial Pritchard v. Papillon* 34 Embark'd in sinistrous and unjustifiable ways. **1717** Wodrow *Corr.* (1843) II. 327 The coming in by this door..is..a proof of..sinistrous designs in entering upon the holy office of the ministry.

**4.** Betokening or attended with misfortune or disaster; ill-omened, inauspicious, unlucky; baleful, malign, etc.

*a* **1575** tr. *Pol. Verg. Eng. Hist.* (Camden, No. 36) 177 Aswaldus..likewise with sinistrus fortune obteined the regall sceptre. **1598** Yong *Diana* 148 Those fauourable or sinistrous successes of Fortune. **1607** Earl Stirling *J. Cæsar* IV. ii, Which to my soule sinistrous signes impart. **1633** Hart *Diet of Diseased* III. v. 244 Some have observed some sinistrous accident to have insued the use of this remedy. **1733** Budgell *Bee* I. 498 Nor Thunder-Crack Sinistrous roar'd Presage. **1775** Johnson *Journ. Hebrides* Wks. 1825 IX. 126 The arrival of a beggar on an island is accounted a sinistrous event. **1832** Southey in *Q. Rev.* XLVIII. 277 An English traveller noticed it, in his journal, as a sinistrous omen. **1873** Browning *Red Cott. Nt.-cap* 1026 Not one grace Outspread before you but is registered In that sinistrous coil.

**II.** †**5.** Of or pertaining to, situated on, the left hand or side. *Obs.*

**1646** Sir T. Browne *Pseud. Ep.* IV. ii. 182 The heart doth seem to incline unto the left,..because its sinistrous gravity is drawne that way. *Ibid.* 191 The distance of the North and Southerne pole..is equall unto the space between the East and West, accounted the dextrous and sinistrous parts thereof. **1678** Cudworth *Intell. Syst.* 221 The Contrarieties and Conjugations of things, such as..Dextrous and Sinistrous, Eaven and Odd, and the like.

†**6.** *fig.* Left-handed; slow. *Obs.*[−1]

**1682** Sir T. Browne *Chr. Mor.* III. xx, Many, who are sinistrous unto Good Actions, are Ambi-dexterous unto bad.

**7.** Of flat-fishes: = SINISTRAL *a.* 7.

**1803** Shaw *Gen. Zool.* IV. 318 Sinistrous Flounder, *Pleuronectes Passer*... Brown Flounder, with eyes toward the left.

**sinistrously** (ˈsɪnɪstrəslɪ), *adv.* [f. prec.]

†**1.** Unfavourably, *esp.* with display of prejudice against a person. *Obs.*

In the first quot. there is connexion with sense 3.

**1560** Whitehorne tr. *Machiavelli's Arte Warre* 90 b, If the Capitaine..in lightynge of his horse fell, it was of yᵉ souldiours interpreted sinisterously. **1639** Drumm. of Hawth. *Magical Mirror* Wks. (1711) 174 Evil-affected and malicious Spirits..may sinistrously interpret and calumniate the Resolution. **1682** Sir T. Browne *Chr. Mor.* I. xvi, To accuse, calumniate,..detract, or sinistrously interpret others. *a* **1733** R. North *Lives* (1826) I. 266 He had his jury to deal with, and if he did not tread upon eggs, they would conclude sinistrously, and be apt to find against his opinion.

**2.** In an erroneous manner; incorrectly, wrongly, perversely; awkwardly.

**1581** *Satir. Poems Reform.* xliv. 223 Scripture perqueir he hes sinistrouslie. *a* **1670** Hacket *Cent. Serm.* 354 Some of them take Scripture to prove it, but most untowardly;..yet more sinistrously from those words 'If I be lifted up'. **1684** tr. *Bonet's Merc. Compit.* VIII. 307 Digestive and abstersive remedies, applied sinistrously and amiss. **1699** Bentley *Phalaris* xiii. 407 Mr. B.'s general Reflections upon the Stability of the Greek Tongue; which he has made so sinistrously, and with so very little Judgment. **1880** S. Cox *Comm. Job* 416 The Critics misconceive Elihu as completely and sinistrously as Job was by his friends.

†**3.** Inauspiciously, unfortunately. *Obs.*

**1607** Earl Stirling *J. Cæsar* III. ii, Pacifie thy brest Lest sorrows but sinistrously presage That which thou would'st not wish. **1611** Cotgr., *Sinistrement*, sinisterously, vnluckily.

**4.** Corruptly; by underhand means.

**1817** Bentham *Parl. Reform* Introd. 209 The promiscuous multitude being by intellectual weakness prepared for the reception of mental poison—the select few, by sinistrously derived strength, for the injecting of it—observe [etc.].

**5.** With a tendency to use the left hand in preference to the right; with the left hand.

**1646** Sir T. Browne *Pseud. Ep.* 190 Many in their infancy are sinistrously disposed, and divers continue all their life.. left handed. **1830** *Blackw. Mag.* XXVIII. 888 We often stand shut up in that sentry-looking canvass box, dexterously, and sinistrously fingering the string.

†**siˈnistruous**, *a.* *Sc. Obs. rare.* [f. L. *sinister*: cf. forms like *monstruous*.] = SINISTROUS *a.*

**1582–8** *Hist. & Life of Jas. VI* (1804) 275 Twa poets of Edinburgh, perceauing his sinistruous dealling, did publish the same to the people. **1671** [R. Mac Ward] *True Nonconf.* 351 A most effectuall corrective, both of sinistruous designes, and evill mixtures. **1687** *Lond. Gaz.* No. 2221/4 Considering that some Oaths are capable of being Wrested by Men of Sinistruous Intentions.

Hence †**siˈnistruously** *adv.* *Obs. rare.*

**1582** in Sir J. Melville *Mem.* (1735) 259 Sinistruously perverting the same. *a* **1615** *Brieue Cron. Erlis of Ross* (1850) 17 He was sinistruously and wrongously put out of the Abbay.

**Sinitic** (sɪˈnɪtɪk), *a.* [f. late L. *Sin-æ* (see SINÆAN) + -ITIC.] Of, pertaining or relating to, the Chinese, or other oriental peoples.

**1895** in *Funk's Stand. Dict.* **1900** *Speaker* 8 Sept. 614/1 The Professor of Sinitic languages replied in our rough Western way.

**sink** (sɪŋk), *sb.*[1] Forms: 5–6 **synke** (5 **cynke**), 6 **syncke, synk**; 6–7 **sin(c)ke, sinck**, 6– **sink**. [f. SINK *v.* Cf. LG. and G. dial. *sinke* a hollow or depression in the ground; Fris. *sink* sinker on a net.

Kilian gives 'Sincke. *vetus.* Cloaca, latrina. *Ang. sincke*'; but there is no independent evidence for this, and the citation of the English word renders the entry suspicious.]

**I. 1. a.** A pool or pit formed in the ground for the receipt of waste water, sewage, etc.; a cesspool; a receptacle for filth or ordure. Now *rare*.

*c* **1440** *Promp. Parv.* 456/2 Synke, for water receyvynge, ..*exceptorium*. **1463** *Bury Wills* (Camden) 20 Yᵉ newe prevy hous ovir the synke. **1515** Barclay *Egloges* II. (1570) B iij, Of a trene vesell then must thou nedely drinke, Olde, blacke and rustie, lately taken fro some sinke. **1589** *Hay any Work* 39 If you would haue a good sauour, you must go to the sincke for it. **1603** H. Crosse *Vertues Commw.* (1878) 117 A Play is like a Sincke in a Towne, where vnto all the filth doth runne. **1662** J. Davies tr. *Olearius' Voy. Amb.* 373 He converted..the Sepulchre into a Sink or common House of Ease. **1726** Leoni *Alberti's Archit.* I. 58/1 Make good large Sinks, and..fill them up with Sand, which will suck up.. the superfluous moisture. **1731** Swift *To Gay* Wks. 1751 X. 204 You want a Hand to clear a filthy Sink; No cleanly Workman can endure the Stink. **1856** Stanley *Sinai & Pal.* iii. 179 The cave within being the sink described in the Talmud as that into which the blood and offal of the sacrifices were drained off.

*fig.* **1567** *Gude & Godlie B.* (S.T.S.) 185 The watter of life we gaif thame neuer to drink, Bot stinkand pulis of euerie rottin synk. **1588** Shaks. *Tit. A.* III. ii. 19 Against thy hart make thou a hole, That all the teares that thy poore eyes let fall May run into that sinke.

**b.** A conduit, drain, or pipe for carrying away dirty water or sewage; an opening specially made for this purpose; a sewer. Now *rare*.

**1499** *Promp. Parv.* (Pynson), Cynke of Lawere, *mergulus*. **1509–10** *Durh. Acc. Rolls* (Surtees) 105 Pro layng le Synkys in lardariis carnium et piscium. **1564** Haward *Eutropius* I. 3 He builded..sinkes also to avoid the filthe & ordure of the city. **1601** Holland *Pliny* II. 582 The vaulted sinks also and draughts..which he deuised, by..cutting through the seuen hils. **1683** Moxon *Mech. Exerc., Printing* ii. ⁋1 The Lye-Trough and Rincing-Trough he places towards some corner of the Room,..and under these he causes a Sink to be made to convey the Water out of the Room. **1719** De Foe *Crusoe* I. 95 To cut a Hole thro' my new Fortification like a Sink to let Water go out. **1774** *Beverley & Hessle Road Act* ii. 9 Ditches, watercourses, sinks or drains. **1847** W. C. L. Martin *The Ox* 96/1 Two sinks, or drains, with iron gratings over them, to catch the fluid refuse from the gutters.

**c.** A basin or receptacle made of stone, metal, or other material, and having a pipe attached for the escape of water to a drain, etc.; *esp.* such a basin fitted in a kitchen or scullery, and having a supply of water connected with it.

**1566** *Eng. Ch. Furniture* (Peacock, 1866) 65, ij alter Stones —One Mr. Sheffield haith made a sinck of in his kitchine.

**1611** Cotgr., *Aiguier*, a sinke, or washing stone, in a kitchin. **1634** in *Archaeologia* XXXV. 197 In the kitchen.. A grate for the sincke. **1726** Leoni *Alberti's Archit.* I. 95/2 A large Kitchen..with an oven, stove, pump and sink. **1827** Faraday *Chem. Manip.* i. 17 So advantageous is the unlimited use of water, and a regular sink with its drain. **1852** Mrs. Stowe *Uncle Tom's C.* xiii. 115 Simeon..was washing his hands at a neat sink, in a little back porch. **1897** *Allbutt's Syst. Med.* III. 759 Attention must be paid to the housemaid's sink.

*fig.* **1893** Sir R. Ball *Story of Sun* 190 Certain [sun-] spots are, as it were, sinks by which cooler gases descend into the Sun's interior.

**2.** *fig.* **a.** A receptacle or gathering-place *of* vice, corruption, etc.

In common use from *c* 1560; sometimes of single persons.

**1526** *Pilgr. Perf.* (W. de W. 1531) 242 Manasses was as the pyt and synke of all fylth & synne. **1547** J. Harrison *Exhort. to Scottes* b v b, Afore I will stirre that vnsauery sinke of treson and trecherie. **1684** tr. *Bonet's Merc. Compit.* VI. 160 Unless that humour be discharged, it will become a sink of many difficult evils. **1707** J. Stevens tr. *Quevedo's Com. Wks.* (1709) 410 The Man..was the very sink of Fraud and Deceit. **1764** Goldsm. *Trav.* 359 Where kings have toil'd.., One sink of level avarice shall lie. **1822** Hazlitt *Table-T.* Ser. II. x. (1869) 196 The low, dull, level sinks of ignorance and vulgarity. **1855** Motley *Dutch Rep.* II. v. (1866) 215 The justice and finance councils were sinks of iniquity. **1879** G. Macdonald *P. Faber* II. x. 185 What vaults of uncleanness, what sinks of deathful horrors, would not the souls of some of us grow!

**b.** A place in which vice or corruption is rank or rampant.

**1550** Bale *Eng. Votaries* II. A ij, Rome hath bene so synnefull a syncke & pernicious puddell. **1587** Golding *De Mornay* xi. (1592) 160 To toyle it selfe..in this sincke here beneath, I meane this elementall world. **1622** Drayton *Poly-olb.* xix. 25 A city's but a sink, gay houses gawdy graves. **1647** Fuller *Good Th. in Worse T.* (1841) 116 This necessary severity doth sweep their state from being the sink of sinners, the rendezvous of rogues. **1691** Norris *Pract. Disc.* 258 Any good that this World, this Sediment and Sink of the Creation, can afford. **1874** Deutsch *Rem.* 247 The wanton and absurd insult expressly thrown in the face of London..as compared to Rome, that sink of sinks. **1884** Sharman *Hist. Swearing* viii. 150 The sinks and hiding-places of a great city.

†**c.** A collective mass of unsavoury or objectionable matters. *Obs.*

**1577–87** Holinshed *Chron.* III. 1047/1 So manie greeuous faults meeting togither in one sinke. **1589** Nashe *M. Marprelate* Wks. (Grosart) I. 160 To leaue furder stirring of this stinking sink. **1657** Sanderson *Serm.* (1674) 29, I irk to rake longer in this sink.

†**d.** The scum or dregs *of* a place or set of persons. *Obs.* (Cf. L. *sentina.*)

**1573** Baret *Alv.* s.v. *Rascals*, The rascall and vile sort of men: yᵉ sinke of the citie.., *sentina, colluuies vrbis.* **1658** Cleveland *Rustic Rampant* Wks. (1687) 407 No less than 5000 of the sink of the People meet ill armed. **1692** R. L'Estrange *Josephus, Wars of Jews* IV. vi. (1733) 702 As to their Quality, they are the very Scum and Sink of Mankind. **1740** in Wordsw. *Scholæ Acad.* (1877) 313, 2 of King's College..happened to meet with some of yᵉ sink of yᵉ Town.

**e.** A place where things are swallowed up or lost.

**1648** J. Beaumont *Psyche* VI. cxciv, That dark Cave Where Sorrows find their sink, and Cares their grave. **1789** B. Rush *Med. Enquiries* 79 Dr. Rush..terms them [*sc.* hospitals], 'The sinks of human life in an army,' and says, 'they robbed the United States of more citizens than the sword'. **1813** Wellington in Gurw. *Desp.* (1838) XI. 76 As the Secretary of State's office is a sink of papers, and these are really curious,..I shall be glad to have them [*sc.* papers] again.

**f.** In semi-proverbial phr. ***a mind like a sink***, an imagination that tends to put an indecent or lewd construction on events. *slang.*

**1932** A. Christie *Thirteen Problems* x. 170 And if one tries to warn them..they tell one that one has a Victorian mind —and that, they say, is like a *sink*. **1949** Wodehouse *Uncle Dynamite* viii. 129 He concluded by saying that it was a pity that some people, whose identity he did not specify, had minds like sinks. **1970** S. Taylor *Murder grows Roots* ii. 16 [She] said he'd probably gone off with some woman. Her mind's like a sink!

**g.** Used *attrib.* of a (school, estate, etc., in a) socially deprived area.

**1972** *Daily Mail* 4 Oct. 25/3 The downward spiral of decline in the 'sink' areas could be broken if the school led the way. **1972** *Guardian* 17 Oct. 17/4 It is a pity..that there is not a 'sink' schools conference, like the Headmasters' Conference of the public schools, to act as a general champion of the rights of urban schools. **1976** *New Society* 18 Nov. 365/2 Somewhere, in every town that has council houses at all, there's a 'sink' estate—the roughest and shabbiest on the books, disproportionately tenanted by families with problems, and despised both by those who live there and the town at large. **1981** *Observer* 8 Feb. 29/4 None of its problems has reduced Callow to a 'sink' school: it has great achievements, including children in its first sixth form about to depart bright-eyed and bushy-tailed to university.

**3.** *transf.* **a.** A receptacle of foul or waste matter.

**1590** Spenser *F.Q.* I. i. 22 She poured forth out of her hellish sinke Her fruitfull cursed spawne of serpents small. **1601** Weever *Mirr. Mart.* C ij b, The sea [is now] a sinke, and riuers to the same Are rotten pipes. **1655** Culpepper, etc. *Riverius* XIII. ii. 363 The Mesentery..is as it were the sink into which the Noble Parts do send their superfluous Excrements. **1684** *Contempl. State of Man* II. vii. (1699) 206 Hell is the Worlds sink, and the receptacle of all the Filth in this Great Frame.

†**b.** ***the sink(s) of the body***, the organs of digestion and excretion. *Obs.*

**1607** Shaks. *Cor.* I. i. 126 The Cormorant belly.., Who is the sinke a th' body. **1649** Jer. Taylor *Gt. Exemp.* III. 102 From the sinks of our body no such sweet or salutary emanations are observed. **1691** Ray *Creation* (1714) 230 It is also observable that the Sinks of the Body are removed as far from the Nose and Eyes as may be.

**II.** †**4. a.** The well or fountain of a lamp. *Obs.*⁻⁰

*c* **1440** *Promp. Parv.* 456/2 Synke, of a lampe (*P.* holdinge the risshe), *mergulus.*

†**b.** *Founding.* ? A hole dug in the ground for placing a gun-mould. *Obs. rare.*

**1541** *Acc. Ld. High Treas. Scot.* VIII. 125 Gevin to v men ..making and drying of the mulde and spindill, casting of the sink. **1542** *Ibid* 126 Clengeing of the sink and rynnyng of the mettell.

†**c.** A waxen tube or pipe for carrying off melted wax from the model of a statue. *Obs. rare.*

**1756** *Chambers' Cycl.* s.v. *Foundery*, When the wax-work is finished and every part corrected, all these pieces are placed again upon the core, in order to fix hollow pipes of wax in them from every part of the figure,..called sinks.

†**5.** The well of a ship. *Obs.* (= L. *sentina.*)

**1611** Cotgr., *Lossec*, the sinke, or well, of the pumpe of a ship. **1638** Heywood *Drown. Royall Ship* 14 Her sinke drew no more water than one man might easily empty by a pumpe. **1687** A. Lovell tr. *Thevenot's Trav.* I. 270 In the lower Deck they had a very convenient Pump; it is an Iron-Chain..that reaches down to the Sink. **1711** *Phil. Trans.* XXVII. 365 A stink, much like that of the Sink of a Ship.

**6.** *Mining.* **a.** A pit-shaft. Now *rare.*

In quot. 1896 the sense may be 'process of sinking'.

**1576** *Reg. Privy Council Scot.* II. 507 To serche out..leid mynes.., to brek the ground and mak sinkis and pottis thairin. *a* **1578** Lindesay (Pitscottie) *Chron. Scot.* (S.T.S.) II. 316 Ane woman..cuist hir sellff in ane coill sink. **1601** *Charter* in Dallas *Stiles* (1697) 769 For..upholding of Sinks, Syers, Gutters, Eyes,..Airholls [etc.]. **1739** Sir J. Clerk in *Mem. W. Stukeley* (Surtees) II. 91 The sink goes down perpendicularly 80 fathoms below the sea. **1896** *Daily News* 14 Jan. 2/6 Have struck a rich body of ore in the sink worth 11 ounces of gold.

**b.** A well or pool *of* water.

**1834** Medwin *Angler in Wales* II. 126 If this man had really seen ore in the bottom of a sink of water in a mine.

**c.** (See quot.)

**1883** Gresley *Gloss. Coal-mining* 224 *Sinks*, natural cavities met with in iron mines.

**7. a.** A flat, low-lying area, basin, etc., where waters collect and form a bog, marsh, or pool, or disappear by sinking or evaporation. Now *U.S.*

**1596** Dalrymple tr. *Leslie's Hist. Scot.* I. 99 Be thir sinkes [*supra* certane difficile myres] wil gang noᵗ only the Reiuers selfes.., bot the horses in lyke maner. **1702** E. West *Mem.* (1865) 186 The way being full of mires, sinks, and snares. [**1753** Hanway *Trav.* (1762) I. III. xxv. 107 Ghilan is generally esteemed the sink of Persia. **1801** Skrine *Rivers Gt. Brit.* 68 This may be called the sink of Yorkshire, the country being deep, and occasionally sandy.] **1850** B. Taylor *Eldorado* xxi. (1862) 223 On the arid plains around the sink of Humboldt's River. **1872** Raymond *Statist. Mines & Mining* 194 Even large rivers, like the Humboldt, spread out into shallow lakes, erroneously called 'sinks', and, exposing thus a large area to evaporation, dry up.

**b.** = sink-hole 2. Chiefly *U.S.*

**1791** W. Bartram *Trav.* 174 Though the waters of these ponds in the summer and dry seasons, evidently tend towards these sinks. **1854** Bartlett *Personal Narr.* I. 110 We stopped to look at some limestone sinks near the road. **1885** *Boston* (Mass.) *Jrnl.* 6 Apr. 2/3 But in some places veins of sand..run through the rock... Water,..percolating through, sometimes causes the entire vein to fall through. When the vein..comprises an acre or two it is called a 'sink'.

**8.** The opposite of *source* in any scientific sense; a place where or a process by which energy (esp. heat) is removed from a system, or some specific component of a system is removed from circulation and either stored or destroyed; a device whose function is to act as a sink.

**1855** J. C. Maxwell in *Trans. Cambr. Philos. Soc.* (1864) X. 32 If the origin of the tube or its termination be within the space under consideration, then we must conceive the fluid to be supplied by a source within that space, capable of creating and emitting unity of fluid in unity of time, and to be afterwards swallowed up by a sink capable of receiving and destroying the same amount continually. **1878** W. K. Clifford *Elem. Dynamic* I. 214 The point *s* is called a source of strength $\mu$ when the fluid streams out in all directions; when $\mu$ is negative, so that the fluid streams inwards, it is called a sink. **1882** Minchin *Unipl. Kinemat.* 208 The problem to find the velocity..due to the given causes (sources, sinks, etc.). **1885** *Electrician* 3 July 134/1 There will..be transfer of energy through the medium from sources to sinks of energy. **1902** *Encycl. Brit.* XXVIII. 18/2 In the case of current flow in plane sheets, we have to consider certain points called sources at which the current flows into the sheet, and certain points called sinks at which it leaves. **1951** *Jrnl. Brit. Interplanetary Soc.* X. 256 The generation of electrical power by means of a heat engine requires that the heat produced at a temperature $T_1$ be conveyed to a 'sink' at a temperature $T_2$. **1966** *Economist* 8 Oct. 180/1 They [*sc.* power stations] could be used as a 'sink' for the gas while the distribution system is geared up to take it elsewhere. **1977** I. M. Campbell *Energy & Atmosphere* viii. 263 The main sink for hydroperoxy radicals in the troposphere appears, at present, to be identified as reaction with nitrogen oxides.

**III.** †**9.** A quantity *of* hemp sunk in a retting-pit. *Obs.*⁻¹

**16..** in *N.W. Linc. Gloss.* (1889) 485 Drowned in a hempe pitt neare a litle sinke of hempe.

†**10.** *Mining.* = chun 1. *Obs.*⁻⁰

**1747** Hooson *Miner's Dict.* s.v., A Sink..is the same thing with a Chun.

**11. a.** *Dancing.* (See quot.)

**1706** J. Weaver *Orchesography* 2 Sinkings are the bending of the Knees. Risings are when we rise from a Sink.

**b.** A dropping or lowering of the voice. *rare*⁻¹.

**1786** Mrs. A. M. Bennett *Juvenile Indiscr.* III. 189 Their ignorance of the subject of the whispering dialogue..was.. owing..to a soft sink in the voice of both Henry and Clara.

**c.** *gen.* An instance or act of sinking. *rare.*

**1818** Keats *Let.* 13 Mar. (1958) I. 240 When a poor devil is drowning, it is said he comes thrice to the surface, ere he makes his final sink.

**d.** *Aeronautics.* Loss of altitude, esp. in gliding flight; the rate of this.

**1943** [see rate *sb.*¹ 7 b]. **1955** A. Welch et al. *Soaring Pilot* iii. 33 Minimum sink will occur at some lower lift coefficient (i.e. a higher speed). **1962** R. C. S. Allen *Theory of Flight for Glider Pilots* iv. 28 When the power is a minimum, the sink is a minimum. **1973** *Sci. Amer.* Dec. 103/3 The effect of the vulture's lower wing loading is that it can turn in much smaller circles at a similar rate of sink.

**12. a.** *U.S.* A kind of oblong boat used in wild-fowl shooting, which becomes submerged to the water-level and serves to conceal the sportsman.

**1857** E. J. Lewis *Amer. Sportsman* 284 It is better..to have two or more double-barrelled guns in the Sink. **1859** Bartlett *Dict. Amer., Battery*, a sort of boat used for duck-shooting... It is also called..a Surface-boat, Sink, or Box. **1874** J. W. Long *Amer. Wild-Fowl* xxv. 252 When done with, the brush may be thrown off, and the labor of towing about the 'sink' avoided.

**b.** = sinker *sb.*¹ 5.

**1865** *Pall Mall G.* 17 Aug. 11/1 You want..nothing else but a good rod, with..a lead sink, and an inch of mackerel by way of bait.

**c.** *Theatr.* A part of the stage constructed to sink and rise by means of machinery.

Cf. *sinking stage*, s.v. sinking *ppl. a.* 3.

**1840** A. Bunn *Stage both before & behind Curtain* III. viii. 280 The scenery..described, in the glowing language of the stage, under the head of flats, wings, side-pieces, borders, sinks, flies, &c.., has been painted..by a Stanfield and Grieve. **1859** *Punch* 5 Feb. 58/2 Gorgeous transformations, ..scruto work, gas-battens, and all the resources of 'sink and fly'. **1859** Sala *Twice round Clock* (1861) 255 The scene-shifters..seeing..the traps greased, and all the 'sinks' and 'flies', ropes and pullies,..in due working order.

**13.** A depression or hollow, esp. one made in a flat surface.

**1875** Knight *Dict. Mech.* 2616/2 *Trap*, a sink or depression in a sewer-pipe. **1884** Britten *Watch & Clockm.* 94 For making square sinks to receive screw heads and the like, a pin drill is used. **1885** C. G. W. Lock *Workshop Rec.* Ser. IV. 215/2 [In electrotyping] any depressions or 'sinks' must be marked with a pair of callipers.

**IV. 14.** *attrib.* and *Comb.* (chiefly in sense 1), as ***sink-cleansing***, †**-*house***, **-*pan***, **-*pipe***, **-*top***, **-*trap***; also **sink-box** *U.S.*, = sense 12 a; **sink-dirt** *dial.* (see quot.); **sink garden**, a miniature garden, comprising a group of small plants (often alpine varieties) grown in an old stone sink or similar container; **sink rate** *Aeronaut.* = *sinking speed* s.v. sinking *vbl. sb.* 4; **sink-room** *U.S.*, a scullery; **sink tidy**, a perforated receptacle for kitchen waste, placed on a sink unit; **sink unit**, a kitchen unit comprising a sink and draining-board, usu. with cupboards below.

**1874** J. W. Long *Amer. Wild-Fowl* xxv. 252 The usual method of taking canvas-back in the West is by the aid of decoys, shooting..from a *sink-box. *a* **1661** Holyday *Juvenal* (1673) 37 Such can turn black to white; hire temples, ports, Rivers, *sink-cleansing, bus'ness of all sorts, And gain by't. **1838** Holloway *Prov. Dict.*, **Sink-dirt*, channel mud. [**1923** *Gardeners' Chron.* 2 June 306/2 Quite a novel feature of the rock gardens [at Chelsea] were the miniature gardens..in stone sinks.] **1935** C. Elliott *Rock Garden Plants* 10, I at first intended to devote chapters to the building of rock gardens, the making of screes, to *sink gardens, [etc.]. **1954** R. Pearson *Town Gardening* xii. 109 (*heading*) Trough and sink gardens. *c* **1614** *Brasenose Coll. Muniments, Harrowden* (MS.), A *sinkehouse with a chamber over it. **1587** Golding *De Mornay* (1592) 38 Rome became the very *sinckpan of all Idolatries of the Worlde. **1793** Smeaton *Edystone L.* §308 The *sink pipe of lead would convey it to the outside. **1966** *National Observer* (U.S.) 21 Feb. 9/3 Attention so far has focused on the 727's *sink rate', or rate of descent as it comes down from its 25,000-foot cruising altitude on an approach to landing. **1978** A. Welch *Bk. Airsports* vi. 92/2 Most Para-Commander 'chutes..have a sink rate of about 13 feet per second. **1869** Mrs. Stowe *Old Town* vi. The conversation was interrupted by a commotion in the back *sink-room. **1951** *Catal. of Exhibits, South Bank Exhib., Festival of Britain* 52/1 Deep *sink tidy. **1958** *New Scientist* 9 Jan. 13/1 Polyethylene..well known in recent years for its use in the manufacture of..sink-tidies, buckets and washing-up bowls. **1981** R. Barnard *Mother's Boys* v. 52 She took out the sink-tidy, with the rubbish from breakfast, and slapped the contents into the dust-bin. **1875** Knight *Dict. Mech.* 2188/1 The *sink-top is of cast-iron. *Ibid.* 2188/2 **Sink-trap*, (Hydraulics), a trap for a kitchen sink, so constructed as to allow water to pass down, but not allow reflow of air or gases. **1939** Martin & Speight *Flat Bk.* 66 Wringer unit which can be fixed permanently to an 'Easiwork' *sink unit in an ideal position between the sink and copper. **1971** R. Rendell *One across, Two Down* v. 45, I would have it painted throughout for you and a sink unit put in.

†**sink**, *sb.*² *Obs.*⁻⁰ [app. ad. L. *cinct-us* girdle.] (See quot.)

**14..** *Lat.-Eng. Voc.* in Wr.-Wülcker 611 *Semicinctorium*, a synk or a lace.

**sink** (sɪŋk), *v.* Pa. t. sank, sunk. Pa. pple. sunk, sunken. Forms: *Inf.* 1 sincan, 3, 5 sinken (*Orm.* sinnkenn), 5 synken, -yn, cynkyn; 3–7 sinke, 4–6 synke (5 synkke), 4, 7 sincke, 6 syncke; 4, 6– sink (5 senk-), 4–5 synk, 4 sinc, 7 sinck. *Pa. t.* α. *Sing.* 1, 3–4 sanc, 5 sanck; 4–5 sanke, 4–5, 8– sank. *Pl.* 5–7 sanke, 6 sancke, 9– sank. β. *Sing.* 1 sonc, 4 sonk. *Pl.* 3–5 sonken, 5–6 sonke, 6 soncke, 6–7 soonke. γ. *Pl.* 1 suncon, 3 sunken, sunke, 5 sunkyn; also *sing.* 6 suncke, 6–7 sunke, sunck, 7– sunk. δ. 5 synked, 7 (9 *dial.*) sinked. *Pa. pple.* α. 1 suncen, 3 i-sunken (*Orm.* sunnkenn), 3– sunken, 4 sunkin, -yn, 6 suncken; 4–7 sunke, 6–7 sunck(e, 7– sunk. β. 4–5 sonken, 5 sonkyn; *Sc.* 5 sonkine, -yne, 6 sonkin; 4 i-sonke, 6 son(c)ke, soonke, 7 soonk. γ. 9 sank, *dial.* sinken. [Comm. Teut.: OE. *sincan* (*sanc*, *suncon*, *suncen*), = OFris. **sinka* (WFris. *sinke*), MDu. *sincken*, *sinken* (Du. *zinken*), OS. *sinkan* (MLG. and LG. *sinken*), OHG. *sinchan* (MHG. and G. *sinken*), ON. *søkkva* (:—**sinkwan*; Icel. *sökkva*, Norw. *søkka*, *søkkja*; MSw. *sionka*, Sw. *sjunka*; Da. *synke*), Goth. *sigqan* (= **sinkwan*). In trans. use the form *sink* takes the place of OE. *sencan*, ME. *senchen* SENCH *v.*

The use of *sunk* as the pa. t. has been extremely common. Johnson (1755) says 'pret. *I sunk*, anciently *sank*'. In sense 21 c the pa. t. was *sinked*, which otherwise is very rarely found.]

**I.** *Intransitive uses.*

The perfect and pluperfect tenses were formerly freq. conjugated with the vb. *to be* instead of *have*.

* **1.** To become submerged in water; to go under or to the bottom; (of ships) to founder.

*c* **975** *Rushworth Gosp.* Matt. xiv. 30 þa [Peter] in-gon sincan, cegde cwęþende 'hæl mec drihten'. *c* **1205** LAY. 4582 Scipen þer sunken, þer þreo & fifti scipen feollen to grunde. *c* **1220** *Bestiary* 538 in *O.E. Misc.*, Đe fir he [the whale] feleð and doð hem sinken. *a* **1300** *Cursor M.* 2904 þai sink in þat wele þar neuer man sank þat was o sele. **1398** TREVISA *Barth. De P.R.* XIII. xxi. (Bodl. MS.), An egge fleteþ in salt water and sinketh downe in fresche watere. *c* **1400** *Destr. Troy* 12525 [Ajax] Hym-seluyn in the sea sonkyn belyue, Swalprit & swam. **1471** CAXTON *Recuyell* (Sommer) I. 279 The boot was full of water and sanck. **1530** PALSGR. 718/2 Some say that a man shall synke thrise or ever he synke to the bottome. **1555** EDEN *Decades* (Arb.) 51 His shyppes were so laden with golde that they soonke. **1641** J. JACKSON *True Evang. T.* III. 209 The other [emblem] is two pots floting on a pond,..with this word, 'If we knock together, we sink together'. **1660** F. BROOKE tr. *Le Blanc's Trav.* 64 Leaving his other ship..to the mercy of the water, which in a moment sunk before his face. **1748** LIND *Lett. Navy* (1757) II. 107 They were resolved to sink rather than to strike. **1767** SIR W. JONES *Seven Fountains* Poems (1777) 35 The light bark, and all the airy crew, Sunk like a mist beneath the briny dew. **1827** D. JOHNSON *Ind. Field Sports* 142 If she sunk, they considered her innocent. **1858** LARDNER *Handbk. Nat. Phil.* 44 Glass sinks in water, but floats in quicksilver; ebony sinks in spirits of wine, but floats in water.

*fig.* **1575** *Mirr. for Mag.*, *Induction* v, Sithe those..Ofte sooniste sinke, in greatest seas of care. **1611** COTGR. s.v. *Nager*, A fauourite..of authoritie, may boldly swimme where another would sinke.

*Phr.* **1825** *Ann. Reg.*, *Chron.* (1826) 98/2 Dubbed a wizard.., Stebbings..proposed at length, of himself, the old-fashioned ordeal of 'sink or swim'.

(*b*) In fig. phr. ***to sink without trace***; usu. *pass.* [tr. Ger.: see SPURLOS VERSENKT.]

**1925** FRASER & GIBBONS *Soldier & Sailor Words* 267 *Spurlos versenkt*, gone entirely. Disappeared. Specifically—sunk without trace, with all on board. **1936** 'D. YATES' *And Berry came Too* viii. 313 'That has gone, sir.'..'Sunk without trace,' said Berry. 'What a very beautiful thought.' **1946** W. S. CHURCHILL *Compl. Speeches* (1974) VII. 7337 He has departed '*spurlos versenkt*' as the German expression says—sunk without leaving a trace behind. **1965** A. FAIRFAX-LUCY in Battiscombe & Laski *Chaplet for Charlotte Yonge* 92 *Kenneth* has sunk without a trace, but *The Little Duke* lives. **1974** 'J. LE CARRÉ' *Tinker, Tailor* xii. 104 'And the third? Viktorov?' 'Sunk without trace... Trained and disappeared.'

**b.** To become partly or completely submerged in quicksand, marshy ground, snow, etc. Also in fig. context; and in phr. ***to sink through the floor***, used to express deep embarrassment.

*a* **1340** HAMPOLE *Psalter* i. 1 Qwik grauel þat gers him synk þat standis þar on. *c* **1380** WYCLIF *Wks.* (1880) 339 Whenne a man synkis in þe myre. *c* **1511** *1st Eng. Bk. Amer.* Introd. (Arb.) 28/1 They muste goo vpon brode trenchers that they falle not & synke [in sand]. **1530** PALSGR. 718/2 Foure great peces of artillery be sonke in yonder maresse. **1610** HOLLAND *Camden's Brit.* 529 It is so throughly wet..with waters, that a mans foote is ready to sinke into it. **1686** tr. *Chardin's Trav. Persia* 242 They sink up to the Belly in the looser snow. **1784** COWPER *Task* I. 272 We..feel at ev'ry step Our foot half sunk in hillocks green and soft. **1821** CLARE *Vill. Minstr.* II. 110 Each footstep sinking ankle-deep in moss. **1860** TYNDALL *Glac.* I. xviii. 127 [The] snow ..was yielding enough to permit the feet to sink in it a little way. **1890** 'EDNA LYALL' *Hardy Norseman* v, Your feet sank into the softest of carpets. **1908** L. M. MONTGOMERY *Anne of Green Gables* xii. 118 She thought she would sink through the floor when she saw you come in all rigged out like that. **1956** 'C. BLACKSTOCK' *Dewey Death* iv. 79 The pause was long enough to make Barbara wish she could sink through the floor. **1969** E. GÉBLER *Shall I eat You Now?* 36 The fear he might suddenly say *anything*—well something really that would make you sink through the floor.

*Comb.* **1632** LITHGOW *Trav.* x. 428 All my dayly solace, was sincke down comfort; whiles Boggy-plunging deepes kissing my horse belly.

**2.** † **a.** To go down, to descend, *into* hell. Also without const. *Obs.*

*c* **1200** ORMIN 13381 All þatt wannteþþ Cristess hald All sinnkeþþ inntill helle. *a* **1225** *St. Marher.* 7 Mi sawle schulde sinken..to sorhen in helle. *c* **1366** CHAUCER *A.B.C.* 123 Whan j me bithinke þat j agilt haue boþe him and þee And þat my soule is wurthi for to sinke. **1377** LANGL. *P. Pl.* B. XIV. 80 þei sonken in-to helle þo citees vchone. **1508** KENNEDIE *Flyting w. Dunbar* 552 Spynk, sink with stynk ad Tertara Termagorum.

**b.** To subside or go down into, to be swallowed up by, the earth, etc. Also const. *in*, *into*, *within*.

*c* **1250** *Gen. & Ex.* 3775 Alle he sunken ðe erðe wið-in, Wið wifes, and childre, and hines-kin. *a* **1300** *Cursor M.* 2810 þou lede þam suith out o þis tun, Are þat hit be sunken don. *c* **1386** CHAUCER *Can. Yeom. Prol.* 193 Somme of hem synke in to the ground. *c* **1400** MAUNDEV. (1839) ix. 101 In to that See sonken the 5 Cytees. *a* **1450** *Knt. de la Tour* 13 God had made mani citees to sinke for the synne that thei delited hem inne. **1508** DUNBAR *Flyting* 13 For and I flyt sum sege for schame sould sink. **1526** *Pilgr. Perf.* (W. de W. 1531) 99 Amonge other of the euylles of Sodom and Gomor, whiche sanke for synne. **1605** SHAKS. *Macb.* IV. i. 106 Let me know. Why sinkes that Caldron? **1611** BIBLE *Lam.* ii. 9 Her gates are sunke into the ground. **1736** GRAY *Statius* ii. 16 The ponderous mass sinks in the cleaving ground.

**3.** To descend to a lower plane or level; to slip, drop, or fall *down*; to pass *in* by falling. Also *spec.* (quot. 1891).

*c* **1000** *Sax. Leechd.* II. 218 3if þæt sie omihte wæte innan onburnenu tyhte hie mon ut mid liþum mettum sincendum. *c* **1290** *S. Eng. Leg.* I. 251 þe coupe ful out of his hond, & anon to grounde sonk. **13..** *Seuyn Sages* 212 (W.), Other ich am of wine dronke, Other the firmament is i-sonke. *c* **1425** *Abraham's Sacr.* in *Non-Cycle Myst. Plays* 42 A! Lord of Heuyn, thy grace let synke. **1563** FULKE *Meteors* (1640) 47 Clouds..by their heavinesse doe by little and little sinke downe lower into the lowest region. **1602** MARSTON *Antonio's Rev.* IV. iii, With that her head sunk down upon her brest. **1651** HOBBES *Leviath.* IV. xlvi. 374 Some kind of bodies sink naturally downwards toward the Earth. *a* **1700** EVELYN *Diary* 8 Feb. 1645, This subterranean grott..is in some places obstructed by the earth which has sunk in. **1711** ADDISON *Spect.* 159 ¶6 Their Footing failed and down they sunk [from the bridge]. **1831** SCOTT *Ct. Robt.* xxxii, Birds, incapable of sustaining themselves, sunk down exhausted out of their native element. **1852** M. ARNOLD *Empedocles* II. 73 He lets his lax right hand..Sink upon his mighty knees. **1891** *Cent. Dict.*, *Sink*, to swim deep, as a school of fish; specifically, to pass below a net.

*transf.* **1878** BROWNING *La Saisiaz* 59 Power that sinks and pettiness that soars.

**b.** To subside; to give way and go *down*, to fall *away*; to be beaten *in*.

**1530** PALSGR. 718/2, I synke in, as a mans harnesse synketh by vyolence of strokes, *je me efondre*. **1563** FULKE *Meteors* (1640) 21 When some part of the land sinketh downe, and in stead thereof arise Rivers, Lakes [etc.]. **1776** SEMPLE *Building in Water* 3 The Cause of this West Side sinking more than the East Side. **1852** MRS. STOWE *Uncle Tom's C.* xix. 189 If the whole country would sink, and hide all this injustice,..I would willingly sink with it. **1897** WATTS-DUNTON *Aylwin* IV. iv, The very airth under your feet seems to be a-sinkin' away.

**c.** Of the sun or moon: To descend in the sky; to move toward or pass beneath the horizon.

**1601** SHAKS. *Jul. C.* V. iii. 61 O setting Sunne: As in thy red Rayes thou doest sinke to night [etc.]. **1637** MILTON *Lycidas* 168 So sinks the day-star in the Ocean bed. **1794** MRS. RADCLIFFE *Myst. Udolpho* i, Sweeter still, when the sun sinks to rest. **1801** SOUTHEY *Thalaba* XI. xxxix, The Moon is sunk; a dusky grey Spreads o'er the Eastern sky. **1860** TYNDALL *Glac.* I. vii. 57 The sun sank behind the neighbouring peaks.

*transf.* **1821** SHELLEY *Ginevra* 106 The day sinks fast, the sun is set. **1850** TENNYSON *In Mem.* cvi[i], A bitter day that early sank Behind a purple-frosty bank Of vapour.

**d.** To pass out of sight, to be lost to view; to disappear.

**1521** in *Bradshaw's St. Werburge* (1887) 201 Make hym domestique Within the heuyns, in whiche that thou art sonke. **1749** FIELDING *Tom Jones* V. x, Caught a view of the lovers just as they were sinking out of sight. **1896** A. E. HOUSMAN *Shropshire Lad* xxxvii, Low in the forsaken west Sank the high-reared head of Clee.

**e.** Of land, etc.: To have a downward lie or slope; to descend gradually; to dip.

**1726** LEONI *Alberti's Archit.* II. 10/2 If the plain be smooth.., not rising or sinking on any side. **1747** *Gentl. Mag.* 208/1 His belly hangs low, being not far from the ground, as it sinks much in the middle. **1825** SCOTT *Betrothed* iv, The hill sinks downward to an extensive plain. **1873** BURTON *Hist. Scot.* I. i. 25 Descending and ascending as the country sinks and swells.

**f.** Of the eye: To glance or look downwards; to droop.

**1834** WHITTIER *Mogg Megone* 374 The eye of Boniton Sinks at that low, sepulchral tone.

**4. a.** Of water, etc.: To go down; to fall to a lower level; to subside. Also *transf.*

*a* **1000** *Cædmon's Gen.* 1437 (Gr.), þa fandode forðweard scipes, hwæðer sincende sæflod þa ȝyt wære under wolcnum. *a* **1400** *Theophilus* ix. in *Engl. Studien* XXXII. 6 Al his wisdam & his good, Ryȝt as doth þe salte flood, It sanc doun to grounde. **1565** COOPER *Thesaurus*, *Flumina subsidunt*, the riuers sinke. **1741–3** POCOCKE *Descr. East* I. 199 That the water may have a fall from them [*sc.* the higher parts] to all other parts, when the Nile sinks.

**b.** Of flames, etc.: To die down; to burn less strongly; to go out.

**1611** BIBLE *Numb.* xi. 2 When Moses prayed.., the fire was quenched [*marg.* sunke]. **1728** POPE *Dunc.* I. 260 Down sink the flames, and with a hiss expire. **1827** SCOTT *Chron. Canongate* i, A flash of intelligence seemed to revive in the invalid's eye—sunk again.

**5.** To drop or fall gradually down to the ground, on a seat, etc., from want of power to remain erect; †to faint *away*.

***to be sinking***, to be ready to drop (with fatigue, etc.).

**1377** LANGL. *P. Pl.* B. XVIII. 67 þe ded bodye..sank with þat til erthe. **1470–85** MALORY *Arthur* I. xvi. 59 The knyght sanke doune to the erthe dede. *Ibid.* XX. xxii. 838 Syr Gauwayn synked doun vpon hys one syde in a swounde. **1592** SHAKS. *Ven. & Ad.* 593 She trembles at his tale, And ..sinketh down, still hanging by his neck. **1608** CHAPMAN *Duke Byron* V. iii, As a savage boar that..keeps off the baying hounds, Though sunk himself. **1697** DRYDEN *Virg. Georg.* III. 735 The Victim Ox, that was for Altars prest,.. Sunk of himself. **1760–72** H. BROOKE *Fool of Qual.* (1809) II. 159, I reached [the house] with much difficulty, and then sunk away on the threshold. **1782** MISS BURNEY *Cecilia* II. iv, If he gets a seat, he never offers to move, if he sees one sinking with fatigue. **1818** SCOTT *Hrt. Midl.* xxxiii, Jeanie sunk down on a chair, with clasped hands, and gasped in agony. **1837** P. KEITH *Bot. Lex.* 274 If the stem of a balsam sinks down for lack of moisture till it touches the earth. **1879** *Cassell's Techn. Educ.* IV. 95/2 He was sinking with hardship, fatigue, and hunger.

**b.** To fall down, fall *in* ruin; to give way through weakness or fatigue. Also of soil: To be soft or yielding.

**1535**, **1597** [see SINKING *ppl. a.* 1 a]. **1608** SHAKS. *Per.* IV. vi. 128 Your house, but for this virgin that doth prop it, Would sink and overwhelm you. **1700** T. BROWN tr. *Fresny's Amusem.* 13 The Ground is Hard in some Places and Sinks in others. **1770** GOLDSM. *Deserted Village* 47 Sunk are thy bowers in shapeless ruin all. **1843** R. J. GRAVES *Syst. Clin. Med.* iii. 403 When the patient attempted to stand up or walk, he was totally unable to do either, his legs sinking under him.

**c.** To drop down in a slow or easy manner into a lying or sitting posture.

**1825** SCOTT *Betrothed* xiii, The hound sunk down to his couchant posture. **1831** *Society* I. 267 'Will you let me repay myself thus,' added he, sinking into the seat beside her and taking her hand. **1885** 'E. GARRETT' *At Any Cost* x, Mrs. Brander.. sank down on a billowy chair, and took possession of Tom.

**6.** Of water or other liquids: To pass into or penetrate a substance, to be soaked up or absorbed. Const. *in*, *into*, *through*, etc. †Also, to ooze *out of* something.

*a* **1300** *Cursor M.* 535 In to þe see all watres sinkes. *c* **1400** MAUNDEV. (Roxb.) xxxiii. 150 þir flodez sinkez doune in to þe erthe. *c* **1440** *Pallad. on Husb.* I. 37 The watir out of gaseyn or of myre Be not ybrought, ner out of metal synke. **1535** COVERDALE *Isaiah* xix. 4 Nilus shal synke awaye, & be dronke vp. **1593** SHAKS. *3 Hen. VI*, V. vi. 62 Will the aspiring blood of Lancaster Sinke in the ground? **1662** J. DAVIES tr. *Olearius' Voy. Amb.* 412 The continual Rains had..sunk through our Tents and cloaths. **1697** DRYDEN *Virg. Georg.* III. 655 In muddy Pools, the Water sinks. **1738** CHAMBERS *Cycl.* s.v. *Paper*, Blotting Paper is paper..in which..ink readily sinks or spreads. **1745** P. THOMAS *Voy. S. Seas* 247 This Ink is..extremely black, and..sinks when the Paper is fine. **1843** WAY *Promp. Parv.* 78 The drain..which allowed the water..to sink into the earth. **1859** GULLICK & TIMBS *Painting* 222 The tendency some colours have, in certain circumstances, to what is called 'sink-in'.

*fig.* **1390** GOWER *Conf.* III. 5, I with love am so bethrowe, And al myn herte is so thurgh sunke, That I am verraliche drunke. **1567** *Satir. Poems Reform.* vii. 120 Gif the poysone in hir hart be sonkin, That sho will not consent he puneist be. **1844** MRS. BROWNING *Drama of Exile* 1977 Those sins Have sunken to all Nature's heart. **1871** R. ELLIS *Catullus* c. 7 Into my inmost veins when love sank fiercely to burn them.

†**b.** Of paper: To cause ink to spread or 'run' on being applied to it; to absorb ink. *Obs.*

**1594** PLAT *Jewell-ho.* 46 If the paper should happen to sinke, which is an especiall fault in many of our late yeere bookes. **1688** MIÈGE *Gt. Fr. Dict.* II. s.v., This Paper sinks, or blots,..*ce Papier boit.* **1797** *Encycl. Brit.* (ed. 3) XIII. 715/2 To hinder paper from sinking, take..rock alum, dissolve it in..water, and apply it to the paper.

**c.** Of an oil painting: to develop dull spots on the surface where the pigments have sunk into the ground. Also const. *in*. Cf. SINKING *vbl. sb.* 1 e.

**1939** H. HUBBARD *Materia Pictoria* 231 During the process of painting, and after completion, Oil Paintings are liable to sink-in and become dull in parts. **1968** M. NOAKES *Prof. Approach to Oil Painting* ii. 12 Linseed oil can be used for 'oiling out' when a picture shows signs of sinking... Varnish seals and protects the surface of a painting, as well as reviving any areas that have sunk.

**7. a.** Of a weapon or blow: To make way *into* or *through* some part, etc. Also with advb. complement.

*c* **1330** *Arth. & Merl.* 5310 (Kölbing), Wawain on þe helme him smot, þe ax sank depe. *Ibid.* 9352 Arthour on þe helme him smot, þe dent sanke þurch. *a* **1400** *Sir Beues* (Kölbing) p. 212 Hit [*sc.* a stroke] sanke þrouȝ helm and basnette. **1611** BIBLE *1 Sam.* xvii. 49 The stone sunke into his forehead.

**b.** To recede, be depressed, *into* something.

**1530** PALSGR. 718/2 As a mans eyes sinke in to his heed for thought, or sycknesse.

** **8. a.** To penetrate *into* (†*to*, *unto*, *through*), enter or be impressed *in*, the mind, heart, etc.

In quot. 1612 it is not clear whether the meaning is 'to enter into the mind', or 'to find acceptance'.

*a* **1300** *Cursor M.* 15170 Mani sari sight, i-wiss, þar sanc vn-til his hert. *Ibid.* 25997 Sua sar þin sakes to for-thingk þat soru thoru þin hert sink. *c* **1374** CHAUCER *Anel. & Arc.* 8 Hit ful depe is sonken in my mynd. *c* **1422** HOCCLEVE *Learn to Die* 604 In-to thyn herte let my wordes synke. **1470–85** MALORY *Arthur* XXI. xi. 858 There kyndenes and myn vnkyndenes sanke so to myn herte that I myȝt not susteyne my self. **1508** DUNBAR *Tua Mariit Wemen* 115 Quhen that the sound of his saw sinkis in my eris, Than ay renewis my noy. *a* **1548** HALL *Chron., Edward IV*, 18 These reasons..so sancke in the Dukes stomacke, that he promised [etc.]. **1612** T. TAYLOR *Comm. Titus* iii. 3 Very fewe assent vnto the truth we teach; it hardly sinketh with men that God should become man. *c* **1645** HOWELL *Lett.* I. vi. I, That which sinks deepest into me is the Sense I have of the Common Calamities of this Nation. **1814** SHELLEY *Stanza written at Bracknell* 1 Thy dewy looks sink in my breast. **1852** MRS. STOWE *Uncle Tom's C.* xix. 185 These things sink into my heart, Tom. **1884** J. QUINCY *Figures of the Past* 250 Then a pause, that the absurdity of the position of his antagonist might sink in and be vividly realized.

**b.** To press or weigh *on* one.

**1764** GOLDSM. *Hist. Eng. in Lett.* I. 337 The sense of his subjection to his own vassals, sunk deep on his mind. **1858** CARLYLE *Fredk. Gt.* x. iv. (1872) III. 250 This misadventure sank heavily on the spirits of Luiscius.

**c.** To descend or fall (*up*)*on* a person or place; to settle down *over* a district.

**1808** SCOTT *Marm.* III. xii, Silence sunk on all around. **1814** —— *Lord of Isles* v. xv, Over Carrick..Had sunk dejection's iron sleep. **1817** SHELLEY *Rev. Islam* I. 638 With clinging charm Sinking upon their hearts. **1865** SWINBURNE *Poems & Ballads* Ded. xiii, Night sinks on the sea.

**9. a.** To be immersed or plunged deeply *in* something; to dip deep *in*; to be absorbed *in* thought, etc. Chiefly in *pa. pple.*

*a* **1300** *Cursor M.* 29037 Quat bote for-bere bath mete and drink, And saul in sulwines to sink? *c* **1375** *Sc. Leg. Saints* xxxiv. (*Pelagia*) 179, I..þat has nocht anerly my-selfe sonkyne in syne vnhapely. *c* **1400** *Rom. Rose* 5113 In gret myscheef and sorwe sonken Ben hertis that of love arn dronken. *c* **1460** *Vrbanitatis* 55 in *Babees Bk.*, To depe in þy cuppe þou may not synke Thowȝ þou haue good wylle to drynke. *c* **1600** SHAKS. *Sonn.* xii. 2 When I..see the braue day sunck in hidious night. **1711** STEELE *Spect.* No. 262 ¶4 No Man is so sunk in Vice and Ignorance, but [etc.]. **1731-8** SWIFT *Polite Conv.* Introd. 24 A great Variety of new Terms, which are annually changed, and those of the last Season sunk in Oblivion. **1794** MRS. RADCLIFFE *Myst. Udolpho* xlv, He pursued his way through the woods sunk in deep thought. **1814** SCOTT *Lord of Isles* v. xiii, In night the fairy prospects sink. **1842** BORROW *Bible in Spain* vi, Where, sunk in dreamy rapture, I sat during a bright sunny hour. *c* **1850** *Arab. Nts.* (Rtldg.) 2 They..were both sunk in the deepest sleep. **1877** L. MORRIS *Epic of Hades* I. 9 The young dear body bathed And sunk in its delight.

†**b.** To fall away *from* one. *Obs.*

*c* **1430** *How the Good Wiif*, etc. 79 in *Babees Bk.*, þo þat ben ofte drunke, þrift is from hem sunke. *a* **1660** *Contemp. Hist. Irel.* (Ir. Archæol. Soc.) II. 174 The well affected would either joine with them..or sincke from them.

**10.** Contrasted with *swim* (or †*flete*), to denote success, prosperity, etc., in contrast to failure or adversity, or (in later use) determination to do something without regard to consequences.

*c* **1368** CHAUCER *Compl. Pite* 110 Ye rekke not whethyr I flete or sinke. *c* **1386** —— *Knt.'s T.* 1539 She..reccheth neuere wher I synke or fleete. **1538** STARKEY *England* I. iii. 85 They care not (as hyt ys commynly sayd) 'whether they synke or swyme'. **1553** BECON *Reliques of Rome* (1563) 53 Our Recluses neuer come out of their lobbeis, sincke or swimme the people. **1637** GILLESPIE *Eng. Pop. Cerem.* Ep. A 2 b, If the Court swimme, he cares not though the Church sinke. **1668** R. STEELE *Husbandman's Calling* iii. (1672) 29, I will be just and honest, sink or swim. **1818** SCOTT *Hrt. Midl.* xxvi, Sink or swim, I am determined to gang to Lunnon. **1889** 'R. BOLDREWOOD' *Robbery under Arms* xxiii, It's sink or swim with all of us.

**11.** To fall, lapse, or degenerate *into* some inferior or unsatisfactory state or condition. Also const. *from* (a better state).

*c* **1310** in Wright *Lyric P.* x. 37 Betere is were thunne boute laste, then syde robes ant synke into synne. **1642** ROGERS *Naaman* To Rdr. 4 Those that are not sunke into a prophane way, yet may be sunke from a zealous. **1711** ADDISON *Spect.* No. 55 ¶2 The Republick sunk into those two Vices.., Luxury and Avarice. **1775** JOHNSON *Tax. no Tyr.* 28 The constitution sunk at once into a chaos. **1839** THIRLWALL *Greece* II. 190 The nation sank into that state of utter corruption and imbecility which Xenophon..has painted. **1859** GEO. ELIOT *A. Bede* xxxi, She could better bear something quite new than sinking back into the old everyday round.

**b.** To pass *into* oblivion, insignificance, etc. Also const. *from* (notice).

**1704** SWIFT *Tale Tub* Author's Apol., Such treatises.. which are already sunk into waste paper and oblivion. **1783** MME. D'ARBLAY *Diary* 6 Apr., I..catch at the first chair in my way, and take possession of it, merely to sink from notice. **1834** MACAULAY *Ess., Pitt* (1897) 302 The favourite of the people rose to supreme power, which his rival sank into insignificance. **1877** BROCKETT *Cross & Crescent* 286 The songs..are so ancient that their authors have sunk into oblivion.

**c.** To change, turn, be transformed *into* some lower form.

*a* **1770** JORTIN *Serm.* (1771) IV. ix. 187 Prudence without piety sinks into knavish craft. **1849** RUSKIN *Sev. Lamps* ii. §xx. 50 It is, indeed, possible..for men to sink into machines themselves. **1888** 'J. S. WINTER' *Bootle's Childr.* i, The afternoon was just sinking into dusk.

**12.** To pass or fall gently *into* (or *to*) sleep, rest, peace, etc.

**1718** *Free-thinker* No. 82. 190, I have observed above Half of his Hearers sunk into Slumbers. **1794** MRS. RADCLIFFE *Myst. Udolpho* xxxvi, She at length sunk to repose. **1850** TENNYSON *In Mem.* xxxiv, 'Twere best at once to sink to peace, Like birds the charming serpent draws. **1868** HOLME LEE *B. Godfrey* xlvi, He..seemed to sink into a doze.

*fig.* **1743** FRANCIS tr. *Hor., Odes* III. iii. 29 Since the long War now sinks to Peace. **1845** BROWNING *How they brought the Good News* i, Behind shut the postern, the lights sank to rest.

**b.** To lapse or fall *into* reverie, contemplation, etc.

**1794** MRS. RADCLIFFE *Myst. Udolpho* xxvii, She was soon recalled from the reverie into which she sunk. **1831** SCOTT *Ct. Robt.* vi, The officer at once reassumed his superiority, and the soldier sunk back..into his wonted silence and reserve. **1891** E. PEACOCK *N. Brendon* I. 121 He turned away from her and sunk into reverie.

**13.** To give way *under* (or *beneath*) misfortune, affliction, etc.; to be weighed down or crushed.

**1592** SHAKS. *Rom. & Jul.* I. iv. 22 Vnder loues heauy burthen doe I sinke. **1602** MARSTON *Ant. & Mel.* IV. Wks. 1856 I. 54 Courage, sweet boy, sinke not beneath the weight Of crushing mischiefe. **1681** DRYDEN *Abs. & Achit.* 822 But sinking underneath his master's fate: In exile with his godlike prince he mourned. **1711** ADDISON *Spect.* No. 163 ¶7 If we sink under such little Stroaks of Fortune. **1737** *Gentl. Mag.* VII. 570/2 Harissa with triumphant smile..left him sinking in despair. **1802** MRS. E. PARSONS *Myst. Visit* II. 69 Such as many with weak spirits must have sank under. **1855** MACAULAY *Hist. Eng.* xx. IV. 433 That France had at length made overtures to him was a sufficient proof that she felt herself spent and sinking. *a* **1862** BUCKLE *Civiliz.* (1873) III. iv. 274 Under this accumulated pressure, we shall assuredly sink, if we imitate the credulity of our forefathers.

**b.** To become depressed or dejected; to droop or languish.

**1605** *1st Pt. Jeronimo* III. ii. 170 Iust at this instant her hart sincks and dies. **1655** in *Nicholas Papers* (Camden) III. 221 My heart as well as pursse being quite sunck. **1727** BOYER *Fr. Dict.* II. s.v., His Courage sinks or lowers,..*son Courage s'abbat, le Cœur lui manque.* **1773** GOLDSM. *Stoops to Conq.* v. iii, My spirits are so sunk with the agitations I have suffered. **1835** THIRLWALL *Greece* I. ix. 350 Their spirit began to sink, and they sought advice from Delphi. **1850** TENNYSON *In Mem.* xx, So much the vital spirits sink To see the vacant chair. **1873** BLACK *Pr. Thule* xi. 167 While she was outwardly calm,..her heart sank within her.

**c.** To decline rapidly; to fail in health or strength; †also, to die. Freq. const. *under* (some trouble or ailment).

**1718** HICKES & NELSON *Life Kettlewell* III. 457 He sunk all of a sudden; for being raised to take some Chocolate for his Re-freshment, he Died in a Moment in that Posture. **1780** *Mirror* No. 106, His health began to sink under the vexations of his mind. **1804** ABERNETHY *Surg. Obs.* 65 The patient being previously much exhausted, sunk under this last complaint. **1829** COOPER *Good's Study Med.* (ed. 3) I. 385 The patient..did not sink till his stomach became disordered. **1892** *Academy* 13 Feb. 161/1 He sank quietly and died on the 1st February.

**14.** To go downwards in the scale of fortune, success, or relative position.

**1599** B. JONSON *Ev. Man out of Hum.* IV. vi, It was his heauie fortune to sinke;..therefore talke no more of him. **1607** SHAKS. *Timon* II. ii. 240 Neu'r speake, or thinke, That Timons fortunes 'mong his Friends can sinke. **1640** BROME *Sparagus Gard.* IV. xi, Now for a trick to rid us of this Clowne, Or our trade sinks. *a* **1700** EVELYN *Diary* 16 May 1681, Lord Sunderland was much sunke in his estate by gaming. *a* **1715** BURNET *Own Time* (1766) II. 200 Who was sinking in his business and began to think that of a witness would be a better trade. **1829** *Sporting Mag.* XXIV. 125 The Clubs appear to be sinking. **1859** *Habits of Gd. Society* iii, The sight of decayed gentility..may call forth our pity ..: 'You have evidently sunken,' we say to ourselves. **1887** JESSOPP *Arcady* I. 17 It would be an immense calamity to the rural population if the clergy were to sink in the social scale.

**b.** To descend to a lower level or type; to degenerate. Also const. *to.*

**1678** CUDWORTH *Intell. Syst.* 269 Such as are..grosly sunk and debauched in their Lives. **1763** J. BROWN *Poetry & Music* xii. 194 Thus the musical and poetic Arts sunk along with the Roman Empire. *a* **1770** JORTIN *Serm.* (1771) I. iii. 57 An understanding sunk beneath the capacity of a brute. **1868** J. H. BLUNT *Ref. Ch. Eng.* I. 427 Intellect as well as holiness had sunk down to a level of low mediocrity. **1894** SIR E. SULLIVAN *Woman* 29, I don't want to see the morality of women sink to the morality of men.

**c.** To diminish, decrease, or fall in estimation; to decline in value or appreciation. Also const. *to.*

**1685** BURNET *More's Utopia* 11 The Reputation of their Wisdom would sink. **1746** FRANCIS tr. *Horace, Epist.* II. i. 58 Shall he..sink with Moderns to Contempt and Shame? **1780** *Mirror* No. 70, He sunk in his own esteem, in being reduced to use the language of solicitation. **1780** *Ibid.* No. 71, Former services..sunk to nothing. **1802** MAR. EDGEWORTH *Moral Tales* (1816) I. v. 32 Flora soon sunk many degrees in his opinion. **1852** THACKERAY *Esmond* II. xv, He had sunk by this time to the very worst reputation. **1855** MACAULAY *Hist. Eng.* xv. III. 516 The Whigs, conscious that they had lately sunk in the opinion both of the King and of the nation.

**15.** To fall low; to diminish or decrease; also, to disappear, to vanish.

**1655** in *Nicholas Papers* (Camden) 221 My..pursse being quite sunck. **1776** ADAM SMITH *W.N.* I. xi. III. (1904) I. 218 The value [of superfluities]..sinks in times of poverty and distress. **1801** *Farmer's Mag.* Jan. 85 Towards the beginning of Harvest, prices sunk much. **1812** SCOTT *Let.* in *Lockhart* (1837) III. i. 7 While my trees grow and my fountain fills, my purse, in an inverse ratio, sinks to zero. **1826** *Art of Brewing* (ed. 2) 1 The abstruseness and difficulty of such research..sink before the mind capable of valuing the importance of general laws.

**b.** Of sounds: To become gradually fainter; to die away.

**1794** MRS. RADCLIFFE *Myst. Udolpho* xxxiii, The sound of her steps soon sunk in distance. **1820** SHELLEY *Prometh. Unb.* II. i. 195 How the notes sink upon the ebbing wind! **1873** BROWNING *Red Cott. Nt.-cap* 169 Chatting and chirping sunk innocuously To silence.

**II.** *Transitive uses.*

*** **16.** To cause (a vessel, etc.) to plunge or go down beneath the water; to submerge by rendering incapable of floating; to destroy in this way. †Also with *up* (quot. 1591).

*a* **1300** *E.E. Psalter* lxviii. 3, I come in heghnes of þe see, And þe storme it sanke me. *a* **1300** *Cursor M.* 26846 A thirl sinkes þe schipp to grund. **1471** CAXTON *Recuyell* (Sommer) II. 677 Many [ships] were drowned and sonken into the see. *a* **1548** HALL *Chron., Hen. V*, 54 After long fight..they toke and sonke almost all the whole nauy of Fraunce. **1591** SPENSER *Vision Bellay* xiii, The storme impetuous Sunke vp these riches..Within the gulfe of greedie Nereus. **1623** BINGHAM *Xenophon* 126 If I take any of you vpon the Sea, I will sinke you. **1687** A. LOVELL tr. *Thevenot's Trav.* I. 17 They hinder any Ship..to pass them without leave, else they would run a danger of being sunk. **1726** SWIFT *Gulliver* II. vii, The largest balls, thus discharged, would..sink down Ships..to the Bottom of the Sea. **1839** THIRLWALL *Greece* xxvi. III. 429 Seven were so disabled, yet none went down, and they sank three of the Corinthians. **1884** *Manch. Exam.* 21 Oct. 5/4 A single well-directed shot would have sunk them because of the absence of watertight bulkheads.

*fig.* and in fig. context. **1613** SHAKS. *Hen. VIII*, II. i. 131 Those you make friends..fall away Like water from ye, neuer found againe But where they meane to sinke ye. *a* **1658** CLEVELAND *On a Fly* 14 Wks. (1687), 'Twas bravely aim'd,..Th' hast sunk the Fable o'er and o'er. **1809** MALKIN *Gil Blas* I. xvii. ¶4 There is no sinking me; I always float on the surface of ill-luck. *Ibid.* IV. vii. ¶11 If you catch any relation..sneaking about him,..trust me for sinking, burning, and destroying him in less than no time. **1848** THACKERAY *Van. Fair* lvii, I think Miss O'Dowd would have done for me,..and when she had sunk me she would have fallen upon you.

**b.** To submerge; to put or thrust under water.

*c* **1330** R. BRUNNE *Chron. Wace* (Rolls) 12292 Ilka tyme þat y him se, Y wilde be sonken, for y ne may fle. **1530** PALSGR. 718/2 Sythe we must nedes be taken, let us synke our letters. **1560** DAUS tr. *Sleidane's Comm.* 406 b, The Archebyshop, fyrste synkynge hys great Artylarie in the Rhyne,..fled awaye, to save hym selfe. **1578** in *N.W. Linc. Gloss.* (1877) 224/1 That no man synke anie hempe..in the North more. *a* **1687** PETTY *Pol. Arith.* (1690) 66, I have heard Wise Men..wish that..that Island were sunk under Water. **1856** 'STONEHENGE' *Brit. Rur. Sports* 251/2 The line is shotted so as just to sink it.

**17.** To cause (a thing) to descend or fall to a lower plane or level; to force, press, or weigh down in any way.

*c* **1250** *Gen. & Ex.* 754 Ðus it is..brent wið brimfir, sunken and shent. *Ibid.* 1108 Siðen loth wente ut of hine, brende it ðhunder, sanc it erðe-dine. *c* **1386** CHAUCER *Frankl. T.* 345 Prey hire to synken euery Rok adoun In to hir owene dirke Regioun Vnder the ground. *a* **1450** *Knt. de la Tour* (1868) 71 Thus the .viij. citeez were sonken and brent. **1610** SHAKS. *Tempest* I. ii. 11, I would Haue suncke the Sea within the Earth. *Ibid.* II. i. 201 Doth it not then our eye-lids sinke? **1678** MOXON *Mech. Exerc.* iv. 71 Keep the Iron in this Posture, without either mounting, or sinking its ends. **1712** J. JAMES tr. *Le Blond's Gardening* 65 The Rain forcing down the Earth, and sinking the Seed. **1787** *Phil. Trans.* LXXVIII. 44 The blast from an air-gun was repeatedly thrown on the bulb of a thermometer, and it uniformly sunk it about two degrees. **1814** SCOTT *Lord of Isles* v. xxx, He raised the page, where on the plain His fear had sunk him with the slain. **1836-41** BRANDE *Chem.* (ed. 5) 169 Mr. Walker succeeded in sinking the spirit-thermometer to −91°. **1889** WELCH *Text Bk. Naval Archit.* I. 11 Finding the weight necessary to sink the ship one inch from the assigned water line.

*fig.* **1670** in *Caldwell Pap.* (Maitland) I. 140 The dead weight of his brethrein..sunk him into his grave.

*refl.* **1833** *Penny Cycl.* I. 66/1 Air-vessels, by means of which the animals can raise or sink themselves in the water.

**b.** To send, let, or push, down from a higher plane or level. Also with *down.*

**1632** LITHGOW *Trav.* v. 229 We found this auncient Well so wondrous deepe, that scarcely all our ropes could sinke our bucket in the water. **1648** HERRICK *Hesper., Oberon's Palace* 103 A Spinners circle is bespread, With Cob-web-curtains: from the roof So neatly sunck [etc.]. **1663** GERBIER *Counsel* 33 A compleat form..which the Grecians and Romans have found to be a Dimension sunk down from above. **1851-4** *Tomlinson's Cycl. Arts* (1866) I. 168/1 The bore-hole is apt to become crooked, so that it is often impossible to sink the pipes required to protect the hole.

**c.** To allow (the hand, etc.) to fall lower.

**1680** MOXON *Mech. Exerc.* xii. 213 Then sink your Right hand somewhat below the Level of the Rest. **1829** SCOTT *Anne of G.* vi, The two combatants sunk the points of their swords. **1831** —— *Ct. Robt.* iii, Each sentinel sunk his weapon. **1850** TENNYSON *In Mem.* lxvii[i], When in the down I sink my head, Sleep, Death's twin-brother, times my breath.

**d.** *Golf.* To hole a ball from (a putt); to hole (a ball) by putting.

**1916** TRAVERS & RICE *Winning Shot* i. 23 After coming up in three and then sinking a ten or a fifteen putt for a four, the situation had suddenly changed. **1933** F. OUIMET *Game of Golf* xiv. 203, I murmured a few mild prayers before putting again, and this time I succeeded in sinking the ball. **1955** KEELER & RICE *Bobby Jones Story* xxi. 119 Mrs. Vanderbeck did sink that putt of 25-feet,..and..Alexa did sink hers for a win. **1971** 'D. HALLIDAY' *Dolly & Doctor Bird* xv. 215 Arrived on the green, he pursued the ball round the pin.. and finally sank it at nine.

**e.** To consume (an alcoholic drink); to drink down (esp. rapidly); = DOWN *v.*[2] 1 c. *colloq.*

**1932** G. HOLT *Drums beat at Night* ii. 30 Let's go out and sink a few beers. We can talk at the pub. **1947** L. MACNEICE *Dark Tower* 157 I'll sink a pint in The Dog Returns. **1953** A. NEAVE *They have their Exits* xii. 144 Each man spoke of what he would do first on arrival in England. 'I shall sink three pints of mild and bitter,' said one. **1962** L. DEIGHTON *Ipcress File* ii. 19, I..sank a quick grappa. **1977** M. KENYON *Rapist* xiv. 182 Get a couple of cups, Sergeant, we'll sink a fast one.

**f.** *Basketball.* To score a goal or basket from (a shot). Also *absol.*

**1935** *N.Y. Times* 24 Feb. III. 4/1 O'Donnell sank a long field goal and Kozloff threw a foul to give Penn a 4–1 lead. **1950** N. HOLMAN *Holman on Basketball* 50 With Norm Mager sinking five and Floyd Layne making four set shots

..the City College five won. **1962** *Sports Illustr. Bk. Basketball* iv. 83 Cousy..leaped into the air and sank a left-hander that won the game. **1972** *Sports Illustr.* 3 Jan. 51/1 The Rainbows' John Pennebacker sank from free throws.

**18.** To excavate (a well, pit-shaft, etc.) by digging vertically downwards; to bore; to lower (ground, etc.) by excavation.

**1358** *Durh. Acc. Rolls* (Surtees) 561 In uno puteo de novo sinkando in campo de Fery. **1571** DIGGES *Pantom.* I. xxxi. Kj, If a well bee soonke. **1680** BOYLE *Scept. Chem.* vi, They dig up iron in the fields by sinking ditches two foot deep [etc.]. **1708** J. C. *Compl. Collier* (1845) 15 To Sink a Pit, we must have a stock of Timber prepared. **1776** SEMPLE *Building in Water* 42 The Men went on with their sinking that Floor. **1863** MRS. GASKELL *Sylvia's Lovers* xxxiii, She saw that the last tenants had had a pump sunk for them. **1879** FROUDE *Cæsar* xxiii. 404 Fresh water was happily found by sinking wells.

*absol.* **1862** ANSTED *Channel Isl.* IV. xx. 471 Water is obtained by sinking..to the surface of the granite. **1875** KNIGHT *Dict. Mech.* 2757/2 This rock was sunk through for 273½ feet.

**19. a.** To excise or cut out; to form (a cavity, etc.) in this way, or by heavy pressure.

**1632** in E. B. Jupp *Carpenters' Co.* (1887) 297 Carved workes either raised or Cutt through or sunck in with the grounde taken out. **1697** DRYDEN *Virg. Georg.* I. 253 On either side the Head produce an Ear, And sink a Socket for the shining Share. **1728** CHAMBERS *Cycl.* s.v. *Dock*, Any Place in the Ouze, out of the Tide's Way, where a Ship may ..dock herself, or sink herself a Place to lie in. **1793** SMEATON *Edystone L.* §331 Words..were sunk into the Moorstone with the point of a pick. **1814** SCOTT *Lord of Isles* v. xxi, See yonder oak, within whose trunk Decay a darken'd cell hath sunk.

**b.** To lower by cutting away; to cut patterns or designs in (a die, etc.).

Implied much earlier in SINKER *sb.*[1] 1.

**1679** MOXON *Mech. Exerc.* ix. 157 Hew away the under-side of that Board.., and so sink it to a flat superficies to comply with the first Board. **1683** *Ibid.*, *Printing* i, The Founder [would] not sinck the Matrices. **1825** JAMIESON *Suppl.*, *To Sink*, to cut the die used for striking money.

**c.** To let in or insert into the substance of a thing by scooping, hollowing, or cutting.

**1825** J. NICHOLSON *Operat. Mechanic* 596 The holes for sinking the heads of..screws. **1834** L. RITCHIE *Wand. by Seine* 84 There is a stone sunk in the wall containing a sculpture in bas-relief. **1884** BRITTEN *Watch & Clockm.* 122 Hollow Fusee,..a fusee in which the upper pivot is sunk into the body of the fusee.

**20.** To lower the level of (ground, water, etc.).

**1627** CAPT. SMITH *Seaman's Gram.* ii. 6 To sinke a Decke is to lay it lower. **1712** J. JAMES tr. *Le Blond's Gardening* 68 Rolling the Surface of it with great Cilinders..to sink and level it as much as possible. **1713** ADDISON *Cato* III. v, You sunk the river with repeated draughts.

**b.** To lose sight of (an object on the horizon) by sailing away.

**1762** FALCONER *Shipwr.* II. 227 Sunk were the bulwarks of the friendly shore. **1810** *Naval Chron.* XXIV. 313 This island was sunk from the deck. **1840** R. H. DANA *Bef. Mast* iv, They were..far off.., and in a few hours we sank them in the northeast. **1888** CLARK RUSSELL *Death Ship* I. 191 At dusk we had sunk the Englishman to his lower yards.

**c.** To descend, move down (a slope, etc.).

**1862** COLLYNS *Chase Wild Deer* 199 She now sank the bottom for Exford and crossed just above the village. **1892** *Field* 27 Feb. 299/1 Captain Helmes' first gorse, which he skirted, to sink the hill for the gorses above Bigbury.

**d.** *Hunting. to sink the wind*: to move downwind of another; *spec.* of a fox: to pass below the line of scent. Cf. WIND *sb.*[1] 4.

**1778** G. CARTWRIGHT *Jrnl.* 26 Sept. (1792) II. 374, I saw a large stag upon the south hill..and I let him pass; crossing his route and sinking the wind, I made all possible speed to the foot of Gravel Hills, where I headed him. **1847** R. S. SURTEES *Hawbuck Grange* v. 96 We..found a hare by Clipstone Clump, who went as straight as an arrow to Gatley Coppice, from whence, sinking the wind all the way, she ran to Silverspring. **1896** T. SMITH *Life of Fox* 299 When men go down wind to hear the cry, it is called sinking the wind of the hounds. **1948** F. PITT *Hounds, Horses & Hunting* 271 *Sink the Wind*, to go downwind.

**** **21.** To reduce or bring to ruin or a low estate; to overwhelm, destroy; to weigh down.

**1599** B. JONSON *Ev. Man out of Hum.* Prol. 9 Black rav'nous ruine,..Readie to sinke us downe, and cover us. **1613** SHAKS. *Hen. VIII*, II. i. 60 If I haue a Conscience, let it sincke me,..if I be not faithfull. **1637** R. ASHLEY tr. *Malvezzi's David Persecuted* 5 The same action which at one time hath reared up a Prince, should at another sink him. **1725** POPE *Odyss.* XXII. 451 Fate, and their crime, have sunk them to the dust. **1749** FIELDING *Tom Jones* XIV. vii, Whether he will sink these wretches down for ever, or.. raise them all from the brink of misery and despair. **1850** SCORESBY *Cheever's Whalem. Adv.* ii. 22 The king was taking huge morsels that would almost sink a common man. **1865** RUSKIN *Arrows of Chace* (1880) II. 72 Such another article would sink the *Gazette*.

*absol.* **1718** PRIOR *Solomon* II. 943, I raise or sink, imprison or set free; And Life or Death depends on My Decree.

*Comb.* **1600** W. WATSON *Decacordon* (1602) 7 [The Jesuits] had discouered themselues..to be..shelues of sinke-downe to all princely regalitie. **1688** BUNYAN *Heavenly Footm.* Wks. 1851 III. 385 The..soul-entangling flatteries of such sink-souls as these are.

**b.** Used as an imprecation. Now *arch.*

Freq. *sink me*, used in quot. 1666 as a quasi-*sb.*

**1630** J. TAYLOR (Water P.) *Dog of Warre* Wks. II. 229 Who make (God sinke 'em) their discourse [etc.]. **1642** R. ANDREWES *Decl.* A j b, The Cavalliers swore 'Damme me and sinke me if we doe not kill all the Puritans..in the towne'. **1666** M. M. *Solomon's Prescr.* 28 Who can scarce speak a sentence without their Dammee's and Sinkmee's. **1710** MRS. CENTLIVRE *Bickerstaff's Burying* 7 Estate! sink the Estate! **1768** GOLDSM. *Good-n. Man* II. i, Sink the public, Madam, when the fair are to be attended. **1821** SCOTT *Pirate* xxxiv, I had rather you tried your saw..upon the ship's knee timbers than on mine, sink me! **1855** TROLLOPE *Warden* iv. 58 Sink them all for parsons.

**c.** *absol.* To use profane language; to imprecate, swear. Now *dial.* or *arch.*

**1663** *Proposal to use no Conscience* 6 We swear like Gentlemen of Rank, Curse, Damn, Sink. **1681** *Trial S. Colledge* 132 'Tis a strange sort of thing to believe..that he should fall a damning and sinking against Colledge. **1704** TRAPP *Abra-Mulé* Prol. 37 Fools..think All Wit and Valour is to damn and sink. **1750** H. WALPOLE *Lett.* (1846) II. 311 He has constantly been damming and sinking. **18..** *Rakes of Mallow* i, Breaking windows, damning, sinking. **1882** *Jamieson's Sc. Dict.* IV. 225/2 *To Sink and Graem*, to curse, to imprecate; Shetl[and].

**22.** To lower; to make of less repute or estimation.

**1601** SHAKS. *All's Well* v. iii. 181 Let your highnes Lay a more noble thought vpon mine honour, Then for to thinke that I would sinke it heere. **1707** ADDISON *Pres. State of the War* Wks. 1721 IV. 301 They catch at all opportunities of.. ruining our trade, and sinking the figure which we make among the nations of Europe. **1779** *Mirror* No. 60, Far from sinking their dignity in our estimation, it adds to it. **1815** JANE AUSTEN *Emma* xlvi, I cannot say how it has sunk him in my opinion.

**b.** To debase or degrade (a person).

**1706** DE FOE *Jure Divino* III. 2 Why..the Rewards of Vertues are possess'd By him that sinks the Man to raise the Beast. **1779** *Mirror* No. 18, To sink the lower orders of men far beneath that station to which by nature they are entitled. **1781** BURNS *Stanzas Prosp. Death* 15 Again I might..exalt the brute and sink the man.

**c.** To reduce *to*, lose *in*, something lower.

**1751** JOHNSON *Rambler* No. 103 ⁋9 The necessity of doing something, and the fear of undertaking much, sinks the historian to a genealogist. **1781** COWPER *Table T.* 415 When a country..In prostitution sinks the sense of shame.

**23. a.** To reduce the inflexibility of (a bow).

**1634** MARKHAM *Art of Archerie* vii, Take your Bow into the Field, shoote in it, sinke it with dead heavy shaftes. **1875** *Encycl. Brit.* II. 378/2 *Sinking a Bow*, reducing its force.

**b.** To cause (a person, the mind, spirits, etc.) to become dejected or depressed.

**1630–50** BRADFORD *Hist. Plymouth Plantation* (Mass. Hist. Soc.) 208 It is a marvell it did not wholy discourage them, and sinck them. **1665** BUNYAN *Holy Citie* (1669) 65 The Walls of the Canaanites..did even sink the Hearts of those that beheld them. **1719** DE FOE *Crusoe* I. (Globe) 177 The Thoughts of this sometimes sunk my very Soul within me. **1730** SHENSTONE *Ode to Health* 52 Nor growing cares could sink my cheerful mind. **1782** MISS BURNEY *Cecilia* IV. ii, I hate a solo; it sinks, it depresses me intolerably.

**c.** To reduce, weaken, or exhaust the strength of (a person). Now *rare.*

*a* **1715** BURNET *Own Time* III. (1724) I. 523 All these things, together with a load of age.., sunk Duke Lauderdale so that he died. **1782** *Med. Comm.* I. 32 Bleeding sunk the patient much. **1818** HENNEN *Princ. Milit. Surg.* (1820) 217 Repeated and copious venous bleedings now came on, which rapidly sunk the patient.

**24.** To reduce in amount, value, or price.

*a* **1700** EVELYN *Diary* 31 Oct. 1645, We invited all..to a feast, which sunk our excellent wine considerably. **1727** POPE & GAY *What passed in London* Swift's Wks. 1751 VI. 261 It being by our greatest Dealers in Stocks, thought only a Court-Artifice to sink them. **1757** WESLEY *Wks.* (1872) IX. 228 Who would have sunk his own market, by telling his customers there would be plenty the next day?

*Comb.* **1822** W. IRVING *Braceb. Hall* (1823) II. 312 I've been a complete sink-pocket, that's the truth of it.

**b.** To drop or lower (the voice) in speaking; to render less audible.

**1821** SCOTT *Kenilw.* xxvi, He..sunk what he had to say in a whisper. **1882** BESANT *Revolt of Man* vi. (1883) 140 She sank her voice, although they were not within earshot of any one. **1889** CONAN DOYLE *Micah Clarke* 261 'It was in this way,' he went on, sinking his voice.

**25. a.** To abandon or cease to use; to give up; to allow to be merged *in* something else.

**1705** ADDISON *Italy* 23 He took upon him the Title of Duke of Suffolk, which had been sunk in the Family. **1776** SIR J. REYNOLDS *Disc.* vii. (1876) 407 [It] must..disqualify him for the practical part of his profession and make him sink the performer in the critic. **1809** MALKIN *Gil Blas* III. vii, I..have not sunk the lover in the husband. **1840** MARRYAT *Poor Jack* iii, She sunk her assumed rank. **1854** THACKERAY *Wolves & the Lamb* (1899) 11 When I come into the property I shall sink the name of Milliken.

**b.** To avoid mentioning or alluding to (a person or matter); to pass over in silence; *spec.* in *Piquet* (see quot. 1885). Also const. *upon* the person or persons spoken to.

**1749** FIELDING *Tom Jones* VI. xi, Mr. Allworthy,..out of modesty, sunk everything that related particularly to himself. **1772** JOHNSON in *Boswell* 21 Mar., He sunk upon us that he was married; else we should have shewn his lady more civilities. **1809** MALKIN *Gil Blas* VIII. iii. ⁋10, I dined at a cheap ordinary, and sunk the secretary upon my messmates. **1849** ROBERTSON *Serm.* Ser. I. xiv. (1866) 240 A certain courtly willingness to sink obnoxious truths. **1860** WHYTE MELVILLE *Mkt. Harb.* (1861) 43 Too small to be put in training, he had fallen into the hands of a steeple-chasing horse-dealer, who sank his pedigree. **1885** *Encycl. Brit.* XIX. 116/1 Experienced players not unfrequently omit to call some small score..in order intentionally to mis-lead you. This manœuvre (called sinking a score) is especially resorted to [etc.].

*Comb.* **1887** T. A. TROLLOPE *What I remember* I. 301 He, as well as I, utterly scouted the stupid sink-the-shop rule of conversation.

**c.** To suppress in pronouncing.

**1742** POPE *Dunc.* IV. 221 To sound or sink in *cano*, O or A. **1760–1** GRAY *Eng. Metre* Wks. 1884 I. 328 To sink the vowel and abridge it, as was usual, according to the necessity of their versification.

**d.** To deduct (the offal) when reckoning the weight of a carcase.

**1798** *Monthly Mag.* Apr. 307 Mutton from 3*s.* 6*d.* to 4*s.* per stone of 8 lb. sinking the offal. **1844** H. STEPHENS *Bk. Farm* II. 470 A calf..weighs from 10 to 11 stones imperial, sinking the offal, as it is called in London. **1895** *Times* 28 Jan. 13/2 This custom of 'sinking the offal' is very old, and originated in the days when this part of the beast possessed comparatively little value.

*ellipt.* **1801** *Farmer's Mag.* Nov. 481 Lean cattle.., if they had been killed immediately, would have come to 10s. per stone (of 14 lib.) sink.

**e.** To set aside; to leave out of consideration.

**1860** F. W. ROBINSON *Grandmother's Money* VI. i, He was sinking self so much, and struggling so hard towards one noble action,..that [etc.]. **1884** *L'pool Mercury* 18 Feb. 5/2 A happy knack of sinking individual opinion. **1888** *Times* (weekly ed.) 17 Feb. 2/1 Sinking minor differences, all parties ought to unite [etc.].

**26.** To make away with; to appropriate (money, etc.) for one's own use. Also *spec.* (quot. 1819).

**1713** ADDISON *Trial of Ct. Tariff* Wks. 1721 IV. 324 That the said Count had either sunk or mis-laid several books, papers, and receipts. **1727** BOYER *Dict. Royal* II. s.v., To sink or keep part of a Sum of Mony. **1760** C. JOHNSTON *Chrysal* (1822) I. 32 By sinking the greatest part of her fortune to my own use. **1819** J. H. VAUX *Mem.* II. 57, I took up..the broaches, and immediately 'sunk' a very handsome one..in my coat-sleeve.

**27.** To pay up or wipe out (a debt, etc.).

**1727** BOYER *Dict. Royal* II. s.v., To sink a Fund, *éteindre, supprimer, amortir un Fond.* **1740** W. DOUGLASS *Disc. Curr. Brit. Plant. Amer.* 16 Their Bills became of less Value than those of New-York; but being yearly in good Faith, sunk, they became equal. **1787** JEFFERSON *Writ.* (1859) II. 102 That impost will suffice to..sink the principal in a very few years. **1895** *Daily News* 18 Apr. 3/1 This windfall should properly go to sink the unfunded debt.

**28.** = INVEST *v.* 9.

**1727** BOYER *Dict. Royal* II. s.v., In..Annuities, the Capital is sunk for the Lender. **1789** BRAND *Newcastle* II. 197 The revenue of the Corporation..including the sums that had been sunk with them for lives. **1797** BURKE *Reg. Peace* iii. (1892) 243 The Grand Junction Company,.. having sunk half a million,..applied to your House, for permission to subscribe half as much more. **1831** *Society* I. 139 It is in my power to add to my own income by sinking my small principal. **1848** MILL *Pol. Econ.* I. vi. §1 (1876) 57 Capital sunk (as the expression is) in permanent improvements of land. **1866** ROGERS *Agric. & Prices* I. xxviii. 672 To these we must add the capital sunk in the mills.

**29.** To invest or spend unprofitably; to lose (money) in unfortunate investment, war, etc.

**1777** J. REED in Sparks *Corr. Amer. Rev.* (1853) I. 388, I found that in two or three years I should probably sink my little fortune. **1780** J. HOWARD *Prisons Eng. & W.* 263 There is an account of several..bequests to prisoners. Whether they be now totally sunk,..I cannot say. **1818** SCOTT *Hrt. Midl.* xxxv, Some stock sunk in the South-Sea funds. **1847** DE QUINCEY *Sp. Mil. Nun* Wks. 1853 III. 16 The unknown amounts of cash, that had been sunk in that unhappy speculation! **1872** YEATS *Growth Comm.* 310 The enormous sums sunk in war.

**sink**, obs. form of CINQUE.

**sink**, var. SYNC.

**sinkable** ('sɪŋkəb(ə)l), *a.* [f. SINK *v.* + -ABLE.] Capable of being sunk.

Cf. *non-sinkable*, of a life-boat, in recent use. (*N.E.D.*)

**1865** *Times* 11 Mar. 8/5 The most seaworthy vessel is but too likely to be the most sinkable.

**sinkage** ('sɪŋkɪdʒ). [f. SINK *v.* + -AGE.] The act of sinking; subsidence; an instance of this. Also, that which sinks or has sunk.

**1883** *Harper's Mag.* Jan. 174/1 When they lean sideways, they admit the mouldering pile beneath, and own to the sinkage. **1889** WELCH *Text Bk. Naval Archit.* i. 11 The sinkage due to putting weights of moderate amount into the ship. **1891** *Pall Mall G.* 23 Oct. 5/1 The buoyancy of the timber in resisting sinkage when butted against.

**sinkanter**, var. SINCANTER *Obs.*

**sinkapace**, var. CINQUEPACE *Obs.*

**sinke**, obs. f. CINQUE.

**sinkefoile, -foyle**, obs. ff. CINQUEFOIL.

‖**sinkeh** ('sɪŋkeɪ). [Malay *singke(h*, a. Hokkien *sinkheh* (also used), f. *sin* new + *kheh* visitor.] In Malaysia, a newcomer (esp. a labourer) recently arrived from China.

**1879** J. D. VAUGHAN *Manners & Customs of Chinese of Straits Settlements* 6 The Chinaman on first landing in the Straits is called a Sinkeh. **1927** R. J. H. SIDNEY *In Brit. Malaya Today* 145 The Secret Societies were really Friendly Societies which each *sinkeh* (new-comer) joined. **1948** V. PURCELL *Chinese in Malaya* iii. 58 The staple article of local commerce was the *sinkheh* (Hokkien), *sankah* (Cantonese), the new recruit from China. **1972** C. M. TURNBULL *Straits Settlements 1826–67* i. 44 The employer obtained full right to their labour for a period usually of one year, during which the *sinkhehs* were fed, clothed, housed and given a small allowance.

**sinker** ('sɪŋkə(r)), *sb.*[1] Also 6 synkker, 7 syn-, 6–7 sincker; 6–7 sinkar (6 *Sc.* sincar). [f. SINK *v.* + -ER[1]. Cf. G. *sinker* (spec. in mining).]

**I. 1.** One who engraves figures or designs on dies. Chiefly *Sc.* (Cf. *die-sinker* s.v. DIE *sb.*[1] 8.)

**1526** *Sc. Acts, Jas. V* (1814) II. 317/1 þe sayaris fe, and þe sy[n]karis of þe Irnis fee. **1582** *Reg. Privy Council Scot.* III. 481 The generall, maister cunyeoure, warden, sincar and assayer. **1605** *Ibid.* VII. 27 The Lords..commands Thomas Foulis, sinkar of His Majesties irones, to mak ane new greit seale. **1656** in Grose *Antiq. Rep.* (1808) II. 411 The offices of under-engraver and sinker of our saide stamps. **1674** in Dallas *Stiles* (1697) 110 Constituting the said T. W. Graver and Sinker of his Majesties said Mint.

**2.** One who sinks a pit-shaft, well, or the like.

**1708** J. C. *Compl. Collier* (1845) 22 Perhaps the Sincker, (or Labourer) has..12d. or 14d. a Day. **1710** *Act 9 Anne* c. 28 §9 No Coal-Owner..shall knowingly employ..any Overman,..Pitman, Sinker, Carriage-man [etc.]. **1816** W. SMITH in Phillips *Mem.* (1844) 81 These stony nodules the sinkers have called rock, but no regular rock has yet been found. **1862** SMILES *Lives Engineers* III. 51 Kit Heppel, who was a sinker at the pit. **1897** *Daily News* 8 Mar. 3/1 Fourteen sinkers.. were at work in the bottom of the Simpson Shaft.

**3.** One who causes (something) to sink.

**1632** SHERWOOD, A Sinker of poore people with exactions, *oppresseur*. **1823** BYRON *Juan* XII. lxxxix, Meantime, read all the national-debt sinkers. **1867** *Morning Star* 25 Feb., Without Scialoja there is a chance for Ricasoli in swimming with the anti-clerical spring tides. The [ship-] sinker has been dropped.

**II. 4.** †**a.** A weight for pressing cheese. *Obs.*

**1568** *Wills & Inv. N.C.* (Surtees, 1835) 282, x ches fatts w[th] ij[o] sinkers, ij[s]. **1596** *Ibid.* (1860) 271, iij sinckers for to couer cheese.

**b.** In a stocking-frame or knitting-machine, a jack-sinker or a lead-sinker.

**1779** in *6th Rep. Deputy Keeper Rec.* App. II. 164 A Machine for Knitting without the use of Jacks or Sinkers. **1839** URE *Dict. Arts*, etc. 652 Fig. 560, where both kinds of sinkers appear in section. **1875** KNIGHT *Dict. Mech.* 1237/2 The sinkers..are at the same time depressed, one after another, by the cam or slur above them.

**c.** A weight attached to the chain or rope of a horse's stall-collar.

**1842** J. AITON *Domest. Econ.* (1857) 251 Have also a ball of wood called a sinker, as a straw wisp and all such slovenly expedients are said to be dangerous. **1844** H. STEPHENS *Bk. Farm* I. 127 A leather stall-collar, having an iron-chain collar-shank to play through the ring.., with a turned wooden sinker at its end, to weigh it to the ground.

**5. a.** A weight of lead, stone, or other material for sinking a fishing-line or -net in the water. Cf. SINK-STONE 2.

**1844** in W. H. Maxwell *Sports & Adv. Scotl.* (1855) 323 The loops in the lower baulk are loaded with sinkers of stone. **1866** LAING *Prehist. Rem. Caithn.* 34 Such grooved stones have also been found in Denmark, where they are supposed to have been sinkers for fishing lines or nets. **1888** GOODE *Amer. Fishes* 7 A large float and heavy sinker and a worm or minnow for bait.

*fig.* **1849** LONGF. *Kavanagh* xx, I perceive you fish with a heavy sinker; down far down in the future.

**b.** A weight of lead or other metal for sinking a sounding-line, buoy, or mine, in water.

**1882** NARES *Seamanship* (ed. 6) 18 Rope supporting the sinker. **1892** *Daily News* 29 July 6/6 It occupied about five minutes to haul in his sinker and compare the indication of his tube with the scale.

**c.** *slang.* A base coin; also *U.S.* a dollar.

**1839** *Slang Dict., Sinker*, bad money. **1864** *Slang Dict., Sinkers*, bad money—affording a man but little assistance in keeping afloat. **1900** FLYNT *Tramps* 342 'Give you a sinker (a dollar),' I said.

**d.** *slang* (orig. *U.S.*). A doughy cake, esp. a doughnut; a dumpling. Now *rare*.

**1870** J. H. BEADLE *Utah* 223 Our favorite dinner, when we could get the meat, was of fried ham and 'sinkers'. **1903** F. B. SMITH *How Paris amuses Itself* 48 The New York Dairy Lunch, with..its elevating Bible texts, and depressing 'sinkers',..would never make a success with Parisians. **1906** *N.Y. Even. Post* 10 Dec. 14 Without 'sinkers', corn cakes, cream puffs, 'cookies', and other standard foodstuffs at reasonable prices to appease the appetite between lectures, it is simply impossible to go on studying. **1926** E. FERBER *Show Boat* xiii. 268 The coffee was hot, strong, revivifying; the sinkers crisp and fresh. **1946** J. IRVING *Royal Navalese* 157 *Sinkers*, dumplings. **1975** *Amer. Speech 1971* XLVI. 172 Round fried cake with hole in the centre..*sinker*.

**6.** A sink, cesspool, or drain. Now *dial.*

**1623** COCKERAM I, *Lauatrine*, a square stone in a Kitchin, with a hole to auoid water, a sincker. **1847** HALLIW., *Sinker*, a cesspool; used in the neighbourhood of Spilsby. *Linc.* **1866** BROGDEN *Prov. Lincs., Sinker*, a drain to carry off dirty water, etc. *Ibid.*, The rat has run down the sinker-hole.

**7.** *attrib.*, as ***sinker-bar***, ***-wheel*** (in a knitting-machine), ***sinker-bar***, ***-rod*** (in boring apparatus).

**1834–6** *Encycl. Metrop.* (1845) VIII. 747/2 The lead sinkers..being all fixed to one bar, called the *sinker bar. **1883** *Century Mag.* July 330/1 The drilling tools consist of the 'bit',..the sinker-bar resembling the auger stem, and the rope-socket. **1875** KNIGHT *Dict. Mech.* 2441/2 *Substitute*,..a short section of *sinker-rod having flanges to ream the hole and keep it straight. *Ibid.* 1237/1 The wings of the..*sinker wheel..press the yarn in between the needles.

**III.** A person or thing that sinks. Chiefly *N. Amer.* **8. a.** One who sinks. *rare.*

**1851** H. MELVILLE *Moby Dick* II. lxxviii. 78 No sign of either the sinker or the diver.

**b.** A sunken or partly submerged log.

**1884** *Redwood & Lumbering in Calif. Forests* (Edgar Cherry & Co.) 95 The well matured heartwood of the base of these trees is so solid as to sink in water—hence designated as 'sinkers'. **1905** *Terms Forestry & Logging* 34 *Deadhead*, a sunken or partly sunken log... Syn[onym]: sinker. **1915** P. B. KYNE *Cappy Ricks* 28 A sinker is a heavy, close-grained clear redwood butt-log, which, if cut in the spring,..is so heavy it will not float in the mill-pond. **1969** *Marine Digest* 4 Jan. 6/2 Ferry manager..blamed the accident on a sinker.

**c.** *Baseball.* A ball which drops markedly after being pitched or hit.

**1932** *Baseball Mag.* Oct. 496/1 Outfield skill depends a lot on the player's quickness in detecting whether it's a 'sailer' or a 'sinker'. **1943** [see OUTCURVE 1]. **1952** *Sun* (Baltimore) 19 Apr. 13/1 A baffling repertoire of sliders and lazy sinkers. **1967** *Boston Traveler* 1 June 31/3 I've developed a good sinker and my fastball and curve are moving. **1975** *Cleveland* (Ohio) *Plain Dealer* 29 Mar. 2-C/5 He's missing bad with his sinker.

Hence **'sinkerless** *a.*, having no sinker (5).

**1891** W. O. STODDARD in *Arkansas Mite* 31 Under that bank the sinkerless line carried..its little green prisoner. **1905** *Westm. Gaz.* 25 Mar. 2/1, I had but to bait my line and cast it, sinkerless, into the water.

**sinker** ('sɪŋkə(r)), *sb.*[2] *Bot.* Also 9 senker. [a. G. *senker* process, shoot, now assimilated to SINKER *sb.*[1]] A process of the root system of a mistletoe that grows radially into the tissues of the stem of the host.

**1863** J. HARLEY in *Trans. Linn. Soc.* XXIV. 176 The young plant [*sc.* mistletoe] first sends into the bark of the nourishing plant a single root, sucker, or *senker*. **1894** SOMERVILLE & WARD tr. *Hartig's Dis. Trees* I. 27 Once a year, very seldom twice, often only each alternate year, a 'sinker' originates on the inner side of the cortex-root near the apex. **1938** J. S. BOYCE *Forest Path.* xv. 347 From the cortical haustoria are developed the sinkers which grow radially through the inner bark to the cambium, later becoming embedded in the wood by the formation of new annual rings. **1970** W. H. SMITH *Tree Path.* xxi. 220 Generally, sinkers are located within the rays of host xylem tissue, where they appear to grow coincidentally with the host.

**sinkfield, -foil(e**, obs. ff. CINQUEFOIL.

**sinkful** ('sɪŋkfʊl). Also sink-full. [f. SINK *sb.*[1] + -FUL.] As much or as many as will fill a kitchen sink.

**1961** 'A. A. FAIR' *Shills can't cash Chips* viii. 148, I hate to come home to a sinkful of dirty dishes. **1976** W. J. BURLEY *Wycliffe & Schoolgirls* iii. 64 The kitchen..had..a sink-full of dirty dishes. **1982** J. B. HILTON *Sunset Law* i. 7 Mock exasperation about the third sinkful of crockery that day.

**sink-hole** ('sɪŋkhəʊl). [f. SINK *sb.* + HOLE *sb.*]

**1.** A hole or hollow into which foul matter runs or is thrown; †a sink, or a hole by which a sink is emptied. Also *fig.* and in fig. contexts.

**1456** in *Cockersand Chartul.* (Chetham) II. i. 471 *note*, Following the said strind to the Sinkehole, and fro' Sinkeholl..into the Black polles. **1548** PATTEN *Exped. Scotl.* D vij b, James of the synk hole (sauyng your reuerence) a frier, forsooth that wrote the Legendaurie. **1576** FLEMING *Panopl. Epist.* 152 Wee satt at y[e] sterne,..but now we haue no place allowed vs, no not scarsely next the pump, or the sinck-hole. *a* **1625** FLETCHER *Wife for Month* v. ii, Thou wilt be hang'd as handsomly..as if thou wert Heir apparent To all the impious Suburbs, and the sink-holes. **1665** M. N. *Med. Medicinæ* 89 Instead of clearing the body of Scorbutick Humors, they drain the best Juices down through the common Sink-hole. **1687** A. LOVELL tr. *Thevenot's Trav.* I. 132 This passage, or rather sink-hole, as being very steep and shelving,..goes sloaping down Seventy six Foot. **1830** GEN. P. THOMPSON *Exerc.* (1842) I. 259 The law is to be made a sink-hole for the storing-up of old abuses. **1847–** in dialect use (Yks., Linc., Derby, Warw., Oxf.). **1949** *Reader's Digest* June 45/1 The French industrialist behaves as if he believed his country were headed toward the sink-hole. **1976** N. THORNBURG *Cutter & Bone* v. 124 'In this world!' Cutter's grin did not believe. .. 'This jailhouse. This sinkhole of piss and misery.' **1978** H. WOUK *War & Remembrance* xlviii. 488 Hollywood's such a sinkhole.

*attrib.* **1895** RYE *E. Angl. Gloss.* 196 *Sink-hole Thief*, a despicable small thief, capable of creeping through a sink-hole (Arderon).

**2.** A hole, cavern, or funnel-shaped cavity made in the earth by the action of water on the soil, rock, or underlying strata, and frequently forming the course of an underground stream; a swallow-hole. Chiefly *U.S.*

**1780** W. FLEMING *Diary* 20 Mar. in N. D. Mereness *Travels in Amer. Colonies* (1916) 639 Springs..appear again either in Sink holes immediately vanishing or bursting out. **1791** W. BARTRAM *Carolina* 174 The vast grotto or bason of transparent waters, which is called by the traders a sink-hole, a singular kind of vortex or conduit, to the subterranean receptacles of the waters. **1812** BRACKENRIDGE *Views of Louisiana* (1814) 106 The number of funnels, or sinkholes, formed by the washing of the earth into fissures of the limestone rock. **1834** M. SCOTT *Cruise Midge* xx. (1863) 330 As for those sink-holes, or caverns in the rock, I can compare them, from their sinuosities, to nothing more aptly than the human ear. **1889** G. F. WRIGHT *Ice Age N. Amer.* 129 What are called sink-holes, frequent in limestone regions, where a great amount of material below the surface is removed in solution.

**3.** *U.S.* **a.** A soft place in a marsh, remaining unfrozen in winter. **b.** An unprofitable undertaking which is carried on in spite of losses.

**1895** *Funk's Stand. Dict.*

**sinking** ('sɪŋkɪŋ), *vbl. sb.* [f. SINK *v.* + -ING[1]. Cf. Fris. *sinking*, Du. *zinking*, G. *sinkung*.]

**1.** The action of the vb. in intransitive senses:

**a.** Denoting an actual downward movement.

*c* **1440** *Promp. Parv.* 78/1 Cynkynge, *dimersio, submercio.* *a* **1500** in *Bernard. de cura rei fam.* (E.E.T.S.) 33 þe barge of bariona [sall] bowne to the senkyne. **1565** COOPER *Thesaurus, Sedimentum*, a sinkyng downe to the botome. **1590** SHAKS. *Com. Err.* I. i. 78 The Sailors..left the ship then sinking ripe to vs. **1630** in Binnell *Descr. Thames* (1758) 74 No Trinck shall stand to fish..at the rising or sinking of any Mother-Fishes. **1662** GERBIER *Principles* 19 To prevent the sinking and bending of their Walls. **1765** FOOTE *Commissary* II. Wks. 1799 II. 22 One, two, three, ha. There are risings and sinkings [of the body in dancing]! **1799** *Med. Jrnl.* II. 460 The alternate swelling and sinking of the brain, during inspiration and expiration. **1837** P. KEITH *Bot. Lex.* 348 The sinking of the one knob and the swimming of the other. **1890** *Q. Jrnl. Geol. Soc.* XLVI. I. 34 The numerous deep crevasses, sinkings in and landslips. **1895** *Outing* XXVII. 203/1 Bend the knees quickly and fall soft—a sinking down is better for the flesh than a downright tumble.

**b.** In various *fig.* or *transf.* uses. Also with *in*.

**1717–8** HEARNE *Collect.* (O.H.S.) VI. 126 This sinking of the value of Money creates abundance of Murmuring. **1727** POPE (*title*), Peri Bathous: or, Martinus Scriblerus his Treatise of the Art of Sinking in Poetry. **1740–1** RICHARDSON *Pamela* (1824) I. 11 These are wonderful sinkings from purpose. *a* **1851** MOIR *Poems* (1852) II. 11 In his soarings he was Heavenly, In his sinkings he was man. **1897** *Daily News* 18 June 4/3 The sinking of the prices paid in the London markets. **1937** W. B. YEATS *Vision* 178 A sinking-in of the body upon its supersensual life.

**c.** A lowering or drooping of the spirits, etc.

**1663** SPENCER *Prodigies* (1665) 326 Those horrors and sinking of spirit in bad men. **1829** SCOTT in *Croker Papers* 30 Jan., Johnson, however indulgent to his own sinkings of the spirits. **1851** JERROLD *St. Giles* xvi. 168 St. Giles, with a sinking of the heart, passed on. **1888** *Times* (weekly ed.) 23 Jan. 13/2, I felt a sinking at my heart, lest..I should find myself unable to go any further.

**d.** Decline or diminution of vital power.

**1730** BAILEY (fol.), *Arythmos*, a Sinking and Failure of the Pulse, so as it can be no longer felt. *a* **1776** JAMES *Dissert. Fevers* (1778) 125 That kind of sensation which patients describe by a sinking. **1813** J. THOMSON *Lect. Inflam.* 169 We may, by too free a detraction of blood, produce a sudden sinking of the powers of life. **1843** R. J. GRAVES *Syst. Clin. Med.* ix. 101 Coldness of the extremities and sinking of the pulse. **1899** *Allbutt's Syst. Med.* VIII. 146 In this form of neurasthenia, pains, sinkings and acidities of the stomach are frequent.

**e.** *Painting.* A dull matt spot on the surface of an oil painting caused by the absorption of the pigments by the ground; the process by which the pigments sink into or become absorbed by the ground. Also ***sinking-in***.

**1915** P. YOUNG tr. *Vibert's Science Painting* ix. 118 Where, in the execution of a picture on account of repeated re-touching, embus or sinkings appear, it is possible..to make them disappear with a light scumbling of re-touching varnish. **1939** H. HUBBARD *Materia Pictoria* 231 The chief causes of sinking-in are: (A) The porousness of the Painting-ground or Priming [etc.]. **1951** R. MAYER *Artist's Handbk. Materials & Techniques* xii. 433 *Embu*, (French), in an oil painting, a dull spot in an otherwise glossy surface, caused by a sinking-in of the oil color. **1971** B. DORF *Beginner's Guide to Painting in Oils* xiii. 158 *Sinking*, dull patches in oil paint, caused by too absorbent ground, wrong medium, or too much dilutant.

**f.** Also *attrib.*, as ***sinking feeling***.

**1890** H. G. HUTCHINSON *Golf* (Badm. Libr.) ix. 246 The nerves and muscles must be fed for the work before them; otherwise there will ensue a dreadful sinking feeling before the end of the round. **1920** *Poster*, Bovril..Prevents that sinking feeling. **1920** C. A. W. MONCKTON *Some Experiences of New Guinea Resident Magistrate* xxv. 302 'Do you feel devilish hungry half an hour before meals?'..'Yes,.. sometimes so hungry that I have a sinking feeling.' **1937** *Discovery* Oct. 295/1 The slight sinking feeling experienced by pedestrian members.., when faced by the considerable uphill trudge. **1961** W. BUCHAN *Helen All Alone* 196, I just have a sinking feeling. **1979** L. MEYER *Fake Front* xiii. 108, I got that nasty sinking feeling again. We..couldn't get the story into the paper.

**2. a.** The action of the vb. in transitive senses.

***sinking and drawing***, a method of angling, in which the hook is allowed to sink and then gently drawn up again. Also called the 'sink-and-draw' style, principle, etc.

**1605** CAMDEN *Rem., Epitaphs* (1623) 322 His conquering of Cyprus, the sinking of the great Galleasse of the Saracens. **1683** MOXON *Mech. Exerc., Printing* xv. ¶1 When I come to the sinking and justifying of Matrices. **1705** J. BLAIR in W. S. Perry *Hist. Coll. Amer. Col. Ch.* I. 150 Some proposing the cancelling of the said Aspersions, other, the sinking of the whole paper. **1856** 'STONEHENGE' *Brit. Rur. Sports* I. v. iii. 251/2 Chub-Fishing... Sinking and drawing is therefore practised, because by this mode the line is not so likely to be entangled. **1890** W. J. GORDON *Foundry* 223 Though rotary presses at £7,000 apiece require a somewhat alarming sinking of capital.

**b.** The process or act of boring or excavating downwards in search of coal, etc.; the pit or shaft thus formed.

**1708** J. C. *Compl. Collier* (1845) 11 The Earth, Minerals and Water, that may be met with in our way of Sinking. **1802** PLAYFAIR *Illustr. Huttonian Th.* 294 The sinking of perpendicular shafts. **1839** MURCHISON *Silurian Syst.* I. ii. 22, I..learned that sinkings in search of coal had been prosecuted..in the district. **1890** 'R. BOLDREWOOD' *Miner's Right* (1899) 16/2 Our party consists of four, which is much the most common number, particularly where the sinking is deepish.

**3.** A depression, or the amount of this; a recess or worked hollow.

**1712** J. JAMES tr. *Le Blond's Gardening* 27 Niches cut for Figures, and two Sinkings for Shells and Buffets of Water. *Ibid.* 137 The Depth or Sinking you would give the Bowling-green. **1797** T. HOLCROFT tr. *Stolberg's Trav.* II. xxxviii. 27 The sinking under the stage is of a great depth. **1825** J. NICHOLSON *Operat. Mechanic* 615 A beech mould is next made..of the profile of the intended cornice,..with the quirks, or small sinkings, of brass or copper. **1863** *Archaeol. Cant.* V. 16 One piece with chamfered sinkings, probably a piece of Norman moulding. **1879** *Cassell's Techn. Educ.* (1894) III. 176/2 A dovetail sinking is cut on the upper surface of the stones at the ends.

4. Special comb.: **sinking speed**, the vertical downward component of the velocity of a gliding body.

**1930** V. W. Pagé *Henley's ABC of Gliding & Sailflying* (1931) ii. 40 The falling or sinking speed depends on the weight of the glider loaded and the skill of the pilot in manipulating the controls. **1953** *New Biol.* XIV. 72 One requirement of a bird which is to soar in upcurrents is that it should have a low 'sinking speed'; that is to say, it must lose height slowly when gliding in still air. **1973** *Sci. Amer.* Dec. 102/2 If the air through which the bird is flying happens to be rising at a speed greater than the sinking speed, the bird is carried up with it and acquires potential energy it can use later to glide through air that is not rising.

**'sinking**, *ppl. a.* [f. sink *v.* + -ing².]

†**1. a.** Of ground: Soft, yielding. ***a sinking sand***, a quicksand. *Obs. rare.*

**1535** Stewart *Cron. Scot.* III. 148 Thair schippis.. drevin vpoun the land, Quhair tha war ebbit on ane sinkand sand. **1597** Shaks. *2 Hen. VI*, iii. ii. 97 The splitting Rockes cowr'd in the sinking sands. **1656** Blount *Glossogr.*, *Slough*, ..a deep, sinking, mudy place.

†**b.** Of paper: Allowing ink to spread. *Obs.*

**1585** Higins tr. *Junius' Nomencl.* 5/2 *Papier qui passe*, blotting or sinking paper. **1638** Junius *Paint. Ancients* 273 A writer purposing to write well,..doth sometimes come short of his intent, if he meeteth with sinking and blotting paper. **1665** Gurnall *Chr. in Arm.* (1669) 393/2 By thy religious duties thou settest a fair copie, O do not write it in sinking paper. **1772** *Gentl. Mag.* XLII. 192 Will any paper match him?—Yes, throughout He's a true *Sinking Paper*, past all doubt. **1799** G. Smith *Laboratory* II. 83 You must take a paper that will bear ink very well for this use, for a sinking paper will separate with the wet, and spoil all.

**2.** That sinks, in senses of the intransitive verb.

**1676** Dryden *Aurengz.* i. i, As Seas and Winds to sinking Mariners. **1725** Pope *Odyss.* xiii. 95 At once they bend,.. And leave the sinking hills, and less'ning shores. **1746** Hervey *Medit.* (1818) 35 Her hands..sometimes stay the sinking head on her gentle arms. **1817** Shelley *Rev. Islam* i. 179 Like a great ship in the sun's sinking sphere Beheld afar at sea. **1863** Ld. Lytton *Ring of Amasis* i. i. ix, He is within but a few arm-lengths of the sinking child. **1897** Watts-Dunton *Aylwin* i. iii, I can see the rim of the sinking sun burning fiery red low down between the trees.

*fig.* **1704** Prior *Celia to Damon* 88 Another Nymph with fatal Pow'r may rise To damp the sinking Beams of Celia's Eyes. **1740** Wesley *'Jesus, the all-restoring Word'* ii, Quicken my soul,..My sinking footsteps stay.

**b.** Lapsing into ruin or decay; failing, losing; declining, decadent.

**1693** Bowles in Dryden *Juvenal* v. (1697) 103 No Man expects..what Piso us'd to send, To raise, or to support a sinking Friend. **1703** Rowe *Ulysses* iii. i, Save the sinking House of thy Ulysses. **1781** Gibbon *Decl. & F.* (1787) III. 67 Amidst the misfortunes and terrors of a sinking nation. **1818** Scott *Br. Lam.* ii, In the civil war of 1689, he had espoused the sinking side. **1821** Shelley *Hellas* 459 Live! oh live! outlive Me and this sinking empire.

**c.** Of the heart, spirits, health, etc.: Drooping, flagging.

**1820** Scott *Monast.* xxi, The hope of which issue has cheered the sinking heart of many a duellist. **1862** Stanley *Jew. Ch.* (1877) I. xvii. 325 Their appearance..roused..the sinking spirit of the army. **1879** Froude *Cæsar* xiv. 212 [They] cowered in their tents with sinking hearts,..and composed last messages for their friends.

**3.** Special uses: **sinking-chain**, part of the apparatus of a pit-shaft boring-rod; **sinking-fire, heart-burn, -jar** (see quots.); †**sinking-lead**, a sounding-lead; **sinking stage** (see quot.).

**1839** Ure *Dict. Arts* 994 The beam centered at *c*, having an arc-head and martingale *sinking-chain. **1881** Raymond *Mining Gloss.*, **Sinking-fire*, a forge in which wrought-iron scrap or refined pig-iron is partially melted or welded together by means of a charcoal-fire and a blast. **1822-7** Good *Study Med.* I. 163 *Cardialgia..syncoptica*, *Sinking heart-burn. The pain or uneasiness extending to the pit of the stomach; with..failure of strength, and great tendency to faint. **1837** *Penny Cycl.* IX. 24/2 After due agitation of the wash three samples should be taken by the dipping cylinder, or *sinking-jar. **1648** Hexham ii, *Een Zinck-loot*, a *Sinking-lead or Plummet to sound the depth of water. **1841** *Civil Eng. & Arch. Jrnl.* IV. 430/1 The stage,..including a considerable portion formed to rise or fall by suitable machinery, and called the *sinking stage.

**sinking fund.** [See sink *v.* 27 and fund *sb.* 4a.] A fund formed by periodically setting aside revenue to accumulate at interest, usually for the purpose of reducing the principal of a national, municipal, or company's debt.

Sinking funds were established by the British Government in 1716, 1786, and 1875 for reducing the National Debt. In the Act 3 George I (1716) c. 7 it is termed 'a General Yearly Fund'.

**1724** *Lond. Gaz.* No. 6232/1 It must be a..great Satisfaction..to see the sinking Fund improved. **1765** Blackstone *Comm.* I. 329 The surplusses..are usually denominated the sinking fund, because originally destined to sink and lower the national debt. **1824** Byron *Juan* xvi. xcix, The Sinking Fund's unfathomable sea..leaves The debt unsunk, yet sinks all it receives. **1862** Ansted *Channel Isl.* iv. 573 No special sinking fund exists; but the general revenue is in excess of the expenditure.

*attrib.* **1846** *Daily News* 21 Jan. 5/5 A loan of 18,840,000 florins is to be raised by the sinking-fund commission. **1906** *Westm. Gaz.* 30 Apr. 9/1 A restoration of Sinking Fund purchases.

**Sink pors**: see Cinque Ports.

**'sinksman.** [f. sink *v.*] = sinker *sb.*¹ 2.

**1887** P. M'Neill *Blawearie* 46 Foul air, completely extinguishing..the lights of the sinksmen.

**sink-stone** ('sɪŋkstəʊn). Also **sinkstone**. [f. sink *sb.*¹ or *v.* + stone *sb.*]

**1.** *dial.* A stone basin or sink, having a pipe attached for the escape of water; a hollowed stone with an opening leading to a drain.

**1766** *Complete Farmer* s.v. *Gravel*, It will be proper to have sink-stones laid by the sides of the walk,..to let off the wet. **1828** Carr *Craven Gloss.*, *Sink-stone*, an excavated stone, with a small grate, to receive the off-scourings of a kitchen. **1877-** in dial. glossaries (Lanc., Yks., Linc.).

**2.** A stone sinker for submerging a fishing-line or -net in water.

**1865** Lubbock *Preh. Times* 76 Many of them were used as sinkstones for nets. **1872** Evans *Anc. Stone Implements* 212 Sink-stones are by no means rare in Ireland, and continue in use to the present day.

**sinky** ('sɪŋkɪ), *a. rare.* [f. sink *v.* + -y.] Of sand or soil: Yielding; = sinking *ppl. a.* 1 a.

**1827** Steuart *Planter's G.* (1828) 249 If the forced-up surface also of the pit be too soft and sinky. **1895** 'G. Setoun' *Sunshine & Haar* vii. 145 It was a heavy enough walk over the 'sinky' sand even in the best of weather.

**sinless** ('sɪnlɪs), *a.* Forms: 1-2 **synleas**, 4 **sinles**, 7- **sinless**; 2 **synneleas**, 4-5 **-les**, 6 **-lesse**; 3 **sinnelæs**, 7 **-lesse**; 4 **senne-**, **sunneles**. [f. sin *sb.* + -less. Cf. OS. *sundilôs*, OHG. *suntilôs*, (MHG. *sundelôs*, G. *sündenlos*), ON. and Icel. *syndalauss* (Sw. *syndalös*, Da. *syndeløs*).] Free from, devoid of, without sin. Also const. *of*.

*c* **897** K. Ælfred *Gregory's Past C.* liv. 423 Swa bið eac swiðe oft synleas yfel ȝeðoht ðæm godum. *c* **1000** *Ags. Gosp.* John viii. 7 Hwylc eower si synleas [*Hatton* synneleas], wurpe ærest stan on hi. *a* **1023** Wulfstan *Hom.* xxiv. 121 Crist þrowade for us synleas. *c* **1200** Ormin 11020 Soþ mann, all þweorrt ut sinnelæs Off bodiȝ & off sawle. *a* **1300** *Cursor M.* 913 O man sinles þan mad i þe. **1362** Langl. *P. Pl.* A. vii. 217 Miht I sunneles don as þou seist? **1532** More *Confut. Tindale* Wks. 525/2 He..beyng synnelesse hymselfe, paynefullye payed for oures. *a* **1639** W. Whateley *Prototypes* i. iv. (1640) 33 Such a Law, as was given to a sinnelesse and immortall creature. **1671** Milton *P.R.* iv. 425 In calm and sinless peace. **1680** in Howell *State Trials* (1816) VII. 1170 Sir Thomas was as sinless of it [the plot] as the child that was unborn. **17..** Ramsay *Lady Somerville's Bk. Songs* 5 If she thy sinless faults forgive. **1738** Wesley *Ps.* vi. vi, Make ev'n me..A sinless Saint below. **1813** Shelley *Q. Mab* i. 11 Hath then the gloomy Power..Seized on her sinless soul? **1877** E. R. Conder *Basis Faith* ii. 66 To pronounce any human being sinless is to pass a positive judgment carrying immense consequences.

Hence **'sinlessly** *adv.*

**1696** Lorimer *Rem. Goodwin's Disc.* vii. 69 To be always Sinlesly Holy in Heart and Life. **1831** *Blackw. Mag.* XXIX. 290 The image of virgin growing up sinlessly to womanhood. **1867** *Contemp. Rev.* IV. 474 A sinlessly holy co-redeemer.

**sinlessness** ('sɪnlɪsnɪs). [f. prec. + -ness.] The quality or state of being sinless; freedom from sin, innocence.

**1661** Boyle *Motives Love of God* Wks. 1772 I. 287 The sinlessness of whose condition will keep them [etc.]. **1849** C. S. Bird *Mariolatry* 32 The original sinlessness of Mary is at length fully developed. **1862** F. Hall *Hindu Philos. Syst.* 127 When man was in a state of sinlessness. **1880** 'Ouida' *Moths* II. v. 126 A sullen reverence for her..sinlessness and her honour.

**sinn**, obs. f. sin *sb.*; Sc. var. sun.

**'sinnable**, *a. rare.* [f. sin *v.* + -able.] Capable of sinning. Hence **'sinnableness**.

**1662** Gurnall *Chr. in Arm.* vii. (1669) 291/2 Though they never sinned, yet they are sinnable. **1863** tr. *Réville's Man. Relig. Instruct.* 205 If our nature was not sinnable. *Ibid.* 202 Original sin..is not sinfulness but sinnableness.

**sinner** ('sɪnə(r)), *sb.* Forms: α. 4 **sin-**, **synȝer**, **zeneȝere**, **sinnier**, 5 **synnyer**. β. 4 **synnere**, 4-7 **synner**, 4- **sinner**. γ. 4 **synnour**, 4-5 (6 *Sc.*) **synnar**, 5 *Sc.* **synar**, 6 *Sc.* **sinnar**. [f. sin *v.* Cf. OFris. *sondere*, MDu. *sondaer* (Du. *zondaar*), MLG. *sunder*, OHG. *suntari* (MHG. *sundære*, G. *sünder*), ON. and Icel. *syndari* (Sw. *syndare*, Da. *synder*).]

**1.** One who sins; a transgressor against the divine law.

α. *c* **1325** *Prose Psalter* i. 1 Blesced be þe man, þat..stode nouȝt in þe waie of sinȝeres. *Ibid.* i. 6 þe sinniers. **1340** *Ayenb.* 33 Sleuþe and uoryetinge blendeþ þe zeneȝeres. **1422** tr. *Secreta Secret., Priv. Priv.* 201 He did so myche for Pagans and Synnyers.

β. *c* **1325** *Prose Psalter* i. 7 þe waye of synners schal perissen. **1382** Wyclif *Mark* ii. 17, I cam not for to clepe iuste men, but synners. *c* **1440** *Alph. Tales* 470 A riche man ..þat was a synner of his bodie. **1509** Fisher *Funeral Serm. C'tess Richmond* Wks. (1876) 298 It perceth my stomacke to se the rest & ease that synners often haue. **1579** in W. Fulke *Heskins' Parl.* 31 Contrition maketh a man more sinner. **1651** Hobbes *Leviath.* iii. xxxviii. 248 Salvation of a sinner, supposeth a precedent Redemption. **1721** Young *Revenge* i. i, Sinners shall..bid the light adieu. **1784** Cowper *Task* iii. 96 Now..they are safe, sinners of either sex. **1820** Shelley *Witch Atl.* lxxvi, Both, like sinners caught, Blushed. **1881** Besant & Rice *Chapl. of Fleet* I. 179 Sir Miles enjoyed the lamentations of a sinner the morning after a debauch.

*fig.* **1610** Shaks. *Temp.* i. ii. 101 Like one Who..Made such a synner of his memorie To credite his owne lie.

*Comb.* **1797** T. Park *Sonn.* 72 She ponders o'er her follies past, And, sinner-like, repents at last.

γ. *a* **1400** *Minor Poems fr. Vernon MS.* xxiii. 183 Olde Adames sone, þe furste synnour [*rime* sauour]. *c* **1400** *Apol. Loll.* 27 þus was Crist callid a synnar and blasfemer. **1567** *Gude & Godlie B.* (S.T.S.) 120 Sinnaris hes thy Celsitude Resistit cruellie.

**b.** *spec.* An unchaste woman.

**14..** *Nom.* in Wr.-Wülcker 695 *Hec fornicatrix*, a sinner. **1630** *R. Johnson's Kingd. & Commw.* 143 The Servants, Pages, Lacquies, and *Filles de joye* (Punkes or pleasant sinners) which follow the Court. **1688** Bunyan *Jerusalem Sinner saved* (1886) 41 They knew that she [the woman of Samaria] was a town sinner, an adulteress.

**c.** In phrase ***as I am a sinner***.

**1682** N. O. *Boileau's Lutrin* iv. 329 As I am a sinner, My eager stomach crokes, and calls for Dinner! ? **1800** Shelley *Verses on a Cat* i, As I am a sinner, It waits for some dinner. **1844** Thackeray *Contrib. to Punch* wks. 1900 VI. 59 My acquaintance..was in the boat with fifteen trunks, as I am a sinner.

**2.** In trivial use: A reprobate, rogue; an offender against some rule or custom.

**1809** Malkin *Gil Blas* iii. x, A thousand broad hints.. seasoned exactly to the taste of these old sinners. **1851** Mayne Reid *Scalp Hunt.* xxx. 231 The smoky old sinner chuckled with delight at the remembrance of his adventure. **1871** Freeman *Norm. Conq.* IV. xxii. 53 The original sinners of the Herefordshire border..were still lords of English soil.

Hence **'sinner** *v.* (with *it*), to act as a sinner.

**1735** Pope *Ep. Lady* 15 Whether the Charmer sinner it, or saint it, If Folly grow romantic, I must paint it. **1880** A. I. Ritchie *Ch. Baldred* 26 He sainted it and sinnered it.

**'sinneress.** *Obs. rare* (now *arch.*). [f. prec. + -ess.] A female sinner.

**1382** Wyclif *Luke* vii. 37 A womman synneresse, that was in the citee. *Ibid.* 39 She is a synneresse. **1647** Hexham i, A Sinneresse, *een sondaresse*. **1929** S. Leslie *Anglo-Catholic* xii. 165 Veronica's card was the tell-tale finger pointing to her as a sinneress.

**sinnerite** ('sɪnəraɪt). *Min.* [See quot. 1964 and -ite¹.] A sulpharsenite of copper, $Cu_6As_4S_9$, found as brittle, grey, triclinic crystals.

**1964** Marumo & Nowacki in *Schweiz. Min. u. Petrogr. Mitt.* XLIV. 440 In the course of the systematical study of the sulfosalt minerals from Lengenbach, Binnatal, a new mineral, a copper arsensulfide was found, which has some similarity to binnite and lautite... The mineral was named sinnerite in honour of the late Rudolf von Sinner, president of the Commission of the Naturhistorisches Museum Bern. **1975** *Amer. Mineralogist* LX. 998/2 Both natural and synthetic crystals of sinnerite are complexly twinned.

**sinnership** ('sɪnəʃɪp). [f. sinner *sb.* + -ship.] The condition of being a sinner.

*c* **1750** J. Nelson *Jrnl.* (1836) 66 Many..told me to my face that I never knew the gospel liberty, nor what it was to enjoy the poor sinnership. **1818** Bentham *Church-of-Englandism* 175 Exists there any scale..by which the sinnership and the miserableness of the Archbishop can be measured? **1868** Browning *Ring & Bk.* iii. 114 Which the more Tends to the reconciling us, no saints To sinnership. **1887** —— *Parleyings, F. Furini* xi, Show saintliness that's simply innocent Of guessing sinnership exists to cure All in good time!

**sinnes** (in dicing): see sines.

**sinnet** ('sɪnɛt). Also 7 **sinnett**, **sinnit**, 8-9 **sinnate**, 9 **cinnet**. Cf. sennit. [A nautical term of obscure origin.] A kind of flat braided cordage formed by pleating together several strands of rope-yarn, coarse hemp, grass, or other fibrous material.

**1611** Cotgr., *Trene*, a threefold rope, cord, string, or twist, called by Marriners, a Sinnet. **1627** Capt. Smith *Seaman's Gram.* v. 25 Sinnet is a string made of rope yarne commonly of two, foure, six, eight or nine strings platted in three parts, which being beat flat they use to sarue ropes or Mats. **1706** E. Ward *Wooden World Diss.* (1708) 28 If he have but Hands enough to Furl, Rief, and make Sinnate. **1840** R. H. Dana *Bef. Mast* xxvi, The boys..laid up grass into sinnet for the men. **1847** H. Melville *Omoo* lxxiv, A roll of grass sinnate (of the kind which sailors sew into the frame of their tarpaulins). **1880** J. S. Cooper *Coral Lands* I. x. 105 They stand about six feet high, the gables being filled in with sinnet. **1884** Turner *Samoa* 165 Everything is fastened in their ancient style, with cinnet plaited from the fibre of the cocoa-nut husk. Cinnet is likely long to prevail in native canoe and boat-building.

*attrib.* and *Comb.* **1856** Kane *Arct. Expl.* II. x. 101 Our sinnet-laid twine would not stand the powerful struggles of the beast. **1894** B. Thomson *South Sea Yarns* x, A man may make many signs by jerking a sinnet cord which another holds.

**sinnet**, variant of sennet.

**Sinn Fein** (ʃɪn 'feɪn). [f. Ir. *sinn féin* we ourselves.] The name of an Irish movement founded in 1905 by Arthur Griffith (1872-1922), Irish journalist and politician, orig. aiming at the independence of Ireland and a revival of Irish culture and language and now dedicated to the political unification of Northern Ireland and the Republic of Ireland. Freq. *attrib.*

**1905** *United Irishman* 18 Mar. 4/4 The Sinn Fein policy which we have propounded for Ireland, will henceforth be the policy of the National Council. **1906** A. GRIFFITH *Sinn Fein Policy* 4 The policy for which the National Council stands is summarised in its title—'*Sinn Fein*'. *Ibid.* 32 Increase of employment, industrial effort and advancement should be everywhere the principal means towards the national aims of Sinn Fein Policy. **1907** *Westm. Gaz.* 31 Aug. 7/1 Sinn Fein is not as yet a movement of much political moment. **1920** *Public Opinion* 16 July 58/3 The intellectual leaders of Sinn Fein can by no means bind the extremists. **1930** W. K. HANCOCK *Australia* x. 213 Labour politicians preached Australia for the Australians and a sort of Sinn Fein exclusiveness. **1936** E. CURTIS *Hist. Ireland* xx. 386 Sinn Fein came out as a political force by winning an election in Roscommon in February 1917. **1944** M. J. MACMANUS *Eamon de Valera* iv. 69 De Valera.. had been co-opted on the National Council of Sinn Fein after his release. **1955** *Times* 16 May 3/5 The fact that Sinn Fein has put forward candidates for West Belfast, Mid-Ulster, [etc.].. may mean that a Unionist gain will be recorded. **1962** A. LURIE *Love & Friendship* ii. 29 He looked over-excited, as if he were about to.. lead a small raid for the Sinn Fein. **1971** *Eire Nua: Soc. & Econ. Programme of Sinn Fein* 3 The Constitution of Sinn Fein advocates not merely the complete overthrow of English rule in Ireland but also the setting up of a Democratic Socialist Republic. **1972** R. KEE *Green Flag* ix. 452 From May 1905 Griffith's new policy generally began to be called the 'Sinn Fein' rather than the 'Hungarian' policy. The suggestion for the new name had been made to him by a young woman named Mary Butler, late in 1904, though the words had long been fairly commonly used as a motto for Irish self-reliance and had in fact been the early motto of the Gaelic League. **1978** P. BOARDMAN *Worlds of Patrick Geddes* vii. 248 The never-ending nemesis of Sinn Fein Rebellion.

Hence **Sinn 'Feiner**, a member or adherent of Sinn Fein; **Sinn 'Feinism**, the methods, aims, or policies of Sinn Fein.

**1907** *Daily Chron.* 13 Aug. 6/2 Sir Thomas Esmonde's action in adopting Sinn Feinism as against Parliamentary agitation. **1907** *Westm. Gaz.* 31 Aug. 7/1 Sinn Feiners further suggest that the Irish representatives, having withdrawn from Westminster, should assemble in Dublin. **1917** A. HUXLEY *Let.* May (1969) 124 The best part of political life after the war will be an unofficial Sinn Feinism. **1928** *Daily Express* 17 Nov. 3/5 The Sinn Feiners desired to strengthen this protest by obtaining the withdrawal from Parliament of the whole O'Brien party. **1945** R. CHANDLER *Let.* 1 Jan. (1981) 41, I have a great many Irish relatives.. some of them Sinn Feiners. **1979** W. NELSON *Minstrel Code* ix. 75 The spot where Sinn Feiners gunned down a British Field-Marshall, Sir Henry Wilson, in 1922, on the doorstep of his home.

**sinning** ('sɪnɪŋ), *vbl. sb.* Forms: α. 1 syngung; 3 sineginge, siniging (4 -yng), sunegunge, -ynge, -ing; 4 seneȝynge. β. 5 cynn-, synnynge, 6 synnyng, 7- sinning. [f. SIN *v.* + -ING[1].] The action of the verb in various senses.

α. *c* **1000** *Ags. Hom.* (Assmann) 149 Us is swiðe þearle to efstanne,.. þæt we.. ðære syngunge ȝeswican. *c* **1220** *Bestiary* 193 No mod ðu ne cune.. Oc swic of sineginge. *a* **1225** *Ancr. R.* 52 Lo hu holi writ.. telleð hu sunegunge bigon. *c* **1315** SHOREHAM I. 669 Ine wyl of seneȝynge. *a* **1400** in *Herrig's Archiv* CIV. 307 God is more greuet of þat defendyng þen of þe furste sinigyng.

β. *c* **1440** *Promp. Parv.* 78/1 Cynnynge, *peccamen*. **1493** *Communycacyon* (W. de W. 1535) A iij, Thou purposed.. To set my people in synnynge. **1526** *Pilgr. Perf.* (W. de W. 1531) 227 Not onely for ones, twyse, or seuen tymes synnyng. **1611** BIBLE *Ecclus.* xviii. 27 In the day of sinning he will beware of offence. **1667** MILTON *P.L.* VI. 661 Spirits of purest light,.. now gross by sinning grown. **1719** DE FOE *Crusoe* II. (Globe) 429 The Blessing of God does not ordinarily follow a presumptuous Sinning against his Command. **1818** BYRON *Juan* I. vii, The regularity of my design Forbids all wandering as the worst of sinning. **1841** BROWNING *Pippa Passes* Poems (1905) 171 To think She would succeed in her absurd attempt, And fascinate by sinning.

*attrib.* **1643** TRAPP *Comm. Gen.* vi. 17 God will not alway serve men for a sinning-stock. **1673** R. HEAD *Canting Acad.* 147 A sinning-house near Whetstones-Park.

**'sinning,** *ppl. a.* [f. SIN *v.* + -ING[2].] That sins or commits transgressions.

**1609** BIBLE (Douay) *Amos* ix. 8 Behold the eyes of our Lord upon the sinning kingdom. **1616** J. LANE *Contn. Sqr.'s T.* VIII. 370 Tis not yond noble kinges intent to kill his sinninge subiectes that repent. **1885** *Athenæum* 5 Sept. 300/2 The implacable wrath which he subsequently felt for the sinning guest at last melted.

Hence **'sinningly** *adv.*, **'sinningness.**

**1647** TRAPP *Comm. 1 John* iii. 9 Sinningly, so as to be transformed into sin's image. **1674** J. B[RIAN] *Harvest-Home* i. 3 Nor shall they offend Sinningly. **1863** tr. *Réville's Man. Relig. Instruct.* 201 The liability to sin may be called sinnableness; the tendency, sinningness.

**sinningia** (sɪ'nɪŋgɪə). [mod.L. (C. G. Nees von Esenbeck 1825, in *Ann. Sci. Nat.* VI. 296), f. the name of Wilhelm *Sinning* (1794–1874), German botanist + -IA[1].] A hairy herbaceous plant of the genus so called, belonging to the family Gesneriaceæ, native to Brazil, and bearing bell-shaped flowers.

*Sinningia speciosa* is the parent of many varieties commonly known as gloxinias.

**1826** *Bot. Reg.* XII. 997 (*heading*) Green Brazilian Sinningia. **1902** L. H. BAILEY *Cycl. Amer. Hort.* IV. 1670/2 The Sinningias are little known horticulturally. **1936** E. SITWELL *Victoria of England* xix. 226 Flowers from the Queen's hothouses at Osborne—the lyonia with its waxlike bells.., the velvety sinningia with dark leaves. **1979** *Homes & Gardens* Feb. 25/1 Gloxinias, or sinningias as they are now called, are old favourites as house and cottage plants.

**si'nnography.** *nonce-word.* [f. SIN *sb.*: see -GRAPHY.] (See quot.)

**1654** WHITLOCK *Zootomia* 495 Sinnography (as I may tearm it), the description or consideration of the kinds & differences of Sin.

†**sinnomon,** obs. form of CINNAMON.

**1609** ARMIN *Maids of More-cl.* (1880) 108 Stuft with sweet sinnomon and cloues.

**sinnon, sinnowe:** see SINEW *sb.*

†**'sinny,** *a. Obs. rare.* In 1 synniȝ, 5 synny. [f. SIN *sb.* + -Y.] Sinful, wicked.

*c* **950** *Lindisf. Gosp.* Matt. xix. 9 He synȝias *vel* synniȝ bið. *c* **1475** *Partenay* 5218 Off his synny crime [he] lefte not more ne lesse.

**sinny,** Sc. variant of SUNNY *a.*

**Sino-**[1] ('sɪnəʊ, 'saɪnəʊ), combining form of Gr. *Σῖναι*, L. *Sinæ* (see SINÆAN *a.*) the Chinese, as in **'Sinogram,** a Chinese written character; **Si'nologer,** = SINOLOGUE; **Sino'logical** *a.*, 'relating to the Chinese language or literature' (Webster *Suppl.* 1879); **Si'nologist, 'Sinologue,** one versed in the Chinese language, or in the customs and history of China; **Si'nology,** the study of things Chinese (*Imp. Dict.* 1882); **'Sinophil** *a.*, fond of the Chinese; **'Sinophile** [-PHILE], a lover of China or things Chinese; also as *adj.* and **Sino'philia,** love of China or that which is Chinese; contrasted with **Sino'phobia,** dread or hatred of these; also **Sino'phobic** and **'Sinophobe** *adjs.*; **Sino-xenic** *a.* [f. XEN- (see XENO-) + -IC], of a language: unrelated to a Chinese language but containing some Chinese linguistic elements.

**1898** E. P. EVANS *Evol. Ethics* viii. 318 *Sinograms, ideograms, and all hieroglyphics and picture-writing. **1857** *Sat. Rev.* 3 Jan. 12/2 One of the greatest living French *Sinologers. **1877** *Trübner's Amer. & Oriental Lit. Record* XI. 2/1 It is significant of the preponderance assigned in *sinological studies to the English language, that Mr. von Möllendorff has thought it desirable to publish his work in English. **1970** *Guardian* 26 Nov. 15/6 This very readable and also scholarly collection.. has all kinds of Sinological goodies too. **1816** P. DU PONCEAU *Let.* 31 July in *Trans. Hist. & Lit. Comm. Amer. Philos. Soc. 1816* I. 400 As I am no *Sinologist, I will not undertake to say that the description which I have attempted to give of this language.. is very accurate. **1838** —— *Chinese Syst. Writing* Introd. 26 Those sinologists who consider ideas to be inseparably inherent in the Chinese characters. **1884** *Harper's Mag.* Sept. 643/2 The Sinologist who read the scratches.. as Chinese! **1853** *North-China Herald* 21 May 167/2 Prince of *Sinologues. **1856** MEADOWS *Chinese* 375 The metaphysical reader, even if no sinologue, will at once decide in favour of my version. **1880** *Sat. Rev.* No. 1306. 581 A gifted young sinologue who bids fair to introduce a new era in the study of Chinese. **1894** *The Liberal* 24 Nov. 50/1 The *Sinophil author of Primitive Civilization. **1900** E. R. SCIDMORE *China* i. 7 One agrees and disagrees, too, with the sinologues, who are usually *sinophiles, that the Chinese are the one great race and flower of all Asia. **1977** R. LUDLUM *Chancellor MS.* xxxiii. 350 He's a Sinophile.. He has one of the most extensive Chinese art collections in the world. **1974** *Daily Colonist* (Victoria, B.C.) 17 July 17/7 Ireland attributed the herbal pill fad to the public's '*sinophilia' or ardent interest in Chinese culture including medicine. **1920** W. J. LOCKE *House of Baltazar* iii. 31 Water-End became divided into two camps—Sinophile and *Sinophobe. **1966** *New Statesman* 22 Apr. 601/2 Siam.. exhibits considerable *Sinophobia. **1977** *New Yorker* 24 Oct. 177/1 The Korean war and the *Sinophobic diplomacy of John Foster Dulles. **1972** *Computers & Humanities* VI. 259 The term 'dialect' in this article refers loosely to all the sources of information in DOC: Middle Chinese,.. 18 modern Chinese dialects, and 3 *Sino-Xenic sources.

**2.** Combined with adjectives of nationality to mean 'Chinese and..' or 'between China or the Chinese and (the country or people designated)', as ***Sino-Albanian, -American, -Australian, -British, -Indian, -Japanese, -Malay, -Mongolian, -Russian, -Soviet, -Tibetan.***

**1976** W. H. CANAWAY *Willow-Pattern War* v. 55 The Sino-Albanian axis. **1931** H. B. MORSE *Far Eastern International Relations* 750 (*caption*) Significance of the Sino-American treaty of 1928. **1978** D. BLOODWORTH *Crosstalk* iii. 28 Sino-American exchanges.. had yielded a private understanding. **1904** *Amer. Naturalist* Sept. 676 The restriction of the Sino-Australian continent to a certain part of the Cretaceous times consequently would meet the postulates of geography and zoögeography. **1977** *South China Morning Post* (Hong Kong) 15 Apr. 2/1 An insight into how Sino-British relations, already good, are likely to develop. **1959** *Listener* 25 June 1093/2 The Sino-Indian agreement of April 1954. **1903** *Burlington Mag.* Oct. 13/1 We must place to the front the fact that Sino-Japanese design is almost exclusively an art of contours. **1978** *Jrnl. R. Soc. Arts* CXXVI. 652/1 The terms of the Sino-Japanese Trade Agreement are, I would judge, likely to prove more beneficial to both parties than the EEC/China Agreement. **1975** 'G. BLACK' *Big Wind for Summer* ii. 22 The girl.. was .. Sino-Malay. **1976** *Times Lit. Suppl.* 20 Feb. 206/2 In Central Asia.. the Sino-Soviet frontier is straddled by a homogeneous Muslim population, while the Sino-Mongolian frontier is similarly straddled by a Mongolian population. **1926** *Glasgow Herald* 23 Jan. 9 The rift in the Sino-Russian lute. **1929** A. J. TOYNBEE *Survey Internat. Affairs 1928* 434 The zone.. had reverted to Chinese administration in virtue of the Sino-Soviet Russian agreement of the 31st May 1924. **1959** *Listener* 2 Apr. 598/3 The Sino-Soviet zone of nations. **1971** H. TREVELYAN *Worlds Apart* x. 125 Sino-Soviet companies were formed to exploit minerals and oil, to develop Sinkiang in which the Soviet Union had a close interest, and to manage civil aviation. **1973** *Times* 14 Nov. 18/3 The Nagas are a group of 20 tribes of Sino-Tibetan origin.

**3.** Used similarly with sbs. to form sbs. (freq. *attrib.*) with the meaning 'a language (family) or subsection of this, characterized by a relationship between Chinese and the language (family) specified', as ***Sino-Japanese, -Korean, -Siamese***; **Sino-Tibetan,** a family of languages comprising the Chinese, Tibeto-Burman, and (according to some scholars) the Tai languages.

**1923** B. KARLGREN *Analytic Dict. Chinese & Sino-Japanese* 7 After the Sino-Japanese readings I often add in parenthesis the Kana spelling. **1954** M. PEI *Dict. Linguistics* 198 *Sino-Japanese*, a term applied to Chinese loan-words in the Japanese language, the spoken form of which is different from the form or forms occurring in any of the spoken Chinese vernaculars. **1975** *Amer. Speech 1973* XLVIII. 122 If Japanese is indeed the source of the term, a more plausible model would be *nemaki*, the colloquial equivalent of *shin-i*, which is the learned or Sino-Japanese term. **1953** Sino-Korean [see HANGUL[2]]. **1975** *Language* LI. 257 Each representing a lexical item with information regarding.. its pronunciation in the 21 major dialects of China and in the Sino-xenic languages, i.e. Sino-Japanese and Sino-Korean. **1948** D. DIRINGER *Alphabet* 402 The Sino-Siamese sub-family of languages. **1954** M. PEI *Dict. Linguistics* 198 Many linguists classify Chinese and Tai into one Tai-Chinese or Sino-Siamese sub-family. **1933** L. BLOOMFIELD *Language* iv. 69 The great *Indo-Chinese* (or *Sino-Tibetan*) family consists of three branches. **1948** R. A. D. FORREST *Chinese Lang.* i. 21 Chinese is reckoned as an independent member of the Sino-Tibetan, Indo-Chinese, or Sinitic family of languages. **1977** C. F. & F. M. VOEGELIN *Classification & Index of World's Langs.* 307 It is the older, more liberal, classifications of Sino-Tibetan that have now come under critical scrutiny.

**sino-**[2] ('saɪnəʊ), comb. form of SINUS.

**sino-atrial** (saɪnəʊ'eɪtrɪəl), *a. Anat.* Also **sinoatrial.** [f. SINO-[2] + ATRIAL *a.*] Of, pertaining to, or designating a small body of tissue (the ***sino-atrial node***) in the wall of the right atrium of the heart that acts as a pacemaker by producing a contractile signal at regular intervals; (so called because it arises in the embryo at the junction of the sinus venosus and the atrium). Cf. SINUATRIAL *a.*

**1913** *Gray's Anat.* (ed. 18) 552 The sino-atrial node is situated on the anterior border of the opening of the superior vena cava. **1962** *Listener* 10 May 810/1 A small mass of specialized muscle cells within the heart, the sino-atrial node, discharges a brief electric 'spark' regularly seventy-two times a minute or thereabouts. **1969** [see *dysrhythmia* s.v. DYS-].

**sino-auricular** (saɪnəʊɔː'rɪkjʊlə(r)), *a. Anat.* [f. SINO-[2] + AURICULAR *a.*] = prec.

**1907** KEITH & FLACK in *Jrnl. Anat. & Physiol.* XLI. 181 We use the term 'sino-auricular' in preference to 'sino-canalar' because, although a true sino-canalar junction exists on the dorsal side in the most primitive hearts,.. yet in all but these the part of the canal between the sinus and the auricle disappears, and the dorsal junction becomes really a sino-auricular junction. **1942** BRAMWELL & KING *Princ. & Pract. Cardiol.* v. 87 Closely related to sinus arrhythmia is the disorder known as sino-auricular heart-block. **1976** *Archives Internationales de Physiologie et de Biochimie* LXXXIV. 81 (*heading*) Chronotropic responses to experimental ischemia of the canine sino auricular node.

**sinod, -al(l, synode,** obs. ff. SYNOD(AL.

**sinodoches,** obs. f. SYNECDOCHE.

**sinody,** var. SYNODY *Obs.*

**'sin-,offering.** [f. SIN *sb.* 6, prob. after G. *sündopfer*, used by Luther to render Heb. *ḥattāth*, f. *ḥāṭā'* to sin.] In the older Jewish religion, an offering (of an animal for sacrifice) made as an atonement for sin. Also *transf.*

See especially *Lev.* iv and vi. The distinction between *sin-offering* and *trespass-offering* has been the subject of much controversy.

**1535** COVERDALE *Lev.* iv. 3 He shall brynge.. a yonge bullocke.. for a synofferynge. **1597** HOOKER *Eccl. Pol.* v. lxxviii. §1 With what sinne-offering once euery yeere they reconciled.. the people vnto God. **1643** J. CARYL *Expos. Job* i. 5–6 Of other Sacrifices, as the Sin-offering,.. there were parts.. reserved for the Priest. **1786** A. MACLEAN *Chr. Commiss.* I. (1846) 39 The sin-offering or sacrifice of expiation. **1819** SCOTT *Ivanhoe* xxxvi, The death of a Jewess will be a sin-offering sufficient to atone for all the amorous indulgences of the Knights Templars. **1865** R. W. DALE *Jew. Temp.* xvii. (1877) 187 In the sin-offering the idea of atonement was supreme.

**sinogram** ('saɪnəʊgræm). *Med.* [f. SINO-[2] + -GRAM.] An X-ray photograph of a sinus into which a contrast medium has been introduced.

**1961** *Lancet* 5 Aug. 296/1 A sinogram showed narrowing of the sagittal sinus anterior to the fontanelle. **1974** J. D. MAYNARD in R. M. Kirk et al. *Surgery* x. 220/1 Such sinograms.. can be repeated regularly until the cavity has decreased until it is the size of the tube it contains.

So **si'nography,** the radiographic examination of sinuses.

**1957** in DORLAND *Med. Dict.* (ed. 23) 1254/2. **1974** A. HENRY in R. M. Kirk et al. *Surgery* xv. 295/2 When a sinus is present it is worth while performing sinography.. in an effort to delineate a communication with an intraosseous abscess cavity possibly containing a sequestrum.

**sinoite** ('saɪnəʊaɪt). *Min.* [f. the chemical symbols for silicon (*Si*), nitrogen (*N*) and oxygen (*O*) + -ITE[1].] Silicon oxynitride, $Si_2N_2O$, found as colourless orthorhombic crystals in some chondritic meteorites.

**1964** C. A. ANDERSEN et al. in *Science* 9 Oct. 257/3 We propose the name *sinoite*, which is derived directly from the chemical formula, for this new mineral. **1966** *Geochimica & Cosmochimica Acta* XXX. 367 Sinoite has only been found in the enstatite chondrites. **1972** *Nature* 22 Dec. 461/2 The relatively high nitrogen content in some enstatite chondrites is partly due to the presence of the mineral sinoite, $Si_2N_2O$, which so far has been found only in two meteorites.

**Sinologer**, etc.: see SINO-[1] above.

**Sinon** ('saɪnən). Also 6-7 **Synon**. [The name of the Greek who induced the Trojans to bring the wooden horse into Troy (Virgil *Æneid* II. 57 sqq.).] One who misleads by false tales; a perfidious person; a deceiver or betrayer.

In *Peele's Jests* viii. Dyce reads *she-Sinon* for *she-sinnow* of the old editions.

**1581** J. BELL *Haddon's Answ. Osorius* 483 b, You come to late gentle Synon with these fables and bables. **1592** ? KYD *Soliman & Pers.* II. i. 95 Heere comes the Synon to my simple heart: Ile frame my selfe to his dissembling art. **1635** NAUNTON *Fragm. Reg.* (Arb.) 38 They decipher him for another Solon, and the Synon of those times. **1638** SIR T. HERBERT *Trav.* (ed. 2) 133 The Ambassador easily descryed him to be a Synon, sent meerly to betray his credulity. **1807** COLLINSON *Thuanus* 82 They are a company of Sinons, who watch opportunities of enriching them-selves by the ruin of others. **1818** SCOTT *Rob Roy* iv, Osbaldistone inveighed.. against the arts of these modern Sinons.

Hence '**Sinonism**.

**1864** *Daily Telegr.* 29 Oct., Another 'dodge'—another Sinonism, if that phrase sounds more agreeably to classical ears—is conceived.

†**sinoper**. *Obs.* Forms: 5 **zinopre**, 5-6 **synopre**, **-pyr** (6 *Sc.* **-pir**), 5-7 **synoper** (6 *Sc.* **-peir**), 6 **syneper**, **synapour** (*Sc.* **-par**, **-pir**, 7 **-per**), 6-8 **sinoper** (6 **seno-**); 6 **cinaper**, 7-8 **cinoper**. [a. OF. *sinopre* (cf. Pg. *sinopera*), var. of *sinople* SINOPLE. Some of the forms may be partly due to confusion with CINNABAR.]

**1.** A colour of some shade of red. Also *attrib.*

**1412-20** LYDG. *Chron. Troy* II. 964 With knottis graue clene, Depeynt with azour, gold, zinopre, & grene. *c* **1450** *Merlin* xxvii. 530 Lo hym ther that thow sechest, with the shelde of synopre. **1513** DOUGLAS *Æneid* XII. Prol. 57 The syluer scalyt fyschis..Wyth fynnis schynand brovn as synopar. **1530** LYNDESAY *Test. Papyngo* 1112 3e..sall knaw hir be hir moste heuinly hewis,—Gold, Asure, Gowles, Purpour, and Synopeir. **1573** *Art of Limming* 5 To temper good Synapour, grind Synapour lake and Synapour topes ech by himselfe. **1688** HOLME *Armoury* I. 13/2 Colours derived from Sanguine..Synaper, or Lake colour.

**2. a.** A kind of red earth used as a pigment (originally one brought to Greece from Sinope in Paphlagonia). **b.** Cinnabar.

The latter may have been the more usual sense.

**1501** *Acc. Ld. High Treas. Scot.* II. 63 Item, ij unce synapir, xvj d. **1510** in Willis & Clark *Cambridge* (1886) II. 199 Ceruse, Synoper, red okyr, yelowe oker. **1565** COOPER *Thesaurus*, *Cinnabaris*, a softe redde stone founde in mines, called in latin *Minium*, in Englysh, Cinoper... The common Cinoper is counterfayted of brimstone and quicke siluer. *Ibid.*, *Sinopis*, a redde stone commonly called Sinoper, or Ruddle. **1599** HAKLUYT *Voy.* II. 229 Great quantitie of quicksilver and Cinaper. **1610** B. JONSON *Alch.* I. iii, You shall deale much, with mineralls,..argaile, alkaly, Cinoper. **1610** MARKHAM *Masterp.* II. viii. 233 Other Farriers take a dramme of Synoper. **1611** COTGR., *Cinabre*, Synoper; Vermillion; or, a kind of Lybian minerall, redder then Vermillion. **1725** *Fam. Dict.* s.v. *Bezoar-Stone*, Others use Cinoper, Antimony, and Quicksilver. **1726** LEONI *Alberti's Archit.* II. 46/1 Sinoper, or Terra Pontica.

**sinopia** (sɪ'nəʊpɪə). [It.; cf. SINOPER, SINOPLE.]

**1.** = SINOPER 2 a.

**1844** MRS. MERRIFIELD tr. *Cennini's Treatise on Painting* xxxviii. 22 There is a natural red pigment, which is called sinopia or porphyry. **1910** A. P. LAURIE *Materials of Painter's Craft* x. 208 *Sinopia*..is one of the many names under which red ochres are mentioned. **1978** *Times Lit. Suppl.* 20 Oct. 1208/3 Trecento fresco painters normally drew direct on the wall in sinopia without preliminary drawings.

**2.** *transf.* The preliminary rough sketch for a fresco, covered by the final work. Pl. *sinopie*.

**1958** *Times* 10 Dec. 3/4 During the process of detaching a fresco from the wall it is often possible to separate it also from the *sinopia*—that is, the preliminary rough sketch. **1969** *Daily Tel.* (Colour Suppl.) 28 Mar. 28/3 Their long hidden *sinopie*, as the preparatory full-size wall-drawings are called, are generally our only witness to the evolution of their ideas. **1975** E. H. GOMBRICH *Let.* 14 Nov. in *Ideas & Idols* (1979) 182 Are the sinopie really better than the frescoes? **1981** M. DELAHAYE *Sale of Lot 236* xxiii. 197 The sinopia..had also to be right technically... He was safe in the materials. Charcoal, ochre, and sinopite were all natural substances.

**Si'nopian**, *a. rare.* = next.

**1611** COTGR. s.v. *Bol*, Sinopean red earth. *Ibid.*, *Rubrique Sinopique*, Sinopian red earth.

**Sinopic** (sɪ'nɒpɪk), *a.* [ad. L. *Sinōpic-us*, a. Gr. Σινωπικ-ός, f. Σινώπη, a Greek colony in Paphlagonia.] Obtained from Sinope or its neighbourhood.

**1748** J. HILL *Hist. Fossils* 61 Theophrastus expressly says, that it was a Cappadocian Earth, tho' call'd Sinopic. **1753** *Chambers' Cycl.* Suppl., *Sinopis*,..the Sinopic ochre, commonly called *rubrica Sinopica*. **1868** DANA *Min.* 477 The sinopic earth of the ancients was brought from Cappadocia, and used as a red paint.

So **si'nopical**. *rare*$^{-0}$.

**1656** BLOUNT *Glossogr.*, *Sinopical*,..of or belonging to that Stone.

**sinopite** ('sɪnəʊpaɪt). *Min.* [ad. G. *sinopit* (Hausmann, 1847), f. L. *Sinōp-is* or *Sinōp-ē* (see next) + -ITE[1] 2 b.] (See quots.)

**1868** WATTS, *Sinopite*, *Bole of Sinope*,..a ferruginous bole occurring in masses with fine earthy fracture, in Cappadocia. **1868** DANA *Min.* 477 *Sinopite*,..a clayey earth of a brick-red color dotted with white, adhering to the tongue.

†**sinople**. *Obs.* Also 5 **cinople**, 6-7 **synople**, 8 **senople**. [a. OF. *sinople* (cf. Sp. *sinople*, Pg. *sinopla*, It. *sin-*, *senopia*), ad. L. *Sinōpis*, a. Gr. Σινωπίς, f. Σινώπη: see SINOPIC *a.*]

**1.** = SINOPER 1.

?*c* **1450** *Lydgate's Chron. Troy* II. (1555) xi. 964 Green Depeynt with asure, golde, cinople, & grene. **1567** MAPLET *Gr. Forest* 98 The Parret hath all hir whole bodie greene, sauing that..she hath a Coller or Chaine naturally wrought like to Sinople or Vermelon. **1569** J. SANFORD tr. *Agrippa's Van. Artes* 159 From hence came the temperatures of Asure, of Cinnaber, of Sinople, of Purple.

*attrib.* **1552** HULOET, Synople coulour or redde.

**2.** = SINOPER 2.

**1548** ELYOT, *Miniaria*, the place where synople is dygged. *Ibid.*, *Minium*, synople or redde leade. **1611** COTGR., *Minion*, Synople, red lead, Vermillion. **1683** PETTUS *Fleta Min.* II. 7 The Common Armoniack he [Pliny] calls Synoper (and we Synople).

**3.** The colour green; *spec.* in *Her.*, vert.

The origin of this use (prominent in French) is not apparent. In quot. 1838-9 used as if the name of a charge.

**1489** CAXTON *Faytes of A.* IV. xvii. 280 That other colour of armoyrie is grene that men calle sinople or verte. **1602** *Palmerin of Eng.* II. lxii, In this was pictured in a field of Sinople the lively and naturall forme of the Princesse. **1611** COTGR., *Synople*, Sinople; Greene, in Blazon. **1728** CHAMBERS *Cycl.*, *Sinople* or *Senople*, in Heraldry, the Green Colour in Armories. [**1838-9** THACKERAY *Major Gahagan* iv, The well known device of Holkar, argent and or gules, between a sinople of the first, a chevron truncated, wavy.]

**b.** *attrib.* or as *adj.* Of a green colour.

**1590** LODGE *Euphues' Gold. Legacy* O 2 b, The Sinople tree, whose blossomes delight the smell. **1610** GUILLIM *Heraldry* I. i. (1660) 5 They beare three Toades, Sable, in a Field Vert, *alias* Sinople. *a* **1649** DRUMM. OF HAWTH. *Sonnets* xliv, The delightful Green Of your fair radiant Een, ..Sinople Lamps of Jove. **1698** T. FROGER *Voy.* 116 A White Flag with a Sinople or green Cross in it.

**4.** *Min.* A variety of ferruginous quartz.

**1796** KIRWAN *Elem. Min.* (ed. 2) I. 313, 4th Family [of Siliceous Genus]—Sinople. It is said to contain 18 per ct. of iron. **1798** JAMESON *Min. Shetland Isles* 34 Frequently also considerable veins of red sinople, intermixed with chalcedony.., run in this rock. **1836** T. THOMSON *Min., Geol.*, etc. I. 71 Sinople, ribbon jasper, Egyptian jasper.

**sinovia(l**, obs. ff. SYNOVIA(L.

**sinow(e, -ie**, obs. ff. SINEW, SINEWY.

**sinque**, obs. f. CINQUE.

**sinque a pace, sinquepace**, varr. CINQUEPACE.

**sinsemilla** (sɪnsə'mɪlə). [a. Amer. Sp., lit. 'without seed'.] A plant belonging to a strain of *Cannabis sativa* having a particularly high narcotic content; also, the narcotic produced from a plant of this kind. Also *attrib.*

**1975** *High Times* Dec. 68/2 Last year a guy bit the dust in Arizona in a PBY—a big-ass World War II Navy amphibian—full of prime Mexican sinsemilla. **1978** *Time* 12 June 22 Studies show that *sinsemillas* weed contains five times more tetrahydrocannabinol (pot's narcotic ingredient) than the common Mexican variety. **1980** *Daily Tel.* 19 Sept. 11/2 This year sinsemilla buds are fetching from $2,200 (£917) to $3,000 (£1,250) a pound. **1982** *Newsweek* 25 Oct. 60 Sinsemilla retails for up to $250 an ounce these days, and every plant produces up to two pounds of marketable buds.

'**sin-sick**, *a.* [SIN *sb.* 6.] Sick with sin.

**1609** DANIEL *Civ. Wars* IV. xlvi, Is there no meanes, but that a sin-sicke Land Must be let bloud with such a boysterous hand? *a* **1618** SYLVESTER *Paradox agst. Libertie* 1068 Wks. (Grosart) II. 64 The poysony humour fell Where-with my sin-sick heart already 'gan to swell. **1760-72** H. BROOKE *Fool of Qual.* (1809) III. 2 The manifold distempers of your sin-sick soul. **1779** COWPER *Olney Hymns* lix, O God, whose favourable eye The sin-sick soul revives. **1845** G. MURRAY *Islaford* 46 The sin-sick heart reposed in hope and prayer.

Hence '**sin-sickness**. *rare*$^{-1}$.

**1633** EARL MANCH. *Al Mondo* (1636) 161 Commonly good men are best at last, even when they are dying; for they seldome dye of a sinne-sicknesse.

**sinsion**, variant of SENCION.

**sin-soiled** ('sɪnsɔɪld), *a.* [SIN *sb.* 6.] Blemished, stained, or soiled by sin.

**1593** NASHE *Christ's T.* Wks. (Grosart) IV. 214 Our costly skinne-cases could keepe vs from..beeing sinne-soyled. **1612** J. DAVIES (Heref.) *Muse's Sacr.* Wks. (Grosart) II. 50/1 If the Heau'ns, sinne-soiled, must not stand, much lesse must Man. *a* **1618** SYLVESTER *Little Bartas* 907 That B'al-blinded, bloud-soild, sin-soild Pair. **1842** MANNING *Serm.* xxiii. (1848) I. 344 No man that is not..repenting of his sin-soiled state. **1891** G. F. X. GRIFFITH tr. *Fouard's Christ the Son of God* I. 294 The depth of degradation from which the Saviour rescued this sin-soiled creature.

**sinsyne** (sɪn'saɪn), *adv. Sc.* and *north.* Forms: α. 7- **sinsyne**, 9 **sin-**, **sin'**, **sin syne**; *north.* 8 **sinsaan**, 9 **sin-seyne**. β. 8-9 **sincesyne**, **since syne**. [f. SIN *prep.* + SYNE *adv.* Cf. the earlier SENSYNE.] Since then, from that time.

α. *a* **1657** SIR J. BALFOUR *Ann. Scotl.* (1825) II. 228 The forme of worschipe..receaued at the reformatione, and vniwersally practissed sinsyne. **1724** RAMSAY *Royal Archers Shooting* ix, Just fifty years sinsyne. **1793** BURNS *Logan Braes* 3, Years sinsyne hae o'er us run. **1802** ANDERSON *Cumbld. Ball.* (*c* 1850) 43 Monie a thousand happier days We beath ha'e kent sin-seyne. **1824** SCOTT *St. Ronan's* ii, Mony a mad measure has been danced sin' syne. **1865** G. MACDONALD *A. Forbes* 43, I hae eaten ower muckle sin syne.

β. **1725** RAMSAY *Gentle Sheph.* v. iii, She has pass'd since-syne As a poor orphan. **1786** *Har'st Rig* lvi, Ay since syne he's tint the way For her to spear. **1823** GALT *R. Gilhaize* xiv, We twa hae forgathered no lang sincesyne. **1891** BARRIE *Little Minister* xxiii, It has been turned sax times since syne.

**sinter** ('sɪntə(r)), *sb.* [a. G. *sinter*, the equivalent of Eng. *sinder* CINDER.]

**1.** A hard incrustation or deposit formed upon rocks, etc., by precipitation from mineral waters; esp. ***siliceous sinter***, geyserite.

**1780** *Von Troil's Iceland* 344 The porous crustated stone, or sinter, which is found in the moor surrounding the border of the bason. **1796** KIRWAN *Elem. Min.* (ed. 2) II. 279 The massive are often called Cobaltic Sinters. **1830** LYELL *Princ. Geol.* I. 213 The hot springs..precipitate vast quantities of siliceous sinter. **1857** J. D. DANA *Min.* (1862) 249 Iron sinter is a yellowish or brownish hydrous arsenate of the peroxyd of iron. **1881** GEIKIE in *Macm. Mag.* Oct. 432 The tendency of each geysir to build up a cylinder of sinter around its vent.

**2. *sinter coal*** [ad. G. *sinterkohle*], cherry coal.

**1854** RONALDS & RICHARDSON *Chem. Technol.* (ed. 2) I. 105 Sinter coal approaches nearest to caking coal, but the fusion of the separate pieces into one is not so perfect.

**3.** Material which has been subjected to sintering; *spec.* iron ore prepared for smelting by sintering the powdered material, usu. together with coke and other materials; (see also quot. 1958).

**1909** *Chem. Abstr.* III. 167 Process of treating metal-bearing ore in a uniformly formed mass of fine particles containing combustible elements to form relatively large agglomerated bodies of sinter by internal combustion. **1926** *Jrnl. Iron & Steel Inst.* CXIV. 61 Both the briquettes and the sinter are crushed to a somewhat coarser size than the lump ore before charging in the furnace. **1956** *Planning* 9 Apr. 64 Sinter has other advantages—it may rid the furnace of unwanted sulphur and volatile constituents and.. increase furnace output while reducing coke consumption. **1958** A. D. MERRIMAN *Dict. Metall.* 323/2 *Sinter*, a term used in reference to the solid waste from smelting or refining operations. It is also used to denote a product of a sintering operation. **1973** *Times* 12 Feb. (Suppl.) p. ii/4 The mixture of foreign and Frodingham ores will produce a sinter containing about 54 per cent iron.

**4.** Special Comb.: **sinter plant**, a furnace for sintering iron ore.

**1938** R. H. SWEETSER *Blast Furnace Practice* I. 57 Three types of sinter plant were erected in this country..all based on the principle of down-draft suction, ignition on the top of a mixture of flue dust, and fine iron pyrites cinder. **1980** *Times* 29 Feb. 2 The coke ovens at Redcar..are part of the steel complex, along with a sinter plant.

**sinter** ('sɪntə(r)), *v.* [f. the sb.] **a.** *intr.* Of particles or particulate material: to coalesce into a solid mass under the influence of heat without liquefaction. Also with *together*. **b.** *trans.* To cause to coalesce in this way.

**1871** [implied at SINTERING *vbl. sb.*]. **1903** *Amer. Chem. Jrnl.* XXIX. 487. On heating, it [*sc.* methylmercapto-thymine] sintered at about 225°. **1907** *Trans. Inst. Mining & Metall.* XVI. 321 The formation of ferrous silicate aids..in sintering the material. **1938** R. H. SWEETSER *Blast Furnace Practice* I. 58 This plant sinters red ore, fines and flue dust. **1948** *Electronic Engin.* XX. 68 To the surface thus formed a nickel powder is sintered to provide a base for brazing materials. **1953** *Sci. News* XXIX. 43 Many small metal components are now made by sintering metal powders, which have previously been pressed into the desired shape. **1973** *Sci. Amer.* Oct. 129/2 At high temperatures the effect is even stronger: metal powders sinter together under pressure. **1976** *Ceramurgia Internat.* II. 90/2 Attempts were made to sinter material which was dried at 125°C and not calcined.

**sintered** ('sɪntəd), *ppl. a.* [f. SINTER *v.* + -ED; cf. SINTERING *vbl. sb.*] That has been subjected to or formed by sintering; ***sintered carbide***, a very hard material manufactured by sintering a pulverized mixture of cobalt or nickel and carbides of metals such as tungsten and tantalum, and used in the cutting parts of tools; ***sintered glass***, a porous form of glass made by sintering glass powder and used esp. in chemical filtration apparatus.

**1877** RAYMOND *Statist. Mines & Mining* 309 To separate the sintered lumps from the well-roasted fine ore. **1907** *Trans. Inst. Mining & Metall.* XVI. 313 The product obtained consists of a porous sintered mass of ferrous silicate. **1937** *Machinery* L. 773 (*heading*) The production of sintered carbides. **1940** *Jrnl. Sci. Instruments* XVII. 139 (*heading*) Sintered glass filters. **1951** O. W. BOSTON *Metal Processing* (ed. 2) v. 103 Sintered-carbide tools were introduced commercially in this country in 1928. **1959** *Economist* 21 Feb. 719/2 The process of manufacturing small pellets of sintered reactor fuel..follows the normal practice of the ceramics industry. **1962** J. T. Marsh *Self-Smoothing Fabrics* xxii. 365 The liquid is then decanted through a weighed sintered-glass crucible. **1964** S. Crawford *Basic Engin. Processes* iv. 104 Sintered carbide is fully hard when cooled to room temperature. **1982** D. Clark *Doone Walk* vii. 147 Front and back wheels have disc brakes with sintered pads to cure the problem of grip on wet roads.

**sintering** (ˈsɪntəɪŋ), *vbl. sb.* [f. sinter *v.* + -ing[1].] The process or action of the vb.; *spec.* as applied to iron ore (see sinter *sb.* 3). Freq. *attrib.*

**1871** *Trans. Amer. Inst. Mining Eng.* I. 225 In reference to Western coals we cannot talk about the sintering or fusion of carbon. **1907** *Trans. Inst. Mining & Metall.* XVI. 314 These ..difficulties are overcome by the use of the sintering process, as the loss is small owing to the ore being wet. **1914** *Iron Trade Rev.* LV. 292 (*heading*) Sintering plant at Pottstown. **1930** *Engineering* 16 May 650/2 Sintering occurs when charges of partially reduced ores are maintained for considerable periods at temperatures above 750 deg. C. **1958** [see sinter *sb.* 3]. **1958** N. Levine *Canada made Me* ii. 78 Above us a steel cable carried large buckets of iron ore from the Mine to the Sintering Plant. **1977** *Western Mail* (Cardiff) 5 Mar. 6/1 South Wales exports about one million tons a year, much of it anthracite duff used in briquetting and sintering in steel production.

**sintery** (ˈsɪntərɪ), *a.* [f. sinter *sb.* + -y.] Consisting of sinter.

**1863** Baring-Gould *Iceland* xxi. 362 The Great Geysir.. is indicated by a mound of sintery deposit like a heap of dry grey leaves. **1897** *Westm. Gaz.* 13 Aug. 2/1 Here and there ..the sintery veneer was broken off in large uneven patches.

**sintheresis**, obs. form of synteresis.

**Sinto(o, Sintu**, etc.: see Shinto, etc.

‖**sintoc.** Also sindoc, sintok, syndoc. [Malay *sintoq.*] (See quot. 1842.) Also *attrib.*

**1842** *Penny Cycl.* XXII. 45/2 Sintoc, or Sindoc, sometimes written Syndoc, is the bark of a species of Cinnamomum,..called C. Sintoc by Blume... It resembles the Calilawan bark, called clove-bark by some. **1861** Bentley *Man. Bot.* 630 Sintoc bark, which has analogous properties, is the produce of *Cinnamomum sintoc.* **1900** W. W. Skeat *Malay Magic* v. 278 In Penang a root called *sintok* is usually preferred to limes. **1972** A. Amin tr. *Ahmad's No Harvest but Thorn* iv. 32 The *sintok*-wood *tajak*-handle.

**sintyr**: see cintre.

**sinu(e**, obs. ff. sinew *sb.*

**sinuate** (ˈsɪnjuːət), *a.* [ad. L. *sinuāt-us*, pa. pple. of *sinuāre*, f. *sinus* sinus; cf. F. *sinué.*]

**1.** *Bot.* Of leaves: Having a margin made wavy or uneven by alternate rounded and somewhat large sinuses and lobes; sinuous. Also similarly in *Ent.* of wing-cases, etc.

**1688** Holme *Armoury* ii. 117/2 Sinuate leaves, such as are crooked, bent or crumpled about the edges. **1760** J. Lee *Introd. Bot.* iii. v. (1765) 179 *Sinuate, hollowed*; when they have broad and spreading Openings in the Sides. **1785** Martyn *Rousseau's Bot.* xii. (1794) 126 The Wild Clary has the leaves serrate, sinuate, and smoothish. **1826** Kirby & Sp. *Entomol.* III. xxxi. 258 The margins of these cases are sinuate. **1871** Garrod *Mat. Med.* (ed. 3) 290 The leaves are large, ovate, smooth, unequally sinuate. **1882** Vines tr. *Sachs's Bot.* 212 A rudimentary branching, as in indented, toothed, and sinuate leaves.

**b.** *Comb.*, as ***sinuate-angular, -dentate, -lobate, -pinnatifid, -runcinate, -serrate, -undulate; sinuate-leaved, -lobed, -toothed.***

**1793** Martyn *Lang. Bot.*, *Sinuato-angulosum*, a sinuate-angular leaf. *Ibid.*, *Sinuato-dentatum*, a sinuate-toothed leaf. **1822** *Hortus Anglicus* II. 152 Sinuate-leaved Mad Wort. **1847** W. E. Steele *Field Bot.* 11 Leaves cordate at base,.. lower sinuate-runcinate. **1870** Hooker *Stud. Flora* 335 Leaves..of branches..sinuate-lobed. *Ibid.*, Leaves..of branches..sinuate-serrate.

**2.** *Ornith.* (See quot.)

**1872** Coues *N. Amer. Birds* 30 The gape is..curved, sinuate, when they [*sc.* rictus and tomia] lie in the same curved or waved line.

**ˈsinuate**, *v. rare*[−1]. [f. ppl. stem of L. *sinuāre*: cf. prec.] *intr.* To creep or crawl in a winding course.

**1848** *Blackw. Mag.* LXIV. 104 When you are sinuating like a serpent towards the especial stag of your heart.

**sinuated** (ˈsɪnjuːeɪtɪd), *ppl. a.* [f. as sinuate *a.* + -ed[1].]

†**1.** Having a sinus or hollow. *Obs. rare*[−1].

**1578** Banister *Hist. Man* i. 36 A round head..is admitted into the..rounde sinuated side of the Boatelyke Bone.

**2.** *Bot.* Of leaves or their margins: = sinuate *a.* 1.

**1727** Bailey (vol. II), A Sinuated Leaf..is that which is cut about the Edges into several long Segments, as in Oak-Leaves. **1757** *Phil. Trans.* L. 68 The radical leaves..are not sinuated on the edges. **1828** J. E. Smith *Engl. Flora* II. 11 The last, from which it differs in being generally more bushy, with more deeply toothed, or sinuated, leaves. **1847** W. E. Steele *Field Bot.* 13 Leaves lanceolate, unequally spiny, sinuated. **1866** *Treas. Bot.* 1062/2.

**b.** Similarly of shells, parts of insects, etc.

*a* **1728** Woodward *Fossils* (J.), Another was very perfect, ..and more sinuated. **1771** *Phil. Trans.* LXI. 233 Its figure is oblong,..and the hinge somewhat sinuated at the opening. **1835** J. Duncan *Beetles* 103 This piece is usually ..sinuated or notched in the middle of its anterior edge. **1851** Woodward *Mollusca* i. 104 Shell rather ventricose;.. outer lip..sinuated near the notch of the anterior canal. **1875** M. C. Cooke *Fungi* (ed. 2) 67 A cellular mass, consisting of the sinuated hymenium and young spores.

**3.** Sinuous, winding.

**1859** R. F. Burton *Centr. Africa* in *Jrnl. Geogr. Soc.* XXIX. 127 The sinuated beds of watercourses and the steep inclines of hills.

**ˈsinuately**, *adv.* [f. sinuate *a.* + -ly[2].] In a sinuate manner.

**1847** W. E. Steele *Field Bot.* 92 Leaves ovate-rhomboid, sinuately toothed. **1874** M. C. Wood *Fresh-Water Algæ* 135 Polar lobe with its apex broadly sinuately excised.

**sinuation** (sɪnjuːˈeɪʃən). [ad. late L. *sinuātio*, f. *sinuāre* to curve, etc.]

**1.** The act or fact of winding about, or pursuing a winding course.

**1653** R. G. tr. *Bacon's Hist. Winds* 80 We call those Accidentall generations of windes, which doe not..beget the impulsive motion of windes, but..by sinuation or winding doe agitate and tumble it.

**2.** A winding or bending in and out; a sinuosity.

*a* **1676** Hale *Prim. Orig. Man.* 65 The humane Brain is in proportion to the Body much..larger than the Brains of Brutes,..and fuller of *anfractus* or sinuations. **1760** J. Lee *Introd. Bot.* iii. v. (1765) 175 The Form of the Circumference of Leaves where there are no Angles or Sinuations. **1832** Southey *Hist. Penins. War* III. 148 A road..winding in numberless sinuations along the edge of a deep precipice. **1877** Huxley *Anat. Inv. Anim.* vi. 351 A median sinuation divides this extremity into two lobes.

**sinuato-** (ˈsɪnjuːeɪtəʊ), used as combining form of sinuate, prefixed to adjectives in the sense 'sinuately', 'sinuate and', as ***sinuato-dentate, -pinnatifid, -undulate; sinuato-contorted, -dentated, -serrated.***

**1753** *Chambers' Cycl.* Suppl. s.v. *Leaf*, Sinuato-dentated leaf expresses a leaf like the former [*sc.* sinuated], but with the lateral lobes of a linear figure. **1775** J. Jenkinson *Brit. Plants* Gloss., *Sinuato-serrated*, serrated and partly sinuated. **1826** Kirby & Sp. *Entomol.* IV. xlvi. 290 Sinuato-Undulate.., when the sinuses are obtuse. **1857** T. Moore *Handbk. Brit. Ferns* (ed. 3) 46 Fr[onds] coriaceous sinuato-pinnatifid, densely scaly beneath. **1887** Phillips *Brit. Discomyc.* 11 The margin is..undulate, sinuato-contorted, and crisped.

**sinuatrial** (saɪnjuːˈeɪtrɪəl), *a.* *Anat.* Also sinu-atrial. [f. L. *sinu-*, stem of sinus + atrial *a.*] = sino-atrial *a.*

**1935** *Gray's Anat.* (ed. 26) 67 The sinu-atrial and atrioventricular nodes, the atrioventricular bundle and its right fasciculus, are supplied by the right coronary artery. **1962** *Ibid.* (ed. 33) 747 The sinuatrial node is a narrow, horse-shoe shaped structure situated in the upper part of the sulcus terminalis of the right atrium. **1968** Passmore & Robson *Compan. Med. Stud.* I. xxviii. 9/2 The part of the heart with the highest spontaneous rate..provides the source of excitation of the whole heart, and this pacemaker is normally the sinuatrial (SA) node.

**sinu-auˈricular**, *a.* *Zool.* [f. *sinu-*, sinus + auricular *a.* 5.] Of or belonging to, situated between, the sinus venosus and the auricle.

**1875** Huxley in *Encycl. Brit.* I. 764/1 The sinu-auricular aperture, by which the sinus and the right auricle communicate,..has an oval form.

**siˈnumbra.** ? *Obs.* [ad. L. *sine umbrā* without a shadow.] ***sinumbra lamp*** (see quot. 1851–3).

**1834** M. Scott *Cruise Midge* (1863) 109 A mild radiance like that cast by the ground glass globe of a Sinumbra lamp. **1851–3** *Tomlinson's Cycl. Arts* (1867) II. 5 In Phillips's Sinumbra lamp..the shadow if not destroyed is rendered imperceptible by the peculiar form given to the circular oil vessel.

Hence **siˈnumbral** *a.*

**1839** *Civil Eng. & Arch. Jrnl.* II. 329/2 Sinumbral and pneumatic fountain lamps. **1854** *Lardner's Museum Sci. & Art* II. 207 The old English ring-lamp called the Sinumbral lamp.

**sinuose** (sɪnjuːˈəʊs), *a.* [ad. L. *sinuōs-us*, f. *sinus* sinus: see -ose[1].] Full of or characterized by bends or windings; sinuous, sinuated.

**1829** Loudon *Encycl. Plants* Gloss. (1836) 1105/1. **1861** Bentley *Man. Bot.* 250 In the Gourd tribe [the anther lobes are]..linear, and sinuose or convoluted.

Hence **sinuˈosely** *adv.*

**1874** M. C. Wood *Fresh-Water Algæ* 84 Thallus membranaceous saccate, obovate, sinuosely-bullose.

**sinuosity** (sɪnjuːˈɒsɪtɪ). [ad. F. *sinuosité* or med.L. **sinuōsitas*: see prec. and -ity.]

**1.** The character, condition, or quality of being sinuous or winding in and out.

**1598** Drayton *Heroical Ep.* Wks. (1810) 58/2 Meander is a river..famous for the sinuosity and often returning thereof. **1728** Chambers *Cycl.* s.v., 'Tis the Sinuosity of the Sea Coasts that forms Bays, Ports, Capes, &c. **1774** Pennant *Tour Scotl. in 1772* 33 The multitude of pretty bays that give such an elegant sinuosity to its shores. **1830** Lyell *Princ. Geol.* I. 170 The extreme sinuosity of the river has caused it to return for a brief space in a contrary direction to its main course. **1873** G. C. Davies *Mount. & Mere* xiii. 100 Owing to the sinuosity of the brook, the pools ..are yet not within fish sight.

*fig.* **1857** M. Pattison *Ess.* (1889) II. 212 The natural difficulty of the German language,..enhanced by the elaborate sinuosity of the period. **1885** *Society in London* 251 Something of the sinuosity of the Oriental.

**2.** (Chiefly *pl.*) A curve or bend, *esp.* one of a series.

**1720** S. Parker *Biblioth. Bibl.* I. 235 There was no need.. of..so much as of a Helm for steering, or indeed of any Sinuosity or Protuberance whatsoever. **1731** Miller *Gard. Dict.* s.v. *Leaves*, The Sinuosities or Circuits, which are found throughout the whole Structure [of the leaf]. **1766** Smollett *Trav.* xxvii. II. 46 So delicately cut, as to shew.. all the swellings and sinuosities of the muscles. **1831** R. Knox *Cloquet's Anat.* 679 It exactly accompanies the phrenic nerve, forming several sinuosities. **1855** Ramsbotham *Obst. Med. & Surg.* 3 A considerable sinuosity or arch, forming, when the bone is joined to the sacrum, a very long notch. **1876** Bartholow *Mat. Med.* (1879) 88 Care being taken to penetrate to all the sinuosities of the sore.

**b.** A curve, bend, or winding in a road, river, valley, etc.

*a* **1774** Goldsm. *Surv. Exp. Philos.* (1776) I. 334 The fewer the sinuosities of the rivers, the farther was he removed from the sea. **1774** J. Campbell *Polit. Surv. Britain* I. 274 The very irregular indented Line, which forms its Shore, comprehends, allowing for those Sinuosities, at least eight hundred Marine Leagues. **1829** Scott *Anne of G.* i, Winding by a narrow path along the sinuosities of the valley. **1835** Sir J. Ross *Narr. 2nd Voy.* xxix. 406 The further point of this sinuosity. **1882** B. Harte *Flip* ii, She..watched Lance's figure as it vanished..in the shadows and sinuosities of the ascent.

**c.** *fig.* A complexity or intricacy.

**1827** Miss Sedgwick *H. Leslie* (1872) II. 180 One accustomed to all the sinuosities of the human mind. **1849** Bright *Sp., Ireland* 2 Apr. (1876) 171, I certainly never heard the right hon. gentleman steer through so many sinuosities in a case. **1864** Burton *Scot Abroad* I. i. 28 The sinuosities of the discussion.

**3.** A sinuous movement.

*a* **1892** Tennyson in *Mem.* (1897) I. 41, I kept a tame snake... I liked to watch his wonderful sinuosities on the carpet.

**sinuˈoso-**, combining form of L. *sinuōsus*, prefixed to adjs. in the sense 'sinuately', 'sinuate and', as ***sinuoso-lobate, -plicate.***

**1846** Dana *Zooph.* (1848) 142 Dilated and profoundly sinuoso-lobate. *Ibid.* 191 Short turbinate, sinuoso-plicate at margin.

**sinuous** (ˈsɪnjuːəs), *a.* Also 7 sinewes (?). [ad. L. *sinuōs-us* (see sinus and -ous) or F. *sinueux*; cf. It., Sp., and Pg. *sinuoso.*]

**1. a.** Characterized by or abounding in turns, curves, or sinuosities; sinuate, curving.

**1578** Banister *Hist. Man* i. 28 It behoued the head of Radius also to be more depressed, and somewhat sinuous. **1626** Bacon *Sylva* §132 It would be tryed, how..the Voice will be carried..in a Trumpet, which is a line Retorted; Or in some Pipe that were Sinuous. **1667** Milton *P.L.* vii. 481 Whatever creeps the ground, Insect or Worme,..Streaking the ground with sinuous trace. **1686** Snape *Anat. Horse* App. i. 11 The Seed-leaf on its outside is sinuous or full of crinkles. **1708** Ozell tr. *Boileau's Lutrin* 20 In a Cap's round sinuous Bottom laid. **1717** Berkeley *Tour Italy* Wks. 1871 IV. 585 Obstinate, deep, and sinuous ulcers. **1822** J. Parkinson *Outl. Oryctol.* 117 The mouth large, widely sinuous. **1843** R. J. Graves *Syst. Clin. Med.* xxiii. 280 The lungs..containing several sinuous cavities. **1862** Darwin *Orchids* i. 12 The slightest touch causes it to rupture transversely, in a sinuous line.

**b.** Of rivers, coasts, roads, routes, etc.

**1633** J. Done *Hist. Septuagint* 51 The Flood Meander running with his Sinewes returnes and windings. **1635** J. Hayward tr. *Biondi's Banish'd Virg.* 179 Roving from Port to Port in that sinuous Region. **1784** Cowper *Task* i. 165 Here Ouse, slow winding through a level plain.., Conducts the eye along his sinuous course. **1797** Coleridge *Kubla Khan* 8 There were gardens bright with sinuous rills. **1810** T. L. Peacock *Genius of the Thames* 7 While Thames impels, with sinuous flow, His silent-rolling stream below. **1854** Hooker *Himal. Jrnls.* I. xviii. 379 Its bold spurs enclosing sinuous river gorges. **1878** Huxley *Physiogr.* xviii. 303 A sinuous band of highlands stretches almost continuously.

**c.** *transf.* Intricate, complex; roundabout.

**1853** Cdl. Wiseman *Ess.* II. 338 The perplexities of this formulary,..its sinuous involutions,..make its character too plain, as a snare to the simple of heart. **1860** O. W. Holmes *Poet Breakf.-t.* ix, I have been sinuous as the links of Forth..; sinuous, I say, but not..hard to follow for a reader of the right sort.

**d.** *fig.* Deviating from the right; not straightforward or direct; morally crooked.

**1850** Whipple *Ess. & Rev.* (1856) I. 207 A man..who has acquired high station by no sinuous path. **1859** Helps *Friends in C.* Ser. ii. II. x. 230 The beginning of a sinuous course of extravagance. **1901** *Scotsman* 28 Feb. 6/3 The end of his sinuous career is in view.

**2.** Of movements: Taking place in curves.

**1877** Rosenthal *Muscles & Nerves* 11 A..whip-like process by the sinuous motions of which these animals move themselves about in the water.

**3.** Of animals: Moving with supple bends of the body. Also of people.

**1897** F. Thompson *New Poems* 143 The stealthy terror of the sinuous pard. **1906** B. Vaughan *Sins of Society* 129 The lithesome, sinuous girl trips with it across the stage to her mother.

**4.** quasi-*adv.* Sinuously.

**1885** Miss Braddon *Wyllard's Weird* I. i. 2 Now the line seems strung like a thread of iron.., now winds sinuous as a snake.

Hence **ˈsinuously** *adv.*, **ˈsinuousness.**

**1684** *Phil. Trans.* XIV. 513 The..Streams which do arise from under the Mountains do evidence the hollowness, and

Sinousness [*sic*] of them. **1727** BAILEY (vol. II), *Sinuousness*, Fulness of Turnings and Windings. **1847** *Proc. Berw. Nat. Club* II. 249 Whence it narrows rather sinuously to the posterior angles. **1880** HODGKIN *Italy & her Invaders* III. v. II. 409 The dragon ensigns floated sinuously to the breeze. **1924** R. MACAULAY *Orphan Island* xiii. §4 Like a sturdy little boy without feminine elegances, or any of Flora's wild-animal sinuousness. **1980** *Early Music* July 308/1 Any actor reciting them..would certainly emphasize the contrast between the biting *sk* sound at the beginning of these two words and the powerful sinuousness of 'l'onde'.

**sinu'pallial, -'palliate,** *adjs. Conch.* [f. *sinu-* stem of SINUS + PALLIAL *a.*, or PALLIATE *a.* 4.] Of certain lamellibranchs: Having the pallial line deeply incurved or inflected beneath the impression of the posterior adductor muscles, for the retraction or expansion of the pallial siphons.

**1863** DANA *Man. Geol.* 192 This division, the Sinupallial, was far less common in the Silurian than the integripallial. **1877** HUXLEY *Anat. Inv. Anim.* viii. 486 The integropalliate are far more numerous than the sinupalliate forms in the older rocks. **1883** *Encycl. Brit.* XVI. 687/1 The valves of the Sinupalliate genus Cytherea.

**sinus** ('saɪnəs). Pl. **sinuses** (7 sinus, 7–9 sinus's, 8 sinusses). [a. L. *sinus* a curve, bend, bay, etc.]

**1.** *Path.* An impostume, abscess, or sore, forming a narrow suppurating tract and having a small orifice; the cavity or hollow caused by this.

**1597** A. M. tr. *Guillemeau's Fr. Chirurg.* 45/1 If the Sinus be in the legge, & the bottome of the same vnder the Knee. **1693** tr. *Blancard's Phys. Dict.* (ed. 2), *Sinus*, is when the beginning of an Abscess or Ulcer is narrow, but the bottom large. **1748** tr. *Vegetius Renatus' Distempers of Horses* 238 When the *Pus*..has been squeezed out, the Sinus itself, which contained it, is washed. **1804** ABERNETHY *Surg. Obs.* 124 Sinuses remained where the abscesses had been. **1881** *Med. Temp. Jrnl.* XLVI. 83 There was a sinus discharging pus on the inside of the right thigh above the knee.

**2. a.** A curvature, flexure, or bend; *spec.* in *Zool.*, a curved recess in a shell.

**1615** CROOKE *Body of Man* 995 The third bone hath two Sinus distinguished by a long knot, whereinto the heads of the second bone are receyued: againe the knub of the third bone entreth into the Sinus of the second [etc.]. **1656** tr. *Hobbes' Elem. Philos.* (1839) 177 Howsoever a line be bowed, it makes always a *sinus* or cavity. **1720** S. PARKER *Biblioth. Bibl.* I. 235 There was no Sinus or Inequality, or perhaps so much as one Pore left open, according to this Hypothesis of the Figure of the Ark. *a* **1728** WOODWARD *Fossils* (1729) II. 73 Another [echinus], depress'd by some external Force, so as to make a large Sinus on one side. **1802** PALEY *Nat. Theol.* iii, The root of this outward ear, the folds, and sinuses thereof..conducting the air towards it. **1822** J. PARKINSON *Outl. Oryctol.* 156 A wing or lobe, having a sinus distinct from the notched canal at the base. **1840** *Cuvier's Anim. Kingd.* 360 There is a broad notch or sinus in the columella.

**b.** *Bot.* One of a series of small rounded depressions on the margin of a leaf.

**1753** *Chambers' Cycl.* Suppl. s.v. *Leaf*, A leaf with sinus's at the sides. **1785** MARTYN *Rousseau's Bot.* xxviii. (1794) 437 The sinuses being opposite. **1830** LINDLEY *Nat. Syst. Bot.* 59 Their sinuses sometimes lengthened into other lobes. **1870** HOOKER *Stud. Flora* 325 Auricles rounded incurved almost enclosing the deep sinus.

**3.** *Anat.* **a.** One or other of various irregular venous cavities, reservoirs, or dilated blood-vessels in different organs or parts of the body; a venous channel or receptacle of blood.

These are frequently distinguished according to their extent, particular form, or position.

**1672** *Phil. Trans.* VII. 5134 Whether there is any sinus or common Trunk, into which all the veins are gathered. **1731** *Ibid.* XXXVII. 92 We found the Veins much distended with Blood, as were also the Veins and Sinuses of the Brain. **1761** *Ibid.* LII. 267 The brain was..no-ways loaded with blood, either in its proper vessels, or in the contiguous sinuses of the dura mater. **1831** R. KNOX *Cloquet's Anat.* 437 Inferior Longitudinal Sinus.., occupying the lower edge of the cerebral falx. **1851** WOODWARD *Mollusca* I. 31 Both the arteries and veins form occasionally wide spaces, or sinuses. **1877** HUXLEY *Anat. Inv. Anim.* i. 58 The venous system presents many large sinuses in the lower vertebrates.

**b.** A natural hole, cell, or cavity in the substance of a bone or other tissue, and either closed or having a relatively small opening.

**1704** J. HARRIS *Lex. Techn.* I. s.v., Any Cavity in or between the Vessels of an Animal Body, the Anatomists call a Sinus. **1741** A. MONRO *Anat.* (ed. 3) 28 *Sinuses*, large Cavities within the Substance of the Bones, with small Apertures. **1767** GOOCH *Treat. Wounds* I. 297 The application of the trepan to the frontal sinuses. **1835–6** *Todd's Cycl. Anat.* I. 434/2 In the bones of the head we find certain cells, called *sinuses*, which contain air, not marrow. **1871** DARWIN *Desc. of Man* I. iv. 121 The frontal sinus, or the projection over the eye-brows is largely developed.

†**4.** A cavity or hole in the earth. *Obs.*

*a* **1676** HALE *Prim. Orig. Man.* (1677) 299 By the excavation of certain *Sinus* and Tracts of the Earth,..the Water subsided into those Caverns..prepared for its reception. **1684** *Phil. Trans.* XIV. 513 They meet with [natural cavities in the earth] very frequently, some.. running away with small Sinus's. **1784** TWAMLEY *Dairying Exemp.* 145 The Earth..abounding every where with canals and sinuses, wherein the Dew and Rain-water..glide.

†**5.** A bay, gulf, or arm of the sea; = SINE[2] I.

**1684** T. BURNET *Theory Earth* I. 110 The promontories and capes shoot into the sea, and the sinus's and creeks..run as much into the land. **1693** RAY *Three Disc.* II. ii. 85 The Sea would rather run into them, and make Sinus's. **1717** BERKELEY *Tour Italy* Wks. 1871 IV. 549 A bridge over a narrow sinus of the sea. **1749** W. DOUGLASS *Summary* I. 399 A salt water sinus, commonly called a continuation of Taunton river. **1789** J. WILLIAMS *Min. Kingd.* II. 163 The great number of friths, sinuses, or arms of the sea.

**6.** *attrib.* and *Comb.*, as ***sinus affection, aneurysm, infection, phlebitis, pyæmia, thrombosis***; ***sinus-like*** adj. Also **sinus gland** *Zool.* [tr. G. *sinusdrüse* (B. Hanström 1937, in *K. Svenska Vetenskapsakad. Handl.* XVI. III. 3)], a structure in the eye stalk or head of crustaceans orig. thought to be a gland but now recognized as a neurohæmal organ in which are stored various hormones concerned with growth, reproduction, and metabolism; **sinus probe** (see quot. 1884); **sinus rhythm**, the normal rhythm of the heart, proceeding from the sino-atrial node; **sinus venosus** [mod.L., f. *venōsus* venous], a part of some vertebrate hearts into which the veins lead and which empties into the atrium.

**1898** *Allbutt's Syst. Med.* V. 940 The presence or absence of sinus aneurysm. **1938** *Arkiv för Zoologi* XXX B. VIII. 1 When investigating the nervous system and the organs of sense of the crustaceans, Hanström found (1931–1935) two organs which he called the blood gland (the sinus gland) and the X-organ. **1972** M. S. GARDINER *Biol. Invertebrates* xvii. 714/1 Molting in decapod crustaceans is also influenced by hormones discharged from the sinus glands. **1936** *Discovery* Dec. 380/1, I was suffering from widespread sinus infection. **1883** *Encycl. Brit.* XVI. 678/1 Sinus-like spaces surrounding the viscera. **1884** KNIGHT *Dict. Mech.* Suppl. 816/2 *Sinus Probe*, a vermicular pointed uterine curved probe, used in its peculiar branch of surgical operations. **1911** T. LEWIS *Mechanism of Heart Beat* xii. 132 The compensatory pause fails; that is to say, disturbance of sinus rhythm may be demonstrated. **1980** *Brit. Med. Jrnl.* 29 Mar. 922/2 Ventricular fibrillation was converted to sinus rhythm with a 'thump' on the chest. **1836–9** R. B. TODD *Cycl. Anat. & Physiol.* II. 579/2 This division of the auricle into proper auricle and sinus venosus is more distinct in the left than in the right auricle. **1926** J. S. HUXLEY *Ess. Pop. Sci.* 199 The ventricle of the frog's heart has its own independent rate of beat when isolated. But in the intact animal this independent rate is all the time being speeded up by the faster-beating sinus venosus. **1970** *Encycl. Biol. Sci.* (ed. 2) 400/2 In the fish, amphibians, and reptiles the contraction starts in the thin muscle wall of the sinus venosus... In birds and mammals the sinus venosus is absent. **1899** *Allbutt's Syst. Med.* VII. 575 The tissue intermediate between the original inflammation and the sinus wall.

**sinusitis** (saɪnə'saɪtɪs). [f. SINUS + -ITIS, prob. ad. F. *sinusite.*] Inflammation of a sinus, esp. a nasal sinus.

**1896** *Jrnl. Laryngol.* X. 37 (*heading*) Treatment of sinusitis. **1935** IMPERATORI & BURMAN *Dis. Nose & Throat* xi. 146 Morning frontal headache increasing in intensity towards afternoon usually indicates maxillary sinusitis. **1951** M. LOWRY *Let.* 25 Aug. (1961) 252 Water..nearly makes him die of dysentery, and milk..gives him sinusitis. **1977** W. MARSHALL *Thin Air* vii. 87 The smell..came up the rickety stairs..like a poisonous cloud of pollen at the height of the sinusitis season.

**sinusoid** ('saɪnəsɔɪd). [a. F. *sinusoïde*, f. L. *sinus* SINUS + -OID.]

**1.** *Math.* A curve of sines (CURVE *sb.* 1).

**1823** LARDNER *Algebraic Geom.* I. 200 A curve, represented by the equation y = sin. x, related to rectangular co-ordinates, is called the curve of sines, or the sinusoid. **1876** *Proc. Lond. Math. Soc.* VII. 213 Prof. Cayley described a surface, depending upon the sinusoid, which was being constructed for him. **1884** tr. *Glaser de Cew's Magn. & Dynamo-electric Machines* 254 If the magnetic field in which the armature rotated were uniform, this curve would be a true 'sinusoid', or curve of sines.

**2.** A blood vessel similar in size to a capillary but irregular in shape and without the continuous endothelial lining of capillaries.

**1900** MINOT in *Proc. Boston Nat. Hist. Soc.* 185 The [blood-] vessels of the first type are true capillaries... The vessels of the second type I propose to name 'sinusoids', on account of their resemblance to true sinus and also to separate them clearly from genuine capillaries. **1920** *Nature* 27 May 411/1 A system of wide sinusoids (renal venous meshwork), which has no connection with the intertubular plexus. **1974** D. & M. WEBSTER *Compar. Vertebr. Morphol.* xiii. 315 In the mammalian adrenal cortex the steroidogenic tissues can be divided into zones on the basis of the arrangement of cells and their relationships to the numerous blood sinusoids.

**sinusoidal** (saɪnə'sɔɪdəl), *a.* [f. prec. + -AL[1]; cf. F. *sinusoïdal.*] Resembling, pursuing, flowing in, the wave-like course of a sinusoid; having the form of a sinusoid; varying periodically (with time, distance, etc.) as a sine varies with an angle; (see also quot. 1910).

**1878** MAYER *Sound* 64 Hold the glass up to the light, and you will see a delicate wavy line, a sinusoidal trace. **1879** G. PRESCOTT *Sp. Telephone* 54 The curve expressive of a simple pendulous vibration—that is a sinusoidal curve. **1900** *Lancet* 1 Dec. 1580/1 These patients have all been treated with the electrical bath and the sinusoidal current. **1910** N. HAWKINS *Electr. Dict.* 400/2 *Sinusoidal alternator*, an alternating current dynamo which generates simple harmonic or sinusoidal currents. **1948** *Nature* 28 Feb. 295/1 Along with the detailed solutions of the differential equations for step velocity input..is given a brief development of the solutions for sinusoidal input. **1957** G. E. HUTCHINSON *Treat. Limnol.* I. v. 357 The height of the wave at first decreases slightly, then increases as the wave approaches breaking. During the final phase of the rise in height, the sinusoidal or trochoidal form is lost. **1975** *Nature* 23 Oct. 674/1 Patterns of alternating light and dark bars with a sinusoidal luminance profile across the bars—sinusoidal gratings—are commonly used to study spatial interactions in the visual system.

Hence **sinu'soidally** *adv.*

**1888** *Philos. Mag.* Ser. v. XXVI. 373 Let *f* vary sinusoidally with the time. **1929** J. A. RATCLIFFE *Physical Princ. Wireless* i. 3 The simplest form of alternating current is one in which the current varies sinusoidally with the time. **1947** *Jrnl. Inst. Electr. Engineers* CXIV. III. 279/1 When the hemispherical end of a reproducing stylus is moved in contact with a sinusoidal surface of comparable curvature, the stylus tip does not itself move sinusoidally. **1974** *Sci. Amer.* Nov. 34/3 Voltages and current vary sinusoidally at a frequency of 60 hertz (cycles per second) in the U.S. and Canada and 50 hertz in most other countries of the world.

**sinward** ('sɪnwəd), *adv.* [f. SIN *sb.* + -WARD.] Toward or in the direction of sin. †Also *to sinward.*

**1377** LANGL. *P. Pl.* B. XIII. 346 Vche a mayde þat he mette he made hir a signe Semynge to-synne-ward. *c* **1440** *Jacob's Well* 111 Feendys noumbre þe steppys of man & womman to synne warde. **1642** ROGERS *Naaman* 45 The thoughts that were roving helward, worldward, and sinward. **1644** T. CASE *Quarrel of Covenant* 74 A people..may enter Covenant with God, with their hearts, Rome-ward, and Earth-ward, and Sin-ward. **1820** MRS. GRANT OF LAGGAN *Mem. & Corresp.* (1844) II. 268 An infirmity always verging sinward.

‖**sion.** *rare.* [L. *sion* water-parsley, a. Gr. σίον some kind of marsh plant.] = LAVER *sb.*[1] 1.

*c* **1000** *Sax. Leechd.* I. 254 Ðeos wyrt þe man sion & oðrum naman laber nemneþ byð cenned on wætum stowum. **1562** TURNER *Herbal* II. (1568) 138 Sion is so muche hote as it is well smelling, when it is tasted. **1861** READE *Cloister & H.* xciv, His remedies were 'womanish and weak'. Sage and wormwood, sion, hyssop,..and Faith, and all in small quantities except the last.

**sion, sioun,** obs. forms of SCION.

**Sion(er,** etc.: see ZION(ER, etc.

‖**siot** (ʃɔt). [Welsh, evidently a loanword from an unrecorded regional sense of SHOT *sb.*[1]] In North Wales, a cereal mash of buttermilk and crushed oat-bread.

**1936** *Farmhouse Fare* 148 *Siot.* ½ cupful oat bread. 1 pint buttermilk. Crush the bread..and put into a basin. Pour in the buttermilk, and let the bread soak for 1 hour, when it will be ready to serve. **1949** 'M. INNES' *Journeying Boy* xiv. 172 For breakfast it was impossible that they should have anything but siot or skirlie-mirlie. **1974** *Country Life* 12 Dec. 1845/2 Siot..was a pint of buttermilk poured on to a half cup of crushed oat bread... The 'mash' was served with bread and butter.

**Siouan** ('su:ən), *a.* and *sb.* [f. SIOU(X *a.* and *sb.* + -AN.] **A.** *adj.* = SIOUX *a.* b. **B.** *sb.* **a.** = SIOUX *sb.* 2 a. Also *Comb.* **b.** = SIOUX *sb.* 1 b.

**1885** J. O. DORSEY in *Smithsonian Inst. Rep. 1883* 919 The term 'Siouan' has been applied to that family of Indians which has been known heretofore as the 'Dakotan Family'. It is unfortunate that we are obliged to use this adjective, which is derived from 'Sioux', as the latter is not a genuine Indian word... In honor of Albert Gallatin, who was the first to classify the Indians of this family as the 'Sioux', the Bureau of Ethnology of the Smithsonian Institution has adopted the new term, 'Siouan', as the name of this family. **1889** *Amer. Naturalist* Jan. 75 The Siouan group had its habitat on the prairies between the Mississippi and Missouri. **1900, 1907** [see CROW *sb.*[4] and *a.*]. **1929** E. SAPIR in *Encycl. Brit.* V. 139/2 Hokan-Siouan... Eastern group (1) Siouan-Yuchi..(2) Natchez-Muskogian. **1937** R. H. LOWIE *Hist. Ethnol. Theory* (1938) vi. 63 [Morgan] recognized the criteria of..the 'Omaha' system and indicated its occurrence among the Algonkian as well as the Siouan family. **1949** B. A. BOTKIN *Treas. S. Folklore* III. ii. 497 Enough Biloxi were left..to enable investigators to identify them..as members of the Siouan linguistic family. **1977** H. LANDAR in T. A. Sebeok *Native Langs. Americas* II. III. 352 Gallatin (1836) assigned the Shyenne language to his Sioux group on the basis of several names of 'Shyennes' who signed a treaty in July, 1825. The signers were possessed of Siouan, not Algonquian, names. **1978** C. CALLENDER in B. G. Trigger *Handbk. N. Amer. Indians* XV. 610/1 The societies that at the time of European contact were established in the upper Great Lakes area..were mostly Algonquian but included the Siouan-speaking Winnebago.

**Sioux** (su:), *a.* and *sb.* Also 8 **Sous,** 9 **Suouex.** [a. N. Amer. Fr., earlier *Nadouessioux*, etc., ad. Ojibwa (Ottawa dial.) *nātowēssiwak*: Fr. pl. termination *-x* replaced the equivalent Ojibwa feature *-ak.*] **A.** *adj.* **a.** Of or pertaining to the Sioux people or their language (see the sb. below). **b.** Formerly, of or pertaining to the Siouan languages or language grouping; = SIOUAN *a.*

**1761** D. CLAUS *Let.* 19 Mar. in J. Sullivan *Papers Sir W. Johnson* (1921) III. 363, I picked up a pair of shoes made by the Sioux Ind[in]. to the Westward. **1805** Z. N. PIKE *Jrnl.* 8 Sept. in *Sources of Mississippi* (1810) I. 14 His design was to winter with some of the Sioux bands. **1824** W. H. KEATING *Narr. Exped. St. Peter's River* I. viii. 376 Account of the Dacotas or Sioux Indians. **1836** A. GALLATIN in *Trans. & Coll. Amer. Antiquarian Soc.* II. 120 The nations which speak the Sioux language may be considered..as consisting of four subdivisions, viz. the Winnebagoes; the Sioux proper and Assiniboins; [etc.]. **1893** L. WAGNER *Significance of Names* 36 The Sioux State [is] the territory of the Sioux tribe of Indians. **1919** S. LEWIS *Free Air* ix. 101 She fancied that on it the Sioux scout still sat sentinel. **1949** *Amer. Photogr.* Jan. 40/1 Following a speech in Sioux language, in which God was asked for rain, the real Sun Dance now started. **1973** *Black Panther* 1 Sept. 17/1 Chief Fools Crow ..damned the Executors in Sioux language.

**B.** *sb.* **1. a.** = DAKOTA *sb.* 1. **b.** Formerly also, more generally, a (member of a) linguistic grouping of North American Indian peoples that includes the Sioux, Crow, Omaha, and others.

**1762** D. CLAUS Let. 2 June in J. Sullivan *Papers Sir W. Johnson* (1921) III. 754 Missisages, Ottawawas, Renards & Sioux, were the Nations assembled at Cataracqui. **1768** [see *hot war* s.v. HOT *a.* 12]. **1785** T. JEFFERSON *Notes on Virginia* xi. 185 Sioux. On the heads of the Mississippi and westward of that river. **1827** J. F. COOPER *Prairie* III. vii. 227 The keen weapon..meeting the naked breast of the impetuous Sioux, the blade was buried to the buck-horn haft. **1836** A. GALLATIN in *Trans. & Coll. Amer. Antiquarian Soc.* II. 120 The Indians..east of the mountains are the Sioux; the Pawnees; the Fall, Rapid, or Paunch Indians; [etc.]. **1908** *Rep. Brit. Assoc.* 851 They [*sc.* the mound-builders] seem to have been followed by the Sioux (Dakotas), Iroquois, who are probably of Aztec origin. **1937** R. H. LOWIE *Hist. Ethnol. Theory* (1938) xiv. 262 The signs of Queenslanders and Sioux lend little support to psychic unity. **1957** P. WORSLEY *Trumpet shall Sound* 222 To the Sioux..the coming of the Dance helped to set off a train of events which culminated in the bloody massacre at Wounded Knee. **1964** MRS. L. B. JOHNSON *White House Diary* 11 Jan. (1970) 40 George Catlin..painted the Sioux... His paintings line the second-floor hall of the White House. **1975** D. PITTS *This City is Ours* xiv. 48 His name was Mick Dull Knife; he was a full-blooded Sioux and a graduate of Princeton.

**2. a.** Formerly, the language family to which the Sioux and related peoples belong; = SIOUAN *sb.* **b.** The language of the Sioux or Dakota Indians.

**1783** J. O. JUSTAMOND tr. *Raynal's Philos. & Polit. Hist. Settlements & Trade of Europeans in E. & W. Indies* VI. xv. 439 Three original languages were spoken in Canada, the Algonquin, the Sioux, and the Huron. **1915** J. BUCHAN *Salute to Adventurers* ix. 141 He said something in Sioux to one of the warriors. **1971** *Guardian* 18 Sept. 10/4 She spoke only Cheyenne and Sioux.

**sip**, *sb.*[1] Also 7 **sippe**. [f. the vb.] A single act of sipping; a small quantity *of* some liquid taken in this way.

It is possible that *sype* in Caxton's text of Chaucer's *Anel. & Arc.* 193 may have been intended for *sip*, but the correct reading is *schipe* reward.

**1633** P. FLETCHER *Poet. Misc.* 131 The wine..did appeare no common grape: my haste could not forbeare a second sippe. **1665** PEPYS *Diary* 19 Aug., A bottle of strong water, whereof, now and then, a sip did me good. **1687** A. LOVELL tr. *Thevenot's Trav.* I. 33 They..bring it to you scalding hot, and so you must drink it, but at several sips, else it is not good. **1715** CHAPPELOW *Right Way Rich* (1717) 169 A sip of some comforting syrup. **1768–74** A. TUCKER *Lt. Nat.* (1834) II. 234 A sip of Daffy's Elixir, in the morning rising, has proved a powerful means of grace. **1828** SCOTT *F.M. Perth* xvi, However Oliver might have relished a moderate sip of the same good wine. **1856** LONGF. *Gold. Leg.* IV. Poet. Wks. (1910) 495/1 Between this cask and the Abbot's lips Many have been the sips and slips. **1887** JEFFERIES *Amaryllis* iii, If it was to be had, a sip of port wine.

**b.** *fig.* A mere taste *of* something.

**1728** YOUNG *Love Fame* VI. 442 Will the great Author us poor worms destroy, For now and then a sip of transient joy? **1852** DE QUINCEY *Sir W. Hamilton* Wks. 1890 V. 307 A sip is all that the public collectively ever care to take from reservoirs of abstract philosophy. **1871** N. SHEPPARD *Shut up in Paris* 246 They take a little sip of a stroll, a little sip of sleep, and a little sip of manual labour.

**Sip** (sɪp), *sb.*[2] Also **sip**. Black English abbrev. of *Mississippi* (cf. MISSISSIPPIAN *sb.* and *a.*); *the Sip*: the State of Mississippi.

**1969** P. CROSS in *Folklore Forum* II. VI. 141 There's this nigga who went to the 'Sip', you know, uh—Mississippi, that is. **1971** *Black Scholar* Jan. 41/1 He loaded up the trunk with all his fine clothes and lit' out for the 'sip'.

**sip**, *v.* Forms: 5 syppy(n, cyppyn, 6 syppe; 5, 7 sippe (5 scippe), 6– sip. [Of obscure origin; possibly a modification of *sup* intended to express a slighter action.

Kilian's '*Sippen*, pitissare, sorbillare' is not otherwise certified, and is rendered suspicious by his citing 'Ang. *sippe*'; but a LG. *sippen* in the same sense is given in the Bremisches Wörterbuch, and appears to be genuine.]

**1.** *intr.* To take up liquid in small quantities with the lips; to drink by a sip or sips; freq. with *of* (a specified liquid, etc.). Also in fig. contexts.

*c* **1386** CHAUCER *Wife of Bath's Prol.* 176 Than maystow chese, wheither thou wolt sippe Of that tonne that I shal abroche. **14..** *Lat.-Eng. Voc.* in Wr.-Wülcker 604 *Potisso*, to syppy. *c* **1440** *Promp. Parv.* 456/2 Syppyn, nowȝt fully drynke, *potisso, subbibo*. **1530** PALSGR. 739/1 Syppe on, Cysse, and tell me what it is. **1584–7** GREENE *Carde Fancie* Wks. (Grosart) IV. 162 Yea, let thy Concubine Castania..to sippe of the same sorrow. **1602** SHAKS. *Ham.* IV. vii. 161 Ile haue prepar'd him A Challice..; whereon but sipping,.. Our purpose may hold there. *a* **1628** PRESTON *Breastpl. Love* (1631) 182 Yee doe here but sippe of this cuppe, but then ye shall drinke up the dreggs of it for ever. **1687** A. LOVELL tr. *Thevenot's Trav.* I. 33 They all drink it sipping for fear of scalding themselves. **1733** POPE *Hor. Sat.* II. i. 47 Ridotta sips and dances, till she see The doubling Lustres dance as fast as she. **1780** COWPER *Progr. Err.* 581 With caution taste the sweet Circean cup; He that sips often, at last drinks it up. **1789** —— *Annus Mem.* 18 As the bee..Assiduous sips at ev'ry flow'r. **1810** SOUTHEY *Kehama* XXIV. v, As a man in social hour Sips of the grateful cup. **1859** DICKENS *T. Two Cities* I. v, Who bent over their shoulders, to sip, before the wine had all run out.

*transf.* **1601** B. JONSON *Poetaster* III. i, As many as haue but the..audacitie to—sip of their lips. **1871** *Athenæum* 26 Aug. 273 The whole French nation..sip in drinking, they sip in reading, and they sip their work.

**2.** *trans.* To drink (liquid, etc.) in very small draughts; to imbibe, or partake of, by sipping. Said also of bees, etc.

**1611** COTGR., *Humé*, supped, sipped, or sucked vp [etc.]. *a* **1650** CRASHAW *Carmen Deo Nostro, Mary Magd.* v, Every morn from hence A brisk Cherub somthing sippes. **1662** R. MATHEW *Unl. Alch.* 191 Drink one quarter of a pint as hot as you can sip it. **1697** DRYDEN *Virg. Georg.* III. 505 Let 'em sip from Herbs the pearly tears Of Morning Dews. **1746** HERVEY *Medit.* (1818) 187 Bees, industrious workmen! that ..sip the mellifluous dews. **1784** COWPER *Task* III. 391 He enjoys..Sweet converse, sipping calm the fragrant lymph Which neatly she prepares. **1825** LAMB *Elia* II. *Wedding*, None told his tale. None sipt her glass. **1848** THACKERAY *Van. Fair* lxii, The knowing way in which he sipped, or rather sucked, the Johannisberger. **1886** PASCOE *Lond. of To-day* xl. (ed. 3) 350 The places where ladies go to eat creams..and sip coffee.

**b.** *fig.* and *transf.*

**1602** MARSTON *Ant. & Mel.* v. Wks. 1856 I. 67 Weele drinke a health, while they two sip a kisse. *c* **1614** SIR W. MURE *Dido & Æneas* I. 274 The shippe..sinking sippes the seas, by weight downe borne. **1632** MILTON *Penseroso* 172 And every Herb that sips the dew. **1769** SIR W. JONES *Palace Fortune* Poems (1777) 13 The maid attentive sips Each word that flows, like nectar, from her lips. **1871** [see sense 1 *transf.*].

**c.** With advs., as *off*, *up*.

**1656** EARL MONM. tr. *Boccalini's Advts. fr. Parnass.* I. (1674) 50 The Macedonians..thought to have sipt up every mans State in less than a moneths time. *a* **1763** W. KING *Polit. & Lit. Anecd.* (1819) 13 Pope had sipped up all the brandy. **1863** W. C. BALDWIN *Afr. Hunting* vii. 278 A large spoonful of mustard in a pint of warm water, which he sipped off like coffee!

**d.** *fig.* To take a mere taste of (something).

**1618** BOLTON *Florus* 105 That he might not seeme to have once sipt or skimd the honour of their Chastity. **1639** FULLER *Holy War* III. xiv. (1840) 139 Pleasures he rather sipped than drank off.

**3.** To take honey from (a flower) by sipping.

**1697** DRYDEN *Virg. Georg.* IV. 76 The winged Nation.. skim the Floods, and sip the purple Flow'rs. **1727** GAY *Beggar's Opera* I. i, My heart..roved like the bee,..I sipt each flower. **1878** J. MILLER *Songs of Italy* 81, I should sip but one, this one Sweet flower underneath the sun.

**4.** *refl.* To bring (oneself) into a certain state by sipping.

**1823** SCOTT *Quentin D.* Introd., I gradually sipped and smoked myself into a certain degree of acquaintance with *un homme comme il faut*.

Hence **'sipping** *ppl. a.*

**1670** EACHARD *Cont. Clergy* 31 That would much better fit some old soker..than his sipping..bibbership. **1871** N. SHEPPARD *Shut up in Paris* 246 This sip, sip, sipping race have been devoured by a race which does nothing by sips. **1898** *Allbutt's Syst. Med.* V. 993 Then peptonized milk.. may be swallowed in sipping fashion.

**sipage** ('saɪpɪdʒ). *Sc.* and *U.S.* [f. SIPE *v.* + -AGE. Cf. SEEPAGE.] Leakage or oozing of water.

**1825** in JAMIESON *Suppl.* **1892** *Trans. Amer. Soc. Civil Engin.* XXVI. 572 The new levees..and..the land behind them [were]..very much affected by sipage.

**sipahee, sipahi**, variants of SEPOY.

**Sipapu** ('siːpæpuː). Also **Shipap(u**. [ad. Hopi *sípâ·pɨ*.] In the beliefs of Pueblo Indians, an opening in the earth, variously located by different tribes, through which their mythical ancestors emerged into the present world; a symbolic representation of this opening, as a hole in the floor of a kiva.

**1891** A. F. BANDELIER in *Jrnl. Amer. Ethnol. & Archaeol.* (1892) III. 111 Cibobe is the same as Shipapu, the lagune where the deceased go to rest. **1896** J. W. FEWKES in *16th Ann. Rep. Bur. Amer. Ethnol.* (1897) 279 The Snake chief at Cipaulovi has no *tiponi*, and consequently no altar. The only objects at the end of the altar..was a row of twenty snake whips leaning against the ledge of the rear wall, behind the *sipapû*. **1931** R. BENEDICT in *U.S. Bur. Amer. Ethnol. Bull.* XCVIII. 3 When the people who came up out of Shipap found these people who had been saved they called them Tsauwan yahana. **1939** E. C. PARSONS *Pueblo Indian Religion* I. iii. 216 On the road to the *sipapu* in the west, the place of emergence where the Hopi dead return..an actual spot in the wall of the Grand Canyon.., the breath body is met by..an Agave spirit sentinel. **1955** PRIESTLEY & HAWKES *Journey down Rainbow* vii. 115 Although the Sun Father was worshipped as the great cosmic power, Pueblo religion was mainly directed downwards towards the realm of the Earth Mother, the realm that was reached by way of the *Sipapu*, the home of the spirits whence the newborn came and the dead returned. **1977** M. JENKINSON *Land of Clear Light* I. 69 Man came up through the opening, the Sipapu, and flourished upon the surface of the earth... The image of the Sipapu has been likened by non-Indians to the birth process.

**sipars**, obs. form of CYPRESS[3].

**sipe** (saɪp), *sb.* Chiefly *Sc.* and *U.S.* Also **sype**. [Related to SIPE *v.* Cf. MDu. *sijp*, *zijp* (Du. dial. *zijp*), MLG. *sîp*, *sipe*, Fris. *syp*, *sipe* a ditch, channel, etc.]

**1.** The act of percolating or soaking through, on the part of water or other liquid; the water, etc., which percolates. (Cf. SEEP *sb.*)

*c* **888** K. ÆLFRED *Boeth.* xxxiii. §5 Seo eorðe hit helt & be sumum dæle swilȝð, & for þam sype heo bið ȝeleht. *a* **1583** in Sir J. Balfour *Minor Pract.* (1754) 588 Gif thair be ony persounis that settis furth under the yeird the sype of thair bark cobill,..or ony sype of kitching, to the King's water or well. **1777** in Cramond *Ann. Banff* (1893) II. 97 By the general sipe of the slating there is no mending of the slating without terring the sclates. **1839** STONEHOUSE *Hist. Isle of Axholme* 25 The water obtained from the wells sunk in the warp..is what is termed ground sype, i.e. water filtering through from the surface. **1894** *Naturalist* 23 There is no inflow or spring here apparently, so the water is only sipe.

*attrib.* **1892** *Trans. Amer. Soc. Civil Engin.* XXVI. 568 The water which thus transpires through the soil is called.. by the Americans of the Mississippi Valley 'sipe-water' (pronounced *seep*).

**2.** A small spring or pool of water.

**1825** JAMIESON *Suppl.*, *Sipe*, *Sype*,..a slight spring of water; *Perths.* **1897** BUTLER *Brit. Birds* iv. 65 Here and there, many small ponds or 'sypes', and birch trees.

**sipe** (saɪp), *v.* Chiefly *Sc.* and *north. dial.* Also **sype**. [OE. *sipian* wk. vb., = Fris. *sypje*, MLG. *sīpen* (pp. *gesypet*): cf. MDu. *sīpen*, *sypen* (Du. dial. *zijpen*), MLG. *sîpen*, MHG. *sīfen* str. vb. Sw. dial. *sipa*, Da. *sive* are prob. from LG.

The length of the vowel in OE. *sipian*, and the relation between this vb. and the OE. sb. *sype*, are not clear. If the vowel was short, the modern representative would normally be SEEP *v.*, and the form *sipe* may really correspond to the continental strong vb.]

*intr.* Of water or other liquid: To percolate or ooze through; to drip or trickle slowly; to soak.

For various dialect modifications of sense, and transitive uses, see the *Eng. Dial. Dict.*

*c* **1000** *Sax. Leechd.* II. 252 Asete þonne on hate sunnan, ..þæt hit sipiȝe & sociȝe .iiii. daȝas oþþe ma. **1398, 1503** [see the *vbl. sb.* and *ppl. a.*]. **1559** MORWYNG *Evonym.* 2 Plinie.. writes of the wode that is called Smilax, how it will let sype through water mixt with wyne, and kiep the wyne still. **1781** J. HUTTON *Tour to Caves* (ed. 2) Gloss. 97. **1825** BROCKETT *N.C. Gloss.*, *Sipe*, to leak, to ooze or drain out slowly through a small crevice. **1891** ATKINSON *Moorland Par.* 446 In this way a considerable amount of water was permitted to ooze and 'sipe' out and away.

**si'peera.** *Bot.* Also sip(e)ira, -(i)era, sipiri. [Native name in Guyana.] **a.** *sipeera-tree*, the greenheart tree (*Nectandra Rodiæi*) of Guyana; = BEBEERU. **b.** The bark of this tree.

**1769** E. BANCROFT *Nat. Hist. Guiana* 333 They contentedly recur to the use of Sipera, or Green-Hart-tree Apples. **1829** *Encycl. Metrop.* (1845) XX. 6/2 The timber of the Green Hart, or Sipiera tree, is very valuable. **1863** *Chambers's Encycl.* V. 92/2 The timber is commonly called Greenheart; the bark is better known as Bebeeru..and Sipiri or Sipeira.

Hence **si'peerine**. *Chem.* [Named by Maclagan in 1843.] (See quot.)

**1868** WATTS *Dict. Chem.*, *Sipeerine*, *Sipirine*, *Sepeerine*, an alkaloid existing, together with bebirine, in the..greenheart-tree... It was discovered by Rodie in 1834.

**siper** ('saɪpə(r)). *north. dial.* Also s(e)yper. [f. SIPE *v.*] An immoderate drinker; a toper.

**1803** R. ANDERSON *Cumbld. Ball.* (*c* 1850) 66 The Hiverby lads at fair drinkin are seypers. **1885** HALL CAINE *Shadow of a Crime* xxv, You're worse than he is, you old sypers.

**sipers**, obs. form of CYPRESS[3].

†**siphac.** *Anat. Obs.* Also α. 5 syphac, 6 cyphac, sifac, 7 siphack. β. 6–7 siphach. [a. med.L. *siphac*, *syphac* (whence also obs. F. *siphach*, Pg. *sifac*), a. Arab. *çafāq*, from the root *çafaqa* to cover.] The peritoneum.

α. **1398** TREVISA *Barth. De P.R.* VII. lv. (Bodl. MS.), Hernia is a skynne in þe wombe and hatte Siphac also and brekeþ somtyme. *c* **1400** *Lanfranc's Cirurg.* 169 For to holde alle þese þingis, þe stomak & þe guttis is ordeyned a skyn, þat is clepid þe siphac. **1541** R. COPLAND *Guydon's Quest. Chirurg.* Bj, The voyde places that are betwene the cyphac and the myrac. **1548** VICARY *Anat.* (1888) 64 That [part] which appeareth next vnder the Sifac is *Omentum*.

β. **1552** UDALL tr. *Germinus' Anat.* C vj, Nexte within thys Abdomen or Mirach is contayned Siphach. **1587** T. THOMAS *Lat.-Eng. Dict.* (1615), *Peritonæum*,..the inner rim of the bellie..: the Anatomists call it Siphach. [Hence in later Eng. Dicts.]

†**siphany.** *Obs. rare.* Also sy-. [Of obscure origin.] The name of some flower.

**1509** *Invent. Plate*, etc. (St. John's Coll., Camb.), Item ij copes of blew satyn..embrodride with Rede rosis and white syphanyes orfreide with rede satyn..embrodrid with portculis and white and blew syphanyes. *Ibid.*, A vestment and ij tunycles..garnyshed with siphanyes and margaretes with my ladies pose.

**sipher**, obs. form of CIPHER *sb.*

†**'sipher**, obs. form of CIPHER *v.* 8.

**15..** in Grose *Antiq. Rep.* (1809) IV. 407 To myche wyndinge of the pipis is not the best, Whiche may cause them to sypher wher armoney shulde rest. *Ibid.*, Wronge handlynge of the stoppis may cause them sipher fro the kynde.

**siphilitic**, obs. form of SYPHILITIC.

**Siphnian** ('sɪfnɪən), *sb.* and *a.* [f. Gr. Σίφνιος, L. *Siphnius* + -AN.] **A.** *sb.* A native or inhabitant of the Greek Cycladic island of Siphnos. **B.** *adj.* Of, pertaining to, or characteristic of Siphnos.

**1709** I. LITTLEBURY tr. *Herodotus' Hist.* I. III. 282 The Siphnians drawing all their forces together, fought a battle, and were defeated by the Samians, who took many prisoners in the pursuit. **1845** *Encycl. Metropol.* XVII. 494/2 The soft stone, whence the ancient Siphnians used to cut pots and cauldrons. **1886** J. H. FRERE *Aristophanes* 18 It appears by what Herodotus says of the oracle addressed to the Siphnians, that the 'red cheeks' must have gone out of fashion in his time. **1895** *Jrnl. Hellenic Studies* XV. 208 The school to which the sculpture of the Siphnian treasury must be assigned has already caused some discussion. **1932** R. Fry *Let.* 1 May (1972) II. 669 The early Ionian sculptures—above all the Siphnian treasure. **1956** Parke & Wormell *Delphic Oracle* I. II. vi. 150 Siphnos had a..rich source of income in gold and silver mines. From the proceeds of these mines the Siphnians became after the mid-sixth century the richest of the islanders. **1977** *Antiquaries Jrnl.* LVII. 348 Chemical tests have shed no further light on the origin of the wares conventionally known as 'Melian' and 'Siphnian'.

‖**sipho** (ˈsaɪfəʊ). *Zool.* [L. *sīpho* SIPHON *sb.*] = SIPHUNCLE 1.

**1888** Rolleston & Jackson *Anim. Life* 458 The chambers are traversed by a tube—the sipho or siphuncle. *Ibid.* 464 The sipho is formed by two free folds.

**siphon** (ˈsaɪfən), *sb.* Also 7–8 **cyphon**, 7– **syphon**. [ad. L. *sīphōn-*, *sīpho* (cf. prec.), ad. Gr. σίφων pipe, tube. Cf. F. *siphon* (1611), Sp. *sifon*, Pg. *sifão*, It. *sifone*.]

**1.** A pipe or tube of glass, metal, or other material, bent so that one leg is longer than the other, and used for drawing off liquids by means of atmospheric pressure, which forces the liquid up the shorter leg and over the bend in the pipe.

α. **1659** Leak *Waterworks* 6 A Syphon..hath that end which is without the vessell longer then the other. **1698** Fryer *Acc. E. India & P.* 306 The Water..forces it self in nature of a Syphon up to the highest Clifts. **1710** J. Clarke tr. *Rohault's Nat. Philos.* (1729) I. 75 If the Water in the Vessel be made to rise up into the Syphon. **1794** Sullivan *View Nat.* I. 283 The ebb and flow of springs..are likewise to be accounted for on the simple principle of the syphon. **1827** Faraday *Chem. Manip.* xxiv. 634 Bend a piece of glass tube into a syphon. **1907** Hodges *Elem. Photogr.* 28 A syphon to carry off the contaminated water.

β. **1660** Boyle *New Exp. Phys. Mech.* xxxv. 263 We resolved, instead of a List of Cotton, or the like Filtre, to make use of a Siphon of Glass. **1661** —— *Examen* vi. (1682) 72 The passage of Water through Siphons. **1745** Franklin *Lett.* Wks. 1887 II. 11, I applied the siphon..to the pipe of a water-engine. **1815** J. Smith *Panorama Sci. & Art* II. 125 Water will not therefore rise in a siphon, any more than in a pump, beyond the height of 33 feet. **1887** *Encycl. Brit.* XXII. 95/2 The siphon has practically a certain minimum diameter for each liquid.

**b.** *transf.* A channel or tube through which water passes on the principle of the siphon.

**1744** Thomson *Autumn* 829 Beneath th' incessant weeping of these Drains, I see the rocky Siphons stretch'd immense. **1756–7** tr. *Keysler's Trav.* (1760) IV. 139 A communication betwixt the caverns that lie one over another, by a kind of natural syphons. **1837** Whittock *Bk. Trades* (1842) 200 A vertical 'syphon' in the embankment of the reservoir composed of well wrought masonry or brick-work. **1878** Stevenson *Inland Voy.* 148 We had to take to the canal..; because, where it crossed the river, there was, not a bridge, but a siphon. **1889** Welch *Text Bk. Naval Archit.* xi. 129 The pump then becomes a syphon, the flow of water continues without further pumping.

**c.** *ellipt.* A siphon-bottle, *esp.* one containing aerated water.

**1875** Knight *Dict. Mech.* 2189/2. **1898** G. B. Shaw *Plays* II. *You never can tell* 307 *Waiter*... Scotch and syphon for you, sir? **1905** Vachell *The Hill* iii, Upon the table were some siphons.

**2.** †**a.** A fire-bucket. *Obs.*$^{-0}$

**1688** Holme *Armoury* III. 296/2 A Fire Bucket, (or a Leather Bucket)... This is also called a Syphon, which is a kind of Vessel made of Tanned Hydes to carry Water in, to quench Fire that is raging amongst Dwelling Houses.

†**b.** (See quot.) *Obs.*$^{-1}$

**1724** Mason in *Abridg. Patent Spec., Shipbuilding* (1862) 10 A new machine called a siphon or an attracting engine,.. composed of two tubes one within the other.

**c.** A form of tube for milking cows.

**1844** Stephens *Bk. Farm* II. 468 He..introduces the small tube of the siphon an inch or more into the teat. **1881** Shelden *Dairy Farming* 58/1 A silver 'syphon' or 'milking tube'.

**3.** *Zool.* **a.** = SIPHUNCLE 1.

**1822** J. Parkinson *Outl. Oryctol.* 174 The partitions, siphon, &c., of this fossil are those which are to be found in every species of *Belemnite*. **1858** Geikie *Hist. Boulder* vi. 107 The inner tube that traverses the centre of the chambers from end to end of the shell is called the syphon.

**b.** A tube-like organ serving as a canal for the passage of water or other fluid; also, a breathing-tube or suctorial organ.

**1826** *Phil. Trans.* 353 The Buccinum, when completely buried, is enabled to communicate with the water by its respiratory syphon. **1840** *Cuvier's Anim. Kingd.* 445 A sucker, or siphon,..occupies the place of the mouth. **1872** H. A. Nicholson *Palaeont.* 217 The margins or lips of these orifices are usually drawn out..into longer or shorter muscular tubes,..termed the siphons. **1888** Rolleston & Jackson *Anim. Life* 449 The mid-foot..forms two lobes which usually fuse together, and constitute the siphon.

**c.** (See quots.)

**1888** Rolleston & Jackson *Anim. Life* 561 In the *Desmosticha* and *Petalosticha* a tube—the siphon—arises from the posterior extremity of the oesophagus and lies closely applied to the inner margin of the intestine into which it opens again at or near the end of the inferior coil. **1896** tr. *Boas' Text Bk. Zool.* 137 The so-called siphon, or accessory intestine, is a very peculiar structure occurring in most Echinoids.

**4.** *Bot.* One or other of a number of elongated cells which surround the large monosiphonous cell in the frond of certain florideous red algæ.

**1889** *Cent. Dict.* s.v. *Monosiphonous*, Certain of the higher algæ..in which the siphons or pericentral tubes are wanting. **1902** *Encycl. Brit.* XXV. 269/1 The species of *Polysiphonia*, the 'siphons' of which may be regarded as one-celled branches.

**5.** *attrib.* In names of apparatus, etc., of which a siphon forms a part, or which involve the principle or use of the siphon, as ***siphon barometer***, ***bottle***, ***can*** (sense 2 c), ***condenser***, ***cup***, ***fountain***, ***gauge***, ***pump***, ***recorder***, ***trap***, etc. Also ***siphon pipe***, ***tube***, = sense 1; **siphon-shell**, a gasteropod having a siphon (3 b); **siphon-worm** (see quot.).

Descriptions of most of these are given by Knight *Dict. Mech.* (1875) 2189–90 and *Suppl.* (1884) 817–8.

**1835** *Penny Cycl.* III. 482/2 The *siphon barometer..was early adopted as more convenient than that of Torricelli. **1856** *Orr's Circ. Sciences, Pract. Chem.* 244, I employ a *siphon bottle such as is here represented. **1875** Knight *Dict. Mech.* 2189/2 An apparatus for filling siphon-bottles with aerated liquids. **1844** Stephens *Bk. Farm* II. 468 The milker sits down as in the common method, fixing the *siphon can (pail) firmly between his knees. **1851** *Official Catal. Exhib.* I. 419 *Syphon douche. **1819–24** *Encycl. Metrop.* (1845) III. 388/1 Of the *siphon-fountain. **1842** *Penny Cycl.* XXII. 47/2 Such are Tantalus's Cup and the siphon fountain. **1819–24** *Encycl. Metrop.* (1845) III. 372/2 The *siphon-gage..differs from the short barometer-gage merely in this circumstance, that [etc.]. **1831** Lardner *Pneumatics* v. 294 The siphon gauge must be regarded as a more direct measure of the elastic force of the air in the receiver than the barometer gauge. **1838** *Civil Eng. & Arch. Jrnl.* I. 237/2 The whole circle of pipes..is supplied with water..by means of the *syphon pipe. **1873** F. Jenkin *Electr. & Magn.* xxiii. §5 Sir William Thomson's *syphon recorder actually draws on paper the curves which we have learnt to construct theoretically. **1884** Knight *Dict. Mech.* Suppl. 788/1 The common *siphon trap as used in most sinks and water-closets. **1688** J. Smith *The Baroscope* §74, I shall endeavour to demonstrate it in a *Cyphon-Tube... Take then a Glass Tube [etc.]. **1880** Bastian *Brain* iv. 75 Other bivalves possessing prolongations of the mantle known as siphon-tubes. **1856** *Eng. Cycl., Nat. Hist.* IV. 802 The Sipunculidæ (*Syphon-Worms) have a retractile proboscis, at the base of which is placed the vent.

**6.** *Comb.*, as ***siphon-bearing***, ***cleaning***, ***-filling***; ***siphon-like*** adj. and adv.; ***siphon-mouthed***, ***-shaped***.

**1688** J. Smith *Baroscope* §74 Let about a Foot of the other End be turned up, Cyphon-like, in the Form of a Fish Hook. **1842** Brande *Dict. Sci.*, etc. 1120 A family of Crustaceans, comprehending those which have a siphon-shaped mouth. **1858** Mayne *Expos. Lex.*, *Siphonostomus*, having a siphon-like mouth. **1875** Knight *Dict. Mech.* 2189/2 *Siphon-filling Apparatus*, an apparatus for filling siphon-bottles with aerated liquids.

**siphon** (ˈsaɪfən), *v.* Also **syphon**. [f. SIPHON *sb.* Cf. mod.F. *siphonner*.]

**1. a.** *trans.* To draw off or bring up (liquid, etc.) by means of a siphon. Const. with advs., as *off*, *out*, or with preps., as *from*, *into*.

**1859** *Jrnl. R. Agric. Soc.* XX. I. 135 The tolerably clear liquid was syphoned off. **1877** Raymond *Statist. Mines & Mining* 394 It is..siphoned off and a fresh charge put in. **1897** *Allbutt's Syst. Med.* III. 558 The contents [of the stomach] may be syphoned out.

**b.** *fig.* To draw off or from, as if by means of a siphon; to divert. Const. advbs. (chiefly *off*: *spec.* illicitly, of money) and preps.

**1940** E. Wilson *To Finland Station* II. i. 75 All the fervor of which they were still capable was siphoned off into the revolutionary army. **1952** *N.Y. Times* 8 Sept. (late City ed.) 45/7 The police said order was gradually restored as the screaming crowd was slowly siphoned out of the stadium. **1955** H. Roth *Sleeper* ix. 69 We are positive he wasn't siphoning out information. **1957** *Economist* 7 Dec. 842/1 If he were to siphon off the more than 20 per cent of the poll which Liberals won at Gloucester and Ipswich..the Tories' majority..would be reduced. **1965** H. I. Ansoff *Corporate Strategy* (1968) iv. 61 This personal objective [of maximum current earnings] can have a shattering effect on a firm when control is taken over by a person or a group with the explicit aim of siphoning out of the firm most of its liquid..assets. **1976** F. Warner *Killing Time* I. ii. 12 Society depends on the integration of those functions that prostitution siphons off. **1979** 'A. Hailey' *Overload* III. xiii. 261 So how about the remainder [of the income of an organization]? The best guess was that Birdsong, who controlled p & lfp totally, was siphoning it off.

**2.** To empty after the manner of a siphon.

**1892** *Pall Mall G.* 15 Feb. 3/1 During this time many gullies and traps have been syphoned, giving free egress for sewer gas.

Hence **ˈsiphoning** *vbl. sb.*

**1895** Parkes *Health* 53 The discharge of one closet may cause the siphoning of the trap of the other.

**siphon-**, combining form of Gr. σίφων before vowels (cf. SIPHONO-), occurring in a few terms of *Zool.* and *Bot.*, of doubtful currency in English, as ***siphonanth***, ***-anthous***, ***-apter***, ***-apterous***. See also SIPHONAPTERAN *a.*

**1858** Mayne *Expos. Lex.* (Siphonanthous, Siphonapterous). **1895** *Funk's Stand. Dict.*

**siphonaceous** (saɪfəˈneɪʃəs), *a. Bot.* [f. SIPHON *sb.* + -ACEOUS.] Characterized by or being an algal thallus that is tubular and largely without septa; = SIPHONEOUS *a.*

**1916** G. S. West *Algæ* I. 223 There are a number of undoubted fossil siphonaceous Algæ, the calcified thallus of various forms having lent itself to preservation. **1933** G. M. Smith *Fresh-Water Algae U.S.* 299 Continued growth of such a coenocyte..would lead to a simple siphonaceous form such as *Protosiphon*. **1969** F. E. Round *Introd. Lower Plants* ii. 30 One of the simplest completely siphonaceous genera is *Bryopsis*.

**siphonage** (ˈsaɪfənɪdʒ). Also **sy-**. [f. SIPHON *sb.* + -AGE. Cf. F. *siphonage*.] The action of drawing off liquid by means of a siphon; also *spec.*, the accidental emptying of a siphon-trap.

**1855** *Orr's Circ. Sci., Elem. Chem.* 353 A heavy yellow liquor..sinks to the bottom, and may be withdrawn by syphonage. **1884** *Century Mag.* Dec. 260/1 Siphonage is due to the rapid movement through the trap of air. **1897** *Allbutt's Syst. Med.* III. 437 The stomach-pump or a free syphonage of the stomach may be promptly used.

**siphonal** (ˈsaɪfənəl), *a.* Also **sy-**. [f. SIPHON *sb.* + -AL[1].] Having the form or character of a siphon; of or pertaining to a siphon. Chiefly *Zool.*

(*a*) **1826** *Phil. Trans.* 353 The syphonal, or posterior extremity of the valves [of *Pholas candida*]. **1851** Woodward *Mollusca* I. 85 The siphonal lappets of Paludina. **1880** Günther *Introd. Study Fishes* 130 The siphonal [stomach of Teleosteans]..presents the form of a bent tube or canal.

(*b*) **1853** Phillips *Rivers Yorks.* iii. 112 Variable pressure on the water, derived from a curved or siphonal passage underground.

**siphonapteran** (saɪfəˈnæptərən), *a.* (*sb.*) [f. mod.L. order name *Siphonaptera* (P. A. Latreille *Familles Naturelles du Règne Animal* (1825) 334), (f. combining form of Gr. σίφων SIPHON- + ἄπτερος wingless) + -AN: cf. APTERAN *a.* and *sb.*] Of or pertaining to a flea of the order Siphonaptera. Also as *sb.*

**1842** Brande *Dict. Sci.*, etc. 1120 (Siphonapterans). **1941** I. Fox in *Proc. Entomol. Soc. Washington* XLIII. 6 (*title*) The siphonapteran thorax. **1962** Gordon & Lavoipierre *Entomol. for Students of Med.* xxxv. 218 The egg is similar to that of other fleas and the larvae which emerge after 3 to 4 days incubation are typical siphonapteran larvae.

‖**siphonaria** (saɪfəˈnɛərɪə). [mod.L. *Siphonaria* (Sowerby, 1824), f. L. *sīphōn-* SIPHON.] A pulmonate gasteropod of the genus *Siphonaria*, distinguished by a siphon passing from the apex to the margin.

**1861** P. P. Carpenter *Lect. Mollusca* 82 (Cent. Dict.), The Siphonarias have solid, conical shells, often overgrown with sea-weeds and millepores... They are found on almost all tropical shores.

**siphonate** (ˈsaɪfənət), *a.* and *sb. Zool.* [f. SIPHON *sb.* + -ATE[2] 2.]

**A.** *adj.* Of molluscs: Furnished with, or characterized by having, a siphon.

**1870** Rolleston *Anim. Life* 61 Representing the inhalant siphon of the siphonate orders. **1883** *Encycl. Brit.* XVI. 686/2 In this way the notches..are in the Siphonate forms converted into two separate holes.

**B.** *sb.* A mollusc furnished with a siphon.

**1877** Le Conte *Elem. Geol.* (1879) 304 Lamellibranchs are divided into siphonates and Asiphonates, i.e. those with and those without breathing siphons behind. The Siphonates are the higher. *Ibid.*, At present the Siphonates are the more abundant.

**ˈsiphonated**, *a. Zool.* [f. prec. + -ED[1] 2.] = SIPHONATE *a.*

**1851** Woodward *Mollusca* I. 13 Most of the siphonated univalves are animal-feeders. **1863** Lyell *Antiq. Man* xxii. 442 A greater number in the lower division, that of entire-mouthed univalves, than in that of the siphonated.

**siphoned** (ˈsaɪfənd), *a.* Also **syphoned**. [f. SIPHON *sb.* + -ED[1].]

**1.** *Zool.* Siphonate.

**1889** Hyatt *Genesis Arietidae* 13 The smaller siphoned species of the genera Endoceras and Sannionites.

**2.** Operated on by means of a siphon.

**1897** *Allbutt's Syst. Med.* III. 512 My first syphoned patient..was admitted into the Leeds Infirmary with benignant pyloric stenosis.

**siphonein** (ˈsaɪfəniːn). *Biochem.* [f. SIPHON(O- + *-ein*, perh. after LUTEIN.] An ester of siphonoxanthin present in certain green algæ.

**1949** H. H. Strain in Franck & Loomis *Photosynthesis in Plants* vi. 162 Siphonein. In most algae containing siphonaxanthin one finds about equivalent amounts of a spectroscopically similar carotenoid which is converted into siphonaxanthin by saponification with alcoholic potassium hydroxide. **1964** [see *siphonoxanthin* s.v. SIPHONO-]. **1969** *Tetrahedron Lett.* No. 59. 5141 Siphonein is an ester of siphonaxanthin characterized by the esterification of the primary hydroxyl group with a fatty acid.

**siphoneous** (saɪˈfəʊnɪəs), *a. Bot.* Also **sy-**. [f. SIPHON *sb.* + -EOUS.] Of the fronds of algæ: Composed of tubes; having a tubular structure; = SIPHONACEOUS *a.*

**1858** Mayne *Expos. Lex.* s.v. *Siphoneus*. **1892** *Athenæum* 14 May 636/2 Spirit specimens of *Ascothamnion intricatum*, an organism described as a siphoneous alga. **1967** I. Morris *Introd. Algae* ii. 21 Multicellular thalli may be regarded as being of five main types: 1. Colonial..2. Aggregatious..3. Filamentous..4. Siphoneous..5. Parenchymatous. **1971** Kumar & Singh *Textbk. Algae* ii. 24 A siphoneous thallus is multinucleate lacking septation except during the formation of reproductive organs.

**siphoner** (ˈsaɪfənə(r)). [f. SIPHON *v.* + -ER[1].] One who draws off (liquid, etc.) by siphoning; *spec.* a petrol-thief.

**1961** E. S. Turner *Phoney War* vii. 44 The scarcity of petrol bred a new type of sneak-thief, the siphoner, who went round with a length of rubber tubing and a can, helping himself to the contents of car tanks. **1979** *Tucson Mag.* Sept. 35/1 Mass cruising [in cars] is dying rapidly. About the only people who can do it anymore are the filthy rich and the skillful siphoners.

**ˈsiphonet.** *Ent.* [f. SIPHON *sb.* + -ET¹.] A small siphon or tube by which an aphis emits a sweet, honey-like fluid; a honey-tube. Now *rare* or *Obs.*, *siphunculus* (q.v., sense 2) or more commonly *cornicle* being used instead.

**1826** KIRBY & SP. *Entomol.* III. xxxiii. 393 *Siphonuli* (the Siphonets). *Ibid.* IV. xl. 120 The Aphides all secrete a fluid excrement.., which is ejected not only at the anal passage, but, in many, by two little siphonets also above it.

**†siˈphonia.** *Obs.* [Of obscure origin.] A light kind of overcoat.

**1853** *Household Words* VIII. 76 Not less can I set down as slang the verbiage by which coats are transformed into bisuniques, alpacas,..and siphonias. **1859** SALA *Gaslight & D.* xxxiv. 391 Incongruously picturesque garments such as ponchos, togas, vicunas, siphonias, Inverness wrappers, &c. **1863** *Morning Star* 21 May, The Derby Days, when blue veils and siphonias..have been the main characteristics of the journey by road.

**siphonic** (saɪˈfɒnɪk), *a.* Also sy-. [f. SIPHON *sb.* + -IC.]

**1.** *Zool.* Of or pertaining to a siphon; siphonal.

**1832** OWEN *Mem. Pearly Nautilus* 63 The siphonic artery. **1836** BUCKLAND *Geol. & Min.* (1837) I. 322 *note*, The siphonic apertures of the transverse plates.

**2.** Of or pertaining to, working by means of, on the principle of, a siphon.

**1884** *Century Mag.* XXIX. 257 The siphonic action, or suction. **1884** *Health Exhib. Catal.* 59/2 Syphonic Water Closets, Urinal and Cistern. *Ibid.* 74/1 Automatic Syphonic System of Ventilation.

**siphoˈniferous,** *a.* *Zool.* [f. SIPHON *sb.* + -(I)FEROUS.] Having a siphon; siphonate.

Brande *Dict. Sci.*, etc. (1842) 1120 gives *Siphonifers* as a rendering of mod.L. *Siphonifera*.

**1835–6** *Todd's Cycl. Anat.* I. 519/1 All the other genera.. are provided..with an internal siphoniferous polythalamous shell. *Ibid.* 700/1 In the siphoniferous acephala having the foot short and rudimentary. **1837** *Penny Cycl.* VII. 432/1 In the siphoniferous branch of the family [*Conchifera*]. **1858** in MAYNE *Expos. Lex.*

**siˈphoniform,** *a.* [f. as prec. + -(I)FORM.] Having the form or shape of a siphon.

**1891** in *Cent. Dict.*

**ˈsiphonless,** *a.* *rare*⁻¹. [f. SIPHON *sb.*] Destitute of a siphon.

**1862** DANA *Man. Geol.* 258 In both groups the species are mostly siphonless.

**siphono-** (ˈsaɪfənəʊ), *a.* Gr. σιφωνο-, combining form of σίφων SIPHON, used in various terms of *Zool.* and *Bot.*, as **ˌsiphonoˈbranchiate** *sb.* and *a.*; **siˈphonogam; ˌsiphonoˈgamic** *a.*; **siphoˈnogamous** *a.*; **siphoˈnogamy; siˈphonoglyph** (-glɪf); **ˌsiphonoˈglyphe** (-ˈglaɪfiː); **siphoˈnophoran** *sb.* and *a.*; **ˈsiphonophore** (-fɔə(r)) *sb.* and *a.*; **siphoˈnophorous** *a.*; **siˈphonopod; siphoˈnopodous** *a.*; **ˈsiphonostele** *Bot.*, a stele consisting of a core of pith surrounded by concentric layers of xylem and phloem; so **ˌsiphonoˈstelic** *a.*; also (*rare*) **ˈsiphonostely,** the state of being or having such a stele; **ˌsiphonoˈstomatous** *a.*; **ˈsiphonostome; siphoˈnostomous** *a.*; **ˌsiphonoˈxanthin** (also **siphona-**), a xanthophyll pigment, $C_{40}H_{56}O_4$, present in certain green algæ; **ˌsiphonoˈzooid**: (see quots.).

Various other combs. of doubtful currency, such as *siphono-cladaceous, -clamydate, -gnathoid*, etc., are given in recent Dictionaries.

**1842** BRANDE *Dict. Sci.*, etc. 1120 **Siphonobranchiates*,.. an order of Gastropods, including those in which the branchial cavity terminates in a tube or siphon more or less prolonged, by which the respiratory current of water is received and expelled. **1849** CRAIG, Siphonobranchiate *a.* **1898** tr. *Strasburger's Text-Bk. Bot.* 431 The pollen-tubes.. conduct the two generative cells to the egg-cell. The Phanerogams have accordingly been termed by Engler, *Siphonogams. **1900** B. D. JACKSON *Gloss. Bot. Terms* 242/1 *Siphonogamic. **1891** *Nature* 17 Sept. 484 From another point of view karyogamy is..*Siphonogamous: karyogamy is effected by a tubular outgrowth from one or both of the gametes. **1900** B. D. JACKSON *Gloss. Bot. Terms* 242/1 *Siphonogamy. **1894** *Jrnl. Marine Zool.* I. 78 The single *siphonoglyph giving attachment to the ventral pair of directive mesenteries. **1883** *Phil. Trans.* CLXXIV. 693 On the Ciliated Groove (*Siphonoglyphe) in the Stomodæum of the Alcyonarians. *Ibid.* 694, I propose to call this groove 'the siphonoglyphe'. **1888** ROLLESTON & JACKSON *Anim. Life* 725 [One end of the mouth] leading into well marked grooves strongly ciliated known as gonidial grooves or siphonoglyphes. *Ibid.* 775 A *Siphonophoran has been variously regarded (1) as an assemblage of organs, or (2) as a colony of polymorphic zooids. *Ibid.* 775 *note*, The Siphonophoran tentacle..is sometimes attached directly to the coenosarc. **1842** BRANDE *Dict. Sci.*, etc. 1120 **Siphonophores*,..a name given by Escholtz to an order of Acalephes, to which he refers those species which have no central digestive cavity, but simply isolated tubes. **1883** *Century Mag.* Sept. 733/2 The vapory, translucent siphonophores..lived contentedly in their glass prison. **1884** *Riverside Nat. Hist.* I. 106 The Siphonophore fauna of the Mediterranean Sea. *a* **1843** *Encycl. Metrop.* VII. 267/1 The *Siphonophorous Order are..distinguished by the absence of any stomach. **1881** *Encycl. Brit.* XII. 555/1 The variously modified units of the siphonophorous colony. *Ibid.* XVI. 684/1 In embryo *Siphonopods..the sucker-bearing lobes of the fore-foot are truly podial structures. *Ibid.* 669/1 *Siphonopodous Cephalopods in which the inflected lateral margins of the mid-foot are fused so as to form a complete tubular siphon. **1902** *Siphonostele [see MESARCH 1]. **1969** F. E. ROUND *Introd. Lower Plants* x. 123 The central tissue in the siphonosteles is often sclerified. **1899** E. C. JEFFREY in *Mem. Boston Soc. Nat. Hist.* V. 160 The two primitive types of stele described above may..be appropriately designated, protostelic and *siphonostelic respectively. **1969** F. E. ROUND *Introd. Lower Plants* x. 123 A simple stele is formed. This consists either of a stellate mass of xylem surrounded by a few rows of simple phloem cells or, in the aerial parts of *Psilotum* and *Tmesipteris*, becoming siphonostelic. **1899** E. C. JEFFREY in *Mem. Boston Soc. Nat. Hist.* V. 160 The primary vascular axes of living Lycopodiales rarely present the phenomena of *siphonostely. **1872** H. A. NICHOLSON *Palaeont.* 244 In a second group the aperture of the shell is notched in front; and the shell is said to be '*siphonostomatous'. **1837** *Penny Cycl.* IX. 460/1 Latreille..admitted into the class *Crustacea* 12 orders,..the Ostrapods, the Xyphosures, and the *Siphonostomes. **1842** BRANDE *Dict. Sci.*, etc. 1120 *Siphonostomes*,..a family of Crustaceans, comprehending those which have a siphon-shaped mouth for suction. *Ibid.*, *Siphonostomes*... By M. de Blainville the term is applied to those gastropods which have the opening of the shell prolonged into a siphon. *a* **1843** *Encycl. Metrop.* VII. 278/1 All the pieces of the mouth can be accounted for in the *Siphonostomous Order. **1855** OGILVIE *Suppl.*, *Siphonostomous*, a designation of animals with a siphon-shaped mouth for suction. **1949** H. H. STRAIN in Franck & Loomis *Photosynthesis in Plants* vi. 162 *Siphonaxanthin. Green algae of the order Siphonales yield significant quantities of this ketonic pigment that closely resembles fucoxanthin with respect to spectral absorption properties. **1964** *Oceanogr. & Marine Biol.* II. 217 Within the Chlorophyta, the Siphonales differ from the other members in possessing siphonein and siphonoxanthin. **1973** V. J. & D. J. CHAPMAN *Algae* (ed. 2) vi. 137 The discoid chloroplasts..lack siphonaxanthin so characteristic of the siphonaceous Chlorophyceae. **1881** H. N. MOSELEY *Corals* in *Rep. Sci. Results Voy. Challenger 1873–76* II. 118, I propose to term in the case of Alcyonarians, in which there are two kinds of zooids,..the aborted polyps (zooids of Kölliker) '*siphonozooids'. *Ibid.* 119 The siphonozooid cavities are only about one-fifth the length of the autozooid cavities. **1896** tr. *Boas' Text Bk. Zool.* 114 The constant presence, in various Alcyonarians, of arrested individuals (siphonozooids).

**ˈsiphosome.** *Zool.* [f. Gr. σίφω-ν siphon + σῶμα body.] The lower part of a siphonophore stem, bearing the reproductive and nutrient organs.

**1891** in *Cent. Dict.* **1898** SEDGWICK *Textbk. Zool.* I. 139 Two parts may be distinguished in it [the coenosome]—an upper part, the nectosome.., and a lower part, the siphosome, bearing the nutritive and reproductive organs.

**siphre, -yre,** obs. forms of CIPHER *sb.*

**siphuncle** (ˈsaɪfʌŋk(ə)l). *Zool.* [ad. L. *siphunculus*, dim. of *sīpho* SIPHON.]

**1.** A small canal or tube traversing and connecting the shell-chambers in certain cephalopods; = SIPHUNCULUS, and SIPHON *sb.* 3 a.

**1822** J. PARKINSON *Outl. Oryctol.* 161 The most important part of this organ, the continuous siphuncle. **1862** KEARLEY *Links in Chain* v. 103 A membranous tube termed the Siphuncle, which originating in the body of the nautilus in the outer chamber passes through all the partitions in succession. **1870** H. A. NICHOLSON *Man. Zool.* li. (1875) 368 The function of the siphuncle is unknown, except in so far as it doubtless serves to maintain the vitality of the shell. *transf.* **1866** BLACKMORE *Cradock Nowell* xxxv. (1883) 213 This flint has traversing it from pole to pole a thread, a spindle, a siphuncle of the richest golden hue.

**2.** *Ent.* A small siphon or suctorial organ; *spec.* = SIPHUNCULUS 2.

**1826** KIRBY & SP. *Entomol.* III. xxxiii. 363 Replaced by an exarticulate retractile tube, which exerts a retractile siphuncle. *Ibid.* xxxiv. 472 The siphuncle, which is the suctorious part, being first retracted within the tubulet. **1899** *Cambr. Nat. Hist.* VI. 589 Another highly peculiar structure [in aphids] is the siphons, frequently called nectaries, honey-tubes, or siphuncles. **1962** G. A. TULLOCH *J. R. de la Torre-Bueno's Gloss. Entomol.* (rev. ed.) 268 *Siphuncle*, the cornicle of the aphids.

**ˈsiphuncled,** *a.* *Zool.* [f. prec. + -ED¹.] Possessing or furnished with a siphuncle.

**1847** in WEBSTER (citing Buckland). **1851** WOODWARD *Mollusca* I. 77 *Shell, mucro* (only known) chambered and siphuncled.

**siˈphuncular,** *a.* *Zool.* [f. L. *sīphuncul-us* + -AR.] Of or pertaining to, acting or serving as, a siphuncle. Also, of or pertaining to a siphunculus.

**1832** OWEN *Mem. Pearly Nautilus* 46 The siphuncular apertures of the septa. **1851** RICHARDSON *Geol.* viii. (1855) 230 An external, many-chambered shell, with a siphuncular tube passing through the chambers. **1888** ROLLESTON & JACKSON *Anim. Life* 464 Siphuncular collars generally directed backwards. **1975** *Jrnl. Zool.* CLXXV. 278 Prodding the abdomen and pinching the legs of a sycamore aphid induces it to produce siphuncular exudate.

**siˈphunculate,** *a.* *Zool.* [f. as prec. + -ATE.] = next.

**1875** BLAKE *Zool.* 244 A shell which is external, many-chambered, and siphunculate. **1877** *Encycl. Brit.* VI. 738/2 The spiral-chambered and siphunculate shell of *Spirula*.

**siˈphunculated,** *a.* *Zool.* [Cf. prec.] Possessing or furnished with a siphuncle.

**1828–32** in WEBSTER (citing Say). **1851** MANTELL *Petrifactions* v. §5. 459 The Phragmocone, or chambered, siphunculated, internal shell. **1877** HUXLEY *Anat. Inv. Anim.* viii. 532 The *Tetrabranchiata* possess an external chambered siphunculated shell.

**‖siˈphunculus.** *Zool.* Pl. -culi. [L. *sīphunculus* a little pipe, dim. of *sīpho* SIPHON.] **1.** = SIPHUNCLE 1.

Anglicized as *siphuncule* by Mayne *Expos. Lex.* (1858).

**1752** J. HILL *Hist. Anim.* 121 A siphunculus carried the whole length of the shell [of the nautilus]. **1764** *Phil. Trans.* LIV. 48 The siphunculus of the Belemnite is always upon the verge of the chamber, or cell. **1822** J. PARKINSON *Outl. Oryctol.* 164 The chambers divided by winding septa, pierced by a siphunculus always placed at the outer side. **1836** BUCKLAND *Geol. & Min.* xv. §3 (1837) I. 332 Families of fossil chambered shells, that possessed siphunculi.

**2.** *Ent.* A tubular appendage on the abdomen of aphids, which lets out a waxy substance when the animal is attacked that acts as an alarm pheromone; (formerly believed to be the tube from which honeydew comes). Usu. called a *cornicle*.

**1939** V. B. WIGGLESWORTH *Princ. Insect Physiol.* x. 233 At the apex of the abdominal tubes or siphunculi of Aphids are ostioles..which allow wax-laden blood cells to escape. **1975** *Jrnl. Zool.* CLXXV. 280 When prodded or attacked by parasites or predators aphids often exude these cells bathed in fluid from their siphunculi.

**sipid** (ˈsɪpɪd), *a.* *rare.* Also 7 sippid. [Back-formation from INSIPID *a.*]

**1.** Savoury; = SAPID *a.* 1.

**1623** COCKERAM I, *Sippid*, sauorie. **1660** F. BROOKE tr. *Le Blanc's Trav.* 237 The flesh of Crocodile..was wholesome, white, and sipid.

**2.** *fig.* = SAPID *a.* 3.

**1908** A. SYMONS in *Sat. Rev.* 17 Oct. 480/2 The music was ..gay, rattling, sipid, voluptuously melodious.

Hence **siˈpidity,** savour, flavour. *rare*⁻¹.

**1880** MISS BIRD *Japan* I. 233 It is..used everywhere..to give sipidity to their otherwise tasteless food.

**siping** (ˈsaɪpɪŋ), *vbl. sb.* Now *dial.* [f. SIPE *v.*] The action of percolating, oozing, etc.; the result of this; also *pl.*, water or other liquid that has oozed or leaked.

**1503** *Eng. Misc.* (Surtees) 30 So that no fylth..discend from the same swynstye..excepte yt it be by sipynge, or casualtie. **1621** GRANGER *On Eccl.* 316 The siping through of waters into the house. **1808** in JAMIESON. **1825–** in dialect glossaries, etc. (Northumb., Yks.). *c* **1880** in Heslop *Northumbld. Gloss.* (1894) 644 Sandy gravel, with a small siping of water.

So **ˈsiping** *ppl. a.* Also as *adv.*

**1398** TREVISA *Barth. De P.R.* VII. lix. (Bodl. MS.), Whanne þe posteme is in state men schal vse temperinge þinges and scheding and naissching and cypingg. **1642** H. MORE *Song of Soul* I. iii. 24 Here fifty Sisters in a sieve do draw Thorough-siping water. **1862** C. C. ROBINSON *Dial. Leeds* 408 A siping wet neet.

**sipirs,** obs. form of CYPRESS³.

**sipling** (ˈsɪplɪŋ), *north.* and *obs. Sc.* Forms: 6 suppline, syplin, syeppaling, 8 sippleing; 7, 9– sipling, 9 siplin', -lin. [perh. ad. OF. *souplin* a shoot of a tree (Godef.); as a mere var. of SAPLING the change of vowel would be difficult to account for.] A sapling.

**1513** DOUGLAS *Æneid* III. i. 47 Quhar hepthorne buskis.. grew hye, And evin syplinnis of myrthus. *Ibid.* VII. xiv. 87 And a haill suppline of a gret myrtre. **1610** *North Riding Rec.* (1884) I. 186 To cutt upp young siplings of asshe & hassells. **1708** J. C. *Compl. Collier* (1845) 35 Young Plants or Sippleings, as we here call them, of Oak, Ash or Aller. **1807** R. ANDERSON *Cumbld. Ball.* (1881) 108 Wid a spur on my heel, a yek [= oak] siplin in han. **1849–** in dialect glossaries (Northumb., Durh., Cumb.).

**sipman,** obs. form of SHIPMAN.

**Siporex** (ˈsɪpɒrɛks). A proprietary name for a type of cement or concrete (see quots.).

**1938** *Trade Marks Jrnl.* 27 July 913/1 *Siporex* 583, 757. Slates, bricks, blocks, beams, piles, pillars, posts, tiles, pipes, drains and shaped pieces, all made of cement or concrete for use in building or construction. *Internationella Siporex Aktiebolaget*..Sweden..24th February 1938. **1943** *Archit. Rev.* XCIV. 68/1 The Mässhallen in Gothenburg —a large covered sports hall in steel, concrete and siporex —is also by Eriksson. **1965** *Economist* 5 June 1176/2 Siporex is an autoclaved lightweight aerated concrete product which was first developed in Sweden some thirty years ago, and is now used all over the world.

**sipper** (ˈsɪpə(r)). [f. SIP *v.* + -ER¹.] One who sips; hence, a drinker or toper.

**1611** COTGR., *Piailleur*, a bibber, sipper, wine-swiller. **1614** B. JONSON *Barth. Fair* III. i, They are all sippers, sippers o' the city; they look as they would not drink off two pen'orth of bottle-ale amongst 'em. **1702** BAYNARD *Cold Baths* II. (1709) 381 Sippers of Brandy and spirituous distill'd Liquors. **1806** SURR *Winter in London* II. 233 Only look..at the difference of beef steak breakfasters, and the sippers of souchong! **1866** MEREDITH *Vittoria* viii. (1889) 62, I promised my Rosellina, my poppy-headed sipper, a red-wine evening. **1891** *Leeds Mercury* 27 May 5/2 Half a dozen gentlemen..sipping tea..; each sipper wears a tall hat.

*fig.* **1850** MᶜCOSH *Div. Govt.* (1852) 206 He is probably an idle dreamer, or a sipper of the sweets of literature.

**sippers** ('sɪpəz). *Naut. slang.* [f. SIP *sb.*: see -ER[6].] A sip (of rum), esp. taken from another's tot, as a reward for some service or in celebration; *spec.* (see quot. 1944).

**1944** J. P. W. MALLALIEU *Very Ordinary Seaman* 99 For his service in measuring the rum the Leading Hand of the mess was entitled to 'sippers' from every man, a 'sipper' being a taste of each tot. **1945** *Penguin New Writing* XXIII. 49 Old three-badge A.B.'s offer him 'sippers' from their tots of rum and protect him from over-zealous killicks. **1956** H. TUNSTALL-BEHRENS *Pamir* 25 A bottle appeared with enough in it to give us all 'sippers'. **1977** R. BAKER *Dry Ginger* viii. 100 Two brothers, one old enough to be allowed his tot of rum, and the other too young.. known respectively as 'Gulpers' and 'Sippers' Young.

**sipper-sauce**, *dial.*: see SIBBER-SAUCE.

† **'sippet**, *sb.*[1] *Obs. rare.* Also 6 syppet. [Cf. SIP *sb.* and -ET[1].] A little sip.

*a* **1529** SKELTON *E. Rummyng* 367 Here is an olde typpet, And ye wyll gyue me a syppet Of your stale ale. **1574** HELLOWES *Gueuara's Fam. Ep.* (1577) 98 Shee drinketh.. but water mixed with wine: in such wise, that with her sippets none may.. kill his thirst.

**sippet** ('sɪpɪt), *sb.*[2] Also 6–7 syppet, 7 sippit, -ett, cippet. [app. intended as a diminutive of SOP *sb.* Cf. *supett* in the earlier Wycl. version *2 Sam.* xiii. 8.]

**1.** A small piece of toasted or fried bread, usually served in soup or broth, or with meat, or used for dipping into gravy, etc.; a small sop.

**1530** PALSGR. 270/2 Syppet a lytell soppe, *tatin.* **1600** SURFLET *Countrie Farme* v. xxi. 720 Some do make sippets or small slices (as they call them) of bread dried vpon the coales. *a* **1655** SIR T. MAYERNE *Archimag. Anglo-Gall.* No. 47 (1658) 41 Serve it up with brown bread, and sippets fryed with butter. **1693** CROWNE *Country Wit* III. iii, See that the mutton broath have white bread sippets in it. **1747–96** MRS. GLASSE *Cookery* v. 42 Lay round them stewed spinage pressed and cut like little sippets. **1764** ELIZ. MOXON *Eng. Housew.* (ed. 9) 71 When you dish it up take off the lid, and ..cut the lid in sippets. **1826** POLWHELE *Trad. & Recoll.* I. 139 The fresh boiled round of beef, with onions and sippets, welcomed my arrival. **1843** *Tait's Mag.* X. 142 Having leisurely buttered his sippets of crisp dry toast. **1887** FENN *Master Cerem.* iii, She threw some of the sippets in, and began tasting the broth in an unpleasant way.

**b.** *transf.* A small piece of something; a mere fragment.

**1613** BEAUM. & FL. *Captain* IV. iii, Come pre'thee leave this sadness,.. This mumps, this Lachrymæ, this love in sippets. **1647** J. C[LEVELAND] *Char. Lond. Diurn.* 1 It is an History in Sippets; the English *Iliads* in a Nut-shell. **1751** LD. COBHAM in Walpole *Geo. II* (1822) I. v. 117 He did not like cutting the government out into sippets. **1761** COLMAN *Prose on Sev. Occas.* (1787) I. 83 A vast variety of thin volumes, containing certain sippets of philosophy, morality, and the arts. **1888** *Athenæum* 30 June 822/2 Those fragments are portions of a whole.., not [to be] doled out in literary sippets.

**2.** *attrib.* and *Comb.*, as ***sippet-brewis***, ***-pudding***, ***-shaped***.

**1653** URQUHART *Rabelais* I. xxi, Store of good minced meat, and a great deal of sippet-brewis. **1830** DOLBY *Cook's Dict.* 452/2 *Sippet Pudding.*—Cut a small loaf into extremely thin slices [etc.]. **1837** BARHAM *Ingol. Leg.* Ser. I. *Leech of Folkestone* (1905) 74 The occasional presentation of a sippet-shaped *billet-doux*.

Hence **'sippet** *v.*, to cut into sippets. *rare.*

**1681** CHETHAM *Angler's Vade-m.* xxxix. §6 (1689) 257 Sippet it and garnish the dish.

**sipping** ('sɪpɪŋ), *vbl. sb.* [f. SIP *v.* + -ING[1].]

**1.** The action of the vb.; drinking by sips; also, a single act of this; a quantity taken at a sip.

*c* **1440** *Promp. Parv.* 78 Cyppynge of drynke, *subbibitura.* **1483** *Vulgaria* 15 b, See now wyth their syppynge what wyne thei haue dronken. **1534** MORE *Comf. agst. Trib.* III. xxvi. (1847) 306 The little sipping that our hearts should have here now. **1597** J. PAYNE *Royal Exch.* 6 O praye for a fore taste and sum sippinge of this greate supper. **1611** COTGR., *Piaison*, a bibbing, sipping, tipling. **1617** MORYSON *Itin.* III. 89 The Weomen of Germany have a custome to helpe their.. Friends, by sipping of the cup. **1822–7** GOOD *Study Med.* (1829) I. 187 A little toast and water alone, taken in small sippings. **1826** F. REYNOLDS *Life & Times* I. 34 The sipping and gurgling of tea.

*transf.* **1886** F. HARRISON *Ess.* 211 How different this from the critic's sipping of new books! **1891** MISS DOWIE *Girl in Karp.* 219 Her aprons were darker than in the other villages of my sipping.

**b.** *attrib.* and *Comb.*, as ***sipping-drink***, etc.

**1589** NASHE *Anat. Absurd.* Wks. (Grosart) I. 61 May not a man as soone surfet by eating a whole sheepe.. as by the sipping taste of sundry dainties? **1648** HEXHAM II, *Een.. Zuyp-dranck*,.. a Sipping-drinke. **1821** SCOTT *Kenilw.* i, If you call on your host for help for such a sipping matter as a quart of sack. **1871** *Athenæum* 26 Aug. 273 Perhaps their sipping disposition has something to do with their fall.

†**2.** = SIPPET *sb.*[2] 1. *Obs. rare.*

**1535** COVERDALE *2 Sam.* xiii. 6 Let my sister.. make me a syppynge or two, and that I maye eate it of hir hande. *Ibid.* 8 She toke floure,.. and made him a syppynge.

**'sippingly**, *adv.* [f. SIPPING *ppl. a.* + -LY[2].] By or in sips. Also *transf.*

**1814** W. TAYLOR in *Monthly Rev.* LXXIV. 275 Theology is sippingly tasted. **1858** *Chamb. Jrnl.* IX. 201 He takes it, not sippingly and with gusto,.. but.. in large quantities.

**sipple** ('sɪp(ə)l), *v.* Also 6 syp-, 7 scipple. [f. SIP *v.* + -LE 3.]

**1.** *trans.* To drink (liquor, etc.) slowly or by small sips; to sip *up*.

**1566** DRANT *Horace, Sat.* I. iii. B v, The man doth sipple up the brothe. **1570** LEVINS *Manip.* 141 To sypple, *sorbillare.* **1683** G. M[ERITON] *Yorkshire Ale* (1685) 7 At the first they did but sipple up This rare Ambrosia. **1748** SMOLLETT *R. Random* xlvi. (1817) II. 96 Improperly applied to the taking of coffee, inasmuch as people did not drink, but sip or sipple that liquor. **1832–53** *Whistle-Binkie* Ser. I. 14, I had not learn'd to sipple tea.

**2.** *intr.* To sip liquor or the like leisurely.

**1607** MARKHAM *Caval.* VII. (1617) 19 Distempered with heate.., which you shall plainely perceiue by his continuall desire to drinke and scipple. **1816** SCOTT *Antiq.* ix, The body had got sic a trick of sippling and tippling wi' the bailies and deacons when they met. **1819** —— in *Lockhart* (1837) IV. ix. 294 You had better drink a bottle of wine on any particular occasion, than sit.. and sipple at an English pint every day.

Hence **'sippling** *vbl. sb.* Also *attrib.*

**1601** HOLLAND *Pliny* xx. xxi. II. 72 The seed of Mallows ..sodden in milk and taken after a sippling sort. **1681** W. ROBERTSON *Phraseol. Gen.* (1693) 1159 To spend all the day in sipling. **1687** A. LOVELL tr. *Thevenot's Trav.* I. 33 They all drink it sipping..; so that being in a Coffee-hane.. one hears a pretty pleasant kind of sippling musick.

† **sippo.** *Obs.*$^{-1}$ [ad. Pg. *sipo.*] A liana.

**1657** S. PURCHAS *Pol. Flying-Ins.* 207 They run among some Sippoes or Withes that run into the tree.

**sipress, -is, -ous**, obs. ff. CYPRESS[3].

**sipunculan** (saɪ'pʌŋkjʊlən), *sb.* and *a.* [f. mod.L. name of phylum *Sipuncula*: see SIPUNCULID.] **a.** *sb.* A burrowing unsegmented worm of the phylum Sipuncula, found in sandy littoral regions. **b.** *adj.* Of or pertaining to a worm of this kind or the group as a whole.

**1975** *Nature* 30 Oct. 818/2 There is convincing evidence that myohaemerythrin, a monomeric protein found in the retractor muscles of the sipunculan worm *Themiste pyroides*, and the protomers of haemerythrin have quite similar tertiary structures. **1977** P. E. GIBBS *Brit. Sipunculans* 7 Whilst sipunculans show clear embryological affinites with the Annelida, it is now generally agreed that.. they are best regarded as a distinct and separate phylum.

**si'puncular**, *a.* *Zool.* [f. SIPUNCUL-US + -AR.] Of or belonging to the genus *Sipunculus* of gephyrean worms.

**1841** FORBES *Hist. Brit. Starfishes* 254 Pallas, in his Miscellanea Zoologica,.. has figured two English Sipuncular worms.

**si'punculid**, *sb.* (and *a.*) *Zool.* [f. mod.L. (Linnæus *Systema Naturæ* (ed. 12, 1766) I. II. 1078); see prec. and -ID[3].] A gephyrean worm of the family *Sipunculidæ*. Also as *adj.*

**1888** ROLLESTON & JACKSON *Anim. Life* 619 A caecum is sometimes present at the commencement of the rectum in Sipunculids. **1893** *Proc. Zool. Soc.* 328 The papillæ.. characteristic of the skin of Sipunculids. **1928** RUSSELL & YONGE *Seas* i. 20 The Sipunculids.. have a protrusible proboscis and a tough leathery body. **1941, 1967** [see ECHIUROID *a.* and *sb.*]. **1974** *Sci. Amer.* Apr. 88/2 Probably a fourth type consisted of unsegmented burrowers that fed on surface detritus and gave rise to the modern sipunculid worms.

**si'punculiform**, *a.* *Zool. rare.* [f. as prec. + -(I)FORM.] Having the form of a small pipe or of a sipunculus.

**1838** *Penny Cycl.* XII. 270/2 The Sipunculiform Holothuriæ. Body more or less suddenly attenuated backwards.

**si'punculoid**, *sb.* and *a.* *Zool.* [-OID.]

**A.** *sb.* Any member of the group *Sipunculoidea* of gephyrean worms.

**1857** AGASSIZ *Contrib. Nat. Hist. U.S.* I. 78 The Sipunculoids appear to be more closely related to the Annulata than to the Holothurioids. **1885** *Encycl. Brit.* XIX. 430 Forming with the Brachiopoda and Sipunculoids an isolated group.

**B.** *adj.* Of or belonging to the group *Sipunculoidea*.

**1881** *Nation* 1 Dec. 435/1 The report on the *Gephyrea*, or Sipunculoid worms. **1885** *Encycl. Brit.* XIX. 431/1 The Sipunculoid Gephyræans.. possessing identically this arrangement.

‖**sipunculus** (saɪ'pʌŋkjʊləs). *Zool.* Pl. -culi. [L. *sīpunculus*, var. of *sīphunculus* SIPHUNCULUS.] A gephyrean annelid with a retractile proboscis, belonging to the typical genus of the family *Sipunculidæ*.

**1841** FORBES *Hist. Brit. Starfishes* 252, I have represented the Sipunculus alive in a Periwinkle shell. *Ibid.* 255 It is very probable that several other minute Sipunculi inhabit the British seas. **1877** HUXLEY *Anat. Inv. Anim.* v. 247 A larval Sipunculus about $\frac{1}{12}$ of an inch long.

**sipylite** ('sɪpɪlaɪt). *Min.* [f. *Sipyl-us*, one of the children of Niobe + -ITE[1] 2 b.] (See quots.)

**1877** MALLET in *Amer. Jrnl. Sci.* 3rd Ser. XIV. 397 On Sipylite, a new Niobate, from Amherst County, Virginia. **1881** WATTS *3rd Suppl.*, *Sipylite*, a niobate,.. associated with albanite and magnetite, and occasionally with a few large crystals of hydrous zircon.

† **siquare.** *Obs.* Also 4 siquar, sequar; 5 *Sc.* sith(t)-, syth(t)ar, -ware. [Origin and precise form doubtful.] Period or point of time; moment. Chiefly in phr. ***in that siquare***.

Very common in the Cotton MS. of the *Cursor M.*, but usually altered in the other MSS. Otherwise recorded only in the *Sc. Leg. Saints*, where the forms should perhaps be written with *sich-*, as in Horstmann's edition.

*a* **1300** *Cursor M.* 5656 He sagh an egypcien ful sare Smit a juu in þat si-quare. *Ibid.* 12301 þe barn frendes fra þat siquar Held iesum in wirscip mar þan ar. *a* **1400** *Sc. Leg. Saints* i. (*Peter*) 631 He saw cryst in þat sythware pas in hewine. *Ibid.* ii. (*Paul*) 306 In þat sithar.

‖**si quis** (saɪ kwɪs), *sb.* Also si-quis, siquis. [L. *sī* if, *quis* any one (sc. *invēnerit*, etc.), the opening words of the notice or bill (see def.) when written in Latin.]

**1.** A public intimation, notice, or bill, freq. one exhibited on a post, door, etc., requesting information, advertising something lost, or the like; in later use only *Eccl.*, a notice, required in certain cases, intimating that a candidate seeks ordination, and asking if any one knows of any impediment.

**1597** BP. HALL *Sat.* II. v, Saw'st thou ever *Siquis* patch'd on Paul's church dore, To seek some vacant Vicarage before? **1599** JONSON *Ev. Man out of Hum.* III. i, Enter Caualier Shift, with two Siquisses in his hand. *Ibid.*, The aduancement of a *Siquis* or two. **1601** WEEVER *Mirr. Martyrs* A 3 b, Set vp a Siquis, giue intelligence, That such a day shall be my Tragedie. **1611** COTGR., *Plaquard*,.. a Bill, Siquis, or Libell stucke vpon a post, &c. **1646** H. MOSELEY in *Beaum. & Fl.'s Plays* I. (1905) p. xiii, Therefore now I put up this *Si quis*, that whosoever hereafter happily meetes with it [etc.]. **1674** MARVELL *Reh. Transp.* II. 48, I understood that he had sent out a general Siquis thorow his own Province. **1817** C. HODGSON *Instr. Candidates Holy Orders* 3 Form of notice or 'Si quis', and of the certificate of the same having been published in the church of the parish where the candidate usually resides. **1843** HOOK *Ch. Dict.* 523 In the case of a Bishop, the Si quis is affixed.. on the door of Bow Church. **1904** WRIGHT & NEIL *Protestant Dict.* s.v. *Ordination*, If the candidate had left the university and is living elsewhere, a notice must be published... This notice is known as a *si quis*.

*attrib.* **1609** DEKKER *Gull's Horn Bk.* Wks. (Grosart) II. 235 The first time that you venture into Powles.., presume not.. to cast an eye to Si quis doore.

**2.** *slang.* (See quot.)

**1864** *Slang Dict.* 231 Si Quis, a candidate for orders.

Hence ‖**si quis** *v. trans.*, to advertise for.

**1713** *Gentleman Instructed* II. x. 186, I must excuse my Depart.., otherwise he may send Hue and Cry after me, and *Si quis* me in the next Gazette.

**sir** (sɜː(r)), *sb.* [Reduced form of *sire* SIRE *sb.*, the shortening being due to the absence of stress before the following name or appellation. The forms *sore*, *sur(e* may represent OF. *sor* or *sieur*, the oblique case of *sire*.]

**A.** Illustration of forms.

**α.** 4– **sir** (6 sirr, 6–7 S[r]), 5–7 **syr.**

**1297–** (see examples in B).

**β.** 3–6 **ser**, 4–5 **sere.**

*a* **1300** *Cursor M.* 27450 Sere biscop, ta god kepe. *c* **1386** CHAUCER *Sir Thopas* 6 (Cambr.), His name was sere Thopas. *a* **1400–50** *Alexander* 182 Seses, seris, of ȝour syte. *c* **1444** CAPGRAVE *Life St. Kath.* IV. v. 441 This grete noyse, seres, what may it bee? **1451** —— *Life St. Gilbert* 112 The fayre tour.. which þou say, Ser Pope, is þe grete excellens of þi dignite. **1509** in *Scott. Jrnl. Topogr.* (1848) II. 120/2 Ser Wilȝeam Synclair of Wairseytt, Kny[ch]t.

**γ.** 5 **sur, sure, sore.**

? *a* **1400** *Arthur* 285 Hys worthynesse, sur Emperour, Passeþ Muche alle ȝowre. *a* **1400** *Sir Degrev.* 289 The doughty knyght sure Degrevaunt. *c* **1410** *Sir Cleges* 443 Sore, for thy corteci, Smyghte me no more! *c* **1425** *Abraham's Sacr.* 435 in *Non-Cycle Myst. Plays*, Lo! sovereyns and sorys, now haue we schowyd [etc.].

**δ.** *Sc.* 4–5 **scher(e**, 5 **schyr**, 5–6 **schir** (5 **shir**).

In later Sc. also STIR (cf. STIRRAH).

**1375** BARBOUR *Bruce* XVII. 494 Till schir Robert the douchty king. **1396** in *Scott. Antiq.* XIV. 217 Scher Henry Synclar, Erle of Orkynnay. *c* **1425** WYNTOUN *Cron.* IX. xviii. 125 Schirris, I thank God and al ȝow. *c* **1459** *Regist. de Aberbrothoc* (Bann.) II. 105 Honorabile and wirschypful schyris. **1473** *Acc. Ld. High Treas. Scotl.* I. 43 A lettre to Schire James Ogilvy of Erly. **1550** *Reg. Privy Council Scot.* I. 84 Schir George Douglas of Pettindreicht Knycht. **1574** *Satir. Poems Reform.* xlii. 6 Schirs, is thair ony heir Quhais lornay lyes unto Dundie?

**B.** Signification.

**I. 1. a.** The distinctive title of honour of a knight or a baronet, placed before the Christian name (†rarely the surname).

**1297** R. GLOUC. (Rolls) 10822 Sir hubert de boru & oþere þat in prison were ido. **13..** *Gaw. & Gr. Knt.* 387 Sir Gawan, so mot I þryue,.. þis dint þat þou schal dryue. *c* **1386** CHAUCER *Sir Thopas* 6 (Lansd.), A knyht was faire and gent.., His name was sir Thopas. *c* **1440** *Contin. Brut* (1908) 437 Sir Henry Beauford, Cardynall, and Bisshop of Winchestre. **1488–94** LD. FITZWALTER in *Paston Lett.* III. 343 Zowir lofyng cosyn, J. Sir Fytz Wauter. **1556** *Chron. Grey Friars* (Camden) 41 The lady Margarete Bowmer wyffe unto sir John Bowmer,.. but she was the wyffe of one Cheyny, for he solde hare unto sir Bowmer. **1596** SPENSER *State Irel.* (Globe) 667/2 [A grant] of New-castell to Sir Henry Harrington, and of.. Fearnes to Sir Thomas Masterson. **1627** HAKEWILL *Apol.* (1630) 272 Sir Drake whom well the worlds end knew. **1645** SYMONDS *Diary* (Camden) 217 Sir Nich. Kemys was governour when Gerard came. **1711** ADDISON *Spect.* No 112 ¶2 My Friend Sir Roger, being a good Churchman [etc.]. **1819** SHELLEY

*Peter Bell 3rd* VI. xv, He never read them;—with amaze I found Sir William Drummond had. **1899** FITZPATRICK *Transvaal fr. within* (1900) 286 Sir Alfred Milner.. commanded the entire confidence of the Uitlanders.

**b.** In *transf.* uses, as ***Sir Harry, John, Sydney, Timothy*** (see quots.). **Sir Berkeley** *coarse slang* [after *Berkeley* Hunt: see BERK], the female genital organs; hence *transf.*, sexual intercourse, 'sex'; **Sir Garnet**: see GARNET[5].

See also BARLEYCORN 1 b and ROGER DE COVERLEY.

*a* **1700** B. E. *Dict. Cant. Crew, Sir Timothy*, one that Treats every Body, and Pays the Reckonings every where. **1808** JAMIESON, *Sir John*, a close stool. **1812** J. H. VAUX *Flash Dict., Sir Sydney*, a clasp knife. *a* **1825** FORBY *Voc. E. Anglia, Sir Harry*, a close-stool. **1937** J. CURTIS *There ain't no Justice* xvii. 175 She gives me plenty of the old Sir Berkeley, but she knows how to look after herself, I guess.

**2.** Applied retrospectively to notable personages of ancient, esp. sacred or classical, history. Now only *arch.*

*a* **1300** *Cursor M.* 4249 Sir putifar wel vndirstod þat ioseph was o gentil blod. *c* **1330** R. BRUNNE *Chron. Wace* 24 Sen þe tyme of sir Noe. *c* **1400** *Sc. Trojan War* (Horstm.) I. 215 Jasone, the gentile, With hys falow, schyr Hercules. *c* **1440** *York Myst.* xxx. 208 We will prese to Sir Pilate. *c* **1475** HENRYSON *Orpheus & Eurydice* 116 At þe last schir orpheus couth heir. **1513** DOUGLAS *Æneid* VII. v. 110 Schir Dardanus, born of this cuntre eik. **1582** STANYHURST *Æneis* III. (Arb.) 71 Woorthye syr Æneas, why.. teare you A caytiefe forlorne?.. I am named syr Polydor. **1598** SHAKS. *Merry W.* I. iii. 83 Shall I Sir Pandarus of Troy become? *Ibid.* II. i. 122 Goe thou like Sir Acteon. **1821** SCOTT *Kenilw.* xxxii, The valiant Sir Pandarus of Troy. **1881** R. F. BURTON tr. *Camoens' Lusiad* IV. 23 The Oriental hordes.. Wherewith Sir Xerxes crost the Hellespont.

**3. a.** Used fancifully, or as a mock title.

**1362** LANGL. *P. Pl.* A. II. 82 þe Deede was a-selet, Be siht of sir Symoni. *a* **1500** *Bernard. de cura rei fam.* (E.E.T.S.) 13 Schir drunkyiness þat syre doys no thing rycht. **1567** JEWEL *Def. Apol.* v. 561 Here, yee saie, 'Sir Defender is pretily seene in humanitie'. **1581** T. HOWELL *Deuises* (1879) 185 Tyll syr Phebus beames shall lose their light. **1592** GREENE *Disput.* Wks. (Grosart) X. 254 Though the other youth beare the charges and was made sir pay for all. **1600** SHAKS. *Merch. V.* I. i. 93 (Qq.), I am sir Oracle, And when I ope my lips, let no dog barke. **1610** —— *Temp.* II. i. 286 This Sir Prudence, who Should not vpbraid our course. **1781** COWPER *Hope* 416 Lowest at the board.. sat Sir Smug. **1822** SHELLEY *Faust* ii. 114 Does not Sir Mammon gloriously illuminate His palace for this festival? *Ibid.* 150 Sir Urian is sitting aloft in the air. **1879** FARRAR in *Expositor* IX. 214 He suddenly confounds the highly self-satisfied Sir-oracle.

**b.** ***Sir Rag*** (see quots.).

**1764** in *N. & Q.* 7th Ser. XII. 29/1 Thomas Hunt, from Leicester (a Sir-Rag to a Waggoner), died at yᵉ George. **1891** *Ibid.* 132/2 A dusty set of tatterdemalions.. constantly attended fairs and race-courses, and these poor scarecrows used to be called in my young days 'Sir-Rags'. *Ibid.*, In the Midland Counties.. the chief of a band of servants or workers, a foreman or overseer,.. is the 'sir-rag'. *Ibid.* 133/1 Sometimes he or she is the 'head sir-rag', or, as some put it, 'head sir-rag, chief cork and bottle-washer'. **1901** J. PRIOR *Forest Folk* ii. 18 He looks at a body as if he were head Sir Rag.

†**4.** Placed before the Christian name of ordinary priests (also that of a pope). *Obs.* (Cf. SIRE *sb.* 1 b, and DAN[1] a.)

It has been supposed that this use arose out of sense 5, but there appears to be no evidence for this, although the title (at least in later times) was clearly used in contrast to *Master*, and denoted that the priest had not graduated in a university. For the generalized use of *Sir John* see JOHN 3.

*c* **1386** [see JOHN 3]. *c* **1425** WYNTOUN *Cron.* VII. vii. 207 Kynge Henry.. wrat richt reuerendly Til þe pape Schir Adryane. **1450** *Paston Lett.* I. 170 Sir John Bukk, Parson of Stratford, physshed my stankys at Dedham. **1511–2** *Rec. St. Mary at Hill* (1905) 277 To sir Robert for Candell to sey his matens in the mornynges. **1550** BALE *Image Both Ch.* II. f vj, The most ragged ronnagate, and idle idiote among theym, is no lesse then a syr, whiche is a Lord in the Latin, as syr John, syr Thomas, syr Wylliam. **1554** HILARIE *Resurr. Masse* A viij, My smered Chaplens.. I make them to be called Syrs euery one. **1573** TYRIE (*title*), The Refutation of ane Answer made be schir Johne Knox. **1595** ? GREENE *George a Greene* 1191 Well preacht sir Iacke, downe with your staffe. **1635** [see JOHN 3].

†**5.** Used (as a rendering of L. *dominus*), with the surname of the person, to designate a Bachelor of Arts in some Universities. *Obs.*

**1557** in Lamb *Collect. Hist. Univ. Camb.* (1838) 229 Mʳ Turner, Father, Syr Whytgyfte the bachelor, Syr Bryges the eldest son. **1575** in Fowler *Hist. C.C.C.* (O.H.S.) 150 Too Sʳ huker of Corpus christie college in Oxforde. **1614** SELDEN *Titles Honor* 54 How *Dominus*.. is now familiar for *Sir* to euery Batchelor of Art in the Schools, all men know. **1655** FULLER *Ch. Hist.* IX. 71 Hall and his Popish faction (whereof Mʳ. Potto, Mʳ. Binnion, and Sʳ. Appleby the Leaders) opposed his admission. **1690** S. SEWALL *Diary* 2 July, Sir Mather in England yet had a Degree conferred on him. **1714** in Aubrey *Lett.* (1814) I. 294 Pray, Sir, will you do so much as send to Sir Wilkinson of Queen's? **1763** in Pierce *Hist. Harvard Univ.* 234 (Cent. Dict.), That Sir Sewall, B.A., be the Instructor in the Hebrew and other learned languages for three years. **1822** NARES s.v. *Sir*, At the Universities.. a bachelor, who in the books stood *Dominus* Brown, was in conversation called *Sir* Brown. This was in use in some colleges even in my memory.

**II. 6. a.** Placed before a common noun, and forming with it a term of address, as ***Sir clerk, king, knight***, etc. Now *arch.*

**1297** R. GLOUC. (Rolls) 10282 Sir king,.. we beþ icome fram verre londe iwis. *Ibid.* 10309 Nou sir clerc, quaþ þe king, ȝe mowe þretni ynou. *c* **1330** *Amis & Amil.* 757 Sir knight,.. Whi seystow euer nay? *c* **1400** *Rom. Rose* 6390 Sir Preest, in shrift I telle it thee, That he.. Hath me assoiled. **14..** *Chaucer's Doctor's Prol.* 10 Sir Doctour of Phisyke.., Telle us a tale. *c* **1440** *York Myst.* xxx. 211 Sir Knyghtis [*sc.* Roman soldiers], þat are curtayse and kynde. **1591** SPENSER *M. Hubberd* 589 Ah! sir Mule, now blessed be the day [etc.]. *Ibid.* 1033 Nay (said the Foxe) Sir Ape, you are astray. **1601** SHAKS. *Twel. N.* III. iv. 298, I am one, that had rather go with sir Priest, then sir knight. **1611** —— *Wint. T.* I. ii. 135 Come (Sir Page) Looke on me with your Welkin eye. **1794** MRS. RADCLIFFE *Myst. Udolpho* xliv, 'Sir knight,' replied the baron, 'how is it possible that' [etc.] ? **1820** SCOTT *Monast.* xxxiii, Saint Mary! what call you yon, Sir Monk? **1842** TENNYSON *Morte d'Arth.* 152 Sir King, I closed mine eyelids, lest the gems Should blind my purpose. **1865** KINGSLEY *Herew.* iv, Now, then, sir priest,.. go on with your story. **1939** *Sun* (Baltimore) 30 Sept. 7/8 We stand here today to watch you, sir knights, just in friendly tournament. **1977** *Belfast Tel.* 19 Jan. 2/4 The Officers and Sir Knights of the United Sons of Ulster R.B.P. 1041, regret the death of the Sister of their esteemed Sir Knight Robert Scott, P.M.

*transf.* **1826** SCOTT *Jrnl.* 14 May, Look where you will, Sir Sun, you look upon sorrow and suffering.

**b.** With contemptuous, ironic, or irate force.

*c* **1386** CHAUCER *Wife's Prol.* 242 (Harl.), Sir [*v.r.* Sire] olde lecchour, let thi japes be. *a* **1529** SKELTON *Against Scottes* 101 Syr skyrgalyard, ye were so skyt [etc.]. **1591** *Troublesome Raigne of King John* (1611) 27 *Lim.* Good words sir sauce, your betters are in place. *Phil.* Not you sir doughtie, with your Lyons case. **1599** SHAKS. *Much Ado* V. i. 83 Come sir boy, come follow me Sir boy, ile whip you from your foyning fence. **1759** STERNE *Tr. Shandy* II. ii, So, Sir Critic, I could have replied; but I scorn it. **1825** SCOTT *Betrothed* xxix, 'How, sir knave!' said the King, angrily, 'is it for such as thou to dictate to our judgment?'

**7. a.** Used as a respectful term of address to a superior or, in later use, an equal (sometimes with additions as *dear*, †*fair*, †*gentle*, *good*); also by schoolchildren in addressing a master, and formally in addressing the Speaker of a legislative assembly.

**1320–30** *Horn Ch.* 721 Sir, miȝtestow hold him to þi nede, .. Batayle miȝt þou bide. *c* **1375** *Sc. Leg. Saints* xli. (*Agnes*) 102 Certis, gud sir, maryt ame I. *c* **1460** *Towneley Myst.* iv. 228 Hir answere bese belife—'nay, sir!' **1509** FISHER *Fun. Serm. C'tess Richmond* Wks. (1876) 307 But ye wyll say vnto me, Syr yf we were sure of this we wolde not be sory. **1535** COVERDALE *Ruth* ii. 13 She sayde: let me fynde fauoure (syr) before thyne eyes. **1590** SHAKS. *Com. Err.* I. ii. 57 The Sadler had it Sir, I kept it not. **1638** CHILLINGW. *Relig. Prot.* I. ii. 97 For Gods sake, Sʳ, tell me plainly. **1662** STILLINGFL. *Orig. Sacræ* Ded. 11 You see, Sir, to what an unexpected length my desire to vindicate [etc.]. **1709** STEELE *Tatler* No. 45 ¶1, I heard a Voice cry, Sir, Sir!—This raised my Curiosity. **1794** MRS. RADCLIFFE *Myst. Udolpho* xliv, 'Dear Sir!' said Henri, 'here is an armchair.. massy with gilding'. **1838** DICKENS *Nickleby* (1839) viii. 69 'Third boy, what's a horse?' 'A beast, Sir,' replied the boy. **1849** THACKERAY *Pendennis* x, 'Sir to you,' said Mr. Foker politely. **1867** SMYTH *Sailor's Word-bk.* 627 'Aye, aye, sir,' is the well-known answer from seamen. **1873** in Hansard *Parl. Deb.* 31 July 1389/1, I rise, Sir,.. to make the Indian Financial Statement. **1899** KIPLING *Stalky & Co.* 108 Please, sir, what am I to do about prep.? *a* **1930** D. H. LAWRENCE *Phoenix II* (1968) 25 Please Sir, do tortoises bite? **1955** E. BLISHEN *Roaring Boys* i. 31 'The cane,' said Sims vaguely. 'Sir can't,' said Pottell.. 'Is it because you're too young, sir?' **1974** 'J. LE CARRÉ' *Tinker, Tailor* xiv. 118 'Sir, please sir, I think he's to do with the church, sir,' said Cole Slaw. 'I saw him, talking to Wells Fargo, sir, after the service.'

**b.** In *pl.*, used in addressing two or more persons. In Scottish use passing into a mere exclamation (see the later quots.).

*c* **1400** *Destr. Troy* 4907 Þerfore, sirs,.. Let make vs a message. **1459** *Rolls Parlt.* V. 369/2 Sirres, be mery, for yet we have moo frendis. *c* **1500** *Adam Bel* cxiv. in Child *Ballads* III. 27/2 Good syrs, of whens be ye? **1615** RUGGLE *Ignoramus* IV. (1736) 50 Goodly, Sirs,.. I shou'd have sworn it had been my Master Antonio. **1766** FORDYCE *Serm. Young Wom.* (1767) I. vii. 304 Have you forgotten, Sirs, that what they see you admire,.. they will be induced to think.. worthy of admiration? **1816** SCOTT *Old Mort.* xxxix, 'But eh, sirs,' she continued,.. 'Eh, sirs! ye're sair altered, hinny'. **1825** JAMIESON *Suppl., Sirs, Sirse, Serse*, interj., a common mode of address to a number of persons, although of both sexes; often pron. q. *Sirce.* **1894** CROCKETT *Raiders* (ed. 3) 96 Eh, sirce, but there's mony wonderfu' things in the warld.

**c.** Used in commencing or subscribing letters.

**1425** *Paston Lett.* I. 19 Right worthy and worshepefull Sir. *a* **1448** *Ibid.* 71 Syr, I recummand me to zow. **1535** STARKEY *England* (1878) p. xiii, Syr, I most hertely commend me vn to you. **1568** *Peebles Burgh Rec.* (1872) 73 His supplicatioun..:—Schirris, baillies, counsale, and communite of the burgh. **1628** USSHER in *Lett. Emin. Lit. Men* (Camden) 138 Deare Sir, I know not who should beginne first [etc.]. **1655** in *Nicholas P.* (Camden) 300 Which I shall desire you to keepe for yᵉ use of, Sir, Your.. humble seruant, Robert Phelipps. **1745** J. ELTON in Hanway *Trav.* (1762) I. v. lxvii. 304 Sirs, I have been acquainted with your resolutions of August last. **1789** BURNS *Let. to Cunningham* 4 May, My dear Sir, Your duty-free favour.. I received two days ago. **1822** LAMB *To J. Taylor* 7 Dec., Dear Sir, I should like the enclosed Dedication to be printed. **1861** BREWSTER in Mrs. Gordon *Home Life* xix. (1869) 345 Sir,—I have only this moment seen.. an advertisement of your picture [etc.].

**8. a.** Used with scornful, contemptuous, indignant, or defiant force. (Cf. SIRRAH.)

**1592** GREENE *Conny Catch.* Wks. (Grosart) XI. 84, I.. account thee no honest man: For sir know I haue learned your pettegree. **1600** SHAKS. *A. Y. L.* I. i. 80 Well sir, get you in: I will not long be troubled with you. **1632** MASSINGER *City Madam* II. ii, *Lacy.* By the city custom, madam? *Lady.* Yes, my young sir. **1675** BAXTER *Cath. Theol.* II. XIII. 283 Sir, the City ringeth of you as one that greatly wrongeth the cause of God. **1782** in *Brit. Tourist* (1809) IV. 119 *Sir!* in a surly tone, [signifies] a box on the ear at your service!—to a dog it means a good beating. **1824** SCOTT *St. Ronan's* xxx, Sir, this is either a very great mistake or wilful impertinence. .. I am Captain Jekyl, sir. **1855** J. D. BURN *Autobiogr. Beggar Boy* (1859) 44 His uniform manner of addressing me was, by the withering and degrading title of 'sir!' **1861** GEO. ELIOT *Silas M.* ix, I've been too good a father to you all.. But I shall pull up, sir.

**b.** ***my dear sir***, in remonstrance or expostulation.

**1768** STERNE *Sent. Journey* I. 38 Figure to yourself, my dear Sir, that in giving you a chaise which would fall to pieces before you had got half way to Paris.. how much I should suffer. **1776** *Critical Rev.* XLII. 89 It is usual, we are told, with the Scots.. to address the person with whom they converse by the appellation My dear Sir. **1825** R. P. WARD *Tremaine* II. xxvi. 238 'And, indeed, my dear Sir—' 'I won't be Sir'd,' cried the Doctor. **1893** G. B. SHAW *Widowers' Houses* II. iii. 43 *Sartorius*: Will you excuse me for ten minutes? *Cokane*: My dear sir!—*Trench*: Certainly. **1983** A. VENTERS *Blood on Rocks* xiii. 122 'You must have something to eat, my dear sir,' he cried.

**c.** ***yes, sir***: an emphatic assertion; ***no, sir***: see NOSSIR. Chiefly *U.S. colloq.*

**1799** *Aurora* (Philadelphia) 8 Aug. (Th.), Yes Sir! and [France] has been successful beyond any former experience. **1889** 'C. E. CRADDOCK' *Despot of Broomsedge Cove* 40 Yes, sir... None like 'em now. **1929** W. FAULKNER *Sartoris* II. v. 124 'Yes sir,' he repeated, 'he's sure some joker.' **1942** J. B. PRIESTLEY in *R.A.F. Jrnl.* 3 Oct. 2, I could take it and I could dish it out. Yes, Sir!

**9.** Applied to women. Now *dial.*

**1578** WHETSTONE *Promos & Cassandra* I. IV. vii, [To Dalia.] Ah syr, you would, be like, let my Cocke Sparrow goe. **1611** BEAUM. & FL. *King & No K.* II. i, *Pan.* [to waiting-women]. Sirs, leave me all. (Exeunt Women.) **1621** FLETCHER *Pilgr.* II. i, *Juletta.* Would you know o' me, Sir? *Alphonso.* O' thee, Sir? ay, o' thee, sir; What art thou, Sir? **1688** CROWNE *Darius* II. Dram. Wks. 1874 III. 411 *Barzana* [to her confidante, Oronte]. How ill you dress me, sir? **1818** MISS FERRIER *Marriage* ii, 'And ye tu bonny sir,' addressing Lady Juliana.

**10. a.** A person of rank or importance (more recently, also *spec.* a knight or baronet); a lord, a gentleman; one who might be addressed as 'sir'.

In early use equivalent to *sire*; in later examples usually by direct transference from sense 7.

**13..** *Coer de L.* 3567 Whos hed it was my seres aske? *c* **1500** *Young Children's Bk.* 88 in *Babees Bk.*, Wer-euer þou commys, speke honestly To ser or dame. **1585** T. WASHINGTON tr. *Nicholay's Voy.* I. xvii. 20 Taking with him to accompanie him the sir of S. Veran. **1601** SHAKS. *Twel. N.* III. iv. 81 A sad face, a reuerend carriage,.. in the habite of some Sir of note. **1611** —— *Cymb.* I. vi. 160 A Lady to the worthiest Sir, that euer Country call'd his. **1698** FRYER *Acc. E. India & P.* 45 In one of their open Pagods.. stands a Venerable Sir at the upper end. **1703** ROWE *Fair Penit.* II. ii, A talking Sir that brawls for him in Taverns. **1740–1** RICHARDSON *Pamela* II. 354 On Tuesday Morning, my dear Sir rode out, attended by Abraham. **1847** TENNYSON *Princ.* Concl. 102 Why should not these great Sirs Give up their parks some dozen times a year? **1854** EMERSON *Lett. & Soc. Aims, Poet. & Imag.*, Our little sir, from his first tottering steps,.. does not like to be practised upon. **1922** W. J. LOCKE *Tale of Triona* i. 9 A proud old Anglo-Indian family, all Generals and Colonels and Sirs and Ladies. **1952** 'W. COOPER' *Struggles of Albert Woods* IV. i. 202 Albert thought .. there must be a connection between Jameson's appointments and his becoming a Sir. **1974** P. GORE-BOOTH *With Great Truth & Respect* 374, I argued hard and explicitly on behalf of my diplomatic colleagues because becoming a 'Sir' is one of the tools of the trade.

**b.** *spec.* a schoolmaster. *colloq.* or *humorous.*

**1955** [see sense 7 a above]. **1961** *Guardian* 1 Dec. 7/2 [The] users will be grateful to Sir for providing.. a smashing set of answers. **1968, 1973** [see MISS *sb.*[2] 3 f]. **1980** *Daily Tel.* 31 Mar. 10/3 Sir never repeated any part of a question.

**11.** A parson or priest. Now *dial.* (Cf. 4.)

**1591** SPENSER *M. Hubberd* 390 But this good Sir did follow the plaine word. **1869** *Lonsdale Gloss.* 74/2 'Here's t' sir cumman' = Here's the clergyman coming.

**sir** (sɜː(r)), *v.* [f. prec.]

**1.** *trans.* To address (a person) as 'sir'. Also with *up.*

**1576** R. PETERSON *Galateo* (1892) 47 He that is wont to be (*Sird*) and likewise (*Sirreth*) other. **1600** *1st Pt. Sir J. Oldcastle* II. i, *Sum.* Sir, I brought it not my lord to eate. *Harp.* O, do you sir me now? **1722** DE FOE *Relig. Courtsh.* I. ii. (1840) 68 Don't worship me and sir me now. **1748** RICHARDSON *Clarissa* (1768) I. viii. 43 My Brother and Sister.. Sirr'd him up, at every word. **1806–7** *Poet. Reg.* 179 Learn.. To frown importance while they cap and sir ye. **1861** LEYS *Mem. J. D. Maclaren* v. 94 In his kind and sincere way he sirred some cabman, porter, or poor man. **1890** L. C. D'OYLE *Notches* 8 'I don't know, sir, I'm sure,' said the stranger... 'Don't *sir* me! don't you know my name?'

**2.** *intr.* To use the term 'sir' in addressing a person.

**1798** SOUTHEY *To M. Hill* 7 Sir-ing and Madam-ing as civilly As if the road between the heart and lips Were.. a weary and Laplandish way.

Hence **ˈsirring** *vbl. sb.*

**1836** W. E. FORSTER in Reid *Life* (1888) I. 76 [He is] remarkably civil to me, and he gives me such quantities of *sirrings*—that is, he says *sir* so often.

**sir,** obs. f. SIRE *sb.*

**sír,** variant of (*Anglo-Ind.*) SEER.

**sirab,** var. SERAB.

**sirah,** obs. f. SIRRAH.

**siratro** (sɪˈrætrəʊ). [f. initial letters (as indicated) of Commonwealth *S*cientific and *I*ndustrial *R*esearch Organization + *atro*(*purpureus* the specific epithet of the parent plants.] A tropical legume of the variety so called, developed at the C.S.I.R.O. Pasture

Research Station, Samford, near Brisbane, by E. M. Hutton in the early 1960s from Mexican strains of *Macroptilium* (*Phaseolus*) *atropurpureum*.

**1962** E. M. Hutton in *Austral. Jrnl. Exper. Agric.* II. 117/1 Two Mexican strains of *P*[*haseolus*] *atropurpureus*.. were crossed, and this resulted in the development of a new bred strain which has been named Siratro. **1975** *Nature* 31 July 409/1 An isolate from nodules of *Trema cannabina*.. is a strain able to nodulate siratro. **1978** *Jrnl. R. Soc. Arts* CXXVI. 628/2 The Legume Siratro is probably the most outstanding example of pasture plant breeding... It is now the most widely grown pasture legume in southern and central Queensland.

**sirbace**, obs. f. SURBASE.

**sircar**: see SIRKAR.

**sirce** (Sc.): see SIR *sb.* 7 b.

**sircot**, obs. f. SURCOAT.

**sircue**, var. CIRCUE *v. Obs.*

**sircule**, obs. f. CIRCULE *v.*

†**sirculey**, var. *circulet* CIRCLET.

**15..** *Bk. of Precedence* in *Q. Eliz. Acad.* 16 The sword borne by an Earle, the cappe and Sirculey borne by an Earle.

**sircumsycion**, obs. f. CIRCUMCISION.

**sircuyte**, obs. f. CIRCUIT *sb.*

‖**sirdar** (ˈsɜːdɑː(r), səˈdɑː(r)). Forms: α. 7, 9 serdar, 7 serdaar. β. 8 sardar, surdâr, 9 surdar. γ. 8 sirdâr, 9 sirdar. [Urdū (Pers.) *sardār*, f. Pers. *sar* head + *dār* possessor.]

**1.** In India and other Eastern countries, a military chief, a leader or general of a force or army; also *spec.* more recently, the British commander-in-chief of the Egyptian army.

α. **1615** Sandys *Trav.* 211 This Ioseph..got to be made Seidar [*sic*] of Damasco (which is Generall of the Souldiery). **1686** tr. *Chardin's Trav. Persia* 256 He has also the Title of Serdar or General of the Army. **1819** F. Hamilton *Nepal* 109 Military officers, named Serdars, frequently are appointed to command over different portions of the country.

β. **1718** Ozell tr. *Tournefort's Voy* II. 349 The Janizaries are there under the Command of a Sardar. **1753** Hanway *Trav.* (1762) I. III. li. 231 The begler-begs have the power of life and death, as have also those sardares, who are on the frontiers. **1800** *Asiatic Ann. Reg.* 178 He is a Sardar of five thousand horse in the Mahratta empire. **1899** P. S. Allen *Let.* 15 Feb. (1939) 19 A Sardar of this neighbourhood whom we met in Khewra station sent us..a present. **1969** S. M. Sadeek *Windswept & Other Stories* 36 An arsenal of life pulsed and throbbed between the harsh rasping orders of the sardars echoing through the native compound.

γ. **1803** Wellington in Owen *Wellesley's Desp.* (1877) 788, I had also a long and difficult negotiation with the Nizam's sirdars. **1815** Elphinstone *Acc. Caubul* (1842) I. 337 There are many other shops which accompany the camp, to supply the sirdars and the soldiers. **1885** *Times* (weekly ed.) 26 June 4/3 The Turcoman shepherds or sirdars, who alone traverse these little frequented routes. **1898** —— 5 Sept. 3/3 The Sirdar's force to day marched to within six miles of Omdurman.

**2. a.** *sirdar-bearer*, an Indian valet or body-servant. (See BEARER 1 d.)

**1782** *India Gaz.* 2 Sept. (Yule), That a gentleman should pay a rascal of a Sirdar Bearer monthly wages for 8 or 10 men. **1859** Lang *Wand. India* 104 A sirdar-bearer (personal attendant, or Indian valet) took charge of my two boxes. **1863** Trevelyan *Compet. Wallah* (1866) 225 There is every reason to believe that he is honest, as Sirdar-bearers go.

**b.** *ellipt.* in the same sense.

*c* **1813** Mrs. Sherwood *Ayah & Lady* xii. 75 'I will also swear,' said the sirdar, 'by Gunga' [etc.]. **1828** *Asiatic Costumes* 27 The barburdar, or surdar, ..keeps the keys, and in fact has charge of every thing in the house. **1845** Stocqueler *Handbk. Brit. India* (1854) 117 The sirdar-bearer, called sirdar in brevity, is, among other things, the valet-de-chambre.

Hence **sirdarship**, the office of Sirdar.

**1898** *Daily Chron.* 10 Oct. 6/3 The statements that Lord Kitchener intends to resign the Sirdarship.

**sirdena**, obs. form of SARDINE *sb.*[2]

**sire** (saɪə(r)), *sb.* Forms: α. 3– sire, 4–5 sir, 6 sier; 4 scire, 7 shire. β. 3–8 syre, 5 cyre, cyyr, syr, syar, 5–6 syer. [a. OF. *sire* (*cyre*), for earlier **sieire*:—pop. L. **seior*, for cl. L. *senior* SENIOR. The oblique case in OF. was *sieur*:—**seiōr-em* for *seniōr-em*.]

**I.** †**1.** Placed before personal names:

**a.** Denoting knighthood. = SIR *sb.* 1. *Obs.*

*c* **1205** Lay. 22485 Wulcume sire Arður, wilcume lauerd. **1297** R. Glouc. (Rolls) 9066 Sire geffray, þat was erl of aungeo. *c* **1330** *Amis & Amil.* 44 He was callid Syre Amys.. at his crystenyng. **1387** Trevisa *Higden* (Rolls) V. 305 þe firste ȝere of þe comynge of sire John, þe secounde kyng Henricus his sone, into Irlond. *a* **1400** *Minor Poems fr. Vernon MS.* xxix. i. 37 þus sone Sire Rollo..Bi-sette þat Citee. **1492** *Paston Lett.* III. 380 To my..frendes, Sire William Knevette, Sire John Paston, Sire Robert Clere, Knyghtes.

*transf.* **1362** Langl. *P. Pl.* A. x. 1 Sire Dowel dwelleþ.. not a day hennes, In a Castel. *Ibid.* 19 Sire seowel and seywel,..And sire Godfrei Gowel, grete lordes alle.

†**b.** Applied to persons of ancient history, or to ecclesiastics: cf. SIR *sb.* 2 and 4. *Obs.*

*c* **1290** *S. Eng. Leg.* I. 21 þe Erchebischope of Caunterburi sire Ode. **1297** R. Glouc. (Rolls) 2009 To þis senatour.. Sire maximian. *c* **1330** R. Brunne *Chron. Wace* (Rolls) 785 Sire Eneas was þer-of fayn. *c* **1380** Wyclif *Wks.* (1880) 192 And þanne strumpatis & þeuys preisen sire iacke or hobbe & williem þe proude clerk. *a* **1400** *Minor Poems fr. Vernon MS.* 407 A frenche romance that sire Robert, Bisschope a lycoln, made.

†**2.** With common nouns, = SIR *sb.* 6. *Obs.*

(*a*) *c* **1290** *S. Eng. Leg.* I. 15 'Sire Aumperour,' he seide. *a* **1300** *Havelok* 2861 Sire erl,.. And þou wile mi consayl tro, Ful wel shal ich with þe do. *c* **1386** Chaucer *Prol.* 837 Sire knyght, quod he, my mayster and my lord. *c* **1400** *Brut* lvi. 50 Þerfore, sire kyng,..we bene comen into ȝoure lande. **1484** Caxton *Fables of Æsop* v. ix, Syre kynge god yeue good helthe. *c* **1500** *Melusine* 264 'By my feyth, sire knight,' said geffray.

(*b*) *c* **1386** Chaucer *Prol.* 840 And ye sire clerk lat be your shamefastnesse. —— *Nun Priest's Prol.* 26 Wherfore sire Monk daun Piers by youre name I pray yow [etc.]. *Ibid.* 44 (Corpus), Come ner sire prest com hider sir Iohn.

†**b.** = SIR *sb.* 6 b. *Obs.*

*c* **1386** Chaucer *Wife's Prol.* 242 Sire [*v.r.* Sir] olde lecchour, lat thy Iapes be. *c* **1500** *Melusine* 28 By my feyth, sire vassal, hit commeth to you of grette pryde [etc.]. *Ibid.* 29 Sire musarde.

**3.** Without following sb. In early use = SIR *sb.* 7. Now only *arch.* (= 'your majesty') or as an echo of French usage.

*a* **1225** *Ancr. R.* 52 Me leoue sire,..is hit nu so ouer vuel uor te toten utward? *c* **1290** *S. Eng. Leg.* I. 49 'A, sire,' quath þe luþere Quiene,..'Furst ichulle to þe drinke'. **13..** *K. Alis.* 2099 (W.), A knyght com sone rennyng, And saide, 'Sire, up on hast!' **1390** Gower *Conf.* III. 301 'Ha, lieve sire,' tho quod sche, 'Now tak the harpe'. **1470–85** Malory *Arthur* VII. xviii. 240 Sire said the reed knyght..al this wil I do as ye commaunde. *c* **1500** *Melusine* 267 Sire, the kyng is departed from hens. [**1672** Temple *Ess., Government* Wks. 1720 I. 100 The peculiar Compellation of the King in France, is by the Name of Sire.] **1768** Sterne *Sent. Journ.* (1778) I. 3 By heaven! Sire, it is not well done. **1820** Shelley *Œd. Tyr.* I. 71 Your sacred Majesty... They are in waiting, Sire. **1845** S. Austin *Ranke's Hist. Ref.* II. 357 'Sire,' said he, 'there has been a battle before Pavia'.

†**b.** = SIR *sb.* 7 b. *Obs.*

*c* **1350** *Will. Palerne* 2248 Herkenes nowe, hende sires, ȝe han herd ofte, wich a cri has be cried. *a* **1375** *Lay-Folks Mass-Bk.* App. IV. 257 Certes, sires; ful good hit is To stonde stille at þe Mes. *c* **1412** Hoccleve *Reg. Princ.* 2747 Considereth, sires, I am oon of þo [etc.]. **1426** Audelay *Poems* (Percy Soc.) 6 Gentyl sires, herkene to me. *c* **1500** *Melusine* 271 After, after, fayre sires.

†**c.** = SIR *sb.* 7 c. *Obs.*

**1426** *Paston Lett.* I. 24. **1490** *Ibid.* III. 363.

**II. 4.** One who exercises dominion or rule; a lord, master, or sovereign. In ME. freq. in phrase *lord and sire*. Now *rare* or *Obs.*

**1297** R. Glouc. (Rolls) 6556 He wende aboute as noble sire fram londe to londe. *a* **1300** *Cursor M.* 440 He..sette him heist in his hall, Als prince and sire ouer oþer all. **13..** *E.E. Allit. P.* B. 1260 Þay..þat sumtyme sete in her sale syres & burdes. **1422** tr. *Secreta Secret., Priv. Priv.* 217 This yonglynge..aftyr be-came a grete Sire in the realme. **1456** Sir G. Haye *Law Arms* (S.T.S.) 42 And sa was Romulus all hale lord and syre. **1513** Douglas *Æneid* IX. iv. 58 Soupyt in wyne and sleip [are] baith man and syre. *c* **1586** Sidney *Ps.* XVIII. iv, Then thundred heav'nly sire. **1608** Topsell *Serpents* (1658) 780 Podagra..quietly laid herself down at the feet of this corsie sire. **1812** Shelley *Devil's Walk* xxviii, With delight its Sire to see Hell's adamantine limits burn.

†**b.** A lord or ruler *of* a specified place. *Obs.*

*a* **1300** *Cursor M.* 22256 A king..þat of þe romain sal Impire Hali lauerd be and sire. **1338** R. Brunne *Chron.* (1810) 14 In Charlemayn courte, sire of Saynt Dinys. **1390** Gower *Conf.* I. 250 Of thilke Empire He was coroned Lord and Sire. **1415** Hoccleve *To Sir J. Oldcastle* 265 Almighty god thow lord of al, and Syre. *c* **1430** Lydg. *Min. Poems* (Percy Soc.) 25 Where is Pirrus, that was lord and sire Of Ynd? **1526** Skelton *Magnyf.* 1491 Syrus, that soleme syar of Babylon. **1535** Stewart *Cron. Scot.* II. 217 For his reward.., Of tha landis tha maid him lord and syre.

**5.** A person of some note or importance; an aged or elderly man. Also generally, man, fellow.

**1362** Langl. *P. Pl.* A. XI. 62 Nou is vche boye bold broþel an oþer, To talken of þe Trinite to beon holden a syre. *c* **1440** *Ipomydon* 1643 He semyd a fole, that queynte syre, Bothe by hede and by atyre. *a* **1500** *Debate of the Carpenter's tools* 241 in Hazl. *E.P.P.* I. 88 The wymbulle spekes lyke a syre. **1508** Dunbar *Tua Mariit Wemen* 145 Fra sic a syre, God ȝow saif, my sueit sisteris deir! **1548** Udall, etc. *Erasm. Par. Matt.* iv. 32 That maliciouse and crafty olde syre. **1600** Hakluyt *Voy.* (1810) III. 388 Our men, regarding his age, began to make much of him;..whereat the olde sier showed himselfe very glad. **1630** *Tincker of Turvey* 41 This smith was a quaint sire, As merry as bird on brier. **1667** Milton *P.L.* XI. 715 At length a Reverend Sire among them came. **1807** Crabbe *Par. Reg.* I. 688 To name an infant meet our village sires. **1814** Scott *Ld. of Isles* v. xxiv, 'What says the monk?' —'The holy Sire Owns, that..She sought his skiff.'

**6.** A father; a male parent; also, a forefather. (Cf. GRANDSIRE 1.) Now chiefly *poet.*

*c* **1250** *Lutel Soth Serm.* 81 in *O.E. Misc.* 190 Hire sire and hire dame þreteþ hire to bete. **1377** Langl. *P. Pl.* B. Prol. 189, I herde my sire seyn..þere þe catte is a kitoun, þe courte is ful elyng. *c* **1385** Chaucer *L.G.W.* 2492 (*Phyllis*), Fals in loue was he rygh as his syre. *c* **1400** *Destr. Troy* 13198 Þat noble he stale Fro the souerain hir Syre, & soght with hir furth. **14..** *Sir Beues* 1283 + 244 He made a fyre And threwe þer yn dam & syre. **1566** Painter *Pal. Pleas.* I. 4 Whose sire was the old earl of Bedford. **1582** Stanyhurst *Æneis* II. (Arb.) 64 Pyrrhus shortlye wyl hither, Thee soon fast bye the syre, thee syre that murthred at altars. **1674** Milton *P.R.* I. 86 His Mother then is mortal, but his Sire He who obtains the Monarchy of Heav'n. **1697** Dryden *Virg. Georg.* III. 282 Nor be with harmful Parsimony won To follow what our homely Sires have done. **1742** Gray *Adversity* 9 When first thy Sire to send on earth Virtue, his darling Child, design'd. **1791** Cowper *Iliad* II. 57 The sceptre of his sires he took. **1814** Scott *Ld. of Isles* II. xxxii, In distant ages, sire to son Shall tell thy tale of freedom won. **1871** B. Taylor *Faust* (1875) II. III. 177 My sire the daughter gave him and the government.

*attrib.* and *Comb.* *a* **1835** Motherwell *Poet. Wks.* (1847) 10 'Tis Harold—'tis the Sire-bereaved—Who goads the dread career. *a* **1849** Mangan *Poems* (1859) 442 Shame to me,..my sire-land, Not to know thy soil and skies!

**b.** *fig.* and *transf.*

**1718** Prior *The Flies*, Sire of Insects, mighty Sol. **1784** Cowper *Task* II. 674 Profusion is the sire. **1821** Shelley *Adonais* iv, He died, Who was the Sire of an immortal strain. **1871** Earle *Philol. Eng. Tongue* vi. 245 The venerable sire of Gothic philology, Jacob Grimm.

**7.** A male parent of a quadruped; *esp.* a stallion. Correlative to *dam.*

**1523** Fitzherb. *Husb.* §68 She shall haue moste comonly a sandy colte,..neyther lyke syre nor damme. **1594** T. B. *La Primaud. Fr. Acad.* II. 54 Beastes haue no other care of their yong ones, but onely..vntill they bee able to feede.. themselues: afterward, both syre and damme and little ones forget one another. **1607** Topsell *Four-f. Beasts* (1658) 229 The Pharsalian Mores evermore bring Foals very like their Syre. **1697** Dryden *Virg. Past.* I. 32 So Kids and Whelps their Sires and Dams express. **1733** Pope *Ess. Man* III. 126 Thus beast and bird their common charge attend; The mothers nurse it, and the sires defend. **1846** J. Baxter *Libr. Pract. Agric.* (ed. 4) I. 423 Although both sire and dam may possess some good points, yet in the offspring these will be lost. **1859** Jephson *Brittany* iii. 30 They must not feed their sires upon straw.

*transf.* **1780** Cowper *Progr. Err.* 568 The mind and conduct..: Each, sire and dam of an infernal race, Begetting and conceiving all that's base.

**sire** (saɪə(r)), *v.* Also 6 syre. [f. SIRE *sb.*] *trans.* To beget or procreate; to become the sire of:

**a.** Of persons, or in general use.

**1611** Shaks. *Cymb.* IV. ii. 26 Cowards father Cowards, & Base things Syre Bace. **1835** Longf. *Outre-mer* Prose Wks. 1886 I. 119 He was a gross, corpulent fellow,..sired by a comic actor. **1891** Zangwill *Bachelors Club* 82 His father had just that measure of talent which so often sires a genius.

*transf.* **1902** Owen Wister *Virginian* xiv, The blamed thing was sired by a whole doggone Dutch syndicate.

**b.** *spec.* Of animals, esp. horses. (The more frequent use.)

**1828–32** in Webster. **1882** *Pall Mall G.* 1 July 6/2 These also are animals with rare pedigrees... Several are sired by Kisber. **1894** Astley *50 Years Life* II. 190 He sired some real good hunters.

**sire**, obs. variant of Sc. SYRE, drain.

**siredon** (saɪˈriːdən). [a. late L. *Sīrēdon*, ad. Gr. Σειρηδών, late form of Σειρήν SIREN. Named by Wagler (1828–33).] The axolotl.

**1842** *Penny Cycl.* XXII. 56/1 *Siredon*, Wagler's name for the Axolotl. **1875** Cope *Check-list N. Amer. Batrachia* 63 The Siredons, or larval *Amblystomae*. **1879** E. P. Wright *Anim. Life* 402 Dumeril has also shown that the Siredons were capable of reproduction.

**siree**, var. SIRREE.

**sireen** (saɪˈriːn). Also syreen. Repr. colloq. (now chiefly *U.S.*) pronunc. of SIREN *sb.* (esp sense 7 b).

**1915** Kipling *Fringes of Fleet* 11 Five damned trawlers with their syreens blowing. **1940** *Economist* 28 Sept. 398/2 The air raids have produced some more new war words... A quite inexplicable new word is the 'sireen', which has widely ousted the siren. Its slight resemblance to Eileen and Doreen suggests that it may have arisen from a desire to give the noise a feminine personality. **1943** G. Greene *Ministry of Fear* I. i. 16 This time of night... It's the sireens. **1957** W. Faulkner *Town* xxiv. 363 Mr. Connors went to his [car] that had the red light and the sireen on it. **1977** J. Cleary *Vortex* i. 20 The siren began to wail again:..'I wish he'd blow up that goddam si-reen.'

**sireland** (ˈsaɪələnd). *nonce-wd.* [f. SIRE *sb.*, punningly after *Ireland.*] The land of one's birth; one's native country or fatherland.

**1922** Joyce *Ulysses* 182 Cranly's eleven true Wicklowmen to free their sireland. **1939** —— *Finnegans Wake* (1964) 428 Sireland calls you.

**sireless** (ˈsaɪəlɪs), *a.* [f. SIRE *sb.* + -LESS.] Having no sire; fatherless.

**1598** Sylvester *Du Bartas* II. i. I. *Eden* 583 The Beast is lust-less, sex-less, sire-less, mute. *a* **1618** —— *Triumph Faith* III. xxiii, That Mother-Maid, Who Sire-lesse bore her Sire, yet ever-Maid. **1790** A. Wilson *To D. Brodie* Poet. Wks. (1846) 9 The sullen midnight tempest roars; Loud o'er my sireless dome it wildly howls. **1814** Byron *Address Caledonian Meeting* 20 The sireless offspring and the lonely spouse. **1850** Blackie *Æschylus* I. 124 Them sireless see in dire starvation's gripe.

**siren** (ˈsaɪərən), *sb.* Forms: α. 4 sereyn, -ayn, 5 -ayne, 6 *Sc.* seryne, syraine. β. 4–7 *pl.* sirenes (5 syrenes); 6–8 syrene, 7 sirene (syriney). γ. 5– siren. δ. 5– syren. [Ultimately ad. Gr. Σειρήν (pl. Σειρῆνες, first mentioned in *Odyss.* xii. 39 ff.), through L. *Sīrēn* and late L. *Sīrēna*; the latter is the source of It. and Sp. *sirena*, *serena*, Pg. *sereia*, *serea*, F. *sirène*, and OF. *sereine*, *seraine*, whence the earliest forms in English.]

**I.** †**1.** An imaginary species of serpent. *Obs.*

This sense is derived from glossarial explanations of L. *sirenes* in the Vulgate text of *Isaiah* xiii. 22, where the Wycliffite versions have 'wengid edderes' and 'fliynge serpentis'.

1340 *Ayenb.* 61 An eddre þet hatte serayn, þet yernþ more zuyþere þanne hors, and oþerhuyl vleþ [etc.]. [1398 TREVISA *Barth. De P.R.* XVIII. ix. (Bodl. MS.), In Arabia beþ serpentes wiþ winges, þat beþ icleped Sirene,..and here venym is so stronge þat deþe comeþ tofore þe biting.] *c* 1520 ANDREW *Noble Lyfe* III. lxxxiii, Ther be also in some places of arabye, serpentis named sirenes, that ronne faster than an horse, & haue wynges to flye.

**2.** *Classical Mythol.* One of several fabulous monsters, part woman, part bird, who were supposed to lure sailors to destruction by their enchanting singing.

In early use frequently confused with the mermaid.

α. *c* 1366 CHAUCER *Rom. Rose* 684 Though we mermaydens clepe hem here,..Men clepen hem sereyns in Fraunce. 1481 CAXTON *Myrr.* II. ix. 88 They be called seraynes or mermaydens. 1572 *Satir. Poems Reform.* xxxviii. 33 With sangis lyke the seryne our lyfis thow allurit.

β. 1387 TREVISA *Higden* II. 369 þe þre Sirenes, þat were half maydens, half foules, and hadde wynges and clawes. 1390 GOWER *Conf.* I. 58 Sirenes of a wonder kynde Ben Monstres,..And in the grete Se thei duellen. *c* 1407 LYDG. *Reason & Sens.* 1772 Hit passed of force and myght Sirenes song,..Which ar meremaydenes of the se. *c* 1430 —— *Misericordias* 83 Syrenes, with warblys of swetnesse Blente ther resouns. *c* 1520 L. ANDREW *Noble Lyfe* III. lxxxiii, Syrene, the mermayde is a dedely beste that bringeth a man gladly to dethe. 1560 DAUS tr. *Sleidane's Comm.* 18 He must ..sayle besydes theyr songes as the enticementes or daungerous rockes of the Sirenes. 1605 DANIEL *Queen's Arcadia* I. i, The Foggs and the Syrene offends us more. 1648 HEXHAM II, *Een Meer-minne*, a Mer-maide, or a Syriney. 1661 LOVELL *Hist. Anim. & Min.* Isagoge a vj b, The fabulous [birds] are, the..harpie, stymphalides, sirenes,..phœnix. 1726 DE FOE *Hist. Devil* (1822) 265 She talked like an angel, sung like a Syrene.

γ. *c* 1400 *Destr. Troy* 13286 When the Sirens this sene, ..þai wyn to the wale ship, & walton all vnder. 1598 J. DICKENSON *Greene in Conc.* (1878) 148 They hauing Sirens tongues and Crocodiles teares, thereby entic'd him to intangle him. 1621 BURTON *Anat. Mel.* I. ii. II. vi, Voluntary solitariness..brings on like a Siren..some Sphinx to this irrevocable gulf. 1682 SIR T. BROWNE *Chr. Mor.* (1716) 24 There is no Damocles like unto self opinion, nor any siren to our own fawning conceptions. 1753 HOGARTH *Anal. Beauty* vi. 32 The sphinx and siren have been admired, and accounted elegant in all ages. 1776 BURNEY *Hist. Music* (1789) I. II. ii. 310 All ancient authors agree in telling us that Sirens inhabited the coast of Sicily. 1831 KEIGHTLEY *Myth. Anc. Gr. & It.* 246 Hesiod describes the mead of the Sirens as blooming with flowers. 1876 A. S. MURRAY *Mythol.* iii. (1877) 38 The Sirens are strictly personifications, not of the sea, but of the dangers of the sea-coast to sailors.

δ. *c* 1400 *Destr. Troy* 13271, I..sailet þurgh a sea þere Syrens were in. 1657 H. PINNELL *Philos. Ref.* 26 Nimphs, Undens, Melosyns, whose Monsters or bastards are the Syrens that swim upon the water. 1688 HOLME *Armoury* II. 364/1 This is one of the kinds of Mermaids.., and is the right Syren; two of them, about..1670, was brought dead, to our City of Chester,..where I..drew them. 1768–74 TUCKER *Lt. Nat.* (1834) I. 315 When Ulysses stopped the ears of his crew with wax, on sailing by the Syrens. 1820 T. S. HUGHES *Trav. Sicily* I. v. 163 It is of the purest gold, and represents a Syren. 1877 *Times* 17 Feb. 4/4 Projecting from the extreme edges..are, first, 15 birds with human faces —syrens.

**3.** *fig.* One who, or that which, sings sweetly, charms, allures, or deceives, like the Sirens.

γ. 1590 SHAKS. *Com. Err.* III. ii. 47 Oh traine me not sweet Mermaide with thy note, To drowne me in..teares: Sing Siren for thy selfe. *c* 1630 MILTON *At a Solemn Music* 1 Blest pair of Sirens,..Sphear-born harmonious Sisters, Voice and Vers. 1653 BINNING *Serm.* (1845) 595 These are Blessed Sirens that..Pipe..some sad and woful ditties of men's sin. 1756 C. SMART *Horace, Sat.* II. iii. (1826) II. 109 That guilty Siren, sloth, must be avoided. 1768–74 TUCKER *Lt. Nat.* (1834) II. 552 Pleasure is..a very siren, attracting only to devour. 1813 SCOTT *Trierm.* III. xxxii, As round the band of sirens trip, He kiss'd one damsel's laughing lip. 1857 HUGHES *Tom Brown* I. i, To accept the oft-proffered invitation of these sirens. 1884 *Christian World* 19 June 453/2 The influence of the sirens of the political boudoir.

δ. 1588 SHAKS. *Titus A.* II. i. 23 This Queene, This Syren, that will charme Romes Saturnine, And see his shipwracke. 1592 GREENE *Groat's W. Wit* (1617) 7 Deceyuing Syrens, whose eyes are Adamants, whose wordes are Witchcrafts. 1627 E. F. *Hist. Edw. II* (1680) 4 This Syren (as some write) came out of Gascoign. 1665 BOYLE *Occas. Refl.* I. iv, Fortune has seldome yet vouchsaf'd to turn Syren to pervert me. 1756 tr. *Keysler's Trav.* (1760) IV. 13 There are too many instances of intrigues..with these wanton syrens, having been revenged with death. 1789 MRS. PIOZZI *Journ. France* I. 176 These pretty syrens were delighted to seize upon us. 1803 H. K. WHITE *Clifton Grove* 108 Why clasp the syren pleasure to his arms. 1848 GALLENGA *Italy* I. p. xxv, A rosy syren before—Hope,..always receding from its embrace.

†**4.** A drone bee. *Obs. rare.*

1601 HOLLAND *Pliny* I. 318 The Drones at the beginning be termed Sirenes or Cephenes. 1658 ROWLAND tr. *Moufet's Theat. Ins.* 930 Of the Sirens there are two sorts, the one lesse all of a duskie colour; the other bigger, black mixt with other colours.

**5.** One or other of the eel-like gradient and tailed amphibians belonging to the family *Sirenidæ*, native to N. America; esp. the mud-iguana, *Siren lacertina*.

So named by Linnæus on account of the statement made to him by Dr. Garden, that it had a sort of singing voice.

[1766 tr. *Linnæus* in *Phil. Trans.* LVI. 192 It must be a new and very distinct genus, and should most properly have the name of *Siren*.] 1791 SHAW *Nat. Misc.* Pl. 61 The genus with which the Siren has evidently the greatest possible affinity is that of Lacerta or Lizard. 1831 GRIFFITH tr. *Cuvier* IX. 414 The Lacertine Siren (*Siren Lacertina*). 1855 OWEN *Skel. & Teeth* 28 In the siren the pelvic arch and limbs are not developed. 1883 *Science* II. 160/2 This siren will eat crayfish.

**6.** *Anat.* (See first quot. and cf. sense 9.)

1839 *Penny Cycl.* XV. 347/2 In another family of [human] monsters, denominated *Symeles*, or Sirens, the two thoracic or abdominal limbs are fused together into a single member. 1902 *Brit. Med. Jrnl.* 15 Mar. 671 His identification of the Siren with the sympodial fetus..seems exceedingly probable.

**7. a.** An acoustical instrument (invented by Cagniard de la Tour in 1819) for producing musical tones and used in numbering the vibrations in any note. Cf. SIRENE.

1820 *Ann. Reg.* II. 1364 The Syren, a new Acoustical Instrument... In consequence of this property of being sonorous in the water the instrument has been called the Syren. 1870 TYNDALL *Heat* viii. App. 256, I placed a syren within a few feet of the singing flame. 1875 KNIGHT *Dict. Mech.* 2191/1 It has been ascertained by means of the siren that the wings of the mosquito move at the rate of 15,000 times a second. 1884 *Encycl. Brit.* XVII. 104/1 The 'siren' ..consists essentially of a circular plate, revolving on an axis through its centre at right angles to its plane.

**b.** An instrument, made on a similar principle but of a larger size, used on steamships for giving fog-signals, warnings, etc. Also, more generally, a device which produces a piercing note (freq. of varying tone), used as an air-raid warning, or to signify the approach of a police car, etc.; the noise itself. Formerly, a motor-horn.

1879 TYNDALL *Fragm. Sci.* (ed. 6) I. x. 332 He..found that when the syren was sounded no echo was returned. 1880 *Daily News* 27 Dec. 2/2 The Siren can be sounded with either steam or compressed air, made to pass through a fixed flat disc fitted into the throat of a long trumpet. 1897 KIPLING *Capt. Courageous* 11 Harvey heard the muffled shriek of a liner's siren. 1907 [see CUT-OUT *sb.* 1 b]. 1917 *Flying* 25 July 2/2 Tests with various sirens were made in Central London in order to ascertain whether they would be audible. 1940 S. O'CASEY *Let.* 20 Aug. (1975) I. 866 We have a kind of a cellar that we are to go to when the siren sounds. 1943 *Times* (Weekly ed.) 18 Aug. 12/3 The Luftwaffe helps the Church Army. How?—every night there isn't a siren, a Church Army friend puts sixpence in her box and when there is she puts 2s. 6d. in as soon as the 'All Clear' goes. 1963 MRS. L. B. JOHNSON *White House Diary* 22 Nov. (1970) 5 We got in [the car]. Lyndon told the agents to stop the sirens. 1969 G. MACBETH *War Quartet* 43 Then the sirens went, Sucking life underground. 1971 *Daily Tel.* (Colour Suppl.) 22 Oct. 19/3 Pursued by cops, lights flashing, siren wailing, up Brighton Road.

**II.** *attrib.* and *Comb.*

**8. a.** Attrib., in sense 'characteristic of, resembling that of, a Siren', as ***siren air***, ***beauty***, ***note***, etc.

*a* 1568 ASCHAM *Scholem.* I. (Arb.) 75 Noble personages,.. whom all the Siren songes of Italie, could neuer vntwyne from the maste of Gods word. 1588 *Marprel. Epist.* (Arb.) 43 Be not led away by the Syren sounds and intisements of yong Iohn. 1598 SYLVESTER *Du Bartas* II. i. III. *Furies* 787 Whose Syren-notes Inchaunt chaste Susans. 1600 SHAKS. *Sonn.* cxix, What potions haue I drunke of Syren teares? 1665 J. SPENCER *Vulg. Proph.* 2 Soft and siren words and periods which..make a pretty sound in the ear. 1728–46 THOMSON *Seasons, Spring* 991 Her syren-voice, inchanting, draws him on To guileful shores. *a* 1743 SAVAGE *Valentine's Day* 19 Far from that shore, where syren-beauty dwells. 1788 BURNS *Written in Friars-Carse Hermitage* iii, Pleasure with her siren air May delude the thoughtless pair. 1827 KEBLE *Chr. Y., Wednesday before Easter*, Be silent, Praise, Blind guide with siren voice. 1879 FARRAR *St. Paul* (1883) 712 The gentle breathing of the south wind..was but a siren song which had lured them to their destruction.

**b.** Appositive, as ***siren daughter***, ***enemy***, ***hag***, etc.

1641 MILTON *Ch. Govt.* II. Wks. 1851 III. 149 The invocation of Dame Memory and her Siren Daughters. *a* 1680 BUTLER *Rem.* (1759) II. 76 How silly were their Sages heretofore To fright their Heroes with a Syren-whore? 1742 POPE *Dunc.* IV. 541 Others the Syren Sisters warble round, And empty heads console with empty sound. 1768–74 TUCKER *Lt. Nat.* (1834) II. 561 Then the siren enemies are busiest about us. 1794 COLERIDGE *Lines on a Friend who died of a frenzy Fever*, Vice, siren-hag! in native ugliness. 1836 NEWMAN *Siren Isles* in *Lyra Apost.*, The craft of Siren choirs. 1871 FARRAR *Witn. Hist.* ii. 76 When..the music of Memory and her syren daughters has been brought low. 1923 E. SITWELL *Bucolic Comedies* 90 Where siren-birds sip Bohea.

**c.** Forming adjs. or advs., as ***siren-haunted***, ***-voiced***; ***siren-like***.

*a* 1617 BAYNE *Lect.* (1634) 235 Siren-like songs. *a* 1704 T. BROWN *Libertine* i. Wks. 1711 IV. 144 No more shall your Voice, Syren-like, charm my Heart. 1819 MRS. HEMANS *Tales & Hist. Scenes, Death of Conradin* 244 Bid him guide Thy steps Those syren-haunted seas beside. 1879 GEO. ELIOT *Theo. Such* ii. 44 The siren-haunted sea.

**9.** In sense 6, as ***siren form***, ***formation***, ***-like***.

1831 SOUTH *Otto's Path. Anat.* I. 32 The most perfect degree of coalescence in the human subject, the syren formation, in which even the whole of the lower extremities are united into one common limb. 1849–52 *Todd's Cycl. Anat.* IV. II. 964/1 *Sympodia* or Siren-like form. 1883 *Encycl. Brit.* XVI. 764/2 Another curious result of defective separation of symmetrical parts is the siren form of fœtus.

**10.** In sense 7 b, as ***siren alarm***, ***signal***, ***-trumpet***; **siren suit**, a one-piece costume resembling overalls or a boiler-suit, orig. designed for wear by women in air-raid shelters; later, worn by either sex, and as a fashion garment.

1950 G. B. SHAW *Farfetched Fables* II. 107 He is interrupted by a siren alarm, followed by an artillery salvo. 1976 LD. HOME *Way Wind Blows* iv. 72 Some time in the early hours of the next morning there was a siren alarm, and we all trooped down to the basement of No. 10. 1899 F. T. BULLEN *Way Navy* 70 Making our presence known to one another by siren signals. 1939 *English* Autumn 346 Ladies' dress-shops ambiguously advertise 'siren suits' for the Air Raid Shelter. 1942 C. KING *Jrnl.* 17 July in *With Malice toward None* (1970) 183 The Prime Minister..was in his blue siren-suit. 1959 R. COLLIER *City that wouldn't Die* vii. 102 In a minute he [*sc.* Winston Churchill] came—black silk dressing-gown embroidered with gold pheasants over the baby-blue siren suit he called 'my rompers'. 1977 *Belfast Tel.* 19 Jan. 18/7 (Advt.), Good reductions in children's coats and fur siren suits. 1879 TYNDALL *Fragm. Sci.* (ed. 6) I. x. 332 The aërial echoes heard when standing behind the syren-trumpet at the South Foreland.

**'siren**, *v.* Also **syren**. [f. prec.]

**1.** *trans.* To allure, entice, persuade. *rare.*

1690 *Secr. Hist. Chas. II & Jas. II*, 50 The advantageous league which she had pleasantly syren'd her brother to make with the French Monarch. 1935 L. MACNEICE *Poems* 14 Two [women] there are, as I drive in the city... The one sirening me to draw up by the kerb. 1960 T. STACEY *Brothers* xxx. 353 They heard brilliant rippling music like some huge wooden xylophone. With this intricate sound still sirening them they found themselves on a hill top.

**2.** *intr.* To make signals with the siren. Also (of a police car, etc.), to proceed with siren blaring; to make *one's way* thus. Also **'sirening** *ppl. a.*

1895 *Westm. Gaz.* 2 Feb. 5/1 The statement that 'it is the custom of the North German Lloyds to run "syrening and flaring" down the North Sea'..was absurd. 1940 'M. INNES' *Secret Vanguard* x. 106 A sirening ambulance or fire-engine. 1951 R. BRADBURY *Silver Locusts* 50 They slammed the police-wagon door and drove him off into the early morning, his face pressed to the rear window, and just before they sirened over a hill, he saw the red fire..on an ordinary Monday morning on the ordinary planet Earth. 1960 *Guardian* 21 Oct. 13/4 He was sirening up the Henry Hudson parkway. 1965 D. S. DAVIS *Pale Betrayer* xxviii. 206 Fitzgerald sirened his way through the crowd, not leaving the car. 1978 J. I. M. STEWART *Full Term* viii. 86 An ambulance went wildly sirening into St. Giles'.

†**Sirenaic.** *Obs. rare.* [irreg. f. SIREN *sb.*] A member of the celebrated Club which met at the Mermaid Tavern.

Due to confusion of the siren with the mermaid: see SIREN *sb.* 2.

1616 CORYAT *Trav. Eng. Wits* 37 Right Generous, Iouiall, and Mercuriall Sirenaicks. *Ibid.* 42 Farewell noble Sirenaicks!

**'sirename.** *rare.* [Alteration of *sirname* SURNAME, after SIRE *sb.*] A patronymic; a family name.

1542 UDALL *Erasm. Apoph.* 305 b, It should bee called our sire name, that is to say yᵉ name of our fathers bloudde. 1552 *Ord. St. Barthol. Hosp.* D iij, Ye shall manifestly declare.. the names and sirenames of so many as that yeare haue died in the house. 1588 GREENE *Perimedes* Wks. (Grosart) VII. 17 Pharao the last king of Memphis of that sirename. 1871 M. COLLINS *Marq. & Merch.* I. iii. 100 Old Reuben Mowbray had an excellent surname or sirename.

‖**sirene.** Now *rare* or *Obs.* Also **sirène**. [F. *sirène.*] = SIREN *sb.* 7.

1830 *Encycl. Metrop.* (1845) IV. 777 This is precisely the principle of the Sirene of Baron Cagniard de la Tour... The Sound produced is clear and sweet, like the human voice. 1850 *Pract. Mech. Jrnl.* III. 149 (*title*), On the Sirene, a new sound producer. 1866 *Chambers's Encycl.* VIII. 745/1 More complex forms, such as Helmholtz's double sirène.

†**sireneal**, *a. Obs. rare*$^{-1}$. In 6 **syreneall**. [irreg. f. SIREN *sb.*] Of or given by sirens.

1592 R. D. *Hypnerotomachia* 53 b, [Nymphs] which..did alter their Musicke and Instruments, and during the banquetting, others with an Angelike and Syreneall consent, did tune the same to their handes.

†**Sireniacal**, *a. Obs. rare.* [Cf. SIRENAIC.] Belonging to the Mermaid Club.

1616 CORYAT *Trav. Eng. Wits* 32 Pray commend me to M. Protoplast, and all the Sireniacall gentlemen. *Ibid.* 37.

**sirenian** (saɪ'riːnɪən), *sb.* and *a.*[1] *Zool.* [f. mod.L. *Sirenia*, f. L. *Sīrēn* SIREN *sb.*]

**A.** *sb.* Any member of the order *Sirenia* of fish-like aquatic mammals.

1883 *Science* I. 346/1 The discovery of a new fossil sirenian in South Carolina. 1884 GOODE *Nat. Hist. Aquat. Anim.* 114 The Sirenians or Sea-Cows. 1894 LYDEKKER *Roy. Nat. Hist.* II. 567 The existing Sirenians resemble the Cetaceans in having their fore-limbs converted into flippers.

**B.** *adj.* Pertaining to or having the characteristics of the order *Sirenia*.

1891 in *Cent. Dict.*

†**sirenian**, *a.*[2] *Obs.* Also **syrenian**. [f. SIREN *sb.* + -IAN.]

**1.** Of or characteristic of a siren; alluring, seductive, deceitful.

1600 TOURNEUR *Trans. Metamorph.* li, To her Syrenian Song the Knight gave eare. 1633 PRYNNE *1st Pt. Histriom.* Ep. Ded., So desperately infatuated with their Syrenian enchantments. 1648 J. BEAUMONT *Psyche* VIII. cxxxiv, No wanton Dress, no Tongue's Sirenian Grace.

**2.** Inhabited or frequented by alluring women.

1659 HOWELL *Lexicon, Ital. Prov.*, In that Syrenian Citty [Naples] 'tis found that one hair of a woman can draw more then a hundred yoaks of Oxen.

**Sirenian**, var. SIRYENIAN *sb.* and *a.*

**sirenic** (saɪ'rɛnɪk), *a. rare.* Also 8–9 **syrenic** (8 -ick). [f. SIREN *sb.* + -IC.]

**1.** Melodious; charming, fascinating, alluring.

*a*1704 T. Brown *Ep. to Ch. Dives* Wks. 1711 IV. 180 Spell-caught by their Syrenick Voice. 1822 T. G. Wainewright *Ess. & Crit.* (1880) 292, I can truly describe her intense power over me as that of the moon on the restless tides;—a Syrenic song [etc.]. 1877 Ruskin *Fors Clav.* lxxxiii. 360 Which satyric dance and sirenic song accomplished.

2. Of persons: Sweet-singing.

1797 Anna Seward *Lett.* (1811) IV. 393 Nor less was he charmed with the vocal duetts and trios of our syrenic friends.

**si'renical**, *a.* Also 6–7 syrenicall, 7 -ical, sirenicall. [f. as prec. + -ICAL.]

1. = SIRENIC *a.* 1. Now *rare.*

1599 *Broughton's Lett.* ii. 11 This is the Syrenicall allurement of your attendant φιλοδοξία. 1609 Sir E. Hoby *Let. to Mr. T.H.* 4 Freeing..my deare countrimen from your Syrenicall deceit. *Ibid.* 92 Bobbing your credulous Ladies with these Syrenicall insinuations. 1662 in Ellis *Orig. Lett.* Ser. iii. IV. 283 They play on loud virginals joyntly to their singing, which..make up a syrenical and spherical harmony. 1900 Upward *Eben. Lobb* 254 There was not much that was sirenical about this instrument.

†2. = SIRENIC *a.* 2. *Obs.*

1604 Marston *Malcontents* iii. iv, But here's a couple of sirenical rascals shall enchant ye: what shall they sing, my good lord?

Hence **si'renically** *adv.*

1888 *Punch* 4 August 53 We loathe deserted wives and sirenically influenced (if we may coin an epithet) husbands.

**si'reniform**, *a. rare.* [f. SIREN *sb.* 6 + -(I)FORM.] Of human monsters: Having the lower extremities abnormally united in a single limb.

1849–52 *Todd's Cycl. Anat.* IV. ii. 965/1 A surgeon.. supposed that the Sireniform monster had been formed during a very difficult delivery.

**'sirenize**, *v.* Now *rare.* Also 6 syranyze. [f. SIREN *sb.* + -IZE.] *trans.* To delight or charm; to allure or enchant. Also *intr.* (quot. 1656).

1584 H. Constable *Diana* vii. viii, Thy transparent eyes ..Whose dumbe conceits diuinely syranyze. 1592 G. Harvey *Four Lett.* iv. Wks. (Grosart) I. 212 That same gentle kindnes,..that abandoned odious Hatred; That Sirenized Furies. 1623 Cockeram i, *Syrenize*, to enchaunt, to bewitch. 1656 Blount *Glossogr.*, *Sirenize*, to play the Siren, to attract or allure, as Sirens do with singing.

b. To charm *out of* a certain state.

1593 Nashe *Christ's T.* (1613) 123 What soule is so metaphusicall subtile, that can humorously sirenize heauens soule, Iehovah, out of the concealments of his Godhead?

**sirenoid** ('saɪrənɔɪd), *a.* (*sb.*). *Ichth.* [See def. and -OID.] Of or belonging to the group *Sirenoidei* of dipnoid fishes. Also *sb.*, a lung-fish of this group (*Cent. Dict.*).

1875 tr. *Schmidt's Desc. & Darwinism* 238 The notably small division of sirenoid fish which breathe air during the dry season of the year.

†**'sireny.** *Obs. rare.* In 6 syrenie. [f. SIREN *sb.* + -Y.] Allurement, fascination.

1600 Tourneur *Trans. Metamorph.* xvi, Disquiet Eriphila; hel's Syrenie. *Ibid.* xxx, Rowze up the watch, lull'd with world's Syrenie.

**sireship** ('saɪəʃɪp). [f. SIRE *sb.* + -SHIP.] The state or condition of being a sire; paternity, fatherhood; also *fig.*, authorship.

1837 C. Lofft *Self-formation* II. 94 The Two Gentlemen must be left at large, to walk abroad and plume themselves in the false bravery of their sireship. 1882 *Standard* 4 Sept. 6/1 His credentials bid fair for the success of his sireship.

**'siress.** *nonce-word.* [f. SIRE *sb.* + -ESS.] A mother; a matron.

1804 Eugenia de Acton *Tale without Words* II. 176 But softly, ye venerable sires and siresses!

**sirex** ('saɪrɛks). *Ent.* Also Sirex. [mod.L. (Linnæus *Fauna Suecica* (ed. 2, 1761) 396), f. Gr. σειρήν siren, a solitary bee or wasp.] A wood-wasp or horntail of the genus *Sirex*, whose larvæ burrow into the trunks of trees. Also *attrib.*

1895 *Cambr. Nat. Hist.* V. 509 The *Sirex* will..attack a perfectly healthy tree immediately after it has been felled. 1908 A. T. Gillanders *Forest Entomol.* v. 190 The female *Sirex*..is armed with a long ovipositor. 1928 *Bull. Entomol. Res.* XIX. 219 (*heading*) The *Sirex* wood-wasps and their importance in forestry. 1958 *N.Z. Timber Jrnl.* Sept. 87/1 The sirex woodwasp..attacks live and freshly felled trees. 1969 *Sun* (Melbourne) 26 June 16/2 The dreaded sirex wasp has been found in pine plantations.

**sirfoot**, obs. Sc. form of SURFEIT *a.*

**sirgirie**, obs. form of SURGERY.

**sirha**, obs. form of SIRRAH.

**Sirian** ('sɪrɪən), *a.* and *sb. Astr.* Also 6–7 Syrian. [f. SIRI-US + -AN.]

1. Of or belonging to Sirius.

1591 Spenser *M. Hubberd* 5 And the hot Syrian Dog on him [*sc.* the sun] awayting,..Corrupted had th'ayre. 1611 Beaum. & Fl. *Philaster* v. iii, The worthier beasts have made their layers, and slept Free from the Syrian Star. 1685 Caryll in *Dryden's Misc. Poems* (1727) I. 306 Thrice happy Swains, guarded from Sirian Beams By sacred Springs. 1874 Proctor *Expanse of Heaven* 246 We must set all the Sirian planets circling much more rapidly than the corresponding members of the solar family. 1885 Clerke *Pop. Hist. Astron.* 417 A spectrum of the Sirian pattern.

2. Having a spectrum like that of Sirius.

1892 *Photogr. Ann.* II. 138 The former star..is more nearly allied to the Sirian stars in the distribution of energy in its spectrum. 1903 A. R. Wallace *Man's Place in Universe* vi. 130 Other astronomers call the first group 'Sirian stars', because Sirius though not the hottest is a characteristic type.

3. *absol.* as *sb.* A star having a spectrum like that of Sirius.

1900 *Edin. Rev.* Apr. 461 Helium or Orion stars merge imperceptibly into Sirians, Sirian into Solar.

‖**siriasis** (sɪ'raɪəsɪs). *Path.* [a. L. *sīriāsis*, a. Gr. σειρίᾱσις, f. σειριᾶν to be hot and scorching.] A disease affecting children, characterized by inflammation of the brain and membranes, and burning fever. Cf. SIDERATION 3.

1601 Holland *Pliny* II. 397 Yong infants many times be tormented with an vnnaturall heat and burning of their head, called Siriasis. 1693 tr. *Blancard's Phys. Dict.* (ed. 2), *Sirricasis* [sic], an Inflammation, or rather great Heat of the Brain and its Membranes, occasion'd by the heat of the Sun. 1879 Lewis & Short *Lat. Dict.* 1710/3. 1898 P. Manson *Trop. Dis.* xii. 203 The very definite and probably specific disease described under the name siriasis.

**siriema**, variant of SERIEMA.

**Sirien**, obs. variant of SYRIAN *sb.*

‖**sirih** ('sɪərɪ). *Bot.* Also seri, sireh, siri. [Malay *sirih.*] **a.** A trailing tropical shrub, *Piper betle*, of the family Piperaceæ, native to Indonesia, where the pungent leaves are chewed with areca nuts; also, the leaves of the shrub; = BETEL 1.

1779 T. Forrest *Voyage to New Guinea* vi. 75 The Malays call the betel leaf, Ciry. 1783 W. Marsden *Hist. Sumatra* 74 The *Seeree*, a creeping plant, whole leaf, of a strong aromatic flavor, they eat with the betel nut. 1795 tr. *C. P. Thunberg's Trav.* (ed. 2) II. 268 The betel leaves, called Siri (*Piper betel*), are therefore brought in fresh every day for sale. 1839 T. J. Newbold *Straits of Malacca* I. ii. 87 The parents.. offer a small present of plantains, sirih, tobacco, etc. 1866 *Treas. Bot.* 1064/1. 1869 A. R. Wallace *Malay Archip.* I. 126 In a small Bamboo case..the Dyak carries his sirih and lime for betel chewing. 1882 De Windt *Equator* 72 Mats were spread out, and siri and betel-nut produced.

**b.** *attrib.*, as *sirih-box, juice, leaf, vine.*

1839 *Chinese Repository* VII. 130 His betel and siri box. 1846 H. Keppel *Exped. to Borneo of H.M.S. Dido* II. i. 13 His majesty chewed his sīrih-leaf and betel-nut. 1864 D'Almeida *Life in Java* II. 104 Chewing tobacco betel, and seri leaf. 1869 A. R. Wallace *Malay Archip.* I. 271 A married woman may not accept..a sirih leaf from a stranger. 1881 *Bock's Head-Hunters Borneo* ii. 19 Other princes.. squatted on the floor, each with his large silver-gilt sirih-box, and a huge brass spittoon in their midst. 1893 F. A. Swettenham *About Perak* 38 Here the Malay lives under his sireh-vine and durian tree. 1939 A. Keith *Land below Wind* xiii. 211, I looked back at the kampong women..; their lips, red with *sireh* juice, like cerise flowers.

**siringe**, obs. form of SYRINGE.

‖**'siris.** *Bot.* Also siriss, sirris. [Hindī *siris.*]

**a.** One or other of several leguminous trees of the genus *Albizzia*, native to tropical Asia and Africa. **b.** A similar tree belonging to the genus *Acacia*, esp. *A. sirissa.*

1874 Stewart & Brandis *Flora N. West India* 176 *A*[*lbizzia*] *Lebbek*,..Siris. *Ibid.* 177 *A*[*lbizzia*] *Julibrissin*,.. Pink Siris. 1883 *Cassell's Fam. Mag.* Oct. 685/1 The *Coccus lacca*..is also found on..the Siriss (*Acacia sirissa*). 1896 *Academy* 28 Nov. 458/1 The broad Mall [of Lahore], embowered in siris and peepul trees.

*attrib.* 1886 Kipling *Departm. Ditties* 114 Ah! *köil*, little *köil*, singing on the *siris* bough.

‖**Sirius** ('sɪrɪəs). *Astr.* Also 6 Ser-, Syrius. [L. *Sīrius*, ad. Gr. Σείριος.] A fixed star of the first magnitude, the chief of the constellation Canis Major or Great Dog, and the brightest in the heavens; the dog-star.

*c* 1374 Chaucer *Boeth.* i. met. v. (1868) 22 þe sedes þat.. arcturus saw ben waxen heye cornes whan þe sterre sirius eschaufeþ hym. 1555 Eden *Decades* (Arb.) 294 *marg.*, Serius is otherwyse cauled Canicula, this is the dogge of whom the Canicular dayes haue theyr name. 1582 Stanyhurst *Æneis* iii. (Arb.) 75 Thee fields cleene fruictlesse thee dogstar Sirius heated. 1697 Dryden *Æneid* x. 382 So Sirius, flashing forth sinister lights, Pale human kind with..famine frights. 1715 tr. *Gregory's Astron.* (1726) I. 512 An Image of the Sun, as bright as Sirius to an Eye given in Position. 1727 W. Broome *Poems* 38 When sultry Sirius..Flames in the Air, and cleaves the glowing Plains. 1756 Mason *Ode Memory* ii. Poems (1774) 20 If Sirius flame with fainting heat. 1847 Tennyson *Princ.* v. 252 As the fiery Sirius alters hue, And bickers into red and emerald. 1883 Jefferies *Story My Heart* i, I prayed..now with the Pleiades, now with the Swan or burning Sirius.

*transf.* 1891 Hardy *Tess* (1900) 83/2 Each gem turned into an Aldebaran or a Sirius—a constellation of white, red, and green flashes, that interchanged their hues with her every pulsation.

‖**sirkar** ('sɜːkɑː(r)). *Anglo-Ind.* Forms: α. 7 sercar(e, -carr, -cor; 7 sarkar, 9 surcar; 8 sircâr, 8–9 sircar, 9 sirkar. β. 7 cercarr, circare, 8–9 circar. [Urdū (Pers.) *sarkār*, f. Pers. *sar* head + *kār* agent, doer.]

†1. The court or palace of a native king or prince. *Obs.*

1619 in Foster *Eng. Factories India* (1906) I. 160 We weare sent for to the Governors to cutt price of our clothes for the Princes sercarr. 1623 *Ibid.* (1908) II. 303 [Three pictures] delivered into the Prince his sercare. 1626 *Ibid.* (1909) III. 141 [A commodity] which beloungeth to our masters cercare.

2. A province; a revenue division. Cf. CIRCAR.

1627 in Foster *Eng. Factories India* (1909) III. 176 The Decies of Surrat Cercare..will not obey the Kings firmaen, though the Divan..seemeth to urge them. 1796 Morse *Amer. Geog.* II. 532 Large provinces called Soubahs, which were subdivided into sircars and Purgunnahs. 1800 *Asiatic Ann. Reg.* II. 15/2 The great failure has occurred in the northern sircars; where..the collections are still attended with difficulty. 1806 T. Maurice *Ind. Antiq.* I. 285 Multan contains 3 sircars, divided into 8 pergunnahs.

3. The State or Government.

1798 Edmonstone in Owen *Wellesley's Desp.* (1877) 61 The allied Sircars look to no other object than the security and tranquillity of their own dominions. 1800 Wellington in Gurw. *Desp.* (1844) I. 54 To make the people pay the circar according to the exchange fixed at Seringapatam. 1883 Mateer *Travancore* (1891) 179 The principal temples ..are under the immediate control of the Sirkar or native Government. 1896 B. M. Croker *Village Tales* 118, I fled to the plains, where I have taken road contracts for the Sirkar, and prospered.

4. A house-steward (usu. native).

1772 Verelst *View Eng. Govt. Bengal* Gloss. p. v, In common usage in Bengal, the under Banyans of European gentlemen are called *Sircars.* 1776 *Trial of Nundocomar* 47/2 The cloth which common sircars tie round their loins. 1796 Eliza Hamilton *Lett. Hindoo Rajah* (1811) II. 187 My English Sircar, who has the uncontrolled disbursement of my money. *c* 1803 Mrs. Sherwood in *Life* (1847) xv. 269 These persons were..stewards, or head servants,—persons in Calcutta called Circars.

5. A native writer or accountant; a clerk employed in a merchant's office for making purchases, etc.

1828 *Asiatic Costumes* 41 The surcars are brokers, agents, and clerks, in all the public offices in Calcutta. 1905 *Statesman* 23 Aug. 3/4 The accused..was a bill collecting sircar in the employ of the complainant.

‖**'sirki.** *Anglo-Ind.* Also 9 sirky, seerky. [Hindī *sirkī.*] **a.** The upper part of the culm of a species of tall reed-grass, *Saccharum Munjia* or *Sara*, native to India. **b.** Matting made of this.

1801 *Asiatick Researches* VII. 463 *Hoogla* or *Sirkee* mats. 1810 T. Williamson *Vade Mecum* I. 489 This *seerky* is composed of the stems of the *surput*, or tassel grass. *Ibid.* 490 In India those itinerants [*sc.* gipsies]..invariably shelter themselves under *seerky.* 1866 *Treas. Bot.* 1064/1 Sirki. 1886 Yule & Burnell *Anglo-Ind. Gloss.* 666/1 It is from the upper part of the flower-bearing stalk of surkunda that sirky is derived.

**sirloin** ('sɜːlɔɪn). Forms: α. 5–8 surloyn, 6–7 -loyne, 7 -loi(g)ne, -line, 8– surloin (8 sur-loin). β. 6 serlyn, 7 sir-loyne, 8 sir-loyn, sirloyn; 7 s^r^loin, 8 sir loin, 8–9 sir-loin, 8– sirloin. [ad. OF. *surloigne, var. of *surlonge*, f. *sur* over, above + *longe* LOIN *sb.* The spelling *sirloin* shows the same tendency as *sirname* for *surname*, *sirples* (obs.) for *surplice*; its final prevalence may have been largely due to the fictitious etymology variously stated in the following quotations.

1655 Fuller *Ch. Hist.* vi. ii. 299 A Sir-loyne of beef was set before Him (so knighted, saith tradition, by this King Henry [the Eighth]). 1732–8 Swift *Polite Conv.* ii. 121 *Miss.* But, pray, why is it call'd a Sir-loyn? *Lord Sparkish.* Why,..our King James First,..being invited to Dinner by one of his Nobles, and seeing a large Loyn of Beef at his Table, he drew out his Sword, and..knighted it. 1822 *Cook's Oracle* 163 Sir-Loin of Beef. This joint is said to owe its name to King Charles the Second, who dining upon a Loin of Beef,..said for its merit it should be knighted, and henceforth called Sir-Loin.]

1. The upper and choicer part of a loin of beef, used for roasting. Also const. *of.*

α. 1554 *Church-w. Acc., St. Marg. Westminster* (Nichols, 1797) 14 A surloyn of beef, 6*s.* 8*d.* 1559–60 *Old City Acc. Bk.* in *Archæol. Jrnl.* XLIII. 175 Paide for a surloyne of beffe, vs iiijd. 1630 J. Taylor (Water P.) *Gt. Eater Kent* 9 A calfe, a surloyne of roast biefe, a pigge. 1661 Pepys *Diary* 21 Nov., We had a good surloyne of rost beefe. 1718 *Free-thinker* No. 9. 57 Many..prefer..a Surloin of Beef, or a Haunch of Venison. 1740 Somerville *Hobbinol* ii. 132 A Spit he seiz'd, Just reeking from the fat Surloyn. 1827 J. F. Cooper *Prairie* II. ii. 23 When he has gotten his surloin or his steak. 1885 *Times* 9 Apr. 9 The production of a perfect shorthorn surloin.

*fig.* 1596 Nashe *Saffron Walden* 48 Let's haue a dozen spare ribs of his rethorique,..and a whole surloyne of his substantiallest sentences and similes.

*attrib.* 1601 in *Househ. Ord.* (1790) 296 The surloine peece of the beefe. 1885 *Times* 9 Apr. 9 A riband-patterned surloin steak.

β. 1525 *Old City Acc. Bk.* in *Archæol. Jrnl.* XLIII. 172 Payd to the Bochsar for a greyt serlyn, xvid. 1623 *Althorp MS.* in Simpkinson *Washingtons* (1860) App. 46 A s^r^loin, a rumpe,..and a rond of beef. 1630 J. Taylor (Water P.) *Wks.* i. 119/1 When..fish is gone,..then these venerable fathers..can take a Sir-loyne of Beefe [etc.]. 1712 Addison *Spect.* No. 517 ¶2 He had lost his Roast-Beef Stomach, not being able to touch a Sirloin. 1760 Sarah Fielding *Ophelia* (1785) II. iv, The first cut of a sirloin of beef was better. 1819 S. Rogers *Human Life* 13 Then the huge ox shall yield the broad sir-loin. 1836 T. Hook *G. Gurney* III. 67, I hold it an article of faith to have a sirloin of beef upon my table on Sunday. 1865 Miss Braddon *Doctor's Wife* xv, A side-table was laid for him, and a great sirloin was brought in.

**b.** *transf.* Of persons.

1648 Mayne *Amorous War* i. i, I doe feele, One of my Surloynes going. 1757 E. Perronet *Mitre* ii. lxxxvii, The news makes all their Sur-loins crack: Down drops each stounded head. 1823 Byron *Age of Bronze* xviii, To see proud Albyn's tartans as a belt Gird the gross sirloin of a city Celt.

**2.** With punning allusion to SIR *sb.* 1. (Cf. the etym. note above.)

**1630** J. TAYLOR (Water P.) *Great Eater of Kent* 10 That he should presently enter combate with a worthy knight, called Sir Loyne of Beefe, and ouerthrow him.

† **sirly**, *a. Obs. rare.* Also 4 serreli, 6 serly, syrlye. [f. SIR *sb.* + -LY[1]. Cf. SURLY *a.*] Lordly, haughty, imperious.

*c* **1350** *Will. Palerne* 3316 Now William..stifli forþ rides, so serreli þurþ þe cite al him-self one, þat eche weiȝh was a-wondred. **1570** LEVINS *Manip.* 100 Serly, *imperiosus.* **1579** SPENSER *Sheph. Cal.* July 203 Sike syrlye shepheards han we none, They keepen all the path. **1600** HOLLAND *Livy* XXXV. xxxviii. 911 Syrly lords (say they) were the Macedonians, and rigorous. **1648** J. BEAUMONT *Psyche* XIX. i, Thine own erected head To far more solid Wretchedness doth bow Than ever made the vilest Reptile be The foot-stool of Contempt to sirly Thee.

**sirmark** (ˈsɜːmɑːk), *sb.* Also 9 surmark. [f. MARK *sb.*[1] The first element is prob. *sur-* over, above, although *sir-* is the earlier and more usual form.] One or other of several marks made upon a mould to indicate where the respective bevellings are to be applied to the frame-timbers of a vessel.

α. **1664** E. BUSHNELL *Compl. Shipwright* 15 Make Sirmarks to them. **1711** W. SUTHERLAND *Shipbuild. Assist.* 26 Then hang up a Ribbon at the Floor Sirmark. *Ibid.* 52 In the Length, 3, 4, or 5 Sirmarks are made, according to the Length of the Piece. **1797** *Encycl. Brit.* (ed. 3) XVII. 401/1 The lowermost diagonal..which is named the lower sirmark, at which place the bevellings are taken for the hollow of the floors. **1833** RICHARDSON *Merc. Mar. Arch.* 4 Length of midship floor 10 feet 3 inches from sirmark to sirmark. **1879** *Cassell's Techn. Educ.* IV. 190/1 A line or batten is stretched from some point in the middle-line of the keel to the corresponding heads or sirmarks on opposite sides.

β. **1846** A. YOUNG *Naut. Dict.* 250 The points, called surmarks, where the respective bevellings are to be applied to the timbers. **1894** *Outing* XXIV. 21/2 A cross..on the staff line and also on the stem..called the surmark.

Hence ˈ**sirmark** *v.* ? *Obs.*

**1664** E. BUSHNELL *Compl. Shipwright* 16 The Moulds being made and Sirmarked to the body of the Vessell.

**sirmyse**, obs. form of SURMISE *v.*

**sirname**, obs. form of SURNAME.

**siroc** (ˈsaɪrɒk, sɪˈrɒk). Forms: α. 8– siroc (9 sirocc). β. 8–9 sciroc. γ. 8–9 siroch. [a. earlier F. *siroc, siroch* (now *siroco*), or ad. It. *sirocco.*] = SIROCCO *sb.* 1.

Freq. written with a capital letter.

α. **1775** in ASH. **1786** *European Mag.* IX. 286 The fierce Siroc prevails! **1800** SOUTHEY in C. C. Southey *Life* (1849) II. 93 A detestable burning blast, a bastard sort of siroc. **1827** MONTGOMERY *Pelican Isl.* III. 25 Every wind From the hot Siroc to the wet Monsoon. **1867** EMERSON *May-Day*, etc. Wks. (Bohn) III. 438 These the siroc could not melt.

β. **1789** [see b]. **1819** W. S. ROSE *Lett.* I. 289, I attribute..this strange influence of perfumes to the Sciroc. **1879** M. D. CONWAY *Demonol.* I. II. vii. 184 Here sciroc, there hurricane, and often tornado.

γ. **1800** HELENA WELLS *Constantia Neville* (ed. 2) I. 261 The grass looked as if it had endured the baleful effects of the blighting Siroch. **1825–9** MRS. SHERWOOD *Lady of Manor* V. xxix. 122 That woody vale,..where no burning siroch blows.

**b.** *attrib.* and *Comb.*

**1789** MRS. PIOZZI *Journ. France* I. 190 A sciroc wind, or a rainy day, or a hard frost. *c* **1808** R. K. PORTER *Russ. & Swed.* (1813) II. xlii. 193 The Siroc sultriness and oppression..increases at every step. **1809** BRYDONE *Tour thro' Sicily* xx. 207 Lest we should be caught by the Siroc winds. **1829** POE *Tamerlane* Poems (1859) 215 Like rain Upon the Siroc-withered plain.

**sirocco** (sɪˈrɒkəʊ), *sb.* Also 7 syrocco, 8 syrocca, serocco; 7, 9 scirocco, 9 scirrocco. [a. It. *sirocco, scirocco* (also *scilocco*), = Sp. *siroco* (also *xaloque*), Pg. *xarouco*, Prov. *siroc*, older F. *siroc, siroch* (also *siloc, sciloque*, etc.), ad. Arab. *sharq* east, f. *sharaqa* (the sun) rose. Cf. prec.]

**1. a.** An oppressively hot and blighting wind, blowing from the north coast of Africa over the Mediterranean and affecting parts of Southern Europe (where it is also moist and depressing). Usually with *the.*

α. **1617** MORYSON *Itin.* I. 211 The South-East winde (which the Italians call Syrocco) did blow very contrary to us. **1667** MILTON *P.L.* x. 706 Forth rush..Eurus and Zephir with thir lateral noise, Sirocco, and Libecchio. **1756–7** tr. *Keysler's Trav.* (1760) II. 96 The woods south of Rome are kept up as a fence against the *Sirocco*, or south-west wind. *a* **1791** WESLEY *Serm.* lxix. Wks. 1811 IX. 251 There will be no Sirocco in Italy. **1818** MRS. ILIFF *Poems sev. Occas.* (ed. 2) 120 When dire Sirocco..From Afric's burning sands mephitic vapours brings. **1859** HAWTHORNE *Marble Faun* xl, Where the sirocco steals away their strength. **1884** F. M. CRAWFORD *Rom. Singer* I. 21 The sirocco was blowing up and down the streets.

*transf.* **1848** J. S. ROBINSON *Sk. Gt. West* 17 The dreaded Sirocco..burns us even through our clothes. **1870** *Weekly Standard* (Buenos Aires) 21 Dec. (Suppl.) col. 6 The Sirocco on Wednesday was so terrible that in the effort to keep cool, the mind reverted to icebergs and Polar travels but all in vain. **1872** E. BRADDON *Life India* ii. 14 From the west blows a scorching wind, the *sirocco* of..the Daodpore desert.

β. **1819** SHELLEY *Lett.* Prose Wks. 1880 IV. 134 My health is better so long as the scirocco blows. **1861** MISS BEAUFORT *Egypt. Sepulch. & Syrian Shrines* II. 223 Under the balmy skies of the early spring, before the horrible scirocco begins to blow. **1866** HOWELLS *Venet. Life* iii. 33 The insidious heat of the scirocco.

**b.** With *a* and pl.

α. **1700** J. JACKSON *Let.* 2 Feb. in *Private Corr. S. Pepys* (1926) I. 278 But the weather being changed and the Sciroccos now blowing into the place of the Tramontains, this design is become impracticable. **1820** BYRON *Mar. Fal.* I. ii. 572 The atmosphere is thick and dusky; 'Tis a sirocco. **1884** *St. James's Gaz.* 11 Dec. 10/2 The storm..was followed by a sirocco, which lasted until noon.

β. **1841** FITZGERALD *Lett.* (1889) I. 71 We have incessant rain, which is as bad as your sciroccos. **1860** MRS. HARVEY *Cruise Claymore* vii. 134 A khamseen was blowing;..this wind, which is an exaggerated scirocco, brings clouds of hot sand from the desert.

**c.** *fig.* A blighting influence; a fiery storm.

**1864** G. A. SALA *Quite Alone* I. ii. 40 Now Scandal's sirocco seized a spiteful anecdote, and twirled and twisted and sent it spinning. **1865** J. H. INGRAHAM *Pillar of Fire* (1872) 401, I..have passed through a sirocco of the soul.

**2.** *ellipt.* A sirocco drying-machine (see 3).

**1890** *Daily News* 2 Sept. 2/5 When the hops have been sufficiently rolled..they are..placed in the drying machine or sirocco. **1892** WALSH *Tea* 105 In the process of 'firing' the leaves are..placed in layers in a hot-air machine, known as a 'Sirocco'.

**3.** *attrib.*, as ***sirocco blast, -dust, fog, gale, weather, wind***; also **sirocco fan**, a fan for forcing a strong current of air into a mine, etc.; **sirocco drying-closet, drying-machine, oven**, a closet, machine, or oven for drying hops or tea-leaves, by means of a hot, moist current of air (cf. 2).

**1894** GLADSTONE *Horace* III. xxiii. 5 Your vines shall mock *scirocco blasts. **1885** C. G. W. LOCK *Worksh. Rec.* Ser. IV. 115/2 About a third of the tea..is cured in Davidson's so-called '*sirocco' drying-closets. **1890** *Pall Mall G.* 1 Oct. 2/3 The first '*Sirocco' drying machine (in which hops are being made into tea). **1879** *Encycl. Brit.* X. 266/1 The dust or sand of dried lakes..borne away into the upper regions of the atmosphere,..may descend again..in the form of 'red-fog', 'sea-dust', or '*sirocco-dust'. **1861** MISS BEAUFORT *Egypt. Sepulch. & Syrian Shrines* II. xxiii. 295 The mountains..were veiled in a dreamy, sad-looking *scirocco fog. **1895** F. M. CRAWFORD *Casa Braccio* xxxvi, Then came November with its pestilent *sirocco gales and its dampness. **1890** *Daily News* 2 Sept. 2/5 The machinery consists of a *Sirocco oven and a patent tea roller. **1897** HUGHES *Mediterranean Fever* v. 193 It [*sc.* ice] will also be needed in warm and *sirocco weather. **1777** A. ADAMS in *Fam. Lett.* (1876) 253 The same effect..which..the *sirocco winds have upon the inhabitants of Sicily. **1794** SULLIVAN *View Nat.* I. 19 An enfeebling and unhinging power, like that of the Sirocco wind.

**siˈrocco**, *v. rare.* Also scirocco. [f. the sb.] *intr.* and *trans.* To blow (about) like the sirocco.

**1921** D. H. LAWRENCE *Let.* 16 Nov. (1962) II. 677 It has blown, the wind, and snowed on Calabria, and sciroccoed till we are all of us in fragments. **1937** J. SQUIRE *Honeysuckle & Bee* vi. 170 The monotonous maudlin refrain of a song about the Isle of Capri... As it faded away, I remembered where, when it had already sciroccoed the world for six months, I had last heard it.

**siˈroccoish**, *a. nonce-word.* In 9 scir-. [f. SIROCCO *sb.* + -ISH.] Somewhat resembling that produced by the sirocco; oppressively hot and moist.

**1837** J. F. COOPER *England* (ed. 2) III. 195 We are more elastic..in a clear bracing air, than in one that is close and sciroccoish.

**siron**, variant of CIRON *Obs.*

The Latin pl. *sirones, syrones* occurs in works of the 17th cent., as the transl. of Mouffet's *Theat. Insects* (1658) 1094.

**1744** tr. *Boerhaave's Inst.* III. 294 The Sirons, as they are called, dwell in these Cells when they cause the Itch.

‖**sirop** (siro, ˈsiːrɒp). [Fr.: see SYRUP *sb.*] (A drink made from) a sweetened fruit-juice concentrate.

**1871** *Monthly Packet* Oct. 369 The sirops and Savoy cakes had been disposed of. **1889** E. SIMCOX in K. A. McKenzie *E. Simcox & G. Eliot* (1961) ii. 55 Ending up..with *sirop* at some café in the small hours. **1933** 'G. ORWELL' *Down & Out* xvii. 126 Two children..sharing a glass of *sirop.* **1966** H. YOXALL *Fashion of Life* xxiii. 206 We consumed *sirops* called *citronade, grenadine, framboise.* **1978** *Times* 22 July 8/7 The continental 'sirops', in mint, grenadine and blackcurrant flavours, are available in good delicatessens..for under £1.50.

**sirope**, obs. f. SYRUP.

**sirp(e)cloth**, varr. of SURPCLOTH *Obs.*

**sirples, -us**, obs. ff. SURPLICE.

**sirrah** (ˈsɪrə). Now *arch.* Forms: α. 6 syra, syrra (syrria?), 6–7 sirra. β. 6 syrha, syrrha, 6–7 sirha, sirrha. γ. 6 sirah, 7 syrrah, 7– sirrah. δ. 6 serea, serray, serrha, 9 *dial.* serrah. See also STIRRAH. [f. SIR *sb.* The additional syllable had probably no definite origin, though explained by Minsheu as the interj. *ah* or *ha.*]

**1.** A term of address used to men or boys, expressing contempt, reprimand, or assumption of authority on the part of the speaker; sometimes employed less seriously in addressing children.

α. **1526** *100 Merry Tales* (Rastell) xlii, Sirra I vnderstand that thou dost ly euery night with my wyfe when I am from home. **1548** CROWLEY *Confut. N. Shaxton* G j b, A, syra, there said you wel! **1605** SHAKS. *Macb.* IV. ii. 30 Sirra, your Fathers dead, And what will you do now? **1641** W. MOUNTAGU in *Buccleuch MSS.* (Hist. MSS. Comm.) I 289 The Bishop saying 'Sir', was mistaken to have said Sirra, and called to the bar.

β. **1553** T. WILSON *Rhet.* 2 Sirha, when our..graundsires were aliue thei spake plainly in their mothers tongue. **1579** G. HARVEY *Two Lett.* ii. 64 Ah Syrrha, and Iesu Lord, thought I, haue we at last gotten one, of whom his olde..Companions may iustly glory. **1592** KYD *Sp. Trag.* II. v. 61 Syrha, sirha, Ile know the trueth of all. **1601** HOLLAND *Pliny* XXXV. x. II. 538 Sirrha, (quoth he) remember you are but a shoemaker.

γ. **1598** B. JONSON *Ev. Man in Hum.* I. i, But, heare you, sirah. **1631** *High Commission Cases* (Camden) 194 Nay, sirrah,..I knowe not what will become of you. **1656** S. HOLLAND *Don Zara* 171 Syrrah, Though I cannot prove how, or where thou attainedst those glorious Arms, yet [etc.]. **1709** STEELE *Tatler* No. 105 ¶3, I assure you Sirrah, I wont go to the Devil for you. **1796** MME. D'ARBLAY *Camilla* IV. 169 Sirrah, I'll break your bones! **1821–2** SHELLEY *Chas. I*, ii. 106 Go, sirrah, and repent of your offence Ten minutes in the rain. **1855** KINGSLEY *Westw. Ho!* vii, 'You mean Captain Drake, your worship?' 'I do, sirrah'.

δ. **1547** HOOPER *Answ. Bp. Winchester* T j, See thy God, knele downe serea and hold upp thy handes. **1566** DRANT *Horace Sat.* I. iii. B iij b, What serray what I say? (Quod he) doste thou not know thy selfe? **1570** LEVINS *Manip.* 1 Serrha, *heus, io.* **1833** CLOSE *Satirist* 164 I'll fetch the, thau idle serrah!

**b.** Used attributively with appellations or proper names.

**1588** SHAKS. *L.L.L.* III. 121 Sirra Costard, I will infranchise thee. **1591** GREENE *Conny Catch.* I. Wks. (Grosart) X. 59 Sirrha collier, know that we are here all assembled as a grand Iurie. **1603** DEKKER & CHETTLE *Grissil* II. i, But, Sirha Rice, when's the day? **1663** COWLEY *Cutter of Coleman Str.* I. ii, I, Sirra Jack-an-apes, if you start when your father speaks to you. **1860** AINSWORTH *Ovingdean Grange* IX. ii. 341 Give me a glass of brandy, sirrah host.

†**2.** Applied to women (seriously or in jest). *Obs.*

**1604** DEKKER *Honest Wh.* II. i, Sirrah Bellafront,..thou shalt sit at the upper end, punk. **1617** FLETCHER *Valentinian* II. iv, Ah Sirrah; And have we got you here? faith Noble Lady, We'l keep you one month Courtier. **1676** ETHEREDGE *Man of Mode* III. i, Adod, sirrah, I like thy wit well. **1710** SWIFT *Jrnl. Stella* vii, You lose all your money at cards, sirrah Stella. **1711** *Ibid.* 11 July, Stella, hussy, don't you remember, sirrah [etc.].

**sirree.** *dial.* Also sur-, sor-, sarree. [f. SIR *sb.* (cf. prec.); prob. a modification of the common dialect *sirry, surry*, etc.] Sir, sirrah. See also NO SIREE, YES SIREE.

**1823** *Knight's Quarterly Mag.* I. 300 Oi say, sirree, where be'st the gwain?

**sirreng**, obs. form of SYRINGE.

**sir-ˈreverence**, *sb. Obs.* exc. *dial.* Also 6 se-, save, 7 sa-reverence. [Alteration of *save* (abbreviated to *sa'*) *reverence*: see SAVE *prep.* 4 and REVERENCE *sb.* 5.]

†**1.** ***sir-reverence of***, with all respect for, with apologies to. (Cf. REVERENCE *sb.* 5.) *Obs.*

**1575** *Gamm. Gurton* v. ii, Sir reuerence of your masterdome, and you were out a-doore [etc.]. **1594** LODGE & GREENE *Looking Gl.* 326 And sir, sir-reuerence of your manhood and genterie, I haue brought home such mony as you lent me. **1614** RICH *Homestie of Age* (1844) 14 His manners, that hauing to tell a sober tale to a Justice of peace, would still begin his speeches with 'Sir reuerence of your worships honesty'. **1634** MASSINGER *Very Woman* II. iii, The beastliest man—..(Sir-reverence of the company)—a rank whoremaster.

†**b.** Without const. *Obs.*

α. **1590** SHAKS. *Com. Err.* III. ii. 91 A very reuerent body: I such a one, as a man may not speake of, without he say sir reuerence. **1592** G. HARVEY *Four Lett.* Wks. (Grosart) I. 171 And, sir reuerence, how lowsy he and the mother of Infortunatus were. **1614** B. JONSON *Bart. Fair* Induct., Hee has (sirreuerence) kick'd me three, or foure times about the Tyring-house. **1654** GAYTON *Pleas. Notes* Pref. Verses, And makes the Country Neighbourhood about Swallow, Sir reverence, what he voideth out. **1687** MRS. BEHN *Lucky Chance* IV. i, Plain Fulbank,—methinks you might have had a Sir-reverence under your girdle, Sir.

β. **1596** HARINGTON *Metam. Ajax* Let. A ij b, A thing that I cannot name wel without saue-reuerence. **1598** DELONEY *Jacke Newb.* x. 115, I was a woman when she was, a se-reverence, a paltrie girle. **1658** BURTON *Comm. Antoninus Itin.* 223 So great was his despite against him, meerly because he was *Sacerdos Maritatus*, which forsooth he cannot name without a Sa-Reverence. **1681** BLOUNT *Glossogr.* (ed. 5), Sa-reverence, *salva reverentia*, saving regard or respect; an usual word.

†**c.** With punning allusion to SIR *sb.* 1. *Obs.*

**1593** G. HARVEY *Pierce's Super.* Wks. (Grosart) II. 270 They neither feare Goodman Sathan,..nor Sir Reuerence, nor milord Gouernement himselfe.

**2.** Human excrement.

**1592** GREENE *Ned Browne* Wks. (Grosart) XI. 33 His face,..and his Necke, were all besmeared with the soft sirreuerence, so as he stunk. **1694** MOTTEUX *Rabelais* IV. lii, For four..Days I hardly scumber'd one poor Butt of Sir-reverence. **1738** BRACKEN *Farriery* (1749) 218 It was a Bolus made of Sirreverence or Human Dung, begging the Reader's Pardon. **1771** SMOLLETT *Humph. Cl.* 30 Apr., As a plate of marmalade would improve a pan of sir-reverence. **1828–** in dial. glossaries (Yorksh., Durham).

**b.** With *a.* A piece or lump of this.

**1592** GREENE *Upstart Courtier* Wks. (Grosart) XI. 235 As far as a hungry sow can smell a sir reuerence. **1683** DRYDEN *Vind. 'Duke of Guise'* Wks. 1725 V. 333 If I cry a Sir-

Reverence, and you take it for Honey, make the best of your Bargain. **1704** N. N. tr. *Boccalini's Advts. fr. Parnass.* III. 174 To try an Important Experiment, whether it was possible for 'em to preserve a Sir Reverence. **1720-1** *Lett. fr. Mist's Jrnl.* (1722) II. 315 To pass by the Sir-reverence, and the good Dousing the Dragon met with. **1836-48** B. D. WALSH *Aristoph. Acharn.* IV. vii, May Providence Send to the hand of this fine shark A newly-born sir-reverence. *a* **1840** FRERE *Aristoph. Acharn.* 1170 Let him grasp for his defence A ponderous sir reverence.

Hence †**sir-'reverence** *v. Obs. rare.*

**1665** HEAD *Eng. Rogue* I. iii. 27 Another time sirreverencing in a paper, and running to the window with it. **1697** CIBBER *Woman's Wit* IV. 52 O Lord Sir! I do Sir-reverence your Person.

**sirrha**, obs. form of SIRRAH.

†**'sirright.** *Obs.*⁻¹ [f. SIR *sb.*] A right pertaining to the male line.

**1623** tr. *Favine's Theat. Honour* VII. ii. 204 Rodolphe alleaged that the Dukedome..was..a Male Fief of the Empire, from which..Daughters were excluded, and so the sirright ceassing, he was the very neerest heire.

**sirring**, obs. f. SYRINGE.

**sirris**, variant of SIRIS.

**sirrup**, obs. f. SYRUP.

**sirse** (Sc.): see SIR *sb.* 7 b.

**sirship** ('sɜːʃɪp). [f. SIR *sb.* + -SHIP.] The position of a Sir; baronetcy.

**1873** *Gentl. Mag.* July 101 A baronet..whose grandfather ..had left his descendants nothing to support the dignity of the hereditary Sirship.

**sirt**, var. SYRT *Obs.*

**sirtes, -is**: see SYRTIS *Obs.*

**sirup**, obs. and U.S. var. SYRUP.

**sirurgien**: see CHIRURGEON and SURGEON.

‖**sirvente** (sirvɑ̃t). Also **syrvente, sirvent.** [a. F. *sirvente* or ad. Prov. *sirventes, serventes* (cf. OF. *serventeis, -ois*, It. *serventese*, Sp. *serventesio*), app. f. *servir* to serve, but the connexion is not quite clear. The French and English form has arisen by taking *sirventes* as a pl.] A form of poem or lay, usu. satirical, employed by the troubadours of the Middle Ages.

**1819** SCOTT *Ivanhoe* xvii, The knight..asked his host whether he would choose a *sirvente* in the language of *oc*, or a *lai* in the language of *oui*. **1840** BROWNING *Sordello* II. 516 To get A notion of the Troubadour's intent In rondel, tenzon, virlai or sirvent. **1878** STUBBS *Study Med. & Mod. Hist.* vi. (1900) 141 Some few sirventes or satiric lays that entitle Richard [I] to the name of a trouvere.

**Siryenian** (sɜː'jiːnɪən), *sb.* and *a.* Also **Sirenian, Syrianian, -jenian, Syryenian, Ziranian, Zyrenian.** [f. mod.L. *Syriænus* (ad. Russ. *zyryánin, -áne* ZYRIAN *sb.* and *a.*) + -IAN.] = ZYRIAN *sb.* and *a.*

**1851** *Illustr. Catal. Gt. Exhib.* III. 552/1 Sirenian St. Matthew. **1878** *Encycl. Brit.* VIII. 700/1 Finnic or Ugrian represented by..Siryenian. **1879** *Ibid.* IX. 291/2 The Permian Finns comprise the Siryenians,..the Permian proper,..and the Votyak. **1908** [see PERMIAN *a.* (*sb.*) 2]. **1910** *Encycl. Brit.* X. 389/1 The Syryenian headquarters are at the town of Ishma on the Pechora. **1911** *Ibid.* XXVI. 317/2 Syryenians (also Sirianian, Syrjenian, Zyrenian, Ziranian, Zyrian and Zirian), a tribe belonging to the Permian division of the eastern Finns. **1930** LIDDELL & SCOTT *Gr.-Eng. Lex.*, *Κάνναβις*..borrowed perh. fr. Ugro-Finnish, cf... Syrianian *piš* 'hemp'.

**sis** (sɪs), *sb.* Also **siss.** Colloq. abbrev. of SISTER *sb.*

**1656** DR. DENTON *Let.* 20 Nov. in M. M. Verney *Memoirs* (1894) III. ix. 315 We had need call a councell for marrynige and givinge in marriage, you for your sis, she for hers, and I for mine. **1808** LADY LYTTELTON *Let.* 18 Dec. (1912) ii. 53 But oh, Bob, pity your poor Mam and Sis, when they will have to set out on a bleak morning, over such rough, splashy, squashy, jolting and jumbling roads as ours. **1835** *Knickerbocker* VI. 293 All the friends called her sister,.. which, as the half was easier to be bandied about than the whole,..soon dwindled into 'sis'. **1859** BARTLETT *Dict. Amer.* (ed. 2), *Siss* and *Sissy*, contractions for sister, often used in addressing girls, even by their parents. **1872** C. M. YONGE *P's & Q's* iii. 19 'I knew you were a jolly old sis,' said Horace with a hug. **1891** M. E. RYAN *Pagan of Alleghanies* 133 Folks call boys 'bud' sometimes, jist like they call girls 'sis'. **1924** LAWRENCE & SKINNER *Boy in Bush* vi. 86 Skippin' up an' down like sis. **1935** Z. N. HURSTON *Mules & Men* (1970) I. x. 220 Sis Cat, we both got a li'l money. **1948** M. ALLINGHAM *More Work for Undertaker* ii. 26 'Who was she? Your only love?' 'Gawd, no! My sis.' **1970** M. WALKER *Prophets for New Day* in S. Henderson *Understanding New Black Poetry* (1973) II. 161, I run down to Sis Avery's. **1974** D. GRAY *Dead Give Away* i. 14 You'll be wearing clothes at the Private View, won't you, Sis?

‖**sis** (siːs, sɪs), *int. S. Afr.* Also †**cess.** [ad. Afrikaans *sies* (also used), perh. ad. Hottentot *si* or *tsi*.] An ejaculation expressing disgust or disappointment.

**1862** A. W. DRAYSON *Tales at Outspan* 67, I have lost more cattle from the attacks of hyænas than I have from lions, or leopards, and as to sheep, *cess*, I've had nearly a whole flock worried by them. **1909** *Cape* 30 Apr. 6 Sis for her. She gave me nothing to eat but semalina and kofee. **1926** E. LEWIS *Mantis* I. iv. 79 'Sis, man!' Hugo had scolded him, 'you go to see one of these private fellows.' **1949** *Forum* 26 Mar. 15 The elegant word 'sies!' is in evidence when persons to whom objection is taken are present or even mentioned. **1972** *Star* (Johannesburg) 15 Nov. 18 The majority of young Afrikaans people..cannot speak English and..have no intention of doing so. Ag sis! Praat English.

**sis**, obs. variant of SICE.

**-sis**, *suffix*, repr. Gr. -σις in nouns of action, as in ANALYSIS, ARSIS, MERISIS, PERISTALSIS, etc. Also in some nouns denoting a specified diseased state, as FILARIASIS, PHTHISIS, PSITTACOSIS, SEPSIS.

**sisal** ('saɪs(ə)l; formerly also 'sɪsəl, sɪ'sɑːl). Also **sissal** and with capital initial. [See def.]

**1.** The name of a port in Yucatan, used attrib. with ***fibre, grass, hemp***, to designate the prepared fibre of several species of *Agave* and *Fourcroya*, which is largely exported from that place for use in rope-making. Also ***sisal plant***, the aloe or other plant from which the fibre is obtained.

**1843** *Penny Cycl.* XXVII. 724/1 None of its agricultural products yield articles of export, except the Sisal hemp. **1859** *All Year Round* No. 32. 126 The sisal hemp, which is the product of the Agave Americana, is also very enticing to the speculator. **1887** *Boston* (Mass.) *Jrnl.* 6 May 4/8 A cargo of sisal grass for the Plymouth Cordage Company. **1889** *Times* 9 Mar. 4/3 The issue was an Act..to give substantial encouragement..to the cultivation of the sisal fibre. **1889** D. MORRIS *Kew Bulletin* No. 27. 60 The true Sisal plant is Agave rigida.

*attrib.* **1878** *Encycl. Brit.* XVI. 36/2 The prosperity which Yucatan in recent years owes to the development of the Sisal hemp trade. **1882** CHRISTY *New Commercial Pl.* No. 6. 43 The Giant Lily or Sisal Hemp Plant of South America (*Fourcroya gigantea*). **1893** *Westm. Gaz.* 27 May 6/2 Some thousands of acres of sisal hemp plantations.

**2.** *ellipt.* = prec. Chiefly *attrib.*

**1883** *Fisheries Exhib. Catal.* 24 White Sisal Rope. White Sisal Lines. **1895** *Daily News* 7 Sept. 2/3 Hemp has shown renewed activity... Sisal also is firmer. **1896** *Pall Mall Mag.* May 65 Almost all the settlers of this island [*sc.* Andros] are engaged in Sisal cultivation.

**3.** Special combs., as **sisalcraft, -kraft**, a waterproof material with a core of sisal fibres.

**1940** *Chambers's Techn. Dict.* 774/1 Sisalcraft. **1945** *Jrnl. R. Army Med. Corps* LXXXIV. 98 The sisalcraft and blankets already sewn up. **1948** *Spectator* 9 Apr. 430/1 The wooden huts in which the occupants of Antarctic bases live are specially designed with layers of tinfoil and sisalkraft between the inner and outer walls. **1961** [see SARK *v.* 2]. **1962** *Economist* 8 Sept. 956/1 The conventional materials..such as bituminised sisalcraft and burlap.

**sis-boom-bah** (sɪsbuːm'bɑː), *int.* and *sb. U.S.* Also **-ah.** [Echoic, repr. the sound of a skyrocket: a hissing flight (*sis*), an explosion (*boom*), and an exclamation of delight from the spectators (*bah, ah*): see SKYROCKET 2.] A shout expressive of support or encouragement to a college team. Hence as *sb.*, enthusiastic or partisan support of spectator sports, esp. football.

[**1867**: see SKY-ROCKET *sb.* 2]. **1924** *Dialect Notes* V. 276 *Sis-boom*: —— ah, —— bah (college yells). **1961** M. BEADLE *These Ruins are Inhabited* (1963) iv. 48 Fresh from the land of sis-boom-bah.., the Americans had a hard time at first learning to applaud good play by *either* team. **1970** *Time* 17 Aug. 64 For the next 2½ years it was girls, flasks and sis-boom-bah. But the public image concealed an all-night reader.

**siscoe**, variant of CISCO.

**siscowet** ('sɪskəʊɛt). Also **ciscoette, ciscovet, siskawitz, -iwit, -owet,** etc. [Odjibwa, meaning literally 'cooks itself' (Goode).] A variety of the great Lake trout of N. America, found in Lake Superior.

**1847** C. LANMAN *Summer in Wildern.* 159 A fish called ciscovet, is unquestionably of the trout genus, but much more delicious. *Ibid.* 161 The white-fish, ciscovet, and lake trout. **1849** H. W. HERBERT *Fish & Fishing* 145 The Siskawitz is rather shorter and stouter than the Mackinaw fish. **1854** C. LANMAN *Adv. Wilds N. Amer.* xxxiv. 253 We cannot leave Mackinaw without making a passing allusion to the fish whose Indian name is *ciscowet*. It is a handsome fish, unquestionably of the trout family. **1884** GOODE *Nat. Hist. Aquat. Anim.* 496 The Siscowet, *Salvelinus Namaycush*. **1888** —— *Amer. Fishes* 468 The amateur is likely to confound the Namaycush with the Siscowet. **1902** *Jrnl. Amer. Folklore* 243 Ciscoette. A name of the lake herring. Apparently a derivative, with French diminutive suffix, from *Cisco* (q.v.), but rather a corruption of *Siskowit*.

*attrib.* **1882** JORDAN & GILBERT *Syn. Fishes N. Amer.* 318 Siscowet Salmon..is probably a local variety rather than a distinct species.

**sise**, obs. variant of SICE, SIZE.

†**siseangle.** *Obs. rare.* [f. *sise* SICE + ANGLE.] A hexagon. So †**siseangled** *a.*

**1551** RECORDE *Pathw. Knowl.* I. Def., Likewyse shall you iudge of siseangles, which haue sixe corners. **1567** —— *Whetst.* C iij, Quadrate, Cinkeangeled, Siseangeled.

**sisel** ('sɪsəl), *sb. Zool.* [ad. G. *ziesel*: cf. ZIZEL.] A kind of ground-squirrel (see quots.).

**1880** *Cassell's Nat. Hist.* III. 93 Of the Old World species the best known is the Sisel, or Suslik (*Spermophilus citillus*), which is abundant in Central and Eastern Europe, and in Siberia. **1894-5** LYDEKKER *Roy. Nat. Hist.* III. 79 The suslik or sisel of North-Eastern Europe and Northern Asia.

†**sisel,** *a. Obs.*⁻¹ [a. ON. *sýsl*, related to *sýsla* sb. work, business, *sýsla* vb. to be busy, etc.] Occupied, engaged.

*c* **1325** *Metr. Hom.* 112 Quen hali kirc bigan newli, Sain Jon was sisel, and bisi, In ordaining of priestes and clerkes, And in casting kirc werkes.

‖**siser.** *Bot. rare.* [L. *siser*, perhaps the same as Gr. σίσαρον (whence mod.L. *sisarum*).] The water-parsnip or skirret (*Sium sisarum*).

**1548** TURNER *Names Herbes* 74 Fuchsius rekoneth that our skyrwort, or skyrwit is a kinde of siser. **1562** —— *Herbal* II. (1568) 139 The roote of Siser sodden is pleasant to the mouth. **1753** *Chambers' Cycl.* Suppl., *Siser*, in botany, a name given to the skirret. **1858** MAYNE *Expos. Lex.*, *Sium Sisarum*, systematic name of the siser or skirret, formerly considered aromatic.

**siser**, obs. form of SIZAR.

**siserary** (sɪsə'rɛərɪ). Now *dial.* Forms: 5 **sessarary**, 7 **sesarara**, 8 **ceserera**; 7 **sas-**, 8-9 **sass-**, **sussarara** (9 **sassaray**); 7 **sursurrara**; 8 **siserari**, 8-9 **-ary**, 9 **-ara**; 7 **sissara**, 8-9 **sisserara**, 9 **-ary**. [Popular corruption of CERTIORARI.]

†**1.** A writ of Certiorari. *Obs.*

**1481-90** *Howard Househ. Bks.* (Roxb.) 196 My Lord payd to the Clerk of the Pece for a sessarary for the Vekery of Wyrmyngforde ij.s. vj.d. **1607** MIDDLETON *Phœnix* C j, Heere a writ of *Demur*, there a *Procedendo*, heere a *Sursurrara*, there a *Capiendo*. **1607** TOURNEUR *Rev. Trag.* G iij, They cannot so much as pray, but in law, that their sinnes may be remou'd, with a writ of Error, and their soules fetcht vp to heauen, with a sasarara. **1620** MELTON *Astrolog.* 67 Sissaras, Writs, Latitats and Procidendos. **1760-1** SMOLLETT *Launcelot Greaves* ii, O! that there was a lawyer here to serve him with a *siserari*.

**2. *with a siserary***, with a vengeance; suddenly, promptly.

**1607** W[ENTWORTH] S[MITH] *Puritan Widow* II[I]. iii, If it be lost or stole..a Cunning Kinsman of mine..would fetcht againe with a Sesarara. **1765** STERNE *Tr. Shandy* VIII. xxi, It was on Sunday in the afternoon, when I fell in love all at once with a *sisserara*. **1766** GOLDSM. *Vic. W.* xxi, 'As for the matter of that,' returned the hostess, '..out she shall pack with a sassarara'. **1770** GOLDSM. *Vicar W.* (ed. 4) xxi, Gentle or simple, out she shall pack with a sussarara [*edd.* 1766, 1767 sass-]. **1829** BENTHAM *Justice & Cod. Petit.*, *Abr. Petit. Justice* 71 I'll fetch you up with a sisserary. **1857** G. W. THORNBURY *Songs of Cavaliers & Roundheads* 55 Tossing off Canary cups, With a Sassarara.

**3.** A severe rebuke or scolding; a sharp blow; a torrent *of* (language).

**1771** SMOLLETT *Humph. Cl.* 15 May, I have gi'en the dirty slut a siserary. **1826** SCOTT *Woodst.* x, Master Holdenough ..attacked it with such a siserary of Latin as might have scared the devil himself. **1850** G. W. REYNOLDS *Myst. of Court* i. 16 He was just inflicting a Sassarara upon the waiter for not keeping up a cheerful fire. **1893** COZENS HARDY *Broad Norfolk* 5 One boy will give another a clip o' the head .., and once I heard a fellow say he had given another a sisserara.

**4.** A loud clanging noise.

*a* **1770** '*Lady Ouncebell*' v. in Child *Ballads* II. 207 He heard the bells of the high chapel ring, They rang with a ceserera. *a* **1850** *Ibid.* 209 They made a loud sassaray. **1884** *Athenæum* 3 May 578/1, I..at last gave such a sussarara on the bell that I thought the deafest person must hear.

**sisers**, obs. f. SCISSORS.

**siserskite**, var. SYSERTSKITE.

**sisham**, var. SHISHAM.

**sisi**, var. SEESEE.

**sisimbrium**, obs. var. of SISYMBRIUM.

**sisith**, var. ZIZITH.

**siskawitz**, var. of SISCOWET.

**siskin** ('sɪskɪn). Also 6 **sysken-**, 7 **sisken.** [ad. G. dial. *sisschen* or *zeischen*, = older Flem. *sijsken*, *cijsken* (Kilian; Du. and Flem. *sijsje*), Da. *sisgen*, a dim. form based on MHG. *zîsec* (also *zîse*; G. *zeisig*), MLG. *ziseke*, *sisek* (Norw. *sisik*, *sisk*, Sw. *siska*), which are app. of Slavonic origin; cf. Pol. *czyżik*, *czyż*, Russ. *chizhek'*, *chizh'*.]

**1.** A small song-bird, in some respects closely allied to the goldfinch; also called ABERDEVINE.

By older writers sometimes identified with the greenfinch.

**1562** TURNER *Herbal* II. (1568) 134 It [sesamum] groweth in Germany..and men fede byrdes with the sede of it there, namelye Syskennes. **1567** MAPLET *Gr. Forest* 80 She most commonlye hatcheth hir yong in the Larkes Nest or Siskins, which Siskin is not much vnlike to the Goldfinch. **1616** SURFL. & MARKHAM *Country Farme* VII. lxx. 731 The Siskins liue, some fiue, others eight yeares. **1661** LOVELL *Hist. Anim. & Min.* Isagoge d j b, All sorts of little birds, as sparrows,..wrens, witwalls, siskens. **1768** PENNANT *Brit. Zool.* II. 512 The Siskin, which is an irregular visitant, said to come from Russia. **1774** GOLDSM. *Nat. Hist.* (1776) III. 169 The Siskin and Linnet only forsake us in severe winters. **1813** MONTAGU *Ornith.* Suppl. s.v. *Siskin*, The Aberdevine or Siskin, is in size between that of the Greater and Lesser

Red-poles. **1841** *Proc. Berw. Nat. Club* I. 252 The siskin (*Carduelis spinus*)..is sometimes very abundant. **1894–5** LYDEKKER *Roy. Nat. Hist.* III. 385 From Japan to the British Isles the common siskin (*Chrysomitris spinus*) is found in suitable localities.

**2.** Applied with defining words to various small birds related to or resembling the siskin.

**1783** LATHAM *Gen. Synop. Birds* II. I. 292 Mexican Siskin ..inhabits Mexico. *Ibid.* 293 Chinese Siskin..inhabits China. **1839** AUDUBON *Ornith. Biog.* V. 46 Black-headed Siskin, *Fringilla Magellanica*. *Ibid.* 85 Arkansaw Siskin, *Fringilla psaltria*. **1874** COUES *Birds N.W.* 116 Arkansas Goldfinch; Mexican Siskin. **1884** —— *N. Amer. Birds* 354 *Chrysomitris pinus*,..American Siskin.

**3.** *attrib.*, as ***siskin finch, group***; **siskin-green**, a light green inclining to yellow; **siskin-parrot**, a small parrot of the genus *Nasiterna* (*Cent. Dict.*).

**1805–17** R. JAMESON *Char. Min.* (ed. 3) 59 Siskin-green forming the connecting link with yellow. **1815** STEPHENS in *Shaw's Gen. Zool.* IX. II. 467 Siskin Finch. *Ibid.* 471 Mexican Siskin Finch. **1879** E. P. WRIGHT *Anim. Life* 260 A peculiar sort of green approaching to sage-green, but so peculiar as to give rise to the name of 'siskin-green'. **1894–5** LYDEKKER *Roy. Nat. Hist.* III. 385 A less well-known member of the siskin group is the citril finch (*Chrysomitris citrinella*).

**siskowet**, variant of SISCOWET.

**sisme**, obs. f. SCHISM.

**sismograph, -meter**, variants of SEISMOGRAPH, -METER.

**sisour(e**, obs. ff. SIZER.

**sisours**, obs. f. SCISSORS.

†**sispar** (also sy-), ? obs. f. *side-spar*.

**1532–3** *Durh. Househd. Bk.* (Surtees) 173 Pro sarracione ½ rod in sparres et sisparres. *Ibid.*, Walplaytts et sysparres.

**siss**, *sb.* [Cf. next.] A hissing sound.

**1870** TALMAGE *Crumbs Swept Up* 397 The chuck and siss and smoke of the bar, as it plunged into the water.

**siss** (sɪs), *v.* Also 4 ciss-, sciss-, syss-. [ME. *cissen, sissen*, = MDu. *cissen*, Du. and LG. *sissen*, of imitative origin: cf. G. *zischen* and SIZZ *v.*] *intr.* To hiss. Now *dial.* and *U.S.*

In dial. use also *trans.*, to hiss (a person), to incite (a dog) by hissing: see *Eng. Dial. Dict.*

**13..** W. DE BIBBESWORTH in Wright *Voc.* (1857) 152 *Serpent ciphele*, scisset [*v.r.* cisses]. *c* **1400** *MS. Bibl. Reg. 12 B. i.* f. 12 (Halliw.), *Sibilus est genus serpentis*,..a syssing. **1590** SIR J. SMYTH *Disc. Weapons* 21 Their peeces.. sometimes lieth sissing in the touchhole or peece. **1828–** in dialect glossaries (Yks., Lanc., Chesh., Linc.). **1828–32** WEBSTER, *Siss*, to hiss; a legitimate word in universal popular use in New England. **1859** in BARTLETT *Dict. Amer.* (ed. 2). **1886** *S.W. Linc. Gloss.* s.v., I've always a sissing noise in my head. *Ibid.*, If a sup o' rain were to fall, it would siss.

**siss** (obs. Sc.): see SITHE, time.

**siss**, var. SIS *sb.*

**sissars, -ers**, obs. forms of SCISSORS.

**sisserskite**, obs. var. SYSERTSKITE.

‖**sissonne.** [F. *sissonne, sissone*: see Littré and Hatzfeld.] (See quot. 1957.)

**1706** J. WEAVER *Orchesography* Table 35 A Table of Sissonnes or Cross leaps. **1892, 1913** [see CISEAUX]. **1930** CRASKE & BEAUMONT *Theory & Pract. Allegro in Class. Ballet* 47 *Sissonne dessus*... Other *sissonnes* are *sissonne dessous, s. en avant, s. en arrière*, etc. **1947** N. NICOLAEVA-LEGAT *Ballet Education* IV. 109 *Sissone* is another step which has many variations. *Sissone simple* on the *cou-de-pied* is taken from V pos., the right leg in front; a spring into the air, pushing from the ground equally with both feet and with straight knees; land on the left leg. **1957** G. B. L. WILSON *Dict. Ballet* 247 *Sissonne*, or *pas de sissonne*, probably from *pas de ciseaux*, a scissor-like movement... With a slight plié, the dancer springs into the air to the fifth position, alighting on one foot with a demi-plié, with the other leg extended to the back, front, or side; the back foot is then closed to the supporting foot (a sissonne fermée)... If the dancer lands on one foot with the other on the coup-de-pied..it is a sissonne simple (or ordinaire). **1968** J. WINEARLS *Mod. Dance* (ed. 2) iii. 87 This sissonne is a combination of the three elements, light—quick—and peripheral.

‖**sissoo** ('sɪsuː). Also seesoo seesu, sissu. [Urdū (Hindī) *sīsū*.]

**1.** A valuable Indian timber-tree, *Dalbergia Sissoo*.

**1810** T. WILLIAMSON *E. India Vade M.* II. 71 This [wood], which is called the *sissoo*, grows in most of the great forests, intermixed with the *saul*. **1854** HOOKER *Himalayan Jrnls.* II. 340 *note*, The Cuttack forests are composed of teak, Sal, Sissoo, ebony,..and other trees of a dry soil. **1876** *Cornhill Mag.* Sept. 318 Studded here and there with tall clumps of *sâl* and *sissu*.

*attrib.* **1810** T. WILLIAMSON *E. India Vade M.* II. 72 Some *sissoo-trees* grow to a great height. **1859** J. LANG *Wanderings in India* 358 The Governor-General..wore his head as high as a seesu-tree. **1874** STEWART & BRANDIS *Flora N.W. India* 149 The Sissoo tree is indigenous in the sub-Himalayan tract.

**2.** The timber obtained from this tree.

**1810** T. WILLIAMSON *E. India Vade M.* II. 71 *Sissoo* is, of late, more employed than formerly for the frame, ribs, knees, &c. of ships. **1834** MEDWIN *Angler in Wales* I. 162 The beams too of the houses, if not of bamboo, sissoo, or teak, are not safe from their devastating fangs. **1874** STEWART & BRANDIS *Flora N.W. India* 150 Sissoo is very elastic, it seasons well, does not warp or split, and takes a fine polish.

*attrib.* **1873** BALFOUR *Cycl. India* (ed. 2) IV. 184/1 Sissoo-wood oil,..an empyreumatic medicinal product. **1874** STEWART & BRANDIS *Flora N.W. India* 150 Sisso wood is esteemed highly for all purposes where strength and elasticity are required. *Ibid.*, Supplies of large Sissoo logs.

**sissors, -oures**, obs. forms of SCISSORS.

**sissy** ('sɪsɪ). *colloq.* [f. SIS *sb.* + -Y[6]; cf. CISSY *sb.* and *a.*] **1.** A sister.

**1846** *Dollar Newspaper* (Philadelphia) 22 Apr. 1/7 'Sissy Jane' smoothed back my hair, and smiled at me. **1854** DICKENS *Hard Times* I. vi. 41 When Sissy got into the school here..her father was as pleased as Punch. **1859** [see SISS *sb.*[1]]. **1865** K. H. DIGBY *Short Poems* 39 The little one grasping, with such a tight hold, The frock of sweet sissy, herself not too bold. **1901** M. FRANKLIN *My Brilliant Career* xiii. 107 Don't be frightened, sissy, I never kiss girls. **1939** JOYCE *Finnegans Wake* 94 It made ma make merry and sissy so shy.

**2.** An effeminate person; a coward.

**1887** *Lantern* (New Orleans) 27 Aug. 3/2 Look and walk too much like sissies to do much fightin'. **1899** T. HALL *Tales* 131 'Well, you are a sissy,' said Blinks contemptuously. **1926** *British Weekly* 9 Sept. 473/3 A religious 'sissy' was anathema to me. **1932** S. GIBBONS *Cold Comfort Farm* xvii. 237, I want red blood. I don't want no sissies, see? **1938** L. MACNEICE *Zoo* iv. 74 The Sealyham, say the older breeders, is becoming a sissy. **1969** C. HIMES *Blind Man with Pistol* ii. 25 The sissies..were colored and mostly young. They all had straightened hair..; long false eyelashes. **1977** *Time* 21 Feb. 40/2 Smokers proved to be sissies when deprived of cigarettes.

**3.** *attrib.* or as *adj.* **a.** Effeminate; cowardly.

**1891** *Harper's Mag.* Aug. 485/2 He approached and sat near me, deep in conversation with a young gentle-man with sissy whiskers. **1893** *Sunday Mercury* (N.Y.) 14 May 15/5 (*heading*) Sissy men in Society.—Powdered, Painted and Laced. They swarm at Afternoon Teas. **1899** T. HALL *Tales* 121 Scotty was, in the newspaper vernacular, 'a sissy boy', or, in other words, a bit effeminate. **1926** *British Weekly* 2 Sept. 452/3 There was nothing 'sissy' about him. He was a born fighter. **1932** S. GIBBONS *Cold Comfort Farm* xvii. 241 Thassa sissy sort of a name, but it'll do. **1941** 'R. WEST' *Black Lamb & Grey Falcon* II. 152 The monuments..had apparently been produced by a pastry-cook under the influence of Persian art. Such sugary little scrolls and swaps, such sissy little flowers in pots, such coy little etchings of swords on the soldiers' tombs. **1959** *Spectator* 25 Sept. 408/2 All the kudos goes to the campaign-scarred, ink-stained veteran: none to the new bug in his sissy clean blazer. **1970** P. DICKINSON tr. *Aristophanes' Wasps* in *Plays* I. 192 That sissy son of Chaireas prances In with his mincing walk. **1977** C. MCCULLOUGH *Thorn Birds* xi. 260 No cutter ever wore gloves. They slowed a man down... Besides, gloves were sissy.

**b. sissy bar**, a metal loop rising from behind the seat of a bicycle or motor-cycle.

**1969** *Daily Colonist* (Victoria, B.C.) 19 June 40/1 (Advt.), The 'Super Cycle' breed with hi-rise handlebars on a cantilever frame...the 36" Sissy bar, [etc.]. **1974** R. B. PARKER *God save Child* vi. 49 Another motorcycle... A big one,..small front wheel, sissy bar behind.

Hence **sissifi'cation**, effeminacy; **'sissified** *a.*, effeminate; **'sissiness**, effeminacy; **'sissyish** *a.*, somewhat effeminate.

**1889** W. D. HOWELLS *Hazard of New Fortunes* II. 64 The New York fellows carried canes..; and they were both sissyish and fast. **1905** J. C. LINCOLN *Partners of Tide* iv. 78 To be seen with girls was not so 'sissified' in his mind as it used to be. **1926** *Harper's Mag.* Feb. 350/2 In spite of his funny sissiness there was not a dog in town that did not love him. **1938** I. GOLDBERG *Wonder of Words* xv. 305 Mr Sokolsky establishes a correlation between high blood-pressure and masculinity, and between low blood-pressure and femininity or sissification. **1959** E. POUND *Thrones* xcix. 57 In statement, answer; in conversation Not with sissified fussiness (chiao') Always want your own way. **1973** *Guardian* 1 June 10/5 The much-publicised Warhol Factory mystique..thinly veils a highly reactionary, bigoted and sissified neo-Nazi boutique. **1975** *N.Y. Times* 12 Sept. 38/6 Mr. Mahan said that the other cowboys on the rodeo circuit had generally accepted his fashion business, and that none of them considered it 'sissyish or effeminate'.

**sist**, *sb.* *Sc. Law.* [f. the vb.] A stay or suspension of some proceeding; *spec.* an 'order or injunction of the Lord Ordinary prohibiting diligence to proceed' (Bell).

**1693** STAIR *Instit.* (ed. 2) IV. lii. 755 Therefore (by Act of Sederunt Nov. 9. 1680) Fourteen Days are only allowed for Sists of Execution, from the Date the Bill was signed. *Ibid.*, That it may be known what Sists are granted, the Clerks of the Bills are ordained to make an Alphabetick Inventar of Bills Refused or Sisted. **1721** WODROW *Corr.* (1843) II. 562 A sist in case of heats and debates in a session, until superior judicatories took up the differences. **1753** *Stewart's Trial* App. 121 He gave notice to the tenants of Ardshiel, that he had procured a sist for them against the decreet of removing. **1765–8** ERSKINE *Inst. Law Scot.* IV. iii. §18 A sist granted on a bill without passing it, expires also in fourteen days. **1800** A. CARLYLE *Autobiogr.* 287 The solicitor..immediately granted the alarmed brethren a sist. **1838** W. BELL *Dict. Law Scot.* 961 Where intimation of the application or sist in the Bill-Chamber has been made to the charger.

*transf.* **1831** SIR W. HAMILTON *Discuss.* (1853) 216 In contempt of a sist on the proceedings by the Elector of Mentz.

**sist**, *v.* *Sc.* [ad. L. *sistĕre* to cause to stand, etc., a reduplicated form corresponding to *stāre* to stand.]

**1. a.** *trans.* To stop, stay, or suspend (some proceeding, etc.), *esp.* by judicial decree.

**1652** *Reg. Commiss. Gen. Assembly* (S.H.S.) III. 553 Their desire and overture for sisting the present differences had beem mett by the Commission. **1679** *Lond. Gaz.* No. 1406/2 We have thought fit hereby to sist and supersede all Execution upon any Letters of Caption. **1716** WODROW *Corr.* (1843) II. 192 The Assembly might now declare, that they did not..design to..rescind a sentence passed in the Commission; but only..had sisted its execution. **1831** *Church Patronage Reporter* Jan. 9 If it [patronage] enjoys the high sanction of the pages of inspiration, we may here sist our procedure. **1881** J. H. STIRLING *Text-bk. Kant* 6 The whole business of metaphysic..is summarily sisted. **1885** *Law Rep. 10 App. Cases* 174 His Lordship sisted the appellant's action until the decision of the action of declarator.

*absol.* **1678** SIR G. MACKENZIE *Crim. Laws Scot.* II. x. §iii, If a pursuit were intented before them, upon a Bond, they behoved to sist, if the Bond was alledged to be false.

†**b.** *intr.* To cease, desist, stop. *Obs.*

*a* **1676** BP. GUTHRIE *Mem.* (1748) 60 An accident which.. fell out upon the second of July, and imported, that the covenanters meant not to sist there. **1676** ROW *Contin. Blair's Autobiog.* xii. (1848) 456 Neither did the persecuting Prelatis rage then sist. *a* **1707** SIR D. HUME *Domestic Details* (1843) 55 My cause being in the roll, I had no mind it shall sist on any account.

**2.** *trans.* †**a.** To present (oneself) *before* a court. Also without const. *Obs. rare.*

**1643** *Sc. Acts, Chas. I* (1870) VI. I. 5 The Convention.. haveing given warrant to Charge the erle..to compeir with all diligence and sist his persone befor thame. *a* **1722** LAUDER *Decisions* (1759) I. 680 Where a prisoner..grants a bond..to sist himself such a day, or else pay the debt.

**b.** To cause or order (one) to appear *before* a court; to summon or cite.

**1721** WODROW *Hist. Suff. Ch. Scot.* III. i. (1830) III. 7 He was sisted before the committee for public affairs. **1752** LOUTHIAN *Form of Process* (ed. 2) p. vi, The Manner of apprehending and sisting Delinquents before the Court. **1801** A. RANKEN *Hist. France* I. 283 On being sisted before the court, security or bail was taken. **1857** GILFILLAN *Life Waller* 16 He..was sisted before the Court of War, and condemned to die. **1868** *Act 31 & 32 Vict.* c. 100 §98 Nothing herein contained shall prevent..the Court from sisting any person upon his own application..as a party to the cause.

**3.** To place or posit. *rare*$^{-1}$.

**1836** SIR W. HAMILTON *Discuss.* (1853) 313 Some..have preposterously sisted nature as the first or generative principle.

†**sistence**[1]. *Obs. rare*$^{-1}$. [aphetic form of ASSISTANCE.] Aid, help.

*a* **1513** FABYAN *Chron.* VI. cxlviii. (1811) 134 With the sistence of the cytezyns of the same, the sayd Cytie was defendyd.

†**sistence**[2]. *Obs. rare*$^{-1}$. [f. L. *sist-ĕre* SIST *v.* + -ENCE.] Stopping.

**1640** HOWELL *Dodona's Gr.* 187 Extraordinary must be the wisdome of him who floateth upon the streame of Soveraigne favour, wherein there is seldome any sistence, twixt sinking and swimming.

**sister** ('sɪstə(r)), *sb.* Forms: *α.* 1 **sweostor, sweoster (swester, swæster, sw-, su-, soester); swostor, -tur; swustor, -tur, -ter; swystor, -tar, -ter, swistor, -ter.** *β.* 1–7 **suster (4 -tir, -tyr).** *γ.* 3–4 **soster (4 zoster).** *δ.* 2– **sister (4 -terre, -tre, -tur), 5, *Sc.* 5–6 sistir (5 -tire, 6 seister); 4 scyster, syister, 4–6 syster (4 -tre, 6 -tur), 4–5 systyr, 5–6 *Sc.* -tir; 4 cistir, 5 -ter, cyster, -tire, -tyr.** [Common Teut.: OE. *sweoster, swuster*, etc. (see above), = OFris. *swester*, OS. *swestar* (LG. *swester*), OHG. *swester, swister* (G. *schwester*), Goth. *swistar*; forms without *w* appear in OFris. *suster, sister* (WFris. *sister, soster*, EFris. *süster*, NFris. *söster, sester*, etc.), MDu. and MLG. *suster* (Du. *zuster*, LG. *suster, süster*), ON. and Icel. *systir* (Norw. and Sw. *syster*, Da. *søster*). Of the three ME. types, *suster* and *soster* represent OE. forms with the *w* absorbed, while *sister* appears to be from Scandinavian. The Teut. stem **swestr-* stands for an original *swesr-*, and has cognates in OSlav. and Russ. *sestra*, Lith. *sesů*, Skr. *svasā* (*svasr-*), L. *soror* (:—**swesor*), OIr. *siur*, Welsh *chwair*.]

**I. 1. a.** A female in relationship to another person or persons having the same parents. (Also applicable to female animals.)

Sometimes loosely used in the sense of HALF-SISTER, and in that of SISTER-IN-LAW.

*α.* *a* **900** *O.E. Chron.* (Parker MS.) an. 658, Hæfde hine Penda adrifenne..forþon he his swostor [*Laud MS.* swustor] anforlet. *Ibid.* an. 888, Sio wæs Ælfredes sweostor cyninges. *c* **925** *Ibid.* an. 922, þa ȝefor Æþelflæd his swystar æt Tame-worþiȝe. *c* **950** *Lindisf. Gosp.* Luke x. 40 Ne is ðe ȝemnise þætte soester min forleort mec [etc.]. *c* **1000** ÆLFRIC *Gen.* xii. 13 Seȝe nu, ic þe bidde, þæt þu min swuster sig. *c* **1100** *O.E. Chron.* (MS. D) an. 1067, Ða begann se cyngc..ȝyrnan his sweostor him to wife. *a* **1122** *Ibid.* (Laud MS.) an. 1048, þa..betæhte hy his swyster to Hwerwillon. *Ibid.* an. 1091, Eadgar..for to þam cynge..& to his swustor.

*β.* *a* **1122** *O.E. Chron.* (Laud MS.) an. 604, Sæberht Ricolan sunu Æðelberhtes suster. **1154** *Ibid.* an. 1140, Eustace..nam þe kinges suster of France to wife. *c* **1200** *Trin. Coll. Hom.* 147 þo two sustres wepen for here broðres deað. *c* **1200** ORMIN 6382 þa susstress..Werenn Labaness dohhtress. *c* **1350** *Will. Palerne* 2643 þat worþi mayden þat was Williams suster. *c* **1400** MAUNDEV. (1839) xxviii. 288 Thei taken hire Doughtres and hire Sustres to here Wyfes. **1470–85** MALORY *Arthur* III. ii. 101 By reson ye ar myn neuew, my susters sone. **1542** BOORDE *Dyetary* xxxvii.

(1870) 298 He dyd kylle his wyfe, and his wyfes suster. ? **1562** *Child-Marriages* 65, I have gevin her xx[8]; and I wilbe as good vnto my suster Katherine. **1610** B. JONSON *Alch.* III. iv, Gods will, my suster shall see him.

γ. **1275** LAY. 25534 þe fader weap a þane sone, soster o þan broþer. **1297** R. GLOUC. (Rolls) 880 Morgan..of þe eldor soster was. *c* **1320** *Sir Tristr.* 720 Ȝour owhen soster him bare. **1390** GOWER *Conf.* II. 308 Fedra hire yonger Soster eke, A lusti Maide. *Ibid.*, To sen hire Soster mad a queene.

δ. *c* **1250** *Gen. & Ex.* 3855 Ðor was moyses sister dead. *a* **1300** *Cursor M.* 2410 þou art my sister and i þi broþer. *c* **1330** R. BRUNNE *Chron. Wace* (Rolls) 2328 þerfore y schal myn heritage Gyue þy sistres in mariage. **1375** BARBOUR *Bruce* I. 51 He was cummyn off the offspryng Off hyr that eldest systir was. *c* **1440** *Promp. Parv.* 78/2 Cystyr, by þe faderys syde oonly, *soror*. *c* **1449** PECOCK *Repr.* III. iv. 298 That ech man ouȝte forbere ouer myche loue to..britheren and sistris. **1535** STARKEY *Let.* in *England* (1878) p. xx, The weyght of such maryage betwyx brother & systur. **1596** SHAKS. *Tam. Shrew* I. ii. 263 Her father..will not promise her to any man, Vntill the elder sister first be wed. **1610** HOLLAND *Camden's Brit.* (1637) 579 The inheritance became divided among the sisters of the said John Tiptoft. **1665** MANLEY *Grotius' Low C. Wars* 423 Prince Maurice, and his Sister, who was marryed to Count Hohenlo. **1741-2** GRAY *Agrip.* 118 Daughter, sister, wife, And mother of their Cæsars. **1794** COLERIDGE *To a Friend (Charles Lamb)*, I, too, a sister had, an only sister. **1821** SCOTT *Kenilw.* xxix, I trust your honour will allow me to speak with my sister? **1877** TENNYSON *Harold* v. ii, There was more than sister in my kiss, And so the saints were wroth.

**b.** In older forms of the plural.

In OE. the plural had either the same forms as the singular, or appears as *sweostra*, *-tru*, etc. These subsequently assumed the pl. *-n* of weak nouns, and gave the common ME. forms *sustren*, *sostren*, *sistren*, etc. (cf. *brethren*). In general literary use these were finally discarded about 1550 in favour of the pl. in *-s*, which is found as early as *c* 1200.

α. *a* **900** *O.E. Chron.* (Parker MS.) an. 718, Hiera swostur wærun Cuenburȝ & Cuþburh. *c* **950** *Lindisf. Gosp.* Matt. xiii. 56 Suoester [*Rushw.* swæster] his alle. *c* **975** *Rushw. Gosp.* Mark vi. 3 Ah ne swester her usih mið sindun? *c* **1000** *Saxon Leechd.* III. 62 Neoȝone wæran Noðþæs sweoster. *c* **1400** *Destr. Troy* 8710 Miche bale hade his brether, and his blithe sister. *Ibid.* 10759 Myche pite was of Priam.., With sobbyng of syster, þat semly were euer. ? **1562** *Child-Marriages* 65 One of my suster is maried alreadie.

β. *c* **950** *Lindisf. Gosp.* Mark vi. 3 Ahne suoestro [*c* **1000** swustra, *c* **1160** swustre] his her mið usic sint? *c* **1100** *O.E. Chron.* (MS. D) an. 1067, Mid his modor & his twam sweostran. [*c* **1160** *Hatton Gosp.* Mark iii. 35 Se is min moder & min broðer & mine swustren.] *c* **1290** *S. Eng. Leg.* I. 435 þat þou sum-ȝware þine sostrene do in-to ane nonnerie. **1297** R. GLOUC. (Rolls) 7560 His moder & is sostren tuo mid him sone he nom. **1340** [see sense 5]. **1387-8** T. USK *Test. Love* III. i. (Skeat) I. 93 As sustern in unitie they accorden. *c* **1400** MAUNDEV. (1839) ix. 102 Sarra..and Melcha..weren Sustren to the seyd Lothe. *c* **1420** *Chron. Vilod.* 2077 Hurre sustron weptone. *c* **1440** *Jacob's Well* 49 Bretheryn or systerynes chylderyn arn in þe secunde degre. *c* **1507** *Plumpton Corr.* (Camden) 202, I recommend me to you,..and to all my brethren and sistren. **1553** T. WILSON *Rhet.* 30b, You have other parentes, other brethren, sisterne, and nephewes. **1580** *Wills & Inv. N.C.* (Surtees, 1835) 432, I will that all the goodes be devyded equallye amongeste my Brethren and systeringe childringe.

**1843-8** [see 5]. *a* **1849**- [see 3b]. **1859** BARTLETT *Dict. Amer.* (ed. 2), *Sistern*, for sisters. A vulgar pronunciation sometimes heard from uneducated preachers at the West.

†**c.** Used to designate the mother-in-law of one's daughter. *Obs.*

**1701** EVELYN *Diary* 28 Mar., I went to the funeral of my sister Draper.

**2.** *fig.* **a.** One who is reckoned as, or fills the place of, a sister. In mod. specific uses: (i) a (fellow) prostitute; (ii) a (fellow) feminist; (iii) among Blacks, a Black woman. ***sisters under the skin***: see SKIN *sb.* 6j.

*c* **950** *Lindisf. Gosp.* Matt. xii. 50 Min broðer & suoester [*Rushw.* swuster] & moder is [he]. *c* **1200** ORMIN 15709 Weppmenn & wifmenn baþe Sinndenn till ure Laferrd Crist Full dere breþre & susstress. **1340** *Ayenb.* 89 He is my broþer and my zoster and my moder. **1382** WYCLIF *Prov.* vii. 4 Sey to wisdam, My sister thou art. *c* **1400** *26 Pol. Poems* 137 Thus sayde I..vnto wormes sekurly,..'My systren all ye bene'. *Ibid.*, I shall call hem sustres. **1604** E. G[RIMSTONE] *D'Acosta's Hist. Indies* v. xxiv. 394 The maidens..that day were called the Sisters of their god Vitzliputzli. **1831** SCOTT *Ct. Robt.* Introd. Addr. ¶19 What do they whisper, thou sworn sister of the Eummenides? **1847** A. HARRIS *Settlers & Convicts* vi. 94 When 'her sister' (so they usually speak in the *sisterhood of sorrow*) came here, she came too. **1870** *Free Lance* 16 Apr. 123/1 The working sisters of this great city are waking up to a sense of what they ought to do in making future provision for themselves. **1889** *Girl's Own Paper* 28 Sept. 824/3 A better day..has dawned ..on our sisters, the working girls of this country. **1899** 'J. FLYNT' *Tramping* I. iv. 94 If he can only have some outcast woman, or 'sister', as he calls her..he is a comparatively happy fellow. **1912** H. ELLIS *Task of Social Hygiene* iii. 104 'La femme libre'..must be a woman of reflection and intellect who, having meditated on the fate of her 'sisters'.. shall give forth the confession of her sex..in such a manner as to furnish the indispensable elements for formulating the rights and duties of woman. **1912** in C. McKay *Songs of Jamaica* 16 Me watch de vine dem grow, S'er t'row dung a de root. **1926** L. HUGHES *Weary Blues* 37, I got a railroad ticket, Pack my trunk and ride. Sing 'em sister! Got a railroad ticket, Pack my trunk and ride. **1935** Z. N. HURSTON *Mules & Men* (1970) I. vii. 164 De cow went bustin' on down de back-road wid de ole man till they met a sister he knowed. **1940** J. CRAD *Traders in Women* v. 130 Then she left her 'selling position' and it was immediately occupied by one of her 'sisters'. **1944** *Publ. Amer. Dial. Soc.* II. 36 *Sister, n.*, a woman. W. N[orth] C[arolina]. **1968** *Ramparts* May 12 Our sisters in Vietnam have taught us many lessons. **1973** *Black World* June 90/2 Sister Williams breaks her book down into three major parts. **1976** R. B. PARKER *Promised Land* xix. 110 When the sisters call you... Talk to them of obligation and sororal affiliation. **1977** C. MCFADDEN *Serial* (1978) iii. 13/1 The sisters weren't invariably as supportive as she'd hoped they'd be. **1979** *Guardian* 5 May 12/2 Becoming Britain's first woman Prime Minister is one [achievement], whatever the sisters may say, that can only change perceptions of what women can aspire to.

**b.** A female holding a similar position to another; a fellow-queen, etc.

**1599** SHAKS. *Hen. V*, v. ii. 2 Vnto our brother France, and to our Sister, Health and faire time of day. **1821** SCOTT *Kenilw.* xvii, If..it was needful to continue some restraint on the person of her unhappy sister of Scotland.

**3. a.** A female member of a religious order, society, or gild; *spec.* a nun.

Also with special designations as ***Sister(s) of Charity***, ***of Mercy***, etc.

(*a*) *c* **900** tr. *Baeda's Hist.* IV. xxiii. (1890) 340 Sumu haliȝu nunne..wæs..restende in sweostra slæperne. *Ibid.*, þa ȝeseah heo oðere sweostor ymb heo restende. **1362** LANGL. *P. Pl.* A. III. 54 þat vche mon schulde seye, Ich were suster of [ȝour] house. *c* **1380** *Antecrist* in Todd *Three Treat. Wyclif* (1851) 125 But take we heede to..nunnes and sustris & see hou þei folowen Crist for þe more partie. **1389** in *Eng. Gilds* (1870) 3 To noriche more loue bytwene þe bretheren and sustren of þe bretherhede. *c* **1440** *Alph. Tales* 174 A sister of þe fraternitie of Oegniez. **1482** in *Eng. Hist. Rev.* XXV. 122 Y[e] kepar of oure y[e] sistrenes librarie. **1530** *Test. Ebor.* (Surtees) VI. 16, I bequeith..to the priorisse of Thikhid and hir systers iijs. **1567** *Gude & Godlie B.* (S.T.S.) 205 The Sisteris gray, befoir this day, Did crune within thair cloister. **1603** SHAKS. *Meas. for M.* II. iv. 18 One Isabell, a Sister. *c* **1660** in J. Morris *Troubles Our Cath. Forefathers* (1872) vi. 257 For Subprioress she appointed Sister Anne Tremaine, one of our old Sisters that came from St. Ursula's. **1796** MRS. M. ROBINSON *Angelina* III. 24 The grey sisters were endowed with five hundred marks an hour, to say masses. **1816** SOUTHEY *Poet's Pilgr.* Proem xvi, Behold the black Beguine, the Sister grey. **1844** *Mem. Babylonian Princess* II. 16 Mass being concluded, each sister departs to pursue her particular employment. **1861** M. ARNOLD *Pop. Educ. France* 112 They regard them..with far less indulgence than the schools of the Sisters.

(*b*) **1841** *Penny Cycl.* XXI. 181/2 There are a Roman Catholic church..and an establishment of the Sisters of Charity. **1871** CARLYLE in Mrs. Carlyle *Lett.* III. 180 We had sick-nurses..Catholic 'Sisters of Mercy'. **1898** C. BELL tr. *Huysmans' Cathedral* viii. 145 Sisters of the Visitation, Sisters of Providence, Sisters of Good Comfort,..all lived in hives close round Chartres.

**b.** A female fellow-member of the Christian Church as a whole, or of some body or association within this.

In quot. 1607 used allusively in bad sense. For the vocative use, which appears earlier, see 5.

*c* **1449** PECOCK *Repr.* I. xiii. 63 Therbi [thou] enhauncidist thi silf aboue thi Cristen britheren and sistren. **1526** *Pilgr. Perf.* (W. de W. 1531) 70 Wyllynge in his herte euery persone as his brother or syster in god, to haue the same graces and glory. **1533** MORE *Apol.* iv. Wks. 849/2 Now was this word taken vp, & walked about abrode among the brethren & sistern. **1577** FULKE *Answ. True Christian* 23 Our deare brethren and sistern begotten in Iesu Christ by the gospell. **1607** DEKKER & WEBSTER *Westw. Hoe* II. ii. Wks. 1873 II. 307 The Seruing-man [has] his Punke, the student his Nun in white Fryers, the Puritan his Sister. **1738** WESLEY *Wks.* (1872) I. 107 The rest of the day we spent with all the brethren and sisters. **1818** SCOTT *Hrt. Midl.* xxix, This is one of the precious sisters, and we'll take her word. *a* **1849** H. COLERIDGE *Ess.* (1851) I. 375 We united brethren and sisteren of the three kingdoms. **1861** N. A. WOODS *Tour Pr. Wales in Canada* 261 The cortège had to be eked out with the Temperance Brethren and Sistren.

†**c.** ***sisters of the bank***, prostitutes. *Obs.*

**1550** CROWLEY *Inform. & Petit.* 472 Immodeste and wanton gyrles haue hereby ben made sisters of the Banck (the stumbling stock of all frayle youth).

**d.** A member of a body of nurses; also *spec.* a head-nurse having charge of a ward in an infirmary or hospital. Also, prefixed as a title to the name of a nurse. ***Sister Dora*** [f. the name of the celebrated nurse Dorothy ('Dora') Pattison, 1832–78], a type of nurse's cap (see quot. 1971).

**1860** [see NURSING *vbl. sb.* 1b]. **1873** MRS. BROOKFIELD *Not a Heroine* II. 158 Two 'Nursing Sisters', from an excellent institution,..took turns day and night to attend upon [him]. **1896** *Allbutt's Syst. Med.* I. 424 The Matron.. who is guided by the reports of the 'sisters' or 'charge-nurses'. **1924** 'R. HALL' *Unlit Lamp* xlvi. 314, I made swabs at the Town Hall at Seabourne... I had a Sister Dora arrangement on my head; we all had, it made us look important. Some of the women wore aprons with large red crosses on their bibs. **1949** N. MITFORD *Love in Cold Climate* II. viii. 276 Doesn't it seem funny to have talcum powder and..boring old Sister waiting..for somebody who doesn't exist? **1971** J. MANTON *Sister Dora* xvi. 266 [Dora Pattison] made herself up a new cap, still tied with a butterfly bow and streamers under the chin but folded smoothly back over her dark hair. It was to be known to generations of nurses as 'a Sister Dora'. **1976** C. STORR *Unnatural Fathers* iii. 34 Kind Sister Tucker..faithful in her professional code of discretion, bustled upstairs..to attend to her interesting patients. **1978** *Church Times* 29 Dec. 11/3 The little white cap worn by nurses everywhere became known within the profession as 'a Sister Dora'. **1979** 'C. AIRD' *Some die Eloquent* i. 11 When Sister Casualty.. had trouble-makers in her patch she would ring down to the police station. *Ibid.* iii. 37 Sister Stork's on the other phone to the delivery ward.

**4. a.** Used to designate qualities, conditions, etc., in relation to each other or to some kindred thing.

*a* **1200** *Vices & Virtues* 29 All ðat hire suster, ðe rihte ȝeleaue, hire seiȝeð, all hie [*sc.* hope] hit fastliche hopeð. *c* **1230** *Hali Meid.* 17 Ah wel is him þat folheð wit godes dohter for ha halt wið meidenhad þat is hire suster. *a* **1300** *Cursor M.* 9547 þe first o þam was cald merci,..Pees þe feirth sister hight. **1399** LANGL. *P. Pl.* C. XII. 98 Ich shal þe kenne to clergie,..hue is sybbe to þe seuen ars and also my soster. **1443** LYDG. in *Pol. Poems* (Rolls) II. 212 In thes seven sustryn was no divisioun; Cheef of ther consayl was Humilitas. **1474** CAXTON *Chesse* III. vi. (1883) 133 Virginite whiche is suster of angellis. **1599** SHAKS. etc. *Pass. Pilgr.* 104 If music and sweet poetry agree,..the sister and the brother. **1604** N. D. *3rd Pt. Three Conversions Eng.* 179 Vayne glory ..with her other sisters, inobedience, boasting, &c. **1667** MILTON *P.L.* VII. 10 Thou with Eternal wisdom didst converse, Wisdom thy Sister. **1817** SHELLEY *Rev. Islam* v. v, Science, and her sister Poesy, Shall clothe in light the.. cities of the free! **1873** HAMERTON *Intell. Life* II. ii. (1876) 58 Inspiration decidedly the sister of daily labor.

**b.** Applied to mythological or imaginary beings; esp. ***the (fatal*** or ***three) sisters***, the Fates or Parcæ.

*c* **1374** CHAUCER *Troylus* III. 733 O fatale sustrin! which, or eny clothe Me shapyn was, my destyne me sponne. *c* **1384** — *H. Fame* III. 1401 The myghty Muse..Caliope, And hir eighte sustren eke. **1402** LYDG. *Compl. Bl. Knt.* 489 Or I was born, my desteny was sponne By Parcas sustren, to slee me, if they conne. *c* **1449** PECOCK *Repr.* II. iv. 155 This opinioun, that iij. sistris (whiche ben spiritis) comen to the cradilis of infantis, forto sette to the babe what schal bifalle to him. *c* **1475** HENRYSON *Orpheus & Eurydice* 388 Scho send hym doun vnto the sisteris thre. **1559** *Mirr. Mag.* (1563) Bij, Whose fatall threde false fortune nedes would reele, Ere it were twisted by the susters thre. **1592** LODGE *Euphues Shadow* (Hunterian Club) 79, I should be confirmed..euen to ouercome the insupportable trauailes of the sisters. **1605** SHAKS. *Macb.* I. v. 8 These weyward Sisters saluted me, and referr'd me to the comming on of time. **1637** MILTON *Lycidas* 15 Begin then, Sisters of the sacred well. **1744** AKENSIDE *Pleas. Imag.* II. 59 The harmonious Muse And her persuasive sisters. **1859** *Habits of Gd. Society* v. 194 Should the weird sisters, in a fit of bad temper [etc.]. **1871** R. ELLIS *Catullus* lxiv. 325 Hark on a joyous day what prophet-story the sisters Open surely to thee.

**5.** In the vocative, as a mode of address, chiefly in transferred senses. Also *colloq.* as a mode of address to an unrelated woman, esp. one whose name is not known.

*c* **1175** *Lamb. Hom.* 5 Leoue broðre and sustre ȝe hi-hered hu [etc.]. *a* **1225** *Ancr. R.* 68 þis nis nout uor ou, leoue sustren, iseid ne uor oðer swuche. **1340** *Ayenb.* 265 Sleȝþe zayþ..'Now broþren and zostren y-hyreþ my red and yueþ youre'. **1451** CAPGRAVE *Life St. Aug.* 31 þan schuld þei pley, as Wiclif disciples played, 'Sistir me nedith'. *c* **1545** COVERDALE *Church in Denmark* Wks. (Parker Soc.) I. 469 My right dear and entirely beloved brethren and sistern in Jesu Christ. **1584** R. SCOT *Discov. Witchcr.* XII. vii. (1886) 181 Thou shalt See sister underneath The grounde with roring gape. **1600** SHAKS. *A.Y.L.* III. v. 75 Will you goe Sister? Shepheard ply her hard. **1603** DEKKER *Batcheler's Banq.* Wks. (Grosart) I. 202 Sister, good morrow, what newes I pray? **1761** GRAY *Fatal Sisters* 51 Sisters, weave the web of death. **1764** — *J.T.* 5 'Lord! sister,' says Physic to Law. **1780** *Mirror* No. 98, And who taught you drinking songs, sister Juddy? **1843** R. CARLTON *New Purchase* I. 203 Brethurn and sisturn, it's a powerful great work, this here preaching of the gospul. **1848** in *Century Mag.* (1882) Apr. 886 Pray for me, brethren! pray for me, sisteren. **1906** H. GREEN *At Actors' Boarding House* 56 He got up and walked over to her bench. 'You up agin it too, sister?' he said, gently. **1926** E. O'NEILL *Great God Brown* I. iii. 40 Blessed are the pitiful, Sister! **1929** W. FAULKNER *Sartoris* II. iii. 97 A voice in the other room boomed in rich rolling waves 'Mawnin', sister,' it said. **1934** 'E. M. DELAFIELD' *Provincial Lady in Amer.* 60 Shouted at by a policeman who tells her: Put your lights on, sister! **1943** *Amer. Speech* XVIII. 88 [New Zealand English] Sister is also used for a girl as a term of address. It is not..a recent adoption from American films, but a relic of the whaling slang of a century ago. **1944** M. LASKI *Love on Supertax* xi. 103 Just waiting for your boy friend, duckie..? You want the best, we got 'em, eh, sister? **1953** H. MILLER *Plexus* (1963) iii. 127 'He doesn't need advice,' she replied. 'He knows what he's doing.' 'O.K. sister, have it your way then!' With this he turned abruptly to me again. **1976** 'R. BOYLE' *Cry Rape* i. 6 Come on, sister. .. Why won't you stay and talk to me? I'm a nice guy.

**6.** *pl.* The seven chief stars in the constellation of the Great Bear. See also SEVEN SISTERS.

*c* **1450** METHAM *Wks.* (E.E.T.S.) 10/266 Hys bryght plowgh of sterrys, and eke the systyrrys at ther stent, The quyche he namyd the sterrys seuyn.

**7. a.** A thing having close kinship or relationship to another.

**1613** DEKKER *Strange Horse Race* Wks. (Grosart) III. 327 There should you behold a Mine of Tynne, (sister to Siluer). **1622** BONOEIL *Art of Making Silke* Title-p, The two renowned and most hopefull Sisters, Virginia, and the Summer-Ilands. **1736** GRAY *Statius* i. 54 The sun's pale sister, drawn by magic strain. **1752** YOUNG *Brothers* I. i, The days of life are sisters. **1789** J. WILLIAMS *Min. Kingd.* I. 176, I am really concerned for the metropolis and her younger sisters. **1812** BYRON *Ch. Har.* I. xxxii, Where Lusitania and her Sister meet, Deem ye what bounds the rival realms divide? **1867** J. L. PORTER *Giant Cities of Bashan* 155 Olivet overtopping its sister [Mt. Moriah] three hundred feet. **1875** JOWETT *Plato* (ed. 2) V. 49 Sparta..in laws and institutions is the sister of Crete.

†**b.** *pl.* The strings of a staircase. *Obs.*$^{-1}$

**1518** *Lett. & P. Hen. VIII*, II. II. 1371 A block to set the systers of the stairs upon, 3 ft. long, 18 inches broad, 10 inches thick.

**c.** One of the cheeks of a cider-press.

**1813** RUDGE *Agric. Surv. Glouc.* 225 The cheeks, or 'sisters', are two strong upright pieces of oak, kept to their places by being let into the ground. **1825** J. NICHOLSON *Operat. Mechanic* 291 An improved cider-press..; B B the cheeks or sisters.

**d.** (See quot.)

**1892** *Pall Mall G.* 18 Feb. 1/3 The term 'sister' used for the stool on which the lace-makers place their pillows.

**8.** *ellipt.* for *sister-line* (see 10b), *-block*.

**1653** R. SANDERS *Physiogn.* 2 The same Signs, with the Sisters relating to the Lines. **1834** MARRYAT *P. Simple* (1863) 29 'What blocks have we below—not on charge?' 'Let me see, sir, I've one sister, t'other we split in half the other day.'

**II.** *attrib.* and *Comb.*

**9.** The old uninflected genitive remained in common use down to the 16th cent. (latterly only in Sc.) in terms of relationship, esp. ***sister son***; rarely in other uses, as ***sister bed, part.*** Now *Obs.* exc. *arch.* in *sister-son.*

(*a*) **835** *Charter* in *O.E. Texts* 448 Đonne ann ic his minra swæstar suna. *c* **900** tr. *Baeda's Hist.* IV. xvi. [xviii.] (1890) 308 Se wæs his sweostor sunu. *c* **1100** *O.E. Chron.* (MS. D) an. 1054, His sunu Osbarn & his sweostor sunu Sihward. **1297** R. GLOUC. (Rolls) 3525 King arthures soster sone þe king howel was. *a* **1300** *Cursor M.* 21130 Iacob..was our lauerd sistur sun. **1375** BARBOUR *Bruce* I. 557 Modreyt his systir son him slew. **14..** *Lat.-Eng. Voc.* in Wr.-Wülcker 575 *Consobrini*, systersones. **1480** WARKWORTH *Chron.* (Camden) 3 One fayre ladye, suster-doughtere to the Kynge of Fraunce. **1483** *Cath. Angl.* 341/1 A Syster husbande, *sororius.* **1529** RASTELL *Pastyme* (1811) 35 Albert..was slayne by his syster sonne. *a* **1578** LINDESAY (Pitscottie) *Chron. Scot.* (S.T.S.) I. 354 The empreouris sister douchtaris. **1596** DALRYMPLE tr. *Leslie's Hist. Scot.* II. 10 Dauid of Abirnethie, his sistir sone. **1680** in *Cloud of Witnesses* (1871) 85 The Earl of Mar's mother and I being sister-bairns. **1955** J. R. R. TOLKIEN *Return of King* vi. 255 Fréalaf, Helm's sister-son. *a* **1973** —— *Silmarillion* (1977) xvi. 136 The King..looked with liking upon Maeglin his sister-son.

(*b*) *c* **1440** *Alph. Tales* 174 Sho purseyvid & saw a multitude of fendis rumyand abowte hur sister bed. **1793** *Statist. Acc. Scotl.* VII. 584 The son got two merks, and the daughter one; hence the sister part, a common proverb in Shetland to this day.

**10.** Appositively, in the sense of 'fellow':

**a.** With designations of persons (or animals).

**1687** T. BROWN *Saints in Uproar* Wks. 1730 I. 77 The kingdom..is ten times as populous as when the legend supposes you and your sister-trollops to have lived there. **1702** ADDISON *Dial. Medals* Wks. 1766 III. 29 The Sister-Graces hand in hand Conjoin'd by love's eternal band. **1708** WYCHERLEY *Let. to Pope* 13 May, Her artful innocence.. will..make her sister rivals of this age blush for spite, if not for shame. **1775** ABIGAIL ADAMS in *Fam. Lett.* (1876) 89 Spending the day with my namesake and sister delegate. *a* **1786** BURNS *Address to Unco Guid* in *Poems* (1968) I. 53 Then gently scan your brother Man, Still gentler sister Woman. **1794** MRS. RADCLIFFE *Myst. Udolpho* xv, With my sister-nymphs I sport. **1820** SHELLEY *Prometh. Unb.* III. iii, To me Shall they become like sister-antelopes. **1839–54** BAILEY *Festus* 226 While six sister goddesses mazily tread The bright fields of air. **1856** DICKENS *Little Dorrit* (1857) xxvii. 243 A woman, who..has a perverted delight in making a sister-woman as wretched as she is. **1862** Q. VICTORIA in Ld. R. Gower *Rec. & Rem.* (1903) 69 Pray express to all these kind *sister widows* the deep and heartfelt gratitude of their widowed Queen. **1939** N. MARSH *Overture to Death* vii. 76, I have judged my sister-woman in my heart and condemned her.

**b.** With names of things.

**1641** MILTON *Reform.* II, We must..come from Schism to Unity with our neighbour reform'd Sister-Churches. **1653** R. SANDERS *Physiogn.* 57 When the sister line of the line of Life is short. **1680** C. NESS *Church Hist.* 92 Those two sister-sins, adultery and idolatry. **1725** POPE *Odyss.* v. 619 Alike their leaves, but not alike they smil'd With sister-fruits. **1727–46** THOMSON *Summer* 1410 The Sister-Hills that skirt her plain. **1777** *Rec. Early Hist. Boston* (1887) XVIII. 285 We are sure, that very large, & much wanted Supplies, the Property of this State & expected here, are now ordered into some of the Sister States. **1787** G. WHITE *Selborne* ix, Wolmer, with her sister forest Ayles Holt. **1808** SCOTT *Marmion* I. Introd. 22 Russet bare Are now the sister-heights of Yair. **1842** TENNYSON *Day Dream* 4 Dreaming on your damask cheek, The dewy sister-eyelids lay. **1870** W. THORNBURY *Tour rd. Eng.* II. xx. 58 Nor did he forget the sister-seat of learning,..Oxford. **1888** BRYCE *Amer. Commw.* II. xlii. 114 Each State recognises the judgments of the courts of a sister State.

**c.** In collocations tending towards specialized uses, as ***sister art, dialect, island, isle, kingdom, language, science, ship, soul, tongue, university***, or the plurals of these.

**1695** DRYDEN *Parallel Poetry & Painting* Ess. (ed. Ker) II. 135 At this time..Poetry is better practised than her *sister-art. **1768** W. GILPIN *Ess. Prints* (1781) 54 The art of scraping mezzotintos is greatly more improved than either of its sister-arts. **1894** PARRY *Stud. Gt. Composers, Mendelssohn* 266 He entered fully into the enjoyment of the numberless masterpieces of the sister art. *c* **1645** HOWELL *Lett.* II. lix. (1892) 475 The *sister-dialects of the Italian, Spanish, and French. **1844** *Proc. Philol. Soc.* I. 217 Similar forms may be found in the sister-dialects. **1816** COLERIDGE *Lay Serm.* (Bohn) 324 The prospective measures in agitation respecting our *sister island. **1838** ARNOLD *Hist. Rome* I. 427 The three sister islands of Sicily, Sardinia and Corsica. **1936** *Discovery* June 187/1 The *waganga*, who specialise in *pepo*-exorcism, go through a special training. The art is at its highest in Pemba, the sister-island of Zanzibar. **1838** T. LANGTON in H. H. Langton *Gentlewoman in Upper Canada* (1950) 58 William Jones is from the *sister isle. **1939** JOYCE *Finnegans Wake* 51 A native of the sisterisle..by his brogue. **1779** *Mirror* No. 30, Our frequent communication with the metropolis of our *sister kingdom [*sc.* England]. **1826** W. COBBETT *Rur. Rides* (1885) II. 246 The Irish Bible-man,..whose family are so very well known in the most unfortunate sister-kingdom. **1846** PRESCOTT *Ferd. & Isab.* I. Introd. 29 The sister kingdom of Aragon. **1748** HARTLEY *Observ. Man* I. iii. §1. 303 The Greek and Latin Tongues I consider as *Sister-Languages. **1842** PRICHARD *Nat. Hist. Man* 246 Other great nations in India whose idioms are sister languages of the people of Tamul. **1901** W. JAMES *Mem. & Stud.* (1911) vii. 169 Whether his name [*sc.* F. Myers'] will have in psychology as honorable a place as their names [*sc.* Cuvier and Agassiz's] have gained in the *sister-science, will depend on whether future inquirers shall adopt or reject his theories. **1840** *Civil Eng. & Arch. Jrnl.* III. 325/2 The 'Vernon', a *sister ship.., made the voyage from Calcutta to Spithead..in 86 days. **1886** *Engineering* 12 Mar., The Edinburgh, a sister ship to the Colossus. **1966** N. NICOLSON in *Diaries & Lett. H. Nicolson* (1966) 56 The airship, R.101, was contracted by the Government in 1925 as a sister-ship to R.100. **1974** E. R. H. IVAMY *Marine Insurance* (ed. 2) xv. 216 This clause is known as the 'sister ship' clause and was introduced to state the legal position where two ships belonging to the same owner come into collision. **1897** J. WARING tr. *Balzac's Lily of Valley* 74 Feeling now that we were twins of the same nurture, she could not conceive of semi-confidences between *sister souls that had drunk of the same spring. **1933** *Times Lit. Suppl.* 16 Nov. 792/2 The influence of the visiting Cousin Nellie, who finds a sister-soul in the comfortable person of an Aug [*sc.* August visitor] of her own age. **1843** *Proc. Philol. Soc.* I. 143 A *sister-tongue to those of which the Hebrew is the oldest literary type. **1679** FELL in Gutch *Coll. Cur.* I. 270 If we are justified, the advantage will extend to our *Sister University. **1849** MACAULAY *Hist. Eng.* iii. I. 378 The emulation of the sister University was moved.

**d.** In scientific or technical terms, as **sister-block, -cell** (see quots.); **sister chromatid** *Biol.*, each of a pair of chromatids derived from a common parent chromosome; **sister-hook, -keelson** (see quots.).

**1794** *Rigging & Seamanship* 156 **Sister-blocks* are made of ash, similar to two single blocks, and are turned out of a solid piece,..one above the other. *c* **1860** H. STUART *Seaman's Catech.* 23 Take it..through the upper sheave of the sister block. **1863** A. YOUNG *Naut. Dict.* (ed. 2) 352 *Sister-blocks*, blocks or bull's-eyes seized between the top-mast shrouds, for the topsail lifts and reef tackles to lead through. **1882** VINES *Sachs' Bot.* 920 A fertile sexual union of *sister-cells takes place regularly. **1887** BENTLEY *Man. Bot.* (ed. 5) 788 By the division of an epidermal cell (the mother-cell) by a partition which extends across and divides the two daughter- or sister-cells. **1942** *Jrnl. Genetics* XLIII. 195 A single chromatid may be broken and fail to rejoin, the chromatid fragment almost always remaining paired to its *sister chromatid. **1975** *Nature* 13 Nov. 122/1 Techniques have been developed which distinguish between sister chromatids without using radioisotopes and autoradiography. **1875** KNIGHT *Dict. Mech.* 2191/2 **Sister hook*, a double hook in which the shanks of the respective portions form mousings for the fellow portions. **1886** R. C. LESLIE *Sea-painter's Log* iv. 74 Un-knotted jibsheets fly out, sister-hooks rattle loose. **1846** A. YOUNG *Naut. Dict.* 176 *Sister keelsons are additional keelsons laid on the floors, one on each side of the main keelson, to afford additional strength and stability, especially to prevent the ship sagging by the weight of the masts. **1869** SIR E. REED *Ship-build.* ii. 45 The forms of keelsons and sister-keelsons used in iron shipbuilding have been almost as various as the forms of keels.

**11.** Attrib., in ***sister-band, -love, -train, -triad, -twin***; **sister act** (see quot. 1952); **sister-fold**, a sisterly embrace (*poet.*); † **sister-right**, a right of sisterhood; **sister tutor**, a nursing sister who teaches trainee nurses; **sister-wife**, a wife who is also the sister of her husband.

**1908** G. V. HOBART *Go to It* 56 Their names were Millie and Tillie, and they..did a *sister act. **1908** *Variety* 18 Apr. 4/4 There may be a number of new 'sister' acts in vaudeville next season. **1952** W. GRANVILLE *Dict. Theatrical Terms* 163 *Sister act*, a variety act performed by two or more sisters; e.g. the famous Dolly Sisters, the singing Green Sisters of the stage and radio. **1786** BURNS *O Thou dread Pow'r*, The beauteous, seraph *Sister-band. **1846** PROWETT *Prometh. Bound* 26 From out our sister-band thou'dst won thy bride. **1813** SCOTT *Trierm.* III. xxx, These maids enlink'd in *sister-fold. **1801** SOUTHEY *Thalaba* III. xxv, Was it *sister-love For which the silver rings Round her smooth ankles and her tawny arms, Shone daily brighten'd? **1467** in *Ripon Ch. Acts* (Surtees) 233 De et super unum *suster right in Collegio S. Trinitatis Pontefract. **1743** FRANCIS tr. *Hor., Odes* IV. vii. 5 The elder Grace, with her fair *sister-Train, In naked Beauty dances o'er the Plain. **1876** B. TAYLOR *Faust* II. iii. (1875) II. 144 In our new *sister-triad what a beauty! **1968** R. RENDELL *Secret House of Death* vi. 62 An even temperature, that's one thing my *sister tutor always impressed on me. **1971** P. D. JAMES *Shroud for Nightingale* iv. 119 I'm not a qualified Sister Tutor. I was only deputizing. **1611** COTGR., *Iumelle*, a female twin, or *sister twin. **1818** SHELLEY *Rev. Islam* VII. xxii. 3 We, on the earth, like sister twins lay down. **1743** FRANCIS tr. *Hor., Odes* III. iii. 64 My Grecians shall victorious prove, By me led on to War, the *Sister-Wife of Jove. *a* **1843** SOUTHEY *Comm.-pl. Bk.* (1851) IV. 4 Mango Capac and Mama Oella his sister-wife. **1853** HUMPHREY *Coin-coll. Man.* x. 118 Ptolemy VII married Cleopatra the sister-wife of his predecessor.

**'sister**, *v.* [f. prec.]

**1.** *trans.* To stand to (a person or thing) in the relationship of a sister or sisters. Chiefly *fig.*

**1608** SHAKS. *Per.* v. Prol. 7 Her art sisters the natural roses. **1748** RICHARDSON *Clarissa* (1811) VI. 407 Whose misfortune [is] to be brother'd and sister'd by a couple of creatures, who are not able to comprehend her excellencies. **1854** S. DOBELL *Balder* xxiv. 158 Seven snowdrops Sister the pleiads.

**2.** To call (one) sister; to address as a sister.

**1663** KILLIGREW *Parson's Wedding* II. iii, You have got one of the best hiders of such a business in the Town; Lord, how he would Sister you at a Play! **1753–4** RICHARDSON *Grandison* (1812) III. 251 How artfully..he reminds her of the brotherly character which he passes under to her. How officiously he sisters her! **1834** MAR. EDGEWORTH *Helen* xxxv, Think what it must be..to be 'dear sistered' by such bodies as these in public.

**3.** To treat in a sisterly manner.

**1871** MRS. WHITNEY *Real Folks* xiv, She could be mothered and sistered, as girls ought to be.

Hence **'sistering** *vbl. sb.* (in sense 2).

**1818** SOUTHEY *Lett.* (1856) III. 97 By..such brothering and sistering he kept up his influence among his people.

**sister-german.** [f. SISTER *sb.* + GERMAN *a.*[1]] A sister through both parents; a full sister.

**1382** WYCLIF *1 Kings* xi. 19 The sister germayn of his wiif Taphnes. *c* **1489** CAXTON *Sonnes of Aymon* vii. 159, I have gyven my suster germayne to Reynawde for his wyff. **1490** —— *Eneydos* xxi. 75 She dyde doo calle anne her suster germayne. **1523** LD. BERNERS tr. *Froiss.* I. xxi. 31 Isabell of Englande..was suster germayne to king Charles last deed. **1570** J. DEE *Math. Pref.* d ij b, Picture and Sculpture, are Sisters germaine.

**†'sisterhead.** *Obs. rare.* [-HEAD.] = next.

**1390** GOWER *Conf.* III. 278 Thei token thanne litel hiede, The brother of the Sosterhiede To wedde wyves. *c* **1400** *Pilgr. Sowle* (Caxton) I. xxxvi. (1859) 40, I doo yow to vnderstande that this lady Misericord, sauynge hyr systerhede, hath caused in this Courte grete annoye. **14..** *Lat.-Eng. Voc.* in Wr.-Wülcker 612 *Sororitas*, a systerhede.

**sisterhood** ('sɪstəhʊd). Also 4 **sosterhode.** [f. SISTER *sb.* + -HOOD.]

**1.** The state or condition of being a sister; sisterly status or relationship. Recently also *spec.* in feminist use.

**1390** GOWER *Conf.* II. 268 That was unto Creusa sent.., For Sosterhode hem was betuene. *Ibid.* III. 278 Thanne.. Sosterhode of mariage Was torned into cousinage. **1609** DANIEL *Civ. Wars* IV. lxxii, She..left to doo the part Of sisterhood, to doo that of a wife. **1611** COTGR., *Demi-lict*,.. brotherhood, or sisterhood, on th' one side only. *a* **1656** BP. HALL *Rem.* (1660) 407 There is a kinde of natural equality in Sisterhood. **1780** S. J. PRATT *Emma Corbett* (ed. 4) III. 10 Her last leave of love and sisterhood. **1820** SCOTT *Monast.* v, I will but salute you with the kiss of sisterhood. *a* **1855** C. BRONTE *Professor* xviii, They acknowledged in her a sisterhood of youth and health. **1968** *Notes from First Year* June 18 Sisterhood is powerful! **1974** *Time* 6 May 80 Sisterhood across class lines is a myth. **1980** J. R. RICHARDS *Sceptical Feminist* i. 28 Basic to much recent feminist practice has been the idea of *sisterhood*, which..involves a determination among members of the women's movement to work together as equals.

*transf.* **1846** GROTE *Greece* I. xxii. (1862) II. 541 Connected by colonial sisterhood with the Chalkidic settlements.

**2. a.** A society of sisters; *esp.* a society of women who have taken certain vows and live together under conventual rule, or who are otherwise devoted to religious life, or to charitable work as a vocation. Also *attrib.*

*c* **1592** MARLOWE *Jew of Malta* III, Let me be one, Although unworthy, of that Sister-hood. **1592** SHAKS. *Rom. & Jul.* v. iii. 157 Ile dispose of thee, Among a Sisterhood of holy Nunnes. **1606** WARNER *Alb. Eng.* XIV. lxxxix. 362 Amongst your Sisterhood I know are amorous Wenches some. **1687** T. BROWN *Saints in Uproar* Wks. 1730 I. 80 Own yourself and the rest of your sister-hood to be cheats. **1711** ADDISON *Spect.* No. 164 ¶3 To look out a Sisterhood of Nuns among whom to place his Daughter. **1794** MRS. RADCLIFFE *Myst. Udolpho* xlvii, When she took the vows,.. few of the present sisterhood, I believe, were witnesses of the ceremony. **1866** *Church Times* 1 Sept. 277/2 The various works of charity which are chiefly conducted by Sisterhoods. **1889** RUSKIN *Præterita* III. 10 The first impression from life at the secluded Sisterhoods was given me at the Convent of St. Michael.

**b.** Used loosely to denote a number of women having some common aim, characteristic, or calling. Often in a bad sense. Recently also *spec.* of feminists.

**1609** MARKHAM *Famous Whore* (1868) 47 You faire creatures of my sister-hoode I wish this my discourse may do you good. **1637** MASSINGER *Guardian* IV. iii, I will build An hospital only for noseless bawds,..and be myself The governess of the sisterhood. **1718** *Free-thinker* No. 71. 103 Have the whole Sisterhood of Canting Females banished to some Desart Island. **1748** SMOLLETT *R. Random* xxiii, One of the sisterhood, a little stale, advised me to take lodgings in a part of the town where I was unknown. **1791** WOLCOTT (P. Pindar) *Ode i to Mrs. Paine* Wks. 1812 II. 440 The Sisterhood of Billingsgate shall throng. **1828** SCOTT *F.M. Perth* xi, She lacked..the decided boldness and effrontery of her sisterhood. **1873** G. C. DAVIES *Mount. & Mere* i. 3 Those members of the female sex..who agitate questions they know nothing about. The *Saturday Review* calls the latter the 'Shrieking Sisterhood'. **1880** 'OUIDA' *Moths* I. 82 Lady Dolly and her sisterhood were audacious but cowardly. **1972** *Newsweek* 9 Oct. 104 That book's stinging attack on the women's lib movement achieved for its author a place in the sisterhood's demonology right next to Hugh Hefner. **1981** *Times* 9 Sept. 9/3 At the age of 24 Sarah Daniels must count as a second generation feminist, and if this first play is a portent of what the sisterhood is now brewing up then male chauvinism can breathe again.

**c.** *fig.* A group, array, association, or number of things imagined as sisters.

**1827** R. POLLOK *Course of T.* II, A little orb [the earth],.. With her fair sisterhood of planets seven. **1839** DONALDSON *New Cratylus* I. iv. 80 The Celtic nations, the claim of whose speech to a place in the Indo-Germanic sisterhood has lately been established. **1883** in Schaff *Encycl. Relig. Knowl.* III. 2038 A sisterhood of churches covering a large section of country.

**sistering** ('sɪstərɪŋ), *ppl. a.* [f. SISTER *v.*] Having a relationship comparable in some way to that of a sister or sisters.

**1597** SHAKS. *Lover's Compl.* 2 From off a hill whose concaue wombe reworded A plaintfull story from a sistring vale. *c* **1625** DRUMM. OF HAWTH. *Fam. Epist.* Wks. (1711) 140 The Roman was almost naked from the Waste upwards, discovering the sistering Apples of her Breast. **1835** *Blackw. Mag.* XXXVII. 856 The soft sistering music of a stream That pilgrimed by. **1880** SWINBURNE *Studies in Song* 13 At his birth the sistering stars were one.

**sister-in-law.** Also 5 **sistir elawe**, 7, 9 *dial.* **sister-law**, etc. [See LAW *sb.*[1] 3 c.] **a.** The sister of one's husband or wife. **b.** The wife of one's brother. **c.** The wife of one's husband's or wife's brother.

*c* **1440** *Promp. Parv.* 457/1 Syster yn lawe, as hows[bondes] syster, or wyfys syster, *glos. Ibid.*, Syster yn lawe, broders wyyf, *fratrissa.* *a* **1450** *Knt. de la Tour* (1868) 35 The ladies husbondes brother was there, and sawe his suster-in-lawe a litelle asyde with a knight in a corner. **1483** *Cath. Angl.* 341/1 A Sistir elawe, *socrus*, *nurus.* **1535** COVERDALE *Ruth* i. 15 Beholde, thy syster in lawe is turned backe vnto hir people. **1552** *Bury Wills* (Camden) 142 Item I geve..to mother Harvy, my syster in lawe, the thurde [gowne] w[ch] I last made. **1676** HOBBES *Iliad* XXII. 467 Her Sister-laws that stood about her nigh. *a* **1721** J. SHEFFIELD (Dk. Buckhm.) *Wks.* (1753) II. 183 He mentions his Sister-in-law's being with child, as no little proof of his brother's kindness. **1779** *Mirror* No. 65, It was my wish to live with my sister-in-law in terms of the strictest friendship. **1820** SHELLEY *Let. to Mary Gisborne* 218 Some dozens of female friends, sisters-in-law, and cousins. **1838** DICKENS *Nickleby* iii, Now for my sister-in-law.

**'sisterize,** *v. rare*[-1]. [f. SISTER *sb.* + -IZE.] In *pass.*: To be provided with a sister or sisters.

**1752** MRS. DELANY *Life & Corr.* (1861) I. 82 It is happy for D., since she is so brotherised and sisterised, that she can make their strange and unnatural behaviour easy to her.

**sisterless** ('sɪstəlɪs), *a.* [f. SISTER *sb.* + -LESS.] Having no sister.

**1856** MRS. CRAIK *J. Halifax* ii, Brotherless, sisterless, and friendless as I was. **1875** W. CORY *Lett. & Jrnls.* (1897) 389 I'd like to end my life that way, motherless, wifeless, and sisterless.

**'sister-like,** *adv.* [f. SISTER *sb.* + -LIKE.] After the manner of a sister. Also **'sisterlike** *a.*, appropriate to sisters; sisterly.

**1576** GASCOIGNE *Philomene* (Arb.) 104 And sister like did louingly Faire Phylomene embrace. **1814** SCOTT *Ld. of Isles* VI. iii, Sister-like in love they dwell. **1839–52** BAILEY *Festus* 205 How sweetly shine the steadfast stars, Each eyeing, sister-like, the earth. **1864** SKEAT *Uhland's Poems* 134 They sat..In sisterlike embrace together wound.

**'sisterliness.** [f. next + -NESS.] The quality of being sisterly; sisterly affection or sympathy.

**1879** G. MEREDITH *Egoist* II. xi. 232 An elegant sisterliness, one might almost say. **1882–3** *Advance* (Chicago) 9 Aug., If you could experience once the brotherliness and sisterliness that warms our Annual [mission] Meetings.

**sisterly** ('sɪstəlɪ), *a.* [f. SISTER *sb.* + -LY[1].]

**1.** Of or pertaining to a sister; also, characteristic of, befitting, becoming, or like a sister.

**1570** LEVINS *Manip.* 100 Sisterly, *sororius.* **1603** SHAKS. *Meas. for M.* V. i. 100 After much debatement, My sisterly remorse confutes mine honour. **1756** WARBURTON *Bolingbroke's Philos.* iii. 158 We shall hear no more of this sisterly resemblance [of Christianity] to Platonism. **1794** MRS. RADCLIFFE *Myst. Udolpho* xlv, A renewal of all the maternal kindness of the abbess, and of the sisterly attentions of the nuns. **1821** SCOTT *Pirate* xix, They.. exchanged a sisterly kiss, and a sisterly good-night. **1848** THACKERAY *Van. Fair* xliii, She..read him lectures with sisterly frankness. **1887** RUSKIN *Præterita* II. 10 Exhibiting in their own lives every joy of sisterly love.

**2.** Of or pertaining to a sisterhood.

**1883** *Women's Suffrage Jrnl.* Nov. 201 The self-devotion of women to the sisterly life arose out of Christ's teaching.

**sisterly** ('sɪstəlɪ), *adv.* [f. as prec. + -LY[2].] In the manner or spirit of a sister.

**1616** J. LANE *Contin. Sqr.'s T.* VIII. 68 Yet if thow die the deathe, I live that liefe Which dieth sisterlie with Algarsife. *a* **1821** KEATS *Hyperion* I. 296 Those silver wings expanded sisterly. **1864** F. W. ROBINSON *Mattie, a Stray* III. 205 She spoke coolly and sisterly now.

**si'sternity.** *rare.* [f. SISTER *sb.*, on the analogy of FRATERNITY.] Sisterhood.

**1603** HARSNET *Pop. Impost.* xxiii. 166 A Sisternity of mimpes, mops, and idle holy women. **1654** GAYTON *Pleas. Notes* IV. ix. 235 Others of their sisternity (very weak headed women, frail vessels) carried not matters so well.

**'sistership.** [f. SISTER *sb.* + -SHIP.] Institutional or conventional sisterhood.

**1840** AGNES STRICKLAND *Queens Eng.* I. 294 *note*, Those favoured ladies who..are fortunate enough to obtain sisterships. **1843** LD. J. MANNERS in *Mrs. Brookfield & her Circle* (1905) 133 They are not to be bound by vows, but during their Sistership to obey all the rules of the House.

**sisters thread.** [perh. from SISTER *sb.* 3 a.] (See quot. 1812.)

**1572** in Feuillerat *Revels Q. Eliz.* (1908) 156 Sisters threade .j. oz. **1586** *Rates of Custome* E viij b, Thred called Sisters thred the li., vs. **1590** *Acct. Bk. W. Wray* in *Antiquary* XXXII. 371, iiii ounce systers thred, vs. **1616** SURFL. & MARKHAM *Countrie Farme* V. xviii. 568 It will make you yarne..for the finest sisters thred that can bee sowed with. **1662** *Act 12 Chas. II*, c. 4 (Rates, inwards), Sisters thred, the pound xvs. **1812** J. SMYTH *Pract. Customs* (1821) 257 All bleached Thread is called Sisters Thread.

**Sistine** ('sɪstiːn), *a.* and *sb.* [ad. It. *sistino* of Sixtus.] **A.** *adj.* Pertaining to Pope Sixtus IV (1471–84); *spec.* as epithet of the chapel built by him; hence, of or belonging to the Sistine Chapel, as *Sistine Madonna*, a picture by Raphael originally hung there. **B.** *sb.* The Sistine Chapel.

[**1769** J. REYNOLDS *Discourse delivered at Opening of Royal Academy* 5 On the sight of the Capella Sistina, he [*sc.* Raphael] immediately..assumed that grand style of painting.] **1771** C. BURNEY *Pres. State Music in France & Italy* p. vi, The Pope's chapel is sometimes called the Sistine chapel, from Sextus Quintus, who built it. **1863** J. A. SYMONDS *Let.* 19 Dec. (1967) I. 435 The Sistine Chapel too gains everything by being seen in the original. **1869** 'MARK TWAIN' *Innoc. Abroad* xxvii. 288 He has shown us the great picture in the Sistine Chapel..by Michael Angelo. **1885** *Encycl. Brit.* XIX. 64/1 San Sisto..lost its chief attraction when Raphael's Sistine Madonna (now in Dresden) was sold by the monks. **1887** 'J. OLDCASTLE' *Leo XIII* vi. 36 The conclave assembled to-day in the Sistine. **1889** GROVE *Dict. Mus.* IV. 122/1 The traditions of the Sistine Choir. **1920** W. B. YEATS *Michael Robartes & Dancer* 2 While Michael Angelo's Sistine roof His 'Morning' and his 'Night' disclose How sinew that has been pulled tight,..Can rule by supernatural right. **1950** *New Yorker* 25 Feb. 82/3 In the vesper Mass, the Sistine's famous boy sopranos let loose their voices. **1968** A. DIMENT *Bang Bang Birds* x. 182 All I could hear was a choir singing in the Sistine Chapel. **1975** 'R. PLAYER' *Let's talk of Graves* iii. 81 The Czar Nicholas the First..was kneeling in the Sistine. *Ibid.* 82 The clouds of Sistine incense around the yellow tapers. **1977** R. L. WOLFF *Gains & Losses* ii. 131 Guy [Morville]..looks like one of the angels in the Sistine Madonna.

**'sistle,** *v. rare*[-1]. [Imitative.] *intr.* To emit a kind of hissing sound.

**1849** H. A. WISE *Los Gringos* 11, I forgive the entire African races for whistling the latest polkas, or rather *sistling* through their closed teeth.

†**'sistre.** *Obs.*[-1] [a. F. *sistre*, or ad. L. *sistrum*: see next.] A sistrum.

*c* **1590** A. HUME *Epist. Montcreif* 30 A loflie troup of Ladies in array, Sum on a luth, sum on a sistre play.

‖**sistrum** ('sɪstrəm). Pl. **sistra** (**sistrums**). Also 8 **systrum**. [L., ad. Gr. *σείστρον*, f. *σείειν* to shake.] A musical instrument consisting of a thin oval metal frame furnished with transverse metal rods loosely fixed in it and a handle by which it was shaken. Also *attrib.*

Originally peculiar to Egypt and the worship of Isis, but subsequently used in other Oriental countries.

**1398** TREVISA *Barth. De P.R.* XIX. cxliii. (1495) 946 It is prouyd that Isis quene of Egypte was the fyrste fynder of Sistrum. **1603** HOLLAND *Plutarch's Mor.* 1312 That brasen Timbrel which they sounded and rung at the sacrifices of Isis, named Sistrum. *Ibid.*, Upon the Absis or rundle of the Sistrum toward the toppe, they engrave the forme of a cat. *a* **1682** SIR T. BROWNE *Tracts* xiii. (1683) 201 A Draught of all sorts of Sistrums, Crotaloes, Cymbals, Tympans, &c. in use among the Ancients. **1698** M. LISTER *Journ. Paris* (1699) 111 A Sistrum or Ægyptian Rattle with three loose and running Wires cross it. **1702** ADDISON *Dial. Medals* ii. Wks. 1766 III. 119 The instrument in her hand is the Sistrum of the Ægyptians. **1792** A. YOUNG *Trav. France* 132 Mademoiselle Le Blanc singing to her systrum. **1842** *Penny Cycl.* XXII. 63/2 Some writers have confounded the sistrum with the cymbals. **1883** V. STUART *Egypt* 206 She held stretched out towards them a sistrum in either hand.

‖**Sisymbrium** (sɪ'sɪmbrɪəm). *Bot.* Also 6 **sisimbrium**. [L., ad. Gr. *σισύμβριον* some sweet-smelling plant.] A genus of herbaceous cruciferous plants (under which water-cress was formerly included); hedge-mustard, garlic-mustard.

**1562** TURNER *Herbal* II. (1568) 140 The seconde kynde of Sisymbrium is called cardamine also, in Englishe water cresses. **1580–3** GREENE *Mamillia* I. Wks. (Grosart) II. 23 The hearbe Sisimbrium growes not to a great braunch in a moment. **1664** EVELYN *Kal. Hort.* (1729) 205 Sisymbrium double and simple. **1753** *Chambers' Cycl.* Suppl. s.v., The smooth rocket-leaved sisymbrium with yellow flowers. **1842** *Penny Cycl.* XXII. 64/1 In Sisymbrium the cotyledons are folded with their back upon the radicle.

**Sisyphean** (sɪsɪ'fiːən), *a.* Also 7 **Sysiphæan**, 9 **Sisyphæan, Sysyphean**. [f. L. *Sīsyphēius*, ad. Gr. *Σισύφειος*, f. *Σίσυφος*, Sisyphus, the name of a king of Corinth, whose punishment in Hades was to roll a heavy stone up a hill; as he reached the top, the stone rolled down again.] Of or pertaining to Sisyphus; like (that of) Sisyphus; resembling the fruitless toil of Sisyphus; endless and ineffective.

**1635** QUARLES *Embl.* III. xv, I barter sighs for tears, and tears for grones, Still vainly rolling Sisyphean stones. **1646** G. DANIEL *Poems* Wks. (Grosart) I. 11 Thus I roll Sisyphean Stones, and play (Which he can never) all my time away. **1858** GANNON *O'Donoghue*, etc. 53 Without this magic bond no power on earth Can raise the ponderous Sysyphean stone. **1871** LOWELL *Study Wind.* (1886) 41 The Sisyphean toil of rolling the clammy balls. **1895** KIDD *Soc. Evol.* ix. 245 Do we only see therein humanity condemned to an aimless Sisyphean labour?

**Sisyphian** (sɪ'sɪfɪən), *a.* [f. L. *Sīsyphius*, ad. Gr. *Σισύφιος*, f. *Σίσυφος*: see prec.] Sisyphean.

**1599** T. M[OUFET] *Silkwormes* 45 Sisyphian soules, betwitched multipliers, Surcease to pitch this neuer pitched stone. **1725** POPE *Odyss.* XI. 734, I..survey'd A mournful vision! the Sisyphian shade. **1863** I. WILLIAMS *Baptistery* II. xxi. (1874) 49 What but this was the Sisyphian stone? **1864** R. A. ARNOLD *Hist. Cotton Famine* 447 A mere labour test —a Sisyphian employment.

**Sisyphism** ('sɪsɪfɪz(ə)m). [f. *Sīsyph-us* + -ISM.] Unceasing and fruitless labour like that of Sisyphus, *spec.* as a characteristic of modern industrial conditions; also, the view that industrial labour is of this nature.

In quot. 1856 the reference is to the use of the crank and similar punishments in prisons.

**1846** G. R. PORTER tr. *Bastiat's Pop. Fall. Gen. Interests* 24 *note*, We beg the reader to excuse us if we designate this system hereafter under the name of Sisyphism. *Ibid.* 26 Industry in practice never admits of Sisyphism. **1856** READE *Never too Late* I. 231 The ancients imagined tortures particularly trying to nature, that of Sisyphus to wit... We have made Sisyphism vulgar. **1884** RAE *Contemp. Socialism* 406 These gloomy views have in France received the name of Sisyphism.

So **'Sisyphist**.

**1846** G. R. PORTER tr. *Bastiat's Pop. Fall. Gen. Interests* 25 It may be thought, perhaps, that I exaggerate, and that there are no true Sisyphists.

**sisyrinchium** (sɪzɪ'rɪnkɪəm). [mod.L. (L. Plukenet *Almagestum Botanicum* (1696) 348), f. Gr. *σισυρίγχιον* a plant name used by Theophrastus.] An annual or perennial herb of the genus so called, belonging to the family Iridaceæ, native to North or South America, and bearing linear leaves and clusters of small blue, yellow, red, or white flowers; = *blue-eyed grass* s.v. BLUE-EYED *a.* and *satin-flower* (*e*) s.v. SATIN *sb.* (and *a.*) 8 b.

**1772** R. WESTON *Universal Botanist* III. 664 (*heading*) Narrow-leaved Virginian Sisyrinchium. **1919** R. FARRER *Eng. Rock-Garden* II. 367 An unknown Sisyrinchium may often prove to be a *Marica* lurking in ambush for the unwary. **1955** L. D. HILLS *Alpine Gardening* v. 137 The Sisyrinchiums are good imitation rushes by the stream side. **1971** B. MILES *Bluebells & Bittersweet* 120/2 Sisyrinchiums will never be accused of flamboyancy [*sic*], but they are darlings.

**siszers**, obs. form of SCISSORS.

**sit** (sɪt), *sb.*[1] [f. the vb. Cf. Fris. *sit*, Du. *zit*, MLG. *sit*, MHG. and G. *sitz* seat, sitting.]

**1. a.** The manner in which an article of dress, or some part of one, is disposed or fits the person.

**1776** MRS. THRALE *Let. Johnson* 16 May, Long lectures about the sit of a cap, which you will not give me a minute to put on as it should be. **1785** MACKENZIE *Lounger* No. 22 ¶9 She looked very narrowly at the Poupée's head-dress, and the particular sit of her tucker. **1837** *Q. Rev.* LIX. 414 Accounting for the sit of a plume by saying that he had fixed it in a moment of enthusiasm. **1861** *Sat. Rev.* 20 July 61 A child..taught to care for nothing but the sit of its frock. **1892** *Gd. Words* Sept. 634/2 Rather concerned about the sit of a couple of folds in her dress.

**b.** Inherent character or tendency.

**1866** DORA GREENWELL *Ess.* 107 Natures the whole bent and sit of which is powerfully attracted to good.

**c.** Manner of sitting. Cf. SEAT *sb.* 2.

**1820** M. EDGEWORTH *Let.* 10 Aug. (1979) 208 Their bodies look as if..they had taken an eternal *sit* from the stiff square stays of former day. **1894** MRS. DYAN *Man's Keeping* (1899) 259 The dignified step of the..black chargers, the rigid sit of the soldiers.

**2. a.** A spell of sitting.

**1832** TENNYSON in *Mem.* (1897) I. vi. 147 After this long sit however I ought certainly to have some interesting passages to tongue. **1852** GLADSTONE in Morley *Life* (1905) I. III. viii. 437, I have had a long sit with Lord Aberdeen to-day. **1971** N. FREELING *Over High Side* I. 8 He wanted a nice cup of tea and a sit.

**b.** *Cant.* (See quot.)

**1907** G. R. SIMS in *Referee* 17 Feb., To be 'at the sit' is to travel by buses and trams for the purpose of picking pockets.

**3.** A sinking or settling down (of a wall, the roof of a mine, etc.).

**1808** JAMIESON, *Sit*, the state of sinking, as applied to a wall. **1879** *Cassell's Techn. Educ.* II. 98/1 If the roof were tender, it would be apt to break away and fill up the passage, which would be a *sit*. **1885** BEVERIDGE *Culross & Tulliallan* II. 234 Many sits or depressions have taken place in the surface.

**4.** The seat of the body.

**1903** HARKER *Rom. of the Nursery* 273, I climbed out of my cot and went downstairs, sit-first, bumpetty-bump on every step.

**sit,** *sb.*[2] *slang* (orig. *Printers'*). Also with point. Abbrev. of SITUATION. Now esp. in *sit(s) vac*, situation(s) vacant (see SITUATION 6 b).

**1853** 'MARK TWAIN' in *Hannibal* (Missouri) *Jrnl.* 8 Sept. 2/1, I shall look out for a sit; for they say there is plenty of work to be had for *sober* compositors. **1878** W. WHITMAN *Daybks. & Notebks.* (1978) I. 110 Applied to Bart Bonsall, for a sit. for Harry. **1888** JACOBI *Printers' Vocab.* 125 *Sit.*, an abbreviation for the word 'situation', an engagement for work. **1896** *Daily News* 15 Feb. 10/6 Compositor..seeks change... Not out of sit. **1901** [see BOVRILIZE *v.*]. **1914** JOYCE *Dubliners* 91 But Hogan has a good sit, hasn't he? **1969** *Guardian* 29 July 4/8 Asians.., with the sort of skills that the 'Sits vac' columns of British newspapers are clamouring for —nurses, motor mechanics, turners, secretaries. **1970** *Ibid.* 14 Nov. 9/2 (*heading*) 'I felt I could do the job.'..Peter Terson on the Sit. Vac. he didn't fill. **1973** *Ibid.* 12 Feb. 11/4 June Moelzer wants..a job... She sifts through the 'sit vac' columns, becoming less and less choosy as the months go by. **1975** *Listener* 8 May 609/3 Raking through the sits. vac., John Timpson..reported an advertisement in a Devon local paper for a person 'to move Earth—about two days' work'. **1980** D. FRANCIS *Reflex* xiii. 161 No rides, no income. You start looking at 'sits vac'.

**sit**, *sb.*[3] Also sitt. Abbrev. of SITTING-ROOM.

**1937** A. CHRISTIE *Dumb Witness* vi. 58 We've a nice bungalow at Hemel End, two bed., one sitt. **1961** [see BED *sb.* 1 f].

**sit** (sɪt), *v.* Forms: (see below). Pa. t. and pa. pple. **sat** (sæt). [Common Teut.: OE. *sittan* (*sæt, sǽton, ȝeseten*), = OFris. *sitta* (WFris. *sitte*), MDu. *sitten, zitten* (Du. *zitten*), OS. *sittian, sittean* (MLG. and LG. *sitten*), OHG. *sizzan, sizzen* (G. *sitzen*), ON. and Icel. *sitja* (Norw. *sitja, sitta, sita*; MSw. *sitia, sittia*, Sw. *sitta*; Da. *sidde*):—Teut. type **sitjan*, for which Goth. had *sitan*. The stem **set-*, pre-Teut. **sed-*, is widely represented in the cognate languages, as in Lith. *sedeti*, Lat. *sedēre*, Gr. ἕζεσθαι (cf. ἕδος seat), etc.

In some senses there has been confusion between *sit* and the corresponding causal verb *set*, analogous to that which has existed between *lie* and *lay*, but in modern use the two verbs are clearly distinguished. Some ME. examples of this confusion, in senses where it does not otherwise occur, are probably no more than scribal errors.]

A. Illustration of forms.

**1.** *Infin.* **α.** 1 sittan (syttan, sitton), 2–4 (7) sitten (3 *Orm.* sittenn), 4–5 sytten, 5 syttyn, cyttyn (6 *erron.* sitting).

*c* **888** K. ÆLFRED *Boeth.* vii. §3 Hu meahtest þu sittan..? **971** *Blickl. Hom.* 237 He ȝeseah..Matheus æ nne sitton. **1154** *O.E. Chron.* (Laud MS.) an. 1137, He ne myhte.. sitten ne lien. *c* **1200** ORMIN 14086 He wollde sittenn þær. **1377** LANGL. *P. Pl.* B. xiv. 218 None..sitten ne mowe þere longe. *c* **1440** *Promp. Parv.* 78/2 Cyttyn, *sedeo. Ibid.* 457/1 Syttyn, on a sete. [**1513** DOUGLAS *Æneid* VIII. vi. 127 He.. mayd him sitting doun. **1642** H. MORE *Song of Soul* III. 26 A lamp, that men do sitten by.]

**β.** 1 sitta, 3–6 sitte (4 zitte), sytte.

*c* **950** *Lindisf. Gosp.* Matt. xx. 23 Sitta..to suiðra minra. *a* **1250** *Prov. Ælfred* 217 in *O.E. Misc.* 116 Syker he may sitte. *c* **1275** *Passion our Lord* 311 *ibid.* 46 Ich ine heuene schal sytte. **1340** *Ayenb.* 264 Riȝtnesse..ssel zitte amydde. **1377** LANGL. *P. Pl.* B. x. 95 þere þe lorde..liketh nouȝte to sytte. **1463** *Bury Wills* (Camden) 39 The peleer there I was wont to sitte. **1470–85** MALORY *Arthur* III. iv. 103 There shall no man sytte therin.

**γ.** 3 siten, 3–4 (6 *Sc.*) site, 4 sijt, siet; 4 sete, 4, 6 *Sc.* seit, 9 *dial.* seet.

*a* **1300** *Havelok* 366 His knictes dede he alle site. *c* **1325** *Prose Psalter* cxxxi. 13 Her childer shul siten. **13..** *Cursor M.* 8291 þan can he seit On þat tre. *Ibid.* 14734 þair setles þat þai in can sete. *Ibid.* 27335 Hu þe man..Sal siet. *Ibid.* 27337 To sijt þe preist fot be-side. **1513** DOUGLAS *Æneid* IV. vi. 6 To site so hie ane charge. *a* **1578** LINDESAY (Pitscottie) *Chron. Scot.* I. 28 To seit with so mony wrangis. **1820** WILBRAHAM *Cheshire Gloss.* 86 *Seet*, to sit.

**δ.** 4–6 syt (5 sytt), sitt, 5– sit (9 *dial.* zit).

*a* **1400–50** *Alexander* 235 Made him to sytt On a sege. *Ibid.* 592 þat folke..May sitt & carpe. **1427** *Acts Privy Council* III. 232 þ at..þei wolde sit upright. **1523** FITZHERB. *Husb.* §18 They wyll folowe those stakes,..and syt by them. *c* **1595** CAPT. WYATT *Dudley's Voy.* (Hakl. Soc.) 47 Beinge suffred to sitt..at libertie. **1886** ELWORTHY *W. Somerset Word-bk.* 852 Plase to zit down.

**2.** *Pres. Indic.* **a.** *1st pers. sing.* 1 *north.* sitto, 1–3, 6 sitte, 4 sitt, 6 syt, 6– sit.

*c* **825** *Vesp. Psalter* xxv. 5 And mid arleasum ic ne sitto. *a* **1000** *Riddles* xxv. 7 þær ic glado sitte. *a* **1225** *Ancr. R.* 358 Hwon ich sitte uorto demen. **13..** *Cursor M.* 20840 Queþer i sitt, or stand. **1530** PALSGR. 719, I syt..amongest other folkes.

**b.** *2nd pers. sing.* **α.** 1 sites, 4 sittes, 4–6 sittis.

*c* **825** *Vesp. Psalter* ix. 5 Ðu sites ofer ðrymseld. *a* **1352** MINOT *Poems* i. 1 Trew king, þat sittes in trone. *a* **1400–50** *Alexander* 1872 þou..sittis..in sege. *a* **1568** A. SCOTT *Poems* (S.T.S.) i. 169 Sen so thow sittis in saitt.

**β.** 1 sitest, 1– sittest, 4–5 sittist, 6 syttest; 1, 6–7 sitst, 7 sit'st, sitt'st; 4 sist.

**971** *Blickl. Hom.* 141 þu þe sitest ofer cherubine. *c* **1000** *Ags. Ps.* (Thorpe) ix. 4 Ðu sitst on ðam hean setle. *Ibid.* lxxix. 2 Ðu ðe..sittest ofer cherubin. *c* **1250** *Owl & Night.* 89 þu sittest a day and flyhst a niht. **1388** WYCLIF *Acts* xxiii. 3 Thou sittist. **1390** GOWER *Conf.* v. 5742 O thou..That hihe sist. **1535** COVERDALE *Ps.* xlix. 20 Thou syttest. **1592** KYD *Sp. Trag.* II. iv. 24 The more thou sitst. **1648** MILTON *Ps.* lxxx. 5 Thou Shepherd..That sitt'st between the Cherubs.

**c.** *3rd pers. sing.* **α.** 1 siteð, sitteð, 1, 4 sitteþ (5 -iþ), 4– sitteth (5 -ethe, -yth); 4 sytteþ, 6 syttethe, -ith, -yth.

*c* **825** *Vesp. Psalter* ix. 29 [He] siteð in searwum. *c* **975** *Rushw. Gosp.* Matt. xix. 28 þonne sitteþ sunu monnes in sedle. **1390** GOWER *Conf.* IV. 2724 Hou he sitteth be the fyr. *c* **1400** *Lanfranc's Cirurg.* 300 þis veine sittiþ ful nyȝ þe gret arterie. **1504** *Bury Wills* (Camden) 102 The which tenement syttyth and lyyth [etc.]. *a* **1530** LUPSET *Treat. Charite* (1539) 8 It..syttethe faste and sure. **1654** WHITLOCK *Zootomia* 160 Where the winde sitteth.

**β.** 1–5 sit (4 zit), 1, 4 sitt, 4 sitte, 7 sith; 1, 4 syt, sytt, 4 sytte.

*c* **888** K. ÆLFRED *Boeth.* xxxix. §13 Sit se hehsta sceoppend on his heahsetle. *c* **1000** *Ags. Gosp.* Matt. xix. 28 þonne mannes sunu sitt [*v.r.* sytt, syt]. *c* **1220** *Bestiary* 701 Bi hire make ȝe [= she] sit o niȝt. **1340** *Ayenb.* 263 He..zit aþe riȝt half of god. *c* **1385** CHAUCER *L.G.W.* 1832 *Lucrece*, She sytte in halle. **1390** GOWER *Conf.* VIII. 2428 So sitte it wel that [etc.]. **1430–40** LYDG. *Bochas* VIII. xxv. (1558) 17 b, Wher he sit crowned. **1609** J. DAVIES (Heref.) *Hum. Heaven on Earth* clxviii, Heere, in a Chimney,..Sith Grimnesse.

**γ.** 1, 4 sites, 4 sitis; 1 sittæs, 1, 4 sittes (5 -ez), 4–5 sittus, 5–6 sittis, 6– sits (7 sitts); 4 syttes, 5–6 syttis.

*c* **950** *Lindisf. Gosp.* Matt. xix. 28 Mið ðy sittes sunu monnes in seðel. **13..** *Cursor M.* 2086 He sittes wit drightin. *Ibid.* 26557 He..Sites [*v.r.* sitis] on his..right hand. *c* **1350** *Will. Palerne* 446 þat he sittus in mi siȝt. *a* **1400–50** *Alexander* 47 As he on dese syttis. *c* **1420** *Wars Alexander* 73 It sittez till hym. **1596** DALRYMPLE tr. *Leslie's Hist. Scot.* I. 37 In fife..sittis the Primat. **1693** LUTTRELL *Brief Rel.* (1857) III. 100 If the wind sitts fair.

**d.** *Plur.* **α.** 1 sittað, 2 sitteð, 3 sittet, sytteþ; 1 *north.* sittas, -es, 6 *Sc.* sittis.

*c* **825** *Vesp. Psalter* cxxxi. 12 Bearn heara..sittað ofer seld min. *c* **950** *Lindisf. Gosp.* Luke i. 79 Ðaðe in ðiostrum..sittas [*c* **1000** sittað, *c* **1160** sitteð]. *c* **1130** *O.E. Chron.* (Laud MS.) an. 1130, Hæge sitteð þa aceres dæleth. *c* **1250** in *O.E. Misc.* 168 ȝe þat sittet [*v.r.* sytteþ] i-schrud wið skarlet. **1508** DUNBAR *Tua mariit Wemen* 440 Thai all, that sittis about [etc.].

**β.** 3–6 (7) sitten; 4 sytten.

*c* **1250** in *O.E. Misc.* 190 [They] sitten þer to-gederes. **1393** LANGL. *P. Pl.* C. xx. 206 Men..þat in merke sytten. **1542** UDALL *Erasm. Apoph.* 34 b, [To] iest vpon the geastes, as they sitten at the table. **1579** SPENSER *Sheph. Cal.* March 1 Why sytten we soe? [**1642** H. MORE *Song of Soul* II. I. iv. 9 They sitten soft.]

**γ.** 4 site, sete, 6 sitte, 6– sit.

**13..** *Cursor M.* 25587 þar we gang and þar we sete [*v.r.* site]. *c* **1586** SIDNEY *Ps.* XXXIV. vii, Gods own eyes on good men sit. **1600** W. WATSON *Decacordon* (1602) 346 They sitte nerer his knee. **1749** GRAY *Installat. Ode* 15 There sit the sainted sage, the bard divine.

**3.** *Pres. Subj.* **α.** *Sing.* 1–7 sitte, 4–6 sytte; 4–5 sitt, 7– sit. **β.** *Plur.* 1–2, 4 sitten (1 sitton, *north.* sitta).

*c* **825** *Vesp. Psalter* c. 6 Ðæt hie sitten. *Ibid.*, *Hymn* iv. 15 Ðæt he sitte. *c* **950** *Lindisf. Gosp.* Mark x. 37 þætte..we sitta [*c* **1000** sitton, *c* **1160** sitten]. *a* **1067** in Kemble *Cod. Dipl.* IV. 226 Sitte his mann ðer ðar he sitte. *a* **1225** *Ancr. R.* 10 þet weneð þet order sitte iðe kurtel. **13..** *Cursor M.* 17583 þof he sitt in heuen hall. *a* **1400–50** *Alexander* 862 þof it vnsemely me sitt. **1502** ARNOLDE *Chron.* C vj, Y[e] the styward ..sytte not from hensforward [etc.]. **1609** BIBLE (Douay) *Deut.* xxix. 20 Al the curses sitte upon him. **1615** G. SANDYS *Trav.* (1637) 57 If the wind sit southward.

**4.** *Imper.* **α.** *Sing.* (later also *Plur.*) 1–4 site, 3–4 sete; 1, 4 sitt, 5 sitte, 4– sit; 4–5 sytte, 5 sytt, 5–6 syt.

*c* **825** *Vesp. Psalter* cix. 1 Site to ðe swiðran minre. *c* **950** *Lindisf. Gosp.* Matt. xxii. 44 Sitt to suiðra min. *a* **1225** *Ancr. R.* 290 Ne lie þu nout..ne site nouðer. *a* **1275** *Prov. Ælfred* 635 in *O.E. Misc.*, Sete þanne..besiden him seluen. **13..** *Cursor M.* 3683 Sitt [*v.r.* sit, sete] vp and ete. **1382** WYCLIF *Isaiah* xlvii. 5 Syt, be stille [**1388** sitte thou]. —— *Matt.* xxvi. 36 Sitte ȝe heer. *c* **1460** *Towneley Myst.* xviii. 68 Com sytt! soyn shall we se. **1535** COVERDALE *Ruth* iv. 2 Syt you downe here.

**β.** *Plur.* 1 sitte, sittað, -aþ, 2–3 sitteð, -eþ, 4 sitteth; 3 sytteþ, 4 syttyþ; 1 *north.* sittas, 4 sittes, sites.

*c* **950** *Lindisf. Gosp.* Matt. xxvi. 36 Sittas [*Rushw.* sittaþ] her. *c* **1000** *Ags. Gosp.* Luke xxiv. 49 Sitte ȝe on ceastre. *c* **1205** LAY. 22827 Sitteð, sitteð swiðe. *c* **1275** *Passion our Lord* 150 in *O.E. Misc.* 41 Sytteþ her þe hwile. **13..** *Cursor M.* 4975 Godmen, sittes [*v.r.* sites] a littel tom. **1303** R. BRUNNE *Handl. Synne* 952 Syttyþ dowun vpp-on ȝoure knees. **1382** WYCLIF *Jer.* xiii. 18 Beth mekid, sitteth.

**5.** *Past Indic.* **a.** *Sing.* (*1st and 3rd pers.*)

**α.** 1, 3–5 set, 4 zet, 4–5 sette.

Instances of *set* in the sense of 'sat' later than the 15th cent. probably belong to SET *v.*[1]

*c* **825** *Vesp. Psalter* xxv. 5 Ic ne set in ȝeðæhte idelnisse. *c* **950** *Lindisf. Gosp.* Matt., Int. 21/2 [He] set ofer assales fola. *c* **1275** *Passion our Lord* 562 in *O.E. Misc.* 53 þe on set at þe heuede. **13..** *Cursor M.* 16025 He sett vte-ouer þam. **1340** *Ayenb.* 96 þer he zet, ase zayþ þet godspel. *c* **1400** *Gamelyn* 790 (Lansd., etc.), Whan þe Iustice sette. **14..** *Sc. Leg. Saints* xxix. (*Placidas*) 876 ȝistyrday in myn In as I set.

**β.** 1, 3 sæt (1 sætt), 3 seat; 2– sat, 3–8 satt, 4–6 satte. Also *2nd pers.* 6 sattest, 7 satst, sat'st.

*c* **888** K. ÆLFRED *Boeth.* xxxv. §7 Se hearpere..sæt on ðæm muntum. *c* **1200** *Trin. Coll. Hom.* 101 He sat ofte and tahte wisdom. *c* **1205** LAY. 2960 þer he on æðelen seat. *Ibid.* 3530 þe swain sæt at hire fæit. *a* **1352** MINOT *Poems* ix. 35 When sir Dauid..satt on his stede. **1390** GOWER *Conf.* VII. 2282 He satte him thanne doun. *c* **1450** *Merlin* xiv. 226 The kynge..satte stille. **1535** COVERDALE *Ezek.* xxiii. 41 Thou sattest vpon a goodly bed. **1579** *Reg. Privy Counc. Scot.* III. 241 [He] satt doun upoun the ground. **1667** MILTON *P.L.* I. 21 Thou..Dove-like satst brooding. **1676** HOBBES *Iliad* I. 101 This said, he sat.

**γ.** (*2nd pers.* 1 sæte, 3 sete, 4 seete,) 4–5 sete, 4 seete, 4, 9 *dial.* seet.

*c* **1000** *Ags. Ps.* (Thorpe) xlix. 21 þu sæte onȝean þinne broþor. *a* **1225** *Ancr. R.* 238 Ich slepte, & tu sete biuoren me. **13..** *E.E. Allit. P.* B. 1171 He sete on Salamones solie. **1382** WYCLIF *Ecclus.* xxxi. 21 If in the myddel of manye thou seete. *c* **1400** *Destr. Troy* 11109 Yet sadly ho sete. **1446** LYDG. *Nightingale Poems* i. 97 She..seet in myddes of the tre. **1886** *Cheshire Gloss.* 306 *Seet*, perf. tense of sit.

**δ.** 4–5 saat (5 saat); 4 (5 *Sc.*) sait, saitt; 4– sate. Also *2nd pers.* 7, 9 satest.

**13..** *Cursor M.* 2768 [He] ras fra þen [*v.r.* þar] he sate. *Ibid.* 8296 þar he sait an. **1387** TREVISA *Higden* (Rolls) III. 339 A ravoun sat [*v.r.* saat] uppon þe riȝht schulder of Valerius. *c* **1400** *26 Pol. Poems* xxvi. 9 Oon byrde..sate on a brere. **1422** tr. *Secreta Secret.*, *Priv. Priv.* 168 He..saate in Iugement. **1611** BIBLE *Gen.* xix. 1 Lot sate in the gate of Sodome. —— *Ezek.* xxiii. 41 Thou..satest vpon a stately bedde. **1761** GRAY *Odin* 18 By the moss-grown pile he sate. **1876** BLACK *Madcap Violet* xxxix, She sate in a corner of the ..waiting room. **1885–94** R. BRIDGES *Eros & Psyche* Oct. xiii, Thou..Satest athirst.

**ε.** 5 sote, 8– 9 *dial.* sot (9 zot).

*c* **1400** *Destr. Troy* 8266 Wayueronde he sote. *a* **1800** PEGGE *Anecd. Eng. Lang.* (1814) 73 London... *Sot*, for *sat*. **1843–** *Sot* in common dialect use (see *Eng. Dial. Dict.*); also *zot* (Som., Dev.). **1861** DICKENS *Gt. Expect.* ii, She sot down, said Joe.

**b.** *Plur.* **α.** 1 sæton, -un, 2–3 sæten (3 -enn); 1 setun, 1, 5 seton, 3–5 seten, 4–5 setyn, 4 seeten, sieten.

*c* **888** K. ÆLFRED *Boeth.* xxvii. §1 þær nane oðre an ne sæton. *c* **950** *Lindisf. Gosp.* John xx. 12 Tuoeȝe engles.. seton [etc.]. *c* **975** *Rushw. Gosp.* Mark iii. 34 Ðaðe vtan ymb heop his setun. *c* **1000** *Ags. Ps.* (Thorpe) lxviii. 12 Ealle þa him sæton sundor. *c* **1200** ORMIN 15560 Menn att bordess sætenn þær. *a* **1225** *Ancr. R.* 258 Unneaðe his moder & Joseph seten þeron. *c* **1320** R. BRUNNE *Medit.* 1139 þy peple ..Whych setyn yn derkenes. **1362** LANGL. *P. Pl.* A. v. 190 [They] seeten so til Euensong. **1390** GOWER *Conf.* III. 1809 Thei sieten alle stille. *c* **1420** *Chron. Vilod.* 3115 Hurre sustren..setone by-sydus herre þo. **1426** LYDG. *De Guil. Pilgr.* 4612 Wher as they setyn on by on. *c* **1450** *Merlin* xiv. 225 The knyghtes..seten..at table.

**β.** 3–4 sete, 4 seete, siete, 8 *dial.* seet; also 7 sitt.

*c* **1205** LAY. 22767 Seoððen sete þa eorles. **1297** R. GLOUC. (Rolls) 2777 þe maistres sete stille ynou. **1390** GOWER *Conf.* v. 3339 Ther they siete and spieke. *Ibid.* VI. 1174 Tofore his oghne bord thei sete. *c* **1400** *Gamelyn* 681 (Harl.), As thei sete and eeten. **1688** in *11th Rep. Hist. MSS. Comm.* App. VII. 109 The..Jury..sitt upp all night about it. **1790** MRS. WHEELER *Westmld. Dial.* (1821) 35 In com thor sougers an seet dawn.

**γ.** 4–5 saten, satyn, 5 soten; 4– sate, 4 saite, 5 *Sc.* sait.

These forms possibly represent ON. *sátu*.

**13..** *Cursor M.* 17845 Sundri þai þam fra oþer saite [*v.r.* sate]. *c* **1400** *Gamelyn* 476 þe grete lordes þat saten in hall. **14 ..** *Sc. Leg. Saints* xxvii. (*Machor*) 1102 Till [= while] þat þai sait at þe burd. **1432–50** tr. *Higden* (Rolls) III. 343 Bees come and sate on the lippes of Plato. *c* **1450** *Gesta Roman.* xcii. 420 (Add. MS.), Such ij..satyn, and dronkyn. **1451** CAPGRAVE *St. Gilbert* 70 On-to hem whech soten aboute him. **1551** ROBINSON tr. *More's Utopia* I. (1895) 114 We came..and sate vs downe.

**δ.** 5 satten, satte.

*c* **1430** *Syr Gener.* (Roxb.) 5435 No man list To speke a word, but satten stil. **1474** CAXTON *Chesse* II. v. (1883) 66 Many flyes satte vpon the soores.

**6.** *Past Subj.* 1 sæte, 3–4 sete.

**971** *Blickl. Hom.* 17 Rihtlic þæt wæs þæt se blinda..sæte wædliende. *c* **1220** *Bestiary* 504 Ðat it..sete one ðe se sond. **1297** R. GLOUC. (Rolls) 4060 þei ech of vs sete al day. *c* **1350** *Will. Palerne* 1622 þeiȝh i sete euer.

**7.** *Past Part.* **α.** 1 ȝeseten, 3 iseten, 2, 5 seten, 4–5 setyn, 5–6 setten; 3–4 isete, 4–5 sete.

*c* **925** *O.E. Chron.* (Parker MS.) an. 922, þæt folc..þe on Mercna lande ȝeseten wæs. *c* **1200** *Trin. Coll. Hom.* 103 Ariseð þanne ȝe hauen seten. *c* **1205** LAY. 18532 þa heo weoren alle iseten [*c* **1275** isete]. **1387** TREVISA *Higden* (Rolls) V. 415 In a tyme he hadde i-sete þere. **1388** WYCLIF *Ecclus.* xxxi. 21 If thou hast sete in the myddis. *c* **1420** *Sir Amadace* (Camden) xvii, This xvi. weke I haue setyn here. *c* **1481** CAXTON *Dialogues* 45 Randolf..hath seten..xxx. yere. **15..** *Adam Bel* 527 in Hazl. *E.P.P.* II. 161 They had not setten but a whyle. **1560** DAUS tr. *Sleidane's Comm.* 21 b, He had muche rather have setten still.

**β.** 4 siten, syten, sytyn; 4– sitten, 5 sitton, 6 (9) *Sc.* sittin (9 *Sc.* sutten); 5–6 sytten, 5 -yn.

The type *sitten* was very commonly used by good writers down to the early part of the 19th cent., but has now in ordinary use been displaced by *sat*.

**13..** *Cursor M.* 11665 Quen sco had sitten [*v.r.* siten, syten] þar a wei. *a* **1340** HAMPOLE *Psalter* cxxvi. 3 Rysis eftire þat ȝe hafe sytyn. *c* **1400** *Destr. Troy* 12222 The sure knightes Hade sitton here. **1470–85** MALORY *Arthur* III. ii. 101 The knyghtes names that had sytten therin. **1526** TINDALE *Rev.* iii. 21 Evyn as I..have sytten with my father. **1596** DALRYMPLE tr. *Leslie's Hist. Scot.* I. 189 Nocht weil sittin doune in the Impire. **1644** DIGBY *Nat. Bodies* xxviii. §7. 253 Strangers haue sitten by him. **1787** BURNS *Let. to W. Nicol* 1 June, I'm sitten down here. **1829** LANDOR *Imag. Conv.*, *Diogenes & Plato* Wks. 1853 I. 467/2 If they had always sitten with their hands before them. **1860** GEN. P. THOMPSON *Audi Alt.* ciii. III. 8 One who might be comfortably sitten down with.

**γ.** 4 satte, 6–7 satt, 6– sat.

*Sot* is also common in dialects (see *E.D.D.*).

*c* **1375** *Cursor M.* 13491 (Fairf.), Doun I walde þe folk ware satte. **1576** GASCOIGNE *Poems* (1869) II. 269 Had she satt in feeld. **1665** *Hatton Corr.* (Camden) 48 The King has satt..at a Councell of Warr. **1711** ADDISON *Spect.* No. 122 ¶6 The Court was sat before Sir Roger came. **1779** *Mirror* No. 60, After having sat a considerable time. **1855** KINGSLEY *Westw. Ho!* xxxiii, Where he had sat when he was a..boy.

**δ.** 6– sate.

**1532** TINDALE *Expos. Matt.* (? 1550) 34 b, As thogh God had sate and eat..wyth them. **1611** BIBLE *Ps.* xxvi. 4, I haue not sate with vaine persons. **1647** COWLEY *Mistr.*, *The Gazers* ii, We have both sate gazing. **1700** S. L. tr. *Fryke's Voy. E. Ind.* 3 Being all sate down, we fell a talking. **1803** *Edwin* II. i. 12 Where..Hermon and his friend were sate. **1848** THACKERAY *Van. Fair* vi, She had sate by him.

**ε.** 6 sytt, sitt, 6–7 sitte, 6–8 (9 *dial.*) sit.

**1528** in Ellis *Orig. Lett.* Ser. I. I. 284 To have sit down. **1540–1** ELYOT *Image Gov.* (1556) 145 After he had sitte a good space. **1565** STAPLETON tr. *Bede's Hist. Ch. Eng.* 81 When..the kinge and the..bishop were sitt doune. **1600** W. WATSON *Decacordon* (1602) 327 Hauing sit enthronized three daies. **1662** HICKERINGILL *Apol. Distressed Innoc.* Wks. 1716 I. 288 The better for being sit upon. **1721** WODROW *Hist. Suff. Ch. Scot.* (1830) III. 109 He..had sit down in a fur. **1888** *Sheffield Gloss.* 216 That milk has sit.

B. Signification.

**I.** *intr.* **1. a.** Of persons: To be or remain in that posture in which the weight of the body rests upon the posteriors; to be seated.

*Beowulf* 500 Hunferð maþelode..þe æt fotum sæt frean Scyldinga. *c* **825** *Vesp. Psalter* xlix. 20 Sittende wið broeðer ðinum ðu teldes. **971** *Blickl. Hom.* 15 þa sæt þær sum blind þearfa be ðon wege. *c* **1200** ORMIN 8933 þære he satt to fraȝȝnenn hemm Off þeȝȝre bokess lare. *c* **1250** *Gen. & Ex.* 279 Ic wile..Min sete norð on heuene maken, And ðor ic wile sitten. **1340** *Ayenb.* 266 Ich yzeȝ oure lhord iesu crist ine riȝt half zittinde. **1387** TREVISA *Higden* (Rolls) III. 297 þe senatoures arayed hem..and so þey seten in here hous. *c* **1400** *Pilgr. Sowle* (Caxton) I. xxi. (1859) 21 Sathanas satt for to wryte. **1470–85** MALORY *Arthur* I. xix. 65 As he satte so hym thoughte he herd a noyse of houndes. **1513** DOUGLAS *Æneid* VI. ii. 42 Sibilla Cumane..Quhair as scho sat rummesing in hir caif. **1585** T. WASHINGTON tr. *Nicholay's Voy.* I. xxi. 26 b, Within it was Victory sitting with two wings. **1673** RAY *Journ. Low C.* 186 After that he hath sitten a while there..he is conducted..to his lodgings. **1757** GRAY *Bard* 45, I see them sit, they linger yet. **1779** *Mirror* No. 26, The rest of the company sat nearer or more remote from him according to their respective ranks. **1824** MISS MITFORD *Village* Ser. I. (1863) 30 It is a beautiful brook, and one that Walton himself might have sitten by and loved. **1855** MACAULAY *Hist. Eng.* xi. III. 94 The clause which permitted scrupulous persons to communicate sitting. **1874** BLACKIE *Self-Cult.* 41 A man may think as well standing as sitting, often not a little better.

*fig.* **1600** W. WATSON *Decacordon* (1602) 346 [I do not believe] that they sitte nerer his knee, or foote stoole, then other penitent sinners doe. **1632** MILTON *Penseroso* 40 Thy rapt soul sitting in thine eyes. **1747** GRAY *Ode Favourite Cat* 28 Malignant Fate sat by, and smil'd. **1818** BYRON *Ch. Har.* IV. i, Venice sate in state, throned on her hundred isles. **1856** AIRD *Poet. Wks.* 307 Beneath her branchless palm must Judah sit.

**b.** Const. *on* or *upon*. Also fig. ***to sit on the*** or ***one's throne***, to reign.

*Beowulf* 286 Weard maþelode, ðær on wicge sæt. *c* **888** K. ÆLFRED *Boeth.* iv, Sittað manfulle on heahsetlum, & haliȝe under heora fotum þrycað. *a* **1122** *O.E. Chron.* (Laud MS.) an. 1079, Se cyng..wearð þær ȝewundod, & his hors ofslaȝen þe he on sæt. *c* **1200** ORMIN 5807 þær he satt onn hiss sæte. *c* **1290** *S. Eng. Leg.* I. 235 þe ston þat ich op-on sitte. **1375** BARBOUR *Bruce* x. 608 Thair ane place thai fand so braid, That thai mycht syt on anerly. *a* **1450** HOCCLEVE *Min. Poems* 2/75 O thynke how..on my knee Thow sat. **1481** CAXTON *Reynard* (Arb.) 18 He satte vpon his hammes. **1542** UDALL *Erasm. Apoph.* 305 He cutte the benche yᵗ Darius had sitten on. **1613** R. HARCOURT *Voy. Guiana* 41 This Idole is fashioned like a man sitting vpon his heeles, holding open his knees. *c* **1670** HOBBES *Dial. Com. Laws* (1681) 65 That in this court the Kings of the Realm have sitten on the high bench. **1734** tr. *Rollin's Anc. Hist.* (1827) VIII. XIX. 276 After he had sitten 24 years on the throne. **1797** *Encycl. Brit.* (ed. 3) XVI. 609 A stone, on which.. Telamon sat to view the Salaminian ships. **1855** SMEDLEY *Occult Sciences* 226 Although the Christian sybils..no longer sat upon a tripod.

**c.** Const. *in* (a seat, throne, saddle, etc.).

*a* **1300** *Cursor M.* 8540 Salamon Was king sittand in his fader tron. *c* **1375** *Sc. Leg. Saints* Prol. 131 Quhen at he suld sit in sege of maieste. *a* **1400–50** *Alexander* 482 As he sat in his sete softly by his qwene. *c* **1420** *Avow. Arth.* xiv, The king in his sadul sete. **1526** *Pilgr. Perf.* (W. de W. 1531) 3 Whiche sawe..a persone syttyng in the trone of god. **1593** SHAKS. *Rich. II*, v. v. 26 Like silly Beggars..sitting in the Stockes. *a* **1648** LD. HERBERT *Hen. VIII* (1683) 215 The said Heralds..presented themselves before Charles, who sate in an high Throne. **1672–5** COMBER *Comp. Temple* (1702) 529 They would not have sitten any longer in their Thrones than the Pope pleased. **1754** in Picton *L'pool Munic. Rec.* (1886) II. 166 Persons who rent seats..after they quitt sitting in them. **1893** HODGES *Elem. Photogr.* 112 The chair in which he sits.

**d.** *spec.* Used of persons seated (usually at a table) for the purpose of, or while engaged in, eating, drinking, gaming, etc. (Cf. 2 a.)

*a* **1300** *Havelok* 2098 Betere is i go miself, and se, Hweþer he sitten nou, and wesseylen. **1377** LANGL. *P. Pl.* B. VI. 265 Sitte nouȝt to longe. Arise vp ar appetit haue eten his fulle. **1494** in *Ordin. Household* (1790) 116 And the Kinge sitt in the chamber, that the board must bee on the left hand;..and at the end must the Bishoppe sitt. **1553** BRENDE *Q. Curtius* X viij, Wyth whom when he had sitten eating awhile, he departed from them out of the feast. **1577** *F. de Lisle's Legendarie* I vj, The Kinge of Spaines embassador slacked his comming to yᵉ Council, because he disdained to sit vnder yᵉ French embassador. **1597** [see SALT *sb.*¹ 7 b]. **1605** *Hist. T. Stukeley* A 3 b, Ber Lady we haue sitten well my host, 'tis one a clock. **1791** BURNS *Tam o'Shanter* 24 That..ilka melder, wi' the miller, Thou sat as lang as thou had siller. **1825** T. HOOK *Sayings* Ser. ii. *Man of Many Fr.* II. 2 Without..recollecting that he had described himself..as engaged to a party likely to sit late. **1845** W. H. G. KINGSTON *Lusitanian Sk.* xxiii. II. 145 We sat but a short time after the hostess and her daughters had retired.

**e.** *ellipt.* To sit up (see 25 b).

**1852** THACKERAY *Esmond* I. i, Little Trix was promised to sit to supper that night.

**f.** To sit down in a public place as a form of protest; to take part in a sit-in.

**1961** *Daily Tel.* 21 Oct. 7/1 A tailor..was yesterday preparing to 'sit' for nine years, if necessary, in the path of a £1,500,000 redevelopment scheme. **1963** G. BUTLER *Coffin for Baby* iii. 49 My boy said to me this morning: Shall I sit or shan't I? You must do as your conscience tells you, I said. **1966** WODEHOUSE *Plum Pie* v. 121 Every now and then we march from Aldermaston, protesting like a ton of bricks... And then we sit a good deal. **1970** P. LAURIE *Scotland Yard* x. 259 The demonstrators..could 'sit' as long as they liked.

**g.** To baby-sit.

**1966** J. GLOAG *Sentence of Life* xxiii. 192 He wondered if Willy would be able to get Mrs Hillman in to sit. Friday was a bad night. **1968** J. UPDIKE *Couples* iii. 247 It was easier for the Saltzes to leave Bernard, who stays up forever reading anyway, to sit for his brother. **1975** M. BRADBURY *History Man* vii. 121 I'll have to get a sitter... I shouldn't have any trouble finding someone to sit. One of the students.

**2.** With prepositional phrases denoting the occupation of the person while seated: **a.** With *at* (table, meat, a meal, etc.).

*c* **975** *Rushw. Gosp.* Matt. ix. 9 Ȝesæh monnu sittende æt ȝæflaes monunȝe. *c* **1000** ÆLFRIC *Exodus* xi. 5 Oð þære wylne frumcennedan sunu, þæt sitt æt þære cweornan. *c* **1205** LAY. 13460 He uondede heom mid worde alse heo seten [*c* **1275** sete] at borde. **1297** R. GLOUC. (Rolls) 1215 þer after hii sete at hor mete, wiþ gret nobleie echon. **13..** *E.E. Allit. P.* B. 1763 Vche haþel..Seten at her soper & songen þer-after. **1382** WYCLIF *Luke* vii. 37 Jhesu hadde sete at the mete in the hous of the Pharisee. *c* **1400** *Pilgr. Sowle* (Caxton, 1483) III. ix. 55 They hadde none other lust but al day syt at the table. **1495** *Act 11 Hen. VII*, c. 22 §4 Laborers..longe sitting at ther brekfast at ther dyner and nonemete. **1535** COVERDALE *Tobit* ix, He founde Tobias syttinge at yᵉ table. **1610** HOLLAND *Camden's Brit.* I. 819 When we had sitten at supper untill it was two houres. **1710** *Tatler* No. 235 ¶3 It was an unspeakable Pleasure to visit or sit at Meal in that Family. **1742** RICHARDSON *Pamela* III. 88 One Day, as she and I sat together, at our Needles. **1806** WORDSW. *Horn Egremont Castle* 74 As good men do, he sate At his board by these surrounded. **1848** DICKENS *Dombey* xviii, They..sit long at meals, making much of their meat and drink. **1880** [see MEAT *sb.* 4 b].

**b.** With *to*.

**1382** WYCLIF *Luke* ix. 14 Make hem to sitte to mete. **1625** in Ellis *Lett. Lit. Men* (Camden) 132 One that hath already been tryed in transcribing of manuscripts, and will sitt close to worke. **1719** DE FOE *Crusoe* II. (Globe) 338 They could hardly sit to their Oars. **1749** FIELDING *Tom Jones* XVIII. xiii, These two therefore sat stoutly to it [*i.e.* drinking] during the whole Evening. **1817** BELOE *Sexagenarian* II. 218 He sat sturdily to work, and produced..an historical performance of several volumes.

**c.** With *through*.

**1889** J. L. TOOLE *Reminisc.* I. viii. 263 Quite different in its acceptance of fun or pathos from the audience that sits through the same piece the next night. **1932** D. L. SAYERS *Have his Carcase* xix. 255 She sat on right through the programme, but when it came to God Save the King, she chucked it. **1981** L. DEIGHTON *XPD* xxix. 236 Sir Sydney ..gallantly sat through another half-hour of finer points of script editing.

**3. a.** With complement denoting the manner (or place) of sitting (on a seat, etc., or on horseback).

*c* **1205** LAY. 25121 Summe heo sæten stille mucle ane stunde. *a* **1225** *Ancr. R.* 266 Nule he nout..wenden ouer, auh wule sitten ful ueste. *c* **1400** *Destr. Troy* 10151 He wauerit þerwith, & weikly he sete. **1423** JAS. I *Kingis Q.* 196 The magnificence Of him that hiest In the hevin sitt. **1530** PALSGR. 719/1, I syt hyest, or uppermoste at a table. **1620** MIDDLETON *Chaste Maid* (1630) 34 Sit you all merry, Ladies. **1662** J. WILSON *Cheats* I. iii, A Woman need not be asham'd to sit Jig by Joule, with the best of the Parish. **1687** A. LOVELL tr. *Thevenot's Trav.* I. 72 They look very well, and sit as close as if they were nailed to the Horse. **1719** DE FOE *Crusoe* II. (Globe) 565 The poor Beast..was no more to be govern'd by his Rider, tho' the Fellow sat well enough too. **1754** SHEBBEARE *Matrimony* (1766) II. 158, I sha'n't dare to sit cross-legg'd for you without offence. **1791–3** *Spirit Public Jrnls.* (1799) I. 74 A fat Whitechapel butcher, seated on the centre of the front bench... The butcher sat very back. **1850** THACKERAY *Pendennis* xl, Old Colchicum.. sitting bodkin between Mademoiselle Coralie and her mother.

**b.** With adj. or advb. complement in figurative phrases (see quots. and the complementary words). ***to sit pretty***: see PRETTY *adv.* 2 a; ***to sit tight***: see TIGHT *adv.* 2 b, etc.

**1427** *Act. Privy Council* III. 232 þat..þei [*sc.* lords of the Council] wolde sit upright and entende hooly to..þe goode of þe King and of his land. **1634** SIR T. HERBERT *Trav.* (1638) 315 The Mogull oft threatens to dethrone him; yet he sits close and keeps his owne. **1694** PENN *Rise & Progr. Quakers* vi. 116 To shew his Disciples it was Good to be Solitary, and sit loose to the World. **1833** G. S. FABER *Recapit. Apostasy* 127 Striving..to sit light to all sublunary matters. **1844** THACKERAY *Contrib. Punch* Wks. 1900 VI. 54, I wish to sit as soft as I can in this life. **1896** BADEN-POWELL *Matabele Campaign* i, They never reckoned that..they would sit tight and strike out hard.

**c.** In other figurative phrases (see quots. and the various sbs.). ***to sit at the feet of*** (a person), to be the disciple or pupil of (a teacher); ***to sit on one's hands***, (*a*) *U.S. colloq.*, to withhold or be sparing of applause; (*b*) to be inactive.

**1560** DAUS tr. *Sleidane's Comm.* 45 b, The Byshoppe, whiche as the master of a shyppe sitteth watching at the Healme. *c* **1580** J. HOOKER *Life Sir P. Carew* (ed. Maclean) 228 Oure enemyes, that have threatened to sitt on my skirts. **1625** MASSINGER *New Way* III. iii, She..sits on thorns till she be private with him. **1632** —— *City Madam* IV. i, He shall not Sit long on Penniless-Bench. **1652** in *Victoria Hist. Dorset* (1908) II. 252 [To] pay v s. or sitt vi houres by the heeles. **1717** PRIOR *Alma* I. 230 Poor Alma sits between two Stools. **1762–71** H. WALPOLE *Vertue's Anecd. Paint.* (1786) III. 23 Between..the dearth of good masters, and a fashionable reputation, Jervas sat at the top of his profession. **1885** H. HARLAND *As it was Written* 153, I had sat on pins during the inquisition. **1887** *Cornh. Mag.* June 626 Those who sit 'on the fence'—men with impartial minds, who wait to see..'how the cat will jump'.

**1535** BIBLE (Coverdale) *Luke* x., Mary..sat hir downe at Iesus fete, and herkened vnto his worde. **1611** *Ibid.* (A.V.) *Luke* x. 39 Mary..also sate at Iesus feet, and heard his word. **1633** D. ROGERS *Treat. of Sacr.* ii. 79 We have sitten at the feet of Christ attentively while we heard. **1907** KIPLING *Sons of Martha*, They sit at the Feet, and they hear The Word—they see how truly the Promise runs. **1926** G. M. TREVELYAN *Hist. England* v. iii. 557 They [*sc.* the Whigs] had sat at the feet of Edmund Burke. **1952** G. SARTON *Hist. Sci.* I. xxi. 547 He came to Athens to sit at Plato's feet. **1971** *Nature* 5 Mar. 2/2 It is clear that there are far more universities per square mile in Britain than are necessary to enable students to sit at the feet of some teacher or other.

**1926** E. FERBER *Show Boat* vi. 106 Well, they were sitting on their hands to-night, all right. Seemed they never would warm up. **1948** *Newsweek* 16 July 19/1 Listlessly, the convention sat on its hands at all mentions of Mr. Truman in the opening speeches. **1959** *Listener* 1 Jan. 4/1 This helped to reduce the number of constituency associations, who had to be persuaded by MacDonald or Gladstone to sit on their hands or, worse still, toil for their ally. **1961** *IUD Digest* Fall 74/1 Organized labour can ill afford to sit on its hands. **1972** *Guardian* 19 May 12/3 Opposition MPs who only yesterday sat on their hands to let Herr Brandt's Ostpolitik treaties through the Bundestag were back on their feet again this morning. **1976** *New Yorker* 8 Mar. 57/1 'Don't clap too hard—it's a very old building,' he cautions the audience, which is sitting on its hands. **1979** M. A. SHARP *Sunflower* xvi. 148, I should have learned *something* by now. I haven't exactly been sitting on my hands.

**4. a.** To occupy a seat in the capacity of a judge or with some administrative function.

***to sit in judgement***: see JUDGEMENT 1 b.

*c* **950** *Lindisf. Gosp.* Matt. xxvii. 19 Mið ðy sæt..he fore hehsedle. *c* **1000** ÆLFRIC *Exod.* xviii. 13 Þiȝ oðre dæȝe sæt Moises, þæt he wolde deman þam folce. *c* **1340** HAMPOLE *Pr. Consc.* 5636 Haly men and parfit, þat with hym in dome þan sal sitt, And wyth hym deme. **1377** LANGL. *P. Pl.* B. Prol. 96 Some..in stede of stuwardes sytten and demen. *c* **1400** *Gamelyn* 790 [He] him be-hette þat he wolde be redy whan þe Iustice sette. **1507** in Leadam *Sel. Cases Star Chamber* (Selden) 257 He..syttith as stuard..and holdith theyre Courtes. *a* **1548** HALL *Chron., Hen. V*, 75 A greate assemble ..in the whiche the two kynges sat as judges. **1681** WOOD *Life* 17 Aug., The judges..went to the Guildhall yard where they sate from 9 to 12. **1835** *Penny Cycl.* III. 376 When the judges of each court sit together upon their several benches. **1896** *Law Times Rep.* LXXIII. 690/1 The summons was heard by the registrar, sitting as Deputy Chancellor.

**b.** To occupy an episcopal, or the papal, see.

**1387** TREVISA *Higden* (Rolls) VII. 151 Gregorie þe sixte, first called Gracianus, after Benet, sat almost foure ȝere. *c* **1425** WYNTOUN *Orig. Cron.* v. 4535 Qwhen Anastace þe pope was dede, Symacus sat in til his stede Fifteyn ȝhere. *c* **1450** *St. Cuthbert* (Surtees) 6531 Tumbertus..Was Eata successour; he sat in hexham ȝeres thre. **1579** FULKE *Confut. Sanders* 540 Peter is sayd first to haue sit at Antioche. **1586** FERNE *Blaz. Gentrie* 128 Clement 5 then sitting in his papacy. **1631** WEEVER *Anc. Funeral Mon.* 132 When he had sitten fourty yeares in his Bishopricke. **1690–1** WOOD *Life* 1 Feb., Pope Ottoboni..died (after he had sate 16 months). *a* **1701** MAUNDRELL *Journ. Jerus.* (1732) 13 It was dignify'd with a Bishop's See. In which sometimes sate Severian. **1862** C. WORDSW. *Misc.* (1879) I. 257 The Roman Bishop of that name, who sate in the episcopal see from A.D. 218 to 223.

**c.** To have a seat in, be a member of, a council or legislative assembly. Also const. *for* (a constituency).

**1382** WYCLIF *Jer.* xv. 17, I sat not in counseil of pleieres. **1535** COVERDALE *Jer.* xxiii. 16 For who hath sytten in the councell of the Lorde? **1545** BRINKLOW *Compl.* 3 b, Them that sytte in the Parlament. **1645** WITHER *Vox Pacifica* 195 Since he hath sitten in this Parlament. **1675** HOBBES *Odyss.* IV. 268 Countries I have seen Many; and oft with Heroes in my life In Councels sitten. **1705–6** LUTTRELL *Brief Rel.* (1857) VI. 9 The clause..about officers sitting in parliament after the queens death. **1828** W. FIELD *Mem. Dr. Parr* II. 305 The third..had sitten in eleven successive parliaments. **1855** MACAULAY *Hist. Eng.* xii. III. 203 Francis Plowden, the Commissioner of Revenue, who sate for Bannow. **1880** TROLLOPE *Duke's Childr.* I. v. 55 You used to sit for Silverbridge.

**5.** Of a legislative or other assembly: To hold a session; to be engaged in the transaction of business.

**1518** *Rec. St. Mary at Hill* (1905) 298 Paid for brede and drynke at the parsonage at syttyng vppon þe Avdytt for the newe byldyng. **1577–87** HOLINSHED *Chron.* III. 924/1 We the aforesaid rector and doctors haue..sitten to dispute these questions. **1601** R. JOHNSON *Kingd. & Commw.* (1603) 57 When the counsell hath sitten seauen or eight houres, the Bassa visier maketh true relation to the Prince, of all that hath bene handled. **1639** *3rd Rep. Hist. MSS. Comm.* 78/1 If the King..go about to break their Parliament, I hear they are resolved to sit without his Majesty's leave. **1712** in Picton *L'pool Munic. Rec.* (1886) II. 6 That the..town's chest be now..inspected, sitting this Councill. **1761** HUME *Hist. Eng.* (1806) IV. lxiv. 725 A convocation..had usually sitten at the same time with the parliament. **1841** *Penny Cycl.* XXI. 177/1 There is also a chief secretary for Ireland, resident in Dublin (except when parliament is sitting). **1863** H. COX *Instit.* I. ix. 136 In the House of Lords the presence of three members is sufficient to enable the House to sit.

**6. a.** To place oneself in a position for having one's portrait painted or for being photographed. Also const. *for* (one's portrait), *to* (a painter, etc.).

**1538** CROMWELL in Merriman *Life & Lett.* (1902) II. 122 It may please you..to sit so longe..that a seruaunt of the kinges highnes..may take your phisionomie. **1584** LYLY *Alex. & Camp.* IV. ii, The misfortune I had with your picture wil put you to some paines to sitte againe to be painted. **1666** PEPYS *Diary* 17 Mar., This day I began to sit; and he will make me, I think, a very fine picture. *a* **1700** EVELYN *Diary* 28 June 1641, I..sate to one Vanderborcht for my picture in oyle. **1742** YOUNG *Nt. Th.* VI. 53 Who can take Death's portrait true? The tyrant never sat. **1840** THACKERAY *Paris Sk. Bk.* I. 115 Simon..painted portraits to admiration, only nobody came to sit to him. **1894** LIDDON *Life Pusey* I. Pref. p. x, Dr. Pusey persistently refused to sit for this portrait.

**b.** To serve as a model *for* a painting or a character in a novel. Also *fig.*

**1673** [R. LEIGH] *Transp. Reh.* 35 Imagining, as he well might, that he had sat for the Coffee-house Sign. **1762** *Ann. Reg.* II. 18 Mr. Young, a learned..friend of..Fielding's, sat for parson Adams. **1784** COWPER *Task* IV. 526 Airy dreams Sat for the picture; and the poet's hand..Impos'd a gay delirium for a truth.

**c.** To present oneself for examination, etc. (also const. *for*); to be a candidate *for* a fellowship.

The latter is a special Cambridge use; at Oxford one is said to *stand* for a fellowship.

**1830** S. BUTLER in *Life* I. 371 Tom will be at Cambridge to sit for a fellowship at St. John's. *Ibid.*, I had only two men to sit at the Classical Tripos. **1929** R. GRAVES *Goodbye to all That* xxvii. 362 My tutor..warned me that I must on no account disparage the eighteenth century when I sat for my final examination. **1955** *Times* 30 June 6/5 Pupils sitting for the examination for entry to secondary schools. **1963** R. Pedley *Comprehensive School* i. 14 In some of the 3900 'modern' schools in England and Wales it is possible for the cleverer pupils to sit for GCE at ordinary level. **1968** G. Maxwell *Raven seek thy Brother* viii. 102, I appealed to my guardian to be allowed to retire..from the scene on the grounds of ill-health... The refusal was absolute..; I was to sit for my degree, no matter what the outcome. **1980** *Radio Times* 1–7 Mar. 16/4 It is possible to take an A-level without having sat for the O-level.

**7. a.** To be, to continue or remain, *in* a certain state. Now *rare* or *Obs.*

In most cases with suggestion of the literal sense.

*c* **825** *Vesp. Psalter* cvi. 10 Sittende in ðeostrum & scuan deaðes. *a* **1000** *Genesis* 2700 Ic þæs færes a on wenum sæt. *a* **1200** *Trin. Coll. Hom.* 103 Ðus sit man on his sinne, swo ich seid haue. *c* **1250** *Gen. & Ex.* 1239 Ðor sat his moder in sik and sor. *c* **1375** *Cursor M.* 15576 (Fairf.), þ ou sal couer & confort ham þat sitis in sorou & site. **1377** Langl. *P. Pl.* B. xx. 198 As I seet in þis sorwe, I say how kynde passed. *c* **1450** Holland *Howlat* 22 Thus sat I in solace, sekerly and sure. **1535** Stewart *Cron. Scot.* I. 30 Than we and tha sall sit in rest and peice. **1628** Gaule *Pract. The.* (1629) 401 Had not our Sunne thus wisely prolonged his course, we had sit still in Darknesse. **1671** Milton *P.R.* ii. 431 While Virtue, Valour, Wisdom sit in want.

**b.** With adjectival or other complement denoting the condition.

*a* **1000** *Deor's Compl.* 24 Sæt secȝ moniȝ sorȝum ȝebunden, wean on wenan. *a* **1035** *Laws Cnut* ii. lxxiii. (Liebermann) 360 Sitte ælc wuduwe werleas twelf-monað. *a* **1250** *Prov. Ælfred* 378 in *O.E. Misc.* 124 þanne myht þu sikerliche sely sytte. **1382** Wyclif *Lam.* iii. 28 He shal sitte solitarie. *c* **1400** *Destr. Troy* 2265 Ye wetyn..þat all Auffrike & Europe..Sittyn to hom subiecte. *c* **1450** *St. Cuthbert* (Surtees) 1006 He was anker and sole satt,..And leued in lyf contemplatyue. **1530** Palsgr. 719/1 Go to the warre who wyll, I wyll sytte styll. *c* **1595** Capt. Wyatt *R. Dudley's Voy.* (Hakl. Soc.) 47 The Indians beinge suffred to sitt afterwarde at libertie. **1638** W. Sclater *Serm. Experim.* 79 That people have now long sitten without a King. *a* **1700** Evelyn *Diary* 23 Sept. 1683, That the French King might the more easily swallow Flanders..whilst we sat unconcern'd. **1760** *Ann. Reg.* i. 9 That haughty power was obliged to sit the impotent spectator of the ruin of her colonies. **1775** Johnson *Tax. no Tyr.* 31 That he can sit secure in the enjoyment of inheritance. **1875** Jowett *Plato* (ed. 2) V. 68 Plato has arrived at the time when men sit still and look on at life.

**c.** With appositive complement denoting the position or occupation of a person. Also *fig.*

*c* **825** *Vesp. Psalter* xxviii. 10 Siteð dryhten cyning in ecnisse. **1382** Wyclif *Isaiah* xlvii. 8, I shal not sitte a widewe. —— *Rev.* xviii. 7 In hir herte she seith, I sitte a queen. **1614** Raleigh *Hist. World* iv. iii. §3. 181 Having sitten Viceroy tenne yeeres. **1629** H. Burton *Babel no Bethel* 124 It is Babylons voyce, *Sedeo Regina*, I sit a Queene. **1634** Milton *Comus* 957 Night sits monarch yet in the mid sky. *a* **1661** Fuller *Worthies* (1840) III. 304 He sate bishop 19 years. **1715** Hearne *Collect.* (O.H.S.) V. 62 Dr. Charlett sate Vice-Chancellor, and ordered ye Sermon to be printed. **1784** Cowper *Task* v. 877 Gods..that sit Amus'd spectators of this bustling stage. **1833** Chalmers *Const. Man* (1835) I. i. 103 Conscience sat mistress over the whole earth. **1859** Reade *Love me Little* vii. (1868) 88 She was sitting sentinel till the carriage should arrive.

**8. a.** To have one's seat, quarters, or place; to abide, dwell, remain (in a place).

*c* **900** *O.E. Chron.* (Parker MS.) an. 855, Her hæþne men ærest on Sceapiȝe ofer winter sætun. *c* **950** *Lindisf. Gosp.* Luke xxi. 35 On allum ðaðe sittað ofer onsione all eorðes. *a* **1122** *O.E. Chron.* (Laud MS.) an. 1036, Man ȝerædde þa þæt Ælfȝifu..sæte on Winceastre. **1154** *Ibid.* an. 1137, Sculdest þu neure finden man in tune sittende. **13..** *K. Alis.* (Laud MS.) 1927 Bitwene tygre & Eufraten, Seten alle þise heþen men. *c* **1380** Wyclif *Sel. Eng. Wks.* I. 149 Hem were beter to sitten at home. *a* **1400–50** *Alexander* 4024 [They have] Nouthire cites in to sytt, cellis, nor na tounes. **1584** *Leycesters Commw.* (1641) 23 If the good Lady had..used his helpe, shee should not have needed to have sitten so pensive at home. **1649** Sclater *Comm. Malachy* (1650) 176 It had better for them, to have sitten by the flesh-pots and garlicke, and onyons of Egypt. **1667** Milton *P.L.* ii. 56 Shall the rest..sit lingring here Heav'ns fugitives? **1721** Kelly *Sc. Prov.* 194 It is hard to sit in Rome, and strive against the Pope.

*fig.* *c* **1350** *Will. Palerne* 446 He sittus in mi siȝt me þinkes euer-more. *c* **1400** *Rom. Rose* 2846 Y-wis, he sit so nere myn herte. To speke of him, at eve or morwe, It cureth me of al my sorwe. **1749** Fielding *Tom Jones* xvii. v, The lady..who sits, indeed, very near my heart.

**b.** To be tenant of, to occupy, a house, farm, etc.; to remain during a lease; to continue a tenancy. Usually const. *at* (a certain rent), or with compl. Also, †to live *at* a certain rate of expense.

**1598** Shaks. *Merry W.* i. iii. 8, I sit at ten pounds a weeke. **1609** W. M. *Man in Moone* (1849) 17 Marke how they will moane their own mischances, how they sit at an unmerciful rent. **1625** Bacon *Ess., Of Usury* (Arb.) 542 As a Farmer cannot husband his Ground so well, if he sit at a great Rent. **1713** in *N. & Q.* 9th Ser. X. 257/1 The Schoolmistress to sit Rent free. **1751** Smollett *Per. Pic.* xci, She found herself ..incapable..of keeping the farm, unless he would..allow her to sit free for a twelvemonth. **1811** Scott in *Lockhart* (1837) II. xi. 356, I now sit a tenant at will under a heavy rent. **1844** W. Cross *Disruption* xxxviii. (E.D.D.), Sit wha like, I'll flitt. **1883** *19th Cent.* Sept. 439 The ryots..claim at times to sit at rates that have long been obsolete.

*Prov.* **1615** W. Lawson *Country Housew. Gard.* (1626) 9 Their Tenants..haue taken vp this Prouerbe, Botch and sit, Build and flit.

**9. † a.** To lie *in* wait or in ambush. *Obs.*

*c* **825** *Vesp. Psalter* ix. 29 [He] siteð in searwum mid ðæm weoligum. *a* **1225** *Ancr. R.* 332 Tristre is þer me sit mid þe greahundes forte kepen þe hearde. *a* **1340** Hampole *Psalter* ix. 30 He sittis in waitis wiþ þe riche in hidels. **1382** Wyclif *Josh.* viii. 9 Thei wenten to the place of the busshement, and thei seten betwixe Bethel and Hay.

**b.** To remain at a siege. Cf. 23 c (*b*).

*c* **900** *O.E. Chron.* (Parker MS.) an. 878, He..him æfter rad oþ þæt ȝeworc, & þær sæt xiiii niht. *a* **1000** *Boeth. Metr.* xxvi. 16 Aulixes mid an hund scipa lædde ofer laȝustream; sæt longe ðær tyn winter full. **1802** James *Milit. Dict.* s.v., To sit before a fortified place; to lie encamped for the purpose of besieging it.

**10. a.** Of birds: To perch or roost; also, to rest the body on the ground or other surface.

*a* **1000** *Phœnix* 208 þær se wilda fuȝel..siteð siþes fus. *a* **1000** *Genesis* 2159 Ac nefuȝlas under beorhhleoþum blodiȝ sittað. *c* **1205** Lay. 2827 An muchel ærn spec a þon castle þer he set. *c* **1250** *Owl & Night.* 89 þu sittest a day and flyhst a niht. **13..** *Coer de L.* 465 (W.), On hys crest sat a raven swart. **1446** Lydg. *Nightingale Poems* i. 97 She a-lyght Ande singynge seet in myddes of the tre. **1486** *Bk. St. Albans* d ij b, All maner of fowlys that syt in trees. **15..** in *Dunbar's Poems* (S.T.S.) App. ii. 12 That bird..satt, & tald me hir intent. **1613** Purchas *Pilgrimage* (1614) 748 The birds sit as thicke, as stones lie in a Paued street. **1696** Tate & Brady *Ps.* cii. 6 Like an Owl that sits all day On barren Trees. **1784** Cowper *Task* vi. 308 The stock-dove..Sits cooing in the pine-tree. **1803** *Gaz. Scotl.* s.v. *Orkney Islands*, The cliffs on which the birds are sitting. **1821–2** Shelley *Chas. I*, v. 4 A widow bird sate mourning Upon a wintry bough. **1901** *Westm. Gaz.* 30 Aug. 1/3 The coveys have grown so wild.. that they will not sit to setters.

**b.** To take up or continue in the posture necessary for the hatching of eggs. Also const. *on.*

In older use freq. *to sit abrood*: see abrood *adv.*

**1483** *Cath. Angl.* 341/2 To Sytt on eggis, *incubare*. **1523** Fitzherb. *Husb.* §146 All hole-footed fowles wyll sytte a moneth. **1602** *2nd Pt. Return fr. Parnass.* i. ii. 173 An old goose that sits hatching vp those eggs. **1658** tr. *Porta's Nat. Magic* ii. xvii. 50 Let them [eggs] be sitten upon, their due time [etc.]. **1759** R. Brown *Compl. Farm.* 71 A hen sits twenty days. **1828** Stark *Elem. Nat. Hist.* I. 303 Until the female begins to sit, the male is frequently heard to make a singular kind of noise. **1855** D. J. Browne *Amer. Poultry Yd.* 108 If a hen is really determined to sit, it is useless..to attempt to divert her from her object.

*transf.* **1608** Topsell *Serpents* (1658) 597 The Serpent having laid her Egge sitteth upon them to hatch them at several times.

*fig.* **1667** Milton *P.L.* i. 21 Thou..Dove-like satst brooding on the vast Abyss And mad'st it pregnant. **1818** Scott *Rob Roy* xxxv, Civil war is like a cockatrice;—we have sitten hatching the egg that held it for ten years.

**11.** Of animals: To rest the body in a manner analogous to that of a seated person.

*c* **1250** *Owl & Night.* 86 þe were icundere to one frogge þat sit at Mulne vnder cogge. **13..** *Pains of Hell* (Vernon MS.) 217 Wormes and serpentes on hem seeten. **1340** Hampole *Pr. Consc.* 4178 'þe Dan' he says 'sal þe nedder be Sitand in þe way als men sal se'. *c* **1420** *Anturs of Arth.* x. (Thornton MS.), Cerkelytt withe serpentes, þat satt by hir sydes. **1486** *Bk. St. Albans* F vij b, A Cony sittyng. **1523** Fitzherb. *Husb.* §18 The sheepe..wyll folowe those stakes, as he flytteth them, and syt by them. **1667** Milton *P.L.* iv. 352 Others on the grass Coucht, and now fild with pasture gazing sat. *Ibid.* v. 25 How the Bee Sits on the Bloom. **1711** Addison *Spect.* No. 115 ¶6 A Hare is not yet safe that Sits within ten Miles of his House. **1856** 'Stonehenge' *Brit. Rural Sports* i. ii. vi. 139 It is very desirable to find the hare sitting, because she may otherwise sit so close as to be 'chopped'.

*fig.* **1749** Fielding *Tom Jones* v. x, This alone must have abundantly satisfied Jones that he was (to use the language of sportsmen) found sitting.

**12.** To rest the body *on* the knees; to be in a kneeling posture. Cf. 19. *Obs.* exc. *dial.*

*c* **893** K. Ælfred *Oros.* iii. ix. 134 þeh þe hie hiene meðiȝne on cneowum sittende metten. *a* **1000** *Daniel* 180 þa hie for þam cumble on cneowum sæton. *c* **1275** *Passion our Lord* 106 in *O.E. Misc.* 40 He hit bitauhte iudas, þat alle hit myhte iseo, þer he wes bivoren him and set on his kneo. *c* **1375** *Sc. Leg. Saints* xiii. (*Mark*) 173 He..prayt for þam ..& sad, sittand one his kne [etc.]. **1390** Gower *Conf.* I. 155 This Maiden, which sat on hire knes Tofore the king. *c* **1440** *Alph. Tales* 15 As he satt in his prayers, hym þoght [etc.]. **1518** in *Yorks. Arch. Trans.* II. 381, iij pure women to sit at ye herse & pray. **1593** in J. Morris *Troubles Cath. Forefathers* (1877) 155 All the time he was before them, the President forced him to sit upon his knees. *c* **1610** Sir J. Melvil *Mem.* (Bann. Club) 120 He sitting vpon his knees before hir, keping a gret grauite. **1652** Boate *Nat. Hist. Ireland* (1860) 125 On that dry place where the mud is poured forth sit certain women upon their knees. **1821** Scott *Kenilw.* xxxii, While he sat on his knees before me, mopping and mowing. **1868** in *Myrc's Instr. Par. Priests* 74 In Durham *sitting on the knees* is an expression still used for kneeling.

**II. 13. a.** Of things: To have place or location; to be situated.

*c* **888** K. Ælfred *Boeth.* xxxix. §13 þæt leohte fyr..up ȝewit, & sio hefiȝe eorðe sit þær niðere. *c* **900** Wærferth tr. *Gregory's Dial.* 245 þæt ȝetacnað, þæt seo rihtȝewittuȝe sawl siteð on þam lichaman. **1362** Langl. *P. Pl.* A. viii. 129, I.. sauh þe sonne sitte souþ euene þat tyme. *c* **1391** Chaucer *Astrol.* ii. §33 The same wyse maistou sen..wheither the sterre sitte est or west or north. *c* **1400** Maundev. (1839) i. 7 The evylle Town, that sytt toward the ende of Hungarye. *c* **1425** *Crafte Nombrynge* (E.E.T.S.) 23 Loke quere sittes 2 in þe lyft side in þe first rewe. *c* **1440** *Astron. Cal.* (MS. Ashm. 391), A table..which will shewe you in what signe þe moone sitteþ euery day. **1504** *Bury Wills* (Camden) 102 The which tenement syttyth and lyyth by ye tenement of John Clerk. **1570** *Satir. Poems Reform.* xxii. 54 The forkit Clauer besyde the Croce that sittis. **1812** *New Bot. Garden* I. 29 The involucre..sits close to the flower. **1867** Augusta Wilson *Vashti* xx, In the room where the coffin sat wreathed with flowers. **1879** Stevenson *Trav. Donkey* (1886) 179 The village of Cocurès, sitting among vineyards and meadows. **1976** M. Machlin *Pipeline* liii. 526 Occasionally a guard was left when equipment sat in the field, but now it was lunch hour. **1977** *Oxford Jrnl.* 10 June 1/5 There were a dozen eggs still sitting on the front porch and the dustbin sat at the back of the house where the binmen had left it. **1978** *Sci. Amer.* May 65/2 The idea of an exploding clump of matter sitting somewhere in space offers no natural way to account for the existence of the cosmic background radiation.

*fig.* **1632** Milton *Penseroso* 40 Thy rapt soul sitting in thine eyes. **1760–72** H. Brooke *Fool of Qual.* (1809) IV. 93 That regardlessness for trifles which then sat at my heart. **1793** Burns *Young Jessie* 13 Love sits in her smile, like a wizard ensnaring. **1821–2** Shelley *Chas. I*, ii. 34 Mark you what spirit sits in St. John's eyes?

**b.** To be situated, to rest or lie, to be supported, *on* or *upon* something. Freq. *fig.*

**971** *Blickl. Hom.* 75 Swa seo hefiȝe byrþen [of the tomb] siteþ on þæm deadan lichoman. *a* **1023** Wulfstan *Hom.* xxxiii. (1883) 162 Us godes yrre hetelice on sit. *a* **1300** *Havelok* 735 þer sat is ship up-on þe sond. **1362** Langl. *P. Pl.* A. vi. 11 An hundred of ampolles on his hat seeten. **1390** Gower *Conf.* II. 23 Which Ring..where it on a finger sat [etc.]. **1494** *Act 11 Hen. VII*, c. 23 The little Bone that sitteth upon the great Fin. **1619** Beaum. & Fl. *Knt. Malta* iv. ii, Art thou a Knight? did ever on that sword The Christian cause sit nobly? **1676** Hobbes *Iliad* ii. 20 That sleep all night upon his eyes should sit. **1766** Goldsm. *Vic. W.* xxviii, A fatal paleness sat upon her cheek. **1796** Withering *Brit. Plants* (ed. 3) IV. 114 Scarlet semi-globules sitting on the sides of the branches. **1820** Scott *Monast.* xxxvii, Your Father and Abbot will not disgrace the mitre which sits upon his brow. **1853** M. Arnold *Sohrab & Rustum* 666 Truth sits upon the lips of dying men. **1885** *Century Mag.* XXIX. 880/2 A little three-legged trivet on which a tankard..might sit with live coals beneath.

**c.** With compl. denoting manner or position.

*c* **1400** *Lanfranc's Cirurg.* 188 It wole make hise heeris longe & make hem sitte faste. **1654** Z. Coke *Logick* To Rdr., The numerous Tomes of the Times, which serve but..to make the world sit straight about you. **1719** De Foe *Crusoe* i. (Globe) 55 The Ship sat upright. **1739** Labelye *Piers Westm. Bridge* 30 We sunk the Caisson a second time, and found it to bed itself, or sit perfectly level upon the hard Gravel. **1878** D. Kemp *Man. Yacht & Boat Sailing* 368/2 Sails are said to 'sit' well when they do not girt, pucker, belly, or shake. **1958** *Listener* 28 Aug. 309/3 Slots must be cut in the bottom half of them [*sc.* the horizontal pieces] where they meet the posts, so that they will sit nicely. **1971** *Good Motoring* Sept. 18/1 Where the 33 tended to hang out its back end on fast corners the 44 sat steadily on the road.

**d.** Of the wind: To blow from, be in, a particular quarter. Now only in fig. phrase.

**1593** Shaks. *Rich. II*, ii. ii. 123 The winde sits faire for newes to go to Ireland, But none returnes. **1596** Danett tr. *Comines* ii. xiv. 78, I wot not whether it were bicause the winde sat that way, or bicause we lodged vpon the riuer. **1610** Holland *Camden's Brit.* 587 When the wind sitteth West, it is alwaies rain. *a* **1654** Selden *Table-T.* (Arb.) 32 A good Miller that knows how to grind which way soever the Wind sits. **1711** Addison *Spect.* No. 10 ¶5 By that Time they are pretty good Judges of the Weather, know which Way the Wind sits [etc.]. **1762** *Gentl. Mag.* 137 The wind sat North.

*fig.* **1599** Shaks. *Much Ado* ii. iii. 102 That she should so dote on Signior Benedicke... *Bene.* Is't possible? sits the winde in that corner? **1605** Chapman *All Fools* i. i, Sits the winde there? blowes there so calme a gale From a contemned and deserued anger? **1706** Mrs. Centlivre *Basset-Table* iv, Ha, Captain, how sits the wind between you and your mistress? **1818** Scott *Br. Lamm.* xv, So soon as the Marquis's political agent found how the wind sat, he began [etc.]. **1834** Whately in *Life* (1866) I. 243 The following straw may serve to show how the winds sits. **1893** Stevenson *Catriona* vi, Is it so the wind sits?

**† e.** Of the tide: To set. *Obs.*⁻¹

**1751** R. Paltock *P. Wilkins* (1884) I. 239 Shooting from shelf to shelf, as the tide sat.

**14.** In fig. phrases: **a.** With *nigh*, *near*, *close to*, *at*, etc.: To affect one deeply.

*c* **1402** Lydg. *Compl. Bl. Knt.* 18 My sekenes sat ay so nigh my herte. **1584** B. R. tr. *Herodotus* 106 There befell unto him another mischiefe, that sate as neere hys skirtes as the death of his dilling. **1603** Shaks. *Meas. for M.* v. 394 Your Brothers death I know sits at your heart. **1611** Speed *Hist. of Gt. Brit.* ix. iii. §19. 443 Whose sinnes beganne to sit so neere his heart..that hee sore repented him of the same. **1622** Mabbe tr. *Aleman's Guzman d' Alf.* ii. 39 Of all my misfortunes, the greatest that ever befell mee, and which sits closest to my heart. **1713** Addison *Cato* i. iv, When discontent sits heavy at my heart. **1821** Scott *Kenilw.* xxx, The anguish and uncertainty which sat heavy at his heart.

**b.** To press or weigh (heavily, lightly, etc.) *on* or *upon* one. Also without const.

**1593** Shaks. *Rich. II*, i. iii. 280 (Q.), Woe doth the heauier sit, Where it perceiues it is but faintly borne. **1643** Milton *Divorce* Wks. 1851 IV. 9 For no effect of tyranny can sit more heavy on the Common-wealth. **1697** Collier *Ess. Mor. Subj.* (1703) ii. 182 These questions well-answered.. will make a man's years sit easy upon him. **1729** Butler *Serm., Balaam* 451 There must therefore be some method of making it sit a little easy upon their minds. **1759** Sterne *Tr. Shandy* ii. xiv, To make reparation..for the insult he had given him, which sat still upon my father's mind. **1861** Hughes *Tom Brown at Oxf.* x, The restless haggard expression sat more heavily than ever on his face. **1875** Jowett *Plato* (ed. 2) III. 196 Old age sits lightly upon you.

**c.** To lie (easily, etc.) *on* the stomach. Also without const., to be easily digested.

(*a*) **1708** W. King *Cookery* 19 You cannot imagine..how much easier they will sit upon your Stomach. **1773** Goldsm. *Stoops to Conq.* iv. i, Good liquor will sit upon a good supper, but a good supper will not sit upon..my conscience. **1822–7** Good *Study Med.* (1829) V. 572 Such preparations of iron as may sit easy on the stomach.

(*b*) **1737** Byrom *Rem.* (1856) II. i. 123 Had a cheesecake.. by the way, which..did not sit so easy, being buttery. **1822–7** Good *Study Med.* (1829) I. 187 A little toast and water alone..will often sit easy when nothing else will remain.

**† 15. a.** With dative of person: To affect (one) in a specified way; to distress, vex, grieve. *Obs.*

*c* **1230** *Hali Meid.* 7 To don al & drehen þat him likeð, ne sitte hit hire se uuele. *c* **1375** *Cursor M.* 24342 (Fairf.), Our sorowing..satte vs baþ in flesshe & bane. **1393** LANGL. *P. Pl.* C. III. 154 Yf he fynde ȝow in defaute..Hit shal sitte ȝoure soules ful soure at þe laste. *c* **1400** *Destr. Troy* 2284 Sothely your suster sittes vs not so harde. *c* **1470** HENRY *Wallace* VI. 24 Ȝeit he desyrd the thing that sat him sar. *a* **1500** *Assembly Ladies* 663 She felt gret displesaunce,..And no wonder; it sat her passing nere. **1535** STEWART *Cron. Scot.* III. 269 In his aige that sat him than full soir. *a* **1542** WYATT *Poet. Wks.* (1861) 24 But pray restore it mannerly,..For to lese it, it sitteth me near.

†**b.** To cost (one) so much. *Obs. rare.*

**1377** LANGL. *P. Pl.* B. III. 48 We han a wyndowe a wirchyng wil sitten vs ful heigh. *c* **1421** *26 Pol. Poems* 85 Mannys loue sat me so sore, Nas neuere bargayn derrere bouȝt.

**16.** Of clothes: **a.** With dative: To fit or suit (a person, etc.). *rare.*

This sense and 17 are due to the influence of AF. *seeir* (mod.F. *seoir*).

*a* **1300** *Cursor M.* 15286 Wit a tuell he belted him His side sitand ful mete. *a* **1764** LLOYD *Poet. Wks.* (1774) II. 38 Suppose For once you wear the begger's clothes;..Bless me, they sit you to a hair. **1827** CARLYLE *Germ. Rom.* III. 129 Her morning-promenade dress of white muslin,..but, adds she, it will not sit her.

**b.** To fit (well, tightly, etc.). Freq. with preps. as *about*, *on*, *to*. Also *fig.*

? **1370** *Robt. Cicyle* 287 Alle men wondurd fro whens he came, So welle hys rayment sate hym on. *c* **1400** *Rom. Rose* 2263 Poyntis and sleves be wel sittand, Right and streight upon the hand. **1470–85** MALORY *Arthur* IX. i. 338 His ouer garment sat ouerthwartly. **1561** HOBY tr. *Castiglione's Courtyer* I. (1577) H ij, Her hose sittynge cleane to her legge. **1594** HOOKER *Eccl. Pol.* Pref. iii. §14 Which cloak sitteth no less fit on the back of their cause, than of the Anabaptists. **1602** *How Chuse Good Wife* III. iii, He is such a sloven, That nothing will sit handsome about him. **1607** DEKKER *Northward Hoe* II. i, How sit our blew-coates on our backes. **1687** MIÉGE *Gt. Fr. Dict.* II. s.v., A Coat that sits close to the Body. **1819** SCOTT *Ivanhoe* iii, A close dress of scarlet which sate tight to his body. **1851** *Eliza Cook's Jrnl.* 19 July 177 Throwing also an occasional look down..his new Californian trowsers, seeing that they 'sit' well. **1884** G. ALLEN *Philistia* I. 52 Now just turn round and show me how it sits behind.

**c.** *fig.* Of airs, opinions, practices, etc.

**1614** D. DYKE *Myst. Self-deceiving* 263 Let his gifts and graces be neuer so excellent, yet they sit but loose about him. **1728** VANBR. & CIBBER *Prov. Husb.* II. i, *Lady Ara.* Do you ever play at hazard, Clarinda? *Clar.* Never; I don't think it sits well upon women. **1786** *Francis the Philanthropist* III. 79 He whose opinions..sat loose upon him, was always deemed a bad, and generally a weak, man. **1821** SCOTT *Kenilw.* vii, Her little air of precision sits so well upon her. **1858** CARLYLE *Fredk. Gt.* XI. i. (1872) IV. 25 A light stoicism sits gracefully on him. **1885** *Spectator* 25 July 970/2 The feudal Conservatism which sat so well upon him.

**d.** *fig.* Without compl.

**1964** G. C. KUNZLE *Parallel Bars* ix. 410 Make certain that you can do an individual movement with perfect technique before you include it in the exercise. Then try it out in minor competitions until it 'sits'. **1971** B. GRAHAM *Spy Trap* ii. 19 It was too pat, too smug, like a well-turned-out radio script. It didn't sit.

**17.** †**a.** Usually *impers.* To suit; to be suitable, fitting, proper, or seemly. *Obs.*

*c* **1330** R. BRUNNE *Chron. Wace* (Rolls) 15558 Þei mette..To conseille þem, & to wyte How þat þyng best mighte site. *c* **1386** CHAUCER *Clerk's T.* 404 But..I seye that yuele it sit To assaye a wyf whan þat it is no nede. **1390** GOWER *Conf.* I. 335 Yit sit it wel that thou eschuie That thou the Court noght overhaste. *c* **1449** PECOCK *Repr.* III. ix. 333 It bisemeth and it is sitting, and therfore it is to be doon. **1579** SPENSER *Sheph. Cal.* Nov. 26 The Nightingale is souereigne of song, Before him sits the Titmose silent bee.

†**b.** Const. *for*, *to*, or with dative. *Obs.*

*c* **1386** CHAUCER *Merch. T.* 1071, I am a kyng, it sit me noght to lye. **1390** GOWER *Conf.* I. 51 It sit a prest to be wel thewed. **14..** in *Hist. Coll. Cit. Lond.* (Camden) 129 As hyt syttythe and semyþe so worthy a prynce and a pryncesse. *c* **1420** *Wars Alexander* 73 It sittez noȝte till an emperour..to lese his men þus. *c* **1460** J. RUSSELL *Bk. Nurture* 392 With pesyn & baken whan sesoun þer-to dothe sitt. **1530** PALSGR. 719/2 It sytteth nat for your estate to weare so fyne furres.

**c.** With *well* as complement. Now *dial.* and *poet.*

? *a* **1366** CHAUCER *Rom. Rose* 750 It sat hir wondir wel to synge. **1375** BARBOUR *Bruce* I. 394 In spek wlispyt he sum deill; Bot that sat him rycht wondre weill. **1399** GOWER *In Praise Peace* 52 It sit hem wel to do pite and grace. **1426** *Acts Privy Council* III. 183 My..lorde of Gloucestre wol as hit sitteth him wel..kepe & restreyne his meyne. **1846** BROCKETT *N.C. Gloss.* (ed. 3) s.v., 'It sits him well,' of a pretentious person. **1878** J. J. AUBERTIN tr. *Camoens' Lusiads* II. VIII. lxiv. 129 With a proud confidence, which sat him well.

**III. 18. a.** To seat oneself; to take a seat; to sit down. Cf. 23 a. Also const. *to.*

*Beowulf* 489 Site nu to symle..swa þin sefa hwette. *c* **1175** *Lamb. Hom.* 105 þet mon..er timan to his borde ne sitte. **1382** WYCLIF *Jer.* xiii. 18 Sei to the king,..Beth mekid, sitteth. **1592** KYD *Sp. Trag.* I. v. 12 [They] sit to the Banquet. *c* **1611** CHAPMAN *Iliad* I. 98 Thus, he sate, and up ..Heroic Agamemnon rose. **1662** J. DAVIES tr. *Olearius' Voy. Amb.* 19 This done, they sate to the Table, and some Gobelets..were drunk about. **1676** HOBBES *Iliad* I. 101 This said, he sat. **1831** SCOTT *Ct. Robt.* xii, Sit then, Brenhilda, since the good man will have it so. **1873** HOLMES *Addr. Opening Fifth Avenue Theatre* 100 The hurrying crowd.. smooths its caudal plumage as it sits.

**b.** In pa. pple. with *is*, *was*, etc. Cf. 23 a (*b*). Now *dial.*

*c* **925** *O.E. Chron.* (Parker MS.) an. 922, Him cierde eall þæt folc to þe on Mercna lande ȝeseten wæs. *c* **1290** *St. Brendan* 281 Þo heo weren alle i-sete þare cam on and seruede. *c* **1300** *Childhood Jesu* 1720 (Horstm.), To þe bord huy beoþ isete. *c* **1380** *Sir Ferumb.* 48 Al on murȝþe was he y-sete wiþ a fair baronye. **1597** SHAKS. *Lover's Compl.* 66 Her ageine desires her, being satte [etc.]. **1655** tr. *Sorel's Com. Hist. Francion* VII. 12 We being sate, and she likewise, Clerantes said [etc.]. **1711** [see A. 7γ]. **1864** RAMSBOTHAM *Lanc. Rhymes* 12 At th' eend o' th' day..aw'm sat at whoam.

**c.** *transf.* To set; to stick; to settle down.

**1621** BP. MOUNTAGU *Diatribæ* 358 He heard the Sunne hisse, sitting in the West Ocean. **1888** ADDY *Sheffield Gloss.* 216 *Sit*, to adhere firmly, to be burnt. 'That milk has sit.' **1901** *Daily Chron.* 28 Dec. 9/2 Henriette (French barque), supposed sat upon her anchor in Astoria Harbour.

†**19.** To go down *on* one's knees. Cf. 23 b. *Obs.*

*c* **1290** *S. Eng. Leg.* I. 63 Ȝwane it saiȝ þe freres sitten a-kneo, kneuli it wolde al-so. *a* **1300** *Havelok* 2709 Þou wost ful wel..Þat Aþelwold þe dide site On knes. **1483** CAXTON *Gold. Leg.* 195 b/2 Assone as the preestys were gone and departed she satte on hir knees. *a* **1533** LD. BERNERS *Huon* xvi. 43 Huon..by force was fayne to syt on one of his knees to the erthe.

**20.** To rise *upright*, *on end*, move or lean *back*, in a sitting posture. Cf. 27.

*a* **1300** *Cursor M.* 19790 Quen sco o petre had a sight, Bi hir self sco satt vp-right. **1822** SCOTT *Nigel* xxv, The female ..sat by the expiring fire with her limbs outstretched...'Do not leave me,'..she said, sitting upright. **1884** T. SPEEDY *Sport Highl.* xiii. 212 It being a habit of the mountain hare ..to run one or two hundred yards, and then, kangaroo-like, sit on end and look back. **1885** *Manch. Exam.* 6 Aug. 5/5 Lord Redesdale beamed benevolently upon his contemporary as he sat back upon his bench.

**IV.** * *With adverbs.*

**21. sit around.** To be idle; to lounge. orig. *N. Amer.*

**1915** N. L. MCCLUNG *In Times like These* iv. 42 Personally I sympathize with the young man and believe it would be a happier home if she were as interested in the paper as he and were reading the other half of it instead of sitting around feeling hurt. **1935** *Time* 29 July 42/2 *Accent on Youth* suffers less than most pieces on translation to the screen, for, although its people sit around and talk a lot, they at least talk with wit. **1939** I. BAIRD *Waste Heritage* xix. 267 A lot of them sat around in shirtsleeves. **1959** J. THURBER *Years with Ross* iv. 61 Ross had asked me..to sit around and talk with him and H. L. Mencken. **1971** C. WHITMAN *Death Suspended* v. 95 All they did was to sit around looking decorative. **1979** *Times* 13 Nov. 2/8, I could not sit around twiddling my thumbs and doing nothing.

**22. sit back.** To be inactive or passive.

**1943** D. POWELL *Time to be Born* xi. 276 One can't sit back and see one's brother..made a monkey of that way! **1953** E. SIMON *Past Masters* III. 156 Harriet is the ideal executive... I can just sit back and let her get on with it. **1970** J. SANGSTER *Touchfeather, Too* ii. 38 Here then was my contact... I sat back and waited for him to make his play. **1982** *Times* 22 Feb. 1/3 We cannot sit back and let them walk all over us.

**23. sit down. a.** (*a*) To seat oneself; to take a seat. Cf. 18.

*c* **1205** LAY. 12958 þe swike set adun alse he wolde holden run. *a* **1300** *Havelok* 2809 Nu wile ich þat ye doun site. **1390** GOWER *Conf.* II. 240 Doun thei seten bothe same. *c* **1470** *Rauf Coilȝear* 177 Doun he sat the King neir, And maid him glaid and gude cheir. *a* **1562** G. CAVENDISH *Wolsey* (1893) 217 He was at the last constrayned for werynes to sitt down in a chayer. **1582** LICHEFIELD tr. *Castanheda's Conq. E. Ind.* 155 A place appointed for yᵉ captain generall to sit down on. **1674** tr. *Martiniere's Voy. N. Countries* 22 We sat down, fed as heartily as we could, and then taking leave [etc.]. **1766** GOLDSM. *Vic. W.* xv, He entered, drew a chair, and sate down. **1782** MISS BURNEY *Cecilia* VIII. v, Mrs. Delville.. made her sit down. **1817** SCOTT in *Lockhart* (1837) IV. iii. 97, I..am often six hours on foot without stopping or sitting down. **1841** LANE *Arab. Nts.* I. 104 He then sat down between the doors. **1890** DOYLE *White Company* iv, He sat down by the roadside to partake of his bread and cheese.

(*b*) In pa. pple. with *is*, *was*, etc. Cf. 18 b.

**1632** J. HAYWARD tr. *Biondi's Eromena* 185 As soon as they were sitten downe. **1641** BROME *Joviall Crew* III. Wks. 1873 III. 402 Yonder they are at peep. And now sitten downe as waiting for my purpose. **1763** *Museum Rust.* I. 23, I am now sat down to give you a few scattered observations. *a* **1774** GOLDSM. tr. *Scarron's Com. Rom.* (1775) I. 273 They were scarcely sat down, before one of the housemaids came [etc.]. **1787** [see A. 7β].

(*c*) Const. *to* (a game, meal, etc.).

**1588** SHAKS. *L.L.L.* II. i. 239 The sixt houre, when..men sit downe to that nourishment which is called supper. **1706** E. WARD *Wooden World Diss.* (1708) 101 He..sits down to the Cards or Hazard. **1710** STEELE *Tatler* No. 148 ¶1 The first who ever sat down to a whole roasted Ox. **1795** *Jemima* I. 206 Quietly submit to sit down to the table at which my late fellow servants are to wait. **1826** LAMB *Pop. Fallacies* xiii, Cannot we like Sempronia, without sitting down to chess with her eternal brother? **1856** C. J. ANDERSON *Lake Ngami* 98 We arrived..just as the family was sitting down to dinner. **1884** *Times* (weekly ed.) 19 Sept. 5/1, I sit down to ham and eggs.

*ellipt.* **1863** *Illustr. Lond. News* 8 Aug. 150/3 The inspection dinner..took place yesterday week... Between forty and fifty gentlemen sat down.

(*d*) To come accidentally to the ground in a sitting posture.

**1859** *Habits Gd. Society* v. 212 To see a man *sit down* in a waltz.

†**b.** To go down *on* one's knees. Cf. 19. *Obs.*

*c* **1290** *S. Eng. Leg.* I. 137 Bi-fore ech ymage he op aros, and eft he sat a-doun a-kne. **1297** R. GLOUC. (Rolls) 1335 þe erl wende to þe emperour & sat adoun a kne. *c* **1375** *Sc. Leg. Saints* xxxii. (*Justin*) 604 With þat befor þe bischape rath he set done one his kneis bath. **1544** *Extr. Aberd. Reg.* (1844) I. 198 To cum..and syt down on hir knees and ask the said Jonat forgifnis. *a* **1578** LINDESAY (Pitscottie) *Chron. Scot.* (S.T.S.) II. 187 [They] passit to the quenis grace and sat doune vpone thair kneis and askit pardone. **1626** *N. Riding Rec.* III. 260 Until such time as she shall sit down upon her knees and submit herself to her mother and crave her blessinge.

**c.** (*a*) To establish oneself in some position or place; to settle, take up one's abode. In later use chiefly *U.S.*

**1535** STEWART *Cron. Scot.* II. 693 Donald Bane..efter his Deid sat doun and rang into his Steid. **1579** *Reg. Privy Counc. Scot.* III. 241 [He] satt doun upoun the ground of the saidis landis,..and upliftit the dewiteis of the samin. **1632** WINTHROP *New Eng.* (1825) I. 87 The Braintree company, (which had begun to sit down at Mount Wollaston). **1637** in *Century Mag.* (1883) Sept. 644 These ten men..shall have liberty to view a place to sit down, and have land sufficient for three-score families. **1764** T. HUTCHINSON *Hist. Mass.* (1765) I. 89 Salt meadows..were an inducement to people to sit down there. **1799** in *Farmer's Mag.* Aug. (1801) 311 On the turn of middle age..the author sat down on a farm in Maryland. **1817** J. BRADBURY *Trav. Amer.* 332 A comparison of their present state with their situation when they first sat down.

(*b*) To encamp *before* a town, etc., in order to besiege it; to begin *to* a siege.

**1607** SHAKS. *Cor.* IV. vii. 28 All places yeelds to him ere he sits downe, And the Nobility of Rome are his. **1632** MASSINGER *Maid of Hon.* I. i, The great Gonzaga,..before we could get time To victual or to man the conquered city, Sat down before it. **1670** COTTON *Espernon* I. I. 6 His Father ..resolv'd to send him..to the Siege of Rochelle, that was then sitting down. **1724** DE FOE *Mem. Cavalier* (1840) 120 They sat down to the siege of Coburgh Castle. **1761** HUME *Hist. Eng.* II. xxix. 155 Had he not..sitten down in the winter season before that city. **1829** SCOTT *Anne of G.* xxxv, The army of Burgundy sat down before Nancy, in a strong position. **1854** MILMAN *Lat. Chr.* IV. ix. (1864) II. 419 With a large force he sat down before Ravenna.

(*c*) *fig.* Of persons or things: To settle down in some way.

**1599** ALEX. HUME *Day Estivall* 182 Great is the calme, for euerie quhair The wind is sitten downe. *a* **1675** LIGHTFOOT *Rem.* (1700) 203 There hath been many a good soul that hath sitten down in much sadness. **1730** T. BOSTON *Mem.* x. 298 In this time it began to sit down on my spirit very much that I was unfit for them. **1780** J. BERINGTON *St. Eng. Cath.* p. viii, Shall I sit down satisfied because the good humour of a magistrate chooses to indulge me. **1818** SCOTT *Hrt. Midl.* iv, We little thought to hae sittin doun wi' the like o' my auld Davie Howden, or you either. **1888** *Times* 26 June 4/6 He [a jockey] did not sit down to ride the horse—*i.e.*, to ride him with his hands and legs. **1897** MARY KINGSLEY *W. Africa* 583 A terrific tornado, which has been lurking growling about, then sits down in the forest and bursts.

**d.** To put up, rest content, *with* (†also in early use *by*), †to acquiesce *in*, something. Cf. 31 a.

(*a*) **1608** DOD & CLEAVER *Expos. Prov.* xi–xii. 117 But men will laugh at our simplicity, if we sit downe by such indignities. **1663** P. HENRY *Diaries & Lett.* (1882) 141, I.. chose rather to sit down by ye loss then displease him.

(*b*) **1614** JACKSON *Creed* III. 126 All were bound vpon paine of death to sit down with their priuate loss. **1674** BOYLE *Corpusc. Phil.* 17 A sober physician..will never sit down with so short an account. **1709** STEELE *Tatler* No. 49 ¶1 We are apt to sit down with our Errors, well enough satisfied with the Methods we are fallen into. **1764** J. RANDALL *Semi-Virgil. Husb.* App. 10, I was obliged to sit down with that loss, great as it was. **1818** SCOTT *Hrt. Midl.* xlvi, He was compelled to sit down with the affront. **1881** MALLOCK *Rom. 19th Cent.* I. 152 He was not a man tamely to sit down with dejection.

(*c*) **1646** SIR T. BROWNE *Pseud. Ep.* I. viii, The major part sit down in his authority.

**e.** *spec.* To sit down on strike in one's place of work; to sit down in a public place as a form of protest.

**1936** *Sun* (Baltimore) 2 Nov. 14/1 Various of the men reporting for picket duty yesterday came from ships where cooks had been the first to 'sit down' in sympathy with the West Coast strikers and hadn't had any food for forty-eight hours. **1942** BERREY & VAN DEN BARK *Amer. Thes. Slang* §528/7 *Sit down*, to go on a 'sit-down strike'. **1962** P. MORTIMER *Pumpkin Eater* xxi. 179 'She paints Ban the Bomb on everything.'..'I suppose she sits down all over the place?' **1963** D. V. BAKER *Door is always Open* ix. 190 Parents sitting down on a dangerous high-way, children sitting down to protect a play-street, workers sitting down to achieve some change in conditions. **1965** J. PORTER *Dover Three* iii. 34 If she's been sitting down again, she'll have to go... Having members of the staff arrested and flung into jail is bad for the school's reputation.

**24. sit in. a.** To have a place as a player *at* a game.

**1599** B. JONSON *Cynthia's Rev.* IV. i, We cannot all sit in at them [the proposed games]; we shall make a confusion.

**b.** To begin in earnest *to* something.

**1736** [CHETWOOD] *Voy. Vaughan* vi. (1760) 91 When our Business was over, we sat in to Drinking. **1749** FIELDING *Tom Jones* XVIII. xiii, The Squire sat in to his Cups.

**c.** *dial.* (See quot.)

**1828** CARR *Craven Gloss.* s.v., 'Sit in,' to adhere, as any extraneous matter does in a recent wound.

**d.** To attend or be present at an event. (*a*) To take part in a game or other event. Also const. *on*, *to*, *with*. Cf. sense a. orig. and chiefly *U.S.*

**1868** S. HALE *Let.* 5 Jan. (1919) ii. 44 Before we got to lunch two Englishmen *sot in*. **1916** C. SANDBURG *Chicago Poems* 63 He didn't sit in with the big thieves. *a* **1922** T. S. ELIOT *Waste Land Drafts* (1971) 5 Sopped up some gin, sat in to the cork game. **1929** WODEHOUSE *Gentleman of Leisure* x. 79 You'll be able to let me sit in on de game, won't you? **1962** D. FRANCIS *Dead Cert* ii. 19, I took ten of Henry's chips and sat in with them. Joan dealt. **1973** 'H. HOWARD' *Highway to Murder* viii. 102 You weren't invited to sit in on this deal, but you elected to take a hand.

(*b*) To attend an event or occasion as a spectator or observer. Also const. *at*, *on*, *with*.

**1919** C. S. PARKER *Amer. Idyll* x. 103, I sat in on a meeting of the Building Trades Board. **1931** *Oil & Gas Jrnl.* 5 Mar. 197/4 Any oil man or state or federal official may 'sit in' on the proceedings of the state wide committee. **1945** A.

Huxley *Time must have Stop* viii. 91 Paul De Vries had already sat in at a number of the old lady's séances. **1949** 'J. Tey' *Brat Farrar* viii. 66 Kevin Macdermott had 'sat in' at one of these office conferences. **1959** *Times Lit. Suppl.* 10 July 411/1 Mrs. Bennett sat in, in 1928, on the experiment which produced Dr. I. A. Richard's *Practical Criticism*. **1962** 'S. Ransome' *Without Trace* iii. 31 'He has something to talk over with me.'.. 'Would he mind if I sat in?' **1965** *Listener* 13 May 703/2, I sat in with a class and saw the *Antigone* and *The Caucasian Chalk Circle* cut up into weekly twenty-minute doses. **1967** *Daily Tel.* 15 May 9/4 To sit in at a play of this sort is to realise quite soon that you are being asked a riddle. **1970** *Morning Star* 11 May 4/4 The headmaster will therefore sit in on some lessons and try to pinpoint the weaknesses so that the teacher is helped. **1977** *Spare Rib* July 17/1 If you sat in on some of the interviews I've been through you'd know.

**e.** To co-operate, to collaborate. Also const. *with*, *on*. (Only in P. G. Wodehouse.)

**1925** Wodehouse *Sam the Sudden* xiii. 96 Do you mean to say..that if Soapy was sitting in with the Archbishop of Canterbury on a plan for skinning a sucker, the archbish wouldn't split Even Stephen? **1937** —— *Lord Emsworth & Others* ii. 96 Can I count on your co-operation?.. Sit in, and I shall be able to marry the girl I adore. Refuse to do your bit, and I drift through the remainder of my life a soured, blighted bachelor. *a* **1975** —— *Sunset at Blandings* (1977) xi. 77 Jeff refused to sit in on your chuckleheaded idea of eloping for a very good reason.

**f.** orig. *U.S.* To join in playing or singing with a (*spec.* jazz) band or orchestra of which one is not a regular member. Also const. *with*.

**1936** *Delineator* Nov. 102/ Those on the drawn-up chairs are *sitting in*; they have dropped in with their instruments to jam. **1937** *New Republic* 24 Nov. 69/2 Jess saw Bix Beiderbecke and sat in with him later. **1943** H. L. Mencken *Heathen Days* vii. 91 Once, when a baron sat in for a few sessions, we called him Count. **1949** L. Feather *Inside Be-bop* i. 8 On these occasions Kansas Fields or Jack Parker might sit in on drums. **1956** E. Delaney in S. Traill *Play that Music* v. 57 Another thing which influences the playing of today is the fact that no longer can one 'sit-in'. Before the war any player could walk into a club and 'sit-in' with the band. **1965** G. Melly *Owning Up* vii. 75 Buying a barrel of cider for the musicians who came along to sit in. **1971** *Melody Maker* 4 Sept. 20 Mungo Jerry, with Joe Rush, of the Country Jug band sitting in on washboard, sounded like a five man Jesse Fuller. **1982** *New Yorker* 30 Aug. 63/2 His unique playing..alienated club owners and other musicians, and he found little work. He even had trouble sitting in.

**g.** orig. *U.S.* (Often written with a hyphen.) To occupy a building as a demonstration of protest.

**1941** *Sun* (Baltimore) 15 Apr. 3/3 More than 700 of the city's brighter-than-average students spurned their Easter Monday holiday today and marched to their city college preparatory school to 'sit in and work' as a protest against Mayor LaGuardia's proposal to close the school. **1961** *Look* 25 Apr. 46/2 Negroes who picket, sit-in, crowd our jails, advance on white schools and otherwise approach prevailing privilege. **1967** *Economist* 8 Apr. 142/2 Young people who.. defend the virtues of marijuana and LSD and march, demonstrate, sit-in or lie-in to prove their faith in assorted causes. **1974** K. Millett *Flying* (1975) v. 517 Rosset had my friends arrested when they sat in at his publishing house. **1976** C. Hollis *Oxford in Twenties* 128 A few [undergraduates]..sit-in, demonstrate, occupy buildings, demand higher grants and more adequate lodgings.

**25. sit on. a.** Also with *to*. (See quots.) Now *dial.*

*c* **1450** *Two Cookery-bks.* 107 Sette al on the fire,..but sterre it well..for sitting to. **1808** Jamieson s.v., Any food, prepared in a pot, is said to *sit to*, when, from not being stirred, it is allowed to burn. **1825** —— *Suppl.* s.v., Broth or soup, which has been boiled too long, especially when burnt in the pot, is said to be *sitten on*. **1828** Carr *Craven Gloss.* s.v., 'To sit on,' to burn to the pan, chiefly applied to milk.

**b.** To continue to sit, to remain, stay on.

**1882** *Jamieson's Sc. Dict.* IV. 228/1 *To sit on*, to remain, to continue to abide in the same house. **1893** Keith *'Lisbeth* II. ii, Isabella was fidgeting..for fear I should be sitting on till the bell rang.

**26. sit out. a.** To sit apart from others, or to remain seated, so as take no part in a game, dance, etc. Cf. 39 a.

**1626** Middleton *Mayor of Queenb.* i. ii, If I see any kneel, and I sit out, That hour is not well spent. **1629** H. Burton *Babel no Bethel* 54 A nimble humour, apt..to play at small play rather than sit out. **1659** *Shuffling, Cutting & Deal.* 7 I'le play at small game, rather then sit out. **1775** Sheridan *Rivals* v. iii, You won't be so cantanckerous as to spoil the party by sitting out. **1827** Scott *Chron. Canongate* i, Some stuck to cards, and though no longer deep gamblers, rather played small game than sat out. **1886** 'Edna Lyall' *Won by Waiting* xxix, [She] only refused him once when she wanted to sit out with Cornelia.

*fig.* **1664** J. Wilson *A. Commenius* ii. ii, Who was the prouder pray; Diogenes, that spurn'd at every thing, Or Alexander, that sate out at nothing?

**b.** To sit in the open air.

**1805** E. Cavanagh *Let.* 20 Aug. in Londonderry & Hyde *Russian Jrnls.* (1934) ii. 179, I sat out & made a Gown while we were going along. **1908** [Miss Fowler] *Betw. Trent & Ancholme* 109, I am now sitting out, for the first time.

**27. sit up. a.** To raise the body from a recumbent to a sitting posture.

*a* **1225** *Leg. Kath.* 1597 þa ha weren iseten up, [ha] sehen as þe engles..smireden hire wunden. *a* **1300** *Cursor M.* 3683 'Fader,' he said, 'sitt vp and ete'. **1377** Langl. *P. Pl.* B. v. 456 þanne sat sleuthe vp and seyned hym swithe. **1526** Tindale *Luke* vii. 15, I saye vnto the aryse. And the deed sate vp. **1687** Miège *Gt. Fr. Dict.* ii. s.v., To sit up in his Bed, *s'asseoir dans son Lit.* **1847** Tennyson *Princ.* v. 69 She heard, she moved,..and up she sat. **1908** R. Bagot *A. Cuthbert* xxvii, Sonia sat up excitedly. 'I will not have a doctor,' she exclaimed.

**b.** To defer the hour for retiring to bed until late; to wait up *for*; to watch through the night (or some part of it) *with* one. Also, *S. Afr.* and *dial.*, to stay up for part of the night (*with* a person) as a sign of or during courtship, to keep company *with*. Cf. opsit *v.*

**1550** Crowley *Epigr.* 624 Our drunkards, that sytte vp so late. **1592** Shaks. *Rom. & Jul.* iv. iii. 10 Let the Nurse this night sit vp with you. **1611** Bible *Ps.* cxxvii. 2 It is vaine for you to rise vp early, to sit vp late. **1672** Villiers (Dk. Buckhm.) *Rehearsal* ii. v. (Arb.) 63, I sate up two whole nights in composing this Air. **1710–1** Swift *Jrnl. to Stella* 9 Mar., The surgeon sat up with him: he is asleep again. **1774** Goldsm. *Nat. Hist.* (1776) VII. 78 He..even sat up two nights together to examine their operations. **1786** J. Woodforde *Diary* 18 Feb. (1926) II. 228 The Captain..did not return till 12 at Night, just as I was going to bed after sitting up for him till that time. **1837** Lockhart *Scott* II. v. 189 'To sit up to supper' was the great reward when they had been 'very good bairns'. **1869** Geo. Eliot *Let.* 15 Nov. (1956) V. 67, I admire your courage and endurance in sitting up for the meteors. **1878** H. A. Roche *On Trek in Transvaal* 136 The question of questions is, whether she will 'sit up and keep company with him!' If she has consented to do this she has virtually consented to 'sit up' with him as long as they both shall live. **1891** E. Peacock *N. Brendon* II. 86 They sat up talking till far into the night. **1892** O. Schreiner *Thoughts on S. Afr.* iv. 181 Having made up his mind which daughter he desires to pay his attention to, it is now necessary he should request the parents' permission to sit up with her. **1893** *West Cumberland Times* (Holiday No.) 6/2 (E.D.D.), The custom being for the lad to sit up with the lass. **1896** *Dial. Notes* I. 424 *Sit up with*, to receive courtship from. **1951** L. Craig *Singing Hills* 99 Then he asked if he could sit up with me that night. He was merely asking for a date so I said yes. **1961** F. G. Cassidy *Jamaica Talk* x. 221 Courting..is still described by the terms to *sit up* or to *walk out*. **1961** D. Rooke *Lover for Estelle* 36 He had solemnly shown a candle which he carried in his pocket as a hint to Estelle that they should sit up together that night. **1974** *Daily Dispatch* (S. Afr.) 29 Mar. 12 Clinton, you've been sitting up with Nellie..an car riding and nothings come of it.

**c.** To be in a sitting posture, in contrast to lying in bed. Also *spec.*, to remain in a sitting posture during an overnight train journey, in contrast to taking a sleeper. ***to sit up and take nourishment***, to be convalescent.

**1727** Boyer *Dict. Royal* ii. s.v., To sit up in one's Bed, *se tenir assis dans son Lit.* **1789** W. Buchan *Dom. Med.* (1790) 165 He may sometimes sit up in bed for a short space. **1843** R. J. Graves *Syst. Clin. Med.* ix. 98 When they attempt to sit up during convalescence. **1858** Geo. Eliot *Scenes Cler. Life, Janet's Repentance* xxvii, The pale wasted form in the easy-chair (for he sat up to the last). **1909** Wodehouse *Mike* lv. 311 'How's Adair?'.. 'Sitting up and taking nourishment once more.' **1918** E. V. Lucas *'Twixt Eagle & Dove* 152 The well-worn phrase 'to sit up and take nourishment'. **1947** L. P. Hartley *Eustace & Hilda* i. ix. 162 'But could you cancel your wagon-lit ticket?' 'I don't need to. I'm going to sit up.' **1953** K. Tennant *Joyful Condemned* xxviii. 277 Now there are no sleepers, you'd have to sit up in the train. **1967** O. Wynd *Walk Softly* vii. 107 'You've got a sleeper reservation?' 'No, I was going to sit up.' **1982** N. Painting *Reluctant Archer* v. 82 'Book a sleeper,' said Reggie airily. There were no sleepers. I sat up all night.

†**d.** *Anglo-Ind.* (See quot. 1780.) *Obs.*

**1777** in Busteed *Echoes Old Calcutta* (1888) 136 Lady Impey sits up with Mrs. Hastings; *vulgo* toad-eating. **1780** Capt. I. Munro *Narr.* (1789) 56 When a young lady arrives at Madras she must, in a few days afterwards, sit up to receive company, attended by some beau as master of the ceremonies, which perhaps continues for a week. **1795** Sir T. Munro in Gleig *Life* (1830) I. 169, I am not to be forced to sit up, and receive male or female visitors. **1810** [see sitting *vbl. sb.* 6 (*b*)].

**e.** (See quot.)

**1856** S. Warner *Hills of Shatemuc* xvi. 162 'Will you sit up, cousin?'..: the meaning of the request being that he should move his chair up to the table.

**f.** *to make* (one) *sit up*, to astonish, startle, have a powerful effect on, one. Also ***to sit up and take notice***, to become suddenly interested, to pay attention.

**1886** H. Baumann *Londinismen* 179/2 *To make a person sit up*, jemand in Erstaunen setzen. **1889** *Daily News* 23 July 5 When her [George Sand's] novels first made the world 'sit up', if we may venture to use such a phrase. **1893** 'Q.' (Quiller Couch) *Delect. Duchy* 323, I am going to tell you a story that..will make you sit up. **1896** Mrs. Hungerford *Lonely Girl* xv, If you had accepted my pink gown..you would have made..[him] sit up. [**1898** Kipling *Stalky & Co.* (1899) 84 If they make such a row now, what will they do when she really begins to look up an' take notice?] **1909** *N.Y. Even. Post* 6 Mar. 1/3 The crowd that fell upon Washington was of such a size that the District authorities sat up and took serious notice. **1929** *Burton Evening Gaz.* 1 Jan. 5/1 By the time that the Oxford English Dictionary compilers reach the 'E' section of additions to that great work..they will have to sit up and take some notice of a new and curious borrowing from the French. **1954** A. Huxley *Let.* 18 Jan. (1969) 694 If you want them to sit up and take notice, prepare your way with a barrage of heavy guns from respectable institutions. **1968** H. C. Rae *Few Small Bones* ii. viii. 141 Look at him..stuffed full of pet theories, praying I'll sit up and take notice of him. **1977** M. Allen *Spence in Petal Park* xvii. 77 When I see him I sit up and take notice.

**g.** *to sit up and beg* (cf. beg *v.* 2 i): used *fig.*; also (with hyphens) as *adj. phr.*

**1917** R. Barnes *Let.* 20 July in M. Gilbert *W. S. Churchill* (1977) IV. Compan. i. 105 Pile up the guns & shells & we will make the Hun sit up & beg, but we haven't got enough yet. **1919** W. H. Berry *New Traffic* (*Aircraft*) viii. 46 Our gallant youth is quite prepared..to make his seventy miles per hour motor-bike sit-up-and-beg as he would put it. **1958** *Listener* 16 Oct. 603/2 In the 'sit-up-and-beg' attitude in which some modern fighter aircraft come in to land. **1961** Partridge *Dict. Slang* Suppl. 1275/1 'He can make it sit up and beg' indicates that a man has become extremely proficient in working some material, e.g. a metal. **1963** Bird & Hutton-Stott *Veteran Motor Car* 215 They were usually endowed with handsome 'sporty' bucket seat bodies in marked contrast to the usual sit-up-and-beg auntification of the time. **1968** *New Scientist* 3 Oct. 8/2 The pilot is thus in a sit-up-and-beg attitude. **1973** G. Talbot *Ten Seconds from Now* xvi. 200 He rode, incongruously, in a vintage, sit-up-and-beg, hearse-like black limousine. **1978** *Lancashire Life* Apr. 65/1 Old Luke's sit-up-and-beg bike was propped against one of the sandstone gateposts. **1978** *Times* 4 July 19/4 Ramirez tucked away a net cord by his opponent that sat up and simply begged. **1980** *Radio Times* 4–10 Oct. 13/1 A midwife in London's dockland, travelling around on a sit-up-and-beg bike.

**h.** *to sit up like Jacky* (Austral.), to sit up straight, to comport oneself in a prim and proper manner.

**1941** Baker *Dict. Austral. Slang* 38 *Jacky, sit up like*, to behave, sit up straight. **1969** P. A. Smith *Folklore Austral. Railwaymen* 180 As we were rattling along north to Darwin I happened to look back out of the guard's van and there they [*sc.* the hoboes] were—sitting up like Jacky in the commissioner's car behind us. **1975** H. Porter *Extra* 139 He's telling Edinburgh, and those writers sitting up like jacky in tiers behind him, about the construction of his next book.

** *With prepositions, in special senses.*

**28. sit on** or **upon. a.** To sit in judgement or council, to deliberate, on (a person or matter).

*c* **1440** *Gesta Rom.* viii. 21 (Harl. MS.), þe domys-man come to þe Cite, for to sitte vp on brekers of þe lawe. **1462** *Paston Lett.* II. 82 It is seyd her that..serteyn jwgys.. schold come downe and syt on syche pepyll as be noysyd ryotous. **1535** Coverdale *2 Macc.* xiv. 21 They appoynted a daye to syt vpon these matters quyetly amonge them selues. **1574** Travers *Decl. Eccl. Discipl.* Table, Deacons which he appointed..to sit vppon the offences that arise in the churches. **1608** Chapman *Byron's Trag.* v. ii, Must I be sat on now, by petty Judges. *a* **1693** Ashmole *Antiq. Berksh.* (1719) I. 153 Her Father..caused her Corps to be taken up, the Coroner to sit upon her, and further Enquiry to be made. **1712** Addison *Spect.* No. 550 ¶3 At which time I intend to sit upon Business. **1798** *Hull Advert.* 13 Oct. 3/2 A coroner's jury has sat on the body, and returned a verdict of lunacy. **1852** Hawker *Diary* (1893) II. 337 The select committee at Ordnance, who..sat on my new military carbine. **1885** *Harper's Mag.* Mar. 547/1 A committee of..friends..'sat' upon our affairs while we were furnishing.

**b.** To have a seat on (a jury, commission, etc.).

**1538** Cromwell in Merriman *Life & Lett.* (1902) II. 134 The kinges maiestye hathe appointed you..to sit vpon the tryall of knell being accused of Treason. **1594** West *2nd Pt. Symbol., Chancerie* §84 When the time came that the same commission was to be sitten on. **1609** Holland *Amm. Marcell.* 282 We find not that there was any..commission sitten upon about their death. **1676** I. Mather *Hist. K. Philip's War* (1862) 48 Indians as well as English sate upon the Jury. **1836** in Barrow *Mirror of Parlt.* 2041/2 Those who sit on courts-martial have a most important office to perform. **1840** Mrs. Carlyle *Lett.* I. 120 My poor man of genius had to sit on a jury. **1895** *Times* 10 Jan. 9/6 He sat on the Royal Commission on Hospitals.

†**c.** To press *sore* or *hard* on (one). Cf. 14 b.

*c* **1470** Henry *Wallace* x. 690 In to fleyng the Sotheroun suttaill ar, Se thai the tym thai wyll syt on ws sar. **1737** L. Clarke *Hist. Bible* (1740) I. ix. 583 He..would never..give that party any favour.., but on the contrary sat hard upon them on all occasions.

**d.** *slang.* To squash, check, snub.

**1865** *Slang Dict.* 231 *Sit-upon*, to overcome or rebuke, to express contempt for a man in a marked manner. **1872** Black *Adv. Phaeton* xviii, 'Bell, what is good for you, when you're sat upon?' 'Patience,' says Bell. **1886** Mrs. Lynn Linton *Paston Carew* xxxiv, My lady felt rebuked, and, as she afterward expressed it, sat upon. **1892** I. Zangwill *Childr. Ghetto* I. xi. 238 'Odious prig!' thought Hannah. 'He actually doesn't see I'm sitting on him.' **1894** Somerville & 'Ross' *Real Charlotte* I. vi. 76 If you're going to sit on me every time I open my mouth, I'd better shut up. **1936** N. Streatfeild *Ballet Shoes* xiv. 225 In the tube going home, Pauline and Petrova pestered Posy for criticism of the production; but the moment she made any, they sat on her, asking her what she thought she knew about it. **1969** *New Yorker* 14 June 46/2 Someone should have sat on him when he was young. **1975** *Guardian* 22 Jan. 1/2 The TUC general secretary..proceeded to sit heavily on the CBI's suggestion.

**e.** To hold back, to keep to oneself without acting upon.

**1906** Kipling *Actions & Reactions* (1909) 203 A three-million pound insurrection caused by a deputy Under-Secretary sitting upon a mass of green-labelled correspondence instead of reading it. **1967** F. Clifford *All Men are Lonely Now* i. iv. 64 Where have all the yellows gone?.. Seriously, who's sitting on them? **1983** M. Hinxman *Corpse Now Arriving* vii. 45 She'd 'sat' on the article..until..a deadline had galvanized her into putting words on paper.

**f.** To suppress, to silence.

**1915** A. Huxley *Let.* Nov. (1969) 85 What an odd business it was about the suppression of Lawrence's book, *The Rainbow*. It is always the serious books that get sat on. **1925** 'R. Hall' *Saturday Life* iv. 51 But she sat on her conscience. **1972** D. McLachlan *No Case for Crown* iii. 39, I want this story sat on till midnight. **1976** M. Machlin *Pipeline* ii. 32 There had to be a scout on that plane—this one's going to be hard to sit on. **1977** *Undercurrents* June–July 18/1 These huge public charivari were sat upon heavily by the police.

**g.** To wait for (something or someone) to change or develop; to observe or trail.

**1958** *Spectator* 11 July 62/2 Two children..were brought to my hospital..suffering from appendicitis, which had been treated conservatively (or in hospital slang 'sat on') for several days. **1966** I. Jefferies *House-Surgeon* vi. 118, I couldn't make up my mind either, so we decided to sit on her and see what happened.

**h.** *to sit on the splice* (Cricket): see SPLICE *sb.* 1 c.

**29. sit over**, to be occupied with (a matter, etc.) while sitting; to pore over (a book). Also, to linger over (a meal, etc.) while sitting.

**1848** THACKERAY *Van. Fair* xlviii, Her daughters sighed, and sate over the Peerage all night. **1861** M. PATTISON *Ess.* (1889) I. 45 The garden..where..the elder merchants sat over their pipe and beaker of Rhine wine. **1952** M. LASKI *Village* x. 156 The dinner was cleared away and they sat over their coffee. **1971** 'E. FERRARS' *Stranger & Afraid* vi. 112 They..had lunch, sitting over it until about two o'clock.

**30. sit under.** To listen to, be a hearer of, attend the church of (a minister or preacher). Also, to listen to (a teacher), to be the pupil of.

**1644** MILTON *Educ.* 6 There would then also appear in Pulpits other visages, other gestures,..then what we now sit under. [**1688** BUNYAN *Jerus. Sinner* (1700) 130 Those that sit under the Glorious sound of the Gospel.] **1754** *Connoisseur* No. 27 ¶5 The..audience that sits under our preachers. **1797** R. STORRY *J. Foster's Poems* To Rdr., The privilege which he enjoyed in sitting under the ministry of the late..Mr. Adam. **1840** THACKERAY *Gt. Hoggarty Diamond* x, She, after a time,..*sat under him*, as the phrase is, regularly thrice a week. **1878** J. A. SYMONDS in Brown *Life* (1903) 338 Your sermon on Faith..makes me wish that I had the privilege of 'sitting under' you. **1899** J. LONDON *Let.* 20 Sept. (1966) 56 Stopped over at Stanford, where I..sat under the various profs. **1952** 'J. TEY' *Singing Sands* iii. 39 He 'sat under' a bank clerk in Glasgow, a chap from Uist, and swotted up some Gaelic.

**31. sit with.** †**a.** *Sc.* To put up with or tolerate, to stand (a wrong, etc.). *Obs.* Cf. 23 d.

*c* **1470** *Gol. & Gaw.* 90 That sege wald sit with none wrang Of berne that wes borne. *a* **1578** LINDESAY (Pitscottie) *Chron. Scot.* (S.T.S.) I. 28 Ane man..nocht willing to seit with so mony wrangis as he had gottin onrewengit. **1635** RUTHERFORD *Lett.* (1862) I. lii. 149 They haue been false to Christ and He will not sit with the wrong. **1678** SIR G. MACKENZIE *Crim. Laws Scot.* I. xxi. §iii. 112 Nor is it probable that the person offended would have sitten long with such a wrong. **1714** in *Cloud of Witnesses* (1778) 5 God will not sit with all the wrongs done to him.

**b.** To be consonant or in harmony with, to agree with, to befit (one). Now only *arch.*

**1555** W. WATREMAN *Fardle Facions* App. 330 It sitteth not with equitie, that the elder should be putte beside the enheritaunce of his father. **1579** SPENSER *Let. to Harvey* Wks. (Globe) 706/1 It sitteth with you now, to call your wits and senses togither. **1590** —— *F.Q.* I. i. 30 With holy father sits not with such thinges to mell. [**1893** STEVENSON *Catriona* i. 2 As for the rapier, nae doubt it sits wi' your degree.]

**c.** To be received in a specified manner by; to be consonant with.

**1961** in WEBSTER s.v. [1]*sit*, Setting an example that may not sit well with the more obedient Communist leaders. **1972** *Listener* 1 June 705/2 In the meanwhile sanctions would be continued, and this did not sit well with right-wing opinion inside the Conservative Party.

V. *refl.* and *trans.*

**32.** *refl.* To seat (oneself).

*c* **888** K. ÆLFRED *Boeth.* xxxvi. §2 Sitte [ðin mod] him on minum hrædwæne;..ic bio his ladðeow. *a* **1300** *Cursor M.* 17845 Sundri þai þam fra oþer saite, And aiþer be himseluen wrate. *c* **1500** *Melusine* 243 Thenne he satte hym at dyner nygh to Eglantyne. **1593** SHAKS. *3 Hen. VI*, III. iii. 16 Sit thee by our side. **1686** J. S[ERGEANT] *Hist. Monast. Conv.* 183 The Prayer of the Mass..being sung, he sat him self again in his seat. **1830** H. ANGELO *Remin.* I. 185 Bach..would sit himself in his place. **1898** RIDER HAGGARD *Dr. Therne* 202 He sat himself upon the marble edge of the basin.

**b.** With *down.* (The more frequent use.) Also, to settle (quot. 1823).

*c* **1450** *St. Cuthbert* (Surtees) 3671 He satt him doune besyde him. *a* **1533** LD. BERNERS *Huon* I. 166 He sat hym down vnder a fayre oke. *a* **1562** G. CAVENDISH *Wolsey* (1893) 104 [He] called for a chayer, & satt hyme self down in the mydds of the table. **1659** PELL *Impr. Sea* 59 In every corner they walk into, or sit themselves down in. **1682** N. O. *Boileau's Lutrin* I. 156 He yields, and sits him down to tast the Creature. **1764** GOLDSM. *Trav.* 32, I sit me down a pensive hour to spend. **1775** FLETCHER *Checks* Wks. 1795 VI. 230 The multitude of professors, who sit themselves down in self imputed righteousness. **1823** COLEBROOKE in *St. Cape Good Hope* 374 The early colonists of South Africa sat themselves down on fertile spots. **1868** F. E. PAGET *Lucretia* 199, I..sat myself down on the ridge. **1888** 'J. S. WINTER' *Bootle's Childr.* xiii, Come and sit you down by the fire.

**33. a.** *trans.* To sit upon, to ride (a horse). Also *transf.*

**1542** UDALL *Erasm. Apoph.* 276 He would not suffre any bodye to sitte hym, or gette up on his backe. **1561** T. HOBY tr. *Castiglione's Courtyer* IV. (1577) S iv b, Hee that sitteth not well a horse. **1613** SHAKS. *Hen. VIII*, IV. ii. 16 He..grew so ill He could not sit his Mule. **1662** J. DAVIES tr. *Olearius' Voy. Amb.* 285 The King return'd..so Drunk, as were also most of his Lords, that they could hardly sit their Horses. **1700** PRIOR *Carm. Sec.* xvi, Hardly the Muse can sit the headstrong Horse. **1762** WESLEY *Jrnl.* 30 Mar., It was difficult to sit our horses. **1814** JANE AUSTEN *Mansfield Park* II. ii. 33 Poor old coachman would attend us..though he was hardly able to sit the box on account of the rheumatism. **1836** MRS. SHERWOOD *H. Milner* III. v, Edgar sits a horse as well as any young man in England. **1891** N. GOULD *Double Event* 230 Wells could not sit the horse better himself. **1977** *New Yorker* 11 July 19/1 She sits a bicycle with the feckless insouciance of an eleven-year-old gliding down a country lane.

**b.** Of a hen or hen-bird: To sit upon, to hatch (eggs). Also *transf.* (quot. 1828).

**1600** SURFLET *Countrie Farme* I. xvi. 107 Geese loue not almost to sit any but their owne egs. **1651** BAXTER *Inf. Bapt.* 51 The Hen gathereth the youngest most tenderly: Yea, how long will she sit the very eggs? **1828** CARR *Craven Gloss.* s.v., 'He wad sit eggs,' said of a person, who sits long in a neighbour's house, when his company might be well dispensed with. **1867** *Jrnl. R. Agric. Soc.* III. II. 525 The hen will sit seventeen of her own eggs.

**c.** To sit in (a boat) in an expert manner, using one's body-weight to adjust its balance.

**1865** *Etoniana* xi. 170 The time-honoured custom of 'sitting a boat'. **1866** *Routledge's Ev. Boy's Ann.* 66 They sit their boat, and keep time as if they were two clock-work figures. **1886** *Illustr. Lond. News* 1 May 448/2 There is a great deal in knowing how to 'sit' and 'trim' a boat.

**34. a.** To cause (a person) to sit; to seat in a certain place or position. Also with *down, up.*

**1470–85** MALORY *Arthur* VII. ix. 225 The grene knyghte took hym and sat hym at a syde table. **1557** NORTH *Gueuara's Diall. Pr.* 379 In the bankets the kings of Persia made, they sate him whom they loved..on the left hand of the prince. *a* **1562** G. CAVENDISH *Wolsey* (1893) 253, I went and sat the wayters to dynner. **1848** DICKENS *Dombey* xi, Taking Paul up in his arms, and sitting him on another little table. **1890** *Chamb. Jrnl.* 21 June 387/1 He promptly sat us down to such entertainment as his vessel furnishes. **1895** *Daily News* 9 Oct. 7/5 The man is so bad that we can't sit him up.

**b.** To place in position for photographing.

**1890** *Anthony's Photogr. Bull.* III. 92 We sit a stranger immediately he comes in, knowing absolutely nothing what manner of man he is of.

**c.** To make or cause (a hen-bird) to sit.

**1891** T. HARDY *Tess* (1900) 62/1 Ought she not..to..know how to sit hens and turkeys?

†**35.** To set or place. *Obs. rare.*

**1530** PALSGR. 719/1 Syt these glasses of rose water a sonnynge. **1798** CHARLOTTE SMITH *Yng. Philos.* IV. 224 If he would sit me down where he found me. **1824** W. TAYLOR in *Monthly Mag.* LVII. 511 When he took his lady from the horse Into his arms, he gently sat her down.

†**36.** *Sc.* (and *north.*). To disregard, neglect, pay no heed or attention to (a command, call, etc.). *Obs.* [So MIcel. *sitja.*]

*a* **1300** *Havelok* 2567 Was non þat euere his bode sat, For he him dredde swipe sore. *c* **1470** *Rauf Coilȝear* 99 Durst scho neuer sit summoundis that scho hard him say. **1513** DOUGLAS *Æneid* IV. vi. 6 Astonist he was to site so hie ane charge. *a* **1585** MONTGOMERIE *Flyting* 67 Sit thou this charge,..The second sall bee something sairer. *c* **1620** Z. BOYD *Zion's Flowers* (1855) 43 Let Cities learne of Ninive the great, For to repent, and not God's summons sit. **1699** T. BOSTON *Art of Man-Fishing* (1900) 61, I did a long time sit the call of the church. **1742** E. ERSKINE *Serm.* Wks. 1871 III. 58 His bowels are shut against me: I have sitten his call so often. **1856** G. HENDERSON *Pop. Rhymes Berwick* 43, I sat that bidding, but I've rued it ay sin syne.

**37.** To sit against, resist; to endure, bear; to put up with, go on with. Now *rare.*

*c* **1400** *Sir Degrev.* 15 (Lincoln MS.), Was never knyghte..Mighte sitt a strake of his hande One his styff stede. **1604** DEKKER *Honest Wh.* Wks. 1873 II. 114, I must sit all stormes. **1625** DONNE *Serm.* cl. Wks. 1839 VI. 56 First God turns their Rivers into blood, Pharaoh Sits that process and more. **1640** tr. *Verdere's Rom. of Rom.* I. 50 Being unable to sit the shock of fowr lances,..he was unhorsed. **1848** NEWMAN *Loss & Gain* xviii. 273 And he's so positive..; it is quite unpleasant, I don't know how to sit it sometimes. **1859** READE *Love me Little* vii. (1868) 88 Ladies, whose hearts are in dress, have no taste for books however frivolous; can't sit them above a second or two.

**38.** †**a.** To hold (a meeting). *Obs.*[−1]

**1635** in *Buccleuch MSS.* (Hist. MSS. Comm.) I. 274 For the meeting..it stood not well with some other occasion to have it sitten at this time.

**b.** = *sit out* (39 b); to stay till the end of.

**1784** *Laura & Augustus* III. 16 We soon after this returned home, not chusing to sit the entertainment. **1845** STILL *Cottar's Sunday* 36 Neebours roun', whan Robin teuk it, Swore he wadna sit his lease.

**c.** To bear (one) company in sitting.

**1828** CARR *Craven Gloss.* s.v., 'To sit a woman,' to keep company with her, to court. **1879** MEREDITH *Egoist* xix, I will undertake to sit you through it up to morning.

**d.** To act as a baby-sitter for (a child). Also *transf.*

**1950** *Here & Now* (N.Z.) Nov. 28/2 He is a nice domestic chap: speaks on international affairs; helps old ladies across the street; can sit a baby. **1971** E. FENWICK *Impeccable People* xx. 110 He can help sit Granny, too. **1976** *Billings* (Montana) *Gaz.* 16 June 9-c/6 (Advt.), 'Grandma' needed to sit 3 pre-school boys, in my home ½ days beginning late August.

**e.** To take (an examination).

**1957** A. WILSON *Bit off Map* 40 With the degree behind me, I shall sit the Administrative in June. **1966** *Rep. Comm. Inquiry Univ. Oxf.* II. 152 Collections are college examinations, usually sat at the beginning of a term. **1980** *Radio Times* 1–7 Mar. 16/4 A child can..enter for and sit an examination without being put forward by the school.

**39. sit out. a.** To remain seated and take no part in (a game or dance). Also *transf.* Cf. 26 a.

**1659** *Shuffling, Cutting & Deal.* 3, I was somewhat scrupulous, whether Play was lawful, or not; and so sate out the last Game. *c* **1869** TAYLOR & DUBOURG in M. R. Booth *Eng. Plays of 19th Cent.* (1973) III. 251, I didn't sit out one dance. **1885** 'F. ANSTEY' *Tinted Venus* 15 I've never had to sit out a waltz before. **1957** *Economist* 19 Oct. 208/2 Only two countries—Holland and Australia—gave a majority in favour of getting involved [in a war with Russia]. In the rest, all but two of which are allies of America, most people said they would rather sit this one out. **1978** G. A. SHEEHAN *Running & Being* xv. 211, I hadn't realized this..until the 1976 Boston Marathon... Any thinking adult would have sat this one out.

**b.** To remain sitting, so as to be present during the course of (something). Also with *it* (quot. 1809), implying endurance of something disagreeable.

**1711** ADDISON *Spect.* No. 101 ¶7 An Audience would sit out an Evening to hear a Dramatical Performance. **1727** SWIFT *Art Polit. Lying* Wks. 1755 III. I. 118 [To] sit out publick prayers with decency. **1809** MALKIN *Gil Blas* VIII. IX. ¶11, I cannot conceive how a clever fellow like you can sit it out with such loutish guests. **1837** TICKNOR *Life, Lett. & Jrnls.* II. vi. 107, I..sat out a part of their family breakfast. **1888** J. JOHNSTON *Cent. Conf. Missions* I. 450 This is the only meeting, except the first, which it has been my privilege to sit out.

**c.** To remain longer than (another) when paying a visit.

**1751** FIELDING *Amelia* II. v. v. 127 She resolved to come to an eclaircissement, and having sat out some company that came in, when they were alone together, [etc.]. **1808** JANE AUSTEN *Let.* 9 Dec. (1952) 237 We found Mrs. Lance at home & alone, & sat out three other Ladies who soon came in. **1845** MRS. CARLYLE *Lett.* I. 344 He stayed till eleven, Craik sitting him out. **1883** W. E. NORRIS *Thirlby Hall* xii, I thought I would sit the other visitors out.

**sit-**, the verbal stem in combs., as †**sit-horse**, a riding-horse; †**sit-house**, *Sc.* a residence; **sit-me-down (-upon)** *colloq.*, the buttocks, the posterior.

*c* **1652** *Verney Mem.* (1894) III. 193 He was not only for my coach, but he paced as easy as any sitt-horse. **1743** *Maxwell's Sel. Trans.* (Jam.), The form of a sit-house, barn, bire, stable, with corn and kitchen yards. **1754** *Forfeited Estates Papers* (S.H.S.) 333 For expenses in building the Sitt house as agreed on. **1926** D. L. SAYERS *Clouds of Witness* ii. 55 He's left the impression of his sit-me-down-upon on the cushion. **1935** 'G. ORWELL' *Clergyman's Daughter* iii. 187 Shift yourself..and make room for my little sit-me-down. **1942** PARTRIDGE *Usage & Abusage* 351/2 Euphemism..is often employed, sometimes in such childish form as *sit-me-down.*

**sital**, obs. form of CITOLE.

**sitar** (ˈsɪtɑː(r), sɪˈtɑː(r)). Also **setar, sitarre.** [Urdū *sitār.*] A long-necked, guitar-like, Indian musical instrument, having from three to seven strings which the player plucks. Also *attrib.* and *Comb.*

**1845** STOCQUELER *Hdbk. Brit. India* (1854) 26 A trio of sitars, or rude violins. **1859** J. LANG *Wand. India* 152 Two or three of the company..played alternately on the sitarre (native guitar or violin). **1879** E. ARNOLD *Lt. Asia* VI. 144 One that twitched A three-string sitar. **1898** SIR G. ROBERTSON *Chitral* i. 7 A sitar-player will sing of love. **1954** *Grove's Dict. Mus.* (ed. 5) IV. 459/1 The *Setar* is the most popular instrument in northern India. **1957** *New Oxf. Hist. Music* I. iv. 224 Another favourite plucked instrument is the *setar*, of Persian origin. **1959** D. COOKE *Lang. Music* ii. 55 A recent improvisation on a *raga*, by one of India's leading sitar-players. **1966** *Melody Maker* 7 May 10 Since George Harrison introduced the sitar on 'Norwegian Wood' on the Beatles' 'Rubber Soul' album there has been an intense interest in this Indian instrument. **1975** D. LODGE *Changing Places* ii. 85 Someone dimmed the lights and turned up the sitar music. **1978** P. GRIFFITHS *Conc. Hist. Mod. Music* ix. 139 The use of sitars in rock bands.

ˈ**sitarch.** *rare*[−0]. [ad. Gr. σιτάρχης or σίταρχος, f. σῖτος corn, food.] (See quots.)

**1656** BLOUNT *Glossogr.*, *Sitark*, he that hath the Office to provide Corn, and Victuals sufficient. **1676** COLES, *Sitarch*, a Pourveyor.

**Sitaris** (ˈsɪtərɪs). *Ent.* [mod.L. (Latreille, 1802), f. Gr. σιτάριον, dim. of σῖτος corn, food.] A genus of beetles belonging to the family *Meloidæ*, the larvæ of which are parasitic in the nests of certain bees; a member of this genus, esp. *S. muralis.*

**1835** *Partington's Brit. Cycl. Nat. Hist.* I. 689 M. Bretonneau of Tours..having found that Sitaris is not vesicant. **1866** DARWIN *Orig. Species* xiv. (ed. 4) 530 The first larval form of a certain beetle, the Sitaris,..is a minute active insect. **1881** *Cassell's Nat. Hist.* V. 337 The female Sitaris..lays her eggs in a mass glued together.

**sitarist** (sɪˈtɑːrɪst). [f. SITAR + -IST.] One who plays the sitar.

**1966** *Guardian* 16 Aug. 6/5 Jayasri..gave her first public recital at the age of 15 accompanying her father, who is himself a well-known sitarist. **1977** *Times* 23 July 9/3 It provides opportunities for the sitarist to engage in musical small-talk with Menuhin's violin and Jean-Pierre Rampal's flute. **1982** *Listener* 18 Nov. 21/2 They were Indian sitarists, and they went at their sitars with a will.

**sitatunga**, var. SITUTUNGA.

**sitch** (sɪtʃ). Now *dial.* Forms: 1 sic, 4, 6 syche, 5–7 siche, 6 sucche, 7 sich, 9 sech, seech; 6 sytche, 7 sytch; 6–7 sitche, 9 **sitch.** [OE. *síc*, giving normally ME. *sich(e, siche* in southern and midland dialects, corresponding to the northern SIKE *sb.*[1]; cf. DITCH and DIKE.]

**1.** = SIKE *sb.*[1] 1.

Chiefly recorded in descriptions of boundaries.

**969** in Birch *Cartul. Sax.* III. 535 Of þam mere west ..þonne innan anne sice þonne andlangc sices þæt cymð to þæm hor pytte. [? *c* **1160** in Dugdale *Mon. Angl.* (1825) V. 584 In viis, et aquis, in sichis et moris.] *c* **1315** SHOREHAM V. 177 Ine flom iordanes syche He was ycrystned. **1410** *Coventry Leet Bk.* 12 Et abhinc vsque Merdonsiche. Et sic per illam siche diuertendo vsque [etc.]. **1523** FITZHERB. *Surv.* 10 b, Some rynning waters be commen, as lytell brokes, and sytches. *Ibid.* 50 Smale ryuers, brokes, sucches, ..and pyttes. **1581** *Coventry Leet Bk.* (E.E.T.S.) 826 A litle waye into the sitche there, called Sisley-hole,..& vnder the bridge vp the sitche to Hyndwell. **1601** in *Ch. Stretton* (1904) II. 195 Thence following the fylde..and then up a sytch called Newe sytch. **1637** in Miss Jackson *Shropsh. Word-bk.* s.v., Half a land in the Barley field near Stafford's siche. **1684** MANLEY, *Sichetum*.., a Sich or small Current of Water that uses to be dry in the Summer. **1826-** in dialect glossaries (Chesh., Northampt., Shropsh., Sheff.).

*attrib.* **1601** in *Ch. Stretton* (1904) II. 196 Over Wittingslow Heath to Dunocke sytch heade.

**b.** = SIKE *sb.*[1] 1 b.

**1888** ABDY *Sheffield Gloss.* 214 It is a gate at the bottom of a *sitch* or ravine.

**2.** = SIKE *sb.*[1] 2.

**1842** W. WOOD *Hist. & Antiq. Eyam* (1848) 114 A gravestone..found in a field which is now called Philip's sitch.

**sitch**, dial. or illiterate f. SUCH *a.*

**sitcom** (ˈsɪtkɒm). orig. *U.S.* Also **sit-com, sit.-com.** Abbreviation of *situation comedy* s.v. SITUATION 11.

**1964** *Life* 18 Sept. 24/2 Even Bing Crosby has succumbed to series TV and will appear in a sitcom as an electrical engineer who happens to break into song once a week. **1970** *Globe & Mail* (Toronto) 25 Sept. 14/4 A domestic sitcom about a pair of newlyweds. **1972** P. BLACK *Biggest Aspidistra in World* III. v. 195 The only sitcom shows to see the possibility of success..were *Dear Dotty* and *Friends and Neighbours.* **1973** *Times* 2 June 8/4 *My Good Woman*, the new peak time sit-com spot on Monday evenings. **1978** *Encounter* Feb. 32/2 The nearest thing is the comedian Les Dawson, when he relies on words and not on sit.-com. conventions. **1980** *Times Lit. Suppl.* 2 May 492/5 His [*sc.* N. Simon's] stage comedy is hardly distinguishable from television sitcom.

**sit-down**, *a.* and *sb.* [The phrase *sit down* (see SIT *v.* 23) used attrib. and as sb.]

**A.** *adj.* **1.** Of a meal: At which persons sit down; somewhat substantial or formal.

**1836-7** DICKENS *Sk. Boz, Tales* xi, Jemima thought we'd better have a regular sit-down supper, in the front parlour. **1897** *Westm. Gaz.* 4 June 3/1 It seems that the Kitchen Committee..will have nothing to do with an organised sit-down banquet.

**2.** Of a fight: Determined, hard.

**1853** JERDAN *Autobiogr.* III. 18 It was a fair sit-down fight and keen encounter.

**3.** Of a strike, demonstration, etc.: in which persons sit down in a work-place, public building, etc.; also *fig.* Of a person: participating in such a strike or demonstration.

**1936** *N.Y. Times* 30 Jan. 7/6, 1000 workers of the Firestone Tire and Rubber Company remained idle in a 'sit down' protest. **1936** *Sun* (Baltimore) 2 Nov. 14/2 Claiming 2,300 men already were affected by a 'sit down' strike on eighteen ships, the insurgent seamen's defense committee tonight set out to extend its work embargo on all United States vessels in this port. **1937** *Times* 25 Jan. 19/4 The General Motors Corporation has decided to remain in possession of such of its plants as are occupied by sit-down strikers. *Ibid.* 22 Nov. 12/5 'Business' says it is hampered by Government interference and unwise taxation; the Government seem convinced that political enmity has provoked capital investors to a sit-down strike. **1940** H. BRIGHOUSE *Man who ignored War* 23 You're on a sit-down strike, sitting there and saying to Hitler, 'Go away, little man, I'm busy creating beauty.' **1948** *Sun* (Baltimore) 8 Apr. 1/6 A small bloc of Republicans is conducting a deliberate 'sit-down strike' on the ECA and other legislation in an attempt to block as much of the Administration's program as it can. **1958** *San Francisco Examiner* 24 Aug. 1. 25/2 (*heading*) New sit-down battle in Jim Crow cafes. *Ibid.* 25/6 The 'sit-down' endeavor at Brown's [luncheonette] was the latest in a series which began Tuesday night. **1959** *Listener* 15 Jan. 118/1 London Transport appeals for an end to sit-down strikes on the underground railways. **1960** *Washington Post* 24 Feb. 33/7 White college students joined Negroes today in 'sitdown' lunch counter protests in Winston-Salem. **1960** *Sunday Express* 18 Dec. 12/8 Bertrand Russell proposes to stage a 'sit-down' demonstration outside the Ministry of Defence. **1961** *Daily Tel.* 18 Oct. 1/1 Four members of the anti-nuclear Committee of 100 staged a sit-down protest for over four hours last night in a sitting-room at the Russian Embassy in London. **1962** *Listener* 15 Mar. 458/2 The reasonable sit-down demonstrator. **1972** G. DURRELL *Catch me Colobus* x. 221 Remember that animals and plants have no M.P. they can write to; they can't perform sit-down strikes..they have nobody to speak for them except us.

**B.** *sb.* **1. a.** An act of sitting down, esp. as an occasion of friendly or social intercourse. Also an opportunity to sit down and relax, and *spec.*, a place where travellers habitually rest (see quot. 1898).

**1861** MRS. STOWE *Pearl of Orr's Island* I. xii. 104, I am come here for a good sit-down by your kitchen-fire. **1878** —— *Poganuc P.* xiii. 111 After tea there came the genial hour of the social sit-down in front of the andirons. **1898** *Jrnl. Sch. Geogr.* (U.S.) Oct. 315 At intervals of two miles [in Burma]..are 'sit-downs', generally a favorite tree selected because of its dense and wide spreading shade, beneath which all native travellers have their sit-down and smoke. **1932** D. L. SAYERS *Have his Carcase* iv. 56 'A nice sit-down in the lounge,' said Wimsey, sitting down. **1937** 'J. BELL' *Murder in Hospital* i. 6 By the nurse's desk a constant stream came in with..heads done up in dirty, blood-stained rags.. some with nerves on edge from witnessing so many.. gruesome sights, some all the better for a good sit down. **1967** N. FREELING *Strike out where not Applicable* 69 The sit-down had done his leg..some good. **1982** J. SHERWOOD *Shot in Arm* iii. 32 If Verney wanted to go back..it would mean a sit-down and a cup of tea.

**b.** *N. Amer. Tramps' slang.* A free sit-down meal.

**1919** *Dialect Notes* V. 42 *Sit-down*, a meal sitting down. 'A sit-down, with hot Java.' **1926** J. BLACK *You can't Win* vi. 67 She'll give you a sit-down for yourself, chances are, but bring back a 'lump' for us. **1927** F. NIVEN *Queer Fellows* iv. 45 There must be houses where we could get a hand-out for sure... We might even get a sit-down. **1936** *New Republic* 15 July 289/1 Upon the occasions referred to, 'sit downs', or invitations to eat at the family table, are more apt to be given.

**c.** A sit-down strike or demonstration.

**1936** *N.Y. Times* 2 Feb. 26/1 The Akron rubber industry's second 'sit-down' of the week was in progress today. **1938** *Times* 23 May 13/4 About 1200 single unemployed men entered three Vancouver buildings..on Friday..and began a 'sit down' in order to obtain immediate work and wages. **1958** *Economist* 1 Nov. 421/1 The Japanese government has long been irked by the failure of the police to deal effectively with demonstrators who stage sit-downs at American air bases and also inside government offices. **1960** *N.Y. Times* 3 Apr. IV. 7/1 (*caption*) Negro students at Southern University in Louisiana apply at registrar's office to withdraw from the university to protest expulsion of classmates for lunch-counter sitdowns. **1961** *Guardian* 3 Feb. 5/6, 1,200 volunteers..have so far agreed to take part in a sitdown outside the Ministry of Defence... The sitdown is in protest against the Polaris agreement. **1967** *Times* 28 Feb. (Canada Suppl.) 34 Young Canadians have joined sit-downs against nuclear arms. **1972** R. THOMAS *Porkchoppers* (1974) xxvi. 228, I spent forty-one days in that place... It was a sit-down and the old man sent me in to sit with them. **1978** *Peace News* 25 Aug. 3/1 The next day, 2,100 workers turned up for a 'sit-down', and another 300 were dismissed. **1982** M. WALLACE *Brit. Govt. N. Ireland* ii. 29 Measures to deal with street sit-downs and the occupation of public buildings.

**2.** ***sit-down-upons***, trousers, breeches. *colloq.* (Cf. SIT-UPON.)

**1840** J. T. HEWLETT *P. Priggins* viii, Some little damage from the splinters and tenterhooks to my sit down-upons. **1844** —— *Parsons & Widows* iv, [He] threatened to lower his sit-down-upons and apply the rod.

Hence **ˈsit-downer**, a participant in a sit-down strike or demonstration.

**1936** *Time* 30 Nov. 15/1 Most of the 4,300 workers obeyed, but 1,100 sit-downers sat pat. **1949** *Sun* (Baltimore) 6 July 9/4 The local Communist association aided the sitdowners. **1960** *N.Y. Times* 15 May 12E/1 (*heading*) Sit-downers score a quiet victory. **1961** *Guardian* 27 Sept. 20/6 Lord Russell..has won the sit-downers' enthusiasm. **1963** D. V. BAKER *Door is always Open* ix. 187 We had finally reached Hyde Park, where the Committee had arranged for the sit-downers to meet before marching to Whitehall.

†**site**, *sb.*[1] *Obs.* Forms: 3-5 **sit**, 4 **site, sijt, syt, siht**, 4-6 **syte**, 5 **sitt, syte, cytte.** [a. ON. **sýt* (cf. Norw. *syt*), variant (properly the original nom. sing.) of *sút* (Norw. *sut*) sorrow, distress. Cf. SITE *v.*[1]]

**1.** Care or sorrow; grief, trouble of any kind.

Common in northern ME. poetry during the 14th cent.; in the 16th cent. in Scottish use only.

*c* **1200** ORMIN 4852 All flæshliȝ care & serrȝhe & sit. *Ibid.* 7967 Wiþþ serrȝhe & sit, wiþþ bitter wop. *a* **1300** *Cursor M.* 1410 Adam..liued..al his liue in site and care. *a* **1352** MINOT *Poems* (ed. Hall) vii. 65 Inglis men with site þam soght, And hastily quit tham thaire hire. *a* **1400-50** *Alexander* 182 Seses, seris, of ȝour syte & soruȝes na mare. *c* **1470** *Gol. & Gaw.* 1202 He has me sauit fra syte throw his gentrice. **1501** DOUGLAS *Pal. Hon.* II. xviii, Tuiching the proces of my panefull site. **1535** STEWART *Cron. Scot.* II. 519 Se ȝe be blyth and glaid, And slaik also of all ȝour syte and sorrow. **1567** *Satir. Poems Reform.* iii. 157 Sa mot hir hart be fillit full of syte.

**b.** With *a* and pl.

**13..** *E.E. Allit. P.* B. 566 He schulde neuer for no syt smyte al at onez. **1357** *Lay Folks Catech.* 88 The secund dedeli syn is hatten enuy, That is a sorowe and a site of the welefare..of our euen-cristen. *c* **1400** *Anturs of Arth.* xvii. (Thornton MS.), Telle me now sothely what may safe thi sytis. *c* **1475** HENRYSON *Poems* (S.T.S.) III. 107 False is this warld,..Besoucht with syn and other sytis mo.

**2.** ***to make site***, to lament, mourn. *rare.*

**1338** R. BRUNNE *Chron.* (1810) 5 Sorow & site he made.. For his sonne & heyre þat so sone was dede. *c* **1350** *Leg. Rood* (1871) 63, I sall mak site and sorows sere.

**site** (saɪt), *sb.*[2] Forms: α. 4- **site**, 6-7 **syte**; 5 **siȝt**, 6 **sight.** β. 6-7 **scyte**, 6-9 **scite** (9 **cite**). [a. AF. *site* (1302-3 in Godef.), or ad. L. *situs* place, position, etc. The mod.F. *site* (for which Cotgr. has *sit*) appears to be ad. It. *sito*).]

†**1. a.** The place or position occupied by some specified thing. Freq. implying original or fixed position. *Obs.* (common in the 17th cent.).

α. *c* **1391** CHAUCER *Astrol.* ii. §17 Fro the Equinoxial may the declinacion..of any body celestial be rikned, after the site north or south. **1412-20** LYDG. *Chron. Troy* II. 3322 Þe clere sterris of Iades so red Whiche han her siȝt in þe Crabbis hed. **1581** G. PETTIE tr. *Guazzo's Civ. Conv.* (1586) I. 22 b, Mariners..learne to knowe..the syte and place of rockes and shelues. **1605** TIMME *Quersit.* III. 184 The fourth difference [in distillation] is by the site and placing of the vessell. **1646** SIR T. BROWNE *Pseud. Ep.* 273 Of the providence and wisdome of God in the site and motion of the Sun. **1691** RAY *Creation* I. (1704) 167 The Chamælion imitates the Woodspite..in the site of his Toes.

β. **1627** DRAYTON *Agincourt*, etc. 154 The Rocks Tumbling downe from their scytes. **1675** ALSOP *Anti-sozzo* 353 A Body is..the result of all the Integral parts put together in their due Scite and proper Order.

†**b.** With *a* and pl. A place or position. *Obs.*

*a* **1400** in Halliwell *Rara Mathem.* (1841) 63 Þan drawe a lyne..in anoþer site, þat es to say, place of þe table. *Ibid.* 69 Calle G þe mark in þe place of þe seconde site, þat es to say, stondynge. **1596** LODGE *Divel Coniured* D iij, Peculiar and determinate obseruances, (as certaine houres, a certaine scite of stars). **1662** MORE *Antid. Ath.* I. xi. §6 There appearing to us but one Animadversion as but one site of things. **1678** CUDWORTH *Intell. Syst.* 165 Supposing all things to arise from the different Compositions of Magnitudes, Figures, Sites, and Motions. **1716** SWIFT *Progr. Beauty* Wks. 1757 III. II. 163 Three Colours,..So graceful in their proper Place Remove them to a diff'rent scite, They form a frightful hideous Face.

†**c.** Without article or other qualification: Place, position, situation. *Obs.*

(*a*) *a* **1400-50** *Bk. Curtasye* 469 in *Babees Bk.*, In syte [*text* syce] ichon from oþer shalle be þe lenghthe of oþer, þat men may se. **1613** PURCHAS *Pilgrimage* (1614) 874 Contrariwise in the Plaines, iust by in site, they haue their summer from October to Aprill. **1657** J. SMITH *Myst. Rhet.* 199 When words..are in site or placing disjoyned.

(*b*) **1620** T. GRANGER *Div. Logike* 67 Site, or situation, as it is the passion of a thing placed, belongeth hither. **1642** H. MORE *Song of Soul* II. II. ii. 6 Site doth confine This point; take site away, it's straight a spark divine. **1697** tr. *Burgersdicius' Logic* I. ix. 29 Site is the order of the parts of the body amongst themselves.

†**d.** Attitude, position, or posture (of the body, etc.). *Obs.*

**1609** ANDREWES *Serm.* (1841) II. 239 Christ's site, that He stood, when He wished it. **1660** SHARROCK *Vegetables* 148 That uprightness and straitness, which is the most useful site of most plants. **1691** RAY *Creation* II. (1692) 4 The conveniency of this Site of our Bodies. **1728-46** THOMSON *Spring* 1022 The semblance of a lover, fix'd In melancholy site, with head declin'd.

**2. a.** The situation or position of a place, town, building, etc., esp. with reference to the surrounding district or locality. Occas. without article.

α. **1579** SPENSER *Sheph. Cal.* June 1 Lo Collin, here the place, whose pleasaunt syte From other shades hath weand my wandring mynde. **1600** HOLLAND *Livy* XXVI. 582 Anniball..rode to the gate Capena, for to view the site of the cittie. **1664** BUTLER *Hud.* II. i. 24 Some force whole Regions, in despight O' Geography, to change their site. **1711** POPE *Temple Fame* 421 A Structure fair, Its Site uncertain, if in Earth or Air. **1781** J. MOORE *View Soc. It.* (1790) I. i. 5 The sublime site of the Castle. **1838** *Murray's Hdbk. N. Germ.* 286 Its Castle,..imposing from its size, its strength, its site. **1869** MARTINEAU *Ess.* II. 70 The loss of health caused by the pestilential site of a dwelling.

β. **1567** FENTON *Trag. Disc.* I. (1898) I. 18 The magnificall scites and scituations of greate men's houses. **1570-6** LAMBARDE *Peramb. Kent* (1826) 374 A man (but meanly exercised in their language) may..readily understand the Scite, or soile, of their townes, by the onely sounde of the name. **1622** DRAYTON *Poly-olb.* xxx. 236 Both in their pleasant Scites, most happily installd. **1665** MANLEY *Grotius' Low C. Wars* 625 His Cannon shot were aimed with that skill from a little rising, whose scite they had tryed, that [etc.]. **1714** *Steele's Poet. Misc.* 292 A House by Scite and Structure warm. **1771** SMOLLETT *Humphry Cl.* (1815) 281 The castle is an instance of the sublime in scite and architecture. **1807** CUMBERLAND *Mem.* II. 150 In this valley, on the banks of the fertilizing Douro, would be the proper scite for the capital of Spain. **1809** PINKNEY *Trav. France* 255 The town has nothing but its scite to recommend it.

**b.** In scientific use, a position or location in or on something, esp. one where some activity happens or is done.

**1950** *Sci. News* XV. 70 Even a perfect crystal will contain a certain number of vacant lattice positions. The proportion of such sites depends only on the temperature. **1954** A. WHITE et al. *Princ. Biochem.* xii. 259 This inhibition may be a result..of combination of the inhibitor with the same site on the enzyme at which the substrate would combine. **1956** M. DEMEREC in *Publ. Carnegie Inst. Washington* No. 612. 2 The specific properties of an allele are determined by changes at a specific part of the gene locus. Thus it is now evident that a gene locus is composed of a number of units, separable by crossing over, which we call 'sites'. **1966** T. S. & C. R. LEESON *Histology* viii. 140/1 In the fetus..blood cells are formed in different sites at different ages. **1968** PASSMORE & ROBSON *Compan. Med. Stud.* I. vii. 2/2 The high specificity of most enzymes..suggests that on the surface of the enzyme molecule there is one or perhaps a few sites specifically adapted for binding the correct substrate and bringing about the reaction. **1971** LEVITAN & MONTAGU *Textbk. Human Genetics* xv. 576 On this view the several factors belonging to the same polypeptide..would be determined by different mutable sites on one of the genes. **1982** K. H. MUENCH in T. M. Devlin *Textbk. Biochem.* xix. 943 (*caption*) Human proinsulin. After cleavage at the two sites indicated..the arginine residues..and the lysine residue..are removed to give insulin and C-peptide.

**3. a.** The ground or area upon which a building, town, etc., has been built, or which is set apart for some purpose. Also, in mod. use, a plot, or number of plots, of land intended or suitable for building purposes, and, in wider use, a piece of ground or an area which has been appropriated for some purpose; the scene of a specified activity. Freq. in comb. with the first element indicating the (intended) use of the area as ***building, caravan, landing, launching, picnic*** (etc.) ***site***: see these words.

***plane of site*** in *Fortif.*: see PLANE *sb.*[3] 1 h.

α. **1461** *Rolls of Parlt.* V. 490/2 Londes..such as been and make the Syte or Sites of any such Abbey, Priory [etc.]. **1547** in *Vicary's Anat.* (1888) App. III. i. 131 The Sightes.. wheruppon the same ij churches Are nowe..buyldyd. **1649** MILTON *Observ. Peace* Wks. 1851 IV. 542 The Sites and Precincts hereby intended, are declared to be the Body of the Abby, one Garden and Orchard [etc.]. **1789** G. WHITE *Selborne* i. 2 The gardens..and small enclosures behind.. may perhaps have been the original site of the town. **1796** H. HUNTER tr. *St.-Pierre's Stud. Nat.* (1799) I. 228, I have seen only countries frequented by Europeans,..but I shall ever recollect with pleasure two of those sites. **1838** J. L. STEPHENS *Trav. Greece* I. 57 Every ruined village on the road stands on the site of an ancient city. **1863** LYELL *Antiq. Man* 18 In rude and unsettled times, these insular sites afforded safe retreats. **1879** *Cassell's Techn. Educ.* I. 38 The costly nature of the work in making good the site, when the soil is not naturally suitable. **1888** [see *nesting-site* s.v.

NESTING *vbl. sb.* b]. **1930** [see *nest-site* s.v. NEST *sb.* 8]. **1953** N. TINBERGEN *Herring Gull's World* xvii. 152 The bird usually developed a clear preference in favour of one of the two nests,..a site-preference. **1963** *Camping* ('Know the Game' Ser.) 43/2 (*heading*) Choosing a camp site. *Ibid.* 46/2 Have consideration for other campers. Do not stroll into someone else's site just as they are in the middle of morning ablutions. **1965** A. J. P. TAYLOR *Eng. Hist. 1914–1945* xvi. 578 The use of the pilotless aeroplanes and of the rockets was delayed.. by bombing their launching sites in France. **1973** E. F. SCHUMACHER *Small is Beautiful* II. iv. 129 There will be a continuous traffic of radioactive substances..from the stations to waste-processing plants; and from there to disposal sites. **1980** J. MCNEIL *Spy Game* xix. 189 It was shoe-horned between the radar assembly sheds, a piece of open ground which had miraculously escaped the rash of building covering the rest of the site.

*β.* **1535** *Act 27 Hen. VIII*, c. 27 Al the scites & circuites of all such religious houses. **1558** in Feuillerat *Revels Q. Eliz.* (1908) 48 Scyte, precinkte, and Compasse of the late dissolved Hospitall. *a* **1647** HABINGTON *Surv. Worcs.* (Worcs. Hist. Surv.) I. III. 499 Lower Wyke with the scyte of the mannor. *a* **1661** FULLER *Worthies, Cornwall* (1662) 202 He conferred on him and his heirs the rich demesne and scite of Middleton. **1718** OZELL tr. *Tournefort's Voy.* I. 167 The Descendants..are still in possession of the Scite of the Castle. **1793** SMEATON *Edystone L.* §130 *note*, Upon this scite the Baths and Long Room have since been erected. **1808** PARSONS *Trav. Asia* iii. 72 A steep road leads to the cite of the celebrated village, formerly called Daphne. **1835** PALGRAVE *Hist. Anglo-Saxons* iv. 89 The entrenchments.. just enable us to trace the scite of the royal residence.

**b.** *transf.* The seat *of* (an industry); the scene *of* (some condition, etc.).

**1637** G. DANIEL *Genius of this Isle* 572 Looke now vpon my Sister Germanie; The Seat of Warre, the Scite of Miserie. **1809** BAWDWEN *Domesday Bk.* 98 There is the site ..of a fishery there. **1872** YEATS *Growth Comm.* 151 In the ninth century Lake Mälar was the site of so prosperous a trade.

**c.** *Archæol.* A place containing the remains of former human habitation; an excavation.

**1911** T. E. LAWRENCE *Let.* Apr. (1954) 149 The dig has proved a failure to the present (tho' there is still hope of one part of the site). **1963** E. S. WOOD *Collins Field Guide Archaeol.* II. ii. 200 Bronze Age sacred sites, such as the circles at Knowlton (Dorset), which has a church inside it, ..indicate continuity of sacred sites. **1977** *Times* 13 Aug. 14/4 More than four fifths of the villa's walls have been destroyed by ploughing and erosion, and Mr Sumpter feels that the site would not have survived another year's ploughing. **1980** *Rescue News* Dec. 7/5 A cliff site near Northskaill. The site is a great kitchen-midden at least 3·5m thick.

**4.** *techn.* A framework of timber forming the foundation or basis of a piece of scaffolding.

**1901** BLACK *Scaffolding* 27 At a suitable distance from the intended wall a 'site' is first planted... This consists of a baulk of squared timbers, frequently about 4 in. square.

**5.** *U.S. Naut. slang.* A job, a situation.

**1930** *Amer. Speech* V. 393 *Site*, a place as fisherman aboard a fishing vessel. **1957** *Maine Coast Fisherman* July 21/1 Skipper Farrell won't offer a site to a cook who will only cook. **1967** *National Fisherman* June 19-c/2 Palmer was to have a steady job ('site') aboard until he quit or was discharged for cause. **1977** *New Yorker* 15 Aug. 46/3 Joe, who generally keeps his own counsel, tells me that he is hoping to get a site—a job—on the Sniktaw.

**6.** *attrib.* and *Comb.*, as (sense 3) ***site clerk, foreman, manager***; **site assembly**, assembly of building components on the site; **site value**, the amount for which a site may be sold (see also quot. 1893).

**1958** *Listener* 6 Nov. 726/2 The mechanization of building and rapid site-assembly of light-weight factory-produced components is a priority item in the current five-year plan. **1961** *Evening Standard* 20 July 18/3 (Advt.), Site Clerk required by..contractors. **1969** T. PARKER *Twisting Lane* 57 I'd got a fairly decent job as a site-clerk with a small firm of builders. **1964** K. G. LOCKYER *Introd. Critical Path Anal.* iii. 27 Departmental managers, site foremen. **1981** J. B. HILTON *Playground of Death* viii. 97 Three site foremen in succession suffered accidents. **1961** *Technology* May 121/3 There was a need..for a new sort of foreman for the larger projects, a site manager. **1976** R. LEWIS *Distant Banner* iii. 85 The bosses had obviously been on the site manager's back. **1893** *Westm. Gaz.* 20 Dec. 7/3 Defining the term 'site value' as 'the annual rent which at the time of valuation might reasonably be obtained for the land..as a cleared site, if let for building'. **1904** G. B. SHAW *Common Sense of Municipal Trading* x. 92 The popular remedy is to tax site values directly. **1941** H. NICOLSON *Diary* 17 Mar. (1967) 152 It gives a magnificent vista of St Paul's... To get that permanently cleared is worth 40 million pounds in site-value. **1973** E. PAGE *Fortnight by Sea* vi. 67 Hunston's had been losing trade..had been glad to sell out in the end for the very considerable site value.

†**site**, *v.*[1] *Obs.*[−1] [a. ON. *sýta* (Icel. *sýta*, Norw. *syta*), f. *sút* sorrow: see SITE *sb.*[1]] *intr.* To grieve.

*a* **1300** *Cursor M.* 11675 Bot i site for an oþer thing, þat we o water has nu wanting.

**site** (saɪt), *v.*[2] [f. SITE *sb.*[2], or back-formation from SITED *ppl. a.*]

**1.** *trans.* To locate, to place. See also SITED *ppl. a.*, SITING *vbl. sb.*

**1598** GRENEWEY *Tacitus, Ann.* XII. xii. (1622) 174 For the Greeks sited Byzance in the vtmost part of Europe, in a very narrow streight, which diuideth Europe from Asia. **1611** SPEED *Hist. Gt. Brit.* VII. ii. §3. 197 And Amianus Marcellinus siteth the Sacæ..to inhabit ouer-grown places ..at the foote of the mountaines Ascanimia and Comedus. **1920** *Discovery* Apr. 116/1 It is advisable to avoid siting a wireless station close to higher ground. **1955** *Times* 29 June 7/1 New proposals for siting Rodin's sculptured group of the Burghers of Calais.

**2.** *intr.* To be situated or placed; to lie.

**1630** *R. Johnson's Kingd. & Commw.* 460 The lower Æthiope, siteth most Southerly of any part of Africke.

**site**, obs. form of CITE *v.*

**sited** ('saɪtɪd), *ppl. a.* Also 7 scited. [f. SITE *sb.*[2] or L. *sit-us* placed, situated.]

**1. a.** Of buildings, countries, etc.: Having a (certain) site or situation; situated. Usually const. with preps. or advs. (Common *c* 1600–1650, and in recent use.)

*α.* *a* **1455** *Rolls of Parlt.* V. 305/2 A mansion for the Dean there, sited betwene the Toure called the Clokhous, and the wall of our seid Palice. **1585** W. WHITAKER *Answ. Rainolds* 283 The garden wherein Adam for a time remained, was sited in the east. **1598** GRENEWEY *Tacitus, Ann.* XIII. xii. (1622) 198 A Riuer..sited in the confines of both their Countries. **1619** in Foster *Eng. Factories India* (1906) I. 72 A little howse..sited in midst of a small wood. **1633** P. FLETCHER *Purple Isl.* I. xxxviii, This fair Isle, sited so nearely neare. **1975** *No Through Road* Automobile Assoc.), This unusually sited lake, halfway up a steep hillside, was created when a glacial overflow channel became blocked. **1979** *Weekend Bargain Breaks* (Trusthouse Forte) 17/1 The hotel..is well sited in this peaceful town.

*β.* **1610** HOLLAND *Camden's Brit.* 122 Ireland, an Isle most fruitful, and fitly scited to endamage Spain. **1655** FULLER *Ch. Hist.* IV. 179 Aix.., scited in the furthermost parts of Provence. *a* **1661** —— *Worthies* II. *London* (1662) 218 The City of Leyden is scited in the very bottom of the Low-Countries.

**b.** Turned, or facing, in respect of site. *rare.*

**1665** J. WEBB *Stone-Heng* (1725) 102 Their Temples were ..sited indifferently towards all Parts of the World.

†**2.** Of things, persons, etc.: Having a particular place or position; placed, seated. *Obs.*

**1609** HOLLAND *Amm. Marcell.* XX. iii. 145 When she [the moon] is sited just against and directly by line opposite, she will shine out at the full. **1624** GATAKER *Wife in Deed* 10 A wart, or a wen,..sited and seated in some conspicuous part. **1624** —— *Transubst.* 98 What should he speake to him as sited elsewhere, when hee hath him corporally there present? **1660** R. COKE *Justice Vind.* 9 Aristotle..makes virtue and vice to be sited in the power of man.

†'**siteful**, *a. Obs. rare.* Also 5 sitfull. [f. SITE *sb.*[1] + -FUL.] Sorrowful, mournful, doleful.

*a* **1300** *Cursor M.* 21513 And spak he wit a siteful care. *c* **1470** HENRY *Wallace* II. 219 Compleyne for him in to that sitfull sell is. **1501** DOUGLAS *Pal. Hon.* II. xxx, Rander louingis..Till Venus, and vnder her guerdoun..Rest at all eis, but sair or sitefull schouris.

Hence †'**sitefully** *adv. Obs.*[−1]

*c* **1470** HENRY *Wallace* VII. 1243 To Dunbar the twa chyftanys couth pass, Full sitfully, for thar gret contrar cas.

**sitellyng**, f. of *citoling* CITOLE *v. Obs.*

**siter**, obs. f. SITTER[1].

**sitesyn**, obs. f. CITIZEN.

'**sit-fast, sitfast**, *sb.* and *a.* Also 7 sitt-. [f. SIT *v.* + FAST *adv.*]

**A.** *sb.* **1.** *Farriery.* A hard excrescence, induration, or tumour, tending to ulceration, produced on the back of a horse by the uneven pressure or chafing of the saddle.

**1611** COTGR., *Mal de corne*, the sitt-fast; a hornie swelling on the backe of a horse. **1639** T. DE GREY *Expert Farrier* 317 An hard knob..formerly a saddle-gald..is converted into a sit-fast. **1708** *Lond. Gaz.* No. 4493/3 A white Gelding full aged,..a Sit-fast lately taken out about the middle of the Saddle-place. **1753** BARTLET *Gentl. Farriery* (1754) 285 A sit-fast proceeds generally from a warble. **1831** YOUATT *Horse* 169 Warbles..will frequently disappear without medical treatment, but they will, at other times, degenerate into sitfasts. **1887** *Sat. Rev.* 19 Nov. 707/2 Whether a warbly back or even a sitfast would be such unsoundness as to constitute breach of warranty.

*fig.* **1661** HICKERINGILL *Jamaica* 11 Arguments.. sufficiently confirm'd by every Marriner, to take of [= off] the greatest sit-fast of incredulity. *a* **1732** BOSTON *Crook in Lot* (1805) 53 He can raise the oldest sit-fast, concerning which there remains no hope with us.

**b.** *dial.* (See quots.)

**1828** CARR *Craven Gloss.*, *Sit-fast*, a false healing of a wound, whereby is made a hard scab or excrescence. **1888** ABDY *Sheffield Gloss.* s.v., He's got a sit-fast in his arm. **1893** HESLOP *Northumbld. Gloss.*, *Sitfast*, a hard substance which sometimes forms in a wound and prevents it from healing.

**2.** *Sc.* **a.** The plants restharrow and creeping crowfoot.

**1765** A. DICKSON *Treat. Agric.* (ed. 2) 114 Of this sort are some species of the thistle, and what the ploughmen call sit-fasts. **1808** JAMIESON, *Sitfasts*, restharrow. **1825** —— *Suppl.*, *Sitfast*, Creeping Crowfoot, *Ranunculus Repens.*

**b.** An earth-fast stone. (Cf. B. 1 a.)

**1813** R. KERR *Agric. Berwick* i. 35 Some [stones] are even of many hundred weights, and are called sit-fasts. *Ibid.* 380.

**3.** *dial.* (See quot.)

**1828** CARR *Craven Gloss.*, *Sit-fast*, a sottish person, one who sits long or is fast bound to his cups.

**B.** *attrib.* or as *adj.* **1. a.** *Sc.* Of stones: Firmly fixed or embedded in the ground (cf. A. 2 b).

**1801** *Farmer's Mag.* Nov. 377 Land that is incumbered with sitfast stones, or with the roots of trees and bushes. **1880** W. MARSHALL *Hist. Scenes Perthshire* (1881) 312 The land contains numbers of sitfast stones.

**b.** Remaining stationary; unmoving.

**1857** EMERSON *Poems* 70 To find the sitfast acres where you left them.

**2.** Marked or characterized by sitting firmly; fixed, firm.

**1807** G. CHALMERS *Caledonia* I. I. iv. 165 Which the cultivators of the soil have not yet been able to dig up from its sitfast hold. **1837** CARLYLE *Fr. Rev.* I. II. vi, For now no man..but will trot *à l'Anglaise*, rising in the stirrups; scornful of the old sitfast method.

**sith**, *adv.*, *prep.*, and *conj.* Now *dial.* or *arch.* Forms: *α.* 1 **siððа**, 2–3 **siððe**, 3–5 **siþþe**, 4 **sitthe**, 5 **sythþe**; 4–5 **siþe**, 4–7 **sithe**, 4 **syðe**, 5–6 **sythe**; 4 **siþ**, 4– **sith** (6 **sigh**), 5 **syghth** (**syght**), 5–6 **syth**. *β.* 1 **soððа, soða**, 3 **soþþe**; 2 **seodðe**, 3 **seoððe, seoþþe**; 2–5 **seþþe** (4 **zeþþe**), 4 **setthe**, 4–6 **sethe** (9 *dial.* **zeeth**), 5 **seþ**, 5–7 **seth**. *γ.* 2 **sydðe, syððe**, 3–5 **suþþe**, 5 **suthþe**, 4 **sutþe, sutthe**, 5 **sutth, suþ**. [Reduced form of OE. *siððan*, etc., SITHEN.]

**A.** *adv.*

†**1.** Then, thereupon; afterwards, subsequently.

*α.* *a* **1000** *Lindisf. Gosp.* John, Postscr., [John] in foresaʒa siððа..ʒisprunt word miððy god ʒisalde. *c* **1150** *Ags. Gosp.* (Royal MS.) John xix. 12 And siððe sohte pilatus hwu he hine for-lete. *c* **1275** LAY. 3060 Þus seide þat maide Gordoille, and siþþe sat stille. *a* **1300** *Havelok* 1814 Þe rith eye..made he fleye, And siþe clapte him on þe crune. *c* **1440** *Pallad. on Husb.* IV. 215 The pith Pike out,..ek do in sith Donge & cucumber seed. *c* **1489** CAXTON *Blanchardyn* v. 22 He stode styl,..and syth demaunded hym of the causes of his..sorowe. *c* **1500** *Robin Hood* IV. 118 To bydde a man to dyner And syth hym bete & bynde. **1512** *Helyas* in Thoms *Prose Rom.* (1828) III. 18 Matrabrune murmured alway..bi wicked detraccion, which she put sith in effect.

*β.* *c* **950** *Lindisf. Gosp.* John xi. 7 Soððа *vel* ðona æfter ðas [he] cuoeð to his ðeʒnum. *c* **1175** *Lamb. Hom.* 49 Þet..he hine icnawe and seodðe hine for-hoʒie. *c* **1205** LAY. 29537 Þa iwende seint Austin..suð and norð, and seoððe þurh ut Englelond. *c* **1275** *Passion our Lord* 149 in *O.E. Misc.* 41 Vre louerd myd heom iwende... Seþþe he to heom seyde [etc.]. *c* **1350** *Will. Palerne* 2997 Whan þei samen hade souped & seþþe whasche after. *a* **1450** *Knt. de la Tour* (1868) 13 So she shroue her and was sethe of holy lyff.

*γ.* *c* **1275** LAY. 28736 Suþþe he nam þane way. *c* **1380** *Sir Ferumb.* 1855 Þow scholdest hem ʒelde aʒeyn; And suþþe to him amendes make. **1393** LANGL. *P. Pl.* C. XII. 171 In a myrour..hue made me to loke, And sutthe seide to me [etc.]. *c* **1430** *Two Cookery-bks.* 113 Boille hem in water, & suththe roste hem on a gridel.

†**b.** Next in succession, order, or place. *Obs.*

*c* **1275** *Passion our Lord* 47 in *O.E. Misc.* 38 Alle men he tauhte to holde treowe luue, Erest to god almyhti,..Seþþe to luuye his euenyng. *c* **1380** WYCLIF *Sel. Wks.* III. 63 Saturnus is þe hiʒeste planete, siþ Jubiter, and siþ Mars. *c* **1385** CHAUCER *L.G.W.* Prol. 228 (Fairf.), First sat the god of love, and syth his quene.

†**2.** Continuously or ever from or since that time (cf. SINCE *adv.* 2, and SITHEN *adv.* 2). Freq. with *ever* or *alway*. *Obs.*

*c* **1205** LAY. 25511 Þat heo..[were] æuer seoððe laðen in auer ælche londe. *c* **1350** *Will. Palerne* 902 For so hard hacches haue hold me seþþe, þat i not in þe world what is me to rede. **1390** GOWER *Conf.* I. 31 For alway siththe the more and more The world empeireth every day. *a* **1547** SURREY *Æneid* II. 120 Ulysses ever sithe With new found crimes began me to affray. **1621** *N. Riding Rec.* (1894) 183 And ever seth the woddes hath beyne kept as they ought to be.

†**3.** At some or any time(s) since; = SINCE *adv.* 3.

*c* **1300** *Harrowing Hell* 49 Ich haue seþþe þoled..hot, cold, honger ant þurst. **1377** LANGL. *P. Pl.* B. v. 441 The kyndenesse þat myne euene-cristene kidde me fernyere, Sixty sythes I sleuthe haue forʒete it sith. *c* **1400** *Beryn* 3287, I also Have enquerid sith..to knowen of his ende. *a* **1533** LD. BERNERS *Golden Bk. M. Aurel.* (1546) B ij, Bycause they erred, wee haue founde sithe the waie. **1549** LATIMER 7 *Serm. bef. Edw. VI* (Arb.) 120 *marg.*, The byshoppes be stirred theym so then, that some of theim were neuer so diligent sythe.

†**4.** Ago; before now; = SINCE *adv.* 4. ***sith ago***, long ago; long since. *Obs.*

*c* **1350** *Will. Palerne* 1647 Elles had i deide for duel many dai seþþe. **1390** GOWER *Conf.* I. 104 And [it] fell bot siththe awhile,..That my Stepmoder..Forschop me. **1430–40** LYDG. *Bochas* III. xxvi. (Bodl. MS.), The deth contagiousli conspired Of Artaxerses sithe go ful yore. *a* **1450** *Knt. de la Tour* 62 As y herde an holy man preche, and not longe sythe. **1545** RAYNOLD *Byrth Mankynde* Prol. C viij, It hath ben long sith tought to speke dutche,..spanish, and dyuers other langages.

**B.** *prep.*

†**1.** Continuously or ever from (a specified time, etc.) till now; = SINCE *prep.* 1. *Obs.*

*β.* *γ.* *a* **1325** tr. *Stat. Westm. I* c. 38 (MS. Rawl. B. 520) lf. 7 b, That the writ[s]..habben the terme suþþe þe furste passage of þe King Henri in to Gascoine. **1362** LANGL. *P. Pl.* A. Prol. 81 Parisch prestes playneþ..þat heore Parisch haþ ben pore seþþe þe Pestilence tyme. **1387** TREVISA *Higden* (Rolls) VI. 161 To þat tyme þe archebisshoppis were of Rome, and seþþe þat tyme þe archebisshoppes were of Engelond. **1442** *Rolls of Parlt.* V. 56/1 Seth which tyme.. the seide Statute hath nat at all tymes be putte in due execution. **1462** *Paston Lett.* II. 90, I have ben so sekelew sethe Crystmasse.

*α.* **1377** LANGL. *P. Pl.* B. xx. 186 Sith whanne was þe way ouer mennes hedes? *c* **1400** MAUNDEV. (1839) vi. 68 Thei seye that it hathe ben there sithe the beginnynge of the World. **1460** *Paston Lett.* I. 536 In dayly experiens sithe bifore the Parlement of Bury. *a* **1548** HALL *Chron., Edw. IV*, 59 His Feuer tercian, of the whiche he had languished sore, sithe his voyage royall into Fraunce.

†**2.** During the period, at some or any time(s), since (a specified time); = SINCE *prep.* 2. *Obs.*

*c* **1275** LAY. 4154 Soch nas neuere..suþþe þe ilke time þat Brutus com her liþe. *c* **1394** *P. Pl. Crede* 158 Swich a bild bold..Say i nouʒt in certeine siþþe a longe tyme. **1426** LYDG. *De Guil. Pilgr.* 21803 A place Wych, syth tyme that I was born, I hadde neuere seyn toforn. **1495** *Act 11 Hen. VII*, c. 57 §2 Your lettres patentes made sith the same iiij[th] daie. **1535** STARKEY *Let.* in *England* p. xiii, Syth our fyrst acquyntance.. many letturys ther hath byn at sundry tymys betwyx vs wryten. **1593** SHAKS. *3 Hen. VI*, II. i. 106, I come to tell you things sith then befalne.

†**b.** ***sith late***, recently. *Obs.*

**1483** CAXTON *G. de la Tour* d vj b, How syth late a hooly man dyd preche therof. **1484** —— *Fables of Æsop* v. v, Of thy thowsand wyles that syth late thow coudest doo, lete me now see.. one of them.

**C.** *conj.*

†**1.** From, subsequent to, or since the time that. Also rarely with *that*. *Obs.*

*α.* *c* **950** *Lindisf. Gosp.* Luke vii. 45 Ðios uutedlice of ðon *vel* siððа in ic foerde ne blann cossetunges foeta mine. **12..** *Prayer our Lady* 30 in *O.E. Misc.* 193 Ich habbe isuneȝet.. mid alle mine lime siððe ich sunehi cuðe. **1377** LANGL. *P. Pl.* B. Prol. 64 For sith charite haþ be chapman.. Many ferlis han fallen. *c* **1400** *Pilgr. Sowle* (Caxton) I. ii. (1859) 3 So hast thou done alwey syth thou began. **1483** CAXTON *Gold. Leg.* 110 b/2 It is longe sith that I knewe that thou dwelledest in this region. *c* **1530** LD. BERNERS *Arth. Lyt. Bryt.* 360, I sawe not you syth I was in your bedde. **1581** RICH *Farew. Milit. Prof.* C c iv, It is long agoe sithe I haue bothe forgiuen and forgotten these causes.

*β.* *c* **950** *Lindisf. Gosp.* Luke xiii. 7 ðero ðrio sint of ðon *vel* soððа ic cuom. *c* **1160** *Hatton Gosp.* Luke vii. 45 Seððe ich inn eode. *c* **1275** *Serving Christ* 52 in *O.E. Misc.* 92 Seynt iohan is þe beste þat euer wes iwrouht Seoþþe god makede Middelerd. **1387** TREVISA *Higden* (Rolls) II. 117 Seþþe þat þe see was first i-ordeyned.. hit chaungeþ neuere his place. **1490** *Plumpton Corr.* (Camden) 100, I had no word seth I parted from Plompton.

*γ.* *c* **1160** *Hatton Gosp.* Mark i. 14 Sydðe [*v.r.* syððe] iohannes ȝeseald wæs com se hælend on galileam. *c* **1250** *Moral Ode* 59 in *E.E.P.* (1862) 26 Eal þat eure ilc man haued i-do sutþe he com to manne. **1297** R. GLOUC. (Rolls) 4778 Among þe brutons.. was euere cristendom Suþþe it verst.. hider com.

†**b.** During which; that. *Obs.*⁻¹

*a* **1533** LD. BERNERS *Gold. Bk. M. Aurel.* (1546) T viij, It is nowe three score and two yeres sith the earth hath susteigned and fedde the earth of my bodie.

**2.** Seeing that; = SINCE *conj.* 4. Now *arch.* or *poet.*

Very common from *c* 1520 to *c* 1670, being freq. used to express cause, while *since* was restricted to time. After 1700 app. obsolete, but revived by early 19th cent. writers.

*α.* *c* **1380** WYCLIF *Sel. Wks.* III. 339 Siþ þei alle been deed in bodi, Cristis wordis may be taken of hem. *c* **1386** CHAUCER *Knt.'s T.* 874 For sith the day is come þat I shal dye, I make pleynly my confession. *c* **1400** *Beryn* 159 Sith yee be in company of honest men & good, Worchith somwhat aftir. *a* **1450** *Le Morte Arth.* 1744 But sythe it is so,.. What were now thy beste consayle? **1523** FITZHERB. *Husb.* §157 Nowe sythe helle is derer than heuen, I aduyse the specyally to bye heuen. **1592** TIMME *Ten Eng. Lepers* C iv b, It was a shame the sonne shoulde haue a beard, sith the father had none. **1640** FULLER *Joseph's Coat* (1867) 237 And yet why so? sith since I call to mind, Than the Clementes none were more unkind, Than Innocents more nocent none I find. **1680** H. MORE *Apocal. Apoc.* 185 The usual Traffick in the Church of Rome.. now ceaseth, sith she herself ceaseth. [**1751** LLOYD *Progr. Envy* Poems (1762) 206 Ah me! unhappy state of mortal wight, Sith Envy's sure attendant upon fame.] **1814** CARY *Dante, Inf.* II. 22 It seems.. well deserv'd: Sith he of Rome.. In heaven's empyreal height was chosen sire. *a* **1850** ROSSETTI *Dante & Circle* I. (1874) 38 Weep, Lovers, sith Love's very self doth weep, And sith the cause for weeping is so great. **1872** BLACKIE *Lays of Highl.* 43 Sith I am the man I am.

*β. γ.* **1340** *Ayenb.* 47 Hue is hit uoul dede zeþþe hit is kendelich? *a* **1375** *Minor Poems Vernon MS.* 500/274 Seþþe hit is vnknowe to vs, We schul preye for alle Fidelibus. **1393** LANGL. *P. Pl.* C. xx. 33 What neodeþ hit þanne a newe lawe to brynge, Sutthe þe furste suffisede. *c* **1450** *Merlin* x. 143 Seth it is so, we shall delyuer yow the rynge. **1502** ATKYNSON tr. *De Imitatione* III. xxxi. (1893) 222 Seth.. worldlye thynges.. doth nat helpe mannes soule.

†**b.** So *sith that*. *Obs.*

**1387** TREVISA *Higden* (Rolls) III. 223 Þat is no body, seþþe þat þe liknesse.. is no body. *Ibid.* VI. 101 Siþþe þat ȝe telleþ [etc.]. *c* **1430** *Syr Gener.* (Roxb.) 8452 Sith that ye haue him forlore, Ye shal haue a richer husbond. *c* **1489** CAXTON *Sonnes of Aymon* vi. 140 Sith that he is not deed, it oughte to suffyse you. **1559** *Mirr. Mag.* (1563) X ij, And in her wealth, sith that such chaunge is wrought, Hope not to much. **1590** SPENSER *F.Q.* I. v. 43 Sith that heauens king From hope of heauen hath thee excluded quight, Why fearest thou? **1651** H. MORE *Second Lash* in *Enthus. Tri.*, etc. (1656) 228 Sith that the Extent of heaven is not acknowledged any higher then the clouds. **1678** GALE *Crt. Gent.* IV. III. 2 And indeed no wonder, sithat corrupt Nature.. has.. been ever aspiring after an Equality to the Deitie.

**sith**, obs. form of SCYTHE *sb.*, SIGHT *sb.*¹

**sitha, sithee** (ˈsɪðə, ˈsɪðiː), repr. dial. pronunciations of *see thou* (see SEE *v.* 5 f), used esp. as an interjection to draw attention or as a conversation filler.

For further material see *Eng. Dial. Dict.*

**1885** [see PLONKER 1 a]. **1887** KIPLING *Plain Tales from Hills* (1888) 62 Now, *sitha*, tak' a *tat* an' a *lookri*, an' ride tha domdest. **1920** D. H. LAWRENCE *Touch & Go* III. ii. 86 See's motor?—comin' up—sithee? **1932** KIPLING *Limits & Renewals* 309 She's proud of hersen!—Sitha! She's tryin' to admire of her own belly! **1969** *Listener* 15 May 700/3 My first awareness of Castleford was as a young sports writer looking round for the press box when an official said: 'Sitha, lad, it's up there, on't top deck.' **1974** J. AIKEN *Midnight is Place* iv. 135 They're needing a place to lodge too, sithee.

†**sithe**, *sb.*¹ *Obs.* Forms: 1–3 **sið**, 2 **syð**, 4 **sid**; 1 **siþ, syþ**, 4–6 **sihþ**; 4–6 **sith** (4 **siþt, siht**), 4–6 **syth**, 6 *Sc.* **syith**; (1) 2–3 **siðe**, (1) 2–4 **siþe** (4 **ziþe**), 3–4 **syþe**, 4–6 **sithe, sythe** (4 **syde**); also *pl.* 5–6 *Sc.* **sis(e), sys(e), syis.** [Common Teut.: OE. *síþ, síð* str. masc., = OFris. **sīth* (in dat. pl. *sethen*), OS. *sîð, sîth*; these represent original **sinþ*, the *n* of which is preserved in Goth. *sinþs*, OHG. *sind* (MHG. *sind-, sint*), ON. and Icel. *sinn* and *sinni* (neut.), related to the vb. **sinþan* (ON. *sinna*) to go, the causative of which is represented in English by SEND *v.*]

**I. 1.** A going, journey, path, way.

This sense is very common in OE. poetry.

*Beowulf* 1278 His modor.. ȝegan wolde sorhfulne sið. **971** *Blickl. Hom.* 173 Hu myccle scipbrocu he ȝebad on þæm siþe. *c* **1000** *Sax. Leechd.* I. 360 Butan fyrhtu þu ðone sið ȝefremest, ac se wulf sorȝað ymbe his sið. *a* **1122** *O.E. Chron.* (Laud MS.) an. 959, His sawle to ȝescyldnesse on langsuman syðe. *c* **1460** *Towneley Myst.* xxviii. 85 The holy gost before vs glad Full softly on his sithe.

**2.** Fortune on a journey; also generally, fortune, hap, luck.

*Beowulf* 1986 Hiȝelac ongan.. fricgean hwylce Sæȝeata siðas wæron. *c* **1000** ÆLFRIC *Hom.* II. 64 Hu lange wilt ðu bewepan Saules sið, þonne ic hine awearp, þæt he leng ofer Israhela ðeode ne rixiȝe? *c* **1100** *O.E. Chron.* (MS. D) an. 1057, þæt wæs hreowlic sið & hearmlic eallre þissere þeode, þæt he swa hraðe his lif ȝe-endade. *c* **1175** *Lamb. Hom.* 79 He hefde þurst and hunger and chele and alle wreche siþe. *a* **1225** *St. Juliana* 47 Nat i hwet vnseli sið makede me her to sechen. *c* **1250** *Gen. & Ex.* 2546 Egipte folc adden nið For ebris adden seli sið.

**b.** Mishap, misfortune, trouble.

*c* **1205** LAY. 25846–7 [Heo] weop for hire wei-sið, wanede hire siðes þæt heo wæs on liues. *c* **1250** *Gen. & Ex.* 274 Wid ðat pride him wex a nyð, Ðat iwel weldeð al his sið. **13..** *St. Gregory* (Vernon MS.) 425 Schome hit is.. longe to liuen in serwe and sihþ. **13..** *Cursor M.* 9456 (Gött.), In soru and sithe to him and his. *Ibid.* 10411 Speke we nou.. Of hir sythe and of hir care.

**3.** One's pilgrimage on earth; life-time; the course *of* one's life.

*c* **1175** *Lamb. Hom.* 55 He haueð to us muchel nið alle þa deies of ure sið. *c* **1290** in Horstm. *Altengl. Leg.* (1881) 217 Hy tolden tales Of hoere auentures fales And of here liwes siþe. *a* **1300** *Cursor M.* 1400 Adam was for þis tiþand blith, Sua glad was he neuer his sith. *Ibid.* 27021 Þou has soght in all þe sith Werldes welth to lijf in pese.

**II.** Time, occasion.

This is the only sense in which the word is recorded in Goth. and OFris.; it is also found in OS., and is prominent in ON. (also MSw. and MDa.). For the sense-development cf. GANG *sb.*¹ 6, GO *sb.* 4, and the similar use of LG. and Du. *reis*, Sw. *resa*.

**4.** With cardinal numbers (or equivalent term), denoting frequency of occurrence, etc.

In OE. the case is either the instrumental, or the accusative governed by a prep. The instr. pl. *síðum* became ME. *siðen*, and finally assumed the same form as the sing. In place of a numeral, an adj. or adv. might be used, as in *eft-sith(es)* EFT *adv.* 4, *fele-sithe(s)* FELE *a.*¹ 4, and OFT-SITHE(S). With the Sc. forms (δ) cf. mod.NFris. *-sis*, as in *twasis* twice, *manningsis* many times.

*α.* *Beowulf* 1579 Oftor micle ðonne on ænne sið. *c* **825** *Vesp. Psalter* lxi. 12 Æne siða spreocende wes God. *c* **1200** ORMIN 1025 Þe bisscopp sellf.. Þær shollde cumenn o þe ȝer Ann siþe. *c* **1250** *Gen. & Ex.* 3093 Bi-sek ȝet god, ðis one siðe, Ðat he vs of ðis pine friðe. *a* **1400** *Minor Poems fr. Vernon MS.* xxxvi. 273, I.. swouhnede mony a siþe. **1595** SPENSER *Col. Clout* 23 The woods were heard to waile full many a sythe.

*β.* *c* **825** *Vesp. Psalter* cxviii. 164 Seofen siðum in deȝe lof ic seȝde ðe. *c* **950** *Lindisf. Gosp.* Luke xvii. 4 ȝif seofo siða ȝesynngiȝa in ðec & seofa siða [*Rushw.* siðum] on dæȝe ȝecerred bið. *c* **1000** ÆLFRIC *Josh.* vi. 15 Hiȝ ferdon seofon siðon embe þa buruh. *c* **1205** LAY. 1188 Niȝen siðen he bi-eode þat weofed. *a* **1225** *Ancr. R.* 38 Aues also er fif siðen. *a* **1300** *Havelok* 2189 Þo was hauelok swiþe bliþe, And þankede God ful fele siþe. *c* **1330** R. BRUNNE *Chron. Wace* (Rolls) 1377 Nyne syþe he ȝede aboute, & kiste þe auter. **1412–20** LYDG. *Chron. Troy* II. 3239 Sche seyde 'allas' more þan an hundrid sythe. *c* **1450** *Mirour Saluacion* (Roxb.) 48 He weshe hym.. in flvmme Jordan seven sithe. **1501** DOUGLAS *Pal. Hon.* I. xxvii, Ʒeildand Venus thankis ane thousand syith. **1590** SPENSER *F.Q.* III. x. 33 The foolish man.. humbly thanked him a thousand sith.

*γ.* *c* **1000** *Ags. Gosp.* Matt. xviii. 21 Mot ic him forȝyfan oð seofon siþas? *c* **1000** *Sax. Leechd.* I. 352 Þare ylcan gate meolc.. on þry siþas drince. *c* **1250** *Gen. & Ex.* 1731 Ten siðes ðus binnen .vi. ȝer, Shiftede iacob hirdenesse her. *a* **1300** *Havelok* 2162 Hise fet he kisten an hundred syþes. **1387** TREVISA *Higden* (Rolls) I. 123 Þat welle chaungeþ hewe and colors foure siþes a ȝere. **1447** BOKENHAM *Seyntys* (Roxb.) 178 Every day.. Sevene sythys into the eyr.. she up lyfted was. *c* **1456** PECOCK *Bk. of Faith* (1909) 232 Verrili thus it fallith in unnoumbrable sithis in Ynglond. *a* **1513** FABYAN *Chron.* v. (1811) 120 He went .v. sythes to Rome and came agayne. **1598** HALL *Sat.* IV. vi. 79 He.. Wishes for home a thousand sithes a day.

*δ.* **1375** BARBOUR *Bruce* xv. 393 That gert him victor haue feill sis. *c* **1425** WYNTOUN *Cron.* IX. ii. 103 He þat day was stad straytly.. And fyve syis [*v.r.* syse] was at gret myscheyf. **1508** DUNBAR *Gold. Targe* 101 Dame Flora.. thay thank a thousand syse. **1567** *Gude & Godlie Ball.* (S.T.S.) 132 Ane thousand syse than sall I pryse Thy halynes.

**b.** *on* (or *in*) *one sithe*, at one and the same time.

*c* **888** K. ÆLFRED *Boeth.* xvi. §4 Neron.. het æt sumum cyrre forbærnan æalle Romeburȝ on anne sið. *c* **1000** *Sax. Leechd.* II. 208 Ne forlæt þu þæs blodes to fela on ænne siþ. *c* **1470** *Gol. & Gaw.* 382 Syne thay.. salust the souerane sone, in ane sith.

**c.** Used to express the multiplication of numbers, *esp.* (so many) times *ten* or *twenty*.

Cf. Da. *tred-sinds-tyve* sixty, *fir-sinds-tyve* eighty.

*c* **950** *Lindisf. Gosp.* Matt. xviii. 22 Ne cuoeðo ic ðe wið seofo siða ah wið hundseofuntiȝ siða seofo siða. **971** *Blickl. Hom.* 79 Ehtatyne syþum hund teontiȝ þusenda hi.. wið feo sealdon. *c* **1055** *Byrhtferth's Handboc* in *Anglia* VIII. 302 Feower siðon seofon ȝear þæt beoð eahta & twentiȝ. *a* **1122** *O.E. Chron.* (Laud MS.) an. 1070 Ða com Turold abbot & æhte siþe twenti Frencisce men mid him. *c* **1205** LAY. 1103 Sixtene siðe tuenti scipen tuhten from hauene. *a* **1225** *Leg. Kath.* 1287 Alle italde bi tale, fif siðe tene. *a* **1300** *Cursor M.* 11345 Anna,.. þat liued had foursith tuenti yeier In viduid. **13..** *Coer de L.* 2096, I will have three sythe double of his [treasure]. **1340** *Ayenb.* 234 Þe tale of zixti,.. þet is of zixziþe ten. **1387** TREVISA *Higden* (Rolls) I. 45 Þe roundenesse of þe worlde aboute is þre hundred siþes and fiftene siþes an hondred þowsand paas.

**d.** Used to express comparison.

**971** *Blickl. Hom.* 147 Heo hæfde seofon siþum beorhtran saule þonne snaw. *a* **1225** *Leg. Kath.* 1665 Seouen siðes brihtre þen beo þe sunne. *a* **1300** *Cursor M.* 702 Þe sun was þat time.. Seuen sith brighter þen þe dai. **1362** LANGL. *P. Pl.* A. Prol. 109 Al þis I sauȝ slepynge & seue siþes more. *c* **1430** LYDG. *Minor Poems* (Percy Soc.) 62 An hundred sithes better than they deserue. **1480** CAXTON *Myrr.* II. xxxi. 126 His cercle is gretter.. than the cercle of the mone.., xii sithes so moche. **1515** BARCLAY *Egloges* I. (1570) A iij, His Church is twenty sith more gay Then all the Churches betwene the same and Kent.

**5.** With ordinal numbers, and indefinite or demonstrative pronouns.

In some cases denoting a space of time (cf. 3); a trace of this appears to survive in Shetland dial. in such expressions as *the night side, the season side*.

*a* **850** *Lorica Prayer* 5 in *O.E. Texts* 174 Do ðonne fiorðan siðe ðin hleor ðriȝa to iorðan. **971** *Blickl. Hom.* 27 Þæt deofol hine þa ȝenam þriddan siþe. *a* **1122** *O.E. Chron.* (Laud MS.) an. 1110, He.. to Pentecosten forman siþe his hired on.. Windlesoran heold. *a* **1225** *Juliana* 64 Us reoweð þat sið þat we so longe habbeð ileuet þine reades. *c* **1250** *Owl & Night.* 325 Ich singe.. þe þridde syþe a middelnyhte. *a* **1300** *Cursor M.* 6421 If he þam slaked ani sith, Sir amalech wan als sith. *Ibid.* 13094 Hu lang siþe Sal he him hide? **1382** WYCLIF *Exod.* x. 17 Also this sithe prey ye the Lord [etc.]. *a* **1400–50** *Alexander* 4204 Þan was he sary in þat sithe & sadly he pleyned. **1421** in Ellis *Orig. Lett.* Ser. II. I. 85 For in this sith in the bailliage of Caux.. ther ys no steryng of none evyl doers. **1590** GREENE *Mourn. Garm.* (1616) 14 He spends the yeare as blyth, As doth the King at euery tyde or syth. **1630** *Tincker of Turvey* 41 This smith was.. Jocund and gleesome at every sith.

**6.** *by sithes*, at various times. *rare.*

**13..** *Gaw. & Gr. Knt.* 17 Where werre, & wrake, & wonder, Bi syþez has wont þer-inne. *a* **1400** HYLTON *Scala Perf.* I. xxxvi. (W. de W. 1494), Vnto some men and wymmen he yeuyth it all theyr lyfe tyme bysythes whan he vysyteth hem.

**sithe**, *sb.*² Now only *dial.* Also 7 **sith**, 9 **sigth.** [var. of SIGH *sb.*, after SITHE *v.*²] A sigh.

**1609** ARMIN *Maids of More-Clacke* E iv, Be smilefull, and expresse no griefe in sithes. **1633** COWLEY *Pyramus & Thisbe* 71 With many a Sith, many a speaking Teare. **1854** MISS BAKER *Northampt. Gloss.* **1890** *Glouc. Gloss.* 139 *Sigth*, a sigh.

Hence †ˈ**sitheful** *a.*, sighful, sad. *Obs.*

**1610** R. NICCOLS *Robt. Dk. Normandy* lxxxix. in *Mirr. Mag.* 650 As bird in cage.. sadly sits and sings,.. Till breath be spent in many a sithfull song.

**sithe**, *sb.*³ *Sc.* and *dial.* Also 6, 9 **syth**, 9 **sythe.** [prob. a var. of SIEVE *sb.* Cf. next and SITHE *v.*³] A sieve; a milk-strainer.

**15..** *Wowing Jok & Jynny* 28 in *Bannatyne MS.* (Hunter. Cl.) 388 Ane milk syth. **1881** *Leicester Gloss.* 240. **1887** *Jamieson's Sc. Dict.* Suppl. 233/2 *Syth, Sythe*, a 'sey', sieve, or strainer for milk.

**sithe**, *sb.*⁴ *rare.* Also 6 **siethe.** [Alteration of *sive, cive* CHIVE *sb.*¹; cf. prec.] *pl.* Chives.

**1573** TUSSER *Husb.* (1878) 94 Seedes and herbes for the Kitchen... Spinage,.. Suckerie,.. Siethes. **1712** W. ROGERS *Voy.* (1718) 13 There's abundance of good herbs, as parsly, purslain, Sithes in great plenty. **1853** PULMAN *Rustic Sketches* Gloss., *Sithes*, chives.

†**sithe**, *v.*¹ *Obs.* In 1 **siþ-, siðian**, 3 **siðen.** [OE. *síðian*, = OS. *sîthôn*, OHG. *sindôn*:—OTeut. **sinþōjan*: see SITHE *sb.*¹] *intr.* To go, travel.

*Beowulf* 808 Scolde.. se ellorgast on feonda ȝewealdfeor siðian. *c* **1000** ÆLFRIC *Lives Saints* I. xvi. 154 Ða se hælend siðode,.. sum man him cwæð to, 'Ic wille siþian mid ðe'. *c* **1205** LAY. 21279 Cheldric.. þohte forð siðen & ouer sæ liðen. *c* **1220** *Bestiary* 698 Ʒef ȝe ones make haueð, fro him ne wile ȝe siðen.

**sithe** (saɪð), *v.*² Now *dial.* Forms: 3 (*pa. t.*) **siþte**, 5–6 **sythe**, 6–7, 9 **sithe** (6 *pa. t.* **sitht**), 7 **sith**; 5 **syghth-**, 6 **sygth-, sigth-, sighth-.** [A variant of SIGH *v.*, prob. originating in the pa. t. *siþte* for *sihte*: see SICHE *v.*] *intr.* To sigh. Also *trans.*, to say with a sigh.

*c* **1275** LAY. 3108 Ʒeo eode in to bure and ofte siþte sore. *a* **1400** *Sir Cleges* 98 As he walkyd vpp and dovn Sore syghthyng. *a* **1400** *Cov. Myst.* (Shaks. Soc.) 361 Why dost thou sythe so sore, & qwake? **1528** in Burnet *Hist. Ref., Rec.* (Pocock) I. 133 The said holiness.. sithed and wiped his eyes. *a* **1548** HALL *Chron., Hen. VIII*, 180 b, Some sighthed and sayd nothyng. **1588** GREENE *Perimedes* Wks. (Grosart) VII. 92 He lookt, he sitht, he courted with a kisse. **1607** MARSTON *What You Will* III. i, So I say sithing and sithing say my end is to paste vp a Si quis. **1685–90** COAD *Wonderful Prov.* (1849) 72 A new born child (that is living) doth sith and sob. *a* **1825** FORBY *Voc. E. Anglia* 303 *Sithe*, to sigh. **1875** *My Opin. & Betsey Bobbets* 91 As the young woman totters along to prison, is it any wonder that she sithes to herself. *Ibid.* 89 'Alas!' sithes the woman to herself.

Hence ˈ**sithing** *vbl. sb.*, *ppl. a.*; ˈ**sithingly** *adv.*

*c* **1530** WOLSEY in Ellis *Orig. Lett.* Ser. II. II. 27 Thys nygth my brethe and wynde by sythyng was so short that I was.. as one that shuld have dyd. **1570** J. DEE *Math. Pref.* a j, What manly vertues, in other noble men.., he Sythingly aspired after. **1609** ARMIN *Ital. Taylor* (1880) 171 The sithing King sayes, Courage man. **1838** HOLLOWAY *Prov. Dict.* s.v., I knew a clergyman who always read 'Sithing', for 'sighing of a contrite heart'.

**sithe**, *v.*³ Now *dial.* Forms: 5 cythyn, 6 syth, 9 sythe; 8 sieth, 9 sithe. [prob. a var. of ME. *cyve, syve* SIEVE *v.* Cf. SITHE *sb.*³ and *sb.*⁴] *trans.* To strain; to pass through a sieve.

c1440 *Promp. Parv.* 79/1 Cyyd, or cythyd and clensyd, as mylke, or oþer lyke, *colatus. Ibid.*, Cythynge or clensynge, *colatura.* 1595 DUNCAN *App. Etym.* (E.D.S.), *Colo*, to syth or passe through a claith. 1756 MRS. CALDERWOOD *Jrnl.* (1884) 84 They sieth it into a brass veshell tinned within. 1825 JAMIESON *Suppl.*, *To Sythe*, to strain any liquid; *Lanarks.* 1854 MISS BAKER *Northampt. Gloss.*, *Sithe*, to strain and purify milk.

**sithe**, obs. form of SCYTHE, SIDE, SIGHT.

**sithement**, variant of SYTHMENT *Sc. Obs.*

†'**sithen**, *adv.*, *conj.*, and *prep. Obs.* Forms: α. 1 sioððan, 1-3 siððan, 2 -on, 3 -en; 1 siþðan, siþþan, -on, 4-5 siþþen (3 *Orm.* -enn), 4-5 siþthen, 5 sythethyn, sitthen; 3 siðen (4 siden, syden), 3-4 siþen (4 -an), 4 syþen, 4-5 siþin; 2-7, 9 sithen (5 -enne, -in, -yn, -un, 7 -ene); 4-6 sythen (5 -ene, -in, -inne, -yn, -on, -un). β. 1-2 seoððan, 3 seoð-, seodþen (soððen); 1 seoþðan, 2 seod-, 3 seoðþan; 1 seoþþan, 3 -þen (2 soþþen); 2 seððan, 2-3 seððen (3 sed-), 4-5 seþþen; 1 seoðan, 3 seoðen, seoþen; 2-3 seðen, 3 seiþin, 4 seþen, -in; 3-6 sethen (5 -enne), 4-5 sethyn, 5-6 sethin (5 -inne, -un). γ. 1 syð-, 2 sydþan, 1-2 syþðan, syððan (2 -on), 2-3 suððen (3 -den), 3 swo-, swu-, souððen; 1 syþþan (syþan), 3-4 suþþen, sut(t)hen. [OE. *siþþon, siþþan*, etc. (see above), for earlier **sīð þon (þan)* 'subsequent to that' (cf. *æfter þon*, and G. *seitdem*), with shortening of the first vowel. The ME. *siþen, sithen*, however, may also represent ON. *síðan* (Da. *siden*), of the same meaning.]

A. *adv.*

**1.** = SITH *adv.* 1.

α. 831 *Charter* in *O.E. Texts* 445 Wes hit becueden Osbearte..& siððan neniʒgra meihanda ma ðes cynnes. 971 *Blickl. Hom.* 59 He þonne siþþon mid sare ʒeswenced bið. 1154 *O.E. Chron.* (Laud MS.) an. 1140, Sithen þerefter sahtleden þe king & Randolf eorl. c1200 ORMIN Ded. 235 He..sennde siþþenn Haliȝ Gast Till hise Lerninngcnihhtess. c1300 *Havelok* 399 Godard stirt up..and siþen sat Bi þe knictes. c1340 HAMPOLE *Pr. Consc.* Prol. 25 Þe sam God sythyn was..þe first maker of alle thyng. 1428 *Eng. Misc.* (Surtees, 1890) 6 And sythen was funden half a duzan fals tyn. 1470-85 MALORY *Arthur* v. ix. 175 Kynge Arthur..entryd in to Lorayne..and sythen retorned in to hault Almayn. 1559 *Mirr. Mag.* (1563) Diij, And sythen In Wygmore land..I caught the ryght heyre of the crowned howse.

β. *Beowulf* 1937 Hraþe seoþðan wæs æfter mundgripe mece ʒeþinged. 971 *Blickl. Hom.* 79 Swa swa hit seoþþan ʒelamp. a1175 *Cott. Hom.* 225 Ga inn seðen mid þine hiwun. c1205 LAY. 26580 Ælc his Rumain of-sloh; & seoððen heore hors wenden. c1320 *Cast. Love* 46 Hou sone he hit for-les, And seþþen hou hit for-bouht wes. 1362 LANGL. *P. Pl.* A. VII. 59, I wol souwen hit my-self and seþþen with ou wende. c1450 LOVELICH *Grail* lv. 451 But Sethen Cam there gret persecucioun To bothe Rewmes.

γ. c1000 *Ags. Gosp.* Matt. iv. 2 Þa ongan hyne syððan hingrian. 1154 *O.E. Chron.* (Laud MS.) an. 1137, Þe Iudeus of Noruuic..him on rode hengen..& sythen byrieden him. c1205 LAY. 3915 His lond he huld half ʒer, and suððen he adun halde. c1300 *Harrow. Hell* (Digby MS.) 17 Ihesu..suþþen was don ful muchel some. 1393 LANGL. *P. Pl.* C. XXII. 143 Iuwes..culled hym on croys-wyse.., And sutthen buriede hus body.

**2.** = SITH *adv.* 2. (In later use = SINCE *adv.* 2.)

(*a*) a900 CYNEWULF *Elene* 507 (Gr.), Him næniȝ wæs..oðer betera under sweȝles hleo syðþan æfre. 971 *Blickl. Hom.* 219 Þa æfter þisse dæde his noma wæs a seoþþan..mære ʒeworden. a1122 *O.E. Chron.* (Laud MS.) an. 963, Se Ælfsi wæs þa abbot syððon fiftiȝ wintre. c1205 LAY. 4257 He makede..monien laʒen gode þe long swuððen stode. c1400 *Destr. Troy* 2897 And o sithen it was said..That Parys was Pryam son.

(*b*) c1250 *Gen. & Ex.* 262 Ihesus..Ros fro ded on ðe sunenday, ðat is forð siðen worðed ay. a1300 *Cursor M.* 1256 Þat gresse gren, þat euer has siþen ben gren. 1338 R. BRUNNE *Chron.* (1810) 2 A grete Daneis felde..þat euer siþen hiderward Kampedene men kalle. c1450 *Mirk's Festial* 22 Euer sethen angeles haue ben frendys..to all good men. 1487 *Act 3 Hen. VII*, c. 11 §1 The seid Clothes ever sythen into this day have been..conveyed out of this realme. 1550 J. COKE *Eng. & Fr. Heralds* §29 Which armes the frenche kynges have ever sythen borne, and yet bere unto this present tyme. 1601 R. JOHNSON *Kingd. & Commw.* (1603) 116 Euer sithene this citty hath declined.

**3.** = SITH *adv.* 3.

a900 CYNEWULF *Crist* 39 Næniȝ efenlic þam, ær ne siþþan, in worlde ʒeweard wifes ʒeeacnung. c1000 ÆLFRIC *Deut.* xxxiv. 10 Ne aras siððan nan witeʒa..swilce Moises wæs. c1300 *Harrow. Hell* (Digby MS.) 33 Suþþen haui þoled..hounger and þurst. ?a1366 CHAUCER *Rom. Rose* 1641 In sory houre Stood I to loken,..For sithen have I sore syked. 1422 tr. *Secreta Secret., Priv. Priv.* 146 The cursid Emperoure Nero, and many otheres Sethyn and in oure dayes. 1495 *Act 11 Hen. VII*, c. 35 The Kyngis Grace..deputed to hym than and sithen offices of charge. c1570 *Pride & Lowl.* (1841) 25 Before thy time men were not half so wyse As sythen in thy schoole they have been taught. 1669 STURMY *Mariner's Mag.* v. xii. 46 Sithen our Country-man Dr. Dee..saith, that an English-man was first Inventor.

**4.** = SITH *adv.* 4.

c1386 CHAUCER *Sqr.'s T.* 536, I..took his herte in chaunge for myn for ay, But sooth is seyd, goon sithen many a day [etc.]. 1471 CAXTON *Recuyell* (Sommer) I. 118 Hit is not longe sythen whan I was in my royame [etc.].

B. *conj.*

**1.** = SITH *conj.* 1.

α. c888 K. ÆLFRED *Boeth.* viii, Ealra ðara arwyrðnessa þe ðu..hæfdest siððan ðu ærest ʒeboren wære oð ðisne dæʒ. 971 *Blickl. Hom.* 23 We..swa wæron siþþon se æresta ealdor..Godes bebodu abræc. c1250 *Gen. & Ex.* 84 Siðen ðat newe werld was boren, Til ihesus crist fro helle nam His quemed. 13.. *Cursor M.* 7993 (Gött.), Siþen god þe ches king of kith, His herte has euer ben þe wid. c1386 CHAUCER *Knt.'s T.* 1244 (Corpus MS.), Neuer siþþen þat þe world bigan..Nas of so fewe so noble a companye. c1450 *Mankind* 265 in *Macro Plays* 10, I was neuer worth a pottfull a wortis, sythyn I was borne. 1477 *Paston Lett.* III. 201 The greet good that ʒe have had in yowyr rewle sythyn yowyr fadyr deyyd. 1555 BRADFORD in *Coverdale's Lett. Martyrs* (1564) 252 My manyfolde synnes, euen sythen I came into prison. 1572 ABP. PARKER *Corr.* (Parker) 405 He was with me sithen Justice Manwood was placed. [1889 F. COWPER *Capt. of the Wight* 3 The price has risen mightily sithen the tolls have been laid on all hawks.]

β. 971 *Blickl. Hom.* 187 Maniʒe ʒear syndon agan nu seoþþan ure bisceopas..to me ʒewreoto sende. c1200 *Trin. Coll. Hom.* 3 Alle þo þe habben ben seðen ure louerd..steh to heuene. c1205 LAY. 338 Moni ʒer was agan seodðen his cun hider com. c1320 *Sir Tristr.* 1139 In sorwe ich haue ben ay Seþþen ich aliue haue ben. 1422 tr. *Secreta Secret., Priv. Priv.* 197 Ho-so will enserche the olde stories Sethyn the worlde began.

γ. *Beowulf* 2474 Þa wæs synn and sacu..syððan Hreðel swealt. c1000 *Ags. Gosp.* Mark ix. 21 Hu lang tid is syððan him þis ʒebyrede. c1205 LAY. 4154 Swulc nes næuere ær on erde swoððen..þe Bruttes come hær liðen. c1300 *Harrowing Hell* (Digby MS.) 32 Almest so muchel hit is agon Suþþen þat i bicom furst mon. 1393 LANGL. *P. Pl.* C. XXI. 138 Sutthen þis barn was ybore, beoþ þritty wynter passed.

**2.** = SITH *conj.* 2.

α. c1200 *Trin. Coll. Hom.* 21 Whu shal þat wurðe, siððen [L. *quoniam*] wapman me ne atrineð? c1220 *Bestiary* 160 Ðis neddre, siðen he nede sal, makeð seld of his bodi. 13.. *Cursor M.* 3167 (Gött.), Quar sal we take þe best,..Siþen we wid vs broght hiþer nan? c1375 *Lay Folks Catech.* (Lamb. MS.) 273 þis ys Iesus oure lord..siþen he made vs of noʒt. c1400 LOVE *Bonavent. Mirr.* (1908) 49 And sithen crist..chas that.., sothely that is best. 1470-85 MALORY *Arthur* I. xxii. 69 Sythen I haue made yow knyghte thow must yeue me a gyfte. 1509 HAWES *Past. Pleas.* XXXI. (Percy Soc.) 153 Thus, sithen Nature hath you well indued With so much beaute,..Exyle Disdayne.

β. c1175 *Lamb. Hom.* 77 Hu scal þat bon, soþþen na Mon mine likame irineð. a1200 *Vices & Virtues* 65 Hu scolde godd..hauen rewðe..of ðe, seððen ðu..ne hafst nu hier none of ðe seluen? c1330 *Arth. & Merl.* 239 (Kölbing), Seþþen þe king yslawe was.., A king þai mosten haue swiþe. c1386 CHAUCER *Knt.'s T.* 545 (Corpus), Siþen his face was so disfigured..He mighte wel..Lyue in Athenes eueremore vnknowe. c1450 LOVELICH *Merlin* 9966 Sethen hit is so as that ʒe seyn. c1500 *Melusine* 163, I beseche you.., sethen I moste departe your presens, to call me ofte in your remembraunce.

β. a1200 *Moral Ode* 205 Suððen God nom swa muchele wrake..we muʒen eðe us adrede. 1393 LANGL. *P. Pl.* C. XX. 272 Suthen charite..chargeþ this so sore.

**b.** So *sithen that.* = SITH *conj.* 2b.

1387-8 T. USK *Test. Love* III. iv. (Skeat) I. 241 Sithen that god al thing thus beforn wot. c1449 PECOCK *Repr.* I. xiv. 73 Holi Scripture is a reuerend thing.., sythen that bi it..the Cristen Chirche of God takith her feith. 1485 CAXTON *Chas. Gt.* 50 For noo thynge I shal suffre the to do that fayte sythen that thou arte not presently in helthe.

C. *prep.*

**1.** = SITH *prep.* 1.

c1200 *Trin. Coll. Hom.* 5 Eche lif..þat is ʒiarked siðen þe biginninge of þes woreld. 13.. *Cursor M.* 5670 (Gött.), Siþen quen was þu vr domesman? 1414 *Rolls of Parlt.* IV. 57/2 Myne adversaries hav..holden me in prison, sithen Seynt Katerynes day twelve Monthes last passed into this tyme. 1500 *Rec. St. Mary at Hill* (1905) 236 Olde dett that was dew sethen the tyme off Iohn Mylton. 1581 NOWELL & DAY in *Conf.* I. (1584) Diij b, The space of a xi. hundred yeeres..sithen the Tridentine Councill.

**2.** = SITH *prep.* 2.

a1122 *O.E. Chron.* (Laud MS.) an. 963, Ðis wæs ʒedon syððon ure Drihtnes acennednesse dcccclxxii⁰. 1377 LANGL. *P. Pl.* B. IX. 164 Many a peire sithen þe pestilence han pliʒt hem to-gideres. 1415 SIR T. GREY in *43rd Rep. Dep. Keeper Rec.* 583, I spake never withe hem sethen yat tyme. 1469 *Paston Lett.* II. 368 Whych appoyntements sythen yourr departyng hath be largely remembryd. 1535-6 *Act 27 Hen. VIII*, c. 42 By an Acte made sithen the begynnyng of this parliament. a1604 HANMER *Chron. Irel.* (1633) 70 And sithen that time, hath sprung not all to the pleasure of God.

'**sithence**, *adv.*, *conj.*, and *prep. Obs.* exc. *arch.* Forms: α. 4 sith-, sytthenes, 4-5 siþ-, sithenes, 5 sythnes; 5-8 (9 *arch.*) sithens (6 -ins, sythens, -yns, -ence), 6 sithence. β. 5-6 sethens, 6 sethence (7 seeth-). [f. prec. + *-es* -s¹: cf. SINCE *adv.*, etc.]

A. *adv.*

†**1.** = SITH *adv.* 1. *Obs.*

In later use with tendency to pass into sense 3.

1377 LANGL. *P. Pl.* B. VI. 65, I wil sowe it my-self and sitthenes wil I wende To pylgrymage. c1400 *Brut* lxix, Merlyn saw þat sterre,..and siþenes he quok and wepte tenderly. ?1479 in *Eng. Gilds* 414 [He] ordeigned by the same fro that tyme sethens, every mayre on Mighelmas daie to be chargid [etc.]. 1632 J. HAYWARD tr. *Biondi's Eromena* 31 The slaves were not sithence seene, by whom they beleived the Prince to bee betraied. 1655 FULLER *Ch. Hist.* II. 94 Certain principall Persons, conceived signall for Sanctity in that Age, and sithence put into the Calender of their Saints. 1757 DYER *Fleece* II. 311 Sithence the Fleeces of Arcadian plains..bore esteem.

†**2.** = SITH *adv.* 2. Freq. with *ever. Obs.*

1560 in Marsden *Cases Crt. Admiralty* (Selden) II. 119 Our said subjectes have feared ever sethence to trime..any shippes of warr. 1599 BUTTES *Dyets Drie Dinner* Fij, Ever sithence, it hath bene a by-word: an Almond for the Parrat. 1610 HOLLAND *Camden's Brit.* I. 684 Ever sithence the British nation hath continued..dutifully in their loyal allegiance. 1671 F. PHILLIPS *Reg. Necess.* 103 The Defendant was in his service before the day given by the Essoin,..and every time sithence.

†**3.** = SITH *adv.* 3. *Obs.*

1529 MORE *Dyalogue* III. Wks. 223 Sythe that time Tyndal hath put out..another booke... And yet hath he sithens put forth a worse. 1570-6 LAMBARDE *Peramb. Kent* (1826) 11 Long since there was an istmus.., although the sea hath sithence fretted the same in sunder. 1607 J. CARPENTER *Pl. Man's Plough* Ep. Ded. p. vi, That..which I have sithence conceived and thus brought forth. 1660 *Trial Regic.* 35 What Goods, and Chattels, he had at the time of committing the said Treason, or at any time sithence.

†**4.** = SITH *adv.* 4. *Obs.*

Very common from c1550 to c1650.

1548 UDALL *Erasm. Par. Mark* i. 9 The Prophetes so many hundred yeares sythens prophecied. 1591 SPENSER *Ruins Rome* ix, Why haue your hands long sithence traueiled To frame this world? 1619 J. KING *Serm.* 11 Apr. 10 Well-nigh fifteene yeeres sithence. 1655 FULLER *Ch. Hist.* II. 135 Seeing Devotion..long sithence hath desisted to expresse itself in such pompous Buildings.

B. *conj.*

†**1.** = SITH *conj.* 1. *Obs.*

1557 in *10th Rep. Hist. MSS. Comm.* App. v. 387 Sethienc [*sic*] the said Colladge was furste..unitid together. 1566 ADLINGTON *Apuleius* (1596) 11 It is a great while paste sithens we two sawe eche other. 1606 *Proc. agst. Late Traitors* 55 Such as were made Priests sithence her Majesty came to the Crowne.

**2.** Seeing that; = SITH *conj.* 2. Now *arch.*

Very common from c1550 to c1650.

1377 LANGL. *P. Pl.* B. XIX. 15 Why calle ʒe hym cryst,..sithenes iuwes calle hym ihesus? c1400 *Beryn* 559 Sithens þow hast hym bete, it were no reson þat I shuld bere þe gilt. 1477 NORTON *Ord. Alch.* v. in Ashm. (1652) 60 Sithens our Tincture must be most pure and faire. 1509 HAWES *Past. Pleas.* XLI. (Percy Soc.) 203 What you avayleth such treasure to take, Sithens by force ye must it now forsake? 1590 SPENSER *F.Q.* I. ix. 8 Sithens silence lesseneth not my fire,.. I will reuele, what ye so much desire. 1626 J. YATES *Ibis ad Cæsarem* II. 1 Well might he say so, sithence none that is sound and Orthodox, professeth any other societie. 1644 J. BERKENHEAD *Serm.* 3 We must be subject, sithence there is no power but of God. c1709 PRIOR *1st Hymn Callim.* 16 Holy Retreat! Sithence no Female hither..Must dare approach. 1798 SOTHEBY tr. *Wieland's Oberon* IV. xlviii, Sithence our Drusi prince is loathsome grown,..she sees him not without disdain. 1898 LD. E. HAMILTON *Mawkin* xiii, It's our plain duty to bide by it, sithens we was sent by Buccleuch to be guided by the hound.

†**b.** So *sithence that*, = SITH *conj.* 2b. *Obs.*

c1400 *Brut* cxcvi, How might Robert Holonde fynde in his hert me to bitraye, siþens þat y haue Louede him so miche? 1535 FISHER *Wks.* (1876) 385 Studiouslie to keepe it, sithens that you haue it once. 1580 LYLY *Euphues* (Arb.) 394 But sithens that sicke men are not to prescribe diets but to keepe them, I am redie to take potions. 1630 LENNARD tr. *Charron's Wisd.* I. x. (1670) 37 For sithence that by their means..we attain to all knowledge [etc.].

C. *prep.*

†**1.** = SITH *prep.* 1. *Obs.*

1483 in Ellis *Orig. Lett.* Ser. III. I. 102 The revenues of the same.., sethens Michilmesse last past. 1556 in *Rep. Hist. MSS. Comm.* Var. Coll. IV. 221 Ever sithens the begynnyng of Kyng Edwarde the VIth untill this tyme. c1585 HOOKER *Serm.* v. ¶8 This hath been the state of the Church sithence the beginning. 1603 OWEN *Pembrokeshire* (1892) 8 For soe much doe I finde to be called Dyuett seethence the conquest. 1628 ABP. WILLIAMS *Serm.* 17 What life you see in me, sithence that happy houre I first applyed to my soule the passion of my Sauiour.

†**2.** = SITH *prep.* 2. *Obs.*

1536 in Fuller *Ch. Hist.* (1655) v. 209 It was never merry in England, sithence the Letany was ordained. 1581 NOWELL & DAY in *Conf.* I. (1584) Db, Sithence the Tridentine Councill, some Popish printers haue left out the ..Prologue. 1601 R. JOHNSON *Kingd. & Commw.* (1603) 29 Sithence the remembrance of later times, a larger Emperie hath not befallen any christian potentate.

**siþer, sither(e**, ob. ff. CIDER.

**sitherope**, obs. f. SIDE-ROPE.

**sithir**, obs. f. CIDER.

**sithment**, var. SYTHMENT *Sc. Obs.*

†'**sithre**, *adv. Obs.* [f. OE. *siþor*, comp. of *siþ* late.] With *of*: At a later time; subsequently.

c1200 ORMIN 322 þatt Daviþ kingess kinness menn..Wiþþ Aaroness kinness menn Off siþre wærenn sammnedd. *Ibid.* 7293 Alle þa þatt herrdenn itt & wisstenn itt off siþre.

**sith(t)ware** (obs. Sc.): see SIQUARE.

†**sithy-coat.** *Obs.*⁻¹ (Meaning obscure.)

1657 REEVE *God's Plea* 125 They must be rents, rags, slashes, Sithy-coats, and sack-cloth people, that must undertake this work.

†'**sitiate**, *v. Obs.*⁻¹ [irreg. f. L. *sitī-re* to thirst + -ATE³.] *intr.* To thirst.

1599 A. M. tr. *Gabelhouer's Bk. Physicke* 130/2 Let him drincke of this water when he Sitiateth.

†**si'ticulous**, *a. Obs.*⁻¹ [ad. L. *siticulōs-us*, f. *sitis* thirst.] Very dry.

1620 VENNER *Via Recta* vii. 116 They engender cholericke and siticulous humors.

**sitient** ('sɪtɪənt), *a. rare.* [ad. L. *sitient-em*, pres. pple. of *sitīre* to thirst.] (See quot. 1656.)

1656 BLOUNT *Glossogr.*, *Sitient*,..thirsting, coveting, desiring much. 1821 *Blackw. Mag.* VIII. 358 Rheumatism doth not seem to have made thee less esurient or sitient.

**sitiles**, obs. form of CITYLESS.

**sit-in**, *a.* and *sb.* orig. *U.S.* [The phrase *sit in* (see SIT *v.* 24 and -IN[3]) used attrib. and as sb.]

**A.** *adj.* Of a strike, demonstration, etc.: in which persons occupy a work place, public building, etc., esp. in protest against alleged activities there. Of a person: participating in such a strike or demonstration. Also, of or pertaining to such a strike or demonstration.

**1937** *Sun* (Baltimore) 3 Apr. 7/2 (*caption*) The Synthetic Yarn Federation Local 2214.. is staging a 'sit-in' strike at Covington. **1938** *Topeka* (Kansas) *Capital* 26 Nov. 12/5 [Daladier] used.. police to eject sit-in strikers from factories. **1941** *Sun* (Baltimore) 15 Apr. 3/3 (*heading*) New York students stage 'sit-in' protest. Spurn holiday to make demonstration against proposed school closing. **1948** *Ibid.* 25 Nov. 1/4 Passengers aboard the strike-bound luxury liner Queen Elizabeth today were ordered to get off by Friday, but approximately 900 said no and voted for a 'sit-in' strike. **1959** *Times* 10 Jan. 6/7 A warning to passengers not to repeat the recent 'sit-in' strikes on the London Underground was given yesterday. **1960** *Time* 14 Mar. 21/1 Negro 'sit-in' demonstrations at segregated lunch counters. **1960** *Guardian* 25 July 7/3 The two men had agreed.. to express 'support for the objectives of the sit-in demonstrators' in the South. **1973** *Black World* Mar. 37 Pressure for opening the main-stream of American life to Blacks mounted in the 1950's—the sit-in kids, the Supreme Court School Desegregation Decision, [etc.]. **1973** *Times* 17 Nov. 8/2 During May [1936] the French Treasury almost ran out of funds... There was.. a great wave of 'sit-in' strikes. **1980** *Washington Post* 1 Feb. A2/1 Their refusal to budge officially launched the sit-in phase of the civil rights movement.

**B.** *sb.* **1.** A sit-in strike or demonstration.

**1937** *N.Y. Times* 29 May 1/7 Fifty members of the Workers Alliance who tried to stage a sit-in at City Hall yesterday were removed.. by a dozen policemen. **1941** *Sun* (Baltimore) 15 Apr. 3/3 He approved the 'sit in' as an 'orderly and dignified protest'. **1960** *Newsweek* 22 Feb. 27 What some Negroes were calling the 'sit-down' and some the 'sit-in'. **1960** *Commentary* June 525/2 The spread of similar picket lines to other cities.. seems to have been as spontaneous as the sit-ins themselves. **1965** MRS. L. B. JOHNSON *White House Diary* 11 Mar. (1970) 250 Some of the Civil Rights marchers had walked into the White House.. and refused to budge. A sit-in in the White House! **1973** *Law Reports: Appeal Cases* Nov. 858 A sit-in per se is not threatening, abusive or insulting behaviour. **1976** *Times* 10 May 20/5 Sit-ins and work-ins are used by employees.. increasingly.. as a tactic in collective bargaining. **1978** *Cornish Guardian* 27 Apr. 1/1 Mothers who last year threatened to stage a sit-in on St. Austell's Truro Road are again worried that a child is going to be knocked down and killed there.

**2.** A participant in a sit-in strike or demonstration. *U.S.*

**1963** R. I. McDAVID *Mencken's Amer. Lang.* 557 Most lay newspapers would simply describe such persons [*sc.* sitters-in] as sit-ins. **1970** *Daily Progress* (Charlottesville, Va.) 19 Mar. 1/8 A group of people willing to commit civil disobedience will sit down on the pavement in front of the building, obstructing the entrance. If these sit-ins are arrested, another group will take their place.

Hence **'sit-inner** = SIT-IN *sb.* 2.

**1946** *Sun* (Baltimore) 26 Oct. 3/1 Sixty American War Department civilian employés.. held to their rooms in the luxury Hotel Excelsior tonight as the midnight deadline approached for them to obey army orders to move out. Officially an army spokesman said no action was contemplated against the defiant 'sit-inners' until after midnight. **1960** *New Left Rev.* Sept.–Oct. 39/2 The police hosed and clubbed the sit-inners.

**sit-in-'ems, sitinems** ('sɪtɪnəmz), *sb. pl. slang* (now *rare* or *Obs.*). [Repr. a colloq. pronunciation of *sit in them* + pl. *-s*.] Trousers.

**1886** in H. BAUMANN *Londinismen* 179/2. **1922** JOYCE *Ulysses* 418 Don't stain my brandnew sitinems.

**siting** ('saɪtɪŋ), *vbl. sb.* [f. SITE *v.*[2]] The action of locating or placing buildings, trenches, etc.

**1902** *Encycl. Brit.* XXVIII. 449/2 Trace or Siting of Trenches—The system on which trenches are laid out [etc.]. *Ibid.*, The siting of the trenches will depend on the ground. **1918** *Cornhill Mag.* June 621 The short-sighted policy adopted in the siting and construction of schools. **1931** *Times Lit. Suppl.* 16 Apr. 310/2 A practical handbook on the siting, construction and upkeep of garden pools. **1946** *Nature* 2 Nov. 600/2 Areas of exceptional natural beauty or great historic interest should be avoided if their character would be impaired by the siting of a town. **1980** *New Age* (U.S.) Oct. 37/2 This arrangement.. has resulted today in more than sixty so-called 'energy wars' going on in this country between utilities or siting authorities and the politically weaker rural people.

**sitio-** (sɪtɪəʊ), combining form of Gr. σιτίο-ν food made from grain, bread, as **siti'ology** [cf. F. *sitiologie*], (see quots.). **sitio'mania, sitio'phobia** [cf. F. *sitiophobie*], morbid repugnance or aversion to food. Cf. SITO-.

**1849** CRAIG, *Sitiology*, a treatise upon aliments. **1858** MAYNE *Expos. Lex.*, *Sitiology*,.. the doctrine or consideration of aliments..; dietetics. **1887** *Cassell's Encycl. Dict.*, Sitiomania. *Ibid.*, Sitiophobia. **1899** *Allbutt's Syst. Med.* VIII. 379 Acute cases with great nutritional disorder, when great insomnia, sitiaphobia [*sic*], or suicidal impulse is present.

†**sitisot.** *Obs. rare.* Forms: sit(t)isott, -sotte, setisot, sitisote. [Of obscure formation; the final element may be SOT *sb.*] Some kind of game (see quots.).

*a* **1300** *Cursor M.* 16623 Wit him þai plaid sitisott, and badd þat [he] suld rede Quilk o þaim him gaf þe dint. *Ibid.* 24027 O clai þai kest at him þe clote, And laiked wit him sitisote. **13..** *St. Alexius* 366 in Horstm. *Altengl. Leg.* (1881) 182 Som keste atte him stone & clotte, Som plaied wiþ him sitti-sotte.

**sitizen**, obs. Sc. form of CITIZEN.

**Sitka** ('sɪtkə). [a. Tlingit *sheet'ká* (town of) Sitka, lit. 'outer side of Baranof Island'.]

**1.** (A member of) a local group of Tlingit Indians formerly living principally in this North American Indian town. Also formerly, the variety of the Tlingit language spoken there. Also *attrib.* or as *adj.*

**1829** J. S. GREEN in *Missionary Herald* (1830) XXVI. 343 The Sitka Indians have built their village under the guns of the fort, so the Russians can easily defend them-selves from their depredations. *Ibid.* 344 The Sitka I think is peculiarly soft and musical. **1836** [see CHILKAT]. **1873** *Alaska Herald* 9 July 4/2 The Hydahs, Chilcats, Tarkous, Ouchanons, and Sitkas participated. **1879** W. G. MORRIS *Public Service of Alaska* 14 In the fall of 1877, a potlatch was given at Sitka by Jack, chief of the Sitkas, and it is estimated correctly he gave away on that occasion 500 blankets. **1910** F. W. HODGE *Handbk. Amer. Indians* II. 582/2 *Sitka*,.. a Tlingit tribe.. on the w. coast of Baranof id., Alaska.

**2.** The name of the town, used *attrib.* or *absol.* to designate trees native to the region, as **Sitka cedar, cypress**, the Alaska cedar, *Chamæcyparis nootkatensis*, of the family Cupressaceæ; **Sitka pine, spruce**, a large conifer, *Picea sitchensis*, of the family Pinaceæ, or its light softwood timber.

**1884** C. S. SARGENT *Rep. Forests N. Amer.* 580 The most valuable tree of this region [*sc.* Alaska] is the Sitka cedar. *Ibid.* 178 *Chamæcyparis Nutkaensis*... Yellow Cypress. Sitka Cypress. **1884** *N.Y. Times* 5 Oct. 5/2 The white spruce, or Sitka pine.. grows to a height of 150 and 175 feet. **1895** FUNSTON & COVILLE in *Contrib. U.S. Nat. Herbarium* III. 328 The great bulk of this forest is composed of Sitka spruce. **1920** *Nature* 29 July 692/1 The Sitka or silver spruce.. might be called the aluminium of timbers. **1928** *Daily Mail* 9 Aug. 13/4 The Duchy estates on Dartmoor, where it is hoped to plant 5,000 acres with sitka, Norway spruce, and Douglas fir. **1948** *Antioch Rev.* Winter 48 This would be the first step toward cutting off the magnificent Douglas fir and Sitka pine from 300,000 acres. **1965** G. MAXWELL *House of Elrig* vi. 98 The needles of unthinned sitka. **1975** W. CONDRY *Pathway to Wild* ix. 151 If that other western American, the Sitka spruce, now planted so multitudinously in Britain, were also going to be given the chance of making forests of giant trees.. then conservationists might be less unhappy with it. **1977** *Chicago Tribune* 2 Oct. I. 39/2 (Advt.), This fine piano was made specially for us. Its quality features include.. solid Sitka spruce soundboard.

‖**sitkamer** ('sɪtkamər). *S. Afr.* Also **sit-kamer, zitkamer, zit-kamer.** [Afrikaans, f. Du. *sit* sitting + *kamer* room.] A sitting-room, a lounge.

**1902** 'INTELLIGENCE OFFICER' *On Heels of De Wet* 88 Those cushions you have on your front seat came out of the Nieuwjaarsfontein *sitkomer* [sic]. **1904** *Argus* (Cape Town) *Christmas Ann.* 12 He saw his mother standing at the door of the *zitkamer*. **1912** F. BANCROFT *Veldt Dwellers* 31 It was smoke-room, bar-room, and general zit-kamer combined. **1929** J. G. VAN ALPHEN *Jan Venter, S.A.P.* 249 The *sitkamer* was packed with visitors. **1935** P. SMITH *Platkops Children* 84 The sit-kamer is so beautiful you know, that Ou-ma Carel never lets the sun shine in it excep' for a little on Sundays. **1955** W. ROBERTSON *Blue Wagon* i. 3 Van Zyl and John.. entered the *sit-kamer*, as the general living-room of the place was called. **1964** J. NEINTJES *Manor House* 7 We entered a lounge on the right, the *sitkamer*—a large room with a high ceiling on beams. **1971** J. A. BROWN *Return* 79 The door of the cuckoo-clock in the *sitkamer* banged in and out.

**sito-** (saɪtəʊ), combining form of Gr. σῖτο-ς food made from grain, bread, as **si'tology**, = SITIOLOGY; **sito'mania, sito'phobia**, = SITIOPHOBIA; hence **sito'phobic** *a.* (*Cent. Dict.* 1891).

**1864** WEBSTER, Sitology. [Hence in recent Dicts.] **1882** *Ogilvie's Imperial Dict.* IV. 93/2 *Sitomania*, morbid repugnance to or refusal of food. *Ibid.*, Sitophobia may consist in repugnance to all food, or merely to particular viands. It is a frequent accompaniment of insanity. **1902** *Brit. Med. Jrnl.* 4 Jan. 1 The gastric condition of twenty insane patients who manifested sitophobia.

**sitol(e**, variants of CITOLE *Obs.*

**sitosterol** (saɪ'tɒstərɒl). *Biochem.* [ad. G. *sitosterin* (R. Burián 1897, in *Sitzungsber. der K. Akad. der Wissensch.* (*Math.-Nat. Classe*) CVI. IIb. 549), f. Gr. σῖτο-ς grain, bread + G. *-sterin* after *phytosterin* (see PHYTO-); cf. PHYTOSTEROL, -STEROL.] Any of a number of closely similar crystalline sterols, most of them isomers of formula $C_{29}H_{50}O$, first isolated from corn oil and widely distributed in plants; *spec.* the most common such substance, *β-sitosterol*, also called CINCHOL.

Before 1926 considered to be a single substance.

**1898** *Jrnl. Chem. Soc.* LXXIV. I. 72 A substance.. is obtained which resembles the cholesterol of bile in external appearance and in composition..; it is named sitosterol. **1926** *Jrnl. Amer. Chem. Soc.* XLVIII. 2986 The substance corresponding in composition to sitosterol.. is not homogeneous. It is a mixture containing at least three isomeric sterols... It is proposed to name these isomers α-, β- and γ-sitosterol. **1943** *Ann. Reg. 1942* 358 Work on algal chemistry showed that sitosterol, the characteristic sterol of the phanerogams, is common to the green algæ. **1962** H. BURN *Drugs, Med. & Man* v. 57 The substance sitosterol can be given which prevents the cholesterol which is in the diet from being absorbed through the wall of the intestine. **1974** M. C. GERALD *Pharmacol.* xxii. 401 Sitosterols enhance the elimination of cholesterol in the feces.

**sitrep** ('sɪtrɛp). *Mil.* Also **Sit. Rep., Sitrep, Sit-rep.** Abbrev. of *situation report* s.v. SITUATION 11.

**1943** J. H. FULLARTON *Troop Target* xxiii. 173 The daily Sit. Rep. had now identified seven Italian and at least three German divisions in the line. **1947** D. M. DAVIN *For Rest of our Lives* 307 He thumbed through his log with its patrol reports, phone messages, sitreps, all the raw material from which he must first form in his mind a clear picture of what the enemy was up to. **1955** E. WAUGH *Officers & Gentlemen* 264 The B.G.S. said: 'We got a sitrep from the Halberdiers three hours ago.' **1961** I. FLEMING *Thunderball* xxiii. 240 I'm going to.. get a signal off to Navy Department, give them a Sitrep. **1968** P. KINSLEY *Pimpernel 60* ii. 37 Look over a couple of Sit-reps which I received yesterday. **1975** D. W. S. HUNT *On Spot* i. 11 In fact what he [*sc.* Wellington] wrote was a succinct report on the fighting of the past four days. It was in the first place the equivalent of the modern 'Sitrep', which a general, or his staff in his name, telegraphs every night.

‖**sitringee** (sɪ'trɪndʒiː). *Anglo-Ind.* Also 7 **citterengee, cittringe, sittron-, sitterne-, siturngee,** 8 **sittringe(e),** 9 **satrin-, sattran-, satrun-, sitringe, sut(t)rin-, -gee, -jee; satrangi, -ji, shatranji.** [ad. Urdū *shaṭranjī*, f. Persian *shaṭranj* chess, with reference to the original chequered pattern.] A carpet or floor-rug made of coloured cotton, now usually with a striped pattern.

**1621** in Foster *Eng. Factories Ind.* (1906) I. 354 [With the help of skins], cittringes, [etc., they saved most of them from harm]. **1688** J. PEACHEY in W. Hedges *Diary* (1888) II. cclxv, 2 Citterengees, charged before. **1698** FRYER *Acc. E. India & P.* 93 They.. seat themselves in Choultries,.. commonly spread with Carpets or Siturngees. **1785** in Seton-Karr *Sel. Calcutta Gaz.* (1864) I. 111 To be sold by Public Auction.. The valuable effects of Warren Hastings, Esquire,.. Carpets and Sittringees. **1785** *Calcutta Gaz.* 3 Mar. 7/2 To be sold by public auction.. The valuable effects of Warren Hastings, Esq... Carpets and Sittringes. **1825** HEBER *Jrnl.* 4 Jan., Sitringees were laid, by way of carpet, on the floor. **1825–9** MRS. SHERWOOD *Lady of Manor* III. xxi. 240 The pavement was spread with a sitringe, or carpet of striped cotton, the manufacture of the country. *Ibid.* V. xxix. 80. **1851** *Illustr. Catal. Gt. Exhib.* IV. 917/2 Cotton carpets (*Satrunjees*) of different sizes—from Bengal. **1858** P. L. SIMMONDS *Dict. Trade Products*, *Sattrangee*, *Satringee*, a kind of fibrous striped mat or carpet made in India. **1859** M. THOMSON *Story of Cawnpore* xii. 189 They provided us with straw to lie upon, and gave us a sutringee each (a piece of carpet) to cover our bodies. **1876** *Encycl. Brit.* V. 129/2 Cotton carpets or *Suttringees* are a cheap substitute for woollen fabrics in almost universal use throughout India. **1881** *Ibid.* XII. 762/1 Carpets and rugs may be classified into those made of cotton and those made of wool. The former, called *satranjis* and *daris*, are made chiefly in Bengal and northern India. **1904** G. WATT *Indian Art at Delhi 1903* 273 If to this list be added.. the rug the *dari* or *satranji*, the series of chief artistic textile articles of Native dress and household use may be regarded as complete. *Ibid.* 446 A larger market might be found in India for *shatranjis* than has as yet been attained. **1969** E. BHARNANI *Decorative Designs & Craftsmanship of India* iii. 33 In North India.. cotton rugs (*Daris* and *Satrangis*) have been produced in several areas since a long time.

**sitryn(e**, obs. forms of CITRINE.

**sits vac**: see SIT *sb.*[2]

**sittell, sittelness**, obs. Sc. ff. SUBTLE(NESS.

‖**sittella** (sɪ'tɛlə). *Austr.* [mod.L. (Swainson, 1837), dim. of *sitta*, ad. Gr. σίττη nuthatch.] A species of small tree-creeping bird, somewhat resembling the nuthatch, native to Australasia; a tree-runner.

**1848** GOULD *Birds Australia* IV. pl. 102 *Sittella Leucocephala*, White-headed Sitella. *Ibid.*, My collection contains three specimens of this new species of *Sittella*. **1890** in Morris *Austral Eng.* (1898) 419 Sittellas. [Close season.] From the first day of August to the 20th day of December.

**sitten** ('sɪt(ə)n), *ppl. a. Sc.* and *north. dial.* [pa. pple. of SIT *v.*]

For various mod. dial. uses, see the *Eng. Dial. Dict.*

†**1.** ***well sitten***, having a good seat (on horseback). *Obs. rare.*

**1500–20** DUNBAR *Poems* xxvii. 70 The tailȝeour that wes nocht weill sittin, He left his sadill. *c* **1560** A. SCOTT *Poems* (S.T.S.) ii. 38 He micht counter Will on horss, For Sym wes bettir sittin Nor Will.

†**2.** ***sitten-up***, settled in habit, not easily stirred or moved. *Obs.*[−1]

**1671** J. LIVINGSTONE *Let. to Parishoners Ancram* 15 Their fire edge might help to kindle-up old sitten-up professours.

**sitter**[1] ('sɪtə(r)). Also 4 **siter, sittere,** 5 **syttarre,** 6 **sittare.** [f. SIT *v.* + -ER. Cf. WFris. *sitter*, MDu. *sitter*, *zitter* (Du. *zitter*), G. *sitzer*.]

**1.** One who sits or occupies a seat:

**a.** In general use.

*a* **1340** HAMPOLE *Psalter* xlix. 5 He.. sall call.. all perfite men to be siters wiþ him and deme. **1388** WYCLIF *Rev.* v. 1 Y say in the riȝthond of the sittere on the trone, a book. *c* **1400** *Destr. Troy* 9140 Hit semyt by sight of sitters aboute, As the moron mylde meltid aboue. *c* **1440** *Promp. Parv.* 457 Syttare, at mete, *conviva*. **1565** COOPER *Thes.*, *Sessor*, one that sitteth: a sitter. **1608** *Dispute Quest. Kneeling* 73 Not kneelers at any distance from the table,.. but sitters at the table. **1626** BACON *Sylva* §740 The Turks are great Sitters and seldom walk. **1650** *Bounds Publ. Obed.* (ed. 2) 47 Few or many sitters in the House, is not a thing of our examination, if they be above forty. **1806** W. TAYLOR in *Ann. Rev.* IV. 561 Oft from the sitter tales fall about; and from the recumbent, lies. **1837** W. B. ADAMS *Carriages* Introd. 18 The seat, for a single sitter, was placed in the centre of the poles. **1897** MISS BROUGHTON *Dear Faustina* xiv, In a quarrel the sitter has always an advantage over the stander.

*fig.* **1862** LOWELL *Biglow P.* Ser. II. Poet. Wks. (1879) 277/1 A large majority.. who hold with Dædalus, the primal sitter-on-the-fence, that [etc.].

**b.** A person who sits to an artist, photographer, or sculptor, for a portrait, etc., or as a model.

**1649** LOVELACE *Poems* 62 As if thou.. didst draw With those brave eyes your Royall Sitters saw. **1816** GALT *Life B. West* 69 [The artist's] youth and the peculiar incidents of his history attracted many sitters. **1841** CATLIN *N. Amer. Ind.* xxxvii. (1844) II. 37, I am going further to get sitters than any of my fellow artists ever did. **1883** *Hardwich's Photogr. Chem.* 297 The roof over the sitter.. must also be opaque.

**c.** A passenger in a rowing-boat, as distinct from the rowers or steersman; *spec.* at Eton (see quot. 1827).

**1653** APPLETON *Fight Legorn-Road* 5 Captain Cox in the Elizabeth's Shallop with nine Oars and four Sitters. **1676** *Lond. Gaz.* No. 1086/3 A single Boat, with but two Sitters, besides the ordinary crew of Rowers. **1725** DE FOE *Voy. round World* (1840) 66 A boat put off.. with four oars and one sitter only. **1827** *Ann. Reg.* 480/2 Mr. Canning was the sitter in the 'ten-oar' at the Eton regatta, a post of honour which is always reserved by the boys for some favoured visitor. **1865** DICKENS *Mut. Fr.* I. i, His boat had no cushion for a sitter, no paint, no inscription.

†**d.** *Cards*, etc. One who actually takes part in a game, as distinct from one who stands by and bets on it. *Obs. rare.*

**1748** SMOLLETT *R. Random* lii, He then explained the difference between the sitters and the betters; characterized the first as old rooks, and the last as bubbles.

**e.** *Sc.* One who has a seat in a church.

**1838** CHALMERS *Wks.* XII. 212 A sitter in the Church of St. John.

**f.** (See quot.)

**1851** in Mayhew *Lond. Lab.* II. 35/1 Five men worked [at 'translating' shoes] and slept there, and three were *sitters*—that is, men who paid 1*s.* a week to sit there and work, lodging elsewhere.

**g.** One who has a sitting with a medium.

**1909** in WEBSTER. **1928** *Daily Mail* 25 July 6/2 If media were unable to get into a trance the sitting was cancelled and the money returned to the sitter. **1961** W. H. SALTER *Zoar* vi. 73 The sitter brings with him marked plates which he gives the medium. **1977** 'L. EGAN' *Blind Search* ii. 32 One of their perennial sitters, Claire Ewing.. a researcher herself, not an emotion-harried sentimentalist seeking reassurance.

**h.** *U.S. slang.* (See quots. 1938, 1948[2].)

**1938** S. HART *New Yorkers* 183 Bowery barkeeps employed homeless men and women as 'sitters' to shiver near the fire on wintry nights and thus evoke the sympathy of cash customers who would treat them to drinks to the great profit of the house. **1948** *Sun* (Baltimore) 7 Aug. 5/4 Violations, particularly of sitters' rules, would mean suspension or barring women from the licensed premises. **1948** H. L. MENCKEN *Amer. Lang.* Suppl. II. 682 Women who frequent taverns or night-clubs, getting a percentage on the drinks they induce male patrons to buy, are.. *sitters.*

**i.** A baby-sitter.

**1943** *Life* 8 Nov. 100/2 (*caption*) Matt Thomson stays home with baby... Once they would have hired capable 'sitter'. Now only inexperienced girls are available. **1951** H. MACINNES *Neither Five nor Three* I. i. 11 She and Jon couldn't come to the party because the baby was sick or they couldn't get a sitter. **1960** *Sunday Express* 26 June 5/3 He has a first-class nurse and a 'sitter' while I am away. **1975** [see SIT *v.* 1 g].

**j.** A participant in a sit-in or sit-down.

**1961** *Britannica Bk. of Year* 537/2 *Sit in*,.. and *sitter*, terms used in connection with the attempts by Negroes to eat in cafés and restaurants from which they were normally excluded. **1961** *Guardian* 22 Sept. 12/4 There are still people who think that marchers and sitters can be dismissed because some are oddly dressed.

†**2.** One who sits on a horse or other animal; a rider. Also *transf. Obs.*

*a* **1340** HAMPOLE *Psalter* xxxii. 17 þe sittere on þat hors sall noght be safe in habundaunce of his vertu. **1382** WYCLIF *Num.* xxii. 25 Whom seynge, the asse ioynede hym silf to the wal, and briside the foot of the sitter. — *2 Macc.* iii. 25 Forsothe sum hors apeeride to hem, hauynge a dreedful sitter. **1515** BARCLAY *Egloges* iv. (1570) ciij b/1, But if this same colte be broken at the last, His sitter ruleth and him refrayneth fast. **1608** TOPSELL *Serpents* (1658) 659 Hornets.. getting upon the poor Bees backs, they use them in stead of a Waggon or carriage: for when the silly Bee laboureth to be discharged of his cruel Sitter: the Hornet.. spareth not to kill.. his.. chief maintainer.

†**3.** A name for the hare. *Obs.*[−1]

**13..** *MS. Digby 86* fol. 168 b, þe sittere, þe gras hoppere, þe Fitelfot, þe fold sittere.

**4.** A female bird, *esp.* a domestic hen, which sits on eggs for the purpose of hatching them.

**1614** MARKHAM *Cheap Husb.* (1623) 137 A Henne will be a good sitter from the second yeare of her laying to the fift. **1707** MORTIMER *Husb.* (1721) I. 256 The oldest [hens] being always reckoned the best Sitters, and the youngest the best Layers. **1836** *Penny Cycl.* VI. 229/1 The plan of giving the eggs to another sitter. **1884** L. F. ALLEN *Amer. Farm Bk.* 493 The hen [turkey].. is an inveterate sitter, and carefully hatches most of her eggs.

**5.** With advs., as ***sitter-by***, ***-out***, ***-up***; ***sitter-in***: (*a*) a baby-sitter; (*b*) one who takes part in a sit-in; (*c*) one who sits in with a band (SIT *v.* 24 f).

(*a*) **1561** T. NORTON *Calvin's Inst.* II. 167 Princes that haue theyr sitters by, to whom they commit theyr office to rule and gouerne in their stede. **1804** CHARLOTTE SMITH *Conversations*, etc. II. 79 It is very dull tho', Mamma, to the sitters-by. **1850** CLOUGH *Dipsychus* II. iv. 89 Life.. still delights to turn The tide of sport upon the sitters-by. **1860** GEN. P. THOMPSON *Audi Alt.* clx. III. 173 He must be excused by the honourable members who complained of something in his pocket injurious to the sitters-by.

(*b*) **1611** BEAUM. & FL. *Philaster* II, Not a bed Ladies? y'are good sitters up. **1822** LAMB *Ess. Elia, Confess. Drunkard*, They were men of boisterous spirits, sitters up a-nights, disputants, drunken. **1872** GEO. ELIOT *Middlem.* lxxi, There's them can pay for hospitals.. choose to be sitters-up night and day.

(*c*) **1829** CAROLINE B. SOUTHEY *Ch. on Churchyards* II. 292 An unwearied sitter out of.. Dr. Hartop's long stories. **1853** MRS. GASKELL *Cranford* i. 14 Miss Jessie could not play cards: but she talked to the sitters-out.

(*d*) **1947** J. L. BURN *Recent Advances in Public Health* ix. 132 To enable husband and wife to go out together, a 'sitters in' service to look after the baby has been established in some areas. **1951** M. KENNEDY *Lucy Carmichael* VII. iv. 330 'We shan't even be able to go to the club.' 'We'll get a sitter-in for them.' **1960** *Guardian* 30 Dec. 10/5 The husband.. [acted] as the sitter-in when his wife was on evening shift. **1962** *Maroon* (Univ. of Chicago) 20 July 1 (*heading*) Convict Cairo sitters-in; fine each $300. **1963** *Economist* 8 June 1013/1 Negro 'sitters-in'.. gather daily to decide who shall court arrest. **1968** *Blues Unlimited* Dec. 12 Jake recorded with his current group.. plus assorted sitters-in. **1976** *Southern Even. Echo* (Southampton) 6 Nov. 7/2 Members of the Jess Roden Band are some of our favourite 'sitters-in'. **1976** J. I. M. STEWART *Memorial Service* vi. 92 There would be eruptions. 'Demos' would be held, buildings sat in by sitters-in.

**6.** Anything easy or (apparently) certain of performance; an easy catch, stroke, or shot; a sitting target; a certain winner; a certainty.

**1898** *Tit-Bits* 25 June 252/3 A 'sitter' is a catch which falls absolutely into the hands. **1903** G. L. JESSOP in H. G. Hutchinson *Cricket* v. 117 The missing of a 'sitter' by some lazy fieldsman whose thoughts were anywhere but on the game. **1908** A. S. M. HUTCHINSON *Once aboard Lugger* I. iv. 50 'You know I got ploughed?'.. 'Bad luck, I suppose? I thought it was a sitter for you this time.' **1917** H. A. VACHELL *Fishpingle* ix. 183 'Down ours,' enjoined Lionel to his [golfing] partner. 'You'll do it, Joyce. It's a sitter.' **1918** *Chambers's Jrnl.* Apr. 239/1 'A sitter, by the Great Hook Block!' cried Carstairs. 'A transport full of Boches!' **1923** WODEHOUSE *Inimitable Jeeves* v. 54 An absolute sitter came unstitched in the second race at Haydock Park. **1927** *Observer* 3 July 18/1 A series of very bad shots, including a double fault by Borotra, the missing of absolute 'sitters' by both players and the driving of many easy balls into the net well over the baseline. **1946** *Sunday Dispatch* 8 Sept. 6/2 Midway through the second half Bradley missed a sitter when Roper centred across an open goal. **1951** N. M. GUNN *Well at World's End* xix. 156 A pheasant showed, an old cock. The bird stood. We stood. 'Granville, my boy,' he said to me, 'I always want you to remember this: Confucius never shot at a sitter.' **1973** A. HUNTER *Gently French* ii. 16 They use two [routes]... The trouble is they just alternate them... So they were sitters for a villain like Quarles. **1977** *Times of Swaziland* 11 Feb. 14/2 When Wire Kunene was given a sitter on a plate by the evergreen Sugar Ray Zulu, Kunene let slip the chance. **1980** *Amer. Speech* 1976 LI. 294 *Sitter*, ball that is soft and easy to return.

**sitter**[2] ('sɪtə(r)). *Oxford University slang.* [-ER[6]: cf. BED-SITTER.] A sitting-room.

**1904** [see -ER[6]]. **1925** *Glasgow Herald* 24 Oct. 6 If lectures are to be broadcast, the temptation to listen to them in the quiet and comfort of one's own sitter will be irresistible.

†**sitterine**, obs. form of CITRINE B. 2.

**1571** in Feuillerat *Revels Q. Eliz.* (1908) 139 Stones called Sitterines and Topiasses with enamellings.

**sittim**, obs. form of SHITTIM.

**sittine** ('sɪtaɪn), *sb.* and *a. Ornith.* [f. mod.L. *Sittinæ.*] **a.** *sb.* A member of the *Sittinæ*, a subfamily of the Linnæan genus *Sitta*. **b.** *adj.* Of or pertaining to this family (*Imp. Dict.* 1882).

**1829** GRIFFITH tr. *Cuvier* VII. 345 The Sittines.. differ only in having the bill a little more compressed.

**sitting** ('sɪtɪŋ), *vbl. sb.* Also 3 sittunge, 4–5 sittyng (4 cyttynge), sytting, 5–6 -yng(e, etc. [f. SIT *v.* + -ING[1].]

**1. a.** The action of the vb. SIT, in various senses; the fact of being seated; an instance of this.

*a* **1225** *Ancr. R.* 156 Hwat oðer god cumeð of þisse onliche sittunge, þet Ieremie spekeð of. *c* **1325** *Prose Psalter* cxxxviii. 1 Lord,.. þou knewe.. my sittyng and my risynge. **1382** WYCLIF *Lam.* iii. 63 The sitting.. and the aȝeen rising of hem see; Y am the salm of hem. *c* **1400** *Destr. Troy* 440 Hit is wonder of the wit of this wise kyng, Wold assent to þat sytting. *c* **1450** in Aungier *Syon* (1840) 325 The lay brethren.. keping the same stondynges and syttyngs that the quer doth. **1526** *Pilgr. Perf.* (W. de W. 1531) 233 b, This syttynge signyfyeth none other but the peace of the soule. **1581** MULCASTER *Positions* xxxix. (1887) 197 Is the skill in sitting of an horse no honour at home? **1671** MILTON *P.R.* IV. 107 Without the highest attain'd Will be for thee no sitting, or not long On David's Throne. *a* **1700** EVELYN *Diary* 30 Nov. 1680, The place of sitting was now exalted some considerable height from the paved floore. **1730** BAILEY (fol.), *A Siege* is the Sitting or Encampment of an Army round a Place. **1874** BLACKIE *Self-Cult.* 41 Why should a student indulge so much in the lazy and unhealthy habit of sitting?

†**b.** Order or place of sitting (at table, etc.).

*c* **1380** *Antecrist* in Todd *Three Treat. Wyclif* (1851) 127 þei wolen sitt ful hiȝe in furst sittyngis at þe sopers. *c* **1386** CHAUCER *Clerk's T.* 902 And eek that euery wight in his degree Haue his estaat in sittyng and seruyse. ? *a* **1400** *Arthur* 51 For no pryde scholde aryse For any degree of syttynge. **1494** in *Ordin. Household* (1790) 112 The sitting of all Dukes, Earles, and Barons sonnes.

†**c.** The fact of being sat in or occupied. *Obs.*[−1]

*c* **1440** LOVELICH *Merlin* 4490 They.. axeden.. why that place was voyde of syttyng, and why that som good man mihte not sytten there.

**d.** Carriage or posture *of* something. *rare.*

**1709** STEELE *Tatler* No. 9 ¶3 Miss.. immediately at her Glass, alters the Sitting of her Head. **1816** JANE AUSTEN *Emma* II. iv. 69 His air as he walked by the house—the very sitting of his hat.

**2. a.** The action on the part of hen-birds of sitting on and hatching eggs; incubation.

**1399** LANGL. *Rich. Redeles* III. 39 In þe somer seson whane sittinge nyeth, þat ich foule with his fere folwith his kynde. *c* **1400** MAUNDEV. (Roxb.) vii. 25 Þe egges bringges furth briddes withouten sittyng of hen. **1611** COTGR., *Couvement*, a brooding, sitting on. **1711** ADDISON *Spect.* No. 128 ¶3 The Male [Bird].. amuses and diverts her [the Hen] with his Songs during the whole Time of her Sitting. **1787** GOUV. MORRIS in Sparks *Life & Writ.* (1832) I. 292 [They] are really the foolishest geese I ever beheld, for they choose all times for sitting but the spring. **1830** SOUTHEY *Young Dragon* I. v. 10 With amianth he [the dragon] lined the nest,.. To bear the fiery sitting. **1854** MEALL *Moubray's Poultry* 425 For sitting, the newest [eggs] are to be preferred.

**b.** A number of eggs placed under a sitting bird for incubation; a clutch.

**1854** MEALL *Moubray's Poultry* 426 The differences of the seasons.. must have a considerable effect upon the chances of hatching a sitting of eggs. **1895** ELWORTHY *Evil Eye* 406 A sitting of eggs is a number just as well known as a baker's dozen—thirteen.

**3. a.** The fact of being engaged in the exercise of judicial, legislative, or deliberative functions; an instance or occasion of this; a meeting of a legislative or other body; the period of time occupied by this.

*c* **1400** *Ywaine & Gaw.* 3446 It es the assyse, Whils sityng es of the justise. **1560** DAUS tr. *Sleidane's Comm.* 240 The eight daye of Aprill was the thirde sytting of the fathers in the Counsell at Trent. **1598** *Child-Marriages* 173 It is fuly Concluded.. at this, her Maiesties generall Sessions, by the said Justices in their open Sessions and full sittinge. **1660** MILTON *Free Commw.* Wks. 1851 V. 452 If all this avail not to remove the Fear or Envy of a perpetual Sitting, it may be easily provided [etc.]. *a* **1700** EVELYN *Diary* 1 Oct. 1678, The Parliament, growing now corrupt and interested with long sitting and court practices. **1764** *Ann. Reg.* I. 50 The speaker was twenty hours in the chair, which was the longest sitting, by three hours, that is remembered to have happened. **1821** SCOTT *Kenilw.* xvii, The brief interval.. betwixt the dismissal of the audience and the sitting of the privy council. **1855** PRESCOTT *Philip II*, II. xi. (1857) I. 269 These discussions occupied many and long protracted sittings of the council. **1896** *Law Times* C. 356/2 The first sitting of the new court was held on the 10th inst.

**b.** *Yorks.* A statute or hiring fair. Now *pl.*

**1641** BEST *Farm. Bks.* (Surtees) 135 Masters that wante servants, and servants that wante masters, have the benefitte of the next sittinge to provide for themselves. *Ibid.* 136 When servants goe to the sittinge, they putte on theire best apparrell. **1788** W. H. MARSHALL *Yorksh.* II. 352 *Sittings*, statutes for servants. **1851** *N. & Q.* 1st Ser. III. 328/2 It is customary once a year for men and women servants out of place to assemble in the market places of Hedon and Patrington.. and there await being hired. This very ancient custom is called Hedon Sittings or Statutes. **1892** M. C. F. MORRIS *Yorks. Folk-Talk* 369 We're off for Pockli'ton sittins.

**c.** Among the Society of Friends, a gathering or meeting for family worship.

**1841** GURNEY *Jrnl.* in Braithwaite *Mem.* II. 261 We were favoured with a very good family sitting after breakfast... I had to minister to them all.

**4.** A thing or place upon or in which one sits; a seat, *esp.* in later use, sitting accommodation for one person in a church or other place of worship. Also *fig.*

*c* **1400** MAUNDEV. *Trav.* (1839) ix. 106 In that Cytee [Samaria] was the syttinges of the [ten] Tribes of Israel. **1607** TOPSELL *Four-f. Beasts* (1658) 119 The nature of these is.. to cast about for the sitting of the Beast, and so having found it, with continual cry to follow after it till it be wearyed. **1828** CARR *Craven Gloss.*, *Sitting*, a single seat or sitting in a pew. **1835** I. TAYLOR *Spir. Despot.* 168 The number of sittings between one wall of a chapel and its opposite. **1874** MICKLETHWAITE *Mod. Par. Churches* 339 From £10 to £12 per sitting is, I think, a fair estimating price.

**5.** A spell of remaining seated:

**a.** In phr. ***at a*** or ***one sitting***, during a single period of sitting; at one time or spell of continuous action, work, or study.

**1596** SHAKS. *Merch. V.* III. i. 117 Your daughter spent in Genowa.. one night fourescore ducats. *Shy.*... Fourescore ducats at a sitting! fourescore ducats! **1691** T. H[ALE] *Acc. New Invent.* 47 To finish this Piece up at one sitting. **1711** ADDISON *Spect.* No. 72 ¶8 Others who have smoaked an Hundred Pipes at a Sitting. **1731–8** SWIFT *Polite Conv.* 198, I was assur'd.. that she lost at one Sitting to the Tune of a hundred Guineas. **1840** DICKENS *Old C. Shop* xlvi, You should question me for half-a-dozen hours at a sitting, and welcome. **1843** *Penny Cycl.* XXV. 76/1 They [turtles].. lay at one sitting to the number of a hundred eggs. **1887** JESSOPP *Arcady* iv. 120 The incredible bulk of food that they will make away with at a sitting.

**b.** In other uses.

**1621** BP. HALL *Heauen upon Earth* §4 [Gorges] who.. can freely carue to themselues large morsels at the next sitting. **1833** T. HOOK *Parson's Dau.* I. ii, The man is a monster, without one redeeming quality that I could discover in a seven hours' sitting. **1848** THACKERAY *Van. Fair* xlv, Every time that he got a headache from too long an after-dinner sitting. **1896** *Allbutt's Syst. Med.* I. 370 The symptom often departs suddenly during the course of the first sitting [for treatment by electricity].

**c.** A spell of sitting to an artist, sculptor, or photographer for a portrait, etc.

**1706** *Art of Painting* (1744) 333 He drew his picture for him at several sittings. **1762–71** H. WALPOLE *Vertue's Anecd. Paint.* (1786) II. 243 He..generally obtained one or two sittings for the completion [of the portrait]. **1829** LYTTON *Devereux* II. viii, I am going to give Kneller my last sitting. *c* **1865** *Wylde's Circ. Sciences* I. 147/2 The muscles of the neck are apt to become fatigued if a long 'sitting' be necessary. **1884** *Harper's Mag.* Sept. 522/2 His ordinary mode of proceeding in the case of a portrait was to make a realistic study during the sitting.

*fig.* **1818** HAZLITT *Eng. Poets* iv. (1870) 106 Dryden recurs to the object often, takes fresh sittings of nature [etc.].

**d.** A séance.

**1880** HARE in W. H. Harrison *Psychic Facts* 14 The medium..gave me another sitting at her own dwelling.

**e.** One in a series of (esp. two) servings of a meal, *spec.* in the restaurant-car of a train.

**1959** P. MOYES *Dead Men don't Ski* i. 13 The lights of the train came on..and..the bell sounded..for First Dinner. Jimmy..was..due to dine at the first sitting. **1962** N. STREATFEILD *Apple Bough* vii. 101 An attendant from the restaurant-car looked in. 'Luncheon tickets?' he asked. The man said: 'Second sitting, please.' **1965** E. BROWN *Big Man* ix. 74 I'll clean up the cabin while you are at lunch. You are second sitting. **1977** C. ALLEN *Raj* i. 25/2 Gongs were sounded to mark the arrival of each course... Older travellers preferred the second sitting.

**6. a.** With advs., as *down, in, out, up.*

For northern dial. uses, see the *Eng. Dial. Dict.*

(*a*) **1535** COVERDALE *Lam.* iii. 63 Thou seist also their sittinge downe and their rysinge vp. *a* **1572** KNOX *Hist. Ref.* Wks. 1846 I. 220 The sitting doun of the schip called the Cardinall..betuix Sanct Colmes Inch and Crawmond, without any occasioun, except negligence. **1617** MORYSON *Itin.* II. 141 Some few shot of the Spaniards offered to disturbe our sitting downe [= encamping], but were soone beaten home. **1667** MARVELL *Corr.* Wks. (Grosart) II. 218 It being now but seven days till the sitting down of the Parliament. **1707** FREIND *Peterborow's Cond. Sp.* 43 The only contrivance by which the sitting down of such a handful of men..could have had the effect of a regular envestment. **1881** MISS YONGE *Lads & Lasses Langley* ii. 67 When there was a sitting down, Frank had been used to.. put his head on his arms and be comfortable.

(*b*) **1547** *Bk. of Marchauntes* e ij, If any woman lye in childbed, they to go to say gospels and to be at the syttyng vp and chirching. **1607** CHAPMAN *Bussy d'Ambois* III. ii, I, watching my lady's sitting up, stole up at midnight from my pallet. **1810** T. WILLIAMSON *E. India Vade-M.* II. 112 This 'sitting up'..generally took place at the house of some lady of rank,..who for three successive nights, threw open her mansion. **1817** JANE AUSTEN *Let.* 22 May (1932) 493 Words ..fail..to describe what a Nurse she has been to me... There was never any sitting-up necessary. **1900** M. BEERBOHM in *Sat. Rev.* 6 Jan. 12/2 Was not a pantomime.. the most brilliant occasion for 'sitting-up'?

(*c*) **1902** MRS. ALEXANDER *Stronger than Love* xi, Nothing short of two valses and one 'sitting-out' can atone for it.

(*d*) **1946** R. BLESH *Shining Trumpets* x. 237 The band instrumentation was kept normal, and men alternated with one another in the process known as *sitting in.* **1977** 'C. AIRD' *Parting Breath* iv. 54 The students..squatted on the floor... 'Sitting-in means sitting down, I reckon,' remarked one student.

**b.** *attrib.* (See quots.)

**1874** W. LENNOX *My Recollections* II. 29 A sitting-down supper was announced. **1893** KEITH *'Lisbeth* II. ii, I hope you'll excuse it's not being a sitting-down tea. **1895** E. F. BENSON *Dodo* II. xi. 232 The music..was quite loud enough to be heard distinctly in a small, rather unfrequented sitting-out room. **1899** *Allbutt's Syst. Med.* VII. 460 A change from the lying-down to the sitting-up position. **1900** *Westm. Gaz.* 11 Apr. 3/2 Thousands of shirts, sitting-up jackets, socks, pyjamas. **1900** *Traveller* 4 Aug. 106/2 On the *Caledonia* there was a minimum of space... There were no sitting-out places. **1902** E. GLYN *Refl. Ambrosine* 53, I went to no more sitting-out places [at a ball]. **1939** *Sun* (Baltimore) 5 Apr. 26/2 An abundance of unoccupied land for playgrounds, sitting-out areas, walks and service streets. **1964** V. J. CHAPMAN *Coastal Veg.* ix. 212 Maritime cliffs are often the haunt of sea birds, either as nesting areas or as 'sitting out' places. **1976** *National Observer* (U.S.) 19 June 17 (Advt.), It gives full pillow support to head and back for firm sitting-up comfort.

**7.** *attrib.* and *Comb.*, as ***sitting apartment, bath, box, -chamber, height, muscle, parlour, part,*** etc.

**1849** D. J. BROWNE *Amer. Poultry Yard* (1855) 89 The partition between the laying and *sitting apartments. **1843** ABDY *Water Cure* 67 Copious water drinking, short *sitting baths, and wet bandages on the body. **1849** D. J. BROWNE *Amer. Poultry Yard* (1855) 87 Laying and *sitting boxes may be placed at either side of the building. **1833** T. HOOK *Parson's Dau.* III. xi, Here was the governor's sleeping-cabin [on board]—his lady's *sitting-cabin [etc.]. **1886** R. F. BURTON *Arab. Nts.* (1887) III. 6 A mansion, wherein were furnished *sitting-chambers. **1665** J. WEBB *Stone-Heng* (1725) 176 These were Stones but of a *sitting height at utmost. **1822–7** GOOD *Study Med.* (1829) IV. 348 A high narrow chair with a straight back that hardly allows of any flexion to the *sitting muscles. **1854** MEALL *Moubray's Poultry* 424 The construction of *sitting-nests on one side of the..night-house. **1789** G. WHITE *Selborne* lxxxvi, Within sight of some window in the common *sitting parlour. **1730** FIELDING *Tom Thumb* II. x, While the two stools her *sitting-part confound, Between 'em both fall squat upon the ground. **1775** ADAIR *Amer. Ind.* 396 After sleeping two hours in a *sitting posture. **1573** in W. H. TURNER *Select. Rec. Oxford* (1880) 350 For chargys aboute the swanes..at the *syttynge tyme and uppynge tyme.

**b.** Special combs.: **sitting-breeches** (see quot.); **sitting-day**, a day on which a legislative or deliberative body sits; **sitting-shot**, a shot taken in a sitting position.

**1785** GROSE *Dict. Vulgar T.*, **Sitting breeches*, one who stays late in company, is said to have his sitting breeches on, or that he will sit longer than a hen. **1664** PEPYS *Diary* 14 July, I went, and found him busy in trials of law in his great room; and it being *Sitting-day, durst not stay. **1894** *Daily News* 6 March 2/1 He was not absent from the House one sitting day. **1874** J. W. LONG *Amer. Wild-fowl.* ix. 151 If it was later in the day, it might be to our advantage to try a *sitting-shot.

**'sitting,** *ppl. a.* [f. SIT *v.* + -ING². In senses 1 and 2 after OF. (*bien*) *seant.*]

†**1. a.** Of garments or articles of apparel: Fitting *well* or closely to the body. *Obs. rare.*

**12..** *Prayer* 42 in *O.E. Misc.* 193 Inne mete & inne drinke ic habbe ibeo ouerdede, & inne wel sittende schon. *a* **1400** *Rom. Rose* 2263 Poyntis and sleves be welle sittande, Right and streght on the hande. *c* **1440** *Promp. Parv.* 457/1 Syttynge clothe, or streythe, *strigium.* *a* **1500** *Flower & Leaf* xxi, In surcotes whyte, of veluet wel sitting.

†**b.** (Well) placed or formed. *Obs.*⁻¹

*c* **1450** *Merlin* xiv. 227 She was sklender a-boute the flankes and the haunche lowe and comly well syttynge.

†**2. a.** Becoming, befitting; proper, suitable; appropriate. Freq. preceded by *well.* Const. *to, unto,* rarely *for,* or *that. Obs.*

? *a* **1366** CHAUCER *Rom. Rose* 986 To hem [the arrows] was wel sitting and able The foule croked bowe hidous. *c* **1400** *Beryn* 1041 Fawnus for Agea, as it was wele sitting, Made ful grete ordenaunce for hir burying. **1412–20** LYDG. *Chron. Troy* I. 1262 A wel beseyn meyne, Lyche as was sytting vnto his degre. *c* **1449** PECOCK *Repr.* III. ix. 333 It bisemeth and it is sitting..that the ȝeuer ȝeue his ȝifte..mediatli. *a* **1513** FABYAN *Chron.* VII. ccxxxii. (1811) 265 It is not vnworthy to the..for to the it is sittynge for noblesse of bloode. **1564** HAWARD *Eutrop.* x. 114 Not all together so hedefull aboute hys affayres as it was sittinge & fitte for soo myghtye a prince. *c* **1575** T. HACKET *Treas. Amadis de Gaule* 284 This ..shall be a thing very well syttyng and convenient to your accustomed graciousnesse.

†**b.** In attributive use. *Obs. rare.*

? *a* **1400** *Morte Arth.* 953 He saluȝede þat sorowfulle with sittande wordez. **1483** CAXTON *G. de la Tour* b iiij b, [The] nose..is the most syttyng membre that a man..may haue.

**3.** That sits in, possesses the right to, or holds, a position, office, or tenancy.

*sitting member*, a Member of Parliament actually holding a seat in the House of Commons at the time referred to.

(*a*) **1706** LUTTRELL *Brief Rel.* (1857) VI. 19 Petitioners against sir Thomas Bellot and Mr. Cotton, the sitting members. **1813** *Exam.* 1 March 139/1 Three of the Sitting Members..were not duly elected. **1890** M. S. WILLIAMS *Leaves of Life* II. v. 44 A property which he had bought when sitting Member for Preston.

(*b*) **1768** *Ann. Reg.* 57 The sitting Magistrates..at the Rotation-office in Whitechapel. **1843** *Chambers's Edin. Jrnl.* 45/2 The case being brought before one of the metropolitan police courts, the sitting magistrate committed the soldier for trial.

(*c*) **1844** H. STEPHENS *Bk. Farm* I. 614 The new conditions will be made as if the sitting tenant were a stranger. **1884** ROGERS *Six Cent. Work & Wages* I. 54 Raising rent on the sitting tenant, to use a modern phrase.

**4.** That sits: **a.** Of animals or birds, *esp.* of hen-birds whilst hatching.

**1611** COTGR., *Couveresse*, a sitting henne. *c* **1709** PRIOR *Dove* xiii, Have You observ'd a sitting Hare, List'ning [etc.]? **1844** H. STEPHENS *Bk. Farm* II. 708 Places should be chosen for placing the sitting hens in. **1883** *Century Mag.* 682 A deep,..elaborate structure, in which the sitting bird sank.

†**b.** *Bot.* Sessile. *Obs.*

**1796** WITHERING *Brit. Plants* (ed. 3) I. 82 Sitting Flowers, are those which have no Fruit-stalk. *Ibid.* 328 In *Leontodon Taraxacum* the down is supported on a long pedicle, in all the other English species it is sitting. **1837** P. KEITH *Bot. Lex.* 17 It is..placed immediately on the ovary or pistil, and is said to be sitting. **1851** RICHARDSON *Geol.* vii. 203 Leaves are..either sessile or petiolate, that is, either sitting or having footstalks.

**c.** Of persons, figures, etc.: Seated.

**1839** *Civil Eng. & Arch. Jrnl.* II. 426 Monument of Maximilian-Joseph I... Colossal sitting figure. **1842** TENNYSON *Vision of Sin* i. 12 Sitting, lying, languid shapes. **1887** MAHAFFY *Gk. Life & Thought* vi. 112 The proposal.. to carve Mount Athos into a sitting figure.

**d.** Of a huntsman's target: stationary, and so easily hit. Freq. *fig.* (orig. *Mil.*) in ***sitting bird, duck,*** etc.

**1867** TROLLOPE *Claverings* I. x. 126 The man who fires at a sitting bird is known to be no sportsman. **1944** *R.A.F. Jrnl.* Aug. 270 Carriers are sitting birds for enemy surface craft. **1944** *Reader's Digest* May 53 (*heading*) Why tankers are no longer sitting ducks. **1948** *Harper's Mag.* Apr. 290/2 Ever since Sinclair Lewis gave the first lessons in marksmanship, men of the Senator's type have been sitting ducks for the opposition. **1949** *Sat. Even. Post* 16 July 23/3 (*caption*) Rescuing downed aviators sometimes got a sitting-duck submarine fired on by our own quick-triggered forces. **1954** J. BLISH in *If; Worlds Sci. Fict.* No. 4. 38/2 You're a sitting duck for a real infection if you abuse your time during convalescence. **1958** 'A. GILBERT' *Death against Clock* vi. 89 'It could be he was financin' another establishment and didn't want Mrs M. to know. And Wife No. 2 might be makin' trouble.' 'Simpler to put *her* light out in that case.' .. 'Ah, but then he'd be a sitting duck for the police. Someone always comes forward in cases like these to say he ..saw the dear departed with a gent.' **1961** B. FERGUSSON *Watery Maze* vii. 183 We had learned that for tanks to land before tank obstacles had been breached was lethal; they would inevitably be halted, and would become sitting ducks. **1977** 'J. D. WHITE' *Salzburg Affair* xiii. 109 Narrow streets, he'd be a sitting target. **1978** J. WAINWRIGHT *Thief of Time* 195, I have no 'gentlemanly' distaste at shooting sitting targets; wood pigeons, rabbits, hares..let them be motionless..and I have meat for supper.

**e.** *fig.* That can hardly be bungled.

**1932** *Evening Standard* 28 Jan. 11/2 They had a hand which contained a 'sitting' game in Spades—one of two had five to the four top honours. **1960** I. PEEBLES *Bowler's Turn* 190 Against these two Dexter with a bit of luck (dropped at square leg at 30 and off a sitting return by Worrell at 32) played confidently.

**5.** *dial.* To which one sits down.

**1889** WESTALL *Birch Dene* I. 251 A 'standing gill' cost a penny, a 'sitting gill' three-halfpence. **1898** COBBAN *Angel* 180 To take a sitting drink..with the Gordon gentlemen.

†**'sittingly,** *adv. Obs.* [f. SITTING *ppl. a.* + -LY².] In a befitting or becoming manner; fittingly; suitably.

*a* **1300** *Cursor M.* 3289 Hir semed all hir werkes wel, Sittandlik hir watur [she] toke. ? *a* **1400** *Morte Arth.* 159 Take kepe..That they bee herberde in haste in thoos heghe chambres, Sythine sittandly in sale seruyde ther-aftyr. *c* **1430** *Pilgr. Lyf Manhode* II. vi. (1869) 78 For she wole no thing sey but sittingeliche and wel ordeyned. *c* **1450** *Mirour Saluacioun* (Roxb.) 114 In gods temple has this angulere two wallis iognt sittingly. **1530** PALSGR. 841/2 Syttyngly, *conuenablement.*

**'sitting-place.** [SITTING *vbl. sb.*]

**1.** A place to sit in; a seat. *rare.*

**1382** WYCLIF *Matt.* xxiii. 6 Sothely thei louen the first sittyng placis [L. *primos recubitus*] in sopers. *c* **1440** *Promp. Parv.* 457/1 Syttynge place, *sedile.* **1587** GOLDING *De Mornay* xxx. (1592) 472 Being required a sitting-place at his right hand or at his left. **1611** BIBLE *2 Chron.* ix. 18 There were sixe steps to the throne.., and stayes on each side of the sitting place. **1841** LANE *Arab. Nts.* I. 59 There is not one among you whose sitting-place is not written by God, whether in the fire or in paradise.

†**2.** The posteriors, the rump. *Obs.*

**1545** RAYNOLD *Byrth Mankynde* 117 A suppositar.. conueyed into the syttynge place of the chylde. **1607** TOPSELL *Four-f. Beasts* (1658) 198 Take the hairs that grow behind on the goats sitting place. **1704** *Lond. Gaz.* 4035/4 A ..Mare,..with two..white Spots in the middle of the Sitting Place.

**'sitting-room.** [SITTING *vbl. sb.*]

**1. a.** A room or apartment used for sitting in, esp. in contrast to a bed-room or kitchen.

**1771** H. PELHAM *Let.* 25 Aug. in *Mass. Hist. Soc. Coll.* (1914) LXXI. 147 The Arches at the sides of the Chimnie in the Sitting Room, I like. **1797** J. WOODFORDE *Diary* 31 Jan. (1931) V. 8 Our sitting Room smoked very much all the Morning. **1806** J. BERESFORD *Miseries Hum. Life* VI. (ed. 3) I. 96 A travelling trap for a sitting room! **1862** MRS. H. WOOD *Mrs. Hallib. Troub.* I. i. 4 The usual sitting-room of his house presented a cheerful appearance. **1894** E. BANKS *Camp. Curiosity* 34 With each sleeping-room was connected a sitting-room, where fires were kept.

*attrib.* **1852** *Beck's Florist* 172 The bouquet with which they are in the habit of daily furnishing their sitting-room table. **1895** CROCKETT *Love Idylls* (1901) 125 Behind the sitting-room door.

**b.** A portion of a poultry-house in which hens sit or hatch eggs.

**1849** D. J. BROWNE *Amer. Poultry Yard* (1855) 89 The ends of the nest box may be shifted, so that she will be in the sitting room, where she may remain..till she hatches her brood.

**2.** Room or space in which to sit or available for sitting.

**1881** 'MARK TWAIN' *Prince & Pauper* xxxii. 365 Trying to find sitting-room in the galleries. **1882** *Imperial Dict.* s.v., Sitting-room could not be got in the hall.

**sitti-sotte,** variant of SITISOT *Obs.*

**sittringee,** variant of SITRINGEE.

**situ,** in L. phr. *in situ*: see ‖IN 26.

**situal** ('sɪtjuːəl), *a. rare*⁻¹. [ad. med.L. *situālis*, f. *situs* site.] Positional.

**1856** A. BUTLER *Hist. Anc. Philos.* I. 351 Campanella.. establishes five separate worlds—situal, material, mathematical, mental, and archetypal.

**situate** ('sɪtjuːət), *ppl. a.* Also 6 situat, sytuate, 6–8 scituate. [ad. late L. *situāt-us*, pa. pple. of **situāre* (used in med.L.), f. L. *situs* site.] = SITUATED *ppl. a.*

**1523** LD. BERNERS *Froiss.* I. Pref. p. i, Mortall folke are marueylously separated, both by lande and water, and right wonderously sytuate. **1553** EDEN *Treat. New Ind.* (Arb.) 8 The Ilandes of Molucca situate in the mayne Easte Indian Sea. **1648** WILKINS *Math. Magic* I. v. 34 Now the body being situate in this rectangular forme, the weight AB must needs be augmented. **1705** tr. *Bosman's Guinea* 336 Popo being an Island Scituate in the midst of the River. **1781** GIBBON *Decl. & F.* xviii. II. 107 This large and populous city was situate about two days journey from the Tigris. **1845** HERSCHEL *Ess.* (1857) 666 A planet situate on its surface and forming a part of it. **1885** MISS BRADDON *Wyllard's Weird* III. 145 The château..was situate on low ground.

**situate** ('sɪtjuːeɪt), *v.* Also 6 situat, cituat, cytuat(e, 7 scituate. [f. ppl. stem of med.L. *situāre*: see prec.]

**1. a.** *trans.* To give a site to; to place, locate. Now often *fig.*, to establish or indicate the place of, to put in a context, to bring into defined relations.

*c* **1532** DU WES *Introd. Fr.* in *Palsgr.* 940 To situat, *colloquer.* **1542** BOORDE *Dyetary* i. (1870) 232 Where a man shulde cytuate or sette his mancyon place. **1632** LITHGOW *Trav.* v. 189 Tripoly..hath three times beene situated, and remoued in three sundry places. **1697** POTTER *Antiq. Greece* II. x. (1715) 292 The rapidness of the Torrent carry'd back those Islands.., not situating them in the same place as at first. **1726** LEONI *Alberti's Archit.* I. 86/1 The Ancients dedicated their Buildings.., and situated them in the best air they cou'd find out. **1953** *Sunday Times* 20 Sept. 5/7 From Baudelaire to Balchin, Swinburne to Sansom, Virginia Woolf to Angus Wilson, he situates us all, and hands out a ticket to the celestial garden-party of modern literature which assigns us to our table. **1961** *Encounter* May 49/2 The key to 'situating' her..is to grasp..that she was not an 'Edwardian natural' at all. **1964** E. PALMER tr. *Martinet's Elem. General Linguistics* ii. 44 Their linguistic behaviour, whereby *maison* appears in exactly the same contexts in which I would situate it myself. **1973** *Mod. Eucharistic Agreement* 74 We have sought..to situate the role of the presiding minister in relation to the sacerdotal ministry of the Church. **1977** *Proc. Roy. Soc. Med.* LXX. 425/2 Since I know less about medicine than about Molière, I have woven into my paper a brief review of his career with a view to situating the seven comedies in which medicine is parodied or satirized. **1982** *Times Lit. Suppl.* 13 Aug. 872/1 The title of John Allett's book indicates that this is where he wishes to situate Hobson.

**b.** With personal object.

**1597** A. M. tr. *Guillemeau's Fr. Chirurg.* 23/2 We must first of all situate the patient towardes the light. **1652** *Persuasive* 4 They meant to situate them in a higher condition then they were themselves. **1790** *Bystander* 178 It was thought proper to situate them between the audience and the stage. **1824** LANDOR *Imag. Conv.* Wks. 1853 I. 1 *note*, As a painter would situate a beggar under a triumphal arch.

*refl.* **1791** PAINE *Rights of Man* (ed. 4) 107 They situated themselves in three separate chambers.

**c.** To subject to circumstances; to place in a certain situation.

**1896** *Harper's Mag.* Apr. 656/2 He would violate his promises, and that would so situate her that she would not be able to keep hers.

†**2.** *intr.* To have, or take up, a certain situation or position. *Obs.*

**1583** STOCKER *Civ. Warres Lowe C.* IV. 46b, The Countries nere aboute Friselande scituatyng betweene Eems, and Lauwers. **1627** HAKEWILL *Apol.* (1630) 286 As many steeles as touch that vertuous stone..Together move themselves, and situate together.

Hence **'situating** *vbl. sb.*

**1726** LEONI *Alberti's Archit.* I. 84/1 The Ancients in the situating of their smaller Temples..turned their fronts so as they might be seen from the Sea.

**situated** ('sɪtjuːeɪtɪd), *ppl. a.* [f. as SITUATE *ppl. a.* + -ED[1].]

**1.** Of places or things: Placed, located.

**1560** DAUS tr. *Sleidane's Comm.* 116 Asperge situated on a verey hyghe mountayne standyng alone. *a* **1586** SIDNEY *Arcadia* III. (Sommer) 299 While he cast his eye about,.. cursing all Ilands in being euill scituated. **1650** T. B[AYLEY] *Worcester's Apoph.* 13 A place so proudly scituated, that you might as well command all the Countrey. **1699** MAUNDRELL *Journ. Jerus.* (1749) 153 It is scituated in the Wilderness. **1780** *Mirror* No. 95, His estate..is situated in an agreeable neighbourhood. **1808** CRUTTWELL *Univ. Gazetteer* (ed. 2) III, *Oxford*, a city..situated on a gentle eminence. **1868** LOCKYER *Elem. Astron.* §83 The great nebula of Orion is situated in the part of the constellation occupied by the sword-handle.

**b.** Used attributively, chiefly with advs.

**1601** CHESTER *Love's Mart.* (1878) 77 What famous towne and situated Seate Is that huge Building that is made by Art? **1854** GREENWOOD *Haps & Mishaps* 120 Belfast is a handsomely-situated and well-built town. **1875** W. MCILWRAITH *Guide Wigtownshire* 94 The..finely-situated ..Endcliffe House.

**2.** Of persons: Placed in relation to, or in respect of, circumstances.

**1702** C. MATHER *Magn. Chr.* VII. 110 There have been some rich Men, that were finely Scituated, and had all things richly to Enjoy. **1806** A. KNOX *Rem.* (1844) I. 74 In one way or other, he will still, as he is situated, cultivate the Communion of Saints. **1857** C. BRONTE *Professor* vi, It was impossible for me to be thus situated, and not feel the angel or the demon of my race at work within me.

**situation** (sɪtjuː'eɪʃən). Also 5 setuacyon, 6 syt-, situacion, sytuation, 6–8 scituation (7 citt-). [a. F. *situation* (†*sit-*, *scituacion*, etc., = Sp. *situacion*, It. *situazione*), or ad. med.L. *situātio*, n. of action f. *situāre*, f. L. *situs* site.]

**I. 1. a.** The place, position, or location *of* a city, country, etc., in relation to its surroundings.

**1490** CAXTON *Eneydos* xii. 44 Haue in mynde..the setuacyon of thy cyte newely fowunded. **1530** PALSGR. 270/2 Sytuacion of a towne, *assiete*. **1553** EDEN *Treat. New Ind.* (Arb.) 8 The situation of the cytie of Saba in Ethiopia vnder Egipt. **1596** WARNER *Alb. Eng.* x. lviii. (1602) 253 France,.. whose Scituation so Spaynes scattred Realmes disioynes. **1636** DAVENANT *Platonick Lovers* I. i, The scituation of this house hath but a while employed his eyes without. *a* **1687** PETTY *Pol. Arith.* (1690) 3 The same must be attributed to the Scituation of the Land. **1719** W. WOOD *Surv. Trade* 5 Our Native Riches and apt Scituation for Commerce. **1796** C. MARSHALL *Gardening* iii. (1813) 26 The situation of a garden should be..rather low than high. **1842** CUNNINGHAM *Revels at Crt.* 223 In one [plan] the situation of the music room is clear enough; viz. at the side of the stage.

**b.** Used without *of* (but implying this).

**1560** DAUS tr. *Sleidane's Comm.* 210b, The Castell was kept agaynst them which for the situation was unprennable. **1610** HOLLAND *Camden's Brit.* 677 The high situation upon an hill. **1665–6** *Phil. Trans.* I. 262 As for the Scituation—he chooses that side or declivity of a Hill. **1781** GIBBON *Decl. & F.* xix. II. 129 Their prison was an ancient palace,..the situation was pleasant, the buildings stately. **1886** *Encycl. Brit.* XXI. 243/2 The situation as a whole is far more beautiful than that of Jerusalem.

**c.** Without article.

**1553** EDEN *Treat. New Ind.* (Arb.) 14 The chiefe cytie.. is in situacion..much lyke vnto the cytie of Milayne. **1611** BIBLE *Ps.* xlviii. 2 Beautifull for situation..is mount Sion. **1635** A. STAFFORD *Fem. Glory* (1869) 76 Places as eminent in scituation as she in sweetnesse of disposition. **1820** MISS MITFORD in L'Estrange *Life* (1870) II. v. 119 Edinburgh is the finest town for situation in Europe.

**d.** With *a* (usually followed by an adj.).

**1565** COOPER *Thesaurus*, *Positio campestris*, a situation in a playne champion countrey. **1610** HOLLAND *Camden's Brit.* I. 429 Westminster..had a pleasant situation amongst fruitfull fields and greene grounds [etc.]. **1663** COWLEY *Verses & Ess.* (1669) 133 We ought in the choice of a Scituation to regard above all things the Healthfulness of the place. **1748** *Anson's Voy.* II. x. 236 Manila itself is in a very healthy situation. **1797** *Encycl. Brit.* (ed. 3) II. 246/1 Such a situation as might be agreeable..to the architect. **1808** J. WEBSTER *Nat. Philos.* 162 A fire burning in an open situation.

**2.** †**a.** The place occupied by something; the site *of* a building, etc. *Obs.*

**1542–3** *Act 34 & 35 Hen. VIII*, c. 25 Having sixtene fote of..the same grounde for the scituacion of the same conduicte heade. **1604** E. G[RIMSTONE] *D'Acosta's Hist. Indies* III. xvi. 172 The Citie of Mexico is seated in the same Lake, although the Spaniards have filled vp the place of the scituation with earth. *a* **1615** *Brieue Cron. Erlis of Ross* (1850) 3 The said Erll founded an abbey at Farne, quhair the situation thereof yit does appeare. **1730** A. GORDON *Maffei's Amphith.* 323 Pilasters of Stone, and Arches, would have taken up a great part of the Situation there.

**b.** A place, locality.

**1610** HOLLAND *Camden's Brit.* 260 The pleasant scituation called Beaulieu. **1667** MILTON *P.L.* I. 60 He views The dismal Situation waste and wilde, A Dungeon horrible. **1716–8** LADY M. W. MONTAGU *Lett.* I. xvi. 53 After passing these dreadful rocks, Dresden appeared to me a wonderfully agreeable situation. **1762–71** H. WALPOLE *Vertue's Anecd. Paint.* (1786) III. 105 Sir William Soames being sent embassador to Constantinople.., Vosterman accompanied him, intending to paint the delights of that situation. **1823** J. F. COOPER *Pioneers* xv, Two chairs were placed by the side of this comfortable situation.

**3. a.** Place or position of things in relation to surroundings or to each other.

*c* **1600** SHAKS. *Sonn.* cxxviii, To be so tikled they would change their state And situation with those dancing chips. **1615** CROOKE *Body of Man* 31 From the scituation some are Anterior, some Posteriour. **1675** *Phil. Trans.* X. 543 The scituation of these two conduits. **1728** CHAMBERS *Cycl.* s.v. *Resistence*, The Resistence of a Body is always equal to the greatest Weight which it will sustain in a vertical Situation, without breaking. **1792** *Baron Munchausen* i. 4, I fell..to the ground with fear; after waiting in this prostrate situation a few seconds, I heard a noise. **1813** SOUTHEY *Nelson* II. 257 Her mizen-top,..in the then situation of the two vessels, was not more than fifteen yards from that part of the deck. **1841** *Penny Cycl.* XXI. 177/1 In the three first situations the separation is sometimes called exhalation.

**b.** A place or locality in which a person resides, or happens to be for the time.

**1615** CHAPMAN *Odyss.* XXIV. 21 Those soules Idols, that the weary dead Gaue vp in earth: which in a flowry Mead Had habitable situation. **1745** P. THOMAS *Jrnl. Anson's Voy.* 18 Boisterous weather..caused us to make all manner of Dispatch to get out of that Situation. **1788** V. KNOX *Winter Even.* I. II. vii. 157 Apply in sickness to the best physician or apothecary within reach of your situation. **1817** MALTHUS *Popul.* Pref. p. iii, It was written..from the few materials which were then within my reach in a country situation. **1825** SCOTT *Betrothed* xi, Educated in a remote situation.

†**4. a.** Direction, course. *Obs.*

**1509** HAWES *Past. Pleas.* I. (Percy Soc.) 7 This is the waye and the sytuacion Unto the toure of famous doctrine.

†**b.** Surface. *Obs.* Cf. GROUND *sb.* 6b.

**1558** WARDE tr. *Alexis' Secr.* (1568) 9 Whan you wil gylte the parchemente, you shal geve it a grounde or sytuatyon wyth the white of an Egge or Gomme.

†**5. a.** The action of situating. *Obs.*

**1589** PUTTENHAM *Eng. Poesie* II. x. (Arb.) 98 By diuersitie of placing and scituation of your measures and concords.

†**b.** Settlement, occupation. *Obs.*

*c* **1650** BRADFORD *Plymouth Plant.* I. x. (Mass. Hist. Soc.) 88 They..found diverse cornfeilds, & litle runing brooks, a place (as they supposed) fitt for situation.

**II. 6. a.** The position in life, or in relation to others, held or occupied by a person.

**1710** STEELE *Tatler* No. 169 ¶4 That the very situation in a country-life does not incline men [etc.]. **1782** PRIESTLEY *Inst. Relig.* I. Pref. p. xliii, In my present situation at Birmingham. **1802** MAR. EDGEWORTH *Moral T.* (1806) I. xiv, His situation, at this printer's, was far better suited to him, than that..at the brewer's. **1831** SCOTT *Cast. Dang.* viii, I am happy that my situation, as a soldier under command, altogether dispenses with my thinking of it at all.

**b.** A post of employment; a position in which one works for wages. ***situations vacant***: jobs to be filled, *spec.* as advertised in a column or page of a newspaper; a newspaper column or page advertising jobs; also *attrib.* Also ***situations wanted***.

**1803** G. COLMAN *John Bull* III. ii. 36 Service? Nonsense.. I'll put you into a situation in town. **1813** *Examiner* 26 Apr. 265/1 He obtained the situation of army-agent. **1847** DE QUINCEY *Sp. Mil. Nun* vii, A gallant young cavalier.. offered to Catalina a situation amongst his retinue. **1885** G. ALLEN *Babylon* xvii, I took a situation. *a* **1911** D. G. PHILLIPS *Susan Lenox* (1917) II. iv. 73 Want ads..closely printed columns of advertisements of help wanted and situations wanted. **1931** M. ALLINGHAM *Look to Lady* xx. 207 I'll be readin' the Situations Vacant before I know where I am. 'E aint even left me a reference. **1944** M. LASKI *Love on Supertax* ii. 14 'Is it Situations Wanted day?'..If so, give me the outside sheet.'.. The Duke pulled his newspaper to pieces. **1949** E. COXHEAD *Wind in West* i. 19 She began to look through the situations-vacant columns in the farming papers. **1967** R. RENDELL *New Lease of Death* ix. 88 Elizabeth Crilling sat..reading the Situations Vacant in last week's local paper. **1971** D. LEES *Rainbow Company* ii. 29 An obvious commercial traveller reading the situations vacant column of the *Telegraph*.

**7. a.** Condition or state (*of* anything). ? *Obs.*

**1710** SHAFTESB. *Charac.* (1737) II. 230 That which we esteem a Happiness in one Situation of Mind, is otherwise thought of in another. **1765** A. DICKSON *Treat. Agric.* (ed. 2) 405 The land, at the end of the nine years, must be in a much better situation than before it was limed. **1793** SMEATON *Edystone L.* §148, I found the work now in the following situation.

**b.** Physical condition; state of health. In later use only *spec.* of women (see quots.).

**1749** SMOLLETT *Gil Blas* (1797) I. 117 Examine the situation of my son, and prescribe what you shall judge proper for his cure. **1780** *Mirror* No. 80, The change of situation from pimples and scales to a blooming complexion. **1792** M. RIDDELL *Voy. Madeira* 95 People in a weak debilitated situation. **1829** SCOTT *Hrt. Midl.* xv. *note*, That the woman should have concealed her situation during the whole period of pregnancy. **1848** THACKERAY *Van. Fair* xxvii, Mrs. Bunny's in an interesting situation..and has given the Lieutenant seven already.

**8.** Position of a person with regard to circumstances.

**1728** T. SHERIDAN tr. *Persius* (1739) Ded. p. iv, You are now in a Situation of taking two the most delightful Prospects that a generous Mind can have. **1768** BLACKSTONE *Comm.* III. 162 Where undue advantage is taken of the plaintiff's situation. **1791** BURKE *Corr.* (1844) III. 353 Your situation is a situation of difficulty, and nothing but great patience can carry you through it. **1830** D'ISRAELI *Chas. I*, III. xvi. 342 How true is it that men in parallel situations necessarily move on similar principles. **1860** MOTLEY *Netherl.* I. i. 1 The difficulties of his situation increased.

**9. a.** Position of affairs; combination of circumstances. Also in mod. usage, preceded by an attributive word or phrase, and designating: (*a*) the state or general circumstances of something at a particular time, as *coal situation*, etc. (and which is acknowledged to change from time to time); (*b*) a particular state of affairs or occasion existing independently, as ***standing credit situation***, ***crisis situation***, etc.

Objections have been raised to both mod. usages, but the latter is often especially decried as an ugly and sometimes tautological formation.

**1750** CHESTERF. *Lett.* ccxix. (1792) II. 343 Suppose that business and situations should..call Mr. Harte away from you. **1777** PITT in Almon *Anecd.* (1812) II. 302 This ruinous and ignominious situation..calls upon us to remonstrate in the strongest..language. **1828** SCOTT *F.M. Perth* ix, He honoured his religion..by the morality which guided his conduct in all ordinary situations. **1845** M. PATTISON *Ess.* (1889) I. 15 In a situation of the utmost difficulty and peril. **1884** *Manch. Exam.* 20 May 5/2 The financial situation is perceptibly clearer. **1934** *Times* 22 Aug. 11/3 A popular dodge at present is to add the word 'situation' or 'position' to a noun; by this means apparently it has been discovered that the most pregnant meanings can be expressed with the least effort. The 'coal situation' remains unchanged; the 'herring position' is grave. **1935** *Jrnl. Pediatrics* VI. 115 The group that is treated at the Children's Hospital,..may be received after an attempt has been made in an outlying home or hospital to make the best of a premature baby situation. **1941** J. S. HUXLEY *Uniqueness of Man* ix. 193 A crab can react to various situations—a food-situation, a hunger-situation, a fear-situation, a sex-situation. **1952** *Amer. Speech* XXVII. 13 Corn-shortage situation, draft-evasion situation. **1966** [see LEAST *a.* 1e]. **1972** *Where* Jan. 18/1 A school hall or playground, festooned with bunting, with colourful stalls and the sound of the tombola rolling, assumes less of an institutional atmosphere and more of a face-to-face primary group situation. **1973** *Art Internat.* Mar. 26/1 What comes to such galleries is filtered through all kinds of art situations. **1975** *N.Y. Times* 17 Sept. 47/3 We can run innovative or traditional programs here, whereas in an old-fashioned building the architecture limited us to traditional teaching situations. **1976** *Local Council Rev.* Summer 3 (Advt.), These chairs are ideally suitable for multiple seating situations for use in Town Halls, Village Halls, Community Centres, etc. **1977** H. FAST *Immigrants* I. 74 This is not a loan but a standing credit situation. **1978** *Oxford Times* 13 Jan. 4/3 Unless catchment areas are re-drawn Lord Williams's school will go through a crisis situation for at least five years.

*Phr.* **1856** MERIVALE *Rom. Emp.* lxiii. (1865) VIII. 3 The senate at last was master of the situation. **1870** MISS BRIDGMAN *R. Lynne* II. v. 111 He was..master of the situation.

**b.** A particular conjunction of circumstances (*esp.* one of a striking or exciting nature) under which the characters are presented in the course of a novel or play.

**1779** *Mirror* No. 31, The novellist who delineates characters by feigned circumstances and situations. **1790** CATH. GRAHAM *Lett. Educ.* 147 The conduct of her story is well conceived, her situations are in general natural. **1830** W. IRVING in *Life & Lett.* (1864) II. 446 It has some striking scenes, but I think the 'situations' are produced by rather extravagant means. **1847** *Illustr. Lond. News* 24 July 59/1 At the head of every scene is a description of the action, as a key to the musical situation. **1864** G. A. LAWRENCE *M. Dering* i, It [a book] is wildly melodramatic, and full of 'situations' from end to end.

**c.** Without article (see quots.).

**1779** SHERIDAN *Critic* III. i, This scene goes entirely for what we call situation and stage effect. *Ibid.*, There's situation for you! there's an heroic group!

**10.** *Horse-racing.* One of the first three places in order of arrival at the winning-post; a place.

**1871** 'M. LEGRAND' *Cambr. Freshm.* 34 Saying that he could lay against Blue Bell,..and that he had a little more to lay out against Whistler for a 'situation'. *c* **1887**

'THORMANBY' *Men of the Turf* 105 The three worst horses, probably, that ever monopolized the Derby 'situations'.

**11.** Special combs.: **situation comedy**, a comedy (serial) in which the humour derives largely from the particular conjunction of characters and circumstances; **situation ethics, morality**, the belief that individual circumstances or particular situations may call for flexibility in the application of moral laws; **situation report** *Mil.* (see quot. 1918); also *transf.*; **situation(s) room**, a room set aside by a military or governmental agency for giving reports on the current state of any action, operation, etc.

**1953** *TV Guide* (N.Y. Metro ed.) 23 Oct. 19/1 Ever since *I love Lucy* zoomed to the top rung on the rating ladder, it seems the networks have been filling every available half-hour with another *situation comedy. **1967** *Listener* 10 Aug. 161/1 The two best situation-comedy shows this country has ever produced are.. *Steptoe and Son* and.. *Till Death Us Do Part.* **1972** *Time* 17 Apr. 39/1 NBC plans *The Little People*, about a Hawaiian pediatrician and his pediatrician daughter, and ABC has *Temperature's Rising*, about the chief surgeon in a big city hospital. Both shows will combine the medical genre with the situation-comedy formula. [**1950** K. RAHNER in *Stimmen der Zeit* CXLV. 330 (*heading*) Situationsethik und Sündenmystik.] **1955** *Cross Currents* Winter 79/2 Father Rahner wished to demonstrate.. that ..*situation-ethics was the most modern and fashionable form of laxity; that it was.. an attempt of half-Christians to dodge the effort demanded by the notion of morality and the rigor of the law, by appealing to 'the situation'. **1966** J. FLETCHER *Situation Ethics* i. 26 Situation ethics goes part of the way with natural law, by accepting reason as the instrument of moral judgment while rejecting the notion that the good is 'given' in the nature of things, objectively. **1979** B. G. SKINNER *Robert Exon* vi. 56 The so-called Situation Ethics, where the Christian in a spirit of prayer and love decides for himself what is the right course of action to take. **1962** *Dict. Moral Theol.* 801/1 *Situation morality, carried to extremes, must not be understood as an escape from the heavy burden of moral integrity. **1918** E. S. FARROW *Dict. Mil. Terms* 561 **Situation reports*, reports designed to keep superior officers and neighboring units informed of the progress of events and any important changes in the situation or movement of their own or enemy troops. **1960** *Mag. Fantasy & SF* (N.Y.) Nov. 58/1, I assume that I will be attacked, and decide to file a situation report. **1970** C. WHITMAN *Death out of Focus* vii. 104 No doubt her precious father had telephoned her and given her the latest situation report. **1977** W. H. SAUMAREZ SMITH *Young Man's Country* ii. 33 One regular chore was the 'fortnightly confidential report' to the District Magistrate, which was a general 'situation report' about anything interesting happening in the subdivision. **1967** *Sunday Times* 21 May 7 The intelligence '*situation room' will keep the 15 permanent ambassadors of the NATO countries and their key military commands more fully up-to-date on Russia's political and military build-up than they have ever been before. **1970** M. KELLY *Spinifex* ii. 28 Hopkins was sitting on the edge of a table in the Situations Room. **1976** *National Observer* (U.S.) 28 Aug. 2/5 In the Situation Room of the White House, Secretary of State Kissinger convened the Washington Special Action Group, a subcommittee of the National Security Council, to plot possible U.S. responses to the deaths.

**situational** (sɪtjuːˈeɪʃənəl), *a.* [f. SITUATION + -AL.] Of or pertaining to a situation or situations; dependent on, determined by, or in relation to position, situation, or circumstances. ***situational analysis, logic*** (see quot. 1977[2]); ***situational ethics, morality*** = *situation ethics, morality* s.v. SITUATION 11.

**1903** *Academy* 27 June 632/1 As situational drama (if we may coin the term) always is rhetorical. **1927** *Observer* 24 Apr. 14/5 The main defect of this book seems to lie in the way in which literary or dramatic or situational clues are allowed to dictate musical judgments. **1935** *Jrnl. Philos.* XXXII. 650 Psychology has an incontestable claim if it will but stake it out and work it properly. By working at a meaningful level—not of physical stimulus and meaningless sensation—its products will be observable meaningful properties of situational things. **1945** K. R. POPPER *Open Soc.* II. xiv. 90 The method of applying a situational logic to the social sciences is not based on any psychological assumption concerning the rationality.. of 'human nature'. **1949** M. MEAD *Male & Female* xiv. 286 It [*sc.* the dating pattern] defines the relationship between a male and a female as situational. **1952** *Essays in Criticism* II. 95 The situational analogies are clear enough by the end of the first episode. **1959** J. L. M. TRIM in R. Quirk et al. *Teaching of English* iii. 87 Nouns, principal verbs, adjectives and adverbs are indefinite in number and therefore subject to primarily situational constraints. **1968** *Meta* XIII. 16 Situational meaning reflects the influence of context on utterances. Asking someone about his troubles is likely to produce different responses in a bank and in a hospital regardless of the speaker's intention. **1969** *Observer* 21 Dec. (Colour Suppl.) 38/3 As for sin—situational ethics could take care of that. **1972** K. R. POPPER *Objective Knowl.* iv. 179 By a situational analysis I mean a certain kind of tentative or conjectural explanation of some human action which appeals to the situation in which the agent finds himself. **1975** *Language for Life* (Dept. Educ. & Sci.) x. 157 It is this 'situational context', as a linguist would term it, that calls for improvisation. **1977** J. D. DOUGLAS in Douglas & Johnson *Existential Sociol.* i. 14 Man is fundamentally grounded, situational—existential. **1977** in Bullock & Stallybrass *Fontana Dict. Mod. Thought* 575/1 *Situational analysis*; *situational logic*.., an approach to the explanation of social action in which a detailed reconstruction of the circumstances of action (including both objective conditions and the participant's aims, knowledge, beliefs, values, and subjective 'definitions' of the situation) is taken as a basis for hypothesizing rational courses of action for the individual involved, through which their observed behaviour may be rendered intelligible. **1978** J. M. GUSTAFSON *Protestant & Roman Catholic Ethics* ii. 48 Rahner's criticisms warned against the radical extension of situational morality. **1980** *English World-Wide* I. 1. 3 Relating linguistic to situational factors.

Hence **situ'ationalism** = SITUATIONISM 2; **situ'ationalist** *a.*, of or pertaining to situation ethics; **situ'ationally** *adv.*, with respect to situation; in a situational manner.

**1935** *Word Study* Feb. 1/2 *Situationally* is a regular adverbial formation from the adjective situational. **1939** P. CHRISTOPHERSEN *Articles* 38 The article is of course situationally determined here. **1964** R. H. ROBINS *Gen. Linguistics* 191 A sentence is by definition grammatically complete (the alleged 'incomplete' or 'elliptical' situationally tied sentences are complete in those situations). **1970** W. K. FRANKENA in Pahel & Schiller *Readings in Contemp. Ethical Theory* 542 Views variously referred to as antinomian,.. existentialist, situationalist, or contextualist. **1971** N. H. G. ROBINSON *Groundwk. Christian Ethics* ix. 242 Nor indeed may we expect any other out-come, unless.. the logical successor to Bonhoeffer is to be found either in secularization or in situationalism. **1977** J. D. DOUGLAS in Douglas & Johnson *Existential Sociol.* i. 60 There are other reasons why we see experience as necessarily problematic, as necessarily free and situationally contingent. **1977** J. M. JOHNSON in *Ibid.* v. 161 This extreme situationalism is perhaps best illustrated by Zimmerman and Pollner's (1970) discussion of the *occasioned corpus.* **1979** *Guardian* 9 June 10/3 Since the Bible was written in a very different age from ours, its commands must be interpreted situationally.

**situationer** (sɪtjuːˈeɪʃənə(r)). [f. SITUATION + -ER[1].] In *Journalism*, an article or report constituting a general essay on a situation.

**1959** *Observer* 15 Nov. 20/5 I.T.V.'s *This Week*.. was struggling to condense an African situationer—ranging from Oxford undergraduates boycotting South African sherry to forecasts of the future of Federation and the White Highlands—and a profile of Mao Tse-tung into a few minutes each. **1972** D. BLOODWORTH *Any Number can Play* xi. 93 Ivansong had written and cabled a one-thousand-word situationer on Mekong. **1977** *Radio Times* 2–8 July 13/2 Newspapers.. had far more word-space than radio.. so newspapers found it easier to accommodate 'situationers'.

**situationism** (sɪtjuːˈeɪʃənɪz(ə)m). [f. SITUATION + -ISM.] **1.** The revolutionary ideas relating to culture associated with the Situationist International (see quot. 1971 s.v. SITUATIONIST *sb.* 1).

**1964** *Times Lit. Suppl.* 3 Sept. 781/4 Our International.. coming after the development both of our philosophy and of our art, at once refuses to proclaim any sort of doctrine and rejects the term 'situationism' as used only by enemies of the situationist programme. **1973** *Listener* 2 Aug. 152/1 The Angry Brigade['s].. communiqués suggest.. a combination of situationism and Syndicalism. **1978** *Radio Times* 28 Jan.–3 Feb. 15/3 One philosophical strain, peculiar to developed countries, was 'Situationism'. At its simplest, its followers believe the working class has been bamboozled out of its legitimate rights by a capitalist conspiracy that 'appropriated' trade unionism and socialism, then 'laundered' and returned them as harmless institutions.

**2.** Adherence to situation ethics.

**1966** J. FLETCHER *Situation Ethics* i. 29 There are various names for this approach: situationism, contextualism, occasionalism, circumstantialism, even actualism. **1977** A. KOLNAI *Ethics, Value, & Reality* vii. 145 The wide variety of reductionist and constructivist types of Ethics ranging, say, from utilitarianism to prescriptivism or from metaphysical perfectionism to situationism.

**situationist** (sɪtjuːˈeɪʃənɪst), *a.* and *sb.* [f. SITUATION + -IST; in sense A. 1 ad. Fr. *situationniste.*] **A.** *adj.* **1.** Of or pertaining to certain revolutionary views about the situation of man in modern culture (see quot. 1971, sense B. 1 below); ***Situationist International***, a movement started in Paris in the 1950s to promote these views.

**1958** *Archit. Rev.* CXXIV. 1/2 Snap judgments on the publications of the Situationist International had best be restrained until the documents have been frisked for hidden persuaders. **1963** *Listener* 31 Jan. 202/2 What she has to say about the uses of diversity seems to derive as uniquely from this particular urban scene as does the Situationist vision from the psychogeography of Paris. **1975** *Observer* (Colour Suppl.) 13 July 26/1 The sergeant discovered that the word 'spectacles' was a concept, an emblem, almost, of a group subscribing to the views of the so-called Situationist International. **1980** *Times Lit. Suppl.* 4 Apr. 387 The walls and statues of the Sorbonne were plastered with posters of Marx, Lenin, Che and Mao, with situationist slogans and Red Flags.

**2.** Dependent on or determined by circumstances; situationalist.

**1970** G. GREER *Female Eunuch* 328 Women's revolution is necessarily situationist. **1972** *Times Lit. Suppl.* 19 May 580/4 His own view involves contextual considerations without being situationist. The relevant context is that of a particular social system.

**B.** *sb.* **1.** An adherent of the Situationist International or of situationism.

**1963** *Listener* 31 Jan. 201/1 The Situationists are best-known as one of the most subversive anti-art groups of the post-war epoch. **1964** *Times Lit. Suppl.* 3 Sept. 781/5 True situationists are much more strongly opposed to all the prevailing mechanisms of culture and information. **1971** R. GOMBIN in Apter & Joll *Anarchism Today* 19 For the situationists, the bureaucratic system of industrial society has considerably increased the sum total of the exploitation and repression of man... The tremendous development of science and technology has led to the individual being completely taken over by the system; the individual is no more than a commodity.. manipulated by the specialists in cultural repression: artists, psychiatrists,.. sociologists and 'experts' of all kinds. To fight against a 'spectacular' society, in which everything is treated as a commodity and in which creative energy spends itself in the fabrication of pseudo-needs, one must attack on all fronts simultaneously. **1977** *It* May 5/1 Debord was (is?) a Situationist—a member of perhaps the most radical group to emerge in France in the years approaching the 1968 eruption: they were radical in the sense that they explored most deeply the critique of modern industrial society, which formed the ideological basis for the French upheaval.

**2.** An upholder of situation ethics.

**1966** J. FLETCHER *Situation Ethics* i. 26 The situationist follows a moral law or violates it according to love's need.

**situla** (ˈsɪtjuːlə). *Archæol.* Pl. situlae, -las. [L., = bucket.] Any of various bucket-shaped vessels. Also *attrib.*

**1897** *Knowledge* 1 Oct. 229/1 Situla (Bucket), of Apulian fabric, with scene representing Dionysos espousing Ariadne. **1905** *Brit. Mus. Guide Early Iron Age* 14 The succeeding (iron-sword) period.. is richly represented by articles decorated in the *situla* style. Such is the name given to a method of ornamenting vessels of the bucket-type.. by means of horizontal bands. **1928** D. RANDALL-MACIVER *Italy before Romans* 61 An early example of the situla or bronze bucket for which Bologna no less than Este was to become famous in future years. **1942** *Oxoniensia* VII. 45 (*caption*) Everted rim; general form approaching carinated situlas of Long Wittenham type. **1970** *Ashmolean Mus.: Rep. Visitors 1969* 14 Luristan bronze situla decorated with a feast scene. **1972** *Times* 18 May (Egypt Suppl.) p. iv/6 (*caption*) A *situla*, or temple ritual vessel.

Hence **'situlate, si'tuliform** *adjs.*, having the form of a situla.

**1937** *Oxoniensia* II. 26 The Iron Age A2 wares also call for some remark. The situliform jar passes through the usual stages of degradation, and finger-tip ornament goes out of use. **1945** *Proc. Prehistoric Soc.* XI. 32 Shouldered and situlate vessels, either plain or with simple finger-tip ornament. **1946** *Ibid.* XII. 125 A tall situliform urn which may owe some features to Iron Age A forms. **1967** *Antiquaries Jrnl.* XLVII. 181 The rim of a coarse, situlate jar with short upright rim and weak shoulder of Early Iron Age affinities.

**sit-up**, *sb.* and *a.* [See SIT *v.* 27.]

**A.** *sb.* **1.** A surprise. *rare*[−1].

**1483** BP. LANGTON in *Christ Ch. Lett.* (Camden) 46, I trow.. thai shal have a sit up or ever the Kyng departe fro York.

**2. a.** An act of sitting up.

**1843** R. CARLTON *New Purchase* I. ix. 64 This sit-up we instantly performed—as well, at least, as we could.

**b.** A physical exercise in which the upper half of the body is raised to a sitting from a supine posture. Also *attrib.*

**1955** V. FALLON *Figure Correction & Beauty for You* xx. 112 Sit-up—2 sets of twenty repetitions. **1960** J. HEWITT *Yoga* III. 56 The well-known 'sit-up' exercise... Paschimatanasana differs from an ordinary sit-up in that the movement is continued until the face comes close to the knees. **1971** A. A. MICHELE *You don't have to Ache* 93 Do five to ten sit-ups in a curling fashion bringing your body straight forward. Then do five sit-ups twisting your body to the left, and five twisting your body to the right. **1977** J. F. FIXX *Compl. Bk. Running* xv. 179 To strengthen your stomach muscles,.. do twenty or so sit-ups with your knees bent.

**B.** *adj.* Used for sitting up in. Also, at or against which one sits up.

**1902** BARNES-GRUNDY *Thames Camp* 178 The lounge chairs are canvas, the sit-up chairs are rush seated. **1960** *Times* 16 Mar. (Canberra Suppl.) p. v/4 A tavern, with a sit-up bar. **1980** L. BIRNBACH et al. *Official Preppy Handbk.* 93 To Buy (or otherwise obtain as soon as possible:.. Sit-up pillow.

**'sit-upon.** *colloq.* [f. SIT *v.*] **1.** In *pl.*: Trousers, breeches. (Cf. SIT-DOWN *sb.* 2.)

**1841** J. T. HEWLETT *Parish Clerk* I. 126 With a pair of the master's sit-upons that wanted reparation. **1857** 'C. BEDE' *Verdant Green* III. x, They weren't dressed in tall hats.. and velvet sit-upons.

**2.** The buttocks, the posterior.

**1920** C. A. W. MONCKTON *Some Experiences of New Guinea Resident Magistrate* xxv. 302 You have a big boil on your sit-upon. **1955** E. WAUGH *Officers & Gentlemen* II. i. 169 Mrs Stitch immediately sat in the place he vacated. 'Hot-sit-upon,' she remarked. **1976** 'J. WELCOME' *Grand National* viii. 130 I've got something to eat off and to put me sit-upon on in the evenings.

‖**situs** (ˈsaɪtəs). [L.] **1.** Situation, position. *rare.*

**1701** RAY *Creation* (ed. 3) II. 229 It was convenient that man should have such a figure or Situs of the parts of his body that he might conveniently look upwards. **1728** CHAMBERS *Cycl.* s.v., Things depending on the Situs of Lines and Figures. **1890** *Pop. Sci. Monthly* XXXVI. 289 The future situs of the cotton manufacture of the United States. **1891** *Tablet* 28 Feb. 334 It enables a Catholic to see as he never otherwise could the precise situs and shape of ultra-Protestant convictions.

**2.** *Law.* **a.** Chiefly *U.S.* The place to which for purposes of legal jurisdiction or taxation a property is deemed to belong.

**1834** J. STORY *Commentaries on Conflict of Laws* xiv. 462 Moveables are, for many purposes, to be deemed to have no *situs*, except that of the domicil of the owner. **1884** R. DESTY *Amer. Law of Taxation* I. v. 97 The legislature has the power to fix the *situs* of property for purposes of taxation. **1926** *Pacific Reporter* CCXLVIII. 341/1 Actual situs of personal property is necessary for taxation... In order to tax the cars in controversy as personal property, they must have actual situs at common law in this state. **1956** *All England Law Reports* 19 Jan. 134 If, however, the situs of the debt be German, he submits that the moratorium law is confiscatory. **1970** *Southwestern Reporter* CCCCXLV. Ser. II. 57/1 Bulldozers, which were regularly moved from one temporary location to another, did not have actual situs of their own, and were not subject to ad valorem taxation. **1977** JOHNS & GREENFIELD *Dymond's Capital Transfer Tax* xxiii. 491 Seven of the agreements provide *situs* codes (for determining the locality of assets).

**b.** *U.S.* A work-site, esp. (***common situs***) one occupied by two or more employers. Freq. *attrib.*

**1950** *Fed. Suppl.* XCI. 698/2 The Act..was intended to keep the situs of a labor dispute confined to actual functions of the parties involved... It is 'stranger picketing', i.e., picketing in aid of a secondary boycott. **1952** *Cornell Law Q.* Winter 247 In such 'common-situs cases' additional criteria necessarily must be invoked. **1959** *Missouri Law Rev.* Jan. 89 Common-premises or common-situs picketing occurs where a labor organization pickets premises where the employees of two or more employers are working and the labor organization has a dispute with only one of the employers. **1977** *Time* 4 July 47/1 With smoothly coordinated pressure, business lobbyists have managed..to defeat organized labor's bid to pass a common situs picketing bill that would have allowed a single union to shut down a construction site.

**situs inversus** ('saɪtəs, 'siːtəs ɪn'vɜːsəs). *Med.* [L., in full *situs inversus viscerum* inverted disposition of the internal organs.] The condition in which the organs of the body are transposed through the sagittal plane (so that the heart lies on the right side, etc.).

**1896** J. T. WHITTAKER in T. L. Stedman *Twentieth Century Pract. Med.* IV. 59 Malformations of individual organs are very rare in typical situs inversus. **1966** WRIGHT & SYMMERS *Systemic Path.* I. xv. 484/2 Situs inversus due to malrotation of the foetal gut..is very rare. **1976** *Sci. Amer.* Sept. 68/2 Patients exhibiting situs inversus frequently suffer from chronic sinusitis and bronchitis.

**situtunga** (sɪtʊ'tʌŋgə). Also **sitatunga**. [Swahili.] A medium-sized brown or greyish antelope, *Tragelaphus spekei*, found in east and central Africa, and distinguished by elongated, splayed hooves that enable the animal to walk on marshy ground, and spiral horns in the male. Also *attrib.*

**1881** F. C. SELOUS *Hunter's Wanderings Afr.* x. 158 These men told me that in some thick beds of reeds near their town were some situtunga antelope. **1899** [see HARNESSED *ppl. a.* 4]. **1920** G. D. H. CARPENTER *Naturalist on Lake Victoria* iv. 80 The thunderous snortings of hippos, the muffled bark of the Situtunga, break in. **1947** L. HASTINGS *Dragons are Extra* viii. 191 The highly specialised sitatunga, lord of the swamps. **1949** *Cape Argus* 11 Aug. 7/6 Lions in the swamp appeared to live on Situtunga bush buck. **1955** P. A. BUXTON *Nat. Hist. Tsetse Flies* vi. 144 On some uninhabited islands in Lake Victoria, Uganda, the sitatunga antelope (*Limnotragus s. spekii*) multiplies and with it *G. palpalis*. **1973** *Stand. Encycl. S. Afr.* IX. 650/1 The sitatunga has coarse, shaggy hair.

**sit vac:** see SIT *sb.*[2]

**Sitwellian** (sɪt'wɛlɪən), *a.* and *sb.* [f. the name *Sitwell* (see below) + -IAN.] **A.** *adj.* Of, pertaining to, or characteristic of the writers Edith Sitwell (1887–1964), and her brothers Osbert (1892–1969) and Sacheverell (1897–1988). **B.** *sb.* An admirer of the Sitwells.

**1923** A. BENNETT in *Adelphi* Aug. 237 This book..is a characteristically Sitwellian beauty. **1927** *Observer* 5 June 4 The Sitwells are known to everyone who has even a casual acquaintance with modern literature, though many who talk of them seem to have read about their doings rather than studied them in their own works. This is a necessary consequence of the Sitwellian methods of publicity. **1937** *Times Lit. Suppl.* 1 May 322/1 Mr. Courtenay's extremely modern simile with its oozy vowels—Sitwellian, surely. **1952** *Scrutiny* Oct. 6 Rajan's examination of Milton's verse keeps turning into Sitwellian clap-trap. **1960** V. SACKVILLE-WEST *Let.* 23 Mar. in H. Nicolson *Diaries* (1968) 382 Edith has built up her personality in many fortuitous ways—her strange appearance,..and all the Sitwellian legend. **1978** J. PEARSON *Façades* xi. 196 The society was conducted with true Sitwellian panache. *Ibid.* 212 Thomas Balston at Duckworth's—himself an enthusiastic Sitwellian—had taken over from Grant Richards as the trio's publisher.

So **'Sitwellism**, the style or behaviour of the Sitwells.

**1927** R. L. MÉGROZ *Three Sitwells* vi. 105 The phenomenon of Sitwellism. **1932** F. R. LEAVIS *New Bearings in Eng. Poetry* ii. 73 The opposition to the Georgians was already..(just after the war) Sitwellism. **1981** V. GLENDINNING *E. Sitwell* v. 80 The Sitwells defence was attack... Sitwellism at its silliest and most inflated.

**sity,** obs. form of SIGHTY *a.*

**sitz bath** ('sɪtsbɑːθ, -æ-). Also **sitz-bath**. [ad. G. *sitzbad*, f. *sitzen* to sit.]

**1.** A bath in which one sits; a hip-bath.

**1849** CLARIDGE *Cold Water-Cure* 54 The Sitz or Sitting Bath. By this is to be understood a hip bath: that used at Gräfenberg is a small flat tub. **1884** *Health Exhib. Catal.* 94/1 Combined Spray and Sitz Bath..Copper Sitz Bath in Cabinet Work.

**2.** A bath taken by means of this.

**1852** BRISTED *Five Years Eng. Univ.* (ed. 2) 165 The daily purgatory of wet sheets, sitz baths, and the like. **1861** GEO. ELIOT in Cross *Life* II. 318 We were..looking slightly blue after our sitz baths. **1899** *Allbutt's Syst. Med.* VII. 750 A hot sitz-bath may be used.

‖**Sitzfleisch** ('zɪtsflaɪʃ). Also **sitzfleisch**. [Ger., f. *sitz-en* to sit + *fleisch* flesh.] The ability to endure or persist in some activity.

*a* **1930** D. H. LAWRENCE *Lovely Lady* (1932) 165 They simply hadn't enough *Sitzfleisch* to squat under a bho-tree. **1971** *Atlantic Monthly* May 106 It takes not only special training but a liberal endowment of *Sitzfleisch* to hear one of his [*sc.* Messiaen's] pieces out from one end to the other. **1975** *Harpers & Queen* May 127/3 Lenny hadn't got the patience, the concentration, the sitzfleisch. **1977** *Time* 26 Dec. 31/1 Some of the games now filtering into the general consciousness are distance runs indeed, taking anything from several hours to several months to play, and requiring formidable *Sitzfleisch* (German for sitting flesh).

‖**Sitz im Leben** ('zɪts ɪm leːbən). *Theol.* Also hyphened. [Ger., lit. 'place in life'.] In Biblical criticism, the circumstances in which a tradition developed, considered as determining the form of that tradition.

**1934** M. DIBELIUS *From Tradition to Gospel* i. 7 The categories enable us to draw a conclusion as to what is called the 'Sitz im Leben', i.e. the historical and social stratum in which precisely these literary forms were developed. **1955** D. E. NINEHAM *Stud. Gospels* 230 They [*sc.* the Form-critics] have shown the importance of the factor they call *Sitz-im-Leben* in the preservation of the material included in our gospels. **1956** *Scottish Jrnl. Theol.* IX. 403 Events in Jesus' life are seen by Mark from the *Sitz im Leben* which they have in the early Church. **1976** *Expository Times* LXXXVII. v. 139/2 We may therefore accept without hesitation the doctrine of *Sitz im Leben*, provided that we clearly understand what it is and what are its limitations.

**sitzkrieg** ('sɪtskriːg). Also **Sitzkrieg**. [Formed on the analogy of BLITZKRIEG, as if f. G. *sitz-en* to sit + *krieg* war.] A war, or part of a war, marked by a (relative) absence of active hostilities; *spec.* that phase of the war of 1939–45 lasting from September 1939 to May 1940; a 'phoney war'. Also *fig.*

**1940** *N.Y. Times* 21 Feb. 4/7 The R.A.F. referred to the war as a 'Sitzkrieg', which it translated as 'sit-down war'. **1940** *Newsweek* 11 Mar. 28/2 The European 'sitzkrieg' has definitely taught the usually turbulent Balkan states that their safety and independence can best be attained through at least a modicum of unity. **1943** *Sun* (Baltimore) 12 Nov. 1/6 (*heading*) Temporary 'sitzkrieg' on Garigliano sector. **1954** W. K. HANCOCK *Country & Calling* vii. 187 The *sitzkreig* had at least given me a golden chance to visit West Africa and had thereby enabled me to finish my book. **1967** B. B. GILBERT *Britain Since 1918* iv. 118 As the German conquest of Poland had been termed a '*blitzkrieg*', a lightning war, the new phase of the war that lasted from the end of September [1939] until the beginning of April was frequently designated a '*sitzkrieg*'. **1970** *Courier-Mail* (Brisbane) 22 Dec. 3/1 (*heading*) Old men prepare for sit-in battle... Thirty-six old men..yesterday settled down to a 'sitzkrieg' in the Battle of Rosebank—the Glebe, Sydney, aged men's home. **1980** *Christian Sci. Monitor* (Midwestern ed.) 4 Dec. 6/1 Most observers think the two armies will become involved in a 'sitzkrieg', meaning a long military waiting game.

**sitzmark** ('sɪtsmɑːk). *Skiing.* [App. f. G. *sitz-en* to sit + MARK *sb.*[1]] The impression in the snow made by a skier falling backwards on his posterior; an act of so falling. Hence **'sitzmark** *v. intr.*, to fall in this manner.

**1935** *Punch* 13 Feb. 176/2 One seems to see as in an inspired flash..the insidious vileness of a sitzmark. [*Note*] Deliberately sitting down in the snow when no other method of stopping seems possible. Very degrading. **1935** *Sierra Club Bull.* Feb. 7 One should be ashamed to make a long descent by 'sitzmarking' at every turn. **1947** F. S. SMYTHE *Again Switzerland* ii. 22 While to fall backwards and *sitzmark* is the hallmark of the craven. **1964** *Harper's Bazaar* Nov. 140/2 The wintersporter who prefers..a bar stool to sitting repeatedly in a *sitzmark*. **1973** P. A. WHITNEY *Snowfire* xvi. 306, I sat down and let my skis go out from under me, sliding a little way on the seat of my pants, leaving sitzmarks behind me. **1977** *Globe & Mail* (Toronto) 16 Nov. 37/6 My rump has had much practice from last winter's skiing—sitzmarks were almost second nature to it.

**siue, siuier,** obs. forms of SIEVE, SIEVIER.

**Siva** ('ʃiːvə, 'siːvə). Also **Shiva**. [a. Skr. *śiva*, lit. 'the auspicious one'.] **1.** The third deity of the Hindu triad, to whom are attributed the powers of reproduction and dissolution. Also *transf.*, a representation of this deity.

**1788** *Asiatick Res.* I. 248 Siva is believed to have *three* eyes. **1862** J. B. SPEID *Our Last Years in India* iv. 73 The horrid Churruckpuja..festival..in honour of Kali, the consort of Siva, the God of Destruction. **1903** J. C. OMAN *Mystics, Ascetics, & Saints of India* vii. 110 Siva, regarded by his special followers as the Supreme Being, commands their adoration in many different and even seemingly contradictory characters. **1931** *Times Lit. Suppl.* 28 May 429/2 Soon he had brought a haunting fear to the minds of several people, turning upon the possession of an old bronze dancing Siva. **1963** *Times* 23 May 14/6 They [*sc.* deformed cattle] are taken as avatars of..the riding bull of the Lord Shiva. **1977** *Jrnl. R. Soc. Arts* CXXV. 583/2 The famous dancing Siva from Ujjain in the Gwālior Museum.

**2.** *attrib.* and *Comb.*, as ***Siva-complex***, ***-worship***.

**1876** *Encycl. Brit.* V. 243/1 The Mahávinayaka Peak..has been consecrated for ages to Siva-worship by ascetics and pilgrims. **1937** H. NICOLSON *Helen's Tower* ix. 191 Was it (as the Viennese might further contend) some Siva-complex, some dread of the destruction-principle? **1967** SPATE & LEARMONTH *India & Pakistan* (ed. 3) vi. 174 Artistically, the best things are a handful of..seals. These..carry an undeciphered script, and their symbolism suggests that some elements in Hinduism, notably Siva-worship, may stem from Harappan culture.

**Sivaism** ('siːvəɪz(ə)m). Also **Shivaism**. [f. Skr. *Siva* 'the auspicious one' (see prec.) + -ISM.] The special worship of Siva, the third deity of the Hindu triad, to whom are attributed the powers of reproduction and dissolution. Cf. *S(h)aivism* s.v. SAIVA.

**1901** *Edin. Rev.* 7 Jan. 32 The lotus of Sivaism and of Isis. **1905** *Q. Rev.* July 200 The temper of Sivaism is not that of Buddhism. **1931** *Times Lit. Suppl.* 19 Mar. 228/2 Vishnuism and Shivaism. **1962** A. HUXLEY *Island* xi. 178 The local brand of Mahayana Buddhism, with a bit of Shivaism, probably, on the side.

**Sivaist** ('ʃiːvəɪst, 'siːvəɪst), *a.* [f. as prec. + -IST.] Of or pertaining to the worship of Siva.

**1937** M. COVARRUBIAS *Island of Bali* I. vii. 173 It was within this period, from the seventh to the ninth centuries, ..that the finest monuments of Java were built, the Buddhist *Borobudur* and the Sivaist *Lora Djongrang* in Prambanan.

**Sivaistic** (siːvə'ɪstɪk), *a.* [f. as SIVAISM + -ISTIC.] Of or pertaining to the worship of Siva.

**1891** in *Cent. Dict.*

**Sivaite** ('siːvəaɪt). Also **Shivaite, shivaite, Sivite**. [f. as prec. + -ITE.] One who specially worships Siva; an adherent of Sivaism. Also *attrib.* (Cf. SIVITE.) Cf. *S(h)aivite* s.v. SAIVA.

**1880** *Encycl. Brit.* XIII. 815/2 Sankara Acharya, the great Sivaite reformer of the 8th century. **1882** *Missionary Herald* (Boston) 8 Feb. 68 Considerable opposition displayed by the Sivites. **1883** *Encycl. Brit.* XV. 185/1 The Sivaites are most numerous in the extreme south and on the west coast. **1892** *Missionary Herald* (Boston) Sept. 369 They answered that they were Sivite boys, and could not say Christian prayers. **1958** A. HUXLEY *Let.* 22 June (1969) 850 The process of turning old Shivaite-cum-Mahayana-Buddhist society into something combining the best features of East and West was inaugurated in the eighteen-forties by a Scottish surgeon. **1962** —— *Island* vi. 82 We're still Buddhists or Shivaites. **1970** *Guardian* 10 Aug. 9/4 A 1,000-year-old shivaite temple ..on the border between Cambodia and Thailand.

Hence **Siva'itic** *a.* (*Funk's Stand. Dict.*).

**Sivan** ('siːvɑːn). Also 4–5 **Ciban, Siban, Siwan**. [a. Heb. *siwān*.] The ninth month of the Jewish year, though named third in the traditional month-list, corresponding to the latter part of May and the earlier part of June.

*c* **1382** BIBLE (Wycliffe) *Esther* viii. 9 The thridde moneth, that is clepid Ciban [*later text* Siban], that is June. **1535** *Ibid.* (Coverdale), In the thirde moneth, that is the moneth Siuan. **1737** W. WHISTON tr. *Josephus' Jewish War* III. vii. §29 This fight happened upon the twentieth day of the month Desius (Sivan). **1816** J. ALLEN *Mod. Judaism* xxi. 386 The feast of Pentecost is on the *sixth* day of the month of *Sivan*, the *fiftieth* of the *Omer*. **1891** M. FRIEDLÄNDER *Jewish Relig.* ii. 393 The Feast of Weeks, the 6th and 7th of *Sivan*, commemorates..an historical event. **1952** *Jewish Q. Rev.* XLIII. II. 181 On Siwan 7..Moses ascended the mountain. **1977** *Jewish Chron.* 20 May 17/1 Friday, May 20 (Sivan 3), Sabbath begins in London at 8.38.

**sivathere** ('sɪvəθɪə(r)). [Anglicized form of next.] = SIVATHERIUM.

**1847** ANSTED *Anc. World* xiv. 334 The Sivathere..had another pair [of horns] placed more towards the back of the head. **1894** LYDEKKER *Roy. Nat. Hist.* II. 337 By far the largest of all Ruminants was the gigantic Indian sivathere.

‖**sivatherium** (sɪvə'θɪərɪəm). *Palæont.* [mod.L., f. *Siva* the Hindu god + Gr. θηρίον wild beast.] A fossil ruminant of great size, with four horns, discovered in the Siwalik or Sub-Himalayan hills in Northern India.

**1835** FALCONER & CAUTLEY in *Asiatic Res.* XIX. I. 2 We have named the fossil, *Sivatherium* [etc.]. *Ibid.* 22 The food of the Sivatherium was less herbaceous than that of existing horned ruminants. **1851** MANTELL *Petrifactions* 457 The living Sivatherium must have resembled an immense Gnu or Antelope. **1886** GEIKIE *Class-bk. Geol.* xxvi. (1903) 393 The *Sivatherium* and *Bramatherium*—colossal, four-horned creatures, allied to our living antelopes and prong-bucks.

**sive** (also 5–6, 9 **syve**, 6 **syue, siue**), variant spelling of *cive* CHIVE *sb.*[1]

*c* **1440** *Promp. Parv.* 457/2 Syvys, herbe. **1562** TURNER *Herbal* II. (1568) 101 The moste parte of the writers of herballes in Germany, teach that our Sive..is porrum sativum. **1580** HOLLYBAND *Treas. Fr. Tong*, *Civot, cive*, or *Civette*, a chiboll, siues, scalions. **1707** MORTIMER *Husb.* (1721) II. 171 Sives are a diminutive kind of Leek. **1874** MRS. WHITCOMBE *Bygone Days in Devon & Cornw.* 47 The fairies had even their musicians, whose hautboys were of syves.

**sive,** obs. form of SIEVE.

† **'sived.** *Obs.* [OE. *sifeþa*, etc., f. the same stem as *sife* sieve.] *pl.* Siftings, bran.

*c* **725** *Corpus Gloss.* F 386 *Furfures*, sifiðan. *c* **888** K. ÆLFRED *Boeth.* xxxiv. § 11 Ðæt meolo ðurgcrypð ælc ðyrel, & þa syfeða [*v.r.* siofoða] weorðað asyndred. *c* **1000** *Sax. Leechd.* II. 250 Oferwylle on þam selfan ecede sifeþan. *c* **1440** *Promp. Parv.* 78/2 Cyuedys, of mele, or brynne, *furfur*, *cantabrum*. *Ibid.* 457/1 Syvedys, or brynne, or palyys, *furfur*.

Hence † **'sivedy** *a.*, full of bran. *Obs.*

**13..** *Metr. Hom.* (Vernon MS.) in *Herrig's Archiv* LVII. 290 Atte laste on Bord was brouht A Lof þat payed him riht nouht; Blac hit was and siuedi.

**siver**, variant of Sc. SYVER, drain.

†**'siver**, *v. Obs. rare.* [Origin obscure.] *intr.* To simmer. Hence **'sivering** *vbl. sb.*

**1601** HOLLAND *Pliny* xx. ix, Colestocke ashes set over the fire untill it siver only, or have one walme at the most, is good for spasmes. *Ibid.* XXIII. ix, If they haue a little siuering or waulm ouer the fire.

† **sivet, sivil.** *Obs.* (See quots.)

**1607** MARKHAM *Caval.* VI. ix. 54 He shall not suffer any holes to be cut through the tree for to passe the stirrop leathers thorowe, but to haue stronge Siuills of yron wel reuited thorow the tree wherein to put your stirrop leathers. **1688** HOLME *Armoury* III. iii. 93/2 The *Sivets*, which are square rings in Plates, three on each side the tree to put the straps too. *Ibid.* ix. 397/1 The Sivett, is a square barr of Iron or square-Buckle, without a tonge, set to the sides of the Sadle-tree,..to hang the Straps at for the Girth, and the Leathers for the Stirrops.

**Sivite**, variant of SIVAITE.

**'sivvens.** *Obs.* exc. *Hist.* Also 8 cevenns, 8–9 sibbens (-ans, -ins), 9 sivens. [ad. local Gael. *suibhean* (commonly *suibheag* or *subhag*) raspberry: see quot. 1776.] An infectious skin disease formerly prevalent in Scotland.

**1762** *Forfeited Estates Papers* (S.H.S.) 235 A Distemper commonly called the Cevenns, which is believed to have been brought originally..by Oliver Cromwell's army. **1776** PENNANT *Tour in Scot.* II. App. 447 A loathsome and very infectious disease of the venereal kind, called the *Sivvens*... Sometimes a fungus appears in various parts of the body, resembling a raspberry, in the Erse language called *Sivven*. **1792** *Statist. Acc. Scot.* V. 146 The disease called Sibbins.. has made its appearance once or twice in this parish. **1798** J. PATERSON in Beddoes *Contrib. Phys. & Med. Knowl.* (1799) 410 The sibbens affecting the surface of the body, more than the common lues. **1810** J. ADAMS *Hunter's Treat. Ven. Dis.* VII. 566 Of this kind [non-syphilitic] is the sivvens of Scotland. **1822–7** GOOD *Study Med.* (1829) III. 167 Yaws have been supposed by some writers to be a species of lues, and especially of that which in Scotland is denominated sibbens or sivens. **1822** HIBBERT *Desc. Shetl. Isl.* 542 There is a great variety of cutaneous complaints... Sibbens, a disease hitherto ill defined, I saw occasionally. **1851** in W. Cramond *Ann. Banff* (1891) I. 369 A case of 'Sibbans' reported by Dr. Whyte in the Gallowhill.

**siw(e**, obs. forms of SUE *v.*

**Siwalik** (sɪ'wɑːlɪk). Also †**Sewalik**; **Sivalik.** [Hind.]

**a.** The name of the southern outlying foot hills of the Himalayas, extending from Sikkim through Nepal and India to Pakistan, used *attrib.* with reference to the thick sequence of fluviatile and lacustrine sediments, rich in fossil vertebrates, of which they are composed and the time in the Pliocene (or late Miocene) to early Pleistocene when they were deposited.

**1836** CAUTLEY & FALCONER in *Asiatic Researches* XIX. xiii. 200 There existed along with the Mastodon, Sivatherium, Fossil Camel, &c. of the Sivalik deposits, a large distinct species of Bear, equalling if not exceeding the largest known of the genus. **1864** *Q. Jrnl. Geol. Soc.* XX. 383 He refers the rocks observed [in the northwestern Himalayas] to the following formations:—1. The fluvio-lacustrine series. 2. The Siwalik series...6. The Palæozoic series. **1902** *Encycl. Brit.* XXV. 466/1 Dr. Dubois.. excavated from a bed, considered by him to be of Sivalik formation (Pliocene), a thighbone which competent anatomists decide to be human. **1908** H. B. C. SOLLAS tr. *Suess's Face of Earth* III. IV. vi. 218 Sediments possibly of Siwalik age. **1955** BROWN & DEY *India's Mineral Wealth* (ed. 3) xix. 697 The outer margin of the Himalayas is formed by a continuous fringe of foot-hills built of the rocks of the Siwalik Series. **1975** A. M. DAVIES et al. *Tertiary Faunas* (ed. 2) II. vi. 359 From the Indian subcontinent the Middle Siwalik succession is of Late Miocene equivalent.

**b.** *absol.* The Siwalik series or period.

**1877** *Rec. Geol. Survey India* X. 121 Upper Siwalik. This division includes the great conglomerates and associated beds which terminate the tertiary series of the country. **1938** *Q. Jrnl. Geol. Soc.* XCIV. 407 The alluvial deposits of the Bannu and Derejat plains probably conceal..a geological record more or less continuous from the latest Siwalik. **1974** *Encycl. Brit. Micropædia* IX. 246/2 Remains of the first clearly hominid forms..are known from the Siwalik. **1978** MITCHELL & READING in H. G. Reading *Sedimentary Environments & Facies* xiv. 464/2 Stratabound deposits of uranium with minor vanadium occur in the late Miocene to early Pliocene Middle Siwaliks.

**Siwash** ('saɪwɒʃ), *sb. N. Amer.* Also **Si-wash, siwash.** [Chinook Jargon, a N. Amer. Fr. dial. form of Fr. *sauvage* (SAVAGE *a.*) in same sense.]

**1. a.** An Indian, *spec.* of the North Pacific Coast. Freq. *attrib.* (Now considered pejorative.)

**1847** J. PALMER *Jrnl. Trav. Rocky Mts.* 150 Si-wash Indians. *a* **1861** T. WINTHROP *Canoe & Saddle* (1883) ii. 18 The three unsavory..mat-haired, truculent siwashes. **1869** [see HAIDA *a.* and *sb.*]. **1870** [see ALEUTIAN *a.* and *sb.*]. **1897** *Outing* XXX. 541/1 As we neared the Narrows other Siwashes in other queer-looking canoes paddled out. **1904** E. ROBINS *Magnetic North* 293 You soon learn it is the Siwash custom. **1949** *Boston Globe* 15 May (Fiction Mag.) 3/2 The Siwash showed him a poke of coarse gold. **1967** C. L. EVANS *Newel Post* 6 He was looking portly in a heavy Siwash sweater, and unselfconsciously wearing the knitted hat to match.

**b.** *transf.* A name of opprobrium; occas. joc.

**1882** *Edmonton Bull.* 3 June 4/3 Does this great chieftain think new settlers are a community of Siwashes or cringing dependants. **1924** C. E. MULFORD *Rustlers' Valley* xiii. 158 So-long, you Siwash! **1964** P. BERTON *Golden Trail* 23, I wouldn't go across the river on that old Siwash's word.

**2.** Chinook Jargon, the lingua franca of the North Pacific Coast Indians.

**1902** *Skagway Daily Alaskan* 23 Aug. 3/1 The governor was forced back upon his ability to talk siwash, hoping thereby to control the Indian vote. **1908** R. E. BEACH *Barrier* 56 Address me in Siwash or in English unless we are alone. **1936** W. B. MOWERY *Paradise Trail* 14 That's what Saghelia means in Siwash—the purty land..paradise.

**3.** *Comb.*, as **Siwash camp**, an open camp with no tent; **Siwash duck**, a scoter of the genus *Melanitta.*

**1922** *19th Cent.* Feb. 267 At night they would build a 'siwash' camp, digging a big hole in the snow, lining it with green spruce boughs and building up a three-foot wall of green spruce trees for a windbreak on back and sides. **1962** M. F. MURIE *Two in Far North* II. x. 197 We had only about twelve miles to travel from our siwash camp to Tramway Bar. **1911** *Daily Colonist* (Victoria, B.C.) 30 Apr. 10/1, I finally caught Mr. Indian just as he was coming ashore with his ducks, he had about 60 or 70 in the canoe, but they were mostly scoter or what is more commonly called Siwash ducks. **1927** *Blackw. Mag.* Aug. 207/2 He could see when any siwash ducks were on a shallow part of the lagoon. **1966** *Daily Colonist* (Victoria, B.C.) 20 Mar. 11/4 It is a rare occurrence for a Siwash duck, as the species [*sc.* surf scoter] is commonly called, to be found on such a shoreline.

**'siwash,** *v. N. Amer.* [f. prec.] **1.** *intr.* To camp without a tent, like an Indian.

**1938** T. C. STANWELL-FLETCHER *Driftwood Valley* (1946) v. 94 Since we can't carry the additional weight of a tent, we'll have to siwash under trees. **1977** *New Yorker* 20 June 64/3 In discrete valleys were a few cabins, and they stayed in them or siwashed (camped on the trail).

**2.** *trans.* To bar (a person) from purchasing alcoholic drink. *colloq.*

**1948** C. W. HOLLIDAY *Valley of Youth* 144 It [*sc.* Painkiller] was in great demand by the old inebriates during the periods when they had been 'Siwashed'—which meant that it was illegal to serve them with a drink over the bar or sell them liquor. **1957** A. R. BARRATT *Coronets & Buckskins* 9 Wen a wite man gets so's no one will sell him drinks—well folks say e's been siwashed.

So (sense 1) **'siwashing** *vbl. sb.*

**1904** *Churchman* 21 May 626, I have a lame shoulder, the result of continuous 'siwashing' and sleeping in the snow. **1938** T. C. STANWELL-FLETCHER *Driftwood Valley* (1946) vi. 110 The day after our siwashing trip, we lounged about the cabin, luxuriating in a paradise of warmth and rest. **1962** M. E. MURIE *Two in Far North* II. ix. 194 South Fork Henry no doubt thought we were young fools to be looking forward to a night of siwashing.

**six** (sɪks), *a.* and *sb.* Forms: α. 1 siox-, siex, 1–5 syx, (1) 5–6 syxe; 1- six (4 zix), 3–7 sixe. β. 1–2 seox, 1–6 (*Sc.* 7–8) sex, 2–4 sexe, 5 cex(e. γ. *Sc.* 5- sax. [Common Teut.: OE. *sex, six, siex, syx*, etc., = OFris. *sex* (WFris. *sêchs*, NFris. *soks*, etc.), MDu. *ses(se, zes(se, zees* (Du. *zes*), OS. *sehs, ses* (MLG. *sês, ses, sos*, LG. *ses, sös, sos*), OHG. and MHG. *sehs* (G. *sechs*), ON. (Icel., Norw., Sw., Da.) *sex* (MSw. *säx, siäx, siax*, etc., MDa. *sæx, siæx*), Goth. *saihs*. Cognate forms occur in all the Indo-European languages (as L. *sex*, Gr. ἕξ, etc.) and indicate an original **sueks*.

In OE. used either without change of form (esp. when attributive) or with plural declension *syxe, syxa, syxum*.]

The cardinal number next after five, represented by the symbols 6, VI, or vi.

**A.** *adj.* **1. a.** In concord with a sb. expressed.

α. *c* **893** K. ÆLFRED *Oros.* II. iv. 70 Siex mila from ðære byriᵹ. *c* **901** *O.E. Chron.* an. 901, Her ᵹefor Ælfred..syx nihtum ær ealra haliᵹra mæssan. *c* **1000** *Ags. Gosp.* Matt. xvii. 1 Æfter six daᵹum. *c* **1124** *O.E. Chron.* an. 1124, Tweᵹen sed-læpas to six scillingas. *c* **1205** LAY. 25979 þa six swin he to-droh. *c* **1300** *Havelok* 2788 Sixe erles weren sone yare. **1340** *Ayenb.* 21 þis zenne him sseaweþ..ine zix maneres. *c* **1400** MAUNDEV. (Roxb.) ix. 37 He had syx wyfes. *c* **1500** *Melusine* 117 The maister had..vytaylled & laden.. six galeys. **1596** SHAKS. *1 Hen. IV*, II. iv. 199 Some sixe or seuen fresh men set vpon vs. **1662** STILLINGFL. *Orig. Sacræ* III. iv. §2 The Creation of the world in the six daies work. **1762** *Ann. Reg.* II. 21 Henry Fielding was in stature rather rising above six feet. **1822** SCOTT *Nigel* xiii, She..had probably completed her six lustres. **1847** W. C. L. MARTIN *The Ox* 152/1 Six drachmas of Barbadoes aloes, six ounces of Epsom salts.

β. **835** *Charter* in *O.E. Texts* 449 An swin oððe sex weðras. *c* **975** *Rushw. Gosp.* Mark ix. 2 Æfter daᵹum sexum. *Ibid.* John ii. 6 Stænene fato sexo. *a* **1122** *O.E. Chron.* (Laud MS.) an. 852, He scolde ᵹife ilca ᵹear..sex foður ᵹearda. *c* **1250** *Gen. & Ex.* 739 Sex ȝer and fiftene mo, Adde Abram on is elde ðo. *a* **1300** *Cursor M.* 7387 His suns sex þat war at hame. *c* **1340** HAMPOLE *Pr. Consc.* 2708 Of þir sex poyntes I wil spek and rede. *c* **1400** *Apol. Loll.* 90 As þe heþun men had sex kyndis of similacris,..so han lordis now sex kyndis of prelatis. *c* **1440** *Promp. Parv.* 67 Cexe, *sex*. **1559** W. CUNNINGHAM *Cosmogr. Glasse* 65 By my computation your table sheweth sexe zones. **1572** *Wills & Inv. N.C.* (Surtees 1835) 348 Sex stone of talow... Sex payre of lyne shets. **1627** *Rep. Parishes Scotl.* (Bann. Club) 3 We walow it to be worth sex bollis ane husband land off rining wictuall. **1722** in *Scottish Jrnl. Topogr.* (1848) II. 62/1 To sex bottles sack.

γ. **1489** *Barbour's Bruce* I. 39 The land sax yer, and moyr perfay, Ley desolat after hys day. **1549** *Compl. Scot.* 107 Sax mulis chargit vitht gold. *c* **1615** SIR W. MURE (*title*), Sax Lynes wpon the Fall of Somersait. **1795** MACNEILL *Scotland's Skaith* xli, Wi' firm intention To drink sax nights out o' seven. **1816** SCOTT *Old Mort.* xlii, Ae night, sax weeks or thereby afore Bothwell Brig.

**b.** Followed by *hundred* or *thousand*, or the ordinals of these. Also *six-sevenths*, six (parts, etc.) out of seven.

*c* **893** K. ÆLFRED *Oros.* I. vii. 38 Pharon hæfde syx hund wiᵹwæᵹna..: þæt wæs syx hund þusenda manna. *a* **1122** *O.E. Chron.* (Laud MS.) an. 657, Æfter ure Drihtnes acennednesse seox hundred wintra. *c* **1205** LAY. 613 In þon castle he dude hende six hundred of his cnihten. *a* **1300** *Cursor M.* 2002 He had sex hundret yeir and an. *c* **1440** *Promp. Parv.* 67 Cex hundryd, *sexcenti*. **1549** *Compl. Scot.* 6 He beand bot sex thousand men. **1647** HEXHAM I. (Numbers), The sixe hundreth, *de ses hondertste*. **1785** BURNS *Death & Dr. Hornbook* xiii, Sax thousand years are near hand fled. **1855** TENNYSON *Lt. Brigade*, Into the valley of Death Rode the six hundred. **1899** *Allbutt's Syst. Med.* V. 13 Six-sevenths of the cases occurred between the ages of 40 and 70.

**c.** Coupled with a higher cardinal or ordinal numeral following, so as to form a compound (cardinal or ordinal) numeral.

*a* **900** *O.E. Martyrol.* 26 Mar. 50 On þone syx & twenteᵹðan dæᵹ þæs monðes. *c* **950** *Lindisf. Gosp.* John ii. 20 Feortiᵹ & sex uintro ᵹetimbred uæs ðis tempel. **1297** R. GLOUC. (Rolls) 233 þre þousend & sixe & twenti þer [*v.r.* ȝer] was fram þe worldes biginninge. *c* **1375** *Sc. Leg. Saints* Prol. 96 Til I had mad þaim redy, in novmer sex & sexty. *c* **1425** *Craft Nombrynge* (E.E.T.S.) 6 As þou seyst by þe comyne speche, Sex & twenty & nouȝt twenty & sex. **1579** FULKE *Heskins' Parl.* 223 The sixe and thirtieth Chapter treateth of the next text. **1605** SHAKS. *Lear* III. vii. 16 Some fiue or six and thirty of his Knights. **1725** DE FOE *Voy. round World* (1840) 164 We sailed again the six-and-twentieth day after we came in. **1779** *Mirror* No. 47 ¶4 Tom is a young man of six-and-twenty. **1855** KINGSLEY *Westward Ho!* x, Six-and-twenty years of travel.

**d.** In special applications. *Six Acts, Articles* (see quots.). *Six Clerks* (see SIX CLERK); *Six Counties*, the Ulster counties of Antrim, Down, Armagh, Londonderry, Tyrone, and Fermanagh, which have since 1920 comprised the province of Northern Ireland; (cf. *twenty-six counties* s.v. TWENTY-SIX *a.*); *Six Dynasties*, a collective term for the Chinese dynasties of Ch'en, Eastern Chin, Liang, Liu-Sung, Southern Ch'i and Wu, belonging to the period A.D. 220–589; freq. used *attrib.* to denote this period of history in China; *Six Nations* (see quots.); *Six Preachers* (in Canterbury Cathedral; hence the sing. *Six Preacher*).

**1834** *Times* 22 Apr. 5/6 Every man that dared to open his mouth against the Castlereagh and Sidmouth despotism must have set the *Six Acts at defiance. **1859** ROSSE *Index of Dates, Six Acts*, severely repressive measures, passed, 1819. **1862** TOUNSEND *Man. of Dates, Six Acts*,..six measures for the prevention of seditious meetings and the regulation of political publications. **1655** FULLER *Ch. Hist.* v. 231 Death being the penalty of such who were made guilty by the *six Articles. **1862** TOUNSEND *Man. of Dates, Six Articles, or Bloody Statute*,..an act (31 Hen. VIII, c. 14) passed June 28, 1539... The six articles enforced were transubstantiation, communion of one kind, celibacy of the clergy, vows of chastity, private masses, and auricular confession. **1647** CLARENDON *Hist. Reb.* I. §112 Sir Julius Cæsar was then Master of the Rolls, and had..the indubitable right and disposition of the *Six-Clerks' places. **1692** *Lond. Gaz.* No. 2771/4 Lost..between St. Paul's Church-yard, and the Six Clerks-Office. **1728** CHAMBERS *Cycl., Six Clerks*, Officers in Chancery of great Account, next in Degree below the Twelve Masters. **1842** *Penny Cycl.* XXII. 70/1 The office of Six Clerks is an office of great antiquity connected with the Court of Chancery, probably as ancient as the Court itself. **1921** *Notes from Ireland* 40/1 The Unionists of the '*Six Counties'. **1922** C. J. C. STREET *Ireland in 1921* ix. 226 The House of Commons contained only Unionist members, who were obviously deeply concerned at the position of affairs while anxious to say nothing which might compromise the position of the Six Counties. **1935** *Frontier Sentinel* (Newry) 22 June 4/4 The Six-County Premier. **1949** [see ENGLISHIZE *v.*]. **1960** J. STROUD *Shorn Lamb* iv. 49 Suppose..she turns out to be some one-eyed horror in the Six Counties looney-bin. **1974** *Irish Democrat* Nov. 5/2 The significance of the six county election results has been widely debated. **1934** K. S. LATOURETTE *Chinese* I. iv. 155 The fall of the Eastern Chin ..is usually said to mark the beginning of the era known to the Chinese as the..Southern and Northern Dynasties, which lasted until 589. Another classification—inclusive of a longer period—employed by Chinese historians is the *Six Dynasties, by which are meant the six kingdoms and dynasties between the downfall of the Han and the reunification of China in 589. **1966** F. SCHURMANN *Ideology & Organization in Communist China* vii. 407 The most ambitious attempt of this sort occurred during the Six Dynasties Period (third to sixth century A.D.). This was a period of serious political and social breakdown. **1973** T. R. TREGEAR *Chinese* i. 26 Monks from India..so impressed the barbarians of the Six Dynasties..that they adopted Buddhism. **1980** E. BEHR *Getting Even* v. 59 A huge 'Six Dynasties' celadon jar and a horseman of the Northern Wei period. **1710** in J. W. Lydekker *Faithful Mohawks* (1938) ii. 28 And as a sure Token of the sincerity of the *six Nations, We do..present Our Great Queen with these Belts of Wampum. **1785** T. JEFFERSON *Notes Virginia* 390 The Mingo or Six-nation Indians. *Ibid.*, The Mingos are a war colony from the six nations. **1895** *Westm. Gaz.* 13 Apr. 6/2 'Which..are the Six Nations?' 'The Mohawks, the Oneidas, the Onondegas, the Cayugas, the Senecas, and the Tuscaroras.' **1900** *Ibid.* 15 Jan. 10/1 The Six Nations Indian Reserve, Ontario... The Six Nation Indians number 3,500 to 4,000 souls. **1841** *Clergy List, Benefices* (219), *Six Preachers. James Reeve M.A. 1816 [etc.]. **1879** CROCKFORD *Cler. Directory* 469/1 Six Preacher of Cant. Cathl. 1874.

**e.** Colloq. phr. *six feet under* and varr.: dead and buried; in or into the grave.

**1942** BERREY & VAN DEN BARK *Amer. Thes. Slang* §117/19 *Dead and buried*..six feet under. **1968** J. SANGSTER *Touchfeather* xv. 184 Bill didn't realise it, but he was as dead now as he would be when they lowered him six feet under. **1976** A. PRICE *War Game* v. 107 He never cared for nobody born... He never did, and he never will. Not till he's six foot under. **1979** J. GERSON *Omega Factor* 78 In Islay.. we make sure the dead are stiff and cold and six feet under.

**2. a.** With ellipsis of sb., which may usually be supplied from the context.

*a* **900** *O.E. Martyrol.* 1 Aug. 134 þa hyra syxe wæron acwealde beforan þære meder. *a* **1225** *Ancr. R.* 298 Nullich of alle [mihtes] siggen, buten sixe. *c* **1330** *Arth. & Merl.* 6842 (Kölbing), þo was þer of .xv. þousand Yleued bot sex bihinde. *c* **1400** *Laud Troy Bk.* 6859 He sles oure men by fyue and six. **1500–20** DUNBAR *Poems* liii. 43 Quhen thair was cum in fywe or sax, The Quenis Dog begowthe to rax. **1567** *Gude & Godlie Ball.* (S.T.S.) 210 Gif God was maid of bittis of breid, Eit ȝe not oulklie sax or seuin. **1601** SHAKS. *Jul. C.* II. i. 277 Heere haue beene Some sixe or seuen, who did hide their faces. **1673** *Humours Town* 95 A Declamation against the Act for Six in the Hundred. **1724** SWIFT *Drapier's Lett.* Wks. 1755 V. II. 60 Wood's half-pence will come to be offered for six a penny. **1780** COWPER *Progr. Error* 161 Let that day be blest,.. Nobly distinguish'd above all the six. **1831** *Wilson's Amer. Ornith.* II. 180 Four inches long, and six in extent. **1895** ZANGWILL *Master* III. vii. 401 Broken lines of foam, which sometimes rolled in six-deep.

**b.** More specifically with ellipsis of *pieces*, *years* (of age), *syllables* or *feet* (in verse), *points* (on a stag's horn), *inches*, or *pence* (as in 'ten and six').

*c* **1420** *Avow. Arth.* lxv, Alle in sundur hit brast, In six or in seuyn. *c* **1440** *Pallad. on Husb.* XII. 420 Ek oon yeer oolde Is good, & so til sixe on wol he holde. **1590** SHAKS. *Mids. N.* III. i. 25 Well, we will haue such a Prologue, and it shall be written in eight and sixe. **1622** FLETCHER *Span. Cur.* II. iii, Let him bear six, and six, that all may blaze him. **1781** COWPER *Table-T.* 507 At Westminster, where little poets strive To set a distich upon six and five. **1818** BYRON *Juan* I. l, At six.. he was a charming child. **1897** MARY KINGSLEY *Trade W. Africa* 329 The average height.. is five feet six to five feet eight.

**c.** With omission of *hours*, as *six o'clock*.

[**1482** *Monk of Evesham* (Arb.) 20 Fro mydnyght tyl sex of the belle yn the mornyng.] **1596** SHAKS. *Merch. V.* II. v. 25 At six a clocke ith morning. *a* **1604** HANMER *Chron. Irel.* (1809) 273 Hee.. tooke shipping.. by sixe a clocke in the morning. **1629** WADSWORTH *Pilgr.* iii. 14 At six they go all to study in a large Hall. **1726** SWIFT *Gulliver* IV. viii, I set sail on the 24th day of September, 1701, at six in the morning. **1834** K. H. DIGBY *Mores Cath.* v. vi. 183 The rule in Du Guesclin's time was to rise and sup at six. **1888** LOWELL *Heartsease & Rue* 127 'Tis striking six! Sure never day Was short as this is!

*attrib.* **1867** AUGUSTA WILSON *Vashti* xxv, I shall go on the six o'clock train. **1899** *Daily News* 7 Dec. 3/4 De Aar has been placed under martial law and a six-to-six curfew established.

**d.** With omission of *horses*.

**1684** [see COACH *sb.* 4]. **1693** TATE in *Dryden's Juvenal* II. (1697) 30 You Nymphs that would to Coach and Six arrive. **1764** GRAY *J.T.* 18 Not I—for a coronet, chariot and six. **1849** MACAULAY *Hist. Eng.* iii. I. 377 A coach and six is.. never seen, except as part of some pageant. **1877** [see COACH *sb.* 4].

**e.** With omission of *shillings*; spec. in *six-and-eightpence* as a lawyer's fee; also *transf.*

*a* **1700** B. E. *Dict. Cant. Crew*, *Six and eight-pence*, the usual Fee given, to carry back the Body of the Executed Malefactor, to give it Christian Burial. **1748** RICHARDSON *Clarissa* VI. 393 Flinging down a Portugal Six-and-thirty [= a Joanese]. **1756** FOOTE *Eng. fr. Paris* I, *Lat.* The Law.. is the Bulwark... *Crab.* Mercy, good Six and Eight-pence. **1785** GROSE *Dict. Vulgar T.*, *Six and eight-pence*, an attorney, whose fee on several occasions is fixed at that sum. **1825** T. HOOK *Sayings* Ser. II. *Man of Many Fr.* (Colburn) 100 The six-and-eightpenny feeling.. was too strong to be resisted. *Ibid.* 151 Cynics tell us, that.. we shall find six-and-eightpence at the bottom of every thought and every action of mankind. **1879** MISS BRADDON *Cloven Foot* x, I have.. the interest of a friend rather than a lawyer. You don't suppose it's for the sake of the six-and-eightpence.

**f.** In phr. *six.. and half-a-dozen..*, denoting that there is little or no difference or choice between two (sets of) persons or things.

**1836** MARRYAT *Pirate* iv, I never knows the children. It's just six of one and half-a-dozen of the other. **1865** H. KINGSLEY *Hillyars & Burtons* xxxviii, 'What do they say about his chance?'.. 'Six and half-a-dozen, sir.' **1870** MISS BRIDGMAN *R. Lynne* II. xii. 256 My verdict is, six of one and half a dozen of the other.

**g.** Naut. slang phr. *six upon four*: (on) short rations (i.e. four men's food shared between six men). ? *Obs.*

**1829** D. JERROLD *Black-ey'd Susan* II. ii. 31 May you live a life of ban-yan days, and be put six upon four for't. **1843** J. F. COOPER *Ned Myers* 78 As to food, we were kept 'six upon four' the whole time I was prisoner. *Ibid.* 86 Put at 'six upon four' again.

**h.** *Cricket.* With omission of *runs*. (i) Six runs, esp. scored by striking the ball clear over the boundary. Cf. sense 6 of the sb., below.

**1857** T. HUGHES *Tom Brown's School Days* II. viii. 392 When you or Raggles hit a ball hard away for six, I am delighted. **1951** G. BRODRIBB *All Round Wicket* vi. 39 A lusty hit for six gives many people intense pleasure... There were.. many outstanding feats of six-hitting. **1979** *Daily Tel.* 29 May 17/3 The ball was hit for six.. into the vicarage grounds.

(ii) Also *transf.* and *fig.* in various colloq. phrases: *to knock* (someone) *for six*, to wrench from a state of composure; to defeat (soundly); to astonish; also in extended uses, and with inanimate obj. Similarly, *to go for six* (see also quot. 1943); *to hit for six*: see HIT *v.* 8 f.

**1902** J. MILNE *Epistles of Atkins* vi. 107 'It knocked me for six', is the statement we have about a bullet in the knee. **1934** A. BERKELEY *Panic Party* iv. 69 It's a crashing bore.. to think of those dim cads knocking us for six like this, but.. it's no use getting strenuous about it. **1941** L. A. G. STRONG *John McCormack* viii. 129 John.. hurled his Santuzza from him with such vigour that she went for six, landing in the wings on the far side of the stage. **1943** C. H. W. JACKSON *It's a Piece of Cake* 32 *Gone for six*, killed, missing. **1949** R. Gow *Ann Veronica* I, in *Plays of Year 1949* I. 240 You're just like an angel yourself sitting there. You knock me for six, if I may borrow a sporting metaphor. **1955** *Times* 6 Aug. 7/4 It is a song that knocks for six the illusion.. that little creatures probably know by instinct how to do their stuffs. **1973** 'B. GRAEME' *Two & Two make Five* vi. 58 A glass of his home-made cider.. knocks you for six.

**i.** Chiefly as Fr. phr. *Les Six* (le sis) a Parisian group of six composers, Louis Durey (1888–1979), Arthur Honegger (1892–1955), Darius Milhaud (1892–1974), Germaine Tailleferre (b. 1892), Georges Auric (b. 1899), and Francis Poulenc (1899–1963), formed after the war of 1914–18, whose music represents a reaction against romanticism and impressionism.

[**1920** H. COLLET in *Comœdia* 16 Jan. 2/6 Les artistes conscients reconnaissent en Satie un maître. Voyons maintenant ce que valent les 'Six' qu'il précéda sur la voie nouvelle.] **1927** *Grove's Dict. Mus.* (ed. 3) II. 662/1 Although a member of the group of French musicians known as the 'Six', he [*sc.* Honegger] is of Swiss parentage. **1934** C. LAMBERT *Music Ho!* III. 194 Chabrier.. may be considered.. the father of the post-war movement associated with the names of Les Six. **1952** B. ULANOV *Hist. Jazz in Amer.* (1958) x. 113 The lessons the composer had learned from.. the music of Ravel and *les six* were poorly applied. **1978** P. GRIFFITHS *Conc. Hist. Mod. Music* vi. 72 Les Six did not exist as a group for more than a few years.

**j.** *the Six*, the group of countries (Belgium, France, the German Federal Republic, Holland, Italy, and Luxembourg) which were the original members of the European Economic Community from 1958 until the admission of others in 1973.

**1957** [see EUROPEAN *a.* 1 c]. **1958** *Economist* 18 Oct. 207/1 The Six are the European Community, fore-runner of the continental political union.. that is to be when General de Gaulle is gone. **1981** *Times* 30 June 7/1 In 1977 Britain.. threatened to bring down the whole European edifice built up painstakingly by the original Six.

**3.** = SIXTH *a.*

*c* **1385** in *Wyclif's Sel. Wks.* III. 506 Oure pope Urban þo sex. *c* **1430** *Brut* ccxliii, And þe vj day come a nother Henauder. **1523** LD. BERNERS *Froiss.* I. cccxlvi. 547 Bartylmewe des Angles.. receyued the papalyte, and was called Vrbayne the sixe. **1586** W. WEBBE *Eng. Poetrie* (Arb.) 62 Make short either the two, foure, sixe, eight, tenne, twelue sillable, and it will.. fall out very absurdly. **1603** PARSONS in *Cath. Rec. Soc. Publ.* (1906) II. 218 This 6 of July.

**B.** *sb.* **1.** The abstract number six, or the symbol denoting this.

**1398** TREVISA *Barth. De P.R.* XIX. cxix. (1495) 922 The nombre of syxe.. is the fyrste perfyghte nombre of the euen partyes therof taken alle togyder. *c* **1425** *Craft Nombrynge* (E.E.T.S.) 6 Write þe digit of þe nombur in þe first place þat is sex. **1565** COOPER *Thesaurus*, *Senarius*, that is of the number of sixe. **1611** COTGR., *Sixiesme*,.. a proportion of six. **1696** PHILLIPS (ed. 5), *Six*, a Primitive Number, compos'd of Four and Two, or Twice Three. **1815** G. BEATTIE *John o' Arnha'* (1826) 13 Scarcely could ye counted sax, Before [etc.]. **1861** F. W. ROBINSON *No Church* II. i, Little boys who wore their hair in 'number sixes' at the temples, when law had left them hair sufficient for such ornamentation.

**2.** Chiefly *pl.* **a.** A set of six spots or pips on a die, domino, or card; also, a card, etc., having six pips or spots. (Cf. SICE.)

**1599** MINSHEU *Percivall's Sp. Dict.* Dial. 26 R. I did lift an ace.—L. I a fower.—M. I a sixe. **1663** COWLEY *Ess.*, *Danger of Procrastination*, 'Tis a hundred to one, if a man fling two Sixes. **1863** WHYTE MELVILLE *Gladiators* I. 410 One more throw for the Sixes and the great game is fairly won. **1878** T. HARDY *Ret. Native* III. viii, Venn lifted the box, and behold a triplet of sixes was disclosed. **1885** *Harper's Mag.* Apr. 734/2 You have thrown double-sixes.

**b.** A set of six persons: (*a*) *gen.*

**1796** *Instr. & Reg. Cavalry* (1813) 36 The standard and its coverer each in the middle of the two center ranks of sixes. **1842** BORROW *Bible in Spain* xxiii, On every road of Spain.. may be seen gangs of fives and sixes of these people. **1874** HARDY *Far fr. Mad. Crowd* ix, He's been courted by Sixes and Sevens—all the girls.. have tried him.

(*b*) *spec.* a group of six Brownie Guides or Cub Scouts.

**1916** R. BADEN-POWELL *Wolf Cub's Handbk.* II. 59 Each Six is called after a Wolf by its colour. **1920** —— *Brownies or Blue Birds* II. 11 The Brownies are divided into parties of six; each 'Six' is under the leader who is called a 'Sixer'. **1972** TRINKY & PETERS *Cub Scout Games* 26 Cubs enjoy Six relays and will compete fiercely for their Six.

**3.** *pl.* In various elliptic uses.

**a.** Lines of six syllables. † **b.** Sixpenny nails. † **c.** ? Spirits. † **d.** *Mus.* Intervals of a sixth. **e.** Gloves, shoes, etc., of the sixth size. **f.** Six-pounder guns. **g.** Some form of cake. **h.** Candles weighing six to the pound. **i.** Large flower-pots, six of which are formed from a cast of clay. **j.** Bonds bearing interest at 6 per cent. **k.** *U.S. slang.* A prison sentence of six months. **l.** A six-cylinder motor car or engine.

**a. 1586** W. WEBBE *Eng. Poetrie* (Arb.) 59 The first [line] hauing eyght sillables, the second sixe, wherof the two sixes shall alwayes ryme. **1891** J. C. PARSONS *English Versification* 36 Sixes and four. Iambic trimeter and dimeter. *Ibid.*, Sevens and sixes.

**b. 1629** *MS. Acc. St. John's Hosp., Canterb.*, For one hundred of fiues and one hundred of sixes xjd.

**c.** *a* **1658** CLEVELAND *Xmas Day* 14 Were ere such dregs mix'd with Geneva sixes?

**d. 1752** tr. *Rameau's Treat. Musick* 44 Observe those two Parts that proceed always by Sixes. *Ibid.* 45 Before we had a Knowledge of these small and great Sixes, it was almost impossible to add two Parts with these Sixes.

**e. 1796** PEGGE *Anonym.* (1809) 97 When.. a shoemaker.. came to take measure of him, he told him, 'O.. long sixes or short sevens will do'.

**f. 1804** *Naval Chron.* XI. 409 A Ship Privateer, carrying sixteen twelves and sixes. **1812** in *Examiner* (1813) 4 Jan. 6/2 Carronades of different calibres, with two long sixes.

**g. 1825** HONE *Every-day Bk.* I. 51 The.. ginger-bread bakers coaxingly insinuate them among their new made sixes.

**h. 1825** T. HOOK *Sayings* Ser. II. *Passion & Princ.* v, A serious injunction 'not to take out sixes for tens'. **1826** LAMB *Pop. Fallacies* xv, Man found out long sixes.—Hail candle-light! **1843** DICKENS *Mart. Chuz.* ii, An imaginary general illumination of very bright short-sixes.

**i. 1824** J. C. LOUDON *Encycl. Gardening* II. 327 The Flower Pot, is a cylindrical tapering vessel of burnt clay, with a perforated bottom, and of which there are ten sorts, distinguished by their sizes thus: the.. third [size has] 6 [to the cast, and are called] sixes [, being] 9 [inches diameter] 8 [inches deep]. **1851** *B'ham. & Midl. Gardeners' Mag.* Apr. 31, I ordered.. 200 pots, (size full sixes).

**j. 1867** *Nation* 10 Oct. 295 The bonds became known as the 'Sixes of 1861'. **1893** *Daily News* 29 June 2/5 Mexican Sixes have dropped further 3¼ per cent.

**k. 1844** J. H. INGRAHAM *La Bonita Cigarera* vi. 27/1 I've served two sixes in her, and that's enough for me to give to the service o' my country! **1928** J. O'CONNOR *Broadway Racketeers* xvii. 182 Even if its only a sixer in the pen, too many sixes are bad for the health.

**l. 1920** *Motor Man.* (ed. 23) 19 The chief constructional difference between the six and the four is in the crankshaft. **1977** *Chicago Tribune* 2 Oct. XIII. 18/2 The use of fours, sixes, and small V-8's is more prevalent in 1978.

**4.** † **a.** Six-shilling beer. In later use *pl.* Also *old six* (see quot. 1890).

**1631** BRATHWAIT *Whimzies* xii. 97 How this threede-bare Philosopher shruggs, shifts, and shuffles for a cuppe of six. **1655** R. YOUNGE *Agst. Drunkards* 3 Nor hath the richest Sherrie, or old Canarie any more operation with them, than a cup of six hath with me. **1785** GROSE *Dict. Vulgar T.*, *Six and Tips*, whisky and small beer (Irish). **1796** *Ibid.* (ed. 3), *Sixes*, small beer, formerly sold at six shillings the barrel. **1810** in *Anc. Brit. Drama* II. 461, I suppose he means small beer, which, among the vulgar, still goes by the cant name of sixes. **1890** BARRÈRE & LELAND *Dict. Slang* II. 98 *Old six* (common), old ale at sixpence a quart. *Spoken*—Look what I've got to do tonight! There's fourteen 'pubs' on my beat.. That means that I've got fourteen pints of old six to get down me. **1898** J. D. BRAYSHAW *Slum Silhouettes* 155 Tell 'er ter send for an hexty pint of old six. *Ibid.* 156 The foaming jug of 'old six' was placed on the table.

**b.** Sixpennyworth.

**1871** 'M. LEGRAND' *Cambr. Freshm.* 107 Nothin'.. but six of pale brandy neat got her round again.

**5.** In phrases with *six and seven*, *sixes and sevens*, etc., originally denoting the hazard of one's whole fortune, or carelessness as to the consequences of one's actions, and in later use the creation or existence of, or neglect to remove, confusion, disorder, or disagreement.

The original form of the phrase, *to set on six and seven*, is based on the language of dicing, and is probably a fanciful alteration of *to set on cinque and sice*, these being the two highest numbers. Subsequent variations arise from the use of *at* for *on*, of *or* for *and*, of other verbs in place of *set*, and of the plurals *sixes* and *sevens*; the latter became the standard form in the 18th cent. To illustrate the development more clearly, the chief types are here grouped in separate paragraphs.

(*a*) *c* **1374** CHAUCER *Troylus* IV. 622 Lat nat this wrechched wo thyn herte gnawe, But manly set the world on sexe and seuene. *c* **1460** *Towneley Myst.* xvi. 128, I shall, and that in hy, set all on sex and seuen. **1535** STEWART *Cron. Scotl.* I. 654 Quha.. settis all his thrift on sax and sevin. **1542** UDALL *Apoph.* 267 b, There is a prouerbe, *omnem jacere aleam*, to cast all dyce, by which is signified, to sette all on sixe & seuen. **1601** WEEVER *Mirr. Mart.* B iv, I'm in a wood,.. Yet o're my head a threatning Rocke still hingeth..; Twixt wood and rocke, I stand on six and seauen. **1611** COTGR. s.v. *Desesperade*, *Iouër à la desesperade*, to set his whole rest, or set all on sixes, and seuens.

(*b*) **1535** JOYE *Apol. Tindale* (Arb.) 43 Yet had he leuer marre and destroy al, and (as they saye) set all at six and seuen, then [etc.]. **1596** NASHE *Saffron Walden* Wks. (Grosart) III. 38 Old Laertes.. caring for all other things else, sets his owne estate at sixe and seauen. **1607** WALKINGTON *Opt. Glass* To Rdr., I haue set all at six and seuen, and I intend by the Muses favour happilie to go on. **1622** JACKSON *Judah* 56 To become cold, carelesse, and negligent, set all at six and seven.

(*c*) **1583** GOLDING *Calvin on Deut.* cxxxvi. 833 Not to runne and scratch for other mens goods, as if they were left at sixe and seuen. **1592** *Repentence R. Greene* G.'s Wks. (Grosart) XII. 179 Then left I her [my wife] at six or seuen, who went into Lincolnshire, and I to London. **1648** T. HILL *Dying Saints* 19 Do not let things lie at six and sevens.. any longer. **1670** G. H. tr. *Hist. Cardinals* II. I. 127 They leave things at sixes and sevens. **1713** SWIFT *Cadenus & Vanessa* 888 The goddess.. Left all below at Six and Sev'n. **1785** GROSE *Dict. Vulgar T.*, *Left at sixes and sevens*, in confusion, commonly said of a room where the furniture, etc. is scattered about, or of a business left unsettled. **1829** SCOTT *Jrnl.* (1890) II. 317, I was sick of the labour by two o'clock and left several of my books and all of my papers at sixes and sevens. **1854** MISS BAKER *Northampt. Gloss.* s.v., He's gone away in such a hurry, he has left everything at sixes and sevens.

(*d*) **1597** BEARD *Theatre God's Judgem.* (1612) 528 He let the affaires of his kingdome runne at six and at sevens. *a* **1610** HEALEY *Cebes* (1636) 151 She doth nothing with discretion, but hurleth all about at six and seven. **1679** ALSOP *Melius Inq.* II. viii. 369 The worship of God lying at sixes and sevens, the Government of the Church meer Anarchy. **1713** ARBUTHNOT *John Bull* II. i, His Affairs went on at sixes and sevens. **1784** R. BAGE *Barham Downs* I. 345 It was owing to the Six-and-seven way of going on of things in the heathen world. **1809** MALKIN *Gil Blas* XII. vii. ⁋ 3 The affairs of the treasurer..are all at sixes and sevens. **1862** HAWTHORNE *Our Old Home* (1883) I. 171 The line of a railway..puts all precedent things at sixes-and-sevens. **1887** *Times* (weekly ed.) 2 Sept. 15/3 [These] differences.. have for a long time kept society in Sofia at sixes and sevens.

(*e*) *a* **1704** T. BROWN *Alsop's State of Conform.* Wks. 1711 IV. 118 His zeal swallowing his concern for his Family, things were run to sixes and sevens. **1782** ELIZ. BLOWER *Geo. Bateman* II. 126 If I was to go from home..every thing would soon go to sixes and sevens. **1846** MRS. CARLYLE in *New Lett.* (1903) I. 219 With her departure everything went to sixes and sevens.

**6.** *Cricket.* A score of six runs made by striking the ball clear over the boundary; a shot which achieves this.

**1920** D. J. KNIGHT in P. F. Warner *Cricket* i. 34 If accurately timed—remember that flick of the wrists at the psychological moment—there goes the easiest six in cricket to your credit! **1933** H. LARWOOD *Body-Line?* 8 Mr. Wyatt again bats well... He ends a fiery rubber with a crashing six! **1949** J. SYMONS *Bland Beginning* 217 The ball sailed high into the air... The umpire signalled a six. **1957** G. LYTTELTON *Let.* 27 June in *Lyttelton-Hart-Davis Lett.* (1979) II. 120 His [*sc.* F. Trueman's] three sixes off consecutive balls were worth seeing. **1976** J. SNOW *Cricket Rebel* 16 Shortly after my six-hitting effort the school was sold and the ground used for building.

**7.** *the deep six*: used in various slang phrs. to denote death or the grave (perh. from the custom of burial at sea, at a depth of six fathoms); also *fig.* Hence as *v. trans.*, to submerge in water; also *fig.*, to reject, abandon, conceal. orig. and chiefly *U.S.*

**1929** M. A. GILL *Underworld Slang* 4/2 Deep six, grave. **1947** S. PALMER *Miss Withers Regrets* (1948) xii. 135 My old lady went over the hill with my bank account before I was out of boot camp. I'd have given her the deep-six if I coulda got a furlough. **1966** T. PYNCHON *Crying of Lot 49* iii. 50 Attack, retaliation, both projectiles deep-sixed forever and the Pacific rolls on. **1973** *Times* 26 July 8/3 Mr Dean has testified that Mr Ehrlichman told him to 'deep six' the documents... He said he threw the documents into the Potomac river. **1975** *Publishers Weekly* 28 July 116/1 They discovered that Americans..have been hung up on the wisdom of Franklin's 'Poor Richard's Almanack'..: 'work hard, be thrifty, don't borrow.'.. They tell their readers to 'deep six' Poor Richard and put his advice into reverse. **1976** *Listener* 28 Oct. 524/3 The more serious charge from Dean that he [*sc.* President Ford] tried to 'deep six' the Watergate investigation. **1977** *Islander* (Victoria, B.C.) 21 Aug. 2/3, I heard later that Bruce had taken them [*sc.* three guns] out into the saltchuck and deep-sixed them. **1978** *Sunday Mail Color Mag.* (Brisbane) 7 May 13 'Fraid the rest of the treasure *and* your gear have gone for the deep six!.. It's over three hundred feet to the bottom of that trench!

**C.** *Comb.* **1. a.** Combining (usually hyphened) with a sb. and forming an attrib. compound, as ***six-ball*** (over), ***six-bar*** (gate), ***six-bit*** (code, row), ***six-bottle*** (man), ***six-cylinder*** (engine, motor vehicle) (also *absol.*), ***six-piece*** (band), ***six-water*** (grog), etc.

Common during the 19th cent., and very freq. in recent use.

**1910** *Blackw. Mag.* Jan. 97/2 He covered something between 250 and 300 yards in the course of each *six-ball over. **1979** *Times* 29 Nov. 19/1 England..made 211 for eight in their 50 six-ball overs. **1711** ADDISON *Spect.* No. 57 ⁋3 She..makes nothing of leaping over a *Six-bar Gate. **1868** *U.S. Rep. Munit. War* 286 Two of the *six barrel, and one of the ten barrel improved guns. **1964** T. W. MCRAE *Impact of Computers on Accounting* i. 9 A computer using a '*six-bit' binary code. **1964** C. DENT *Quantity Surveying by Computer* vi. 72 These word trains, forming blocks of data, are directed to the tape via the tape control unit, which breaks them into six-bit rows. **1807** E. S. BARRETT *Rising Sun* I. 102 A *six-bottle-man, that is to say, one who can make such a tun of his corporation, as to carry off six bottles of wine at one sitting. **1812** SIR J. SINCLAIR *Syst. Husb. Scot.* I. 303 On land that will carry beans, he thinks a *six-course shift the best. **1905** G. B. SHAW in *Grand Mag.* Feb. 116 An old crock of a 1904 *six-cylinder car. **1938** *New Statesman* 22 Jan. 142/2 At one period the Morris interests were building a couple of dozen six-cylinders, all different. **1977** 'D. RUTHERFORD' *Return Load* iv. 83 Under the shiny cellulose lid..lurked a six-cylinder engine. **1822–7** GOOD *Study Med.* (1829) II. 131 Five-day ague... *Six-day ague. **1684** T. BURNET *Theory Earth* III. 45 It does not agree with the scheme of the *six-days creation. **1890** *Pall Mall G.* 6 Feb. 1/2 An eight hours day and a six days week stand in the forefront of the workman's programme. **1812** SIR J. SINCLAIR *Syst. Husb. Scot.* II. 132 A *six-ell ridge about 19½ feet broad. **1801** BUSBY *Dict. Mus.*, *Trimeters*, ancient lyrical verses of a *six-feet measure. **1709** *Lond. Gaz.* No. 4515/3 A *six gun Privateer taken by the Crown. **1794** T. DAVIS *Agric. Wilts.* 112 The lowest size of a Wiltshire down farm, that can be managed to advantage, is a good *six horse business. **1892** E. REEVES *Homew. Bound* 114 Cobb & Co.'s line of six-horse coaches. **1848** THACKERAY *Van. Fair* xxxii, The entire repulse of the French under Ney after a *six hours' battle. **1761** in Sir J. Picton *L'pool Munic Rec.* (1886) II. 276 Carts to have *six-inch Wheels. **1890** W. J. GORDON *Foundry* 23 This six-inch gun is stopped dead in eighteen inches. **1863** TREVELYAN *Compet. Wallah* (1866) 30 The sun was low enough to allow me to venture on a *six-mile walk. **1884** BRITTEN *Watch & Clockm.* 268 *Six month Clocks have two extra wheels and pinions between the great and centre wheels. **1887** I. R. *Ranche Life Montana* 46 From a *six-months' calf to very old cows. **1948** A. BARON *From City from Plough* 39 On the dais at the end of the ballroom a *six-piece band thumped and brayed. **1959** *Encounter* Oct. 49/1 In the dining-room a six-piece dance-band plays. **1839** URE *Dict. Arts* 580 A ground plan..of a *six-pot furnace. **1856** MORTON *Cycl. Agric.* II. 725/3 **Six-quarter-cattle*, (Fife), from eighteen months to two years old. **1852** SURTEES *Sponge's Sp. Tour* (1893) 203 He is a *six-season hunter. **1614** B. JONSON *Bart. Fair* I. i, Give me the man can start up a justice of wit, out of *six shillings beer. **1679** EVELYN *Pomona* (ed. 3) Pref., When..our Citizens..shall come to drink it [cider] moderately diluted, (as now they do six-shilling Beer, in London and other places). **1898** *Westm. Gaz.* 17 Nov. 5/1 The length requisite for a six-shilling novel. **1832** J. RENNIE *Butterfl. & Moths* 23 *Six Spot Burnet. **1813** T. DAVIS *Agric. Wilts.* Gloss. s.v. *Sheep*, [Sheep are called] *six-teeth [wethers or ewes] from the shear-time after three years old. **1872** *Routledge's Every Boy's Ann.* 134/2 The difference between a four and a six tooth wether. **1669** STURMY *Mariner's Mag.* v. i. 3 A *six Thred-line or small Belch. **1829** D. JERROLD *Black-Ey'd Susan* II. i. 27 May I be put on *six-water grog for a lubber. **1833** MARRYAT *P. Simple* (1863) 267 You'll make a wry face upon six-water grog. **1874** *Slang Dict.* 292 *Six-water Grog*, ..the weakest grog possible—six portions of water to one of rum. **1851** *Westm. Rev.* July 368 A *six wheel tank engine. **1898** *Hutchinson's Arch. Surg.* IX. 293, I find that practical dentists are in the habit of speaking of the first permanent molar tooth as 'the *six year molar'.

**b.** In phr. ***six-year(s)-old*** used attrib. or absol.

**1630** M. GODWYN tr. *Bp. Hereford's Ann. Eng.* 220 The six yeare old Queene. **1707** *Lond. Gaz.* No. 4342/3 A Plate ..shall..be run for..by Six Years old Mares. **1850** THACKERAY *Pendennis* lviii, My wife..wears shoes for a six-years-old child. **1897** *Daily News* 15 Feb. 2/3 This six-year-old has a very light weight to carry.

**c.** In various attributive combs.

**1858** HOGG *Life Shelley* II. 158 Thrice in the week did the six-inside coach plough its reluctant course to town. **1889** *Daily News* 22 Jan. 2/5 The minister never came down out of his six-by-four pulpit to be cross-examined. **1895** *Times* 10 Sept. 4/2 The Football Association..[is] prohibiting all six-a-side competitions.

**2.** Parasynthetic, as ***six-angled***, ***-arched***, ***-barred***, ***-holed***, ***-membered***, ***-pointed***, ***-toothed***, ***-wheeled***, etc.; sometimes in specific names of animals, birds, etc., as ***six-banded***, ***-belted***, ***-lined***, ***-plumed***, ***-striped*** (see quots.).

Many examples of this type occur in recent use.

**1509** HAWES *Past. Pleas.* XXI. (Percy Soc.) 99 With knottes *sixeangled, gay and glorious, The rofe did hange. **1681** GREW *Musæum* I. ii. i. 18 Not of triangular, but six-angl'd and square pieces. **1893** 'MARK RUTHERFORD' *C. Furze* i, A *six-arched stone bridge. **1800** SHAW *Gen. Zool.* I. i. 189 *Six-banded Armadillo. **1879** E. P. WRIGHT *Anim. Life* 213 The Six-banded Armadillo..is a native of Brazil. **1760–72** H. BROOKE *Fool of Qual.* (1809) IV. 58 They met with a *six-barred gate. **1881** *Times* 15 Jan. 5/6 The *six-barrelled Gatling..fired 267. **1908** R. SOUTH *Moths Brit. Isles* II. 358 *Six-belted Clearwing... The body of the male has seven yellow belts, and that of the female one less. **1958** W. J. STOKOE *Caterpillars Brit. Moths* II. 244 The Six-belted Clearwing..*Dipsosphecia scopigera*. The haunts of this moth are on chalk downs. **1877** W. BLACK *Green Past.* xi. 89 He.. took out a *six-chambered revolver. **1552** HULOET, *Sixe cornered. **1610** HOLLAND *Camden's Brit.* 239 Pointed with sixe cornerd or foure cornerd smooth sides. **1800** *Asiatic Ann. Reg.* 271/1 Peduncles very short, solitary, *six-flowered. **1846** *Ecclesiologist* V. 164 The window..consists of two trefoiled lights, with a *sixfoiled circle in the head. **1602** *2nd Pt. Return fr. Parnass.* v. iv, And art thou there *six footed Mercury? **1820** T. MITCHELL *Aristoph.* I. 231 Words of six-footed dimension. **1606** SHAKS. *Tr. & Cr.* Prol. 15 Priams *six-gated City. **1862** COUCH *Brit. Fishes* I. 21 *Six-Gilled Shark... Grey Shark. **1955** E. POUND *Classic Anthol.* II. 135 With *six-holed flutes That were bamboo shoots. **1821** SCOTT *Kenilw.* i, During the emptying of a *six-hooped pot. **1651** OGILBY *Æsop* (1665) 12 The Vulgar shout to see their *six-inch'd King. **1828** STARK *Elem. Nat. Hist.* II. 181 Body *six-jointed, the last segment largest. **1753** *Chambers' Cycl.* Suppl. s.v. *Convolvulus*, The smaller five or *six-leav'd hairy bindweed of Ceylon. *a* **1711** KEN *Hymnotheo* Poet. Wks. 1721 III. 11 The *Six-legg'd Nation [*sc.* ants] in the Fields appears. **1874** LUBBOCK *Metam. Ins.* i. 16 The larva is minute, six-legged, and very active. **1802** SHAW *Gen. Zool.* III. i. 240 *Six-lined Lizard. **1956** I. L. FINAR *Org. Chem.* II. viii. 252 Bicyclic monoterpenes contain a *six-membered ring and a three-, four-, or five-membered ring. **1978** A. J. BIRCH in *Further Perspectives Organic Chem.* (Ciba Symposium) 6 A similar cyclization to a six-membered ring from the $C_{20}$-precursor geranyl-geranyl pyrophosphate would not yield this group. **1685** *Lond. Gaz.* No. 2023/4 A *six Oared Barge never used above four or five times. **1809** BRYDONE *Tour Sicily* xiii. 155 This is a small six-oared boat, made entirely for speed. **1880** *Cassell's Nat. Hist.* IV. 25 The *Six-plumed Bird of Paradise. **1764** T. H. CROKER et al. *Compl. Dict. Arts & Sciences* I. s.v. *Diamond*, These [diamonds] the jewellers call *six-pointed stones. **1864** BOUTELL *Her. Hist. & Pop.* xxiv. (ed. 3) 405 Its six-pointed mullets charged upon a field of Warrenne. **1888** RUTLEY *Rock-forming Min.* 193 A small *six-rayed star has been developed. **1721** BRADLEY *Philos. Acc. Wks. Nat.* 24 The other has its Stems *six-rib'd. **1890** 'R. BOLDREWOOD' *Col. Reformer* (1891) 423 A neat *six-roomed cottage. **1762** MILLS *Syst. Pract. Husb.* I. 419 Both the four rowed and the *six rowed barley. **1856** MORTON *Cycl. Agric.* I. 183 The six-rowed barley is said to be hardy and prolific. **1805** R. W. DICKSON *Pract. Agric.* I. Pl. ix, A *six-shared horse-hoe. **1596** HARINGTON *Metam. Ajax* D ij, The king..saued him from the ierke of the *six string'd whip. **1897** WATTS-DUNTON *Aylwin* III. ix, This obsolete six-stringed instrument. **1907** R. SOUTH *Moths Brit. Isles* I. 227 The *Six-striped Rustic..is also generally distributed over our islands. **1696** PATRICK *Comm. Exod.* xxvii. (1697) 524 These Hangings..were made of simple fine *sixthreded Linen. **1742** W. ELLIS *Mod. Husbandman* Sept. xxvi. 124 The Sheep..are generally *six-toothed Wethers. **1812** W. STEVENSON *Agric. Dorset* 411 They..are called by the name of two-toothed, four-toothed, and six-toothed ewes. **1856** *Farmer's Mag.* Jan. 29 The old plan of keeping flocks until six-toothed is become quite obsolete. **1841** *Civil Eng. & Arch. Jrnl.* IV. 90/2 The question of four and *six-wheeled engines. *a* **1976** A. CHRISTIE *Autobiogr.* (1977) VIII. i. 372 It was at this time of day when the big *six-wheeled cars most often went off the track. *a* **1711** KEN *Hymnotheo* Poet. Wks. 1721 III. 204 Some cast on *Six-wing'd Seraphs envious eye.

**3.** In comb. with sbs. ending in *-er*, as ***six-bitter*** [BIT *sb.*² 8 b], ***-footer***, ***-roomer***, ***-seater***, ***-wheeler***.

Other examples, as *six-incher*, etc., occur in recent use.

**1928** *Coast Guard* Aug. 6/1 (*caption*) A fleet of '*six-bitters', or 75-footers, at maneuvers. **1964** M. F. WILLOUGHBY *Rum War at Sea* vii. 88 Many six-bitters were used offshore to picket larger rum vessels. **1844** HEWLETT *Pars. & W.* xxxiii, I..inquired of a second *six-footer. **1887** BLACK *S. Zembra* 192 Scarcely a man of the family less than a six-footer! **1897** *Outing* XXX. 144 Some of the big six-footers (commonly called 'old sojers' or 'old man kangaroos'). **1853** DICKENS *Bleak Ho.* lxiv. 612 'It's a *six roomer, exclusive of kitchens,' said Mr. Guppy, 'and in the opinion of my friends, a commodious tenement.' **1894** A. MORRISON *Mean Streets* 115 A remnant of land too small for another six-roomer. **1932** T. S. ELIOT *Sweeney Agonistes* 24 There's no motor cars No two-seaters, no *six-seaters. **1977** *Herald* (Melbourne) 18 Jan. 2/2 A six-seater antique dining table, and two antique chairs were among the $4000 haul. **1890** W. J. GORDON *Foundry* 158 The longest *six-wheeler is fifty-four feet [long].

**4.** In advb. sense, = 'in six parts', as ***six-cleft***, ***-parted***, ***-partite***.

**1785** MARTYN *Rousseau's Lett. Bot.* xxviii. 439 The corol is six-parted; and the stamens are usually eighteen. **1832** RENNIE *Butterfl. & Moths* 231 The Six-cleft Plume.. appears early in spring. **1861** HULME *Wild Fl.* Introd. p. viii, Perianth campanulate, six-partite. **1866** *Treas. Bot.* 167/2 A very short six-cleft somewhat spreading limb.

**5.** Miscellaneous, as **six-ale** (see quot. 1898); **six-bar**, a six-barred gate; **six-branchial** *a.*, six-gilled; **six by six** *U.S. Mil. slang* (see quot. 1966); also written *6 × 6*, *6 by 6* and *ellipt.* as **six-by**; **six chamber**, a six-chambered revolver; also in full **six chamber revolver**; **Six Day(s) War**, an Arab—Israeli war that lasted from 5 to 10 June 1967; †**six-double** *a.*, sixfold; **six-eight tempo, time** *Mus.*, time or rhythm having a bar length of six quavers' duration divided into two equal beats; also *ellipt.* and as $\frac{6}{8}$; **six-figure** *a.*, (*a*) evaluated to or containing six significant figures or six decimal places; (*b*) containing or represented by six digits; *spec.* worth hundreds of thousands (of pounds, dollars, etc.); also in phr. ***in six figures***; **six-four** (see quot.); **six-four measure, meter, time** *Mus.*, time or rhythm having a bar length of six crotchets' duration divided into two equal beats; also *ellipt.* and as $\frac{6}{4}$; **six-gun** *N. Amer.* = SIX-SHOOTER; cf. *six-chamber* (*revolver*); **six-oar**, a six-oared boat; **six o'clock**: see sense 2 c of the adj.; also denoting any position resembling that of the hands of a clock at six o'clock; **six-pack** orig. and chiefly *U.S.*, a package containing six cans or bottles of a drink; **six-shot, six-stroke**, a stroke in billiards counting six points; **six-tooth** (cf. *six-tooth* C. 1 and *six-toothed* C. 2); **six-two time** *Mus.*, time or rhythm having a bar length of six minims' duration divided into two equal beats; also written $\frac{6}{2}$.

**1871** *N.Y. Almanac* 40/1 And a glass of '*six ale', punctually every morning at eleven o'clock, was absolutely necessary to his existence. **1898** *N. & Q.* 9th Ser. I. 132 'Six ale' is a mixture of one at fourpence a pot with one at eightpence a pot in equal proportions. **1841** LYTTON *Night & M.* I. iv, We will..take the gate yonder—the old *six-bar. **1862** COUCH *Brit. Fishes* I. 21 *Six-Branchial Shark. **1942** *Infantry Jrnl.* Sept. 41/1 A group of upturned faces stands out to an aerial observer like a *6 × 6 in a flock of jeeps. **1943** *Yank* 3 Sept. 7/2 I'm herding a 6 by 6. **1966** *Sunday Times* (Colour Suppl.) 4 Dec. 73/4 GI Jargon. *Six by six*, six wheel truck with six-wheel drive. **1973** D. FAIRBAIRN *Shoot* xiv. 109, I want you to load everything onto a six-by, and I want you to have the six-by all gassed up and ready to go. **1898** *Tit-Bits* 9 July 289/1, I slipped..a neat..*six-chamber into my hip-pocket. **1922** JOYCE *Ulysses* 642 The sixchamber revolver anecdotes verging on the tropical. **1967** *Times* 14 June 1/3 The purpose of this move is clearly to have the Assembly condemn Israel and demand that she withdraw her armed forces to the armistice demarcation lines as they existed before the *six-day war that started on June 5. **1967** *Listener* 17 Aug. 196/3 In the euphoria that followed the Six Days War, the Israelis appear to be convinced that they can work miracles. **1977** P. JOHNSON *Enemies of Society* xviii. 241 The impetus which created the political terrorism of the 1970s was undoubtedly provided by the Arab defeat in the 1967 Six Day war. **1552** HULOET, *Sixe dowble, *sexcuplus*. **1873** *Illustr. London News* 2 Aug. 114/2 'Sleep, baby darling,' a lullaby..is in the '*six-eight tempo conventionally associated with slumber-songs. **1884** GROVE *Dict. Mus.* IV. 119/1 Six-eight time..with two Beats in the Bar, each represented by a dotted Crotchet—or its equivalent, three Quavers. **1936** F. G. HAWKES *Stud. in Time & Tempo* xii. 74, $\frac{3}{4}$, $\frac{6}{8}$, and $\frac{6}{4}$ are much alike so far as the movements of the baton are concerned. **1965** *New Yorker* 8 May 173/1 McFarland's rhythms are full of stop-times, double time-passages, six-eight time, and shuffle rhythms. **1978** G. READ *Mod. Rhythmic Notation* v. 158 In essence, the $\frac{6}{8}$ violin part constitutes triplets in duple time. **1840** R. FARLEY (*title*) Tables of *six-figure logarithms. **1873** 'MARK TWAIN' & WARNER *Gilded Age* xiii. 123 He always talked in six figures. It was as natural for the dear boy to be rich as it is for most of us to be poor. **1963** P. DRACKETT *Motor Rallying* iii. 40 To illustrate, let's take a six-figure reference, the type normally employed. It may be, say 386 443. **1970** J. MCN. DODGSON *Pl.-Names Cheshire* I. p. xliv, A four- or six-figure National Grid reference to the location of the principal hamlet. **1971** *Daily Tel.* 7 July 14, 64 pictures in 75 minutes, three in the six-figure class, and Monet's great painting..not far behind. **1981** R. ADAMS *Girl in Swing* (rev. ed.) xxi. 291 If you were to decide to put it into auction it would be almost bound to go for a very large sum—in the six-figure range. **1873** H. C. BANISTER *Music* 70 The second inversion, consisting of a note with its 4th and 6th, is termed the Chord of the *Six-four. **1884** GROVE *Dict. Mus.* IV. 119/1 Six-four Time..with two Beats in the bar, each represented by a dotted Minim—or its equivalent, three Crotchets. **1936** Six-four [see *six-eight* above]. **1938** *Oxf. Compan. Mus.* 409/1 If the fifth [is in the bass] it is a Second Inversion (also spoken of as 'six-four' chord). **1968** *Listener* 6 June 748/3 An un-metrical vocal line in six-four against an accompaniment in four-four. **1978** G. READ *Mod. Rhythmic Notation* v. 159 Combining two $|\frac{3}{4}$ measures into one $|\frac{6}{4}$ measure does not simplify the issue, nor would altering the $|\frac{6}{4}$ meter to $|\frac{5}{2}$. **1912** W. M. RAINE *Brand Blotters* 336 My carbine was gone. It was too far for a *six-gun. **1968** E. MCCOURT *Saskatchewan* v. 61 The Canadian cowboys rode un-armed, the Americans carried six-guns. **1979** G. SWARTHOUT *Skeletons* 30 I'll..order a shot of red-eye and lay my six-gun on the bar. **1856** LEVER *Martins of Cro' M.* vii. 57 Where [were] the fellows who could tool a team or steer a *six-oar? **1684** *Phil. Trans. R. Soc.* XVII. 672 The Courses [i.e. veins of ore] usually lying from East to West, or at *Six a Clock as their Term is. **1915** 'I. HAY' *First Hundred Thousand* vii. 82 He..touched 'six o' clock' on the distant bull..and took the second pull for the last time. **1927** W. E. COLLINSON *Contemp. Eng.* 92 Expressions I learnt.. when doing target-practice..viz. the six o'clock aim (from position on target focussed). **1961** *Wall St. Jrnl.* 19 Oct. 1/5 One leading brand which retailed for $2·09 a *six-pack last January now is sold for $1·79. **1972** M. J. BOSSE *Incident at Naha* iii. 138, I took her a pound of bacon and a six-pack of diet cola. **1981** *TV Picture Life* Mar. 46/2 'I went out and borrowed a pickup truck and wore my hat out in the rain for a couple of days, got a six-pack of beer and didn't shower,' John remembers. **1861** *Chambers's Encycl.* II. 98/2 A *six-stroke is made by playing at the red, and pocketing it and your own. **1878** *Wilts. Arch. Mag.* XVII. 303 We have wether hogs.., and four-tooths, and *six-tooths. **1884** GROVE *Dict. Mus.* IV. 119/1 *Six-two time, $|\frac{6}{2}$; with two beats in each Bar; each represented by a dotted Semibreve —or its equivalent, three Minims. **1978** G. READ *Mod. Rhythmic Notation* ii. 9 In more traditional symbology, $\frac{3}{1}$ or $\frac{3}{1}$.

**sixain** ('sɪkseɪn, ‖sizɛ̃). Also 6 **syx-, sixaine, sizeine.** [a. F. *sixain* (OF. *sisain, sizain*), f. *six* six.]

**1.** A stanza of six lines. (Cf. SEXTAIN.)

**1575** GASCOIGNE *Notes of Instruction* Wks. 1907 I. 472 There are Dyzaynes, & Syxaines,..commonly used by the French. *Ibid.* 473 Dizaynes and Sixaines [serve] for shorte Fantazies. **1589** PUTTENHAM *Eng. Poesie* (Arb.) 79 The first proportion..of a staffe is by *quadrien* or foure verses... The third by *sizeine* or sixe verses. *Ibid.* 101 The *Sixaine* or staffe of sixe hath ten proportions. **1656** in BLOUNT *Glossogr.* **1841** BORROW *Zincali* III. i. 6 Occasionally, sixains or stanzas of six lines, are to be found. **1881** SAINTSBURY in *Academy* 15 Jan. 40 The tendency of a sonnet to split into a huitain and a sixain.

†**2.** *Mil.* (See quot.) *Obs.*⁻⁰

Merely copied from some French work, such as Furetière's Dict., and never actually used in English. Hence in later Dicts., as Harris, Kersey, James, etc.

**1702** *Milit. Dict.* (1708), *Sixain*, an ancient Order of Battle for six Batalions... Twelve Batalions will make two Sixains, eighteen will make three, and so on.

**sixareen**: see SIXERN.

**Six Clerk.** Now only *Hist.* Also **Six-Clerk.** [See SIX *a.* 1 d.] One of the six official clerks formerly connected with the Court of Chancery.

The office was abolished in 1843; for a full account of its history see the *Penny Cycl.* (1842) XXII. 70–72.

**1625** WOTTON *Lett.* (1907) II. 316 A Moiety of a Six Clerk's place in Chancery. **1659** *England's Conf.* 11 Mr. Smith a Six Clerk. *a* **1734** NORTH *Lives* (1826) II. 189 A good natured six-clerk took a fancy to the young man. **1813** *Act 53 Geo. III*, c. 129 Any Office or Offices of a Six Clerk or Six Clerks of the Court of Chancery in Ireland. **1842** *Penny Cycl.* XXII. 70/2 In 1630 the office of Six-Clerk was, if not a sinecure, at least an appointment of great value.

**sixer** ('sɪksə(r)). *colloq.* [f. SIX *a.* + -ER¹. Cf. G. *sechser.*]

**1.** Anything that counts as six (as a hit for six runs at cricket).

**1870** *Routledge's Every Boy's Ann.* 452 It is not difficult to hit sixers to leg. **1905** VACHELL *Hill* xii, Never before in an Eton and Harrow match have two 'sixers' been hit in succession.

**2.** *slang.* **a.** Six months' hard labour. Also, six months' imprisonment.

**1849** *Session Papers* 1 Feb. 324 The prisoner said he should not mind if he got off with a *sixer*—that means six months' imprisonment. **1869** *Temple Bar* Apr. 75 The next bit I did was a 'sixer'. **1887** J. W. HORSLEY *Jottings from Jail* i. 23 Neddie, from City Road, smugged for attempt up the Grove, expects a sixer..and is reconciling himself to an absence from his oriental home for half a year. **1900** *Daily News* 6 Nov. 9/1 The prisoner..said, 'It don't matter whether I get a sixer or a stretch'. **1903** [see CARPET *sb.* 7]. **1926** J. BLACK *You can't Win* xii. 161 We'll both get a 'sixer' in the morning if we go in front of the judge. **1955** D. W. MAURER in *Publ. Amer. Dial. Soc.* xxiv. 151 Maybe he will get off with a *bit*..or a *sixer*, which is six months in jail.

**b.** A sixth term of imprisonment.

**1872** [see FIVER 3].

**c.** A six-ounce loaf.

**1877** *Five Yrs. Penal Servitude* iii, He keeps a sharp eye on that man to see he does not 'filch' a 'sixer', as the six ounce loaf served with dinner, is called. **1899** *Westm. Gaz.* 29 Nov. 3/1 The 'sixers' of old..had become eight-ounce loaves for men.

**d.** Six strokes of the cane administered as punishment in school. Cf. *six of the best* s.v. BEST *a.* 10 d.

**1927** *Chambers's Jrnl.* 10 Sept. 645/2 About a dozen boys ..ranged up in front of the Doctor, who, stepping off his pedestal, administered a 'sixer' to each of the culprits with a long and stout cane. **1977** C. MCCULLOUGH *Thorn Birds* ii. 29 They all got sixers, but Meggie was terribly upset because she thought she ought to have been the only one punished.

**3.** A Brownie Guide or Cub Scout in charge of a six.

**1916** R. BADEN-POWELL *Wolf Cub's Handbk.* III. 216 The average Cub when promoted to Sixer does not carry so much authority. **1920** [see SIX *sb.* 2 b (*b*)]. **1965** G. MCINNES *Road to Gundagai* x. 161, I was promoted to be Sixer of the Whites. **1978** *Lochaber News* 31 Mar. 7/5 On Thursday, March 23 the sixers and seconds went to Raigmore Hospital to present a cheque to Dr John Burton for the kidney unit at the hospital.

**sixern** ('sɪksən). *Shetland.* Also **sexern, sixareen, sixereen,** etc. [repr. ON. *sexæringr* (Norw. *seksæring, seksring*), f. *sex* six + *ár* oar.] A six-oared boat.

**1866** EDMONSTON *Gloss. Shetl.* 103 *Sixareen*, a six-oared Norway skiff. **1881** *Standard* 9 Aug. 6/3 The 'Sixern'..will not on the average exceed 19 ft. in length by about 5 ft. or 6 ft. in breadth and 4 ft. in depth. **1883** *Fisheries Exhib. Catal.* 46 Model of a 'Sixern', 'Sixareen', or six-oared yawl. **1906** H. W. SMYTH *Mast & Sail* 114 *note*, Very few 'sexerns' are now being built.

'**sixfoil.** *Arch.* and *Her.* [f. SIX, after *quatre-, cinquefoil.*] An ornamental design (or opening) having the form of six leaflets or petals radiating from a common centre.

**1849** RUSKIN *Seven Lamps* ii. §21. 53 The double sub-arch decorated..with quatrefoils, sixfoils, and septfoils, in the transept towers of Rouen. **1864** [see CINQUEFOIL *sb.* 2 b]. **1864** BOUTELL *Her. Hist. & Pop.* xv. 194 In early blazoning but little difference appears to have been recognized between sixfoils and roses.

**sixfold** ('sɪksfəʊld), *a.* Also 1 **sixfeald,** 5 **sex(e)fold,** 6–7 **sixefolde,** 7 **-fold, sixfould.** [f. SIX *a.* + -FOLD. Cf. ON. *sexfaldr*, MSw. *siäxfald*, Da. *sexfold*, MHG. *sehsvalt.*] Consisting of six together; comprising six things, kinds, etc.; also, six times as great or as numerous; sextuple.

*a* **1000** in Wr.-Wülcker 230 *Exagonum*, sixfeald. *Exametro heroico*, sixfealdum leoþcræfte. **1447** BOKENHAM *Seyntys* (Roxb.) 10 This sexefold propyrte Of the margaryte. **1497** *Naval Acc. Hen. VII* (1896) 91 Sex fold takle with a robenett. **1552** in HULOET. **1557** RECORDE *Whetst.* B ij, Sextupla. 6 to 1 : 12 to 2..Sixefolde. **1609** [J. MELTON] (*title*), A Sixe-folde Politician; together with a Sixe-folde Precept of Policy. **1641** 'SMECTYMNUUS' *Vind. Answ.* xiv. 182 Wee shewed a sixfold difference. **1733** E. ERSKINE *Serm.* Wks. 1871 II. 206, I have given you a sixfold View of that Christian fortitude. **1776** PENNANT *Brit. Zool.* III. 94 The mouth of this fish is furnished with (sometimes) a sixfold row of teeth. **1823** H. J. BROOKE *Introd. Crystallogr.* 59 The primary planes of those forms which possess fourfold or sixfold cleavages. **1882** FARRAR *Early Chr.* II. 29 The sixfold woe of Isaiah (Is. v. 1–30) on greed, and luxury, and unbelief, and pride, and injustice, and the reversal of moral truths.

'**six-foot,** *a.* [See SIX C. 1.]

**1.** Measuring six feet in length, breadth, or height.

*a* **1683** OLDHAM *Par. Horace* II. xiv. 4 To have but the small pittance of a six-foot Grave. **1733** TULL *Horse-Hoeing Husb.* xi. 113 To make a Six-Foot Ridge very high, will sometimes require more Furrows. **1808** SCOTT *Marm.* I. viii, Each one a six-foot bow could bend. **1823** BYRON *Juan* IX. xlvi, But they were mostly nervous six-foot fellows. **1872** RAYMOND *Statist. Mines & Mining* 301 The pump.. worked on a six-foot stroke.

**b.** ***six-foot way***, the space between two parallel railway lines; also with ellipse of *way*.

**1861** *Star & Dials* 21 Oct., The third [truck] was simply knocked into the six-foot. **1878** F. S. WILLIAMS *Midl. Railw.* 559 The distance between the two pairs of rails (popularly called the six-foot) is here wider than usual.

**2.** Containing six (metrical) feet.

**1891** J. C. PARSONS *English Versification* 98 The existence [in Shakspere] of occasional six-foot lines is generally admitted. [Cf. *six-feet* s.v. SIX C. 1.]

**six-footer**: see SIX C. 3.

‖**sixieme.** *Obs. rare.* Also **sixiesm.** [F. *sixième* (†*sixiesme*, etc.), f. *six* six.] A sequence of six cards at piquet. ***sixieme major***, one consisting of ace, king, queen, knave, ten, and nine.

**1663** DRYDEN *Wild Gallant* IV. i, 'Twas won fairly: a Sixieme, and Fourteen by Aces. *Ibid.*, 14 by Aces, and a Sixieme Major. **1674** COTTON *Compl. Gamester* (1680) 60 You must reckon..for a Sixiesm sixteen.

**sixpence** ('sɪkspəns). Also *Sc.* 8- **saxpence.** [f. SIX *a.* + PENCE.]

**1.** A sum of money equal in value to six pennies.

*c* **1380** WYCLIF *Wks.* (1880) 36 Wheþer þis be charite to curse a man for sexe pans. *c* **1440** *Alph. Tales* 273, I sall pray my moder to gif me vjd & þat I sall giff you. **1486** *Rec. St. Mary at Hill* (1905) 6 For the vnder Clerk vj d for euer. **1590** SHAKS. *Mids. N.* IV. ii. 20 Thus hath he lost sixepence a day, during his life; he could not haue scaped sixpence a day. **1641** HAKEWILL *Libertie of Subject* 70 There shoulde be paid ..six pence of the pound upon all other Merchandizes. **1705** HICKERINGILL *Priest-cr.* I. (1721) 44 In hopes of Sixpence and their Dinners. **1752** HUME *Ess. & Treat.* (1777) I. 444 Every person in England is computed by some to spend sixpence a day. **1807** CRABBE *Par. Reg.* I. 83 That Bible, bought by sixpence weekly saved. **1846** DICKENS *Cricket on Hearth* ii. 65 As near the real thing as sixpenn'orth of halfpence is to sixpence.

*Comb.* **1780** J. WOODFORDE *Diary* 20 June (1924) I. 286 Gave on going—O.I.O. For which you have 6d worth of anything at the Bar. **1828** SCOTT *Jrnl.* 22 April, An extra sixpence worth of snuff. **1875** A. R. HOPE *My Schoolboy Fr.* 76 We bought sixpenceworth of chocolate.

**2. a.** *Hist.* A British silver (subsequently cupro-nickel) coin worth six pennies.

**1598** [see MILL *sb.*¹ 12]. **1659** [see MILLED *ppl. a.* 2]. *c* **1675** R. CROMWELL in *Eng. Hist. Rev.* XIII. 93 As much as will lye upon a sixpence. **1707** SIBBALD *Scotland* (1739) I. 24 The Size of the late Coin'd English Sixpence. **1758** *Phil. Trans.* L. 551, I found the peritonæum..to be of the thickness of a six-pence. **1800** MRS. HERVEY *Mourtray Fam.* I. 294 Lady Bell protested she had not a six-pence in her pocket. **1833** T. HOOK *Parson's Dau.* I. xi, I have no assurance..that Emma Lovell cares one single sixpence about me. **1886** PASCOE *London of To-day* iv. (ed. 3) 65 The 'Zoo' on Monday,.. when a sixpence opens the gate to the neediest.

**b.** Applied to Spanish coins. In later use *U.S.*

**1563** *Child Marriages* 58 Well she remembres he send her a Spanish vjd. **1818** H. B. FEARON *Sk. Amer.* 13 A beggar came in, and was relieved with a Spanish silver piece called a six-pence. **1859** BARTLETT *Dict. Amer.* (ed. 2), *Sixpence*, the New York name for the Spanish half-real. **1891** S. M. WELCH *Home Hist.* 169 It was common, particularly in New England, to call a sixpence or a half dime, a *fip*.

**c.** *transf.* Used familiarly as a nickname or designation.

**1600** NASHE *Summers Last Will & Test.* 857 Young sixpence, the best page his master hath, playes a little, and retires. **1899** WESTCOTT *David Harum* vii, Ann and Jeff are just the same old sixpences as ever.

**d.** *colloq.* (See first quots.)

**1772** R. GRAVES *Spir. Quixote* (1783) I. 225 Beginning to spit six-pences (as his saying was), he gave hints to Mr. Wildgoose to stop at the first public-house. **1799** BEDDOES *Contrib. Phys. & Med. Knowl.* 419 Expectoration of a little frothy mucus, such as are vulgarly called sixpences. **1889** A. G. MURDOCH *Sc. Readings* Ser. III. 60 See if ye can bring us in half-a-mutchkin, for I'm spittin' white sixpences.

**sixpenny** ('sɪkspənɪ), *a.* and *sb.* [SIX *a.*]

**1.** ***sixpenny nail***, a nail originally costing sixpence per hundred. (See PENNY 10.) Also *fig.*

**1426–7** [see PENNY 10]. **1486** *Naval Acc. Hen. VII* (1896) 16, cc vj peny nailes xijd. **1494–5** *Sarum Churchw. Acc.* (ed. Swayne) 43 Pro clauis voc' sixpeny nayle iijd. **1607** WALKINGTON *Opt. Glass* 128 Rap at the wicket with the six-penny nayle of modesty. **1703** MOXON *Mech. Exerc.* 244 Four Penny, and Six Penny Nails, used for Pantile Lathing. **1730** *Phil. Trans.* XXXVI. 309 A prepared Six-penny (or.. a Ten-penny) Nail. **1833** *Penny Cycl.* I. 119/1 A six-penny nail, 73 to the lb., 2½ inches long. **1869** RANKINE *Machine & Hand-tools* App. 46 The force required to draw a 'sixpenny nail' of 73 to the lb.

**2.** Of persons: That may be hired for sixpence; earning no more than sixpence; worth only sixpence; paltry, petty. Also of things.

Common as a depreciatory term *c* 1590–1630.

**1561** PRESTON *K. Cambyses* B iij, *Ruff.* I will giue thee sixpence to lie one night with thee. *Mer.* Gogs hart, slaue, doost thinke I am a sixpeny Jug? **1589** NASHE *Anat. Absurd.* Epist., The birthright of euerie six pennie slaue. **1596** SHAKS. *1 Hen. IV*, II. i. 82, I am ioyned with no Footland-Rakers, no Long-staffe six-penny strikers. **1632** MASSINGER *City Madam* III. i, Swaggering, suburbian roarers, Sixpenny truckers. **1633** FORD *Love's Sacr.* II. iii, The poorest peasant that ever was yok'd to a sixpenny strumpet. **1788** BURNS *Let. to Mrs. Dunlop* 21 Jan., Lately I was a six-penny private, and, God knows, a miserable soldier enough. **1878** H. H. JACKSON *Travel at Home* 11 She didn't never want to see any o' them sixpenny towns agin. **1911** G. B. SHAW *Doctor's Dilemma* p. xxvi, The sixpenny doctor, with his low prices and quick turnover of patients, visibly makes much more than you. **1927** KIPLING *Limits & Renewals* (1932) 164 When I was a sixpenny doctor at Lambeth.

**3. a.** Costing, or priced at, sixpence.

**1591** NASHE *Pref. Sidney's Astr. & Stella*, An Asse is no great statesman..though he..look as demurely as a six-penny browne loafe. **1614** B. JONSON *Barth. Fair* II. ii, Bring him a sixpenny bottle of ale. **1678** *Lond. Gaz.* No. 1348/4 Eight pieces of Six-peny broad black taffaty Ribon. **1711** SWIFT *Jrnl. to Stella* 27 Apr., I went to town in the sixpenny stage to-day. **1760–72** BROOKE *Fool of Qual.* (1809) III. 110 A shilling, to buy two six-penny loaves. **1904** *Daily Chron.* 11 Mar. 3/5 It is generally accepted..that the six-penny reprint has come to stay.

**b.** Bringing in sixpence; having a subscription of sixpence; selling articles at sixpence.

**1673** *Humours Town* 29 To make the Voyage of the Strand ..in search of some Six-penny Adventure. **1807** SYD. SMITH *P. Plymley's Lett.* iv, I hear from some persons in Parliament, and from others in the sixpenny societies for debate [etc.]. **1888** *Daily News* 23 Nov. 7/2 A 'sixpenny bazaar', an emporium where any article on sale was to be had for a sixpence.

**c.** As *sb.* A book (*esp.* a novel) or magazine published at sixpence.

**1840** *Knickerbocker* XV. 138 The larger newspaper establishments, satirically termed by their Lilliputian rivals, 'the respectable sixpennies'. **1894** *Literary World* 30 Nov. 432/1 Has the knell of the solid Sixpennies been sounded?

**d.** As *sb.* A cinema seat that costs sixpence.

**1958** *Listener* 4 Dec. 927/2 A small boy sitting in the sixpennies at the Bijou Cinema.

**4.** Amounting to, having the value of, sixpence.

***sixpenny bit*** or ***piece*** (now *Hist.*), = SIXPENCE 2.

**1592** GREENE *Groat's W. Wit* (1617) 3 A sixepenny reward in signe of my superficiall liberality. **1605** *London Prodigal* v. i. 72 Ile not let a sixepennie-purse escape me. **1712** H. PRIDEAUX *Direct. Ch.-Wardens* (ed. 4) 99 This is done for the base Lucre of a Six-penny or Twelve-penny Fee. **1842** BISCHOFF *Wool Manuf.* II. 157 A sixpenny duty on the import. **1852** BRISTED *Five Yrs. Eng. Univ.* (ed. 2) 335 Non-reading men play..for the lowest possible (sixpenny) points. **1897** M. H. KINGSLEY *Travels in W. Afr.* xxvi. 589 A piece of ground the size of a sixpenny piece. **1899** *Allbutt's Syst. Med.* VIII. 837 It is round or oval, the size of a threepenny or sixpenny piece.

**sixpennyworth** (sɪks'pɛnɪwɜːθ). Also **sixpenn'orth** (sɪks'pɛnəθ), **sixpennorth**. [f. SIX *a.* + PENNY + WORTH *sb.*] As much as is worth sixpence; an amount which is or may be bought for sixpence.

*c* **1450** *Godstow Reg.* 502 Sixe peny worthe of yerely rente. **1711** SWIFT *Jrnl. to Stella* 5 Apr., This rain ruins me in coach-hire; I walked away sixpennyworth. **1836–7** DICKENS *Sk. Boz, Characters* viii, Ninety-seven sixpenn'orths of gin-and-water. **1884** *Graphic* 13 Sept. 278/1 A marvellous Sixpennyworth. **1933** [see BACCO, BACCY].

**six-pounder** ('sɪkspaʊndə(r)). [f. SIX *a.* + POUNDER *sb.*[4]]

**1.** A cannon throwing shot six pounds in weight.

**1684** J. PETER *Relat. Siege of Vienna* 108 Six pounders, 2. **1748** *Anson's Voy.* II. iv. 169 Four six pounders, four four pounders, and two swivels. **1790** BEATSON *Naval & Milit. Mem.* II. 166 A light brass six-pounder to be fixed in the bow of their long-boat. **1838** *Civil Eng. & Arch. Jrnl.* I. 347/1 The report was smart like that of a six-pounder. **1876** BANCROFT *Hist. U.S.* V. xx. 568 Cornwallis planted..some six-pounders on his own left.

*fig.* **1797** in Lockhart *Scott* (1837) I. viii. 263 Clerk and I are continually obliged to open a six-pounder upon him in self-defence.

*attrib.* **1810** WELLINGTON in Gurw. *Desp.* (1838) VI. 220 The Portuguese six pounder brigade.

**b.** A shot weighing six pounds.

**1855** MACAULAY *Hist. Eng.* xvi. III. 628 He was himself hit by a second ball, a sixpounder.

†**2.** (See quot.) *Obs.*[−0]

**1785** GROSE *Dict. Vulgar T., Six pounder*, a servant maid, from the wages formerly given to maid servants, which was commonly six pounds.

**'sixscore**, *a.* Now *arch.* [f. SIX *a.* + SCORE *sb.* 16.] Six times twenty, one hundred and twenty.

*a* **1300** *Cursor M.* 5353, I am sex scor and ten yeir ald. **1393** LANGL. *P. Pl.* C. IV. 183 Hue may ney as moche do in a mounthe one As ȝoure secret seel in sexscore dayes. **1489** *Mater. Reign Hen. VII* (Rolls) II. 445 Diverse summes of money amounting to the sum of sex score poundes sterlinges. **1535** COVERDALE *1 Kings* ix. 14 And Hiram sent vnto the kynge sixe score hundreth weight of Golde. **1604** E. G[RIMSTONE] *D'Acosta's Hist. Indies* v. xiii. 363 There was a staire of stone of sixscore steppes. *a* **1704** T. BROWN *Two Oxford Scholars* Wks. 1730 I. 9 His living was commonly reputed worth sixscore pounds a year. **1814** SOUTHEY *Carmina Aulica* ii. 2 Sixscore full years have pass'd. **1870** BRYANT *Iliad* I. II. 59 Fifty were their barks and each Held sixscore youths of the Bœotian race.

**'six-ˌshooter.** [See SIX C. 3.] A revolver capable of firing six shots without reloading; a six-chambered revolver. Also *fig.*

**1844** *Nauvoo* (Illinois) *Neighbor* 24 July 3/1 Joseph.. opening the door..discharged one barrel of a six shooter (Pistol) in the entry. **1856** KANE *Arct. Expl.* II. xxv. 250 The imaginary powers of the angekok-soak and the marvellous six-shooter which attested them. **1865** LOWELL *Wks.* (1890) V. 267 Every senator seems to carry..a sort of legislative six-shooter. **1883** *Harper's Mag.* Jan. 207/2 A valiant wielder of the brush brought up the rear with a six-shooter.

*attrib.* *a* **1894** C. H. PEARSON in Stebbing *Life* (1900) 134 There were only two laws..in Julesburg—lynch law and six-shooter law.

Hence **'six-ˌshooting** *vbl. sb.* and *ppl. a.* Also **'six-ˌshooter** *v.*; **'six-ˌshootering** *vbl. sb.*

**1858** T. VIELE *Following Drum* 224 A belt full of pistols, .. and a six-shooting rifle. **1887** *Illustr. Lond. News* 2 Apr. 370 The Home Secretary sees no reason for legally interfering with the unrestricted enjoyment of six-shooting. **1896** *Daily News* 24 Jan. 3/4 By his side was a six-shooting revolver. **1904** P. FOUNTAIN *Great North-West* xx. 242, I never was so near six-shootering myself as I was that night. **1909** 'O. HENRY' *Roads of Destiny* xxii. 371 We heard a yelling and a six-shootering.

**six-sided**, *a.* [f. SIX *a.* + SIDE *sb.*[1]] Having six sides; hexagonal.

**1693** *Phil. Trans.* XVII. 756 Some were pyramidal, constituted on a six-sided Basis. **1797** *Encycl. Brit.* (ed. 3) IX. 739/2 Prisms, terminated by six-sided pyramids. **1821** JAMESON *Man. Min.* 194 Its most frequent crystallization is the acute six-sided pyramid. **1859** HUXLEY *Oceanic Hydrozoa* 65 Hydrophyllium six-sided. **1877** —— *Physiogr.* 58 These shapes usually look like little six-sided towers.. terminated at one end..by a short six-sided spire.

Hence **six-sidedness.**

**1883** DRUMMOND *Nat. Law Spir. W.* 371 There is a six-sidedness, as it were, in the very nature of this substance.

**sixsome** ('sɪkssəm). Chiefly *Sc.* Also 5 **sex sum**, 5–9 *Sc.* **saxsum**. [f. SIX *a.* + -SOME. Cf. OFris. *sexasum* (WFris. *sechstesum*, *seizesum*).]

**1. a.** As one of six; with five others. *Obs.* **b.** Six in all; six together. Now *rare* or *Obs.*

*c* **897** K. ÆLFRED *Oros.* I. i. 18 þara he sæde þæt he syxa sum ofsloȝe syxtiȝ on twam daȝum. **1375** BARBOUR *Bruce* VI. 231 And syne his suerd he swappit out, .. And slew sex sum weill soyn and ma. ? *a* **1400** *Morte Arth.* 471, I am sengilly here, with sex sum of knyghtes. **1470** HENRY *Wallace* IX. 703 Saxsum thar com, and brocht bot cartis thre. **1825** JAMIESON *Suppl.* s.v. *Sum.*

**2.** As *adj.* Performed by six persons together.

**1888** SAXBY *Lads of Lunda* 216 The set began a sixsome reel.

† **six-square**, *a.* and *sb. Obs.* [f. SIX, after *three-*, *four-*, *five-square*.]

**A.** *adj.* **1.** Having six (linear) sides; hexagonal.

*c* **1530** in Gutch *Coll. Cur.* II. 305 A Challes withe a patten gilte, the foote of vj square. **1577** GOOGE *Heresb. Husb.* IV. (1586) 175 Their Celles, or lodgings, made every one sixe square. **1688** HOLME *Armoury* III. 456 He beareth Gules, a six Square Tower. **1699** MAUNDRELL *Journ. Jerus.* 7 Below the Castle Hill..stands a noble old Monument. It is six square. **1713** WARDER *True Amazons* 59 Cells..which are Mathematically Six Square.

**2.** Having six superficial sides; of the form of a cube; cubical.

**1594** BLUNDEVIL *Exerc.* III. I. (1636) 273 Made like a six-square Dy. **1598** BP. HALL *Sat.* IV. iii, Upon a six-square piece of ivory.

**B.** *sb.* A hexagon.

**1680** *Lond. Gaz.* No. 1499/4 The hours engraven in a six-square.

**sixt(e**, obs. forms of SIXTH.

‖ **sixte** (sɪkst). [F. *sixte* sixth.] A particular position in fencing.

**1885** E. CASTLE *Schools & Masters of Fence* 138 It is.. probable that seven out of the eight modern parries, 'prime, seconde, tierce, quarte, sixte..' were practised..in the early days of Louis XIV.'s reign. **1889** POLLOCK *Fencing* (Badm.) p. xi, Time Thrust in Sixte.

**sixteen** (sɪk'stiːn, 'sɪkstiːn), *a.* and *sb.* Forms: α. 1 **syx-**, **sixtyne**, 3–4 **sixtene**, 5–6 **syxtene**, 6–7 **sixteene**, 7– **sixteen** (7 **-tein**). β. 1– 6 **sextene** (5 **cex-**), 4–6 **sexten**, 4 **sextiene**, 5 **sex-**, **cexteyn(e**; *Sc.* 5 **saxten**, 6 **-tine**, 7 **sextine**. [OE. *syx-*, *six-*, *sextyne* (see SIX *a.* and -TEEN), = OFris. *sextine*, *-tene* (WFris. *sêchstjin*, NFris. *sokstain*, etc.), MDu. *sestien* (Du. *zestien*), OS. *se(h)stein* (MLG. *sestein*, LG. *ses-*, *sös-*, *sostein*), OHG. *seh(s)zên* (G. *sechzehn*, †*sechszehn*), ON. and Icel. *sextán* (Sw. *sexton*, Da. *sexten*).] The cardinal number composed of ten and six, represented by the symbols 16, XVI, or xvi.

**A.** *adj.* **1.** In concord with a sb. expressed.

α. *a* **900** *O.E. Martyrol.* 4 Mar., Sixtyne monað hi wæron somod. *c* **1205** LAY. 26658 Arður þider hafde isend sixtene þusund baldere Brutten. *c* **1290** *S. Eng. Leg.* I. 115 Sixtene bischopus al-so þis dede to ende bringue. **1382** WYCLIF *2 Kings* xv. 33 Sixtene ȝeer he regned in Jerusalem. **1495** *Trevisa's Barth. De P.R.* IX. ix. 354 Ianuarius hath longe nyghtes of syxtene houres. **1535** COVERDALE *Gen.* xlvi. 18 She bare vnto Iacob these sixtene soules. **1591** SHAKS. *Two Gentl.* IV. i. 21 Some sixteene moneths. **1653** H. COGAN tr. *Pinto's Trav.* xxix. 113 Two Mayes, which amounts to about sixteen pence of our Money. **1700** DRYDEN *Ovid's Metam., Acis, Pol. & Galatea* 7 Now sixteen Summers the sweet Youth had seen. **1784** COWPER *Tiroc.* 210 There shall he learn, ere sixteen winters old [etc.]. **1847** W. C. L. MARTIN *Ox* 178/2 A full dose averages twelve, fourteen, or sixteen ounces. **1889** GRETTON *Memory's Harkback* 123 The man had the sixteen miles to Gloucester to cover.

β. *a* **900** *O.E. Martyrol.* 30 July, þonne bið seo niht eahta tida lang, & se dæg sextene tida. *c* **1200** ORMIN 572 Forr þatt Eleazar Sextene suness haffde. **1390** GOWER *Conf.* III. 120 Cancer..hath unto his retienance Sextiene sterres. *c* **1470** HENRY *Wallace* IX. 63 Sowthest he saw..Saxten salis arayit all on raw. **1483** *Cath. Angl.* 332/1 Sexten sythe, *sedecies*. **1549** *Compl. Scotl.* 93 To the nummer of sexten scoir of the maist nobillis of the cuntre. **1596** DALRYMPLE tr. *Leslie's Hist. Scot.* I. 82 A thousand a hundir and saxtine ȝeiris.

**2. a.** With ellipsis of sb., which may usually be supplied from the context.

*a* **1225** *Ancr. R.* 298 þe uorme o six stucchenes, þe oðer o sixtene. **1338** R. BRUNNE *Chron.* (1810) 37 þe date was nien hundreth sexti & sextene. *c* **1375** *Sc. Leg. Saints* xxxvi. (*Baptist*) 31 Of þis nowmir sexten were of þe kyne of Eleazare. *c* **1470** HENRY *Wallace* V. 799 Sexteyn with him that worthi was in wer.

**b.** With ellipse of *years* (of age).

**1607** SHAKS. *Timon* IV. i. 13 Sonne of sixteen, Plucke the lyn'd Crutch from thy old limping Sire. **1794** MRS. RADCLIFFE *Myst. Udolpho* xxxviii, Several of sixty tripped it with almost as much glee and airy lightness as those of sixteen. **1891** HARDY *Tess* (1900) 73/2 Why didn't you stay and love me when I—was sixteen?

†**3.** = SIXTEENTH *a.* 1. *Obs.*

*c* **1400** *Destr. Troy* 10639 The sextene day sothely..The bold men to bent bounet full þicke. **1412–20** LYDG. *Chron. Troy* II. 3338 When Tytan..hadde take his se, Of þe Bole in the sixtene degre. **1536** BELLENDEN *Cron. Scot.* Headline, The sextene buke. **1653** *Apol. for Goodwin* 3 Take a taste.. of his sixteen Querie. **1680** in *Proc. Berw. Nat. Club* II. 179 Twesday the sixtein of the said moneth.

**B.** *sb.* **1.** The abstract number sixteen.

*c* **1055** *Byrhtferth's Handboc* in *Anglia* VIII. 318 To-dæl þa syxtyne, þonne byð se an dæl eahta. *c* **1425** *Crafte Nombrynge* (E.E.T.S.) 6 Compositys ben nomburs þat bene componyt of a digyt & of an articulle as..fyftene, sextene, & such oþer.

**2.** A sheet of sixteen leaves; a book in sixteenmo.

? **1606** BODLEY in *Reliq. B.* (1703) 62 If Mr. Principal shall want Strings for the lesser sort of Books in Octavo, and Sixteens. **1688** HOLME *Armoury* III. xv. (Roxb.) 23/2 Whether they be large or small octavo's, sixteens, or twenty foures. **1715** M. DAVIES *Athen. Brit.* I. 11 Bound in Twelves, Sixteens, or Twentyfours. **1888** JACOBI *Printers' Vocab.* 125.

†**3.** *pl.* A kind of ale. *Obs. rare*[−1].

**1584** COGAN *Haven Health* (1636) 251 That kinde of ale which at Oxford is called sixteenes.

**4.** A girl of sixteen.

*c* **1840** O. W. HOLMES *The Dilemma* 2 Now, by the bless'd Paphian queen, Who heaves the breast of sweet sixteen.

**5.** A medium-sized flower-pot, sixteen of which are formed from a cast of clay.

**1802** W. FORSYTH *Treat. Culture & Managem. Fruit-Trees* viii. 114 The 1st size of 8 in the Cast is called Eights. 2[nd size of] 12 [in the Cast is called] Twelves... Sixteens... Twenty-fours. **1852** G. W. JOHNSON *Cottage Gardener's Dict.* 392/2 Nine-inch pot..16s. [= sixteens]. **1895** *Culture of Veg. & Flowers* (Sutton & Sons) (ed. 6) 323 Small 60..2¾ [inches]. Mid. 60..3. Large 60..3½... 16..8½... 6..12½. **1955** W. E. SHEWELL-COOPER *Pot Plants* ii. 19 The tendency is to use smaller pots and, whereas years ago we grew all our late Chrysanthemums in 12's, we try to do them today in 16's or even 24's. **1962** [see SIXTY *sb.* 4 c].

**C.** *Comb.* **1.** With sbs., forming attributive compounds, as ***sixteen-ounce***, ***-page***, etc. **sixteen millimetre,** (more usually) **16mm**, a cine film which is sixteen millimetres wide; in full **sixteen millimetre film**; also *attrib.*

**1774** *Ann. Reg., Chron.* 165/1 [On Nov. 30 there was] executed at Tyburn,..John Rann, alias Sixteen-String Jack. **1780** *New Newgate Cal.* V. 139 [He obtained] the appellation of Sixteen-strings Jack, by wearing breeches with eight strings at each knee. **1849** NOAD *Electricity* (ed. 3) 50 Common sixteen-ounce phials of white glass. **1865** 'CUTHBERT BEDE' *Rook's Gard.* etc. 269 Their Sixteen-shilling Reversible Trousers. **1888** *Encycl. Brit.* XXIV. 464/2 In weaving, say a sixteen-leaf satin. **1890** W. J. GORDON *Foundry* 204 To print a sixteen-page paper in duplicate. **1926–7** *Army & Navy Stores Catal.* 971/1 The Bell Howell 'Filmo' automatic camera..Accommodates newly standardized 16 m/m films. **1951** R. SPOTTISWOODE *Film & its Techniques* i. 9 The producer must also make up his mind whether to shoot in color or black and white, in standard theater 35 mm. film, or nontheatrical 16 mm. film. **1969** G. GREENE *Travels with my Aunt* I. viii. 82 The films, of course, had all been shot on sixteen millimetre, and..they were enlarged practically to cinerama size. **1977** *New Yorker* 29 Aug. 66/2 Travelling, then, at almost six hundred miles an hour, we watch this innovative sixteen-millimetre movie, projected with infinite difficulty at thirty-six feet a minute.

**2.** Parasynthetic, as ***sixteen-sided***, etc. Also ***sixteen-square*** adj. and vb.

**1611** COTGR. s.v. *Rang*, A sixteene-stringd Lute. **1794** *Rigging & Seamanship* 29 It is trimmed sixteen-square. *Ibid.* 33 The yard is then sixteen-squared. **1895** SWETTENHAM *Malay Sketches* 157 A sixteen-sided stand.

**3.** With sbs. in *-er*, as ***sixteen-pounder***.

**1695** *Lond. Gaz.* No. 3112/3 We found in the Castle..69 Pieces of Cannon, viz...3 sixteen Pounders [etc.].

**sixteener** (sɪk'stiːnə(r)). [f. prec. + -ER[1].]

**1.** One of a body of persons sixteen in number.

**1801** W. TAYLOR in *Monthly Mag.* XII. 574 On the decease of one sixteener or alderman, the remainder filled up the vacancy.

**2.** A youth of sixteen.

**1824** MISS MITFORD *Village* Ser. I. (1863) 41 For Joe is a less boy than many of his companions, some of whom are fifteeners and sixteeners. **1966** *Daily Tel.* 5 Nov. 7/6 The world's biggest organization of young motor-cyclists.. launched a petition against the sixteener ban.

**six'teenmo.** [English reading of the symbol 16mo; cf. *twelvemo*, *eighteenmo*.] = SEXTODECIMO.

**1847** *Chambers's Jrnl.* 6 Feb. 87/2 Duodecimo, post-octavo, eighteenmo, sixteenmo, and a hundred other vos and mos. **1903** *Publishers' Circular* 28 Mar. 353/2 In folio, octavo, and duodecimo the water-lines are vertical; in quarto and sixteenmo horizontal.

**sixteensome** (sɪk'stiːnsəm). [f. SIXTEEN *a.* + -SOME[2].] A group of sixteen persons. Usu. *attrib.* in ***sixteensome reel***, a Scottish dance performed in sets of sixteen persons. Also *absol.*

**1926** [see EIGHTSOME *a.*]. **1938** *St. Andrews Citizen* 13 Aug. 9 He is much in request to teach..eightsomes, sixteensomes, and thirty-twosomes. **1954** H. A. THURSTON *Scotland's Dances* 51 The same process can be applied to the eightsome reel: the result is the *double eightsome* or *sixteensome reel*. **1964** J. & T. FLETT *Trad. Dancing* i. 18 Mr Reid taught..the Eightsome Reel, and the Sixteensome Reel. **1979** *Harper's & Queen* July 157/3 They led the sixteensome of Atholl Highlanders down the stairs two by two.

**sixteenth** (sɪk'stiːnθ, 'sɪkstiːnθ), *a.* and *sb.* Forms: α. 1 **sexteȝða**, **sex-**, **syxteoða**, 3 **sixteoþe**, 3–4 **sixteþe** (4 **syx-**). β. 2 **sixtenðe**, 4–5 **-tenthe**, 6 **-tenth**, 6– **sixteenth**; 5 **syxtenethe**, 6 **-tenth**, **-teenth**; 4 **sextenþe**, **-tenthe**, 4, 6 **-tenth**; *Sc.* 5 **sextend**, 6 **-teint** (9 **saxteent**). [f. SIXTEEN + -TH[1], replacing OE. *syxtéoða*, etc. Cf. OFris. *sextinda*, *-tenda*, *-tiensta* (WFris. *sechstjinde*), MDu. *sestiende* (Du. *zestiende*), MLG. *sesteende* (LG. *sesteinste*), MHG. *seh(s)zehende* (G. *sechzehnte*, †*sechszehnte*), ON. and Icel. *sextándi* (Sw. *sextonde*, Da. *sekstende*).] The ordinal numeral belonging to the cardinal sixteen.

**A.** *adj.* **1.** In concord with a sb. expressed or implied.

α. *a* **900** *O.E. Martyrol.* 16 Jan. 18 On þone sexteoðan dæȝ þæs monðes. *c* **1000** ÆLFRIC *Gram.* (Z.) 283 *Sextus decimus*, se syxteoða. **1297** R. GLOUC. (Rolls) 5244 In þe sixteþe [*c* **1430** sixtene] ȝere of þe kinges kinedom. *c* **1300** *St. Swithin* 81 in *E.E.P.* (1862) 45 Eiȝte hondred ȝer and in þe sixteoþe ȝere. **1387** TREVISA *Higden* (Rolls) V. 145 In þe sixteþe ȝere he was i-made knyȝt.

β. *a* **1220** *Juliana* 79, I þe Sixtenðe dei of feouerreres moneð. *c* **1380** WYCLIF *Wks.* (1880) 221 þe sextenþe [article is] þat þei ben verrey..myrrours of mekenesse. **1390** GOWER *Conf.* I. 3 The yer sextenthe of kyng Richard. **14..** *Lat.-Eng. Voc.* in Wr.-Wülcker 610 *Sedenus*, the syxtenethe. **1473** *Rental Bk. Cupar-Angus* (1879) I. 180 Wil Smith and John eldar a ilkane of thir a sextend pairt. **1579** FULKE *Heskins' Parl.* 188 The sixteenth Chapter endeth the exposition. **1589** in *Exch. Rolls Scotl.* XXII. 27 The fewferm of the sexteint pair of the landis. **1611** COTGR., *Seziesme*, the sixteenth in ranke, number, &c. *a* **1700**

EVELYN *Diary* 15 July 1669, I went towards home the sixteenth. **1728** CHAMBERS *Cycl.* s.v. *Bible*, The New Latin Translations, done..in the 16th Century. **1850** J. H. NEWMAN *Difficulties Anglicans* I. xii. (1891) 388 The shadow of the fifth century was on the sixteenth. **1866** MISS YONGE *Dove in Eagle's Nest* xi, Within a week of their sixteenth birthday.

**2.** ***sixteenth note***, the sixteenth part of a semibreve; a semiquaver.

**1861** J. S. ADAMS *5000 Mus. Terms* 92.

**B.** *sb.* **1.** A sixteenth part.

**1611** COTGR., *Seziesme*, a sixteenth; a sixteenth part. **1769** *St. James's Chron.* 14–16 Sept. 3/3 The Tickets..are..divided into Halves, Quarters, Eighths and Sixteenths. **1832** J. RENNIE *Butterfl. & M.* 31 Wings of the male one inch to one inch one-sixteenth. **1867** DENISON *Astron. without Math.* 176 The fourth a quarter as wide, or one sixteenth as large. **1897** *Allbutt's Syst. Med.* III. 742 One thirty-second to one sixteenth of a grain of periodide.

**2.** *Mus.* **a.** The interval of two octaves and a second. **b.** A sixteenth note.

**1876** HARDY *Ethelberta* xlii, He'll keep me there while he tweedles upon the Twelfth and Sixteenth.

Hence **six'teenthly** *adv.*, in the sixteenth place.

*a* **1642** SIR W. MONSON *Naval Tracts* III. (1704) 322/1 Sixteenthly, They ought to appoint a Surveyor. **1691–8** NORRIS *Pract. Disc.* (1711) III. 170 And Sixteenthly, the Glory that Virtue casts about the Head of those who suffer this little Martyrdom. **1819** SCOTT *Leg. Montrose* xiv, Never..was a sermon listened to with more impatience... The Captain heard 'sixteenthly'—'seventeenthly'—'eighteenthly', and 'to conclude'.

†**sixter.** *Obs.*$^{-1}$ In 5 syxter. [ad. OF. *sex-, sestiere*:—L. *sextāri-us*.] A certain measure.

**1491** CAXTON *Vitas Patr.* (W. de W. 1495) I. xxxvii. 44/1 He lyued sobrely: And in thre yere he ete not but onely a syxter of wortes medled in a lytyll colde water.

**sixth** (sɪksθ), *a.* and *sb.* Forms: α. 1 **sexta (sesta, seista)**, 2–5 **sexte** (2–4 **seste**), 3 **sæxte**, 3–6 **sext**, 5– *Sc.* **saxt** (6 **saxte**). β. 1 **siexta, sihsta, sixta**, 2–6 **sixte** (2–3 **siste**, 4 **zixte**), 3–7 **sixt** (4 **sixst**); 1 **syxta**, 3–6 **syxte**, 5 **zyxst**, 6 **syxt**. γ. 6 **syxthe**, 7– **sixth**. [OE. *sexta, sixta, syxta*, etc. (see SIX *a.*), = OFris. *sexta* (WFris. *sechste*, NFris. *sokst*), MDu. *seste* (Du. *zesde*), OS. *se(h)sto* (MLG. *seste, soste*, LG. *seste, söste, soste*), OHG. *sehsto* (MHG. *sehste*, G. *sechste*), Goth. *saihsta*; also OHG. *sehto* (MHG. *sehte*), ON. *sétti* (Icel. *sjötti*, Norw. *sette*, Sw. and Da. *sjette*).] The ordinal numeral belonging to the cardinal six.

**A.** *adj.* **1. a.** In concord with a sb. expressed or implied (freq. occurring earlier in the context).

α. *a* **900** *O.E. Martyrol.* 6 Jan. 14 On þone sextan dæᵹ þæs monðes. *c* **950** *Lindisf. Gosp.* Mark xv. 33 Miððy awarð tid ðio seista. *c* **1205** LAY. 13909 Þæ sæxte [god] hæhte Appollin. *a* **1225** *Ancr. R.* Pref. p. xxiii, The seste dale is of penitence. **13..** *K. Alis.* 2736 (Laud MS.), Þe sexte he slouȝ of Nauere he was. *c* **1320** *Deb. Body & Soul* in *Map's Poems* (Camden) 348 The seste day ayen the dom shule foure aungles stonde. **1390** GOWER *Conf.* III. 121 After Leo Virgo the nexte Of Signes cleped is the sexte. *c* **1400** *Destr. Troy* 2047 Here begynnes the Sext Boke. **1549** *Compl. Scotl.* 35 Virgil..in the sext beuk of his eneados. *c* **1570** *Satir. Poems Reform.* xliv. 302 That saxt chapter of Iohne. **1609** SKENE *Reg. Maj.* 43 The saxt day of November.

β. *c* **893** K. ÆLFRED *Oros.* I. vii. 38 þæt syxte [wonder] wæs þæt eall þæt folc wæs on blædran. *c* **900** *O.E. Chron.* (Parker MS.) an. 827, Siexta [cyning] wæs Oswald se æfter him ricsode. *c* **1000** *Sax. Leechdoms* II. 298 Syxte mæᵹen is þæt drycræft þam men ne dereþ. *c* **1175** *Lamb. Hom.* 43 Þe forme [wave] wes snaw,..þe siste smorðer. *a* **1225** *Ancr. R.* 14 Þe sixte dole is of penitence. **1297** R. GLOUC. (Rolls) 5018 He deide after martin masse riȝt þe sixte day. **1340** *Ayenb.* 17 Þe uerste boȝ of prede is ontreuþe,..þe zixte, ypocrisie. **1387** TREVISA *Higden* (Rolls) IV. 59 Þe sixte tyme þe consuls of Rome..were sent aȝenst Hanibal. **1523** FITZHERB. *Husb.* §75 The syxte [property] is, to haue great nosethrylles. **1579** FULKE *Heskins' Parl.* 336 The sixt Chapter declareth, that Manna was a figure. **1611** BIBLE *Transl. Pref.* ¶6 Yea, there was a fift and a sixt edition. **1667** MILTON *P.L.* VII. 449 The Sixt [day], and of Creation last arose.

γ. **1526** *Pilgr. Perf.* (W. de W. 1531) 14 b, Saynt Brigitte..in the syxthe boke of her reuelacyons. **1611** BIBLE *Gen.* i. 31 And the euening and the morning were the sixth day. **1662** PLAYFORD *Skill Mus.* II. (1674) 92 The first [string]..is called the Treble;..the Sixth, the Bass. **1726** SWIFT *Gulliver* II. vi, His Majesty, in a sixth audience,..proposed many doubts. *a* **1771** GRAY *Dante* 74 E'er the sixth Morn Had dawn'd. **1837** P. KEITH *Bot. Lex.* 404 Among anatomists we sometimes hear of a sixth sense. **1884** *Jrnl. Education* 1 Sept. 351/1 A classical Sixth Form.

**b.** Following on the names of kings, popes, etc.

Very commonly, and now usually, expressed by the symbol VI, *e.g.* James VI.

**1387** TREVISA *Higden* VII. 151 Gregorie þe sixte,.. after Benet. **1423** in *Rep. Hist. MSS. Comm.* Var. Coll. IV. 83 The ȝere of Kyng Harry the zyxst the furste. **1456** SIR G. HAYE *Law Arms* (S.T.S.) 2 Charles the Sext of that name. **1549** *Compl. Scotl.* 86 Ther eftir henry the saxt lossit his liyf. **1588** LAMBARDE *Eirenarcha* II. iv. 160 The late K. Henry the sixt. **1641** 'SMECTYMNUUS' *Vind.* xiv. 174 All the Bishops in King Edwards the sixt time. **1674** BREVINT *Saul at Endor* 227 Nothing to Pope Sixtus the 4th, nor to Alexander the sixt. **1788** GIBBON *Decl. & F.* xlviii. V. 57 To nominate for her successor Michael the sixth. **1857** *Willis's Current Notes* Jan. 4/2 King James the Sixth.

**2.** *ellipt.* With omission of *day, house, form, former*, etc.

**1573** *Cath. Tractates* (S.T.S.) 14 Writtin at Paris the sext of December. **1592** tr. *Junius on Rev.* xi. 7 In the Sixt of the Decretals. **1631** WEEVER *Funeral Mon.* To Rdr., The sixt of May. **1647** LILLY *Chr. Astrol.* xliv. 258 Any malevolent in the sixt,..shews great danger. **1857** HUGHES *Tom Brown* Pref., By getting not only the Sixth to put it down but the lower fellows to scorn it. *c* **1898** W. LEWIS *Let.* (1963) 6 First a fellow got a 'sixth licking' (stripes from every sixth in the house). **1906** R. BROOKE *Let.* 3 Feb. (1968) 39 [He] has been discovered..showing up proses done for him by a wee & terrified Sixth. **1914** 'I. HAY' *Lighter Side School Life* i. 5 The Head..probably takes the Sixth for an hour or two a day. **1963** *Sunday Times* 8 Sept. 29/3 Cool Shakespeare thrives in the sixth and phrases like 'Pox on't'..are in present usage. **1977** R. RENDELL *Judgement in Stone* vi. 50 You're no longer the naughtiest girl in the sixth.

**B.** *sb.* **1.** A sixth part.

**1557** RECORDE *Whetst.* B ij b, A sixte more. **1611** COTGR., *Sixain*, a sixt, a sixt part. **1728** CHAMBERS *Cycl.* s.v. *Measure*, The Viertel, or Verge, consists of five Mingles, and one Sixth of a Mingle. **1828** SIR J. E. SMITH *Eng. Flora* II. 345 Some flowers are deficient in a sixth of all their parts. **1842** *Penny Cycl.* XXIII. 418/2 One-sixth of its width. **1866** *Treas. Bot.* 588/2 In some Indian species the pores are one-sixth of an inch across.

**2.** *Mus.* A tone on the sixth diatonic degree above or below another; the harmonic combination of two such tones; an interval comprising six diatonic degrees of the scale.

Different varieties are distinguished by the epithets *added, augmented, French, greater, Italian, minor, Neapolitan, sharp, small.*

**1597** T. MORLEY *Introd. Mus.* 70 A third, a Fift, a Sixt, and an eight. **1609** J. DOWLAND *Ornith. Microl.* 29 Those which sound thirds, sixts, or other imperfect Concords. **1706** A. BEDFORD *Temple Mus.* ix. 178 In this Tune they might ascend gradually unto a Sixth. **1752** tr. *Rameau's Treat. Mus.* i. 3 The Third becomes a Sixth,..and..the Seventh becomes a Second. **1801** BUSBY *Dict. Mus.* s.v., There are four kinds of sixths, two consonant and two dissonant. **1873** H. C. BANISTER *Music* 70 The first inversion of the Triad, consisting of a note with its 3rd and 6th, is termed the Chord of the Sixth.

**3.** *Fencing.* = SIXTE.

**1885** E. CASTLE *Schools & Masters of Fence* Introd. 10 There can be as many guards as there are parries, although in modern days, carte, tierce, and sixth are almost exclusively used.

**4.** *Anat.* A nerve of the sixth cranial pair.

**1899** *Allbutt's Syst. Med.* VII. 117 Double ptosis has been frequently noted, and paralysis of both sixths sometimes.

**C.** *Comb.* **1.** With sbs., forming an attributive compound, as ***sixth-floor, -form, -rate*** (also *absol.* of a former class of warships).

**1820** T. MITCHELL *Aristoph.* I. 232 A tub-and-cask tenant,—vulture-lodg'd—*sixth-floor man. **1807** SYD. SMITH *P. Plymley's Lett.* vi, The *sixth-form effusions of Mr. Canning. **1879** L. STEPHEN *Hours Library* III. 273 Landor is precisely a glorified..edition of the model sixth-form lad. **1694** *Lond. Gaz.* No. 3014/4 A *Sixth Rate Frigat of 26 Guns called the *Drake*. **1747** LIND *Lett. rel. Navy* (1757) I. 22 Captains of sloops [have] the same [pay] with captains of a sixth rate. **1858** SIMMONDS *Dict. Trade, Sixth-rate*, a British vessel of war bearing a captain.

**2.** ***sixth day***, the name given to Friday by members of the Society of Friends; ***sixth form***: see FORM *sb.* 6 b; hence ***sixth-former***: see -FORMER; ***sixth-form college***, a college for pupils over the age of sixteen, chiefly providing A-level courses.

**1655** G. FOX *Jrnl.* (1694) 152 On the Sixth day of that Week I had a meeting near Colchester. **1858** M. TUCKETT *Diary* 26 Sept. in H. Fox *Mariana's Diary* (*c* 1975) 8 Sixth day morning was bright and fine. **1976** *Minutes Ohio Yearly Meeting of Friends* 30 (*heading*) Sixth day afternoon session, eighth month 27th. **1938** C. MORGAN *Flashing Stream* 31 He who wrote the Sonnets, or Hamlet's bidding to Ophelia..had no moderation, no smell of the sixth form, no sense of humour. **1967** *Listener* 18 May 645/1 The eighteen-year-old emerging from our sixth forms has a level of knowledge as good as a second year student in a North American university. **1965** H. L. ELVIN *Educ. & Contemp. Soc.* II. vii. 134 There is little doubt that the sixth form college would be welcomed by most of the young people who would go to it. **1976** *Times* 18 Aug. 3/2 Tameside council has decided not to introduce two proposed sixth form colleges.

**'sixthly**, *adv.* [f. prec.] In the sixth place.

α. *c* **1532** DU WES *Introd. French* in *Palsgr.* 929 Sixtely, *sixtement*. **1579** FULKE *Ref. Rastel* 770 Sixtly, that..[he] had not..ben iudged for an heretike. **1608** DOD & CLEAVER *Expos. Prov.* ix–x. 15 Sixtly, we are simple men and want vnderstanding. **1657** AUSTEN *Fruit Trees* II. To Rdr., Sixtly in boasting of their Parts.

β. **1556** OLDE *Antichrist* 42 Sixthely, how farre [etc.]. **1648** D. JENKINS *Wks.* 37 Sixthly, we maintained the counterfeiting of the great Seale to be high Treason. **1681** H. MORE *Expos. Dan.* App. III. 297 Sixthly, If one require a Reason why Christ is described [etc.]. **1725** *Fam. Dict.* s.v. *Rules*, Sixthly, Racking. **1832** W. PALMER *Orig. Liturg.* I. 25 Sixthly, one of the MSS...contains a prayer taken from Basil's liturgy. **1876** *Clinical Soc. Trans.* IX. 93 Sixthly and lastly, as to the use of phosphorus.

**sixth sense** (sɪksθ sɛns). [f. SIXTH *a.* + SENSE *sb.*] A supposed intuitive faculty by which a person or animal perceives facts and regulates action without the direct use of any of the five senses. Hence **sixth-sense** *v. trans.*, to discover by means of a sixth sense; **sixth-sensed** *a.*, possessing a sixth sense.

[**1687** W. DOMVILE tr. *B. de Fontenelle's Plurality of Worlds* III. 50 It has been thought that we want a sixth natural Sense, by which we might know many things more than we do.] **1761** L. STERNE *Tristram Shandy* IV. i. 75 There seems in some passages to want a sixth sense to do it rightly. **1807** R. SOUTHEY *Lett. from England* II. xl. 176 It was surprising to see them [*sc.* the blind] move about the room,..as if they had possessed that sixth sense, which experimental naturalists..are said to have discovered in bats, when they have put out their eyes. **1841** DICKENS *Barnaby Rudge* xxxiii. 122 People..doing exactly the same things for a great many years, acquire a sixth sense, or some unknown power of influencing each other. **1903** *Science Siftings* 31 Oct. 46/1 The 'sixth sense' by which blind persons perceive certain objects. **1958** R. GODDEN *Greengage Summer* xvi. 199 Did she have some sixth-sense warning? **1967** *Punch* 25 Oct. 609/2 This, I sixth-sensed, could well be it. **1976** J. CROSBY *Nightfall* xxx. 176 About Elf I am second-sighted, sixth-sensed, magicked. **1979** R. JAFFE *Class Reunion* (1980) II. iii. 199 There was something about living together and being very close that gave people a sort of sixth sense.

**sixtieth** ('sɪkstɪɛθ), *a.* and *sb.* Forms: 1 **syx-, sixtiᵹeþa, sixteoᵹoða**, 4 **zixtiaȝte, sixtithe, sextid**, 6 **syxteth, sixteth**, *Sc.* **saxtieth**, 6– **sixtieth**. [OE. *sixteoᵹoða*, etc., f. *sixtiᵹ* SIXTY.]

**A.** *adj.* The ordinal numeral belonging to the cardinal sixty.

*c* **960** *Rule of St. Benet* (Schröer) 37 Ðy feorþan dæᵹe se þreo and syxtiᵹeða and se feower and syxtiᵹeþa [sealm]. *c* **1000** ÆLFRIC *Gram.* (Z.) 283 *Sexagesimus*, se sixteoᵹoða. **1340** *Ayenb.* 234 Þo þet byeþ in wodewe-hod habbeþ þet zixtiaȝte frut. **1382** WYCLIF *1 Macc.* x. 1 In the hundrid and sixtithe ȝeer Alisaundre..stiede vp. **1530** PALSGR. 372 *Soixantiesme*, syxteth. **1579** FULKE *Heskins' Parl.* 527 The Sixtieth Chapter treateth vpon this text. *a* **1700** EVELYN *Diary* 30 Oct. 1680, Now I ariv'd at my sixtieth year. **1755** JOHNSON, *Second*,..the sixtieth part of a minute. **1879** *St. George's Hosp. Rep.* IX. 77 The temperature became normal by the sixtieth [day]. **1892** GLADSTONE in *Pall Mall G.* 24 June 7/2 In this, the sixtieth year of my public life.

**B.** *sb.* A sixtieth part.

**1800** *Phil. Trans.* XCI. 61 It would be expected that the image should be diminished about one-sixtieth. **1823** J. BADCOCK *Dom. Amusem.* 145 The addition of..potash..in the proportion of one-sixtieth is always necessary. **1841** *Penny Cycl.* XXI. 320/1, 48-sixtieths of a minute.

**Sixtine** ('sɪkstɪn), *a.* [ad. mod.L. *Sixtin-us*, f. the papal name *Sixtus*.] Of or pertaining to the pope Sixtus V (1585–1590), or to the edition of the Vulgate published by him in 1590.

More rarely used as a variant of *Sistine*, the special epithet of the chapel and bridge built by Sixtus IV (1471–1484).

**1843** *Penny Cycl.* XXVI. 465/2 The true Sixtine Vulgate is now of excessive rarity. **1845** in Kitto *Cycl. Bibl. Lit.* (1849) II. 924/1 The Sixtine and Clementine Bibles. **1863** WESTCOTT in Smith *Dict. Bible* III. 1707/2 The critical value of the Sixtine readings.

**six-tooth(ed**: see SIX C. 1, 2, and 5.

**sixty** ('sɪkstɪ), *a.* and *sb.* Forms: α. 1 **siexteᵹ**, 2–4 **sixti** (4 **zixti**), 4– **sixty**, 5 **-sty**, 6 **sixtye**, 6–7 **sixtie**; 1–2 **syxtiᵹ**, 3–6 **syxty** (5 **syxti**). β. 1 **sexteiᵹ, -tih, -deih, -diᵹ**, 1–2 **sextiᵹ**, 4–6 **sexti**, 4–6 **sexty** (5 **cexty**, *Sc.* **saxtie, sexte**); *Sc.* 5 **saxte**, 6 **-tie**, 9 **-ty**. [OE. *siex-, syx-, sextiᵹ*, = OFris. *sextich, -tech* (WFris. *sechstich*), MDu. *sestich* (Du. *zestig*), OS. *sehstic* (MLG. *sestich*, LG. *sestig, söstig*), OHG. *sehszug*, etc. (MHG. *sehzic, -zec*, G. *sechzig*), ON. *sextigir* (MSw. *säxtighi*, MDa. *sexti*; Icel. *sextíu*, Sw. *sextio*).] The cardinal number equal to six times ten, represented by the symbols 60, LX, or lx.

**A.** *adj.* **1. a.** In concord with a sb. expressed or implied.

α. *c* **893** K. ÆLFRED *Oros.* IV. vi. 172 Æfter siexteᵹum daᵹa ðæs þe ðæt timber acorfen wæs. **971** *Blickl. Hom.* 35 On þæm ᵹeare bið þreo hund daᵹa & fif & syxtiᵹ daᵹa. *a* **1122** *O.E. Chron.* (Laud MS.) an. 852, He scolde ᵹife ilca ᵹear into þe minstre sixtiᵹe foðra wuda. *c* **1200** *Trin. Coll. Hom.* 51 On þralshipe hie wuneden two and sixti wintre. **1297** R. GLOUC. (Rolls) 7260 In a þousend ȝer of grace & sixe & sixti riȝt. **1377** LANGL. *P. Pl.* B. v. 441 Sixty sythes I..haue forȝete it sith. **1495** *Trevisa's Barth. De P.R.* VIII. ix. 306 Syxty secondes make one mynute, syxty mynutes one gree. **1560** BIBLE (Genevan) *Gen.* v. 20 So all the days of Iered were nine hundreth sixty and two yeres. **1606** SHAKS. *Ant. & Cl.* III. vii. 50, I haue sixty Sailes, Cæsar none better. **1611** BIBLE *Numb.* vii. 88 The rammes sixtie, the hee goates sixtie. **1816** SCOTT *Let.* in *Lockhart* (1837) IV. i. 33 Longman's people had then only sixty copies. *a* **1860** ALB. SMITH *Med. Student* (1861) 39 Some sixty of these small pieces of paper.

β. *c* **950** *Lindisf. Gosp.* Matt. p. 19 Bisin [he] cueð wæstm[es] ðrittiᵹes, sexteiᵹes, & hundrades. *Ibid.* Mark iv. 20 [Hia] wæstmiað an ðrittiᵹ & an sextiᵹ. *c* **1250** *Gen. & Ex.* 663 Twelwe and sexti men weren ðor-to. **1330** R. BRUNNE *Chron. Wace* (Rolls) 10197 In þat louh ar sexti iles. **1393** LANGL. *P. Pl.* C. IV. 234 Ich saued my-self and sexty þousand lyues. *c* **1470** HENRY *Wallace* VI. 827 Sexty thai slew. *Ibid.* x. 878 Off his best men saxte was brocht toded. **1589** MONTGOMERY *Misc. Poems* lviii. 6 Tuyse sax and saxtie ȝeirs he livd. **1816** SCOTT *Antiq.* xxiii, I hae kend this auld kirk, man and bairn, for saxty lang years.

†**b.** Sixtieth. *Obs.*$^{-0}$

**1483** *Cath. Angl.* 332/1 Sexty,..*sexagesimus*.

**2. a.** Followed immediately by a lesser numeral, as ***sixty-one***, etc.

**1597** SKENE *De Verb. Sign.* s.v. *Serplath*, Ane thousand, three hundreth, sextie aucht zeires. **1728** CHAMBERS *Cycl.* s.v. *Star*, Reducing the..Number of Knights [of the Star] to Sixty-two. **1777** ROBERTSON *Hist. Amer.* (1783) III. 177 The most valuable of these was published by Purchas in sixty-six plates. **1848** THACKERAY *Van. Fair* xi, The actress, who was sixty-five years of age. **1868** *Rep. U.S. Commiss. Agric.* (1869) 191 The new building..is one hundred and seventy feet long by sixty-one feet deep.

**b.** ***sixty-six***, a card-game in which a point is gained by scoring sixty-six; ***sixty-nine***, **69** = SOIXANTE-NEUF.

**1857** T. Frere *Hoyle's Games* 4 The German game of 'Sechs und Sechszig', or Sixty-six, has never before, that we are aware of, been dressed in an English garb. **1888** [see SOIXANTE-NEUF]. **1897** *Daily News* 22 Feb. 9/2 The game was called '66'. **1973** D. Lang *Freaks* 90 We spent many hours lying on her bed, more or less in the classical 69 position, but motionless. **1978** *Guardian Weekly* 23 Apr. 21/5 When I first met him, I thought 69 was a bottle of Scotch.

**3. a.** Forming part of an ordinal number.

**1647** *Form for Ch. Govt.* Prop. 12 The sixtie one Canon of the sixth generall Synode. **1777** Robertson *Hist. Amer.* (1783) II. 395 The sixty-second year of his age. **1821** Byron *Cain* II. ii. 71 As The sixty-thousandth generation shall be. **1879** *St. George's Hosp. Rep.* IX. 77 The patient was out of bed on the sixty-second [day].

**b.** With *part*, or used absol. in this sense, esp. ***sixty-fourth***; hence ***sixty-fourther***, one who owns a sixty-fourth part of a vessel.

**1768** Dr. Chauncy *Lett.* 74 It was but the sixty-thousandth part. **1811** Miss L. M. Hawkins *C'tess & Gertr.* I. 269 A favor in the form of sixty-fourths of lottery-tickets. **1889** *Whitby Gaz.* 14 June 3/3 A shipowning port, in which the disease of the sixty fourther exists in an aggravated form. **1899** Werner *Capt. Locusts* 76 The minutest fraction of European blood,..one thirty-second, perhaps, or one sixty-fourth.

**B.** *sb.* **1. a.** The abstract number sixty.

**1340** *Ayenb.* 234 þe tale of zixti þet is wel gratter, þet is of zixziþe ten. *a* **1400** *Pistill of Susan* 91 Turtils troned on trene By sixti I say3. *c* **1425** *Crafte Nombrynge* (E.E.T.S.) 4 þere he [the figure 6] schuld tokyne but sexty. **1594** Blundevil *Exerc.* I. (1636) 84 Which [numbers] maketh two sixties to bee kept in mind. **1728** Chambers *Cycl.* s.v. *Character*, The same Characters are sometimes us'd, where the Progression is by Tens; as 'tis here by Sixties. **1755** Johnson, *Second*,.. the second division of an hour by sixty. **1886** Pendlebury *Arithm.* (1897) 5 The number in six groups of ten is called sixty.

**b.** ***like sixty***, with great force or vigour; at a great rate. *colloq.* or *slang.* (Cf. FORTY A. b.)

**1848** Lowell *Biglow Papers* Poems (1890) II. 135 Though like sixty all along I fumed an' fussed. **1860** *Slang Dict.* 215 'To go like sixty,' i.e. at a good rate, briskly. **1910** *Dialect Notes* III. 445 That child cuts up like sixty. **1975** J. D. Fitzgerald *Great Brain does it Again* ii. 20 We ran like sixty to the front porch.

**c.** ***sixty per cent***, a usurer. *colloq.*

**1853** Reade *Gold* i. 1 What you do on the sly, I do on the sly, old sixty per cent. **1897** Marsh *Crime & Criminal* xii, Was he going to develop into a sixty per cent, and offer me a loan?

**2.** Sixty years of age. Also ***sixty-one***, ***-two***, etc.

**1717** Prior *Alma* III. 503 We find ourselves at Sixty wise. **1780** *Mirror* No. 103, He seemed to be about sixty, but retained a..florid complexion. **1842** Borrow *Bible in Spain* xxvi, He appeared to be about sixty-five. **1872** Calverley *Fly Leaves* (1903) 30 Although I am but sixty-three Or four. **1890** *Spectator* 11 Oct. 473/2 An old lady over sixty.

**3.** *pl.* The years from 60 to 69 in a century or in a person's life. Now *spec.* the period 1960–9.

**1886** Besant *Childr. Gibeon* II. xxi, The old patter, that spoken by himself in the early sixties, was unknown. **1889** R. B. Anderson tr. *Rydberg's Teut. Mythol.* 9 A series of works published in the fifties and sixties. **1964** M. McLuhan *Understanding Media* II. xxxi. 320 TV in the Fifties and Sixties spread to the entire population. **1978** *Listener* 3 Aug. 145/1, I was, alas, one of those who spent the Sixties sneering at the notion of parish-pump broadcasting. **1981** 'D. Shannon' *Murder most Strange* ii. 34 They were both in the sixties, middle-sized, sandy coloring. **1983** D. Gethin *Wyatt* xiv. 99 An ageing sixties swinger with the elegant mannerisms of a professional hotelier.

**4. a.** *pl.* A particular quality of wool. **b.** A certain size of sewing-cotton.

**1894** *Daily News* 23 Jan. 2/6 Medium sixties are a shade weaker. *Ibid.* 2 Feb. 2/6 Super 60's and the finer crossbreds ..are steady. **1907** H. Wales *The Yoke* xix, Three reels of white cotton—one eighty and two sixty.

**c.** A small flower-pot, sixty of which are formed from a cast of clay.

**1802** W. Forsyth *Treat. Culture & Managem. Fruit-Trees* viii. 114 There are some [pots] smaller than sixtys, for seedlings and heaths. **1895** [see SIXTEEN *sb.* 5]. **1962** A. J. Huxley *Garden Terms Simplified* 69 Above are shown, to scale top row from left to right, an 8½ in. pot (16),..and a 3½ in. pot (large 60).

**C.** *Comb.* **a.** With sbs., forming attributive compounds, as ***sixty-gun***, or with nouns in *-er*, ***sixty-pounder***; ***sixty-miler*** (*Austral.*), a small cargo vessel which transports coal along the coast from Newcastle to Sydney; also ***sixty-sized*** adj.

**1747** Dr. Lind *Lett. rel. Navy* (1757) I. 35 *note*, None who had not commanded..60 gun ships, would have a right [etc.]. **1756–7** tr. *Keysler's Trav.* (1760) I. 317 The French had erected a battery of twenty-four sixty pounders [etc.]. **1828** Cunningham *N.S. Wales* II. 257 Why could not the fellow..have had his sixty-guinea hoard taken from him? **1851** Glenny *Handbk. Flower Garden* 155 When they have taken good root, pot them into sixty-sized pots. **1882** *U.S. Rep. Prec. Met.* 123 A new 60-stamp mill has been under course of construction. **1933** I. Hamilton *Nights Ashore* 29 The *Five Stars* was a few tons larger than the average ancient sixty miler. *Ibid.* 210 During the slack 'sixty-miler' season. **1940** Blunden *Poems 1930–40* 202 And as the stream's last murmer stilled, Our sixty-pounders started talking. **1948** *Sydney Morning Herald* 28 Jan. 1/7 Sydney's gas supply now depends on the '60-milers'.

**b.** Similarly when followed by a lesser number.

**1860** *All Year Round* No. 73. 547 The gun was designed for a sixty-eight pound shot. *Ibid.*, No sixty-eight pounder in the service. **1896** *Godey's Mag.* Apr. 407/1, I..returned ..holding the sixty-one day record. **1899** *Westm. Gaz.* 2 Aug. 7 The sailing yacht *Vendetta*, a well-known sixty-five rater.

**c.** ***sixty-fourmo*** (see quot.). Also called ***sixty-fours***.

**1805** in E. Howe *London Compositor* (1947) ii. 92 Forty-eights to be paid two shillings per sheet extra, and sixty-fours two shillings and sixpence per sheet extra. **1888** Jacobi *Printers' Vocab.* 126 *Sixty-fourmo*, a sheet folded into sixty-four leaves—written shortly, 64mo.

**d.** ***sixty-four dollar question***, ***$64 question***, orig. the question posed at the climax of a U.S. radio quiz for a prize of sixty-four dollars, used *transf.* to denote a difficult or crucial question; also ***sixty-four dollar answer***, ***sixty-four thousand dollar question***, and varr.

**1942** J. R. Tunis *All American* vii. 240 Here's the sixty-four dollar question. Will the team go to Miami? **1942** *Time* 18 May 22/3 The Jap..could still sweat over the $64 question. **1955** M. Gilbert *Sky High* xii. 176 'What have these receivers got to do with us?..'That's the sixty-four dollar question.' **1957** R. Hoggart *Uses of Literacy* vi. 150 All the time he had the sixty-four dollar answer but did not know it. **1957** *Observer* 21 July 1/3 Mr. Macmillan said.. there was only one answer to the 64,000-dollar question—to increase production. **1958** *Listener* 4 Dec. 930/1, I come now to what you probably feel is the sixty-four-dollar question. How is all this to be paid for? **1963** *N.Y. Times* 2 Dec. 37/1 Mr. Baker..left the air, to return in 1942 as master of ceremonies on 'Take it or Leave it'... He posed 'the $64 question', a term that became part of everyday language. **1967** *N.Y. Rev. Bks.* 7 Dec. 27/1 On June 1, 1955, 'The $64,000 Question' was born and commercial television was never the same again. **1979** *Jrnl. R. Soc. Arts* CXXVII. 143/2 Like his predecessor on this rostrum he left it to Mr. Tyrrell Burgess, our lecturer tonight, to tackle the sixty-four dollar question—What now? **1981** B. Healey *Last Ferry from Lido* vi. 101 It still leaves the sixty-four thousand dollar question. Where do we go from here?

**sixtyfold** ('sɪkstɪfəʊld), *a.* (and *sb.*). [f. SIXTY + -FOLD.] Sixty times as great or as much.

*c* **1000** Ælfric in Assmann *Ags. Hom.* ii. 175 Sum berð þrittigfealdne wæstm, sum syxtigfealdne. *Ibid.* 182 þa habbað eft æt him syxtigfealde mede. *c* **1230** *Hali Meid.* 23 Wedlac haueð hire frut þritti-fald in heuene; widewehad, sixti fald. **1382** Wyclif *Matt.* xiii. 8 But other seedis ..3auen fruyt; sum an hundred fold, another sexti fold. [So in later versions.] **1865** Ruskin *Sesame* ii. §82 It gave you income sixtyfold instead of fourfold.

**sizable**, variant of SIZEABLE.

**sizar** ('saɪzə(r)). Also 6–9 sizer (7 cizer). [f. SIZE *sb.*[1] 7 + -ER[2], -AR[3].] In the University of Cambridge, and at Trinity College, Dublin, an undergraduate member admitted under this designation and receiving an allowance from the college to enable him to study.

The name probably indicates that the person so admitted received his 'sizes' free. Formerly the sizar performed certain duties now discharged by college servants.

α. **1588** Burghley in Ellis *Orig. Lett.* Ser. I. III. 27 Under the pain of six shillings and eight pence for everye tyme that any..Fellow, Scholer, Pensioner, or Sizer shall offende in any of the foresaid Orders. **1638** Mede *Wks.* (1672) 835 My Sizer being not yet come with a candle, I will transcribe a passage of Eusebius. **1674** Blount *Glossogr.* (ed. 4) *Sizer*, is a Servitor or Attendant in our Universities. **1745** Mrs. Delany *Life & Corr.* (1861) II. 377 The dean said, if his parents would consent to his entering the college of Dublin as a sizer..he would take care he was treated with a particular regard. **1809** Byron *Bards & Rev.* (ed. 2) Postscr. There is a youth.., a sizer of Emanuel College. **1856** Lever *Martins of Cro' M.* vii, As he sauntered along the silent alleys of the College Park..some solitary sizer might be met with.

β. **1670** Eachard *Cont. Clergy* 16 They took..heretofore a very good method to prevent sizars over heating their brains: bed-making, chamber-sweeping, and water-fetching. **1694** Motteux *Rabelais* IV. lxvii, Which..I had snatched up..as thievishly as any sizar of Montague college could have done. *c* **1780** in Willis & Clark *Cambridge* (1886) I. Introd. p. xcvi, My Father..entered me a Sizar. **1804** H. K. White *Lett.* I. 117 Somebody, perhaps, has been hinting that there are servile offices to be performed by sizars. It is a common opinion, but perfectly erroneous... The sizars at Cambridge only differ from the rest in name. **1868** Helps *Realmah* v. (1876) 83, I was a poor man, a sizar, and had to make my way in the world. **1902** *Student's Hdbk. Cambridge* v. 92 The emoluments of a Sizar take the form of various allowances, the annual value of which may be estimated at about £40.

*attrib.* **1859** Farrar *J. Home* ix, I'll pay you and your sizar friend there for this, depend upon it.

**sizars**, obs. form of SCISSORS.

**sizarship** ('saɪzəʃɪp). Also 8 sizership. [f. SIZAR.] The position or status of being a sizar.

**1782** Burke *Penal Laws agst. Irish Cath.* Wks. VI. 282 Your lordship mentions a proposal..of erecting a few sizerships in the college. **1803** H. K. White *Lett.* I. 96, I have not heard from Cambridge yet, and it is very doubtful whether there be a vacant sizarship in Trinity. **1850** Kingsley *A. Locke* xiii, These sizarships, now, were meant for—just such cases as yours. **1902** *Student's Hdbk. Cambridge* v. 77 Exhibitions, Sizarships and Subsizarships limited to candidates who can show that they are in need of pecuniary assistance.

*transf.* **1877** J. Morley *Robespierre* in *Crit. Misc.* Ser. II. 31 He proceeded with a sizarship to the college of Louis-le-Grand in Paris.

**size** (saɪz), *sb.*[1] Forms: 3–7 syse (*Sc.* 5 siys, 6–7 syis, 7 sys), 3–7 sise; 5 (8) syze, 6– size; 5 cyse, 5–7 cise, 7–8 cize; 5 syce, 7 sice. [a. OF. *sise*, *cise*, aphetic forms of *assise* ASSIZE *sb.* probably due to *l'assise* being apprehended as *la sise*. Cf. med.L. *sisa*, *cisa*, MDu. *sise*, *sijs*, MLG. *sise*, MDa. *sise*, *sisæ*. The currency of the form in Eng. may have been subsequently increased by *assize* being taken as *a size*.]

**I. 1. a.** An assize for the administration of justice. = ASSIZE *sb.* 11, 12, 13. Now *dial.*

In later use commonly in the pl. form *sizes*.

(*a*) *a* **1300** *Body & Soul* in *Map's Poems* (Camden) 337 W3an 3e hadden set your sise. ye thre traytours, sore I wep. **1393** Langl. *P. Pl.* C. III. 178 Gyle..shope þat a shereyue sholde bere mede Softliche in saumbury fram syse to syse. *c* **1440** Capgr. *Life St. Kath.* I. 894 They sette the shire, þe cessyons and the Cyse Ryght as hem lest. *c* **1486** *Plumpton Corr.* (Camden) 68 As touching the matters he hard at the syse, I caused some to be thyn at this time. **1509** Barclay *Shyp of Folys* (1570) 4 There shall be no bayle nor treating of mainprise,.. There shall be no delayes vntill another Sise. **1581** T. Howell *Deuises* (1879) 187 Like as the captiue Wight..hopes at Sise to be releast, is then condemde to dye. *a* **1631** Donne *Sat.* II. Poems (1654) 123 You said if I return'd next size in Lent, I should be in remitter of your grace. **1749** Fielding *Tom Jones* XVIII. vi, He sent for a writ against me and had me to size.

*attrib.* **1630** J. Taylor (Water P.) *Wks.* II. 14 'Twas Size time there, and hanging was a brewing.

(*b*) *a* **1513** Fabyan *Chron.* VII. (1811) 344 Iudgys [were] ordeyned to kepe a cyrcuyte, as nowe they kepe the syzys in the tyme of vacacyon. **1538** Starkey *England* II. ii. 190 In the sessyonys and sysys at scyre townys appoyntyd. *a* **1616** Beaum. & Fl. *Wit without M.* III, The Sattin..will serve you at a Sizes yet. *Ibid.* IV. [iii], Some Dunce that..admires nothing but a long charge at Sizes. **1673** Temple *Ess. Ireland* Wks. 1720 I. 114 Sometimes one Share of that Money is paid to a single Pretender at the Sizes or Sessions. **1703** De Foe *Reform. Manners* Misc. 81 A Brace of Female-Clients meet him there, To help debauch the Sizes and the Fair. **1760–72** H. Brooke *Fool of Qual.* (1809) III. 145, I will never..bring you to the sizes or sessions. **1847–** in dial. glossaries (see *Eng. Dial. Dict.*). **1861** Geo. Eliot *Silas M.* viii, There had been one tried at the 'sizes, not so long ago.

†**b.** *Sc.* A jury. *Obs.* = ASSIZE *sb.* 13 b.

*c* **1470** Henry *Wallace* IV. 124 The siys of this couth say to him rycht nocht. **1535** Stewart *Cron. Scot.* III. 489 This governour..Corruptit judgis thair with him he brocht, And syis also that knew richt weill his thocht. *a* **1586** Montgomerie *Misc. Poems* xliv. 29 In dout vhat wyse that feirfull syse Pronunce thair sentence wald.

†**2.** An ordinance or regulation. *Obs.*

*a* **1425** *Cursor M.* 9427 (Trin.), Lawes two were set on sise To Adam in paradise. **1474** *Coventry Leet Bk.* 401 The sise of a Corriour is þat he corry no maner of lether but yf it be thorowe tanned. *Ibid.*, The sise is that no mercer, Grocer, Draper, Smyth nor no other crafty man by nor sell no maner thyng..but yf ther weyghtes and mesures be sised & sealed.

†**3.** The established order of things. *Obs.*

*c* **1400** *Sc. Trojan War* (Horstm.) I. 570 Thyr war þe wordys of Denyse Quhene þat he saw againe þe syse The sonne Eclyps.

†**4.** An ordinance fixing the amount of a payment or tax. Also *attrib.*, as ***size-boll***, ***-money***. *Obs.*

*a* **1300** *Cursor M.* 28438 Toll and tak, and rent o syse, Withalden i haue wit couettise. **1543** *Extr. Aberd. Reg.* (1844) I. 199 Robert Ratray..resignit..in the prouestis handis..the haly dais fische of Dee, and syise boll. **1633** *Sc. Acts, Chas. I* (1817) V. 94 For bruiking of the said burgh lands.., tolles, customes, sys bolles. **1641** *Ibid.* 627 To apply to þe vse of þe said brucht with the syis boll and syistrie. **1733** P. Lindsay *Interest Scot.* 206 The Payment of their Size-money, which they reckon so great a Hardship.

†**5.** A fixed standard of quality or quantity for articles of food or drink, or other commodities. *Obs.* = ASSIZE *sb.* 5.

? **1479** in *Eng. Gilds* 424 The Maire..to do calle byfore hym..all the Bakers of Bristowe, there to vndirstand whate stuff they haue of whete. And after, whate sise they shall bake. **1485** *Rolls of Parlt.* VI. 364/2 The Office of Cise of Ale in the same Towne, in the Countie of Glamorgan. **1529** Rastell *Pastyme* (1811) 194 The mayre toke brybes of the bakers & suffred them to sell brede under the syse. **1559** *Fabyan's Chron.* VII. (1811) 705 An acte of parliament for wood and coal to kepe the fulle sise,..that no man shall bargaine, sell, bryng, or conueigh of any other sise. **1641** Baker *Chron.* (1653) 15 He made a Law, ordaining a size, by certain pins in the pot, with penalty to any that should presume to drink deeper then the mark. *c* **1680** Shaftesbury in Christie *Life* (1871) I. App. I. p. xii, The senior fellows.. articled with us never to alter the size of our beer. **1688** Holme *Armoury* III. 308/1 The Bakers cannot without [scales] make and perform that just Size put upon them.

†**6.** A proper manner or method; a standard of action or conduct; a limit. *Obs.*

*c* **1420** *26 Pol. Poems* 66 He may not stonde, þat haþ no toon [= toes], Lepe ne renne, ne ryde in syse. **1470–85** Malory *Arthur* X. lii. 500 Of syre Tristram came..alle the syses and mesures of blowynge of an horne. **1526** Skelton *Magnyf.* 854 My persone prest Beyonde all syse. **1550** Crowley *Last Trumpet* 400 Though..he were wicked past al sise. **1574** Hellowes *Gueuara's Fam. Ep.* (1584) 63 In our talke or in any other thing no syse is suffered, but in sermons which muste not passe above an howre.

†**7. a.** A quantity or portion *of* bread, ale, etc.; *spec.* in Cambridge use (see quot. 1617); an allowance.

**1555** W. Watreman *Fardle Facions* II. xii. 285 That in so smalle a syse of breade and wine, the infinite..Christe.. shoulde be comprehended. **1592** Nashe *P. Penilesse* 20 The Maister Butler of Pembrooke Hall,..one that sheweth more discretion in setting vp a syse of Bread, than thou in all thy whole booke. **1605** Shaks. *Lear* II. iv. 178 Tis not in thee.. to cut off my Traine,..to scant my sizes. **1617** Minsheu *Ductor* s.v., A size is a portion of bread and drinke: it is a farthing which schollers in Cambridge haue at the buttery: it is noted with the letter *S* as in Oxford with the letter *Q* for halfe a farthing. **1691** Ray *S. & E. Co. Words* 113 A *Size* of Bread, and a Cue of Bread, Cambridge. The one signifies half, the other one fourth part of a Half-penny Loaf. **1785**

GROSE *Dict. Vulgar T.* s.v., Size of Ale, half a pint; Size of bread and cheese, a certain quantity.

*transf.* **1606** SHAKS. *Ant. & Cl.* IV. xv. 4 Our size of sorrow Proportion'd to our cause, must be as great As that which makes it.

†**b.** *size-q(ue)*, the half of an ordinary allowance. Cf. CUE *sb.*[1] 2 b. *Obs.*

**1602** *2nd Pt. Return fr. Parnassus* IV. iii. 1838 You are at Cambridge still with sice kue. **1670** EACHARD *Cont. Clergy* 31 He never drunk above size-q: of Helicon.

†**8.** *to pay size*, to pay heavily. *Obs.*[−1]

**1662** PEPYS *Diary* 4 Sept., My Lady Batten and her crew, at least half a score, came into the room, and I believe we shall pay size for it.

**9.** †**a.** A device for measuring pearls.

**1728** CHAMBERS *Cycl.* s.v. [Hence in later Dicts.]

**b.** A gauge used in wire-drawing.

**1763** W. LEWIS *Phil. Comm. Arts* 55 A brass plate called a size, on which is measured by means of notches..the increase which a certain length of wire should gain in passing through a fresh hole.

**II. 10. a.** The magnitude, bulk, bigness, or dimensions *of* anything.

*a* **1400–50** *Alexander* 26 For þai þe mesure & þe mett of all þe mulde couthe, þe sise of all þe grete see. **1530** PALSGR. 270/2 Syse of a mannes body, *corpulence. Ibid.*, Syse of any thyng, *moyson.* **1621** DONNE *Anat. World* I. 12 When, as the age was long, the sise was great; Mans grouth.. recompenc'd the meat. *a* **1676** HALE *Prim. Orig. Man.* (1677) 65 The humane Brain is..much..larger than the Brains of Brutes, having regard to the size and proportion of their Bodies. **1707** NORRIS *Treat. Humility* x. 376 The cloathing of humility does as it were conform itself to the size of the wearer. **1796** C. MARSHALL *Gardening* xiii. (1813) 181 The size of a hot bed, as to length and breadth. **1846** J. BAXTER *Libr. Pract. Agric.* (ed. 4) I. 111 The size of some stems is truly astonishing. **1880** BESSEY *Botany* 146 The absolute size of leaves varies greatly also.

**b.** Preceded by *of*, or in later use with ellipse of this. *of a* (or *one*) *size*, of the same magnitude or dimensions.

*c* **1400** *Destr. Troy* 3815 Protheselus the pert kyng was of pure shap, Semely for sothe, & of Syse faire. **1470–85** MALORY *Arthur* V. viii. 173 Now arte thow better of a syse to dele with than thou were. **1560** BIBLE (Genevan) *Exod.* xxxvi. 9 The curtaines were all of one cise. [Also *1 Kings* vi. 25.] **1598** BARRET *Theor. Warres* V. i. 124 Of the Size royall, is that peece which shooteth a bullet from seuenteene pound waight vpward. **1657** AUSTEN *Fruit Trees* I. 63 Young trees of a smaler sise. **1677** PLOT *Oxfordshire* 108 Of different colours, figures, cizes. **1767** *Phil. Trans.* LVII. 490 The crystals of this salt were in general..more of a size, than those of the gooseberry. **1781** COWPER *Ep. Lady Austin* 95 A seed of tiny size. **1840** DICKENS *Old C. Shop* v, 'Why don't you hit one of your own size,' said the boy. **1884** PAE *Eustace* 13 The two men were about a size. **1893** HODGES *Elem. Photogr.* 115 A frame the exact size of the window.

**c.** In abstract use: Magnitude.

**1667** MILTON *P.L.* VI. 352 They Limb themselves, and colour, shape or size Assume. **1701** GREW *Cosmol. Sacra* I. i, The mixture of cize and figure, can beget nothing but cize and figure. **1781** COWPER *Retirem.* 67 Whose shape would make them, had they bulk and size, More hideous foes [etc.]. **1845** PATTISON *Ess.* (1889) I. 12 The church of St. Julian, equal in size to most cathedrals. **1848** DICKENS *Dombey* v, The books precisely matched as to size. **1886** RUSKIN *Præterita* I. vi. 199, I had always a quite true perception of size, whether in mountains or buildings.

**d.** Suitable or normal dimensions. *rare* exc. in phr. *to cut* (*chop*, etc.) *down to size*: see CUT *v.* 54 h. *colloq.*

**1842** *Penny Cycl.* XXII. 65/1 The plants..should be thinned, and..may be used as they attain size till August. **1953** *Time* 20 July 40/3 He kept Stalin down to size. **1962** *Listener* 17 May 883/1 The complexity and psychological depth abandoned in hacking the novel down to size. **1972** *N.Y. Times* 3 Nov. 39/6 Once the warlord armies supporting him were chopped down to size.., he was content to fade away.

**e.** Thickness or thinness (of a liquid mixture); consistency (cf. SIZE *v.*[1] 4 c).

**1863** WISE *New Forest* Gloss., 'The size of the gruel' means its consistency. **1889** C. T. DAVIS *Bricks & Tiles* (ed. 2) 147 The temperer having secured the proper plasticity, or 'size' for the clay.

**f.** In colloq. phr. *that's* (*about*) *the size of it*, etc.: that is what it amounts to, that is the situation.

**1860** WHYTE MELVILLE *Mkt. Harb.* 30 Nothing to do, and lots of time to do it in! that seems to be about the size of it. **1880** 'MARK TWAIN' *Tramp Abroad* viii. 71 'Bloodshed!' 'That's about the size of it,' I said. **1914** G. ATHERTON *Perch of Devil* I. 89 That's the size of it, only I couldn't ever say it like that. **1922** JOYCE *Ulysses* 305 Talking about the Gaelic league and the antitreating league and drink, the curse of Ireland. Antitreating is about the size of it. **1966** D. FRANCIS *Flying Finish* ii. 21 'He just went to Italy and didn't come back?' 'That's about the size of it,' Simon agreed. **1973** 'M. INNES' *Appleby's Answer* xv. 134 It's money that's really in his head... That's about the size of it, wouldn't you say?

**11. a.** A particular magnitude or set of dimensions; *esp.* one of a series in the case of various manufactured articles, as boots, gloves, etc.

**1591** PERCIVALL *Span. Dict.*, *Punto*,..the sise of a shoo. *c* **1610** DONNE *Lett.* xxxii. Wks. 1839 VI. 338 There is not a size of paper in the palace, large enough to tell you how much I esteem myself honoured in your remembrances. **1706** E. WARD *Wooden World Diss.* (1708) 104 He is certainly a Size above ordinary in his own Conceit. **1711** *Lond. Gaz.* No. 4899/4 Another silver Mazarene, a size larger. **1828** CARR *Craven Gloss.*, *Size*, a term of measure amongst shoemakers, equal to one third part of an inch. **1836–7** DICKENS *Sk. Boz, Scenes* xx, Her white satin shoes being a few sizes too large. **1846** GREENER *Sci. Gunnery* 329 It appears also that there is a size which meets with less resistance from atmospheric influence than others. **1872** CALVERLEY *Fly Leaves* (1903) 9 To haste..to..the glover, Having managed to discover what is dear Neæra's 'size'.

*fig.* **1879** HUTTON in *Bagehot's Lit. Studies* I. p. lxii, He was 'between sizes in politics'.

**b.** Used *ellipt.* with a sb. following.

**1769** MRS. RAFFALD *Eng. Housekpr.* (1778) 41 Cut your sturgeon into what size pieces you please. **1771** LUCKOMBE *Hist. Print.* 215 The Writings of that Father [St. Augustine] were the first Works done on that size Letter. **1846** BRITTAN tr. *Malgaigne's Man. Oper. Surg.* 308 After this first trial you can judge what size eye will do next. **1886** CAULFEILD *Seamanship Notes* 3 Different size cables. **1889** *Anthony's Photogr. Bulletin* II. 159 A large size plate.

**c.** *to try* (something) (*on*) *for size*: to consider (an idea, theory, etc.) to see whether it fits the facts. Also *loosely*, to try out or sample. *colloq.* (orig. *U.S.*).

**1956** 'E. MCBAIN' *Cop Hater* (1958) viii. 70 'Try this for size,' Bush said. 'I'm listening,' Carella said. **1967** 'E. QUEEN' *Face to Face* xxix. 127 'All right,' said the Inspector. 'Let's try this on for size: You knew what Spotty had to sell, didn't you?' **1969** 'J. FRASER' *Cock-pit of Roses* x. 81 'I know some bugger's been pinching 'em, if that's what you're getting at.' Try that on for size, you devil, his look seemed to say. **1979** A. BOYLE *Climate of Treason* (1980) viii. 258 Trying his boss's desk for size, Philby noticed the untidy array of memoranda and pending files in the in-tray. **1980** J. MCCLURE *Blood of Englishman* xxiv. 221 She was shaking the sardines into a saucer. 'There, kitty! Try those for size.'

**12. a.** Magnitude, extent, rate, amount, etc., as a standard of immaterial things. Also in phrases (see later quots.).

*a* **1530** HEYWOOD *Love* 1509 (Brandl), As the horse feleth pleasure in syse..aboue the tre, So feleth he..aboue ye. **1579** SPENSER *Two other Lett.* i. 56, I hope you will vouchsafe mee an answeare of the largest size. **1597** SHAKS. *Lover's Compl.* 21 Shriking vndistinguisht wo, In clamours of all size both high and low. **1613** PURCHAS *Pilgrimage* III. xii. 257 Although those dayes shall be of a larger size then these. **1701** SWIFT *Contests Nobles & Commons* Wks. 1755 II. I. 25 The power of these princes..was much of a size with that of the kings in Sparta. *a* **1715** BURNET *Own Time* (1766) I. 133 He understood well the size of their understandings. **1780** COWPER *Progr. Error* 283 Errors, of whatever size. **1828** CARR *Craven Gloss.* s.v., 'He talks at a fearful size;' i.e. he talks big. **1836–8** HALIBURTON *Clockm.* (1862) 299 One day I was adrivin' out at a'most a deuce of a size, and he stopped me. **1883** GRESLEY *Gloss. Coal Mining* 224 *Size*, in reference to a *fault*; this word means the extent of the displacement or the *throw*.

**b.** Of persons in respect of mental or moral qualities, rank or position, etc.; †hence, class, kind, degree, order.

**1679** PENN *Addr. Prot.* II. v. (1692) 151 Which showeth.. that Christians of all sizes, great and small, are but Brethren. **1699** BENTLEY *Phalaris* 497 Our Mock Phalaris is a Sophist of that size, that no kind of Blunder is below his Character. **1719** SWIFT *To a Young Clergym.* Wks. 1755 II. II. 5 A plain sermon intended for the middle or lower size of people. **1722** WOLLASTON *Relig. Nat.* ix. 207 Can we impute to God that, which is below the common size of men? **1746** FRANCIS tr. *Horace, Art Poet.* 506 But God, and Man, and letter'd Post denies, That Poets ever are of midling Size. **1844** EMERSON *Ess.* Ser. II. vi, The cause is reduced..to suit the size of the partisans. **1872** MORLEY *Voltaire* (1886) 8 There are things enough to be said of Voltaire's moral size.

**c.** *pl.* As adv. Many times, far.

**1861** EMILY DICKINSON *Lett.* (1897) II. 241 All our Lord demands, who sizes better knows than we.

**13.** Special combs., as **size-bone**, whalebone of the length of six feet or above; **size distribution**, the way in which size varies among members of a population of particles; **size effect**, an effect due to size; **size-fish**, a whale yielding size-bone; **size-group**, those constituents of a population whose sizes fall within a specific range; †**size-land**, a narrow strip of ploughed land; **size-range**, a range of sizes; a size group; **size-roll**, (*a*) a military roll showing the size of each man; (*b*) 'a piece of parchment added to a roll' (Simmonds, 1858); **size-slate**, a slate having certain definite dimensions or measurements; **size-stick** (see quot.).

**1820** SCORESBY *Arct. Regions* II. 419 The *size-bone or such pieces as measure six feet or upward in length is kept separate from the under-size. **1888** *Encycl. Brit.* XXIV. 527/2 The figures given are the values of 'size-bones',.. which is twice the value of whalebone under that length. **1925** *Trans. Faraday Soc.* XXI. 381 (*heading*) A simple method of obtaining the *size distribution of particles in soils and precipitates. **1966** D. G. BRANDON *Mod. Techniques Metallogr.* v. 250 In the past, size-distribution analysis has usually involved time-consuming measurements on individual grains or particles. **1943** *Ann. Appl. Biol.* XXX. 216/2 The loss in weight increases progressively from *I* to *IV* indicating the existence of a *size effect. **1968** C. G. KUPER *Introd. Theory Superconductivity* v. 92 The discrepancy between the experiments and the London theory has been interpreted as a size effect, arising from the scattering of normal electrons by the n-s boundary. **1820** SCORESBY *Arct. Regions* II. 419 The captain and some of the officers..having a premium on every *size fish. **1867** SMYTH *Sailor's Word-bk.* 628 The harpooner gets a bonus for striking a 'size-fish'. **1944** J. S. HUXLEY *On Living in Revolution* 110 The total population can be separated into four *size-groups, corresponding to the produce of the four successive years that each grub lives in the soil before it turns into a beetle. **1971** I. G. GASS et al. *Understanding Earth* ix. 132/2 They contain both filamentous and globular structures, and the latter occur in more than one size-group. **1750** W. ELLIS *Mod. Husb.* I. i. 75 [In Middlesex] they plow two, three, or four of these *size-lands into one broad-land. **1924** *Industr. & Engin. Chem.* XVI. 930/2 The figures given ..for the *size range were calculated in this way. **1955** *New Biol.* XIX. 95 Some particles in the mitochondrial size-range appear to be proplastids. **1962** *Science Survey* III. 296 Shoals of large salmon were observed to remain inactive at the tail of the pool while a smaller size-range of salmon and trout ascended successfully. **1757** WASHINGTON *Lett.* Writ. 1889 I. 473 Nor shall I delay to send the companies' *size-rolls, when they come to my hands. **1832** *Regul. & Instr. Cavalry* II. 16 Each Troop forms on its own parade, in rank entire according to the size-roll. **1844** *Regul. & Ord. Army* 155 The form of Size Roll..is so arranged as to sub-divide the three divisions for each height,—'small,' 'middling,' and 'large,'—each into three classes. **1865** BOWER *Slate Quarries* 31 The average price of *size slates, tons, and slabs. **1875** KNIGHT *Dict. Mech.* 2192/1 **Size-stick*, the shoemaker's measuring-stick to determine the length of feet.

**size** (saɪz), *sb.*[2] Forms: 5 cyse, 5–7 syse, 6 syes, 6–7 sise, syze, 7– size. [Possibly the same word as prec., but the history is not clear.

Cf. Sp. *sisa*, given by Minsheu (1599) as 'solder for golde', but explained in later Sp. dicts. in accordance with sense 1. Florio (followed as usual by Torriano) gives both It. *sisa* and *assisa* in the sense of size 'that painters use', but later It. dicts. do not confirm this.]

†**1.** A glutinous or viscid wash applied to paper, parchment, etc., to provide a suitable ground for gilding, painting, or other work. *Obs.*

*c* **1440** *Promp. Parv.* 456/2 Syse, for bokys lymynynge. *c* **1485** *E. Eng. Misc.* (Warton Club) 73 To make a cyse to gyld unburned gold on bokys. **1573** *Art of Limming* Title-p., The maner how to make sundry sises or grounds to laye silver or gold upon. **1601** HOLLAND *Pliny* II. 595 Whatsoeuer is to be pargetted with this Maltha..ought first to be rubbed throughly with a size of oile. **1669** STURMY *Mariner's Mag.* VII. xxxiv. 49 Take Red Lead..or Yellow Oker, well ground with Oyle of Spike or Turpentine; this is the Sise: Then draw with that the Figure you would have in Gold. **1728** CHAMBERS *Cycl.* s.v. *Limning*, There are always applied two Lays of hot Size e'er the Colours..are laid on. **1763** W. LEWIS *Phil. Comm. Arts* 62 For gilding on wood, &c. with what is called water-size, the parchment or leather size above-mentioned is mixed with whiting, and several layers of the mixture spread upon the piece.

**b.** *Printing.* (See quot.)

**1888** JACOBI *Printers' Vocab.* 126 *Size*, the preparation used for printing with bronze.

**2.** A semi-solid glutinous substance, prepared from materials similar to those which furnish glue, and used to mix with colours, to dress cloth or paper, and for various other purposes.

**1530** PALSGR. 270/2 Syse for colours, *colle de cvir.* **1565** COOPER *Thesaurus* s.v. *Color, Liquidus*... Moyste, tempered with sise as peynters vse. **1582** in Feuillerat *Revels Q. Eliz.* (1908) 359 Paste bord, paper, and paste, white, sise, verte, syneper. **1658** W. SANDERSON *Graphice* 78 Old rotten size, to bind the Colours together. **1714** MANDEVILLE *Fab. Bees* (1733) I. 234 What size is to white walls, which hinders them from coming off, and makes them lasting. **1747** FRANKLIN *Conjecture* Wks. 1887 II. 107 Paper wet with size and water will not dry so soon as if wet with water only. **1800** *Phil. Trans.* XC. 367 The various degrees of viscidity and tenacity which characterize mucilage, size, and glue. **1843** HOLTZAPFFEL *Turning* I. 63 The outer face of the veneer and the surface of the table are wetted with very thin glue, or with a stiff size. **1883** HALDANE *Workshop Rec.* Ser. II. 302/1 Size of very different qualities is made at glue-works.

**3.** The buffy coat on the surface of coagulated blood in certain conditions. Cf. SIZY *a.*

**1770** *Phil. Trans.* LX. 387, I shall next..enquire into the formation of the inflammatory crust, or size, as it is called.

**4.** *attrib.*, as **size-colour**, **-gelatin**, **-manufactory**, **-manufacturer**, **-water**.

**1603–4** *Act 1 Jas. I*, c. 20 §1 As well with Oyle Colours as Size Colours. **1728** CHAMBERS *Cycl.* s.v. *Limning*, That the Size-Colours hold the best. **1738** *Ibid.* s.v. *Book-binding*, The leaves being wetted with the size-water. **1858** SIMMONDS *Dict. Trade*, *Size-manufacturer*, a boiler down of skins, etc., and maker of size. **1869** E. A. PARKES *Pract. Hygiene* (ed. 3) 20 Substances..from size, horn, and isinglass manufactories. **1873** T. H. GREEN *Introd. Pathol.* 123 Others are softer, more resembling size-gelatin.

†**size**, *sb.*[3] *Obs.* Forms: 5 sise, 6 sys(s)e, syce, 5–7 size, 6–7 syze. [perh. ad. OF. *sis*, *siis* six: cf. *size* SICE and SIX B.] A certain kind or size of candle, used esp. at court and in churches.

*a* **1483** *Liber Niger* in *Househ. Ord.* (1790) 22, x candells wax, for the sizes of the chamber. *Ibid.* 41 He setteth up the sises in the King's chambre. **1518** *Lett. & Papers Hen. VIII*, II. II. 1515 Pure wax for morters, quariers, prikettes and sysys. **1560** *Acc. Fratern. Holy Ghost, Basingstoke* (1882) 13 Item paid for tapers & Syces at whitsontyde, ij *s.* **1570** GOOGE *Pop. Kingd.* III. 37 To whome [Christ] if that they light a syse, his mother hath six againe. **1611** COTGR., *Bougie*,..a size or small round candle vsed in churches. **1659** HEYLIN *Examen Hist.* I. 288 Upon the Communion Table they..never set more then two fair Candles with a few small Sizes neer to them.

*attrib.* **1552** HULOET, Size candle. **1559** *Ludlow Churchw. Acc.* (Camden) 91 Payd upon Easter day in the mornynge for a sysse candle, j[d].

**size**, variant of SICE (six in dice).

**size** (saɪz), *v.*[1] Forms: 5 syse, 5–8 sise, 8 cise, 6– size. [f. SIZE *sb.*[1], or, in early use, aphetic for ASSIZE *v.*]

†**1.** *trans.* To regulate or control, *esp.* in relation to a fixed standard. *Obs.*

*a* **1400–50** *Alexander* 4654 Many seerties we seet [*read* he set] þat sysed all þe werde. **1467** *Coventry Leet Bk.* 335 þat þe Mair ordeyn iiij assisours to sise þe watir at all Milles within þis Cete. **1579** in W. H. Turner *Select. Rec. Oxford* (1880) 402 All other measures..to be vewed, tryed, sised, allowed, and sealed. **1580** LYLY *Euphues* (Arb.) 247 Ye coyn they vse is either of brasse or els rings of Iron, sised at a certein weight in steede of money. **1613** in W. M. Williams *Founders' Co.* (1867) 23 The said Weights..shall..be sized by the Standard at Founders' Hall. **1656** W. WEBB in D. King *Vale Royall* II. 213 This Maior..sized the Wines,—Muscadine at 7d. the quart, Sack at 10d. and other Wines at six pence. **1698–9** *Act 11 Will. III*, c. xv. §1 A Vessel.. made, sized, and equalled unto the said Standard. **1766** ENTICK *London* IV. 79 All makers of brass weights..are obliged to have their..weights sized by the Company's standard. **1771** *Phil. Trans.* LXI. 467 My weights were most accurately sized.

**2. a.** In University use (at Cambridge, Harvard, and Yale): To enter as a 'size' upon the buttery or kitchen books; to score (an amount) against oneself in this manner. Also *transf.*

**1598** E. GUILPIN *Skial.* (1878) 47, I knew thee when thou war'dst a thred-bare gowne: Siz'd eighteene pence a weeke. **1602** *2nd Pt. Return fr. Parnassus* V. ii. 2048, I vse to size my musicke, or go on the score for it, Ile pay it at the quarters end. **1630** RANDOLPH *Aristippus* Wks. 1875 I. 14 Drinking college tap-lash..will let them have no more learning than they size, nor a drop of wit more than the butler sets on their heads. **1790** *Laws of Harvard Coll.* 38 They may be allowed to size a meal at the kitchen. **1811** *Laws of Yale Coll.* 31 The Butler shall make up his bill against each student, in which every article sized or taken up by him at the Buttery shall be particularly charged.

**b.** *intr.* To order 'sizes', or have them entered against one.

**1598** E. GUILPIN *Skial.* (1878) 11, I have sized in Cambridge, and my friends a season, Some exhibition for me there disburst. **1602** *2nd Pt. Return fr. Parnassus* IV. ii. 1691 You that are one of the Diuels fellow commoners, one that sizeth in the Deuils butteries. **1617** MINSHEU *Ductor* s.v., To size is to set downe their *quantum*, i.e. how much they take in their name in the Buttery-booke. **1706** PHILLIPS (ed. 6), *To Size*,..to Score as Students doe in the Buttery-Book of a College at Cambridge. **1852** BRISTED *Five Yrs. Eng. Univ.* (ed. 3) 19 Soup, pastry, and cheese can be 'sized for', that is, brought in portions to individuals at an extra charge. **1859** *Slang Dict.* 93 If a man asks you to supper, he treats you; if to size, you pay for what you eat.

†**c.** *trans.* To allowance (oneself); to eke *out* with something extra. *Obs.*

**1607** TOPSELL *Serpents* (1658) 727 It is said, they eat earth by measure, for they eat so much every day as they can gripe in their fore-foot, as it were sizing themselves. *c* **1614** FLETCHER *Wit at Sev. Weap.* II. i, To be so strict A Nigard to your Commons, that you are fain To size your belly out with Shoulder Fees.

†**3.** To state the size of (something). *Obs.*$^{-1}$

*a* **1661** HOLYDAY *Juvenal* (1673) 250 The pygmies..being but one foot high (as some size them).

**4. a.** To make of a certain size; to give size to; to adjust in respect of size. Also with *out.*

**1609** C. BUTLER *Fem. Mon.* iii. (1623) 4 They serue to size out the Summer-doore to his due space of foure square inches. **1691** T. H[ALE] *Acc. New Invent.* 21 Pieces of Lead sized to, and nailed over the said Bolts. **1701** GREW *Cosmol. Sacra* I. i, That the parts of the organ be fitly cized, shaped and set together. **1793** SMEATON *Edystone L.* §290 The smaller end of it being sized as near as possible to the manholes of the floors. **1862** *Trans. Ill. Agric. Soc.* (1865) V. 233 There is no provision made for 'sizing the gavels' [in reaping]. **1897** F. C. MOORE *How to build Home* 90 The first-story beams are to be sized and leveled upon the sill and upon the foundation wall. **1981** *Sci. Amer.* Apr. 30/1 Second, says Dr. Derry, the book was sized to fit into a briefcase.

*fig.* **1733** *Revolution Politicks* VII. 44 Sizing his Words at such a rate as one yet willing to be understood that he had not stray'd from his Brethern in Point of Loyalty. **1742** RICHARDSON *Pamela* IV. 284 He is so exactly siz'd and cut out for a Town Fop, Coxcomb, or pretty Fellow. **1899** [see PANHANDLER 1].

**b.** *Agric.* (See quots.)

**1707** MORTIMER *Husb.* (1721) I. 53 You must not let it lie long before you strick, sise, or plow it up into small Ridges. **1808** *Young's Ann. Agric.* XLV. 342 [He] sizes the field, as it is styled, that is, draws out new ridges or stitches nearly in the direction of the old original ones. **1844** *Jrnl. R. Agric. Soc.* V. I. 5 These..are what is termed sized; that is,..the ploughman sizes them by going one bout, or by once going and returning up the field.

**c.** To reduce (clay) to the proper consistency for moulding.

**1889** C. T. DAVIS *Bricks & Tiles* (ed. 2) 147 It is necessary to grind the same clay..several times..before it comes to the proper degree of plasticity for moulding; this operation is called 'sizing the clay'.

**5. a.** To classify or arrange according to size. Also *transf.* to class or rank (*with* others).

*a* **1635** RANDOLPH *Townsmen's Petition* Wks. 1875 II. 658 With proctors and with testers grave Our bailiffs you may size. **1649** BLITHE *Eng. Improv. Impr.* (1653) 197 Size your Horses or Oxen equal. **1677** YARRANTON *Eng. Improv.* 46 They sort and size all the Threads so, that they can apply them to make equal Cloaths. **1735** SOMERVILLE *Chase* I. 82 The Multitude Dispers'd, to size, to sort their various Tribes. **1805** *Edin. Rev.* VI. 463 Instead of being scientifically classified, and (if we may so speak) accurately sized, we may expect to find them [i.e. facts] tossed together with little judgment. **1886** *Law Times' Rep.* LIII. 696/2 The said broken products were then sized and separated.

**b.** *Mil.* To arrange or draw up (men) in ranks according to stature.

**1802** JAMES *Milit. Dict.* s.v., The flank troops of a squadron must be sized in the following manner. **1847** *Infantry Man.* (1854) 46 In this formation companies are to assemble.., being sized from flanks to centre. **1868** *Regul. & Ord. Army* §857 All guards are..to be inspected and sized by the adjutant.

**c.** To single (plants). *rare.*

**1660** [see SIZING *vbl. sb.*[1] 3]. **1764** *Museum Rusticum* III. lvii. 241 It would be adviseable, at the time of first sizing the plants, to leave more than are necessary.

†**6.** *U.S.* (See quot. 1836–9) *Obs.*

**1836–9** HALIBURTON *Clockm.* (1862) 442 Come, I'll size your pile... Plank down a pile of dollars..of any size you like, and I'll put down another of the same size. **1853** J. G. BALDWIN *Flush Times Alabama* 113 The jury shortly after returned into court with a verdict which 'sized their pile'. **1873** J. H. BEADLE *Undevel. West* xii. 198 They are satisfied to 'size your pile' and take quarter of it. **1889** 'MARK TWAIN' *Conn. Yankee* 300, I was resolved he should have at least one [bath]..if it sized up my whole influence and bankrupted the pile.

**7. a.** *colloq.* (orig. *U.S.*). Usually with *up*: To take the size or measure of; to regard so as to form an opinion of; to make an estimate of. Hence **'size-up** *sb.*, an estimate (*U.S.*).

**1884** *Cent. Mag.* Nov. 54 Such a stranger..would have 'sized them up'..simply as a pair of poverty-stricken Mexicans. **1891** MARRIOTT-WATSON *Web of Spider* xi, It was dark when I seized her, and I hadn't time to 'size' her. **1896** NEWNHAM DAVIS *Three Men & a God* 148 The grey-haired..man who met us..mentally sized me up at once. **1924** E. O'NEILL *All God's Chillun got Wings* 103 John scrutinizes their faces keenly, sizing up the situation. **1945** E. S. GARDNER *Case of Golddigger's Purse* v. 35, I always like to plan my campaign after I've sized up my man. **1949** *Security* (Charlottesville, Va.) May 1/2 Reminded him how wrong a bright man can be in his size-up of other folks. **1952** *Sun* (Baltimore) 22 Oct. 19/7 Casey's size-up of Woodling as a pinch-hitter was verified in the eighth inning. **1978** *N.Y. Times* 30 Mar. B3/1 A teen-ager in sneakers, sizing up the drinkers in the darkened bar as easy marks, whispered to a friend, 'I wonder if they've got any change.'

**b.** With *down*: (*a*) To arrange in sizes downwards; (*b*) to size up; to comprehend.

**1896** W. MORRIS in Mackail *Life* (1899) I. 229 The stone slates are 'sized down', the smaller ones to the top, the bigger towards the eaves. **1896** *Chambers' Jrnl.* 25 Jan. 57 There's just one thing I don't size down. I know why I am here:.. but why are you? **1912** A. CONAN DOYLE *Lost World* vi. 87, I want a man I can bank on. So I sized you down, and I'm bound to say that you came well out of it.

**8.** *intr.* **a.** To be on an equality *with*; to match *with*; also with *up.*

**1639** MAYNE *City Match* IV. viii, Her birth Not being so high she will more size with you. **1902** O. WISTER *Virginian* v, It was a letter which..'sized up' very well with the letters written in my part of the United States.

**b.** To assume size; to increase in size.

*a* **1631** DONNE *Poems* (1633) 63 So As they waxe lesser, fall, as they sise, grow. **1818** KEATS *Endymion* III. 206 The gulphing whale was like a dot.., Yet look upon it, and 'twould size and swell To its huge self. *c* **1866** G. M. HOPKINS *Poems* (1967) 36 That a quince I pore upon? O no it is the sizing moon. **1926** *Daily Colonist* (Victoria, B.C.) 13 July 4/5 Pears and apples are sizing well and developing nicely. **1940** *Sun* (Baltimore) 5 Sept. 7/5 Sweet potato tubers are developing and sizing in Western Maryland.

**c.** With *up*: to develop or take shape; to amount (*to* something); to reach the necessary standard. Cf. *to measure up to* s.v. MEASURE *v.* 4 c. *U.S.*

**1884** E. W. NYE *Baled Hay* 126 Time, at last, makes all things size up in proper shape. **1905** *N.Y. Even. Post* 21 Nov. 1 If the President does not think that Mr. Halpin sizes up as chairman of the County Committee, [etc.]. **1910** J. HART *Vigilante Girl* ii. 28 Burke isn't a bad sort—he sizes up about as well as most of them. **1917** H. JAMES *Ivory Tower* II. i. 89 The question of what Gray's 'interest'..might size up to.

**size** (saɪz), *v.*[2] Also 7 sise. [f. SIZE *sb.*[2] Cf. Sp. *sisar* (1739), It. *sisare* (Florio).] *trans.* To cover, smear, prepare, treat, or stiffen with size.

Cf. the earlier OVERSIZE *v.*[2], and *blood-sized* in Beaum. & Fl. *Two Noble K.* I. i. 105.

**1667** PRIMATT *City & C. Builder* 103 For Lathing, Plaistering, Rendring and sizing the Partition. **1703** *Art's Improv.* I. 65 Cold-clear it, i.e. Size it over. **1721** C. KING *Brit. Merch.* II. 268 A Liquor is there prepared for sizing or gumming every Sheet. **1857** MILLER *Elem. Chem., Org.* ii. §4. 93 In order to fit it [paper] for the ink, it is *sized*, or coated with a mixture of weak fine glue and alum. **1885** *Encycl. Brit.* XVIII. 225/1 The paper..is then sized by passing the spurs through a strong solution of gelatin.

*fig.* **1633** J. ADAMS *Exp. 2 Peter* ii. 10 Uncleanness is a deep stain, sized into the soul by her dwelling in the body.

**sizeable** ('saɪzəb(ə)l), *a.* Also sizable. [f. SIZE *v.*[1] + -ABLE.] Of a fair (†proper or convenient) size; fairly large.

In very common use from *c* 1680; *sizeable* has always been by far the more frequent spelling.

*α.* **1613** J. MAY *Decl. Clothing* iii. 16 His charge not to set that seale but vpon perfect and sizable cloth. **1681** R. KNOX *Hist. Ceylon* 16 The trees are not very great but sizable. **1703** DAMPIER *Voy.* III. I. 115 A Fish about 8 inches long, broad and sizable. **1783** COWPER *Let. to Newton* 30 Nov., I swallow ..a dozen good sizable cakes. **1855** HALIBURTON *N. & H. Nature* II. 193 Halifax is a sizable place and covers a good deal of ground. **1893** *Times* 12 June 13/5 Prices continue to show increasing firmness, especially for sizable and hard wood.

*β.* **1677** YARRANTON *Eng. Improv.* 185 The Wyer must be ..drawn and made sizeable and fit to make all sorts of Pins. **1686** PLOT *Staffordsh.* 293 Having taken up at a time 3 sizeable men. **1710** ADDISON *Tatler* No. 220 ¶3 A more modern Virtuoso..invented that sizeable Instrument which is now in Use. **1789** *Trans. Soc. Arts* II. 238 The people are fond of purchasing sizeable trees for building. **1818** *Blackw. Mag.* III. 147 We find the cerebellum sizeable, but not remarkable. **1882** *Good Words* Sept. 606 Presently we come upon quite a sizeable stream.

Hence **'sizeableness** (Bailey, 1727, vol. II).

**size-boll** (obs. Sc.): see SIZE *sb.*[1] 4.

**sized** (saɪzd), *ppl. a.*[1] [f. SIZE *sb.*[1] or *v.*[1]]

**1.** Having a specified or indicated magnitude or size: **a.** In predicative use.

**1582** STANYHURST *Æneis* III. (Arb.) 82 A strange sow mightelye sized. **1602** SHAKS. *Ham.* III. ii. 180 As my Loue is siz'd, my Feare is so. **1693** NORRIS *Pract. Disc.* (1711) III. 17 Certain Particles of Matter so and so sized, so and so figured. **1759** B. MARTIN *Nat. Hist. Eng.* I. 121 Differently sized, from the Bigness of a Pheasant. **1766** CANNING *Anti-Lucretius* II. 89 If in it's motion one should chance to strike Against another, shap'd and siz'd alike.

**b.** Attributively, with qualifying words denoting relative size, as ***fair-***, ***full-***, ***great-***, ***large-***, ***middle-sized.***

In later use also with advs., as *fairly-*, *moderately-sized.* **1606** SHAKS. *Tr. & Cr.* V. x. 26 Thou great siz'd coward. **1611** COTGR. s.v. *Poincte*, The middle-sized wax-candle vsed in Churches. *a* **1678**– Large-sized [see LARGE A. 15]. **1725** *Fam. Dict.* s.v. *Cock*, A Dunghil Cock..should be..of a large and well-siz'd Body. **1796** C. MARSHALL *Gardening* xiv. (1813) 204 One plant or at most two will be now under one full-sized light. **1801** *Med. Jrnl.* V. 225 A moderate sized garden pea. **1883** F. DAY *Indian Fish* 46 Large drag-nets,..having fairly-sized meshes. **1888** *Encycl. Brit.* XXIV. 528/2 The average-sized bottlenose whale yields 22 cwts. of oil.

**c.** With qualifying words of the types *same*, *such*, *this*; *different*, *several*, etc.

**1626** SIR E. CECIL in *J. Glanville's Voy. Cadiz* (Camden) p. xliii, The Commissioners are much to be commended for such sized shippes as they have made. **1656** DUCHESS OF NEWCASTLE *Nature's Picture* XI, Like several sized candles, are longer or shorter ere they come to a snuff. **1680** MOXON *Mech. Exerc.* xiii. 224 They have different sized Grooves in the Slate for that purpose. **1806** A. HUNTER *Culina* 189 This sized pie will require three hours baking. **1857** T. MOORE *Handbk. Brit. Ferns* (ed. 3) 28 Re-pot in the same sized pot. **1879** NOAD & PREECE *Electricity* 221 A series of experiments made..with different-sized platinum electrodes.

**d.** With *the*, = the size of.

**1824** J. JOHNSON *Typographia* II. 139 Having..decided upon the sized type most suitable for the principal one. **1875** BEDFORD *Sailor's Pocket Bk.* x. (ed. 2) 362 Table showing the Sized Chain or Wire Rope which is used as a Substitute for Hempen Rope. **1897** MARY KINGSLEY *Trav. W. Africa* 547, I should say this is about the sized one you find..in your chicken-house.

**2.** Matched in size. *rare*$^{-1}$.

**1700** DRYDEN *Pal. & Arc.* III. 569 Such Bodies built for Strength, of equal Age, In Stature siz'd;..The nicest Eye cou'd no Distinction make.

**3.** Of a fair, proper, or standard size. ***sized fish***, a size-fish (see SIZE *sb.*[1] 13).

**1737** BRACKEN *Farriery Impr.* (1757) II. 33 [He] writ to me to buy him a sized Gelding for Hunting. **1771** BERENGER *Horsem.* I. 170 As the riders were cloathed in..armour.. Great and sized horses were..required. **1778** PRYCE *Min. Cornub.* 217 Taking off the sized Tin from time to time on another shovel. **1845** J. COULTER *Adv. Pacific* ii. 12 A sized fish that any Waltonian might well stare at! **1865** BOWER *Slate Quarries* 30 Sized tons, various breadths, and irregular lengths.

**sized** (saɪzd), *ppl. a.*[2] [f. SIZE *v.*[2]] Treated or prepared in some way with size.

**1771** *Encycl. Brit.* II. 713/1 This sized paint must be laid on with a stiff brush. **1815** *Hist. John Decastro* II. 199 As worthy a gentleman as ever walked between sized felt and neats leather. **1825** J. NICHOLSON *Operat. Mechanic* 747 If the varnish be applied to a sized colour. **1878** ABNEY *Photogr.* xxv. (1881) 172 Sized paper is floated in potassium dichromate.

**b.** With qualifying term.

**1864** R. A. ARNOLD *Hist. Cotton Famine* 513 The wearers of this heavily sized cloth. **1888** JACOBI *Printers' Vocab.* 126 A certain proportion of size.., according to instructions for a 'hard' or 'soft' sized article.

**sizel**, variant of SCISSEL.

**sizeless** ('saɪzlɪs), *a.* [f. SIZE *sb.*[1] + -LESS.] Devoid of magnitude.

**1874** *Edin. Rev.* No. 285. 76 An immeasurably small speck or size-less point. **1896** L. T. HOBHOUSE *Theory Knowl.* 47 Can we now stigmatise the sizeless, figureless, positionless extension in the same way? **1935** W. DE LA MARE *Early One Morning* xv. 195 A universe that was nothing but a sizeless point.

†**sizely**, *adv. Obs. rare.* Also syzely. [? f. SIZE *sb.*[1]] Nicely, daintily.

Cf. Ray's northern word '*Sizely*, nice, proud, coy'.

**1575** LANEHAM *Let.* (1871) 23 Three prety puzels..before the Bryde, Syzely, with set countenauns, and lips so demurely simpring, az it had been a Mare cropping of a thistl. *Ibid.* 33 The coorsez wear not so orderly serued, & sizely set dooun, but wear by and by az disorderly wasted & coorsly consumed.

†**sizer**[1]. *Obs.* Forms: 4 sisour(e, 4–5 sysour(e, 5 cysour, 7 sizer. [aphetic form of *assisour* ASSIZER.] An assizer.

**1303** R. BRUNNE *Handl. Synne* 1336 What shul we sey of þys dytours, þys fals men, þat beyn sysours. *c* **1380** WYCLIF *Wks.* (1880) 234 Lordis wolen not mekely here a pore mannus cause.., but suffre sisouris of contre to distroie hem. *c* **1440** *Jacob's Well* 131 þe ferthe inche is, whan false cysourys gon vp-on qwestys, & puttyn a man fro his ryȝt thrugh a fals verdyȝte. *a* **1450** MYRC 1665 Alle fals sysourus and okererus. **1614** in W. M. Williams *Founders' Co.* (1867)

30 Persons..that shall be Auditors, Clerk, Bedell, Sizer, Searcher, or Searchers, shall take the severall Oathes.

**sizer**[2] ('saɪzə(r)). [f. SIZE *v.*[1]] A device for testing the size of articles, or for separating them according to size.

**1677** MOXON *Mech. Exerc.* iii. 52 Making a true round hole in a thin peece of Brass,..you may try if the cast bullet will just..fill that hole..This thin peece of Brass, with a round hole in it, is call'd a Sizer. **1858** SIMMONDS *Dict. Trade, Sizers,* machines used in Ceylon made of perforated sheet zinc or wire gauze, for separating the coffee into three sizes.

**sizer**[3] ('saɪzə(r)). [f. SIZE *v.*[2]] One who applies size to any article.

**1863** *Chambers's Encycl.* III. 276/1 Average weekly wages: ..Sizers,..25*s.* *c* **1890** W. H. CASMEY *Ventilation* 8 The reason why so many old sizers are found with joints twisted out of all natural shape by rheumatism.

**sizer**, variant of SIZAR.

**sizers**, obs. form of SCISSORS.

**siziness** ('saɪzɪnɪs). Also 8 sizyness. [f. SIZY *a.*] The quality or state of being sizy or glutinous; viscosity.

Common in the 18th cent. with reference to the blood.
**1701** FLOYER *Cold Baths* I. 25 Windiness or Siziness of the Humours. **1756** P. BROWNE *Jamaica* 226 Disorders arising from the sizyness of the juices. **1797** J. DOWNING *Disord. Horned Cattle* 3 This medicine..thins the blood, and dilutes its siziness.

**sizing** ('saɪzɪŋ), *vbl. sb.*[1] [f. SIZE *v.*[1]]

**1. a.** In University use: The action or practice of procuring 'sizes' from the buttery or kitchen; a portion or quantity so obtained; a size.

**1596** NASHE *Saffron Walden* Wks. (Grosart) III. 104 The Butler or Manciple of Trinitie Hall..trusted him for his commons and sizing. **1628** SHIRLEY *Witty Fair One* IV. ii, I have had a head in most of the butteries of Cambridge, and it has been sconced to purpose. I know what belongs to sizing. **1661** BLOUNT *Glossogr.* s.v. *Size,* In Cambridge they call it Sizing. **1736** in *Athenæum* (1906) 20 Jan. 76/2 Commons, 10 weeks, £1 3*s.* 4*d.* Sizings, £1 11*s.* 6*d.* **1785** GROSE *Dict. Vulgar Tongue, Sizings,* Cambridge term for the college allowance from the buttery, called at Oxford battles. **1833** PIERCE *Hist. Harvard Univ.* 219 We were allowed at dinner a cue of beer, which was a half-pint, and a sizing of bread. **1834** in Cottle *Rem. Coleridge & Southey* (1847) 304 What little suppers, or sizings, as they were called, have I enjoyed. **1852** BRISTED *Five Yrs. Eng. Univ.* (ed. 3) 20 Two tables..which..go through a regular second course instead of the 'sizings'.

**b.** *transf.* A share or allowance.

**1822** BYRON *Werner* IV. i, As for merriment And sport,.. our sizings were Even of the narrowest. **1885** *Sat. Rev.* 3 Jan. 1/1 There appears to have also been a..tendency..to stint the metropolitan counties of their sizings.

†**2.** = ASSIZING *vbl. sb. Obs.*[−1]

*c* **1640** in *Roxb. Ballads* II. 181 A health unto the Baker that never was misled Nor yet put into the pillorie for sizing of his bread.

**3.** The action of separating and arranging according to size; also, singling of plants.

**1660** SHARROCK *Vegetables* 119 It may be proper here to speak of weeding and sising. The latter operation is the plucking up roots or plants that are..offensive to others in the same beds, by reason of their nearness. **1710** J. HARRIS *Lex. Techn.* II, *Sizing,* is a curious way of Dressing the Tin Ore, after it comes from the Launder of the Stamping-mill; which is by sifting it thro' an Hair-Sieve. **1802** JAMES *Milit. Dict.* s.v. *Size,* In all regiments the sizing begins from flanks to centre [etc.]. **1877** RAYMOND *Statist. Mines & Mining* 425 A previous accurate sizing of the stuff to be treated is necessary. **1894** *Daily News* 30 Jan. 3/4 It is most especially in the inferior sizing or assorting of fruit that reform is needed.

*attrib.* **1875** KNIGHT *Dict. Mech.* 2192/1 Sizing-apparatus, -cistern. **1882** *U.S. Rep. Prec. Met.* 650 The ore is..carried ..through the sizing-screens into a series of eighteen settling-tanks. **1884** *Bath Herald* 27 Dec. 6/5 The middlings..are carried now to the sizing machines.

**4.** *sizing up*, the process of assessing or evaluating.

**1967** *Coast to Coast 1965–6* 136 No doubt he guessed I'd been doing a bit of sizing up and decided he had better help me get my ideas into order.

**sizing** ('saɪzɪŋ), *vbl. sb.*[2] [f. SIZE *v.*[2]]

**1.** The action of applying size, or of preparing in some way with size.

**1635** *Church-w. Acc. Pittington,* etc. (Surtees) 98 Item siseing and oyling of the new window, 8 d. *a* **1667** PETTY in Sprat *Hist. Royal Soc.* (1667) 294 When we treat of Sising and Stiffening. **1797** *Encycl. Brit.* (ed. 3) XIII. 715/1 The sizing of this paper must also be moderate. **1839** URE *Dict. Arts* 927 For printing paper, the sizing is given in the beating engine. **1883** *Hardwich's Photogr. Chem.* (ed. 9) 229 The Photographic properties of the paper are much affected by the mode of sizing adopted.

**2.** Size prepared for use; also, the materials from which size is prepared.

**1825** J. NICHOLSON *Operat. Mechanic* 470 A strong lie of soft soap, called *sizing.* **1828** CARR *Craven Gloss., Sizing,* glutinous matter used by weavers to stiffen the warp, or to make it more smooth. **1878** ABNEY *Photogr.* (1881) 177 The sizing should be removed by immersion in boiling water.

*fig.* **1855** BAGEHOT *Lit. Studies* (1879) I. 289 No great painter of English life can be without a rough sizing of strong sense.

**3.** *attrib.*, as *sizing-box*, *-house*, *-machine*, etc.

**1799** *Hull Advertiser* 1 June 1/1 Paper-mill..comprises.. four vatts,..and sizing-house adjoining. **1835** URE *Philos. Manuf.* 370, I have since seen the sizing machine in action, dressing warp. **1880** J. DUNBAR *Pract. Papermaker* 55 Strain through a fine wire into the sizing box. **1887** MOLONEY *Forestry W. Africa* 405 It has..been recommended as a sizing material for photographic prints.

**sizing**, yeast: see SIZZING.

**sizors**, obs. form of SCISSORS.

**sizy** ('saɪzɪ), *a.* Also 8 sizie, sizey. [f. SIZE *sb.*[2]] Resembling size; having the consistency of size; thick and viscous; glutinous.

Very common in the 18th cent., esp. of blood.
**1687** *Phil. Trans.* XVI. 552 The Interstices of the Muscles ..where the Blood is very sizy. **1707** MORTIMER *Husb.* (1721) II. 321 The most flowery parts of it [boiling malt] run whitish, glewy and sizie, like Sadler's Paste. **1763** GOLDSM. *Misc. Wks.* (1837) II. 539 Those which lay them in the waters, place them..generally in a sizy substance. **1797** J. DOWNING *Disord. Horned Cattle* 17 This medicine.. disperses pituitous skins, and the sizy blood. **1827** *Lancet* 8 Dec. 390/2 The blood drawn yesterday is slightly buffed and sizy.

**sizz** (sɪz), *v.* Also 8 siz. Chiefly *dial.* or *U.S.* [Imitative: cf. SISS *v.*, and WFris. *size, siizje.*]

†**1.** *trans.* To burn, brand. *Obs.*[−1]

*a* **1700** B. E. *Dict. Cant. Crew* s.v. *Neck-verse,* The Women are of course sizz'd in the Fist, without running the risque of a Halter.

**2.** *intr.* To give out a hissing sound; to hiss, sizzle. Also *fig.*

**1788** W. H. MARSHALL *Yorksh.* II. 352 *To Siz,* to hiss. **1861** MRS. CHESNUT *Diary fr. Dixie* 27 June, If, when water is thrown on them, they do not sizz, they won't do. **1887** *The Voice* (N.Y.) 1 Sept., Touch any one of the 900 delegates.. and he (or she) will sizz.

Hence **'sizzing** *vbl. sb.* Also *attrib.*

**1890** *Nature* 16 Oct. 595 Mention has been made..of a peculiar 'singing' or rather 'sizzing' noise on the wire. **1907** *Scribner's Mag.* Feb. 145 The monotonous sizzing of cicadas.

**sizzars, -ers**, obs. forms of SCISSORS.

**'sizzing.** *dial.* Also 6 sizing, 8 siesin, 9 sizzen, etc. [See quot. 1674.] Yeast, barm.

Given in 19th c. glossaries as current in Kent, Surrey, Sussex, and Hampshire.
**1594** LYLY *Mother Bombie* II. i, My wits worke like barme, alias yest, alias sizing, alias rising, alias Gods good. **1674** RAY *S. & E. Co. Words, Sizzing,* yeast or barm, *Suss.*; from the sound Beer or Ale make in working. [Hence in Grose, etc.] **1736** LEWIS *Hist. Thanet* (ed. 2) 38 *Siesin.*

**sizzle** ('sɪz(ə)l), *sb.* [from the vb.] **1.** A hissing sound, *esp.* one produced by the action of frying or roasting; also, broiling heat. Also *fig.*

**1823** E. MOOR *Suffolk Words* 351 *Sizzle,* the half hiss, half sigh of an animal; of an owl for instance. **1880** *Scribner's Mag.* June 222 The sizzle and delectable flavor of the deer's juicy ribs roasting in those ashes. **1901** *Munsey's Mag.* XXIV. 510/2 The match..ended a wasted life in a sizzle of despair. **1964** *Economist* 1 Feb. 400/1 The Jesuit sanctuary at Loyola..was a sizzle of sex-appeal. **1976** *National Observer* (U.S.) 17 July 6/1 You've reached middle age, and your marriage has lost its sizzle.

**2.** *Comb.*, as **sizzle cymbal**, a cymbal, used chiefly in jazz and dance bands, with several small rivets set loosely through it to make a sizzling sound when the cymbal is struck.

**1944** W. APEL *Harvard Dict. Mus.* 198/1 Various modifications are used in jazz bands, e.g., the Choke cymbal, the Sizzle cymbal. **1964** R. BURNS *Selection, Care, & Use of Cymbals* 7 Sizzle cymbals are immensely popular with drummers playing with jazz groups. **1967** *New Yorker* 21 Jan. 52/2 Marsala told me just to play with wood-blocks and a sizzle cymbal.

**sizzle** ('sɪz(ə)l), *v.* Also 7 sizle, 8 sizel. [Imitative: cf. SIZZ *v.* and FIZZLE *v.*]

**1.** *trans.* To burn or scorch so as to produce a hissing sound; to burn *up* with intense heat.

**1603** HARSNET *Pop. Impost.* xxiii. 165 Having his taile wel sizled with brimstone or scalded soundly with Holy water. **1624** J. GEE *Foot out of Snare* 47 Hath none read of..the holy potion, to scald, broil, and to sizle the Diuell? **1715** *Cotton's Scarron.* IV. (ed. 10) 92 To sizel thy Tail instead of Paper. **1823** E. MOOR *Suffolk Words* 351 If we heen't rain in another week we shall be all sizzled up.

**2.** *intr.* To make a kind of hissing sound, esp. in the process of frying, roasting, or burning.

*a* **1825** FORBY *Voc. E. Anglia* 303 *Sizzle,* to dry and shrivel up with hissing, by the action of fire on some greasy or juicy substance. **1861** O. W. HOLMES *Elsie V.* v. 66 In it the hot iron being then allowed to sizzle, there results a peculiar singed aroma. **1883** E. H. ROLLINS *New Eng. Bygones* 67 From its ends sizzled and dropped its sap.

*fig.* **1859** BEECHER *Life Thoughts* Ser. II. 91 This question is sizzling everywhere. **1880** 'MARK TWAIN' *Tramp Abroad* I. 245, I simply sat still..and sizzled,—for I was being slowly fried to death in my own blushes. **1928** 'BRENT OF BIN BIN' *Up Country* xv. 266 As Little River was in the same direction he sizzled away to old Healey at the point of the spur. **1966** *Daily Tel.* 15 Nov. 13/3 Some colours vibrate when they are used together and I often use them to make a dull corner sizzle. **1979** *Fisherman's Weekly* 21 July 27/1 When a run comes, line can sizzle off the reel, so be sure to use an open bale-arm plus indicator.

Hence **'sizzling** *vbl. sb.* and *ppl. a.* Also *fig.*

**1845** S. JUDD *Margaret* 159 (Bartlett), From the ends of the wood the sap fries and drips on the sizzling coals below. **1877** E. G. SQUIER *Peru* (1878) 234 There is a gentle and constant sizzling of frying meats. **1884** *Harper's Mag.* Sept. 526/2 We could..hear the sizzling of our cutlets. **1890** HALL CAINE *Bondman* xxvi, Instantly a sizzling and bubbling sound came up from below. **1923** [see PICTURE *sb.* 2 j]. **1947** *Sporting Mirror* 7 Nov. 8/1 His intended tap back to goalkeeper Hesford, from a long way out, became a sizzling shot which won the game for Charlton. **1977** *Time* 30 May 51/2 The sizzling increases [in personal income] of February and March.

**sizzler** ('sɪzlə(r)). *colloq.* [f. SIZZLE *v.* + -ER[1].]

**1.** *U.S.* A sizzling heat, day, etc.; a 'scorcher'.

**1901** *Emporia* (Kansas) *Gaz.* 1 July 9 The drought which is a sizzler and frier and boiler is a good thing for Kansas. **1904** G. H. LORIMER *Old Gorgon Graham* ii. 37 Satan may be down in Arizona cooking up a sizzler for the corn belt.

**2. a.** Something salacious or *risqué.* Cf. SCORCHER 3 d.

**1957** 'N. BLAKE' *End of Chapter* xi. 169 A lot of morons who only wanted to curl up with a nice sizzler by Elinor Glyn. **1977** *News of World* 17 Apr. 9/9 A blue movie being shown to a judge in court was a real sizzler. In fact, it was so hot that it began to melt.

**b.** A very fast shot or hit. Cf. SCORCHER 3 c.

**1960** E. W. SWANTON *West Indies* iii. 51 The one chance he gave..was a sizzler to the gully. **1976** *Sunday Times* (Lagos) 26 Sept. 1/3 Buffaloes goalkeeper Chilongwe positioned himself to record an amazing save off a sizzler.

**sizzlingly** ('sɪzlɪŋlɪ), *adv.* [f. prec. + -LY[2].] So as to sizzle. Used to give emphasis to expressions of warmth, intensity, etc.

**1956** *Essays in Crit.* VI. 204 You, too, were once not allegoric But blazed with passions sizzlingly phosphoric. **1963** *Listener* 21 Feb. 327/2 Unless one has some sizzlingly hot contributions to make, one somehow feels that a mere dialogue is perhaps not enough.

**sizzly** ('sɪzlɪ), *a.* [f. SIZZLE *v.* + -Y[1].] Sizzling, effervescent, exciting.

**1936** J. DOS PASSOS *Big Money* 17 The sizzly smell of champagne and welshrabbit. **1948** D. BALLANTYNE *Cunninghams* xii. 70 Carole Plowman..was the most beautiful girl in the hall... 'A few good-looking girls here,' he said. 'About three,' Phil said. 'That Plowman tart's sizzly.'

**sizzors**, obs. form of SCISSORS.

‖**sjambok** ('ʃæmbɒk), *sb.* Also 8 chanboc(k), 9 samboc, sambock, sambok, schambok, shambo, shambok, sjambock, jambok. [a. Cape Du. *sam-, tjam-, sjambok,* a. Malay *samboq, chamboq,* ad. Urdū *chābuk*: see CHABOUK and CHAWBUCK.] A strong and heavy whip made of rhinoceros or hippopotamus hide, used in South Africa for driving cattle and sometimes for administering chastisement.

α. **1790** E. HELME tr. *Le Vaillant's Trav. Interior Parts Afr.* I. xxi. 412 The next day my men employed themselves in cutting the skin off the Hippopotamus, to make what, in this country, the[y] call *Chanboc,* which are whips, used to drive the oxen. **1804** J. BARROW *Trav. Interior S. Afr.* II. ii. 96 One of those infernal whips, made from the hide of a rhinoceros or sea-cow, known by the name of *sambocs.* **1808** J. READ in G. E. Cory *Rise of S. Afr.* (1921) I. vii. 203 Terribly flogged with a sambok or whip made of the skin of a rhinoceros. **1830** S. BANNISTER *Hum. Policy* 126 Sambocks of rhinoceros and sea-cow skins. **1842** MISS MOFFAT *Tour S. Africa* vi. 86 On their punishing him with a sambock, he seized a gun. **1850** T. SHONE *Diary* III. 19 Mar. in *Voorloper* (1976) 717 Lost my Samboc, the Horse Broke his bridle. **1852** M. B. HUDSON *S. African Frontier Life* I. 40 No coaxing nor threats, after sambok persuasion, Could cure him of sulks on the present occasion.

β. **1791** tr. *Le Vaillant's Trav. Interior Parts Afr.* I. 195 My people were busied in cutting to pieces the hide of the hippopotamus, to make what the country folks call *chanboc.* **1801** J. BARROW *Trav. S. Afr.* iii. 145 These sort of whips which they call *shambos* are most horrid instruments. **1812** A. PLUMPTRE tr. *Lichtenstein's Trav. S. Afr.* I. I. vii. 98 The skin is the only thing valuable to the colonists, to cut into strips for making the driving whips known here by the Malay name of Schamboks. **1822** W. J. BURCHELL *Trav. Interior S. Afr.* I. 86 Some-times encouraged by good words, at other times terrified into exertion by ten blows of the *shambok.* **1834** PRINGLE *Afr. Sk.* iv. 175 Large whips of rhinoceros and hippopotamus hide (termed sjamboks). **1856** ANDERSSON *Lake Ngami* 61 We also carried away a goodly supply of the beast's hide, for the purpose of converting it into 'shamboks'. **1893** SELOUS *Trav. S.E. Africa* 99 To.. take some of his hide for sjamboks. **1911** L. COHEN *Reminisc. Kimberley* xviii. 320 'All right,' he replied... 'Bring me a shambok.'

γ. **1850** R. G. CUMMING *Hunter's Life S. Africa* (1902) 144/2 Every ox had been most unmercifully flogged with both waggon-whips and jamboks. **1867** MAYNE REID *Giraffe Hunters* II. xix. 225 The Makalolo were constantly wielding their huge 'jamboks' to induce them to go quicker.

Hence **'sjambok** *v. trans.*, to strike or flog with a sjambok. Hence **'sjambokker**, one who uses a sjambok; **'sjamboking, -bokking** *vbl. sb.*: also *fig.*

**1881** *Blackw. Mag.* Dec. 756/1 To associate or have anything to do with blacks, except to make them work, or *sjambook* them if they don't work hard is an unpardonable offence in a Boer's eyes. **1894** E. GLANVILLE *Fair Colonist* xv. 116, I would cheerfully sjambok a stock-lifter until he dropped. **1899** G. H. RUSSELL *Under the Sjambok* ix. 92 Then I will sjambok them first, and hang them after. *Ibid.* xxxiv. 247, I have given him many a sjamboking. **1900** *Daily Graphic* 8 Feb. 3/1 To be sjambokked within an inch of his life. **1908** D. BLACKBURN *I came & Saw* 208 Your sjambokking of Sixpence gave me the idea for the Humanitarian Company. **1953** *Cape Times* 30 Mar. 1/1 A police investigation into the alleged sjambokking of two United Party canvassers. *Ibid.* The sjambokker came outside and hit..Mr. Eddy..on the legs. **1980** *Listener* 17 Apr. 487/3 Lilford, landowner and power behind Smith and the Rhodesian Front, gave me a verbal sjambokking over the telephone.

**Sjögren** (ˈʃɜːgrən). *Path.* [The name of H. S. C. *Sjögren*, Swedish ophthalmologist, who described the condition in 1933 (*Acta Ophthalm.* Suppl. No. 2. 1–151); used after G. *Sjögrens-syndrom* (Weber & Schlüter 1937, in *Deutsch. Arch. für klin. Med.* CLXXX. 333).] ***Sjögren's disease*** or ***syndrome***: a condition characterized by chronic inflammatory swelling of the salivary and lachrymal glands and by auto-immune antibodies in the blood.

**1938** *Proc. R. Soc. Med.* XXXII. 255 (*heading*) Sjögren's syndrome associated with pigmentation and sclerodermia of the legs. **1954** [see *keratoconjunctivitis* s.v. KERATO-]. **1961** *Lancet* 26 Aug. 456/2 The diagnosis of Sjögren's disease was made from the case-history and clinical condition, supported by positive Schirmer and rose-bengal tests. **1974** PASSMORE & ROBSON *Compan. Med. Stud.* III. xxv. 18/2 Sjögren's syndrome rivals systemic lupus erythematosus in the multiplicity of auto-antibodies present in the serum.

**sjögrenite** (ˈʃɜːgrənaɪt). *Min.* [f. the name of S. A. Hjalmar *Sjögren* (1856–1922), Swedish mineralogist + -ITE[1].] A hydrated basic carbonate of iron and magnesium found as yellowish or brownish thin transparent plates formed by hydrothermal action.

**1941** C. FRONDEL in *Amer. Mineralogist* XXVI. 303 The hexagonal mineral commonly admixed with pyroaurite is described on a following page under the name sjögrenite. **1968** *Acta Crystallographica* B. XXIV. 972/1 The carbonate-hydroxides $Mg_6M_2^{III}(OH)_{16}CO_3.4H_2O$ ($M^{III}$ = Fe, Al, or Cr) are known to occur in two dimorphic forms: the hexagonal sjögrenite group has $a \sim 3{\cdot}1$ and $c \sim 15{\cdot}5$ Å; the rhombohedral pyroaurite group has the same *a* value but *c* is about 23·2 Å. **1973** *Mineral. Mag.* XXXIX. 378 Two sub-groups could be distinguished, which would today be described as polytypes differing only in layer stacking; these are represented by pyro-aurite and sjögrenite respectively.

**sk-**, in ME. and older Sc. a frequent variant of SC-, as in *skab* scab, *skabard* scabbard, *skable* scabble, etc.

For variant forms not entered under SK- see SC-.

**ska** (skɑː). [Origin unknown, perh. echoic.] A kind of popular music of Jamaican origin, characterized by a fast tempo and emphasis of the off-beat. Also, a dance to such music. Cf. REGGAE, ROCKSTEADY.

**1964** [see GAME *sb.* 3 b]. **1969**, etc. [see ROCKSTEADY]. **1971** *Guardian* 25 Feb. 10/4 West Indian ska or blue beat music, latterly taken up by skinheads. **1980** *Rolling Stone* (Austral.) 26 June 16/5 'We don't see it as a ska revival,' Davies says, 'because we don't play pure ska.'.. The group is also quick to point out the differences between the various 'ska' bands.

**skaal**: see SKOAL.

**skaapsteker** (ˈskɑːpsteɪkə(r)). Also scarpsticker, scha(a)psteeker, -steker, -sticker. [Afrikaans, f. Du. *skaap* sheep + *steker* stinger.] A venomous but usually harmless snake of the genus *Psammophylax*, esp. the spotted skaapsteker, *P. rhombeatus*, or the striped skaapsteker, *P. tritæniatus*, which are both greyish-brown with darker markings.

**1818** C. I. LATROBE *Jrnl. Visit S. Afr.* xxii. 353 Our good-natured Hottentots, perceiving that I had begun to collect serpents, brought me several kinds, among which were the ..schaapsteker, (sheep-stinger); and copra di capella. **1834** T. PRINGLE *Afr. Sketches* 280 There are several species of snakes..such as the nacht-slang (night adder), the schaap-steeker (sheep-stinger), [etc.]. **1856** F. FLEMING *S. Afr.* 406 The 'Scarpsticker' of the Dutch, or Night-Adder; a small dingy-brown Adder, spotted with black, about eighteen inches long. **1887** *Encycl. Brit.* XXII. 197/1 The second African snake of this family is the 'schapsticker' (Sheep Stinger). **1915** *Chambers's Jrnl.* June 437/2 The schaap-sticker..is a short, silvery snake about the thickness of a man's finger. **1931** *Discovery* Mar. 73/2 We have droves of skaapstekers, night-adders, and house snakes. **1952** *Cape Argus* 7 June (Mag. Sect.) 2/4, I..'bagged' a good collection of the local snakes; mostly of a harmless variety, such as mole snakes, water snakes, herald snakes, schaapstekers. **1973** *Stand. Encycl. S. Afr.* IX. 651/2 The name skaapsteker is quite misleading and unfortunate, as there is certainly no truth in the widespread belief that these snakes are in the habit of biting and killing sheep.

**skabe, skab(e)d**, obs. ff. SCAB *sb.*, SCABBED *a.*

**skaberge, -berk(e, -bord, -brek**, obs. ff. SCABBARD *sb.*[1]

**skable**, obs. f. SCABBLE *v.*

**skace**, obs. f. SCARCE *adv.*

**skad**, var. SCAD[7].

†**skaddle**, app. a var. of (or error for) STADDLE.

**1635** L. FOX *North-West Fox* 210 The Salv[age] inhabitants had lately bin there, & left the skaddles of their fire.

**skaddon**, variant of SCHADON *Obs.*

**skade**, Sc. var. of SCALD *a.*[1]; dial. form of SCATHE *sb.*

**skadle, skadylle**, obs. ff. SCADDLE *a.*

**skaerd**, obs. pa. pple. of SCARE *v.*

**skafemaster**: see SCAFFMASTER.

**skaffel(l**, varr. of SCAVEL, spade.

**skaffell**, obs. f. SCAFFOLD *sb.*

**skaffie**, var. SCAF.

**skafrie, skaif(f)ry**, varr. SCAFFERY *Sc. Obs.*

**skag**, var. SCAG.

**skaid**, var. Sc. f. SCALD *a.*[1]

**skail** (skeɪl), *sb. north. dial.* and *Sc.* Also 4 skaile, 8 skyle; 4, 7 scaill, 9 scail, scale. [f. the vb.]

**1.** A dispersal or separation; a scattering.

**13..** *Cursor M.* 15541 (Gött.), þis ilke night sal be a skaile bi-tuix ȝu and me. **1625** in Lang *Hist. Scot.* (1904) III. i. 8 There would be a scaill among our Counsellors and the Sessioners. **1808** JAMIESON s.v., The skail of the kirk. **1837** *Voluntary Church Mag.* Jan. 12 The skail of the kirk and the dismissal of the court happening at the same time. **1871** J. RICHARDSON *Cummerland Talk* Ser. I. 47 They wad mak a bonnie scail o' thur scrafflen things 'at git silver cups.

**2.** A dispersed company; a scattered party.

**1375** BARBOUR *Bruce* xv. 337 He Saw bot the fleand scaill, perfay, And thame that sesyt in the pray. **1819** W. TENNANT *Papistry Storm'd* (1827) 160 Within the yetts, that stood unlockit To catch the skails, that..Cam' rushin' in.

**3.** *Mining.* (See quots.)

**1860** *Eng. & For. Mining Gloss.* (ed. 2) 62 *Scale of air*—a small portion of air abstracted from the main current. **1883** GRESLEY *Gloss. Coal-m.*, *Scale*, a small portion of the ventilative current in a mine passing through a certain-sized aperture.

**skail** (skeɪl), *v. north. dial.* and *Sc.* Forms: 4–6, 9 scail (6 scaile), 5–6 scaill (6 schaill), scayl; 4– skail, 4–6 skaill (6 skeill), 4–7 skaile, 4–6, 9 skayl, 9 *Sc.* skell; 4– scale, skale, 9 scaale; 9 skyle (scyle), skile, etc. [Of obscure origin; the correspondence in form and meaning with OIr. *scáilim* (later Ir. *sgaoilim*) to scatter, is prob. accidental, as the early adoption and extensive use of a Gaelic word of this type would be very remarkable.

A more likely source would be an OScand. **skeila*, related by ablaut to ON. *skilja* to separate, divide; but there appears to be no trace of such a form.]

**I. 1.** *trans.* To scatter or disperse (a thing or collection of things).

*a* **1300** *Cursor M.* 26021 þis reuth es like a castand gin, Scailand a hepe es samen o sin. *Ibid.* 27899 For all þat euer festis wiit, Drunkennes þan skailes it. *c* **1375** *Sc. Leg. Saints* ii. (*Paulus*) 378 Here slane has bene mony men, Of quham þe hedis in placis sere ar scalyt. *c* **1425** WYNTOUN *Cron.* VIII. 2443 Qwha skalis his thoucht in syndrynes, In althynge it is þe les. **1456** SIR G. HAYE *Law Arms* (S.T.S.) 123 Gif the vassallis be nocht with thair lord, thai ar agaynis him, and scailis his gudis. *c* **1500** KENNEDY *Passion of Christ* 14 Haill, beyme to skaill of ded þe dirk vmbrakill! **1596** DALRYMPLE tr. *Leslie's Hist. Scot.* II. 453 Lyk a certane sone, new risen to skail and skattir the Cloudis of al tumulte. **1826** GALT *Lairds* i, It has skail't the daunert wits o' the master. **1839** URE *Dict. Arts* 990 This is termed skailing the air; for otherwise the gas would kindle at the furnace. **1853** G. JOHNSTON *Nat. Hist. E. Bord.* I. 125 The pains that Nature takes to 'scale' her species.

*absol.* **1456** SIR G. HAYE *Law Arms* (S.T.S.) 123 He that gaderis nocht with him scaylis.

†**b.** To spread (a rumour, tale, etc.). *Obs.*

**1375** BARBOUR *Bruce* v. 447 Bot the tithandis var scalit sone, Of the deid Douglas had done. *c* **1470** HENRY *Wallace* XI. 1300 Throuch braid Bretane the woice tharoff was scalyt. **1513** DOUGLAS *Æneid* IV. v. 32 This ilk wenche..Glaidlie this rumour gan throw the peple skaill.

**c.** To scatter or spread (hay, manure, mole-hills, etc.) over the ground. Also, to clear (land) of mole-hills by scattering them.

(*a*) **1641** BEST *Farm. Bks.* (Surtees) 78 Then att night.. hee..scaled the hey aboute in little heapes. **1764** *Museum Rust.* II. 247 They lead out their fold-garth manure, and *scale*, or spread it immediately from the waggon. **1781** J. HUTTON *Tour to Caves* (ed. 2) Gloss. 95 *Skale*, or *Skail*, to scatter or throw abroad, as molehills are when levelled. **1789** D. DAVIDSON *Seasons* 143 Some..skail, Wi' eager nebs, the dusky frozen turf. **1893** HESLOP *Northumbld. Gloss.* s.v. *Scale*, Manure is dropped on land from a cart in isolated little heaps which are subsequently *scaled*, that is, scattered evenly over the surface.

(*b*) **1822** BEWICK *Mem.* 14 To 'scale' the pastures and meadows, that is to spread the mole hills over the surface of the ground. **1827** E. MACKENZIE *Hist. Newc.* II. 713 They are also required to scale, mole, and dress the Cow Hill.

**d.** *dial.* To rake out; to clear with a poker.

**1790** GROSE *Prov. Gloss.* Suppl. s.v. *Scale*, Scale the Oven. **1867** BRIERLEY *Marlocks* I. i, The youth with the poker commenced 'scaling' the fire.

**2.** To pour out; to shed; to spill.

**1513** DOUGLAS *Æneid* IV. iii. 59, I sall vpon thaim a mirk schour doun schaill Of weit and wynd. **1549** *Compl. Scotl.* iii. 27 Them that settis ther felicite to skattir & to skail blude. **1578** *Reg. Privy Council Scot.* II. 695 [They] skaillit and sparpallit the meill..in the said burne. **1728** RAMSAY *Robt., Richy, & Sandy* 80 Red-yards, ye ken.., Had skail'd of ours, but mair of his ain blood. **1828** MOIR *Mansie Wauch* xix, Scores of folks driving about with pitcherfulls of water, and scaling half of it on one another and the causeway. **1894** A. LAING *Poems* 17 (E.D.D.), Then glaiket things may scale their tea Upon oor Sunday braws.

*fig.* **1637** RUTHERFORD *Lett.* (1862) I. cxx. 299 Alas! I have skailed more of Christ's grace,..than I have brought with me.

*absol.* **1641** FERGUSSON *Scot. Prov.* No. 51, An old seck is ay skailing. **1896** BARRIE *Tommy* xxxvii. 441 It's a small offence to skail on a clarty floor.

**b.** To rend, spoil. *rare*[−1].

**1768** ROSS *Helenore* 28 Her gartens tint, her shoon a' skelt and torn.

†**3.** To spread out, distend. *Obs.*[−1]

**1513** DOUGLAS *Æneid* VIII. xii. 83 Scaland schetis, and haldand rowme at large.

**4.** To separate, remove. *rare*[−1].

*a* **1833** *Queen's Marie* vi. in Child *Ballads* III. 393/1 The king is to the Abbey gane, To pu the Abbey-tree, To scale the babe frae Marie's heart.

**II. 5.** To break up (an assembly, school, etc.) by dismissal; †to disband (an army).

*a* **1300** *Cursor M.* 13850 Wit þis þai scaild þair semble, Bot iesus went fra þat cite. *c* **1425** WYNTOUN *Cron.* IX. 1440 Ay þai qwhit ȝow lil for lal, Or þat þai skail þar marcat all. **1487** *Sc. Acts, Jas. III* (1814) II. 177/2 The Shereff sal..charge þaim to cess, & skale þair gadering. **1582** *St. Papers Hen. VIII*, IV. 510 *note*, Unto suche tyme as the Kyng retorne homewardes, and scail his host. **1541** *Ibid.* V. 199 We ar contentit þat baith ye armyis in all partis be skalit. **1598** *Extr. Aberd. Reg.* (1848) II. 174 Gif the said schooll be dissolvit and skaillit, it will tend to the preiudice of the youth of this town. **1791** LEARMONT *Poems* 43 Stick baith the sermon an' the tune, An' skale the kirk. **1886** 'H. HALIBURTON' *Horace* 11 Then Patie's waukened wi' a kick, An' skells the meetin'.

*refl.* **1375** BARBOUR *Bruce* XII. 465 ȝe sall se als soyne at thai ..sall brek aray, And scale thame, our harness to ta.

†**b.** To break up (one's home). *Obs.*

*c* **1550** ROLLAND *Crt. Venus* I. 551 Men & wemen hes skalit thair hale houshald. **1567** *Reg. Privy Council Scot.* I. 516 Diverse..landis are laid waist, and mony honest houshaldis constrenit to skaill thair houssis. **1637** RUTHERFORD *Lett.* I. clxxxii. (1664) 352 Were it not that want paineth me, I should have skailed house & gone a begging long since.

†**c.** To annul (a proclamation). *Obs.*[−1]

*a* **1583** SIR J. BALFOUR *Practicks* (1754) 345 To proceid aganis ony persoun that aucht to keip proclamatioun, the samin standand vndischargit or skaillit.

†**6.** To compel (an army, etc.) to scatter or disperse; to put to flight, to rout.

**1375** BARBOUR *Bruce* VI. 428 And Douglas..full egirly Assalit, and scalit thame hastely. *Ibid.* VII. 299 Fortoun has traualit vs this day, That scalit vs so suddandly. *c* **1425** WYNTOUN *Cron.* IX. 1492 Befor þe laif þai knychtis þen.. Pressit þaim fast to skayl þat rowt. **1482** CAXTON *Trevisa's Higden* III. xiv, And there his men were beten..and skayled euery from other. **1533** BELLENDEN *Livy* I. x. (S.T.S.) I. 57 To skail þame in sindry partis he began to fle. **1581** *Satir. Poems Reform.* xliv. 328 Iudas sall Iuge ȝou, and God sall scale ȝour nest. *a* **1600** *Floddan F.* viii. (1664) 73 The gray gooswing did work such greif, And did the Scots so skoure and skaile. **1732** EBEN. ERSKINE *Serm.* Wks. 1871 I. 485 By the fall of Adam the family was skailt. **1843** *Coquetdale Fishing Songs* (1852) 109 Deil scale the byke frae Redlees Syke.

†**b.** To raise (a siege). *Obs.*

*c* **1425** WYNTOUN *Cron.* IX. 2970 Sa sall we pruff þat sege to skail, or gar remuff. **1533** BELLENDEN *Livy* II. vi. (S.T.S.) I. 147 How Caius mucius..causit porsena to scale his sege. **1573** *Satir. Poems Reform.* xxxix. 60 To Glasgow [they] past with mony trapit steid, Thair skalit the sege.

**III. 7.** In passive: To be in a scattered or dispersed condition.

*a* **1300** *Cursor M.* 22304 Cummen I am to gedir yow þat has been scaild ai to nu. **1375** BARBOUR *Bruce* XII. 466 Quhen we se thame scalit swa, Prik we than on thame hardely. *c* **1470** HENRY *Wallace* v. 282 The chas was gret, scalyt our breid and lenth. **1513** DOUGLAS *Æneid* VI. xi. 58 The byssy beis..On diuers colorit flouris scalit wyde. *a* **1578** LINDESAY (Pitscottie) *Chron. Scot.* (S.T.S.) I. 45 Money of the earleis freindis being skailed of the toune.

**8.** *intr.* Of persons, assemblies, etc.: To separate, disperse, break up, scatter.

*a* **1300** *Cursor M.* 2524 þair folk scaild ai-quare a-boute. **1375** BARBOUR *Bruce* v. 93 Thai scalit throu the toune in hy. **1498** *Extr. Rec. Burgh Edin.* (1869) 75 That all scuillis scail and nane to be haldin. **1542** *St. Papers Hen. VIII*, V. 215 *note*, He mette..thayme of Lowdean scayllande and goinge homewarde. *a* **1578** LINDESAY (Pitscottie) *Chron. Scot.* (S.T.S.) II. 120 This airmie skailled and passit na forder at that tyme. **1637** RUTHERFORD *Lett.* (1675) I. cxlvii. 287 How soon will this House skail! **1724** *Ramsay's Tea-t. Misc.* (1733) II. 211 Ay Jeany, Jeany, ye gade to the kirk; But when it skail'd where could thou be? **1822** GALT *Provost* xxxii, The grammar school was at the time skailing. **1858–61** RAMSAY *Remin.* (1870) p. x, I was just stan'ing till the kirk had scaled. **1897** CROCKETT *Lad's Love* xvii. 179 A miscellaneous pour of lads and lasses almost like a kirk skailing.

*Prov.* **1641** FERGUSSON *Scot. Prov.*, Bread's house skaild never. **1721** KELLY *Scot. Prov.* 20 'A Bread House skail'd never'... Spoken when we have Bread, and perhaps want something finer. **1862** HISLOP *Prov. Scot.* 40 Bread's house skail'd never. A full or hospitable house never wants visitors.

**9.** Of things: To spread or disperse; to pour down or be spilled.

*a* **1300** *Cursor M.* 18836 His hare..Apon his sculdres ligand wele, Bi his eres skailand sumdele. *Ibid.* 26995 Quat es man lijf bot fam, And a rek þat..skailles wit a windes blast. *c* **1470** HENRY *Wallace* VII. 467 The stynk scalyt off ded bodyis sa wyde. **1513** DOUGLAS *Æneid* XIII. Prol. 22 The recent dew begynnis doun to scaill. **1599** ALEX. HUME *Day Estivall* 62 The clouds of raine From tops of mountaines skails. **1895** N. ROY *Horseman's Word* xxxiv, It wantit little till it would be skailin' ower the tap on's [= top of us].

Hence **skailed** *ppl. a.*, scattered, spilled.

*c* **1470** HENRY *Wallace* x. 691 Feill scalyt folk to thaim will son ranew. **1500–20** DUNBAR *Poems* xiii. 30 Sum standis besyd and skaild law keppis.

**skail-**, the verbal stem in combination, as **skail-door, -water** (see quots.); †**skail-wind**, a scattering wind.

**1709** M. BRUCE *Serm.* 13 (Jam.), You shall all be scattered. .. You are sure enough now, but beware of the next blast that is to blow, it will make a skealwind among you. **1825** JAMIESON *Suppl.*, *Skail-Water*, the water that is let off by a sluice before it reaches the mill. **1883** GRESLEY *Gloss. Coal-m.*, *Scale Door*, .. a door in the mine, the opening or closing of which regulates the supply of ventilation to a district.

**skail(e), skaille**, obs. forms of SCALE.

**skailes**, variant of SKAYLES *Obs.*

**skailing** (ˈskeɪlɪŋ), *vbl. sb.* [f. SKAIL *v.*]

**1.** The action of the verb in various senses; dismissal, dispersion.

?*c* **1450** in *Ratis Raving* 16 Tyme of scalynge, tyme of gaderinge. **1497** *Acc. Ld. High Treas. Scot.* I. 354 To Johnstoune,.. that brocht tithingis of the skaling of the Inglismen, iij *s.* **1523** *St. Papers Hen. VIII*, VI. 206 He [Burbon] myght.. percace have ben redy, leng before the tyme of ther skaling. **1569–70** *Extr. Burgh Rec. Edin.* (1875) 269 To enter euerye day at the skaling of the nycht wasche. **1651** in Z. Boyd *Zion's Flowers* (1855) Introd. 53 Mr... Boyd to be spoken to about the soon scaling of the Barony Kirk on Sunday afternoon. *a* **1670** SPALDING *Troub. Chas. I* (1850) I. 190 The Erll Marschall haveing sure intelligens of the skailling of the barronis army. **1805** J. NICOL *Poems* II. 158 (Jam.), It sall soon get a scailin! **1881** *Blackw. Mag.* Apr. 527/1 They were discussed and pulled to pieces at the 'scaling of the kirk', as the parishioners trudged homewards.

**2.** *Mining.* An opening through which the ventilating current passes.

**1850** ANSTED *Geol.*, etc. IV. xix. 490 The current of air once obtained, is conducted through the passages of the mine by various contrivances, consisting of.. partitions, and partial orifices or *scalings*.

**skaillie** (ˈskelɪ). *Sc.* Forms: 5 scailȝee, 6 skal-, skelȝe, skail-, 6–7 scailyie, 7 -yee, scailzie, 8 scaillie, skailly, 7– skaillie; 8 skell(e)y, 9 skeelie, skyl(l)ie. [a. MDu. *schaelie* (mod.Du. *schalie*), or ad. OF. *escaille* (mod.F. *écaille*): see SCALE *sb.*[2]]

†**1.** Blue roofing-slate. *Obs.*

Frequently mentioned along with *slate*; on the distinction see quot. 1808.

**1496** *Acc. Ld. High Treas. Scot.* I. 275 To the man that brocht vp the scailȝee. **1516** *Ibid.* V. 115 To Johne Kelsaucht, sklatter of Striveling, to by skalȝe for the castel in Edinburgh. **1584** *Reg. Privy Council Scot.* III. 678 To carie the sklaittis, skailyie, lyme, sand, and tymmer. **1621** *Sc. Acts, Jas. VI* (1816) IV. 626 To thaick þe same agane with Sklait or skailyee. **1681** *Ibid.*, *Chas. II* (1820) VIII. 357 To be theiked with lead, sclait, scailyie or tyle. **1707** MIEGE *St. Gt. Brit.* ii. 7 Slates.. of a blue colour, which they call *Skelley*, and are made use of for covering the Houses of People of Quality. **1715** PENNECUIK *Tweeddale* 5 Here is to be found Marle,.. Slait and Skailly. **1808** JAMIESON s.v., The name *skaillie* [in the north of Scotland] being confined to blue slates, while the flat stones, commonly used instead of them, are called *brown sklates*.

**2.** Slate-pencil. Also *skaillie pen*.

**1808** JAMIESON, *Skaillie Pen*, a sort of pencil of soft slate, used for taking memorandums, or writing accounts on a slate. **1871** ALEXANDER *J. Gibb* ix. 69 A bit sclattie an' skaillie. **1885** STRATHESK *More Bits* iii. 42 To sharpen their slate-pencil or 'skeelie', as they call it.

**skailly**, obs. Sc. form of SCALY *a.*

**skain(e**, obs. forms of SKEIN, SKENE[1].

†**skains mate.** *Obs.*$^{-1}$ (Origin and exact meaning uncertain.)

**1592** SHAKS. *Rom. & Jul.* II. iv. 162 Scuruie knaue, I am none of his flurt-gils, I am none of his skaines mates.

**skair** (skɛə(r)), *sb. Sc.* and *north. dial.* Also 6 scair, 8–9 skare. [var. of SHARE *sb.*, but the *sk-* is difficult to account for.] A share, portion.

*c* **1573** *Satir. Poems Reform.* xlii. 556 That ressoun is bot vane, To say a man may do na mair, But serue a kirk vntil his skair. **1585** JAS. I *Ess. Poesie* (Arb.) 43 Six hundreth yeares and fourtie was her scair, Which Nature ordained her for to fulfill. *c* **1650** R. SEMPILL *Piper of Kilbarchan* xiv, For of his springs I gat a skair, At every play, race, feast and fair. **1721** RAMSAY *Poet's Wish* iii, May he then but gie then Those blessings for my skair. **1819** W. TENNANT *Papistry Storm'd* (1827) 115 And chang'd her camstane for a skair O' belly-timber sweet. **1858** M. PORTEOUS *Real Souter Johnny* 31 In a tuilzie.. to tak your skair.

**skair** (skɛə(r)), *v.*[1] *Sc.* and *north. dial.* [Cf. prec.] *trans.* and *intr.* To share.

**1720** RAMSAY *Wealth* 114 Thrice lucky pimps,.. That can in a' his wealth and pleasure skair. **1725** —— *Gentle Sheph.* III. iii, Had I fifty times as mickle mair, Nane but my Jenny shou'd the samen skair. **1773** FERGUSSON *Caller Water* xiii. (1789) II. 41 Caller burn.. That gars them a' sic graces skair, And blink sae bonny. **1858** M. PORTEOUS *Real Souter Johnny* 31 To seek wi' fremmit folk, to skair A safer beild.

†**skair**, *v.*[2] *Obs.* Also 3 skeȝȝrenn, 4 skayre. [Of obscure origin.] *trans.* To scatter, disperse; to send *out* in various directions.

*c* **1200** ORMIN 16451 Forr þatt all Adamess stren Todrifenn wass & skeȝȝredd Inntill þiss wide middellærd. ?*a* **1400** *Morte Arth.* 2467 Thane the price men.. skyrmys a lytill; Skayres thaire skottefers, and theire skowtte-waches. *c* **1400** *Destr. Troy* 1089 [They] Skairen out skoute-wacche for skeltyng of harme.

**skair**, Sc. variant of SCAR *sb.*[1]

**skait**, obs. form of SCAT *sb.*[3], SKATE.

†**skaitbird.** *Sc. Obs.*$^{-1}$ (Meaning uncertain.)

Guessed by Jamieson on insufficient grounds to be 'the Arctic Gull'. The first element might be Norw. and Sw. *skata* (Da. *skade*) magpie.

**1508** KENNEDIE *Flyting w. Dunbar* 37 Skaldit skaitbird, and commoun skamelar.

**skaitgyld**: see SCAT *sb.*[3] c.

**skaith, skaithless**, Sc. varr. of SCATHE *sb.* and *v.*, SCATHELESS.

**skål**, var. SKOAL *sb.*

†**skalbert**, obs. Sc. form of SCABBARD *sb.*[1]

**1534** *Acc. Ld. High Treas. Scot.* VI. 194 Veluet to be ane skalbert to the Kingis suerd.

**skald, scald** (skɔːld, skæld). Also 8 scalld. [a. ON. and Icel. *skáld* neut., occurring as early as the 9th cent.; no satisfactory etymology has yet been proposed. Hence also mod.Norw. and Sw. *skald*, Da. (incorrectly) *skjald*, †*sk(i)alder*, *sk(i)aldre.*] An ancient Scandinavian poet. Also sometimes in general use, a poet.

Usually applied to Norwegian and Icelandic poets of the Viking period and down to *c* 1250, but often without any clear idea as to their function and the character of their work.

α. **1763** PERCY *5 Pieces Runic Poetry* Pref. A 5 b, It was the constant study of the northern Scalds to lift their poetic style as much as possible above that of their prose. *Ibid.* 49 The Ransome of Egill the Scald. **1775** WARTON *Hist. Eng. Poetry* I. 60 It is supposed, that Rollo carried with him many scalds from the north. **1830** SCOTT *Ivanhoe* xxxii. *note*, It will readily occur to the antiquary, that these verses are intended to imitate the antique poetry of the Scalds. **1869** FREEMAN *Norm. Conq.* (1875) III. 267 The inspiration of the scald comes upon him.

β. **1780** VON TROIL *Iceland* 198 In ancient times there was no king, or any other man of note, who had not his own skald or poet. **1818** E. HENDERSON *Iceland* II. 356 Before taking the field of battle, it was the office of the Skald to compose a poem suited to the occasion. **1886** *Athenæum* 24 Apr. 551/2 The skill with which the author has reproduced.. the alliterative verse of the Skalds.

Hence **ˈskaldship**, the office of skald.

**1879** E. W. GOSSE *North. Studies* 117 There was no young man so fit to be considered heir-apparent of the skaldship as Runeberg.

**skald(e**, obs. forms of SCALD *v.*, SCOLD *sb.*

**skaldic** (ˈskɔːldɪk, ˈskældɪk), *a.* Also scaldic. [f. SKALD + -IC.] Of or pertaining to the skalds or their poetry.

**1775** WARTON *Hist. Eng. Poetry* I. Diss. i. e 3, The old scaldic fables and heroes. **1784** JERNINGHAM *Scand. Poetry* Advt., The system of the Scaldic mythology. **1808** FINLAY *Scot. Hist. & Rom. Ball.* I. p. xxx, The Skaldic remains preserved in the Edda. **1861** MAX MÜLLER *Sci. Lang.* v. 180 One of the chief features of this artificial or skaldic poetry. **1894** *Nation* 21 June 471/3 Here and in the other Sagas the scaldic verses are such a component part of the text that they cannot.. be eliminated without serious loss.

**skales**, variant of SKAYLES *Obs.*

**skalesse**, obs. form of SCALELESS.

**skalfatting**, obs. Sc. form of SCAFFOLDING.

†**ˈskalfering**, *vbl. sb.* and *ppl. a.* Also 6 scalf-, scelf-, skelf-. [f. LG. *schalfer* or Du. *schelfer*, var. of *schilfer*: see SKILFER.]

**a.** *vbl. sb.* Scurfiness. **b.** *ppl. a.* Scurfy.

**1561** HOLLYBUSH *Hom. Apoth.* 2 He yᵗ hath a scalfering head let the same take yᵉ course branne.. & put a litle vinegre thereto..: yᵗ doth driue the scelfering away. **1579** LANGHAM *Gard. Health* (1633) 674 Head skalfering, cast seething hot water into Wheat branne [etc.].

†**skalk**, obs. variant of SCALP *sb.*[1]

*a* **1340** HAMPOLE *Psalter* lxvii. 23 God sall breke þe.. skalke of thare of gangand in þaire trespas. *Ibid.* cxxviii. 4 Lord of riȝtwys shal hew downe þe skalkys of synful.

**skallade, -ader, -ado**, var. ff. SCALADE, SCALADO.

**skallewag**, var. form of SCALLYWAG.

**skalling**, obs. f. SCALING *vbl. sb.*[2]

**skaloun**, obs. f. SCALLION.

**skaltre**, var. SHALTREE *Obs.*

**skam(e)lar**, obs. ff. SCAMBLER.

**skammel, skamyll**: see SCAMBLE *sb.*[1] and *v.*

**skance** (skæns), *a.* [aphetic f. ASKANCE *adv.*] Of a look, glance, etc.: Oblique, sidelong.

**1866** BLACKMORE *Cradock Nowell* xliii, The cunning skance gleam from the black, deep-ambushed squinters. **1872** LE FANU *In a Glass Darkly* I. 56 With a skance look, all the time, watching the movements of the beast.

‖**skandalon** (ˈskændəlɒn). *Theol.* Also scandalon. [Gr. σκάνδαλον stumbling-block; cf. *I Cor.* i. 23 Χριστὸν ἐσταυρωμένον, Ἰουδαίοις μεν σκάνδαλον Christ crucified, to the Jews a stumbling-block.] A stumbling-block, cause of offence, scandal (sense 1 b).

**1945** *Theology* XLVIII. 104 Any particular 'Thou' may become a *skandalon* at any time. **1948** *Scott. Jrnl. Theol.* I. 113 It is not a truth which can be arrived at by scientific investigation, and on that account it is a *scandalon* to the scientist, and to this scientifically minded generation. **1957** *Ibid.* X. 86 The scandalon of Christian faith is accepted, and the essay aims at being the account which biblical thinking must give of itself, taking itself seriously and simply. **1972** *Times Lit. Suppl.* 28 Jan. 105/4 Belief in God is *the* skandalon barring men and women in their thousands from a secular faith in Jesus Christ.

†**ˈskander**, *sb. Obs. rare.* Also 4 schaundre. [ad. OF. *escandre*, var. of *esclandre*: see SLANDER *sb.*] Slander, scandal.

**1338** R. BRUNNE *Chron.* (1810) 336 Of.. Tomlyn,.. and of Sir Alisandere,.. þat boþe com in skandere for dedes þei did þore. **1387** TREVISA *Higden* (Rolls) III. 421 He putte of þe schaundre of his moder.

†**ˈskander**, *v. Obs. rare.* Also 5 skaunder. [ad. OF. *escandrer*, var. of *esclandrer*: see SLANDER *v.*] *trans.* To bring into discredit; to slander.

*a* **1300** *Cursor M.* 26221 For bath gain man, man seis him wirk, And þof skander hali kyrk. **1424** *Paston Lett.* I. 17 Walter.. hath noysed and skaundered the seyd William.

**skane**, obs. f. SKENE[1].

**skanking** (ˈskæŋkɪŋ), *sb.* (and *a.*) [f. *skank* of unknown origin + -ING[1].] A style of West Indian dancing to reggae music, in which the body bends forward at the waist, and the knees are raised and the hands claw the air in time to the beat; dancing in this style. Also as *adj.*, of music suitable for skanking.

**1976** *New Musical Express* 31 July 29/3 One of the best instrumental sequences is the prelude to her 'Wild Bird' —the bit *before* the skanking starts. **1981** *Westindian World* 11 Sept. 4/5 The last track on side one is 'Pocket Money', an excellent Skanking tune. **1982** *Spectator* 13 Feb. 14/2 One young man, dreadlocks poking from his hat, danced across the floor in the style known as 'skanking'. **1984** *Sounds* 1 Dec. 16/6 Songs like the skanking 'Stop, Look 'N' Listen' and the crunching 'Army Song' show a lot more thought and ideas than earlier offerings from them.

Also **skank** = SKANKING; music for this.

**1974** [see DUB *sb.*[7] 1]. **1985** *Sounds* 27 July 14/4 UB40 turn out a creamy swank of a skank here, but one's bound to ask, what for?

**skans**, var. SCHANSE.

**skap(e**, obs. Sc. ff. SCALP.

**skarale**, obs. Sc. f. SQUIRREL.

**skard, skarrit**, obs. pa. t. of SCARE *v.*

**skarn** (skɑːn). *Geol.* Also scarn. [a. Sw. *skarn* lit. 'dung, filth', in same sense, f. ON. *skarn* (cf. north. dial. *scarn* dung (E.D.D.)).] Orig. applied to the silicate gangue of certain Archæan iron-ore or other mineral deposits, esp. where these occur in limestone or dolomite; now extended to any lime-bearing siliceous rock produced by metamorphism (esp. of limestone or dolomite) and the introduction of new elements. Freq. *attrib.*

**1901** H. LOUIS in *Trans. Inst. Mining & Metallurgy* X. 49, I have of late years adopted a very convenient Scandinavian word, *skarn*, for the zone of altered rock, usually calcareous, that contains such minerals as epidote, schorl, idocrase, at times augite, hornblende, mica, etc., and I speak of these altered rocks as epidote skarn, etc. **1911** *Econ. Geol.* VI. 708 Very characteristic of this zone, especially in connection with ore deposits, are the 'scarn' rocks—iron-rich silicate rocks produced by the addition of iron and silica to limestones. **1932** A. HARKER *Metamorphism* ix. 129 The skarn type of metasomatism is found at numerous British localities, but usually as a narrow belt and with little of the impregnation with sulphides. **1954** *Econ. Geol.* XLIX. 633 The skarn is a hard dense green rock characterized by the presence of quartz, green ferro-magnesian silicates.. and garnet. **1966** [see SAKHAITE]. **1978** [see SERENDIBITE].

**skarschliche**, obs. f. SCARCELY *adv.*

**skarsinarie**, obs. f. SCORZONERA.

**skarste**, obs. form of SCARCITY.

**skarth**: see SCART *sb.*[1], SCARTH *sb.*[1] and *sb.*[2]

**skat** (skɑːt). Also scat. [a G. *skat* (recorded from at least 1838), ad. It. *scarto* (F. *écart*) cards laid aside.] A three-handed card-game of German origin, with bidding for contract.

**1864** *Athenæum* 27 Aug. 269/3 Even to the present day, the game [Ombre] is to be met with, although it has powerful rivals to contend against in Whist and Scat. **1889** E. LEMCKE (*title*), Skat: an Illustrated Grammar of the German Game of Cards. A Complete Treatise How to Play Scat.

**skatable**, variant of SKATEABLE.

**skate** (skeɪt), *sb.*[1] Forms: α. 4–5 schat(e, 4–9 scate, 7 scaite. β. 6 skete, 6–8 skeat(e, 7 skeite; 6, 8 skait(e, 7– skate (7 skatt). [a. ON. *skata* (still in Norw. and Icel. use; Færöese *sköta*).]

**1. a.** A fish of the genus *Raia*; esp. the common species *Raia batis*, a very large, flat, cartilaginous fish much used for food.

α. *c* **1340** *Durh. Acc. Rolls* (Surtees) 36, j Schat. *Ibid.*, x schat. *c* **1375** *Ibid.* 46 In vij scates. *c* **1440** *Promp. Parv.* 443/1

Scate, fysche, *ragadies*. *c* **1475** *Pict. Voc.* in Wr.-Wülcker 764/39 *Hic garus*, a schate. **1530** PALSGR. 266/1 Scate fysshe, *raye*. **1570** LEVINS *Manip.* 39/11 A Scate, fishe, *batis, raia*. **1601** CHESTER *Love's Mart.* lxxxii, The Skate, the Roch, the Tench, the pretie Wincle. **1646** SIR T. BROWNE *Pseud. Ep.* 119 Yet is it commonly contrived out of the skins of Thornebacks, Scaites or Maids. **1737** *Ochtertyre House Bk.* (S.H.S.) 27 For scate and flounders [£]o. o. 7. **1800** COLQUHOUN *Comm. Thames* xv. 440 Haddock, Scate, fresh Ling.

β. **1538** ELYOT *Dict.*, *Raia*, a see fysshe called Raye or skete. **1596** DALRYMPLE tr. *Leslie's Hist. Scot.* I. 13 Mony kyndes of fische, cheiflie in thrie, Killine, Skait, and Makrell. **1601** HOLLAND *Pliny* II. 439 The fresh gall of a Ray or Skeat..is an excellent medicine for the eares. **1634** SIR T. HERBERT *Trav.* 213 One fish like to a Skate we caught. **1701** WOLLEY *Jrnl. New York* (1860) 61 In shape like a Skate or Flare as we call them in Cambridge. **1752** HILL *Hist. Anim.* 308 The variegated Raia, with the middle of the back smooth.., The Skaite. **1836** YARRELL *Brit. Fishes* II. 422 There is reason to believe that the true Skate produces its young later in the season than either the Thornback or the Homelyn. **1884** GOODE *Nat. Hist. Aquat. Anim.* 667 Of the Skates, *Raiidæ*, there are five species on our Atlantic coast.

**b.** With distinguishing adjs.

**1611** COTGR., *Raye estelée*, the starrie Skate. **1668** CHARLETON *Onomast.* 130 *Raia Fullonica*,..the Fuller-Scate. *Ibid.*, *Spinosa*,..the Card-scate. **1836** YARRELL *Brit. Fishes* II. 421 The Skate. Blue Skate, and Grey Skate, *Scotland*. **1882** JORDAN & GILBERT *Syn. Fishes N. Amer.* 40 *Raia erinacea*, Common Skate; Little Skate. *Raia ocellata*,.. Big Skate. **1883** *Fisheries Exhib. Catal.* (ed. 4) 104 Crab-eating Skate, Rhina Skate.

†**2.** The angel-fish. *Obs.*

**1668** WILKINS *Real Char.* 133 Scate, *Angel-fish*. **1681** GREW *Musæum* I. v. i. 96 The Scate, or Angel-Fish.

**3.** *attrib.* and *Comb.*, as ***skate-fish***, ***-liver oil***, ***soup***, ***-tailed***, ***-toothed***; **skate-barrow**, the egg-case of a skate; **skate-bread** (see quot.); **skate-leech**, a leech which infests the skate; **skate maid** (see MAID *sb.*[1] 7); **skate-rumple**, the hinder quarters of a skate; **skate-shears** (see quot.); **skate-sucker**, = *skate-leech*.

**1851** THOREAU *Jrnl.* 27 July in *Writings* (1906) VIII. 354 Skates' eggs, called in England *skate-barrows from their form, on the sand. **1884** *Evang. Mag.* Aug. 344 The so-called 'Mermaid's-Purses'..the fishermen call..'Skate-barrers'. **1681** in Macfarlane *Geogr. Coll.* (S.H.S.) III. 191 *Skatebread, which is a small fish, an inch and a half long. **1596** NASHE *Saffron Walden* O iv b, Like restie bacon, or a dride *scate-fish. *a* **1801** R. GALL *Poems & Songs* (1819) 69 Our wames e'en to our rigging-bane Like skate-fish clapping. **1882** *Encycl. Brit.* XIV. 404 The best-known example is the *skate-leech (*Pontobdella muricata*, L.), which is olive-coloured and dusted with whitish grains. **1858** SIMMONDS *Dict. Trade*, **Skate-liver oil*, a fish oil often sold for the same purposes as cod-liver oil. **1836** YARRELL *Brit. Fishes* II. 422 Fishermen distinguish the females..by the names of *Skate Maid, Thornback Maid, and Homelyn Maid. **1824** SCOTT *St. Ronan's* iii, [An] auld fule.., that may hae some judgment in cock-bree or in *scate-rumples. **1810** NIELL *List Fishes* 27 (Jam.), The male..possesses long sharp-edged appendages on the lower part of his body..; and fishers call these appendages *skate-sheers. **1710** P. LAMB *Royal Cookery* 25 *Scate or Thornback-Soupe. **1829** *Encycl. Metrop.* (1845) XX. 289/1 The type of the genus is *Hirudo muricata*, Lin., well known to fishermen under the name of *Skate-sucker. **1882** *Cassell's Nat. Hist.* VI. 242 The Skate-sucker belongs to the genus Pontobdella. **1713** *Phil. Trans.* XXVIII. 181 *Scate-tail'd Sicilian Amaranth. **1836** YARRELL *Brit. Fishes* II. 393 The..*Skate-toothed shark. **1883** DAY *Fishes Gt. Brit.* II. 296 Smooth-hound,.. skate-toothed dog, in allusion to its dentition.

**skate** (skeɪt), *sb.*[2] Also α. 7 **scats**, **schate**, 7–8 **scate**, 7–9 **skait**. β. 7 **skeate**, **skeete**, **skite**, **scheet**, 8 **skeet**. [Orig. in pl. *schates*, *scates*, etc., ad. Du. *schaats* (pl. *schaatsen*), MDu. *schaetse*, ad. ONF. *escache* (mod. *écache*) stilt: see SCATCH[1].

The alteration of sense from 'stilt' to 'skate' in Du. has not been clearly traced. In English the *s* was from the first apprehended as a plural ending, there being only one example of the pl. *scatses*: cf. however the Sc. verb *sketch*, *skeetch*. The spelling *skait* was not uncommon in the earlier part of the 19th cent.]

**1. a.** A device consisting of a steel blade mounted in a wooden sole, and fixed to the boot by means of a screw and straps, used for the purpose of gliding over ice; in later use a similar device made entirely of steel and clamped, strapped, or otherwise attached to the boot. Also = ROLLER-SKATE *sb.* Chiefly used in *pl.*

The blades are of varying length and curved or rounded at the toe.

α. [**1648** HEXHAM II, *Rijdt-schoenen*, Riding shoes upon yce, called in Holland Schates.] **1684** *Ballads Gt. Frost* (Percy Soc.) 11 The Rotterdam Dutchman with fleet-cutting scates. **1688** W. CARR *Rem. Govt. United Prov.* 113 The nimble Duchmen on their Scatses. **1701** WOLLEY *Jrnl. New York* (1860) 60 Upon the Ice its admirable to see Men and Women as it were flying upon their Skates from place to place. **1710** SWIFT *Jrnl. to Stella* 31 Jan., Rosamond's Pond full of the rabble sliding, and with Skates, if you know what those are. **1777** WATSON *Philip II* (1793) II. XII. 72 The Hollanders transport themselves..over the ice, with scates. **1806** J. BERESFORD *Miseries Hum. Life* III. i, Learning to cut the outside edge, on skaits that have no edge to cut with. **1856** 'STONEHENGE' *Brit. Rural Sports* 522/2 After seeing that the strap is properly crossed,..buckle it sufficiently tight to fasten the skate on securely. **1876** J. A. HARWOOD *Rinks & Rollers* iii. 39 The skates used had four wheels of iron placed in one line from the foot to the heel. **1892** 'F. ANSTEY' *Voces Pop.* Ser. II. 121 Several persons are having their skates put on. **1925** *Sears Roebuck & Co. Catal.* 751 Children's Extension Skates With Steel Self Contained Ball Bearing Rolls. **1959** *Ice & Roller Skating* 20 Wooden wheels are essential for rink skating and the skate should be screwed onto the boot by an expert. **1975** *Man. Artistic Roller Skating* 24 The change-of-edge..should be as short as possible, not materially longer than the length of the skate.

β. **1662** PEPYS *Diary* 1 Dec., Over the Parke, (where I first in my life..did see people sliding with their skeates, which is a very pretty art). **1688** HOLME *Armoury* III. xx. (Roxb.) 239/2 A Dutch Skite, this is a kind of wooden paten. *a* **1700** EVELYN *Diary* 24 Jan. 1684, Sleds, sliding with skeetes, a bull-baiting.

*fig.* **1719** BAYNARD *Health* (1740) 20 Life on smooth skeets slides swiftly by.

(*b*) In slang (orig. *Mil.*) phr. ***to get*** (or ***put***) ***one's skates on***, to hurry up (see also quot. 1925).

**1895** W. C. GORE in *Inlander* Dec. 113 *Get your skates on*, hurry up. **1919** *War Slang* in *Athenæum* 8 Aug. 727/2 To evade duty or get clear, you 'put your skates on'. **1925** FRASER & GIBBONS *Soldier & Sailor Words* 260 *Skates, to put on*, to hurry up. Also to evade duty. To desert. **1938** F. D. SHARPE *Sharpe of Flying Squad* xxvi. 263 'Jack, guy for your b—— life. The Squad are here.'.. Said Jack: 'I very soon put my skates on.' **1969** G. LYALL *Venus with Pistol* ix. 54 It was Carlos telling me to get my skates on and down to the Doelen plenty chop-chop. **1976** W. J. BURLEY *Wycliffe & Schoolgirls* i. 33 I'd better be getting my skates on, I'm catching the night train and I haven't done a thing about getting ready.

**b.** *pl.* = SKI *sb.* 1.

**1698** A. BRAND *Embassy China* 57 They make use of Scates, by the help of which they pass over the Snow with great Agility. **1774** GOLDSM. *Nat. Hist.* (1776) II. 215 They make use of skates, which are made of fir, of near three feet long, and half a foot broad. **1820** SCORESBY *Acc. Arctic Reg.* I. 242 There is no difficulty in travelling over them, even without either snow skaits or sledges. **1849** [see 3].

**c.** *U.S.* A sledge runner.

**1781** S. PETERS *Gen. Hist. Connecticut* 320 In the winter, the sleigh is used; a vehicle..carrying six persons in its box, which hangs on four posts standing on two steel sliders, or large scates. **1907** *St. Nicholas* July 781/1 You make a framework of timbers..and stick a skate or runner at each corner.

**d.** *transf.* A device with a set of rollers or wheels on which something moves; a device which can be placed under a heavy object to facilitate its movement.

**1905** *Engineering Rev.* XIII. 103/1 The Dolter system.. consists of a skate suspended from the under part of the car; this makes contact with a small iron block embedded in the road. **1940** *Chambers's Techn. Dict.* 774/2 *Skate, sidetracking*. (1) A device to move an aeroplane sideways on the ground, for manoeuvring in confined spaces, as when packing into sheds. (2) A shoe for slipping beneath the wheels for handling an aeroplane on soft snow. **1961** *Daily Tel.* 4 Oct. 15/2 An engineering firm has offered to supply skates for the Arch. *Ibid.*, The skates, or tracked skids, are made of steel plates. **1972** *Police Rev.* 10 Nov. 1477/1 It appears that the 'skates' shown in..last week's *Police Review* (page 1405) would combat the above criticisms. **1976** *Southern Even. Echo* (Southampton) 18 Nov. 17/7 Terry Maine..invented a 'skate' to go under the damaged wheel—which enables the aircraft to be moved quickly into a hangar for repairs.

**e.** *N. Amer.* A set of tackle for halibut-fishing, etc., used chiefly on the Pacific Coast of N. Amer.

**1882** J. W. COLLINS in *Fishermen's Own Book* 96 We set twenty skates of trawl—the whole string. **1897** KIPLING *Captains Courageous* iii. 75 'How many skates you reckon we'll need?' 'Baout three. Hurry!' 'There's three-hundred fathom to each tub,' Dan explained. **1960** M. SHARCOTT *Place of Many Winds* vii. 127 Either the night before or in the morning before the skates of gear are set they must be baited. *Ibid.* 129 Trolling fishermen often curse the skates of halibut gear. **1972** F. FORD *Atush Inlet* ix. 85 The marker, then the anchor, then two-three hundred yards of halibut line with a baited hook every ten feet, then another anchor and a marker. That's a skate.

**2.** [from the vb.] An act or spell of skating; one of a series of turns in figure-skating.

**1853** KANE *Grinnell Exped.* xxvi. (1856) 214 Took a skate this morning, over some lakelets recently frozen over. **1860** *All Year Round* No. 38. 277 He ceases to complete his skates, he passes from one to the other too rapidly. **1889** *Advance* (Chicago) 11 Apr. 294 Bound for the smooth sheet of ice..for a skate.

**3. a.** *Comb.*, as ***skate-grinder***, ***-lender***, etc.

**1849** LONGF. *Kavanagh* xxviii, In his imagination arose images of the Norwegian Skate-Runners. **1858** SIMMONDS *Dict. Trade*, *Skate-maker*, a manufacturer of iron sliding shoes. **1860** C. A. COLLINS *Eye-witness* vi. 84 What becomes of icemen and skate-lenders in summer? **1875** KNIGHT *Dict. Mech.* 2192/2 *Skate-grinder*, a machine for grinding skates.

**b.** *attrib.*, as ***skate-blade***, ***-iron***; **skate key**, a key for tightening roller-skates; **skatepark**, a park or rink for skateboarding; **skate-sail**, a sail rigged up on a skater's back so that the wind may carry him along.

**1895** *Outing* XXVII. 202/1 The *skate-blades are fixed to plates which are screwed fast to heel and sole of the skating-boots. **1838** J. H. INGRAHAM *Burton* I. x. 143 It was placed on runners sixteen inches high, shaped like *skate-irons. **1868** LOSSING *Hudson* 277 Three sled-runners, having skate-irons on their bottoms. **1962** 'E. MCBAIN' *Like Love* xiv. 193 A little girl..was sitting on the steps tightening her skates with a *skate key. **1977** *Montgomery Ward Catal.* Spring-Summer 509/1 Clamp-on sidewalk skates... Skate key included. **1976** *N.Y. Times Mag.* 12 Sept. 85/2 A $60,000 15 thousand-square-feet-of-concrete *skatepark. **1977** *Sunday Times* 27 Nov. (Colour Suppl.) 27/4 Use purpose-built skate-parks as they have a variety of bowls and slaloms which allow you freedom to develop tricks away from other skaters and spectators. **1882** *Standard* 1 Dec. 5/4 Skimming over the frozen lakes by the aid of the Danish *skate-sail.

**skate** (skeɪt), *sb.*[3] *slang* (chiefly *U.S.*). [Origin uncertain.] **1.** A poor, worn-out, decrepit horse.

**1894** KIPLING in *Cent. Mag.* Dec. 295/2 This yaller-backed skate comes to our pastur'. **1923** E. HEMINGWAY *Three Stories* 29 They'd kill that bunch of skates for their hides and hoofs up at Paris. **1935** H. DAVIS *Honey in Horn* vi. 61 Joel Hardcastle's horses were underfed, badly shod, and skates. **1978** E. TIDYMAN *Table Stakes* I. iv. 68 The man was a gambler... A pony player. Used to bet thousands on the worst-looking skates you've ever seen.

**2. a.** A mean or contemptible person. Esp. in ***cheap skate*** (also *attrib.* or as *adj.*).

**1896** Cheap skate [see HORSE *sb.* 18]. **1898** F. P. DUNNE *Mr. Dooley in Peace & War* 198 If th' skate fr'm Oklahoma is allowed f'r to belch anny in this here assimblage, th' diligates fr'm th' imperyal Territ'ry iv New Mexico'll lave th' hall. **1904** J. C. LINCOLN *Cap'n Eri* xxi. 383 Offered me a hundred dollars a week, the skate! **1935** D. L. SAYERS *Gaudy Night* xix. 399 'It would suit them very well,' thought Harriet, 'the cheap skates!' **1947** *Partisan Rev.* XIV. 259 Samuel lost his temper and told the boss what he thought of him, what a cheap skate he was. **1958** *New Statesman* 4 Oct. 444/2 A cheapskate doctor he employed to save a few dollars gave his wife, Mary, morphine to ease her pains after delivering her youngest son, Edmund, and she has become an addict. **1960** H. PINTER *Caretaker* I. 9 *Aston*: I saw him have a go at you. *Davies*:..The filthy skate, an old man like me. **1973** J. PORTER *It's Murder with Dover* xii. 119 They were hardened women of the world and knew a cheap skate when they saw one.

**b.** *labour skate* (U.S.), a trade-union official.

**1930** *Amer. Mercury* Dec. 456/2 *Labor-skate*, an official of a labor union. **1978** *Washington Post* 27 Jan. D7/3 Most of the crowd consisted of labor skates, members of Jewish groups, and friends of Jackson and Moynihan.

**skate** (skeɪt), *v.* Also 7–8 **scate**, 9 **skait**; 8 **skeit**, **skete**. [f. SKATE *sb.*[2]]

**1. a.** *intr.* To glide over ice upon skates; to use skates as a means of exercise or pastime. Also with *over* (cf. ROW *v.*[1] 1 f).

**1696** S. SEWALL *Diary* 30 Nov., Many Scholars go in the Afternoon to Scate on Fresh-pond. **1730** THOMSON *Winter* 632 With him who slides; Or sketing sweeps, swift as the winds, along. **1768** WILKES *Corr.* (1805) III. 223, I scate almost every day; and amuse myself much with so noble an exercise. **1833** HT. MARTINEAU *Vanderput & S.* ii. 38 Because I cannot shoot and skait and swim? **1842** HAWTHORNE in *Longfellow's Life* (1891) I. 450, I get up at sunrise to skate. **1890** *Field* 11 Jan. 65/3 One Mile Race. G. C. Tebbutt.. skated over.., Verspijk being absent.

**b.** *transf.* To slide or glide along; to move lightly and rapidly.

**1775** C. & F. DAVY tr. *Bourrit's Journ. Glaciers* (1776) 221 Driving his heels more or less into the snow, he skaited, if I may so call it, to the bottom. **1782** MRS. COWLEY *Bold Stroke for Husband* v. ii, Those new shoes! they have made me skate all day, like a Dutchman on a canal. **1847** EMERSON *Poems* Wks. (Bohn) I. 425 The train along the railroad skates. **1891** *Nature* 10 Sept. 457/1 Other insects merely dive into the water..or skate upon the surface.

**c.** *fig.*, esp in phr. (*a*) ***to skate over*** (or ***on***) ***thin ice***; (*b*) ***to skate over*** or ***round*** (a fact, subject, etc.), to pass by or over hurriedly, to avoid mentioning.

**1841–4** EMERSON *Ess.*, *Experience* Wks. (Bohn) I. 179 We live amid surfaces, and the true art of life is to skate well on them. **1897** *Church Times* 17 Sept. 283 Cardinal Vaughan is an adept at skating over thin ice. In his address..there were many points which every one knows were weak, but he glided over them with surprising deftness. **1897** A. BEARDSLEY *Let.* 15 Sept. (1970) 368, I hardly like to think now of all the thin ice I must have skated over since March 31st—a miraculous patinage! **1926** P. GUEDALLA *Palmerston* V. iii. 356 Even *Punch* regaled its readers with a princely figure of slightly sinister aspect skating perilously on the thin ice of foreign affairs. **1928** *Manch. Guardian Weekly* 30 Mar. 243/1 The Premier did not do more than skate round the problem. **1945** E. WAUGH *Brideshead Revisited* I. v. 98 He..could talk at length of..how this or that Jesuit or Dominican had skated on thin ice or sailed near the wind in his Lenten discourses. **1948** 'N. SHUTE' *No Highway* v. 123 We both skated over the implications of that. **1957** *Economist* 7 Dec. 860/1 The reason for the outbreak of the second Balkan war in 1913..is gracefully skated over. **1965** *New Statesman* 16 Apr. 622/3 Mr Brown's latest paper on prices and incomes skates carefully around this point. **1971** *Where* Sept. 266/1 It also skates over the fact that it is an offence to be in possession of the drugs listed if they have not been legally prescribed. **1978** H. CARPENTER *Inklings* IV. i. 216 He skated on thin ice in the opening chapter of *The Problem of Pain*, where he offered his readers a 'proof' of the existence of God which..tackled this immense issue 'on the scale of a pamphlet in a church porch'. **1979** C. MOULE in M. Goulder *Incarnation & Myth* v. 135 It has been claimed that Mark's christology is authoritative and as much part of the New Testament as Paul's... But this is to skate over the question, What was Mark's intention?

**d.** *colloq.* To depart speedily.

**1915** in C. Johnson *Battleground Adventures* liv. 418 Holt met the ol' man comin' from the barn as hard as he could run. Oh! he was comin' from thar skatin'. *c* **1926** 'MIXER' *Transport Workers' Song Bk.* 31 Well, I'm skating. Coming, 'Slasher'? **1937** G. FRANKAU *More of Us* v. 63 When one's happy—well, time simply flies. Me for the hay. Let's get our bill, and skate.

**e.** *U.S. slang.* (See quots.)

**1945** L. SHELLY *Jive Talk Dict.* 17/1 *Skate*, to get away with something. **1977** *Amer. Speech* 1975 L. 66 *Skate vi*, shirk duties. 'The new pledges are really skating this week.' **1979** *Observer* 18 Mar. (Colour Suppl.) 56 I'm not a woman's libber but I don't want to skate (shirk).

**2.** *trans.* **a.** To knock (one) *down* in skating; to contest (a match), to compete with (some one), by skating.

**1788** MME. D'ARBLAY *Diary* April, To skate a man down is a very favourite diversion among a certain race of wags.

**1847** MRS. GORE *Castles in Air* xxxiii, A match was skated upon the lake. **1890** *Field* 1 Feb. 143/2 Whether a race is skated or not.

**b.** To cause (something) to slide or glide over a smooth surface.

**1883** *Daily News* 29 Sept. 3/3 They..turn up on deck early in the morning to 'skate the chairs'.

**c.** To slide or glide over. Also *fig.*

**1900** [see FENNER]. **1970** G. F. NEWMAN *Sir, you Bastard* i. 22 Sneed skated the passing out examination with the highest marks on record. **1971** B. PATTEN *Irrelevant Song* 27 Quick as the autumn marigold Skates the borders of whitening grass.

**skateable** ('skeɪtəb(ə)l), *a.* [f. SKATE *v.* + -ABLE.]

**1.** Fit for skating upon.

**1890** *Daily News* 23 Dec. 3/2 The River Cam is covered with thick ice, and is skateable from the university town to some distance below Ely. **1893** *Star* 7 Jan. 3/5 Above Hampton Court..there is absolutely no skateable ice.

**2.** Capable of being skated.

**1891** *Field* 7 Mar. 334/3, I have a design for a cross-cut in which the lines are crossed five times; it is quite 'skateable'.

**skateboard** ('skeɪtbɔəd), *sb.* orig. *U.S.* Also skate board. [f. SKATE *sb.*$^{2}$, after *surfboard.*] A narrow platform mounted on roller-skate wheels, on which the rider coasts along, usu. in a standing position (orig. developed from surf-riding, chiefly as a pastime). Also *attrib.*

**1964** *Life* 5 June 89 Skateboards appeared last fall in southern California. **1964** *Surfer* Sept. 72 No one, except possibly the skateboard manufacturers, took them seriously until recently. *Ibid.* 76 When they can't go out in the water and surf, they can do it on land with a skate-board. **1965** *Globe & Mail* (Toronto) 21 Apr. 5/6 Hundreds of vacationing teen-agers..wheeled to City Hall yesterday on their skate boards to demand an off-the-street area to carry on their latest fad. **1974** *Daily Colonist* (Victoria, B.C.) 21 Aug. 18/6 He was..a legless cripple whose only means of locomotion was a skate board. **1976** A. CASSORLA *Skateboarder's Bible* i. 9 Already in the works are extensive skateboard parks. **1976** C. WESTON *Rouse Demon* (1977) xxi. 96 A boy on a skateboard whirled by on the sidewalk. **1978** K. AMIS *Jake's Thing* xx. 204 The local authorities wanted ..a skateboard park built on the site. **1978** *Cornish Guardian* 27 Apr. 23/1 (Advt.), Used Car Parts (fronting the quay, adjoining skateboard rink). **1980** P. HARCOURT *Tomorrow's Treason* I. i. 28 An even smaller boy..seemingly unable to get off his skate-board..was careering straight into the path of my car.

Hence **'skateboard** *v. intr.*, to ride on a skateboard; **'skateboarder**; **'skateboarding** *vbl. sb.*

**1964** *Life* 5 June 89 Skateboarding requires only a tapered piece of wood flexibly mounted on roller-skate wheels and a stretch of pavement. *Ibid.*, A good skate-boarder can do all a surfer's tricks and more. **1964** *Surfer* Sept. 74 Some of the skateboarders have set up slalom courses, timing each other from stand-still starts. **1968** W. WARWICK *Surfriding in N.Z.* 19/1 To skateboard properly the rider should have a reasonable sense of balance. **1976** *National Observer* (U.S.) 3 July 12/2 They're..'taking it to the limit': skateboarding up the sides of empty swimming pools and pipelines. **1977** *Times* 15 Oct. 24/2 The odd skateboarder en route for the adventure playground. **1978** *Morecambe Guardian* 14 Mar. 4/5 Coun. Mrs Taylor said that if any children still felt strongly about having no skateboarding park they should contact her so that a united effort could be made. **1979** V. S. NAIPAUL *Bend in River* xv. 249 A wise, sloping avenue.. with boys skateboarding.

**'skateless**, *a. rare*$^{-1}$. [f. SKATE *sb.*$^{2}$] Having no skates. In quot. *absol.*

**1826** HONE *Every-day Bk.* II. 98 The skateless hire the '*best* skates' for a shilling.

**skater** ('skeɪtə(r)). Also 8 scater, 8–9 skaiter. [f. SKATE *v.* + -ER.] One who skates. Occas. = SKATEBOARDER.

**1700** S. PARKER *Six Philos. Ess.* 57 The next Generation, believe me, shall all be Scaters. **1768** WILKES *Corr.* (1805) III. 228 Ice-boats sailing up and down, the scaters, the booths, &c. All Holland is now alive. **1796** MORSE *Amer. Geogr.* II. 334 They are the best skaters upon the ice in the world. **1841** L. HUNT *Seer* II. (1864) 19 Now skaiters are on the alert. **1892** 'F. ANSTEY' *Voces Pop.* Ser. II. 121 Practised Skaters being irritable and impatient. **1977** *Times* 19 Nov. 26/6 Many a skate park, rightly, refuses admittance unless skaters wear protective helmets and pads. **1977** [see *skatepark* s.v. SKATE *sb.*$^{2}$ 3 b].

**skating** ('skeɪtɪŋ), *vbl. sb.* [f. SKATE *v.* + -ING$^{1}$.]

**a.** The action of the verb.

**1723** *Present St. Russia* I. 30 Their chief Delight was in scating. **1753** HANWAY *Trav.* (1762) II. I. vi. 29 When the water is frozen,..it also furnishes them the amusement of skeiting. **1842** E. MIALL in *Nonconf.* II. 27 The exercise and recreation of scating. **1876** J. A. HARWOOD *Rinks & Rollers* iv. 63 There are few more lively..sights than..the young engaged in skating and flirting, while the elder ones sip tea between the trees. **1886** MABEL COLLINS *Prettiest Woman* x, Are you coming to the skating? **1948** C. BEASTALL *Int. Roller Skating Annual* 15 The RSROA, who banned metal wheels, introduced skating and proficiency tests..in their rinks. **1975** *Man. Artistic Roller Skating* 38 The candidate is required to compose..an original dance..suitable for skating in public skating sessions.

*transf.* **1849** LONGF. *Kavanagh* v, Another long silence, broken only by the skating of the swift pen over the sheet.

**b.** *attrib.*, as *skating-book, -boot, -match, -rink* (also *fig.*), *skirt.*

**1763** *Brit. Mag.* IV. 104 A skating match from hence to Whittlesea. **1867** *N. & Q.* 3rd Ser. XII. 171/1 'A skating rink' is a meadow, on to which water is let in winter to a slight depth, for the purpose of skating. **1875** BURNIE *Mem. Thomas* 54 The idle world is frantic on skating-rinks; they are springing up everywhere. **1875** *Building News* 19 Nov. 579/1 Skating Rinks. The [roller-]skating rink is an institution that has rapidly grown in..popularity. **1895** *Outing* XXVII. 206/2 A little intelligent study of the diagrams in your skating-book. **1895** Skating-boot [see SKATE *sb.*$^{2}$ 3 b]. **1903** Skating pond [see *live wire* s.v. LIVE *a.* 9]. **1926** MAINES & GRANT *Wise-Crack Dict.* 14/2 *Skating rink for flies*, baldheaded man. **1958** *Roller Dance Skating Man.* 32 (Advt.), Skating Rinks at: Skating Rink & Cafeteria, Granby Halls, Leicester. **1968** J. IRONSIDE *Fashion Alphabet* 62 *Skating skirt.* Traditionally this is cut circular and very short, worn with tights. **1971** *Petticoat* 24 July 3/4 They'll be taking hemlines just about as high as they can go, even to skating-skirt length. **1976** *Flintshire Leader* 10 Dec. 2/8 Freezing conditions this week turned a road in Carmel near Holywell into a skating rink. **1981** *Northeast Woods & Waters* Jan. 24/3 Osborndale in Derby even offers a large skating pond, lighted for night skating.

**skatist** ('skeɪtɪst). [f. SKATE *v.*] One who is fond of skating.

**1876** *All Year Round* XVI. 18 Even in Chicago,.. persistent and fanatical 'skatists'..have shown a decided preference for rollers. **1885** *Kendal Mercury* 30 Jan. 5/2 The skatists rubbed their hands gleefully.

**skatol** ('skætɒl). *Chem.* Also scatol, skatole. [f. Gr. σκατ-ός, gen. of σκῶρ dung + -OL.] An aromatic substance produced by the decomposition of albumen in the intestinal canal.

**1879** *Academy* 11 Jan. 34 Bruger has found a new substance skatol. **1881** WATTS *Dict. Chem.* 3rd Suppl. 1803 Skatole forms the chief constituent of the volatile aromatic portion of human fæces. **1887** A. M. BROWN *Anim. Alkaloids* 13 The products become simpler,..as phenol or phenic acid, indol and skatol.

**ska'toxyl.** *Chem.* [f. as prec. + OX(Y)- 2 + -YL.] A product of the oxidation of skatol. Also *attrib.* and *Comb.*

**1890** J. CAGNEY tr. *Jaksch's Clin. Diagnosis* vii. 244 It is assumed that skatol..is oxidised to skatoxyl within the body, appearing in the urine as skatoxyl-sulphuric acid. **1897** *Allbutt's Syst. Med.* IV. 287 The indoxyl and skatoxyl sulphates of copper.

†**skaunce.** *Obs.* Also 5 skawnce. [Formed by a false analysis of ASKANCE(S) *conj.*] A jest.

It is doubtful whether quot. 1483 belongs here.

*c* **1440** *York Myst.* xxx. 291 But þis is but a skaunce. *c* **1460** *Towneley Myst.* ii. 401 Peasse, man, for godis payn! I saide it for a skaunce. *Ibid.* xxi. 353 Sir, we do it for a skawnce. **1483** *Cath. Angl.* 341/2 A Skaunce, *vbi* a wylte.

**skaunt**, aphetic form of *askaunt* ASKANT.

**1791** W. TAYLOR tr. *Lessing's Nathan* (1887) 35 This fellow does not follow me for pastime. How skaunt he eyes his hands!

**skawburn(e**, obs. forms of SCABBARD *sb.*$^{1}$

**skawde**, obs. north. form of SCOLD *v.*

†**skawte.** *Obs.*$^{-1}$ (Meaning uncertain.)

*c* **1460** *Towneley Myst.* xxx. 559 Sir, I Wold cut thaym a skawte and make theym be knawne.

**skayle, skaylle**, obs. ff. SCALE *sb.* and *v.*

†**skayles.** *Obs.* In 6 skailes, 6–7 skayles, scailes, skales, 7 scales. [app. a variant of KAYLES, but the origin of the *s-* is not clear; cf. *kittle-pins* and *skittles.*] A form of the game of skittles or ninepins; also, one of the pins with which this game is played.

α. *a* **1566** W. WAGER *Longer thou livest* 781 You taught me first to play at blow pointe,..At skayles, and the playing with a sheepes ioynte. **1579–80** NORTH *Plutarch* (1895) II. 91 He played at skayles in the middest of the streete. **1598** FLORIO, *Sbrigli*, a play called ninepins or keeles or skailes. **1628** *Maldon Docs.* (Bdle. 199 No. 4), Playinge at..skayles, bowles, or anie other unlawfull games. **1647** PEACHAM *Worth of a Penny* 31 The most ordinary recreations of the Countrey are foot-ball, skales, or nine pins.

β. **1579** RICE *Invective agst. Vices* D ij b, Tennis balles or bowles, horse bones for scailes, nor kniues for muggle pricke. **1600** NASHE *Summers Last Will* Wks. (Grosart) VI. 105 It is against my profession to vse any scales, but such as we play at with a boule. **1613** PURCHAS *Pilgrimage* (1614) 257 To them that doubt of Wine, of chesse, scailes, and of Tables, thou shalt say that such sports and such drinkes are a great sinne.

Hence †**'skayler; 'skayling; skayle-pins.**

**1579** RICE *Invective agst. Vices* C iv, Giuen to Bowlyng,.. Tennis plaiyng, scailyng, and such like. *Ibid.* F j, Dicers, Bowlers, Carders, Scailers, Crossers and Pillers. **1656** *New Almanack* 8 That antient Olympick game called scale pins, in memorie of nine of those gallant lads.

**skaymlis**, obs. pl. f. SCAMBLE *sb.*$^{1}$

**skayne**, obs. form of SKEIN, SKENE$^{1}$.

**skayre**, obs. form of SCARE *v.*

**skayth**, obs. Sc. form of SCATHE.

†**skayved**, *a. Obs.*$^{-1}$ (Meaning uncertain.)

**13..** *Gaw. & Gr. Knt.* 2167 þe skwez of þe scowtes skayued hym þoȝt.

‖**skaz** (skaz). [Russ.] First-person narrative in which the author assumes a persona. Also *attrib.*

**1926** D. S. MIRSKY *Contemp. Russ. Lit.* vii. 311 Michael Zoshchenko..is a more narrative writer: he is also an ornamentalist, but his ornamentalism is a purely colloquial skaz, which proceeds from Leskov. **1957** W. E. HARKINS *Dict. Russ. Lit.* 360 *Skaz*, a Russian word designating a narrative told by a fictitious narrator, rather than by the author directly. **1967** *Russ. Review* XXVI. 177 In succeeding works Solzhenitsyn resorts to *skaz* only occasionally. **1974** MOORE & PARRY *Twentieth-Cent. Russ. Lit.* i. 10 Remizov was a sharp stylist who often wrote in the vein of folklore; he carried on Nikolai Leskov's tradition of *skaz*, an attempt to reproduce the exact idiom of each speaker in a story. **1980** *Times Lit. Suppl.* 7 Nov. 1264/4 The narrator [is] a typically Russian busybody in the 'skaz' tradition.

**skeal(l**: see SCALE *sb.*$^{2}$ and *sb.*$^{4}$, SKAIL-.

†**skealt.** *Obs.*$^{-1}$ In 6 skealte, skelte. [prob. ad. Irish *scéalta*, pl. of *scéal* tale, story.] Story, talk, rumour.

*c* **1580** J. HOOKER *Life Sir P. Carew* in *Archaeol.* XXVIII. 130 This was not onely her talke; but it was also the comon skealte and speache throught the whole lande.

**skean**: see SKENE, Irish dagger.

**skean(e**, var. SKEIN *sb.*

**skear**, dial. f. SCARE *v.*

**skeary(e**, obs. or dial. ff. SCARY *a.*

**skeat**, var. of SCEAT.

**skeat(e**, obs. ff. SKATE *sb.*$^{1}$

**skeath**, obs. f. SCATHE *sb.*

**skeating**, *vbl. sb.*: see SKEET *sb.*$^{1}$

†**skeck**, *sb. Obs. rare.* In 3–4 skec, skek(ke, scek. [ad. OF. *eskec*, var. of *eschec* spoil, booty.] An attack made for the sake of plunder; a petty raid. Cf. SKEG *sb.*$^{3}$

**1297** R. GLOUC. (Rolls) 5131 Bote hii þus mid scolkinge vpe þe englisse wende, & doþ eni skek feble ynou & abbeþ þe worse ende. *c* **1330** *Arth. & Merl.* 4324 (Kölbing), Kepe we þe strait wais Ouer alle in þe cuntrays & robben hem her sustenaunce Wiþ skec. *Ibid.* 4501 þat..Binomen mani painems her liif & wiþ skekes & wiþ fiȝt þe wayes loked wele a pliȝt.

†**skeck**, *v. Obs. rare.* In 4 skecken, skekke. [f. prec. Cf. SKICK *v.*]

**1.** *intr.* To make a raid *on*; to spoil, plunder.

*c* **1330** *Arth. & Merl.* 7409 (Kölbing), þai hem hidden a litel þer bi, For to aspien, sikerli, þe route of þe Sarrazins.., For to skecken on hem on hest, When þai seiȝe time best. *a* **1400** *Relig. Pieces fr. Thornton MS.* 82 Thyne executurs Of þe ne will rekke, but skikk ande skekke Full baldely in thi boures.

**2.** *trans.* To seize as spoil.

*c* **1325** *Body & Soul* 244 in *Map's Poems* (Camden) 243/1 Uche to pyke that he con skekke, Scheep or swyn..or net.

Hence †**'skecking** *vbl. sb. Obs.*

**13..** *K. Alis.* 3563 (Laud MS.), Many proude gome.. Willeþ wenden in þe morowenyng And vpon vs maken a skekkyng. **1387** TREVISA *Higden* (Rolls) III. 257 Half þe peple stood i-armed wiþoute þe cite forto defende þe cite, and þe workmen for resynge and stekkynge [*v.r.* skekkynge] of straunge naciouns.

**skecon**, obs. form of SCUTCHEON.

**sked** (skɛd), colloq. abbrev. (orig. *U.S.*) of (*a*) SCHEDULE *sb.*; (*b*) SCHEDULE *v.*; (*c*) SCHEDULED *ppl. a.*; also *ellipt.*, a scheduled flight.

**1929** *Amer. Speech* IV. 289 A 'sked' (schedule) is a message to the central office briefly sketching the contents of a story offered for transmission. **1942** BERREY & VAN DEN BARK *Amer. Thes. Slang* §597/5 *Bill* [verb]; *schedule*, sked. **1949** *Daily Progress* (Charlottesville, Va.) 26 Aug. 12/3 (*heading*) W[illiam] & M[ary] skeds tour for court team. **1953** SCOTT & FISHER *Thousand Geese* ix. 103 If we were to get back for our radio sked..we thought we should start home. **1972** *Sat. Rev.* (U.S.) 4 Mar. 33/2 The ultimate answer..is for the skeds to become competitive with the charters. **1977** *New Day* Summer 6/1 All mission stations [in Papua New Guinea] are connected by radio, and different times (skeds) are assigned for their use. The Post Office has radio skeds for Government traffic. **1981** *Beautiful Brit. Columbia* Fall 22 Near the Dean, at Eliguk or Gatcho lakes you can be flown out to Nimpo Lake at Highway 20; thence by car, 'sked-flight' (a Cariboo phrase for a scheduled flight). **1981** L. LEAMER *Assignment* i. 8, I don't mind when it's skedded right..but..I don't ever want to work with Henderson again.

**skedaddle** (skɪ'dæd(ə)l), *sb. colloq.* [f. the vb.] A hasty or precipitate retreat or flight; a scurry.

**1870** M. COLLINS *Vivian* I. xvii. 267 There was a rapid skedaddle of small legs all in one direction. **1884** GORDON *Jrnls.* (1885) 128 One feels such a mean brute to go egging on men to fight, and then to let it end with a skedaddle.

**b.** Without article.

**1871** *Daily News* 27 Jan., Although the movement was directed by the noble sentiment of wisdom, it must be described by the undignified name of skedaddle. **1885** *Pall Mall G.* 14 Feb. 2/2 In advocating a policy of skedaddle he only represents himself.

**skedaddle** (skɪ'dæd(ə)l), *v. colloq.* Also skeedadle, skiddaddle. [prob. a fanciful formation.

'Said to be of Swedish and Danish origin, and to have been in common use for several years throughout the Northwest, in the vicinity of immigrants from those nations' (Webster, 1864); but there are no forms in Sw. or Da. sufficiently near to be seriously taken into acount. There is some slight evidence of the currency of the word in English and Scottish dialect use before it became prominent in

America, but it is doubtful how far this is of importance for its origin.]

**1.** *intr.* Of soldiers, troops, etc.: To retreat or retire hastily or precipitately; to flee.

Orig. U.S. military slang, introduced during the Civil War of 1861–5.

**1861** *N.Y. Tribune* 10 Aug. 5/5 No sooner did the traitors discover their approach than they 'skiddaddled', (a phrase the Union boys up here apply to the good use the seceshers make of their legs in time of danger). **1862** in Post *Soldiers' Lett.* II. xxxii. 90 As soon as the rebs saw our red breeches (the Zouaves) coming through the woods they skedaddled. **1863** J. Russell *Diary North & S.* II. 421 For their men skedaddled, and the Secession cavalry slipping after them, had a very pretty chase. **1875** Buckland *Log-Book* 246 The enemy skedaddled without coming to the scratch. **1894** H. Nisbet *Bush Girl's Rom.* xxvii. 260 So that those honest fellows..might have the less temptation thrown in their way to skedaddle.

**2. a.** In general use: To go away, leave, or depart hurriedly; to run away, 'clear out'.

**1862** *Illustr. Lond. News* 24 May 540/3, I 'skeedadled' from the capital of the dis-United States. **1867** Trollope *Chron. Barset* I. xxxi. 260 Mama, Major Grantly has—skedaddled. **1878** Besant & Rice *Celia's Arb.* xxxix, The middies swiftly creep over the seats and skedaddle.

**b.** Of animals: To run off, stampede.

**1879** F. Pollok *Sport Brit. Burmah* I. 166 There were several hundred elephants about, and they all skedaddled, making for the hills. **1888** J. Inglis *Tent Life in Tigerland* 66 An untried elephant will not unnaturally turn tail and incontinently 'skedaddle' as hard as it can lay legs to the ground.

**3.** *trans.* To spill (milk, etc.). *dial.*

**1862** Ld. Hill in *Times* 13 Oct. 10/3 You blind buzzard, don't you see you are skedaddling all that milk?

Hence **ske'daddler**.

**1864** *Index* 9 June 359/3 If the emigration of skedaddlers from the field of battle continues to increase. **1869** *Routledge's Ev. Boy's Ann.* 507 Consolation to skedaddlers in general.

**skee**, var. SKI *sb.* and *v.*

**Skee-Ball** ('ski:bɔ:l). Also **skeeball**. [f. SKI *sb.* or *v.* + BALL *sb.*¹] An indoor game in which balls set rolling down an alley are projected over a hump or otherwise into targets. Also *attrib.*

*Skee-Ball* is a proprietary term in the U.S.

**1923** *Daily Mail* 11 June 3 The game of Skeeball is an American invention which has been in increasing operation in the United States for some six years. It is the latest development of the game of bowls, sharply distinguished from all similar games by a hump in the centre of the alley which causes the ball to leap high in the air and enter a target. **1930** A. P. Herbert *Water Gipsies* xviii. 258 Ernest played skeeball because it was the nearest thing to skittles, and he won a china dog. **1974** J. Wainwright *Evidence I shall Give* xxiv. 121 A Skee-Ball set-up with six lanes.

**skeed**, obs. f. SKID *sb.*

**skeel** (ski:l). Now *dial.* Forms: 4–6 **skele**, 6 **skelle**, 6–9 **skeil**, 6 **skeill**, **skeyll**, 7 **skeele**, 7– **skeel**; 7 **skile**, 8–9 **skiel**, etc. [a. ON. (now Icel.) *skjóla* pail.]

**1.** A wooden bucket, pail, tub, or similar vessel used for some domestic purpose, chiefly for holding milk or water, and usually having a handle or handles formed by staves rising above the rim.

In early use freq. in inventories and similar documents; now only dial., chiefly Northern and West Midland.

The precise purpose for which a skeel is used varies in different localities, and this is occas. denoted by a defining word prefixed, as ***bread***, ***butter***, ***dough***, ***washing skeel***.

*c* **1330** *Durh. Acc. Rolls* (Surtees) 518 In Erthening, Chese-clathe, Meles, et Skeles,..iij*s.* ij*d.* **1387–8** *Ibid.* 314 In iij skelys empt. pro lacte, ix*d.* **1459** *Ibid.* 89, j caldrun, ij skelez, j kyrn. **1483** *Cath. Angl.* 341/2 Skele, *emicadium.* **1508** Dunbar *Flyting* 231 Fische wyvis cryis, Fy! and castis doun skillis and skeilis. **1570** *Durham Deposit.* (Surtees) 186 This examinate brought water in a skeill to be maid in holly water. **1629** *Mem. Fountains* (Surtees) 365 The greater milkinge skeele, one stone trough. **1641** Best *Farm. Bks.* (Surtees) 145 A little two gallon skeele to fetch water in. **1766** *Museum Rust.* VI. 169 She must either quit her place, or break the *skeel*; the vessel in which water is brought from the well. **1789** W. H. Marshall *Glouc.* I. 269 Skeels..are broad shallow vessels; principally for the purpose of setting milk in. **1790** Grose *Prov. Gloss.*, *Skiel*, a beer-cooler, used in brewing. **1805** R. W. Dickson *Pract. Agric.* II. 1008 Part of the butter is spread on the bottom of another bason or *skeel*. **1825–** in dial. glossaries (Cumb., Durh., Glouc., Heref., Northampt., Warw., Worc., Yorks.). **1864** A. Leighton *Myst. Leg. Edin.* (1886) 3 Mrs. Hyslop's head was over the skeil, wherein lay one of the linen shirts of Mr. Dallas.

**2.** *Coalmining.* (See quot.)

**1883** Gresley *Gloss. Coal-m.* 224 *Skeel*, a kind of cage in which coals are lowered down the cuts or staples.

Hence '**skeelful**, a bucketful, pailful.

**1575–6** *Durham Deposit.* (Surtees) 296 This examinate had bein at St. Oswald's well for a skeil full of wayter. **1863** in Robson *Bards of Tyne* 237 But wi' skeelfuls o' wetter he brightened his jaw.

**skeel**, variant of SCALE *sb.*²

**skeel-duck, -goose:** see SKEELING (quot. 1806).

**skeeler** ('ski:lə(r)). [Perh. f. SKI *sb.* + ROL)LER *sb.*¹] (See quots.) Hence '**skeeling** *vbl. sb.*, skating on skeelers.

**1968** *Daily Tel.* 28 Dec. 23/4 (*caption*) 'Skeelers', a cross between ice and roller skates. *Ibid.* 23/6 The skates, called 'Skeelers'.., are just part of the fun for the children at the *Daily Mail* New Year Show. **1969** *Ibid.* 31 Jan. 17/5 Skeeling, launched last autumn, gives some of the exhilarating feeling of skating—but without ice. Skeelers are like ice skates but three wheels replace the blade; they will slide on any hard surface. **1972** *Kingston* (Ontario) *Whig-Standard* 13 June 15/6 Skeeling, according to the publicity releases, is iceless skating; a summer hockey equivalent. Skeelers are a cross between roller skates and ice skates and were originally developed by the Russians to help condition speed skaters during the off-season.

'**skeeling.** *Orkney dial.* Also 6 **skilling**. [prob. of Scandinavian origin.] ***skeeling-goose***, the sheldrake.

**1578** [see ROUT *sb.*⁷]. **1684** Sir R. Sibbald *Scotia* III. 21 *Skeeling-goose*, de quo fama est, in ejus Ventriculo Grana Piperis reperiri, de quo tamen non constat. **1806** Neill *Tour Ork. & Shetl.* 195 *Skeel-goose*, Shieldrake, *Anas Tadorna.* In Orkney it is sometimes also called skeeling-goose or skeel-duck. **1866** Edmonston *Gloss. Shetl. & Orkney* 104.

**skeely**, variant of SKILLY *a. Sc.* and *north.*

'**skeeman.** *Naut.* [ad. Du. *schieman* (hence G. *schiemann*, F. *esquiman*) 'boatswain's mate', formerly also *schimman* (so in LG. of 1557), possibly for *schipman* SHIPMAN.] (See quot.)

**1820** Scoresby *Acc. Arctic Reg.* II. 306 The line-managers, together with the 'skeeman' [*note*, the officer who has the direction of operations conducted in the hold], the cooper, and..a few others, are employed in breaking out the hold.

**skeemish**, obs. or dial. form of SQUEAMISH.

**skeen** (ski:n). Also **skin**, **skyn**. β. **sakeen**, **sakin**. [ad. Tibetan *skyin.*] The Himalayan ibex (*Capra himalayana*).

α. **1825** J. D. Herbert in *Asiatic Researches* XV. 397 A curious animal, which had been killed in hunting and which these people called Skin. **1842** Vigne *Trav. Kashmir* II. 385 Several Skyn or Ibex had been seen. **1867** A. L. Adams *Wand. Naturalist India* 233 The ibex (*Capra himalayana*).. is known to the natives by the names 'skeen' and 'kail'.

β. **1836** *Jrnl. Asiatic Soc. Bengal* V. 242 Capra Ibex? called Sakeen in Kanáwar. **1852** Gray *Catal. Specim. Mammalia Brit. Mus.* III. 150 Capra Himalayana. The Sakeen or Skyn.

**skeen:** see SCHEME *sb.*², SKENE¹.

**skeer**, dial. f. SCARE *v.*; var. of SKERE *a. Obs.*

**skeer**, *v.*¹ Now *dial.* Also 7 **skeere**. [Cf. SKIRR *v.*] *trans.* = SKIRR *v.* 4.

For intransitive uses, current in Somerset and Wiltshire, see the *Eng. Dial. Dict.*

**1636** R. James *Minucius Felix* 8 Children sportfully contending who should skeere shells farthest upon the top of the sea. **1880** *Cornwall Gloss.* 51/1 *Skeer*, to skim a stone on the surface of the water.

**skeer**, *v.*² *dial.* Also **skare**. [a. ON. *skara* (still in Icel., Norw., and Sw. dial.), in the same sense. For the form *skeer* cf. SCARE *v.*] *trans.* To poke out (ashes), clear out (a fire) by poking.

**1674** Ray *N.C. Words* 17 *Skeer the Esse*: Cheshire. Separate the dead ashes from the Embers. **1791–6** Pegge *Derbicisms* Ser. II, *Skare*, 'to skare the fire,' to stir it at the bottom and potter the dust out. **1865–** in dial. glossaries (Derby, Cheshire, Sheffield).

**skeer-devil**, variant of SCARE-DEVIL 2.

**skeery**, variant of SCARY *a.*

**skeesicks**, var. SKEEZICKS.

†**skeet**, *adv.* and *a. Obs.* Forms: 3–5 **sket** (4 **schet**, **skette**, 4–5 **skit**), 4–5 **skete** (4 **schete**, **sckete**), **skeet** (5 **skeete**). [a. ON. *skjótt* (Icel. *skjótt*, Norw. *skjott*; MSw. *skót*, *skyt*, *skit*) quickly, neut. of *skjótr* (Icel. *skjótur*, Norw. *skjot*; MSw. *skioter*, *skiuter*) swift, quick, related to ON. *skjóta*, = OE. *scéotan* to shoot. The corresponding OE. adj. *scéot* occurs once, with the variant *ʒescéot*.]

**A.** *adv.* **1.** Quickly, hastily, immediately.

Very common in metrical texts *c* 1300–1400.

*c* **1200** Ormin 1266 ʒiff þu..ʒeornesst tatt tu mote sket Uppcumenn inntill heoffne. *a* **1300** *Havelok* 1960 Mi dore he broken up ful sket, And wolde me binden hond and fet. **13..** *Coer de L.* 5488 (W.), The ryche Sawdon, al so skete, A noble clerk he sente for thenne. **13..** *E.E. Allit. P.* C. 195 Þenne ascryed þay hym sckete, & asked ful loude [etc.]. *c* **1400** *St. Alexius* (Laud 622) 493 Þe sergeauntz stirten out skeet, Þai founden hym, & kisten his feet. *c* **1460** *Towneley Myst.* vii. 221 Thay were dampned, sone and skete, Vnto the pyne of hell.

**2.** Readily, easily. *rare.*

*c* **1200** Ormin 2900 Forr mann maʒʒ sket to soffte ben ʒæn þa þatt Drihhtin wraþþenn. *Ibid.* 4716.

**B.** *adj.* Swift, active.

*c* **1400** *Destr. Troy* 13434 This Askathes, the skathill, had sket sones thre. *Ibid.* 13672 Ascatus þe skete, for skath of his sones, Miche water he weppit.

Hence †'**skeetly** *adv. Obs.*⁻¹

*a* **1400–50** *Alexander* 5040 Þen bownes agayn þe bald kyng, baldly he wepis, Þat he so skitly suld skifte.

**skeet** (ski:t), *sb.*¹ Also 5 **skete**, 9 **skeat**. [Of obscure origin.] A long-handled scoop or shovel; in later use *Naut.* (see quots. 1769, 1846). Also *fig.*

*c* **1440** *Jacob's Well* 168 A skete is opyn a-forn, redy to deluyn in-to þe nesch wose, & redy to delyuere it out. A skete also sumdel, in þe heuyd, is raysed & reryd on bothe sydes... Also a skete hath a long handle. *Ibid.* 178 Lo, how þis skeet of perfyʒt sorwe sauyd þe chanoun fro wordly schame. **1662** *Ir. Stat. at Large* (1765) II. 465 Skeets for whitsters, the skeet 1ˢ. **1719** De Foe *Crusoe* II. (Globe) 476 That the Men in the Boats might be ready with Skeets and Buckets to put out any Fire these Savages might endeavour to fix to the Outside of the Ship. **1750** Blanckley *Naval Expos.* 152 Skeets are for weting Yachts Sails, or the Ship's Sides. **1769** Falconer *Dict. Marine* (1780), *Skeet*, a..long scoop..used to wet the decks and sides of a ship in hot weather... This instrument..is also employed in small vessels to wet the sails, to render them more..efficacious in light breezes. **1846** A. Young *Naut. Dict.* 284 *Skeet*, a piece of wood or iron with a groove in it, used for throwing water over the planks of a ship's sides. **1885** Lady Brassey *The Trades* 13 A man stood on the gunwale throwing water into the sail with a long-handled metal 'skeet'.

Hence **skeet** *v.*¹ *trans.*, to throw (water) over sails, etc., with a skeet; to wet (sails) in this way; '**skeeting** *vbl. sb.*¹

**1885** Lady Brassey *The Trades* 17 The men on board still 'skeeting' the water on to the sails. **1890** *Outing* XXIV. 470/2 Our British-made sails were..kept decently flat only by drenching the luffs with water, a process called 'skeating'.

**skeet** (ski:t), *sb.*² orig. *U.S.* [Proposed for the name of the sport (see quot. 1926) as an 'old' form of SHOOT *v.*] A form of clay-pigeon shooting in which targets are projected at a variety of shooting angles in a semicircular range. Also, in some *attrib.* uses (see below), a clay pigeon; so ***to shoot skeet***.

**1926** *National Sportsman* (U.S.) May 18 (*heading*) Skeet, the new sport. *Ibid.*, Since the prize of $100 was offered for the most suitable name for the new shooting sport.., nearly 10,000 suggestions have been received... After careful consideration, the name that seemed to apply itself the best was '*skeet*', a very old form of our present word 'shoot'... Mrs. Gertrude Hurlbutt, Dayton, Montana, sent in the suggestion. **1931** *Daily Progress* (Charlottesville, Va.) 26 Oct. 3/2 Skeets [*sic*] is unlike regular trap-shooting in that the birds come from oppositely located houses and that, in one position two birds come at once. **1931** L. B. Smith (*title*) Better trapshooting. With a section on skeet. **1939** *Country Life* 11 Feb. p. xxi/3 (Advt.), Clay bird shooting.—Practice and Coaching; every flight imitated; skeet; automatic traps. **1955** R. Churchill *Game Shooting* III. i. 173 In 1927, I myself introduced the game of skeet to England. **1976** *Webster's Sports Dict.* 395/1 A round of skeet consists of 25 shots. **1979** R. Jaffe *Class Reunion* II. ii. 139 He liked to dance, play golf, drink, shoot skeet, and laugh.

**b.** *attrib.* and *Comb.*, as ***skeet championship***, ***contest***, ***ground***, ***gun***, ***match***, ***range***, ***shoot***, ***shooter***, ***shooting***.

**1942** *Tee Emm* (Air Ministry) II. 75 He has won the *Skeet championship several times. **1975** *Oxf. Compan. Sports & Games* 927/1 The first U.S. national skeet championships were held in 1935. **1952** *Times* 14 July 5/5 Colonel C. T. Edwinson..won the *skeet (clay pigeon) contest in the world shooting championships here yesterday. **1926** *National Sportsman* (U.S.) Sept. 22 (*heading*) News from the *skeet grounds. **1975** *Oxf. Compan. Sports & Games* 925/2 On a skeet ground layout there are two spring-release traps. **1976** *Shooting Times & Country Mag.* 9–15 Dec. 5/1 (Advt.), David Price..can testify to the suitability of his Miroku 800SW *Skeet gun for game shooting. **1970** *Cape Times* 28 Oct. 24/4 Evgeny Petrov, of Russia, set an unofficial world record here, breaking 200 straight targets in the International *skeet match of the world shooting championships here. **1942** *Tee Emm* (Air Ministry) II. 75 We had an article on Training with Clay Targets and the *Skeet Range in our April, 1942, issue. **1970** G. Jackson *Let.* 21 May in *Soledad Brother* (1971) 255 Quietly..I would have my fronts open as many skeet, trap, rifle, and pistol ranges as I could rent space for in and around the black community. **1926** *National Sportsman* (U.S.) June 18 A group of about twenty good sportsmen in the town of Maynard, Mass. held their first *skeet shoot. **1959** *Times* 1 Aug. 9/5 In addition to tests which simulate the different types of game-shooting, 'skeet' and 'down the line' shoots are held. **1926** *National Sportsman* (U.S.) June 18 If the *skeet shooter were in hot competition..he would probably choose small shot. **1967** *Boston Sunday Herald* 26 Mar. VI. 6/5 A rifle range for the skeet shooter. **1926** *National Sportsman* (U.S.) May 19/2 (Advt.), The Western Practice Trap is ideal for '*Skeet' shooting, or for any kind of shotgun practice. **1971** *Courier-Mail* (Brisbane) 11 June 7/3 Winner..was Graham Bailey, ..who took the final of the Winchester Australia skeet shooting championship at the Belmont range.

Hence '**skeeting** *vbl. sb.*², participating in the sport of skeet, skeet shooting.

**1926** *National Sportsman* (U.S.) May 18/2 It is as easy to say *skeet*, *skeeting*, *skeeter* as it is to say shoot, shooting, shooter. *Ibid.* Sept. 22/3 The game of *skeeting* is just like a ball game. *Ibid.*, Hunt's Club and *skeeting* field is a public place. **1968** *Daily Mail* 23 Oct. 16/7 Skeeting is a precise form of shooting which is in the Olympic Games for the first time.

**skeet**, *v.*¹: see SKEET *sb.*¹

**skeet** (ski:t), *v.*² *dial.* [Alteration of (esp. *U.S.*) SCOOT *v.* or (esp. *Sc.*) SKITE *v.*² or SKATE *v.*]

**1.** *intr.* To move swiftly; to hurry; to run. Usu. with advbs.

**1838** J. C. Neal *Charcoal Sk.* 97 You must skeete, even if you have to cut high-dutchers with your irons loose. *a* **1855** J. F. Kelly *Humors of Falconbridge* (1856) 251, I skeeted down them steps into the Common to let off my corked up risibilities. **1861** in L. C. Baker *Hist. U.S. Secret Service* (1867) v. 101 Burn the letter..and then get in your hole and skeet for Dixie. **1877** G. Stewart *Fire-side Tales* 89 Skeet howe hame, guid folk! **1922** JOYCE *Ulysses* 748 That icy wind skeeting across from those mountains. **1924** C. GREER-PETRIE *Angeline of Hill Country* 18 Here comes a mighty impudent lookin' darky a-skeetin' towards us. **1929** L. ROBINSON in *Lett. Sean O'Casey* (1975) I. 358 Johnny Perrin..got married yesterday and skeeted off to Wales for a few days.

**2.** *trans.* To squirt, to eject (fluid). Also *absol.*

**1880** COURTNEY & COUCH *Gloss. Words in Use in Cornwall* 51/2 *Skeet, v.*, to eject saliva through the teeth. **1886** J. J. H. BURGESS *Shetland Sk. & Poems* 114 Every platch 'at he med skeetit it up and doon ower every ane 'at cam' near. **1908** *Dial. Notes* III. 370 *Skeet, v. tr.*, to scoot (water), spew out of the mouth, especially between the teeth. **1912** J. NICOLSON *Hame-Spun* 45, I was skeetit frae head ta foot, sae 'at I'm not onlookin'. **1935** Z. N. HURSTON *Mules & Men* I. iii. 64 Julius spat out into the yard, trying to give the impression that he was skeeting tobacco juice like a man. **1946** C. MCCULLERS *Member of Wedding* I. 48 She loved to ..lightly meddle with their things—with Mrs Marlowe's atomizer which skeeted perfume, the grey-pink powder puff, [etc.].

**'skeeter**, *sb.*[1] Colloq. form (chiefly U.S. and Austr.) of MOSQUITO.

**1839** *Spirit of Times* 21 Dec. 495/2, I was fas asleep, and dreaming dat a big skeeter was a biten me. **1852** MRS. STOWE *Uncle Tom's C.* xx, Miss Feely whip!—wouldn't kill a skeeter, her whippins. **1882** LEES & CLUTTERBUCK *Three in Norway* xvii. 131 In this happy spot the 'skeeter' is unknown. **1893** J. A. BARRY *Steve Brown's Bunyip* 14 Making up the fire, and throwing some green bushes on it to drive the skeeters away.

**skeeter** ('ski:tə(r)), *sb.*[2] [f. SKEET *sb.*[2] + -ER[1].] One who participates in the sport of skeet, a skeet shooter.

**1926** *National Sportsman* (U.S.) May 18/1 From this station Skeeter faces each trap in turn and shoots at the target coming directly over his head. **1968** *Daily Mail* 23 Oct. 16/8 The skeeter loses a point if he fails to destroy the pigeon as it passes invisibly over his head.

**skeeter** ('ski:tə(r)), *v.* Var. SKITTER *v.*[2] 1.

**1964** J. HILLABY *Journey to Jade Sea* 101 Three geese promptly took off, skeetering up into a gust of wind. **1971** C. MCCULLERS in *Redbook* Oct. 196/1 She had one of those grotesque little imaginings... She saw herself and Marshall. .. Skeetering angrily up and down the cold blank glass like minute monkeys. **1972** *Observer* (Colour Suppl.) 23 Apr. 35/4 Fiennes and Stanley Cribbett skeeter through the savage waters of the Bridge River rapids.

†**skeeth**, obs. or erron. f. SHEATH (of a plough).

**1614** MARKHAM *Eng. Husb.* I. i, The head thicke and large, the skeeth broad, strong, and well sloping. *Ibid.*, A slender skeeth.

**skeeze** (ski:z), *v. rare.* [Origin uncertain.] *intr.* ? To peer, to glance obliquely.

**1922** JOYCE *Ulysses* 298 Old Garryowen started growling again at Bloom that was skeezing round the door.—Come in, come on, he won't eat you, says the citizen. *Ibid.* 731 Hes mad on the subject of drawers..always skeezing at those brazenfaced things on the bicycles with their skirts blowing up to their navels.

**skeezicks** ('ski:zɪks). *U.S. slang.* Also **skeesicks, -zacks, -zecks.** [? Fanciful.] A good-for-nothing, a rascal, a rogue. (Now usu. playfully of children.)

**1850** *Frontier Guardian* (Kanesville, Iowa) 2 Oct. 3/5 Though Kister that skeezecks with Hall at his back, Should come again thieving [etc.]. **1869** B. HARTE in *Overland Monthly* June 572/1 Thar aint nobody but him within ten mile of the shanty, and that 'ar d——d old skeesicks knows it. **1875** J. G. HOLLAND *Sevenoaks* iii. 40 If there's anything awful bad..in [the word] Skeezacks—I should say that Tom Buffum was an old Skeezacks. **1908** *Everybody's* Dec. 796/2 This is a poor skeezicks that's got nothing to eat but an onion. **1939** P. A. ROLLINS *Gone Haywire* v. 117 Eb Hawkins, that ol' skeesicks you met on th' railway train an' liked, is th' feller that's acted as th' owners' agent in sellin' rights to your uncle.

**Skeffington's daughter:** see SCAVENGER'S DAUGHTER.

**skefold**, obs. form of SCAFFOLD.

**skeg**, *sb.*[1] Also 6 skeygg, 7 skegge, scegg, 7, 9 skegg. [a. ON. *skegg* (Icel. *skegg*, Norw. *skjegg*, Sw. *skägg*, Da. *skjæg*) beard (of men, also transf. of a ship, of grain, etc.). Sense 2, however, may be directly from Du. *scheg, schegge* (hence G. *schegg, schech*), which represents the same Scand. word.]

**1.** *local.* A species of bearded oat, of inferior quality (see quots.). Also *attrib.* in ***skeg-oat.***

**1598** I. R. *Fitzherbert's Husb.* §14 These [rough oats] are for the most barranest Heath or forrest ground that may be, as in Darbishiere, where they call them Skeyggs, and not Oates. **1607** MARKHAM *Caval.* III. (1617) 18 The Oates being good, sound and full, and not like your Southerne Oates light and empty, which in the North we call skegs. **1794** R. LOWE *Agric. Notts.* 9 It was usual to get five crops running; oats or pease, barley, rye, oats, and lastly skegs. **1804** A. HUNTER *Georgical Ess.* (ed. 4) VI. 259 Upon such land he may profitably obtain a crop of skegs. **1832** WHITE *Notts.* 44 *Skegs*, a species of oats, are the '*Avena stipiformis*' of Linnæus. They grow where nothing else will, and..yield a sweet nourishing food.

*attrib.* **1607** MARKHAM *Caval.* v. (1617) 9 Now there is a fourth kinde of Oate, which is a Skeg-oate, which is a small light naughtie Oate. **1613** —— *Eng. Husb.* I. xvii, The skegge Oate..with a beard at the small end like a wilde Oate.

**2. a.** *Shipbuilding.* (See quots.) Also *attrib.*

*a* **1625** *Nomencl. Navalis* (Harl. MS. 2301), *Skegg*, is that little parte of the Keele which is cutt slaunting, and is lefte a little without the Sternepost. [Hence in Boteler, Phillips (1658), and later Dicts.] **1664** E. BUSHNELL *Shipwright* 21 The little round piece of an Arch, in the Scegg of the Vessell. **1711** *Milit. & Sea Dict.* (ed. 4) s.v., These Skegs are very useless and inconvenient, for they are apt to snap off, and so endanger the Stern-Post. **1846** A. YOUNG *Naut. Dict.* 284 *Skeg-shores*, pieces of plank put up endways under the skeg of a heavy ship, to steady her after part a little at the moment of launching. **1875** KNIGHT *Dict. Mech.* 2193/2 *Skeg*,..a knee which unites and braces the stern-post and keel of a boat.

**b.** *Surfboarding.* The fin of a surfboard.

**1962** T. MASTERS *Surfing Made Easy* 65 *Skeg*, the rudder or fin of a surfboard. **1964** *Sunday Mail Mag.* (Brisbane) 17 May 1 These were the now famous Malibu boards. 10 feet long, and made of balsa, with a fin or skeg for greater control. **1968** *Surfer Mag.* Jan. 73/2 He showed them skeg-first take offs.

**skeg**, *sb.*[2] Now *dial.* Also 7 skegg(e. [Of obscure origin: cf. SCAD[2].] A species of wild plum, esp. the bullace (*Prunus insititia*) or the sloe (*P. spinosa*).

**1601** HOLLAND *Pliny* II. 278 *marg.*, Some take them for Damascen plums, or rather for Bullois, Skegs, or such like wilde Plums. **1611** FLORIO, *Bulloi*, bulloes, slowne, or skegs. **1657** W. COLES *Adam in Eden* cclx, The Sloes and Skegges grow in Hedges and Copses. **1838** HOLLOWAY *Prov. Dict.*, *Skeg*, a wild plum of a reddish colour, growing in hedges. **1851** STERNBERG *Northampt. Dial.*, *Skeg*, the wild damson. *c* **1895** in *Eng. Dial. Dict.* s.v., He laughed at me for calling berries skegs.

*attrib.* **1601** HOLLAND *Pliny* I. 511 That kind of Peaches or Abricots..love better to bee graffed either upon a skeg or wild Plum-stocke, or Quince. *Ibid.* 554 Skeg trees, Brambles, the little wild Bulbous Crow-toes.

†**skeg**, *sb.*[3] *Obs.* In 6 skegg(e. = SKECK *sb.*

**1542** *St. Papers Hen. VIII*, V. 211 His Majeste meaneth not that suche revenge shall procede uppon every skegge or thefte, but uppon a notable rode or hurte. **1545** *Ibid.* 434 Upon the courrage wherof the Scottes shall perchaunce attempt somme skegg upon the frontiers.

**skeg**, *sb.*[4] Now *dial.* Also 7 sceg. [Of obscure origin: the form *skag* is also current in south-western dialects.] (See quot. 1839.)

**1625** J. TAYLOR (Water P.) *Arrant Thiefe* B 4, A nayle, or sceg, by chance his breech did teare. **1839** SIR G. C. LEWIS *Gloss. Heref.*, *Skeg*, the stump of a branch; also a rent in a piece of cloth such as would be made by a stump of a branch.

Hence **skeg** *v. trans.*, to tear (cloth) jaggedly or as with a snag.

**1890-** in dial. glossaries (Glouc., Wilts.).

**skegger** ('skegə(r)). Also 7 skeggar, 8 scegger, 9 scagger. [Of obscure origin.] A young salmon, a samlet; salmon fry.

**1653** WALTON *Angler* vi. 141 There is more than one sort of them [salmon], as namely, a Tecon, and another called in some places a Samlet, or by some, a Skegger. **1658** FRANCK *North. Mem.* (1694) 255 In the South they call him Samlet; but if you step to the West he is better known there by the name of Skeggar. **1661** WALTON *Angler* (ed. 3) vii. 135 Those little Salmons called Skeggers, which abound in many Rivers relating to the sea. **1740** R. BROOKS *Art of Angling* I. iv. 19 The Salmon-Fry, or Scegger, call'd in some Countries a Salmon-Smelt. **1818** J. HASSELL *Rides & Walks round Metrop.* II. 58 There is excellent fly-fishing for a small fish called a scagger. **1836** YARRELL *Brit. Fishes* II. 48 A Salmon or a Skegger in the Thames is now but rarely seen. **1882** DAY *Fishes Gt. Brit.* II. 68 [Salmon] from one to two years old; before it has gone to the sea, it is known as a shed, skegger [etc.].

*attrib.* **1653** WALTON *Angler* iii. 85 A little Trout called a Samlet or Skegger Trout;..these [are] by some taken to be young Salmons.

**skeʒʒren**, var. SKAIR *v. Obs.*

**skeigh** (skix), *a.* and *adv. Sc.* Forms: 6-7 skeich, 9 skiech, skeech; 8 skiegh, 8- skeigh. [Related to OE. *scéoh* shy (= MHG. *schiuhe, schiech-*, G. *scheuch*), but the origin of the *sk-* is not clear: cf. SKEY *a.*]

**A.** *adj.* **1.** Of horses: inclined to shy; skittish, mettlesome, spirited.

**1508** DUNBAR *Tua Mariit Wemen* 357 He is nought skeich, na ʒit sker, na scippis nought on syd. **1513** DOUGLAS *Æneid* XII. vi. 134 Thymetes..Castyn from hys staffage, skeich and hedstrang hors. *c* **1610** SIR J. MELVIL *Memoirs* (Bann. Cl.) 34 My skeich horse ran throw them.., against my will. **1786** BURNS *To Auld Mare* viii, When thou an' I were young an' skiegh,..How thou wad prance, an' snore, an' scriegh, An' tak the road! **1822** SCOTT *Nigel* iv, The loupin here and there of the skeigh brute of a horse. **1891** N. DICKSON *Kirk Beadle* 62 The minister remarked as he saw the mare a little friskier than usual, 'She's a little skiech the day'.

**2.** *transf.* Of persons, esp. women. Hence, shy, coy, disdainful, proud.

*c* **1560** A. SCOTT *Poems* (S.T.S.) xxvii. 34 Quhen scho growis skeich, I byd on beich, To lat hir in the brydill bend. **1568** CHARTERIS *Pref. to Lyndesay's Wks.* Aij b, Now Courteouris cum hidder! Thocht ʒe be skeich, and skip abone the skyis. **1715** RAMSAY *Christ's Kirk Gr.* II. vi, And vow gin she was skeigh And mim that day. **1789** D. DAVIDSON *Seasons* 90 The lasses turned skeigh, man, They hid themsels amang the corn. **1822** *Blackw. Mag.* Jan. 33/2 There's nae need for being sae skeigh on a night like this. **1861** J. BARR *Poems* 235 (E.D.D.), There should be something done anent her, She'll turn ower skeigh.

**B.** *adv.* Proudly, disdainfully.

**1792** BURNS *Duncan Gray* 6 Maggie coost her head fu' high, Looked asklent and unco skiegh. **1813** PICKEN *Poems* I. 153 Wi' guid plain fare we'll leuk fu' skeigh, Haud up our nose fu' bauld, ay.

Hence **skeigh** *v. intr.*, to shy, startle; **'skeighish** *a.*, somewhat skittish.

**1513** DOUGLAS *Æneid* VII. xiii. 152 Harlyt wyth hors that caucht affray And skeichit at ane meirswyne by the way. **1827** W. TAYLOR *Poems* 12 (E.D.D.), The capering skeighish jade Made him owre the rumple fly, In dirt that day.

**skeil(l**, obs. forms of SKEEL.

**skein** (skeɪn), *sb.*[1] Forms: α. 5-7 skeyne, 7- skein. β. 5 skayn(e, 6-7 skaine, 6-8 skain; 6 scayne, 7 sc(h)aine, 8 scain. γ. 6 scan (*Sc.* sc-, skanʒe), skane, 7 scane. δ. 6 sken(e, *Sc.* skenye, -ʒe, 7 skiene, skeane, 9 skean. [ad. OF. *escaigne* (1354 in Godefroy; mod.Picard dial. *écaigne, écagne*), of obscure origin. Cf. med.L. *scagna* (1294 in Du Cange).]

**1. a.** A quantity of thread or yarn, wound to a certain length upon a reel, and usually put up in a kind of loose knot.

A skein of cotton consists of eighty turns of the thread upon a reel fifty-four inches in circumference.

α. *c* **1440** *Promp. Parv.* 457/2 Skeyne, of threde, *filipulum, versofilum.* *a* **1529** SKELTON *E. Rummyng* 310 Some for very nede Layde downe a skeyne of threde, And some a skeyne of yarne. **1619** in Foster *Eng. Factories India* (1906) I. 116 [We] send you two skeynes [of silk] hearewith. **1681** FLAVEL *Right Man's Ref.* 249 Like a ravelled skeyn of silk, so entangled and perplexed. **1704** DE FOE *Giving Alms no Charity*, For every skein of worsted these poor children spin, there must be a skein the less spun by some poor family. **1772** M. CUTLER in *Life*, etc. (1888) I. 39 They spun forty-two and a half skeins of line, worsted, and tow-yarn. **1825** J. NICHOLSON *Operat. Mechanic* 392 The silk is imported into this country thus wound off into skeins. **1884** W. S. B. MCLAREN *Spinning* (ed. 2) 179 Woollen yarn is reckoned in skeins, the scale being based on the number of yards per dram.

β. **1442** in Willis & Clark *Cambridge* (1886) I. 387, xvj Skaynys of grete packethrede. **1486** *Naval Acc. Hen. VII* (1896) 13, vj skaynes of Saile Twyne. **1579** in *Rel. Ant.* I. 255 For 4 scaynes yelow sylke, 6*d.* **1628-9** *Sarum Churchw. Acc.* (ed. Swayne) 313, 2 skaines of silke to sewe y[e] cushin, 2*d.* **1688** HOLME *Armoury* III. xxi. (Roxb.) 253/1 This is an other kind of engine..by which silk skaines or hanks..are vnwound. **1765** *Phil. Trans.* LV. 205 The manufacturers usually distinguish and denominate the fineness, by the number of skains which go to the pound.

γ. **1523** SKELTON *Garl. Laurel* 798 Reche me that skane of tewly sylk. **1527** *Dunmow Churchw. MS.* lf. 6 b, For ii scanys of whyte threde for the copys, iid. **1675** in Wiseman *Surg. Treat.* 300, I kept the Ulcer..open with a Scane of Silk.

δ. **1541** *Acc. Ld. High Treas. Scot.* VIII. 23 Foure skenʒe pakin threid, price xij *d.* **1546** *Yatton Churchw. Acc.* (Som. Rec. Soc.) 159 Payd for a skene of sylke to mend the second cope, ij[d]. **1591** in *Antiquary* XXXII. 79 A sken of black stychinge silke, i *d.* **1622** MABBE tr. *Aleman's Guzman d'Alf.* 54 The Skeane there breaketh soonest, where the Threed is finest. **1649** DAVENANT *Love & Hon.* II. iii, A skeane of brown thread. **1816** SCOTT *Antiq.* i, She sold tape, thread, needles, skeans of worsted.

**b.** *fig.* (esp. with *ravelled, tangled*, etc.).

**1606** SHAKS. *Tr. & Cr.* v. i. 35 Thou idle, immateriall skiene of Sleyd silke. **1625** B. JONSON *Staple of N.* v. ii, My parts depend Vpon the vnwinding this so knotted skeane. **1636** T. COLE in *Ann. Dubrensia* (1877) 39 Detraction will be ready to undoe, And ravell out my skaines, ere they can well Bee stretch't upon the Loome. **1784** COWPER *Task* III. 145 They disentangle from the puzzled skein..The threads of politic and shrewd design. **1797** *Enquirer* I. xi. 95 In the tangled skein of human affairs. **1831** SCOTT *Ct. Rob.* xxxi, The unwinding of the perilous skein of state politics. **1884** *Spectator* 2 Aug. 999/2 The appointment..might introduce order into the confused skein of our policy there. **1932** W. B. YEATS *Words for Music* 26 For love is but a skein unwound Between the dark and dawn. **1935** T. S. ELIOT *Murder in Cathedral* I. 37 You hold the skein: wind, Thomas, wind The thread of eternal life and death. **1939** DYLAN THOMAS *Map of Love* 16, I with a living skein, Tongue and ear in the thread, angle the temple-bound Curl-locked and animal cavepools of spells and bone.

†**c.** A certain length or quantity *of* girth-web made up like a skein. *Obs.*[−1]

**1566** in Hay Fleming *Mary Q. of Scots* (1897) 499 Tuay skenyeis of girdis to bind up the bedde.

**2.** *transf.* **a.** A small cluster or arrangement resembling a skein.

**1687** *Death's Vision* x. (1713) 51 *note* 13 The Glands are found to be nothing but a Clew or Skain of most fine and slender Pipes. **1818** KEATS *Endym.* III. 757 Ah, gentle! 'tis as weak as spider's skein. **1874** T. HARDY *Far fr. Mad. Crowd* I. xxiii. 256 Her red cheeks and lips contrasting lustrously with the mazy skeins of her shadowy hair. **1878** J. MILLER *Songs of Italy* 117 Far And near red lightning in ribbon and skein Did write upon heaven Jehovah's name.

**b.** A flight of wild fowl.

**1851** G. H. KINGSLEY *Sp. & Trav.* (1900) 119 Skeins of wild geese fly clanking over our heads. **1860** WHYTE MELVILLE *Holmby House* I. 53 A skein of wild fowl..were winging their airy flight. **1889** H. M. DOUGHTY *Friesland Meres* 182 Only one skein of geese passed over us.

†**c.** *Cytology.* The chromosomal strands in a cell undergoing mitosis; used *attrib.* to denote the stage of mitosis now known as PROPHASE; = SPIREME. *Obs.*

**1889** *Q. Jrnl. Microsc. Sci.* XXX. 164 The first stage of karyokinesis, the so-called 'dense skein' ('dichter Knäuel'). *Ibid.* 173 Rable says definitely that he has always found the longitudinal splitting of the chromatic threads to be completed at the end of the skein phase. **1904** *Science* 4 Mar. 393/1 No sign of chromatin thread (linin or skein) is apparent.

**3.** *attrib.*, as ***skein-silk***, ***wool***, etc.; ***skein-winder***.

**1764** *Jackson's Oxf. Jrnl.* 17 Mar., Scain and Barrel Pig-Tail, and Shagg Tobaccoes. **1858** SIMMONDS *Dict. Trade*, *Skein-silk Dyer*, a dyer of raw silk. **1868** *Rep. U.S. Commiss. Agric.* (1869) 289 Skein sewing-silk is made of three to ten threads twisted together, and two of these latter doubled. **1875** W. MORRIS in Mackail *Life* (1899) I. 318 A great heap of skein-wool has come for me. **1920** L. HOOPER *Weaving for Beginner* x. 76 A skein winder..is only required if the weft is supplied to the weaver in skeins. **1964** O. G. TOD *Joy of Hand Weaving* (ed. 2) xviii. 87 If winding from a skein, place the skein around an adjustable *skein-winder*.

**skein** (skeɪn), *sb.*[2] Also skain. [ad. Du. *scheen* (MDu. *scheene*), = G. *schiene* in the same senses (see Grimm, s.v.), cognate with SHIN *sb.*[1]]

**1.** A split of osier after being dressed for use in fine basket-work.

**1837** HEBERT *Eng. & Mech. Encycl.* I. 154 The osiers are divided into four parts, lengthways, which are called splits, and these are afterwards reduced to various degrees of fineness, when they are called skeins. **1851–4** *Tomlinson's Cycl. Useful Arts* (1867) I. 109/1 By passing the splits between the two edges, they are reduced to skains. **1875** *Encycl. Brit.* III. 423/1 The skains are frequently smoked and dyed either of dull or brilliant colours.

**2.** *U.S.* A metal head or thimble protecting the spindle of a wooden axle.

**1862** T. HUGHES in Ludlow *Hist. U.S.* 345 One of the free-state settlers went to the blacksmith's shop unarmed, carrying a waggon skein to be repaired. **1875** KNIGHT *Dict. Mech.* 2193/2 The ordinary skein consists of three straps, let into slots in the arm.

**skein** (skeɪn), *v.* Also 8 skain. [f. SKEIN *sb.*[1]] *trans.* To make into skeins. Also *fig.*

**1775** ASH, *Skain*, to wind and make up threads in knots or small parcels. **1864** *Intellect. Obs.* No. 34. 303 The men skeining the cotton. **1899** *Academy* 11 Feb. 184/1 Flax was ....spun into thread, skeined, and bleached in butter milk. **1955** E. BOWEN *World of Love* xi. 219 Water skeined the landscape. **1971** 'D. HALLIDAY' *Dolly & Doctor Bird* v. 62 The Florida coast. Flat land skeined with sheets of flat water.

Hence **skeined** *ppl. a.*; **'skeiner**, one who or that which makes yarn into skeins.

*c* **1885** G. M. HOPKINS *Poems* (1967) 98 Let life, waned, ah let life wind Off her once skeined stained veined variety upon, all on two spools. **1977** P. SCUPHAM *Hinterland* 8 When Vulcan beat new armour out for Rome..Skeined cupids hooded their toy bacchanals. **1921** *Dict. Occup. Terms* (1927) 169/1 *Skeiner* (twine); minds skein or rand machine, which winds finished twine into skeins. *Ibid.* 367/2 *Bundler* (flax and hemp); *skeiner*; puts together necessary number of hanks of yarn to form a bundle. **1931** M. L. DAVIES *Life as we have known It* 74 As a 'skeiner' her work was to separate and twist up the skeins from the 'bond' (on a silk mill). **1969** E. H. PINTO *Treen* 318/2 The niddy-noddy was a combined measure and skeiner.

**skein(e**, var. forms of SKENE[1].

**skeith** (ski:θ), local var. of *skeef* SCAIFE.

**1851** *Jrnl. R. Agric. Soc.* XII. II. 369 The Yorkshire two-horse swing-plough, furnished with a 'skeith' instead of a straight coulter. **1884** *Impl. & Mach. Rev.* 1 Dec. 6727/1 The skeith or wheel-coulter..divides the slice into two parts.

**'skelder**, *v.* *Obs.* exc. *arch.* [A cant term of obscure origin.]

**1.** *intr.* To beg; to live by begging, esp. by passing oneself off as a wounded or disbanded soldier.

**1601** B. JONSON *Poetaster* I. ii, An honest decayed commander, cannot skelder, cheat, nor be seene in a bawdie house, but he shall be straight in one of their wormewood comœdies. **1611** L. BARRY *Ram Alley* I. i, You see how I must skelder for your good. **1633** MARMION *Fine Companion* III. iv, Wandering abroad to skelder for a shilling. **1822** SCOTT *Peveril* xxxviii, Such a wife would save thee from skeldering on the public.

**2.** *trans.* To swindle, cheat, defraud (a person); also, to obtain (money) by cheating.

**1601** B. JONSON *Poetaster* III. iv, A man may skelder yee, now and then, of halfe a dozen shillings, or so. **1609** DEKKER *Gull's Horn Bk.* Wks. (Grosart) II. 246 He shall now and then light vpon some gull..whom he may skelder..of mony. **1822** SCOTT *Nigel* xxxiv, I could not skelder one piece out of them, without risk of hue and cry.

Hence **'skeldering** *vbl. sb.*

**1599** B. JONSON *Ev. Man out of Hum.* Introd., His profession is skeldring and odling. **1602** DEKKER *Satirom.* Wks. 1873 I. 203 If Skeldring fall not to decay, thou shalt flourish. **1606** —— *Seven Deadly Sins* Ded., That art of Skeldring I studie not; I stand vpon stronger Bases.

**'skeldering**, *ppl. a.* *Obs.* exc. *arch.* [f. prec. + -ING[2].] Begging, sponging, swindling.

**1601** B. JONSON *Poetaster* I. i, There was the madde skeldring captaine, with the veluet armes. **1606** DEKKER *Seven Deadly Sins* vi. (Arb.) 41 The Meanie are..skeldring soldiers, and begging schollers. **1611** MIDDLETON & DEKKER *Roaring Girl* v. i, You skeldering varlet! hold, stand. **1822** SCOTT *Nigel* xvii, Such base, skeldering, coistril propositions. **1826** —— *Woodst.* xx, I have lived in a skeldering sort of way myself.

†**skeldock**. *Obs. rare.* Also 7 skaldock, 8 scaldrick. [Obscurely related to KEDLOCK; see also SKELLOCH *sb.*[1]] (See quots.)

**1673** WEDDERBURN *Vocab.* 18 (Jam.), *Rapistrum arvorum*, skaldocks. **1747** R. MAXWELL *Bee-Master* (1750) 71 There are two Sorts of wild Mustard, the one commonly called Skeldocks, the other Runches... Skeldocks yield Yellow, Runches very white Honey. **1791** *Statist. Acc. Scotl.*, *Cramond* I. 217 The long continued use of the town dung has filled the soil full of every kind of annual weeds, particularly..wild mustard, called here scaldricks.

**skeldraik, -drake**: see SCALEDRAKE.

†**skele**. *Obs. rare.* [? ad. OF. *escuele*: see ESQUELE.] A dish or platter.

**13..** *E.E. Allit. P.* B. 1405 When alle segges were þer set, þþen seruyse bygynnes,..Burnes berande þe bredes vpon brode skeles.

**skele**, obs. form of SKEEL *sb.*

**'skelet**. *Obs.* exc. *dial.* Also 6 skelette, 7 scelet. [ad. older F. (16th cent.) *sc-*, *sk-*, *squelete* (also *sch-*, *squelet*, etc.; mod.F. *squelette*), or Gr. σκελετ-ός, -όν: see SKELETON *sb.*]

**1.** A skeleton. Also *fig.*

**1565** COOPER *Thesaurus*, *Forma ossea*,..a skelette. **1603** HOLLAND *Plutarch's Mor.* Explan. Words, *Scelet*..is taken also for a dead carcasse of man or woman, represented with the bones onely, and ligaments. **1621** S. WARD *Life of Faith* 24 For what should I cast away speech vpon scelets and skulles, carnall men I meane. **1707** SIR J. LAUDER *Decis.* Suppl. (1826) IV. 673 The Lords thought this decreet had not so much as the visage and scelet of a decreet. **1720** PENNECUIK *Helicon* (ed. 2) 146 The Skelet now hath got his Breast-Plate on. *a* **1904** in *Eng. Dial. Dict.* (Cornwall), She's nothing but a walking skelet.

†**2.** A mummy. *Obs. rare.*

**1603** HOLLAND *Plutarch's Mor.* 328 To bring in place..at their feasts a Scelet, that is to say, a drie and withered anatomie of a dead man.

**skelet**, obs. form of SKILLET[1].

**skeletal** ('skɛlɪtəl, skɛ'li:təl), *a.* [f. SKELET-ON *sb.* + -AL[1].] **a.** Of or belonging to, forming or formed by, forming part of, or resembling, a skeleton.

**1854** OWEN in *Orr's Circ. Sci.*, *Org. Nat.* I. 168 The skeletal framework..does not go beyond the fibrous stage. **1872** HUMPHRY *Myology* 8 The skeletal formations in the sternal region of the visceral wall.

**b.** ***skeletal muscle***, a muscle attached to and controlling a part of a skeleton or transmitting force to connective tissue sheets, and in most cases under voluntary control; striated muscle other than cardiac muscle.

**1877** M. FOSTER *Physiol.* I. ii. (1879) 37 All the ordinary striated skeletal muscles are connected with nerves. **1936** L. B. AREY *Developmental Anat.* (ed. 3) xiii. 361 With the exception of those muscles of the head and neck which differentiate out of the branchial arches, the skeletal muscles originate from that portion of the mesodermal segment designated a myotome, or muscle plate. **1978** D. R. LAMB *Physiol. of Exercise* ii. 15 The skeletal muscles consume most of the oxygen and require most of the body's blood during heavy exercise. **1982** *Sci. Amer.* June 48/2 It was found that in skeletal and cardiac muscle (which is called striated muscle because of its striped appearance in a micrograph) calcium binds to a protein called troponin *c*.

**c.** ***skeletal soil*** = *lithosol* s.v. LITHO-.

[**1928** *Proc. 1st Internat. Congr. Soil Sci.* IV. 31 [Soils] developing in a normal way..whose profile is imperfect wholly because of lack of time to complete their development have never been given any designation covering them as a whole. They have been designated as *skeleton soils* but this term is not applicable to the group as a whole.] **1932** G. W. ROBINSON *Soils* xvi. 320 Immature skeletal soils are found in the south [of Germany]. **1939** [see *lithosol* s.v. LITHO-]. **1977** J. C. F. TEDROW *Soils of Polar Landscapes* xxii. 568 Ohsumi reviewed the characteristics of the alpine soils in Japan and established four varieties: (1) Alpine grassland soils, (2) Alpine podzols, (3) Alpine wet meadow soils, and (4) Skeletal soils.

**d.** Having or consisting of only a framework or outline; bare, meagre.

**1961** W. BROWN *Bedeviled* 106 Once Dr. Hazel had pieced together this skeletal tale, he notified Captain Brill. **1967** T. KENEALLY *Bring Larks* II. 17 She stood business-like against the skeletal tracery of her master's sick vines. **1967** A. N. SHERWIN-WHITE *Racial Prejudice in Imperial Rome* Pref. p. vii, They have been printed much as delivered, with the addition only of source references, a skeletal bibliography, and translations of most quotations. **1971** *Physics Bull.* Aug. 462/1 Some body can be given to these skeletal facts by an order-of-magnitude calculation.

Hence **'skeletally** *adv.*, as regards the skeleton.

**1956** *Nature* 18 Feb. 342/2 The history of the Amphibia Salientia can readily be traced back to the Jurassic when it appears that, skeletally at least, they were already typical, modern Anura. **1974** *Ibid.* 13 Sept. 137/2 In Detroit.. serum antirachitic activity..was significantly less in symptomatic osteoporotic subjects than in the skeletally normal.

**'skeleto-**, combining form of Gr. σκελετός, -όν, used in a few scientific terms as **skele'togenous** *a.*, producing, or helping to form, a skeleton; **skele'tography**, **skele'tology**, **,skeleto'trophic** *a.* (see quots.).

**1851** DUNGLISON *Med. Dict.*, *Skeletology*,..a treatise on the solid parts of the body. **1876** *Ibid.*, *Skeletography*, a description of the skeleton. **1878** BELL *Gegenbaur's Comp. Anat.* 427 The tissue..which has been called the 'skeletogenous layer' or 'skeletogenous tissue', on account of its relations to the future skeleton. **1883** *Encycl. Brit.* XVI. 634/1 The skeletal and blood-containing and -producing tissues in fact form one..continuous whole, which may be called the skeleto-trophic system of tissues.

**skeleton** ('skɛlɪtən), *sb.* Forms: α. 6–8 sceleton (7 scell-, scal-). β. 7 skelliton (-itan), skelle-, skel(i)ton, skeleten, 7– skeleton. [a. mod.L. *sceleton*, *skeleton*, ad. Gr. σκελετόν (sc. σῶμα), neut. of σκελετός dried up, f. σκέλλειν to dry up. The Gr. masc. form σκελετός also occurs in this sense, whence late L. *sceletus* (Appuleius). Cf. F. *squelette* (see SKELET), Sp. and Pg. *esqueleto*, It. *scheletro*.]

**1. a.** The bones or bony framework of an animal body considered as a whole; also, more generally, the harder (supporting or covering) constituent part of an animal organism.

α. **1578** BANISTER *Hist. Man* Biiij, I haue found some of Galens Sceletons in sundry pointes. *a* **1616** B. JONSON *Masques* Wks. (1616) 966 Whose very sceleton boasts so much worth. **1665** HUBERT *Catal. Rarities* 4 A Scelleton of a little Marmoset. **1688** HOLME *Armoury* II. 408/1 The Scaleton of a Man..is the emblem of Mortality. **1768** CHESELDEN *Anat.* 50 The sceleton of a child twenty months old. *Ibid.* 59 A sceleton of an adult.

β. **1611** COTGR., *Scelete*,..a carkasse whereof nothing is left but the bones, which we call a Skelton, or Skeliton. **1643** SIR T. BROWNE *Relig. Med.* I. §38 By continuall sight of Anatomies, Skeletons, or Cadaverous reliques. **1719** DE FOE *Crusoe* II. (Globe) 338 These poor Wretches look'd like Skeletons. **1756–7** tr. *Keysler's Trav.* (1760) I. 498 At the entrance hang the skeleton and some other parts of a whale. **1836** MACGILLIVRAY *Trav. Humboldt* xix. 279 All the skeletons are bent, and so entire that not a rib or a bone of the fingers or toes is wanting. **1845** GOSSE *Ocean* ii. (1849) 84 Even the muscles [of the crab] becoming detached from skeleton. **1884** DAY *Fishes Gt. Brit.* I. p. xiv, The skeleton or endoskeleton of fishes differs widely in the various orders.

*fig.* **1874** SAYCE *Compar. Philol.* ix. 347 Grammar is not only the skeleton of a language but the very life-blood of it as well.

**b.** ***a skeleton in the closet, cupboard***, etc.: A secret source of shame or pain to a family or person.

Brought into literary use by Thackeray, but known to have been current at an earlier date.

**1845** THACKERAY *Punch in the East* Wks. 1886 XXVI. 112 There is a skeleton in every house. **1855** —— *Newcomes* lv, Some particulars regarding the Newcome family, which will show us that they have a skeleton or two in *their* closets, as well as their neighbours. **1859** W. COLLINS *Q. of Hearts* (1875) 62 Our family had a skeleton in the cupboard. **1881** E. J. WORBOISE *Sissie* ix, She regretted having ever unveiled for her benefit the family skeleton. **1883** *Harper's Mag.* Dec. 51/1 A household that..possessed no closeted skeleton.

**c.** ***a skeleton at the feast*** (or ***banquet***), a reminder of serious or saddening things in the midst of enjoyment; a source of gloom or depression.

An allusion to the practice of the ancient Egyptians, as recorded by Plutarch in his *Moralia*.

**1857** G. A. LAWRENCE *Guy Livingstone* iii. 18 The skeleton of ennui sat at these dreary feasts; and it was not even crowned with roses. **1893** VIZETELLY *Glances Back* I. iv. 86 He was..the general skeleton at all banquets. **1896** MRS. HUNGERFORD *Lonely Girl* xiv, To give him leisure to act the skeleton at the feast.

**d.** *Hist.* A member of a 'skeleton army' (see sense 7 d below).

**1882** *Eastern Post* 4 Nov. 3/3 There was nothing to fear from the latest born army; there would be 'skeletons' enough in it. **1950** R. SANDALL *Hist. Salvation Army* xxxiii. 196 The police..dispersed the 'skeletons'. **1981** C. SCOTT *Heavenly Witch* viii. 120 The Judge of Assize..condemned the Skeletons as the aggressive party.

**2. a.** *transf.* A very thin, lean, or emaciated person or animal.

**1629** MASSINGER *Picture* III. i, Who haue we heere? What skelliton's this?..A Ghost! or the image of famine! **1649** J. TAYLOR (Water P.) *Wand. West* 2, I gave 2s. 6d. for the hire of the Skelliton or Anatomy of a Beast to carry me ten miles. **1699** BENTLEY *Phal.* iii. 65 He came out half starved, a mere Sceleton. **1715** J. CHAPPELOW *Right way Rich* (1717) 55 We are become an army of mere skellitons. **1797–1805** S. & HT. LEE *Canterb. T.* II. 213 The sad sense of impending evil.. wore him down to a skeleton. **1819** BYRON *Juan* II. cii, A mother had not known her son Amidst the skeletons of that gaunt crew. **1847** W. E. FORSTER in Reid *Life* (1888) I. vi. 193 Men gaunt skeletons; women in cabins too weak to stand.

**b.** *fig.* A mere outline; a thing having a bare, meagre, unattractive character.

**1607** BREWER *Lingua* III. ii, Such a Rawbond Skelton as Memory. **1642** LD. BROOKE *Disc. Episc.* Ep. Ded. 3 How much lesse then, when presented only in a bare and naked Sceleton? *c* **1685** BURNET *Own Time* Suppl. (1902) I. 3 He laid all the Scriptures relating to any point together, but it was but a skeleton of bones. **1857** RUSKIN *Arrows of Chace* (1880) I. 49 The systems [men] learn are nothing but skeletons to them. **1878** STUBBS *Const. Hist.* III. xx. 376 Scarcely a skeleton of the proceedings of the earlier sessions.

**3. a.** The supporting framework of anything, as of buildings, etc.

*a* **1658** CLEVELAND *Wks.* (1687) 32 So by an Abbey's Skeleton of late I heard an Eccho supererogate. **1688** HOLME *Armoury* III. 109/2 *Carcase*, is (as it were) the Skeleton or Frame of an House new raised. **1759** MILLS tr. *Duhamel's Husb.* I. iii. (1762) 5 The plant would indeed die..: without earth, not even a skeleton of it would remain. **1792** in Picton *L'pool Munic. Rec.* II. 266 The Skeleton or Carpentry of the Dome. **1817** J. BRADBURY *Trav. Amer.* 48 We noticed this day the skeleton or frame of a skin canoe. **1857** MILLER *Elem. Chem.*, *Org.* xiii. 727 The obvious use of the saline matters is to furnish a skeleton or support for the plant. **1880** HAUGHTON *Phys. Geogr.* iv. 168 The mountain chains which form the skeleton of Europasia.

**b.** *Chem.* The basic atomic framework of a molecule, disregarding substituents (and sometimes also side chains or bond type).

**1907** J. B. COHEN *Org. Chem. Adv. Students* I. xiii. 472 It will be at once perceived how very large a number of possible menthadienes can be derived from these two skeleton structures. **1910** *Jrnl. Physiol.* XLI. 29 The carbon-skeleton of β-phenylethylamine is..identical with that of adrenine. **1926** [see *isoprene unit*]. **1956** I. L. FINAR *Org. Chem.* II. viii. 310 The nature of the sesquiterpene skeleton is also characterised by the number of double bonds present in the molecule. **1975** *Jrnl. Chem. Soc. Dalton Trans.* 31/1 Internal vibrations of nitrate, the imidazole ligands.., and the $ML_6$ skeleton.

**4. a.** The bare outlines or main features, the most necessary elements, *of* something.

**1647** *Case of Kingdom* 2 The bare bones, the very Skeleton of a Monarchie. *a* **1661** FULLER *Worthies* I. (1662) 2 This bare Sceleton of Time, Place, and Person, must be fleshed with some pleasant passages. **1721** AMHERST *Terræ Fil.* No. 42. 222 They have the skeletons of all the arts or sciences, in which they are to be examined. **1765** BLACKSTONE *Comm.* I. 175 Being indeed only the sceleton of the bill. **1796** MME. D'ARBLAY *Lett.* 10 July, What did you write of it here?.. Did you finish any part? or only form the skeleton? **1836** H. ROGERS *J. Howe* ii. 27 It may be useful..to look even on the skeleton of the Scriptures. **1858** HAWTHORNE *Fr. & It. Note-bks.* I. 164 The sterner features remain, the skeleton of thought.

**b.** The outlines, plan, or scheme of a sermon.

**1724** R. WODROW *Life of J. Wodrow* (1828) 125 He took in the performances he termed skeletons. *c* **1799** J. BUNTING in *Life* (1859) I. vii. 102 My stock of skeletons is yet so small, that I should find it difficult..to avoid sameness and repetition. **1808** SIMEON (*title*), Helps to Composition: or, Six hundred skeletons of sermons.

**5.** *Mil.* The small number of men (and officers) representing a regiment which is far short of its full strength. (Cf. 7 c).

**1802** JAMES *Milit. Dict., Skeleton*,..frequently applied to regiments..extremely reduced in their number of men. **1812** *Ann. Reg., Chron.* 77 Having on board part of the skeleton of the 16th regiment of foot,..consisting of 10 officers, and 62 rank and file. **1837** COL. THOMPSON in Barrow *Mirr. Parl.* III. 1805/2 A fat soldier..said, 'I am the skeleton of the 101st regiment'. **1867** SMYTH *Sailor's Word-bk.* 628 *Skeleton of a Regiment*, its principal officers and staff. **1876** VOYLE & STEVENSON *Milit. Dict.* 387/2.

**6.** *ellipt.* **a.** *pl.* A skeleton suit.

**1879** MRS. EWING *Jackanapes* iii, It was when he had just been put into Skeletons (frocks never suited him).

**b.** A skeleton key.

**1884** *Times* (weekly ed.) 24 Oct. 8/1, 300 implements for house-breaking,..skeletons and other keys.

**c.** A skeleton toboggan.

**1904** *Field* 6 Feb. 204/1 There were sixteen entries on skeletons... Eight skeletons (four gentlemen and four ladies) ran in the second heat.

**d.** A skeleton forme.

**1938** F. T. BOWERS in *Library* XIX. 315 When the term skeleton is used it will indicate the imposed cross-bars, furniture, and running-titles of a forme. **1950** *Studies in Bibliography* III. 246 The first five sheets of the play were printed with three skeletons used in a pattern some-what different from that in *Lear*. **1978** *Studies in Eng. Lit.: Eng. Number* (Tokyo) 22 Skeleton II was used for the outer forme of sheets B, C, D.

**7.** *attrib.* That is, or has the character of, a skeleton:

**a.** In sense 1, as *skeleton-chief*, *-hand*, etc.

**1811** SHELLEY *St. Irvyne* III. xvi, Her skeleton form the dead Nun reared Which dripped with the chill dew of hell. **1831** HOWITT *Seasons* (1837) 288 The plants which waved their broad, white umbels.., like skeleton-trophies of death. **1850** DICKENS *Dav. Copp.* xv, He was high-shouldered and bony;..and had a long lank, skeleton hand. **1894** MRS. DYAN *Man's Keeping* (1899) 82 It was an army of skeletons —a skeleton chief at their head and skeleton horses to bear them onward!

**b.** In sense 4, as *skeleton map*, *note*, *plan*, *sermon* (cf. 4 b), etc.

**1802** JAMES *Milit. Dict.*, Skeleton plan. **1829** I. TAYLOR *Enthus.* viii. 202 The skeleton-machinery of his individual existence. **1830** HERSCHEL *Study Nat. Phil.* 134 The circulation of printed skeleton forms, on various subjects. **1856** DOVE *Logic Chr. Faith* III. §2. 138 Skeleton maps of knowledge. **1864** D. G. MITCHELL *Sev. Stor.* 35, I have but filled in the little skeleton notes in the musty memoranda of travel. **1867** FREEMAN *Norm. Conq.* (1877) I. v. 260 A sort of skeleton biographies of the leading men. **1868** HELPS *Realmah* xvii. (1876) 475 A series of skeleton sermons.

**c.** In sense 5, as *skeleton battalion*, *company*, *crew*, *regiment*, etc. Also, in wider use, applied to any staff, company, etc., of the minimum size for carrying on the work to be done; so *skeleton service*, a service reduced to a bare minimum.

**1778** A. HAMILTON *Wks.* (1886) VII. 546 Owing to the skeleton state of our regiments. **1809** A. HENRY *Trav.* 183 With my skeleton-battalion, therefore, I proceeded to the fort. **1829** BESTE *Mem.* 177 A skeleton regiment, such is the phrase, arrived from the West Indies. **1830** MARRYAT *King's Own* xxxv, To fill up the skeleton ranks of the different Companies. **1833** *Regul. & Instr. Cavalry* II. 38 The Skeleton Squadron will be composed of non-commissioned officers, or privates, with their coverers. **1881** *Daily News* 21 Jan. 5/6 The brigade depot at Chester, consisting of four skeleton companies of the 22nd Regiment. **1914** in W. S. Churchill *World Crisis* (1923) xix. 445 There is only a skeleton force of patrol vessels available on the East Coast. **1925** *Strand Mag.* Sept. 255/2 A skeleton staff were working nervously under the direction of a chartered accountant. **1926** *Times* 6 May 3/1 On the railways skeleton services were run on main and suburban lines, and more trains are promised to-day. **1928** *Daily Mail* 7 Aug. 2/5 The establishment of skeleton air defence formations on the northern coast. **1937** W. H. SAUMAREZ SMITH *Let.* 23 Jan. in *Young Man's Country* (1977) ii. 53 All my officers have gone out to the mofussil..and all the clerks except 6, a mere skeleton staff to keep the work going. **1938** *Sun* (Baltimore) 20 Jan. 6/3 A skeleton crew of 125 men will take the ship to Scotland. **1957** P. KEMP *Mine were of Trouble* ii. 29 Skeleton crews whose task was to train Spaniards in the use of their weapons. **1973** 'I. DRUMMOND' *Jaws of Watchdog* xviii. 255 A skeleton staff was still on duty, juniors, message-takers. **1976** *S. Wales Echo* 25 Nov. 4/2 Buses will not run in Cardiff for three consecutive days over Christmas despite a last-ditch effort to have a skeleton service on one day.

**d.** In miscellaneous uses, as *skeleton ball*, *beam*, *clock*, *dial*, *frame*, *framework*, *key*, etc.; also applied to a vehicle or other conveyance of basic or light construction, as *skeleton bob* [BOB *sb.*[1] 2 e], *brake*, *break* [BREAK *sb.*[2]], *car*, *gig*, *sleigh*, *wagon*; also **skeleton army** *Hist.*, a group of people attempting to disrupt the activities of the Salvation Army or Church Army; **skeleton brass**, a memorial brass representing a skeleton; **skeleton construction** (see quot.); **skeleton drill** *Mil.*, infantry drill for the instruction of officers, in which a small number of men represents a battalion; also *fig.*; **skeleton forme** (see quot. 1972); **skeleton larva**, **shrimp**, **suit** (see quots.); **skeleton weed**, a perennial herb, *Chondrilla juncea*, of the family Compositæ, native to the Mediterranean region and naturalized in Australia, where it is a troublesome weed of cereal crops.

**1881** *War Cry* Christmas No. 6/2 The chief officers of 'The *Skeleton Army', raised to oppose us at Exeter, were converted. **1888** C. M. YONGE *Beechcroft at Rockstone* I. iii. 64 The Salvation Army was marching that way, and..yells and cat-calls behind showed that the Skeleton Army was on its way to meet them. **1920** H. BEGBIE *Life W. Booth* I. xxix. 482 'Skeleton Armies'..set themselves up to break up the processions of the Salvation Army. **1950** R. SANDALL *Hist. Salvation Army* xxxiii. 196 These skeleton armies carried flags usually bearing a skull and crossbones device. **1980** F. K. PROCHASKA *Women & Philanthropy in 19th-Cent. England* vi. 193 A 'Skeleton Army' of rowdies often shadowed volunteers of the Church Army and..pelted them. **1860** *Merc. Mar. Mag.* VII. 125 A new Beacon has been erected.., having a *Skeleton Ball at the top. **1869** RANKINE *Machine & Hand-tools* App. 23 The first case explained will be that of a *skeleton beam, composed of a framework of slender bars of the simplest possible construction. **1954** R. MARTIN *Your Ski Holiday* xiii. 91 Racing on the 'skeleton bob' is a very different affair... The '*skeleton bob' is a steel chassis with two steel runners, about 3 feet long and about 13 inches apart. On this chassis is a sliding seat. **1963** I. FLEMING *On H.M. Secret Service* xii. 133 A little 'garage' that housed the bob-sleighs and one-man skeleton-bobs. **1898** *Carriage Builders' Jrnl.* Nov. p. viii/2 (Advt.), Wanted, Pair-horse *Skeleton Brake. **1935** *Automobile & Carriage Builders' Jrnl.* Apr. 68/2 The skeleton brake has a high driving seat with the fore and hind carriages connected by a perch only. **1890** H. W. MACKLIN *Monumental Brasses* i. 17 Shroud and *skeleton brasses came into general use. **1956** A. C. BOUQUET *Church Brasses* vii. 147 There is a skeleton brass at Weybridge, Surrey, with three effigies. **1972** R. LE STRANGE *Compl. Descriptive Guide Brit. Monumental Brasses* 9 Between the two, the shroud and skeleton brasses, lay the cadavers. **1974** S. WALROND *Encycl. Driving* 237 *Skeleton Break... This vehicle..was used for breaking and training when a youngster would be put in alongside an older school-master. **1936** *'ABC' Brit. Columbia Lumber Trade Directory* 73 Elco Logging Co. Ltd. .. Three High Leads;..45 *Skeleton Cars. **1942** R. L. HAIG-BROWN *Timber* 253 *Skeleton car*, a railroad car made up of two sets of four wheels joined by a heavy timber across which the steel bunks are set to carry the logs. **1842** FRANCIS *Dict. Arts* s.v., A *skeleton clock is one which is without the usual case, and so fitted up, that the interior wheel-work is visible. **1870** MISS BRIDGMAN *R. Lynne* II. ii. 23 On the mantelpiece was a skeleton-clock. **1891** *Archit. Record* Oct.-Dec. 228 Within the past three or four years a new method of constructing very high buildings in New York has come into vogue. It is known as the *skeleton construction and consists in the use of iron or steel columns, with thin curtain walls between, in place of solid thick brick walls. **1874** MICKLETHWAITE *Mod. Par. Churches* 176 A *skeleton dial of cast iron gilt. **1876** VOYLE & STEVENSON *Military Dict.* 387/2 **Skeleton drill*, which is a method of instructing officers and non-commissioned officers in drill, when a sufficient number of men cannot be collected to form a battalion in single rank. **1897** HARDY *Well-Beloved* III. v. 278 Pierston..could consider, and practise thoroughly a species of skeleton-drill in receiving visitors when the pair should announce themselves as married. **1888** JACOBI *Printers' Vocab.* 126 **Skeleton face*, thin-faced letter used for jobbing purposes. *Ibid.*, **Skeleton forme*, a special forme —usually of a broken and open nature. **1964** F. BOWERS *Bibliogr. & Textual Crit.* I. i. 10 An examination of the running-titles..discloses that the text of the play in sheet B was imposed in two different skeleton-formes. **1972** P. GASKELL *New Introd. Bibliogr.* 109 All these re-usable parts, the typographical parts which left their mark upon the paper, and the chase, quoins, and furniture which did not, are known collectively today as the 'skeleton forme'. **1951** KOESTLER *Age of Longing* iv. 84 Towers of wood and towers of metal, towers which had merely a *skeleton-frame and towers that were panelled in from all sides. **1897** *Building Construction* (new ed.) I. 17 The combination of columns and girders which form the '*skeleton' framework. **1867** 'T. LACKLAND' *Homespun* II. 181 At all hours of the day..a fly, a sulky, or a *skeleton gig could be seen somewhere about the yard. **1974** S. WALROND *Encycl. Driving* 238 *Skeleton gig*, a light gig with a curved open stick-back seat which is suspended by iron stays on two side and one cross-spring. The shafts run outside the bootless body. **1810** *Ann. Reg.* 296 The locks might have been picked with *skeleton-keys. **1842** FRANCIS *Dict. Arts* s.v., Skeleton keys are thin light keys, with almost the whole substance of the bits filed away. **1854** *Pereira's Polarized Light* (ed. 2) 156 The aquatic larvæ of a gnat, commonly called *skeleton larvæ, form a very amusing exhibition. **1839-52** BAILEY *Festus* 194 Distinct.. as is the *skeleton leaf Whose green hath fretted off its fibrous frame. **1861** BENTLEY *Man. Bot.* 147 This double layer..is readily seen in what are called skeleton leaves, namely, those in which the parenchyma between the veins has been destroyed. **1884** F. J. BRITTEN *Watch & Clockm.* 29 A bar movement is sometimes called a '*skeleton' movement. **1803** *Sporting Mag.* XXI. 327 *Skeleton packs are made by taking three or four cards out of the pack. **1897** MARY KINGSLEY *W. Africa* 493 A *skeleton platform which is filled in with withies and made flat. **1833** LOUDON *Encycl. Archit.* §766 A *skeleton roof..is formed of long poles [etc.]. **1882** *Cassell's Nat. Hist.* VI. 212 The popular name of Spectre, or *Skeleton Shrimp, seems very appropriate to *Caprella*. **1902** *Hub* Aug. 172/1 The *skeleton sleigh as seen last winter had a black body, cream gear and black irons. **1955** E. A. COLLARD *Canadian Yesterdays* 232 Next comes a stunner—a skeleton sleigh, red as fire, drawn by a trotter black as coal. **1836-7** DICKENS *Sk. Boz.* (1850) 46 A patched and much-soiled *skeleton suit; one of those straight blue cloth cases in which small boys used to be confined. **1852** *Househ. Wds.* V. 190/1 Those premier pantaloons were snuff-coloured, buttoning over the jacket, and forming, with an extensive shirt frill, what was then called a 'skeleton suit'. **1868** H. WOODRUFF *Trotting Horse Amer.* x. 112 If the race is to be run in harness, it will be advisable to change the sulky for a *skeleton wagon occasionally. **1974** S. WALROND *Encycl. Driving* 238 *Skeleton waggon*, an American four-wheeled single-seat vehicle which was built for racing. **1935** ROSS & TAYLOR in *Agric. Gaz. N.S.W.* XLVI. 16/1 *Skeleton weed is well liked by sheep, especially when it is in the young stages. **1965** *Austral. Encycl.* IX. 225/2 Skeleton weed..is a close relative of the dandelion and chicory, having a spindly habit of growth.

**8.** *Comb.*, as *skeleton-gaunt*, *-producing*, *-strewn* adjs.; *skeleton-wise* adv.

**1888** ROLLESTON & JACKSON *Anim. Life* 726 The skeleton-producing cells appear to be derived from the ectoderm. **1888** *Amer. Jrnl. Psychol.* I. 382 To have pencil and paper at hand and jot down the dream, at least skeletonwise. **1895** SHAND *Life Gen. Hamley* I. iv. 94 On the skeleton-strewn plateau. **1929** W. B. YEATS *Winding Stair* 3 When withered old and skeleton-gaunt.

**'skeleton**, *v.* [f. prec.]

**1.** *trans.* To outline or mark after the manner of a skeleton.

**1861** *Athenæum* 23 Feb. 262/1 The swarthy wood-marge, skeleton'd with snow. **1897** *Daily News* 23 June 15/4 The.. thirty miles of shipping will be skeletoned in lights.

**2.** To construct in outline.

**1880** 'MARK TWAIN' *Tramp Abroad* I. 202 The true Black-Forest novel, if it is ever written, will be skeletoned somewhat in this way. **1883** *Pall Mall G.* 26 Nov. 6/2 He skeletons his act, then clothes it with language.

**3.** To convert into a skeleton.

**1888** *Scientific American* LVIII. 203 A recipe for skeletoning and bleaching leaves.

**'skeletoned**, *ppl. a.* [f. SKELETON *sb.* or *v.*] Reduced to a skeleton; skeletonized.

**1850** S. G. OSBORNE *Gleanings* 53 This little blanched piece of skeletoned humanity. **1891** F. ADAMS *J. Webb's End* 233 The empty, skeletoned hide of a bullock.

**'skeletoness.** *nonce-word.* A female skeleton.

**1840** *P. Parley's Ann.* I. 9 A marvellously lean lady, called the 'living skeletoness'.

**skele'tonian**, *a. rare.* [f. SKELETON *sb.*] Pertaining to or resembling a skeleton; skeletal.

**1801** R. WARDLAW *Let.* in *Life* (1856) iii. 51 The skeletonian method of sermonising. **1879** *Temple Bar* Oct. 258 His skeletonian hands outstretched, his parched lips suing for mercy.

**skeletonic** (skɛlɪ'tɒnɪk), *a.* [f. SKELETON *sb.* + -IC.] = SKELETON *sb.* 7; also, skeleton-like.

**1880** W. S. GILBERT *Pirates of Penzance* II, Take your file and your skeletonic keys. **1883** *Scotsman* 6 Sept. 5/3 In its later days the meetings of the Club became more and more skeletonic. **1897** *Westm. Gaz.* 5 Feb. 5/2 The huge beast will subsequently be preserved in stuffed, skeletonic form.

**skeletonize** ('skɛlɪtənaɪz), *v.* Also 7 skellitonize, 8 sceletonise. [f. SKELETON *sb.* + -IZE.]

**1.** *trans.* To reduce to a skeleton. Also *fig.*

**1644** J. TAYLOR (Water P.) *No Merc. Aulicus* 7 Thus.. I have anatomized and skellitonized your railing Pamphlet. **1720** W. STUKELEY in *Mem.* (1882) I. 32, I likewise sceletonisd several different sorts of birds. **1747** *Gentl. Mag.* XVII. 488/1, I would propose that the bodies..should be made skeletons, and plac'd in..his own proper chaise, which shall be first skeletoniz'd by a coachmaker. **1807** P. GASS *Jrnl.* 246 Captain Lewis had four of those animals skeletonized. **1865** PARRISH (*title*), The Phantom Bouquet: a popular treatise on the art of skeletonizing leaves and seed vessels. **1885** HORNADAY *2 Yrs. Jungle* v. 51 We skinned and skeletonized many a gavial and large bird.

**2.** To draw up in outline; to sketch out.

**1865** MASSON *Rec. Brit. Philos.* 128 We but skeletonize an unknown and unknowable cause in the form of some of its effects. **1882** MOZLEY *Remin.* (ed. 2) I. 75 Long before Simeon was skeletonising our sermons.

*absol.* **1869** SHEDD *Homiletics* iv. 94 This homiletic habit will appear in a disposition to skeletonize.

**3.** *intr.* To become a skeleton.

**1831** *Lincoln Herald* 23 Dec. 3/6 Are our shipwrights skeletonising on air? **1879** *Scribner's Monthly* XIX. 182 His brethren gathered to bear him down, And lay him away to skeletonize.

Hence **,skeletoni'zation**, reduction to a skeleton; **'skeletonized** *ppl. a.*, reduced to a skeleton; drawn up in outline; also, possessing or having developed a skeleton; **'skeletonizer**, an insect which reduces leaves to a skeleton; **'skeletonizing** *vbl. sb.* (also *attrib.*).

**1795** SOUTHEY *Let.* in C. C. Southey *Life* (1849) I. 252 Perhaps the climate may agree with me, and counteract a certain habit of *skeletonisation. **1834** *Gentl. Mag.* CIV. I. 185 The *skeletonized Death, with all the animation of a living person. **1857** TAYLOR *Hist. Antiq. Cupar* 17 The Revolution consigned the skeletonised remains to their present resting place. **1885** SIR P. PERRING *Hard Knots* 215 Yet have we here..a skeletonized sentence, or rather a succession of skeletonized sentences. **1976** *Nature* 29 Jan. 271/1 Some 500 million years ago..all but two of the living phyla that are well skeletonised had already appeared. **1978** *Sci. Amer.* Sept. 108/1 These durable skeletonized invertebrates seem to have one thing in common: they all originally lived on the sea floor rather than burrowing in it. **1891** *Cent. Dict.* s.v., The apple-leaf *skeletonizer, *Pempelia hammondi.* **1869** SHEDD *Homiletics* viii. 186 *note*, *Skeletonizing is to sermonizing what drawing is to painting. **1884** COUES *N. Amer. Birds* 48 Complete skeletonizing of a bird is a special art of some difficulty. **1885** *Athenæum* 14 Nov. 640/2 Observations as to definite layers [in leaves] and the relation of these to the skeletonizing process.

**'skeletonless,** *a.* [f. SKELETON *sb.* + -LESS.] Having no skeleton.

**1883** W. S. KENT in *Fisheries Bahamas* 38 The skeletonless Slime-sponge (*Halisarca Dujardinii*). **1888** *Amer. Nat.* Oct. 894 Its soft and skeletonless body.

**'skeletonly,** *adv. rare*⁻¹. [f. SKELETON *sb.* + -LY².] Like a skeleton.

**1847** MEDWIN *Life Shelley* II. 242 Byron.., at Genoa, had become skeletonly thin.

†**skeletontal,** *a. Obs. rare*⁻¹. In 7 sceletantall. [irreg. f. SKELETON *sb.* + -AL¹.] Skeleton-like.

**1651** BIGGS *New Disp.* ¶192 His sceletantall fabrick appear'd as a pale statue of exanguinality.

**skeletony** ('skɛlɪtənɪ), *a.* [f. SKELETON *sb.* + -Y¹.] Skeleton-like. Also *Comb.*

**1852** M. CAMPBELL in *Mem.* (1877) I. vii. 242 For the first half-hour it [the address] was dry and skeletony. **1860** *All Year Round* No. 38. 280, I was still examining the atrophied arm,..feeling..its dark nails and bent skeletony fingers. **1884** A. PUTNAM *Ten Yrs. Police Judge* xii. 104 The cattle.. were a skeletony-looking herd.

**skeleto-trophic:** see SKELETO-.

**skelett(e,** obs. forms of SKILLET¹, SKELET.

**skelf.** *Sc.* (and *north. dial.*). Also 4–5 skelfe. [prob. ad. Du. or LG. *schelf*, related to SHELF *sb.*] A shelf (see also quot. 1802).

**1396–7** *Durh. Acc. Rolls* (Surtees) 214, j skelfe pro caseo. **1408** *Ibid.* 223, ij skelfes. *c* **1480** HENRYSON *Fables, Town & C. Mouse* xv, Baith cheis and butter vpoun thair skelfis hie. **1725** RAMSAY *Gentle Sheph.* III. ii, On skelfs foregainst the door. **1768** ROSS *Helenore* II. 71 On skelfs a' round the wa's the cogs were set. **1802** FINDLATER *Agric. Peebles* 41 Above it, lying against the slaunt of the roof, is the *skelf*, or frame, containing shelves. **1837** R. P. GILLIES *Recoll. Sir W. Scott* III. ix. 200 The whole of the *skelves* cam to an accident and fell down. **1871** W. ALEXANDER *Johnny Gibb* (1873) 169 He has a hantle o' rael gweed claith upo' yon back skelfs.

**skelȝe,** obs. f. SKAILLIE *Sc.*

**skell.** *north. dial. rare.* [a. ON. *skel*, = OE. *scell* SHELL *sb.*] A shell.

*c* **1330** R. BRUNNE *Chron. Wace* (Rolls) 14683 Luytel notes þey toke, &..dide y[n] þe schelles [*v.r.* skellis] fyr & tunder. *c* **1440** *York Myst.* II. 65 þe see now will I set within..Othir fysch to flet with fyne, sum with skale and sum with skell. **1878** DICKINSON *Cumbld. Gloss.* s.v., Borrowdale nuts hes thin skells.

**skell,** variant of SCALE *sb.*⁴

**skellach** ('skɛləx). *Sc.* Also 7 skelloche. [Alteration of next.] A small bell. Also *attrib.*

**1653** in R. S. Fittis *Eccl. Annals Perth* (1885) 43 On the Skelloche littill Bell, anno dom. 1400. **1851** D. WILSON *Preh. Ann.* II. IV. ix. (1863) 474 The recovery of another iron skellach..which lay buried..alongside a group of stone cists.

**skellam,** var. of SKELM.

**'skellat.** *Sc.* and †*north.* Now *rare.* Forms: 4 skellet, 6– skellat, 9 skellit, skillet, -at. [ad. OF. **eskelette* (*escalete, esqualette*), var. of *eschelette*, etc., dim. of *esquelle, eschelle* (cf. med.Lat. *scella, scilla*, It. *squilla*, Sp. *esquila*, Prov. *esquella*), ad. OHG. *scella, scilla* (MHG. and G. *schelle*), related to the verb *scellan* (G. *schellen*) to sound, resound, ring.]

**1.** A small bell, a hand-bell, used for ecclesiastical purposes, or by a bellman. Also *transf.*, a scolding, railing woman.

Also, 'a sort of iron rattle, used for the same purpose as a hand-bell, for making proclamations on the street' (Jamieson).

**1398–9** *Durh. Acc. Rolls* (Surtees) 268 In j corda de canabo emp. pro skellet, ij *d.* **1500–20** DUNBAR *Poems* xxxiii. 50 Vnto no mess pressit this prelat, For sound of sacring bell nor skellat. *a* **1810** R. TANNAHILL *'Come hame to your lingels'* 5 Guidwife, ye're a skillet, your tongue's just a bell. **1856** J. STRANG *Glasgow & its Clubs* 214 The triple tinkle of his skellat was heard. **1883** R. M. FERGUSSON *Rambling Sk.* 11 The small bell, called the skellat or shrill-toned bell, also called the fire bell, is not hung.

**2.** *attrib.*, as ***skellat-bell, -bellman, -tongue.***

**1578** in R. S. Fittis *Eccl. Annals Perth* (1885) 43 The Assembly ordains..to buy an Tow to the Little Skellet Bell. **1806** J. GRAHAME *Birds of Scot.* 37 Skillet tongue, Shrilly reviling. **1827** W. TAYLOR *Poems* 112 (E.D.D.), Here lies Maggie, a skillat bell,..Rail'd on her neibours air and late. **1864** A. MCKAY *Hist. Kilmarnock* 114 A hand-bell, called the skellat-bell and by some the passing-bell, was rung through the streets.

**skeller** ('skɛlə(r)), *v. north. dial.* [Of obscure origin.] *trans.* To cause to warp, twist, shrivel, or blister, esp. with heat. (Cf. SKELLOW *v.*)

**1691** RAY *N.C. Words* (ed. 2) 63 Skellerd, warpt, cast, become crooked; *Darbish.* **1818** WILBRAHAM *Chesh. Gloss.*, *Skellerd*, crooked, out of the perpendicular. **1828** CARR *Craven Gloss.*, *Skeller*, to warp, to cast. **1876** F. K. ROBINSON *Whitby Gloss.* s.v., It's all skeller'd to one side. **1883** *Almondb. & Huddersf. Gloss.* s.v., Paint blistered with heat is also said to be skellered.

**skellet, -it,** variants of SKILLET¹.

†**skellett.** *Obs.*⁻⁰ (See quot.)

**1688** HOLME *Armoury* III. xxi. (Roxb.) 251/2 He beareth Gules a weavers skellett, Or: wyered Argent... This is part of the Loome and is a long square of wood, made after the maner of an Embrautherers tent to slip up and down.

**'skellied,** *a. Sc.* [Cf. SKELLY *v.*] Squint-eyed; squinting.

**1821** HOGG *Jacobite Relics* Ser. II. 40 There's gentle John, and Jock the slorp, And skellied Jock, and bellied Jock. **1870** J. K. HUNTER *Studies Char.* 257 Willie had a real earnest servant-lass, who was skellied in one eye.

**skelloch** ('skɛləx), *sb.*¹ *Sc.* Also 9 skellach, skellock, skillock. [Obscurely related to *kellock* KEDLOCK: cf. also the earlier SKELDOCK. The Gael. *sgeallag* is prob. from Sc.] Wild mustard, *Sinapis arvensis.* Also, wild radish (Jamieson).

**1743** MAXWELL *Sel. Transact.* 80 This Ground, if it is much dunged, runs excessively to Runches, Skellochs, etc. *c* **1800** H. MACNEILL *Poems* (1844) 55 The skelloch bright 'mang corn sae green. **1817** *Blackw. Mag.* II. 235 He sows his barley early, and it is choked by runches and skelloch. **1871** W. ALEXANDER *Johnny Gibb* (1873) 202 His patches of corn bloomed a bright yellow with the ancient 'skellach'.

**skelloch** ('skɛləx), *sb.*² *Sc.* Also skellock. [Cf. SKELLOCH *v.*] A shrill cry; a scream, shriek.

**1808** JAMIESON, *Skelloch*, a shrill cry, a squawl. **1824** SCOTT *Redgauntlet* let. xi, Bang gaed the knight's pistol, and Hutcheon, that held the ladder, and my gudesire.., hears a loud skelloch. **1894** CROCKETT *Raiders* (ed. 3) 166 Did ye think the bit stot was the Foul Thief himsel' that ye gied that skelloch!

**skelloch** ('skɛləx), *v. Sc.* [prob. imitative.] *intr.* To shriek, yell; to resound shrilly.

**1808** JAMIESON, *To Skelloch*, to cry with a shrill voice. **1819** W. TENNANT *Papistry Storm'd* (1827) 180 [He] skelloch'd at ane awfu' rate, As onie man in sic a state Would do. **1901** G. DOUGLAS *House w. Green Shutters* 124 Her laugh went skelloching up the street.

**skelloche,** obs. variant of SKELLACH.

**skellow,** to warp: variant of SKELLER *v.*

**1888** *Pall Mall G.* 31 Jan., Not without fear and trembling lest the wood should prove perverse and 'skellow'.

**'skellowed,** *ppl. a.* (See quots. and prec.)

**1607** MARKHAM *Caval.* VI. (1617) 56 If it be not iust and euen, but longer or wider one way then another, which of Sadlers is called a skellow'd tree, then it..will hurt a horse. *a* **1796** PEGGE *Derbicisms* Ser. II, *Skellowed*, warped.

**skellum,** var. SKELM.

**'skelly,** *sb.*¹ *Sc. rare.* [Of doubtful origin: cf. Irish *sceilg* reef, rock.] A rock, a skerry.

**1513** DOUGLAS *Æneid* V. iv. 89 On the scherp skelleis, to hir wanhap, [she] Smat with sic fard the airis in flenderis lap. **1819** W. TENNANT *Papistry Storm'd* (1827) 102 The storm that dang him frae the deep, Upon our tangly skellies steep. **1839** T. CHALMERS in Hanna *Mem.* (1852) IV. v. 81 The rocks not high; but having more the character of skellies projecting into the sea.

**skelly** ('skɛlɪ), *sb.*² *north.* Also 8 schell(e)y, 9 skilly. [? f. SKELL *sb.* + -Y.]

**1.** The gwyniad, the fresh-water herring, *Coregonus clupeoides.*

**1740** R. BROOKES *Art of Angling* I. xiii. 40 The Schelley is bred in..Ulles-Water... In shape it is more like a Herring than a Trout. **1787** J. CLARKE *Surv. Lakes Cumbld.* 38 The skelly is remarkable for this, no bait has ever been found which they will take. **1805** DOROTHY WORDSWORTH *Jrnls.* (1897) II. 156 Hundreds of fish were leaping in their prison. They were all of one kind, what are called Skellies. **1899** J. WATSON *Lake District Fisheries* vii. 91 The gwyniad (locally skelly) occurs in Ullswater.

**2.** The chub, *Cyprinus cephalus.*

**1769** PENNANT *Brit. Zool.* III. 268 *note.* **1794** HUTCHINSON *Hist. Cumbld.* I. 33/1 Chub or Skelly... The skelly is plentiful in almost all our rivers. **1836** YARRELL *Brit. Fishes* I. 358 It [the Chub] is the Skelly of Cumberland, so called on account of the large size of its scales. **1894** in *Eng. Dial. Dist.* s.v., That they no longer employ a man to kill skellies, but that the members devote one week to a competition in skelly catching.

**3.** The roach, *Leuciscus rutilus.* [Cf. Da. *skalle.*]

**1846** BROCKETT *N.C. Gloss.* (ed. 3) s.v.

**4.** The dace or dare, *Leuciscus vulgaris.*

**1846** BROCKETT *N.C. Gloss.* (ed. 3) s.v. **1904** in *Eng. Dial. Dict.* s.v., The Petteril skellies were hated of the single-hair trout-fisher.

**skelly** ('skɛlɪ), *v. Sc.* and *north. dial.* Also 8 scalie. [ad. ON. **skjelga* (cf. Norw. *skjegla*), refl. *skjelgask*, f. *skjalgr* (MSw. *skälgh, skielgh*, Norw. *skjegl*), adj., = OHG. *scelah, sceleh* (MHG. *schelch*), OE. *sceolh*, squint, skew.] *intr.* To squint.

Cf. SKELLIED *a.*; the noun and adj. *skelly*, and the comb. *skelly-eyed*, are also in dialect use.

**1776** HERD *Scottish Songs* (ed. 2) II. 171 Sae proud was he o' his Maggie, Tho' she did baith scalie and squint. **1816** SCOTT *Old Mort.* iv, 'It is the very man!' said Bothwell;—'skellies fearfully with one eye?' **1829–** in dial. glossaries (Northumb., Durh., Cumb., Yks.).

**skelm** ('skɛlm), *sb.* and *a.* Also 7 skelum, scellum, schellam, 7– skellum, skelm, 7–9 schellum, 9 skellam, 9– schelm, 20 skilum. For examples attributed to German speakers see SCHELM. [ad. Du. *schelm* ('sxeləm), a. G. *schelm* rascal, devil, pestilence, carcase, etc. (MHG. *schelme*, OHG. *scelmo*): cf. SCHELM. ON. *skelmir*, Da. *skelm*, Sw. *skälm* are from LG.]

**A.** *sb.* **1.** A rascal, scamp, scoundrel, villain. Now *arch.* (except in S. Africa).

**1611** B. JONSON *Coryat's Crudities* Introd. Verses, Going to steal 'em He findeth soure graspes and gripes from a Dutch Skelum. **1663** PEPYS *Diary* 3 Apr., He ripped up Hugh Peters (calling him the execrable skellum). *a* **1693** *Urquhart's Rabelais* III. xlviii. 386 Pander, Knave, Rogue, Skelm, Robber or Thief. **1723** *Trickology* 22 A Piece of Villainy peculiar to a finisht Skellum, or consummated Scoundrel. **1790** BURNS *Tam o' Shanter* 19 She tauld thee weel thou was a skellum, A blethering, blustering, drunken blellum. **1814** SCOTT *Wav.* lxxi, That schellum Malcolm. **1827** *Scenes & Occurrences in Albany & Caffer-Land* ii. 38 The Caffer flew into a violent passion, and said that he was no *schelm*:—that a *schelm* was a man that ought to be strangled. **1858** A. W. DRAYSON *Sporting Scenes* xviii. 314 A thorough Cape 'schelm' would..beat the best English swindler living. **1888** BEVIS CANE *Haunted Tower* 194 What then ye skellum? What then? **1910** D. FAIRBRIDGE *That which hath Been* xxiii. 281 That poor nervous woman called out in Dutch: 'I will open the door, you schelms'. **1916** J. BUCHAN *Greenmantle* iii. 35, I got into German territory all right, and then a *skellum* of an officer came along, and commandeered all my mules. **1939** S. CLOETE *Watch for Dawn* i. 7 A thieving skelm of a Hottentot. **1950** *Cape Argus* 26 July 2/5 There are very few fools in Johannesburg, but a lot of skelms. **1956** E. U. T. HUDDLESTON *Naught for your Comfort* ii. 29 As for Absalom—he is a 'skellum', a 'tsotsi'—the kind of Kaffir who ought to be sjambokked every day: it would teach him sense. **1961** L. VAN DER POST *Heart of Hunter* I. v. 95 'Moren!' he said hoarsely, 'you're more of a skelm than any spirit.' **1976** J. MCCLURE *Rogue Eagle* v. 90 Vorster pardoned that *skelm* who was always breaking out of jail and shooting policemen.

**2.** In S. African use applied to animals.

**1827** G. THOMPSON *Travels in S. Afr.* 467 Both the lion and the saddle had disappeared, and nothing could be found but the horse's clean picked bones. Lucas said he could excuse the schelm for killing the horse. **1850** R. G. CUMMING *Hunter's Life S. Afr.* (1902) 8/2 Move yourselves forward, there, you skellums! **1887** RIDER HAGGARD *Jess* i. 6 But I am glad that you have killed the *skellum* (vicious beast). **1909** P. FITZPATRICK *Jock of Bushveld* 260 The natives told us it was quite useless to follow it up as it was a real 'schelm'. **1939** S. CLOETE *Watch for Dawn* v. 67 'I am not dead,' Kaspar said, having quieted his horse, 'and I do not think anything is broken,..but your horse is a skelm.'

**B.** *attrib.* or as *adj.* Rascally, villainous; sly; untrustworthy; of an animal: vicious, bad-tempered. Chiefly and now only *S. Afr.*

**1673** DRYDEN *Amboyna* I. i, A certain Plot, which I have long been brewing, against these Skellum English. **1801** G. M. THEAL *Records Cape Colony* (1899) IV. 442 Owing to the present hostile disposition of the Skellam Hottentots.., I sent the Euphrosyne with the Dispatch. **1827** *Scenes & Occurrences in Albany & Caffer-Land* vii. 151 Diederik.. determined on shooting it, declaring, that no *schelm* beast should kill his horse. **1828** T. PRINGLE *Ephemerides* 114 'Tis his lair—'tis his voice! from your saddles alight, For the bold skelm-beast is preparing to fight. **1829** C. ROSE *4 Yrs. in S. Africa* 115, I joined a party of Schelm (robber) Hottentots and Kaffers, and we had horses, and arms, and we would attack the boors' houses. **1852** M. B. HUDSON *S. Afr. Frontier Life* I. 16 We had in our drove a most skellum young mare. *c* **1902** I. VAUGHAN *Diary* (1958) 3 Joseph it is my feet that are skelm. They go by themselves, before I know. **1911** L. COHEN *Reminisc. Kimberley* xxiii. 397 'Hi, skilum Pontac!' (crack) 'Ah! you verdompt England!' (crack, whack, bang) and poor England would plunge into the yoke mad with pain and terror. **1972** *Sunday Tribune* (Natal) 25 June 23 You've got to be 'skelm' (sly) when you're working on a project like this.

**skelp,** *sb.*¹ Chiefly *north.* and *Sc.* Also 6 scelpe. [Related to SKELP *v.*¹] A blow, *esp.* one given with the flat of the hand, or with something having a flat surface; a slap or smack; also, the noise made by a blow of this kind.

Also, in East Anglia, a strong kick (cf. the vb.). For other variations of meaning see the *Eng. Dial. Dict.*

*c* **1440** *York Myst.* xxxiii. 35 [He shall be] with schath of skelpys yll scarred. *Ibid.* 370 Fra oure skelpes not scatheles he skyppes. *c* **1460** *Towneley Myst.* iii. 323 Yit for drede of a skelp help well thi dam. *Ibid.* xii. 425 Now, in payn of a skelp This sang thou not lose. *c* **1550** BALE *K. Johan* (Camden) 26 He regardyth no more the pope than he dothe a whelpe. Well lett hym alone, for that wyll I geve hym a scelpe. ? **1555** LYNDESAY *Satyre* 127 (Bann. MS.), I sowld haif revin thame all in raggis, And laid on skelp for skelp. *a* **1600** *Burel's Pilgr.* in Watson *Coll. Sc. Poems* (1709) II. 48 Quhyls luking comfort to resaue, Quhyls luking for a skelp. **1794** BURNS *Contented wi' Little* 3, I gie them a skelp as they're creepin' alang. **1808** JAMIESON s.v., The water is said to come with a *skelp* on a boat, when its shock is sudden and violent. **1823** E. MOOR *Suffolk Words* 352 *Skelp*, a blow. **1833** M. SCOTT *Tom Cringle* xvii, They came crack down on their bottoms with a loud skelp on the seats. **1887** *Schoolmaster* 15 Jan. 104/1 He got two skelps on the side of the head.

*fig.* *a* **1774** R. FERGUSSON *Drink Eclogue* Poems 1789 II. 75 Wi' skelps like this fock sit but seenil down To wether-gammon.

**skelp**, *sb.*[2] Also scelp. [? f. SKELP *v.*[1] 1.]

**1.** A thin narrow plate or flat strip of iron or steel, which by twisting and welding is converted into the barrel of a gun.

**1811** *Patent* (Bradley) No. 3437, The manufacturing of iron skelps (for the making of barrels for fire-arms)..by rollers instead of by forge hammers. **1833** J. HOLLAND *Manuf. Metal* II. 96 When a common musket barrel is made, the maker inserts the thicker end of a skelp in the fire. **1881** GREENER *Gun* 219 He made the barrels by twisting a scelp with bevelled edges round a mandril.

**2.** *attrib.* and *Comb.*, as ***skelp-bender, -bending*** adj., ***-forger, -iron, -twist, -welding***.

**1804** *Aris's Gaz.* (Birmingham) 23 Apr. 3/3 (Advt.), Wanted a good skelp-forger, who has a perfect knowledge of drawing skelps for all kinds of binding, military, and African gun barrels. **1845** *Penny Cycl.* Suppl. I. 672/1 A strike among the skelp-forgers. **1846** GREENER *Sci. Gunnery* 147 A barrel made from threepenny skelp iron. **1853** URE *Dict. Arts* (ed. 4) I. 724 This method has entirely superseded the skelp-welding by hand. **1892** GREENER *Breech-Loader* 4 The cheapest kind of twist barrels is that called scelp twist.

†**skelp**, *a.* *Obs.*[−1] [f. next.] Good for galloping on (cf. SKELPING *vbl. sb.*).

**1607** MARKHAM *Caval.* III. (1617) 30 But if he haue not sweat at all, then you shall vpon some faire skelpe earth gallop him till you make him sweat.

**skelp**, *v.*[1] Chiefly *north.* and *Sc.* Also 5–6 skelpe, 9 scelp. [prob. imitative.]

**1.** *trans.* To strike, beat, slap, smack, in later use *spec.* on the breech.

*a* **1400–50** *Alexander* 1924 Ledis me him hedire, þat I may him skelp with a skorge. *c* **1440** *York Myst.* xxxiii. 338 Skelpe hym with scourges and with skathes hym scorne. **1526** SKELTON *Magnyf.* 2207, I shall skelpe the on the skalpe; lo, seest thou that? **1725** RAMSAY *Gentle Sheph.* v. iii, I'm friends wi' Mause,..Altho' they skelpit me. **1797** BRYDGES *Hom. Trav.* II. 348 Euripylus, who saw them skelp him, Resolved at any rate to help him. **1861** READE *Cloister & H.* lii, Why not take 'em by twos across thy knee, and skelp em till they cry Meculpee? **1888** F. HUME *Madame Midas* I. iii, They should hae been skelped for their idleness.
*absol.* **1837** R. NICOLL *Poems* (1843) 133 She scolds at the lasses, she skelps at the bairns.

**b.** To drive with blows.

**1824** in Mactaggart *Gallovid. Encycl.* 126 Mons Meg we'll drag out, and we'll thunner him down, We'll skelp him to hell. **1861** R. QUINN *Heather Lintie* (1863) 131 My fair opponents skelp me aff. **1876** SMILES *Sc. Natur.* i. 17 A byke was regarded as a glorious capture,..because of the fun the boys had in skelpin' out the bees.

**2.** *E. Anglia.* To kick violently.

*a* **1825** FORBY *Voc. E. Anglia* 303 *Skelp*, to kick with violence. **1895** RYE *E. Angl. Gloss.*

**3.** *intr.* To skip, trip, walk, or run rapidly; to hurry. Also with *it*.

**1721** RAMSAY *Rise & Fall of Stocks* 68 Instead of coach, on foot they skelp it. **1786** BURNS *Holy Fair* ii, Three hizzies, early at the road, Cam skelpan up the way. **1790** —— *Tam o' Shanter* 81 Tam skelpit on thro' dub and mire. **1816** SCOTT *Bl. Dwarf* vi, If he will not take warning,..and no keep skelping about here. **1828** CARR *Craven Gloss.*, *Skelp*, to move quickly, to skelp away. **1902** BELLOC in *Academy* 3 May 453/1 Two hundred leagues and a half Marched I, skelped I, slipped I.

**skelp**, *v.*[2] [? f. SKELP *sb.*[2], or a special use of prec.] *trans.* To beat out into a skelp. Hence **'skelping** *vbl. sb.*[2] (in quot. *attrib.*).

**1803** *Aris's Gaz.* (Birmingham) 26 Dec. 2/4 (Advt.), Lot 1. A forge and mill..recently used as a plating or skelping forge. **1831** J. HOLLAND *Manuf. Metal* I. 139 The sheet, when drawn from the furnace, is skelped upon the floor, or on an iron plate.

**'skelper**[1]. *dial.* [f. SKELP *v.*[1]] One who slaps or smacks; also, a specially large thing or tall person.

**1790** BURNS *To a Gentleman*, etc. 7 That vile doup-skelper, Emperor Joseph. **1790** GROSE *Prov. Gloss.*, *Skelper*, a large thing of any kind. **1854** MISS BAKER *Northampt. Gloss.*, *Skelper*, a tall, lanky youth.

**'skelper**[2]. [f. SKELP *v.*[2]] A hammer used in forging skelps.

**1831** J. HOLLAND *Manuf. Metal* I. 139 Which was formerly done almost exclusively by the forge-hammer or skelper.

**skelpie-limmer.** *Sc.* [f. SKELP *v.*[1]] A jade, hussy.

**1785** BURNS *Halloween* xiv, Ye little Skelpie-limmer's-face! I daur you try sic sportin. **1819** W. TENNANT *Papistry Storm'd* (1827) 13 And brewsters tongues, wi' dads and dabs, Rome's skelpie-limmer thumpet.

**'skelping**, *vbl. sb. dial.* [f. SKELP *v.*[1]] The action of the verb in various senses. Also ***skelping earth*** (see quot. 1607 and cf. SKELP *a.*).

**1607** MARKHAM *Caval.* III. (1617) 29 More, Medow, Heath, greenswarth, or grasse leyes, all of which my countrymen of the North call skelping earths, because a horse may..gallop smoothly thereupon. **1818** SCOTT *Hrt. Midl.* xvii, He must have been a great villain, indeed,..and I wish I had the skelping o' him. **1820** —— *Monast.* iv, I reckon their skelping back and forward..has been a main cause of a' the breach between us and England. **1895** CROCKETT *Men of Moss-Hags* xxxiii, We were but silly boys that needed skelping.

**'skelping**, *ppl. a. dial.* [f. as prec.] That skelps, in various senses; also, big, large, lusty.

**1607** MARKHAM *Caval.* VI. (1617) 3 If the fierce Horse have in his skelping course either upwithes, inwithes, or downewithes. **1785** BURNS *Jolly Beggars* 22 And aye he gies the tozie drab The tither skelpin' kiss. **1787** GROSE *Prov. Gloss.*, *Skelping*, full, bursting, very large. **1828** CARR *Craven Gloss.*, *Skelping*, stout, lusty. 'That's a skelping lass'. **1866** BROGDEN *Prov. Lincs.*, *Skelping*, large or fine.

†**skelt**, *v.* *Obs.* [Of obscure origin.]

**1.** *intr.* To hasten; to be diligent.

**13..** *St. Erkenwolde* 278 in Horstm. *Altengl. Leg.* (1881) 272 For as he [God] says in his sothe,..þe skilfulle & þe vnskathely skeltone ay to me. **13..** *E. E. Allit. P.* B. 1554 Scoleres skelten þeratte þe skyl forto fynde, Bot þer was neuer on so wyse coupe on worde rede.

**2.** *trans.* ? To spread or scatter hurriedly.

**13..** *E.E. Allit. P.* B. 1186 þenne was þe sege sette þe Cete aboute, Skete skarmoch skelt, much skaþe lached. *Ibid.* 1206 Hiȝe skelt was þe askry þe skewes an-vnder.

Hence †**'skelting** *vbl. sb.* *Obs.*

*c* **1400** *Destr. Troy* 1089 The Grekys..Skairen out skoute-wacche for skeltyng of harme. *Ibid.* 6042 With skowte wacche for skathe & skeltyng of harme.

**skelter** ('skɛltə(r)), *v.* [f. the second element in HELTER-SKELTER.] *intr.* To dash along, hurry, rush, scurry.

**1852** R. F. BURTON *Falconry Valley Indus* i. 8 Those that were on the wing began skeltering in headlong flight. **1868** WALLACE *Malay Archip.* 65 Numbers of women skeltered away as I walked through the village. **1899** *Daily News* 24 Nov. 4 They will come skeltering back fast enough.

Hence **'skeltering** *ppl. a.*

**1869** BLACKMORE *Lorna D.* xxii, After the long dry skeltering wind of March.., there had been a fortnight of soft wet.

**skelton**, obs. form of SKELETON.

**Skel'tonian**, *a.* [-IAN.] = SKELTONICAL.

**1867** HALES in H. & Furnivall *Bp. Percy's MS.* I. 211 Some Skeltonian doggrel about the famous fight. **1889** LOWELL *Latest Lit. Ess.* (1891) 139 Did not Skelton borrow his so-called Skeltonian measure from France?

**Skel'tonic**, *a.* and *sb.* [-IC.] **a.** *adj.* = next.

**1843** DYCE in *Skelton's Wks.* I. p. cxxix, A poem called *Philargyrie*..has been frequently mentioned as a 'Skeltonic' composition. **1938** L. MACNEICE *Mod. Poetry* 190 Witness his [*sc.* Auden's] Skeltonic polemic. **1954** C. S. LEWIS *Eng. Lit. in Sixteenth Cent.* I. i. 72 *Pars Prima* is in rough trimeters of Skeltonic type. *Ibid.* ii. 137 There would be no problem if all Skelton's Skeltonic poems had been on this level.

**b.** *sb. pl.* Skeltonical lines. Also *sing.*

**1908** G. SAINTSBURY in *Camb. Hist. English Lit.* II. 212 Irregular octosyllables, sometimes approaching 'Skeltonics'. **1923** A. HUXLEY in *Athenæum* 12 Nov. 655/2 Skelton, whose..variations on the decasyllable are mostly..rough skeltonics. **1936** *N. & Q.* 21 Nov. 362/1 The Skeltonic consists of short verses of two, three or four accents..varying in syllabic content..and rhyming in groups of anything from two to five or more lines at a time. **1954** C. S. LEWIS *Eng. Lit. in Sixteenth Cent.* I. ii. 136 The problem about the source of Skeltonics sinks into insignificance beside the critical problem. **1976** *Times Lit. Suppl.* 12 Mar. 295/3 [Hood's] 'A Public Dinner' catches exactly in its breathless Skeltonics the noise and hurry of the occasion.

**Skeltonical** (skɛl'tɒnɪkəl), *a.* [f. the name *Skelton* (see def.) + -ICAL.] Of verse: Pertaining to, or characteristic of, John Skelton (*c* 1460–1529); consisting of short irregular lines with frequent running on of the same rime.

**1589** in Warton *Hist. Eng. Poetry* xxxiii, A Skeltonicall salutation..Of the Spanish nation. **1601** MUNDAY *Downf. Earl of Hunt.* III. iii. I ij, You fall into your vaine, Of ribble rabble rimes, Skeltonicall. **1630** J. TAYLOR (Water P.) *Wks.* II. 245 A Skeltonicall salutation to those that know how to reade. **1843** DYCE in *Skelton's Wks.* I. p. cvii, Examples of the metre called Skeltonical. *Ibid.* p. cxxix, Which has some Skeltonical lines. *Ibid.*, Various Skeltonical passages. **1873** MORLEY *Eng. Lit.* (1886) 217 This form of verse, which has been called Skeltonical, appeared in the delicately playful *Boke of Phyllyp Sparowe*.

**'Skeltonize**, *v. rare*[−1]. [f. as prec. + -IZE.] *intr.* To compose Skeltonical verse.

**1822** SCOTT *Nigel* v. *motto*, Skelton Skeltonizeth.

**skelum**, obs. form of SKELM *sb.*

**skeluolliche**, obs. form of SKILFULLY.

**'skelvy**, *a. Sc.* [f. SKELF: cf. *shelvy*.] Full of shelves or ledges.

**1787** BURNS *Bruar Water* iv, Here, foaming down the skelvy rocks, In twisting strength I rin.

**skelyng**, obs. f. SKILLING, hut.

**skem(e**, obs. ff. SCHEME, SKIM.

**skemble**, var. of SCAMBLE *v.*

**skemere**, obs. f. SKIMMER *sb.*

†**skemler**, variant of SCAMBLER *Sc.*

**1595** DUNCAN *App. Etym.* (E.D.S.), *Assecla*, a skemler, a page, a lackay.

**skemmel, -il, skemmle**, var. ff. SCAMBLE.

**skemp**, Sc. variant of SCAMP.

**skemting**, variant of SKENTING *Obs.*

**sken**, *v. dial.* [Of obscure origin: perh. related to the stem of ASKANCE.] *intr.* To squint; to give a side-look; to glance.

**1611** COTGR., *Bigle*, skenning, squinting, looking askew, or nine waies at once. *Ibid.*, *Vuarlouque* squinteyed, skenning, askew-looking. **1688** HOLME *Armoury* II. 427/1 *Squint Eyed*, to sken or look awry. **1694** CROWNE *Married Beau* Epil., Then on her cullies she begins to sken; She pats their cheeks, and calls 'em—pretty men. **1781** J. HUTTON *Tour to Caves* (ed. 2) Gloss. 95 *Sken*, to squint. **1818-** in northern and north-midland dialect glossaries, etc. **1861** WAUGH *Birtle Carter's T.* 14 Skens a bit, lass!..He skens ill enough to crack a lookin'-glass.

**skene**[1] (skiːn). Now *Hist.* or *arch.* Forms: α. 6–7 skayne (6 scayne), skaine, 8 skane. β. 6–7 (9) skeyne, 6 skeyn, 6–7 skeine, 7- skein. γ. 6–7, 9 skene (7 skine), 7–8 skeen (7 -e), 9 skien. δ. 6–7 skeane, 7- skean. ε. 8–9 skian. [a. Irish (and Sc.) Gaelic *scian*, *sgian* (genitive *sceine*, *scine*) knife (cf. W. *ysgien*). The α and β forms prob. represent the Gaelic ones with *ei*, and the others those with *ia* or *i*.]

**1.** A form of knife or dagger, in former times one of the chief weapons of the Irish kerns, and also in use among the Scottish Highlanders.

The word was also loosely applied by writers of the 16th and 17th centuries to a dagger or small sword of any kind.

α. **1527** *Will of Bolde* (Somerset Ho.), My blak sattyn doblet, my skayne, & a paire of blak hoses. *a* **1548** HALL *Chron., Hen. V*, 60, xvi. hundreth Ireshmen armed in mayle with dartes and skaynes after the maner of their countrey. **1567** GOLDING *Ovid's Met.* v. 220 Persey thrust him through the hart with Hermes hooked skaine. **1600** HOLLAND *Livy* XXII. xlviii. 461 Short daggers or skaines hidden under their cuirasse and harnesse. **1622** DRAYTON *Poly-olb.* xxii. 1579 For their weapons [they] had but Irish Skaines and Darts. **1735** *Phil. Trans.* XL. 426, I was called to Thomas Conway, who had received a Wound with a Skane or great Knife.

β. **1530** PALSGR. 271/1 Skeyne a knyfe. **1534** WHITINTON *Tullyes Offices* III. (1540) 128 Therof rose bearyng of skeynes and murderers. **1586** J. HOOKER *Hist. Irel.* in *Holinshed* II. 42/2 The bill against the spar, and the sword against the skeine. **1609** HOLLAND *Amm. Marcell.* 431 A certaine shag-haired fellow..drawing out his skeine or short curtle-axe. *a* **1661** FULLER *Worthies, Kent* II. 74 To him all the Irish Nobility made their solemn submission.., laying aside their Girdles, Skeines, and Caps. **1750** CARTE *Hist. Eng.* II. 828 The Irish were armed only with darts and skeins. **1852** MISS YONGE *Cameos* I. xxii. (1877) 160 Melachlin sent with her..sixteen young men armed with skeynes, or long knives. **1872** ELLACOMBE *Bells of Ch.* in *Ch. Bells Devon* vii. 181 They were found in a bog..along with a variety of skeynes, celts, ..and other relics of antiquity.

γ. **1592** KYD *Sol. & Pers.* I. iii. 22 Against the light foote Irish haue I serued, And in my skinne bare tokens of their skenes. **1606** HOLLAND *Sueton.* Annot. 15 Caivs..was stabbed treacherously with a knife or short skeene. **1633** T. STAFFORD *Pac. Hib.* II. xiii. (1821) 143 Whereupon with their skenes they instantly murdered him in the place. *c* **1680** in Somers *Tracts* (1748) II. 254 They kill'd poor Infants,.. tossing some upon their Swords, Skeens, and other Instruments of Cruelty. **1694** MOTTEUX *Rabelais* v. ix. (1737) 34 Poinadoes, Skenes, Penknives, Puncheons. **1821** SCOTT *Kenilw.* xvii, A stout soldier before he was so mangled by the skenes of the Irish clan MacDonough. **1865** KINGSLEY *Herew.* iv, Their black skenes and light darts were no match for the Danish swords and battle-axes. **1895** SIR H. MAXWELL *Duke of Britain* viii. 106 A short skene in his belt.

δ. **1596** SPENSER *State Irel.* Wks. (Globe) 631/2 He may under his mantell goe privilye armed,..carrying his head-peece, his skeane, or pistoll yf he please. **1600** HOLLAND *Livy* VII. Arg. 249 The young man..drew his skeane and forced him to sweare unto him. **1646** VICARS *Parl. Chron.* IV. 163 Inhumane whores, with Skeans or long Irish knives about them. **1690** J. MACKENZIE *Siege London-Derry* 2/2 Not only the Men, but the Women and Boys too began to furnish themselves with skeanes, and half-pikes. **1720** SWIFT *Irish Feast* in Misc. (1735) V. 16 They rise from their Feast, And hot are their Brains, A Cubit at least The Length of their Skeans. **1855** MACAULAY *Hist. Eng.* xii. III. 156 The very women were exhorted by their spiritual directors to carry skeans. **1879** *Cassell's Techn. Educ.* IV. 275/1 The good claymores, the dirks, skeans, and pistols.

ε. **1774** D. GRAHAM *Hist. Reb.* Writ. 1883 I. 135 With durks and skians they fell a sticking. **1878** A. HUME *Antrim Dial.* 23 (E.D.D.), There is no appearance of a skian or any other weapon. **1897** A. LANG *Pickle the Spy* 6 Well knowing that the skian was sharpened for his throat if he were detected.

**2. a.** ***skene-dhu*** [Gael. *sgian dubh* black knife], a small dagger carried by Highlanders (now only as an ornament), frequently thrust into the stocking.

**1819** SCOTT *Let.* in *Lockhart* (1839) III. 353 A very formidable knife which when opened becomes a sort of skene-dhu or dagger. **1874** R. TYRWHITT *Our Sketching Club* 37, I..struck him [a deer] just right with the skean-dhu at the root of the neck. **1897** A. L. HUMPHREYS *Private Libr.* (ed. 2) 16 Some employ mediaeval daggers, or skene dhus, but the edges spoil a book.

**b.** ***skene-ochles, -ochil, -occle*** [Gael. *achlais* armpit]: (see quot. 1754).

**1754** BURT *Lett. N. Scotl.* (1818) II. 119 Some of them carry a sort of knife which they call a skeen-ochles from its being concealed in the sleeve near the arm-pit. **1814** SCOTT *Wav.* xxix, Her ain sell..could..kittle his quarters wi' her *skene-occle*. **1828** —— *F.M. Perth* ii, The skene-occle is an ugly weapon. **1829** HOGG *Sheph. Cal.* xiii, So saying, the beldam plunged a skeinochil into my breast.

**Skene**[2] (ski:n). *Anat.* The name of Alexander Johnston Chalmers *Skene* (1838–1900), Scottish-born U.S. gynæcologist, used in the possessive to designate two small, blind ducts which open into the female urethra and the glands which they drain, homologous to the ducts of the male prostate gland; (described by Skene in 1880).

**1890** BILLINGS *Med. Dict.* II. 543/2 *Skene's tubules*, small blind canals, 3 to 6 mm. in length, lying along the urethra of the female and opening near the meatus. **1910** *Practitioner* Mar. 393 Two of these spots..probably represent the opening of Skene's ducts. **1932** C. J. MILLER *Clin. Gynecol.* ii. 35 The cure of a chronic urethritis cannot be expected while there remains an active infection in Skene's glands. **1963** *Lancet* 5 Jan. 23/2 The urethra is often tender on palpation, and thick yellow mucus can be expressed from Skene's glands.

**skene**, variant of SCHEME *sb.*[2], SKEIN.

**skenis**, var. of ME. *(s)kinnes*: see KIN *sb.*[1] 6 b.

**'skenningly**, *adv. rare*$^{-0}$. [f. SKEN *v.*] With a squint.

**1611** COTGR., *Biglement*, squintingly, skenningly, askew.

**skeno-**: see SCENO-.

†**skent**, *v. Obs.* Also 3 skemt-. [ad. ON. *skemta*, f. *skamm-r* short. For the change of *mt* to *nt* cf. SCANT *a.*] *trans.* To entertain, amuse.

*a* **1250** *Owl & Night.* 449 þe more ich singe þe more ich may & skente hi myd myne songe. *Ibid.* 1085 Ic..sori was for hire sore And skente hi mid myne songe.

Hence †**skenting** (**skemting**) *vbl. sb.*

α. *c* **1200** ORMIN 2165 þatt doþ uss tunnderrstanndenn wel þatt nass ȝho nohht tær ute I skemmtinng & inn idelleȝȝc. *c* **1220** *Bestiary* 434 He bit us..eten & drinken wið unskil, & in ure skemting he doð raðe a foxing.

β. *c* **1205** LAY. 19167 þis iherde þe king þer he læi an skentting. *a* **1250** *Owl & Night.* 446 þe rose..Bit me þat ich schulle singe For hire luue one skentynge. *Ibid.* 532.

**skenus**, var. of ME. *(s)kinnes*: see KIN *sb.*[1] 6 b.

**skenye**, obs. Sc. form of SKEIN *sb.*[1]

**skeo** (skjo:). *Ork.* and *Shetl. dial.* Also 9 skio, skoe. [a. Norw. *skjaa* a shed.] (See quot. *a* 1688.)

**1602** in J. MILL *Diary* (S.H.S.) 181 Sawndie Smyth awner of the skeo. *a* **1688** WALLACE *Orkney* (1693) 93 *Skeos*, little houses built of dry stones without any Morter, that the wind may have free passage through them, in which they dry their fishes and fleshes. **1795** J. MILL *Diary* (S.H.S.) 101 [She] murdered the child and concealed the body in a skeo. **1821** SCOTT *Pirate* xi, He would substitute better houses for the skeoes. *Ibid.* xxix, A deserted *Skio*, or fisherman's hut. **1897** *Shetl. News* 3 July (E.D.D.), The old skoes for preserving meat or vivda in, existed to my time.

*Comb.* **1822** HIBBERT *Descr. Shetl. Isl.* (1891) 259 The tables labouring..under the weight of skeo-dried vivda.

**skeow-ways** (skɪ'aʊweɪz), *adv. Ir. dial.* [f. SKEW *a.* and *adv.* + -WAYS.] = ASKEW *adv.*

**1869** P. KENNEDY *Evenings in Duffrey* xii. 108 Down I flew *Skeow ways* across the river. **1922** JOYCE *Ulysses* 99 Horse looking round at it with his plume skeowways. **1947** P. C. O'NEILL *North-County Dublin Gloss.* xvii. 279 He went skeow-ways down the field.

**skep**, *sb.* Forms: α. 1 sceppe, 4 scep, 4, 7 scepp, 5 scappe, 8 *Sc.* scape; 4–6 skeppe, 5–7 skepp, 4– skep (9 skape, skeb). β. 4–7 skepe, 6 skeipp, 8 scepe. γ. 4, 7 skippe, 5 skyppe, skype, 7– skip (9 skib). [a. ON. *skeppa* (Norw. *skjeppa*, Sw. *skäppa*, Da. *skæppe*) basket, bushel, obscurely related to OS. *scepil*, MLG. and MDu. *schepel* (Du. *schepel*), OHG. *sceffil* (G. *scheffel*), of the same meaning.

In early documents the Eng. word also appears in the Latinized forms *sceppa*, *(e)scheppa*, *eskeppa*, etc.]

**1.** A specific quantify *of* grain, malt, charcoal, etc., being the amount contained in a basket or other vessel of a certain size; a skepful.

α. **1100** in Napier *Contrib. O.E. Lex.* 55 þæt is iii sceppe mealtes & healf sceppe hwæte. *Ibid.*, An sceppe malt & iii hund hlafe. [**1216** *Acc. Exch. K.R.* (Bd. 505 No. 5), Item Brasium pro dominicis. De Penred xviij. schepp[e]. **1225** *Whitby Cartul.* (Surtees) I. 220 Solvere annuatim..sex sceppas pacabilis farinae de avena. **1234** *Pipe Rolls Cumberland & Westm.* (1905) 55 Reddit compotum..de xxxiiij. escheppis et viij. strakes avene. **1353** in *Test. Karleol.* 2 Item..duas eskeppas farinæ, duas eskeppas ordei. **1371** in *York Minster Fabric Rolls* (Surtees) 9 In vj scheppis de charcole emptis.] *c* **1380** WYCLIF *Sel. Wks.* I. 22 He seide he ouȝte an hundrid skippis of corn. þis mesure of corn is more þan a quarter. [**1470–1** *Mem. Ripon* (Surtees) III. 216 Et in ij skeppis carbonum vocatorum charcole.] **1496** *Nottingham Rec.* III. 295 For a skep of light brede. **1523** FITZHERB. *Husb.* §166 Fyue barley loues, wherof was lefte .xii. coffyns or skyppes of fragmentes. **1570** LEVINS *Manip.* 70 *A Skeppe*, a measure of corne. **1669** GURNALL *Chr. in Arm.* lxi. 437/1 And for every skep of sand did he not come upon Gods ground? **1824** *Examiner* 9/1, 3 skeps of vegetables besides potatoes. **1846** J. BAXTER *Libr. Pract. Agric.* (ed. 4) II. 119 A hogshead is then placed by the copper, and one or two skeps of chaff thrown in.

*attrib.* **1859** A. JEFFREY *Roxburghshire* III. vii. 125 The skep measure is said to have been borrowed from the English practice. It contained twelve bushels.

**2.** A basket or hamper, varying in form and use in different localities.

Also, in local use, a coal-scuttle.

α. *a* **1300** *Cursor M.* 4741 Len vs sumquat o þi sede,..Len vs sumquat wit þi scep. *c* **1340** *Nominale* (Skeat) 533 *Bolenge et corbelchon*, Bultyngcloth and skeppe. **1419** *Durh. Acc. Rolls* (Surtees) 228, j skepp de virgis. *c* **1440** *Pallad. on Husb.* III. 209 A better craft is for this besinesse: Let make a skeppe of twygge a foote in brede. **1519** *Maldon* (Essex) B. 160 Oon quarte pott, ii[o] pynt potts, ii[o] skepps to bere malte in. **1573** TUSSER *Husb.* (1878) 35 A pitchfork, a doongfork, seeue, skep and a bin. **1600** HOLLAND *Livy* 46 A great number of people sent thither at once to carrie it away in baskets and skeps. *c* **1680** W. LINNETT in Willis & Clark *Cambridge* (1886) II. 493 Wheelbarrows, skepps, ladders, sieves, and other necessaries. **1787** W. H. MARSHALL *E. Norfolk* (1795) II. 388 *Skep*, a coarse round farm-basket. **1823–** in many dialect glossaries. **1863** MRS. GASKELL *Sylvia's Lovers* (ed. 2) I. 34 The skeps and baskets and three-legged stools were all cleared away. **1893** COZENS-HARDY *Broad Norf.* 37 Bullock-tenders always call their baskets skeps.

*Comb.* *c* **1440** *Promp. Parv.* 457/2 Skeppe makere, *corbio*.

β. *c* **1375** *Sc. Leg. Saints* xviii. (*Egipciane*) 1257 He let hyre se sic met as with hyme had he In a skepe. **1397** in *Finchale Priory Charters* (Surtees) p. cxviii, Item j skepe pro elemosyna. **1483** *Cath. Angl.* 341 A Skepe, *canistrum, cofinus*. **1563** *Wills & Inv. N.C.* (Surtees, 1835) 207 One mavnde, j straw skeipp & j hopper. **1669** WORLIDGE *Syst. Agric.* Gloss., *A Skepe*, or *Scuttel*, a flat and broad Basket, made to carry Corn withal.

γ. **1435** *Tintinhull Church-w. Acc.* (Som. Rec. Soc.) 176 Item pro uno skyppe, iiij[d]. *c* **1460** *Promp. Parv.* (Winch.), Mawnd, skype, *sportula*. **1604** E. G[RIMSTONE] *D'Acosta's Hist. Indies* IV. viii. 231 Mettall..tied together in a cloth in manner of a skippe. **1691** RAY *S. & E.C. Words* 114 A *Skip*.., a Basket, but not to carry in the Hand. **1854** MISS BAKER *Northampt. Gloss.*, *Skip*,..a wicker basket, wider at top than bottom, almost uniformly a bushel measure. **1887** BYRRNE *Heir without Heritage* I. vii. 122 Silky bundles of finished work lay in skips by the side. **1894** *Jrnl. R. Agric. Soc.* June 237 Increased demand for crates, skips, and baskets.

**b.** *Mining.* (See quots. and cf. SKIP *sb.*[2])

**1860** *Mining Gloss.* (ed. 2) 44 *Skep*, or *Skip*, a square box (usually wrought iron) in which the coals are sent up to the pit's mouth. **1883** GRESLEY *Gloss. Coal-m.* 224 *Skep*, a bucket or tub a pit-horse drinks out of.

**3.** A beehive. Also *fig.*

**1494** *Deed* (P.R.O., A 6660), The same Kateryne shall have fre yssve to goo and come to hyr hyve skeppys beyng w[t]in the Meese and Yards. **1585** JAS. I *Ess. Poesie* (Arb.) 45 Euen as they do swarme about their king The hunnie Bees, ..When he delyts furth of the skepps to spring. **1622** MALYNES *Anc. Law-Merch.* 231 The making of conuenient Skepes or Bee-hyues. *a* **1640** J. DAY *Parlt. Bees* (1881) 21 Honey and waxe I will bequeath to build A skep. **1716** *Hist. MSS. Comm., Moray P.* 150 Being informed that your Lady wanted some huny I have caused smoak a scepe. *a* **1774** FERGUSSON *Ode to Bee* Poems (1789) II. 31 Yet thir, alas! are antrin fock That lade their scape wi' winter stock. **1818** SCOTT *Rob Roy* xvii, Andrew..often cast a parting glance upon the *skeps*, as he called the beehives. **1842** BORROW *Bible in Spain* 119 He conducted us to a place where there were several skeps of bees. **1884** *Pall Mall G.* 21 Aug. 2/2 A rustic who keeps his bees in a flat-topped straw skep.

**skep**, *v.* [f. prec.]

**1.** *trans.* To cause (bees) to enter a skep; to hive. Also *fig.*

**1825** in JAMIESON *Suppl.* **1866** G. EASTON *Autobiogr.* (1867) x. 135 Whist! we are skepping the bees. **1891** *Scott. Leader* 21 Oct. 7 If they put a hive over them they would.. have 'skepped' nine-tenths of so-called Liberal Unionists of Scotland.

**2.** *intr.* Of bees: To enter a skep. *rare*$^{-1}$.

**1842** *Dumfries Herald* Oct., Flowers as thick as swarms of bees a-skepping.

Hence **'skepping** *vbl. sb.*

**1883** J. MARTIN *Remin. Old Haddington* 322 The keeping and skeping of bees.

**skepe**, obs. pa. t. SCAPE *v.*

**skepen, -on**, obs. forms of SCHEPEN.

**'skepful**. Also -full. [f. SKEP *sb.* + -FUL[2].] The fill of a skep; as much as a skep will contain. Also *fig.*

*c* **1570** *Durh. Deposit.* (Surtees) 195 She borre one skepfull of sande to the buyldynge of the aulter. *Ibid.*, 2 skepfull of clay. **1832** J. WILSON *Noct. Ambr.* lxii. in *Blackw. Mag.* Sept. 402 Why, the ballads swarm out every morning by the skep-full. **1855** [ROBINSON] *Whitby Gloss.* s.v. *Skep*, The tithes of certain grain were paid to Whitby Monastery in 'Skepfuls', but the specific amount of a skepful does not appear. **1906** *N. & Q.* Ser. x. V. 45/1 A log of wood, a bushel of corn, or a skepful of some farm produce.

†**'skepper**. *Obs.* Also 6 scepper. [f. SKEP *sb.*] A maker of skeps.

**1499** *Nottingham Rec.* III. 300 Edmund Bartlet, skepper. **1527** in *Non-Cycle Myst. Plays* p. xxx, Bagmakers, Sceppers, Wyerdrawers & Cardmakers.

**skepping**, variant of SKIPPING *vbl. sb.*[2]

‖**skepsel** ('skɛpsəl). *S. Afr. colloq.* Also **schepsel**. [Afrikaans *skepsel*, Du. *schepsel*, f. *scheppen* to create.] A creature; freq. used as a derogatory designation for a Black or Coloured person. Also *attrib.* or as *adj.*

**1844** J. BACKHOUSE *Narr. Visit to Mauritius & S. Afr.* xxxiv. 620 The coloured, who are generally styled Heathens, Schepsels, *Creatures*. **1899** B. MITFORD *Weird of Deadly Hollow* 125 Your baas? Confound you, it's my buck. Leave it alone, you schepsel. **1920** R. Y. STORMBERG *Mrs. Pieter de Bruyn* 96 Swartz was called a Hottentot, a Shangaan, a skepsel and a few other elegant compliments, and being a full-blooded and very proud Basuto his eyes rolled at the insult. **1943** J. BURGER *Black Man's Burden* 67 The Boer farmer treats his workers in a kindly and tolerant fashion; he does not refer to them as 'bloody niggers', but as *skepsels*. **1951** P. ABRAHAM *Wild Conquest* I. I. ii. 48 All they are going to do is to stop working for us. So that *skepsel* Johannes says. **1953** M. MURRAY *Fire Raisers* xiv. 131 How can we bring up our children decently when there are skepsels like that about? **1968** K. MCMAGH *Dinner of Herbs* 32 You know how the volk love meat and don't mind where it comes from. Poor skepsels! **1975** W. M. MACMILLAN *My S. Afr. Years* 143 There was I remember one terrible case of a horrible old rascal who sold his step-daughter to a Hottentot. I remember that the *schepsel* was soundly punished.

**skeptic, skeptical**, etc.: see SCEPTIC, etc.

**skepyn**, obs. form of SCHEPEN.

†**sker**. *Obs.*$^{-1}$ [prob. of Scand. origin: cf. Norw. *skjera*, MSw. and Sw. *skära*.] ? A sickle.

? **1340** *Durh. Acc. Rolls* (Surtees) 203, iij bemes pro aratris .., j par de bustyngs. It[em] ij skers, i hacke.

†**sker**, in phr. *o sker*, ? aslant. *Obs.*

*c* **1330** R. BRUNNE *Chron. Wace* (Rolls) 4421 Bot Nemny bar þe scheld o sker, & Iulius smot his swerd ouer fer.

**sker**, obs. or dial. var. SCAR *a.*, SKIRR *v.*

†**skerche**, obs. Sc. form of SCARCE *a.*

**1500–20** DUNBAR *Poems* xli. 5 Be nocht a wreche, nor skerche in ȝour spending.

†**skere**, *a.* and *adv. Obs.* Forms: 3–4 sker (4 scker), 3–5 skere, 4 skeer, 5 *Sc.* skeyr. [a. ON. *skærr* (Norw. *skjær*, Da. *skær*, Sw. *skär*) bright, clean, pure: cf. ME. *scēre*, *schēre* SHEER *a.*]

**A.** *adj.* **1.** Pure, purified; cleansed or free from sin or guilt.

*a* **1225** *Ancr. R.* 350 Whoa is þeonne skerre, & more ut of þe worlde þen beoð pilegrimes? *c* **1275** *Sinners beware* 28 in *O.E. Misc.* 73 Makie we us clene and skere þat we englene ivere Mawe beon o buten ende. *c* **1330** *Amis & Amil.* 843 Darstow into bataile go, Al quite and skere you make? *c* **1395** *Plowman's Tale* 987 Of the bishop he hath powere To soyle men..; His absolucion may make hem skere.

**b.** Const. *of* sin, etc.

*c* **1290** *S. Eng. Leg.* I. 424/140 Ich am her In mi purgatorie, forte ich beo of mine sunnes scker. **13..** *Ibid.* (MS. Bodl. 779) in Herrig's *Archiv* LXXXII. 311/238 [Christ] was bore of þe mayde þat was of sinne skere. **1387** TREVISA *Higden* (Rolls) VI. 203 He schulde be skeer of his synnes.

**2.** Free from injury, harm, or molestation; unhurt, unmolested; also const. *of*. Freq. in ***quit and skere***.

*a* **1225** *Juliana* 50 We schulen sechen efter wrake..þat ne schulen ha beon sker of ure weorre. *c* **1275** *Passion of Our Lord* 372 At eure Muchele feste euervyche yere Schal ich þere gywene kyng lete gon al skere. *c* **1330** R. BRUNNE *Chron. Wace* (Rolls) 7936 þe kyng þankede God þo, þat so quit & sker had lat hym go. *a* **1400** *Lybeaus Disc.* 297 For love of swete Jhesus, Now let us passe skere.

**3.** Destitute, devoid, *of* something.

*c* **1250** *Doomsday* 78 in *O.E. Misc.* 166 Goð awariede gostes, feondes ifere, In-to berninde fur; of blisse ȝe beoþ skere.

**4.** ***Skere Thursday***, = SKIRE THURSDAY. *Sc.* Cf. Norw. *skjær-*, Da. *skær-*, Sw. *skärtorsdag*.

**1498** *Acc. Lord High Treas. Scot.* I. 384 To serue the pur men of thair siluir on Skeyr Thursday at the seruice. **1498** in *Rec. Old Aberdeen* (1899) 15 Nundinas..in Cena Domini ante Pascha vulgariter nuncupata Skeyrthursday.

**B.** *adv.* Quite; entirely; altogether.

*a* **1225** *Leg. Kath.* 867 Al ich forsake her, & cweðe ham al sker up. *c* **1275** *Moral Ode* 159 in *O.E. Misc.* 63 He myhte helle fur..schonye, And lete sker al þes worldes weole. *a* **1400** *Lybeaus Disc.* 1914 Maboun..To-karf that sworde.. A twynne quyt and skere.

†**skere**, *v. Obs.* Also 3 skeren, 4 skeri, -y, sckere, skiere. [Related to prec.: cf. MSw. and Sw. *skära*, MDa. *skiære*, to cleanse, purify, clear (a person), etc.]

**1.** *trans.* To free (a person) from blame or accusation; to acquit (one) *of* a penalty or charge; to clear, exculpate.

*a* **1225** *Ancr. R.* 308 3if þu wreiest þe wel her, God wule unwreien þe þer, and skeren mid alle. *c* **1275** *Fragm. Song* 7 in *O.E. Misc.* 101 He vs skere of þe typing, þat sunfule schulle an-vnderfon. *c* **1400** *Launfal* 795 They seyden..Hyt was long on the quene, and not on Launfal, Therof they gonne hym skere.

**2.** *refl.* To clear (oneself) *of* a charge, etc.

*a* **1250** *Owl & Night.* 1302 Bute hit of wicchecrafte were þar of þu wrecche most þe skere. **13..** *K. Alis.* 3995 (Laud MS.), Of traisoun me wil I skere. *c* **1320** *Pol. Songs* (Camden) 156 Of scathe y wol me skere. *c* **1425** *Seven Sages* (P.) 3398 Bot thou may the fayrer skere Of that thyn sone haves tolde here.

**b.** Without construction, or with clause.

*c* **1275** *Lutel soth Sermun* 85 (Jesus Coll. MS.), Euer heo wule hire skere ne com hire no mon neyh. *c* **1290** *S. Eng. Leg.* I. 99 He tormentede þare-fore manie Men þat ne miȝten heom nouȝt skere. **13..** *K. Alis.* 3998 (Laud MS.), Antiochus seide, 'þou ne miȝth þe skere'.

**c.** To defend or save (oneself).

**1390** GOWER *Conf.* I. 58 In this wise himself he skiereth, So that he hath the wordes weyved And thurgh his Ere is noght deceived. *Ibid.* 175 Sche lieveth noght al that sche hiereth, And thus fulofte hirself sche skiereth.

Hence †**'skering** *vbl. sb. Obs.*

**1297** R. GLOUC. (Rolls) 6885 Ac ȝif..heo hire skeringe do after mi lokinge. *a* **1400** *R. Gloucester's Chron.* (Rolls) 6958 To do my penaunce [MS. a. sckeringe].

**skere**, obs. f. SCARE.

**skerel(e**, varr. of SCARLE *Obs.*

**skerf**: see SCARF *sb.*[2]

**skerl**, var. SCARLE *Obs.*; obs. f. SKIRL *v.*

**skerling**, var. SKIRLING *sb.*

**skerlyt**, obs. form of SCARLET *sb.* and *a.*

‖**skerm** (skɛrm). *South Africa.* Also **skarm**, **scherm**, **schirm**. [Afrikaans *skerm*, a. Du. *scherm*, = G. *schirm* screen, protection.]

**a.** A screen or barrier constructed of brushwood or the like, to serve as a protection for troops, as an ambuscade from which to shoot game, or to prevent cattle from straying. **b.** A temporary dwelling used by nomads.

**1835** A. SMITH *Diary* 4 Nov. (1940) II. 272 Have neither cattle nor chiefs, cut all the hair off, use red clay, have no fixed residence, make skerms under a bush. **1861** C. J. ANDERSSON *Okavango* xxv. 262 A few bushes having been cut down, and a sort of skarm constructed, we both ensconced ourselves at night-fall therein. **1864** T. BAINES *Explor. in S.-W. Afr.* 131 Two or three scherms for night-shooting had been thrown up. **1885** RIDER HAGGARD *Solomon's Mines* iv, We went to work to build a scherm. **1894** E. GLANVILLE *Fair Colonist* xxiv. 186 The gentlemen, you know, will take a tent, and our dining-room will be a skerm. 'Good gracious! what is that?' 'A large canvas drawn over the waggon-top and stretched out to some trees, with canvas sides and an open front.' **1905** *Outlook* 29 July 124/1 With a terrific crash a mob of cattle burst from their scherm of thorns. **1936** C. BIRKBY *Thirstland Treks* x. 118, I saw white men living in *skerms*—huts made of matting laid over frames of thorn-bush boughs. **1943** D. REITZ *No Outspan* 70 Lion roared about our skerm. **1960** *Africa* 4 Oct. 343 It always amuses me to speak of residence when I visualize the nomadic !Kung..building their nest-like grass shelters (scherms) for a stay of a few weeks. **1963** R. LEWCOCK *Early 19th Cent. Architecture in S. Afr.* viii. 137 In the small frontier farmhouses cooking was done in the open air, behind a simple screen shelter, or 'skerm'.

**skermish(e**, etc., obs. ff. SKIRMISH.

**skerre**, obs. f. SCAR *sb.*[1], SCARE *v.*

**skerret, -it**, obs. ff. SKIRRET[1].

**skerrick** (ˈskɛrɪk). Now chiefly *Austral. colloq.* (orig. *dial.*). Also **skerrik**, *Sc.* **skourick**; 9 **scurrick**, **skirrack**, **skirrick**, **skurrick**. [Origin uncertain: cf. SCUDDICK.] †**1.** (See quot.) *Obs.*

**1823** *Grose's Dict. Vulgar T.* (ed. Egan), *Scurrick*, a half-penny. *Cant.*

**2.** A small amount; a small fragment; the slightest bit. Usu. in neg. contexts.

**1825** JAMIESON *Etym. Dict. Sc. Lang.* Suppl. 407/2, I care nae a *skourick*. **1841** R. W. HAMILTON *Nugae Literariae* 359 *Skerrick*, the smallest thing or fraction. 'Not a skerrick remaining.' 'Not worth a skerrick.' **1859** W. DICKINSON *Gloss. Words & Phr. Cumberland* 104 Nay, *aal* nut give a *skurrick* mair. **1863** *Bairnsla Foak's Annual* 14 A son ov hiz woddant gie a skirrick a nowt ta noabdy. **1873** *Halifax Orig. Illuminated Clock Almanack* 11 He cooarted a lass 'at didn't care a skirrack fur him. **1890** J. D. ROBERTSON *Gloss. Dial. & Arch. Words used in County of Gloucester* 135 You shan't use a *scurrick* of anything that belongs to me. **1916** *Bulletin* (Sydney, N.S.W.) 16 Mar. 47/1 Nothing found at all of them? Not a skerrick. **1936** F. CLUNE *Roaming round Darling* xxv. 269 These wadless blokes of the Never-Never have to pay road, car, petrol, State, Federal and Unemployment Relief taxes, and never get a skerrick in exchange. **1947** H. DRAKE-BROCKMAN *Fatal Days* 116 Eddie had rushed off without leaving a skerrick of kindling; he often did. **1962** A. UPFIELD *Will of Tribe* i. 13 'And no tracks ..you said.' 'Not a skerrik of a track.' **1969** D. CLARK *Nobody's Perfect* v. 139 'Any luck?' 'Not a skerrick,' said Green. **1972** *South China Morning Post* 18 Aug. 5/2 The felon was made to pick up every skerrick of refuse. **1977** C. MCCULLOUGH *Thorn Birds* vii. 143 If I had paid you a skerrick of attention it would have been all over Gilly in record time.

†**skerry**, *sb.*[1] *Obs.* Also 6 skerrey. [Of obscure origin.] (See later quots.)

**1540–1** *Will W. Coney* (Somerset Ho.), A little boote otherwyse callyd a Skerrey. **1610** HOLLAND *Camden's Brit.* I. 531 Little punts or boats that will carry but two apeece (which they call Skerries). **1851** STERNBERG *Northampt. Dial.*, *Skerry*, a small boat, formerly much used in the fenny districts. **1861** SMILES *Engineers* I. 25 Islands..to which the Croyland men went in their boats or skerries to milk the cows—the boats being so small that they could carry only two men and their milk-pails.

**skerry** (ˈskɛrɪ), *sb.*[2] [Orkney dial., f. ON. *sker* (Norw. *skjer*, Sw. *skär*, Da. *skær*), whence also Gael. *sgeir*.] A rugged insulated sea-rock or stretch of rocks, covered by the sea at high water or in stormy weather; a reef.

**1. a.** With reference to Scotland, esp. those parts of it formerly under Scandinavian influence.

**1612** *Sc. Acts, Jas. VI* (1816) IV. 481/1 Ony landis, annuel-rentis, Iles, skerreis, holmes..within the erldome of Orknay. **1654** BLAEU *Atlas Scotia* 135 Minimæ partes vocantur Scopuli (vulgari apud Incolas Orcadum nomine Skerries). *a* **1688** T. WALLACE *Descr. Orkney* (1693) 93. **1795** *Statist. Acc. Scot.* XV. 300 Near this Pentland Skerry, there are two or three other skerries or rocks, on which there is not nourishment for any tame living creature. **1805** BARRY *Orkney Islands* 18 There are several [islands] which are overflowed at high water, and have scarcely any soil... These..are called *Skerries*. **1823** SCORESBY *Jrnl. Whale Fish.* 373 The islands, or skerries, which..skirt the forbidding coast on the western side of the Hebrides. **1875** W. MCILWRAITH *Guide Wigtownshire* 62 The rocks stretch seaward in rugged ledges and skerries.

**b.** In general use.

**1853** KANE *Grinnell Exp.* v. (1856) 40 Rocky islets known to the Danes as 'skerries'. **1870** MORRIS *Earthly Par.* II. III. 512, I see his black bows strike The hidden skerry. **1885** S. TROMHOLT *Aurora Borealis* II. 251 Between islands and tiny skerries, the steamer speeds on.

**2.** Without article.

**1847** H. MILLER *Test. Rocks* i. (1857) 19 Rock and skerry are brown with sea-weed. *a* **1856** —— *Rambles Geologist* in *Cruise of 'Betsey'* (1858) 273 The tempest weltered round reef and skerry. **1896** KIPLING *Seven Seas, Coastwise L.* i, From reef and rock and skerry—over headland, ness, and voe.

**skerry** (ˈskɛrɪ), *a.* and *sb.*[3] [Of uncertain origin.]

**1.** *adj.* Of the nature of shale; shaly, slaty.

*a* **1800** PEGGE *Suppl. Grose*, *Skerry*, shaley... *Derb.* Spoken of coals. **1829** *Glover's Hist. Derby* I. 59 Brown skerry stone. **1876** PAGE *Adv. Text-bk. Geol.* xvi. 296 Grey shale and thin skerry laminae.

**2.** *sb.* Earth or stone of a shaly nature.

**1844** H. HUTCHINSON *Pract. Drainage Land* 140 From this depth..was nine feet to the water, then one foot of yellow skerry and sand. **1881** *Leicester Gloss.* 240 *Skerry*, the thin, grey, partially laminated bands occurring in the red brick earth near Bosworth. **1883** GRESLEY *Gloss. Coal-m.* 224 *Skerries*, greenish-white micaceous sandstone.

**skerry**, Sc. variant of SCARRY *a.*[1]

*a* **1830** *Thomas Rymer* x. in Child *Ballads* I. 325/1 It's dont ye see yon broad broad way, That leadeth down by yon skerry fell?

**skers, skersytye**, obs. ff. SCARCE, SCARCITY.

**skerth.** *dial.* [? a. ON. *skarð*: see SCARTH *sb.*[1]] A small watercourse.

**1851** *Jrnl. R. Agric. Soc.* XII. II. 291 [Lincolnshire], The river..is augmented by numerous highland streams, 'delphs and skerths', on each side. *Ibid.* 302 A network of drains, dykes, eaus, and skerths.

**sketch** (skɛtʃ), *sb.* Also 7 **scetch**, **schetch** (**schetse**, **schytz**). [ad. Du. *schets* or G. *skizze* (†*skitze*, *skize*), neither of which is recorded before the 17th cent., ad. It. *schizzo*, whence also Sp. *esquicio*, F. *esquisse* (†*esquiche*): the source of the It. word is supposed to be L. **schedius* (cf. *schedia* raft, *schedium* extemporaneous poem), Gr. σχέδιος done or made off-hand, extempore.

In the following examples the foreign origin of the word is still indicated by the spelling: **1691** T. H[ALE] *Acc. New Invent.* p. xlvii, A Schytz or hasty Piece of Painting done by a great Hand is of great Value. **1693** P. PETT *Barlow's Rem.* Pref. A viij b, Intending only what the Dutch Painters call a Schytz, and not a perfect Delineation or Draught. **1697** W. POPE *Life Bp. Ward* 149 The first *Schetse* of a Comedy calld the *Paradox*.]

**1. a.** A rough drawing or delineation of something, giving the outlines or prominent features without the detail, esp. one intended to serve as the basis of a more finished picture, or to be used in its composition; a rough draught or design. Also, in later use, a drawing or painting of a slight or unpretentious nature.

α. **1668** [see 2]. **1682** WHELER *Journ. Greece* Pref., Both he that designed it from my Scetch, and the Engraver after him. **1694** *Phil. Trans.* XVIII. 179 This..moulding.. would be far better exprest by a Scetch that should.. represent the bottom and top of two of them.

β. **1687** A. LOVELL tr. *Thevenot's Trav.* II. 145, I have made a little Sketch of this which will serve to give an Idea of those of Tschehel-minar. **1709** POPE *Ess. Crit.* 23 As the slightest sketch, if justly trac'd, Is by ill-colouring but the more disgrac'd. **1751** HOLLIS in *Lett. Lit. Men* (Camden) 380 The Designs that have been taken of them hitherto, have been rather Sketches..than accurate and exact Plans. **1794** MRS. RADCLIFFE *Myst. Udolpho* xxxii, In these little sketches she generally placed interesting groups characteristic of the scenery they animated. **1819** SCOTT *Let.* in *Lockhart* (1837) IV. viii. 246 Constable has offered Allan three hundred pounds to make sketches for an edition of the Tales of My Landlord. **1863** GEO. ELIOT *Romola* xviii, All about the walls hung pen and oil sketches of fantastic sea-monsters.

*transf.* **1713** *Guardian* No. 149, We have a kind of sketch of dress, if I may so call it, among us, which..is called a Dishabille. **1831** SCOTT *Ct. Robt.* iii, But in this respect his fancy probably filled up the sketch which his conjectures bodied out. **1864** LOWELL *Fireside Trav.* 242 His [*sc.* the donkey's] bray is..an experimental sketch for the neigh of her finished animal.

†**b.** (See quot.) *Obs.*[−0]

**1688** HOLME *Armoury* III. 149/1 *Schetches*, are touches on a Paper with the point of a Charcoal in drawing out of any Figure, and so by little and little running over the whole Work.

**2. a.** A brief account, description, or narrative giving the main or important facts, incidents, etc., and not going into the details; a short or superficial essay or study, freq. in *pl.* as a title.

**1668** CHARLETON *Ephesian & Cimm. Matrons* II. 76 Whereof I have here drawn no perfect Picture, but only a rude Scetch. **1715** BENTLEY *Serm.* x. 366 After this short but true sketch of Popery. **1744** HARRIS *Three Treat.* Wks. (1841) 5 Thus..have you had exhibited to you a sketch of art. You must remember, however, it is but a sketch. **1780** *Mirror* No. 66, I offer you a small sketch of an incident, supposed to have happened in the times of our forefathers. **1831** D. E. WILLIAMS *Sir T. Lawrence* II. 301 [This] renders necessary some sketch of the establishment of the Academy of painting in Ireland. **1867** FREEMAN *Norm. Conq.* (1877) I. 7 Here our narrative, even as the merest sketch, comes to its natural close.

(*b*) **1758** L. TEMPLE *Sketches* Preface, The Author of the following Papers chuses to call them *Sketches.* **1835–6** DICKENS (*title*), Sketches by Boz. **1876** D. DONOVAN (*title*), Sketches in Carbery, Co. Cork; its Antiquities [etc.].

**b.** The general plan or outline, the main features, of anything. *rare.*

**1697** DRYDEN *Virgil, Ess. Georgics* (1721) I. 207 We are beholden to him [Theocritus] for the first rough Sketch of a Georgic. **1796–7** JANE AUSTEN *Pride & Prej.* xxvii, Everything..was finally settled according to Charlotte's first sketch. **1803** G. ELLIS *Let.* in Lockhart *Scott* (1837) I. xi. 394 If the sketch of that story was previously known.

**3.** *Mus.* **a.** A short piece, usu. for the pianoforte, either slight in construction or vividly descriptive.

*c* **1840** SIR W. S. BENNETT (*title*), Three Musical Sketches.

**b.** A preliminary study made during the progress of, or in preparation for, a finished work or composition.

**1883** *Grove's Dict. Mus.* III. 528 The Movement..affords us examples both of preliminary sketches and an amended whole. *Ibid.* 529 The volume presents some intensely interesting sketches for an Andante.

**4.** A short play or performance of slight dramatic construction and usually of a light or comic nature (see quot. 1892); also, a musical performance by one person, in which playing, singing, and talking are combined.

**1789** W. DUNLAP *Darby's Return* (title-page), A comic sketch. As performed..for the benefit of Mr. Wignell. **1829** H. FOOTE *Compan. to Theatres* 74 Satirical sketches, or slight comic pieces on the follies of the day, have likewise been produced here with good effect. **1861** MAYHEW *Lond. Lab.* (ed. 3) III. 132/2 We always did a laughable sketch entitled Billy Button's Ride to Brentford. **1881** *Daily Telegr.* 27 Dec., Mr. Corney Grain..now gives a supplementary musical sketch, entitled 'Master Tommy's Theatricals'. **1892** *Daily News* 3 June 2/2 'Sketches'—the new name for small or condensed, and in some cases, mutilated stage plays, the acting time of which shall not be more than 40 minutes, and the performers in which shall not be more than six.

**5.** *slang.* A small quantity; a drop.

**1894** ASTLEY *Fifty Years Life* II. 258, I have had..just a sketch of whisky with water from the burn.

**6.** A ridiculous sight, a very amusing person; so ***hot sketch***, a comical or colourful person. *slang.*

**1917** S. LEWIS *Job* xx. 299 You women cer'nly are a sketch! **1921** H. C. WITWER *Leather Pushers* x. 269 This Roberts is a hot sketch for a fighter, anyways! **1925** E. HEMINGWAY *In Our Time* (1926) 84 You're a hot sketch. Who the hell asked you to butt in here? **1926** MAINES & GRANT *Wise-Crack Dict.* 9/2 *He's a sketch*, he's comical. **1930** J. DOS PASSOS *42nd Parallel* v. 399 'He's a hot sketch,' said one of the girls to the other. **1930** J. B. PRIESTLEY *Angel Pavement* xi. 604 You do look a sight, Dad... I never saw such a sketch.

**7.** *attrib.* and *Comb.*, as ***sketch-block***, ***-map***, ***-pad*** [PAD *sb.*[3]], ***-plan***.

**1782** R. CUMBERLAND *Anecd. Painters* (1787) I. 194 His figures..are slight and sketch-like. **1872** W. W. SMYTH *Mining Stat.* 38 The geological sketch-map, which accompanies this paper. **1886** *Guide Exhib. Galleries Brit. Mus.* 235 A sketch-plan of the Battle of Aboukir. **1892** *Daily News* 19 May 2/4 The practice of sketch artists, sketch authors, and sketch managers has been..to pay copyright fees. **1893** *Photogr. Ann.* 281 You must..practise with a pencil and sketch-block the..foreshortening of objects. **1961** M. SPARK *Prime of Miss Jean Brodie* iii. 64, I went to get a new sketch pad. **1981** *Listener* 5 Nov. 546/2 The drawings..offering imaginative ideas to any child with a sketch-pad.

**sketch** (skɛtʃ), *v.* Also 7 scetch. [f. prec. or ad. Du. *schetsen*, G. *skizziren*.]

**1.** *trans.* To describe briefly, generally, or in outline; to give the essential facts or points of, without going into details; to outline.

**1695** DRYDEN *Dufresnoy's Art Paint.* Pref. p. xii, To contemplate those Idea's, which I have onely sketch'd, and which every man must finish for himself. **1751** J. HARRIS *Hermes* I. ii. (1786) 19 Now a Sentence may be sketch'd in the following description. **1814** SCOTT *Let.* in *Lockhart* (1837) III. x. 312 The language most animated and poetical; and the characters sketched with a masterly enthusiasm. **1841–4** EMERSON *Ess.* xix. Wks. (Bohn) I. 237 The history of the State sketches in coarse outline the progress of thought. **1868** FREEMAN *Norm. Conq.* (1877) II. 285 The history of the city will be more fittingly sketched at another stage.

**b.** With *out* (cf. 2 a).

**1694** SALMON *Bate's Dispens.* Ded., Could I but scetch out a faint Idea of Your Glorious Actions. *a* **1779** WARBURTON *Wks.* (1811) X. 201, I have at present nothing to do with its various abominations, here sketched out. **1847** L. HUNT *Men, Women, & B.* II. xii. 302 To sketch out..what we conceive to be a better mode of supplying some account of Madame de Sévigné. **1867** RUSKIN *Time & Tide* xxiii. §154, I have sketched out this scheme for you somewhat prematurely.

**2.** To draw the outline or prominent features of (a picture, figure, etc.), esp. as preliminary or preparatory to further development; to make a sketch or rough draught of (something); to draw or paint in this manner.

**a.** With advs., as *in*, *out*, *over*.

**1725** WATTS *Logic* (J.), Some admirable design sketched out only with a black pencil, though by the hand of Raphael. **1801** *Farmer's Mag.* Jan. 66 For this purpose, a map of the soil is sketched out—we presume, from imagination. **1831** D. E. WILLIAMS *Sir T. Lawrence* I. 331 The pupil confined himself to pen and ink drawings, sketched over with Indian ink and bistre. **1886** G. ALLEN *Maimie's Sake* i, He sketched in lightly the face and figure.

*transf.* **1818** HAZLITT *Charac. Shaks. Plays* (1838) 244 This is little more than the first outlines of a comedy loosely sketched in.

**b.** Without qualifying term.

**1786** REYNOLDS *Notes Mason's tr. Dufresnoy* xi, The method of Rubens was to sketch his compositions in colours. **1807** HUTTON *Course Math.* (ed. 3) II. 73 Sketching on the sides the shape or resemblance of the fences or boundaries. **1855** TENNYSON *The Brook* 102 Sketching with her slender pointed foot Some figure..On garden gravel. **1860** TYNDALL *Glac.* I. xxvii. 213, I sketched some of the crystals.

*transf.* **1847** DE QUINCEY *Sp. Mil. Nun* vi, She had soon sketched and finished a dashing pair of Wellington trousers.

**c.** *intr.* To admit of sketching.

**1883** HOLME LEE *Loving & Serving* I. ii. 27 Those poke bonnets..sketched well.

**3.** *intr.* or *absol.* To practise sketching; to draw or paint sketches.

**1874** R. TYRWHITT *Our Sketching Club* 29 If you will only practise measuring heights and distances with thumb and pencil, whenever you sketch.

**b.** To proceed in a sketchy manner. (Cf. prec. 4.)

**1888** HOWELLS *Annie Kilburn* xv, We have to cut some of the business between Romeo and Juliet, because it's too long, you know... But we sketch along through the play.

**sketch**, Sc. f. SKATE *sb.*[2] and *v.* (see *Eng. Dial. Dict.*); dial. f. SCATCH *sb.*[1] (a stilt).

**sketcha'bility.** [f. as next + -ITY.] The quality of being sketchable; suitability as a subject for a sketch.

**1840** T. A. TROLLOPE *Summer in Brittany* I. 253 To..try the sketchability of a water-mill. **1883** H. JAMES *Portraits of Places* 48 In the wonderful..Genoese alleys the traveller is really up to his neck in the old Italian sketchability.

**sketchable** ('skɛtʃəb(ə)l), *a.* [f. SKETCH *v.*] Suitable for being sketched; effective as the subject of a sketch.

**1862** H. MARRYAT *Year in Sweden* II. 182 Wyk, a place most sketchable, situated on a branch of the fiord. **1877** A. B. EDWARDS *Up Nile* 533 Thinking to find a sketchable point of view inland, we struck down towards the plain.

**'sketch-book.** [f. SKETCH *sb.*]

**1.** A book having leaves of drawing-paper specially reserved or adapted for making sketches in.

**1837** LOCKHART *Scott* IV. vi. 197 Encountering some odd figure, armed with a sketch-book, evidently bent on a peep at the Great Unknown. **1848** THACKERAY *Van. Fair* lxii, Dobbin used to carry about for her her stool and sketch-book. **1884** *Harper's Mag.* Feb. 338/2 My friends take their sketch-books.

**b.** As the title of a book containing essays or studies of a more or less descriptive nature.

**1820** IRVING (*title*), The Sketch Book of Geoffrey Crayon. **1843** THACKERAY (*title*), The Irish Sketch-Book.

**2.** A note-book containing a composer's preliminary sketches or studies.

**1883** *Grove's Dict. Music* III. 528 Beethoven..left behind him a whole library of Sketch-books. *Ibid.* 529 Some of the Sketch-books in the Royal Library at Berlin.

**sketcher**[1] ('skɛtʃə(r)). [f. SKETCH *v.* + -ER[1].]

**1.** One who sketches a picture, portrait, etc.

**1812** COMBE *Syntax, Picturesque* II. 128 I'll do as other sketchers do—Put any thing into the view. **1831** D. E. WILLIAMS *Sir T. Lawrence* I. 234 As a sketcher of likenesses, he disclosed the future power of the President. **1840** T. A. TROLLOPE *Summer in Brittany* I. 70 As perfect a little domestic landscape as a sketcher could desire. **1888** W. P. FRITH *Autobiog.* III. v. 137 Creswick, though by nature a lazy fellow, was a pretty constant sketcher.

**b.** One who writes an outline sketch, or who jots down preliminary memoranda.

**1851** J. H. NEWMAN *Posit. Cath. Eng.* 311 Those who write books about a people or a school are hardly more than extempore sketchers; or they paint from memory. **1883** *Grove's Dict. Mus.* III. 526 Others, again—the Sketchers, *par excellence*—began even their greatest works by noting down a few scraps of Subject, which they afterwards modified, enlarged, and improved.

**2.** An implement for sketching.

**1894** BARING-GOULD *Des. S. France* I. 159 With a sketcher of flint,..a primeval man amused himself in delineating..such animals as he pursued in the chase.

**'sketcher**[2]. *Sc.* Also 8 skytcher, 9 skatcher. [f. *sketch*, Sc. form of SKATE *v.*] A skate.

For the Sc. *sketcher*, etc., a skater, see *Eng. Dial. Dict.* **1790** A. WILSON *Rabby's Mistake* Poet. Wks. (1846) 101 Owre the loch's clear frozen face, On skytchers thrang, in airy chase, Flew mony a cheery chiel. **1824** SCOTT *St. Ronan's* iii, I thought sketchers were aye made of airn. **1865** G. MACDONALD *A. Forbes* xxvi, A new strap for my skatcher.

**sketchily** ('skɛtʃɪlɪ), *adv.* [f. SKETCHY *a.* + -LY[2].] In a sketchy manner; without elaboration or detail.

**1825** T. HOOK *Sayings* Ser. II. *Passion & Princ.* iii, The character of the lieutenant was sketchily given. **1870** *Daily News* 5 Dec., Her account of the country is lightly and sketchily written. **1886** G. ALLEN *Maimie's Sake* i, A few stray lines made to do duty sketchily for a rough idea of the imaginary picture.

**sketchiness** ('skɛtʃɪnɪs). [f. as prec. + -NESS.] The state or condition of being sketchy.

**1843** RUSKIN *Mod. Paint.* I. II. viii. 119 His modes of treatment are alike removed from sketchiness or incompletion, and from exaggeration. **1885** *Athenæum* 6 June 719 The tendency to sketchiness is not great where the materials..lie..ready to the hand.

**b.** *techn.* (See quot.)

**1890** W. J. GORDON *Foundry* 173 Sketchiness is the technical term for the tendency of patterns to show lines of spacing across the cloth in a way that is objectionable.

**sketching** ('skɛtʃɪŋ), *vbl. sb.* [f. SKETCH *v.*]

**1.** The action of the verb SKETCH; something sketched, a sketch. Also with *down*.

**1824** W. IRVING *Life & Lett.* (1864) II. 226, I enjoy the first conception and first sketchings down of my ideas. **1840** HOOD *Up Rhine* 215 You remember poor George's fondness for picturesque views and sketching. **1884** *Athenæum* 5 Jan. 20/1 It was a crazy oddity with much scribbling and even schoolboy-like sketching by some one in the last century.

**2.** *attrib.*, as ***sketching-basket, -block, -book, -case, -club, -pencil, -ramble, -stool, -tour, -umbrella***, etc.

**1806–7** J. BERESFORD *Miseries Hum. Life* VI. xxxv, In a sketching ramble—a charming morsel of the picturesque breaking out upon you. **1812** COMBE *Syntax, Picturesque* III. 212 His well-stuff'd bags, with all their hoard Of sketching-tools. *Ibid.* XVIII. 70 He..from his pocket took His pencil and his sketching-book. **1843** D. G. ROSSETTI *Let.* 7 July (1965) I. 16 There have been two meetings of the Sketching Club since your departure. **1848** DICKENS *Dombey* xiv, A set of sketching materials. **1852** C. M. YONGE *Two Guardians* i. 9 They set off..Marian carrying her little sketching-basket. **1861** G. MUSGRAVE *By-Roads France* 45 Folding up my sketching stool and strapping it on to the havresac. **1865** G. M. HOPKINS *Jrnls. & Papers* (1959) 86 Shewing a sketching-block, he asked if there would be any objection to his sketching there. **1874** R. TYRWHITT *Our Sketching Club* 67 Get..a good sketching-block. **1890** C. M. YONGE *More Bywords* viii. 269 There's..our sketching tour in August. **1902** A. BENNETT *Anna of Five Towns* x. 247 Beatrice, with easel and sketching-umbrella. **1939–40** *Army & Navy Stores Catal.* 375/1 *Sketching umbrellas.* Cream cover, lined green, wind valve, jointed stick, and spike, closes up to 34½ in.—42/-.

**'sketching,** *ppl. a.* [f. SKETCH *v.* + -ING[2].] That sketches; occupied with sketching. Hence **'sketchingly** *adv.*

**1824** SCOTT *St. Ronan's* iv, A sketching gentleman that lives..at the Cleikum of Aultoun yonder. **1869** *Pall Mall G.* 16 Aug. 10 Telling..how he himself had been guide to Horace Vernet as he rode sketchingly along to his namesake's dwelling-place.

**'sketchist.** *rare.* [f. SKETCH *sb.* 2 + -IST[1], after *novelist*, etc.] A writer of literary sketches.

**1837** *Tait's Mag.* IV. 576 The phrase might have been restricted to essayists, or, were the term admissible, sketchists. **1893** *Star* 22 June 1/8 The popular legal sketchist.

**sketch-map:** see SKETCH *sb.* 3.

**sketchy** ('skɛtʃɪ), *a.* [f. SKETCH *sb.* + -Y.]

**1.** Giving only a slight or rough outline of the main features, facts, or circumstances without going into details: **a.** Of writings or authors.

**1805** *Edin. Rev.* VII. 136 These two extremes, of meagre copying, and of imitation so free and sketchy as to leave no likeness, are to be found in our two translations of Homer. **1828** J. STERLING *Ess.* (1848) II. 50 Sketches of society,—very sketchy indeed,—..make up the miscellany. **1854** S. LOVER *Handy Andy* (ed. 4) Pref., A story thus originated could not be other than sketchy and desultory. **1884** *Law Times* LXXVI. 358/1 On particulars of breaches and of objections he is very sketchy.

**b.** Of style, etc. (in writing or painting).

**1811** *Self Instructor* 527 This style of painting is intended to be light and sketchy. **1852** MOTLEY *Corr.* (1889) I. v. 137 The thin, sketchy, and slight manner in which the whole was executed. **1871** *Athenæum* 3 June 686 In the second volume ..The style is not so sketchy, but we have rather a fragment of a picture than the picture itself.

**2.** Of pictures, etc.: Of the nature of, or resembling, a sketch; consisting or composed of outline without much detail.

**1859** GULLICK & TIMBS *Painting* 288 A sketchy generalized resemblance of an object. **1864** I. TAYLOR in *Good Words* 231 These sketchy portraits, inserted..in the very midst of the reported speeches. **1884** *19th Cent.* Jan. 31 The well-known column..around which Landseer's very sketchy lions watch.

*fig.* **1817** KEATS *Lett.* Wks. 1889 III. 96 It [Wordsworth's 'Gipsy'] is a kind of sketchy intellectual landscape. **1826** DISRAELI *Viv. Grey* V. xv, A party of this kind should be more sketchy in its style; the outline more free, and less detail.

**3.** *colloq.* Of a light, flimsy, unsubstantial or imperfect nature. Also *fig.*

**1878** H. S. WILSON *Alpine Ascents* i. 16 A scrappy sort of sketchy fragmentary breakfast. **1897** MARY KINGSLEY *W. Africa* 563 A house with no doors, and only very sketchy wooden window-shutters. **1943** E. B. WHITE *Let.* 13 Mar. (1976) 238, I am hoping that my health (which has been rather sketchy lately) will improve. **1977** *Horse & Hound* 14 Jan. 7/3 He survived some decidedly sketchy jumps in the early stages.

‖**skete** (ski:t). [ad. mod. Gr. σκῆτος, f. Gr. ἀσκητής monk, hermit.] An association of hermits belonging to the Greek Church.

**1869** TOZER *Highl. Turkey* I. 68 When a number of these retreats are assembled round a central church, a skete (ἀσκητήριον) is formed, which in some cases differs from a monastery only in not possessing an independent constitution. **1887** RILEY *Athos* 79 The sketes, or priories, have no voice in the government of the community.

**skete,** var. SKEET *sb.*[1], SKEET *adv.* and *a.*

**skethill,** var. SCATHEL *a.*

**skeuomorph** ('skju:əʊmɔ:f). [f. Gr. σκεῦος vessel, implement + μορφή form.] **1.** An ornament or ornamental design on an artefact resulting from the nature of the material used or the method of working it.

**1889** H. COLLEY MARCH in *Trans. Lancs. & Cheshire Antiq. Soc.* VII. 166 The forms of ornament demonstrably due to structure require a name. If those taken from animals are called zoomorphs, and those from plants phyllomorphs, it will be convenient to call those derived from structure, skeuomorphs. **1979** *Nature* 6 Dec. 632/2 So-called 'skeuomorphs' in architecture that involve conversion of originally necessary features into purely decorative patterns.

**2.** An object or feature copying the design of a similar artefact in another material.

**1938** *Proc. Prehistoric Soc.* IV. 82 This necklace type is best known in jet from northern Britain, where it has.. provided the type of which the gold lunula is a skeuomorph. **1943** *Antiquity* XVII. 7 Stone skeuomorphs of wooden fences. **1977** [see SKEUOMORPHIC *a.* below]. **1981** *Chartered Mechanical Engineer* Sept. 20/3 'Skeuomorphs' seem to be very common in motor car design, particularly where changes are made from ferrous metals to non-ferrous metals or plastics.

Hence **skeuo'morphic** *a.*, of, pertaining to, decorated with, or having the character of a skeuomorph or skeuomorphs.

**1889** H. COLLEY MARCH in *Trans. Lancs. & Cheshire Antiq. Soc.* VII. 168 The transfer of thong-work from the flint axe, where it was functional, to the bronze celt, where it was skeuomorphic. **1895** A. C. HADDON *Evol. Art* 6 The reader is referred to the section on skeuomorphic pottery. **1905** [see ANTHROPOMORPHIC *a.* 2]. **1928** R. A. S. MACALISTER *Archaeol. Ireland* vi. 277 Celtic interlacement ..is *skeuomorphic*; that is, it is derived from the patterns produced by a technical process—in this case, by weaving. **1930** J. L. MYRES *Who were Greeks?* viii. 464 When a potter, working in red clay..fashions clay vessels so that..they resemble metal work or leather work or basketry..his style is 'skeuomorphic'. **1951** B. Z. SELIGMAN *N. & Q. Anthropol.* (ed. 6) III. 311 Note whether the design is.. skeuomorphic. **1959** J. D. EVANS *Malta* iii. 127 The skeuomorphic carving of some of the inner halls of the rock-cut monument of Hal Saflieni. **1977** T. SHAW *Unearthing Igbo-Ukwu* 15 When something is originally made in one material and is then translated into another, but by its form and decoration reveals the original model which it imitates, this is called a 'skeuomorph', and the object in the new material is said to be 'skeuomorphic'. Thus the bronze pot described is skeuomorphic of an ordinary pottery vessel.

**skeut,** obs. f. SCOUT *sb.*[3]

†**skevin.** *Obs.* In 4 skeuayne, skeuyn, skyueyn, 5 skyveyne; 4 skyuen, 5 skywen. [ad. ONF. *eskevein*, var. of OF. *eschevin* (mod.F. *échevin*): see ECHEVIN and SCABINE.] A steward of a gild.

**1389** in *Eng. Gilds* (1870) 46 To chesen an Aldirman..and foure skeuaynes, trost men and trewe, for to kepyn and reseyuen þe goodes..of þe gilde. *Ibid.* 64 To chesyn alderman and skyueynys that ben profitable for the Gylde. *c* **1440** *Promp. Parv.* 458 Skyveyne, of a gylde (*S.* skywen).

†**skevinage.** *Obs.* Also skun-, scunage. [ad. ONF. *eskevinage*, var. of OF. *eschevinage* mod.F. *échevinage*): see prec.] A district under the jurisdiction of a local magistrate.

In English use only with ref. to the precincts of Calais. **1449** *Rolls of Parlt.* V. 149/2 Withoute the Towne, in the Procincte longing to the same, called the Skevinage. **1487** *Ibid.* VI. 404/2 Th' Office of Baillyve of the Scunage of Calais. **1529** *Lett. & Pap. Hen. VIII* (1876) IV. III. 2392 A house place..within the scunage of Calais.

**Skevington's daughter, gyves, irons:** see SCAVENGER'S DAUGHTER.

†**skew,** *sb.*[1] *Obs.* Also 4 skewe, skwe, skiu, scue. [prob. of Scand. origin and related to SKY *sb.*[1]]

**1.** The sky or heaven.

*a* **1300** *E.E. Psalter* xvii. 13 Mirke watres þat ware ofe hewe In þe kloudes of þe skewe. **13..** *E.E. Allit. P.* B. 483 Ho [*sc.* the dove] skyrmez vnder skwe & skowtez aboute. *c* **1375** *Cursor M.* 1341 (Fairf.), Þis tree was of sa mykil in siȝt, þat to þe skew raȝt þe top. *c* **1400** *Destr. Troy* 10182 The skew [*MS.* skewe], for þe skrykyng & skremyng of folke, Redoundet with dyn.

**2.** *pl.* The skies, heavens, or clouds.

*c* **1320** *Cast. Love* 1494 Þe wey he made vs to lede þorw þe skewes [F. *nuwes*], þer he eode. **13..** *E.E. Allit. P.* B. 1206 Hiȝe skelt was þe askry þe skewes an-vnder. *c* **1400** *Destr. Troy* 9637 That day was full derke..With a Ropand Rayne rut fro the skewes.

**skew** (skju:), *sb.*[2] Forms: 3 sc(u)we, 5 scue; 3 scyue, skyue, 4 skewe, 7– skew (9 *Sc.* skeu). [ad. OF. *escu* (mod.F. *écu*):—L. *scūtum* shield.

Both the OF. *escu* and L. *scutum* occur in this sense in early accounts (1253) of Westminster Abbey: see G. Scott *Westm. Abbey* (1863) 239. The OF. word may also be the source of *scu*, a screen or partition, given in *Promp. Parv.* 450/2 and 468/2.]

**1.** †**a.** A stone specially intended or adapted for being placed with other similar ones to form the sloping head or coping of a gable, rising slightly above the level of the roof. *Obs.*

**1278** *Bursar's Rolls, Merton Coll.* in *Archæol. Jrnl.* II. 143 Item eidem iij.*s.* iij.*d.* per xx pedibus in longitudine de quibusdam lapidibus qui vocantur scuwes et ponuntur in opere in tecto parve domus retro coquinam. **1288** *Ibid.*, Item in xviij ped' de skyues empt' xviij.*d*, precium pedis j.*d.*

**1359–60** *Ely Sacr. Rolls* II. 193 In iiij$^{xx}$ iiij ped. de skewes empt., prec. pedis j.*d.* [**1445–6** in Willis & Clark *Cambridge* (1886) I. 392, 45½ feet of 'Scuez'..are bought for the construction of the walls.] **1635** in Paterson *Hist. Musselburgh* (1857) 146, vij$^c$ double and single treis, and about j$^m$, skewis.

*collect.* **1428** in Heath *Grocers' Comp.* (1869) 6 Ashler, coyne, skew, ragge, chalke, flint, tyles, and estriche boarde. **1533** in Bayley *Tower of London* (1821) I. App. p. xxix, In skew and crests to the same spacys on the west side. *Ibid.*, At the Juell Hows doore, iij. spacys covered w$^t$ skew and crest.

**b.** The line of coping on a gable. Chiefly *Sc.*

**1789** D. Davidson *Seasons* 43 High on the sklentin skew, or thatched eave, The sparrow..Seeks out a dwelling-place. **1823** Galt *Entail* xlix, I paid..the Glasgow mason..for the count o' his sklater that pointed the skews o' the house. **1861** Stephens & Burn *Farm-Buildings* §279 There are no skews [in this gable], the slating projecting over the walls.

**c.** A skew-corbel (see 2).

The genuineness of this sense is somewhat doubtful.

**1845** Parker *Gloss. Archit.* (ed. 4) I. 340 The term skew is still used in the north for a stone built into the bottom of a gable or other similar situation to support the coping above.

**2.** *attrib.*, as ***skew-corbel***, ***-put***, ***-stone***, ***-table***.

Parker appears to have formed *skew-table* out of *scutable*, which is given by J. T. Smith *Antiq. Westm.* (1807) 207 in a translated document of 1330; on the same page occurs *sencrestes*, which may be a misreading of *scu-crestes*.

**1833** Loudon *Encycl. Archit.* §947 The gables are to be slated over, and the skew-stones (the coping-stones of the gables, called barge-stones in England) are to be laid over the slates, but to project 3 inches over..the walls. **1845** Parker *Gloss. Archit.* (ed. 4) 340 Skew-table was probably the course of stone weathered, or sloped, on the top, placed over a continuous set-off in a wall. **1850** Ogilvie, *Skew-corbel, Skew-put*, a stone built into the bottom of a gable to support the coping above. **1851** Turner *Dom. Archit.* II. ii. 31 The spring stones or skew-tables of the gables.

**3.** A slate used in forming the gutter of a roof.

**1899** *Evesham Jrnl.* 1 Apr. (E.D.D.), The centre one is the 'bottomer', on either side are two 'tie-lyes', and above and below in the next course two 'skews'.

**skew** (skjuː), *sb.*³ Also 7 scew. [f. skew *a.* or *v.*²]

†**1.** A side-glance. *Obs. rare.*

**1622** S. Ward *Christ All in All* (1627) 29 Whateuer good workes we doe with an eye from his, and a skew vnto our owne names,..the more penaltie of pride belongs vnto vs. **1884** G. Forbes in W. Thomson *Molecular Dynamics* 289 So the coefficients sighed and gave a last tangential skew And *a* shook hands with *b* & *c* and S and T and U, And with a tear they parted.

**2. a.** A slant; a deviation from the straight line; an angle, esp. that at which a bridge spans a road or river; a sideward movement.

**1688** Holme *Armoury* III. 261/2 Scew or Campher, is the cutting off of a corner of a Wall. **1840** *Civil Eng. & Arch. Jrnl.* III. 232/2 The projections of all the lines of pressure are equal to..each other,..whatever may be the angle of the skew. **1885** *Scientific American* 1 Aug. 64 In the completed structure there are..no two skews alike. **1903** *Daily Chron.* 18 Feb. 3/3 The skew in the chancel he attributes..to an alteration having been carried out by rule of thumb.

**b.** *transf.* A slip, an error.

**1869** Furnivall in *Bk. Precedence* Pref. p. xvii, Thus one of the many skews in the Harleian Catalogue was set straight.

**c.** ***on the*** (or ***a***) ***skew***, on the slant, slantwise.

**1881** Young *Every Man his own Mechanic* §399. 175 All these bits are secured in the main stock on a skew. **1891** C. James *Rom. Rigmarole* 174 Birds that flew dead straight, birds that seemed to work on the skew. **1894** *Times* 22 Sept. 13/4 Over the Lune, which is crossed on the skew, the span is 350 ft.

**3.** *Mining.* (See quots.)

**1789** T. Williams *Min. Kingd.* I. 27 Skews and backs are only local joints of an irregular curved figure, which often resemble hitches. *Ibid.* 330 A skew is an irregular discontinuous mineral fissure,..which generally lies in a very slanting irregular position. **1883** Gresley *Gloss. Coal-m.* 224 *Skews*,..irregularities in the roof indicating danger from falls.

**4.** *Statistics.* Skewness.

**1974** *Listener* 7 Nov. 595/2 The skew in the graph is at both ends. **1978** *Nature* 2 Mar. 39/1 The distribution is not symmetrical but displays positive skew, a feature held in common with observations at lower frequencies.

†**skew**, *sb.*⁴ *Cant. Obs.* [Of obscure origin.] A cup; a wooden dish.

**1561** Awdelay *Frat. Vacab.* (1869) 83 A skew, a cuppe. **1641** Brome *Joviall Crew* II. F iv b, This is Bien Bowse, this is Bien Bowse, Too little is my Skew. *a* **1700** B. E. *Dict. Cant. Crew*, *Skew*, a Begger's Wooden Dish. **1754** *Song* in Farmer & Henley *Slang* s.v., To thy Bugher [= dog] and thy Skew, Fitch and Jybes, I bid adieu.

**skew** (skjuː), *sb.*⁵ *Cornish dial.* [? Cornish.] A drizzling rain; a driving mist. Also *fig.*

**1839** W. E. Forster in Reid *Life* (1888) I. v. 128, I am in a regular Cornish skew as to the future,..can't see an inch before me. **1880–** in Cornish glossaries.

**skew** (skjuː), *sb.*⁶ *Harrow slang.* [Cf. skew *v.*⁵]

**a.** A difficult passage for translation or explanation. **b.** An entrance examination held at the end of a term. Also *attrib.*

**1866** *Routledge's Ev. Boy's Ann.* 757 One examination paper..was popularly known as 'Skew-paper'. **1890** *Daily News* 14 Aug. 4/8 To explain hard passages, or 'skews', as they are technically styled.

†**skew**, *sb.*⁷ *Sc. Obs.*⁻¹ (Meaning doubtful.)

Perhaps a back-formation from *reskew*, but cf. skew *v.*²

*c* **1470** Henry *Wallace* v. 835 Hardy and hat contenyt the fell melle, Skew and reskew off Scottis and Inglis als.

†**skew**, *sb.*⁸ *Obs.*⁻¹ [Cf. scow *sb.*² 2.] A coracle.

**1577** Harrison *Descr. Brit.* iv. in *Holinshed* I. 5/2 These Scots..vsed..to steale ouer into Britaine in leather skewes.

**skew** (skjuː), *a.* and *adv.* Also 7 skue, scue. [Cf. skew *v.*² and askew *adv.*]

**A.** *adj.* **1. a.** Having an oblique direction or position; turned to one side, slanting, squint.

**1609** Holland *Amm. Marcell.* xxx. xi. 397 He had with his gray eyes a skew cast at all times, and looked sterne. **1639** *Crabtree Lect.* 106 Thy skew legges are so distant one from another, that it is unpossible that thou shouldest ever gall thine Ankles. **1651** H. More *Enthus. Tri.* (1712) 44 It is far easier for her to..fetch in some odd skue conceit from some remote obscure corner, than to think of what is nearer. **1684** Burnet *Theory Earth* I. 195 Its right and parallel situation ..was chang'd into an oblique; in which skew posture it hath stood ever since. **1850** Parker *Gloss. Archit.* I. 429 The common coping of a wall, which consists of a sloped or skew surface surmounted by a roll moulding. **1860** Wraxall *Life in Sea* v. 130 The skew mouth running vertically, make[s] their appearance something frightfully odious. **1881** E. B. Tylor *Anthropology* 63 The Tatar and Japanese faces show the skew eyelids of the Mongolian race.

†**b.** Distorted, perverted; macaronic. *Obs.*

**1607** Brewer *Lingua* III. v, I remember about the yeare 1602. many vsed this skew kind of language.

**c.** *Statistics.* Of a statistical distribution: not symmetrical about its mean. Cf. skewed *a.*² 2.

A distribution is said to be *skew* (or *skewed*) *positively* or *to the right* if its third moment about its mean is positive, so that its larger tail lies to the right; and conversely.

**1894** *Phil. Trans. R. Soc.* CLXXXV. 107, I have succeeded in resolving this mortality-curve into components which are not..all of the normal type, but become, as we approach infinite mortality, of the skew form. **1905** *Drapers' Co. Res. Mem.* (Biometric Ser.) II. 22 The theory of skew variation will give regression curves.. containing product terms in *x* and *y*. **1929** *Jrnl. du Conseil* IV. 219 The area of the curve has been reduced to about half its original dimensions, but it has not been rendered very skew. **1936** *Bot. Rev.* II. 229 The distributions of the less common grasses are markedly skew. **1968** *Brit. Med. Bull.* XXIV. 210/2 The first is fairly symmetrical but discloses one outlying value; the second is notably skew to the right.

**2. a.** In special collocations, denoting that the thing in question deviates from a straight line, or has some part not at right angles with the rest, as ***skew arch***, ***bridge***, ***girder***, etc., or ***skew bevel***, ***chisel***, ***facet***, ***former***, ***iron***, etc.; ***skew gearing***, gearing consisting of two cog-wheels having non-parallel, non-intersecting axes; so ***skew gear***; ***skew nail***, ***nailing*** (cf. *skew-nail* vb., sense 3).

**1845** Ford *Hdbk. Spain* I. 257 First observe a singular Moorish *skew arch. **1857** Whewell *Hist. Induct. Sci.* (ed. 3) II. 447, I speak of what are called Skew Arches, in which the courses of stone or brick of which the bridge is built run obliquely to the walls of the bridge. **1846** Holtzapffel *Turning* II. 668 They fulfil the office of bevil wheels, or rather of *skew-bevil wheels. **1879** *Cassell's Techn. Educ.* I. 349/2 The teeth have then a peculiar form, and the wheels are called *skew-bevels*. **1838** Southey *Lett.* (1856) IV. 546, I have found a good story of a *skew bridge at Caen. **1872** Yeats *Techn. Hist. Comm.* 245 The art of building oblique or skew bridges appears to have been known on the Continent as early as 1530. **1872** *Routledge's Ev. Boy's Ann.* 354/1 One *skew, or corner chisel. **1881** Young *Every Man his own Mechanic* §644. 296 The tools used in carving are the chisel, the gouge, the skew-chisel, the parting tool. **1751** Jeffries *Treat. Diamonds & Pearls* (ed. 2) Gloss., In Brilliants, there are two sorts, **skew* or *skill* facets and *star* facets. **1678** Moxon *Mech. Exerc.* iv. 74 The *Skew-Former ..is seldom used by Joiners, but for cleansing accute angles. **1908** J. Richardson *Mod. Steam Engine* ix. 159 Fig. 150 shows the usual bevel gear, and Fig. 151 the *skew gear now used in preference. **1929** *Times* 2 Nov. 4/7 The oil pump, driven by skew gear from the camshaft, is in the sump. **1975** Ryder & Bennett *Mechanics of Machines* iv. 112 Skew or spiral gears (which are helical gears of differing helix angles forming a mating pair) are used to transmit motion between non-intersecting shafts. *a* **1877** Knight *Dict. Mech.* III. 2194/2 **Skew-gearing*, cog-wheels with teeth placed obliquely, so as to slide into each other and avoid clashing. **1902** A. C. Harmsworth et al. *Motors & Motor-Driving* x. 191 Another plan..substitutes for the bevel gearing what is known as skew or screw gearing. **1838** Simms *Publ. Wks. Gt. Brit.* 8 In the *skew girders the proper wind must be preserved. **1875** *Carpentry & Join.* 27 The iron is sometimes set at right angles to the sole of the plane and sometimes at an acute angle, when it is called a *skew iron. **1954** W. E. Kelsey *Carpentry, Joinery & Woodcutting Machinery* xiv. 394 In practice, *skew nails are driven in various places..to prevent any movement. **1958** *Times* 27 Mar. 5/2 In one case there was a double skew nail. **1929** T. Corkhill in R. Greenhalgh *Joinery & Carpentry* VI. 1561 **Skew nailing*, nails driven with an inclination to the surface to give greater security. **1958** *Times* 27 Mar. 5/2 Double skew nailing was an old traditional practice. **1973** P. Hutchinson *Home Carpenter* ii. 13 (*caption*) Skew nailing locks timber framing firmly in place. **1846** Holtzapffel *Turning* II. 485 The obliquity is then given to the iron, which is inserted at an angle, as in the *skew-rebate and fillister. **1822–7** Good *Study Med.* (1829) IV. 214 In *skew-sight or lateral vision, the axis of the eye affected usually coincides with that of the sound eye. **1850** *Engineer & Mach. Assist.* 74 That variety of toothed-geer known as *skew-wheels.

**b.** *Math.* (see quots.) ***skew field***, a ring whose non-zero elements form a group with respect to multiplication; a set which satisfies the axioms for a field except that multiplication is not commutative.

**1848** Cayley *Math. Papers* I. 378 Passing to the general case where the lines and points in question are not identical, which I should propose to term the theory of 'Skew Polars'. **1867** Brande & Cox *Dict. Sci.*, etc. III. 467 *Skew Surface*, a ruled surface of which two successive generators do not in general intersect. **1873** Cayley *Math. Papers* IX. 65–6 Before going further it will be convenient to establish the definition of 'skew anti-points'. **1873** Maxwell *Electr. & Magn.* (1881) I. 384 When they are not satisfied it is called a Skew system. **1965** Patterson & Rutherford *Elem. Abstract Algebra* iii. 75 In certain cases we encounter systems which satisfy all the required properties for a field with one exception, the commutative law of multiplication. Such systems are known as..skew fields. **1969** F. M. Hall *Introd. Abstr. Algebra* II. iv. 114 The only skew field of any importance is the set of quaternions.

**3.** *Comb.*, as ***skew-eyed*** adj. and adv., ***-fisted*** adj.; ***skew-nail*** vb.; ***skew-wise*** adv.

**1658** Rowland tr. *Moufet's Theat. Ins.* 1074 They are not one-ey'd, nor horrid skew-ey'd. *a* **1700** *Dict. Cant. Crew*, *Skew-fisted*, awkward, ungainly. **1875** Morris *Æneid* v. 445 He..his body swift writhed skew-wise from the fall. **1881** Young *Every Man his own Mechanic* §743. 340 The edge of the shelf may be skew-nailed to the support behind. **1922** Joyce *Ulysses* 30 And skeweyed Walter sirring his father. **1976** I. Levin *Boys from Brazil* ii. 57 He..smiled skew-eyed at him.

**b. skew-symmetric** *a. Math.*, (of a matrix or other square array of elements) having all the elements of the principal diagonal equal to zero, and each of the remaining elements equal to the negative of the element in the corresponding position on the other side of the diagonal; more generally, applied to an array of any dimension in which every element having a repeated subscript is zero and every other element is equal to the negative of elements having an odd permutation of the same subscripts; also **skew-symmetrical** *a.*; hence **skew-symmetry**.

[**1849** A. Cayley in *Jrnl. für die reine und angewandte Math.* XXXVIII. 93 On a $\lambda_{r,s} = -\lambda_{s,r}$ $(r \neq s)$; $\lambda_{r,r} = 0$. Ces déterminants peuvent être nommés 'gauches et symmétriques'.] **1911** T. Muir *Hist. Determinants* II. ix. 255 Any skew determinant is expressible in terms of *skew symmetric determinants and those of the original determinant which are not included in the latter. **1955** W. Pauli *Niels Bohr* 45 The vectors and skew-symmetric tensors transform just like the analogous electromagnetic quantities. **1967** [see bilinear *a.* 2]. **1980** A. J. Jones *Game Theory* i. 44 Thus a matrix game is symmetric if its matrix is skew-symmetric. **1911** T. Muir *Hist. Determinants* II. 269 The identity..is the twin theorem to one given in his previous paper regarding a bordered *skew symmetrical determinant of even order. **1927** *Proc. R. Soc.* A. CXVI. 249 In any example the quickest way of showing the *skew-symmetry is to write T symbolically as a determinant. **1980** A. J. Jones *Game Theory* i. 46 Skew-symmetry of the matrix is preserved by this operation.

**B.** *adv.* Obliquely, askew. *rare.*

**1706** Phillips (ed. Kersey) s.v., To *look skew*, or *a-skew*, to squint or leer, to look shy, or with an evil Eye upon one. **1815** *Zeluca* I. 305, I hope you don't think, Ma'am, that I have looked skew at not being paid my last week.

†**skew**, *v.*¹ *Obs.*⁻¹ [f. skew *sb.*¹] *intr.* To become overcast.

*c* **1400** *Siege Jerusalem* (E.E.T.S.) 53 Þe welcon wanned anon & þe water skeweþ, Cloudes clateren gon, as þey cleue wolde.

**skew** (skjuː), *v.*² Also 5–6 skewe, 7 scew, scue, 7–8 skue, 9 'skew. [ad. ONF. *eskiu(w)er*, *eskuer*, *escuer*, var. of OF. *eschuer*, *eschever*, etc.: see eschew *v.*¹ The later development of sense is curious, as well as the apparent use of the verb-stem in the adv. askew and the adj. skew.]

†**1.** *intr.* To escape, to slip away. *Obs.*

? *a* **1400** *Morte Arth.* 1562 Skilfulle skomfyture he skiftez as hym lykez, Is none so skathlye may skape, ne skewe fro his handez.

**2. a.** To take an oblique course or direction; to turn *aside*, move sideways.

*c* **1470** Henry *Wallace* IX. 148 Crawfurd drew saill, skewyt by, and off thaim past. **1567** Drant *Horace, Ep.* I. i. C ij, He, that..chearelye wills the to be bould not once to skew a syde. **1637** N. Whiting *Albino & Bellama* Author's Apol., And should they see us on our knees for blessing, They'd scue aside, as frighted at our dressing. **1703** Brand *Descr. Orkney & Zetland* 9 We judged it safest, to keep as near it [the land] as we could, and scued away by the coast. **1706** Phillips (ed. Kersey), To *Skue* or *walk skuing*, to waddle, to go sideling along. **1811** Willan in *Archaeologia* XVII. 158 *Skew*, to go aside, or obliquely. **1813** D. Anderson *Poems* 112 (Jam.), Contemplating ilk foppish brat,..To see them skew and skip about. **1845** S. Judd *Margaret* I. xvii, They skewed, bustled, and bumped along.

**b.** To shy (as a horse), to swerve. Also *fig.*

**1679** Alsop *Melius Inq.* II. viii. 370 When the Magistrate is settling the Civil peace of his Dominions, he needs not concern himself whether the people will skew or no. *a* **1825** Forby *Voc. E. Anglia* 304 *Skew*, to start aside, as a horse, at some object which scares him. **1851–** in dialect glossaries (Northampt., Linc., etc.).

**3.** To squint *at*, to look *at* (or *upon*) sideways, esp. in a suspicious or slighting manner; hence, to make side-hits *at*, reflect *upon*, something.

**1570** Levins *Manip.* 94 To Skewe, *limis oculis spectare.* **1618** Fletcher *Loyal Subj.* II. i, Our service Neglected, and look'd lamely on, and skew'd at. **1638** Sanderson *Serm.* (1681) II. 111 We find our selves ready..to skew at the infirmities of others. **1692** R. L'Estrange *Fables* 460 'Tis dangerous skewing upon the errors of the age a man lives in. **1827** Clare *Sheph. Cal.* 173 The cows stood round her in a wondering way,..Skewing at her. **1862** Borrow *Wild Wales* III. 74 Now looking to the left, now to the right,.. now skewing at an object, now leering at an individual.

†**4.** *trans.* To turn (the eyes) sidewards. *Obs.*

**1577** STANYHURST *Descr. Ireland* in Holinshed *Chron.* (1587) II. 17/1 Pleaseth you to skew your eie towards the margent. **1582** —— *Æneid* II. (Arb.) 67 Nor backward skewd I myn eyesight..tyl that my burden I lighted.

**5.** To cut *off*, set *back*, insert, etc., in an oblique manner.

**1611** COTGR., *Embraser*, to skue, or chamfret off the Iaumbes of a doore, or window. **1703** R. NEVE *City & C. Purchaser* 11 The springing of the Arch is skew'd back from the upright of the Jambs. **1777** GOSTLING *Walk Canterb.* (ed. 2) 181 The way was skewed off with an angle. **1886** MRS. CADDY *Footsteps of Jeanne D'Arc* 109 The lower room has a narrow window..skewed into the thickness of the wall.

**6.** To depict or represent unfairly. Also, to distort, bias.

**1872** C. KING *Sierra Nevada* x, What has he done but twist and skew and distort and discolor..this whole doggonned country? **1975** *Amer. Speech 1972* XLVII. 284 If he sings the song, he pronounces the name and possibly skews the results. **1979** *Sci. Amer.* Feb. 105/2 Whatever was skewing the eye-color ratio had its effect only in the course of sperm formation, not in egg formation. **1981** *Amer. Speech* LVI. 45 If we count those informants using both *big daddy* and *big mamma* only once, to avoid falsely skewing the data, fully 39 percent of the 38 different informants..are black.

**7.** *dial.* To throw, hurl, cast, fling.

**1824-** in dialect glossaries, etc. (Northumbld., Yks.).

**8.** *Statistics.* To make skew (SKEW *a.* 1 c).

**1929** *Jrnl. du Conseil* IV. 219 The frequency curve has been reduced to a very small proportion of the original, the mode has been shifted 1⅜ cms., and the group has been distinctly 'skewed'. **1931** *Brit. Jrnl. Psychol.* XXII. 85 The raising of the level of difficulty of test *A* will tend to skew the score-scatter positively.

Hence **'skewing** *vbl. sb.* (*a*) the action of the verb; (*b*) bias, distortion; **'skewing** *ppl. a.*

**1611** COTGR., *Biseau*, a bezle, bezeling, or scuing; such a slopenesse, or slope forme, as is in the point of an yron leauer, chizle, &c. **1692** L'ESTRANGE *Josephus, Life* (1733) 807 He prepar'd the people for his Purpose by a skewing discourse upon the Matter then in Question. **1821** CLARE *Vill. Minstr.* II. 8 Jane's 'skewing cow was struck with fear. **1969** *Language* XLV. 487 In reality the transfer at the kernel level can generally be made with far less danger of skewing than if one follows the highly involved processes. **1975** *Nature* 13 Mar. 139/2 The degree of skewing would depend on factors such as the length of time between the act of volunteering and actual participation in the experiment.

**skew**, *v.*[3] *techn.* [Of obscure origin.] (See quots.) Also **'skewing** *vbl. sb.*

**1688** HOLME *Armoury* III. 149/1 *Skew*, a term in Herald-Painting, which is with a Wing or Hares Foot [to] brush away all the loose edges of Silver and Gold that remains of the working of them. **1851-4** *Tomlinson's Cycl. Useful Arts* (1866) I. 758 A brush, with which every part is carefully gone over, superfluous gold being removed from some parts, and worked into others..The process is called *skewing*, and the particles of gold collected from it, are sold under the name of *skewings*. **1870** *Eng. Mech.* Jan. 487/1 Go over the frame with a *skewing* brush to remove all loose particles of gold. **1875** KNIGHT *Dict. Mech.* 2194/2.

**skew**, *v.*[4] [f. SKEW *sb.*[5]] In *pass.* with *up*: To have the vision obstructed by mist.

**1842** W. E. FORSTER in Reid *Life* (1888) I. v. 149 Walking I know not where—all mist before my vision, 'skewed up', nothing certain.

**skew**, *v.*[5] [? a special use of SKEW *v.*[2] Cf. SKEW *sb.*[6]] **a.** *to be skewed*, to fail in repetition. **b.** To fail in doing (a repetition).

**1859** FARRAR *Eric* 53 He would laugh when any one told him how he had escaped 'skewing' (i.e. being turned) by reading it off. **1899** 'MARTELLO TOWER' *At School & at Sea* 36 *Skew*..signified failure in a lesson, as: 'I skewed my rep (repetition) this morning'. **1905** H. A. VACHELL *The Hill* iii, It doesn't pay to be 'skewed'.

†**skewage**, obs. variant of SCAVAGE.

**1444** *Rolls of Parlt.* V. 68/1 Thei pay Skewage for the same merchaundises atte Suthampton. **1503** *Ibid.* VI. 550/2 An Act concerning Skavage or Skewage.

**skew-back.** [f. SKEW *sb.*[3] or *v.*[2] + BACK *adv.*]

**1.** *Arch.* The springing-line of an arch; the sloping surface on which either extremity of an arch rests; a course of stone or brickwork, an iron plate, etc., immediately supporting the foot of an arch.

**1703** MOXON *Mech. Exerc.* 279 According to the breadth of the Piers between the Windows, so ought the Skew-back or Sommering of the Arch to be. *Ibid.* 280 The line AC, which is vulgarly called the Skew-back for the Arch. **1725** W. HALFPENNY *Sound Building* 36 Set off the Skew-Back from *f* to *E*, and..*I* will be the Centre to which the Skew-Backs..are directed. **1837** *Civil Eng. & Arch. Jrnl.* I. 34/1 The arching for the support of the stairs is to be..springing from cut skew backs, and properly keyed in. **1842** *Penny Cycl.* XXII. 87/1 A plate of cast-iron is usually laid upon the stone skew-backs, extending the whole width of the bridge. *a* **1878** SIR G. SCOTT *Lect. Archit.* II. 40 The arches are turned in Roman bricks,..a steep skewback being formed for their springings.

**b.** A ring on the inside wall of a blast-furnace, by which the area is diminished.

**1884** KNIGHT *Dict. Mech.* Suppl. 820/1.

**2.** *Mech.* A cap or other casting made to receive the end of a diagonal rod or brace.

**1884** KNIGHT *Dict. Mech.* Suppl. 820/1.

Hence **skew-backed** *a.* (see quot.).

**1905** BOND *Goth. Archit.* 259 The upper surface of the top springer..against which the first voussoir of the real arch..starts, is said to be skewbacked.

**skewbald** ('skju:bɒld, -bɔ:ld), *a.* and *sb.* Also 7 **skewbal'd**, 8–9 **-ball**, 9 **squebald.** [Cf. SKEWED *a.*[1] and PIEBALD.]

**A.** *adj.* Of animals, esp. horses: Irregularly marked with white and brown or red, or some similar colour.

Properly distinct from PIEBALD (see quot. 1866), which is sometimes inexactly used for it.

**1654** J. CLEVELAND *Poems* 38 Th' Apparatour upon his skew-bal'd horse. **1692** *London Gaz.* No. 2777/4 A skew-bald Gelding about 14 hands. **1702** *Ibid.* No. 3870/4 A Strawberry Gelding.., with a skew bald Face (the white coming over his off Eye). **1789** MRS. PIOZZI *Journ. France* II. 20 Yesterday however shewed me what I knew not had existed—a skew-ball or pyeballed ass. **1825** HONE *Every-day Bk.* I. 992 Captain, a fallow and white dog, with skewbald face. **1866** W. WATSON *Youatt's Horse* xv. 346 When the white is mixed with black it is called 'pie-bald', with bay the name of 'skew-bald' is given to it. **1876** *World* V. 19 A middle-aged gentleman of hermit habits on a skewbald cob. **1884** *Liverpool Echo* 2 May, Thoroughbred Horse,..beautifully spotted red roan, squebald and piebald.

**B.** *sb.* A skewbald horse.

**1863** G. A. SALA *Capt. Dangerous* I. iii. 47 She was to have her pony, with John coachman on the skewball, sent to fetch her every Saturday. **1883** *Times* 30 May 5/1 Mr. Frisby's skewbald was at some disadvantage in this class.

**skewed** (skju:d), *a.*[1] ? *Obs.* Also 5 **scued, skevyd,** 5–7 **skued,** 7 **skude, skewd.** [Of doubtful origin: perh. f. OF. *escu* shield (cf. L. *scutulātus* as a colour of a horse, f. *scutula* platter), but there is also close resemblance in form and sense to Icel. *skjóttr*, the history of which is equally obscure.] Skewbald.

In quot. 1495 the reading of the Bodleian MS. is *scawed*, translating *maculosum* of the original.

*c* **1440** *Pallad. on Husb.* I. 703 (E.E.T.S.), The skewed goos, the brune goose as the white Is not fecounde. *Ibid.* IV. 810 The gray [horse], the goldenhered and the skued [*v.r.* scued]. **1481–90** *Howard Househ. Bks.* (Roxb.) 507 Item, payd to Richard Wayfer..for a skevyd nagg iiij.*s.* **1495** *Trevisa's Barth. De P.R.* XVIII. lxxvi. 830 Some Catte is whyte, some red, some blacke, some skewed and speckled. *a* **1529** SKELTON *E. Rummyng* 142 Some be flybytten, Some skewed as a kytten. **1577** B. GOOGE *Heresbach's Husb.* III. (1586) 116 b, The yelowish and the skued or pied horses are discommended almost of all men. **1611** COTGR., *Pecile*, a pide, or skude colour of a horse. **1616** J. LANE *Contn. Sqr.'s T.* XI. 323 Skewd was his horse, of manie colors chaunginge. *a* **1800** PEGGE *Suppl. Grose* s.v., A skew'd horse, one of two colours.

**skewed** (skju:d), *a.*[2] [f. SKEW *sb.*[3] or *v.*[2]] **1. a.** Set obliquely or aslant; skew. Also *Comb.*

**1611** BIBLE *1 Kings* vi. 4 *marg.*, Windowes broad within and narrow without; or skewed and closed. **1619** FLETCHER *Wild Goose Chase* IV. i, As I live I am asham'd, this wench has reach'd me,..This skew'd ey'd Carrion. **1840** *Civil Eng. & Arch. Jrnl.* III. 109/1 It is in the construction of railroads that the skewed arch meets with its most important application. **1895** C. R. B. BARRETT *Surrey* iii. 95 The eastern half of the chancel is skewed internally.

**b.** *fig.*

**1960** *Economist* 25 June 1330/1 This triple structure [of a book] is a magnificent achievement,..but its magnificence is ..skewed at its foundation... The skewness derives from Professor Hayek's perfectly legitimate definition of freedom. **1977** *New Yorker* 17 Oct. 78/2 She quickly came to share her husband's feelings about the skewed state of the world.

**2. a.** *Statistics.* = SKEW *a.* 1 c.

**1940** *Brit. Jrnl. Psychol.* XXX. 259 A difficult test tends to produce a positively skewed score-scatter. **1953** E. MAYR et al. *Methods & Princ. Systematic Zool.* vii. 134 A skewed curve is a curve in which the mode..is above or below the mean. **1977** *Lancet* 5 Feb. 311/1 In our hands, the crude breath-test results are highly skewed, but logarithmic transformation does produce a distribution which is indistinguishable from normal. **1977** R. E. MEGILL *Introd. Risk Analysis* iii. 22 The distribution shown in Fig. 3.1 is skewed to the right; i.e. it has more values to the right of its highest frequency (mode) than to the left.

**b.** Of a sample or data: biased, not representative.

**1975** *Amer. Speech 1973* XLVIII. 6 Since the data used for restructuring would have been external and skewed, one would expect attempts at restructuring to be only partially successful. **1977** *Times* 12 May 23/2 Quotas..are at present heavily skewed in favour of those countries which were economically powerful when the [International Monetary] Fund was set up.

**3.** Distorted; shifted in emphasis or character.

**1935** G. K. ZIPF *Psycho-Biol. of Lang.* iii. 105 A range of frequency where the skewed phoneme *t* in *ts* would be most stable. **1965** E. HAUGEN *Norwegian Eng. Dict.* 40/1 The typical East Norwegian (Oslo) [vowel] system is markedly skewed (in the same direction as Swedish)... The whole system has undergone a counterclockwise movement. **1980** *Nature* 17 Jan. 234/1 Critics..argued that the military control of research meant such research would inevitably be skewed towards the production of weapons of mass destruction. **1981** *Time* 7 Dec. 79/2 The wildness of the cat, its..skewed version of reality.

†**skewel.** *Obs.*[−1] [prob. a. OF. *escuele* (mod.F. *écuelle*).] ? A dish, platter.

**1567** *Wills & Inv. N.C.* (Surtees, 1835) 278, iiij litle wood skewells, xij[d]; v laten bassings.

**skewer** ('skju:ə(r)), *sb.* Also 7 scure, scuer, 8 scewer. [A variant of SKIVER *sb.*[1], which is prob. the more original form: cf. *kever*, *kiver*, and *cure* as variants of COVER *v.*, and *newt* from earlier *evet*.

In the *Nottingham Recs.* II. 86 (an entry of 1411) it is probable that *skuer* should be read as *skumer*, scummer.]

**1. a.** A long wooden or metal pin, used especially to fasten meat or the like together, to keep it in form while being cooked.

**1679** EVELYN *Sylva* (ed. 3) xxi. 100 The Wild Cornel or Dog-wood good to make Mill-Cogs, Pestles,..Butchers Skewers, &c. **1688** HOLME *Armoury* III. 292/2 A Butchers Cambril, Or, between two Scuers. *Ibid.* 315/1 He beareth Azure, two Skewers or Flesh pricks. **1704** SWIFT *Batt. Bks.* Misc. (1711) 266 He with Iron Skewer, pierces the tender Sides of both, their Legs and Wings close pinion'd to their Ribs. **1729** —— *Direct. Serv.* ii, Send up your Meat well stuck with Scewers, to make it look round and plump. **1809** *Asiat. Researches* IX. 60 These leaves are..used all over India to make baskets, and made fast together, with skewers, from the fibres of the *bambu*. **1837** WHITTOCK *Bk. Trades* (1842) 33 [Bleacher], To these pieces of canvass, the ends of the web of calico..may be fastened by wooden 'skewers'. **1881** YOUNG *Every Man his own Mechanic* §79. 33 It is the wood used by butchers for making wooden skewers.

*fig.* **1872** BLACK *Adv. Phaeton* xii, Transfixed by the red-hot skewers of jealousy.

**b.** A metal pin used to fasten an article of dress or to secure the hair.

**1771** SMOLLETT *Humph. Cl.* (1815) 234 A fringed blanket, fastened about her shoulders with a copper skewer. **1825** BENTHAM *Ration. Reward* 303 The buckles of the Romans, and the skewers employed by Queen Elizabeth. **1840** HOOD *Up Rhine* 222 Two plaited bands of hair..fastened up with a flat silver or gilt skewer.

**c.** A pin on which a bobbin is placed.

**1835** URE *Philos. Manuf.* 158 But single bobbins are set on skewers in the reel in correspondence with the single spindles on the copping rail. **1875** KNIGHT *Dict. Mech.* 315/1 The bobbins..are mounted..on a creel which has skewers for their reception.

**d.** Applied contemptuously to a weapon.

**1838** JAMES *Robber* vii, Let us look at your skewer in a handle, my Lord. **1848** *Sinks of London Laid Open* 124/2 *Skewer*, sword. **1934** A. RUSSELL *Tramp-Royal in Wild Australia* xxxviii. 254 There'd be 'skewers' flying in all directions. Rotten wounds they'd make—barbed, you know.

**2.** *attrib.* and *Comb.*, as ***skewer-full***, ***-machine***, ***-maker***; **skewer-piece** (see quot. 1867); **skewer tree, wood,** the spindle-tree, from the wood of which skewers are made.

(*a*) **1782** J. SCOTT *Poet. Wks.* 95 The green skewerwood seeds of scarlet shows. **1863** PRIOR *Brit. Pl.*, *Skewer-wood*, from skewers being made of it, a shrub called in the Western counties Skiver-wood, *Evonymus Europæus*. **1894** *Cornh. Mag.* Feb. 164 The square berries of the skewer tree little known except to the birds and the gipsies.

(*b*) **1832** MARRYAT *N. Forster* xl, Strung together like what we call 'skewer pieces' on board of a man-of-war. **1867** SMYTH *Sailor's Word-bk.* 629 The meat being then divided into messes, the remnants are cut into small pieces termed skewer-pieces. **1875** KNIGHT *Dict. Mech.* 2194/2 Skewer-machine. **1880** *Times* 10 Dec. 3/4 Tempting the hungry passers-by to purchase a skewer-full of the dainty roast. **1885** *Instr. Census Clerks 1881* 46 Skewer Maker.

**skewer** ('skju:ə(r)), *v.* Also 8 skuer. [f. the sb.]

**1.** *trans.* To fasten (meat, etc.) with a skewer; to pierce with a skewer or skewers. Also const. *together*, *up*, *upon*.

**1701** WOLLEY *Jrnl. New York* (1860) 29 Some be of Bears Skins and Rackoon Skins sewed or skuered together. **1741** *Compl. Fam.-Piece* I. ii. 147 Skewer them and roast them or stove or bake them, just as you please. **1769** MRS. RAFFALD *Eng. Housekpr.* (1778) 69 Skewer your hare with the head upon one shoulder. **1806** A. HUNTER *Culina* (ed. 3) 69 Skewer the fillet as close as possible. **1834** MARRYAT *P. Simple* v, A piece of stick..upon which were skewered..pieces of beef and pork.

*refl.* **1821** SCOTT *Kenilw.* xxxiii, If thou takest all that trouble of skewering thyself together, like a trussed fowl.

*fig.* **1850** DICKENS *Dav. Copp.* xliv, Britannia, that unfortunate female.., skewered through and through with office pens and bound..with red tape. **1871** *Member for Paris* II. 10 He..served him up every day to the readers of the *Pavois*, skewered through and through with an epigram.

**b.** To run through, transfix, with a sword or other weapon.

**1837** CARLYLE *Fr. Rev.* II. III. iii, Perhaps *not* to part, but to fall mutually skewered through with iron. **1861** C. READE *Cloister & H.* xliii, He felt his arm hot, then cold, and there was an English arrow skewering it. **1870** MISS BRIDGMAN *R. Lynne* I. xiii. 214, I thought I was being skewered by a horrid savage.

*refl.* **1865** TYLOR *Early Hist. Man.* xi. 311 The bird alighted there, and skewered itself upon the lance.

**c.** To place upon skewers. Cf. SKEWER *sb.* 1 c.

**1835** URE *Philos. Manuf.* 379 There are 1656 under 18 years of age, of whom..108 [are employed] in..skewering cops.

**2.** To fix, fasten, or secure to or into something else with, or as with, a skewer or skewers; to truss. Const. *in*, *into*, *to*, also *down*, *up*.

**1777** SHERIDAN *Trip to Scarborough* v. ii, Why should you ..suffer the rascals thus to skewer down my arms like a rabbit! **1799** W. TAYLOR in *Monthly Mag.* VII. 139 We'll see what fare the butler's foresight Has skewer'd into my knapsack. **1815** *Hist. J. Decastro* III. 331 He saw a great long thing lying on the ground skewered up in a white cloth. **1840** *P. Parley's Ann.* 364 The grenadier turned down his bayonet, and skewered him to the ground. **1890** *Nature* 30 Oct. 641 The mats are skewered on to two long bamboos.

*fig.* **1838** COLERIDGE in *Lit. Rem.* III. 174 When so strict a Calvinist..could skewer such frippery patches..on the sober gown and cassock of a Reformed and Scriptural Church!

**3.** To fix or thrust (*into* or *through* something) like a skewer or skewers.

**1869** BLACKMORE *Lorna D.* xxvi, He skewered his great eyes into mine. **1876** A. J. EVANS *Through Bosnia* iv. 135 They took a sharp stake..and..skewered it right through the carcase.

Hence **'skewered** *ppl. a.*; **'skewering** *vbl. sb.*

**1794** T. WEDGE *Agric. Chester* 58 The more perfectly the whey is got out of the cheese, by skewering, thrusting, and pressing, the less air will be left in it. **1806** A. HUNTER *Culina* (ed. 3) 237 Take the steaks,..then roll them up, and secure their form by skewering. **1839** *Mag. Dom. Econ.* IV. 243 The cheese..is turned and the pressure and skewering continued. **1868** *Daily Tel.* 29 May, The Chinese belles, with their crimped..and skewered hair.

**Skewes** ('skjuːɪz, skjuːz). *Math.* The name of S. *Skewes* (b. 1899), South African born mathematician, used *attrib.* and in the possessive to designate an extremely large number, relevant in the theory of the distribution of prime numbers, having the value exp(exp (exp 79)).

The first pronunc. is that used by the Skewes family.

In 1933 (*Jrnl. London Math. Soc.* VIII. 277) Skewes claimed that, for some value of *a* less than this number, the number of primes less than *a* exceeds $\int_0^a dx/\ln x$.

**1949** KASNER & NEWMAN *Math. & Imagination* ii. 32 A veritable giant is Skewes' number, even bigger than a gogolplex. **1955** *Math. Rev.* XVI. 676/1 In a previous paper ..the author has obtained a larger value of $X_1$ (the so-called Skewes number) on the assumption of the Riemann hypothesis.

**skewgy-mewgy**, var. SOOGEE-MOOGEE.

†**skewing.** *Obs.*$^{-1}$ = SKEWAGE.

**1312** in Sharpe *Cal. Lett. Bk. D.* (1902) 280 [Citizens of York to pass free from payment of murage, pavage,] skewynge [or] skewenge, [and other customs].

**skewing**, *vbl. sb.*: see SKEW *v.*$^{2}$ and *v.*$^{3}$

**'skewly**, *adv. rare.* [f. SKEW *a.* 2b + -LY$^{2}$.] In a skew manner.

**1896** W. W. R. BALL *Math. Recreations* (ed. 3) 137 Two cells in complementary rows and columns are said to be skewly related.

**'skewness.** [f. SKEW *a.* + -NESS.] The quality of being skew.

**1894** *Phil. Trans.* CLXXXVI. 357 While their frequent skewness sufficiently indicates that the neglect of X'r + ½ as compared with *a* is unjustifiable. **1901** *Nature* 3 Oct. 569/1 The polygon with the lower mode has a skewness of +0.48. **1905** K. PEARSON in *Biometrika* IV. 173 The chief physical differences between actual frequency distributions and the Gaussian theoretical distribution are:...(ii) The ratio of this separation between mean and mode to the variability of the character—a quantity I have termed the skewness. **1935** G. K. ZIPF *Psycho-Biol. of Lang.* iii. 99 The varying degrees of difficulty in the articulation of a phoneme resulting from the different combinations in which it occurs, together with the various relative frequencies of occurrences of the phoneme in its different combinations, may introduce a modification in the normal distribution of speech-sounds about the phonemic norm which, it seems, may well be termed *skewness.* **1936** *Hereditas* XXI. 330 The difference is probably not significant (the standard error could not be calculated owing to a marked skewness in both series). **1965** *Language* XLI. 189 A 'sound system'..of a complexity and skewness out of line with anything attested by languages known to us. **1968** *Economist* 30 Nov. 63/1 The latest crisis ..has been about the skewness of certain European currencies and not about the dollar or gold at all. **1970** *Watsonia* VIII. 124 A similar distribution of this character was found in most of the plants included in Table 1; in only four of them was the skewness more markedly positive.

**skewse**, obs. f. SCUSE *v.*

**skewt**, var. SCOOT *v.*$^{1}$

**skew-whiff** (skjuː'wɪf, -'hwɪf), *a.* and *adv. dial.* and *colloq.* Also **skew-wiff, -wift,** etc.; 8 **scew-.** [f. SKEW *a.* and *adv.* + WHIFF *sb.*$^{1}$ or *v.*$^{1}$] Askew, awry (*lit.* and *fig.*).

**1754** *Scots Mag.* July 337/2 Behind, with a coach-horse short dock, cut your hair; Stick a flower before, scew-whiff, with an air. **1839** W. HOLLOWAY *General Dict. Provincialisms* 154/1 *Skew-whift, adj.* (Askew, from Skef, Belg. oblique; and perhaps Whiffed, blown.) Awry. **1854** A. E. BAKER *Gloss. Northamptonshire Words & Phrases* II. 239 *Skew-whiff*, awry, aslant. 'It's all *skew-whiff*.' Probably blown on one side by a whiff or puff. **1879** G. F. JACKSON *Shropshire Word-Bk.* 386 *Skew-wiff*,..*adv.* awry; irregular; zigzag. **1895** J. T. CLEGG *Stories, Sketches, & Rhymes in Rochdale Dialect* 228 Her judgment's getten thrut skew-wift. **1899** *Shetland News* 20 May 7/2, I hed ta geng skewquieff. **1935** A. P. HERBERT *What a Word!* iv. 101 Go on cackling..until the orator has to stop and ask you why you cackle. Then tell him. He won't get *Frankenstein* skew-whiff again. **1946** D. L. SAYERS *Unpopular Opinions* 59 When Neptune shouldered Britain out of the sea, he did not make a neat engineering job of it. Characteristically, Britain came up skew-wiff, with one edge thick and hard and the other soft and thin, like a slice of wedding-cake. **1959** I. & P. OPIE *Lore & Lang. Schoolch.* iii. 47 If a boy's cap is on skew-whiff: 'Are you wearing that cap or just walking underneath it?' **1959** *N.Z. Listener* 12 June 20/3 A breaker turned the bow skew-wiff. **1974** J. CLEARY *Peter's Pence* iii. 82 Our plans seem to have gone a bit skew-wiff, don't they? That's the trouble with the Irish. **1977** *Lancashire Life* Feb. 53/4 Thi tie's put on skew-wiff.

**skewy** ('skjuːɪ), *a. colloq.* [f. SKEW *a.* and *adv.* + -Y$^{1}$.] Somewhat askew, awry, or twisted. So **'skewiness**, the quality of being skewy.

**1862** 'G. HAMILTON' *Country Living* 62 Though freedom from foreign growth discovered an intention of straightness, the most casual observer could not but see that skewiness had usurped its place. **1898** A. T. SLOSSON *Dumb Foxglove* 71 Narrer an' p'inted like a pear, or skewy an' knobby like a quince. **1940** *Amer. Speech* XV. 131/2 They have the same meaning as awry or 'skewy'. **1960** E. H. GOMBRICH *Art & Illusion* viii. 248 The right-hand one is really a distorted, skewy object which only assumes the appearance of a chair.

†**skey**, *sb.*$^{1}$ *Obs. rare.* A kind of boat.

**1507** *Will of Gorman* (Somerset Ho.), A boote otherwise called a Skeye. **1542** *Admir. Ct. Warrant Bks.* 1 Sept., Navicula vocata a skey.

‖**skey** (skeɪ), *sb.*$^{2}$ *S. African.* Also **skea.** [Du. *schei* tie-piece.] One of a pair of wooden bars passing through each end of an ox-yoke, to which the neckstraps are fixed.

**1850** R. G. CUMMING *Hunter's Life S. Afr.* (1902) 7/1 In inspanning, the yoke is placed on the back of the neck of the ox, with one of these skeys on either side. *Ibid.* 10/2 The oxen..spring about in the yoke,..invariably snapping the straps and yoke-skeas. **1863** W. C. BALDWIN *Afr. Hunting* iv. 103 From the beams hung Kaffir ropes,..old saddles, yokes, skeys, neckstraps, and all apparatus for wagoning.

†**skey**, *a. Obs.*$^{-0}$ [var. of SKEIGH *a.*] Skittish.

Cf. the vb. *skey* (of a horse) in Brockett (1829).

*c* **1440** *Promp. Parv.* 444/2 Schey, or skey, as hors, or styȝtyl. *Ibid.* 457/2 Skey, as hors, *umbraticus.*

†**skey**, *v. Sc. Obs. rare.* [Of obscure origin; perh. two different words.]

**1.** *intr.* To get clear, to sheer *off.*

*c* **1470** HENRY *Wallace* x. 873 Bot fra the Scottis thai mycht nocht than off skey, The clyp so sar on athir burd thai wey.

**2.** *trans.* ? To startle, come upon suddenly.

**1539** in Pitcairn *Crim. Trials* I. 220* Ȝe slew his serwandis doggis þat skeyit ȝou quhare ȝe lay.

**skey**, obs. f. SKY.

**skeymishe, -mows(e**, obs. ff. SQUEAMISH.

**skeyn(e**, obs. ff. SKEIN, SKENE.

**skeyr**, obs. Sc. f. SKERE.

‖**skhod** (sxod). [Russ.] In the U.S.S.R. (and pre-Revolutionary Russia), an assembly of villagers. Also ***selskii skhod*** (see quot 1972).

**1877** D. M. WALLACE *Russia* viii. 120 All important communal affairs are regulated by the *Selski Skhod*, or Village Assembly. **1914** H. W. WILLIAMS *Russia of Russians* xi. 348 The affairs of the community are managed by a *skhod*, or mote of which all the adult males are members. **1948** J. TOWSTER *Political Power in U.S.S.R.* x. 201 In small rural settlements the place of a village soviet was to be taken by a *skhod*—a general meeting of electors. **1959** E. H. CARR *Socialism in One Country* II. 307 The *skhod*, which dated from Tsarist times, was the village meeting... It was not, strictly speaking, a public body. It had no constitutional status, no officially recognized duties..but it sometimes performed primitive functions of local government. **1972** T. SHANIN *Awkward Class* ix. 164 A 'rural gathering' (*sel'skii skhod*) was to be established in parallel with the 'land gathering'. The 'rural gathering' would consist of all the inhabitants with Soviet electoral rights within the area of a Rural Soviet.

**ski** (skiː), *sb.* Pl. **skis** (now *rare*) **ski.** Also **she, skee.** [a. Norw. *ski* (*skji, sjii,* also written *skid*) neut.:—ON. *skið* snow-shoe, billet of cleft wood, = OE. *scíd* SHIDE *sb.* In some Norw. dialects also *skida* (*skjia, skjie*) fem., = Sw. *skida* (pl. *skidor*):—ON. *skíða.* In mod.Norw. and Sw. *sk* before palatal vowels has the value of (ʃ).

The form *skid*, and the Sw. pl. *skidor*, have occasionally been used in English context, but have not obtained general currency.]

**1. a.** One of a pair of long slender pieces of wood fastened to the foot and used as a snow-shoe, enabling the wearer to slide down hill with great speed. Also *fig.*

The length and breadth of skis vary, but the average dimensions are eight feet long and four inches broad; they are usually pointed and curved at the toe, sometimes curved at the heel. In the 20th c., the use of skis as a means of exercise or sport has spread from Norway and Sweden to Switzerland and other places.

Quot. 1755 is an isolated early use.

*α.* **1755** *Monthly Rev.* XII. 451 He says they have *skies*, or long and thin pieces of board, so smooth, that the peasants wade through the snow with them. **1885** TROMHOLT *Aurora Borealis* I. 136 The Ski are pointed and slightly curved at one end, and the edges rounded. **1893** *Daily Graphic* 28 June 13 Fourteen pairs of ash and sycamore ski of special pattern, some being 10 feet in length. **1923** D. H. LAWRENCE *Birds, Beasts & Flowers* 177 So she..goes off in slow sad leaps On the long flat skis of her legs. **1933** *Illustr. London News* 9 Dec. 942/1 A German soldier named Schuhmacher, said to have belonged to an infantry battalion training on ski in the Bavarian Alps, was shot dead by Austrian frontier guards. **1960** A. S. NEILL in *Id* III. 4 The snow was deep and we all had to go out on skis.

*β.* **1889** *Montreal Daily Star* Carnival No. 4/3 Snowshoes, skees, and tugues were hung about the arch in stars. **1900** *Westm. Gaz.* 28 Aug. 2/1 Tobogganing, sleighing, and skee-ing (on long, narrow, snow-shoes called 'skees').

**b.** Each of two or three runners forming part of the landing gear of an aeroplane designed to land on snow or ice. Cf. *ski-plane*, sense 2b below.

**1912** *Flight* 17 Feb. 137 (*caption*) Note the special skis attached for landing purposes. **1931** F. D. BRADBROOKE *Light Aeroplane Man.* vi. 96 For work on ice and snow skis are fitted to the undercarriage instead of wheels. **1948** 'N. SHUTE' *No Highway* ii. 41 They flew up in a Norseman fitted with skis and landed in deep snow. **1959** GREEN & POLLINGER *World's Fighting Planes* (ed. 3) 21 The Otter may be fitted with wheels, floats or skis.

**c.** *transf.* = WATER SKI. Usu. *pl.*

**1930** *Literary Digest* 11 Oct. 48/3 Many games have been introduced this summer for those who walk on water with skis. **1964** G. McDONALD *Running Scared* xii. 160 Tom suggested water skiing... Tom's skis surfaced easily and beautifully. **1974** *Encycl. Brit. Micropædia* X. 574/3 Typical all-purpose skis are of wood 6½ inches wide and 5 feet 9 inches..long, with a stabilizing fin on the bottom near the heel.

**d.** A launching site for flying bombs. Freq. *attrib.*

**1953** P. C. BERG *Dict. New Words* (ed. 2) 146/1 *Ski*, the launching apparatus for the flying bomb, from its fancied resemblance to a gigantic ski. (1944.) **1957** P. J. DE LA FERTE *Rocket* vi. 89 The Allied Air Forces launched a massive assault on the ramps, ski constructions and preparation huts. **1958** C. B. SMITH *Evidence in Camera* ix. 224 A launching site..which also matched up with the foundations for ramps at the ski sites... The ski buildings provided storage space for twenty flying bombs on each site. **1978** R. A. YOUNG *Flying Bomb* ii. 27 (*caption*) The left-hand 'ski' has not yet been roofed. *Ibid.* 30 When components arrived at the sites they could be most easily stored in one of the 'ski' buildings.

**2.** *attrib.* and *Comb.*, as ***ski-climber, -runner; ski-excursion, -jumping, -racing, -running***; (= *ski-ing* vbl. sb.), as ***ski boot, -cap, centre, chalet, clothes, club, goggles, -hut, instructor, -jacket -lodge, pants, parka, -race, resort, -room, school, shop, slope, -staff, suit, track, trail, troops, trousers, -wear.***

**1907** E. C. RICHARDSON *Ski-Running* 48 In the Black Forest *ski boots are often made of dog or calf skin. **1972** *Guardian* 31, Oct. 11/3 Ski boots are now injection-moulded plastic shells lined with foam padding. **1937** *Sierra Club Bull.* Feb. 46 There follows, however, our usual clothing list ..ski-boots and *ski-caps. **1975** E. HILLARY *Nothing Venture, Nothing Win* ii. 39, I had an icicle about five inches long hanging from the strap of my ski-cap. **1942** *Ski center [see *ski trail* below]. **1948** [see ORIENTEERING]. **1960** *Sunday Express* 27 Nov. 15/5 On the same railway line..there are nine other ski centres. **1971** *Country Life* 23 Dec. 1814/4 (Advt.), *Ski Chalets. Top resorts in France, Switzerland and Austria. **1975** *Times* 2 Jan. 4/7 President Ford continued to study a report he received at his ski chalet. **1965** 'J. LE CARRÉ' *Looking-Glass War* i. 3 A group of children... Some wore *ski clothes. **1913** F. H. HARRIS *Dartmouth out o' Doors* 104 In our own country *ski clubs are flourishing. **1963** *Ski-ing* ('Know the Game' Series) 12 There are a number of ski clubs which are affiliated to the Ski Club of Great Britain. **1971** C. BONINGTON *Annapurna South Face* 244 *Ski-goggles..proved ideal in bad weather conditions. **1958** E. DUNDY *Dud Avocado* I. vi. 93 Dressed for the Select as for a *ski-hut..in a checkered wool-shirt, G.I. pants and ski-boots. **1973** *Times* 8 Jan. 5/1 The party.. had arrived back at a skihut at Abisko. **1959** P. MOYES *Dead Men don't Ski* iv. 45 It is..traditional for *ski instructors to be handsome. **1978** S. SHELDON *Bloodline* ii. 28 On her thirty-fifth birthday Anna had gone to Kitzbühel, in Austria, and there she had met Walther Gassner, a ski instructor thirteen years younger than she. **1968** M. WOODHOUSE *Rock Baby* xxiv. 234 He was wearing a blue *ski-jacket and denim trousers. **1966** —— *Tree Frog* xii. 86 A hunting-lodge modernised to make a *ski-lodge. **1978** *Chicago* June 36/1 Once a ski lodge, then a theatre, this rural listening room now provides one of the most relaxed settings for good pop, jazz, and folk. **1937** *Sierra Club Bull.* Feb. 46 There follows..our usual clothing list... *Ski-pants. **1977** C. FORBES *Avalanche Express* xxv. 267 Six men clad in ski-masks and ski-pants. **1974** *Amer. Speech 1970* XLV. 180 A variety of wearing apparel, such as children's clothes, men's slacks, *ski parkas and sweaters. **1936** C. M. DOLE *Amer. Ski Ann.* 53 There should be a competent course patrol for all ski races made up from the personnel of the club *ski patrols. **1973** D. FRANCIS *Slay-Ride* ii. 23 He used to win across-country *ski races. **1898** *Encycl. Sport* II. 379/1 About a hundred competitors come from various parts of the country to strive for these blue ribbons of the *ski-racing world. **1975** *Times* 19 Dec. 9/5 In ski racing..one's position in the starting order is based on one's previous results. **1965** 'J. LE CARRÉ' *Looking-Glass War* iii. 33 The town..feeds the main *ski resorts. **1972** D. HASTON *In High Places* vi. 72 We ..tried to be as inconspicuous as four laden climbers can be in a ski resort. **1963** I. FLEMING *On H.M. Secret Service* xii. 129 There was a *ski-room and workshop to the left of the exit. **1887** *Appleton's Ann. Cycl. 1886* XI. 805/1 The distance covered by an expert *skee-runner is from fifty to sixty miles a day. **1888** *Times* 16 Nov. 10/1 At a concourse in Christiania he became champion ski-runner. **1854** LATHAM *Native Races Russ. Emp.* 84 The most characteristic..of their habits..is what we may call by a name coined for the occasion—*she-running. **1911** A. BENNETT *Card* xi. 273 No sport was true sport save the sport of ski-running. **1969** H. MACINNES *Salzburg Connection* ii. 37 We have no ski lift here..no special slopes. But there is good ski-running. That is the best sport anyway... Let me show you on this map... You can ski for thirty kilometres. **1934** *Leisure* Jan. 23 This run..will probably be used by the official *Ski School of the U.S. Eastern Amateur Ski Association. **1954** R. MARTIN *Your Ski Holiday* vi. 44 Some people nowadays go to one of the 'dry ski schools' which are being set up in several of the large towns of England. **1980** J. CARTWRIGHT *Horse of Darius* iii. 42 She..made her way along to the office of the ski school. **1969** H. MACINNES *Salzburg Connection* viii. 114 Just beyond Bad Aussee.. where Johann Kronsteiner has his *ski-shop. **1934** *Discovery* Oct. 297/2 (*caption*) The new 'tower-hotels' at Colle di Sestrières in the Italian Alps, with a background of *ski-slopes. **1976** A. WHITE *Long Silence* xi. 104 A fall of snow at the wrong time can start an avalanche on the ski slopes. **1896** *Idler* Mar. 307/2 He thrust out his *ski staff and tripped up his companion. **1956** R. Braddon *Nancy Wake* vi. 55 She accordingly bought herself a new *ski suit. **1978** J. A. Michener *Chesapeake* 809 They walked together, bundled in ski suits, to all corners of their estate. **1948** H. Innes *Blue Ice* vii. 194 Three *ski tracks ran off at an angle, crossing the tracks we were following. **1975** D. Bagley *Snow Tiger* xxxii. 281 Here is an enlargement of the breakaway point of the avalanche. There is a ski track going into it. **1942** *Economic Geogr.* July 318/2 Lack of overnight accommodations, or their location at inconvenient distances from the *ski trails and slopes, has, and will, retard the popularity of many otherwise excellent ski centers. **1973** P. A. Whitney *Snowfire* vi. 108 The immediate problem of getting myself down a ski trail without breaking my neck. **1934** S. Spender *Vienna* iii. 32 Like diving mono-planes.. curled down on them the *ski-troops. **1974** *Encycl. Brit. Macropædia* XVI. 835/1 Ski troops were..used in Sweden as early as 1452. **1946** P. Bottome *Lifeline* vii. 71 Ida, dressed in long *ski trousers and a black pullover. **1969** N. Freeling *Tsing-Boum* xxii. 158 Tight black ski trousers and excessively brilliant orange sweater. **1961** *Sports & Camping Goods Dealer* Nov. 9/1 Big demand for *Ski-wear... Sales of skiwear continue to rise. **1980** L. Birnbach et al. *Official Preppy Handbk.* 152/2 The latest and most expensive skiwear and equipment.

**b.** Special Combs. **ski-boat**, (*a*) *S. Afr.*, a raftlike boat with two outboard motors used esp. for offshore fishing; (*b*) a small powerboat used for towing water-skiers; **ski-bob** [BOB *sb.*[1] 2 d, e], a vehicle resembling a bicycle with skis instead of wheels, which slides quickly over snow; hence as *v. intr.*, to ride a ski-bob; **ski-bobber**, one who ski-bobs; **ski-bobbing** *vbl. sb.*, the action of riding a ski-bob, esp. as a sport; **ski bum** *N. Amer. slang*, a skiing enthusiast who works casually at a resort in order to ski; hence **ski bumming**; **ski carrier** = *ski rack* below; **ski flying** (see quot. 1974); **skijamas** *N. Amer.*, a pair of pyjamas in the style of a ski suit; **ski-jump**, (*a*) the artificial structure built on a natural slope, from which a ski-jumper takes off; also *transf.* and *fig.*; (*b*) a leap made by a ski-jumper; **ski-jumper**, one who takes part in ski-jumping; **ski-jumping**, a winter sport in which skiers 'jump' from the end of a snow-covered chute built high on a slope, marks being usu. awarded for style and distance covered by the leap; also, this action; **ski-lift**: see LIFT *sb.*[2] 10 b; **ski-mask**, a protective covering for the face, of the type worn by skiers (and adopted by others to conceal identity); hence **ski-masked** *a.*; **ski pack**, an arrangement whereby a tour company offers holiday facilities and the hire of skiing equipment at one inclusive price; **ski patrol** *N. Amer.*, a group of expert skiers who patrol ski slopes to check on conditions and assist skiers in difficulties; hence **ski patrolman**, a member of a ski patrol; **ski-plane**, an aeroplane having its undercarriage fitted with skis (sense 1 b above) for landing on snow or ice; **ski pole** *U.S.* = *ski stick* below; **ski rack**, a frame (usu. fixed to the roof of a car) on which skis are placed for transportation; **ski ramp**, a ramp constructed for skiing practice; also *transf.*; **ski run**, (*a*) a spell of travelling on skis; (*b*) a skiing piste; **ski stick**, one of two long sticks held by a skier to assist in propulsion or braking and in balancing; **ski tour**, a tour made by cross-country skiing; hence **ski-tourer**, **ski-touring**; **ski tow**, (*a*) a mechanical device for conveying skiers up a slope, in the form of an endless moving rope or of bars or seats suspended from an overhead cable; (*b*) a tow-rope for water-skiers; hence **ski-tow** *v. trans.*, to pull with a ski tow; **ski-walking**, cross-country skiing (cf. NORDIC *a.* b); so **ski-walk** *v. trans.*, to travel over by ski-walking; **ski-wax**, wax applied to the undersides of skis to improve performance; **ski-wheel**, on the undercarriage of an aircraft: a combination of ski and wheel (see quots.); hence **ski-wheeled** *a.*, having a ski-wheel landing gear.

**1964** A. Trew *Smoke Island* ii. 43 José brought the *ski-boat round and Andy recovered some of the lost line as he scrambled into the fighting-chair. **1971** 'D. Halliday' *Dolly & Doctor Bird* viii. 103 The holidaymakers..hissing past.. in the ski boat. **1974** *Argus* (Cape Town) 2 Aug. 11/4 Many of the ski-boats operating in that area had 60, 80 or 100 snoek. **1966** *Skier* Sept. 7/1, 1962: I became German and Bavarian Women's *ski-bob Champion. **1968** *Guardian* 21 Sept. 10/3 The ski-bob is a small bicycle on skis with short skis for the feet with braking claws on them. **1969** *Winter Sports Ann.* 20/1 One can learn to ski-bob very quickly. **1976** *Daily Tel.* (Colour Suppl.) 6 Aug. 6/2 A ski-bob can exceed speeds of 80mph on a steep, straight run. *Ibid.* 6/3 Captain John Beckett..who once taught a lady journalist to ski-bob in one-and-a-half hours. **1967** *Ski bobber [see *mini-ski* s.v. MINI-]. **1976** *Daily Tel.* (Colour Suppl.) 6 Aug. 6/1 Ski-bobbers are now eligible for grants from the National Council for Physical Recreation. **1966** *Skier* Sept. 6/2 *Ski-bobbing has come a long way since those first laughing days. **1971** *Daily Tel.* 30 Jan. 7/5 Ski-bobbing (not yet so popular in France as elsewhere, but rapidly catching on). **1976** *Ibid.* (Colour Suppl.) 6 Aug. 6/1 In 1971, the Army included ski-bobbing in their own skiing championships. **1960** *Washington Post* 4 Mar. C5/3 John Kerr..is firmly settled in the picturesque ex-mining town of Aspen, Colo., and happily pursuing one of the world's newest professions—ski bumming... By *ski bum standards, John Kerr has struck it rich. **1978** *N.Y. Times* 16 Jan. C8/1 (*headline*) Ski-bum shortage shakes the resorts. **1978** S. Sheldon *Bloodline* ii. 34 'What can a ski bum contribute to Roffe and Sons?' he asked. **1965** 'D. Shannon' *Death-Bringers* xiv. 187 It was the right Anglia. It had ski *carriers on its roof. **1970** *Globe & Mail* (Toronto) 25 Sept. 32/7 (Advt.), 100 Accessories..from ski carriers to repair bases, we have them all at spectacular savings. **1952** *Sun* (Baltimore) 3 Mar. (B ed.) 15/7 Toivo Lauren..won the international '*ski-flying' contest today with a jump of approximately 429 feet 9 inches. **1974** R. Scharff *Ski Magazine's Encycl. Skiing* 420/2 *Ski flying*, a form of jumping on hills where distances of 100 meters or more can be reached. **1958** L. Whishaw *As Far as you'll take Me* vii. 104, I..then, dressed in my *skijamas, ate my dinner in peace. **1964** *N.Y. Times* 29 Nov. 132 Reis 'ski-jamas' are set for winter slumber. **1907** E. C. Richardson *Ski-Running* 89 The outlook from the top of a *ski-jump of any magnitude is indeed alarming. **1922** E. E. Cummings *Enormous Room* i. 18 A face all ski-jumps and toboggan slides. **1948** H. Innes *Blue Ice* x. 250 He was going to do a ski jump..on to the top of the moving train. **1953** X. Fielding *Stronghold* 42 At last I reached a scree, as long and steep as a ski-jump. **1960** C. H. Gibbs-Smith *Aeroplane* 3/5 A later illustration shows a long 'ski-jump' ramp. **1971** L. Koppett *N.Y. Times Guide Spectator Sports* xvi. 222 One of the most spectacular sights in any sport is the ski jump. **1978** *Navy News* Aug. 40/4 The invention of the Ski Jump take-off ramp to be fitted in Royal Navy ships carrying Harrier aircraft has won an award of £25,000. **1894** *Engineering News* 1 Mar. 169/3 *Ski-jumpers..have for some time been holding tournaments in Minnesota. **1981** 'E. Lathen' *Going for Gold* i. 15 People.. were taking up stations from which they could watch the last of the ski jumpers. **1904** *Sandow's Mag.* Mar. 200 (*caption*) A *ski-jumping competition. **1927** A. Huxley *Let.* 14 Feb. (1969) 283 We had an international ski jumping competition here last week. **1960** *Guardian* 8 Dec. 10/6 In 1950 and 1951 there was ski jumping..on Hampstead Heath. **1973** *Country Life* 29 Nov. 1807 Ski-jumping and cross-country (*lang-lauf*) racing. **1973** 'D. Shannon' *No Holiday for Crime* xiv. 208 It had been a professional job: *ski-masks, a look-out at the door. **1980** J. Ball *Then came Violence* xiii. 103 Since ski masks had been used..there were no descriptions. **1976** *Time* 20 Dec. 7/2 Graziella Quartuccio, 43, was snatched away in her nightgown..by a machine-gun-toting gang of *ski-masked Mafiosi. **1969** *Guardian* 11 Oct. 10/6 See which holidays give the best value in terms of *ski packs. **1936** C. M. Dole *Amer. Ski Ann.* 52 A definite organization is necessary. The *Ski Patrol has been suggested..and..has been instituted in one locality. **1963** *Amer. Speech* XXXVIII. 204 The warning signs erected in ski areas by the ski patrol. **1978** *Globe & Mail* (Toronto) 8 Feb. 31/1 The Canadian Ski Patrol system is again this season doing on-the-slopes testing of bindings for skiers. **1957** *Today's Health* Jan. 54/3 Two *ski patrolmen..lashed their skis together to make an emergency toboggan. **1930** O. H. Kneen *Everyman's Bk. Flying* xiii. 231 The Fairchild Airplane Company and others use the term **ski-plane* for Canadian machines, convertible to seaplanes in the summer. **1936** J. Grierson *High Failure* xiii. 281 For Canadian conditions the most useful machines are seaplanes in summer and ski-planes in winter. **1964** G. Lyall *Most Dangerous Game* xxi. 172, I came in from Spitzbergen, in an old Noorduyn Norseman ski-plane. **1975** E. Hillary *Nothing Venture, Nothing Win* vi. 82 Access to the mountains is often long and difficult—or used to be before the development of ski-planes and helicopters. **1920** *Literary Digest* 14 Feb. 115, I need not describe these poles to you, as any dealer will know what you mean by *ski-poles. **1978** W. F. Buckley *Stained Glass* xv. 155 The accordion player, without ski poles, and making music all the way, began the three-mile ski down the mountain. **1968** *Globe & Mail* (Toronto) 5 Feb. 26/8 (Advt.), 67 Austin Cooper, tachometer, *ski rack. **1980** L. Birnbach et al. *Official Preppy Handbk.* 204/2 In the winter, the car is heading north, topped with a ski rack. **1973** *Houston Post* (Spotlight Suppl.) 14 Oct. 9/5 The fair is free, including hourly ski demonstrations by Ed Williams on a *ski ramp. **1976** *Southern Even. Echo* (Southampton) 11 Nov. 17/2 Ships with 'ski-ramps' at the bow for the launching jump-jet aircraft were forecast by the chief designer of the Harrier at Southampton University last night. **1924** O. Poulsen *Skiing* 72 It is on one of these long *ski-runs alone that a man can think out his problems best. **1951** M. Kennedy *Lucy Carmichael* V. iii. 222 The next few seconds had been as good as a first class ski run. **1953** Dylan Thomas *Let.* 27 Feb. (1966) 395 We could go anywhere on that, except Laughlin's heart and ski-run. **1977** N. Freeling *Gadget* II. 92 The climb..was steep as a downhill ski-run. **1907** E. C. Richardson *Ski-Running* 46 (*caption*) Disc for bottom of *ski stick. **1924** E. Hemingway in *Transatlantic Rev.* Dec. 635 Nick knocked his clamps loose with one of his ski sticks. **1970** N. Fleming *Czech Point* (1971) i. 7, I hooked my skisticks on to the T-bar. **1949** E. Coxhead *Wind in West* vii. 180 Ilse knew..nothing of nature except what she could see from a *ski-tour. **1972** *Guardian* 11 Mar. 13/1 The standard yardstick for these *ski-tourers and ski-mountaineers has been..a mountain obstacle race between..Chamonix, and Zermatt. **1960** *Ibid.* 24 Oct. 11/4 In Scotland..after April only high-level *ski-touring is possible. **1972** Dean & Smith *Wisconsin* 161/1 Call it ski touring, Nordic skiing,.. or simply X-C, but it all boils down to the same thing—the art of walking on skis. **1942** *Economic Geogr.* July 307/2 The invention of the *ski tow at about this time..gave great impetus to the growing interest in skiing. **1967** *Spectator* 15 Sept. 301/1 One laird explained his resistance..to.. building a ski tow in the snowy heights he owned—by saying simply, 'Look what happened to Switzerland.' **1971** J. Yardley *Kiss a Day* vii. 121 He..trailed the ski-tow over the side for her to catch. Five minutes later they were cutting a white wake across the lagoon. **1976** P. Cave *High Flying Birds* iii. 28 Ski-towing a hang-glider is reckoned on being a pretty dangerous sport at the best of times. **1970** R. Lowell *Notebk.* 148 We *ski-walked the eggshell at the Mittersill. **1974** *Observer* 3 Nov. 34/2 The age-old Nordic ski-ing that is both easier to learn and cheaper to enjoy. Essentially it is walking, or running, on skis over undulating country side... Ski-walking, Nordic ski-ing, *Skiwandern*, *ski de vandonnée*, *Ski du fond*, *Langlauf*—the variety of names given to the sport perhaps causes confusion. **1910** W. R. Rickmers *Ski-ing* 35 *Ski-wax can be obtained hard or in tubes. **1979** R. Fiennes *Hell on Ice* v. 68, I needed feeling in my fingers to..feel for my map, change the ski-wax and many other things. **1938** C. Winchester *Wonders of World Aviation* 979/2 It sometimes happens that flights to the northern parts of Canada necessitate a take-off fit only for wheels and a destination with ground fit only for skis. This indicates that there is a need for a *ski-wheel combination. **1958** *Edmonton* (Alberta) *Jrnl.* 24 June III. 17/8 A pilot on ski-wheels who runs into trouble will pick a lake or river, set down parallel to the shore, and ski neatly up onto the beach before his aircraft loses its forward momentum and sinks. **1976** *Jrnl. R. Soc. Arts* CXXIV. 634/2 Two ski-wheeled de Havilland Twin Otter aircraft are operational in the Antarctic between November and March.

**ski**, *v.* [f. the sb.] **1.** *intr.* To travel on skis.

[**1893** Implied in SKI-ING *vbl. sb.* 1.] **1904** *Times* 4 Mar. 9/2 They skied down to Chamonix.

**b.** To water-ski.

**1947** *Life* 17 Feb. 7/3 Lumber dealers..have seen pictures of her skiing among the cypresses and want to know how they can purchase the trees. **1956** Peterson & Fisher *Wild Amer.* ix. 101 A girl came by at breakneck speed on one water ski,..then three daredevil young men..skied up and jumped over an inclined platform. **1970** 'D. Halliday' *Dolly & Cookie Bird* viii. 130 'Does Louie ski?' He swooped away, the spray flying.

**2.** *trans.* To travel over (a slope, etc.) on skis; to ski at (a place).

**1973** P. A. Whitney *Snowfire* xii. 236 It's easier to ski a steep slope than a gentle one. **1980** *Sunday Times* 21 Sept. 8 Ski the top resorts in Europe..and now the U.S.A.

**skiable** ('skiːəb(ə)l), *a.* [f. SKI *v.* + -ABLE.] Of a slope, snow, etc.: capable of being skied on; fit for skiing.

**1961** in Webster. **1963** *Amer. Speech* XXXVIII. 205 Inferior..heavy snow that is hardly 'skiable' for the average skier. **1969** *Observer* 14 Sept. 35/1 In every skiable side-valley, new resorts have sprouted. **1979** *United States 1980/81* (Penguin Travel Guides) 486 This..blown-out volcano is skiable from late October.

**skiagram** ('skaɪəgræm). Also **skiogram**. [f. Gr. σκιά shadow + -GRAM.]

**1.** An outline of the shadow of an object filled in with black (see quot. 1801); a picture painted or produced in this style.

**1801** Fuseli *Lect. Paint.* i. 9 The first essays of the art were Skiagrams, simple outlines of a shade, similar to.. Silhouettes; without any other addition of character or feature but what the profile of the object thus delineated, could afford. **1843** *Blackw. Mag.* LIV. 694 To trace back the more perfect art through its stages—the 'Polychrom', the 'Monochrom', the 'Monogram', and 'Skiagram'. **1848** Wornum *Lect. Paint.* 351 *note*, Vases, or those with the black figures (skiagrams) on the stained reddish-yellow terra cotta, are the most ancient.

**2.** A skiagraph, radiograph.

**1896** *Brit. Med. Jrnl.* 29 Feb. 557 In another case of suspected tuberculous disease of the foot I obtained a very good skiogram. **1899** *Athenæum* 2 Sept. 324 The first series of skiagrams..published with the design of showing the development of the bones of the hand and wrist.

Hence ˌ**skiagraˈmmatic** *a.*, skiagraphic (*Cassell's Suppl.*). Also ˌ**skiagraˈmmatically** *adv.*, skiagraphically.

**1901** *Lancet* 26 Jan. 251/1 It often happened that a limb though not skiagrammatically perfect, was yet functionally so.

**skiagraph** ('skaɪəgrɑːf, -æ-), *sb.* Also **skio-**. [See SCIAGRAPH.] A photograph obtained by means of the Röntgen rays; a radiograph. = SCIAGRAPH 3.

**1896** *Daily News* 11 Apr. 6/4 On a skiagraph being taken ..an obscure..form of partial dislocation was easily discovered. **1897** *Allbutt's Syst. Med.* III. 362 Skiagraphs taken by means of the X Röntgen rays. **1925** [see *roentgenological* adj. s.v. ROENTGEN-, ROENTGENO-]. **1940** E. F. Benson *Final Edition* x. 208 When..one of them suggested that an X-ray skiagraph should be taken, it showed osteo-arthritis in an advanced stage.

Hence ˈ**skiagraph** *v. trans.*, to photograph by means of the Röntgen rays. **skiˈagrapher**, (*a*) a radiographer (Gould *Dict. Med.* Suppl.); (*b*) = SCIAGRAPHER; ˌ**skiaˈgraphic** *a.*, of or pertaining to skiagraphy; radiographic. ˌ**skiaˈgraphically** *adv.*, after the manner of a skiagraph; by means of, with respect to, skiagraphy.

**1896** *Brit. Med. Jrnl.* 29 Feb. 587 Photograph of a patient being *skiographed. *Ibid.* 18 Apr. 997 It is now possible.. to skiagraph the foreign body. **1957** V. Nabokov *Pnin* iv. 98 Lads..would spend years grinding colors in the workshop of some great Italian *skiagrapher. **1896** *Brit. Med. Jrnl.* 22 Feb. 491 All this was ascertained by means of the *skiographic method. **1899** *Allbutt's Syst. Med.* VI. 135 Skiagraphic investigation..in the diagnosis of intra-thoracic growths. **1892** *Speaker* 5 Mar. 285/2 Through the blinds of the saloon below various pairs of lovers are seen —*skiagraphically embracing. **1896** *Brit. Med. Jrnl.* 22 Feb. 490 A case of osseous ankylosis skiographically diagnosed.

**skiagraphy** (skaɪˈægrəfɪ). [See SCIAGRAPHY.]

**1.** (See quot.)

**1859** Gullick & Timbs *Paint.* 37 Painting is said to have passed through several stages in Greece, commencing with simple skiagraphy or shadow-painting: by which is meant giving the exterior outline, or shape of the shadow of an object, without any intermediate lines.

**2.** (See first quot.)

**1858** Gladstone *Homer* I. 235 The fundamental distinction between his [i.e. Homer's] Inner and Outer, his practical and poetical geography. In order to mark that distinction more forcibly, I would..even call..the latter his territorial skiagraphy. *Ibid.* III. 343 There is a great mass of fabulous and imaginative skiagraphy.

**3.** Radiography.

**1896** (*title*), Archives of Clinical Skiagraphy [continued as, Archives of the Roentgen Ray]. **1898** *Allbutt's Syst. Med.* V. 768 Skiagraphy has been employed for the diagnosis of pericardial effusion.

**skian**, var. SKENE[1].

**skiascopy** (skaɪˈæskəpɪ). *Med.* [ad. F. *skiascopie* (Chibret 1886, in *Arch. d'Ophthalmol.* VI. 147), f. Gr. σκιά shadow: see -SCOPY.] Retinoscopy, esp. by means of a skiascope.

**1886** *Amer. Jrnl. Med. Sci.* XCII. 248 Chibret proposes to employ the term 'skiascopy', in place of the terms keratoscopy, retinoscopy, pupilloscopy, and phantoscopy.. to designate this..method of determining the ocular refraction based upon the examination of the shadows which are formed in the eye when light is thrown into it. **1933** *Arch. Ophthalmol.* X. 689 Cycloskiascopy is more difficult than the classic method of cylinder skiascopy. **1958** *Ophthalmic Lit.* XII. 557 The term 'skiascopy' was proposed by Chibret instead of retinoscopy, as the retina is not normally in focus. **1976** *Ophthalmic Res.* VIII. 115 Data of skiascopy are not very exact because of the difficult procedure of measurement.

Hence **ˈskiascope**, an instrument that directs light into a patient's eye along the line of sight of the examiner, so that the latter can judge the refraction of the eye from the movement of the illuminated area and the shadows as the light source is moved; **skiaˈscopic** *a.*, of or pertaining to skiascopy; **skiaˈscopically** *adv.*

**1892** *Arch. Ophthalmol.* XXI. 422 A skiascope is now used at the Utrecht Clinique with glasses on each side which by combinations make a series of plus and minus D from 1 to 10. **1897** *Ibid.* XXVI. 598 A new hand at the sciascopic test. **1903** E. CLARKE *Errors Accommodation & Refraction of Eye* vi. 77 Marple's skiascopes, made by Meyrowitz of New York, are very useful, and obviate the necessity for keeping a separate test case in the dark room. **1930** *Amer. Jrnl. Ophthalmol.* XIII. 102/1 Jackson measured skiascopically the symmetrical aberration in one hundred eyes. **1958** *Ophthalmic Lit.* XII. 557 Four important skiascopic fields are to be considered. **1971** *Biol. Abstr.* LII. 5247/1 (*heading*) Focal ophthalmoscopy with the help of a modified electric skiascope.

**skiatic**, obs. var. SCIATIC *a.*[2]

**Skiatron** (ˈskaɪətrɒn). *Electronics.* Also **skiatron.** [f. Gr. σκιά shadow + -TRON.] A proprietary name for a type of cathode-ray tube in which the electron beam produces a dark trace. Also *attrib.*, esp. as ***Skiatron tube***.

**1940** A. H. ROSENTHAL in *Electronics & Television & Short-Wave World* XIII. 52 (*heading*) The Skiatron—a new scophony development towards large-screen television projection. **1946** *Trade Marks Jrnl.* 26 June 330/2 *Skiatron*... Scientific apparatus and instruments, electrical apparatus and instruments included in Class 9. Scophony Limited... 17th Sept. 1945. **1947** L. J. HAWORTH in L. N. Ridenour *Radar Systems Engin.* xiii. 483 The alkali halides..have the property of darkening for a time at a point where they have been struck by an electron beam of sufficient energy. This phenomenon has been made use of in one form of cathode-ray tube, known as the 'skiatron'..used for projection purposes. **1948** *Electronic Engin.* XX. 21/2 (*caption*) Large screen plan position indicator with 'Skiatron' tube, as used by the Admiralty. **1953** *Official Gaz.* (U.S. Patent Office) 3 Nov. 21/2 *Skiatron*..for cathode ray tubes... Claims use since Aug. 1, 1942. **1966** H. H. POOLE *Fund. Display Systems* ii. 32 The dark trace tube, also referred to as the Skiatron tube, is currently manufactured by National Union. It is available in screen sizes of 5, 7, 10, and 12 inches. **1973** C. J. RICHARDS *Electronic Display & Data Systems* iii. 76 During the Second World War..the skiatron projection tube was used... Today a family of 'deformographic' tubes exists which can project a picture several metres across.

**ˈskibbet.** Now *dial.* Forms: 4–5 **skybet, skibet,** 5 **skebett,** 9 **skibbet, skivet.** [Of obscure origin: cf. SKIPPET[1].] A small box; a small compartment in a chest, etc. Also *transf.*

**1398** TREVISA *Barth. De P.R.* v. xxxix. (Bodl. MS.), And what is hoote and drye..is resceyued proprelich in þe skybet of þe galle. *Ibid.*, þe skibet of the splene, þe melt. *c* **1500** in *Rep. Hist. MSS. Comm.* Var. Coll. IV. 25 De diuersis pixidibus, hampers, skebettis, et aliis locis, ut hoc patet sequenter. **1880** *W. Cornwall Gloss.* 51/2 *Skibbet*, a small covered compartment in a large chest, always near the top. **1895** QUILLER COUCH *Wandering Heath* 81 My grandfather kept his fishing lines in a little skivet under the stern-sheets.

**skice**, *v.*[1] Now *dial.* Also 6–7 **skise,** 9 **skeyse.** [Of obscure origin.] *intr.* To move quickly; to skip or frisk about; to run, etc.

**1591** FLETCHER *Russe Commw.* (Hakl.) 14 They skise a large space, and seeme for to flie withall, and therefore they call them..flying squirrels. **1641** BROME *Joviall Crew* IV. i, He is..up at five a Clock in the morning..; Skise out this away, and skise out that away; (He's no Snayle, I assure you). **1790** GROSE *Prov. Gloss.*, *To skice*, to play and frolick about. **1846** W. SANDYS *Spec. Corn. Dial.* 19 Then a passel of maidens..beginn'd for to skeyce and to fade so friskis. **1867** HARLAND & WILKINSON *Folk-lore Lanc.* 181 To Lapland, Finland, we do skice. **1875-** in dial. glossaries (Sussex, Hampshire, Isle of Wight, etc.).

†**skice**, *v.*[2] *Obs. rare.* [? Alteration of *sclice* SLICE *v.*] *trans.* To slice, cut.

**1600** HOLLAND *Livy* II. lv. 829 The more fiercely he cryed on still, the more cruellie fell the Lictor to cut and skice his apparrell. **1601** —— *Pliny* I. 544 To skice and scrape their bark round about, in maner of scarification.

†**skick**, *v. Obs. rare.* Also 4 **skyke,** 5 **skikke.** [var. of SKECK *v.*] = SKECK *v.* Hence †ˈ**skicking.**

**13..** *K. Alis.* 6077 (W.), And into theo mores they heom drowe,..For to skyke, and for to slene, Of kyng Alisaundris men. *Ibid.* 6142 The kyng was sory..That he no myghte geve heom bataile, Bote here and there, with skykyng. *Ibid.* 6276 By robbery they liveth, and skickyng. *a* **1400** [see SKECK *v.* 1].

**skid** (skɪd), *sb.* Also 7 **skidde,** 8–9 **skeed,** 9 **skidd.** [Of doubtful origin: both form and sense suggest some connexion with ON. *skíð* (see SKI) and OE. *scíd* SHIDE, but *skid* does not phonetically represent either of these.]

**1. a.** A beam, plank, or piece of timber, *esp.* one of a number upon which something rests or is supported, or by which a thing is held in position.

**1609–10** *Cranbrook Churchw. Acc.* in Stahlschmidt *Bells of Kent* (1887) 239 It. pd for two Skiddes for the frame of the bells, vs iiijd. **1759** *Phil. Trans.* LI. 292 This tub was fixed upon skids (pieces of timber) about six inches thick. **1809** W. IRVING *Knickerb.* (1861) 76 He had not a little the appearance of a beer barrel on skids. **1850** HOLTZAPFFEL *Turning* III. 93 The block..is then mounted upon square pieces of wood called skids. **1859** F. A. GRIFFITHS *Artil. Man.* (1862) 63 There is..a skid, or transom, placed across the last step of the carriage.

**b.** One of a number of beams, or pieces of stone, on which a vessel is built, or placed during repair.

**1856** *Illustr. Lond. News* 2 Feb. 110/1 This [dry] dock.. was 191 feet long on the stone skids at bottom. **1867** SMYTH *Sailor's Word-bk.* 629 *Skids*,..beams resting on blocks, on which small craft are built. **1888** *Daily Telegr.* 27 June 5/2 Boats which will float from their skids when waterborne.

**c.** *Oil Industry.* A skid beam (see sense 5 below).

**1975** *Offshore Engin.* Oct. 66/1 The order for the skids went to Hopson, Co Durham. **1976** *Offshore Platforms & Pipelining* 20/2 Major items of drilling equipment represent skid sizes of available components.

**2.** †**a.** A kind of sledge. *Obs.*

**1712** J. JAMES tr. *Le Blond's Gardening* 182 You must have ..a Kind of Skid or Sledge, upon which the tree is set a little leaning.

**b.** *Naut.* (See quot. 1750.)

α. **1743** BULKELEY & CUMMINS *Voy. S. Seas* 8 There broke a Sea in the Ship, which..bilg'd the Cutter, and canted her off the Skeets [*sic*]..athwart the Barge. **1769** FALCONER *Dict. Marine* (1780) D 2, The main skeeds, for hoisting in the boats clear of the ship's side. **1823** W. SCORESBY *Jrnl.* 303 It cleared all our boats, and occasioned only a trifling injury to some of the skeeds in its progress.

β. **1750** BLANCKLEY *Naval Expos.* 152 Skids are wooden Fenders fay'd on the Outside of the Ship, for the Conveniency of hoisting in Boats, Provisions, etc. **1769** FALCONER *Dict. Marine* (1780), *Skids*, or *Skeeds*, are long compassing pieces of timber, formed so as to answer the vertical curve of a ship's side. **1846** A. YOUNG *Naut. Dict.* 284. **1893** J. A. BARRY *Steve Brown's Bunyip* 92 The boats on the davits and the long-boat on the skids.

**c.** A plank or roller on which a heavy thing may be slid or pushed along.

**1782** 'J. H. ST. JOHN DE CRÈVECOEUR' *Lett. from Amer. Farmer* iii. 110 The logs were placed with skids, and the usual contrivances: thus the rude house was raised. **1846** YOUNG *Naut. Dict.* 284 The name of Skids is also given to pieces of plank put under a vessel's bottom, for the purpose of launching her off when she has been driven ashore. **1848** BARTLETT *Dict. Amer.*, *Skid*, a piece of light timber from ten to twenty feet in length, upon which heavier timber is rolled or slid from place to place. **1868** *Regul. Army* ¶1167 As it may become necessary to disembark without the aid of a platform, some strong skids not less than 15 feet long, should always be carried.

**d.** *Lumbering.* One of a set of peeled logs or timbers, partially sunk into the ground, and forming a roadway along or down which logs are drawn or slid; also, one of the logs forming a skidway (see 5). *U.S.*

**1851** *Harper's Mag.* III. 518 New skids are nicely peeled ..and plentifully as well as calculatingly laid along the road. **1880** *Lumberman's Gaz.* 14 Jan., Some of the lumber-men have from 8,000,000 to 10,000,000 [logs] on the skids. **1893** *Atlantic Monthly* Feb. 194/2 Then the load itself, three logs tandem,..slid over the greased skids with a gliding, majestic motion.

**e.** *Coalmining.* (See quot.)

**1883** GRESLEY *Gloss. Coal-m.*, *Skids*, slides or slippers upon which certain coal-cutting machines travel along the faces whilst at work.

**f.** A runner attached to the underside of an aircraft. Cf. *tail skid, wing skid.*

**1909** *Aëronaut. Jrnl.* XIII. 119/2 The tail of the machine rests on a small skid fixed to the frame. *Ibid.* 120/1 The wing tips are provided with light wheels and skids. **1909** A. BERGET *Conquest of Air* II. iii. 194 The planes rest upon two skids which form a kind of sleigh. **1947** A. C. DOUGLAS *Gliding & Advanced Soaring* x. 259 Very close to the usual position of the release, will be the nose fitting of the skid. **1981** 'A. HALL' *Pekin Target* i. 11 We put the chopper down ..on one skid and a rotor tip.

**g.** *pl.* In *fig.* phrases describing impending downfall or defeat; the way to failure or ruin: ***to put the skids under*** (a person or thing), to arrange the downfall of; to remove or oust (esp. from office), to get rid of; to cause to fail; ***to hit the skids***, to enter a rapid decline or deterioration; ***on the skids***, on the way to defeat or ruin; in a steadily worsening state. *colloq.* (orig. *U.S.*).

**1918** H. C. WITWER in *Collier's* 9 Mar. 16/3 Me and Jeanne is gonna have a flat over in Brooklyn as soon as we put the skids under the Kaiser. **1920** —— in *Ibid.* 5 June 36/3 Kane Halliday, as the butlers was wonted to announce him previous to the time he hit the skids, was merely engaged to this gold mine. **1921** A. G. EMPEY *Madonna of Hills* lxi. 363 As yet it would be too dangerous to flaunt Davis openly, even if he was on the 'skids'. **1929** D. HAMMETT *Red Harvest* xii. 119 'What did Noonan put the skids under you for?' 'Skids? What skids? I quit.' **1938** A. J. LIEBLING *Back where I came From* 48 The men on the Bowery..had taken to hanging around saloons, drinking on empty stomachs. Eventually they had hit the skids and been forced to abscond from the genteel communities where their wives still lingered. **1943** M. MCCARTHY *Company she Keeps* v. 128 Capitalism was on the skids, and everybody ought to know about it. **1954** A. MELVILLE in *Plays of Year 1954* (1955) XI. 26 You're too pigheaded to realise that the skids are well and truly under you. **1962** 'K. ORVIS' *Damned & Destroyed* ix. 61 I'm on the skids. For good, it looks like. **1975** J. SYMONS *Three Pipe Problem* xvi. 165 A plan by one gang to put the skids under another. **1976** *Daily Mirror* 12 Mar. 23/4 They were only 378p when the £ hit the skids a week ago. **1977** *Irish Press* 29 Sept. 12/6 The Irish shoe industry, after being on the skids for six years, may be finding its feet again.

**3. a.** A device for locking the wheel of a vehicle or for retarding its motion in descending a hill or slope; *esp.* an iron shoe chained to the vehicle and placed in front of the wheel so as to be caught between it and the ground.

**1766** *Compl. Farmer*, *Skid*, the chain by which the wheel of a waggon is fastened, so as to prevent its turning round, upon descending a steep hill. **1824** BURCHELL *Trav.* I. 151 The *remschoen* (lock-shoe or skid) is a log of wood..having a groove in it to receive the felly of the wheel. **1836** SIR G. HEAD *Home Tour* 87 As the laden carriages are thus raised, an iron skid is attached to the last, to prevent accident. **1874** M. COLLINS *Transmigr.* I. vi. 95 We began to descend a hill so steep that the skid was necessary.

*transf.* **1866** E. C. RYE *Brit. Beetles* 114 This development ..acts as a 'skid' or 'break' upon the base of the elytra.

**b.** *fig.* or in fig. context. A retarding influence or agency.

**1841** HOOD *Tale of a Trumpet* 591 Backsliding in spite of all moral skid. **1865** *Daily Telegr.* 12 Apr. 6 It is for ever the function of Tories to be the skid, and not the wheel. **1874** *Slang Dict.* 292 It is often said that a talkative person might put the skid on, with advantage to his listeners. **1884** *Contemp. Rev.* Aug. 193 Legislation does not require to have a skid on the wheels continuously.

**4. a.** [From the vb.] An act of skidding; also, a side-slip.

**1907** A. BENNETT *Grim Smile of Five Towns* 192 At the bottom they had a severe skid. **1933** KIPLING in *Strand Mag.* Feb. 131 The Cars put up an average bag of twenty dead per diem... And so began, in skid and stink, the real blood-sport of Britain. **1972** 'H. CALVIN' *Take Two Popes* xi. 111 The cars touched gently at 100 kph, went into a skid together and slid on to the roadside verge.

**b.** *Aeronaut.* A movement of an aircraft that includes a sideways component, esp. away from the centre of curvature of a turn. Cf. SLIP *sb.*[3] 9 j.

**1916** H. BARBER *Aeroplane Speaks* 83 The velocity of the 'skid', or sideways movement. **1942** *Tee Emm* (Air Ministry) II. 65 Do a quick barrel half roll with plenty of skid. **1952** A. Y. BRAMBLE *Air-plane Flight* xiii. 199 Some pilots use the term 'slip' loosely to mean a skid. It is important to note the difference. A side-slip may occur whilst flying straight or *inwards* during a turn, but 'skidding' of the machine can occur only during yawing motion, and strictly, is always in the direction outwards, away from the turn.

**5.** *attrib.* and *Comb.*, as **skid beam,** (see quot. 1846); also *transf.*, a horizontal beam supporting a deck on an oil or natural gas platform; **skid-lid** *slang*, a motor-cyclist's crash-helmet; **skid mark,** the mark made on the road by the tyre of a skidding vehicle (usu. *pl.*); **skid-mounted** *a.*, mounted on runners; **skid-pan,** (*a*) (see quot. 1838; (*b*) a slippery road surface prepared to enable drivers to practise skid-correction; also *transf.*; **skid-proof** *a.*, of a road, etc.: on which one cannot skid or slip (esp. in wet conditions); designed to prevent skidding; hence as *v. trans.*, to render skid-proof; **skid road,** (*a*) a way or track formed of skids (2 d) along which logs are hauled; (*b*) N. Amer., orig. a downtown area frequented by loggers; now *gen.* = SKID ROW; **skid-way** (see quot. 1893); also, an inclined way formed of skids (2 d).

**1846** YOUNG *Naut. Dict.* 290 Spar-deck properly signifies a temporary deck laid in any part of a vessel; and the beams whereon it rests get the name of *skid-beams. **1895** *Daily News* 31 Jan. 6/2 Lifting the heavy boats into their positions on the skid-beams over the upper deck. **1976** *Offshore Platforms & Pipelining* 23 The distance between skid beams is the first dimension to consider when designing a platform rig. **1958** *Oxf. Mail* 8 Feb. 8/7 *Skid-lids' importance stressed. **1968** R. V. BESTE *Repeat Instructions* vii. 71 He wore the leather jacket and round skid-lid..usual to ton-up tearaways. **1977** C. WATSON *One Man's Meat* xiii. 120 This bird in motor-cycle get-up..with that great skid-lid hiding half her face. **1937** M. ALLINGHAM *Dancers in Mourning* iv. 59 The *skid marks were easily discernible on the flint road. **1978** M. GILBERT *Empty House* v. 47 There were no skid marks, which would..indicate that he made no attempt to brake. **1960** *Farmer & Stockbreeder* 16 Feb. Suppl. 24/2 Being *skid-mounted, it can readily be moved to a new site. **1975** *Petroleum Rev.* XXIX. 135/1 AOT will provide complete prefabricated skid mounted systems into which are built flowmeters, [etc.]. **1838** HOLLOWAY *Prov. Dict.*, *Skid-pan*, the iron, used to Skid with. **1884** *C.T.C.*

*Monthly Gaz.* Nov. 347/1 These roads being composed of soft stone, and all waggons coming down with skidpans on. **1958** *Times* 17 June 9/6 On the skid pan (which is equivalent to a road covered with wet ice). **1959** *News Chron.* 12 Oct. 1/4 Rain turned many roads into skid-pans and caused hundreds of accidents. **1972** C. MUDIE *Motor Boats & Boating* 108 The control of a car is exact and direct whereas a boat is on the skid pan of the sea. **1976** *Norwich Mercury* 17 Dec. 10/3 This thrilling game played at a terrific pace.. on a greasy treacherous skidpan at Skinners Lane on Saturday. **1980** *Sunday Times* (Colour Suppl.) 21 Sept. 58/2 The first days of the course are instruction in evasive driving, done on a nearby skidpan. **1937** *Daily Express* 20 Feb. 10/2 Some roads are practically *skid-proof, others not. **1958** *Washington Post* 25 Oct. B10/1 To skidproof concrete porch steps, it has long been the custom to sprinkle sand on freshly painted surfaces. **1880** *7th Rep. Topogr. Surv. Adirondack Reg.* 176 Advised that lumbermen had cut '*skid-roads' on which logs were drawn [etc.]. **1906** *Log of 'Columbia'* 1. 8/1 'We'll likely see him in town.'.. 'He'll be in the Skid road somewhere.' **1925** *Amer. Speech* I. 135 When the logger of to-day speaks of the 'skid-road' he means the place where loggers gather when they are in town. **1940** *Amer. Mercury* Dec. 412 Most of the skid-road bars provide either a floor show..or a hill-billy band. **1962** E. LUCIA *Klondike Kate* iii. 98 Arriving in Dawson like some little tramp from Seattle's Skid Road. **1971** *Daily Colonist* (Victoria, B.C.) 15 May 5/5 Young heroin users are replacing the Skid Road addicts in British Columbia. **1980** *Washington Post* 1 Mar. A13/4 In Seattle, where the 'Skid Row' term originated 'from flophouses built along the 'Skid Road' of lumber being 'skidded' to the water front', reminders of that age remain. **1879** *Lumberman's Gaz.* 24 Dec. 9 The *skidways through the woods are piled full of logs. **1893** *Scribner's Mag.* June 707/1 The skidway consists of two logs or timbers about ten feet apart, laid perpendicular to the log-road.., upon which a tier of logs is placed ready to be loaded on the sleighs.

Hence **'skidded** *a.*, provided with a skid or skids.

**1935** *Charlottesville* (Va.) *Daily Progress* 22 Feb. 1/1 He streaked off into the stratosphere at dawn today on a 2,447 mile flight to New York City where he planned to land on the wood skidded belly of the ship. **1961** *Flight* LXXX. 471/2 The lift platform was variously adjusted to handle simple cargo, general 'skidded' cargo and fully loaded vehicles.

**skid** (snow-shoe): see SKI.

**skid** (skɪd), *v.*[1] [f. SKID *sb.*]

**1. a.** *trans.* To apply or fasten a skid or brake to (a wheel) in order to retard its motion; to lock (a wheel) in this way.

**1674** RAY *S. & E.C. Words* 77 To *Skid* a wheel: *Rotam sufflaminare*, with an iron hook fastned to the Axis to keep it from turning round upon the descent of a steep hill, *Kent*. [Hence in later Dicts.]. **1859** DICKENS *Two Cities* I. ii, The guard got down to skid the wheel for the descent. **1860** *Proc. Inst. Civ. Engineers* XIX. 495 If it is required to put on the breaks harder, and to skid the wheels. **1879** *Man. Artill. Exerc.* 133 In order that the wheels may be skidded when necessary to check the recoil.

**b.** To push or drag (a person) *along*.

**1881** *Times* 2 Feb. 4/5 He was skidded along in front of the wheel of the cab.

**2.** *Lumbering.* To haul (logs) on or along skids; to pile or place on a skid-way. Also *absol.*

**1878** *Lumberman's Gaz.* 6 Apr., Not one-fifth of the logs cut and skidded..have been banked. *Ibid.* 18 Dec. 426 Operators have been cutting and skidding for the past thirty or forty days. **1888** *Scribner's Mag.* Dec. 655/2 The logs are then 'skidded' by horses or oxen into skidways.

**3. a.** *intr.* Of a wheel: To slip or be dragged along without revolving, esp. as the effect of having a skid or brake applied to it.

**1838** *Civil Eng. & Arch. Jrnl.* I. 160/2 An engine always gets through its work better upon a wet day than a dry one... It is true, the wheels skid more. **1854** *Trans. Philol. Soc.* 84 A roller *skids*, when in a sharp turn it cuts up the turf. **1894** A. ROBERTSON *Nuggets*, etc. 200 We..would suddenly skid, with the break on, down a steep hill.

*transf.* **1862** JACOMB in *Peaks, Passes, & Glac.* Ser. II. I. 244 We left at noon, and glissaded down the slopes to the Maison Blanche again. Mr. Mathews..skidded down with all his wonted agility.

**b.** To slip obliquely or sideways, esp. owing to the muddy, wet, or dusty state of the road; to side-slip. Usually said of cycle or motor-car wheels, but also of horse-vehicles or persons. Also, of the vehicle itself.

**1884** *Pall Mall G.* 12 May 10/2 While the steam-engine.. was on its way to the fire the wheels 'skidded' against the kerb. **1886** *C.T.C. Gaz.* IV. 137 Enough weight on the steering-wheel to prevent it skidding at all. **1892** *Liverpool Daily Post* 4 July, The back wheel of their machine skidded, throwing the lady under the vehicle. **1907** G. B. SHAW in *Neolith* Nov. 3 'The bus skidded.' 'So would any bus skid in this mud, going at that rate.' **1926** E. F. SPANNER *Naviators* i. 13 A car that looks as though it is going straight can be dodged, but one that skids about like a demented dog chasing its tail is not to be faced with assurance. **1927** KIPLING *Limits & Renewals* (1932) 159 It was raining hard, and the car skidded badly. **1966** G. GREENE *Comedians* III. iii. 280 The car because of my momentary inattention skidded sideways.

**c.** *Aeronaut.* Of an aircraft: to move sideways, esp. away from the centre of curvature while turning. Cf. SLIP *v.*[1] 9c.

**1911** *Daily Colonist* (Victoria, B.C.) (Mag. Section) 9 Apr. 9/5 If the rag points up, the operator knows his machine is going down..but if it points to the side, the operator knows he is 'skidding'. **1916** H. BARBER *Aeroplane Speaks* 22 When an aeroplane is turned to the left or the right the centrifugal force of its momentum causes it to skid sideways and outwards away from the centre of the turn. **1942** *R.A.F. Jrnl.* 3 Oct. 35 He lost speed suddenly and skidded to the starboard. **1965** C. N. VAN DEVENTER *Introd. Gen. Aeronaut.* x. 233/2 If the ball moves in the direction of the turn, it indicates that the airplane is slipping toward the inside of the turn... If the ball moves in the opposite direction, the airplane is skidding toward the outside of the turn.

**d.** *fig.* To follow an incorrect or unprofitable course; to make a mistake, to err or fail. Also of prices, etc.: to fall or decline rapidly. *colloq.* (chiefly *U.S.*).

**1920** *Literary Digest* 22 May 120 Time was when the unsuccessful man merely failed, but these days, in a world scurrying about in motor-cars and breathing gasoline, he is said to 'skid'. **1937** G. FRANKAU *More of Us* vi. 67 Next morning woke a damsel heavy-lidded To wonder had she not, or had she, skidded. **1962** K. ORVIS *Damned & Destroyed* iv. 29 He had skidded until he had become merely a brilliant young pianist. **1970** *Computers & Humanities* V. 11 Alabama Populists..tended mainly to be unsuccessful yeoman farmers who were skidding toward tenancy. **1976** *National Observer* (U.S.) 21 Aug. 8/6 A good investment.. if some unforeseen misfortune causes currencies to skid.

**4.** *trans.* To cause (a vehicle, its wheels, etc.) to skid; to turn (a corner, etc.) by means of a skidding movement.

**1924** 'J. SUTHERLAND' *Circle of Stars* xxiii. 238 Carter skidded the Ford to a standstill. **1928** *Sunday Express* 19 Aug. 1/1 Viscount Curzon..was cheered as he skilfully skidded the corners. **1931** G. LE Q. MARTEL *In Wake of Tank* 84 A turn through to a right angle absorbed so much power in skidding the track round that it was usually necessary to change down to first gear on the machine.

Hence **'skidder**, (*a*), a lumberman who hauls logs along the skids to the skidway; (*b*) a tractor or other machine for skidding logs. **'skidding** *ppl. a.*

**1870** *Overland Monthly* V. 56/1 Another, called the 'skidder', skids the road. **1883** in *Cent. Dict.*, The skidders haul the logs to the pile. **1897** *Daily News* 31 Dec. 3/1 Skidding 'buses, and the fog silence. **1905** [see BUMMER 4]. **1945** B. MACDONALD *Egg & I* (1946) 184 These toots were the signals given by the 'whistle punk' to direct the operations of the skidder bringing in the logs. **1965** *Weekend Mag.* 2 Oct. 3/3 Then it lays the denuded trunk on the ground and another machine, called 'a skidder', takes it to a landing area where it is cut into pulpwood lengths. **1976** *New Yorker* 3 May 52/2 The skidder, which vaguely resembles a pair of tractors coupled together..replaced the horse not long ago as the means of 'twitching' a tree..from the cutter to the truck.

**skid** (skɪd), *v.*[2] *rare.* [variant of SCUD *v.*[1]] **1.** *intr.* To run or go quickly, to scud. Also, = SCUD *v.*[1] 2.

**1815** MME. D'ARBLAY *Diary* (1876) IV. lxiv. 311 They ran skidding down the aisle of the chapel..like frightened hares. **1891** KIPLING *Barrack-Room Ball., Screw Guns* i, You can skid up the trees, but you don't get away from the guns! **1940** L. MACNEICE *Last Ditch* 32 Toy sail skidding on Whitestone Pond at the peak of London.

**2.** *trans.* = SCUD *v.*[1] 5 a.

**1891** in *Eng. Dial. Dict.* **1897** G. B. SHAW *Let.* 1 Mar. in *Ellen Terry & Shaw* (1931) 159 Get ten sovereigns and skid them out from the beach into the sea.

**skiddaddle**, var. SKEDADDLE *v.*

**Skiddavian** (skɪ'deɪvɪən), *a. Geol.* [f. *Skiddav-*, stem of latinized form of next + -IAN.] = SKIDDAW *b.* Also *absol.*

**1905** J. E. MARR in *Q. Jrnl. Geol. Soc.* LXI. p. lxxxi, The time-divisions which I would..propose to adopt for the rocks of this [Ordovician] system are as follows:—Ashgillian. Caradocian. Llandeilian. Skiddavian. *Ibid.* p. lxxxii, The beds tabulated above may..be taken as defining the upper and lower limits of the Skiddavian Series. *Ibid.* p. lxxxiii, *Didymograptus bifidus*..belongs to the top of the Skiddavian. **1929** W. W. WATTS in Evans & Stubblefield *Handbk. Geol. Brit. Isles* 63 The Skiddavian fauna includes many species of *Didymograptus*. *Ibid.*, The Manx Slates of the Isle of Man are probably in part of Skiddavian age. **1955** G. G. WOODFORD tr. *Gignoux's Stratigr. Geol.* iii. 83 (*caption*) Upper Skiddavian: shales and sandstones of the upper Arenig. Lower Skiddavian: basal sandstone of the Arenig.

**Skiddaw** ('skɪdɔː). *Geol.* The name of a mountain in the English Lake District, used *attrib.*: (*a*) in **Skiddaw slate(s)** (or **Slate(s)**), a thick group of slates, flags, and mudstones that outcrops in the northern part of the Lake District and out of which Skiddaw and neighbouring mountains have been eroded; (*b*) to designate the lowest division of the Ordovician in Britain, esp. in the Lake District.

**1832** *Proc. Geol. Soc.* I. 401 Skiddaw slate.—The author briefly describes the range and extent of this group. **1855** J. PHILLIPS *Man. Geol.* vi. 108 These..occupy a long range of mountains parallel to the Skiddaw slates. **1897** *Index Vols. I.-L. Q. Jrnl. Geol. Soc.* 357/1 Skiddaw age of Easdale Slates. **1900** *Proc. & Trans. R. Soc. Canada* VI. IV. 200 There is a remarkable similarity between the Ordovician of ..Quebec and New Brunswick and the Ordovician of western Europe as developed in Great Britain: The Skiddaw and Arenig, the Hartfell and Llandeilo formations, being easily recognized in Canada. **1933** H. H. SYMONDS *Walking in Lake District* x. 255 Thus came the 'Skiddaw slate', that earliest rock of Cumberland, found *par excellence* in Skiddaw himself. **1969** BENNISON & WRIGHT *Geol. Hist. Brit. Isles* v. 102 The Skiddaw Slates have been slightly metamorphosed..by later intrusions... However, the early Ordovician seems to have been devoid of igneous activity —unlike Wales—and only late in Skiddaw times did it commence. **1977** R. PROSSER *Geol. explained in Lake District* i. 13 The oldest rocks [of the Lake District massif], the Skiddaw Slates.., have their main exposures north of a line from Ennerdale Water, past Derwentwater to Troutbeck and include the hill masses of the Skiddaw range.

**skidding** ('skɪdɪŋ), *vbl. sb.* [f. SKID *sb.* or *v.*[1]]

**1.** *concr.* Timber or planks used as a support for a gun, etc., or to facilitate its removal.

**1859** GRIFFITHS *Artill. Man.* (1862) 123 One piece of short skidding, $4\frac{1}{2}$ feet long, five..inches square. *Ibid.* 124, 4.. assists 2 at the lever and skidding. **1879** *Man. Artill. Exerc.* 513 The frame..[is] supported..by two upright oak skids, ..and by coins, scotches, or skidding, inserted between it and the fore carriage.

**2.** *Lumbering.* (See quot. 1878.) Also *attrib.* in *skidding-team, -tongs*.

**1877** *Lumberman's Gaz.* 22 Dec., Pevys Skidding Tongs always on hand. **1878** *Scribner's Mag.* XV. 147 Skidding is hauling logs together and placing them on skids convenient for loading. **1893** *Ibid.* June 707/1 The skidding-team is brought in and the log is..hauled away. *Ibid.*, In the case of small logs, it is grappled with 'skidding-tongs', which seize the log like a pair of pinchers.

**3.** The action of the verb SKID (esp. sense 3).

**1889** *Hull & E. Yorks. Times* 27 Apr., Bump on the roadway, through the skidding of the wheels over the wet stones. **1889** *Daily News* 21 June 6/3 There was no skidding of the wheels, and there was no appearance of the brake having been applied.

**'skiddy, 'skiddy-cock**, *sb. dial.* (See quots.)

**1787** GROSE *Prov. Gloss.*, *Skiddey*, or *Skiddey-cock*, a water-rail. **1886** NEWTON in *Encycl. Brit.* XX. 223/1 The Water-Rail, locally known as the Skiddy or Billcock, is the *Rallus aquaticus* of Ornithology.

**skiddy** ('skɪdɪ), *a.* [f. SKID *v.*[1] + -Y[1].] Of surfaces, etc.: on which one is liable to skid; treacherously slippery. Also, characterized by skidding.

**1902** *Car* 4 June 72/2 The state of a road which constitutes a 'skiddy' and a 'non-skiddy' surface. **1928** *Daily Express* 10 Dec. 19 Motorists drove with caution on skiddy roads. **1935** *Punch* 27 Mar. 358/3 Drive frightfully cautiously and go slowly round the corners.., because you *know* how skiddy it is these days. **1947** A. C. DOUGLAS *Gliding & Soaring* 56 Another range of difficulties..caused by..dislike of being out of normal position in the air, resulting in flat skiddy turns, and so on. **1977** D. MURPHY *Where Indus is Young* xi. 233 Skiddy mud making it impossible to keep upright.

**skidoo** (skɪ'duː), *v. N. Amer. slang.* Also skiddoo. [Orig. uncertain, perh. f. SKEDADDLE *v.*] **1.** *intr.* To go away, leave, or depart hurriedly. Freq. *imp.*

**1905** 'H. MCHUGH' *You can search Me* i. 13 Skidoo, skidoo, and quit me, Mr. Josheimer! **1911** G. B. SHAW *Shewing-up of B. Posnet* 404 Outside, Nestor. Out you go... Skiddoo, Nestor. **1949** *New Yorker* 2 Apr. 26/3, I skiddoo and take a trip. **1963** B. MALAMUD *Idiots First* 135 'If you skidoo now..you'll get spit.' 'Who's skidooing?'

**2.** In catch-phrases. **a.** Used as an exclamation of disrespect (*for* a person). Esp. in nonsense association with *twenty-three*. (*temporary*.)

**1906** J. F. KELLY *Man with Grip* (ed. 2) 99 As for Belmont and Ryan and the rest of that bunch, Skidoo for that crowd when we pass. *Ibid.* 118 'I can see a reason for 'skidoo',' said one, 'and for '23' also. Skidoo from skids and '23' from 23rd Street that has ferries and depots for 80 per cent. of the railroads leaving New York.' **1911** *Maclean's Mag.* Oct. 348/1 Surrounded by this conglomerate procession as I went on my way, the urchins would yell 'Skidoo,' '23 for you!'

**b.** *spec.* as ***twenty-three skidoo***: formerly, an exclamation of uncertain meaning; later used *imp.*, go away, 'scram'.

**1926** C. T. RYAN in *Amer. Speech* II. 92/1, I really do not recall which appeared first in my vocabulary, the use of 'some' for emphasis or that effective but horrible '23-Skiddoo'—perhaps they were simultaneous. **1929** *Amer. Speech* IV. 430 Among the terms which the daily press credits Mr. Dorgan with inventing are:..twenty-three skiddoo (go away). **1957** W. FAULKNER *Town* iii. 56 Almost any time now Father would walk in rubbing his hands and saying 'oh you kid' or 'twenty-three skidoo'. **1978** D. BAGLEY *Flyaway* xi. 80 This elderly, profane woman..used an antique American slang... I expected her to come out with 'twenty-three, skidoo'.

**Ski-doo, Skidoo** (skɪ'duː, 'skiːduː), *sb.* orig. *N. Amer.* Also skidoo. The proprietary name of a motorized toboggan; hence *gen.* (with small initial), any motorized toboggan.

**1961** *Time* (Canada ed.) 29 Dec. 10/1 To hear the Eskimos tell it, the Ski-doo is the greatest thing to hit the north since stripped blubber. **1963** *Globe & Mail* (Toronto) 2 Mar. 30/2 Fishermen..were getting to the choice spots the easy way, using skidoos. **1964** *Star Weekly* (Toronto) 19 Dec. 13/1 The first of these open-air snowmobiles was the Skidoo, originated by the late Armand Bombardier of Valcourt, Que., seven years ago. **1966** *Beaver* Winter 29/2 A trapper with a fast skidoo is able to cover his lines in a third of the time that it took him to do it by dog-team. **1969** *Trade Marks Jrnl.* (Canada) 23 July 961/2 Ski-doo... Filing date: Oct. 31 1968. Bombardier Limited, Valcourt, Quebec. **1969** *Guardian* 30 Aug. 4/5 It was this valley which one had originally proposed to travel along with the skidoos. **1973** C. BONINGTON *Next Horizon* xvii. 238 Do you want to go by Skidoo, or dog-team? **1977** *Courier-Mail* (Brisbane) 8 Mar. 5/5 One man..gave me a thrilling but hair-raising lift on his skidoo.

Hence as *v. intr.*, to travel by Skidoo; **ski'dooing** *vbl. sb.*, **ski'dooer**.

**1966** *North* (Ottawa) Nov.–Dec. 38 She now substitutes skidooing under the Midnight Sun for surfing on sub-tropical seas. **1968** J. G. VERMANDEL *So Long at Fair* xvii. 129 It was near one of those small hills that a ski-dooer came upon the body. **1975** W. S. AVIS in *Occasional Papers Dept.*

*English R. Military Coll. Canada* (1978) No. 2. 25 To skidoo. **1979** R. Fiennes *Hell on Ice* viii. 120 Charlie and I skidooed back to our abandoned tents. **1980** *Beautiful British Columbia* Winter 9 (*caption*) Skidooing near Fort St. John.

**skid row** (skɪd rəʊ). Chiefly *N. Amer.* Also with capital initials. [Altered f. *skid road* (*b*) s.v. skid *sb.* 5.] **a.** Any run-down area of a town where the unemployed, vagrants, alcoholics, etc., tend to congregate. Also *fig.*

**1931** G. Irwin *Amer. Tramp & Underworld Slang* 170 *Skid row*, the district where workers congregate when in town or away from their job. **1935** A. J. Pollock *Underworld Speaks* 107/1 *Skid row*, district in a city where tramps (bums) congregate. **1942** *Crisis* Oct. 314/1 Here, a short walk up from 'Skid Row',..is haven for men of all races. **1944** *N. & Q.* Nov. 120/2 A skidrow..is a district (mostly in western cities) where unskilled workers..gather to look for jobs—a district of employment agencies, cheap flop-houses, etc. **1953** W. Burroughs *Junkie* viii. 80 When the time came for my sendoff shot, I was assigned to Ward B—'Skid Row', it was called. **1959** *New Statesman* 26 Dec. 899/2 Described in a report by a church mission as the nearest thing to 'Skid Row' that we have, it is a festering slum hidden in a narrow valley between the backs of lush shops in Firth Street, and Caxton Hill. **1963** *Economist* 13 July 125/1 The grisly inhabitants of the numerous urban 'skid rows'. **1977** D. M. Smith *Human Geogr.* xi. 338 The concentration of social deviants in the local 'Skid Row' produces freak figures.

**b.** *attrib.*

**1948** *Sun* (Baltimore) 18 Sept. 3/2 Salisbury was a skid-row alcoholic when he was committed to Eloise. **1962** *Times* 1 Feb. 5/3 The 'skid-row' pictures painted in Seattle. **1973** E. B. Ritson in Howe & Loraine *Environmental Med.* xvi. 216 The grim environment of the skid-row districts of cities tends to attract social misfits. **1980** N. Marsh *Photo-Finish* i. 18 He disguises himself..like a Skid Row drop-out.

**skie**, obs. form of sky *sb.*$^{1}$

**skied** (skaɪd), *ppl. a.* [f. sky *sb.*$^{1}$ or *v.*$^{1}$]

**1.** Seeming to touch or reach the sky; lofty. *rare*$^{-1}$.

**1730–46** Thomson *Autumn* 1097 Wide the pale deluge floats, and streaming mild O'er the sky'd mountain to the shadowy vale.

**2.** As second element in combs.: Having a sky of a specified kind.

**1839–52** Bailey *Festus* 270 In the bright, hot, blue-skied East. **1903** L. C. Smithers *Burton's Arab. Nts.* 7 The..sensuousness of the hot-skied East glows from every tale.

**3.** *Cricket.* Of a ball: Hit or sent up high in the air. Also *transf.* of a stroke.

**1868** *Morning Star* 19 June, Judging the bound of the ball when it lands after a high throw or skied hit.

**skief**, variant of scaife.

**skier** ('skiːə(r)). [f. ski *sb.* + -er$^{1}$.] **a.** One who uses or travels on skis; a ski-runner; **b.** a water-skier. See also ski-ing *vbl. sb.*

**1895** *Advance* (Chicago) 4 Apr. 967/2, I have seen an expert skeer go down a long steep hill with the swiftness scarcely equaled by a bird. **1924** K. Furse *Ski-Running* 56 By his tracks shall a Ski-er be judged! **1941** *Life* 4 Aug. 54/1 In water-skiing the skiers hang on to a 75-ft. rope behind a speeding motorboat and skim along the water as fast as 45 m.p.h. **1959** P. Moyes *Dead Men don't Ski* iv. 48 Not a bad skier... Could have used him in the Team in the old days. **1973** V. Canning *Finger of Saturn* v. 97 The boat was moving into the small quay now. Its speed slackened and the skier dropped low into the water.

**skier**, variant of skyer.

**skier**, var. skyr; see also ski *v.*

**skieve**, var. skive *sb.*

**skiey**, variant of skyey *a.*

**skiff** (skɪf), *sb.*$^{1}$ Forms: α. 6–7 **skiph, skiffe,** 6 **skyfe, skyffe,** 6– **skiff.** β. **sciffe,** 7 **sciph.** γ. 7 **schiff(e, schiph.** [ad. F. *esquif* (1549), Sp. and Pg. *esquife*, or It. *schifo*: the source of the Romanic word is prob. OHG. *scif* ship, boat.]

**1.** A small sea-going boat, adapted for rowing and sailing; esp. one attached to a ship and used for purposes of communication, transport, towing, etc. Hence, a small light boat of any kind.

α. **1575** Laneham *Lett.* (1871) 13 The hoounds harroing after [deer], az they had bin a number of skiphs too the spoyle of a karuell. **1578** T. N. tr. *Conq. W. India* 8 The Currant..was so fierce, that he could not get in with his Skiffe, because he had no helpe to row. **1587** Greene *Euphues* Wks. (Grosart) VI. 243 Hee sent secretly one of his sonnes in a little skyfe to Pisandros. **1627** Capt. Smith *Seaman's Gram.* vi. 26 Great ships haue also other small boats called Shallops and Skiffes, which are with more ease ..rowed to an[d] againe. **1652** Needham tr. *Selden's Mare Cl.* 228 Those scouting Skiphs which were joined with the bigger sort of Pinnaces or light Vessels. **1719** De Foe *Crusoe* II. (Globe) 328 Their Long-Boat, and a great Shallop, besides a small Skiff. **1791** W. Gilpin *Forest Scenery* II. 96 The port of Lymington..is chiefly frequented by light skiffs, rigged in the cutter-form, with a jib and boom. **1840** R. H. Dana *Bef. Mast* xx. 61 We took a little skiff that lay on the beach, and paddled off. **1875** W. McIlwraith *Guide Wigtownshire* 95 In later times Lochryan was frequented by the skiffs of the Gaelic tribes.

*transf.* **1646** Sir T. Browne *Pseud. Epid.* 66 If in two skiphs of cork, a Loadstone and steele be placed.

*attrib.* **1798** Coleridge *Anc. Mar.* vii. iii, The skiff-boat neared: I heard them talk.

β. **1589** T. B. *La Primaud. Fr. Acad.* i. 259 Themistocles sent Sicinnus his childrens schoolemaster secretly in a Sciffe towards the Persians. **1656** Blount *Glossogr.*, *Skiff* or *Sciph*, a Ship-boat, properly all of one peece.

γ. **1594** R. Ashley tr. *Loys le Roy* 46 To see him hidden in a little Schiffe, whom but a little before the whole Sea could not suffice. **1653** Holcroft *Procopius, Goth. Wars* ii. 51 Where leaving their ships they took their journey, putting their schiffs upon waynes to passe the Poe with. **1670** *Relat. Siege of Candia* 11 We found 3 Schiffs, or wherrys, drawn up upon rowlers.

**2.** *spec.* **a.** A kind of clinker-built sculling- or pleasure-boat (see quot. 1886). Also, a long narrow racing-boat for one oarsman, outrigged, usually fitted with a sliding-seat, and covered in fore and aft with canvas.

**1793** in Quiller-Couch *Rem. Oxford* (O.H.S.) 200 Various vessels, moored in view, Skiff, gig, and cutter, or canoe. **1845** in Sherwood *Oxford Rowing* (1900) 26 All skiffs or boats constructed for less than four oars..are to be fitted.. with a sufficient deck or covering made of wood or waterproof canvass. **1883** *Boats of the World* 26 Edward Hanlan's paper skiff, which..has been sent along faster than any one-man boat of either hemisphere. **1886** Bourne in *Encycl. Brit.* XXI. 31/2 The skiff is wider and longer than the gig and of greater depth, and, rising higher fore and aft, with rowlock placed on a curved and elevated gunwale,.. rows lighter than the gig.

*attrib.* **1886** *Pall Mall Gaz.* 46 Aug. 4/1 With rowlocks rising high from the gunwales, on the well-known skiff system still preferred on the Thames. **1895** *Daily News* 6 July 10/1 The Skiff Club inaugurated its first season with a successful series of races in Teddington Reach.

**b.** A light kind of sailing-boat in use on the St. Lawrence. Also *attrib.*

**1891** *Harper's Weekly* 19 Sept. 713/4 High winds and heavy seas have no terrors for the skiff sailors. *Ibid.*, The manner of sailing these skiffs is unique.

Hence **'skiffless** *a.*, without a skiff or skiffs; **'skiffman**, one who mans a skiff.

**1829** H. Miller *Scenes & Leg. N. Scotl.* (1834) 50 Behind spreads wide a skiffless shore. **1868** Gorrie *Summers & Winters Orkneys* vii. 231 The skiffmen make good bargains.

**skiff**, *sb.*$^{2}$ Chiefly *Sc.* [f. skiff *v.*$^{2}$]

**1.** A slight gust *of* wind or shower *of* rain, etc. Also, a light flurry or cover *of* snow.

**1819** W. Tennant *Papistry Storm'd* (1827) 56 Whan skiffs o' wind blaw aff the brae. **1870** in *Public Opinion* 23 July 110 An occasional skiff with the syringe, to keep the foliage free from dust. **1895** *N.B. Daily Mail* 20 June 4 Notwithstanding a slight skiff of rain. **1928** *Dialect Notes* VI. 88 *Skiff or skift* as applied to snow..means a thin coating. **1959** E. Collier *Three against Wilderness* xix. 193, I saw the track in a skiff of snow, half a mile from the cabin. **1966** M. & O. Murie *Wapiti Wilderness* iv. 44 We were glad enough to have a skiff of snow, it made study and counting of tracks so much easier. **1975** *Budget* (Sugarcreek, Ohio) 20 Mar. 10/5 The weather..has been colder with skiffs of snow here and there.

**2.** A slight sketch, trace, touch, etc., *of* something.

**1839** Moir *Mansie Wauch* xxvii. (ed. 2) 363 Wait a moment, till I give a skiff of description of our neighbour Reuben. **1884** Stevenson *Lett.* (1901) I. vi. 320 I have had a skiff of cold and was finally obliged to take to bed.

**skiff** (skɪf), *v.*$^{1}$ [f. skiff *sb.*$^{1}$]

**1.** †**a.** *trans.* To cross, row, or sail over (a river) in a skiff. *Obs.*$^{-1}$

*a* **1625** Beaum. & Fl. *Two Noble Kinsmen* i. iii, Perill and want contending, they have skift Torrents, whose roring tyranny and power I'th least of these was dreadfull.

**b.** *refl.* To row or scull (oneself) in a skiff. In quot. *fig.*

**1865** Dickens *Mut. Fr.* iv. xvii, I hope she steered herself, skiffed herself, paddled herself to the ceremony.

**2.** *intr.* To row or scull in a skiff; to go on the river in a pleasure-skiff. Hence **'skiffing** *vbl. sb.*

**1869** Bp. McDougall in Morgan *Univ. Oars* (1873) 314 They..should..confine themselves to mild four-oars and skiffing. **1885** M. Pattison *Mem.* i. 151 We were together every day, skiffing, walking, teaing. **1898** T. Arnold in *19th Cent.* Jan. 106 We used often to go skiffing up the Cherwell.

**skiff**, *v.*$^{2}$ *Sc.* [Perhaps an alteration of skift *v.*$^{2}$, but cf. scuff *v.*]

**1.** *intr.* To move lightly and quickly, esp. so as barely to touch a surface; to glide, run, etc., in this manner. Hence **'skiffing** *vbl. sb.*

**1725** Ramsay *Gentl. Sheph.* i. i, Neat she was..As she came skiffing o'er the dewy green. *a* **1758** —— *Guardians of the Fair*, Watchful guardians of the fair, Who skiff on wings of ambient air. **1791** A. Wilson in *Poems & Lit. Prose* (1876) II. 19 See Sweet Peggy skiffin' ow'r the lee. **1819** W. Tennant *Papistry Storm'd* (1827) 66 He saw the Vicar.. Fast scamperin' and skiffin'. **1866** R. Chambers *Ess.* Ser. ii. 31 A hurrying across upper floors, and a skiffing up and down stairs.

**2.** *trans.* To touch lightly in passing over; to skim.

**1807–10** Tannahill *Poems* (1846) 83 Rude storms assail the mountain's brow That lightly skiff the vale below. **1843** Nicholson *Hist. & Tradit. Tales* 234 [They] skiff the water on the wing.

**skiffle** ('skɪf(ə)l). orig. *U.S.* [Origin unknown.]

**1.** Formerly (*U.S.*), a style of jazz music popular at rent parties, deriving from blues, ragtime, and folk music, and played on standard and improvised instruments. Later, a form of popular music developed from this in the 1950s (esp. in the United Kingdom), in which the vocal part is supported by a rhythmic accompaniment of guitars or banjos and other more or less conventional instruments; a song written in this style. Cf. washboard.

**1926** (*jazz-music title*) Chicago skiffle. **1930** *Paramount Dealers' List* Apr. 2/1, 12886—Home Town Skiffle—Part I. Descriptive Novelty—All Star. **1946** in Carey & McCarthy *Jazz Directory* (1949) 167 Dan Burley and his Skiffle Boys.. Skiffle Blues. **1948** *N.Y. Age* 9 Oct. 2/7 Fletcher insisted on looking over the Skiffler's shoulder trying to dig the riffle that make the skiffle. **1957** *Times* 3 May 13/4 Earnest young women will not consent to hear even skiffle, unless they are sure of the reverberation factor of the sitting room. **1959** *Times* 27 June 7/3 Skiffle is a form of Do it Yourself that depends entirely on song and has the supreme merit of persuading its devotees to make music for themselves. **1966** P. J. Kavanagh *Perfect Stranger* xiv. 199 It was the age of skiffle but the ethos had reached Djakarta before the technique. **1973** 'J. Marks' *Mick Jagger* (1974) 55 Chris Barber and Ken Colyer were the leaders of the skiffle movement. I was with the very first Barber-Colyer Skiffle Band, and when they split up, I left because I didn't actually enjoy skiffle. **1976** *Jrnl. R. Soc. Arts* CXXIV. 603/2 One of the most cheering things that came out of skiffle was the fact that it got children singing, because they sang in groups.

**2.** *U.S. Blacks.* = *rent party* s.v. rent *sb.*$^{1}$ 4 c. (Perhaps the original sense.)

**1946** [see percolator c]. **1956** S. Longstreet *Real Jazz Old & New* 126 You could always get together and charge a few coins and have a skiffle... The money paid the rent. **1974** [see percolator c].

**3. a.** *attrib.*, as ***skiffle band, group, music.***

**1957** *Sing Out!* Spring 30 In the first decade of the 20th Century, these New Orleans boys called themselves a 'Skiffle' band. **1981** *Washington Post* 8 Jan. dc7 The Sunshine Skiffle Band..has become a favorite at area folk festivals. **1953** *Melody Maker* 10 Oct. 15/1 London Jazz Club..Ken Colyer's Sensational Jazzmen and Skiffle Group. **1957** C. Brooke-Rose *Languages of Love* 215 A skiffle group—consisting of two guitarists, a thimble-fingered drummer with a wooden washboard, and a man sweeping a carpet-brush rhythmically over three metal strings drawn taut across a saucepan. **1976** *Dumfries & Galloway Standard* 25 Dec. 7/8 The 'Vipers' comprise five well-known artistes in their own right who get together to form a skiffle group. **1948** *Record Changer* June 5/2 The Jazz Room..will feature only the best of jazz and opening night featured..Freddy Moore, Kansas Fields, Dan Burley and his skiffle music. **1958** J. Asman in P. Gammond *Decca Bk. Jazz* xiv. 173 The phenomenon of skiffle music, peculiar only to Britain as yet, is well under way. **1978** *New York* 3 Apr. 73/2 Lonnie Donnegan was already a veteran performer in England when, in 1961, his recording of 'Does Your Chewing Gum Lose Its Flavor on the Bedpost Overnight?' introduced skiffle music to America.

**b.** General *attrib.* uses.

**1946** [see sense 1 above]. **1948** *Record Changer* Aug. 5 Dan Burley, the skiffle man, is now a disc jockey. **1953** *Melody Maker* 19 Sept. 15/2 Club Calendar... London Jazz Club. .. Ken Colyer's Sensational Jazzmen, every Monday, with skiffle party. **1957** *Universe* 30 Aug. 8/3 There were lots of children's playclothes..'skiffle out-fits' of jersey and jeans. **1965** G. Melly *Owning Up* xi. 135 He [*sc.* Ken Colyer] called these interludes 'Skiffle Sessions', to differentiate them from the more serious activity of playing blues, rags, [etc.].

Hence as *v. intr.*, to play skiffle music; **'skiffler**, one who plays skiffle; a devotee of skiffle; **'skiffling** *vbl. sb.*$^{2}$

**1948** *N.Y. Age* 9 Oct. 3/2 The skiffler's Club is one in which members control the titles of records selected for such programs. **1956** *Observer* 21 Oct. 13/3 The clientele whom the skifflers serve are almost wholly under-thirty, non-drinkers.., mainly middle-class. **1957** *Auckland* (N.Z.) *Weekly News* 2 Oct. 5 'Skiffling' is the latest craze to come to New Zealand. **1957** [see rock and roll *v.*]. **1959** H. Hobson *Mission House Murder* iii. 21 Anybody with floppy hair, a pair of tight jeans and a cheap guitar can be a skiffler in three easy lessons. **1974** *Times* 9 Jan. 12/7 That was the time when..those who did not rock skiffled away merrily.

**skiffling** ('skɪflɪŋ), *vbl. sb.*$^{1}$ [Cf. scabbling, scaffling, scappling *vbl. sbs.*] (See quot. *a* 1877.)

*a* **1877** Knight *Dict. Mech.* III. 2195/1 *Skiffling*, knobbing. Knocking off the rough corners of ashlar in the preliminary dressing. **1901** J. Black *Masonry* 23 For ragstone ashlar work, the stone, when quarried, has its rough projections knocked off with a heavy double-pointed hammer... This operation is locally [*sc.* in Kent] called 'skiffling', and is the same as that known in the neighbourhood of London and other parts of the country by the term of 'knobbling'.

**'skiffy.** *Sc. rare*$^{-1}$ (See quot.)

**1795** *Statist. Acc. Scotl., Campsie* XV. 331 There were employed at least two men at the windlass, putting up the coals in skiffies, termed hutches.

**skift**, *sb.*$^{1}$ *Obs.* Also **skiffte, skyft(e.** [a. ON. *skipti* (MSw. *skipte*; Norw., Sw., Da. *skifte*) distribution, shift, etc.: cf. skift *v.*$^{1}$] A shift, in various senses; a change; a division or share; an artifice, device, or trick.

*c* **1400** *Sc. Trojan War* (Horstm.) ii. 1719 Now as hillis hie it schawis, Now set laich with ane noþir skift, That þai may se nocht bot þe lift. *c* **1440** *York Myst.* xxvi. 130 At oure soper as we satte,..My skiffte come to scathe. *c* **1450** *Bk. Curtasye* 198 in *Babees Bk.*, Yf any man haue part with þe in gyft, With hym þou make an euen skyft. *c* **1460** *Towneley Myst.* xxiv. 392 Is ther none other skyfte Bot syfte, lady, syfte? **1470–85** Malory *Arthur* vi. xvii. 211 Make ye as good skyfte as ye can; ye shal bere this lady with you on horsbak vnto the pope of Rome. **1532** More *Confut. Tindale* Wks. 481/2 He will haue a clappe on the tone cheke or the tother, make what skyfte he can.

† **skift**, *sb.*$^{2}$ *Obs.*$^{-1}$ (See quot.)
**1783** W. GORDON *Livy* I. iv. (1823) 20 The water had subsided and left the trough or skift [L. *alveus*], in which the infants had been exposed, on dry ground.

**skift**, *sb.*$^{3}$ Variant (chiefly *N.Amer.*) of SKIFF *sb.*$^{2}$
**1808** B. HUNT *Diary* 25 Dec. in *Chester Co.* (Pa.) *Hist. Soc. Bull.* (1898) 17 May be call'd green Christmass: a small skift of snow. **1877** MAY LAFFAN *Hon. Miss Ferrard* I. vii. 191 The autumn leaves rustling under foot and flying off in sudden skifts across the dry ruddy grass. **1927** *Amer. Speech* II. 364 *Skift of snow*, a small amount of snow. **1947** *Canad. Cattlemen* (Winnipeg) Dec. 148 Farmers regard 'a skift o' rain' as an adjunct to the fermentation of the natural juices in the semi-green corn blown into the [silo]. **1970** I. PETITE *Meander to Alaska* iv. 34 We had seen practically every rock, headland, light, skift of sea birds rising, tree, and deserted beach cabin.

**skift** (skɪft), *sb.*$^{4}$ Var. SKIFF *sb.*$^{1}$ *U.S. dial.*
**1656** *Suffolk Co.* (Mass.) *Deeds* (1880) I. 2 [We are] desired by Jno. Blackman to App[rize] a smale skifte taken vp adrift. **1807** J. R. BEDFORD in *Tenn. Hist. Mag.* (1919) V. 118 They would board us in their skift without the inconvenience to us of going to shore. **1816** U. BROWN *Jrnl.* 12 Sept. in *Maryland Hist. Mag.* (1916) XI. 222 Wm. Wells ..prevails with me to go with him down the River 1¼ Miles to what he called a skift. **1885** *Century Mag.* Aug. 505/2 Visitors call it a skiff, natives a skift. **1935** G. SANTAYANA *Last Puritan* III. x. 395 You were perfectly happy here, sculling in your skift.

**skift**, *v.*$^{1}$ *Obs.* exc. *dial.* Forms: 4–6 **skyft**, 4–5 **-e** (5 **scyfft**), 4–5, 9 **skift** (8 *Sc.* **skifft**), 5 **-e**. [a. ON. *skipta* (MSw. *skipta*; Norw. and Sw. *skifta*, Da. *skifte*) to divide, change, etc., = OE. *sciftan*, SHIFT *v.*]
**1.** *trans.* To shift, change, or move (something).
**13..** *Cursor M.* 23678 (Edinb.), Sun and mon, and stern on lift, þat ai wit stiring er nu skift,..Fra þat tim stil sal þai stand. **13..** *E.E. Allit. P.* B. 709 Now haf þay skyfted my skyl & scorned natwre. *c* **1440** *Alph. Tales* 389 He wolde nevur skyfte his clothis bod ons in a yere. **1470–85** MALORY *Arthur* IX. xl. 405 Lete see now yf ye can skyfte it with your handes. **1828–** in many north. dial. glossaries, etc. (see *Eng. Dial. Dict.*).
†**2.** To arrange, devise, manage, or order (something). *Obs.*
**13..** *E.E. Allit. P.* A. 569 'Þus schal I,' quoth kryste, 'hit skyfte, þe laste schal be þe fyrst þat strykez.' ? *a* **1400** *Morte Arth.* 32 Scathylle Scottlande by skylle he skyftys as hym lykys. *Ibid.* 1643 Loke ȝe skyfte it so þat vs no skathe lympe.
†**3.** To divide, distribute, or make division. *Obs.*
*c* **1420** *Sir Amadas* 644 (W.), Bot skyfte me evon,..Gyffe me my parte, Y wyll awey. *Ibid.* 656 Oderwyse skyft wyll not wee, Bot at yor wyll schall hit bee. *c* **1425** *Cast. Persev.* 108 in *Macro Plays* 80 His good..he wolde þat it were scyfftyd a-mongis his ny kynne.
†**4.** *intr.* To ordain; to act, devise. *Obs.*
*c* **1325** *Metr. Hom.* 61 Bot Godd that skilfulli kan skift, Mad them alle serely spekand. *c* **1500** MEDWALL *Nature* I. (Brandl) 574 Well enured men, suche as..can best for you in tyme of nede skyft.
**5.** To undergo shifting, change, or removal; to change one's place, etc. *Obs.* exc. *dial.*
**13..** *Gaw. & Gr. Knt.* 19 Oft boþe blysse & blunder Ful skete has skyfted synne. *a* **1400–50** *Alexander* 467 To skyre skarlet hewe skyftis hire face. *Ibid.* 5040 Baldly he wepis, þat he so skitly suld skifte. **1791** J. LEARMONT *Poems* 67 The sun now frae the twal hour point Had nearly skifftit twa hours yont. **1847** E. & A. BRONTE *Wuthering Heights* xxiv, He mad ye skift properly. **1848** *Tales of Kirkbeck* 155 A huge carved oak rocking chair 'fearfu' lubbardly for skifting'.
†**b.** To escape, get away *from*. *Obs.*
*c* **1440** *York Myst.* xxvi. 41 Why, sir, to skyfte [*pr.* skyste] fro his skath We seke for youre socoure þis sesoune.
Hence †'**skifting** *vbl. sb.*, division, distribution.
*c* **1440** *Alph. Tales* 249 So þer fell a grete debate..for skiftyyng of þis money betwix þaim.

**skift**, *v.*$^{2}$ *Sc.* [Perhaps only a special use of prec.; see also SKIFF *v.*$^{2}$] *intr.* To move lightly and quickly; to skip, run, glide, etc.
*a* **1586** SIR R. MAITLAND *Poems* (Maitl. Club) 30 Use not to skift athort the gait. **1640** *Canterburians Self-Conviction* Postscr. 13 But ye skift out here much further to an extravagance. **1790** A. WILSON *To W. Mitchell* Poet. Wks. (1846) 112 High ower my head the sheep in packs, I see them mice-like skift. **1819** W. TENNANT *Papistry Storm'd* (1827) 182 And Arnold's nakit ghaist was seen Loupin'..And skiftin' owr the roofs like fire.

'**skifter**, *v.* (See quot. and cf. prec.)
**1887** MRS. C. READE *Maid o' the Mill* xxii, He murmurs spasmodically and skifters off down the stairs.

'**skifting**, Sc. variant of SKIRTING *vbl. sb.* 4.
**1842** AITON *Domest. Econ.* (1857) 223 Then take stone, hewn and well jointed, and set it as a skifthing round the whole wall. **1844** H. STEPHENS *Bk. Farm* I. 119 The floor.. is..finished with a neat skifting board..round the walls of the barn.

†**skig**, *a. Obs.*$^{-1}$ In 4 **skyg**. [Of Scand. origin: cf. Norw. and Sw. dial. *skygg*.] Fastidious.
**13..** *E.E. Allit. P.* B. 21 He is so clene in his courte,..Nif he nere scoymus & skyg & non scaþe louied, Hit were a meruayl to much.

'**ski-ing**, *vbl. sb.* Also **skiing**. [f. SKI *v.*]
**1.** The action of travelling or running on skis, esp. as a sport.
**1893** *Daily News* 31 Jan. 5/3 If we had winter worth speaking of here, ski-ing would soon take a prominent place among our field sports. **1895** *Advance* (Chicago) 4 Apr. 967/2, It must be a very funny sight, that of the skeeing down hill. **1911** A. BENNETT *Card* xi. 273 Ski-ing became the rage... The Captain said 'skee', but he did not object to 'shee'... People with no shame..said brazenly 'sky'. **1927** E. HEMINGWAY in V. W. Brooks *Amer. Caravan* 46 In the Silvretta the ski-ing had been all right, but it was spring ski-ing. **1975** *New Yorker* 21 Apr. 40/3 It has been raining a lot, ruining the skiing.
**2.** Water-skiing.
**1971** 'D. HALLIDAY' *Dolly & Doctor Bird* xii. 161, I have never yet met..a man who with greater clarity could teach me to water-ski... I made a reasonable success, for a beginner, at skiing.
**3.** *attrib.*
**1921** A. LUNN *Alpine Ski-ing* 16 (*caption*) Ski-ing slopes at Scheidegg. **1932** AUDEN in *Rev. Eng. Stud.* (1978) Aug. 283 A waxen sandboy in skiing kit. **1946** G. MILLAR *Horned Pigeon* xx. 306 The first passengers to arrive..wore ski-ing clothes. **1951** 'J. WYNDHAM' *Day of Triffids* vi. 107 She had chosen a dark-blue skiing suit. **1961** 'J. LE CARRÉ' *Call for Dead* xviii. 191 She met Dieter on a skiing holiday in Germany. **1978** S. SHELDON *Bloodline* ii. 30 He skipped skiing lessons in order to go into the village with Anna.

**ski-joring** (skiːˈdʒɔərɪŋ). Also **skijoring**. [Semi-naturalized alteration of Norw. *ski-kjøring*, f. *ski* SKI *sb.* + *kjøring* driving (f. *kjøre* to drive).] A winter sport in which a skier is pulled over the snow by a horse or horses (or by a motorized vehicle).
**1920** *Punch* 17 Mar. 204/1 Skating, sliding, curling and yodelling in the intervals of ski-ing, skijoring, skilacking and skihandlung. **1927** *Sunday Times* 13 Feb. 17/2 In the skijoring races on the Lake,..the well-known Swiss hockey player fell. **1946** G. STIMPSON *Bk. about Thousand Things* 473 The winter sport in which a person on skis is drawn over the snow or ice by a horse is called *skijoring*. **1963** *Guardian* 13 Feb. 13/3 Every type of winter sport..skating, skijöring, bob-sledding. **1980** G. M. FRASER *Mr. American* xvi. 296 Ski-joring..is when you have horses to pull you along on skis.
Also **ski-'jorer**, a skier who engages in ski-joring.
**1936** 'F. BEEDING' *Nine Waxed Faces* 193 Then..I led it back to where Granby was bending over the skijörer.

†**skikart**. *Obs.* [? f. SKICK *v.*] An old name for the hare.
*a* **1325** in *MS. Digby 86* fol. 168 b, þe scotewine, þe skikart.

**skil** (skɪl). [a. Haida *sqil*.] = SABLEFISH. Also '**skilfish**.
**1886** *Encycl. Brit.* XX. 170/1 Halibut, herring, salmon, cod, and coal-fish or 'skil' (this last also rich in oil and a valuable food-fish) are likewise abundant [off the coast of British Columbia]. **1897** C. R. TUTTLE *Golden North* 124 One of the most delicious of deep water fish is the skil, or black cod, as it is sometimes called. **1910** F. W. HODGE *Handbk. Amer. Indians* II. 591/1 Skil. A local name of the black candle-fish. **1923** D. K. TRESSLER *Marine Prod. Commerce* 736/2 Skilfish (*Anoploma fimbria*). A common food fish from Unalaska to Monterey. **1964** G. C. CARL *Some Common Marine Fishes Brit. Columbia* 48 The giant skilfish..may attain a weight of 200 pounds.

†'**skilfer**. *Obs. rare.* [a. Du. *schilfer* (†*schelfer*) fragment, scale; cf. SKALFERING.]
**1.** A small piece; a splinter.
**1597** A. M. tr. *Guillemeau's Fr. Chirurg.* 10/2 If you perceave anye skilfers or splinters by the which that membrane might be pricked. **1599** —— tr. *Gabelhouer's Bk. Physicke* 342/2 If..there weare one little skilfer, or smale bone.
**2.** *pl.* Scurf; dandruff.
**1599** A. M. tr. *Gabelhouer's Bk. Physicke* 3/1 It expelleth alsoe the skilfers of youre heade. *Ibid.* 47/1 This doth not onlye expelle all skilfers of the heade.

**skilful** ('skɪlfʊl), *a.* and *adv.* Forms: 4 **sceluol**, **skileful**; 4–6 **skylful**, 5–6 **-full(e**, 6 **skyllfull**; 4–5 **skilfulle**, 4–7 **-full**, 4– **skilful** (6, 9– (chiefly *U.S.*) **skillful**, 9 *Sc.* **skeelfu'**). [f. SKILL *sb.* + -FUL.]
†**1. a.** Endowed with reason; rational; also, following reason, doing right. *Obs.*
*a* **1300** *Cursor M.* 21334 Mai na skilful man þis wern. **13..** *St. Erkenwolde* 278 in Horstm. *Altengl. Leg.* (1881) 272 For as he says in his sothe psalmyde writtes: þe skilfulle & þe vnskathely skeltone ay to me. *c* **1380** *Lay Folks Catech.* 19 (Lamb. MS.), He made skylful creaturis as angelys and man. *c* **1440** *York Myst.* iii. 22 A skylfull beeste þan will y make, Aftir my shappe and my liknesse.
†**b.** Intellectual, mental. *Obs.*$^{-1}$
**1387–8** T. USK *Test. Love* III. vii. (Skeat) I. 43 Dul ben thy skilful understandinges; thy wil hath thy wit so amaistred.
†**2. a.** Reasonable, just, proper. *Obs.*
**1340** *Ayenb.* 169 Mochel is riȝtuol þing and sceluol þet ich yeue mi lif..uor him þet his lif..yaf uor ous. **1387** TREVISA *Higden* (Rolls) IV. 215 He was nevere so wroþ wiþ man þat he ne wolde forȝeve ȝif he seigh skilful occasioun. *c* **1400** HYLTON *Scala Perf.* I. lxx. (W. de W. 1494), Neuertheles it was worthy and skylfull that our lorde sholde shew as he is. *c* **1460** ASHBY *Dicta Philos.* 831 It is nat lefull..to be serued, but serue skylful Thinges.
†**b.** Of stature or distance. *Obs.*
**1387** TREVISA *Higden* (Rolls) VII. 315 Kyng William was of skilful stature, to greet and fat of body. *c* **1410** *Master of Game* (MS. Digby 182) xxv, þei ought tary till þei are were þat he be entered two skylfull boweshotes. *a* **1513** FABYAN *Chron.* VII. ccxxii. (1811) 247 A man of skylfull stature, but somedele fat in yᵉ bely.
†**3.** Sufficient, ample. *Obs.*
*a* **1350** *St. Nicholas* 190 in Horstm. *Altengl. Leg.* (1881) 13 In þat ȝere þai had none nede, Bot skilfull both to mete and sede.
**4. a.** Having practical ability; possessing skill; expert, dexterous, clever. Also const. *to*.
**1338** R. BRUNNE *Chron.* (1810) 311 At conseil & at nede he was a skilfulle kyng. *c* **1375** *Cursor M.* 27156 (Fairf.), Prest agh be..skilful to knaw þe pliȝt, quilc is heui & quilk is liȝt. **1560** DAUS tr. *Sleidane's Comm.* 82 b, A Captaine of the Sea, moste skylfull. **1587** GOLDING *De Mornay* v. (1592) 49 Of men themselues, the skilfullest make Lawes, & take vpon them to rule others. **1606** SHAKS. *Tr. & Cr.* I. i. 7 The Greeks are strong, & skilful to their strength. **1660** W. SECKER *Nonsuch Prof.* Pref. 15 Where there are any faults men are more skilful to find them, then careful to mend them. **1750** tr. *Leonardus' Mirr. Stones* 44 Many other deceptions may be effected..which are all known to the skilful. **1796** MORSE *Amer. Geogr.* I. 21 Having always his descriptions from the most skilful persons in every country. **1813** SHELLEY *Q. Mab* vii. 25 Human pride Is skilful to invent most serious names To hide its ignorance. **1875** JOWETT *Plato* (ed. 2) I. 85 One who had been trained and exercised under a skilful master. **1891** J. W. STEVENS *Leather Manuf.* vii. 75 There are several machines for this work each of which will perform satisfactory work when managed by skillful hands.
*absol.* **1837** CARLYLE *Fr. Rev.* I. I. iii, In these delicate circumstances..the skilfullest may falter.
**b.** Const. *in* a matter.
**1555** EDEN *Decades* (Arb.) 72 If he had byn skilfull in Astronomye. **1594** HOOKER *Eccl. Pol.* Pref. ii. §8 The perfectest divines were judged they, which were skilfullest in Calvin's writings. **1662** STILLINGFL. *Orig. Sacræ* I. vi. §1 Among the Ægyptians who are supposed most skilfull in the account of the year. **1879** *Cassell's Techn. Educ.* I. 174/2 The Chinese are very skilful in this kind of work.
†**c.** Having a good knowledge *of* a subject. *Obs.*
**1596** SPENSER *F.Q.* VI. v. 16 [He] vpon him set, of perill nought adrad, Ne skilfull of the vncouth ieopardy. **1609** BIBLE (Douay) *Daniel* comm., Daniel skilful of times, a studious historiographer. **1631** WEEVER *Anc. Funeral Mon.* 251 Very skilfull of the Greeke and Latine tongues.
**5.** Displaying or requiring skill.
*c* **1586** C'TESS PEMBROKE *Ps.* XLVII. iii, With skilfull tunes his praises sing. **1598** SYLVESTER *Du Bartas* II. i. I. *Eden* 322 For..he made only sweet Essayes in that, Of skilfull industry. **1757** W. WILKIE *Epigoniad* Pref. p. xvi, He should magnify them likewise by a skilful management of outward circumstances. **1794** BURNS '*My Chloris! mark*' 9 Let minstrels sweep the skilfu' string In lordly lighted ha'. **1805** *Med. Jrnl.* XIV. 416 The skilful manner in which they treated their patient. **1856** KANE *Arct. Expl.* I. xxiii. 309 It was made of the bone of a whale, and worked out with skilful labor. **1895** *Gentl. Mag.* July 581/2 Irony..is one of those edged tools which require skilful handling. **1952** G. SARTON *Hist. Sci.* I. ix. 225 The power of Athens was based..also.. upon the skillful use of all the resources that such places as Delos and Delphi offered. **1969** R. BUCKMINSTER FULLER *Operating Man. Spaceship Earth* i. 19 The myriad of physical, muscle, and craft-skill specializations which their intellect and their skillful swordplay commanded. **1972** P. H. KOCHER *Master of Middle-Earth* ii. 25 Their skillful blending as achieved by Tolkien requires some sophistication of understanding.
†**6.** As *adv.* = SKILFULLY. *Obs.*
*a* **1400–50** *Alexander* 645 Þus skilfull lange he scolaid & þe scole vsed. *a* **1425** *Cursor M.* 3742 (Trin.), Skilful is iacob his nome, þat is to say in riȝt langage Putter out of heritage.

**skilfully** ('skɪlfʊlɪ), *adv.* Also 4 **skeluolliche**, **skilfulliche**, **skil-**, **schilfuli**, **skilefully**, 4–5 **skylfully**, etc. [f. prec. + -LY$^{2}$.]
†**1.** Reasonably; with good reason; naturally.
*c* **1325** *Metr. Hom.* 46 Ful schilfuli and wit resoun Mai men ask this questioun. **1340** *Ayenb.* 6 Me may zuerie wyþ-oute zenne,..in oþre guode skele and clenliche and skeluolliche. *c* **1386** CHAUCER *Second Nun's T.* 320 Men myghten dreden wel and skilfully This lyf to lese. *c* **1400** LOVE *Bonavent. Mirr.* (1908) 176 Who so wole..byholde how oure lorde Jesu wepeth,..skilfully he may be stired to compassioun and wepynge. **1412–20** LYDG. *Chron. Troy* IV. 3198 As deth for deth is skilfully guerdoun. *c* **1460** ASHBY *Dicta Philos.* 403 To..ly not for his profett in suche guise That it shuld harme any man skilfully.
†**b.** To a reasonable extent; in a moderate degree. *Obs.*
**13..** *Minor Poems fr. Vernon MS.* xxxvii. 553 Þerfore I rede..þat vche Mon skilfuli of his god [= good] mak him glad. **1387** TREVISA *Higden* (Rolls) III. 35 He techeþ alle men to be skilfulliche scars. *c* **1430** *Chev. Assigne* 47 She sente aftur a man..That hadde serued her-seluen skylfully longe. *c* **1450** *Two Cookery-bks.* 101 Drawe it thorgh a streynour skilfully thik.
**2.** In a skilful manner; with skill; cleverly, adroitly, dexterously.
**1565** COOPER *Thesaurus*, *Scienter*, cunnyngly: skilfully. **1588** SHAKS. *L.L.L.* II. i. 253 Thou art an old Loue-monger, and speakest skilfully. **1631** GOUGE *God's Arrows* v. §6. 414 Choice persons are instructed..wisely to encampe, and skilfully to embattaile. **1695** LD. PRESTON *Boethius* I. 16 Thou didst skilfully read upon all Divine and Humane Learning. **1774** GOLDSM. *Nat. Hist.* (1824) I. xv. 100 The one being laid against the other so skilfully, that there is a just equipoise of the whole globe. **1839** JAMES *Louis XIV*, I. 105 He skilfully availed himself of those threats to pretend that his life was in danger. **1861** BUCKLE *Civiliz.* (1873) II. viii. 547 The scheme, secretly prepared, was skilfully accomplished.
**b.** With pa. pples. used attributively.
**1821** CRAIG *Lect. Drawing*, etc. iv. 245 In a skilfully executed picture. **1848** BUCKLEY *Iliad* 164, I rushed forth, having burst the skilfully-joined doors. **1863** LYELL *Antiq. Man* 11 The more skilfully worked weapons of a later stage of the same period.

**skilfulness** ('skɪlfʊlnɪs). Also 5-6 skylful-, 7 skilfulnesse, 8 skill-. [f. as prec. + -NESS.]

†**1.** The quality of being reasonable. *Obs.*⁻⁰

*c* **1440** *Promp. Parv.* 457/2 Skylfulnesse, *racionabilitas*.

**2.** The quality of being skilful; dexterity.

**1561** EDEN tr. *Cortes' Arte de Navigar* Pref., The experte skylfulnesse of so excellent a Pilot. **1611** BIBLE *Ps.* lxxviii. 72 He..guided them by the skilfulnesse of his hands. **1660** R. COKE *Power & Subj.* 262 So little avails the skilfulness of the Pilot. **1709** *Brit. Apollo* II. Supernum. No. 1. 2/2 He outstrip'd the Starter in the skillfulness of War. **1768** TUCKER *Lt. Nat.* I. II. xxxv. 336 For want of skilfulness in the pilots. **1885** *Manch. Exam.* 7 Aug. 5/2 A panegyric upon the skilfulness of their administration.

†**3.** Knowledge *of* a thing. *Obs.*

*a* **1656** USSHER *Ann.* (1658) 853 The Iberians had the better of it, through their skilfulness of the places.

**skill** (skɪl), *sb.*¹ Forms: α. 2 skele, 4 sckele, 9 *Sc.* skeel; 2-5 skile, 3-5 skyle; 2-7 skil, 3-4 sckil, 4-6 skyl (skylle), 5-6 skyll, 3- skill (4-6 skille). β. 3 scule, 4 scele, 5 schele, schyle; 3-4 schil, 4 schyl, 4-5 scill(e, scylle. [a. ON. *skil*, neut. (Icel. and Norw. *skil*, Sw. *skäl*, Da. *skjel, skel*) distinction, difference, etc., related to MLG. and MDu. *schele* (LG. *schele, schel*), MDu. and Du. *geschil*, *verschil*, LG. *schill*: cf. SKILL *v.*¹]

The great variety of usage in ME. often renders it difficult to assign particular examples to a definite sense.

†**1. a.** Reason as a faculty of the mind; the power of discrimination. *Obs.*

*c* **1200** ORMIN 1210 ȝiff þu follȝhesst skill & shæd & witt i gode þæwess. *a* **1225** *Ancr. R.* 204 Mid skilles ȝettunge, þet is, hwonne þe schil & te heorte ne wiðsiggeð nout. **1303** R. BRUNNE *Handl. Synne* 645 þyn inwyt, þyn owne skyle, Aȝen þe seyþ and euermore wylle. *c* **1340** HAMPOLE *Pr. Consc.* 273 Swylk men er noght led with skylle, Bot þai folow, ay, þair awen wille. **1375** *Sc. Leg. Saints* xxxii. (*Justin*) 709 þane þu ma se be kyndly skil þat na man suld gyf treutht þaim til. *c* **1440** *Promp. Parv.* 457/2 Skyl, *racio*. *a* **1500** *Ratis Raving* I. 1763 He disspendyt his resone In wycis agan kindly skill.

†**b.** Discrimination or discretion in relation to special circumstances. *Obs.*

*a* **1200** *Vices & Virtues* 139 Ða þinges ðe ne sculen ben iȝiuen, þa bieð to wiðhealden mid michele skele. *c* **1250** *Gen. & Ex.* 193 Hadde he wel loked him wið skil, Ilc beste sulde don his wil. **1375** BARBOUR *Bruce* XII. 260 Me think it suld accorde till skill To set stoutness agane felony. *c* **1375** *Cursor M.* 12807 (Fairf.), John ansquared þes men vntille wiþ milde wordes & wiþ skille. ?*a* **1400** *Morte Arth.* 32 Skathylle Scottlande by skylle he skyftys as hym lykys. *c* **1470** *Gol. & Gaw.* 1325 Sa that the cause may be kend, and knawin throw skill.

†**c.** A sense of what is right or fitting. *Obs.*

**1338** R. BRUNNE *Chron.* (1810) 245 He praied to hold him stille,..& he suld do his wille, in alle þat skille mot se. **1377** LANGL. *P. Pl.* B. XIX. 279 Ne sholde no scorner ne scolde oute of skyl hym [*sc.* Temperance] brynge. ?*c* **1470** ASHBY *Active Policy* 649 Do theim to be lettred right famously Wherby thei shall reule bi Reason and skele. *a* **1536** *Songs, Carols*, etc. (E.E.T.S.) 26 Grant thow me myn askyng, As reason wold, & skyll.

†**2. a.** That which is reasonable, proper, right, or just. *Obs.*

α. *c* **1175** *Lamb. Hom.* 61 God..ȝife us to him god iwil, and to alle men riht and skil. *c* **1330** R. BRUNNE *Chron. Wace* (Rolls) 971 Sire kyng, we aske þe bot skyle. **1375** BARBOUR *Bruce* I. 214 Thai dempt thaim eftir thar will, Takand na kep to rycht na skill. *c* **1460** *Towneley Myst.* ii. 260, I did hym neuer yit bot skill.

β. *a* **1300** *Cursor M.* 13938 O yur vn-witt qui ne wald yee blin,..And herken scil and hald resun? **1340** *Ayenb.* 53 þe ilke ne hyealdeþ scele ne mesure. *c* **1400** *Ywaine & Gaw.* 968 It es oft wemens will Tham forto blame that sais tham scill.

†**b.** In predicative use (= reasonable, right); also with adjs. as *good, great*. *Obs.*

*c* **1250** *Gen. & Ex.* 1425 Siðen men hauen holden [it] skil, first to freinen ðe wimmanes wil. *a* **1300** *Assump. Virg.* 312 Now when it is my sones wille to hym y come, and that is skyle. *c* **1320** *Sir Tristr.* 2635 As lord he þer abade, As gode skil wald be. **1375** BARBOUR *Bruce* IX. 751 It is gret skill at men chasty Thi prowd vourdis. *c* **1400** *Pilgr. Sowle* (Caxton) I. viii. (1859) 6 In euery ryghtwys court skyle is that the actour be admytted to maken his compleynt. *c* **1470** *Gol. & Gaw.* 147 To mak you lord of your avne, me think it grete skill. *c* **1520** SKELTON *Magnyf.* 106 It is reason and skyll, We your pleasure fulfyll. *c* **1550** ROLLAND *Crt. Venus* I. 784 Madame, that is bot skill, To thair counsall hartlie applie I will.

†**c.** In prepositional phrases, denoting that something is in accordance with, or contrary to, what is reasonable or right. *Obs.*

(*a*) *c* **1250** *Owl & Night.* 186 May vr eyþer hwat he wile Mid rihte segge & myd skile. **13..** *Seuyn Sages* 3750 (W.), When thou haues said to tham thi will, And gifen the dome, by right and scill. **1375** BARBOUR *Bruce* VIII. 436 Me think men suld him luf of skill. *c* **1400** *26 Pol. Poems* 24 Let eche man serue his charge in skylle. *c* **1470** HENRY *Wallace* VI. 893 This is a lord..; To salus him ye may be propyr skill.

(*b*) *a* **1300** *Cursor M.* 18274 Qui gaf þou rede þis ilk iesu to crucifi, Wit-vten skil, vn-rightwisli? **1303** R. BRUNNE *Handl. Synne* 5825 He meked hym self ouer skyle, Pottes and dysshes for to swele. *Ibid.* 7293 Dyners are oute of skyl and resun On þe Sunday, or hye messe be doun. *c* **1375** *Sc. Leg. Saints* vii. (*Jacobus Minor*) 358 For til escuse hym of þe Ill, þat he had don agannis skill. *c* **1420** *Chron. Vilod.* 4010 Bot þou toke hurr lond from hurre withouȝt ony reson or skyll.

†**3. a.** Cause, reason, or ground. Also with *a* and pl.

α. *a* **1300** *Cursor M.* 14833 He has vs wonnen wit maistri, And we sal sceu yow sckil for-qui. *c* **1340** HAMPOLE *Pr. Consc.* 1767 Bodily dede here dredes ful many, For twa skilles principaly. **1390** GOWER *Conf.* I. 358 To make werres and to pile For lucre and for non other skyle. *c* **1400** *Pilgr. Sowle* (Caxton) I. xiii. (1859) 9 And that I preue by this skile. *c* **1440** *Gesta Rom.* i. 2 (Harl. MS.), Goode Sir, tell me why and what skile, þat þou so beholdest me? **1537** *State P. Hen. VIII*, I. 551 We haue, for sundry skylles, thought it more convenyent to..differre our journey. **1563** *Homilies* II. *Rogation Week* II. 3 P iv b, For many other skils it is wisedom to knowe..that all goodes..be of God. **1611** SHAKS. *Wint. T.* IV. iv. 152, I thinke you haue As little skill to feare, as I haue purpose To put you to't. **1642** ROGERS *Naaman* 280 Thinking the Lion to be couchant for a skill, that he might be rampant after.

β. *c* **1300** *Cursor M.* 9389 Yon was a rightwis dom, Als yee sal se wit rightwis scill. **1340** *Ayenb.* 11 This heste uorbyet wyl to habbe oþre manne þing by wyckede scele. *c* **1400** *Ywaine & Gaw.* 293, I sayd, How so? tel me thi scill. *c* **1430** LYDG. *Min. Poems* (Percy Soc.) 229 The secounde schyle ys that thou shalle dye.

†**b.** A statement made by way of argument or reasoning. *Obs.*

**1303** R. BRUNNE *Handl. Synne* 4263 þan ys þys Terlyncels skylle, 'Slepe þou long, and y shal hele'. *Ibid.* 11581 Seynt Austyn seyþ þys skyl, Do þyr-aftyr who so wyl. **1390** GOWER *Conf.* I. 104 For ye have told me such a skile Of this ensample. *c* **1400** *Ywaine & Gaw.* 3451 When the king had tald this scill. *c* **1425** *Cast. Persev.* 2532 in *Macro Plays*, Coueytyse, þou seyst a good skyl..; al þi byddynge don I wyl.

†**4. a.** One's case or cause. *Obs. rare.*

*a* **1300** *E.E. Psalter* xlii. 1 Deme me,..and schede mi skil [L. *causa*] Fra men þat noght be hali wil. *Ibid.* lxxiii. 23.

†**b.** An arrangement, ordinance. *Obs.*⁻¹

**13..** *E.E. Allit. P.* B. 709 Now haf þay skyfted my skyl & scorned natwre.

†**c.** A wise or sensible act. *Obs.*⁻¹

**15..** *Doun by ane rever* 63 in *Dunbar's Poems* (S.T.S.) II. 307 Wyismen said, he did nane skill.

†**5. a.** In the phr. ***can*** (or ***could***) ***skill***, to have discrimination or knowledge, esp. in a specified matter. Usually const. *of*, *in*, or *to* with inf. *Obs.*

The phr. is an adoption of the ON. *kunna skil*. In later use, when not accompanied by an adj., *skill* was probably in most cases apprehended as a vb. (cf. SKILL *v.*¹ 4b). The construction with *of* is extremely common *c* 1525–1640.

(*a*) *c* **1340** HAMPOLE *Pr. Consc.* Prol. 198 Ilk cristen man and weman þat has witte and mynd, and skille can,..Suld be bughsom ay [etc.]. **1489** CAXTON *Faytes of A.* II. xxiv. 137 By the aduys of them that best can skyle thees pale-bordes shal be sette. **1526** SKELTON *Magnyf.* 1377 But some man wolde conuey, and can not skyll. **1581** LAMBARDE *Eiren.* I. i. (1588) 5 Let them iudge that can skill.

(*b*) **1387** TREVISA *Higden* (Rolls) II. 345 [Saturnus] kouþe skile of vynes and in repynge and in telyenge of feeldes. *a* **1450** *Knt. de la Tour* (1868) 34 It is a gret perille to beginne to haue langage with suche men that canne skille of the worlde. **1526** TINDALE *Luke* xii. 56 Ye can skyll of the fassion of the erth, and of the skye. **1561** T. HOBY tr. *Castiglione's Courtyer* III. (1577) O j b, Many..that coulde as well skill in ruling Cities and armies, as men can. **1577** *Test. 12 Patriarchs* (1604) 153 A holy man..passeth not how men dishonour him; neither can he skill in any fraud or guile. **1647** TRAPP *Comm. 2 Cor.* xii. 19 But Saint Paul could not skill of those arts.

(*c*) **1542** UDALL *Erasm. Apoph.* 269 Thei have not a capitain that can skill how to use victorie, when he hath it. **1590** GREENE *Never too late* Wks. (Grosart) VIII. 72 Seigneur Francesco..coulde well skill to court all kinde of degrees. **1601** DENT *Pathw. Heaven* 75 Many such men as you are, can skill to giue good words. **1675** EVELYN *Terra* (1729) 11 We could skill to modify also the Air about them. **1869** JEAN INGELOW *Lily & Lute* i. 82 Could he skill to make it seen As he saw?

†**b.** With adjs., as *good, no, some*, etc.

*c* **1350** *Leg. Rood* (1871) 71 þai trowed to turn life him vntill, For þai kowth þan none oþer skill. *c* **1400** *Beryn* 1628 Ascaunce þat þey were lewde, And coude no skill of marchandise. *c* **1450** *Merlin* ii. 27 Thei can knowe many thinges be force of clergie that we ne can no skyle on. **1479** *Paston Lett.* III. 244 He can good skylle to helpe in this mater of the benefice of Oxned. **1523** FITZHERB. *Husb.* §52 Let the wol be..wounden with a woll-wynder, that can good skyll therof. **1540** HEYWOOD *Four P.P.* in Hazl. *Dodsley* I. 359 Yet in lying I can some skill, And if I shall be judge I will. **1587** GOLDING *De Mornay* (1592) 105 Their greatest Philosophers could lesse skill of the nature..of the Tydes.

**6. a.** Capability of accomplishing something with precision and certainty; practical knowledge in combination with ability; cleverness, expertness. Also, an ability to perform a function, acquired or learnt with practice (usu. *pl.*). Freq. const. *to* with inf.

*a* **1300** *Cursor M.* 26181 Ga Til a wijser to sceu þi wond, þat skill has for to mak it sond. **1553** *Respublica* I 109 Will ye beleve People that hath no manier of skill to iudge or to descerne what thing is good or yll? **1596** DRAYTON *Legends* ii. 34 Though..pleasing be his Rime, Yet all his skill cannot excuse her Crime. **1628** COKE *On Litt.* 3 b, If these..bee granted to a man that is unexpert, and hath no skill and science to exercise..the same. **1671** MILTON *P.R.* IV. 552 To stand upright Will ask thee skill. **1738** WESLEY *Psalms* cxxxix. 4 Heav'n, Earth, and Sea,..Shew me thy wond'rous Skill. **1784** COWPER *Task* III. 407 No works..but such as may amuse.., demanding rather skill than force. *Ibid.* VI. 619 That oft we owe our safety to a skill We could not teach. **1849** MACAULAY *Hist. Eng.* v. I. 543 Utterly destitute of the skill necessary to the conduct of great affairs. **1874** GREEN *Short Hist.* viii. §i. 452 The boy inherited his father's skill on lute and organ. **1932** H. G. WELLS *Work, Wealth & Happiness of Mankind* xvi. 808 Unforgettable memories, obstinate prepossessions, life-worn traditions, obsolete skills and responses. **1938** *English* II. 20 It is the function of the educator..to enable the pupils to appropriate and use all that preceding generations have learnt, the useful skills, the practical knowledge, the social organizations, the moral principles. **1945** *Times* 29 Sept. 4/6 There is a sizeable body in Congress which believes..that this country should secure the greatest possible political advantage from its present monopoly of the actual manufacturing skills. **1958** *Listener* 12 June 976/2 There are ages of maturation at which it is appropriate to teach children skills like reading. **1964** P. STREVENS *Papers in Lang.* (1965) ii. 25 The national needs for foreign language skills in the nineteen-sixties are of a different order. **1975** *Language for Life* (Dept. Educ. & Sci.) xiii. 198 The advocates of this form of organisation say that these conditions lead to an assured attention to the 'basic skills'. **1980** *Times* 29 Feb. 19 For the advertising agencies a restricted market means that their skills will be needed more than ever.

**b.** Const. *in* (also arch. *of*) a subject, practice, etc.

**1553** EDEN *Treat. New Ind.* (Arb.) 9 Whiche viage is sufficiently knowen to suche as haue any skyll in Geographie. **1590** *Plain Perc.* 9 Euery cut-purse vseth them..that hath had any skill in his miniken Handsaw. **1662** STILLINGFL. *Orig. Sacræ* II. ii. §6 Their great skill in Astronomy is attested by Diodorus. **1676** RAY *Corr.* (1848) 122 This author..hath good skill in the feeding and ordering of singing-birds. **1709** STEELE *Tatler* No. 78 ¶9 Who shows as much Liberality in his Practice as he does..Skill in his Profession. **1828** SCOTT *F.M. Perth* v, His professional jealousy, personal strength, and skill in the use of arms, brought him into many quarrels. **1887** SWINBURNE *Locrine* I. i. 29 No skill of speech have I. **1889** BARRIE *Window in Thrums* xx. 195 He had little skill in talk.

†**c.** An art or science. *Obs.*

**1570** DEE *Math. Pref.* a iiij, Of the former knowledge Geometricall, are growen the Skills of Geographie, Chorographie, and Stratarithmetrie. **1613** HEYWOOD *Brazen Age* II. ii, Those hidden skils, Ascrib'd vnto the infernall Proserpine. **1647** FULLER *Holy War* III. vi. (1840) 118 Richard..quickly got money, the sinews of warre, by a thousand princely skills. **1667** *Decay Chr. Piety* v. §27. 241 And certainly, the skill of Christian suffering is not the easiest of all trades or sciences.

†**d.** A skilled person. *Obs.*⁻¹

*a* **1657** R. LOVEDAY *Lett.* (1663) 77 You will much oblige me to propound it to as many skills as you shall converse with, and to send me their several judgements.

**7.** Knowledge or understanding *of* something. Now *arch.*

**1587** GOLDING *De Mornay* xxvii. (1592) 425 If thou eate of the tree of the skill of good and euill. **1638** FEATLY *Strict. Lyndom.* I. 157 Surely that Priest..could not have skill of brachygraphy, nor well spell Latine. **1685** BURNET tr. *More's Utopia* Pref. 3 If he..has a competent skill of the one tongue, and is a master of the other. **1818** SCOTT *Hrt. Midl.* v, Since ye say ye hae skeel o' the law. **1887** MORRIS *Odyssey* XI. 463 Thereof I have no skill, Whether he liveth or dieth.

†**8.** ***no skill***, it matters not. *Obs.*⁻¹

**1575** R. B. *Appins & Virg.* in Hazl. *Dodsley* IV. 128 Though shame or defame do happen, no skill.

**9.** *attrib.* and *Comb.* (in sense 6), as ***skill-pride***, ***-thirst***; ***skill-contending***, ***-wrought*** adjs.; **skill centre** orig. *U.S.*, a local training institution providing instruction in practical and technical skills, *spec.* in U.K. (**Skillcentre, skillcentre**), one sponsored by the government (cf. *job centre* s.v. JOB *sb.*² 7); **skill facet** (see quot. 1850).

**1591** SYLVESTER *Du Bartas* I. i. 664 With curious Skill-pride, and vaine dreames. **1593** SHAKS. *Lucr.* 1018 Busy yourselues in skill-contending schools. **1598** SYLVESTER *Du Bartas* II. i. II. *Imposture* 539 Too-curious-Skill-thirst, Envie, Felony. **1615** H. CROOKE *Body of Man* 197 To reueyle the veyle of Nature, to prophane her mysteries for a little curious skil-pride. **1751** JEFFRIES *Treat. Diamonds & Pearls* (ed. 2) Gloss., In Brilliants, there are two sorts, *skew* or *skill* facets and *star* facets. **1850** HOLTZAPFFEL *Turning* III. 1330 These triangular facets are called skill facets, from the difficulty of placing them correctly. *Ibid.* 1336 A row of double skill facets are then arranged around the girdle. **1887** R. BROWN *Trilogy* 72 For ever dart-struck was his casque Skill-wrought. **1963** *Amer. Vocational Jrnl.* Dec. 33/2 The industrial situation assures the future of the area schools, but two problems involved are: (a) a common agreement on the type of regional education programs (i.e. state vocational schools,..vocational departments in comprehensive high schools, state skill centers), [etc.]. **1975** *Manpower Services Commission Ann. Rep. 1974–75* 8/3 The government training centres under their new name of 'skillcentres' were to be expanded. **1976** *Ibid. 1975–76* 16/3 These services include sponsored training at Skillcentres designed to enable firms to send employees to be trained to meet the firms' own precisely defined needs. **1977** *Daily Tel.* 12 Sept. 11 Technicians from the Government Skillcentres, who are of much higher standard. **1978** *Church Times* 27 Jan. 2/2 Skill centres and other training provisions for school-leavers and the young unemployed.

**b.** In *pl.*

**1967** COULTHARD & SMITH in Wills & Yearsley *Handbk. Management Technol.* 196 Techniques of management by objectives, performance planning, and skills analysis are being more widely applied as they become increasingly effective in contributing to success. *Ibid.* 212 *Skills analysis*, the setting down of the underlying knowledge and dexterity which an operative will require in order to perform a given industrial operation. **1971** R. N. EVANS *Foundations of Vocational Education* III. xiv. 231 Unlike earlier manpower and anti-poverty training programs, Skills Centers could accept trainees whenever a training slot was open. **1976** *National Observer* (U.S.) 17 Apr. 14/5 The English teaching profession..has progressed..well beyond thinking of writing instruction solely or principally in terms of basic skills instruction. **1977** P. STREVENS *New Orientations Teaching of English* vi. 78 Shortcomings in demonstration and practice facilities affect the skills component.

†**skill**, *sb.*² *Obs. rare.* ? A skillet.

**1600** *Shuttleworth's Acc.* (Chetham Soc.) 128 One skille xj[d]; one brazen ladle viij[d]. **1603** *Ibid.* 150, ij skilles xix[d].

**skill**, obs. variant of SKULL *sb.*² basket.

**skill** (skɪl), *v.*¹ Now *arch.* Forms: 3 skelien, skilen, 4 skile; 4-5 scil, 5-7 skil, 6 skyl; 5-6 skyll, 6 skille, 6- skill. [a. ON. *skilja* to divide, distinguish, etc., or *skila* to decide, expound, related to MDu. and MLG. *schillen* and *schelen* to differ, make a difference, etc. Cf. SKILL *sb.*[1]]

†**1. a.** *intr.* To separate, part *from*. *Obs.*$^{-1}$

*a* **1200** *Vices & Virtues* 17 Du..noldest þenchen of ðine forðsiðe, þat tu fram ðine lichame scoldest skelien, and tefore me cumen.

†**b.** *trans.* To separate, divide, take *out*. *Obs.*

*c* **1200** ORMIN 16860 Unnlic all oþerr lede, & skiledd ut all fra þe follc þurrh haliȝ lif & lare. *a* **1300** *Cursor M.* 9291 Wel sal he cun knau quilk es quilk, Fra the wick þe god to scil.

†**c.** To make free or quit *of*. *Obs.*

**1481** CAXTON *Reynard* xvii. (Arb.) 44 The kynge hath skylled hym quyte of alle his brokes and forgyuen hym all his trespaces and mysdedes.

**2.** †**a.** *intr.* To cause a distinction or difference.

*c* **1200** *Trin. Coll. Hom.* 119 Swo þe holie gost hem fulde of him seluen, and sette þe word on hem þe þere speken, and skilede on hem þat hie herden.

**b.** *impers.* In negative or interrogative clauses: To make a difference, to be of importance, to matter. †Also with dat. of person. Now *arch.*

Extremely common from *c* 1525 to *c* 1670.

**1460** CAPGRAVE *Chron.* (Rolls) 306 If thei mad question to what entent thei schuld rise, this answere had thei:—'It skil you not, so ye have good wagis, and treuly payed'. **1509** HAWES *Past. Pleas.* xxxiv. (Percy Soc.) 173 What skilleth you though that he dye this nyght? *a* **1530** HEYWOOD *Weather* (Brandl) 443 What yᵉ deuyll shold skyl though all yᵉ world were dum. **1580** LYLY *Euphues* (Arb.) 245 Whether he be now lyuing, I know not, but whether he be or no, it skilleth not. **1614** JACKSON *Creed* III. 16 It skils not how infallible the truth in it selfe or the proposer be. *c* **1680** HICKERINGILL *Hist. Whiggism* II. Wks. 1716 I. 118 From the Court or Queen, what skills it? I commend him. **1837** CARLYLE *Fr. Rev.* II. I. ii, Blow the brains or thinking-faculty quite out of him for the time: it skills not; he.. revives on the morrow. **1861** LYTTON & FANE *Tannhäuser* 94 Hence! Whate'er I am it skills not.

**c.** *impers.* To avail, help. Now *arch.*

**1528** in Strype *Eccl. Mem.* (1822) V. 368 If you have any wast mony, give yt to poore pepull and tarye at home, for it shall not skyll to go on pilgremages to Ipiswiche. **1814** BYRON *Lara* I. ii, It skills not, boots not step by step to trace His youth through all the mazes of its race. **1848** K. H. DIGBY *Broadstone of Honour* III. *Morus* 220 It may not skill repeating the names of holy men forgotten by the moderns. **1880** MCCARTHY *Own Times* lii. IV. 103 But what skills talking?

**d.** To care, reck. *rare*$^{-1}$.

**1821** SCOTT *Kenilw.* xi, Whether he was the devil's crony or no I skill not.

†**3.** To allege in argument. *Obs.*$^{-1}$

**1390** GOWER *Conf.* III. 343 For al that evere I skile may, I am concluded with a nay.

**4.** To understand, comprehend. Now *dial.*

*a* **1500** *How the wise man taught his son* in Hazl. *E.P.P.* I. 170 Skyll fully what thou pray. **1555** PHAER *Æneid* I. 16 Encompast with the cloud he goes (a wondrous thyng to skyll). **1573** G. HARVEY *Letter-bk.* 18 Truly I cannot scil what is procurare malum socio. **1632** J. FEATLY *Hon. Chast.* 9 Who skils not the cunning of those delicate imposters, in their wretched devices? **1657** J. WATTS *Vind. Ch. Eng.* 115 Seeing you are unlettred, and skill not the Original languages. *a* **1677** BARROW *Serm.* (1686) I. xiii. 191 The speaker little skilleth the use of speech, or the rule of conversation. **1828** CARR *Craven Gloss.*, *Skill*, to know, to understand... 'I nivver could skill him.'

†**b.** *intr.* To have knowledge *of*, or skill *in*, something. *Obs.* (Cf. SKILL *sb.* 5.)

**1540** HYRDE tr. *Vives' Instr. Chr. Wom.* (1592) K vij, Or what woman now adaies, that is sad & wise, wil be known to skill of daunsing. **1561** in Strype *Ann. Ref.* (1709) I. xxii. 230 Lest the unlearned should say, they did not skill of such books. **1628** J. DOUGHTY *Serm. Ch. Schismes* 16 More shifts besides they skill of to obscure their malitious drifts. **1662** EVELYN *Chalcogr.* 132 That they might the better skill in the works of Embrodery. **1691** RAY *Creation* I. (1704) 198 To vilifie those Studies which themselves skill not of.

**c.** With inf.: To know how *to* do something. Also with *how*. Now *arch.*

*a* **1586** SIDNEY *Arcadia* lxx. Wks. (Grosart) II. 157 They now skild not how from him to wend. **1671** EVELYN *Let. to Father Patrick* 27 Sept., He would be thought a thick-skinn'd doctor..who skill'd not to discern how a thing might be real, and yet spiritual. *a* **1677** BARROW *Wks.* (1830) I. 462 Not skilling to get his suit quietly, he would extort it by force. **1859** S. R. HOLE *Tour Irel.* 13 He who skilleth not to brew it.., may thank me, perhaps, for thus instructing him. **1865** NEALE *Hymns Paradise* 46 If there be that skills to reckon All the number of the Blest.

†**d.** *trans.* To order, dispose. *Obs.*

*c* **1610** SIR J. MELVIL *Mem.* (1683) Pref., A man may many times, if he skill it aright, give his Prince good counsel, contrary to his inclinations.

†**5.** *intr.* To get along, to subsist. *Obs.*$^{-1}$

**1537** *State P. Hen. VIII*, II. 449 The pore Englishe erth tillers in the English pale cannot skyll upon penury nor wredchidnes, as the Irishe tenantes doo sustayne.

**6.** *trans.* To teach, instruct. *rare*$^{-1}$.

*a* **1813** A. WILSON *Foresters* Poet. Wks. (1846) 218 Not he who guides the legs, or skills the clown To square his fist, and knock his fellow down.

†**skill,** *v.*[2] *Obs.*$^{-1}$ [Of obscure origin.] *intr.* To mount, ascend.

*a* **1400** *Lybeaus Disc.* 1844 Lybeauus wyth goodwyll Into hys sadell gan skyll, And a launce yn hond he hent.

**skilled** (skɪld), *ppl. a.* Also 6 skild. [f. SKILL *sb.*[1] + -ED[2].]

**1.** Of persons: Possessed of skill or knowledge; properly trained or experienced.

**1552** ELYOT s.v. *Calleo*, To be well skilled in the law. **1591** SHAKS. *Two Gentl.* III. ii. 92 Gentlemen, well skil'd in Musicke. **1662** STILLINGFL. *Orig. Sacræ* II. ii. 127 The parts of the Egyptian learning, in which the Scripture tells us Moses was skill'd. **1698** FRYER *Acc. E. India & P.* 291 The Persians are skill'd..to shoot flying. **1743** FRANCIS tr. *Horace, Odes* I. xv. 31 And Sthenelus, in Battle skill'd; Or skill'd to guide with steady Rein..his Chariot. **1770** GOLDSM. *Des. Vill.* 148 More skilled to raise the wretched than to rise. **1806** BERESFORD *Miseries Hum. Life* II. Concl., We are..skilled both in active and sedentary recreations. **1855** MACAULAY *Hist. Eng.* xvii. IV. 76 Sarsfield..was little skilled in the administration of war, and was still less skilled in civil business. **1870** BRYANT *Iliad* IV. I. 114 Some hand Skilled to bend the bow.

**b.** In attrib. use. (Now common.)

**1843** *Penny Cycl.* XXVI. 484/2 An unusual influx of skilled labourers into any employment. **1856** BOND *Russia at Close of 16th c.* (Hakl. Soc.) Introd. 18 Furnishing him with warlike ammunition and with skilled engineers. **1857** J. W. DONALDSON *Christian Orthod.* 436 A general designation of professional or skilled workmen. **1875** JOWETT *Plato* (ed. 2) V. 475 Every physician and every skilled artist does all things for the sake of the whole.

**2.** Of work: Requiring or showing skill.

**1776** ADAM SMITH *W.N.* I. x. (1904) I. 113 The policy of Europe considers the labour of all mechanics, artificers, and manufacturers, as skilled labour. **1860** MILL *Repr. Govt.* 91 Every branch of public administration is a skilled business. **1876** A. S. MURRAY *Mythol.* iii. (1877) 43 He..seems more the patient god of skilled metal-working.

**skilless** ('skɪllɪs), *a.* Also 3 skilllæs, 9 skillless; 6 skilles, 6–7 skillesse, 6 skyllesse. [f. SKILL *sb.*[1] + -LESS.]

**1.** Devoid of (†reason or) knowledge; ignorant.

*c* **1200** ORMIN 3715 Wiþþ mannkinn þatt wass stunnt, & dill, & skilllæs swa summ asse. **1561** NORTON & SACK. *Gordobuc* II. ii, Lest skilles rage throwe doune with headlong fal Their lands. **1577** HOLINSHED *Chron.* IV. 661 Writing the dooings of other persons in a toong wherein I am skillesse. **1601** SHAKS. *Twel. N.* III. iii. 9 [Through] iealousie, what might befall your trauell, Being skillesse in these parts. **1627** MAY *Lucan* x. (1631) 595 The skillesse people run Through the vast pallace scatter'd vp, and downe. **1814** CARY *Dante, Purg.* IX. 100 A heavenly dame, not skilless of these things. **1818** KEATS *Eudym.* III. 909 A little patience, youth! 'twill not be long, Or I am skilless quite.

**2.** Lacking skill; unskilled, unskilful.

**1573** TUSSER *Husb.* (1878) 204 From cities ioy, to countrie care, To skillesse folke is homelie change. **1592** SHAKS. *Rom. & Jul.* III. iii. 132 Like powder in a skillesse Souldiers flaske Is set a fire. *a* **1649** DRUMM. OF HAWTH. *Poems* Wks. (1711) 55/1 Some young Phaeton; Whose skilless and unstaved Hand May prove the Ruin of the Land. *a* **1661** FULLER *Worthies, Yorks.* (1662) 203 But Swords and Guns have not made more mortal wounds, than Probes in the hands of carelesse and skillesse Chirurgeons. **1821** BYRON *Sardanap.* v. i. 101 Let me see the wound; I am not quite skilless. **1862** LYTTON *Str. Story* II. 379 A mind, not ignoble, not skillless, not abjectly craven. **1890** *Spectator* 18 Oct., [To] organise a brigade of poor gentlemen to replace these arrogant and skilless dockers.

**b.** Of things: Showing a lack of skill; badly made, crude, inartistic.

**1830** GODWIN *Cloudesley* I. x. 156 The crude and skill-less impositions of the Turk. **1846** TRENCH *Mirac.* i. (1862) 119 In their skill-less delineations the artists could not manage to find room for more. **1860** LD. LYTTON *Lucile* II. iv. 5 What matter though the skilless the lay be, and rude?

Hence **'skillessness,** want of skill.

**1823** *Blackw. Mag.* XIV. 183 He had messed the mouth of a loose-fish by his awkward and impotent skillessness.

**skillet**[1] ('skɪlɪt). Forms: α. 5 skelet(t, 6–7, 9 skellet (7, 9 -it), 8 scellet. β. 6 skyllet, 7 skillett, 6– skillet. [Of obscure origin.

The sense is against connexion with OF. *eschelette*, etc., a little bell (see SKELLAT), and both form and sense differ from OF. *escuelete*, *esculette*, a small plate. The ending *-et*, however, and the culinary associations of the thing itself, make it probable that the source was AF. or OF.]

**1.** A cooking utensil of brass, copper, or other metal, usually having three or four feet and a long handle, used for boiling liquids, stewing meat, etc.; a saucepan, stew-pan. (See also quot. 1866.) Now chiefly *N. Amer.*, a frying-pan, a (heavy) cooking-pan.

α. **1403** *Nottingham Rec.* II. 20 Unius skelett aeneae, iij d. *c* **1450** *M.E. Med. Bk.* (Heinrich) 131 Take crownes of whitsour bred, smal myed on a gratour, & do hit in a skelet. **1530** PALSGR. 271/1 Skellet with a handell, *poillon*. **1576** BAKER *Jewell of Health* 144 b, These after putting into a possenet or skellet, set..over the fyre. **1616** SURFL. & MARKH. *Country Farme* II. xix. 174 Then put it into a verie cleane sweet pipkin or skellet. **1669** STURMY *Mariner's Mag.* v. xii. 67 Take an Iron Pot or Skellet,..set it on the Fire. **1719** *Will of J. Hirst* (Yorks.), A dozen of trenchers, a skellet, a spit and racks. **1838** HOLLOWAY *Prov. Dict.*, *Skellit*, a small pot with a handle. **1866** BROGDEN *Prov. Lincs.*, *Skellet*, ..a funnel shaped vessel, used principally for heating beer and milk.

β. **1519** *Maldon* (Essex) *Liber B.* fol. 160 b, iiiᵉ ketills, a skillet, ixᵉ platers. **1540** PALSGR. *Acolastus* M ij b, He shall gyue a lydde or couer worthy for the skyllet or lyttell panne. **1578** LYTE *Dodoens* II. xlii. 201 The juyce of the leaves boyled..in a brasen pipkin or skillet is very good to heale.. old ulcers. **1600** SURFLET *Countrie Farme* II. l. 541 Boile them in fresh water in some skillet. **1658** R. WHITE tr. *Digby's Powd. Symp.* (1660) 118 In boyling the milk it swells so high that it sheds over the brim of the skillet. **1707** SLOANE *Jamaica* I. p. lxii, I have seen some try to boil Cane-juice to sugar in an ordinary Skillet. **1757** *Phil. Trans.* L. 108 The lightning..melted an old copper skillet. **1801** WOLCOT (P. Pindar) *Epist. Ct. Rumford* Wks. 1812 V. 136 Whose tinkers form..Skillets and saucepans. **1859** JEPHSON *Brittany* v. 55 The dressers were resplendent with immense brass skillets. **1881** *Cornh. Mag.* Mar. 364 Armed with a skillet she happened..to have been scouring. **1917** C. MATHEWSON *Second Base Sloan* vi. 73 [Nearby lay] an iron skillet with the handle broken off. **1932** W. FAULKNER *Light in August* xvii. 382 He stands, tall, mis-shapen, lonely in his lonely and illkept kitchen, holding in his hand an iron skillet in which yesterday's old grease is bleakly caked. **1959** A. SEXTON in *Audience* Autumn 31, I have found the warm caves in the woods, filled them with skillets, carvings, shelves, closets. **1968** *Globe & Mail Mag.* (Toronto) 13 Jan. 16/3 Cook, stirring constantly, over medium heat, until slightly thickened. Add frankfurters. Cover skillet, simmer 8 to 10 minutes. **1979** *Arizona Daily Star* 5 Aug. (Parade Suppl.) 12/4 Heat oil in paella pan or wide skillet.

**2.** *dial.* (See quot.)

**1823** E. MOOR *Suffolk Words* 353 *Skillet*, the thin brass perforated implement used for skimming or fletting the cream off milk.

**3.** *attrib.* and *Comb.*, as ***skillet-maker, pan, soot***; also ***skilletful***.

**1552** in *Bury Wills* (Surtees) 142 Too brasse pannys, to kattylls, one skyllet panne. **1611** COTGR., *Poislier*,..a Skellet-maker, or Frying-panne maker. **1641** MILTON *Animadv.* 67 Your confutation hath..left nothing upon it, but a foul taste of your skillet soot. **1888** *Cent. Mag.* Jan. 373/2 Mrs. Pearson..had baked a skilletful of hot biscuits.

**'skillet**[2]. [Of obscure origin; there is no obvious connexion with prec.]

**1.** (See quot. 1888.) Also in more general applications.

**1888** *Pall Mall G.* 31 July 3/1 Here a block is being cut into the right length and shape for 'skillets', the wooden strips of which matchboxes are made. **1959** *Gloss. Terms Packaging (B.S.I.)* 19 *Skillet*, a piece of scored timber rotarily cut into veneers which forms part of the finished punnet. **1968** *Guardian* 18 Nov. 6/4 Mr Moreland keeps a selection of 'skillets' (flattened out matchboxes) in his wallet to pass round at social gatherings.

**2.** A thick flat piece of silver or other precious metal (*Cent. Dict.*).

**skillet,** variant of SKELLAT, bell.

**skillful,** chiefly U.S. var. SKILFUL *a.* and *adv.*

**'skillick.** *rare*$^{-1}$. = SKILLIGALEE 2.

Cf. Devonshire *skiddick* in similar uses.

**1835** MARRYAT *Olla Podr.* (Rtldg.) 322, I havn't a skillick till quarter-day.

**skilligalee** (ˌskɪlɪgə'li:). *slang.* Also **skilla-, skillo-, skilly-,** and **-golee, -glee.** [prob. a purely fanciful formation.]

**1.** = SKILLY *sb.*

**1819** J. H. VAUX *Mem.* I. xviii. 202 Tolerable flour, of which the cook composed a certain food for breakfast, known among sailors by the name of skilligolee, being in plain English, paste. **1859** SALA *Gaslight & D.* xxx. 353 In some [Unions] they gives you bread and cheese, and in some broth, and in some skillygolee. **1872** M. COLLINS *Pr. Clarice* II. ii. 22 Aren't you afeard of being..committed for seven days on a diet of skilligalee?

**2.** With negative: A single coin of the smallest value.

**1833** MARRYAT *P. Simple* xii, But this is all nothing, except to prove satisfactorily that I am not worth a skillagalee.

**3.** *attrib.* Worthless, trifling.

**1883** *Christian World* 13 Dec. 870/1 The parsons were a poor skillygalee lot.

**skilling** ('skɪlɪŋ), *sb.*[1] Forms: 4–5 skelyng, 7–9 skeeling, 9 skeling; 8– skillin, skilling, etc. 9 skillen. See also SKILLION. [Of obscure origin.]

**1. a.** A shed or outhouse, *esp.* a lean-to, a penthouse.

Current in the south of England, from Surrey to Dorset.

**1389** *New Coll. Accs.* in Wood's MS. D. 2, fol. 272 In laborem facient. unius Skelyng pro sept. 2*s.* 6*d.* **1448–9** *Abingdon Abbey Accs.* (1892) 124 In j skelyng siue coquina facta in tenemento dicti Henrici Baret. *a* **1722** E. LISLE *Husb.* (1757) II. 93 If I put cows or oxen under skillins, or penthouses. **1831** *Devizes Gaz.* 8 Aug. (E.D.D.), A barn and extensive skilling was burnt down. **1862** *Morning Advertiser* 8 Sept., Mr. Fowle was in his yard..when the storm first burst, and ran for shelter under a skilling. **1874** JEFFERIES in *Toilers of the Field* (1893) 167 A portion of the Court is roofed in and is called the skilling.

**b.** In Australasian use. (Cf. SKILLION.)

**1799** R. JOHNSON *Let.* 26 Aug. in *Evangelical Mag.* (1800) July 299 Blood was discovered in different parts, particularly in a small skilling, where, as afterwards appeared, my friend was dragged. **1826** J. ATKINSON *Acct. State of Agric. & Grazing in N.S.W.* 100 The barn may be built with lean-to's or skillings all round. **1837** GOODRIDGE *Voy. S. Seas* (1832) 172 Many houses have been built.. consisting of two rooms in front, and two sheds or skillings as they are called. **1849** M. RUSSELL *Polynesia* ix. 353 Three substantial weather-board dwelling-houses..with skilling at the back. **1890** 'R. BOLDREWOOD' *Col. Reformer* (1891) 351 At the back a skilling, a lower roofed portion of the building.

*attrib.* **1852** *Colonial Church Chron.* VI. 294 As is usually the case with bush houses, two skillen-rooms were to be added behind. **1900** H. LAWSON *On Track* 79 There were two unfinished skilling rooms built on to the back of the hut.

**2.** (See quots.)

**1674** RAY *S. & E.C. Words* 77 *Skeeling*, an Isle or bay of a barn, *Suss[ex]*. **1838** HOLLOWAY *Prov. Dict.*, *Skeeling* or *Skilling*,..the side of a garret or upper room, where the slope of the roof interferes with the upright.

‖**'skilling,** *sb.*[2] [In sense 1 ad. Du. *schelling*; in sense 2 a. Da., Sw., or Norw. *skilling*.]

†**1.** = SCHELLING. *Obs.*$^{-1}$

**1700** S. L. tr. *Fryke's Voy. E. Indies* i. 6 The Cash-keeper paid us.. three Dutch Skillings every day while we stayed on Shoar.

**2.** A small copper coin and money of account formerly in use in Scandinavia.

**1793** *Encycl. Brit.* (ed. 3) XII. 232/2 [In] Denmark.. and Norway.. 16 Skillings = a Marc [= 9*d*]. **1802** ACERBI *Trav.* I. 220 The poor mendicant finished by asking.. some.. skillings in charity. **1839** *Penny Cycl.* XV. 326/1 *Ryksort*, a Danish silver coin at 24 skillings. **1875** JEVONS *Money* xi. 126 The skilling [of Norway] being nearly equal in value to an English halfpenny.

**skilling** (wild goose), obs. var. SKEELING *Sc.*

**'skilling,** *vbl. sb. rare*[−1]. [f. SKILL *v.*[1]] †The operation of reasoning.

*c* **1374** CHAUCER *Boeth.* IV. pr. vi. (1868) 137 Swiche comparisoun as it is of skilynge [L. *ratiocinatio*] to vndirstondyng and of þing þat is engendred to þing þat is.

**skillinger** ('skılıŋgə(r)). *East Anglian local.* [f. corruption of *Terschelling*, the name of one of the West Frisian Islands in north-western Netherlands + -ER[1].] An East Anglian oyster smack operating off the north-western coast of Holland (see quots.).

**1933** *Yachting Monthly* Aug. 265 Used for oyster dredging off the Terschelling light on the Dutch coast they [*sc.* large Brightlingsea smacks] were known locally as 'Skillingers'. **1959** P. NORTON *End of Voyage* xv. 107 Many of these larger smacks were ketch rigged... They were called 'Skillingers'. **1970** E. MARCH *Inshore Craft Gt. Brit.* I. vi. 192 Another ground lay off the Terschelling Light on the Dutch coast, which gave its name to the vessels working there—'Skillingers'.

**skillion** ('skıljən). *Austral.* and *N.Z.* Also 9 skilion. [Alteration of *skillin* SKILLING *sb.*[1]] **1.** A lean-to, serving as a shed or as a small room.

**1843** C. ROWCROFT *Tales of Colonies* I. vii. 120 At the back of the long room of twenty feet, a skillion, to serve as a kitchen, &c. **1864** ELIZ. MURRAY *Ella Norman* I. 163 This led into a 'skillion', or shed built against the house. **1870** HONEY *Glaucus* I. i. 5 The farm.. together with the three Skillions at the end of the Retreat are.. his property. **1889** 'R. BOLDREWOOD' *Robbery under Arms* 12 The harness-cask, which stood in a little back skillion.

*attrib.* **1866** MRS. N. CHEVALIER *Reminisc. Journey* 23 The house consisted of a front room.. a skillion kitchen with big fire, and one end of this skillion had a kind of shed. **1885** MRS. C. PRAED *Australian Life* 73 A verandah, and a skillion room opening off it.

**2.** (See quot. 1933.) Now *Hist.*

**1846** C. P. HODGSON *Reminisc. Austral.* 39 Skillions formed by a sloping verandah to receive the sheep in from the fold as required. **1863** S. BUTLER *First Year Canterbury Settlement* x. 158 The wool-shed.. [has] a large central space, and an aisle-like partition on each side.. for holding the sheep at night... In a wool-shed, the aisles would be called skilions. **1871** M. A. BROOME *Christmas Cake in Four Quarters* IV. iii. 279 There was the skillions standing empty, and the shearers lounging about idling when Christmas Day came. **1933** L. ACLAND in *Press* (Christchurch, N.Z.) 2 Dec. 15/7 *Skillion.* In old Australian and New Zealand books (up to about 1880) it is common and means the sheep-holding part of a wool-shed.

**3.** Special Comb. **skillion roof**, a roof sloping from the side of a building; hence **skillion-roofed** *a.*

**1911** J. NANGLE *Australian Building Practice* 171 *Lean-to Roof.* This kind (sometimes called a *Skillion Roof).. is generally used only in rear buildings, or verandahs where no ceilings are required. **1977** *N.Z. Jrnl. Science* XIX. 312 A skillion roof and other thin roof forms. **1967** J. MORRISON in *Coast to Coast 1965–66* 136 It was little more than a *skillion-roofed shack.

**†skillwise**, *a. Obs.* Forms: 3 scel-, scilwis; 3–4 skilwis(e, 4 skillwise, -wyse, skyllwyse. [a. ON. *skilvíss* (MSw. *skäl-*, MDa. *skælvis*) reliable, trustworthy, etc., f. *skil* SKILL *sb.*[1]]

**1. a.** Intelligent, discerning, clever.

*a* **1300** *Cursor M.* 4677 Depe selers.. thoru es aun scel-wis [*v.r.* witti] red, He fild wit wines. *Ibid.* 6528 If þai war þat tim sa vn-wise, Yeit er þai noght all skilwise. *a* **1340** HAMPOLE *Psalter* lvii. 11 A man þat is skilwise sall thynke þat it falles þaim not of chawnce.

*absol. a* **1300** *Cursor M.* 33 Bot be the fruit may scilwis se, O quat vertu is ilka tre.

**b.** Endowed with reason; rational.

**1357** *Lay Folks Catech.* (T.) 12 He made skillwise creatures, angel and man. *Ibid.* 330 To tham that he wate er of skill-wise elde.

**2. a.** Just, equitable, fair.

*a* **1300** *Cursor M.* 28781 Godd of heuen.. es rightwise, & til alle men ilik skilwis.

**b.** Reasonable; not excessive.

*a* **1340** HAMPOLE *Psalter* xxvii. 11 When thai.. entice him fra scilwis penaunce. **1357** *Lay Folks Catech.* (T.) 324 Bot if thai forbere it be skilwise cause. *c* **1400** *Rule St. Benet* 1435 And who so askes hir skilwis thyng, Sche sal not greue þam with groching.

**†skillwisely,** *adv. Obs.* [a. ON. *skilvísliga*: see prec. and -LY[2].] Reasonably; rationally; with understanding.

*a* **1300** *Cursor M.* 4747 He salde ilkman his porcion, Sua þat þai moght scilwisli.. liue þar-bi. *Ibid.* 8347 Scilwisli and scort He tald þat him lai apon hert. *a* **1340** HAMPOLE *Psalter* xi. 9 Sonnes of men þat lifis skilwisly and in rightwisnes. **1357** *Lay Folks Catech.* (T.) 446 If we lyff skillwisely als the lawe techis.

**†skillwiseness.** *Obs.* Also 3 sckele-, 4 schil-. [Cf. prec. and -NESS.] Discretion, intelligence, reason.

*a* **1200** *Vices & Virtues* 149 Þe is god þat þu beseke at gode one mihte ðe hatte discrecio, þat is, sckelewisnesse. *a* **1300** *Cursor M.* 567 It has als schilwisnes o will þe god to tak and leue þe ill. *c* **1325** *Metr. Hom.* 1 Thou made manne, And gaf him gast of schilwisnes.

**skilly** ('skılı), *sb.* Also 9 skilley. [Abbreviation of SKILLIGALEE.] **1.** A kind of thin, watery porridge, gruel, or soup, commonly made from oatmeal, and traditionally used especially in prisons and workhouses.

**1839** *Slang Dict.* 33 *Skilley*, nickname for a broth given on board the hulks. **1846** *Camp & Barrack-Room* ii. 16 Jack Skilly, a title given in consequence of his being the dispenser of skilly to patients. **1865** *Daily Telegr.* 27 Oct. 4/5 That 'skilly' formed the traditional staple of workhouse dietary under the New Poor Law, we are well aware. **1894** D. C. MURRAY *Making of a Novelist* 97 Gentlemen who have tasted workhouse skilly and soup.

**2.** *transf.* An insipid beverage; tea or coffee. Also *attrib.* and *Comb.* Chiefly *Naut. slang.*

**1927** [see MADAM *sb.* 3 c(*e*)]. **1933** J. MASEFIELD *Bird of Dawning* 214 The skilly-can, which may have contained a hot drink of some sort, was rolling with the whack-pots. **1935** —— *Victorious Troy* 37 There was a big old battered tin coffee pot containing skilly, or a brown, hot liquid, which the crew called 'tea' at night, and 'coffee' in the morning. **1936** B. M. ADAMS *Ships & Women* iii. 59 They said it was tea. Skilly, they called it. **1953** J. MASEFIELD *Conway* (ed. 2) III. 250 A cup of skilly completed the repast.

**skilly** ('skılı), *a. Sc.* and *north. dial.* Also 9 skeely, skeily. [f. SKILL *sb.*[1] + -Y.] Skilled, skilful; having considerable skill in some respect.

*a.* **1768** ROSS *Helenore* II. 90 Upo' your milk your skilly hand ye'll try, An' gees a feast o't as we're coming by. **1790** SHIRREFS *Poems* 51 Her apron shortens to the skilly ee. **1837** R. NICOLL *Poems* (1843) 91 A gash skilly body, weel kent near and far. **1903** *Daily Record & Mail* 10 July 5 For the past few weeks Greenock has been the happy hunting ground of the skilly cracksman.

*β. a* **1803** *Sir P. Spens* i. in Scott *Minstrelsy*, O whare will I get a skeely skipper, To sail this new ship of mine? **1829** BROCKETT *N.C. Gloss.* (ed. 2) s.v., The doctress of a country village is skeely. **1863** J. L. W. *Bygone Days* 42 Tibbie.. confessed he was a 'skeely' man, John; for he cured her cow.

**skilly-pot, skilpot.** *U.S.* [ad. Du. *schildpad* turtle.] The slider or red-bellied terrapin.

**1807** W. IRVING *Salmagundi* (1824) 58 Famous place for *skilly-pots*—Philadelphians call 'em tarapins.

**skilts.** *U.S.* (See quot.)

**1845** S. JUDD *Margaret* I. ii, A sort of brown tow trousers, known at the time.. as skilts; they were short, reaching just below the knee, and very large, being a full half yard broad at the bottom.

**skilum**, var. of SKELM.

**skim,** *sb.* Also 6 skymme, 6–7 skimme. [f. SKIM *v.* In earlier use taking the place of SCUM *sb.*] **1. †a.** = SCUM *sb.* 2 b. *Obs.*

**1539** ELYOT *Cast. Helthe* 33 That [water].. wherof cometh leest skymme or frothe, whan it doth boyle. *a* **1591** H. SMITH *Serm.* (1622) 444 Like a skimme which seetheth into the broth. **1594** PLAT *Jewell-ho.* III. 70 Continue.. your skimming so long as any skim doth arise. **1703** *Art & Myst. Vintners* 57 Boyl it in a Pan of Iron, take off the skim. **1764** ELIZA MOXON *Eng. Housew.* (ed. 9) 171 Boil it over a slow fire, and skim it whilst any skim rises.

**†b.** = SCUM *sb.* 3 b. *Obs.*

**1606** BRYSKETT *Civ. Life* 108 Although Philip took delight in this skim of men [flatterers], yet could they neuer draw him.. to incurre those vices.

**c.** *Amer.* A thin layer *of* ice.

**1807** J. R. BEDFORD *Jrnl.* 22 Jan. in *Tennessee Hist. Mag.* (1919) V. 50 Nothing worth noting.. but the intense severity of the cold.. occasioning a very thin skim of ice on the river. **1869** 'MARK TWAIN' *Innoc. Abr.* xx. 206 It never has even a skim of ice upon its surface. **1897** *Daily News* 10 Sept. 8/3 A frost that produced a skim of ice beyond Winnipeg.

**d.** The fraction of latex which is poor in globules of rubber and is separated from the cream by centrifugation in the manufacture of rubber.

**1928** *Brit. Pat. 319,410* 2/1 The concentrate contained approximately 0·07 and the skim about 0·14 per cent of ammonia. **1937** H. BARRON *Mod. Rubber Chem.* v. 57 Latex is separated into two portions, one containing about 60 per cent of rubber and very little serum constituents, while the 'skim' contains about 6 per cent rubber and nearly all the serum constituents. **1952** *Ann. Rep. Progress of Rubber Technol.* xvi. 21 A producer of latex concentrate has described a procedure for recovering the residual rubber from centrifuge skim or cream under-layer. **1972** *Materials & Technol.* V. xiv. 471 The whey or skim obtained after the concentration of latex still contains small amounts of rubber, which can be recovered as skim rubber.

**2. a.** A form of horse-hoe; a shim. *rare*[−1].

**1795** VANCOUVER *Agric. Essex* 99 Horse-hoes or skims.. answer particularly well for cleaning the fallows.

**b.** An addition to the coulter of a plough by which the surface of the ground is pared off.

**1799** A. YOUNG *Agric. Linc.* 141 The turnips were ploughed for once, with Duckett's skim coulter plough, without the skim. **1812** SIR J. SINCLAIR *Syst. Husb. Scot.* I. 416 If you attach the skim to bury the surface. **1837** *Brit. Husb.* II. 18 (L.U.K.), A double skim, which can be either added to the plough or removed at pleasure. **1904** *Eng. Dial. Dict.* s.v., There is sometimes a skim in front of the coulter which serves to turn in the weeds.

**3.** *ellipt.* = SKIM-MILK 1. Also *fig.*

**1885** *Daily News* 1 Dec. 2/1 The milk is manufactured into butter and cheese,.. and the 'skim'.. is not exactly the most nourishing stuff in the world. **1886** *All Year Round* 14 Aug. 34 But there is skim and skim, just as there is butter-milk and butter-milk. **1895** *Westm. Gaz.* 30 Dec. 3/1 The owners of pictures are in the habit of proffering a certain proportion of skim with their cream.

**4. a.** The act of skimming or moving lightly.

*a* **1851** MOIR *Castle of Time* xxiii, For clouds on the blue air, with shadowy skim, Were rolling their faint billows. **1891** HARDY *Tess* (1900) 73/2 The buoyancy of her tread, like the skim of a bird which has not quite alighted.

**b.** A hasty sketch or survey.

**1889** *Pall Mall G.* 19 Oct. 3/3 As a careful political study, it [the book] is of little value. Delightful skims are apt to be full of fables.

**5.** *attrib.* and *Comb.*, as ***skim ice***; **skim-board**, a type of surf-board used for riding shallow water; **skim money** *slang*, a portion of the takings at a casino illicitly diverted in order to evade taxes; **skim-net**, a net used with a kind of skimming action; **skim-plough**, a plough having a skim attached, a skim-coulter plough; hence ***skim-plough*** vb.

**1965** P. L. DIXON *Compl. Bk. Surfing* 143 Riding a *skim board is simple to define, difficult to accomplish. **1972** *National Geographic* Nov. 688 Riding a skim-board, a youth glides over a comber-laved beach. **1938** W. FAULKNER *Unvanquished* 211 It lay with its body on the land and its head fixed in the *skim ice like it was set into a mirror. **1974** J. KEATS *Of Time & Island* v. 74 You can see them [*sc.* fish] lying under skim ice in the shallows in the spring. **1973** W. MCCARTHY *Detail* iii. 144 They used her as a courier for *skim money. **1884** KNIGHT *Dict. Mech.* Suppl. 820/2 **Skim Net* (Fishing), a large dipping net. **1887** GOODE *Fisheries U.S.* 802 Prior to 1872, shrimp were taken in this locality only with skim-nets. **1891** C. L. MORGAN *Anim. Sketches* 135 An efficient skim-net, wherewith to capture insects on the wing. **1813** A. YOUNG *Agric. Essex* I. 137 The *skim-plough of the late Mr. Ducket,.. and other skim coulters. **1837** *Brit. Husb.* II. 17 (L.U.K.), Trench and skim ploughs. **1844** H. STEPHENS *Bk. Farm* III. 765 The land has been recently skim-ploughed.

**skim,** *a. rare.* [By inference from *skim-milk.*] Skimmed; made of skim-milk.

**1794** DARKE in Marshall *Rev.* (1810) II. 373 Where they make the skim cheese, the land is deemed too rich for one meal. **1866** *Intellect. Observer* No. 56. 126 Milk scant and skim. **1893** *Daily News* 25 Dec. 5/5 Then the problem of branding skim cheese will be solved.

**skim** (skım), *v.* Also 5 skem(e, skym(e, 7 skeam-, 6–7 skimme. [prob. ad. OF. *escumer*: see SCUM *v.* The vowel may be partly due to SKIMMER, in which the narrowing would be assisted by the original stress on the final syllable.]

**I. 1. a.** *trans.* To clear (a liquid or a liquid mass) from matter floating upon the surface, usually by means of a special utensil; to deprive (milk) of cream by this method; to deal with (a pot, etc.) in this way. Also *absol.* (Cf. SCUM *v.* 1.)

*c* **1420** *Liber Cocorum* (1862) 50 Þou shalt hit frye, In buttur wele skymmet wyturly. *c* **1430** *Two Cookery-bks.* 22 Caste alle on a potte, & skym yt. *c* **1450** *M.E. Med. Bk.* (Heinrich) 71 Þe þridde part of hony, boiled and skemed. **1548** ELYOT, *Despumo*, to skimme or clarifie any licour. **1570** LEVINS *Manip.* 131 To Skimme, *despumare.* **1590** SHAKS. *Mids. N.* II. i. 36 Are you not hee That.. Skim milke, and sometimes labour in the querne? **1611** COTGR., *Escumer*,.. to skimme, or clarifie, liquor. **1744** BERKELEY *Siris* §1 The clear water, having been first carefully skimmed. **1771** MRS. HAYWOOD *New Present for Maid* 32 When it boils, skim it clean. **1826** *Art Brewing* (ed. 2) 114 Boil the first mash one hour... Then skim and cleanse. *c* **1850** *Arab. Nts.* (Rtldg.) 643 Morgiana.. put the pot on the fire to make the broth, but while she was skimming it the lamp went out. **1879** *Cassell's Techn. Educ.* IV. 49/1 When the lead is all melted it is skimmed, and then drawn off into the mould.

*fig.* **1618** BOLTON *Florus* II. vi. (1636) 105 He might not seeme to have once sipt or skimd the honour of their chastity so much as with beholding them. **1673** *S'too him Bayes* 115 He had rak'd hell and skim'd the devil for it. **1704** in *Pennsylv. Hist. Soc. Mem.* IX. 350, I wish we may ever be skimmed so as to leave anything pure behind.

**b.** *Agric.* To plough (land) very lightly.

**1799** A. YOUNG *Agric. Linc.* 163 Skim it with plough very thin to make it fine. **1805** R. W. DICKSON *Pract. Agric.* I. 468 A few surface weeds appearing, he skimmed the land, without turning a furrow.

**2. a.** To remove or collect by skimming. Also in fig. context.

**1651** HOBBES *Leviath.* IV. xlvii. 387 Fairies.. Feast upon the Cream, which they skim from the Milk. **1697** DRYDEN *Virg. Georg.* I. 393 She.. Boils in Kettles Must of Wine, and skims, With Leaves, the Dregs that overflow the Brims. **1778** HAN. MORE *Florio* I. Dramas, etc. 176 He lik'd those literary cooks Who skim the cream of others' books. **1887** RUSKIN *Præterita* II. 141 We bought three cows, and skimmed our own cream. **1894** W. J. DAWSON *Making of Manhood* 30 We forget that the newspaper skims the scum of life.

**b.** To take *off* or *away* by skimming. Also *fig.*

**1670** W. SIMPSON *Hydrol. Ess.* 86 Upon these waters.. is found a kind of white cremor..; this being skim'd off [etc.]. **1744** BERKELEY *Let. on Tar Water* §8 The oil that floated on the top and was skimmed off. **1799** G. SMITH *Laboratory* I. 379 Skim off the skin which will appear on the surface. **1820** SCORESBY *Acc. Arctic Reg.* II. 403 The most pure part is skimmed off, and becomes fine oil. **1857** MILLER *Elem. Chem., Org.* ii. §3. 81 The lighter and decayed seeds float, and are skimmed off.

*fig.* 1676 HOBBES *Iliad* xx. 456 And with his Sword he skim'd his head away Helmet and all. 1780 COWPER *Progress of Error* 343 To purge and skim away the filth of vice. 1926 W. R. INGE *Lay Thoughts of Dean* II. x. 157 Civilisation tends to sterilise the ablest part of a nation. In each generation it skims off the cream and leaves the milk thinner.

†**c.** To scoop *up* as if by skimming. *Obs.*—1

1665 Fox in Bickley *Life* (1884) xviii. 264 The water.. ran about the room so that I was fain to skim it up with a platter.

**d.** To conceal or divert (some of one's earnings or takings, freq. from gambling) to avoid paying tax on them; also *absol.* Also with *off*. *U.S. slang.*

1966 *Nat. Observer* (U.S.) 5 Sept. 7/3 Certain Las Vegas gamblers have been 'skimming' millions of dollars in casino winnings—taking a cut of the receipts before the tax collector had a chance to get his share. 1973 *Sun* (Baltimore) 24 July A7/8 Noting the frequent discrepancies in amounts of cash transferred between people and the huge sums involved, he asked: 'Do you have any information, Mr Strachan, of anyone skimming?' 1978 M. PUZO *Fools Die* xviii. 194 Gronevelt felt that hotel owners who skimmed money in the casino counting room were jerks, that the FBI would catch up with them sooner or later.

**3. a.** To cover with a thin layer, as with scum.

1666 DRYDEN *Annus Mirab.* cxiii, Where the false tides skim o'er the cover'd Land, And Sea-men with dissembled Depths betray. 1859 HAWTHORNE *Marble Faun* xli, The Fountain of Trevi skimmed almost across with a glassy surface.

**b.** *intr.* To put on a thin layer.

*c* 1865 MRS. SPOFFORD *Pilot's Wife* in *Casquet of Lit.* IV. 25/2 The chocolate skimmed all over with a coat of cold oil at last. 1896 KIPLING in *Sat. Rev.* Christmas Suppl. 1/1 The beach-pools cake and skim.

**4.** To throw lightly *over* or *upon* the surface of something.

1774 FOOTE *Cozeners* III. Wks. 1799 II. 187 Some saffron, or snuff, just skimmed over his face. 1831 HOLLAND *Manuf. Metal* I. 141 Water, during the the operation, being frequently skimmed upon the surface to displace the scales.

**II.** †**5.** To scour (the sea, etc.); = SCUM *v.* 2.

*c* 1440 *Brut* ccxlv. 383 þe erle toke his meyne, and went to schyppe, and skimmed the see,.. þat no maner enymys durste rowte vpon þe see. *a* 1513 FABYAN *Chron.* VII. (1811) 573 The whiche scowryd and skymmyd ye see ryght well and manfully.

**6. a.** To deal with, treat, or study, in a slight and superficial manner. Also with *over* (cf. 9 c).

*a* 1586 SIDNEY *Arcadia* II. (1605) 179 Who, (but skimming any thing that came before him) was disciplined to leaue the through-handling of all to his gentle wife. 1665 GLANVILL *Def. Van. Dogm.* 51 Such as love only to skim things, and have not the patience to keep their minds to a deep and close attention. 1727 BOYER *Dict. Royal* II, To skim a thing over, (to pass it over slightly) *effleurer une matière* [etc.]. 1809 MALKIN *Gil Blas* I. i. ¶2 He had never skimmed the first principles of it [Latin]. 1850 ROBERTSON *Serm.* Ser. II. vi. (1864) 88 They skim the surface of the thought. 1876 GLADSTONE in *Contemp. Rev.* June 3 Parliament dived into the question, which the Bench had only skimmed.

**b.** *esp.* To read rapidly or carelessly; to glance over without close attention.

1799 HAN. MORE *Fem. Educat.* (ed. 4) I. 187 The kind of books here recommended, if thoroughly studied, and not superficially skimmed. 1820 BYRON *Blues* i. 22 Where I just had been skimming a charming critique. 1833 T. HOOK *Parson's Dau.* I. xii, The London paper.., which Harvey undertook to skim for the benefit of his friend. 1884 G. ALLEN *Philistia* II. 75 He.. was skimming the telegrams in an unconcerned manner.

**7. a.** To move, glide, fly or float, lightly and rapidly over or along (the ground, etc.).

1697 DRYDEN *Virg. Georg.* IV. 76 Then stooping on the Meads and leafy Bow'rs, They skim the Floods. 1716 GAY *Trivia* II. 232 The Ball now skims the Street. 1735 SOMERVILLE *Chase* III. 101 Smooth as Swallows skim The new-shorn Mead. 1774 GOLDSM. *Nat. Hist.* (1776) VI. 143 One of the most rapacious little animals that skims the deep. 1809 CAMPBELL *Gert. Wyom.* I. ii, The happy shepherd swains.. skim, perchance, thy lake with light canoe. 1849 M. ARNOLD *Resignation* 71 The red-grouse.. Skims, now and then, the shining ground. 1878 J. BULLER *New Zealand* I. ii. 27 Wild fowl skim the surface of the water.

*fig.* 1884 *Pall Mall G.* 4 Apr. 5/1 Lady Duffus-Hardy.. has skimmed a large expanse of country in order to cull these blossoms for our delectation.

**b.** To pass over (a surface) with close approach or very slight contact.

1796 MORSE *Amer. Geogr.* I. 42 On that day the sun, when lowest, skims the horizon without setting. 1822 IMISON *Sci. & Art* I. 414 If you now turn to the north you will find that some just skim the horizon. 1826 F. REYNOLDS *Life & Times* II. 111 The oar, instead of deeply entering the water, only slightly skimming the surface.

**8.** To cause to fly lightly; to throw (a thing, esp. one having a flat surface) so that it maintains an evenness of balance or poise in its flight.

1611 COTGR., *Ricochet*, the sport of skimming a thinne stone on the water. 1748 RICHARDSON *Clarissa* (1811) IV. 138, I skimmed my hat after him to make him afraid for something. 1768 *Woman of Honor* III. 245, I took the guinea, and.. the window being open, I skimmed it out. 1816 SCOTT *Antiq.* xliii, He skimmed his cocked-hat in the air. 1818 —— *Hrt. Midl.* i, Hearing the.. voice of the guard as he skimmed forth for my grasp the expected packet. 1887 MARY COWDEN CLARKE *Girlhood Shaks. Heroines* vii. 174 To skim both bread and trencher to the other end of the hall.

**9. a.** *intr.* To sail, glide, float, fly, run, etc., with a light and easy motion, on or close to some surface, or through the air.

In very frequent use from *c* 1700.

1591 T. ELIOT *Disc. Warre* 18 The little Pyrate, that did but skimme vp and downe the sea in a litle Brigandine. 1630 *R. Johnson's Kingd. & Commw.* 7 The winds skimming over the face of them, fannes the coole vapour all over those quarters. 1697 DRYDEN *Virg. Georg.* I. 497 Sportful Coots run skimming o'er the Strand. 1705 BERKELEY *Cave of Dunmore* Wks. 1871 IV. 507 A rivulet.. skims along the side of the cave. 1740 SOMERVILLE *Hobbinol* III. 287 As the slick Lev'ret skims before the Pack. 1794 MRS. RADCLIFFE *Myst. Udolpho* xv, The barges were seen skimming along the moon-light sea. 1848 DICKENS *Dombey* xxiii, The hard glazed hat in question skimmed into the room like a bird. 1865 W. G. PALGRAVE *Arabia* II. 302 An English-built yacht skimmed by. 1886 *Manch. Exam.* 8 Jan. 6/1 The sleighs skim along very smoothly and lightly as long as the ponies keep their feet.

*fig.* 1704 NORRIS *Ideal World* II. iii. 151 Others who are for skimming over the surfaces of a great many things, without going to the bottom of anything. 1768 TUCKER *Lt. Nat.* I. I. x. 271 They skim lightly over the surface and never touch the greater part lying at the bottom. 1820 SCOTT *Monast.* xxxi, I hate the judgment that, like the flesh-fly, skims over whatever is sound, to detect and settle upon some spot which is tainted. 1874 H. R. REYNOLDS *John Bapt.* iii. §2. 187 The science of comparative religion skims round the outside of the region.

**b.** To glance *over*, without reading closely.

1738 MRS. PENDARVES in Mrs. Delany *Lett. & Corr.* (1861) I. 30 Your last letter, which.. I skimmed over to satisfy myself of your health. 1741 WATTS *Improv. Mind* I. iv, Plumeo skimmed over the pages, like a swallow over the flowery meads. 1800 MRS. HERVEY *Mourtray Family* I. 89 Why in such a hurry? Let me first just skim over the paper. 1843 LE FEVRE *Life Trav. Phys.* I. I. i. 14 He was skimming over my introductory epistle.

**c.** To pass *over* lightly, without dwelling upon or treating fully.

1741 WATTS *Improv. Mind* II. viii. Wks. (1801) 234 They skim lightly over the arguments. 1765 TUCKER *Lt. Nat.* (1834) II. 430 Our blemishes and foibles.., which the eye does not willingly fix upon, but is apt to skim lightly over. 1824 J. H. NEWMAN *Hist. Sk.* (1873) II. II. v. 263 He skims over rather than dives into the subjects of which he treats. 1884 *Spectator* 4 Oct. 1319/2 He is skimming over a real difficulty, which is not to be evaded by eloquent talk.

**d.** To go *over* lightly with the scythe.

*c* 1830 *Glouc. Farm Rep.* 26 in *Husb.* III. (L.U.K.), The rank grass.. is 'skimmed over' or mown, and made into hay for young stock in the winter.

**10.** To glance *round* the horizon.

1817 KEATS *I stood tip-toe* 17 There was wide wandering for the greediest eye,.. Far round the horizon's crystal air to skim.

**ˈskimback.** *U.S. local.* [? f. SKIM *v.*] A North American river-fish (see quots.).

1882 JORDAN & GILBERT *Syn. Fishes N. Amer.* 119 *Carpiodes cyprinus*, Quillback; Spear-fish; Sail-fish; Skimback. 1888 GOODE *Amer. Fishes* 437 *Carpiodes velifer*, the .. 'Skim-back' of the Ohio River, is a fish often seen in the markets.

**ˈskimble-ˌskamble**, *a.*, *sb.*, and *adv.* Also 7 scimble, and 6–7, 9 scamble, 7 scemble. [f. SCAMBLE *v.*, with usual variation of vowel in the first element: cf. *clitter-clatter*, *tittle-tattle*, etc.]

**A.** *adj.* **1.** Confused, incoherent, nonsensical, rubbishy.

In modern use only after the Shakspere passage.

1596 SHAKS. *1 Hen. IV*, III. i. 154 Such a deale of skimble-scamble Stuff, As puts me from my Faith. 1630 J. TAYLOR (Water P.) *Wks.* II. 111/2 Here's a sweet deale of scimble scamble stuffe. 1822 BYRON *Vis. Judg.* Pref., Hence all this 'skimble-scamble stuff' about 'Satanic'. 1864 DASENT *Jest & Earnest* (1873) II. 69 He talks a deal of 'skimble skamble' stuff about 'askance'. 1880 RUSKIN *Arrows of Chace* II. 281 My belief is they scarcely sang a piece of pure Rossini all night, but had fitted in modern skimble-skamble tunes.

**2.** Accompanied by confusion or disorder.

1826 HONE *Every-day Bk.* II. 995 They skurry, In a skimble skamble hurry.

**B.** *sb.* Confused or worthless discourse. Also, writing of this nature.

1619 J. TAYLOR (Water P.) *Kicksey Winsey* B 7, He.. askes ..where's the wind.. With such fine scimble scemble, spitter spatter. 1818 BYRON *Let.* 1 June in *Works* (1900) IV. xvii. 238 Did you read his skimble-skamble about Wordsworth being at the head of his own profession, in the eyes of those who followed it? 1855 MOTLEY *Dutch Rep.* II. ii. (1866) 159 After a good deal of skimble-skamble of this nature.

**C.** *adv.* Confusedly; in confusion.

1775 in ASH. 1845 S. JUDD *Margaret* I. xvii. (1871) 140 The flakes shaded and mottled the sky, and fell twirling, pitching, skimble-scamble.

**ˈskim-ˌcoulter.** *Agric.* [f. SKIM *v.*] A coulter fitted with a plate of iron or steel which shaves off the top-layer of the ground and turns it into the furrow.

1797 *Monthly Mag.* Dec. 447/1 Mr. Ducket was the original inventor of the skim-coulter... It consists of a thin plate of iron, with a sharp edge, fixed horizontally to a common coulter. 1803 A. YOUNG in Hunter *Georg. Ess.* III. 163 This is entirely prevented by the skim-coulter, which is applicable to every sort of soil. 1825 COBBET *Rural Rides* 26 There was a skim coulter that turned the sward in under the furrow. 1881 ELEANOR ORMEROD *Manual of Injurious Insects* 81 A skim-coulter attached to the plough.

**b.** *attrib.* in ***skim-coulter plough***; also used as *vb.*

1799 A. YOUNG *Agric. Linc.* 74 Two skim-coulter ploughs, two drill markers. 1832 *Planting* iii. 23 (L.U.K.), To have the surface scarified, horse-hoed, or skim coulter ploughed. 1834 *Brit. Husb.* I. 264 (L.U.K.), Skim-coulter ploughs have been used to obviate this inconvenience.

Hence **ˈskim-ˌcoultered** *a.*

1805 R. W. DICKSON *Pract. Agric.* I. 542 It may be better to follow the practice adopted in some districts of using a skim-coultered plough. 1812 SIR J. SINCLAIR *Syst. Husb. Scot.* I. 416 No plough ever yet invented will effect this object so well as a skim coultered plough.

**skime**, *v. north. dial.* Also 8–9 **skyme**. [perh. a. ON. *skima* to peer, look about one, = OE. *scimian* (of the eyes) to be dim or dazzled. Cf. also Norw. dial. *skimla* to squint.] *intr.* To squint, look askance.

1691 RAY *N.C. Words* 63 To *Skime*, to look a squint, to glee. 1788– in dialect glossaries (Yks., Linc., Notts.).

**skimi**, var. SHIKIMI.

**skimish** (ˈskɪmɪʃ). *slang.* [ad. Shelta *škimis* to drink, *škimišk* drunk.] Alcoholic drink; liquor. Also **ˈskimished** *a.*, drunk.

1908 W. H. DAVIES *Autobiogr. Super-Tramp* xxiv. 211, I seldom lie down at night but what I am half skimished (half drunk), for I assure you I never go short of my skimish. 1936 J. CURTIS *Gilt Kid* iv. 40 He had been drinking all that skimish without having had a bite to eat.

**skimiter**, obs. form of SCIMITAR.

**skimmed** (skɪmd), *ppl. a.* [f. SKIM *v.*]

**1. a.** Cleared of impurities by skimming.

1558 WARDE tr. *Alexis' Secr.* 44 Adde to it twoo vnces of skimmed Honnye.

**b.** ***skimmed milk***, = SKIM-MILK 1.

1623 [see SKIM-MILK]. *a* 1722 LISLE *Husb.* (1752) 275 We in Leicestershire give them skimmed-milk and whey. 1743 R. MAXWELL *Sel. Trans. Agric.* 347 Sour Milk, as it is commonly called, skimmed Milk, Whey, and the like. 1815 SMITH *Panorama Science & Art* II. 813 Another mode of varnishing plaster,.. is to brush it over with skimmed milk. 1862 MRS. H. WOOD *Mrs. Hallib. Troub.* I. xxiv, They had a quart of skimmed milk, and were glad to get it. 1868 *Rep. U.S. Commiss. Agric.* (1869) 438 In every instance, except one, the milk sold as pure milk was skimmed milk.

*Comb.* 1837 *Flemish Husb.* 62 in *Husb.* III. (L.U.K.), Some skimmed-milk cheese for family use. 1842 J. AITON *Domestic Econ.* (1857) 215 Milk is also manufactured into butter, and what is called skimmed-milk cheese.

**c.** Of cheese: Made from skimmed milk.

1881 *Chicago Times* 16 Apr., This compound can be used only in the manufacture of skimmed cheese. 1893 *Daily News* 25 Dec. 5/5 A cheese with no brand on it will be classed as skimmed cheese.

**2.** Removed or collected by skimming.

1599 B. JONSON *Cynthia's Rev.* II. iii, He speakes all creame, skimd, and more affected then a dozen of waiting women.

**skimmer** (ˈskɪmə(r)), *sb.* Forms: α. 4 **skemour**, 5 **skemere**. β. 4–5 **skymour(e**, 5 **skymere**, 5–6 **skymer**, 7 **skimer**. γ. 4 **skymmoure**, 6 **skymber**, 7 **skymmer**; 5– **skimmer** (8 **schimmer**). [In older senses ad. OF. *escumoir* and *escumeur* (*esquemeur*): see SCUMMER *sb.* In later use also f. SKIM *v.* + -ER1.]

**1. a.** A shallow utensil, usually perforated, employed in skimming liquids; also, any utensil or implement by means of which skimming or some analogous process is performed.

α. 1392 *Earl Derby's Exp.* (Camden) 153, j skemour, j ladell. *Ibid.* 154, ij skemours de laton emptis, iij s. 14.. *Lat.-Eng. Voc.* in Wr.-Wülcker 613 *Spumatorium*, a skemere. *c* 1440 *Douce MS.* 55, fol. 24 b, Bete on the clothe with a skemere or a ladell to make it sadde and flatte.

β. *c* 1430 *Two Cookery-bks.* 17 Gader it to-gederys with a ladelle or a Skymoure. 1459 *Paston Lett.* I. 490, ij. ladels and ij. skymers of brasse. 1542 in Harrison *Ann. Old Manor House* (1893) 211, ij brase ladyls and ij skymers of laten. 1607 *Althorp MS.* in Simpkinson *Washingtons* (1860) App. 6 Brasen skimers v. 1686 in *Essex Rev.* (1906) XV. 172 Two pestls, one brass skimer.

γ. 1481–90 *Howard Househ. Bks.* (Roxb.) 66 Item, a skimmer, iiij d. *a* 1553 UDALL *Royster D.* IV. iv, I with our skimmer will fling him one flappe. 1589 [? LYLY] *Pappe w. Hatchet* C iiij, Giue me my skimmer, Martins mouth hath sod vnskimde these twelue months. 1600 HOLLAND *Livy* XXIII. xix. 487 Great store of nuts.. which floated downe the channell unto Casilinum, and with grated skimmers of wicker were taken up. 1658 ROWLAND tr. *Moufet's Theat. Ins.* 913 Take away the froth that riseth, twice a day, with a wooden skimmer that hath holes in it. 1707 *Curios. in Husb. & Gard.* 124 You may take off with a Skimmer, the Corn that Swims on the Water. 1750 BLANCKLEY *Naval Expos.* 153 Skimmers, made with a round Hoop of Iron,.. are used by the Scavengers for clearing Chips, etc. which float on the Surface of the Water. 1820 SCORESBY *Acc. Arctic Reg.* II. 403 Shallow tinned iron or copper ladles, called skimmers. 1843 HOLTZAPFFEL *Turning* I. 345 Some persons judge of the heat proper for pouring, by applying the skimmer to the surface of the metal. 1883 'ANNIE THOMAS' *Mod. Housewife* 76 As soon as this is melted, take out the oysters with a skimmer.

**b.** (See quot.)

1887 GOODE *Fisheries & Fish. Industr. U.S.* 559 As soon as the oysters are opened they are placed in a flat pan with a perforated bottom, called a skimmer, where they are drained of their accompanying liquor.

**c.** *U.S.* A clam or scallop, the shell of which may be used for skimming milk, etc. Esp. the black clam, *Cyprina islandica*

1881 E. INGERSOLL *Oyster Industry* 248 *Skimmer*, the *Cyprina islandica*, or big beach clam. (South shore of Long Island.) 1891 in *Cent. Dict.* 1949 R. J. SIM *Pages from Past* 65 The big surf clam, or skimmer (Mactra solidissima Chemn.), lies bedded down in great colonies off shore.

**d.** A device or craft designed to collect oil spilled on water.

1971 *Petroleum Rev.* May 203/2 (*caption*) The skimmer straddles the boom and the suction box is about to be immersed to suck up the oil floating on the surface of the water. 1976 M. Machlin *Pipeline* li. 516 Heavy duty floating skimmers will be deployed to recover as much oil as is feasible. 1977 *Times* 25 Apr. 1/4 A fleet of skimmers is steaming from Stavanger to suck up the oil and transfer it to waiting tankers.

†2. = scummer *sb.* 2. *Obs. rare.*

1387 Trevisa *Higden* (Rolls) I. 261 Men of Saxonia..beeþ boþe liȝter and strenger þan oþer skymours of þe see.

3. a. One who skims a liquid. *rare.*

1611 Cotgr., *Escumeur*,..a scummer, or skimmer of liquor.

b. One who conceals or diverts some of his earnings or takings in order to avoid paying tax on them. *U.S. slang.* Cf. skim *v.* 2 d.

1970 *Wall St. Jrnl.* 23 Mar. 13/1 Some skimmers..give themselves away by keeping track of their true earnings. A New York dentist, for instance, devised a dot-dash code for his office records. 1978 S. Brill *Teamsters* vi. 241 The cash was being split, some to be counted for taxes and the rest to go to the skimmers.

4. One who skims in reading.

1751 Skelton *Deism Rev.* viii. (ed. 2) II. 302 There are.. different degrees of Skimmers: first, he who goes no farther than the Title-page. 1864 *Realm* 15 June 6 Nor is it quite fair to newspaper readers or skimmers to expect them [etc.] 1907 *Outlook* 9 Nov. 605/1 For the judicious skimmer there is in these handsomely illustrated volumes a rich store of entertainment.

5. *Ornith.* A bird of the North American genus *Rhyncops*, esp. the black skimmer (*R. nigra*).

The name has reference to the manner in which these birds obtain their food, by skimming small fish, etc., from the surface of the water with the lower mandible.

1785 Latham *Gen. Synop. Birds* III. ii. 347 Black Skimmer, *Rynchops nigra.* 1826 Stephens in Shaw *Gen. Zool.* XIII. 135 The Skimmers are distinguished from all other birds by the very extraordinary form of their beak. 1838 Audubon *Ornith.* IV. 204 The hoarse cries of the Skimmers never ceased more than an hour. 1883 *Cent. Mag.* Sept. 651 The number of birds on Cape Cod is very great, and among them are many rare ones for the North, such as the black skimmer, or shear-water.

6. a. A form of horse-hoe; a shim.

1801 *Farmer's Mag.* Nov. 375 The hand-hoes destroy those that are too near the beans for this skimmer or horse-hoe.

b. *U.S.* A form of skim-coulter (*Cent. Dict.* Suppl.).

c. A metal hook for trundling a child's iron hoop. Now chiefly *Hist.*

1891 R. Pearse Chope *Dial. Hartland, Devonshire* 70 *Skimmer*, a hooked iron rod used by children for trundling iron hoops without striking them. 1953 L. Daiken *Children's Toys* iii. 38 In Victorian times the old-fashioned metal hoop was controlled by a 'skimmer', the vernacular name for the hook-and-handle apparatus held in the hand. 1961 *Listener* 12 Oct. 549/2 For boys they [*sc.* hoops] were of iron, driven along and steered by an iron hook we called a skimmer. 1979 *This England* Winter 66/3 The tool used to both drive and check the hoop had a hook at the end of a short length of steel with a wooden handle, and was called the 'skimmer'.

7. a. One who scours, or passes lightly and quickly over, the sea, land, etc.

1831 *Fraser's Mag.* III. 436 The poor skimmers over sea and land whom our friend so justly denounces. 1863 Janet Hamilton *Poems & Ess.* 75 The cooing dove, the cawing rook, The skimmers of the lake and brook. 1893 McCarthy *Red Diamonds* II. 47 Skipper Borringer.., a persistent skimmer of the seas.

b. Applied to vessels, *spec.* to a particular type of yacht. Hence also, a hydroplane, hydrofoil, hovercraft, or other vessel that has little or no displacement at speed.

1844 Mrs. Houston *Yacht Voy. Texas* II. 235 Thou 'Skimmer' of the untamed sea. 1862 *London Rev.* 16 Aug. 139 Only at the yachting stations will the tapering spars and the snowy wings of the skimmers of the seas be found. 1896 *Westm. Gaz.* 11 Sept. 7/2 The skimmer..is the only type which can be driven at abnormal speeds with a small sail area. 1909 J. I. Thornycroft in *Engineering* 12 Mar. 365/1 Vessels which greatly reduce their displacement when travelling at high speeds are generally called 'hydro-planes', but this name is not altogether satisfactory, as the surfaces on which they glide are not always planes. To call such vessels 'gliders' or 'skimmers' has been suggested as more appropriate... The latter word will be used to describe boats which at high speeds are heavier than the water they displace. 1920 *Yachting Monthly* XXIX. 20 Owing to the fact that she was an unballasted skimmer she had an unfortunate habit of capsizing at moorings. 1945 J. J. Fahey *Pacific War Diary* 308 The General, Admiral, Captain and a few other officers left the ship in a skimmer for a picnic. 1967 (*title*) Jane's surface skimmer systems 1967–68. 1971 *Morning Star* 30 Mar. 9/1 Soviet sea-going skimmers type Kometa-M are furnished with log, radio, radar and other navigation safety instruments. 1975 *Sunday Mail Mag.* (Brisbane) 22 June 5/1 They are not hovercraft or hydrofoils but 'skimmers'—ships which can take off from the water and thunder along a few score cm above it, supported on huge airliner-type wings.

c. A hat; a broad-brimmed boater, esp. of straw. Formerly, ***skimmer hat.*** *slang* (chiefly *U.S.*).

1830 J. F. Watson *Annals of Philadelphia* 176 Other articles of female wear..[include] a 'skimmer hat',..of a very small flat crown and big brim, not unlike the present Leghorn flats. 1929 *Amer. Speech* IV. 430 Among the terms which the daily press credits Mr. Dorgan with inventing are: ..skimmer (hat). 1939 M. B. Picken *Lang. Fashion* 73/3 *Skimmer*, flat-crowned sailor, usually of straw, having wide, straight brim. Worn and so-called by students at Eton College. 1946 *Sun* (Baltimore) 14 Jan. 12/1 New Yorkers who patronize such places pay several times over the original cost of their skimmers, in tips alone, during the course of a year. 1974 P. de Vries *Glory of Hummingbird* ii. 13 The thoroughly incompatible straw hat... The brightly banded boater, or 'skimmer' or 'katy'.

d. A sheath-like dress that fits closely to the lines of the body. Chiefly *U.S.*

1964 *N.Y. Times* 9 Dec. 5 Irish linen skimmer with a flirty scalloped hemline! 1968 *Tel.* (Brisbane) 2 Feb. 14/7 Cotton crepe skimmers..finished with set-in sleeves and a self bow trim. 1974 *News & Press* (Darlington, S. Carolina) 25 Apr. 3 (Advt.), Our large collection includes wraps, skimmers, pleated coat dresses, fit 'n flares [etc.].

8. a. *Golf.* A particular kind of low stroke.

1903 *Westm. Gaz.* 11 Sept. 4/2 The shot was a sliced skimmer off a wooden club.

b. *Cricket*, etc. A ball that travels with a low trajectory.

c 1868 in H. Chadwick *Scrapbks.* XI. 5/1 An over-throw of Hatfield allowed Wilkins to seize second; he then stole to third, and ran in on Fisler's 'skimmer' to left field. 1897 K. S. Ranjitsinhji *Jubilee Bk. Cricket* iii. 119 Strawyard promptly drives it just as expected—a real 'skimmer' 6 feet over extra-cover's head. 1908 *N.Y. Even. Jrnl.* 11 June 17/1 Twice Honus dug up slashing skimmers that Mike shot past Leach. 1911 P. F. Warner *Bk. of Cricket* v. 114 Haigh was bowling, and..Palairet batting, when a 'skimmer' came towards the pavilion straight for me. 1930 A. P. F. Chapman in Lonsdale & Parker *Game of Cricket* vii. 114 The catches sent him are a varied assortment—'skiers and skimmers'—but he rarely gets an easy one. 1980 *Amer. Speech 1976* LI. 294 Tennis slang...*skimmer*, ball gliding lightly and rapidly over the net.

9. *attrib.*, as **skimmer-cake** (see quot. 1863); †**skimmer hat**: see sense 7 c above; **skimmer shell** *U.S.*, the shell of a clam or scallop (cf. sense 1 c).

1795 J. Woodforde *Diary* 9 Feb. (1929) IV. 172 Dinner to day, boiled Beef & a Skimmer-Cake. 1863 Wise *New Forest* Gloss., *Skimmer-cake*, a small pudding made up from the remnants of another, and cooked upon a 'skimmer', the dish with which the milk is skimmed. 1880 *Golden Hours* XII. 520/1 Two pretty shells of the kind that children call 'skimmer shells'. 1889 Hardy *Wessex Tales* 25 Helping himself to a cut piece of skimmer-cake.

**skimmer** ('skɪmə(r)), *v.* [Northern var. of shimmer *v.* The *sk-* suggests a Scand. origin, but there is no trace of the form in ON., and mod.Sw. *skimra* may be from German.]

1. *intr.* To shimmer, glitter, gleam.

c 1440 [implied in the *vbl. sb.*]. 1788 W. H. Marshall *Yorksh.* II. 353 *To Skimmer*, to shine, to glitter. 1835 *New Monthly Mag.* XLIII. 68 Weeds..which, now black, now tipped with light, skimmered and danced in the night air. 1845 *Proc. Berw. Nat. Club* II. 234 It skimmers from the play of light upon those numerous..crystals. 1863 Miss Yonge *Hist. Christian Names* I. 255 The pale pure electric light that skimmers on the topmast.

2. To flutter, move rapidly.

For other dialect variations of sense, see *Eng. Dial. Dict.*

1824 Hogg *Wks.* 1865 I. 464 He was bounding over the heads of the maidens, and making his feet skimmer against the ceiling. a 1825 Forby *Voc. E. Anglia* 304 *Skimmer*, to flutter or frisk about lightly. 1845 S. Judd *Margaret* I. xvii, Some were..skimmering away through the bright air. 1891 in *Pall Mall G.* 28 Sept. 7/3 The hawk darted down, skimmered along the ground a distance, and was then lost in a wood.

Hence '**skimmering** *vbl. sb.* and *ppl. a.*

c 1440 *York Myst.* xvii. 123 Be ony skymeryng [*v.r.* skemeryng] of the skye When ȝe shulde knawe owthir kyng or knave? a 1800 Pegge *Suppl. Grose*, *Skimmer*, a skimmering light, i.e. glimmering. 1825 Jamieson *Suppl.*, *Skimmerin*, the flickering of the rays of light. 1855 [Robinson] *Whitby Gloss.* s.v., 'A fine skimmering morning,' a splendid dawn betokening a fine day.

†**skimmer**, obs. Sc. form of scumber *v.*

a 1585 Polwart *Flyting w. Montgomerie* 780 Leane limmer, steale gimmer! I sall skimmer in thy mouth.

**skimmi**, var. shikimi.

'**skimmia.** *Bot.* [mod.L. (C. P. Thunberg *Nova Genera Plantarum* (1783) III. 57), f. Jap. (*mijama-*) *skimmi*, the name of the plant.] An evergreen shrub of the genus so called, belonging to the family Rutaceæ, native to Japan, China, or the Himalayas, and bearing panicles of small white flowers followed by red berries. Cf. shikimi.

1853 *Curtis's Bot. Mag.* LXXIX. 4719 (*heading*) Japan Skimmia. 1866 *Treas. Bot.* 1064/2 *Skimmia*, the name of a genus of evergreen shrubs, with oblong entire stalked leathery dotted leaves, and flowers in terminal panicles. 1882 *Garden* 1 Apr. 210/1 These Skimmias are excellent evergreens. 1908 G. Jekyll *Colour in Flower Garden* xi. 104 Here are green Aucubas and Skimmias. 1925 A. J. Macself *Flowering Trees & Shrubs* xi. 179 Cuttings of Skimmias root very well in sandy peat under bell-glasses. 1960 *Times* 24 Sept. 9/3 There are..the skimmias, but here we have to be ..more careful, because some of them are monosexual. 1980 *Plantsman* I. 237 Skimmias prefer deep heavy fertile acid moist soils.

'**skim-milk.** [f. skim *v.* + milk *sb.*]

1. Milk with the cream skimmed off or otherwise removed. Also in fig. context.

1596 Shaks. *1 Hen. IV*, II. iii. 36 (Qq.), I could deuide my selfe, and go to buffets, for mouing such a dish of skim milke [1623 *folio* skim'd Milk] with so honorable an action. a 1712 W. King *Misc. Poems, The Old Cheese*, This is Skim-milk, and therefore it shall go. 1799 A. Young *Agric. Linc.* 297 He ..gives first new, then skim milk. 1808 Curwen *Econ. Feeding Stock* 63 The skim-milk was included in the butter account. 1851 Mayhew *Lond. Lab.* I. 382/1 He lived principally upon 'parritch' and skim milk. 1897 *Allbutt's Syst. Med.* III. 132 If fat be removed from the milk as in 'skim' milk, rickets follows.

*fig.* 1778 *The Love Feast* 11 Craft's blue skim-Milk is best for Tools to lap. 1872 *Punch* 4 May 180/2 The genuine outpouring of the milk and cream, and none of the skim-milk of human kindness. 1898 *Westm. Gaz.* 14 Nov. 7/1 The idea prevailed that the cream had been extracted from the.. revelations, leaving little but skim milk behind.

2. *attrib.*, as ***skim-milk cheese***, etc.

1805 R. W. Dickson *Pract. Agric.* II. 1012 In making skim-milk-cheeses the milk is set in the leads or pans as usual. 1836 Haliburton *Clockm.* (1862) 220 It's no skim-milk story, I do assure you. 1837 *Penny Cycl.* VII. 15/2 On the whole it is a better cheese than our Suffolk skim-milk cheese. 1876 *Clinical Soc. Trans.* IX. 38 On the adoption of the skim-milk treatment.

'**skimminess.** *rare*$^{-1}$. [f. skimmy *a.* + -ness.] Resemblance to skim-milk.

1887 F. W. Robinson *In Bad Hands* III. 90 The general skimminess of the fluid [*sc.* milk].

'**skimming,** *vbl. sb.* [f. skim *v.*]

1. That which is removed or obtained by skimming. Usually *pl.*

c 1450 *M.E. Med. Bk.* (Heinrich) 198 Put hyt in a panne ouer þe fuyr, & skem hyt wel as long as eny skemmyng wol aryse. 1603 Owen *Pembrokeshire* (1891) 250 The smoake that the people reported to see and the skyminges of potts. 1658 Rowland tr. *Moufet's Theat. Ins.* 1096 Apply that skimming of the air, that is, those cobwebs that are scattered in Autumn. 1750 Ellis *Mod. Husb.* V. III. 57 (E.D.D.), The skimmings [of soaked wheat] he sowed by themselves. 1777 *Cook's Voy.* (1784) I. I. vii. 130 They relished the very skimmings of the kettle. 1846 J. Baxter *Libr. Pract. Agric.* (ed. 4) I. 211 The last skimmings are termed fleetings, and are generally reserved for the use of the servants. 1858 Simmonds *Dict. Trade*, *Skimmings*,..thick syrup or scum in sugar-boiling.

*fig.* 1553 *Respublica* 98 The skimmynges, the gubbins of booties and praies. 1838 Thackeray in *Fraser's Mag.* Mar. 353 Skimmings from 'The Diary of George IV'. 1845 Huxley in *Life* (1900) I. I. 14 These are but the top skimmings of these five years' living. 1883 Pennell-Elmhirst (*title*), The Cream of Leicestershire: Eleven seasons' skimmings; notable runs and incidents of the chase.

2. a. The action of removing floating matter from the surface of a liquid, etc. Also *fig.*

1611 Cotgr., *Escumement*,..a scumming, or skimming. 1642 Rogers *Naaman* 252 After a short skeaming off a little of the sweet of their will. 1774 Pennant *Tour Scotl. in 1772* II. 299 The great scallop-shell is made use of in the dairies of this country for the skimming of milk. 1826 *Art Brewing* (ed. 2) 115 Repeat the skimming until no yeast rises. 1828 Scott *F.M. Perth* xxxii, I..will return in the skimming of a bowie. 1857 Miller *Elem. Chem., Org.* ii. §1. 65 The impurities, which are afterwards removed by skimming.

b. The practice of concealing or diverting some of one's earnings or takings to avoid paying tax on them. *U.S. slang.* Cf. skim *v.* 2 d.

1966 *Economist* 10 Sept. 1023/3 The report ascribed the allegations of skimming and underworld connections to excessive zeal displayed by the department. 1966 *Wall St. Jrnl.* (Eastern ed.) 23 Nov. 32 The term 'skimming' refers to the alleged practice of some casino operators of failing to report the full amount of their gambling revenues to state and Federal tax authorities, and often distributing this unreported income to alleged secret interests in their casinos. 1970 *Ibid.* 23 Mar. 13/1 A few years ago in Philadelphia, the owner of a large pizza parlour was suspected of skimming. 1976 *National Observer* (U.S.) 23 Oct. 2/4 To correct the common practice of 'skimming' (underreporting the income from bingo games), the commission suggests that all states require operators to report the percentage of the take that actually goes to the intended charity. 1982 *Daily Tel.* 24 Aug. 11/2 Charged in connection with a 'skimming' operation—siphoning off money to avoid tax—at a Las Vegas casino.

3. a. The action of reading (*over*) hastily.

1711 Gay *Pres. St. Wit* in Arber *Garner* VI. 506 A lively instance of those Wits who..'will endure but one skimming'. 1751 Skelton *Deism Revealed* viii. (ed. 2) II. 302 They run over a book with all imaginable haste [etc.]: this they call skimming. 1862 Helps *Organiz. Daily Life* 85 The skimming over [of the pamphlet] was effected in half an hour.

b. The action of causing to skim through the air.

c 1745 in Lees *Hist. Inverness-shire* (1897) xi. 169 Such loud huzzas and schimming of bonnets up into the air..was not heard of for a long time.

4. *attrib.*, as ***skimming-gate***, ***-iron***, ***-ladle***, etc. **skimming net**, a fishing-net with a handle, a dip-net.

1639 *12th Rep. Hist. MSS. Comm.* App. IX. 8 One Skiminge spoone with holes in it. 1801 *Farmer's Mag.* Nov. 375 They use a kind of skimming plough..having a flat share, somewhat like a mason's trowel, with two long wings projecting backwards. 1806 Lewis & Clark *Orig. Jrnls. Lewis & Clark Exped.* (1905) IV. xxv. 292 Those people have a number of buffalow robes. They have great number of skimming nets. 1813 Ellis *Brand's Pop. Antiq.* II. 111 Mr. Douce derives it from the Skimming-Ladle. 1837 *Penny Cycl.* VII. 14/2 When the curd is properly formed, it is cut horizontally in thin slices by the same skimming-ladle. 1839 Ure *Dict. Arts* 578 A scum on the surface, which is removed with skimming irons. 1843 Holtzapffel *Turning* I. 344 The pot is now lifted out..and carried to the skimming-place. 1862 Ansted *Channel Isl.* II. viii. 194 *note*, Taken with the skimming net. 1884 W. H. Greenwood *Steel & Iron* 201 The recess..for the skimming of the metal is known as the *skimming gate.*

'**skimming,** *ppl. a.* [f. skim *v.*]

1. Moving lightly along or close to a surface; flying in an easy gliding manner, etc.

*a*1685 OTWAY *Epist. to Mr. Duke* 33 Where skimming swallows o'er the surface fly. **1783** BURNS '*Now Westlin Winds*' iv, Thick flies the skimming Swallow. **1821** CLARE *Vill. Minstr.* I. 7 Like skimming bees That fly and flirt about. **1859** MAURY *Phys. Geog.* §432 We know that it is not such a skimming current as the geologist would make, which runs from one lake to another. **1894** *Outing* XXIV. 223/1 The dead leaves lift and whirl as though from an earth-skimming cannon shot.

**2.** *fig.* Touching merely the surface of a subject; not deep or thorough.

**1728** MORGAN *Algiers* II. v. 307 A bare superficial, skimming knowledge in the French. **1844** H. STEPHENS *Bk. Farm* II. 181 There are more ways than one of grooming a horse, as may be witnessed by the skimming and careless way in which some ploughmen do it. **1899** *Westm. Gaz.* 20 June 1/3 With all this light and skimming talk.

**3.** Serving to skim a thing over.

**1843** *Civil Eng. & Arch. Jrnl.* VI. 211/1 The first, or 'skimming' coat of the covering being laid on of a thickness of $\frac{3}{16}$ inch.

**4.** *Cricket.* Of a bowler: that bowls the ball with a low trajectory (*obs.*). Also, of a shot which carries low and fast. Cf. SKIMMER 8 b.

**1851** W. CLARK in W. Bolland *Cricket Notes* 132 Suppose you have what I call a skimming Bowler. **1888** A. G. STEEL in Steel & Lyttelton *Cricket* iii. 165 The low skimming fast bowler is generally an easy man to play. **1930** *Morning Post* 9 Aug. 14/1 Woolley..made a low skimming drive over the ring at long-on for 6 off S. Staples.

**'skimming-dish.** [SKIMMING *vbl. sb.* 4.]

**1.** A dish suitable for skimming with; *esp.* one used in skimming milk or in cheese-making.

**1688** HOLME *Armoury* III. 333/1 A little broad flat Dish made of Wood, called by Dairy Women a Scimming Dish. **1713** ADDISON *Guardian* No. 124, Who on her skimming-dish carves her name. **1785** W. W. PEPYS in Roberts *Mem. Han. More* (1835) I. 384 To send you a skimming-dish,.. towards setting-up housekeeping. **1805** R. W. DICKSON *Pract. Agric.* II. 1017 The operator stirs up the unbroken curd from the bottom with the skimming-dish. **1859** GEO. ELIOT *A. Bede* ix, Have you become an amateur of damp quarries and skimming-dishes?

**b.** *fig.* Something comparable to a skimming-dish in respect of shallowness.

**1861** GEO. ELIOT *Silas M.* x, The adherents of the inexplicable more than hinted that their antagonists were.. mere skimming-dishes in point of depth. **1885** *Sat. Rev.* 3 Jan. 11/1 The Englishman not inaptly calls the American's boat a 'skimming dish'.

**c.** *U.S.* A shallow yacht-built type of boat used on the coast of Florida.

**1884** J. A. HENSHALL *Camping in Florida* ii. 15 The boats are..of light draught and center-boarders. There are the 'skimming-dish', the 'pumpkin-seed' and the 'flat-iron' models.

**2.** *attrib.* in †*skimming-dish hat.*

**1766** SMOLLETT *Trav.* I. vi. 99 That unshaken patriot still appears in the same..skimming-dish hat, and slit sleeve. **1773** J. BERRIDGE *Wks.* (1864) 193 A dozen skimming dish hats, such as gentry wear. **1855** *Willis's Current Notes* V. 58/2 The Skimming-Dish Hat.

**'skimmingly,** *adv.* [f. SKIMMING *ppl. a.*] In a skimming manner; *esp.* lightly, carelessly, superficially.

**1847** WEBSTER, *Skimmingly*, by gliding along the surface. **1863** COWDEN CLARKE *Shaks. Charac.* xiv. 361 How skimmingly he relates that, 'having flown over many knavish professions, he settled down in rogue.' **1900** *Pilot* 16 June 494/2 Of all these..men he gossips in an easy, skimming style; too skimmingly, indeed, for the most part.

**skimmington** ('skɪmɪŋtən). Also skyming-, skimmen-, skimmerton; skimmiting, -ity, etc. [Possibly from *skimming* (see quot. 1639 in sense 1) + *-ton* as in *simpleton*, with the object of simulating a personal name.]

†**1.** The man or woman personating the ill-used husband or the offending wife in the procession (see 2) intended to ridicule the one or the other. Also *transf.*, a husband whose wife is unfaithful to him; a shrewish woman. *Obs.*

**1609** BUTLER *Fem. Mon.* iv. (1623) Ij, Yet when they haue it [*sc.* their desire], let them use poore Skimmington as best they may, especially in publike, to hide his shame. **1634** HEYWOOD & BROME *Lanc. Witches* H.'s Wks. 1874 IV. 234 Enter..a Skimington, and his wife on a horse. **1639** *Divers Crabtree Lectures* Frontispiece [representing a woman beating her husband with a skimming-ladle], Skimmington, and her Husband. **1813** ELLIS *Brand's Pop. Antiq.* II. 110 If they stopped at any other door and swept there too, it was a pretty broad hint that there were more Skimmingtons, *i.e.* Shrews in the town than one.

**2.** A ludicrous procession, formerly common in villages and country districts, usually intended to bring ridicule or odium upon a woman or her husband in cases where the one was unfaithful to, or ill-treated, the other. Also *attrib.* (cf. b).

For varying accounts of the reasons for, and the character of, the procession, see the *Eng. Dial. Dict.*

**1634** HEYWOOD & BROME *Lanc. Witches* H.'s Wks. 1874 IV. 230 Hearke ye, do you heare it? There's a Skimington towards, gentlemen. *c*1679 OLDHAM *Wks.* (1854) 125 Like pageants of Lord Mayor, or Skimmington. **1714-5** BAGFORD in *Leland's Collect.* I. p. lxxvi, I might here mention the old Custom of Skimington, when a Woman beats her Husband. **1753** MISS COLLIER *Art Torment.* Concl. (1811) 221 Where the strength of arm is with the wife, she generally uses it in a manner to excite her neighbours to lampoon her by a Skimmington. **1865** *St. James' Mag.* July 511 The 'skymington' is still in use for henpecked husbands and shrewish wives. **1886** HARDY *Mayor of Casterbr.* xxxix, The rude music of the skimmington ceased. *Ibid.* xl, He knew nothing of the skimmington-ride.

**b.** In phrase ***to ride* (*the*) *skimmington***, to hold a procession of this kind.

**1697** *View Penal Laws* App., A Table of..Misdemeanors, Offences and Nusances... Riot and Riding Skinnington [*sic*]. *a*1712 W. KING *Monarch* 1 When the young people ride the Skimmington, There is a general trembling in a town. **1796** *Grose's Dict. Vulgar T.*, Riding Skimmington. **1822** SCOTT *Nigel* xxi, You would do well not to forget whose threshold was swept when they last rode the Skimmington upon such another scolding jade as yourself. **1831** *Examiner* 396/2 One of those scenes called 'riding skimmerton', or rustic country justice, took place on Monday evening last at Bitterne.

**3.** A row, quarrel. *rare*$^{-1}$.

**1753** H. WALPOLE *Lett.* (1846) II. 479 The Speaker..was so misrepresented by the Attorney-general, that there was danger of a skimmington between the great wig and the coif.

**'skimmy,** *a. rare*$^{-1}$. [f. SKIM *v.*] Of the nature of skimming; superficial.

**1893** *Critic* 7 Jan. 6/2 A sketchy and 'skimmy' study of the romance as distinguished from the novel in the United States.

**'skimmy-dish.** *rare*$^{-1}$. = SKIMMING-DISH.

**1823** W. COBBETT *Rural Rides* (1830) I. 347 What! young gentlemen go to plough! They become clerks or some skimmy dish thing or other.

**skimobile** ('skiːməbiːl). *N. Amer.* [f. SKI *sb.* + -MOBILE.] **1.** A car or chain of cars used to carry skiers up a mountain; a ski-lift.

**1946** *Richmond* (Va.) *News Leader* 9 Jan. 4/2 A ski-mobile ascends Mount Cranmore, near North Conway, N.H., taking skiers to the top of a 2,052 foot rundown. **1979** *United States 1980/81* (Penguin Travel Guides) 483 Its oddball skimobile is one of the oldest lifts in New England.

**2.** A small vehicle for travelling over snow, with caterpillar tracks at the back and steerable skis in front. Cf. SNOWMOBILE. (Now the usual sense.)

**1955** *Kingston* (Ont.) *Whig-Standard* 6 Apr. 25/3 With the advent of snowmobiles and skimobiles, most dog teams are now used for dog races. **1969** 'R. STARK' *Blackbird* (1970) xx. 127 There were a couple of skimobiles down there, little open scooters with skis in front and treads in back. **1974** R. B. PARKER *God save Child* ii. 8 Shopping centers, a fish market, a skimobile shop.

**skimp,** *a.* [Of obscure origin: not in general use until late 19th c.] Scanty; = SCRIMP *a.*

**1775** *Songs & Poems Costume* (Percy Soc.) 255 Then the fops are so fine, With lank waisted chine, And a skimp bit of a hat. **1890** *Athenæum* 9 Aug. 189/3 Breaking up other measures, especially those of the ode, into skimp lengths of like sort. **1926** [see *love-curl* s.v. LOVE *sb.*[1] 16]. **1970** G. F. NEWMAN *Sir, You Bastard* viii. 244 Sneed turned his attention to considering the skimp possibles; there were no probables for the job.

**skimp** (skɪmp), *sb.* Chiefly *dial.* and *colloq.* [f. the adj.] A small or insignificant piece *of* something; a small or scanty article, esp. a fashionably skimpy garment.

**1862** C. C. ROBINSON *Dial. Leeds* 118 He thowt 'at t' moin was necessary tul his existence, and..he hed one mäade o' white päaper, an' oiled here an' thear, so as to resemble skimps o' cloud, as seen to the physical eye. **1925** *Bulletin* (Glasgow) 11 Apr. 10/2 She surreptitiously dabbed a little skimp of a handkerchief in her eyes. **1966** *Seventeen* June 92 A skimp..of stinging green French cotton. **1979** B. MALAMUD *Dubin's Lives* vi. 211 She wore a yellow skimp, her bosom snug in the fabric, her legs..good to see in short dresses.

**skimp,** *v.* [Cf. SKIMP *a.*] = SCRIMP *v.*

**1879** in WEBSTER *Suppl.* **1880** R. G. WHITE *Every-Day English* 13 The *a* in *catch* is moderately broad;..and consequently it is 'skimped' by all who are inclined to be slovenly. **1888** RIDER HAGGARD *Col. Quaritch* i, In those ages men did not skimp their flint, and oak, and mortar. *absol.* **1888** EGGLESTON *Graysons* xix, The woman who has ..schemed and skimped to achieve her attire.

**skimped** (skɪmpt), *ppl. a.* Also 9 scimpit. [Cf. SKIMP *v.*] = SCRIMPED *ppl. a.*

**1839** CARLETON *Fardorougha* v. (1848) 55 Only your cothamore's too scimpit for me. **1860** MAYNE REID *Hunters' Feast* i, Bradley's garments, on the contrary, were tight-fitting and 'skimped'. **1884** LANG in *Cent. Mag.* Jan. 323/1 Stone walls can never seem so squalid and skimped as the London houses of dirty, yellowish brick.

**skimper-scamper,** *adv.* [f. SCAMPER *v.*, with usual variation of vowel.] In hurry and confusion.

**1778** MISS BURNEY *Evelina* xlvi, And there all the lamps are broke,—and the women run skimper scamper.

**skimpily** ('skɪmpɪlɪ), *adv.* [f. SKIMPY *a.* + -LY[2].] In a skimpy manner or style.

**1859** W. H. GREGORY *Egypt* I. 314 She would..have dressed herself more becomingly, and less skimpily. **1866** *Contemp. Rev.* II. 487 They are carelessly and 'skimpily' got up goods. **1887** FENN *Master Cerem.* iii, She recrossed the skimpily furnished drawing-room.

**'skimpiness.** [f. SKIMPY *a.* + -NESS.] The quality of being skimpy.

**1879** MISS BRADDON *Vixen* xxxi, The faded and unknown hue of the substantial brocade, the skimpiness of the satin. **1884** *Punch* 2 Feb. 53 [A female] who had tried to make up for the skimpiness of her figure by the breadth of her hat-brim.

**'skimping,** *ppl. a.* [f. SKIMP *a.* and *v.*] Skimpy; marked by skimpiness.

**1775** S. J. PRATT *Liberal Opin.* xcv. (1783) III. 193 Sir, what a *skimping* waistcoat is here! neither cut, nor turn, nor slope, nor figure. **1803** MARY CHARLTON *Wife & Mistress* III. 213 He was downright tired of the Skimping out-of-the-way doings as is here. **1862** SALA *Seven Sons* I. vi. 125 A little milliner's girl in a skimping plaid shawl. **1889** 'R. BOLDREWOOD' *Robbery under Arms* xxii, The miserable, scrambling, skimping life we had lately been used to.

Hence **'skimpingly** *adv.*

**1853** LYTTON *My Novel* III. xv, The Squire and his son Frank were large-hearted, generous creatures in the article of apology, as in all things less skimpingly dealt out.

**'skimping,** *vbl. sb.* [f. SKIMP *v.* + -ING[1].] The action of the verb.

**1898** A. BEARDSLEY *Let.* Jan. (1970) 425, I must try and boil the book down but it's so rich and full of chances that skimping would be a sin. **1977** *Hot Car* Oct. 125/3 (Advt.), No skimping to cut cost.

**'skimpings.** *Mining.* [? alteration of *skimmings.*] (See quots.)

**1778** PRYCE *Min. Cornub.* 222 The water is poured off from the surface of the Tin, and the light waste upon it is skimmed off and laid by itself, to be buddled over again by the name of the Skimpings. *Ibid.* 238 The Ore swims uppermost, and is skimmed off in the manner of Tin skimpings. **1839** DE LA BECHE *Rep. Geol. Cornwall*, etc. xv. 577 If divided into three, the two upper portions were termed top and bottom skimpings. **1860** *Eng. & Foreign Gloss.* (ed. 2) 23 (Cornwall terms), *Skimpings*, skimmings of the light ores, &c., in the dressing process.

**'skimpling.** *rare*$^{-1}$. [f. SKIMP *a.*] A stunted, not properly developed, person.

**1890** G. ALLEN in *Universal Rev.* May 53 Let her parents marry her to no matter what rich fool, what undersized skimpling, what hereditary *crétin.*

**skimpy** ('skɪmpɪ), *a.* [f. SKIMP *a.* + -Y.] Of a scrimp, scanty, meagre, or spare character; stinted or stunted in some respect; lacking the proper fulness or size.

**1842** C. RIDLEY *Let.* 9 Oct. in *Cecilia* (1958) viii. 101 She had on her wedding dress which was very skimpy. **1847** *Mary, Star of the Sea* xxii. (1878) 325 Her grand-mother.. pulled a *skimpy* curtain one way across the window, in order to exclude the light. **1859** *Blackw. Mag.* LXXXV. Apr. 450/1 Contrasting advantageously with the pitiful skimpy garments of the English foot-soldier. **1883** MRS. LYNN LINTON *Ione* I. viii. 197 You must give me a whole hour to-morrow to make up for this skimpy call to-day.

**skimshander.** = SCRIMSHAW.

**1850** SCORESBY *Cheever's Whaleman's Adv.* xiii. 182 *Mux* and *skimshander* are the general names by which they express the ways in which whalemen busy themselves..in working up sperm whales' jaws and teeth and right whale bone into boxes [etc.].

**skin** (skɪn), *sb.* Forms: 3- **skin** (3, 7 **skinn**), 4-6 **skyn** (4 **skiyn**, 5 **sckyn**), **skynn**, 3-6 **skynne**, 4-7 **skinne**; 4-6 **skine**, **skyne**; 4 **schin(ne**, **scinne**, **scyn**, 4-5 **scin**. [a. ON. *skinn* (Icel., Norw., and Sw. *skinn*, Da. *skind*) neut., for earlier **skinþ*, related to OHG. *scindan* (MHG. *schinden*, *schinten*, G. *schinden*), MLG. *schinden*, *schinnen*, Du. *schinden* to flay, peel, etc. Cf. also G. dial. *schind*, *schinde* skin of fruit, obs. Flem. *schinde* bark, rind (Kilian).]

**I. 1. a.** The integument of an animal stripped from the body, and usually dressed or tanned (with or without the hair), or intended for this purpose; a hide, pelt, or fur; also occas., an article made of this.

In technical use the *skins* of the smaller animals (as sheep, calves, etc.) are distinguished from the *hides* of the larger (as oxen).

*c*1200 ORMIN 3210 Hiss girrdell wass off shepess skinn. *a*1300 *Cursor M.* 3677 Wit a rugh skin sco hidd his hals. *a*1340 HAMPOLE *Psalter* cl. 4 Taburn is made of a dryid scyn. **1390** GOWER *Conf.* II. 359 His gulion, Which of the Skyn of a Leoun Was mad. **1474** CAXTON *Chesse* III. iii. (1883) 93 The Notayres skynners coryours and cardewaners werke by skynnes and hydes. **1526** *Pilgr. Perf.* (W. de W. 1531) 276 These be wolues in lambes skynnes. **1592** TIMME *Ten Eng. Lepers* K ij, They have the skinne of the Hyena, which..will drawe the haire from the skinne of other beastes to it. **1617** MORYSON *Itin.* I. 173 Guilded leather.., three skins whereof were commonly sold for a Crowne. **1697** DRYDEN *Virg. Georg.* III. 588 Skins of Beasts, the rude Barbarians wear. **1750** tr. *Leonardus' Mirr. Stones* 82 Some say, it should be wrapt in the skin of a calf. **1837** W. IRVING *Capt. Bonneville* II. 72 In a little while the skins began to make their appearance, a few at a time; they were laid down in the lodge. **1879** *Cassell's Techn. Educ.* IV. 349/1 Beneath is stretched a leather apron, or 'skin', to catch the filings.

**b.** In phrases, esp. those (*a*) denoting premature action or too confident anticipation.

(*a*) **1567** *Cal. Scott. Papers* (1900) II. 392 Theye coulde not marchaundyze for the beares skynne before they had hym. **1577** *F. de Lisle's Legendarie* E viij, Selling the beares skinne which yet they had not taken. **1599** SHAKS. *Hen. V.* IV. iii. 93 The man that once did sell the Lyons skin While the beast liu'd, was kill'd with hunting him. **1641** in Rushw. *Hist. Coll.* (1721) IV. III. 436 We must not dispose of the Bears Skin till the Bear be Dead. **1835** LYTTON *Rienzi* V. iii, Are ye dividing the skin while the lion lives? **1858** COSTELLO *Millionaire Mincing Lane* xvii. 146 That reckoning which sells the skin of the bear before the beast is captured. **1899** *Westm. Gaz.* 30 Nov. 5/2, I do not like to divide the skin before we have caught the bear.

(*b*) **1570** *Cecil Papers* (Hist. MSS. Comm.) I. 489 You can have no more of the cat but the skin. **1582** T. WATSON *Poems* (Arb.) 96 Besides his Skinne, the Fox hath nought to pay. **1647** TRAPP *Comm. Rom.* iv. 6 Every Fox must pay his own skin to the flaier.

**c.** *slang.* (See quots.)

**1785** GROSE *Dict. Vulgar T., Skins,* a tanner. *a* **1790** H. POTTER *New Dict. Cant & Flash* (1795) 53 *Skin,* a purse. **1812** J. H. VAUX *Flash Dict., Skin,* a purse, a money bag. [Hence in later slang Dicts.] **1821** HAGGART *Life* 15 Young McGuire had taken some skins with a few shillings in each. **1856** MAYHEW *Gt. World London* iii. (Farmer), Abstracting skins from gentlemen's pockets. **1902** S. CLAPIN *New Dict. Americanisms* 365 *Skin*... A purse; a pocket-book. **1935** A. J. POLLOCK *Underworld Speaks* 107/1 *Skin,* a pocketbook or wallet. **1936** J. CURTIS *Gilt Kid* xii. 137 Proper jobs I mean. Not nicking skins from blokes what are lit up. **1955** D. W. MAURER in *Publ. Amer. Dialect Soc.* xxiv. 114 Synonymous terms [of billfold] are *hide, skin,* or *poke.*

**d.** The integument of a bird or mammal, which is preserved but not mounted.

**1840** W. SWAINSON *Taxidermy* I. iii. 84 The preservation of birds in skins, or, more properly, in an unmounted state, is, above all others, the best for scientific purposes. **1888** *Encycl. Brit.* XXIII. 90/1 Powders consisting of tannin, pepper, camphor, and burnt alum are sometimes used for 'making skins', but they dry them too rapidly for the purposes of 'mounting'... When 'skins' only are to be made for the cabinet, it is sufficient to fill the head and neck with chopped tow, [etc.]. **1964** G. CORBET in H. N. Southern *Handbk. Brit. Mammals* I. 117 There are two current methods of preparing study skins, resulting in 'round' and 'flat' skins respectively. The round skin, in which the skin is filled to simulate the shape of the body, is the traditional method.. but flat skins are now usually preferred.

**e.** *spec.* A piece of sealskin or the like attached to the running surface of a ski to prevent slipping backwards during climbing. Also called ***climbing skin.*** Usu. *pl.*

**1924** E. C. RICHARDSON *'Shilling' Ski-Runner* (ed. 3) 11 Sealskins.. are useful where long, unbroken ascents are to be made. By far the best kind are those which are stuck temporarily to the bottom of the ski... They are called, after their inventor, 'Sohm' skins. **1924** K. FURSE *Ski-Running* 39 Skins are used for climbing uphill on tour. They consist of long strips of sealskin, which are attached to the running surface of the Skis. **1948** H. INNES *Blue Ice* vii. 192 The Norwegians use different waxes, not skins, for climbing through snow. **1966** M. WOODHOUSE *Tree Frog* xvi. 123 The back room, damp and musty with stored rugs and climbing skins. **1980** J. CARTWRIGHT *Horse of Darius* xii. 175 He fastened his skis, attached some skins and made the climb.

**2. a.** A complete hide of a sheep, calf, etc., or a part of one, specially prepared as parchment or vellum and used for writing or painting upon.

Cf. Icel. *skinn* parchment, and *-skinna* used in the names of manuscripts.

**1340** *Ayenb.* 44 Betere may ech man rede þe ilke zenne and þe oþre ine þe boc of his inwyt þanne ine ane ssepes scinne. *a* **1375** *Minor Poems Vernon MS.* xlvii. 308 He wrot so faste til þat he want, For his parchemyn-skin was so scant. *c* **1489** CAXTON *Sonnes of Aymon* xi. 280 This Pygwade had well herde all that the kyng yon had sayd, & wrote it in a skynne of parchemente. **1583** STUBBES *Anat. Abus.* II. (1882) 32 A whole skin of parchment, and some-times 2. or 3. skins will hardly serue. **1649** BP. HALL *Cases Consc.* III. x. (1654) 274 It is not a small skin that would containe that Tome. **1679–88** *Secr. Serv. Money Chas. & Jas.* (Camden) 65 Writing, flourishing, and embellishing one large skinn of vellom with his said Majesties armes. **1738** CHAMBERS *Cycl.* s.v. *Parchment,* The Persians of old.. wrote all their records on skins. **1861** READE *Cloister & H.* lx, The very skin of vellum Gerard had longed for. **1870** E. PEACOCK *Ralf Skirl.* I. 1 The ponderous deed of eight skins of parchment.

**b.** *U.S. slang.* A dollar.

**1930** [see BY *prep.* 33 e]. **1950** [see LIP *sb.* 3 d]. **1976** R. B. PARKER *Promised Land* xx. 121, I got a buyer with about a hundred thousand dollars.. a hundred thousand skins.

**3.** A vessel made of the hide of a small animal, such as a sheep or goat, and used for holding or carrying liquids, etc.

**1547** BOORDE *Introd. Knowl.* xxx. (1870) 199 You shall draw your wyne out of one of the legges of the skyne. **1683** *Lond. Gaz.* No. 1867/6 His Coach [was] visited, and a little Skin of Wine.. taken out of it. **1745** P. THOMAS *Jrnl. Anson's Voy.* 54 We brought.. Tar one Skin. **1835** SIR J. ROSS *Narr. 2nd Voy.* xl. 530 A native drawing two skins of oil. **1846** *Edin. Rev.* LXXXIV. 175 The best Xeres that ever smacked of the skin. **1879** FROUDE *Cæsar* iv. 40 [The army] carried its water supplies with it in skins.

*fig.* **1874** G. C. HUTTON in Oliver *Life* (1910) viii. 82 You cannot keep Christianity in the old bottles of Constantine. It is continually bursting the legislative skins.

**4.** Chiefly *Jazz.* (*a*) A drum-head; (*b*) *slang,* a drum. Usu. *pl.*

**1927** *Melody Maker* Aug. 756/1 Moisture from the breathing of the dancers will also condense on your side drum and the skins absorb this immediately. **1938** *Manch. Guardian Weekly* 2 Sept. 188/3 The swing musicians called 'cats' play.. 'skins' (drums) and 'woodpiles' (xylophones). **1945** L. SHELLY *Jive Talk Dict.* 21 *Beatin' the skins,* striking the drums. **1980** *Musicians Only* 26 Apr. 12/5 They come in with skins with holes in.

**II. 5. a.** The continuous flexible integument forming the usual external covering of an animal body; also, one or other of the separate layers of which this is composed, the derma or epidermis.

**1340** *Ayenb.* 81 Ac oure eȝen byeþ fyeble, þet ne zyeþ bote þet skin wyþ-oute. *c* **1384** CHAUCER *H. Fame* III. 1229 Marcia that lost her skyn Bothe in face, body, and chyn. *c* **1430** *Two Cookery-bks.* 11 Pyke a-way clene þe bonys an þe Skyn, an bray hym in a morter. **1486** *Bk. St. Albans* e iij b, All [animals] that bere skyne and talow and Rounge. **1508** DUNBAR *Tua Mariit Wemen* 93 To see him scart his awin skyn grit scunner I think. **1542** BOORDE *Dyetary* xvii. (1870) 276 Refrayne from etynge of the skynnes of fysshe and flesshe, & bornet meate. **1600** J. PORY tr. *Leo's Africa* v. 237 Their women are white, hauing blacke haires and a most delicate skinne. **1661** LOVELL *Hist. Anim. & Min.* Isagoge b, The skinne in the seahorse is so thick, that speares may be made thereof. **1704** F. FULLER *Med. Gymn.* (1711) 201 The true Skin, and all its innumerable Glands. **1774** GOLDSM. *Nat. Hist.* (1776) II. 56 The skin of children newly brought forth, is always red. **1845** BUDD *Dis. Liver* 92 By circumscribed œdema, or a slight blush on the skin. **1880** DAY *Fishes Gt. Brit.* I. p. xx, The skin or tegumentary system may be entirely or partially scaleless.

*Prov.* **1419** *26 Pol. Poems* 70 It is worthy he smerte and be wo, þat of his owen skyn wole kerue a thong.

**b.** *fig.* (See quots.)

Quot. 1579 echoes Persius *Sat.* v. 116 'veterem pelliculam retines', which Cooper (1565) renders 'thou art the olde man still; thou hast still thine olde skinne'.

**1579** TOMSON *Calvin's Serm. Tim.* 133/1 We shall be alwayes in part lead away with our old skin, and there will be great remnants of the old man in vs. **1632** MASSINGER & FIELD *Fatal Dowry* II. ii, They skip into my lord's cast skins some twice a year. **1828** LYTTON *Pelham* xxxiv, That great epoch, when vanity casts off its first skin. **1856** MAYHEW *Gt. World London* 39 The wealth in which the merchants of Rag Fair deal.. is merely the offal of the well-to-do—the skins sloughed by gentility.

**c.** Without article, as a material.

**1813** SIR H. DAVY *Agric. Chem.* (1814) 88 When skin is exposed to solutions containing tannin, it slowly combines with that principle.

**d.** The bare (human) skin.

**1922** JOYCE *Ulysses* 748, I in my skin hopping around. **1956** H. GOLD *Man who was not with It* (1965) xvi. 142, I asked her to bring her swimming clothes.. because we were not to swim in our skins today. **1976** *Western Mail* (Cardiff) 27 Nov., The great day dawned, Wales v Africa, Wales in skins and Jack Sharkey's and S. Africa in white (skins meant no jerseys).

**e.** *U.S. Blacks' slang.* The skin of the palm of the hand, as making contact in shaking or slapping hands in friendship or solidarity. Freq. in phr. ***to give (some) skin,*** imp. ***gimme some skin*** (also as *sb.*).

**1942** Z. N. HURSTON in A. Dundes *Mother Wit* (1973) 223/2 'Gimme some skin!' 'Lay de skin on me, pal!' Sweet Back grabbed Jelly's outstretched hand and shook hard. **1944** D. BURLEY *Handbk. Jive* 85 The act of 'Gimme-some-skin' involves some theatricals, an intricate sense of timing, plenty of gestures. **1967** *Harper's Mag.* Nov. 62/2 Once—when I came in on the break behind him at precisely the right point—Pops gave me some skin. He reached out his dark old hand.. and I turned my hand, palm up... Pops lightly brushed my open palm in a half-slap, the jive set's seal of approval. **1972** B. G. COOKE in T. Kochman *Rappin' & Stylin' Out* 33 The gestural expressions of 'giving skin' and 'getting skin' are very common in the black community. **1974** H. L. FOSTER *Ribbin', Jivin', & Playin' Dozens* iv. 119 The viewer of TV sporting events will often observe black athletes, and whites too now, giving skin after a home run, a touch-down, or at the start of a basketball game.

**6.** In allusive phrases: **a.** Denoting oppressive or severe treatment, or summary punishment.

*c* **1380** WYCLIF *Wks.* (1880) 73 þus, as god seiþ of tyrauntis, þei taken here skyn fro þe bak. **1399** LANGL. *Rich. Redeles* II. 32 þey plucked the plomayle from þe pore skynnes. *Ibid.* 126 ȝe.. plucked and pulled hem anon to þe skynnes. **1549** LATIMER *3rd Serm. bef. Edw. VI* (Arb.) 96 She can bringe the Iudges skynne ouer hys eares. *Ibid.* 97 He wyll for wyddowes sakes.. plucke ye Iudges skinnes ouer theyr headdes. **1621** T. WILLIAMSON tr. *Goulart's Wise Vieillard* 55 Many.. who in regard of their age,.. being esteemed as dead men, haue made young men to tremble and quake, who earst purposed to plucke their skin ouer their eares.

**b.** ***skin and bone(s),*** denoting extreme emaciation or leanness. Also, a very lean person. Hence ***skin-and-bony*** adj. Also ***skin and grief.***

*c* **1430** *Hymns Virgin* (1867) 73 Ful of fleissche Y was to fele, Now.. Me is lefte But skyn & boon. *a* **1548** HALL *Chron., Edw. V,* 16 b, In.. whose reigne she dyed, when she had nothyng but a reueled skynne and bone. **1562** J. HEYWOOD *Prov. & Epigr.* (1867) 134 Yet art thou skyn and bone. **1617** MORYSON *Itin.* I. 251 My self being nothing but skin and bone, as one that languished in a Consumption. *c* **1643** LD. HERBERT *Autobiog.* (1824) 22 She languished and pined away to skin and bones. **1748** RICHARDSON *Clarissa* VII. 201 Her features are so regular.. that were she only skin and bone, she must be a beauty. **1827** *Perils & Captivity* (Constable's Misc.) 224 We arrived, extenuated and reduced to skin and bone. **1886** H. BAUMANN *Londinismen* 180/2 *Skin-and-bones.., skin-and-grief..* haut und knochen, dürre Person. **1888** W. D. LIGHTHALL *Young Seigneur* 73 'Heh, heh, heh!' cried an old skin-and-bones. **1906** [see GRAMOPHONE]. **1912** D. H. LAWRENCE *Let.* 24 Dec. (1962) I. 172 They want me to have form: that means, they want me to have *their* pernicious ossiferous skin-and-grief form, and I won't. **1935** C. DAY LEWIS *Time to Dance* 61 You silly great fulminating bogeyman! You're nothing but a laugh and a daft skin-and-bony man. **1955** G. GREENE *Loser takes All* I. vii. 43 The horse was all skin and bone and I had forgotten that the road was uphill. **1981** B. GRANGER *Schism* i. 9 The old man.. was just skin and bones. Maybe they could fatten him up.

**c.** ***to sleep in a whole skin,*** etc., to escape being wounded, to remain uninjured.

**1555** J. PROCTOR *Hist. Wyat's Rebellion* 45 The common saiynge, Good to slepe in a whole skinne. **1596** NASHE *Saffron Walden* Wks. (Grosart) III. 114 The foole is crafty inough to sleepe in a whole skin. **1600** HOLLAND *Livy* XXXII. xxi. 823 b, To enter into no armes at all, to sit still and sleepe in a hole skin. **1694** ECHARD *Plautus* 110 Begon in a moment, as you hope to sleep in a whole skin. **1704** J. PITTS *Acc. Moham.* ii. 16 The Algerines are a very timorous sort of People, willing to sleep in a whole Skin. **1813** SOUTHEY *March to Moscow* x, He was besides in a very great fright, For a whole skin he liked to be in. **1897** W. E. NORRIS *Marietta's Marriage* xliii, We'll assume.. that your anxiety to keep a whole skin justified you in taking to your heels.

†**d.** ***as the skin between one's brows,*** etc., used to emphasize the force of an adjective. *Obs.*

**1575** *Gamm. Gurton* V. ii. 121, I am as true, I wold thou knew, as skin betwene thy browes! **1599** B. JONSON *Ev. Man out of Hum.* II. i, *Punt.* Is he magnanimous? *Gent.* As the skin between your brows, sir. **1614** —— *Barth. Fair* IV. iii, Tou shalt be as honesht as the skin between his hornsh. *a* **1643** CARTWRIGHT *Ordinary* V. iv, I am as honest as the skin that is Between thy Brows.

**e.** ***to the skin,*** through all one's garments; hence, thoroughly, completely. Also, leaving no clothing on the body.

(*a*) **1582** ALLEN *Martyrdom Campion* (1908) 84 After these iiij had been searched unto their skinnes, and nothing found upon them. **1605** SHAKS. *Lear* III. iv. 7 This contentious storme Inuades vs to the skin. **1611** COTGR., *Traversé,*.. wet through, or (as we say) to the skinne. **1764** FOOTE *Mayor of G.* I. (1783) 14, I don't believe.. that they were ever wet to the skin in their lives. *c* **1885** A. W. PINERO in M. R. Booth *Eng. Plays of 19th Cent.* (1973) IV. 338, I'm wet to the skin and frightfully hungry! **1938** R. D. FINLAYSON *Brown Man's Burden* 60 It was useless to try and find shelter, and the two runaways were soaked to the skin in a minute. **1974** S. MILLIGAN *Rommel* 128 The rain had temporarily stopped... We were all soaked to the skin and bloody miserable.

(*b*) **1613** PURCHAS *Pilgrimage* (1614) 749 The Sauages.. giuing all to their naked skinne.. for the trifles he gaue them. **1634** MASSINGER *Very Woman* V. v, We were boarded, pillaged to the skin, and after Twice sold for slaves. *a* **1639** W. WHATELEY *Prototypes* II. xxxiv. (1640) 181 The Egyptians would rather sell themselves to the skinne, yea sell themselves and all, then they would.. take corne by force.

**f.** ***out of one's skin,*** denoting excessive exertion, or more usually (with *jump,* etc.) extreme delight, excitement, high spirits, or surprise.

(*a*) **1584** B. R. tr. *Herodotus* I. 38 Hymselfe as one ready to leape out of hys skynne for joy,.. declared [etc.]. **1616** R. C. *Times' Whistle* (1871) 94 The marchant, if his gaines doe safe come in, Is with joy ready to leape out on's skinne. **1668** H. MORE *Div. Dial.* III. xxxvi. (1713) 283 How transported are my Spirits, that I am ready even to skip out of my skin for Joy! **1732** FIELDING *Miser* V. i, I am ready to leap out of my skin for joy. **1798** COLMAN *Blue Devils* I. i, 'Twould make me jump out of my skin with joy. **1809** MALKIN *Gil Blas* X. vii, Scipio.. was ready to jump out of his skin for joy at the sight of me. **1860** TROLLOPE *Castle Richmond* III. xiii. 246 So is we all ould frinds, an we're all glad—out of our skins wid gladness. **1891** N. GOULD *Double Event* xv. 101 The horse.. looked in splendid condition, 'fit to jump out of his skin', to use a racing term.

(*b*) **1592** NASHE *P. Penilesse* Wks. (Grosart) II. 40 The souldiour may fight himselfe out of his skinne. **1865** TROLLOPE *Belton Est.* vii, Why should he be made.. to drive the poor beast out of its skin?

**g.** ***by*** (or ***with***) ***the skin of one's teeth,*** with difficulty, narrowly, barely.

In the original form *with,* etc., the phrase is a literal translation from the Hebrew text of *Job* xix. 20; the Vulgate and Septuagint render the passage differently.

**1560** BIBLE (Geneva) *Job* xix. 20, I haue escaped with the skinne of my tethe. **1647** CLARENDON *Contempl. Ps.* Tracts (1727) 510 He reckoned himself only escaped with the skin of his teeth, that he had nothing left. **1825** J. NEAL *Bro. Jonathan* I. 109 Skin o' my teeth, I guess, if it hadn't been for Watty boy. **1893** *Nation* 9 Feb. 99/2 His eldest son was implicated in the robbery.., and came off by the skin of his teeth. **1894** SALA *Lond. Up to Date* 66, I got in by the skin of my teeth.

**h.** ***to save one's skin,*** to save oneself from loss or injury.

**1642** ROGERS *Naaman* Index, Æquivocating with our conscience.. for the saving of our owne skin, is abominable. **1692** R. L'ESTRANGE *Fables* liv. 54 Dangerous Civilities.., wherein 'tis a Hard Matter for a Man to Save, both his Skin, and his Credit. **1890** W. STEBBING *Peterborough* viii. 155 A poltroon who was ever considering how to save his skin. **1898** DOYLE *Tragedy Korosko* v, He was taken prisoner.. and had to turn Dervish to save his skin.

**i.** Miscellaneous phrases (see quots.).

For the Sc. *skin and birn,* see BURN *sb.*[3] 2 b.

*a* **1592** GREENE *Jas. IV,* III. i, Thou shalt both have thy skin full of wine and the rest of thy money. **1630** LENNARD tr. *Charron's Wisd.* II. ii. (1670) 236 We must discern the skin from the shirt. *c* **1680** SOUTH *Serm.* (1715) I. 36 If Mens Religion lies no deeper than their Skin. **1731–8** SWIFT *Pol. Conv.* 46 Why where should she be? You must needs know; she's in her Skin. **1770** *Gentl. Mag.* XL. 560 To express the Condition of an Honest Fellow.. under the Effects of good Fellowship, it is said that he [has].. Got his Skin full. **1790** MME. D'ARBLAY *Diary* Feb., I shall pity those men when the book comes out!—I would not be in their skins! **1796** *Grose's Dict. Vulg. T., In a bad skin,* out of temper, in an ill humour. **1828** CARR *Craven Gloss.* s.v., 'To be in another's skin,' to be in his place or situation. *a* **1850** ROSSETTI *Dante & Circle* I. (1874) 221 Him who sticks so in his skin. *Ibid.* 224 Messer Angiolieri's slipped his skin. **1858** CARLYLE *Fredk. Gt.* XVI. ii. (1872) VI. 142 It is certain Voltaire was a fool.. not to have a thicker skin. **1860** WHYTE MELVILLE *Holmby House* I. xi. 151 Lady Carlisle laughed under the skin. **1886** G. B. SHAW *How to become Musical Critic* (1960) 115 The one [*sc.* actor] gets into the skin of one character: the other only puts on the clothes of twelve. **1896** *Daily News* 1 June 3/2 Mr. Tree may be said.. to have got into 'the skin of the part', as the French have it. **1916** J. R. TOWSE *Sixty Years of Theater* xxiii. 361 In the church scene, Miss Rehan won her audience by a fine display of honest womanly indignation, but she never really 'got into the skin' of Beatrice. **1959** M. SUMMERTON *Small Wilderness* i. 11 He got under the skin of the rôle and lived it... He was given a small part in the spring production. **1963** *Listener* 28 Mar. 564/2 Those who enjoy the fun of getting inside someone else's skin.

**j.** ***under the skin,*** in reality, as opposed to superficial appearances. Esp. in phr. ***sisters under the skin*** (after quot. 1896).

**1896** KIPLING *Seven Seas* 193 For the Colonel's lady an' Judy O'Grady Are sisters under their skins! **1946** A. CHRISTIE *Hollow* iii. 31 They were the same, sisters under the skin, Mrs. Pearstock from Tottenham and Mrs. Forrester of Park Lane. **1959** [see IMPULSE *sb.* 6 c]. **1960** P. GALLICO *Mrs Harris goes to New York* ii. 24 Mrs Schreiber poured it all forth to her sympathetic sister-under-the-skin, Mrs Harris. **1960** *Economist* 8 Oct. 149/1 The old ladies who booed him..are sisters under the skin to the dockers who met him with a placard curtly advising him to 'drop dead, you bum'. **1975** D. FRANCIS *High Stakes* xi. 160 Merchant bankers are pirates under the skin. **1977** *Times* 19 Apr. 14/2 *Sub specie aeternitatis*, you might say, the Richmond dustmen and Jimmy Edwards are brothers under the skin.

**k.** ***to get under*** (a person's) ***skin***, (*a*) to affect the deep feelings of; to irritate, to annoy; (*b*) to come to an understanding of, to empathize with.

**1896** ADE *Artie* vi. 54 Say, Miller, if I was to beat his whole face off I could n't ketch even. He got way under the skin on me. **1927** H. T. LOWE-PORTER tr. *T. Mann's Magic Mountain* I. v. 300 What's the matter? Has any-thing got under your skin? **1927** H. CRANE *Let.* 12 Sept. (1965) 307, I think I really succeed in getting under the skin of this glorious and dying animal [*sc.* the Indian]. **1933** F. BALDWIN *Innocent Bystander* (1935) vii. 132 That pleased her, she had got under his skin, he had at least admitted something. **1938** E. BOWEN *Death of Heart* I. viii. 143 'That is why she annoys me so.' 'You once said she'd been very kind.' 'Indeed she has— that's her way of getting under my skin.' **1942** A. CHRISTIE *Five Little Pigs* I. iv. 32, I think you are interested in—character, shall we say?.. To get under the skin, as it were, of your criminal. **1948** L. A. G. STRONG *Trevannion* xvi. 297 'Aren't you perhaps afraid the inadequacy may be on your side?'.. 'Damn you, Walter. You do get under a man's skin.' **1972** D. DELMAN *Sudden Death* iii. 58 Do I bug you, Mr Mathews? Do I get under your skin? **1977** C. MCCULLOUGH *Thorn Birds* xvii. 455, I can keep you, because I'll never let you get under my skin.

**l.** ***no skin off one's nose*** and varr. (*colloq.*), a matter of indifference to one.

**1920** S. LEWIS *Main Street* xxv. 312 Go to it. No skin off my ear, Nat. Think I want to be fifth wheel in the coach? **1926** —— *Mantrap* viii. 95 If you think..that it's any skin off my nose to lose the pleasures of your company..you got another think coming. **1930** *Amer. Mercury* Dec. 420/1 It ain't no skin off of Hymie's bugle. **1934** J. O'HARA *Appointment in Samarra* vi. 158 Okay. No skin off my ass. **1938** D. BAKER *Young Man with Horn* I. iv. 30 It was no skin off Jeff what color his old lady painted the piano. **1955** A. MILLER *View from Bridge* 102 Don't thank me... It's no skin off me. **1960** D. LYTTON *Goddam White Man* v. 113 But it was no skin off my nose that she was dead. **1963** *Australasian Post* 14 Mar. 51/2 If you want to yap on like a drongo in the DTs it's no skin off *my* bugle. Go ahead: be a gig! See if I care! **1966** J. PORTER *Sour Cream* v. 60 Our arrival was no skin off her nose and she didn't pay all that much attention to us. **1971** B. MALAMUD *Tenants* 35 Make it like eight [o'clock] or around that if it's no skin off you. If I miss a day don't fret on it. **1972** R. MILNER in W. King *Black Short Story Anthol.* 378 Then Clyde said it was no skin off his ass. **1978** L. MEYNELL *Papersnake* xiv. 188 It was no skin off my nose... My heart wasn't hurt, even if my pride was.

**m.** (***here's to the***) ***skin off your nose*** and varr.: used as a toast.

**1925** FRASER & GIBBONS *Soldier & Sailor Words* 260 *Here's to the skin off your nose*: Your good health! **1936** WODEHOUSE *Young Men in Spats* ii. 42 'Well, skin off your nose,' said Pongo. 'Fluff in your latchkey,' said Barmy. **1949** [see MUD *sb.*[1] 3]. **1959** D. EDEN *Sleeping Bride* ix. 85 Philip handed her a drink and she added, 'Here's the skin off your nose.'

**n.** ***skin and blister***, sister. *Rhyming slang.*

**1925** FRASER & GIBBONS *Soldier & Sailor Words* 260 *Skin and blister*, sister. (Rhyming slang.) **1935** G. INGRAM *Cockney Cavalcade* x. 170, I saw your skin and blister last night. **1972** G. F. NEWMAN *You Nice Bastard* 348 *Skin and blister*, sister.

**7.** A membrane covering any internal part of an animal body.

***gold-beater's skin***: see GOLD-BEATER 1 b.

*c* **1400** *Lanfranc's Cirurg.* 169 þe stomak & þe guttis is ordeyned a skyn, þat is clepid þe siphac. *a* **1425** tr. *Arderne's Treat. Fistula*, etc. 69 Swynez grese wele y-clensed of þe litel skynnez and smal y-kutted. *c* **1475** *Pict. Voc.* in Wr.-Wülcker 749 *Hoc fren*, the sckyn of the brayne. **1590** BARROUGH *Meth. Physick* II. ix. (1639) 84 If the skins [pleuræ] which be joyned all the length of the breast within be inflammate. **1668** CULPEPPER & COLE *Barthol Anat.* Introd., The internal Skin of the inner Cavities. **1702** J. PURCELL *Cholick* (1714) 7 The two Skins of the Mesentery. **1897** *Allbutt's Syst. Med.* II. 1138 Skins may be expectorated abundantly.

**8.** Anything which resembles skin in nature or use; an outer coat or covering of anything.

**a.** The outer covering of certain fruits and vegetables; the peel or rind; also, the bark or rind of a tree or plant.

**1398** TREVISA *Barth. De P.R.* XVII. clv. (Bodl. MS.), Plinius..seiþ þat frute of siliqua is swete:..and þe skynne þerof is y3ete. **1558** WARDE tr. *Alexis' Secr.* 22 b, You shal take the rootes of..wilde Mallow, and scrape from them cleane their skinne or barke. **1599** SHAKS. *Hen. V*, v. i. 56 The skinne [of the leek] is good for your broken Coxcombe. **1657** R. LIGON *Barbadoes* (1673) 81 The body of this plant is soft,..and between the skins, water issues forth as you cut it. **1687** A. LOVELL tr. *Thevenot's Trav.* II. 34 The Cucumbers are so good in Aleppo, that..the Francks also eat them green. skin and all. **1733** W. ELLIS *Chiltern & Vale Farm.* 116, I have often seen the very Skin, or Rind of the young Roots left behind in drawing. **1826** *Art of Brewing* (ed. 2) 190 The moment the skin [of the apple] is first cut. **1862** MILLER *Elem. Chem. Org.* iii. §1 (ed. 2) 160 Red grapes may be made to yield a 'white' wine..; but if the skins be left in the fermenting mass [etc.]. **1874** RAYMOND *Statist. Mines & Mining* 511 Yellow pine timber..placed at first skin to skin, and afterward 2 feet apart.

**b.** A pellicle, a film. Also *fig.*

**1576** FLEMING *Panopl. Epist.* 64 Those remedies whiche ought..to drawe a skinne ouer my wound. **1671** GREW *Anat. Pl.* I. ii. (1684) 15 The Cuticle becomes a Skin; as we see in the growing of the Coats of Cheeses, of the Skin over divers Liquors, and the like. **1678** HOBBES *Decam.* viii. 98 For the skin of the Bubble is Water. **1758** REID tr. *Macquer's Chem.* I. 385 In the same manner take off a second skin that will form on the surface of the Lead. **1793** T. BEDDOES *Calculus*, etc. 279 The heat of boiling water would not.. produce a skin upon milk without the presence of air. **1831** BREWSTER *Optics* xiii. 110 Covered with gauze or muslin, or with a skin of dried skimmed milk. **1878** HUXLEY *Physiogr.* 81 It is this white solid substance which forms the thin skin on the surface of the water.

**c.** In miscellaneous uses (see quots.).

**1611** SHAKS. *All's Well* II. ii. 29 As fit..as the pudding to his skin. **1677** *Descript. Diamond Mines* in *Misc. Curiosa* (1708) III. 243 The Diamonds..are very well spread, large Stones.., they have generally a bright Skin. **1763** *Museum Rust.* I. 94 It enables the land..to come speedily to a good skin (as we term it), or coat of grass. **1875** DAWSON *Dawn of Life* ii. 12 If they [Laurentian hills] could be flattened out they would serve as a skin much too large for mother earth in her present state. **1894** *Nature* 26 July 289 Observations hitherto made in the earth's outer skin.

**d.** The surface of a piece of cast or rolled metal.

**1840** *Civil Eng. & Arch. Jrnl.* III. 425/1 The removal of the exterior *skin* of a casting greatly increases the corrosive action of salt water and its combined air. **1869** RANKINE *Machine & Hand-tools* App. 54 It is used to form a hard and impenetrable *skin* to a piece of grey cast iron by the process called *chilling*.

**e.** *Arch.* The facing of a wall, in contrast to the material in the heart of it.

**1884** *Mil. Engin.* I. II. 84 To have only a thin skin on the outside which could readily be knocked out by a crowbar. **1897** *Daily News* 23 Nov. 6/5 The disintegrated condition of the inner masonry..rendered impossible the project..of replacing the inside masonry without disturbing the 'skin'.

**f.** The outermost layer of a pearl.

**1885** *Encycl. Brit.* XVIII. 446/2 A pearl of the first water should possess, in jewellers' language, a perfect 'skin' and a fine 'orient'. **1935** L. KORNITZER *Pearls & Men* xix. 165 Keep on inspecting your pearl... When the blemish has been removed and a clean bright skin shows up, the worst is over. Smooth the skin with the finest emery paper you can obtain. **1976** B. W. ANDERSON *Gemstones for Everyman* xxiii. 300 The finest cultured pearls have come from waters off the north Australian coast... The oyster used here is the large *pinctada maxima*. The resultant cultured pearls are also large and have very thick skins.

**g.** The outer or surface layers of a conductor, in which alternating current tends to be concentrated at high frequencies.

**1891** [see *skin effect*, sense 16 below]. **1891** [see *skin resistance*, sense 16 below]. **1893** J. J. THOMSON *Recent Res. Electr. & Magn.* iv. 260 When the vibrations are very rapid the currents are practically confined to a thin skin on the outside of the conductor. **1943** C. L. BOLTZ *Basic Radio* vii. 121 As the frequency is increased, the current is concentrated more and more in the outer layer—the 'skin' —of a conductor. **1958** J. SHEPHERD et al. *Higher Electr. Engin.* vii. 182 The effect increases with frequency, until at high frequencies the current is almost entirely in the 'outer skin' of the conductor.

**h.** *slang.* A tyre.

**1954** *Rocky Mountain News* (Denver) 2 Sept. in *Amer. Speech* (1956) XXXI. 305 *Skin*, a tire. **1977** *Hot Car* Oct. 62/1 The answer is to run at the *same pressure* as the standard tyres, as by dropping the pressure any more than two pounds, you could cause sidewall failure, even in the big American skins.

**i.** A duplicating stencil; *spec.* the part that actually goes on the duplicator.

**1965** G. M. BEER *Machines for Office Workers* iv. 73 When the [correcting] fluid is applied [to the stencil] it will..seep through the incisions and make the carbon..adhere to the wax sheet; subsequently, at the duplicator, the carbon and backing sheets are removed, and in doing this it is..possible that the re-formed skin will also be detached so that both the incorrect letter, and the correction over it, appear on the duplicated sheet. **1972** T. LILLEY *'K' Section* xl. 203 She had typed the 'skin'; he would check it and then run off about four hundred copies. **1973** *Daily Tel.* 25 Apr. 13/8 It was then discovered that one foolscap duplicating skin could produce only 10,000 copies. Four skins had to be typed and 'run off'.

**9.** *Naut.* **a.** The planking, or iron plating, covering the ribs or frame of a vessel.

(*a*) **1769** FALCONER *Dict. Marine* (1780), *Planking* is sometimes called 'laying on the skin', by the artificers. **1814** *Phil. Trans.* CIV. II. 287 The ribs are covered by a skin of greater or less substance from the extreme ends of them to the keel or back bone. **1856** KANE *Arct. Expl.* I. xxxii. 444 The entire bulkhead was in a blaze, as well as the dry timbers and skin of the brig. **1867** SMYTH *Sailor's Word-bk.* 629 *Skin*, this term is frequently used for the inside planking of a vessel, the outside being the *case*. **1886** *Pall Mall G.* 26 Aug. 4/1 The boat is most substantially constructed;..the skin being of mahogany three-eighths of an inch thick.

(*b*) **1862** *Times* 7 Mar., The 18 inches of wood between the armour and iron skin. **1883** NARES *Constr. Ironclad* 5 The plates forming the outer and inner bottoms or *skins* are rivetted on.

**b.** (See first quot.)

**1841** TOTTEN *Naval Text Bk.* 394 *Skin*, that part of a sail, when furled, which remains outside and covers the whole. *c* **1860** H. STUART *Seaman's Catech.* 49 What cloth will you take for furling the spanker in a skin? The third from the leech. **1882** NARES *Seamanship* (ed. 6) 134 Gather up the skin, shaking the slack sail well down into it.

**c.** *transf.* The outer covering of any craft or vehicle (or a constituent layer of this); esp. of an aircraft or spacecraft.

**1921** *Flight* XIII. 247/2 The skin below the chines is formed of two thicknesses of mahogany planking... One ply of varnished cotton fabric is laid between the mahogany skins. **1937** *Jrnl. R. Aeronaut. Soc.* XLI. 846 It is proposed to form the skin of the wing from two separated sheets of plywood. **1948** 'N. SHUTE' *No Highway* iii. 64 Here in the aircraft everything was firm and steady and secure; the even tremor of the engines, the faintly heard rush of air over the outer skin, these bred confidence. **1962** G. COOPER in *Into Orbit* 29 The crews are equipped with..a fire axe for cutting through the capsule's skin. **1973** *Times* 3 May 4/1 They found that the whole of the skin of the caravan was full of blocks of cannabis. **1973** TERRY & BAKER *Racing Car Design & Development* vi. 135 Increasing safety-consciousness caused the FIA to stipulate that, for 1972, the outer skins of all Formula 1 monocoques had to have a maximum thickness of 16 swg. **1977** D. BEATY *Excellency* i. 8 The company to which it [*sc.* an aircraft] belonged had been painted out... What remained against the silver duralumin skin was AN——.

**10. a.** Used as a term of contempt.

**1825** JAMIESON *Suppl.*, *Skin*, a term applied to a person, as expressive of the greatest contempt; as 'Ye're naething but a nasty skin'. **1889** *Century Mag.* Dec. 227 Occasionally he would refer to the president of the Off-shore Wrecking Company, his former employer, as 'that skin'.

**b.** *U.S. slang.* = SKINFLINT.

**1900** ADE *More Fables* 30 Some of the Folks..used to say that Henry was a Skin, and was too Stingy to give his Family enough to eat.

**c.** Without contemptuous implications: a person (of a specified kind). Chiefly *Anglo-Ir.*

**1914** JOYCE *Dubliners* 152 Ah, poor Joe is a decent skin. **1939** 'F. O'BRIEN' *At Swim-Two-Birds* 166 A decent skin if ever there was one, said Slug with warmth, a man that didn't stint the porter. **1958** B. BEHAN *Borstal Boy* III. 258 These were lies..that Cragg was muttering about the Colonel, who wasn't a bad old skin at all,..since he got to know us. *Ibid.* 266 He seemed a decent old skin. **1966** F. SHAW et al. *Lern Yerself Scouse* 22 *Ee's a good skin*, he is an agreeable fellow.

**d.** *slang.* A horse or mule.

**1923** E. HEMINGWAY *Three Stories & Ten Poems* 32 They take the first batch of skins out to gallop. **1925** FRASER & GIBBONS *Soldier & Sailor Words* 260 *A skin*, a horse: mule. **1941** BAKER *Dict. Austral. Slang* 67 *Skin*, a horse, 'generally the property of a professional wayfarer'.

**e.** *slang.* = SKINHEAD 2 (*b*).

**1970** *Daily Progress* (Charlottesville, Va.) 15 Apr. 7/1 You gotta decide what family you are going to join, the hairies or the skins. **1978** R. WESTALL *Devil on Road* iv. 26 Those Midland sods must be crazy... I shouted the rudest things you can shout at skins. **1981** *Times* 22 July 11/3 'There's good and bad skinheads,' is as far as he will go... The picture is complicated: there are black skins, and there are non-violent skins... Certainly, many of the skins are thugs.

**11.** *U.S.* A card game in which each player has one card which he bets will not be the first to be matched by a card dealt from the pack.

**1925** *Messenger* Dec. 386/1 Playing 'skin' for matches. **1935** Z. N. HURSTON *Mules & Men* I. iii. 72 Ah played skin wid de Devil for mah life. **1973** J. SCARNE *Scarne's Encycl. Games* xvi. 310/1 The game of Skin is dead even; that is, dealer and player have exactly equal chances of winning. **1978** MOORE & LEVINE *Big Paddle* (1979) i. 15 Larsen loves skin. He'll go all over looking for a skin game.

**12.** ***the Skins***, the nickname of the 5th Royal Inniskilling Dragoon Guards or, formerly, the Royal Inniskilling Fusiliers [properly a corruption of *Inniskilling*, assimilated to the sb.].

**1938** R. HAYWARD *In Praise of Ulster* 235 The Indian Mutiny, South Africa and the Great War brought fresh glories to the valiant 'Skins'. **1949** ST. J. ERVINE *Craigavon* II. xlvi. 233 The history of 'the Skins', the nickname of the Inniskilling Fusiliers, is rich with the jewels of courage. **1954** L. MACNEICE *Autumn Sequel* 67 The Skins have gone to Kenya with their trousers smartly creased. **1981** J. JOHNSTON *Christmas Tree* 25 Did you have a brother in the Skins?

**III.** *attrib.* and *Comb.*

**13.** Attrib. **a.** In sense 'of, in, connected with, the skin', as ***skin care***, ***colour***, ***-disease***, ***-flake***, ***-furrow***, ***-tint***, ***-tissue***, etc.

**1615** H. CROOKE *Body of Man* 349 Betwixt the fleshy membrane and the skinne runne certaine vessels called *Skin-veines.* **1676** MARVELL *Mr. Smirke* Wks. (Grosart) IV. 16 'Tis a pitiful giddy..insect, ingendered..in every marish, can but run a pore thorow and give but a skinne-wound. **1769** MRS. RAFFALD *Eng. Housekpr.* (1778) 57 Lay the feet over them the skin side up. **1864** W. T. FOX *Skin Dis.* 15 The unchangeable elements, in the teaching of skin pathology. **1865** *Chambers's Encycl.* VII. 363/1 Pellagra, at one time, the name of a loathsome skin-disease. **1880** *Nature* 28 Oct. 605 On the Skin-furrows of the Hand. **1896** *Peterson's Mag.* VI. 231/2 The skin-tints are less clear and warm than the same painter's 'Bubbles'. **1930** E. POUND *XXX Cantos* xv. 66 Skin-flakes, repetitions, erosions. **1944** *Horizon* Mar. 172 The grey matter of the brain-rind was originally skin-tissue. **1949** M. MEAD *Male & Female* i. 19 The sensitivity of our skin-tissues. **1954** V. DENGEL *All about You* vi. 141 There are four points to proper, daily skin care. **1969** V. J-R. KEHOE *Technique Film & Television Make-Up* (ed. 2) iii. 40 (*heading*) Skin care products. **1972** *Sat. Rev.* (U.S.) 27 May 18/2 The idea of discrimination based on skin color is beyond their comprehension.

**b.** In sense 'made, or consisting, of skin', as ***skin-bag***, ***skin-boat***, ***-bottle***, ***-canoe***, ***-case***, ***-cover***, etc.

**1593** NASHE *Christ's T.* Wks. (Grosart) IV. 214 Our costly skinne-cases could keepe vs from consuming to dust. **1647** J. TRAPP *Comm. Luke* i. 59 A skin-bottle hanging in the smoke of filthy desires. **1761** *Ann. Reg.* 128 This plate is to be moved round,..rubbing it with a small skin cushion. **1804** W. CLARK in *Orig. Jrnls. Lewis & Clark Expedition* (1904) I. 87 The Indians pass this river in Skin Boats which is flat and will not turn over. **1808** PIKE *Sources Mississ.* (1810) II. 155 We..nearly compleated the frame of a skin Canoe. **1827** J. HOLMES *Hist. United Brethren* i. (ed. 2) 7 The skin-boat is..from forty to fifty feet long, and proportionally broad and deep. **1860** Skin-bag [see ATTA].

1871 W. MORRIS in Mackail *Life* (1899) I. 246 Skin shoes tied about the ankle with neat thongs. 1895 SCULLY *Kafir Stories* 123 He carried a small skin wallet slung to his waist. 1910 W. DE LA MARE *Three Mulla-Mulgars* xxviii. 237 Having cut one of their skin-bags to pieces. 1954 J. R. R. TOLKIEN *Fellowship of Ring* ix. 408 They drew the skin-covers over their boats. 1968 G. JONES *Hist. Vikings* I. i. 17 These hunters, fishermen, and food-gatherers from the south..developed the skin-boat.

**14.** Objective. **a.** With pres. pples., as ***skin-breaking***, ***-clipping***, ***-fitting***, ***-piercing***, ***-plastering***, etc.

1593 NASHE *Christ's T.* Wks. (Grosart) IV. 226 Those skin playstring Painters. 1599 —— *Lenten Stuff* ibid. V. 229 The curtaild skinclipping pagans. 1611 COTGR., *Ratoire*,..a skinne-breaking oyntment. 1784 COWPER *Task* v. 141 Arrowy sleet, Skin-piercing volley, blossom-bruising hail. 1889 J. J. THOMAS *Froudacity* 40 The skin-discriminating policy induced..since the abolition of slavery. 1891 MISS DOWIE *Girl Karp.* 244, I listened open-eyed to the herd's bear statistics, literally skin-clamming as these were. 1915 D. H. LAWRENCE *Rainbow* iv. 91 She wore an elegant, skin-fitting coat. 1947 *Science News* IV. 11 The men who went into enemy ports during the war wore skinfitting dresses.

**b.** With verbal sbs., as ***skin-cutting***, ***-grafting***, ***-healing***, etc.

1829 SCOTT *Anne of G.* xxvii, The other three are picked men, who will not fear their skin-cutting. 1860 TOMLINSON *Arts & Manuf.* Ser. II. *Leather* 25 When they are in the state of pelt, they are split... This is effected by means of a.. machine called the 'skin-splitting machine'. 1870 *Lancet* 27 Aug. 306/2 (*heading*) Skin-grafting. *Ibid.* 22 Oct. 566/2 Mr. Francis Mason has performed the operation of skin grafting on granulating surfaces in nine instances. 1876 *Clinical Soc. Trans.* IX. 30 During this period skin grafting was practised continuously. 1896 *Allbutt's Syst. Med.* I. 380 Manipulations cannot be begun upon wounded surfaces until skin-healing is complete.

**c.** With agent-nouns, as ***skin-dealer***, ***-dresser***, ***-hunter***, ***-preserver***.

1858 SIMMONDS *Dict. Trade*, *Skin-dealer*. *Ibid.*, *Skin-dresser*, a currier, or furrier. 1890 *Daily News* 9 Sept. 7/1 A brother..who carried on business as a furrier and skin-dresser. 1893 *Scribner's Mag.* June 794/1 Wholesale slaughter by skin-hunters has nearly destroyed the Platypus in some districts. 1893 *Daily News* 16 Feb. 5/5 No fewer than three taxidermists or skin preservers.

**15. a.** With past pples., as ***skin-built***, ***-clad***, ***-covered***, ***-peeled***, ***-spread***.

*a* 1661 HOLYDAY *Persius* (1673) 294 Who without heed.. praise thee so, That (skin-peel'd asse!) thy self dost first cry, Hoe! 1823 JOANNA BAILLIE *Poems* 260 Whilst travellers from their skin-spread couches rise. 1846 H. G. ROBINSON *Odes of Horace* II. vi, Galesus' tide, Sweet to the skin-clad flocks. 1883 *Boats of World* 27 Two examples of skin-built canoes. 1886 *Encycl. Brit.* XXI. 113/2 Stilicho..planted the cruel Goths, his 'skin-clad' minions, in the very sanctuary of the empire. 1897 YEATS *Secret Rose* 1 A large house with skin-covered wattles for the assembly. 1977 *Proc. R. Soc. Med.* LXX. 234/1 Any open lesion is more dangerous than a skin-covered one.

**b.** Misc., as ***skin-like***, ***-thin*** adjs., (*to the*) ***skinward*** adv.

1699 R. L'ESTRANGE *Erasm. Colloq.* (1711) 302 That wears Linen above, and woollen to the Skinward. 1796 WITHERING *Brit. Plants* (ed. 3) I. 82 *Skinny*, or *Skin-like*.., tough, thin, and semi-transparent, like gold beater's skin. 1847-9 *Todd's Cycl. Anat.* IV. I. 9 Gelatinous skin-like integument of the compound body. 1946 W. DE LA MARE *Traveller* 12 Their skin-thin gills. 1966 P. SCOTT *Jewel in Crown* IV. 171 The tough little shell of skin-thin masculinity that used to harden the outward appearance of the British military wives.

**16.** Special combs.: **skin-beater** *slang* (now *Obs.* or *rare*), in a jazz- or dance-band: a drummer; **skin beetle** *U.S.*, a greyish-brown beetle of the genus *Trox* or a brown, hairy beetle of the family Dermestidæ, feeding on carrion or other organic material; **skin-bone**, an ossification in or of the skin; **skin-book**, a book made of parchment or vellum; **skin-bound** *a.*, having the skin tensely drawn; hide-bound; **skin-changer**, one supposedly able to metamorphose himself or herself; **skin cream**, an oleaginous cosmetic preparation for care of the skin; **skin depth** *Electr.* [cf. sense 8 g], the distance from the surface of a conductor at which an electromagnetic wave of a given frequency is attenuated by a factor of $1/e$ ($e$ = 2·718...); also *fig.*; **skin-drying** *vbl. sb.* (*Founding*), drying of the surface of a greensand mould before casting; so **skin-dried** *a.*; **skin-eater**, a moth or beetle which infests and destroys prepared skins or furs; **skin effect** *Electr.*, the tendency of an alternating current of high frequency to flow through the outer layers only of a conductor, resulting in an increase in effective resistance; **skin-faro**, *U.S.* (see quot. and *skin game*); **skin-finish**, a particular style of chasing in bronze; **skin flap** *Surg.*, a portion of living skin attached to the body by one edge so that it remains alive while it is used to close a wound after amputation, or in plastic surgery; **skin-flick** *slang*, a film of a pornographic type; **skin-food**, a preparation for improving the skin; **skin friction**, the friction developed between a solid and a fluid or gaseous body; *esp.* the friction between the surface of an aircraft or the like and the air; **skin game**, (*a*) (see quots. 1882, 1897); also *transf.* and *fig.*; (*b*) the pornography trade; (*c*) = sense 11 above; a game of this; **skin graft**, a piece of living skin which has been surgically transferred to a new site or to a different individual; also, the process of making such a transfer; also as *v.*, to subject to the process of skin-grafting; **skin house** *slang*, (*a*) a gambling establishment; (*b*) an establishment providing pornographic entertainment; **skin magazine** *colloq.*, a magazine containing nude photographs, a pornographic magazine; **skin-man**, a skin-dresser or skin-dealer; **skin-mark**, a merchant's mark; **skin-merchant**, a skin-dealer (see also quot.); **skin packaging**, a method of packaging in which the article, placed on a backing plate which is to form part of the package, has a plastic film cover thermoformed on to it; **skin pass** *Metallurgy*, a final cold-rolling, effecting a small reduction in thickness, given to heat-treated strip steel in order to improve surface and mechanical properties; **skin-plating**, metal plating forming the skin of a vessel; **skin-pop** *v. intr.* (*slang*, orig. *U.S.*), to inject a drug subcutaneously (cf. MAIN-LINE *v.*); so as *sb.*, the action of skin-popping; also *fig.*; hence **skin-popper**; **skin-popping** *vbl. sb.*; **skin potential**, the electrical potential between different points on the skin, esp. as exhibited in the galvanic skin response; †**skin-prints**, tattoo-marks; **skin resistance**, †(*a*) = *skin friction* above; †(*b*) the resistance of the skin (sense 8 g) of an electrical conductor; (*c*) the electrical resistance of the skin of an organism; **skin-scraper**, a skin-scraper, a strigil; **skin-search** *sb.* and *v.* (*slang*) = *strip-search* sb. and vb. s.v. STRIP *v.*[1] 27 a; **skin-sensory** *a.*, of or pertaining to the skin together with the sensory apparatus; **skin test** *sb.*, a test to see whether an immune reaction is elicited when a substance is applied to or injected into the skin; so **skin-test** *v. trans.*, **skin testing** *vbl. sb.*; **skin tonic**, a cosmetic astringent for the skin; **skin trade** (orig. *U.S.*), commerce in animals' skins; also *fig.*; also = *skin game* (*b*) above; **skin-vision**, the power of perceiving distinctions of light by means of the skin; **skin-wool**, wool taken from the skin of a dead sheep; **skin-worm**, the Guinea worm; **skin-yard**, a yard used for the working of skins.

1936 *Amer. Mercury* XXXVIII. p. x/2 *Skin beater, the drummer man. 1953 *N.Y. Times Book Rev.* 13 Sept. 33/3 Red, the reefer-smitten skin beater. 1842 T. W. HARRIS *Treat. Insects New Eng. Injurious to Vegetation* 11 *Skin-beetles.., bone-beetles..act the useful part of scavengers. 1895 J. H. & A. B. COMSTOCK *Man. Study Insects* 559 The skin-beetles..are small or of medium size. 1942 [see *larder beetle* s.v. LARDER[1] 3]. 1972 SWAN & PAPP *Common Insects N. Amer.* xx. 436 Skin beetles feed on carrion, skin, feathers, and dung. 1862 COCKAYNE *St. Marherete* Title-p., Now First Edited from the *Skin Books. 1883 G. STEPHENS *Bugge's Stud. North Myth. Examined* 33 The oldest known Swedish skin-book dates after 1250. 1799 UNDERWOOD *Dis. Childhood* (ed. 4) I. 130 Of which [tightness of the skin] further notice will be taken under the article of *Skin-bound. 1803 BEDDOES *Hygëia* IX. 136 Except in a very close room, I feel as if skin-bound for days together. 1927 E. V. GORDON *Introd. Old Norse* 224 Berserks were probably named 'bear-shirts' from a superstition that they were '*skin-changers'. 1937 J. R. R. TOLKIEN *Hobbit* vi. 121 He is a skin-changer. He changes his skin: sometimes he is a huge black bear, sometimes he is a great strong black-haired man with huge arms and a great beard. 1907 *Yesterday's Shopping* (1969) 537/1 Violet oatmeal *skin cream. 1979 P. FERRIS *Talk to me about England* III. 133, I appear to be missing a pot of special vitamin skin-cream. 1941 J. A. STRATTON *Electromagn. Theory* ix. 536 One may assume for conductors of arbitrary cross section that the field and current distributions near the surface differ negligibly from those near the surface of an infinite plane provided the radius of curvature is very much greater than the *skin depth. 1962 CORSON & LORRAIN *Introd. Electromagn. Fields* x. 338 The skin depth decreases if either the conductivity $\sigma$, the permeability $K_m$, or the frequency $f$ increases. 1966 *Listener* 5 May 653/3 Myshkin's apparent niceness and gentleness, his ridiculousness, are the surface, the skin depth of his assumed role. 1954 *Skin-dried [see *skin-drying* vbl. sb. below]. 1970 E. PARKES et al. in K. Strauss *Appl. Sci. in Casting Metals* ix. 321 (*heading*) Skin dried and dry sand moulding. 1888 *Lockwood's Dict. Mech. Engin.* 324 *Skin drying effects the removal of a portion of the moisture and diminishes the risk of a blown or a scabbed casting. 1954 J. E. GARSIDE in A. J. Murphy *Non-Ferrous Foundry Metall.* v. 171 Pouring should be completed as soon as possible after skin-drying owing to the fact that the moisture from the backing sand slowly penetrates towards the skin-dried mould face. 1891 *Electrician* 29 May 91/1 Sir William Thomson recalled attention to the tendency of alternating currents to avoid the central portions of metallic conductors, thereby giving rise to an increase of resistance which has been occasionally alluded to under the name of the '*skin effect'. 1965 *Wireless World* Aug. 401/1 The h.f. resistance is increased partly by skin effect, and more significantly by eddy currents induced in the lossy magnet system. 1882 MCCABE *New York* xxxix. 545 *Skin-faro..offers no chance whatever to the player. 1884 C. G. W. LOCK *Workshop Rec.* Ser. III. 19/2 This mode of chasing, called..in English '*skin-finish', is..only found on work of the best class. 1873 *Brit. Med. Jrnl.* 15 Mar. 286/2 He took a large *skin-flap from the front below the knee, a smaller flap behind, and left just enough of the bones to fit an apparatus. 1974 R. M. KIRK et al. *Surgery* v. 73/2 Skin flaps are used to close large defects in situations where sound healing is essential, when good quality of skin is desirable and when the local blood supply would not sustain free grafts. 1968-70 *Current Slang* (Univ. S. Dakota) III-IV. 110 **Skin flick*, *n.* A pornographic movie. 1969 *Daily Colonist* (Victoria, B.C.) 7 June 13/3 We ran family movies for nine years and almost went broke. For the last three years, we've been showing skinflicks and doing much better financially. 1975 P. WEBB *Erotic Arts* viii. 280 In the '60s..film-makers became aware of the commercial possibilities of the voyeur film, or 'skin-flick'. 1898, etc. *Skin-food [see FOOD *sb.* 2 b]. 1977 B. PYM *Quartet in Autumn* ix. 81 Turning her attention to the wash basin she noted..a jar of skinfood and a tube of Steradent tablets. 1881 *Encycl. Brit.* XII. 518/2 The two principal causes of the resistance to the motion of a ship are the *skin friction and the production of waves. 1907 F. W. LANCHESTER *Aerodynamics* vi. 220 In actual planes it is impossible to do away with thickness, so that in addition to skin friction there must be the possibility of a longitudinal pressure component due to the shape of the plane. 1919 R. H. GODDARD *Method of Reaching Extreme Altitudes* 9 The resistance, R, may be taken as independent of the length of the rocket by neglecting 'skin friction'. 1948 *Sci. News* VII. 24 In the same way a body moving through air loses energy by skin friction (analogous to conduction). 1978 *Jrnl. R. Soc. Arts* CXXVI. 683/1 During acceleration to supersonic speeds the external surface of the structure becomes hotter due to skin friction from the air flow. 1868 M. H. SMITH *Sunshine & Shadow in New York* 405 The square game..is played only by gentlemen, and in first-class houses;..the *skin game..is played in all the dens and chambers, and in the thousand low hells of New York. 1882 MCCABE *New York* xxxix. 545 The 'skin game' is used, with the majority of the visitors, for the proprietor is determined from the outset to fleece them without mercy. 1897 R. F. FOSTER *Compl. Hoyle* 623 *Skin Games*, those in which a player cannot possibly win. 1904 W. H. SMITH *Promoters* 98 We built the bridges finally,..for we weren't really working a skin game. 1920 GALSWORTHY *Skin Game* I. 19 She wants to sell, an' she'll get her price, whatever it is. *Hillcrist.* (*With deep anger*) If that isn't a skin game..I don't know what is. 1958 *Economist* 1 Feb. 398/2 The..ironies of German political life: the strange mixture of elements..that mingle in the Bonn skin game. 1970 *Times Educ. Suppl.* 18 Dec. 1/1 The censor and the skin game. 1973 J. SCARNE *Scarne's Encycl. Games* xvi. 308 (*heading*) The skin game. 1973 E. MCGIRR *Bardel's Murder* i. 10 As a very small [antiques] dealer, I was no opposition... His business is rather a skin game. 1976 *Globe & Mail* (Toronto) 7 Jan. 10/3 The long-respected publication had been sold and new publishers had changed big game to the skin game. 1978 Skin game [see sense 11 above]. 1871 *Lancet* 22 Apr. 535/1 On taking off the plaster the *skin-grafts were found adhering. 1900 *Brit. Med. Jrnl.* 12 May, Epit. Med. Lit. 74 The wound should be allowed to granulate and subsequently be skin grafted. 1930 A. H. DAVIS *Burns* xxi. 195 Most surgeons..find that heteroplastic skin grafts are universally unsuccessful. 1935 P. H. MITCHINER *Mod. Treatment of Burns & Scalds* v. 54 Riverdin's or Thiersch's skin grafts give excellent results. 1977 D. BAGLEY *Enemy* xxxi. 251 Gillian..had just had the operation for the first of the skin grafts. 1871 *Galaxy* XII. 61 A '*skin' house, as the dens where cheating games are played are called. 1902 FARMER & HENLEY *Slang* VI. 227/1 *Skin-house*, a gambling den. 1970 *Harper's Mag.* July 34 The skin houses were mostly playing short subjects—a girl taking a bath in a sylvan stream, a volley-ball game in a nudist camp. 1972 *Dict. Contemp. & Colloq. Usage* (Eng. Lang. Inst. Amer.) 27/1 *Skin house*, a theater featuring nude women or films of nude women. 1972 J. WAMBAUGH *Blue Knight* (1973) i. 29 Some gunsel I'd heard was hanging out in the skin houses and taxi-dance joints. 1968 *Rat* 13-16 May 11/1 Two prophylactics and a *skin magazine was found in President Kirk's drawer. 1980 *Cosmopolitan* May 319/1 Men often use pictures as stimulation when they masturbate (hence the popularity of so-called skin magazines), but women do so much less often. 1788 BIDDLE *Autobiogr.* (1883) 227 *Skinmen, breechesmakers and glovers. 1829 P. EGAN *Boxiana* 2nd Ser. II. 220 At a proper age, JEM turned out to earn an honest penny, and was apprenticed to a *skyver*, or skinman, in Newcastle-upon-Tyne. 1970 M. TARMEY *Skinman* vi. 128 He sat hunched and helpless in the chair..., a skinman without any skins. 1736 H. BOURNE *Hist. Newcastle* 89 There are higher up this Isle..other Three Characters, which are the Merchants *Skin-mark. 1789 BRAND *Hist. Newcastle* I. 278 *note*, Skin marks were not used instead of arms, but rather as distinct insignia appropriated to the profession of merchandise. *a* 1792 BURGOYNE *Lord of Manor* III. ii. (D.), I am..vulgarly called a recruiting dealer, or more vulgarly still, a *skin-merchant. 1962 A. L. GRIFF *Plastics Extrusion Technol.* vi. 122 In *skin-packaging, the coated board can now be the base, while coated flexible film can be the skin. 1971 *Engineering* Apr. 63/2 Two commercial systems of skin packaging are in general use. The Soag-Stanley process uses an uncoated board, the other a coated and perforated board. 1939 J. DEARDEN *Iron & Steel Today* x. 149 A single pass through a *skin pass mill then brings it to its final thickness. 1977 R. B. ROSS *Handbk. Metal Treatments & Testing* 351 On the production side, the Skin pass will be used to produce the final surface finish and simultaneously achieve slightly improved mechanical properties. 1869 SIR E. REED *Shipbuild.* ix. 174 The fastenings of the stringer angle-irons connecting it with the *skin-plating. 1953 KRAMER & KARR *Teen-Age Gangs* i. 35 You get a big fat mouth every time you give that leg of yours a *skin-pop. *Ibid.* 243 *Skin-pop*, to inject drugs, usually heroin, under skin into body. 1959, 1964 [see MAIN-LINE *v.*]. 1971 'D. HALLIDAY' *Dolly & Doctor Bird* xvi. 242 You can't deny we gave your social habits a skin-pop. 1970 *Daily Tel.* 30 Jan. 19/1 She had also '*skin-popped' (injected drugs just below the surface of the skin) and taken a vast assortment of pills. 1953 KRAMER & KARR *Teen-age Gangs* i. 35 A very expert *skin-popper, Hoppy is. 1970 H. WAUGH *Finish me Off* 48 No marks. She must be a skin-popper. 1952 *Sunday Times* 3 Feb. 5/4 '*Skin popping'..consists of scratching open a place in the skin and injecting heroin or morphine there. 1970 *Observer* 3 May 3/1 When the addicts run out of veins to inject, because of scars and ulcers, they try skin-popping—injecting just under the skin or into a muscle. 1936 *Amer. Jrnl. Physiol.* CXVII. 189 (*heading*) *Skin potential and impedance responses with recurring shock stimulation. 1967 VENABLES & MARTIN *Man. Psychophysiol. Methods* ii. 58 The permeability of the cell membrane is a physiological phenomenon, and measurements of skin resistance and skin potential must be made within physiological limits. **1650** BULWER *Anthropomet.* 237 The chief men and women have *skin-prints, as a brave kind of Gallantry. **1875** *English Mechanic* 3 Sept. 634/3 We have sufficient data from which the *skin-resistance [of a ship's hull] can be determined. **1891** *Jrnl. Inst. Electr. Engineers* XX. 479 When we deal with conductors of about a centimetre in diameter there is no apparent effect of this skin resistance. **1895** H. LAMB *Hydrodynamics* xi. 575 The frictional or 'skin-resistance' experienced by a solid of 'easy' shape moving through a liquid. **1904** *Jrnl. Franklin Inst.* CLVII. 248 The skin resistance of copper bonds increases with time. **1927** *Brain* L. 231 We have learned that the skin resistance is invariably decreased both by pain and by elevation of body temperature. **1942** S. R. HATHAWAY *Physiol. Psychol.* xi. 236 The level of skin resistance has a low inverse correlation with neuroticism. **1971** *Jrnl. Gen. Psychol.* LXXXV. 88 Each record was analyzed by recording the averaged skin resistances for the last two minutes of the resting period and for each minute of the stimulus film period. **1875** *Encycl. Brit.* II. 555/1 Blunted strigils or *skin-scrapers. **1935** A. J. POLLOCK *Underworld Speaks* 107/2 **Skin search*, an arrested person who is stripped naked and his body thoroughly searched for narcotics. **1970** G. JACKSON *Let.* 4 Apr. in *Soledad Brother* (1971) 212 Our cells were being invaded by the goon squad: you wake up, take your licks, get skin-searched. **1973** *Time* 26 Mar. 64 So far, none of the three new guards in California's state prison system for men have been assigned to conduct 'skin searches' of nude prisoners for contraband. **1979** F. FORSYTH *Devil's Alternative* xvii. 386 If you are thinking of giving me a weapon, don't bother. On my return I am to be skin-searched. **1879** tr. *Haeckel's Evol. of Man* I. ix. 270 The first of the secondary germ-layers, the *skin-sensory-layer. **1925** W. W. DUKE *Allergy* xv. 207 She gave positive *skin tests to a number of extracts including wheat. **1943** W. C. BOYD *Fund. Immunol.* xi. 424 Patients should not be skin tested without previous adequate history and physical examination. **1961** *New Scientist* 16 Mar. 696/1 All the components cause a positive reaction in the skin tests commonly used for allergic responses. **1971** R. SCOTT *Wedding Man* ii. 65 Every Asian child was skin-tested [for tuberculosis] as soon as possible after arrival. **1925** W. W. DUKE *Allergy* xv. 206 One's first impression of *skin testing is likely to be one of disappointment. **1963** L. V. CRAWFORD in F. Speer *Allergic Child* xxvii. 420 Although the mechanics of skin testing are simple, considerable experience is required for proper interpretation. **1906** *Daily Colonist* (Victoria, B.C.) 27 Jan. 5/1 (Advt.), Special Sales. Toilet Goods..*Skin Tonics. Perfumes. **1971** M. LEE *Dying for Fun* xxxiv. 167 The fragrance of Lapsang Souchong, mingled with the tang of skin tonic. **1710** W. BYRD *Secret Diary* (1941) 186 About 5 o'clock Robin Hix and Robin Mumford came to discourse about the *skin trade. **1885** *List of Subscribers, Classified* (United Telephone Co.) (ed. 6) 101 (*heading*) Fur and skin trade. *a* **1953** DYLAN THOMAS (*title*) Adventures in the skin trade. **1977** *Time* 19 Sept. 41/1 The city [*sc.* Boston] set aside this seedy downtown area three years ago for X-rated movies, porn shops and other facets of the skin trade—in hopes of being able to contain them. **1883** *Nature* XXVII. 399 Experiments with regard to the '*skin-vision' of animals. **1805** LUCCOCK *Nature of Wool* 340 The *skin-wool is not usually found most plentiful where the stock of sheep is most heavy. **1884** W. S. B. MCLAREN *Spinning* (ed. 2) 71 With short wool, especially if it be skin wool, the rollers should be closed up. **1857** tr. *Küchenmeister's Anim. & Veg. Parasites* I. 398 Amongst the Germans it is known as..the *skin worm,..leg-worm,..and Pharaoh's-worm. **1879** E. R. LANKESTER *Advancem. Sci.* (1890) 40 The skin-worm (*Demodex folliculorum*). **1885** *Manch. Exam.* 7 Apr. 4/7 A fire occurred..in Mr. Pryce Parry's *skinyard and wool warehouse.

**skin**, variant of SKEEN.

**skin**, *v.* Also 6–7 skyn, skinne (6 scinne). [f. SKIN *sb.* Cf. Norw. *skinna* to cover with skin.]

**I. 1. a.** *trans.* To furnish or cover with skin; to cause skin to form or grow on; to heal by the formation of skin. Also with *over*.

**1547** BOORDE *Brev. Health* cix. 41 b, After that incarnat the place and so skyn it. **1597** A. M. tr. *Guillemeau's Fr. Chirurg.* 39/2 We must..with an exsiccating plaster cure them, and soe skinne them. **1614** W. B. *Philosopher's Banquet* (ed. 2) 55 Fresh-Butter skinnes the rawnesse of the throate. **1697** DRYDEN *Ded. Æneid* Ess. (Ker) II. 210 The wound was skinned; but the strength of his thigh was not restored. **1872** GEO. ELIOT *Middlem.* I. x, He looks like a death's head skinned over for the occasion.

*absol.* **1601** HOLLAND *Pliny* II. 272 It [aloe] is..a great healer, and that which vniteth & skinneth quickly.

**b.** In fig. contexts. †Also with *up*.

**1602** SHAKS. *Ham.* III. iv. 147 It will but skin and filme the Vlcerous place. *a* **1659** BP. BROWNRIG *Serm.* (1674) II. xx. 253 They had skin'd up the sore, and yet, it breaks out in their Soul again. *c* **1750** WARBURTON *Serm.* ii. Wks. 1811 IX. 47 The wounds, our own earth hath formerly received,..which though skinned over by time and human culture, are seen. **1796** COLERIDGE *The Destiny of Nations* 410 Short Peace shall skin the wounds of causeless War. **1880** MCCARTHY *Own Times* lx. IV. 337 He does not seem to have considered the difference between skinning over a wound and healing it.

**c.** *fig.* To cover (*over*) in some slight or superficial manner.

**1603** SHAKS. *Meas. for M.* II. ii. 136 Authoritie..Hath yet a kinde of medicine in it selfe That skins the vice o' th top. **1650** *Nicholas Papers* (Camden) 191 It is to be feared your Amsterdam affaires are rather skinned than cured. **1658–9** SIR A. HASLERIGGE in *Burton's Diary* (1828) III. 104 It may be skinned over for a time, but will break out. The people are not pleased. **1796** BURKE *Regic. Peace* Wks. 1842 II. 289 It is only their assured and confident expectation..that skins over their mischievous dispositions with a momentary quiet. **1833** T. HOOK *Parson's Dau.* I. x, The objects of which (so thinly were they skinned over) were just as evident to Emma as to Lady Frances. **1850** MERIVALE *Rom. Emp.* ix. (1865) I. 372 This open rupture was with difficulty skinned over at the last moment.

**2. a.** *fig.* To clothe, attire. *rare*.

**1599** B. JONSON *Cynthia's Rev.* II. iv, You never skin'd a new [? = anew] beautie more prosperously in your life. **1610** BEAUM. & FL. *Scornf. Lady* II. ii, Off with your husks; I'le skin you all in Sattin.

**b.** To cover with a skin or skins. *rare*$^{-1}$.

**1618** in Foster *Eng. Factories India* (1606) I. 10 The jarres are all fild, stoped close, skyned, and marked with the distinction of the fruits.

**c.** *absol.* To put a good skin on cattle. *rare*$^{-1}$.

**1765** *Museum Rust.* IV. 190 The largest pasture..will neither *skin* nor *tallow*, or, in other words, is fit for nothing but young stock.

**d.** *Naut.* (See quots.)

**1815** BURNEY *Falconer's Dict. Marine* s.v., *To Skin up a Sail in the Bunt*, is to make that part of the canvas which covers the sail when furled, smooth and neat, by turning the sail well up on the yard. **1841** TOTTEN *Naval Text Bk.* 394 To skin the sail up smooth is to turn it well up, and so as to cover the sail neatly and smoothly.

**e.** *Shipbuilding*. (See quot.)

*c* **1850** *Rudim. Nav.* (Weale) 141, Planking is often termed *skinning* the ship.

**3.** *intr.* To form skin; to become covered with skin; to grow a new skin; to heal *over* in this way. Also *fig.*

**1579** LYLY *Euphues* (Arb.) 181 The sooner it skinneth, the sorer it festereth. **1654** H. L'ESTRANGE *Chas. I* (1655) 124 Her excoriated carkasse began to skin again. **1763** MILLS *Pract. Husb.* IV. 345 All suckers must be cut away from the root, and the place..smoothed with a knife; for then it will soon skin over. **1829** SOUTHEY *Lett.* (1856) IV. 129 If the ulcer skins over in that way, the quacks will exult in having wrought a cure. **1843** R. J. GRAVES *Syst. Clin. Med.* xxix. 392 The centre [of the ulcer] granulated and skinned naturally. **1891** RIDER HAGGARD *Nada* xxxv, The hole in his skull skinned over.

**II. 4. a.** *trans.* To strip or deprive of the skin; to flay; to peel.

**1591** PERCIVALL *Span. Dict.*, *Desollar*.., to skin, to pul off the skin. **1687** A. LOVELL tr. *Thevenot's Trav.* I. 246 The Crocodile is very strong, and one day as I caused one of them ..to be skinned [etc.]. **1725** *Fam. Dict.* s.v. *Pears*, When they are off the Fire, stir, skin them, and squeeze about half a Lemon upon them. **1791** BOSWELL *Johnson* 3 Apr. 1779, A fishmonger who was skinning an eel alive. **1853** SOYER *Pantropheon* 167 It was necessary to skin the bird very carefully. **1875** JOWETT *Plato* (ed. 2) I. 210 They may skin me alive, if they please.

**b.** To rub or scrape the skin off; to bark. Also *transf.*

**1855** JARVES *Art Hints* 383 Almost every one of his pictures have been more or less skinned, to use an expressive term, by the carelessness of cleaners. **1856** KANE *Arct. Expl.* I. xiii. 167 It is the same hummock you skinned your shins upon. **1891** C. ROBERTS *Adrift Amer.* 97 My feet were already skinned in several places.

**c.** In phrases denoting excessive meanness or desire for gain, esp. *to skin a flint*.

**1694** MOTTEUX *Rabelais* v. vii, May I be broil'd like a Red-herring, if I don't think they are wise enough to skin a Flint. **1834** MARRYAT *P. Simple* (1863) 195 Report says, that she would skin a flint if she could. **1851** MAYHEW *Lond. Labour* I. 134 They'd skin a flea for his hide and tallow. **1859** LEVER *D. Dunn* iv, I was..brought up amongst fellows would skin a cat. **1884** [see FLINT *sb.* 4].

**d.** *to skin the cat* (*U.S.*), to perform a gymnastic exercise involving passing the feet and legs between the arms while hanging by the hands from a horizontal bar and so drawing the body up and over the bar; also *transf.* and *fig.*

**1845** S. JUDD *Margaret* II. i. 199 Their several diversions, snapping-the-whip, skinning-the-cat, racing round the Meeting-house, or what not. **1888** 'C. E. CRADDOCK' *Story of Keedon Bluffs* v. 88 He did not wait a second but 'skinned the cat' among the rafters. **1905** *N.Y. Even. Post* 14 Oct., We have learned how to hide behind the back log of 'environment' or to 'skin the cat' in morality on the score of 'heredity'. **1907** C. E. MULFORD *Bar-20* viii. 80, I used to shinny up this here wall an' skin th' cat getting through that hole up there. **1931** *Sun* (Baltimore) 29 May 12/7 You saw them skin the cat On the high trapeze. **1946** B. TREADWELL *Big Bk. Swing* 125/2 Skin he cat; ride, brother, ride.

**e.** To keep (one's eyes) open. *U.S. colloq.*

**1865** *N.Y. Herald* in Farmer & Henley *Slang* (1891) II. 361, Keep a padlock on yer mouth and skin yer weather eye. **1875** J. G. HOLLAND *Sevenoaks* x. 133 Skin yer eyes, now, Mr. Balfour, we're comin' to a lick.

**f.** *fig.* To beat or overcome completely. *U.S. slang.*

**1862** *Charleston* (S. Carolina) *Mercury* 9 Aug. 1/5 They were 'skinning' the soldiers of other regiments the 'tallest kind'. **1911** H. QUICK *Yellowstone Nights* iv. 110 'Purty good little places,' said he, 'but the home place skins 'em all.' **1981** *Verbatim* VII. III. 7/2 Puns ('Eagles *skin* Washington').. offer limitless possibilities to the enterprising sports journalist.

**5.** To strip or pull *off* (a skin, etc.); to remove by drawing off inside out.

**1658–9** in *Burton's Diary* (1828) IV. 228 They skin off your skin. **1683** MOXON *Mech. Exerc.*, *Printing* xxiv. ¶ 11 Having carefully skinned off the Film with the edge of the Slice. **1759** MARTIN *Nat. Hist.* I. 28 Turf of the Ground, skinned off, and burnt to Ashes. **1861** DICKENS *Gt. Expect.* xxxi, Skin the stockings off,..or you'll bust 'em.

*transf.* **1896** LILLARD *Poker Stories* ii. 59 Many a time I've seen a game player just skin off his watch and ring..and play them in.

**6.** *intr.* To shed or cast the skin; to lose the skin by rubbing.

**1772** *Ann. Reg.* 96/2 It skins every year; and its skin is said to be a remedy against the cramp. **1908** GILBERT MURRAY tr. *Aristoph., Frogs* I. ii, When all my shoulder's skinning, simply skinning.

**7.** *slang.* **a.** *trans.* To clean out (a person) at play.

**1812** J. H. VAUX *Flash Dict.* s.v., To strip a man of all his money at play, is termed *skinning* him. **1864** *Daily Telegr.* 19 Oct., The gamblers did their best to give us fits; but in less than half an hour, sir, the little squaw she skinned the crowd. **1889** H. O'REILLY *Fifty Yrs. on Trail* 343 In less than two or three hours [to] be skinned out of every cent.

**b.** To strip (*of* clothing or money); to fleece by exactions or swindling.

**1819** *Massachusetts Spy* 24 Mar. 3/1 They will not be able to skin the people as deep as they did during their former reign. **1839** C. F. BRIGGS *Harry Franco* II. vi. 76, I wish I may be blown into a gin shop if I warnt skinned clean O! The young woman had..picked my pockets of every cent. **1851** MAYHEW *Lond. Labour* II. 71 Perhaps he gets 'skinned' (stripped of his clothes and money from being hocussed, or tempted to helpless drunkenness). **1892** *Spectator* 12 Mar. 364/2 Suppose the Emigration Trusts skin the emigrants until they stop emigration. **1898** *Eclectic Mag.* LXVII. 607 Some new device is invented for enmeshing and skinning the investor.

**c.** *skin the lamb* (see quots.).

**1864** *Slang Dict.* 232 *Skin the Lamb*, a game at cards, a very expressive corruption of the term lansquenet... When a non favourite wins a race 'bookmakers' are said to skin the lamb. **1883** *Graphic* 21 Apr. 410/2 The Ring are enormous winners on the race, the majority having 'skinned the lamb'.

**8.** To exhaust or impoverish by excessive fishing, cropping, etc.

**1867** F. FRANCIS *Angling* vii. (1880) 274 He does not want to skin the stream. **1895** *Forum* (N.Y.) Sept. 8 To renovate the soil which had been 'skinned' in the days of slavery.

**9.** *U.S. slang.* †**a.** *trans.* and *intr.* To copy or crib. *Obs.*

**1835** J. TODD *Student's Manual* (ed. 3) 115 Should you allow yourself to think of going into the recitation-room, and there trust to 'skinning', as it is called in some colleges. **1837** *Yale Lit. Mag.* Feb. 138 A student is said to skin a problem, when he places the most implicit faith in the correctness of his neighbor's solution of it, or at least sufficient to warrant bestowing upon it the rites of adoption. **1849** *Yale Lit. Mag.* XV. 81 Never skin a lesson which it requires any ability to learn. **1851** BRISTED *Five Yrs. Eng. Univ.* (1852) 381 Classical men were continually tempted to 'skin' (copy) the solutions of these examples. **1851** B. H. HALL *College Words & Customs* 430 'At Yale College,..in our examinations,' says a correspondent, 'many of the fellows cover the palms of their hands with dates, and when called upon for a given date, they read it off directly from their hands. Such persons *skin*'.

**b.** *intr.* To abscond, make off, slip away; (*U.S.*) with *out*, to depart hastily. Also with *through*, to slip through, to pass by a narrow margin.

**1876** BESANT & RICE *Gold. Butterfly* (1877) 254 You jest gether up your traps and skin out of this. **1894** *Outing* XXIV. 442/1 The hero..would never have been one could he have skinned for cover in time. **1902** G. H. LORIMER *Lett. Self-Made Merchant* xi. 141 If you would make a downright failure or a clean-cut success once in a while, instead of always just skinning through this way. **1920** W. CAMP *Football without Coach* 57 The best a runner can hope for is a chance to skin through that opening before it ceases to exist.

**c.** With *out*: To produce, display.

**1873** J. MILLER *Life amongst Modocs* iv. 44 Four aces! and what else? Skin 'em out, skin 'em out! *c* **1895** *Thompson St. Poker Cl.* 42 Mr. Williams proudly skinned out three jacks and a pair of kings.

**d.** To glance over, examine.

**1895** *Cornh. Mag.* Aug. 174 Each man skinned his cards and tried his hardest to look disappointed.

**10.** In phrases used as adjs.

**1869** W. MORRIS in Mackail *Life* (1899) I. 203 If you had passed a week at this skin-'em-alive place. **1891** MISS MACEWEN *Three Women in One Boat* 87 A good old skin-your-nose encounter.

**III. 11.** *trans.* and *intr.* To inject (a drug) subcutaneously. Cf. *skin-pop* v. s.v. SKIN *sb.* 16. *slang.*

**1953** W. BURROUGHS *Junkie* vi. 57 He had to shoot in the skin about half the time. But he only gave up and 'skinned' a shot after an agonizing half-hour of probing and poking and cleaning out the needle, which would clog up with blood. **1970**, **1972** [see MAIN *v.* 2].

**skinch** (skɪntʃ), *v.* and *int.* *north* and *Midland dial.* [Origin unknown.] **A.** *v. intr.* To encroach, to cheat. **B.** *int.* A formula used by children in a game to demand a truce.

**1891** S. O. ADDY *Gloss. Words Sheffield* Suppl. 52 *Skinch*, *v.* to encroach, to shorten distance. When a boy playing at marbles moves his taw nearer to the ring than he ought to do he is said to *skinch*, *i.e.*, to encroach unfairly. **1893–4** O. HESLOP *Northumberland Words* II. 649 *Skinch!* the cry for parley in a boys' game. **1914** D. H. LAWRENCE *Prussian Officer* 262 Willy could hear the endless calling and shouting of men's voices. 'Tha'rt skinchin!' **1959** I. & P. OPIE *Lore & Lang. Schoolch.* viii. 150 'Croggie' is..general in West Hartlepool although the usual term in County Durham is 'skinch'.

**skin-coat.** Also 6 skyn coit, skincote, -coate. [f. SKIN *sb.* + COAT *sb.*]

**1.** A coat made of skin.

**1533** *Acc. Lord High Treas. Scotl.* VI. 181 To begary the samyne doublet, and to begary ane skyn coit, v ½ quarteris veluot. **1589** GREENE *Menaphon* (Arb.) 76 Am not I a Gentleman, though tirde in a shepheardes skincote.

†**2.** *transf.* A person's skin. *Obs.*

**1589** *Hay any work* (1844) 9, I will lay on load on your skincoat for this geare anon. *a* **1592** GREENE *Jas. IV*, I. Proh., Ay engraued the memory of Boughon on the skin-coate of some of them. **1611** COTGR., *Escailler*,..to beat, bethwacke, belabor the skin-coat of. **1653** URQUHART *Rabelais* II. xvii, I will have their skin-coat shaken once yet before they die.

†**skind**, *v. Obs.*$^{-1}$ [a. ON. *skynda* (so mod.Icel., Norw., and Sw.; Da. *skynde*), = OE. *scyndan*, OS. *skundian*, etc.] *trans.* To hasten.

*c* **1250** *Gen. & Ex.* 1989 Ðe chapmen skinden here fare, In to egipte ledden ðat ware.

**skin-deep**, *a.* and *adv.* [f. SKIN *sb.* 5 + DEEP *a.* and *adv.*]

**A.** *adj.* Penetrating no deeper than the skin; superficial, shallow, slight: **a.** As a proverbial limitation of beauty, or in similar connexions.

*a* **1613** OVERBURY *A Wife*, etc. Wks. (1856) 37 All the carnall beauty of my wife, Is but skin-deep. **1687** BOYLE *Martyrd. Theodora* iv. (1703) 49 Nor any of our sex ought to think skin-deep beauty as great a blessing, as 'tis an applauded one. **1725** RAMSAY *Gentle Sheph.* IV. ii, Beauty that's only skin deep Must fade like the gowans of May. **1740–1** RICHARDSON *Pamela* (1824) I. xcix. 484 Beauty is but a specious..recommendation, a mere skin-deep perfection. **1854** SPENCER *Personal Beauty* Ess. (1891) II. 394 The saying that beauty is but skin-deep, is but a skin-deep saying. **1869** MCLAREN *Serm.* Ser. II. v. 79 Moses' face shone, but the lustre was but skin deep.

**b.** Of wounds, incisions, etc. Also *transf.*

*a* **1613** OVERBURY *Charac., Ordinary Fencer* Wks. (1856) 112 His wounds are seldome above skin-deep. **1805** JEFFERSON *Writ.* (1830) IV. 30 The skin-deep scratches, which we can make or find on the surface of the earth. **1841** EMERSON *Method of Nat.* Wks. (Bohn) II. 222 But the thunder is a surface phenomenon, makes a skin-deep cut. **1877** A. B. EDWARDS *Up Nile* xix. 566 As for his wounds, they were literally skin-deep.

**c.** *fig.* in various contexts.

**1657** TRAPP *Comm., Ps.* xvi. 9 Their joy is but skin-deep. **1677** HORNECK *Gt. Law Consid.* vii. (1704) 399 A few slight and skin-deep reflexions. **1730** T. BOSTON *Mem.* xii. 434 Denoting the skin-deep joy of ungodly men. **1766** FORDYCE *Serm. Yng. Women* (1767) II. x. 130 Skin-deep and short-lived allurements. **1825** LADY GRANVILLE *Lett.* (1894) I. 362 The little faults are all skin-deep, and she is excellent. **1889** GRETTON *Memory's Harkback* 251 The effect upon the hearers was, after all, but skin-deep.

**B.** *adv.* To the depth of the skin; in a superficial manner; superficially, slightly.

**1633** P. FLETCHER *Purple Isl.* VII. xiv, Caro, cursed damme of sinne,..Yet seems (skin-deep) most fair. **1660** F. BROOKE tr. *Le Blanc's Trav.* 218 They have little horns which grow but skin-deep, mooving them as their ears. **1702** STEELE *Funeral* II, When I know her further than Skin-deep, I'll tell you more of my mind. **1796** BURKE *Regic. Peace* Wks. 1842 II. 288 Stings that have penetrated more than skin-deep into my mind. **1864** KINGSLEY *Rom. & Teut.* iv. (1875) 100 He was but a wild man of the woods..polished over skin-deep with Roman civilization.

**skin-diver.** [f. SKIN *sb.* + DIVER.] One who dives or swims underwater without a full diving suit or a fixed line to the surface. Hence **skin-diving** *vbl. sb.* and *ppl. a.*; [as back-formation] **skin-dive** *v. intr.*, to dive or swim underwater as a skin-diver; also as *sb.*, an act or instance of skin-diving.

**1932** *Blackw. Mag.* Jan. 20/1 They relied solely upon their skin divers—the divers' technical term for a naked man. **1938** D. LONG *Sailing all Seas in Idle Hour* ix. 121 The finest 'skin' divers in the world come from lonely atolls such as Penrhyn, where only 'skin' diving is allowed. **1950** SCHENK & KENDALL *Shallow Water Diving* iv. 74 This equipment is used in the sport commonly known as 'Goggling' or 'Skindiving'. **1951** *Skin Diver* Dec. 2 The name of *The Skin Diver* was picked because it includes everyone interested and participating in underwater fishing and hunting. *Ibid.*, We want to publish any and all items of interest to our skin diving readers. **1952** *Time* 17 Nov. 50/3 Bucher, poised on the rail of the small ship bobbing in the rough water, was aiming to become the first man ever to 'skin-dive' (*i.e.*, without the aid of artificial breathing apparatus) deeper than 115 ft. **1953** J. Y. COUSTEAU *Silent World* i. 9 Vanity coloured our early skin dives. We plumed ourselves at the thought that we latecomers could attain the working depths of pearl and sponge divers who had made their first plunges as infants. *Ibid.*, Dumas's skin-diving technique consisted of floating face under water and breathing through a schnorkel tube. **1959** L. SMITH *One Hour* v. 69 For hours, we'd engage in this philosophical skin-diving. **1964** M. MCLUHAN *Understanding Media* xxiii. 233 The smarter advertisers have made free with fur and fuzz, and blur and buzz. They have, in a word, taken a skin-dive. For that is what the TV viewer is. He is a skin-diver, and he no longer likes garish daylight on hard, shiny surfaces. **1966** T. PYNCHON *Crying of Lot 49* iii. 57 There stood Di Presso, in a skin-diving suit and wraparound shades. **1970** *Daily Colonist* (Victoria, B.C.) 14 Oct. 7/6 At Taveuni, the prince took time off to swim and skindive. **1973** J. LEASOR *Host of Extras* vii. 127 He adjusted his mask and went over backwards in the way of the trained skin-diver. **1975** *N.Y. Times* 6 Nov. 20/2 Skindiving Israeli scientists are exploring the sunken fortifications of the city of Acre. **1977** B. PYM *Quartet in Autumn* iv. 37 'It's the swimming that would attract me.' 'You mean skin-diving and that sort of thing?'

**'skinflint.** Also 7–9 **skin-flint.** [f. SKIN *v.* 4 c + FLINT *sb.*] One who would skin a flint to save or gain something; an avaricious, penurious, mean or niggardly person; a miser.

*a* **1700** B. E. *Dict. Cant. Crew, Skin-flint*, a griping,..close-fisted Fellow. **1761** A. MURPHY *Citizen* II. i. An old miserly good for nothing skin-flint. **1791** A. WILSON *Laurel Disputed* Poet. Wks. (1846) 125 How skin-flint graned his pocks o' goud to loss. **1816** SCOTT *Antiquary* xi, It would have been long..ere my womankind could have made such a reasonable bargain with that old skinflint. **1840** THACKERAY *Catherine* x, It is a pity that old skinflint should be in the way of both your fortunes. **1891** C. ROBERTS *Adrift Amer.* 226 Which sum the captain, who was a regular skinflint, said was far too much.

**b.** *attrib.* or as *adj.* Miserly, mean.

**1789** PARKER *Life's Painter* xiv. 114 The miser, that skin-flint old elf. **1854** H. MILLER *Sch. & Schm.* v. (1857) 86 The skin-flint wife of a 'paper minister'. **1895** ZANGWILL *Master* II. vii, By persuading some small skinflint dealer to cheat him.

Hence **'skinflinty** *a.*, niggardly; **'skinflintily** *adv.*, in a niggardly manner; **'skinflintiness**, **'skinflintism**, niggardliness, parsimony.

**1861** *Lond. Rev.* 16 Feb. 170 Love of approbation,..for the time, conquers her native skinflintiness. **1886** F. R. STOCKTON *Casting away of Mrs. Lecks & Mrs. Aleshine* II. 122 If he undertook to be skinflinty he'd better try it on somebody else besides us. **1893** *Columbus* (Ohio) *Disp.* 10 July, The rewards of 'skinflintism' are not great in the long run. **1899** *Daily News* 19 Sept. 6/1 He behaved skin-flintily to Max Müller. **1901** *Munsey's Mag.* XXV. 431/2 The man with the skinflinty heart.

**skin fold.** *Med.* Also **skin-fold, skinfold.** [f. SKIN *sb.* + FOLD *sb.*[3]] A fold of skin and underlying fat formed by pinching, as a measure of nutritional status; freq. *attrib.*, as ***skinfold thickness***; **skinfold cal(l)iper(s)**, a pair of callipers for measuring the thickness of such a fold.

**1921** *Amer. Jrnl. Physical Anthrop.* IV. 224 For the estimate of the quantity of the skin and of the subcutaneous fat, the writer uses the thickness of the skin fold on the upper arm, above the biceps; on the forearm..and on the abdomen. **1950** *Nutrition Abstr. & Rev.* XX. 250 Pinching a skinfold to obtain a rough estimate of the thickness of the subcutaneous adipose tissue and, by inference, of the fatness or leanness of a subject, is an old clinical procedure. **1954** *Jrnl. Lab. & Clin. Med.* XLIII. 969 The skinfold thickness is read to the nearest half millimeter on the slide scale. *Ibid.* 970 A skinfold caliper..which is easily manipulated with one hand. **1961** L. MARTIN *Clin. Endocrinol.* (ed. 3) ii. 54 Measurements by skin-fold calipers have shown that from birth until three months..there is a rapid increase in fat deposition. **1973** *Times* 17 May 20/1 Using skinfold calipers, designed by and for doctors working on obesity, the thickness of the fat layer at four sites on the body is measured. **1977** *Lancet* 1 Jan. 17/2 Skinfold thickness measurements provide a non-invasive and reproducible means of measuring subcutaneous fat in newborn babies.

**'skinful.** Also 9 **-full.** [f. SKIN *sb.* + -FUL.]

**1.** The quantity contained within the skin.

**1650** HOWELL *Lett.* III. 4, I could willingly..return this small skinfull of Bones to my common Mother.

**2.** A quantity that fills a skin vessel.

**1802** SOUTHEY *King Ramiro* xii, So he gave him..a skinful of wine to quench his thirst. **1863** KINGLAKE *Crimea* II. 195 That simple skinful of water which..is the life of men passing a desert. **1885** *Century Mag.* XXIX. 652/1 Well do I remember how at each well the first skinful [of water] was tasted all around.

**3.** As much as the skin can hold: **a.** As much as any one can drink.

**1788** *Columbian Mag.* Oct. 557/2 Determined, as they said, once more to get a *skin-full of liquor*. **1824** W. IRVING *T. Trav.* II. 234 When he has no liquor at all, or when he has a skinfull. **1839** THACKERAY *Fatal Boots* (1869) 348 On this night I had my little skinful,—for there was no stinting. **1886** W. GRAHAM *Social Problem* 203 Why should I work, when I..can get my skinful?

**b.** *transf.* A full allowance; as much as one wants or cares for.

*a* **1779** D. GRAHAM *Leper the Taylor* I. Writ. 1883 II. 116 Poor Sandy went home with a skinful of terror. **1869** W. S. GILBERT *Bab Ball., Sir Macklin* v, He wept to think each thoughtless youth Contained of wickedness a skinful. **1897** *Pall Mall Mag.* Dec. 501 His men had had a skinful of fighting and short commons just before.

**'skinhead.** *colloq.* [f. SKIN *sb.* + HEAD *sb.*[1]]

**1.** (A person with) a bald head.

**1953** BERREY & VAN DEN BARK *Amer. Thes. Slang* (1954) §430/5 Bald-headed man,..cue ball, skinhead, turret top. **1957** M. SHULMAN *Rally round Flag, Boys!* vi. 66 Oscar was a bow-legged, barrel-chested man with a skin head. **1976** 'O. JACKS' *Assassination Day* v. 85 'Ow long you gonna be, skinhead?.. Your wig's slipping.

**2.** A person with a shaven head or closely cropped hair; *spec.* (*a*) a recruit to the U.S. Marine Corps; (*b*) in the U.K., a youth (often one of a gang), also typically characterized by wearing workman-like clothing and heavy boots, and by a tendency to aggressive behaviour.

**1953** BERREY & VAN DEN BARK *Amer. Thes. Slang* (1954) §825/2 Cue ball, skinhead, a fellow with a crew haircut. **1956** *Amer. Speech* XXXI. 190 He will administer a royal chewing out (tongue lashing) to the hapless skinheads (recruits; so-called because of their completely shaven heads). **1969** *Daily Mirror* 3 Sept. 12/1 A group of teenagers ..wear tight and rather short jeans, collarless T-shirts, exposed braces, big steel-capped boots and hair erased almost to their scalps. The lack of hair is what gives them their generic names..crop-heads, skin-heads or peanuts. The boots are good for kicking. **1971** *Daily Tel.* 13 Apr. 1 Gangs of Hell's Angels and skinheads marred Easter Monday seaside outings. **1973** C. MULLARD *Black Britain* IV. xi. 131 According to an eye-witness a gang of white skinheads savagely attacked a black youth who today is nearly blind as a result. **1975** I. SHAW *Nightwork* vii. 84 The skinheads are preparing the ground... One morning we'll wake up and the tanks will be rolling down Pennsylvania Avenue and the machine guns will be on every roof. **1978** *Lancashire Life* Apr. 27/1 The index can be visualised: Beats, Jesus Freaks, Groupies, Skinheads, Punks..the procession seems endless, and to many is evoked by one word—Hippies. **1980** *Herald* (Melbourne) 9 Apr. 5/3 Thousands of skinheads shouting Nazi slogans invaded the resort in special trains.

**skink** (skɪŋk), *sb.*[1] *Zool.* Forms: α. 6, 9 **scinc**, 7, 9 **scinck**, 7–9 **scink**. β. 7 **skinke**, 8 **skinc(k**, 6– **skink**. [a. older F. *scinc* (now *scinque*), or ad. L. *scincus*, ad. Gr. σκίγκος.] A small lizard (*Scincus officinalis*) common in northern Africa and Arabia, formerly regarded as of great value in medicine for its stimulative qualities; also, any lizard belonging to the same family (the *Scincidæ*).

α. **1590** BARROUGH *Meth. Physick* 182 Also the parts of scinces which embrace the reines. **1608** TOPSELL *Serpents* (1658) 693 There have been some that have reckoned Scinks and Lizards among worms. **1681** GREW *Musæum* I. iii. 48 The Scink..hath..short Legs, a flat and broad Foot like a Hand, with very short Toes. **1775** *Phil. Trans.* LXV. 246 Gulls, the scink, the leech,..&c. are all said to feel.. approaching changes of weather. **1802** SHAW *Gen. Zool.* III. I. 281 The Scink is one of the middle-sized or smaller lizards. **1854** *Orr's Circ. Sci., Org. Nat.* I. 275 Herbivorous ..scinks, called, on account of the shape of the teeth, *cyclodus*. **1872** HUMPHRY *Myology* 37 In the Scinc this portion..is quite separate in its whole length.

β. **1591** SYLVESTER *Du Bartas* I. vi. 200 Th' horned Cerastes, th' Alexandrian Skink. **1601** HOLLAND *Pliny* II. 316 Much like to this kind is the Skink (whom some haue named the land Crocodile). **1718** QUINCY *Compl. Disp.* 171 Skincks.—Some Authors have ascribed much to these as Alexipharmicks. **1831** GRIFFITH tr. *Cuvier* IX. 237 The skink of pharmacopolists..does not exceed the length of six or eight inches. **1880** *Cassell's Nat. Hist.* IV. 296 The Skink inhabits the western and northern parts of Africa.

*attrib.* and *Comb.* **1790** J. WHITE *Jrnl. Voy. N.S. Wales* 242 The Scincoid, or Skinc-formed Lizard. **1896** LYDEKKER *Roy. Nat. Hist.* V. 166 The skink tribe..are a very numerous family.

**skink**, *sb.*[2] Now *rare.* Also 7 **skinck, skinke.** [In sense 1 ad. early mod.Du. or LG. *schenke*, repr. MDu., MLG., and MHG. *schenke* (rarely *schinke*), OS. *skenkio*, OHG. *scenko*, *scencho*, etc. In sense 2 from SKINK *v.*]

**1.** A skinker; a tapster or waiter. In later use only *spec.* (see quot. 1847).

**1603** J. DAVIES (Heref.) *Microcosmos* Wks. (Grosart) I. 21/1 O Skinck, how blessed wert thou in his loue That drue thee on. **1786** *Francis the Philanthropist* I. 172 Mr. Francis and his companion had friends of every rank, from the humble skink to the dignified..doctor. **1847** HALLIW. s.v., In a family the person latest at breakfast is called the *skink*, or the *skinker*, and some domestic office is imposed or threatened for the day, such as ringing the bell, putting coal on the fire, or, in other cases, drawing the beer for the family.

**2. a.** *Sc.* Drink, liquor. (In contemptuous use.)

**1824** SCOTT *St. Ronan's* xxxii, The wine!..puir, thin, fushionless skink it was. **1844** BALLANTINE *Miller Deanhaugh* xvi. 247 Jail beer was poor, thin skink for gentlemen who had drank claret after dinner every day for twenty years.

**b.** *pl.* (See quot.)

**1888** JACOBI *Printers' Vocab.* 126 *Skinks*, an old term applied to drink—or drinking around the imposing stone in order to celebrate some auspicious occasion.

**skink**, *sb.*[3] *Sc.* Now *Obs.* exc. *Hist.* Also 7 **skinck.** [prob. ad. MLG. *schinke* (see next), either with ellipse of some word for 'broth', or with simple transference from the meat to the liquid.] A kind of soup made from shin of beef. Also *attrib.*

*c* **1575** BALFOUR *Practicks* (1754) 235 The air sall haue.. ane butter-plait, ane skink-plait, ane beif plait, ane luggit disch. **1602** in Henderson *Old World Scotl.* (1893) 14 Ane dische of bruise, and ane uther of skink or kaill. **1626** BACON *Sylva* §45 Wee finde also that Scotch Skinck (which is a Pottage of strong Nourishment,) is made with the Knees, and Sinewes of Beefe, but long boiled. *a* **1682** SEMPILL *Blythsome Wedding* 72 There will be meal-kail and castocks, And skink to sup till you rive. **1790** SHIRREFS *Poems* 210 Guid barley broth and *skink* came next. **1844** H. STEPHENS *Bk. Farm* II. 169 It was of this piece that the old favourite soup of Scotland, called *skink*, was made. **1893** HENDERSON *Old World Scotl.* 57 Its quality was very similar to that of the strong Lowland soup called skink.

†**skink**, *sb.*[4] *Obs.*$^{-1}$ [ad. LG. *schinke* (G. *schinken*), OHG. *scinca*, *scinco*.] Ham.

**1630** J. TAYLOR (Water P.) *Gt. Eater Kent* 12 He cares not for..the sawsedge of Bolognia, the skink of Westphalia.

†**skink**, *sb.*[5] Obs. variant of SKUNK *sb.*

**1774** GOLDSM. *Nat. Hist.* III. ix. 381 The skink.. resembles a polecat in shape and size. **1809** *Spirit Public Jrnls.* XIII. 2 Where'er the skink-ey'd Gallic pest Flings taint and uproar o'er the ball. **1824** COLERIDGE *Aids Refl.* (1848) I. 90 As..the skink and squash are treated by American woodmen, who turn their backs upon the fetid intruder.

**skink**, *v.* Now *dial.* or *arch.* Forms: 4 **skynke**, 6–7 **skinke** (6 **skincke**, 7 **scinke**); 6 (9) **skynk**, **skinck**, 6– **skink**. [ad. MDu. or MLG. *schenken* (cf. OFris. *skenka*; ON. *skenkja*, Sw. *skänka*, Da. *skænke*), corresp. to OE. *scencan* SHENCH *v.*]

**1.** *trans.* To pour out or draw (liquor); to offer, present, serve (drink, etc.).

*c* **1386** CHAUCER *Merch. T.* 478 Bacus the wyn hem skynketh al aboute. **1513** DOUGLAS *Æneid* VII. iii. 90 In flacon and in skull Thai skynk the wyne. **1607** W. BARKSTED *Mirrha* (1876) 45 The Queen of loue..forc'd her to skinke so much, the iuice ran ore. **1635** SHIRLEY *Lady of Pleas.* IV.

ii, A drawer is my Ganymede: he shall skink Brisk nectar to us. **1667** DAVENANT & DRYDEN *Tempest* IV. iii, Hem! skink about his grace's health again. **1728** RAMSAY *Last Sp. Miser* xxvii, And like dub-water skink the wine. **1806** R. JAMIESON *Pop. Ballads* I. 221 They skinked the mead, and they skinked the wine. **1899** LUMSDEN *Edin. Poems & Sangs* 130 Stout Scots drink to me skynk.

†**2.** To fill with liquor; to pour liquor into. *Obs.*

**1513** DOUGLAS *Æneid* VII. iii. 62 Now skynk, and offer Jupiter, coupis full. **1558** PHAER *Æneid* VII. S iv b, Now skinke your cups to Ioue, and great Anchises cheerely cal. **1594** GREENE & LODGE *Looking Gl.* H, Ile haue them skincke my standing bowles with wine.

**3.** *absol.* To draw, pour out, or serve drink; to wait on a company (see quot. 1785).

**1591** FLETCHER *Russe Commonw.* (Hakl. Soc.) 17 For that cause [they] called this newe citie by the name of Naloi, that is skinck or poure in. **1594** GREENE & LODGE *Looking Gl.* Wks. (Grosart) XIV. 93 Villaines, why skinck you not vnto this fellow? **1630** J. TAYLOR (Water P.) *Penniless Pilgr.* Wks. I. 123/2 And No-body did drinke, and winke, and scinke. **1676** HOBBES *Iliad* I. 562 And then the Gods laught.. outright, To see the lame and sooty Vulcan skink. **1755** SMOLLETT *Don Quixote* IV. xiv. II. 425 Truce with your compliments and skink away, honest Tosilos. **1785** GROSE *Dict. Vulgar T.*, To *skink*, is to wait on the company, ring the bell, stir the fire, and snuff the candles; the duty of the youngest officer in a military mess. *a* **1825** FORBY *Voc. E. Anglia* 304 *Skink*, to serve at table; particularly to serve the guests with drink. **1845** S. JUDD *Margaret* II. vi. (1871) 260 Come crush a glass with.. all this nice company. You have skinked quite long enough.

†**4.** *Sc.* To make a present of; to make *over* to another. *Obs. rare.*

**1508** *Burgh Rec. Edin.* (1882) I. 117 Vpoun his gude warkmaneschip and gyding thai skynk him the tymmer of the auld ruf. **1637** RUTHERFORD *Lett.* (1848) lxxxv. 156 If this had not been, I would have skinked over and foregone my part of paradise and salvation, for a breakfast of dead, moth-eaten earth. *Ibid.* lxxxviii. 163 Do we not sit far in our own light, to make it a matter of bairn's play, to skink and drink over paradise.

Hence '**skinked** *ppl. a.*

**1598** FLORIO, *Mesciuto*, skinkt, powred or filde wine.

†'**skinkard.** *Obs. rare.* Also 7 skinkird. [f. SKINK *v.* + -ARD.] A tapster.

**1615** BRATHWAIT *Strappado* (1878) 11 To be a drudge.. Vnto the base-borne Skinkird bred in Hell. **1632** MARMION *Holland's Leaguer* II. iii, Thou hast a noble wit and spirit, wench, That never was ordained for any skinkard T'engender with.

**skinker** ('skɪnkə(r)). Now *arch.* or *dial.* Also 6 scincker, skincker, skynker. [ad. MDu. or MLG. *schencker* (*schincker*), or f. SKINK *v.* + -ER[1].]

**1.** One who draws, pours out, or serves liquor; a tapster; (see also quot. 1847 s.v. SKINK *sb.*[2] 1).

**1586** *Praise of Musicke* 51 That banquet of the gods where Vulcan plaid the skinker. **1603** HOLLAND *Plutarch's Mor.* 444 The butler or skinker asked him how much he should poure out for everie one. **1647** C. HARVEY *Schola Cordis* vi. 3 See how the hellish skinker plies his bowle. **1681** T. FLATMAN *Heraclitus Ridens* No. 15 (1713) I. 98 From rebellious Taps, and Tapsters and Skinkers, *Libera nos.* **1702** S. PARKER tr. *Cicero's De Finibus* II. 63 My Skinker perceives himself.. agreably affected in filling me out a Glass when he has no Inclination to drink. **1813** J. HOGG *Queen's Wake* 24 Thrice did they drain th' allotted store And wondering skinkers dun for more. **1830** LAMB *Let. to W. Wordsworth* Wks. 1900 XII. 128 [Vulcan] the two-handed skinker. **1852** HAWTHORNE *Blithedale Rom.* II. xi. 206 Some old-fashioned skinkers and drawers.. were spreading a banquet. **1887** BROWNING *Parleyings* Wks. 1896 II. 733/2 The skinker fast brimmed Their glass with rare tipple's enticement.

†**b.** The constellation Aquarius. *Obs.*

**1591** SYLVESTER *Du Bartas* I. iv. 278 Mean-while the Skinker, from his starry spout, After the Goat, a silver stream pours out. *Ibid.* II. ii. IV. *Columnes* 418 On th' Azure steep Our Parents plac't a Skinker: and by him, Two silver Fishes in his floods to swim.

†**2.** A jug or similar vessel used for skinking with. Also *attrib. Obs.*

**1594** *Wills & Invent. N.C.* (Surtees, 1860) 245 The butterye.. ij hodgsheads,.. j quarte potte, j skinker. **1600** *Will of Sir R. Bedingfeild* (Somerset Ho.), Silver wine pot called a Skynker. **1639** *12th Rep. Hist. MSS. Comm.* App. IX. 7 Four great flagons... 10 Skinker potts. 7 Tankards. **1646** *Will of Estcourt* (Somerset Ho.), A deepe silver bason with a silver skinker.

'**skinking,** *vbl. sb.* [f. SKINK *v.*] The action of pouring out or serving liquor. Also *attrib.*

**1592** R. D. *Hypnerotomachia* 57 The skinking pottes.. were all of pure fine Gold. **1598** FLORIO, *Versatione*,.. a skinking. **1611** *Ibid.*, A powring or skinking forth. **1631** MABBE *Celestina* ix. 105, I know no better office at the board, then to fall a skinking. **1819** W. TENNANT *Papistry Storm'd* (1827) 102 Had Bacchus sell been there,.. for skinkin', He couldna weil hae blam'd the drinkin'.

'**skinking,** *ppl. a.* [f. SKINK *v.*]

**1.** That skinks; wine-giving.

**1582** STANYHURST *Æneis* III. (Arb.) 74 With nauye we passed By mounts of Nazon too skincking Bacchus alotted.

**2.** *Sc.* Thin, watery. (Cf. SKINK *sb.*[2] 2.)

**1786** BURNS *To a Haggis* viii, Auld Scotland wants nae skinking ware That jaups in luggies. *a* **1894** STEVENSON *St. Ives* xxvii, A pint of skinking claret.

**skinkle** ('skɪnk(ə)l), *v. Sc.* [perh. a frequentative f. ON. *skína* to shine.] *intr.* To glitter, glisten, sparkle; to have a showy appearance.

**17..** *Lord Thomas* xix. in Percy *Reliques*, It skinkled in their een. **1791** A. WILSON *Laurel Disputed* Poet. Wks. (1846) 127 Ae night the lift was skinkling a' wi' starns. **1888** *Glasgow Evening Times* 15 Oct. 2/6 A handful of flame which.. merely skinkles on the window-panes.

Hence '**skinkling** *ppl. a.*

**1790** A. WILSON *Poems* 205 Row't in a skinklan plaid. *c* **1795** ? BURNS *Poem on Pastoral Poetry* iv, Squire Pope but busks his skinklin patches, O' heathen tatters! **1819** W. TENNANT *Papistry Storm'd* (1827) 30 Or flee about on skinklin' wing, Like butterflies. **1849** SYMINGTON *Harebell Chimes* 104 Death lurks in its skinkling fire.

**skinless** ('skɪnlɪs), *a.* Forms: 5 skin-, skynles, 6 skinne-, 6–7 skinlesse, 8– skinless. [f. SKIN *sb.* + -LESS.] Destitute or deprived of skin; having only a very thin skin; *spec.* of sausages and similar meats.

*c* **1340** HAMPOLE *Med. Pass.* in Horstman (1895) I. 98 þe fleisch þere þe cros sittith is skinles & ouer-runne wiþ bloodrowis. **1484** CAXTON *Fables of Æsop* v. ix, The wulf ranne aweye skynles. **1594** T. B. *La Primaud. Fr. Acad.* II. 59 The head woulde bee very deformed if it were skinnelesse, where it is couered with haire. **1600** *Hosp. Incurable Fooles* A iv, Those skinlesse Snailes that lift vp their hornes for nothing. **1611** COTGR., *Fricandeaux*, short, skinlesse, and daintie puddings. **1706** LONDON & WISE *Retir'd Gard.* I. vii. 28 The.. skinless Pear is a kind of Russelet in Shape and Taste. **1738** *Gentl. Mag.* VIII. 310/1 What is it that's born Skinless, flies Wingless, and goes roaring to Death? **1850** KINGSLEY *A. Locke* xxi, He was looking.. at the skinless cast on the chimney-piece. *Ibid.*, He looked round again at the skinless man. **1891** ATKINSON *Last of Giant-killers* 78 He [the raven] pranced about on his [the wolf's] scraggy skinless carcase. **1954** *Food Manufacture* 1 Nov. p. xi (Advt.), Visking food and sausage casings are.. available through Viskase Limited... Visking Nojax for skinless sausages. **1959** E. H. CLEMENTS *High Tension* vi. 119 'He'd bring.. *cevabcici*—'... 'Sausages, you mean.' 'Oh yes... Special skinless ones.. from a shop in Soho.' **1968** R. CLAPPERTON *No News on Monday* v. 52, I helped myself to a couple of skinless sausages from the refrigerator. **1972** D. BLOODWORTH *Any Number can Play* xvii. 170 He.. had.. eaten a tin of skinless frankfurters with a purée of mashed yam.

*fig.* **1859** *Sat. Rev.* 19 Mar. 331/2 There was nothing in it to make the most skinless man in existence wince.

Hence '**skinlessly** *adv.*

**1859** BOYD *Recreat. Country Parson* (1862) 86 Not only are they themselves skinlessly sensitive [etc.].

'**skinlet.** *rare.* [f. SKIN *sb.* + -LET.] A thin skin; a membrane.

**1598** FLORIO, *Cuticula*, a filme, a skin or skinlet, a thin rinde or pill. *Ibid.*, *Milza*,.. a filme or skinlet.

**skinned** (skɪnd), *ppl. a.* [f. SKIN *sb.* and *v.*]

**I. 1. a.** Having a skin, *esp.* of a specified kind.

*c* **1400** MAUNDEV. (1839) xix. 206 In another Yle ben folk, that gon upon hire Hondes and hire Feet, as Bestes: and thei ben alle skynned and fedred. **1611** COTGR., *Marmote*,.. a little muddie fish, headed, skinned, and finned, like an Eele. **1641** BROME *Joviall Crew* III, Oh here they come. They are delicately skin'd and limb'd. **1655** MOUFET & BENNET *Health's Improv.* (1746) 260 Skate is skin'd like a File. **1727** *Philip Quarll* (1754) 3 These Fish are.. skinned like a Mackerel.

**b.** With defining term prefixed, as ***clean-***, ***dark-***, ***fox-***, ***hard-***, ***loose-***, etc.

See also THICK- and THIN-SKINNED.

**1450–80** tr. *Secreta Secret.* 32 Kepe the fro fische þat is hard skynned. **1523** FITZHERB. *Husb.* § 56 Se that he [an ox] haue a brode ryb, and a thycke hyde, and to be lose-skinned. **1598–** [see ROUGH-SKINNED *a.*]. **1611** COTGR., *Poire d'amiot*, a yellow, and hard-skind Peare. **1665** BRATHWAIT *Comment. Two Tales* (1900) 45 What Sir Raynard, ye fox-skin'd Chuffe. **1827** [see FAIR *a.* 18]. **1893** F. ADAMS *New Egypt* 58 An English official,.. having a lean, clean-skinned body. **1897** WATTS-DUNTON *Aylwin* III. vi, A bright-eyed, dark-skinned little girl.

**2.** Of wounds, etc.: Covered with skin. Also with *over*.

**1640** BP. REYNOLDS *Passions* xxvii. 288 Which like a skinn'd wound doth wrankle inwardly. **1739** S. SHARP *Surg.* p. xxx, The Edges of it in process of time, tuck in, and growing skinn'd and hard, give it the Name of a callous Ulcer. **1760–72** H. BROOKE *Fool of Qual.* (1809) IV. 90 My wounds, though not skinned, were healing apace. **1809** MALKIN *Gil Blas* XI. ix. ¶6 A wound imperfectly skinned over.

**3.** Covered with a layer (of something).

**1684** T. BURNET *Theory Earth* I. 145 When the earth grows discolour'd and skin'd over. **1837** WORDSW. *Musings near Aquapendente* 193 From pavement skinned with moss.

**II. 4. a.** Stripped of the skin.

**1673** RAY *Journ. Low C.* 404 Their [frogs'] flesh shows white and lovely as they lie in the markets skin'd and ready prepared. **1826** SCOTT *Woodstock* xxxii, The boy, whose appearance [was] not much dissimilar to that of a skinned rabbit in a livery. **1861** *Macm. Mag.* June 131 Birds and their eggs, skinned animals, and insects.

**b.** *colloq.* In phr. ***to keep one's eye skinned***, etc., to keep a sharp look-out.

**1833** *Political Examiner* (Shelbyville, Kentucky) 22 June 4/1, I wish I may be shot if I dont think you had better keep your eyes skinned so that you can look powerful sharp, lest we get rowed up the river this heat. *a* **1859** *Traits Amer. Humor* (Bartlett), Keep your eye skinned for sign. **1887** FARRELL *How He Died* 22 The reverend josser.. kept his eye skinned. **1898** KIPLING *Fleet in Being* iii, We kept a skinned eye on her.

**c.** Beaten, bested, overcome completely; esp. in *to have* (*got*) (a person or object) ***skinned.*** *colloq.* (orig. *U.S.*).

**1904** 'O. HENRY' *Cabbages & Kings* iii. 56, I guess you've got us skinned on the animal and vegetation question. **1908** 'YESLAH' *Tenderfoot S. Calif.* ii. 22 When it rains in California, it's got all the rest of the country skinned to death. **1913** R. BROOKE *Let.* c 23 July in *Coll. Poems* (1918) Mem. p. lxxxiv, 'Sir, I may tell you that in my opinion you have Mr. Noyes skinned.' That means I'm better than him. **1927** E. WALLACE *Feathered Serpent* iv. 47, I came down here to make a few inquiries... I've got these reporter guys skinned to death!

**d.** = SKINT *a.* Also with *out. colloq.*

**1935** A. J. POLLOCK *Underworld Speaks* 107/1 *Skinned out*, broke; without funds. **1957** C. MACINNES *City of Spades* I. xii. 93 Why's he left me skinned in hopeless destitution? **1958** *Observer* 14 Dec. 7/8 I'm skinned, I know I can always count on someone helpin' me.

**skinner**[1] ('skɪnə(r)). Forms: 5 scynner(e, schynnere, skynnar(e, 6 skynar, 5–7 skynner, 6– skinner. [f. SKIN *sb.* or *v.* + -ER[1]. Cf. ON. *skinnari*, MSw. *skinnare*, Norw. *skinnar.*]

**1.** One whose work or business is concerned with the preparation of skins for commercial purposes.

**1398** TREVISA *Barth. De P.R.* XVIII. lxxv. (Bodl. MS.), [The cat] is ofte for his faire skynne itake of þe skynner and islayne & ihuylded. **1418** *Nottingham Rec.* II. 116 Johanne Crophyll, skynner. **1484** CAXTON *Fables of Æsop* v. xvii, Theyr skynnes were good for to make mantels with, yf skynners myght haue them. **1542** BOORDE *Dyetary* (1870) 249 Let your skynner cut both the sortes of the skynnes in smale peces tryangle wyse. **1592** GREENE *Upst. Courtier* Wks. (Grosart) XI. 268 He began to tell me that by his art he was a Skinner. **1600** SURFLET *Countrie Farme* 873 The skinners are woont to make stomachers to lay ouer the stomacke. **1675** OGILBY *Britannia* Introd., The Principal Companies are the Mercers,.. Skinners. **1859** C. BARKER *Assoc. Principle* ii. 45 One Hinde, a citizen and skinner of London, lent to Henry IV. the sum of £2000. **1882** *Encycl. Brit.* XIV. 852/2 Seven of the livery companies of London.., the Mercers',.. the Salters',.. and the Skinners'.

*attrib.* **1794** R. GRAY in Scott *Stat. Acc. Perth* (1796) 38 This corporation has a very convenient skinner-work.

**2. a.** One who removes the skin; a flayer.

**1699** DAMPIER *Voy.* II. II. iii. 98 Then the Hockser immediately Mounts, and Rides after more Game, leaving the other to the Skinners, who are at hand, and ready to take off his Hide. **1884** *Good Words* June 391/1 In districts where the game is abundant more skinners were enlisted.

**b.** An implement used for skinning animals.

**1872** *Amer. Naturalist* VI. 223 The specimen could have been used as a knife, or 'skinner', although now its edge is too irregular and dull for skinning.

**3.** *U.S.* One of a number of marauders who committed depredations on the neutral ground between the British and American lines during the War of Independence.

**1775–83** [see COW-BOY 2]. **1821** J. F. COOPER *Spy* i, This poor opinion of the Skinners was not confined to Mr. Cæsar Thompson. **1825** J. NEAL *Bro. Jonathan* III. 290 Who knows but you are one o' the tories yourself.. or one o' the skinners? **1857** [see COW-BOY 2]. **1882** LECKY *Engl. in 18th Cent.* IV. 129 The loyalist banditti called the Skinners.

**4. a.** (See quot.)

**1856** MAYHEW *Gt. World London* 46 'Skinners,' or women and boys who strip children of their clothes.

**b.** A fleecer. Also in racing slang (see quot. 1874 and cf. SKIN *v.* 7 c); esp. common in Australia to mean (*a*) a horse that wins a race at very long odds; (*b*) any betting coup.

**1856** DORAN *Knights & their Days* ix. 142 They are constituted the legal skinners of all sojourners among them. **1874** *Slang Dict.* 293 *Skinner*, a term among bookmakers. 'May we have a skinner,' i.e., may we skin the lamb. **1893** *Westm. Gaz.* 13 Apr. 5/2 Yesterday's race.. resulted in what the sporting public, high and low, graphically describe as a 'skinner'. The bookmakers.. do the skinning. **1903** A. M. BINSTEAD *Pitcher in Paradise* xii. 292 A skinner!—great-balls-of-fire! a skinner! **1907** A. WRIGHT *Keane of Kalgoorlie* 66 Although he had gone up in the weights considerably, his owner decreed that he should win the Rosehill handicap, and give the 'shop' another 'skinner'. **1930** *Technique of Betting* 7 Frequently a race is won by a horse against which the bookmaker has not laid any bet, and the book then shows a profit of 100%—the bookmaker has what he calls a 'skinner'. **1934** T. WOOD *Cobbers* viii. 96 Charles.. would lay two to one port-wine jelly, five to apple-pie... Tonight we had college pudding and jam tart. Charles.. said it was a skinner for the books. **1974** *Sydney Morning Herald* 8 Oct. 17 Skinner for bookmakers. **1977** A. C. H. SMITH *Jericho Gun* v. 60 At twelve to one, which is the forecast SP here, it's a skinner.

**5.** One who makes skin to grow. In quot. *fig.*

**1660** GAUDEN *Slight Healers Publick Hurts* 43 Pretenders to heal, superficial skinners.

**6.** (See quots.)

**1881** DAY *Fishes Gt. Brit.* I. 278 Poullach.. In the Channel those the size of a whiting are termed codlings and skinners. **1881** *Cassell's Nat. Hist.* V. 59 When Cod are of the size of Whiting they are termed Codlings and 'Skinners'.

**7.** A driver of a team of horses or mules; occas. also, a lorry driver. *N. Amer.*

**1870** [see *mule skinner* s.v. MULE[1] 5 c]. **1910** E. FERGUSON *Janey Canuck in West* 91 The teamsters are called 'skinners'. I met them all on the log road. **1924** *Scribner's Mag.* Dec. 645/1 The skinner with the longest words travels the fastest. **1929** *Amer. Speech* V. 147 Since the driver of the old time orecar was called a *mule-skinner* or *mule-whacker*, the driver of the modern motor-propelled car is a *motor-skinner*, sometimes just a *trammer*. **1939** J. STEINBECK *Grapes of Wrath* ii. 14 A guy that never been a truck skinner don't know nothin' what it's like. **1954** E. F. HAGELL *When Grass was Free* 3 A single line attached to the next leader's bit and passed back along the teams to the teamster or 'skinner'.

**8.** ***a skinner*** semi-adj.: 'skint', broke; empty. *N.Z. colloq.*

**1943** *New Writing* XVIII. 68 So I paid for the pair of us, which left me practically a skinner. **1967** *Landfall* XXI. 241 Sure you're a skinner? Not a drop in the place, I mean? **1981** *Macquarie Dict.* (s.v. *skinner*), The beer's a skinner.

**Skinner**[2] ('skɪnə(r)). The name of the American psychologist, B. F. *Skinner* (b. 1904), used *attrib.* to indicate the theories or methods concerned with conditioning human or animal behaviour associated with him; esp. as ***Skinner box***, a box in which an animal is isolated, equipped essentially with a bar or other device that it learns to use either to obtain a reward or to escape punishment.

**1938** *Jrnl. Exper. Psychol.* XXIII. 507 A modified form of the Skinner apparatus. **1940** *Ibid.* XXVI. 614 (*heading*) The variability of extinction scores in 'Skinner-box' experiments. **1951** E. R. HILGARD in S. S. Stevens *Handbk. Exper. Psychol.* 530/1 It is possible to train animals in the Skinner box to do what the experimenter wishes. **1962** *Listener* 13 Sept. 390/1 The technique for measuring the pressure applied to a lever by a rat in a Skinner-box. **1973** *Nature* 27 July 241/3 The method of 'operant conditioning' in a Skinner box can be used to investigate physiological changes that accompany habit formation. **1980** BROWN & WALLACE *Physiol. Psychol.* xv. 457 Most of the principles of learning were derived from studies on a single animal (the white rat) in a single learning situation (instrumental conditioning in the Skinner box).

**Skinnerian** (skɪ'nɪərɪən), *a.* and *sb.* [f. prec. + -IAN.] **A.** *adj.* Of or pertaining to B. F. Skinner's behaviourist theories or methods. **B.** *sb.* A follower or adherent of B. F. Skinner.

**1958** *Psychol. Bull.* LV. 148/2 The studies to be reviewed in this paper follow this Skinnerian paradigm. **1964** H. J. EYSENCK *Exper. Behav. Therapy* II. 187 One possible reason why Skinnerians have restricted them-selves in this fashion. **1965** *Language* XLI. 98 The extreme Skinnerian view that the correct inductive generalization can be accomplished with no need for anything more than positive instances. **1977** H. J. EYSENCK *You & Neurosis* v. 168 Skinnerian behaviourism has become a 'school', in the same way as Freudianism did many years earlier. Skinnerians concentrate exclusively on a very small area of psychology. **1979** *Nature* 29 Nov. 440/1 The sales techniques used in Iran, and no doubt they are now being used in other Third World countries, were a balanced compound of Skinnerian Psychology and gangsterism.

So **'Skinnerism**, Skinnerian behaviourism.

**1969** *Times Educ. Suppl.* 16 May 1640/2, I fear the growth of Skinnerism and its rats and pigeons. **1979** *Nature* 24 May 355/1 They bring us a metatheoretical commitment to a hard-line Skinnerism, according to which even the editorial policy of the *Journal of the Experimental Analysis of Behavior* is dangerously revisionist.

**skinnery** ('skɪnərɪ). Also 5 **skynnery**. [f. SKIN *sb.* + -ERY.]

†**1.** Skins or furs collectively. *Obs.*

*c* **1460** J. RUSSELL *Bk. Nurture* 946 To drapery & skynnery euer haue ye a sight.

**2.** A place where skins are dealt with for commercial or other purposes; the working premises of a skinner.

**1480** *Wardr. Acc. Edw. IV* (1830) 131 Canvas in the Skynnery j. *Ibid.* 146 A lb' of threde delivered into the Skynnery for skynners to wirk with. **1483** *Cath. Angl.* 342/1 A Skynnery, *pelliparium.* **1827** MACKENZIE *Hist. Newcastle* II. 716 There are some extensive tan-yards and skinneries in Newcastle. **1883** J. MARTIN *Reminis. Old Haddington* 84 There was long ago a tannery and skinnery at its termination.

**'skinniness.** [f. SKINNY *a.*] The quality of being skinny; leanness, emaciation.

**1727** BAILEY, vol. II. [Hence in later Dicts.]

**skinning** ('skɪnɪŋ), *vbl. sb.* [f. SKIN *v.*]

**1. a.** The action or process of covering with skin, or of forming a new skin; cicatrization, healing. Also with *over*, and *fig.*

**1547** BOORDE *Brev. Health* 49 For skynnynge of a place there is nothing shal skyn so sone as it wyl. **1633** WOTTON *Lett.* (1907) II. 341 But whether these be perfect cures or but skinnings over..will appear hereafter. **1638** A. READ *Chirurg.* ix. 66 We are not to goe about the skinning of the wound before the flesh bee somewhat higher than the naturall skin. **1739** S. SHARP *Surg.* Introd. 2 The first Stage of Healing..is by Surgeons call'd Digestion;..and the last, or skinning-over, Cicatrization. **1793** J. HUNTER *Treat. Blood*, etc. Wks. 1837 III. 496 Therefore contracting and skinning are probably effects of one cause. **1813** J. THOMSON *Lect. Inflam.* 455 The parts towards the centre may be so long kept from skinning, that the granulations may become weak.

**b.** *Naut.* (See quots.)

**1846** A. YOUNG *Naut. Dict.* 284 *Skinning*, a term used for planking a vessel. *c* **1850** *Rudim. Nav.* (Weale) 138 *Planking*, covering the outside of the timbers with plank; sometimes.. called 'skinning'.

**2. a.** The removal, or stripping off, of skin; the fact of having the skin removed or rubbed off. Also *fig.*

**1775** in ASH. **1837** W. IRVING *Capt. Bonneville* I. 141 These..are bound to exert themselves..in taking beavers, which, without skinning, they render in at the trader's lodge. **1878** SPURGEON *Serm.* XXIV. 699 The skinning of flints and the driving of screws are practised by many people as if they were positively meritorious. **1891** C. ROBERTS *Adrift Amer.* 105 My feet were not yet quite well, after the skinning they had got coming over the trail from Wallace.

†**b.** Fleecing, plundering. *Obs. rare*$^{-1}$.

**1686** tr. *Chardin's Trav. Persia* 347 Places for the skinning of strangers, who are reputed to be rich.

**c.** Impoverishing, exhausting.

**1856** *Trans. Michigan State Agric. Soc.* VII. 171 The old plan of constant cropping without manure, or 'skinning', will ruin the land. **1888** *Harper's Mag.* Mar. 559 The skinning of the land by sending away its substance in hard wheat is an improvidence of natural resources.

**d.** A physical or verbal beating; a hammering. *U.S. slang.*

**1929** *Chicagoan* 17 Aug. 22/2 In this period he [*sc.* Carl Sandburg] wrote the poetic denunciation of the Rev. Billy Sunday that..remains as the most thorough skinning that the evangelist ever received. **1972** J. W. THOMPSON in W. King *Black Short Story Anthol.* 260 Daddy..has taught me several different ways to skin a cat, and that redhead doesn't know it yet, but he's got a skinning coming.

**3.** (See quot.) *slang.* Cf. SKIN *v.* 11.

**1973** *Daily Mail* 3 Apr. 19/4 *Skinning*, injecting drugs under the skin.

**4.** *attrib.*, as ***skinning-apparatus***, ***knife***, ***process***, ***table***.

**1835–6** *Todd's Cycl. Anat.* I. 602/2 The skinning process takes place in this stage. **1859** G. A. JACKSON *Diary* 8 Jan. in F. Hall *Hist. Colorado* (1890) II. 521 Dug and panned to-day until my belt knife was worn out; so will have to quit or use my skinning knife. **1864** WHEELWRIGHT *Spring Lapl.* 296 Hoping soon to see it lying on his skinning table! **1875** KNIGHT *Dict. Mech.* 2196/1 *Skinning-apparatus*, a mechanical appliance for removing the hides from animals. **1884** *Good Words* June 391/1 The skinning knives did duty as table knives.

**skinnis**, var. of ME. *kinnes*: see KIN *sb.*[1] 6 b.

**'skinnum.** [See quot. 1854.] A variety of domestic pigeon.

**1854** MEALL *Moubray's Poultry* 277 It is perhaps owing to the loose *skinny* eyes and bill..that they are vulgarly called 'Skinnums'. **1867** TEGETMEIER *Pigeons* ix. 100 My skinnum was in his hand. Hurrah! the prize was mine.

**skinny** ('skɪnɪ), *a.* and *sb.* [f. SKIN *sb.* + -Y[1].]

**A.** *adj.* **1.** Consisting or formed of skin; resembling skin or film; cutaneous, membranous.

**1573** BARET *Alv.* s.v. *Flie*, To flie with skinny winges. **1601** HOLLAND *Pliny* XXIII. Proem, The bones charged with purulent and skinnie matter. **1615** CROOKE *Body of Man* 236 Heere is also to be obserued a skinny Ligament. **1657** S. PURCHAS *Pol. Flying-Ins.* 6 The Bee hath four dry pellucid skinny wings. **1753** N. TORRIANO *Gangr. Sore Throat* 94 Those loosened Pieces of skinny Membranes. **1796** WITHERING *Brit. Plants* (ed. 3) III. 734 The middle row of scales the largest, all more or less membranaceous and skinny. **1805** *Med. Jrnl.* XIV. 71 Whirls..surrounded by a skinny sheath. **1875** JOWETT *Plato* (ed. 2) III. 660 So the hair sprang up in the skin, being of a skinny and stringy nature.

*fig.* **1641** MILTON *Ch. Govt.* I. Wks. 1851 III. 11 Settling in a skinny congealment of ease and sloth at the top.

*Comb.* **1822** *Hortus Anglicus* II. 351 *L. Scariosa*, Skinny cupped Liatris.

**2. a.** Of, pertaining to, or affecting, the skin. *rare.*

**1611** COTGR., *Peaucier*, skinnie; of, in, or belonging to, the skinne. **1737** BRACKEN *Farriery Impr.* (1756) I. 186 In cutaneous or skinny Distempers. *Ibid.* 246 An excellent Medicine in Skinny Disorders.

**b.** Lying next the skin.

**1675** HAN. WOOLLEY *Gentlew. Comp.* 114 Take the rump-end of the Back-bone, and lay it with the skinny side upward.

**3.** Having the skin prominently shown; lacking flesh; thin, lean, emaciated.

**1605** SHAKS. *Macb.* I. iii. 45 Each at once her choppie finger laying Vpon her skinnie Lips. **1724** RAMSAY *Health* 118 With skinny cheek, pale lips, and blood-run eyes. **1781** SIR J. REYNOLDS *Journ. Flanders* Wks. 1797 II. 29 The daughter of Herod..is rather beautiful, but too skinny and lean. **1812** SIR J. SINCLAIR *Syst. Husb. Scot.* II. 127 Skinny shrivelled grain produces food weak and unsubstantial. **1857** HUGHES *Tom Brown* II. iii, His long skinny arms all covered with anchors and arrows and letters. **1879** *Sat. Rev.* 4 Oct. 415 A chicken..sometimes skinny and often ill-kept.

**4.** Mean, miserly, niggardly, stingy.

**1833** HOOD *Public Dinner* 152 The subscription still skinny. **1838** HOLLOWAY *Prov. Dict.*, *Skinny*, mean; inhospitable. **1890** *Lancet* 2 Aug. 246/2 As a rule, the whole of the men in a factory would contribute, and 'skinny' ones were not let off easily.

**5.** Of clothing: tight-fitting.

**1970** 'D. HALLIDAY' *Dolly & Cookie Bird* vii. 96 Janey's friends..in skinny sweaters and bell-bottomed corduroy trousers. **1972** *Vogue* Feb. 63 Long skinny jacket over beautifully cut pants. **1982** *Times* 2 Apr. 10/3 Teddy bear fur over skinny suede skirts.

**6.** Special collocations, as **Skinny Liz**, a thin girl or woman (see also quot. 1940); **skinnymalink, -links, -linky** (chiefly *Sc.*), a thin or emaciated person or animal; also *attrib.* or as *adj.*; **skinny-rib** *a.*, of a sweater, etc., fitting tightly across the ribs [the apparent connection with *rib stitch* is accidental]; also *ellipt.* as *sb.*

**1940** M. MARPLES *Public School Slang* 190 St. Bees..used *wimp* (a corruption of *women*) and the Arabic *bint* of women in general, while **skinny liz* was applied, almost as a nickname, to any elderly woman. **1959** I. & P. OPIE *Lore & Lang. Schoolch.* ix. 169 Thin people..skin and bones, skinny,..skinny guts, Skinny Liz, skinny-malink. **1961** N. FITZGERALD *Black Welcome* iv. 95 She takes no interest in.. eatin'. That's why she's such a Skinny Liz. **1892** *Brechin Advertiser* 6 Sept. 3 Twa *skinamalinks o' the genus horse. **1904** 'H. FOULIS' *Erchie* iii. 15 Wee skina-malink craturs dottin' up the passages in U.F. kirks carryin' the books. **1916** *Dialect Notes* IV. 280 *Skinny-malink*, a very thin person. 'O, she's a regular skinny-malink.' Usage jocular. **1935** S. BECKETT *Echo's Bones*, The chagrin of the old skinnymalinks. **1956** *Sunday Times* 22 Jan. 2/5 There used to be a children's song in Aberdeen relating the adventures of a thin man called 'Skinamalinky Lang Legs', which is still sung as a skipping song, etc.: Skinamalinky lang legs Umbrella feet. **1979** L. DERWENT *Border Bairn* vi. 71 A skinnymalink of a laddie with holes in his stockings. **1973** *Tucson* (Arizona) *Daily Citizen* 22 Aug. 48/2 (Advt.), Men's fashionable, *skinny-rib..acrylic pullover. **1976** *Milton Keynes Express* 25 June 11/1 (Advt.), Skirts, blouses, and skinny ribs.

**B.** *sb.* **1. a.** *Austral.* A girl or woman. ? *Obs.* **b.** A thin person.

**1941** BAKER *Dict. Austral. Slang* 67 *Skinny*, a girl or young woman. **1959** [see *Skinny Liz*, sense A. 6 above]. **1977** *Time* 6 June 48/2 The skinnies of the world have, in effect, righteously established fitness standards that reward their own strengths and forgive their weaknesses.

**2.** Information; rumour (see also quot. 1959). *slang* (chiefly *U.S.*).

**1959** *Amer. Speech* XXXIV. 156 *What's the skinny* means 'What's up?' **1974** E. BRAWLEY *Rap* (1975) II. xxiii. 363 Come to lay some skinny on you that I picked up off the vine. **1979** D. ANTHONY *Long Hard Cure* xxi. 162 Who killed her, Butler? Let's have the skinny. **1980** L. CODY *Dupe* xxiii. 165 Give them the skinny but keep the kudos.

**'skinny**, *v.* [f. the adj.] *intr.* To lose flesh; to become skinny or skinnier. Usu. with *down.*

**1939** J. STEINBECK *Grapes of Wrath* xxii. 423 She thinned out and she skinnied out, an'—she dropped that baby, dead. **1976** *Billings* (Montana) *Gaz.* 30 June 6-B/3 She joined TOPS after a neighbor started skinnying down to the system. **1981** *TV Picture Life* Mar. 61/1 (Advt.), All the difficult 'skinnying-down' has been done for you while you slept.

**'skinny-dip**, *v. slang* (orig. *U.S.*). [f. SKINNY *a.* 3 + DIP *v.* 8.] *intr.* To swim naked. So as *sb.*, a naked swim; **'skinny-dipper**, a person who swims naked; **'skinny-dipping** *vbl. sb.*

**1966** *Punch* 12 Oct. 557/2 Nearly a year has passed since three members of the San Francisco Sexual Freedom League went skinny-dipping in the San Francisco bay. **1967** WENTWORTH & FLEXNER *Dict. Amer. Slang* Suppl. 704/2 *Skinny-dip*, to swim in the nude. **1970** J. HOWARD *Please Touch* 14 Except for a couple of furtive midnight skinny-dips I had never taken off my clothes in public. **1971** *Daily Colonist* (Victoria, B.C.) 26 May 19/4 It was never resolved if the chickens got over the light problem or the skinny dippers were apprehended by the constable. **1971** *Daily Progress* (Charlottesville, Va.) 17 July 1/7 Two young men decided to skinny-dip near Rexburg, Idaho and left their clothes in their sail boat, but the boat sailed out of reach. **1975** *Sunday Mail* (Brisbane) 9 Mar. 30/6 *Perth.*—Skinny-dippers breathed a collective sigh of relief last week when Police Minister Ray O'Connor said..they could carry on stripping. **1977** *Times* 11 Apr. 5/7 His guests took skinny-dips in baths of champagne. **1980** L. BIRNBACH et al. *Official Preppy Handbk.* 190/1 Once every summer, teenagers are caught skinny-dipping after dark. **1981** *Times* 20 Apr. 4/8 One weekend no less than 36 people were arrested for 'skinny-dipping'.

†**'skinster.** *Obs.* In 3 **skinnestere.** [f. SKIN *v.* + -STER.] A female skinner.

**1270** *Close Roll 2 Edw. I*, memb. 7d, [Agnes] the skinnestere.

**skint** (skɪnt), *a. colloq.* [Var. SKINNED *ppl. a.* (see sense 4 d).] Penniless, broke.

**1925** FRASER & GIBBONS *Soldier & Sailor Words* 260 *Skint, to be*, hard up. **1935** G. INGRAM *Cockney Cavalcade* vii. 97 Edina [*sic*] offered him a shilling. 'That's all right... I ain't "skint" yet.' **1955** G. FREEMAN *Liberty Man* III. iv. 158 If he had enough to pay, it would just about leave him skint. **1962** *New Statesman* 18 May 708/3 All I want is a bike and ten pounds a week in me pocket—there's one thing I can't stand and that's being skint. **1977** S. MILLIGAN in *Observer* (Colour Suppl.) 6 Nov. 32/2 McGonagall.. journeyed on foot (he was skint) from Dundee to Balmoral. **1981** *Times* 27 Aug. 17/3 Are the British really as skint as we tend to make out?

**skin-tight** ('skɪntaɪt), *a.* and *sb.* [SKIN *sb.*]

**A.** *adj.* Fitting tightly to the skin; close-fitting. Also *fig.*

**1885** *Pall Mall G.* 14 Apr. 4/2 The skin-tight bodice which forbids all graceful, easy movements. *a* **1891** T. C. CRAWFORD *English Life* 91 (Cent.), Pink skin-tight breeches met his high patent-leather boots at the knee. **1895** *Outing* Dec. 202/1 When these boots are on they are skin-tight everywhere. **1916** JOYCE *Portrait of Artist* v. 280 They.. gave orders to jarvies in highpitched provincial voices which pierced through their skintight accents. **1977** *Sounds* 9 July 31/1 'Cathedral', 'Dark Star', 'Cold Rain' and 'In My Dreams' are all skintight songs, questioning, but personal and without pretension.

**B.** *sb. pl.* Close-fitting nether garments.

**1899** *Daily News* 6 Apr. 7/4, I should have to admit some who go along the Portsmouth road in skin tights.

**skintle** ('skɪnt(ə)l), *a.* and *sb.* [? f. SKINTLE *v.*] (See quots.)

**1889** C. T. DAVIS *Bricks, Tiles*, etc. (ed. 2) 135 The straight courses, pillar, hangers, and skintle bricks. *Ibid.* 136 The 'skintles' are the bricks set diagonally in order to tie the over-hangers together.

**skintle** ('skɪnt(ə)l), *v.* Also scintle. [perh. for *squintle*, f. SQUINT *a.*] *trans.* To separate and reset (half-dried bricks) at angles to each other, so as to complete the drying.

**1876** *Encycl. Brit.* IV. 280/2 When half dry the bricks are separated somewhat (*scintled*), to allow free access of the air. **1904** A. GRIFFITHS *Fifty Yrs. Public Serv.* 236 They dried slowly, and were regularly 'skintled', or rearranged so that the air might get all round them.

So **'skintling** *vbl. sb.*; also as *adv.*

**1836** *Penny Cycl.* V. 408/2 After the bricks are partially dried, another operation takes place, called 'skintling'. **1841** *Civil Eng. & Arch. Jrnl.* IV. 341/1 *note*, When the bricks have stood a few days, they are reset with a greater space between them, which operation is called *scintling*. **1889** *Science* XIII. 335/2 When dry, they [the bricks]..are carried in wheel-barrows and set 'skintling', or at angles across each other.

**skio**: see SKEO.

**skiogram, -graph**, etc.: see SKIAGRAM, -GRAPH, etc.

**skip** (skɪp), *sb.*[1] Also 5 **skyp(pe**, 5–7 **skippe** (6 **szkippe**). [f. SKIP *v.*[1]]

**1. a.** An act of skipping; a slight bound or spring. ***hop, skip, and jump*** (see HOP *sb.*[2] 3).

*c* **1440** *Promp. Parv.* 290/2 Lawnche, or skyppe, *saltus*. *c* **1450** *Mir. Saluac.* (Roxb.) 165 The ydicus [*sic*] made a skippe fro heven to the anone. **1508** DUNBAR *Gold. Targe* 19 For mirth of May, wyth skippis and wyth hoppis, The birdis sang vpon the tender croppis. **1647** TRAPP *Marrow Gd. Authors* in *Comm. Ep.* 655 Father Latimer..suddenly gave a skip in the floor for joy. **1768** STERNE *Sent. Journ., The Address*, Nor did I mount them [the steps] with a skip and a couple of strides. **1807–8** IRVING *Salmag.* (1824) 80 She was a young lady of most voluminous proportions, that quivered at every skip. **1886** STEVENSON *Kidnapped* ii, The woman..turned with a skip, and was gone.

*fig.* **1650** BULWER *Anthropomet.* Pref., Whether by Art's rude force, or Natures skip I know not. **1667** PEPYS *Diary* 26 Apr., And hath come into his place..with a great skip over the heads of a great many. **1817** SCOTT in *Lockhart* (1837) IV. iii. 84, I..had hoped..to have indulged myself with a skip over the Border.

**b.** = LEAP *sb.*[1] 3.

**1844** H. STEPHENS *Bk. Farm* II. 478 Two or three thorough skips are quite sufficient for the purposes of conception.

**2. a.** An act of passing from one thing or point to another with omission or disregard of what intervenes.

**1656** EARL MONM. tr. *Boccalini's Advts. fr. Parnass.* I. v. (1674) 8 Not conferring places upon her Nobility by skips and leaps, but by degrees and gradation. **1665** HOOKE *Microgr.* 127 Nor do I imagine that the skips from the one to another will be found very great. **1853** KANE *Grinnell Exped.* v. (1856) 36 To avert the disastrous consequences of a twelve hours' skip in their polar reckonings. **1883** S. C. HALL *Retrospect* I. 197 It is a long skip between 1789 and 1807.

**b.** *Mus.* A passing from one note to another at a greater interval than one degree.

**1730** *Treat. Harmony* 29 It is only in the foresaid Skips that we can make use of Discords upon the accented Part of the Bar. **1869** OUSELEY *Counterp. Canon & Fugue* vii, In three-part counterpoint skips are always to be avoided. **1873** H. C. BANISTER *Music* 53 Two successive wide skips in the same direction being generally undesirable.

**c.** Matter in a book which may be skipped in reading.

**1833** MACAULAY *Ess., Walpole* (1897) 275 In his books there are scarcely any of those passages which, in our school days, we used to call *skip*. **1889** HANNAY *Capt. Marryat* viii. 122 The scenes in which his heroines are on the stage are skip. Amine's appearances, however, are not skip.

**d.** *Poker.* = ***skip straight*** s.v. SKIP *v.*[1] 8.

**1880** J. BLACKBRIDGE *Compl. Poker-Player* vii. 48 'Skips' consisting of alternate cards in sequence for instance, 3, 5, 7, 9, Jack. **1905** R. F. FOSTER *Practical Poker* 75 A skip is almost twice as difficult to get as any other straight, the exact odds against it being 423 to 1.

**e.** *Radio.* The phenomenon of the poor or non-existent reception of signals from a particular station which occurs between points where signals propagated directly from the station become undetectable and points where signals begin again to be received owing to reflection in the upper atmosphere. Also applied to the silent region itself, and to radio signals received from beyond it.

**1925** [see *skip region*, sense 5 below]. **1927** O. F. BROWN *Elem. Radio-Communication* xvi. 203 The existence of the skip is explained by there being insufficient electrons to bring the wave down again until the angle of incidence becomes that corresponding to the 500 range. **1931** *Observer* 8 Nov. 18/5 Because of 'skip' it will hardly ever be audible in this country. **1965** B. SWEET-ESCOTT *Baker St. Irregular* iv. 114 The 'skip' was explained..as being the heavenward arc made by the path of the waves emitted by the short-wave transmitters. **1976** PERKOWSKI & STRAL *Joy of CB* vii. 68 The FCC purposely limited CB operations to distances under 150 miles to preclude the use of skip. **1976** *S9* (N.Y.) Feb. 88/2 When CB skip starts rolling in, he says that's the time to start tuning 25 to 50 MHz.

**f.** In automatic data processing, the action of a machine (e.g. a punch) in passing over material not requiring the functioning of the machine; a computer instruction or routine specifying such action.

**1946** [see *skip bar*, sense 5 below]. **1962** *Gloss. Terms Automatic Data Processing* (*B.S.I.*) 91 Machines in current use can perform the function called skip wherein a field in which no punching is required is rapidly passed under the punch knives, which are not active at the time. **1966** H. P. HARTKEMEIER *Data Processing* iv. 199/1 All functions of the machine are stopped while a skip is taking place. **1969** P. B. JOURDAIN *Condensed Computer Encycl.* 468 An unconditional skip is a computer instruction demanding that the next *n* instructions be ignored. **1976** KERNIGAN & PLAUGER *Software Tools* iii. 80 Skip produces n blank lines.

**3.** [prob. short for SKIP-KENNEL.] A footman, lackey, or manservant. In later use *spec.* at Trinity College, Dublin, a college-servant, a scout.

**1698–1700** WARD *London Spy* VII. Wks. 1706 I. 157 As a Courtiers Footman when he meets his Brother Skip. **1716–20** *Lett. fr. Mist's Jrnl.* (1722) I. 142, I was surprized to see a Skip transformed so speedily into a Trumpeter. **1732** DODSLEY *The Footman* 91 Then to the hall I guide my steps, Amongst a crowd of brother skips. **1839** LEVER *H. Lorrequer* xiii, Call your own skip.., damn me if I'll be your skip any longer. **1884** *Punch* 22 Mar. 141/2 A good man once, now, so his skip informs me,..smokes six or seven pipes of strong tobacco..every night.

**4.** *N. Amer. colloq.* One who absconds, *spec.* to avoid paying debts; one who defaults in payment.

**1915** J. R. FOOTE *Mod. Collection Methods* 32 In some lines of business, much, and in some, most of the collection department work is the tracing of skips. A skip is a handy term used to describe a debtor who finds it easy to forget to leave any tracks when he moves his earthly possessions. **1939** *Amer. Speech.* XIV. 240 *Skip*, guest who leaves without paying his bill. **1949** *Collier's* 8 Jan. 27/1 Kleinman's book of procedures lists exactly 110 ways to trace a skip. **1978** *Detroit Free Press* 14 Apr. 2C/2 Jean Phelan traces all kinds of hard-to-locate 'skips'—the defaulters who have 'skipped' out.

**5.** *attrib.* and *Comb.*, as (sense 2e) ***skip distance, region, zone***; (sense 2f) ***skip bar***; (sense 4) ***skip-trace, -tracer, -tracing*** vbl. sb.

**1946** *Ann. Harvard Computation Laboratory* I. 274 Cards may be punched containing a function in the first columns of the cards and a serial number in the last columns of the cards. After the function is punched, a duplicating card and *skip bar control the punch. **1926** *Physical Rev.* XXVII. 189 Larmor's theory of refraction due to the electrons of the Kennelly-Heaviside layer does not explain the '*skip distances' for short radio waves. **1977** T. ALLBEURY *Man with President's Mind* vii. 75 The radiated strength was fifty kilowatts..a power of about seventy-five kilometres due east. It would be the skip distance that carried it to Washington, or a relay from London. **1925** *Proc. IRE* XIII. 680 An uncertain region not far from the transmitter has been introduced between 100 and 350 miles during the summer night range and a *skip, or entirely-missed, region, occurs in the winter night ranges between 100–350 miles. **1970** K. CONWAY *Naked Nemesis* ii. 18 The last one hadn't paid me... There wasn't enough involved for me to start a *skip-trace on him. **1980** J. GARDNER *Garden of Weapons* II. i. 119 The Yanks think we need it [*sc.* a safe house] for a skip-trace outfit. They think we've lost somebody. **1953** BERREY & VAN DEN BARK *Amer. Thes. Slang* (1954) §460/18 **Skip tracer*, a tracer of defaulting debtors. **1960** P. S. BEAGLE *Fine & Private Place* i. 12 You ran away from it [*sc.* life] nineteen years ago, and it follows you like a skip-tracer. **1978** *Globe & Mail* (Toronto) 14 Sept. 3/2 Mr. Lillie testified that he is a skip-tracer who tracks down persons who default on their debts then change addresses. **1960** J. BLISH *Galactic Cluster* 124 If he has rebuilt..the Universe to accommodate a private *skiptracing firm..I..see no reason why we can't countercheck him. **1977** B. GARFIELD *Recoil* xi. 134 This is ..better than repossessing cars and skip-tracing. **1926** *Physical Rev.* XXVII. 192 The *skip zone was not very sharply defined. **1946** *Richmond* (Va.) *Times-Dispatch* 27 Jan. I. 16/6 The skip zone is one of the knottiest problems of present-day radio communications.

**skip**, *sb.*[2] Also **skipp**. [var. of SKEP *sb.* (q.v. for *skip* in other senses).] In mining or quarrying, a bucket, box, basket, cage, or wagon, in which materials or men are drawn up or let down. Also *gen.*, a large container for the reception and conveyance of materials or rubbish.

**1815** *Ann. Reg., Chron.* 86 Some colliers were descending into a coal pit,..five in one skip and four in the other. **1841** in HARTSHORNE *Salop. Ant.* Gloss. **1884** *Building News* 15 Aug. 283/3 The mortar and other rubbish was also lowered in skips. **1940** *Chambers's Techn. Dict.* 775/2 *Skip*,..a bucket used for the transport of spoil or materials and hung for this purpose from a crane or cableway. **1950** *Landfall* (N.Z.) IV. 125 We start loading seasoned timber into one of the skips. **1972** *Daily Tel.* 17 Jan. 3/3 Householders who leave builders' skips—large containers which can be hired to take away rubble—at the kerbside for collection by a special vehicle face fines of up to £100 under a law coming into force today. **1978** *Cornish Guardian* 27 Apr. 8/8 There will be a skip placed at the Town Hall, St. Columb and at the entrance to Halloon Avenue, St. Columb Road, on Friday, 28th. April, and at the Town Hall and Public Conveniences, Indian Queens on Friday, 12th. May, 1978 for Bulk Household refuse collections.

*attrib.* **1875** J. H. COLLINS *Met. Mining* 75 A plan of a shaft with double skip-road adapted for wheels. **1875** KNIGHT *Dict. Mech.* 2196/2 *Skip-shaft* (Mining), one boxed off by itself for the skip to ascend and descend in. **1951** J. CLEMO in D. V. Baker *One & All* 260 He had worked as a loader in a clay-pit near Pengarth, and one winter's day he had been crushed by a skip-waggon. **1972** CONYUS in A. Chapman *New Black Voices* 219 Shoveling straw Into the mouth of the skip loader. **1976** *Star* (Sheffield) 29 Nov. 12/5 (Advt.), Sale, TK skip lorry. 12 months' test.

**skip**, *sb.*[3] Orig. *Sc.* [abbrev. of SKIPPER *sb.*[2]] The director or captain of a curling or bowling team or side. Also *gen.*, a captain, a commanding officer, a manager, a boss.

**1830** *Memorab. Curl. Maben.* 29 The other skips having arranged among themselves, the boards were selected [etc.]. **1862** *Chambers's Encycl.* III. 368/1 Sides are made up, usually consisting of four against four, with a director styled *skip* for each. **1881** *Sat. Rev.* No. 1318. 138 A great moorland farmer having to figure as skip on the one side. **1921** *Amer. Legion Weekly* 28 Jan. 7 The skip wanted to investigate. **1930** T. FREDENBURGH *Soldiers March!* xxv. 201 Better get into a wagon somewhere..in case the Skip starts prowling. **1948** M. ALLINGHAM *More Work for Undertaker* xiii. 163 I've been chinning with the old Skip and he says Bang on, jolly good show. **1955** *Times* 15 Aug. 8/5 In rink games the 'skip', or captain, of each side stands near the jack to direct his men by voice or signal where their next shot should arrive. **1968** *Globe & Mail* (Toronto) 3 Feb. 35/5 In addition to winning several minor bonspiels, the Thornhill skip is in the last 16 for the Ontario Curling Association Championship. **1970** *Wall St. Jrnl.* 8 July 18/6 If you're ever called up to play baseball in the big leagues, be sure to call the manager 'Skip'. Managers like to be called Skip. **1973** D. KYLE *Raft of Swords* (1974) viii. 81 On the flight deck..the young navigator said, 'I don't really understand what we're looking *for*, skip.' 'Just Russian warships.' **1977** *N.Z. Herald* 8 Jan. 1–10/3 Who are Arthur Connew's great heroes in all those many years and thousands of ends of bowling? J. S. Martin in the singles and Jimmy Mingins and Mort Squire as skips. **1977** *S. Wales Guardian* 27 Oct. 4/5 Skip Mr. Cliff Davies invested new members to the scout troop.

**skip**, *sb.*[4] [f. SKIP *v.*[2]] (See quots.)

**1858** SIMMONDS *Dict. Trade*, *Skip*, in sugar-making in the West Indies, a charge or strike of syrup from the coppers. **1885** C. G. W. LOCK *Workshop Rec.* Ser. IV. 163/2 The difficulty is determining the exact moment when the boiling of the 'sling' in the striking-teach must cease, i.e. when to make a 'skip'.

†**skip**, *sb.*[5] *Obs.*$^{-0}$ (See quot.)

**1688** HOLME *Armoury* III. 260/2 Goat skins are reckoned by the skip, which is 50 Skins.

**skip**, *sb.*[6] Abbrev. of SCHIPPERKE.

**1895** *Our Dogs* I. 128/2 The best class of Skips ever seen in England.

**skip** (skɪp), *sb.*[7] orig. *Sc.* [Origin obscure.] The peak of a cap.

**1888** A. G. MURDOCH *Scotch Readings* (Ser. 2) 29 Ye're surely no ettlin' to put on that ugly twa-faced kep..wi' the skip baith back an' fore? **1969** M. PUGH *Last Place Left* ii. 11 He adjusted his American fatigue cap so that the skip almost covered his eyes. **1974** H. MACINNES *Climb to Lost World* xi. 207 'Hiya, Jo. Did you make it?' asked Don, peering up from beneath his cap skip.

**skip**, *v.*[1] Forms: 4–6 **skippe** (4 **schippe**), 4–7 **skyppe** (5 **sckyppe**), 6 **skype**; 4– **skip** (4 **schip**, ?**scep**, 4–6 **scip**), 5 **skyp(p**, 6–7 **skipp**. [app. related to MSw. *skuppa, skoppa* in the same sense (cf. also SCOPE *v.*[1]), but the history of the vowel is not clear.]

**I.** *intr.* **1. a.** To raise oneself off the ground by a light and graceful movement; to spring or leap lightly and easily, *spec.* in the exercise of skipping with a rope.

*a* **1300** *Cursor M.* 23569 For to skip and for to rin, Quen it war better for to blin. **1390** GOWER *Conf.* II. 95 With such gladnesse I daunce and skippe, Me thenkth I touche noght the flor. **1406** HOCCLEVE *La Male Regle* 120 Seeknesse.. paieth me my wage, So þat me neithir daunce list, ne skippe. *c* **1460** *Wisdom* in *Macro Plays* 54 For ioy, I sprynge, I sckyppe. **1530** PALSGR. 719 Are you nat ashamed to skyppe thus in your daunsynge, lyke a gyrle of the countray? **1576** FLEMING *Panopl. Epist.* 227 The grassehopper..skipped, leapt and chirpte, in her kinde. **1632** LITHGOW *Trav.* I. 27 [These nymphs] would oft run races, skipping like wanton Lambes. **1706** E. WARD *Wooden World Diss.* (1708) 54 Up he skips upon his legs, as manfully as a Taylor upon a Shop-Board. **1792** MME. D'ARBLAY *Diary* 24 Sept., Sophia skipped with joy, and Cecilia was all smiles. **1844** HOOD *Skipping* i, Little Children skip, The rope so gaily gripping. **1877** A. B. EDWARDS *Up Nile* x. 259 He skips, and screams, and grins like an ubiquitous goblin.

*fig.* **1647** N. BACON *Disc. Govt. Eng.* I. Concl. (1739) 201 If at any time he skipped higher, he afterwards fell lower.

**b.** With cognate accusative. *rare.*

**1602** MARSTON *Antonio's Rev.* V. iv, Force the plump lipt god, Skip light lavoltaes in your full sapt vaines.

**2. a.** To spring or leap lightly in a certain direction or to a certain point; to move or advance by a skip or skips. Const. with advs. and preps.

*a* **1300** *K. Horn* 1361 (Ritson), The knyht to Horn gan skippe, And in his armes clippe. **13..** *K. Alis.* (Laud MS.) 1108 Hym to awreke, kyng Philipp Ouer þe table gan to skipp. **1382** WYCLIF *Acts* xiv. 13 Barnabas and Poul.. scipten out into the cumpanyes. *c* **1450** *Merlin* xxvii. 552 Gaheries toke the horse..to Gueheret his brother, and made hym skippe in to the sadell. **1548** UDALL, etc. *Erasm. Par. Mark* Pref. 4 Hou uncomely a thing it were if a Philosophier would..scip about the stage. **1582** STANYHURST *Æneis* I. (Arb.) 23 On sands from vessels dooth skippe thee coompanye cheereful. **1634** SIR T. HERBERT *Trav.* 158 Thus burthened, [he] shal trauell till hee come where he can skip into Paradice. **1676** HOBBES *Iliad* (1677) 266 Let none from hence again retire..Nor any man before the rest skip out. **1726** CAVALLIER *Mem.* I. 58 He was very much surprised to see Eighteen young Men skipping one after another into his House. **1786** tr. *Beckford's Vathek* (1883) 110 She skipped along with the alertness of an antelope. **1841** B. HALL *Patchwork* III. 146 Our walker skipped from rock to rock at a great rate. **1898** *Allbutt's Syst. Med.* V. 955 They skip up stairs two at a time.

*fig.* **1388** WYCLIF *Ecclus.* xxxviii. 37 And thei schulen not skippe ouer in to the chirche. **1583** GREENE *Mamillia* II. Wks. (Grosart) II. 282 Insomuch that they say when the gods made beautie, they skipt beyond their skill. **1692** S. PATRICK *Answ. Touchstone* 58 The Faith of the Gospel (unto which he now skips).

**b.** To hasten, hurry, move lightly and rapidly; to make off, abscond. Also with *out* and as *to skip it*. Now *colloq.*

**1338** R. BRUNNE *Chron.* (1810) 255 To Paris gan he skip, & held his parlement. *c* **1400** *Laud Troy Bk.* 2920 Eche man ..with his god schippes And alle here good thedur skippes. **1479** *Paston Lett.* III. 257 Ye had ned to be ware that th' Exchetor skyppe not from you, when he comyth to London. **1586** J. HOOKER *Hist. Irel.* in *Holinshed* II. 142/2 The foresaid rebels, who skipped to and fro in such sort, that in no case could he find them at any aduantage. **1590** GREENE *Orl. Fur.* (1599) 8 What is Orlando, but a stragling mate, .. Skipt from his countrey. **1830** MARRYAT *King's Own* xix, By Jove, you'd better skip for it, or you'll have what Captain M— says. **1865** M. GRIGSBY *Diary* 3 Jan. in *Smoked Yank* (1888) xxi. 179 Thirteen [paroled men] .. skipped out to-day. **1890** L. C. D'OYLE *Notches* 107 So, to throw her father off the scent, on the appointed night we 'skipped' and went by way of Fort James. **1902** 'MARK TWAIN' in *Harper's Mag.* Jan. 265/2 Skip out for the coast some night. **1959** I. & P. OPIE *Lore & Lang. Schoolch.* x. 193 Juvenile language is well stocked .. with expressions inviting a person's departure, for instance: .. skip it, sling your hook, [etc.]. *a* **1966** 'M. NA GOPALEEN' *Best of Myles* (1977) 308 The son turned out to be a very bad bit of work, sold all the furniture to buy drink and then skipped it to America. **1969** G. LYALL *Venus with Pistol* xxxv. 231 He tells Dona Margarita we seem to have skipped out together. **1977** J. THOMSON *Case Closed* ii. 21 Bibby hadn't turned up. He wondered if he had skipped out.

**3. a.** To pass from one point, matter, etc., to another with omission of what intervenes; in mod. use *spec.* to do this in reading.

*c* **1385** CHAUCER *L.G.W.* 622 *Cleopatra*, The weddynge & the feste to deuyse .. It were to longe, .. And for thy to thefeect thanne wele I skyppe. **1559** in Strype *Ann. Ref.* (1824) I. App. xi. 35 He that woulde challenge kyndred of Constantyne the Great, and woulde from his father skippe upp streight to Constantyne. **1611** SHAKS. *Cymb.* IV. ii. 199, I had rather Haue skipt from sixteene yeares of Age to sixty. **1864** BURTON *Scot Abroad* II. ii. 150, I must really spare the reader two thirds of this portentous list, and skip for him to the conclusion. **1873** HAMERTON *Intell. Life* IV. iv. 163 The art of reading is to skip judiciously.

**b.** Similarly with *over*. Also sometimes, to pass *over* with very slight or superficial treatment.

**1412–20** LYDG. *Chron. Troy* III. 4417 Late him be with sorwe, And skippeth ouer wher ȝe list nat rede. **1548** ELYOT, *Prætereo*, .. to make no mencion of, to skippe ouer, to leaue out a thyng, that shulde be spoken of. **1654** WHITLOCK *Zootomia* 454 The nimble Perfunctorinesse of some Commentators (that skip over hard Places). **1725** WATTS *Logic* 344 They skip over, and but lightly touch the drier part of their theme. **1843** MAITLAND *Dark Ages* xv. (1890) 274 As I am not writing history, .. let us skip over rather more than a century. **1871** L. STEPHEN *Playgr. Eur.* (1894) x. 248, I might have skipped over these difficulties like the proverbial chamois.

**4. a.** Of things, in literal or fig. senses.

*c* **1386** CHAUCER *Pars. T.* ¶ 361 In this wise skippeth venial in to deedly synne. **1500–20** DUNBAR *Poems* liv. 8 Quhou hir schort catt noiss vp skippis. **1568** *Like Will to Like* in Hazl. *Dodsley* III. 331 The barrel was turned to a ship, Which me-thought the wind made nicely to skip. **1610** G. FLETCHER *Christ's Vict.* I. lxxxv, Bright Palestine, Whose woods drop honie, and her rivers skip with wine. **1663** S. PATRICK *Parab. Pilgr.* (1667) 330 Just as the Loadstone draws Iron to it, and makes it skip into its Bosome. **1728** POPE *Dunc.* II. 212 Quick sensations skip from vein to vein. **1840** DICKENS *Old C. Shop* xviii, The landlord stirred the fire, sending the flame skipping and leaping up.

**b.** *Mus.* To pass from one note to another at an interval of more than one degree.

**1868** OUSELEY *Harmony* iii. (1875) 52 The seventh may skip sometimes to the fifth on the same bass.

**II.** *trans.* **5. a.** To pass over in reading, or in going through a book, etc. Also with *over*, and in fig. context.

**1526** *Pilgr. Perf.* (W. de W. 1531) 158 Not sparing your voyces, not clipping the syllables, nor skyppyng ony worde. **1597** MIDDLETON *Wisd. Solomon* i. 7 Christ skips thy faults, only thy virtue reads. **1604** —— *Father Hubbard's T.* Wks. 1885 VIII. 54 To skip it over and say that line were naught. **1660** BOYLE *New Exp. Phys. Mech.* Preface p. iv, Those that are well versed in the New Philosophy .. may skip what was design'd. **1753** RICHARDSON *Grandison* (1781) IV. ii. 21 The Doctor looked so earnestly at me, when he skipped two sides of it. **1823** LAMB *Let. to Barton* 17 Feb., I do not think that I skipped a word of it [*sc.* a book]. **1875** R. F. BURTON *Ultima Thule* I. xii, Let the reader 'skip' such photos if he likes.

**b.** To pass over without mentioning, dealing with, taking into account, etc.; to omit.

**1531** ELYOT *Governor* II. xiv. (1557) 141 Oftentimes a .. loker on espieth a default, that the doer forgetteth or skyppeth ouer. **1593** BILSON *Govt. Christ's Ch.* 232 How childish an oversight was it for Paul to skip the whole bench of them. **1669** BP. HOPKINS *Serm. 1 Peter* ii. (1685) 66 A day it was, that .. we might well wish that the Year would skip it over. **1684** T. BURNET *Theory Earth* II. 180 In reckoning up the chief patrons of it, he always skips Justin Martyr. **1787** MME. D'ARBLAY *Diary* Apr., I shall skip useless recollections upon unpleasant subjects. **1875** JOWETT *Plato* (ed. 2) III. 52 Two virtues remain; shall we skip one and go to the other? **1893** W. FORBES-MITCHELL *Rem. Mutiny* 2, I intend to skip much that has already been recorded in the pages of history.

**c.** To pass over, pass by, without touching or affecting in any way. Also with *over*.

**1599** B. JONSON *Ev. Man out of Hum.* IV. v, He, making a reverse blow, .. enters the linings [of a doublet] and skips the flesh. **1607** SHAKS. *Timon* IV. iii. 110 Let not thy sword skip one: Pitty not honour'd Age for his white Beard. **1626** MIDDLETON *Women Beware W.* II. ii, All means to come by riches or advancement Miss me, and skip me over! **1778** BP. LOWTH *Transl. Isaiah* Notes xxxi. 162 He passed over, or skipped, those houses, and forbore to smite them. **1886** G. ALLEN *Darwin* ii. 25 It is fashionable to say .. that the mental energy skips a generation. **1898** MANSON *Trop. Dis.* viii. 155 Sometimes it [the plague] skips a house, a village, or a district.

**d.** To miss, escape from. *rare*$^{-1}$.

**1630** J. TAYLOR (Water P.) *Wks.* II. 132/2 Ther's nothing of him that doth hanging skip Except his eares.

**e.** Phr. ***skip it, let's skip it***: an exhortation or command to drop a subject or forget something. orig. *U.S.*

**1934** M. H. WESEEN *Dict. Amer. Slang* 395 *Skip it*, drop the matter. **1939** R. CHANDLER *Big Sleep* xiii. 97, I started to say: 'What the hell—!' 'Oh, skip it,' Eddie Mars sighed. **1943** M. MCCARTHY *Company she Keeps* vi. 195 'Oh, Dr James,' she sighed. 'Let's skip it this time.' **1945** E. WAUGH *Brideshead Revisited* 17 Oh, very conscientious, I'm sure. Skip it and get a move on. **1955** E. CADELL *Lark shall Sing* x. 116 'I hate to seem to butt in on your——' 'Skip it. Go ahead and help me.' **1971** R. DENTRY *Encounter at Kharmel* ii. 31 At home .. we cope and never give it a second thought. Out here we——oh, skip it! **1977** *New Yorker* 3 Oct. 40/3 Forgive me... Let's skip it, then, she says.

**f.** To forgo, to abstain from; to omit to take part in or to do.

**1961** in WEBSTER s.v. [1]*skip*, The president skipped his regular Thursday press conference. **1970** K. H. COOPER *New Aerobics* ix. 137 Women suffering from cramps find exercise extremely uncomfortable. Common sense alone tells them to skip exercise during those days. **1979** R. JAFFE *Class Reunion* II. ix. 209 They picked at their dinner, unable to eat the roast pigeon .. or the salad, and skipping dessert.

**6. a.** To jump or leap lightly over (something); to go off, leave (rails).

*a* **1732** SWIFT *Tom Mullinex & Dick* vii, Tom could move with lordly grace, Dick nimbly skip the gutter. **1821** CLARE *Vill. Minstr.* I. 121 Nelly lightly skipt the stile. **1903** *Daily Chron.* 18 May 6/5 A little later another car skipped the rails.

**b.** To absent oneself from, stay away from.

*c* **1810** W. HICKEY *Memoirs* (1960) ii. 28, I had intended to skip school, and take the usual march with the Guards to Kensington. **1824** SOUTHEY in *Life & Corr.* (1849) I. 141 Having one day skipped school to attend a concert. **1951** J. D. SALINGER *Catcher in Rye* xxv. 270 If I let you skip school this afternoon and go for a little walk, will you cut out the crazy stuff? **1976** *National Observer* (U.S.) 17 Jan. 1/2 School phobia is a fairly common reason why some kids skip school.

**c.** *U.S. colloq.* To flee (a place).

**1884** *Milnor* (Dakota) *Teller* 12 Sept., The granger school master .. skipped the country this week. **1885** *Santa Fé Weekly New Mexican* 10 Sept. 4/7 George Handley, a laundryman at Albuquerque, has skipped the town. **1906** U. SINCLAIR *Jungle* xxv. 307 The offending gambler had got wind of what was coming to him, and had skipped the town. **1977** *Detroit Free Press* 11 Dec. 11-B/1 Cliff won't go along with Molly's scheme to take Olive's $10,000 and skip town.

**d.** ***to skip (one's) bail*** = ***to jump (one's) bail*** (see JUMP *v.* 10 a).

**1900** *Congr. Rec.* 5 Feb. 1521/2, I should like the gentleman to know that one lot of those ballot-box stuffers are in jail and every one of the others has skipped his bail. **1930** P. W. SLOSSON *Great Crusade* (1931) 88 The I.W.W. leader who had 'skipped bail' and fled abroad. **1973** *Black Panther* 16 June 3/3 Eldridge Cleaver .. skipped bail to avoid prosecution.

**7.** To cause to skip, bound, or jump.

**1683** MOXON *Mech. Exerc., Printing* xxiv. ¶ 13 He skips his Balls both at once from the first and third Row to the second and fourth Row. **1841** CATLIN *N. Amer. Ind.* (1844) II. lv. 194 The usual friendly invitation however was given .. by skipping several rifle bullets across the river. **1894** H. GARDENER *Unoff. Pat.* 26 He had skipped pebbles on it and waded across it at low tide.

*fig.* **1867** F. H. LUDLOW *Little Briggs & I* 217 Retired merchants, who had a passion for skipping away their hard dollars on the bottomless pond of fancy cattle-breeding.

**III. 8.** The verbal stem in comb., as **skip-bombing** (see quot. 1973); also *attrib.*; **skip-bone**, = SKIPJACK 3; **skip-brain** *a.*, flighty, hare-brained; †**skip-frog**, the game of leap-frog; **skip-louse**, a tailor; **skip mackerel** *U.S.*, the blue-fish or skipjack; **skip-read** *v. trans.* and *intr.*, to read (a book) while skipping the passages of less importance; so **skip-reader**; **skip-rope**, a skipping-rope (*Cent. Dict.*); **skip straight** *Poker*, a straight (STRAIGHT *sb.* 5) consisting of cards of alternate values; **skip-tail**, a spring-tail; **skip-tooth** (see quot. 1875).

**1943** *Time* 18 Jan. 68/3 A U.S. Flying Fortress thundered into the Jap Harbor at Rabaul .. to make the first test in the South Pacific of a new technique—'*skip-bombing'. **1944** W. W. ELTON et al. *Guide Naval Aviation* ix. 172 A skip-bombing airplane must be fast and maneuverable... Tanks and ships are often attacked with skip bombing. **1964** D. MACARTHUR *Reminisc.* VI. 171 Special preparations were made to carry out a new technique of skip-bombing in the event of unfavorable weather and low cloud formations. **1973** J. QUICK *Dict. Weapons & Mil. Terms* 401/2 *Skip bombing*, a method of aerial bombing in which the bomb is released from such a low altitude that it slides or glances along the surface of the water or ground and strikes the target at or above water level or ground level. **1901** E. L. ARNOLD *Lepidus* 33 As he finished a drum-stick, or pitched a clean-picked *skip-bone into the ferns. **1603** J. DAVIES (Heref.) *Microcosmos* Wks. (Grosart) I. 30/1 This *skipp-braine Fancy moves these easie Movers To loue what ere hath but a glimpse of good. **1727** BOYER *Fr. Dict.* II, Skip-Frog, (a sort of Play, amongst Boys), *La Poste.* **1807** J. BERESFORD *Miseries Hum. Life* xx. (ed. 3) 271 We laugh that win, Since we pay but for one, tho' nine *Skip-lice get in. **1884** GOODE *Nat. Hist. Aquat. Anim.* 433 About New York they are called '*Skip Mackerel'. **1977** M. T. BLOOM *13th Man* (1978) p. ii, *Skip-read all you want through the book, but go through the last page word by word. **1977** *Modern Railways* Dec. 490/1 Once taken up it is not a book which can be skip-read, for every page is packed solid with information. **1973** *Howard Jrnl.* XIII. 342 A very clear and easy to read book which should present no difficulties to the *skip-reader. **1887** J. W. KELLER *Game of Draw Poker* 17 Efforts have been made to introduce into the game of Draw Poker what is known as the '*skip' straight—a sequence of alternate cards. **1944** A. H. MOREHEAD *Mod. Hoyle* 31 *Skip straight*, a sequence of cards once separated in rank. Examples: A—Q—10—8—6, or J—9—7—5—3. **1839** *Penny Cycl.* XV. 188/1 The small insect called *Podura Plumbea*, the common *Skiptail. **1875** KNIGHT *Dict. Mech.* 2196/2 **Skip-tooth Saw*, a saw in which alternate teeth are cut out.

**skip**, *v.*[2] [ad. Du. *scheppen* (G. *schöpfen*) to ladle, bale, dip, draw (water), etc.] *trans.* To transfer (sugar) from one vessel to another in the process of manufacture.

*a* **1818** M. G. LEWIS *Jrnl. W. Ind.* (1834) 87 Till it becomes sufficiently free from impurities to be skipped off, that is, to be again ladled out of the coppers and spread into the coolers. **1843** G. R. PORTER *Sugar Cane* (ed. 2) 211 When the sugar is perfectly clarified it is skipped off, or passed into another vessel.

**skip**, *v.*[3] [f. SKIP *sb.*[3]] *trans.* To command or direct (a team in curling or bowling) as skip.

**1900** *Ardrossan & Saltcoats Herald* 2 June 5/2 President and Vice-President skipped rinks pitted against each other.

**skiph**, obs. form of SKIFF *sb.*

**skipjack** (ˈskɪpdʒæk), *sb.* and *a.* Also 6 scipjacke, -jake, 6–7 skipiack(e, 7 -jacke. [f. SKIP *v.*[1] + JACK *sb.*[1]]

**A.** *sb.* **1.** A pert shallow-brained fellow; a puppy, a whipper-snapper; a conceited fop or dandy. Now *arch.*

**1554** T. MARTIN *Marr. Priests* Ll ij b, A way was opened to euery skipiack that lusted to make hymselfe a priest. **1586** J. HOOKER *Hist. Ireland* in *Holinshed* II. 106/1, I trust to see the daie, when .. your children .. shall disdaine the companie of anie such shipiacke. **1604** ROWLANDS *Looke to it* (Hunterian Cl.) 38 You nimble skipiacke, turning on the toe, As though you had Gun-pouder in your tayle. **1653** W. RAMESEY *Astrol. Restored* To Rdr. 18 Our shoes and fantastical stockins speak us rather Skip-jacks, Whifflers or Antics, then sober and solid men. **1806** SURR *Winter in Lond.* III. 230 How few of our fashionable skip-jacks .. possess a spark of that spirit. **1869** *Daily News* 12 June, Noble bronze faces, which contrast rather strongly with the countenance of the simpering skipjack who has preceded them.

†**2.** A horse-dealer's boy; a jockey. *Obs.*

**1608** DEKKER *Lanth. & Candle Lt.* x, The boyes, striplings, &c., that haue the Riding of the Iades vp and downe are called Skip-Iacks. **1674** STAVELEY *Romish Horseleech* (1769) 215 If friars should wear short habits they would look more like Jockeys and Millers than Friars... And then, .. will it not be a rare sight for us to go like skipjacks and Millers? *a* **1700** B. E. *Dict. Cant. Crew*, *Skip-jacks*, youngsters that Ride the Horses for Sale. [Hence in later Dicts.]

**3.** A toy made of the merrythought of a fowl, and so contrived that it can be made to skip automatically; also, the merrythought itself.

**1797** MAR. EDGEWORTH *Early Lessons* I. 253 This is as tight and strong as the stick and string in my skip-jack. **1805** *Poet. Reg.* 179 Thy bony breast Shall featly frisk it o'er the cottage floor, A strange automaton, by village hinds A Skip-Jack nam'd. **1825–1895** in dialect glossaries (Northumbld., Yks., Northampt., E. Anglia, etc.).

**4.** The name of various fishes which have a habit of leaping out of the water, *esp.* the blue-fish (*Temnodon* or *Pomatomus saltator*) of tropical and subtropical seas. Also *attrib.*, esp. in **skipjack tuna**, a tropical pelagic food fish, *Katsuwonus pelamis*, of the family Scombridæ, distinguished by its large size and striped body.

In American use the name is also given to the horse-mackerel, Ohio shad, and brook silverside (1882 Jordan & Gilbert *Fishes N. Amer.*), the bonito, jurel, runner, leather-jacket, butter-fish, cutlass-fish, etc. (1884 Goode *Nat. Hist. Aquat. Anim.*).

**1703** DAMPIER *Voy.* III. I. 115, I saw also some Boneta's and some Skipjacks, a Fish about 8 Inches long, broad and sizable, not much unlike a Roach. **1734** *Phil. Trans.* XXXVIII. 317 *Saltatrix.* The *Skip-Jack.* It hath obtained its Name from its frequent Skipping out of the Water. **1775** *Ibid.* LXVIII. 393 [The] sea was covered with Portuguese men of war, of which [we] took up several; also some pilot-fish and skip-jacks. **1815** *Sporting Mag.* XLVI. 225 That species of whale, called by sailors skip jacks. **1871** KINGSLEY *At Last* vi, Pelicans .. fell into the water with wide-spread wings, and after a splash, rose with another skipjack in their pouch. **1888** GOODE *Amer. Fishes* 76 Snapper-fishing is usually carried on with a bottom bait of skip-jack, bluefish, or young shark. **1920** BLUNDEN *Waggoner* 2 Where flock and shine the skip-jack dace. **1936** P. S. BARNHART *Marine Fishes S. Calif.* 36 Skipjack .. a pelagic fish of a wide range. **1937** L. A. WALFORD *Marine Game Fishes Pacific Coast* 17 The skipjack is the smallest of the tunas, rarely exceeding 25 inches in length. **1949** THOMAS & LOVETT in Vesey-Fitzgerald & Lamonte *Game Fish of World* II. 132 There are the oceanic bonito, known locally as the skipjack, and the California bonito. **1961** E. S. HERALD *Living Fishes of World* 229 (*caption*) Skipjack Tuna .. world-wide in tropical waters. **1973** *Sunday Times* 10 June (Colour Suppl.) 44/3 The most valuable fish in Papua New Guinea waters are skipjack tuna.

**5. a.** A beetle belonging to the family *Elateridæ*; a click-beetle (see CLICK *sb.*[1] 4) or spring-beetle. Also *attrib.*

**1817** KIRBY & SP. *Entomol.* xxiii. (1818) II. 317 The numerous species of the elastic beetles (*Elater*, L.), skip-jacks as some call them, perform this motion by means of a pectoral process or mucro. **1868** *Rep. U.S. Commiss. Agric.* (1869) 93 From this habit of suddenly springing into the air, these insects are known in Europe by the common name of 'skip-jacks'. **1871** KINGSLEY *At Last* i, The Elaters—fire-fly, or skip-jack beetles.

**b.** A kind of trout-fly.

**1867** F. FRANCIS *Angling* vi. (1880) 233 There is a smaller fly .. called the Skipjack.

**6.** *U.S.* A kind of sailing-boat (see quot. 1976). Also *attrib.*

**1887** *Forest & Stream* IX. 75 The 'skip-jack' is a connecting link between the skiff and the round-bottom boat. **1941** H. I. CHAPELLE *Boatbuilding* i. 36 The well-known Chesapeake Bay Skipjacks may be taken to represent the next type, having a good deal of beam and more dead rise than the modified sharpies. **1968** *Washington Star* 27 May B-1/2 They were watching last October's Chesapeake Appreciation Day skipjack races, off Annapolis. **1976** *Oxf. Compan. Ships & Sea* 807/2 *Skipjack*, a work-boat of the east coast of the U.S.A., sloop-rigged with a jib-headed mainsail and a foresail set on a bowsprit. They were hard-chined boats with a large wooden centreboard. **1978** J. A. MICHENER *Chesapeake* 725 In winter months he labored aboard a white man's skipjack dredging oysters... In spring he helped the skipjack captain haul timber to Baltimore.

**B.** *adj.* **1. a.** Having the trifling, petty, or flighty qualities of a skipjack; puppyish, foppish.

**1598** E. GUILPIN *Skial.* (1878) 19 The world finds fault with Gellia, for she loues A skip-jack fidler. **1645** *Arraignment Persecution* Ep. Ded. 2 Such a Quagmire of croaking skip-jacke Presbyters. **1696** VANBRUGH *Relapse* v. iii, I verily believed miss had got some pitiful skip-jack varlet or other to her husband.

**b.** *transf.* Of things.

**1597** *Return fr. Parnass.* I. i. 464 Why, I cannot abide these scipjake blanke verses. **1650** H. MORE *Enthus. Tri.* etc. (1656) 75 Meer vagrant imaginations seated in your own subsultorious and skip-jack phansie onely. **1686** GOAD *Celest. Bodies* II. xiv. 360 These petty Skip-Jack Aspects which have to do.. where ever the Sun hath to do.

**2.** Hopping, jumping, skipping.

**1605** P. WOODHOUSE *Flea* (1877) 18 For I shall make it very plaine appeare, This little skip-iack beast, his worth is small. *c* **1626** *Dick of Devon* IV. i. in Bullen *Old Pl.* II. 60 What with your skip Jacke fleas, the nap of my sleepe was worne off.

Hence **'skipjackly** *a. rare*$^{-1}$.

**1674** N. FAIRFAX *Bulk & Selv.* 135 Now 'tis but odde to think how such a flicketing skipjackly thing as that is.. should be bound to the behaviour of such a grave stayd thing as time is.

† **skip-kennel.** *Obs.* [f. SKIP *v.*[1] + KENNEL *sb.*[2]] One who has to jump or skip over the kennels or gutters; a lackey, a foot-boy, a footman. (Cf. SKIP *sb.*[1] 3.)

**1668** R. L'ESTRANGE *Vis. Quev.* (1708) 155 Yet every Draggle-Tail'd Wench, and Skip-kennel, shall be better us'd than We. *c* **1680** *Roxb. Ball.* VII. 18 A Mountebank with-out his fools, and a Skip-kennel turn'd out of place. **1721** AMHERST *Terræ Fil.* No. 13. 63 It is peculiar to these learned head-pieces to shew more respect.. to their skip-kennels, than to their students or fellows. **1729** SWIFT *Direct Serv., Footman*, You have no professed enemy but the rabble and my lady's waiting-woman, who are sometimes apt to call you skip-kennel. **1828** *Blackw. Mag* XXIV. 39 The grid-iron whizzing, The skip-kennels quizzing.

**skippable** ('skɪpəb(ə)l), *a.* Also **skipable**. [f. SKIP *v.*[1] + -ABLE.] That may be skipped, omitted, or passed over in reading.

**1820** MISS MITFORD in L'Estrange *Life* (1870) II. 94 Sir Philip's English sapphics or dactylics—which are, to be sure, the most unreadable and skippable things ever written. **1858** CARLYLE *Fredk. Gt.* XI. viii. (1872) IV. 98 A fifth part of it consists of 'Documents' proper, which are skippable.

**skipper** ('skɪpə(r)), *sb.*[1] Also 5 **skyppare**, 6 **skyppar**. [f. SKIP *v.*[1] + -ER[1].]

**1.** One who or that which skips or jumps.

*c* **1440** *Promp. Parv.* 458/1 Skyppare, *saltator, saltatrix.* **1530** PALSGR. 271/1 Skyppar, *saultevr.* **1601** HOLLAND *Pliny* I. 264 Many a time the fishers twitch vp their hooks, and see a number of these skippers [fleas] and creepers [lice] setled thicke about their baits which they laied for fishes.

**b.** Applied contemptuously to a youth. *rare*$^{-1}$.

**1596** SHAKS. *Tam. Shrew* II. i. 341 *Tra.* Greybeard, thy loue doth freeze. *Gre.* But thine doth frie. Skipper stand backe, 'tis age that nourisheth.

**2.** *spec.* As a name for various insects:

† **a.** A locust. *Obs. rare.*

*c* **1250** *Gen. & Ex.* 3087 Ðis wind hem broȝte ðe skipperes, He deden on gres and coren deres. **1599** T. MOUFET *Silkwormes* 25 Springs not from egges that.. bloudy Crocodile, Fish, Lyzards, Snakes, and Skippers African?

**b.** A skipjack or spring-beetle.

**1796** MORSE *Amer. Geogr.* I. 225 Skipper, *Elater oculatus.* **1813** BINGLEY *Anim. Biogr.* (ed. 4) III. 143 The Night-Shining Skipper. In the savannas of most of the warmer parts of America, these insects are to be seen in great abundance.

**c.** A butterfly of the family *Hesperiidæ*.

Also used with various distinguishing epithets, as *chequered, clouded, dingy, Lulworth, pearl skipper*, etc. **1817** KIRBY & SP. *Entomol.* xxiii. (1818) II. 305 A butterfly, called by Aurelians 'The large skipper' (*Hesperia Sylvanus*, F.), when it alights.. always turns half-way round. **1868** *Rep. U.S. Commiss. Agric.* (1869) 314 The family of skippers, *Hesperians*, are rather small, thick-bodied butterflies, having the antennæ hooked at the end like a shepherd's crook. **1896** LYDEKKER *Roy. Nat. Hist.* VI. 92 To *Pamphila* and the following genera belong all the small, quick-flying butterflies, known as the skippers, properly so called.

*attrib.* **1903** A. C. P. HAGGARD *Sporting Yarns* 126 A butterfly of the skipper tribe.

**d.** *dial.* and *U.S.* A cheese-maggot, or other small maggot, etc., of similar habits.

**1828–32** in WEBSTER. **1882–** in dial. glossaries (Cornwall, Cumberland).

**3.** *spec.* As a fish-name: **a.** The saury pike.

**1674** RAY *Coll. Words, Fishes* 104 Skipper, *Acus minor.* *a* **1705** —— *Synop. Pisc.* (1713) 109 In Mari Britannico duæ Acus species inveniuntur, ut nobis retulerunt piscatores Cornubienses, quarum alteri *Girrocks*, alteri *Skippers* nomen indiderunt. **1836** YARRELL *Brit. Fishes* I. 394 The Saury Pike. Skipper, *Scomberesox saurus.* **1865** COUCH *Brit. Fishes* IV. 141 Skipper.. is a migratory fish, which comes to our coasts at the beginning of summer.

**b.** The hopping-fish of Australia.

**1898** MORRIS *Austral Eng.* 419.

**4.** One who omits passages in reading.

Cf. the earlier *overskipper* (1377) and *forskipper*.

**1824** MISS FERRIER *Inher.* lxvi, He never had skipped in his life, and had such a thorough contempt for skippers. **1856** *Titan Mag.* Nov. 415/1 Our service is spoil'd by.. The trippers—the clippers—the impudent skippers. **1888** *Athenæum* 11 Feb. 178/1 He has.. compiled a useful and interesting monograph, especially for the judicious skipper.

**skipper** ('skɪpə(r)), *sb.*[2] Also 4, 7 **skypper**, 6 **skyppar**, 5–7 **skippar** (6 **-are**), 7 **sckipper**, **skiper**, 7–8 **scipper**, 8 **schipper**. [ad. MDu. or MLG. *schipper* (cf. Fris. and Da. *skipper*, Sw. *skeppare*, ON. *skipari*; also OF. *eskipre, eschipre*), f. *schip* SHIP *sb.*]

**1. a.** The captain or master of ship, esp. of a small trading, merchant, or fishing vessel; †a shipman, seaman.

In the 15th and 16th cent. chiefly in Sc. use.

**1390** *Earl Derby's Exped.* (Camd.) 37 Item Herman, skypper de Dansk. **1496** *Acc. Ld. High Treas. Scot.* I. 310 The skippar of the schip callit the Ros. **1506** in *Charters*, etc. *Edinb.* (1871) 190 That na skipperis nor maisters of schippis saill furth of our realme [etc.]. **1594** NASHE *Unfort. Trav.* 16 My rapier pendant like a round sticke fastned in the tacklings for skippers the better to climbe by. **1624** in Foster *Eng. Factories Ind.* (1909) III. 19 The murder of one of our people ther by a scipper of theirs. **1656** BLOUNT *Glossogr.* s.v. *Scipper*, But we usually take *Skippers* for common Seamen or Mariners. **1677** W. HUBBARD *Narrative* II. 65 Eight of them went a shore, leaving two Indians aboord with the English Skipper. **1721** RAMSAY *Prospect of Plenty* 154 The north-sea skippers are leal-hearted men. **1767** T. HUTCHINSON *Hist. Mass.* II. i. 110 A French man of war.. met one of our fishing vessels.. [and] sent for the skipper to come on board. **1822** SCOTT *Nigel* iii, A rank, as well as manners, highly superior to the skippers (or Captains, as they called themselves) of merchant vessels. **1878** JEVONS *Polit. Econ.* 29 The skipper starts when wind and tide are in his favour.

*fig.* **1673** S. PARKER *Reproof Reh. Transp.* 481 As if you were the Skipper of the State.

*Comb.* **1848** DICKENS *Dombey* iv, Here he lived too, in skipper-like state, with his nephew Walter.

**b.** *skipper's daughters*, high white-crested waves.

**1888** STEVENSON *Across the Plains* vi. (1905) 130 Out in the open there were 'skipper's daughters'.

**2.** The captain or director of a sporting team or side.

In curling and bowling the Sc. term is now SKIP *sb.*[3], which is also used generally as a colloq. abbreviation.

**1830** *Memorab. Curl. Maben.* 100 The sweeping department to be under the exclusive control of the skipper. **1838** in *Chambers's Inform. People* (1849) II. 651/1 The skippers shall have the exclusive regulation and direction of the game [in curling]. **1893** *Star* 30 May 1/7 He.. afterwards acted as skipper of the Cambridgeshire Eleven.

**3.** *Gun-making.* (See quot.)

**1851–4** *Tomlinson's Cycl. Arts* (1867) I. 821/1 From [the screwer-together the gun] passes to the *skipper* and *finisher*, who takes the whole to pieces, and corrects any trifling errors of the preceding workmen.

**4.** *Services' slang.* A commanding officer in the army; the captain of an aircraft or squadron.

**1906** *Soldier Slang* in C. McGovern *Sarjint Larry an' Frinds, Skipper*, the commanding officer. **1926** *Sat. Even. Post* 6 Mar. 154/3 The skipper told us to look after yuh. **1929** *Papers Mich. Acad. Sci., Arts & Lett.* X. 323 *Skipper*, the squadron commander in the Royal Naval Air Service. **1958** P. KEMP *No Colours or Crest* v. 86 The Skipper wondered if you'd like to go forward to the flight deck for a look around. **1977** *R.A.F. News* 11–24 May 9/1 The headmaster.. will join his wartime Whitley skipper, Gp Capt Leonard Cheshire.

**5.** *slang* (orig. *U.S.*). A police captain or sergeant; a police chief.

**1929** HOSTETTER & BEESLEY *It's a Racket!* 238 *Skipper*, a police captain in command of a police station, bureau, or district. **1930** *Amer. Mercury* Dec. 457/2, I goes to the skipper and fronts for the mutt. **1962** *John o' London's* 25 Jan. 82/2 A police sergeant is called *skipper*. **1976** D. BARNES *Yesterday is Dead* (1977) II. 262 Good piece of police work. .. I'll fill the skipper in. I'm sure he'll be pleased.

Hence **'skippership**, the office of skipper; the management or handling of a ship.

**1828** *Examiner* 1/1 If skippership went to the highest bidder,.. we should have a still greater proportion of bad pilots. **1894** *Daily Chron.* 4 Aug. 3/5 In recognition of his skippership of the Trafalgar.

**'skipper**, *sb.*[3] *Cant.* Also 6 **skypper**. [A canting term, possibly ad. Cornish *sciber* or W. *ysgubor* a barn.] **1.** † **a.** A barn, outhouse, or shed, used as a sleeping-place by vagrants. *Obs.*

**1567** HARMAN *Caveat* (1869) 83 A skypper, a barne. *Ibid.* 85, I couched a hogshead in a Skypper this darkemans. **1641** BROME *Joviall Crew* II. Wks. 1873 III. 392 Now let each Tripper Make a retreat into the Skipper. *a* **1700** B. E. *Dict. Cant. Crew, Skipper*, a Barn. [Hence in later Dicts.]

**b.** Any sleeping-place for a vagrant.

**1925** *Flynn's* 3 Jan. 661/2 *Skipper*,.. a lodging house; a tramp. **1935** 'G. ORWELL' *Clergyman's Daughter* ii. 101 We ain't got a brown between us, and we.. got to tap for our tommy and skipper at nights. **1939** J. WORBY *Spiv's Progress* i. 9 I'm going north. Do you know any good skippers up the road? **1978** *Country Life* 20 July 189/2 He had painfully to learn the rudiments of vagrant survival; to make sure of his 'skipper' or kip before dark.

**2.** A vagrant; one who sleeps rough.

**1925** [see sense 1 b above]. **1965** *Guardian* 9 Dec. 9/1 It was the night of the big Government census of the 'skippers'—the people who sleep rough. **1977** *Listener* 28 July 103/3 On the rubble-strewn redevelopment sites of central Glasgow, you find the groups of 'skippers', the men who live rough... These are the ones who admit that alcohol has won.

**3.** An act of sleeping rough; esp. in *to do a skipper*.

**1935** H. NEVILLE *Sneak Thief on Road* 347 *Skipper*, a liedown in a spinney or anywhere where no rent is paid. **1937** J. CURTIS *You're in Racket Too* i. 9 It would be no fun doing a skipper on a November night. **1962** *Observer* 11 Mar. 35/1 There are not enough beds. Many will be turned away and have to do a 'skipper' in station, park or ruin.

† **'skipper**, *sb.*[4] *Obs. rare*$^{-1}$. [ad. Du. *schepper* scoop, ladle: cf. SKIP *v.*[2]] (See quot.)

**1688** HOLME *Armoury* III. xxii. (Roxb.) 280/1 A Skipper or Sugar ladle.

**'skipper**, *v.*[1] [f. SKIPPER *sb.*[2]] *trans.* To act as skipper or captain of (a vessel, team, etc.).

**1893** *Westm. Gaz.* 25 July 5/2 The former is to skipper his yacht *Meteor.* **1950** *Sport* 7–11 Apr. 14/1 Dick skippered the City side who, in 1938, wrote a chapter of Cup history. **1951** N. M. GUNN *Well at World's End* xxvi. 239 The idea.. was to get the old man to skipper her for a couple of seasons. **1977** *R.A.F. News* 27 Apr.–10 May 5/1 Brian, then a flight lieutenant, had skippered the Sunderland on three flights.

*absol.* **1883** *Harper's Mag.* Aug. 445/2 The owner skippers for himself.

**'skipper**, *v.*[2] *Cant.* [f. SKIPPER *sb.*[3]] *intr.* To sleep in a barn or outhouse, or in the open. Also with *it*.

**1851** MAYHEW *Lond. Lab.* I. 478 They.. frequently 'skipper it' in the open air, when the weather is fine and warm. **1894** D. C. MURRAY *Making of a Novelist* 107 In the language of the road, to sleep in the open is to 'skipper'.

*Comb.* **1851** MAYHEW *Lond. Lab.* I. 310 Here is the best places in England for 'skipper-birds'; (parties that never go to lodging-houses, but to barns or outhouses, sometimes without a blanket).

**'skipper**, *v.*[3] *rare*$^{-1}$. [freq. of SKIP *v.*[1]] *intr.* To skip or hop.

**1845** S. JUDD *Margaret* I. xiv, A grass-finch skippered to the top of a stump.

**'skippery**, *a. dial.* and *U.S.* [f. SKIPPER *sb.*[1] 2 d.] Of cheese, etc.: Full of maggots.

**18..** DOW *Serm.* II. 258 (Bartlett), The earth [will] appear as animated as a plate of skippery cheese. **1899** *Cumbld. Gloss.* 170/2 *Skippery*,.. said of bacon and cheese when full of 'jumpers'.

† **skippeson.** *Obs. rare.* In 5 **skyppeson**. [ad. OFr. *eskip(p)eson*, f. *eskipper, esquiper* to EQUIP.] Equipment, provision of necessaries.

**1444** *Coll. Hist. Staff.* (1891) XII. 318 With skyppeson and reskyppeson reasonable for him, is seid men and horses. *Ibid.* 320 The seid Sir Phelip shall have skyppeson and reskyppeson resonable for him.

**'skippet**[1]. [Cf. SKIBBET.] A small round wooden box, used for the preservation of documents or seals. Also *transf.* (quot. 1398).

**1398** TREVISA *Barth. De P.R.* IV. x. (Tollemache MS.), The toþer party of colera, þat is drawen to þe skipet of galle [L. *ad cistam fellis*]. *c* **1400** *Pilgr. Sowle* (Caxton) I. xxxiv. (1859) 37 In her hond she brought a skypet,.. and she took forth the Charter. **1864** E. EDWARDS *Libr. & Founders Libr.* ix. 223 Skippets (or boxes turned on a lathe). **1871** *Athenæum* 11 Feb. 179 A 'skippet' found in the parvise of Bodmin Church, and a leather-covered case. **1886** *Ibid.* 11 Dec. 783/2 The seals of the different parties being preserved in silver skippets attached to the volumes by silken cords.

**'skippet**[2]. *rare.* Also 5 **skeppette**. [dim. of *skip* SKEP *sb.*]

**1.** A basket. Now *dial.*

*c* **1450** *Mirour Saluacioun* (Roxb.) 44 Hym closid in a skeppette sho laide be the Ryvere syde. **1890** *Gloucester Gloss.* 141 *Skippet*, the same as Kipe [= a bushel basket].

† **2.** A small boat or skiff. *Obs.*$^{-1}$

Prob. due to association with *ship* or *skiff*.

**1590** SPENSER *F.Q.* II. xii. 14 Vpon the banck they sitting did espy A daintie damzell,.. By whom a little skippet floting did appeare. [Cf. stanza 15.]

**'skippet**[3]. Now *dial.* Also 8 **skippit**. [var. of SCUPPET.] (See quots.)

**1764** *Museum Rust.* II. 194 Help the water out of the ruts with scoops or skippits. **1866** BROGDEN *Prov. Lincs.*, *Skippet*, a wooden shovel used for lifting water. **1879** MISS JACKSON *Shropshire Word-Bk.* 386 *Skippet*, a long-handled, spoon-shaped implement used by drainers. **1893** *Wiltshire Gloss.*, *Skippet*, the long-handled ladle used for filling a water-cart, emptying a hog-tub, &c.

**'skipping**, *vbl. sb.*[1] [f. SKIP *v.*[1]]

**1.** The action of the verb skip, in literal senses.

*c* **1440** *Promp. Parv.* 246/1 Hoppynge, or skyppynge, *saltacio.* **1590** BARROUGH *Physick* I. xxxviii. (1639) 60 The diseases which come by skipping in of stones or chips.. into the Eyes. **1611** COTGR., *Resiliment*, a leaping, skipping, rebounding, backe. **1800** *Infant's Library* IX. 7 Skipping. This is a very healthful play in winter; it will make you nice and warm in frosty weather. **1844** HOOD *Skipping* i, Little Children skip,.. All are fond of skipping!

*attrib.* **1736** AINSWORTH s.v., In a skipping posture, *saltabundus.* **1894** *Daily News* 14 June 6/4 Among the 'sports' for girls being a skipping contest and various races. **1898** *Allbutt's Syst. Med.* V. 827 Her first attack cut short prolonged and severe skipping effort. **1959** I. & P. OPIE *Lore*

& *Lang. Schoolch.* ii. 38 Norman Douglas gives it as a skipping rhyme in 'London Street Games'. **1977** N. Freeling *Gadget* II. 70 How many skipping rhymes do I know? Sixty? A hundred?

**2.** The action of skipping, in transferred senses.

**1560** *1st Bk. Discipline* xi. (1836) 69 This skipping and divagation from place to place of Scripture. **1597** T. Morley *Introd. Mus.* 7, I know not how to tune them [*sc.* notes] by reason of their skipping. **1674** N. Fairfax *Bulk & Selv.* Contents, Stirring of Ghost is like skipping of thought. **1824** Scott *Redgauntlet* II. i. 15 Such as are addicted to the laudable practice of *skipping*. **1863** *Reader* 5 Dec. 660 We remember, of course, that skipping is fair play in novel-reading. **1885** *Manch. Exam.* 22 July 3/2 The reader ..can always have recourse to judicious skipping.

**'skipping**, *vbl. sb.*[2] Also skepping. [f. skip *v.*[2]] In sugar-making: (see quots.). Also *attrib.*

**1824** *Mech. Mag.* No. 60. 58 Whether the new boiler can improve the grain of inferior West Indian sugars. Two charges, or skeppings, as they are technically termed, were run off in 13½ minutes. **1826** Henry *Elem. Chem.* II. 196 Of this solution about fifty gallons, called a skipping, are put into a copper pan. **1839** Ure *Dict. Arts* 1202 Each finished charge is called a skipping, because it is skipped or laded out. **1860** Tomlinson *Arts & Manuf.* Ser. II. *Sugar* 16 Sometimes the last and largest copper contains a skipping-teach, a smaller vessel of the same shape with a valve at the bottom worked by a handle.

**'skipping**, *ppl. a.* [f. skip *v.*[1]]

**1.** That skips. Also *spec.* in ***skipping stickleback*** (see quot. 1803).

**1560** Bible (Genevan) *Wisdom* xvii. 19 The running of skipping beastes, that colde not be sene. **1596** Shaks. *1 Hen. IV*, III. ii. 60 The skipping King hee ambled vp and downe. **1601** B. Jonson *Poetaster* III. iv, Hee's a good skipping swaggerer. **1661** K. W. *Conf. Charac.* (1860) 81 A designe to make your skipping suiters hop away and leave you. **1733** Fielding *Intriguing Chambermaid* I. v, Indeed, with your little, pert, skipping beaux, I don't know what may happen. **1791** Cowper *Yardley Oak* 25 A skipping deer, With pointed hoof dibbling the glebe. **1803** Shaw *Gen. Zool.* IV. 609 Skipping Stickleback, *Gasterosteus Saltatrix*... Stickleback with eight dorsal spines connected by a membrane. **1893** F. Adams *New Egypt* 95 A she-goat..with her two little black fantastically-skipping kids.

*transf.* **1596** Shaks. *Merch. V.* II. ii. 196 Allay with some cold drops of modestie Thy skipping spirit. **1602** Marston *Ant. & Mell.* I. Wks. 1856 I. 13 A short finger, and a naked chinne, A skipping eye. **1801** Busby *Dict. Mus.*, *Skipping-Notes*, notes which do not proceed by conjoint degrees, nor in any regular course, but which lay at awkward and unexpected distances from each other.

**2.** Characterized by skips.

**1596** *Edw. III*, I. ii, In their vild, vnseuill, skipping giggs. **1615** G. Sandys *Trav.* 172 An Æthiopian..who..doth dance in their processions with a skipping motion.

**'skippingly**, *adv.* [f. prec. + -ly[2].] In a skipping manner; by skips.

**1572** Huloet *Alv.*, Skippingly, or by skippes and leapes. **1642** Howell *For. Trav.* (Arb.) 23 If one read skippingly and by snatches, and not take the threed of the story along. **1656** W. Du Gard tr. *Commenius' Gate Lat. Unl.* §639 The third [the rash man] rambling over businesses skippingly. **1842** *Tait's Mag.* IX. 605 Hart on the hill never bounded more skippingly. **1889** *Times* 13 Aug. 4/3 Readers who get through a book skippingly.

**'skipping-rope.** [f. skipping *vbl. sb.*[1]] A piece of rope, sometimes with a wooden handle at each end, used in the pastime of skipping.

**1802** F. Burney *Jrnl.* (1975) V. 388 He interests himself warmly about them, since he has seen the Cuttings, especially of the skipping ropes. **1836** T. Hook *G. Gurney* III. 318 Stretching to catch two things like skipping-ropes. **1853** R. S. Surtees *Sponge's Sp. Tour* ix. 45 Just as a girl throws her skipping-rope. **1887** R. N. Carey *Uncle Max* x, I showed her a new skipping-rope that I had bought on my way.

*attrib.* **1888** Rolleston & Jackson *Anim. Life* 798 The peculiar 'skipping rope' fibres, i.e. filaments with a knob at each end, which occur..in the mesogloea of certain Ceratine sponges.

†**'skippish**, *a. Obs.*[−1] [f. skip *v.*[1] + -ish[1].] Inclined to skip; given to skipping.

**1576** A. Fleming tr. *Caius' Eng. Dogs* (1880) 16 A Hare (being a wilde and skippishe beast).

**skipple** ('skɪp(ə)l). *U.S.* Also 7 **skiple**. [ad. Du. *schepel* (also MDu. and MLG.; OS. *scepel*), = G. *scheffel* (OHG. *sceffil*) bushel.] A measure of three pecks. Also *attrib.*

**1685** *Pennsylv. Arch.* I. 95 One Skiple Salt. **1701** Wolley *Jrnl. N. York* (1860) 34 Long Island Wheat three shillings a Skipple (a Skipple being three parts of a Bushel). **1769** *Cont. Narr. Ind. Charity School Lebanon* 18 Corn [maize] and wheat at the German Flats are from six shillings to a dollar a skipple. **1901** *N. & Q.* Ser. IX. VIII. 283/2 The Skipple-measure or Short Bushel of New England.

†**skippound.** *Obs. rare.* [ad. Du. *schippond*, or LG. *schippund* (cf. ON., MSw., etc., *skippund*.] = shippound.

**1622** Malynes *Anc. Law-Merch.* 30 The Skippound is vsed in many places..: the Skippound is taken for the lading of corne in a ship, *Quasi Shippond*, as a diuident of a Last of corne. **1674** S. Jeake *Arith. Surv.* (1696) 126 At Antwerp.. A Stone is 8 lb. The Skippound 300 lb.

**skippy** ('skɪpɪ), *a.* [f. skip *v.*[1] + -y[1].] Characterized by skipping.

**1883** Jane G. Austin *Nantucket Scraps* 178 The beach-grass long and tangled, swarmed with all things of a crawly, skippy, venomous nature.

†**skire**, *a. Obs.* Forms: 3, 5 skir, 5, 8–9 **skire**; 4–6, 9 skyre, 5 skyr. [a. ON. *skírr* (Norw. and MSw. *skir*) clear, pure, = OE. *scír* shire *a.* In later use only *Sc.*]

**1.** Clear *of*, free *from*, something morally bad.

*c* **1200** Ormin 8015 þatt genge þatt wass milde & meoc, ..& off galnesse skir & fre. *Ibid.* 12194 All þatt ahhte off eorþliȝ þing þatt Godess þeowwess haffdenn..i þiss middell ærd Iss all skir fra þe deofell.

**2. a.** Of water: Pure, clear.

**13..** *E.E. Allit. P.* B. 1776 þay..Asscaped ouer þe skyre watteres & scaþed þe walles. *a* **1400–50** *Alexander* 2119 Scamandra þe slire [*read* skire: *Dubl.* skyr] flode þe scriptour it callis.

**b.** Of colours, flames, etc.: Clear; bright.

*a* **1400–50** *Alexander* 467 To skyre skarlet hewe skyftis hire face. *c* **1400** *Destr. Troy* 12500 [The lightning] skirmyt in the skewes with a skyre low. *a* **1585** Polwart *Flyting w. Montgomerie* 533 With flying fyreflaughts burning bright and skyre [*v.r.* schyre].

**3.** Conspicuous or notable, esp. in respect of harmful qualities.

This sense, which appears only in the *Destr. Troy* (cf. also ll. 12700 and 13616) is prob. due to the requirements of alliteration.

*c* **1400** *Destr. Troy* 8897 In anythyng..þat hase skapet vs to skathe, ne to skyre harme. *Ibid.* 13397 Ascatus the skir, þat skathill was in elde.

**4.** (See quot. and cf. skire *adv.*)

**1825** Jamieson *Suppl.*, *Skire*, *Skyre*, pure, mere; as 'a skire fool'.

†**skire**, *v. Obs.*[−1] In 4 skir. [a. ON. *skíra* (Norw. and MSw. *skira*), f. *skírr* adj.: see prec.] *refl.* To cleanse, clear, or purify (oneself).

*a* **1300** *Cursor M.* 28058 þat þai ripe wele þair aun boke, And skir þam sua wit þair in-sight þair conscience..clene and bright.

**skire**, *adv. Sc.* Also 6 **skyr**, 8 **skier**, 9 **skyre**, **scyre**. [See skire *a.*] Sheer; quite; altogether. Also *ellipt.* quite mad.

**1581** J. Hamilton in *Cath. Tract.* (S.T.S.) 85 Sum in Angus exponing the same ran skyr daft. **1766** A. Nicol *Poems* 95 (E.D.D.), Our land is now quite skier naked made. **1822** Howden in Edwards *Mod. Sc. Poets* Ser. II. (1881) 35 'The man's gane skire', muttered Matt. **1825** Jamieson *Suppl.* s.v. *Skeir*, In Fife..the phrase is *skyremad*, i.e., quite insane.

**skiret**, obs. form of skirret[1].

**Skire Thursday.** *Sc.* and *north. dial.* ? *Obs.* Forms: α. 5 Skire, 5–6 Skyre, 6 Skir, 7 Sky(i)r, Skier, Sky. β. 5 Skyrys, 6 Skyris, Skiris, 9 Skiers, Scarce; 7 Skis, Skies. See also Thursday. [ad. ON. *Skíri-þórsdagr* (Norw. *Skirtorsdag*), f. *skír* skire *a.* Cf. also skere *a.* 4.] The day next before Good Friday; Maundy Thursday; = Sheer Thursday.

α. *c* **1450** *St. Cuthbert* (Surtees) 2277 So..walde he passe To Skyre thuresday, þan walde he his fete waschyn and clensyd be. **1474** *Acc. Ld. High Treas. Scot.* I. 72 Almous on Skire Thurisday. **1562** *Invent. R. Wardrobe* (1815) 156 Item, fourty drying claithis of all sortes—Deliverit xii..on skir-furisday at the wesching of the pure folkis fete. **1621** *Sc. Acts, Jas. VI* (1816) IV. 642 Thrie ȝeirlie faires, Viz. the first ..vpoun skyirthurisdaye, the secund..at Lambes. **1670** *Churchw. Acc. Pittington*, etc. (Surtees) 228 For wine att the Communion upon..Sky Thursday.

β. **1489** *Acc. Ld. High Treas. Scot.* I. 108 On Skyrys Thursday, giffin for the Kingis almus clathis, xvij merkis. **1630** in Brand *Hist. Newcastle* (1789) II. 343 *note*, Skis-Thursday being our Lady-Day in Lent. **1677** *Churchw. Acc. Pittington*, etc. (Surtees) 241 For bread and wine att the Communions of Palme Sunday, Skies Thursday, Good Friday, Easter Day, and the Sunday after.

**b.** *Sc.* Used as the name of local fairs or markets held on this day.

In quot. 1864 the date is correct by Old Style.

**1825** Jamieson *Suppl.* s.v. *Skeir*, *Scarce-Thursday*, the name of a fair held at Melrose on the Thursday before Easter. **1864** *Glasgow Her.* 15 Apr., 'Skiers' Thursday.—This important concluding market was held yesterday.

**skiriwort**, obs. form of skirret[1].

**skirl** (skɜːl), *sb. Sc.* and *north. dial.* Also 6 **skyrl**, 8 **skirle**. [f. the vb.]

**1.** A shrill cry, a shriek; shrill talk.

**1513** Douglas *Æneid* II. xi. 1 With skirlis and with skrekis thus sche beris. **1549** *Compl. Scotl.* vi. 40 The botis man.. cryit vitht ane skyrl, quod he, i see ane grit schip. **1718** Ramsay *Christ's Kirk Gr.* III. xix, Mony an unco skirl and shout. **1791** A. Wilson *Laurel Disp.* Wks. 1876 II. 18 Her skirle Sets my twa lugs a ringing like a gir'le. **1816** Scott *Antiq.* xxxv, That silly fliskmahoy..has..done naething but laugh and greet, the skirl at the tail o' the guffa, for twa days successfully. **1853** Mrs. Gaskell *Ruth* xxiv, The skirl of the grey sea-birds.

**2.** A shrill sound, *esp.* that characteristic of the bagpipe.

**1860** Russell *Diary India* I. xv. 238, I hear the skirl of the bagpipes which announces that we are not far from the Highlanders. **1892** Jane Barlow *Irish Idylls* iv. 78 A skirl of vocal music rose up suddenly close by.

**b.** ***skirl-in-the-pan***, something prepared for eating by frying in a pan.

**1816** Scott *Old Mort.* v, I trow ye dinna get sic a skirl-in-the-pan as that at Niel Blane's. **1825** in Jamieson *Suppl.*

**skirl** (skɜːl), *v.*[1] *Sc.* and *north. dial.* Also 5 scrille, skrille, 6, 8 skirle, 6 skyrl, 8 skerl. [prob. of Scand. origin: the early form *skrille* corresponds to a Norw. dial. *skrylla*, with variants *skrella* and *skrolla* in the same sense.]

**1.** *intr.* To scream, shriek, cry out shrilly.

*c* **1400** *Anturs Arth.* 536 Thenne his lemmon on lofte scrilles [*v.r.* skirles] and scrykes. *Ibid.* 619 Ho scrilles [*v.r.* skrilles] and scrikes. **1508** Kennedie *Flyting w. Dunbar* 39 Baith Iohne the Ross and thow, sall squeill and skirle. *a* **1513** Fabyan *Chron.* VII. (1811) 593 Whan he was borne towarde his moders chare, he skyrlyd and cryed so feruently. **1645** Sir T. Hope in *Misc. Sc. Hist. Soc.* I. 131 Quhen I preis to tak any of the barnes in my armes, he skirlis for impatiencie. **1785** Burns *Halloween* vi, He grippet Nelly hard an' fast; Loud skirl'd a' the lasses. **1818** Scott *Br. Lamm.* xi, Stay where ye are, and skirl as loud as ye can. **1889** Barrie *Window in Thrums* xi. 100 The women-folk fair skirled wi' fear.

**b.** Of the bagpipe (or its music): To produce the shrill sounds by which it is characterized; to sound shrilly.

*a* **1665** R. Sempill *Piper of Kilbarchan* 44 He gart his pipe, when he did play, Baith skirl and skreed. **1791** Burns *Tam o' Shanter* 123 He screw'd the pipes and gart them skirl, Till roof and rafters a' did dirl. **1873** Black *Pr. of Thule* iv, The wild and ominous air that was skirling upon the hill-side.

**c.** Of other inanimate things.

**1827** Scott *Chron. Canongate* iv, On the painted board that is skirling and groaning at the door. **1891** Barrie *Little Minister* iii, Blasts from the north..skirled through the manse. **1894** Crockett *Raiders* 388 It was comfortable too at meal-times to hear the bacon skirling in the pan.

**2.** To play the bagpipe.

**1828** Moir *Mansie Wauch* ii, Three fiddlers..and a piper ..all skirling, scraping and bumming away throughither. **1879** C. Keene *Let.* in *Life* x. (1892) 296 [He] had a sort of piper skirling away in his garden.

**3.** *trans.* To sing, utter, play, etc., in loud and shrill tones.

**1786** Burns *Ordination* iii, O' double verse come gie us four, An' skirl up the Bangor. **1818** Scott *Hrt. Midl.* xvii, If he suld hear her skirling her auld ends o' sangs. **1844** W. H. Maxwell *Sports & Adv. Scotl.* i. (1855) 23 His piper 'skirling a gathering'.

**b.** To cause (the bagpipe) to sound shrilly.

**1885** G. Fraser *Poems* 219 Pate Clauchan o' this toon, Wha skirled his pipes.

**skirl** (skɜːl), *v.*[2] [Of obscure origin; also current in northern dial. as *scurl.*] *intr.* To fly with a sweeping or whirling motion.

**1859** H. Kingsley *G. Hamlyn* xxxi, A pretty white curlew skirled over the housetop to settle on the sheepwash dam. **1869** *Daily News* 18 Aug., Butterflies white, butterflies blue, are on all sides trooping and skirling in the shine.

**skirlie** ('skɜːlɪ). *Sc.* Also **skirley**. [Shortened dim. form of *skirl-in-the-pan* s.v. skirl *sb.* 2 b: see -y[6], -ie.] A dish of oatmeal and onions, etc., fried together.

**1914** *Trans. Banffshire Field Club* 26/27 June 26 Crackens, bayheads, and skirlie are formed of fish livers and oatmeal cooked together. **1929** F. M. McNeill *Scots Kitchen* 205 *Skirlie*... Chop two ounces of suet finely. Have a pan very hot and put in the suet. When..melted, add one or two finely chopped onions and brown them well. Now add enough oatmeal to absorb the fat. **1947** *Sc. Women's Rural Inst. Cookery Bk.* x. 184 *Skirley*..3 handfuls of oatmeal.., ½ lb. suet, 2 onions.., pepper, salt. **1969** *Observer* 12 Jan. 33/4 *Skirley* (oatmeal, onions, suet, seasoned and fried in a cake).

**'skirling**, *sb. local.* Also scar-, scur-, skerling. [Of obscure origin.] A young salmon; a samlet, sparling.

**1776** Pennant *Brit. Zool.* (ed. 2) III. 266 [Samlets] are also common in the Wye, where they are known by the name of Skirlings, or Lasprings. **1801** W. Coxe *Tour Monmouth.* i. 2 The only fish not common in the English rivers, are the skerling and the sewin. **1844** *Zoologist* II. 527 *note*, Scarling or scurling,..smolt, &c. all denote the same fish. **1891** *Fishing Gaz.* 14 Feb. 88/3 The Severn Board of Conservators have successfully prosecuted those found with these skirling in their possession.

**'skirling**, *vbl. sb.* [f. skirl *v.*[1]] Shrill crying, shrieking, etc.

**1820** Scott *Monast.* xxx, She could find voice enough to tell the women and children without, to 'leave their skirling, and look after the cows'. **1855** [Robinson] *Whitby Gloss.* s.v. *Skerl*, The skirling of the sea-gulls is said to be the forerunner of a gale. **1893** Stevenson *Catriona* v. 53 It heartens me..like the skirling of the Highland pipes.

**'skirling**, *ppl. a.* [f. skirl *v.*[1]] Crying or sounding shrilly, screaming, etc.

**1785** Burns *Scotch Drink* xii, When skirlin weanies see the light. **1818** Scott *Hrt. Midl.* xvi, Haud your tongue, ye skirling limmer! **1819** —— *Leg. Montrose* iii, Their damnable skirlin' pipes. **1894** *Field* 1 Dec. 828/1 The skirling cry of the snipe.

†**skirm**, *sb. Obs. rare.* [f. the vb. Cf. F. *escrime*, OF. *escremie*, *eskermie*, etc.] Movement as in fencing or fighting; skirmish.

*c* **1400** *Destr. Troy* 13541 Thus I skope fro the skathe with skyrme of my hondes. **1534** *Primer in English* F v, Syr, lo: here are two swerdes, thynk ye not these two be sufficient for this scyrme.

†**skirm**, *v. Obs.* Forms: 3 scurmen, 3–4 skirmen, 4 skyrmen; 3 scerem-, schirme, 4–5 skirme, 4 sckyrme, 5 skyrme. [ad. OF. *eskirmir*, *eskermir*, *eschermir*, etc. (also *escremir*: see skrim *v.*), f.

OHG. *skirman, scirman* (G. *schirmen*) to defend, f. *scirm, scerm* shield, defence. Cf. SKIRMISH *v.*]

**1.** *intr.* To fence, to skirmish.

c **1205** LAY. 8144 þeos tweien cnihtes bi-gunnen mid sceldes to scurmen. *a* **1225** *Ancr. R.* 212 þe wreðfule biuoren þe ueonde skirmeð mid kniues. *c* **1330** R. BRUNNE *Chron. Wace* (Rolls) 4745 Oþer bachelers skirmede faste, Wrastlede, lepen, stones caste. *c* **1380** *Sir Ferumb.* 2227 Somme for to sckyrme asay with swerd & bokelere. *c* **1430** *Pilgr. Lyf Manhode* II. cxxi. (1869) 120 Now j wole telle of the staf;..I skirme therwith and defende me. ? *c* **1450** HOLLAND *Houlat* 67 (Bann. MS.), Sum bird will bay at my beke,..sum skyrme at myn e.

**b.** *trans.* To engage with (one) in fight. *rare*$^{-1}$.

*c* **1400** *Destr. Troy* 13601 þow has britnet my brether..; And now Aschatus with skath wold skirme to þe deth.

**2.** *intr.* To dart about, move rapidly.

**13..** *E.E. Allit. P.* B. 483 Ho skyrmez vnder skwe & skowtez aboute, Tyl hit was nyȝe at þe naȝt. *c* **1400** *Destr. Troy* 12500 Hit skirmyt in the skewes with a skyre low.

Hence **'skirming** *vbl. sb.*

In *Wars Alex.* 5157 the form *skirmand* prob. stands for *skremand* screaming.

*c* **1275** LAY. 8144 þeos twei cnihtes bi-gonnen to sceremigge [*read* -inge]. *a* **1300** *Havelok* 2323 Buttinge with sharpe speres, Skirming with taleuaces þat men beres. **13..** *K. Alis.* 672 (Laud MS.), Now can Alisaundre of skirmyng, As of stedes derayeyng.

† **'skirmery.** *Obs. rare.* [ad. OF. **eskirmerie* (var. of *escrimerie*), f. *eskirmir*: see prec.] Skirmishing, fencing.

*c* **1450** *Merlin* xxi. 368 The kynge Bohors, that moche cowde of skirmerie, resceyved the stroke on his shelde. *Ibid.* xxviii. 571 Dodinell caste a stroke of skirmerye to monevall.

**'skirmish** ('skɜːmɪʃ), *sb.* Forms: α. 4 skarmuch, 4, 6 -moch, 5 -moche, -masche, 6 -musch(e, -mouch; 4 scharmoch, -mus; 5 scarmuche, -musche, -musshe, 6 -muss, -mouch(e, -moge; 6 skaramouche, scaramoche, -moshe. β. 4–5 skarmich, 4 -myssh, 6 -mische; 4 scarmich, -mych(e, 5 -mysshe. γ. 4–6 skyrmysshe, 5–6 -mysh, 6 -myshe, -mish; 4–6 skirmysshe (5 scir-, 6 schyr-), 6 -mysche, -mishe, 6– skirmish; 5 skermyshe, 6 -mysche, 7 -mish. δ. 6 skyrmosh, skyr-, skirmush. ε. 5–6 skermyche; 6 scir-, 6–7 skirmige, 8–9 *dial.* -idge; 6 scir-, 6–7 skirmage. [The earlier forms are ad. OF. *escar(a)moche, -muche, -musche*, etc., ad. It. *scaramuccia* (cf. Sp. *escaramuza*, Pg. *-muça*), of doubtful origin. The later forms *scar-, sker-, skirmish* (cf. SCRIMISH *sb.*) have been influenced by those forms of the vb. which are derived from OF. *eskirmiss-*; with the obsolete variants of these in *-iche, -ige, -age*, cf. SCRIMMAGE *sb.* and the forms of RUBBISH.]

**1.** An irregular engagement between two small bodies of troops, esp. detached or outlying portions of opposing armies; a petty fight or encounter. Also occas. without article, as a mode of fighting.

α. **13..** *E.E. Allit. P.* B. 1186 þenne was þe sege sette þe Cete aboute, Skete skarmoch skelt. *c* **1374** CHAUCER *Troylus* II. 934 (Campsall MS.), Now late..we oure tales holde Of Troylus þat is to palays ryden Fro þe skarmuch. *c* **1475** *Harl. Contin. Higden* (Rolls) VIII. 533 They..made there many skarmuches. **1481** CAXTON *Godfrey* cliv. 228 And there was the skarmoche grete & fiers. **1562** J. SHUTE tr. *Cambini's Turk. Wars* 33 They helde them contynually occupied.. with scaramoshes, alarmes, and false assaultes. **1590** SPENSER *F.Q.* II. vi. 34 Not this rude kind of battell, nor these armes Are meet,..Such cruell game my scarmoges disarmes. **1601** J. CHAMBERLAINE *Lett.* (Camden) 115 Slaine there with a shot in an obscure scarmouch.

β. *c* **1374** CHAUCER *Troylus* II. 611 Ascry aros at skarmyssh [*v.r.* scarmich] al with oute. *c* **1400** *Destr. Troy* xx. Title, Of ..Skarmiches Lastyng xxx dayes Betwene the Towne & the tenttes. **1489** CAXTON *Faytes of A.* I. xxiv. 75 To haue them fyrst at a scarmysshe ayenst the aduersaryes.

γ. *c* **1400** *Brut* ccxxxiv. 324 Pryns Edward,..with sore skyrmisshes & fightyng and grete assautes, fought with hem. *c* **1440** *Partonope* 911 To profer Skyrmyssh to this Castell. *a* **1513** FABYAN *Chron.* v. cxviii. (1811) 94 By dayly skyrmysshes & assautes he loste moche of his people. **1560** DAUS tr. *Sleidane's Comm.* 267 b, The Prince..had offered them the skermysche with the light horsemen. **1592** KYD *Sp. Trag.* I. ii, While they maintaine hot skirmish too and fro, Both battailes ioyne. **1688** J. S. *Art of War* 2 Distances for intire Doublings or Skermishes between rank and file is 3 foot. **1761** HUME *Hist. Eng.* (1806) IV. lv. 276 In many counties, where the people were divided, mobbish combats and skirmishes ensued. **1810** WELLINGTON in Gurw. *Desp.* (1837) VI. 496 Our cavalry had a skirmish with the enemy ..in which they had the advantage. **1874** GREEN *Short Hist.* iii. §5. 141 At this critical moment..the Earl fell in an Irish skirmish.

δ. **1514** in Ellis *Orig. Lett.* Ser. II. I. 313 Who hathe had manye skyrmoshys withe hyme. **1560** WHITEHORNE *Ord. Souldiours* (1588) 352 Y^e^ assaultes..which be called skirmushes be easilie withstood.

ε. **1556** *Chron. Grey Friars* (Camden) 45 Thys yere..was a grete skermyche in the northe abowte Carlelle. **1567** DRANT *Hor. Ep.* I. i. B viij, The valiant man of warre May..liue at lengthe a parte from scirmage farre. **1581** RICHE *Farew.* (1846) 8 The orders of sondrie battailes, and the maner of skirmiges. **1623** in Foster *Eng. Factories Ind.* (1908) II. 240 In the heate of scermadge. **1680** C. NESS *Ch. Hist.* 96 Save onely two poor spirts, or small skirmages. *c* **1746** J. COLLIER (Tim Bobbin) *View Lanc. Dial.* Wks. (1775) 46 While the Skirmidge lastut. *a* **1825** FORBY *Voc. E. Anglia* 305 *Skirmidge*, a skirmish. **1854** MISS BAKER *Northampt. Gloss.*

†**2.** A body of skirmishers. *Obs.*

**1562** J. SHUTE tr. *Cambini's Turk. Wars* 23 b, Minutius forthwith sent forthe his lighte armed men and attacked the scaramoche.

**3.** *transf.* **a.** Any contest or encounter.

**1576** FLEMING *Panopl. Epist.* 43 Bitter bruntes and shrewde skyrmishes of aduersitie. **1599** SHAKS. *Much Ado* I. i. 64 They neuer meet, but there's a skirmish of wit between them. **1615** G. SANDYS *Trav.* 58 Incountring still in loues sweete skirmiges. **1690** C. NESS *Hist. O. & N. Test.* I. 300 His violent wrestling was not..a short skirmish of a few day-hours. **1724** DE FOE *Mem. Cavalier* (1840) 74, I had a new skirmish with him whose the money should be. **1823** LAMB *Elia* II. *Poor Relations*, Many and hot were the skirmishes on this topic. **1853** KANE *Grinnell Exp.* l. (1856) 472 In two days more, after a closing skirmish with the ice-pack, we headed homeward.

**b.** An action or proceeding of a slight character; a slight display *of* something.

**1651** N. BACON *Disc. Govt. Eng.* II. xxvi. (1739) 114 By light skirmishes of borrowing smaller sums of money,..and paying them again, thereby to gain credit for greater sums. **1681** FLAVEL *Right. Man's Ref.* 166 The fury of his anger, not some light skirmish of his judgment.

**c.** A scamper, scramble.

**1835** T. ARNOLD in *Life & Corr.* (1844) I. vii. 428, I never have regarded a regular walk along a road..as exercise... A skirmish over the country is a very different thing.

**4.** *attrib.*, as ***skirmish-drill, -line.***

**1868** UPTON *Inf. Tactics* §638 In the skirmish-drill the officers..will constantly aim to impress each man with the idea of his individuality. **1876** *N. Amer. Rev.* CXXIII. 241 The wonderful exploits on the skirmish-line and at the outposts.

**skirmish** ('skɜːmɪʃ), *v.* Forms: α. 5 scarmuche, -mushe, 5–6 -musshe, 6 -musch, -mush, -muss, -mosh; scarmuss. β. 5–6 scarmysshe, 5 -myshe, -mish, 6 -missh, -mesh; 5 scarmiss, -mys; 5 skarmysshe, 6 -misch, -mis. γ. 5 scermish, 5–6 skyrmysshe, 6 -myshe, -mish, skirmishe, -misch, 6– skirmish (7 scir-). δ. 6 skyrmyche, 9 *dial.* -mage. [The α-forms are ad. OF. *escar(a)mucher, -mucier*, ad. It. *scaramucciare* (cf. Sp. *escaramuzar*, Pg. *-muçar*), f. *scaramuccia*: see prec. The forms in *-ish* are influenced by, or directly based on, OF. *eskirmiss-, eskermiss-*, the lengthened stem of *eskermir*, etc.: see SKIRM *v.*]

**1. a.** *intr.* To engage in a skirmish or irregular encounter; to fight in small parties. Freq. const. *with.*

α. *c* **1470** *Contin. Brut* cclix. 528 þe Duke..gat peple to him, which come out & scarmusshed [1482 *Caxton* scarmuched] with þame of Caleys. **1562** J. SHUTE tr. *Cambini's Turk. Wars* 33 They salied forth daiely and scaramoshed with them. **1598** BARRET *Theor. Wars* III. ii. 46 Any part of shot or pikes..set to defend any straight, or to scarmush.

β. *c* **1420** *Chron. Vilod.* 282 þus men bygonne & scarmysshute fast, þe twey hostes bothe y-fere. *c* **1475** *Partenay* 2079 On a day he went, to scarmish with thaim.

γ. *a* **1513** FABYAN *Chron.* VII. (1811) 512 He..issuyd boldly agayne y^e^ foresayd persones and skyrmysshed with them. *a* **1548** HALL *Chron., Hen. IV*, 21 Thei with light horses began to skirmishe with his hoste. **1617** MORYSON *Itin.* II. 141 Sir John Barkeley..skirmishing with them, killed some dead in the place. **1683** *Brit. Spec.* 88 Next Morning the Britains..skirmished with the Roman Horse. **1796** MORSE *Amer. Geogr.* I. 123 Thence to Acomac, where he skirmished with some Indians. **1855** MACAULAY *Hist. Eng.* xv. III. 607 Some of his ships should skirmish with the enemy: but the great body of his fleet should not be risked.

δ. **1530** PALSGR. 720/1 They dyd skyrmyche togyther syxe dayes or ever the batayles joyned. **1841** HARTSHORNE *Salop. Ant.* Gloss., *Skirmage*, to skirmish.

**b.** In fig. uses or contexts.

**1587** TURBERV. *Trag. Tales* 17 Bebrusht with bryers her broosed body bled, The brambles skirmishte had with every vayne. **1601** WEEVER *Mirr. Mart.* A viij b, But inward Senses skirmish in the night. **1648** CRASHAW *Delights of Muses* 20 Awakes his Lute,..and ere the warre begin, He lightly skirmishes on every string. **1751** JOHNSON *Rambler* No. 96 ¶11 [Falsehood] sometimes waited the attack; but always endeavoured to skirmish at a distance. **1886** GLADSTONE in *Times* 9 Apr. 5/5 We should no longer fence or skirmish with this question... We should come to close quarters with it.

**c.** *colloq.* (orig. *U.S.*). To make excursions in order to see what one can find; to scout *round* in search of something.

**1864** 'MARK TWAIN' in Harte & 'Twain' *Sk. Sixties* (1926) 129 His first cousin..is a skirmisher and is with the parson —he goes through the camp-meetings and skirmishes for raw converts. **1869** —— *Innocents Abroad* ix. 86 When the commissary department fails they 'skirmish', as Jack terms it in his sinful, slangy way. **1893** M. HOLLEY *Samantha at World's Fair* xix. 608 The males, from creation down, have been left free to skirmish round and git a livin' for themselves. **1894** 'R. ANDOM' *We Three & Troddles* xxiii. 220 He left the room to skirmish after a clean handkerchief. *Ibid.* xxiv. 231 We had them downstairs and into the cab before they could skirmish after more substantial fare. **1907** S. E. WHITE *Arizona Nights* 17 We skirmished around and found a condemned army pack saddle with aparejos.

†**2.** To fence; to make flourishes with a weapon.

**1387** TREVISA *Higden* (Rolls) IV. 399 þan Nero made oon skirmysshe above Seneca his heed with a bryght swerd. *c* **1450** *Merlin* xxxii. 648 He myght not se where to smyte, and be-gan to scarmyshe and to grope a-boute hym with his staffe. **1582** N. LICHEFIELD tr. *Castanheda's Conq. E. Ind.* I. vii. 18 b, Then were in sight the number of twentie Moores skirmishing with their dartes. **1763** J. BROWN *Poet. & Music* xxxvi. 97 After skirmishing for some time with their Swords, one of them (as wounded) fell down.

†**3. a.** *trans.* To engage or attack (an enemy) in or with a skirmish. Also *fig. Obs.*

*c* **1500** *Melusine* 273 Yonder is the kyng vryan.., that scarmyssheth theire nauye. *a* **1578** LINDESAY (Pitscottie) *Chron. Scot.* (S.T.S.) II. 109 They..fell to the Inglischemen, and skirmischit thame so haitlie that they caussit thame reteir. **1599** HAKLUYT *Voy.* II. I. 83 The great quantity of artillery..skirmished them so well [etc.]. **1679** ALSOP *Melius Inq.* II. iii. 245 To war with God or skirmish the Scripture is no approved method to secure Peace.

†**b.** *fig.* To win by skirmish. *Obs.*$^{-1}$

*a* **1797** WALPOLE *Geo. II* (1847) II. viii. 271 Fox even skirmished his borough from Dr. Hay.

**skirmisher** ('skɜːmɪʃə(r)). [f. prec. + -ER.] One of a number of soldiers taking part in a skirmish or acting in loose order apart from the main body of an army or battalion.

**1565** COOPER *Thesaurus, Excursor*, a skirmishar. **1579** DIGGES *Stratiot.* 156 That his Skirmishers and light armed be beaten in. **1622** PEACHAM *Compl. Gentl.* xx. (1634) 246 If this be exactly done the Skirmishers will never be above the length of one File behind the body of your Pikes. **1642** FULLER *Holy & Prof. St.* IV. xvii. 329 Skirmishers are scouts for the discovery of the strength of an army, before battel be given. **1799** *Cavalry Instr.* (1813) 269 Skirmishers are to be very attentive..in instantly obeying the signals made for their direction. **1844** H. H. WILSON *Brit. India* III. 199 A detachment of whom..were employed as skirmishers and marksmen. **1875** KINGLAKE *Crimea* V. ii. 382 Our skirmishers gained the edge of the bank.

**b.** *transf.* and *fig.* Something sent out in advance.

**1820** SCOTT *Monast.* Introd. Ep., As you usually throw out a few lines of verse (by way of skirmishers, I suppose) at the head of each division of prose. **1890** *Pall Mall G.* 18 Jan. 1/3 We have four advertising cars, which go one, two, three and four weeks ahead. These we call 'skirmishers'.

**skirmishing** ('skɜːmɪʃɪŋ), *vbl. sb.* Forms: (see the vb.). [f. SKIRMISH *v.*] The action of engaging, or taking part, in a skirmish or skirmishes.

α. β. *c* **1385** CHAUCER *L.G.W.* 1910 *Ariadne*, So hyt happed, that at a skarmysshynge [*v.r.* scarmuchyng, etc.], She caste hir hert vpon Mynos the kynge. **1489** CAXTON *Faytes of A.* I. xviii. 54 Whan prisouners be taken in scarmyshyng or otherwyse. *c* **1500** *Melusine* 131 Thenne bygan the scarmusshing of strong & grete and moche mortal. **1533** BELLENDEN *Livy* I. xx. (S.T.S.) I. 116 The fulich gabynis.. straik sindri small skarmischingis and batallis aganis þe romanis. *a* **1600** *Hist. Jas. VI* (Bann. Cl.) 128 He fell in the hands of the said capten efter a light scarmeshing.

γ. **1592** *Soliman & Pers.* IV. i, The self same musick that in auncient daies Brought Alexander..from skirmishing to kissing. **1603** KNOLLES *Hist. Turks* (1638) 180 Wearied with the heat of the day and long skirmishing. **1724** DE FOE *Mem. Cavalier* (1840) 259 An infinite number of party skirmishings..happened. **1839** JAMES *Louis XIV*, I. 307 Merely the skirmishing of light troops before the commencement of a general battle. **1855** MACAULAY *Hist. Eng.* xiii. III. 333 Mackay, meanwhile, wasted some weeks ..in indecisive skirmishing.

*attrib.* **1858** BROCK *Havelock* xiii. 210 Advance was made in skirmishing order on the entrenched quadrangles.

*fig.* **1656** *Artif. Handsom.* 42 Which are but light skirmishings, and not serious contendings in matters of Religion. **1687** in *Magd. Coll. Collect.* (O.H.S.) 166 All this was but skirmishing in respect of what was done on Saturday. **1864** BOWEN *Logic* x. 338 Little is to be hoped for from the skirmishings..and desultory movements of the intellect.

**skirmishing** ('skɜːmɪʃɪŋ), *ppl. a.* [f. as prec.] Engaging in a skirmish or skirmishes; designed for skirmishing.

**1781** in Simes *Milit. Guide* (ed. 3) 8 [The Adjutant-general] gives and signs all the orders for skirmishing parties. **1799** *Cavalry Instr.* (1813) 269 Skirmishing detachments are usually made of a flank division or subdivision. **1873** TRISTRAM *Moab* i. 9 The wild fellows were thrown out on all sides, and formed a skirmishing front all the way.

Hence **'skirmishingly** *adv.*, in a skirmishing manner.

**1848** DICKENS *Dombey* xxxv, The upholsterer's foreman ..skirmishingly measuring expensive objects. **1889** *Chamb. Jrnl.* 5 Oct. 638/1 What loading-up he did was very skirmishingly effected from the rear.

**skirp,** *v. rare.* Now *Sc.* [a. ON. *skirpa* (also Icel. and MSw.), to spit.]

†**1. a.** *intr.* To behave with contempt. **b.** *trans.* To mock, deride. (Cf. SCRIP *v.*[2]) *Obs. rare.*

*c* **1200** ORMIN 7393 ȝiff þeȝȝ herenn ohht off Godd, & skirrpenn þær onnȝæness. *Ibid.* 7389. ? *c* **1450** HOLLAND *Howlat* 67 (Bann. MS.), Sum bird will..skirp me with scorne.

**2.** *trans.* To splash up on; to bespatter.

**1871** W. ALEXANDER *Johnny Gibb* (1873) 18 The boat rising up and down on its very ends, and leaning over till the spray actually 'skirpit' her face.

**skirr** (skɜː(r)), *sb.* Also scurr, skurr. [f. the vb.] A sound of a grating, rasping, or whirring character.

*c* **1870** M. CLARKE in *Mem. Vol.* (1884) 127 How many nights in that humble shelter have I listened to the skirr of the wild cats. **1874** T. HARDY *Far fr. Mad. Crowd* I. xx. 219 The scurr of whetting [*sc.* shears] spread into the sky. **1887** —— *Woodlanders* III. ii. 44 The occasional skirr of a halter in Melbury's stables.

**skirr** (skɜː(r)), *v.* Forms: α. 6 skyr, 6–7, 9– skir, 7 skirre, 7, 9– skirr; 6, 9 *dial.* sker. β. 7, 9 scur (9 *dial.* skur), 9 scurr. [Of doubtful origin; the form *scur* could represent OF. *escorre*, *escourre*:—L. *excurrĕre*, but the existing evidence indicates the priority of *skir*.]

**1.** *intr.* To run hastily (*away*); to flee, make off; = SCOUR *v.*[1] 1 c.

α. *a* **1548** HALL *Chron., Rich. III*, 54 b, Your..bragging adversaries.. wil flee, ronne, & skyr out of the felde. **1599** SHAKS. *Hen. V*, IV. vii. 64 We will come to them, And make them sker away. **1602** *Life Ld. Cromwell* III. ii, So many battles have I overpass'd And made the French skir when they heard my name.

β. **1887** CAINE *Deemster* xxxvii, From their confusion in scurring away, I knew that the sheep had indeed been there.

**2.** To move, run, fly, sail, etc., rapidly or with great impetus. Sometimes implying a whirring sound accompanying the movement. Usu. const. with advs. or preps.

α. **1567** TURBERV. *Epit.*, etc. 7 Let Zeuxis Grapes not make him proude at all, Though Fowles for them did skyr against a wall. *a* **1656** USSHER *Ann.* (1658) 315 Seleucus with an hundred ships,.. in a scornful manner, skirred along under the noses of them. **1674** tr. *Scheffer's Lapland* 5 From their skirring along, or gliding upon the snow. **1827** J. F. COOPER *Prairie* II. xii. 198 Suddenly one of the.. most ferocious of them all broke out of the ring, and skirred away in the direction of her victims. **1872** BLACKIE *Lays Highl.* 113 The black-maned clouds, like Furies on the wing, Skir past.

β. *a* **1616** BEAUM. & FL. *Bonduca* I. i, The light shadows, That in a thought scur o'r the fields of Corn. **1842** BORROW *Bible in Spain* xxii, The animal, who was scurring over the field,..instantly returned. **1866** *Reader* 17 Feb. 173/1 A picture..of the wind and the rain, as the first scurs at its fiercest speed.

**b.** *dial.* To slide or skate swiftly.

**1811** WILLAN in *Archaeologia* XVII. 158 *Sker*, to slide swiftly, to skait. **1825-** in dial. glossaries (Northumb., Lancs., Devon, Cornwall).

**3.** *trans.* To pass or go rapidly over (a stretch of land or water), esp. in search of something or some one. (Cf. SCOUR *v.*[1] 2.) †Also, to ride rapidly *through*.

**1605** SHAKS. *Macb.* V. iii. 35 Send out moe Horses, skirre the Country round. *a* **1625** FLETCHER *Love's Cure* II. ii, Whil'st I with that, and this well mounted, scurr'd A Horse-troope through, and through. **1816** BYRON *Siege Corinth* xxii, Mount ye, spur ye, skirr the plain, That the fugitive may flee in vain. **1826** SCOTT *Kelly's Reminisc.* Misc. Wks. 1870 XX. 234 An adventurous little schooner of this kind skirring the coast in search of its own peculiar objects. **1877** BLACKMORE *Cripps* ii, The broader puddles, though skirred by the breeze, found the network of ice veiling over them.

*fig.* **1821** BYRON *Cain* III. i. 64, I had..skirr'd extinguish'd worlds; And, gazing on eternity, methought [etc.].

**4.** To throw with a rapid skimming motion. Cf. SKEER *v.*[1]

*a* **1652** BROME *Mad Couple* I. i, None dare venture so neare you as a Man hurles a Die or Skirrs a Card. **18..** in *Eng. Dial. Dict.* s.v., 'See me skirr this stone.' A word used only ..in connection with this boyish test of skill. **1894** BLACKMORE *Perlycross* xxxv. 358 Polwarth..skirred his flat hat into the middle of the sawdust.

Hence **'skirring** *ppl. a.*

**1573** TWYNE *Æneid* XII. Mm ij b, As the swallow..With tendre houeringe winges her skirringe flight swift forward takes. **1827** J. WILSON *Noct. Ambr.* Wks. 1855 I. 277 *North*. Have you had any snow yet James, in the forest? *Shepherd*. Only some skirrin sleets.

**skirrack**, obs. var. SKERRICK.

**skirret**[1] ('skɪrɪt). Forms: α. 4 **skyrwate**, 5-6 **skyrwyt** (5 **-wytte**, **skerwyth**, **scyrwyȝth**, **schirewyt**), 6 **skyrwit**; 4 **skirwhite**, 4-5 **-whit**, 5-7 **-wit**, 6 **-wike**, 7 **-wicke**. β. 6 **skyrwort**, **-wurt**, 6-8 **skirwort**, 6 **-wurt**, 7 **-wirt**; 7 **skir(r)iwort**. γ. 6 **skyrrit**, 6- **skirret** (6 **skiret**), 7 **skirrot**; 7 **skerret**, 8 **-ett**, **-it**. [ME. *skirwhit(e*, app. an alteration by popular etymology (? simulating *skire white* pure white) of OF. *eschervis* (mod.F. *chervis*), which is closely related to Sp. *chirivia*, Pg. *cherivia*, and appears to be a variant of OF. *carvi* CARAWAY. The later Eng. *skirret* is a natural development from *skirwhit*, while *skirwort* represents a further attempt to make the word intelligible.]

**1. a.** A perennial umbelliferous plant, *Sium sisarum*, a species of water parsnip, formerly much cultivated in Europe for its esculent tubers; the root of this plant.

In one or two 15th cent. glossaries *skyrwyt* renders L. *eruca*, prob. in error.

α. **1338** in Dugdale *Monasticon* (1846) II. 585/1 In flore, *jd*. In skirwhittes, *jd*. *a* **1387** *Sinon. Barthol.* (Anecd. Oxon.) 12 *Baucea*, skirwhit. *Ibid.* 33 *Pastinaca*, skirwhite. *c* **1440** *Promp. Parv.* 458/1 Skyrwyt, herbe or rote. **1530** PALSGR. 271/1 Skyrwyt, an herbe. **1579** LANGHAM *Gard. Health* (1633) 600 Skirwits: The roots boiled are good for the stomacke. **1639** HORN & ROB. *Gate Lang. Unl.* xii. §126 The rape.., the navew, parsnip, carret, skirwit.

β. **1548** TURNER *Names Herbes* (E.D.S.) 74 Fuchsius rekoneth that our skyrwort or skyrwit is a kynde of siser. Persnepes and skirwortes are commune in Englande. **1578** LYTE *Dodoens* 605 Skirwurtes are hoate and drie in the seconde degree. **1611** SPEED *Theat. Gr. Brit.* xxxix. (1614) 78 Pomfret..brings forth liquorice and great plenty of skiriworts. **1725** *Fam. Dict.*, *Skirret* or *Skirwort*.

γ. **1573** TUSSER *Husb.* (1878) 94 Herbes and rootes for sallets and sauce... Skirrets. **1608** MACHIN *Dumbe Knight* I, Roasted potatoes, or boil'd skerrets, are your only lofty dishes. **1699** EVELYN *Acetaria* 64 Skirrets..exceedingly nourishing, wholsome and delicate. **1732** ARBUTHNOT *Rules of Diet in Aliments*, etc. I. 250 Skirrets, useful in bloody Urine, and Spitting of Blood. **1803** A. HUNTER *Georg. Ess.* I. 416 Half a pound of skirrets, an ounce and a half of pure sugar. **1855** DELAMER *Kitchen Gard.* (1861) 33 The Skirret. .. A native of China, with the root composed of fleshy tubers..growing together something like a dahlia root.

*attrib.* **1728** E. SMITH *Compleat Housewife* (ed. 2) 113 (*heading*) To make a skirret-pye. **1840** AINSWORTH *Tower of London* (1864) 85 A skirret pasty; an apple tansy; and a prodigious marrow pudding.

**b.** With distinguishing terms, as *garden*, *wild*; also applied to other species of *Sium* (quot. 1796).

*c* **1450** *Alphita* (Anecd. Oxon.) 30 *Carui agreste*, wyldeschirewyt. **1580** HOLLYBAND *Treas. Fr. Tong*, *Chervis sauvages*, wild Skirwike. **1601** HOLLAND *Pliny* II. 41 To come more particularly to the garden Skirwort. **1713** *Phil. Trans.* XXVIII. 42 Garden Skirrets. **1796** WITHERING *Brit. Pl.* (ed. 3) II. 299 *Sium latifolium*.., Broad-leaved Skerrett. Great Water Parsnep. *Ibid.*, *S. angustifolium*.., Upright Water Parsnep. Narrow-leaved Skerret.

†**c.** ***skirret of Peru***, the potato. *Obs.*

**1597** GERARDE *Herbal* II. cccxxxiv. 780 This plant which is called of some *Sisarum Peruuianum*, or Skyrrits of Peru, is generally of vs called Potatus or Potatoes.

**2.** ***skirret-root***, the edible root of the plant *Sium sisarum*, or, more frequently, the plant itself.

**1565** COOPER *Thesaurus* s.v. *Siser*, One kinde of it is the roote that is called Skirwike rootes. **1601** HOLLAND *Pliny* XIX. v. II. 18 The Skirwirt root or white Parsnip, (which indeed would be written among other Physicke plants). **1655** MOUFET & BENNET *Health's Improv.* (1746) 326 Skirret-roots were so sweet and delicate in ancient times, that [etc.]. **1736** AINSWORTH II, *Siser*,..the skirret root.

**'skirret**[2]. *Freemasonry.* (See quots.)

**1825** *Republican* 29 July 123 The skirret is an implement which acts on a centre pin, from whence a centre line is drawn, chalked and struck, to mark out the ground for the foundation of the intended structure. **1853** G. OLIVER *Dict. Symb. Masonry* 339 The skirret acting on a centre pin is used to mark out the ground of a new building. As the skirret has a chalked line attached to it [etc.]. **1877** K. R. H. MACKENZIE *Roy. Masonic Cycl.* 677 *Skirret*.—One of the working tools of a Master Mason. It is an instrument usually made of wood, shaped like the letter **T**, acting on a centre-pin.

**skirrh**, var. SCIRRHE *Obs.*

**skirr(h)ous**, obs. ff. SCIRRHOUS *a.*

**skirrick**, obs. var. SKERRICK.

**skirring**, *ppl. a.*: see SKIRR *v.*

**skirry**, var. SCURRY *v.* (Cf. SKIRR *v.*)

**1869** 'OUIDA' *Tricotrin* I. 260 She is no more dead than that mouse that skirries over the floor.

**skirt** (skɜːt), *sb.* Forms: 4-7 **skirte** (6 **-the**, 7 **scirte**), 4- **skirt** (6 **schirt**, 7 **skeart**); 4-6 **skyrte** (5 **-tte**, **scyrtte**), 5-6 **skyrt**; 5-6 **skurte**, 8 **scurt**; 6 **skort**. [a. ON. *skyrta* (Icel. *skyrta*, Norw. *sjørte*, *sjorte*, *sjurte*; MSw. *skiurta*, *skiorta*, Sw. *skjorta*, Da. *skjorte*) shirt, = OE. *scyrte*: see SHIRT *sb.* The development of the Eng. sense is obscure, but the corresponding LG. *schört* has in some districts the sense of 'woman's gown'.]

**I. 1. a.** The lower part of a woman's dress or gown, covering the person from the waist downwards; also, esp. in modern use, a separate outer garment serving this purpose. †In ME. occas. = LAP *sb.* 4 b.

*divided skirt*, a form of skirt divided in the middle and presenting the appearance of full knickerbockers; also, a skirt made in two widths and open back and front, used in riding or cycling.

*a* **1300** *Cursor M.* 8963 Sco lift hir skirt wit-vten scurn, And bar-fote wode sco þat burn. *c* **1440** *Gesta Rom.* xlvi. 188 (Add. MS.), The woman..toke his hede into her skirthe, and he began strongely for to slepe. *c* **1440** *Alph. Tales* 398 When þe childe was born it was broght & layd in hur skurte. **1535** COVERDALE *Lam.* i. 9 Ierusalem synned euer more & more... Hir skyrtes are defyled, she remembred not what wolde folowe. **1590** SPENSER *F.Q.* II. ix. 37 In a long purple pall, whose skirt with gold Was fretted all about, she was arayd. *a* **1625** BEAUM. & FL. *Two Noble Kinsmen* II. ii, This is a pretty colour, wi'lt not do Rarely upon a skirt, wench? **1670** in *12th Rep. Hist. MSS. Comm.* App. V. 21 Upon the Queene's Birthday most wore embraudered bodys with plaine black skirts of Morella Mohair and Prunella. **1845** S. JUDD *Margaret* I. xiv, She put on her white muslin tunic and pink skirt. **1885** 'V. LEE' *Let.* in P. Gunn *V. Lee* (1964) x. 127 A very bright blue paper dress suggestive of divided skirts and ulster to match. **1890** *Pall Mall Gaz.* 2 Sept. 7/1 A divided skirt..is the clumsiest..article that a woman can put on. **1899** CONAN DOYLE *Duet* (1909) 105/2 With a swift rustle of skirts, she was between the door and his chair.

*fig.* **1857** W. T. MATSON *Resurgam* Poems (1858) 142 When Darkness gathers up the skirts of gloom.

**b.** A woman; *the skirt*, women collectively. ***a bit of skirt***: a woman; esp. an attractive one. Now *slang*.

**1560** ROLLAND *Seven Sages* 52 Now thow thy tale hes tauld,..Bot not gottin thow wald, licht skirt for all thy skippis. **1899** HYNE *Further Adv. Capt. Kettle* xii. 298 If any of you rats of men shove your way down here..before all the skirt is ferried across [etc.]. **1914** S. LEWIS *Our Mr. Wrenn* iv. 55 Pete was..singing hoarsely, 'Dey was a skoit and 'er name was Goity.' **1916** C. J. DENNIS *Doreen & Sentimental Bloke* 89 *Skirt, or bit of skirt*, a female. **1928** D. H. LAWRENCE *Woman who rode Away* 283 And what about your American skirt?—I told him, there was nothing to say about her. **1934** J. BROPHY *Waterfront* ii. 42 A nice juicy bit of skirt, eh? **1958** 'N. CULOTTA' *They're a Weird Mob* 190 'Reckon we better stick ter beer?' 'Until them other two skirts turn up.' **1974** K. MILLETT *Flying* (1975) v. 469 The two patriarchs, never tired of chasing twenty-year-old skirts in their old age. **1977** J. I. M. STEWART *Madonna of Astrolabe* xx. 280 They mustn't quarrel over a bit of skirt.

**c.** An underskirt or petticoat.

**1862** *Catal. Internat. Exhib., Industr. Dept., Brit. Div.* II. No. 3674 Counterpanes, toilette-covers, skirts. *Ibid.* No. 4935 Spiral Crinoline Steel and Bronze for Ladies' Skirts. **1908** M. E. MORGAN *How to dress Doll* v. 51 The flannel skirt is cut from a straight piece of fine white flannel.

**2. a.** The lower part of a man's gown or robe. Now chiefly *Hist.* or with reference to Eastern countries.

*c* **1330** R. BRUNNE *Chron. Wace* (Rolls) 7884 þe kyng.. anon vp stirt, Bot Hengist laughtym by þe skirt, & held hym as stille as ston. **13..** *Gaw. & Gr. Knt.* 865 [A robe] þat sete on hym semly, wyth saylande skyrtez. ? *a* **1400** *Morte Arth.* 3473 Many schredys and schragges at his skyrttes hynnges. *c* **1440** *Alph. Tales* 65 He grapid in his bosom & fand xij d of gold, & he keste þaim in þis wude preste skyrte. **1535** COVERDALE *Ps.* cxxxii[i]. 2 It..ranne downe vnto the beerd, ..& wente downe to the skyrtes of his clothinge. **1598** BP. HALL *Sat.* IV. i, Or wilie Cyppus, that can winke and snort Whiles his wife dallyes on Mæcenas skort. **1784** COWPER *Task* II. 822 In the skirts Of the rob'd pedagogue. **1797** MRS. RADCLIFFE *Italian* vii, I saw the skirts of his garments ascending up those steps in the rock. **1841** LANE *Arab. Nts.* I. 105 He stretched forth his hand, and lifted up the skirts of his clothing.

*fig.* **1884** *Fortn. Rev.* June 754 He proudly lifts his skirts lest they should trail in the mire of antiquated Conservatism.

**b.** The bottom, lower portion, or tail of a coat or similar garment. Chiefly *pl.*

**1598** SHAKS. *Merry W.* I. i. 29 If he ha's a quarter of your coat, there is but three Skirts for your selfe. **1632** J. HAYWARD tr. *Biondi's Eromena* 92 Because he could not come to kisse his hand, he reverently kissed the skirt of his armour. **1659-60** PEPYS *Diary* 1 Jan., I rose, put on my suit with great skirts, having not lately worn any other clothes but them. **1711** STEELE *Spectator* No. 145 ¶7 The Skirt of your [men's] fashionable Coats forms as large a Circumference as our Petticoats. **1802** JAMES *Milit. Dict.* s.v., The whole of the British army formerly wore skirts to their coats. **1848** THACKERAY *Van. Fair* xxiv, 'For God's sake, what is it?' Mr. Chopper said, catching the Captain by the skirt.

**3.** In various phrases, denoting close approach or adherence to some person or thing; in earlier use esp. ***to sit on*** (***upon*** or ***in***) ***one's skirts***, to press hard upon one, to deal heavily with, to punish severely. ***to hide behind the skirts of***, to take refuge behind, to use for protection.

(*a*) **1546** HEYWOOD *Prov.* (1867) 10, I shall to reveng former hurtis..syt on theyr skurtis That erst sate on mine. **1577** STANYHURST *Descr. Irel.* in *Holinshed* (1808) VI. 32 They would not..forget nor forgive so horrible a murther, but were fullie resolved..to sit in their skirts. *c* **1630** BP. SANDERSON *Serm.* II. 271 Adversaries; who..might sit closer upon their skirts than formerly, and do them a shrewder turn for it another day. **1654** H. L'ESTRANGE *Chas. I* (1655) 184 Many began..to sit upon the Bishops skirts, that is, to controvert the motes and bounds of their authority. **1706** E. WARD *Wooden World Diss.* (1708) 12 He'll be sure to sit like Pitch on his Skirts. **1755** SMOLLETT *Quix.* II. III. xv. (1803) IV. 75 If my government holds,..I will sit upon the skirts of more than one of these men of business.

(*b*) **1579** G. HARVEY *Letter-bk.* (Camden) 67 To have everyon in continuall ielouzye lest he sitt over neere there schirtes. **1584** [see SIT *v.* 14 a]. **1809** MALKIN *Gil Blas* v. i. ¶65 A Sicilian gentleman..determined to stick in my skirts, and either ruin or marry me. **1813** *Examiner* 24 May 335/2 He..need not come skulking in under the skirt of a borough-monger. **1840** DICKENS *Old C. Shop* xxxvi, That amiable virgin, having clung to the skirts of the Law from her earliest youth. **1867** LONGF. *Dante, Inf.* xv. 40 Therefore go on; I at thy skirts will come. **1938** G. GRAHAM *Swiss Sonata* 356 Is *she* hiding behind your skirts too? **1975** *Current Hist.* Dec. 230/2 In terms of foreign dominance, Thailand asserted her independence from China only as she was able to hide behind the skirts of the Western giants, Great Britain, France and, most important, the United States.

**II. 4. a.** One of the flaps or lower portions of a saddle. Also ***saddle skirt***, SADDLE *sb.* 12.

**13..** *Gaw. & Gr. Knt.* 601 þe apparayl of þe payttrure, & of þe proude skyrtez, þe cropore, & þe couertor, acorded wyth þe arsounez. *c* **1450** *Merlin* xxiii. 683 [He] smote the horse with the spores on bothe sides faste by the skirtes of his sadell, for his legges were so shorte. **1688** HOLME *Armoury* III. 94/1 The Skirts, the covers of the side of the [saddle] tree, which are Fringed and wrought, and sometime plain. **1723** *Lond. Gaz.* No. 6136/3 A brown quilted Saddle marked J. H. on the near Side Skirts. **1736** CARTE *Life Ormonde* II. 13 This letter was sowen up in the skirt of a saddle. **1866** *Chambers's Encycl.* VIII. 415/1 A saddle consists of the wooden frame or saddle-tree, the skirts or padded under-flaps [etc.].

**b.** The rim or base of a bell or bee-hive.

**1555** *Inv. Ch. Goods* (Surtees) 147 One lytle bell..being.. xxx[th] ynces about the skyrtes. **1609** C. BUTLER *Fem. Mon.* iv. (1623) K ij, The Bees..otherwise might be prest to death betweene the two skirts. **1688** HOLME *Armoury* III. 462/1 The Skirt, the bottom of the Bell. **1707** MORTIMER *Husb.* (1721) I. 275 Some reckon it better to place the Hive..into another, in a place that the skirts may be uppermost. **1736** BAILEY *Househ. Dict.* s.v. *Bees*, When you buy a new hive, try it..whether there be not a hollowness some where or other in the skirt.

**c.** The border, rim, outer portion, extremity, or tail-end of anything. Also *techn.* (see later quots.) and *fig.*

**1566** in *Sidneiana* (Roxb.) 4 A Post-script by my Lady Sidney, in the skirts of my L. Presidents Letter. **1617** MORYSON *Itin.* III. 174 Shasses, that is, striped linnen.. wound about the skirts of a little cap. **1642** FULLER *Holy & Prof. St.* v. xix. 436 Onely the skirts of their lungs were tainted. **1679** MOXON *Mech. Exerc.* ix. 169 *Skirts*, Projecting of the Eaves. **1725** E. W. *Amorous Bugbears* 18, I began to noch down my Observations upon the Skirts of my Memory. **1805** WORDSWORTH *Waggoner* III. 58 And to the waggon's skirts was tied The Creature. **1829** P. NICHOLSON in *Encycl. Metrop.* (1845) VI. 237/2 In the seven diagrams [of roofs] here referred to, the side BC is supposed to be the skirt next to the wall. **1875** KNIGHT *Dict. Mech.* 2196/2 The skirt or external periphery of a millstone; *e.g.* from the eye to the skirt the leader-furrows run. **1951** *Gloss. Aeronaut. Terms (B.S.I.)* III. 15 *Skirt*, the lower portion of the canopy [of a parachute]. **1962** J. GLENN et al. in *Into Orbit* 245 Parachutes used on Mercury capsules are reefed by means of ropes tied around the skirt of the parachute. **1964** J. L. NAYLER *Dict. Astronautics* 252 *Skirt*, the lower outer part of a rocket vehicle. It acts as a fairing to the rocket motor or booster. **1969** *Times* 22 July (Moon Rep. Suppl.) p. iii/7 There's one picture I'm taking now of the right rear of the spacecraft looking at the skirts of the descent stage. **1970** *Gloss. Aeronaut. & Astronaut. Terms (B.S.I.)* VI. 2 *Skirt*, an ærodynamic fairing to influence the airflow in the vicinity of the propelling nozzles.

**d.** *Naut.* A side or leech of a sail.

**1627** CAPT. SMITH *Seaman's Gram.* v. 23 The Leech of a saile is the outward side of a skirt of a saile. **1711** *Milit. & Sea Dict.* (ed. 4) s.v. *Brayls*, Brayls..are fasten'd to the Creengleys at the Skirt of the Sail. **1743** BULKELEY & CUMMINS *Voy. S. Seas* 119 We hoisted a skirt of the Mainsail, and edged further off. **1851** KIPPING *Sailmaking* (ed. 2) 4 In all quadrilateral sails..the sides, or skirts, are called the leeches.

**e.** A surface that conceals or protects the wheels or underneath of a vehicle or aircraft; *spec.* (*a*) a detachable panel concealing part of the wheel of a car and fitted flush with the bodywork; (*b*) a surface designed to deflect the air so as to produce a downward force on the car aerodynamically.

**1912** C. B. HAYWARD *Practical Aeronautics* 286 There are six landing wheels forward, three on each side of the center and enclosed in what is termed a 'skirt'. **1953** FRAZEE & SPICER *Automotive Collision Work* i. 55 Sometimes fender skirts are used on the rear fenders of cars. These skirts cover the wheel opening and are attached to the fender by clamps. **1965** M. C. OAKS *Fell's Guide to Mobile Home Living* vi. 97 Many mobile home owners enclose the space beneath their mobile homes with skirts or siding. These skirts..provide enclosed storage space, protect your tires from the sun, and ..provide extra insulation. **1974** *Country Life* 21 Mar. 659/1 The Triumph Dolomite Sprint..is recognized by its.. discreet spoiler beneath the front skirt. **1981** *Times* 5 Feb. 13/1 The South African Grand Prix will take place at Kyalmi... The cars will be equipped with skirts, almost certainly for the last time. **1981** *Sci. Amer.* Aug. 25/3 Most new main battle tanks have lightly armored 'skirts' to cover vulnerable treads and wheels.

**f.** *Mech.* The lower part of the curved surface of a piston in a piston engine, below the grooves for piston rings. Also *piston skirt*.

**1913** W. E. DOMMETT *Motor Car Mech.* 12 For the sake of lightness and more particularly for use on racing cars, holes are drilled around the lower part or skirt of the piston and two rings only may be used. **1929** NEWTON & STEEDS *Motor Vehicle* vi. 57 In order that finer clearances may be used without risk of seizure, many different designs of semi-flexible skirt have been introduced. **1970** K. BALL *Fiat 600, 600 D Autobook* i. 14/2 In each case, the number is on the opposite side to the slot in the piston skirt.

**g.** A flexible surface that projects downwards underneath a hovercraft to contain or divide the air-cushion.

**1962** *Daily Tel.* 12 Apr. 15/7 The cushion of pressurised air can take any proportion of the weight off the wheels. It is in an adjustable synthetic rubber 'skirt' below the waist-line of the vehicle. **1968** *Economist* 7 Sept. 81/1 The skirt of the hovercraft is one of its most sensitive parts. If the design is not right, the ride is uncomfortable and skirt edges flap up and down on the surface of the sea causing excessive wear. **1977** *Hovering Craft & Hydrofoil* XVII. 18/2 SEDAM, the French manufacturer, claims that their skirt is better than ours, but these claims will be put to the acid test when the N 500 and the SR.N4 Mk 3 run alongside each other on the Channel next year.

**5.** A rim or border; an edging. *rare.*

**1576** BAKER *Jewell of Health* 30 One of the vessels hath a skirte or edge, wythin which the other is receyved. **1688** HOLME *Armoury* III. 325/2 By these Pincers two edges or Skirts of Lead are turned one over the other. **1713** ADDISON *Guard.* No. 118 ¶3 This consists of a narrow lace, or a small skirt of fine ruffled linnen, which runs along the upper part of the stays before.

**6. a.** The diaphragm or midriff of an animal, *esp.* as used for food.

[In the following quotation the sense is not clear:—**1486** *Bk. St. Albans, Hunting* f iij b, Than shall ye kyt the skyrtis the teeth euen fro.]

**1725** *Family Dict.* s.v. *Hog's Tongues*, Drain them a little, and having cut some Hog's Skirts, according to the Length of the Tongues, let every one be put into its Case, made of those Skirts. **1771** MRS. HAYWOOD *New Present for Maid* 18 Then the skirt and tripe. **1844** H. STEPHENS *Bk. Farm* II. 241 The diaphragm or skirt is also cut off. **1868** *Daily News* 19 June, A considerable portion of the livers and skirts are purchased wholesale by retail dealers in low neighbourhoods. **1888** 'R. BOLDREWOOD' *Robbery under Arms* (1890) 121 We had a hearty breakfast off the 'skirt'.

**b.** (See quot. 1886.)

**1881** *Dr. Gheist, An Autobiogr. fr. Midlands* 66 His menu is varied enough, and ranges from 'skirts of casalty mutton' up to the primest joints. **1886** ELWORTHY *W. Somerset Word-bk.* 674 *Skirts* or *Skirting*. Used by butchers. The trimmings or loose pieces taken off from the carcass after being 'dressed'. Also the loose pieces of wool mixed with dung on a fleece.

**c.** Chiefly *pl.* = SKIRTING *vbl. sb.* 5.

**1851** F. A. WELD *Hints to Intending Sheep-Farmers N.Z.* 8 The Merino has the more valuable wool, being finer, and particularly superior in the 'skirts', which are remarkably deficient in the crossed sheep. **1886** [see sense b above]. **1965** J. S. GUNN *Terminol. Shearing Industry* II. 23 *Skirt, skirting.* This word is generally used in the plural and refers to the wool round the edge of the fleece which is pulled off by the 'skirter'..or woolroller... In original English practice the skirts were handled by the 'wool sorter'..and not processed quite so carefully as in Australia.

**III. 7. a.** The border, boundary, or outlying part *of* a territory, country, kingdom, etc. Chiefly in *pl.*

*sing.* c **1470** HENRY *Wallace* v. 905 Rycht at the skyrt off Quenysbery befell,..Schir Jhone the Grayme [etc.]. **1610** HOLLAND *Camden's Brit.* 627 In the very utmost skirt of this Shire. **1847** TENNYSON *Princess* v. 210 Upon the skirt and fringe of our fair land.

*pl.* **1570–6** LAMBARDE *Peramb. Kent* (1826) 216 He and his sonnes abroade ransacked, herried, and spoiled, the skirts, and outsides of the whole shyre. **1592** *Soliman & Perseda* I. v, From the other skirts of Christendome Call home my Bassowes. **1615** G. SANDYS *Trav.* 139 They hang about the skirts of the habitable countries. **1708** J. CHAMBERLAYNE *St. Gt. Brit.* I. I. iii. (1710) 19 The Soil [is] not very fertile towards the middle, but rich in the Skirts. **1821** BYRON *Sardanap.* I. ii. 165 The far shores And skirts of these our realms. **1870** ROSSETTI *Poems* 31 Lilith stood on the skirts of Eden.

**b.** *pl.* The outskirts or outlying parts *of* a town or city; the suburbs. Also rarely *sing.*

**1598** B. JONSON *Ev. Man in Hum.* IV. vii, As I haue walkt alone, in diuers skirts i' the towne, as Turne-bull, White-chappell, Shore-ditch. **1621** in Foster *Eng. Factories Ind.* (1906) I. 247 It proseeded estward unto the veryе scirtes of the towne. **1673** RAY *Journ. Low C.* 72 Collen,..a free city. .. The middle part of it is well built of Stone.., the Skirts meaner and of Wood. **1728** BERKELEY *Wks.* (1871) IV. 149 Inquire in some other skirt or remote suburb. **1774** PENNANT *Tour Scotl. in 1772* 51 The Derwent washes the skirts of the town.

**c.** *pl.* The parts *of* an army furthest distant from the centre or main body; the edge, border, or fringe *of* a crowd, etc.

**1533** BELLENDEN *Livy* II. xxv. (S.T.S.) I. 232 þai saw..þe vtir skirtis of þare armye discomfist with grete slauchter. **1577–87** HOLINSHED *Chron.* I. 26/2 They would ride about the sides and skirts of the enemies host. **1600** HOLLAND *Livy* XL. xxxix. 1085 The charge was alreadie given in the utmost skirts of the armie. **1764** WESLEY *Jrnl.* 22 Apr., The skirts of the congregation could not hear. **1838** PRESCOTT *Ferd. & Is.* (1846) I. v. 237 Squadrons of light cavalry, hovering on the skirts of the Portuguese camp. **1894** HALL CAINE *Manxman* VI. xix, An old fisherman on the skirts of the crowd.

**8. a.** The edge, margin, verge *of* a wood, lake, cloud, etc.; the foot or lower slopes *of* a mountain or hill.

*sing.* **1611** COTGR. s.v. *Rive*, The skirt, edge, or side of a wood. **1632** LITHGOW *Trav.* III. 86, I passed along the skirt of Mount Ida. **1719** DE FOE *Crusoe* I. (Globe) 237, I came to the Skirt of the Wood. **1796** H. HUNTER tr. *St.-Pierre's Stud. Nat.* (1799) II. 197 Seated under their shade on the skirt of a meadow. **1817** J. BRADBURY *Trav. Amer.* 20 *note*, Colter..succeeded in gaining the skirt of the cotton wood trees. **1847** GROTE *Greece* II. lii. (1862) IV. 438 Landing at the skirt of the island.

*pl.* **1598** MANWOOD *Lawes Forest* i. (1615) 19 Meeres and boundaries to know the Ring and uttermost Skirtes of the Forest by. **1608** WILLET *Hexapla Exod.* 294 The people are forbidden to goe vp to the mountaine or to come neere the skirts of it. **1667** MILTON *P.L.* XI. 878 To binde The fluid skirts of that same watrie Cloud. **1750** G. HUGHES *Barbados* 69 Those which feed in the miry skirts of muddy ponds or rivers. **1789** J. WILLIAMS *Min. Kingd.* I. 142 The coals and coal metals trend away in a south-east direction to the skirts of the Moorfoot hills. **1839** DE LA BECHE *Rep. Geol. Cornw.*, etc. iii. 93 Gray or brown argillaceous slates that range from the skirts of the granite. **1873** HAMERTON *Intell. Life* I. iv. 26 After the first ten minutes on the skirts of the wood.

**b.** *Mining.* (See quot.)

**1747** HOOSON *Miner's Dict.* Pj, However, that which bounds and limits its [*i.e.* the vein's] breadth, we never call Sides but the Skirts, or Scurts.

**c.** The lower sloping portions of a peak or rise on a graph, esp. of one representing electrical resonance.

**1940** *Chambers's Techn. Dict.* 775/2 *Skirt*, the lower side portions of a resonance curve. **1962** SIMPSON & RICHARDS *Physical Princ. Junction Transistors* xiv. 341 This would be partly overcome if the top of the amplitude response curve were made flatter and the 'skirts' made steeper. **1965** *Wireless World* Sept. 33 (Advt.), Bandwidth skirts are better than 80-dB down. **1970** J. EARL *Tuners & Amplifiers* ii. 43 In such sets..the element is arranged in the form of a bandpass coupling or filter, giving sharp response skirts while handling signals in the required bandwidth.

**9. a.** In figurative use, after senses 7 and 8.

**1629** WHITLOCK in Rushw. *Hist. Coll.* (1659) I. 688 Now we are but upon the brink and skirts of the Cause. **1648–9** *Eikon Bas.* 135 The differences are but the skirts and suburbs of Religion. **1820** KEATS *Isabella* xxxix, I am a shadow now, alas! alas! Upon the skirts of human-nature dwelling. **1839** J. H. NEWMAN *Par. Serm.* IV. xxiii. 383 It sees the skirts of powers and providences beyond this world.

**b.** The beginning or end *of* a period of time. Chiefly *pl.*

**1624** B. JONSON *Neptune's Triumph* Wks. (Rtldg.) 642/2 To draw down a cup of nectar, in the skirts of a night. **1686** GOAD *Celest. Bodies* II. ix. 285 Snow..may fall..on the Day, or upon the Skirts of the Day, upon the precise Aspect. **1823** GALT *R. Gilhaize* III. xxiv. 222 It was then the skirt of the afternoon. **1857** HEAVYSEGE *Saul* (1869) 55 Seven days I waited,—ay, till the skirts o' the term Had disappeared.

**10. a.** A tract or piece of land forming a border, edge, or side of a river, country, etc. ? *Obs.*

**1599** NASHE *Lenten Stuff* Wks. (Grosart) V. 227 The skirt or lappet of earth whereon it stands. **1669** GALE *Crt. Gentiles* I. iv. 25 The Canaanites..were crouded up in that narrow skirt of Phenicia. **1677** W. HUBBARD *Narrative* (1865) II. 70 Spots and Skirts of more desireable Land upon the Banks of some Rivers.

**b.** A number of trees, etc., surrounding or bordering a place.

**1617** MORYSON *Itin.* III. 74 They call it a Towne, when they have compassed a skirt of wood with trees cut down. **1835** W. IRVING *Tour Prairies* xxiv, A skirt of thickets hid the approach of the supposed enemy from our rear. **1885** G. ALLEN *Babylon* xxix, A broad skirt of unoccupied hillocks.

**11.** *attrib.* and *Comb.* (in sense 1 or 2), as ***skirt-braid, -clasp, -fold, -guard, -length, -lining, -pocket***, etc.; ***skirt-like*** adj.; **skirt-board,** (*a*) = SKIRTING-BOARD; (*b*) a board to iron skirts on; **skirt-chaser** *slang*, one who pursues women with amorous attentions; hence **skirt-chase** *v. intr.*; **skirt-chasing** *vbl. sb.*; **skirt-dancing,** a form of ballet dancing in which the steps are accompanied by the manipulation of long flowing skirts or drapery; so ***skirt-dancer, skirt-dance*** sb. and vb.; **skirt duty** *slang*, (*a*) acting in a way designed to attract men; (*b*) keeping company with women, regarded as a military duty; †**skirt-foist,** a female cheat; **skirt-knicker(s)** (see quot. 1913); **skirt-land,** land having skirt soil (see below); **skirt patrol** *slang* (orig. *U.S.*) (see quot. 1941); **skirt soil,** a loam composed of a mixture of peat and clay or sand or silt (cf. SKIRTY *a.*).

**1690** LEYBOURNE *Curs. Math.* 901 Other Works about a Building..: As, Contaliver Cornice,..*Skirt board,..&c. **1861** MRS. BEETON *Bk. Househ. Managem.* 1013 The skirts of muslin dresses should be ironed on a skirt-board covered with flannel. **1932** D. C. MINTER *Mod. Needlecraft* 107/2 Almost indispensable to successful dress-making are.. sleeve and skirt board for pressing, [etc.]. **1851** MAYNE REID *Scalp Hunt.* xxi, A row of entire skins of that animal hung from the *skirt border. **1882** CAULFEILD & SAWARD *Dict. Needlwk.* 451/1 *Skirt braids..are made of Alpaca and Mohair. **1942** BERREY & VAN DEN BARK *Amer. Thes. Slang* §438/2 Lascivious man... **Skirt* or *woman chaser.* **1962** L. PETERS *Snatch of Music* iii. 45 He had always despised..the indiscriminate skirt-chaser. **1974** L. LAMB *Man in Mist* xvi. 106, I don't suppose that Settle is a skirt chaser. He probably wanted to frighten the girl away. **1943** J. B. PRIESTLEY *Daylight on Saturday* xi. 70 Don't be a dam' fool, Percy. I'm not *skirt-chasing. **1950** 'S. RANSOME' *Deadly Miss Ashley* xiv. 167, I always told you you'd regret your skirt-chasing... A man should stick with his wife and family. **1981** D. BOGGIS *Time to Betray* vii. 40 Chevalier went skirt-chasing at a disco. **1875** KNIGHT *Dict. Mech.* 2196 [*Skirt-clasp, -elevator, -protector, etc.] **1894** *Cornh. Mag.* Feb. 206 The girls who could not *skirt-dance yawned behind their fans. **1895** G. B. SHAW *Let.* 1 Nov. in *E. Terry & B. Shaw* (1931) 17 Mrs Pat Campbell entrances all London as Juliet, with a skirt dance. **1961** WODEHOUSE *Ice in Bedroom* vi. 47, I feel like dancing a skirt dance. **1974** D. SMITH *Look back with Love* xii. 113 There was usually one skirt-dance, during which the boys lolled..looking tolerant and slightly cynical. **1895** G. B. SHAW in *Sat. Rev.* 6 Apr. 445/1 Our *skirt dancers are all petticoats. **1922** Skirt-dancer [see *high-kicker* s.v. HIGH *a.* 21]. **1892** *Pall Mall G.* 24 Mar. 1/2 It should be the very thing for *skirt-dancing. **1922** JOYCE *Ulysses* 758 He was throwing his sheeps eyes at those two doing *skirt duty up and down. **1925** in *Amer. Speech 1972* (1975) XLVII. 102 That evening, Jim detailed himself to some more 'skirt duty'. *a* **1652** A. WILSON *Inconstant Ladie* IV. ii, I do not like that *skirtfoist. Leave your bouncing! **1932** C. MORGAN *Fountain* II. ii. 100 A woman's bicycle with the broken strings of its *skirt-guard dangling in a melancholy fringe over its spokes. **1982** J. HONE *Valley of Fox* vii. 105 A big, black old-fashioned woman's bicycle, with cord skirt-guards forming a fan over the back wheel. **1908** in C. W. Cunnington *Eng. Women's Clothing in Present Cent.* (1952) ii. 84 The *skirt-knickers which the up-to-date maiden delights in. **1913** *Queen* 13 Dec. 1091/2 The tango and peg-top fashion between them are responsible for an entirely new form of skirt-knicker... The characteristic of the new garment..is that it is formed entirely of one length of material falling from the waist in front to the knees and up again to the waist at the back, slits or openings occurring at the sides through which the legs are passed. **1946** J. W. DAY *Harvest Adventure* x. 145 Those cows are fed for more than nine months of the year on by-products of the farm—such as beet-tops, beet-pulp, kale—and on *skirt-land, and marsh grazings. **1981** P. SALWAY *Roman Britain* 268 The skirtlands of the southern Fens were the worst hit by these troubles. **1920** *T. Eaton & Co. Catal.* Spring & Summer 1/1 *Skirt Lengths 35 ins. 37 ins. 38 ins. **1980** L. LEWIS *Private Life Country House* xii. 166 Skirt lengths remained what you had been wearing for some time. **1862** W. C. BRYANT *Tale of Cloudland* in *Poet. Wks.* (1883) II. 315, I plainly saw a chariot cushioned deep With sides that seemed of down, and *skirt-like wings On which they nestled. **1980** *Motor* 16 Feb. 31/1 Deep, 'skirt-like' door sills. **1882** CAULFEILD & SAWARD *Dict. Needlwk.* 451/2 As a rule, alpaca and silecia are the principal materials in use for *Skirt Linings. **1941** *Amer. Speech* XVI. 168/2 **Skirt patrol*, search for feminine companionship. **1967** Skirt patrol [see *OAO* s.v. O 5 d]. **1838** DICKENS *Nickleby* xxi, The knife—..an inconvenient and dangerous article for a *skirt-pocket. **1960** *Times* 5 July (Suppl. on Agric.) p. vi/3 Lying between the areas of silt and peat there are indeterminate areas of what are now called '*skirt' soils. The soil physicist has classified them as organic silty clay loams. **1968** *Economist* 27 Apr. 52/2 Only two-thirds of the original acreage of peat in the fens—over 300,000 acres—are now covered with more than a 'skirt soil'.

**skirt** (skɜːt), *v.* [f. the sb.]

**I.** *trans.* **1.** Chiefly of, or with reference to, natural features, scenery, or surroundings:

**a.** To form the skirt or edge of; to lie alongside of; to bound or border.

**1602** CAREW *Cornwall* II. 127 b, The little parish called Temple, skirteth this Hundred, on the waste side thereof.

1734 tr. *Rollin's Anc. Hist.* (1827) II. 2 [They] dragged them headlong with them, down the precipices which skirted the road. 1748 *Anson's Voy.* I. vi. 69 The western coast is of less extent..by reason of the Andes which skirt it. 1820 W. IRVING *Sketch Bk.* II. 254 Those vast and trackless forests that skirted the settlements. 1843 PORTLOCK *Geol.* 520 The granite appears to skirt the great mass of altered schists and hornblendic rocks. 1879 DIXON *Windsor* II. vii. 73 The gardens skirted the river-side.

*fig.* 1817 CHALMERS *Astron. Disc.* iv. (1852) 92 That boundary which skirts and which terminates the material field of his contemplations.

**b.** In pa. pple., const. *with* or *by*.

1717 ADDISON tr. *Ovid's Met.* III. *Death Pentheus*, A spacious circuit..Level and wide, and skirted round with wood. 1748 *Anson's Voy.* II. i. 121 A very narrow path skirted on each side by precipices. 1818 SCOTT *Hrt. Midl.* viii, A fair and fertile champaign country..skirted by the picturesque ridge of the Pentland Mountains. 1872 COUES *N. Amer. Birds* 107 In the fall, the black feathers of the crown of the adult are skirted with ash.

*fig.* 1847 EMERSON *Poems, Dæmonic Love*, So is man's narrow path By strength and terror skirted.

**2.** To surround, edge, or border, *with* something.

1667 MILTON *P.L.* v. 282 The middle pair Girt like a Starrie Zone his waste, and round Skirted his loines and thighes with downie Gold. 1746 J. HERVEY *Medit.* (1818) 209 See how the declining sun has beautified the western clouds..and skirted them with gold. 1769 FALCONER *Dict. Marine* (1780) s.v. *Sail*, The edges of the cloths,..of which a sail is composed, are generally sewed together with a double seam: and the whole is skirted round at the edges with a cord. 1828 CAMPBELL *Lines on Departure Emigrants N.S. Wales* 27 To skirt our home with harvests widely sown.

**b.** To provide with an edging or border.

1787 *Builder's Price-bk.* 39 Dado..level, skirted, and caped.

**c.** To turn *up* at the skirts.

1848 CLOUGH *Bothie* ii. 96 With blue cotton gown skirted up over striped linsey-woolsey.

**3.** Of persons, ships, etc.: To go or pass along the border, edge, or side of (a country, district, etc.); to go round, in place of crossing.

1735 SOMERVILLE *Chase* II. 204 The Covert's utmost Bound Slily she skirts. 1808 SCOTT *Marm.* II. viii, And now the vessel skirts the strand. 1865 W. G. PALGRAVE *Arabia* II. 182 Near sunset we skirted a large reedy swamp. 1877 A. B. EDWARDS *Up Nile* xxii. 684 Skirting some palm-groves and crossing the dry bed of a canal.

*fig.* 1817 COLERIDGE *Biogr. Lit.* (Bohn) 70 They..enabled me to skirt, without crossing, the sandy deserts of utter unbelief.

**b.** To scour or search the outskirts of (a wood, etc.). *rare.*

1724 DE FOE *Mem. Cavalier* (1840) 231 They past..by us, without skirting or searching the wood. 1828 SCOTT *F.M. Perth* xxxii, All who have gone out to skirt the forest..bring back the same news.

**4.** *dial.* **a.** To plough in a certain manner (see SKIRTING *vbl. sb.* 2).

*c* 1795 WOLCOT (P. Pindar) *Rights of Kings* vii. Wks. 1816 II. 193 Time.., Who, with that ease a farmer skirts his land, Furrows so cruelly o'er the fairest face. 1796- [see SKIRTING *vbl. sb.* 2]. 1848 *Jrnl. R. Agric. Soc.* IX. II. 462 In the South Hams the land is skirted (ploughed so as to miss a portion).

**b.** To trim (a hedgerow); to dress (a fleece) by removing the ragged edges.

1879 *Norfolk Archæol.* VIII. 173 The sides of the highways are skirted in autumn. 1883 *Leisure Hour* 244/1 This is called 'skirting' the fleece... The fleece, when skirted, is rolled up, and we now follow it to the classer's table.

**II.** *intr.* **5. a.** Of persons: To travel, move, hang about, etc., on the outskirts or confines of something, or in a casual manner.

1623 tr. *Favine's Theat. Hon.* v. i. 37 [He] made himselfe Master of Denmarke and Norway, whence he went and skirted on [F. *aborder*] the Gaules. 1768 G. WHITE *Selborne* xiii, [He] passed through that kingdom on such an errand; but he seems to have skirted along in a superficial manner. 1827 J. F. COOPER *Prairie* I. xvii. 245 Lest the sons of the squatter should be out skirting on our trail. 1837 CARLYLE *Fr. Rev.* III. I. vii. Brunswick is skirting and rounding, laboriously, by the extremity of the South. 1869 BLACKMORE *Lorna Doone* xliv, Then I set off up the valley, skirting along one side of it.

*fig.* 1900 *Westm. Gaz.* 31 Jan. 2/1 It may have been due to the fact that he had to skirt round under the bluff of Mr. Henry Chaplin.

**b.** Of hunting-dogs: To leave the pack when following the scent or in a chase.

1781 BECKFORD *Thoughts Hunting* (1802) 61 Should a favourite dog skirt a little, put him to a thorough line-hunting bitch. 1842 APPERLEY *Life Sportsman* xvii, The two most acknowledged faults [of a hound] are running mute and skirting. 1856 'STONEHENGE' *Brit. Rural Sports* I. II. iv. 119 The defects which should especially be avoided are..mute running,..skirting, or a tendency to leave the rest of the pack.

**6. a.** Of roads, rivers, etc.: To lie or run *along* or *round* the edge or border of a place, etc.

1776 GIBBON *Decl. & F.* i. (1782) I. 30 A sandy desert..skirts along the doubtful confine of Syria. 1859 SIR E. TENNENT *Ceylon* II. VII. ii. 138 As the path ascends it skirts round scarped acclivities. 1863 HAWTHORNE *Our Old Home* (1879) 56 The Leam..skirts along the margin of the Garden.

**b.** Of strata: To crop *out*.

1806 FORSYTH *Beauties Scotl.* III. 84 Many of the strata below it..have skirted out at the surface, and are no longer found.

**ˈskirted**, *ppl. a.* [f. SKIRT *sb.* or *v.* + -ED[1].]

**1. a.** Wearing a skirt or skirts. Freq. in modern use in ***skirted rider***.

1598 SHAKS. *Merry W.* I. iii. 93 French-thrift, you Rogues, my selfe, and skirted Page. 1895 K. GRAHAME *Golden Age* 113 The public voice was against the admission of the skirted animal. 1898 *Girl's Own Paper* 19 Nov. 120 There are five distinct methods of mounting for skirted riders.

**b.** Of garments: Having a skirt.

1842 LOVER *Handy Andy* v, Heavy-caped and skirted frieze coats streamed behind the full-grown. 1893 *Westm. Gaz.* 15 Dec. 6/3 That the present skirted dress of women is unfit for cycling and other outdoor pursuits.

**c.** Of a hovercraft, having a skirt. Cf. SKIRT *sb.* 4 g.

1967 *Jane's Surface Skimmer Systems 1967–68* 1/2 The relative sophistication of the 80 knot skirted hovercraft.

**2.** Having a skirt, edge, or border of a specified kind, as ***dewy-***, ***long-***, ***sky-***, ***wide-***, ***willow-skirted***.

1605 SHAKS. *Lear* I. i. 66 With plenteous Riuers, and wide-skirted Meades. 1730–46 THOMSON *Autumn* 959 The dewy-skirted clouds imbibe the sun. 1807 WORDSW. *The Mother's Return* 35 Far as the willow-skirted pool. 1812 CRABBE *Tales* vi. 430 Does that long-skirted drab, that over-nice And formal clothing prove a scorn of vice? 1856 EMERSON *Eng. Traits, Stonehenge*, In the sea-wide, sky-skirted prairie.

**skirter** (ˈskɜːtə(r)). [f. SKIRT *v.* + -ER[1].]

**1.** *Hunting.* **a.** A hound which leaves the pack while following scent.

1781 BECKFORD *Thoughts Hunting* (1802) 86 They should not be skirters, but, on the contrary, should be fair-hunting hounds. 1842 APPERLEY *Life Sportsman* xvii, What are called left-handed hounds, not exactly skirters, but apt to run wide of the pack. 1856 'STONEHENGE' *Brit. Rural Sports* I. II. v. 131 Inveterate skirters, also, and conceited babblers, by all means hang.

**b.** A hunter who skirts or goes round an obstacle instead of over or through it.

1827 *Sporting Mag.* XX. 37 One more proof how often riders and skirters bring on mischief. 1856 KINGSLEY *Poems, The Find* ii, Leave cravens and skirters to dangle behind.

**2.** *Austr.* A horseman who rides on the flank or side of a body of riders, party of travellers, etc.

1890 'R. BOLDREWOOD' *Col. Ref.* (1891) 209 The couple on the trail ensured its being neither lost nor overlooked; the skirters, by riding straight on either side, picked up the tracks when any deviation was made.

**3.** *Austr.* One who trims fleeces.

1883 *Leisure Hour* 243/1 Near the skirters' table there is a very much shorter table.

**skirting** (ˈskɜːtɪŋ), *vbl. sb.* [f. SKIRT *v.*]

†**1.** The action or fact of treating lightly or superficially. *Obs.*[−1]

1687 R. L'ESTRANGE *Brief Hist. Times* I. 164 A little Skirting now and then, upon the Narratives; and Bantering, betwixt Jest and Earnest, upon the Credit of the Witnesses.

**2.** *Devon dial.* (See quot. 1796.)

1796 W. H. MARSHALL *W. Eng.* I. 144 For Skirting, the common share is used; but made, perhaps, somewhat wider than when it is used in the ordinary operation of plowing. In this mode of using the plow, little more than half the sward is pared off; turning the part raised, upon a line of unmoved turf [etc.]. 1813 VANCOUVER *Agric. Devon* 115 When skirting is required, the wing of the share is considerably enlarged. 1856 MORTON *Cycl. Agric.* II. 725/3.

**3. a.** A border, edge, edging, or margin.

1764 *Museum Rust.* III. 88 The ploughman..leaving the skirtings near the hedges to be last finished. 1825 HONE *Every-day Bk.* I. 1530 This latter boundary and skirting of Assam. 1872 COUES *N. Amer. Birds* 171 Very young birds have rufous skirting of many feathers.

**b.** The lower part or skirt of a garment. Also *pl.*

1821 CLARE *Vill. Minstr.* II. 68 With slop-frock suiting to a ploughman's taste, Its greasy skirtings twisted round his waist. 1829 TENNYSON *Timbuctoo* 177 Wherefrom The snowy skirting of a garment hung.

**c.** Material used for the skirts of saddles; saddle-skirts collectively.

1852 C. MORFIT *Tanning & Currying* (1853) 150 The smaller and lighter ones [*sc.* hides] are used for 'skirting' and for enamelling.

**d.** Cloth or material suitable for women's skirts or underskirts (see quot.).

1882 CAULFEILD & SAWARD *Dict. Needlwk.* 451/1 *Skirting*, strong thick woollen, worsted, cotton, or mixed fabrics, woven of certain dimensions, so as to be suitable in length and width for women's underskirts, and to preclude the necessity of making gores and seams.

**4.** *Carp.* The narrow boarding, edging of slate or cement, etc., placed vertically along the base of the wall of a room, or other place in a building, next to the floor. Also *collect.*, material suitable for this. ***skirting radiator***, a radiator running along a wall at the level of the skirting. Cf. SKIRTING-BOARD.

1825 J. NICHOLSON *Operat. Mechanic* 603 Skirting, when wide, is also measured by the foot superficial. *Ibid.* 626 It [*sc.* slate] makes excellent skirtings of all descriptions. 1863 WHYTE MELVILLE *Gladiators* II. 242 The walls were of polished citron-wood, heavily gilded round the skirting and edges. 1881 YOUNG *Ev. Man his own Mechanic* §886. 414 There is a skirting round the room which must not be cut away. 1970 *Home & Garden* Mar. 94/4 Skirting radiators have a great deal to recommend them. 1978 *Cornish Guardian* 27 Apr. 16/6 (Advt.), Superbly renovated cottage with full central heating, unobtrusive skirting radiators [etc.].

**5.** *Austr.* The trimmings or inferior portions of a fleece. Also, ***skirting table***, the table at which these are removed.

1881 GRANT *Bush Life Queensland* I. vii. 85 The roller-up, with a rapidity which is the result of long practice, separates the skirtings. 1890 *Melbourne Argus* 20 Sept. 13/7 At the 'skirting table' we will stand for a little while, and watch while the fleece..is opened out by the 'roller' and the inferior portions removed.

**ˈskirting**, *ppl. a.* [f. SKIRT *v.*] That skirts, in senses of the vb.

*c* 1735 HARTE *Eulogius* Poems (1810) 383/1 On skirting heights thick stood the clust'ring vine. 1817 J. SCOTT *Paris Revisit.* (ed. 4) 77 Beyond the city..a black skirting outline ran along a ridge of high ground. 1829 P. NICHOLSON in *Encycl. Metrop.* (1845) VI. 237/2 Every supporting bar ought to be fixed at each extremity to opposite parts of the skirting frame. 1858 FROUDE *Hist. Eng.* III. 131 Skirting parties meantime scoured the country far and near.

Hence **ˈskirtingly** *adv.*

1882 PROCTOR in *Longman's Mag.* Dec. 184 The earth can pass through, centrally or skirtingly, but a very minute proportion of the meteor systems.

**ˈskirting-board.** [Cf. SKIRTING *vbl. sb.* 4.] The narrow board placed round the wall of a room, etc., close to the floor.

1759 *Phil. Trans.* LI. 291 The floor, joints and projections of the skirting-board. 1771 MRS. HAYWOOD *New Present for Maid* 256 Rubbing the skirting-boards with a piece of oily flannel. 1814 SOUTHEY in *Q. Rev.* XII. 185 The skirting board of the room was painted of that colour. 1861 WYNTER *Soc. Bees* 25 A cracked window or a shrunken skirtingboard.

*fig.* 1859 SALA *Gaslight & D.* xxiii. 268 A woful skirting-board of crouching Irish paupers.

**skirtless** (ˈskɜːtlɪs), *a.* [f. SKIRT *sb.* + -LESS.]

**a.** Of garments: Having no skirt. **b.** Of persons: Wearing no skirt.

1809 BYRON *Bards & Rev.* 599 For skirtless coats and skeletons of plays Renown'd alike. 1896 *Daily News* 14 Jan. 6/5 Baggy trousers, such as skirtless feminine bicyclists adopt. 1899 *Blackw. Mag.* Sept. 372 The traveller was in livery—skirtless fawn and silver coat.

**ˈskirty**, *a. Linc.* [f. SKIRT *sb.*] (See quots.)

1851 *Jrnl. R. Agric. Soc.* XII. I. 282 These fens..being 'skirty', *i.e.* a mixture of peat and alluvial silt or clay, forming a deep black loam. 1851 H. STEPHENS *Bk. Farm* (ed. 2) I. 490 The fen land adjoining the hard lands partaking of the characters of both, is called *skirty land.*

**skirty** (ˈskɜːtɪ), *sb. colloq.* [f. SKIRT *sb.* + -Y[6].] A skirt or underskirt.

1922 JOYCE *Ulysses* 47 A woman and a man. I see her skirties. Pinned up, I bet. 1977 *Sounds* 9 July 18/2 I'd like to dirty up Their little skirties up.

**skirvie, -vye**, obs. ff. SCURVY *sb.* and *a.*

**skirwhit(e, -wike**, etc., obs. ff. SKIRRET[1].

†**skirwingle.** *Obs.*[−1] [Of obscure origin.] Some kind of bird.

1610 W. FOLKINGHAM *Art of Survey* IV. iii. 83 Churre, Peeper, Grindle, Skirwingle, Sea and Land Larkes.

**skirwit, -wort, -wurt**, obs. ff. SKIRRET[1].

**skise**, obs. or dial. form of SKICE *v.*[1]

**skish** (skɪʃ). *U.S.* [perh. f. SK(EET *sb.*[2] or SK(ILL *sb.*[1] + F)ISH *sb.*[1]] A game in which participants use fishing tackle to cast a plug or fly at a target on dry land. Also *attrib.*

1940 *Outdoor America* Jan. 11/3 *Skish*—the new name chosen for the casting game originally known as Fish-O was selected on January 6 by the judges of the Fish-O change-of-name contest. 1942 *Sun* (Baltimore) 8 July 13/3 He said the best score he ever made in 'skish'—dry-land 'fishing' in which participants cast at thirty-inch rings at distances from forty to eighty feet—was in the eighties out of a possible 100 points. 1965 *Richmond* (Va.) *Times-Dispatch* 5 Feb. 25/2 Skish..is a game devised for indoor anglers who want to improve their casting techniques by casting at targets rather than for fish. 1976 *Webster's Sports Dict.* 399/1 There are 3 different skish events: skish bait, skish spinning, and skish fly casting.

**skister** (ˈʃiːstə(r), ˈskiː-). [f. SKI + -STER.] One who uses ski; a ski-runner.

1898 CONWAY *With Ski & Sledge* xi. 194 The..expertness attained by the best Norwegian and Swedish skisters (to coin a needed word).

**Skis Thursday**, obs. var. of SKIRE THURSDAY.

**skit**, *sb.*[1] Now *dial.* Also 4 **skitte, skyt**, 5 **skytt(e.** [Of Scand. origin: cf. Norw. *skit* dirt, filth, Norw. and Icel. *skita* diarrhœa. The corresponding native form is SHIT *sb.*]

**1.** *fig.* Dirt, trash. *rare*[−1].

*c* 1330 R. BRUNNE *Chron. Wace* (Rolls) 16714 But for to schewe his mykel wyt, On my spekynge þat ys but skyt [*v.r.* skitte].

**2.** Diarrhœa in animals, esp. sheep; scouring.

*c* 1440 *Promp. Parv.* 458/1 Skytte, or flyx,..*fluxus*,..*dissenteria.* 1741 *Compl. Fam.-Piece* III. 491 To cure the Skit or Looseness in Sheep. 1799 A. YOUNG *Agric. Lincoln.* 376 They die of the *skit*, or scouring. 1805 R. W. DICKSON *Pract. Agric.* II. 986 A sort of indigestion..which, when it proceeds to any great length, is termed the *skit.* 1865 *Jrnl. R. Agric. Soc.* I. II. 289 Something more than common 'skit', or diarrhœa.

**3.** *attrib.* and *Comb.*, as ***skit-brains***, ***-brained***, in opprobrious use.

**1553** *Respublica* 1812 Stande styll, skitbraind theaff, or thy bonds shall be coilled. *Ibid.* 1818 The skitbraines nold not bee roilled ner sens ye wente.

**skit**, *sb.*[2] [Related to SKIT *v.*[2], but the earlier history is not clear.]

**1. a.** A female of a vain, frivolous, or wanton disposition. Chiefly *Sc.*

**1572** *Buchanan's Detect. Mary Q. Scots* M ij, That haynous offence,.. that at the banquet of her domesticall parasite, sche had nat played the dauncing skit. **1583** EARL NORTHAMPTON *Defensatiue* S ij, At the request of a dauncing skitte [Herod] stroke of the head of Saint Iohn the Baptist. **1808** JAMIESON s.v., *Skit* is still used for a vain, empty creature; sometimes, *proud skit*.

**b.** *Sc.* 'A young capering or restive horse.'

**1882** *Jamieson's Sc. Dict.* IV. 254/2.

**2.** A quizzing or satirical reflection *upon*, or hit *at*, a person or thing; a remark of this nature.

**1727** BAILEY (vol. II), *Skit*, a Caprice, Whimsey. **1779** MRS. H. COWLEY *Who's the Dupe?* II. ii, Come, come, none of your tricks upon travellers. I know you mean all that as a skit upon my edication. **1820–2** PYNE *Wine & Walnuts* (1824) II. xi. 174 No more of your skits at my right noble country. **1861** *Times* 22 Mar. 8/6 Mr. Cobden could afford to reply to the compliments of a Mayor without a skit at the press. **1878** E. FITZGERALD *Lett.* (1889) I. 421 He did not deserve your skit about his 'Finsbury Circus gentility'.

**b.** A literary or artistic production intended as a piece of light satire, parody, or caricature.

**1820** COMBE *Syntax, Consol.* VII. (Chandos) 243 A Manuscript with learning fraught, Or some nice, pretty little skit Upon the times. **1884** *Athenæum* 19 Jan. 91/1 The German skit on the Shapira forgeries.. is about to be translated in English verse. **1884** SHARMAN *Hist. Swearing* iv. 60 The British bull-dog has figured again and again in pictorial skits.

**c.** A trick; a hoax; a practical joke; = SKITE *sb.* 2. Chiefly *dial.*

**1815** SCOTT *Guy M.* xxxii, If he really shot young Hazlewood—But I canna think it, Mr. Glossin; this will be some o' your skits now. **1865–** in dialect glossaries.

**3.** A slight shower (*of* rain or snow).

**1847** in HALLIW. **1865** MRS. CARLYLE *New Lett.* (1903) II. 336 It is blowing hard to-day, with a dull grey sky, and skits of rain. **1880** BLACKMORE *Mary Anerley* III. ii. 18 Soon the first snow of the winter came, the first abiding earnest snow, for several skits had come before.

*transf.* **1877** BLACKIE *Wise Men* 334 Plagues, frosts and mildews, and the lashing hail,.. Are all but skits of crudely mingled air.

**b.** A squirt or small jet of water.

**1877** BLACKIE *Nat. Hist. Atheism* ii. 31 No more.. than a skit of a boy's squirt can put out the sun.

**4.** A slight stroke.

**1860** EMERSON *Cond. Life, Wealth* Wks. (Bohn) II. 351 In the city, where money follows the skit of a pen,.. it comes to be looked on as light.

**skit**, *sb.*[3] (See quot.)

**1885** C. G. W. LOCK *Workshop Rec.* Ser. IV. 277/1 The rods, or willows, as they are termed in the trade, comprise several varieties, as the skit willow, the gold-stone.

**skit** (skɪt), *sb.*[4] *colloq.* [Origin obscure.] A large number, a crowd; *pl.* 'lots'.

**1913** C. MACKENZIE *Sinister St.* I. II. ix. 287, I met an odd sort of chap.. who told me a skit of things—you know—about a bad life. **1925** A. S. M. HUTCHINSON *One Increasing Purpose* III. ix. 268 'What was that little red rosette he had on his left arm? I see skits of people with it.' 'Been vaccinated, of course.' **1927** *Blackw. Mag.* Nov. 594/1 The Kachins were in the jungle, a skit of them, trying to stop us at the ford.

**skit**, obs. var. SKATE *sb.*[2]

**1688** HOLME *Armoury* III. 484 What to term them I know not, (except Dutch skits, to Slide withal).

†**skit**, *a.*[1] *Obs.*$^{-1}$ In 6 skyt. [? Back-formation from SKITTISH *a.*] Precipitate, over-hasty.

*a* **1529** SKELTON *Agst. Scottes* 101 Syr Skyrgalyard, ye were so skyt, Your wyll than ran before your wyt.

**skit** (skɪt), *a.*[2] *Anglo-Ir.* [App. colloq. adjectival use of Ir. *sciót* cut, bit, laugh.] Amusing; ***to be right skit***, to be a great laugh (cf. LAUGH *sb.* 4 b).

**1914** JOYCE *Dubliners* 26 Mahoney said it would be right skit to run away to sea on one of those big ships.

**skit**, *v.*[1] *rare*$^{-1}$. [Related to SKIT *sb.*[1]] *intr.* To void thin excrement; = SKITTER *v.*[1]

**1805** R. W. DICKSON *Pract. Agric.* II. 985 If the milk be given over cold, it is apt to cause the calf to *skit* or purge.

**skit** (skɪt), *v.*[2] [Of doubtful origin: perh. only a back-formation from SKITTISH *a.* It might, however, represent an ON. ***skytja* (cf. *flytja* flit), f. **skut-*, the weak grade of *skjóta* to shoot. In sense 2 perh. from SKIT *sb.*[2] 2.]

**1.** *intr.* To shy or be skittish; to move lightly and rapidly; to caper, leap, or spring.

**1611** CHAPMAN *May Day* II. ii, I hope my friend will not loue a wench against her will;.. if shee skit and recoile,.. away he goes. **1621** MOLLE *Camerarius' Liv. Lib.* IV. xiii. 278 The daughters of Prætus.. persuaded themselues that they were changed into cowes, and thereupon began to low, and skit vp and downe the fields. **1807–10** TANNAHILL *Poems* (1846) 11 She skits and flings like ony towmont filly. **1860** PIESSE *Lab. Chem. Wonders* 3 Innumerable insects may be seen at sunset skitting and dancing in the air. **1894** BLACKMORE *Perlycross* viii. 64 The man.. skitted back into a bush, very nimble and clever.

**2. a.** *trans.* To cast indirect reflections or light satire upon (a person, etc.); to ridicule or caricature by means of a skit.

**1781** J. HUTTON *Tour to Caves* (ed. 2) Gloss., *Skit*, to reflect on. [Similarly in later northern dial. glossaries.] **1892** *Star* 24 Mar. 2/4 These meetings were skitted by Elkanah Settle in 'The New Athenian Comedy'. **1904** *Daily Chron.* 20 Feb. 3/4 The first occasion on which Mr. Roberts has 'skitted' Mr. Beerbohm Tree.

**b.** *intr.* To make satirical hits *at* a person or thing.

**1821** *Londsdale Mag.* II. 247 Then nobody dare skit at me for being a tailyer. *c* **1840** H. COLERIDGE *Ess.* (1851) II. 84 Warburton.. had too much learning to skit at Bentley as Pope has done. **1885** MOZLEY *Rem.* I. 130 When people have condoled with me.. or have skitted at commercial gentility.

**skite** (skaɪt, *Sc.* skeit), *sb.* In senses 1–3, *Sc.* and *north. dial.* Also skyte. [Related to SKITE *v.*[2]]

**1.** A sudden, vigorous stroke or blow, esp. one given in an oblique direction; an oblique impact, or one which causes a rebound.

**1785** BURNS *Jolly Beggars* i, When hailstanes drive wi' bitter skyte, And infant frosts begin to bite. **1825** JAMIESON *Suppl., Skite*,.. a smart and sudden blow, so as to make what strikes rebound in a slanting direction. **1895–** in *Eng. Dial. Dict.* (Sc., N. Irel., Northumb.).

**2.** A trick; a skit. Cf. SKIT *sb.*[2] 2.

**1804** W. TARRAS *Poems* 60 He's play'd my dochter Meg a skyte, Which weel has coft the gibbet. **1825** JAMIESON *Suppl.* s.v., He's played me an ill skite. **1899** LUMSDEN *Edin. Poems* 89 This Club.. Enjoy'd thy witty 'Tory' skites Wi' hearty glee.

**3.** A person who on some account or other is regarded with contempt. (Cf. *blatherskite*.)

**1790** W. MACLAY *Jrnl.* 28 June (1890) x. 310 Hamilton has a very boyish, giddy manner, and Scotch-Irish people could well call him a 'skite'. **1808** JAMIESON s.v. *Skyte.* **1818** SCOTT *Rob Roy* xxvii, But I maun speak to this gabbling skyte too, for bairns and fules speak at the Cross what they hear at the ingle side. **1850** MRS. CARLYLE *Lett.* II. 136 Oh, such a withered up skite poor Mac is become.

**4.** *Austral.* and *N.Z. colloq.* **a.** Boasting, boastfulness; ostentation, show; conceit.

**1860** C. THATCHER *Victoria Songster* v. 160 You don't often see a chap given to the 'skite, Can do very much when it comes to a fight. **1910** E. W. HORNUNG *Boss of Taroomba* 180 'Then none o' your skite, mate,' said Bill, knocking out a clay pipe against his heel. **1918** G. WALL *Lett. Airman* 85 This notepaper is a part of it, quite unnecessary skite. I thought you might like a sample of it, though. **1933** N. LINDSAY *Saturdee* 115 Ponk's the bloke to take the skite outer him. **1958** I. CROSS *God Boy* vi. 44 You started us off with your skite about not caring about fifty bangs and now you say shut up. **1965** S. T. OLLIVIER *Petticoat Farm* ii. 31 'Alister Bridgeman says it's mostly skite,' Sarah said breezily. **1972** P. NEWTON *Sheep Thief* xviii. 149, I thought I had a good district run but you've taken the skite out of me.

**b.** A braggart, a boaster; a conceited person.

**1906** 'T. COLLINS' in *Barrier Truth* (Broken Hill, N.S.W.) 1 June, In spite of Rigby's very complimentary insinuation that I'm a skite and a liar, the wagon was gone. **1928** *Bulletin* (Sydney) 29 Feb. 21/1 To the mug, the skite and the liar, to the nark and the hypocrite A fellow can always jerry. **1941** S. J. BAKER *N.Z. Slang* vii. 61 Our borrowings [from Australia] of what might be described as 'social' slang ..[include] *skite*. **1952** D. NILAND in *Coast to Coast 1951–1952* 198 And what a skite! You should have seen him. **1958** I. CROSS *God Boy* i. 8 I'm not a skite but if I was fighting a man it would be the same. **1965** G. MCINNES *Road to Gundagai* ii. 30 He had no time for 'skites', that is, boastful know-it-alls. **1969** *Australian* 23 Sept. 2 Australians should not see themselves as boastful, arrogant skites, the Governor-General, Sir Paul Hasluck, said yesterday.

**5.** Orig. and chiefly *Sc.* A jollification, a spree, a binge. Freq. in phr. ***on the skite***.

**1869** *St. Andrews Gaz.* 27 Nov. 3/6 A correspondent.. sends the following.. catalogue of synonyms of whisky and whisky drinking in the West of Scotland:— .. on the skyte. **1895** W. STEWART *Lilts* 65 When ye went on the 'skite' an' sent railway things glee'd. **1909** J. J. BELL *Oh! Christina* xiv. 112 You an' me's gaun to ha'e an' awfu' skite, eh, auntie? **1946** J. IRVING *Royal Navalese* 158 *Skite* (*skyte*), *on the*, indulging in an orgy; on 'the tiles'. **1954** *Times* 16 Nov. 4/1 The Bejant skite (the party of the first-year students). **1972** N. SMYTHE in E. Berman *Ten of Best* (1979) 113, I was a bit too fond of the old jar, Went on the skite once too often.

**skite** (skaɪt), *v.*[1] *Sc.* and *dial.* Also 5 (9 *Sc.*) skyte. [a. ON. *skíta* (Icel. *skíta*, Norw. and Sw. *skita*, Da. *skide*), or MLG. *schîten*, MDu. *schijten*, = OE. *scítan* SHITE *v.*] *intr.* To void excrement. Hence **'skiting** *ppl. a.*

**1449** *Paston Lett.* I. 85, I cam abord the Admirall, and bade them stryke in the Kyngys name.., and they bade me skyte in the Kyngs name. **1508** DUNBAR *Flyting* 194, I warne the it is wittin, How, skyttand skarth, thow hes the hurle behind. **1596** HARINGTON *Metam. Ajax* Prol. B, In further contempt of his name, vsed a phrase that he had lerned at his being in the lowe countries, and bad Skite vpon Aiax. **1808** in JAMIESON. **1823** E. MOOR *Suffolk Words* 353.

**skite** (skaɪt), *v.*[2] Also 8 skyt, 9 skyte. [perh. f. ON. *skýt-*, umlauted stem of *skjóta* to shoot.]

This verb, and the corresponding sb., have much currency in dial. use; fuller illustration of the various senses may be found in the *Eng. Dial. Dict.* For further material see also *Sc. Nat. Dict.*

**1.** *intr.* To shoot or dart swiftly, esp. in an oblique direction; to run lightly and rapidly; to make *off* hastily. *Sc.* and *dial.*

**1721** RAMSAY *Rise & Fall of Stocks* 112 Like a shot starn, that thro the air Skyts east or west with unko glare. **1859** BARTLETT *Dict. Amer.* (ed. 2) s.v., To skite about is to go running about. **1895** JANE BARLOW *Strangers at Lisconnel* 325 It's a.. young villain her son must be.. to skyte off and lave her that-a-way.

**2.** To slip suddenly. *Sc.* and *dial.*

**1871** W. ALEXANDER *Johnny Gibb* (1873) 225 The 'blower' skytit oot o' Samie's mou'. **1881** J. BALLANTINE in Edwards *Mod. Sc. Poets* Ser. I. 29 Our feet skyted back on the road freezing hard.

**3.** *Austral.* and *N.Z. colloq.* To brag, to boast.

**1857** C. R. THATCHER *Colonial Songster* 18 If ever you get into a fight, Of course you'll not forget to skite. **1896** E. TURNER *Little Larrikin* xxiv. 295 It used to make me a bit sick sometimes to hear him skite, knowing how much chance I had. **1902** *N.Z. Illustr. Mag.* V. 486 They had him skiting about his moonlight stroll with someone. **1940** F. SARGESON *Man & his Wife* (1944) 79, I suppose he went back to his ship and skited about the time he'd had. **1956** G. CASEY in *Coast to Coast 1955–56* 82 Spent most of the forty-eight hours skiting to his wife and young Les that he had got old Spend's goat thoroughly. **1968** A. HOLDEN *Death after School* xxv. 181 They did save my life... I don't mind *how* much they skite. **1978** P. GRACE *Mutuwhenua* xiv. 102 Everyone laughing, hugging Nanny who was skiting about her hat.

Hence (sense 3) **'skiter**; **'skiting** *vbl. sb.*

**1898** *Bulletin* (Sydney) 17 Dec. (Red Page) An incessant talker is a *skiter* or a *fluter*. **1916** *Anzac Bk.* 99 If there's one thing I hate, it is skiting... So you won't think I boast when I tell you. **1936** F. CLUNE *Roaming round Darling* ix. 77 A fellow, fed up with city skiters, came out west to the edge of beyond, and began this village, where he could do his own skiting. **1957** R. LAWLER *Summer of Seventeenth Doll* III. 113 Lyin' comes as natural to him as skiting.

†**skitegate.** *Obs. rare.* Also skyt-. [ad. Du. *schiet-gat*, f. *schieten* to shoot + *gat* hole.] An opening or loop-hole in a wall for a cannon or other piece of artillery.

**1677** EARL ORRERY *Treat. Art War* 118 Great Cannon Gabions well fill'd with Earth, or Skite Gates thorow the Flanks and Faces of the said Works. **1685** COTTON tr. *Montaigne* (1877) I. 93 Captain Julius.. being so astonish'd with fear as to throw himself and his fellows out at a skyt-gate [Fr. *une canonniere*], was immediately cut to pieces by the enemy.

**skither**, var. SKITTER *v.*[2]

**skitly**: see SKEETLY *adv.*

**'skitter**, *sb.*[1] Chiefly *Sc.* and *dial.* Also 9 *dial.* skitta. [f. the vb.]

**1.** Diarrhœa; looseness or laxity of the bowels. Now freq. in *pl.* (Also *colloq.*)

*a* **1585** POLWART *Flyting w. Montgomerie* 244 To heale thee of thy skitter. **1823–** in dialect glossaries (Sc., Yks., Lanc., Linc., Suff.). **1939** J. STEINBECK *Grapes of Wrath* xxii. 431 They et green grapes. They all five got the howlin' skitters. Run out ever' ten minutes. **1940** M. MARPLES *Public School Slang* 159 *Skitters, squitters*, diarrhœa. **1948** PARTRIDGE *Dict. Forces' Slang* 180 *Squitters, skitters*, a symptom of dysentery and other stomach troubles.

**2.** Thin excrement. Also *Comb.*

**1692** *Sc. Presbyt. Eloq.* (1738) 118 A Cake unturn'd, that is, it's stone-hard on one Side, and skitter raw on the other. **1721** KELLY *Sc. Prov.* 16 A Spoonful of Skitter will spill [= spoil] a Potful of Skink.

**'skitter**, *sb.*[2] [f. SKITTER *v.*[2]] A light scampering or skipping movement or the sound caused by this.

**1905** *Scribner's Mag.* July 1 The slim shell trailed with dying headway to the skitter of the resting oars. **1959** E. ALLEN *Man who chose Death* xiii. 130 A quick skitter of footsteps like mice in the rafters. **1961** S. BUNCE *No Sainted City* xxiii. 170 A confusion of sounds. A skitter of light footfalls.

**'skitter**, *v.*[1] *Sc.* and *dial.* Also 4 skiter-, 5 skyter-. [A frequentative of SKITE *v.*[1]] *intr.* To void thin excrement. Hence **'skittering** *vbl. sb.*[1] and *ppl. a.*[1]

**13..** *Langtoft's Chron.* (Rolls) II. 252 Skiterende Scottes, Telle i for sottes, And wrecches unwar. *a* **1585** MONTGOMERIE *Flyting* 499 It skittered and skarted; they skirled ilk ane. *c* **1610** SIR J. MELVIL *Mem.* (1683) 14 Seeing there was but a Skittering Lass between him and the Crown. **1683** *Yorkshire Dial.* 5 Thur Yowes are Clow-clagg'd, they skitter sayr. **1721** KELLY *Prov.* 20 A skittering Cow in the Loan would ay have many Marrows. **1825–** in dialect glossaries (Northumb., Cumb., Yks., Som., Dev.).

*transf.* **1682** MARTINDALE in Houghton *Coll. Lett. Impr. Husb.* No. 11, Some, when the strength of Marle is worn out by long Tillage, strengthen it with a new Supply, but then they ordinarily set it thin (which they call *skittering*).

**'skitter**, *v.*[2] Also skither. [app. a frequentative f. SKITE *v.*[2]]

**1. a.** *intr.* To move or run rapidly; to hurry about; to scamper off. Freq. with advbs.

**1845** S. JUDD *Margaret* (1871) 149 On they flew, skittering, bowling, sluice-like, mad-like. **1875** *Toxie, a Tale* I. vi. 100 Neither did he and I skitter at sixty miles an hour. **1882** BLACKMORE *Christowell* lii, Up on the first horse we could lay hold of, and skittered on the heels of the rest of them. **1903** KIPLING in *Windsor Mag.* Sept. 363/2 She skittered about in the bracken, being a 'citable child. **1922** H. QUICK *Vandemark's Folly* viii. 143, I remembered.. how she had skithered back to the carriage. **1929** S. LEACOCK *Iron Man* v. 205 When we drive the ball.. skithers off sideways. **1935** M. EBERHART *Cases of S. Dare* 64 The monkey darted out from under the sofa and was suddenly skittering across the room again. **1946** C. MCCULLERS *Member of Wedding* III. 178 Frances watched the Portuguese who.. played a mock piano on the counter to the music-box tune. He swayed as he played and his fingers skittered up and down the counter. **1949** B. MARSHALL *To Every Man a Penny* xlix.

151 The limousines, the taxicabs, the lorries and the buses roared round the church, skittering away to Neuilly, Auteuil and Montmartre. **1968** B. HINES *Kestrel for Knave* 57 The boys began to swallow their Adam's apples, their eyes skittering about in still heads. **1976** *Church Times* 26 Nov. (Bk. Suppl.) p. iv/2 He skittered through a fantastic mass of scientific evidence for the scarcely believable and downright unbelievable. **1977** *Meanjin* (Austral.) XXXVI. I. 68, I skither down barefeet first. **1977** *Listener* 17 Feb. 215/3 Not only is the tenor-saxophonist playing his usualy devious game but..Basie is joining in... Both men skittering around the melody line in high good humour. **1977** *New Yorker* 24 Oct. 33/1, I found, skittering in nervous computer printout across the bottom of my bill, the words 'Thank you very much for your prompt payment'.

**b.** Orig. *dial.* To skip or skim *along* a surface, with occasional rapid contact. Also with other advbs. and advb. phrases.

**1847** J. O. HALLIWELL *Dict. Archaic & Provincial Words* II. 750 A countryman who was leading me up a steep hill, when we came to a place which was inaccessible, said 'We had better *skitter* under here, and it won't be so steep.' (Kent). **1885** T. ROOSEVELT *Hunting Trips* 56 Some kinds of ducks in lighting strike the water with their tails first, and skitter along the surface for a few feet before settling down. **1904** *Eng. Dial. Dict.* V. 483/1 Leeak at mah scoperil, hoo it skithers across teeable. **1931** W. FAULKNER *Sanctuary* xxv. 298 A second man flew out and skittered along the floor on his back. **1951** J. C. FENNESSY *Sonnet in Bottle* II. i. 40 The little whitish-silver flying fish skittering over the ship's bow wave. **1956** C. EVANS *Kanchenjunga* xii. 121 Fragments of snow kept skittering down the slope and bombarding the tent. **1969** *New Yorker* 12 Apr. 127/1 The astronauts will start back to the LM—first tossing the universal handling tool..across the black *mare*, where it may skitter to rest inside a small crater. **1970** *Globe & Mail* (Toronto) 28 Sept. 21/7 His long blast was deflected by defenseman Jim McKenny's glove and skittered past a surprised Bruce Gamble in goal who was moving the opposite way to cover. **1978** M. PUZO *Fools Die* ii. 15 He was tired of the glittering red dice skittering across green felt.

**2. a.** *trans. U.S.* In angling, to draw (a spoon-bait or hook) with a jerking or skipping motion over the surface of the water. Also *absol.*

**1883** *Cent. Mag.* July 383/2 The angler, standing in the bow, 'skitters' or skips the spoon or bait over the surface just at the edge of the weeds. **1897** *Outing* XXX. 221 In skittering with a spoon, some of the fly-fisher's skill..comes into play.

**b.** In various senses, with reference to the impartation of a rapid or sliding motion (see quots.).

**1902** KIPLING *Just So Stories* 61 Let's say things to the bunnies, and watch 'em skitter their tails! **1907** *Harper's Mag.* Feb. 460 The younger boy skittered rocks at a chicken-hawk. **1919** J. MASEFIELD *Reynard* 112 The great hooves skittered The Blood Brook's shallows to sheets that glittered. **1968** A. DIMENT *Bang Bang Birds* ii. 22 She produced a 6 × 4 glossy..and skittered it across the desk to me. **1972** M. J. BOSSE *Incident at Naha* i. 54 Edgar Gear blinked and skittered his hand through his hair.

Hence **'skittered** *ppl. a.*; **'skittering** *vbl. sb.*$^{2}$ and *ppl. a.*$^{2}$

**1883** *Cent. Mag.* July 383/2 Skittering..is practised with a strong line..to which is affixed a small trolling-spoon. *a* **1888** in Goode *Amer. Fishes* 37 When taken with a skittered minnow or bright fly on a light rod. **1893** M. GRAY *Last Sentence* II. viii, The skittering feet and minute shriek of mice.

† **skitterbrook.** *Obs. rare.* [ad. Du. *schijtebroek*, with the first element assimilated to SKITTER *v.*$^{1}$] One who befouls his breeches; a coward.

**1632** BROME *Crt. Beggar* IV. ii, The Devill fright him next for a spurging skitterbrooke. *a* **1652** —— *Novella* IV. ii, Like to make a skitter brooke Of you in your Dutch slops.

**'skittery,** *a.* [f. SKITTER *v.*$^{2}$] **1.** Trifling.

**1905** M. DEANE *Little Neighbour* 124 'She is just a little fool,' said Roger—'a skittery little fool, with no sense, and not much to look at'.

**2.** Skittish, restless.

**1941** *Sun* (Baltimore) 29 Aug. 17/2 The little fellers—the skittery moths, and the 11½-foot penguin dinghies, complete the list. **1974** D. SEARS *Lark in Clear Air* x. 123 You can see that kind of eye in a skittery horse. **1976** *Gramophone* Oct. 607/1 The only two points at which I was aware of any lack of finish were in the finale of Op. 13 (sometimes a bit skittery) and the 'Dance' of Op. 14.

**3.** *Textiles.* Producing or taking on an undesired speckly appearance in dyeing.

**1955** *Jrnl. Soc. Dyers & Colourists* LXXI. 707/1 A dye which is selective, i.e. skittery, in dyeing behaviour, however, will show marked differences in the rate of exhaustion. **1970** E. R. TROTMAN *Dyeing & Chem. Technol. Textile Fibres* (ed. 4) xvii. 442 It [*sc.* water solubility] increases the tendency to give 'skittery' shades, caused by the emphasis of variations in affinity from one fibre to another.

Hence **'skitteriness.**

**1952** *Jrnl. Soc. Dyers & Colourists* LXVIII. 306/1 *Skitteriness*, an undesired speckled effect in a yarn or fabric arising from differences in colour or depth of dyeing between adjacent fibres or portions of the same fibre. **1955** *Ibid.* LXXI. 707/1 Skitteriness is a specific property of the dye... Skitteriness comes about through selective dyeing of different wool fibres. **1964** *Dyeing of Polyester Fibres* (I.C.I.) (ed. 3) viii. 237 Although the..dyes recommended..are those with superior levelling properties, it is still essential to ensure initial level application of the wool dye if excessive 'skitteriness' is to be avoided.

**skittish** ('skɪtɪʃ), *a.* Also 6 **skyttys(s)he, skytysshe, scittish.** [Of obscure origin: perh. f. a Scand. base **skyt-* (see SKIT *v.*$^{2}$) + -ISH.]

**1.** Of disposition, etc.: Characterized by levity, frivolity, or excessive liveliness.

*c* **1412** HOCCLEVE *De Reg. Princ.* 590 Whan þat þou hast assayde boþe two, Sad age, I seye, after þi skittish youþe. **14..** *Six Ballads* (Percy Soc.) 10 My dere is off a skyttyshe brayne. *a* **1513** FABYAN *Chron.* VII. (1811) 339 Lewelyn..rebellyd agayne the kyng; for so moche as syr Edwarde his sone..wolde haue chaungyd some of theyr skyttyshe condycyons. **1594** T. B. *La Primaud.* II. 230 Fancie, being very turbulent and skittish,..is the cause that wee liue in the middest of marueilous troubles in respect of our affections. **1611** COTGR., *Perversité*, a skittish, giddy, or vntoward humor to doe an vnlawfull, or ill, thing. **1678** BUTLER *Hud.* III. ii. 479 He still resolv'd..T' adhere and cleave the obstinater; And still the skittisher and looser Her Freaks appear'd, to sit the closer. **1748** RICHARDSON *Clarissa* II. 135 If you think you can part with her for her skittish tricks. **1784** COWPER *Task* II. 470 T' address The skittish fancy with facetious tales. **1882** TENNYSON in *Life* (1897) I. 95, I considered it [a critique] at the time as somewhat too skittish and petulant. **1894** J. KNIGHT *Garrick* iv. 68 Macklin claims to have supplied a curiously unconventional and skittish rhymed apology.

*Comb.* **1605** BRETON *Soules Immortal Crowne* I. xlii, How Fancie like a Flea, Can skip about a skittish humour'd hart.

**2.** Of horses, etc.: Disposed or apt to start or be unruly without sufficient cause; given to shying or restiveness through high spirits or playfulness; unduly lively or spirited.

*c* **1510** MORE *Picus* Wks. 14/2 These great fortunes lift vp a man hie,..but oftentymes, as a fierce and a skittish horse, thei cast of their maister. **1519** HORMAN *Vulg.* 37, I had a sore falle of a skytysshe horse. **1635** JACKSON *Creed* VIII. xviii. 202 The old asse..became resty and skittish, ready to kick. **1642** FULLER *Holy & Prof. St.* III. ii. 178 Great is the difference betwixt a swift horse, and a skittish, that will stand on no ground. **1707** tr. *Wks. C'tess D'Anois* (1715) 638 The skittish Beast being affrighted..gave two Starts and threw the Prince to the Ground. **1758** JOHNSON *Idler* No. 33 ¶24 Horse skittish and wants exercise. **1801** MAR. EDGEWORTH *Fr. Governess* Wks. 1832 II. 138 The ass is sometimes skittish and playful. **1882** B. D. W. RAMSAY *Rough Recoll.* I. i. 8 A very skittish, and at times vicious, thoroughbred colt.

*fig.* and *transf.* **1655** FULLER *Ch. Hist.* VI. 370 These skittish Lands will dismount all that bestride them. **1841** CATLIN *N. Amer. Ind.* (1844) II. lvi. 208 Balancing our skittish bark upon the green waters.

**b.** Similarly of other animals.

**1600** *Maids Metam.* I. i, A heard of skittish Deere. **1639** FULLER *Holy War* 198 A trick to stroke the skittish cow to get down her milk. **1837** HOOD *Ode to R. Wilson* 241 Exactly as a skittish Scottish bull Hunts an old woman in a scarlet cloak.

**3.** Fickle, inconstant, changeable; tricky, difficult to deal with or manage.

**1601** SHAKS. *Twel. N.* II. iv. 18 Such as I am, all true Louers are, Vnstaid and skittish in all motions else. **1606** —— *Tr. & Cr.* III. iii. 134 How some men creepe in skittish fortunes hall. **1639** HAMMOND *Serm.* Wks. 1683 IV. 547 What skittish things popular benevolence and popular applause have been always found to be. **1844** N. P. WILLIS *The Lady Jane* II. 411 A 'scribbler's' is a skittish reputation. **1872** GEO. ELIOT *Middlem.* xv, The management and training of the most skittish or vicious diseases.

**4.** Spirited, active, lively; frolicsome.

*a* **1592** GREENE *Jas. IV*, IV. iii, She is like a frog in a parsley-bed, As skittish as an eel. **1619** FLETCHER *Wildgoose Chase* II. iii, He slights us As skittish things... May be my free behaviour turns his stomach. **1665** PEPYS *Diary* 26 July, [He] is the most skittish leaping gallant that ever I saw, always in action. **1709** PRIOR *Let. to Sir T. Hanmer* 4 Aug., If you hear of a Welch widow..that has her goings and is not very skittish. **1813** H. & J. SMITH *Home in London* 131 One night at the British, We grew rather skittish, And sallied out fighting the rabble. **1887** JESSOPP *Arcady* v. 166 Sobriety of dress must be enforced, and skittish widows protected from their own volatile tastes.

**5.** Inclined to show coyness or reserve.

**1648** *Merc. Publicus* No. 2 ¶9 The Irish wench hee thought to hold By force, but she was skittish. **1700** DRYDEN *Ovid's Art Love* I. 822 Name not yourself her Lover, but her Friend. How many skittish Girls have thus been caught? **1774** J. ADAMS *Fam. Lett.* (1876) 42 They are, therefore, jealous of each other—fearful, timid, skittish. **1840** MRS. TROLLOPE *Widow Married* ii, So skittish that she would never let one speak to her. **1865** CARLYLE *Fredk. Gt.* XXI. iv. (1872) X. 31 Kaunitz and his Empress are extremely skittish in the matter, and as if quite refuse it at first.

**'skittishly,** *adv.* [f. prec. + -LY$^{2}$.] In a skittish or lively manner.

**1598** FLORIO, *Ritrosamente*, waywardly, frowardly, skittishly. **1611** COTGR., *Sauvagement*,..skittishly. **1683** [LD. COLERAINE] *Situat. Paradise* 93 The Beasts were very plump, and skittishly played as they passed by. **1873** MRS. WHITNEY *Other Girls* xxxiv, The animal made a half parenthesis of himself, curving skittishly..as he went by the frightsome pile. **1882** A. EDWARDES *Ballroom Repentance* I. 19 Skittishly tapping the young man's arm with her fan.

**'skittishness.** [f. as prec. + -NESS.] The quality of being skittish, in various senses.

**1607** MARKHAM *Caval.* II. (1617) 12 Skittishness or fearefulness proceedeth..either from nature, youth, custome, or imperfectness of sight. **1692** *D'Urfey's Marriage-Hater Match'd* A iij, The Skittishness of Miss Margery, and the freakishness of Berenice. **1721** STEELE *Const. Lover* III. i, Then, Phillis, consider how I must be reveng'd..of all your skittishness, shy looks, and at best but coy compliances. **1778** MME. D'ARBLAY *Lett.* 5 July, He would fain have discovered the reason of my skittishness. **1863** N. HAWTHORNE *Our Old Home* 134 Something akin to feminine skittishness. **1874** M. COLLINS *Transmigr.* I. vi. 110 The old roan plodded along, his skittishness quite lost.

*transf.* **1871** EARLE *Philol. Eng. Tongue* iv. 183 Young sprigs of language have a levity and skittishness which render them unworthy of literature.

**skittle** (skɪt(ə)l), *sb.* Also 7 *pl.* **skittolles, sketells (skyttals).** [Of uncertain origin: forms without initial *s-* (see KITTLE-PINS) appear a little later in the 17th cent., whereas in the case of KAYLES and SKAYLES the *s-* form is the later of the two.

Phonetically *skittle* answers exactly to the Scand. word represented by Da. and Sw. *skyttel*, occurring in the senses of 'shuttle, child's marble, movable bar in a gateway', but there is no evidence to connect this in any way with the game of skittles.]

**1. a.** *pl.* A game traditionally played with nine pins set in a square upon a wooden frame, an angle of which is directed towards the player, who endeavours to bowl down the pins in as few throws as possible; = NINE-PINS 1.

**1634** in Footman *Hist. Parish Ch. Chipping Lambourn* (1894) 120 William Gyde..for playing at skittolles on Sunday. **1666** WOOD *Life* (O.H.S.) II. 96 Dice, cards, sketells, shuffle-boords, billiard tables. **1748** WESLEY *Wks.* (1872) II. 120, I was one day playing at skittles with some of these. **1773** A. JONES (*title*), The Art of Playing at Skittles; or the Laws of Nine-Pins displayed. **1807** CRABBE *Par. Reg.* I. 64 All the joys that ale and skittles give. **1865** LUBBOCK *Preh. Times* xiii. (1869) 443 The Feegeeans..have also a game resembling skittles.

**b.** In the phrase *(not) all beer and skittles*, or variants of this, used to denote that something is (not) unmixed enjoyment.

**1837** DICKENS *Pickw.* xli, It's a reg'lar holiday to them—all porter and skittles. **1857** T. HUGHES *Tom Brown's School Days* I. ii. 46 Life isn't all beer and skittles. **1870** MANSFIELD *School-life Winch. Coll.* 138 But Football wasn't all beer and skittles to the Fags. **1897** 'OUIDA' *Massarenes* v, Life isn't all skittles and swipes... You always seem to think it. **1931** A. CHRISTIE *Sittaford Mystery* xxvi. 211 'It's an experience, isn't it?' 'Teach him life can't be all beer and skittles,' said Robert Gardner maliciously. **1963** D. OGILVY *Confessions Advert. Man* (1964) i. 12 Managing an advertising agency isn't all beer and skittles.

**c.** *colloq.* Nonsense; rubbish. Also used interjectionally.

**1864** *Orchestra* 12 Nov. 104/1 *Se faire applaudir* is not 'to make onesself applauded', and 'joyous comedian' is simply skittles. **1886** KIPLING *Departmental Ditties* (ed. 2) 43 'Where is your heat?' says he, 'Coming,' says I to Pagett. 'Skittles!' says Pagett, M.P. **1904** F. T. BULLEN *Creatures of Sea* xxiv. 354 [He told me] That they never ate and never rested because they had no feet, and other skittles of the kind. **1905** *Author* 1 Feb. 149 *Mag.* A man has..more self-restraint. *Char.* Skittles! That's the last thing he's got.

**d.** *colloq.* Chess played without serious application.

**1856** C. TOMLINSON *Chess Player's Ann.* 61 Nor will our royal Game less royal sound, If shallow men play skittles on the ground, Where first-rate Chess sedately sits in state, And spends long hours accomplishing a mate. **1894** *Daily News* 30 May 3/6 There is, as every experienced chessist knows, all the difference in the world between what is known as off-hand play or 'skittles' and chess. **1940** PRINS & WOOD tr. *Euwe's Meet Masters* i. 14 Every game of chess, serious or 'skittles'.

**2.** One of the wooden pins with which this game is played. Cf. NINE-PINS 2.

**1680** *Merry Milkmaid Islington* I. B, To cleave you from the scull to the Twist, and make nine Skittles of thy bones. **1866** *Chambers's Encycl.* VIII. 758/1 The player..tries to knock down the whole of the skittles in a given number of throws. **1884** KNIGHT *Dict. Mech.* Suppl. 820/2 A crucible taking the shape of a skittle.

**3.** *attrib.* and *Comb.* **a.** Attrib., in sense 'used in, or for playing at, the game of skittles', as ***skittle-alley, -ball, -bowl, -frame, -ground, -pin.***

**1755** *Connoisseur* No. 68 ¶2 Every *skittle-alley half a mile out of town is embellished with green arbours and shady retreats. **1822–7** GOOD *Study Med.* (1829) V. 319 The bronchocele had increased to the size of a *skittle-ball. **1733** TULL *Horse-Hoeing Husb.* xxiii. (Dubl.) 378 A piece of Wood of the shape of a *Skittle-Bowl. **1801** STRUTT *Sports & Past.* Introd. §38 All the *skittle-frames in or about the city of London. **1737** *London Mag.* Sept. 477/2 Such days would still be much better employed in that Way, than in sotting at an Ale-House, or loitering in a *Skettle or Nine-Pine Ground. **1771** MISS BURNEY *Early Diary* (1889) I. 131 Pray get the skittle ground marked out. **1971** *Country Life* 9 Dec. 1673/3 In 1773, the spring was covered over, and the site reverted to a simple public house with a skittle-ground attached. **1801** STRUTT *Sports & Past.* III. vii. 203 The kayle-pins were afterwards called..kittle-pins, and hence ..*skittle-pins. **1664** COTTON *Scarron.* IV. Wks. (1725) 109 Nor did I e'er make *skittle Pin-bones, Or Bobbins, of Anchises shin-bones.

**b.** Miscellaneous, as ***skittle-maker, -player, pool, -sharp, swindle; skittle-playing, -sharping; skittle-shaped;*** **skittle-pot**, a jeweller's crucible fashioned like a skittle (Knight, 1875).

**1858** SIMMONDS *Dict. Trade*, **Skittle-maker*, a turner who shapes wooden skittles. **1822** HAZLITT *Table-t.* Ser. II. vii. 158 As the *skittle-player bends his body to give a bias to the bowl. **1767** A. CAMPBELL *Lexiph.* (1774) 63 During a season of *skittle-playing. **1884** *Sat. Rev.* 7 June 758/1 *Skittle pool and other minor games. **1869** A. R. WALLACE *Malay Archip.* I. 374 They are all *skittle-shaped, larger in the middle than at the base. **1851** MAYHEW *Lond. Lab.* I. 345/2, I was not..a *skittle sharp, for I never entered into a plot to victimise any person. **1881** *Daily News* 23 Dec. 5/6 The..victim of the skittle-sharp is..told that a man..who is very silly, is coming to play..and that if the dupe will 'make one' in the pitiful robbery he shall share in the proceeds. **1862** MAYHEW *Lond. Lab.* IV. 309 Others betake themselves to card-sharping and *skittle-sharping. **1851** *Ibid.* I. 345/2 Getting into a hobble relative to a *skittle swindle.

**skittle** (skɪt(ə)l), *v.* [f. prec.]

**1.** *intr.* To play at the game of skittles.

**1865** *Good Words* 125/2 On 'Saint Monday' they go 'pigeoning', 'skittling', or after some other amusement.

**2. a.** *trans.* With *down*: To spend or lose (money) prodigally; to squander.

**1883** *Contemp. Rev.* XLIV. 609 There are many ways in which the Australian..can skittle down his money... He can lose £10,000 in a night at cards [etc.].

**b.** To knock down (skittles, etc.); *Cricket*, to bowl out (batsmen) in rapid succession. Also *fig.*, to kill, defeat easily.

**1880** *Wisden's Cricketers' Almanack* 18 Mr. Chatterton 'skittled' the wickets down so rapidly. **1919** W. H. Downing *Digger Dial.* 45 *Skittled*, killed. **1928** *Daily Express* 31 Mar. 3/4 Mine host and Mr. Herbert swung their arms, flung the cheeses, and skittled the pins. **1977** *World of Cricket Monthly* June 92/3 The Warwickshire bowling attack..skittled the students for a mere 59 in just 2¼ hours.

**c.** *Cricket.* Similarly with *out.* Also, to dismiss (a team) cheaply.

**1906** A. E. Knight *Compl. Cricketer* v. 172 Jim Jones thinks Sir Arthur Squire a rotten captain, who never gives him a chance to 'skittle the rabbits out'. **1949** J. Symons *Bland Beginning* 216 Now that Anthony had found a length, he began to skittle out the batsmen. **1979** *Daily Tel.* 9 Aug. 1/3 Somerset's West Indian fast bowler, Joel Garner, took five wickets for 11 runs, helping to skittle out Kent for 60.

Hence **'skittling** *vbl. sb.* Also *attrib.*

**1890** F. W. Robinson *Very strange Family* 71 Throwing one piece of furniture at another in a skittling fashion.

**skittle-dog.** *local.* (See quot.)

**1862** Couch *Brit. Fishes* I. 49 Spur Dog;..in Cornwall the male is called Skittle Dog.

**'skittler.** *rare.* [f. skittle *v.*] **1.** One who plays at the game of skittles. Also *fig.*

**1836** *Fraser's Mag.* XIII. 200 He suffered himself to be bowled down in such a cause by such a beggarly skittler as Willis, as if he had been a penny ninepin. **1958** G. Usher *Death in Bag* vii. 64 He'd go and see how the skittlers was doin'.

**2.** One who plays chess without serious application.

**1868** *Westminster Chess Club Papers* I. 87 We consider it quite possible to diffuse the game [of chess] without affording encouragement to the mere 'skittler'. **1911** *Daily News* 24 Apr. 4 The spread of chess literature, which has made every 'skittler' a book player.

**'skitty.** *dial.* [Cf. skiddy *sb.*] The moorhen.

**1813** Montagu *Ornith.* Suppl. s.v. *Gallinule*, Skitty, Spotted Rail, or Lesser spotted Water-Rail. **1888** in Elworthy *W. Somerset Word-bk.* 675.

**skitty-bats, -boots.** *dial.* (See quot. 1886.)

Halliwell (1847) gives *skilty-* and *skitter-boots* in this sense.

**1882** T. Hardy *Two on Tower* xxxviii, His corduroys and skitty-boots in which he had been gardening. **1886** Elworthy *W. Somerset Word-bk.* 675 *Skitty-bats*, boots laced in front, but not so high in the leg as *half-bats.*

**skiu,** variant of skew *sb.*[1] *Obs.*

**skiv.** *slang.* A sovereign.

**1858** Thomson *Almæ Matres* i. 4 A slight peculiarity of habit, contracted..from constantly losing 'skivs' at cards. **1871** *Punch* 14 Oct. 160/2 They tip you half a skiv now, instead of half a cartwheel.

**skive** (skaɪv), *sb.*[1] Also skieve. [ad. Du. *schijf* (sxɛɪf), MDu. *schîve*: see shive *sb.*] A revolving iron disk or wheel used with diamond powder in grinding, polishing, or finishing diamonds or other gems; a lap, a diamond-wheel. Cf. scaife 2.

**1843** Holtzapffel *Turning* I. 176 The diamonds are lastly polished upon an iron lap or skive, charged with diamond powder. **1862** *Catal. Intern. Exhib., Brit.* II. xxxiii. 53 Large diamonds are not exposed to the risk of cutting, but are polished from the rough on the skieve. **1884** F. J. Britten *Watch & Clockm.* 241 Gently pouring a little powder between the edge of the skive and the stone.

**skive** (skaɪv), *sb.*[2] [f. the vb.] The surface part of a sheet of leather cut off by a skiving-machine; a skiver.

**1875** Knight *Dict. Mech.* s.v. *Leather-skiving Machine*, The knife *C*, whose position..determines the thickness of the leather which passes between the knife and roller, the skive passing above the knife.

**skive** (skaɪv), *sb.*[3] *slang.* [f. skive *v.*[3]] An act of shirking; an opportunity for avoiding a difficult or unpleasant task, an easy option.

**1958** F. Norman *Bang to Rights* iii. 90 Not many of us wanted to learn english and only went on the class for a skive. **1960** [see chuffed *a.* a]. **1968** *Guardian* 1 Oct. 6/1 'Isn't just a skive,' he told them. 'At any time, any time, you may be parachuted behind the Russian lines.' **1976** *Times Higher Educ. Suppl.* 26 Mar. 7/1 I'd always thought that science degrees with a non-scientific element would be attractive but perhaps students associate them with the general studies they do in the sixth form and think of them either as a skive or a nuisance. **1980** J. Ditton *Copley's Hunch* i. ii. 68 He thought the sentry was on the skive. Thought he'd come down..for a cup of coffee.

**skive** (skaɪv), *v.*[1] Also skyve. [a. ON. *skífa* (Norw. *skiva*), related to ME. *schîve* shive *sb.*] *trans.* To split or cut (leather, rubber, etc.) into slices or strips; to shave or pare (hides).

*a* **1825** Forby *Voc. E. Anglia* 305 *Skive*, to pare off the thicker parts of hides, to make them of uniform substance, in order to their being tanned. **1875** Knight *Dict. Mech.* 1280/2 Leather is also skived for making lap-joints in round work and belting. **1884** *Health Exhib. Catal.* 115/1 One Machine for skyving or paring the edges of leather.

**b.** To pare or cut *off.*

**1875** Knight *Dict. Mech.* 1277/2 [A] Machine..for skiving off the edge of a piece or strip of leather.

Hence **skived** *ppl. a.*

**1875** Knight *Dict. Mech.* 1280/2 The lap-seam..is sometimes formed with skived edges to avoid a ridge. **1893** *Westm. Gaz.* 30 Nov. 7/2 Pneumatic tyres, which are made from 'skived' rubber.

**skive** (skaɪv), *v.*[2] *dial.* [Of obscure origin.] *intr.* To move lightly and quickly; to dart.

**1854** Miss Baker *Northampt. Gloss.* s.v. *Skave*, Thus we say, 'skiving like a lapwing', in allusion to the manner in which that bird skims over the surface of a sheet of water. **1857** J. G. Holland *Bay Path* xxvi. 334 Don't you want a little tot, Hugh, to be skiving round the cabin here? **1893** Cozens-Hardy *Broad Norf.* 49 Can't they skive under water when they want tu?

**skive** (skaɪv), *v.*[3] *slang* (orig. *Mil.*). Also scive, skyve. [perh. ad. Fr. *esquiver*, to dodge, slink away, but cf. skive *v.*[2]] *intr.* To evade a duty, to shirk; to avoid work by absenting oneself, to play truant. Also with *off.*

**1919** *Athenæum* 1 Aug. 695/1 'To skive,' to dodge a fatigue. **1925** Fraser & Gibbons *Soldier & Sailor Words & Phrases* 260 *To skive*, to dodge a duty or fatigue. **1960** *Twentieth Cent.* Nov. 390 Who hasn't bought black-market, possibly stolen goods, who hasn't skived off work? **1960** J. Birley *Time of Cuckoo* 139 'But a second is what you aimed for, isn't it? I mean one has to be pretty brilliant for the other, anyway, and if not, why work all that hard?' 'Oh, yes, yes, I dare say... I've been skyving all my life, certainly, if that's what you mean.' **1961** *New Statesman* 21 July 82/2 If one of the other cleaners offered advice, it was usually on how to scive off better. **1962** *Listener* 27 Dec. 1104/3 Anyone who thinks of the Fire Service as a soft option that literary types skived into during the war ought to have watched 'Fire Rescue'. **1965** [see *free period* s.v. free *a.* D. 2]. **1971** *Times Educ. Suppl.* 25 June 69 People work—and skyve—openly at any time. **1973** J. Mann *Only Security* vi. 58 The girls who dig are always glad of an excuse to skive off and have a rest. **1976** *Sunday Post* (Glasgow) 26 Dec., A Dundee bus conductor was chatting to three young boys as he took their fares last Monday. He asked if they were on holiday. They replied they were 'just skiving'. **1982** *Sunday Times* 31 Jan. 3/6 These people work, skive and fiddle in packs.

Hence **'skiving** *vbl. sb.*[2]

**1958** *Daily Mail* 18 July 3/3 You do two hours' work a day and spend the rest of the time dodging. In the Army we called it swinging the lead, but on the railway it's called skiving. **1974** *New Society* 19 Sept. 727/1 It is among managerial and professional workers that sponging, skiving and malingering is epidemic. **1977** *Ibid.* 25 Aug. 381/3 Some of the overseers connive at, even join in, this skyving. **1978** P. Marsh et al. *Rules of Disorder* ii. 33 Skiving was not infrequent—the pupils slipping out once the register had been called.

**skivel** ('skɪv(ə)l). *dial.* = skiver *sb.*[1]

**1790** E. Nairne *Kentish Tales* (1824) 76 No pains or cost's required to paint a devil Down in a trice, with black ink and a skivel. **1868-** in dial. glossaries (Sussex, Kent).

**skiver** ('skɪvə(r)), *sb.*[1] Chiefly *dial.* Also 9 sciver, skivver, skivor. [See note to skewer *sb.*] A skewer. Also *fig.*

**1664** J. Wilson *Projectors* iv, The frugal Spaniard!..that shall..carry a pound of Mutton in triumph on a Skiver! **1685** Boyle *Effects Motion* ix. 121 A little Bodkin or skiver of wood. **1699** Dampier *Voy.* II. i. 31 Little bits of Pork, spitted 5 or 6 of them at once, on a small skiver, and roasted. **1746** *Gentl. Mag.* XVI. 491/1 With a skiver From love's quiver I am spitted. **1838-** in dialect glossaries, etc. (Yks., Som., Cornw., Irel.).

*attrib.* **1847** Halliw., *Skiver-wood*, dogwood, of which skewers are made. **1886** Elworthy *W. Somerset Word-bk.* 675 *Skiver-timber*, the spindle-wood;..*Euonymus europæus.*

**skiver** ('skaɪvə(r)), *sb.*[2] Also skyver. [f. skive *v.*[1] + -er.]

**1.** A thin kind of dressed leather split from the grain side of a sheep-skin and tanned in sumach, used for bookbinding, lining hats, and other commercial purposes.

**1800** *Hull Advertiser* 12 Apr. 2/2 Various kinds of leather, ..red and brown skivers. **1851** Mayhew *Lond. Lab.* I. 443/2 The skin is 'split'... That known as the 'grain'..is very thin, and is dressed into a 'skiver'. **1880** Leland *Minor Arts* i. 32 Now make a dragon..out of papier mâché..., cover it with skiver.

*attrib.* **1845** G. Dodd *Brit. Manuf.* V. ix. 205 The other half being alumed or tawed for 'skiver' leather.

**2.** One who or that which skives; *esp.* a workman who pares or splits leather.

**1829** P. Egan *Boxiana* 2nd Ser. II. 220 At a proper age, Jem turned out to earn an honest penny, and was apprenticed to a *skyver*, or skinman, in Newcastle-upon-Tyne. **1850** *Rep. Comm. Patents 1849* (U.S.) I. 313, I claim ..the application of a guage or gauges to a skiver. **1875** Knight *Dict. Mech.* 2197/1 *Skiver*, a paring tool for leather. **1894** J. Macintosh *Ayrshire Nts. Entert.* xxi. 397 The shapes are then handed to the skivers, the fitters, and the sewers.

**skiver** ('skaɪvə(r)), *sb.*[3] *slang.* Also sciver, skyver. [f. skive *v.*[3] + -er[1].] One who avoids work; a shirker; a truant.

**1941** G. Kersh *They die with their Boots Clean* 219 Well, mud in your eye, old skivers! **1942** —— *Nine Lives Bill Nelson* xi. 71 You end up like them old skivers that mooch about the Naffy Library. **1959** I. & P. Opie *Lore & Lang. Schoolch.* xvii. 372 A few children in Kirkcaldy give 'sciver' as a name for a truant. **1961** *New Statesman* 26 May 830/1 As it was day-time, everyone in the coffee bar was a sciver, on the dole or on the fiddle or just plain hopeful. **1971** [see *fruit gum* s.v. fruit *sb.* 9]. **1977** *Daily Tel.* 24 Nov. 8/6 A Labour-controlled council is to crack down on 'skivers' following a report which alleges large scale absenteeism and sick leave among its manual workers. **1982** *Times* 20 Apr. 4/8, I frequently came across cases at depots where there were skivers galore.

**skiver** ('skɪvə(r)), *v.*[1] [f. skiver *sb.*[1]] *trans.* To pierce or stab with or as with a skewer; to fasten with a skewer.

**1832** *Blackw. Mag.* Mar. 432/2 Nor was that abject delusion destroyed even by the bayonets that skivered the Invincibles. **1874** Mahaffy *Soc. Life Greece* ix. 280 *note*, The head doctors would skiver him, if they caught him taking a fee. **1886** Elworthy *W. Somerset Word-bk.* 675 Mind you skiver up the bag.

**skiver** ('skaɪvə(r)), *v.*[2] [f. skiver *sb.*[2]] *trans.* To cut or pare (leather).

**1875** Knight *Dict. Mech.* 2197/1 *Skiver*,..a machine.. adjustable to skiver counters to any desired width of scarf.

**skiver,** *v.*[3] *U.S.* [Cf. skive *v.*[2]] (See quot.)

*a* **1891** *Shore Birds* 33 (Cent. Dict.), At the report of a gun the frightened flock will dart about in terror, *skiver*, as it is technically called.

**skivet,** variant of skibbet.

**skivie** ('skaɪvɪ), *a. Sc.* Also skaivie. [Of obscure origin: cf. Du. *scheef*, ON. *skeifr* askew, asquint.] Harebrained; mentally deranged.

**1808** Jamieson, *Skaivie*, harebrained; applied to one who acts as if in a delirium, or on the borders of insanity. **1824** Scott *Redgauntlet* ch. vii, 'He means *mad*,' said the party appealed to... 'Ye have it—ye have it', said Peter, 'that is, not clean skivie, but—'.

**'skiving,** *vbl. sb.*[1] [f. skive *v.*[1]]

**1.** (See quots.)

*a* **1825** Forby *Voc. E. Anglia* 305 *Skivings*, the parings of hides, to be boiled into glue. **1875** Knight *Dict. Mech.* 1281/2 By splitting so as to preserve the grain side, one sheet of very fair leather may be obtained, while the other (*skiving*) is fit for trunk-covers, etc.

**2.** The action of splitting leather, etc.

**1884** Knight *Dict. Mech.* Suppl. 820/2 *Skiving*, the act of removing the rough fleshy portion from the inner surface of a skin. **1893** *Westm. Gaz.* 30 Nov. 7/2 'Skiving' has hitherto been thought impracticable, but specimens of this process applied to the Surrey pneumatic tyres were shown by the patentee.

**3.** *attrib.*, as ***skiving-knife, machine, process, -tool.***

**1875** Knight *Dict. Mech.* 1277/1 It is a skiving process, and is usually performed on a skiving or shaving machine. *Ibid.* 2197/1 Skiving-knife; skiving-tool.

**skiving,** *vbl. sb.*[2]: see skive *v.*[3]

**skivvy** ('skɪvɪ), *sb.*[1] *colloq.* (usu. *derogatory*). Also scivey, skivey. [Of obscure origin.] A female domestic servant, esp. a maid-of-all-work. Also *transf.*

**1902** H. Baumann *Londinismen* (ed. 2) 211/2 *Skivey*,.. slav(e)y. **1913** C. Mackenzie *Sinister St.* I. ii. iv. 195 The ball had landed twice..on the same balcony to the great annoyance of the 'skivvy', who was..invited to bung it down. **1915** W. Owen *Let.* 23 Nov. (1967) 367, I never thought myself capable of such strenuosities as to do skivvy's drudgery. **1938** L. Durrell *Black Book* 240 Gwen, that dirty little skivvy, smelling of..grease from the sink! **1947** E. Wilson *Europe without Baedeker* viii. 206 You were waited on by slovenly skivvies so pallidly unappetizing that they made the meager food seem more tasteless. **1961** 'F. O'Brien' *Hard Life* vii. 52 The young people of today think the daddy is a tramp and the mammy a poor skivvy. **1974** *Times* 1 May 4/5 This represents a change in the nurses' attitude. No longer will you be the skivvies of the health service. **1977** *Punch* 31 Aug.–6 Sept. 331/1 Blossom, the strikingly handsome new scivvy, is mixing her a posset.

Hence **'skivvy** *v. intr.*, to work as a skivvy; **'skivvying** *vbl. sb.*

**1931** R. Campbell *Georgiad* ii. 44 Every Nellie, Gertie Or Daisy that..ever left her own unlettered stews To skivvy in the kitchen of the Muse. **1968** *Punch* 21 Feb. 287/1 There are now better jobs than skivvying to look for, and wages sometimes comparable with what the job-seeking housewife herself might be earning. **1973** J. Thomson *Death Cap* ii. 33 It wasn't no skivvying job... Mrs King treated me like a friend. **1974** W. Foley *Child in Forest* ii. 156 She come up to skivvy in the same place as you, then?

**skivvy** ('skɪvɪ), *sb.*[2] Also scivvy, skivie, skivvie. [Of unknown origin.] **1.** *N. Amer. slang* (orig. *Naut.*). **a.** An undershirt, a vest. Also ***skivvy shirt.*** **b.** *pl.* Underclothes.

**1932** J. L. D'Esque *Count in Fo'c'sle* 216 He cut away the unconscious engineer's shirt and skivie with his jack-knife. **1942** Berrey & Van den Bark *Amer. Thes. Slang* §900/6 *Skivvie shirt*, an undervest. **1944** C. Mackenzie *Sailors of Fortune* 95 The Red Cross woman brought me khaki trousers, scivvy shirt and a left shoe. **1945** *Seafarers' Log* 9 Nov. 6/3 Chips appeared, also gassed up, in his skivvies. **1946** T. Heggen *Mister Roberts* 7 It now contained a soiled scivvy shirt. **1953** S. Bellow *Adventures Augie March* 28

We had to brush our teeth with salt..and sleeping in skivvies, was outlawed; we had to wear pajamas. **1967** 'J. CROSS' *To Hell for Half-a-Crown* ii. 36 The..biceps straining at the white skivvy shirt. **1972** R. WHITE *Be not Afraid* xvii. 206 We jumped out of our sleeping bags.., only realizing after we had recovered the gear that we were barefoot and in skivvies in subzero weather. **1978** W. HJORTSBERG *Falling Angel* xxxviii. 184 Ethan Krusemark, wearing boxer shorts and a skivvy, lay on his back..doing leg presses.

**2.** A high-necked lightweight pullover or jumper.

**1967** *Telegraph* (Brisbane) 27 Feb. 14/4 (*caption*) This waistcoat should be a winner on the winter scene teamed with white long-sleeved skivvy. **1972** *New York* 8 May 20/1 (Advt.), Sleeveless skivvy (shown under the cardigans) in peach or pale blue. **1972** D. SALE *Love Bite* xix. 239 She was wearing a navy-blue jump suit over a black skivvy, so that she wouldn't be seen in the dark.

**skladdyt**, obs. pa. pple. of SCALD *v.*

**sklait(t, sklate**, obs. Sc. forms of SLATE *sb.*[1]

**sklander**, etc.: see SLANDER, etc.

**skla(u)nt, sklave, sklavin**: see SLANT, etc.

†**skleir**, *sb. Obs.* Also 4 scleire, scleyre, sklayre, skleire, sleyre, slaire. [a. MLG. *sleier, sleiger*, = MHG. *sleier*, mod.G. *schleier*, Du. *sluier*, of obscure origin.] A veil.

**13..** *Minor Poems fr. Vernon MS.* xxxvii. 280 þis wymmen..Wiþ hornes on heore hed Pinned on vch a syde ..Wiþ selk scleyres I-set aboue. **1362** LANGL. *P. Pl.* A. VII. 7 'þat weore a long lettynge' quaþ a ladi in a skleir [*v.rr.* scleire, sklayre, slaire, etc.].

Hence †**skleir** *v. trans.*, to veil. *Obs.*

**1387-8** T. USK *Test. Love* II. xiv. (Skeat) 25 And with fayre honyed wordes heretykes and mis-meninge people skleren and wimplen their errours.

**sklent**, *sb. Sc.* Also sclent. [Sc. var. of SLENT *sb.* Cf. the earlier ASKLENT *adv.*] A slant or slope; a slanting or sideward movement; a side-look, etc.

**1768** ROSS *Helenore* 16 With easy sklent, on every side the braes..wi' scatter'd busses raise. **1786** BURNS *To J. Smith* vii, This while my notion's taen a sklent, To try my fate in guid, black prent. **1818** HOGG *Brownie of Bodsbeck* xiv, I gae a sklent wi' my ee. **1891** *Blackw. Mag.* CL. 712/1 Not descended indeed in direct line from..Wordsworth.., but striking off from him in a sort of sklent, if we may use such a word.

**sklent**, *v. Sc.* and *north. dial.* Also sclent. [var. of SLENT *v.*]

**1.** *intr.* To move, dart, or fall, obliquely; to lie aslant; to give a side-look, etc.

**1513** DOUGLAS *Æneid* VII. vii. 87 As sum tyme sclentis the round top of tre, Hit with the twynit quhyp. *Ibid.* X. xiii. 51 The casting dart..That fleand sclentis on Eneas scheyld. **1629** SIR W. MURE *True Crucifixe* 1668 The honour.., streight sent back, is vpwards driven, And by Reflexe doth sklent hye way to Heauen. **1808-1901** in *Eng. Dial. Dict.* (Sc. and Northumb.).

**b.** *fig.* To deviate from a straightforward course, or from the truth.

**1581** N. BURNE in *Cath. Tract.* (S.T.S.) 155 Bot becaus ye se your self conuict,..ye ar constranit to sklent and mak the act of Parliament ane buclar for your defence aganis al argumentis. **1785** BURNS *2nd Epist. J. Lapraik* xi, Do ye envy the city-gent, Behint a kist to lie an' sklent. **1864** in *Eng. Dial. Dict.*

**2.** *trans.* To direct obliquely.

**1785** BURNS *To W. Simpson* ii, Ironic satire, sidelins sklented, On my poor Musie. **1785** —— *Addr. Deil* xvii, Ye ..sklented on the man of Uzz, Your spitefu' joke.

Hence '**sklenting** *vbl. sb.* and *ppl. a.*

**1568** *Satir. Poems Reform.* xlvii. 83 Tha peure winschis ȝe wranguslie suspect For sklenting bowttis. *a* **1572** KNOX *Hist. Ref.* Wks. 1846 II. 321 He was a large quarter of myle from the schote and sklenting of boltis. **1785** BURNS *Addr. Deil* vii, The stars shot down wi' sklentan light.

**skleroclase**, variant of SCLEROCLASE.

**sklice**, obs. or Sc. form of SLICE.

**sklither**, obs. variant of SLITHER *a.*

**sklodowskite** (sklə'dɒvskaɪt). *Min.* [a. F. *sklodowskite* (A. Schoep 1924, in *Compt. Rend.* CLXXIX. 415), f. *Skłodowska*, maiden name of Marie Curie (1867-1934), Polish-born chemist and co-discoverer of radium: see -ITE[1].] A hydrated uranyl magnesium silicate, $Mg(UO_2)_2Si_2O_7.6H_2O$, which occurs as a secondary mineral, forming lemon-yellow monoclinic crystals.

**1924** *Chem. Abstr.* XVIII. 3577 (*heading*) Sklodowskite, a new radioactive mineral. **1957** *Amer. Mineralogist* XLII. 617 Sklodowskite, which is considered iso-structural with uranophane, and beta-uranophane may have structures based on uranophane. **1972** *Canad. Mineralogist* XI. 562 A mixture of uranophane and sklodowskite forms a coating on a specimen of quartz with magnetite.

†**skluce.** *Obs.*[−1] [Cf. MDu. *sluus* pulp (of an apple).] A pulpy mass.

*c* **1430** *Two Cookery Bks.* 25 Boyle it, & plante þin skluce with Rosys, & serue forth.

**skn-**, occas. ME. variant of SN-.

**skoal**, var. SKOL *sb.* and *v.*

**skocche, skoch(e**, obs. ff. SCOTCH *sb.*[1] and *v.*[1]

**Skoda** ('skəʊdə). The name of the Czech engineer and industrialist Emil von *Skoda* (1839-1900), used *attrib.* and *ellipt.* to designate guns manufactured in the factories established by him.

**1902** *Encycl. Brit.* XXIX. 166/1 In the Hotchkiss and also in the Skoda systems the mechanism is of the vertical breech block type. **1933** J. BUCHAN *Prince of Captivity* I. 78 Skoda mountain howitzers which had once been destined for the Hedjaz. **1973** J. QUICK *Dict. Weapons & Mil. Terms* 402/1 The first Skoda machine gun appeared in 1888 and was a delayed-blowback weapon.

**skodaic** (skəʊ'deɪɪk), *a. Path.* [f. the name of the Austrian physician Joseph *Skoda* (1805-81).] The specific epithet of the resonant percussion note heard in cases of pleuritic effusion.

**1882** *Quain's Dict. Med.* II. 1187 This resonance, called Skodaic resonance, is a very characteristic sign. **1897** *Allbutt's Syst. Med.* II. 1137 If a layer of lung intervene.. a Skodaic note may be elicited. **1898** *Ibid.* V. 338 The resonance becoming..of that character which is generally known under the name of 'skodaic resonance'.

**skoe, skogy**: see SKEO, SCUGGY *a.*

‖**skoff** (skɔf). *S. Afr.* Also schoft, skof, skoft. Pl. skoffs, skofte. [Afrikaans *skof*, f. Du. *schoft* (see SCOFF *sb.*[2]).] A stage of a journey, a period of travel between outspans.

**1785** G. FORSTER tr. *Sparrman's Voyage to Cape of Good Hope* I. 132 Four such hours with a horse, or with eight oxen, are reckoned to make one *skoft*. **1801** J. BARROW *Acct. Trav. S. Afr.* I. ii. 55 Each day's journey is called a *skoff*; and the length of these is generally regulated by local circumstances, being from five to fifteen hours. **1835** H. I. VENABLE in D. J. Kotzé *Lett. Amer. Missionaries* (1950) 70 The Dutch call a day's journey a *schoft*. For oxen in good condition a schoft is from twenty to twenty-four miles. **1892** R. CHURCHILL *Men, Mines & Animals in S. Afr.* ix. 134 We have done twenty-five miles from Silika in three 'skoffs', which is excellent trekking. **1932** L. FOUCHE in C. Fuller *Louis Trigardt's Trek* p. xv, It became imperative to ascertain the value of Trigardt's unit, the length of a 'skof'. **1969** A. FUGARD *Boesman & Lena* I. 2 That last skof was hard. Against the wind... Heavier and heavier. Every step. **1972** L. G. GREEN *When Journey's Over* (1973) v. 50 The normal day on the road was made up of two or three stages known as *skofte*.

**skoff**, var. SCOFF *sb.*[2] and *v.*[2]

†**skoke.** *Obs.* [ad. MDu. or MLG. *schok*: see SHOCK *sb.*] A certain quantity (see quot.).

**1545** *Rates of Customs* bj, Double Iron plates called doubles the skoke xx.*s.* Doubles the bondel, iij.*s.* iiij.*d.* and vj. bondels to the skoke.

**skokiaan** ('skɒkɪɑːn). *S. Afr.* Also skokian. [Poss. of Nguni origin.] An intoxicating home-brewed liquor fermented with yeast. Also *attrib.*

**1926** S. G. MILLIN *S. Africans* VII. ii. 223 Sometimes a group of Kaffirs are found drinking a rapidly fermenting preparation called *skokiaan* in the outbuilding of a European's home. **1936** WILLIAMS & MAY *I am Black* IV. xvii. 175 The white men call me a skokiaan queen. **1946** P. ABRAHAMS *Mine Boy* xi. 135 He knew she was one of the foremost Skokiaan Queens—for that is what they call the women who deal in illicit liquor. **1953** D. LESSING *Five* 286 Skokian is a wicked and dangerous drink, and it is illegal. It is made quickly, in one day, and may contain many different substances. On this night it has mealie-meal, sugar, tobacco, methylated spirits, boot polish and yeast. Some skokian queens use magic, such as the limb of a dead person. **1970** G. LORD *Marshmallow Pie* iv. 33 He didn't hate the blacks. .. All they wanted was a quiet life and some *skokiaan* on Saturday nights. **1976** *Globe & Mail* (Toronto) 13 Nov. 16/5 The rougher shebeens lack refinements and sell often-questionable products, ranging from commercial and homemade beers to a variety of moonshine liquors, including the legendary skokiaan.

‖**skol** (skɒl, older skəʊl), *sb.* Also skal, skoal, sköl; 7 scol, scoll, skole, scoill, scoall. [ad. Da. and Norw. *skaal*, Sw. *skål*, repr. ON. *skál* bowl.] A health in drinking; a toast. Also *Comb.*

In early use only Sc., perhaps introduced through the visit of James VI to Denmark in 1589. In recent use the Scandinavian spelling *skaal* is sometimes retained.

**1600** *Scot. Acts, Jas. VI* (1816) IV. 204 He was directit frome his ma[tie] To drink his scoll to my lord diuk and the rest of the companie. *Ibid.*, Immediatlie after the scoill had passit about. **1649** *Ibid.*, *Chas. II* (1814) VI. II. 174 All those who under whatsoever name..Drink healthes and scoalles. **1678** CALDERWOOD *Hist. Ch. Scot.* 787 Sir William Beyer.. stayed the taking away of the centries..till the Kings skole were drunk at that part of the bridge. **1840** LONGF. *Skel. in Armour* xx, There from the flowing bowl Deep drinks the warrior's soul, *Skoal!* to the Northland! *Skoal!* **1857** LD. DUFFERIN *Lett. High Lat.* (ed. 3) 62 With the peculiar manners used in Scandinavian skoal-drinking I was already well acquainted. **1924** *Vogue* late Jan. 64/2 If only I could make out why nobody dared touch his glass before someone else had said 'Skål', and why you yourself were at it the whole time. **1935** J. D. CARR *Death-Watch* xix. 187 'Skoal,' wheezed Dr. Fell absently. He pushed his glass away. **1948** F. BROWN *Murder can be Fun* (1951) ii. 24 'Skoal!' he said. They drank. **1961** *Guardian* 8 Feb. 12/5 'Skol' which we imagine to be a jolly kind of 'Cheerio' on lifting a glass, is an essential part of Swedish etiquette. **1961** M. BEADLE *These Ruins are Inhabited* (1963) ix. 116 We..learned the etiquette of *sköl*. The Swedes are enthusiastic drinkers. **1973** D. FRANCIS *Slay-Ride* i. 17 '*Skol*' they said. '*Skol*' I repeated. They watched interestedly while I drank.

**skol**, *v.* In 6-7 scoll, 7 scole, scoall, 20 skoal, skol. [f. prec.] **a.** *intr.* To drink healths; to drink deeply. orig. *Sc.*

*a* **1598** [implied in SKOLING *vbl. sb.*]. **1624** *Extr. Aberdeen Register* (1848) II. 391 That nane presume..to vrge thair nichtbouris to waught or scole farder nor thair plesour. **1909** E. POUND *Personae* 17, I skoal to the eyes as grey-blown mere..Wineing the ghosts of yester-year.

**b.** *trans.* To drink the health of.

**1935** G. GREENE *England made Me* I. 1 She swallowed it at a draught.. skoal, skoal, but there was no one to skoal. **1963** *Times* 23 Jan. 12/7 There was ample time to *skol* one another. **1980** P. HARCOURT *Tomorrow's Treason* I. iv. 67 We had skolled in champagne the bonfires being lit around the fjord.

Hence '**skoling** *vbl. sb.*

*a* **1598** ROLLOCK *Serm.* Wks. 1849 I. 395 He is harling them to harlatrie,..to scolling and drinking. **1649** *Sc. Acts, Chas. II* (1814) VI. II. 174 Healthing and scoalling is the occasion of much drunkennesse. **1928** H. CRANE *Let.* 27 Mar. (1965) 320 Many bottles of dubious gin and whiskey —with much 'skoling'.

**skolder**, obs. Sc. f. SCOWDER *v.*

**skole**, obs. f. SCALE *sb.*[1], SCHOOL, SKOAL.

**skolecite**, obs. f. SCOLECITE.

**skolion**, var. SCOLION.

**skolkerye**, obs. var. SKULKERY.

**skolly** ('skɒlɪ). *S. Afr.* Also scolly, -ie. [a. Afrikaans, prob. ad. Du. *schoelje* scoundrel, rascal.] A Black or Coloured African hooligan, gangster, hoodlum; a vagrant. Also *attrib.*, as ***skolly boy***. Hence '**skollydom**, the condition or activity of a skolly; '**skollyism**, the way of life of a skolly.

**1934** *Cape Argus* 8 Jan. 10/6 The accused..were actually several degrees lower than the average 'scolly-boy' who commits most of the crimes of violence and theft in the Peninsula. **1934** *Cape Times* 12 Jan. 9/7 The 'scollie' boys could be rounded up and sent to labour colonies. **1949** *Ibid.* 10 Sept. 8/8 The cure for skollydom is not mollycoddling. **1954** R. ST. JOHN *Through Malan's Africa* v. 32 Experts say that dagga is one of the least harmful of the narcotics, and yet in District 6 it leads to the shebeens and skollyism. **1961** *Cape Times* 28 Jan. 11/1 Don't you realize that your son is becoming a White skolly?.. He is going to land in gaol unless you do something about him. **1972** *East Cape Post* 14 Mar., Tsotsis and skollies who lurk in street corners, waiting to assault and rob innocent people. **1980** J. MCCLURE *Blood of Englishman* ix. 82 Look at the clientele... All the top-notch... You won't find skolly boys in here.

**skons(e**, obs. ff. SCONCE.

**skonschon**, obs. f. SCUNCHEON.

**skoob** (skuːb). [Reversal of *books*: not in general use (see quots.).] A pile of books assembled in order to be destroyed as a gesture against the proliferation and undue veneration of the printed word (see quot. 1967); the ceremonial burning of a book or books.

**1963** *Guardian* 14 Feb. 6/5 The Skoob Image—the mangled books. **1966** *Archit. Rev.* Dec. 441/2 A skoob tower by John Latham—a construction of art books destined to be detonated. **1967** *Listener* 18 May 654/3 Latham's earlier works were assemblages of torn and paint-covered books... His 'skoob' (books spelt backwards) are a cathartic topsy-turvying of the natural reaction of horror at the destruction of the printed word. **1968** *Guardian* 14 Sept. 3/3 Mr. Stone said it was the first time that a 'skoob', the burning of a book, had taken place in Kensington Church Walk.

**skookum** ('skuːkəm), *sb.* and *a. N. Amer.* Also †scocum, scokum, etc. [a. Chinook Jargon.]

**A.** *sb.* An evil spirit; a disease. *Obs.* exc. *Hist.*

**1838** S. PARKER *Jrnl. of Exploring Tour beyond Rocky Mts.* 336 Evil spirit, skookoom. Hell, skookoom. **1844** LEE & FROST *Ten Yrs. in Oregon* xvi. 180 He [*sc.* the medicine man] transfers the 'sko-koms', or 'tam-an-a-was', or disease, wholly or in part from the patient to himself. **1846** JOHNSON & WINTER *Route Across Rocky Mts.* iii. 54 Several loud shouts are uttered in as frightful a manner as they are able. They then open their fingers gradually, to allow the terrified Scocum, (evil spirit,) to make his escape. **1900** *Oregon Hist. Soc. Q.* I. 185 The benefits of his fishery had gone, not to the people, but to the wicked skookum.

**B.** *adj.* **a.** Strong, stout, brave; fine, splendid.

**1847** J. PALMER *Jrnl. Trav. Rocky Mts.* 151/1 *Skokum*, strong, stout. **1891** H. W. SETON-KARR *Bear Hunting in White Mts.* viii. 83 He believed that a bear would hold out its paw towards a man at a distance and feel whether he was *skookum*—brave. **1901** *Daily Colonist* (Victoria, B.C.) 29 Oct. 6/3, I would have gone up myself but could not stand the five days' tramp with 40 or 50 pounds on my back. It takes a 'skookum' man to stand a trip like that. **1913** [see ROUGH LOCK, ROUGH-LOCK]. **1941** J. SMILEY *Hash House Lingo* 50 *Skookum*, good; all right. **1949** *Sierra Club. Bull.* (San Francisco) June 105 Billy and Pete were skookum, and I was pretty good myself in those days. **1962** E. LUCIA *Klondike Kate* 12 As Klondike Kate, she was a mighty skookum gal. **1975** *Islander* (Victoria, B.C.) 6 July 4/2 Ted, by this time a skookum young fellow of 20, then turned his eyes further west.

**b.** Special collocations. **skookum chuck** [CHUCK *sb.*[6]], a fast-moving body of water, a torrent, rapids; an ocean; **skookum house**, a gaol.

**1888** LEES & CLUTTERBUCK *B.C. 1887: Ramble in British Columbia* xvii. 184 We arranged to meet at the Skookumchuck Creek ('the stream of the rapid torrent').

**1899** *Bull. U.S. Fish Comm. 1898* XVIII. 73 The passage is a 'skookum chuck', through which the water runs in whirls and rapids almost constantly and with great velocity. **1911** E. P. JOHNSON *Legends of Vancouver* 47 You have listened to the call of the Skookum Chuck, as the Chinook speakers call the rollicking, tumbling streams that sing their way through the canyons. **1940** K. S. PINKERTON *Three's Crew* x. 102 A tidal rapids is a 'skookum chuck'. **1959** *Times* (Queen in Canada Suppl.) 18 June p. xii/1 This is the salt chuck, the skookum chuck.. in fact the Pacific. **1873** R. C. L. BROWN *Klatsassan* 165 It was only after much *waw-waw* (parley) and sundry threats of the skookum-house (gaol).. that one of them was got to undertake to carry him. **1901** *Daily Colonist* (Victoria, B.C.) 5 Oct. 3/2 There were no less than fourteen inmates of the 'skookum house' on Cormorant Street last night. **1965** *Islander* (Victoria, B.C.) 9 May 6/2 In 1872, Frederick Brent was appointed Justice of the Peace and a skookum-house (jail) was built on his land.

**skooter**, obs. var. SCOUTER.

**skop(e, -ppe**, obs. ff. SCOOP.

**skopster.** *local.* The saury pike.
*a* **1705** RAY *Syn. Pisc.* (1713) 165 *Skipper* Cornubiensium (corruptione vocis) *skopster.* **1865** COUCH *Brit. Fishes* IV. 141 Skipper. Saury. Skopster.

**skoptophilia**, var. SCOPOPHILIA.

**Skoptsi** ('skɒptsɪ), *sb. pl.* Also occas. **Skoptzi, Skopzy**, etc. [Russ., pl. of *skopéts*, eunuch, member of Skoptsi.] An ascetic Russian Christian sect, known since the eighteenth century and now forbidden, given to self-mutilation (see quots.). Also *rarely* as *sing.* Hence '**Skoptsism**, the faith and practice of the Skoptsi.
**1856** [see KHLIST]. **1874** J. H. BLUNT *Dict. Sects* 564/1 *Skoptzi*, a name signifying 'eunuchs', given to a Russian sect of the Bezpopoftschin Dissenters, and derived from their practice of self-mutilation, which they supposed to be warranted by Scripture (Matt. xix. 12). **1887** A. F. HEARD *Russ. Ch. & Russ. Dissent* xi. 270 Notwithstanding their precautions, the Skoptsi are betrayed by their pale, sallow complexion, their scanty beard, shrill voice, effeminate, peculiar gait, and hesitating, wavering look. **1888** 'STEPNIAK' *Russ. Peasantry* II. iii. 439 The *Skopzy* or *Castrati*, founded by Selivanov at the close of the eighteenth century. **1911** *Encycl. Brit.* XXV. 194/1 Skoptsism was, however, not exterminated, and grave scandals constantly arose. **1957** *Ibid.* XXIII. 873/1 The Skoptsi.. settled in Yakut in the 1860s and introduced agriculture... The clean, well-built Skoptsi villages were a striking contrast to the dirty Yakutsh settlements. **1960** O. MANNING *Great Fortune* I. 25 A *Skopit.* One of the sights of the city. The *Skopits* belong to a Russian sect. **1970** B. WALKER *Sex & Supernatural* ix. 84 The best known of the modern castrant cults called the Skoptsi, or 'eunuchs', a mystical Russian sect which first came into prominence in the middle of the 18th century but which was said to have been in existence for at least three centuries before that.

**skoray**, var. SCAURIE.

**skord(e**, obs. pa. pple. SCORE *v.*

**skorodite**, var. SCORODITE.

**skorrie, skory**, varr. SCAURIE.

**skorza**, var. SCORZA.

**skose**, obs. f. SCORSE *v.*[1]

‖**skothending** ('skɒthɛndɪŋ). *Pros.* [ON.] Chiefly in Scaldic verse: rhyme formed with the same consonant or consonant cluster preceded by differing vowels; half-rhyme.
**1838** G. P. MARSH *Compendious Gram. Old-Northern or Icel. Lang.* IV. 144 The same consonants with different vowels (skothending, *half-rhyme*, or *assonance*). **1860**, **1873-4** [see *half-rhyme* s.v. HALF- II. n]. **1945** L. M. HOLLANDER *Skalds* 10 The *skothending* in the odd, and the *adalhending* in the even, half-line always involve the second but last syllable. **1977** J. MILROY *Lang. G. M. Hopkins* v. 144 We are not accustomed to notice *skothending* (end-consonant rhyme) when it occurs in English. Hopkins uses it very liberally.

**skotophil(e**, var. SCOTOPHIL *a.*

**skouchin**, obs. f. SCUTCHEON *sb.*[1]

**skough, skowg**, obs. ff. SCUG *sb.*[1]

**skoukinge**, obs. f. SKULKING *vbl. sb.*

**skoulk-, skoute-wacche**, obs. varr. SCOUT-WATCH.

**skourick**, Sc. var. SKERRICK.

**skoverour**, obs. f. SCOURER[1].

**skowe**, var. SCOGH, wood. *Obs.*

**skowke**, obs. form of SCULK *v.*

**skowlt**, obs. f. SCOUT *sb.*[4]

**skowre**, obs. f. SCORE *sb.*, SCOUR *v.*

**skoymus, -mys**, obs. ff. SQUEAMOUS, -MISH.

†**skoyse**, ? obs. variant of SKICE *v.*
**1616** J. LANE *Contn. Sqr.'s T.* VII. 411 Instantlie kinge Cambuscan skoysd to campe in th' aier.

**skrae-fish.** *local.* (See quots. and SCRAE *sb.*[2])
**1867** SMYTH *Sailor's Word-bk.* 630 *Skrae-fish*, fish dried in the sun without being salted. **1881** DAY *Fishes Gt. Brit.* I. 295 Coal-fish,.. also locally.. skrae-fish.

**Skraeling** ('skreɪlɪŋ). *Scandinavian Hist.* Also †**Schrelling, Skrelling, Skrælling**, etc.; **Skræling.** [ad. ON. *Skræling(j)ar* pl., the Norse name for the inhabitants of Greenland at the time of the Norse settlement.] A member of a savage people encountered by the early Norse settlers on Greenland, of uncertain origin but often considered to be of Eskimo descent. Also applied similarly to the inhabitants of Vinland (sometimes identified with the NE. coast of N. America). Usu. *pl.*
**1767** tr. *Crantz's Hist. Greenland* I. III. i. 132 The Greenlanders call themselves.. *Innuit*... The Icelanders, who many hundred years ago discovered.. this country and the neighbouring coasts of America, called them in form *Skrællings*, because they are little of stature. **1797** *Encycl. Brit.* VIII. 129/2 This nation, called *Schrellings*, at length prevailed against the Iceland settlers who inhabited the western district [of Greenland]. **1875** *Ibid.* I. 706/2 They had some intercourse.. with a people who came in leathern boats, and were called *Skrælings*, from their dwarfish size... The Skrælings were of course Esquimaux... The hostilities of the Skrælings was no doubt the principal cause of the abandonment of the colony [of Vinland]. **1891** KIPLING in *Contemp. Rev.* July 21 He.. said:—'When they heard *our* bulls bellow the Skrælings ran away!' **1921** G. M. GATHORNE-HARDY *Norse Discoverers of Amer.* II. iv. 172 In so far.. as the descriptions of the Skrælings of Wineland are realistic, and differ materially from anything which can have been derived from Eskimo sources, these descriptions form probably the most convincing proof of the historical accuracy of these stories. **1979** N. DAVIES *Voyagers to New World* 227 When spring came the skraelings once more appeared.

†**skrange**, ? misprint for *skragge* SCRAG *sb.*[2]
**1607** *Barley-Breake* D iv b, Amongst the rest, a blacke and filthie bird Sate on a skrange, and cries, A rope, a rope.

**skrap(p)le**, obs. forms of SCRAPPLE *sb.*[1] and *v.*

**skraule**, obs. form of SCRAWL *v.*

**Skraup** (skraʊp). *Chem.* The name of Zdenko Hans *Skraup* (1850–1910), Czech chemist, used *attrib.* and in the possessive to denote a reaction which he discovered (*Sitzungsber. der K. Akad. der Wissensch.* (*Math.-Nat. Classe*) (1880) LXXXI. II. 593), in which a quinoline is synthesized by heating a primary aromatic amine with glycerol, sulphuric acid, and an oxidizing agent.
**1886** *Jrnl. Chem. Soc.* L. 79 Chloromethylquinoline.. is prepared by Skraup's method from parachlorometa-toluidine. **1935** L. F. MAREK in P. H. Groggins *Unit Processes in Org. Synthesis* vii. 350 Quinoline is prepared from aniline and glycerol by the Skraup reaction. **1954** I. L. FINAR *Org. Chem.* (ed. 2) I. xxxi. 691 Alizarin Blue.. may be prepared by first reducing Alizarin Orange to the corresponding amino-compound and then heating this with glycerol, sulphuric acid and nitrobenzene (Skraup's synthesis). **1975** R. F. BROWN *Org. Chem.* xxviii. 908 The Skraup synthesis involves a dehydration, a Michael addition, an electrophilic substitution (the ring-closing reaction), and an oxidation, all occurring in one flask during a relatively short period of refluxing.

**skreef**, obs. var. SCREEF *sb.*

**skreigh** (skrix), *sb.*[1] *Sc.* Forms: 6 **skrech**, 8 **skriech**, 9 **skreich**; 7- **skreigh**, 9 **skriegh, skreegh, screigh**, etc. [Alteration of *screik* SCREAK *sb.*, in order to imitate a more prolonged or harsher sound.] A shriek or screech; a loud shrill cry or scream. Also *fig.*
**1549** *Compl. Scot.* vi. 39 The herrons gaif ane vyild skrech as the kyl hed bene in fyir. *c* **1614** SIR W. MURE *Dido & Æneas* III. 395 The skreigh is rais'd, with many rewfull cries. **1715** RAMSAY *Christ's Kirk Gr.* II. vi, He gripped Kate, And gar'd her gi'e a skreigh. **1790** BURNS *Tam o' Shanter* 200 The witches follow Wi' mony an eldritch skriech and hollo. **1816** SCOTT *Antiq.* vii, 'The skriegh of a Tammie Norie,' answered Ochiltree, 'I ken the skirl weel'. **1818** —— *Rob Roy* xxiii, The skreigh of duty, which no man should hear and be inobedient.

**skreigh** (skrix), *sb.*[2] *Sc.* Also **skrieh, skregh, screigh**, etc. [Alteration (after prec.) of *skreek*, *skriek*, etc. (see SCREAK *sb.* 3), for earlier CREEK *sb.*[2]] The break *of* day.
**1802** LEYDEN *Lord Soulis* viii, The page he look'd at the skrieh of day. **1816** SCOTT *Bl. Dwarf* x, I wad.. be on and awa' to Mucklestane wi' the first skreigh o' morning. **1879** *Yachtsman's Holidays* 53 The watchful Lachlan called all hands by 'skreigh o' day'.

**skreigh** (skrix), *v. Sc.* Also 8 **skriegh**, 9 **skreegh, skriech, skreich**; 8 **scriegh**, 8–9 **screigh**, 9 **scriech**, etc. [Alteration of *screik* SCREAK *v.*: cf. SKREIGH *sb.*[1]]
**1.** *intr.* To screech or shriek; to utter a loud shrill cry; to make a screeching noise.
**1715** RAMSAY *Christ's Kirk Gr.* II. vii, And fouk wad threep, that she did green For what wad gar her skirle And skreigh some day. **1786** BURNS *To Auld Mare* viii, How thou wad prance, an' snore, an' scriegh. **1816** SCOTT *Antiq.* xi, I would hae skreigh'd out at once, and raised the house. **1894** LATTO *Tam. Bodkin* ii, The tempest.. whistlin' and skreeghin' amang the.. trees.
**2.** *trans.* To utter in a screeching tone.
**1786** BURNS *Earnest Cry* ii, Scriechan out prosaic verse, An' like to brust! *c* **1800** MACNEILL *Poems* (1844) 60 Rebellion loud.. Skreighed wild her cry.
Hence '**skreighing** *vbl. sb.*
**1816** SCOTT *Antiq.* xi, I doubted Mary wad waken you wi' her skreighing.

**skrene**, obs. form of SCREEN *sb.*[1]

**skreyme**, obs. f. SCREAM *sb.*

**skrich(e**, obs. ff. SCRITCH.

‖**skrik** (skrɪk). *S. Afr. colloq.* Also **schreik, schrick, schrijk, schrik, scrick.** [Afrikaans, f. Du. *schrik* fright.] A sudden fright, start; a shock or *frisson.* Freq. in phr. ***to get, have*** or ***give*** (someone) ***a skrik.***
**1887** A. A. ANDERSON *Twenty-Five Years in Waggon* i. 21 They heard the rattling of wheels in a manner which made them think that the oxen must have had a 'scrick' (scare) from a lion. **1896** H. A. BRYDEN *Tales of S. Afr.* 68 It gave me a very nasty *schrijk* at the time. **1897** E. GLANVILLE *Tales from Veld* xxiii. 173 Lor' bless yer, the *schreik* he gave me. **1899** D. BLACKBURN *Prinsloo of Prinsloosdorp* 30 Piet had a bad schrick, but he thought out a plan. **1913** J. J. DOKE *Secret City* xxx. 255 How you do frighten me. You gave me quite a schrik. **1942** S. CLOETE *Hill of Doves* xxxi. 440 'It's Reuter,' someone said. 'What are you doing to give us a skrik like this? It is a joke. It is Reuter.' **1969** A. FUGARD *Boesman & Lena* I. 7 Remember that night the water came up so high?.. You got such a skrik you ran the wrong way. **1975** *Darling* 12 Feb. 119 'Who, me?' I tune him, meantime, feeling the skriks running up and down my spine.

**skrike** (skraɪk), *sb.* Now only *dial.*: see *Eng. Dial. Dict.* s.v. *scrike.* For forms see the vb. [f. SKRIKE *v.* Cf. SCREAK *sb.*]
**1.** A shrill cry, a screech; = SCREAK *sb.*
**13..** *Coer de L.* 4709 The Crystene men gunne make a scryke: Anon they wunnen ovyr the dyke. *c* **1400** *Destr. Troy* 910 A wonderfull noyse Skremyt vp to the skrow with a skryke ffelle. *c* **1425** *Seven Sag.* (P.) 491 A grete scryke up he nam. **1500–20** DUNBAR *Poems, Fenȝeit Freir* 97 The ja him skrippit with a skryke. **1548** UDALL *Erasm. Par., Mark* xv. 37 Jesus.. gaue a great skryke, and therwith yelded vp the ghost. **1631** *Celestina* xix. 190 You will haue mee fill my Fathers house with cryes and skrikes. **1891** ATKINSON *Last of Giant-Killers* 107 The savagest scrike ever uttered by a raving giant.
**2.** ***skrike of day***, the dawn. Cf. SCREAK *sb.* 3.
**1746** COLLIER (Tim Bobbin) *View Lanc. Dial.* Wks. (1862) 41, I geet up be skrike o Dey. **1866** BROGDEN *Prov. Lincs.*

**skrike** (skraɪk), *v.* Now only *dial.*: see *Eng. Dial. Dict.* s.v. *scrike.* Forms: 4–6 **scryke, skryke**, 4–7, 8–9 *dial.* **scrike, skrike**; *pa. t.* 4 **skryȝte.** [Prob. of Scandinavian origin: cf. Norw. *skrika* (str. vb.), Da. *skrige.* See also SHRIEK.]
**1.** *intr.* To utter a shrill harsh cry; = SCREAK *v.* I.
**1340** HAMPOLE *Pr. Consc.* 7347 Þe devils ay omang on þam salle stryke, And þe synfulle þare-with ay cry and skryke. *c* **1340** *Nominale* (Skeat) 744 *Senge braie*, Ape scrikith. *c* **1380** *Sir Ferumbr.* 1609 Loude þay cryede & skryȝte an hye: 'Mahoun wat is þy red?' *c* **1420** *Chron. Vilod.* 1671 He woke w[t] pat & scrykede for fere. *c* **1420** *Anturs of Arth.* 129 (Douce MS.) Þe birdes in þe bowes, þat one þe goost glowes, þei skryke [*Ireland* scryken] in þe skowes. *c* **1460** *Towneley Myst.* iii. 232 For all if she stryke, yit fast will she skryke. **1590** GREENE *Never too late* (1600) 98 Hee is such a sneaking fellowe, that.. touch him and he will scrike. **1596** SPENSER *F.Q.* VI. iv. 18 The litle babe did loudly scrike and squall. *a* **1600** *Flodden Field* i. (1664) 8 Their names make.. children skrike.
**2.** To weep, cry.
**1905** *Eng. Dial. Dict.* V. s.v., Hoo skrite't so when hur mother deed I thow't hoo'd ne'er ha done. *Ibid.*, I can tell by yur een as yo'n bin skrikin'. **1977** P. CARTER *Under Goliath* xxvi. 142, I stood there.. skriking my eyes out like a mammy's boy... I really cried my eyes out in the loft. **1978** *Lancashire Life* Apr. 42/3 Second un poor little soul Did nuthin' else but skrike.
Hence **skriking** *vbl. sb.* and *ppl. a.*; **skriker**, one who skrikes.
**1340** HAMPOLE *Pr. Consc.* 7352 Þare salle be swilk rareyng and ruschyng.. And skrykyng of synfulle. *c* **1400** *Destr. Troy* 10182 The skrew for þe skrykyng & skremyng of folke, Redoundet with dyn drede for to here. *c* **1440** *Promp. Parv.* 450/2 Scrykynge, of chyldyr, *vagitus.* **1599** HAKLUYT *Voy.* II. II. 112 Notwithstanding his pitifull lamentation and skrikings. **1631** R. BOLTON *Comf. Affl. Consc.* (1640) 241 They shall never more be heard, though with much violence they throw their scrikings into the Aire. **1632** LITHGOW *Trav.* IX. 401 A scriking noyse, as if it had beene the chirking of Frogs. **1891** ATKINSON *Last of Giant-Killers* 149 Others used to call it the 'Scriker' because of the awful scrikes (shrieks) it uttered. **1937** J. R. R. TOLKIEN *Hobbit* iv. 76 The yells and yammering, croaking, jibbering and jabbering; howls, growls and curses; shrieking and skriking, that followed were beyond description. **1959** I. & P. OPIE *Lore & Lang. Schoolch.* x. 186 In the area of Blackburn, Bolton, Manchester, Stockport, and Halifax the term 'skriking' [*sc.* for 'crying'] is common, the noun being 'skriker'.

**skrim**, *v. Sc.* In 5–6 **scrym, skrym.** [ad. OF. *scrimir*, var. of *escremir, eskermir*, etc.: see SKIRMISH *v.*] *intr.* To skirmish; to dart. Hence '**skrimming** *vbl. sb.*
For possible traces of the vb. in modern Sc. see Jamieson's Dict., s.v. *Scrim* and *Skrim.*

**1375** BARBOUR *Bruce* XIX. 521 Thar wes ilk day Iustyng of wer, And scrymmyng maid full apertly. *c* **1450** HOLLAND *Howlat* 67 Sum skripe me with scorne, sum skrym at myn E. **1513** DOUGLAS *Æneid* XII. v. 68 Ane gret flycht or ost Of fowlis..Quhilk on thar wyngis..Skrymmys heir and thar. **1535** STEWART *Cron. Scot.* II. 610 Ane lang quhile thair he la, With greit scrymmyng and carmusche euerie da.

**skrine**, obs. form of SCREEN *sb.*[1]

**skua** ('skjuːə). *Ornith.* [Adopted by Hoier (*c* 1604) from the Færoese *skúgvur* (earlier **skúvur*), = ON. *skúfr* (in mod.Icel. *skúmur*), of uncertain origin.] A predatory gull belonging to the genus *Stercorarius*, esp. the largest European species, *S. catarrhactes*, which breeds in Shetland, the Færöes, and Iceland.

**1678** RAY *Willughby's Ornith.* 349 Hapning to read over the description of Hoier's Skua..I find it exactly agrees with ours, so that I do not at all doubt but this Bird is the Skua of Hoier. **1768** PENNANT *Brit. Zool.* II. 417 They hold a knife erect over their heads, on which the Skua will transfix itself. **1777** FORSTER *Voy. round World* I. 109 We saw a bird ..which proved to be the skua or great northern gull. **1826** STEPHENS in Shaw *Gen. Zool.* XIII. I. 214 The Skuas are more partial to fish..than the Jagers. *Ibid.* 216 Pomarine Skua. **1896** J. SKELTON *Summers & W. Balmawhapple* I. 216 The tarrock skims lightly along, and screams as the skua comes prowling round the cape.

**b.** *attrib.* in *skua-gull.*

**1768** PENNANT *Brit. Zool.* (1776) II. 447 *headline*, Skua Gull. **1820** SCORESBY *Acc. Arctic Reg.* II. 370 Solan geese, skua-gulls and land birds on the wing. **1872** COUES *N. Amer. Birds* 26 A sort of false cere occurs in some water birds, as the jaegers, or skua-gulls.

**skuddiller**, variant of SCUDLER, scullion.

**skue**, obs. form of SKEW *a.*

†**skue**, *v. Obs.*[−0] (See quot.)

**1611** COTGR., *Raser les eaux*, to skimme ouer, to skue [? *read* skud] or sayle vpon, the water.

†**skuett.** *Obs.*[−1] [app. related to SKEWER *sb.* Cf. SCUET.] (See quot.)

**1728** E. SMITH *Compleat Housewife* (ed. 2) 35 To make Skuetts. Take fine, long, and slender Skewers; then cut Veal Sweet-breads into pieces, like Dice, and some fine Bacon into thin square bits;..and then spit them on the Skewers [etc.].

**skugry**, obs. Sc. form of SCUGGERY.

**skul**, obs. form of SCULL, SKULL *sb.*[1]

**skulduggery.** orig. *U.S.* Also 9 scullduggery; skullduggery. [altered f. SCULDUDDERY.] Underhand dealing, roguish intrigue or machination, trickery.

**1867** A. D. RICHARDSON *Beyond Mississippi* xi. 134 From Minnesota had been imported the mysterious term 'scull-duggery', used to signify political or other trickery. **1890** *N. & Q.* Ser. VII. X. 224/1 Some two or three years ago one of the New York papers..announced that a missionary on the Congo intended to return to America and blow up the whole sculduggery; meaning, apparently, to expose the false pretences on which money had been collected for the mission. **1892** *Boston* (Mass.) *Jrnl.* 7 Nov. 7/4 Unfounded Charges of Skulduggery. **1893** *Columbus* (Ohio) *Dispatch* 22 Dec., The United States Courts..are now very busy affixing the penalties for violations of the national banking laws and for general skulduggery in the management of the institutions. **1911** H. QUICK *Yellowstone Nights* ix. 239 It began to look to me like Hen was up to some skulduggery. **1929** M. A. GILL *Underworld Slang* 11/1 *Skull duggery*, dirty work. **1936** H. HAGEDORN *Brookings* iii. 49 America at..its worst in financiering, political machination and the skullduggery of the stock market. **1949** J. STEINBECK *Russian Jrnl.* ix. 215 The political skulduggery of the Kremlin. **1957** A. GRIMBLE *Return to Islands* vii. 130 Disgraceful stories of all the skulduggeries he had got away with by suborning government officials. **1962** D. FRANCIS *Dead Cert* ix. 108 The skulduggery that goes on in respectable little old Brighton. **1980** *Times* 3 Jan. 10/2 Watergate was such a sensational piece of skulduggery.

Hence [as back-formation] '**skuldug** *v. trans.*, to extract by trickery. *nonce-wd.*

**1936** W. FAULKNER *Absalom, Absalom!* vi. 178 This Faustus who..skuldugged a hundred miles of land out of a poor ignorant Indian.

**skulk** (skʌlk), *sb.* Also 4–5 sculke, 6 scoulke, sculck; 5 skulke. [f. the vb.]

**1.** One who skulks or hides himself; a shirker.

*c* **1320** LANGTOFT *Chron.* (Rolls) II. 248 The roghe raggy sculke Rug ham in helle! **1838** *Knickerbocker* XI. 448 Spotswood had told the middie that Tudor was a great 'skulk', and would probably be reluctant to turn out. **1847** H. MELVILLE *Omoo* iv, 'Where's that skulk, Chips?' shouted Jermin down the forecastle scuttle. **1894** BLACKMORE *Perlycross* 107 You are an honest fellow, Jemmy, whatever skulks and sneaks may say.

†**2.** A number, company, or gathering (of persons or animals given to skulking). *Obs.*

Chiefly in echoes of a list of 'proper terms', and having at no time much real currency.

*c* **1450** in *Trans. Philol. Soc.* (1909) 25 A Skolke of freris. A Skolke of thewys. A Skolke of foxys. **1486** *Bk. St. Albans* f vj b, A Skulke of Theuys [etc.]. **1502** ARNOLDE *Chron.* (1811) 90 Ony persone or persones..that make ony sculke or be a receyuer or a gederar of euyl company. **1532** MORE *Confut. Tindale* Wks. 502/1 He shall doe [miracles] in hys catholike church, and suffereth none to be done among all the scoulkes of heretykes. **1582** STANYHURST *Æneis*, etc. (Arb.) 138 An armoure..wheare scaals be ful horriblye clincked Of scrawling serpents, with sculcks of poysoned adders. **1594** O. B. *Quest. Profit. Concern.* 10 Notwithstanding all this, there remained a sculke of such, as neither care nor castigation could amend. [**1706** PHILLIPS (ed. Kersey), *Sculk*, (among Hunters) a Company, as A Skulk of Foxes. **1801** STRUTT *Sports & P.* I. i. 17. **1820** W. IRVING *Sketch Bk.* (1821) II. 50 We say a flight of doves.., a skulk of foxes. **1883** E. PENNELL-ELMHIRST *Cream Leicestersh.* 380 A cloud of foxes..(the term, an old book told me years ago, should be a sculk of foxes).]

**3.** An act of skulking.

**1858** WRAXALL *Wild Oats* xxv, [He] preferred being locked in till twelve, 'doing a skulk', as he elegantly termed it.

**skulk** (skʌlk), *v.* Forms: *α.* 3 sculkin, 4 sculke, 4– sculk, 7 sculck. *β.* 4 skulc, 4– skulk, 4, 7 skulke. *γ.* 3 scolk-, 5 *Sc.* scowk-, 6 scowlke, scoulk, 7 scouke, skowke. [app. of Scand. origin: cf. Norw. *skulka* to lurk, lie watching, Da. *skulke*, Sw. *skolka* to shirk, play truant.]

There is app. a remarkable lack of evidence for the currency of the word in the 15th and 16th centuries, compared with its frequency in earlier and later use.

**1.** *intr.* To move in a stealthy or sneaking fashion, so as to escape notice. Usually with advs. and preps., as *about*, *away*, *into*, etc. †Also *refl.*

*α.* *a* **1225** *Ancr. R.* 400 Nis non þet muwe etlutien [*v.r.* auuey sculkin] þet heo ne mot him luuien. *a* **1300** *Cursor M.* 13741 Ne wist þai neuer quat to sai; Bot ilkan sculked þaim awai. *c* **1340** HAMPOLE *Pr. Consc.* 1788 Alle thyng it brestes in sonder, Als it sculkes by diverse ways. **1642–4** J. VICARS *God in Mount* (1844) 149 Lord Paulet..took his way toward Myneard, and so to sculk over into Wales. **1691** WOOD *Ath. Oxon.* II. 24 He was..forced to..creep and sculk into every place for fear of being taken and hanged. **1773** JOHNSON in *Boswell* (1831) II. 484 It is a poor thing for a fellow to get drunk at night, and sculk to bed. *c* **1825** MRS. SHERWOOD *Houlston Tracts* II. No. 32. 6 The three servants sculked by her to get out of the room. **1849** MACAULAY *Hist. Eng.* v. I. 525 Plotters and libellers by profession,..who were forced to sculk in disguise through back streets.

*β.* *a* **1300** *E.E Psalter* cxviii. 158, I sagh wemmand and skulked awai. **1390** GOWER *Conf.* II. 93 Awey he skulketh as an hare. *c* **1400** *Sowdone Bab.* 2651 Take withe the .iij. hundred knightes..Leste þat lurdeynes come skulkynge oute. **1419** *26 Pol. Poems* 69 þe glosers skulked away, for shame of here sooles. **1677** W. HUBBARD *Narrative* (1865) I. 209 The Enemy..killing a Man at Weymouth, another at Hingham, as they lay skulking up and down in Swamps and Holes. *c* **1720** PRIOR *True's Epitaph* 19 He..Ne'er skulk'd from whence his sovereign led him. **1804** *Naval Chron.* XII. 338 The enemy..skulking out of Toulon for a mile or two, and then..skulking into port again. **1850** D. G. MITCHELL *Reveries Bachelor* 245, I went up at night, and skulked around the buildings. **1883** S. C. HALL *Retrospect* II. 382 The peasant, when drunk, skulks to his home from the public-house through by-ways.

**b.** *transf.* and *fig.*

**1665** HOOKE *Microgr.* liv. 211 Some mischief that makes it [a louse] oftentime sculk into some meaner and lower place, and run behind a mans back. *a* **1694** TILLOTSON *Serm.* clii. (1748) VIII. 369 As if things..did break forth into being and sculk again into nothing..'at the beck of his will'. **1800** COLERIDGE *Piccolom.* I. iii, Beware you do not think That I by lying arts..have skulk'd into his graces. **1865** RUSKIN *Sesame* i. §16 There are masked words droning and skulking about us in Europe just now.

**2.** To hide or conceal oneself, to keep out of sight, to avoid observation, esp. with some sinister motive or in fear of being discovered; to lurk.

*α.* *a* **1300** *E.E. Psalter* cxi. 9 Sinful sal se,..And sal sculke to be awai. *c* **1330** R. BRUNNE *Chron. Wace* (Rolls) 15887 Al þat ilke day he sculked; Among þe pouere men he hulked. **1484** in *Litt. Cantuar.* (Rolls) III. 311 Sculkynge in wodys be day and lyinge a wayte to robbe the Kynges lyege people. **1615** G. SANDYS *Trav.* 217 A Leopard that sculkt in the aforesaid thicket. **1641** J. JACKSON *True Evang. T.* I. 15 Man is a yong Lyon,..lurking and sculking to doe mischiefe. **1736** FIELDING *Pasquin* v, The fox, Wise beast, who knows the treachery of men, Flies their society, and sculks in woods. **1806** H. SIDDONS *Maid, Wife, & W.* I. 108, I..must sculk, a dishonourable, an abandoned fugitive. **1894** GLADSTONE *Horace* III. xii. 22 Sculking where the woods are thick.

*β.* *a* **1300** *E.E. Psalter* xxxviii. 15 To skulke als irain þou made saule his. *c* **1330** R. BRUNNE *Chron. Wace* (Rolls) 8287 Hengist byforn had don hem skulke In wodes, in hilles, to crepe in hulke. **1615** G. SANDYS *Trav.* 129 Our Ianizaries discharged their harquebuses, lest some should haue skulkt within. **1709** DAMPIER *Voy.* III. II. 165 She [a boat] seeing us coming that way,..skulked behind a point a while. **1834** MARRYAT *P. Simple* (1863) 42 They told me that they had seen two sailors skulking behind the piles of timber. **1884** GILMOUR *Mongols* 265 Most Mongols would prefer to endure two or three years' imprisonment, to being compelled to skulk for life.

*transf.* **1664** H. POWER *Exp. Philos.* II. 117 The spontaneous Dilatation..of that little remnant of Ayr skulking in the rugosities thereof. *c* **1750** SHENSTONE *Ruin'd Abbey* 293 The bigot pow'r Amidst her native darkness skulk'd secure. **1838** DICKENS *Nickleby* XIX, A smile, which seemed to skulk under his face.

*γ.* **1530** PALSGR. 699/2 A daye tale he scoulketh in corners and a nyghtes he gothe a thevyng. **1533** MORE *Debell. Salem* Wks. 994/2 Heretikes..wont but to crepe together in corners, and secretly scoulk together in lurkes lanes. **1611** COTGR., *Blotir*, to squat, skowke, or ly closе to the ground. **1659** TORRIANO *Eng.-Ital. Dict.*, To scouke, *nascondersi.*

**b.** To hide, to withdraw or shelter oneself, in a cowardly manner. Freq. with *behind.*

**1621** G. SANDYS *Ovid's Met.* XIII. 256 Reuoke the foe, thy wounds, and vsuall feare; Behind my target sculk. **1681** DRYDEN *Span. Friar* IV. ii, Should a common Soldier sculk behind, And thrust his General in the Front of War. **1781** COWPER *Conversation* 375 But counterfeit is blind, and skulks through fear, Where 'tis a shame to be asham'd t'appear. **1840** DICKENS *Barn. Rudge* li, They shall not find us skulking and hiding, as if we feared to take our portion of the light of day. **1877** W. BLACK *Green Past.* xi, I'll fight any one of you—ah! skulk behind the women, do!

*transf.* **1681** DRYDEN *Abs. & Achit.* 207 He stood at bold Defiance with his Prince;..and sculk'd behind the Laws. **1771** SMOLLETT *Humph. Cl.* (1815) 122 Every rancorous knave..may skulk behind the press of a newsmonger.. without running the least hazard of detection or punishment. **1866** G. MACDONALD *Ann. Q. Neighb.* xxvii, But my love did not long remain skulking thus behind the hedge of honour.

**c.** To shirk duty; *spec.* to malinger.

**1781** COWPER *Table-T.* 312 Let magistrates alert perform their parts, Not skulk or put on a prudential mask. **1826** HUTCHISON *Pract. Obs. Surg.* 191 The sick list having been ..delivered in to the captain, with a particular mark against the name of every man either sculking or suspected of sculking. **1843** H. GAVIN *Feigned Diseases* 23 Marines.., much more than sailors, are found frequently skulking, owing to the severity of their exercise. **1887** BESANT *The World Went* iv, [He] is not one who will skulk, or suffer his crew to skulk.

**3.** *trans.* **a.** To shun, keep away from, avoid, in a skulking manner.

*c* **1620** Z. BOYD *Zion's Flowers* (1855) 8 I'le skulk the place where God hath sent me to. **1835** *Tait's Mag.* II. 377 What school-boy would dare to skulk a fight? **1847** *Fraser's Mag.* XXXVI. 561 Southey, in his wonted mode, skulks the affair of the Bay of Naples.

**b.** 'To produce or bring forward clandestinely or improperly.'

**1846** WORCESTER, citing *Eclectic Rev.*

**skulker** ('skʌlkə(r)). Also 4, 6 sculker(e, 4 scolker, 5 sculcare, *Sc.* scoukar. [f. prec. + -ER[1]. Cf. MSw. *skulkare*, Norw. *skulkar.*]

**1.** One who skulks, in various senses. †Also as a name for the hare.

**13..** *Names of Hare* in *MS. Digby* 168 b, þe wint-swifft, þe sculkere, þe hare-serd, þe heg roukere. **1387** TREVISA *Higden* (Rolls) VII. 491 He haþ wiþ hym flemed men and scolkers aboute. ? *a* **1400** *Morte Arth.* 3119 Than skyftes þes skouerours,..Diskoueres for skulkers that they no skathe lymppene. *c* **1470** HENRY *Wallace* IX. 180 Skour weyll about for scoukaris in the se. *c* **1530** *Pore Helpe* 384 in Hazl. *E.P.P.* III. 266 A man that wyl not vary, And one that is no sculker. **1728** *Wodrow Corr.* (1843) III. 401 The numbers that are for laying him aside.., too often hedgers and skulkers. **1800** COLERIDGE *Wallenstein* I. vii, Did we confine thee not to let that skulker..pass the gates of Pilsen! **1841** C. MACKAY *Pop. Delusions* II. 30 He..was now a solitary skulker in the forests. **1870** DICKENS *E. Drood* xv, It's good advice, whichever of you skulkers gave it.

**b.** *spec.* (See quot. 1785.)

**1785** GROSE *Dict. Vulgar T.*, *Skulker*, a soldier who by feigned sickness or other pretences evades his duty, a sailor who keeps below in time of danger [etc.]. **1826** HUTCHISON *Pract. Obs. Surg.* 191 The plan I adopted, when serving afloat, to lessen the sick list of sculkers, as they are technically termed in the navy. **1887** *Spectator* 9 July 932/1 Serjeant Lawrence..was particularly hard on skulkers.

**2.** A moth, *Graphiphora latens.*

**1832** RENNIE *Butterfl. & Moths* 54 The Sculker..appears in summer. Rare. South of Scotland.

**3.** *Ornith.* (See quots.)

**1867** H. SPENCER *Princ. Biol.* VI. viii. §349 'Skulkers' is the descriptive title applied to the Water-Rail, the Corn-Crake, and their allies, which evade enemies by concealment. **1872** COUES *N. Amer. Birds* 241 Their shy retiring habit of skulking among the rushes has caused them to be sometimes called *Latitores* (skulkers).

†'**skulkery.** *Obs.* Also 5 sculkery, scolcurye, skolkerye, skoulkery. [f. SKULK *v.* + -ERY.] The practice of skulking.

*c* **1400** *Laud Troy Bk.* 7602, I may not longe it suffry Off that Achilles with his sculkery. *Ibid.* 8360. ? *a* **1400** *Morte Arth.* 1644 For na skomfitoure in skoulkery is skomfite euer.

**skulking** ('skʌlkɪŋ), *vbl. sb.* [f. SKULK *v.* + -ING[1].] The action of the verb, in various senses.

**1297** R. GLOUC. (Rolls) 5130 Bote hii þus mid scolkinge vpe þe englisse wende. **1338** R. BRUNNE *Chron.* (1810) 3 þei went tille Snawdone..To purueie þam a skulkyng, on þe Englis eft to ride. **1375** BARBOUR *Bruce* VII. 130 Thai var fayis to the kyng, And thoucht to cum in-to scowkyng [*v.r.* sculking], And duell with hym. *c* **1440** *Promp. Parv.* 451/1 Sculkynge, *cleptura.* **1611** COTGR., *Tapissement*,..a crooching, skowking, or ducking downe. **1659** HAMMOND *On Ps.* lxxxviii. 18 The lying hid, and sculking of friends. **1751** J. BROWN *Shaftesb. Charac.* 9 These hussars..by sudden evolutions and timely skulking, can do great mischiefs. **1805** *Med. Jrnl.* XIV. 415 Intemperance and skulking were never so little practised in any fleet as in this. **1867** F. FRANCIS *Angling* ix. (1880) 333 The artifices of salmon are multifarious... 'Skulking' is a common one.

**b.** *attrib.*, as *skulking hole*, *place.*

**1535** COVERDALE *1 Macc.* ix. 40 Then Ionathas and they that were with him, rose out of their skoukinge places agaynst them. **1655** GURNALL *Chr. in Arm.* xiv. (1669) 301/1 The Quakers..have their skulking hole to which they run from the Scripture. **1831** SCOTT *Ct. Robt.* ii, The light-footed Grecian..dodged his pursuer from one skulking place to another.

'**skulking**, *ppl. a.* [f. as prec. + -ING[2].]

**1.** That skulks or hides; sneaking, lurking.

**1619** FLETCHER *False One* I. i, I bought it Of a skulking Scribler for two Ptolomies. **1639** *Lismore Papers* Ser. II. (1888) IV. 37 The malignitie of some Skulkinge enviers of my preferment. **1728** MORGAN *Hist. Algiers* II. v. 320 What have we to do with the History of a Crew of starving, beggarly, skulking Pyrates? **1755** *Gentl. Mag.* XXV. 571 The Moravians..are apprehensive of a visit from some of their skulking parties. **1803** *Naval Chron.* X. 82 The skulking French row-boats..make sure work of taking prizes. **1828** L. M. HAWKINS *Annaline* I. 171 You gave that skulking rascal..money when you spoke to him. **1878** Bosw. Smith *Carthage* 208 A few skulking marauders.

*fig.* **1654** H. L'Estrange *Chas. I* (1655) 110 An old skulking statute long since out of use.

**2.** Characterized by skulking.

**1658** W. Burton *Itin. Antoninus* 39 Such as by stealth, and in a skulking way, did what they did. **1674** Marvell *Reh. Transp.* II. 38 That anonymous and sculking method both of Writing and Licensing. **1742** Young *Nt. Th.* VIII. 487 But thy Great Soul this skulking glory scorns. **1826** Scott *Woodst.* xx, That skulking and rambling mode of life.

Hence **'skulkingly** *adv.*

**1847** in Webster. **1878** C. J. Vaughan *Earnest Words for E. Men* 118 The good thing [presented itself] timidly, skulkingly.

**skull** (skʌl), *sb.*[1] Forms: α. 3–5 **scolle**, 4–5 **scol, scoll**, 5 **scole**; 5 **skolle**, 5–6 **skoll**, 6 **skol**. β. 3, 5 **schulle**, 4–7 **sculle** (6 **scoulle**, 7 **scoule**), 6–7 **scul**, 6–9 **scull**. γ. 4–6 **skulle**, 6–7 **skul**, 5– **skull**. [Of obscure origin: first prominent in south-western texts of the 13–14th centuries, usually in the form *scolle*.

A foreign origin is indicated by the initial *sc-*, *sk-*, but the locality of the early examples is against connexion with ON. *skoltr* (Norw. *skolt*, *skult*, Sw. *skult*, dial. *skulle*) skull, poll, or with Norw. dial. *skul*, *skol* shell (of nuts or eggs). There is correspondence of form with Du. *schol*, MLG. *schulle*, MHG. (and G.) *scholle* (OHG. *scolla*, *scollo*) earthy crust, turf, piece of ice (cf. also Sw. *skolla* metal plate), but there is no evidence that these were ever used in the sense of 'skull'. The same difficulty applies to OF. *escuelle*, *escule* dish, nor would this readily have assumed the early form *scolle*.]

**1. a.** The bony case or frame containing or enclosing the brain of man or other vertebrate animals; the cranium; also, the whole bony framework or skeleton of the head.

α. *c* **1290** *S. Eng. Leg.* I. 168 Robert de brok..þoruȝ þe scolle smot is swerd. *c* **1330** *King of Tars* 521 Summe pleyed of the heved, And summe heore scolles icleved. **1387** Trevisa *Higden* (Rolls) I. 115 Golgotha is to menynge a baar scolle. For whan..mysdoeres were þere byheded, þe hedes were i-left þere. *c* **1400** *Lanfranc's Cirurg.* 216 Watir þat is gaderid in children hedis, ouþer it is wiþinne þe scolle or wiþoute þe scolle. *c* **1450** *Two Cookery-bks.* 79 Take a plouer, and breke his skoll, and pull him dry. **1506** *Kal. Sheph.* (Sommer) 102 In the skol ben two bones which ben called parietalles that holdeth the brayne close and stedfast.

β. *a* **1225** *Ancr. R.* 296 Ne ȝif him neuer inȝong auh tep him oðe schulle, uor he is eruh ase beore þeron. *c* **1340** *Nominale* (Skeat) 8 *Greue, fountayne, et haterel*, Sched, molde, and sculle. **1382** Wyclif *2 Kings* ix. 35 Thei founden not, no bot the scul, and the feet, and gobitis of the hond. *c* **1440** *Promp. Parv.* 450/2 Sculle, of the heede, *craneum*. *c* **1450** *Two Cookery-bks.* 80 Lete the sculle be hole. **1555** Eden *Decades* (Arb.) 238 They haue the bones of the sculles of theyr heades foure tymes thycker..then owres. **1578** Lyte *Dodoens* II. xxvii. 180 Small rounde heades..with little hooles in them, like to a dead scull. **1615** Crooke *Body of Man* 548 All these muscles are seated on the backe-side of the Eye within the cauity of the Scull. **1725** N. Robinson *Th. Physick* 34 The Carotid Arteries..after they have enter'd the Scull. **1781** Cowper *Convers.* 780 That truth itself is in her head as dull, And useless, as a candle in a scull. **1824** W. Irving *T. Trav.* II. 236 Ghosts being seen about.. at night, with bare sculls and blue lights in their sockets.

γ. **1387** Trevisa *Higden* (Rolls) V. 371 Þis Albuinus had.. overcome þe kyng of Gispides, and i-made hym a cuppe of his skulle forto drinke of. **1390** Gower *Conf.* I. 128 The kyng in audience aboute Hath told it was hire fader Skulle. **1579** G. Baker *Guydo's Quest.* 11 b, Other [bones] be..saw-wise, as y[e] skul of the head. **1615** Crooke *Body of Man* 440 The skull or cranium is all that bone which compasseth the braine and after-brain like a helmet. **1653** H. Cogan tr. *Pinto's Trav.* xxxi. 124 There were also other vessels laden with dead mens skuls. **1756–7** tr. *Keysler's Trav.* (1760) IV. 428 A piece of a skull, which had belonged to..Oliver Cromwell. **1830** R. Knox *Béclard's Anat.* 209 The great veins of the skull or the sinuses. **1877** J. A. Allen *Amer. Bison* 454 Variations in the form of the skull are often strikingly apparent.

**b.** The head as the proper seat of thought or intelligence. Commonly with allusion to dullness of intellect.

**1523** Skelton *Garl. Laurel* 82 Better a dum mouthe than a brainles scull. **1601** Shaks. *Twel. N.* I. v. 121 Thou hast spoke..as if thy eldest sonne should be a foole: whose scull, Ioue cramme with braines. **1632** Lithgow *Trav.* x. 488 Your Sexe, Whose empty Sculles..your selues peruersely vexe. *a* **1795** Cowper *Pairing Time* 8 Ev'n the child who knows no better..Must have a most uncommon skull. **1823** in Cobbett *Rur. Rides* (1885) I. 338 It has at last been hammered into their skulls, that the interest cannot be paid in full, if wheat sells low. **1857** Reade *Course True Love* 99 We..have not an idea of our own in our sculls.

(*b*) In slang phr. ***out of one's skull***, out of one's mind, crazy. Also succeeding pa. pple., as ***bored out of one's skull***, beside oneself with boredom, bored stiff.

**1967** *Listener* 7 Dec. 740/2, 12 good men and true, glumly spruce, resigned to a long haul and bored, bored out of their skulls. **1968** T. Wolfe *Electric Kool-Aid Acid Test* xv. 205 They [*sc.* the Beatles] have brought this whole mass of human beings to the point where they are..out of their skulls. **1973** W. Sheed *People will always be Kind* II. v. 301 You'd have had to be out of your skull not to in those days. **1978** G. Vidal *Kalki* iii. 83, I thought that Kalki was out of his skull.

†**c.** *slang.* The head of an Oxford College or Hall. *Obs.* Cf. GOLGOTHA 2.

**1721** Amherst *Terræ Fil.* No. 11 (1726) 55 The Sculls.. clapp'd a Degree upon his back. *Ibid.* No. 30. 167 Another gentleman..who has lately given a certain learned Scull great offence. **1864** *Slang Dict.* 223 *Scull* or *Skull*, the head or Master of a College,..but nearly obsolete.

**d.** A representation of a human skull, as an emblem or reminder of death or mortality. Also ***skull and crossbones***, a representation of a bare skull with two thigh-bones crossed beneath it as an emblem of death, esp. as depicted on a pirate's flag. Cf. *the Jolly Roger* s.v. ROGER[2] 4. Also *attrib.* and *fig.* Hence ***skull-and-cross-boned*** adj.

**1826** Miss Mitford *Village* Ser. II. (1863) 898 She was a perpetual *memento mori*; a skull and cross-bones would hardly have been more efficacious. **1875** W. McIlwraith *Guide Wigtownshire* 40 Here are the typical marrow-bones, skull, and sand glass. **1911** D. H. Lawrence *Let. c* 11 May (1979) I. 268 I've got a grinning skull-and-crossbones headache. **1924** Wodehouse *Bill the Conqueror* xvii. 254 This was open rebellion. This was hoisting the skull and cross-bones. **1928** J. M. Barrie *Peter Pan* in *Plays* v. 73 We see what is happening on the deck of the *Jolly Roger*, which is flying the skull and crossbones. **1930** *Times Lit. Suppl.* 5 June 481/4 The pirates on the Spanish Main in the old skull-and-crossbones days were pleasant and picturesque fellows. **1931** A. Ransome *Swallowdale* iii. 50 A small varnished dinghy..was sailing in between the headlands. At the masthead was a black flag with the skull and crossbones on it in white. **1955** J. Kenward *Suburban Child* xxxii. 94 Further down the street where I lived there lived a pirate five years old, the very thing in appearance as in temperament, with a cutlass (silver painted) and a black triangular hat (skull-and-cross-boned) both home-made by his understanding parents. **1982** *Times* 5 July 4/3 The nuclear submarine..[was] flying the Jolly Roger to denote their success in sinking the Argentine cruiser... The Skull-and-Crossbones denotes a 'kill'.

**e.** *slang.* (So much) ***a skull***, per person. Cf. HEAD *sb.*[1] 7 b.

**1922** Joyce *Ulysses* 299 They chop up the rope after and sell the bits for a few bob a skull. **1950** *Chambers's Jrnl.* Apr. 213/2 'What difference would the five of clubs make? Sure he had a cast-iron hand.' The Sergeant drew slow caressing fingers along his jaw. 'That'll be two bob a skull, boys,' he reminded them pleasantly.

†**2. a.** The crown or top of the head; the sconce, the (bare) scalp. *Obs.*

*c* **1380** *Sir Ferumb.* 353 Loke þat þou be armed sad, & hele þy bare scolle. *c* **1386** Chaucer *Reeve's T.* 15 As piled as an Ape was his skulle. **14..** *Voc.* in Wr.-Wülcker 586 *Glabella*, the schulle. **1611** Cotgr., *Calvaire*, the (bare) skull, or skalpe of the head. **1634** Sir T. Herbert *Trav.* (1638) 16 A third..shaves here and there, the bald scull appearing in many places.

†**b.** Used to render L. *cervix*, the back of the neck. *Obs.*

**1382** Wyclif *Deut.* xxviii. 48 He shal put on an yren ȝok vpon thi scol. —— *1 Sam.* iv. 18 He felle fro the litil seet.., and the scullis brokun, he is deed.

†**3.** A skull-cap of metal or other hard material; a close-fitting head-piece. *Obs.*

α. **1522** *Galway Arch.* in *10th Rep. Hist. MSS. Comm.* App. V. 400 No kynde of armor, as shorte of maylle, ne skoll. **1536** in W. H. Turner *Select. Rec. Oxford* (1880) 136 [He] had a paire of brexen journeys on his backe,..and a skoll on his head.

β. **1530** Palsgr. 268/1 Scull harnesse for the heed, *segrette*. **1557** *Act 4 & 5 Phil. & Mary* c. 2 §2 One Murrien or Sallet, ..and one Steele Cappe or Sculle. **1611** Cotgr., *Secrete*, a thinne steele cap, or a close scull worne vnder a hat, &c. *a* **1674** Milton *Hist. Mosc.* Wks. 1851 VIII. 478 Thir Armour is a Coat of Plate, and a Scull on thir Heads.

γ. *a* **1548** Hall *Chron., Hen. VIII*, 235 Suche as should beare Morysh Pyckes..had no harnesse but skulles. **1600** Dymmok *Ireland* (1843) 7 Armed with a shert of maile, a skull, and a skeine. *a* **1674** Milton *Hist. Mosc.* Wks. 1851 VIII. 517 They saw the Emperor and his Son..each with a Skull of Pearl on thir bare Heads.

**4.** A crust of solidified steel or other metal formed on a ladle, etc., by the partial cooling of the molten material. Also without article.

**1773** *Wright's Pat.* in *6th Rep. Dep. Kpr. Rec.* App. II. 161 Making Malleable Iron..from Scull and Cinder Iron or other Cast Metal. **1880** *Encycl. Brit.* XIII. 326/2 To keep the blown metal in fusion and prevent 'skulls' forming when it is run out into a casting ladle. **1894** *Daily News* 12 Feb. 6/6 The process does not produce 'skull', and small quantities can therefore be dealt with without in any way chilling the metal.

**5.** *attrib.* In sense 'of or pertaining to, belonging to or connected with, the skull', as ***skull-bone***, ***-eye***, ***-form***, ***-neck***, ***-pan***, ***-piece***, ***-skin***, ***-wall***, etc.

**1615** Crooke *Body of Man* 575 The muscle of the eare springing from the *pericranium* or skull [s]kin. **1746** W. Thompson *R. Navy Adv.* (1757) 39 The Scull Pieces of Oxen and Hogs. **1866** *Chambers's Encycl.* VIII. 759/2 The skull-bones are freely supplied with blood. **1891** *Archaeol.* LIII. 212 A heavy stroke through the crown into the side of the skull-pan. **1899** *Allbutt's Syst. Med.* VII. 239 The pressure of the cranial contents against the skull-wall. *Ibid.* 644 A tympanitic note on skull-percussion. **1922** Joyce *Ulysses* 509 His eye agonising in his flat skullneck. **1928** Blunden *Retreat* 32 The stone skull-eyes look down most drearily.

**b.** In sense 'in which skulls are reposited', as ***skull-box***, ***-house***.

**1628–9** *Sarum Churchw. Acc.* (Swayne, 1896) 312 Henge for the skulle howse dore. **1654–5** *Ibid.* 330 Locke for y[e] skull house dore. **1859** Jephson *Brittany* vi. 67 In the apertures between the uprights which supported the roof [of the charnel-house] were heaped up skull-boxes.

**c.** In sense 'formed or made of a skull', as ***skull-cup***, ***-goblet***, ***wine-cup***.

**1825** Hogg *Q. Hynde* 280 Their skull-cups fill'd unto the brim. **1854** G. Greenwood *Haps & Mishaps* 27 The housekeeper took from a costly cabinet the famous and fearful skull wine-cup. **1856** Hawthorne *Eng. Note-bks.* (1870) II. 221 Where..the skull goblet has often gone its rounds.

**6.** *Comb.* **a.** With pa. or pres. pples., as ***skull-built***, ***-covered***, ***-crowned***, ***-dividing***, ***-hunting***; also ***skull-like*** adj.

**1594** Nashe *Unfort. Trav.* Wks. (Grosart) V. 145 A scull cround hat of the fashion of an olde deepe porringer. **1641** W. Hooke *New England's Tears* 10 Their instruments are.. skul-dividing Halberds. **1805** Southey *Madoc* II. xxii, The skull-built towers, the files of human heads. **1809–10** Shelley *Bigotry's Victim* 2 Dares the lama..The lion to rouse from his skull-covered lair? **1839–52** Bailey *Festus* 523 The charnel-house of Time—where skull-like orbs.. Defiled the purview. **1898** C. S. Horne *Story L.M.S.* 407 The teachers had themselves been skull-hunting cannibals.

**b.** With agent-nouns, as ***skull-cracker***, ***-hunter***, ***-slinger***, ***-thacker***, ***-thatcher***.

**1706** Baynard *Cold Baths* II. 394 Rats-bane [a physician] .., who was but a young Skull-slinger then. **1719** Ramsay *2nd Answ. Hamilton* ii, But me ye ne'er sae crouse had craw'd Ye poor scull-thacker! **1852** Mundy *Antipodes* (1857) 181 A splendid green-stone Meri, heirloom of her deceased lord, and the skull-cracker no doubt of a hundred foes. **1859** *Slang Dict.* 94 *Skull thatchers*, straw bonnet makers,—sometimes called 'bonnet-builders'. **1863** Miss Braddon *A. Floyd* xxiv, 'I'll find my skull-thatcher if I can,' said Captain Prodder, groping for his hat amongst the brambles. **1866** 'Mark Twain' *Lett. from Hawaii* (1967) 62 In spite of the depredations of 'skull hunters', we rode a considerable distance over ground..thickly strewn with human bones. **1902** J. Chalmers in *Life* (1905) xx. 98/2 That they are skull-hunters I do not doubt.

**7.** Special combs.: **skull-buster** *U.S. slang*, something that taxes the mind; a complicated problem; † **skull butterfly** (see quot.); **skull-eel**, the sharp-nosed eel, *Anguilla vulgaris*; **skull-fish**, † (*a*) some fish supposed to resemble a skull; (*b*) a whalebone whale above two years of age; † **skull-man** (see quot.); † **skull-moss**, a greenish kind of moss growing on skulls long exposed to the air; † **skull-seam**, a suture on the skull; **skull session** *U.S. slang*, a discussion, conference; **skull-vein** (see quot.).

**1926** *University Mag.* (Univ. Va.) Oct. 17 **Skull-buster*, a particularly hard course. **1946** Mezzrow & Wolfe *Really Blues* i. 18 Most of my skullbusters got solved at The School. **1797** *Encycl. Brit.* (ed. 3) XIII. 721/2 The *skull butterfly is another singular species, so called from its head resembling in some degree a death's head or human skull. **1883** Day *Fishes Gt. Brit.* II. 243 Eel, *skull-eel, or brown-eel. **1668** Charleton *Onomast.* 154 *Orbis*,..the Globe, or *Scull-fish. **1725** *Phil. Trans.* XXXIII. 257 After this, they [whales yielding whalebone] are term'd Scull-fish, their Age not being known, but only guess'd at by the Length of the Bone in their Mouths. **1858** Simmonds *Dict. Trade*, *Skull-fish*, the technical name among whalers for..a whale which is more than two years old. **1659** Torriano, *Capellétti*, certain soldiers serving on horse-back with steele-caps, called with us *skull-men, or black-skulls. **1631** W. Foster *Hoplocrisma-Spongvs* 40 **Scull-mosse* or bones,..Mummy and the Fat of Man..comprehend the corporeall perfection of Man. **1681** Grew *Musæum* II. III. iv. 237 Of the same Species with the Skull-Mosse. **1598** Sylvester *Du Bartas* I. vi. 576 The Nose..serveth as a Gutter To void the Excrements of grossest matter; As by the *Scull-seams and the Pory Skin Evaporate those that are light and thin. **1959** J. Blish *Clash of Cymbals* iv. 97 Web and Estelle..had become accepted silent partners at such *skull-sessions. **1973** 'D. Jordan' *Nile Green* xi. 49 Joe was ready for the skull session. **1838** *Civil Eng. & Arch. Jrnl.* I. 98/2 The peculiar character of the veins commonly called *scull veins, from their strong resemblance to the sutures of the scull, which traverse the blocks of white limestone.

**skull, scull** (skʌl), *sb.*[2] *Sc.* and †*north.* Forms: α. 6 **skill, skyll**. β. 6– **skull**. γ. 8– **scull**. [Of obscure origin.] A strong, shallow basket (now sometimes made of iron wire) of a circular or oval form and considerable size, used esp. for farm produce, fish, and fishing-lines.

α. **1508** Dunbar *Flyting* 231 Fische wyvis cryis, Fy! and castis doun skillis and skeilis. **1516–7** *Durh. Acc. Rolls* (Surtees) 106 Pro le Skyll' pro bobus pascent ij d.

β. **1513** *Acc. Ld. High Treas. Scot.* IV. 496 Item, for skullis, vj d. **1634–46** Row *Hist. Kirk* (1842) 288 To the Judas, whose skill..was knowen to be far greater in making of skulls nor either in praying or preaching. **1724** *Dunbar's Flyting* xxiii. in Ramsay *Evergreen*, Fish Wyves..cast down Skulls and skeils. **1821** *Blackw. Mag.* X. 395 She seized her empty skull, and beat it unmercifully about..poor John. **1840–1** *Q. Jrnl. Agric.* XI. 112 The large ozier or willow basket..in some parts of the country known by the name of 'skulls'. **1882** *Jamieson's Sc. Dict.* s.v., The fisherman's skull is..deep at one end for the line, and shallow at the other for the baited hooks.

γ. **1752** *Rec. Elgin* (New Spald. Cl.) I. 465 All riddles, sculls, creels, mauns, beescaps. **1794** *Statist. Acc. Scotl.* XIII. 401 She recollected that she was..rocked in a fisher's scull instead of a cradle. **1816** Scott *Antiq.* xxvi, She maun get the scull on her back, and awa wi' the fish to the next burrows-town. **1851** H. Stephens *Bk. Farm* (ed. 2) I. 261 The most common practice of carrying the turnips is by the stalls in baskets, called *sculls*.

Hence **'skullful, 'scullful**, the fill of a skull.

**1844** H. Stephens *Bk. Farm* II. 122 Each skulful [ed. 2 scullful] will contain rather more than 32 lb. [of turnips].

†**skull**, *sb.*[3] *Obs. rare.* Also scull. [Of obscure origin.] A drinking-bowl or -vessel.

**1513** Douglas *Æneid* III. i. 125 We keist of warme mylk mony a scull [L. *cymbium*]. *Ibid.* VII. iii. 89 In flacon and in skull [L. *cratera*] Thai skynk the wyne.

**skull** (skʌl), *v.* [f. SKULL *sb.*[1]] **1.** *trans.* (with *up*) and *intr. Metallurgy.* Of molten metal: to freeze and form a skull (in). Cf. SKULL *sb.*[1] 4.

**1941** *Engineers' Digest* II. 409/2 Very low sulphur iron, or slow-running iron, would skull up the ladles if much scrap were used. **1953** D. J. O. BRANDT *Manuf. Iron & Steel* xxiii. 174 Neither may the ladle be emptied too slowly, for if it is the steel will get too cold and will 'scull' [*ed.* 2: skull], i.e., freeze.

**2.** *trans.* To strike (someone) on the head. *slang* (chiefly *U.S.*).

**1945** BAKER *Austral. Lang.* viii. 157 *Skull*, to strike (someone). **1952** B. MALAMUD *Natural* 32 My father? Well, maybe I did want to skull him sometimes. **1956** F. CASTLE *Violent Hours* vii. 58 'You didn't get skulled backing away from him,' Webb said dryly. **1975** A. BERGMAN *Hollywood & Le Vine* (1976) viii. 97 My waking came in drugged stages... I had been skulled.

**skull**, variant or obs. form of SCULL *sb.* and *v.*

**skullbanker**, var. SCOWBANKER *slang.*

**skull-cap** (ˈskʌlkæp). Also 7–9 scull-cap. [f. SKULL *sb.*[1] + CAP *sb.*[1]]

**1. a.** A light, close-fitting cap, usu. of silk, velvet, or other soft material, for covering the head.

α. **1682** LUTTRELL *Brief Rel.* (1857) I. 182 About 30 persons,..clad in Indian stuffs, with sculp [*sic*] caps on their heads. **1687** MIÈGE *Gt. Fr. Dict.* II. s.v., A Scull-cap, that some wear under the Perwig. **1753** HANWAY *Trav.* (1762) I. III. xlii. 194 They also use scull-caps of paper, or a cabbage-leaf under their hats. **1819** SCOTT *Leg. Montrose* xi, A Presbyterian clergyman,..wearing a black silk scull-cap. **1869** TOZER *Highl. Turkey* II. 206 Their black and greasy scull-caps..might once have been red.

β. **1704** STEELE *Lying Lovers* II. i, I suppose I was used like other Children. They clap'd me on a Skul-cap. *a* **1734** NORTH *Lives* (1826) I. 59 He wore commonly a little leather cap, which sort was then called skull caps. **1848** LAYARD *Nineveh* vii. (1850) 141 The women wore small embroidered skull-caps. **1888** BURGON *Lives 12 Gd. Men* I. iii. 355 He commonly wore a black silk skull-cap.

**b.** *fig.*

**1960** S. BECKER tr. *A. Schwarz-Bart's Last of Just* (1961) VI. 305 Everything under the skullcap of the heavens that called itself a democracy. **1978** *Amer. Poetry Rev.* July/Aug. 35/2, I remember the moon is a skullcap not placed properly on the head.

**2.** *Hist.* A steel or iron cap, a form of casque or helmet fitting closely to the head; = SKULL *sb.*[1] 3.

**1820** SCOTT *Monast.* ix, An iron skull-cap, none of the brightest, bore for distinction a sprig of the holly. **1824** W. IRVING *T. Trav.* (1849) 174 There was a ferocious tyrant in a skullcap like an inverted porringer, and a dress of red baize. **1834** PLANCHÉ *Brit. Costume* 98 Skull-caps.., with or without nasals, are common amongst esquires, archers and men at arms.

**3.** *Bot.* One or other of various species of plants belonging to the genus *Scutellaria*, in which the calyx finally assumes the appearance of a helmet.

α. **1760** J. LEE *Introd. Bot.* App. 326 *Scull-cap*, see Skull-cap. **1777** LIGHTFOOT *Flora Scot.* I. 320 *Scutellaria*,..Little red Scull-cap or Willow-herb. **1821** BARTON *Flora N. Amer.* I. 5 *Scutellaria hyssopifolia.* Hyssop-leaved Scull-cap. *Ibid.* 78 *Scutellaria laterifolia.* Side-flowering Scull-cap... Blue Scull-cap. **1845–50** MRS. LINCOLN *Lect. Bot.* 172 The scull-cap, (*Scutellaria*,)..has been said to be a remedy for the hydrophobia.

β. **1760** J. LEE *Introd. Bot.* App. 327 Skull-cap, *Scutellaria.* **1786** ABERCROMBIE *Arr.* 67 in *Gard. Assist.*, Skull-cap, or helmet flower. **1855** MISS PRATT *Flowering Pl.* IV. 205 Common Skull-cap..received its name from the singular impalement of its calyx, which, when inverted, resembles a helmet with its visor raised.

**b.** *Amer.* (See quot.)

**1846–50** A. WOOD *Class-bk. Bot.* 406 *Veronica scutellata*, Skull-cap or Marsh Speedwell,..[grows] in swamps and marshes, N. Eng. and Western States, and Brit. Am[erica].

**4.** *Geol.* (See quots.)

**1839** *Civil Eng. & Arch. Jrnl.* II. 375/2 The skull cap [in certain quarries in the island of Portland] is irregular in texture; it is a well-compacted limestone, containing cherty nodules. **1860** DAMON *Geol. Weymouth* 88 The term 'skull cap', applied to the solid layers constituting the lowest bed of the Purbeck formation, is intended to denote its position in relation to other beds below. **1885** R. ETHERIDGE *Stratigr. Geol. & Palæontol.* 478 *note*, The lower Purbeck beds are known as the '*cap*' and the '*skull cap*'. They are botryoidal limestones or indurated calcareous tuffs, possibly derived from the denudation of the Portland rocks.

**5.** *Anat.* The bony structure covering the brain; the top or roof of the head.

**1855** L. HOLDEN *Human Osteology* 94 The skull-cap is composed of the expanded arches of three of the cranial vertebræ, and forms a beautiful oval dome for the protection of the brain. **1866** *Chambers's Encycl.* VIII. 760/1 These fossæ are marked, as is the whole skull-cap, by the cerebral convolutions.

**skullduggery**, var. SKULDUGGERY.

**skulle**, obs. f. SCULL *sb.*, oar.

**skulled** (skʌld), *a.* [f. SKULL *sb.*[1] + -ED[2]. Cf. *thick-skulled*, etc.] Of certain vertebrates: Possessing or furnished with a skull.

**1879** tr. *Haeckel's Evol. Man* II. xvii. 97 The whole Vertebrate tribe may primarily be divided into the two main sections of the Skull-less and the Skulled Vertebrates.

**skullen**, obs. form of SCULLION.

**skullery** (ˈskʌlərı). [f. SKULL *sb.*[1] + -ERY 2.] A collection of skulls; a place for skulls.

**1818** *Blackw. Mag.* IV. 327 The effect of the water dropping from the jaw-bones and eyeholes... It is not to be thought that an Irishman could contemplate such a skullery with unmoved imagination. **1908** *Westm. Gaz.* 31 July 1/3 On his excavating expeditions an annexe, usually known as the 'skullery', is almost invariably brought into use.

**skullian, -ion**, obs. forms of SCULLION.

**ˈskull-less**, *a.* [f. SKULL *sb.*[1]] Having no skull; not furnished with a skull.

**1879** tr. *Haeckel's Evol. Man* II. xvii. 97 Of the earlier and lower section, that of the Skull-less, the Amphioxus is alone extant.

**ˈskully**, *a. rare.* [f. SKULL *sb.*[1]] Containing skulls; having skulls about.

**1896** E. A. KING *It. Highways* 218 A damp and skully place..is the crypt.

**skulp**, obs. form of SCALP *v.*[2]

**skumer, -our(e**, obs. forms of SCUMMER.

**skumfite, skunfit**, obs. forms of SCOMFIT.

**skun**, occas. pa. t. or pa. pple. of SKIN *v. dial.* and *colloq.* (chiefly *U.S.*). (See also Wentworth *Amer. Dial. Dict.*)

**1917** R. FROST *Let.* 3 Dec. (1972) 20 They might have skun him alive if he had been a mere pupil in their classes. **1927** *Bulletin* (Glasgow) 26 Sept. 12/3 When it comes to breakfast foods America has got Great Britain skun a mile. **1936** J. G. BRANDON *Pawnshop Murder* xxvi. 260 The toff Wibley is working for might be connected with the old dame Widgett skun for her 'ice'? **1942** W. FAULKNER *Go down, Moses* 23 You run a hard race and you run a good one, but you skun the hen-house one time too many.

**skunage**, variant of SKEVINAGE *Obs.*

**skundrell**, obs. form of SCOUNDREL.

**skunge**, var. SCUNGE *sb.*

**skunk** (skʌŋk), *sb.* Also 7 squnck, squunncke, 8 skunck. See also SKINK *sb.*[5] [ad. Amer. Indian (Abenaki) *seganku* or *segongw*; variant forms occur in many other dialects.]

**1. a.** A North American animal of the weasel kind, *Mephitis mephitica*, noted for emitting a very offensive odour when attacked or killed.

**1634** W. WOOD *New Eng. Prosp.* (1865) 25 The beasts of offence be Squunckes, Ferrets, Foxes. **1674** JOSSELYN *Two Voy.* 85 The Squnck is almost as big as the Racoon. **1701** C. WOLLEY *Jrnl. New York* (1860) 31 Musquashes, Skunks, Deer and Wolves, they bring upon their backs to New-York. **1775** A. BURNABY *Trav.* 11 *note*, There is a species of pole-cat in this part of America, which is commonly called a skunk. **1800** SHAW *Gen. Zool.* I. II. 395 A smell as insufferable as that of some of the American Weesels or Skunks. **1835** W. IRVING *Tour Prairies* xi, He was advised to wear the scalp of the skunk as the only trophy of his prowess. **1877** COUES *Fur-Bearing Anim.* vii. 196 The Skunk is a stoutly built animal, with a small head, low ears, and short limbs..; the tail long and very bushy.

**b.** *ellipt.* The fur of the skunk.

**1862** B. TAYLOR in *Life & Lett.* (1884) I. xvi. 404 Sables are so expensive as to be vulgar and Skunk..is infinitely handsomer. **1884** *Daily News* 23 Sept. 6/1 Skunk is to be very much worn this winter. It can be deodorised to a very great extent.

**2.** *colloq.* A thoroughly mean or contemptible person. Also in playful use.

**1841** [W. G. SIMMS] *Kinsmen* I. 171 He's a skunk—a bad chap about the heart. *a* **1859** in Bartlett *Dict. Amer.* (ed. 2) s.v., Now, Tom, you skunk, this is the third time you've forgot to set on that switch. **1891** N. GOULD *Double Event* 42 That miserable old skunk you've engaged to take my place.

**b.** Something unpleasant or rotten; rubbish, nonsense.

**1929** D. H. LAWRENCE *Pansies* 148 Once and for all, have done with it, all the silly bunk of upper-class superiority; that superior stuff is just holy skunk. **1976** *Daily Times* (Lagos) 8 Oct. 7/6 However, for throwing away the skunk of a national anthem that was unashamedly saddled to this federation for 16 long years, a thousand cheers to the father of this nation, late Murtala Muhammed.

**c.** *U.S. Mil. slang.* An unidentified surface craft. Cf. BOGY[1], BOGEY[1] 6.

**1945** J. BRYAN *Diary* 24 Mar. in *Aircraft Carrier* (1954) 112 'Skunk' is code for a surface contact, a companion term to 'bogey' in the air. **1952** *N.Y. Times Mag.* 19 Oct. 14/4 The cruiser is..useful at times for coastal bombardment or to seek out and destroy enemy 'skunks' (surface craft). **1957** *Ibid.* 19 May 22/3 A Skunk is an unidentified surface ship, as opposed to a Bogie, which is an unidentified aircraft.

**3.** *attrib.* and *Comb.*, as *skunk-fur*, *-robe*, *-skin*; *skunk-like* adj.; **skunk bear** = WOLVERENE, -INE, 1; **skunk-bird, -blackbird** *U.S.* (see quots.); **skunk currant** *U.S.*, the fetid or mountain currant, *Ribes prostratum*; **skunkhead** *U.S.* (see quot.); **skunk porpoise** *U.S.* (see quot. and PORPOISE *sb.*); **skunk spruce**, one of several aromatic North American spruces, esp. the eastern *Picea glauca* or the western *Picea engelmannii*; **skunk weasel**, = SKUNK *sb.* 1; **skunk-weed** *U.S.*, = SKUNK-CABBAGE.

**1876** G. B. GRINNELL in W. Ludlow *U.S. Army Corps of Engineers Rep. Reconn. to Yellowstone Nat. Park* i. 65 *Gulo luscus*... In this region, they were spoken of as the '*Skunk-bear'. **1911** J. E. ROGERS *Wild Animals* 112 The wolverine, largest of all the weasels, looks more like a bear and a skunk combined. 'Skunk-bear' is one of his many nicknames. **1961** *Tamarack Rev.* Spring 9 He slouched..but never preventing the fear from settling in him, never preventing it from turning his eye wary and cruel as any skunkbear's. **1836** *Penny Cycl.* V. 30/1 [The male bobolink's] variegated dress, which, from a resemblance in its colours to that of the quadruped, obtained for it the name of '*skunk-bird' among the Cree Indians. **1855** H. W. BEECHER *Star Papers* (1873) 192 We followed that old Polyglott, the *skunk blackbird, and heard [etc.]. **1859** BARTLETT *Dict. Amer.* (ed. 2), *Skunk blackbird*, the common marsh blackbird, so called in the rural districts of New England, New York, and Canada West. **1893** *Scribner's Mag.* June 771/1 The bobolink's chief name was suggested by..his song; but another, skunk-blackbird, alludes to the skunk-like color and pattern of his dress. *a* **1817** T. DWIGHT *Trav. New Eng.* (1821) II. 312 Three sorts of currants are found in the forest: the red, the black, and a peculiar kind, called *Skunk currants. **1846–50** A. WOOD *Class-bk. Bot.* 273 A small shrub,.. ill-scented, and with ill-flavored berries—sometimes called Skunk Currant. **1882** CAULFEILD & SAWARD *Dict. Needlwk.* 451/2 *Skunk Fur..is of a dark brown colour, rather long in the hair, and rough. **1848** BARTLETT *Dict. Amer.* 305 **Skunkhead*, the popular name, on the sea-coast, of the Pied Duck of ornithologists. **1847** DARLINGTON *Amer. Weeds*, etc. (1860) 346 This plant—so readily known by its *skunk-like odor. **1884** GOODE *Nat. Hist. Aquat. Anim.* 16 The best known species on the Atlantic coast are the '*Skunk Porpoise', or 'Bay Porpoise'. **1851** G. H. KINGSLEY *Sp. & Trav.* (1900) v. 144 A good *skunk robe is a very pretty bit of peltry. **1862** B. TAYLOR in *Life & Lett.* (1884) I. xvi. 404 With my pelisse of racoon and my cap of *skunk-skin. **1894** *Amer. Folk-Lore* VII. 99 *Picea alba*,..*skunk-spruce. **1921** P. B. KYNE *Go-getter* iii. 32 Have you ever had any experience selling skunk spruce?.. It's coarse and stringy and wet and heavy and smells just like a skunk. **1948** *Sun* (Baltimore) 21 Dec. 14/2 They are not, it seems, 'real Christmas trees: only skunk spruce'. **1771** PENNANT *Synop. Quad.* 233 *Skunk Weasel. **1738** *Phil. Trans.* XL. 348 *Arum Americanum, Betæ folio.* The *Scunk-weed. **1855** *New Cycl. Bot.* II. 708 *Dracontium fœtidum*... It is a native of North America, where it is called Scunk Cabbage or Scunk Weed.

Hence **ˈskunkdom**, (*a*) skunkish character; (*b*) skunks collectively; **ˈskunkish** *a.*, resembling a skunk; contemptible; **ˈskunklet**, a young skunk; **ˈskunky** *a.*, befitting a skunk; nasty; evil-smelling.

**1839** J. BROWN *Lett.* (1907) 49 My skunkdom requires only to be known to be felt. *Ibid.*, I wish you would write poor Isabella. In this you are more skunkish than I. **1851** G. H. KINGSLEY *Sp. & Trav.* (1900) v. 144, I was meditating on skunkdom and keeping a look-out for willow grouse. **1894** *Westm. Gaz.* 2 Feb. 3/1 The five or six little skunklets remain *en famille* with their parents until the following spring. **1897** BLACKMORE *Dariel* xl, You try to shove him into any skunky corner.., and he lets you know. **1946** D. C. PEATTIE *Road of Naturalist* i. 21 Nicolletia with off-shade yellow-pinks and mustardy green-yellows and a skunky odour that simply would not wash off the fingers. **1960** *Tamarack Rev.* Winter 127 He called..'Skunky small one?' Tommy Moore turned his soapy face upward. He was used to being summoned this way. **1973** *Globe & Mail* (Toronto) 3 July 28/1 The thousands of blue-jeaned teenagers..drink beer in the sun, drinking it fast so it doesn't go skunky. **1981** P. THEROUX *Mosquito Coast* xxi. 277 In very hot weather.. the jungle odour is skunky and as strong as garbage.

**skunk** (skʌŋk), *v. slang* (orig. and chiefly *N. Amer.*). [f. the sb.] **1. a.** *intr.* To fail. *rare.*

**1831** *Constellation* 1 Jan. 54/1 It is a common expression in New-England, to say of a person, who does not get a king in the game of chequers, he *skunked*.

**b.** *trans.* To defeat or get the better of; to inflict defeat upon.

In some quots. in passive = 'defeated without making any score'.

**1843** *Quincy* (Illinois) *Herald* 24 Nov. 2/1 The Legislature will be Democratic by an overwhelming majority; it is more than probable that the Whigs have been skunked. **1845** *Spirit of Times* 9 Aug. 273/2 In the second hand of the third game, I made high, low, game, and 'skunked' him, outright. **1848** BARTLETT *Dict. Amer.* 409 In games of chance, if one of the players fails to make a point, he is said to be *skunked.* A presidential candidate who fails to secure one electoral vote is also skunked. **1876** W. WRIGHT *Big Bonanza* lxxi. 541 'Skunked, by the holy spoons', cried he. **1898** N. BROOKS *Boys of Fairport* ii. 37 Their only hope now was to 'skunk' the White Bears, who were coming to bat. **1904** F. CRISSEY *Tattlings* xvii. 365 A certain trio of choice scamps from the city hall gang would make a strong committee that could skunk the enemy. **1921** *Daily Colonist* (Victoria, B.C.) 18 Oct. 10/1 Very few hunters who went after the pheasants ..did not get some at any rate, and the man who was 'skunked' probably would be very hard to find. **1939** *Sun* (Baltimore) 4 Dec. 18/1 The outcome of that battle..was Navy 10, Army 0... 'Which means,' one of them explained to his girl friend, 'We got 10 and they got skunked.' **1944** DUNCAN & NICKOLS *Mentor Graham* xvi. 170 Lincoln, with a short, logical speech in which no words were wasted, 'skunked' his adversary. **1948** *Field & Stream* June 86/2, I have fished on opening day in the snow.., only to get skunked. **1971** D. CONOVER *One Man's Island* 33 When the Colonel comes home from fishing, by his vociferous oaths we know that he was skunked. **1972** D. DELMAN *Sudden Death* (1973) vi. 64 She'll skunk Nell Duncan today, and win.

**2. a.** *trans.* To fail to pay (a bill or a creditor).

**1851** B. H. HALL *College Words* 284 *Skunk*, at Princeton College, to fail to pay a debt; used actively; e.g. to skunk a tailor, i.e. not to pay him. **1859** BARTLETT *Dict. Amer.* (ed. 2) s.v., A student who leaves college without settling up, is said to skunk his bills. **1961** WEBSTER s.v., Made a practice of skunking hotels.

**b.** To cheat; in *pass.*, to be cheated *out of.*

**1890** C. W. Haskins *Argonauts of Calif.* xvii. 250, I got skunked once out of a good claim. **1971** E. Fenwick *Impeccable People* iii. 21 I'm beginning to think we skunked you over the price.

**skunk-cabbage.** *N. Amer.* Also **skunk's cabbage.** [f. skunk *sb.*] A perennial stemless plant of the arum family, *Symplocarpus fœtidus*, giving out an offensive odour, especially when bruised. Also used, esp. on the Pacific Coast, to designate *Lysichiton camtschatcense*, another member of the family Araceæ, or a false hellebore of the genus *Veratrum*, of the family Liliaceæ.

**1751** J. Eliot *Ess. Field-Husbandry* iii. 66 Take the Roots of Swamp Hellebore, sometimes called Skunk Cabbage, Tickle Weed. **1762** Eliot in Mills *Syst. Pract. Husb.* I. 156 The roots of swamp hellebore (known in different places by the several names of skunk cabbage, tickle weed, bear root). **1792** Belknap *Hist. New-Hampsh.* III. 127 The *arum*, or skunk cabbage, has been found very efficacious in asthmatic complaints. **1830** Lindley *Nat. Syst. Bot.* 287 The root and seeds of the Skunk Cabbage, *Symplocarpus fœtida*, are powerful antispasmodics. **1849** N. Kingsley *Jrnl.* 3 May (1914) 15 The fruit grows on the extreme top with a blow or flower resembling our Skunks Cabbage. **1868** H. W. Beecher *Norwood* 91 The great, succulent leaves of the skunk's cabbage were fully expanded. **1878** Mrs. Stowe *Poganuc P.* xvii. 147 The honest, great green leaves of the old skunk cabbage, most refreshing to the eye in its hardy, succulent greenness, though an abomination to the nose. **1906** *Atlantic Monthly* Oct. 495 The first flower to bloom in this latitude when the winter frost loosens its grip upon the sod is the gross, uncouth, and noisome skunk cabbage. **1950** *Chicago Tribune* 28 Mar. 14/3 Some watch for skunk cabbages poking mottled brown snouts thru the swamp muck. **1968** Peterson & McKenny *Field Guide to Wildflowers* 368 Skunk Cabbage... The sheathing, shell-like spathe, mottled and varying from green to purple-brown, envelops the heavy rounded spadix. **1976** *Hortus Third* (L. H. Bailey Hortorium) 1148/1 *Veratrum.. californicum* E. Durand. Corn lily, skunk cabbage.

**skunte**: see scum *v.* 5 b.

**skuppat**, obs. form of scuppet *sb.*

‖**Skupština** ('skʊpʃtiːnə). Also 9 **Scubsch'tina, Skoupschina**, etc.; **Skupshtina.** [Serbo-Croatian *skupština*, f. *skupa* together, *skupiti* to assemble.] The national assembly of Yugoslavia; formerly, of Serbia or Montenegro.

**1847** A. Kerr tr. *von Ranke's Hist. Servia* x. 190 Soon after New Year's Day, all the Woiwodes, with their suites, assembled at a Diet called Skupschtina. **1862** W. Denton *Servia & Servians* xii. 241 Immediately after the Servians had succeeded in liberating themselves from the Turkish rule they set about forming political institutions for themselves. Among the earliest is the assembly called the Skoupschina. **1866** *Chambers's Encycl.* VIII. 629/2 Each circle.. sends a deputy to the *Scubsch'tina.* **1883** *Encycl. Brit.* XVI. 781/2 In 1851, Danilo.. prevailed on the 'skuptchina' to declare Montenegro a secular state with the hereditary government of a prince. **1902** *Ibid.* XXX. 821/1 A *Skupshtina*, or popular assembly, is summoned on rare occasions of national importance. **1911** R. W. Seton-Watson *Southern Slav Question* ix. 194 The Skupština had sufficient self-restraint and sanity to decide against war. **1923** [see *Serbo-Bulgarian* adj. s.v. Serbo-]. **1940** C. Sforza *Fifty Years of War & Diplomacy in Balkans* iv. 22 In the elections.. Pashich won a complete victory. In the Skupshtina, an imposing majority was ready to follow him. **1968** F. W. Hondius *Yugoslav Community of Nations* ii. 74 This Constitution.. created a precedent by recognizing the concept of popular sovereignty, reflected in a powerful one-chamber Skupština. **1976** F. Singleton *Twentieth-Cent. Yugoslavia* I. iv. 48 The regency introduced constitutional reforms which provided for a Skupština of 120 members.

**skur(r**: see scour *v.*[2]; skirr *sb.* and *v.*

†**skure**, *v. Obs.* (Meaning doubtful.)

Not likely to be either *secure* or *skewer*.

**1587** M. Grove *Pelops & Hipp.* (1878) 129 As the Puttoke doth surpasse eche winged foule perdy, By egernesse to skure her pray, once seene with greedy eye.

**skurn(e**, obs. ff. scorn *v.*

**skurrick**, obs. var. skerrick.

**skurt**, var. squirt *sb.*

**skuruie, -uy**, obs. ff. scurvy *sb.* and *a.*

**skut**, obs. f. scout *sb.*[3], scut *sb.*[1]

**skut**, var. scut *sb.*[4]

**skute**, var. scoot *v.*[1]; obs. f. scute.

**skutterudite** ('skʊtərədaɪt). *Min.* [ad. G. *skutterudit* (W. von Haidinger *Handb. der bestimm. Mineral.*, etc. (1845) iv. 560), f. *Skutterud*, name of a village in SE. Norway (now called *Skotterud*): see -ite[1].] An arsenide of cobalt, ideally $CoAs_3$, that commonly contains other elements, esp. nickel, iron, bismuth, and sulphur, and is found as grey cubic crystals with a metallic lustre.

**1850** J. D. Dana *Syst. Mineral.* (ed. 3) 474 Skutterudite. .. Lustre bright metallic. Color between tin-white and pale lead-grey, sometimes iridescent. **1892** [see *nickel-skutterudite* s.v. nickel *sb.* 3 b]. **1902** H. A. Miers *Mineralogy* 332 It is remarkable that there is another arsenide of cobalt of quite different composition, $CoAs_3$, known as skutterudite, which is also cubic and pyritohedral. **1947** *Bull. Geol. Soc. Amer.* LVIII. 317 In spite of repeated attempts, varying the conditions of temperature and using different fluxes, no higher cobalt arsenide other than skutterudite $CoAs_3$ was obtained. **1968** I. Kostov *Mineral.* 135 Skutterudite, smaltite, and chloanthite are typical intermediate- or high-temperature hydrothermal minerals.

**skuyer**, obs. f. squire.

**skuys**, obs. f. scuse *sb.*

**skwar**, obs. f. square.

**skwe**, var. skew *sb. Obs.*

**skwff**, obs. Sc. f. scoff *sb.*[1]

**skwsacion**, obs. f. scusation.

**sky** (skaɪ), *sb.*[1] Forms: 3-4 (6) ski (4 scki, schi); 3 skei, 4 skey; 3 skiȝe, 4-7 skie, skye (5 schye), 4- sky (7 *pl.* skyne). [a. ON. *ský* (Icel. *ský*, Norw., Sw., Da. *sky*) neut., cloud (:—original **skiuja*), directly related to OS. *skio* masc., OE. *scéo* (doubtful), and more remotely to OE. *scuwa*, ON. *skugge* shade, shadow, whence scug *sb.*[1] See also skew *sb.*[1]]

†**1.** A cloud. *Obs.*

*c* **1220** *Bestiary* 66 Up he teð, til ðat he ðe heuene seð, ðurȝ skies sexe and seuene til he cumeð to heuene. *c* **1250** *Gen. & Ex.* 3255 Bi-foren hem fleȝ an skiȝe briȝt ðat niȝt hem made ðe weiȝe liȝt. *c* **1384** Chaucer *H. Fame* iii. 1600 A certeyn wynde.. blewe so hydously and hye That hyt ne left not a skye In alle the welkene. **1390** Gower *Conf.* II. 50 Al sodeinly Sche passeth, as it were a Sky, Al clene out of this ladi sihte. *c* **1407** Lydg. *Reson & Sens.* 1007 As sterris in the frosty nyght, Whanne walkne is most bryght, With-oute cloude or any skye. *c* **1430** —— *Min. Poems* (Percy Soc.) 161 The somerys day is.. seelden seyn, With so cleer hayr, but that ther is som skye. **1500-20** Dunbar *Poems* lxix. 3 Quhone sabill all the hewin arrayis, With mystie vapouris, cluddis and skyis. ? *a* **1550** *Sterne of Redempt.* 31 in *Dunbar's Poems* (1893) 329 To the superne eternall regioun, Quhair noxiall skyis may mak no sogeorn.

*fig.* **14..** *Epiph.* in *Tundale's Vis.* (1843) 121 Thus.. trw menyng darketh with a skye That we in Englysch callon flaturye. *a* **1529** Skelton *Replyc.* 165 Ye soored ouer hye.., Your names to magnifye, Among the scabbed skyes Of Wycliffes flesshe flyes.

**2. a.** *the skies*, the clouds (*obs.*); the upper region of the air; the heavens. Chiefly *poet.*

*a* **1300** *XV Signa* in *E.E.P.* (1862) 11 þe holi man telliþ .. þat þe skeis so sal spec þan.. in steuen as hit wer man. **1390** Gower *Conf.* II. 261 Sche drof forth bothe char and whel Above in thair among the Skyes. *c* **1400** *Destr. Troy* 6016 The day was done, dymmet the skyes. **1508** Dunbar *Gold. Targe* 25 The skyes rang for schoutyng of the larkis. **1590** Shaks. *Mids. N.* iv. i. 121 The skies, the fountaines, euery region neere, Seeme all one mutuall cry. **1614** C. Brooke *Ghost Rich. III*, Poems (1872) 103 To.. curle his leauie hayres The more in bows, and armes, that kisse the skyne. **1697** Dryden *Virg. Georg.* iii. 248 Late at Night, when Stars adorn the Skies. **1754** Gray *Pleasure* 51 The common Sun, the air, the skies To him are opening Paradise. **1784** Mickle *Cumnor Hall* ii, Now nought was heard beneath the skies, The sounds of busy life were still. **1837** Carlyle *Fr. Rev.* i. vii. ix, With uplifted right hand.. to these pouring skies. **1860** Ld. Lytton *Lucile* i. iv. 12 There was war in the skies!

*transf.* and *fig.* **1562** Winȝet *Wks.* (S.T.S.) I. 20 We exhort ȝow, and adiuris ȝow also,.. to descend from the hie skyis. **1585** Higins tr. *Junius' Nomencl.* 190/2 *Machina*,.. the skies or counterfet heauen ouer the stage.

**b.** Used without *the*, in limited sense.

**1503** Dunbar *Thistle & Rose* 41 Illumynit our with orient skyis brycht. **1748** Gray *Alliance* 55 A brighter Day and Skies of azure Hue. **1781** Cowper *Truth* 138 The rude inclemency of wintry skies. **1907** H. Wyndham *Flare of Footlights* xxx, It was a dismal day, with leaden skies overhead.

**3. a.** *the sky*, the apparent arch or vault of heaven, whether covered with cloud or clear and blue; the firmament.

*a* **1300** *Cursor M.* 1341 Him thoght.. þat to þe sky it raght þe toppe. **1390** Gower *Conf.* I. 312 The Sky wax derk, the wynd gan blowe, The firy welkne gan to thondre. *c* **1470** *Gol. & Gaw.* 610 Quhen the day can daw,.. And the sone in the sky was schynyng so schir. **1508** Dunbar *Golden Targe* 50, I saw approch agayn the orient sky, A saill. **1546** J. Heywood *Prov.* (1867) 9 When the sky fallth we shall have larks. **1594** Shaks. *Rich. III*, v. iii. 283 The sky doth frowne, and lowre vpon our Army. **1635** R. N. tr. *Camden's Hist. Eliz.* ii. 221 The skye being extreame cold with snow and frost. **1672** R. Wild *Poet. Licent.* 34 If the Skie fall, down-comes the price of Larks. **1728** Pope *Dunc.* i. 178 As.. lead itself can fly, And pond'rous slugs cut swiftly thro' the sky. **1774** M. Mackenzie *Maritime Surv.* 5 A dark Flag on that [pole] which appears between you and the Sky. **1843** Ruskin *Mod. Paint.* I. ii. i. §5. 204 The sky is to be considered as a transparent blue liquid, in which.. clouds are suspended. **1876** Mozley *Univ. Serm.* vi. 135 No people have ever existed to whom the sky has not suggested one set of ideas.

**b.** With descriptive or limiting term.

**1613** Chapman *Maske Inns Court*, Ouer this.. in an Euening sky, the ruddy Sunne was seen ready to be set. *a* **1700** Evelyn *Diary* 1 Nov. 1660, The Sunn represented by a face and raies of gold, upon an azure skie. **1798** Coleridge *Anc. Mar.* ii. vii, All in a hot and copper sky, The bloody Sun.. did stand. **1814** Wordsw. *Yarrow Visited* 17 A blue sky bends o'er Yarrow vale. **1855** Tennyson *Maud* v. ii, With her.. wild voice pealing up to the sunny sky. **1869** E. Dunkin (*title*), The Midnight Sky: Familiar Notes on the Stars and Planets.

**c.** Without article.

**1596** Spenser *F.Q.* iv. iii. 13 Into a starre in sky. **1611** Shaks. *Cymb.* v. v. 146 A Nobler Sir ne're liu'd 'Twixt sky and ground. **1649** Jer. Taylor *Gt. Exemp.* ii. 93 But the greatest part of this paisage and Landtskip is sky. **1725** Pope *Odyssey* iii. 411 A length of Ocean and unbounded sky. **1805** Wordsw. *Prelude* iii. 107, I.. perused The common countenance of earth and sky. **1855** Tennyson *Maud* i. xviii. v, The countercharm of space and hollow sky. **1884** *Jrnl. R. Meteorol. Soc.* (1885) XI. 231 There was a portion of blue sky between the Helm cloud and the Bar.

**d.** *fig.* or in fig. phrases. Also, *out of a clear* (or *blue*) *sky* and varr. = *out of the blue* s.v. blue *sb.* 5 a; (*b*) *to the sky* or *skies*, to the highest possible degree, enthusiastically, extravagantly; (*c*) *in the skies*, in an ecstasy, in the realms of fancy; (*d*) *the sky's the limit*, there is no apparent limit.

(*a*) *c* **1586** C'tess Pembroke *Ps.* lxxx. i, O God,.. Display thy faces skie on us thine owne. **1597** Shaks. *2 Hen. IV*, iv. iii. 56, I, in the cleare Skie of Fame, o're-shine you. **1793** Cowper *To Mary* i, The twentieth year is well-nigh past, Since first our sky was overcast. **1878** Browning *La Saisiaz* 61, I bid him—at suspicion of first cloud athwart his sky.. die! **1875** Tennyson *Q. Mary* v. iii. 264 So from a clear sky falls the thunderbolt! **1897** W. E. Norris *Marietta's Mar.* xxxi. 224 He dropped upon me suddenly out of a clear sky and began asking questions which I had to answer. **1903** Wodehouse *Tales of St. Austin's* 2 To spring an examination on you in the middle of the term out of a blue sky, as it were, was underhand and unsportsmanlike. **1924** E. O'Neill *Welded* i, in *All God's Chillun got Wings* i. 98 It was revelation, then—a miracle out of the sky! **1958** G. Greene *Our Man in Havana* iii. ii. 115 She's had two unhappy *coups de foudre* herself. They came quite suddenly, out of a clear sky.

(*b*) **1617** Moryson *Itin.* i. 104 Italians.. alwaies extoll their owne things to the skie. **1670** G. H. *Hist. Cardinals* ii. iii. 191 Those of any Piety or Religion, commended it to the Skyes. **1731-8** Swift *Polite Conv.* 71 You were extoll'd to the Skies I assure you. **1815** W. H. Ireland *Scribbleomania* 25 Rhymsters who praise 'em to the skies, And meanest actions eulogize. **1915** W. S. Maugham *Of Human Bondage* xlii. 198 Red-nosed comedians were lauded to the skies for their sense of character. **1955** D. Garnett *Golden Echo* II. i. 16 If he had praised it to the skies or damned it, or even told the truth, not much harm would have been done. **1973** P. J. Seybold *Revolutionary Educ. in China* xiv. 156 At one time they shouted 'Long live the teachers'.., praising them to the skies.

(*c*) **1869** Mrs. H. Wood *R. Yorke* xx, Roland was in the skies at once.

(*d*) **1920** *Current History* (U.S.) Oct. 142/2 (*caption*) The sky is now her limit. **1933** *Daily Mirror* 26 Oct. 12/4 To say 'the sky was his limit' definitely adds something to the usual 'he succeeded' or 'he rose in the world'. **1934** Webster s.v. *sky*, The sky is the limit. **1936** C. Sandburg *People, Yes* 160 'Did you say the sky is the limit?' 'Yes, we won't go any higher than the sky.' **1942** E. Paul *Narrow St.* xxiv. 211 Every municipality, excepting small villages, had its official Mont-de-Piété, and the sky was the limit. **1952** W. R. Burnett *Vanity Row* vii. 68 If there's ever anything we can do for you... You know. Sky's the limit, as people say. **1961** L. Mumford *City in History* ii. 52 The cult of power exulted in its own boundless display... The sky was the limit. **1977** H. Fast *Immigrants* ii. 97 As far as the Pacific passage is concerned, rates are going up and the sky's the limit.

**4.** *poet.* or *rhet.* **a.** The celestial regions; heaven; the heavenly power, the deity.

**1590** Shaks. *Mids. N.* v. i. 308 Now am I dead, now am I fled, my soule is in the sky. **1634** Milton *Comus* 242 So maist thou be translated to the skies. **1697** Dryden *Alex. Feast* 179 He rais'd a Mortal to the Skies; She drew an Angel down. **1731** Swift *Judas* Wks. 1755 IV. i. 165 The just vengeance of incensed skies. **1781** Cowper *Charity* 70 Thou that hast.. dared despise Alike the wrath and mercy of the skies. **1810** Shelley *Despair* 8 In the eternal mansions of the skies. **1868** Lynch *Rivulet* cli. ii, Time loses his scythe When he enters the skies.

**b.** The sky (sense 3) of a particular region; hence, climate, clime.

**1701** Addison *Let. to Ld. Halifax* 136 We envy not the warmer Clime that lies In ten Degrees of more indulgent Skies. **1842** Tennyson *You ask me why* vii, I seek a warmer sky. **1856** Kane *Arctic Explor.* II. xxi. 207 Strange that these famine-pinched wanderers of the ice should rejoice in sports .. like the children of our own smiling sky.

**c.** In joc. phr. *the* (or *that*) *great* —— *in the sky*: with personal subj., God considered as the omniscient exponent of an earthly art or profession; of a place or structure, the type of a paradise especially suited to the deceased.

**1977** McKnight & Tobler *Bob Marley* v. 62 Chuck Willis, the 'Sheik of the Stroll' became one of the first members of the great rock group in the sky. **1979** *Times* 24 Nov. 15/7 It is up to that Great Film Critic in the sky to deal with *Life of Brian* in His own way. **1980** D. Bloodworth *Trapdoor* xvii. 107 There's a Director of Central Intelligence up there in that great Langley in the sky. **1982** *Times* 26 Jan. 10/3 Daphne, the pelican, has gone to that great aviary in the sky after 25 years residence.. in St James's Park.

**5. a.** The colour of the sky; sky-blue.

**1667** Dryden *Maiden Queen* ii. i, Those knots of sky do not So well with the dead colour of her face. **1668** Etheredge *She wou'd if she cou'd* iii. ii, A whole bevy of damsels in sky, and pink, and flame-coloured taffetas. **1851** *Illustr. Catal. Gt. Exhib.* iii. 506/2 Pink, white, sky, and maize gros de Naples for ladies' bonnets. **1894** [see helio[2]]. **1923** *Weekly Dispatch* 11 Feb. 14 (Advt.), Will not Fade... Silky finish. Ivory, Biscuit, Sky, Coral [etc.]. **1949** *Radio Times* 15 July 44/3 Lovely pastel shades—Peach, Apple, Sky. **1976** *National Observer* (U.S.) 22 May 17/4 (Advt.), The plain shades... Rust, Beige, Tan, Sky, White, Black.

**b.** The representation of a sky in a painting, etc.

**1747** Francis tr. *Horace, Art P.* 34 *note*, It is chiefly in this View, that Ruisdale's Waters, and Claude Lorrain's Skies are so admirable. **1815** J. Smith *Panorama Sci. & Art* II. 746 For a pure mid-day sky,.. vermilion and white as the sky approaches the horizon. **1878** Ruskin *Notes* 43 The sky is unusually careless.

**6.** 'The upper rows of pictures in a gallery; also, the space near the ceiling' (*Cent. Dict.* 1891).

**7.** The small opening in the roof of a cab, used as a means of communication.

**1907** *Daily Chron.* 18 Oct. 4/4, I did..steal the..box from his hansom-cab, and the driver was looking through the sky.

**8.** *Rhyming slang. ellipt.* for sky-rocket *sb.* 3: pocket.

**1890** in Barrère & Leland *Dict. Slang* II. 248/2 The Oof Bird's scarce and the landlady's fly, And there isn't a mash with a mag in his sky. **1898** A. M. Binstead *Pink 'Un & Pelican* xi. 237 After thirty-six 'ands 'ad bin all over him, tore his trowseys an' left 'im as naked as Barth-Sheber—why, even *then* we never found his sky! **1928** E. Wallace *Gunner* xviii. 140 'Put that in your sky... In your pocket,' she said impatiently. **1979** P. Hill *Washermen* lx. 132 Said 'ee found it [*sc.* a gun] on the rattler. Put it in 'is sky when 'ee got off at Leicester Square.

**9.** *attrib.* and *Comb.* Now chiefly *Lit.* and *poet.*

**a.** Attrib., in sense 'of or in the sky', as ***sky-children, -glare, -pebble***, etc.

**1582** Stanyhurst *Æneis* I. (Arb.) 18 Shee pouts, that Ganymed by Ioue too skitop is hoysed. **1634** Milton *Comus* 83, I must put off These my skie robes spun out of Iris Wooff. **1653** H. More *Conject. Cabbal.* (1713) 53 The Sun and the Moon (according to this Hypothesis) will prove the two great Lights, and the Stars but scatter'd sky-pebbles. *a* **1821** Keats *Hyperion* I. 133 Beautiful things made new, for the surprise Of the sky-children. **1865** Dickens *Mut. Fr.* III. viii, In the sky-glare of the lights of the little town. **1882** Jefferies *Bevis* I. 251 It was a sky-storm, and the lightning was at least a mile high. **1904** W. B. Yeats *Pot of Broth* in *Hour-Glass* 78 Give me some vessel till I give this sky-woman a taste of it. **1916** Blunden *Harbingers* 64 He stells the meadows in similitude Of stars in black sky-spaces. **1920** D. H. Lawrence *Lost Girl* xiv. 320 White clouds, in the sort of hollow sky-dome. **1930** W. H. Auden *Poems* 9 Though heart fears all heart cries for, rebuffs with mortal beat Skyfall, the legs sucked under, adder's bite. **1946** L. B. Lyon *Rough Walk Home* 11 Lift arm or lift an eyebrow, He'll weave his sky-brow Spell round the offender. **1959** D. Davie *Forests of Lithuania* vi. 59 Fires cluster and dart Cross over, light over light Overarches the sky-round. **1979** D. Williams *Genesis & Exodus* vii. 127 He enjoyed the wide sky-sweep of the fens.

**b.** With agent nouns, as ***sky-flyer, -gazer, -holder***, etc.

**1812** Colman *Br. Grins, Fire* xlviii, The monarch of Olympus spake; It made his petty tenants quake, And the large sky-holders obedient bowed. **1838** 'T. Treddlehoyle' *Ben Bunt* 19 Bein a bit an a ski-peepar ma sen. **1891** *Times* 5 Oct. 3/5 Splendid buildings..—veritable 'sky-piercers', as most modern American aspiring business houses are. **1897** *Daily News* 3 June 5/6 There would be hardly a point..where at least the pyrotechnic sky-flyers could not be seen. **1930** V. Woolf *On being Ill* 19 Pedestrians would be impeded and disconcerted by a public sky-gazer.

**c.** With pa. pples., as ***sky-blasted, -born, -bred, -capped, -cast, -dyed***, etc.

Similar combs. are common in the 19th and 20th cent.

**1589** R. Greene *Menaphon* Sig. F1ᵛ, A Skie borne forme. **1595** Spenser *Friend's Passion* 31 The skiebred Egle roiall bird. **1599** J. Davies *Immort. Soul, Introd.* xi, What is this Knowledge, but the Sky stoll'n Fire? *c* **1611** Chapman *Iliad* VII. 346 He held his scepter vp, to all the skie thron'd powres. **1611** Shaks. *Cymb.* v. iv. 96 The Thunderer, whose Bolt..Sky-planted, batters all rebelling Coasts. **1667** Milton *P.L.* v. 285 The third his feet Shaddowd from either heele with featherd maile Skie-tinctur'd grain. **1725** Pope *Odyss.* XI. 727 There figs sky-dy'd, a purple hue disclose. **1742** Young *Nt. Th.* VI. 418 Sky-born, sky-guided, sky-returning race! **1747** Collins *Ode Pity* ii, Let the nations view Thy skyworn robes. **1807** J. Barlow *Columbiad* III. 110 Far beneath, the sky-borne waters ride, Veil the dark deep and sheet the mountain's side. *a* **1821** Keats *Hyperion* I. 310 Earth-born And sky-engender'd, Son of Mysteries! **1878** B. Taylor *Deukalion* III. ii. 108 The sky-cast shadow of a Hebrew chief. **1887** Bowen *Æneid* III. 291 Soon thy sky-capped towers, Phæacia, vanish from view. **1923** D. H. Lawrence *Birds, Beasts & Flowers* 17 And sipped down, perhaps, with a sip of Marsala So that the rambling, sky-dropped grape can add its music to yours. **1934** L. B. Lyon *White Hare* 14 Wind-scoured and sky-burned The fell was. **1946** Dylan Thomas *Deaths & Entrances* 27 May his hunger go howling on bare white bones Past the statues of the stables and the sky roofed sties. **1977** *Hongkong Standard* 12 Apr. 3/3 Aides say Mr. Peres originated and pushed the idea of last July's skyborne rescue from Uganda of 100 hostages.

**d.** With pres. pples., as ***sky-aspiring, -cleaving, -falling, -measuring, -pointing, -reaching***, etc.

This type is also common in the 19th and 20th cent.

**1593** Shaks. *Rich. II*, I. iii. 130 Sky-aspiring and ambitious thoughts. **1596** Spenser *F.Q.* VI. x. 22 They are the daughters of sky-ruling Ioue. **1600** Nashe *Summer's Last Will* 1492 Skie-measuring Mathematicians. **1612** Drayton *Poly-olb.* ix. 66 Mighty Raran shooke his proud sky-kissing top. **1633** Drumm. of Hawth. *Speeches to Pr. Chas.* Wks. (1711) 39/1 Nero's Sky-resembling Gold-ceil'd Halls. **1743** Francis tr. *Horace, Odes* III. x. 21 Thy Threshold hard-hearted, and sky-falling Rain. **1788** P. Freneau *Hermit of Saba* in *Misc. Works* 31 When thou, sky-pointing Saba, Shall tremble on thy base most fearfully! **1796** Eliza Hamilton *Lett. Hindoo Rajah* (1811) II. 117 Whose trees have their sky-touching heads overshadowed by..mountains. **1819** Sky-aspiring [see balmily *adv.*]. **1820** Shelley *Prometh. Unb.* II. iii. 28 The keen sky-cleaving mountains. **1837** Carlyle *Fr. Rev.* I. IV. iv, Amid skyrending *vivats*, and blessings from every heart. **1844** J. R. Lowell *Poems* 274 They tell us that our land was made for song, With its huge rivers and sky-piercing peaks. **1887** *Times* 29 Aug. 4/4 Endless sky-reaching spires. **1922** Joyce *Ulysses* 563 Stephen with hat ashplant frogsplits in middle highkicks with skykicking mouth shut hand clasp part under thigh. **1933** C. Day Lewis *Magnetic Mountain* 9 Void are the valleys..And dumb the sky-dividing hills. **1957** L. MacNeice *Visitations* 42 Felt suddenly harassed, a sky-splitting headache with nothing to cause it. **1977** *New Scientist* 24 Feb. 478/1 A spiky, sky-piercing crenellation of buildings running down the Royal Mile from the hunched bulk of the castle to the rounded towers of the Palace of Holyroodhouse.

**10.** Special combs.: **sky bear** *N. Amer. slang*, (an officer in) a police helicopter (cf. Smokey Bear 2); **sky-blink,** = ice-blink 1; **sky-blotch,** the dark outline of a building against the evening sky; **sky border** *Theatr.*, a border of painted cloth, used both to represent sky and to conceal the top of the stage from the audience; **skycap** *N. Amer.* [after redcap 5], a porter at an airport; **sky-clad** *a. slang*, nude, unclothed (esp. in *Witchcraft*); **sky-clear** *a.*, clear as the sky; **sky cloth** *Theatr.*, a backcloth painted or coloured to represent the sky (cf. *sky border* above); **sky-clothed** *a.* = *sky-clad* adj. above; **sky-diving,** the sport of parachuting from an aeroplane with a long period of (freq. acrobatic) free fall before the parachute is opened; also as adj., **sky-diver** and (as back-formation) **sky-dive** *v. intr.*; **sky-drop** *Theatr.* = *sky cloth* above; **sky fighter,** an aeroplane or airman that engages in aerial combat; hence **sky-fight; sky filter,** a filter (usu. yellow and denser at the top than at the bottom) for improving the rendering of a bright sky in black and white photography; **sky-fire** (see quot. 1710); **sky-flower,** a shrub or small tree, *Duranta repens*, of the family Verbenaceæ, native to Central and South America and bearing clusters of pale blue flowers followed by yellow berries (cf. pigeon-berry 1); **sky-flyer,** an ambitious person; **sky-gazer** (see quots.); **sky-god** *Religion* and *Mythol.*, a god of or in the sky; also **sky-goddess; skyman** *Journalists' slang*, a paratrooper; **sky-mark,** a thing standing out against the sky (*nonce-use*); **sky-marker** *Mil.*, a parachute flare used by raiding aircraft to mark a target (cf. parachute *sb.* 5); also Comb., as ***sky-marker bomb***; also ***sky-marking***; **sky marshal** *U.S.*, a plain-clothes armed guard on an aeroplane employed to counter hi-jacking; **sky-organ,** the wind (*nonce-use*); **sky-path,** a route taken through the sky, a skyway; **sky pilot** *slang* (see quot. 1893); also, a chaplain in any of the armed forces, prison service, etc., and *gen.*, a priest or parson, a clergyman; **sky-pipit** *U.S.*, = skylark *sb.* 2; **†sky-puppy** (see puppy *sb.* 3c); **†sky race,** in British India, an amateur steeplechase; **sky-ride** *U.S.*, a device for conveying passengers at a considerable height above ground, spec. one at the World Fair at Chicago in 1933–4; **sky screen,** an array of photocells used to record or detect the travel of an aircraft, projectile, etc.; **†sky-setting** *Sc.*, sunset; **sky shade** *Photogr.* (see quots.); **sky-ship,** a very large craft for air or space travel; **sky-shouting,** the sending of advertisements or messages from an aircraft to the ground by means of a loudspeaker; also as adj. and **sky-shouter; sky-stone,** a meteorite; **sky-surfing** *U.S.* = *hang-gliding* s.v. hang-; hence **sky-surfer; skywatch** orig. *U.S.*, the process or activity of watching the sky for aircraft or other phenomena; hence **skywatcher; sky wave,** a radio wave reflected back towards the earth's surface by the ionosphere (cf. *ground wave* s.v. ground *sb.* 18 a).

**1975** L. Dills *CB Slanguage Dict.* 54 **Sky bear*, police helicopter. **1977** *Daily Colonist* (Victoria, B.C.) 3 July 1/2 (*heading*) Sky bear keeps eye on Island's drivers. **1837** MacDougall tr. *Graah's E. Coast Greenl.* 134 This *sky-blink, or ice-blink, as it is usually termed by English navigators, is a whitish luminous appearance seen above ice. **1879** *Cassell's Techn. Educ.* I. 311/2 The aspect of the '*sky-blotch' of an architectural edifice is very important. **1846** G. A. A'Beckett *Quizziology Brit. Drama* 16 Pointing with a property sword to the *sky borders. **1896** W. Archer *Theatr. World of 1895* iv. 28 Above it hang mathematically horizontal 'sky-borders', apparently representing a flat layer of fog in the upper air. **1918** G. B. Shaw in *Nation* 22 June 310/1 The scenery made Old Drury feel young again. Wings, sky-borders, set pieces: nothing was missing. **1950** *Official Gaz.* (U.S. Patent Office) 26 Dec. 1066/2 *Sky Cap. For General Porter Service. **1966** *National Observer* (U.S.) 7 Nov. 6/5 They would reduce the number of Negro 'sky caps' employed at the airport. **1972** T. Kenrick *Tough One to Lose* ii. 33 He took a job as a skycap at the International Airport. **1977** J. Wambaugh *Black Marble* (1978) xv. 342 He spotted a skycap carrying some bags towards the front. **1909** Webster, *Sky-clad. **1970** R. Buckland in K. Singer *Tales from Unknown* 296 Witches always work naked or, as they call it, *skyclad*. **1868** Gladstone *Juv. Mundi* x. (1869) 386 His soul and actions are *sky-clear. **1933** *Sky-cloth [see batten *sb.*¹ 1 b]. **1981** *Times Lit. Suppl.* 4 Sept. 998/3 Instead of a naturalistically painted backcloth he used a plain sheet of colour (what we should call a sky cloth). **1924** Earl of Ronaldshay *India* xxiv. 305 The Digambara, or *sky-clothed ascetic, must live stark naked. **1965** *N.Y. Times* 24 Apr. 21 Mary Cushing..snorkles, surfs, skis and *sky-dives. **1961** *Times* 3 July 6/4 The screech of the *skydiver was heard above Hereford this weekend as..people saw a demonstration of the latest 'official' British Army sport. **1970** *Daily Tel.* 5 Oct. 1/1 Two women sky-divers and a man were injured when they parachuted at 2,500 ft from a De Havilland aircraft..last night. **1979** P. Niesewand *Member of Club* xii. 84 A flypast might be nice. .. How about some sky-divers? Everyone likes them. **1959** *News Chron.* 8 July 4/7 The sport..of '*sky-diving' in which certain adventurous types turn somersaults in the air before opening their parachutes. **1962** *Daily Tel.* 7 Aug. 11/7 A sky-diving team will leave London Airport today..to compete in the sixth world sport parachuting championships. **1979** R. Jaffe *Class Reunion* (1980) II. ix. 275 Apparently she's taken up skydiving... She's going to kill herself. **1901** C. Morris *Life on Stage* xii. 84 In this tableau the circular opening in the flat, backed by a *sky-drop and with blue clouds hanging about the opening, represented heaven. **1969** G. Macbeth *War Quartet* 36 He was dead to this Antarctic *sky-fight. **1937** *Sun* (Baltimore) 2 Mar. 1/3 The first of the army's super *sky-fighters, a four engined Boeing bomber, dropped to a perfect landing on snow-covered Langley Field at 2.09 P.M. today. **1943** R. Whelan *Flying Tigers* ix. 97 George Paxton..moved to break up this shocking attack on a helpless airman, which violated the code of sky fighters. **1930** G. E. Brown *Clerc's Photogr.* xi. 83 *Sky filters are made in the shape of a long rectangle, which is carried in a mount, allowing it to be raised or lowered. **1970** M. J. Sethna *Photogr.* v. 102 Where the sky is light and bright, but the landscape is less bright or is dark, the balance of tones can well be secured through the use of what is known as 'the graduated sky filter'. **1710** P. S. *Wks.* II. 262 *Sky-Fire is that in the Body of the Sun, and other Heavenly Lights. **1906** Sky-fire [see *night-web* s.v. night *sb.* 13 a]. **1938** D. Wyman *Hedges, Screens & Windbreaks* II. 77 Tall Broad-leaved Evergreens... *Duranta plumieri*, *Skyflower. **1971** Sky-flower [see pigeon-berry 1]. **1887** *Daily News* 30 Nov. 3/4 Such a work, by a young *sky-flyer of eighteen. **1854** Badham *Halieut.* 127 The name of this fish, *uranoscopus*, or '*sky-gazer', is derived from the position of the eyes, which are singularly planted on the crown of the head. **1867** Smyth *Sailor's Word-bk.* 630 *Sky-gazer*,..a sail of very light duck, over which un-nameable sails have been set, which defy classification. **1907** H. M. Chadwick *Orig. Eng. Nation* x. 245 On the strength of this passage [in *Gylfaginning*] it has been supposed that Frey was originally a *sky-god or sun-god. **1938** E. Bevan *Symbolism & Belief* ii. 30 The belief in the Sky-God may have, of course, two forms according as the sky itself is personified, is identified with the Person up there, or as the Person is conceived more anthropomorphically. **1948** B. G. M. Sundkler *Bantu Prophets in S. Afr.* i. 24 The lightning-magician, the priest of the sky-god, arrives much sooner..at proficiency in his particular speciality. **1979** *N.Y. Rev. Bks.* 25 Oct. 19/3 Now the Heavenly Father, or Aryan sky-god, is found to be..simply irrelevant. **1959** *New Larousse Encycl. Mythol.* 23/2 *Hathor*... A *sky-goddess, she was originally described as the daughter of Ra and the wife of Horus. **1982** N. Frye *Great Code* iii. 70 Zeus..third in a line of sky-gods. The earth-mother..tends to take on the characteristics of a sky-goddess. **1952** *John o' London's Weekly* 18 Jan. 54/1 The failure of Fleet Street to make paratroopers into *skymen. **1958** *Daily Mail* 18 July 1/2 Skymen saved Hussein's life... But for the arrival of our paratroops yesterday,..Hussein..would almost certainly have been assassinated. **1964** *Sunday Tel.* 14 June 3/4 (*heading*) Skymen hit the target. **1856** Miss Mulock *J. Halifax* (1857) 101 The four tall poplars..were our landmarks, and *skymarks too. **1943** *Times* 31 Dec. 4/6 The Pathfinder force used parachute flares known as '*sky-markers' which drift downwards very slowly, to mark the target area. **1944** *Times* 17 Feb. 4/4 Flak was so violent when the first sky-marker bombs were dropped that it was evident that the main night fighter force was late. **1946** *R.A.F. Jrnl.* May 169 The red, yellow and green T.I.s and the skymarker flares, remained the principal weapons of P.F.F. throughout the war... The 'wanganni' skymarkers went down over Germany and load after load of destruction followed. **1944** R. Dimbleby in *War Report* (B.B.C.) (1946) 281 Our job was to replenish the flares already dropped by the Pathfinders ahead... This was '*sky-marking'. **1968** *Sunday Mail* (Brisbane) 23 June 32/6 He is a member of a new elite breed of law enforcement officers in America—the *sky marshals. His job is to prevent airliner hi-jacking... All the sky marshals are volunteers from the ranks of the F.A.A.'s regular inspectors. **1971** *Daily Colonist* (Victoria, B.C.) 13 Mar. 25/6 A number of women trained in marksmanship and hand-to-hand combat will join the men assigned to the skymarshal force recently created to protect U.S. airliners from hijackers. **1837** Ht. Martineau *Soc. Amer.* II. 20 The next moment, the *sky-organ began to blow in our rigging. **1931** F. Simpich in *Nat. Geogr. Mag.* Jan. 1 (*heading*) *Skypaths through Latin America. **1958** *Times* 27 Oct. 10/1 Nearly 400 Glacier dry bearings assist each Comet 4 on its smooth skypath. **1883** G. W. Peck *Peck's Bad Boy* 177 Look-a-here you *sky-pilot, this thing has gone far enough. **1888** Churchward *Blackbirding* 22 A dock missionary (we called him sky-pilot). **1893** *Spectator* 30 Dec. 952/2 A 'Sky-pilot', in sailor's parlance, is a clergyman generally, and specially a clergyman who has a spiritual charge among seamen. **1910** *Busy Man's Mag.* Mar. 71/1, I was hailed as a 'sky pilot' by the trio and invited to be sociable over a whisky bottle. **1922** Joyce *Ulysses* 305 One or two sky pilots having an eye around that there was no goings on with the females. **1935** Auden & Isherwood *Dog beneath Skin* II. v. 114 Ort ter 'ave bin a sky pilot, you ort! **1973** B. Broadfoot *Ten Lost Years* xii. 140 At the missions you would get a sermon, say 15 minutes of religion from a sky pilot. **1982** *New Scientist* 18 Mar. 740/3 The first issue includes an attack on the accuracy of radiocarbon dating by an English skypilot called Charles Foley. **1884** Coues *N. Amer. Birds* 286 *Neocorys*, *Sky Pipits. **1858** G. F. Atkinson *Curry & Rice* (ed. 2) xviii, The *Sky Races, which to the uninitiated may be explained as a meeting for horses that have enjoyed no specific training beyond what could be accomplished during the interval of the 'get-up' and the 'come-off'. **1885** Lady Dufferin *Jrnl.* 11 June in *Our Viceregal Life in India* (1889) I. iv. 157 The Simla sky races began today. **1933** *Sun* (Baltimore) 22 July 10/3 Two Concordia women, who attended the World's Fair at Chicago recently ventured on the '*sky ride', the device which carries passengers across the grounds at a height of

200 feet. **1966** E. McCullogh *World's Fair Midways* viii. 93 One of the features of the fair [*sc.* Century of Progress Exposition] was the Sky Ride, a monorail structure whose two giant towers stretched up sixty-four stories... They were connected at the twenty-fourth story by cables, from which so-called rocket cars were suspended. **1945** L. E. Simon *German Sci. Establishments* (PB Rep. No. 19849) ii. ii. 48 One thing that was particularly notable was a large number of photoelectric '*sky screens'. **1969** *New Scientist* 2 Oct. 25/3 The accuracy of the sky screens is said to be two metres in azimuth, and 1·5 metres in elevation. **1731** *Gentl. Mag.* I. 31 On the last Monday of Nov. 1730, about *sky setting. **1889** E. J. Wall *Dict. Photogr.* 177 **Sky shade*, a piece of wood or card used to shade the lens during exposure, to prevent reflections from the sky or sun. **1909** G. L. Johnson *Photographic Optics & Colour Photogr.* ii. 152 Skyshades are of great value in colour photography..as without some such screen the skies are invariably spoilt through overexposure. **1930** G. E. Brown *Clerc's Photogr.* xi. 83 The most usual form of commercial sky shade..consists of a uniformly graduated filter of gelatine or glass. **1973** D. A. Spencer *Focal Dict. Photogr. Technol.* 568 *Sky shade*, any form of shield attached to the lens mount for preventing direct rays of the sun reaching the camera lens. In USA, the term is sometimes used as another name for lens hood. **1923** L. Pauer *Day of Judgment* 16 If possible..we are going to board that *sky-ship. **1960** *Analog Science Fact/Fiction* Dec. 10/1 When we first heard of the Sky Ship, we were on an island whose name..was Yarzik. **1975** *Times* 18 Apr. 6/3 The Sky Ship, with a diameter of 30ft and in the shape of a flying saucer..is a scaled-down prototype of a planned vehicle..which will be 700 ft in diameter..able to carry a payload of up to 400 tons. **1932** *Children's Newspaper* 23 Jan. 6/1 The inventor..can now quote terms for Sky Shouting or Sky Advertising. Concerning the *sky-shouters a really alarming invention has been successfully tried. **1932** *Flight* 8 July 638/1 They recommend that *sky-shouting (by means of a loud speaker) should be prohibited by law for all private purposes. **1955** *Times* 9 June 8/2 The withdrawal of the surrender offer was being conveyed to the terrorists by all possible means, including radio and sky-shouting aircraft. **1962** *Engineering* 26 Oct. 564 The practicability of long range speech transmission was seen during British army operations in Malaya when a 'sky-shouting' installation in an aircraft was used for propaganda purposes. **1973** *Times* 15 May 8/4 Last year 2,285 hours were logged by aircraft flying 'sky-shouting' patrols in which recorded propaganda messages were relayed to Africans living in the bush. **1797** Southey *Lett. fr. Spain* (1808) II. 78 Let the heavier *sky-stones come whence they may, these must have been formed in the atmosphere. **1972** *Popular Mechanics* June 102/2 How long a *sky surfer can stay in the air depends on wind strength and skill. **1972** *Popular Sci.* June 94/2 Today's hang-glider pilots like to call their sport '*sky-surfing'. **1974** *Sci. Amer.* Dec. 138/1 The rapidly evolving sport, which is known as sky surfing or hang gliding, makes about equal demands on the enthusiast's skills as a pilot and as an aerodynamicist. **1952** *Sun* (Baltimore) 17 July B7/5 (*heading*) 18,000 in Britain serve on *skywatch. **1958** A. Budrys in Aldiss & Harrison *Decade 1950s* (1976) 68, I made it. Got to this Navy skywatch station. **1972** *Oxford Times* 21 Jan. 3/7 A full house is expected for next week's UFO convention in Banbury... 'Many of those attending are the people who made sightings over North Oxon last year which ended with us having a skywatch, which was unfortunately rained off.' **1973** *Daily Tel.* 30 July 1/5 Skylab, at present, is not visible to British *sky-watchers since its orbital track does not take it over Britain. **1928** Sterling & Kruse *Radio Manual* xiv. 524 The day signal which reappears at 850 miles may be considered the *sky wave. **1944** *Proc. IRE* XXXII. 668/1 Design of directional antennas for broadcast stations to prevent skywave interference to another station. **1971** K. Kent in C. Bonington *Annapurna South Face* 277 The near-link radios had to be h/f sets capable of voice/cw and able to utilize a sky-wave and surface-wave mode of operation.

**sky**, *sb.*² *Orkn.* and *Shetl.* ? *Obs.* [repr. ON. *skeið*: cf. mod.Norw. *skeid* foot of a plough (Aasen).] A small board in the place of a mould-board in a plough.

**1793** *Statist. Acc. Scot.* VII. 585 A square hole is cut through the lower end of the beam, and the *mercal*, a piece of oak about 22 inches long, introduced, which..holds the sock and sky.

**sky** (skaɪ), *sb.*³ *slang.* (See quots.)

**1860** *Slang Dict.* 216 *Sky*, a disagreeable person, an enemy. **1869** Stanley *Westm. Abb.* (ed. 3) 471 The..conflicts between the Westminster scholars and the 'skys' of London, as the outside world was called.

**sky** (skaɪ), *v.*¹ Also skie. [f. sky *sb.*¹]

**1.** *trans.* **a.** *slang.* To throw or toss up (a coin). Also used of other objects, as a hat, etc.; spec. ***to sky the wipe*** Austral. Boxing slang = ***to throw up the sponge*** s.v. sponge *sb.*¹ 1 c.

**1802** Mar. Edgeworth *Irish Bulls* 129 Billy (says I) will you sky a copper? **1860** *Slang Dict.* 216 *Skie*, to throw upwards, to toss 'coppers'. **1872** *Punch* 3 Feb. 53/2 Sufficient for that indeed would have been 'skying a copper'. **1898** A. M. Binstead *Pink 'Un & Pelican* x. 215 He skied his tile in the most approved fashion..literally beaming with good-nature as he shook his jockey by the hand. **1916** C. J. Dennis *Songs of Sentimental Bloke* xi. 87 Fer 'arf a mo' I 'as a fight; Then conscience skies the wipe... Sez I 'Orright'. **1933** *Bulletin* (Sydney) 14 June 27/2 It is generally understood that a boxer must consider himself beaten when his seconds 'sky the wipe'.

**b.** *Cricket.* To strike (a ball) into the air. Also in *Golf*, etc.

**1868** *J. Lillywhite's Cricketers' Compan.* 102 He..sometimes gets deceived by a short one, and 'skies' it. **1873** *Routledge's Young Gentlem. Mag.* 378/1 The ball did not 'travel' on the sand, and when 'skied' was at once secured. **1880** *Times* 28 Sept. 11/5 He skied the ball to cover-point, where it was easily held. **1909** [see fluff *v.*¹ 5 e]. **1922** E. F. Benson *Miss Mapp* iii. 73 Major Flint drove, skying the ball to a prodigious height. **1976** *Morecambe Guardian* 7 Dec. 8/1 Worksop came back into the attack when Wall started a good move but Joe Johnson skied the ball high over.

*absol.* **1882** *Daily Telegr.* 27 May, His eleventh proved disastrous to Abel, who skyed up to Spofforth at point.

**c.** At an auction: to raise the price of (an item) by high bidding; to raise (the bidding) by a considerable amount.

**1892** Stevenson & Osbourne *Wrecker* ix. 146 All of a sudden he appeared as a third competitor, skied the *Flying Scud* with four fat bids of a thousand dollars each, and then as suddenly fled the field. **1928** D. L. Sayers *Ld. Peter views Body* x. 236 Wimsey, entering into the spirit of the thing, skied the bidding with enthusiasm. The dealers,..fancying that there must be some special excellence about the book.., joined in.

**2.** To hang (a picture, etc.) high up on the wall or near the ceiling, *esp.* at an exhibition.

**1865** *Slang Dict.* 233 Artists say that a picture is skyed when it is hung on the upper line at the Exhibition of the Royal Academy. **1882** *Harper's Mag.* Dec. 70/2 Skied up over a door of the hall is the portrait of a..maiden dressed as a shepherdess. **1885** *Truth* 28 May 848/2 A good sea-piece, and one which is undeservedly skied.

*transf.* **1884** *Pall Mall G.* 3 Oct. 3/1 The members of the press are regarded as unwelcome intruders and are shamefully 'skied'.

**3.** To cover like the sky; to overshadow.

**1844** Mrs. Browning *Crowned & Buried* 3 Napoleon!—years ago, and that great word..skied us overhead—An atmosphere whose lightning was the sword.

**4.** To catch sight of (an outline) against the sky.

**1900** H. Lawson *Over Sliprails* 95 He stooped,..with his hands on his knees, to 'sky' the loom of his big shed and so get his bearings.

**5.** *intr.* To paint a sky in a picture. *nonce-use.*

**1862** Thornbury *Turner* I. 139 If any one calls, I can't be seen—I'm skying.

**6.** *Boating.* To lift the blade of an oar too high.

**1883** *Cambridge Staircase* vi. 94 He knows..when men are cocking or skying, or swinging out of or into the boat.

Hence **'skying** *vbl. sb.* (in sense 2).

**1869** *Echo* 23 Jan., In the new rooms a much larger number of pictures will find places... The 'skying' and 'grounding' so much complained of will be avoided.

**sky**, *v.*² [Of doubtful origin; connexion with prec. is not apparent in either sense.]

**1.** *intr.* To run swiftly.

**1837** J. E. Murray *Summer in Pyrenees* II. 153 They sky along, breast high, causing the woods to ring again.

**2.** *trans.* At Harrow: To charge and overthrow in a game of football.

**1905** Vachell *The Hill* iv. 83 Jolly well played, Cæsar!—Sky him!—Well skied, sir!

**sky-**, common ME. var. of ski-.

**'skybald.** *Sc.* and *north. dial.* Forms: 6, 8–9 **skybald**, 6 **schy-**, 9 **skybauld**, **-belt**; 6 **skay-**, **skybell**, 9 **skybal**, **-bel**, **-ble**, **skebal**, **-bel**, **scybel**, **-ble**, etc. [Of obscure origin.] A low, rascally, or contemptible fellow; a lean or worn-out person or animal; a worthless article, etc.

*a* **1572** Knox *Hist. Reform.* Wks. 1848 II. 11 Fy, lett us never leive efter this day, that we sall recule for Frenche schybaldis. **1580** *Extr. Burgh Rec. Glasgow* (1876) I. 77 Geveand to him money iniurius wordis, sick as knayf, skaybell, matteyne, and lowne. *c* **1587** Montgomerie *Sonnets* xxiv, A skurvie skybell for to be eshued. **1728** Ramsay *General Mistake* 154 Poor skybalds! curs'd with more of wealth than wit. **1804** R. Anderson *Cumbld. Ball.* (*c* 1850) 115 Oft did he wish aw sec skeybels were hang'd. **1825–** in *Eng. Dial. Dict.* (Sc. and N. Irel.).

*attrib.* *a* **1585** Polwart *Flyting w. Montgomerie* 126 Learne, skybalde knaue, to knaw thy sell.

**sky-blue**, *sb.* and *a.* [sky *sb.*¹]

**A.** *sb.* **1. a.** A pure blue colour like that of the sky; a fabric of this colour.

**1738** Chambers *Cycl.* s.v. *Dying of silks*, Sky blues are begun with orchal, and finished with indigo. **1778** Mme. D'Arblay *Evelina* (1791) II. 245 He may lay that your nose is a sky-blue, if he pleases. **1840** Thackeray *Shabby-genteel Story* ii, A guitar, with a riband of dirty skyblue. **1899** W. T. Greene *Cage-Birds* 63 Followed by a narrow line of sky-blue.

**b.** Comb., as ***sky-blue-pink***, a fantasy colour. Also as adj. *joc.*

**1942** G. Kersh *Nine Lives Bill Nelson* xi. 66 Bill could swear that black was white, or green was sky-blue-pink. **1967** L. J. Braun *Cat who ate Danish Modern* xv. 131 What colours do you mix to get sky-blue-pink? **1982** S. T. Haymon *Ritual Murder* xvii. 116 Caught him out red-handed... Not to say green and yellow an' sky-blue-pink.

**2.** Thin or watery milk, having a bluish tint.

**1798** Bloomfield *Farmer's Boy* 254 Its name derision and reproach pursue, And strangers tell of 'three times skimm'd sky-blue'. **1827** Hood *Retrospective Review* 68 Oh! for that small, small beer anew! And..that mild sky-blue That wash'd my sweet meals down. **1886** *All Year Round* 14 Aug. 34 'Sky-blue' is not always the result of over-creaming and dilution.

†**3.** *slang.* **a.** Gin. *Obs.*

**1755** *Connoisseur* No. 53 ⁋4 Madam Gin has been christened by as many names as a German princess; every petty chandler's shop will sell you Sky-blue. **1796** in *Grose's Dict. Vulgar T.*

**b.** Barley broth (*Naut.*); any vegetable soup.

**1887** S. Samuels *Forecastle to Cabin* iv. 53 Sky-blue (boiled barley), hard tack, and tea sweetened with treacle was Jack's fare for the morning meal. **1908** J. M. Sullivan *Criminal Slang* 23 *Sky-blue*, vegetable soup. **1910** H. Y. Moffat *Ship's Boy to Skipper* xiii. 204 Once a week we had for dinner what we called 'Sky Blue'. It was made by putting a small quantity of barley into a large quantity of water.

**B.** *adj.* Of the blue colour of the sky; azure.

**1728** Chambers *Cycl.* s.v. *Silver*, The Spirit of Wine assumes a beautiful Sky-blue Colour. **1773** M. Browne *Pisc. Eclog.* viii. 117 'Twas there gay Phylla..Glanc'd the soft passion from her sky-blue eye. **1821** R. Turner *Arts* 235 The lapis lazuli is of a beautiful sky-blue colour. **1888** *Truth* XXIV. 99/2 The carriage..is in sky-blue plush and silver.

**Skybus** ('skaɪbʌs). *U.S.* Also **skybus, sky bus.** [sky *sb.*¹] **1.** The proprietary name of a regular air service for which passengers need not book in advance. Cf. skytrain 2.

**1945** *Aviation* Feb. 132 Douglas Skybus. Designed for feeder line operations, seating 24 passengers. **1966** *Official Gaz.* (U.S. Patent Office) 8 Feb. TM 65/1 New York Airways, Inc... *Skybus* for air service for passengers, mail, and freight. First use Oct. 15, 1952. **1972** *Times* 28 Sept. 1/1 Trans International Airlines today proposed to the Civil Aeronautics Board a daily New York to London 'sky bus' service at a fare of $75. **1977** *Time* 10 Oct. 5/1 Trans International Airlines..borrowed a leaf from Laker's book and last month proposed a 'Skybus' service from the U.S. to Tokyo and Hong Kong.

**2.** (See quots.)

**1966** *Daily Tel.* 21 Apr. 16/4 (*caption*) In Pittsburgh..tests are being carried out with a Skybus... The bus itself is a lightweight aluminium car with light rubber wheels, which run on two small concrete rails. It picks up current from a centre beam. **1967** *Guardian* 2 Feb. 3/3 Westinghouse Electric Corporation, of Pittsburgh..have developed a driverless 'skybus' for the US Government... The skybus is a cross between a bus and a train and can run in tunnels, on the ground, or elevated.

**sky-colour.** [sky *sb.*¹] A (blue) colour like that of the sky. Also as *adj.*, = next.

**1552** Elyot, *Cærulus & Cæruleus*, blewe of colour lyke the skye in a clere wether, skie colour. *a* **1586** Sidney *Arcadia* i. xii. (1891) 50b, Vpon her bodie she ware a doublet of skie colour sattin. **1594** T. B. *La Primaud. Fr. Acad.* ii. 71 For this cause some are red, others yellow, these greene, those skie-color, others gray, or blew. **1631** Widdowes *Nat. Philos.* 24 It is of a greene, yellow, and a skye colour. *a* **1691** Boyle *Hist. Air* (1692) 149 Within an hour..the sky-colour reached to the lower part of the liquor. **1771** *Encycl. Brit.* II. 962/1 Dying of Leather... A pure sky colour. **1865** Swinburne *Chastelard* i. ii. 39 They say men dying remember..Some garment or sky-colour. **1889** Jefferies *Field & Hedgerow* 21 The innumerable other flowers and wings and sky-colours.

**sky-coloured,** *a.* [sky *sb.*¹] Of the (blue) colour of the sky.

**1585** T. Washington tr. *Nicholay's Voy.* iv. xxxvi. 160b, The tulbant of the merchant must be skie coloured. **1614** Sylvester *Bethulia's Rescue* iv. 59 Her Robe, Sky-colour'd Silk, with curious Caul Of golden Twist. **1668** H. More *Div. Dial.* iii. xxviii. (1713) 251 The Figure thereof was..drawn with Lines of a Sky-coloured blew. **1769** *De Foe's Tour Gt. Brit.* (ed. 7) II. 189 They wore a Sky-coloured Habit after the Manner of the Hermits. **1827** Griffith tr. *Cuvier* V. 214 The Sky-coloured Rat of Pennant.

**Skye** (skaɪ). [Gaelic *Sgith* (skiː), recorded in OIcel. as *Skíð*.] **a.** The name of the largest island of the Inner Hebrides used attributively, esp. in ***Skye terrier***, a small breed of dog, long-haired, long-bodied, and short-legged.

**1847** H. D. Richardson *Dogs* vii. 71 The Skye Terrier, so called from its being found in greatest perfection in the Western Isles of Scotland, and the Isle of Skye in particular. **1856** 'Stonehenge' *Brit. Rural Sports* iv. ii. i. 571/1 In shape he is more like the English than the Skye variety. *Ibid.* 571/2 The Skye dog. **1871** M. Collins *Marq. & Merch.* II. x. 290 A blue Skye-terrier lay on his back. **1971** F. Hamilton *World Encycl. Dogs* 478 The show Skye Terrier's profuse, well groomed coat.., its veil of thick hair shielding fore-face, and the silky feathering of ears and tail, are not attained and maintained without considerable trouble.

**b.** *ellipt.* A Skye terrier.

**1851** Mayhew *Lond. Lab.* II. 53/1 A small Isle of Skye terrier—but few, I was informed, know a 'real Skye'. **1863** Ouida *Held in Bondage* (1870) 40 A setter, a retriever, and a couple of Skyes, were on the hearthrug.

**skyer** ('skaɪə(r)). Also **skier.** [f. sky *v.*¹ + -er.] A lofty hit at cricket.

**1853** *Bell's Life in London* 24 July 6/2 Mr Walker gave a few 'skyers' in scoring 20, for which number he brought out his bat. **1867** *Australasian* 26 Jan. 107/4 Fowler hit a skyer to leg, no one in the road. **1882** *Daily Telegr.* 12 June, Being grandly caught from a skyer behind the wickets. **1883** F. M. Peard *Contrad.* xxi, You should have seen Henderson caught at slip from a 'skyer'. **1893** *Times* 12 July 11/5 The fieldsman soon had the satisfaction of seeing the batsman..taken at mid-on from a skier.

**skyer**, obs. form of squire *sb.*

**skyey** ('skaɪɪ), *a.* Also 7 **skyie**, 8–9 **skiey.** [f. sky *sb.*¹ + -(e)y.]

**1.** Of or pertaining to the sky; emanating from the sky: **a.** In the phr. ***skyey influence***(*s*), due to Shakspere.

α. **1603** Shaks. *Meas. for M.* iii. i. 9 A breath thou art, Seruile to all the skyie-influences. **1799** *Spirit Public Jrnls.* III. 129 Subject to the 'skiey influences'. **1832** Lytton *Eugene Aram* iii. ii, The skiey influences seem to tincture the animal life with their own..spirit of change. **1851** *Illustr. Lond. News* 18 Oct. 491/3 The skiey influences were decidedly sympathetic.

β. **1820** Scott *Monast.* xix, Upon whose complexion the 'skyey influences'..had blended the red and white into the purely nut-brown hue. **1847** Miller *First Impr. Eng.* viii. (1857) 123, I was eager to ascertain whether it had not stood its testing century better under the skyey influences. **1882** C. F. KEARY *Prim. Belief* 128 Almost all the Vedic hymns are concerned with the skyey influences.

**b.** In other contexts. Also, lofty.

*a.* ?**1793** COLERIDGE *Lines on Autumn. Evening* 74 The skiey deluge, and white lightnings glare. **1814** CARY *Dante, Purg.* III. 28 In the skiey element One ray obstructs not other. **1885–94** R. BRIDGES *Eros & Psyche* Aug. xxviii, From their skiey haunt Fell to their feast the great birds bald and gaunt.

*β.* **1818** KEATS *Endym.* IV. 558 No charm Could lift Endymion's head, or he had view'd A skyey mask. **1826** H. N. COLERIDGE *Six Months in W. Ind.* (1832) 167 The mountains..are of skyey height. **1887** T. HARDY *Woodlanders* I. xiii. 234 Beside him sat Marty, also straining her eyes towards the skyey field of his operations.

**2.** Resembling the sky in colour; azure.

**1816** SOUTHEY *Lay of Laureate* lxx, A virgin clad in skiey blue. *a* **1851** MOIR *Poems* (1852) II. 305 Skiey robes, The tincture of the young Year's finest blue. **1884** *Harper's Mag.* Aug. 392/1 The soft skyey tone of the turquoise.

*Comb.* **1797** WALDRON *Virg. Queen* IV. i, Apt to soil our skiey-tinctur'd wings.

**sky-farmer.** [SKY *sb.*$^1$]

†**1.** *Cant.* (See quots.) *Obs.*

**1753** *Disc. J. Poulter* (ed. 2) 36 Sky Farmers, are People that go about the Country with a false Pass,..under Pretence of sustaining Loss by Fire, or the Distemper amongst the horned Cattle. **1756** *Gentl. Mag.* XXVI. 566 A set of cheats who..impose on the benevolence and compassion of the charitable; these are called sky-farmers. **1785** GROSE *Dict. Vulgar T.*, *Sky-farmers*, cheats who pretend they were farmers in the isle of sky, or some other remote place,..or else called sky farmers, from their farms being in..the clouds.

**2.** In Ireland, a contemptuous name for a class of tenant-farmers.

**1763** *Museum Rust.* I. 8 The sky-farmers (those who hold at rack-rents) are mostly so greedy for gain, that [etc.]. *Ibid.* 371 Of late years the hard-hearted sky-farmers, that is, the inferior sort,..drive the poor into the mountains. **1780** YOUNG *Tour Irel.* I. 73 The sky farmers,..that is the petty ones, let potatoe ground. **1910** P. W. JOYCE *English in Ireland* 326 *Sky farmer*, a term much used in the South.., is a farmer without land, or with only very little.

**skyful.** Also sky-ful, -full. [SKY *sb.*$^1$] As much, or as many, as the sky can hold.

**1649** BP. REYNOLDS *Hosea* vi. 99 Contented to part with a skie-full of Starrs for one Sunne. **1874** T. HARDY *Far fr. Mad. Crowd* I. xxviii. 309 A firmament of light,..resembling a sky-full of meteors close at hand. **1910** KIPLING *Rewards & Fairies* 152 Presently I heard guns... I stopped fiddling to listen, and I heard a whole skyful o' French up in the fog. **1966** D. VARADAY *Gara-Yaka's Domain* xiii. 146 They slept under the trees, with a skyful of stars for their blankets.

**sky-gazer**: see SKY *sb.*$^1$ 9.

**sky-high**, *adv.* and *a.* [SKY *sb.*$^1$]

**A.** *adv.* As high as the sky; very high. Freq. *fig.* Also in phr. ***to blow sky-high***; *fig.*, to refute utterly; = EXPLODE *v.* 3.

**1818** LADY MORGAN *Autobiog.* (1859) 208 Opinions which would make the bench of bishops jump sky-high! **1840** R. H. DANA *Bef. Mast* xviii, We..should probably have been knocked to pieces and blown sky-high. **1845** A. JACKSON *Let.* 6 June in M. James *A. Jackson* (1937) xxiii. 498 Put your veto upon them both, or you and your Secretary will be blown sky high. **1887** SIMS *Mary Jane's Mem.* 62 Always up sky-high or down in the dumps. **1948** *Daily Tel.* 29 May 2/6 [He] blew sky-high the complacent superstition of a wartime 'renaissance'. **1951** N. MITFORD *Blessing* I. viii. 83 At this dinner Grace's preconceived ideas about the French..were blown sky high. **1955** *Times* 26 May 3/3 Matters which had been put forward in the course of that case had either fallen by the wayside or had been blown 'sky-high'.

**B.** *adj.* Reaching to the sky. Also *fig.*, very high.

**1840** CARLYLE *Heroes* i. (1904) 39 Utgard with its skyhigh gates..had gone to air. **1959** *Times* 7 Sept. 11/6 The current miracle of labour-saving flats, sky-high wages, and welfare state. **1975** A. BERGMAN *Hollywood & Le Vine* (1976) v. 67 We don't pay writers whatever sky-high figures their agents talk them into demanding.

**sky-hook.** Also sky hook, skyhook. [SKY *sb.*$^1$]

**1. a.** orig. *Aeronaut.* An imaginary contrivance for attachment to the sky; an imaginary means of suspension in the sky.

**1915** *Aeroplane* 10 Mar. 222 The battery signaller sent a message: 'Battery out of action for an hour, remain aloft awaiting orders.' Back came the reply with remarkable promptitude: 'Submitted; that this machine is not fitted with sky-hooks.' **1933** *Ibid.* 11 Jan. 47/1 They [*sc.* slots] have in fact been used as..sky-hooks on the wing tips. **1948** *Register* Sept. 262 Mr. Shaw's plea..is, at bottom, a plea for a skyhook. For that common agreement which it assumes hung from a skyhook and was broken when we severed it from its support. **1960** R. W. MARKS *Dymaxion World of B. Fuller* 28/1 With each thrust of his wings, the duck generates a momentary vacuum sky-hook above each wing. **1970** D. WATERFIELD *Continental Waterboy* i. 6, I..was prepared to..fetch him a left-handed wrench, a skyhook, anything.

**b.** Applied to various devices or craft capable of lifting something into the air, as: a hook on an aircraft; an aerial cableway; a balloon, helicopter, etc., designed for lifting. orig. *U.S.*

**1935** MEIER & LINDBERGH in *Sci. Monthly* (N.Y.) Jan. 5 An instrument new to transatlantic airplanes..which, being untried, was noncommitally called the 'sky hook'. **1945** *Collier's Mag.* 27 Jan. 38/4 He tried building a model of one of these seed pods, blowing it up to the size of a man and loading its hollow container with cargo. It spiraled down vertically and could safely bring 100 pounds to earth from any height... The device, now nicknamed the 'skyhook', is fluttering down on many Allied battlefields. **1949** *Sun* (Baltimore) 13 Aug. 12/3 That long renowned but hitherto incredible gadget, the sky-hook, is now a reality... It is known as 'The Aerial Track Airport: a cable runway for landing and launching airplanes'. **1951** *N.Y. Times* 13 Feb. 1/7 The balloons, called skyhooks by the Navy researchers, were released at many points in the country. **1966** *Science* 11 Feb. 682 (*heading*) Satellite elongation into a true 'sky-hook'. **1970** [see *dogman* s.v. DOG *sb.* 20a]. **1982** *Monitor* (McAllen, Texas) 25 Mar. 1-A/1 The shuttle's robot arm lifted a space environment monitor out of the payload bay today in an important 'first' that proved the remotely controlled skyhook will be able to launch satellites.

**2.** *Mountaineering.* A hook fixed into a rock-face, from which ropes, etc., may depend.

**1957** *Appalachia* 15 Dec. 452 On the one occasion when I carried a 'skyhook' among my pitons I was no less than delighted to find it really could be used to circumvent the placing of a bolt. **1968** P. CREW *Encycl. Dict. Mountaineering* 108/2 *Sky-hook*..consists of a flattened hook of high quality steel... Sky-hooks have a small eye, to which a sling and étrier can be attached... They are particularly useful on loose flakes..which would probably break off if a piton was used. **1976** [see RURP].

**skyhoot**, *v.* ? Fanciful perversion of SCOOT *v.* Freq. as pres. pple.

**1888** *Boy's Own Paper* Summer 38/1 Something's sky-hooted in my shoulder... That brute threw me on my head. **1900** H. F. DAY *Up in Maine* 56 That air pessle..come sky-hootin' like a ten-inch bomb. **1911** [see LICKETY *adv.*]. **1928** E. WALLACE *Double* i. 7 Why I'm sky-hooting down to Brighton for two days, heaven knows!

**skyish** ('skaɪɪʃ), *a.* [f. SKY *sb.*$^1$ + -ISH.]

**1.** Lofty; approaching the sky.

**1602** SHAKS. *Ham.* v. i. 276 To o're top old Pelion, or the skyish head Of blew Olympus. [**1816** BYRON *Let. to Moore* 5 Jan., The skyish top of blue Olympus.] **1844** *Blackw. Mag.* LVI. 78 The distant spires Of skyish hills.

**2.** Resembling that of the sky.

**1818** LD. JEFFREY *Let. to C. Wilkes* 5 Aug., The whole landscape took a strange silvery skyish tint.

**skyjack** ('skaɪdʒæk), *v.* Also sky-jack. [f. SKY *sb.*$^1$ + HI)JACK *v.*] *trans.* To hijack (an aeroplane). Also const. *to* (a destination).

**1961** *N.Y. Mirror* 10 Aug. 1 (*heading*) Pan Am Jet skyjacked to Havana. **1968** *Tel.* (Brisbane) 13 Mar. 24/7 Over the years scores of light planes, in addition to larger passenger airliners, have been skyjacked and flown to Cuba. **1970** *Time* 12 Oct. 38/3 Aboard the plane was Leila Khaled, 24, the Palestinian guerrilla who attempted to skyjack an El Al airliner over Britain last month. **1971** *Daily Tel.* 1 Feb. 20/3 Sentence of death on a Lithuanian..for trying to skyjack a Soviet airliner to Sweden, has been commuted. **1977** *Whitaker's Almanack 1978* 604/2 A Russian engineer who skyjacked a Soviet airliner surrendered to Swedish police when the plane landed at Stockholm.

Hence **'skyjacked** *ppl. a.*, **'skyjacking** *vbl. sb.*

**1961** *N.Y. Mirror* 5 Aug. 3 (*heading*) Rush stiff skyjacking law. **1969** *Daily Tel.* 1 Nov. 1/1 All air traffic was warned..to avoid the sky-jacked airliner as special preparations were made at Shannon Airport to receive the Trans-World airliner. **1977** D. E. WESTLAKE *Nobody's Perfect* (1978) 227 Listen to this. We fake a skyjacking, but what we *really* do—.

**skyjack** ('skaɪdʒæk), *sb.* [f. the vb.] An instance of skyjacking.

**1968** *Tel.* (Brisbane) 13 Mar. 24/7 In the third skyjack in 16 days, a U.S. National Airlines DC8 with 59 people aboard landed at Havana, Cuba, today. **1969** *Cavalier Daily* (Univ. Va.) 5 Feb., United Airlines Tuesday reported an unsuccessful skyjack attempt. **1975** A. OSMOND *Saladin!* I. v. 39 The wars and the riots, the skyjacks and terrorists' bombs. **1978** R. JANSSON *News Caper* iv. 46 This is a skyjack. We have a hostage at either end of the plane.

**skyjacker** ('skaɪˌdʒækə(r)). Also sky-jacker. [f. SKY *sb.*$^1$ + HI)JACKER.] One who hijacks an aeroplane.

**1961** *N.Y. Mirror* 4 Aug. 1 (*caption*) JFK directed capture of skyjackers. **1970** *Pacifist* Sept. 5/2 The death of hostages will not necessarily lead to the release of..the woman sky-jacker, Leila Khaled. **1976** P. HENISSART *Winter Quarry* ix. 91 You're probably a skyjacker or a bigamist on the run. **1982** *Daily Tel.* 24 July 4/6 The skyjackers..were said to have threatened crew members.

**skyke**, variant of SKICK *v. Obs.*

**Skylab** ('skaɪlæb). [f. SKY *sb.*$^1$ + LAB *sb.*$^2$] The name of a space laboratory launched into earth orbit by the U.S. in 1973. Freq. *attrib.* Occas. (with small initial) in *gen.* use.

The laboratory itself was more precisely designated *Skylab 1*; *Skylabs 2, 3,* and *4* were the spacecraft which successively ferried crews to it. The laboratory was manned until 1974, and disintegrated in the atmosphere in 1979.

**1970** *Nature* 13 June 1001/2 There are now only four journeys to the Moon before autumn 1972 when the engineers at the Cape and in Houston turn their attention to the Skylab programme—the renamed Apollo applications programme. *Ibid.* 22 Aug. 774/1 Cancelling two of the [Apollo] flights so as to conserve the Saturn V launcher vehicles for ambitions nearer home, such as Skylab and the space station project. **1972** *Daily Progress* (Charlottesville, Va.) 19 Jan. B9/8 The first three-man crew is scheduled to spend 28 days aboard the Skylab mission starting next May. **1973** *Guardian* 11 Apr. 4/3 Preparations are precisely on schedule at Cape Kennedy for the launching on May 14 of Skylab-1, the first US experimental space station. **1975** *McGraw-Hill Yearbk. Sci. & Technol.* 43 With the recovery of the *Skylab 4* command module and crew on Feb. 8, 1974, the active operational phase of the Skylab Program was brought to a successful conclusion. **1979** *Guardian* 12 July 1/8 Skylab fell to earth last night... Its debris scattered into the sea and on to a sparsely inhabited Australian desert. **1982** M. DUKE *Flashpoint* xiii. 98 Scientifically equipped satellites and sky labs.

**skylark** ('skaɪlɑːk), *sb.* [SKY *sb.*$^1$]

**1.** The common lark of Europe, *Alauda arvensis*, so called from its habit of soaring towards the sky while singing.

**1686** R. BLOME *Gentlem. Recreat.* II. *Fowling* xxxi. 168 The Sky-Lark is more hardy than the Wood-Lark, and less troublesom to keep. **1754** GRAY *Pleasure* 13 The Sky-lark warbles high His trembling thrilling ecstacy. **1802** MONTAGU *Ornith.* s.v., It has been asserted that the Sky Lark never perches. **1833** TENNYSON *Miller's Dau.* 40 Some wild skylark's matin song. **1876** SMILES *Sc. Natur.* vii. (ed. 4) 128 After the Skylark and Blackbird have heralded the coming day.

**2.** *U.S.* The Missouri pipit, *Anthus* or *Neocorys spraguei*; the prairie lark or sky pipit.

**1872** COUES *Birds N.W.* 42 The Missouri Skylark..is one of the most abundant and characteristic birds of all the region along the forty-ninth parallel of latitude.

**3.** With initial capital in catch-phr. ***any more for the Skylark?*** (from a boatman's cry at seaside resorts), used to offer an open invitation, usu. for a ride or lift.

**1931** M. ALLINGHAM *Look to Lady* x. 107 What a good job there's no more for the Skylark... I love riding in other people's motor-cars. **1977** E. DEWHURST *Curtain Fall* v. 46 You hoping for a lift, Miss Rhoda?.. Come along, then, ducky. Any more for the *Skylark*?

**skylark** ('skaɪlɑːk), *v.* [f. prec.: see the vbl. sb., quots. 1815–19.]

**1.** *intr.* **a.** To frolic or play; to play tricks; to indulge in rough sport or horse-play. In early use chiefly *Naut.*

**1809** *Naval Chron.* XXI. 84 By kicking R. Nelson.., when 'skylarking'. **1835** MARRYAT *J. Faithful* xxxviii, Every evening the hands were turned up to skylark, that is, to play and amuse themselves. **1857** S. OSBORN *Quedah* iv. 51 My Malays skylarked, joked, and played about. **1872** W. BLACK *Adv. Phaeton* xxii, The chief administrator of justice..was up here skylarking in a phaeton.

**b.** With *it*: (See quot.)

**1822** W. IRVING *Braceb. Hall* v. 46 Listening to a lady amateur skylark it up and down through the finest bravura of Rossini or Mozart.

**2.** *trans.* **a.** To trick, cheat.

**1824** SCOTT *St. Ronan's* v, 'I'll fly a cheque on Meiklewham.' 'See it be better than your last,' said Sir Bingo, 'for I won't be skylarked again'.

**b.** To leap in a frolicsome manner.

**1825** HONE *Every-day Bk.* I. 292, I begin skylarking the gates and setting into wind to follow the foxhounds.

Hence **'skylarking** *vbl. sb.* and *ppl. a.*; also **'skylarker**, (*a*) one who skylarks; † (*b*) *Cricket* = SKYER (*Obs.*).

**1809** *Naval Chron.* XXI. 84 An admonition against 'skylarking'. **1815** BURNEY *Falconer's Dict. Marine* 484 *Skylarking*, a term used by seamen, to denote wanton play about the rigging, and tops, or in any part of the ship, particularly by the youngsters. **1819** *Metropolis* II. 204, I heard [him] say to a friend, 'I say Baronet, let us have a *lark*'. I asked our Scapegrace..what this meant? He told me that it was a term in low life, for kicking up a *row*,..at break of day; it being the short term for *sky-larking*. **1829** MARRYAT *F. Mildmay* iv, Fond of displaying my newly-acquired gymnastics, called by the sailors 'sky larking'. **1839** *Bell's Life* 30 June 4/1 Wells..soon retired, giving a 'skylarker', which Button caught. **1889** GRETTON *Memory's Harkback* 76 Sundry fast sky-larkers amused themselves with horse-racing. *Ibid.* 221 To the wonderment of the citizens, the skylarking barrister drops down upon them as the Simeonite Vicar of St. Peter's.

**skyle**, obs. form of SKILL *sb.*

**'skyless**, *a.* [f. SKY *sb.*$^1$] Without visible sky; dark, cloudy.

**1848** KINGSLEY *Yeast* i, A soulless, skyless, catarrhal day. **1871** *Athenæum* 9 Sept. 337 A large boundless sea, skyless and sunless. **1888** GISSING *Life's Morning* III. xxii. 208 In what black, skyless, leafless town was she pursuing her lonely life?

**skylight** ('skaɪlaɪt), *sb.* Also sky-light.

**1. a.** Light from the sky; light coming into a room, etc., from above.

**1679** MOXON *Mech. Exerc.* ix. 152 It being intended that a Skie-light shall fall through the Hollow Newel upon the Stairs. **1683** —— *Mech. Exerc., Printing* ii. ¶ 1 Not..so low that the Sky-light will not reach into every part of the Room. **1780** JOHNSON *Lett. to Mrs. Thrale* 1 May, The pictures, for the sake of a sky-light, are at the top of the house. **1781** *Phil. Trans.* LXXII. 96 *note*, I found, that I could..perceive a bright object, such as white paper, against the sky-light. **1879** TYNDALL *Fragm. Sci.* (ed. 6) I. iv. 110, I now..direct attention to..the polarisation of skylight.

†**b.** *Sc.* The light of the night-sky. *Obs.*

**1730** in Marshall *Hist. Scenes Perthshire* (1880) 199 It [a ghost] appeared to me again, just after daylight, betwixt day and skylight.

**c.** = DAYLIGHT 3 b. ? *Obs.*

**1816** T. L. PEACOCK *Headlong Hall* v, Push about the bottle:..No heel-taps. As to sky-light, liberty-hall. **1824** SCOTT *St. Ronan's* x, Come, Mick, no skylights—here is Clara's health.

**2.** A small opening in a roof, or in the ceiling of a room, filled in with glass, for admitting daylight; the framework and glass fitted to an opening of this kind.

**1690** C. Nesse *Hist. & Myst. O. & N. Test.* I. 111 For the finishing of its roof and sky-light. **1707** J. Stevens tr. *Quevedo's Com. Wks.* (1709) 257 A Sky-light that was over a Kitchen. **1774** *Phil. Trans.* LXV. 113 The second and third rooms were square, and both furnished with a sky-light. **1834** Marryat *P. Simple* (1863) 239, I smelt a very strong smell, blowing in at the weather port, and coming down the skylight which was open. **1886** *Manch. Exam.* 9 Jan. 5/5 The *débris* fell with a crash through a skylight into the offices below.

*transf.* and *fig.* **1833** M. Scott *Tom Cringle* iii, His other skylight had been shut up ever since Aboukir. **1871** R. H. Hutton *Theol. Ess.* I. 13 Skylights opened to let in upon human nature an infinite dawn from above.

**3.** A light in the sky; a rocket.

**1898** T. Hardy *Wessex Poems* 70 Three sky-lights then from the girdling trine Told 'Ready!'

**4.** Special Comb.: **skylight filter**, a pale filter for use when taking colour photographs to counter excessive blueness from skylight.

**1955** G. R. Sharp tr. *Lorelle's Colour Bk. Photogr.* 77 A pale yellow haze or skylight filter may be desirable for shots of people or groups in the shade under a blue sky. **1965** *Focal Encycl. Photogr.* I. 615/2 General correction filters for colour include haze and skylight filters, which mainly absorb ultraviolet and a certain amount of blue light. **1978** *SLR Camera* Sept. 45/1 In addition to performing this very useful warming task, the Skylight filter also gets rid of a lot of UV and gives a mild degree of haze penetration.

Hence **'skylight** *v. trans.*, to furnish with a skylight or skylights; **'skylighted** *ppl. a.*, furnished with a skylight or skylights; lighted from above; **'skylighty** *a.*, having the characteristics of being lighted from above.

**1837** Dickens *Pickw.* xiii, If the Buffs proposed to new sky-light the market-place, the Blues..denounced the proceeding. **1848** *Man in Moon* III. 248 Perhaps you may know the room—large, square, skylighty. **1849** Dickens *Dav. Copp.* (1850) xxiii. 246 The sky-lighted offices of Spenlow and Jorkins. **1880** L. Wallace *Ben Hur* 136 As these were now raised, the compartment had the appearance of a skylighted hall. **1884** *Athenæum* 29 Mar. 410/2 The mezzanine floor and skylighted gallery..will be devoted to the Department of Prints and Drawings.

**sky-like,** *a.* [sky *sb.*[1]] Resembling the sky in colour or shape.

**1591** Sylvester *Du Bartas* I. iii. 912 The sky-like Turquez, purple Amethists. **1649** Lovelace *Ode to Lucasta, The Rose* i, Sweet serene skye-like Flower. **1652** Bp. Hall *Invis. World* II. §5 Some glister with a sky like, others with a star-like, clearness. **1822** Milman *Martyr of Antioch* 136 Down through the round and sky-like dome.

**sky-line.** [sky *sb.*[1]] **1. a.** The line where earth and sky meet; the horizon. Also, the representation of this in painting or another art.

**1824** Scott *St. Ronan's* I. iv. 84 Some boy's daubing, I suppose... Eh! What..is this?.. Who can this be?.. Do but see the sky-line—why, this is.. an exquisite little bit. **1849** Lytton *Caxtons* III. xiv. ii. 10 Seeing only the roof of that palace boldly breaking the sky-line, how serene your contemplations! **1860** G. H. K. *Vac. Tour* 126 The blue hare ..running up hill, and seating himself on the sky-line. **1871** Whyte Melville *Sarchedon* 23 The sun was sinking.. behind the level sky-line of the desert. **1897** Mary Kingsley *W. Africa* 384. I see two lumps of land on the sky-line.

**b.** The outline or silhouette of a building or number of buildings or other objects seen against the sky.

**1896** G. B. Shaw in *Sat. Rev.* 10 Oct. 386/2 A tall and beautiful figure, rising like a delicate spire above a skyline of city chimney-pots. **1928** *Daily Mail Year Bk.* 48/1 A traveller returning to the metropolis after some years' absence has difficulty in recognising some of our famous streets; the sky-line is different, salients have disappeared. **1932** *News Chron.* 5 July 9/5 The city's skyline of roofs was silhouetted against a blaze of gold. **1962** *Economist* 27 Oct. 347/1 The decision to free London from the sixty-year-old 100-foot ceiling which cramped ground space and deadened the skyline. **1971** P. Gresswell *Environment* 230 Consideration of skylines should be one of the prerequisites of planning.

**2.** *Forestry.* An overhead cable for the transport of logs.

**1925** A. Philip *Crimson West* 144 Preparing the spar-tree for 'high-lead' or 'sky-line' rigging, is the most spectacular and thrilling performance in the logging industry. **1942** R. L. Haig-Brown *Timber* 254 In the case of a yarder the sky line is the same as the main-line, going from the spar tree through a block attached to a tree stump at the back of the setting. **1958** W. F. McCulloch *Woods Words* 168 Perhaps the first skyline in the Northwest was rigged by Bob Barr at the Bridal Veil Lumber Company in Oregon in 1899. **1963** *Press* (Vancouver) Apr. 9 There's where the donkeys puff and strain As they pull the logs on the road And the skyline moans, as if in pain As it bears its heavy load.

Hence **'skylined** *ppl. a.*, visible or silhouetted on the skyline.

**1946** G. Millar *Horned Pigeon* ii. 33 We heard trucks behind us. When we dropped flat we saw them sky-lined. **1969** 'J. Fraser' *Cock-pit of Roses* xvi. 126 Out past the hedge you'll be sky-lined, flashing like neon. **1978** L. Heren *Growing up on The Times* v. 170 The bear was briefly skylined on another false crest, and I fired..and finally killed it.

**skylit** ('skaɪlɪt), *ppl. a.* [Pa. pple. of skylight *v.*] = skylighted *ppl. a.*

**1923** A. E. Housman *Shropshire Lad* xli. 62 And like a skylit water stood The bluebells in the azured wood. **1978** *Jrnl. R. Soc. Arts* CXXVI. 237/2 It occupies eight of the Royal Academy skylit galleries. **1979** *United States 1980/81* (Penguin Travel Guides) 191 Rooms full of medieval and Renaissance art,..ranged around a skylit, plant-filled courtyard.

**skyll,** obs. f. skill; obs. var. skull, basket.

**Skylon, skylon** ('skaɪlɒn). *Archit.* [f. sky *sb.*[1], prob. after pylon.] The name of a spindle-shaped filigree spire, illuminated at night, forming a prominent feature of the South Bank exhibition at the Festival of Britain in 1951. Also used *transf.* of other similar structures.

**1950** *Times* 11 Nov. 4/4 Mrs. A. G. S. Fidler, the wife of the chief architect to the Crawley Development Corporation, was informed yesterday that her suggestion of the name of 'Skylon' for the vertical feature of the Festival of Britain exhibition had been accepted. **1951** *John o' London's Weekly* 11 May 280/2 Skylon..denoting something streamlined and precariously poised. **1959** I. & P. Opie *Lore & Lang. Schoolch.* ix. 169 The term Skylon.. was found two years later [*sc.* after the Festival of Britain] to be a name for the lanky not only in London but as far away as Ruthin. **1961** *Daily Tel.* 9 Nov. 28/5 The centrepiece of decoration is, perhaps, a gold skylon on the road from the airport [in Accra]. **1966** *Guardian* 5 Nov. 7/5 There is an elegant skylon with a revolving restaurant on top. **1977** *Times* 9 Feb. 16/3 Dominating the exhibition will be a Skylon-type structure recalling the Festival of Britain.

**skymer(e, skymour,** obs. ff. skimmer *sb.*

**skyn,** variant of skeen.

**skynd,** variant of schynd *Obs.*

**skynes, skynnes** = *kinnes*: see kin *sb.*[1] 6b.

**sky-parlour.** [sky *sb.*[1]]

**1.** An attic, a garret.

**1785** Grose *Dict. Vulgar T.*, *Sky parlour*, the garret, or upper story. **1805** *Naval Chron.* XIII. 7, I remained six weeks in this Sky parlour. **1859** W. Collins *Q. of Hearts* (1875) 14 The necessary order was also despatched to the carpenter and glazier to set them at work on Morgan's sky-parlour in the seventh story.

**2.** The gallery in a theatre.

**1807–8** W. Irving *Salmag.* (1824) 27 The advice so often given by the illustrious tenants of the theatrical sky-parlour.

**skyphos** ('skaɪfɒs). *Gr. Antiq.* [Gr. σκύφος scyphus.] A large drinking-cup or bowl, having two handles not extending above the rim, and no foot.

**1858** S. Birch *Anc. Pottery* II. 103 The Heraclean *scyphos* had its handle ornamented with the Heraclean knot. **1921** *Brit. Museum Return* 61 in *Parl. Papers 1921* XXVII. 555 Attic black-figure skyphos. **1942** J. D. Beazley *Attic Red-Figure Vase-Painters* xii. 301 The vases..are by Makron, whose name appears on his masterpiece, the Boston skyphos. **1960** *Oxf. Univ. Gaz.* 4 Mar. 805/2 From Cyprus:..a painted skyphos imitating a class of pottery made at al Mina under East Greek influence (8th century B.C.). **1979** *Nature* 29 Feb. 643/2 Samples were taken from the base, sides and handles of an Attic skyphos which had been fired between 440 and 425 bc.

**sky-pilot:** see sky *sb.*[1] 9.

‖**skyr** (skɪə(r)). [Icel.] A dish prepared from curdled milk; a kind of curd.

**1857** Dufferin *Lett. High Lat.* (ed. 3) 122 Not to mention reindeer tongues, skier,—a kind of sour curds, excellent when well made. **1868** Whittier *Dole of Jarl Thorkell* 77 Make dole of skyr and black bread That old and young may live. **1890** Hall Caine *Bondman* II. vii, He supped on the porridge and skyr they set before him.

**skyr(e,** varr. skire *a.* and *adv.*, skirr *v.*

**skyrby,** obs. form of scurvy *sb.*

†**skyre,** *sb. Sc. Obs.* (Meaning uncertain.)

**1508** Dunbar *Flyting* 122 Ffy! skolderit skyn, thow art bot skyre and skrumple.

**skyre** (*Sc.* skaɪr), *v. Sc.* [Of obscure origin.] *intr.* To be bright or glaring; to flaunt. Hence **'skyring** *ppl. a.*, bright or loud in colour; glaring; conspicuous.

**1677** Nicolson in *Trans. Roy. Soc. Lit.* (1870) IX. 318 *Skire*, to shine. **1724** Ramsay *Tea-Table Misc.* (1733) I. 25 Nae skyring gowk, my dear, can see Or love, or grace, or heaven in thee. **1760** J. Barclay *Battle of Sheriffmuir* in *Jacobite Songs* (1871) 35 Had ye seen the philabegs And skyrin tartan trews. **1831** *Blackw. Mag.* XXX. 107 They do not wonder even at meteors, for the air is full of them, and they go skyring through the stars. **1871** W. Alexander *Johnny Gibb* (1873) 169 That braw French merino 't she's been skyrin in.

†**skyred,** *a. Sc. Obs.*[−1] [Cf. skire *adv.*] ? Slightly crazy.

**1581** *Satir. Poems Reform.* xliv. 207 As he vas vyse, the vther planelie skyrit, Gar paint thair baigis: to Geneue haist vith speid.

†**skyrgaliard.** *Obs.* Also 6 skyre-. [f. galliard *sb.*[1], with obscure first element.] A wild or dissipated fellow.

*a* **1529** Skelton *Agst. Scottes* 101 Syr skyrgalyard, ye were so skyt, Your wyll than ran before your wyt. —— *Dk. Albany* 168 Suche a proude palyarde, Suche a skyrgaliarde. [**1826** Hor. Smith *Tor Hill* (1838) I. 26 The quarrel of these wild rufflers and skyr-galliards.]

**sky-rocket,** *sb.* [sky *sb.*[1]] **1.** A rocket which ascends high into the sky before exploding. Also *fig.*

**1688** Luttrell *Brief Rel.* (1857) I. 454 There are various reports how the late fire..began: some say by carelessnesse; others, by a sky rocket falling amongst hay. **1690** Dryden *Prol. to 'Mistakes'* 15 He's no high Flyer—he makes no sky Rockets, His Squibbs are only levell'd at your Pockets. **1702** *Lond. Gaz.* No. 3805/8 The Ships..made a very Glorious Show at Night,..some firing several Sky-Rockets. **1765** R. Jones *Fireworks* iv. 136 Six sky rockets, fixed on one stick, and fired together, make a grand and beautiful appearance. **1834** Marryat *P. Simple* (1863) 79 At last I obtained a grumbling assent to my going on shore, and off I went like a sky-rocket. **1846** Greener *Sci. Gunnery* 230 The composition in a sky-rocket, which is required to burn on a graduated scale. **1862** Mrs. Carlyle *Lett.* III. 108, I should be back like a returned sky-rocket.

*attrib.* **1893** *Advance* (Chicago) 3 Aug., Such successors seldom report in such sky-rocket style after about six months.

**2.** *transf.* An enthusiastic cheer, raised esp. by college students; = sis-boom-bah. *U.S. slang.*

**1867** *Ball Players' Chron.* (N.Y.) 25 July 2/2 After cheers had been interchanged, and the Nationals had let off a 'sky rocket'—namely a sort of finish to three cheers, with a 'hiss —boom—ah!'—an adjournment was had to the clubhouse. **1894** R. H. Davis *Eng. Cousins* 120 An American misses the rah-rahs, and the skyrocket cries. **1947** G. S. Perry *Cities of Amer.* 222 He is such a stimulating lecturer that many of his classes are preceded by a 'skyrocket': a Wisconsin yell reserved for its heroes.

**3.** *Rhyming slang* for 'pocket'. Cf. sky *sb.*[1] 8.

**1879** *Macmillan's Mag.* Oct. 502/1 A slavey piped the spoons sticking out of my skyrocket (pocket), so I got smugged. **1898** [see outer colloq. var. out of *prep. phr.*]. **1936** J. Curtis *Gilt Kid* ix. 98 There's no sense in hanging around in the West End with a cane and Christ knows what else in my sky-rocket. **1962** F. Norman *Guntz* i. 8 He put the letter in an envelope and..handed it to me. I took it and stuffed it in my sky rocket. **1973** 'B. Mather' *Snowline* xv. 180 Ten trouble-free runs..and you're back in England with five thousand quid in your skyrocket.

Hence **sky-rockety** *a.*

**1890** *Voice* (N. York) 23 Jan., I began to ask myself questions about this sky-rockety assemblage of words. **1896** *Godey's Mag.* April 348/2 That the sudden and sky-rockety increase last year was unnatural is generally admitted.

**'skyrocket,** *v.* [f. the sb.] **1.** *trans.* In *Cricket*, = sky *v.*[1] 1b. *rare*[−1].

**1851** W. Clarke *Pract. Hints Cricket* in W. Bolland *Cricket Notes* 134 It's enough to make you bite your thumbs to see your best balls pulled and sky-rocketed about.

**2. a.** *intr.* To rise abruptly and rapidly; to increase dramatically (in number, amount, etc.). Cf. rocket *v.* 2c. Chiefly *U.S.*

**1895** in *Funk's Stand. Dict.* **1923** *Nation* (N.Y.) 22 Aug. 181 The supply runs short and prices go skyrocketing. **1935** *Motion Picture* Nov. 40/2 Frances Dee..sky-rockets to new importance with an amazingly fine performance. **1936** M. Mitchell *Gone with Wind* xii. 217 Even the cheapest cotton goods had skyrocketed in price. **1943** J. Steinbeck in *N.Y. Herald Tribune* 29 Sept. 21/8 The incidence of GI dysentery skyrocketed. **1951** E. Paul *Springtime in Paris* iv. 80 After World War I,..the mark skyrocketed from 100 to the dollar to 3,000,000 or more. **1968** Mrs. L. B. Johnson *White House Diary* 14 Mar. (1970) 638 The headlines ran:—'Mad Rush in Europe'..'Gold Buying Skyrockets'. **1974** 'E. Lathen' *Sweet & Low* xviii. 173 It had taken only twenty-four hours in the hinterland for his opinion of Milan to sky-rocket.

**b.** To jump or fly up suddenly, in the manner of a sky-rocket. *rare.*

**1907** G. B. Shaw *John Bull's Other Island* II. 30 Here! where are you jumpin to? Wheres your manners to go skyrocketin like that out o the box in the middle o your confession? **1946** J. W. Day *Harvest Adventure* iv. 48 Partridges sky-rocketed and screwballed overhead and fled to safety.

**3. a.** *trans.* To destroy utterly; = explode *v.* 3. **b.** To cause to rise abruptly and rapidly: to propel rapidly forward or upward; to increase sharply.

**1928** *Daily Express* 24 Nov. 3/5 A careful 'once-over' of some of London's most prominent public men has..sky-rocketed the popular American idea that all Englishmen are snappy dressers! **1950** Blesh & Janis *They all played Ragtime* v. 102 His 1896 success at Keith's and Tony Pastor's in New York skyrocketed him into the public eye. **1976** *National Observer* (U.S.) 31 Jan. 6/1 If I had a disease that skyrocketed my chances of dying early.., would I take the drugs that would control my disease.

So **'skyrocketing** *vbl. sb.* and *ppl. a.* Cf. rocketing *ppl. a.*

**1849** Poe *Marginalia* in *Compl. Wks.* (1902) XVI. 166 The German 'Schwärmerei'—not exactly 'hum-bug', but 'sky-rocketing'—..that peculiar style of criticism which has lately come into fashion, through the influence of certain.. people who live..about Boston. **1933** *Sun* (Baltimore) 18 Aug. 16/5 Skyrocketing of all grain values immediately ensued. **1962** [see explosion 4b]. **1979** *Vole* 8 Nov. 26/1 Land-prices..are a key element in the sky-rocketing costs of both housing and food.

**skyrre,** obs. form of scar *sb.*[1]

**skyrrhus,** obs. form of scirrhus.

†**skyrsay.** *Sc. Obs.*[−1] (Meaning uncertain.)

*c* **1425** Wyntoun *Cron.* II. xii. 1104 (Cott. MS.), Withe aulde hoyis [= hose] and rewyn schoyn, And mowlyt breid in skyrsays [*v.rr.* cartis, baggis] don.

**skyruie,** obs. form of scurvy *sb.*

**skyrwate, -wyt(te,** obs. ff. skirret *sb.*[1]

**sky-sail.** *Naut.* Also skysail. [sky *sb.*[1]] In square-rigged vessels, a light sail set above the royal.

**1829** Marryat *F. Mildmay* xv, I set and took in every sail, from a sky-sail to a try-sail. **1840** R. H. Dana *Bef. Mast* x,

The sun came out bright, and we set royals, sky-sails, and studding-sails. **1891** C. ROBERTS *Adrift Amer.* 230 She was a full-rigged ship, carrying three skysails.

**b.** *attrib.* with *mast, pole, yard.*

**1829** MARRYAT *F. Mildmay* iii, White hammock-cloths, skysail masts. **1846** A. YOUNG *Naut. Dict.* 284 Either of these poles gets the name of the skysail pole. **1885** *Daily Telegr.* 26 Nov. (Cassell), A length of mast continued above the royal mast, upon which a skysail-yard may be crossed.

**ˈskyscape.** [f. SKY *sb.*[1], after *landscape, seascape.*] A view of the sky; also in painting, etc., a representation of part of the sky.

**1817** SOUTHEY *Let.* in *Life* (1850) IV. 283 It was the unbroken horizon which impressed me,..and the skyscapes which it afforded. **1861** C. J. ANDERSON *Okavango* x. 137 The beautiful and striking skyscapes and atmospheric coruscations attendant on these storms. **1878** GROSART *More's Poems* Introd. p. xli, The great ancient Painters, whose backgrounds of portraits..rather than land-scape, or sea-scape, or sky-scape proper, assure us [etc.].

**sky-scraper.** [SKY *sb.*[1]]

**1.** *Naut.* A triangular sky-sail.

**1794** *Rigging & Seamanship* 135 *Sky-scrapers.* These sails are triangular... The foot spreads half of the royal yards. **1797** S. JAMES *Narr. Voy.* 52 Four vessels hove in sight.. with..royals and skyscrapers set. **1860** *Slang Dict.* 217 The light sails which some adventurous skippers set above the royals in calm latitudes are termed sky-scrapers and moon-rakers. **1883** A. KNOX *New Playground* 113 Studding-sails and sky-scrapers did not produce the smallest effect.

**2.** *colloq.* **a.** A high-standing horse. [A horse named Skyscraper, sired by Highflyer, won the Epsom Derby in 1789:

**1788** *Racing Calendar* 269 Mr. Dutton named the D. of Bedford's c. Skyscraper, by Highflyer. **1810** T. H. MORLAND *Geneal. English Race Horse* 147 Skyscraper mare produced Brainworm by Buzzard. *Ibid.* 160 [Death] Skyscraper, 1807.]

**1826** HONE *Every-day Bk.* II. 461 The huntsmen were all abroad.., trotting..down the road, on great nine-hand sky-scrapers. **1827** *Sporting Mag.* (N.S.) XX. 48, I should like to see him upon one of the crack Sky-scrapers of the day.

**b.** A very tall man.

**1857** *Slang Dict.* 19, I say, old sky-scraper, is it cold up there?

**c.** A rider on one of the high cycles formerly in use.

**1892** *Daily News* 7 Mar. 6/6 Riders of the ordinary [cycle] ..are few and far between, and are often derisively styled 'sky-scrapers'.

†**d.** A tall hat or bonnet. *Obs.*

**1800** W. SCOTT *Let.* 5 Apr. (1937) XII. 159 The trumpets call me to swagger in a cockd skyscraper and sword. **1847** J. A. EAMES *Budget of Lett.* 397 She gave me a black silk bonnet ..which stuck right up in the air after the fashion of the old 'sky scrapers'.

**e.** In *Baseball, Cricket,* etc., a ball propelled high in the air; a towering hit, a skyer.

**1866** *N.Y. Herald* 27 June 5/5 Goodspeed made three handsome fly catches; Mehl, Sweet and Dupignac each paying their share of attention to the 'skyscrapers'. **1907** *St. Nicholas* (N.Y.) Sept. 996 A 'skyscraper' throw to first. **1943** *Amer. Speech* XVIII. 104 Fly balls include the *skyscraper,* the *cloud-buster,* [etc.]. **1963** *Times* 28 Feb. 3/6 Alabaster's skyscraper to Titmus at midwicket demonstrated only the extraordinary sureness of Titmus in the field.

**3.** An exaggerated or 'tall' story. *nonce-use.*

**1841** LEVER *C. O'Malley* xxxiii, My yarn won't come so well after your sky-scrapers of love.

**4.** A high building of many stories, *esp.* one of those characteristic of American cities.

[**1883** J. MOSER in *Amer. Architect & Building News* 30 June 305 The capitol building should always have a dome. I should raise thereon a gigantic 'sky-scraper', contrary to all precedent in practice.] **1888** *Inter-Ocean* 30 Dec. 10/5 The 'sky-scrapers' of Chicago outrival anything of their kind in the world. **1891** *Boston* (Mass.) *Jrnl.* Nov., How the sky-scrapers are built. **1893** *Daily News* 15 May 5/5 It does not look like a typical skyscraper, though I suppose a thirteen-story house is one. **1903** O. KILDARE *My Mamie Rose* xix. 288 We reach our stoop in the yawning dark cañon of the skyscrapers. **1928** W. A. STARRETT *Skyscrapers & Men who build Them* i. 1 The skyscraper is the most distinctively American thing in the world. **1942** *Short Guide Gt. Brit.* (U.S. War Dept.) 7 London has no skyscrapers. **1951** *Manch. Guardian Weekly* 19 Apr. 5 Theatres will have skyscrapers superimposed on them. **1976** *Sunday Mail* (Glasgow) 28 Nov. 20/2 Babs Marchant..lives 18 storeys up in an Ibrox, Glasgow, skyscraper.

Hence **sky-scrapered** *a.*, characterized by the presence of or full of sky-scrapers; surrounded by sky-scrapers; built very tall.

**1947** *Ann. Reg. 1946* 212 The new home [for the U.N.] would be sky-scrapered, congested and expensive. **1963** *Harper's Bazaar* Jan. 21/2 Cagliari..is now a busy sky-scrapered seaport. **1963** C. L. COOPER *Black!* x. 151 The skyscrapered trillion-bricked dwellings. **1965** *Guardian* 4 Oct. 9/4 Salisbury is brittle, skyscrapered, centralised, and carefully zoned into European and African residential areas.

**sky-scraping,** *a.* [SKY *sb.*[1]] High enough to appear to touch the sky; hence, remarkably high or lofty.

**1840** MARRYAT *Poor Jack* i, He..saw my mother with her sky-scraping cap at the back of her head. **1884** *Chicago Daily Tribune* 9 Mar. 19/1 The sky-scraping buildings that have been and will be erected down-town will never endanger human life, because they will only be occupied by people wide awake. **1891** *Boston* (Mass.) *Jrnl.* Nov., When entire streets are built with sky-scraping buildings. **1897** MARY KINGSLEY *W. Africa* 550 It [the mountain] revealed itself.. from its surf-washed plinth to its sky-scraping summit. **1904** *N.Y. Even. Post* 12 Mar. 10 (*heading*) Sky-scraping prices at last Brandus picture sale. **1905** KIPLING *Actions & Reactions* (1909) 123 What under the stars are you doing here, you sky-scraping chimney-sweep? **1961** P. FLEMING *Bayonets to Lhasa* xviii. 230 The force camped..less than a mile from the sky-scraping Potala. **1973** *Washington Post* 13 Jan. C1/1 Man's most wondrous, skyscraping community, the 110-story Brobdingnagian shafts stand..at the western edge of Manhattan island.

**sky-sign.** [SKY *sb.*[1]]

**1.** *poet.* A celestial sign or portent.

**1880** BROWNING *Idyls, Pietro* 8 Where [there] was..Star to name or sky-sign [to] read. **1940** C. DAY LEWIS tr. *Virgil's Georgics* I. 23 Well for us that we watch the rise and fall of the sky-signs And the four different seasons that divide the year equally.

**2. a.** A sign of the nature of an advertisement, so constructed and placed that the letters, etc., stand out against the sky. Also *spec.* an electrically illuminated sign or message similarly placed.

**1890** *Spectator* 30 Aug., We entirely agree with him as to the hideous horror of these 'sky-signs', as he terms them. **1893** *Daily Telegr.* 27 Mar. 5/4 A large board on the roof of a house is a great deal more to be dreaded than any sky-sign yet invented. **1903** *Building News* 10 Apr. 510/2 Mr Caudwell..contended..that a sky sign was any sign which could be seen against the sky by a person standing beneath. **1916** A. BENNETT *Lion's Share* ix. 64 They crossed a thoroughfare that twinkled and glittered from end to end with moving sky-signs. **1926** *Socialist Rev.* June 13 In Piccadilly a large crowd—mostly strikers—watched a *Daily Dispatch* news bulletin thrown up on a huge sky-sign. **1938** F. BRETT YOUNG *Dr. Bradley Remembers* iii. 121 He was to see the dim, discreet streets of the city centre..garish with neon lights and sky-signs. **1954** *Times* 17 Dec. 9/4 London County Council gives notice of a Bill..'To repeal the provisions of the London Building Acts, 1930 to 1939, prohibiting the erection of sky signs.' **1966** *Punch* 16 Mar. 368/2 There's to be one of those electric sky-sign newscasters in Piccadilly Circus at last. But remember how easy it is to get hold of the wrong end of those revolving messages.

**b.** An advertisement or other message in sky-writing.

**1922** *Flight* XIV. 330/2 This week has witnessed the first practical application of the invention of Major J. C. Savage, by means of which chemical smoke trailing from an aeroplane can be used for writing words or tracing figures in the sky... His first 'sky sign' took the form of the word 'Castrol'. **1931** C. DAY LEWIS *From Feathers to Iron* 53 Now shall the airman vertically banking Out of the blue write a new sky-sign.

**skytrain** (ˈskaɪtreɪn). Also with hyphen and as two words. [SKY *sb.*[1]] **1.** *U.S.* A convoy consisting of a number of gliders towed in line by an aeroplane, and used for the transport of freight, etc. and in *Mil.* applications. (*temporary.*)

**1934** *Sun* (Baltimore) 4 Aug. 4/2 Glider lands from air-mail 'train' in pioneer flight... Lustig sky trains. **1935** *Evening Sun* (Baltimore) 14 May 1/7 The sky-train..—two gliders towed by an airplane—took off at Miami on its one-stop flight under perfect weather conditions. **1944** C. MILBURN *Diary* 18 June (1979) 221 Wounded men..are evacuated from Normandy by 'sky trains', which carry a flight nurse and two medical officers. **1946** A. LEE *German Air Force* xii. 165 The fighter units in Western Germany.. carried out only one or two thrusts against the long sky train of tempting Dakotas and their gliders.

**2. Skytrain.** Also **skytrain.** The name of a privately-owned passenger air service seeking to provide regular, low-cost, transatlantic travel facilities. (No longer in operation.)

A proprietary name in the U.S.

**1971** *Daily Tel.* 20 Oct. 2/6 Laker Airways applied yesterday..for permission to operate a 'sky train' service to New York for a winter single fare of £32.50 per passenger. **1972** *Ibid.* 27 Sept. 1 Mr Freddy Laker..said last night: 'Skytrain is a walk on, walk off, no frills, no reservation service similar to a train service.' **1977** *Arab Times* 14 Dec. 6/2 Freddie Laker, creator of the cut-rate London-New York Skytrain air service, said Monday his airline has applied to operate a similar Skytrain service between London and Los Angeles. **1978** *Official Gaz.* (U.S. Patent Office) 23 May 345/2 Laker Airways Limited..*Skytrain*.. For air passenger services—namely, the transportation of passengers by air.

†**skyvald.** *Obs.*[−1] (Meaning obscure.)

**13..** *E.E. Allit. P.* B. 529 Þerwyth he blessez vch a best, & bytaȝt hem þis erþe. Þen was a skylly skyualde, quen scaped alle þe wylde.

**skyve, -er, -ing,** varr. SKIVE *v.*[3], SKIVER *sb.*[3], SKIVING *vbl. sb.*[2]

**skyward** (ˈskaɪwəd), *adv.* and *adj.* Also 6 skies ward. [SKY *sb.*[1]]

**A.** *adv.* Towards, in the direction of, the sky. In early use *to (the) skyward.*

**1582** STANYHURST *Æneis* I. (Arb.) 20 To skyward his claspt hands heauelye lifting. *Ibid.* II. 65 Mounting his sight to the skyward. **1586** W. WEBBE *Eng. Poetrie* (Arb.) 76 Swift buckes shall flie for foode to the skies ward.

**1821** CLARE *Vill. Minstr.* I. 80 One glances sky-ward with affright. **1840** HOOD *Kilmansegg, Courtship* ii, The grieving Angel had skyward flown. **1871** PALGRAVE *Lyr. Poems* 17 A blaze shot skyward from the crystal mere.

*fig.* **1884** 'H. COLLINGWOOD' *Under Meteor Flag* 33 Our hopes..began once more to soar skyward.

**B.** *adj.* Leading to the sky; going towards the sky; heavenward.

**1831** W. HOWITT *Bk. of Seasons* 325 The sky-ward and inaccessible pinnacles. **1838** MOIR *Casa Wappy* Poems (1852) I. 21 Thy little feet have trode The skyward path. **1839-48** BAILEY *Festus* Proem p. v, Ere..granite wrought Its skyward impulse from earth's hearth of fire. **1935** C. DAY LEWIS *Time to Dance* 22 Speak up, speak up, you skyward man, Speak up and tell us true.

Hence **ˈskywardly** *adv.*

**1893** *Nat. Observer* 11 Mar. 413/1 The corks have broken forth and shot skywardly.

**ˈskywards,** *adv.* [Cf. prec.] Towards the sky.

**1811** W. R. SPENCER *Poems* 54 Skywards were spread his wings of feathery snow. **1853** MISS E. S. SHEPPARD *Ch. Auchester* I. 275 The smoke looked beautiful..as it swelled skywards. **1888** 'J. S. WINTER' *Bootle's Childr.* ix, Mrs. Landover's nose went sky-wards, and her short upper lip curled itself in the same direction.

**skyway** (ˈskaɪweɪ). Chiefly *U.S.* [SKY *sb.*[1]]

**1.** The sky as a medium of transport or a route used by aircraft; = AIRWAY 2.

**1919** *Pearson's Mag.* Dec. 547/1 The letters will tell..the nationality of the ship passing along the world's skyways. **1928** L. THOMAS (*title*) European skyways. The story of a tour of Europe by aeroplane. **1934** *Sun* (Baltimore) 15 May 1/3 Theirs is the great-circle route over the North Atlantic —the skyway emblazoned by Byrd, Acosta, [etc.]. **1952** *N.Y. Times* 7 Aug. 39/8 The team of precision flyers will fly the skyway route on the way to their home base at Corpus Christi, Tex. **1967** M. CRAVEN *I heard Owl call my Name* xi. 68 High in the skyways wild geese called exultantly on their first early passages back from the south.

**2.** An overhead motorway. Also *transf.* (see quot. 1960).

**1940** *Sun* (Baltimore) 6 Sept. 13/4 It has been suggested that a skyway be built along Pratt street from Monroe to the Fallsway, the western end to connect with the route to Washington. **1958** *Wall St. Jrnl.* 10 Nov. 18/3 A reduction in toll rates charged on the Sunshine Skyway..is expected to be approved by the State Road Department Board. **1960** *Daily Tel.* 10 Feb. 20/6 The system, known as Skyway, runs on a concrete way 15 ft above ground. It has a speed of 50 m.p.h. and it is estimated operates for as little as a penny a mile. **1972** J. GORES *Dead Skip* (1973) i. 7 Heslip unlocked the chain-link storage lot under the concrete abutments of the skyway adjacent to the DICA office.

**3.** Chiefly in Minneapolis: (see quot. 1975[1]); an aerial walkway between buildings. *U.S.*

[**1968** *Archit. Forum* Jan.-Feb. 83/2 The first pedestrian bridge of an elaborate second-story network has been completed in downtown St. Paul. Part of the 12-block urban renewal project, the 'Skyway' will eventually comprise an elevated system of bridges and concourses.] **1969** *Ibid.* Jan.-Feb. 75/3 The overpass idea, now called a 'Skyway', is being carried out several blocks to the east. **1970** *Business Week* 26 Dec. 48/2 Shelter from summer heat and winter weather is one advantage of skyways—especially in Minneapolis, where it is below or near freezing for five months of the year. **1975** *Country Life* 2 Jan. 36/3 There has been a great incentive to construct the Skyway system... Skyways are broad, carpeted, heated, air-conditioned, glass-covered corridors, linking the main city buildings at first-floor level. **1975** *New Yorker* 24 Mar. 106/2 Walking there is a pleasure —down the carless mall, or through a glazed 'skyway' system if snow starts to fall. **1979** *United States 1980/81* (Penguin Travel Guides) 266 The most extraordinary feature of downtown Minneapolis is its internal skyway, an inter-connected belt of pedestrian malls and escalators.

**sky-writing,** *vbl. sb.* [SKY *sb.*[1]] The tracing of legible signs in the sky, esp. for advertising purposes, by means of smoke trails made by aircraft or (occas.) by letters and devices projected by searchlight. Also, the writing so produced.

**1923** *Western Gaz.* 16 May 8/4 Sky-writing..did not commend itself to the general body of advertisers. **1926** H. BARR in *Mod. Advertising* I. 9/1 Invented in 1910 by John Clifford Savage, it was not until twelve years later that sky-writing became an accomplished fact. *Ibid.* 9/2 The corporation..is stated to have spent £320,000 on sky-writing publicity alone. **1932** *Flight* 8 July 638/1 Night sky-writing, by projection of light on to clouds at night, was considered at no little length. **1935** H. G. WELLS *Things to Come* ix. 91 Sky writing by the new planes. **1959** *Belfast Tel.* 9 Oct. 7/1 It is believed to be the first time skywriting has been used in a general election. **1966** *Punch* 13 July 54/1 Long ago You fancied many wonders that we know, The 'Telephonoscope', for one, 'Sky Writing', and the Long Range Gun. **1978** F. ROSS *Sleeping Dogs* 157 He couldn't have made his intentions universally clearer if he'd spelled them out in sky-writing.

So as *ppl. a.* and hence [as back-formation] **sky-write** *v.* (*a*) *intr.*, to practise sky-writing; (*b*) *trans.*, to trace in the sky by means of smoke trails; **sky-writer; sky-written** *ppl. a.*

**1922** *Daily Mail* 8 Aug. 5/3 The Daily Mail sky-writing aeroplane was over Margate and Folkestone yesterday. **1926** *Mod. Advertising* I. 9/2, 1,450 sky-written demonstrations were carried out by eight pilots. **1927** *Pictorial Weekly* 17 Sept. 198 A window sign which reproduces in miniature the work of the sky-writer. **1932** *Times Educ. Suppl.* 22 Oct. p. iv/3 A battery of sky-writing projectors will be installed on the roofs of buildings. **1934** WEBSTER, Skywrite. **1941** B. SCHULBERG *What makes Sammy Run?* xii. 219 Feeling his words fade off into the air like a sky-writer's. **1959** J. CARY *Captive & Free* xlvii. 203 She was always calling him on the telephone with new ideas—aeroplanes sky-writing the message..; pavement-writing;..and loudspeaker vans. **1960** *Guardian* 29 Dec. 3/2 Sky-written slogans. **1973** J. DRUMMOND *Bang! Bang!* i. 2 The plane swooped... The smoke spurted... People wondered if it was possible for a sky-writer to dot his 'i's. *Ibid.* 3 They've been sky-writing to advertise their shows.

**sla(a,** obs. ff. SLAY, SLOE, SLOW.

**slaap,** obs. f. SLAPE.

**slaar(e,** obs. north. ff. SLAYER.

**slaathorn**, obs. f. SLOE-THORN.

**Slaavic**, var. of SLAVIC.

**slaa-worm**, obs. f. SLOW-WORM.

**slab** (slæb), *sb.*[1] Also 3 sclabbe, 4, 6 slabbe, 7 slabb. [Of obscure origin: the form does not accord with OF. *esclape* splinter, shiver (of wood).]

**1. a.** A flat, broad, and comparatively thick piece or mass of anything solid.

In early use of metal, later also of stone and wood, and finally of any substance capable of having this form. For some technical uses see quots. 1674, 1825, and 1964.

*c* **1290** *S. Eng. Leg.* I. 315 Ase ȝif a man nome ane sclabbe [*Harl. MS.* slab] of Ire, þat glowynde were a-fuyre. **1354–5** *Ely Sacr. Rolls* (Surtees) II. 164 In M de grossis spykinge, 7s 6d. In viij slabbes empt. 1s 8d. *c* **1380** *Sir Ferumb.* 3313 Grete slabbes of styl & yre to þe walles þo wern y-slente. **1556** RECORDE *Castle Knowl.* a viij, The Grounde of Artes who hathe well tredd, And noted well the slyppery slabbes. **1665** J. WEBB *Stone-Heng* (1725) 198 One only simple Circle of about twelve Slabbs of Stone. **1674** RAY *Coll. Words, Preparing of Tin* 124 When they have a sufficient quantity of the melted metal, they cast it into oblong, square pieces in a mould made of moore-stone. The lesser pieces they call *slabs*, the greater *blocks*. **1771** CUMBERLAND *West Indian* III. iv, A large cargo of..sugars, rum-puncheons, mahogany slabs. **1796** H. HUNTER tr. *St.-Pierre's Stud. Nat.* (1799) II. 452 An arch enclosed on every side with large slabs of stone. **1825** J. NICHOLSON *Operat. Mechanic* 637 The large piece [of glass] with the knot, still retains the name of *table*; the smaller piece is technically called a *slab*. **1840** DICKENS *Old C. Shop* l, A little slab of plum cake. **1856** KANE *Arct. Expl.* II. xiv. 141 The walrus..was cut into flat slabs half an inch thick. **1871** TYNDALL *Fragm. Sci.* (1879) I. x. 316 Our slabs of gun-cotton also emit waves of different densities in different parts. **1881** *Encycl. Brit.* XII. 839/1 The rubber is glossy, of a bright pink colour and mottled appearance, and occurs in the form either of small balls pressed together or of irregular masses called 'slabs or 'loaf' rubber. **1903** *Imperial Inst. Techn. Rep.* 153 The 'slabs' of blackish rubber alone being worth 1*s.* 11*d.* per pound. **1964** *Amer. Speech* XXXIX. 274 *Slab*, a solid piece of rubber used as an ingredient to be melted and mixed with solvents to form rubber cements or to be milled and stripped off.

*transf.* **1882** *Harper's Mag.* July 32/2 From one of our exchanges..we chip off the following slab of scientific knowledge. **1896** MRS. CAFFYN *Quaker Grandmother* 171 He was a pampered slab of propriety from his youth up. **1951** PARTRIDGE *Dict. Slang* (ed. 4) Add. 1172/2 *Slab*..a long paragraph. **1958** *Listener* 14 Aug. 249/3 The conventional slabs of Brahms, Beethoven, and Tchaikovsky. *a* **1974** R. CROSSMAN *Diaries* (1976) II. 623 When I started, I used to dictate slabs without any real preparation.

**b.** *spec.* in *Metallurgy*, such a piece of metal produced from an ingot for subsequent rolling into sheet or plate.

**1863** *Chambers's Encycl.* V. s.v. *Iron*, Puddled balls which have undergone shingling are called *slabs* or *blooms*. **1910** [see BILLET *sb.*[2] 9]. **1931** *Economist* 21 Mar. 608/1 The biggest decline occurring in billets, blooms and slabs. **1968** D. R. CLIFFE *Technical Metallurgy* iv. 70 Ingots are broken down into blooms or slabs, as a hot working process, in a cogging mill. **1972** *Times* 18 Sept. 21/6 Production of slab zinc was 35,000 tons.

**c.** = *slab-cake*, sense 6 below.

**1908** J. KIRKLAND *Mod. Baker* III. 462 Rice Slab at 6d. per lb... Lemon Madeira at 3d. per lb... Fruit Slab at 3d. per lb. **1948** *Good Housek. Cookery Bk.* 580 Cut the Genoese slab into 2-inch squares. **1974** W. FOLEY *Child in Forest* I. iii. 39 Plain slab was a delicate luxury and this was no plain slab!

**d.** *Archit.* A rectangular block of pre-cast, reinforced concrete used in building, esp. in multi-storey constructions.

**1927** *Archit. Rec.* Dec. 452/2 A number of experimental houses have been built with 'textile-block slab construction'... The system consists of concrete block slabs about two or three inches thick of unit sizes which can be handled, laid on end with interlocking grooves, reinforced horizontally and vertically by means of steel rods. **1930** *Amer. Architect* Apr. 32/2 A type of floor and ceiling construction light in weight, quickly erected..is being used... The system consists of two types of slabs, one for floors and another for ceilings, used in conjunction with the ordinary supporting members of steel construction. **1938** *Archit. Rev.* LXXXIII. 223 (*caption*) One of the two 'porte-cochères', in reinforced concrete column and slab construction. **1951** *Ibid.* CX. 92 The café terrace, which disappears beneath its lightly supported slab roof to become a two-level café-bar. **1973** D. FRANCIS *Slay-Ride* x. 122 A modern square-built glass and slab affair a mile out of the city centre.

**e.** *Archit.* A high-rise block of impersonal aspect.

[**1933** L. MUMFORD in *New Yorker* 23 Dec. 29/2 What does one find? First, a gigantic slab of a building.] **1952** *Archit. Rev.* CXI. 119/1 As is well known, the term 'slab' was coined in the 1930's in connection with publicity on the RCA Building at Rockefeller Center. **1958** *Listener* 20 Nov. 827/1 A point block of government offices is now going up at Wellington..and other high-rise slabs for offices and flats. **1969** BURCHARD & BUSH-BROWN *Archit. of Amer.* IV. 353 The early skyscrapers were massive blocks... The new characteristic form became the slab, a term applied to the buildings erected at the Rockefeller Center beginning about 1930. The slab form had appeared briefly in the early history of the skyscraper, notably in the Monadnock Building... It remained for the architects of Rockefeller Center..to modernize the slab, to make it thinner in relation to its height, to simplify it and to treat it with characteristic but underemphasized setbacks.

**2. a.** A rough outside plank of timber cut from a log or a tree-trunk preparatory to squaring the main portion, or sawing it into planks.

**1573** TUSSER *Husb.* (1878) 33 Sawne slab let lie, for stable and stie. *Ibid.* 42. **1663** GERBIER *Counsel* 25 [He must watch] the Sawyers at their Pit, that they waste no more than needs in Slabs. **1669** WORLIDGE *Syst. Agric.* (1681) 332 *Slab*, the out-side sappy Planck or Board sawn off from the sides of Timber. **1833** LOUDON *Encycl. Archit.* §549 A marine character may be given by shells;..that of a Russian log-house by the outside slabs of trees. **1886** *Encycl. Brit.* XXI. 345/1 The waste of the log, consisting of the 'slabs' and edgings.

**b.** *Austr.* and *N.Z.* A coarse, axe-hewn plank, two or three inches in thickness.

**1829** H. WIDOWSON *Present State Van Diemen's Land* 86 Logs, or as they are more commonly called, slabs, for erecting barns or small buildings are erected in the same manner. **1845** [see 5 a]. **1861** MRS. MEREDITH *Over the Straits* iv. 130 A bare, rough, barn-like edifice, built of slabs. **1886** HENEY *Fortunate Days* 71 Built was the house of slabs, long and thick and rudely planed by the hatchet. **1905** W. B. *Where White Man Treads* 259 It is a low whare of split slabs, adzed over, and sunk into the earth as closely as the inequalities of adze-jointing will permit. **1950** *N.Z. Jrnl. Agric.* Apr. 375/2 Floors [in very early milking sheds] were of wooden slabs, bricks, stones, or even clay. **1957** P. WHITE *Voss* vi. 154 She was standing in front of a house, or hut, of bleached slabs, that melted into the live trunks of the surrounding trees.

**3. a.** A flat piece of wood or stone used as a table, counter, etc.; a small table hinged to the wall in the passage or hall of a house.

**1739** R. BULL tr. *Dedekindus' Grobianus* 16 Throw Chairs about; the Slab in pieces beat. **1836–7** DICKENS *Sk. Boz, Tales* xi, Four..wine-glasses..were on the slab in the passage. **1883** *Fisheries Exhib. Catal.* p. xxxiii, The most luxurious slab of a fishmonger's shop.

**b.** A flat piece of stone, etc., on which colours are ground, or printing-ink distributed.

**1859** GULLICK & TIMBS *Paint.* 199 The Slab and Muller, for grinding pigments, figures in a painter's paraphernalia far less frequently now than formerly. **1882** SOUTHWARD *Pract. Printing* 383 *Ink Slabs*... Metal being injurious to many kinds of coloured inks, slabs of various kinds are used.

**c.** A porcelain palette divided into compartments, usually with sloping surfaces, for mixing and holding water-colours.

**1888** FIELD & DAVIDSON *Gram. Colouring* (ed. 4) 158 Mix the colour in three degrees of depth, in as many different compartments of the slab.

**d.** A flat piece of stone, etc., immediately in front of a fire-place; a stone hearth.

**1876** *Encycl. Brit.* IV. 466/2 The slab is that part of the floor of a room which is immediately before the fireplace, and along the extent of its front. In basement rooms, this slab is supported by a brick wall brought up from the ground; but in upper rooms the slab is supported by a flat half brick arch called a brick trimmer. **1883** R. L. STEVENSON *Treasure Is.* xix. 153 Little had been left beside the framework of the house; but in one corner there was a stone slab laid down by way of hearth, and an old rusty iron basket to contain the fire. **1963** B. GOODSON *Pract. Guide to House Repairs* iv. 50 The tiled hearth slab is bedded in about ½ in. of mortar on the existing hearth. **1977** J. S. CURL *Eng. Archit.* 154/1 *Slab*..the hearth of a fireplace.

**e.** The stone on which a corpse is laid in a mortuary. Also *transf.* and *fig.*

**1903** A. H. LEWIS *Boss* viii. 101 I've seen a bloke take a slab in th' morgue for less. It was Benny the Bite; he gets a knife between his slats. **1924** G. C. HENDERSON *Keys to Crookdom* 417 Slab... Undertaker's table. **1930** H. C. BAILEY *Mr. Fortune Explains* 111 On a slab in the mortuary the woman's body lay and the divisional surgeon turned from it to nod at Reggie. **1932** E. WALLACE *When Gangs came to London* ii. 26 My best friend is a forty-five..and the day he puts you on the slab I'm going to put diamonds all round his muzzle. **1977** 'C. AIRD' *Parting Breath* x. 127 Pathologists had hobbyhorses, too, and obesity was..Dr. Dabbe's. He was always having a go at Sergeant Gelven..about his weight. 'See you soon,' was his favourite form of greeting to the portly detective, 'on my slab.'

**4.** *attrib.* **a.** In sense 'constructed of slabs', as *slab-cottage*, *-fence*, *whare* [WHARE], etc.; (sense 2 b) *slab-and-bark house*, *hut*; *slab-and-shingle hut*.

**1826** LONGF. in *Life* (1891) I. vii. 86 No slab-fences; no well-poles. **1846** STOKES *Disc. in Australia* I. ix. 266 The house..was what is called a Slab Hut, formed of rough boards and thatched with grass. **1862** R. HENNING *Let.* 18 Oct. (1966) 111 It is not much to move a slab house; all the woodwork takes down and puts up again. **1869** TOWNEND *Rem. Australia* 155 We passed through Studley Park, with here and there a slab house or tent. **1890** 'R. BOLDREWOOD' *Col. Reformer* (1891) 97 A very small slab cottage. **1901** M. FRANKLIN *My Brilliant Career* i. 5 Our comfortable, wide-veranda'ed..slab house..was ever full to overflowing. **1905** W. B. *Where White Man Treads* 293 He..who lives in a slab whare, and on a fare which his dainty collie sniffs at and rejects. **1908** E. J. BANFIELD *Confessions of Beachcomber* I. i. 12 According to the formula neatly printed in official journals, the building of a slab hut is absurdly easy. **1933** *Bulletin* (Sydney) 25 Jan. 20 A good three-roomed slab-and-shingle hut that had been vacated by a white family. **1945** *Salt* 12 Feb. 4/1 His earliest years were spent in a slab-and-bark hut. **1949** F. SARGESON *I saw it in my Dream* 100 A slab *whare* in a narrow valley. **1959** J. WRIGHT *Generations of Men* 53 A slab-and-bark house in lonely fever-ridden country. **1969** F. SARGESON *Joy of Worm* i. 7 It then became pleasant to look forward to hot food, the shelter of the farmer's slab hut, and talk with the man himself.

**b.** In sense 'having the form of a slab or slabs', as *slab-board*, *-deal*, *-slate*, etc.; (sense 2 a) *slabwood*.

**1844** H. STEPHENS *Bk. Farm* II. 133 The slab-slices..may of course vary, but all are free of the smallest portion of waste. **1875** KNIGHT *Dict. Mech.* 2197/2 The waney portions of the slab-boards are removed by the Edger. **1877** RAYMOND *Statist. Mines & Mining* 412 Slab-wood answering all purposes. **1881** YOUNG *Every Man his own Mechanic* § 157. 54 When the slab deals or outsides have been cut away. **1889** SEDDON *Builder's Work* (ed. 2) 231 The work upon slab slates, or slate-mason's work. **1921** *Daily Colonist* (Victoria, B.C.) 2 Oct. 10/1 (Advt.), Cordwood, Slabwood, Blockwood, Dry Kindling. **1962** M. E. MURIE *Two in Far North* I. ii. 20 Off at one side, a lean-to bedroom built of slab wood. **1976** *Newmarket Jrnl.* 16 Dec. (Advt.), Hardwood and softwood, slabwood and off-cuts for sale.

**c.** Misc., as *slab-car*, *-pit*, *-saw*.

**1879** *Lumberman's Gaz.* 19 Dec., Getting the slabs and clippings into the slab-pit. *Ibid.*, The refuse will be run to the slab-saw and cut up, and from there it will fall into the slab-car.

**5.** *Comb.* **a.** With pa. pples., as *slab-bridged* (fig.), *-built*, *-roofed*, *-walled*. Cf. SLAB-SIDED *a.*

**1845** *Voy. of Port Philip* 52 His slab-built hut, with roof of bark. **1859** *Atlantic Monthly* Nov. 642/1 Anyone who has driven over a mountain-stream by one of those bridges made of *slabs* will feel the force of a term we once heard applied to a parson so shaky in character that no dependence could be placed on him,—'A slab-bridged kind o' feller!' **1860** G. H. K. *Vac. Tour* 119, I suspect that he confounded those mysterious slab-built *uags* with the real hour-glass tower. **1866** LOWELL *Biglow P.* Ser. II. *Introd.* Poet. Wks. (1884) 280 The picturesque force of the epithet *slab-bridged* applied to a fellow of shaky character. **1896** MRS. CROKER *Village Tales* 99 The little slab-roofed dwelling. **1930** L. G. D. ACLAND *Early Canterbury Runs* 1st Ser. viii. 213 The slab-walled, earthen-floored hut.

**b.** With agent-nouns, as *slab-burner*, *-grinder*.

**1875** KNIGHT *Dict. Mech.* 2197/2 *Slab-grinder*, a machine used for grinding up the refuse slabs in a..saw mill. **1886** *Encycl. Brit.* XXI. 345/2 The 'slab-burner' or 'hell', a large circular brick furnace..erected conveniently near the saw-mill.

**c.** *slab-like* adj.

**1899** W. JAMES *Talks to Teachers* 214 The even forehead, the slab-like cheek, the codfish eye, may be less interesting for the moment. **1970** R. J. SMALL *Study of Landforms* iv. 122 On the high valley slopes above Glen Rosa great slab-like outcrops of granite, tilted at between 30° and 60°, are developed where glacial erosion and frost weathering have exposed dilatation joints.

**6.** Special combinations: **slab avalanche**, an avalanche in which a sheet of snow breaks cleanly away along a fracture line; **slab bacon**, unsliced bacon; **slab-cake**, (a) cake baked in a large rectangular tin (cf. sense 1 c above).

[**1920** A. LUNN in G. W. Young *Mountain Craft* ix. 431 The wind-slab is the most treacherous of all avalanches. **1936** G. SELIGMAN *Snow Structure & Ski Fields* vii. 160 If this 'slab' of snow has formed on a steep slope it will shatter into countless blocks of hardened snow, and these, sliding downhill, will precipitate the most insidious of all avalanches—the wind-slab avalanche.] **1953** *Avalanche Handbk.* (U.S. Dept. Agric. Forest Service) iv. 34 (*caption*) Major *slab-avalanche. Depth of fracture: 10 feet. **1978** C. FRASER *Avalanches & Snow Safety* v. 79 Criterion 1 is the form of break which started the avalanche and this leads to the broad division of all avalanches into two types: 'loose-snow avalanches' and 'slab avalanches'. **1932** *Even. Sun* (Baltimore) 7 Nov. 12/7 (Advt.), Boneless *Slab Bacon lb 13½c. **1975** L. & S. LOBEL *All about Meat* vii. 115 Take the trouble to hunt for unsliced slab bacon. **1902** J. T. LAW *Grocer's Man.* (ed. 2) 854/1 *Slab Cakes, or Cut Cakes (sold by the pound).—The introduction of these ready-made cakes, as an extension of the birthday, wedding, and Christmas cake system, appears to be displacing or supplanting much of the old-fashioned retail business in currants, raisins,..spices, etc. **1935** *Economist* 22 June 1439/1 Scribbans and Company, the well known makers of slab cake, find their activities in fields where steady progress ..is the natural order of things. **1974** W. FOLEY *Child in Forest* I. v. 57 A slice of bright slab cake.

**slab** (slæb), *sb.*[2] Also 7 slabb(e. [app. of Scand. origin: cf. older Da. *slab* mud, mire, Icel., Norw., and Sw. *slabb* wet filth, slops, etc. Ir. and Sc. Gael. *slab*, *slaib* mire, mud, dirt, are prob. from English.]

**1.** A muddy place; a puddle. Now *dial.*

**1610** HOLLAND *Camden's Brit.* I. 532 A fairer towne, than a man would looke to finde in this tract among such slabbes and water-plashes. **1756** *Phil. Trans.* XLIX. 392 The bottom of the harbour, which is all a slab, was much altered, the mud being washed from some places, and deposited in others. **1847** HALLIW., *Slab*, a puddle, a wet place. *North.* **1895** RYE *E. Anglian Gloss.*, *Slab*, a puddle or collection of surface drainage.

**2.** Wet and slimy matter; ooze, sludge.

**1622–3** *Sarum Churchw. Accs.* (Swayne, 1896) 175 A Barrowe full of Lyme Slabb, 8d. **1671** *St. Foine Improved* 4 The Slabb and Mud which remains after the Water is drawn off the Ground. **1867** EMERSON *May-Day* Wks. (Bohn) III. 408 And upward pries and perforates Through the cold slab a thousand gates.

*fig.* **1868** BROWNING *Ring & Bk.* IV. 733 Throw in abuse..: shake all slab At Rome, Arezzo for the world to nose.

**slab** (slæb), *sb.*[3] *Naut.* [Cf. SLAB-LINE.] (See quots.)

**1882** NARES *Seamanship* (ed. 6) 12 *Slab*, any slack part of a sail hanging down. **1886** *Encycl. Brit.* XXI. 604/2 *Slab of a sail*, the slack part which hangs down after the leech-lines are hauled up.

**slab** (slæb), *a.*[1] [Related to SLAB *sb.*[2] Cf. older Da. *slab* slippery.] Semi-solid; viscid.

In modern use entirely as an echo of Shakspere, frequently *fig.*, and usually accompanied by *thick*.

(*a*) **1605** SHAKS. *Macb.* IV. i. 32 Make the Grewell thicke, and slab. **1844** DICKENS *Mart. Chuz.* xvi, Whatever the chance contributions that fell into the slow caldron of their talk, they made the gruel thick and slab with dollars. **1870**

FRISWELL *Mod. Men of Lett.* vii. 126 Various adventures and thoughts, poured out thick and slab. **1894** RALEIGH *Eng. Novel* viii. (1903) 234 His ['Monk' Lewis's] taste was rather for horrors, thick and slab.

(*b*) **1841** SEALY *Porcelain Tower* 154 Where the air is slab and hath got no sky. **1849** AINSWORTH *Lanc. Witches* I. vi, The slab, salt waves of the Dead Sea. **1868** E. EDWARDS *Ralegh* I. xvii. 351 The embroilment would seem to be now slab enough.

Hence **'slably** *adv.*; **'slabness**.

**1881** *Academy* 7 May 334 All these materials are mixed thickly and slably by the aid of a very clumsy style. **1892** *Sat. Rev.* 13 Aug. 206/2 If these ingredients are not thick and slab enough for readers, they must, indeed, be fanatics of thickness and slabness.

†**slab**, *a.*² (or *adv.*). *Obs.*⁻¹ (See quot.)

*c* **1682** J. COLLINS *Salt & Fishery* 13 With Scotch Salt, he cured the whole Lading of Cod, having none that were weak or slab salted.

†**slab**, *v.*¹ *Obs.*⁻¹ [Of doubtful origin: connexion with SLAB *sb.*² is perhaps possible.] *intr.* ? To wallow.

*c* **1315** SHOREHAM VII. 442 Hou yst þet hy ine helle slabbeþ, And þare-tou none grace nabbeþ To repente?

**slab**, *v.*² Now *dial.* or *Obs.* [prob. of Du. or LG. origin: cf. MDu., Du., and LG. *slabben* (G. *schlabben, schlappen*), Fris. *slabje*, Norw. and Sw. *slabba*, in the same sense.] To eat or drink in a hasty or untidy manner: **a.** *trans.* with *up*. **b.** *intr.* with *at*.

**1553** *Respublica* 853 Suche hongrye doggs will slabbe vp sluttishe puddinges. **1729** in Macfarlane *Genealog. Collect.* (S.H.S.) I. 111 The Laird of Grant..was for Diversion's Sake brought to see the Orphans slabbing at their Trough. **1787** W. TAYLOR *Scots Poems* 173 Lang may ye blow the reamin ale,..While I slab up my barefit kail.

**slab** (slæb), *v.*³ [f. SLAB *sb.*¹]

**1. a.** *trans.* To dress (timber) by removing the outside slabs; to clear of bark-wood.

**1703** [R. NEVE] *City & C. Purchaser* 237 They will cut none smaller, neither will they Slab any, unless they are paid for it by Measure. **1811** *Self Instructor* 137 For cutting a piece of timber..and slabbing it, i.e. cutting off the outside pieces. **1812** J. SMYTH *Pract. Customs* 234 A paling Board..being slabbed or feather-edged and dubbed on the sappy side. **1875** KNIGHT *Dict. Mech.* 2028 *Sapping-machine*, a circular saw for slabbing balks.

**b.** *U.S.* With *off*: 'To throw aside as useless, like the outside piece of a log' (Bartlett, 1859).

**1835** COL. CROCKETT *Tour* 212 You must take notice that I am slabb'd off from the election.

**2.** To convert into a slab or slabs.

**1868** LOSSING *The Hudson* 70 There are also several mills for slabbing the fine black marble of that locality. **1893** *Advance* (Chicago) 11 May, A section of one thirty feet in diameter is to be slabbed, and the slabs..are to be set up to form a house.

**3. a.** To lay or pave with slabs.

**1832** *Lincoln Herald* 7 Feb. 4/4 The expense of slabbing the sides of the Market-place. **1874** SYMONDS *Sk. Italy & Greece* (1898) I. ii. 46 The parapet is broad, and slabbed with red Verona marble. **1891** BARING-GOULD *In Troubadour Land* xvi. 230 The roof is slabbed with stone, so as to form a terrace.

**b.** To support (the sides of a shaft) with slabs. In quot. *absol.*

**1871** J. J. SIMPSON *Recit.* 24 So dig away, drive away, slab and bail.

**4.** To stick or plaster in slabs.

**1886** TUPPER *My Life* 21 They had slabbed on the underside of the tables masses of bread and butter supposed to have been eaten-out.

**5.** *trans.* Of a path, climber, etc.: to traverse (the side of a slope) horizontally or at a gentle angle. *U.S.*

**1889** FARMER *Americanisms* 492/2 *To slab*, to make roads round the sides of mountains. **1892** *Outing* Jan. 268/1 So we started blindly up the bank and into the forest, continuing for an hour and a half to 'slab' the mountain, as the backwoodsmen say. **1907** *Guide Paths & Camps White Mountains* (Appalachian Mountain Club) 62 The path now slabs the east side. **1916** *Ibid.* (ed. 2) 265 The path..rises by easy zigzags slabbing the S.W. flank of Eagle Cliff. **1963** *Appalachian Trailway News* Sept. 43/2 We zigzagged and slabbed mountains, finally coming..down a beautiful grassy glade where stood Big Stamp Shelter. **1968** *Ibid.* Sept. 43/2 Route slabs northwestern slope of ridge.

†**slabbard.** *Obs.*⁻⁰ (See quot.)

The sense does not correspond to that of MDu. *slabbaerd-, slabbaert*, glutton, foul-mouthed person.

*c* **1440** *Prompt. Parv.* 458/1 Slabbarde,..*morosus, tardus.*

**slabbed** (slæbd), *ppl. a.* [f. SLAB *sb.*¹ or *v.*³ + -ED.] Formed, or made, of or into slabs; protected by, paved with, slabs.

**1818** KEATS *Endym.* I. 870 The slabbed margin of a well. **1820** —— *Lamia* I. 381 A silver lamp, whose phosphor glow Reflected in the slabbed steps below. **1883** SYMONDS *Ital. Byways* v. 99 A fine inner court, with sumptuous staircases of slabbed stone.

**slabber** ('slæbə(r)), *sb.*¹ [Related to SLABBER *v.* Cf. G. *schlabber* slaver, slush, street-mud; older Da. *slabber* muddy ground.]

**1.** Slaver; excessive saliva. Also *slabber-like.*

**1718** OZELL tr. *Tournefort's Voy.* I. 193 This Surface is supple, cover'd with a gluey slabber-like Liquor. **1737** BRACKEN *Farriery Impr.* (1757) II. 140 The Slabber which may distil out of his Mouth.

**2.** Slobbering talk.

**1840** R. H. DANA *Bef. Mast* xvi. 44 The language of these people..is the most brutish and inhuman language..that could well be conceived of. It is a complete *slabber*.

**3.** *Sc.* Soft mud; slop, slush.

**1887** *Jamieson's Dict.* Suppl. 221/2.

**slabber** ('slæbə(r)), *sb.*² [f. SLAB *v.*³ + -ER¹.] **a.** A saw or machine for removing the outside slabs from timber, or dressing the outer portion of logs. **b.** A machine for dressing nuts or bolts.

**1875** KNIGHT *Dict. Mech.* 2197/2.

**c.** A workman who cuts or forms materials into slabs.

An early form of the word may occur in the proper name *Ric. Sclaber* (1327), *Ric. le Sclabber* (1333): see *N. & Q.* (1963) July 256/1.

**1921** *Dict. Occup. Terms* (1927) §118 *Slabber*, cements together tiles and other shaped articles for hearths, kerbs, etc. *Ibid.* §159 *Slabber*,..cuts blocks of gelatine..into slabs. **1977** *New Society* 25 Aug. 387/1 His heavy manual work as a fireplace 'tile slabber'.

**slabber** ('slæbə(r)), *v.* Now chiefly *dial.* Also 6 slabour, 7 slabbor. [prob. of Du. or LG. origin: cf. Du. *slabberen*, LG. *slabbern* (G. *schlabbern, schlappern*), Fris. *slabberje*, older Da. *slabre*, a frequentative of *slabben*, etc.: see SLAB *v.*², and cf. SLOBBER, SLUBBER. The compound *bislaberen* occurs in ME.]

**1.** *trans.* To wet or befoul with saliva; to beslaver or beslobber.

**1579** W. FULKE *Conf. Sanders* 657 This was no great honouring of that holy yron, to put it to bee champed and slaboured in an horse mouth. **1619** HARRIS *Drunkard's Cup* 28 A Spaniell..will leape vpon him, slabber his cloathes. **1650** WELDON *Crt. Jas. I*, I. 102 The K[ing] hung about his neck, slabboring his cheeks. **1712** ARBUTHNOT *J. Bull* III. vi, He..slabber'd me all over from Cheek to Cheek, with his great Tongue. **1753** SMOLLETT *Ct. Fathom* (1784) 64 He..began to slabber his companions, with a most bear-like affection. **1818** HAZLITT *Eng. Poets* vi. (1870) 151 How Gargantua mewls, and pules, and slabbers his nurse. **1865** ATKINSON *Prov. Danby* (MS.), *Slabber*, to wet the thread with saliva in the process of spinning.

*refl.* **1668** PEPYS *Diary* 26 Mar., Eating of sack posset, and slabbering themselves.

*fig.* **1637** J. WILLIAMS *Holy Table* 86 So as you eat cleanly, & do not slubber & slabber your quotations of those books.

**2.** To wet in a dirty or disagreeable manner.

**1573** TUSSER *Husb.* (1878) 106 Her milke pan and creame pot, so slabbered and sost. **1630** J. TAYLOR (Water P.) *Wks.* II. 22/1 We were enclosed with most dangerous sands. There were we sowsd & slabberd, wash'd & dash'd. **1675** HOBBES *Odyss.* VI. 49 A pure and undecaying firmament, Which..Nor wet nor slabber'd is with showr of rain. **1822** SCOTT *Nigel* xvii, A huge book..whose leaves, stained with wine, and slabbered with tobacco juice [etc.]. **1901** *Stafford Chron.* 25 Oct. (E.D.D.), Cyclists on a wet day get slabbered.

**3.** To gobble *up*, swallow *down*, in a hurried or unrefined manner. Cf. SLAB *v.*²

**1573** BARET *Alv.* s.v., To Slabber vp potage halfe hoate & halfe colde. **1682** T. FLATMAN *Heraclitus Ridens* No. 53 (1713) II. 85 Their Leading-men..void Pamphlets..so thick, that their hungry Spectators cannot slabber them up fast enough. **1689** G. HARVEY *Curing Dis. by Expect.* vii. 48 A course of Waters slabber'd down..do undoubtedly very much prolong the interval of fits.

**4.** *intr.* To let saliva flow or fall from the mouth; to slaver, dribble; to disgorge water.

**1648** HEXHAM II, *Zeeveren*, to Slabber like young children. **1678** *Lond. Gaz.* No. 1272/4 He is..given to slabber in his speech. **1712** J. JAMES tr. *Le Blond's Gardening* 217 Two young Tritons, and three Dolphins, that slabber into the same Bason. **1748** RICHARDSON *Clarissa* (1811) I. xlii. 322 How did he use to hang, till he slabbered again, poor doting old man! **1793** WOLCOT (P. Pindar) *Odes to Pope* Wks. 1812 III. 220 Slabbering, whining, crying.

**5.** To flow in a viscid or sloppy manner.

**1650** BULWER *Anthropomet.* ix. (1653) 164 Their spittle slabbering forth. **1683** MOXON *Mech. Exerc., Printing* xix. ¶1 The Mettal may spill or slabber over the Mouth of..the Mold.

**6.** *Sc.* To work in a sloppy manner.

**1831** SCOTT *Jrnl.* (1890) II. 369 This morning, when I came down-stairs, I found Mr. Macdonald [a sculptor] slabbering away at the model. **1894** [see the *vbl. sb.* 1].

Hence **'slabbered** *ppl. a.*

**1609** J. DAVIES (Heref.) *Hum. Heaven on Earth* vi. Wks. (Grosart) I. 6 Ouer all, he ware a slabberd Gowne. **1638** RANDOLPH *Hey for Honesty* IV. iii, The rugged wrincles of her slabber'd face. **1742** YOUNG *Nt. Th.* III. 337 For what live ever here?.. To see what we have seen? Hear, till unheard, the same old slabber'd tale? **1818** SCOTT *Rob Roy* xxvii, A hadden tongue..makes a slabbered mouth. **1857** THOREAU *Maine W.* i. (1864) 46 A few..slabbered slices of pork.

**slabber-chops.** *rare*⁻⁰. [f. prec.] (See quot.)

**1727** BOYER *Dict. Royal* I, *Baveur*, one that slabbers, a slabber Chops.

†**slabberdegullion.** *Obs. rare.* [Cf. SLABBER *v.*] = SLUBBERDEGULLION. Also *attrib.*

**1653** URQUHART *Rabelais* I. xxv, Slapsauce fellows, slabberdegullion druggels, lubbardly lowts. **1694** MOTTEUX *Rabelais* v. xv. (1737) 60 The Scabby Slabberdegulions still waited for us.

†**'slabberer.** *Obs.* [f. SLABBER *v.* + -ER¹. Cf. G. *schlabberer.*] One who slabbers; a driveller; a slobberer.

**1611** COTGR., *Patouillard*, a padler, dabler, slabberer; one that tramples with his feet in plashes of durtie water. **1660** WOOD *Life* (O.H.S.) I. 370 *note*, You may know him by his red beard, a slabberer of Boyes. **1744** OZELL tr. *Brantome's Sp. Rhodom.* 99, I have observed a great many of your gigantic People..to be mere Dolts, Slabberers and Oafs.

**slabbering** ('slæbərɪŋ), *vbl. sb.* [f. SLABBER *v.*]

**1.** The action of the verb, in various senses.

**1611** COTGR., *Patouil*, a padling, dabling, slabbering. **1630** J. TAYLOR (Water P.) *Wks.* II. 169/2 Call not your Laundresse slut or slabb'ring queane, It is her slabb'ring that doth keepe thee cleane. **1698** FRYER *Acc. E. India & P.* 223 Glasses of Rose-Water poured on our Garments to excessive slabbering. **1766** *Compl. Farmer* s.v. *Staggers*, It is a good sign if he..drinks freely without slabbering. **1894** CROCKETT *Raiders* v. 55 All his work was only slabbering with paint.

**2. a.** *slabbering-bib*, a bib, esp. for a child, to protect the clothes from falling saliva.

**1648** HEXHAM II, *Een Zeever-doeck*, a Slabbering-bibb. **1673** *Humours Town* 27 They are but petty Striplings, scarce out of their Slabbering-bibs. **1714** MANDEVILLE *Fable Bees* (1733) II. 176 We say, that a man wants a slabbering-bibb, when he behaves very sillily. **1782** MISS BURNEY *Cecilia* VI. viii, Lady Honoria..seized one of the napkins, and protested she would send it to Mortimer for a slabbering-bib.

*transf.* **1796** *Grose's Dict. Vulgar T.* (ed. 3), *Slabbering bib*, a parson or lawyer's band.

**b.** *slabbering-bit*: (see quot.).

**1753** *Chambers' Cycl.* Suppl., *Mastigadour*, or *Slabbering-Bit*, in the manege, is a snaffle of iron, all smooth, and of a piece [etc.].

**'slabbering**, *ppl. a.* [f. SLABBER *v.*]

**1.** Characterized by slabbering.

**1583** STUBBES *Anat. Abus.* I. (1879) 78 They get many a slabbering kisse. **1747** *Gentl. Mag.* 191 I've now and then a slabb'ring kiss. **1808** JAMIESON, *To Slaik*,..to kiss in a slabbering manner. **1840** R. H. DANA *Bef. Mast* xvi. 44 A continual *slabbering* sound is made in the cheeks.

**2.** That slabbers, in various senses.

**1630** [see the *vbl. sb.* 1]. **1681** W. ROBERTSON *Phraseol. Gen.* (1693) 1045 He all to bespattered him with his railing and slabbering tongue. **1764** *Museum Rust.* I. 451 Aukward slabbering sky-farmers. *a* **1774** GOLDSM. tr. *Scarron's Com. Romance* (1775) I. 42 Set down that slabbering milksop..and let her shift for herself.

**'slabberish**, *a.* *rare*⁻⁰. [f. SLABBER *sb.*¹] Of the nature of slabber.

**1648** HEXHAM II, *Zeeverachtigh*, Slabberish, or Slabbie.

†**'slabberment.** *Obs.*⁻¹ [f. SLABBER *v.* + -MENT.] A slabbery application.

*a* **1620** J. DYKE *Sel. Serm.* (1640) 160 All these slabberments will never ease the paine.

†**slabber-sauce.** *Obs.* [f. SLABBER *v.* Cf. the earlier SLIBBER-SAUCE.] A sauce, or similar preparation, composed of various ingredients mixed in a sloppy mass. Also *fig.*

**1577** FULKE *Confut. Purg.* 27 Which will not be filled vp with the slabbersawce of mens merits and satisfactions. **1581** *Test. 12 Patriarches* 10b, The Egiptian woman did much to him..by offering him slabersawces. **1621** SANDERSON *Serm.* I. 202 As absurd..as it would be for a man to accustome himself to no other diet but slabber-sauces, and druggs. **1788** FALCONBRIDGE *African Slave Trade* 21 A sauce, composed of palm-oil, mixed with flour, water, and pepper, which the sailors call slabber-sauce.

†**'slabbery**, *sb.* *Obs.*⁻¹ [f. SLABBER *sb.*¹ or *v.*] *fig.* An outpouring of abuse.

**1596** NASHE *Saffron Walden* 134 She..calls mee rampant beast in formidable hide, with I wot not what other Getulian slabberies.

**slabbery** ('slæbərɪ), *a.* Now chiefly *dial.* [f. SLABBER *sb.*¹ or *v.* Cf. LG. *slabbrig*, G. *schlabb(e)rig.*] Sloppy, slabby, slushy.

**1600** HOLLAND *Livy* XXI. xxxvi. 413 They were faine to go upon the bare yce underneath, and in the slabberie snow-broth. **1654** FLECKNOE *Ten Years Trav.* 95 The sudden rain having rendred the ways so slabbery, and me so dirty. **1711** SWIFT *Jrnl. Stella* 31 Dec., Our frost is broken,..and it is very slabbery. **1874** T. TAYLOR *Leic. Sq.* viii. 177 Hard frost was passing into 'slabbery' thaw.

**slabbiness** ('slæbɪnɪs). [f. SLABBY *a.* + -NESS.] The quality, condition, or state of being slabby; wetness; sloppiness.

**1555** EDEN *Decades* (Arb.) 310 All iorneys incumbered with continuall waters and myrie slabbynesse. *a* **1656** USSHER *Ann.* VI. (1658) 251 Alexander got on land, where he could hardly stand, for the slabbinesse of the ground. **1684** BUNYAN *Pilgr. Prog.* II. 183 The Way also was here very wearysom thorow Dirt and Slabbiness.

**'slabbing**, *sb.* [f. SLAB *sb.*¹] Slabs collectively; slab-work.

**1893** J. A. BARRY *Steve Brown's Bunyip* 76 The slabbing..had rotted away and fallen down.

**slabbing** ('slæbɪŋ), *vbl. sb.* [f. SLAB *v.*³ + -ING¹.] The action of the vb., in various senses.

**1703** [R. NEVE] *City & C. Purchaser* 237 If the Carpenter will have any pieces clear'd by Slabbing..they will..be paid by Measure for it. *Ibid.* 239 Slabbing..is cutting off the outside pieces. **1896** *Daily News* 21 Nov. 7/4 Much interest was taken in the 'slabbing' of an ingot for H.M.S. Glory.

**b.** *attrib.*, as *slabbing-gang, -mill, -roll, -saw.*

**1863** P. BARRY *Dockyard Econ.* 258 Engine-houses with engines driving slabbing rolls. **1875** KNIGHT *Dict. Mech.* 2197/2, Slabbing-saw. *Ibid.*, Slabbing-saw. **1886** *Encycl. Brit.* XXI. 344/2 In the 'slabbing' gang [of saws], the outsides or slabs were cut from one log. **1903** J. H. BRIDGE *Hist. Carnegie Steel Co.* 33 The slabbing-mill now turns out thirty thousand tons of steel slabs a month.

**'slabbish**, *a. rare*⁻⁰. Somewhat slabby.
1647 HEXHAM I, Slabbish way, *slijckachtige wegh.*

**slabby** ('slæbɪ), *a.*[1] [f. SLAB *sb.*[2] + -Y.]
**1.** Wet, miry, muddy, slushy, sloppy. Now *dial.*
**a.** Of roads, etc. (Common in 17th cent.)
1542 *Lamentable & Piteous Treat.* in *Harl. Misc.* (1745) IV. 512 The poore Souldyers..fynding the Way, by which they shuld go, so slabby and slyppery. 1555 EDEN *Decades* (Arb.) 321 The citie is very large and wyde and also very slabby and myrie. 1600 HOLLAND *Livy* XXI. xxxvi. 413 To tumble..upon the slipperie and glassie yce, and the molten slabbie snow. 1690 C. NESS *Hist. & Myst. O. & N. Test.* I. 418 They oft pass through a strait, long, slabby lane. 1716 GAY *Trivia* II. 92 When waggish boys the stunted beesom ply To rid the slabby pavement. 1737 BRACKEN *Farriery Impr.* (1757) II. 78 Deep or slabby roads. 1806 J. BERESFORD *Miseries Hum. Life* IV. xxxvii, By stamping close at your side on the slabby pavement. 1825- in dial. glossaries (N. Cy., Northampt., Suff.).
*fig.* 1610 COOKE *Pope Joane* 106 You..make that the ground of your conclusion. Now that is a slabbie ground. 1650 H. MORE *Observ.* in *Enthus. Tri.*, etc. (1656) 79 This latter is more clean and sober, the other more slabby and fantasticall.
**b.** Of weather.
1653 W. RAMESEY *Astrol. Restored* 291 [It] denotes,..in winter, grievous cold, and snowy slabby weather. 1675 EVELYN *Terra* (1729) 14, I am only to caution our labourer, ..that he do not stir the Ground in over-wet and slabby weather. 1713 SWIFT *Jrnl. to Stella* 7 Jan., Very warm slabby weather, but I made a shift to get a walk.
**2.** Of liquids, etc.: Thick, ropy, viscous.
*a* 1654 SELDEN *Table-t.* (Arb.) 86 They present you with a Cup, and you must drink of a slabby stuff. 1676 WISEMAN *Surg. Treat.* II. iii. 173 In the Cure of an Ulcer with a moist Intemperies slabby and greasy Medicaments are to be forborn. 1725 *Family Dict.* s.v. *Tart*, You must drain off the Milk, or else the mass will be too slabby. 1810 W. TAYLOR in *Monthly Mag.* XXIX. 148 In order to render palatable the bitter herbs.., it was usual..to sprinkle over them a thick slabby sauce. 1865 *Pall Mall G.* 17 June 10 Pawing at the corners of the mouth to free it from thick slabby saliva.

**slabby** ('slæbɪ), *a.*[2] [f. SLAB *sb.*[1]] Of the nature of a slab; covered with slabs.
1853 *Chamb. Jrnl.* XX. 308 It is remarkable for clean, broad, and handsome streets; for slabby terraces and a broad-sweeping beach. 1879 RUTLEY *Study Rocks* xii. 224 Some of the quartz-trachytes show a fissile, slaty, or slabby structure.

**slabby** ('slæbɪ), *sb. N.Z. colloq.* [f. SLAB *sb.*[1] 2 a.] A timber worker dealing with slabs of timber.
1907 'G. B. LANCASTER' *Tracks We Tread* vi. 87 The.. clumsiest slabby that lumped in the mill. 1916 G. THORNTON *Wowser* v. 72 Barnabas the slabby (the man who wheels away the unused portions of timber).

**slabline** ('slæblaɪn). *Naut.* [prob. ad. Du. *slaplijn* (G. *schlappleine*), f. *slap* slack.] (See quots. 1769 and 1846.) Also *attrib.*
1647 N. WARD *Simple Cobler* 46 When Kings are haleing up their top-gallant, Subjects lay hold on their slablines. 1769 FALCONER *Dict. Marine* (1780), *Slab-line*, a small cord passing up behind a ship's main-sail or fore-sail... It is used to truss up the sail. 1846 A. YOUNG *Naut. Dict.* 285 *Slab-line*, a rope used to haul up the slack of a course, in order to prevent it from shaking, or being split in the act of hauling up the sail. *c* 1860 H. STUART *Seaman's Catech.* 25 The quarter slabline block on the jackstay. *Ibid.* 47 The inner slabline is..brought abaft the sail.

**slably, slabness**: see SLAB *a.*[1]

**slab reef.** *Naut.* (See quot. and SLAB-LINE.)
1882 NARES *Seamanship* (ed. 6) 125 There are the same number of slab reef lines.., and they are used for hauling up the slab reef or slack part of sail which hangs down abaft all when a reef is taken in.

**slab-sided** ('slæbsaɪdɪd), *a.* Orig. *U.S.* [f. SLAB *sb.*[1]] Having sides like slabs; flat-sided; long and lank. Also in *Archit.*: see SLAB *sb.*[1] 1 d.
1817 J. K. PAULDING *Lett. from South* II. 122 He was what is usually called a tall slab-sided Virginian. 1825 J. NEAL *Bro. Jonathan* II. 145 Great, long, slab-sided, simple gawkeys. 1840 R. H. DANA *Bef. Mast* xxv. 79 Her captain was a slab-sided, shamble-legged Quaker. 1874 J. W. LONG *Amer. Wild-fowl* v. 94 The silky, thin-haired, narrow-chested, and slab-sided animal so fashionable nowadays. 1927 A. CONAN DOYLE *Case-Bk. Sherlock Holmes* iii. 89 The prize-fighter, a heavily built young man with a stupid, obstinate, slab-sided face. 1933 *Flight* 23 Mar. 268 The fuselage is not quite 'slab-sided'. 1964 L. DEIGHTON *Funeral in Berlin* v. 32 The large slab-sided department store. 1981 E. CORLETT *Revolution in Merchant Shipping* 35/1 High slab-sided deckhouses.

**'slab-stone.** Also slabstone. [SLAB *sb.*[1]] A stone having the form of a slab.
1851 STERNBERG *Northampt. Dial.*, *Slab-stones*, broad and thin stones. 1891 *N. & Q.* 3 Jan. 8 A slabstone was discovered in the Court aisle. 1897 CHETWYND-STAPYLTON *Stapeltons of Yorks.* 191 Torre also saw four monumental slabstones.

**slachtir**, obs. Sc. form of SLAUGHTER.

**slack** (slæk), *sb.*[1] *north.* and *Sc.* Forms: 5 slac, slakke, slake, 5-6 slak, 6- slack. [a. ON. *slakki* (Icel. *slakki*, Norw. *slakke*) in sense 1.]
**1. a.** A small shallow dell or valley; a hollow or dip in the ground; a depression in a hill-side or between two stretches of rising ground.
1375 BARBOUR *Bruce* XIV. 536 Till the hill thai tuk the way. In a slak thame enbuschit thai. *c* 1400 *Rowland & O.* 1418 Doun þay dange þaire Baners brade Bothe in slakkes & in slade. *c* 1450 *St. Cuthbert* (Surtees) 7418 Slike paynes suffird all þe pak þat wer broght in to þat slak [= a vale of depnes 7407]. 1470-85 MALORY *Arthur* VI. v. 189 Ther by a lytyl slake syr launcelot wounded hym..nyghe vnto the deth. 1513 DOUGLAS *Æneid* VIII. x. 91 Sitand into ane holl valle or slak. *a* 1560 ROLLAND *Crt. Venus* III. 146 Quhite as the snaw that euer lay in slak. 1615 *Extr. Aberd. Reg.* (1848) II. 326 The samen is mercheit be stanes..quhill it come to the end of the Gallow slackis. 1682 O. HEYWOOD *Diaries* (1885) IV. 85 My danger upon Clifton common..; in a slack full of snow my horse got fast. 1718 *Records of Elgin* (New Spald. Cl.) I. 402 Ane stripe that rins in ane slack. 1788 W. H. MARSHALL *Yorksh.* II. 353 *Slack*, a valley, or small shallow dale; a dip. 1813 HOGG *Queen's Wake* (1871) 60 O'er slope and slack She sought her native stall. 1825- in northern glossaries. 1891 J. C. ATKINSON *Moorland Par.* 186 A series of short banklets, hillocks, mounds, and peaks, with intertwining gullies, slacks, and hollows.
†**b.** A pit, a hole. *Obs.*⁻¹
*a* 1500 in *Ratis Raving* (1870) 23 Mony man makis a slak in an vthir manis vay, and fall fyrst thar in.
**2.** A hollow in the sand- or mud-banks on a shore. Also, a depression among sand-dunes.
?*a* 1400 *Morte Arth.* 3720 Thane was þe flode passede; Thane was it slyke a slowde in slakkes fulle hugge, That let þe kyng for to lande. 1570 *Satir. Poems Reform.* xxiv. 39 Had not bene ane slack was in the sands, Weill had he payit ȝow tratouris for ȝour tressoun. 1901 *Pall Mall Mag.* Sept. 138 The 'slacks' I have mentioned are fresh-water pools which extend just inside the outer sandhills [of the estuary of the Mersey]. 1929 [see LOW *sb.* 3 a]. 1934 *Geogr. Jrnl.* LXXXIII. 498 The question that always comes to my mind in looking at dune formations is what is the primary cause of the rhythmical or ripple effect, the succession of ridges and slacks. 1963 *Times* 27 Feb. 11/6 In the lee of the high dunes lie wet slacks and attractive freshwater pools out of which grow strands of reed and reed-mace. 1964 V. J. CHAPMAN *Coastal Vegetation* vi. 153 The damp soil of the slacks is colonized by a carpet of the Creeping Willow.
**3.** A soft or boggy hollow; a morass.
1719 in Cramond *Annals Cullen* (1888) 79 The magistrates appoint..that none cast above two spades casting in the common moss or Chamar Slack without liberty. 1815 SCOTT *Guy M.* xxv, A deep morass, termed in that country a slack. *c* 1880 J. LUCAS *Stud. Nidderdale* 278 *Slack*, a hollow boggy place. 1897 LD. E. HAMILTON *Outlaws* xxviii. 310 The yellow slack that feeds the Blackburn, and in which horse and rider might readily disappear for ever.

**slack** (slæk), *sb.*[2] Also (now *dial.*) sleck. [Of doubtful origin: cf. older Flem. *slecke*, Du. *slak*, LG. *slak(ke*, G. *schlacke* dross of metals.] Small or refuse coal. Also *attrib.*
α. *c* 1440 *Pallad. on Husb.* II. 152 Vndonged sleck wole make hem lene, as preue is. 1665 DUDLEY *Metallum Martis* (1854) 8 These Colliers must cast these coles and sleck or drosse out of their wayes. 1677 *Phil. Trans.* XII. 898 The Men..hid themselves as well as they could in the loose sleck or small Cole. 1800 *Hull Advertiser* 29 Nov. 2/1 For every chaldron of coals, sleck, cinders, culm, coke. 1857 WAUGH *Lanc. Life* 197 Nearly every cottage had its stock of coals piled up under the front window,..the 'cobs' neatly built up into a square wall, and the centre filled up with the 'sleck an' naplins'.
β. 1729 SWIFT *Let. on Irish Coal* Wks. 1841 II. 110 In every half barrel of coals you have the one-half of it slack, and that slack of little use. 1795 J. PHILLIPS *Hist. Inland Navig.* Add. 173 For all slack or small and inferior coal for the purpose of burning lime-stone or bricks,..six-pence per ton. 1825 J. NICHOLSON *Operat. Mechanic* 358 The fire is now slackened, and a quantity of slack, or refuse pit-coal, thrown into the furnace. 1881 YOUNG *Every Man his own Mechanic* §1420. 649 The fuel used is fine coal generally called 'Smith's coal' or 'slack'. 1881 *Census Instr.* (1885) 84/3 Slack-picker, -washer.

**slack** (slæk), *sb.*[3] Also 6 -e. [f. SLACK *a.* or *v.*]
†**1.** The passing or spending *of* time. *Obs.*
*a* 1533 LD. BERNERS *Gold. Bk. M. Aurel.* (1559) R iij b, All onely for slacke of time, and driuyng of one houre to a nother.
**2. a.** A cessation in the strong flow of a current or of the tide. (Cf. SLACK-WATER.)
1756 *Phil. Trans.* XLIX. 531 During the time of the water flowing, the strength of the current going down was greatly abated, almost to a slack. *Ibid.*, He met an unexpected slack in Greenwich-reach. 1892 *Law Times Rep.* LXVII. 251/1 The tide was low water slack, and the weather was fine and clear. 1902 LD. AVEBURY *Scenery of England* 456 They are the debris of the Yorkshire and Lincolnshire coast, and are deposited at the slack of highwater.
**b.** A stretch or reach of comparatively still water in a river.
1825 BROCKETT *N.C. Gloss.*, *Slack*, a long pool in a streamy river. 1889 in *N.W. Linc. Gloss.* 1902 *Daily Chron.* 28 Jan. 8/3 Some perch and pike have also been taken out of the eddies and slacks.
**3. a.** An interval of comparative inactivity; a lull in business or in action of any kind.
1851 MAYHEW *Lond. Lab.* II. 83/1 An ingenious..coster-monger, during a 'slack' in his own business [etc.]. 1861 HUGHES *Tom Brown at Oxf.* xliv, Though there's a slack, we haven't done with sharp work yet, I can see.
**b.** A slackening of speed.
1899 *Daily News* 14 Sept. 7/6 The 23½ miles..are covered in 21½ minutes; and this though there is a relaying slack at Farnborough.
**c.** In critical path analysis, the length of time by which a particular event can be delayed without delaying the completion of the overall objective.
1962 *NASA PERT & Compan. Cost System Handbk.* (U.S. Nat. Aeronaut. & Space Admin.) B-3 The accomplishment of event #3 could be delayed by three weeks without jeopardizing meeting the expected date for the end objective. This difference or cushion is called slack. 1964 K. G. LOCKYER *Introd. Critical Path Anal.* v. 46 A different expression of the ability of activities to move is given by considering the head and tail events. These have 'earliest' and 'latest' times, and slack is the difference between these times. 1970 O. DOPPING *Computers & Data Processing* xxii. 346 After the critical path has been found, it may be possible to transfer resources from activities with a big slack to certain critical activities.
**4. a.** That part *of* a rope, sail, etc., which is not fully strained, or which hangs loose; a loose part or end. Also *fig.*, esp. in phr. ***to take up the slack***, to use up a surplus or make up a deficiency, thereby maintaining or returning to a stable condition; ***to hold on the slack***, to skulk; to be lazy (1864 *Slang Dict.*).
1794 *Rigging & Seamanship* 95 Topsails are allowed 3 inches slack in every cloth in the foot. 1825 J. NICHOLSON *Operat. Mechanic* 437 When the sledge is in motion,..it pulls up the slack of the rope from the bottom of the rope-walk. 1867 F. FRANCIS *Angling* viii. (1880) 281 Gathering the line up..so that no slack hangs about. 1899 F. T. BULLEN *Log of Sea-waif* 89, I sat on the poop beside the tiller, hauling back the slack of the wheel-ropes. 1915 J. LONDON *Jacket* viii. 63 Jones was forcing his foot into my back in order to cinch me tighter, while I was trying with my muscle to steal slack. 1930 *Economist* 21 June 1391/2 There is general agreement that the termination of the Stevenson Scheme left the industry with much more 'slack' to take up than was realised two years ago. 1933 *Sun* (Baltimore) 12 Sept. 1/6 The American Federation of Labor..was framing demands for further..wage-boosting to take up employment slack. 1957 *Economist* 16 Nov. 610/2 Sir Alexander Fleck's investigations may show just how much slack has crept into an organization that should be, if anything, over-cautious. 1967 *Times* 28 Feb. (Canada Suppl.) 33 There is the feeling that slack will develop as the year progresses. 1972 A. MACVICAR *Golden Venus Affair* vi. 61 It was a comfort having somebody like Mary Jo to take up the slack of decision-making. 1980 B. PAUL *First Gravedigger* v. 60 We'd no longer be handling his speciality. ..Our new rare books department in London would take up the slack.
**b.** *colloq.* The seat *of* a pair of trousers.
1848 LOWELL *Biglow P.* Ser. I. ii, To take a feller up jest by the slack o' 's trowsis. 1879 WAUGH *Chimney Corner* 229, I took it bi th' slack o'th' breeches, an' chuck't it into th' poand.
**c.** Phr. ***to give*** (or ***cut***) (a person) ***some slack***, to show (a person) understanding or restraint, to give (one) a chance. *U.S. slang* (chiefly *Blacks'*).
1968 M. F. JACKMON in Jones & Neal *Black Fire* (1969) 555 Say, baby, light'n up on me—gimme some slack. 1969 H. RAP BROWN *Die Nigger Die* ii. 29 Now, if the brother couldn't come back behind that, I usually cut him some slack. 1971 *Current Slang* (Univ. S. Dakota) VI. 3 *Cut me some slack!*, to give one a chance (imperative). 1973 *Black World* May 39/1 Tradesmen give them no slack in the unfamiliar bargaining processes.
**5.** *pl.* Trousers. Now *spec.* loosely-cut trousers for informal wear, esp. those worn by women.
1824 in *Spirit Publ. Jrnls.* (1825) 346 His inexpressibles (drab slacks) were napless. 1853 R. S. SURTEES *Sponge's Sp. Tour* (1893) 232 Formidable in 'slacks', as he called his trousers. 1889 *Pall Mall G.* 28 Sept. 7/2 Eight nice little British sailors, in eight nice little pairs of white pants, called slacks. 1932 D. L. SAYERS *Have his Carcase* ii. 31 He wore a pair of old flannel slacks, and a khaki shirt. 1937 *Night & Day* 29 July 22/2 Deeply to be deplored are such things as sandals..slacks and sun-top dresses. 1942 A. CHRISTIE *Body in Library* xii. 139 She was wearing grey slacks and an emerald jumper. 1947 W. S. MAUGHAM *Creatures of Circumstance* 303 He changed from his business clothes into slacks and an old coat. 1956 A. H. COMPTON *Atomic Quest* i. 32 Dressed casually in slacks and a sweater, he invited me cordially into his study. 1966 J. BETJEMAN *High & Low* 56 The debs may turn disdainful backs On Pearl's uncouth mechanic slacks. 1968 *Listener* 10 Dec. 790/3 In Jordan, girls at Amman University have been instructed not to wear ..slacks either, and, moreover, to keep off heavy make-up. 1979 R. JAFFE *Class Reunion* (1980) I. i. 27 Nor could you wear slacks or any other sort of pants to class, even in the snow.
**6.** *dial.* and *U.S. colloq.* Impertinence, cheek.
1825 J. NEAL *Bro. Jonathan* I. 156 'None o' your slack,' says I..'none o' your pokin' fun at me.' 1842 H. J. DANIEL *Bride of Scio*, etc. 177 Howld tha slack! Yer tongue young chap's too saucy. 1876 T. HARDY *Ethelberta* (1890) 357 Let's have none of your slack. 1901 *Munsey's Mag.* XXIV. 481/2 I've taken a lot of your slack for a month or two, and I'm.. gettin' somewhat peevish.
**7.** *Pros.* A syllable or part of a foot which does not receive stress.
*c* 1883 G. M. HOPKINS *Poems* (1967) 45 Every foot has one principal stress or accent, and this or the syllable it falls on may be called the Stress of the foot and the other part, the one or two unaccented syllables, the Slack. 1970 J. MALOF *Man. Eng. Meters* i. 2 In the freer varieties of accentual verse, meter is determined simply by counting the number of stresses in the line.., ignoring the relatively unemphatic or unstressed syllables, which we call slacks. 1973 *Word* 1970 XXVI. 56 None or as many as six slacks may appear between such isochronous accents, though one, two, or three slacks are more normal.
**8.** A street-walker or prostitute. *slang.*
1959 *Encounter* May 24 *Slack*, which is the call-girls' word for a street-girl. 1963 *Observer* 29 Sept. 31/4 A young master was asked by a boy..'Can a slack (prostitute) work hard enough to earn a living?' 1965 W. YOUNG *Eros Denied* xiv. 141 The slack is afraid of disease, and afraid of the sex maniac who thinks it'd be fun to strangle her.
**9.** *Comb.* **slack suit**, a pair of slacks with a matching jacket, as a fashionable garment for women; **slack variable** *Math.*, a variable which

expresses the difference between the two sides of an inequality.

**1940** R. CHANDLER *Farewell, my Lovely* xxvii. 203 Miss Anne Riordan stood there, in a pale green *slack suit. **1973** H. NIELSEN *Severed Key* viii. 91 She had..changed into a lime-green knitted slack-suit. **1953** COOPER & HENDERSON *Introd. Linear Programming* I. ii. 6 These values $\lambda_i$ ($i$ = 10,11, ...16) so introduced may be referred to as *slack variables. .. The requirement that the slack variables be non-negative merely extends the range of the subscript. **1974** ADBY & DEMPSTER *Introd. Optimization Methods* v. 156 At least some evidence exists which suggests that the use of slack variables is an effective method for handling inequality constraints, both linear and non-linear.

**slack** (slæk), *a.* and *adv.* Forms: 1 **sleac, slæc,** 3–5 **slac,** 4–6 **slak** (5 **sclak**), **slakke,** 4–7 **slacke,** 5– **slack.** [Common Teut.: OE. *sleac, slæc,* = MDu. *slac, slack-* (Du. and Flem. dial. *slak*), MLG. *slak* (LG. *slakk, slack*), OHG. and MHG. *slach* (G. dial. *schlach,* also *schlack*), ON. *slakr* (Icel. *slakur,* Norw. and Sw. *slak,* Da. †*slag*). The stem is related to that of L. *laxus.*]

**A.** *adj.*

**I. 1. a.** Of persons: Lacking in energy or diligence; inclined to be lazy or idle; remiss, careless; negligent or lax in regard to one's duties.

*Beowulf* 2187 Ᵹeata bearn..wendon, þæt he sleac wære, æðeling unfrom. *c* **897** K. ÆLFRED *Gregory's Past. C.* xvii. 125 Ðæt he..ne sie to stræc on ðære lare, ne to slæc on ðære mildheortnesse. *c* **1055** *Byrhtferth's Handboc* in *Anglia* VIII. 317 Þæt þam sleacan preoste ne þince to mycel ȝeswinc þæt he undo his eaȝan herto. **1340** *Ayenb.* 32 Huanne he is sleuuol,..uoryetinde, slak, and fallinde. *c* **1386** CHAUCER *Shipm. T.* 413 Ye han mo slakkere dettours than am I. *c* **1400** *Gamelyn* 711 Allas! seide Gamelyn, þat euer I was so slak That I ne hadde broke his nekke. **1492** *Bury Wills* (Camden) 78 Yf he se othyr be slakke or necligent. **1535** COVERDALE *Hab.* ii. 3 For in very dede he wil come, and not be slacke. **1577** HARRISON *England* II. i. (1877) I. 18 If they haue been found to be slacke, their negligence is openlie reprooued. **1621** BURTON *Anat. Mel.* III. ii. VI. v. (1651) 576 Many slack and careless Parents..measure their childrens affections by their own. **1665** DRYDEN *Ind. Emp.* III. i, The Truce will make the Guards more slack. **1741** WESLEY *Wks.* (1872) I. 304, I put those of the women who were grown slack, into distinct Bands. **1793** MANN in *Lett. Lit. Men* (Camden) 438 A Government unhinged, an exhausted Treasury, and slack Allies. **1826** DISRAELI *V. Grey* VI. ii, When you complained that you and meat had been but slack friends of late. **1888** BRYCE *Amer. Commw.* II. xlix. 255 In such parts of the West.., if the sheriff is distant or slack, lynch law may usefully be invoked.

**b.** With various constructions, esp. *in* with gerund or sb., and *to* with inf. Also † ***slack of***, short of (quot. 1605).

*c* **1000** ÆLFRIC *Hom.* II. 100 Se ðe on oðrum daȝum sleac wære to godnysse. *c* **1000** in *Anglia* XI. 117 Handa mine.. synd..sleace to æniȝ wyrcenne god. **1535** STARKEY *Let.* in *England* (1878) p. xxiv, I perceyue you haue byn slakker in wrytyng bycause you mor lokyd for ferther instructyon. **1535** COVERDALE *Eccl.* v. 4 Yf thou make a vowe vnto God, be not slacke to perfourme it. **1605** SHAKS. *Lear* I. iii. 9 If you come slacke of former seruices, You shall do well; the fault of it Ile answer. **1681** H. MORE *Exp. Dan.* II. (1782) 97 Thy purged eye will see God is not slack..to fulfil his word. **1703** *Clarendon's Hist. Reb.* VI. §235 II. 96 Neither the King, nor the Parliament, being slack in pursuing the business by the Sword. **1753** WASHINGTON *Jrnl.* Writ. 1889 I. 33 The French were not slack in their Inventions to keep the Indians this Day also. **1828** SCOTT *F.M. Perth* iv, The sturdy armourer was not.. slack in keeping the appointment. **1867** S. SMILES *Huguenots Eng.* ix. (1880) 145 Louis was not slack to obey the injunction. **1867** FREEMAN *Norm. Conq.* (1877) I. App. 711 Florence was not slack at attributing crimes to Eadric.

**c.** Slow in coming; tardy, late. *rare*$^{-1}$.

**1694** ECHARD *Plautus* 53 An empty Belly and a slack Guest, makes one as mad as the Devil.

**2.** Not busy; having little work, etc. (Cf. 6.)

**1834** *Tait's Mag.* I. 421/2 There are plenty of empty or slack hotels in Edinburgh that would answer your purpose. **1861** DICKENS *Gt. Expect.* xv, As we are rather slack just now, if you would give me a half-holiday. **1870** BARTLEY *Sq. Mile E. London* 54 He would not mind when in work, but when slack he thought they should go free.

**II. 3.** Of conduct, actions, etc.: Characterized by remissness or lack of energy.

*c* **900** tr. *Baeda's Hist.* v. xv. 442 Ðiode he swiðe druncennisse & monȝum oðrum unalefednessum ðæs slæcran lifes. *c* **960** *Rule St. Benet* (Schröer) xviii. 44 Hit is ealles to sleac munuca þeowdom..ȝif hie læsse singað on þære wucan. *c* **1000** ÆLFRIC *Hom.* I. 602 We sceolon asceacan ðone sleacan slæp us fram. **1534** MORE *Treat. Passion* ii. Wks. 1312/2 Their fastynges were also verye paynefull and precyse: and ours neglygent, slacke, and remysse. **1579** NORTHBROOKE *Agst. Dicing* (1843) 20 The cause of my slacke and seldome comming to the church. **1608** TOPSELL *Serpents* (1658) 689 If they will decipher..a slow and slack victory, they picture a Scorpion. **1611** BIBLE *Prov.* x. 4 He becommeth poor that dealeth with a slacke hand. **1809** W. IRVING *Knickerb.* VII. i. (1849) 382 The slack though fitful reign of William the Testy. **1855** MACAULAY *Hist. Eng.* xxi. IV. 566 The correspondence gradually became more and more slack. **1857** BUCKLE *Civiliz.* I. xiv. 820 Some very great men have effected absolutely nothing, not because their labour was slack, but because their method was sterile.

**4.** Of pace: Slow; not smart or hurried.

*c* **1000** ÆLFRIC *Hom.* II. 138 Sum oðer munuc..mid sleaccre stalcunge his fotswaðum filiȝde. *c* **1386** CHAUCER *Knt.'s T.* 2043 The nobleste of the grekes..caryeden the beere With slak paas. **1682** DRYDEN *Medal* 44 Their pace was formal, grave, and slack. **1719** DE FOE *Crusoe* I. (Globe) 243 As he came nearer, I found his Pace was slacker, because he had something in his Hand. **1844** DICKENS *Mart. Chuz.* v, His companion slackened the slack pace of the horse.

**5. a.** Comparatively weak or slow in operation; deficient in strength or activity; dull.

*c* **1374** CHAUCER *Boeth.* III. met. ii. (1868) 68 Wiþ slakke and delitable soun of strenges. **1398** TREVISA *Barth. De P.R.* v. xxxvi. (Bodl. MS.), Whanne þe vertu is feble and slake it may nought sprede þe woosen and veynes into euerich place and side of þe body. **1547** BOORDE *Brev. Health* §50 This infirmite doth come thorowe euyll, slacke, or slowe digestion. **1678** BUTLER *Hud.* III. ii. 32 Rebellion now began for lack Of Zeal and Plunder to grow slack. **1688** PRIOR *Seneca Dying* 3 The moral Spaniard's ebbing Veins, By Study worn, and slack with Age. **1786** MME. D'ARBLAY *Diary* 7 Aug., I pretended not to understand him. I am forced to that method of slack comprehension continually. **1802–12** BENTHAM *Ration. Judic. Evid.* Wks. 1827 IV. 81 It may be imagined whether imitation is in danger of being slack. **1826** *Art of Brewing* (ed. 2) 15 Many brewers hesitate in applying what are called slack liquors, lest their worts should be foul. **1865** M. ARNOLD *Ess. Crit.* v. (1875) 201 The culture of Germany—so wide,..that it is apt to become slack and powerless.

**b.** Of heat, etc.: Not strong or excessive; gentle, moderate.

**1495** *Trevisa's Barth. De P.R.* IX. xv. 356 Thys monthe [July] the heete is stronge in the begynnynge and slacker in the ende. **1662** J. CHANDLER *Van Helmont's Oriat.* 57 They give the greatest coldness to the water, with a slack or mean moystness. **1735** *Dict. Polygraph.* s.v. *Varnish,* Harden it.. first with a slack heat, the next with a warmer, and the third with a very hot one. **1741** *Compl. Fam.-Piece* I. iii. 228 Set them in a slack Oven till they are tender. **1892** *Daily News* 11 Mar. 5/8 Three-fourths of the blast furnaces have been put on slack blast.

**c.** Of wind, or tide: Blowing, or running, with very little strength or speed.

**1670** MILTON *Hist. Eng.* II. Wks. 1851 V. 38 Cæsar.. about sun sett, hoysing saile with a slack South-West, at mid-night was becalm'd. **1817** COLERIDGE *Biogr. Lit.,* *Satyrane's Lett.* i, The wind continuing slack. **1853** SIR H. DOUGLAS *Milit. Bridges* (ed. 3) 218 Pontoons used as row-boats, when the tide was slack. **1892** W. C. RUSSELL *List Ye Landsmen* xi, The breeze has fallen slack.

**6. a.** Of work, etc.: Not brisk or active.

**1813** *Sporting Mag.* XLII. 119 When betting became slack. **1821** CLARE *Vill. Minstr.* I. 17 Discourses..'Bout work being slack, and rise and fall of bread. **1873** C. ROBINSON *N.S. Wales* 50 The work..is not always continuous as the demand is sometimes slack.

**b.** Of times: Characterized by inactivity or dullness in work or business.

**1828** CARR *Craven Gloss.* s.v., Slack times. **1833** HT. MARTINEAU *Manch. Strike* ix. 99 A slack season in which many workmen remain unemployed. **1894** *Field* 1 Dec. 838/2 There would be a slack three weeks between two of the fruit crops.

**III. 7. a.** Not drawn or held tightly or tensely; relaxed, loose.

**13..** *K. Alis.* 1252 (W.), The stedes ronnon with slak bridel. *c* **1386** CHAUCER *Merch. T.* 605 The slakke skyn aboute his nekke shaketh. *c* **1440** *Promp. Parv.* 317/2 Lusch, or slak, *laxus.* **1530** PALSGR. 324/1 Slacke, nat fast togyther, *lasche.* **1579** SPENSER *Sheph. Cal.* Mar. 83 His..siluer bowe, which was but slacke. **1621** in Foster *Eng. Factories Ind.* (1906) I. 272 In the morning wee bore a slack saile. **1687** A. LOVELL tr. *Thevenot's Trav.* II. 4 The Stays were very slack, being loosened by the force of the Wind the day before. **1798** LANDOR *Gebir* VII. 52 The slack cordage rattles round the mast. **1826** S. COOPER *First Lines Surg.* (ed. 5) 136 It was an invariable rule with me to be sure that the bandage was slack. **1879** BEERBOHM *Patagonia* iii. 29 The slack canvas being no longer water-tight, little pools of water gathered round the furs and saddle-cloths.

**b.** In fig. contexts.

**1590** R. HITCHCOCK *Quint. Wit* 13 Wicked men let slacke their raines with liberty to follow vice. **1648** *Nicholas Papers* (Camden) 104 To reward merritt and punish offenders.., not letting slacke the raignes. **1873** BROWNING *Red Cott. Nt.-cap* 1530 Somewhere must a screw be slack!

**c.** Free from confinement. *rare*$^{-1}$.

**1565** GOLDING *Ovid's Met.* I. (1593) 9 Eche one of them unloosed his spring, and let the water slacke.

**d.** Not contracted; open, wide. *rare*$^{-1}$.

**1577** B. GOOGE *Heresbach's Husb.* II. (1586) 74b, You must take heed..that the cleft be not to slacke nor to strait.

**e.** *Phonetics.* Of a vowel: = LAX *a.* 5c.

**1909** H. C. WYLD *Elem. Lessons Eng. Gram.* ii. 28 Vowels formed with the tongue tense we call Tense Vowels, those with the tongue soft we call Slack Vowels. **1934** C. DAVIES *Eng. Pronunc. from 15th to 18th Cent.* 8 It was probably a slack, round mid-back, vowel. **1970** B. M. H. STRANG *Hist. Eng.* 285 The letter *æ* represents a long, low, slack front vowel /æ:/ in *dælan.*

**8.** Lacking cohesiveness or solidity; not compact or firm; crumbling, loose; soft.

*c* **1440** *Pallad. on Husb.* IX. 72 Slak [*v.r.* sclak] sonde, lymous and lene, vnswete & depe. **1608** TOPSELL *Serpents* (1658) 785 Of these Cobwebs..some..are loose, weak, slack, and not well bound: other contrary-wise well compacted. **1830** M. DONOVAN *Domest. Econ.* I. 91 When malt which has been thus sprinkled remains some time in store, it grows soft, or *slack,* as it is called. **1897** *Daily News* 29 Dec. 4/7 The mud, which was a cake during the frost, became slack dough with the thaw.

**9. a.** Of the hand: Not holding or grasping firmly. Also in fig. context.

**1667** MILTON *P.L.* IX. 892 From his slack hand the Garland wreath'd for Eve Down drop'd. **1722** DE FOE *Col. Jack* (1840) 158 A slack hand had..been held upon them. **1726** POPE *Odyss.* XIX. 548 Down dropp'd the leg, from her slack hand releas'd. **1856** BRYANT *Hymn to Death* 57 His slack hand Drops the drawn knife. **1871** PALGRAVE *Lyrical Poems* 120 Some finish'd thing, Ere the slack hands at eve Drop, should be his to leave.

**b.** Similarly of one's hold of anything.

**1836** MRS. BROWNING *Poet's Vow* II. i, A somewhat slacker hold. **1876** SMILES *Sc. Natur.* ii. (ed. 4) 29 Her hold getting a little slacker, he made a sudden bolt.

**10.** Special collocations. ***slack barrel, cask,*** one made to hold dry goods; ***slack-course*** (see quot. 1875); ***slack helm*** (see quot. 1867); ***slack key*** (Mus.) [tr. Hawaiian *kī hō'alu,* f. *kī* key + *hō'alu* slack], used *absol.* and *attrib.,* esp. as ***slack-key guitar,*** with reference to a style of guitar-playing originating in Hawaii, in which the strings are slightly relaxed to produce strong bass resonances; ***slack lip,*** = SLACK-JAW; ***slack party*** (Naut. slang) (see quots.); ***slack wire,*** a wire not drawn tight, on which an acrobat performs.

**1877** *Encycl. Brit.* VI. 338 *Slack barrels are..extensively employed. *Ibid.,* Tight or wet and dry or *slack cask manufacture. **1875** KNIGHT *Dict. Mech.* 2197/2 **Slack-course* (Knitting-machine), a range of loops or stitches more open than those which precede them. **1867** SMYTH *Sailor's Word-bk.* 630 **Slack helm,* if the ship is too much by the stern, she will carry her helm too much *a-lee.* **1975** G. S. KANAHELE in *Ha'ilono Mele* Jan. 2/2 Our first concert [in 1972] was memorable. It featured the *slack key guitar, the first time that an entire concert was devoted to this unique style of playing. **1976** *Guitar Player* Apr. 14/2 The original style is kept alive solely by those guitarists who insist on playing only slack key. **1977** *Zigzag* Mar. 20/1 Could you explain about slack-key guitar? **1899** F. T. BULLEN *Log of Sea-waif* 104 No man durst give him '*slack lip' on pain of being instantly knocked endways. **1933** J. MASEFIELD *Conway* IV. 145 For official punishments there was an institution known as '*slack party', which meant employment upon every available job..from morning till night. **1945** 'TACKLINE' *Holiday Sailor* 133 Jimmy's pet form of punishment was his 'slack party'. Hands tardy in going on watch or performing some allotted task with lack of zeal were enrolled in the slack party. And the slack party did not lead an especially restful existence. **1753** *N.-Y. Mercury* 20 Aug. 3/3 The Surprizing Performances of the celebrated Anthony Joseph Dugee..On a *Slack Wire scarcely perceptible and without a Balance. **1825** HONE *Every-day Bk.* I. 1185 Another female danced on the slack-wire. **1866** M. MACKINTOSH *Stage Reminisc.* xi. 138 Andrew was at once a good tight-rope dancer and slack-wire vaulter. **1977** E. AMBLER *Send no more Roses* viii. 183 A slack-wire baggy-pants act out of a third-rate circus.

**IV. 11.** *Comb.* **a.** Parasynthetic adjs., as ***slack-backed, -fingered, -haired, -hammed, -handed, -jawed, -mouthed,*** etc.

**1642** ROGERS *Naaman* 301 Debaucht and slacke hayred companions. *a* **1661** HOLYDAY *Juvenal* (1673) 20 O, there's a monstrous league between these soft And slack-ham'd pathicks! **1674** FLAVEL *Husb. Spiritualized* i. 22 What, now slack-handed, when so neer to my everlasting rest! **1796** *Grose's Dict. Vulgar T., Slag,* a slack-mettled fellow, one not ready to resent an affront. **1822** MANBY *Voy. Greenland* 130 In what are called slack-backed fish. **1881** G. MEREDITH *Tragic Comed.* 92 This time if I let you slip, may I be stamped slack-fingered! **1897** RHOSCOMYL *White Rose Arno* 25 A slack-lipped specimen of the young blood of the period. **1901** KIPLING *Kim* iii. 76 Our colonel used to send for slack-jawed down-country men who talked too much. **1936** W. FAULKNER *Absalom, Absalom!* 44 Wild-eyed and considerably slack-mouthed. **1942** —— *Go down, Moses* 32 He stood for perhaps ten seconds, slackjawed with amazed and incredulous comprehension. **1976** J. CARROLL *Mortal Friends* II. iii. 170 The people were Catholics nearly to a person, and they stared slack-jawed at the line of nuns. **1976** P. CAVE *High Flying Birds* iii. 42, I continued to gaze at Sonya with slack-mouthed adoration.

†**b. slack-grace,** one who has little grace. *Obs.*

**1623** R. CARPENTER *Consc. Christian* 29 Weaklings and slacke-graces, set not their hands to the worke.

**B.** *adv.* **a.** In a slack manner; loosely, slackly.

**1641** MILTON *Reform.* I. Wks. 1851 III. 7 Persecuting the Protestants no slacker then the Pope would have done. **1658** A. FOX *Würtz' Surg.* v. 357 It is better they [the joints] be bound slack a whole week, than too hard one hour. **1712** J. JAMES tr. *Le Blond's Gardening* 81 Makes the Joint go stiffer, or slacker, at Pleasure. **1854** MISS BAKER *Northampt. Gloss.* s.v., Tradesmen..say, 'Money comes in very slack'.

**b.** With pa. pples., as ***slack-done, -dried, -laid, -salted, -sized, -spun, -tethered.***

**1669** WORLIDGE *Syst. Agric.* (1681) 153 A handful of slack-dried Hops will mar and spoil many pounds. **1794** *Rigging & Seamanship* 56 Slack-laid means slack-twisted. *Ibid.* 59 If slack-spun, it will break. **1854** MISS BAKER *Northampt. Gloss.* s.v., Anything dressed before a slack fire, or in a slow oven, as 'slack-done meat'. **1862** RAWLINSON *Ancient Mon., Chaldæa* I. v. 91 A third [brick], the coarsest of all, is slack-dried, and of a pale red. **1922** JOYCE *Ulysses* 98 On the towpath by the lock a slacktethered horse.

**slack** (slæk), *v.* Also 6–7 **slacke,** 6 *Sc.* **slak.** [f. SLACK *a.,* in some senses taking the place of the earlier SLAKE *v.* Cf. MDu. and older Flem. *slacken,* Flem. dial. *slakken,* Norw. *slakka.*]

**I.** *trans.* **1.** To be slack or remiss in respect of (some business, duty, etc.); to leave undone or not properly attended to.

**1530** PALSGR. 720/2 Whye slacke you your busynesse thus? **1549** LATIMER *7th Serm. bef. Edw. VI* (Arb.) 201 What a remorse of conscience shall ye haue, when ye remembre howe ye haue slacked your dutye. **1573** TUSSER *Husb.* (1878) 88 Who slacketh his tillage, a carter to bee, for grote got abrode, at home lose shall three. **1605** SHAKS. *Lear* II. iv. 248 Why not my Lord? If then they chanc'd to slacke ye, We could comptroll them. **1621** QUARLES *Hadassa* §2 Wks. (Grosart) II. 48/2 But in contempt, she slacks our dread behest, Neglects performance of our deare Request. *a* **1659** BP. BROWNRIG *Serm.* (1674) I. i. 16 Fear had made him.. slack the performance of what he had promised. **1831** SCOTT *Cast. Dang.* viii, My duty has limits, and if I slack it for a day [etc.]. **1886** C. SCOTT *Sheep-Farming* 76 Breeding ewes that are kept too well..seldom acquit themselves so well..as those that have been slacked a little in winter.

†**b.** To neglect (an opportunity, etc.); to allow to slip or pass by. *Obs.*

*a* **1548** HALL *Chron., Hen. VII*, 27 b, The occasion of so glorious a victory..was..putte by and shamefully slacked. **1597** DANIEL *Civ. Wars* III. lxxiv, This good chaunce, that thus much favoureth, He slackes not. **1612** T. TAYLOR *Comm. Titus* iii. 1 Slacke not this thy tearme-time, but get.. knowledge of God. **1697** DRYDEN *Æneid* v. 834 Time calls you now,..Slack not the good Presage.

†**c.** To lose or waste (time). *Obs.*

*a* **1548** HALL *Chron., Hen. VI*, 161 Like a spedy purvior, whiche slacketh not time. **1591** SIR H. SAVILE *Tacitus, Hist.* II. xlviii. 82 Lest by slacking the time they prouoked his further displeasure. **1633** A. STAFFORD *Pac. Hib.* I. v. (1821) 72 Slack not time..to prosecute him freshly in the Reare-ward.

**2.** To cease to go on with, or prosecute, in a vigorous and energetic manner; to allow to fall off or decline. Also *to slack one's hand(s)*, to diminish one's exertions or activity.

**1520** *State Papers, Hen. VIII*, VI. 63 Though the preparacions here bene slacked, because moche money nedith. **1596** DALRYMPLE tr. *Leslie's Hist. Scot.* II. 143 The king of clemencie tha besocht, to slak the seige a lytle. **1638** JUNIUS *Paint. Ancients* 15 Neither is there any reason why we should slacke our endeavours. **1687** MIÉGE *Gt. Fr. Dict.* II, To slack his hand, in point of Liberality, to give less liberally, *être moins liberal*. **1697** DRYDEN *Virg. Georg.* I. 292 If they slack their Hands, or cease to strive, Then down the Flood with headlong haste they drive. **1790** WESLEY *Jrnl.* 1 Jan., I do not slack my labour. I can preach and write still. **1835** WILLIS *Melanie* 57, I did not slack my love of life and hope of pleasure.

**b.** To allow to mitigate or abate. *rare.*

**1560** DAUS tr. *Sleidane's Comm.* 161 Consideryng how the Turke slacketh nothyng of his fiersenes. **1596** SPENSER *F.Q.* IV. ix. 25 Yet neither would their fiendlike fury slacke, But euermore their malice did augment. **1609** TOURNEUR *Funeral Poem Sir F. Vere* 231 With their obedience he did slacke the bent of his severitie in punishment.

**3.** To reduce the force or strength of; to make less active, vigorous, or violent.

**1589** NASHE *Anat. Absurd.* 36 There be three things which are wont to slack young Students endeuor. **1610** *Histrio-mastix* vi. 149 To waile our want, let speaking slacke the paine. **1639** S. DU VERGER tr. *Camus' Admir. Events* 155 The boiling heate of your love will be..at least something slackt. **1719** DE FOE *Crusoe* I. (Globe) 122, I slack'd my Fire gradually. **1791** COWPER *Iliad* XXI. 399 Nor slack thy furious fires 'till with a shout I give command, then bid them cease to blaze. **1812** W. TAYLOR in *Monthly Mag.* XXXIV. 234 You ringers, slack the knell.

**b.** To slake (one's thirst).

**1631** GOUGE *God's Arrows* V. x. 420 So much as might somewhat slacke their thirst. **1663** *Aron-bimn.* 29 Here is a Julip will slack his thirst. **1750** BEAWES *Lex Mercat.* (1752) 1 A neighbouring spring slacked their thirst. **1864** NEALE *Seatonian Poems* 52 One drop to find, his maddening thirst to slack. *a* **1904** A. ADAMS *Log Cowboy* v. 65 It was a novelty to see them reach the water and slack their thirst.

**4.** To make lax, neglectful, or remiss.

**1597** MARLOWE *Ovid's Elegies* I. i, Love slack'd my Muse, and made my numbers soft. *a* **1631** DONNE *Lett.* (1651) 30 Not to slack you towards those friends which are religious in other clothes then we. **1659** W. BROUGH *Sacr. Princ.* 441 Hold thy foot when he hath thus slackt thy heart.

*refl.* **1881** RUSKIN *Love's Meinie* Pref. p. viii, Languages called living, but which live only to slack themselves into slang, or bloat themselves into bombast.

**5.** To delay or retard; to render slower in respect of motion or progress. Also with *up*. Now *rare.*

**1577** *F. de Lisle's Legendarie* I vj, When..the Kinge of Spaines embassador slacked his comming to ye Council. **1592** SHAKS. *Rom. & Jul.* IV. i. 3, I am nothing slow to slack his hast. **1625** N. CARPENTER *Geogr. Del.* I. iv. (1635) 80 All other bodies are slacked by the medium or Aire by which they are to moue. **1638** RAWLEY tr. *Bacon's Life & Death* (1650) 6 This..conserveth the greenness and slacketh the Dessication of it. **1891** *Cent. Dict.*, *To slack up*, to retard the speed of, as a railway-train.

**b.** To allow (one's pace, course, etc.) to become less rapid.

**1633** HART *Diet of Diseased* Ep. Ded. 1 It did not become one that was running a race, to intermit or slacke his pace. **1675** OTWAY *Alcibiades* III. i, But you, Sir,..Missing your Game, can easily slack the Flight. **1704** SWIFT *Battle Bks.* Misc. (1711) 264 But Wotton..began to slack his Course. **1760–72** H. BROOKE *Fool of Qual.* (1809) I. 152 Here, slacking our pace, we found ourselves growing extremely sick. **1826** HOOD *Fall of the Deer* 23 Slacking Pace at last From runninge slow he standeth faste.

**6.** To make slack or loose; to render less tense or taut; to loosen, relax.

**1530** PALSGR. 720/2, I slacke a knotte,..I lowse a thynge that was to strayte tyed, *je lasche*. *Ibid.*, Slacke his gyrdell. **1596** SPENSER *F.Q.* V. ii. 14 Ne ever Artegall his griple strong For any thing wold slacke, but still vppon him hong. **1608** SHAKS. *Pericles* III. i. 43 Slack the bolins there! **1633** P. FLETCHER *Purple Isl.* VIII. i, The Sunne began to slack his bended bow. **1695** *New Light Chirurg. put out* 53 As often slacking the Turneke. **1753** *Chambers' Cycl.* Suppl., *Slack the hand*, is to slack the bridle, or give a horse head. **1816** SCOTT *Old Mort.* xli, Tak the gentleman's horse to the stable, and slack his girths. **1867** SMYTH *Sailor's Word-bk.* 630 Slack the laniard of our main-stay.

**b.** With advs., as *back, down, off*, etc.

**1806** *Port of London Bye-Laws* xxvii. (1807) 34 If the person..shall not..slack off the breastfasts of such ship. **1867** SMYTH *Sailor's Word-bk.* 631 Slack up the hawser. **1869** RANKINE *Machine & Hand-tools* Pl. Q 7, The saw can be instantly stopped by slacking back one of the slides. **1883** *Cent. Mag.* Sept. 654 With..the peak of the foresail slacked down. **1893** F. M. CRAWFORD *Children of King* i. 8 A hand forward to slack out the cable.

*fig.* **1876** BESANT & RICE *Gold. Butterfly* (1877) 280 Jack Dunquerque was to 'Slack off' his visits to Twickenham.

**c.** *absol.*

**1828** SCOTT *F.M. Perth* v, Give her line enough; but do not slack too fast. *c* **1860** H. STUART *Seaman's Catech.* 27 Slack back two or three turns. **1884** *Law Reports* 9 App. Cases 426 They slacked astern about 25 feet.

**7.** To cause (lime) to disintegrate by the action of water or moisture; to slake.

**1703** MOXON *Mech. Exerc.* 258 When you slack the Lime, take care to wet it every where a little. **1758** REID tr. *Macquer's Chym.* I. 40 It..takes the form of a fine powder, and the title of 'Lime slacked in the air'. **1812** SIR J. SINCLAIR *Syst. Husb. Scot.* I. 177 Lime, if exposed to rain, ..and slacked like mortar, loses half its effect. **1905** *Daily Mail* 2 Jan. 5/6 Where 150 sacks of lime, slacked by the inrushing water, burst into flame and were destroyed.

**II.** *intr.* †**8.** To delay, tarry. *Obs. rare.*

**1530** PALSGR. 720/2 You have slacked to longe, you shulde have come afore. *a* **1553** UDALL *Royster D.* II. i, I woulde not haue slacked for ten thousand poundes. **1611** COTGR., *Tardiver*, to linger, foreslow, slacke, delay.

**9.** To be inactive or idle; to fail to exert oneself in a due manner. In mod. use *colloq.*

**1543** *Necess. Erudit. Chr. Man* B iii, Those men..slacking in suche care and desyre, as they shulde haue to please god. **1582** BENTLEY *Mon. Matrones* II. 6 Thou..also didst put hir [the soul] within this bodie, not for to slacke with sloth. *c* **1586** C'TESS PEMBROKE *Ps.* XLIV. xi, Up, O Lord,.. Sleepe not ever, slack not ever.

**1904** *Daily Chron.* 27 June 8/2 It is far better for any eleven to possess a duffer,—..provided he is a thorough 'goer'—than a good player, however great, if he slacks.

**b.** To neglect, to be backward or dilatory, *to* do something. Now *rare.*

*c* **1560** E. G. in Farr *S.P. Eliz.* (1845) II. 505 Thy word to offer thou doest not slacke. **1582** STANYHURST *Æneis* II. (Arb.) 66 Slack not my woords to remember. **1609** BIBLE (Douay) *Ecclus.* v. 8 Slacke not to be converted to our Lord. **1611** BIBLE *Deut.* xxiii. 21 When thou shalt vow a vow vnto the Lord..., thou shalt not slacke to pay it. **1886** CHRISTINA ROSSETTI *Poems* (1904) 146 The kind Physician will not slack to treat His patient.

**10.** Of persons (or animals): To become less energetic, active, or diligent.

**1560** DAUS tr. *Sleidane's Comm.* 323 b, After they..found in manner nothing, they begin somewhat to slack. **1607** MARKHAM *Caval.* III. (1617) 83 If..after a traine or two more they slacke againe the second time. **1623** BINGHAM *Xenophon* 30 In case any man appointed to worke seemed to slacke,..he chastised and put him off. **1779** T. FORREST *Voy. N. Guinea* 13 We rowed with fourteen oars, and continued so most part of the day, slacking at times when it was very hot. **1875** MORRIS in Mackail *Life* (1899) I. 319, I have somewhat slacked from the Virgil translation.

**b.** Similarly with *off*.

**1864** MISS YONGE *Trial* xvi. (1882) 243 If he slacks off in his respect or affection for you. **1884** *Bazaar* 17 Dec. 647/2 This young artist..has not slacked off, as so many do when a certain..standard is reached.

**11.** To diminish in strength or speed; to become weaker or slower; to moderate in some respect.

*c* **1580** in Hakluyt *Voy.* (1598) I. 453 The storme began to slacke, otherwise we had bene in ill case. **1601** HOLLAND *Pliny* II. xvi. I. 11 For that naturall motions doe either hasten or slacke. *a* **1635** NAUNTON *Fragm. Reg.* (Arb.) 37 If the fire chance to slack which I have kindled. **1726** SHELVOCKE *Voy. round World* 69 Just as we had gained somewhat more than mid passage, the tide slack'd. **1788** M. CUTLER in *Life*, etc. (1888) I. 394 Rain slacked about six, and we set out. **1865** W. G. PALGRAVE *Arabia* II. 313 The breeze slacked, and we slowly worked up to the north. **1880** 'MARK TWAIN' *Tramp Abr.* 274 One expected to see the locomotive pause, or slack up a little.

**b.** Of affairs, business, etc.: To fall off; to go more slowly; to be less brisk.

**1606** SHAKS. *Tr. & Cr.* III. iii. 24 Their negotiations all must slacke, Wanting his mannage. **1831** R. SHENNAN *Tales* 37 When business had begun to slack.

**12.** To become less tense, rigid, or firm.

**1577** HARRISON *England* II. v. (1877) I. 117 Hir garter, which slacked by chance and so fell from her leg. **1592** J. DAVIES *Immort. Soul* III. vii. (1714) 33 When the Body's strongest Sinews slack, Then is the Soul most active. **1773** FERGUSSON *Poems* (1789) II. 87 How maun their weyms wi' sairest hunger slack! **1820** SCORESBY *Acc. Arctic Reg.* I. 215 The ice slacked, and the ship was towed..to the east-ward. **1825** JAMIESON *Suppl.*, *To Slack*,..to become flaccid. *Ibid.*, A tumour is said to *slack*.

**13.** Of lime, etc.: To become disintegrated under the action of moisture.

**1703** MOXON *Mech. Exerc.* 242 Lime..appears to be cold, but Water excites it again, whereby it Slacks and crumbles into fine Powder. **1760** R. BROWN *Compl. Farmer* II. 46 Good marle in hot weather will slack with the heat of the sun like lime. **1874** RAYMOND *Statist. Mines & Mining* 15 It.. often crumbles to powder, even the pebbles of a certain sort 'slacking' to a sandy consistency.

**slack-baked,** *a.* [SLACK *adv.*] Of bread: Imperfectly or insufficiently baked.

**1823** J. BADCOCK *Dom. Amusem.* 32 Those loaves are invariably slack-baked. **1844** DICKENS *Mart. Chuz.* viii, That particular style of loaf which is known to housekeepers as a slack-baked, crummy quartern. **1884** SALA *Journ. South* I. xxiv. (1887) 318 A board covered with squat round loaves of bread, somewhat slack-baked in appearance.

*fig.* **1840** DICKENS *Barn. Rudge* xli, One beaming smile, from his nut-brown face down to the slack-baked buckles in his shoes. **1882** *Daily Telegr.* 8 Apr., Such a slack-baked slop-made little atomy as he is.

Hence **slack-bake** *v.*

**1836** DICKENS *Sk. Boz* iv. (1850) 14 Men..who had mis-managed the workhouse, ground the paupers, diluted the beer, slack-baked the bread.

**slacked** (slækt), *ppl. a.* [f. SLACK *v.*]

**1.** Retarded; rendered slower.

**1628** FELTHAM *Resolves* II. lxxi. 201 A graue Poem..wings the Soule vp higher, then the slacked Pace of Prose.

**2.** Of lime: Slaked.

**1700** MAUNDRELL *Journ. Jerus.* (1749) 152 The Body instantly dissolv'd and fell into Dust like slack'd Lime. **1733** W. ELLIS *Chiltern & Vale Farm.* 367 Slack'd or powdered Stone Lime must be by degrees sifted on. **1813** SIR H. DAVY *Agric. Chem.* (1814) 318 Slacked lime is merely a combination of lime, with about one third of its weight of water. **1875** *Encycl. Brit.* I. 645/2 It falls to powder, like slacked quicklime.

‖**'slacken,** *sb.* Also 8 **slaken**, 9 **-in.** [ad. G. *schlacken*, var. *schlacke* dross of metal, etc.] Slag.

There is no evidence that the word has ever had any real currency in English.

**1670** *Phil. Trans.* V. 1197 They ordinarily melt it..by the help of Iron-stone..and Slacken (a scum or cake taken off from the top of the pan, into which the melted Minerals run). **1693** SIR T. P. BLOUNT *Nat. Hist.* 233 To this..they add Limestone and Slacken, and Melt them together. *a* **1744** LUCAS in *Trans. Cumb. & Westm. Archaeol. Soc.* VIII. 36 Slaken as the Germans call them, or old Cinders, which they here call Forest Cinders. [**1753** *Chambers' Cycl.* Suppl., *Slacken*, in metallurgy, a term used by the miners to express a spungy and semivitrified substance (etc. Hence in later Dicts.). **1837** HEBERT *Engin. Encycl.* II, *Slakin*, a term used by smelters to express a spongy, semi-vitrified substance, which they mix with the ores of metal, to prevent their fusion. (Hence in Francis, Knight, etc.)]

**slacken** ('slæk(ə)n), *v.* [f. SLACK *a.* Cf. the rarer SLAKEN *v.*, and Icel., Norw., and Sw. *slakna* (older Da. *slagne*).]

**I.** *trans.* **1.** To cause to become slower; to delay or retard.

**1580** HOLLYBAND *Treas. Fr. Tong*, *Tarder*, to hinder, to slacken. **1632** SIR T. HAWKINS tr. *Mathieu's Unhappy Prosp.* 283 That the Sunne denyeth her his beames, that her presence slackneth his rising. **1656** tr. *Hobbes' Elem. Philos.* (1839) 406 Some alteration..of vital motion, by quickening or slackening..the same. **1726** LEONI *Alberti's Archit.* II. 113/2 You may slacken the current of the Water, by making it run winding. **1794** T. DAVIS *Agric. Wilts.* 91 The 'clinginess'..may tend to slacken the step of the Wiltshire ploughman. **1833** HT. MARTINEAU *Briery Creek* ii. 42 The production of the one will be slackened, and that of the other quickened, till they are made equal. **1878** HUXLEY *Physiogr.* 130 As the river approaches its mouth, the flow becomes slackened.

**b.** To allow (one's pace, etc.) to become slower; to diminish or lessen (speed).

**1749** FIELDING *Tom Jones* XII. v, Partridge being unable any longer to keep up with Jones,..begged him a little to slacken his pace. **1796** MME. D'ARBLAY *Camilla* IV. 103 Neither quickening nor slackening his pace as he approached. **1853** MRS. CARLYLE *Lett.* II. 213, I..slackened my steps, till they were clear off. **1863** W. C. BALDWIN *Afr. Hunting* vi. 186, I gave him a bullet.., which soon caused him to slacken his pace. **1896** *Law Times Rep.* LXXIII. 615/1 [The engine-driver] did not slacken speed.

*fig.* **1837** T. JONES *Christian Warrior* IV. ii. 84 Do not slacken your pace in religion because of reproaches.

**2.** To render less vigorous or eager; to cause to fall off or decline.

*a* **1631** DONNE *Select.* (1840) 35 Such a rest..as shall slacken our endeavour to make sure our salvation. *a* **1677** BARROW *Serm.* Wks. 1716 I. 10 Religion seemeth to smother or to slacken the..alacrity of men in following Profit. **1718** *Free-thinker* No. 87. 222 Riches had no Allurements to slacken their Enquiries. **1807** JOEL BARLOW *Columb.* IV. 422 Thy freeborn sons..Nor sloth can slacken, nor a tyrant bind. **1839** FR. A. KEMBLE *Resid. Georgia* (1863) 26 The sight of which..is enough to slacken the appetite. **1896** TOUT *Edw. I*, iii. 47 The best and the worst of motives combined to slacken crusading enthusiasm.

**b.** To allow to become less vigorous, etc.

*a* **1631** DONNE *Select.* (1840) 197 If we slacken our holy industry in making sure our salvation, we..may be cast out. **1665** TEMPLE *Let. to Ld. Arlington* Wks. 1720 II. 6, I know him to be a Man too firm to be diverted from his Point, or slacken it without some such Maim. **1841** ELPHINSTONE *Hist. Ind.* I. 541 The Hindús..first slackened their efforts, and at last gave way and dispersed. **1857** BUCKLE *Civiliz.* I. xiv. 784 In the heat of their new warfare they slackened their opposition to the church.

**3.** To relax in point of strictness or severity.

**1605** BACON *Adv. Learn.* I. vii. §9 The temperate use of the Prerogative, not slackened, nor much strayned. **1643** MILTON *Divorce* II. i, In matters not very bad or impure, a human law giver may slacken something of that which is exactly good. **1697** BURGHOPE *Disc. Relig. Assemb.* 180 The laws for coming to church have been slackned in favour to the scrupulous dissenters.

**b.** To render (a person) less severe or stern.

**1685** F. SPENCE tr. *Varilla's Ho. Medicis* 168 There was some glimmering of hope, that..it would not be impossible to slacken and mollifie him if he gave him audience.

**4.** To give relaxation to (one's thoughts, etc.).

**1643** DENHAM *Cooper's Hill* 242 When great Affairs Gave leave to slacken, and unbend his cares. **1805** WORDSW. *Prelude* I. 63 Where down I sate Beneath a tree, slackening my thoughts by choice, And settling into gentler happiness.

**5.** To moderate, make less intense.

**1685** LADY R. RUSSELL *Lett.* I. xxii. 58 That consideration should in reason slacken the fierce rages of grief. **1747–96** MRS. GLASSE *Art of Cookery* xxv. 377 Make a pretty brisk fire,..then slacken it so as just to have enough to keep the still at work.

**6.** To render, to allow to become, less tense, taut, or firm; to reduce the tension of.

**1611** COTGR., *Lascher*, to slacken, wyden, loose, vnbend, let out. **1668** MARVELL *Corr.* xcviii. Wks. (Grosart) II. 251 Yesterday Harman was brought to the House to give account of slackning saile in the first victory. **1760–72** H. BROOKE *Fool of Qual.* (1809) III. 86 Slackening our sail, and heaving out a small boat. **1797–1805** S. & HT. LEE *Canterb. T.* II. 246 She slackened the reins. **1823** GALT *R. Gilhaize* xxii, Being then somewhat slackened in the joints of the right side by a paralytic. **1900** *Jrnl. Soc. Dyers* XVI. 12 The yarn is alternately stretched and slackened.

**b.** In fig. contexts.

*c* **1645** HOWELL *Lett.* I. VI. liii, Nor shall this storm slacken a whit that firm ligue of love, wherin I am eternally tied unto you. **1647** CLARENDON *Hist. Reb.* I. §191 A Superior.. who having the Reins in his hand, could Slacken them according to his own humour. **1861** BUCKLE *Civiliz.* II. viii. 467 In Spain, directly government slackened its hold, the nation fell to pieces. **1865** DICKENS *Mut. Fr.* III. xvi, Most of its money mills were slackening sail, or had left off grinding for the day.

**c.** To cause to relax; to weaken.

**1663** COWLEY *Complaint* vii, Thou slacknest all my Nerves of Industry. **1697** J. COLLIER *Ess. Moral Subj.* I. (1703) 63 Such a Partiality will slacken the Nerves of Industry. **1778** LOWTH *Transl. Isaiah* xiii. 7 Therefore shall all hands be slackened.

**7.** To make loose, to loosen. Also *refl.*

**1815** J. SMITH *Panorama Sci. & Art* I. 54 By slackening the screws.. the puppets are at liberty to slide horizontally. **1869** RANKINE *Machine & Hand-tools* Pl. P 11, The rotation of the mandril is continued until the tyre is slackened by the continued action of the rollers. *Ibid.* P 13, The vice gradually slackens itself from the severe shake and strain it is receiving.

**II.** *intr.* **8.** Of persons: To become lax, remiss, or negligent; to grow less energetic or eager.

**1641** MILTON *Reform.* II. Wks. 1851 III. 47 When the people slacken, and fall to loosenes and riot. **1800** WORDSW. *Michael* 443 Meantime Luke began To slacken in his duty. **1854** FREEMAN in *Ecclesiologist* XV. 320 At this point I feel that I must begin to slacken. **1860** MOTLEY *Netherl.* iii. (1868) I. 81 Preventing them.. from slackening in their determined hostility to Spain.

**9.** To diminish in respect of strength, vigour, intensity, etc.

**1651** HOBBES *Leviath.* II. xxx. 178 Their Obedience (in which the safety of the Common-wealth consisteth) slackened. **1671** MILTON *Samson* 738 My penance hath not slack'n'd, though my pardon No way assur'd. *a* **1738** SWIFT *Will. II*, Wks. 1768 IV. 265 In a few years the piety of these adventurers began to slacken. **1794** NELSON 20 July in Nicolas *Disp.* (1845) I. 451 Our exertions must not slacken. **1823** LAMB *Elia* II. *Old Margate Hoy*, In a poor week, imagination slackens. **1876** FREEMAN *Norm. Conq.* IV. xviii. 116 The assault must have begun to slacken; for he feared a sally of the besieged.

**b.** Of fire, wind, tides, or other natural forces or processes.

**1666** PEPYS *Diary* 9 Nov., By and by comes news that the fire is slackened. **1687** A. LOVELL tr. *Thevenot's Trav.* II. 155 The Wind slackened so at this place, that we scarcely made any way at all. **1794** G. ADAMS *Nat. & Exper. Phil.* III. xxxi. 287 When the impulse slackens, the fly communicates part of its motion. **1820** tr. *Legrange's Chem.* II. 309 When the distillation begins to slacken, unlute the apparatus. **1832** DE LA BECHE *Geol. Man.* (ed. 2) 99 The currents run with the wind.. and slacken in September. **1885** *Manch. Exam.* 12 Jan. 6/1 The intensest heat is white, if it slackens it becomes faintly coloured.

**c.** Of business, etc.: To become less active or brisk. (See also quot. 1828.)

**1745** *De Foe's Eng. Tradesm.* ii. (1841) I. 14 Markets slacken much on this side. **1828** CARR *Craven Gloss.*, *Slacken*, to fall in price. 'Corn begins to slacken.' **1832** HT. MARTINEAU *Hill & Valley* iv. 63 When the demand for iron slackens. **1874** RUSKIN *Fors Clav.* xlviii. 267 Faster and faster slackens the demand for tea.

**10.** To diminish in speed; to become slower.

*a* **1721** KEILL *Maupertius' Diss.* (1734) 65 In those distant parts, the velocity of the Comet slackens. **1784** COWPER *Task* I. 155 How oft upon yon eminence our pace Has slacken'd to a pause. **1822** SCOTT *Nigel* xvi, As he approached the entrance to that den of infamy,.. his pace slackened. **1893** TRAILL *Social Eng.* Introd. p. xxxiv, Through the first half of the ensuing century the rate of progress in the sciences a little slackens.

**b.** To begin to go more slowly.

**1837** CARLYLE *Fr. Rev.* I. I. iv, At a high trot, they start; and keep up that pace. For the jibes.. do not tempt one to slacken. **1850** S. DOBELL *Roman* vi. Poet. Wks. (1875) 84 The tired ox slackens in the furrow. **1865** DICKENS *Mut. Fr.* III. xv, 'That was well done!' panted Bella, slackening in the next street, and subsiding into a walk.

**11.** Of lime: To become slaked.

**1703** [R. NEVE] *City & C. Purchaser* 206 Bricklayers.. let the Lime slacken and cool before they make up their Mortar.

**12.** To become less tense or firm.

**1850** SCORESBY *Cheever's Whaleman's Adv.* ix. (1858) 120 The line for an instant slackened. **1892** LOW *Machine Draw.* 20 When in this condition the nut has no tendency to slacken back. **1894** HALL CAINE *Manxman* III. vii, Her clenched hands slackened away from his neck.

**slackened** ('slæk(ə)nd), *ppl. a.* [f. prec.]

**1.** Rendered less tense or firm.

?*c* **1640** WALLER *Chloris* Poems (1711) 146 Wind up the slacken'd Strings of thy Lute. **1725** POPE *Odyss.* v. 522 Fear seiz'd his slacken'd limbs and beating heart. **1762** FOOTE *Orator* I. Wks. 1799 I. 204 He reanimates their slackened nerves with the mystic picture of an apple-tree. **1801** SOUTHEY *Thalaba* III. xxiii, The slacken'd bow, the quiver, the long lance. **1869** RANKINE *Machine & Hand-tools* Pl. P 16, In the slackened state of the key.

**2.** Abated, mitigated; relaxed.

**1736** GRAY *Statius* i. 51 The circle sped; It towers to cut the clouds;.. Anon, with slacken'd rage comes quiv'ring down. **1791** MME. D'ARBLAY *Diary* 20 Aug., 'Tis best, therefore, to think of these matters till they occur with slackened emotion. **1833** ARNOTT *Physics* II. 83 During the moment of slackened combustion. **1848** THACKERAY *Van. Fair* ix, He began to reform the slackened discipline of the hall.

**'slackener.** [f. as prec.] One who, or that which, slackens or slakes.

**1861** LYNCH *Lett. to Scattered* (1872) 516 The common slackener of our thirst.

**'slackening,** *vbl. sb.* [f. as prec.] The action of making or becoming slack, in various senses. Also with *off*.

**1611** COTGR., *Relaschement*,.. a relenting, or slackening. **1648** SANDERSON *Serm.* II. 225 By the slackning, loosening, or disjoynting whereof, the body.. cometh to be as much weakned. **1706** STANHOPE *Paraphr.* III. 266 There may too in the Soul be great Slacknings of Zeal. **1765** A. DICKSON *Agric.* II. 248 Tho' it may be known when the foremost neglects his work by the slackening of his traces. **1860** GEN. P. THOMPSON *Audi Alt.* cxiv. III. 45 But there are great slackenings in the tide. **1869** FREEMAN *Norm. Conq.* (1875) III. 335 Nothing is described as taking place.. to cause any slackening in the levies. **1903** CONRAD *Romance* v. i. 402, I wanted rest, woman's love, slackening off. **1951** J. M. FRASER *Psychol.* xiv. 157 It is rather more usual for a slackening-off process to take place.

**'slackening,** *ppl. a.* [f. as prec.] Making or becoming slack.

**1593** Q. ELIZ. *Boeth.* v. metr. i. 104 What so seame by slakning ranes [= reins] to slip. **1887** RUSKIN *Præterita* II. 42 One really began sometimes to think of the slackening wheels of Pharaoh. **1892** *Daily News* 24 May 7/1 Some still more general cause of slackening traffic.

**'slacker.** [f. SLACK *v.*]

**1.** (See quot. 1877, and cf. SLAKER 2.)

**1797** *Trans. Soc. Arts* XV. 155 An oak head and slacke[r] is placed on the end [of the drain] next the land. **1877** *N.W. Linc. Gloss.*, *Slacker*, a shuttle or stopgate to hinder the passage of water.

**2.** *colloq.* A person who shirks work, or avoids exertion, exercise, etc. Also, *spec.* used in *Mil.* contexts in the war of 1914–18.

**1898** *Westm. Gaz.* 7 Apr. 4/1, I said it was a silly thing to do, and they retorted that I was a 'slacker'. **1914** 'BARTIMEUS' *Naval Occasions* v. 37 What about a song, you slacker! **1917** 'TAFFRAIL' *Sub* ii. 62 An habitual slacker at Osborne, however, was soon sized up, and if repeated warnings did not cause him to mend his ways, he generally got the Order of the Boot at the end of his third term. **1921** H. WILLIAMSON *Beautiful Years* 217 He was a little slacker, the kind that used cribs later on in school life. **1933** H. C. BAILEY *Mr. Fortune Wonders* 109 Eston strode past him with a laugh, 'Had enough already?' and Cicely pattered after crying, 'Slacker!' **1964** A. WHITEHOUSE *Epics & Legends of First World War* vi. 134 The.. League.. rendered important service in.. handling the 'slacker' and conscientious-objector groups. **1969** R. MAUGHAM *Link* II. 16 'You're a slacker and you're a shirker,' he said. 'You're a little runt in many ways. But you're the best of the lot of them.'

**'slacking,** *vbl. sb.* [f. SLACK *v.*] The action of the vb., in various senses.

**1542** UDALL *Erasm. Apoph.* 287 Our countree.. to be desolated through our slouthfulnesse or slackyng. **1577–87** HOLINSHED *Chron.* I. 26/1 They wanted their horssemen which were yet behind, & through slacking of time could not come to land. **1607** HIERON *Wks.* I. 135 Sith there is no slacking of Gods kindnes, why should there be any intermission of our duty? **1665** MANLEY *Grotius' Low C. Wars* 488 The other Ship.. was hindred by the slacking of the wind. **1707** MORTIMER *Husb.* (1721) I. 292 With Quick-lime, which slacking will make it as hard as a Stone. **1812** SIR J. SINCLAIR *Syst. Husb. Scot.* I. 175 The slacking of lime completely is a most important operation. **1905** H. A. VACHELL *The Hill* ix. 189 How about work, eh? Lot o' slacking last term.

*attrib.* **1855** J. R. LEIFCHILD *Cornwall* 222 The water of the slacking pits and buddles.

**'slacking,** *ppl. a.* [f. as prec.] That slacks, in senses of the vb.

*a* **1625** *Nomenclator Navalis* 126 When it is slacking water. **1811** A. T. THOMSON *Lond. Disp.* (1818) 459 A white brittle substance, having the peculiar odour of slacking quick-lime. **1855** SINGLETON *Virgil* II. 366 Many watch The ebbing motions of the slacking sea. **1882** *U.S. Rep. Prec. Met.* 642 It resists the solvent and slacking action of water.

**'slackingly,** *adv.* [Cf. prec.] Slackly.

**1578** BANISTER *Hist. Man* II. 39 [The eyelids] by their meanes are stifly supported, and not slackyngly or losely borne.

**'slack-jaw.** [f. SLACK *a.* Cf. JAW *sb.*[1] 6.] Tiresome or impertinent talk.

**1797** MRS. M. ROBINSON *Walsingham* IV. 14 *Ayes* and *noes* settle the affairs of the nation,.. as well as all the slack-jaw of modern orators. **1821** SCOTT *Pirate* xxxv, A sort of nautical eloquence, which his enemies termed slack-jaw. **1833** *Fraser's Mag.* VII. 10 All manner of blarney, slack-jaw, fudge, and gossip. **1864** *Realm* 6 July 7 The platitudinous sham-antique slackjaw, all words and no thought, of.. worthless pedants.

**slack-lime.** [? f. SLACK *v.*] Lime in the state of being slacked.

**1840** POE *Balloon Hoax* Wks. 1865 I. 92 A coffee-warmer, contrived for warming coffee by means of slack-lime.

**slackly** ('slæklɪ), *adv.* Forms: 1 **sleaclice,** 4 **slacli,** 5–6 **slakly,** 6 **slacklie, -lye,** 6– **slackly;** 5 **slackelich,** 5–7 **-ly.** [f. SLACK *a.* + -LY[2].]

**1.** In a remiss or negligent manner; without due diligence or energy.

*c* **960** *Rule St. Benet* (Schröer) xliii. 68 Wen is, þæt sume .. sleaclice laȝon and slepon. **1388** WYCLIF *2 Macc.* xii. 14 These that weren with ynne, tristiden to the stablenesse of wallis,.. and diden slacliere. **1422** *Secreta Secret.*, *Priv. Priv.* 160 For-als-moche that he his Sonnes.. slackely reprowid and not chastid. **1531** TINDALE *Exp. 1 John* (1537) 99 Therfor is that office so slackly executed. **1596** SPENSER *State Irel.* Wks. (Globe) 622/2 The same Statutes are soe slacklye penned.. that they are often.. wrested to the fraud of the subject. **1621** BURTON *Anat. Mel.* II. v. II. iii. (1651) 387 They use them rashly, unprofitably, slackly, and to no purpose. **1665** MANLEY *Grotius' Low C. Wars* 627 Descending suddenly to assault Voorne Island, if it were slackly guarded. **1727** POPE, etc. *Art of Sinking* 72 Their laws.. have ever been slackly executed. **1816** SCOTT *Old Mort.* xxvi, The summons was very slackly obeyed. **1876** GEO. ELIOT *Dan. Der.* xxiii, You would find—after your education in doing things slackly for one-and-twenty years—great difficulties in study.

**2.** Without due vigour or force; slowly.

**1398** TREVISA *Barth. De P.R.* v. xxxix. (Bodl. MS.), By openyng þereof þe vertu passith and þe lyuour worcheþ þe more slackelich. **1511** *Guylforde's Pilgr.* (Camden) 58 We sayled forth slakly and easely ayenst the wynde. **1586** J. HOOKER *Hist. Irel.* in *Holinshed* II. 32 When he dooth set foorth on his iournie verie slacklie and slowlie. **1648** HEXHAM II. s.v. *Slappelick*, To go Slackly, Faintly, or Slowly to worke. **1850** TENNYSON *In Mem.* lxxxvii. 7 When one would aim an arrow fair, But send it slackly from the string.

**b.** Not busily or briskly.

**1884** *American* IX. 148 Times are dull and labor slackly employed. **1892** GISSING *New Grub Street* I. 5 When one kind of goods begins to go slackly, he is ready with something new.

**3.** Not tightly or firmly; loosely.

**1486** *Bk. St. Albans* B vj, Tho saame lewnes [= lunes for hawks] þou shalt fastyn slackely as a bowstryng vnocupyede. **1532** MORE *Confut. Tindale* IV. Wks. 591/2 So god agayne-warde vseth hymselfe towarde hym, in holdynge hym the more slackely. **1597** SHAKS. *Lover's Compl.* 35 Some in her threeden fillet still did bide,.. Though slackly braided in loose negligence. **1730** *Phil. Trans.* XXXVI. 454 A Piece of Muslin.. tied slackly about the Neck. **1805** *Naval Chron.* XIII. 243 This accident happened from her being.. slackly rigged. **1879** DIXON *Royal Windsor* II. i. 6 The gown was caught in slackly by a belt.

**Slack-ma-girdle** ('slækmə'gɜːd(ə)l). Also **Slack-my-girdle.** [f. phr. *slack my girdle*: cf. SLACK *v.* 6.] A variety of cider apple (see quots.).

**1885** HOGG & BULL *Herefordshire Pomona*, *List of other Cider Apples*, Slack-My-Girdle, or Slack-my-girl.—A striped Somersetshire apple of large size. It is also much grown in Devonshire. **1967** [see HANG-DOWN *sb.* and *a.*]. **1981** *Countryman* LXXXVI. III. 42 Others.. use only true cider apples, from trees with names as evocative as.. Slack-ma-Girdle.

**slackness** ('slæknɪs). Forms: 1 **sleacnes, -nys, slecnys,** 4 **slacnesse, slaknes** (5 **-nesse**), 5 **slakenes,** 6 **slacke-,** 6–7 **slacknesse,** 6– **slackness.** [f. SLACK *a.* + -NESS.]

**1. a.** Lack of diligence or energy; tendency to idleness or sluggishness; remissness.

*c* **897** K. ÆLFRED tr. *Gregory's Past. C.* xl. 289 Oft eac sio godnes ðære monnðwærnesse bið dieȝellice ȝemenged wið sleacnesse. **1340** *Ayenb.* 33 Efterward comþ slacnesse.. þet bint zuo þane man þet onneaþe he him yefþ to done wel. *c* **1386** CHAUCER *Pars. T.* ¶680 He dooth alle thyng with.. slaknesse and excusacion, and with ydelnesse, and vnlust. **1555** EDEN *Decades* (Arb.) 55 Who maye herein woorthely accuse vs for the slackenesse of owre dewtie towarde hym. **1592** W. WEST *1st Pt. Symbol.* §38 B iiij, Deley.. which happeneth by the slacknesse either of the creditor, or debtor. **1642** in Clarendon *Hist. Reb.* IV. §346 He said, 'he should wash his hands.. from the least imputation of slackness in that.. pious work'. **1667** MILTON *P.L.* XI. 630 From Mans effeminate slackness it begins. **1713** YOUNG *Last Day* I. 107 Not folded arms, and slackness of the mind, Can promise for the safety of mankind. **1803** MALTHUS *Popul.* (1817) II. 408 The slackness of its neighbours in manufacturing, or any other cause. **1849** MACAULAY *Hist. Eng.* viii. II. 313 His slackness drew on him a sharp reprimand from the royal lips. **1869** FREEMAN *Norm. Conq.* III. 327 Their interest and their duty were too nearly the same to allow of any slackness.

**b.** Laxity; want of strictness.

**1674** *Essex Papers* (Camden) I. 213 Y[e] slackness of dicipline used in England towards Soldiers. **1699** BURNET *39 Art.* xxv. (1700) 280 A slackness in Doctrine.. will always bring with it a much greater corruption in practice.

**2.** Slowness; tardiness.

*c* **1000** *Saxon Leechd.* III. 264 Swa swa þære sunnan sleacnys acenð ænne dæȝ.. swa eac þæs monan swiftnes awyrpð ut ænne dæȝ. *c* **1000** ÆLFRIC *Hom.* II. 282 Ðam ȝemettum wæs beboden þæt hi sceoldon caflice etan, forðan ðe God onscunað þa sleacnysse on his ðeȝnum. *c* **1055** *Byrhtferth's Handboc* in *Anglia* VIII. 301 Nu wolde ic þæt þa æðela clericas asceocon fram heora andȝites orðance ælce sleacnysse. **1611** BIBLE *Transl. Pref.* ¶ 14 In a businesse of moment a man feareth not the blame of conuenient slacknesse. **1635** SWAN *Spec. M.* i. §3 (1643) 14 These who mocked at the slacknesse of Christs coming to judgement. **1739** S. SHARP *Surg.* (J.), There is a slackness to heal, and a cure is very difficultly effected.

**3. a.** Lack of vigour or strength; absence of tension or tightness.

**1398** TREVISA *Barth. De P.R.* IX. xxiv. (Bodl. MS.), Poores of bodies.. closeþ for slakenes of heete in the euetide. *c* **1440** *Promp. Parv.* 458/1 Slaknesse, *laxatura*. **1743** BLAIR *Grave* 284 Man.. knowing well the Slackness of his Arm, Trusts only in the well-invented Knife. **1755** JOHNSON, *Laxity*,.. slackness; contrariety to tension.

**b.** *concr.* The slack part *of* anything.
**1898** CROCKETT *Red Axe* (1903) 157 Lifting him unceremoniously up by the slackness of his back covertures, I turned him over.

**4.** Absence of briskness; dullness (of trade, etc.).
**1851** HELPS *Comp. Solit.* iv. (1874) 51 Whenever he speaks of the slackness of trade. **1884** *Manch. Exam.* 9 June 4/1 In the Stock Exchange the tone was mostly flat, in consequence of the slackness of business.

**5.** *Naut.* (See quot. 1877.)
**1877** W. H. WHITE *Man. Naval Archit.* 484 The contrary condition, where the resultant resistance acts abaft the resultant wind pressure, and makes the head of the ship fall off from the wind, is termed 'slackness', and can only be counteracted by keeping the helm a-lee. **1922** E. L. ATTWOOD *Theoret. Naval Archit.* (ed. 8) xi. 380 If the centre of effort is forward of the C.L.R. the bow of the ship tends to fall off from the wind (which is termed 'slackness').

**ˈslack-rope.** [SLACK *a.* 7.]
**1.** A rope, loosely stretched, on which an acrobat performs. (Contrasted with TIGHT-ROPE.)
**1749** CHESTERF. *Lett.* (1774) I. 388 There are fewer people who walk well upon that line, than upon the slack rope. **1808** PIKE *Sources Mississ.* (1810) III. 263 In the evening we went to see some performers on the slack rope. **1848** THACKERAY *Van. Fair* vi, The signal which announced that Madame Saqui was about to mount skyward on a slack-rope ascending to the stars. **1892** KIPLING & BALESTIER *Naulahka* 199, I have danced on the slack-rope before the mess-tents of the officers.
**2.** *Naut.* (See quot.)
**1820** SCORESBY *Acc. Arctic Reg.* II. 456 These anchors being likewise connected with the ice, by means of a slack-rope.

**ˈslackster.** [f. SLACK *v.*] = SLACKER 2.
**1901** *Daily Chron.* 6 Nov. 4/5 There are 'slacksters', as the slang of the schools and universities has it, in all professions.

**†slackstone.** *Obs. rare.* [ad. G. *schlackstein* (see quot. in Grimm).] A form of slag.
**1683** PETTUS *Fleta Minor* I. xiv. 41 How a Slackstone or Copper-stone is to be made. *Ibid.*, Slackstones (as the Philosophers do judg) are Sulphur and Arsnick mingled with a subtil Earth.

**slack-trough.** [f. SLACK *v.*] A water-trough in which a blacksmith cools heated metal. (Cf. SLAKE- and SLECK-TROUGH.)
**1854** MISS BAKER *Northampt. Gloss.*, *Slack-trough*, the trough which is used for quenching the iron in a blacksmith's shop. **1884** C. G. W. LOCK *Workshop Rec.* Ser. III. 285/2 Lay rod on edge of slack trough.

**slack-twisted,** *a.* [f. SLACK *adv.*] Of a rope: Not tightly twisted. Hence *fig.*, of a loose, unsatisfactory character; lazy, inactive.
**1794** *Rigging & Seamanship* 56 Slack-laid means slack-twisted. **1802** *Sporting Mag.* XX. 292 The slack-twisted operations of a certain pack of hounds. **1887** *Proc. Soc. Antiquaries* XII. 16 One Dr. Barlow, a notable trimmer even in those slack-twisted times. **1891** T. HARDY *Tess* (1900) 17/2 Durbeyfield was what was locally called a slack-twisted fellow.

**slack-water.** Also slack water, slackwater. [f. SLACK *a.*]
**1.** The time at high or low water when the tide is not flowing visibly in either direction.
Occurs earlier as ***slake water***: see SLAKE *a.* 3.
**1769** FALCONER *Dict. Marine* (1780), *Slack-water*, the interval between the flux and reflux of the tide;..during which..the water apparently remains in a state of rest. **1832** MARRYAT *N. Forster* xviii, The ebb-tide was..over; a short pause of 'slack water' ensued. **1875** BEDFORD *Sailor's Pocket Bk.* v. (ed. 2) 170 This long period of nearly slack water is very valuable to the traffic of the port.
*fig.* **1883** *19th Cent.* May 896 We are in a period of 'slack water' so far as politics are concerned.
**2.** A stretch of comparatively still water in the sea, due to the absence of currents.
**1853** KANE *Grinnell Exp.* x. (1856) 76 A portion of the interval between the eastern and western coasts is the seat of a partial slackwater, or even rotating eddy. **1862** ANSTED *Channel Isl.* I. iv. 65 The north of Herm is the point of land where there would be slack water.
**3.** A part of a river lying outside of the current, or one in which the flow is lessened by a lock or dam. Also *fig.*
**1837** J. M. PECK *Gazetteer Illinois* (ed. 2) III. 264 Fox river is susceptible of improvement by slack water at small expense. **1867–77** CHAMBERS *Astron.* 258 There is no 'slack-water', as is ordinarily the case in other rivers. **1886** *Pall Mall G.* 14 July 1 [To] swim..into the current, get swept down by it a quarter of a mile, and paddle slowly back again in the slackwater. **1901** *Scotsman* 25 Mar. 7/3 The House again fell into the slack water of small talk.
**4.** *attrib.*, as ***slack-water basin, deposit, period, stream***; **slack-water navigation,** navigation carried on by the use of locks or dams on a river.
**1836** J. HALL *Statistics of West* 38 At low stages the [Ohio] river becomes resolved into a succession of ripples, with extensive slack water basins between them. **1842** *Civil Eng. & Arch. Jrnl.* V. 75/2 It was concluded that the time had arrived for changing the navigation of the Lehigh into a slackwater navigation. **1860** HOLMES *Elsie V.* ii, This slack-water period of a race, which comes before the rapid ebb of its prosperity. **1877** BURROUGHS *Taxation* 28 It is difficult to see how the advantages of slackwater navigation..can be brought within the range of local objects. **1889** F. G. WRIGHT *Ice Age North Amer.* 358 The Ohio above Cincinnati was a slack-water stream. **1894** *Pop. Sci. Monthly* June 196 The ice-dam accounts most naturally for the slack-water deposits.

**ˈslacky.** *Sc. rare.* Also slackie. [Of obscure origin.] A form of sling.
**1653** URQUHART *Rabelais* I. xxv, The other shepherds and shepherdesses came with their slings and slackies following them. *Ibid.* xxxii, He..found..that Marquet's head was broken with a slackie or short cudgel. **1825** JAMIESON *Suppl.* s.v., The *slackie*, it is believed, is that kind of sling, which is made of an elastic rod, or piece of wood, split at one end, for receiving the stone.

**sladang,** var. SELADANG.

**slade** (sleɪd), *sb.*[1] Forms: 1 slead, sled, 1–3 slæd, 9 *dial.* slad (sled); (1–3 *dat.*) 4– slade (3–4 sclade), 5–6 *Sc.* slaid, 6 slaide. [OE. *slæd* (*slead, sled*) neut., = Norw. dial. *slad* neut. (also *slade* masc.), a slope, hollow; cf. also Da. dial. *slade* a piece of level ground (16th cent. in Kalkar), G. dial. (Westph.) *slade* dell, ravine.
The OE. nom. and acc. *slæd* is represented by the mod. dial. form *slad*, current chiefly in western counties. The usual *slade* is from inflected forms, esp. the dat. sing.]
A valley, dell, or dingle; an open space between banks or woods; a forest glade; a strip of greensward or of boggy land.
The precise application of the word varies in different localities: see the *Eng. Dial. Dict.*
*c* **893** K. ÆLFRED *Oros.* II. iv. 76 Hio..beforan þæm cyninge farende wæs,..oð hio hiene ʒelædde on an micel slæd. **944** in Earle *Land Charters* 179 Andlang dic oð ðone weʒ þe scyt to fealuwes lea on þam slade. **956** *Ibid.* 192 þonne on þæt slæd, þonne of ðan slæde [etc.]. *c* **1205** LAY. 8585 He ferde..in to ane muchele slæde, & slahliche his folc hudde. *Ibid.* 28365 þe niht heom to-delde, ȝeond slades & ȝeon dunen. **13..** *Guy Warw.* 3475 Wiþ strengþe þe helde þai vnder-nome, Wiþ strengþe þai wene þe slade ouer-go. **1390** GOWER *Conf.* II. 93 Hou he clymbeth up the banckes And falleth into Slades depe. *c* **1440** *Pallad. on Husb.* IX. 176 In conditis descende into the slade Hit may, and on that other side arise. **1470–85** MALORY *Arthur* VI. xiii. 203 Ther by in a slade he sawe four knyghtes houyng vnder an oke. **1513** DOUGLAS *Æneid* XI. xi. 84 In dern sladis and mony scroggy slonk. **1555** W. WATREMAN *Fardle Facions* I. vi. 97 The Ethiopians..gather together into a long slade betwixte two hilles, a great deale of rubbeshe. **1606** J. REYNOLDS *Dolarnys Primerose* (1880) 62 Thus as the medowes, forests and the feelds, In sumptuous tires, had deckt their daynty slades. **1649** BLITHE *Eng. Improv. Impr.* (1653) 81 If you consider that all your Common Fields were never under Tillage neither, As great part Slades and Hade wayes, and a great part Meadow. **1700–1** GOUGH *Hist. Myddle* (1875) 37 You will finde it more unlevell with banks and deep slades, than any other low grounds in the Lordship. **1811** WILLAN in *Archaeologia* XVII. 158 *Slade*, a breadth of green-sward in plough'd land, or in plantations. **1855** BAILEY *Mystic*, etc. 137 Lovers there she saw, arm-twining, in the wild wood's shadowy slade. **1899** A. MORRISON *To London Town* 5 Over the slade they took their way, where the purple carpet was patterned with round hollows.
*transf.* *a* **1300** *Cursor M.* 1258 Quen we war put o paradis vn-to þis wreched warld slade. **1598** DRAYTON *Heroical Ep.* I. 115 When as the Sunne hales tow'rds the Westerne slade.

**slade** (sleɪd), *sb.*[2] Now *dial.* Also 6–7 *Sc.* slaid. [var. of SLEAD or SLED *sb.*[1]] A sledge.
*a* **1585** MONTGOMERIE *Flyting* (Tull.) 86 Thow cwmelie conductit thy termes on ane slaid. **1661** *Reg. Privy Counc. Scotl.* Ser. III. I. 44 [Indwellers in Restalrig..thrust the complainer's servants off his said land,..and with carts and] slaids [carried away the whole crop]. **1688** HOLME *Armoury* III. 339/1 A Slade..and a Tumbrell..are things used by Carters and Husbandmen, for the carriage of Commodities from place to place. **1787** W. H. MARSHALL *E. Norfolk* (1795) II. 388. **1799** YOUNG *Agric. Linc.* 157 They load it on slades, and carry it for grassing to an eaten eddish. *a* **1825** FORBY *Voc. E. Anglia* 306. **1879** MISS JACKSON *Shropsh. Word-bk.* 387.

**slade** (sleɪd), *sb.*[3] [Of obscure origin: perh. related to SLIDE *v.*] The sole of a plough.
**1867** J. & F. HOWARD *Catal. Steam Cultivators*, etc. 38 The wear of plough slades or soles, by sliding on the roads, is obviated [by the use of a wheeled sledge]. *Ibid.* 39 When a new breast is put on, a new slade should be put on also, or the plough will not stand level.

**Slade** (sleɪd), *sb.*[4] The name of Felix Slade (1790–1868) used: **a.** *attrib.* to designate the School of Fine Art (founded 1871) at University College London and its members, and scholarships and professorships in fine art endowed by him at Oxford, Cambridge, and London.
**1869** *Proc. A.G.M.* (U.C.L.) 13 At their Session on May 2nd the Council received notice of the bequest of £45,000 made by the late Mr Felix Slade, for the purpose of founding 'three or more Professorships for promoting the study of Fine Arts, to be termed the Slade Professorships of Fine Arts..one..in..Oxford, another..in..Cambridge, and one more in the University College of London'. **1872** *U.C.L. Calendar, 1871–1872* 44 Slade Scholarships. Under the will of the late Mr Felix Slade, six Scholarships of £50 per annum each..have been founded in the College. **1885** KIPLING *Let.* 18 Dec. in C. Carrington *Rudyard Kipling* (1955) iv. 71 Do you ever come to know anything about the Slade Art School and the students there—the female ones. **1925** E. BUDGE *Mummy* (ed. 2) p. vii, In the year 1892, on the recommendation of J. H. Middleton, Slade Professor of Fine Art in the University of Cambridge, the Syndics..commissioned me to make a Catalogue. **1958** *Observer* 15 June 15/2 Joan Mitchell's rather beautiful painting..which has a sensitive, tight-lipped, almost Slade School quality. **1964** K. CLARK *Ruskin Today* I. 11 In 1869 he [*sc.* John Ruskin] was appointed Slade Professor at Oxford. **1978** *Ann. Rep. 1977–78* (U.C.L.) 19 The College acknowledges ..the co-operation of the Fine Art Society Gallery.., which put on an exhibition of work by Slade artists.
**b.** *absol.* with *the*: the School of Fine Art itself.
**1890** C. M. YONGE *More Bywords* 249 There are the art classes at the Slade, and the lectures I am down for. **1904** R. FRY *Let.* 22 June (1972) I. 222 You will..be as much disappointed, almost, as I am about the Slade. It is a very serious blow to my hopes... They have long ago realized that Waldstein was a failure as Slade Professor. **1928** R. CAMPBELL *Wayzgoose* i. 10 And surely from the stir that this one made He might have been a student at the Slade. **1961** G. SPENCER *Stanley Spencer* v. 102 His entry into the Slade proved to be a most far-reaching and valuable decision. **1980** I. MURDOCH *Nuns & Soldiers* 201 Tim described the Slade and his early experiments in painting.

**slade** (sleɪd), *v.*[1] *dial. rare.* [app. related to SLIDE *v.*] **a.** *intr.* To slide. **b.** With *down*: (see quot. 1787).
**1787** W. H. MARSHALL *E. Norfolk* (1795) II. 388 To *Slade down*, to draw back part of the mould into the inter-furrow, with the plow dragging, or slading upon its side. **1895** P. H. EMERSON *Birds*, etc. *Norf. Broadlands* 186 They don't move their wings much—kind of slade along.

**slade** (sleɪd), *v.*[2] *dial. rare.* [f. SLADE *sb.*[2]] *trans.* To carry on a sledge.
*a* **1825** FORBY *Voc. E. Anglia* 306 Heavy weights are easily sladed on level ground.

**slade,** obs. or Sc. pa. t. of SLIDE *v.*

**slae,** north. and Sc. var. SLOE.

**slaer,** obs. f. SLAYER.

**†slaffart.** *Sc. Obs.* (Meaning doubtful.)
See *Sclaffert* in Jamieson and the *Eng. Dial. Dict.*
**1609** in R. M. Fergusson *A. Hume* (1899) 195 Vilipending of Johne Scherare, baillie,..in saying he wald nocht gif ane slaffart for his kyndnes.

**slag** (slæg), *sb.*[1] Also 6 slagge, 6–9 slagg. [a. MLG. *slagge* (whence also Sw. *slagg*), = G. *schlacke* (also *schlack*), of obscure origin.]
**1.** A piece of refuse matter (see 2) separated from a metal in the process of smelting.
**1552** in P. H. Hore *Wexford* II. (1901) 236 At the furst melting of the after Gripple..was mad therof 288 lbs. of lead besids the slaggs and stones. **1581** in *Trans. Jewish Hist. Soc.* (1903) IV. 98 When it cometh to the smeltinge the copper cometh forth so easelie, without such quantitie of slagges or drosse. **1668** *Phil. Trans.* III. 771 They sometimes find Slaggs 3, 4, or 5 feet under ground, but such as they judge cast aside heretofore. **1691** RAY *Coll. Words* 177 The slags or cinders of the first smelting they beat small with great stamps. **1787** WESLEY *Wks.* (1872) IV. 398 It [a chapel] is composed wholly of brazen slags. **1832** BABBAGE *Econ. Manuf.* xxiii. (ed. 3) 236 Others remain in the form of melted slags, floating on the surface of the iron. **1869** *Daily News* 30 Mar., Two hundred,..with bludgeons and iron slags, attacked the lecturer and the audience.
**2. a.** A vitreous substance, composed of earthy or refuse matter, which is separated from metals in the process of smelting, often used in the construction of roads; any similar product resulting from the fusion or distillation of other substances. (Cf. SCORIA 1.)
**1620** *Patent Office Rec.* (1858) 71 Which Slag, Scorious or Sinder is by our Founders at Furnaces wrought again and found to contain much Yron. **1678** *Phil. Trans.* XII. 1051 If the Stuff be hard to flux, they throw in some slag (which is the Recrement of Iron) to give it fusion. **1763** W. LEWIS *Phil. Comm. Arts* 22 The metal and slag, melting and dropping down through the coals, are collected in the bottom. **1778** PRYCE *Min. Cornub.* 274 The slag is skimmed or drawn off through the hole of the furnace. **1803** *Phil. Trans.* XCIII. 82 The emery was reduced to a dark gray or blackish slag, which occupied the upper part of the crucible. **1862** MILLER *Elem. Chem.*, *Org.* ix. (ed. 2) 644 The ashes of the peat melt and form a slag. **1884** C. G. W. LOCK *Workshop Rec.* Ser. III. 4/1 A small amount of calcined borax is added, which makes the slag more liquid. **1951** *Sources of Road Aggregate in Gt. Brit.* (Dept. Scientific & Industrial Research) (ed. 2) 4 Slags from smelting operations form a valuable source of roadstone in England and Wales... With one exception the slags are derived from iron smelters or steel works. **1955** I. D. MARGARY *Roman Roads in Britain* I. i. 15 In districts where iron was being worked the hard slag provided an almost ideal metalling [for Roman roads]. **1958** *Optima* Mar. 14/1 At Maresfield Hempstead, near Benenden, and at Slinfold, Roman roads are partly constructed of slag, and large quantities of slag have since been used.
*fig.* **1870** LOWELL *Among my Books* Ser. I. 295 All through his life..he never quite smelted his knowledge clear from some slag of learning. **1878** E. JENKINS *Haverholme* 2 The hard slag of a cold, sagacious cynicism.
**b.** With specific epithets, as *basic, grey, sharp.*
**1811** FAREY *Derbyshire* I. 389 This tapped or white [lead] Slag..received the name of Macaroni Slag. *a* **1876** W. H. GREENWOOD *Man. Metall.* II. 37 From the sharp edges of the fractured fragments it [metal slag] is sometimes called sharp slag. **1881** RAYMOND *Mining Gloss.*, *Gray slag*, the slag from the Flintshire lead furnace. It is rich in lead. **1888** [see BASIC *a.* 2d]. **1889** A. B. GRIFFITHS *Manures & Uses* 101 Finely ground basic slag must be considered an important fertilizer for wheat crops. **1937** *Nature* 20 Feb. 318/2 The Industrial Research Council of the British Iron and Steel Federation will show..the applications of foamed slag as an aggregate for lightweight concrete. *c* **1957** *Story of Slag* (Brit. Slag Federation) 16 (*caption*) Airfield, showing main runway coated with three-quarter inch graded bituminous slag. *Ibid.* 17 Dry slag makes excellent rail track ballast. *Ibid.* 18 Dry slag is used by many local authorities as filter-bed media. *Ibid.* 21 Foamed slag building blocks used in

construction of houses at Gateshead and Middlesbrough. **1971** *Arable Farmer* Feb. 69/2 Dressings of basic slag, potassic basic slag or PK compound fertiliser at the beginning and near the end of the ley break should prove sufficient to carry three successive corn crops.

**3.** *Geol.* A rough clinker-like lump of lava (see quot. 1879); lava in this form. (Cf. SCORIA 2.)

**1777** FORSTER *Voy. round World* II. 307 Easter Island.. produces..vegetables and useful roots, without any other soil than slags, cinders, and pumice-stones. **1789** E. DARWIN *Bot. Gard.* I. 103 Break into clays the soft volcanic slaggs. **1857** LD. DUFFERIN *Lett. High Lat.* (ed. 3) 106 Bare cinder-like hills, that rose round..in a hundred uncouth peaks of ash and slag. **1879** *Encycl. Brit.* X. 243 When the ejected fragment of lava has a rough irregular form, and a porous structure like the clinker of an iron-furnace, it is known as a *slag*.

**4.** *local.* (See quots.)

**1828** CARR *Craven Gloss.*, *Slag*, the cinder of a bad, spurious, kind of coal. **1883** GRESLEY *Gloss. Coal-m.* 225 *Slag*,..a thin bed or band of coal mixed with lime and iron pyrites. **1891** *Labour Commission Gloss.*, *Small coal*,..the duff, slag, or waste, which arises from the sorting of the large coal into nuts.

**5.** *slang.* **a.** A worthless or insignificant person (freq. used as a term of contempt): *spec.* (*a*) a coward; (*b*) a rough or brutal person; (*c*) any objectionable or contemptible person; (*d*) a vagrant or a petty criminal; also, such persons collectively; (*e*) (the most usual sense) a prostitute or promiscuous woman; a slattern.

(*a*) **1788** GROSE *Dict. Vulgar Tongue* (ed. 2), *Slag*, a slack-mettled fellow, one not ready to resent an affront. **1958** F. NORMAN *Bang to Rights* II. 62 You'v got the guts of a slag. (*b*) **1934** P. ALLINGHAM *Cheapjack* xix. 237 The Newcastle 'slag' is the sort of man who makes up the personnel of the race-gangs, and..he will pick a fight with anyone. **1961** *New Statesman* 14 Apr. 576/2 As the underworld put it, 'he steamed in like a slag and roughed them up as he topped them.' (*c*) **1943** W. BUCHANAN-TAYLOR *Shake It Again* xxi. 199 It seemed slaggy to me. (A *slag* is a person who is not much *bottle*—not much good;..for whom you have no respect or time.) **1958** M. PUGH *Wilderness of Monkeys* 89 Sit down.. you slag. **1962** PARKER & ALLERTON *Courage of his Convictions* iv. 159 When I got out there was some slag on the door, all gold braid and nose in the air, wouldn't let me in! **1981** *Daily Tel.* 8 July 3/1 As sentence was announced, the dead boy's father..shouted: 'I hope you rot in it, you slag.' (*d*) **1955** P. WILDEBLOOD *Against Law* III. 120 Several different kinds of burglars..the rank amateurs or 'slags' who had stolen paltry sums. **1962** R. COOK *Crust on its Uppers* iii. 43 Marchmare lent it to this hatful of slag. **1962** D. WARNER *Death of Bogey* I. ii. 14 In my day, the strong-arm boys were slags. Nobody in the big-time would look at 'em. **1963** T. & P. MORRIS *Pentonville* xi. 227 Pentonville also contains at any given time a number of vagrants, drunks and similar social derelicts... Prison argot classifies them all as *slags*. **1968** J. LOCK *Lady Policeman* xii. 108 Only prostitutes, their friends, layabouts, tom watchers, petty criminals and the like are left—'the slag' we call them. **1970** P. LAURIE *Scotland Yard* vi. 141, I could get them up the nick and take their prints with ink, but that's really for slag. (*e*) **1958** *N.Z. Listener* 10 Oct. 6/3 A 'slag' is a white girl who lives with or is friendly with coloured people of either sex. **1959** ANON. *Streetwalker* iv. 87 It's my pride he hurts, with his little slags. **1966** *New Statesman* 23 Dec. 934/2 You have to wear glasses these days if you don't want to be called a slag. **1970** 'D. CRAIG' *Young Men may Die* x. 72 Does anyone care what happens to a slag? **1973** J. SEABROOK *Loneliness* 185, I went out with a girl called Angie, who was really a bit of a slag.

**b.** Worthless matter, rubbish; nonsense.

**1948** V. PALMER *Golconda* v. 35 'Listen,' he said... 'There's some men in every camp will get a kick out of throwing dirt. Who's been filling you up with slag about me? That old crank up on the mountain, was it?' **1970** *New Yorker* 12 Sept. 32/3 It is very depressing to think about the wonderful..letters people used to get..and then look at the slag on one's desk.

**6.** *attrib.* **a.** In sense 'consisting or composed of slag', as ***slag-bed***, ***-brick***, ***-cement***, ***slag-dump***, ***-heap*** (also *fig.*), ***inclusion***, ***-mound***, ***-tip***, ***wool***, etc.

**1877** RAYMOND *Statist. Mines & Mining* 385 The workmen clean up the *slag-bed and tend to the fire. **1875** KNIGHT *Dict. Mech.* 2198/1 *Slag-brick. **1879** H. REID *Nat. & Art. Concrete* (new ed.) 123 An hospital..was built..of these slag bricks. **1884** C. G. W. LOCK *Workshop Rec.* Ser. III. 436/2 The *slag-cement undergoes a similar change to that..in Portland or Roman cements. **1923** KIPLING *Irish Guards in Gt. War* I. 109 It was a jagged, scarred and mutilated sweep of mining-villages, factories, quarries, *slag-dumps, pit-heads, chalk-pits and railway embankments. **1974** *Times* 11 Jan. 16/6 Various stages of iron-working are represented by ore-roasting areas, three slag dumps, 36 smelting furnaces [etc.]. **1880** SIR E. BECKETT *Book on Building* (ed. 2) 220 That new *slag-felt which I mentioned. **1884** C. G. W. LOCK *Workshop Rec.* Ser. III. 431/2 *Slag-glass, owing to its toughness, is specially suitable for manufacturing into tiles,..slates, &c. **1917** A. G. EMPEY *Over Top* 308 **Slag heap*, a pile of rubbish, tin cans, etc. **1931** C. DAY LEWIS *From Feathers to Iron* xxix. 54 Wherever radiance from ashes arises—Willow-herb glowing on abandoned slagheaps. **1963** *Times* 24 Jan. 6/2 It was not enough to put one or two council houses near the slag heaps. **1974** F. WARNER *Meeting Ends* II. ii. 39 What a bore the slagheap of matrimony! **1913** *Slag inclusion [see INCLUSION 2]. **1934** *Jrnl. R. Aeronaut. Soc.* XXXVIII. 249 Thirteen micro-photographs show forms of slag inclusion and distortion of films in butt welding. **1945** GREAVES & WRIGHTON *Practical Microsc. Metallogr.* vi. 96 Of commercial wrought irons, Swedish Bar Iron is most free from slag inclusions. **1955** J. R. R. TOLKIEN *Return of King* 374 Frodo reaches the *slag-mounds. **1841** HARTSHORNE *Salop. Antiq.* Gloss., **Slagg pigs*, flat pigs of lead of a smaller size and inferior quality to the common ones. **1797** *Encycl. Brit.* (ed. 3) XII. 142/2 *Slag-sand or ashes... This is thrown out from volcanoes in form of..grains. **1884** C. G. W. LOCK *Workshop Rec.* Ser. II. 433/1 The united action.. scatters, as it were, the molten slag in the water into the material called slag-sand. *Ibid.* 432/2 When perfectly cold, it is tipped from the waggons, and falls into small-sized pieces, called '*slag-shingle'. **1960** C. DAY LEWIS *Buried Day* vii. 130 The prevailing wind brought the acrid smell of *slag-tips from the Mansfield collieries. **1862** KINGSLEY in *Macm. Mag.* Aug. 275 Plodding along the dusty road, between black *slag walls. **1878** J. DEBY *Rep. Iron & Steel Industries Foreign Countries* II. i. 13 The manufacture of blast furnace *slag wool has recently been established commercially for the first time in America. **1884** *Health Exhib. Catal.* 83/2 'Silicate Cotton', or 'Slag Wool', a pure mineral fibre manufactured from blast furnace slag. **1979** *Nature* 19 July 183/2 The fibres are produced from glass, rock, slag and metallic oxides and include fibreglass and rock and slag wools which are widely used for home insulation as a substitute for asbestos.

**b.** In other uses, as ***slag-car***, ***-furnace***, etc. **slag notch**, a hole in a furnace, above the level of the molten metal, which can be unstopped to let out slag.

**1875** KNIGHT *Dict. Mech.* 2198/1 *Slag-car*, a wrought-iron car..used to contain and carry off the slag of a furnace. *Ibid.*, Slag furnace. *Ibid.*, The slag-pots are of cast-iron. **1877** RAYMOND *Statist. Mines & Min.* 269, 14 inches from tuyeres to slag-tap. **1890** W. J. GORDON *Foundry* 99 The slag being drawn off..by a channel-way into the slag-waggons. **1895** E. L. RHEAD *Metallurgy* 96 In the top of the dam is a groove, the 'slag-notch', through which the slags flow continuously, after reaching that level, and through which the blast blows to keep it clear. **1929** W. LISTER *Practical Steelmaking* xxxviii. 392 A 'Dewhurst' ladle can stand under the middle door in order to catch the slag running over the slag notch.

**7.** *Comb.*, as ***slag-burner***, etc.; ***slag-molten*** adj.

**1582** STANYHURST *Æneis* III. (Arb.) 89 Stoans hudge slag molten he rowseth. **1782** *Phil. Trans.* LXXII. 320 A Hessian crucible..melted into a slag-like substance. **1881** *Census Instr.* (1885) 164/2 Slag-burner, -felter, -tipper [etc.].

† **slag** (slæg), *sb.*[2] *Obs. Criminals' slang.* [Prob. f. SLANG *sb.*[4], under influence of SLAG *sb.*[1]] = SLANG *sb.*[4] I.

**1857** 'DUCANGE ANGLICUS' *Vulgar Tongue* 19 *Slag, n.* Chain, a gold or silver one. **1926** *Clues* Nov. 159/1 Then we'll take the hot hoops and slags up to the block dealers. **1929** *Detective Fiction Weekly* 2 Mar. 694/2 One 'nips the slag' when one cuts the watch chain, a practice practically defunct now.

**slag**, *a. rare.* [Of obscure origin: cf. MLG. *schlagge* rainy or dirty weather, Sw. *slagg* sleet, Norw. *slagg* slaver, and see the *Eng. Dial. Dict.* s.v. *Slag(g* adj.] Slippery with mud; muddy.

*c* **1440** *Promp. Parv.* 458/1 Slag, or fowle wey,..*lubricus, lutosus, limosus.*

**slag** (slæg), *v.* [f. SLAG *sb.*[1]]

**1.** *trans.* To free (ore) from slag; to convert into slag; to scorify.

**1882** *U.S. Rep. Prec. Met.* 580 The ore must first be slagged. *Ibid.*, A cord of wood will slag several tons of ore.

**2.** *intr.* To form into a slag; to become a slag-like mass.

**1891** in *Cent. Dict.*

**3.** *trans.* To abuse or denigrate (a person); to criticize, insult. Also with *off*. *slang.*

**1971** J. MANDELKAU *Buttons* v. 75 He was doing a good job of bad mouthing and slagging me to a number of the Angels. **1972** *Guardian* 17 Aug. 1/1 Mr Jack Jones, general secretary of the Transport and General Workers' Union, was 'slagged off'—in dockland jargon—several times during the day. A gang of furious dockers invaded his press conference. **1974** G. F. NEWMAN *Price* v. 156 She always put out warnings, invariably slagging Terry. **1976** E. DUNPHY *Only a Game?* v. 150 When the game starts, if things start going wrong, everyone blames them. Everyone slags them off. **1978** *Broadcast* 29 May 2/2 There's been a growing tendency for some sales organisations to slag the [television] company which used to be..the brand leader in British sales. **1981** *Daily Tel.* 25 Feb. 17/6 He followed me down the street, slagging me off.

Hence (or from the sb.) **slagged** *ppl. a.*; **'slagging** *vbl. sb.* Also **'slagger** *sb.*

**1824** MCCULLOCH *Highlands Scot.* I. 285 The walls are more or less perfectly slagged or scorified. **1877** RAYMOND *Statist. Mines & Mining* 317 A hearth for slagging purposes. **1892** *Labour Commission Gloss.*, *Slagger*, those in the blast furnace industry who attend to the slag as it is run down the trough... Their work is called slagging. **1971** *News-Advocate* (Barbados) 20 Mar. 9/6 You get so much slagging of bands nowadays. **1977** *Zigzag* Aug. 20/3 The gig met with quite a bit of slagging in the rock press.

**'slagger**, *v.* Now *dial.* [Of obscure origin.] *intr.* To loiter, lag, walk slowly or lamely. Also *fig.* Hence **'slaggering** *vbl. sb.*

**1622** R. PRESTON *Godly Man's Inquisit.* ii. 47 It is not leaden heeles, but faint and dead hearts that makes vs slagger. *Ibid.* 62 Fie on this slaggering and staggering of Christians. **1809** BATCHELOR *Anal. Eng. Lang.* 144. *c* **1821** MASTERS *Dick & Sal* xxxii. (Kent. Gl.), An so we slagger'd den, ya know, An gaapt an stared about. **1887** in *Kentish Gloss.*

**slaggy** ('slægɪ), *a.* Also 8 slaggey. [f. SLAG *sb.*[1] + -Y[1].] **1.** Of the nature of slag; pertaining to or resembling slag.

**1688** HOLME *Armoury* III. 266/1 Slateing, is a covering of Houses with a kind of Blew Slaggy Marble. **1757** tr. *Henckel's Pyritologia* 170 A slaggey and stoney body. *Ibid.* 176 It also often appears slaggy, and run. **1797** *Encycl. Brit.* (ed. 3) XII. 133/2 This is..of a slaggy texture. **1805** R. JAMESON *Min.* II. 49 Slaggy Mineral Pitch. **1833** LYELL *Princ. Geol.* III. 219 Some of the bones were found adhering to the slaggy lava. **1881** JUDD *Volcanoes* ii. 12 Stromboli is a great mass of cinders and slaggy materials.

*Comb.* **1863** RAMSAY *Physical Geogr.* 13 An arrangement in slaggy-like layers.

**2.** *slang.* **a.** Of a person or thing: objectionable, unpleasant, offensive.

**1943** [see SLAG *sb.*[1] 5 a (*c*)]. **1962** R. COOK *Crust on its Uppers* x. 82 That slaggy basement of yours. **1972** R. QUILTY *Tenth Session* I. 20 Some sort of hippie, maybe? No roadie, he could swear to that, having tangled with some real slaggy ones.

**b.** Of a woman: promiscuous, 'cheap'; slatternly.

**1973** H. MILLER *Open City* xiv. 160 The writer and his slaggy girl friend. **1980** R. CONNOLLY *Sunday Kind of Woman* ii. 22 He thought about some of the slaggy models he had known.

**'slag-hearth.** [SLAG *sb.*[1]] A furnace for treating the slag-products of lead-smelting.

**1778** PENNANT *Tour Wales* (1883) I. 79 These artless slag-hearths are very frequent in the dingles of our country. **1839** URE *Dict. Arts* 756 The whole may then be..introduced without any preparation into the slag-hearth. **1868** JOYNSON *Metals* 101 By the aid either of the reverbatory furnace, the slag hearth, or the cauldron furnaces.

**slaght**, variant of SLAUGHT *Obs.*

**slaght-boome:** see SLAUGHT-BOOM *Obs.*

**slaghter**, obs. form of SLAUGHTER *sb.*

**'slag-lead.** [SLAG *sb.*[1]] Lead obtained by resmelting grey slag.

**1668** CHARLETON *Onomast.* 294 *Plumbum Nigrum*,.. Common Lead, & Slagg Lead. **1729** *Phil. Trans.* XXXVI. 32 This Slag is afterwards smelted again,..and the Lead obtained from it is called Slag-lead. **1811** FAREY *Derbyshire* I. 391 For Red-Lead making..the Hard or Slag-Lead is preferred. **1858** GREENER *Gunnery* 436 Slag-lead is lighter than other lead, but it is much harder.

**slagless** ('slæglɪs), *a.* [f. SLAG *sb.*[1] + -LESS.] Of iron, steel, etc.: free from slag. Hence **'slaglessness.**

**1902** *Encycl. Brit.* XXIX. 571/1 (*in table*) Slagless or 'Ingot-metal' Series. *Ibid.* 571/2 But the former lack the essential quality—slaglessness—which makes the latter steel.

**slaht**, var. of SLAUGHT *Obs.*

**slaid**, Sc. pa. t. SLIDE *v.*

**slaie**, var. of SLAY *sb.*[1]; obs. f. SLAY *v.*[1]

**slaigh**, dial. var. of SLOE.

**slaight**, obs. f. SLEIGHT.

**slain** (sleɪn), *sb. north. dial.* Also **slane, sleean.** [f. SLAIN *ppl. a.* 3.] Smut in grain; also *concr.*, smutty grains.

**1703** THORESBY *Lett. Ray* (E.D.S.) 103/1 *Leyse*, to pick the slain and trucks out of wheat. **1788** W. H. MARSHALL *Yorksh.* II. 358 *Sleean* (that is, *slain*), the smut of corn. **1829–** in northern glossaries.

**slain** (sleɪn), *ppl. a.* [See SLAY *v.*[1]]

**1.** That has been slain; killed, slaughtered.

*a* **1225** *Leg. Kath.* 199 As te keiser stod bimong þat sunful slaht of þat islein ahte deouele to lake [etc.]. *c* **1225** *Ancr. R.* 118 So schulen eft acwikien hire isleiene briddes. **1382** WYCLIF *Lev.* vii. 8 The preest that offreth the slawn offryng of brent sacrifice. **1388** —— *Ps.* ci. 21 For to vnbynde the sones of slayn men. **1535** COVERDALE *1 Chron.* xxii. 26 Dauid ..offred burntofferynges & slaynofferynges. **1579** LODGE *Def. Poetry* 22 In all the Romaine conquest, hardest thou euer of a slayne Poete? **1628** in Foster *Eng. Factories India* (1909) III. 292 Our people, who wanted not will to have revenged the slaine mans cause. **1697** DRYDEN *Virg. Georg.* IV. 784 From the slain Victims pour the streaming Blood. **1776** MICKLE tr. *Camoens' Lusiad* Introd. 151 *note*, Homer and Virgil's lists of slain warriors. **1831** SCOTT *Cast. Dang.* vii, The slain game affording a plentiful supply for roasting or broiling. **1872** RUSKIN *Eagle's Nest* §223 The wearing of the skins of slain animals.

**b.** *absol.* Usually *pl.*

*c* **1340** HAMPOLE *Psalter* 522 Of the blode of slayne. **1382** WYCLIF *Numb.* xxxv. 19 The nyȝ kynne of the slayn. **1535** COVERDALE *Ezek.* xxxii. 30 All the prynces of the north, with all the Sidonians, which are gone downe to the slayne. **1671** MILTON *Samson* 439 Their God who hath deliver'd Thee Samson..into thir hands..who slew'st them many a slain. *a* **1700** EVELYN *Diary* 8 July 1685, The slaine were most of them Mendip-miners. **1837** CARLYLE *Fr. Rev.* I. v. vii, In hot frenzy of triumph, of grief and vengeance for its slain. **1870** BRYANT *Iliad* I. vii. 231 For the slain, I give consent to burn them.

**2.** *letter(s) of slains*, in older Scots Law, 'letters subscribed by the relations of a person who had been slain, declaring that they had received an assythment, and concurring in an application to the Crown for a pardon to the offender' (Bell). Now only *Hist.*

**1473–4** *Acc. Ld. High Treas. Scot.* I. 4 Componit wytht Will Scot for a remissione for the slachter of Johnne Crossate, for the quhilk he schew a lettre of slanys of the partj. **1546** *Reg. Privy Council Scot.* I. 34 To gif ane plane letter of slains to the said Capitane for the slauchteris committit upoun him and his freindis. **1661** *Ibid.* Ser. III. I. 10 The said Barbra Turner, her only dochter, who hes granted the foresaid letter of slayans and discharge. **1678** SIR G. MACKENZIE *Crim. Laws Scot.* II. xxviii. §iv, If the party doth willingly grant a discharge of all grudge, or revenge in the Crime of Murder, this discharge is called a letter of Slanes. **1765-8** ERSKINE *Inst. Law Scot.* IV. iv. §105 In the case of slaughter, it behoved the wife or executors of the deceased..to subscribe letters of slains, acknowledging that they had received satisfaction. **1769** ROBERTSON *Chas. V*, I. 301 By the letters of Slanes, the heirs and relations of a person who had been murdered, bound themselves..to forgive, pass over, and forever forget, and in oblivion interr all rancour, malice [etc.]. **1814** SCOTT *Wav.* xlviii, You are aware the blood-wit was made up..by assythment, and that I have since expedited letters of slains.

**3.** *dial.* Of grain: Affected by smut or blight. **1641** H. BEST *Farm. Bks.* (Surtees) 53 When your barley is infeckted with slaine corne yow must endeavour by all meanes possible to leade it dry. **1788** W. H. MARSHALL *Yorksh.* II. 353 An ear which is smutty is called a 'slain ear'. **1800** TUKE *Agric. N. Riding* 111 In order to prevent wheat from being smutty or slain, brine..has been generally used. **1825-** in northern glossaries.

‖**slainte** ('slɑːntʃə), *int.* Also slainté. [a. Gael. *sláinte*, lit. 'health'.] A Gaelic toast: good health! **1824** SCOTT *Redgauntlet* II. vii. 159 He then took up the tankard, and saying aloud in Gaelic, '*Slaint an Rey*', just tasted the liquor. **1880** A. P. GRAVES *Irish Songs & Ballads* 71 Here's a health to you, Father O'Flynn, Slainté, and slainté, and slainté agin. **1922** JOYCE *Ulysses* 44 Well: *slainte!* **1949** E. COXHEAD *Wind in West* iv. 114 '*Slainte mhor*, Rory!' cried Kurt, who knew what was necessary in every language. **1952** 'J. TEY' *Singing Sands* vii. 105 '*Slainte!*' he said, and took a swig of it. **1966** S. FORBES *Terror touches Me* iv. 43 'Here, Brendan. Slainté.' Brendan's hand trembled as he took the full glass. **1980** M. MCMULLEN *My Cousin Death* (1981) vi. 78 Upshaw gave him his drink..'*Slainte.*'

**slaire**, variant of SKLEIR, a veil. *Obs.*

**slaister** ('sleɪstə(r)), *sb. Sc.* and *north. dial.* [Cf. the vb.] A dirty or disgusting mess or compound; the act of working at or making this. **a1774** FERGUSSON *Election* Poems (1845) 43 Ye louns! that troke in doctor's stuff, You'll now hae unco slaisters. **1824** SCOTT *St. Ronan's* ii,'Ay, and are you at the painting trade yet?' said Meg; 'an unco slaister ye used to make with it lang syne'. **1832** CARLYLE in Froude *Life* (1882) II. 268 They are painting the dining-room, lobby, and staircase; and, to avoid such a *slaister* for the future, doing it in oil. **1857-** in *Eng. Dial. Dict.*

**slaister** ('sleɪstə(r)), *v. Sc.* and *north. dial.* Also slester, etc. [Of obscure origin.] **a.** *intr.* To eat, work, etc., in a slobbering, wet, or dirty manner. **b.** *trans.* To plaster in this fashion.

For fuller illustration of forms and senses see the *Eng. Dial. Dict.*

**1756** MRS. CALDERWOOD *Jrnl.* (1884) 64 The maids..have nothing to do but slester and wash. **1773** FERGUSSON *Auld Reekie* 124 Look at that head, and think if there The pomet slaister'd up his hair! **1816** SCOTT *Antiq.* x, Ye'll be for your breakfast?..hae, there's a soup parritch for ye—it will set ye better to be slaistering at them and the lapper-milk than meddling wi' Mr. Lovel's head. **1819** TENNANT *Papistry Storm'd* (1827) 89 Loud gaups o' laughter shook the bank, As Johnnie slaister'd throu' the stank.

**slait**, obs. Sc. var. SLATE *sb.* and *v.*; var. of SLEIGHT *sb.*[3]; pa. t. SLITE *v.*

**slake** (sleɪk), *sb.*[1] Also 4 **slak**. [f. SLAKE *v.*[1]]

**1.** The act of slacking or slackening in some respect; an instance of this. **a1300** *Cursor M.* 23618 Sua sal þe wreches..for þair sak, Be stad in pine wit-vten slak. **16..** *Robin of Portingale* in *Percy's Folio MS., Ball. & Rom.* I. 238 At the wakening of your first sleepe your sorrowes will haue a slake. **1787** W. H. MARSHALL *E. Norfolk* (1795) II. 388 'To be at slake,' to be at leisure. **1837** CARLYLE *Fr. Rev.* I. III. iii, Such side-questions..as, in the heat of the main-battle, he..could not get answered; these also he takes up, at the first slake. **1865** —— *Fredk. Gt.* XIV. iii. V. 184 Some slake occurring..in that interminable Honsbruck Lawsuit.

**2.** A source or cause of slaking. *rare*⁻¹. **a1300** *Cursor M.* 24592 His lijk ful lath was þe to þarn, þat slak was o þi site.

**slake** (sleɪk), *sb.*[2] *Sc.* and *north. dial.* Also *Sc.* 5 **slak**, 7, 9 **slaik**. [Obscurely related to the synonymous SLAWK and SLOKE.] A name given to several species of Algæ, including marine and edible kinds as *Ulva* and *Porphyra*, and also the freshwater sorts, as *Enteromorpha* and *Conferva*. **c1475** HENRYSON *Poems* (S.T.S.) III. 151 Ane sleiffull of slak, þat growis in the sluss. **1623** *Orkney Witch Trial* in Dalyell *Darker Superst. Scotl.* (1834) 389 And giving him a 'cogfull of slaik' to be eat raw on a cake, he recovered daily. **1710** RUDDIMAN *Gloss. Douglas' Æneis* s.v. *Slike*, Scot. Bor. call a kind of Sea-weed, very soft and slippery, Slake, which they also eat. **1793** *Statist. Acc. Scotl.* VII. 201 The green slake which grows in the river. **1853** G. JOHNSTON *Terra Lindisfarnensis* I. *Bot. E. Borders* 287 The Enteromorphæ fill the bed of the lower part of the Tweed during the summer, and are well known to our fishermen under the name of Slake. **1901** *Trans. Stirling Nat. Hist. Soc.* 68 The Bannock at this point was filled with slake, and so deep that none could ride over it.

**slake** (sleɪk), *sb.*[3] Chiefly *north. dial.* [? Related to SLIKE *sb.*]

**1.** Mud, slime. **c1800** *Rep. Agric. Surv., Cumb.* 30 (Britten), Slake or mud left by the tide. **1883** *Pall Mall G.* 10 Nov. 4/1 At low tide a large area of river slake is left exposed on each side to the influences of the weather.

**2.** A stretch of muddy ground left exposed by the tide; a mud-flat. **1828** G. YOUNG *Geol. Surv. Yorks. Coast* 39 The morass at Hartlepool is evidently a continuation of the slake. **1868** MAIDMENT *Sc. Pasquils* 4 *note*, The slakes are waste lands bordering on the sea shore, which are covered with water when the tide comes in. **1889** *Athenæum* 16 Mar. 348/3 Adventures..in a gunning punt along the 'slakes' off Holy Island.

†**slake**, *sb.*[4] *Obs.* [Of obscure origin.] A flake. **a1608** DEE *Relat. Spirits* I. (1659) 357 They knock their wedges..and so break off great Slakes of Stone, like Slate. **1610** FOLKINGHAM *Art of Survey* I. x. 32 Columbine or Pidgeon Marle lies in lumpes and cloddes, but with Sunne and Frost, it resolues and cleaues into thinne slakes or flakes. **1721** *Post-master* 9 June 264 The Slakes of Fire were wafted by a strong Wind upon the Roofs of the Houses.

**slake** (sleɪk), *sb.*[5] *Sc.* and *north. dial.* [f. SLAKE *v.*[2]] A splashy daub; a smear; a lick, wipe, soft stroke, etc. **1721** KELLY *Sc. Prov.* 396 I'll give you a Gob Slake. **1818** SCOTT *Hrt. Midl.* xvii, Maybe a touch o' a blackit cork, or a slake o' paint. **1829** *Blackw. Mag.* XXVI. 144 Wafered to the pane with three wafers of divers colours, and a slake of starch. **1855** ATKINSON *Whitby Gloss.*, A *Slake*, a mere wipe, not a thorough cleansing. 'A lick and a slake',..as a slut gets over certain of her household duties.

**slake**, obs. variant of SLACK *sb.*[1]

†**slake**, *a. Obs.* [var. of SLACK *a.*, representing OE. disyllabic forms.]

**1.** Loose, relaxed; not tight. = SLACK *a.* 7. **13..** *K. Alis.* 1251 (Laud MS.), þe stedes rennen wiþ slake bridlen. **c1374** CHAUCER *Boeth.* I. met. i. (1868) 4 þe slake skyn tremblep vpon myn emty body. **1422** tr. *Secreta Secret., Priv. Priv.* 221 Flesshe in tempure neshe, noght slake, tokenyth good vndyrstondynge. **a1586** SIDNEY *Astr. & Stella* xxviii, The raines of Loue I loue, though neuer slake. **1643** STEER tr. *Exp. Chyrurg.* xv. 60 It sheweth holes, by whose benefit the ring is made straight, or slake, according as need requireth.

**2.** Slack, remiss. *rare*⁻¹. **1538** STARKEY *England* II. iii. 214 For my parte, I wyl neuer be slake in thys behalfe.

**3.** *slake water*, = SLACK-WATER. **1580** BURROUGH in Hakluyt *Voy.* (1598) I. 436 Diligently note the time of..the slake or still water of full sea. **1635** in Foxe *North-west Fox* 124 It was then slake-water. **1793** R. MYLNE *Rep. Thames* 34 From the strong current on the Bucks side, to the slake water on the Berks side.

**slake** (sleɪk), *v.*[1] Forms: 1 sleac-, slacian, 3 slakien, 5 slakeen (?); 2-3 slakie (3 scl-), 3- slake (5 scl-), 4 slak; *Sc.* 5-7 slaik (5 slalk, 6 sclaik), 6 slaike. [OE. *sleac-*, *slacian*, f. *slæc* SLACK *a.* Cf. MDu. and Du. *slaken* to make slack, relax, diminish, etc., mod.Icel. *slaka* to give way, Norw. *slaka* to slacken. OE. had also the compound *aslacian*: see ASLAKE *v.*]

**I.** *intr.* †**1.** Of persons: To diminish the intensity of one's efforts; to become less energetic or eager; also, to undergo or manifest a weakening or decrease in some specified respect. *Obs.*

In some cases the sense approaches that of 'cease'.

**c1000** ÆLFRIC *Exod.* xvii. 11 ðif he þonne lithwon slacode, þonne hæfde Amalech sige. **a1310** in Wright *Lyric P.* xvi. 54 For hire love in slep y slake, For hire love al nyht ich wake. **c1400** tr. *Secreta Secret., Gov. Lordsh.* 110 If þou fynde hem yn hem slakand or failland, comforte here hertes. **a1400-50** *Alexander* 3050 Als sone as þe son vp soȝt þe slaȝtere begynnes, And so to þe son-sett slakid þai neuire. **1596** DALRYMPLE tr. *Leslie's Hist. Scot.* II. 214 Quhen the peple, throuch the dinn and cry tha maid, slaiket nocht lytle.

†**b.** Const. to with inf. *Obs.* **a1225** *Leg. Kath.* 2136 Swa þat ich slakie to ofseruin heouenriche. **c1250** *Moral Ode* 38 in *O.E. Misc.* 59 Ne scholde nomon don a virst ne slakien wel to donne. **13..** *Minor Poems fr. Vernon MS.* xxi. 112 ȝif me grace from synne to fle, And him to loue let me neuer slake. **c1440** *Pol. Poems* (Rolls) II. 206 Alas! for to sorow how shuld I slake.

†**c.** Const. *of* something. *Obs.* **c1375** *Cursor M.* 13054 (Fairf.), Bot þou of suche dedis slake, þou wil noȝt dey wiȝ-outen wrak. **c1386** CHAUCER *Clerk's T.* 649 They kan nat stynte of hire entencion,..They wol nat of that firste purpos slake. **c1470** HENRY *Wallace* v. 656 Prefand giff he mycht off that languor slalk [= slaik]. **a1578** LINDESAY (Pitscottie) *Chron. Scot.* (S.T.S.) I. 398 The Inglischemen..slaikit of thair curage. **1621** in *Gude & Godlie Ball.* App. I. 232, I will ȝow exhort..To slaik of ȝour sleuth.

†**d.** To fall *away* from one; to depart. *Obs.*⁻¹ **c1400** *Sir Cleges* 80 (W.), His men..Gan slake awaye on euery syde; With hym there wold dwell non. **c1440** *Pallad. on Husb.* XI. 248 Wyne dreggis wole make hem [ants] thennes slake.

**2.** †**a.** To become relaxed, slack, or loose. *Obs.* **c1000** ÆLFRIC *Exod.* xvii. 12 Aaron and Ur underwriðedon Moises handa..and hiȝ ne slacedon nan þing syððan. **c1220** *Bestiary* 126 [The serpent] fasteð til his fel him slakeð. **c1420** LYDG. *Assembly of Gods* 1244 The bende of your bowe Begynneth to slake. **1599** SIR J. DAVIES *Immort. of Soul* III. vii, When the Body's strongest Sinews slake.

**b.** Of lime: To become hydrated or slacked. **1766** *Compl. Farmer* s.v. *Lucern*, The chalk slakes, when thaws and rains come on. **1857** MILLER *Elem. Chem., Org.* iii. §1. 122 The lime gradually slakes and falls to powder. **1895** *Bloxam's Chem.* 332 Air-slaked lime has slaked by simple exposure to air.

**3.** To decrease in force or intensity; to become less violent, oppressive, or painful; to abate, moderate. Now *rare*. **a1300** *Cursor M.* 3772 Sco send him son in-til aran,..þar to suiorn..Til þat his broþer wreth suld slake. **a1352** MINOT *Poems* v. 4 Wald he salue vs sone, mi sorow suld slake. **a1400** *Rom. Rose* 3108 In me fyve woundes dide he make, The soore of whiche shalle nevere slake. **c1440** *Generydes* 4190 Atte last the wynde beganne to slake. **1553** in Hakluyt *Voy.* I. 248 The winter..doth still..increase by a perpetuitie of cold: neither doth that colde slake, until [etc.]. **1581** W. STAFFORD *Exam. Compl.* iii. (1876) 93 That the indignation against them shortly will slake of it selfe. **c1605** ? ROWLEY *Birth of Merlin* I. ii, No man leaves physic when his sickness slakes. **1648** J. BEAUMONT *Psyche* VI. xvii, Custom..can make The dint and edge of any strangeness slake. **1837** CARLYLE *Fr. Rev.* IV. vi, It tolled One when the firing began; and is now pointing towards Five, and still the firing slakes not.

**b.** Of fire: To burn less strongly; to die down, die away, go out. Also *fig.* **c1340** HAMPOLE *Pr. Consc.* 6224 þe synful..sal wende Until helle fire, þat never sal slake. **1387** TREVISA *Higden* (Rolls) II. 23 þere þe fuyre slakeþ, it chaungeth into stony clottes. **a1400** *Minor Poems fr. Vernon MS.* xxxiii. 14 Poul sayh bi-foren helle ȝates Brennynge tres þat neuer slakes. **1603** DRAYTON *Odes* i. 93 'Tis possible to clyme, To kindle, or to slake, Although in Skelton's Ryme. **1613** BROWNE *Brit. Past.* I. i, She perceiving that his flame did slake [etc.]. **1648** HERRICK *Hesper.*, ''*Tis not ev'ry day*' 10 Look how next the holy fier, Either slakes or doth retire.

†**4.** To become weaker or fainter; to lessen, fall off. *Obs.* **c1315** SHOREHAM I. 806 ȝef mannes deuocioun slakeþ..By-þenche hym Of þe uertue þat þer hys. **a1400** *Hymns to Virgin* 71 þi siȝte and heeryng bigynneþ to slake. **1470-85** MALORY *Arthur* XVIII. i. 726, I see and fele dayly that thy loue begynneth to slake. **1573** TUSSER *Husb.* (1878) 6 When ioie gan slake, then made I change. **1579** TOMSON *Calvin's Serm. Tim.* 114/2 When we see the honour of God slake, or bee in daunger to be darkened. **1614** DYKE *Myst. Selfe-Deceiving*, His forwardnesse slaked.

†**b.** To come to an end; to cease. *Obs.* **a1300** *Cursor M.* 12886 þe ald testament hir-wit nu slakes, And sua þe nei bigining takes. *Ibid.* 23794 Als wreches [we] wid vr will forsakis þat selines þat neuer slakis. **13..** *Gaw. & Gr. Knt.* 244 Al stouned at his steuen, & stonstil seten,..As al were slypped vpon slepe, so slaked hor lotez in hyȝe.

†**5.** To become or grow less in number, quantity, or volume; to fall or subside. *Obs.* **c1380** *Sir Ferumb.* 2595 Now is þe þridde day a-gon þat our vitaile gunne to slake. **1387** TREVISA *Higden* (Rolls) I. 411 They leueþ in more pees, By cause of hir riches. For hir catel schulde slake, And þey vseþ ofte wrake. **1577** HANMER *Anc. Eccl. Hist.* 421 This misery..fell and slaked by a litle and litle, vntill at length all was ended. **1593** SHAKS. *Lucr.* 1677 No floud by raining slaketh. **1601** HOLLAND *Pliny* I. 42 The tides swell, and anon again..they slake. **1613** PURCHAS *Pilgrimage* (1614) 580 Nilus slaking, the Windes then blowing,..the Winter approaching.

**II.** *trans.* †**6.** To make slack or loose; to lessen the tension of; to allow to become slack or relaxed. *Obs.* **c1175** *Lamb. Hom.* 51 Mon sunfulle þet lið in heuie sunne and þurh soðe scrift his sunbendes nule slakien. **c1275** LAY. 21922 Louerd Arthur þe king slake oure bendes. **a1300** *Cursor M.* 6421 Quils moyses heild vp his hend..Had godds folk þe hale maistri; Bot if he þam slaked ani sith, Sir amalech wan als suith. **1390** GOWER *Conf.* III. 341 The See was plein, Hem nedeth noght a Riff to slake. **c1430** *Pilgr. Lyf Manhode* IV. xxviii. (1869) 190 But summe of þe hoopes weren slaked for defaute of oseres. **1489** CAXTON *Faytes of A.* I. xxiv. 77 Syn cam a rayne that slaked the cordes of theyre bowes. **1513** DOUGLAS *Æneid* X. v. 34 Takyll thy schippis, and thy schetis sclaik. **1581** PETTIE tr. *Guazzo's Civ. Conv.* (1586) III. 157b, The father must somewhat slake the bridle hand, and giue her more libertie.

†**b.** To let or set loose; to set free, release. *Obs.* **13..** *Evang. Nicod.* 518 in Herrig *Archiv* LIII. 401 At pasch of Iewes þe custom was Ane of preson to slake. **c1374** CHAUCER *Boeth.* III. metr. ii. (1868) 68 þei [lions]..slaken hir nekkes from hir cheins vnbounden.

†**c.** To pour (*on* something). *Obs. rare.* **c1440** *Pallad. on Husb.* XII. 540 Of aysel oon emyne on hit they slake. *Ibid.* 582 Aysel theron and hony wol they slake. [L. *superfundere.*]

**d.** To disintegrate or slack (lime). **1662** GERBIER *Principles* 20 Did not make use of their Lime at the same time it was slakt. **1823** P. NICHOLSON *Pract. Builder* 331 Let the lime be slaked, by plunging it into a butt filled with soft-water. **1837** J. T. SMITH tr. *Vicat's Mortars* 198 The Lyonese builders..slake the lime by aspersion.

†**7.** To make smaller or less in amount or size; to reduce, diminish, lessen. *Obs.* **a1300** *Cursor M.* 26269 Ai quen nede es for to slak [*v.r.* slake] þe sett penance. **c1400** *Rule St. Benet* (Verse) 2343 ȝit sall þai not þam-self it [*sc.* their task] slake, Bot suffer it for godes sake. **a1425** tr. *Arderne's Treat. Fistula*, etc. 49 þe 3 day, forsoþ, remeuyng þe emplatstre, þe bolnyng in party was slaked. **1530** H. RHODES *Bk. Nurture* 618 in *Babees Bk.*, If that thou spent past thy degree, thy stock thou soone shalt slake. **1578** LYTE *Dodoens* 749 Taken in the same maner they slake the bellyes of suche as have the dropsie. **1612** WOODALL *Surgeon's Mate* Wks. (1653) 80 Wheat bran..doth slake and swage the hard swellings.

**8.** To render less acute or painful; to abate, mitigate, or assuage. Now *rare*. **a1300** *Cursor M.* 9641 þat sua þou wald his sorus slak, þat he moght dom be-for þe tak. **1387** TREVISA *Higden* (Rolls) III. 11 He fonde up also halsynge coniuresouns for to slake wiþ siknesse. **a1400** *Stockholm Med. MS.* i. 84 in *Anglia* XVIII. 297 þis drinke xal..slakyn þe terys euerychon. **c1440** *Alph. Tales* 212 His brethir þoght þai wuld somwhat slake his truble. **1509** HAWES *Past. Pleas.* XXVII. (Percy) 120 Dame Venus..all thy payne may sone redresse and slake.

**1578** LYTE *Dodoens* 317 The roote..slaketh the gryping paynes of the belly. **1682** N. O. *Boileau's Lutrin* II. 57 Hope of Lawful gain might slake my Anguish. **1821** SHELLEY *Adonais* 192 Wake thou,..and slake..A wound more fierce than his, with tears and sighs.

†**b.** To relieve (one) *from* or *of* sorrow, etc.; to comfort. *Obs.*

*a* **1300** *E.E. Psalter* xciii. 13 þat þou slake him fra daies ille. *c* **1330** *King of Tars* 733 That ilke lord ful of miht, Of serwe he may me slake. *c* **1375** *Sc. Leg. Saints* xxxix. (*Cosme & D.*) 254 Prayand þame for goddis sake hyme of his sorou for to slake. **14..** *Sir Beues* 711 So him solaste [*v.r.* slaked] þat mai, þat al is care wente awai. **1570** *Satir. Poems Reform.* xxiii. 28 Thow knawis thy self gif he was diligent To get thy peax, and slaik the of that weir. *a* **1585** POLWART *Flyting w. Montgomerie* 230, I want wares And salues, to slake thee of thy saires.

†**9.** To make less vehement, violent, or intense; to diminish the force or fury of. *Obs.*

*a* **1300** *E.E. Psalter* lxxxviii. 10 Stiringe of his stremes slakes þou. *c* **1386** CHAUCER *Clerk's T.* 746 And eek the pope, rancour for to slake, Consenteth it. *c* **1470** HENRY *Wallace* VII. 672 He thocht to slaik Makfadȝanys hie curage. **15..** in *Q. Eliz. Acad.*, etc. 45 þat schall sclake hym of hys mode. **1600** HAKLUYT *Voy.* (1810) III. 501 Who of his great goodnesse..vouchsafed a little to slake the tempest. **1628** WITHER *Brit. Rememb.* I. 453 She often makes Our peace with God, and his displeasure slakes. **1664** H. MORE *Myst. Iniq.* vii. 126 The just chastisements of their offended Consciences being slaked.

**b.** To allow to diminish in vehemence or vigour; to moderate (one's anger, etc.). Now *rare.*

*a* **1300** *Cursor M.* 18357 þou þat þi wreth sua suetli slakes, And fra þi folk þair sinnes takes. **1390** GOWER *Conf.* II. 96 Hire oghte of mercy forto slake Hire daunger. *a* **1400** *Pilgr. Sowle* (Caxton) I. xxxviii. (1859) 42 To this she hath goodly agreed hyr selue, slakyng hyr ryghtwys rygour. **1591** LYLY *Endym.* I. ii, He shall slake that loue which he now voweth to Cynthia. **1596** DALRYMPLE tr. *Leslie's Hist. Scot.* II. 356 The Quene for her humanitie and gentlenes, slaiket her seueritie. **1664** H. MORE *Myst. Iniq.* Apol. 558 If there be any that would slake their zeal in this point. **1887** MORRIS *Odyss.* I. 73 But Poseidon Girdler of Earth his anger will not slake.

**10.** To appease, allay, or satisfy (desire, thirst, †hunger).

Said either of the person or of the means.

(*a*) *c* **1325** *Metr. Hom.* 80 He umthoght him..How he might this ilk nonne fange To slake his lust that was so strange. **1538** BALE *God's Promises* I, Plages of coreccyon Most grevouse and sharpe, hys wanton lustes to slake. **1594** SHAKS. *Lucrece* 425 His rage of lust by gazing qualified; Slakt, not supprest. **1608** HIERON *Wks.* I. 722 Crucifie my lustes,..slake and quench in me this vnlawfull heate. **1817** SHELLEY *Rev. Islam* IV. iv, In life and truth, Might not my heart its cravings ever slake? **1839–52** BAILEY *Festus* 188 Each, apart, too soon will tire; Altogether slake desire. **1894** S. WEYMAN *Lady Rotha* iv, All who could not get into the house to slake their curiosity or anger.

(*b*) *c* **1374** CHAUCER *Boeth.* III. pr. ii. (1868) 71 Ryche men han y-nouȝ wher wiþ þei may staunchen her hunger, and slaken her þrest. **1377** LANGL. *P. Pl.* B. XVIII. 366 May no drynke me moiste ne my thruste slake. **1615** CHAPMAN *Odyss.* XI. 796 Tormented Tantalus..could not slake His burning thirst. **1713** ADDISON *Cato* I. iv, Amidst the running stream he slakes his thirst. **1784** COWPER *Task* II. 509 A crystal draught Pure from the lees, which often more enhanc'd The thirst than slak'd it. **1869** PHILLIPS *Vesuv.* viii. 213 Here wild boars and deer slake their thirst in small lakes. **1876** GLADSTONE *Homeric Synchr.* 28 Fine springs..slaked the thirst of the Explorer's workmen during the excavations.

(*c*) *c* **1385** CHAUCER *L.G.W.* 2006 *Ariadne*, In to the bestis throte he shal hem [i.e. balls] caste To slake his hungir. *c* **1450** *St. Cuthbert* (Surtees) 1820 þar with þair hungyr forto slake. **1568** *Jacob & Esau* II. ii, Give me somewhat, wherwith to slake mine honger. **1590** SPENSER *F.Q.* III. i. 52 They slaked had the feruent heat Of appetite with meates of euery sort. **1610** HOLLAND *Camden's Brit.* 492 Men may..eat to slake hunger and content nature.

**11.** To quench or extinguish (fire); to cause to burn less strongly. Also in fig. contexts.

*c* **1566** *Merie Tales of Skelton* in S.'s Wks. (1843) I. p. lxvii, The fire being quickly slaked, Skelton cam in with his frendes. **1611** BIBLE *2 Esdr.* v. 8 The fire shalbe oft..[*marg.* slaked] agaïne. **1657** J. WATTS *Vind. Ch. Eng.* 125, I hope I have slaked your flame, and stopt your mouth with a..better ordinance. *a* **1800** PEGGE *Suppl. Grose* s.v., To slake a fire is to put on small coals, that it may not burn too fast. **1842** LOVER *Handy Andy* xxvi, 'Only for two days,' said Charlotte, trying to slake the flame she had raised. **1868** MILMAN *St. Paul's* vii. 144 By mitigating..the pains of inevitable Purgatory, slaking the penal fires [etc.].

**12.** To cool or refresh by means of water or other fluid. Also *fig.*

**1387** TREVISA *Higden* (Rolls) VII. 311 He boorded soo for kyng William hadde i-slaked his greet wombe wiþ a drynke þat he hadde i-dronke. **1527** ANDREW *Brunswyke's Distyll. Waters* A ij, Sorell water..slaketh all hote thynges bothe within the body and without. **1592** KYD *Sp. Trag.* I. i, Ere Sol had..slakte his smoaking charriot in her floud. **1749** SMOLLETT *Regicide* II. vii, In the blood that warms Thine heart, perfidious, I will slake mine ire! **1822** LAMB *Elia* II. *Conf. Drunkard*, When a draught from the next clear spring could slake any heats which summer suns..had power to stir up in the blood. **1850** WHITTIER *All's Well*, The clouds, which rise with thunder, slake Our thirsty souls with rain. **1871** L. STEPHEN *Playgr. Eur.* (1894) x. 235, I reached a little patch of snow, and managed to slake my parched lips.

*refl.* **1873** DIXON *Two Queens* XXI. v. IV. 152 The great passion of the age began to slake itself with blood.

**b.** To moisten, wet, soak. (Cf. 6 d.)

**1810** SCOTT *Lady of L.* II. xiv, A mass of ashes slaked with blood. **1820** —— *Monast.* xxxv, Oatmeal slaked with cold water. **1824** L. M. HAWKINS *Annaline* III. 35 The rebels retraced their steps, leaving this fertile province slaked in blood and ashes.

†**13.** To render less active or vigorous. *Obs.*

**1549** UDALL, etc. *Erasm. Par. Phil.* II. 9 Howbeit your good wil was not slaked,..yet you wanted oportunitie to sende the thinges. *a* **1578** LINDESAY (Pitscottie) *Chron. Scot.* (S.T.S.) I. 121 James Earle of Douglas..past fordwart with displayit banner to slake the kingis airmie lyand at the seige of Abercorne. **1608** SHAKS. *Per.* III. Prol. 1 Now sleep yslaked hath the rout.

†**b.** To remit or slacken (exertion, etc.). *Obs.*

**1586** DRAKE in Ellis *Orig. Lett.* Ser. I. II. 304 We then slaked no possyble travel or dyllygence. **1594** R. CAREW *Tasso* (1881) 22 Vnto some Frigate light get thee aboord, And towards Greekish soyle no sayling slake.

†**14. a.** To put off, delay. *Obs.*$^{-1}$

**1544** *St. Papers Hen. VIII*, X. 48 It seamith that the Bushop slakith the sending of the Cardinals to thEmperour.

†**b.** To neglect, allow to pass. *Obs.*

**1560** FRAMPTON *Narr.* in Strype *Ann. Ref.* (1709) I. 230 They asked me, Why I did so slake the time, and not declare the truth.

**slake** (sleɪk), *v.*[2] *dial.* Also 6, 9 **slaik**, etc. [a. ON. (Icel. and Norw.) *sleikja* (MSw. *slekia*) to lick.] *intr.* and *trans.* To lick with the tongue; to smear, daub, wet slightly, etc.

Common in Sc. and north. dial. use; for variations of sense see the *Eng. Dial. Dict.*

**1535** LYNDESAY *Satire* 2173 Set thou not by, howbeit scho kisse and slaik it. **1808** JAMIESON, *To Slaik*,..to bedaub. **1811** WILLAN in *Archaeologia* XVII. 158 *Slake*, to smear, to wet, or bedaub. **1824** MACTAGGART *Gallovid. Encycl.* 5 Adders rough, and gruesome horrid,..gluey tongues did slake and feed. **1871** C. GIBBON *Lack of Gold* xxx, The mischievous ones were busy..'slaking' neighbour's doors with sowens.

*transf.* **1807–10** TANNAHILL *Poems* (1846) 68, I never had an itchin' To slake about a great man's kitchen, And like a spaniel lick his dishes.

**slaked** (sleɪkt), *ppl. a.* [f. SLAKE *v.*[1] + -ED[1].]

†**1.** Loosened; slackened. *Obs.*$^{-1}$

*c* **1374** CHAUCER *Boeth.* v. met. i. (1868) 152 Fortune, þat semeþ as þat it fletiþ wiþ slaked or vngouernede bridles.

**2.** Of lime: Hydrated; slacked.

**1611** COTGR. s.v. *Fusé, Chaux fusée*, slaked, or sleckt lime. **1813** SIR H. DAVY *Agric. Chem.* i. (1814) 20 Slaked lime was used by the Romans for manuring the soil. **1837** J. T. SMITH *Vicat's Mortars* 79 The heat given out by a large quantity of slaked lime. **1871** TYNDALL *Fragm. Sci.* (1879) I. v. 173 Adjacent to these reservoirs are others containing pure slaked lime.

**slakeless** ('sleɪklɪs), *a.* [f. SLAKE *v.*[1] + -LESS.] Incapable of being slaked, quenched, or mitigated; insatiable.

**1596** R. LINCHE *Diella* (1877) 36 My slakelesse payne hells horror doth exceede. **1819** BYRON *Proph. Dante* i. 115 The ..slakeless thirst of change. **1832** *Fraser's Mag.* V. 361 To glut her slakeless thirst for blood. **1842** *Gentl. Mag.* Jan. 26 *note*, This wholesale spiller and slakeless thirster of blood.

†'**slaken**, *v. Obs.* Also 4 **slakyn**. [f. SLAKE *a.* + -EN[5]: cf. the later SLACKEN *v.*]

**1.** *intr.* To grow slack; to abate.

**1303** R. BRUNNE *Handl. Synne* 5993 Here synne shal noþer be forȝyuen ne slakyn Vn-to þey ȝelde þat þey haue takyn. *c* **1330** —— *Chron. Wace* (Rolls) 9473 When he was ded, his side gan slaken; Lightly was þen þe castel taken. *a* **1352** MINOT *Poems* ix. 49 þe pride of sir Dauid bigon fast to slaken. **1633** T. JAMES *Voy.* 103 The Storme began to slaken. **1675** *Essex Papers* (Camden) I. 308 Least any may pretend ignorance or thinke we should slaken therein.

**2.** *trans.* To assuage, mitigate.

**1629** SIR W. MURE *True Crucifix* Wks. I. 275 Till God thy Dolours slaken, in some sort.

**slaker** ('sleɪkə(r)). *rare.* [f. SLAKE *v.*[1] + -ER[1].]

**1.** One who slakes, assuages, or quenches.

**1514** BARCLAY *Cyt. & Uplondyshm.* (Percy Soc.) 34 Where be subduers and slakers of all vyce! **1554–9** *Songs & Ball. Phil. & Mary* (Roxb.) 3 He ys owr swete savyor and slaker of sadnes. **1611** COTGR., *Estancheur*, a..slaker, quencher (of hunger, thirst, &c.).

**2.** A sluice or stop-gate; = SLACKER I.

**1664–5** *Act 16–17 Chas. II*, c. 11 §11 The Slakers to take off the Surplusage of Waters. **1767** *Hull Navigation Act* 1072 Leave open any of the gates, doors, or slakers.

**slake-trough.** [f. SLAKE *v.*[1] 12.] = SLACK-TROUGH.

**1843** HOLTZAPFFEL *Turning* I. 228 He then dips the hammer in the slake trough, and lets fall upon the anvil a few drops of the water it picks up. **1875** KNIGHT *Dict. Mech.* 2198.

**slakin:** see SLAKEN *sb.*

**slaking** ('sleɪkɪŋ), *vbl. sb.* [f. SLAKE *v.*[1] + -ING[1].] The action of the verb in various senses.

*c* **1400** in J. R. Boyle *Hedon* (1875) App. 120 In slakyng dicte calcis xj. d. *a* **1425** tr. *Arderne's Treat. Fistula*, etc. 11 þe slakyng or esyng of the akyng and brennyng. **1580** HOLLYBAND *Treas. Fr. Tong*, *Estanchement de soif*, slaking of thirst. **1587** A. FLEMING *Contin. Holinshed's Chron.* III. 1548/2 With the slaking of the one followed the forgetfullness of the other. **1620** *Church-w. Acc. Pittington*, etc. (Surtees) 78 Item payed for a foother of lyme, iij s. iiij d. .. Item for bearing it in and slaking, iiij d. **1815** J. SMITH *Panorama Sci. & Art* I. 200 That sort of lime..which heats the most in slaking.

**slaky** ('sleɪkɪ), *a.* [f. SLAKE *sb.*[3] + -Y.] Muddy.

**1841** *Proc. Berw. Nat. Club* I. 250 The low and slaky shore that extends from Berwick Bay to Fenham Flats. **1901** *Trans. Stirling Nat. Hist. Soc.* 70 The swampy ground had assumed a different aspect. Its slaky condition had disappeared.

**slalom** ('slɑːlɒm). [a. Norw. *slalåm*, f. *sla* sloping + *låm* track.] **1.** A downhill race in which skiers, descending singly, describe a zigzag course between artificial obstacles, usu. flags. Freq. *attrib.*

**1921** *British Ski Year Bk.* 274 Slalom race on Inner-Arosa practice slopes. **1927** A. LUNN *Hist. Skiing* xviii. 227 However, the Slalom was worth a trial, and in 1922 the Alpine Ski Challenge Cup became a Slalom race. **1950** *Times* 13 Feb. 7/5 The Kandahar Ski Club, which originated the modern downhill racing movement (the slalom is a British invention worked out at Mürren), still insists that its candidates shall pass a test in soft snow. **1966** L. DEIGHTON *Billion-Dollar Brain* I. vii. 58 Three sets of skis..one set of which were slalom skis. **1972** C. SHORT *Naked Skier* i. 2 She did a slalom turn... I stood for a while looking at the ski tracks she had left. **1980** *Daily Tel.* 26 Jan. 32 The shadow of Switzerland's Marie-Therese Nadig, who beat her in both the downhill and giant slaloms in the 1972 Winter Games.

**2.** *Water-skiing.* A run along a zigzag course defined by buoys. Also *attrib.*

**1949** *Sun* (Baltimore) 25 July 14/1 Mary Lois Thornhill.. yesterday added the slalom to the trick riding and jumping titles she won on Martin Lagoon. **1963** *Newsweek* 23 Sept. 66/3 Billy Spencer, the youngest of the 99 competitors in the world water-skiing championship at Vichy, France, finished his first slalom run. **1978** G. WRIGHT *Illustr. Handbk. Sporting Terms* 154/1 In Slalom—a timed run through two lines of buoys—half a point is awarded for every buoy successfully rounded and also for returning to within the boat's wake before the next buoy.

**3.** A race in which canoeists weave between obstacles, esp. along a course of rapid water. Freq. *attrib.*

**1956** N. MCNAUGHT *Canoeing Man.* vii. 86 Most local slaloms take place on weir-type courses. *Ibid.* 88 Slalom organizers must ensure that a rescue boat is always manned and ready. **1964**, **1969** [see KAYAKING *vbl. sb.*] **1969** *Publ. Amer. Dial. Soc.* LI. 7 *Slalom kayak*,..a highly maneuverable kayak constructed with more curve rocker in the keel than a downriver or combination kayak. **1973** R. FIENNES *Headless Valley* vii. 111 Then in 1969 two Russians, expert slalom canoeists, set out to navigate the Liard. **1977** *Herald* (Melbourne) 17 Jan. 2/5 Kaine had a junior kayak for a year, but found it did not perform as well as the slalom boat his father built.

**4.** An exercise or contest in which a motor vehicle is driven along a zigzag course defined by markers. Also *attrib.*

**1965** *Listener* 15 Apr. 578/1 There is a keen following of motor racing among the Swiss: entries are not lacking in their speed hill climbs, rallies, and slaloms (or 'wiggle-woggles' between pylons). **1972** *National Observer* (N.Y.) 27 May 19/2 Next came a *slalom* exercise through a long row of traffic cones. You must swerve the car to the right of the first cone, to the left of the second, back right around the third. .. It teaches braking and shows how much more your car can take and 'do' than you thought. **1974** *Rules of Game* 297/1 Slalom, or autotest, competitions are a test of maneuverability. Cars attempt the course singly. Each car starts with 0 points and receives 1 point for each second taken and 10 points for each marker touched. The winner is the driver with the fewest points at the finish.

**5.** A similar race or activity in *Skateboarding.* (See also quot. 1976[2].) Also, a track suitable for this.

**1976** A. CASSORLA *Skateboarder's Bible* 11 Slaloms could not be held on a steep grade or be set up with widely spread cones because of the poor turning capacity of the boards. **1976** *National Observer* (U.S.) 3 July 12/3 Slalom, as in skiing, going downhill and weaving around markers. **1978** *Skatcat's Quiz Bk.* (R. Soc. Prevention of Accidents) 2/1 You need a 6" wide deck to start with. Flexi for slalom. Stiffer for free-style. **1978** *Cornish Guardian* 27 Apr. 13/4 The playgrounds were flat and the youngsters wanted the excitement of bowls and slaloms which the Polkyth park would have.

Hence as *v. intr.*, to perform or compete in a slalom, to make frequent rapid (slalom) turns; '**slalomer**, '**slalomist**, one who slaloms; '**slaloming** *vbl. sb.*

**1956** N. MCNAUGHT *Canoeing Man.* vii. 90 An individual slalomist who overturns is disqualified on that particular run. *Ibid.*, Strength and skill are needed for successful slaloming. **1973** *Times* 28 Sept. 36/5 Forty miles of pistes where you can schuss, trek, slalom, langlauf. **1976** *Daily Tel.* (Colour Suppl.) 30 July 9/1 What they are all doing is skateboarding—zooming and slaloming and 'hanging ten' and catamaraning on four-wheeled boards. **1977** *Skateboard Special* Sept. 5/1 The best slalomists still use wide wheels to prevent the board wobbling at high speed. **1978** *Guardian Weekly* 12 Feb. 24/3 Whether he is the world's greatest ever slalomer no-one can say.

**slam** (slæm), *sb.*[1] Also 7 **slamm**. [Related to SLAM *v.*[1]]

**1. a.** A severe blow; a violent impact.

**1672** J. BLAKESTON *Lazarillo* II. ix, He gave me half a dozen..punches with his knee, and as many slamms with his girdle. **1829** A. W. FONBLANQUE *Under 7 Administr.* (1837) I. 306 Their whole career is a series of tumbles, back-slidings, and cogent slams of the head against the wall.

**b.** A violent blow administered to a ball. *slang* (chiefly *U.S.*).

**1931** *Lit. Digest* 18 Apr. 40, I remember when a hit was a ..clout,..slam..but never..just a hit. **1978** *Chicago* June 274/1 Engrossed as each team was in setting up the ball for a slam, the players' concentration was marred by the explosion of tear-gas canisters some distance away.

**2. a.** A violent closing of a door, etc., producing a loud resounding noise; the noise so made, or a noise of this nature.

*a* **1817** JANE AUSTEN *Persuasion* (1818) IV. viii. 147 The various noises of the room, the almost ceaseless slam of the door. **1837** DICKENS *Pickw.* xxxiv, Both the slam and the scowl were lost upon Sam. **1861** J. PYCROFT *Agony Point* (1862) 334 A slam was heard at the hall door. **1871** BP. FRASER in Hughes *Life* (1887) 204 Closing his prayer-book with an angry slam. **1898** MUNRO *J. Splendid* xi. 109 The crack of the musket..falling away in a dismal slam that carried but a short distance.

**b.** *dial.* (See quot.)

**1854** MISS BAKER *Northampt. Gloss.*, *Slam*, a peculiar mode of ringing the bells.

**3.** An insult or 'put-down'. *U.S. slang.*

**1884** I. M. RITTENHOUSE *Jrnl.* in *Maud* (1939) 296 Oh! did I tell you that Mr. Hough to atone for his 'slams', said, 'I did want to make one gallant speech, but I hardly dared, about how remarkably well you looked Tuesday night.' **1944** B. A. BOTKIN *Treas. Amer. Folklore* III. 410 Certain formulae are identified with disparaging or insulting wisecracks, or 'slams'. **1980** R. L. DUNCAN *Brimstone* I. 22, I don't take that description as a slam. I was a great piece of ass.

**4.** = SLAMMER 3. Usu. with *the.* Chiefly *U.S. slang.*

**1960** R. G. REISNER *Jazz Titans* 164 *Slam*, jail. **1965** A. LURIE *Nowhere City* (1966) xi. 118 That was really thinking fast. I guess you saved me a night in slam. **1972** J. WAINWRIGHT *Requiem for Loser* vi. 132 Reginald Drover. Escapee from one of Her Majesty's slams. **1972** S. GREENLEE in W. King *Black Short Story Anthol.* 95 Uncle Benny told him that getting a bad teacher for a year was like being in the slam, and you just did your time and didn't let it bug you. **1978** J. GORES *Gone, no Forwarding* vii. 40 You're going to the slam for fifteen.

**5.** Special *Combs.* **slamdunk** *U.S. Basketball* [cf. DUNK *v.*], a forceful shot in which a player jumps and slams the ball down into the basket.

**1976** *N.Y. Times* 25 May 35 The only one-eyed candidate who would know how to put in a slamdunk on a New York playground has new financial life. **1981** *Washington Post* 25 Feb. E7/3 Robinson had 32 points and Jones put on a slam-dunk show to finish with 17.

**slam** (slæm), *sb.*[2] Also **slamm.** [Of obscure origin.]

†**1.** The card-game ruff and honours. *Obs.*

**1621** J. TAYLOR (Water P.) *Motto* D4 Ruffe, slam, Trump, nody. **1648** HERRICK *Hesp.*, *Upon Tuck* 281 At Post and Paire, or Slam, Tom Tuck would play. **1674** COTTON *Compl. Gamester* (1680) 82 At Ruff and Honours, by some called Slamm, you have in the Pack all the Deuces.

**2. a.** The fact of losing or winning all the tricks in a game of cards, esp. in whist.

**1660** in Wilkins *Polit. Ball.* (1860) I. 148 Thus all the while a Club was trump,.. Until a noble General came, And gave the cheaters a clear slam. **1674** HICKMAN *Quinquart. Hist.* (ed. 2) 229 The Doctor hath one Card more left to play, which if it hit not, he will have a perfect Slam. *a* **1700** *Dict. Cant. Crew*, *Slam*, a Trick; also a Game entirely lost without getting one on that side. **1755** J. SHEBBEARE *Lydia* (1769) II. 435 Notes upon Hoyle, who is vastly erroneous in many places, particularly in calculating the slam. **1850** *Bohns' Hdbk. Games* 85 When a player calls, and his partner refuses to answer, although he has the power, they cannot gain a slam. **1864** *Reader* 827/1 He lost a slam—that is to say, he did not win a single trick.

**b.** With the qualifying terms *grand* and *little*, *small* or *minor*, chiefly in Bridge.

**1814** C. JONES *Hoyle's Games Improved* 188 These declarations will supersede that of Boston simply... The highest, called Grand Slam, is undertaking to get 13 tricks. **1892** *Pall Mall G.* 14 May 3/1 In two of the 'hands' to be played the 'grand slam' is won. **1897** R. F. FOSTER *Compl. Hoyle* 623 (Bridge), Little Slam, winning 12 out of 13 possible. **1899** A. MAINWARING *Cut Cavendish* 48 'Grand slam', *i.e.* taking every trick [at bridge], or 'minor slam', every trick but one. **1921** F. IRWIN *Compl. Auction Player* i. 25 To take all, or all but one, of the tricks is to make a slam. The former is called a grand slam, and is worth 100 above the line. The latter is called a small slam, and is worth 50. **1937** N. DE V. HART *Slams à la Culbertson* I. vi. 53 If he has his maximum count.., he will bid Small Slam even without a five-card suit. **1959** *Listener* 15 Jan. 146/2 West might then content himself with the small slam. **1977** *Times* 3 Sept. 7/2 South made an overtrick in the small slam.

**c.** ***grand slam*** (transf.): (*a*) a complete success; *spec.* victory in all of a series of matches or competitions; (*b*) an attack in force; forceful or decisive behaviour; (*c*) in Baseball, ***grand slam (homer, home run)***: (see quot. 1974).

(*a*) **1920** D. H. LAWRENCE *Let.* 5 Feb. (1962) I. 619, I feel that this is the time to make our grand-slam. **1966** D. F. GALOUYE *Lost Perception* viii. 86 We're going to try for a grand slam—knock them all out at once with nuclear stuff the next time we pin down their locations. **1967** *Boston Sunday Herald* 26 Mar. II. 7/1 He was the world's No. 1 amateur in 1962 and only the second player in history to accomplish the 'Grand Slam'. **1976** *Scottish Daily Express* 24 Dec. 14/1 We are the Home International champions after a Grand Slam of victories against England, Wales and Northern Ireland.

(*b*) **1933** F. RICHARDS *Old Soldiers never Die* ix. 123 Dawn broke..and we were anxiously waiting for the time when the Grand Slam commenced. **1959** *Times Lit. Suppl.* 29 May 322/5 Churchillian impetuosity and grand-slam rashness. **1963** *Times* 7 Mar. 8/3 The most persuasive argument for retaining *Checkmate* in the Royal Ballet's repertory..is the opportunity for grand slam acting it offers to its protagonist, the malevolent Black Queen.

(*c*) **1953** *Sport* June 58/1 Bill Carr knocked his pitch over the fence for a grand-slam homer. **1961** *Sports Illustr.* 2 Oct. 10/2 Baltimore's Jim Gentile hit a grand slam homer off Don Larsen in Chicago one rainy night last week. **1967** *Boston Sunday Herald* 30 Apr. I. 8/2 (Advt.), It's as exciting as a ninth inning grand-slam! **1974** *Rules of Game* 168/3 A grand slam home run is a home run hit when the bases are loaded, i.e. when three men are on base. It scores four runs, the maximum possible from one hit. **1978** *Detroit Free Press* 16 Apr. E 3/1 The Pirates finally put it together and broke a five-game skid with a little help from a pair of homers from Bill Robinson, one a grand slam.

**3.** *attrib.* in *Bridge*, as ***slam bid(ding), contract, hand.***

**1929** M. C. WORK *Compl. Contract Bridge* p. xi, The partner..must jump if his hand warrant it—either one step ..or a vault toward a *slam bid. **1947** E. KLEIN *Enjoy your Bridge* II. xiii. 114 Be content to win a perfectly safe contract and leave your slam bids for a later stage. **1927** *Work-Whitehead Auction Bridge Bull.* Feb. 141 Contract in its original form, minus the recently introduced 'vulnerable' feature and *slam bidding, made its first appearance abroad some fifteen years ago. **1974** *Times* 16 Feb. 13/2 Slam bidding is treated in most text books as if it..cannot be covered by ordinary approach bidding. **1938** *Slam contract [see CONTROL *sb.* 3 e]. **1959** *Listener* 8 Jan. 84/2 There is every reason to hope for a slam contract in some suit. **1977** *Times* 16 Apr. 11/8 He..bid Three Diamonds which..in conjunction with the cue-bids, produced a slam contract in the wrong suit. **1937** J. CRANE *Crane Syst. Contract Bidding* 78 (*heading*) Examples of a bidding game and *slam hands from matches. **1979** REESE & FLINT *Trick 13* 17, I didn't know anything was wrong till that slam hand near the finish.

†**slam,** *sb.*[3] *Obs.* [a. LG. *slam* (whence Sw. *slam*), = G. *schlamm* mud, slime.] Refuse matter separated from alum in the preparation of this.

There appears to be no evidence for the currency of the word later than the 17th cent.; the entries in various technical dictionaries of the 19th cent. are app. derived from Bailey (1728).

**1650-1** *North Riding Rec.* V. 65 Throwing the slam of allome into the water-course. **1678** *Phil. Trans.* XII. 1054 That which they call Slam, is first perceived by the redness of the Liquor when it comes from the Pit. **1681** GREW *Musæum* III. III. i. 343 Certain Nitrous and other parts call'd Slam.

**slam,** *sb.*[4] *rare.* [Cf. next, and mod.Yks. *slam* a slovenly person.] ? An ill-shaped person.

**1697** VANBRUGH *Relapse* V. v, *Hoyden.* I don't like my lord's shapes, nurse. *Nurse.* Why, in good truly, as a body may say, he is but a slam.

†**slam,** *a.* *Obs.*[−1] (See quot.)

**1691** RAY *N.C. Words* 137 A *slam* or *slim* Fellow is a skragged, tall, rawboned Fellow.

**slam** (slæm), *v.*[1] [Possibly of Scand. origin: cf. Sw., Norw., and Icel. *slamra* (also MSw. and Icel. *slambra*), Sw. dial. *slämma*, Norw. *slemma* (*slemba*), to slam.]

**1.** *trans.* To beat or slap vigorously. *dial.*

**1691** RAY *N.C. Words* 137 To *Slam* one, to beat or cuffe one strenuously. **1825-56** in *Eng. Dial. Dict.*

**2. a.** To shut (a door, window, etc.) with violence and noise; to bang; to close with unnecessary force. Also with advs., as *down, to, up.*

**1775** ASH, *Slam* (*v.t.* a colloquial word), to shut with a noise. **1809** W. IRVING *Knickerb.* VII. viii. (1820) 504 He.. slammed down the window. **1816** SCOTT *Antiq.* vi, The clang of several doors which he..slammed with force behind him. **1873** BLACK *Pr. of Thule* ix. 142 He would slam the door to again. **1892** GREENER *Breech-Loader* 186 The practice of slamming the gun up is dangerous.

**b.** Freq. with *in one's face*; often *fig.*

**1786** in Mrs. Delany *Life & Corr.* (1861) Ser. II. III. 421, I hear..that you squander away your money..and then slam the doors in the King's face! **1826** SCOTT in *Lockhart* (1839) VIII. 238, I propose to slam the door in the face of all and sundry for these three years to come. **1851** MAYHEW *Lond. Lab.* I. 348 They always wait where they think there's the slightest chance of effecting a sale, until the door is slammed in their face.

**c.** To dash, throw, push, etc., with some degree of violence or force. Also *fig.*

**1870** 'MARK TWAIN' *Lett. to Publishers* (1967) 49, I can slam you into the lecture field for life and secure you ten thousand dollars a year as long as you live. **1899** GARDINER *Cromwell* 192 One of them slammed an overturned cream-tub on the head of another. **1899** *Westm. Gaz.* 24 Oct. 5/3 Slamming every available man into the firing line. **1902** CORNISH *Naturalist Thames* 150 When the winter storms slam the roaring billows against the cliff faces.

**d.** ***to slam on the brakes***, to apply the brakes of a motor vehicle, etc. suddenly; also *fig.*

**1958** L. URIS *Exodus* IV. iii. 501 Zev slammed on the brakes and pulled over to the side of the road. **1975** *Business Week* 1 Sept. 23 The rule is designed to prevent a truck from jackknifing or jumping a lane when drivers slam on the brakes at 20 mph to 60 mph. **1975** *Economist* 4 Oct. 11 Can the driver [*sc. contextually* General Franco] be persuaded to look forward instead of back, or can someone else intervene to slam on the brakes? **1976** *Business Week* 11 Oct. 96 A radar unit in the nose..that warns the driver of road hazards ahead—and slams on the brakes if he fails to do so. **1982** *Chr. Sci. Monitor* 13 Apr. 7 Inflation has dropped dramatically as the quasi-independent Federal Reserve Board slams on the brakes of high interest rates.

**3.** *intr.* Of doors, etc.: To shut, or strike against anything, with violence and resounding noise. Also with advs., as *down, to,* etc.

In recent use freq. employed to denote any violent action or loud noise.

**1823** E. MOOR *Suffolk Words* 359 To shut a door violently, or to let it slam to of itself. **1837** CARLYLE *Fr. Rev.* I. v. vi, The huge Drawbridge slams down. **1858** DICKENS *Lett.* (1880) II. 52 Big doors slam and resound when anybody comes in. **1893** *Jrnl. R. Agric. Soc.* Mar. 58 The gates are so hung that, if carelessly left open, they will always slam to and fasten.

**4.** Used with adverbial force: With a slam or heavy blow; suddenly and violently.

**1726** G. ROBERTS *Four Yrs. Voy.* 320, I no sooner rais'd my Head in Sight, but slam came three or four Stones at me. **1755** SMOLLETT *Quix.* (1803) II. 129 Slam went his head to the ground. **1796** WOLCOT (P. Pindar) *Middlesex Election* Wks. 1816 IV. 178 Slam off a [= he] went, without more ado; Nort could his bacon save. **1914** G. B. SHAW *Misalliance* 42 Theyre coming slam into the greenhouse. **1930** E. POUND *XXX Cantos* xviii. 82 An' he run damn slam on the breakwater.

**5. a.** To be severely critical, to utter insults. *U.S. slang. rare.*

**1884** I. M. RITTENHOUSE *Jrnl.* in *Maud* (1939) 291 When I and Mr Hough arrived late Dr Benson and Mr Parsons slammed right and left at the tardiness.

**b.** *trans.* To criticize severely. *colloq.* (orig *U.S.*).

[**1914** 'HIGH JINKS, JR.' *Choice Slang* 18 *Slamming contest*, a condition where two or more individuals are engaged in criticism. 'A Knockfest.'] **1916** H. L. WILSON *Somewhere in Red Gap* ii. 57 Couldn't even agree on the same kind of cocktail. Both slamming the waiter. **1932** G. ATHERTON *Adventures of Novelist* VI. xiii. 380 She took care I should constantly be slammed. **1958** 'N. SHUTE' *Rainbow & Rose* 252 They come with bright and tinkling vivacity until I slam them down. **1962** J. SYMONS *Killing of Francie Lake* ii. 19 You go on the air and slam negro landlords and they'll be saying you're anti-negro. **1978** J. IRVING *World according to Garp* v. 89 A long, cocky letter, quoting Marcus Aurelius and slamming Franz Grillparzer.

**6.** *intr.* Const. *prep.* To move violently, to crash.

**1973** *Times* 2 Nov. 13/6 Rosa..savagely slamming around the kitchen. **1976** M. MACHLIN *Pipeline* lvi. 566 The lifeboat was now slamming through the choppy two and three foot high waves at over twenty knots. **1979** R. JAFFE *Class Reunion* (1980) II. iv. 209 She didn't even see the small stone wall until she had slammed into it.

Hence **'slamming** *vbl. sb.* (*spec.* of boats: see quot. 1948) and *ppl. a.*

**1796** WOLCOT (P. Pindar) *Wks.* (1816) IV. 186 One scoundrel..with a slammin stick, Com'd souse upon my sconce. **1868** J. R. GREEN *Lett.* (1901) II. 204 There was a great slamming of pew doors. **1892** *Daily News* 29 Apr. 5/4 The wing of a slamming door shut in front of him. **1893** *Jrnl. R. Agric. Soc.* Mar. 58 Formerly the posts, both hanging and slamming posts, were made of oak. **1935** *Engineering* 18 Jan. 55/1 'Pounding' or 'slamming' damage is looked upon as no more than a normal circumstance..of cargo vessels trading across the North Atlantic. **1948** R. DE KERCHOVE *Internat. Maritime Dict.* 685/1 Slamming almost always takes place forward... Slamming damage is usually ascribed to dynamic pressures arising from impact of the ship's hull upon the surface of the water, and from the actual impulsive displacement of water caused by the downward movement of the ship when pitching. **1972** C. MUDIE *Motor Boats & Boating* 17 If such a craft were to be taken to sea she would rapidly be found to be..apt to break her back from slamming when pitching.

**slam** (slæm), *v.*[2] [f. SLAM *sb.*[2]]

**1.** *trans.* To beat by winning a slam; also *dial.*, to trump. Hence *transf.*, to beat completely.

**1746** HOYLE *Whist* 80, D having seven Spades in his Hand wins them, and consequently Slams A and B. **1907** *Daily Mail* 5 Sept. 6/1 He [a race-horse] absolutely slammed his field.

**2.** *intr.* To win a slam.

**1833** W. H. MAXWELL *Field Bk.* 489.

†**slam,** *v.*[3] *Obs. rare.* A substitution for DAMN *v.* 5, perh. suggested by SLAM *sb.*[2]

*a* **1657** N. WALLINGTON *Notices Chas. I* (1869) II. 94 They returned only burning and slamming themselves in rage and malice. **1760** FOOTE *Minor* I. Wks. 1799 I. 243 Slam me, but the man's mad! **1797** BRYDGES *Hom. Trav.* I. 321 But ev'ry syllable is true, Or slam me if I'd tell it you!

**slam-bang,** *adv.*, *a.*, and *v.* Also **slam bang.** [f. SLAM *v.*[1] 4 + BANG *v.* 8. Cf. SLAP-BANG *adv.*, *a.*, and *sb.*]

**A.** *adv.* With a slam and a bang; with noisy violence.

**1840** R. M. BIRD *Robin Day* 25 Five or six hundred field pieces blazing away slambang. **1847** in Halliw. **1853** HAWTHORNE *Tanglewood T.* (Chandos) 201 He would fetch his club down, slam bang, and smash the vessel into a thousand pieces. **1887** F. R. STOCKTON *A Borrowed Month* 159, I sent an arrow slam-bang into the lantern.

**B.** *adj.* **1.** Noisy, violent.

**1823** 'J. BEE' *Dict. Slang* 158 *Slam-bang shops*, places where gourmands of the fourth rate regale;..probably, from ..the 'slam-banging' of the doors, plates, and tools. **1889** *Advance* (Chicago) 14 Mar., The friends of the Sabbath are not what some..slam-bang reformer would have the world believe. **1957** *Economist* 28 Sept. 999/1 With all the diplomatic finesse of a runaway bulldozer, the governments of the major powers are conducting a slambang exchange of public accusations. **1981** H. R. F. KEATING *Go West, Inspector Ghote* ii. 25 Fred Hoskin's slam-bang voice broke in on his thoughts.

**2.** In weakened use: exciting, impressive, first-rate. Also, vigorous, energetic. *colloq.*

**1939** *Sun* (Baltimore) 4 Dec. 13/4 The balance of the card will be made up of some real slam-bang preliminaries. **1942** *Ibid.* 17 June 1/8 American heavy bombers have entered the Mediterranean sea war in slambang fashion. **1952** B. MALAMUD *Natural* 20 A slambang young pitcher who'd soon be laying them low in the big leagues. **1965** *Times Lit. Suppl.* 25 Nov. 1061/2 We have this plot for a slam-bang topical novel about the Johnson administration. **1972** D. DELMAN *Sudden Death* (1973) v. 126 You were good today. I watched you. Slam-bang. **1975** *Publishers Weekly* 2 June 49/1 A very cerebral English mystery, with..a finale that is full of slambang action. **1979** *Radio Times* 5-11 May 23/2 It was described by Judith Crist as a 'slam-bang top-quality grown-up adventure which thumbs its nose at authority and morality'.

**C.** *vb.* **1.** *intr.* To slam and bang.

**1837** MISS SEDGWICK *Live & Let Live* (1876) 110 She slam-bangs about the house. **1896** KIPLING *Seven Seas* 51 My engines Through all the seas, slam-bangin' home again, Slam-bang too much.

**2.** *trans.* To assail violently.

**1888** *The Voice* (N.Y.) 12 July, You might as well denounce the legal profession because of the shysters.. as to slam-bang newspapers because there are recreant editors.

Hence **'slam-,banging** *vbl. sb.*

**1823** [see sense 1 of the adj., above]. **1843** *Knickerbocker* XXII. 41 The creaking on its rusty hinges and slam-banging of the sign of the Devil-Tavern. **1889** *The Voice* (N.Y.) 1 Aug., When you take up a Prohibition organ, you will find it full of political slang and slambanging.

**slammable** ('slæməb(ə)l), *a. rare.* [f. SLAM *v.*[1] + -ABLE.] Of a door, etc.: capable of being slammed (shut).

**1976** T. STOPPARD *Dirty Linen* 9 Separate table with good slammable drawers for *Maddie*.

**'slammakin, 'slammerkin,** *sb.* and *a.* Chiefly *dial.* Also 9 **slammockin, slomm-, slummackin,** etc.; 9 **slommacking, -icking, -ocking,** 20 **slummocking.** [Of obscure origin; the shorter forms *slammack(s, slommack(s* occur widely in dialect, but are not recorded before the 19th century.

Mrs. Slammekin, who is described as affecting a careless undress, is a character in Gay's *Beggars' Opera* (1727). It is more probable that the colloquial word suggested the name than that it was subsequently derived from it.]

**A.** *sb.* †**1.** A loose gown or dress. *Obs.*[−1]

**1756** *Connoisseur* No. 134 ⁋7 A burgess's daughter.. who appeared in a Trolloppee or Slammerkin, with treble ruffles to the cuffs.

**2.** A slovenly female, a sloven, a slattern.

α. **1785** GROSE *Dict. Vulgar T.*, *Slammakin*, a female sloven, one whose clothes seem hung on with a pitch fork, a careless trapes. **1808** JAMIESON, *Slammikin*, a drab, a slovenly woman; Loth[ian]. **1839** SIR G. C. LEWIS *Gloss. Heref.*, *Slammockin*, a slattern.

β. **1822** W. IRVING *Braceb. Hall* (1823) I. 103 A brisk, coquettish woman; a little of a shrew, and something of a slammerkin.

**B.** *adj.* Untidy, slovenly.

Ash *Suppl.* (1775) gives '*Slammerkin* (a droll word), irregular in motion, making a sudden transition'; the existence of this sense is very doubtful.

α. **1794** WOLCOT (P. Pindar) *Soldier of Tilbury* Wks. 1812 III. 241 So slammakin, untidy, ragged, mean, Her garments all so shabby and unpinn'd. **1864** LE FANU *Uncle Silas* III. 157 Holding out with finger and thumb.. her slammakin old skirt. *Ibid.* 261 The vainest and most slammakin of women.

β. **1837** THACKERAY *Professor* Wks. 1900 XIII. 499 That saucy, slammerkin, sentimental Miss Grampus. **1863** *Examiner* 14 Nov., His Minerva is a tawdry slammerkin slattern. **1887** MISS BRADDON *Like & Unlike* xxxvii, The slammerkin Irish housekeeper.

γ. **1841** HARTSHORNE *Salop. Ant.* Gloss., *Slommacking*,.. unwieldy, clumsy. ?*c* **1850** H. & A. MAYHEW *The Good Genius* xvi, A nasty slommicking bit of goods, with her things all hanging about her anyhow. **1873** *Daily News* 30 Aug. 5/6 His high cheek bones and slommocking gait. **1960** R. COLLIER *House called Memory* iv. 53 A big slummocking girl with cropped hair and braying laugh. **1978** S. RADLEY *Death & Maiden* iv. 37 They're a slummocking family.. always have been.

**slammer** ('slæmə(r)). [f. SLAM *v.*[1]]

**1.** A violent gust (of wind).

**1891** *Field* 7 Mar. 344/4 A strong westerly wind.. came off the Barn Elm grounds in regular slammers at times.

**2.** One who slams (doors, etc.).

**1892** *Chamb. Jrnl.* 11 June 372/1 He is a quiet neighbour —no slammer or tramper.

**3.** Prison, gaol. Usu. with *the*: occas. ***the slammers.*** Cf. SLAM *sb.*[1] 4. *slang* (orig. *U.S.*).

**1952** G. MANDEL *Flee Angry Strangers* 358 I'm hip what you was doin wit Ange while I was in the slammer. **1961** RIGNEY & SMITH *Real Bohemia* p. xvii, *Slammer*, jail. **1970** E. BULLINS *Theme is Blackness* (1973) 177 I'm into a heavy petty criminal thing, man. The Man is always ready to vamp on you and take you off 'round here or put you in the slammers. **1975** B. GARFIELD *Death Sentence* (1976) v. 31 Less than one per cent of Chicago's crimes are solved, in the sense that some joker gets tried and convicted and sent to the slammer. **1977** D. BAGLEY *Enemy* xv. 131 This one's not for the slammer. He'll go to Broadmoor for sure.

†**slamp.** *Obs.*[−0] (See quots.)

**1611** COTGR., *Chinfreneau*, a slampe, iert, wipe; thumpe. *Ibid.*, *Truellée*,.. a clap, slat, or slamp with a Trowell.

**slampaine, -pam:** see SLAMPANT.

†**slampamb.** *Obs.*[−1] (Meaning obscure.)

Halliwell's explanation appears very unlikely.

*a* **1573** *New Custom* II. iii, I will never staye, Tyll I finde meanes to ridde the beaste out of the waye. I wyll cut him of the slampambes,.. Where so ever I meete him.

†**slampamp.** *Obs. rare* [Of obscure formation: cf. Du. *slampampen* to revel.] (See quots.)

**1593** G. HARVEY *New Lett.* Wks. (Grosart) I. 282 A homely gallimaufry of little Art, to requite her dainty slaumpaump of little wit. **1593** —— *Pierce's Super.* ibid. II. 277, I haue seldome.. tasted a more vnsauory slaumpaump of wordes. **1596** NASHE *Saffron Walden* Wks. (Grosart) III. 79 Let them look to it..for the course they take in commending this course Himpenhempen Slampamp, this stale Apple-squire.

†**slampant.** *Obs. rare.* Also 6 **slampaine, -pam.** [Of obscure origin and doubtful form.] A trick. *to give one the* (or *a*) *slampant*, to play a trick on, to circumvent or hoodwink, one.

Cotgrave prob. copied North's rendering of Fr. *trousse*.

**1577** STANYHURST *Descr. Irel.* in *Holinshed* (1808) VI. 30 The townesmen being pinched at the heart, that one rascal in such scornfull wise should give them the slampaine. **1579–80** NORTH *Plutarch* (1595) 805 Polyperchon,.. meaning to giue Cassander a slampant and blurt,.. sent letters Pattents vnto the people at Athens. **1582** STANYHURST *Æneis* IV. (Arb.) 116 Shal a stranger geue me the slampam? With such departure my regal segnorye frumping? **1611** COTGR., *Trousse*,.. a cousening tricke, blurt, slampant.

**slan** (slæn). [Invented word, from the novel by A. E. van Vogt: see quot. 1940.] In works of Science Fiction: a being of superior intelligence, physique, etc.; a superman. Hence used *gen.* among fans of this type of literature.

**1940** A. E. VAN VOGT *Slan* in *Astounding Sci. Fiction* Oct. 27/1 They.. accuse Samuel Lann, the human being and biological scientist who first created slans, and after whom slans are named—Samuel Lann: S. Lann: Slan—of fostering in his children the belief that they must rule the world. **1955** KOESTLER *Trail of Dinosaur* 143 Fen gather in clubhouses called slanshacks, 'slan' meaning a biologically mutated superman. **1969** H. WARNER *All Our Yesterdays* ii. 42 'Fans are slans!' became the rallying cry of the Cosmic Circle. **1975** E. WEINSTEIN *Fillostrated Fan Dict.* 119 *Slan shack*, a place where more than two fans live. **1980** *Verbatim* Autumn 10/1 'He's a slan' is the fannish equivalent of 'He's a helluva guy'.

**slan,** dial. variant of SLOE.

**slanchways,** var. SLAUNCHWAYS, -WISE *adv.* and *a.*

**slander** ('slɑːndə(r), -æ-), *sb.* Forms: α. 3–6 **sclaundre,** 4–6 **-der** (4 **-dire,** 5 **-dir**); 4 **sclawndire,** 5 **-dre, -dyr, -der;** 4–6 **sclander, -dre** (6 **-dir**), 4 **sclondre.** β. 4–6 **sklaunder** (4 **-dere, -dir,** 4–5 **-dre,** 5 **-dur, -dyre**); 5 **sklawnder** (5–6 **-dyr**); 5 (*Sc.* 6–7) **sklander** (**-dyr,** 6 *Sc.* **-dir, -dre**). γ. 4–7 **slaunder** (4–5 **-dre,** 5 **-dere**), 4 **slawndire;** 5 **slandyre,** 6– **slander.** [ad. AF. *esclaundre*, OF. *esclandre*, an alteration of *escandle*, ad. L. *scandalum*: see SCANDAL *sb.*]

**1.** The utterance or dissemination of false statements or reports concerning a person, or malicious misrepresentation of his actions, in order to defame or injure him; calumny, defamation.

α. *c* **1290** *S. Eng. Leg.* I. 165 Þov mis-seist mi louerd þe king;.. ho miȝte soffri swuch sclaundre bote he nome þar-of wreche? *a* **1325** *Prose Psalter* xlix. 21 Þou.. spak oȝain þy broþer, and þou settedest sclaundre oȝains þe sones of þy moder. **1340** *Ayenb.* 6 Þe ilke þet zuereþ zoþ.., naȝt kueadliche, ake liȝtliche and wyþ-oute sclondre. *c* **1450** *Mirk's Festial* 27 Þay þoghten forto take hym wyth som wordes of sclawndyr yn God. **1486** *Bk. St. Albans* f v, Ther be iiii. thyngs principall to be drad of euery wise man... The iiii. is sclaunder & the mutacion of a comynalte. **1526** *Pilgr. Perf.* (W. de W. 1531) 138 b, The spiryte of falsnes, the spiryte of sclaunder.

β. *c* **1375** *Lay Folks Catech.* (T.) 489 Sklaundir for to fordo a mannes gode fame. *c* **1384** CHAUCER *Ho. Fame* III. 1580 His other clarioun That hight sklaundre in euery toun With whiche he wonte is to diffame hem that me liste. *c* **1400** *Cursor M.* 27683 (Cott. Galba), Of enuy cummes oft grete grocheing, Missaw, sklander, and bacbiteing. **1500–20** DUNBAR *Poems* xlii. 100 That nobill king.. Chest Sklander to the west se cost. **1609** SKENE *Reg. Maj.*, *Acts Jas. VI*, 137 Any purpose of reproch, or sklander of his Majesties person, estate, or governement.

γ. *c* **1440** *Promp. Parv.* 458/2 Slaunder,.. *calumpnia*. *a* **1548** HALL *Chron.*, *Hen. VI*, 84 b, Whose mother susteyned not a litle slaunder and obloquye of the common people. **1589** PUTTENHAM *Eng. Poesie* I. xvi. (Arb.) 50 The Poets being in deede the trumpetters of all praise and also of slaunder (not slaunder, but well deserued reproch). **1629** CARLIELL *Deserving Favourite* 833 Though heretofore the company of a Father Were a sufficient buckler to beare off slanders darts. **1649** JER. TAYLOR *Grt. Exemp.* II. Disc. ix. 124 He that kills a mans reputation by calumnies or slander, or open reviling. **1727** GAY *Fables* I. xxv, Who deals in slander, lives in strife. **1794** COLERIDGE *Lines on a Friend* 19 Shall Slander squatting near Spit her cold venom in a dead man's ear? **1817** W. SELWYN *Law Nisi Prius* (ed. 4) II. 1161 Falsehood and malice, either express or implied, are of the essence of the action for slander. **1872** GEO. ELIOT *Middlem.* lxxiv, How much is only slander and false suspicion?

†**b.** Fame, report, rumour. *Obs.*[−1]

Here used for the sake of the rime; but in some other ME. examples the idea of rumour is perhaps more prominent than that of falsity.

**13..** *K. Alis.* 4797 (Laud MS.), The lijf of Alisaunder, Of whom fleiȝ so riche sklaunder. *Ibid.* 6066 Þe folk of þe londe herden þe sclaunder þat to hem com kyng Alisaunder.

**2.** A false or malicious statement or utterance intended to injure, defame, or cast detraction on the person about whom it is made.

α. β. **1297** R. GLOUC. (Rolls) 6851 Þer was vpe þe quene emme.. ydo A luþer sclandre. *c* **1320** *Sir Tristr.* 2145 Vngiltles er ȝe In swiche a sclaunder brouȝt. **1393** LANGL. *P. Pl.* C. III. 86 To scornie and to scolde, sclaundres to make. *a* **1450** *Knt. de la Tour* 2 Of the whiche there come to diuerse gret defames and sclaundres withoute cause and reson. **1508** FISHER 7 *Penit. Ps.* cii. Wks. (1876) 155 There was neuer creature borne.. that myght escape the sclaundres and backbytynges of them whiche are backbyters. **1560** DAUS tr. *Sleidane's Comm.* 13 b, If he beynge tyckled wyth false complaintes and sklaunders [L. *criminationibus*], should come into Germany. **1562** J. HEYWOOD *Prov. & Epigr.* (1867) 69 It maie be a sclaunder, but it is no lie.

γ. *c* **1375** *Lay Folks Catech.* (L.) 1338 Slaundrys for to fordo a mannys good fame. *c* **1380** *Sir Ferumb.* 132 Þe Emperour.. askeþ þan What ys riȝte name was þat made such a slaundre. 'Sire,' said he, 'sir Fyrumbras, þe kyng of Alysaundre'. **1590** SHAKS. *Much Ado* II. i. 144 His gift is, in deuising impossible slanders. **1611** B. JONSON *Catiline* III. i, Where it concernes himselfe Who's angrie at a Slander, makes it true. *a* **1656** BP. HALL *Rem. Wks.* (1660) 122 Your tongues.. run ryot in.. spightful slanders. **1727** GAY *Fables* I. xxv, One slander must ten thousand get. **1794** MRS. RADCLIFFE *Myst. Udolpho* lvi, Count de Villefort has detected the slanders that have robbed me of all I hold dear on earth. **1855** MACAULAY *Hist. Eng.* xviii. IV. 172 His slanders were monstrous: but they were well timed. **1875** JOWETT *Plato* (ed. 2) V. 302 The envious.. reduces his rivals to despair by his unjust slanders of them.

†**3.** Discredit, disgrace, or shame, incurred by or falling upon a person or persons, *esp.* on account of some transgression of the moral law, unworthy action, or misdemeanour; evil name, ill repute, opprobrium. *Obs.* Cf. SCANDAL *sb.* 2.

In some cases not clearly separable from sense 1.

α. **1297** R. GLOUC. (Rolls) 7287 Haraldes broþer, þat he drof in to flaundre,.. him sulf to grete sclaundre. *c* **1375** *Lay Folks Mass Bk.* (MS. B.) 377 To hom þat are in ille lyue, In sclaunder, myscounforth, or in stryue. *c* **1400** *Rom. Rose* 5074 And she of hirs may hym, certeyne, With-oute sclaundre, yeven ageyn. *a* **1450** *Knt. de la Tour* 35, I will telle you of a lady that caught a gret blame and sclaundre atte iusting withoute cause. **1565** *Reg. Privy Council Scot.* I. 340 Quhilk taill and brute, besydis the sclandir that it importis to thame.., is to hir Hienes self verie prejudiciall.

β. **1362** LANGL. *P. Pl.* A. XII. 17 Hit were boþe skaþe and sklaundre to holy cherche. **1377** *Ibid.* B. XII. 47 Felyce hir fayrnesse fel hir al to sklaundre. *c* **1425** AUDELAY *XI Pains of Hell* 139 in *O.E. Misc.* 215 Þese.. neuer wold shryue hem of þat trespase, Fore dred of sklawnder and penans doyng. **1470–85** MALORY *Arthur* XVIII. i. 726 He withdrewe hym from the companye and felaushyp of Quene Gueneuer for to eschewe the sklaunder and noyse. **1508** DUNBAR *Flyting* 21 It is.. tinsale baith of honour and of fame, Incres of sorrow, sklander, and evill name.

γ. *c* **1375** *Sc. Leg. Saints* xxi. (*Clement*) 618 With þat al schot sone one hyme,.. & huntyt hym owt of þare towne with slandyre & confusione. *a* **1548** HALL *Chron.*, *Edw. V*, 15 b, Muche matter was deuised in the same proclamacion to the slaunder of the Lord Hastynges. **1583** STUBBES *Anat. Abus.* II. (1882) 75 Some [ministers] fall to one mischiefe, some to another, to the great slander of the Gospell of Iesus Christ. **1678** SIR G. MACKENZIE *Crim. Laws Scot.* I. xvii. §iii, When they are suspected of Adultery, and thereby gives slander to the Kirk,.. they are excommunicat.

†**b.** Const. *of* the person, etc. *Obs.*

*c* **1385** CHAUCER *L.G.W.* 2231 *Philomene*, Why madist thow on to the Slaundere of man, Or.. Whi sufferist thow that tereus was bore. *c* **1400** *Rom. Rose* 3972 To me it is gret hevynesse, That the noyse so ferre is go, And the sclaundre of us twoo. **1428** in *Surtees Misc.* (1890) 3 In.. ryght gret sklaundre of ye cite of York, and agayne ye course of trewe marchandise. **1500–20** DUNBAR *Poems* lxxxii. 21 Think ȝe nocht schame, Sa litill polesie to wirk In hurt and sklander of ȝour name.

†**c.** A source of shame or dishonour; a discreditable act; a disgrace; a wrong. *Obs.*

**1390** GOWER *Conf.* III. 189 If the lawe be forbore.. It makth a lond torne up so doun, Which is unto the king a sclandre. **1470–85** MALORY *Arthur* XVIII. iv. 731 That shalle be a grete sklaunder for yow in thys Courte. **1480** CAXTON *Myrr.* III. xiii. 162 A grete lady whiche to fore had don to hym a grete sklaundre and dysplaysir. **1529** MORE *Dyaloge* III. Wks. 218/1 And that wer a sore sclaunder to the word of god, that men should se him whom thei heare preache well, so proude an ypocryte. **1540** *Act 32 Hen. VIII*, c. 30 The whiche is thought as well a greate sclaunder to the said common lawe of this Realme.

†**d.** A person who is a discredit, disgrace, or scandal to some body or set of persons. *Obs.*

**1529** MORE *Suppl. Souls* Wks. 306/2 They should be of the worst sort, & such as now be sklaunder of their order. **1547** J. HARRISON *Exhort. Scottes* a v, These.. reputed heddes of the Churche, bee the onely shame and slaunder of the Churche. **1596** SPENSER *F.Q.* IV. viii. 35 That shame-full Hag, the slaunder of her sexe.

†**4.** A cause of moral lapse or fall; a stumbling-block. = SCANDAL *sb.* 1 b, OFFENCE *sb.* 2. *Obs.*

*c* **1340** HAMPOLE *Psalter* xlviii. 13 Þis way, þat is, þis life of þa, for it ledis þaim til hell, is slawndire til þaim. **1382** WYCLIF *Matt.* xiii. 41 Mannes sone shal sende his angels, and thei shulden gedre of his rewme alle sclaundris, and hem that don wickidnesse. *a* **1400** *Apol. Loll.* 57 Go o bak after me Sathanas, and þu art sclaunder to me. *c* **1449** PECOCK *Repr.* III. xi. 348 He was not so perfit that he couthe bere beggerie at ful withoute sclaundre. **1533** GAU *Richt Vay* 30 Ve prech Iesu Christ crucifeit, sclander to the Iowis and folie to the gentils. **1586** A. DAY *Eng. Secretary* II. (1625) 126 He that desirith to be good indeed ought not so much as to become an occasion or slander of evill.

**5.** *attrib.* and *Comb.* (in sense 1), as ***slander action, -bearer, currency, law; slander-beaten, -mouthed*** adjs.

**1600** LANE *Tom Tel-troth* 114 Whole volumes gainst their slander-bearers. **1622** BP. HALL *Serm.* (1627) 492 A slander-beaten crosse, a crucified Sauiour. **1700** CONGREVE *Way of World* III. v, A Slander-mouth'd Railer. **1777** SHERIDAN *Sch. Scandal* II. ii, In all cases of slander currency, whenever the drawer of the lie was not to be found. **1897** *Westm. Gaz.* 29 Nov. 5/3 Our slander law is still uncivilised. **1900** *Daily News* 1 June 7/4 Rumours had been spread about the village, on which the slander action was begun by him.

**slander** ('slɑːndə(r), -æ-), *v.* Forms: α. 4–6 **sclaundre, -der** (4 **-dir,** 5 **-dyr**), 4 **schlaundre,** 5 **sclawndre,** 4–6 **sclandre, -der** (5 **-dir**). β. 4–6 **sklaundre, -der** (5 **-dir, -dur**), 5 **sklawnnder,** 4–7 **sklander** (6 **-dir**). γ. 4–7 **slaundre, -der,** 5 **-dir,**

slawnder, 5- slander. [ad. OF. *esclandrer* (and *esclandrir*), f. *esclandre*: see prec.]

†**1.** *trans.* In or after Biblical use: To be a stumbling-block to; to offend; to cause to lapse spiritually or morally. *Obs.*

**a.** In passive; also *refl.* (see first quot.).

*a* **1300** *Cursor M.* 13109 þat man sal for-blisced be þe quilk him sclanders noght for me. *c* **1325** *Metr. Hom.* 35 Ful bliced..es he That es noht sclaunderd in me. **1382** WYCLIF *Mark* iv. 17 Afterward tribulacioun sprongen vp,..anoon thei ben sclaundrid. *c* **1400** N. LOVE *Bonavent. Mirr.* xxviii. (1908) 146 Wherfore they were gretely sclaundred and stired aȝenst hym. *c* **1449** PECOCK *Repr.* v. vi. 513 The persoon sclaundrid (that is to seie, prouokid and putt into synne). **1563** WINȜET *Wks.* (S.T.S.) I. 67 That the waik and infirm be nocht slanderit be our vngodly silence in tyme of persequtioun.

**b.** Used actively. (Cf. SCANDALIZE *v.*[1] 2.)

**1382** WYCLIF *Malachi* ii. 8 Forsothe ȝe wenten awey fro the weye, and sclaundren ful many men in the lawe. *c* **1400** *Apol. Loll.* 40 He þat puttiþ forþ þis þing noiþer drediþ ne schamiþ to lette ne sclaunder oþer men. **1483** CAXTON *Cato* C vj, If thyne eye sclaunder or shame thy self put hit fro the. **1526** *Pilgr. Perf.* (1531) 61 Yf thyne eye sclaunder the, or be to the occasyon of synne.

†**2.** To bring into discredit, disgrace, or disrepute. *Obs.*

*c* **1375** *Sc. Leg. Saints* xxxii. (*Justin*) 430 þe feynde.. thocht to fyle hyre gud name, & sclandir hyr, & gere thol scham. **1387** TREVISA *Higden* (Rolls) IV. 23 þe prisoners þat were i-sent aȝe were i-sclaundred for evermore. *c* **1440** *Alph. Tales* 125 þies synnes er grevus, and þerfor I enione þe to penance at þou schryfe þe noght of þaim vnto no noder man, for þai may gretlie sklander þe. *c* **1477** CAXTON *Jason* 128 b, I entende not that by me ye sholde be sclawndrid. **1538** STARKEY *England* II. iii. 209 Now a days the precharys sklaunder the word of God, rather then teche hyt, by theyr contrary lyfe. **1592** KYD *Sp. Trag.* II. i, Yet might she loue me for my valiancie: I, but thats slaundred by captiuitie. **1603** DRAYTON *Bar. Wars* v. lviii, Least in that place the sad displeased earth, Doe loathe it selfe as slandered with my birth.

**3.** To defame or calumniate; to assail with slander; to spread slanderous reports about, speak evil of, traduce (a person, etc.).

α. *c* **1340** HAMPOLE *Pr. Consc.* 4252 Thurgh pride he sal ogayn God ryse And hym sclaunder and his law dispise. **1397** *Rolls of Parlt.* III. 379/1 In that that I sclaundred my Loord, I knowleche that I dede evyll. *a* **1450** *Knt. de la Tour* 21 After these wordes, she wepte and saide he had sclaundred her, and that it shuld not abide unponisshed. **1468** *Paston Lett.* II. 314 W. Barker sclaundred me yn certeyn maters of gode... Wold Jesu Barker had seyd true. *a* **1569** KINGESMYLL *Godly Advise* (1580) 10 The finest clothe maie be soonest stained, the honestest maie bee soonest sclaundered. **1599** SANDYS *Europæ Spec.* (1632) 74 Their art of sclaundering their opposites,..misreporting their actions [etc.].

β. **13..** *Evang. Nicod.* 421 in Herrig *Archiv* LIII. 398 Wha sklaunders god, yhe wate he mon Be staned to ded for syn. *c* **1340** HAMPOLE *Pr. Consc.* 7415 þus in helle salle þai far ay, And þar-with sklaundre God. *c* **1425** AUDELAY *XI Pains of Hell* 77 in *O.E. Misc.* 213 þo..Bakbidit here neȝtbore for enuy, And sklaundird hem in erþ ful falseley. **1483** CAXTON *Gold. Leg.* 84 b/1, I..haue leuer to deye than to dyffame & sklaundre my moder so fowly. **1581** J. HAMILTON in *Cath. Tract.* (S.T.S.) 83 Gif they..sklander and blaspheme lauful magistrats. **1596** DALRYMPLE tr. *Leslie's Hist. Scot.* I. 187 Throuch the inuie of sum persounis he had bene sklanditret to the Emperour.

γ. *c* **1425** *Hampole's Psalter* Metr. Pref. 55 Thus þei seyd ..And slaundird foule þis holy man. *c* **1440** *Promp. Parv.* 458/2 Slawnderon, *scandalizo, calumpnior.* **1530** PALSGR. 720/2 Have alwayes a good tonge in your heed, for it is both synne and shame to slaunder any bodye. **1560** DAUS tr. *Sleidane's Comm.* 16 To slaunder any man, before he be convicte of Heresye. **1621** BP. SANDERSON *Serm.* (1637) 51 It is deepliest slandered and hotliest opposed. **1653** W. RAMESEY *Astrol. Restored* 307 One shall abuse and slander the other. **1735** POPE *Prol. Sat.* 374 Full ten years slander'd, did he once reply? **1735** POOLE *Dialogue* 82 You slander us in this Point. **1864** TENNYSON *Aylmer's F.* 350 Some one, he thought, had slander'd Leolin to him. **1888** G. MASSON *Med. France* (1897) 42 Bertram de Born..spent his life in warring against his neighbours..and..slandering them in his *sirventes.*

†**b.** To accuse (unjustly or otherwise) *of*, charge or reproach *with*, something discreditable. Also with *that* and clause. *Obs.*

*c* **1400** *Destr. Troy* 834, I am ferd..þat hit lede..me harme for to haue of thy hegh wille, To be sclaundret of þi skathe. *c* **1430** *Chev. Assigne* 234 She was sklawnndered onhyȝe þat she hadde taken howndes. **1526** TINDALE *Titus* i. 6 Havynge faythfull children which are not sclandred off royote. **1591** SHAKS. *Two Gentl.* III. ii. 38 The best way is, to slander Valentine With falsehood, cowardize, and poore discent. **1603** OWEN *Pembrokeshire* (1892) 128 That are (truelie) slaundred with eating fyve meales a day. **1607** B. JONSON *Volpone* IV. i, O, Sir, proceed: I'll slander you no more of wit, good Sir.

†**c.** *Sc.* To charge *with*, accuse *of*, a crime or offence. *Obs.*

**1504** *Acc. Ld. High Treas. Scot.* II. 436 Men that wes sclanderit with finding of ane hurd. **1579** *Reg. Privy Council Scot.* III. 158 Personis sclanderit or suspect of treasoun salbe tane and remane in firmance. **1609** SKENE *Reg. Maj., Act Jas. II*, 132 Gif any person is sklandered, or suspect of treason, he sal remaine in firmance.

†**4.** To speak or write evil of, to misrepresent or vilify (a thing). *Obs.*

**1401** *Pol. Poems* (Rolls) II. 94 Thou wenest thou saist soth whan thou liest most lewde, and sclaunderist the truthe. **1549** *Compl. Scotl.* xx. 183 Thir freuole sophistaris that marthirs and sklandirs the text of aristotel, deseruis punitione. **1569** ROGERS *Glasse of Godly Love* 178 Make such ashamed as would sclaunder the holy Gospell. **1623** LISLE *Ælfric on O. & N. Test.* Pref. 11 It hath beene slandered for heresie and new doctrine to have the Scripture in vulgar.

**5.** *intr.* or *absol.* To speak or utter slanders.

**1426** AUDELAY *Poems* 6 Ne say no word to hym sklaunderyng. **1428** in *Surtees Misc.* (1890) 6 He was counseld and biddyn noght to sclandyr in na maner bot say fully ye treuthe. **1500–20** DUNBAR *Poems* xli. 22 Be ȝe so wyiss that vderis at ȝow leir, Be nevir he to sklander nor defame. **1621** BURTON *Anat. Mel.* II. iii. vii, Let them rail, then, scoff, and slander. **1855** TENNYSON *Maud* I. IV. iv, I keep but a man and a maid, ever ready to slander and steal.

†**6.** *trans.* To publish or spread abroad. *rare.*

*c* **1375** *Cursor M.* 27425 (Fairf.), Atte wiser squa his rede aske he, þat na man shrift sklaunderet be. *c* **1470** HENRY *Wallace* VII. 919 Tharfor I will bot lychtly ryn that cace, Bot it be thing that playnly sclanderit is.

Hence **'slandered** *ppl. a.* Also *absol.*

**1602** COLLETON (*title*), A Ivst Defence of the Slandered Priestes. **1819** SHELLEY *Cenci* III. i. 285 We Are now..man to man;..The slanderer to the slandered; foe to foe. **1881** MISS BRADDON *Asphodel* II. 230 They all preferred the slandered to the slanderer; but they listened all the same.

**slanderer** ('slɑːndərə(r), -æ-). Also 4–6 sclaund- (6 sclaunderour, *Sc.* sclanderar); 4 sklaund-, 6–7 *Sc.* sklend- (6 -erar); 5–7 slaunderer. [f. SLANDER *v.* + -ER[1].]

**1.** One who slanders, one who devises or utters false or malicious statements about a person, etc.; a defamer or calumniator.

α. *c* **1380** WYCLIF *Wks.* (1880) 14 It semeþ þat þei ben.. sclaunder[er]is of crist, puttyng on hym siche worldly pompe and ypocrisie. **1388** —— *Titus* ii. 3 Olde wymmen in hooli abite, not sclaunderers. *c* **1515** *Cocke Lorell's B.* 11 Spyes, lyers, and grete sclaunderers. **1560** DAUS tr. *Sleidane's Comm.* 468, I saye they be sclaunderers, and ennemies of the common countrie. **1647** HEXHAM I, A sclaunderer, *een lasterder.*

β. *c* **1340** HAMPOLE *Pr. Consc.* 7042 þe domes salle þan be redy Tille þe sklaunderers of God alle myghty. **1585** *Reg. Privy Council Scot.* IV. 40 The sklenderaris of his Hienes. **1609** SKENE *Reg. Maj.*, *Burrow Laws* 155 Gif there be any sklenderers, rebelles, or nicht walkers within the burgh.

γ. **1535** COVERDALE *Ps.* xliii. 15 The voyce of the slaunderer & blasphemer. **1560** DAUS tr. *Sleidane's Comm.* 467 b, The slanderer afterwarde, loste his head, as he deserved. **1603** SHAKS. *Meas. for M.* v. i. 260 Stir not you till you haue Well determin'd vpon these Slanderers. **1660** MILTON *Free Commw.* Wks. 1851 V. 425 To be ourselves the slanderers of our own just and religious Deeds. **1749** FIELDING *Tom Jones* XI. i, Much of it will probably seem too severe, when applied to the slanderer of books. **1777** SHERIDAN *Sch. Scand.* I. i, The male slanderer must have the cowardice of a woman before he can traduce one. **1829** LYTTON *Devereux* I. iii, Ye are both my foes and slanderers. **1869** FREEMAN *Norm. Conq.* (1875) III. 50 The slanderers were ready with long tales of rapine and sacrilege.

†**2.** A source of discredit or disrepute. *Obs.*[−1]

**1558** KENNEDY *Compend. Treat.* (Wodrow Soc.) 151 Are thay not oppin sclanderaris of the Congregatioun, quhilkis sulde be myrouris of gude lyfe?

†**'slanderful,** *a. Obs. rare.* Also 5 sclandirful, 6 sklaunder-. [f. SLANDER *sb.* + -FUL.] = SLANDEROUS *a.*

**1453** *Epist. Acad. Oxon.* (1898) I. 320 The first publisheris of the seide sclandirful noysyng. **1663** DRYDEN *Wild Gallant* III. ii, Come, come, you're a slanderful huswife.

Hence †**'slanderfully** *adv. Obs. rare.*

**1550–1** *Acts Privy Council* (1891) III. 213 He had at all tymes..used him self unreverentlie to the Kinges Majestie, and very sklaunderfullie towardes the Counsaill.

**slandering** ('slɑːndərɪŋ, -æ-), *vbl. sb.* Now *rare.* [f. SLANDER *v.* + -ING[1].] The utterance of slander(s).

*c* **1380** WYCLIF *Wks.* (1880) 18 In..muche sclaundrynge and cursynge and oþere peynes ynowe. *Ibid.* 264 For as þei seyn þis is bacbitynge or detraction & sclaundrynge. **1560** DAUS tr. *Sleidane's Comm.* 48 To teache the treuth, and to abstaine from sklaundering of others. **1586** W. WEBBE *Eng. Poetrie* (Arb.) 89 The olde manner of Commedies decayde, by reason of slaundering which therein they vsed against many. **1647** HEXHAM I, A sclaundering, *een lasteringe.*

So **'slandering** *ppl. a.*, **'slanderingly** *adv.*

**1402** HOCCLEVE *Letter of Cupid* 140 A sclaundryng [*v.r.* sclaundrous] tong is his grete aduersarye. **1599** H. PORTER *Angry Women Abingdon* (Percy Soc.) 56 A iealious slandering spitefull queane she is. **1648** HEXHAM II, *Lasterlicken*, Calumniously, Sclaunderingly. **1716** *Loyal Mourner* 50 No sland'ring Tongue.

**slanderous** ('slɑːndərəs, -æ-), *a.* Forms: α. 5–7 sclaunderous (5 -drous(e), 6 sclandero(u)s. β. 6 skla(u)nderous(e), *Sc.* sklanderus. γ. 5–7 slaunderous (6 -erus), 7 slandrous, 6– slanderous. [ad. AF. *esclandrus, = OF. *esclandreux* (1455), f. *esclandre* SLANDER *sb.*: see -OUS.]

†**1.** **a.** Of bad repute; discreditable, disgraceful, shameful. *Obs.* (Freq. in 16th cent.)

**1402** HOCCLEVE *Letter of Cupid* 67 Now ys it good, confesse him a traytoure, and bringe a woman to a sclaundrouse name. **1535** COVERDALE *Prov.* ii. 15 Whose wayes are croked, and their pathes slaunderous. **1560** DAUS tr. *Sleidane's Comm.* 35 That filthy and sklaunderous life of pristes. **1589** WARNER *Alb. Eng.* Prose Addit. (1602) 335 Our effeminate abode here is vaine and slanderous.

†**b.** Forming a source of shame or disgrace *to* some one. *Obs. rare.*

**1592** *Arden of Feversham* III. v, Tis thou hast..made me slanderous to all my kin. **1595** SHAKS. *John* III. i. 44 If thou .. wert grim, Vgly, and slandrous to thy Mothers wombe, Full of vnpleasing blots [etc.].

†**c.** Giving cause or occasion for slander. *Obs.*[−1]

**1601** SHAKS. *Jul. C.* IV. i. 20 Though we lay these Honours on this man, To ease our selues of diuers sland'rous loads.

**2.** Of words, reports, language, etc.: Of the nature of, characterized by, or containing slander or calumny; calumnious, defamatory.

α. β. **1424** in *Cal. Pat. Rolls, Hen. VI*, II. (1907) 31 Non of the xxiiij aldermen sai..supporten..no maner of persone ..in spekyng of sclaundrous wordes. *c* **1500** in Leadam *Star Chamber Cases* (Selden Soc.) 101 It is allegid by the seid Complaynaunt in his seducyous and sclaunderous bill [etc.]. **1535** STARKEY *Lett.* in *England* (1870) p. xx, Where as sklanderouse fame & mysreport may perauentur put you in suspycyon of the contrary. **1566** *Reg. Privy Council Scot.* I. 481 Quhat sclanderous brute and rumour is spred.

γ. **1485** *Rolls of Parlt.* VI. 288/2 An inordinate, seditious and slaunderous Acte..made ayenst..King Herrie the VI[th]. **1529** in *Vicary's Anat.* (1888) App. xiv. 256 Yt ys ordeyned that no man of the sayde Felyshippe shall..speke any Slaunderus wordes yn disablyng hym of hys science. **1573** L. LLOYD *Marrow of Hist.* (1653) 44 He was openly beheaded by decree of all the Senate, and a slaunderous Epitaph set upon his grave. **1600** E. BLOUNT tr. *Conestaggio* 229 Some had giuen out most slaunderous speeches against him. **1667** MILTON *P.L.* XII. 536 Truth shall retire Bestuck with slandrous darts. **1801** *Med. Jrnl.* V. 267 This part of Mr. W's reply, I call slanderous personal abuse. **1858** FROUDE *Hist. Eng.* IV. xix. 114 His supposed offences were slanderous expressions used against the king. **1883** *Law Rep.* 11 *Q.B.D.* 597 The highest judge in the land is answerable in damages for slanderous language.

**3.** Of persons, etc.: Given to the use of slander or calumny; employing slander as a means of defaming or injuring others. Also *absol.*

α. β. **1521** FISHER *Serm. agst. Luther* ii. Wks. (1876) 327 The sklaunderous mouthe & cruel tethe that Martyn luther hath set vpon them [*sc.* Sacraments]. **1567** *Satir. Poems Reform.* viii. 2 Skorner of poitis and sklanderus knaif! **1647** HEXHAM I, Sclaunderous lippes, *lasterlicke lippen.*

γ. **1559** in Strype *Ann. Ref.* (1709) I. viii. 116 To stop the mouths of evil and slaunderous reporters. **1564** *Brief Exam.* *ij, He wyll not be slaunderous to any man. **1622** in Foster *Eng. Factories Ind.* (1908) II. 88 Lyinge, slanderouse rogues. **1653** LD. VAUX tr. *Godeau's St. Paul* 210 Nor covetous persons, nor envious, nor slanderous,..shall enter into the kingdom of heaven. **1769** *Junius Lett.* ii. (1780) 40 They find no notice taken of, or reply given to, these slanderous tongues and pens. **1838** ARNOLD in *Life & Corr.* (1844) II. viii. 114 Zealous,..and pious, but narrow-minded in the last degree, fierce and slanderous.

*transf.* *a* **1616** BEAUMONT *Bridal Song* iv, The crow, the slanderous cuckoo, nor The boding raven.

†**4.** Of the nature of a scandal or offence, = SCANDALOUS 1. *Obs.*

**1553** HOOPER *Let.* in Foxe *A. & M.* (1583) 1513/2 These men..may be kept by one sclaunderous stumbling blocke or other, that they neuer come vnto Christ.

**'slanderously,** *adv.* [f. prec. + -LY[2].]

**1.** In a slanderous manner; with slander; calumniously; also, unjustly, falsely.

**1429** in *Cal. Pat. Rolls, Hen. VI* (1907) II. 31 That same persone of the xxiiij aldermen so spoken of sclaundrously. ? **1500** in Leadam *Sel. Cases Star Chamber* (Selden Soc.) 104 That the seid John shuld sedicyously and sclaunderously put yn his bill of complaynt. **1545** BRINKLOW *Lament.* (1874) 118, I knowe the papystes and their flocke shall sclaunderouslye report me. **1611** BIBLE *Rom.* iii. 8 As wee be slanderously reported. **1647** HEXHAM I, Sclaunderously, *lasterlicken.* **1675** SHARP *Serm.* (1754) I. 47 So far it is from abridging us of any of our earthly delights, (as its enemies slanderously represent it) that it abundantly heightens them. **1875** JOWETT *Plato* (ed. 2) I. 462 Men..slanderously affirm of the swans that they sing a lament at the last.

†**2.** Scandalously; shamefully. *Obs.*

**1563** ABP. PARKER *Articles* §24 Any couples maried that liue not together, but slaunderously liue apart. **1631** *Conf. Faith* in Sternhold & H. *Ps.* R r vij b, He was guiltles condemned vnder Pontious Pilate,..and most slandrously hanged on the Crosse.

**'slanderousness.** [f. as prec. + -NESS.] Inclination to slander.

**1577** *Test. 12 Patriarchs* (1706) 119 Teaching slanderousness, war, wrong, and abundance of all mischief. **1727** BAILEY (vol. II), *Slanderousness*, reproachfulness. **1810** BENTHAM *Packing* (1821) 101 Impropriety... Slanderousness... Ill-nature. **1882** FARRAR *Early Chr.* II. 247 Breathing the atmosphere of faction, slanderousness and hate.

**slane** (sleɪn). *Anglo-Irish.* Also slean. [ad. Ir. *sleaghán.*] A long-handled spade, having a wing at one or both sides of the blade, used in Ireland for cutting turf.

**1750** W. ELLIS *Mod. Husb.* IV. iv. 40 Dig your trench with slanes. **1778** *Phil. Surv. S. Irel.* 96 They are cut by an instrument called a slane, which is..a spade of about four inches broad, with a steel blade of the same breadth, standing at right angles to the edge of the spade. **1847** *Paddiana* I. 307 Two or three slanes..being propped up against it [the door]. **1902** *Blackw. Mag.* Aug. 265/1 They brought me a spade and a slane for turf-cutting. **1951** *Engineering* 6 Apr. 389/2 'Sleans' are used to cut the peat. **1976** J. HAYES *Missing* (1977) v. 203 The man's had his slean out for me since we cut the turf together... Had me unfrocked, he did. **1977** J. HODGINS *Invention of World* iii. 74 When some turf-cutter drives his slean into the peat in that desolate valley [etc.].

*Comb.* **1892** JANE BARLOW *Irish Idylls* 172 There isn't a spade-load of good slane turf.

**slane,** var. of SLAIN *sb.*; obs. pl. SLOE.

†**slang,** *sb.*[1] Chiefly *Sc. Obs.* Also 6 slaing. [a. MDu. or MLG. *slange* (Du. *slang*, G. *schlange*) serpent, cannon, etc.] A species of cannon; a serpentine or culverin. (Cf. SLING *sb.*[2])

**1521** LD. DACRE in *Archaeologia* XVII. 205 A Saker, two Faucons,.. viij. small Serpentyns.., a grete Slaing of Irn. **1539** in *Archaeologia* XI. 439 Four score shotte of leade for a slang, 16 shotte of leade for a saker. **1549** *Compl. Scot.* vi. 41 Mak reddy 3our.. slangis, & half slangis, quartar slangis. *c* **1600** R. BANNATYNE *Memor.* (1836) 133 Small brasen peices, slanges of irone, and vtheris mae peices that was tane fra the toun.

**slang** (slæŋ), *sb.*[2] *dial.* [Of obscure origin. Some dialects have the form *sling*; further variations are *slanget* (*slanket*) and *slinget* (*slinket*).] A long narrow strip of land.

The precise sense varies a little in different localities.

**1610** HOLLAND *Camden's Brit.* I. 715 There runneth forth into the sea a certaine shelfe or slang, like unto an out-thrust tongue. **1764** in *Rep. Comm. Inq. Charities* XXVIII. 145 Two slangs of ground. **1804** J. EVANS *Tour S. Wales* 300 Formerly the lands of this district [near Fishguard] were divided into very narrow slangs, which were unenclosed. **1839-** in dialect glossaries (Northampt., Shropsh., Heref.). **1885** *Field* 4 Apr. 426/2 He struggled across a couple of grass fields into the slang adjoining Brown's Wood.

**slang** (slæŋ), *sb.*[3] [A word of cant origin, the ultimate source of which is not apparent. It is possible that some of the senses may represent independent words. In all senses except 1 only in slang or canting use.

The date and early associations of the word make it unlikely that there is any connexion with certain Norw. forms in *sleng-* which exhibit some approximation in sense.]

**1. a.** The special vocabulary used by any set of persons of a low or disreputable character; language of a low and vulgar type. (Now merged in c.)

In the first quot. the reference may be to customs or habits rather than language: cf. the use of SLANG *a.* 2 b.

**1756** TOLDERVY *Hist. 2 Orphans* I. 68 Thomas Throw had been upon the town, knew the slang well. **1774** KELLY *School for Wives* III. ix, There is a language we [bailiffs] some-times talk in, called slang. **1809** E. S. BARRETT *Setting Sun* I. 106 Such grossness of speech, and horrid oaths, as shewed them not to be unskilled in the slang or vulgar tongue of the lowest blackguards in the nation. **1824** SCOTT *Redgauntlet* ch. xiii, What did actually reach his ears was disguised.. completely by the use of cant words, and the thieves-Latin called slang. *a* **1839** PRAED *Poems* (1864) II. 117 And broaches at his mother's table The slang of kennel and of stable.

**b.** The special vocabulary or phraseology of a particular calling or profession; the cant or jargon of a certain class or period.

**1801** *Encycl. Brit.* Suppl. I. 723/1 A studied harangue, filled with that sentimental slang of philanthropy, which costs so little, promises so much, and has now corrupted all the languages of Europe. **1802-12** BENTHAM *Ration. Judic. Evid.* (1827) IV. 306 Giving, in return for those fees, scraps of written lawyer's slang. **1834** H. J. ROSE *Apol. Study of Divinity* (ed. 2) 15 However tempting the scientific *slang*, if I may so term it, of the day may be. **1857** KINGSLEY *Lett.* (1878) II. 43, I have drawn, modelled in clay and picture fancied, so much in past years, that I have got unconsciously into the slang. **1872** GEO. ELIOT *Middlem.* xi, Correct English is the slang of prigs who write history and essays. And the strongest slang of all is the slang of poets.

**c.** Language of a highly colloquial type, considered as below the level of standard educated speech, and consisting either of new words or of current words employed in some special sense.

**1818** KEBLE in Sir J. T. Coleridge *Mem.* (1869) 75 Two of the best [students] come to me as a peculiar grinder (I must have a little slang). **1848** THACKERAY *Van. Fair* xliii, He was too old to listen to the banter of the assistant-surgeon and the slang of the youngsters. **1868** DORAN *Saints & Sinners* I. 107 He [Latimer] occasionally employed some of the slang of the day to give force to his words. **1887** R. N. CAREY *Uncle Max* xv, If I had ever talked slang, I might have said that we chummed together famously. **1914** J. M. BARRIE *Admirable Crichton* IV. 227 In the regrettable slang of the servants' hall, my lady, the master is usually referred to as the Gov. **1925** T. DREISER *Amer. Tragedy* (1926) I. II. i. 156 Don't say 'swell'. And don't say 'huh'. Can't you learn to cut out the slang? **1937** PARTRIDGE *Dict. Slang* p. ix, *A Dictionary of Slang and Unconventional English*, i.e. of linguistically unconventional English, should be of interest to word-lovers. **1976** *Times Lit. Suppl.* 30 Apr. 520/4 In Australia, slang simply has a quite different status from slang in England. It is a *part* of 'Standard English' there, not outside 'Standard English'. Slang words are used informally, casually and naturally by all Australians regardless of class or education.

*attrib.* and *Comb.* **1846** MRS. GORE *Engl. Char.* (1852) 139 Like a door from which some slang-loving roué has wrenched the knocker. **1850** *N. & Q.* Ser. I. 369/2 That great slang-manufactory for the army, the Royal Military College, Sandhurst. **1856** G. MEREDITH *Let.* 15 Dec. (1970) I. 28 Have you.. a book of Hampshire Dialect?.. Also a slang Dictionary, or book of the same with Gloss. **1926** *Variety* 29 Dec. 5/3, I was hep that the slang slingers were not crowding each other. **1977** K. F. KISTER *Dictionary Buying Guide* II. 240 The more substantial slang dictionaries provide detailed word histories and thus complement the etymological dictionaries.

**d.** Abuse, impertinence. (Cf. SLANG *v.* 3, 4.)

**1805** T. CAMPBELL *Let.* 9 Feb. in W. Partington *Private Letter-bks. W. Scott* (1930) 100 In five weeks, however, her slang broke out, and within the seventh she discovered the whole catalogue of Vices of which a very ugly woman can be guilty. **1825** LOCKHART in *Scott's Fam. Lett.* (1894) II. 297 This Mr. H. gave grand slang to the Porters, etc., who crowded the vessel on our anchoring: 'Your fingers are all thumbs, I see', etc.

†**2.** Humbug, nonsense. *Obs.*[−1]

**1762** FOOTE *Orator* I. Wks. 1799 I. 192 Have you seen the bills?.. What, about the lectures? ay, but that's all slang, I suppose; no, no. No tricks upon travellers.

†**3.** A line of work; a 'lay'. *Obs.*[−1]

*c* **1789** G. PARKER *Life's Painter* 120 How do you work now?.. O, upon the old slang, and sometimes a little lully-prigging.

**4.** A licence, *esp.* that of a hawker.

**1812** J. H. VAUX *Flash Dict.*, *Slang*,.. a warrant, license to travel, or other official instrument. **1865** *Slang Dict.* 234 'Out on the slang,' i.e. to travel with a hawker's licence. **1896** *Westm. Gaz.* 9 Dec. 2/1 You don't want for much to start with;..½ sovereign.. for a (slang) licence is plenty.

**5. a.** A travelling show.

**1859** *Slang Dict.* 94 *Slang*, a travelling show. **1873** LELAND *Egypt. Sketch Bk.* 63 There is a great deal of the Rommany or Gipsy element.. wherever the 'slangs' or exhibition affairs show themselves.

**b.** A performance.

**1861** MAYHEW *Lond. Lab.* III. 101, I am talking of a big pitch, when we go through all our 'slang', as we say.

**c.** *attrib.*, as **slang cove, cull**, a showman.

*c* **1789** G. PARKER *Life's Painter* 130 To exhibit any thing in a fair or market,.. that's called slanging, and the exhibiter is called the slang cull. **1851** MAYHEW *Lond. Lab.* I. 353 We did intend petitioning.., but I don't suppose it would be any go, seeing as how the slang coves (the showmen) have done so, and been refused.

**6.** A short weight or measure. (Cf. SLANG *a.* 3.)

**1851** MAYHEW *Lond. Lab.* I. 32/2 There's plenty of costers wouldn't use slangs at all, if people would give a fair price. *Ibid.* II. 90/1 Some of the street weights, a good many of them, are slangs.

**slang** (slæŋ), *sb.*[4] *Cant.* [app. a. Du. *slang* snake, etc.: see SLANG *sb.*[1]]

**1.** A watch-chain; a chain of any kind.

G. *schlange* is similarly used in canting language.

**1812** in J. H. VAUX *Flash Dict.* *c* **1866** VANCE *Chickaleary Cove* (Farmer), How to do a cross-fan for a super or slang. **1884** *Pall Mall G.* 29 Dec. 4/2 The slang (chain) should be taken with the watch, if possible, by snipping.. the button-hole that it is fixed in.

**2.** *pl.* Fetters, leg-irons.

**1812** J. H. VAUX *Flash Dict.*, *Slangs*, fetters, or chains of any kind used about prisoners. **1823** 'J. BEE' *Dict. Turf*, *Slangs* are the greaves with which the legs of convicts are fettered. **1883** *York & York Castle* 276 Each set of these slangs or leg irons, weighing perhaps from twelve to fifty pounds.

So **slanged** *ppl. a.*, fettered.

**1812** in J. H. VAUX *Flash Dict.*

**slang** (slæŋ), *a.* (and *adv.*). [Related to SLANG *sb.*[3]]

**1.** Of language, etc.: Having the character of, belonging to, expressed in, slang.

**1758** *J. Wild's Adv. to Successor* (Hotten), The master who teaches them should be a man well versed in the cant language, commonly called the slang patter. **1798** *Anti-Jacobin* 5 Mar., The following stanzas.. in the Slang or Brentford dialect. **1810** *Ann. Reg.* 296 The police-officers are of opinion that the robbery.. is what is called, in slang language, *a put-up robbery*. **1817** *Edin. Rev.* XXVIII. 512 Now this style is the reverse of one made up of slang phrases. **1861** *Q. Rev.* No. 220. 468 The translation.. is studded with the colloquialisms, and sometimes even slang expressions, of Charles II's time. **1892** STEVENSON *Across the Plains* 24 Set phrases, each with a special and almost a slang signification.

**2.** Given to the use of slang; of a fast or rakish character; impertinent.

**1818** MOORE *Diary* 1 Dec., The conversation to-day of rather a commoner turn than usual on account of these slang bucks. **1858** TROLLOPE *Dr. Thorne* xxiv, The set with whom he lived at Cambridge were the worst of the place. They were fast, slang men, who were fast and slang, and nothing else. **1862** WHYTE MELVILLE *Ins. Bar* xi, Forgetting in his indignation to be either slang or cool. **1864** *The Realm* 30 Mar. 7 Daring, saucy girls, slang and fast.

*Comb.* **1856** WHYTE MELVILLE *K. Coventry* xii, A slang-looking man with red whiskers.

**b.** Of dress: Loud, extravagant; more showy or obtrusive than accords with good taste. ? *Obs.*

**1828** *Sporting Mag.* XXII. 444 Without the slightest appearance of slang or flash toggery about him. **1849** ALB. SMITH *Pottleton Legacy* (1854) 11 A smart scarf, a very new hat, a slang coat, and a massive watch-chain. **1858** WHYTE MELVILLE *Interpreter* x, His dress was peculiarly neat and gentlemanlike, not the least what is now termed 'slang'.

**c.** Of tone, etc.: Slangy, rakish.

*a* **1834** COLERIDGE *Notes & Lect.* (1849) I. 47 Let some wit call out in a slang tone,—'the gallows!' and a peal of laughter would damn the play. **1840** HOOD *Up Rhine* 62 A slang air.. and the use of certain significant phrases.. current in London. **1847** ALB. SMITH *Chr. Tadpole* xxix. (1879) 263 The slang tone in which these words were uttered produced another burst of laughter.

**3.** *Costers' slang.* Of weights and measures: Short, defective.

**1812** J. H. VAUX *Flash Dict.*, *Slang weights* or *measures*, unjust, or defective ones. **1851** MAYHEW *Lond. Lab.* I. 32/2 The slang quart is a pint and a half. *Ibid.*, The slang pint holds in some cases three-fourths of the just quantity.

**b.** *adv.* So as to give short measure.

**1851** MAYHEW *Lond. Lab.* I. 32/2 He could always 'work slang' with a true measure.

**slang** (slæŋ), *v. colloq.* or *slang.* [f. SLANG *sb.*[3] or *a.*, in various senses.]

**1.** ? *intr.* To exhibit at a fair or market.

*c* **1789** [see SLANG *sb.*[3] 5 c].

**2. a.** *trans.* To defraud, cheat. **b.** *intr.* (also with *it*). To employ cheating; to give short measure.

**1812** J. H. VAUX *Flash Dict.*, *Slang*, to defraud a person of any part of his due, is called *slanging* him; also to cheat by false weights or measures, or other unfair means. **1812** *Sporting Mag.* XXXIX. 284 He *slanged* the *dragsman*,.. which means that he sneaked away from the coach. **1851** MAYHEW *Lond. Lab.* I. 32/2 So the men slangs it, and cries '2*d.* a pound', and gives half-pound. *Ibid.* 474/2 What he's made by slanging, and what he's been fined.

**3.** *intr.* To utter, make use of, slang; to rail in abusive or vulgar language.

**1828** LYTTON *Pelham* xlviii, We rowed, swore, slanged with a Christian meekness and forbearance. **1842** LD. HOUGHTON in Wemyss Reid *Life* I. 285 Having so furiously slanged against the wickedness of war. **1868** W. R. GREG *Lit. & Soc. Judgm.* 141 Mr. Carlyle slangs like a blaspheming pagan; Mr. Kingsley like a denouncing prophet.

**4.** *trans.* To abuse or scold violently.

**1844** ALB. SMITH *Adv. Mr. Ledbury* i, He could.. slang coal-heavers.. better than anybody else in London. **1853** R. S. SURTEES *Sponge's Sp. Tour* v, His off-hand way of blowing up and slanging people. **1888** BURGON *Lives 12 Good Men* II. xi. 314 He sent for the offender.. and in the most slashing style 'slanged', even threatened him.

Hence **'slanging** *vbl. sb.* **slanging match**: an exchange of abuse; a vituperative argument.

**1856** LEVER *Martins of Cro' M.* 250, I feel certain that I could stand any.. quantity of what is genteelly called 'slanging'. **1864** MISS YONGE *Trial* xvii, I never had such a slanging in my life! **1895** *Athenæum* 7 Sept. 316/3 The slanging all round which they give one another. **1896** T. E. TAYLOR *Running Blockade* vi. 74 A slanging match went on between us, like that sometimes to be heard between two penny steamboat captains on the Thames. **1936** *Sun* (Baltimore) 14 Oct. 12/3 They [*sc.* the speeches] were made by the man who commands the highest authority and the greatest power in all the Reich, and they provoked an international slanging match. **1938** 'G. ORWELL' *Homage to Catalonia* xii. 243 The slanging-match in the newspapers. **1978** J. PORTER *Dead Easy for Dover* xiv. 140 Mrs Vincent very sensibly decided not to get involved in a slanging match with Dover. Their views on unmarried mothers were poles apart.

**slang,** obs. or Sc. pa. t. of SLING *v.*

†**'slangam.** *Obs. rare.* [Cf. SLANG *sb.*[2] and SLANGREL.] ? A lanky person.

**1611** COTGR., *Longis*,.. a tall and dull slangam, that hath no making to his height, nor wit to his making. **1653** URQUHART *Rabelais* I. xxv, Codshead loobies, woodcock slangams,.. and other such like defamatory epithetes. *Ibid.* II. i, The little Grammar school-boyes.. called those leg-grown slangams Jambus.

**slangily** ('slæŋılı), *adv.* [f. SLANGY *a.* + -LY[2].] In a slangy (†or flashy) manner; in language of the nature of slang.

**1858** R. S. SURTEES *Ask Mamma* lxvii, It is not every baggy-corded fellow that rolls slangily along in top-boots.. that is a groom. **1864** *Daily Telegr.* 7 Nov., There would be an opening for clever workmen,.. but none for what are slangily but very expressively known as 'duffers'. **1895** *Strand Mag.* 724 'Thanks awfully,' I said, slangily but firmly.

**slanginess** ('slæŋınıs), *sb.* [f. as prec. + -NESS.] Slangy character or quality.

**1865** *Lond. Rev.* 7 Oct. 392/1 An exaggerated and caricatured account of the slanginess.. of the American nature. **1877** MRS. FORRESTER *Mignon* I. 15 Courteous, well-bred, and utterly devoid of slanginess. **1891** *Spectator* 23 Mar., The predominant slanginess and flippancy of her style.

**slangish** ('slæŋıʃ), *a.* [f. SLANG *sb.*[3] 1 + -ISH.] Somewhat slangy.

**1813** J. B. S. MORRITT *Let.* 3 Apr. in W. Partington *Private Letter-bks. W. Scott* (1930) 110 Poems of their own which are dull and slangish. **1828** *Blackw. Mag.* XXIII. 380 'A great school-boy'.. is a sort of slangish expression. **1851** H. NEWLAND *The Erne, its Legends*, etc. 102 The slangish looks.. and knowing demeanour of the men. **1894** BLACKMORE *Perlycross* 278 That extremely low slangish way.

Hence **'slangishly** *adv.*

**1820** *Blackw. Mag.* VIII. 261 Living on the town, as it is slangishly called. **1822** *Ibid.* XI. 723 The 'Northamptonshire peasant,' as he is somewhat slangishly called.

**'slangism.** [f. SLANG *sb.*[3] 1.] A slang expression. Also **'slangist, 'slangster**, one who uses slang. **'slanguage**, slangy speech; a form of slang (*jocular*). **'slangular** *a.*, pertaining to slang (*jocular*).

[The following passage is the source of the adj. *slangous* given in some Dicts:—**1823** J. BEE *Dict. Turf* p. vi, The irons were *the slangs*, and the *slang*-wearers' language was of course *slangous*, or partaking much, if not wholly, of the *slangs*.]

**1853** *Household Wds.* Sept. 76/2 Frivolous little foreign *slangisms hovering about fashionable cookery and fashionable furniture. **1866** E. YATES *Kissing Rod* I. i. 6 A 'cool card', a 'long-headed chap',.. and.. other complimentary slangisms. **1885** *Harper's Mag.* Dec. 83/1 She did not exactly say with the modern *slangist, 'That's rather an extensive order'. *c* **1830** in *N. & Q.* 1st Ser. I. 369 Gentlemen cadets wishing to achieve a notoriety as wits and *slangsters. **1926** *Variety* 29 Dec. 5/4 Most slangsters use the exaggerated simile when breaking into print. **1933** *Times Lit. Suppl.* 16 Nov. 781/4 Rhoda Broughton.. would probably have thought Galsworthy far too much of a 'slangster'. **1945** *Gen* 5 May 24/1 His [*sc.* Walter Winchell's] slangster column.. in the New York Daily Mirror. **1965** *English Studies* XLVI. 465 A *slangster* [is] a user of slang. **1879** *Harvard Lampoon* 21 Nov. 88/1 (*title*) *Slanguage on Angele. **1892** LELAND in *Chambers's Encycl.* IX. 496 A congress 'at which a language, or rather slanguage, was deliberately constructed and adopted'. **1899** *Sport. Life* 4 Sept. 5/3 In 'slanguage' current on the Turf and amongst the young bloods of the Stock Exchange. **1911** *Daily Colonist* (Victoria, B.C.) 7 Apr. 4/2 The 'slanguage' of a sporting reporter is a fearful and wonderful thing. **1926** *Irish Statesman* 18 Dec. 355/1 (*heading*) The American slanguage. **1926** *Variety* 29 Dec. 7/4 Every phase of our complex civilization, and every class have contributed something to what is fast becoming a national slanguage. **1927** *Vanity Fair* XXIX. 67/2 Jack Conway..is conceded to be the ace 'slanguage' hurler in the world. **1935** [see CAT *sb.*[1] 2 c]. **1958** *Inside the ACD* (Amer. College Dict.) Nov. 2/1 Max Shulman shows in *Rally Round the Flag, Boys*, a new novel, that he can capture and record living speech including the 'slanguage' of the current cool crop of hipsters. **1963** [see CUBE, *sb.*[1] 1 c]. **1974** *Trailer Life* Nov. 92 Our slanguage is so offbeat that during World War II American military men were able to foil the enemy by resorting to American vernacular. **1853** DICKENS *Bleak Ho.* xi, Being asked what he thinks of the proceedings, [he] characterises them (his strength lying in a *slangular direction) as 'a rummy start'.

† **'slangrel**, *sb.* and *a. Obs. rare.* [Cf. SLANG *sb.*[2] and SLANGAM. Mod. Warwick dial. has *slang* adj. in the same sense.] **a.** *sb.* A lanky person (? or thing). **b.** *adj.* Long and narrow.

**1592** GREENE *Upst. Courtier* Wks. (Grosart) XI. 250 The third was a long leane old slauering slangrell. **1598** FLORIO, *Bislongo*, twice long, a slangrell. **1643** tr. *Diodati's Annot. Bible* Gen. vi. 14 A great Vessell, on the inside like a great chest, of a slangrell forme.

**slangwhang** ('slæŋhwæŋ), *v.* Chiefly *U.S.* [f. SLANG *sb.*[3] 1 + WHANG *v.*] *trans.* and *intr.* To assail with, to make use of, violent language, abuse, or vituperation. Also **'slang,whanging** (also **slangwanging**) *vbl. sb.* and *ppl. a.*

**1809** *Essex Register* (Salem, Mass.) 20 May 2/2 (*heading*) Federal Slang-whanging..or, a new comical, heroic, quizzical, serio farcical melo-drama. **1829** H. MURRAY *N. Amer.* II. III. iii. 366 The expression 'slangwhanging', which signifies making violent political harangues to the multitude. **1841** in *J. Q. Adams' Conn. w. Monroe Doctrine*, etc. (1902), This french proverb applies to all such slang whanging rascals like yourself. **1880** *Punch* 11 Sept. 117/1 Over the Census Bill Honourable Members got senselessly incensed.., Orthodoxy and the other Doxies slang-whanging each other just as if they were really in earnest. **1890** *Melbourne Punch* 14 Aug. 107/4 That Eminent Personage immediately began to slangwhang the umpire. **1959** *Listener* 19 Feb. 325/2 A slang-wanging, stump speaker.

† **slangwhang** ('slæŋhwæŋ), *sb. U.S. Obs.* Also **slang-wang.** [f. as prec. + WHANG *sb.*[2]] Violent or abusive language.

**1834** H. M. BRACKENRIDGE *Recollections* xvi. 183 The young lawyer..who has acquired nothing of the ordinary slangwhang. **1859** *Harper's Mag.* July 164/1 Don't allow their vulgar slang-wang to have the slightest effect upon you.

**'slang,whanger.** Chiefly *U.S.* [Cf. SLANGWHANG *v.*] A noisy or abusive talker or writer.

**1807** W. IRVING *Salmag.* (1824) 109 These knights, denominated editors, or *slang-whangers*,..may be said to keep up a constant firing 'in words'. **1836** HALIBURTON *Clockm.* (1862) 203 Candidate, Slangwhanger, and Member. **189.** T. & ANNA FITCH *Better Days* 304 The Tucson Star which used to be the chief of slangwhangers.

**slangy** ('slæŋɪ), *a.* [f. SLANG *sb.*[3] 1.]

**1.** Of persons: **a.** Of a flashy or pretentious type. **b.** Given to the use of slang.

**1850** KINGSLEY *A. Locke* vi, He appeared to me merely a tall, handsome, conceited, slangy boy. **1860** *Slang Dict.* 217 *Slangy*, flashy, vulgar; loud in dress, manner, and conversation. **1870** FRISWELL *Mod. Men Lett.* ix. 149 A 'Varsity man, as the slangy people of to-day call those educated at Oxford or Cambridge.

**2. a.** Of dress: Somewhat loud or vulgar.

**1861** *Times* 30 May 9/3 A queer-looking man, whose attire, though good, is 'slangy', and suggestive somehow of the stable. **1884** *Ibid.* (weekly ed.) 3 Oct. 13/3 Fellows in smart, though slangy attire.

**b.** Of language, etc.: Pertaining to, of the nature of, slang.

**1842** R. H. DANA *Jrnl.* 14 Nov. (1968) I. 103 His letters have been careless, pretentious, & with a kind of off-hand, slang-ey, defying tone. **1864** *Daily Telegr.* 3 Sept., A slangy vulgarity which savours even more of the bar-room than of the camp. **1876** *World* V. 4 The conversation of Society is as slangy..as its ethics are dubious. **1883** *Fortn. Rev.* Sept. 381 Their style is always smart,..sometimes slangy.

**slank** (slæŋk), *a.* Now *Sc.* and *north. dial.* [prob. a. Du. or LG. *slank* (MDu. and MHG. *slanc*, G. *schlank*) thin, slender.] Of persons, parts of the body, the hair: Lank, thin.

The quotation dated 1656 in Davies reads *flank* in the original edition, but this may be a misprint for *slank*.

**1668** WILKINS *Real Char.* 33 Slim, lank, slank, slight. **1715** CHAPPELOW *Right Way Rich* (1717) 119 They wound religion through his slank sides. **1825** in JAMIESON *Suppl.* **1865** MELLOR *Uncle Owdem* 4 (E.D.D.), It ratched him eawt an' made him lunger an' slanker. **1882** in *Lanc. Gloss.*

[**slank**, error for *slauk* SLAWK.

The mistake appears to have originated in ed. 1552 of Elyot's Latin Dict. (s.v. *Bryon*), and is continued by Cooper, Cotgrave, etc.]

**slant** (slɑːnt, -æ-), *sb.*[1] Also 7, *Sc.* 9 **slaunt.** [Connected with SLANT *adv.*, *a.*, and *vb.* See also SLENT *sb.*[1]]

**1. a.** The slope *of* a hill, piece of ground, etc.; a sloping stretch of ground; an inclined plane or surface.

**1655** MOUFET & BENNET *Health's Improv.* (1746) 87 The best Situation of a House or City, is upon the Slaunt of a South-west Hill. **1728** PEMBERTON *Newton's Philos.* 84 If this globe be drawn along the slant DF, less force will be required to raise it, than if it were lifted directly up. **1757** J. H. GROSE *Voy. E. Indies* 92 Returning then to the foot of the hill, you ascend an easy slant. **1802** [see SKELF]. **1838** PRESCOTT *Ferd. & Is.* (1846) II. xiv. 41 Ferdinand..kept along the southern slant of the coast as far as Almeria. **1860** WARTER *Sea-board* II. 33 His dog..brought back some stray sheep to the sunny side of the slant.

**b.** A small surface, a short line, having an oblique position or direction.

*c* **1711** PETIVER *Gazophyl.* x. §98 Luzone Olive Whelk, with white Slants and Spots. **1787** BEST *Angling* (ed. 2) 10 First cut the pieces with a slope, or slant,..and then spread a thin layer of shoemaker's wax over the slants. **1873** BROWNING *Red Cott. Nt.-cap* 122 Each pullet-egg Of diamond, slipping flame from fifty slants.

**c.** A sloping beam or ray *of* light.

**1855** DICKENS *Dorrit* iv, Pale slants of light from the yard above. **1862** THORNBURY *Life Turner* I. 20 Crimson fog-suns and misty slants of sunshine. **1865** DICKENS *Mut. Fr.* I. i, A slant of light from the setting sun.

**d.** *Mining.* (See quot. 1881.)

**1881** RAYMOND *Mining Gloss.*, *Slant*, a heading driven diagonally between the dip and the strike of a coal-seam; also called a *run*. **1892** *Pall Mall G.* 27 Aug. 5/1 He succeeded in penetrating the mine a hundred yards into the main slant.

**e.** *Typogr.* = OBLIQUE *sb.* 5, SOLIDUS[1] 2. Used esp. of either of a pair of lines enclosing the representation of a linguistic (esp. phonemic) element.

**1962** *Gen. Systems* VII. 299/2 Its mate is suffixed with a slant (virgule), thus: 4006 How to Silence. 4006/ How to Sound. **1964** E. PALMER tr. *Martinet's Elem. Gen. Linguistics* i. 24 This [*sc.* a significans] we represent between slants (/ʒ e mal a la tet/, /ʒ e mal/, /mal/). **1972** HARTMANN & STORK *Dict. Lang. & Linguistics* 172/1 Phonemic transcription is usually written between slants, e.g. /haus/.

**2.** A course or movement in an oblique direction.

**1712** E. COOKE *Voy. S. Sea* 313 Kept plying to Windward not far from the Land, sometimes making good Slants. **1889** T. E. BROWN *Manx Witch* 2 Lek didn want The Pazon to know her, and made a slant.

**3. a.** Slope, inclination, obliquity. ***on the slant***, aslant, obliquely. Also ***on a slant.***

**1817** H. T. COLEBROOKE *Algebra*, etc. 97 Where the length of the cavity, owing to the slant of the sides, is measured [etc.]. **1880** 'MARK TWAIN' *Tramp Abr.* 258 The slant of a ladder that leans against a house. **1884** Q. VICTORIA *More Leaves* 97 Not a bad road, but on the steeper side of the hill, and quite on the slant. **1951** E. PAUL *Springtime in Paris* xv. 286 Busse..leaped quickly, hit the lower level of the street pavement on a slant, and almost turned his ankle. **1957** D. LESSING *Going Home* ii. 35 The night was magnificent; the Southern Cross on a slant overhead.

**b.** *Microbiol.* A sloping surface of culture medium, usu. prepared by letting it solidify in a sloping test-tube, and used for the culture of micro-organisms. Cf. SLOPE *sb.*[1] 3 a.

**1899** T. BOWHILL *Man. Bacteriol. Technique* ii. 60 Take three freshly prepared tubes of oblique surface agar-agar —usually called 'agar-slants'—with plenty of water of condensation in the bottom. **1924** *Jrnl. Bacteriol.* IX. 398 Loops were transferred, at intervals up to four hours, to agar slants, and these were incubated overnight. **1949** *Amer. Jrnl. Path.* XXV. 7 Growth on plated media, while not unlike that on slants, was somewhat slower. **1972** *Sci. Amer.* Sept. 187/1 Dried yeast is typically sealed in an airtight envelope filled with nitrogen. Cultures can be perpetuated by inoculating slants of fresh nutrient agar under sterile conditions every 90 days.

**4.** *techn.* **a.** A receptacle having a sloping bottom in which paint-brushes are placed in order to keep them moist.

**1875** FIELD & DAVIDSON *Grammar of Colouring* 168 The brushes..may be dipped in nut-oil and laid in a tin slant until wanted again. *c* **1896** *Rowney's Price List* 20 Oil Slant and Smutch Pan.

**b.** A slab having shallow sloping compartments or depressions for water-colours.

**1897** *Army & Navy Stores List* 817 Round China Slants and Basins.

**5.** *dial.* and *U.S.* A sly hit or sarcasm.

Occurs much earlier in the form SLENT.

**1825** BROCKETT *N.C. Gloss.*, *Slant*, sly jokes, or petty lies. **1828–32** WEBSTER, *Slant*, an oblique reflection or gibe; a sarcastic remark. (In vulgar use.) **1856** MRS. STOWE *Dred* I. xxi. 274 Had the slant fallen upon himself, personally, Old Tiff would probably have given a jolly crow. **1897** HOWELLS *Landlord at Lion's Head* 94 Whitwell felt an ironical slant in the words.

**6.** *slang.* An occasion, chance, opportunity; also, an opportunity of going somewhere.

**1837** *Fraser's Mag.* XVI. 49, I boldly entered myself on board a privateer, with the determination of playing them a slippery trick the very first slant I had. **1859** CORNWALLIS *New World* I. 140 It was n't any wonder, when we did get a slant into town, if we took a drop too much. **1868** H. WOODRUFF *Trotting Horse Amer.* iii. 58, I have known many that will be always watching slants to get an extra quart of oats for their colts.

**7.** *Austr. slang.* (See quot.)

**1897** P. WARUNG *Tales Old Regime* 217 Pedder had got tired of things in general, and had organized that movement which was popularly known in Norfolk Island and Port Arthur as a 'slant', that is, he had planned a murder or a mutiny on purpose to obtain a trial in Hobart or Sydney.

**8.** A way of regarding something, a point of view or 'angle'; an interpretation; a bias. orig. *U.S.*

**1905** *N.Y. Even. Post* 28 Jan. 5 The titles of articles on this subject bear an extremely pessimistic slant. **1927** C. CONNOLLY *Let.* 26 Jan. in *Romantic Friendship* (1975) 230 The slant at which I write betrays an unbearable optimism. **1935** M. M. ATWATER *Murder in Midsummer* xv. 138 Mentally he was going over his 'story'..to change the slant of some of the phrases. **1948** *Sunday Pictorial* 18 July 12/3 A new and intriguing slant on the Borgias by Nigel Balchin. **1965** *Amer. N. & Q.* Mar. 99/2 The book has a pro-Galvão slant showing the man as a romantic hero. **1973** J. WOOD *North Beat* ii. 19 New slant—timing the lunch-hour, eh? When did we have that one before?

**9.** *U.S. colloq.* A glance, look.

**1911** E. FERBER *Dawn O'Hara* viii. 109 You're supposed t'take a slant at th'things an' make up your mind w'at you want. **1934** [see PETTING *vbl. sb.* 3].

**10.** *U.S. slang.* A slant-eyed person, *spec.* used as a term of contempt for one of Oriental stock. Cf. *slant-eye(s)* s.v. SLANT *a.* 3.

**1942** BERREY & VAN DEN BARK *Amer. Thes. Slang* §385/19 Oriental..*slant.* **1969** *Time* 5 Dec. 26/1 To the G.I. the Vietnamese..is a 'gook', 'dink', 'slope' or 'slant'. **1976** M. MACHLIN *Pipeline* vii. 79 And the fuckin' Eskimo slants are tryin' to get the rest of it. **1978** J. GORES *Gone, no Forwarding* (1979) 191 He took me back to the slant broad... A slant or a Buddha-head.

**slant** (slɑːnt, -æ-), *sb.*[2] *Naut.* [Later form of SLENT *sb.*[2]] A slight breeze or spell *of* wind, etc.

**1823** SCORESBY *Jrnl.* 381 Having a slant of wind from the eastward, we fetched the coast of Ireland. **1867** TROLLOPE *Chron. Barset* II. lxii. 195 Trimming his sails, so as to catch any slant of a breeze. **1871** *Daily News* 16 Mar., We got a slant of bad weather, which, however, did not prevent other balloons from starting. **1892** CLARK RUSSELL *List, Ye Landsmen* i, Should there come a slant of wind, I'm off.

**b.** Used without the genitive phrase.

**1833** M. SCOTT *Tom Cringle* xii, Having had a slant from the land wind in the night previous. **1865** DICKENS *Mut. Fr.* I. xii, The wind coming against them in slants and flaws. **1876** R. F. BURTON *Gorilla Land* II. 15 There was no wind except a slant at sunset.

**slant** (slɑːnt, -æ-), *adv.* and *a.* Also 5 **slonte**, 7 **slaunt.** [Aphetic for ME. *a-slonte*, *o-slante*, etc.: see ASLANT *adv.* It is not clear in what way these forms are related to the early sb. and vb. SLENT.]

**A.** *adv.* In a slanting, sloping, or oblique manner or direction; slantingly, aslant.

**1495** *Trevisa's Barth. De P.R.* VIII. ix. 306 Zodiacus is a cercle that passith slonte [*Bodl. MS.* aslonte]. **1612** BRINSLEY *Lud. Lit.* 29 Cut the nebbe first slant downewards to make it thinne, and after strait ouerthwart. *c* **1700** CELIA FIENNES *Diary* (1888) 294 Encompassing ye maze, in which are some slaunt cut wayes. **1795** SOUTHEY *Joan of Arc* VII. 625 The mighty Talbot came, And smote his helmet: slant the weapon fell. **1804** *Wolcot's* (P. Pindar) *Beauties Eng. Poetry* II. 11 A bridge, that cuts From Richmond Ferry slant to Brentford Butts. **1878** BAYNE *Purit. Rev.* v. 185 The sunbeams fell slant through the church windows.

**B.** *adj.* **1.** Of wind, etc.: Blowing or coming from the side; moving obliquely.

*c* **1618** MORYSON *Itin.* IV. viii. (Roxb.) 136 Beholding an English Shipp woorke into the harbor with a very slant and boysterous gayle of wynde. **1667** MILTON *P.L.* x. 1075 The slant Lightning, whose thwart flame driv'n down Kindles the gummie bark of Firr or Pine. **1790** *Naval Chron.* XXIV. 49 A slant wind..brought me..in with the island. **1819** SHELLEY *Prometh. Unb.* I. 318 Trampling the slant winds on high.

**2. a.** Having an oblique or sloping position or direction; inclined from the perpendicular or horizontal; falling, lying, placed, etc. slantwise.

**1776** MICKLE tr. *Camoens' Lusiad* VI. 260 On the wide mountain-wave's slant ridge. **1784** COWPER *Task* VI. 59 The southern side of the slant hills. **1793** SMEATON *Edystone L.* 194 Hatched with slant lines. **1863** B. TAYLOR *H. Thurston* xviii, The sun threw softer and slanter lights over the beautiful picture of the valley. **1883** PROCTOR *Great Pyramid* ii. 56 The slant tunnel would give the direction of the true north.

**b.** Of direction: Oblique.

**1793** W. ROBERTS *Looker-on* No. 47 (1794) II. 188 Those fine obliquities of his genius began to expand, and, taking a thousand slant and cross directions [etc.]. **1807** SOUTHEY *Espriella's Lett.* II. 173 Across which we had about three leagues to sail in a slant direction. **1871** *Daily News* 25 Jan., The French began to retreat, and in a slant direction right in front of us.

**3.** In special collocations, as ***slant fire***, ***height***, ***side***, ***tack***, ***vein*** (see quots.); **slant-drill** *v. intr. Oil Industry*, to drill a bore hole at an angle to the vertical; also *trans.*; so **slant-drilling** *vbl. sb.*; **slant-eye(s)** *slang* (orig. *U.S.*), a slant-eyed person, *spec.* an Asian (cf. SLANT *sb.*[1] 10); **slant-line** = SLANT *sb.*[1] 1 e; **slant-rhyme** = *half-rhyme* s.v. HALF- II. n.

**1969** *New Scientist* 24 Apr. 169/1 They suggest the search for oil..should be restricted to *slant-drilling from the shore. **1975** *Offshore* Sept. 244/2 Much of the area covered by the sale can be *slant-drilled from the shoreline or the barrier islands. **1976** L. ST. CLAIR *Fortune in Death* i. 8 We've wasted enough time fishing drill pipe out of this hole. Let's plug back and slant-drill. **1977** *Time* 28 Feb. 17/2 Two weeks ago the Israelis began sinking another hole on the shore at El Tur, slant-drilling into the waters whose ownership it disputes. **1929** *Amer. Speech* IV. 344 **Slant eye*, an oriental. **1962** E. SNOW *Red China Today* (1963) xii.

85 One might assume that contempt for American imperialism would by now have produced Chinese equivalents of insulting American epithets such as slopeys, slant-eyes and chinks. **1966** *Publ. Amer. Dial. Soc. 1964* XLII. 31 A few terms [for Orientals] reflect stereotype racial characteristics, i.e., *yellow-belly, yellow-man, slant eyes.* **1972** *Times* 20 May 3/4, I have engaged in campaigns against blacks, yellows and slant-eyes. Why should we have one rule for the whites and one for coloureds? **1974** *Times Lit. Suppl.* 26 July 795/4 And those Jap Ph.D.'s, their questionnaires! (Replying 'Sod off, Slant-Eyes' led to friction.) **1977** 'J. LE CARRÉ' *Hon. Schoolboy* i. 36 Renting a cottage in the New Territories, he..proposed to expire under a slanteye heaven. **1851** J. S. MACAULAY *Field Fortif.* 43 *Slant fire [is] when the shot strikes the interior slope of the parapet, forming with it a horizontal angle not greater than 30°. **1798** HUTTON *Course Math.* II. 42 To find the Surface of a Pyramid or Cone. Multiply the perimeter of the base by the *slant height, or length of the side [etc.]. **1873** J. PRYDE *Pract. Math.* 156 The slant height of a cone. **1954** F. G. CASSIDY *Robertson's Devel. Mod. Eng.* (ed. 2) iv. 61 Phonemic symbols are placed between virgules (or '*slant-lines', or 'diagonals'). **1966** *Publ. Amer. Dial. Soc.* XLVI. 16 In line with Haugen's procedure..*slant lines*..used in this article perform double duty for phonemic and diaphonic representations. **1944** *Mod. Lang. Q.* V. 324 Traditional prosodists have discussed rhyme as a degree of likeness in word sounds and have catalogued its approximations, alliteration, assonance, *slant rhyme, eye rhyme, [etc.]. **1976** *Times Lit. Suppl.* 16 Jan. 50/2 Wilfred Owen and Yeats opted for slant-rhyme because it suited their poetic purposes; Fry seems to chime because sometimes he cannot rhyme. *a* **1823** HUTTON *Course Math.* (1828) II. 138 Suppose the same cone to be cut by a plane parallel to one of the *slant sides, entering the other slant side at 4 inches from the vertex. **1873** J. PRYDE *Pract. Math.* 156 A line from the vertex of a right cone to any point in the circumference of its base, is called its slant side. **1867** SMYTH *Sailor's Word-bk.* 631 **Slant tack*, that which is most favourable to the course when working to windward. **1747** HOOSON *Miner's Dict.* Qj, Having duly weighed its randome and Inclination either Way, whether any Cross or *Slant Vein appears. **1828** CARR *Craven Gloss.*, *Slant-vein*, one vein crossing another at an acute angle.

**4.** *Comb.*, as *slant-eyed, -shouldered.*

**1865** *Daily Telegr.* 17 Nov. 5/2 A slant-eyed, saffron-coloured race. **1870** WHITTIER *Miriam* 126 The slant-eyed sages of Cathay. **1897** FLANDRAU *Harvard Episodes* 103 That hatchet-faced, slant-shouldered,..comic valentine.

**slant** (slɑːnt, -æ-), *v.* Also 6 skla(u)nt. [Later variant of SLENT *v.*[1], the vowel having probably been influenced by ASLANT *adv.*]

**1.** *intr.* To strike obliquely *on, upon,* or *against* something.

**1521** FISHER *Serm. agst. Luther* Wks. (1876) 323 For the sonne shooreth so lowe by the grounde that his bemes thanne sklaunteth vpon the grounde. **1711** in *10th Rep. Hist. MSS. Comm.* App. V. 132 The ball..slanted upon the right shoulder of the Prince..and struck off the skin. **1777** *Ann. Reg.* 161 Mr. Bates's sword bent and slanted against the Captain's breast-bone. **1873** SMILES *Huguen. France* II. ii. (1881) 342 The shot..slanted on the King's right shoulder, [and] took a piece out of his coat.

**2. a.** To be in, to have or take, an oblique direction or position; to deviate from a straight line or course; to slope.

**1698** FRYER *Acc. E. India & P.* 37 The Governor's House in the middle overlooks all, slanting diagonally with the Court. **1766** J. CUNNINGHAM *Poems, Inscription Imit.* iii, Where the green hill so gradual slants, Or flowery glade extends. **1797** COLERIDGE *Kubla Khan* 12 That deep romantic chasm which slanted Down the green hill. **1810** SCOTT *Lady of L.* I. xvii, An aged oak, That slanted from the islet rock. **1853** J. H. NEWMAN *Hist. Sk.* (1873) II. I. i. 24 The Tartar eyes are not only far apart, but slant inwards. **1860** TYNDALL *Glac.* I. xxvii. 218 A range of minor peaks ran slanting downwards.

**b.** Of light or shadow: To fall obliquely.

**1795** COWPER *Moralizer Corrected* 15 And from the trees ..Shades slanting at the close of day Chill'd [etc.]. **1804** GRAHAME *Sabbath* 371 The sunbeam slanting through the cedar grove. **1837–42** TENNYSON *St. Agnes' Eve* 6 The shadows of the convent-towers Slant down the snowy sward. **1863** GEO. ELIOT *Romola* xvii, A sickening sense of the sunlight that slanted before him.

**3. a.** Of persons: To travel, move, sail, etc. in an oblique direction; to diverge from a direct course. Also *U.S.*, to move off.

**1692** L'ESTRANGE *Josephus, Antiq.* XVI. xii. (1733) 443 And so by a side-Wind he slanted all the way upon Pheroras. **1719** DE FOE *Crusoe* I. (Globe) 143, I stretch'd a-cross this Eddy slanting North-west. **1776** CARROLL *Jrnl.* (1845) 74 From *La Prairie* you go slanting down the river to Montreal. **1861** DICKENS *Gt. Expect.* xlviii, We went along Cheapside, and slanted off to Little Britain. **1897** HOWELLS *Landlord at Lion's Head* 12 The father and the elder brother came out, and..slanted away to the barn together.

**b.** Of things: To take an oblique course.

*a* **1849** H. COLERIDGE *Poems* (1850) II. 11 The thunder roar'd, the sharp rain slanted. **1874** LISLE CARR *J. Gwynne* I. iii. 69 From this her mind would slant off into a sideway. **1885** C. E. CRADDOCK *Prophet of G.S.M.* vii, Her rebuking glance slanted beyond him from under her half-lifted lashes.

**c.** *fig.* To be inclined, have a bent, *towards* something.

**1850** LOWELL *Unhappy Lot of Mr. Knott* I. xi, I've always heard our poor friend somewhat slanted Tow'rd taking liquor overmuch.

**4.** *trans.* To cut with a slant.

**1771** LUCKOMBE *Hist. Print.* 439 We venture to disapprove the custom of slanting Quoins on both sides, and planing their edges and corners off. *Ibid.*, It would deserve the name of an improvement, were Quoins slanted on one side only.

**5. a.** To give an oblique or sloping direction to (something); to cause to slope.

**1805** SOUTHEY *Madoc* II. xviii. 63 The evening glories which the sun Slants o'er the moving many-colour'd sea. **1812** MME. D'ARBLAY *Diary* (1876) IV. lx. 206, I turned suddenly from my walk..to slant my steps close to where he sat. **1871** B. TAYLOR *Faust* IV. ii. (1875) II. 254 Their inky sails are hither slanted. **1891** *Sportsman* 8 July 8/1 The rain came down in torrents, slanted by the wind.

**b.** *fig.* To give a slant (SLANT *sb.*[1] 8) or bias to (something). orig. *U.S.*

**1939** *Writer's Digest* Sept. 26/2 These types of articles are exceptionally valuable in slanting the writing for certain magazines and trade journals. **1951** H. MACINNES *Neither Five nor Three* II. xi. 166 Did that fool Weidler see that Blackworth was 'slanting' his use of material? **1960** *New Left Rev.* May–June 66/1 There is no suggestion..that Mr. Bullock is deliberately slanting the picture he paints. **1980** M. BABSON *Dangerous to Know* vi. 41 'I suppose it *could* be slanted that way.' It was obvious that May had been considering a different slant.

**6.** Of a path: To ascend in a sloping direction.

**1850** TENNYSON *In Mem.* xxii, Where the path we walk'd began To slant the fifth autumnal slope.

**'slanted,** *ppl. a.* [f. SLANT *v.* + -ED[1].] **1.** Having an oblique or sloping direction; cut, placed, or driven aslant.

**1771** LUCKOMBE *Hist. Print.* 439 The slanted side of a Quoin. **1818** KEATS *Endym.* IV. 333 In less time Than shoots the slanted hail-storm. **1851** TRENCH *Poems* 24 The slanted columns of the noon-day light. **1891** *Pall Mall G.* 12 Jan. 7/1 The flames rise from the furnace and pass..in between the slanted tubes.

**2.** Biased, tendentious.

**1959** *Listener* 2 Apr. 580/2 A consistently slanted picture of Soviet policy. **1967** 'R. SIMONS' *Taxed to Death* v. 80 Why are you asking me all these slanted questions about Nathin? **1978** *Detroit Free Press* 16 Apr. E8/1 'The material coming our way is so slanted on gun control and hunting's role in wildlife management, I can't, in good conscience, pass it on to our youngsters,' he had said.

**slanter,** var. SCHLENTER *sb.* and *a.*

**slantindicular** (ˌslɑːntɪnˈdɪkjʊlə(r), -æ-), *a.* (*sb.*) and *adv.* Also slanting-, slantendicular, slantindiclar, -dickelar, slantendikular. [f. SLANTING, after *perpendicular.* Orig. *U.S.* and chiefly colloq. or humorous.]

**A.** *adj.* **a.** Slanting, sloping, oblique; neither perpendicular nor horizontal.

α. **1840** J. T. HEWLETT *P. Priggins* ii, I took particular care to slew the buttons at the knees well forward in a slanting-dicular direction. **1868** *Hurst Johnian Mag.* Feb. 341 Put your arm quite straight at an angle of about 45° with your body, (that is in a 'slantingdicular' direction).

β. **1832** *Mem. of Nullifier* iv. 37 This is sorter a slantindickelar road, stranger. **1835** P. H. NICKLIN *Lett. Descr. Virginia Springs* 30 [He] makes his bivouac among the trees..under a slantindicular shed. **1855** SMEDLEY *H. Coverdale* liv, Jumping off the ground all four feet at once in a slantindicular direction.

*fig. c* **1863** *U.S. Newspaper* in Bright *Sp.* (1868) II. 239 He walked uprightly *before the world*, but when he was *not* before the world his walk was slantindicular. **1872** DE MORGAN *Budget of Paradoxes* 289 And he must not put himself [in the calendar] under the first saint with a slantendicular reference to the other.

**b.** As *sb.*, with *the.*

**1843** MRS. ROMER *Rhone, Darro,* etc. II. 305 What the Doctor termed 'the slantingdicular' of our position obliged me to be secured in my place by a rope.

**B.** *adv.* = next.

**1831** *Daily Louisville Public Advertiser* 17 Oct. 2/3 He looked up at me slantindicler [*sic*], and I looked down on him slantindiclar. **1866** BUCKLAND *Curios. Nat. Hist.* Ser. III. I. 73 They [ducks] open their web feet, come down, as the Yankees say, 'slantindicular'. **1873** C. H. SMITH *Bill Arp's Peace Papers* xxx. 202 If we could have slid into it quietly and slantendikular, if slavery could have sorter tapered out and freedom sorter tapered in, everybody could have got used to it.

**slantin'dicularly,** *adv.* [See prec.] In a slanting or sloping direction or position; obliquely. Also *fig.*, indirectly.

α. **1839** MARRYAT *Diary Amer.* Ser. I. I. 110 Others mounting slantingdicularly and Paul-Prying into the bedroom windows. **1869** *Eng. Mech.* 19 Nov. 230/1 He sits *slantingdicularly*, as he does on the..bicycle. **1880** 'WILDFOWLER' *Mod. Wildfowling* 66 The shoulder guns were resting 'slantingdicularly'.

β. **1834** DE QUINCEY in *Tait's Mag.* I. 86 For..a sunrise and a sunset, ought to be seen from the valley or horizontally,—not, as the man of Kentuck expressed it, slantindicularly. **1844** DICKENS *Mart. Chuz.* xxi, Glancing —however slantin'dicularly—at the subject in hand, I would say [etc.]. **1884** *Punch* 22 Nov. 245/2 Some 'gees'..Who go slantindicularly down the street.

**'slanting,** *vbl. sb.* [f. SLANT *v.* + -ING[1].] The action of the verb; in quot. *a* 1618 = PERSPECTIVE *sb.* 3.

*a* **1618** RALEIGH *Rem.* (1644) 136 Painted Tables (in which the art of Slanting is used) appear to the Eye, as if the parts of them were some higher, and some lower than the other. **1959** *Times* 15 May 6/7 It is still an even chance that any University production of [Shakespeare's plays] one samples will not be heavily flavoured with gimmickry or slanting. **1980** M. MCMULLEN *My Cousin Death* (1981) 7 Not a gentle ..rain..but an ill-natured heavy slanting from the northeast.

**'slanting,** *adv.* and *ppl. a.* [f. SLANT *v.* + -ING[2].]

**A.** *adv.* In a sloping direction; slantingly.

*a* **1625** *Nomencl. Navalis* (Harl. MS. 2301), *Skegg*, is that parte of the keele, which is cut slanting [etc.]. **1664** EVELYN *Kal. Hort.* (1729) 190 Cut off slanting above the Bud, with a very sharp knife. **1893** HODGES *Elem. Photogr.* 33 A thin nail driven slanting through the support..will make the framework quite firm.

**B.** *ppl. a.* That slants or slopes; lying, situated, or directed, obliquely.

**1688** MIÉGE *Gt. Fr. Dict.* II, To give a slanting blow. **1760–72** H. BROOKE *Fool of Qual.* (1809) III. 63 Hills, some of which were slanting, some headlong and impending. **1797–1805** S. & HT. LEE *Canterb. T.* I. 353 The returning sun now shot a bright and slanting ray. **1807** G. CHALMERS *Caledonia* I. II. ii. 240 It continues a south-east course, in a slaunting form, across Allan-water. **1859** REEVE *Brittany* 75 The slanting dilapidated roof of the chancel. **1876** M. FOSTER *Physiol.* II. ii. (1879) 302 All the ribs have a downward slanting direction.

**b.** *Needlework.* (See quots.)

**1882** CAULFEILD & SAWARD *Dict. Needlwk.* 32/1 *Slanting Gobelin Stitch*, a name sometimes given to long or satin stitch. *Ibid.* 125/1 *Slanting Stitch*, a variety of Double Crochet.

**slantingdicular(ly:** see SLANTINDICULAR(LY.

**'slantingly,** *adv.* [f. SLANTING *ppl. a.* + -LY.] In a slanting direction or position; with a slope or inclination; aslant, obliquely.

**1570** BILLINGSLEY *Euclid* XII. prop. xvii. 380 Which it will the more aptly doo, if ye do abate slauntingly the contrary arasses of the slitt of it. **1683** SNAPE *Anat. Horse* II. viii. (1686) 85 The septum of a Hog's Heart slantingly pervious in several places with great..pores. **1708** BERKELEY *Commonpl. Bk.* Wks. 1871 IV. 489 The extension of a plain, look'd at straight and slantingly. **1786** ABERCROMBIE *Gard. Assist.* 184 Cut it slantingly, half way through up towards the next joint. **1817** KEATS '*Lo! I must tell a tale of chivalry*' 12 The lance points slantingly Athwart the morning air. **1866** G. MACDONALD *Ann. Q. Neighb.* xiii. (1878) 247 The afternoon sun as it shone slantingly through the stained window.

**b.** *fig.* Indirectly.

*a* **1677** BARROW *Pope's Supremacy* Wks. 1859 VIII. 9 It little mattereth, if he may strike princes, whether it be by a downright blow, or slantingly. **1694** STRYPE *Cranmer* I. xxvi. 111 Slantingly through their Sides, striking at the Arch-bishop himself.

**'slantingness.** *rare*[−0]. (See quot.)

**1727** BAILEY (vol. II), *Slopingness*, Slantingness, going diagonally.

**slantingways** (ˈslɑːntɪŋweɪz, -æ-), *adv. rare.* [f. SLANTING *ppl. a.* + -WAYS.] Slantwise. Cf. SLANTWAYS *adv.*

**1899** H. G. WELLS *When Sleeper Wakes* vi. 59 He walked slantingways across the room. **1916** —— *Mr. Britling* II. iv. 332 We were busy..pushing our trench out from an angle slantingways forward.

**†'slantling,** *adv. Obs.*[−1] In 6 sklantlynge. [f. SLANT *a.* + -LING[2].] Slantingly, obliquely.

**1521** FISHER *Serm. agst. Luther* Wks. (1876) 323 Whan a bowle is throwen sklantlynge vpon a wall it slydeth forwarde.

**'slantly,** *adv.* [f. SLANT *a.* + -LY[2].] Slantingly, obliquely.

**1727** BOYER *Dict. Royal* II, Slantingly, or slantly, *obliquement*. **1851** R. H. STODDARD *Serenade* Wks. (1880) 49 The yellow Moon looks slantly down, Through seaward mists, upon the town. **1876** LANIER *Poems, Clover* 105 Champs and chews, With slantly-churning jaws.

**slantways** (ˈslɑːntweɪz, -æ-), *adv.* [f. SLANT *a.* + -WAYS.] = next.

**1826** MISS MITFORD *Village* Ser. III. (1863) 497 A new street standing slant-ways to one of the entrances of the town. **1854** H. MILLER *Sch. & Schm.* (1858) 128 The two clouds..went rolling slantways on the wind towards the west. **1895** TRISTRAM *Japan* 19 The four main islands of Japan stretch slantways through sixteen degrees of latitude.

**slantwise** (ˈslɑːntwaɪz, -æ-), *adv.* and *a.* [f. SLANT *a.* + -WISE.]

**A.** *adv.* In a slanting or sloping direction or position; slantingly, obliquely.

**1573** TUSSER *Husb.* (1878) 98 Some maketh a hollownes, halfe a foote deepe, with fower sets in it, set slant wise a steepe. **1751** J. BARTRAM *Observ. Trav. Pennsylv.*, etc, 38 In the mean time we were setting poles slantwise in the ground. **1760–72** tr. *Juan & Ulloa's Voy.* (ed. 3) II. 333 Three streets, which run slantwise up the eminence. **1843** F. W. FABER *Lett.* (1869) 194, I think of..how the sun is coming slant-wise out of Langdale. **1882** J. HAWTHORNE *Fort. Fool* I. xvi, The waggon lying slantwise across the road.

*fig.* **1869** *Fortn. Rev.* June 637 When..they have an opportunity of looking slantwise at their own merits, and of praising themselves by implication.

**B.** *adj.* Slanting, oblique.

**1856** HAWTHORNE *Eng. Note-bks.* (1870) II. 129 From our windows we have a slantwise glimpse of the walls of St. John's College. **1858** WHITTIER *Telling the Bees* viii, The slantwise rain Of light through the leaves. **1891** MISS DOWIE *Girl in Karp.* 101 Its slantwise band across the chest.

**slap** (slæp), *sb.*[1] [a. LG. *slapp* (also *slappe*; G. *schlapp* and *schlappe*), of imitative origin: cf. SLAP *adv.* Older Da. *slap* is also from LG.]

The apparent instances in *Arthur & Merlin* (1838) 8084, *Pallad. on Husb.* (1873) IV. 763, Palsgr. 563, and Milton *Colasterion*, are errors for *flap*: see FLAP *sb.* 1 and 1 b.

**1. a.** A smart blow, esp. one given with the open hand, or with something having a flat surface; a smack; an impact of this nature. ***slap on the back*** (or ***shoulder***): as a hearty gesture of friendship or congratulation. Also *fig.* Cf. BACK-SLAPPING *ppl. a.* and *vbl. sb.*

**1648** HEXHAM II, *Flabbe*, a Slash, or a Slap with a sword on the face. **1709** STEELE *Tatler* No. 45 ¶7 One..got behind me in the Interim, and hit me a sound Slap on the Back. **1726–46** THOMSON *Winter* 627 The leap, the slap, the haul. **1767** BICKERSTAFFE *Love in the City* I. ii, If we had not been in church, I would have hit her a slap in the face. **1820** W. IRVING *Sketch Bk.* VI. 94 His hospitable attentions were brief, but expressive, being confined to a shake of the hand, a slap on the shoulder..and a pressing invitation to 'reach to, and help themselves'. **1831** SCOTT *Cast. Dang.* xviii, Not believing, that the knowledge..can be at once conferred by the slap of the flat of a sword. *c* **1850** *Arab. Nts.* (Rtldg.) 294 She seized her nurse's head, and gave her repeated slaps and blows. **1863** G. MEREDITH *Let.* 19 Feb. (1970) I. 193 Did you say in it you are sorry for your virulent offensive letter that I received?.. If so, a slap on the back and we're friends again. **1882** B. D. W. RAMSAY *Rough Recoll.* I. ix. 216, I felt a slap on my back which nearly sent me down the companion-ladder. **1883** STEVENSON *Treasure Isl.* viii. 62 He seemed in the most cheerful spirits..with a merry word or a slap on the shoulder for the most favoured of his guests. **1929** L. MACNEICE *Blind Fireworks* 5 There are lines which may, by the incautious, be (wrongly) read in a merry slap-on-the-back fashion.

**b.** A cut or stroke *of* something. *rare*$^{-1}$.

**1688** HOLME *Armoury* III. xxi. (Roxb.) 267/1 They can cutt through many wyers together at one slap of the sheares.

**c.** ***at a slap***, all at once.

**1753** *Gray's Inn Jrnl.* No. 59, Loosing Ten Thousand Pounds at a Slap. **1820** *Blackw. Mag.* VII. 676 But we are losing our time in describing, Here at a slap we throw the whole tribe in.

**d.** A gust *of* wind.

**1890** CLARK RUSSELL *Marriage at Sea* v, A slap of wind carried pretty nigh half the mast over the side.

**e.** ***slap and tickle***: (a bout of) light amorous play.

**1928** E. ROBERTSON *Cullum* ix. 178 She gave me a playful push... She was one of the dreadful type that Cullum called 'slap-and-tickle' girls. **1936** N. COWARD *To-Night at 8.30* 77 She won't [come back]—she's out having a bit of slap and tickle with our Albert. **1958** 'N. SHUTE' *Rainbow & Rose* vi. 243 When I want a bit of slap and tickle I'll arrange it for myself, thank you. **1977** C. MCCULLOUGH *Thorn Birds* x. 236 He'd woo her the way she obviously wanted, flowers and attention and not too much slap-and-tickle.

**f.** *Mech.* = *piston slap* s.v. PISTON *sb.* 4.

**1930** *Engineering* 7 Mar. 304/1 Large engines..used,.. until recently,..cast-iron pistons. This is because of required durability..and because of expansion troubles—slap, leakage, &c.

**2.** *transf.* **a.** A reprimand, reproof; a spoken or written attack or censure; a side-hit. Esp. in phrs. ***a slap in*** (or †***on***) ***the face, in the eye, on the wrist.***

**1736** DUCHESS OF MARLBOROUGH *Opin.* in *Corresp.* (1838) II. 207, I could easily forgive him [Swift] all the slaps he has given me and the Duke of Marlborough. **1791** BURKE *Corr.* (1844) III. 30 You see on what topics they chose to magnify him [Foxe] at York. It is a slap at me. **1853** DARWIN in *Life & Lett.* (1887) II. 41, I much enjoyed the slaps you have given to the provincial species-monger. **1861** T. A. TROLLOPE *La Beata* II. 135 [He] could not help feeling severely the very vigorous slap on the face which had been administered to him. **1895** LLOYD GEORGE *Let.* 3 June (1973) 85 So there's another slap in the eye for the Bryn party. **1898** G. B. SHAW *Philanderer* I. 96 I'll have to apologize for her... Her going away is a downright slap in the face for these people. **1914** *Dialect Notes* IV. 112 *Slap on the wrist*, mild rebuke or criticism. **1920** D. H. LAWRENCE *Touch & Go* 5 How much will you give me for my syllogism? Not a slap in the eye, I hope. **1932** L. GOLDING *Magnolia Street* II. iii. 308 The Great War was..a slap in the face, quite simply. **1966** *Economist* 26 Feb. 801/1 The Administration has been trying to choke off North Vietnam's supplies for some time... The latest move—a 'slap on the wrist', according to the dockers—has been to blacklist ships which visit Haiphong. **1970** P. CARLON *Death by Demonstration* vi. 73 All she said was, 'I don't want to talk about it.' That was as good as a slap in the eye. **1977** *Rolling Stone* 7 Apr. 17/3 We think we can get Anita off with a fine and a slap on the wrist, but the thing with Keith is much more serious. **1979** *Guardian* 17 Jan. 1/4 Industry will regard action to tighten price control..as a slap in the face.

**b.** An attempt, venture, go, *at* something.

**1840** A. BUNN *Stage before & behind Curtain* III. 38 Enabled me to have a slap at the pretenders. **1855** SMEDLEY *H. Coverdale* i. 5 We mean to have a slap at the rabbits. **1884** 'H. COLLINGWOOD' *Under Meteor Flag* 270 Come, lads!.. take another slap at them; we must get on deck somehow. **1890** 'R. BOLDREWOOD' *Col. Reformer* (1891) 417 He dashed off to Adelaide for a slap at copper.

**c.** A quick trip or dash.

**1901** P. FOUNTAIN *Deserts N. Amer.* ix. 163, I..collected the wherewithal for another slap across country.

**slap**, *sb.*² *Sc.* Also 5–7 slop, 5–6 slope. [a. MDu. or MLG. *slop*: cf. Du. and LG. *slop*, LG. *slup(p*, MG. *slupf*, G. *schlupf* (dial. *schluff*, *schloff*), opening, gap, narrow passage, hiding-place, etc. The change of *o* into *a* before *p* is normal in Sc.; cf. *drap* drop, *tap* top, etc.]

It is possible that *slope* and *sloppes* in the alliterative *Morte Arthure* 2977 and 3923 belong to this word, but in neither passage is the sense quite clear.

**1.** A breach, opening, or gap in a wall, fence, hedge, etc.

α. **1375** BARBOUR *Bruce* VIII. 179 Bot sloppis in the vay left he, So large, and of sic quantite, That fyffe hundir mycht sammyn ryde In at the sloppis, syde for syde. *c* **1425** WYNTOUN *Chron.* V. xi. 3256 þan þar fais..Sloppis in syndry placis made. **1513** DOUGLAS *Æneid* II. viii. 77 He.. throw the ȝet ane large wyndo mackis; By the quhilk slop the place within apperis. **1549** *Compl. Scot.* xvi. 140 Lyik.. scheip that vil nocht pas throucht the slop of ane dyik.

β. *a* **1575** *Diurn. Occurr.* (Bann. Cl.) 264 [They] dischargit the said cannone oft tymes thairat and maid greit slappis in the wall. **1629** *Orkney Witch Trial* in *County Folk-Lore* III. (1903) 110 Quhen he was cuming to Birssay with hir out of the slap. **1686** *Records of Elgin* (New Spald. Cl.) I. 339 Throwing down ane slap in the Trinity Churchyard dyke lately builded up be the magistrats. **1762** BP. FORBES *Jrnl.* (1886) 241 Here you see a Slap, then a Stone hanging over, as portending its Speedy Fall. **1783** BURNS *Poor Mailie* 37 To slink thro' slaps, an' reave an' steal, At stacks o' pease. **1815** SCOTT *Guy M.* i, His guide..then broke down a *slap*, as he called it, in a dry-stone fence. **1875** W. MCILWRAITH *Guide Wigtownshire* 140 Slaps in the dykes admit easy ingress and egress.

**b.** An opening or passage left in a salmon-cruive from Saturday evening to Monday morning, in order to allow the fish to pass; the period during which this is left open; the weekly close time for salmon. Freq. in ***Saturday('s) slap***.

**1424** *Scott. Acts* (1814) II. 5 þai þat has crufis in fresche watteris þat þai ger keip þe lawis anentis þe setterday slop, and suffer þaim nocht to stande in forbodyne tyme. **1597** SKENE *De Verb. Sign.* S ij, The Setter-dayis slop, is ane space of time, within the quhilk it is nocht leasum to take Salmonde fish. **1622** MALYNES *Anc. Law-Merch.* 246 And albeit some are permitted to lays nets, and to make weares, yet must he keep the Saturdaies slop, that is, to lift the same from Saturday in the afternoone vntill Monday. **1851** G. H. KINGSLEY *Sp. & Trav.* (1900) 275 On Sunday afternoon, when the 'Slaps' are open. **1876** MAXWELL in Francis *Angling* x. (ed. 4) 349 The Luce is terribly netted; the fish slaps are sometimes built up. **1900** *Westm. Gaz.* 7 Aug. 2/1, 'I should like to have your opinion on the weekly close time.' 'The "Saturday slap", I suppose you mean.'

**c.** ? A break in the clouds; a patch of sky.

**1508** DUNBAR *Golden Targe* 26 The purpur hevyn our scailit in silvir sloppis Ourgilt the treis.

**d.** A narrow pass between hills or mountains.

**1715** PENNECUIK *Tweeddale* 10 The Water of Line hath its first Spring near the Coldstaine Slap. **1721** RAMSAY *Ode to the Ph——* i, O'er ilka cleugh, ilk scar and slap. **1897** CROCKETT *Lads' Love* xiv, They passed through the 'buchts' and 'slaps' of the Galloway hills.

**2.** *transf.* A breach in, or way *through*, a body of troops; a gap *in* the ranks.

*c* **1470** HENRY *Wallace* IX. 949 Sloppys thai maid throu all that chewalry, The worthy Scottis thai wrocht so worthely. *Ibid.* X. 310 A slop thai maid, quhar thai set on a syd. **1533** BELLENDEN *Livy* II. xxi. (S.T.S.) I. 218 Be force of al þare bodyis and wapynnys..þai made ane slop throw þare Inemyis. **1867** A. DAWSON *Rambling Recoll.* (1868) 38 These triumphs made many slaps in the ranks of the regiment.

†**3.** A gash or wound. *Obs. rare.*

*c* **1375** *Sc. Leg. Saints* Prol. 72 Longius..mad ȝet þare in cristis syd a slope, þat ves bath lang & vyd. *Ibid.* xlv. (*Christine*) 300 With ane arrow in hire syd he mad a slope.

†**slap**, *sb.*³ *Obs.*$^{-1}$ [f. SLAP *v.*³] A single act of lapping or licking up; a lap.

**1589** R. HARVEY *Pl. Perc.* 3 As for my spoons, those I brought, that I..might haue one slap at the Spoone meat.

†**slap**, *sb.*⁴ *Obs.* App. a var. of SLOP *sb.*

**1600** BRETON *Pasquil's Fooles Cap* lxxxiv. D iij b, Hee that puts fifteene elles into a Ruffe And seauenteene yards into a swagg'ring slappe. **1605** —— *Olde Man's Lesson* C iv, A thousand times more contentiue, then to buye it in a Shoppe, and to weare it in Slappe.

†**slap**, *sb.*⁵ (Origin and meaning uncertain.)

**1648** GAGE *West Ind.* xv. 99 Under which [market] the poore Indian wives meet at five a clock at evening to sell what slap and drugges they can prepare most cheape for the empty Criolian stomackes.

**slap**, *sb.*⁶ *Sc.* [Of obscure origin. Jamieson also gives *slap* as a vb. 'to separate grain', etc.] 'A riddle for separating grain from the broken straw, &c.' (Jam. 1808). Also *slap-riddle*.

**1844** H. STEPHENS *Bk. Farm* II. 271 The rougher part that is left in the slap-riddle is..passed again through the mill. *Ibid.* 333 The slap-riddles are $\frac{3}{4}$ inch, and 1 inch in the meshes.

**slap**, *sb.*⁷ *Coalmining.* Slack. Also *attrib.*

**1865** *Morning Star* 27 Feb., While one [coal-waggon] was being lowered by the machinery so that it might be brought near the slap-heap. **1883** in GRESLEY *Gloss. Coal-m.* 225.

**slap**, dial. form of SLOP *sb.* and *v.*

**slap** (slæp), *v.*¹ [f. SLAP *adv.* or *sb.*¹]

**1. a.** *trans.* To strike or smack (a person or thing) smartly, esp. with the open hand or with something having a flat surface; to hit (one) *on*, *upon*, or *over* (a certain part) in this way. Also ***to slap*** (someone) ***on the back***: to clap (someone) on the back as a gesture of goodwill or congratulation; to treat in a hearty or jovial manner.

**1632** SHERWOOD, To slappe, *frapper. Voyez* to flap. **1676** WYCHERLEY *Pl. Dealer* III. i, I should hate, man, to have my father's wife kissed and slapped..by another man. **1690** CROWNE *Eng. Friar* 111, Must I be slap'd over the lips by every fellow? **1747** RELPH *Poems* Gloss., *To slap*, to beat. **1766** GOLDSM. *Vic. W.* xxvi, He slapped his forehead as if he had hit upon something material. **1829** LYTTON *Devereux* I. ii, Sir William slapped the calf of the leg he was caressing. **1852** MRS. STOWE *Uncle Tom's C.* xxix. 271, I was trying on Miss Marie's dress, and she slapped my face. **1887** SIR R. H. ROBERTS *In the Shires* viii. 135 He slapped the palm of her hand very vigorously. **1908** E. M. FORSTER *Room with View* x. 173, I said, 'Hooray, old boy!' and slapped him on the back. **1914** A. C. BENSON *Jrnl.* in D. Newsome *On Edge of Paradise* (1980) x. 320 M. F. was always the sort of man who slapped everyone on the back. **1931** R. CAMPBELL *Georgiad* iii. 54 Nicolson who in his weekly crack Will slap the meanest scribbler on the back. **1941** 'R. WEST' *Black Lamb & Grey Falcon* I. 496 The stocky little men were..lifting their glasses to him and slapping him on the back.

*refl.* **1836** W. IRVING *Astoria* III. 45 The gigantic chief.. slapping himself upon the breast, gave Mr. Crooks to understand [etc.].

**b.** To drive *back*, beat *down*, knock *to* the ground, etc., with a slap.

**1819** TENNANT *Papistry Stormed* (1827) 17 Fun at the door-stane stands, And slaps him [Care] back wi' baith his hands. **1842** LOVER *Handy Andy* li, Oonah slapped down the hand that barred her progress. **1889** GUNTER *That Frenchman!* ix, Louise is coming to-night to see me slap the masked fellow to the dust.

**c.** *techn.* To work (clay) in a certain manner: (see SLAPPING *vbl. sb.* b).

**1786** WEDGWOOD in *Phil. Trans.* LXXVI. 397 What we call handing or slapping the clay, an operation by which its different parts are intermixed, and the mass rendered of an uniform temper throughout. **1839** URE *Dict. Arts* 577 The clay is made into lumps, is equalized, and slapped much in the same way as for making Pottery.

**d.** *U.S. slang.* To play (a double-bass) without a bow in jazz style, *spec.* to pull the strings so as to let them snap back on to the fingerboard.

**1933** [see DOG-HOUSE 2 b]. **1935** *Swing Music* June 83/1 The lyric, which was a masterpiece of fatuity.., had to do with the vogue of 'picking and slapping' the double bass. **1958** *Times Lit. Suppl.* 11 Apr. (Children's Literature Suppl.) p. iii/3 He takes up the violin, viola and cello, but happily stays just the right size for the double-bass, which he 'slaps' with such proficiency that he ends up in a famous jazz orchestra.

**2.** To write or jot *down* quickly or smartly.

**1672** VILLIERS (Dk. Buckhm.) *Rehearsal* I. i, But as soon as any one speaks, pop I slap it down, and make that, too, my own. **1673** [R. LEIGH] *Transp. Reh.* 37 Pop, he slaps them down. **1884** 'MARK TWAIN' *Huck. Finn* xvii. 158 She could rattle off poetry like nothing... She would slap down a line, and if she couldn't find anything to rhyme with it she would just scratch it out and slap down another one.

**3. a.** To strike, bring down (one's hand, etc.) *on* or *upon* something with a slap; to clap (the hands) *together*.

**1717** PRIOR *Alma* I. 346 Dick..Then slapp'd his Hand upon the Board. **1791** MME. D'ARBLAY *Diary* 4 June, The Duke slapped his hand violently on the table, and called out [etc.]. **1860** HOLLAND *Miss Gilbert's Career* xviii. 332 He suddenly slapped his hand upon his forehead. **1885** *Manch. Exam.* 10 July 5/5 The Chancellor of the Exchequer slapped his palms together.

**b.** To put or place *on* or *into*, to fling or throw *down*, etc., with a slap or clap.

**1836** MARRYAT *Midship. Easy* xiii, The grating was slapped on again by Jack. **1847** ALB. SMITH *Chr. Tadpole* vii. (1879) 65 Long planks were drawn from waggons and slapped down on one another. **1898** G. B. SHAW *Plays* II. *Man of Destiny* 161 He slaps the cloth on the table and deftly rolls it up.

*fig.* **1839–40** W. IRVING *Wolfert's R., Mountjoy* (1855) 63 The moment I make my appearance in the world, a little girl slaps Italian in my face. **1922** *Collier's* 1 July 26/1 Judge Tuckerman..slapped on the fines and costs with a lavish hand. **1924** E. M. FORSTER *Passage to India* vii. 61 The College itself had been slapped down by the Public Works Department, but its grounds included an ancient garden. **1968** J. WAINWRIGHT *Web of Silence* 12 A 'D Notice' gets slapped on the inquiry... The newspapers are gagged from the word 'go'. **1976** *Milton Keynes Express* 23 July 38/5 The Berks and Bucks FA have slapped a severe six-week ban on Hurrell following his sending off in a charity match.

**c.** To place, put, or set (one's hat) *over* the face, etc. so that it lops down or overhangs; to jam *down* firmly. ? *Obs.*

**1782** MISS BURNEY *Cecilia* IX. ii, [He] slapped his hat over his face. **1796** —— *Camilla* II. 168 Lionel slapped his hat over his eyes. **1801** CHARLOTTE SMITH *Lett. Solit. Wand.* I. 162 His hat was slapped quite down, as if to keep it from being carried away by the wind.

**4.** To shut (a door, gate, etc.) sharply or with a slap. Also with *to*.

**1708** MRS. CENTLIVRE *Busie Body* IV. ii. *Sir Jeal.* There, go, and come no more within sight of my Habitation... (Slaps the Door after her.) **1762** *Ann. Reg.*, *Chron.* 133/1 The daughter..slapped to the door. **1818** SCOTT *Rob Roy* xxiv, I..contented myself with slapping the door of my bedroom in his face. **1847** C. BRONTE *J. Eyre* v, The door was slapped to,..and on we drove.

**5.** *intr.* Of a door, etc.: To slam. *rare.*

**1796** *Black Giles* (Cheap Reposit. Tracts) 4 They are very apt to let the gate slap full against you, before you are half way through. *a* **1882** ROSSETTI *Ballad of J. Van Hunks* i, You might hear the hall-door slap.

**6.** Of waves, water, etc.: To beat or strike *on* or *against* something with a slapping sound.

**1840** MARRYAT *Poor Jack* xxii, We could..hear the water slapping against the bends. **1883** SYMONDS *Ital. Byways* v. 86 The sea slapped and broke..on our windward quarter. **1897** FLANDRAU *Harvard Episodes* 169 The fellows could hear the rain slapping in gusts against the window-panes.

**7.** To move or walk quickly; to go *along* in this manner. *dial.* or *colloq.* Also *poet.*

**1827** *Mirror* II. 36/2 Always slap along at a desperate rate through the streets. **1828–** in *Eng. Dial. Dict.* (Yorks., Lancs., Northants.). **1966** S. HEANEY *Death of Naturalist* 57 And one Was scaresome for there, out of ferns and tall Foxgloves, a rat slapped across my reflection.

**8.** To strike or fire *at* a person. Also *trans.*, to throw (in quot. *fig.*)

**1842** LOVER *Handy Andy* ii, I'll keep no terms with him; —I'll slap at him directly, what can you do that's wickedest? *Ibid.* iii, Slap at him, Morty, my boy, the minute you get the word, and if you don't hit him itself, it will prevent him dwelling on his aim. **1957** [see *prisoner's dilemma* s.v. PRISONER² 1 b].

**9.** *trans.* To punish (someone) *with* a penalty, sentence, etc. *N. Amer.*

**1968** *Globe & Mail* (Toronto) 13 Jan. 37/2 Late in the contest coach John Petrushchak and centre Bruno Marcocchio were slapped with technical fouls for disagreeing with the referees. **1972** *Newsweek* 10 Jan. 17/3 For his indiscretion, he is slapped with a stiff $17,000 fine. **1973** *Tucson* (Arizona) *Daily Citizen* 22 Aug. 4/1 Two young stepbrothers involved in a drug-crime.. were slapped with five years partial probation.

**10.** In *fig.* phrs. ***to slap*** (a person or thing) ***down***: to snub, suppress, or rebuke; ***to slap*** (a person's) ***wrist***: to scold or reprimand; ***to slap*** (a person's) ***face***: to administer a sharp reproof or rebuff.

**1938** 'E. Queen' *Four of Hearts* xi. 153 She's been.. leading me on just so she could turn around and slap me down. **1949** L. A. G. Strong *Maud Cherrill* 40 Any hint of affectation or pretentiousness she would have slapped down hard. **1960** 'E. McBain' *See them Die* xvi. 209 You're God, and there isn't anyone who's going to slap your wrist, no matter how you do it. **1973** *Times* 13 Aug. 4/2 Sales of this have gone up in recent years and we cannot think that the Government is going to slap the face of a very large number of users to save a little money. *Ibid.* 17 Oct. 20/3 The police sergeant who conducted the prosecutions was often slapped down by the clerk of the court for leading his witnesses. **1977** E. Ambler *Send no More Roses* iii. 53 Thinking that he was about to deliver the admonition, I let him go ahead. He didn't even slap her wrist. **1978** *Lancashire Life* July 63/2 His seniors might well have felt he was a publicity-seeker who needed slapping-down.

**11.** *Comb.* **slap-bass**, a double-bass played in jazz style (see quot. 1956); **slap-you-on-the-back** *attrib. phr.*, hearty, jovial.

**1949** *Sun* (Baltimore) 22 Jan. 6/3 The *slap-bass virtuoso who accidentally kicks a hole in his instrument in the middle of a jam session. **1956** S. Traill *Play that Music* iv. 46 This was the era of the slap bass: so called because the strings were pulled away from the fingerboard of the bass and.. let smartly back to the fingerboard—thereby making a loud clicking sound. **1932** B. Worsley-Gough *Public Affairs* x. 182 'Lord,' said Venetia, 'I had forgotten the Bishop. What is he like?' 'Jovial. Jolly. *Slap-you-on-the-back-for-tuppence.' **1957** *Times Lit. Suppl.* 22 Nov. 708/4 Mr Matthews has a jolly, slap-you-on-the-back approach. **1962** *Listener* 28 June 1114/2 Newbolt himself was no hearty, bluff, slap-you-on-the-back sort of man.

**slap**, *v.*[2] *Sc.* Also 6 slop. [f. slap *sb.*[2]]

**1.** *trans.* To make gaps or breaches in (a wall, etc.).

**1513** Douglas *Æneid* ix. viii. 110 The Volscenaris assemblit in a sop, To fyll the fowseis and the wallis to slop. *a* **1575** *Diurn. Occurr.* (Bann. Cl.) 211 The men of weare.. slappit all the pendis of the kirk, for keiping thairof aganis my lord regent. **1767** in Cramond *Ann. Cullen* (1888) 106 The wall is slapt to make a slit to give air to the criminal prison. **1805** *State Fraser of Fraserfield* 216 (Jam.), The remains of an old dyke or bulwark, much slapped and broken.

†**2.** *transf.* To make breaks or breaches in (a body of troops). *Obs.*

**1513** Douglas *Æneid* x. viii. 6 The quhilk Turnus.. The myd routis went sloppand heir and thair. **1533** Bellenden *Livy* i. xv. (S.T.S.) I. 86 þai nocht alanerlie dang and sloppit þe Sabynis legiounis, bot als put þame to flicht.

**slap**, *v.*[3] Now *dial.* [ad. LG. *slappen* (G. *schlappen*) in the same sense.]

**1.** *intr.* To lap.

**1603** Holland *Plutarch's Mor.* i. 4 The other [dog] ranne straight to slap in the platter.

**2.** *trans.* To lap or gobble *up*.

**1608** H. Clapham *Errour Right Hand* 19 They haue slapt vp his Vomite. **1637** Heywood *Pleas. Dial.* iv. Wks. 1874 VI. 191 With his long finger having scrap'd the dish, And slapt up all the sauce of flesh or fish. **1828** Carr *Craven Gloss.* s.v., 'To slap up,' to swallow greedily, to dispatch a meal. *Ibid.*, He slapt up his porridge in a trice.

**slap** (slæp), *adv. colloq.* [ad. LG. *slapp* (G. *schlapp*), of imitative origin.]

**1.** With, or as with, a slap or smart quick blow; quickly, suddenly, without warning or notice: **a.** In general use (frequently parenthetic); also with *off*, *down*.

**1672** Villiers (Dk. Buckhm.) *Rehearsal* iii. i, First one speaks, then presently t'others upon him slap, with a Repartee. **1706** Vanbrugh *Mistake* iii, You han't been married eight-and-forty hours, and you are slap—at your husband's beard already. **1733** Fielding *Quix. in Eng.* ii. iv, There is no laying down anything eatable, but if you turn your back, slap, he has it up. **1736** —— *Pasquin* i., I defy you to guess my couple till the thing is done, slap, all at once. **1852** Reade *Peg Woff.* (1889) 123 Let us be serious and finish this comedy slap off. **1865** Dickens *Mut. Fr.* iii. xiii, 'The money must be paid.' 'In full and slap down, do you mean?' asked Fledgeby.

**b.** With *come*, *go*, *run*, etc.

In later use freq. implying sense 2.

**1676** Etheredge *Man of Mode* iv. ii, Slap down goes the glass, and thus we are at it. **1713** Arbuthnot *John Bull* ii. v, If they offered to come into the warehouse, then strait went the yard slap over their noddle. *a* **1766** Mrs. F. Sheridan *Sidney Bidulph* IV. 10 You were but twelve hours in my house,.. when slap comes down an express to hurry you away. **1831** Trelawny *Adv. Younger Son* II. 280, I was determined to run slap ashore. **1890** 'R. Boldrewood' *Col. Reformer* (1891) 259, I'm blessed if I didn't ride slap into that drain. **1894** Astley *Fifty Yrs. Life* I. 226 A ball had passed slap through his body.

**c.** With verbs denoting violent impact.

**1825** Westmacott *Eng. Spy* I. 291 Let fly.. slap at my smeller. **1851** Hawthorne *Twice-told T.* I. vii. 140 A ball, of the consistence of hasty pudding, hit him slap in the mouth. **1861** G. Meredith *Evan Harrington* xli, Andrew pushed through the doorway, and.. delivered a punch slap into Old Tom's belt.

**2.** Directly; straight.

**1829** Marryat *F. Mildmay* iv, I, and my Noah's Ark, lay slap in the way. *a* **1845** Barham *Ingol. Leg.* Ser. iii. *The House-Warming* ii, The shaft.. ne'er glanced from a limb Of a tree.., but was aimed slap at him. **1852** Dickens *Bleak Ho.* x, A turnstile leading slap away into the meadows. **1889** 'R. Boldrewood' *Robbery under Arms* xxv, We walked slap down to the hotel.

**slap**, *a. slang.* Ellipt. for slap-up.

**1840** H. Cockton *Valentine Vox* xiv. 108 But it's a werry nice place; werry private and genteel. None o' your public 'uns!—everything slap and respectable! **1851** Mayhew *Lond. Lab.* II. 107/1 People's got proud now,.. and must have everything slap.

**'slap-back.** *U.S.* Also slapback. [f. slap *v.*[1] + back *adv.*] A counter-attack, retaliation.

**1931** *Sun* (Baltimore) 31 Mar. 10/7 The working of Canada's tariff slap-back against our beloved Smoot-Hawley law. **1941** *New Yorker* 27 Dec. 37/1 A resounding Allied slapback at the enemy in the Pacific.

**slap-bang**, *adv.*, *a.*, and *sb.* Also slap bang. [f. slap *adv.* + bang *v.* 8.]

**A.** *adv.* With, or as with, a slap and a bang; without delay, immediately; without due consideration or regard to the consequences. Also of position: directly or precisely (*in the* centre); completely, absolutely. Cf. bang *adv.* a.

**1785** [see B. 1 a]. **1829** Brockett *N.C. Gloss.* (ed. 2), *Slap-bang*, violently, headlong—slap-dash. **1833** T. Hook *Parson's Dau.* i. vii, After fooling a man like a child in leading-strings for half a year, to let him go slap-bang, as I call it, in a minute, is an infernal shame. **1885** Rider Haggard *K. Solomon's Mines* (1889) 34 Over they went slap bang; whether they were China or woolen goods they met with the same treatment. **1963** A. Smith *Throw out Two Hands* xiv. 143 That gas was contentedly holding over three-quarters of a ton 1,500 feet above a lake and slap bang in the middle of the sky.

**B.** *adj.* † **1. a.** ***slap-bang shop***, an eating-house or cook-shop (see quot. 1785). *Obs.*

**1785** Grose *Dict. Vulgar T.*, *Slap-bang shop*, a petty cook's shop where there is no credit given, but what is had must be paid down with the ready slap-bang, i.e. immediately. This is a common appellation for a night cellar frequented by thieves, and sometimes for a stage coach or caravan. **1823** *Spirit Publ. Jrnls.* 83 So I *vauks* myself to a slap-bang shop, for half a pound o' beef. **1838** *New Monthly Mag.* LIV. 214 Cow-heel or hot alamode from the slap-bang shop.

† **b.** ***slap-bang coach*** (cf. prec., quot. 1785). *Obs.*

**1797** Mrs. M. Robinson *Walsingham* IV. 9, I invented the slap-bang coaches, and sported the tandem.

**2.** Marked or characterized by carelessness, heedlessness, or haste.

**1815** W. H. Ireland *Scribbleomania* 53 Still I dare this slap bang assertion dispute. **1873** *Routledge's Yng. Gentl. Mag.* Apr. 283/1 A bold 'slap-bang' method. **1878** Fr. A. Kemble *Rec. Girlhood* I. 98 The careless, slap-bang style in which overtures were performed.

**3.** = slap-up *a.* 1.

**1866** *Routledge's Every Boy's Ann.* 209 We don't intend to send you out in the tip-top, slap-bang, gentleman's-son style at first.

**C.** *sb.* **1.** A slap-bang shop.

**1836–7** Dickens *Sk. Boz* (1837) III. 36 They.. dined at the same slap-bang every day, and revelled in each other's company every night. **1860** Mayhew *Upper Rhine* iii. 106 Refreshments served with no more style than at what we term a 'slap-bang'. **1865** *Athenæum* No. 1950. 341/1 Cook-shops, or 'slap-bangs', as street-boys call such odorous places.

**2.** Some kind of liquor.

**1845** Disraeli *Sybil* (1863) 77 What shall I call for? glass of the Mowbray slap-bang? No better; the receipt has been in our family these fifty years.

**slap-dab**, *adv. N. Amer. dial.* and *colloq.* [f. slap *adv.* + dab *adv.*] = slap-bang *adv.* (see also quot. 1896). Cf. smack-dab *adv.*

**1886** *Turf, Field & Farm* XLII. 174/3 He was goin' that fas' he run slap-dab agin me afo' he seed me. **1896** *Dialect Notes* I. 399 *Slap-dab*.., violently or awkwardly. 'He rushed in slap-dab and broke things.' **1949** *Publ. Amer. Dial. Soc.* xi. 11 It jumped slap-dab in the middle. **1973** *Victorian* (Victoria, B.C.) 1 Aug. 1/1 It occurred slap dab in the middle of what is now Centennial Square.

**slap-dash**, *adv.*, *a.*, and *sb.* Also slap dash, slapdash. [f. slap *adv.* + dash *adv.*]

**A.** *adv.* With, or as with, a slap and a dash; in a hasty, sudden, or precipitate manner; *esp.* without much consideration, thought, ceremony, or care; hurriedly and carelessly.

**1679** Dryden *Limberham* iii. i, Down I put the notes slap-dash. **1693** Congreve *Old Bach.* iv. iv, Now am I slap dash down in the mouth, and have not one word to say! **1729** Byrom *Rem.* (1855) I. ii. 331 A way of printing letters or anything slap-dash. **1748** Richardson *Clarissa* (1811) III. xxvii. 167 These denunciations come so slap-dash upon one, so unceremoniously,.. that they overturn one! **1787** 'G. Gambado' *Acad. Horsem.* 42 He.. rode slap-dash at Gimcrack, hoping to effect it by a broadside. **1838** Macaulay in Trevelyan *Life & Lett.* (1883) II. 37, I cannot plunge, slap dash, into the middle of events and characters. **1871** Carlyle in *Mrs. Carlyle's Lett.* II. 40 Record of the tour, written slapdash after my return.

**B.** *adj.* **1.** Marked or characterized by haste, carelessness, or want of due preparation or consideration; done, performed, etc. in a dashing and haphazard manner or style.

*c* **1792** Milner in Sidney *Rowland Hill* (1834) 96 'Tis this slap-dash preaching.. that does all the good. **1833** T. Hook *Parson's Dau.* i. xi, The Yahoos, who invariably couple noise with smartness, had, in their slap-dash manner, arranged the table and placed the chairs for the guests. **1862** Grattan *Beaten Paths* II. 70 The slapdash mass of censure, sarcasm, philosophy, and fiction contained in those remarkable pages. **1883** F. M. Peard *Contrad.* xiii, I thought it rather a mad proceeding.. to come off in this slap-dash fashion.

**2.** Of persons: Given to acting in this way.

**1833** M. Scott *Tom Cringle* xii, You right hearted but thoughtless slapdash vagabond. **1893** Jessopp *Stud. Recluse* v. 181 To study history.. is always.. abhorrent to men who belong to the slapdash classes.

**C.** *sb.* † **1.** Slapping, cuffing, or beating. *Obs.*$^{-1}$

**1712** Mrs. Centlivre *Perplexed Lovers* iii, Hark ye, Monsieur, if you don't march off I shall play you such an English Courant, of slap-dash, presently, that shan't out of your Ears this Twelvemonth.

**2. a.** Roughcast.

**1796** W. H. Marshall *W. Eng.* I. 330 *Slapdash*, rough-cast, or liquid coating of buildings. **1853** *Exeter Dioc. Archit. Soc.* IV. 166 Masons actually laying slapdash thickly on the exterior. **1886** *Cent. Mag.* July 423 The gray slap-dash is filled with red granite pebbles.

**b.** *north. dial.* (See quot.)

**1825** Brockett *N.C. Gloss.*, *Slab*, or *Slap-dash*, a cheap mode of colouring rooms [**1829** by dashing them with a brush], in imitation of paper.

**3. a.** Carelessness, roughness, or want of finish in style or workmanship; writing or work done in this style.

**1826** *Examiner* 73/1 We are to be flabbergasted for some time to come with slap-dash in support of the commercial wisdom of our ancestors. **1876** W. White *Holid. in Tyrol* ix. 74 English folk are too fond of slap-dash in their writing. **1889** *Athenæum* 2 Feb. 146/3 As a specimen of newspaper 'slapdash' we may point to the description of General Ignatieff.

**b.** With reference to painting: (cf. 2).

**1884** *Athenæum* 6 Dec. 739/2 The energetic slap-dash of the landscape and sky. **1886** *Ibid.* 14 Aug. 215/3 Curing our water-colourists of the too prevalent tendency to mere slap-dash as the only way of expressing strength.

**4.** *north. dial.* (See quot.)

**1828** Carr *Craven Gloss.*, *Slapdash*, a thoughtless, impetuous fellow.

Hence **'slap-dash** *v. intr.*, to write, work, etc. in a slap-dash or offhand manner or style; *trans.* (see quot. 1828). Also **slap'dashery**, (*rare*) **slapdasherie**; (in *nonce use*) **slap-'dashically** *adv.*; **slap'dashness**.

**1820** T. G. Wainewright *Ess. & Crit.* (1880) 99 'Come,' said he,.. with that, slap-dashing into the thickest of any question that started itself. **1828** Carr *Craven Gloss.*, *Slap-dash*, to rough-cast. 2. To colour rooms by dashing them with a brush. **1836** E. Howard *R. Reefer* lii, These latter friends of mine were, as our Transatlantic brethren say, pretty considerably, slap-dashically right. *a* **1871** De Morgan *Newton*, etc. (1885) 105 One of the most stinging warnings which a biographer had ever received against what I must call the slapdashery of assertion. **1872** *Dublin Rev.* April 380 Many novelists have taken the Crimean war for their theme;.. but they do not 'slapdash'. **1908** Kipling *Lett. of Travel* (1920) 144 Here and there the people are infected with the unworthy superstition of 'hustle', which means half-doing your appointed job and applauding your own slapdasherie for as long a time as would enable you to finish off two clean pieces of work. *a* **1913** F. Rolfe *Desire & Pursuit of Whole* (1934) vii. 60 That really huge romance.. which his friend.. wrote with such reprehensible slapdashery. **1929** *Daily Tel.* 15 Jan. 7 If he has the defects of his virtues—a certain slap-dashness visible enough in one or two of these stories—he has also the virtues of his defects. **1965** *Punch* 27 Jan. 146/2 By halfway I was finding the slapdashness of the overall pattern rather self-indulgent and the separate delights were suffering from this. **1966** *New Statesman* 14 Oct. 547/2 Sensibility and earthiness, obsession with detail and romantic slapdashery. **1982** *Times* 28 July 11/3 What it loses in slapdashery it gains in exuberance.

**slape** (sleɪp), *a. north. dial.* [a. ON. *sleip-r* (Icel. *sleipur*, Norw. *sleip*) slippery.]

**1.** Slippery; smooth. Also *fig.*, crafty, cunning, deceitful.

*c* **1460** *Towneley Myst.* ii. 414 Who so will do after me Full slape of thrift then shal he be. **1671** Skinner *Etymol. Angl.*, *Slape*, quod agro nostro Linc. lubricum & mollem signat. **1691** Ray *N.C. Words* (ed. 2), *Slape*, slippery. **1788** W. H. Marshall *Yorksh.* II. 353 *Slape*, slippery; as ice, or a dirty path. **1811–** in dial. glossaries (N. Cy., Linc., Notts.). **1835** *Blackw. Mag.* XXXVIII. 562 Doff it, and lo! the slape sconce of the Doctor. **1901** Marq. Lorne *V.R.I.* 48 The gardener warned her to be careful, as the ground was 'slape'.

**2.** Of ale: (see quots.).

**1671** in Skinner *Etymol. Angl.* [with Latin explanation, translated by Ray]. **1674** Ray *N.C. Words*, *Slape-ale*: Lincoln. Plain ale as opposed to Ale medicated with Wormwood or Scurvy-grass, or mixed with any other liquor. **1742** Gale in *Mem. W. Stukeley* (Surtees) I. 338 His old companions say they will in a little time bring him back again to slape-ale. **1787** Grose *Prov. Gloss.*, *Slape-yale*, rich, soft or smooth ale. **1866** Brogden *Prov. Lincs.*, *Slape*, strong, soft and sweet (applied to ale).

**3.** *attrib.* and *Comb.*, as ***slape-faced***, ***-fingered***, ***-haired***, etc.; **slape-face** (see quot. 1847); also, a smooth-faced man.

For other combs. of this type, see the *Eng. Dial. Dict.* **1803** R. Anderson *Cumbld. Ball.* (*c* 1850) 75 Left-handed Sim, slape-finger'd Sam. **1839** Rayson *Poems* (1858) 63 For slape-finger'd art he is equall'd by neane. **1847** Halliw., *Slape-face*, a soft-spoken, mealy-mouthed hypocrite. **1884**

W. Black *J. Shakespeare* i, If he..have a red beard, I will not have him... If he be a slape-face, I will have none of him. **1890** *Cornhill Mag.* Oct. 392 There were..two distinct breeds [of dogs]: the slape-haired and the rough-haired.

**slape**, obs. form of SLEEP.

**ˈslap-happy**, *a.* *colloq.* (orig. *U.S.*). Also **slaphappy**. [f. SLAP *sb.*$^1$ + -HAPPY.]

**1.** Dazed, punch-drunk; dizzy (with happiness).

**1936** J. Tully *Bruiser* x. 89 A slap-happy bum. **1938** *Newsweek* 23 May 22/1 A sample [of talk] designed to knock philologists slap-happy. **1940** *Detective Tales* Apr. 8/1 He was a little slap-happy from a decade of slug-festing. **1947** [see PUNCH-DRUNK *a.*]. **1973** *Maclean's Mag.* (Toronto) Feb. 32/2 It was so exhilaratingly ludicrous..that I felt quite slaphappy.

**2.** Carefree, casual; careless, thoughtless, irresponsible.

**1937** *N.Y. Herald Tribune* 28 Aug. 14/1 After the dust had settled he and Ernest Hemingway, the slaphappy litterateur, toured Spain together. **1940** *Nation* 6 Apr. 448/1 Unless production [of television programmes] is slap-happy, the costs promise to compare with those of Broadway shows. **1951** R. Hoggart *Auden* iii. 78 This is Auden's characteristic 'Love' again, allied to his leftism—a lyrical but vague coda to a slap-happy knocking-down of many old guys. **1958** E. H. Clements *Uncommon Cold* i. 26 The irresponsible slap-happy manners of extreme modern youth. **1977** *Meanjin* XXXVI. I. 131 The real point is that Sydney—slap-happy and extroverted— is the favoured haunt of the cultural bureaucrats.

Hence **slap-ˈhappily** *adv.*, **slap-ˈhappiness**.

**1958** S. Hyland *Who goes Hang?* xiv. 63 The impression of boisterous slap-happiness. **1968** M. Bragg *Without City Wall* II. xxvii. 249 Spray the world with froth of slap-happiness. **1969** *Guardian* 20 Oct. 22/2 He is unlikely to display himself so slap-happily before those surging crowds.

**slapjack** (ˈslæpdʒæk). Also **slap-jack, slap jack**. [f. SLAP *v.* + JACK *sb.*$^1$]

**1.** *N. Amer.* A griddle-cake. Cf. FLAPJACK 1.

**1805** 'An American Lady' *New Amer. Cookery* 60 *Indian Slapjack*. One quart milk, 1 pint of Indian meal, 4 eggs, 4 spoons of flour. **1820** W. Irving *Sketch Bk.* (1865) 438 Dainty slapjacks, well buttered, and garnished with honey or treacle. **1836** Haliburton *Clockm.* (1862) 97 A dish of real Connecticut Slap Jacks, or Hominy. **1867** J. K. Lord *At Home in Wilderness* viii. 132 Then I can bake bread in my frying-pan, make and fry pancakes, or 'slap-jacks', as trappers call them. **1872** C. King *Sierra Nevada* vii. 148 Such dainties as thrice-turned slap-jacks. **1895** W. Elkington *Five Years in Canada* xiii. 111 Another favourite dish..is also made of flour and water, mixed into a batter and fried in fat; it is eaten with syrup or sugar, and is called 'slap-jack'.

**2.** A card-game in which a player gains by being the first to slap a jack when played.

**1887** Miss Braddon *Like & Unlike* v, He would labour with sublime patience at the perplexity of 'Muggins' or 'Slap-Jack', two games of cards, to enliven the dulness of a purely literary evening.

†**slappaty-pouch**. *Obs.*$^{-1}$ [f. SLAP *v.*$^1$] ? Slapping of the hands against the sides in order to warm oneself.

*c*1700 T. Brown *Lett. fr. Dead* Wks. 1720 II. 151 We have even tired our Palms and our Ribs at Slappaty-pouch, and..I [*sc.* Charon] had almost forgot to handle my Sculls.

**ˈslappel**. *dial.* (See quot.)

**1674** Ray *S. & E. Co. Words*, A *Slappel*, a piece, part, or portion, *Suss*[*ex*]. [Hence in Grose, etc.]

**slapper**$^1$ (ˈslæpə(r)). [f. SLAP *v.*$^1$ + -ER.]

**1.** *dial.* A large thing or object; a big, strapping, or overgrown person.

**1781–** in northern dial. glossaries. **1825** Jamieson *Suppl.*, *Slapper*, any large object; as a big salmon, *Roxb.* **1854** Miss Baker *Northampt. Gloss.*, *Slapper*,..applied to persons and things, but most frequently to over-grown females. *Ibid.*, 'She's a slapper.'

**2. a.** One who slaps; *spec.* in *Pottery*.

**1860** Tomlinson *Arts & Manuf.* Ser. II. *Pottery* 32 The workman called the slapper takes a mass of the paste, weighing from sixty to seventy pounds, and dashes it down on a bench before him. **1880** C. Mason *Forty Shires* 159 When the clay is to be used, the slapper does his work.

**b.** In jazz, one who plays the double-bass (see SLAP *v.*$^1$ 1 d).

**1934** S. R. Nelson *All about Jazz* vi. 126 So a race of pickers and slappers..sprang into being. **1936** *Swing Music* Mar. 9/2 Steve Brown, that tremendous string-bass slapper.

**3.** An implement used for slapping with.

*a*1886 H. S. Brown *Autobiog.* (1887) iv. 18 Mr. Stowell had on his desk a broad wooden slapper, to be smitten with which we were commanded to hold out our hands.

**ˈslapper**$^2$. *rare*$^{-0}$. [f. SLAP *v.*$^3$] (See quot.)

**1611** Cotgr., *Licheur*, a licker, lapper, or slapper vp of.

**ˈslappet**, *sb.* *Derby mining.* Also **slap(p)it**. [? dim. of OF. *esclape* shiver, splinter.] A splinter or shiver of ore, etc.

**1768** Mettam in Whitehurst *Form. Earth* (1778) 188 They fly out in such slappits, smooth on one side. **1811** Farey *Derbyshire* I. 250 Large Slapits, Spels or fragments fly off, sometimes with loud explosions.

Hence **ˈslappet** *v.*

**1811** Farey *Derbyshire* I. 367 On his return, [he] finds all the Vein-stuff so furrowed, spelled, or slappeted off.

†**ˈslappiness**. *Obs.*$^{-1}$ [Cf. Du. *slap* soft.] Softness, flabbiness.

**1668** Culpepper & Cole *Barthol. Anat.* III. vi. 142 For this cause Infants do not presently speak nor reason, because the slappiness of their brain gives not passage to the Idea's.

**ˈslapping**, *vbl. sb.*$^1$ [f. SLAP *v.*$^1$] **a.** The action of the vb., in various senses; an instance of this.

**1632** in Sherwood. **1682** T. Flatman *Heraclitus Ridens* No. 67 (1713) II. 166 Our Author's next Charge..is the slapping of the Pew-doors in Prayer-time. **1682** Bunyan *Holy War* (1905) 378 The Town made answer with the slapping of their slings. **1865** Tylor *Early Hist. Man.* iii. 51 The pattings and slappings of the Fuegians. **1897** Kipling *Capt. Courageous* 70 There was an incessant slapping and chatter at the bows now, varied by a solid thud.

*attrib.* **1851** Hawthorne *Twice-told T.* I. viii. 154 That smart, slapping sound, produced by an open hand upon tender flesh. **1897** *Allbutt's Syst. Med.* III. 44 The loud, vibrating, prolonged, presystolic bruit and slapping first sound [of the heart].

**b.** *spec.* in *Pottery.* (See quots.)

**1825** J. Nicholson *Operat. Mechanic* 460 When the clay is required for the thrower the process of *slapping* follows next. This is performed by a strong man, who places a large mass..upon a..bench. He then..cuts the mass through, and taking up the piece thus cut off, he..casts it down again on the mass below. **1880** Janvier *Pract. Keramics* iv. 44 Just before using, the paste for this often undergoes the process of 'slapping'.

**c.** In jazz, the action of playing a double-bass (see SLAP *v.*$^1$ 1 d).

**1931** *Melody Maker* Dec. 1029/3 Slapping, too, becomes next to impossible with a high bridge. **1959** 'F. Newton' *Jazz Scene* 289 *Slapping* for pizzicato playing.

**ˈslapping**, *vbl. sb.*$^2$ [f. SLAP *v.*$^3$] (See quot.)

**1611** Cotgr., *Lichement*, a licking; lapping, or slapping vp.

**ˈslapping**, *ppl. a.* [f. SLAP *v.*$^1$ + -ING$^2$.]

**1.** Of pace, etc.: Extremely fast; rapid, rattling.

**1812** *Sporting Mag.* XXXIX. 124 The first run was at a slapping pace. **1842** Lover *Handy Andy* xxii, Billy gave the little black mare her head, and away she went at a slapping pace. **1863** W. C. Baldwin *Afr. Hunting* ix. 428 One giraffe-cow, going at a slapping gallop a long way ahead over a villainous country.

**2.** Of horses: Big, powerfully built (sometimes implying ability to travel quickly).

**1828** *Sporting Mag.* XXI. 277 One by Comus, and the other by Jonathan, both slapping colts. **1852** R. S. Surtees *Sponge's Sp. Tour* ix. 38 Nor did the great slapping brown horse..turn out less imposingly than his master. **1856** H. H. Dixon *Post & Paddock* i, The Yorkshiremen..try to breed great slapping carriage-horses.

**b.** Of persons or things: Unusually large or fine; excellent, very good; strapping.

**1825** Jamieson *Suppl.* s.v., *A slappin chiel*, a tall fellow. **1829–** in dial. glossaries (N. Cy., Berks., Somerset, Cornw., etc.). **1849** Cupples *Green Hand* ii. (1856) 23, I really couldn't help laughing to see the slapping, big-bearded fellows..showing off in this manner.

**3.** That slaps, in senses of the vb.

**1898** *Allbutt's Syst. Med.* V. 750 The large and slapping pulse which he has frequently observed in pericardial effusions. **1899** *Triad* vii. 12/1 We swam on in the face of the slapping seas.

**ˈslappy**, *sb.* [f. SLAP *v.*$^1$] Some indoor game.

**1868** Holme Lee *B. Godfrey* xxxvi, Everybody was willing..to engage in 'Post' or 'Slappy'.

**slappy** (ˈslæpɪ), *a.* *U.S. slang.* [f. SLAP(-HAPPY *a.* + -Y$^1$.] = SLAP-HAPPY *a.* Also as *sb.*

**1937** [see PUNCHY *a.*$^4$]. **1942** Berrey & Van den Bark *Amer. Thes. Slang* §151/9 *Foolish*; *silly*;..slappy. *Ibid.* §702/32 '*Punch-drunk*'; *dazed*..slappy.

**slap riddle**: see SLAP *sb.*$^6$

†**slapsauce**. *Obs.* [f. SLAP *v.*$^3$ + SAUCE *sb.*]

**1.** One who is fond of good eating; a greedy or gluttonous person. Also *attrib.*

**1573** Tusser *Husb.* (1878) 188 At dinner and supper the table doth craue good fellowly neighbour good manner to haue. Aduise thee well therefore, ere tongue be too free, or slapsauce be noted too saucie to bee. **1611** Cotgr., *Leschard*, a lickorous, or sweet-mouthed slapsawce. **1653** Urquhart *Rabelais* I. xxv, Slapsauce fellows, slabberdegullion druggels, lubbardly lowts.

**2.** A slabber-sauce. *rare*$^{-1}$.

**1709** O. Dykes *Eng. Prov. & Refl.* (ed. 2) 12 Her Chocolate, her Gellies, and her Sweet-meats; or such like liquorish Slap-sawces, which pall the Appetite and disrelish the Palate for the whole Day.

†**slap-shoe**. *Obs.*$^{-0}$ (See quot.)

**1688** Holme *Armoury* III. 14 Slap shooes, or Ladies shoes, are shooes with a loose Sole.

**slap shot**. *Ice Hockey*. Also **slapshot**. [f. SLAP *v.*$^1$ + SHOT *sb.*$^1$] A shot made with a sharp slapping movement of the stick, which usu. lifts the puck off the ice. Hence **ˈslapshoot** *v. trans.*, to hit (a puck) in this manner.

**1942** E. Jeremiah *Ice Hockey* iii. 12 A slap shot..is very effective because its suddenness has a valuable surprise element. **1956** *Roy. Canad. Air Force Coach's Manual Hockey* 40 The slap shot can be made by stopping the puck first, then teeing off on it. **1968** *Globe & Mail* (Toronto) 3 Feb. 35/1 Athlete-columnists are more common than writers who can also skate and slapshoot a hockey puck. **1972** 'E. Lathen' *Murder without Icing* (1973) ii. 18 Billy Siragusa, the Huskies' new center, was practicing slap shots. **1974** *Los Angeles Times* 13 Oct. III. 2/3 Rene Robert got Buffalo's only goal at 14:06 of the opening period with a 30-foot slapshot.

**ˈslapstick**. orig. *U.S.* Also **slap-stick**. [f. SLAP *v.*$^1$ + STICK *sb.*$^1$] **1.** Two flat pieces of wood joined together at one end, used to produce a loud slapping noise; *spec.* such a device used in pantomime and low comedy to make a great noise with the pretence of dealing a heavy blow (see also quot. 1950).

**1896** *N.Y. Dramatic News* 4 July 9/3 What a relief, truly, from the slap-sticks, rough-and-tumble comedy couples abounding in the variety ranks. **1907** *Weekly Budget* 19 Oct. 1/2 The special officer in the gallery, armed with a 'slap-stick', the customary weapon in American theatre galleries, made himself very officious amongst the small boys. **1925** M. W. Disher *Clowns & Pantomimes* 13 What has caused the playgoers' sudden callousness? The slapstick. Towards the end of the seventeenth century Arlequin had introduced into England the double-lath of castigation, which made the maximum amount of noise with the minimum of injury. **1937** M. Covarrubias *Island of Bali* iv. 77 Life-size scarecrows are erected, but soon the birds become familiar with them... Then watchmen circulate among the fields beating bamboo drums and cracking loud bamboo slap-sticks. **1950** *Sun* (Baltimore) 10 Apr. 3/1 The 50-year-old clown..said that when he bent over another funnyman accidentally hit him with the wrong side of a slap-stick. He explained that a slap-stick contains a blank ·38-caliber cartridge on one side to make a bang.

**2. a.** *attrib.* passing into *adj.* Of or pertaining to a slapstick; of or reminiscent of knockabout comedy.

**1906** *N.Y. Even. Post* 25 Oct. 10 It required all the untiring efforts of an industrious 'slap-stick' coterie..to keep the enthusiasm up to a respectable degree. **1914** *Photoplay* Sept. 91 (*heading*) Making slap-stick comedy. **1923** *Weekly Dispatch* 4 Mar. 9 He likes good comedies.. but thinks the slapstick ones ridiculous. **1928** *Daily Sketch* 7 Aug. 4/3 The jokes..are rapier-like in their keenness, not the usual rolling-pin or slapstick form of humour. **1936** W. Holtby *South Riding* IV. v. 258 She took a one-and-threepenny ticket, sat in comfort, and watched a Mickey Mouse film, a slapstick comedy, and the tragedy of Greta Garbo acting Mata Hari. **1944** [see POCHO]. **1962** A. Nisbett *Technique Sound Studio* x. 173 Decidedly unobvious effects, such as the cork-and-resin 'creak' or the hinged slapstick 'whip'. **1977** R. L. Wolff *Gains & Losses* II. iv. 296 The prevailing tone of the book is highly satirical, with strong overtones of slapstick farce.

**b.** *absol.* Knockabout comedy or humour, farce, horseplay.

**1926** *Amer. Speech* I. 437/2 *Slap-stick*, low comedy in its simplest form. Named from the double paddles formerly used by circus clowns to beat each other. **1930** *Publisher's Weekly* 25 Jan. 420/2 The slapstick of 1929 was often exciting. The Joan Lowell episode was regarded as exposing the gullibility of the critics... The popularity of 'The Specialist' made the whole book business look cockeyed. **1955** *Times* 6 June 9/1 A comic parson (Mr. Noel Howlett) is added for good measure, mainly to play on the piano while other people crawl under it. Even on the level of slapstick the farce seemed to keep in motion with some difficulty and raised but moderate laughter. **1967** M. Kenyon *Whole Hog* xxv. 253 A contest which had promised..to be short and cruel, had become slapstick. **1976** *Oxf. Compan. Film* 640/1 As it developed in the decade 1910–20..slapstick depended on frenzied, often disorganized, motion that increased in tempo as visual gags proliferated.

**ˈslap-tongue**, *v.* Also **slaptongue, slap tongue**. [f. SLAP *v.*$^1$ + TONGUE *sb.*] *intr.* To produce a staccato effect in playing the saxophone by striking the tongue against the reed. So **ˈslap-tonguing** *vbl. sb.*; hence **ˈslap-tongue** *a.*, playing or played with this technique.

**1926** Whiteman & McBride *Jazz* ix. 203 Slap tonguing is accomplished by sucking on the reed, thus creating a vacuum, then hitting the vacuum with the tongue, causing a pop. **1927** *Melody Maker* May 503/1 How to slap-tongue is not the easiest thing to explain in words. **1954** *Grove's Dict. Mus.* (ed. 5) VII. 433/2 Tongued staccato playing.. was at one period developed by dance musicians into a curious explosive effect termed 'slap-tonguing'. **1963** *Down Beat* 3 Jan. 20 His first solo with Henderson, a clownlike, slap-tongue effort. **1969** *Listener* 12 June 838/1 Experimentation was limited to exploiting its [*sc.* the saxophone's] agility..or producing comic effects by slap tonguing. **1971** *Daily Tel.* 18 Sept. 7/8 Henderson's Columbia sessions..despite occasional farmyard noises and slaptongue reeds offer good Redman and Charlie Green.

**slap-up**, *a.* *slang* and *colloq.* [SLAP *adv.*] Very or unmistakably good or fine; of superior quality, style, etc.; first-rate, first-class, grand. (Common in 19th cent.) **a.** Of things. Now used esp. of meals.

**1823** 'J. Bee' *Slang* 161 *Slap-up*, used for 'bang-up'. 'Tis *northern.* **1827** *Sporting Mag.* XX. 147 Send them to that slap-up work, the Sporting Magazine. **1858** Dickens *Lett.* (1880) II. 66 A trim, sparkling, slap-up Irish jaunting-car. **1889** J. K. Jerome *Three Men in Boat* iv. 53 We'll have a good round, square, slap-up meal at seven. **1931** W. S. Maugham in *Nash's Pall Mall Mag.* Dec. 24/1 A bottle of pop tonight, my pet, and a slap-up dinner. **1977** *Lancashire Life* Nov. 74/2 There was a slap-up tea at the institute.

**b.** Of persons.

**1829** *Caricature Title*, The Slap-up Swell wot drives when hever he likes. **1840** Thackeray *Paris Sk.-bk.* (1869) 17 He had made some slap-up acquaintances among the genteelest people at Paris. **1876** J. Saunders *Lion in Path* xx, I'm a little sweet on her maid, slap-up creature, I can tell you.

**slare** (slɛə(r)), *v.* *dial.* [prob. of Scand. origin: cf. Norw. *slara* to stagger; also NFris. *slare* to drag the feet. *Slare* or *slair* in other senses (see

*Eng. Dial. Dict.*) is current in all northern and eastern dialects.] *intr.* (See quot. 1877.)

**1726** S. WESLEY in Southey *Life J. Wesley* (1820) I. 445 My man, who lay in the garret, heard some one come slaring through the garret to his chamber. **1726** HOOLE *Ibid.* 457 We ..heard, at the broad stairs head, some one slaring with their feet. **1877** *N.W. Linc. Gloss.* 227/1 *Slare*, to make a noise by rubbing the boot-soles on an uncarpeted floor.

**slart** (slɑːt). *dial.* [Origin unknown: for related senses see *Eng. Dial. Dict.*] *pl.* Left-overs, scraps.

**1913, 1917** [see ORT]. **1977** SCOLLINS & TITFORD *Ey up, mi Duck!* III. 50 *Slarts*, left-overs, scraps of food.

**slash** (slæʃ), *sb.*[1] [f. SLASH *v.*[1]]

**1. a.** A cutting stroke delivered with an edged weapon or instrument, or with a whip.

**1576** FLEMING *Panopl. Epist.* 297 *marg.*, Because euery one was ready to cutte his throte as to haue a slash at his fleshe. **1597** A. M. tr. *Guillemeau's Fr. Chirurg.* 13b/2 A great hewe or slashe, by which the eare hangeth by the heade. **1617** MORYSON *Itin.* III. 26 Sometimes they fight after their fashion, which is a slash or two with the edge of the sword. **1652** COTTERELL tr. *Calprenède's Cassandra* III. (1676) 43 Cut the straps of his Cask, with a slash of his sword. **1726** SWIFT *Gulliver* II. i, I observed it had yet some life, but, with a strong slash across the neck, I thoroughly despatched it. **1818** SCOTT *Rob Roy* xxxix, He..had only taken this recumbent posture to avoid the slashes, stabs, and pistol-balls, which..were flying in various directions. **1868** FREEMAN *Norm. Conq.* (1877) II. 431 There seemed a prospect of the English crown passing, without slash or blow, to the brow of the Norman.

*transf.* **1858** CARLYLE *Fredk. Gt.* V. vii. (1872) II. 119 Capable of rough slashes of sarcasm when he opens his old beard for speech. **1867** LATHAM *Black & White* 3 Listening to the angry slash with which each wave's crest swished like a scourge across the ship.

**b.** In *Cricket*, any unorthodox attacking stroke played with a great swing of the bat.

**1906** A. E. KNIGHT *Complete Cricket* ii. 78 A slash at the ball, the bat slicing the ball instead of meeting it with the full face. **1948** *Sporting Mirror* 21 May 7/1 The first shot he made after arriving at the wickets was a glorious 'slash' to the boundary. **1977** *Daily Express* 29 Jan. 35/1 Yajuvendra, never looking the part in his first Test innings, took a full-blooded slash outside off stump at a short one from Willis.

**c.** *fig.* A reduction; a (swingeing) cut. Cf. SLASH *v.*[1] 1 d.

**1950** *N.Y. Times* 20 Apr. 2/1 (*heading*) House group bars overall 50% slash in wartime excises. **1951** [see CONSUMER 2c]. **1973** *Tucson* (Arizona) *Daily Citizen* 22 Aug. 1 This would be the second wave of base slashes in about a year. **1983** *Guardian Weekly* 6 Mar. 14/1 A 50 per cent slash in the army's budget.

**2. a.** A long and deep or severe cut; a gash; a wound of this character.

**1580** HOLLYBAND *Treas. Fr. Tong* s.v. *Taillade*, He gaue him a slashe or cutte on the legge. **1603** KNOLLES *Hist. Turks* (1621) 986 Three great slashes [were] made on his backe, where they began to flea him. **1634** SIR T. HERBERT *Trav.* 10 In adding to their beauties, they have two or three slashes in the face. **1717** PRIOR *Alma* II. 445 Scarr'd with ten thousand comely Blisters,..Distinguish'd Slashes deck the Great. **1829** SCOTT *Rob Roy* Introd., A slash or two, or a broken head, was easily accommodated. **1890** DOYLE *White Company* xxx, The Bohemian knight..bleeding from a slash across the forehead.

**b.** *Bot.* (See quot.)

**1866** *Treas. Bot.* 654/1 *Lacinia*,..a slash. A deep taper-pointed incision.

**3. a.** A vertical slit made in a garment in order to expose to view a lining or under garment of a different or contrasting colour.

**1615** MARKHAM *Country Contentm.* I. xi. (1633) 75 Let your apparel be plain..without any new fashioned slashes, or hanging sleeves, waving loose, like sails about you. **1627** in Birch *Crt. & Times Chas. I* (1848) I. 261 A swain..was suspected..and..searched, and a poisoned knife found in one of his slashes. **1711** STEELE *Spect.* No. 109 ¶5 Observe the small Buttons,..the Slashes about his Clothes. **1831** SCOTT *Cast. Dang.* i, The colour of the traveller's doublet was blue, and that of his hose violet, with slashes which showed a lining of the same colour with the jerkin. **1882** CAULFEILD & SAWARD *Dict. Needlwk.* 451/2 *Slashes* or *Panes*, a term used by tailors and dressmakers, to signify a vertical cutting in any article of dress [etc.].

**b.** *attrib.* with *cuff*, *pocket*. Also *absol.* (see quot. 1839).

**1799** WASHINGTON *Lett.* Writ. 1893 XIV. 149 To you I submit..whether the coat shall have slash Cuffs (with blue flaps passing through them), and slash pockets. **1839** H. BRANDON *Poverty, Mendicity & Crime* 165/1 *Slash*, outside coat pocket. **1969** *Sears Catal.* Spring/Summer 47 No-iron reversible jacket... Plaid side has two slash pockets. **1973** W. HALLAHAN *Ross Forgery* iii. 3 The watchman pushed his hands into the slash pockets of his jacket.

**4. a.** An open tract or clearing in a forest, esp. one strewn with debris resulting from felling or logging, high wind, or fire. Cf. SLASHING *vbl. sb.* 4b. *N. Amer.*

**1825** A. ANDERSON *Diary* 30 Aug. in G. Sellar *Narr.* (1916) vii. 102 We have been here scarce three months and there is a great slash. **1849** J. E. ALEXANDER *L' Acadie* I. 272 After various difficulties..getting with our horses into 'slashes' or parts of the forest cut down..we at last reached the small wooden hostel. **1923** H. E. WILLIAMS *Spinning Wheels & Homespun* 154 Raspberries are found oftenest in what are called 'slashes' in the woods, where the older timber has been cut down, and the new has not yet grown up to replace it. **1963** *Sun* (Vancouver) 23 Nov. 21/1 The rolling hills along the..rivers are parklike with their copses of fir, tamarack, poplar and willow..left standing in old log slashes or burns.

**b.** Felled trees and other debris left in a forest after logging or the clearing of a tract, or resulting from high wind or fire. Cf. SLASHING *vbl. sb.* 4c. orig. and chiefly *N. Amer.*

In mod. use, *slash* denotes the branches and other trimmings cut from trees preparatory to removing the logs from a forest.

**1841** *Bytown* (Ottawa) *Gaz.* 17 Feb. 1/3 To end of month clearing up old 'slash', which term has previously been defined. **1917** F. D. ADAMS in J. O. Miller *New Era in Canada* 85 In Quebec and British Columbia, settlers who desire to burn their slash must now obtain permits from the Government forest ranger, who supervises the burning. **1928** *Indian Forest Rec.* XIII. VII. 3 Comprehensively defined, *chir* slash includes all débris resulting from operations involving the felling and utilization of *chir* trees, and also from the destruction of trees of this species by such agencies as wind, snow, fire, lightning, floods, landslips, insects and fungi. **1952** P. W. RICHARDS *Tropical Rain Forest* xvii. 379 Soil impoverishment will in turn depend on ..the quantity of debris and 'slash' left on the ground after clearing. **1965** *Wildlife Rev.* Mar. 19/2 Cougars travel over long ranges and are found in various ecological types of terrain such as slash, mature forest and second growth. **1980** *Search* XI. 71/1 Planting of tubed stock on corridors cleared of slash may be another means of establishing eucalypt seedlings.

**c.** *attrib.* and *Comb.*, as ***slash area, fire***.

**1971** *Islander* (Victoria, B.C.) 30 May 12/3 After about a third of a mile you break out into a *slash area where logging operations have been carried out. **1949** *Pacific Discovery* Jan.-Feb. 4/1 The river knew well the flashing draft of lightning fires in the grass but not the consuming roar of a *slash fire. **1980** *Search* XI. 69/1 Slash fires result in mobilisation of large amounts of nutrients both during the fire..and subsequently as a result of stimulated biological mineralisation in the soil.

**5.** A thin sloping line, thus /; = OBLIQUE *sb.* 5, SOLIDUS[1] 2. *U.S.* Also ***slash-mark***.

**1961** in WEBSTER. **1964** *Amer. Speech* XXXIX. 103 The number to the right of the slash is the total number of occurrences of that type of clause. **1976** T. ALLBEURY *Only Good German* x. 76 Reference SC49 slash two. **1979** C. E. SCHORSKE *Fin-de-Siècle Vienna* vii. 331 Breaking the phrase with slash marks at unsuspected nodes. **1980** *Maledicta* III. II. 206 Although it is true that . , : ; () - [] - ! ? / and * have names—in the case of /, several names: solidus, virgule, slash-mark, diagonal—there is a gap in the naming of #.

**slash**, *sb.*[2] [Of obscure origin: cf. Sc. *slash* a large splash of liquid, etc., perh. ad. OF. *esclache* (Godef.).] †**1.** A drink, draught. *Obs. rare.*

**1614** W. HORNBY *Sco. Drunkennesse* (1859) 18 But if to pledge a slash hee doth refuse They'l take the pot, and throw the drinke in's face. *c* **1783** *Roxb. Ball.* (1890) VII. 94 Flounders, the younger,..So prim on his stallion and fond of his slash.

**2.** *slang.* An act of urination.

**1950** P. TEMPEST *Lag's Lexicon* 192 *Slash, to go for a*, to visit the urinal. **1953** *Chambers's Jrnl.* June 325/1 'I'm leaving my turret for a moment. I want a slash.' 'Okay, kid, you know where to find it?' 'I should do. I've had to empty them often enough!' **1977** N. J. CRISP *Odd Job Man* i. 5 He decided to risk a quick slash, which..he needed.

**slash** (slæʃ), *sb.*[3] *U.S.* [Of obscure origin: cf. FLASH *sb.*[1] and PLASH *sb.*[1], also Eng. dial. *slashy* wet and dirty, miry.] **a.** Swampy ground; a swamp.

**1652** in N. M. Nugent *Cavaliers & Pioneers* (1934) I. 239/2 Neer a wett slash, running N.N.W. to an Easternmost branch of Richard Cr. **1717** *Prince George County* (Virginia) *Deed Bk.* 202 in *Amer. Speech* (1940) XV. 393/1 A white Oake Standing in a round Slash. **1799** WASHINGTON *Writ.* (1893) XIV. 232 Excepting the ground now in and designed for lucerne, south of the slash by the Barn. **1837** P. H. GOSSE in *Life* (1890) 106 The first quarter of a mile lay through a very rough slash. *a* **1859** in Bartlett *Dict. Amer.* s.v., Between this and Edenton there are many whortleberry slashes. **1890** *Cent. Mag.* June 221/2 The camp was in a cypress slash. You could cut the miasma with a knife. **1897** *Geogr. Jrnl.* IX. 538 There are many successive ridges of shingle running in varying directions, and often with narrow strips of marsh enclosed between successive ridges. Such bands of marsh have been given the very appropriate name of 'slashes' in New Jersey. **1903** *Dialect Notes* II. 330 [S.E. Missouri] *Slash*, wet bottom land. A slash differs from a slough in having no perceptible channel. **1966** *Publ. Amer. Dial. Soc.* XLVI. 29 *Slash*, a swamp.— 'It was in that slash down on the river.'

**b.** *Comb.* **slash-pine**, a pine growing in a slash or low-lying coastal region, esp. *Pinus caribæa*, the principal native pine of south-eastern North America; also, the wood of this tree.

**1882** HOUGH *Elem. Forestry* 328 Varieties [of *Pinus taeda*] are known in North Carolina as 'Swamp Pine', '*Slash Pine'. **1884** C. S. SARGENT *Rep. Forests N. Amer.* 516 The slash pine (*Pinus Cubensis*) of the Florida coast. **1934** *Sun* (Baltimore) 7 Dec. 3/2 Dr. Herty recently made newsprint from slash and other southern pine. **1949** *Clarke County Democrat* (Grove Hill, Alabama) 28 July 1/3 Both have plots on which they have set out slash pine seedlings. **1974** *Calhoun Times* (St. Matthews, S. Carolina) 18 Apr. 2/1 Loblolly and slash pines are most susceptible [to rust galls].

**slash** (slæʃ), *sb.*[4] *local.* [Later form of SLATCH 1.] (See quots.)

**1839** MURCHISON *Silur. Syst.* 376 Besides 'sloughs' there occur in Broadhaven and elsewhere, small but very deep troughs of finely fractured culm, which are called 'slashes'. These (as far as my knowledge goes) are peculiar to Pembrokeshire. **1849** —— *Siluria* (1854) 275 The stone-coal..has been for the most part shivered into small fragments, and is frequently accumulated in small troughs or hollows, the 'slashes' of the miners. **1916** [see SLATCH 1].

**slash** (slæʃ), *v.*[1] Also 4 **slasch**, 6–7 **slassh**. [perh. ad. OF. *esclachier* to break; used once in the Wycliffite Bible, but otherwise recorded only from the middle of the 16th cent.]

**1. a.** *trans.* To cut or wound with a sweep or stroke of a sharp weapon or instrument; to gash, †hew.

**1382** BIBLE *1 Kings* v. 18 (MS. Bodl. 959), The grete stones..which þe masownys of Salamon..han slascht [*altered to* ouerscorchyd]. **1587** TURBERV. *Trag. Tales* (1837) 42 Slashing the Lady with his fauchion fell. **1596** NASHE *Saffron Walden* Wks. (Grosart) III. 114 Hewd and slasht he had beene as small as chippings, if he had not played ducke Fryer. **1605** SYLVESTER *Du Bartas* II. iii. III. *Law* 664 Alas! some of us shall with Scythes be slasht. **1685** COTTON tr. *Montaigne* (1877) I. 14 Where all their confederates and neighbours..cut and slashed their fore heads in token of sorrow. **1716–8** LADY M. W. MONTAGU *Lett.* I. xxxviii. 152 Some slashed their arms with sharp knives, making the blood spring out. **1791** COWPER *Iliad* II. 518 The thighs with fire consumed, they..slash'd the remnant, pierced it with spits [etc.]. **1850** SCORESBY *Cheever's Whaleman's Advent.* v. (1858) 67 The mincer with a two-handed knife slashes it nearly through into thin slices. **1881** BESANT & RICE *Chapl. of Fleet* II. xviii, There are few things a woman ..would not do to save two friends from hacking and slashing each other.

*refl.* **1652–62** HEYLYN *Cosmogr.* IV. (1682) 64 Most hideously to slash themselves in all parts of their bodies.

**b.** To cut *off* or *out* with a sweeping or sharp stroke.

**1599** GREENE *Alphonsus* 597 Therefore Fabius, stand not lingring, But presently slash off his trayterous head. **1625** PURCHAS *Pilgrimes* II. 1724 Their owne flesh..they slash off in morsels. **1821** SCOTT *Kenilw.* xix, I will slash the eyes out of his head with my poniard! **1837** CARLYLE *Fr. Rev.* I. v. vii, Already one poor Invalide has his right hand slashed off him.

**c.** To clear (land) of vegetation, to cut (trees or undergrowth) *down*, esp. preparatory to burning off the resulting slash. Chiefly *N. Amer.*

**1821** T. MCCULLOCH *Stepsure Letters* (1960) 20 He had slashed down a large piece of wood; and now he determined to raise a crop. **1849** C. HURSTHOUSE *Acct. Settlement New Plymouth* vii. 93 The cane-like fern stalks..should be cut at once,..and the 'Tutu' slashed down with a bill-hook. **1889** W. H. WITHROW *Our Own Country* 362 The native forest had been 'slashed' in that particular locality. **1931** *Beaver* Sept. 276 Five acres of virgin land were slashed. **1962** A. FRY *Ranch on Cariboo* 66 Sometimes we built fence or slashed brush to extend the yard.

**d.** *fig.* To reduce (something) severely in size or quantity. Freq. used with reference to prices, payments, etc.

**1906** *Washington Post* 29 Apr. 6 A disposition was manifested in the Senate Committee to slash the salaries of members of the commission. **1910** *Springfield* (Mass.) *Weekly Republican* 8 Dec. 8 It is not a pleasant thing to slash a presidential message to this extent. **1931** *Evening Standard* 4 Aug. 10/1 The big department stores have not merely reduced their prices; they have 'slashed' them. **1958** *Listener* 13 Nov. 777/2 After that I stuck to one garage and slashed expenditure by 50 per cent. at a single stroke. **1976** *Daily Mirror* 16 July 1/1 Labour held their seat in yesterday's vital Thurrock by-election. But their majority was slashed.

**2. a.** *intr.* To deliver or aim cutting blows (also const. *at*); to make gashes or deep wounds.

**1548** PATTEN *Exped. Scotl.* H iv, Euen so..was Syr Arthur Darcy slasht at with swoordes, and..hurt vppon the weddyng fynger of hys righte hande. **1590** SPENSER *F.Q.* II. ix. 15 The knights..Broke their rude troupes,..Hewing and slashing at their idle shades. **1616** J. LANE *Contn. Sqr.'s T.* VIII. 261 Swoordes flew out, most feircelie hissinge, percinge, cuttinge, slasshinge. **1678** BUTLER *Hud.* III. I. 349 Knights..when they slash, and cut to pieces, Doe all with civillest addresses. **1709** HEARNE *Collect.* (O.H.S.) II. 317 Yᵉ Spatæ were us'd both to push and slash. **1794** MRS. RADCLIFFE *Myst. Udolpho* xxxi, The enemy..will fall to, cutting and slashing, till he makes them all rise up dead men. **1846** LANDOR *Exam. Shaks.* Wks. II. 291 Then did he slit them with his thumbnail, and then did he pare and slash away at them again. **1880** 'MARK TWAIN' *Tramp Abr.* 44 In the fights..these lads hacked and slashed with the same tremendous spirit.

*fig.* **1596** NASHE *Saffron Walden* Wks. (Grosart) III. 114 He would needs..hewe and slash with his Hexameters. **1865** CARLYLE *Fredk. Gt.* XIX. vii. (1872) VIII. 225 The Austrians..will not go, till well slashed into, and torn out by sheer beating.

**b.** To strike violently or at random; to lay about one with heavy blows; to move rapidly and violently, etc. Also with *down*, *out*. Also in cricket, to play a vigorous attacking stroke. Occas. *trans.* (in quot. with bowler as object).

*a* **1654** SELDEN *Table T.* (Arb.) 88 They that do drudgery-work, slash, and puff, and swear. **1819** *Sporting Mag.* IV. 236 Boshell came up rather distressed,..and endeavoured to slash out. **1880** 'MARK TWAIN' *Tramp Abr.* 159 We.. came slashing down with the mad current into the narrow passage between the dykes. **1901** *Scotsman* 10 Sept. 7/3 Williamson..slashed to the enclosure. **1955** [see GULLY *sb.*[1] 2d]. **1974** *Plain Dealer* (Cleveland, Ohio) 26 Oct. 7-D/7 Tailback Mike Newman slashed across from two yards out to cut Westlake's margin to 7-6 with 8:42 left. **1977** C. MARTIN-JENKINS *MCC in India* iii. 51 Viswanath slashed, snicked and was caught by Knott. **1977** *World of Cricket Monthly* June 87/1 The self-appointed England exile slashed Sarfraz for two boundaries in the first over.

**3.** *trans.* To cut slits in (a garment) and so expose to view an under-garment or a lining of a contrasting colour; to vary *with* another material or colour in this way.

**1698** FRYER *Acc. E. India & P.* 9 A Coat slasht to hang back to shew their Sleeves. **1820** SCOTT *Monast.* xviii, A carnation-velvet doublet, slashed and puffed out with cloth of silver. **1831** CARLYLE *Sart. Res.* I. vii, Those enormous habiliments, that were..slashed and galooned. **1898** *Stratford-on-Avon Herald* 11 Feb., A morning dress was made with..cuff sleeves to match, slashed with bright colour.

*transf.* **1889** DOYLE *Micah Clarke* 26 The sun sinking slowly behind a fog-bank had slashed the whole western sky with scarlet streaks.

4. To cut with a scourge or whip; to lash, whip, thrash severely.

**1614** B. JONSON *Bart. Fair* IV. iv, You know where you were taw'd lately, both lash'd, and slash'd you were in Bridewell. **1688** HOLME *Armoury* III. 266/1 Here I stand, with whip in hand To slash all those that do oppose Good Husbandry. **1710** *Medley* No. 12, These the Emperor order'd to be daily beaten and slash'd in the Market-place with cudgels, whips, and scourges. **1823** SCOTT *Quentin D.* xxxiii, Drag him to the market-place!—slash him with bridle-reins and dog-whips! **1896** A. J. C. HARE *Story Life* I. iii. 173 He was very hot-tempered, and slashed our hands with a ruler.

5. To rebuke or assail cuttingly; to criticize severely or mercilessly. Also *absol.*

**1653** A. WILSON *Jas. I*, Pref. 4 History must not cauterise, and slash with Malice, those Noble Parts. **1659** PELL *Impr. Sea* Ded. a 5 b, Because you have Authority..to cut the comb of that, which this Book so sharply slashes, and reproves in the Sea. *a* **1734** NORTH *Examen* II. iv. §55 If we would see him in his Altitudes, we must go back to the House of Commons... There he cuts and slashes at another Rate. **1771** GRAY in *Corr. w. Nicholls* (1843) 121, I do not think myself bound to defend the character of even the best of kings. Pray slash them, and spare not. **1830** LYTTON *P. Clifford* v, Criticism is a great science and may be divided into three branches: viz. 'to tickle, to slash, and to plaster'.

6. To crack (a whip); to bring down in a slashing manner.

**1660** H. MORE *Myst. Godl.* VI. ii. 220 She slash'd a whip which she had in her hand; the cracks thereof were..loud and dreadful. **1695** BLACKMORE *Pr. Arth.* IX. 305 He slashed his breaded whip. **1852** MRS. STOWE *Uncle Tom's C.* iii. 13 Slashing his whip so near the horse that the creature was frightened. **1899** WERNER *Capt. Locusts* 113 She brought her switch down on the old grey's flank; and then..slashed it sharply across her own shoulders.

7. To beat, tread *down*.

**1841** CATLIN *N. Amer. Ind.* (1844) II. xxxiii. 18 Where the herds have slashed down the high grass.

8. Used adverbially to denote action or sound.

*a* **1654** SELDEN *Table T.* (Arb.) 71 A Whip that cry'd Slash. **1839** *John Bull* 11 Aug., Here, said he, and slash went the knife.

9. *Comb.* **slash-hook** = SLASHER 2 b.

**1891** R. WALLACE *Rural Econ. Austral. & N.Z.* xv. 231 Vines, creepers, supplejacks, and small saplings..require to be carefully cut by *slash-hooks. **1930** BLUNDEN *Poems* 188 Some harsh slash-hook Slit my skull and poured out all the fountains of my senses. **1942** [see FAGGING *vbl. sb.*[2]].

**slash** (slæʃ), *v.*[2] *slang.* [f. SLASH *sb.*[2] 2.] *intr.* To urinate.

**1973** M. AMIS *Rachel Papers* 189 If you can slash in my bed (I thought) don't tell me you can't suck my cock.

**slash-and-burn.** *attrib. phr.* Also **slash and burn, slash-burn, slash, burn.** [f. phr. *to slash and burn*: see SLASH *v.*, BURN *v.*[1]] Designating a method of shifting cultivation in which vegetation is cut down in an area of virgin or rejuvenated forest, allowed to dry, and then burned off before seeds are planted. Also occas. in non-*attrib.* use.

**1942** CHAPPLE & COON *Princ. Anthropol.* viii. 189 Linton has a theory that the development of confederacies by the Maya and the Indians of the southeastern States was a consequence of this aspect of the slash-and-burn system. **1951** [see SWIDDEN 2]. **1969** G. CLARK *World Prehistory* (ed. 2) vi. 126 The rapidity of their spread..was due in part to their use of slash and burn agriculture,..and in part to the lack of opposition. **1973** J. J. MCKELVEY *Man against Tsetse* iii. 190 The Kibori River eradication program..obviated the need to continue with a slash-burn program. **1976** *Conservation News* Sept./Oct. 5/1 The slash, burn, short-term cultivation and migration habit of tribal populations has been forced for centuries by the intractable fact that when an area of forest is cleared crops can be grown in it for only two or three seasons before the soil nutrients are exhausted. **1977** G. CLARK *World Prehistory* (ed. 3) III. 126 The regime of slash and burn, involving the shift of cultivation every few years and the clearance of new patches of forest, inevitably implied the temporary abandonment of settlements. **1978** *Guardian Weekly* 2 Apr. 13/1 Eking out a living by fishing, picking fruit and berries and by slash-and-burn farming.

Hence **slash and burn** *v. trans.*; **slashed and burnt** *ppl. a.* Also **slash-'burning** *vbl. sb.*, the process or practice of slash-and-burn agriculture.

**1919** *Jrnl. Forestry* XVII. 277 It is proposed..to conduct slash-burning operations under control in selected localities [in Canada] and observe the establishment of natural regeneration through a period of years. **1949** *Malayan Forester* XII. 83 The plot was established in order to ascertain the extent of soil erosion..and to study natural plant succession of the slashed and burnt..areas. **1954** *Brit. Columbia Lumberman* Mar. 78 Slash burning in a good seed year should precede seedfall, if possible. **1955** J. D. FREEMAN *Iban Agric.* VI. 128 Deleterious results..ensue when healthy, young vegetation..is slashed and burnt before proper regeneration..has taken place. *Ibid.* 129 Three sample plots were established to study 'natural plant succession', on (*a*) the slashed and burnt area [etc.]. **1980** *Search* XI. 71/2 Since slash-burning has been widely used [in Australia] only for the last 20–25 years, there has been no opportunity in Australian native forests to observe its effect on the productivity of successive forest rotations. **1981** P. THEROUX *Mosquito Coast* xii. 137 Slash and burn the whole area and we've got four or five acres of good growing land.

**slashed** (slæʃt), *ppl. a.* [f. SLASH *v.*[1] + -ED[1].]

1. Of garments: Having vertical slits to show a contrasting lining; in mod. use, having a piece of material of a different colour inserted.

**1633** SHIRLEY *Triumph of Peace* Plays (1888) 441 Confidence in a slashed doublet parti-coloured. **1649** QUARLES *Virgin Widow* III. i, Like a Cavalier, in a slasht suit. **1762–71** H. WALPOLE *Vertue's Anecd. Paint.* (1786) V. 79 Charles I. with ruff, ribband, and slashed habit. **1802** JAMES *Milit. Dict.* s.v., Slashed sleeves and pockets, which are peculiar to the British cavalry, when the officers or men wear long coats. **1887** *The Lady* 20 Jan. 37 Another [costume] of black velvet and white silk, with slashed sleeves.

2. Gashed, cut; deeply wounded. Also *absol.*

**1825** SCOTT *Betrothed* iii, A sound skin is better than a slashed one. *c* **1850** KINGSLEY *Misc.* (1860) II. 143 Chopping into small pieces the already slashed and slain.

3. *Bot.* Deeply cut; laciniate.

**1839** LINDLEY *Introd. Bot.* 138 Where leaves are extremely divided,..we say..that the leaf is multifid, laciniated, decomposed, or slashed. **1856** HENSLOW *Bot. Terms* 174 *Slashed*, where a surface is divided by deep and very acute incisions.

4. Of timber: felled, esp. in an unplanned or destructive manner. *N. Amer.*

**1843** *Yale Lit. Mag.* VIII. 332 His eye wandered far away over acres of slashed timber.

5. *Cricket.* Played with or resulting from a slash (SLASH *sb.*[1] 1 b).

**1974** *Observer* 9 June 24/8 A slashed catch to first slip accounted for Johnson. **1976** *S. Wales Echo* 27 Nov. 18/6 Reaching his half century in 138 minutes, he gave one difficult chance off a slashed stroke when he was 55, but Glenn Turner could not hold the ball at slip.

**slasher** ('slæʃə(r)). [f. SLASH *v.*[1] + -ER[1].]

1. a. One who slashes; a fighter, a bully; a slashing fellow.

**1559** *Mirr. Mag.*, *The Blacksmith* xxxii, With slashers, slaues and snuffers so falshod is in price, The simple faith is deadly sinne, and vertue counted vice. **1593** G. HARVEY *Pierce's Super.* Wks. (Grosart) II. 57, I..behold the glorious picture of that most-threatning Slassher. **1611** COTGR., *Chamailleur*, a slasher,..swash-buckler. **1785** GROSE *Dict. Vulgar T.*, *Slasher*, a bullying riotous fellow. **1830** LYTTON *P. Clifford* vi, The worn-out acerbity of an old slasher [= reviewer]. **1836** in C. K. Sharpe *Corr.* (1888) II. 495 Mrs. Villiers, in galloping to cover.., was pitched off, and frighten'd even the hard-hearted Melton Slashers. **1859** *Slang Dict.* 95 *Slasher*, a powerful roisterer, or pugilist. **1885** RUNCIMAN *Skippers & Shellbacks* 291 We'll make a slasher of him in a little bit.

b. *pl.* (See quot. 1802.)

**1802** JAMES *Milit. Dict.*, *Slashers*, a nickname which was given during the American war to the 28th regiment of foot. **1848** THACKERAY *Let.* 28 July, The other regiment in garrison at Canterbury, the Slashers if you please. **1898** *Times* 10 Jan. 11/6 When my original regiment, the 28th Gloucestershire, the gallant 'Slashers', arrived home from India in 1865.

2. a. A sword; a weapon for slashing.

**1815** SCOTT *Guy M.* xxxiii, 'Had he no arms?' asked the Justice. 'Ay, ay, they are never without barkers and slashers.' **1901** *Munsey's Mag.* XXIV. 445/2 The creese.. makes a frightful wound, whether used as a slasher or a sticker.

b. A billhook.

**1858** J. A. WARDER *Hedges & Evergreens* 98 The slasher with a wooden handle set at an angle with the edge of the blade. **1882** HAY *Brighter Brit.* I. 186 A billhook, or slasher, ..for the purpose of clearing all the undergrowth. **1883** *Pall Mall G.* 25 Oct. 10/3 One..was armed with a 'slasher', used for cutting hedges. **1916** J. B. COOPER *Coo-oo-ee* xi. 147 Cathead ferns and bracken..soon sprang up if he neglected to use the 'slasher', a large broad half-moon knife fixed to a stout ash handle. **1947** J. BERTRAM *Shadow of War* 70 Native convicts kept the lawns trimmed with formidable slashers.

c. An implement used in brick-making to detect stones in the clay.

**1889** C. T. DAVIS *Bricks & Tiles* v. 129 The hand-temperer then cuts through the small pile of clay with a tool termed a 'slasher'.

d. A form of circular saw used to cut logs into predetermined lengths, usu. having several blades mounted on the same shaft.

**1892** P. BENJAMIN *Mod. Mechanism* 777 A power-feed slab slasher, which differs greatly from the ordinary type of slabbing machines..has but one saw. **1915** *Saw in Hist.* III. 38 Then there are Slashers—Circular Saws used in a gang, and averaging four or more to each set. **1947** N. C. BROWN *Lumber* ii. 108 The slasher consists of a set of circular cut-off saws, generally arranged 49" apart on a single shaft, to cut slabs, edgings, and other sawmill refuse into suitable lengths for lath stock, broomhandle stock, fuelwood, or other purposes. **1963** R. R. A. HIGHAM *Handbk. Papermaking* v. 111 It will be assumed that they [*sc.* the logs] have already arrived at the slasher.

3. A severe criticism or review.

**1849** *Ainsworth's Mag.* Dec. 535 Writing squibs or slashers for electioneering purposes. **1858** THACKERAY *Let.* 27 Dec., A request for a notice might bring a slasher down upon you.

4. A form of sizing-machine for yarn, so called on account of its rapid working.

**1862** *Catal. Brit. Exhib.*, *Brit. Div.* I. §1515 Sizing Machine, commonly called Slasher, for sizing or dressing, and afterwards drying the warp preparatory to being woven. *Ibid.*, Slasher-sizing machine. **1875** KNIGHT *Dict. Mech.* 2199/1 In the slasher..the yarn runs through boiling size.

**'slashing,** *vbl. sb.* [f. SLASH *v.*[1] + -ING[1].]

1. The action of the verb; cutting; gashing.

**1596** NASHE *Saffron Walden* Ep. Ded., Discoursing of his fraies and deep acting of his slashing and hewing. **1649** MILTON *Eikon.* iv, Onely to turne his slashing at the Court Gate, to slaughtering in the Field. **1653** W. RAMESEY *Astrol. Restored* 13 We were at slashing and pelting with the Hollanders, and they with us. **1782** CREVECŒUR *Lett.* 81 How do you go on with your new cutting and slashing? **1855** MACAULAY *Hist. Eng.* xxi. IV. 655 Special orders were given ..that the swords should be made rather for stabbing than for slashing.

*attrib.* **1670** AUBREY *Miscell.* (1890) App. 214 Their servants..(in that slashing age) did commonly bang one another's bucklers.

2. a. The action of making a slit in a garment in order to show the lining or an under-garment of a contrasting colour; the opening thus made.

**1834** PLANCHÉ *Brit. Costume* 221 The elegant fashion of slashing makes its appearance about this time. **1882** CAULFEILD & SAWARD *Dict. Needlwk.* 451/2 Pieces of stuff of a different material being sewn under the Slashings.

b. A piece of material inserted in a garment of a different colour to form a contrast.

**1842** *Illustr. London News* 14 May 9/1 The slashing being fully studded..with diamonds, rubies, emeralds. **1887** *Sporting Life* 2 July 3/1 A dress of creamy white material with a pale pink slashing. **1888** *Athenæum* 27 Oct. 551/3 Brocaded trains gleaming fitfully with slashings of exquisite pink.

3. A heavy downpour of rain.

**1828** MRS. S. C. HALL *Sketches Irish Char.* (1842) 74 The rain fell in slashings, like hail.

4. *N. Amer.* a. The action of felling trees, esp. as a preliminary to clearing a tract of forest by burning.

**1822** *Port Folio* XIII. 68 The act of hewing down the timber is called *slashing*. **1833** A. FERGUSSON *Pract. Notes* 42 A mode of chopping is in use hereabouts, termed slashing. It consists in merely prostrating the trees, without any further operation for a season, and then at leisure consuming the whole by fire. **1899** W. A. MACKAY *Pioneer Life in Zorra* 167 There were three ways by which the first settlers cleared the land. The first was called 'slashing'. **1963** E. C. GUILLET *Pioneer Farmer & Backwoodsman* I. 309 Another easy and cheap method was 'slashing'..felling the trees and allowing them to stay where they fell for a season or two.

b. = SLASH *sb.*[1] 4 a.

**1840** *Jamestown* (N.Y.) *Jrnl.* 1 July 2/5 On Monday, the body of Mr. Brown was found in a slashing. **1894** *Outing* XXIV. 186/2 When we got into a spruce thicket or an old 'slashing'—the track of a hurricane. **1912** 'R. CONNOR' *Corporal Cameron of N.W. Mounted Police* 269 At the 'slashing' the wagon ruts faded out and the road narrowed to a single cow path.

c. = SLASH *sb.*[1] 4 b. Freq. *pl.*

**1864** T. WEED in T. L. Nichols *40 Yrs. Amer. Life* II. 215 Cattle..were turned out to 'browse' in the 'slashings'. **1928** P. A. TAVERNER *Ornithol. Invest. near Belvedere, Alberta* 104 *Mountain Bluebird*, not uncommon in the burnt spruce and slashings, but scarce elsewhere. **1964** *Islander* (Victoria, B.C.) 20 Sept. 5/2 Another small fire was burning in slashing on the west side of Reef Point. **1980** *Northeast Woods & Waters* Dec. 7/3 It headed into a small swamp made up of very thick and very low alders, criss-crossed with blowdowns and slashings.

5. The sizing of yarn by means of a slasher (sense 4) (see also quot. 1960).

**1895** R. MARSDEN *Cotton Weaving* 514 Blackburn prices for Tape-sizeing or Slashing. **1921** *Dict. Occup. Terms* (1927) §369 *Dresser*,..one who prepares delicate and fine yarns by passing them through sizing or slashing frame. **1960** *Textile Terms & Definitions* (Textile Inst.) (ed. 4) 136 *Slashing*,..(1) A synonym for slasher sizing. (2) This term has also been adopted to indicate the process which is used to reduce the extensibility of rayon yarns... The process consists in stretching the yarn in the wet state and then drying it while maintaining the stretched length.

**'slashing,** *ppl. a.* [-ING[2].]

1. Severely critical; cuttingly sarcastic.

**1735** POPE *Prol. Sat.* 164 From slashing Bentley down to pidling Tibalds. **1841** DE QUINCEY *Homer* i. Wks. 1857 VI. 312 The Alexandrian critics, with all their slashing insolence, showed themselves sons of the feeble. **1868** M. PATTISON *Academ. Organ.* §5. 306 Slashing style, and daring assertion,..are falling into discredit. **1895** *Tablet* 23 Mar. 457 A deliberate and slashing attack upon the Catholic Church.

2. That slashes or cuts severely. Also of weapons with cutting edges.

**1827** ROBERTS *Voy. Centr. Amer.* 70 Being 'called out' by one of these slashing gentlemen. **1863** *Reader* 31 Oct. 502 The way in which he cramps up his calves and toes as the next slashing blow is about to come down. **1890** W. J. GORDON *Foundry* 121, In every mill there are other saws.., such as 'slashing' saws for cutting slabs. **1950** H. L. LORIMER *Homer & Monuments* i. 34 To give better protection against the slashing sword. **1964** C. WILLOCK *Enormous Zoo* ix. 162 Their wrists adorned with semi-circular slashing knives and their fingers with the slashing blades they mount on rings.

3. a. Spirited; dashing; full of vigour. Now used esp. of horses.

**1828** SCOTT *F.M. Perth* viii, There goes the pride of Perth —there go the slashing craftsmen. **1852** BRISTED *Five Yrs. Eng. Univ.* (ed. 2) 276 They were mostly what would be called slashing men, who could do a great deal and do it well. **1862** *Illustr. Lond. News* 10 May 492/3 The Stockwell colt.. was a slashing horse. **1951** *Sport* 16–22 Mar. 20/2 A big slashing powerful chestnut with powerful limbs to support his considerable weight, he is equally good in front and behind the saddle. **1976** *Horse & Hound* 10 Dec. 8/1 Fred Winter was able to give Bula the run he needed..in Wednesday's Sundew 'Chase, named after the fine, big, slashing chestnut whom he rode to victory in..1957.

b. Of actions; *esp.* of pace, rapid.

**1824** W. IRVING *Tales Trav.* I. 54 My grandfather rode jollily along, in his easy slashing way. **1837** T. HOOK *Jack*

*Brag* iii, They all went off at a slashing pace. **1882** *Daily Tel.* 19 May, Making a slashing drive to the off for 4.

**c.** *spec.* in *Cricket*, playing or played in a vigorous or unrestrained manner. Cf. SLASH *v.*[1] 2 b.

**1832** P. EGAN *Bk. Sports* 346/1 A free slashing hitter, who holds it a crime To get any less than six runs a time. **1849** *Boy's Own Bk.* 69 Such implements as these [*sc.* the old bats] were but ill adapted even for what is termed 'slashing hitting'. **1885** [see FREE *a.* 8 f].

*Comb.* **1857** HUGHES *Tom Brown* II. viii, A long-armed, bare-headed, slashing-looking player coming to the wicket.

**4.** Very large or fine; splendid. Now chiefly *Austral.*

**1854** DICKENS *Hard T.* II. vii, Some fair creature with a slashing fortune at her disposal. **1861** *Harper's Mag.* Mar. 470/1 Capin Clapp..relaxed his rigid features..as he thought of the 'slashin' cargo we had aboard. **1969** *Telegraph* (Brisbane) 16 May 15/4 Elke Sommer in some slashing fashions takes up crime in this study of computerised skullduggery. **1973** *Ibid.* 16 Aug. 26/3 Who'll win a slashing $700 wardrobe just for looking her smart, bright self?

Hence **'slashingly** *adv.*, in a slashing manner; vigorously; severely.

**1659** TORRIANO, *A-slàscio*, slashingly, riotously. **1843** *Tait's Mag.* X. 743 He goes slashingly to work. **1893** *Review of Rev.* Dec. 626 Told so vividly and slashingly.

**slashy** ('slæʃɪ), *a. rare.* [f. SLASH *v.*[1]] Of a slashing nature.

**1862** CARLYLE *Fredk. Gt.* XI. iii. (1872) IV. 54 Its wit is very copious, but slashy, bantery.

**slat** (slæt), *sb.*[1] Forms: α. 4–7 sclat, 5 sklat, 6 sklatt(e, 6–7 sclatt. β. 4–7, 9 slatt, 6–7 slatte, 5– slat. [ad. OF. *esclat* (mod.F. *éclat*) splinter, shiver, piece broken or split off anything, related to OF. *esclater* to burst, of doubtful origin (cf. ÉCLAT *sb.*).]

With the following example, in which the sense is not clear, cf. *slate-incense* s.v. SLATE *sb.*[1] 7.—**1345–6** *Ely Sacr. Rolls* II. 133 In xxxiiij libris de slatt' pro incens' empt. 5[s]. 8[d].

**1. a.** A roofing-slate; a thin slab of stone used for roofing. Now *dial.*

**1382** WYCLIF *Luke* v. 19 By the sclattis thei senten him doun with the bed in to the myddil. **1387** TREVISA *Higden* (Rolls) I. 399 There lyme is copious, And sclattes also for hous. *c* **1440** *Promp. Parv.* 449 Sklat, or slat stone, *latericia, ymbrex.* **1521** in *10th Rep. Hist. MSS. Comm.* App. V. 399 No man shall buld..anny straue or tache housse..unlesse they be covered with sklattes. **1565** *Wills & Inv. N.C.* (Surtees, 1835) 234 For ij. foder of sclatts caring frome plawsworth. **1627** DRAYTON *Nymphidia* vi, The Roofe, instead of Slats, Is couer'd with the skinns of Batts. **1662** J. DAVIES tr. *Olearius' Voy. Amb.* 391 All the houses of the Village were cover'd with slats or tiles. **1823–** in many dialect glossaries (chiefly Midland and Southern). **1842** FRANCIS *Dict. Arts*, *Slatt*, a thin slab of stone used to cover buildings, distinct from what are called slates.

*transf.* **1387** TREVISA *Higden* (Rolls) VI. 55 He unheled chirches roves and coppes þat were i-heled wiþ slattes of bras, and took awey þe slattes.

**b.** Used to denote a certain shape.

**1634** *Lowe's Chirurg.* 354 Part of the bone is superficially separated like unto a little spelch or sclat. **1665** HOOKE *Microgr.* 81 The Figure of them is for the most part flat, in the manner of Slats. **1676** J. COOKE *Marrow Chirurg.* (1685) 377 Sediment like Meal, is ill. If like Slats, worst.

**c.** A large slab of stone. *rare.*

**1894** CROCKETT *Mad Sir Uchtred* v. 61 The burn comes down over broad slats of granite.

**2.** A writing-slate. Now *dial.*

*c* **1390** ? CHAUCER *Merciles Beaute* 34 Love hath my name y-strike out of his sclat. **1669** STURMY *Mariner's Mag.* V. xii. 63 Draw a Circle on a Slat or Paper. **1823** [see 3].

**3. a.** Slate used for roofing buildings. Now *dial.*

*c* **1400** *Laud Troy Bk.* 18362 Thei caste al doun thes worthi wones, Led & tyle, sclat & stones. **1412–3** *Abingdon Rolls* (Camden) 76 Et in ij M[l] sclat emptis. **1581** in W. H. Turner *Select. Rec. Oxford* (1880) 413 He shall..cover the same..w[th] slatt. **1598** SYLVESTER *Du Bartas* II. ii. IV. *Columnes* 43 Built but of Brick, of rusty Tiles, and Slat. **1823** E. MOOR *Suffolk Words* 360 *Slat*, slate, either that used at school, or to roof houses, or what is found among coals.

†**b.** Slate, or some slaty substance, used in the form of powder, esp. as a medicine; *Irish slat*, alum-slate. (Cf. SLATE *sb.*[1] 4 b.) *Obs.*

**1639** T. DE GRAY *Expert Farrier* 265 Take of black or blew slat, and make it into fine powder. **1643** SIR B. GRENVILE *MS. Letter*, I am something sore, and did spitt bloud two daies... I had no slatt, neither do I now need it. **1665** SIR R. HOWARD *Committee* 111, Go in and take some Irish slat by way of Prevention, and keep your self warm. **1684** in *Phil. Trans.* XX. 271 Irish Slat Pulveriz'd, and infus'd in Water.., would impart its Vitriolick Quality.

†**c.** Slate as a variety of stone or rock. *Obs.*

**1591** SYLVESTER *Du Bartas* I. iii. 896 Slat, Jet, and Marble shall escape my pen, I over-pass the Salt-mount Oromene. **1681** GREW *Musæum* III. II. ii. 329 A Metalline Slat from the Tin-Mines. **1697** in *Phil. Trans.* XXVII. 467 The Slat above this Coal afforded only Stalks of Plants.

**4. a.** A long narrow strip of wood or metal, used for various purposes.

**1764** *Museum Rust.* II. 189 Nailing of slats, old hoops, or laths, on the two sides and fore end of the cart. **1828–32** WEBSTER s.v., The slats of a cart or a chair. **1866** *Harvard Mem. Biogr.*, *R. Ware* I. 242 The bulk of those now in bed must have lain on the slats of the bedstead. **1885** C. F. HOLDER *Marvels Anim. Life* 28 Arranged in transverse rows, like slats on a blind. **1890** HALLETT *1000 Miles* 277 When the floors are of split bamboo..the interstices between the slats are many and often large.

**b.** In vehicles: (see quots.).

**1794** W. FELTON *Carriages* (1801) I. 31 The side pieces are called Slats, which are..hung on a centre pin or bolt to the elbow-rails. **1854** MISS BAKER *Northampt. Gloss.*, *Slats*, the sleepers or rails to support the bed of a cart. **1875** KNIGHT *Dict. Mech.* 2199/1 *Slat*,..a bent strip which bows over the seat and forms one of the ribs of the canopy.

**c.** *pl.* The ribs. *slang* (orig. and chiefly *U.S.*).

**1898** H. E. HAMBLEN *General Manager's Story* 33 There's nothing much the matter with him; few of his slats stove in, that's all. **1911** J. MASEFIELD *Everlasting Mercy* 11 Billy bats Some stinging short-arms in my slats. **1916** C. J. DENNIS *Ginger Mick* 28 Why don't ole England belt 'em in the slats? **1928** *New Yorker* 3 Nov. 44/2 When Mr. Kaplan pokes M. de Vos in the slats he (or it) [*sc.* the crowd] halloos rapturously for Mr. Kaplan. **1944** W. STEVENS *Let.* 12 Sept. (1967) 473, I want to give the office a kick in the slats. **1976** *Observer* (Colour Suppl.) 29 Feb. 33/1 The crunch probably came with the V & G report where, to my mind unfairly, certain civil servants got a real kick in the slats.

**d.** *Aeronaut.* The part of an aeroplane wing that is forward of a slot near the leading edge, or that can be moved forward to create such a slot and so provide additional lift. Cf. SLOT *sb.*[2] 2 d.

**1931** *Man. Rigging for Aircraft* (H.M.S.O.) (ed. 3) i. 12 Slots are a device for varying the air flow over the surface of an aerofoil, by the use of an auxiliary aerofoil, or slat, set parallel to and in front of the leading edge of the main aerofoil. **1935** C. G. BURGE *Compl. Bk. Aviation* 451/2 The slat behind which the slot itself lies is mounted so that it swings forward automatically when an angle of incidence some few degrees below stalling point is reached. **1960** C. H. GIBBS-SMITH *Aeroplane* I. xiii. 104 The slotted wing, matured in 1919,..was a device consisting of a curved slat (at first manually operated and then automatic) which was made to project from the leading edge of the wing and thus force air through the resulting slot and over the upper surface of the wing: the effect was to..postpone stalling.

**5. a.** *Basket-making.* (See quots.) Cf. SLATH.

**1837** HEBERT *Engin. & Mech. Encycl.* I. 153 The larger ones [*sc.* osiers] forming the slat and skeleton of the basket. **1851–4** *Tomlinson's Cycl. Useful Arts* (1867) I. 109/1 In this way the foundation of the basket, called the *slat* or *slate*, is formed.

**b.** *dial.* A hurdle.

**1883** C. R. SMITH *Retrosp.* I. 4 Some open hurdles, or slats as they are called in Kent.

**6.** *attrib.* and *Comb.* **a.** In senses 1–3, as ***slat-coal, -pen, -pin, -stone.***

**1412–3** *Abingdon Rolls* (Camden) 76 In sclatpynnes emptis xx d. **1436–7** *Ibid.* 114 Et in sclatpynnes et tyȝlpynnes emptis iiij s. *c* **1440** [see 1]. **1669** STURMY *Mariner's Mag.* IV. xii. 195 If you make it upon a Slat Stone, ..you may wipe the Arch, that is lightly drawn by a Slat Pen.., off at pleasure. **1713** *Phil. Trans.* XXVIII. 222 This resembles a Slat-Coal of a Lead colour.

**b.** In sense 4, as ***slat-awning, -bar, -bottom, -matting***; **slat-back** *a.* orig. and chiefly *U.S.*, of a chair: having a back constructed of several horizontal ribs (cf. *ladder-back* (*chair*) s.v. LADDER *sb.* 6); also *absol.* as *sb.*; **slat conveyor** (see quot. 1957); **slat fence** *U.S.*, a fence made of slats.

Various other combs. are given by Knight *Dict. Mech.* **1875** KNIGHT *Dict. Mech.* 2199/1 A corrugated iron *slat-awning. **1891** I. W. LYON *Colonial Furnit. New England* 165 They were called in their day 'bannister back', 'split back', 'slit back', and sometimes '*slat back' chairs. **1904** W. B. WARE *Seats of Colonists* 12 *Slat-back Chair*: Now often known as *Shaker Chair*, is the simplest expression of the *Turned Chair.* **1952** J. GLOAG *Short Dict. Furnit.* 434 *Slat back*, a name sometimes used for a primitive form of ladder back chair, with four or five slats between the seat and the top rail: a type made in the countryside. **1976** *Billings* (Montana) *Gaz.* 30 June 4-c/1 (Advt.), Slat-back rocker is constructed of selected hardwoods with an antique pine finish. **1876** VOYLE & STEVENSON *Milit. Dict.* 388/2 **Slat Bar*, the bar of a siege howitzer limber between the splinter bar and bolster. **1883** *Cent. Mag.* Oct. 819/2 The olives are first dried in trays with *slat bottoms. **1916** G. F. ZIMMER *Mech. Handling & Storing* (ed. 2) vii. 101 *Slat conveyors are used largely to carry substance in bags, also general merchandise packed in boxes and crates. **1957** J. A. W. HUGGILL in H. W. Cremer *Chem. Engin. Practice* III. 413 The slat conveyor, for packages, sacks and similar unit loads, has its carrying surface made of wooden or metal slats.., each attached to the chain links. **1790** W. BENTLEY *Diary* 22 June (1905) I. 180 The Principal Garden is in three parts divided by an open *slat fence painted white. **1938** M. K. RAWLINGS *Yearling* xxxiii. 424 He came to the slat fence. He felt his way along it. **1875** KNIGHT *Dict. Mech.* 2202/1 **Slat-matting*, a floor covering of wooden slats or veneers on a flexible fabric, which may be rolled like a carpet.

**slat** (slæt), *sb.*[2] [f. SLAT *v.*[2]]

**1.** A slap; a slapping blow. Now *dial.*

**1611** COTGR., *Truellée*, a trowell-full; or, a clap, slat, or slamp with a Trowell. **1746** *Exmoor Scolding* (E.D.S.) 101 Ad! chell gi' tha..a zlat in the chups. **1837–** in Devon and Somerset use (see *Eng. Dial. Dict.*). **1898** T. HARDY *Wessex Poems* 47 Such snocks and slats since war began Never saw recruit or veteran.

**2.** A sudden gust or blast *of* wind.

**1840** R. H. DANA *Bef. Mast* xxv, The sail..by a slat of the wind blew in under the yard with a fearful jerk.

**slat,** *sb.*[3] *rare*$^{-1}$. In 8 slatt. [a. Irish *slat* rod, measuring stick.] (See quot.)

**1780** YOUNG *Tour Irel.* I. 348 Frize..at a slatt or measure, four feet two inches long, and 20 to 23 inches wide.

**slat** (slæt), *sb.*[4] [? Irish.] A salmon out of season; a spent salmon.

**1870** *Daily News* 16 Feb., An unclean and unseasonable salmon of the species called 'kelts' in Scotland and 'slats' in Ireland. **1882** DAY *Fishes Gt. Brit.* II. 69 After spawning this fish [salmon] is a kelt or slat. **1886** *Field* 27 Feb. 261/1 These 'slats' would then escape, and the cause of a great injury to the fishing be prevented.

**slat** (*Cant*): see SLATE *sb.*[2]

**slat** (slæt), *v.*[1] Also 7 slatt. [f. SLAT *sb.*[1]] *trans.* To cover with slates. Now *dial.*

*c* **1475** *Crabhouse Reg.* (1889) 61 Sche made the cloystir.. and slattyd it. **1615** SIR R. BOYLE in *Lismore Papers* Ser. I. (1886) I. 79, I compounded with Iohn Lambert to slatt my new stable in yoghall. **1667** in Earwaker *E. Cheshire* (1877) I. 114 Paid for slatting the Lych porch. **1881** in EVANS *Leic. Gloss.*

**slat** (slæt), *v.*[2] Also 3 sclatte, 9 *dial.* sclat. [Of doubtful origin. Some of the senses resemble those of ON. *sletta* to slap, splash, etc., but this would not readily account for the currency of the word in south-western dialects. In sense 4 perh. partly imitative: cf. SLATTER *v.*[2]]

**1.** *trans.* To flap, cast, dash, impel quickly and with some force. Const. *down, against, on*, etc.

*a* **1225** *Ancr. R.* 212 Hwon heo ihereð þet god, heo sleateð [*v.r.* sclattes] adun boa two hore earen. **1611** COTGR. s.v. *Flacquer*, He squasht, slat, or squat her downe there. **1787** GROSE *Prov. Gloss.*, *To slat on*, to dash against, or cast on any thing. **1850** SCORESBY *Cheever's Whaleman's Adv.* xiii. (1858) 186 The danger from a whale's flukes and fins, as the monster slues and slats them round. *c* **1866** STATON *Rays fr. Loominary* 37 If he comes this way ogen..aw'll slat some watter on him. **1897** HOWELLS *Landlord at Lion's Head* 95 She'll slat the letters down every which way, and you've got to hunt 'em out for yourself.

**b.** To knock *off* by impact or pulling.

**1871** DE VERE *Americanisms* 545 Fishermen on the Eastern coast, who disengaged mackerel and other delicate-gilled fish by slatting them off the hook.

**2.** To strike, beat; to knock *out.*

**1577–87** HOLINSHED *Chron.* III. 1034/2 A butcherlie knaue named Fulks..slat him in the head with a club. **1604** MARSTON *Malcontent* IV. iii, *Men.* How did you kill him? *Mal.* Slatted his braines out. **1837–** in south-western dialect (see *Eng. Dial. Dict.*).

**3.** *intr.* (See quots.) *dial.*

**1838** HOLLOWAY *Prov. Dict.*, *To slat* or *sclat*, to beat with violence against any thing, as rain against a window. **1854** MISS BAKER *Northampt. Gloss.* s.v., What's the water's slatting off your hat on to your coat.

**4.** *Naut.* Of sails: To flap violently.

**1840** R. H. DANA *Bef. Mast* v, The great jib flying off to leeward and *slatting* so as almost to throw us off the boom. **1865** MRS. WHITNEY *Gayworthys* xxvi, The canvas slatting out and in, in great bights. **1881** CLARK RUSSELL *A Sailor's Sweetheart* III. vi. 256 The sail slatted so violently that it was as much as we could do..to get the canvas up to leeward.

**b.** In other contexts: To flap or slap.

**1889** 'MARK TWAIN' *Yankee at Court of K. Arthur* I. 120, I couldn't seem to stand that shield slatting and banging.. about my breast. **1897** —— *Man that corrupted Hadleyb.*, etc. (1900) 333 The removable desk-boards had been taken away, and nothing left for disorderly members to slat with.

Hence **'slatting** *vbl. sb.* and *ppl. a.*

**1883** *Cent. Mag.* Oct. 942/1 All hands..jumping aloft like monkeys to roll up the slatting canvas. **1888** CLARK RUSSELL *Death Ship* I. 46 Every moment this terrible slatting threatened her other spars.

**slat** (slæt), *v.*[3] Now *dial.* [prob. ad. OF. *esclater* to break in pieces: cf. SLAT *sb.*[1]] *intr.* and *trans.* To split.

**1607** TOPSELL *Four-f. Beasts* 415 It [the nail] slatteth and shiuereth in the driuing into two parts. **1609** HOLLAND *Amm. Marcell.* 424 Both head-peeces and habergeons were slat and dashed a peeces. **1702** *Burlesque of R. L'Estrange's Vis. Quevedo* 72 If his Horns had not been Flatted Perhaps my Head he might ha' Slatted. **1825–** in dialect glossaries (chiefly south-western).

†**slat,** *ppl. a. Obs.*$^{-1}$ [f. SLEAT *v.*[1]] Baited.

*c* **1300** *Pol. Songs* (Camden) 154 He sitteth ase a slat swyn that hongeth is eren.

**slatch** (slætʃ). ? *Obs.* [A derivative of OE. *slæc* SLACK *a.*, with normal palatalization.]

**1.** = SLASH *sb.*[4] *rare.*

**1603** OWEN *Pembrokeshire* (1892) 91 A slatch they call a peece of coal by itselfe found in the erthe and is quicklie digged about and no more to be found of that peece. **1916** T. C. CANTRILL et al. *Geol. S. Wales Coalfield* XII. xii. 116 It is probable that the circular or elliptical pockets of coal known as 'slatches' or 'slashes' are the remains of short closed synclinal masses of coal abnormally swollen out by the squeezing-down of the two sides of the syncline.

**2.** *Naut.* †**a.** The slack of a rope. *Obs.*

*a* **1625** *Nomencl. Navalis* (Harl. MS. 2301) 126 When.. parte of a Cabell or Roape doth hang slack,..then they said hale the Slatch of the Roape or Cabell. [Hence in Boteler, Holme, Harris, etc.] **1627** CAPT. SMITH *Seaman's Gram.* ix. 39 Hale vp the slatch of the Lee-boling. By Slatch is meant the middle part of any rope hangs ouer boord.

**b.** A brief respite or interval; a short period or spell (*of* some kind of weather, etc.).

*a* **1625** *Nomencl. Navalis* (Harl. MS. 2301), When it hath beene a sett of foule weather and that there comes an Interim ..of faire weather,..they call it a little Slatch of faire weather. [Hence in Boteler, Holme, Harris, etc.] **1633** T. JAMES *Voy.* 79 Wee could neuer haue a cleere slatch from Ice, to haue it vp. **1703** SIR H. SHERE *Medit. Sea* in *Ld. Halifax's Misc.* 9 At certain times in the Winter Season, they take their Slatches of Flood and Ebb according to their Occasions. **1730** WRIGLESWORTH *Jrnl. of the Lyell* 7 Apr., This morning it blowing Hard,..so [we] must wait for a slatch of fair Weather. **1769** FALCONER *Dict. Marine* (1780), *Slatch*, is generally applied to the period of a transitory breeze of wind, or the length of it's duration. [Hence in later Dicts.]

**slate** (sleɪt), *sb.*[1] Also (chiefly *north.* and *Sc.*) 4– **sclate** (5 **sclathe**), **sklate** (9 **sklet**); 5–9 **sclait** (6 **sclayt**), 5 **sklaytt**, 6 **sklaitt**, 6–9 **sklait**. [ad. OF. *esclate* fem., in the same sense as *esclat* masc., whence SLAT *sb.*[1] After *c* 1630 the forms with *scl-*, *skl-* are exclusively northern and Scottish.

The earliest example of the form occurs in sense 3, but the development of the senses must have been the same as in SLAT *sb.*[1]]

**1. a.** A thin, usually rectangular, piece of certain varieties of stone which split readily into laminæ (see 4), used especially for the purpose of covering the roofs of buildings.

Also freq. called a *roofing-slate*, and with distinguishing terms, as *blue, green, grey, white slate(s)*. For the older Sc. use of the word see SKAILLIE.

α. **1455** *Anc. Cal. Rec. Dublin* (1889) 284 Sclatys, bordes, gottorys, schall ly upon the key be the spase of xx. dayes. **1456** SIR G. HAYE *Law Arms* (S.T.S.) 228 As a sclate fell of a hous and slewe a man. *c* **1540** BOORDE *The Boke for to Lerne* B ij, Many tyles or sklates. **1584** *Reg. Privy Council Scot.* III. 678 Becaus thair is sklaittis, lyme, sand and tymmer to be transportit..to his said palice. **1832** CARRICK in *Whistle-Binkie* (1890) I. 213 Some o' them gaed ower the sklates As weel's your dainty dow.

β. **1530** PALSGR. 706/1, I sclate a house with stone slates. **1570** LEVINS *Manip.* 39/12 A Slate, tyle, *tegula, later.* **1600** J. PORY tr. *Leo's Africa* III. 202 The roofe is couered with certaine blacke stones or slates. **1662** GERBIER *Principles* 36 The Roof..should be covered either with Lead or blew Slates. **1745** *Season. Advice Protestants* 17 The Houses, that were formerly in good Repair, and cover'd with Slates, decay. **1758** J. S. *Le Dran's Obs. Surg.* (1771) 65 A Slate fell upon her Head from the Top of an House. **1811** FAREY *Derbyshire* I. 428 At Sheffield these white and grey Slates are exclusively used. **1841** JAMES *Brigand* xix, The house was built of cold grey stone, with a roof of slates. **1889** H. C. SEDDON *Builder's Work* (ed. 2) 231 Ordinary roofing slates are sold by the number... Some of the largest sized slates are..sold by the ton, and hence are called ton slates or weight slates.

**b.** A slab of slate, †or other stony substance; a laminated rock.

**1601** HOLLAND *Pliny* XVII. viii. I. 506 It [the Columbine marl] will resolve and cleave into most thin slates or flakes. **1601** R. JOHNSON *Kingd. & Commw.* 27 The Irish Ocean, a sea so shallow, and so full of rocks and slates [etc.]. **1876** *Encycl. Brit.* IV. 500 He [the slater] supplies sawn slates for shelving in larders and dairies.

**c.** In phr. ***to have a slate loose*** or ***off***, to be weak in intellect. (Cf. TILE *sb.*)

**1854** J. E. MILLAIS *Let.* 25 May in M. Lutyens *Millais & Ruskins* (1967) 216 Ruskin..is certainly *mad* or has a slate loose. [**1857** W. COLLINS *Dead Secret* III. i, The college tutor ..facetiously likened his head to a roof, and said there was a slate loosened in it.] **1860** *Slang Dict.* 218 He has a slate loose. **1862** *Athenæum* 27 Sept. 397 On too good terms with himself to think that..there is a 'loose slate', in his intellectual covering. **1867** MISS BROUGHTON *Cometh up as a Flower* xxxv, You must have a slate off this morning, Nell!

**d.** A flat piece or plate of some other material used for the same purpose as a roofing-slate.

**1887** *Archit. Soc. Dict.* VII. 87 'Glass slates' in roofing to lofts are sometimes used to admit light. *Ibid.* 89 Slating with very strong zinc slates. **1893** SPON *Mechanic's Own Book* (ed. 4) 617 Shingles, or wooden slates, are made from hard wood.

**2. a.** A tablet of slate, usually framed in wood, used for writing on.

*c* **1391** CHAUCER *Astrol.* II. §44 Consider thy rote furst,..& entere hit in-to thy slate. *Ibid.* §45 Take alle the signes,..& wryte hem in þy slate. **1571** DIGGES *Pantom.* I. xxviii, Ye must search Angles of position agayne, and marke them in the table or slate. **1635–56** COWLEY *Davideis* I. Wks. 1710 I. 315 Letters..painfully engrav'd in thin wrought Plates, Some cut in Wood, some lightlier trac'd on Slates. **1698** FRYER *Acc. E. India & P.* 112 A Board plastered over, which with Cotton they wipe out, when full, as we do from Slates or Table-Books. **1752** FOOTE *Taste* I, I can't remember her name, but 'tis upon the slate. **1768** TUCKER *Lt. Nat.* II. I. iii. 39 We proceed in the same manner a person would who should undertake to draw any plan assigned him upon a slate. **1826** *Art Brewing* (ed. 2) 53 We will now work a brewing according to the example in the instructions, on a slate. **1874** JEVONS *Princ. Sci.* (1900) 96, I have used a slate of this kind, which I call a Logical Slate, for more than twelve years.

*transf.* **1897** *Army & Navy Stores List* 750 Opal Slates in Leather Frame. *Ibid.* 757 Porcelain Menu Slate.

**b.** *fig.* A record of any kind concerning or against a person; esp. in phr. ***a clean slate***. Also in phrs. ***to wipe*** (***off***) ***the slate***, ***to wipe the slate clean***: to obliterate or cancel a record, usu. of a debt, misdemeanour, etc.; hence *loosely*, to make a fresh start.

**1868** E. YATES *Rocks Ahead* II. ii, He had passed the wet sponge over the slate containing any records of his early life. **1888** *Pall Mall G.* 27 Sept. 9/1, I can conceive nothing more desirable in the interests of these embarrassed tenants than that they should have a clean slate. **1899** [see ACTIVE *a.* 4]. **1921** G. B. SHAW *Back to Methuselah* p. lxix, We are helpless before a slate scrawled with figures of National Debts..the sensible thing to do is to wipe the slate and let the wrangling States distribute what they can spare. **1937** A. HUXLEY *Ends & Means* iv. 27 Where violence is pushed to its limits and the victims are totally exterminated, the slate is wiped clean and the perpetrators of violence are free to begin afresh on their own account. **1960** *Times* 2 Mar. 14/1 Tactically, Wolves must bank on all-out attack to wipe the slate clean. **1973** *Times* 28 Apr. 11/4 What I try to do each year is to wipe the slate clean. 'Now what can I do this year?'

**c.** Orig. and chiefly *N. Amer.* A list of candidates proposed for election or appointment to an official (esp. political) post; also *transf.*, the group of candidates so nominated; a group of candidates (occas. also of electors) with a set of shared political views.

**1842** *N.Y. Tribune* 24 Jan. 3/1 The Regency are obliged to put them on the *slate* to be rid of them, and then rub names out at leisure. **1877** *Ibid.*, 1 Mar. (Farmer), The facts about the latest Cabinet slate..are interesting as showing..the course of President Hayes in choosing his advisers. **1884** *American* VIII. 232 In dictated nominations, in the making of 'slates' for obedient party acceptance. **1888** BRYCE *Amer. Commw.* III. lxiii. II. 457 Some leading man..sketches out an allotment of places; and when this allotment has been worked out fully, it results in a Slate, *i.e.* a complete draft list of candidates to be proposed for the various offices. **1913** R. M. LAFOLLETTE *Autobiogr.* 12 Well, the fraternities made their slate and put it through. **1931** W. G. MCADOO *Crowded Years* xii. 182 The Governor had Brandeis on the slate as Secretary of Commerce. **1952** *Manch. Guardian Weekly* 1 May 2/2 There were..nine contests between slates of delegates pledged to Taft and slates pledged to Eisenhower. **1963** *Economist* 2 Nov. 18/1 Electors were originally independent agents, not bound to any party. However, 'slates' of electors soon appeared, usually, though not always, pledged..to one or other of the parties. **1968** *Globe & Mail* (Toronto) 13 Feb. 3/2 The Eglinton Federal Liberal Association last night..selected a complete slate of delegates pledged to vote for Finance Minister Mitchell Sharp at the national Liberal leadership convention. **1970** *New Yorker* 15 Aug. 78/3 Only three slates, or thirty candidates, can be elected. **1972** R. THOMAS *Porkchoppers* (1974) xxvi. 230 Cubbin voted without hesitation for himself and his slate. **1976** *National Observer* (U.S.) 12 June 2/2 Uncommitted slates led the voting in the Democratic Presidential primary. **1977** *N.Y. Rev. Bks.* 23 June 19/3 Eliav..who abandoned Labor in 1975, led a socialist and dovish slate ('Sheli') in this election. **1979** *Observer* 27 May 9/2 It was possible to see lists—Labour back-benchers are great ones for lists—giving the 'slates' of the Tribune and Manifesto Groups for the Shadow Cabinet elections.

**d.** A written record of a debt made when purchase of goods is allowed on credit. Also *fig.*, esp. in phr. ***on the slate***, on account. (See also quot. 1909.)

**1909** J. R. WARE *Passing Eng.* 188/1 *On the slate* (*Lower Peoples'*), written up against you—from the credit-slate kept in chandlers' shops. **1922** JOYCE *Ulysses* 369 Lose your customers that way. Pubs do. Fellows run up a bill on the slate and then slinking around the back streets into somewhere else. **1954** *Sun* (Baltimore) 30 Oct. 1/5 [London] Many food stores are putting the bills 'on the slate' until the men go back to work. **1966** 'J. HACKSTON' *Father clears Out* 114 The Site Committee..made history by going on the slate and ticking up a few rounds of drinks. **1973** J. MARKS *Mick Jagger* (1974) 39 He let them run a slate because they seemed like good sorts. **1980** *Observer* 7 Dec. 3/3 He knew of pharmacists who had been asked to put the bill 'on the slate' by families needing four or five prescriptions.

**3.** Roofing-slates collectively, or the material from which these are made.

α. *a* **1340** HAMPOLE *Psalter* civ. 23 þai..did treson [to the Israelites] forto less þaim in werke of mortere and sclate. **1392** *Mem. Ripon* (Surtees) III. 116 In sal. Simonis Sklater cooperantis et ponentis lapides de sklate. *a* **1513** FABYAN *Chron.* v. (1811) 113 He buylded a royall mynstre of lyme and stoone, and coueredit with platis of syluer in stede of sclate or leade. **1571** *Mem. Ripon* (Surtees) I. 309 Ten lode of sclait.

β. **1530** PALSGR. 720/2, I slate a house, I cover it with slate. **1555** EDEN *Decades* (Arb.) 194 Many also [are covered] with slate or other stone. **1582** N. LICHEFIELD tr. *Castanheda's Conq. Ind.* I. xl. 94 A greate citie, consisting of houses made of Earth, and couered ouer with broade stone or slate. *c* **1630** RISDON *Surv. Devon* (1810) 8 Of late days quarries of slate are found out, wherewith they cover houses. **1667** PRIMATT *City & C. Builder* 72 A Penthouse..covered with Tyles, Lead or Slate. **1725** *Fam. Dict.* s.v. *Slating*, Roofs cover'd with Slate, must be first Boarded over. **1841** *Penny Cycl.* XXI. 181/2 Houses of respectable appearance, roofed with slate.

**4. a.** An argillaceous rock of sedimentary origin, the different varieties of which have the common property of splitting readily into thin plates.

Many varieties are distinguished, esp. in *Geol.*, by special terms, as *clay, hornblende, mica, talc slate.*

**1653** COGAN tr. *Pinto's Trav.* (1663) 254 The extream trouble his people were at in planting their ladders against the walls by reason of their bad scituation which was all of Slate. **1676** *Phil. Trans.* XI. 764 There is also a sort of Mineral we call a Slate, which is partly Coal, partly Alum-stone, partly Marcasite, which being laid up in heaps and burnt, are used for hardening the Coal-ways. **1738** CHAMBERS *Cycl.* s.v., The same impressions are also frequently found on other substances, as on the black slate that lies over veins of coals. **1796** KIRWAN *Elem. Min.* (ed. 2) II. 19 This [slaty alum] is the stone called Black Slate, celebrated among the vulgar for its medicinal properties. **1811** A. T. THOMSON *Lond. Disp.* (1818) 24 The ore is first calcined with a low heat, so as to destroy the bituminous matter of the slate. **1852** LYELL *Elem. Geol.* (ed. 4) 266 The slate of Stonesfield..is a slightly oolitic shelly limestone. **1872** RAYMOND *Statist. Mines & Mining* 254 The quartz is divided by a horse of slate into two parts.

†**b.** ***Irish slate***, alum-slate, formerly used medicinally in the form of powder. *Obs.*

*a* **1704** T. BROWN *Wks.* (1720) III. 99 You must give him Irish Slate *quantum sufficit*. **1741** *Compl. Family-Piece* I. i. 22 Take of Irish Slate, *Sperma Ceti*, of each half a Dram.

**c.** With *a* and pl. A kind or variety of slaty rock.

**1704** *Dict. Rust.* (1726) s.v., Some Directions..whereby the..lasting Goodness of any Slate may be Experimented. **1728** CHAMBERS *Cycl.* s.v., Besides the Blue Slate, we have in England a Greyish Slate, call'd also Horsham Stone. **1841** *Penny Cycl.* XXI. 171/2 Undulations on slates and sandstones of every geological age. **1860** TYNDALL *Glac.* II. App. 430 The cleavage of slates is therefore not a question of stratification. **1903** MARR *Agric. Geol.* 234 Mudstones which, owing to the subsequent impress of cleavage, usually occur as slates.

**5.** A bluish-grey colour like that of slate.

**1813** JANE AUSTEN *Let.* 16 Sept. (1952) 327 There was but 2 yd and a qr of the dark slate in the Shop, but the Man promised to match it. **1882** SIR W. CROOKES *Dyeing & Tissue-Printing* 144 Light Slate. *Ibid.* 145 Slate on Cotton Wool. **1897** *Westm. Gaz.* 12 Nov. 1/3 Far to the south, where the slate of the sea and the grey of the sky wove together.

**6.** *attrib.* and *Comb.* **a.** Attrib. in the senses 'made or consisting of slate', 'having the character of slate', as ***slate-band***, ***-bed***, ***-belt***, ***-book***, etc., ***slate-clay***, ***-coal***, ***-marl***, ***-spar*** (see quots.).

**1810** S. SMITH *Agricultural Survey of Galloway* 20 *note*, The proper schistus,..called by English miners shiver, and in Galloway *slate-band. *Ibid.* 21 Strata of a soft shivering argillaceous stone, which..is called in the country slate-band. **1839** DE LA BECHE *Rep. Geol. Cornw.* vi. 184 The *slate-beds in the valley between Milton and Maristow. **1858** SIMMONDS *Dict. Trade* s.v., A billiard-table with a slate-bed. **1882** *U.S. Rep. Prec. Met.* 458 On the eastern or *slate belt great activity is manifested. Most of the mines are situated near the contact of the slate and the granite. **1858** SIMMONDS *Dict. Trade*, **Slate-book*, two or more slabs of framed slate bound together for writing on. **1804** R. JAMESON *Min.* I. 312 *Slate clay, shale. **1839** URE *Dict. Arts* 962 The strata of this section contain numerous varieties of ..slate-clay. **1805** R. JAMESON *Min.* II. 72 *Slate-Coal... Colour intermediate between velvet-black and dark greyish-black. **1883** GRESLEY *Gloss. Coal-m.* 225 *Slate Coal*, a hard, dull variety of coal, not unlike Cannel. **1803** A. HUNTER *Georgical Ess.* I. 233 A drachm of a friable *slate-marl afforded a residuum of eighteen grains of yellow sand. **1805** R. W. DICKSON *Pract. Agric.* I. 238 Where this sort of marle has a thin laminated structure.., it is frequently denominated *slate marle.* **1796** KIRWAN *Elem. Min.* (ed. 2) I. 344 The aggregate of quartz and mica..is, when it is slaty, called *slate mica, or shistose mica, or slaty mica. **1793** W. H. MARSHALL *W. Eng.* (1796) II. 344 The *slate-rock waters of this District are superior to those of any others. **1813** COLERIDGE *Remorse* II. i, There where the smooth high wall of slate-rock glitters. **1860** TYNDALL *Glac.* II. App. 432 Fossil shells are found in these slate-rocks. **1578–9** *Reg. Privy Council Scot.* III. 99 [They] enterit in the said hous, ..and thaireftir tuke doun the *sklait ruife. **1875** KNIGHT *Dict. Mech.* 2200/1 The pitch of a slate roof should not be less than 1 in h[e]ight to 4 of length. **1821** SCOTT *Kenilw.* xx, A devil's ally, that can change *slate-shivers into Spanish dollars. **1858** SIMMONDS *Dict. Trade*, **Slate slab*, a sheet or plate of slate. **1804** R. JAMESON *Min.* I. 508 *Slate Spar... Its colour is milk, greenish and reddish white. **1858** J. NICOL *Elem. Mineral.* 203 *Slate spar*, thin, lamellar,..with a shining white pearly lustre and greasy feel. **1877** RAYMOND *Statist. Mines & Mining* 65 The character and features of this *slate-stratum. **1855** J. R. LEIFCHILD *Cornwall* 81 The *slate-system [of rocks] has obtained its full share of such attention. **1531** *Lett. & Papers Hen. VIII* (1880) V. 183 Payment to John Cornelis of Handwarp, for..making of *slate tyle. **1778** *England's Gaz.* (ed. 2) s.v. *Padstow*, The trade in slate-tiles. **1867** MUSGRAVE *Nooks & Corners Old France* II. 6 A lofty domicile..exhibiting laths, timbering and *slatework.

**b.** Instrumental, as ***slate-floored***, ***-formed***, ***-hung***, ***-pointed***, ***-roofed***, ***-spired***, ***-strewn***; ***slate-thatcher***.

**1648** HEXHAM II, *Een Schalie-decker*, a Slate-thatcher, or Coverer. **1789** J. WILLIAMS *Min. Kingd.* I. 235 The thin slate-formed argillaceous strata of the coal metals. **1862** H. MARRYAT *Year in Sweden* I. 238 Leckö Slott with her grand slate-spired towers. **1890** 'R. BOLDREWOOD' *Miner's Right* xxv. (1899) 116, I had crossed more than one crest of the slate-strewn ranges. **1930** J. DOS PASSOS *42nd Parallel* IV. 292 The shining gray slate-pointed roofs of Quebec. **1948** J. BETJEMAN *Sel. Poems* 116 The slate-hung, goodly-builded house. **1960** *Times* 26 Mar. 9/5 Indeed, everything here recalls France—the squares and cobbled streets, the whitewashed walls and dormered slate-pointed houses. **1978** J. L. HENSLEY *Killing in Gold* (1979) xi. 151 The slate-floored entrance hall. **1981** V. GLENDINNING *Edith Sitwell* xi. 151 A whitewashed slate-roofed village.

**c.** Objective, as ***slate-cutter***, ***-maker***, ***-picker***, etc.; ***slate-cutting***, ***-dressing***, etc.

(*a*) **1780** *Westm. Mag.* Suppl. 730/1 Slate-mak[er]. **1833–4** J. PHILLIPS *Geol.* in *Encycl. Metrop.* (1845) VI. 703/1 The slate-workers of Stonesfield. **1875** KNIGHT *Dict. Mech.* 2200/2 *Slate-cutter*, a machine for cutting the edges of roofing or other slates.

(*b*) **1839** URE *Dict. Arts* 329 The stone slag, or copper cinder, resulting from the slate-smelting. **1875** KNIGHT *Dict. Mech.* 2200/2 Slate-beveling, -cutting, -making, -trimming, Machine. **1894** *Daily News* 13 June 5/2 Collecting data as to the methods of slate-dressing.

**d.** With names of colours, as ***slate-blue***, ***-brown***, ***-grey***. Also *attrib.*, of a slate colour.

(*a*) **1796** KIRWAN *Elem. Min.* (ed. 2) I. 152 Leek green, or slate blue. **1839** URE *Dict. Arts* 619 For several other shades as..slate-gray. **1871** KINGSLEY *At Last* vii, A slate-blue heron rose lazily off a dead bough. **1883** *Cent. Mag.* Sept. 729 Latticed porticoes, and slate-brown paint. **1937** *Discovery* Dec. 384/2 Its black or slate-grey body. **1976** *National Observer* (U.S.) 6 Nov. 21 (Advt.), Generously cut in quality wool gabardine—Mid-Fawn, Slate Grey or Lovat.

(*b*) **1872** COUES *N. Amer. Birds* 233 Tail..entirely black, or with only a slight slate tipping. **1889** SAUNDERS *Brit. Birds* 646 The adult in summer has a slate or greyish-black hood.

**7.** Misc. and special combs., as ***slate-like*** adj., ***slate-merchant***, ***-mine***, ***-pit***, ***-quarry***, etc.; **slate-axe** (see quots.); **slate-board**, **-boarding** (see quot. 1833); **slate club**, a sharing-out club, whose accounts are nominally kept on a slate;

**slate-frame** (see quot.); **slate-galiot**, a vessel carrying slates; **slate house** *Sc.*, a house with a slated roof; † **slate-incense**, ? (cf. note to SLAT *sb.*[1]); **slate-knife**, a knife used for splitting slates; **slate-land** (see quot.); **slate-nail, -peg, -pin**, a nail, peg, or pin used to fix a slate on a roof; **slate-saw** (see quot.); **slate-writer**, a person who practises slate-writing; **slate-writing**, in spiritualism: writing performed on a slate, attributed to the agency of a medium, but without physical contact of the medium and the writing instrument.

**1828–32** WEBSTER, **Slate-ax*, a mattock..used in slating. **1858** SIMMONDS *Dict. Trade, Slate-axe*, a mattock for shaping slates for roofing, and making holes in them to fasten them to the roof. **1842** *Civil Eng. & Arch. Jrnl.* V. 242/2 The *slate-boards are supported by five purlins 4 ft. apart. **1833** LOUDON *Encycl. Archit. Gloss.*, **Slate-boarding*, boards placed on the roof, on which to nail the slates. **1888** *Daily News* 27 Dec. 7/5 He would pay her in the evening, as he was in a *slate club. **1891** J. F. WILKINSON *Mutual Thrift* 60 Taking London, we have a large number of old dividing clubs located in the East End, and known as 'Birmingham societies' or 'Slate clubs'. **1858** SIMMONDS *Dict. Trade*, **Slate-frame*, the narrow wood border for a writing-slate or slate-book. **1887** DOWDEN *Shelley* I. v. 235 When at length they set sail in a *slate-galiot, a storm whirled them quite up to the north of Ireland. **1554** *Reg. Mag. Sig. Scot.* 198 De domo tegulata, vulgo ane *sklait hous. **1815** in *Pennecuik's Wks.* 243 *note*, A wild and solitary site for a slate house, yet proper for a hunting seat. **1470–1** *Mem. Ripon* (Surtees) III. 217 In incenso vocato *Sclate-incense empto ad deserviendum in choro festis duplicibus principalibus, nil hoc anno. **1484–5** *Ibid.* 222. **1825** J. NICHOLSON *Operat. Mechanic* 622 The instruments used in splitting and cleaning slates are, *slate-knives, axes, bars, and wedges. **1733** TULL *Horse-Hoeing Husb.* xiv. 196 (Dublin ed.), Poor **Slate* Land [*note*, lying upon Slate or Stone]. **1898** *Pop. Sci. Monthly* 523 Impressions..have been left upon *slate-like rocks. **1858** SIMMONDS *Dict. Trade*, **Slate-merchant*, an importer or wholesale dealer in slates. **1648** HEXHAM II, *Een Schalie-myne*,..a *Slate-mine. **1880** A. MCKAY *Hist. Kilmarnock* (ed. 4) 300 He now, with the forefinger of his left hand, got hold of a *slate-nail. **1875** KNIGHT *Dict. Mech.* 2201/1 **Slate-peg*, a kind of nail used in securing slates on a roof. **1579** in Willis & Clark *Cambridge* (1886) I. 312 Lathe, ..*slatepyne, and nayles. **1736** DRAKE *Eboracum* I. ii. 64 At the end of each tile is a hole that would receive a common slate pin. **1611** COTGR., *Ardoisiere*, a *slate-pit, *slate quarrey. **1829** SCOTT *Bl. Dwarf* Introd., He was the son of a labourer in the slate-quarries of Stobo. **1846** TENNYSON *Golden Year* 75, I heard them blast The steep slate-quarry. **1875** KNIGHT *Dict. Mech.* 2201/2 **Slate-saw*, a machine for trimming the edges of slate-slabs to shape. **1858** SIMMONDS *Dict. Trade*, **Slate-works*, a yard, etc. where slate is sawn or shaped. **1902** F. PODMORE *Mod. Spiritualism* II. IV. ii. 221 Professional *slate-writers. **1949** G. B. SHAW *Buoyant Billions* 7 They have a cohort of Slate Writers and Writing Mediums. **1885** *Century Mag.* July 382/2 She can do the trance business, and knocks, and *slate-writing, and all that sort of thing. **1898** *Sci. Amer.* 8 Oct. 229/2 There has probably been nothing that has made more converts to spiritualism than the much talked of 'Slate Writing Test'. **1930** H. CARRINGTON *Story of Psychic Science* VI. 147 The majority of messages..have been upon *slates*—hence the former popularity of 'slate-writing' mediums. **1977** B. INGLIS *Natural & Supernatural* xxviii. 277 Slade was one of the practitioners of the new technique: slate-writing. **1860** TYNDALL *Glac.* I. I. 6, I..visited *slate-yards and quarries.

† **slate**, *sb.*[2] *Cant. Obs.* (See quots.)

a. **1567** HARMAN *Caveat* (1869) 61 Some of these goe with slates at their backes, which is a sheete to lye in a nightes. *Ibid.* 76 Their mothers carries them at their backes in their slates, whiche is their shetes. [Hence in later works; in the *Dict. Cant. Crew* (*a* 1700) given as *slat.*] **1622** FLETCHER *Beggar's Bush* III. iii, To Mill from the Ruffmans, commision and slates.

b. *a* **1700** B. E. *Dict. Cant. Crew, Slate*, a half Crown.

**slate** (sleɪt), *sb.*[3] [f. SLATE *v.*[2]] A severe criticism; a slating.

**1887** LANG *Books & Bookmen* 19 'Slate' is a professional term for a severe criticism. **1889** HANNAY *Marryat* 157 Carlyle's savage 'slate' of him [Marryat] is unjust.

**slate**, *sb.*[4] *Sc. rare.* [Of obscure origin.] A slovenly, dirty person.

**1715** RAMSAY *Christ's Kirk Gr.* II. vi, Had aff [= hold off], quoth she, ye filthy slate. **1806** JOHN HOGG *Poems* 74 (Jam.), The blether-lipped drunken slate!

**slate** (sleɪt), *v.*[1] Also 6 **sclate, slaytt**, 7 *Sc.* **skleat**. [f. SLATE *sb.*[1]]

**1.** *trans.* To cover or roof with slates.

**1530** PALSGR. 706/1 It is better to sclate a house with stone than to tyle it. **1554** in Willis & Clark *Cambridge* (1886) II. 470 Covenaunted wyth Odam to slaytt the new Buylding. **1605** *Ibid.* 491 Thomas Yates to slate yᵉ Hall. **1624** CAPT. SMITH *Virginia* IV. 108 Houses..built..warme and defensiue..as if they were tiled and slated. **1637–50** ROW *Hist. Kirk* (Wodrow Soc.) 471 Walls were not repaired nor the roofe skleated till three yeares after. **1708** S. SEWALL *Diary* 23 Aug., I pleaded that Mr. Dudley had been at great Charge to Slate his House. **1833** LOUDON *Encycl. Archit.* §947 The gables are to be slated over. **1883** *Law Times Rep.* XLIX. 138/2 The defendant..had on several occasions employed S. to slate houses for him.

*absol.* **1727** SWIFT *Vanbrugh's House* Wks. 1755 III. II. 64 A lyrick ode wou'd slate; a catch Wou'd tile; an epigram wou'd thatch. **1941** *Cross & Plough* Ladyday 9/2 To shelter him, man had to fell timber,..to burn bricks and tiles, to thatch and to slate.

**2. a.** To put down (a name, etc.) on a writing-slate; to set down, book, *for* something; also const. *to* with *inf.* Also, to plan, propose, or schedule (an event). Chiefly *U.S.*

**1883** *Daily News* 18 Sept. 6/2 He had been 'slated' for a month—that is, his name was entered upon a slate in the porter's lodge, which indicated that he was dangerously ill. **1896** *Harper's Mag.* XCIII. 25/1 So the Professor was unconsciously slated for the office of hero. **1904** F. LYNDE *Grafters* xxvii. 343 Griggs was on for the night run eastward with the express; and 'Dutch' Tischer had found himself slated to take the fast mail west. **1936** WODEHOUSE *Laughing Gas* ix. 94 You ought to be thanking me on your knees for warning you. Yes, sir, unless you pull up mighty quick, you're slated to get yours. **1944** *College Topics* (Univ. of Virginia) 30 Mar. 3 No one has been slated for the 220, but Wenger may run in that event. **1960** *Times* 14 Sept. 12/6, I was intrigued to see this heading in a Charleston paper 'Church Tour slated'... It turned out to be nothing more than the announcement of an annual plantation tour..to raise funds for the local Protestant Episcopal Church. **1966** [see LOCOMOTIVE *sb.* 4]. **1971** *Wall St. Jrnl.* 22 July w1/2 The Treasury is offering new 7%, 10-year bonds... Other cash-raising moves are also slated. **1973** *Oxf. Mag.* 4 May 10/1 When Americans mean to do something they *slate* it, rather than timetable or table it. When they do *table* it, they don't mean to do it. **1979** *Farmington* (New Mexico) *Daily Times* 27 May 3A/3 Gov. Bruce King and..Navajo Tribal Chairman Peter MacDonald are slated to attend the ceremony.

**b.** *spec.* to propose or nominate a candidate for political office; to form a slate (SLATE *sb.*[1] 2 c) of candidates. *U.S.*

**1804** J. PEARSON *Let.* 26 Nov. in J. Steele *Papers* (1924) I. 441 The Federalists have not, nor do they intend slating a candidate. **1912** T. DREISER *Financier* xxvii. 297 Stener, although he had served two terms, was slated for re-election. **1961** T. H. WHITE *Making of President 1960* iv. 100 On one huge ballot the Charlestonian was offered *fifty-three* individual choices of candidates if he wished to ponder his selections. Such a mystifying ballot requires simplification ..supplied by 'slating'. The local bosses, the union chiefs, the statewide candidates, the education-board candidates, even the veterans organizations, all make cross-alliances to settle on, then print, a 'slate' of approved candidates among the multitude of names.

**3.** To scrape (a skin or hide) with a slater to remove loosened hairs.

**1885** C. T. DAVIS *Manuf. Leather* xxxii. 527 Upon removal from the bate the skins are 'slated', which is the removal of the fine hair remaining upon the skins after the unhairing operation.

**slate** (sleɪt), *v.*[2] *slang* and *colloq.* [app. f. SLATE *sb.*[1] Sense 2 appears to have originated in Ireland.]

**1.** *trans.* (See quot. 1865.) ? *Obs.*

**1825** C. WESTMACOTT *English Spy* II. 158 Another point of amusement is *flying a tile* or *slating* a man as the phrases of the Stock Exchange describe it. **1865** *Slang Dict.* 234 *Slate*, to knock the hat over one's eyes, to bonnet.

**2.** To beat or thrash severely.

**1825** KNAPP & BALDW. *Newgate Cal.* IV. 149/1 Slate him, the Dublin word for an unmerciful beating. **1857** KINGSLEY *Two Y. Ago* III. 159 Putting his head in cautiously for fear of drunken Irishmen, who might be seized with the national impulse to 'slate' him.

**b.** *Mil.* To punish (an enemy) severely.

**1854** CHAMPION in Kinglake *Crimea* (1877) V. 375 'Slate 'em, slate 'em, my boys!' was his exulting..adjuration. **1885** WILSON *From Korti to Khartum* (1886) 163 Now we shall get 'slated', I thought..; a few good shots might have picked off every one on deck. **1902** 'LINESMAN' *Words Eyewitness* 107 Their smaller guns..kept it up far into the night, slating the reverse slopes of the Krantz with wonderful accuracy.

*transf.* **1883** *Harper's Mag.* Apr. 688/1 A billiard table in an overcrowded hotel, even with a railway rug around one, is apt to 'slate' the sleeper before morning.

**3.** To assail with reproof or abuse; to rate or reprimand; to scold severely.

**1840** *Blackw. Mag.* XLVIII. 210, I weep over the realm's decay, and have some notion of *slating*—excuse me for borrowing a word from the vocabulary of the new ministerial and courtly party of Ribandism—Lord Palmerston. **1860** *Slang Dict.* 218 *Slate*, to pelt with abuse. **1866** BROGDEN *Prov. Lincs.*, *Slate*, to scold. **1881** MRS. LYNN LINTON *My Love* II. 306 Val slated me hard enough. So we may cry quits over that.

**b.** To criticize (a book or author) severely; to castigate, cut up.

**1848** A. WATTS in *Life* (1884) II. 258 And, when they'd been by critics slated, Had always the review to show 'em. **1870** 'OUIDA' *Puck* xvi, That wretched Mouse, when he wants to slate a very good novel. **1890** SAINTSBURY *Ess. Eng. Lit.* p. xxv, You slated this [book], and it has gone through twenty editions.

**slate** (sleɪt), *v.*[3] *north.* and *Sc.* Also 4–5 **slayt**, 6–7 *Sc.* **slait**. [ad. ON. **sleita*, corresponding to OE. *slǣtan*: see SLEAT *v.*[1]]

**1.** *trans.* To incite or set on (a dog). Also const. *on, at, against* (a person, etc.).

**13..** *Metrical Hom.* (Vernon MS.) in Herrig *Archiv* LVII. 266 þei sayh beestes..and þei hem bayted Wiþ houndes þat þei on hem slayted. *c* **1375** *Sc. Leg. Saints* xxx. (*Theodora*) 657 þat feynd..slaytyt þaim full fellonly, & bad þai suld þat hure wery. **1501** DOUGLAS *Pal. Hon.* I. xxii, Diane..him in forme hes of ane hart translatit. I saw (allace) his houndis at him slatit. *a* **1568** BALNEVIS in *Bannatyne MS.* 393 Thairfoir had bound thocht scho be found, Or dreid thy doggis be slaittit. **1787** GROSE *Prov. Gloss.* s.v., To slate the dog at any one. **1796** in Pegge *Derbicisms* (E.D.S.) 63. **1828** CARR *Craven Gloss.*, *Slate*, to set on, to incite. **1876** *Mid-Yorksh. Gloss.* 126 I'll slate my dog against thine.

**2.** To bait, assail, or drive, with dogs. Also *fig.* Hence **'slating** *vbl. sb.*

**13..** *K. Alis.* 200 (Laud MS.), þer was..Of lyons chace, of bere baityng, A-bay of bore, of bole slatyng. **1684** *Yorkshire Dial.* (ed. 2) 43, I did Slate him back than with our Dog. *Ibid.* 106 *To slate a Beast*, is to hound a Dog at him. **1755** *Guthrie's Trial* 143 (Jam.), It is much to be lamented, that people professing his name, should be so slaited and enslaved by transgression as many are.

**'slate-colour.** [SLATE *sb.*[1]] The bluish-grey colour of slate.

**1799** in M. Edgeworth *Parent's Assistant* (1800) VI. 119 Mr. Davis, slate-colour and straw. **1826** KIRBY & SP. *Entomol.* III. xxxii. 303 The abdomen of the male is usually slate-colour. **1835** *Ladies' Cabinet* Nov. 338 Fashionable colours,..slate-colour and myrtle green. **1889** SAUNDERS *Brit. Birds* 642 The mantle is slate-colour. **1919** E. O'NEILL *Rope* in *Moon of Caribbees* 180 The sea is a dark slate color.

**'slate-coloured**, *a.* [SLATE *sb.*[1] Cf. prec.] Of the colour of slate, usually bluish-grey.

**1801** SHAW *Gen. Zool.* II. II. 319 Slate-coloured Antelope. **1811** *Ibid.* VIII. I. 261 Slate-coloured Creeper. **1812** A. WILSON *Amer. Ornith.* VI. 13 Slate-colored Hawk, *Falco Pennsylvanicus*. **1836–7** DICKENS *Sk. Boz* (1850) 135/2 Grandmamma in a high cap, and slate-coloured silk gown. **1871** DARWIN *Desc. Man* II. xvi. (1890) 481 Young swans are slate-coloured. **1874** COUES *Birds N.W.* 162 *Passerella Townsendii*,..Slate-coloured Sparrow.

**slated** ('sleɪtɪd), *ppl. a.*[1] Also *Sc.* **sclated, sklaitit**. [f. SLATE *v.*[1] + -ED[1].] Covered with slate or slates. Used *pred.* and *attrib.*

*pred.* **1611** COTGR., *Ardoisé*, slated, couered with slates. **1634** BRERETON *Trav.* (Chetham Soc.) 50 Here..a brave fish-market, the stalls curiously slated. **1719** DE FOE *Crusoe* II. (Globe) 411 His House was as dry as if it had been til'd or slated. **1806** *Gaz. Scotl.* 600 There were 72 houses, of which 35 were slated. **1834** *Brit. Husb.* (L.U.K.) I. 104 The house and buildings are brick, and slated.

*attrib.* **1798** HUTTON *Course Math.* II. 90 The content of a slated roof. **1843** THACKERAY *Irish Sk.-bk.* xi, A dismal, rickety building, with a slated face. **1886** RUSKIN *Præterita* I. v. 168 The houses..with high and steep slated roof.

**slated** ('sleɪtɪd), *ppl. a.*[2] [f. SLATE *v.*[2]] Reproved, scolded; severely criticized or attacked.

**1872** E. PEACOCK *Mabel Heron* I. 80 Think how he went away like a slated dog—rated I should have said. **1897** *Daily News* 13 Jan. 6/4 One of the consolations of the 'slated' author. **1899** *Westm. Gaz.* 18 Apr. 2/3 The athletic friends of the 'slated' authoress.

**'slateful.** [f. SLATE *sb.*[1] 2.] As much or as many as can be written on a slate.

**1836** E. HOWARD *R. Reefer* xxvi, A slatefull of..*x, y, z*'s. **1866** E. B. ELLIOTT *Mem. Ld. Haddo* xviii. (1868) 350 A slateful of names had been gone through.

**'slate-pencil.** [SLATE *sb.*[1]]

**1.** A pencil, made of soft slate or other material, used for writing on a slate.

**1759** *Phil. Trans.* LI. 483 Some wear, at their nostrils, slate pencils, about four inches long. **1810** *Risdon's Surv. Devon* p. xv, A manufactory of slate pencils has of late been established. **1875** KNIGHT *Dict. Mech.* 2201/1 The common irregularly shaped black slate-pencils..are made in Germany.

**2.** The material of which slate-pencils are made.

**1801** *Phil. Trans.* XCI. 436 Children..often introduce.. pieces of slate-pencil, and even pins into their ears. **1838** DICKENS *Nickleby* i, Putting out at good interest a small capital of slate-pencil and marbles.

*attrib.* and *Comb.* **1882** BRET HARTE *Flip* ii, A greyish slate-pencil pallor. **1894** *Proc. Geol. Assoc.* XIII. 364 Slate-pencil-coloured strings of clay.

**slater**[1] ('sleɪtə(r)). Also 5, *Sc.* 7–9 **sclater**, 5 *Sc.* **sclatar(e**; 6, *Sc.* 9 **sklater**, 6 *Sc.* **skläittar, skleattar**; 6 **slaiter**. [f. SLATE *sb.*[1] or *v.*[1]]

**1.** One whose work consists in laying slates.

α. **1408** *Mem. Ripon* (Surtees) III. 137 In sal. Will. Fyscher sclater operantis et emendantis. **1488** *Acc. Ld. High Treas. Scot.* I. 89 To a sclatar for the poyntin of al the place off Stirling. **1561** *Dunfermline Reg.* (Bann. Cl.) 454 To ye sklaittar and his servandis. *c* **1600** *Chester Pl., Banes* 92 You wrightes and sklaters, with good players in showe. **1808** JAMIESON Addit., *Sclater*. **1823** GALT *Entail* xlix, His sklater that pointed the skews o' the house.

β. **1562–3** *Act 5 Eliz.* c. 4. §xxiii, Tharte or Occupation of a..Tyler, Slater, Healyer, Tilemaker. **1591** *Wills & Inv. N.C.* (Surtees, 1860) 200 Thre slaiters and a boye. **1663** GERBIER *Counsel* 50 When some of the slates are broke, the Slater mends them with little charge. **1723** *Lond. Gaz.* No. 6222/9 Thomas Hookam,..Slater and Plasterer. **1823** P. NICHOLSON *Pract. Builder* 399 All quarry slates require this preparation from the slater. **1893** EARL DUNMORE *Pamirs* I. 46 Silvery roofs..deftly fitted by some cunning slater.

*attrib.* **1813** J. THOMSON *Lect. Inflam.* 241 A slater boy, dwelling in the village of Hamegecourt. **1844** H. STEPHENS *Bk. Farm* I. 196 The slater-work is then covered.

**2.** A wood-louse. *Sc., north. dial., Austral.*, and *N.Z.*

α. **1684** SIBBALD *Scot. Illustr.* II. III. vii. 33 *Millepes Asellus, nostratibus* the Sclater. **1824** MACTAGGART *Gallovid. Encycl.* 361 He is also fond of eating *sclaters*. *c* **1873** G. JOHNSTON in *Hist. Berwick. Nat. Club* (1876) VII. 32 'Sclaters' were crawling on the paved floor.

β. **1802** *Eng. Encycl.* V. 627/2 *Millepedæ*,..Wood-lice, hog-lice, or slaters. **1873** DAWSON *Earth & Man* iii. 44 Modern slaters or wood-lice, which are not very distant relatives of these old crustaceans. **1876** SMILES *Sc. Nat.* vi. 97 Hosts of night-wandering insects,..slaters, centipedes and snails. **1951** J. FRAME *Lagoon* 45 She collected things, slaters and earwigs and spiders. **1965** *Austral. Encycl.* IX. 349/2 The best-known isopods are the terrestrial forms commonly called wood-lice, slaters, carpenters, or sow-bugs. **1979** *Sunday Mail Color Mag.* (Brisbane) 23 Sept. 21/3 (Advt.), Snails slugs slaters millipedes. Now Baysol kills them all.

**3.** A blade of slate or the like used for slating skins and hides.

**1885** C. T. DAVIS *Manuf. Leather* xxxii. 527 The 'slater' is a tool closely resembling a 'slicker'; but the edge of the 'slater' is ground sharp.

†**'slater**². *Obs.*⁻¹ [f. SLATE *v.*³] (See quot.)

**1774** GOLDSM. *Nat. Hist.* IV. ii. (1862) I. 394 There are two varieties of this kind [the land-spaniel]; namely the slater, used in hawking to spring the game; and the setter, that crouches down when it scents the birds, till the net be drawn over them.

**Slater**³ ('sleɪtə(r)). *Physics.* [The name of John C. *Slater* (1900–76), U.S. physicist.] *Slater determinant*: a determinant which expresses the total wave function of an atom and is totally anti-symmetric with respect to an interchange of electrons, the elements being single-electron wave functions.

Described by Slater in *Physical Rev.* (1929) XXXIV. 1293.

**1952** *Jrnl. Chem. Physics* XX. 769/1 The wave function of the ³E*u*− state is $|\phi_0\phi_0\phi_1\phi_1\phi_{-1}\phi_{-2}|$ or $|\phi_0\phi_0\phi_{-1}\phi_{-1}\phi_1\phi_2|$, where |...| means a Slater determinant, and the spin is assumed to be suitable for each state. **1964** L. WILETS *Theories Nucl. Fission* iv. 56 A Slater determinant of plane waves replaces the highly correlated true wave function. **1976** *Nature* 28 Oct. 804/2 Such determinants have ever since been known as Slater determinants and have found applications in many fields.

**'slate-stone.** Also 4, *Sc.* 8–9 **sklate**, 5 **sklaytt**, **sclathe**, 6–7 (9 *Sc.*) **sclate**. [SLATE *sb.*¹]

**1.** A single piece of slate, or of thin stone serving the same purpose.

*c* **1440** *Alph. Tales* 307 He tuke þe knyght be þe nekk & drew hym oute þurgh þe thakk of þe howse..& his bowels cleuyd on þe sclathe stonys. **1493** *Mem. Ripon.* (Surtees) III. 164 Pro xxiiij sklaytt stonys pro prædictis cameris. **1530** PALSGR. 271/1 Slate stone, *ardoyse*. **1610** HOLLAND *Camden's Brit.* 514 The neighbour inhabitants use to digge great plenty of sclate stones for their buildings. *a* **1618** RALEIGH *Invent. Shipping* 7 All that have Corne beate it in Morters, and make Cakes, baking them upon Slatestones. **1720** RAMSAY *Rise & Fall of Stocks* 156 'Tis a' sklate-stanes instead of money. **1778** W. PRYCE *Min. Cornub.* 74 The famous Delabole Slate-stones. **1818** SCOTT *Hrt. Midl.* xviii, The folk might see men deliver up their silver to the state's use, as if it had been as muckle sclate stanes. **1842** BORROW *Bible in Spain* xxiv, The huts were built of slate stones.

**2.** Stone of the nature of slate.

**1392** *Mem. Ripon* (Surtees) III. 116 Pro coopertura cujusdam domus..cum sklatestane. **1748** J. HILL *Hist. Fossils* 446 Blueish glittering slate Stone. **1764** *Phil. Trans.* LIV. 51 In the slate-stone, they are generally crushed. **1796** W. H. MARSHALL *Econ. W. Eng.* II. 320 The material of building being a coarse schistus, or slate stone. **1871** TYNDALL *Fragm. Sci.* (1879) I. xii. 360 These flags are employed for roofing purposes..and receive the name of 'slatestone'.

*attrib.* **1796** W. H. MARSHALL *Econ. W. Eng.* II. 65 The materials of these hills appear to be chiefly rotten slate, or rusty slate-stone rubble.

**slath** (slæθ). = SLAT *sb.*¹ 5 a.

**1875** *Encycl. Brit.* III. 423/1 The whole now forms what is technically called the slath, which is the foundation of the basket. **1906** M. CORELLI *Treasure of Heaven* 288 He..was now patiently mastering the technical business of forming a 'slath'. **1949** K. S. WOODS *Rural Crafts of England* III. x. 162 A base is woven first, called in the Midlands a 'slath'. **1968** J. ARNOLD *Shell Bk. Country Crafts* 257 A round or oval one [*sc.* base] is started with the 'slath', an interlaced cross-work of rods of at least four each way, around which the weaving begins.

**slather** ('slæðə(r)), *v.* Chiefly *dial.* and *U.S.* [Of obscure origin.] **1.** *intr.* To slip or slide; to move in a sliding or trailing manner.

**1818** WILBRAHAM *Chesh. Gloss.*, *Slather*,..to slip or slide. **1809** *Glouc. Gloss.* s.v., The plank slathered away. **1909** KIPLING *Actions & Reactions* 115, I hate slathering through fluff.

**2. a.** *trans.* To spill or slop; to scatter. Also, to use in large quantities; to squander; to paste, spread, or smear liberally. Usu. with advbs.

**1866** 'MARK TWAIN' *Sk. Sixties* (1926) 210 You have slathered too many frivolous sentimental tales into your paper. **1875** —— *Let.* 26 Jan. (1917) I. 247 The partialities of Providence do seem to be slathered around (as one may say). **1876** C. C. ROBINSON *Gloss. Words Dial. Mid-Yorks.* 126/1 *Slather*.., to spill. **1877** F. ROSS et al. *Gloss. Words used in Holderness* 128/2 Leeak at him! he's *slatherin* pig-meeat all across hoose fleear. **1895** J. T. CLEGG *Stories, Sk., & Rhymes* 43 Some carless chilt had bin a buyin peawdher blue an' slatthert it. **1904** G. ADE *True Bills* 131 A very Rich Man who wishes to be Respected must fill his Clothes with Currency and go out and slather it around. **1928** PEASE & FAIRFAX-BLAKEBOROUGH *Dict. Dial. N. Riding Yorks.* 118/2 'Eh bud things is slather'd aboot i' that hoos!' 'T'hay an' strae war blawn clean oot o' t'stagarth an' slather'd aboot t'field ayont.' **1937** M. HILLIS *Orchids on your Budget* v. 82 You can get a good make-shift facial by slathering cream on your face after a shampoo. **1954** *Columbia* (S. Carolina) *Record* (Sat. Comic Suppl.) 27 Nov. 6, I got some American toast here, an' I'll gladly slather some jam on to sweeten it up. **1967** E. B. NICKERSON *Kayaks to Arctic* iii. 24 Slather it [*sc.* mosquito repellent] on where common sense indicates, and have confidence. **1978** J. IRVING *World according to Garp* xvii. 363 Perfume, which he remembered Roberta slathering over him.

**b.** To besmear; to spread or splash liberally on. Usu. with *with*.

**1941** W. A. PERCY *Lanterns on Levee* xvi. 184 Another rest-camp, half completed, leaking the ample French rain, slathered with mud, awaited us. **1961** WEBSTER s.v. ²*slather*, Slathering the cars with paint. **1977** *Time* 25 Apr. 17/1 His top chef offers such specialties as veal tongue slathered with *foie gras*. **1979** R. GILLESPIE *Crossword Mystery* iii. 53 She burned painfully. Rocky slathered her externally with Solarcaine.

**3.** *slang.* To thrash, defeat thoroughly, castigate.

**1910** O. JOHNSON *Varmint* viii. 112 He turned on the Coffee-colored Angel and slathered him, drove him hither and thither with terrific blows. *c* **1926** 'MIXER' *Transport Workers' Song Bk.* 36 And all their Simon Puritans Are infused with great delight When an officer is slathered As chair-warmer, parasite. **1968** *Globe & Mail* (Toronto) 13 Feb. 27/1 Canadians can get slathered in Olympic hockey.

**slather** ('slæðə(r)), *sb.* [f. prec.] **1.** *U.S. colloq.* Usu. *pl.* A large amount, lots, lashings.

**1857** M. D. SANFORD *Jrnl.* 30 Mar. in D. F. Danker *Mollie* (1959) 6, I believe there are 500 passengers, lots and 'slathers' of young men. **1876** 'MARK TWAIN' *Tom Sawyer* vii. 68 They get slathers of money—most a dollar a day. **1906** *N.Y. Globe* 20 Aug. 6 There is the same slather of indefinite charges. **1966** 'E. LINDALL' *Time too Soon* (1967) vii. 69 What he's giving her I don't want anyway. A whole slather of animal passion. **1970** —— *Gathering of Eagles* vi. 63 They ..ate the damper with slathers of sweet, brown treacle.

**2.** *north.* and *Sc. dial.* Thin mud; a sloppy mass.

**1876** C. C. ROBINSON *Gloss. Words Dial. Mid-Yorks.* 126/1 *Slather*, puddle, in a thin state. **1928** PEASE & FAIRFAX-BLAKEBOROUGH *Dict. Dial. N. Riding Yorks.* 118/2 *Slather*.., mud and mess. **1939** A. BORTHWICK *Always Little Further* vi. 126 Two big slabs o' breed wi' a slather o' jam in atween. **1980** J. GARDAM *Sidmouth Lett.* 134 Wear yer wellies or you'll get in a slather int yard.

**3.** *open slather* (*Austral.* and *N.Z. colloq.*), freedom to operate without interference, a free-for-all.

**1919** J. V. MARSHALL *World of Living Dead* 71 They say she's an open slather up there. Not a demon [*sc.* a policeman] in the burg. **1949** J. MORRISON *Creeping City* xxviii. 227 You're asking to be allowed an open slather at an essential public service without being challenged. **1959** G. SLATTER *Gun in Hand* xiii. 180 It's worth a go. Come round, she said, it'll be open slather. **1974** *Sunday Sun* (Brisbane) 1 Sept. 5/1 The beef was marked and butcher shop customers had the opportunity to check the grading... Now it's open slather. **1979** *Financial Rev.* (Austral.) 9 May 5 A problem..was how to prevent an 'open slather' in the sale of tickets.

**slath sword:** see SLAUGH-SWORD.

**'slatiness.** *rare*⁻⁰. [f. SLATY *a.*] 'The quality of being slaty; slaty character.'

**1882** in *Imperial Dict.* (Annandale).

**slating** ('sleɪtɪŋ), *vbl. sb.*¹ [f. SLATE *v.*¹]

**1.** The fixing of slates (on a roof or elsewhere); the business of fixing slates.

**1579** in Willis & Clark *Cambridge* (1886) I. 312 They.. shall perfectlye and workmanlye finishe the slateinge off the sayd rouffe. **1583** *Shuttleworths' Acc.* (Chetham Soc.) 18 Wylliam Broune for slatynge seven dayes ijˢ iiijᵈ. **1663** GERBIER *Counsel* 63 Slating with blew Slates the workmen finding all, will cost seven pence per foot. **1825** J. NICHOLSON *Operat. Mechanic* 626 Slating is performed in several other ways. **1889** H. C. SEDDON *Builder's Work* (ed. 2) 231 The slating of roofs is paid for by the square of 100 feet super.

*attrib.* **1572–3** in Willis & Clark *Cambridge* (1886) II. 120 A hundreth sclaiting latthes. **1863** SMILES *Indust. Biogr.* 237 As the slating trade did not keep him in regular employment.

**2.** *collect.* The slates covering a roof.

**1816** J. SCOTT *Vis. Paris* (ed. 5) 24 The ancient slating reposes in venerable grey amongst moss and grass. **1838** in Col. Hawker *Diary* (1893) II. 142 The shot rattled on the slating of my house. **1867** MUSGRAVE *Nooks & Corners Old France* II. 6 The slating here and there imitating scales.

**3.** The action of covering with a composition imitating slate; a kind of wash for blackboards.

**1884** KNIGHT *Dict. Mech.* Suppl. 822/1 Black-board Slating may be accomplished with the following mixture. **1885** SPON *Mechanic's Own Book* 435 Black-board wash, or 'liquid slating'. *Ibid.*, To apply the slating, have the surface smooth.

**4.** The process of removing hairs from skins or hides with a slater. Freq. *attrib.*

**1885** C. T. DAVIS *Manuf. Leather* xvi. 313 In many.. tanneries fleshing machines have been tried..in..other tanneries experiments were made to convert them into slating..machines. **1903** L. A. FLEMMING *Pract. Tanning* 12 In some cases it is necessary to work the skins through the slating machine, or upon the beams.

**slating** ('sleɪtɪŋ), *vbl. sb.*² [f. SLATE *v.*²]

**1.** A severe punishment; a beating.

**1860** P. H. RATHBONE in *Trades' Societies & Strikes* 368 The society defended all men prosecuted for trade assaults or 'slatings', as the term was. **1872** *Echo* 4 Sept., The Kilkenny Militia..really did..get a fearful slating to-day.

**2.** A severe reprimand or scolding.

**1881** MRS. LYNN LINTON *My Love* II. 307 After that first 'slating', as the vulgar little creature called it, Valentine said no more. **1894** *Tablet* 24 Aug. 304, I hear the good nuns got a bit of a 'slating' from the Chaplain as a reward for their anxiety.

**3.** A severe criticism or literary castigation.

**1870** 'OUIDA' *Puck* xix, Extinguished by means of journalistic slating. **1890** *Literary World* 22 Aug. 145 It must be admitted that the slating was well deserved.

†**slating,** *vbl. sb.*³ *Obs.*⁻⁰ [f. OF. *esclater*: see F. *éclater* (sense 7) in Littré.] (See quot.)

**1688** HOLME *Armoury* III. 91/1 Slat-ing of Inamell, is taking Inamell off a Ring, and Inamelling it with another colour.

**slating** ('sleɪtɪŋ), *ppl. a.* [f. SLATE *v.*²] Severely critical or condemnatory.

**1885** *Longm. Mag.* V. 499 A 'slating' article was in type for publication. **1900** *Daily News* 7 Dec. 7/1 A question whether 'booing' was more damaging than a 'slating' notice.

**slatish** ('sleɪtɪʃ), *a.* [f. SLATE *sb.*¹ + -ISH.] Somewhat resembling the colour of slate.

**1860** WRAXALL *Life in Sea* i. 11 The colour of the back is slatish grey with white spots. **1884** *Chambers's Jrnl.* Nov. 703/2 The musk-rat is..of a slatish-blue colour. **1887** CLARK RUSSELL *Frozen Pirate* I. ix. 134 The clouds..had taken a slatish tinge.

‖**slatko** ('slætkəʊ). [Serbo-Croatian, lit. sugared fruit.] (See quots.)

**1941** 'R. WEST' *Black Lamb & Grey Falcon* II. 111 The gallery, here walled in though it is open in most monasteries, where the visitors are given slatko, the ceremonial offering of sugar or jam and glasses of cold water. **1961** *Times* 9 Sept. 11/3 In the hostelry guests..are offered *slatko*, the ceremonial offering of sugar or jam.

†**'slat-stone.** *Obs.* Also 4 **skalt-**, 6 **slatte-**. [f. SLAT *sb.*¹] = SLATE-STONE.

**1391** *Mem. Ripon* (Surtees) III. 108 In cc skaltstanes [*sic*] emp. pro emendacione j cameræ. *c* **1440** *Promp. Parv.* 458/1 Slat stone,..*ymbrex*. **1516** in *Wilts. N. & Q.* July (1905) 90 Too lodes of slattestone fro the Quarre of Cotteswolde. **1648** B. PLANTAGENET *Descr. New Albion* 6 Building and Slatstone. **1669** STURMY *Mariner's Mag.* v. xii. 46 In a Morter covered with a Slat-stone.

**slatted** ('slætɪd), *a.* [f. SLAT *sb.*¹ or *v.*¹ + -ED², -ED¹.] Made or furnished with slats.

**1886** C. SCOTT *Sheep-Farming* 66 The hay-rack is slatted so closely that the sheep cannot put their heads through the bars. **1948** W. FAULKNER *Intruder in Dust* ix. 180 The truck (it was another pickup; they..had commandeered it, with a slatted cattle frame on the bed). **1960** *Farmer & Stockbreeder* 2 Feb. 82/1 Calves..were housed in individual slatted-floor boxes until seven or eight weeks old. **1968** C. BROOKE-ROSE *Between* 30 The light pours through the slatted shutters making a slatted pattern on the left pale green wall. **1972** *Daily Tel.* 11 July 3/2 A vertically slatted radiator grille..and an XJ12 motif at the back distinguish the new car from the XJ6. **1980** *Amat. Gardening* 4 Oct. 31/3 An advantage of slatted benching against solid trays is that the slats can be opened out to permit better air circulation between the plants.

**'slatter,** *sb.* Also 4–5 **sclatter**, 5–6 **sklatter**, 6 **sklattar**. [f. SLAT *sb.*¹ or *v.*¹]

**1.** = SLATER¹ 1. Now *dial.*

**1379** in *Yorks. Archæol. Jrnl.* V. 43 Henricus Sclatter & vxor, Sclatter, vjᵈ. *c* **1400** *Laud Troy Bk.* 1793 Sklatteres, Masons, and Carpenter, And other Men of alle mister. **1444** *Act 23 Hen. VI*, c. 12, Les gages ascun..maistre Tiler ou Sclatter. **1539** in W. H. Turner *Select. Rec. Oxford* (1880) 160 William Bybe, sklatter. Waltar Cuddesdon, sklattar. **1621** BURTON *Anat. Mel.* III. ii. VI. v. (1651) 575 As slatters sort their slattes, do they degrees and families. **1669** *Phil. Trans.* IV. 1009 The Sects (the hewing instrument of the Slatters). **1881** *Leic. Gloss.*, *Slatter*, one who 'slats' generally, but more particularly a slater.

†**2.** A wood-louse. = SLATER¹ 2.

**1739** DR. CLARKE in Graham *Soc. Life Scotl. in 18th c.* (1899) I. i. 50 Give him twice a day the juice of twenty slatters squeezed through a muslin bag.

†**'slatter,** *v.*¹ In 5 **slat(e)re**. [Cf. SLAT *v.*³]

**1.** *trans.* To slash or slit (clothes).

*a* **1400** *Hymns Virgin* (1867) 62 Slatre þi clothis boþe schorte & side. **1480** CAXTON *Cron. Eng.* ccxxvi. 233 Short clothes and streyte..on euery syde slatered [*Brut* 297 desslatered] and botened with sleues and tapytes of surcotes.

**2.** To split, to shiver.

*c* **1400** *Turnament Tottenham* 159 Ther were flayles al to slatred [*v.r.* flatred],..Bollys and dysches al to schatred.

**slatter** ('slætə(r)), *v.*² [Imitative: cf. SLAT *v.*² 4.] *intr.* To clatter. Also **'slattering** *vbl. sb.*

**1661** K. W. *Conf. Charac.* (1860) 20 The slattering of a cadent brickbat. **1830** *Blackw. Mag.* XXVII. 588 At first a low muttering is heard,..then a sort of sliding slattering noise, and finally a reverberating thundering crash. **1870** *Daily News* 1 Oct., The Prince might ride by with his escort slattering over the paved street.

**'slattering,** *ppl. a. rare.* [f. the dialect verb *slatter* to spill or splash awkwardly, to slop, to waste, etc., of obscure origin.] Careless, slovenly.

**1674** RAY *N.C. Words*, A *Dawgos* or *Dawkin*, a dirty, slattering woman. *a* **1677** BARROW *Serm.* I. vii. 79 All persons who would not lead a loose and slattering life, but design..to prosecute an orderly course of action. **1889** in *N.W. Linc. Gloss.* (ed. 2).

**slattern** ('slætən), *sb.* and *a.* Also 7 **slaterne**, 7–8 **slatern**. [Related to prec.]

**A.** *sb.* A woman or girl untidy and slovenly in person, habits, or surroundings; a slut. (See also quot. 1639.)

**1639** J. SMYTH in *Glouc. Gloss.* (1890) 199 A slaterne, i.e. a rude ill bred woman. *a* **1668** DAVENANT *Play-Ho. to be Let* Wks. (1673) 118 Good Housewife in House, not sauntering young slatern. **1669** DRYDEN *Royal Martyr* Epil., Here Nelly lies, who, though she liv'd a Slattern, Yet dy'd a Princess, acting in St. Cathar'n. **1710** ADDISON *Tatler* No. 243 ⁋3 That Species of Women which we call a Slattern. **1766** FORDYCE *Serm. Yng. Women* (1767) I. ii. 76 Butterflies one day, and slatterns the next. **1845** MRS. NORTON *Child of Islands* (1846) 110 His wife a shrew and slattern. **1883** S. C. HALL *Retrospect* II. 314 The young girls were tawdry slatterns.

**b.** Applied to a man. *rare*⁻¹.

**1849** THACKERAY *Pendennis* v, He was now..as great a dandy as he before had been a slattern.

**B.** *adj.* Slovenly, untidy, slatternly. Said of appearance, etc., or of persons.

(*a*) **1716** GAY *Trivia* III. 270 Beneath the Lamp her tawdry Ribbons glare, The new-scower'd Manteau, and the slattern Air. **1784** J. BARRY *Lect. Art* vi. (1848) 208 Works formed out of trite, vulgar, slattern matter. **1822** W. IRVING *Braceb. Hall* xvii. 146, I could not but admire a certain degree of slattern elegance about the baggage. **1861** D. COOK *Paul Foster's Daughter* ii, At the best his room has a slattern air.
(*b*) **1824** W. IRVING *T. Trav.* I. 340, I recognised..in his slattern spouse, the once trim and dimpling columbine. **1846** J. BAXTER *Libr. Pract. Agric.* (ed. 4) II. p. xlix, He plods his way to a fireless hut, where a slattern wife and ragged children receive him.
*transf.* **1896** *Westm. Gaz.* 16 Dec. 4/3 The slipshod writer and the slattern thinker.

**slattern** ('slætən), *v.* [f. prec.]

**1.** *trans.* To fritter or throw *away* (time, opportunity, etc.) by carelessness or slovenliness.

**1747** CHESTERF. *Lett.* (1774) I. ci. 242 Every fool, who slatterns away his whole time in nothings. **1755** —— in *World* No. 148, I have known many a passion..(if I may use the expression) wholly slatterned away, by an unguarded and illiberal familiarity. **1785** *Town & Co. Mag.* Nov. 594 This class..frequently slattern away a reputation for the sake of idolatry. **1878** *N. Amer. Rev.* CXXVII. 103 The mournful folly with which they slatterned away the noblest opportunity.

**2.** To work *over* in a slovenly manner.

**1807** E. S. BARRETT *Rising Sun* II. 4 Many of our great men in office..generally slattern over what they are obliged to do, by proxy.

**3.** *intr.* To play the slattern.

**1856** MASSON *Ess.* vi. 246 [They] and the niece are slatterning about the house.

**'slatternish,** *a.* [f. SLATTERN *a.* + -ISH.] Somewhat slatternly.

**1833** LYTTON *Godolphin* 10 Then, came a gentleman's wife, a pretty, slatternish woman, much painted.

**'slatternliness.** [f. next + -NESS.] The quality or fact of being slatternly.

**1811** MISS L. M. HAWKINS *C'tess & Gertrude* II. 172 She ..was shocked to see the effect of domestic slatternliness. **1847** L. HUNT *Men, Women, & B.* I. vii. 126 Evidences that the esteem of a life is preferred to the slatternliness of the moment. **1869** TROLLOPE *He Knew* xlviii, [She] put down the deficiency to the charge of domestic slatternliness.

**slatternly** ('slætənlɪ), *a.* [f. SLATTERN *sb.*]

**1.** Of persons: Having the condition or habits of a slattern; slovenly; untidy.

*c* **1680** COTTON *Ep. to Sir C. Clifton* 49 One that had since bin her Maid;..a slatternly ill-favour'd toad. **1753-4** RICHARDSON *Sir C. Grandison* (1781) VI. vi. 21 She..looked so shy! so silly! so slatternly! **1847** C. BRONTË *J. Eyre* vi, I am ..slatternly; I seldom put, and never keep things in order; I am careless. **1865** E. C. CLAYTON *Cruel Fortune* I. 143 The tatterdemalion, slatternly, slipshod women who lounge.. against the door-posts.
*Comb.* **1847** H. MELVILLE *Omoo* i, She turned out to be a small, slatternly-looking craft.

**b.** *transf.* Of artists or authors in respect of their work.

**1762-71** H. WALPOLE *Vertue's Anecd. Paint.* (1786) IV. 70 The time he wasted on his works, in which at least he was the reverse of his slatternly cotemporaries. **1812** SCOTT *Let.* in *Lockhart* (1837) III. i. 21 When you have twenty things to tell, it is better to be slatternly than tedious.

**2.** Of appearance, etc.: Appropriate to, characteristic of, a slattern.

**1776** MME. D'ARBLAY *Early Diary* 5 Apr., We saw the young and handsome Duchess..walking in such an undressed and slaternly manner. **1801** MAR. EDGEWORTH *Angelina* iv, The slatternly, dirty appearance of Araminta's dress. *a* **1853** ROBERTSON *Lect.* i. (1858) 33 A home made wretched by a wife's slatternly conduct. **1877** A. B. EDWARDS *Up Nile* xxii. 702 The rooms were untidy; the general aspect of the place was slatternly and neglected.

**slatternly** ('slætənlɪ), *adv.* [f. SLATTERN *a.* + -LY[2].] In a slovenly way.

**1750** CHESTERF. *Lett.* (1792) III. ccxxxiv. 68 A fine suit, ill-made and slatternly or stifly worn,..only exposes the aukwardness of the wearer. **1841** TUPPER *Twins* iii, [She] lay slatternly abed, to nurse a head-ache till noon.

**slatternness** ('slætənnɪs). Also **slatterness.** [f. SLATTERN *a.* + -NESS.] Slatternliness.

**1745** ELIZA HEYWOOD *Female Spect.* No. 16 (1748) III. 166 To give the artful stepmother an opportunity of accusing her of ill housewifry and slatterness. **1886** *New York Herald* IX. 196 You cannot expect neatness and order in any house where the daughters see nothing but slatterness.

**† slatter-pouch.** Also **slatter de pouch.** *Obs. rare.* Some kind of dance or game.

*c* **1600** *Grobiana's Nuptialls* I. iii. (MS. Bodl. 30), Noe daunceinge unlesse it be the old slatter de pouch or y^e^ beares masque. **1654** GAYTON *Fest. Notes* III. iv. 86 Much did they suffer, but what did they? much When they were boyes at Trap, or slatter-pouch; They'd sweat untill they stank.

**'slattery,** *a. rare*$^{-1}$. [Cf. SLATTER *v.*[1]] Of a brittle or shivery character.

**1829** GLOVER *Hist. Derby* I. 58 This last mentioned coal is slattery and often sulphureous.

**'slatting,** *vbl. sb. rare.* Also 6 **sclattynge.** [f. SLAT *v.*[1]] = SLATING *vbl. sb.*[1]

**1532** in W. H. Turner *Select. Rec. Oxford* (1880) 109 Excepte sclattynge and tymber owerhedde. **1583** in Hutton *St. John's Coll.* (1898) 62 Item for slatting of y^e^ lofer. **1757** *Phil. Trans.* L. 504 The slatting of the house cracked.

**† 'slatty,** *a. Obs.* [f. SLAT *sb.*[1] + -Y.] Slaty.

**1661** J. CHILDREY *Brit. Baconica* 74 In a Clayie and slatty Countrey. **1686** PLOT *Staffordsh.* 120 They have harder, stony, slatty sorts of Marles. **1758** BORLASE *Nat. Hist. Cornw.* 59 The black and gritty, the shelfy slatty Soil, and the stiff reddish Soil.

**slaty** ('sleɪtɪ), *a.* Also 7 **slatie,** 8 **slatey.** [f. SLATE *sb.*[1] + -Y.]

**1.** Composed of slate; resembling slate; having the nature or properties of slate. Also of land: Lying upon slate (quot. 1733).

In the earliest quots. the sense is perhaps 'stony, rocky'.
*a* **1529** SKELTON *E. Rummyng* 258 Some go streyght thyder, Be it slaty or slyder; They holde the hye waye [etc.]. **1538** LELAND *Itin.* (1768) I. 62 An exceding..strong Castelle on a stepe Rok, having but one way by the stepe slaty crag to cum to it. **1611** COTGR., *Ardoisin*,..slatie, or, of slate. **1670** W. SIMPSON *Hydrol. Ess.* 65 Blew slate..and other slaty stone mixed therewith. **1708** J. C. *Compl. Collier* (1845) 19 [The stone-coal] is subject to be a little Slaty. **1733** TULL *Horse-Hoeing Husb.* xiv. 199 These Estates consisted of Thin Slatey Land. **1796** KIRWAN *Elem. Min.* (ed. 2) II. 153 Slaty Copper ore, or Cupriferous Marlite. **1820** KEATS *Hyperion* II. 16 Hard flint they sat upon, Couches of rugged stone, and slaty ridge. **1865** J. T. F. TURNER *Slate Quarries* 5 From Newquay to above Boscastle the rocks..are of a slaty character.

**2.** Characteristic or typical of slate. ***slaty cleavage***: see CLEAVAGE 1 c.

**1796** KIRWAN *Elem. Min.* (ed. 2) I. 83 Of a slaty fracture. **1837** WHEWELL *Hist. Induct. Sci.* (1857) III. 445 The slaty cleavage never coincides with the direction of the strata. **1854** RONALDS & RICHARDSON *Chem. Techn.* (ed. 2) I. 45 The principal fracture is straight, slaty.

**3. a.** Slate-coloured.

**1822-7** GOOD *Study Med.* (1829) II. 176 The slaty or purplish and granular saburra thrown up from the stomach. **1868** G. MACDONALD *Seaboard Parish* II. v. 77 The sun had disappeared under a cloud, and the sea had turned a little slaty. **1893** LYDEKKER *Horns & Hoofs* 202 A slaty patch extending from the shoulder and hip to the legs.

**b.** ***slaty gum***: (see quots.).

**1889** MAIDEN *Useful Pl.* 470 *Eucalyptus largiflorens*... Also called 'Slaty Gum', from the grey and white patches on the bark. *Ibid.* 524 *Eucalyptus tereticornis*... Called..'Slaty Gum' in New South Wales and Queensland.

**4.** Smacking of slate.

**1824** HENDERSON *Anc. & Mod. Wines* 226 The better sorts [of Moselle wines]..sometimes contract a slaty taste from the strata on which they grow. **1981** *Woman's Jrnl.* Mar. 135/3 Duck is..on the fatty side, so we need a dry, even slaty, wine to accompany it.

**5.** *Comb.* **a.** With names of colours, as ***slaty-black, -blue, -green, -grey.***

**1818** SCOTT *Rob Roy* xxx, A broken track along the precipitous face of a slaty grey rock. **1826** STEPHENS in Shaw *Gen. Zool.* XIII. II. 164 Slaty-black Graucalus with the head and neck..black. **1854** [see JACINTH 1 e]. **1859** DARWIN *Orig. Species* i. (1860) 25 The rock-pigeon is of a slaty-blue, with white loins. **1874** T. HARDY *Far fr. Mad. Crowd* v, A coat..approximating in colour to white and slaty grey. **1975** H. R. F. KEATING *Remarkable Case of Burglary* i. 1 The slaty-blue eyes in his thin pale face.

**b.** Misc., as ***slaty-headed, -like, -looking,*** etc.

*a* **1866** R. DICK in Smiles *Life* (1878) 91 The cliffs—now yellowish, then reddish—now thin and slaty-like. **1876** *Nature* XIV. 580/1 A Slaty-headed Parrakeet. **1882** *Cent. Mag.* XXV. 241 Gray, slaty-looking little towns.

**slauchter, -ir,** obs. Sc. forms of SLAUGHTER.

**slaue,** obs. form of SLAVE *sb.*[1] (and *a.*) and *v.*

**slauen, -eyn,** variants of SLAVIN *Obs.*

**† slaugh,** obs. variant of SLAWK.

**1743** BULKELEY & CUMMINS *Voy. S. Seas* 44 Most Part of our People eat a Weed that grows on the Rocks; it is a thin Weed of a dark green Colour, and called by the Seamen, *Slaugh. Ibid.* 62 Eat Slaugh and Sea-weed fry'd with Tallow-Candles.

**† slaughmess.** *Obs.*$^{-1}$ [ad. older Flem. *slachmes*, f. *slach* (*slag*) blow, stroke + *mes* knife: cf. next.] A large knife used as a weapon; a dagger.

*a* **1548** HALL *Chron., Hen. V*, 47 b, The fierce Brabanders and strong Almaines with long pykes and cuttyng slaughmesses.

**† slaugh-sword.** *Obs.* Also 6 **slawght-, slath-,** 7 **slaug-.** [ad. older Flem. *slachsweerd* (Du. *slagzwaard*; Da. *slagsværd*, Sw. *-svärd*), or G. *schlachtschwert*.] A large two-handed sword.

*a* **1548** HALL *Chron., Hen. VIII*, 235 b, Euery man hauing a iauelyn or slaughsword to keepe the people in aray. *a* **1575** tr. *Pol. Verg. Eng. Hist.* (Camden, No. 36) 11 A brode slawght swerde, and a dager sharpe onelie on the one side. **1590** SIR J. SMYTH *Disc. Weapons* 6 b, A fewe slath swords for the gard of their Ensignes. **1614** GORGES *Lucan* VI. 226 Those rough Tewtons..That vse long slaug-swords [*printed* slang-] in their mart.

**† slaught,** *sb. Obs.* Forms: 3 **slaht,** 3-4 **slaȝt** (4 **slaȝte, slaȝþe, sclaȝt**), 4-5 **slaght** (5 **-te, sIagh**); 4 **slawȝt, slawhte,** 5 **slawþe,** 6 **slawght;** 4 **slauht,** 5 **slauȝt,** 4-5 **slauȝte** (4 **-tte**), 4-7 **slaughte.** [Early ME. *slaht*, *slaȝt*, app. repr. OE. **sleaht* (cf. gen. pl. *wælsleahta*), var. of *slæht*, *sleht*, *sliht*, etc.: see SLEIGHT *sb.*[2] The unmutated vowel corresponds to that of OFris. *slachte* (Fris. *slacht*), MDu. and Du. *slacht*, OS. *-slahta*, OHG. *slaht* (G. *schlacht*) and *slahta* (MHG. *slahte*), ON. and Icel. *sláttr* masc. and *slátta* fem.]

**1.** Slaying; slaughter.

*c* **1205** LAY. 4263 Alken farinde mon, ȝef slaht oþer hæfde þeofðe idon [etc.]. *a* **1225** *Leg. Kath.* 198 Þe keiser stod bimong þat sunful slaht. **13..** *E.E. Allit P.* A. 801 As a schep to þe slaȝt þer lad was he. **1390** GOWER *Conf.* I. 362 Be wel avised..Of slawhte er that thou be coupable. **1422** tr. *Secreta Secret., Priv. Priv.* 142 Yf the slaght be vnryghtfull, god shal answere, 'Who-So sleyth, he shal be slayne'. **1469** in *10th Rep. Hist. MSS. Comm.* App. V. 307 All suche slaghts and kyllyng done in defennce. *a* **1586** SIDNEY *Arcadia* (1622) 298 Where shee had made a scaffold,..and there caused them to be kept, as ready for the slaughte. **1610** HEALEY *St. Aug. Citie of God* II. xi, Bad [spirits] are delighted with slaughtes and tragicall invocations.

**2.** *fig.* A stroke (of sorrow), spell (of sleep). *rare.*

**13..** *E.E. Allit. P.* A. 59, I slode vpon a slepyng slaȝte. *Ibid.* C. 192 [They] Arayned hym..what raysoun he hade In such slaȝtes of sorȝe to slepe so faste.

**3.** A flash (of lightning). Cf. FIRE-SLAUGHT.

*a* **1300** *Cursor M.* 17372 His cher lik was slaght o fire. *Ibid.* 22680 All þe stanes..Sal smitt togedir wit sli maght Als thoner dos wit firen slaght.

**† slaught,** *v. Obs. rare.* [f. prec., or ad. Du. (and LG.) *slachten* or G. *schlachten*.] *trans.* To kill, slaughter. Hence **† 'slaughting** *vbl. sb.*

**1535** COVERDALE *Prov.* ix. 2 Wysdome..hath slaughted, ..and prepared hir table. —— *Jer.* xii. 3 Take them awaye, ..and apoynte them for the daye off slaughtinge. **1647** HEXHAM I. s.v., The time of slaughting beasts, *den slaghtijdt.*

**‖ slaught-boom.** *Obs.* In 7 **slaught bome, slaght-boome.** [ad. Du. or LG. *slagboom* (hence Da. and Sw. *slagbom*), = G. *schlagbaum*, f. *slagen* to strike, fall, and *boom* beam, tree.] A beam used as a barrier.

**1637** MONRO *Exped.* 7 The Castell..with Moates, Draw-bridges, and slaught bomes without all. **1642** *Relat. Action before Cirencester* 4 Each end of the high street..was secured against Horse with strong slaght-boomes which our men call Turne-pikes.

**slaughter** ('slɔːtə(r)), *sb.* Forms: α. 4 **slahter, -tir,** 4-5 **slaȝter** (4 **-tter**), **slaghter** (5 **-tre, -tur**); 4 **slauh-, slauȝter,** 5- **slaughter** (5 **slawghtir,** 6 **-ter**); 4 **sclawtur, sclauter,** 6 **sklaut(t)er;** 5 **slawter, -tyr, slauther,** 6 **slauter.** β. *Sc.* 5-6 **slachtir** (5 **-tyr, -ter**), **slawchtir** (5 **-tyr,** 6 **-ter**), **slauchtir** (5 **-tyr**), 5-7 **slauchter** (6 **-tre**). [a. early ON. **slahtr* neut. (ON. and Icel. *slátr* butcher-meat, Norw. dial. *slaater* cattle for killing), f. the stem **slah-*: see SLAY *v.*[1]]

**1. a.** The killing of cattle, sheep, or other animals for food. (See also 4.)

*a* **1300** *E.E. Psalter* xliii. 24 Als schepe of slaghter wend er we. **1398** TREVISA *Barth. De P.R.* XVIII. i. (1495) 741 Fysshe fleeth..the place of wasshyng and of slaughter of other fysshe. *c* **1440** *Promp. Parv.* 458/2 Slawtyr, of beestys, *mactacio*. **1487** *Act 4 Hen. VII*, c. 3 The Slaughter of Beasts ..had and done in the Butchery. **1697** DRYDEN *Virg. Georg.* IV. 794 From his Herd he culls, For Slaughter, four the fairest of his Bulls. *a* **1704** T. BROWN *Dial. Dead* Wks. 1711 IV. 77 A Son of Slaughter at White-Chapel converted to the observation of Fish-days. **1868** *Standard* 15 Dec. 6 The laws ..that have traditionally been handed down with respect to the slaughter of cattle.

**b.** The skins of killed beasts. *rare*$^{-1}$.

**1789** BRAND *Hist. Newcastle* II. 317 The ordinary of the tanners..enjoined..That each brother should have but one butcher to buy slaughter of.

**2.** The killing or slaying of a person; murder, homicide, esp. of a brutal kind.

α. *a* **1300** *Cursor M.* 6752 If þe son be risen þan, It sal be slaghter telld o man. *c* **1325** *Metr. Hom.* 38, I wille you telle Hou it of his slahter felle. *c* **1422** HOCCLEVE *Jereslaus's Wife* 882 No wight but shee Mighte of this slaghtre and murdre gilty be. *c* **1450** *Mirour Saluacioun* (Roxb.) 4 Dauid after the slaghter of Golie. **1587** *Mirr. Mag., Porrex* vii, I procur'd hir wrath by slaughter of hir sonne. **1592** *Arden of Feversham* II. ii, The villaine hath sworne the slaughter of his maister. **1652** BURROUGHES *Exp. Hosea* vii. 142 It is a fruit, I say, of the slaughter of Christ and of his blood. *a* **1722** SIR J. LAUDER *Decis.* (1759) I. 13 Our law concludes all it finds with cold steel..guilty of the slaughter. **1820** SCOTT *Monast.* xxvii, He felt..indignant at the supposed slaughter of young Glendinning. **1825** —— *Betrothed* xxxi, So singular were the tidings of the Constable's slaughter.
β. *c* **1375** *Sc. Leg. Saints* ii. (*Paulus*) 457 And þai..throw browthir slawchtir cun þe file. *c* **1470** HENRY *Wallace* VI. 215 The saklace slauchter off hir. **1570** BUCHANAN *Admonit.* Wks. (S.T.S.) 23 Sum of þame ar counsalouris of þe kingis slauchter. **1596** DALRYMPLE tr. *Leslie's Hist. Scot.* I. 288 Throw counsell of his wyf he inuented the kings slauchtre.

**3. a.** The killing of large numbers of persons in war, battle, etc.; massacre, carnage.

α. *a* **1338** R. BRUNNE *Chron.* (1810) 91 Sen þis greuance hard, þe slauhter & þe drede,..sone afterward þe kyng to ȝork ȝede. **1387** TREVISA *Higden* (Rolls) V. 307 Þat ȝere was þe grete slauȝter of Saxons. **1420-22** LYDG. *Thebes* III. (MS. Laud 557), He made of hem..So grete slaughter and occisioun, That as þe deth fro his swerd þey fled. *c* **1489** CAXTON *Blanchardyn* xxiv. 92 The grete damage and grete slawghtir that he had don of his folke. *a* **1533** LD. BERNERS *Huon* cxliii. 637 There was on both partyes such slauter that it was marueyle to behold it. **1597** J. KING *On Jonas* (1618) 199 What slaughter and hauocke it caused, what profusion of blood between the nobles and the commons. **1665** DRYDEN *Ind. Emp.* v. ii, Slaughter grows murder when it goes too far, And makes a Massacre what was a War. **1713** ADDISON *Cato* I. i, The field Strow'd with Rome's citizens, and drench'd in slaughter. **1750** GRAY *Elegy* 67 To wade through slaughter to a throne. **1835** W. IRVING *Tour Prairies* 122 The chief..cut his way through the enemy with great slaughter. **1849** GROTE *Greece* II. lxix. (1862) VI. 224 These Greeks repelled the Persian assailants with considerable slaughter.

*fig.* **1526** *Pilgr. Perf.* (W. de W. 1531) 37 b, In oppression & slaughter of all true soules that resisteth hym. **1621** BURTON *Anat. Mel.* III. iv. I. iii, They make a slaughter of Scriptures.

*transf.* **1748** *Anson's Voy.* II. iv. 160 The slaughter [by scurvy] would have been..terrible. **1971** *Rand Daily Mail* 27 Mar. 5/3 The slaughter on our roads and damage to property are apparently accepted with equanimity.

*β.* **1375** BARBOUR *Bruce* XIX. 567 A felloun slauchtir maid thai thair. *c* **1470** HENRY *Wallace* v. 930 On Sotheron men full gret slauchter thai maid. **1513** DOUGLAS *Æneid* v. xiii. 98 Sic multitude Of slauchter he maid. **1596** DALRYMPLE. tr. *Leslie's Hist. Scot.* I. 193 This, in the secunde ȝeir of his regne, maid gret slachter amang the Pechtes.

**b.** Personified.

**1595** SHAKS. *John* III. i. 237 They were besmear'd and ouer-staind With slaughters pencill. **1735** SOMERVILLE *Chase* II. 496 Grim Slaughter strides along, Glutting her greedy Jaws. **1840** WHITTIER *'Maiden, with the fair brown tresses'* 129 When the red right-hand of slaughter Moulders with the steel it swung.

**c.** Persons slain in battle, etc. *rare.*

**1757** W. WILKIE *Epigoniad* v. 122 Some, 'midst the heaps of slaughter, sought their dead. **1764** GOLDSM. *Hist. Eng. in Lett.* (1772) I. 210 His body being found amidst a heap of slaughter.

**4.** In the phrases *to* or *for the slaughter.*

*a* **1400** N. T. (Paues) *Acts* viii. 32 As a schepe vnto þo slawghter was he ledde. **1535** COVERDALE *Ezek.* ix. 2 Euery man [had] a weapen in his honde to the slaughter. **1611** BIBLE *Ps.* xliv. 22 Wee are counted as sheepe for the slaughter. **1650** TRAPP *Comm. Num.* xxxv. 21 Wilful murtherers..should..be taken from the altar to the slaughter. **1719** DE FOE *Crusoe* I. 238 Two miserable Wretches..were now brought out for the Slaughter. **1784** COWPER *Task* VI. 421 Witness the patient ox,.. Driv'n to the slaughter. **1911** M. BEERBOHM *Zuleika Dobson* viii. 137, I.. am going to die for the love I bear this woman. And let no man think I go unwilling. I am no lamb led to the slaughter. **1926** W. R. INGE *Lay Thoughts of Dean* II. ii. 98 The Russians..were driven like sheep to the slaughter, in some cases unarmed, and always insufficiently protected by artillery. **1955** J. MASTERS *Coromandel!* iii. 203 They are on their way now... They will be goats for the slaughter. **1982** *Daily Tel.* 10 Feb. 16/5 The rank-and-file membership of the union are meekly following their so-called leaders like lambs to the slaughter.

**5.** A particular instance or occurrence of slaying or massacre.

**1483** *Cath. Angl.* 342/2 A Slaghter, *cedes.* **1535** COVERDALE *Numb.* xxxv. 6 Ye shall geue them sixe fre cities, that he which committeth a slaughter, maie flye thither. **1630** *R. Johnson's Kingd. & Commw.* 33 The slaughters made by the gunne. **1665** MANLEY *Grotius' Low C. Wars* 131 There was a horrible slaughter, for..those that fled could not escape their pursuers. **1722** DE FOE *Col. Jack* (1840) 229 We made a..terrible slaughter. **1836** THIRLWALL *Greece* III. xxii. 215 Of those who escaped this slaughter most met with death in some other form. **1855** MACAULAY *Hist. Eng.* xxi. IV. 575 They next resolved..that the slaughter was a murder.

†**6.** *Mil.* (See quots.) *Obs. rare.*

**1581** STYWARD *Mart. Discipl.* I. 45 These..be placed in the heart of the battaile, vsuallie called the slaughter of the field, or execution of the same, who commonlie doe not fight but in verie great extremitie. **1598** BARRET *Theor. Wars* III. ii. 47 Halberdes or billes..we call..the gard of the ensignes, and slaughter of the field.

†**7.** A cut or slash; a wound. *Obs. rare.*

**1592** GREENE *Upst. Courtier* Wks. (Grosart) XI. 274, I pray you how many slaughters do you make in a poore Calues skin? **1606** G. W[ODCOCK] *Hist. Ivstine* II. 12 This man, after innumerable slaughters receiued in the Battayle, as also hauing pursued the Enemy [etc.].

**8.** *fig.* **a.** An excessive cutting down *of* trees.

**1657** W. COLES *Adam in Eden* cxv. 167 There hath been of late dayes, Such a Slaughter of Oaks, and other Trees, all over this Land.

**b.** A sweeping reduction in the price of goods in order to effect a clearance.

**1891** in *Cent. Dict.*

**9.** *attrib.* and *Comb.* **a.** Attrib., in sense of 'intended or set aside to be killed for food', as ***slaughter cattle, cow, lamb, ox, sheep, stock.***

**1535** COVERDALE *Zech.* xi. 7, I myself fedde yᵉ slaughter shepe. **1607** TOPSELL *Four-f. Beasts* (1658) 496 Such as are killed they call the skins of slaughter-lambs. **1612** *Extr. Burgh Rec. Stirling* I. 132 Ilk slauchter kow passing langis the brig,..tua pennies. **1645** RUTHERFORD *Tryal & Tri. Faith* (1845) 43 It should be but the logic of a beast, if the slaughter ox should say [etc.]. **1863** W. C. BALDWIN *Afr. Hunting* vii. 301 Slaughter oxen or cows, and milch cows, are not to be had for money. **1899** C. J. CUTCLIFFE HYNE *Further Adventures of Captain Kettle* v. 123 The foreign crew of the lifeboat, limp with scare, would have been mere slaughter-pigs on board, even if they could have been lured there. **1958** *Johannesburg Sunday Times* 14 Dec. 7/1 The highest price for slaughter stock at the Ladysmith Farmers' Association stock sale last week was £52 10s. **1968** *Globe & Mail* (Toronto) 13 Feb. B10/3 Slaughter cattle of mixed quality. **1977** *West Briton* 25 Aug. 6/1 (Advt.), We have received Ministry approval under this Order for the sale of slaughter sheep and store and breeding sheep on the same day. **1978** *Morecambe Guardian* 14 Mar. 22/1 (Advt.), Usual Sale of Livestock including..Fat Cattle and Slaughter Cows.

**b.** Attrib., with words denoting a place used for slaughtering, as ***slaughter-pen, -pit, -place, -room, -shop, -yard.***

**1688** BUNYAN *Jerusalem Sinner Saved* (1886) 13 Jerusalem was now become the shambles, the very slaughter-shop for saints. **1796** *Deb. Congress U.S.* 28 Dec. (1849) 1720 Georgia was a slaughter-pen during the war. **1819** SCOTT *Leg. Montrose* vi, Ere we reach yon fatal slaughter-place. **1833** *Penny Cycl.* I. 8/2 Slaughter-rooms, built of stone. **1856** W. G. SIMMS *Charlemont* ii. 27 These lads..raise hogs for the slaughter-pen. **1878** *Rep. Indian Affairs* (U.S.) 151 For the first time in the history of this agency Indians have been induced..to perform the labor of the slaughter-pen. **1890** 'R. BOLDREWOOD' *Col. Reformer* (1891) 218 All that's a turn too good for making slaughter-yard bacon, does for the Chinamen. **1897** *Daily News* 24 Feb. 5/2 The troops who have just entered the city found many of these slaughter pits. **1928** BLUNDEN *Undertones of War* iv. 37 The casualties caused by the mine were sixty or more. Cuinchy..was a slaughter-yard. **1968** T. KINSELLA *Nightwalker* 28 Pigs in a slaughteryard that turn and savage each other.

**c.** Objective, as ***slaughter-breathing, -dealing, -threatening*** adjs.

**1777** POTTER *Æschylus, Supplicants* 131 Pursuit's alarms, And slaughter-threat'ning arms. **1814** *Sporting Mag.* XLIII. 259 The slaughter-breathing lad in the blue coat. **1870** BRYANT *Iliad* II. XVIII. 214 His slaughter-dealing hands.

**10.** Misc. and special combs., as ***slaughter-feast, -market, -stack, -weapon, -work***; **slaughter-master,** = SLAUGHTERER 3; **slaughter price** (see quot. and cf. 8 b); **slaughter shop,** = SLAUGHTER-HOUSE 4 b; **slaughter-skin** (see quot.) ? *Obs.*; †**slaughter-slave,** a vile executioner; †**slaughter sword** (see SLAUGH-SWORD); **slaughter-year** (see quot.).

**1606** SYLVESTER *Du Bartas* II. iv. I. *Tropheis* 201 This savage Beast, Which in his Fold would make a *Slaughter-feast. **1847** W. C. L. MARTIN *The Ox* 59/1 The cottier or small farmer, who could not pretend to rear beasts for the *slaughter market. **1841** GREENER *Sci. Gunnery* 181 The *slaughter-master..is a cormorant, who swallows the food of the weak. **1893** *Daily News* 27 Jan. 7/4 The bank premises had been written down to what was called in the north '*slaughter prices'—that was to say, not what they would fetch in the market, but as mere bricks and mortar. **1841** GREENER *Sci. Gunnery* 180 Tradesmen..whose establishment bears the euphonious titles of the '*slaughter shop' and 'blood house'. **1753** *Chambers' Cycl.* Suppl., **Slaughter-skins*, a term used by our curriers..for the skins of oxen, or other beasts, when fresh, and covered with the hair. **1555** in Foxe *A. & M.* (1684) III. 512/1 The common Cut-throat and general *Slaughter-slave to all the Bishops of England. **1593** NASHE *Christ's T.* Wks. (Grosart) IV. 72 The clowde-climing *slaughter-stack of thy dead carkases. **1569** *Irish Act 11 Eliz.* Stat. III. c. 1 Preamble, The Scotts..with their *slaughter swords hewed him to pieces. **1611** BIBLE *Ezek.* ix. 2 Euery man a *slaughter weapon in his hand. **1818** SCOTT *Hrt. Midl.* x, The hand-waled murderers, whose hands are hard as horn wi' haudin the slaughter-weapons. **1598** BARRET *Theor. Wars* I. i. 4 Our nation hath performed round *slaughter-worke therewith. **1728** P. WALKER *Life Peden* Pref. (1827) 32 The two bloody *Slaughter-years.., 1684, 1685, wherein 82 of the Lord's suffering People were ..cruelly murdered.

**slaughter** ('slɔːtə(r)), *v.* [f. prec. Cf. ON. and Icel. *slátra*, Norw. dial. *slaatra*, in sense 1.]

**1.** *trans.* To kill (cattle, sheep, or other animals), *spec.* for food.

**1535** COVERDALE *Isaiah* xxii. 13 But they..slaughter oxen, they kyll shepe. **1727** BAILEY s.v. *Diipolia*, A number of Oxen.., of which if any eat of the Cakes he was slaughtered. **1774** GOLDSM. *Nat. Hist.* (1776) III. 165 During the winter, the rein-deer are slaughtered as sheep with us. **1833** *Act 3 & 4 Will. IV*, c. 46 §112 It shall not be lawful for any flesher ..to slaughter cattle..elsewhere than in the shambles. **1856** KANE *Arctic Expl.* I. xxvii. 362 The fire was lit up, and one of our birds slaughtered forthwith. **1890** L. C. D'OYLE *Notches* Introd. p. viii, English and Eastern hunters, who came out and slaughtered game by thousands.

*absol.* **1844** H. STEPHENS *Bk. Farm* II. 167 He should learn to slaughter gently, dress the carcass neatly [etc.].

**2. a.** To kill, slay, murder (a person), esp. in a bloody or brutal manner.

**1582** STANYHURST *Æneis* I. (Arb.) 21 Wheare lyes strong Hector slaughtred by manful Achilles. **1592** *Soliman & Pers.* v. iv, In slaughtering him thy vertues are defamed. **1630** *R. Johnson's Kingd. & Commw.* 357 The Prince himselfe hath hardly escaped from being taken or slaughtered. **1746** FRANCIS tr. *Horace, Art Poet.* 268 Let not Medea.. Slaughter her mangled Infants on the Stage. **1825** J. NEAL *Bro. Jonathan* III. 427 She slaughtered our child on the spot. **1865** LECKY *Ration.* (1870) II. 154 They said it was not lawful for a single unauthorised individual to condemn and slaughter the consecrated ruler of the nation.

*fig.* **1632** LITHGOW *Trav.* IX. 389 The circumstances.. were very plausible, if time did not slaughter my goodwill. **1845** BROWNING *Time's Revenges* 5 He slaughters you with savage looks Because you don't admire my books.

**b.** To destroy by excessive felling.

**1896** *Vermont Agric. Rep.* XV. 85 Our lumber forests are being slaughtered. **1903** S. E. WHITE *Blazed Trail Stories* 27 Fitzpatrick would not have the pine 'slaughtered'.

**c.** To defeat or demolish completely. *colloq.*

**1903** *N.Y. Even. Post* 5 Oct. 3 McLaughlin's lieutenants are openly declaring that they will 'slaughter' the McClellan-Grout-Fornes ticket. **1929** C. E. MERRIAM *Chicago* 280 He was hopelessly beaten..in the primaries of 1907; and again slaughtered..in the primaries of 1915.

**3.** To kill or slay (persons) in large numbers; to massacre.

**1589** WARNER *Alb. Eng.* Prose Addit. (1602) 341 Troy is sacked, and her people for the most part slaughtered. **1671** MILTON *P.R.* III. 75 What do these Worthies, But rob.., slaughter, and enslave Peaceable Nations. **1692** DRYDEN *St. Euremont's Ess.* 69 To know simply how to slaughter Men.. is to excel in a very fatal Science. **1792** A. YOUNG *Trav. France* 405 Frederic, who attained the title of Great, on account of his superior skill in the arts of slaughtering men. **1819** SCOTT *Ivanhoe* xxxvi, He shall..slaughter the infidels, even heaps upon heaps. **1853** J. H. NEWMAN *Hist. Sk.* (1873) II. I. iii. 138 The Latins were slaughtered in their own homes and in the streets.

*fig.* **1611** SHAKS. *Wint. T.* I. ii. 93 One good deed, dying tonguelesse, Slaughters a thousand wayting vpon that. **1842** LOVER *Handy Andy* x, Fanny went on slaughtering the S's as fast as Furlong ruined R's.

*absol.* **1718** POPE *Iliad* XI. 199 Still slaughtering on, the king of men proceeds.

†**4.** To gash or slash (a hide). *Obs. rare.*

**1603-4** *Act 1 Jas. I*, c. 22 §1 No Butcher..shall gash, slaughter, or cut any Hide..in flayinge thereof.

**5.** *fig.* To sell at low prices or at a sacrifice.

**1896** *Daily News* 9 June 9/6 In that case,..we should have to slaughter our stock and lose our money.

**slaughterable** ('slɔːtərəb(ə)l), *a.* [f. SLAUGHTER *v.* + -ABLE.] That may be slaughtered; fit for slaughter.

**1911** *Daily News* 25 Sept. 4 There will simply be a dearth of slaughterable cattle. **1966** *Punch* 17 Aug. 261/3 Even the angriest demon drivers are reduced to the status of slaughterable black sheep.

**'slaughterage.** [f. SLAUGHTER *sb.*] All that is connected with the slaughtering of animals for food.

**1854** *Bentley's Misc.* Oct. 323 It is astonishing with what art..we have succeeded in hiding..the slaughterage, the sutlerage, and the sewerage.

**'slaughterdom.** *rare.* [f. as prec.] Slaughter, massacre; slaughtered condition.

**1592** G. HARVEY *Four Lett.* ii, What cruell bloudshed, what horrible slaughterdome haue bene committed, for the point of Honour. **1593** NASHE *Christ's T.* (1613) 11 How much more shall the King of all kings reuenge the death and slaughterdom of his Embassadors. **1860** *All Year Round* No. 74. 575 On either hand, lie the carcases and bones of horses in different stages of slaughterdom.

**slaughtered** ('slɔːtəd), *ppl. a.* [f. SLAUGHTER *v.*]

**1.** Of animals (or flesh): Killed for food, etc.

**1588** SHAKS. *Tit. A.* II. iii. 223 Lord Bassianus lies embrewed heere, All on a heape like to the slaughtred Lambe. **1597** A. M. tr. *Guillemeau's Fr. Chirurg.* 48/1 Water wherinne slaughtered fleshe hath binn washed. *a* **1639** CAREW *A Cruel Mistress* 5 A slaughter'd bull will appease angry Jove. **1814** SCOTT *Ld. of Isles* III. xvii, Underneath yon jutting crag Are hunters and a slaughter'd stag. **1837** P. KEITH *Bot. Lex.* 390 The muscle of slaughtered animals.. forms also an agreeable..food for man.

*transf.* **1746** FRANCIS tr. *Horace, Epist.* I. xii. 29 Whether slaughter'd Onions crown your Board, Or murder'd Fish an impious Feast afford.

**2.** Of persons: Killed, slain; massacred.

**1593** SHAKS. *Lucr.* 1376 A weeping tear, Shed for the slaughter'd husband by the wife. **1669** HOPKINS *Serm. 1 Pet.* ii. 13 (1685) 4 Our most unfeigned mourning for a slaughtered Monarch. **1697** DRYDEN *Virg. Georg.* IV. 117 Heaps of slaughter'd Soldiers bite the Ground. **1743** FRANCIS tr. *Horace, Odes* III. iii. 68 Thrice shall her Matrons ..Deplore their slaughter'd Sons. **1849** MACAULAY *Hist. Eng.* viii. II. 316 Another had marched.., over heaps of slaughtered Moslem, to the sepulchre of Christ.

*absol.* **1826** SCOTT *Woodst.* xiv, I have heard..that the spirits of the slaughtered have strange power over the slayer.

**3.** *slang.* (See quot.)

**1892** *Star* 19 Dec. 2/5 Furniture made by 'slaughtered' (i.e., extra sweated) cabinet makers.

**slaughterer** ('slɔːtərə(r)). [f. SLAUGHTER *v.*]

**1.** One who slaughters or kills.

**1591** SHAKS. *1 Hen. VI*, II. v. 109 Thou do'st then wrong me, as yᵗ slaughterer doth, Which giueth many Wounds, when one will kill. *c* **1611** CHAPMAN *Iliad* XIII. 593 At his slaughterers Incensed Paris spent a lance. **1679** C. NESS *Antichrist* 191 Nations all that time warring against those slaughterers. **1864** BURTON *Scot Abroad* II. i. 98 The slaughterers of St. Bartholomew.

**b.** A powerful fighter or boxer.

**1896** C. DOYLE *R. Stone* xvii, I've seen Jack Harrison fight five times, and I never yet saw him have the worse of it. He's a slaughterer, and so I tell you.

**2.** A killer of animals; a butcher.

**1648** HEXHAM II, *Een slager der beesten*, a Slaughterer. **1668** R. STEELE *Husbandman's Calling* vi. (1672) 161 The Lamb looks cheerfully on the slaughterer. **1795** SOUTHEY *Joan of Arc* IV. 352, I saw the cattle start..And with a piteous moaning vainly seek To fly the coming slaughterers. **1828** MAITLAND *Let. to Simeon* 28 One perhaps has been a singer in the synagogue;..a third, a slaughterer. **1868** *Standard* 15 Dec. 6 The [Jewish] slaughterer is not a butcher in the accepted sense of the term. **1881** *Nation* (N.Y.) XXXII. 428 A tremendous slaughterer of the brute creation.

**3.** *slang.* A dealer who buys from small makers at extremely low prices.

**1851** MAYHEW *Lond. Lab.* I. 333 The 'slaughterers'..buy at 'starvation prices'.., the artificer being often kept waiting for hours. *Ibid.* II. 303 The slaughterer cared only to have them viewly and cheap.

**'slaughter-house.** [SLAUGHTER *sb.*]

**1. a.** A house or place where animals are killed for food.

*c* **1374** in *Scriptores Tres* (Surtees) App. p. cxli, Primo Lardariam, quæ vocatur Sclauterhus. **1441-2** *Durh. Acc. Rolls* (Surtees) 79 Pro cust. boum gros. apud le Slautherhouse. **1471-2** *Ibid.* (Surtees) 93 Pro una magna corda pro le Slaughterhous. **1535** in W. H. Turner *Select. Rec. Oxford* (1880) 133 The bochers..shall have the voyde grounde..to make a sklautter housse. **1593** SHAKS. *2 Hen. VI*, IV. iii. 6

They fell before thee like Sheepe and Oxen, & thou behaued'st thy selfe, as if thou hadst beene in thine owne Slaughter-house. **1675** Brooks *Golden Key* Wks. 1867 V. 340 A lamb..goeth as quietly to the shambles or the slaughter-house as if it were going to the fold. **1709** Steele *Tatler* No. 21 ¶13 The Second is a Butcher's Daughter and sometimes brings a Quarter of Mutton from the Slaughter-house. **1811** *Sporting Mag.* XXXVII. 86 The butchers men who work in the slaughter-houses. **1860** Emerson *Conduct of Life* Wks. (Bohn) II. 310 You have just dined, and, however scrupulously the slaughter-house is concealed.., there is complicity.

*fig.* **1819** Scott *Ivanhoe* xxvi, Permit him to go freely about his task of preparing these Saxon hogs for the slaughter-house. **1894** Drummond *Ascent of Man* 25 The world has been held up to us as one great..slaughter-house resounding with the cries of a ceaseless agony.

**b.** *attrib.*, as ***slaughter-house style, talk***.

**1850** Ht. Martineau *Hist. Peace* II. vi. viii. 576 The rise of Young Ireland, with its political ignorance, its slaughter-house talk, and its bullying boasts. **1854** Emerson *Lett. & Soc. Aims, Immortality* Wks. (Bohn) III. 279 Where there is depravity there is a slaughter-house style of thinking.

**2.** *transf.* **a.** A place or scene in which persons are killed or slaughtered.

**1578** T. N. tr. *Conq. W. India* 103 [They] beganne openly to say Cortes meant to carrie them to the slaughter house. **1597** Middleton *Wisdom of Solomon* viii. 15 A reign, not blood, An empire, not a slaughter-house of lives. **1646** Trapp *Expos. John* x. 40 Jerusalem was then as Rome is now, the saints' slaughter house. **1673** Stillingfl. *Serm.* v. 86 Those whose malice goes beyond their power, and want only enough of that to make the whole World a Slaughter-house. **1790** Merry *Laurel of Liberty* (ed. 2) 24 Yet, haughty France, my verse could never claim, For deeds that suit the slaughter-house of fame. **1814** Scott *Ld. of Isles* ii. xv, This ancient fortress of my race Shall be..No slaughter-house for shipwreck'd guest. **1868** Tennyson *Lucretius* 84 The lust of blood That makes a steaming slaughter-house of Rome.

*fig.* **1797** Godwin *Enquirer* i. iii. 17 It is the great slaughter-house of genius and of mind. **1918** [see *cutting-room* s.v. cutting *vbl. sb.* 10].

**b.** A house injurious to health.

**1899** *Atlantic Monthly* LXXXIII. 769/1 Rear tenements, to the number of nearly 100, have been condemned as 'slaughter houses', with good reason.

†**3.** A part of a fortification. *Obs.*

**1552** Edw. VI *Jrnl.* (Roxb.) 439 It was agreed the wall shuld stond, and tow slaughter houses to be made upon to skowre the utter cutiners. *Ibid.*, Another walle within that, with tow other slaughter houses, and a rampere within that again.

**4.** *slang.* **a.** (See quot.)

**1809** *Sporting Mag.* XXXIII. 73 The houses called by sharpers Slaughter-Houses, are those where persons are uniformly employed by the proprietors to affect to play at hazard for large sums of money.

**b.** A shop where goods are bought from small makers at very low prices. Also *attrib.*

**1851** Mayhew *Lond. Lab.* I. 333 This was owing to..the unwillingness of the small master to carry it to another slaughter-house in the rain. **1861** *Ibid.* III. 233 A special race of employers, known by the significant name of 'slaughter-house men'.

**c.** A cheap brothel.

**1928** E. Sutton tr. *Londres' Road to Buenos Ayres* vii. 55 She had got into a slaughter-house at two dollars instead of five. **1962** W. Faulkner *Reivers* viii. 164 Both of you get to hell back to that slaughterhouse.

**slaughtering** (ˈslɔːtərɪŋ), *vbl. sb.* [f. slaughter *v.*] The action of the verb in various senses.

**1597** J. King *On Jonas* (1618) 646 By trecheries, poisonings, slaughtering, and such like Scythian kindnesses. **1649** Milton *Eikon.* iv. Wks. 1851 III. 367 To turne his slashing at the Court Gate, to slaughtering in the Field. **1711** in *10th Rep. Hist. MSS. Comm.* App. V. 165 The slaughtering of a great number. **1819** Shelley *Cyclops* 387 Axes for Aetnean slaughterings. **1875** *Encycl. Brit.* I. 7 Since the opening of the public abattoir, all private slaughtering..is strictly prohibited.

**b.** *attrib.*, as ***slaughtering-house, stock***, etc.

**1845** Darwin *Voy. Nat.* iii. (1873) 56 The estancias and slaughtering-houses. **1870** Morris *Earthly Par.* II. iii. 280 His slaughtering stock before the knife would pine. **1891** *Month* LXXII. 18 Ice-houses, slaughtering-yards.

ˈ**slaughtering**, *ppl. a.* [f. as prec.]

**1.** That slaughters; killing, slaying.

**1588** Shaks. *Tit. A.* v. iii. 144 Hither hale that misbelieuing Moore, To be adiudg'd some direfull slaughtering death. **1592** *Soliman & Pers.* iii. i, Inforce me sheath my slaughtering blade In the deare bowels of my countrimen. **1625** Milton *On Death Fair Infant* 68 To..drive away the slaughtering pestilence. **1679** C. Ness *Antichrist* 211 Ministers have..ever been the sacrifices for slaughtering tyrants.

**b.** *transf.* or *fig.* (Cf. killing *ppl. a.*)

**1811** *Sporting Mag.* XXXVIII. 184 Having thus far described the slaughtering rounds of this fight. **1851** Mayhew *Lond. Lab.* II. 303 A little master, working, as he called it, 'at a slaughtering pace,' for a warehouse. **1867** F. Francis *Angling* (1880) 298 The most slaughtering way of fishing for grayling is with the grasshopper.

**2.** Of prices: Of the nature of a sacrifice; lower than is profitable.

**1898** *Daily News* 29 Mar. 9/4 In the export yarn trade there is a turn for the worse in values, owing to sales at slaughtering prices from stock.

Hence ˈ**slaughteringly** *adv.*

**1836** E. Howard *R. Reefer* xxxvii, They waxed..cuttingly polite, then slaughteringly sarcastic.

ˈ**slaughterman.** Also 4 slaghter-, 4–5 slawter-, 6 slauter-. [f. slaughter *sb.*]

**1.** One who kills or slays; an executioner.

*a* **1350** *St. Matthew* 307 in Horstm. *Altengl. Leg.* (1881) 135 He þat was þaire slaghter man Vnto þe appostell playnly ran And bare him thurgh with-owten let. *c* **1550** Bale *K. Johan* (Camden) 92 To slea that beaste & slauterman of the devyll. **1577** Bullinger *Decades* (1592) 64 He suffered..the torments of the slaughtermen, and death it selfe. **1611** B. Jonson *Catiline* v. iv, All his aides Of ruffians, slaues, and other slaughter-men. **1680** C. Ness *Church Hist.* 39 Some savage slaughter-men..to drown those males. **1869** Spurgeon *Treas. David* Ps. ix. 12 Before the slaughtermen are permitted to smite the Lord's enemies. **1899** *Contemp. Rev.* Sept. 439 Adventurers who had been hired on both sides as slaughter-men.

*fig.* *a* **1658** Cleveland *Poems* (1677) 118 O he's a terrible Slaughter-man at a Thanksgiving Dinner! **1711** Shaftesbury *Charac.* (1737) I. 270, I know not whether it be from this killing disposition..that our satirists prove such very slaughter-men. **1784** Berridge *Wks.* (1864) 412 Mr. Newton has fallen into the hands of a slaughter-man.. Dr. Mayhew, who will certainly cleave him down the chine.

**2.** One whose work or occupation it is to kill cattle, etc., for food.

**1389** *Durh. Acc. Rolls* (Surtees) 49 Stipendia famulorum ...: Slawterman, iis vjd. **1416–7** *Ibid.* 613 Item in feodo del Slawterman. **1548** Elyot, *Bouicida*, a slaughter man. **1624** J. Davies *Ps.* xliv, Like sheep which Slaughter-men cull out to kill. **1677** Yarranton *Eng. Improv.* 153 Houses for the Slaughter-men, Sea-men, and Fishers. **1722** *Lond. Gaz.* No. 6048/4 Richard Gilbert,..Butcher and Slaughter-man. **1810** *Sporting Mag.* XXXVI. 124 No bullock ever fell so clean from the hands of an experienced slaughterman. **1851–3** *Tomlinson's Cycl. Useful Arts* (1866) I. 3/1 To give space for one slaughterman to dress a bullock.

**slaughterous** (ˈslɔːtərəs), *a.* [f. slaughter *sb.* + -ous.] Murderous, destructive.

**1582** Stanyhurst *Æneis* i. (Arb.) 20 What fortun vnhappye Mee fenst from falling wyth thy fierce slaughterus handstroke. **1605** Shaks. *Macb.* v. v. 14 Direnesse familiar to my slaughterous thoughts Cannot once start me. **1634** Canne *Necess. Separation* 20 Many will rather submit to those slaughterous and inhuman courses than seek to redeem their precious liberty. **1798** *Progress of Man* 96 in *Anti Jacobin* (1852) 74 The slaught'rous arms that wrought thy woe. **1817** J. Scott *Paris Revisit.* (ed. 4) 97 The place where the slaughterous but immortal struggle was waged. **1839** James *Louis XIV*, II. 367 After various slaughterous conflicts,..the Spanish troops were obliged to withdraw. **1853** Mrs. Gaskell *Cranford* x, Some accident might occur from such slaughterous and indiscriminate directions.

Hence ˈ**slaughterously** *adv.*, 'destructively; murderously' (1847 Webster).

ˈ**slaughtery** (ˈslɔːtərɪ). [f. slaughter *sb.*, after *butchery*.]

**1.** Slaughter.

**1604** Drayton *Moses Map Miracles* 62 Death is discern'd triumphantlie in Armes, On the rough Seas his slaughterie to keepe. **1610** Marcelline *Triumphs Jas. I*, 9 That slaughtery, butchery, and all their massacres..are to him most horrid and hateful. **1648** [see sense 2]. **1904** Hardy *Dynasts* I. vi. iii. 196 If it indeed must be That this day Austria smoke with slaughtery, Quicken the issue as Thou knowest how.

**2.** A slaughter-house.

**1648** Symmons *Vindic.* 191 Masters of a Slaughtery will they be called, because they delight so much in the slaughtery of mankind. **1665** J. Webb *Stone-Heng* (1725) 181 A Slaughtery for killing of Beasts. **1917** G. J. Nicholls *Bacon & Hams* 26 The exporting slaughteries or factories. *Ibid.*, There is appointed to each slaughtery at least one veterinary officer who acts as inspector.

**slauk(e**, variants of slawk.

**slaum** (slɔːm), *v. dial.* Also **slorm**. [perh. related to slime *sb.*, *v.*[1]; for other uses see *Eng. Dial. Dict.*] *intr.* To slobber, to blubber; also, to flatter obsequiously. Hence ˈ**slauming** *ppl. a.*, (*a*) muddy, sticky; (*b*) slobbering, obsequiously flattering. Also *vbl. sb.*

**1787** W. Taylor *Scots Poems* 99 He has a dreadfu' drouth, Whilk *slawmin* canna put awa'. **1904** in *Eng. Dial. Dict.* V. 506/2 The wet maks the road a bit slaumin'. *Ibid.*, Yer needn't come slawmin 'ere, for a don't believe yer. (Notts.) **1911** A. Warrack *Scots Dict.* 527/1 *Slaum*, v., to slobber; to blubber; to smear. **1920** D. H. Lawrence *Lost Girl* xi. 278 I'd rather have him than your smarmy slormin sort.

**slaunchways, -wise** (ˈslɔːntʃweɪz, -waɪz), *adv.* and *a. U.S. colloq.* Also **slanch-, slawnch-**. [Alteration of slantways *adv.*, slantwise *adv.* and *a.*] Slanting(ly), oblique(ly); out of true. Also *fig.*

**1913** H. Kephart *Our Southern Highlanders* xiii. 294 Slaunchways denotes slanting. **1923** *Dialect Notes* V. 236 *Slawnch-wise*, adj., slantwise, slanting, out of true. **1933** *Amer. Speech* VIII. iii. 82 A Texas colleague of mine..said he wanted a full-width bed so that he could lie *slaunchwise* part of the time. **1941** *Sat. Even. Post* 5 Apr. 23/2 The race tide would slap him slanchways pronto. **1944** *Publ. Amer. Dial. Soc.* ii. 61 'The road runs *slaunchways* across the field.' "Don't hold your cup *slaunchways*; you'll spill your coffee.' **1981** *N.Y. Times Mag.* 19 Apr. 10 If you think Professor Cassidy's ideas are slaunchwise or skewhiffy, harass him directly.

**slaunder, -ir, -re**, obs. ff. slander *sb.* and *v.*

‖**slauntiagh.** *Obs.* Also slanteghe. [In form app. a. Ir. Gael. *sláinteacha*, pl. of *sláinte* health, but the sense is that of *slán, slánadh*, or *slánaidheacht* surety, guarantee.] A pledge or surety.

**1535** *State Papers Hen. VIII*, II. 266 Chaier Ochonor..is sworne and bounde by suirties and slauntiaghs of Omore and others, to take the Kingis parte against his broder. **1538** *Ibid.* III. 44 The said ODonyll and ONeile were bounde and sworne togethers.., and have fond suerties, otherwise callid slanteghe.

**slauth(e**, obs. forms of sloth *sb.*

**Slav** (slɑːv, slæv), *sb.* and *a.* Forms: α. 4 **Sclaue**, 4, 9 **Sclave**. β. 8–9 **Slave**. γ. 9 **Slav**. [In early use ad. med.L. *Sclavus* (recorded from *c* 800), corresponding to late Gr. *Σκλάβος* (*c* 580): cf. older G. *Sklave, Sclav(e, Schlav(e*, MHG. *Schlaff*. The later forms in *Sl-* correspond to mod.G. and F. *Slave*, med.L. *Slavus* (951), and are closer to the OSlav. and Russian forms: see Slovene.]

**A.** *sb.* **1.** A person belonging by race to a large group of peoples inhabiting eastern Europe and comprising the Russians, Bulgarians, Serbo-Croats, Slovenes, Poles, Czechs, Slovaks, etc.

α. **1387** Trevisa *Higden* (Rolls) IV. 417 Cirillus, apostel of þþe Sclaves. *Ibid.* VI. 249 He chastede þe Saxons and þe Sclaves. **1398** —— *Barth. De P.R.* viii. xxii. (Tollem. MS.), þþe contre and londe of sclaues. *c* **1835** *Encycl. Metrop.* (1845) XXIII. 631/1 Pomerania was originally peopled by the Sclaves. **1876** A. J. Evans *Through Bosnia* i. 15 The Croatian dress resembles that of all the Southern Sclaves.

β. **1788** Gibbon *Decl. & F.* lv. V. 544 The national appellation of the Slaves has been degraded by chance or malice from the signification of glory to that of servitude. **1861** J. G. Sheppard *Fall of Rome* vii. 349 The particular inroad in which the Slaves participated was signalized by the last triumph of the veteran Belisarius. **1889** I. Taylor *Orig. Aryans* 21 Linguistically the Slaves are closely related to the Letts.

γ. **1866** *Chambers's Encycl.* VIII. 383/2 The Eastern Slavs, the ancestors of the Russians. **1880–1** Morfill in *Trans. Phil. Soc.* 74 A very full account of the North-Western Slavs. **1883** —— *Slavonic Lit.* ii. 31 We find Slavs settled between the Danube and the Balkan.

**2.** = Slavonic *sb.* (Cf. Fr. *slave.*) Also *Comb.*

**1924** G. G. Walsh *Emperor Charles IV* iii. 34 The right of the monks, in his presence, to recite the Offices in Slav. **1935** Huxley & Haddon *We Europeans* vii. 203 The Slav-speaking population of central Europe. **1972** D. Dakin *Unification of Greece* 265 The Greek Church and the Greek communities had maintained schools where even the Slav-speaking Orthodox could acquire a knowledge of Greek.

**B.** *adj.* Belonging to, characteristic of, or originating with the Slavs; Slavic; Slavonian.

**1876** A. J. Evans *Through Bosnia* i. 10 The twin pigtails of maidenhood are far more characteristically Sclave than German. **1878** *N. Amer. Rev.* CXXVII. 403 The Slav trap prepared for her in Bosnia. **1903** G. F. Abbott *Tour Macedonia* 110 Through great part of Central Macedonia one finds the Slav language predominating in the open country.

Hence ˈ**Slavdom**, the Slavonic race generally; Slavs collectively.

**1881** *Times* 19 Jan. 9/5 A general casting off of the Turkish yoke from all Slavdom. **1889** *Ibid.* 15 Aug. 3/4 Outside Slavdom Russia has no politics whatever.

‖**slava** (ˈslɑːvə). [Serbo-Croatian, lit. honour, renown.] A festival of a family saint in Yugoslavia, a name-day.

**1900** 'Odysseus' *Turkey in Europe* viii. 372 The Slava, or festival of the family saint. **1920** *Glasgow Herald* 6 July 9 They told us of that country beyond, with its mountains and rivers, its peasant homes, its Slavas and songs of heroes—an Arcadia in truth. **1970** J. Brown *Un-melting Pot* v. 76 The household gods have had a central place in Yugoslav life since pre-Christian times and families today still have their household saints and keep their slava—their annual family days. **1976** *New Yorker* 22 Mar. 68/3 He remembers the priest blessing the house on his father's *slava*, or name day.

**slave** (sleɪv), *sb.*[1] (and *a.*). Forms: α. 4–6 **sclaue**, 5 **sclave**, 6 **sklaw, sklaue, sklave**, *Sc.* **sclayff**. β. 6 *Sc.* **slawe, slaif**, 6–7 **slaue**, 6– **slave**. [ad. OF. *esclave* (also mod.F.), sometimes fem. corresponding to the masc. *esclaf, esclas* (pl. *esclaz, esclauz, esclos*, etc.), = Prov. *esclau* masc., *esclava* fem., Sp. *esclavo, -va*, Pg. *escravo, -va*, It. *schiavo, -va*, med.L. *sclavus, sclava*, identical with the racial name *Sclavus* (see Slav), the Slavonic population in parts of central Europe having been reduced to a servile condition by conquest; the transferred sense is clearly evidenced in documents of the 9th century.

The form with initial *scl-* is also represented by older G. *schlav(e, sclav(e*, G. *sklave*. In English the reduction of *scl-* to *sl-* is normal, and the other Teut. languages show corresponding forms, as WFris. *slaef*, NFris. *slaaw*, MDu. *slave, slaef* (Du. *slaaf*), MLG. and LG. *slave* (hence Da. and Norw. *slave*), older G. *slaf(e*, Sw. *slaf*).

The history of the words representing *slave* and *Slav* in late Gr., med.L., and G., is very fully traced in Grimm's *Deutsches Wörterbuch* s.v. *Sklave*.]

**I. 1. a.** One who is the property of, and entirely subject to, another person, whether by capture, purchase, or birth; a servant completely divested of freedom and personal rights.

α. *c* **1290** *S. Eng. Leg.* I. 106 He was sone i-nome, Ase a sclaue forth i-lad and i-don in prisone. *c* **1374** Chaucer *Troylus* iii. 391, I wol þe serue Right as þi sclaue. **1513** Douglas *Æneid* ix. v. 114 My fader..Twelf chosin matronis sall ȝou geif all fre, To be ȝour sclavis in captiuite. *aa* **1533** Ld. Berners *Huon* xlviii. 161 It is a sclaue, a crysten woman, whom we bought at Damiet. **1590** Spenser *F.Q.* ii. vii. 33, I..rather choose..to be Lord of those that riches haue, Then them to haue my selfe, and be their seruile sclaue.

*β.* **1538** Elyot *Dict.*, *Seruiliter*, lyke a bondman or slaue. **1562** Winȝet *Wks.* (S.T.S.) I. 50 As thai war slawes, presoneris, and captiues in a raip. **1568** Grafton *Chron.* II. 2 Before the commyng of the sayde William there were no slaues or bondmen. **1610** Shaks. *Temp.* I. ii. 308 Wee'll visit Caliban, my slaue, who neuer Yeelds vs kinde answere. **1667** Milton *P.L.* xii. 167 Of guests he makes them slaves Inhospitably. **1717** Lady M. W. Montagu *Lett.* II. xlvi. 35 You will expect I should say something.. of the slaves. **1764** Goldsm. *Trav.* 388 The wealth.. Pillag'd from slaves to purchase slaves at home. **1809–10** Coleridge *Friend* (1865) 73 They were preparing us to give up.. the children of free ancestors to become slaves, and the fathers of slaves! **1878** H. M. Stanley *Dark Cont.* (1889) 204 The Arabs bring cloth, beads, and wire, to buy ivory and slaves.

**b.** Used as a term of contempt. Now *arch.*

**1537** *St. Papers Hen. VIII* (1834) II. 448 Emonges 200 of them [galloglasses] shalbe skaunt 8[th] that are gentilmen.., and all the residue sklawes. *c* **1560** *Durham Deposit.* (Surtees) 64 Thou art a slave and a knave to fynd fault with me. **1607** Shaks. *Cor.* I. vi. 39 Where is that Slaue Which told me they had beate you to your Trenches? **1780** Cowper *Progr. Error* 615 Though the deist rave, And atheist, if earth bear so base a slave. **1819** Scott *Ivanhoe* xxii, 'And what is to be my surety?' said the Jew... 'The word of the Norman noble, thou pawnbroking slave', answered Front-de-Bœuf.

*transf.* **1607** Shaks. *Timon* IV. iii. 33 This yellow Slaue [*sc.* gold] Will knit and breake Religions.

†**c.** In less serious use: Rascal; fellow. *Obs.*

**1592** R. D. *Hypnerotomachia* 87 Dyvers persons wondering at the force of such a little slave [Cupid]. **1601** Sir W. Cornwallis *Ess.* xv, I come now from discoursing with an Husbandman—an excellent stiffe slave. **1607** Shaks. *Cor.* IV. v. 181 Oh Slaues, I can tell you Newes, News you Rascals.

**d.** *Slave of the Lamp*, in the story of Aladdin in the *Arabian Nights*: a genie summoned by rubbing a magic lamp and bound to perform the wishes of the lamp's possessor; hence, allusively, one who performs swift miracles, or one who is under an inescapable obligation.

*c* **1840** Lady Wilton *Art of Needlework* xv. 238 The accommodations provided for the king.. on this occasion [*sc.* The Field of Cloth of Gold] were more than magnificent; a vast and splendid edifice that seemed.. to rise almost with the celerity of that prepared by the slaves of the lamp. **1841** Dickens *Let.* 1 July (1969) II. 319, I am bound to be.. constant to my plans. I am a poor Slave of the Lamp. **1853** C. Brontë *Villette* II. xxi. 90, I almost looked to see if a huge, dark, cloudy hand—that of the Slave of the Lamp—were not.. guarding its wondrous treasure. **1897** Kipling *Stalky & Co* (1899) 38 (*title*) Slaves of the Lamp. **1953** E. Coxhead *Midlanders* v. 120 Their working life was a deadening one. They were as near as possible machines themselves, slaves of the implacable lamp. **1959** *Encounter* Aug. 67/2 The physical scientist.. is the magician. He is the contemporary equivalent of that old friend of our children, the Slave of the Lamp. Which means that he is very much an underling: he makes his magic at the command of his masters.

**2. a.** *transf.* One who submits in a servile manner to the authority or dictation of another or others; a submissive or devoted servant.

**1521** *Bradshaw's St. Werburge* (1887) 203 Be nowe beniuolent, whan I shall on the call, Vnto thy slaue. **1596** Shaks. *Tam. Shrew* I. i. 224 Let me be a slaue, t' atchieue that maide. **1647** Cowley *Mistr.*, *The Thraldom* iv, I am thy slave then; let me know, Hard Master, the great task I have to do. *a* **1700** Evelyn *Diary* 31 Oct. 1685, He.. is of nature cruel and a slave of the Court. **1794** Mrs. Radcliffe *Myst. Udolpho* i, I'd be her slave no longer. **1849** Macaulay *Hist. Eng.* ii. I. 163 Oliver, the head of a party, and consequently, to a great extent, the slave of a party. **1880** 'Ouida' *Moths* I. 2 She had her adorers and slaves grouped about her.

**b.** *fig.* One who is completely under the domination *of*, or subject *to*, a specified influence.

**1559** *Mirr. Mag.*, *Jack Cade* xxiv, Therefore Baldwin warne men folow reason, Subdue theyr wylles, and be not Fortunes slaues. **1596** Dalrymple tr. *Leslie's Hist. Scotl.* I. 240 Sergius, a mounk and sclaue of the Nestorian and Heretical Impietie. **1602** Shaks. *Ham.* III. ii. 77 Giue me that man That is not Passions Slaue. **1620** T. Granger *Div. Logike* 102 He is the slaue of muddy Mammon. **1684** *Scanderbeg Rediv.* iii. 37 Well knowing that the Tartars are a People that use not to be very much slaves to their words. **1746** Francis tr. *Horace*, *Epist.* I. i. 53 The Slave to Envy, Anger, Wine or Love. **1780** *Mirror* No. 87, The slaves of a weak, a childish, or a gloomy superstition. **1848** Dickens *Dombey* xxvi, I am the slave of remorse. **1875** Jowett *Plato* (ed. 2) III. 174 [He] is the slave of his inveterate party prejudices.

*transf.* **1596** Shaks. *1 Hen. IV*, v. iv. 81 But thought's the slaue of Life, and Life, Times foole. **1602** —— *Ham.* III. ii. 198 Purpose is but the slaue to Memorie. **1817** Shelley *Rev. Islam* VI. xvii, O War! of hate and pain Thou loathed slave.

**3.** One whose condition in respect of toil is comparable to that of a slave.

**1774** Goldsm. *Nat. Hist.* (1776) II. 121 The women, therefore, of these countries, are the greatest slaves upon earth. **1801** Mrs. Sherwood in *Life* (1847) xii. 214 We called the slave-of-all-work to inquire the cause of all this tintamara. **1889** G. B. Shaw in *Fabian Ess.* 192 The white slaves of the sweater.

**4.** *Ent.* An ant captured by, and made to serve, ants of another species.

**1817** Kirby & Sp. *Entomol.* (1818) II. 75 Certain ants are affirmed to sally forth.. for the singular purpose of procuring slaves to employ in their domestic business. **1859** Darwin *Orig. Species* vii. (1860) 220, I opened fourteen nests of F. sanguinea, and found a few slaves in all. **1879** Lubbock *Sci. Lect.* iii. 77 If the colony changes the situation of its nest, the masters are all carried by the slaves to the new one.

**5.** Applied to a thing. **a.** *Naut.* = *slave jib*, sense 10 below.

**1934** *Yachting Monthly* LVII. 119/2 These craft [*sc.* Bristol Channel pilot cutters], when in the pilot service, carried a heavy mainsail roped up the leech, a heavy staysail with two sets of reef points, and a working jib, generally known as 'the slave'. **1970** E. March *Inshore Craft* II. vii. 263 A 'slave' slightly larger [than the storm jib] and so called because it was almost permanently set.

**b.** A slave device (see sense 6 c below).

**1940** F. Hope-Jones *Electr. Timekeeping* (1942) xvi. 156 Using a remontoire impulse as a synchronizing signal to control a Graham dead-beat escapement clock employed as a slave. **1965** *Jrnl. Scientific Instruments* XLII. 444/2 The whole seconds of the slave and chronometer can be matched regardless of the position of synchronization. **1969** J. J. Sparkes *Transistor Switching* v. 129 Which flip-flop is called the master and which the slave is quite arbitrary. **1975** D. Pitts *Target Manhattan* (1976) xxix. 126 'The first move is to get hold of that master computer.'.. 'That would stop the explosion?' 'It will if they haven't given final instructions to the slave.'

**II.** *attrib.* and *Comb.*

**6. a.** Appositive, as ***slave-boy, -girl, -labourer, -martyr, -pander, -soldier, -subject, -wife, woman***, etc.

**1607** Tourneur *Rev. Trag.* II. iv, Where's this slave-pander now? **1711** Shaftesb. *Charac.* (1737) I. 105 'Twas difficult to apprehend.. what publick [subsisted] between an absolute prince and his slave-subjects. **1813** Shelley *Q. Mab* v. 206 The slave-soldier lends His arm to murderous deeds. **1837** Ht. Martineau *Soc. Amer.* III. 110 Slave wives and mothers. **1839** Miss Maitland *Lett. Madras* (1843) 278 Four wives and seven slave-girls were burnt with him. **1848** Mill *Pol. Econ.* I. II. v. 294 No slave-labourers are worse fed, clothed, or lodged, than the free peasantry of Ireland. **1897** M. Kingsley *Trav. W. Afr.* iii. 70, I have myself seen.. slave women who had suffered for theft. **1900** *Dublin Rev.* July 205 The honour that was paid to the slave-martyrs. **1920** J. Masefield *Enslaved* 13 They took my lady with them as a slave-girl to be sold. **1957** H. Roosenburg *Walls came tumbling Down* iv. 79 The Nazis had used Russian and Polish POWs as slave labourers. **1962** H. R. Loyn *Anglo-Saxon England* i. 34 From this district [of Yorkshire] came the slave-boys seen and questioned by Pope Gregory in the Roman slave-market. **1977** P. Johnson *Enemies of Society* ii. 15 We find the great fourth-century senator, Symmachus.., asking a Danubian official to buy him twenty slave-boys, 'because on the frontier it is easy to find slaves and the price is usually tolerable'. **1980** F. Warner *Light Shadows* ii. 10, I gave the Emperor that slave-girl, Acte.

**b.** Used predicatively as *adj.*

*a* **1576** Pilkington *Wks.* (Parker Soc.) 225, I will.. make thee more vile and slave.. than any people round about thee. **1850** Carlyle *Latter-d. Pamph.* i. (*c* 1900) 35 Algiers, Brazil or Dahomey hold nothing in them so authentically slave as you are.

**c.** *techn.* Used to denote a subsidiary device, *esp.* one which is controlled by, or which follows accurately the movements of, another device.

**1904** D. Gill in *Rep. H.M. Astronomer at Cape of Good Hope for 1903* 7 The Clock consists of two separate instruments:—(a) A pendulum... (b) The 'slave-clock' with a wheel train and dead-beat escapement, the pendulum of which has a period of vibration slightly shorter than one second. **1930** *Engineering* 11 Apr. 466/2 A micrometer.. bearing against a 'slave' micrometer introduced to allow of the main one being set to a zero reading anywhere over a considerable range. **1938** *Jrnl. R. Aeronaut. Soc.* XLII. 907 This is a double acting liquid pressure remote control system having a number of slave cylinder units fed from a common source of pressure... The slave cylinders are arranged to effect a number of operations in a predetermined sequence when pressure is fed through one pipe line. **1945** *Electronics* Nov. 94/1 (*caption*) Master and slave stations transmit synchronized pulses, and the difference in their times of arrival determines the position of the ship or aircraft. **1963** *Wall St. Jrnl.* 13 Feb. 20/1 The 'slave' locomotive.. is being tested... The 'slave' would ride in the middle of a train perhaps 200 cars long; automatic sensing devices would keep it pulling the back end of such a train in rhythm with the manned master locomotive up front. **1972** *Amat. Photographer* 12 Jan. 41/1 (*caption*) A slave flash... This gun can be clipped anywhere and will trigger its own bulb, being actuated by the flash from another bulb gun. **1976** *Pract. Householder* Nov. (Heating Suppl.) 2/1 A houseful of remote slave units (electronic, of course) and a central control system is no longer eccentric gadgetry. **1977** *Grimsby Even. Tel.* 27 May 3/9 (Advt.), 100 watt slave amplifier, £40. **1980** Keene & Haynes *Spyship* xiii. 152 With this information, beamed off a slave satellite.., set and drift can be measured.

**7. a.** Attrib. in various senses, as ***slave-bargain, -bill, -blood, -hunt, -labour, -master, song, work***, etc.

**1808** Eleanor Sleath *Bristol Heiress* III. 283 You have.. found a respectable purchaser for your plantations, and have disposed of your *slave-bargain on your own terms? **1791** Cowper *Let. to Lady Hesketh* 27 May, As for politics, I reck not, having no room in my head for any thing but the *Slave-bill. **1612** Chapman *Rev. Bussy d'Ambois* IV. iii, He had bought his bands out With their *slave bloods! **1864** Webster, **Slave-hunt*, 1. A search after persons to make slaves of. *Barth.* 2. A search after fugitive slaves. **1890** *Spectator* 3 May, The leaders of the slave-hunts, the Arab desperadoes. **1820** *Deb. Congr. U.S.* 9 Feb. (1855) 1213 Free labor and *slave labor cannot be employed together. **1842** Dickens *Amer. Notes* II. i. 16 The system of employing a great amount of slave labour in forcing crops. *a* **1859** *Voice from South* 19 (Bartlett), I hear you avowing that slave labor shall not come in competition with free labor. **1871** Kingsley *At Last* xvi, Exclusive sugar cultivation had put a premium on unskilled slave-labour. **1822** *Sunday Times* 20 Oct. 1/4 The Continental Monarchs were but so many *slave-masters. **1869** Mill *Subj. Women* iii. 142 Servitude, except when it actually brutalizes, though corrupting to both, is less so to the slaves than to the slave-masters. **1924** W. Deeping *Three Rooms* ii. 16 His manner towards women was Oriental, playfully and tolerantly casual, but behind it was the thick hand of the slave-master. **1971** *Black Scholar* June 11/1 We were so abhorrent to our slavemasters that legal barriers were instituted to prevent the natural process of assimilation. **1894** H. Gardener *Unofficial Patriot* 2 The direct results of having been born to *slave-ownership. **1860** Pusey *Min. Proph.* 135 The inducement to *slave-piracy among the Cilicians. **1884** *Pall Mall G.* 25 Apr. 2/1 On the western side of Africa there are no *slave raids. **1881** *Harper's Mag.* May 818/2 The plaintive *slave songs.. have won popularity wherever the English language is spoken. **1939** *Jrnl. Negro Educ.* VIII. 641/2 The slave song was an awesome prophecy, rooted in the knowledge of what was going on and of human nature, and not in mystical lore. **1973** *Advocate-News* (Barbados) 19 Feb. 4/4 He sang an old slave song his grandmother had taught him. **1852** J. M. Ludlow *Hist. U.S.* 195 The tendency of the *slave-system being to divide the white population. **1796** H. Hunter tr. *St.-Pierre's Stud. Nat.* (1799) III. 651 The violent remonstrances of our traders in favour of the inhuman *slave-traffic. **1838** Whittier *Farew. of Virginia Slave Mother* 3 Where the *slave-whip ceaseless swings. **1916** D. H. Lawrence *Twilight in Italy* 303 Life is now a matter of selling oneself to *slave-work. **1926** J. Pedersen *Israel, its Life & Culture* I. II. 381 They.. set him to the ignominious slave-work of grinding in the prison house.

**b.** With words denoting places, buildings, etc., in some way connected with slaves or slavery, as ***slave-barge, block, -cabin, camp, -country, house, pen, pit, quarter***, etc.

**1865** J. H. Ingraham *Pillar of Fire* (1872) 218 A *slave-barge passed down the Nile. **1907** Kipling *Actions & Reactions* (1909) 188 The Hajji had often gloatingly appraised his skill.. at five thousand rupees upon any *slave block. **1966** *Keystone Folklore Q.* XI. 74 She was only eight when she was sold on the slave block. **1878** Morley *Diderot* II. 228 Black Toussaint Louverture in his *slave-cabin at Hayti. **1953** K. Tennant *Joyful Condemned* xxii. 208 Men all over the world making weary marches to prison camps and *slave camps. **1973** R. Dougall *In & out of Box* xi. 127 The great bulk of the work was carried out manually by wretched, scarecrow figures dressed in rags... They were gangs from the notorious Stalin slave camps in the Arctic. **1845** Darwin *Voy. round World* (ed. 2) xxi. 499, I thank God, I shall never again visit a *slave-country. **1939** J. Masefield *Live & Kicking Ned* 145 Inside the *slave-house. **1943** H. T. Kane *Bayous of Louisiana* III. 256 A barn and a few slave houses are all that can be found today of the former grandeur of the Durands, among the trees. **1890** Henty *With Lee in Virginia* 76 A warrant to search your *slave-huts.. for a runaway negro. **1855** Bailey *The Mystic*, etc. 70 The desert heart of *slave-land. **1860** Pusey *Min. Proph.* 135 The great *slave-mart at Delos. **1845** Coulter *Adv. in Pacific* ii. 15 One large kind of storehouse attracted my attention;.. it was a *slave-pen. **1901** W. Churchill *Crisis* I. iv. 35 A score of miserable human beings waiting to be sold at auction. Mr. Lynch's slave pen had been disgorged that morning. **1951** E. M. Graham *My Window looks down East* x. 86 In the cellar they have a slavepen. **1931** *Times Lit. Suppl.* 4 June 440/3 Characteristic.. are the winding entrance gangways, a feature.. in the.. '*slave pits'. **1959** J. D. Clark *Prehist. Southern Africa* xi. 302 These pits have been popularly referred to as 'Slave pits' suggesting that they were the places where slaves were confined on their journey from the interior to the coast. This explanation is, however, more fanciful than factual. **1982** *Evening Post* (Bristol) 19 Jan. 12 (Advt.), 2 further rooms and basement, with slave pit. **1837** H. Martineau *Society in America* II. i. 49 The *slave-quarter is large. **1911** G. B. Shaw *Getting Married* Pref. 160 The people whose conception of marriage is a farm-yard or slave-quarter conception are always more or less in a panic lest the slightest relaxation of the marriage laws should utterly demoralize society. **1956** G. P. Kurath in A. F. C. Wallace *Men & Cultures* (1960) 152 The hot rhythms of jazz.. have emerged from slave quarters.. to respectable society. **1981** P. Mallory *Killing Matter* vii. 82, I bought some groceries.. and, once inside my undistinguished slave-quarter, made myself a drink. **1796** H. M. Williams *Lett. on France* IV. 177 (Jod.), The faithful historian of a *slave-ship. **1842** Longf. *Witnesses* iii, There the black Slave-ship swims. **1897** Mary Kingsley *W. Africa* 219 The *slave villages.. are away down the north face of the island.

**c.** Consisting of slaves, as ***slave-caravan, -caste, -class, -coffle, -drove***.

**1840** Macaulay *Ess.*, *Ranke's Hist.* (1897) 558 The marts of the African slave-caravans. **1865** *Atlantic Monthly* June 752 The last slave-coffle that shall ever tread the streets of Richmond. **1872** Yeats *Growth Comm.* 348 The slave-droves of an African prince. **1895** C. S. Horne *Story L.M.S.* 95 Members of the poor slave-castes must not approach nearer than ninety paces to a Brahmin. **1935** Huxley & Haddon *We Europeans* ix. 279 A slave-class.. of markedly different ethnic type from their masters. **1977** W. M. Spackman *Armful of Warm Girl* 108 No birthright Philadelphia Quaker ever bothered his head over their slave-class preoccupation with the safety of their unappetizing souls.

**8.** Objective. **a.** With agent-nouns, as ***slave-auctioneer, -broker, -catcher, -dealer***, etc.

**1861** Gen. P. Thompson *Audi Alt.* III. clxxviii. 216 Give up your sons to slaughter, that *slave-auctioneers may still handle female flesh. **1893** *Dublin Rev.* April 295 The son of a *slave-broker in Cairo. **1852** Mrs. Stowe *Uncle Tom's C.* ix. 77 Are you the man that will shelter a poor woman and child from *slave-catchers? **1601** Holland *Pliny* II. 110 The root is.. well known to these *slaue-coursers. **1776** G. Sharp *Law Liberty* Title-p., Slave-holders and *slave-dealers. **1874** Green *Short Hist.* i. 17 'They are English, Angles!' the slave-dealers answered. **1856** Olmsted *Slave States* 196 The *slave employer.. has no remedy but to solicit.. a deduction from the price. **1776** G. Sharp *Law Retrib.* Title-p., Tyrants, *Slave-holders, and Oppressors. **1861** *Sat. Rev.* 23 Nov. 525 An intention of alarming the slaveholders of the coast. **1973** *Black World* Oct. 68/2 Unable to live in the slave-holder's kingdom, Walker fled to Boston. **1982** *English World-Wide* III. i. 19 A majority of the planters attempted to surmount the moral conflict inherent in being a slave-holder. **1889** *Academy* 24 Aug.

112/2 Our hero's capture by a band of ruthless *slavehunters. **1861** J. G. SHEPPARD *Fall Rome* xiii. 628 Fortune-tellers, *slave-mongers, gladiators. **1848** THACKERAY *Van. Fair* xx, Her father was a German Jew—a *slave-owner they say. **1939** J. MASEFIELD *Live & Kicking Ned* 71 A white slave who knew medicine might be worth double that to a slave-owner. **1957** V. W. TURNER *Schism & Continuity in Afr. Soc.* vi. 193 The mechanisms which formerly maintained the norms governing the relations of slave-owners and slaves could no longer operate. **1884** *Pall Mall G.* 20 Feb. 1 The *slave raider has extended his operations far and wide. **1946** *Nature* 2 Nov. 607/2 Slave-raiders were exhausting a wasting asset, the chief export of tropical Africa. **1601** HOLLAND *Pliny* I. 162 A merchant *slaue-seller. **1854** MILMAN *Lat. Chr.* III. v. (1864) II. 16 Barbarian or Jewish *slave-venders.

**b.** With pres. pples., as ***slave-carrying***, ***-collecting***, ***-dealing***, ***-holding***, ***-making***, ***-owning***, etc.

**1799** *Hull Advertiser* 13 July 4/2 The *slave carrying ships were pestilential jails. **1817** KIRBY & SP. *Entomol.* xvii. (1818) II. 88 Both species of the *slave-collecting ants. *Ibid.* 75 None of the *slave-dealing ants appear to be natives of Britain. **1864** *Q. Jrnl. Sci.* Jan. 10 The slave-dealing king of Dahomey. **1798** *Deb. Congr. U.S.* 29 June (1851) 2058 At present the *slaveholding parts of the State are burdened with the heaviest part of the State taxes. **1837** HT. MARTINEAU *Society in Amer.* II. 77 This brought in an accession of slave-holding settlers. **1959** D. K. WILGUS *Anglo-Amer. Folksong Scholarship* 353 White songs in the slave-holding areas. **1735** THOMSON *Liberty* I. 32 Extended in her hand the Cap, and Rod, Whose *Slave-inlarging touch gave double life. *a* **1628** F. GREVIL *Life Sidney* xv. (1652) 205 These *slave-making conjunctions betweene the Spaniard, and his Chaplaine. **1817** KIRBY & SP. *Entomol.* xvii. (1818) II. 81 Another of the slave-making ants. **1928** Slave-making [see DULOSIS]. **1944** J. S. HUXLEY *On Living in Revolution* 61 The raids of the slave-making ants are..a curious combination of predation and parasitism. **1977** RICHARDS & DAVIES *Imms' Gen. Textbk. Ent.* (ed. 10) II. III. 1243 Slave-making ants are confined to the northern hemisphere and are members of four genera only. **1828** J. F. COOPER *Notions of Americans* II. xiii. 296 The confederation is nearly equally divided into *slave-owning, and what are called free states. **1852** J. M. LUDLOW *Hist. U.S.* 195 A slave-owning oligarchy. **1934** E. O'NEILL *Days without End* I. 34 They..had supplanted Him [*sc.* Almighty God] with the slave-owning State—the most grotesque god that ever came out of Asia! **1971** *Black Scholar* June 3/1 The human capital of the slave-owning class.

**c.** With vbl. sbs., as ***slave-catching***, ***-dealing***, ***-holding***, ***-hunting***, ***-raiding***, etc.

**1864** WEBSTER, **Slave-catching*, the business of searching out and arresting fugitive slaves. **1873** P. H. COLOMB (*title*), Slave-catching in the Indian Ocean. **1835** J. E. ALEXANDER *Sk. in Portugal* ix. 212 Many of the governors have held office solely for the purpose of enriching themselves by *slave-dealing. **1845** MARG. FULLER *Wom. 19th Cent.* (1862) 25 Room for a monstrous display of slave-dealing and slave-keeping. **1841** J. STURGE *Let.* 30 June in *Visit to U.S. in 1841* (1842) 33 If *slave-holding were to be justified at all, the slave-trade must be also. **1863** SPEKE *Discov. Nile* p. xxvi, The whole system of slave-holding..is exceedingly strange. **1863** W. PHILLIPS *Sp.* v. 75 The pulpit preached *slave-hunting. **1845** *Slave-keeping [see *slave-dealing*]. **1933** A. N. WHITEHEAD *Adv. of Ideas* iii. 34 Mediaeval wars were dissociated from *slave-raiding expeditions. **1855** MACAULAY *Hist. Eng.* xvi. III. 715 The law which made *slavetrading felony. **1957** V. W. TURNER *Schism & Continuity in Afr. Soc.* p. xx, The slave-trading and -raiding of the nineteenth century.

**9. a.** With pa. pples., as ***slave-cultured***, ***-deserted***, ***-got***, ***-grown***, ***-peopled***.

**1763** CHURCHILL *Duellist* I. Poems 1767 II. 11 Some slave-got Villain. **1788** COWPER *Morning Dream* 26 To a slave-cultur'd island we came. **1809–10** SHELLEY *'Oh! take the pure gem,'* etc., ii, Where patriotism..Plants Liberty's flag on the slave-peopled shore. **1817** —— *Rev. Islam* IX. x, Their many tyrants sitting desolately In slave-deserted halls. **1848** MILL *Pol. Econ.* III. vi. §3 I. 571 Slave-grown will exchange for non-slave-grown commodities in a less ratio [etc.]. **1860** GEN. P. THOMPSON *Audi Alt.* III. cxli. 120 The supply of slave-grown cotton.

**b.** Similative, as ***slave-like***.

**1607** SHAKS. *Timon* IV. iii. 205 This Slaue-like Habit. **1845** LD. CAMPBELL *Chancellors* lii. (1857) III. 19 He would have addressed her in the most fulsome and slave-like strain. **1896** *Daily News* 13 Apr. 3/1 A slave-like obedience.

**10.** Special combs.: **slave ant** = sense 4; **slave bangle, bracelet** orig. *U.S.*: formerly, a slave's identity bracelet worn on the wrist or ankle; now, a bangle of metal, glass, bone, etc., worn for ornament, freq. above the elbow; **slave-captain**, the captain of a slave-vessel; **Slave Coast**, a part of the west coast of Africa (see quot. 1875) from which slaves were exported; **slave-fork**, a forked branch of a tree secured to the neck of a slave to prevent escape; **slave jib** *Naut.* (see quot.); **slave king** *Indian Hist.*, one of a dynasty founded by a former slave, Qutb uddin Aibak, which ruled the Delhi Sultanate from 1206 to 1290; usu. *pl.*; **slave-maker**, an ant belonging to a species that uses ants of a different species as slaves; **slave market**, a market at which slaves are bought and sold; also *fig.*, esp. (*N. Amer. slang*) an employment exchange; **slave morality** [tr. G. *sklaven-moral* (Nietzsche, *Jenseits von Gut und Böse* (1886) 231)], a morality characteristic of the weak, and rooted in resentment of the powerful, that exalts the lowly virtues of meekness, obedience, etc.; **slave-power**, a power based upon, or recognizing, slavery as an institution; **slave state**, one or other of the southern United States of America, in which slave-holding was legal; **slave-stick**, = *slave-fork*; **slave worker**, in the war of 1939–45: a person put to enforced labour by the German Nazi regime, esp. a foreigner deported to Germany for this purpose.

*Slave-wood*, given in various Dicts., etc., as a name for the Simaruba tree, is an error for *stave-wood*.

**1862** *Chambers's Jrnl.* 15 Feb. 97/2 Reaumur discovered how the ants of South America sally forth to kidnap hundreds of the black '*slave ants'. **1895** J. H. & A. COMSTOCK *Man. Study Insects* 641 The Slave-ant, *Formica subsericea*..is usually a dark-brown or ash-colored ant with reddish legs. **1923** U. L. SILBERRAD *Lett. Jean Armiter* ii. 33 A green-glass *slave bangle. **1931** N. CUNARD *Black Man & White Ladyship* 4 The thick old Congo ivories she thinks, are slave bangles. **1975** D. GRAY *Ride on Tiger* ii. 20 She wore ..a silver slave bangle on her right arm. **1934** WEBSTER, *Slave bracelet. **1940** R. CHANDLER *Farewell, My Lovely* xxi. 164 An emerald..that..managed to look as phony as a dime-store slave bracelet. **1976** BOTHAM & DONNELLY *Valentino* xxii. 169 Her special gift for her husband—a platinum slave bracelet. **1808** CLARKSON *African Slave-Trade* I. 378 Norris had been formerly a *slave-captain, but had quitted the trade. **1778** *Encycl. Brit.* (ed. 2) II. 1110/2 Benin,..in Africa, has..the *Slave Coast on the west. **1837** *Penny Cycl.* VII. 299/1 The most eastern districts [of the Gold Coast] are often distinguished by the name of the Slave Coast. **1875** *Encycl. Brit.* I. 269 The Slave Coast extends from the river Volta to the Calabar river. **1883** ANNANDALE *Imperial Dict.*, *Slave-fork. **1898** *Daily Telegr.* 11 Apr. 4/7 Many poor wretches fighting in fetters or in slave-forks. **1948** R. DE KERCHOVE *Internat. Maritime Dict.* 685/2 **Slave jib*, a term used by yachtsmen to denote a working jib, almost permanently set. **1841** M. ELPHINSTONE *Hist. India* II. VI. I. 1 (*heading*) *Slave kings. **1882** W. W. HUNTER *Indian Empire* ix. 223 Kutab-ud-dín had started life as a Túrkí slave, and several of his successors rose by valour or intrigue from the same low condition to the throne. His dynasty is accordingly known as that of the Slave Kings. **1958** O. CAROE *Pathans* i. 17 The slave-kings who followed them in Delhi were, every one, a Turk. **1971** *Illustr. Weekly India* 11 Apr. 55/1 Following Mohammed Ghori's establishment in Delhi, we had several dynasties of Muslim rulers like the so-called Slave Kings. **1859** DARWIN *Orig. Species* vii. (1860) 223 Ants which are not *slave-makers. **1915** H. ST. J. K. DONISTHORPE *Brit. Ants* 282 *Formica sanguinea*, the blood-red Robber Ant, our only slave-maker, is one of the most interesting species, showing great intelligence in adapting its habits to varying circumstances. **1978** *Nature* 16 Mar. 209/1 Wilson surveys a range of behaviour including that of 'slavemaker' ants who have become dependent on workers of other species. **1835** W. E. CHANNING *Slavery* iv. 87 *Slave-markets..turn to mockery the language of freedom in the halls of Congress. **1838** STEPHENS *Trav. Turkey* 52/1 In the slave-market..it required no great effort of the imagination to make her decidedly beautiful. **1871** FREEMAN *Norm. Conq.* (1876) IV. 92 Since Gregory had beheld the angelic children of Deira in the Roman slave-market. **1911** G. B. SHAW *Getting Married* Pref. 179 We are in the slave-market, where the conception of our relations to the persons sold is..simply commercial. **1931** 'D. STIFF' *Milk & Honey Route* 214 *Slave market*, that part of the main stem where jobs are sold. **1960** *Voice of Idle Worker* (Vancouver) 8 Feb. 2/2 The chances are that he will be a regular customer at the slave market for a few months. **1907** H. ZIMMERN tr. *Nietzsche's Beyond Good & Evil* ix. 227 In a tour through the many finer and coarser moralities which have hitherto prevailed or still prevail on the earth, I found certain traits recurring regularly together and connected with one another, until finally two primary types revealed themselves to me, and a radical distinction was brought to light. There is *master-morality* and **slave-morality*. **1907** G. B. SHAW *Major Barbara* Pref. 153 Nietzsche..regarded the slave-morality as having been..imposed on the world by slaves making a virtue of necessity and a religion of their servitude. Mr Stuart-Glennie regards the slave-morality as an invention of the superior white race to subjugate the minds of the inferior races whom they wished to exploit. **1960** J. O. URMSON *Conc. Encycl. Western Philos.* 282/2 It deals at length with slave morality which contrasts good and *evil*. **1859** BARTLETT *Dict. Amer.* 413 **Slave power*, the political power of slaveholders; the body of slaveholders. **1861** GEN. P. THOMPSON *Audi Alt.* III. clxxvii. 214 The martyrdoms a victorious Slave-power may in its tenderness impose. **1812** BRACKENRIDGE *Views Louisiana* (1814) 94 Buffaloe robes.. will be found of much use in the *slave states, as a cheap and comfortable bedding for negroes. **1888** BRYCE *American Commw.* III. liii. II. 334 New States had been admitted substantially in pairs, a slave State balancing a free State. **1899** WERNER *Capt. Locusts* 244 Once before I saw him there with people tied in *slave-sticks. **1946** *Ann. Reg. 1945* 185 The all-overshadowing event after the collapse of Nazi Germany was the liberation of the concentration camps and the huge army of foreign *slave-workers in Germany. **1956** I. SERRAILLIER *Silver Sword* vii. 47 Everyone over twelve had to register, and he would almost certainly have been carried off to Germany as a slave worker. **1971** P. D. JAMES *Shroud for Nightingale* viii. 264 [They] were Jewish slave workers in Germany..they were given lethal injections.

**Slave** (sleɪv), *sb.*[2] Also Slavey; 9 Slavé, Slavi. [tr. Cree *awahkān* captive, slave; the disyllabic Eng. forms reflect a local jargon var. with Fr. suffix *-ais*.] (A member of) a grouping of Athapascan-speaking North American Indians living in the boreal forest region of northwestern Canada; the language of this people. Also *attrib.* or as *adj.*

**1789** A. MACKENZIE *Let.* 22 May in L. R. Masson *Les Bourgeois de la Compagnie du Nord-Ouest* (1889) 30 (*Récits* section), Mr. Leroux arrived on the 22nd March from the other side of Slave Lake where he had seen a great number of Red Knives and Slave Indians. **1801** —— *Voyages from Montreal* (1903) I. viii. 340 When this country was formerly invaded by the Knisteneaux, they found the Beaver Indians inhabiting the land about Portage la Roche; and the adjoining tribe were those whome they called slaves. They drove both these tribes before them; when the latter proceeded down the river from the Lake of the Hills, in consequence of which that part of it obtained the name of the Slave River. **1851** J. RICHARDSON *Arctic Searching Exped.* I. viii. 242 The comfort, and not unfrequently the lives, of parties of the timid Slave or Hare Indians are sacrificed. **1862** R. G. LATHAM *Elements Comparative Philol.* lv. 391 The *Beaver* Indian is transitional to the Slave and the Chepewyan proper. **1875** H. H. BANCROFT *Native Races Pacific States* III. 587 A greater divergence from the stock language is observable in the dialect of the Tutchone Kutchin, which, with those of..the Slavé of Francis Lake.. might almost be called a dialectic division of the Tinneh language. **1890** W. C. BOMPAS (*title*) Hymns in the Tenni or Slavi language. **1907** F. W. HODGE *Handbk. Amer. Indians N. of Mexico* I. 440 Petitot restricted the term [*sc.* Etchareottine] to the Etcheridiegottine, whom he distinguished from the Slaves proper. **1932** D. JENNESS *Indians of Canada* xxiii. 390 In summer the Slave lived in conical lodges covered with brush or spruce bark. **1938** E. M. NORTH *Bk. Thousand Tongues* 870/1 *Slave*... Spoken by Indians living along the Mackenzie River, northwestern Canada. **1946** J. J. HONIGMANN *Ethnogr. & Acculturation of Fort Nelson Slave* 16 He is married to a Slave woman and in his cultural affiliations and back-ground is more Slave than Cree. **1959** E. TUNIS *Indians* x. 132 There was a group, the Etchaottine (Slaves), who were kind to old people. **1974** *Sunday Tel.* 18 Aug. 5/5 In the Territorial Capital of Yellowknife barmen have noticed a substantial reduction in the number of Dogribs seeking drink—and a corresponding increase in the number of Indians claiming to be members of the Chepeweyan and Slavey tribes. **1979** M. E. KRAUSS in Campbell & Mithun *Languages of Native Amer.* 862 These are all to a significant degree mutually intelligible, with Dogrib being the most divergent (not counting Slavey). **1981** *Handbk. N. Amer. Indians* VI. 79 No convenient name for this language exists, although Slave or Slavey was in 1980 commonly used as a self-designation by most speakers of Mountain, Bearlake, and Hare, as well as of Slavey proper.

**slave** (sleɪv), *v.*[1] Also 6–7 slaue. [f. SLAVE *sb.*[1] Cf. ENSLAVE *v.*; also (M)Du. and (M)LG. *slaven*, G. *sklaven*, chiefly in sense 4.]

**1.** *trans.* To reduce to the condition of a slave; to enslave; to bring into subjection.

**1602** MARSTON *Antonio's Rev.* II. ii, Thou canst not slave Or banish me. **1644** BERKENHEAD *Serm.* 21 Princes protect us from evill doers, who would..mercilesly slave our children. **1691** J. WILSON *Belphegor* II. i, I lend a Hand to Slave my Country!—No. **1881** MRS. A. R. ELLIS *Sylvestra* II. 60 Why did he go on board a Bristol ship, if not for slaving men?

*fig.* **1605** SHAKS. *Lear* IV. i. 71 Let the..Lust-dieted man, That slaues your ordinance,..feele your powre quickly. **1639** G. DANIEL *Ecclus.* xlviii. 30 Who could never stoope To slave his vertue, for a servile Hope.

**b.** Const. *to* (a person, etc.).

**1559** AYLMER *Harborowe* L iij b, Subiected and slaued to the proudest..nacion. **1608** MACHIN *Dumb Kt.* I. i, My recreant soule, Slaved to her beauty, would renounce all warre. **1652** C. B. STAPYLTON *Herodian* 76 It slav'd them unto Macedon and Rome. **1850** BLACKIE *Æschylus* II. 39, I first slaved to the yoke Both ox and ass.

*refl.* *c* **1613** ROWLANDS *Paire of Spy-Knaves* (Hunterian Cl.) 3 A Sicophant, that slaues himselfe to all. **1620** E. BLOUNT *Horæ Subs.* 439 If they hope to obtaine any thing by their fauour..they must..slaue them-selues to Flatterie.

**c.** *Croquet.* (See quot.)

**1868** WHITMORE *Croquet Tactics* 21 To 'slave'..a ball is to take it on with you in the game.

**d.** *techn.* To subject (a device) to control or regulation by another device. Const. *to* the device.

**1952** [see MANIPULATOR 2 f]. **1958** C. C. ADAMS *Space Flight* v. 132 The camera is synchronized with the National Bureau of Standards radio transmitter WWV, whose chief function is to broadcast time signals of incredible accuracy. .. It does this by means of a crystal clock..which is 'slaved' to WWV. **1978** *Broadcast* 21 Aug. 5/3 (Advt.), Picture stabilization provided by an oscillating mirror slaved to the film perforations.

**2.** To treat as a slave; to employ in hard or servile labour.

**1699** M. LISTER *Journ. Paris* 218 The Ægyptian Kings built them Monuments, wherein they slaved their whole Nation. **1737** BRACKEN *Farriery Impr.* (1756) I. 179 Brought on..by hard Riding and Slaving the Horse afterwards. **1820** SCOTT *Monast.* xxxvi, A man were better dead than thus slaved and harassed. **1925** E. O'NEILL *Compl. Wks.* II. 154 Didn't he slave Maw t' death?

**b.** To abuse by the name of slave.

**1719** LONDON & WISE *Compl. Gard.* p. iii, The Nursery man is presently slaved and condemned for a cheating Knave.

**3.** *intr.* (with *it*). **a.** To practise slavish imitation. **b.** = next.

**1589** NASHE *Anat. Absurd.* E ij, Some proude spirited princocks..gets him a liuerie Coate of their cloth, and slaues it in their seruile sutes. **1852** THACKERAY *Esmond* II. vii, He found himself presently..slaving it like the rest of the family.

**4.** To toil or work hard like a slave.

**1719** D'URFEY *Pills* (1872) V. 77 There's many more who slave and toil, Their living to get. **1766** ANSTEY *New Bath Guide* viii. 80 She slav'd all the Day like a Spitalfields Weaver. **1806** BERESFORD *Miseries Hum. Life* II. x, Slaving to drag up each separately out of its deep bed. **1848** DICKENS *Dombey* xi, Poor Berry drudged and slaved away as usual. **1870** LOWELL *Among my Bks.* Ser. I. (1873) 55 While he was still slaving at these bricks without straw.

**b.** To plod *through* something in reading.

**1806** BERESFORD *Miseries Hum. Life* VIII. xvi, Reading newspaper poetry;—which..you occasionally slave through.

**c.** *trans.* To wear *out*, etc., by severe toil.

**1864** MISS BRADDON *Doctor's Wife* ii, I may slave my life out, and there isn't one of you will..help me. **1880** —— *Just as I am* xlix, You will slave yourself to death. **1891** *Harper's*

*Mag.* July 184/1 What a hideous place was Pentonville to slave away one's life in.

**5.** *intr.* To traffic in slaves. *rare*$^{-1}$.

1726 G. Roberts *Four Yrs. Voy.* 1, I made a contract..to buy a Cargo to slave with on the Coast of Guinea.

†**slave**, *v.*[2] *Obs. rare.* [Related to sleave *v.* or slive *v.*] *intr.* To tear away or split.

1523 Fitzherb. *Husb.* §127 Cutte the settes..a lyttel from the erth, the more halfe a-sonder, and lette it slaue downewarde, and not vpwarde. *Ibid.* §133 That causeth the bowes to slaue downe the nether parte.

**slaveage** (ˈsleɪvɪdʒ). *nonce-word.* [f. slave *sb.*[1], after *peerage*.] Slaves collectively.

1831 *Blackw. Mag.* XXIX. 428 His ignorance of the British Peerage is equal to his ignorance of the American slaveage.

**ˈslave-born**, *a.* [slave *sb.*[1] 9 a.] Born of a slave parent or parents; born in the condition of a slave.

*a* 1586 Sidney *Arcadia* III, The obstinate cowards, the slave-born tyrants. 1594 *Selimus* (Temple ed.) 551 The mighty Emperor of Russia Sends in his troops of slave-born Muscovites. 1616 Drumm. of Hawth. *Poems* D iv b, A sable Stage Where slaue-borne Man playes to the scoffing Starres. 1765 Francis tr. *Horace, Odes* I. xxvii. 19 Thy breast no slave-born [*earlier edd.* slavish] Venus fires.

**slaved** (sleɪvd), *ppl. a.* [f. slave *v.*[1] + -ed[1].]

**1.** Enslaved.

1639 G. Daniel *Vervic* 515 As coldly Dull As the slaved Russian.

**2.** Of a vessel: Loaded with slaves. *rare*$^{-1}$.

1796 Z. Macaulay in Visc'tess Knutsford *Life & Lett.* (1900) vi. 141 Some of which he had already sent off fully slaved.

**3.** With prep., as ***slaved-for***. *rare.*

1952 Dylan Thomas *Coll. Poems* 132 My paid-for slaved-for own.

**slavedom** (ˈsleɪvdəm). [f. slave *sb.*[1] + -dom.]

**a.** Slavery. **b.** The position of a slave.

1562 Phaer *Æneid* x. Dd ij b, Than may your grace condempne al Italy to great Carthage, In slauedome vnder Moores. 1605 T. Bell *Motives Romish Faith* 8 [He] shal becom a Papist, and yeilde himselfe to the slauedome of popish religion. 1839–48 Bailey *Festus* xxvii. 324 A throne, at which earth's puny potentates May sue for slavedoms. 1863 Dicey *Federal St.* I. 165 The tyrants of slavedom have borne the sway here for forty years.

**ˈslave-drive**, *v.* [Back-formation from slave-driver.] *intr.* To exploit slave labour; to demand hard or servile labour. Also *trans.*, to demand an excessive amount of work from (a person). So **ˈslave-driven** *ppl. a.*, **ˈslave-driving** *ppl. a.* and *vbl. sb.*

1830 *Reg. Deb. Congr. U.S.* 10 May 939/1 Here they may live and flourish, until some slave-driving politician and planter of South Carolina..again chains them to a miserable dependence on South Carolina cotton and British looms. 1836 *Blackw. Mag.* Oct. 562/1 Ye slave driving hosts of factory and poor law commissioners. 1859 J. B. Jones *Wild Southern Scenes* vi. 46 The reason alleged was his alliance with the 'slave-driving' Blounts of the South. 1878 G. Meredith *Lett.* (1970) II. 565, I hope to propose myself to you for a night in January. At present I have the Devil behind me slave-driving. 1888 G. B. Shaw in *Star* 1 June 4/1 Bully him; slave-drive him. 1889 —— in *Fabian Ess.* 23 Its ferocious sweating and slave-driving. 1933 Slave-driven [see *medium close-up* s.v. medium B. 3 d]. *a* 1935 T. E. Lawrence *Mint* (1955) II. xiv. 136 Corporal Hemmings again supervised the gymnasium-work today. He slave-drove us as usual. 1952 E. O'Neill *Moon for Misbegotten* I. 13 He's gone like Thomas and John before him to escape your slave-driving. 1957 W. Camp *Prospects of Love* II. v. 61 You're not to let her slave-drive you. 1982 P. Fitzgerald *At Freddie's* iv. 32 There was no need for her to go back... Indeed it was probably a mistake, and might give Freddie the notion that slave-driving encourages slavery.

**ˈslave-driver.** orig. *U.S.* [slave *sb.*[1] + driver.] An overseer of slaves; *transf.* an exacting taskmaster.

1807 *Salmagundi* 13 Feb. 42 Beautiful, Oh most puissant slave-driver, as are my wives, they are exceeded by the women of this country. 1828 *Athenæum* 29 Feb. 162/2 The scourge shall no longer sound among the Antilles, nor the image of God be trampled by the slave-driver into the likeness of the beasts that perish. 1830 R. Walsh *Notices of Brazil* II. 480 A ferocious looking fellow with a scourge.. who was the slave-driver of the ship. 1854 Thoreau *Walden* 10 It is..worst of all when you are the slave-driver of yourself. 1857 T. B. Gunn *Physiol. N.Y. Boarding-Houses* xv. 127 He'd been an overseer—or, as they termed it, *slave-driver*— down South. 1889 G. B. Shaw in *Fabian Ess.* 193 The sweater himself, a mere slave driver paid 'by the piece'. 1901 Merwin & Webster *Calumet 'K'* x. 189 Do you think it would be worth something to the men who hire you for a dirty slave-driver to be protected from a strike? 1922 E. O'Neill *Hairy Ape* iii. 32 Bloody slave-driver! 1948 H. L. Mencken *Amer. Lang.* Suppl. II. 674 The [prison] guards are *shields, screws,..slave-drivers* or *herders.* 1975 *Investors Chron.* 28 Feb. 589/1 He is not a slave driver but somehow generates an extremely hard-working atmosphere.

**slave-holder**, etc.: see slave *sb.*[1] 8.

**slaveless** (ˈsleɪvlɪs), *a.* [f. slave *sb.*[1] + -less.] Not possessing slaves.

1852 J. M. Ludlow *Hist. U.S.* 195 An ignorant and helpless mass of slaveless freemen.

**slave-like** *a.*: see slave *sb.*[1] 9 b.

**slaveling** (ˈsleɪvlɪŋ). [f. slave *sb.*[1] + -ling[1].] A submissive or servile person.

1884 *Contemp. Rev.* May 688 The most independent of these slavelings..degenerated into a place-hunter.

†**ˈslavely**, *adv. Obs.*$^{-1}$ [f. slave *sb.*[1] + -ly[2].] After the manner of slaves; oppressively.

1553 W. Turner in Strype *Eccl. Mem.* III. I. iv. 49 If ye saw..how slavely and bondly they handle the rest of the Clergy.

**slave-merchant.** [slave *sb.*[1] 7.] One who traffics or deals in slaves; a slave-dealer.

1747 Dunkin in *Francis's Horace, Ep.* II. ii. 7 *note*, This was probably the usual Language of Slave-Merchants. 1792 *Gentl. Mag.* LXII. I. 2 The slave-merchants..brought forward several persons as witnesses. 1808 Clarkson *African Slave-Trade* I. 385 Slave-merchants..came in. 1876 Bancroft *Hist. U.S.* III. vi. 85 The slave-merchant supplied laborers on credit.

†**slaven**, *ppl. a. Obs. rare.* [irreg. f. sleave *v.* or slive *v.* Cf. slave *v.*[2]] Split.

1688 Holme *Armoury* III. xvii. (Roxb.) 116/2 In the bent of this Bow..is placed an arrow slaven; halfe an arrow it cannot properly be termed, but the side of an arrow.

**slaveocracy, -crat**: see slavocracy.

**slaver** (ˈslævə(r)), *sb.*[1] Forms: 4 slavere, 5 slavyr, 6–7 slauer, 6– slaver. [Related to slaver *v.* Cf. Icel. *slafur* in the same sense.]

**1.** Saliva issuing or falling from the mouth.

*c* 1325 *Gloss. W. de Bibbesw.* in Wright *Voc.* 143 *Pur sauver ses dras de baavure*, from slavere. *c* 1440 *Promp. Parv.* 458/2 Slavyr, *orexis.* 1562 Turner *Herbal* II. (1568) 79 The leafe is hote: and holden vnder ones tethe, bryngeth furth slauer. 1575 Laneham *Let.* (1871) 17 To shake hiz earz twyse or thryse wyth the blud & the slauer aboout hiz fiznamy. 1601 Holland *Pliny* II. 329 The froth or slauer of an horse mouth. 1646 Sir T. Browne *Pseud. Ep.* 136 That a Toad communicates its venom..by the humiditie and slaver of its mouth. 1735 Pope *Prol. Sat.* 106 Of all mad creatures..It is the slaver kills, and not the bite. 1774 Goldsmith *Nat. Hist.* (1862) II. 400 A venomous slaver, which, they suppose, issues from the Salamander's mouth. 1820 Byron *Blues* I. 47 I'd inoculate sooner my wife with the slaver Of a dog when gone rabid. 1834 Disraeli *Rev. Epick* I. xlix, It spat, and washed With burning slaver from my front the cross. 1904 M. Hewlett *Queen's Quair* II. iv, Ruthven, with the slaver of his rage upon his mouth.

**b.** *fig.* Drivel, nonsense; also, gross flattery.

1825 Coleridge *A Character* 68 The coward whine and Frenchified Slaver and slang of the other side. 1862 *Times* 2 Apr., A modest man, one to whom such slaver must be loathsome. 1893 Cozens Hardy *Broad Norf.* 55 Some people may look upon this correspondence as a lot of squit and slaver (nonsense).

**2.** Mucus-slime of fish or worms. *rare.*

1650 Earl Monm. tr. *Senault's Man bec. Guilty* 293 She got nothing but the slaver of worms, or scum of fishes. 1657 S. Purchas *Pol. Flying-Ins.* 46 In the Eele..is no Sex visible, yet by their slaver..do they produce their young.

**slaver** (ˈsleɪvə(r)), *sb.*[2] [f. slave *sb.*[1] + -er[1].]

**1.** A vessel engaged in slave-traffic.

1830 R. Walsh *Notices of Brazil, 1828–9* II. 482 This was opposed by the mate of the slaver. 1863 H. Cox *Instit.* III. viii. 722 The proceeds of ships..condemned as slavers. 1886 *Athenæum* 13 Nov. 627/3 They were in the boats creeping up to a slaver.

*attrib.* and *Comb.* 1886 *Athenæum* 13 Nov. 627/3 The story of his slaver hunting carries one back to boyish recollections. 1897 *Daily News* 30 Dec. 5 As stout a slaver-skipper as ever kept niggers under hatches.

**2.** One who deals or traffics in, or owns, slaves.

1842 Longf. *Quadroon Girl* iv, The Slaver's thumb was on the latch. 1862 *Industrial Mag.* Feb. 52 In America the slavers themselves make it an open boast. 1889 *John Bull* 2 Mar. 145/2 That there was no worse slaver than the present Sultan of Turkey.

**slaver**, variant of sliver *sb.*

**slaver** (ˈslævə(r)), *v.* Forms: 4– slaver, 5 slawer, slavyr, 6–7 slauer. [app. of Scand. origin: cf. Icel. *slafra* in the same sense, related to LG. *slabbern*, etc., slabber *v.*]

**1.** *intr.* To let the saliva run from the mouth; to slabber. Also *fig.*

*c* 1325 *Gloss. W. de Bibbesw.* in Wright *Voc.* 143 *L'enfaunt bave de nature*, slaveryt of kynde. *c* 1340 Hampole *Pr. Consc.* 784 His mouthe slavers, his tethe rotes. *c* 1425 *Voc.* in Wr.-Wülcker 668 *Salmare*, to slawer. *c* 1440 *Promp. Parv.* 458/2 Slaveron, *orexo.* 1530 Palsgr. 720/2 Fye on the knave, arte thou nat a shamed to slaver lyke a yonge chylde. 1576 Turberv. *Venerie* 224 He driueleth and slauereth at the mouth commonly. 1607 Markham *Caval.* I. (1617) 83 You shall euer haue a Horse that is so cut,..continually slauering, because the moysture which commeth into his mouth, cannot bee held in. 1667 H. More *Div. Dial.* III. vi, It may be also, when they take Tobacco, they slaver on the shorn side of their Chin. 1751 *Phil. Trans.* XLVII. 194 All of them slaver'd and frequently chang'd colour. 1797 T. Wright *Autobiog.* (1864) 87 He chewed tobacco, and sitting next my companion, slavered and spat upon his coat. 1841 Thackeray *Men & Coats* Wks. 1886 XXIII. 366 The man was bleeding at the nose, and slavering at the mouth. 1874 Holland *Mistr. Manse* xxvi. 228 With lips that slavered with their hate.

**b.** *fig.* To drivel; to fawn. Also with *it*.

1730 Swift *Wks.* (1755) IV. I. 122 Why must he sputter, spawl, and slaver it In vain against the people's fav'rite? 1753 Smollett *Ct. Fathom* (1784) 13/1 Where humour turns changeling, and slavers in an insipid grin. 1862 Wraxall tr. *Hugo's Les Miserables* IV. xxvii, It is a..frog-like language which crawls, slavers. 1894 Hall Caine *Manxman* 135 He thought..of his uncle and how he had snubbed and then slavered over him.

**2.** To issue as or like slaver.

1582 Stanyhurst *Æneis* III. (Arb.) 90, I saw flesh bluddye toe slauer, When the cob had maunged the gobets. 1614 B. Jonson *Barth. Fair* II. vi, Still the bottle-ale slauereth, and the tabacco stinketh! 1650 Bulwer *Anthropomet.* ix. 103 Their gums are seen..with spittle slavering forth.

**3.** *trans.* To wet with saliva; to slobber.

1591 Harington *Orl. Fur.* xxx. xcix, That [meat] they left they did so file and slaver As few could brook the sight. *a* 1601 ? Marston *Pasquil & Kath.* II. 209 Thou wast not made to slauer her faire lips With thy dead rewmy chops. 1693 Dryden, etc., tr. *Juvenal's Sat.* vii. 144 With white Froth his Gown is slaver'd o'er. 1819 Southey *Lett.* (1856) III. 135 Provided it be slavered over with a froth of philosophy. 1865 Miss Braddon *Only a Clod* i, To..slaver his hand with its flapping tongue.

**b.** *fig.* To fondle, to flatter, in a disgusting or sycophantic manner.

1794 Mrs. A. M. Bennett *Ellen* III. 183 She wondered Mr. Runnington was not ashamed to be slavering such a great girl. 1832 A. W. Fonblanque *Eng. under 7 Administr.* (1837) II. 238 This eagerness to slaver the arch-foe of the cause. 1856 Mrs. Browning *Aur. Leigh* VI. Wks. (1904) 484/2 Is it that the Devil slavers them So excellently, that we come to doubt Who's stronger?

**4.** To utter in a slavering fashion. Also with *out*.

1599 Broughton *Lett.* i. 7 You will needes..slauer out your follies in view of the world. 1847 Disraeli *Tancred* II. xii, Slavering portentous stories about malcontent country gentlemen.

Hence **ˈslaverer**, one who slavers; also *fig.*, a servile flatterer.

1618 Holyday *Technogamia* III. v, My Slauerer was at his Tobacco. 1843 *Blackw. Mag.* LIII. 71 Fashionable life has been exalted above its just and proper level, and depressed below it, by the slaverers and the vituperators.

**slavering** (ˈslævərɪŋ), *vbl. sb.* [f. slaver *v.*]

**1.** The action of allowing saliva to run from the mouth.

*c* 1325 *Gloss. W. de Bibbesw.* in Wright *Voc.* 143 *De baavure*, fro slavering. *c* 1425 *Voc.* in Wr.-Wülcker 668 *Hec salmacio*, slaveryng. *c* 1480 Henryson *Fables, Wolf & Lamb* iii, How durst thow be sa bald to fyle this bruik..with thy foull slauering? 1611 Cotgr., *Baverie*, a..slauering, or driuelling at the mouth. *a* 1827 Good *Study Med.* (1829) I. 107 In vulgar language it is denominated Drivelling or Slavering. 1878 Meredith *Teeth* 61 Slavering; imperfect speech; inflamed gums.

**b.** *pl.* That which is emitted as slaver; also *fig.*, drivellings.

1535 Coverdale *1 Sam.* xxi. 13 His slauerynges ranne downe his beerd. 1616 J. Lane *Contn. Sqr.'s T.* (Chaucer Soc.) 237 *note*, [They] doe pronounce such waer, slaveringes, not poems rare. 1684 *Contempl. State of Man* I. iii. (1699) 28 Silk [was nothing] but the slaverings of Worms.

**c.** *fig.* Extreme longing or desire. *rare.*

1642 H. More *Song of Soul* I. iii. 15 Strutting-in knowledge, Egre slavering-After hid-skill, with every inward uncouth thing. 1678 Butler *Hud.* III. II. 1201 Your greedy slav'ring to devour, Before 'twas in your Clutches, Pow'r.

**2.** *fig.* Kissing. *rare*$^{-1}$.

1607 Topsell *Four-f. Beasts* (1658) 183 An old lecherous fellow which could not keep his lips from slavering of women.

**3.** *attrib.*, as ***slavering-bib, -bit, -cloth, -clout.***

*c* 1325 *Gloss. W. de Bibbesw.* in Wright *Voc.* 143 *Une bavere*, a slavering-clout. *c* 1425 *Voc.* in Wr.-Wülcker 668 *Hoc salmarium*, slaveryngclout. 1530 Palsgr. 271/1 Slaveryng clothe for chyldren, *bauette.* 1648 Hexham II, *Een Slabbe*,..a childs Bib, or Slavering clout. 1704 *Dict. Rust.* (1726) s.v. *Bits*, The Masticadour or Slavering-Bit. 1823 E. Moor *Suffolk Words* 358 *Slaaverin bib*, a bit of cloth under a child's chin. 1899 *Allbutt's Syst. Med.* VIII. 244 The provision of slavering-bibs in some cases.

**slavering** (ˈslævərɪŋ), *ppl. a.* [f. as prec.]

**1.** Characterized or accompanied by the emission of slaver. Also *fig.*

1576 Turberv. *Venerie* 224 The fifth..kynde of madnesse is called the Rewmatike or slauering madnesse. *a* 1586 Sidney *Arcadia* II. (1622) 118 Miso..came with skowling eyes to deliuer a slauering good morrow to the two Ladies. 1603 H. Crosse *Vertues Commw.* (1878) 109 In one slauering discourse or other, [to] hang out the badge of his follie. 1664 Cotton *Scarron.* (1675) 56 A kind of slav'ring Letchery. *c* 1830 Coleridge in *Lit. Rem.* (1838) III. 48 In the slavering times of our Scotch Solomon. 1871 E. Peacock *R. Skirlaugh* I. 192 Let's have no slaverin talk like that.

**2.** That slavers; allowing saliva to fall.

1592 Greene *Upst. Courtier* Wks. (Grosart) XI. 250 The third was a long leane old slauering slangrell. 1602 *How to Choose a Good Wife* II. iii, Money can make a slavering tongue speak plain. 1630 *R. Johnson's Kingd. & Commw.* 56 An old sheep-biter..with a slavering lip. 1700 Dryden *Cymon & Iphigenia* 179 The slavering Cudden, prop'd upon his Staff. 1703 Rowe *Ulyss.* I. i, What Crowds Of Slav'ring, ..shameful Ideots. 1857 Trollope *Barchester T.* (1861) 240 She is proud of having this slavering, greedy man at her feet. 1883 *Fortn. Rev.* 1 Aug. 188 The lowing and slavering droves that one sees on the roads.

Hence **ˈslaveringly** *adv.*

1736 Ainsworth, Slaveringly (foolishly), *ineptè, insulsè.* 1834 *Fraser's Mag.* X. 113 The muscles of the lips [have been] slaveringly relaxed.

**slavery** (ˈsleɪvərɪ), *sb.* Forms: 6–7 slauerie, 6–8 slaverie, 7 slauery, 7– slavery. [f. slave *sb.*[1] + -ery. Cf. MDu. *slaverie* (Du. *slavernij*), LG.

*slaverei* (Da. *slaveri*, Sw. *slafveri*), G. *scl-*, *sklaverei* (†*skl-*, *schlaverey*).]

**1.** Severe toil like that of a slave; heavy labour, hard work, drudgery.

**1551** ROBINSON *More's Utopia* II. v. (1895) 161 In this hal, all vyle seruice, all slauerie, .. is done by bondemen. **1603** OWEN *Pembrokeshire* (1891) 43 Digginge of Coles, and other slaueryes and extreame toyles. **1698** FRYER *Acc. E. India & P.* 34 Asses which they use .. to carry Packs, .. and any other Slavery. **1712** J. JAMES tr. *Le Blond's Gardening* 65 To give them continual Waterings .. is a very great Slavery and Expence. **1897** *Daily News* 13 Sept. 6/7 Such people .. ought never to keep servants, but do their own slavery.

†**2.** Conduct befitting a slave; ignoble, base, or unbecoming behaviour. *Obs. rare.*

**1553** WILSON *Rhet.* 73 But if an officer .. should vse any slauerie, we are much more greeued. **1581** PETTIE *Guazzo's Civ. Conv.* (1586) A vj, If there bee anie .. which seeketh to .. benefit himselfe by flatterie, by briberie, by slauerie.

**3.** The condition of a slave; the fact of being a slave; servitude; bondage.

**1604** SHAKS. *Oth.* I. iii. 138 Being taken .. And sold to slauery. **1665** SIR T. HERBERT *Trav.* (1677) 9 Seeing the gain by their slavery is more aim'd at than the conversion of their souls to Christ. **1717** LADY M. W. MONTAGU *Lett.* II. xlvi. 36 Their slavery is, in my opinion, no worse than servitude all over the world. **1841** SPALDING *Italy & It. Isl.* I. 211 A barbarian killing his wife and himself to escape slavery. **1863** MILL in *Sat. Rev.* 302 Foremost among all things which injure and dishonour a country stands the personal slavery of human beings.

**b.** *fig.* The condition or fact of being entirely subject to, or under the domination of, some power or influence.

**1577** tr. *Bullinger's Decades* (1592) 114 The redemption of all yᵉ world .. from the slauerie of sinne. **1644** MILTON *Education* 3 Instilling their barren hearts with a conscientious slavery. **1724** WATTS *Logic* (1736) 223 This is .. as shameful a Slavery of the Soul. **1794** MRS. RADCLIFFE *Myst. Udolpho* xix, If you will not release yourself from the slavery of these fears. **1855** H. REED *Lect. Eng. Lit.* ii. (1878) 68 The slavery to chance is a worse evil than slavery to authority. **1873** HAMERTON *Intell. Life* X. x. 393 A kind of slavery—a minute obedience to the clock.

**c.** A state of subjection or subordination comparable to that of a slave; also with *pl.*, an instance of this.

**1586** MARLOWE *1st Pt. Tamburl.* v. ii, No hope of end To our infamous monstrous slaueries. **1621** BURTON *Anat. Mel.* III. iv. I. ii, 'Tis a wonder .. what slavery King Henry II. endured for the death of Thomas à Beckett. *a* **1700** EVELYN *Diary* 17 June 1683, The extream slavery and subjection that courtiers live in. **1724** SWIFT *Drapier's Lett.* iv. Wks. 1761 III. 74 All government without the consent of the governed, is the very definition of slavery. **1844** H. H. WILSON *Brit. India* II. 208 The feeling which pervaded the native states, their anxiety to be rescued .. from the miserable slavery to which they had been reduced.

**4.** The fact of slaves existing as a class in a community; the keeping of slaves as a practice or institution.

**1728** CHAMBERS *Cycl.* s.v. *Slave*, As Slavery was not abolished by the Gospel, the Custom .. lasted a long Time. **1764** BURN *Poor Laws* 122 The notion of slavery was not unknown to our laws, so early as the reign of king Edward the sixth. **1832** HT. MARTINEAU *Demerara* ii. 22 Why, then, has there been slavery in all ages of the world? **1852** MRS. STOWE *Uncle Tom's C.* xix. 188 On this abstract question of slavery there can, as I think, be but one opinion. **1873** SPENCER *Stud. Sociol.* vi. 143 Slavery, under which .. certain men held complete possession of others.

*personif.* **1794** COLERIDGE *To La Fayette*, Slavery's spectres shriek and vanish from the ray! **1880** E. KIRKE *Life Garfield* 53 There lies Slavery, a black marble column at the head of its grave.

**5.** *attrib.*, as ***slavery-fetters***, ***question***, etc.

**1824** *Batavian Anthol.* 103 While on our friends No slavery-fetters hang. **1851** CARLYLE *Sterling* I. xii, There are Blacks, and the Slavery Question to be investigated. **1860** LOWELL *Election in Nov.* Prose Wks. 1890 V. 40 The demand of the slavery-extensionists.

**slavery** ('slævərɪ), *a.* [f. SLAVER *sb.*[1] + -Y[1].] Like slaver; befouled with slaver; characterized by slaver; given to slavering.

*c* **1430** *Pilgr. Lyf Manhode* III. xlvii. (1869) 160, I am foule, old, and slavery. **1646** in *Jubilee of W. Orr* (1880) 11 For calling one of ye elders a mansworne slaverie loun. **1730** *Phil. Trans.* XXXVI. 453 A constant weeping of a thin slavery Liquor. **1845** S. JUDD *Margaret* I. vi, Thrusting his slavery lips close to her ear. **1895** KIPLING *2nd Jungle Bk.* 234 He drove the dholes .. from yells to hoarse slavery ravings.

**'slave-trade**, *sb.* [SLAVE *sb.*[1] 7.] Traffic in slaves; *spec.* the former transportation of African Negroes to America. Also *attrib.*

**1734** SNELGRAVE (*title*), A New Account of some Parts of Guinea, and the Slave Trade. **1772** WESLEY *Jrnl.* 12 Feb., A very different book .. on that execrable sum of all villanies, commonly called the Slave-trade. **1834** DE QUINCEY in *Tait's Mag.* I. 18/2 Of the kidnapping, murdering slave-trade, there cannot be two opinions. **1849** LYELL *2nd Visit U.S.* II. 322 The efforts made by the English and United States' fleets to put down the slave-trade. **1876** BANCROFT *Hist. U.S.* II. xxvii. 186 That America should benefit the African, was always the excuse for the slave-trade.

Hence **'slave-trade** *v. intr.*, to traffic in slaves.

**1818** R. THORPE *View Slave Trade* 68 By enabling the great body of factors to discover, that .. they might slave-trade with impunity.

**'slave-trader.** [Cf. prec. and SLAVE *sb.*[1] 8 a.]

**1.** One who trades in slaves; a slaver.

**1813** *Examiner* 22 Mar. 184/2 The .. conviction of three slave-traders at Sierra Leone. **1876** BANCROFT *Hist. U.S.* II. xxxv. 390 For the English colonies, her Britannic majesty .. was the exclusive slave-trader.

**2.** A ship engaged in the slave-trade.

**1875** BEDFORD *Sailor's Pocket Bk.* vi. 232 The most ordinary slave-trader of all .. flies no flag.

**slavey** ('sleɪvɪ). *colloq.* [f. SLAVE *sb.*[1] (and *a.*) + -Y.]

**1.** A male servant or attendant.

**1812** J. H. VAUX *Flash Dict.*, *Slavey*, a servant of either sex. **1852** SMEDLEY *L. Arundel* xii. 91 The slaveys [= waiters] will swallow that or anything else for Persian. **1855** THACKERAY *Newcomes* xi, The slavey has Mr. Frederick's hot water, and a bottle of soda water on the same tray. He has been instructed [etc.]. **1901** M. FRANKLIN *My Brilliant Career* xvii. 141 Harold Beecham kept a snivelling little Queensland black boy as a sort of black-your-boots, odd-jobs slavey or factotum. **1967** *Atlantic Monthly* Apr. 103/2 All his years a loyal slavey he had worked his heart out for peanuts.

**2.** A female domestic servant, *esp.* one who is hard-worked; a maid of all work.

**1821** EGAN *Life in London* 174 'He is only fond of the Slaveys!' (*Note.* A slang term for servant maids.) **1837** T. HOOK *J. Brag* i, Four guineas per annum, and a tip to the slavey. **1893** VIZETELLY *Glances back* I. xiii. 249 A young lodging-house slavey .. bade me follow her upstairs.

**Slavey**, var. SLAVE *sb.*[2]

**Slavi**, obs. var. SLAVE *sb.*[2]

**Slavian** ('slɑːvɪən, 'slævɪən), *a. rare.* [f. SLAV *sb.* + -IAN.] Slavonian, Slavic.

**1836** *Partington's Brit. Cycl. Lit.*, etc. III. 520/1 Its principal ingredient is the Sclavian language. **1854** MILMAN *Lat. Chr.* v. viii. II. 426 Among the Slavian tribes the Greek missionaries had penetrated into regions of unmingled Barbarism. **1865** *Reader* No. 119. 391/1 Greek, Romain, and Slavian newspapers.

**Slavic** ('slɑːvɪk, 'slævɪk), *a.* and *sb.* Also **Sclavic**, **Slaavic.** [f. SLAV *sb.* + -IC.]

**A.** *adj.* Of or pertaining to the Slavs; Slavonian; Slavonic.

*a* **1813** *Q. Rev.* Oct. 256 Classes and families of languages. .. Indoeuropean .. Sclavic. *Ibid.* 281 The connexion of the Sclavonian, and Lithuanian, which we have comprehended in the title of Sclavic family. **1864** *Athenæum* 2 Apr. 467/3 The 'Sclavic Athens' [as] she [Ragusa] was named in the seventeenth century.

*β* **1842** PRICHARD *Nat. Hist. Man* 184 The Slavic, or Sclavonic race, is a 4th Indo-European family. **1849** PATON *Highl. & Isl. Adriatic* I. xii. 157 The most advanced of all the Slaavic nations of central Europe. **1866** *Chambers's Encycl.* VIII. 389/2 The author of a Slavic Grammar. **1882** W. B. WEEDEN *Soc. Law Labor* 11 The Slavic development differs from other Aryan experience.

**B.** *sb.* **a.** A Slavonic form of speech.

**1812** A. MURRAY *Let.* 8 Aug. in T. Constable *A. Constable* (1873) I. 333, I wish, however, to have about 100 or 150 printed pages additional on the Latin, Slavic, Persic, and Celtic. **1850** [see *Church Slavic* s.v. CHURCH *sb.* 18]. **1866** *Chambers's Encycl.* VIII. 389/2 The lines of distinction .. between old Slavic and Russian. **1876** WHITNEY *Language and its Study* vi. 214 Old Slavonic, or the Church Slavic, having been adopted by a large part of the Slavonian races as their sacred language.

**b.** *Comb.*, as ***Slavic-speaking*** adj.

**1942** *Amer. Council of Learned Societies Bull.* No. 34. 58 (*heading*) The Slavic-speaking groups of the United States and Canada. **1980** *Word 1979* XXX. 19 Albanians in Yugoslavia are classified as a nationality (*narodnost*) within a population consisting predominantly of Slavic-speaking peoples.

Hence **'Slavicize** *v. trans.*, to render Slav-like, to convert into Slavs.

**1887** *Pall Mall G.* 22 Dec. 8/1 The Servian individuality cannot be Germanized, but it might be Slavicized. **1898** *Contemp. Rev.* Feb. 172 Any attempt to Slavicise the Germans of Bohemia.

**Slavicist** ('slɑːv-, 'slævɪsɪst). [f. SLAVIC *sb.* + -IST.] = SLAVIST[2].

**1930** K. MALONE in *Stud. in Honor of H. Collitz* 328 *Slavist* .. actually has two meanings: .. (2) an authority on Slavic, and for the second meaning *Slavicist* would be a more appropriate term. **1964** *Slavic Rev.* XXIII. 707 There does not seem to be an organized correlation between trained Slavicists and potentially available posts. **1976** *Language* LII. 108 Most Slavicists agree on two cardinal classes of denominal qualitative adjectives.

**Slavifi'cation.** [f. SLAV *a.* + -(I)FICATION.] The action or process of Slavicizing.

The verb *slavify* also occurs in recent use.

**1883** C. ABEL *Slavic & Latin* Contents, The Slavification of the Finnish area.

**slavikite** ('slævɪkaɪt). *Min.* [ad. Czech. *slavikit* (Jirkovský & Ulrich 1926, in *Věstník Státního Geol. Ústavu Česk. Repub.* II. 345), f. the name of František *Slavík* (1876–1957), Czech mineralogist: see -ITE[1].] A trigonal greenish-yellow hydrated basic sulphate of ferric iron found as an oxidation product of pyrite and usu. containing additional magnesium and sodium.

**1927** *Mineral. Abstr.* III. 365 This mineral, named slavikite (after the abstractor), forms minute, almost microscopic, crystals with the rhombohedron (1011) and the base (0001) equally developed, or tabular parallel to (0001). **1957** *Ibid.* XIII. 369 Slavikite .. associated with gypsum, pickeringite, and jarosite, occurs in Belgium at Stavelot on Revinian phyllites and at Val-Dieu on Famennian sandstone. **1968** I. KOSTOV *Mineral.* 500 Slavikite is trigonal, found in minute uniaxial negative crystals tabular on {0001}.

†**slavin.** *Obs.* Forms: *α.* 3–4 sclaueyn (5 sklaueyne), 5 -ayne; 4 sclaveyn, 5 -ayn, -ene. *β.* 3 scl-, 4 sklauin; 3, 5 sclauyne, 5 scl-, sklauyn; 3 sclavyne, 3–4 sclavyn (4 skl-). *γ.* 4–5 slaueyn, 5 -aine; 4–5 slaveyne, 5 -eyn. *δ.* 5 slaw-, slavyne (-yn), slauyn(e. [ad. OF. *esclavine*, = Sp. *esclavina*, It. *schiavina*, med.L. *sclavina*, *-inia*, app. f. *sclavus* slave or *Sclavus* Slav. Cf. also MDu. *slavine*, *-ijn*, MHG. *slavenîe*.] A pilgrim's mantle.

*α.* *c* **1290** *S. Eng. Leg.* I. 419 Cam þare a Man in o sclaueyn. *c* **1325** *Orfeo* 222 To him a sclaveyn anon he toke. **13..** *Octouian* 394 Ther com a palmer old In a sklaueyne. *c* **1430** *Life St. Kath.* (1884) 25 An oold fader .. wyth an oold sclauayn uppon hym. *c* **1475** *Pict. Voc.* in Wr.-Wülcker 773 *Hec sarabarda*, a sclavene.

*β.* *a* **1300** *K. Horn* (Camb. MS.) 1054 Haue her cloþes myne, And tak me þi sclauyne. *c* **1320** *Sir Beues* 2066 [He] ȝaf him is hors, þat he rod in, For is bordon and is sklauin. **1483** CAXTON *Gold. Leg.* 185/1 The crosse that he bare and sklauyn that he ware. **1491** —— *Vitas Patr.* (W. de W. 1495) I. xxxvi. 42 b/1 A mantel, in maner of a sclauyne.

*γ.* **1399** LANGL. *Rich. Redeles* III. 236 His slaueyn was of þe olde schappe. **1430–40** LYDG. *Bochas* IX. xxxiv. (1554) 214 One Bulgare, clad in slaueyn olde. *c* **1440** *Jacob's Well* 157 A pylgrym ȝaf his slaveyn for to drynke myȝty wyne.

*δ.* ? *a* **1400** *Morte Arth.* 3474 With scrippe, ande with slawyne, and skalopis i-newe. *c* **1440** *Alph. Tales* 198 How þer was a pylgram at .. seld his slavyn. **1481** CAXTON *Reynard* (Arb.) 10 He shewd me his slauyne and pylche and an heren sherte ther vnder.

**slaving** ('sleɪvɪŋ), *vbl. sb.* [f. SLAVE *v.*[1]]

**1.** The practice of capturing or trading in slaves.

**1862** J. STEWART in *Stewart of Lovedale* ix. 88 From the Zambesi to Lake Nyassa there is nothing but slaving. **1865** LIVINGSTONE *Zambesi* 593 The members of the same tribes who .. have never engaged in slaving. **1887** *Pall Mall G.* 28 June 2/1 Though slaving was never our business, it did occasionally happen that we bought a few slaves.

**2.** The automatic control or regulation of one device by another.

**1960** *How TV Works* ii. 17/2 This technique—known by the jargon of 'slaving'—ensures that the programmes sent out from the transmitters are no less excellent in quality when they originate from very distant studios. **1974** *Some Technical Terms & Slang* (Granada Television), *Slaving*, interlocking electronic signals between disparate sources.

†**'slaving**, *sb. Obs.*[−1] [f. SLAVE *v.*[2]] A slip of a tree; = SLEAVING.

**1523** FITZHERB. *Husb.* §130 Dyuerse apple-trees, that haue knottes in the bowes, .. and suche other, that wyll growe on slauynges.

**slavish** ('sleɪvɪʃ), *a.*[1] Also 6 slau(e)ishe, 6–7 slauish. [f. SLAVE *sb.*[1] + -ISH[1]. Cf. Du. *slaafsch*, G. *scl-*, *sklavisch* (†*schl-*, *slavisch*).]

**1.** Of, belonging to, or characteristic of, a slave; befitting a slave; servile, abject.

**1565** COOPER *Thesaurus*, *Vernilitas*, .. slauishe behauour. **1568** GRAFTON *Chron.* II. 3 To submit themselues vnto slauish seruitude. **1576** FLEMING *Panopl. Epist.* 83 The victorie .. which .. had brought you in slaueishe subiection. **1632** LITHGOW *Trav.* II. 66 There was .. twelue thousand Christians deliuered from their slauish bondage. **1671** MILTON *Samson* 122 See how he lies .. In slavish habit, ill-fitted weeds. **1763** J. BROWN *Poetry & Music* xi. 188 The Player .. was generally of slavish Birth at Rome. **1770** *Lett. Junius* xxxix. (1788) 214 The house of lords have imposed a slavish silence upon themselves. **1812** BYRON *Ch. Har.* II. lxxxiii, The bondsman's peace, who .. with smooth smile his tyrant can accost, And wield the slavish sickle. **1874** GREEN *Short Hist.* viii. §2. 468 The spirit of slavish submission which pervaded the Houses.

**b.** Toiling, toilsome, laborious.

**1828** A. CLARKE in *Life* (1840) xiii. 472 Winter is a dangerous and slavish time for the Shetland preachers. **1850** MARSDEN *Early Purit.* (1853) 100 A slavish life, busied with a succession of fretful observances, has no attractions.

**2.** Having the character (†or status) of slaves; of a submissive, unmanly disposition.

**1565** COOPER *Thesaurus*, *Vernaculi*, slauysh and naughtie condicioned men, eyther in flatteryng or in ill speach. **1598** BP. HALL *Sat.* IV. ii. 126 They racke their rents vnto a treble rate; .. And clogge their slauish tenant with commaunds. **1612** T. TAYLOR *Titus* ii. 3 We may not become slauish vnto them. **1632** LITHGOW *Trav.* IV. 152 [They] cause the poore slauish subiected Christians, surrender all they haue. **1662** J. DAVIES tr. *Olearius' Voy. Amb.* 114 The Muscovites how submissive and slavish soever they may be, will endeavour the recovery of their freedom. **1715** POPE *Iliad* I. 306 Scourge of thy people, .. Sent in Jove's anger on a slavish race. **1781** COWPER *Truth* 228 Th' omniscient Judge Scorns the base hireling, and the slavish drudge. **1850** MAURICE *Mor. & Theol. Philos.* (ed. 2) 131 The thoughtless, slavish victim of inclination.

**3.** Vile, mean, base, ignoble.

**1593** SHAKS. *Rich. II*, I. i. 193 The slauish motiue of recanting feare. **1607** CHAPMAN *Bussy d'Ambois* IV. i, The princely author of the slavish sin. *a* **1680** BUTLER *Rem.* (1759) I. 202 To free itself from slavish Prepossession. **1700** ASTRY tr. *Saavedra-Faxardo* I. 89 To lye is a slavish Vice. **1737** SWIFT in Scoones *Four Cent. Eng. Lett.* 169 The slavish, hellish principles of an execrable prevailing faction. **1839** THIRLWALL *Greece* VI. 35 The slavish counsels of those who only calculated the expense of a war. **1845** MAURICE *Mor. Philos.* in *Encycl. Metrop.* II. 547/1 A slavish dread of the powers of nature.

**4.** Implying or involving slavery.

**1593** SHAKS. *Rich. II*, II. i. 291 If then we shall shake off our slauish yoake, .. Away with me. **1648** GAGE *West Ind.* 17

Hee had run away from his master by reason of hard and slavish usage. **1709** WATTS *Hymn*, '*How sad our state by nature is!*' i, Satan binds our captive souls Fast in his slavish chains. **1781** COWPER *Anti-Thelyphth.* 112 For British nymphs..Feel all the meanness of your slavish lot. **1831** SCOTT *Ct. Robt.* i, The slavish and despotic constitution introduced into the empire.

**5.** Servilely imitative; lacking originality or independence.

**1753** TORRIANO *Gangr. Sore Throat* 87 In the Translation ..I have not confined myself to a slavish and literal one. **1861** BROUGHAM *Brit. Const.* xix. i. 307 In preparing this great work there was no slavish adherence to the old law.

**b.** Of persons.

**1756** C. LUCAS *Ess. Waters* III. 294 We have not a few of these slavish followers. **1863** BARRY *Dockyard Econ.* 73 Slavish copyists of the English dockyard system.

**Slavish** (ˈslɑːvɪʃ, ˈslævɪʃ), *a.*² and *sb.* [f. SLAV *sb.* + -ISH¹. Cf. G. *Slavisch*, †*Sclavisch*.]

**a.** *adj.* Pertaining to or characteristic of the Slavs. **b.** *sb.* The Slavonic language.

**1834** *Penny Cycl.* II. 473/2 Some nations of Slavish origin inhabiting Asia. **1843** in *Proc. Philol. Soc.* I. 101 As they relate to the Slavish languages. **1844** *Ibid.* 273 In the old Slavish, or language of the church. **1899** R. MUNRO *Prehist. Scot.* x. 380 Slavish pottery is always well burnt.

**slavishly** (ˈsleɪvɪʃlɪ), *adv.* Also 6–7 **slauishly,** 7 **slaueishly, slauishlie.** [f. SLAVISH *a.*¹ + -LY².]

**1.** In a servile or slavish manner.

**1565** COOPER *Thesaurus, Verniliter*, lewdly:..slauishly. **1593** NASHE *Christ's T.* (1613) 23 Most slauishly thou kissest and embracest them. **1621** BURTON *Anat. Mel.* I. ii. III. xi, It is a wonder to see, how slavishly these kind of men subject themselves. **1698** FRYER *Acc. E. India & P.* 362 Some.. content themselves to live slavishly..for a Morsel of Bread. **1727** GAY *Fables* xii. 21 She never slavishly submits, She'll have her will, or have her fits. **1796** KIRWAN *Elem. Min.* (ed. 2) I. Pref. p. xvi, Not slavishly addicted to any new system. **1840** THACKERAY *Catherine* xi, He was slavishly gentle to Catherine. **1884** *Contemp. Rev.* Oct. 502 A nation.. slavishly devoted to foreign models.

*Comb.* **1821** *Examiner* 659/1 A very slavishly-inclined talker of Kings.

†**2.** Oppressively, tyrannically. *Obs.*

**1621** in Foster *Eng. Factories Ind.* (1906) I. 349 To this missery hath tirannie inthrald us all and slaveishly caused us to stoope to the demaund of even base infidells. **1632** LITHGOW *Trav.* I. 26 The women of the better sort are slauishly infringed from honest and lawfull liberty.

**slavishness** (ˈsleɪvɪʃnɪs). Also 7 **slauishnes, slavishnesse,** *Sc.* **slawischnes.** [f. SLAVISH *a.*¹]

**1.** Slavish quality or characteristics; servility.

**1622** FOTHERBY *Atheom.* I. 120 His willingnesse to serue such base things, is the great brand of his slauishnes. *a* **1683** OLDHAM *Wks.* (1686) 10 To scare The senseless rout to slavishness and fear. *a* **1768** T. SECKER *Wks.* (1771) V. 140 Making a Language absurd, and imprinting a Character of Slavishness upon it. **1830** SIR J. MACKINTOSH *Progr. Eth. Philos.* Wks. 1846 I. 185 Blackstone,..whose writings are not exempt from the charge of slavishness. **1878** BAYNE *Purit. Rev.* ii. 45 This will now strike our readers as a doctrine of utter slavishness.

†**2.** A state of slavery; bondage. *Obs.*

**1622** FOTHERBY *Atheom.* I. 113 Thus detaining them in more than Egyptian slauishnes. **1655** FULLER *Ch. Hist.* IV. xiv. 111 These bemoaned the slavishnesse of these poore servants.

†**3.** Oppression, tyranny. *Obs.*

**1684** E. CHAMBERLAYNE *Pres. St. Eng.* I. 48 For putting any to the rack..it is by the English believed to savour too much of slavishness.

**Slavism** (ˈslɑːvɪz(ə)m, ˈslævɪz(ə)m). [f. SLAV *sb.* + -ISM.] The collective qualities or racial character of the Slav peoples.

**1880** *Daily News* Nov., Its recent effusive article on Slavism. **1897** *Westm. Gaz.* 12 Mar. 5/1 Fearful lest Hellenism should be effaced, more especially by Slavism.

**slavist**¹ (ˈsleɪvɪst). [f. SLAVE *sb.*¹ + -IST. Cf. *anti-slavist* (1832).] One who favours or upholds slavery; *spec.* a member of the former pro-slavery party in the United States.

**1889** H. O'REILLY *50 Yrs. on Trail* 15 The border warfare between the slavists and free-soilers.

**Slavist**² (ˈslɑːvɪst, ˈslævɪst). [f. SLAV *sb.* + -IST.] One skilled in the Slav languages and literature; a Slavonic scholar.

**1863** *Reader* 17 Oct. 444/3 The celebrated Slavist, Paul Safarik. **1883** MORFILL *Slavonic Lit.* v. 115 Professor Jagić, of St. Petersburg, one of the most eminent of modern Slavists.

**Slavistic** (slɑːv-, sləˈvɪstɪk). [f. SLAV *sb.* + -ISTIC.] Slavonic research. In *pl.*, Slav linguistic studies.

**1883** MORFILL *Slavonic Lit.* ii. 31 The orthodox and well-grounded decisions of Slavistic. **1956** *Archivum Linguisticum* VIII. II. 176 Slavic synchronic comparative grammar, a branch of Slavistics which does not yet exist. **1965** [see JAT' *sb.*²].

**slavite** (ˈsleɪvaɪt). *U.S. rare.* [f. SLAVE *sb.*¹ + -ITE¹ I.] = SLAVIST¹.

**1831** GARRISON *Liberator* I. 115/1 Undoubtedly the most abominable and surprising spectacle which the wickedness of war presents in the sight of Heaven is a reverend slavite.

**Slavize** (ˈslɑːvaɪz, ˈslævaɪz), *v.* [f. SLAV *sb.* + -IZE.] *trans.* To Slavicize.

**1887** *Eng. Hist. Rev.* II. 676 Bigleniza may have been slavised from Vigilantia or Biglantia. **1909** *Edin. Rev.* July 142 The Bulgarians..have become wholly Slavised both in language and in sentiment.

**Slavo-** (ˈslɑːvəʊ, ˈslævəʊ), combining form (on Greek analogies) of Slav: **a.** Used parasynthetically with terms denoting other peoples or countries, as ***Slavo-Germanic, -Hungarian, -Lettic, -Lithuanian, -Phœnician,*** etc.

**1839** DONALDSON *New Cratyl.* §97 (1850) 141 The old Pelasgian or Slavo-Phœnician language of the South. **1874** H. BENDALL tr. *Schleicher's Compar. Gram.* I. 7 Teutonic and Sclavo-Lithuanian. **1875** WHITNEY *Life Lang.* x. 182 This branch is often called the Slavo-Lettic. **1888** STRONG tr. *Paul's Princ. Lang.* ii. 29 We assume..a Slavo-Germanic, a Slavo-Lettic, an original Germanic..language. **1889** I. TAYLOR *Orig. Aryans* 35 Roots peculiar to Slavo-Lithuanian and Teutonic.

**b.** Objective, in adjs. or sbs. denoting tendency to admire or favour the Slavs, Slavonic ideals, etc., as **ˈSlavophil(e, Slaˈvophilism**; or morbid dread of these, as **ˈSlavophobe, Slaˈvophobist.**

**1877** WALLACE *Russia* ix. 139 They agreed..with the *Slavophils. **1881** *Athenæum* 8 Jan. 54/1 He poses as an incurable Slavophile. *Ibid.* 55/1 The history of the Slavophile movement. **1892** H. D. TRAILL *Marq. Salisbury* xiii. 183 Their Slavophil opponents were jubilant. **1877** WALLACE *Russia* xxvi. 418 The characteristic traits of genuine *Slavophilism. **1883** *Times* 3 May 4 The second part of the volume is a manifesto of 'Slavophilism'. **1887** *Pall Mall G.* 8 July 1/1 Hungarians are, as a rule, *Slavophobes.

**slavocracy** (sleɪˈvɒkrəsɪ). Also **slaveocracy.** [f. SLAVE *sb.*¹ + -OCRACY, but with erroneous application.] The domination of slave-holders; slave-holders collectively as a dominant or powerful class.

**1840** *Illinois State Reg.* (Springfield) 22 Jan. 2/2 The reign of the slaveocracy is hastening to a close. **1848** *N. Y. Express* 4 Sept. (Bartlett), An exhortation to curb the slaveocracy. **1863** W. PHILLIPS *Sp.* xxiv. 526 Union means a submission to the old slavocracy. **1896** E. B. GORDON *Biogr. A. J. Gordon* 68 The devouring indignation against the slavocracy which possessed the soul of Theodore Parker.

So **ˈslavocrat,** a member of the slavocracy.

**1842** S. M. GATES *Let.* 24 Jan. in J. G. Birney *Lett.* (1938) II. 666 Some Slaveocrats in Georgia have lately attempted to cast odium upon Mr. Adams. **1859** BARTLETT *Dict. Amer.* 413. **1882** H. VON HOLST *Calhoun* ix. 308 The slavocrats.. were not such doctrinaires as to risk their bones in charging windmills.

**ˈSlavon,** *sb.* and *a.* Now *rare* or *Obs.* Also 6–7 **Scl-, Slauon.** [ad. older F. *Esclavon* (whence also older Flem. pl. *Sclavoenen*, mod.Flem. *Slavonen*), = It. *Schiavone*, med.L. *Sclavonius*: cf. next.]

**A.** *sb.* **1.** A Slavonian.

**1555** EDEN *Decades* (Arb.) 290 The Sclauon dooth pleynly vnderstande the Moscouite. *Ibid.* 306 Vnder the dominion of the Slauons and vsyng the same tonge. **1606** G. W[OODCOCKE] *Lives Emperors* in *Hist. Ivstine* Ii vj, He ouercame the Hungars, and Subiected the Sclauons. **1802** PINKERTON *Mod. Geogr.* I. 341 In the seventh century the Slavons..were ruled by chiefs, or dukes, seemingly hereditary. **1836** *Partington's Brit. Cycl. Lit.*, etc. III. 501/1 [They] were followed by the Sclavons, a Sarmatian people.

**2.** The Slavonic language. *rare*⁻¹.

**1635** PAGITT *Christianogr.* I. iii. (1636) 128 The Slavon is their vulgar tongue.

**B.** *adj.* Slavonic. Also *Comb.*

**1555** EDEN *Decades* (Arb.) 318 The Slauon tounge whiche at this day is sumwhat corruptly cauled Sclauon. **1563** FOXE *A. & M.* 344/1 In oure Slauon language, it hath bene vsed of old. **1565** JEWEL *Repl. Harding* Wks. III. 266 [The Bible] in the Sclavon tongue. **1850** *New Monthly Mag.* April 449 The proposed union of the Slavon tribes—Slavon-Poles, Slavon-Bohemians, and Slavon-Servians.

**Slavonian** (sləˈvəʊnɪən), *sb.* and *a.* Also 6–7 **Sclauonian,** 7–9 **Sclavonian.** [f. med.L. *S(c)lavonia* the country of the Slavs, f. *S(c)lavus* SLAV. *Slavonia* is *spec.* the name of a region of Croatia.]

**A.** *sb.* **1.** The language of the Slavs; Slavic; Slavonic.

*α.* **1577** DEE *Memor. Navig.* 62 Far-Forreyn-Languages: As..the Sclauonian, or Moschouite, the Arabik Vulgar, the Turkish [etc.]. *a* **1700** EVELYN *Diary* 17 Nov. 1644, In the Church are confession-seates for all languages, Hebrew, Greek,..Welsh, Sclavonian, Dutch, &c. **1716** LADY M. W. MONTAGU *Lett.* xlv[i]. II. 28 In Pera they speak Turkish, Greek, Hebrew,..Russian, Sclavonian. **1839** DONALDSON *New Cratylus* §88 (1850) 130 The resemblance of Sclavonian to Latin and the oldest element of Greek.

*β.* **1842** *Penny Cycl.* XXII. 107/1 The works of St. Ambrosius..were translated into Slavonian. **1906** PRINCE KROPOTKIN *Mem. Revolutionist* (1908) II. viii. 125 A useless mixture of Russian and old Slavonian obscured the sense.

**2.** A person of Slavonic origin; a Slav.

*α.* **1601** HOLLAND *Pliny* I. 181 One Dando a Sclauonian, who liued 500 yeres. **1648** HEXHAM II, *De Sclavoenen*, the Sclavonians. **1756** MACLAINE tr. *Mosheim's Eccl. Hist.* XII. I. i. §5 The Sclavonians, a rough and barbarous people. **1845** KITTO *Cycl. Bibl. Lit.* s.v. *Gog*, Beyond the Tartars and Sclavonians. **1876** A. J. EVANS *Through Bosnia* ii. 77 The Sclavonians of the Austrian side.

*β.* **1614** BREREWOOD *Lang. & Relig.* 58 Among which the principall in Europe, are the Slauonians themselues. **1782** *Encycl. Brit.* (ed. 2) IX. 6896/2 The Slavi, or Slavonians, corruptly called the *Sclavonians*. **1842** *Penny Cycl.* XXII. 101/1 Jornandes, the first writer who mentions the Slavonians. **1883** MORFILL *Slavonic Lit.* i. 20 The Slavonians were glad that they heard the great things of God in their language.

**B.** *adj.* **1.** Of or pertaining to the Slavs; Slavonic; Slavic.

*α.* **1605** CAMDEN *Rem.* 40 *Alan* is thought by Iulius Scaliger..to signifie an hownd in the Sclavonian tongue. **1617** MORYSON *Itin.* III. 75 The Hermonduri and Sorabi of the Sclavonian Nation. **1662** J. DAVIES tr. *Olearius' Voy. Amb.* 4 The Highdutch, the Sclavonian, and Curland Language. **1724** WATERLAND *Athan. Creed* vi. 94 Cyrill and Methodius, who are said to have invented the Sclavonian letters, and to have translated the Scriptures into the Sclavonian tongue. **1788** GIBBON *Decl. & F.* lv. V. 550 The Hungarian language stands alone..among the Sclavonian dialects. **1830** H. G. KNIGHT *Eastern Sketches* Pref. p. xxix, Of Sclavonian or Illyrian extraction. **1847** MRS. A. KERR tr. *Ranke's Hist. Servia* i. 5 In reviewing the history of the various Sclavonian tribes.

*β.* **1613** M. RIDLEY *Magn. Bodies* 66 To have three teeth, like a Slavonian T. **1614** BREREWOOD *Lang. & Relig.* 59 Of the Turks dominion onely Epirus..speake vulgarly the Slauonian tongue. **1788** GIBBON *Decl. & F.* lv. V. 543 The original stock of the Sclavonian, or more properly Slavonian, race. **1842** *Penny Cycl.* XXII. 101/1 The Slavonian or Slavic race..comprehends about 70,000,000 inhabitants. **1876** A. J. EVANS *Through Bosnia* ii. 80 Here a Slavonian gentleman intervened.

**2.** Of or pertaining to Slavonic countries. In the bird-names ***Slavonian falcon, grebe.*** Also, ***Slavonian oak,*** the silvery timber of a European oak, esp. *Quercus robur* or *Q. petræa*, grown in the Slavonian region of Yugoslavia.

**1809** SHAW *Gen. Zool.* VII. I. 171 Sclavonian Falcon. *Falco Sclavonicus.* **1843** YARRELL *Brit. Birds* III. 308 The Sclavonian Grebe..is rather a rare bird here in summer. **1889** H. SAUNDERS *Brit. Birds* 705 The Slavonian Grebe is a northern species. **1938** E. H. P. BOULTON *Dict. Wood* 127 Oak, Slavonian... Similar to English Oak but softer. **1956** *Handbk. of Hardwoods* (Forest Prod. Res. Lab.) 167 Slavonian oak, from Yugoslavia, is typically of slow, even growth, has a uniform colour and straight grain, and is mild and easy to work. **1966** A. W. LEWIS *Gloss. Woodworking Terms* 106 Slavonian oak (throughout Europe).

**3.** Coming from Slavonic regions.

**1812** CARY *Dante, Purg.* xxx. 88 As snow..closely piled by rough Sclavonian blasts.

Hence **Slaˈvonianize** *v. trans.*, to Slavicize.

**1885** *Science* VI. 303 They [the Bulgarians] are not of pure Slavic descent, but are a Slavonianized race.

**Slavonic** (sləˈvɒnɪk), *a.* and *sb.* Also 7 **Slauonique,** 7–9 **Sclavonic.** [ad. med.L. *S(c)lavonic-us*, f. *Slavonia*: see SLAVONIAN.]

**A.** *adj.* Of, belonging or pertaining to, the Slavs or their language; Slavic; Slavonian.

*α.* *c* **1645** HOWELL *Lett.* (1650) I. 382 The Sclavonic tongue hath abolished her [the Greek tongue] in Epire and Macedon. **1728** CHAMBERS *Cycl.* s.v., A Greek, Latin and Sclavonic Dictionary. **1788** GIBBON *Decl. & F.* lv. V. 564 The Sclavonic city of Julin. **1831** SCOTT *Ct. Robt.* ix. *note*, Teutonic Germany, or Celtic Gaul, or Sclavonic Illyria. **1876** A. J. EVANS *Through Bosnia* i. 2 A Sclavonic tongue begins to be heard around. *Ibid.* 4 The headings over the shops are almost entirely Sclavonic.

*β.* **1614** BREREWOOD *Lang. & Relig.* 59 Yet is not the Slauonique tongue..the vulgar language of the Turkish Empire. **1656** EARL MONM. tr. *Boccalini's Advts. fr. Parnass.* I. lxxiii. (1674) 91 Terms, which..seemed rather to be Slavonick words. **1802** PINKERTON *Mod. Geogr.* I. 299 The Slavonic tribe of Rossi. **1845** S. AUSTIN tr. *Ranke's Hist. Ref.* I. 309 In those districts where the Germanic and Slavonic elements are intermingled. **1883** MORFILL *Slavonic Lit.* i. 21 The introduction of the Roman ritual into the Southern Slavonic countries.

**B.** *sb.* The language of the Slavs.

**1668** WILKINS *Real Char.* 3 The Slavonic is extended, though with some variation, through many large Territories. **1728** CHAMBERS *Cycl.* s.v., Each..have their particular Dialect; only the Sclavonic is the common Mother of their several Languages. **1791** BOSWELL *Johnson* 23 Mar. 1772, He [Johnson] observed, that the Bohemian language was true Sclavonick. **1848** SOAMES *Latin Church* i. 4 Their converts worshipped in Sclavonic, the language which those people spoke. **1883** MORFILL *Slavonic Lit.* i. 7 The modern Bulgarian language shows Slavonic in a very corrupted form.

Hence **Slaˈvonicize** *v. trans.*, to Slavicize.

**1883** *Encycl. Brit.* XVI. 194/1 The Slavonic or Slavonicized population.

†**Slavonish,** *a. Obs. rare.* Also **Sclavonish.** [f. SLAVON + -ISH¹. Cf. Du. and G. *Slavonisch*.] Slavonian.

**1560** DAUS tr. *Sleidane's Comm.* 254 b, Two Frenche, fyve Spanishe, and one Slavonishe. **1614** BREREWOOD *Lang. & Relig.* 58 Many are the nations that haue for their vulgar language the Slauonish tongue. *a* **1700** EVELYN *Diary* 20 Nov. 1644, An altar of the Madona..and divers Sclavonish Saints.

**ˈSlavonism.** *rare.* Also 9 **Scl-.** [f. SLAVON(IC + -ISM.] Slavism.

**1839** DONALDSON *New Cratylus* §78 (1850) 113 The Scandinavian tribes..were much less tainted with Sclavonism than the Lithuanians. **1854** R. G. LATHAM *Native Races Russian Emp.* 332 The two separate nationalities being merged under the great generality of Slavonism.

**Slavoniˈzation.** [f. next.] The process of Slavonizing or of becoming Slavonized.

**1897** *Pop. Sci. Monthly* Nov. 68 This Slavonization of Germany is indicated upon..our large..map.

**'Slavonize,** *v.* Also 9 Scl-. [f. SLAVON(IC + -IZE.] *trans.* To render Slavonic in language, character, political feeling, etc.

**1839** DONALDSON *New Cratylus* §78 (1850) 113 The Low Germans who were thus Sclavonized. **1861** J. G. SHEPPARD *Fall of Rome* iii. 121 The Slavonized portion of the second. **1876** A. J. EVANS *Through Bosnia* i. 30 They have been Sclavonised by the multitude of their subjects.

**slaw** (slɔː). *N. Amer.* Also **slaugh.** [ad. Du. *sla*, shortened form of *salade* SALAD.] A salad made of sliced cabbage, etc. Also, any dish the main ingredient of which is sliced cabbage.

**1794**, etc. [see COLD-SLAW]. **1861** T. WINTHROP *Cecil Dreeme* 157 Pad of butter. Plate of slaw, ready vinegared. **1864** *Daily Telegr.* 9 Feb., Salted cucumber, beetroot and cold slaugh. **1890** *Daily News* 23 Dec. 5/2 Salsify, cold slaw (sliced cabbage) with rich mayonnaise dressing. **1905** *N.Y. Even. Post* 23 Sept. 2 Mince pie, hokey-pokey ice cream, over-ripe watermelon, frankfurters with hot slaw—all the less expensive and less desirable articles of diet go to stunt the gamin's growth. **1916** *Chambers's Jrnl.* Feb. 143/1 In Canada it [*sc.* celery cabbage] is used for cold slaw. **1944** *Sun* (Baltimore) 1 Nov. 10/7 It was customary in his family in his boyhood to serve a 'hot slaw' with turkey, the slaw consisting of cabbage cooked with vinegar and sugar. **1977** *National Observer* (U.S.) 22 Jan. 9/1 If she craves tossed salad when the price of lettuce is high, she resolutely buys cabbage and makes slaw instead.

**slaw,** obs. or dial. f. SLOW.

**slawe(n,** obs. ff. pa. pple. SLAY *v.*[1]

**slawethe,** obs. f. SLOTH.

**slawk** (slɑk). *north dial.* and *Sc.* Also 5, 8 **slauk,** 6–7, 9 **slauke,** 6 **slawke,** 9 **slaak.** [Probably ad. Ir. *slabhac, sleabhac* (also dim. *sleabhacán*, Sc. Gael. *slabhgan*) in sense 1: cf. the Gaelic origin of DULSE. For variant forms see SLAKE *sb.*[2], SLAUGH, and SLOKE.

In older Dicts. frequently misprinted *slank(e.*]

**1.** An edible sea-weed (see quot. 1892).

*c* **1450** *MS. Ee. 4. 20* (Camb. Univ. Lib.) fol. 283, Hec herba vocatur a vulgo slauk. **1548** TURNER *Names Herbes* 21 The other kynde is described..to haue leaues lyke letties, and thys kynde is called in englishe slauke. **1562** —— *Herbal* II. (1568) 76 The bryon thalassion of Theophrastus and Pliny is called in Northumberland slauke: whych in lent the poore people sethe..and eat it. **1577** HARRISON *Descr. Brit.* x. in *Holinshed* 41 Having well doonged it in the meane time with slawke of the sea, they sowe barleie. **1758** BORLASE *Nat. Hist. Cornw.* 236 *Lichen marinus*, the laver, slauk, and by the Irish called Slukane. **1892** HESLOP *Northumb. Gloss.*, *Slauke*, the seaweed green laver, *Ulva lactuca* and *U. latissima*.

**2.** A kind of brook- or river-weed.

**1824** MACTAGGART *Gallovid. Encycl.* 135 His haurns wi' slawk and sludge war muddy. **1861** H. MACMILLAN *Footnotes fr. Nature* 127 That green slimy matter..to which in Scotland the expressive name of *slaak* has been applied. **1884** STREATFEILD *Linc. & Danes* 360 *Slawk*, slimy weeds found in drains.

**slawly,** obs. form of SLOWLY.

**†slawm.** *Obs. Mining.* (See quot.)

**1747** HOOSON *Miner's Dict.* Tj, A remarkable Joynt in the Stone, Ore, &c. and filled with Clay, and this Clay..is very soft and Greasy,..and these are called by the name of Slawms.

**slawn,** obs. pa. pple. SLAY *v.*[1]

**slawnchwise,** var. SLAUNCHWAYS, -WISE *adv.* and *a.*

**slawnes(se,** obs. forms of SLOWNESS.

**slaworm,** obs. or dial. form of SLOW-WORM.

**†'slawsy.** *Sc. Obs.* A ludicrous term of endearment. Also **slawsy-gawsy.**

**1500–20** DUNBAR *Poems* lxxv. 39 My hwnygukkis, my slawsy gawsy. *Ibid.* 41 Tak gud confort, my grit-heidit slawsy.

**slawth(e,** obs. forms of SLOTH.

**slay, sley** (sleɪ), *sb.*[1] Forms: α. 1 **slege,** 5 **sleye,** 7 **sleie,** 6– **sley,** 8–9 **sleigh (slea).** β. 4– **slay,** 5–7 **slaye,** 6 **slai-,** 8–9 **slaie.** [OE. *slege* stroke, striking, slaying, etc., = OS. *slegi*, f. the stem of the vb. SLAY. The related forms in the other Teut. languages retain the vowel *a*, as MDu. and MLG. *slach* (Du. and LG. *slag*), OHG. *slag* (G. *schlag*), ON. *slagr* masc., *slag* neut., Goth. *slahs*; cf. also OS. *slaga* (MLG. *slage*, LG. *slâge, slâe*), OHG. *slaga* (G. *schlage*) fem., stroke, striking implement.

A variant OE. form appears in the Corpus Gloss. P 376 '*Pectica*, slahae', in a later vocab. (Wr.-Wülcker 262) written 'slae'.]

**1.** An instrument used in weaving to beat up the weft; = REED *sb.*[1] 10.

α. *c* **1050** *Suppl. Ælfric's Gloss.* in Wr.-Wülcker 188 *Insubula*, webbeamas. *Percussorium*, slege. **14..** *Lat.-Eng. Voc.* Ibid. 601 *Pecten*,..a sleye. **1530** PALSGR. 13 A sley. **1599** MINSHEU, *Lízos para texér*, the owfe or threed..which the sleie doth weaue vp and downe. **1615** MARKHAM *Eng. Housew.* II. v. (1668) 128 Warp is spun close..because it runs through the sleies. **1656** W. DU GARD tr. *Comenius' Gate Lat. Unl.* 109 [He] weaveth the woof into the warp, and with the sley drawn-to thickeneth the linen cloath. **1701** *Minute Bk. New Mills Cloth Manuf.* (S.H.S.) 238, 800 Spanish Reids long lithed for broad lomb sleas. **1796** *Trans. Soc. Arts* XIV. 278 The sleigh is made in the same manner as stocking-frame sleighs are made. **1890** R. BEAUMONT *Woollen & Worsted Cloth Manuf.* (ed. 2) 139 The sley is fixed vertically in the going-part of the loom. **1894** HALL CAINE *Manxman* 368 Rocking the child..to and fro like the sleigh of a loom.

β. **1316** in Rock *Text. Fabr.* (1870) 96 Item in j slay pro textoribus viij d. *c* **1340** *Nominale* (Skeat) 340 A webbe.. Wouyn thorue slay Made of yrede (*sic*) and of birche. **1404** *26 Polit. Poems* 15 At þe last it goþ,..As ende of web out of slay. **1442** *Rolls of Parlt.* V. 60/2 The Slayes and Yern therto belangyng. **1523** SKELTON *Garl. Laurel* 791 To weue in the stoule sume were full preste, With slaiis, with tauellis, with hedellis well drest. **1591–2** *Proclamation* 20 Jan., Some by using of false slaies, and false weauing of their clothes, making the muster ende thereof..closely wouen. **1602** *Knaresborough Wills* (Surtees) I. 241 My new lynnen loame with all the slayes. **1677** YARRANTON *Eng. Improv.* 53 Thou mayest have the Looms, Wheels, and Slayes at first out of Germany and from Haerlem. **1717** CROXALL *Ovid's Met.* VI. 178 The woof and warp..press'd by the toothy slay. **1806** W. TAYLOR in *Ann. Rev.* IV. 773 The slay, or file of reeds, with which the weaver approximates the threads of shoot. **1879** ASHENHURST *Weaving Des. Text. Fabr.* (1893) 305 There are numerous rules and formulae..for determining the setting of warps in the slay.

**2.** *attrib.* and *Comb.*, as *slay-hook, -maker*; also **slay-bar,** the reed of a stocking-frame, etc.; **†slay-bred:** (see quot. and BRED *sb.*); **slay sword,** each of the supports upon which the slay of a loom oscillates during the process of weaving.

**14..** *Lat.-Eng. Voc.* in Wr.-Wülcker 591 *Lama*, sley-brede. **1583** in Wadley *Bristol Wills* (1886) 236 John Wallys, slaymaker and weaver. **1723** *Lond. Gaz.* No. 6196/8 John Rew, late of Exon, Slea-maker. **1834–6** *Encycl. Metrop.* (1845) VIII. 734/1 The warp..is drawn through the reed by an instrument called a sley or reed hook. **1843** *Mechanics' Mag.* XXXIX. 428 The sley bar has a new and peculiar motion given to it for bringing the work over the needle heads. **1895** R. MARSDEN *Cotton Weaving* v. 166 The shaft is cranked, and by means of arms from these cranks is attached to the 'slay' or lathe..which oscillates upon the 'slay-swords'. **1963** A. J. HALL *Textile Sci.* iii. 142 This reed is fastened to the sley sword *S*, which is pivoted..so that as required it can swing to and from position *X* after the insertion of each weft thread.

**†slay,** *sb.*[2] *Obs.*[−1] Some kind of fabric.

**1745** P. THOMAS *Voy. S. Seas* 58 The plunder..consisted in..fine Linens and Woollens, Britannia's, Slays, and the like.

**slay,** obs. form of SLEIGH *sb.*

**slay** (sleɪ), *v.*[1] Pa. t. **slew** (sluː). Pa. pple. **slain** (sleɪn). Forms: (see below). [Common Teut.: OE. *sléan*, north. *slán, slá* (pa. t. *slóg, slóh*, pl. *slógon*, pa. pple. *slægen, slegen, slagen*), = OFris. *slân, slâ* (WFris. *slaen*, EFris. *slô*, NFris. *slaa, slô, slû*), MDu. *slaen* (*sclaen*, Du. *slaan*), OS. *slahan* (MLG. *slân*, LG. *slân, slagen*), OHG. *slahan, sclahan* (MHG. *slahen, slachen*, etc., G. *schlagen*), ON. *slá* (Icel. *slá*, Norw. and Da. *slaa*, Sw. *slå*), Goth. *slahan*. The relations of the pre-Teut. stem *slak-* are somewhat uncertain.

All parts of the verb exhibit a great variety of OE. and ME. forms, partly through natural phonetic development, and partly by assimilation to each other. The normal ME. infinitives are *slē(n* from OE. *sléan*, and *slā(n, slō(n* from northern OE. *slán* or from ON. *slá*; the later forms *sley, slay* are due to the influence of the pa. pple.]

**A.** Illustration of forms.

**1.** *Infin.* α. 1–3 **slean** (3 **sclean, sclein),** 4–5 **sleen;** 3 **slæn,** 3–5 **slen,** 5 **slene.**

*c* **888** [see B. 3]. *a* **1122** *O.E. Chron.* (Laud MS.) an. 1086, Nan man ne dorste slean oðerne man. *c* **1200** ORMIN 8040 Herode..Let slæn þa little barrness. *a* **1225** *Juliana* 49 þe an to sclein þen oþer. *c* **1250** *Gen. & Ex.* 3729 Ðor ðrette god hem alle to slen. *c* **1275** LAY. 3943 Raþir ich wolle þe slean. *c* **1374** CHAUCER *Boeth.* II. pr. vi. (1868) 53 Busirides þat was wont to sleen hys gestes. *c* **1440** *Promp. Parv.* 459/1 Slen, or kyllyn beestys. *a* **1470** HARDING *Chron.* CVIII. x, The Christen folke [they] did brenne, wast and slene.

β. 1, 3 **slæ,** 3–6 **sle** (5 **scle),** 4–6 **slee** (5 **sclee),** 3–6 **slea.**

*c* **950** *Lindisf. Gosp.* Matt. xxiv. 49 [He] ongann slae heafudlinges his. *c* **1205** LAY. 17952 þu scalt beien slæ þer. *c* **1275** *Ibid.* 16052 þou lettest slea Constance. **1340** *Ayenb.* 223 Ham uor to slea. *c* **1375** *Cursor M.* 4392 (Fairf.), þat wife ..þoȝt him to slee. *c* **1400** *Beryn* 816 þouȝe men wold sclee hym. *c* **1400** *Laud Troy Bk.* 15576 We schal scle hem In fight. *c* **1450** *Merlin* ii. 25 It were beste for vs to sle hym. **1485** CAXTON *Paris & V.* (1868) 28, I shal slee myself. *a* **1553** UDALL *Royster D.* IV. viii, She shall not slee mee. **1575** R. B. *Appius & Virginia* in Hazl. *Dodsley* IV. 153 He ..did sle himself outright. **1587** GROVE *Pelops & Hipp.* (1878) 28 He thinks to slea..his daughter.

γ. (*north.* and *Sc.*) 1, 3–4 **slan,** 4 **slane;** 1, 5 **slaa,** 1, 3–7 **sla** (5 **scla),** 6–7 **slae, slea.**

*c* **950** *Lindisf. Gosp.* Luke xii. 45 [He] onginneð..slaa ða cnæhtas. *c* **975** *Rushw. Gosp.* Matt. xxiv. 49 [He] onginnaþ slan efnþeu his. *c* **1200** ORMIN 19921 To slan þatt mann. *a* **1300** *Cursor M.* 832 þe strang þe weker for to sla. *Ibid.* 13952 þan soght þai iesu for to slan. *c* **1400** tr. *Secreta Secret., Gov. Lordsh.* 48 We purpos to slaa þam alle. **1456** SIR G. HAYE *Law Arms* (S.T.S.) 157 He may sla him at his awin will. **15..** in *Dunbar's Wks.* (S.T.S) II. 318 Thair is nocht thair bot tak and slae. **1583** *Leg. Bp. St. Androis* Pref. 56 To slea the sanctis of God. **1603** *Philotus* civ, Themselues to slea. **1609** SKENE *Reg. Maj.* 40 That the husband did slea hir. *Ibid.*, That he did not slae hir.

δ. 3–5 **slon,** 4–5 **slone;** 3–6 **slo** (5 **sclo),** 4–6 **sloo,** 5–7 **sloe.**

*c* **1250** *Gen. & Ex.* 1328 Abraham..was redi to slon him. *a* **1300** *Havelok* 512 He may me waiten for to slo. *c* **1330** R. BRUNNE *Chron. Wace* (Rolls) 844 Fader & moder scholde he sloo. *a* **1400** *Launfal* 837 To..dampny hym to sclo. *c* **1440** *Promp. Parv.* 274/2 Kyllyn, or slone. **1489** SKELTON *Death Earl Northumbld.* 35 To slo their owne lord. **1526** —— *Magnyf.* 2354 Thyselfe that thou wolde sloo. *a* **1585** MONTGOMERIE *Misc. Poems* xxxiv. 13 To slo me, but offence.

ε. 4 **slaȝe,** 5 **slayn,** 5– 6 **slaye,** 6 **slaie;** 4–7 **sley** (6 **sleye),** 5– **slay** (6 **sleay).**

**1340** *Ayenb.* 8 þou ne sselt slaȝe nenne man. *c* **1380** WYCLIF *Sel. Wks.* I. 139 Some wole..sley sheep of Holy Chirche. *a* **1400–50** *Alexander* 1766 (Dubl. MS.), I sall.. slaye þe with my handez. *c* **1460** *Promp. Parv.* (Winch.), Kyllyn, or slayn. **1479** *Barbour's Bruce* II. 205 [He] bad him ..byrn, and slay. *a* **1535** FISHER *Wks.* (1876) 405 So death doth sleay their soules. **1535** COVERDALE *Gen.* iv. 14 Who so fyndeth me, shal slaye me. **1560** DAUS tr. *Sleidane's Comm.* 219 b, To go & slaie them.

**2.** *Pres. Indic.* **a.** *1st pers. sing.* (also *Subj.*) 1 **slea,** 1, 3 **slæ,** 4 **sle,** 6 **slee;** 6 **sley(e, slaye,** 7– **slay.**

*c* **825** *Vesp. Hymns* vii. 77 Ic..slea & ic ȝehaelu. *c* **950** *Lindisf. Gosp.* Matt. xxvi. 31 Ic slæ hiorde. *c* **1205** LAY. 3943 Ær ich þe slæ mid mine spere. **13..** *Cursor M.* 7632 (Gött.), þat i him sle it es noght gode. **1508** DUNBAR *Flyting* 235 Cry grace,..or I the chece and sley. *a* **1533** LD. BERNERS *Huon* xvi. 43 Better it were..or I slee thee.

**b.** *2nd pers. sing.* α. 1 **sles, slaes,** 5 **slees;** 4 **slaas, slos.**

*c* **825** *Vesp. Psalter* cxxxviii. 19 Hweðer sles ðu..synfulle. *c* **950** *Lindisf. Gosp.* John xviii. 23 Forhuon mec slaes ðu? *a* **1300** *E.E. Psalter* cxxxviii. 18 If þou slaas..sinful. *a* **1300** *Havelok* 2706 þat þou..mine gode knihtes slos.

β. 1 **slehst, slæȝst,** 3 **sleast,** 3–4 **sleest;** 3–4 **slast,** 6– **slayest** (*poet.* **slay'st).**

*a* **900** *Kentish Glosses* in Wr.-Wülcker 79 ȝif ðu slehst. *c* **975** *Rushw. Gosp.* Matt. xxiii. 37 þu þe slæȝst witȝa. *c* **1200** ORMIN 6752 þa slast tu..þin aȝhenn flæsh. *c* **1275** LAY. 5017 ȝif þou sleast þine broþer. **1382** WYCLIF *Matt.* xxiii. 37 Jerusalem, that sleest prophetis. *c* **1440** *Jacob's Well* 46 þou sleest him in þat [etc.]. **1535** COVERDALE *Matt.* xxiii. 37 Thou that slayest the prophetes.

**c.** *3rd pers. sing.* α. 1 **sliehð, slihð, slyhð, slæhð,** 2 **slehð,** 4 **slekþ.**

*c* **897** K. ÆLFRED *Gregory's Past. C.* xlvi. 347 Ðonne hit mon sliehð [*v.r.* slihð]. *c* **900** tr. *Baeda's Hist.* I. xvi. (1890) 78 Seo haliȝe æ mid deaðe slæhð [*v.r.* slyhð]. *c* **1160** *Hatton Gosp.* Luke vi. 29 þam þe þe slehð on þam wange. **1303** R. BRUNNE *Handl. Synne* 1527 He slekþ hym þat trowyþ hys lesyng.

β. 1 **slaeð,** 3 **sleað, slað;** 1 **sleð,** 4–5 **sleþ,** 4–6 **sleth,** 5 **slethe;** 4–5 **sleeþ,** 5–6 **sleeth;** 1 **slaes,** 4 **sles(e,** 4–5 **slees,** 7 **sleas.**

*c* **825** *Vesp. Psalter* lxxvii. 34 Ðonne he sleð hie. *c* **950** *Lindisf. Gosp.* Matt. v. 39 ȝif hua ðec slaes in suiðra ceica. *Ibid.* Luke vi. 29 Seðe ðec slaeð on cece. *c* **1230** *Hali Meid.* 29 Cwalm slað [*Bodl.* sleað] þat ahte. *a* **1300** *Cursor M.* 29386 [He] þat sles his fo. *c* **1330** R. BRUNNE *Chron. Wace* (Rolls) 13890 As þe lyon..sleþ þe best. **1377** LANGL. *P. Pl.* B. XIV. 90 Shrifte of mouth sleeth synne. **1450–80** tr. *Secreta Secret.* 18 He that slethe the creature. *Ibid.*, Who so sleth any man. **1526** *Pilgr. Perf.* (W. de W. 1531) 238 The lawe sleeth the gylty man. **1539** ELYOT *Image Gov.* (1541) 46 He that sleath his prince.

γ. (*north.* and *Sc.*) *3rd pers. sing.* 3 **slaþ;** 4–5 **slas,** 5 **slase,** 5–6 **slaes, slais.** Also 3 **sloð,** 5 **sloys.**

*c* **1200** ORMIN 2092 He slaþ hiss aȝhenn sawle. *c* **1220** *Bestiary* 431 þer he us sloð. *a* **1300** *Cursor M.* 29348 He slas him-seluen. *a* **1400–50** *Alexander* 3883 He..Slaes of þa serpentis many..hundreth. *c* **1400** *Cursor M.* 29386 (Cott. Galba), Him þat slase Preste or clerk. *c* **1400** tr. *Secreta Secret., Gov. Lordsh.* 88 It slas þe souerayn vertu. *c* **1460** *Towneley Myst.* ii. 372 He that sloys yong or old. **1500–20** DUNBAR *Poems* xlix. 44 Evir quhill he be slane he slais. **1596** DALRYMPLE tr. *Leslie's Hist. Scot.* II. 2 *marg.*, He slaes the Inglismen.

δ. 4 **slaȝþ,** 5 **sleith,** 5–6 **sleyth,** 6 **sleythe, sleayeth,** 6– (now *poet.*) **slayeth;** 6–7 **slayes** (*Sc.* **slayis),** 7– **slays.**

**1340** *Ayenb.* 34 He..himzelue slaȝþ. **1422** tr. *Secreta Secret., Priv. Priv.* 143 Who-So sleyth, he shal be slayne. *c* **1450** *Cursor M.* 6673 (Laud MS.), Who sleith eny man with wille. **1535** COVERDALE *Gen.* iv. 15 Who so euer slayeth Cain. **1578** LYTE *Dodoens* 348 In fine it sleayeth the partie. **1607** SHAKS. *Timon* IV. iii. 435 He slayes Moe then you Rob.

**d.** *Plur.* α. 1–2 **sleað;** 4–5 **slen, sleen** (5 **scleen);** 4–6 **slea, sle,** 5–6 **slee** (5 **sclee);** also *north.* 5 **slees.**

*c* **888** [see B. 3]. *a* **1200** *Vices & Virtues* 61 [They] sleað here aȝene saule. **1303** R. BRUNNE *Handl. Synne* 1349 þey sle hem alle. **1388** WYCLIF *2 Kings* xvii. 26 Lo! liouns sleen hem. *c* **1400** MAUNDEV. (1839) xxviii. 288 Theise Serpentes slen men. **1559** MORWYNG *Evonymus* 236 Poysones which slee.

β. 2 **slaȝe(ð,** 6 **sleye, slaye,** 7– **slay.**

*c* **1175** *Lamb. Hom.* 51 þenne slaȝe we ure sunne. *Ibid.* 53 Heo slaȝeð heore aȝene saule. **1535** COVERDALE *1 Esdras* iv. 5 They..slaye (other men) them selues. **1611** BIBLE *1 Esdras* iv. 5 They slay and are slaine.

γ. (Also *Subj.*) 4–5 **sla, slaa,** 5 **slo(e.**

*a* **1300** *E.E. Psalter* lxi. 3 Vnto yhe sla. **1375** BARBOUR *Bruce* I. 487 Thai sla our folk. *a* **1400–50** *Alexander* 3198 Slaa ȝe me þus sudanly? *a* **1425** *Cursor M.* 16328 (Trin.), Till þat þei þe slo.

**3.** *Pres. Subj.* (*2nd* and *3rd pers. sing.*). α. 1 **slae,** 1, 3 **slea,** 4–6 **sle,** 5 **slee.**

*a* **901** *Laws Alfred* Pref. §16 (Liebermann), ȝif hwa slea his ðone nehstan mid stane. *c* **975** *Rushw. Gosp.* Matt. v. 39 ȝif hwa ðec slae. *c* **1000** ÆLFRIC *Exod.* xxi. 15 Se þe slea his fæder. *c* **1325** *Prose Ps.* cxxxviii. 18 ȝif þou sle þe synȝers. **1382** WYCLIF *Job* xiii. 15 If he sle me.

β. *north.* 3–5 **sla,** 4–5 **slo.**

*a* 1300 in *O.E. Misc.* 200/5 Loke þat tu ne sla na man. *c* 1310 in Wright *Spec. Lyric P.* vii. 29 Er thou me slo. *c* 1400 tr. *Secreta Secret., Gov. Lordsh.* 61 Suffre þat he sla. *c* 1460 *Towneley Myst.* ii. 371, I will that no man other slo.

γ. 6 **slaye**, 6– **slay**.

1500–20 DUNBAR *Poems* xxxvi. 15 That..No wicht ane vder slay. 1535 COVERDALE *Deut.* xix. 6 Lest the auenger..slaye him. 1607 SHAKS. *Cor.* IV. iv. 24 If he slay me He does faire Iustice.

**4.** *Imper.* α. 1 **sleh**, 2 **sleih**, 4–5 **sle**, 4–6 **slee**, 6 **sley**; 1 **sleah**, **sleaȝe**, 4–5 **slea**; 1 **slyh**, 2 **slyȝh**. Also *plur.* 1 **slæð** (**slæh**), **sleað** (**slea**), 3 **s(c)leaþ**, **sleoþ**, 4 **sleth**, 5 **sleeth**, **sleeþ**; 4 *north.* **sles**.

*sing.* *c* 825 *Vesp. Psalter* lviii. 12 Ne sleh ðu hie. *c* 1000 *Ags. Gosp.* Mark x. 19 Ne slyh þu. *a* 1200 *Vices & Virtues* 67 Ne sleih, ne ne stell. *a* 1225 *Ancr. R.* 206 Slea hit mid dedbote. *c* 1325 *Prose Ps.* lviii. 11 Lord, ne sle hem nouȝt. 1377 LANGL. *P. Pl.* B. III. 264 What þow fyndest þere, slee it. 1422 tr. *Secreta Secret., Priv. Priv.* 162 Go thou and Sle the Synners. 1480 *Robt. Devyll* 24 Slea me, she sayde. 1539 CRANMER *Luke* xix. 27 Slee them before me.

*plur.* *c* 1000 *Andreas* 1300 Sleað synniȝne ofer seolfes muð. *c* 1205 LAY. 28726 Slæð..al þat ȝe findeð. *c* 1275 *Ibid.* 4222 Sleoþ ham mid swerde. 1297 R. GLOUC. (Rolls) 4855 Sleþ hom hastiliche anon. *c* 1330 R. BRUNNE *Chron. Wace* (Rolls) 1163 Spares non, bot sles on fast. 13.. *Cursor M.* 6634 (Gött.), Sles vp ȝone caytifes. 1382 WYCLIF *Exod.* i. 16 If it be a maal, sleeth hym.

β. *Sing.* 2–4, 6 **sla**; 3–4 **slo**, 7 *Sc.* **sloe**. *Plur.* 4 **slas**, **slays**; **slo**, **slos**.

*c* 1160 *Hatton Gosp.* Luke iii. 14 Ne sla ȝe nanne man. *c* 1250 *Gen. & Ex.* 3505 Ne slo ð u noȝt. *a* 1300 *Havelok* 2596 Slos up-on þe dogges. *a* 1300 *Cursor M.* 6634 Slas vþ yon caitefs. *a* 1400 *R. Brunne's Chron. Wace* (Rolls) 1163 (Petyt MS.), Spares non bot slo all faste. 1611 SIR W. MURE *Wks.* (S.T.S.) I. 10 Save then or sloe ane captiue.

γ. 6 **slaye**, 7– **slay**.

1535 COVERDALE *Judges* viii. 20 Stonde vp, & slaye them. 1611 BIBLE *1 Kings* iii. 27 In no wise slay it.

**5.** *Past Indic.* α. *1st* and *3rd pers. sing.* 1, 3–4 **sloh**, 4 **slohw**; 1 **sloȝ**, **sloȝh**, 4 **sloȝ**, **slooȝ** (3 **sloþ**), 4–5 **sloȝe**; 3–4 **slog**, 4–5 **slogh** (5 **sloght**), **sloghe**, **sloch**; 4–5 **slo**. *2nd pers.* 1 **sloȝe**, 3 **sloȝe**. *Plur.* 1–2 **sloȝon** (1 **-un**), **sloȝan**, 1 **sloȝen**, 2 **sloȝhen**, 3–4 **sloȝen**, 5 **sloghen**; 4 **sloghe**, 5 **sloȝe**; 4 **slogh**.

*sing.* *Beowulf* 421 þær ic..sloȝ niceras nihtes. *Ibid.* 1565 He..yrringa sloh. *c* 825 *Vesp. Psalter* iii. 8 Ðu sloȝe alle wiðerbrocan. *c* 1200 ORMIN 3590 Daviþþ king sloh Goliat. *c* 1205 LAY. 10999 þa þu sloȝe Asclepidiot. *c* 1275 *Ibid.* 1290 Manie he sloþ. *a* 1300 *Cursor M.* 6120 þat he ne slo an. *a* 1300 *E.E. Psalter* c. 9, I slogh with hand Alle þe sinful. *c* 1325 *Prose Ps.* c. 9 Ich sloȝe..alle þe synȝers. 13.. *Cursor M.* 1046 (Gött.), His aune broþer abel he slohw. 1382 WYCLIF *Isaiah* xxvii. 7 As he slooȝ the slayne men. *c* 1400 *Destr. Troy* 9728 Deffibus..oure folk sloght. *c* 1450 *Mirk's Festial* 193 He yn þat maner sloch hymself. *c* 1460 *Towneley Myst.* ii. 395, I slogh my brother. *Ibid.* 433 He that slo his brother.

*plur.* *c* 893 K. ÆLFRED *Oros.* I. x. 46 þa wif..sloȝon þa hysecild. 971 *Blickl. Hom.* 23 Hie hine..mid bradre hand sloȝan. 1154 *O.E. Chron.* (Laud MS.) an. 1138, [They] sloȝhen suithe micel of his genge. *a* 1300 *K. Horn* 195 Hi sloȝen..Cristenemen inoȝe. *a* 1340 HAMPOLE *Psalter* xxvii. 5 þe iowes sloghe crist. *a* 1400–50 *Alexander* 3213 (Dubl. MS.), þees warryd wightez..þat Sloghen [*v.r.* sloȝe] so þair souerent.

β. *Sing.* 3–5 **slowe** (5 **sclowe**), 4–5 **sloue**; 4–5 **slow** (5 **sclow**), 4 **sloow**, **slou** (**sclou**). *Plur.* 3–5 **slowen**, 5 **slowyn**, 4 **slouen**; 4–5 **slowe**, **slow** (5 **sclow**).

*sing.* *c* 1205 LAY. 4355 Seoððen þu hine slowe. 1297 R. GLOUC. (Rolls) 458 Corineus..slou hom to gronde. *a* 1300 in *E.E.P.* (1862) 116 Slowe þu þe holi prophete? 13.. *E.E. Allit. P.* B. 1221 þe kynges sunnes..he slow euer vchone. 13.. *Cursor M.* 14431 (Gött.), Dauid..sclou golias. 1382 WYCLIF *Isaiah* xiv. 20 Thou the puple sloow. ?*a* 1400 *Arthur* 528 Engystis Men þat..sclow þeyre kyn. 1422 tr. *Secreta Secret., Priv. Priv.* 174 The pepill..he slow. *c* 1450 *Knt. de La Tour* (1868) 102 Husbondes, whiche the deuelle slow.

*plur.* *c* 1205 LAY. 1608 Alle heo slowen þat heo neih comen. *a* 1300 *Havelok* 2432 Euerilk fot of hem [they] slowe. 13.. *Cursor M.* 2502 (Gött.), þair fas foluand þaim slow. 1382 WYCLIF *Matt.* xxiii. 35 Zacharie,..whom ȝee slowen. *c* 1400 *Laud Troy Bk.* 16666 Thei sclow ten thousand. *c* 1425 AUDELAY *XI Pains of Hell* 135 in *O.E. Misc.* 215 [They] slowyn here childer. 1483 CAXTON *Gold. Leg.* 228 b/2 Where they slowe..many men.

γ. *Sing.* 3–4 **slouh**, 4–5 **slowh**, **slouȝ**, 5 **slowȝ(e**; 4–5 **slough**, 5 **sloughe**, **slowgh(e**. *Plur.* 5 **sloughen**; 4 **slowȝe**, 4–5 **slowhe**, 5 **sloughe**; 4 **slouȝ**, **slough**.

*c* 1225 *Ancr. R.* 136 Iudit, þet slouh Oloferne. 1310 *St. Brendan* (Bälz) 441 þis luþer best sone he slouȝ. *c* 1330 R. BRUNNE *Chron. Wace* (Rolls) 7280 Of þe Peytes þat he slough. *c* 1386 CHAUCER *Knt.'s T.* 1608 (Lansd. MS.), I slowhe Sampson schakinge þe piler. ?*a* 1400 *Morte Arth.* 4046 He..þat hym slowghe. *a* 1425 *Cursor M.* 162 (Trin.), Heroude..slowȝe childer ȝonge. *c* 1450 *Merlin* xx. 352 Many thei sloughen. 1474 CAXTON *Chesse* III. i. (1883) 76 For this cause he slough abel.

δ. *Sing.* 3 **sluȝ**, 5 **sluȝe**, 6–7 **slue**; 5 **slewȝ**, *Sc.* **sleuch** (**sleucht**), 6 **scleuȝe**; 4– **slew**, 5–6 **slewe**. Also *2nd pers.* 6–7 **slew'st**. *Plur.* 3 **sluȝen**, 5–7 **slue** (5 *Sc.* **sleuch**); 4 **slewen**, 5– **slew** (5 **sclew**), 6 **slewe**.

*sing.* *c* 1250 *Gen. & Ex.* 2685 He..sluȝ ðor maniȝe. 1375 BARBOUR *Bruce* I. 557 Modreyt..him slew. 1382 WYCLIF *1 Kings* ii. 25 The which slewȝ hym. *c* 1420 *Avow. Arth.* lxv, There hit sluȝe him als. 14.. *Sc. Leg. Saints* xxv. (*Julian*) 231 þat fadyr & modir bath sleucht. 1470–85 MALORY *Arthur* x. xxxiv. 468 Kynge Marke slewe hym. *a* 1500 *Pol., Rel., & Love Poems* 124, I scleuȝe my selue. 1559 *Mirr. Mag., Clifford* iii, That slue duke Richardes childe. 1592 KYD *Sp. Trag.* III. vii, I slew him for your sake. 1592 SHAKS. *Rom. & Jul.* III. iii. 138 But thou slew'st Tybalt. *a* 1641 BP. MOUNTAGU *Acts & Mon.* (1642) 323 Saxa..slue himselfe. 1671 MILTON *Samson* 439 Who slew'st them many a slain.

*plur.* *c* 1250 *Gen. & Ex.* 3916 Oc he sluȝen king of basaan. 1382 WYCLIF *Matt.* xxi. 39 Thei kesten [him] out..and slewen. *a* 1400–50 *Alexander* 2043 (Dubl.), þai..Slew downe..seges. *c* 1489 CAXTON *Blanchardyn* xlviii. 187 They kylled and slue..many one. 1490 *Acc. Ld. High Treas. Scot.* I. 131 Men..that sclew a man. 1585 T. WASHINGTON tr. *Nicholay's Voy.* I. xix. 22 They slue foure of the best runners. 1632 LITHGOW *Trav.* III. 104 They scaled the walles, [and] slue the watches.

**6.** *Past Subj.* 1 **sloȝe**, *pl.* **sloȝen**, 2, 5 **sloȝe**, 3 **sluȝe**, 4 **slowe**.

*c* 897 K. ÆLFRED *Gregory's Past. C.* xxviii. 196 Ðæt hie sloȝen..kyning. *a* 1122 *O.E. Chron.* (Laud MS.) an. 1086, Swa hwa swa sloȝe heort. *c* 1250 *Gen. & Ex.* 3976 Had ic an swerd, ic sluȝe ðe. *c* 1380 *Sir Ferumb.* 467 þoȝ y slowe þe her in fiȝt. *a* 1400–50 *Alexander* 5351 If we þis lede sloȝe.

**7.** *Past Part.* α. 1 **ȝeslæȝen**, **ȝesleȝen**, 3 **i-slæȝen**, **i-sleien**, **i-slein**, 4 **i-**, **y-slayn**, 5 **y-sclayn**, **y-slayne**, 6 **y-slaine**; 1 **slæȝen**, **sleȝen**, 4–5 **sleyn**, 6 **sleyne**; 2–3, 6–7 **slaine**, 4–7 **slayne**, 5 **slayen**, 4–6 **slayn** (4–5 **sclayn**, 4 **sclain**), 4, 7– **slain**.

(*a*) *a* 900 *O.E. Chron.* (Parker MS.) an. 823, þær wæs micel wæl ȝeslæȝen. *c* 900 tr. *Baeda's Hist.* III. xi. (1890) 190 þa wæs ȝesleȝen..sum leornungmon. *c* 1205 LAY. 5584 Summe heore men [had] i-slæȝene. *a* 1225 *Ancr. R.* 156 Gostliche isleien. 1387 TREVISA *Higden* (Rolls) VII. 103 If alle fiȝte and alle [be] i-slayn. 1422 tr. *Secreta Secret., Priv. Priv.* 162 Al the grecans..yslayne thay moght. ?*a* 1400 *Arthur* 566 Arthoures nevew..was þere y-sclayn. 1590 SPENSER *F.Q.* III. v. 9 Of a forreine foe He is yslaine.

(*b*) *c* 725 *Corpus Gloss.* P 287 *Percellitur*, bið slaeȝen. *c* 825 *Vesp. Psalter* ci. 5 Sleȝen ic eam. *c* 1200 *Trin. Coll. Hom.* 103 Leirede and slaine. *a* 1300 *Cursor M.* 23964 Hu þai haf þat saccles sclain. *a* 1320 *Sir Tristr.* 830 Ȝif tristrem be now sleyn. *c* 1340 HAMPOLE *Pr. Consc.* 4612 þar sal he be slayn. 1399 LANGL. *P. Pl.* C. I. 113 Hus sones [being] slayen. *a* 1425 *Cursor M.* 4168 (Trin.), þat we haue sleyn him. 1470–85 MALORY *Arthur* XVIII. xvi. 754 There..I was nere slayne. *a* 1548 HALL *Chron., Hen. VIII*, 159 b, Al they that folowed hym..were sleyne. 1584 POWEL *Lloyd's Cambria* 2 Who was slaine by his owne men. 1655–60 STANLEY *Hist. Philos.* (1687) 48/2 Men slain By cruel Men.

β. 3 **i-**, **hii-sleȝe**, **i-slehȝe**; 4 **sleie**, **sleye**, **slaye**, 5 **slay**, **scley**.

*c* 1275 LAY. 10932 He hadde islehȝe moche of hire cunne. *Ibid.* 13602 Hii-sleȝe we habbeþ þane king. *c* 1350 *Will. Palerne* 379 Sche wold haue sleie hire-self. 1393 LANGL. *P. Pl.* C. XVIII. 275 Seynt thomas..in holychurche was sleye. ?*a* 1400 *Arthur* 223 þu hast scley frolle in fraunce.

γ. 1 **ȝeslaȝen**, 3 **i-slaȝen**, **i-sclawen**, **i-slawen**, 4 **y-slawen**; 3 **slaȝen**, 4 **slawen**, **slaun**, 5 **slawn**.

*c* 1000 ÆLFRIC *Hom.* II. 124 Se ȝeslaȝena bið mid deaðe ȝegripen. *c* 1205 LAY. 965 Heora kun we habbet islaȝen. *Ibid.* 1047 Mine men ȝe habbeð isclawen. *c* 1250 *Gen. & Ex.* 591 Ðo was ilc fleis on werlde slaȝen. *a* 1300 *Havelok* 2681 þer were a þousind knihtes slawen. 13.. *Guy Warw.* (A.) 4715 þo he hadde hem slaun ichon. 1382 WYCLIF *Lev.* vii. 8 The slawn offryng of brent sacrifice.

δ. 3 **i-**, 4 **y-slaȝe**, 3–4 **i-slawe**, 4–6 **y-slawe**; 6 **y-slaw**; 4–5 **slawe** (5 **sclawe**).

*c* 1250 *Owl & Night.* 1142 Hwenne þu hongest islawe. *c* 1275 LAY. 322 He his fader adde islaȝe. 1297 R. GLOUC. (Rolls) 889 þe stude þat he was on slawe. 1340 *Ayenb.* 223 Alle were y-slaȝe of þe dyeule. *c* 1374 CHAUCER *Troylus* IV. 884 Both it hadde vs slawe. *c* 1420 *Chron. Vilod.* 4308 Harald..was y-slawe at Hastyngus. *c* 1440 *Gesta Rom.* xvii. 61 How that he had slawe this brid.

ε. 3 **i-slæn**, 5 **sleen**, 6 **slene**.

*c* 1205 LAY. 8326 þine men we habbeð islæn. 1486 *Bk. St. Albans* d j/2 She hath sleen the fowle. *a* 1563 MACHYN *Diary* (Camden) 92 Ther wher dyvers of boyth partes slene.

ζ. *north.* and *Sc.* 4 **slan**, 4–6 **slane**, 6 **y-slane**.

*a* 1300 *Cursor M.* 905 þou sal be slan wit duble dedd. 13.. *Ibid.* 4141 (Gött.), Wit his fader þat he be slane. *c* 1470 HENRY *Wallace* I. 190 Thai had slane mony ane. 1513 DOUGLAS *Æneid* XIII. ii. 3 Sepulturis Of his folkis yslane. 1567 *Satir. Poems Reform.* v. 31 Nouther..hurt nor slane.

η. 4–5 **slon**, 5–6 **slone**, 5 **sloon**.

*c* 1375 *Lay-Folks Mass-Bk.* App. IV. 587 God þat on þe Rode was slon. *a* 1425 *Cursor M.* 1075 (Trin.), Whenne Caym had his broþer sloon. *c* 1440 *Alph. Tales* 516 Whar þer fadur was slone. *c* 1485 *Digby Myst.* I. 361 He hath our children sloon!

**B.** Signification.

**I.** † **1. a.** *trans.* To smite, strike, or beat. *Obs.*

*c* 825 *Vesp. Psalter* lxxvii. 20 Forðon [he] sloȝ stan & fleowun weter. *c* 950 *Lindisf. Gosp.* Mark xiv. 65 Ða embehtmenn mið fystum hine sloȝon. *c* 1000 ÆLFRIC *Exod.* vii. 17 Nu ic slea mid þisse ȝirde..þises flodes wæter. *c* 1250 *Gen. & Ex.* 3964 [Balaam] wurð ðo for anger wroð, And ðis [ass] prikeð and negt [? *read* next] sloð. *a* 1300 *Havelok* 2633 þe þredde so sore he slow, þat he made up-on the feld His lift arm fleye.

† **b.** *absol.* To deal a blow or blows (freq. with *on*); to knock; to strike. *Obs.*

*Beowulf* 1565 He ȝefeng þa fetelhilt,..yrringa sloh. 971 *Blickl. Hom.* 141 Michael..sloȝ on þæs huses duru. *c* 1205 LAY. 797 Ohtliche heom slæð on. *Ibid.* 16488 Aldolf his gode sweord adroh, & uppen Hengest sloh. *a* 1300 *Havelok* 2596 Helpes me..And slos up-on þe dogges swiþe. 1390 GOWER *Conf.* I. 311 And as the fisshere on his bait Sleth, whan he seth the fisshes faste.

† **c.** To strike or cut *off* (a limb). *Obs.*

*a* 1000 *Laws of Ine* §18 Slea mon hond of oððe fot. *c* 1205 LAY. 3856 þer he of-toc Morgan.., & sloh he him of þat hæued.

† **2.** To strike (a spark, fire) from flint or other hard substance. *Obs.*

*c* 1000 *Saxon Leechd.* II. 290 Ȝif mon on his weȝe biþ ȝedwolod slea him anne spearcan beforan. 1375 BARBOUR *Bruce* XIII. 36 Men herd nocht ellis bot granys & dyntis, That slew fire, as men dois on flyntis. *c* 1400 *Ywaine & Gaw.* 2039 Flynt and fir-yren bath he hade, And fir ful sone thar he slogh. *c* 1470 HENRY *Wallace* IV. 285 A gret hart has he slayne; Slew fyr on flynt, and graithit thaim at rycht. 1513 DOUGLAS *Æneid* I. iv. 33 First Achates slew fire of the flynt.

† **3.** To throw or cast; to bring *down* heavily. *Obs.*

*c* 888 K. ÆLFRED *Boeth.* xxxv. §5 Ȝif wit ȝiet uncru word tosomne sleað. *Ibid.* xxxviii. §1 þæt hio sceolde..þa men..slean on þa racentan. *c* 1000 *Daniel* 344 He on andan sloh fyr on feondas for fyrendædum. *c* 1205 LAY. 2312 Corineus up ahof, & his eax adun sloh. *c* 1430 *Syr Gener.* (Roxb.) 90 The bodie among hem was hent; At the steres thei slough it doun.

† **4.** To pitch (a tent). *Obs.*

*c* 1000 ÆLFRIC *Gen.* xxxi. 25 Iacob sloh his ȝeteld on þære dune. *c* 1205 LAY. 7865 Heo sloȝen heoren teldes, wide ȝeond þa feldes.

**II. 5. a.** To strike or smite so as to kill; to put to death by means of a weapon; also generally, to deprive of life by violence.

In this sense (which is copiously represented in the illustration of forms above), and in other surviving uses, *slay* is now mainly confined to literary and rhetorical language, the common word being *kill*.

*Beowulf* 421 Ic..on yðum sloȝ niceras nihtes. *c* 893 K. ÆLFRED *Oros.* I. x. 46 Hi..on ðæt folc winnende wæron, & þa wæpnedmen sleande. 971 *Blickl. Hom.* 151 On þa ilcan tid þa englas..ongunnan slean þa Iudeas. 1154 *O.E. Chron.* (Laud MS.) an 1138, [They] flemden þe king æt te Standard, & sloȝhen suithe micel of his genge. *c* 1200 ORMIN 8089 He..badd tatt mann hemm shollde slæn, Son summ he shollde deȝenn. 1297 R. GLOUC. (Rolls) 3630 þo þe king arþure ysey þat me is men so uaste slou. *c* 1330 R. BRUNNE *Chron. Wace* (Rolls) 13890 As þe lyon for hunger snacches & sleþ þe best þat he first lacches. *c* 1380 WYCLIF *Wks.* (1880) 55 Men þat turmenten & slen þe bodi. *c* 1450 *Merlin* ii. 25 And so xij made hem redy,..and ran on hym with swerdes and knyves, and slowe hym. 1470–85 MALORY *Arthur* v. iv. 165 The bore that the dragon slough. 1560 DAUS tr. *Sleidane's Comm.* 280 The nombre of them that were slaine..was accompted a thousand. 1635 PAGITT *Christianogr.* 215 Two fel at discord between themselves, and the one slue the other. 1781 COWPER *Charity* 619 Slaying man would cease to be an art. 1849 MACAULAY *Hist. Eng.* v. I. 633 Two persons..were found murdered; and it was universally believed that they had been slain by Kirke's order. 1888 MASSON *Med. France* 180 The order given by King Philip to slay the Genoese mercenaries.

*refl.* *c* 1340 *Ayenb.* 34 He..himzelue slaȝþ ase despayred. *c* 1374 CHAUCER *Troylus* II. 462 If this man her[e] sle hemself..In my presence. 1430–40 LYDG. *Bochas* VIII. xvii. (1558) 11 b, Arbogast slough him selfe for drede. 1565 GOLDING *Ovid's Met.* IV. (1593) 83 Thy love (she said) hath made the slea thy selfe. 1628 in Foster *Eng. Factories India* (1909) III. 240 Their mother..slew hirselfe, dying with them.

(*b*) *fig.*; *esp.* To overwhelm with delight, to convulse (someone) with laughter. Cf. KILL *v.* 6 a.

*a* 1340 HAMPOLE *Psalter* vii. 14 Goed wordis, þe whilk slas men fra synne, and makis þaim lifand til god. 1593 SHAKS. *Lucr.* 1110 Sad souls are slain in merry company. 1848 THACKERAY *Van. Fair* xxii, Shooting death-glances at all the servant-girls who were worthy to be slain. 1863 G. MEREDITH *Let.* May (1970) I. 203, I have lately been slain by a pretty face. 1927 L. MAYER *Just between Us Girls* i. 2 Well, anyways, my dear, it simply slayed me. 1937 *Amer. Speech* XII. 181 (*heading*) Satchelmouth slays 'em. 1943 H. A. SMITH *Life in Putty Knife Factory* xiii. 225 The boys who slay me..are the ones who have set pieces to recite when they answer the phone. 1953 R. CHANDLER *Long Good-Bye* xi. 68 A hoodlum with sentiment... That slays me. 1958 *Spectator* 21 Nov. 728/1 Frost,..reading naturally and roughly but with a high degree of contrivance, slaying them into calls for encores and favourite poems. 1965 D. FRANCIS *Odds Against* xi. 150 'Oh God, Dolly, you slay me,' said Chico, laughing warmly. 1975 D. O'SULLIVAN in D. Marcus *Best Irish Short Stories* (1977) II. 98 They're fun... They'll slay you! 1977 *Guardian Weekly* 23 Oct. 4/3 The earliest comment on these lines that I can find comes from Denis Thatcher in October, 1970. 'Who could meet Margaret..without being completely slain by her personality and intellectual brilliance?'

† **b.** *to slay up* or *down*, to kill completely or outright; to annihilate. *Obs.*

*a* 1300 *Cursor M.* 6634 Slas vp yon caitefs al bidene! *a* 1400–50 *Alexander* 2043 (Dubl.), Manly þai feghtyn, Slew downe on ather syde seges owt of nowmbre. 1545 ASCHAM *Toxoph.* (Arb.) 82 The Spanyardes..were quyte slayne vp of the Turkes arrowes. 1549 *Compl. Scot.* 145 Gunnis ande cannons to sla doune the pepil. 1596 DALRYMPLE tr. *Leslie's Hist. Scot.* I. 161 That same tyme..he slawe doune monye of the Nobilitie.

† **c.** To kill the inhabitants of (a country). *Obs.*

*c* 1330 *Arth. & Merl.* 4734 (Kölbing), þis four heþen kinges..þe cuntre aboute Lounde Slowen & brent to þe grounde.

**6.** *absol.* To commit slaughter or murder.

*c* 893 K. ÆLFRED *Oros.* II. viii. 92 Hie wæron þa burȝ herȝende & sleande buton ælcre ware. *a* 901 *Laws K. Ælfred* Introd. §5 Ne sleah ðu. *c* 1000 *Ags. Gosp.* Mark x. 19 Ne slyh [*v.r.* sleh] þu. *c* 1250 *Gen. & Ex.* 2668 Folc ethiopienes on egipte cam, And brende, & sluȝ, & wreche nam. 1297 R. GLOUC. (Rolls) 5215 Hii ne kepte hit holde noȝt bote..destrue & berne & sle. *a* 1352 MINOT *Poems* (ed. Hall) iii. 61 Ful fast þai slogh and brend. 1390 GOWER *Conf.* III. 207 His moste gloire Was forto sle and noght to save. *c* 1440 in *Househ. Ord.* (1790) 450 A castel that the Kyng and the Qwhene comen in for to see how Seint Jorge slogh. 1535 COVERDALE *Ezek.* ix. 5 Go ye..thorow the cite, slaye, ouersee none, spare none. 1589 PUTTENHAM *Eng. Poesie* III. xvi. (Arb.) 188 The Nubiens..sleaing a farre with venim and with dartes. *c* 1700 PRIOR *To a Lady* viii, The Parthian turn'd his Steed,..and as He fled, He slew. 1781 COWPER *Charity* 49 The hand that slew, till it could slay no more. 1817 SHELLEY *Rev. Islam* x. x, We were slaying still without remorse. 1849 AYTOUN *Poems, Heart of Bruce* xxiii, The Moors have come from Africa To spoil and waste and slay.

**7. a.** Of the Deity: To deprive (man, etc.) of life; to bring death upon, to destroy.

*c* **825** *Vesp. Psalter* lxxvii. 51 [He] sloȝ ylc frum-bearn on eorðan [of Egypt]. *c* **897** K. ÆLFRED tr. *Gregory's Past. C.* xxxvi. 251 Ðonne God hie sloȝ, ðonne sohton hie hine. *c* **1055** *Byrhtferth's Handboc* in *Anglia* VIII. 322 God ælmihtiȝ ferde on egiptena lande, hi sleande & alysende Israela bearn. *a* **1300** *Cursor M.* 6122 At þe king-self he be-gan, þe forbirth slou o beist and man. *a* **1340** HAMPOLE *Psalter* ix. 33 Sloand þaim in body noght in saule; [the] riche he sall sla in saule. **1552** *Bk. Com. Prayer, Litany*, O Almightie God, whiche..didst slea with the plague of pestilence, lx and ten thousand. **1611** BIBLE *Hosea* ii. 3 Lest I..set her like a drie land, and slay her with thirst.

*absol.* *c* **1000** ÆLFRIC *Deut.* xxxii. 39 Ic slea and ic hæle. *a* **1340** HAMPOLE *Psalter* 521, I sall sla and i sall make to lif. **1535** COVERDALE *1 Sam.* ii. 6 The Lorde slayeth, and geueth life.

**b.** Of natural forces, accidents, etc.

'Still in current use in Lincolnshire dialect.' *N.E.D.*

*c* **1000** ÆLFRIC *Exod.* ix. 25 Se haȝol sloh..ealle þa þing, þe ute wæron, æȝðer ȝe men ȝe nytenu. **1382** WYCLIF *Dan.* iii. 22 Flawme of the fijre slewȝ tho men. *c* **1420** *Sir Amadace* xli, Thay were..With wild waturs slone. **1486** *Bk. St. Albans* c viij b, The leest mysdyetyng and mysentendyng sleth her. **1611** *Stranton Par. Reg.* 26 June, Agnes..was buried, being slayne with a coupe wayne in the field. **1686** *Merrington Par. Reg.*, She was suddenly slaine with a sled in hay time. **1697** DRYDEN *Virg. Georg.* III. 724 Th' Infection grew, Tame Cattle, and the Beasts of Nature slew. **1708** J. C. *Compl. Collier* (1845) 45 There was above thirty Persons ..slain by a Blast. **1865** *N. & Q.* 3rd Ser. VII. 31 His poor father was sla'ain [by a stay falling]. **1877** in *N.W. Linc. Gloss.*

*absol.* **1559** MORWYNG *Evonymus* 236 There be certaine poysones which slee with the only touching. **1611** BIBLE *Job* ix. 23 If the scourge slay suddenly. **1904** MISS CORELLI *God's Good Man* xxxii, She was undergoing the operation, which was to save or slay.

†**8.** To put to death as a criminal; to execute.

*c* **1200** ORMIN 13782 [The Jews] sloȝhenn himm..All gillte-læs o rode. *a* **1340** HAMPOLE *Psalter* xvi. 12 When þai sloghe crist. *c* **1375** *Sc. Leg. Saints* vii. (*James Minor*) 430 þat al þai þat sclew dere Ihesu, I sal sla. *c* **1420** *Chron. Vilod.* 4756 Ihesu suffrede þe Iuys hym to slen. **1526** *Pilgr. Perf.* (W. de W. 1531) 238 So the lawe sleeth the gylty man, and not the iudge. **1611** BIBLE *Acts* x. 39 Iesus.., whom they slew and hanged on a tree. **1667** MILTON *P.L.* XII. 414 Naild to the Cross By his own Nation, slaine for bringing Life.

**9. a.** To kill (a domestic animal or beast of game), *esp.* for food or as a sacrifice; to slaughter. †Also, to take (fish).

*c* **1000** ÆLFRIC *Deut.* xxviii. 31 Mann slihð þinne oxan beforan þe and þu his ne abitst. *a* **1122** *O.E. Chron.* (Laud MS.) an. 1086, Swa hwa swa sloȝe heort oððe hinde. *c* **1205** LAY. 8105 Islaȝene weoren to þon mele, twælf þusend ruðeren sele. *a* **1300** *Cursor M.* 3019 Quen he was spaned fra þe pap, His fader slou bath scepe and nete. *c* **1400** *Apol. Loll.* 48 Wan prestis slow þe offringis, and bests blod was remissioun of synnis. *c* **1460** FORTESCUE *Abs. & Lim. Mon.* ii. (1885) 111 As the Hunter takyth the wilde beste for to sle and ete hym. **1535** COVERDALE *Exod.* xxix. 20 As for the other ramme, thou shalt slaye him. **1597** SKENE *De Verb. Sign.* s.v. *Assisa*, Everie Boat that passis to the draue, and slayis herring. **1611** BIBLE *Lev.* iv. 29 And he shall..slay the sin offering in the place of the burnt offering. **1728** CHAMBERS *Cycl.* s.v. *Sacrifice*, When the Victim was slain, they flead him. **1837** W. IRVING *Capt. Bonneville* III. 257 While a hunter is..cutting up the deer or buffalo he has slain. **1863** W. C. BALDWIN *Afr. Hunting* ix. 419, I have.. slain this morning..the last rabbit within a circle of eight miles.

*absol.* *a* **1300** *Cursor M.* 19869 Petre,..þou sla and ete. **1535** COVERDALE *Acts* x. 13 And there came a voyce vnto him: Ryse Peter, slaye, & eate.

*transf.* **1483** *Presentmts. Juries* in *Surtees Misc.* (1890) 29 Flech..þat was sclayn of Setterday afor.

†**b.** To destroy (vermin, etc.) by some means. Also in fig. context. *Obs.*

*a* **1225** *Ancr. R.* 206 þe scorpiunes cundel þet heo bret in hire boseme,..slea hit mid dedbote. *a* **1400-50** *Stockh. Med. MS.* 101 To slen lees [= lice]. *c* **1440** *Pallad. on Husb.* I. 912 Elebur blak with fatte..commyxt and offrid hem [mice and rats] wol sleen. **1495** *Trevisa's Barth. De P.R.* VII. xxv. (W. de W.) 241 Wormes of the teeth ben slayne [*Bodl. MS.* kilde] wyth Myrre and Opium. **1578** LYTE *Dodoens* 415 The same is good agaynst wormes,..for it slayeth them.

**III.** †**10.** To bring to spiritual death; to destroy with sin. *Obs.*

*c* **1175** *Lamb. Hom.* 53 Heo slaȝeð heore aȝene saule, and bringeð heom in to þare eche pine of helle. *c* **1200** ORMIN 2092 Whase nile trowwenn þiss He slaþ hiss aȝhenn sawle. *a* **1225** *Ancr. R.* 156 Mest al þe world, þet is gostliche isleien mid deadliche sunnen. *a* **1300** *Cursor M.* 25697 Wit his ded he boght again, Vr sauls þat wit sin war slain. **1382** WYCLIF *Wisdom* i. 11 The mouth forsothe that lieth, sleth the soule. *a* **1529** SKELTON *Bk. Three Foles* Wks. 1843 I. 202 O Enuy, ..thou brennest the desyres, and sleeth the soule in the ende. **1573** TUSSER *Husb.* (1878) 199 What daily watch is made, the soule of man to slea. **1611** BIBLE *Rom.* vii. 11 For sinne taking occasion by the commandement,..by it slew me.

*refl.* **1303** R. BRUNNE *Handl. Synne* 1526 þe bakbyter fyrst hym self sles.

*absol.* **1382** WYCLIF *2 Cor.* iii. 6 The lettre sleith, forsoth the spirit quykeneth. **1387-8** T. USK *Test. Love* III. ix. (Skeat) l. 107 The letter sleeth; the spirit yeveth lyfelich understanding.

†**11.** To overcome with affliction or distress. *Obs.*

*c* **1386** CHAUCER *Squire's T.* 454 (Hengwrt MS.), Ye sleen me with youre sorwe verraily. —— *Frankl. T.* 165 Thise Rokkes sleen myn herte for the feere. *c* **1400** *Rom. Rose* 2593 It makith me fulle of joyfulle thought, It sleth me that it lastith noght. *c* **1425** AUDELAY *XI Pains of Hell* 90 in *O.E. Misc.* 213 ȝif þai ferd wel her hertis hit slow, And of here losse were glad and fayne. **1526** SKELTON *Magnyf.* 2311, I am wery of the worlde, for vnkyndnesse me sleeth. *a* **1568** A. SCOTT *Poems* (S.T.S.) xxiii. 6, I am with sorrow slane, And dyis nicht & day.

**12. a.** To destroy, extinguish, put an end to, suppress completely (*esp.* something bad). Cf. KILL *v.* 4.

(*a*) *c* **1175** *Lamb. Hom.* 51 þe we beoð sari in ure heorte þet we isuneȝed habbeð, þenne slaȝe we ure sunne. *c* **1200** ORMIN 6752 þa slast tu swa þin aȝhenn flæsh & hire fule wille. **1377** LANGL. *P. Pl.* B. XIV. 90 For shrifte of mouth sleeth synne, be it neuere so dedly. *c* **1391** CHAUCER *Astrol.* Prol. (1872) 2 With this swerd shal I slen envie. *a* **1450** MYRC 36 But sle þy lust for any thynge. **1538** BP. BALE *God's Promises* I, Her sede shall..Slee hys suggestyons, & hys whole power confounde. **1560** BECON *Comm.-pl. Holy Script.* Wks. II. III. 68 To reconcile both vnto God in one body thorow the Crosse, and slewe hatred therby. **1763** J. GREGG in *Bk. Praise* (1866) 349 Thoughts must be slain that disobey. **1868** LYNCH *Rivulet* CXLIX. v, O heavenly Lord, whose mercy can..Both slay the sins and save the man.

(*b*) *c* **1200** *Trin. Coll. Hom.* 103 þe rihte bileue and þe soðe luue..ben leirede and slaine on his heorte. *a* **1300** *Cursor M.* 24692 þo þou haf oþer vertus slain, In þe þou mai þam couer again. **1539** ELYOT *Image Gov.* (1549) 99 As pride sleeth loue [etc.]. **1592** SHAKS. *Rom. & Jul.* II. iii. 26 For this..Being tasted slayes all sences with the heart. **1819** SHELLEY *Cenci* V. ii. 144 To slay The reverence living in the minds of men Towards our ancient house. **1884** *Pall Mall G.* 9 July 1/1 In the very act of slaying the Bill.

†**b.** In phr. *to slay care*. *Obs.*

**13..** *Minor Poems fr. Vernon MS.* 695 But make we murie & sle care. *a* **1400** *Siege of Troy* 185 in *Archiv neu. Spr.* LXXII. 16 To Grece þey comen hom And maden murþe and slowe care. *c* **1420** *Avow. Arth.* xlix, The king with a blythe chere Bade hom sle care! *a* **1529** SKELTON *E. Rummyng* 111 Let vs sley care.

†**13. a.** To blight or destroy (vegetation). *Obs.*

*c* **1325** *Prose Ps.* lxxvii. 52 He sloȝe [L. *occidit*] her uines wyþ hail. *c* **1440** *Pallad. on Husb.* III. 453 Tholiues hit forsake; The rootes wol their oyl or slen [L. *necat*] or slake. *Ibid.* 1078 The rootes ek of reed and rish thei ete. When wynter sleth their fedyng, yef hem meete. **1500-20** DUNBAR *Poems* xiv. 63 Quhilk slayis the corne and fruct that growis grene. **1574** HYLL *On Weather* i, Extreme cold doth slea the trees.

**b.** *intr.* Of grain: To become affected by smut, blight, or the like. (Cf. SLAIN *ppl. a.* 3.)

**1641** BEST *Farm. Bks.* (Surtees) 55 But it is observed in wheate, that if the seed bee not chainged once in fower or five croppes it will slay extreamely. **1875** *Encycl. Brit.* I. 360/2 On muiry soils this [oat] crop is also not unfrequently lost by what is called '*slaying*'. This seems to result from the occurrence of frosty nights late in spring. *Ibid.*, This tendency to *slaying* in the oat crop.

†**14.** *Med.* **a.** To resolve (an impostume, etc.). *Obs.*

*a* **1400** *Stockh. Medical MS.* ii. 650 in *Anglia* XVIII. 323 þe powdir on ded flesch who so leye, Anon it sleth it. *a* **1425** tr. *Arderne's Treat. Fistula*, etc. 98 þis medicyne.. wonderfully sleeþ þe antrax and vtterly cureþ it.

†**b.** To destroy the vitality of (a part of the body). *Obs.*[−1]

**1578** LYTE *Dodoens* 348 It choketh and troubleth all the inwarde partes,..and in fine it sleayeth the partie.

**slay**, *v.*[2] Also sley. [Back-formation from SLAYING *vbl. sb.*[2]] *trans.* To set (a warp).

**1828-32** WEBSTER, *Sleid*, to sley or prepare for use in the weaver's sley. **1888** R. BEAUMONT *Woollen & Worsted Cloth Manuf.* 139 The proper method of sleying any particular warp or specific make of cloth.

**'slayable**, *a. rare.* [f. SLAY *v.*[1]] That may be (justly) slain.

**1887** *Edin. Rev.* July 39 Alexander was a tyrant and therefore in all justice slayable.

**slayd**, obs. Sc. pa. t. SLIDE *v.*

**slayer**[1] ('sleɪə(r)). Forms: α. 4-5 sleer, 4-6 sleere, 5-6 slear, 6 *Sc.* sleyar. β. 4 -slaer, -sloer, 5-6 slaar(e, slaer (5 sclaer). γ. 6- slayer (6 *Sc.* slayar). [f. SLAY *v.*[1] + -ER[1]; the compound MANSLAYER is found a little earlier. Cf. MDu. and Du. *slager*, MLG. *slegere* (LG. *släger*), OHG. *slagari* and *slahari* (G. *schläger*).] One who slays or kills. Also in fig. context.

α. *c* **1380** WYCLIF *Wks.* (1880) 151 þei schullen be dampnyd..for sleeris of crist wiþ þe wickid iewis. **1387** TREVISA *Higden* (Rolls) V. 373 Whan þe kyng was i-slawe, þe sleere fliȝ. *c* **1400** *Apol. Loll.* 54 Opun slears and traytors of þe schep. **1432-50** tr. *Higden* (Rolls) III. 227 Then Hispias ..commaundede the sleer of his brother to be taken. **1500-20** DUNBAR *Poems* ix. 50 God for till honour,..no sleyar to be. **1581** LAMBARDE *Eirenarcha* II. vii. 239 Any other, betweene whom and the slear there is no speciall ligeance.

β. *a* **1400-50** *Alexander* 967 It gladis me..to ga þus to deth, To se my slaare..be sa sone ȝolden. *c* **1470** HENRY *Wallace* XI. 1278 The fyrst has bene a gret slaar off men. **1533** BELLENDEN *Livy* II. xviii. (S.T.S.) I. 200 Sum allegis his fader was þe slaar of him. **1596** DALRYMPLE tr. *Leslie's Hist. Scot.* II. 210 The slaers of Drumm sulde be banist to France.

γ. **1547-64** BALDWIN *Mor. Philos.* (Palfr.) 185 Men ought not to weepe for him that guiltles is slain, But for the slayer. *c* **1575** *Diurn. Occurr.* (Bann.) 121 Ane of the alledgit slayaris of the king. **1631** GOUGE *God's Arrows* III. § 14. 211 When he slayeth a malefactour he is not to be counted a slayer of men, but a destroyer of evill men. **1737** WHISTON *Josephus, Hist.* VI. viii, The slayers left off at the evening. **1791** COWPER *Iliad* IV. 536 The slayer o'er the maim'd Exulting. **1815** W. H. IRELAND *Scribbleomania* 217 Each pestle's displayer, Who, living by drugs, proves humanity's slayer. **1884** *Manch. Exam.* 10 May 5/5 The mutilators and slayers of pigeons.

**slayer**[2] ('sleɪə(r)). [f. SLAY *v.*[2] + -ER[1].] One who sets warps.

**1881** *Census Instr.* (1885) 64. **1899** *Daily News* 12 Jan. 2/1 Father,..Blacksmith. Boy,..Slayer.

†**'slayeress.** *Obs.*[−1] In 4 sleeresse. [f. SLAYER[1].] A female slayer.

**1382** WYCLIF *Tobit* iii. 9 See wee no more of thee sone or doȝter vp on erthe, thou sleeresse [*v.r.* sleestere] of thi men.

**slaying** ('sleɪɪŋ), *vbl. sb.*[1] Forms: α. 4 sleing, 5 sle(i)yng, 5-6 sleynge; 4-5 sleaynge, 6 sleaing. β. 4 slaing. γ. 6- slaying. [f. SLAY *v.*[1] + -ING[1].]

**1.** The action of the vb. SLAY; killing, slaughter.

α, β. *c* **1375** *Cursor M.* 6784 (Fairf.), Qua þat honoures goddis new, of his slaing [*Gött.* sleing] sal na mon rew. *c* **1400** *Apol. Loll.* 65 Sampson slow himsilf in sleyng of þe Philisteis. **1450** in *Catal. Publ. Rec. Office* IV. 327 That he wase never gelty of sleyng of the do [= doe]. *a* **1533** LD. BERNERS *Huon* cxxxiv. 495 Then he commaundyd to sece the sleynge.

*fig.* *c* **1450** *Godstow Reg.* 9 The balance of vertues I haue mysweyed, With sleyng of tonge, or with wilfulnesse.

γ. **1528** TINDALE *Obed. Chr. Man* Wks. 129 The slaying & murtheryng of Christen men. **1601** SHAKS. *Jul. C.* V. v. 4 *Clitus.* He is or tane, or slaine. *Brutus.* Slaying is the word, It is a deed in fashion. **1647** HEXHAM I. s.v., A slaying of parents. **1819** SCOTT *Ivanhoe* xxxv, As a man zealous to slaying for every point of the Nazarene law. **1865** A. SMITH *Summer in Skye* I. 219 Their forefathers had a grand slaying of their enemies.

†**2.** *Path.* Mortification. *Obs.*

*a* **1425** tr. *Arderne's Treat. Fistula*, etc. 37 After þe sleyng of flessh putred. *Ibid.* 91 It is best remedi to þam þat haþe ..þe fistule or oþer sleiyng.

**slaying** ('sleɪɪŋ), *vbl. sb.*[2] Also sleying. [f. SLAY *sb.*[2] + -ING[1].] (See quot. 1879.)

**1613** J. MAY *Decl. Est. Clothing* v. 25 In slaying of their warps they will cast the yarne to proue fine about a foot broad by the listes. **1759** BARBOUR *Constr. Sleying Tables*, The disposing of the warp threads in the loom is termed sleying. **1839** URE *Dict. Arts*, etc. 1056 The names of *examining*, *setting*, or *sleying*,..are used indiscriminately, and mean exactly the same thing. **1879** ASHENHURST *Weaving & Designing Text. Fabr.* (1893) 304 The slaying or setting of warps are terms used to denote the proportioning of the counts of warp to the different sets of slay, so as to preserve a uniformity of fabric in similar species of cloth.

*attrib.* **1759** R. BARBOUR (*title*), Essay on the Construction of Sleying Tables. **1793** *Trans. Soc. Arts* V. 235 Mathematical Sleaing Tables, or the..Mystery of weaving Linen Cloth, explained.

**'slaying,** *ppl. a.* Also 5 sleeng(e, sleing(e, 6 sleayng, slayeng. [f. SLAY *v.*[1] + -ING[2].] That slays or kills. Also *transf.* and in fig. context.

**1398** TREVISA *Barth. De P.R.* V. xxi. (Bodl. MS.), Some beestes haue tunges medicinable,..and some haue sleing tunges and venemous. *Ibid.* XVIII. x, þis sleinge addre [Aspis]. **1561** T. NORTON *Calvin's Inst.* I. 19 Certain giddy brained men, which..do scorn their simplicitie which still follow the dead and slayeng letter. **1581** DERRICKE *Image Irel.* C iv b, When as by Ioue eche sleayng beast abstracted thence shalbe. **1858** GLADSTONE *Studies Homer* III. 11 Achilles seems to refer with stinging, nay rather with slaying irony to this claim.

†**'slayster.** *Obs.*[−1] In 5 sleestere. [f. SLAY *v.*[1] + -STER.] A female slayer.

**14..** [see SLAYERESS].

**slayt(t,** obs. forms of SLATE *v.*

**sle,** obs. form of SLAY *v.*[1], SLY *a.*

**slead** (sliːd), *sb.* Now *dial.* Forms: 4-6 slede, 7 sleede (9 sleed), 6-7 sleid(e, 6 sleydd, sleade, 6- slead (9 sleead). [a. MDu. or MLG. *slede* (Du. *slede, slee*, LG. *slede, släde, slee*), = ON. and Icel. *sleði* (Norw. *slede*, Sw. *släde*, Da. *slæde*), OHG. *slito, slita* (MHG. *slite*): the stem *slid-* is the weak grade of the vb. SLIDE.] = SLED *sb.*[1]

*c* **1374** CHAUCER *Boeth.* IV. met. i. 110 þou..by my sledes shalt mowen retourne hool and sounde in to þi contre. **1382** WYCLIF *1 Chron.* xx. 3 The puple..he ladde out, and maad vpon hem pestelis, and sledis, and prowd yren charis, to gon ouer. **1406-7** *Durh. Acc. Rolls* (Surtees) 606, 1 slede empt. pro cariac. decimarum. *c* **1440** *Promp. Parv.* 458/2 Slede to draw wythe,..*traha.* **1555** EDEN *Decades* (Arb.) 292 They trauayl in wynter on sleades. **1591** SYLVESTER *Du Bartas* I. iv. 808 Those that in Ivory Sleads on Ireland Seas (Congeal'd to Crystall) slide about at ease. **1607** TOPSELL *Four-f. Beasts* (1658) 459 They are not drawn upon wheels, but like drays and sleads upon the earth. **1644** PRYNNE & WALKER *Fiennes' Trial* App. 64 The streets blocked up with caskes, carts, sleids, stooles. **1745** tr. *Columella's Husb.* II. xxi, You may make use of the cart or dray made of rough boards, or of a slead. **1877-89** in Linc. and Chesh. glossaries.

**b.** *Rope-making.* (Cf. SLEDGE[2] 3.) Also *attrib.*

**1688** HOLME *Armoury* III. 272/1 A Ropers Slead, a thing by which they Twist their Ropes. *Ibid.*, By the first is the Rope Yarn Spun, or turned in the Slead, when it is Laid for the making of a Cable; and is generally termed a Slead Hook.

Hence †**slead** *v. intr.* (with *it*), to travel in a sledge. *Obs.*[−1]

**1689** C. COTTON *Winter* xxxiii, Look where Mantled up in White, He sleads it like the Muscovite.

**sleahþe,** obs. form of SLEIGHT *sb.*[1]

**sleak** (sliːk), *v.*[1] Now *dial.* and *rare.* Also 4-5 sleke. [var. of SLECK *v.*: cf. *reke, reak* RECK *v.*]

**1.** *trans.* To quench, extinguish, assuage.

13.. *Cursor M.* 18020 (Gött.), Aisel haue i blend wid gall, For to sleke his threist wid-all. 13.. *E.E. Allit. P.* B. 708 Luf lowe hem bytwene lasched so hote, þat alle þe meschefez on mold moȝt hit not sleke. *a* 1400 in *Polit., Relig., & L. Poems* (1903) 135 þou may þaim sleke, als is a sparke when it is put in myddes þe see; & þar may no man sleke my myse bot þou. *c* 1440 *Gesta Rom.* xxxvii. 120 (Add. MS.), As watir sleketh fire, so almesdede sleketh synne. 1781 J. Hutton *Tour to Caves* (ed. 2) Gloss. 96 *Sleak*, to quench. 1884 *Lays & Leg. N. Irel.* 76 Feelin' his drouth stud in need av a sleakin'.

2. To slake (lime). Hence **sleaked** *ppl. a.*

*c* 1450 *M.E. Med. Bk.* (Heinrich) 217 Tak arpment, & slekyd lyme, & argoyle. 1676 *Phil. Trans.* XI. 714 They mix it with Chalk well sleaked.

3. *intr.* To give over or stop raining. *dial.*

1781 J. Hutton *Tour to Caves* (ed. 2) Gloss. 96.

**sleak** (sliːk), *v.*[2] *dial.* [var. of slake *v.*[2]]

1. *trans.* (See quot.)

1674 Ray *N.C. Words* 41 To *Sleak* out the tongue, to put it out by way of scorn, *Chesh.* [Hence in Bailey, Grose, etc.] 1886–7 in Cheshire glossaries.

2. To lick.

1846 *Ballads & Songs of Ayrshire* I. 112 (E.D.D.), He louped up an' sleak'd her cheek.

**sleak(e**, obs. forms of sleek *a.* and *v.*

**slealie**, obs. Sc. form of slyly *adv.*

**slean**, var. slane.

**slear**, obs. variant of slayer *sb.*[1]

[**slear**, error for *sleay* slay *sb.*[1]

1597 Gerarde *Herbal* I. xxiv. §6 The great reede or cane ..is esteemed to make slearres for weauers. 1694 Westmacott *Script. Herb.* 164 Of Cane-Reed are our.. Angling-Rods or Canes made, also Slears for Weavers.]

**sleasie, sleasy**, obs. ff. sleazy *sb.* and *a.*

**slea-silk**, variant of sleave-silk *Obs.*

**sleat** (sliːt), *v.*[1] *Obs.* exc. *dial.* Forms: 1 slǣtan, 3 slæten, slat-, 3, 7 slete, 8–9 sleet, 9 sleeat. Also *pa. t.* 1 slætte, 3 sle(a)tte, 9 slett; *pa. pple.* 4 slat. [OE. *slǣtan*, f. *slāt-* pret. stem of *slītan* slite *v.*, corresponding to ON. **sleita*, whence slate *v.*[3]]

†1. *trans.* To bait (an animal) with dogs. *Obs.*

*c* 1000 Ælfric *Lives Saints* xii. 72 Man slætte þa ænne fearr feringa þær-ute, and se fear arn him toȝeanes. *a* 1225 *Juliana* 52 (Royal MS.), Heo..sletten him wið hundes ant leiden to wið honden. *a* 1300 *Vox & Wolf* 289 in Hazl. *E.P.P.* I. 67 Tho hede the wreche fomen i-nowe, That weren egre him to slete Mid grete houndes.

†2. *intr.* To hunt *after* something. *Obs.*[−1]

*c* 1200 Ormin 13485 þatt time þatt teȝȝ [the apostles] tokenn swa To slætenn affterr sawless.

3. *trans.* To incite, set on (a dog, etc.).

*a* 1225 *Juliana* 53 (Bodl. MS.), Heo..sleatten on him hundes. 14.. *26 Polit. Poems* ix. 22 Synne to bay many a folde On soules helle houndes slete. 1674 Ray *N.C. Words* 43 To *Slete* a dog, is to set him at anything as swine, sheep, &c. 1703 Thoresby *Let. to Ray*, To Sleat a Dog. 1878 *Yorkshireman* Nov. 394 (E.D.D.), I tuke a delight i' sleatin' 'em at one another. 1886 *Rochdale Gloss.* 80 *Sleat*, to send or urge, as a dog at cattle, particularly sheep.

Hence '**sleating** *vbl. sb.*, hunting; also *fig.*, baiting, instigation.

*a* 1122 *O.E. Chron.* (Laud) an. 1087, Ælc unriht ȝeold he forbead, & ȝeatte mannan heora wudas and slætinge. *c* 1205 Lay. 12326 þus Gratien þe king for ut an slæting. *Ibid.* 29170 Hit was in ane dæie, þat Gurmund mid his duȝeðe.. riden a slatinge. *c* 1400 *Destr. Troy* 196 Pelleus..printed in hert Iff he might sleghly be sleght & sletyng of wordes, Gar Iason..the iorney vndertake.

†**sleat**, *v.*[2] *Obs.*[−1] ? var. of slat *v.*[2]

*a* 1225 *Ancr. R.* 212 Hwon heo ihereð þet god, heo sleateð adun boa two hore earen.

'**sleathy**, *a. rare.* Also 9 sleethy. [? f. ON. *slǿða* to drag, trail (so Norw. *slöda*; also, to work carelessly); cf. ON. *slóði* (Norw. *slode*) sloven, sluggard, whence perh. north-eastern Sc. *sleeth*.] Slovenly, careless.

1649 Blithe *Eng. Improv. Impr.* 52 The combination of labourers and poor people may very much prejudice, besides their slothfull and sleathy slubbering of it. *a* 1904 in *Eng. Dial. Dict.* s.v. *Sleath* (Kentish dial.), He is a bit sleethy.

**sleave** (sliːv), *sb.* [See next and sleave-silk.]

†1. A slender filament of silk obtained by separating a thicker thread; silk in the form of such filaments; floss-silk. *Obs.*

1591 Sylvester *Du Bartas* I. v. 955 Those slender sleaves (On ovall clews) of soft, smooth, Silken flakes. 1611 Cotgr., *Cadarce pour faire capiton*, the tow, or coursest part of silke, whereof sleaue is made. 1622 Drayton *Poly-olb.* xxiii. 318 Fair Benefield.., Which bears a grass as soft as is the dainty sleave. 1635 [Glapthorne] *Lady Mother* I. i, Her faire haire; no silken sleave Can be so soft the gentle worm does weave.

2. *transf.* and *fig.* (In modern use only as an echo of the Shaksperean passage.)

1605 Shaks. *Macb.* II. ii. 37 Sleepe that knits vp the rauel'd Sleeue of Care. 1868 G. Macdonald *Seaboard Parish* III. ix. 190 He..began to smooth out the wonderful sleave of dusky gold. 1876 Miss Braddon *Dead Men's Shoes* i, She has not seen the fair and shining fabric in life's loom, but the ragged sleave thereof. 1904 J. C. Collins *Stud. Shaks.* 317 To smoothe the tangled sleave of Shakespearean expression.

**sleave** (sliːv), *v.* Now *dial.* Forms: 6 sleyve, sleue, 7 sleeue, 9 sleeve; 7– sleave. [OE. *slǣfan* (recorded in the comb. *toslǣfan*, Napier *Holy Rood-tree* 32/2), f. *slāf-*, pret. stem of *slīfan* slive *v.*]

It is possible that the pa. t. *slefte* (cf. sleft *ppl. a.*) should be read in the *Gest of Robyn Hode* III. st. 146, where the early editions have *sleste*, *slet*, and *cleft*.

1. *trans.* To divide (silk) by separation into filaments. Also *transf.* and *absol.*

*a* 1628 F. Grevil *Cœlica* I. (1633) 24 When light doth beginne These to retaile, and subdiuide, or sleeues Into more minutes. 1654 Whitlock *Zootomia* 362 The more subtle, (and more hard to Sleave a two) Silken thred, of self-seeking. 1654 Flecknoe *Ten Years Trav.* 71 They use to sleave and spin to what finesse they please. 1890 Lowell *Biglow P.* Ser. II. *Introd.* Poet. Wks. 1890 II. 165 To sleeve silk means to divide or ravel out a thread of silk with the point of a needle till it becomes floss.

2. *dial.* To cleave, split, rend, tear apart.

1828– in dialect glossaries (Yks., Chesh., Heref.).

Hence **sleaved** *ppl. a.* (also 7 sleyd), in *sleaved silk* (see sense 1).

1577–86 Holinshed *Chron.* III. 835 Eight wildmen all apparelled in greene mosse, made with sleued silke. 1592 in Ellis *Orig. Lett.* Ser. III. IV. 103 Sleyved Silk, the lb. 1623 *Shakespere's Tr. & Cr.* v. i. 35 (fol.), Thou idle, immateriall skiene of Sleyd silke. 1706 Phillips (ed. Kersey), *Sleaved*, as Sleaved Silk, *i.e.* such as is wrought fit for Use.

†**sleave-silk.** *Obs.* Also 6 slaye-, 7 slea-, 8 sleeve-. [f. sleave *v.* 1.] Silk thread capable of being separated into smaller filaments for use in embroidery, etc.

α. 1588 in *Antiquary* XXXII. 373, ii ounce of slaye sylke, xvid. 1676 Rainbow *Funeral Serm. C'tess Pembroke* (1677) 38 A Prime..Wit [*marg.* Dr. Donne]..is reported to have said of this Lady..That she knew well how to discourse of all things, from Predestination, to Slea-silk.

β. 1598 Florio, *Capitone*, a kinde of course silke called sleaue-silke. 1600–2 in Whitaker *Hist. Craven* 315 Paid for sleave silk, xxxiiis. 1672–3 Grew *Anat. Pl., Roots* (1682) 66 The Threds..stand collateral together; as the several Single Threds of the Silkworm do in Sleave-Silk. 1703 *Lond. Gaz.* No. 3924/3 Sleeve and Twisted Silk.

*Comb.* *a* 1631 Donne *Poems* (1633) 190 Let..curious traitors, sleave silke [*pr.* sicke] flies Bewitch poore fishes wandring eyes.

*transf.* and *fig.* 1649 Lovelace *Poems* (1864) 36 In the sleave-silke of her haire 'Twas hard bound up and wrapped. 1649 G. Daniel *Trinarch., Hen. IV*, lxxxv, When..all faculties In yᵗ sleave-silke of Sleep soft-fettered Lay.

'**sleaving.** *rare.* Now *dial.* [f. sleave *v.* Cf. slaving *sb.*] A slip taken from a tree by splitting or pulling.

*c* 1440 *Pallad. on Husb.* III. 163 Yf thow sette a plaunte or a sleuyng, Putte in a lytel moysty molde amonge. 1839 Sir G. C. Lewis *Gloss. Heref.*, *Sleaving*, a twig sleaved off.

**sleaze** (sliːz), *sb. slang.* [Back-formation from sleazy, sleezy *a.*] 1. Squalor; sordidness, sleaziness; dilapidation; (something of) inferior quality or low moral standards. Also *attrib.*

1967 *Listener* 14 Sept. 326/2 For all its brazen sleaze, Soho is a pretty fair working model of what a city neighbourhood should be. 1975 *Publishers' Weekly* 29 Dec. 68/2 Obviously written to cash in on 'Mandingo', this isn't even readable sleaze: the plot's sloppy, Gilchrist hasn't the knack for writing commercial sex, and the hero is too despicable to be seductive. 1976 *National Observer* (U.S.) 17 July 16 (*heading*) At home with the sleaze king. 1981 *New Yorker* 9 Mar. 104/1 These stores are vast, computerized sleaze centers, where you can buy almost anything—pills, toys, candy, liquor, stockings, pillows, and gadgetry.

2. A person of low moral standards.

1976 *Telegraph* (Brisbane) 3 Aug. 10/3 When I made the mistake of calling them 'sleazy' to their faces, their reaction was outrage. 'Don't call me a sleaze,' said Miss Currie. 1977 *Time* 28 Feb. 48/1 Oh God, red nail polish—I look like a sleaze.

**sleaze, sleeze** (sliːz), *v.* [Prob. f. as prec.]

1. *dial.* (See quots.) ? *Obs.*

1777 in *Eng. Dial. Dict.* 1825 J. Jennings *Observations on Some of Dialects in W. of England* 69 *To sleeze*,..to separate; to come apart: applied to cloth, when the warp and woof readily separate from each other. 1904 *Eng. Dial. Dict.* V. 513/1 *Sleeze*,..*v.* Of loosely or badly woven cloth: to separate, part asunder; to wear away; also with *away*.

2. *slang.* To move in a sleazy fashion.

1964 *Punch* 30 Dec. 986/2 Other plays, sleazing across the West End boards. 1978 W. F. Buckley *Stained Glass* xxii. 211 The depressing, unseasonal föhn that sleazes over Europe with dumpy barometric pressures that enervate and depress. 1978 *Whig-Standard* (Kingston, Ontario) 31 Mar. A-6 When not thumping.., they [*sc.* a rock group] just kind of sleaze along, a little like Lou Reed at his best.

'**sleazily**, *adv.* [f. sleazy, sleezy *a.* + -ly[2].] In a sleazy manner.

1959 *Listener* 5 Nov. 793/2 A bloated society staggering sleazily towards decay. 1974 M. Fido *Kipling* 119/2 Huneefa and her sleazily exotic magic. 1976 *Listener* 14 Oct. 486/4 Despising and envying the order and bourgeois contentment of the new ménage, sleazily growling in her basement flat.

'**sleaziness.** [f. sleazy *a.*] The fact or quality of being sleazy.

1727 in Bailey (Vol. II.). 1891 Lang in *Illustr. Lond. N.* 7 Mar., Mr. Lanier with his sleaziness condoning the immortal speeches of Achilles and Odysseus. 1959 *Guardian* 3 Dec. 7/2 The pop-eyed sleaziness of a Master Elliot's night-boy. 1978 *Fortune* 18 Dec. 107 The classifieds represent a sleaziness of practice that I hope will be corrected by the more ethical newspapers and publishers.

**sleazo** ('sliːzəʊ), *a.* and *sb. U.S. slang.* [f. sleazy, sleezy *a.* + -o[2].] (Something) sleazy, (something) pornographic.

1972 E. Sanders *Family* iii. 68 Manson used to hang out on the Sunset Strip using the name Chuck Summers. There were a bunch of sleazo bars and cafés on or near the Sunset Strip. *Ibid.* 69 What was it that caused Manson's death-trip? The factors that seem to have fed the violent freak-out shall be termed here sleazo inputs. 1975 *Guardian Weekly* 2 Aug. 20 Her sleazo routines seem half-rehearsed. Her dirty jokes sound almost like last-gasp fill-ins for the cleaner lines she was supposed to deliver but forgot. 1978 *Courier-Mail* (Brisbane) 4 Jan. 16/2 Norman Mailer said he liked sex movies, especially 'love pornies' and 'the sleazos'.

†'**sleazy**, *sb. Obs. rare.* In 7 Sleasie, 8 Slesey. [Abbreviated f. silesia.] = silesia 1.

1670 Blount *Glossogr.* (ed. 3) s.v. *Sleasie Holland*, That only is properly Sleasie or Silesia Linen cloth, which is made in [and] Comes from the Country Silesia in Germany. 1696 J. F. *Merch. Wareho. laid open* 36, I shall now begin according to my promise to treat of Sleasie Lawns, it being a very useful Linnen here with us, it takes its name from a town called Slesia in Hamborough, and not for its wearing Sleasie, as a great many do imagine. 1706 *Lond. Gaz.* No. 4226/4, 8 Pieces of Norwich Druggit,..4 Pieces of Hambrough Cloth, 1 Piece of Slesey.

**sleazy, sleezy** ('sliːzɪ), *a.* Forms: α. 7 sleasie, sleazie, 7–8 sleasy (9 *dial.* -ey), 8– sleazy (9 *dial.* slazy). β. 7 slezie, 8 slesy, 9 sleezy. [Of uncertain origin; the evidence seems to be against any original connexion with prec.

The mod. dial. verb sleaze, sleeze, to wear badly, may be merely a back-formation from the adj.]

1. (See quots.)

1644 Digby *Nat. Bodies* xxxiv. §1. 288 Some drye partes of such liquors, are of themselues as it were hairy or sleasy, that is, haue litle downy partes, such as you see vpon the legges of flies. 1875 Knight *Dict. Mech.* 2192/1 It smooths down the sleezy and fuzzy fibers of the twisted rope. *Ibid.* 2207/1 *Sleezy*,..rough from projecting fibers, as yarn or twine made of inferior material.

2. a. Of textile fabrics or materials: Thin or flimsy in texture; having little substance or body.

α. 1670 Blount *Glossogr.* (ed. 3) s.v., *Sleasie Holland*, common people take to be all Holland, which is slight or ill-wrought. 1696 J. F. *Merch. Wareho. laid open* 21 It..will not wear near so well.., by reason it is made of more sleasie thread than the former is. 1718 Ozell tr. *Tournefort's Voy.* I. 258 'Tis a sleasy sort of stuff, but thickens and contracts by being well pressed on the sea-sand. 1757 Washington *Let.* Writ. 1889 I. 424 They were presented each with a suit made of thin, sleazy cloth without lining. *a* 1825 Forby *Voc. E. Anglia* 306 *Slazy*, of loose and open texture, easily torn, and soon worn out. 1866 Sala *Trip to Barbary* 365 You know that Sleazy calico was made in a mill and by steam power. 1876 C. D. Warner *Winter on Nile* i. 20 Their one sleazy skirt giving little protection against the keen air.

β. 1670 in *12th Rep. Hist. MSS. Comm.* App. V. 15 The silke sleizie and not Naples, which will soone grow rough, gather dust and sullie. 1706 Dr. Baynard *Cold Baths* II. 376 A thin slesy Coat of Sarsenet. 1856 *Househ. Wds.* XIII. 99 A sleezy, cobwebby, hairy genus of coverlets. 1893 Mrs. T. Coke *Gentlewoman at Home* vii. 102 'Sleezy' silks, wispy surahs, or cottony velvets.

b. *transf.* and *fig.* Slight, flimsy, unsubstantial.

*c* 1645 Howell *Fam. Lett.* (1650) II. 2, I cannot well away with such sleazie stuff, with such cobweb compositions. 1648 *Petit. Eastern Ass.* 26 Their vain, and sleasy opinions about Religion. 1860 Emerson *Cond. Life* ii. (1861) 51 You shall not conceal the sleezy, fraudulent, rotten hours you have slipped into the piece. 1880 Blackmore *Erema* xvi. 96, I have only to deal with very little things, sometimes too slim to handle well, and too sleezy to be woven.

c. Dilapidated, filthy, slatternly, squalid; sordid, depraved, disreputable, worthless.

1941 J. Faulkner *Men Working* i. 31 Gwendolin..had been hanging on to her dress and peering around her wide sleazy hips. 1941 W. A. Percy *Lanterns on Levee* x. 111, I was always happening on a Hermaphrodite, in some discreet alcove, and I would examine the sleazy mock-modest little monster. 1946 'P. Quentin' *Puzzle for Fiends* 248 Her glamour dissolved... Suddenly Selena seemed sleazy. 1951 S. Kaye-Smith *Mrs Gailey* iv. xvi. 211 In her now was a real distaste for the sleazy comforts of Mrs Turner's kitchen. 1956 L. McIntosh *Oxford Folly* viii. 128 Beyond it was the cemetery and some sleazy suburb whose name Adrian did not know. 1958 *Punch* 27 Aug. 286/2 A kind of sleazy, leering sex for its own sake. 1959 F. Usher *Death in Error* x. 145 I've seen all the sleasy joints of Paris. 1966 *Listener* 30 June 947/2 He scratches a middle-aged living in Paris as a gigolo in a sleazy night club. 1971 B. W. Aldiss *Soldier Erect* 46 Some sleezy and probably malevolent god. 1976 *National Observer* (U.S.) 1 May 19/1 The methods used to slur the innocent grew sleazier. 1977 *Listener* 3 Mar. 282/1 The entrance of Salomé is greeted by the world's sleaziest tune, 'La Paloma'. 1979 R. Jaffe *Class Reunion* I. iv. 42 Scollay Square, an area that was sleazy, neon lit, and disreputable.

**sle-band**, obs. f. slee-band *Sc.*

**slech**: see sletch *v.*

**sleck** (small coal); var. slack *sb.*[2]

**sleck**, *sb. dial.* [Cf. MLG. and LG. *slick*, G. *schlick, schlich*.] Soft mud; ooze.

It is very doubtful whether *slec* (v.r. *slech*) in *Leg. Kath.* 1662 can be regarded as an early example of this.

1840 Hodgson *Hist. Northumb.* III. II. 319/2 The main sewer or drain..was about one-third filled up with that sort of ammoniacal sleck or sludge which comes from kitchens.

**1894** HESLOP *Northumb. Gloss.* 654 A slake is a large expanse of *sleck.* 'Sludge' is wet, muddy deposit, but not necessarily fine and smooth as *sleck.*

**sleck** (slɛk), *v.*[1] Now *dial.* Forms: 3 slecken(n, 5 sleckyn, 6 slecke, 5- sleck; 4 slekk-, 5 slekkyn, sclekke, 5–6 slek. [The northern form repr. OE. *sleccan* (see SLETCH *v.*), f. *slæc* SLACK *a.* See also SLEAK *v.*[1]]

**1.** *trans.* To extinguish or quench (a fire); to allay, assuage (thirst, etc.).

*c* **1200** ORMIN 5689 All hiss hunngerr & hiss þrisst Shall ben þurrh Drihhtin sleckedd. *c* **1250** *Gen. & Ex.* 1230 Ðe water sleckede ðe childes list. *a* **1400** HYLTON *Scala Perf.* III. xiii. (W. de W. 1494), The preest.. shall put vnder styckes, so that it be not sleckyd. *c* **1400** *Laud Troy Bk.* 12667 Troyle bad faste the fir be bet, But Thelamon bad his men hit slek With water of broke or of bek. **1523** FITZHERB. *Husb.* §169 As water slecketh fyer, soo dothe almesdede slake synne. **1530** PALSGR. 720/2 Whan you slecke a hoote fyre with water, it maketh a noyse lyke thunder. **1674** RAY *N.C. Words* 43 *To Sleck*,.. to quench or put out the fire, v.g., or one's thirst. **1781-** in northern dialect glossaries.

*fig.* *c* **1200** ORMIN 10124 Forr allmess dedess hafenn mahht To sleckenn þine sinness. *a* **1400** HYLTON *Scala Perf.* I. lxix. (W. de W. 1494), That the grounde of synne myghte ..somwhat be slecket in the. **1435** MISYN *Fire of Love* 118 All temptacion þou sall ouercum, & all malesse slek.

†**2.** To alleviate, moderate. *Obs. rare.*

**13..** *St. Erkenwolde* 331 in Horstm. *Altengl. Leg.* (1881) 273 þe fyrst slent þat on me slode slekkyd al my tene. *c* **1400** *Laud Troy Bk.* 5489 Ector sorow myght no man sclekke.

**3.** To cool by means of water, etc.

*c* **1420** *Liber Cocorum* (1862) 6 Tak a gad of stele..; And in goode wyne sleck hit I say. **1825** BROCKETT *N.C. Gloss.*, *Sleck*, to cool in water. *a* **1900** in *Eng. Dial. Dict.* s.v., The blacksmith is slecking a piece of iron.

**4.** To slack or slake (lime).

**1530** PALSGR. 720/2, I slecke lyme, I put water to it, *je destayns.* **1548** in E. Green *Somerset Chantries* (1888) 75 The churche yarde..wherin lyme is slekked. **1617** *Shuttleworth's Acc.* (Chetham Soc.) 219 Sleckinge and spreadinge six score lode of lyme, ijˢ vjᵈ. **1849-** in *Eng. Dial. Dict.*

Hence **slecked** *ppl. a.*, **'slecking** *vbl. sb.*

*c* **1440** *Promp. Parv.* 459/1 Slekkynge, or qwenchynge, *extinctio.* *a* **1533** LD. BERNERS *Golden Bk. M. Aurel.* (1546) H vj b, The morter..ought not to be medled with sande and slecked lyme. **1572** MASCALL *Plant. & Graff.* 41 Ye must meddle it well also with..slekt Sope ashes about the roote. **1611** COTGR. s.v. *Fusé, Chaux fusée*, slaked, or sleckt lime. **1675** *Phil. Trans.* X. 447 The consistence of slecked lime.

†**sleck**, *v.*[2] *Obs. rare.* [var. of SLEEK *v.*] *trans.* To make smooth.

**1530** PALSGR. 720/2, I slecke, I make paper smothe with a sleke stone, *je fais glissant.* You muste slecke your paper if you wyll write Greke well.

**'slecken**, *v.* Now *dial.* Forms: 4–6 sleken, 4–5 slekyn, sleckun, 9 slecken. [f. SLECK *v.*[1] + -EN[5]. In some examples perh. *slēken* is intended, f. *sleke* SLEAK *v.*[1]] = SLECK *v.*[1]

*c* **1340** HAMPOLE *Pr. Consc.* 3101 Alle þe waters, þat men may rekken, A spark þar-of may noght sleken. *a* **1340** —— *Psalter* xii. 4 þe lyght of godis luf es grauen and slekynd in vs. *c* **1400** *Apol. Loll.* 98 Taking þe scheld of þe feiþ, in þe wilk we may sleckun all þe firun dartis of the enemy. **1422** tr. *Secreta Secret., Priv. Priv.* lvii. 79 Cold water dronkyn yn wynter slekyns þe naturell hete. **1570** LEVINS *Manip.* 61/35 To Sleken, *extinguere.* **1876** *Whitby Gloss.* s.v., 'I ha'n't slecken'd mysel yet,' my thirst is not yet abated.

**sleck-trough.** Now *dial.* [SLECK *v.*[1]] = SLACK-TROUGH.

**1716** T. WARD *Eng. Reform.* 38 One who Anointed Had never been, unless his Dad Had in the Sleck-trough wash'd the Lad. **1825** BROCKETT *N.C. Gloss.*, *Sleck-trough*, the trough containing the water in which smiths cool their iron and temper steel. **1863** in Robson *Bards of Tyne* 413 A' wesh thersels clean i' the sleck troughs.

**sled** (slɛd), *sb.*[1] Now chiefly *dial.* and *U.S.* Also 4–7 sledde, 5–7 sledd. [a. MFlem. or MLG. *sledde* (= MHG. *slitte*, G. *schlitten*), related to *slede* SLEAD *sb.*]

**1. a.** A drag used for the transport of heavy goods, etc., = SLEDGE *sb.*[2] 2.

**1388** WYCLIF *1 Chron.* xx. 3 He..made breris,.. and sleddis, and irone charis, to passe on hem. *c* **1400** MAUNDEV. F viij, They cary theyr vytayles vpon the yce on sleddes. *c* **1450** *St. Cuthbert* (Surtees) 6001 On a sledd it sulde be layde. **1535** COVERDALE *2 Sam.* XXIV. 22 There is an oxe for a burnt offerynge, and sleddes. **1573** TUSSER *Husb.* (1878) 37 A sled for a plough, and another for blocks. **1601** HOLLAND *Pliny* II. 573 Some write, that Satyrus..conueied it to Alexandria by means of flat bottoms or sleds. **1677** YARRANTON *Eng. Improv.* 68 Fetching the Water being ready filled in Copper Tubs upon Sleds. **1726** LEONI *Alberti's Archit.* I. 42/1 Of Stones..some are big and unweildy, so that a Man..cannot manage them..without the assistance of Sleds. **1808** PIKE *Sources Mississ.* I. 62 Those sleds are made of a single plank turned up at one end .., and the baggage is lashed on in bags and sacks. **1887** COX *Cycl. Common Things* (ed. 6) 542 In Canada the Indians make a kind of sled which they call a 'toboggan'.

†**b.** Used for dragging condemned persons to execution. *Obs.*

**1576** FOXE *A. & M.* (ed. 3) 1901/2 He was layde vpon a Sled with an Hurdle on it, and drawen to the place of execution. **1655** GURNALL *Chr. in Arm.* ix. §1 (1669) 268/1 If..he should meet some of his fellow-Traytors on sleds, as they are dragging..to execution. **1667** L. STUCLEY *Gospel-Glass* xii. (1670) 107 How many have you seen drawn on Sleds, led to shameful and violent Deaths?

**c.** Any of various devices made to be towed along the sea bed.

**1939** *Sun* (Baltimore) 25 Jan. 3/4 As the sled passes over a buried cable both coils develop electric current which is wired to the mother ship above. **1967** *Petroleum* XXX. 158/2 The jets and suction dredge are mounted on a sled lowered from a frame at the stern of the vessel and straddle the pipe, along which they move as the barge proceeds. **1978** *Nature* 9 Mar. 156/2 This hypothesis is consistent with..the detection of a large ³He excess in a 'thermal plume' (thermal anomaly ~0.1°C, sampled using a deep-tow sled) over the Galapagos Spreading Centre.

**2. a.** A sledge or sleigh used as a vehicle in travelling or for recreation.

**1586** MARLOWE *1st Pt. Tamburl.* I. ii, With milke-white Hartes vpon an Iuorie sled Thou shalt be drawen. **1613** PURCHAS *Pilgrimage* IV. xvii. 431 He departed with Russes and Permacks for Slebotca in a sledde drawne with two deare. **1667** *Lond. Gaz.* No. 124/2 On Monday last their Imperial Majesties had their divertisements upon the Ice, attended by 76 Sleds. **1726–46** THOMSON *Winter* 773 Eager, on rapid sleds, Their vigorous youth, in bold contention, wheel The long resounding course. **1756** NUGENT *Gr. Tour, Netherl.* I. 89 There is a greater number of sleds, which are a heavy unpleasant carriage, and fit for none but old women. **1857** B. TAYLOR *North. Trav.* viii. 75 The postilions fastened our sleds behind their own large sledges, with flat runners, which got through the snow more easily than ours. **1873** 'SUSAN COOLIDGE' *What Katy did at Sch.* x. 168 To help him to get down his sled, because he thinks it is going to snow.

**b.** Also ***rocket sled.*** A rocket-propelled vehicle running on rails for subjecting things to controlled high accelerations and decelerations.

**1948** *Richmond* (Va.) *Times-Dispatch* 13 Jan. 9 The rocket-powered sleds moved over a standard-gauge railroad track.., covering the 2,000 feet in less than two seconds. **1956** L. MALLAN *Men, Rockets & Space* vi. 84 When he decelerated from 421 m.p.h. on the new sled, he reached a peak of only 22 G's. **1967** *Technology Week* 20 Feb. 18/1 Feasibility of a new segmented solid rocket sled motor designed for multiple re-use in sled testing has been shown in recent tests. **1974** *Encycl. Brit. Macropædia* XV. 942/1 Braking is accomplished by a parachute or, more often, by extending a scoop beneath the sled into a trough of water beneath the track rails.

**3.** *Rope-making.* (See SLEDGE *sb.*[2] 3.)

**1875** KNIGHT *Dict. Mech.* 364/1 As the yarns are twisted into a strand they become shorter and draw the sled towards the head of the walk.

**4.** *U.S.* A kind of river-boat used on the Ohio.

**1884** *Harper's Mag.* June 124/2 Of smaller vessels there were 'covered sleds', 'ferry flats', and 'Alleghany skiffs'.

**5.** *attrib.* and *Comb.*, as ***sled-car, -dog*** (N. Amer.), ***-load, -man, -mark, -runner***, etc.; also **sledful**, as much as a sled can hold.

*c* **1440** *York Myst.* xl, The Sledmen. *a* **1674** MILTON *Hist. Mosc.* ii. Wks. 1851 VIII. 484 In whatever place they find enough of white Moss to feed thir Sled-Stags. *Ibid.* v. 506 Chancelor had now gon more than half his journey, when the Sled-man sent to Court meets him on the way. **1692** H. KELSEY *Indian Belief* in *Kelsey Papers* (1929) 21 Now as for a woman they do not so much mind her for they reckon she is like a Slead dog or Bitch when she is living & when she dies they think she dyes to Eternity. **1701** in *Select Biog. Wodrow Society* (1846) II. 489 Two sledfuls of Sand. **1729** SWIFT *Answ. to Sev. Lett.* Wks. 1841 II. 93 The turf, which is now drawn upon sled-cars with great expense. **1777** G. CARTWRIGHT *Jrnl.* 18 Dec. in *Trans. Labrador* (1792) II. 277 Finding my sled-dog lame, I defered my journey. **1805** PIKE *Sources Mississ.* (1810) I. 53 Broke one sled runner, and were detained by other circumstances. *Ibid.* II. 179 Obliged to halt and send back for the sled loads. **1857** THOREAU *Maine W.* (1894) 42 The solitary sled-track running far up into the ..wilderness. **1868** *Harper's Mag.* XXXVI. 422 The sled-tender is ready to raise the huge bodies of the fallen upon his sled. **1869** BLACKMORE *Lorna D.* xiii, I followed the track on the side of the hill..where the sledd-marks are. **1914**, **1966** Sled dog [see MUSH *v.*[3]]. **1980** *Beautiful British Columbia* Winter 9 (*caption*) Sled dogs at Atlin's Long Distance Dog Sled Race.

†**sled**, *sb.*[2] *Obs.*⁻¹ [Alteration of SLEDGE *sb.*[1]] A sledge-hammer.

**1616** W. BROWNE *Brit. Past.* II. iii, They haue beheld the frolicke marriners..Pitch bars of silver, and cast golden sleds.

**sled**, *v.* Chiefly *U.S.* [f. SLED *sb.*[1] Cf. MFlem. *sledden* in sense 2.]

**1.** *intr.* To travel in a sledge.

**1780** A. ADAMS in *Fam. Lett.* (1876) 377 The Bay has been frozen so hard that people have walked, rode, and sledded over it to Boston. **1784** P. OLIVER in *T. Hutchinson's Diary* II. 406 In March they sledded across the Delaware. **1910** *Blackw. Mag.* Nov. 586/1 We had sledded down the cobble road and got on board.

**2.** *trans.* To convey on a sled or sleds.

**1718** in *Hist. Northfield* (Mass.) (1875) 148 Each man with his team shall cart or sled wood one day yearly for Mr. Doolittle. **1852** HAWTHORNE *Blithedale Rom.* xxiv. (1885) 243 Logs..piled up square, in order to be carted or sledded away. **1857** THOREAU *Maine W.* (1894) 207 Some widow's thirds, from which her ancestors have sledded fuel for generations.

**3.** *absol.* To admit of being sledded.

**1869** MRS. H. B. STOWE *Oldtown* xxxvii, P'r'aps, ef you'd jest tighten up the ropes.., the hull load would sled easier.

**'sledded**, *a. rare.* [f. SLED *sb.*[1]] **a.** Mounted on sleds. **b.** Made like a sled.

**1602** SHAKS. *Haml.* I. i. 63 So frown'd he once, when in an angry parle He smot the sledded Pollax on the Ice. **1821** JOANNA BAILLIE *Metr. Leg.*, *Wallace* lvi, Huge waggon, sledded car, and wain.

**'sledder.** [f. SLED *sb.*[1] or *v.*]

**1.** One who conveys heavy articles by means of a sled.

**1649** *Sc. Acts, Chas II* (1819) VI. 482 Haveing agriet with maissons, quarriouris, and sledderis. **1708** J. C. *Compl. Collier* (1845) 39 Fourteen Pence a Day for the other Banck's-Man, or Sledder.

**2.** A horse that draws a sled.

**1869** BLACKMORE *Lorna D.* ii, Smiler (our youngest sledder) had been well in over his withers.

†**'sleddier.** *Obs.*⁻¹ [f. SLED *sb.*[1] or *v.*] One who drives a sledge.

**1654** WHITELOCKE *Swed. Ambassy* (1772) I. 289 The ladyes and their sleddiers are very gallant.

**'sledding**, *vbl. sb. N. Amer.* [f. SLED *v.*]

**a.** The action of using a sled; conditions favourable for this.

**1755** T. SMITH *Jrnl.* (1849) 272 Several falls of snow, and some sledding. *Ibid.* 284 Fine sledding; true winter since the 17th. **1828–32** WEBSTER s.v., Sometimes in New England, there is little or no good sledding during the winter. **1873** *Wisconsin Rep.* XXXI. 422 Scott is to..continue them as long as good sledding continues.

**b.** *fig.* With qualifying adj: work or progress in any sphere of action.

**1839** H. GREELEY in *Corr. Griswold* (1898) 26 Payments are slack still, and we have rather hard sledding. **1898** *N. York Evening Post* 21 Oct. 1 Professional labor agitators do not always have smooth sledding in the field of politics. **1908** R. E. BEACH *Barrier* 127 Now them kind of places is all right for married men but they're tough sleddin' for single ones. **1939** L. M. MONTGOMERY *Anne of Ingleside* xxvii. 185 Ye *can* keep a house without a woman, but it's hard sledding. **1954** T. P. KELLEY *Black Donnellys* 57 Damnation—had he somehow, unknowingly, revealed himself? If so, he could sure expect some rough sledding ahead. **1968** M. WOODHOUSE *Rock Baby* iii. 20 It was hard sledding, but after a while I got him to say something definite. **1979** *Arizona Daily Sun* 19 Apr. 4/2 This part of the administration's plan likewise faces tough sledding on Capitol Hill.

**slede**, obs. form of SLEAD.

**sledge** (slɛdʒ), *sb.*[1] Forms: α. 1 slecg, slegc, 4–6 slegge, 5–6 slege, 7 sleage. β. 6–7 sleadge, 7 sledg, 6- sledge. [OE. *slecg* fem., = MDu. and Du. *slegge*, closely related to ON. (also Norw. and Icel.) *sleggja* (MSw. *sleggia, släggia*, Sw. *slägga*; older Da. *slegge, slægge*). The stem **slagj-* is derived from that of the vb. SLAY.] A large heavy hammer usually wielded with both hands, especially the large hammer used by a blacksmith; a sledge-hammer. (See also quot. 1548.)

α. *a* **1000** in Cockayne *Narrat.* (1861) 21 We hit uneaþe mid isernum hamerum and slecgum ȝefyldon. *a* **1000** *Colloq. Ælfric* in Wr.-Wülcker 100 Hwæt sylst us on smiþþan þinre, buton..sweȝincga beatendra slecgea. *c* **1380** *Sir Ferumb.* 1308 To brynge with him anon anuylt, tange & slegge. **1387** TREVISA *Higden* (Rolls) VI. 199 Slegges and hameres, wiþ þe whiche smythes smyteþ..gaddes of iren. *c* **1475** *Partenay* 3000 In hys bosom [the giant] put thre gret slegges wrought. **1485** *Naval Acc. Hen. VII* (1896) 40 Slegges of Iren, ij. **1549** *Privy Council Acts* (1890) II. 350 Sleges, xxx; shovelles and spades, xvᶜ. **1573** in J. C. Jeaffreson *M'sex County Rec.* (1886) I. 79 Duo mallua ferri vocata slegges.

β. **1548** ELYOT *Fistuca*, an instrument, wherwith piles of wood be dryuen into the ground, called a water pile sledge. **1598** BARRET *Theor. Wars* V. iii. 135 Eight great iron sledges to breake rocks. **1603** OWEN *Pembrokeshire* viii. (1892) 62 They make holes and with a woaden sleadge they sett these hurdels fast in the grounde. **1686** PLOT *Staffordsh.* 390, I saw a Smith make a Horse-shooe..almost as quick as if another had struck the Sledg to him. **1778** PRYCE *Min. Cornub.* 236 The solid Ore should be further disunited from the stony part, by spaling with sledges, or cobbing with hammers to a proper size. **1847** LONGF. *Ev.* I. ii. 106 Nothing is left but the blacksmith's sledge. **1882** *Worc. Exhib. Catal.* iii. 8 Some of the samples..stood 300 blows from a 39 lb. sledge before bending.

**b.** Used for throwing, as an athletic exercise.

**1578** LYTE *Dodoens* 217 A yong wenche called Crocus, went forth into the fieldes with Mercurie to throw the sledge. **1600** *Maids Metam.* III. i, Among the games, myselfe put in a pledge, To trie my strength in throwing of the sledge. **1636** W. DENNY in *Ann. Dubrensia* (1877) 16 Some throw the Sledge, and others spurne the Barre. **1795** H. MACNEILL *Will & Jean* ii, Wha wi' Will cou'd..Throw the sledge, or toss the bar?

**sledge** (slɛdʒ), *sb.*[2] Also 7 sledg. [a. MDu. *sleedse* (mod.Du. dial. *sleeds*), related to *slede* SLEAD.

The Du. forms are peculiar to Friesland and North Holland, and may be of Frisian origin.]

**1. a.** A carriage mounted upon runners instead of wheels, and generally used for travelling over snow or ice; a sleigh. Cf. SLED *sb.*[1] 2.

**1617** MORYSON *Itin.* I. 42 We hired a sledge for eight stivers, and were drawne thither over the yce and snow. **1662** J. DAVIES tr. *Olearius' Voy. Amb.* 63 For Winter Travelling, the Muscovites make use of Sledges, made very low. **1709** *Lond. Gaz.* No. 4507/2 The Diversions of the Carnaval began by a Course of Sledges. **1756** NUGENT *Gr. Tour, Germany* II. 208 The ladies take their recreation in sledges of different shapes. **1810** CLARKE *Trav. Russia* (1839) 6/1 They were liable to be..thrown into a sledge, and hurried off to the frontier, or to Siberia. **1886** MABEL COLLINS *Prettiest Woman* xi, Arthur accepted a seat in a sledge for the drive to the lake.

**b.** = SLED *sb.*[1] 2 b.

**1957** *New Scientist* 20 June 16/3 The isolation of such a fault may lead to simpler performance studies on restricted imitative devices... They may be built into the man-carrying centrifuge or rocket sledge to observe changes due to acceleration.

**2. a.** A simple form of conveyance, having runners instead of wheels, employed in the transport of goods over ice or snow or in heavy traffic unsuited to wheeled vehicles; = SLED *sb.*$^{1}$ 1. Rarely, a similar vehicle with low wheels; a trolley.

**1684** *Lond. Gaz.* No. 1904/1 The same Letters add, that 40 Sledges laden with Provisions, had in the night got into Newheusel. **1733** W. ELLIS *Chiltern & Vale Farm.* 89 Take up the Tree..and carry it on a Sledge, or other Carriage, to the Place designed. **1760** R. BROWN *Compl. Farmer* II. 45 In Lancashire they use a sort of sledge that is made with thick wheels to bring their marle out with. **1867** W. W. SMYTH *Coal & Coal-mining* 146 The sledges have to be still commonly used in *putting* the coal along the face of the workings to the better roads. **1884** *Cent. Mag.* Jan. 446/2 Two skids fastened together make a 'drag', or 'sledge'.

**b.** Formerly used for conveying condemned persons to execution. Cf. SLED *sb.*$^{1}$ 1 b.

**1651** G. W. tr. *Cowel's Inst.* 258 Being laid upon a Sledg in straw, he is drawn by a Horse to the place of Execution. *a* **1700** EVELYN *Diary* 22 May 1685, Oates..was this day plac'd on a sledge,..and dragg'd from prison to Tyburn. **1780** *New Newgate Cal.* V. 81 They were drawn to the gallows on a sledge, as is usual in the case of coiners. **1828** SCOTT *F.M. Perth* xxiii, The sledge is even now preparing to drag thee to the place of execution.

**c.** A form of drag or skid. *Obs.*$^{-1}$

**1839** *Civil Eng. & Arch. Jrnl.* II. 122/2 The sledge or retarder..is formed like a wedge.

**3.** *Rope-making.* A travelling structure of considerable weight to which the rope-yarns are attached at one end.

**1794** *Rigging & Seamanship* 56 *Sledges* are frames made of strong oak, clamped with iron... These sledges are loaded to such a degree as the rope in making requires. **1825** J. NICHOLSON *Operat. Mechanic* 437 In some cases the rope is made to haul the sledge backwards, by fastening one end of it to the sledge. **1851–4** *Tomlinson's Cycl. Usef. Arts* (1867) II. 465/1 The sledge is pulled backwards to stretch the yarns tight.

**4.** *attrib.* and *Comb.*, as ***sledge-boat***, ***-crank***, ***-dog***, ***-driver***, ***-head***, etc. **sledge-meter**, a wheel and counting device towed behind a sledge to measure the distance travelled.

**1808** *Sporting Mag.* XXXI. 22 Sailing on the ice in a *sledge-boat. **1797** *Encycl. Brit.* (ed. 3) XVI. 486/1 (Rope-making), By the motion of the *sledge crank the top is forced away from the knot. **1856** KANE *Arctic Expl.* I. xxix. 377 The instinct of a *sledge-dog makes him perfectly aware of unsafe ice. **1819** *Theatrical Inquisitor* Apr. 314 Of the literary talent of the stage manager, we have never thought highly, and his 'Land Storm; or the *Sledge Driver and his Dogs' seems only a little alteration from a piece, called 'Lowina of Tobolski'..by the same author. **1896** *Idler* 306/2 Becoming a proficient 'kayaker' and sledge-driver. **1924** A. J. SMALL *Frozen Gold* i. 15 A..human thunderbolt which hurled at him... A *sledge-head knocked up from nowhere and connected with his chin. **1966** S. HEANEY *Death of Naturalist* 41 The cap juts like a gantry's crossbeam, Cowling plated forehead and sledgehead jaw. **1708** J. C. *Compl. Collier* (1845) 37 One of these two Men that guides the *Sledge-Horses. **1845** [C. H. J. ANDERSON] *Swedish Brothers* 14 The Norwegian looked in vain for a purchaser for his sledge-horses. **1856** KANE *Arctic Expl.* I. viii. 84 A position which might expedite our *sledge journeys in the future. *Ibid.* xxiii. 288 Their *sledge-load of provisions. **1601** in *The Phœnix* II. 227 *Sledgmen, Carmen, Boatmen. **1856** KANE *Arctic Expl.* I. xv. 179 Too cold still..for our sledgemen to set out. **1902** R. F. SCOTT *Jrnl.* 18 Nov. in *Voyage of 'Discovery'* (1905) II. xiii. 24 A dull day.., but we plodded on... Starting at 11 A.M., we pushed on for two and a half miles by our *sledge-meter. **1929** J. G. HAYES *R. E. Peary* x. 166 Peary never used a sledgemeter on the Arctic pack, saying it would have been smashed by the rough surface. **1958** *Times* 2 Jan. 6/5 During last night's painful run the tractors were biting down 2 ft... The 12-hour haul wound a laborious 22 miles through the sledgemeter. **1856** KANE *Arctic Expl.* I. xx. 251 All the *sledge-parties were now once more aboard ship. **1762** LLOYD *Epist. Churchill* Poems 191 So have I seen, amidst the grinning throng, The *sledge procession slowly dragg'd along. **1678–82** in R. M. Fergusson *Logie* (1905) II. 65 Thence northward by a *sledge road up the brae. **1856** KANE *Arctic Expl.* I. xv. 176 A secure and level sledge-road. **1852** *Zoologist* X. 3379 From its tusks are made..*sledge-runners. **1856** KANE *Arctic Expl.* I. 380 The breach was large enough to admit a *sledge-team. **1796** MORSE *Amer. Geogr.* II. 81 The *sledge-way.. becomes so well beaten.

**sledge** (slɛdʒ), *v.*$^{1}$ [f. SLEDGE *sb.*$^{1}$] **a.** *intr.* To use a sledge-hammer. **b.** *trans.* To break or drive in (something) with a sledge-hammer.

**1654** *Queen's Coll. Oxford Acc.* (MS.), Given to D.L. upon a barg for sledgeing. **1815** *Ann. Reg., Chron.* 4 By their continued firing and sledging the door, they at last entered. **1863** B. TAYLOR *H. Thurston* iv. 51 Miss Dilworth little suspected how many rocks she had sledged into pieces.. through Bute Wilson's arm.

**sledge** (slɛdʒ), *v.*$^{2}$ [f. SLEDGE *sb.*$^{2}$]

**1.** *intr.* (See quot.)

**1708** J. C. *Compl. Collier* (1845) 34 We must haue two more Horses of a less Value, bought to sledge out with, or draw the Corves as they come out of the Pit on a Sledge.

**2.** To travel in a sledge. Also with *it.*

**1853** KANE *Grinnell Exp.* vi. (1856) 45 They boat or sledge it from post to post. **1882** H. SEEBOHM *Siberia in Asia* 17 We sledged up one hill and down another.

**3.** *trans.* To carry or convey on a sledge.

**1864** WHEELWRIGHT *Spring Lapl.* 204 We left him, intending to sledge him home the next day. **1900** *Jrnl. R. Archæol. Inst.* LVII. 73 The stone having been sledged down the hill.

Hence **'sledging** *vbl. sb.*$^{1}$

**1853** KANE *Grinnell Exp.* xxix. (1856) 256 The crew had an hour of sledging. **1876** *Daily News* 30 Oct. 5/2 The wearisome sledging of a mile a day.

**'sledge-hammer**, *sb.* [SLEDGE *sb.*$^{1}$] A large heavy hammer used by blacksmiths.

**1495** *Naval Acc. Hen. VII* (1896) 194 Slege hamers of yron. **1791** BENTHAM *Panopt.* I. Postsc. 163, I would arm another part with another gentleman's sledge-hammers. **1818** SCOTT *Hrt. Midl.* vi, The door was instantly assailed with sledge-hammers. **1844** H. STEPHENS *Bk. Farm* II. 398 Smiths will not care how long they detain horses, provided they can get the assistance of the ploughman at the sledge-hammer. **1894** CROCKETT *Raiders* 317 The strikers with the sledge hammer were swept away.

*attrib.* **1843** DICKENS *Let.* 24 Sept. (1974) III. 572, I sent Miss Coutts a sledge-hammer account of the Ragged schools. **1844** HOOD *Forge* 238 Some cumbrous sort Of sledge-hammer retort At Red Beard. **1887** R. N. CAREY *Uncle Max* iii, I was used to this sort of sledge-hammer form of argument.

*fig.* **1799** T. HOLCROFT *Jrnl.* 13 Jan. in *Memoirs* (1816) III. 123 Yet having read mine, you come with a sledge hammer of criticism, describe it as absolutely contemptible. **1874** L. STEPHEN *Hours Libr.* (1892) II. i. 18 Johnson's sledge hammer smashes his flimsy platitudes to pieces. **1890** *Spectator* 12 July, The author demolishes his opponents, sometimes, with almost too heavy a sledge-hammer.

Hence **'sledge-hammer** *v. trans.*, to strike, work at, as with a sledge-hammer. Also **'sledge-hammering** *vbl. sb.*

**1834** SIR G. C. LEWIS *Lett.* (1870) 32, I send you..an admirable letter written by Sedgwick, in order that you may see what is meant by *sledge-hammering* a man. **1840** WHATELY *Let.* in *Life* (1866) I. 473, I have been to-day sledge-hammering your idea about Simeon into a sermon. **1852** DICKENS *Bleak Ho.* xv, I grant a sledge-hammering sort of merit in him. **1884** *Contemp. Rev.* Dec. 796 The concluding pages of one of his sledge-hammerings on the heads of his adversaries. **1963** A. SMITH *Throw out Two Hands* xvi. 167 Sledge-hammering a steel spike into the ground. **1976** *CRC Jrnl.* July 19/1 It is perfectly possible to understand what is going on on stage without having the point sledgehammered home.

**'sledgeless**, *a.* [f. SLEDGE *sb.*$^{2}$ + -LESS.] Without a sledge.

**1853** KANE *Grinnell Exp.* xxix. (1856) 250 All expected to betake ourselves sledgeless to the ice.

**'sledger.** [f. SLEDGE *sb.*$^{2}$ or *v.*$^{2}$] One who drives or draws a sledge.

**1661** *Justiciary Rec.* (S.H.S.) I. 13 Thomas Neilson, sledger in Leith, indyted for stealling of a Horse. **1876** *Daily News* 28 Oct. 5/4 Greenland was explored far to the eastward. The sledgers all suffered from scurvy.

**'sledging**, *vbl. sb.*$^{2}$ *Austral. Cricket slang.* [f. SLEDGE *sb.*$^{1}$ + -ING$^{1}$.] (See quot. 1982.)

**1977** *World of Cricket Monthly* June 5/1 Lillee had his views on intimidating batsmen on Melbourne television. And on *sledging*—the term comes from *subtle as a sledge-hammer.* **1979** *Age* (Melbourne) 2 July 9/6 A year or so earlier the Australian team coined 'sledging' for needling or gamesmanship. **1982** *London Portrait Mag.* May 68/3 *Sledging*, trying to disrupt batsmen's concentration by abusing, teasing them. **1983** *Guardian* 8 Feb. 23/1 Geoff Howarth says he intends to complain about the amount of swearing, sledging and unchecked short-pitched bowling New Zealand have faced.

**'sledgy**, *a. rare.* [f. SLEDGE *sb.*$^{2}$] Sledge-like.

**1798** MISS H. M. WILLIAMS *Tour Switz.* II. 293 Her sledgy-car, with sparkling frost-work bright.

†**sledo.** *Obs.*$^{-1}$ Some article of dress.

**1719** D'URFEY *Pills* I. (ed. 4) 354 Next then the slouching Sledo, and our huge Button, And now our Coats, flanck broad, like Shoulder Mutton.

**slee**, obs. or dial. var. SLAY *v.*$^{1}$, SLOE *sb.*, SLY *a.*

†**'sleeband.** *Sc. Obs. rare.* (See quot. 1825.)

**1535** STEWART *Cron. Scot.* III. 274 Ane husband man.. Vpoun ane nycht his awin pleuch irnis staw, Baith sok and some, culter and sle-band. **1813** W. LESLIE *Surv. Nairne & Moray* Gloss., *Sleeband*, the ancient muzzle of the plough. **1825** JAMIESON *Suppl.*, *Sleeband*, a band of iron which goes round the beam of a plough, for the purpose of strengthening it at the place where the coulter is inserted.

**sleech** (sliːtʃ), *sb. dial.* Also 8–9 **sleetch**, *Sc.* **sleitch.** [app. a later form of SLITCH.]

**1.** Mud deposited by the sea or a river; soil composed of this.

**1587** FLEMING *Contn. Holinshed* III. 1540/1 Wher the slub or sleech is fifteene foot deepe at the least, and the maine rocke immediatlie vnderneath it. **1623** *Tract Parlt.* in *Hartlib's Legacy* (1655) 288 Then would all..the barren lands [be] mended by Marle, Sleech, Lime, Chalk, Seasand, and other means. *c* **1682** J. COLLINS *Making of Salt* 19 The Ground..ought to be a Sea-Mud, Oase or Sleech. **1764** *Museum Rust.* II. 103 As the sea left the marshes by degrees, the tides brought up the mud with them..; which mud we call sleech. **1799** J. ROBERTSON *Agric. Perth* 298 The soil is composed of a heavy, moist sleech. **1844** LD. COCKBURN *Circuit Journ.* 27 Sept. (1888) 254 But when the sea.. shrinks back, what a change! It becomes a world of sleech. **1899** G. NEILSON *Annals of Solway* 44 The salty particles glittering on the sleech like hoar frost.

**2.** A stretch of mud on a shore.

**1902** *Scotsman* 11 Feb. (E.D.D.), There were near Bo'ness wide expanses of flat muddy foreshore, known as 'sleeches', or 'slob-lands',..covered at high tide.

Hence **'sleechy** *a.*, slimy, muddy.

**1792** *Statist. Acc. Scotl.* IV. 138 A very flat, clay or sleetchy shore. **1844** LD. COCKBURN *Circuit Journ.* 27 Sept. (1888) 254 Dismal swamps of deep sleechy mud. **1877** G. FRASER *Wigtown* 192 The lands, fishings, sleechy grounds, and shores mentioned in the summons.

**sleech** (sliːtʃ), *v. Cheshire dial.* [Of obscure origin.] (See quot.)

**1674** RAY *N.C. Words* 43 *To Sleech*, to dip or take up water. [Hence in Grose, etc.]. **1886–7** in Cheshire glossaries.

Hence **'sleeching-net** (see quot. 1886).

**1665** *Chesh. Farm Accs.* in *Sheaf* (1882) II. 333 For the iron frame for the sleeching nett. **1886** HOLLAND *Cheshire Gloss.*, *Sleeching-net*, a net fixed at the end of a long pole, for catching fish.

**sleek** (sliːk), *sb.*$^{1}$ *Sc.* Also **slick, slieck.** [prob. short for *sleek measure*: cf. SLEEK *v.* 1 c, and MFlem. *sleec, sleic* (mod.Flem. *sleek, sleik*) adj., even with the top of the vessel.] A measure for fruit, etc. (see later quots.).

**1705** in W. Hector *Judic. Rec. Renfrewshire* (1876) 42 Ten slicks of keeping apples, such as his lady shall choyce. **1793** in Ure *Hist. Rutherglen* 45 Each Slieck of Fruit, ½d. **1808** JAMIESON Addit., *Sleek*, a measure of fruits, or roots, &c., containing forty pounds. **1820** CLELAND *Rise & Progr. Glasgow* 167 Fruit is sold by the sleek of 20 Scotch pints. **1856** MORTON *Cycl. Agric.* II. 1126 *Sleek* (Clydesdale), of apples or pears, a peck = 2¼ gallons.

**sleek** (sliːk), *sb.*$^{2}$ *Sc. rare.* Also 8 **sleik.** [? Related to SLEECH *sb.* or SLECK *sb.*] Mud; a mud-bank.

**1774** D. GRAHAM *Hist. Rebell.* Wks. 1883 I. 206 The pilot run her into a creek, Got past the breakers, 'mong sand and sleik. **1875** A. SMITH *New Hist. Aberdeenshire* I. 31 The sleeks of the estuary of the Ythan.

**sleek** (sliːk), *sb.*$^{3}$ *Naut.* [f. SLEEK *a.*] (See quot. and cf. SLICK *sb.*$^{1}$ 3 a.)

**1840** F. D. BENNETT *Narr. Whaling Voy.* II. v. 202 Broad oily tracks, or 'sleeks' on the surface of the water, (produced by the recent passage of a party of cetaceans).

**sleek** (sliːk), *a.* and *adv.* Forms: 6 **sleke, slieke, sleake,** 6–7 **sleik, sleeke,** 7– **sleek.** [Later variant form of ME. *slike* SLICK *a.*]

**1.** Of animals, their limbs, etc.: Having, or covered with, hair or fur which lies close and smooth, usually a sign of good condition or careful attention.

**1590** SHAKS. *Mids. N.* IV. i. 3 While I..sticke muske roses in thy sleeke smoothe head. **1634** HEYWOOD & BROME *Lanc. Witches* IV. H.'s Wks. 1874 IV. 223 You may see by his plump belly and sleeke legs he hath not bin sore travail'd. **1714** GAY *Sheph. Week* Monday 36 See this Tobacco Pouch that's lin'd with Hair, Made of the Skin of sleekest fallow Deer. **1774** GOLDSM. *Nat. Hist.* (1776) IV. 91 No quadrupede is fatter, none has a more sleek or glossy skin [than the mole]. **1822** W. IRVING *Braceb. Hall* ii. (1877) 16 She rode a sleek white pony. **1859** CAPERN *Ball. & Songs* 148 The sleek and dappled kine.

**b.** Of hair, etc., in this condition.

**1829** LYTTON *Disowned* 7 Bright were the eyes and sleek the tresses of the damsel. **1841** —— *Night & M.* I. vi, His hair short, dark, and sleek. **1859** DICKENS *T. Two Cities* I. iv, He wore an odd little sleek crisp flaxen wig.

**2.** Of surfaces: Entirely free from roughness; perfectly smooth or polished.

**1589** PUTTENHAM *Eng. Poesie* III. (Arb.) 251 Her bosome sleake as Paris plaster. *a* **1601** ? MARSTON *Pasquil & Kath.* III. (1878) 136 With a soft sleeke hand I'le clap thy cheeke. **1665** HOOKE *Microgr.* 100 A very smooth and sleek surface, almost like the surface of black sealing wax. *a* **1722** LISLE *Husb.* (1757) 218 In hot dry weather the oat-straw will be so sleek, that it will be troublesome loading and tying it together so as not to slide off from the cart. **1754** GRAY *Lett.* (1900) I. 254 The rock is cut up till it is as smooth and as sleek as sattin. **1807** J. BERESFORD *Miseries Hum. Life* XX. xii, Using once more a discarded nutmeg-grater or a sleek file! **1842** PRICHARD *Nat. Hist. Man* 306 Their skin, though but an indifferent black, is always sleek and smooth.

**b.** Of the sea or sky: Unruffled, tranquil. *rare.*

**1603** DRAYTON *Bar. Wars* III. xlvii, On the sleeke waters waft her sayles along. **1611** MIDDLETON & DEKKER *Roaring Girl* D.'s Wks. 1873 III. 181 After a storme the face of heauen looks sleeke. **1837** CARLYLE *Fr. Rev.* II. I. iii, What sulphur-cloud is that that defaces the sleek sea?

**3.** Oily, fawning, plausible, specious.

**1599** B. JONSON *Cynthia's Rev.* I. ii, Slieke flatterie and shee Are twin-borne sisters. **1605** CHAPMAN, etc. *Eastw. Hoe* II. ii, They be the smoothest and sleekest knaves in a country. **1613** SHAKS. *Hen. VIII*, III. ii. 241 How sleeke and wanton Ye appeare in euery thing may bring my ruine! *a* **1789** MICKLE *Siege of Marseilles* II. iv, With sleek adulterous smiles. **1821** SHELLEY *Hellas* 541 After the war is fought, yield the sleek Russian That which thou canst not keep. **1850** KINGSLEY *A. Locke* iv, Being the sleek, subtle, religious sins they are.

**b.** Dexterous, skilful. = SLICK *a.* 4.

**1822** HAZLITT *Table-t.* Ser. II. i, The waiter who is a sleek hand.

**4.** Of persons: Having a smooth skin, esp. as the result of being in good condition; plump.

**1637** MILTON *Lycidas* 99 On the level brine, Sleek Panope with all her sisters play'd. **1699** GARTH *Dispens.* I. 7 How sleik their looks, how goodly is their Mien, When big they strut behind a double Chin. **1714** N. ROWE *Hor. Ep.* I. iv, Me..Batt'ning in Ease you'll find, sleek, fresh, and fair. **1746** FRANCIS tr. *Hor. Ep.* I. iv. 28 Here, in sleek and joyous Case, You'll find..An Hog by Epicurus fed. **1820** LAMB *Elia* I. *Christ's Hospital*, Sleek well-fed blue-coat boys. **1877** L. MORRIS *Epic of Hades* 91 What were it to lie Sleek, crowned with roses.

*fig.* **1843** CARLYLE *Past & Pres.* II. xi, Monarchism itself.. lies sleek and buried. **1878** GEO. ELIOT *Coll. Breakf. P.* 367 In a sleek and rural apathy.

**5.** *Coal-mining.* (See quot.)

**1883** GRESLEY *Gloss. Coal-m.* 225 *Sleek*, soft and troublesome, as applied to the state of the floor in steep seams.

**6.** As *adv.* In a smooth or sleek manner.

**1602** MARSTON *Antonio's Rev.* IV. i, The chub-fac't fop Shines sleeke with full cramm'd fat of happinesse. **1735** SOMERVILLE *Chase* II. 494 Nor can his spotted Skin, Tho' sleek it shine,.. Save the proud Pard from unrelenting Fate. **1774** GOLDSM. *Nat. Hist.* (1776) V. 161 The feathers, which lie so sleek and in such beautiful order. **1859** DICKENS *T. Two Cities* I. iv, His brown stockings fitted sleek and close.

**7.** *Comb.*, as ***sleek-browed***, ***-faced***, ***-haired***, ***-headed***, ***-looking***, ***-skinned***.

**1601** SHAKS. *Jul. C.* I. ii. 193 Let me haue men about me, that are fat, Sleeke-headed men. **1602** MARSTON *Ant. & Mel.* I. Wks. 1856 I. 11 With most obsequious sleek-brow'd intertain. **1604** MIDDLETON *Father Hubburd's T.* Wks. (Bullen) VIII. 107 A fair sleek-faced courtier. **1661** BRATHWAIT *Comment. Two Tales* (1901) 49 You say a sleek-skinn'd Cat will ever go a Caterwawing. **1760–72** H. BROOKE *Fool of Qual.* (1809) III. 41 The advice of his sleek-headed ministry. **1823** COBBETT *Rural Rides* (1885) I. 290 This school-master was a sleek-looking young fellow. **1840** DICKENS *Barn. Rudge* iv, An old-fashioned, thin-faced, sleek-haired,.. small-eyed little fellow. **1853** JAMES *Agnes Sorel* (1860) II. 221 Were I.. a sleek-faced negotiator.

**sleek** (sliːk), *v.* Also 5 slekyn, 6 sleke, 6–7 sleak, 7 sleeke, sleik. [Later variant form of ME. *slīke(n* SLICK *v.*]

**1. a.** *trans.* To make sleek or smooth by rubbing or polishing.

*c* **1440** *Promp. Parv.* 459/1 Slekyn, *licibricinnulo.* **1615** G. SANDYS *Trav.* 72 They curiously sleeke their paper, which is thick. **1683** PEPYS *Diary at Tangier* in *Life* (1841) I. 422 When dry, they sleek it [calico] with smooth shells, and roll it up. **1771** LUCKOMBE *Hist. Print.* 33 The paper.. was sleeked with a tooth or shell. **1852** MORFIT *Arts of Tanning*, etc. 375 The skin is.. sleeked with a round-knife. **1879** *Cassell's Techn. Educ.* IV. 175 A hide of leather is.. sleeked down till the surface is perfectly smooth.

**b.** To reduce to smoothness; to invest with a smooth unruffled appearance.

**1513** [see SLEEKED *ppl. a.* 1]. **1619** DRAYTON *Bar. Wars* III. 47 Sleek eu'ry little Dimple of the Lake: Sweet Syrens, and be readie with your Song. **1813** HOGG *Queen's Wake*, *Kilmeny* xii, The moon that sleeks the sky. **1834** AIRD *Churchyard Eclog.* 119 Forth looks the sun,.. and sleeks the slippery hills.

**c.** *Sc.* To fill to, make level with, the brim or top.

**1863** R. QUINN *Heather Lintie* (ed. 2) 126 Although the tears I shed behin' her Wad sleek a sheuch. **1882** *Jamieson's Sc. Dict.* s.v., 'Noo, sleek the stimpart,' i.e. smooth or level the grain in the measure.

**2. a.** To make (the skin, hair, etc.) smooth and glossy.

**1508** *Mayd Emlyn* 49 in Hazl. *E.P.P.* IV. 85 Ofte wolde she sleke To make smothe her cheke, With redde roses therin. **1609** DEKKER *Gull's Horn Bk.* Wks. (Grosart) II. 212 A round face sleekt and washt ouer with whites of egges. **1634** MILTON *Comus* 832 Fair Ligea's golden comb, Wherwith she sits.. Sleeking her soft alluring locks. **1720** POPE *Iliad* XXIII. 350 That wont to deck Their flowing manes, and sleek their glossy neck. **1786** *Pogmologia* 133 Thick beards sleeked in the same manner as their hair is. **1830** TENNYSON *A Character* ii, He smooth'd his chin and sleek'd his hair. **1895** A. NUTT *Voy. Bran* I. 238 Two great eagles come and sleek the great bird with their bills.

*refl.* **1891** C. E. NORTON *Dante's Purgat.* viii. 51 Licking like a beast that sleeks itself.

**b.** *to sleek up*, to make presentable, or of attractive appearance.

**1618** FLETCHER *Chances* III. i, Sleek up your self, leave crying, For I must have ye entertain this Lady With all civility. *a* **1639** W. WHATELEY *Prototypes* I. xix. (1640) 241 There is such a man's servant, she is exceedingly sleeked up, see.. what a dress shee hath.

**c.** To lay *back*, to flatten.

**1894** CROCKETT *Raiders* vi, The poor beast.. stood most pitifully still, sleeking back its ears.

**d.** To draw (a comb) through hair with a smoothing effect.

**1959** *Listener* 21 May 904/1 The boys sleeking combs through their hair. **1967** G. B. MAIR *Girl from Peking* vii. 73 The Admiral.. was sleeking a comb through his thinning hair.

**3.** *transf.* or *fig.* To render sleek or smooth, in various senses: **a.** Denoting removal of agitation, disturbance, deep thought, etc.

**1605** SHAKS. *Macb.* III. ii. 27 Gentle my Lord, sleeke o're your rugged Lookes, Be bright and Iouiall. **1640** YORKE *Union Hon., Commend. Verses*, So much fancy, as may sleeke My Lords brow, and dimple my Ladies cheeke. **1859** TENNYSON *Merlin & V.* 748 To sleek her ruffled peace of mind. **1864** CARLYLE *Fredk. Gt.* XVII. ii. (1865) VII. 19 So very possible to sleek them down into peace, thought Majesty's Ministry.

**b.** Denoting the assumption of friendly or flattering looks or speech. Cf. SLEEKED *ppl. a.* 2.

**1607** DEKKER & MARSTON *Northw. Hoe* I. D.'s Wks. 1873 III. 17 Ile candy o're my words, and sleeke my brow. **1671** MILTON *P.R.* IV. 5 The perswasive Rhetoric That sleek't his tongue. **1876** MORRIS *Sigurd* II. 109 So I wrapped my heart in guile And sleeked my tongue with sweetness.

*refl.* **1877** TENNYSON *Harold* I. i. 80 He hath learnt.. To sleek and supple himself to the king's hand.

**c.** To polish (a composition). Also with *over.*

**1630** T. CAREW *To Ben Jonson*, Repine not at the taper's thrifty waste, That sleeks thy terser poems. **1635** PEMBLE *Grace & Faith* Pref. 1 Unto my apprehension, such Prologues, however sleeked over, doe yet feele rough and uneven.

**d.** To gloze *over*, put in a favourable light.

**1871** TENNYSON *Last Tourn.* 391 Musing how to smoothe And sleek his marriage over to the Queen.

**4.** *intr.* To move, glide, sweep *on* smoothly.

**1818** L. HUNT *Foliage, Nymphs* ii, For as the racks came sleeking on, one fell With rain into a dell.

Hence **'sleeking** *vbl. sb.* (also *attrib.*) and *ppl. a.*

**1579** LYLY *Euphues* (Arb.) 116, I loath almost to thincke on.. the sleeking of their faces. **1632** MARMION *Holland's Leaguer* III. iv, Wherefore are all your sleekings and your curlings.. composed by art? **1827** HOOD *Hero & Leander* lix, His sleeking hair Creeps o'er her knees. **1873** O'CURRY *Lect. Ancient Irish* III. 116 The sleeking stick or bone which weavers still use. **1883** R. HALDANE *Workshop Rec.* Ser. II. 368/1 After washing the grain with the grass-brush, it is followed by the sleeking-iron.

**sleeked** (sliːkt), *ppl. a.* [f. prec. + -ED[1].]

**1.** Smoothed; having a glossy skin, etc.

**1513** DOUGLAS *Æneid* VI. xii. 15 All fischis.. doith repair Ondir the sleikit see of marbill hew. **1611** FLORIO, *Cartêlla*, a kind of sleeked pasteboord. **1616** B. JONSON *Forest* viii, Sleeked limmes, and finest blood. **1653** URQUHART *Rabelais* III. viii, By reason of their.. curled, frisling, sleeked smoothness. **1785** BURNS *To a Mouse* i, Wee, sleeket, cowran, tim'rous beastie. **1818** KEATS *Endym.* I. 468 As a dove Trembling its closed eyes and sleeked wings About me. **1861** MISS YONGE *Stokesley Secret* (1880) 199 Captain Merrifield's fine sleeked cows were licking each other.

**2.** *Sc.* Specious, flattering; artful; plausible.

*c* **1400** *Sc. Trojan War* (Horstm.) II. 1838 Oetus.. Told a foule fenȝeit fortoune fals.. With sleked wordis subtelly. **1513** DOUGLAS *Æneid* I. x. 27 Now him withaldis the Phenitiane Dido, And cuilȝeis him with slekit wordis sle. *a* **1585** MONTGOMERIE *Cherrie & Slae* 547 With sleikit sophismis seiming sweit. **1776** C. KEITH *Farmer's Ha'* xxvii, His sleekit speeches pass for true With ane and a'. **1823** GALT *R. Gilhaize* I. xii. 131, I did nae think the sleekit sinner had art enough to play 't. **1895** 'H. HALIBURTON' *Dunbar* 92 Sleekit he was, an' carefu' to conceal.

Hence **'sleekedness.** *rare*[−1].

*a* **1693** *Urquhart's Rabelais* III. xiii. 109 If that the polish'd sleekedness thereof be darken'd by gross Breathings.

**sleeken** ('sliːk(ə)n), *v.* [f. SLEEK *a.* + -EN[5].] *trans.* To make smooth and glossy. Also *fig.*

**1621** BURTON *Anat. Mel.* II. iv. I. iv, The Eban stone which Goldsmiths use to sleeken their gold with. **1688** HOLME *Armoury* II. 41/2 The Sleek stone, a ball made of glass, which Landresses and Drawers of Cloath use to polish or sleeken their Linnen with. **1824** MACTAGGART *Gallovid. Encycl.* 150 Young gorbs which he did fin'.. Whilk sleekened his skin. *c* **1844** MRS. BROWNING *Portrait* xviii, All voices that address her, Soften, sleeken every word. **1862** *Temple Bar* VI. 132 Society.. sleekens the boy into a machine well-oiled, and superfinishes the girl.

**sleeker** ('sliːkə(r)). [f. SLEEK *v.* + -ER[1].] One who sleeks; an implement used for sleeking leather, cloth, etc.

**1611** COTGR., *Estire*, the yron toole wherwith a Currier draynes the skins he receiues from the Tan-pit; some call it a Sleeker. *Ibid.*, *Polisseur*, a polisher;.. sleeker, smoother. **1883** R. HALDANE *Workshop Rec.* Ser. II. 368/1 The skin is.. worked with a 'sleeker' or stretching-iron.

**sleekish** ('sliːkɪʃ), *a.* [f. SLEEK *a.* + -ISH[1].] Somewhat sleek.

**1850** *New Monthly Mag.* Nov. 265 Drawn by a pair of sleekish horses.

**sleek-leaf.** *U.S.* [SLEEK *a.*] The sand-myrtle, *Leiophyllum buxifolium.*

**1845–50** MRS. LINCOLN *Lect. Bot.* App. 219/2. **1855** J. DARBY *Bot. S. States* 421.

**sleekly** ('sliːklɪ), *adv.* [f. SLEEK *a.* + -LY[2].] In a sleek manner. Also *fig.*, smoothly.

**1730** RAMSAY *Fables, Ape & Leopard* 12 My fur sae delicate and fine, With various spots does sleekly shine. **1826** HOOD *Irish Schoolm.* xxvii, The verdant sod, With tender moss so sleekly overgrown. **1877** 'SAXON' *Galloway Gossip* 245 Things didn't move so sleekly in that house after.

**sleekness** ('sliːknɪs). [f. SLEEK *a.*] The quality of being sleek.

**1628** FELTHAM *Resolves* I. xxxii, I confesse, we may liue to .. the sleekenesse of the declining crowne. **1751** JOHNSON *Rambler* No. 138 ¶10 They [*sc.* the horses] lost their sleekness and grace, and were soon purchased at half the value. **1771** H. MACKENZIE *Man of Feeling* xxi. 75 This coat .. spoke of the sleekness of folly, and the threadbareness of wisdom. **1811** *Self Instructor* 561 The glare and sleekness of the sattin. **1868** GEO. ELIOT *Felix Holt* 31 He.. was especially addicted to black satin waistcoats, which carried out the general sleekness of his appearance. **1897** MARY KINGSLEY *W. Africa* 322 The beautiful little gazelles.., white underneath, and satin-like in sleekness all over.

**'sleekstone.** *Obs.* exc. *dial.* Also 5 slek(y)-, 5–6 sleke-, 6–7 sleeke-. [f. SLEEK *a.* or *v.* Cf. SLICKSTONE.]

**1.** A smooth stone used for smoothing and polishing.

**14..** *Nom.* in Wr.-Wülcker 696 *Hoc lacinatorium*, a slekstone. *c* **1440** *Promp. Parv.* 458/2 Slekyston,.. *linitorium.* **1530** PALSGR. 720, I make paper smothe with a sleke stone. **1563** T. GALE *Antidot.* II. 64 Stripe them [clouts] wyth a sleeke stone and make them smouthe. **1580** LYLY *Euphues* (Arb.) 220 Shee that wanteth a sleeke-stone to smooth hir linnen, wil take a pebble. **1612** PEACHAM *Graphice* 94 Take of the fairest and smothest pastboord you can get, which with a sleeke stone rubbe as smooth, and as euen as you can. **1641** MILTON *Animadv.* Wks. 1851 III. 191 A toothlesse Satyr is as improper as a toothed sleekstone. **1688** [see SLEEKEN *v.*]. **1893–4** HESLOP *Northumbld. Gloss.* 656 *Sleekstone*, a polishing stone.

**2.** *transf.* (See quot.)

*a* **1610** HEALEY *Theophrastus* (1636) 19 A Sleeke-stone or Smooth-boot (as we terme him) is hee, that saluteth a man as farre off as his eye can carry levell.

**sleeky** ('sliːkɪ), *a.* [f. SLEEK *a.* + -Y.]

**1.** Marked by sleek condition.

*c* **1725** THOMSON *Soporif. Doctor* 1 Sweet sleeky Doctor! dear pacific soul! **1757** DYER *Fleece* I. 669 All intent to.. wind the sleeky Fleece. *Ibid.* III. 323 The grazier's sleeky kine obstruct the roads. *a* **1814** *Love, Honor & Interest* I. i. in *New Brit. Theatre* III. 265 Like a sleeky snail That climbs into a hive. **1839** *Blackw. Mag.* XLVI. 654 We feel him rubbing his sleeky person against our dexter leg.

**2.** = SLEEKED *ppl. a.* 2.

*a* **1800** in Cromek *Nithsdale Song* (1810) 187 Gane he has wi' the sleeky auld carle. **1822** HOGG *Perils of Man* II. 314 Sleeky Tam possesses both his own and his neighbour's farm at this day. **1863** HOLME LEE *A. Warleigh* III. 3 The most sleeky evil countenance she had ever beheld.

**sleely:** see SLYLY *adv.*

**sleeness**, Sc. variant of SLYNESS.

**sleep** (sliːp), *sb.* Forms: α. 1 slæp, 1, 3–4 (6 *Sc.*) slep (3 sclep), 1, 4– sleep; 1, 3 *dat.* slæpe 3 *dat.*, 6 sleape, 1–3 *dat.*, 4–6 slepe (5 sclepe, sleppe), 5–7 sleepe; 6 *Sc.* sleip(e. β. 1, 3 slap, 2, 4 slape, 4 slope. [OE. *slǽp* (*slāp*), *slēp*, = OFris. *slêp* (WFris. *sliep*, NFris. *slîp*), MDu. *slaep* (Du. *slaap*), OS. (MLG. and LG.) *slâp*, OHG. *slâf*, *sclâf*, *sclâph* (MHG. *slâf*, G. *schlaf*), Goth. *slēps* (wanting in Scandinavian), the sb. corresponding to SLEEP *v.*

On the relation of the rare OE. *slāp* to the usual *slǽp* see the note to the verb. The form is also scantily represented in ME., the following being the more important examples of it (cf. also the rimes in *King & Hermit* 196, 286):—

*a* **1000** in *Englische Stud.* IX. 40 Slape, *somno.* *c* **1200** *Trin. Coll. Hom.* 77 [He] mineȝeð us.. bidden þat he.. weche us of ure heuie slape. *c* **1200** ORMIN 1903 Crist ras upp off dæþess slap. *a* **1300** *Cursor M.* 7201 Sampson wakkend of his slape. *c* **1350** *Will. Palerne* 1995 My lady lis ȝit a-slape. *a* **1400** *Bone Flor.* (R.) 1632 When he wyste they were on slope, To Betres throte can he grope.]

**1. a.** The unconscious state or condition regularly and naturally assumed by man and animals, during which the activity of the nervous system is almost or entirely suspended, and recuperation of its powers takes place; slumber, repose.

Also, a similar state artificially induced, as ***hypnotic*** (or ***magnetic***) ***sleep***. For *dead sleep* see DEAD *a.* 2 b. The word is further applied to the more inert condition of certain animals during hibernation.

*c* **825** *Vesp. Ps.* cxxvi. 2 Ðonne seleð scyldum his slep. *c* **897** K. ÆLFRED tr. *Gregory's Past. C.* xxxix. 283 Sio slæwð ȝiett slæp on ðone monnan. *c* **950** *Lindisf. Gosp.* Luke v. 9 Slep.. ymb-salde hine & Alle ðaðe mið him weron. *c* **1000** ÆLFRIC *Gen.* xv. 12 On æfnunge befeoll slæp on Abram. *c* **1205** LAY. 15707 Þenne ich wæs on bedde iswaued mid soft mine slepen. **12..** *Prayer our Lady* 9 in *O.E. Misc.* 192 Slep me hað mi lif forstole richt half oðer more. *c* **1369** CHAUCER *Dethe Blaunche* 137 Goo.. to Morpheus, Thou knowist hym well, the god of slepe. **1430–40** LYDG. *Bochas* I. viii. (1544) 15 She gaue him milke, yᵉ slepe fell in his hede. **1513** DOUGLAS *Æneid* VIII. vii. 84 The plesand naturall slep.. can he tak. **1596** SPENSER *F.Q.* VI. viii. 38 Sleepe they sayd would make her battill better. **1617** MORYSON *Itin.* II. 46 My selfe being at all howers (but time of sleepe) admitted into his chamber. **1658** *Whole Duty of Man* ix. §i. 75 Sleep comes as a medicine to weariness, as a repairer of decay. **1742** GRAY *Propertius* ii. 17 If sinking into Sleep she seem to close Her languid Lids. **1774** GOLDSM. *Nat. Hist.* (1776) II. 139 Sleep is,.. to some, a very agreeable period of their existence. **1821** BYRON *Sardanap.* IV. i, If Sleep shows such things, what may not death disclose? **1884** DAY *Fishes Gt. Brit.* I. p. xix, Does sleep or a periodical season of repose for the organs of the senses, ever visit fish?

*transf.* **1818** SHELLEY *Rosalind & H.* 1207 Then a dead sleep fell on my mind. **1876** *Encycl. Brit.* IV. 716 Among other notions which they had imbibed, was that of a sleep of the soul after death.

**b.** Freq. in prepositional phrases, as *to*, *in* or † *on*, *out of* or † *of*, *sleep*. (Cf. also ASLEEP *adv.*)

In some of the phrases with *to* it is not always clear whether the noun or verb is intended.

(*a*) *Beowulf* 1251 Siȝon þa to slæpe. *a* **1300** *Cursor M.* 20496 All þar fell to slepe. **1390** GOWER *Conf.* I. 271 The nyht, whan he was leid to slepe. *c* **1450** *St. Cuthbert* (Surtees) 3347 When þai etyn and to slepe ȝode. **1634** SIR T. HERBERT *Trav.* 5 The Sailers, who.. commonly goe to sleepe.. in their wet clothes. **1764** REID *Inquiry* v. §7 A child that has a good musical ear, may be put to sleep.. by the modulation of musical sounds. **1837** DICKENS *Pickw.* iv, Damn that boy, he's gone to sleep again. **1885** MRS. LYNN LINTON *C. Kirkland* II. ii. 68 You.. went happily to sleep.

*transf.* *c* **1440** *Pallad. on Husb.* XIII. 42 His fruyt in picched pottis me may kepe, In drosse of grape or applis leid to slepe.

(*b*) *c* **897** K. ÆLFRED tr. *Gregory's Past. C.* xxviii. 195 Ðonne hnappað he oð he wierð on fæstum slæpe. *c* **1200** ORMIN 8352 He comm till himm o nahht & fand himm þanne o slæpe. *a* **1300** *Cursor M.* 2974 Bot godd on night com to þe king, In slepe. *c* **1450** *Merlin* i. 10 She fill on slepe on her bedde. **1566** *Pasquine in Traunce* 62 To wake the waspes of Germaine, that were on sleepe. **1640** *Plymouth Col. Rec.* (1855) I. 156 In the morneing he found them on sleep by the fyer. **1651** HOBBES *Leviath.* II. xxvii. 156 Dreams be naturally but the fancies remaining in sleep. **1780** *Mirror* No. 73, A particular train of thought impressed upon us in sleep. **1819** SCOTT *Ivanhoe* xxix, The bold and buoyant spirit which forsakes them not even in sleep!

(*c*) *a* **900** CYNEWULF *Elene* 75 He of slæpe onbrægd. *c* **960** *Rule St. Benet* (Schröer) 2 Nu is tima, þæt we of slepe arisan.

c 1200 ORMIN 3136 Josæp..ras himm upp off slæpe anan. 1310 *St. Brendan* (Bälz) 457 Þe fisches sturt up vor hor song, as hi awoke of slepe. 1388 WYCLIF *Gen.* xxviii. 16 Whanne Jacob hadde wakyd of sleep. 1526 TINDALE *John* xi. 11, I goo to wake him out of slepe.

**c.** Personified (after L. *Somnus*, Gr. Ὕπνος).

1390 GOWER *Conf.* II. 101 Sche bad Yris..To Slepes hous that sche schal wende, And bidde him [etc.]. c 1460 SIR R. ROS *La Belle Dame* 2 Halfe in a dreme..The golden slepe me wrapt vndir his wyng. 1563 *Mirr. Mag.* Q iv, By him lay heavy slepe, the cosin of death. 1651 DAVENANT *Gondibert* I. vi. 80 Kind Sleep, Nights welcome Officer. 1718 POPE *Iliad* XIV. 265 The cave of Death's half-brother, Sleep. 1842 TENNYSON *Gardener's D.* 263 Night..in her bosom bore the baby, Sleep.

**d.** The effects or signs of sleep. Also *spec.*, the solid substance found in the corners of the eyes and along the edges of the eyelids after sleep.

1864 LOWELL *Fireside Trav.* 103 A drowsy maid with the sleep scarce brushed out of her hair. 1905 in *Eng. Dial. Dict.* 1922 'R. WEST' *Judge* I. iv. 195 Richard was sitting in front of the fire, rubbing the sleep out of his eyes. 1951 L. MACNEICE tr. *Goethe's Faust* 241 Children, you have scarcely scrubbed your eyes of sleep—and bored already? 1955 J. D. SALINGER in *New Yorker* 29 Jan. 27/1 He began to massage the side of his face.., removing..a bit of sleep from one eye. 1973 P. WHITE *Eye of Storm* vii. 300 The girl stood..washing the sleep out of her eyes.

**e.** *to lose sleep over*, etc.: see LOSE *v.*[1] 3 b.

**2. a.** With possessive pronouns, freq. in adverbial phrases, as ***in his sleep***, etc. Also, in hyperbolic phrase ***could do something in one's sleep*** and varr.

c 825 *Vesp. Ps.* lxxv. 5 Slypton slep heara & nowiht ȝemoettun. c 1100 *Canterb. Ps.* lxxv. 6 Hie slepon sleep *vel* swefne hiræ. 1297 R. GLOUC. (Rolls) 328 Him þoȝte þe ymage in is slep tolde him is chance. c 1386 CHAUCER *Nun's Pr. T.* 188–9 This man out of his sleepe for feere abrayde; But whan that he was wakened of his sleepe [etc.]. c 1400 LOVE *Bonavent. Mirr.* (1908) 64 The aungel of god apered to Joseph in his slepe. c 1450 *St. Cuthbert* (Surtees) 6259 When he of his slepe wakynd. 1573 G. HARVEY *Letter-bk.* (Camden) 131 In my very sleepe, I was adrempt in this wise. 1651 HOBBES *Leviath.* I. iii. 9 To hinder and break our sleep. 1667 MILTON *P.L.* v. 3 His sleep Was Aerie light, from pure digestion bred. 1712 M. HENRY *Daily Comm. w. God* (1822) 372 That will break a worldly man's heart, which will not break a godly man's sleep. 1820 KEATS *Eve St. Agnes* xxxiv, She still beheld, Now wide awake, the vision of her sleep. 1852 M. ARNOLD *Tristr. & Iseult* 59 Hark! he mutters in his sleep. 1953 E. COXHEAD *Midlanders* viii. 187 There's no difficulty. We could make them in our sleep. 1970 J. BRAINE *Stay with me till Morning* i. 9 His job didn't claim much of his energy. He could, as they say, do it in his sleep.

†**b.** In *pl.*, of more than one person. *Obs.*

1586 J. HOOKER *Hist. Irel.* in *Holinshed* II. 160/1 Taking aduantage of the time, when men were wearie and in their sleepes. 1603 DEKKER *Wonderfull Yeare* Wks. (Grosart) I. 105 All his famiy destroied in their sleepes by the mercilesse fire. 1653 HOLCROFT *Procopius, Gothic Wars* I. 25 The people of Rome..being put also to guard the walls, and want their sleepes.

†**c.** With allusion to sleeping together. *Obs.*$^{-1}$

1612 WEBSTER *White Devil* II. i, Fare you well, Our sleeps are sever'd.

**3. a.** A period or occasion of slumber. Also, in phr. ***to have*** or ***get one's sleep out***, to sleep until one wakes naturally.

c 1200 ORMIN 3152 And tær he ras upp off þatt slæp. *Ibid.* 7043 Cristess resste & Cristess ro & Cristess swete slæpess. 1340 *Ayenb.* 31 Hi hedden leuere lyese vour messen þanne ..ane slep. c 1374 CHAUCER *Boeth.* II. metr. 5. ȝoþei slepen holesom slepes vpon þe gras. a 1400–50 *Alexander* 375 Qwen..folke was on þaire firste slepe. 1535 COVERDALE *Ps.* lxxxix. 5 They are euen as a slepe, and fade awaye sodenly like the grasse. 1579 W. WILKINSON *Confut. Fam. Love* 17 b, All your fantasies are but as..the sleepes of a sick man. a 1619 DANIEL *Coll. Hist. Eng* (1626) 56 His owne sleepes.. are saide to haue beene very tumultuous, and full of affrightments. 1685 C. GARDINER *Let.* in M. M. Verney *Mem.* (1899) IV. ix. 341 Your grandsons shall have their sleep out beefore they goe. 1692 PRIOR *To Charles Montague* Wks. (Bell) I. 46 So, whilst in feverish sleeps we think We taste what waking we desire. 1706 E. WARD *Wooden World Diss.* (1708) 69 His Sleeps are moderate enough, just to suffice Nature. 1764 *London Mag.* 417/1 She fell into a sleep which held four days. 1863 W. C. BALDWIN *Afr. Hunting* iii. 91 Towards morning I got a good sleep. 1899 *Allbutt's Syst. Med.* VIII. 412 Between the sleeps the general tendency is to quiet indifference. 1911 F. H. BURNETT *Secret Garden* xvii. 183 'You must go back and get your sleep out,' she said. 1930 A. BENNETT *Imperial Palace* lvii. 434 She had told him to call her. He had refused; she must have her sleep out.

**b.** As an indication or division of time.

1131 *O.E. Chron.* (Laud MS.) an. 1131, On an Mone-niht æt þe forme slæp. c 1500 *Melusine* 186 They departed about the first slepe. 1670 N. CARTERET in *S. Carolina Hist. Soc. Coll.* (1897) V. 166 The Caseeka..was within one sleep of us. 1702 C. MATHER *Magn. Christi* III. App. (1852) 559 Their [the Indians'] division of time is by sleeps, and moons, and winters. 1893 *Arena* Mar 495 Time is divided by them into 'sleeps', and in the same way they [the Indians] estimate distances and journeys. 1896 C. WHITNEY *On Snow-Shoes to Barren Grounds* 182 The one 'sleep' did not bring us up to the caribou, but it took us north to the lodge of another Indian. 1919 CODY & COOPER *Memories of Buffalo Bill* 312 It was many sleeps away. 1953 D. CUSHMAN *Stay away, Joe* 53 From three-four sleeps came riders to the tepee of our father.

**c.** *fig.* A prison term, usu. comparatively short. *slang* (orig. *U.S.*).

1911 D. LOWRIE *My Life in Prison* vi. 63 A year sentence is known as a 'sleep'. 1931 'D. STIFF' *Milk & Honey Route* vi. 65 Any time you want to retreat to some such place for a short or long rest or 'sleep', just go to the social worker displaying the proper symptoms. 1938 J. PHELAN *Lifer* xix. 202, I wasn't interested myself [in escaping]. Three years was nothing—just a sleep, as you chaps put it. 1971 D. BAGLEY *Freedom Trap* iii. 59 In prison jargon, a 'sleep' is a sentence from six months to two years; a 'cut' is from two to four years, and a 'stretch' is anything over four years.

**4.** *fig.* **a.** The repose of death. (Usually with qualifying terms or phrases.) ***to put to sleep***, to kill, esp. painlessly; also *fig.*

a 900 CYNEWULF *Crist* 890 Byman..hatað hy upp astandan sneome of slæpe þy fæstan. c 1200 ORMIN 19254 He ras..Off dæþess slæp to life. a 1400 *Minor Poems fr. Vernon MS.* xxiii. 1130 Þe geaunt..þat wel a-wakeþ þe slepynge Of sleep of deþ so long. 1567 *Gude & Godlie Ball.* (S.T.S.) 89 Help me..That suddand sleip of deide do me na teine. 1579 SPENSER *Sheph. Cal.* Aug. 170 Till my last sleepe Doe close mine eyes. 1810 SCOTT *Lady of Lake* I. xxxi, Sleep the sleep that knows not breaking! 1860 PUSEY *Min. Proph.* 378 They slept the sleep from which they shall not awake until the Judgment Day. 1942 R. GODDEN *Breakfast with Nikolides* v. 118, I want you simply to give him an injection and put him to sleep. I will muzzle him. 1966 K. A. SADDLER *Gilt Edge* ii. 37, I had to have the Allard [*sc.* a car] put to sleep... She started coughing up oil... I couldn't bear to see her in agony. 1967 A. LEWIN *Unaltered Cat* II. vi. 134 Her cousin's Siamese cat..had..a litter of four adorable seal-point kittens. Ethel's husband was for putting them to sleep, but Ethel wouldn't hear of it. 1970 *Women's Household* July 10/1 She had started to suffer, so the humane thing to do was to put her to sleep. 1975 tr. *Melchior's Sleeper Agent* (1976) III. vii. 154 The Führer's Alsatian dog, Blondi..had been ordered put to sleep. Dr. Haase had given her poison.

**b.** A state of inactivity or of sluggishness (in persons or things).

*Beowulf* 1742 He þæt wyrse ne con..; bið se slæp to fæst. c 897 K. ÆLFRED tr. *Gregory's Past. C.* lvi. 431 Be ðæs modes slæpe wæs ær awriten on ðære ilcan Salomonnes bec. c 1200 ORMIN 3148 þatt wass þurrh wanntrowwþess slæp. a 1225 *Ancr. R.* 272 Þis nis buten ine slepe of ȝemeleaste & of slouhðe. 1710 NORRIS *Chr. Prud.* v. 250 The Agreement and Proportion that is between Sleep and Sin,..so that Sin is a kind of Spiritual Sleep. 1718 *Freethinker* No. 83, Many.. begin to slumber in their Manhood; and drop into a sound Sleep in their Age. 1781 COWPER *Expostulation* 637 Ere nature rose from her eternal sleep. a 1822 SHELLEY *With a Guitar* 46 While on the steep The woods were in their winter sleep. 1874 H. R. REYNOLDS *John Bapt.* iv. §5. 259 Men who had laid their ethical sense to sleep. 1889 A. SERGEANT *Esther Denison* I. v. 51 He had put his doubts to sleep.

**c.** The condition of being quiet and peaceful; complete absence of noise or stir.

1807 WORDSW. *Song Brougham Castle* 164 The sleep that is among the lonely hills. 1821–2 SHELLEY *Chas. I*, II. 239 The innocent sleep Of templed cities. 1872 BLACK *Adv. Phaeton* xix. 274 The deep sleep of the landscape.

**5. a.** *Bot.* A condition assumed by many plants, esp. during the night, marked by the closing of petals or leaves.

After L. *Somnus Plantarum*, the title of a pamphlet published by P. Bremer in 1755.

1757 J. HILL *Sleep of Plants* 30 What is called the sleep of plants is the effect of the absence of light alone. 1796 WITHERING *Brit. Pl.* (ed. 3) II. 419 This species is a notable instance of what is called the *Sleep of Plants*—for every night the leaves approach in pairs. 1842 *Penny Cycl.* XXII. 129/2 During sleep the leaves of the sensitive-plant lose their peculiar sensibility. 1877 DARWIN *More Lett.* (1903) II. 414 The cotyledons of Cassia go to sleep, and are sensitive to a touch.

**b.** A state of numbness in a limb, produced by prolonged pressure upon it. (Cf. ASLEEP *adv.* 4.)

1859 PRINCESS ROYAL *Let.* 12 Dec. in R. Fulford *Dearest Child* (1964) 212 Wegner..pinches his arm to see whether he feels it... He feels just a little but not much, like a part that is gone to sleep. 1882 *Quain's Dict. Med.* II. 1649 There is numbness in the hands and forearms, with a sensation of 'going to sleep' in the fingers. 1893 ECCLES *Sciatica* 18 In the cases of external pressure..the patients noticed that the limb had 'gone to sleep'.

**6.** *attrib.* and *Comb.* **a.** Attrib., as ***sleep deprivation, -disturbance, -land***, etc. Also ***sleep-like*** adj.

1966 I. JEFFERIES *House-Surgeon* xii. 230 Those who are still not weakened sufficiently are eroded remorselessly by *sleep-deprivation. 1980 E. BEHR *Getting Even* i. 18 We tried another tactic... Truth drugs... Even some subtle sleep deprivation. Inconclusive. 1834 *Good's Study Med.* (ed. 4) III. 49 Fatuity, mania, melancholy and *sleep-disturbance. 1874 LISLE CARR *Judith Gwynne* I. v. 149 Then her wandering mind went off into *sleepland. 1826 KIRBY & SP. *Entomol.* IV. xliii. 193 At night they regularly muster in a state of *sleep-like silence. 1887 MORRIS *Odyss.* XI. 331 And now anigh it doth draw To the *sleep-tide. 1889 BROWNING *Asolando*, At the midnight, in the silence of the *sleep-time.

**b.** With agent-nouns, vbl. sbs., and pres. pples., as ***sleep-bringer, -dispeller; sleep-bringing, -causing, -compelling, -desiring, -producing***, etc.

1591 SYLVESTER *Du Bartas* I. iv. 718 *Sleep-bringer, Pilgrim's guide, Peace-loving Queen. 1616 W. BROWNE *Brit. Past.* II. iii, *Sleepe-bringing poppy. 1611 COTGR., *Somnifique*, *sleepe-causing. 1762 FOOTE *Orator* I. Wks. 1799 I. 205 Where the *sleep-compelling power will be experimentally demonstrated. 1874 L. CARR *J. Gwynne* I. i. 15 Surrounded..by drowsy, sleep-compelling influences. 1878 B. TAYLOR *Deukalion* I. iv. 34 Dull gleams from *sleep-desiring eyes. 1860 G. H. K. *Vac. Tour* 116 Tub, *sleep-dispeller, welcome! 1816 H. G. KNIGHT *Ilderim* 407 Onward the *sleep-disturbing triumph roll'd. 1847 HELPS *Friends in C.* I. vi. 88 The *sleep-inducing weavings and unweavings of political combination. 1748 THOMSON *Castle Indol.* I. lviii, Where purls the brook with *sleep-inviting sound. 1611 COTGR., *Soporifere*, soporiferous, *sleepe-procuring. 1844 E. A. POE in *Godey's Lady's Bk.* Apr. 177/2 This *rapport* extended beyond the limits of the simple *sleep-producing power... At the first attempt..the mesmerist entirely failed. 1907 W. JAMES in *Amer. Mag.* Nov. 64/2 The best sleep-producing agent which his practice had revealed to him was *prayer*. 1625 K. LONG tr. *Barclay's Argenis* IV. xviii. 306 *Sleepe-provoking poppy and soft paces. 1845 JAMES *Smuggler* III. 37 Any *sleep-resisting powers of the human frame. 1748 THOMSON *Castle Indol.* I. iii, *Sleep-soothing groves, and quiet lawns between.

**c.** With past pples., as ***sleep-bedeafened, -bound, -created, -dazed, -dewed, -drowned, -twisted***, etc.; also with ppl. adjs., as ***sleep-drunk***.

1605 P. WOODHOUSE *The Flea* (1877) 11 The glut'nous Wolfe; and the sleep-fatted Beare. 1605 SYLVESTER *Du Bartas* II. iii. I. *Vocation* 563 Blew Gladiol's juyce, Where-with her sleep-swoln heavy lids she glews. 1631 QUARLES *Samson* Wks. (Grosart) II. 146/1 Whose softer language, by degrees, did wake His father's sleepe-bedeafned eares. 1648 J. BEAUMONT *Psyche* VI. ccxlii, To break her sleep-inthralled Spouse's chains. 1792 CUMBERLAND *Calvary* (1803) II. 57 'Twas the voice As of a spirit..sleep-created in the troubled ear Of conscience. 1820 SHELLEY *Prometh. Unb.* I. 12 Three thousand years of sleep-unsheltered hours. 1839–48 BAILEY *Festus* viii. 82 The recovering breath of earth, sleep-drowned. 1841 J. G. WHITTIER in *Knickerbocker* May 369 Bend o'er us now, as over them, And set our sleep-bound spirits free. 1889 *Cent. Dict.*, Sleep-drunk. 1894 H. NISBET *Bush Girl's Rom.* 148 While his sleep-filled eyes looked on.. the morning. 1938 E. BOWEN *Death of Heart* III. v. 417 He ..saw in a sleep-bound way how specious wisdom was. 1951 KOESTLER *Age of Longing* I. iii. 41 Sleep-drunk and frightened, Hydie begins to cry. 1954 —— *Invisible Writing* IV. xxxvii. 394 Sleep-dazed, he is unable to decide which of the two hostile dictators is reaching out for him this time. 1960 T. HUGHES *Lupercal* 21 Our lantern's little orange flare Made a round mask of our each sleep-dazed face. 1960 S. PLATH *Colossus* 39 Sleep-twisted sheets.

**7.** Special combs.: **sleep apnœa**, apnœa occurring in sleep; **sleep-awake** adj., in a state between sleeping and waking (*nonce-word*); **sleep-coat**, a knee-length front-fastening night-shirt or dressing-gown; **sleep disease**, the sleeping sickness of Africa; **sleep-drink** [cf. Du. *slaapdrank*, G. *schlaftrunk*], a portion of liquor taken just before bed-time; also *fig.*; **sleep-learn** *a.*, pertaining to sleep-learning; **sleep-learning, -teaching** *vbl. sbs.*, learning, teaching, during sleep, esp. by exposure to radio, tape-recordings, etc. (cf. HYPNOPÆDIA); **sleep movement** *Bot.*, a movement of a part of a plant, esp. a leaf, that occurs each nightfall and, in reverse, each daybreak; **sleep-palsy, -paralysis**, paralysis caused by pressure on a nerve during sleep; †**sleeprife** *a.*, bringing sleep, soporiferous; **sleep-shorts**, shorts as an item of nightwear; **sleep-sick** *a.*, excessively given to sleep; **sleep sofa** *U.S.*, a sofa which may be used as a bed; **sleep-stour** *Sc.* (*lit.* sleep-dust), signs of sleep; **sleep-stuff**, an opiate; **sleep-talk** *v. intr.*, to speak (as) during sleep; **sleep-talker**, one who speaks during sleep; **sleep-talking**, speaking during sleep; **sleep-teaching** *vbl. sb.*: see *sleep-learning* vbl. sb. above; **sleep-thorn** [tr. ON. *svefnþorn*], in Scandinavian legend, a thorn imagined as inducing sleep; **sleep-trap**, a church-pew readily inducing sleep (*nonce-word*); **sleep-waker**, a mesmerized or hypnotized person; **sleep-waking**, a mesmeric or hypnotic state; †**sleepward** *adv.* (see quot.); **sleep-wear**, night wear.

1976 *National Observer* (U.S.) 18 Dec. 16/4 *Sleep apnea has three forms: central apnea [etc.]. 1980 *Brit. Med. Jrnl.* 29 Mar. 895/2 Sleep apnoea was defined as cessation of airflow at the nose and mouth lasting for at least 10 seconds. 1614 SYLVESTER *Bethulia's Rescue* VI. 77 For (*sleep-awake, blinde-seeing) while hee plyes T'untrusse his Points, them (fumbling) faster tyes. 1948 *Sun* (Baltimore) 11 Feb. 3/5 (Advt.), Rayon knit *sleep-coats... What young, gay, pretty and practical sleepers! 1966 *Punch* 23 Feb. 290/2 The nearest Hardy Amies equivalent is a..short-sleeved garment called a 'sleep-coat', designed for warm climates and centrally heated homes... It is a loose negligé, fastening with a sash. 1976 *National Observer* (U.S.) 6 Nov. 21 (Advt.), Sleepcoats for cool knights. 1897 MISS KINGSLEY *W. Africa* 401 Among these are the smallpox, and the *sleep disease. a 1700 SHIELDS *Faithf. Contendings* (1780) 308 That *sleep-drink of the Antichristian intoxicating toleration was then brewed in hell. 1861 THACKERAY *Four Georges* i, Every evening they shall have their sleep, and at night their sleep-drink. 1968 *Punch* 4 Dec. 804/2 Two new '*sleep-learn' devices. 1972 D. LEES *Zodiac* 151 By using an adaptation of the sleep-learn technique we can turn you into anything we want. 1953 M. L. COYNE in *Jrnl. Exper. Psychol.* (1956) LI. 97/1 (*heading*) Some problems and parameters of *sleep learning. 1966 *Listener* 8 Dec. 852/3 Equally dangerous might be so-called 'sleep-learning' courses which try to teach you something special, like a new language, while you sleep. 1972 J. GORES *Dead Skip* (1973) iii. 18 Through his mind, like a sleep-learning tape, reeled Bart's words. 1880 C. & F. DARWIN *Movem. Pl.* 262 The periodical movements of leaves thus provided have generally been amplified into so-called *sleep-movements. 1906, etc. [see NYCTINASTIC *a.*]. 1965 BELL & COOMBE tr. *Strasburger's Textbk. Bot.* 391 *Mimosa* also shows sleep movements, and at nightfall appears almost as if stimulated by mechanical shock. 1896 *Allbutt's Syst. Med.* I. 367 The commonest types of paralysis from injury to nerves are *sleep palsy, crutch palsy [etc.]. 1899 *Ibid.* VI. 659 Hence it is a common form of *sleep paralysis. 1513 DOUGLAS *Æneid* IV. ix. 28 Strynkland to hym the wak hony sweit, And *sleipryfe chesbow seid.

**1964** *Women's Wear Daily* 30 Nov. 50 A pair of *sleepshorts in all sleepwear colors to be sold separately, worn with anything the consumer wishes. **1976** *National Observer* (U.S.) 29 May 2/6 (Advt.), Classic travel shave coat & matching sleep shorts. **1591** SYLVESTER *Du Bartas* I. vii. 129 Thou rather sleep'st, thy self, When thou did'st forge thee such a *sleep-sick Elf. **1973** *Washington Post* 13 Jan. A13/3 (Advt.), Elegant traditional sleeper. Refined traditional *sleep sofa from Waynline. **1888** BUCHANAN *Heir of Linne* viii, I see the *sleep-stour in his eyes already. **1880** BROWNING *Dram. Idyls, Clive* 77 Let alone that filthy *sleep-stuff. **1960** S. PLATH *Colossus* 48 The *sleep-talking virgin. **1980** *Times Lit. Suppl.* 23 May 578/5 She has a tendency to over-point,..and I can feel death around too, very little hope or heart—'although I admit I desire', she intones, sleep-talking. **1794** *Sleep talker [see SLEEP-WALKER]. **1972** R. ADAMS *Watership Down* x. 44 His voice sank and became that of a sleep-talker. **1981** *Maledicta* V. 287 Each sleeptalker was asked..a series of some 25 questions and sub-questions about his/her verbalizations. **1829** *Good's Study Med.* (ed. 3) IV. 173 *marg.*, Hence *sleep-talking, sleep-walking, or somnambulism. **1899** [see *somniloquy* s.v. SOMNILOQUACIOUS *a.*]. **1939** JOYCE *Finnegans Wake* 459 She's a fright, poor old dutch, in her sleeptalking. **1981** *Maledicta* V. 286 There has always existed the phenomenon of somniloquy, commonly known as sleeptalking. **1932** *Sleep-teaching [see HYPNOPÆDIA]. **1957** A. HUXLEY *Let.* 12 Dec. (1969) 837 A dictator..could, by the use of drugs, sleep-teaching, hypnosis, subliminal projection..establish a high degree of control over his subjects. **1970** *Times* 19 Sept. 13 In Russia more than 180 educational institutes..are now fully equipped for sleepteaching. **1889** R. B. ANDERSON *Rydberg's Teut. Mythol.* 164 Castles, where goddesses pricked by *sleep-thorns are slumbering. **1895** *Daily Telegr.* 9 Aug. 5/3 These *sleep-traps were in time superseded by high-backed pews. **1840** *Sleep-waker [see MESMERIZE *v.* b]. **1844** E. A. POE in *Columbian Mag.* Aug. 70/2 As the sleep-waker pronounced these latter words..I observed upon his countenance a singular expression. **1884** *19th Cent.* May 807 The sleep-waker will continue to listen and reply. **1840** C. H. TOWNSHEND *Facts Mesmerism* II. i. 47 Mesmeric Somnambulism, or, more properly, *Sleepwaking. **1886** MYERS *Phantasms of Living* I. Introd. p. xlii, Induced somnambulism or the sleep-waking state. **1562** BULLEYN *Bulwarke, Sickmen & Med.* 55 b, Sometime medicen is giuen to *slepe-warde, or before slepe. **1935** A. P. HERBERT *What a Word!* iv. 115, I have been implored by many to attack..'*sleep-wear', and 'swim-wear'. **1964** [see *sleep-shorts* above]. **1979** N. HYND *False Flags* xxiv. 213 You travel light... Just..some sleepwear.

**sleep** (sliːp), *v.* Pa. t. and pa. pple. slept. Forms: (see below). [OE. *slápan, slǽpan, slépan* (pa. t. *slép, slépon*, pa. pple. *-slápen*, etc.), = OFris. *slêpa* (WFris. *sliepe*, EFris. *slepe*, NFris. *slêp, slîp*), MDu. and Du. *slapen*, OS. *slâpan* (MLG. and LG. *slapen*), OHG. *slâfan* (MHG. *slâfen*, G. *schlafen*), Goth. *slêpan* (pa. t. *saislêp, -zlêp*, pa. pple. *slêpans*); wanting in Scandinavian. Besides the strong conjugation (with reduplicated pa. t.) OE. also had the weak forms *slǽpte, slépte*, and after the 14th cent. the strong conjugation disappears from the literary language. A similar change has taken place in WFris., where the pa. t. is now usually *slepte*, pa. pple. *slept*. The ME. *slēped* (mod.Sc. *sleepit*) may represent the northern OE. forms *slépade*, pl. *slépedon* (WS. inf. *slápian*).

It is possible that the weak forms *slǽpte, slépte*, properly belonged to a causative verb corresponding to MHG. (*ent*)-*slæfen*, older or dial. G. *schläfen*, although no trace of this usage appears in OE. texts. The infinitive of this would have had the form **slǽpan*, Merc. and Angl. **slépan*, and would consequently have been identical with the inf. of the strong verb, except where the latter had the special West Saxon form *slápan*. The strong pa. t. is frequent in ME., and the strong pa. pple. is occasionally found (cf. also ASLOPEN); traces of strong conjugation appear in some mod. dialects, but it is possible that these are new formations.]

A. Illustration of forms.

**1.** *Inf.* (and forms connected with this): *α.* **1 slapan, 2 slapen, 4 slape.**

*c* **888** K. ÆLFRED *Boeth.* xxxiv. §11 þonne we slapað. *c* **893** —— *Oros.* IV. vi. 178 þæt he..slapan ne mehte. *c* **1000** *Ags. Gosp.* Matt. xxvi. 45 Slapað..& restað eow. *Ibid.* Luke xxii. 46 Hwi slape ȝe? *c* **1100** *Canterb. Ps.* xl. 9 Se þe slapð. *c* **1200** *Trin. Coll. Hom.* 7 Werie men is lief to slapen. **13..** *Seuyn Sages* 929 (W.), He..gan to slape. *c* **1350** in Horstm. *Altengl. Leg.* (1881) 145 Sum men in kirk slomers and slapes.

*β.* **1 slǽpan, 3 slæpen, 3, 6, sleape.**

*c* **888** K. ÆLFRED *Boeth.* xlii, Ne slæpð he næfre. **971** *Blickling Hom.* 235 Swa he slæpende wære. *c* **1000** *Ælfric's Gr.* (Z.) 211 (Harl.), Me lyste slæpan. *c* **1160** *Hatton Gosp.* Matt. xxvi. 45 Slæpeð..& resteð eow. *Ibid.* Luke xxii. 46 Hwi slæpe ȝe? *c* **1205** LAY. 733 Leteð slæpen þene king. *c* **1275** *Ibid.* 18409 Suþþe hii solle sleape. **1565** COOPER *Thes.* s.v. *Somnus*, To sleape quietly.

*γ.* **1 slepan (slepp-), 2–3 slepen (3 sclepen, sleop-), 5 slepyn; 3–6 slepe, 4 sclep(e, 5 scleppe; 5–6 *Sc.* sleip(e, 5–7 sleepe, 6– sleep.**

*c* **825** *Vesp. Ps.* lxvii. 14 ðif ȝe slepað. *Ibid.* cxx. 4 Ne slepeð se. *c* **897** K. ÆLFRED tr. *Gregory's Past. C.* lvi. 431 Swelce se stiora slepe. *c* **950** *Lindisf. Gosp.* Matt. ix. 24 þæt maiden..slepes. *c* **1000** *Ags. Ps.* (Thorpe) lxxv. 5 [Hi] ongunnon..ȝeorne slepan. *c* **1100** *Canterb. Ps.* xliii. 23 Forwæn slepest þu? *c* **1160** *Hatton Gosp.* Mark v. 39 þis mæden..slepð. *c* **1205** LAY. 966 In eorðe heo sleopeð. *Ibid.* 25582 Agan ich forto slepe. *c* **1275** *Prov. Ælfred* 468 in *O.E. Misc.* 131 Litil sal he sclepen. *a* **1300** *E.E. Ps.* iv. 9 In pees..Sal i slepe. **1340–70** *Alex. & Dind.* 344 We nolle sclepe in no sclowþe. *c* **1440** *Promp Parv.* 459/1 Slepyn, *dormio*. *c* **1450** *Cov. Myst.* (Shaks. Soc.) 41 What man in synne doth..scleppe. *c* **1470** HENRY *Wallace* v. 347 Quhar he suld sleipe. **1570** LEVINS *Manip.* 70 To sleepe, *dormire*. **1596** DALRYMPLE tr. *Leslie's Hist. Scot.* I. 314 Quhen he sleipis. **1617** MORYSON *Itin.* II. 46 He used to sleepe in the afternoones.

**2.** *Past Tense.* **a.** *Strong.* **1–4 slep (1 sclep), 1, 3 slæp, sleap, 2 sliep, 4 sleep, slepp, slepe (9 *dial.* slape).** *Plur.* **1 slepon, -un, -an, 1, 3–4 slepen (4 slupen), 4 slepe.**

The common dial. form *slep* is prob. for *slept*.

*c* **888** K. ÆLFRED *Boeth.* xv, Hi slepon ute. **971** *Blickling Hom.* 235 Se halȝa Andreas þa slep. *c* **1000** *Ags. Gosp.* Matt. xxv. 5 Hnappudon hiȝ ealle & slepun [*c* **1160** slepen]. *c* **1100** *Canterb. Ps.* lvi. 5 Ic slæp ȝedrefed. *a* **1200** *Vices & Virt.* 51 He..reste and sliep. *c* **1205** LAY. 26009 þe eotende lai and slæp [*c* **1275** sleap]. *c* **1220** *Bestiary* 771 Ðre daies slep he. *a* **1300** *Havelok* 2128 He slepen faste alle fiue. *a* **1300** *E.E. Psalter* iii. 5, I slepe [*v.r.* slep] And I ras. **1387** TREVISA *Higden* VIII. 227 He sleep in his studie. **1393** LANGL. *P. Pl.* C. XVI. 272 Seuene slepen [*v.r.* slupen].

**b.** *Weak.* *α.* **1 slypte, 1, 3 slæpte, 1, 3–6 slepte (1 slepde), 3 slapte, sleapte, 6– slept, 7 slep'd.**

*c* **825** *Vesp. Ps.* lxxv. 6 Hneapedun (*vel* slypton) slep heara. *c* **897** K. ÆLFRED *Gregory's Past. C.* xvi. 101 Ða he æt ðæm stane slæpte. *c* **950** *Lindisf. Gosp.* Luke viii. 23 Rowundum..ðæm [he] slepde. *c* **975** *Rushw. Gosp.* Matt. xiii. 25 þa hie..sleptun. *c* **1205** LAY. 25622 þer ich lai and slapte [*c* **1275** sleapte]. *Ibid.* 26024 Lai and slæpte. **1390** GOWER *Conf.* I. 24 As Nabugodonosor slepte. **1535** COVERDALE *Gen.* xli. 5 And he slepte agayne. **1617** MORYSON *Itin.* I. 259 When we slept. **1648** BEAUMONT *Psyche* VII. ccvii, Our tender Flock, which slep'd.

*β.* **4, 6 slepped, 4 sleppet, 5 sleppit.**

*a* **1300** *Cursor M.* 2551 Abram..Slepped. *c* **1375** *Ibid.* 3796 (Fairf.), Ful soft..he sleppet þat niȝt. *c* **1400** *Destr. Troy* 8225 He..sleppit euer after. **1513** BRADSHAW *St. Werburge* II. 863 As she slepped.

*γ.* **4–5 sleped, 7 sleep'd, 7–8 (9) sleeped; *Sc.* 5–6 slepit, 6 sleipet, 9 sleepit; 9 *dial.* sleept.**

*a* **1300** *Cursor M.* 6333 þar he sleped þat morntide. **1375** BARBOUR *Bruce* VII. 188 He slepit as foul on twist. **1596** DALRYMPLE tr. *Leslie's Hist. Scot.* I. 93 Thay..sleipet sound. **1648** BEAUMONT *Psyche* VIII. xlvi, When they wak'd and sleep'd. **1763** *Phil. Trans.* LIV. 18 He sleeped but indifferently. **1818** SCOTT *Hrt. Midl.* xlv, When I sleepit ayont the hallan. **1834** SOUTHEY *Doctor, T' Terrible Knitters e' Dent* (1848) 559 T' woman's doughter sleept we' us.

**3.** *Past Part.* *α.* **4 y-slape, y-slepe, i-slepe, slepe; 9 *dial.* slepen, sleppen, slippen.**

*c* **1310** *St. Brendan* 130 (Harl.), þo hi hadde alle islepe ynouȝ. *c* **1330** *Arth. & Merl.* 2367 (Kölbing), He hadde litel yslape. **1390** GOWER *Conf.* II. 99, I wolde have leie and slepe stille.

*β.* **4 i-sleped, 4–6 sleped, 5 scleped, -yd, *Sc.* slepyt; 5 sleppit, 4 i-slept, 4– slept, 9 *dial.* slep.**

**1362** LANGL. *P. Pl.* A. v. 4 þat I nedde sadloker I-slept [*v.r.* slept, sleped]. *c* **1400** *Destr. Troy* 817 As he hade fast sleppit. *c* **1400** *Laud Troy Bk.* 12963 When thei hadde scleped. *c* **1470** HENRY *Wallace* VI. 629 Quhen..the Scottis had slepyt. **1548** R. HUTTEN *Sum Divin.* R vij b, Them..whych haue sleped.

B. Signification.

I. *intr.* **1. a.** To take repose by the natural suspension of consciousness; to be in the state of sleep; to slumber. Also occas., to fall asleep. ***to sleep rough***: see ROUGH *adv.* 1 b; ***to sleep tight***: see TIGHT *adv.* 1.

*c* **825** *Vesp. Psalter* iii. 6 Ic hneappade & slepan ongon. *c* **888** K. ÆLFRED *Boeth.* xlii, Symle he bið lociende, ne slæpð he næfre. *c* **900** tr. *Baeda's Hist.* III. ix. (1890) 186 þa ȝeswiȝade he semninȝa & his heafod onhylde, swa swa he slapan wolde. **971** *Blickling Hom.* 149 þa æfter þon þa arison ealle þa þe þær slepan. **1154** *O.E. Chron.* (Laud MS.) an. 1137, He ne myhte..sitten ne lien ne slepen. *c* **1250** *Gen. & Ex.* 1065 He..slep and saȝ an soðe drem. *a* **1300** *Cursor M.* 14206 If he mai slepe, hele es at hand. *c* **1386** CHAUCER *Clerk's T.* 168 She wolde noght been ydel til she slepte. *a* **1425** tr. *Arderne's Treat. Fistula*, etc. 32 Aftir refetyng of mete and drink, he went into his bedde and sleped wele all þe niȝt. **1483** CAXTON *Gold. Leg.* 126/1 How many ben there..that slepen in the market place. **1530** PALSGR. 721/1 He that drinketh well slepeth well, and he that slepeth well thynketh no harme. **1590** SHAKS. *Mids. N.* III. ii. 38, I tooke him sleeping..And the Athenian woman by his side. **1621** BURTON *Anat. Mel.* II. iii. v, We are never better or freer from cares than when we sleep. **1686** tr. *Chardin's Trav. Persia* 86 Nor do they ever sleep without their swords by their sides. **1746** FRANCIS tr. *Horace, Epist.* I. xviii. 66 Strange Hopes and Projects fill his Breast; He sleeps 'till Noon. **1774** GOLDSM. *Nat. Hist.* (1776) VI. 124 The feathers of this bird..make the softest and the warmest beds to sleep on. **1841** THACKERAY *Gt. Hoggarty Diam.* xi, I wonder whether the man sleeps easily and eats with a good appetite? **1880** *Encycl. Brit.* XI. 788 The tenrec..sleeps for three months in its burrow during the hottest period of the year.

*Prov.* **1581** PETTIE *Guazzo's Civ. Conv.* I. (1586) 13 b, He which sleepeth with the dogges, must rise with the fleas.

*fig.* **1592** KYD *Sp. Trag.* I. 23 Ere Sol had slept three night in Thetis lap. **1596** SHAKS. *Merch. V.* v. i. 109 Peace, how the Moone sleepes with Endimion.

**b.** Implying sexual intimacy or cohabitation. Also, with *around*: to engage in sexual intercourse casually with a variety of partners; to be sexually promiscuous (*colloq.*).

*a* **900** *Laws Ælfred* Introd. §29 (Liebermann), ðif hwa fæmnan beswice unbeweddode, and hire mid slæpe. *c* **1000** ÆLFRIC *Gen.* xxxix. 7 His hlæfdiȝe lufode hine and cwæð to him: Slap mid me! *c* **1250** *Gen. & Ex.* 967 Forð siðen ȝhe bi abram slep, Of hire leuedi nam ȝhe no kep. *c* **1386** CHAUCER *Sir Thopas* 78 An elf queene shal my lemman be, And slepe vnder my goore. *a* **1400** *Trevisa's Higden* (Rolls) VII. 143 A clerk of þe court hadde i-sleped wiþ hire. **1819** SHELLEY *Cenci* I. iii. 63 Whilst she he loved was sleeping with his rival. **1898** *Sessions Paper of Central Criminal Court* Feb. 266 He has been sleeping with my wife. How would you like it? **1928** A. HUXLEY *Point Counter Point* xxvii. 445 'Sleeping around'—that was how he had heard a young American girl describe the amorous side of the ideal life, as lived in Hollywood. **1936** R. LEHMANN *Weather in Streets* II. 185 A child's out of the question now, they don't sleep together any more. **1940** W. FAULKNER *Hamlet* II. 92 All we want anyway is to keep her out of trouble until she gets old enough to sleep with a man without getting me and him both arrested. **1952** M. LASKI *Village* xvi. 218, I don't think for a minute she's been sleeping around..but you know what gossip is. **1967** J. POTTER *Foul Play* xiii. 161 He's only interested in George and Freda and whether Johnnie and Freda slept together. **1975** P. LORAINE *Wrong Man in Mirror* 78 Rose Maddox was not a loose girl; she did not sleep around with just anybody.

**c.** With *upon* or *on* (a matter), denoting the postponement of a decision till the following day.

In mod. use also with *over* in the same sense.

**1519** *State Papers Hen. VIII*, I. I. 3 His Grace..sayd thatt he wold slepe and drem apon the matter, and geff me an answer apon the mornyng. **1600** HOLLAND *Livy* XLII. xxv. 1129, I will sleepe upon it and bee well advised what to doe for the best. **1668** H. MORE *Div. Dial.* III. xl. Wks. (1713) 289 It will not be amiss to consult with one's Pillow, as the Proverb is, and sleep upon 't. **1755** *Mem. Capt. P. Drake* I. xvi. 161 The Countess..assured him, that she would not let them sleep upon it. **1818** SCOTT *Br. Lamm.* x, The deil of ony master's face he shall see till he has sleepit and waken'd on't. **1889** FROUDE *Chiefs Dunboy* xiii. 185 Colonel Goring slept upon his problem, and woke the next morning resolute. *a* **1907** F. THOMPSON *St Ignatius Loyola* (1909) x. 192 He discussed all measures with his brethren; and ever enjoined them to sleep on the matter, and pray the next morning before decision. **1926** V. MCNABB *Church & Land* 83 My friend rose from his seat. 'I see—we must do things ourselves. I must sleep on this.' **1959** S. SALTON-VANE *Black Whippet* ii. 32 Sleep on it. Think it over, and come and see me early tomorrow morning. **1962** P. GREGORY *Like Tigress at Bay* ix. 99 Let me think about it, though. I'd like to sleep on it. **1983** 'W. HAGGARD' *Heirloom* viii. 90 He simply looked at a problem hard and then slept on it.

**d.** In phrases denoting freedom from anxiety.

**1637** MASSINGER *Guardian* II. ii, Sleep you Secure on either ear. **1677** W. HUGHES *Man of Sin* II. viii. 126 Doubt not a perfect cure:..I am secure that you may sleep on either side.

**e.** ***to sleep like a top*** (cf. 3 c).

**1693** CONGREVE *Old Bachelor* I. 8 Should he seem to rouse, 'tis but well lashing him, and he will sleep like a Top. **1793** *Gentl. Mag.* Oct. 893/2 He sleeps like a top. **1819** BYRON *Juan* II. cxxxiv, Juan slept like a top, or like the dead.

**f.** With *it*: To spend one's time in sleep. Also with *out*.

*a* **1652** BROOME *Queenes Exch.* III, We'l..have him put in bed before he wakes.., and there, When he has slept it out, he will perhaps Be cur'd. **1760–72** H. BROOKE *Fool of Qual.* (1809) I. 58 These have nothing to do but to sleep it.

**g.** With *in*: To sleep in the house, or on the premises, where one is employed (contrasted with 'to sleep out'); also *Naut.*, to remain in one's berth all night; (orig. *Sc.*) to oversleep; also, to lie in (LIE *v.*[1] 23 d), to sleep late.

**1827** C. I. JOHNSTONE *Eliz. de Bruce* I. iii. 56 Ye whiles sleep in on a morning. **1840** R. H. DANA *Bef. Mast* iii, The steward..and..the cook..are allowed to 'sleep in' at night, unless all hands are called. **1883** W. AITKEN *Lays of Line* 58 A'e mornin' last March, when Rab Black sleepit in. **1888** G. MACDONALD *Elect Lady* 138, I had to be up early, and I was feared I would sleep-in. **1931** *Amer. Speech* VII. 20 *Sleep in*, to sleep late. 'I'm going to sleep in tomorrow.' **1931** D. L. SAYERS *Five Red Herrings* i. 16 Shall I tell Mrs. McLeod to let you sleep in, as they say? And call you with a couple of aspirins on toast? **1935** *Beaver* Dec. 66/2 On Sundays the chief guide usually allows his voyageurs to sleep in, which means that instead of getting up at four o'clock they get up about six-thirty. **1967** E. TAYLOR *Second Thursday* ii. 31 Susan dear, you *must* have slept in this morning. **1975** J. GRADY *Shadow of Condor* v. 90 Because he slept in and had an appointment, Malcolm excused himself from the exercises.

**h.** With *in*, in passive, of a bed. Also as *ppl. adj.*

**1848** THACKERAY *Van. Fair* xvi, The bed ain't been slep in. **1861** FLOR. NIGHTINGALE *Notes Nursing* (ed. 2) 55, I assure you the bed has been well slept-in. **1939** W. FORTESCUE *There's Rosemary, There's Rue* xi. 79 We crawled up to our bedroom..and got under our bed-quilts, *not* between those slept-in sheets. **1966** N. FREELING *King of Rainy Country* 140 He..changed his slept-in suit. **1976** J. CROSBY *Snake* (1977) xi. 53 She pulled the crinkly blue-and-white striped blouse as taut as she could..trying to make it look a little less slept-in.

**i.** With *on*: to continue sleeping, to sleep late.

**1739–40** RICHARDSON *Pamela* (1741) I. 267 I'll wake her,—said I.—No, don't,—said she,—let her sleep on; we shall lie better without her. **1939** 'J. BELL' *Death at Half-Term* v. 92, I let our lot sleep on, but the other four came over from the San, and woke them up. **1958** P. SCOTT *Mark of Warrior* I. ii. 44 In four hours Hussein would wake him... Esther would sleep on. **1969** J. FRASER *Clap Hands if you believe in Fairies* iv. 48 Don't worry too much if he's not sleepy. I'll let him sleep on in the morning.

**j.** With *over.* †(*a*) to sleep late (*obs.*); (*b*) to spend the night at a place other than one's own residence (chiefly *U.S.*).

**1827** *Harvard Reg.* Sept. 202 They have indulged in the luxury of 'sleeping over'. **1871** L. H. BAGG *Four Years at Yale* 570 On Sunday mornings, too, there is an unusual amount of 'sleeping over',—breakfast being often cut as well as chapel by the votaries of Morpheus. **1975** *Sunday Advocate-News* (Barbados) 15 June 7/2 The sleep-overs will be the night of the last Thursday of each session. On that night campers sleep-over if they choose to do so. **1977** D. ANTHONY *Stud Game* iii. 23, I begged him to sleep over... But he had an early appointment the next day. **1978** M. PUZO *Fools Die* xxviii. 331 Those were nights I'd hop a plane to Vegas for the evening, sleep over and come back in the early morning.

**k.** With *out*: to spend the night in the open air; also, to sleep away from the premises on which one is employed.

**1852** [implied at SLEEPING *vbl. sb.* 1 c]. **1890** KIPLING *Departmental Ditties, Barrack-Room Ballads* 56 'E's sleepin' out an' far to-night,' the Colour-Sergeant said. **1908** R. BROOKE *Let.* 18 Aug. (1968) 139, I should love to sleep out with nothing but a few extra socks on. **1912** [in *N.E.D.*, sense 1 g]. **1936** 'J. TEY' *Shilling for Candles* xiv. 159 He might have been sleeping out, the first three nights. But you know what last night was like. Torrents... He must have found shelter. **1974** *Whig-Standard* (Kingston, Ontario) 11 Jan. 7/1 There are more dossers sleeping out in London today than there were at the turn of the century.

**l.** Of a bed or mattress: to afford sleep of a specified quality.

**1942** W. FAULKNER *Go down, Moses* 83 This here pallet sleeps all right to me. **1977** *Austral. House & Garden* Jan. 115/1 A foam mattress is generally lighter, is non-allergenic and resists mildew... Foam sleeps cooler in warm temperatures, it is claimed, and warmer in cool temperatures.

**m.** With *up*: to catch up on one's sleep, to stop for a sleep.

**1951** *Manch. Guardian Weekly* 1 Feb. 3/3 The General.. would say nothing more than that he was off for a rest. He headed..for the..hotel to sleep-up until Wednesday. **1968** *Listener* 11 July 50/2 It was..so full and exhausting..that, at the end of term..we used to sleep up for several days before venturing out onto the streets. **1968** in P. G. Hollowell *Lorry Driver* vii. 183 You want to give your mate a bit of a shaking up. What you do is to spot him 'sleeping up' and go quietly by him and turn your wagon round... Then hold your hands on the horn.

**n.** With *through*: esp. of a baby, to sleep uninterruptedly through a period of time, usually the night.

**1967** 'L. EGAN' *Nameless Ones* i. 3 She's the most beautiful baby ever... Sleeping right through. God, when I think——. **1971** O. NORTON *Corpse-Bird Cries* ii. 33, I.. slept through until nearly ten o'clock on Sunday morning. **1976** 'J. CHARLTON' *Remington Set* xx. 104 'Baby going to be all right in the guest room?' 'She'll sleep right through,' Fran said.

**2.** *fig.* To lie in death; to be at rest in the grave.

*c* **950** *Lindisf. Gosp.* Matt. xxvii. 52 And byrȝenna.. untyned weron &..lichoma halȝa wæra ða ðe slepdon arison. *c* **1000** ÆLFRIC *Hom.* II. 566 Hwi sind ða deadan slapende ȝecwedene?.. Ealle hi moton slapan on ðam ȝemænelicum deaðe. *a* **1300** *E.E. Psalter* xii. 4 Ne euer þat I slepe in dede. *c* **1340** HAMPOLE *Pr. Consc.* 878 In pouder sal slepe ilk man, And wormes sal cover hym þan. **1382** WYCLIF *Isaiah* xiv. 18 Alle the kingus of Jentilis, eche slepten in glorie. *c* **1400** *Destr. Troy* 8225 He slode doun sleghly, & sleppit euer after. **1548** R. HUTTEN *Sum Divin.* R vij b, Euen so wil god bring them wyth him whych haue sleped. **1567** *Gude & Godlie Ball.* (S.T.S.) 164 The bodie sleipis, quhill Domisday. **1634** SIR T. HERBERT *Trav.* 29 His owne people..buried him, where not a stones cast further, sleepes Tom Coriats bones. **1726** AYLIFFE *Parergon* 172 A Person is said to be dead to us,..though he only sleeps unto God. **1750** GRAY *Elegy* 16 Beneath those rugged elms.. The rude Forefathers of the hamlet sleep. **1837** CARLYLE *Fr. Rev.* I. I. ii, Charlemagne sleeps at Salzburg, with truncheon grounded. **1888** BURGON *Twelve Good Men* I. Pref. p. xxviii, He sleeps..in Holywell cemetery.

**3.** *transf.* **a.** Of limbs: To be numb, to be devoid of sensation, esp. as the result of pressure.

*c* **1000** ÆLFRIC *Hom.* I. 490 Ȝif we to lange sittað, us slapað ða lima. *a* **1000** *Saxon Leechd.* II. 66 Ȝif þeoh slapan, adelf nioþoweardne secg,..læt reocan on þæt lim þætte slape. *c* **1340** *Nominale* (Skeat) 595 For drede my fote slepith. *a* **1533** LD. BERNERS *Golden Bk. M. Aurelius* (1546) Gg vj, In moyste wethers one of my fyngers slepeth. **1562** TURNER *Baths* 3 b, It is good for..suche membres as are num or slepe. **1895** 'SARAH TYTLER' *Macdonald Lass* xvii. 208 Oh, to be walking there, though our feet were frozen and our fingers sleeping.

**b.** Of plants: To be in a quiescent or drooping condition. (Cf. SLEEP *sb.* 5 a.)

[**1613** PURCHAS *Pilgrimage* IX. iv. (1614) 843 There are hearbes which seeme to sleepe all night.] **1797** *Encycl. Brit.* (ed. 3) XVII. 274/2 Plants are said to sleep when the flowers or leaves are..folded together. **1837** P. KEITH *Bot. Lex.* 325 These positions are not the same in the case of all leaves that sleep... Simple leaves that sleep are affected in their totality. **1880** C. & F. DARWIN *Movem. Pl.* 111 In all such cases the cotyledons may be said to sleep. **1899** G. MASSEE *Plant-Dis.* 328 When this stage is reached the plant droops, or 'sleeps'.

**c.** Of a top: (see quot. 1854).

**1854** MISS BAKER *Northampt. Gloss.* 245 A top sleeps when it moves with such velocity, and spins so smoothly, that its motion is imperceptible. **1879** THOMSON & TAIT *Nat. Phil.* I. I. § 106 It is the case of a common spinning-top, ..not sleeping upright, nor nodding.

**4.** *fig.* **a.** To be dormant, inert, inactive, inoperative, or quiescent. *spec.*, to act as a sleeping partner (see SLEEPING *ppl. a.* 5) or as a sleeper (sense 2 d).

Very common during the 19th cent. in various contexts.

*c* **897** K. ÆLFRED tr. *Gregory's Past. C.* lvi. 431 Swa hit ȝebyreð ðæt ðæt mod slæpð ðæs ðe hit wacian sceolde, & wacað ðæs ðe hit slapan scolde. *a* **1225** *Ancr. R.* 272 Hwon þe olde unwine isihð ure skile slepen. *a* **1300** *Cursor M.* 25855 Let þi sin noght wit þe slepe. **13..** *Polit. Songs, Song of Husbandman* (Camden) 152 Mi lond leye lith ant leorneth to slepe. *c* **1425** LYDG. *Assembly of Gods* 1258 For he demyd sewerly hys sorow shuld nat slepe. **1526** *Pilgr. Perf.* (W. de W. 1531) 183 Not withstandynge yᵗ this errour hath sleped thus longe,..these presumptuous heretykes now of dayes wolde renewe yᵉ same. **1597** SKENE *De Verb. Sign.* s.v. *Annexation*, Induring the time of the quhilk dissolution, the annexation ceases & sleepis. **1610** HOLLAND *Camden's Brit.* 353 This title slept and lay as dead untill the time of King Edward the Second. **1650** E. W. *Virginia* (1844) 32 A man and a boy, if their hands be not sleeping in their pockets [etc.]. **1784** COWPER *Task* v. 204 Violence can never longer sleep Than human passions please. **1855** BAIN *Senses & Int.* III. iv. § 10 When any emotion not entirely wanting is yet allowed to sleep in the character. **1869** FREEMAN *Norm. Conq.* (1875) III. 113 The restless enmity of the Angevin never slept. **1949** D. LEON *Ruskin* I. i. 8 Telford supplied adequate capital and otherwise 'slept' most gracefully. **1975** J. HONE *Sixth Directorate* II. 48 Once they were sure the man was with the KGB..they had watched him... And no one had come near him... They assumed the man was sleeping.

**b.** Of business, etc.: To cease to go forward; to remain in the same state.

**1550** *Reg. Privy Council Scot.* I. 98 The said mater had slepit of langtyme. **1560** DAUS tr. *Sleidane's Comm.* 221 That tyme was the king occupyed with affaires of warre, & therfore the matter slept. **1649** *Nicholas Papers* (Camden) 165 There is a bussines hath slept some while in my hands, but I have not beene idle in itt. **1683** TEMPLE *Mem. 1672–9* Wks. 1720 I. 380 That Matter slept for the present. **1712** ADDISON *Spectator* No. 297 § 10 He should certainly never let his Narration sleep for the sake of any Reflections of his own. **1821** SCOTT *Kenilw.* xvi, My suit should sleep there,.. and with my suit my revenge. **1855** MACAULAY *Hist. Eng.* xiii. III. 256 The question, having slept during eighteen years, was suddenly revived by the Revolution.

**c.** To rest peacefully and quietly; to remain calm, still, or motionless.

**1596** SHAKS. *Merch. V.* v. i. 54 How sweet the moone-light sleepes vpon the banke. **1700** DRYDEN *Cymon & Iph.* 342 The giddy ship..stops, and sleeps again. **1781** COWPER *Retirement* 536 Then, all the world of waters sleeps again. **1826** DISRAELI *V. Grey* v. viii, The blue..sea was sleeping beneath a cloudless sky. **1852** THACKERAY *Esmond* III. vii, Past the river, on which a mist still lay sleeping. **1867** SMYTH *Sailor's Word-bk.* 631 A sail sleeps when, steadily filled with wind, it bellies to the breeze.

**5.** *fig.* To be careless, remiss, or idle; to live thoughtlessly or carelessly.

**1387** TREVISA *Higden* (Rolls) V. 57 Ȝif eny..putteþ errour aȝenst us, he may take hede þat þe grete Homerus slepeþ somtyme. *a* **1548** HALL *Chron., Hen. VI*, 86 The duke of Yorke and his adherentes..determined..no lenger to slepe in so waightie a businesse. *c* **1600** MONTGOMERIE *Cherrie & Slae* 1560 Then let us remuve, And sleip nae mair in sleuth. **1624** MASSINGER *Renegado* I. i, So shall you find me Most ready to assist you; neither have I Slept in your great occasions. *a* **1731** ATTERBURY (J.), We sleep over our happiness, and want to be rouzed into a quick thankful sense of it.

**II.** *trans.* **6. a.** With cognate object: To take rest in, continue in (sleep).

*to sleep a dog-sleep*: see DOG-SLEEP 1.

*c* **825** *Vesp. Ps.* lxxv. 6 Hneapedun (*vel* slypton) slep heara. *a* **1300** *E.E. Psalter* lxxv. 5 Þai slepe þair napping. **1382** WYCLIF *Jer.* li. 39 Y shal drunkne them, that thei..slepen an euere durende slep. *c* **1475** *Partenay* 5463 He ther slepte no slepe, manly waked ryght. **1552** ELYOT s.v. *Edormiscere*, Whyle he dooeth sleape one sleape. **1611** BIBLE *Ps.* xiii. 3 Lighten mine eyes, lest I sleep the sleepe of death. **1791** COWPER *Retired Cat* 48 She left the cares of life behind, And slept as she would sleep her last. **1810** SCOTT *Lady of L.* I. xxxi, Sleep the sleep that knows not breaking! **1848** THACKERAY *Van. Fair* xliii, Sir Michael was sleeping the sleep of the just. **1897** WATTS-DUNTON *Aylwin* IX. vi, Turning into bed, [I] slept my first peaceful sleep since my trouble. **1927** R. LEHMANN *Dusty Answer* III. i. 139 Jennifer's peaceful flushed countenance and regular breathing greeted her astonished senses. She was sleeping the sleep of the slightly intoxicated just. **1944** W. S. MAUGHAM *Razor's Edge* vii. 276 Gray's conversation was composed of clichés... He never went to bed, but hit the hay, where he slept the sleep of the just. **1977** *Lancashire Life* Dec. 57/3 Tired and ready to go home, we went back to the river where Edith's father was still sleeping the sleep of the just.

**b.** *to sleep a wink*, usually with negative.

**1542** UDALL *Erasm. Apoph.* 316 A good vigilaunt Consul ..whiche neuer slept one wynke duryng..his Consulship. **1609** HOLLAND *Amm. Marcell.* 260 Not one of us durst either sit downe, or sleepe one winke for very feare. **1711** SWIFT *Jrnl. to Stella* 13 Nov., I slept not a wink last night for hawking and spitting. **1818** SCOTT *Hrt. Midl.* xlvi, I shall not sleep a wink the less sound. **1840** THACKERAY *Shabby-genteel Story* ix, He..did not sleep one single wink all night.

†**7.** To put off or delay; to disregard, pay no attention to. Also with *out*. *Obs.*

**1470** *Paston Lett.* II. 398, I pray yow let not thys mater be slept. **1523** LD. BERNERS *Froiss.* I. cclxi. 385 So these companyons..slept nat their purpose, but rode in a day and a night. *a* **1548** HALL *Chron., Hen. VI*, 123 These valeaunt capitaines, not myndyng to slepe their busines, environed the toune with a strong siege. **1600** HOLLAND *Livy* XXIII. xiv. 482 They might not sleepe their affaires and go slowly about their businesse. **1624** HEYWOOD *Gunaik.* IV. 179 To persuade men to too much remisnes in wincking at and sleeping out the adulteries of their wives. **1792** T. PAINE *Writ.* (1895) III. 79 It appeared to me extraordinary that any body of men..should commit themselves so precipitately, or 'sleep obedience'.

†**8.** To digest by means of sleep. *Obs.*$^{-1}$

**1481** CAXTON *Reynard* (Arb.) 63 Is your bely ful?..haue ye slepte your dyner?

**9. a.** With *off* or †*out*: To get rid of, remove the effects of, by sleeping.

**1552** ELYOT, *Edormire crapulam*, to sleape out a surfet. **1611** SHAKS. *Wint. T.* IV. iii. 31 For the life to come, I sleepe out the thought of it. **1760** C. JOHNSTON *Chrysal* (1822) II. 29 He had scarce slept off his debauch. **1780** *Mirror* No. 106, Thus were Clavius's nights spent in getting intoxicated, and his mornings in sleeping off that intoxication. **1852** THACKERAY *Esmond* III. viii, In the morning, after he had slept his wine off, he was very gay. **1871** G. MEREDITH *H. Richmond* xiii, This piece of nonsense helped us to sleep off our gloom.

**b.** With *away*: To remove, get rid of, lose, or waste by sleeping.

**1565** COOPER *Thesaurus* s.v. *Crapula*, To vomitte or sleape away his dronkennesse. **1592** KYD *Sp. Trag.* III. xv, Thou art ill aduisde To sleepe away what thou art warnd to watch. **1687** MIÉGE *Gt. Fr. Dict.* II. s.v., To sleep away Sorrow. *Ibid.*, To sleep his Head-ake away. *a* **1716** SOUTH in Chambers *Cycl. Eng. Lit.* (1844) I. 444/1 He..may possibly go to bed with a wonderful stock of good-nature over-night, but then he will sleep it all away again before the morning. **1819** SCOTT *Bl. Dwarf* xiii, I am tired of a party that does nothing but form bold resolutions over night, and sleep them away with their wine before morning. **1828** H. BLUNT *Lect. Hist. Jacob* (1832) 160 He will no more permit his children..to *sleep* away their souls, than..to *sin* them away.

**c.** *refl.* To make (oneself) *sober* by sleeping. Also simply, to sleep.

**1565** COOPER s.v. *Crapula*, To sleape him selfe sober. **1619** HARRIS *Drunkard's Cup* 19 Hee hath slept himselfe sober. **1720** DE FOE *Duncan Campbell* v. § 2 Whensoever he is drunk and has slept himself sober. **1821** SCOTT *Kenilw.* xxxiii, He retreated down to his own den to conclude his lamentations, or to sleep himself sober. **1888** *Pall Mall G.* 25 Oct. 3/2 [The cats] philosophically slept themselves through the two exhibition days.

**10. a.** With *out* or *away*: To pass or spend (a certain time) in sleep.

**1565** COOPER s.v. *Edormiscere*, To sleape out one sleape. **1601** SHAKS. *All's Well* v. iii. 66 Shamefull hate sleepes out the afternoone. **1649** J. TAYLOR (Water P.) *Wand. West* 20, There I sleeped out the later end of the whole Moneth of Iuly. **1766** C. BEATTY *Tour* (1768) 37 Sleeped and waked the night away as well as we could. **1778** PRYCE *Min. Cornub.* 178 When a pair of men went under-ground formerly, they made it a rule, to sleep out a candle, before they set about their work.

**b.** Without adverb. *rare.*

**1613** SHAKS. *Hen. VIII*, Epil., Some come to take their ease, And sleepe an Act or two. **1647** J. ELIOT *Day-Breaking Gosp.* 17 None of them slept Sermon or derided Gods messenger. **1721** BRADLEY *Philos. Acc. Wks. Nat.* 77 These Birds, which sleep the Winter.

**c.** In nonce-uses (see quots.).

**1606** SHAKS. *Ant. & Cl.* II. ii. 181 We did sleepe day out of countenaunce. **1655** VAUGHAN *Silex Scint.* (1900) 57 Yet never sleep the Sun up.

**11.** To cause to sleep or fall asleep.

**1815** SOUTHEY *Common-Pl. Bk.* IV. 402 He was in such pain that the doctors *sleeped* him to death. **1850** LATHAM *Eng. Lang.* (ed. 3) xvii. 445 When we say, *the opiate slept the patient*, meaning thereby, *lulled to sleep*. **1861** [see *mother's blessing* s.v. MOTHER *sb.*¹ 16 a]. **1923** *Daily Mail* 24 Feb. 7 A gasworks foreman..said that at present the gas included 13 per cent of carbon monoxide... 'One per cent is sufficient to kill. It sleeps you to death.'

**12.** To provide with sleeping accommodation.

**1848** BARTLETT *Dict. Amer.* 306 She could eat fifty people in her house, but could not sleep half the number. **1883** *Gringo & Greaser* (Manzano, New Mexico) 1 Sept. 2/1 If we can find some other philanthropist who will kindly hash, beer and sleep us, we'll be there. **1884** *Local Govt. Chron.* 8 Mar. 181 The new Patent Sanitary Hammock is superseding every other mode of sleeping Vagrants. **1895** *Sun* 29 Dec. 3/3 The parents, owing to poverty, had to sleep their children in the same bed as themselves. **1919** MENCKEN *Amer. Lang.* i. 24 A sleeping-car sleeps thirty passengers. **1941** W. A. PERCY *Lanterns on Levee* i. 12 Welcome, messieurs, I can eat you but I cannot sleep you. **1949** *Spectator* 11 Nov. 631/2 During August some hotels were sleeping four or five guests to a room. **1965** E. O'BRIEN *August is Wicked Month* xi. 113 Oh we got beds, we can sleep ..eighty. **1977** *Western Mail* (Cardiff) 5 Mar. 10/7 (Advt.), Farmhouse holiday flat. Sleeps six.

**C.** *Comb.*: **sleep-away** *a.* (*U.S.*), at which one sleeps away from home. See also SLEEP-IN, -OUT, -OVER, *sbs.* and *adjs.*

**1976** *Woman's Day* (U.S.) Nov. 244/2 Diana is told she must go to a sleep-away camp because the doctor says she needs more exercise. **1978** *Chicago* June 157/2 All the sleep-away camps have separate living quarters for boys and girls, but the tennis itself is mixed.

**sleep-at-noon.** (See quots.)

**1779** *Gentl. Mag.* XLIX. 127 The common yellow goat's-beard of our meadows, which by old authors was called Sleep at Noon, or, Go to bed at Noon. **1863** PRIOR *Brit. Pl.*, *Sleep-at-noon*, from its flowers closing at midday, the goat's beard.

**sleeper** (ˈsliːpə(r)), *sb.* Also 3–5 slepar(e, 4–5 sleper(e, 6 sleaper. [f. SLEEP *v.* + -ER¹. Cf. Fris. *slieper*, (M)Du. *slaper*, (M)LG. *slaper*, *sleper*, MHG. *slâf-*, *slæfære*, G. *schlafer*. With the transferred applications of the word in branch II cf. DORMANT *a.* 3 and *sb.* 1 and DORMER 3.]

**I. 1. a.** One who is inclined to sleep, or spends much time in sleep; one who sleeps (well or ill, etc.); also *fig.*, an indolent or inactive person.

*a* **1225** *Ancr. R.* 258 Aȝean slowe & slepares is swuðe openlich his earlich ariste from deað to liue. *c* **1290** *S. Eng. Leg.* I. 319 Ho-so hath of þe watere mest, he schal beo..gret slepare and slovȝ þar-to. *c* **1386** CHAUCER *Nun's Pr. T.* 71 Ye been a verray sleper, fy for shame! **1422** tr. *Secreta Secret., Priv. Priv.* 229 Heuy ey-liddys tokenyth good slepere. *c* **1440** *Alph. Tales* cclxxxv. 197 Cesarius tellis of ane olde monk þat was a grete sleper. *a* **1548** HALL *Chron., Edw. I*, 13 b, The protectour came in emong theim about nyne of yᵉ cloke,..saiyng merely that he had bene a sleper that daye. **1611** COTGR. s.v. *Regnard*, Morning sleepers seldome thriue. *a* **1711** GREW (J.), He must be no great eater, drinker, nor sleeper, that will discipline his senses, and exert his mind. **1838** DICKENS *Nickleby* xxii, The sound of ineffectual knocking at the doors of heavy sleepers. **1848** THACKERAY *Van. Fair* xxx, Being a great sleeper, and fond of his bed. **1897** WATTS-DUNTON *Aylwin* XV. i, I was always a sound sleeper.

†**b.** Used predicatively: Asleep. *Obs.*⁻¹

**1530** PALSGR. 441 Whan he thynketh leste, he may happe to be taken sleper.

**2. a.** One who is asleep. Also *fig.*, a dead person.

**1590** SPENSER *F.Q.* I. i. 43 He bids thee to him send.. A fit false dreame, that can delude the sleepers sent. **1606** SHAKS. *Ant. & Cl.* IV. ix. 31 Hearke the Drummes demurely wake the sleepers. **1610** —— *Temp.* V. i. 49 Graues at my command Haue wak'd their sleepers. **1725** POPE *Odyss.* x. 667 Full endlong from the roof the sleeper fell. **1855** MACAULAY *Hist. Eng.* xvi. III. 639 Before the early dawn of midsummer, the sleepers were roused by the peal of trumpets. **1865** TROLLOPE *Belton Est.* viii. 90 To place themselves at such a distance from the sleeper, that their low words could hardly disturb her.

**b.** *spec.* in *pl.* (See SEVEN *a.*)

**1827** JEFFREY *Let.* xcvii. in Ld. Cockburn *Life*, I shall come back to you like one of the sleepers awaked. **1868** FREEMAN *Norm. Conq.* (1877) II. x. 518 By his orders the tomb of the holy sleepers at Ephesos were opened.

**c.** A sleeping partner.

**1901** *Edin. Rev.* Apr. 385 If.. a director can be treated as a purely sleeping partner, it can do that company no harm that.. the sleeper, on becoming a Minister, should cease to be a director. **1983** 'W. HAGGARD' *Heirloom* xi. 122, I might fix that. At a price... No consortium takes in a sleeper for nothing.

**d.** A spy, saboteur, or the like, who remains inactive for a long period before engaging in spying or sabotage or otherwise acting to achieve his ends; *loosely*, any undercover agent.

**1955** H. ROTH *Sleeper* ix. 66 Hollister.. was a sleeper—a member of the Communist Party whose whole life was dedicated to the one big moment. **1963** J. JOESTEN *They call it Intelligence* I. iv. 45 A 'sleeper' is an agent planted in a strategic place for a specific purpose only. **1966** M. WOODHOUSE *Tree Frog* xxv. 187 Bought, or brainwashed? Or had he been a sleeper for years, waiting for just this job? **1975** *Daily Mail* 16 Aug. 2/1 They had been responsible for a year-long campaign of bombings in the city... When police cleaned up the cell, the IRA activated a reserve unit of 'sleepers'. **1976** *Times* 7 June 12/5 There almost certainly exists within our political establishment, what is known as a 'sleeper'—a high level political figure who is in fact a Soviet agent, infiltrated into the system many years ago. **1981** *Observer* 29 Mar. 15 Key members of the.. Committee concluded that only the existence of a 'mole' or 'sleeper' (the preferred 'trade' word) could explain the many leaks and failures of the 1950s and 1960s.

**3.** *Zool.* **a.** A dormouse. Now chiefly *dial.*

**1693** RAY *Syn. Quad.* 220 *Mus Avellanarum Minor*... The Dormouse or Sleeper. [Hence in Chambers, Pennant, etc.] **1804** CHARLOTTE SMITH *Conversat.*, etc. I. 74 To make you ample amends, and add a little sleeper, as the country people call it, to your collection of minor poetry. **1827** GRIFFITH tr. *Cuvier* V. 221 Dormouse or Sleeper. **1880** MRS. O'REILLY *Sussex Stories* I. 4 Ralph the woodman had brought home a nest of 'sleepers'.

**b.** As the name of various fishes (see quots.). Also *attrib.*

**1668** CHARLETON *Onomast.* 135 *Excætus.. Adonis*; the Sleeper. **1854** *Eng. Cycl., Nat. Hist.* I. 502 *E[leotris] dormatrix*, the Sleeper, is a large fish. It is found in the West Indian marshes. **1882** JORDAN & GILBERT *Syn. Fishes N. Amer.* 15 *Somniosus microcephalus*, Sleeper Shark; Nurse. *Ibid.* 631 *Eleotris gyrinus*,.. Sleeper. *Ibid.* 632 *Dormitator maculatus*, Sleeper. **1884** GOODE *Nat. Hist. Aquat. Anim.* 675 The Nurse Shark or Sleeper.

**4. a.** A thing in a dormant or dead state.

**1625** BACON *Ess.*, *Of Judicature*, Let Penall Lawes, if they haue beene Sleepers of long,.. be by Wise Iudges confined in the Execution. **1823** E. MOOR *Suffolk Words* 360 *Sleeper*, the dead stub of a tree, in a bank, etc. **1854** MISS BAKER *Northampt. Gloss.*, *Sleepers*,.. such grains of barley as do not vegetate whilst undergoing the process of malting.

**b.** *Gambling.* (See quots. 1864, 1897.)

**1856** *San Francisco Bulletin* 4 Dec. 2/2 Some were waiting for 'sleepers', others were telling some other betters a certain card was going to win, dead 'sure'. **1864** W. B. DICK *Amer. Hoyle* 208 A bet [in faro] is said to be a sleeper, when the owner has forgotten it, when it becomes public property, any one having a right to take it. **1897** R. F. FOSTER *Compl. Hoyle* 623 *Sleeper*, a bet left or placed on a dead card at Faro. **1939** P. A. ROLLINS *Gone Haywire* 16 A Dakota miner had been detected attempting to steal 'sleepers' from the faro table. **1944** [see HEAVE HO b].

**5. a.** A railway sleeping-car; a train made up of or including sleeping-cars. Also *attrib.*

**1875** *Chicago Tribune* 11 Sept. 3/2 Every item of wood, iron, or upholstery which enters into the make-up.. of a Pullman sleeper is Selected with Skilled Care. **1880** W. WHITMAN *Daybks. & Notebks.* (1978) I. 188 On a first-class sleeper. **1881** 'MARK TWAIN' *Speeches* (1910) 258, I.. must change cars there and take the sleeper train. **1882** G. A. SALA *Amer. Revisited* II. 2 The Cerberus of the 'sleeper' is always bringing you the wrong boots. **1892** HOWELLS *Mercy* 214 He recalled the long, all-night ride without a sleeper, which he had once made on that route. **1950** O. S. NOCK *Brit. Locomotives from Footplate* vi. 118 The run with No. 46235 on the Inverness 'sleeper'.. shows how great sometimes is the gulf between maximum locomotive capacity under ideal conditions and practical application on the road. **1952** 'J. TEY' *Singing Sands* iv. 62 A friend who came across him on the train. Saw his name on the sleeper list, or noticed him in passing. **1967** O. WYND *Walk Softly, Men Praying* vii. 106 'You've got a sleeper reservation?' 'No, I was going to sit up.' 'All right... How about the eleven o'clock express.' **1969** M. PUGH *Last Place Left* xxi. 164 He made out sleeper tickets for us.. and we shared a two-berth compartment. **1970** R. ADAM *Stalk to Kill* xi. 158 A restless night in the sleeper train from London. **1979** P. THEROUX *Old Patagonian Express* iv. 53, I was glad to be on this sleeper to the coast.

**b.** Used *attrib.* and *absol.* to designate a vehicle with sleeping facilities.

**1939** *Nat. Geogr. Mag.* Feb. 133/2 Their covered wagons are now shiny streamliners (40 hours from Chicago), or mammoth sleeper buses (which they still call 'stages'). **1951** *Amer. Speech* XXVI. 308/2 *Sleeper*, any truck or tractor that is equipped with a sleeping berth. **1969** *Sydney Morning Herald* 24 May 9/7 Mr Ferrier plans to buy a sleeper-van and, with his wife, spend the next 18 months travelling around Australia. **1971** M. TAK *Truck Talk* 146 *Sleeper cab*, a tractor in which an adjoining bunk area is located behind the driver's seat. **1976** *Eastern Daily Press* (Norwich) 19 Nov. 14/2 (Advt.), *Scania* 32-ton tractor, sleeper cab.

**6.** Something whose quality or value proves to be greater than was generally expected; a 'dark horse'. orig. *U.S.*

**1892** *Outing* (U.S.) Mar. 454/2 Williams won the high and low hurdles in record time,.. and Harmar a second in the mile, being beaten by Wells, a 'sleeper' from Amherst. **1903** J. P. PARET *Lawn Tennis* III. vi. 350 Sleeper, a slang expression meaning a player who is much better than was thought. **1926** *Clues* Nov. 162/2 *Sleeper*, something of value that has been overlooked. **1945** *Richmond* (Va.) *Times-Dispatch* 31 July 7/4 In film parlance, this is a *sleeper*—a picture made with the thought that it would be just another light Summer item, but which has turned out to be a surprisingly popular box-office success. **1962** W. & M. MORRIS *Dict. Word & Phrase Origins* I. 267 A sleeper is a stamp more rare—and thus more valuable—than the catalogue listings indicate. **1968** J. D. WATSON *Double Helix* xx. 141 Bill's appearance was the sleeper of the three-day gathering... As soon as he had finished his unassuming report.. everyone in the audience knew that a bombshell had exploded. **1978** *Detroit Free Press* 5 Mar. B. 12/2 In any given week of new book arrivals, there occasionally is a sleeper, a book which comes in virtually unannounced with 'best seller' written all over it. **1981** J. D. MACDONALD *Free Fall in Crimson* v. 49 He made a couple of motion pictures .. on a very small budget, and they were what is called sleepers. They made a lot of money, considering what they cost.

**7.** Miscellaneous uses. **a.** An unbranded calf which has had a notch cut in its ear. *U.S.*

**1893** O. WISTER *Jrnl.* 31 Dec. (1958) 198 *Sleeper*, a cow with earmark and no brand. **1933** J. V. ALLEN *Cowboy Lore* I. 12 *A sleeper* is a calf ear-marked by a cattle thief who intends to come back later and steal the animal. **1949** *Boston Sunday Globe* 1 May (Fiction Mag.) 2/1 He.. gave a tally of the sleepers and mavericks he had branded.

**b.** An earring, esp. one in the form of a simple hoop, worn not primarily as ornament but to keep the hole in a pierced ear-lobe open.

**1896** G. F. NORTHALL *Warwickshire Word-bk.* 215 *Sleepers, sb. pl.*, fine, small rings of gold, first put into the ears after boring, and afterwards worn whenever the larger ear-rings, or 'droppers', are inconvenient. Their use is to prevent the closing of the perforations of the lobes. **1959** *News Chron.* 6 Oct. 6/2 That ghastly business of turning sleepers in a fresh and often painful wound. **1971** R. SCOTT *Wedding Man is Nicer than Cats, Miss* i. 38 Even quite small girls had had their ears pierced... No one wore sleepers, but the ear-rings could be taken out and the holes plugged with tiny pieces of wood. **1978** J. UPDIKE *Coup* (1979) vii. 293 Substituting for her great hoop earrings little sleepers of agate.

**c.** A sleeping-suit for a baby or a small child. Also *pl.* orig. *N. Amer.*

**1921** *Daily Colonist* (Victoria, B.C.) 12 Oct. 7/1 (Advt.), Children's sleepers at $1.95 a suit. Made of strong quality flanelette in neat colored stripe. **1944** C. HIMES *Black on Black* (1973) 247 Norma sat on the side of the bed and helped Lucy into her sleepers. **1970** *Toronto Daily Star* 24 Sept. 23/1 (Advt.), Minute imperfections should not affect wear, appearance or comfort of these cosy sleepers. **1975** *Daily Tel.* 14 Feb. 15/3 (*caption*) Lucy is in her Mothercare sleeper with vinyl feet.

**d.** A particle of sleep (SLEEP *sb.* 1 d).

**1942** BERREY & VAN DEN BARK *Amer. Thes. Slang* §251/1 *Sleepers*, particles in the eyes after a sound sleep. **1944** H. CROOME *You've gone Astray* i. 9 He had sleepers in his eyes, ugh!

**e.** A sleeping-pill. *slang.*

**1961** RIGNEY & SMITH *Real Bohemia* p. xvii, *Sleepers*, barbiturates (sedatives), usually seconal, nembutal, amytal, etc. **1967** M. M. GLATT et al. *Drug Scene* vii. 91 A lot of addicts are taking liquid Methedrine with 'sleepers' now —it is getting worse. **1979** C. DALE *Helping with Inquiries* I. 11 Take a sleeper, I would, put yourself right out.

**II. 8. a.** A strong horizontal beam or balk supporting a wall, joist, floor, or other main part of a building.

**1607** MARKHAM *Caval.* v. 4 All along as your sleepers lye to which you pinne downe the boards, must a trench or sinke be digged. **1675** V. ALSOP *Anti-sozzo* 356 Had he used only Sycamores, they had never been turned into Cedars by being Sleepers in the wall. **1717** in *Trans. Cumb. & Westm. Archæol. Soc.* III. 199 For binding yᵉ sleepers about yᵉ eastermost pillar, 0.3.0. **1794** T. DAVIS *Agric. Wilts.* 97 The .. material for barn-floors in this district is, two-inch oak plank, laid on oak sleepers. **1805** R. W. DICKSON *Pract. Agric.* I. 47 In this way floors are made more secure, and freer from damps, than where they are nailed down to sleepers. **1851** J. S. MACAULAY *Field Fortif.* 154 The sleepers and joists which bear on the walls should be shored up, so that.. the partial fall of the walls may not of necessity be followed by that of the several floors. **1879** *Cassell's Techn. Educ.* I. 79/2 The heads of the piles are cut off at one level; sleepers are laid across and fastened to them.

†**b.** A valley-rafter in a roof. (See also quot. 1688.) *Obs.*

**1688** HOLME *Armoury* III. 450/1 Sleepers [are] the two out pieces of the Dormant, which carrieth the Roof to overseil the Gable end, to secure it from Weather. **1703** R. NEVE *City & C. Purchaser* 166 Hips and Sleepers, are almost the same; only the Sleepers lie in the Vallies. **1753** *Chambers's Cycl.* Suppl. App., *Sleeper*, in building, a name used for the oblique rafter that lies in a gutter. **1811** *Self Instructor* 137 In sawing bevil work, as hipps, sleepers, &c. [**1842** GWILT *Encycl. Arch.* 1049 The old writers called the valley rafters *sleepers*.]

**9. a.** *Shipbuilding.* A strong internal timber in a ship (see quots.).

**1626** CAPT. SMITH *Accid. Yng. Seamen* 9 For clamps, middle bands and sleepers, they be all of 6. inch planke for binding within. **1627** —— *Seaman's Gram.* ii. 3 The sleepers run before and after on each side the keeleson, on the floore well bolted to the Foot-hookes. **1750** BLANCKLEY *Naval Expos.* 153 Sleepers are commonly three Strakes of Foot Waaling thicker than the rest, wrought over the Wrung-heads. **1769** FALCONER *Dict. Mar.* (1780), *Sleepers*, a name formerly given by shipwrights to the thick-stuff placed longitudinally in a ship's hold, opposite to the several scarfs of the timbers. It is now properly applied to the knees, which connect the transoms to the after-timbers on the ship's quarter. **1846** A. YOUNG *Naut. Dict.* 285 *Sleepers*, or *Engine-bearers*,.. pieces of timber placed between the keelson or keelson-riders in a steam ship, and the boilers of the steam-engine to form a proper seat for the boilers and machinery. *c* **1850** *Rudim. Navig.* (Weale) 148 *Sleepers*, pieces of compass timber fayed and bolted upon the transoms and timbers adjoining, withinside, to strengthen the buttock of the ship. **1867** SMYTH *Sailor's Word-bk.* 631 Sleepers.. are particularly used in Greenland ships, to strengthen the bows and stern-frame.

**b.** *Naut.* (See quot. 1882.)

*c* **1860** H. STUART *Seaman's Catech.* 76 The whole tops have the crosstrees, tops, and sleepers, bolted and secured before sending aloft. **1882** NARES *Seamanship* (ed. 6) 8 *Sleepers*.—Two cross-pieces over the top, to secure it down to the crosstrees and trestletrees.

**10. a.** *Mil.* A piece of timber forming one of the rests of a wooden platform for artillery.

**1688** CAPT. J. S. *Fortification* 69 Platforms.. where Timber and Wood is reasonable, are all made of Plank and Sleepers [and] Joyces to lay them upon. **1702** *Milit. Dict.* s.v. *Battery*, It is laid with Planks and Sleepers for them [*sc.* the cannon] to rest on. **1794** NELSON 9 July in Nicolas *Disp.* (1845) I. 431 If sleepers can be got, the platforms are undoubtedly much the better for them. **1802** JAMES *Milit. Dict.* s.v. *Platform*, Planks of oak or elm.. nailed or pinned on.. beams, from 4 to 7 inches square, called sleepers. **1879** *Man. Artill. Exerc.* 82 Where sleepers are used,.. the five sleepers are laid at right angles to the hurter.

**b.** A piece of timber or other material used to form a support (usually transverse) for the rails of a tramway or railway.

In early railways ***longitudinal*** or ***continuous sleepers*** were frequently employed.

**1789** BRAND *Newcastle* II. 687 *note*, After the road is formed, pieces of timber,.. called sleepers, are laid across it. .. Upon these sleepers other pieces of timber, called rails,.. are laid. **1798** *Term Rep.* VII. 599 To the sleepers or dormant timbers they affixed railways or waggon ways. **1837** *Civil Eng. & Arch. Jrnl.* I. 1/1 (Railways), The rails are.. fixed in cast-iron chairs,.. which are spiked down to the sleepers. *Ibid.* 2/1 Longitudinal timber sleepers. **1862** *Chambers's Jrnl.* Apr. 216 The pony roads.. are laid with sleepers, on which rails are placed for the corves to travel over. **1889** G. FINDLAY *Hist. Eng. Rlwy.* 46 The permanent way consists of wooden sleepers, laid transversely.

**c.** A strong longitudinal beam in a wooden bridge, supporting the transverse planks or logs.

**1823** COOPER *Pioneers* xxi, A little bridge, formed of round logs laid loosely on sleepers of pine. **1841** EMERSON *Ess.*, *Spiritual Laws*, One piece of the tree is cut for a weather-cock, and one for the sleeper of a bridge.

**d.** In general use: A horizontal beam, plank, etc., used to support any weighty body.

**1848** LAYARD *Nineveh* xii. (1850) 290 These were placed upon sleepers or half beams,.. laid on the ground parallel to the sculpture. **1879** *Man. Artill. Exerc.* 407 Skids should be supported on soft ground by laying sleepers of planks or fascines for them to rest on.

**11.** In miscellaneous techn. uses: (see quots.).

**1662** MERRETT tr. *Neri's Art of Glass* 364 *Sleepers* are the great Iron bars crossing smaller ones which hinder the passing of the coals, but give passage to the descent of the ashes. **1854** MISS BAKER *Northampt. Gloss.*, *Slats*, the sleepers or rails to support the bed of a cart. **1875** KNIGHT *Dict. Mech.* 2206/2 *Sleeper* (Weaving), the upper part of the heddle of a draw-loom through which the threads pass. **1892** P. H. EMERSON *Son of Fens* xviii. 181 We got inter the lock all right, shut the doors, and hulled up the sleepers to let the water out again.

**12.** *attrib.*, as ***sleeper-beam***, ***-block***, ***-wood***.

**1884** *Health Exhib. Catal.* 93/2 Air Bricks, Sleeper Blocks, &c. **1937** *Discovery* Dec. 377/2 The house had been divided into rooms by lath and plaster walls, the sleeper-beams for which were let into shallow trenches in the chalk or gravel floors. **1970** BRAY & TRUMP *Dict. Archæol.* 213/2 In early timber-framed buildings, Roman, Saxon and medieval, the framing was often erected not on a wall foundation but directly on a horizontal beam resting on or slightly recessed into the ground. From its recumbent position this is known as a sleeper beam.

**III. 13.** Special combs., as **sleeper agent** = sense 2 d above; **sleeper pass** *N. Amer. Football*, a pass unexpectedly involving a player hitherto ignored; **sleeper seat**, a reclining seat on which one can sleep during a journey; **sleeper wall** *Building*, a low wall built under a ground floor to support joists where there is no basement; so **sleeper walling**.

**1973** *TV Times* (Austral.) 3 Feb. 11/1 A *sleeper agent is someone who, over the years, has worked himself up into a position of trust. **1977** H. KAPLAN *Damascus Cover* (1978) v. 54 Operative Sixty-six is a member of the Syrian Parliament. He was a sleeper agent for twelve years. **1954** *Sun* (Baltimore) 4 Dec. (B ed.) 11/3 The Rams pulled the old corner lot '*sleeper' pass on the first running play of the new season for a touchdown. **1966** *Globe Mag.* (Toronto) 20 Aug. 7/3 Part of Canadian football folklore is the sleeper pass Keith Spaith threw.. in 1948. **1960** *Times* 11 Feb. 9/5 Whether *sleeper-seats and bunks should be provided. **1980** *Sunday Times* 21 Sept. 11 (Advt.), TWA's First Class Sleeper-Seats make it easy to lie back and relax peacefully.

**1836** PARKER *Gloss. Archit.* (1850) I. 429 The walls which support these timbers are called *sleeper-walls. **1893** *Archæologia* LIII. 551 The corresponding sleeper wall of the eastern colonnade. **1972** S. SMITH *Brickwork* viii. 37 The sleeper walls supporting the floor are built 'honey-comb', that is, with holes left through them to permit through ventilation. **1971** *Power Farming* Mar. 9/1 The latest aid to producing a 12ft-high stack at Kexby—a 50ft square of *sleeper walling—is illustrated.

Hence **'sleepered** *a.*, furnished with sleepers.

**1894** *Times* 13 Sept. 8/8 He does not think the accident could possibly have happened if the newly-sleepered portion of the line had become firm. **1900** *Daily News* 12 Mar. 5/4 The blundering of the mules along the sleepered platform.

**'sleeper**, *v. rare.* [f. the sb.] **1.** *trans.* To mark (a calf) with a notch in its ear.

**1910** C. E. MULFORD *Hopalong Cassidy* xii. 79 Either the H2 was sleepering Bar-20 calves for their irons later on, or rustlers were at work.

**2.** *intr.* To travel in a railway sleeping-car.

**1978** A. FRASER *Wild Island* xvii. 155 Beauregard was off..on the overnight sleeper to London. 'Flying visit... Back in the morning. Sleepering both ways.'

Hence **'sleepering** *vbl. sb.*

**1910** C. E. MULFORD *Hopalong Cassidy* xii. 80 'I saw a H2 sleeper, up just above th' Bend.'.. 'Lazy trick, that sleepering.'

**Sleeperette** (sliːpə'rɛt). Also **sleeperette.** [f. SLEEPER + -ETTE.] The proprietary name of a kind of reclining seat; = *sleeper seat* s.v. SLEEPER 13.

**1950** *Official Gaz.* (U.S. Patent Office) 11 July 443/2 Pan American Airways Inc., New York... Sleeperette. For transportation of passengers by aircraft. **1959** *Radio Times* 2 Jan. 28/2 (Advt.), Travel by sleeperettes on the 'Austropa Express'. **1966** *Punch* 31 Aug. 341/1 We could put Emma, who is three.., beside a VIP in his long-lie sleeperette. **1968** *Guardian* 27 Apr. 10/2 (Advt.), Fred Olsen car ferry from Harwich; single sleeperette fare £8 5s. **1982** *Daily Tel.* 24 Dec. 11/5 British Airways' new first class 'sleeperette' service.

**'sleepery**, *a. north.* and *Sc.* Now *rare.* Forms: 6 slep(e)rie, -ry, sleipry, 6–7 slipp(e)rie, 9 sleep(e)ry, -'ry. [prob. ad. MLG. *sleperich*, *slaperich*, or MDu. *slaperich* (Du. *slaperig*), = OHG. *slâfarag* (MHG. *slâf-*, *slæfric*, G. *schlafrig*).]

†**1.** Inducing sleep; soporiferous; characterized by a tendency to sleep. *Obs.*

**1513** DOUGLAS *Æneid* v. xiv. 52 This god smat baith his tymplis twane With a full slepry..grane. **1561** HOLLYBUSH *Hom. Apoth.* 4 b, A slouggish or slepery disease.

**2.** Of persons: Inclined to sleep; sleepy.

**1535** COVERDALE *Isaiah* v. 27 There is not one faynt nor feble amonge them, no not a slogish nor slepery parsone. **1556** LAUDER *Tractate* 287 ȝe sulde nocht chuse vnto that cure..No sleprie hird. *a* **1598** ROLLOCK *1 Thess.* (1606) 127 Of all sorts of men in the world a slipprie pastor, a carelesse man in the ministrie, is the worst. *c* **1802** SURTEES in Scott *Minstrelsy* I. 186 Sleep'ry Sim of the Lamb-hill,..my wae wakens na you. **1815** SCOTT *Guy M.* iii, If you..are not very sleepry. **1894** in Heslop *Northumbld. Gloss.*

**'sleepful**, *a.* [f. SLEEP *sb.* + -FUL.]

**1.** Of persons or animals: Sleepy. *rare.*

**1398** TREVISA *Barth. De P.R.* v. iii. (Bodl. MS.), Bestes þat haue to gret brayne been slepeful. **1635** W. SCOTT *Ess. Drapery* 138 Distrust will cure a Lethargie, of a sleepfull man it makes a wakefull one.

**2.** Marked by sleep; restful through sleep.

**1827** MRS. OPIE in Brightwell *Life* (1854) 200 Had a sweet sleepful and favoured night. **1860** N. MCMICHAEL *Pilgr. Psalms* 101 Sleep is more sleepful for long tortures sore. **1884** MRS. S. C. VENN *Dailys of Sodden Fen* iii, Busy days and sleepful nights.

Hence **'sleepfulness**, sleepiness.

**1818** TODD, *Sleepfulness*, strong desire to sleep. **1853** MISS E. S. SHEPPARD *Ch. Auchester* I. 281 The feeling of a knife and fork you cannot manage for sleepfulness. **1890** *Illustr. Lond. News* 30 Aug. 266/1 Dissipating..the last mists of my sleepfulness.

**'sleepifying**, *ppl. a.* [f. SLEEP *sb.*] Inducing or causing sleep.

**1662** J. CHANDLER *Van Helmont's Oriat.* 338 Why are not hot things judged to be alike Stupefactive and Dormitive or Sleepifying? **1695** T. TRYON *Dreams* App. 288 Madness is nothing but an Erring Sleepifying Power, because every Madman dreameth waking. **1835** BECKFORD *Alcobaça & Batalha* 4 The old Marquis of Marialva's most sleepifying dormeuse, which had been lent to him expressly for this trying occasion.

**sleepily** ('sliːpɪlɪ), *adv.* [f. SLEEPY *a.* + -LY².] In a sleepy manner, drowsily; also, calmly, quietly.

**1607** S. HIERON *Wks.* I. 117 If it be heard idlely, carelesly, scornefully, sleepily. **1688** *Answ. Talon's Plea* 9 He carries himself sleepily, and as if he were in a Lethargy, towards the Quietists. **1856** KANE *Arctic Expl.* I. xxix. 384 The renewed chorus..mingling itself sleepily in my dreams. **1873** BLACK *Pr. Thule* x. 161 That great extent of wooded plain, lying sleepily in its pale mists.

**'sleep-in**, *sb.* and *a.* **A.** *sb.* **1.** [-IN³.] A form of protest in which the participants sleep overnight in premises which they have occupied.

**1965, 1971** [see -IN³].

**2.** [f. vbl. phr. *to sleep in*: see sense 1 g of the vb.] An act of sleeping later than usual, a lie-in.

**1977** P. G. WINSLOW *Witch Hill Murder* II. 67 Those bells do make the damnedest racket. Nobody..can have a sleep-in on Sunday.

**B.** *attrib.* or as *adj.* [SLEEP *v.* 1 g.] Of a person: that sleeps on the premises, resident. Of a place: at which one stays overnight, residential.

**1961** in *Webster* s.v., Five sleep-in servants. **1970** L. SANDERS *Anderson Tapes* xxi. 56 Apartment Four A... A sleep-in maid. **1974** H. L. FOSTER *Ribbin', Jivin', & Playin' Dozens* vii. 329 The first was a three-week sleep-in camp experience for 62 children and their teachers in June, 1947, at Life Camps. The second was a three-day sleep-over school camping experience..at Hudson Guild Farm, Nokong, New Jersey. **1981** J. D. MACDONALD *Free Fall in Crimson* x. 106 He managed to hustle me into bed... I told him I had to quit. I wasn't going to be a sleep-in secretary.

**sleepiness** ('sliːpɪnɪs). [f. as SLEEPILY *adv.* + -NESS.]

**1.** The state of being sleepy; drowsiness; inclination to sleep; sluggishness, indolence.

**1580** HOLLYBAND *Treas. Fr. Tong, Endormissement*, sleepinesse, sluggishnesse. *a* **1586** SIDNEY *Arcadia* III. Wks. 1724 II. 680 Presenting a heavy sleepiness in her countenance. **1662** R. MATHEW *Unl. Alch.* 91 There is a sleepiness or dulness the next day in many that takes it. **1671** SALMON *Syn. Med.* I. xliii. 97 Sleepiness shews Cold and Moisture of the Brain. **1773** WILKES *Corr.* (1805) IV. 147 The symptom of her sleepiness is very alarming. **1860** SENIOR *Conversat.* (1880) I. 112, I have pitied poor little things of four or five years old dying from sleepiness, but kept up till nine. **1874** L. STEPHEN *Hours Libr.* (1892) II. vii. 233 [He] is mentally contrasting the sleepiness of the bishops with the virtues of Newton or Whitefield.

**2.** Numbness; absence of sensation. *rare*⁻⁰.

**1647** HEXHAM I, Sleepinesse or benummednesse of membres, *slaperigheyt der leden*.

**3.** Of cream: (see SLEEPY *a.* 1 c, quot. 1885).

**1885** J. LONG *Brit. Dairy-Farm.* 85 What other change of the cream is connected with the 'sleepiness' he has not found out.

**sleeping** ('sliːpɪŋ), *vbl. sb.* [f. SLEEP *v.*]

**1. a.** The fact, state, or condition of being asleep; an instance or occasion of this.

*a* **1300** *Cursor M.* 11583 þar ioseph on his sleping lai. **1362** LANGL. *P. Pl.* A. Prol. 10, I slumberde in a slepyng. *c* **1400** tr. *Secreta Secret., Gov. Lordsh.* 57 Wille þou noght folowe þy delyces yn etynge and drynkynge,..ne longe slepynge. *c* **1440** *Alph. Tales* 91 þis womman layde hur down..& slepyd, & in hur slepyng sho dyed. **1526** *Pilgr. Perf.* (W. de W. 1531) 126 The visyons..& inspiracyons of the holy goost, eyther in slepynge or wakynge. **1576** FLEMING *Panopl. Epist.* 221 As I say of this, so I say of nightly sleepings taken abusiuely. *a* **1613** OVERBURY *A Wife*, etc. (1638) 285 Often sleepings are so many tryals to dye. **1651** R. CHILD in *Hartlib's Legacy* (1655) 66 That you may better understand their severall sicknesses or sleepings. **1719** DE FOE *Crusoe* I. (Globe) 270 The Fellow..was between sleeping and waking. **1796** *Plain Sense* (ed. 2) III. 189 These frequent sleepings, exposed to the open air,..made more substantial cloathing necessary. **1886** GURNEY *Phantasms of Living* I. 389 These experiences, which occur on the borderland of sleeping and waking.

**b.** In *tranf.* or *fig.* senses.

**1398** TREVISA *Barth. De P.R.* VII. lvii. (Bodl. MS.), þey [that] haue þe stone in þe reynes feleþ in that place tyngling and slepyng for stopping of þe senewe. **1483** *Cath. Angl.* 344/2 Slepynge in yᵉ lymmes, *artesis*. **1613** SHAKS. *Hen. VIII*, II. iv. 163 You euer Haue wish'd the sleeping of this busines. **1838** W. BELL *Dict. Law Scot.* 919 *Sleeping of Process.* In the..Court of Session, a process..is said to be asleep, when a year and day have elapsed [etc.].

**c.** With advbs. as *around* (see SLEEP *v.* B. 1 b), *out* (see SLEEP *v.* B. 1 k).

**1852** *Rep. Committee on Criminal & Destitute Juveniles* App. III. 427 in *Parl. Papers* VII. 389 It is his fourth committal; his offence being, 'sleeping out'. **1945** S. LEWIS *C. Timberlane* xxiv. 155 Going to be none of this 'modern civilized, urbane' sleeping around and getting complicated in *our* house. **1957** J. BRAINE *Room at Top* xxv. 204 I'm glad you've decided to settle down. You're too old for sleeping around. **1973** E. J. BAHR *Nice Neighbourhood* xiii. 137 Her mother..did some sleeping around to help make ends meet. **1974** 'M. INNES' *Appleby's Other Story* ix. 73 One very large bush has been curiously hollowed out... The badgers use it as a sleeping-out place. **1976** V. CANNING *Doomsday Carrier* iv. 68 A sleeping-out pass until six tomorrow. **1976** *Howard Jrnl.* XV. I. 43 It seems wrong to assume..that non-indictable assaults, malicious damage, begging and sleeping out [etc.],..are all associated with social dereliction, homelessness, or disturbed behaviour.

**2.** *attrib.* **a.** With words denoting places used for sleeping in, as ***sleeping apartment***, ***-berth***, ***-box***, ***-cabin***, ***-car***, ***-chamber***, ***-place***, ***-platform***, ***-porch***, ***-quarters***, ***-room***, etc.

**1825** SCOTT *Betrothed* Concl., Receiving Damian de Lacy into her *sleeping apartment. **1834** *Chambers's Edin. Jrnl.* III. 316/2 The Calais boats being small, and mounting few *sleeping berths. **1939** AUDEN & ISHERWOOD *Journey to War* v. 123 The bugs must have been nesting in the upholstery of the shabby old Belgian sleeping-berths. **1979** O. SELA *Petrograd Consignment* 259 The..relative comfort of a first-class sleeping berth..all the way to Stockholm. **1847** H. MELVILLE *Omoo* i, Into a wretched 'bunk' or *sleeping-box. **1833** T. HOOK *Parson's Dau.* III. xi, Here was the governor's *sleeping-cabin. **1839** *Mechanic's Mag.* 5 Jan. 240 The introduction of the newly-invented *sleeping cars on our railroads. **1872** Sleeping-car [see PULLMAN a]. **1903** MRS. H. WARD *Lady Rose's Daughter* xviii. 313, I will go and get a sleeping car for you to Calais. **1954** T. S. ELIOT *Confidential Clerk* I. 32, I shall go and rest now. In a sleeping-car it is quite impossible To get one's quiet hour. **1978** J. SIMMONS *Railway in England & Wales 1830–1914* I. viii. 195 The first sleeping cars in Britain appeared in 1873, on trains running between London and Glasgow. **1814** SCOTT *Diary* 30 July in *Lockhart* (1837) III. iv. 137 Then the kitchen of the people, ..then their *sleeping-chamber. **1852** THACKERAY *Esmond* I. iv, A small chamber where..Harry Esmond [had] his *sleeping closet. **1889** *Pall Mall G.* 7 Feb. 7/1 The passengers say than an axle first broke under a *sleeping coach. **1656** PHILLIPS *Purch. Pattern* (1676) 11 *Sleeping holes to defend them from..the weather. **1688** STRADLING *Serm.* (1692) 185 What are Church-yards but κοιμητήρια, *Sleeping-houses. **1870** EMERSON *Soc. & Solitude* v. 98 An eating-house and sleeping-house for travellers. **1869** WALLACE *Malay Archip.* (ed. 10) 272 The skeleton of his little *sleeping-hut remained. **1565** COOPER *Thesaurus, Dormitorium*, a dortour: a *slepaynge place. **1688** MIÉGE, *Dortoir*,..the sleeping Place in a Monastery. **1840** *Cottager's Manual* 35 in *Husb.* III. (L.U.K.), To keep the pigs dry, a sufficient slope must be given..to the floor of the ..sleeping-place. **1910** W. DE LA MARE *Three Mulla-Mulgars* 52 Let us hobble on, Mulla-mulgars, until we find a quieter sleeping-place. **1957** P. WORSLEY *Trumpet shall Sound* viii. 150 Existing huts were to be..replaced by communal houses..one as sleeping-place for the men and one for the women. **1935** *Discovery* Dec. 361/2 Mr E. W. Savory did not actually see any of these apes in the district, but the presence of their *sleeping-platforms is proof of their residence there. **1940** R. FINNIE *Lure of North* 199 His original excavation, from which most of the snow blocks needed for the house had been taken, now constituted the floor, and the rest of that space—more than half—was the sleeping platform, a foot or so higher. **1915** J. WEBSTER *Dear Enemy* 44, I want two hundred feet of *sleeping-porch running along the outside of our dormitories. **1971** *Sunday Express* (Johannesburg) (Homefinder) 28 Mar. 2/2 (Advt.), Flats 6 × 2 plus sleeping porch. **1919** E. O'NEILL *Moon of Caribbees* 117 A door leading to the captain's *sleeping quarters. **1944** J. S. HUXLEY *On Living in Revolution* 111 Many people have to share crowded sleeping-quarters. **1982** V. MEHTA *Vedi* iii. 52 Mrs. Ras Mohun marched me up to her sleeping quarters. **1727** BOYER *Dict. Royal* I, *Dortoir*,.. the *Sleeping Room in a Monastery. **1789** J. MAY *Jrnl. & Lett.* (1873) 125, I often find..the air of the sleeping-rooms thick and ropy. **1833** *Chambers's Edin. Jrnl.* I. 386/1, I..was shown to my sleeping-room by the waiter. **1903** W. B. YEATS in *Fortn. Rev.* Apr. 752 Maeve walked through that great hall, and with a sigh Lifted the curtain of her sleeping-room. **1978** *Chicago* June 135/2 He..leads me into a small sleeping room, which has a cot, a small desk, and a chair. **1753** HANWAY *Trav.* II. xi. (1762) I. 52, I provided myself with a *sleeping waggon, and..took post for St. Petersburg.

**b.** With names of articles used for sleeping in, on, or with, as ***sleeping-bag***, ***-chair***, ***-gear***, ***-mask***, ***-mat***, etc.; **sleeping dictionary** *slang*, a foreign woman with whom a man has a sexual relationship and from whom he learns her language.

Hexham (1648), rendering Du. combs. in *slaep-*, has *sleeping-bank*, *-bed*, *-cap*, *-coif*, *-kerchief*, etc.

**1850** S. OSBORN *Jrnl.* 11 Oct. in *Stray Leaves from Arctic Jrnl.* (1852) 147 Friday morning, at seven o'clock, we rolled up our beds, or rather *sleeping-bags. **1856** KANE *Arctic Expl.* I. xvi. 196 We crawled into our reindeer sleeping-bags. **1933** *Discovery* Sept. 284/1 We retired to sleep in our sleeping-bags in the tiny room allotted us. **1978** *Times* 22 Nov. 5/4 She had put him..in his carrycot wrapped in a sleeping bag, romper suit and cardigan. **1675** in J. Gloag *Short Dict. Furnit.* (1969) 619 For a *sleeping chaire to fall in the back of Iron Worke. *a* **1877** KNIGHT *Dict. Mech.* I. 481/2 Car-seats..made reclining, for night travel..are termed 'sleeping-chairs'. **1924** MACQUOID & EDWARDS *Dict. English Furnit.* I. 215 In the Queen's Closet at Ham House are two winged 'sleeping chairs'..with ratchets to let down the backs. **1928** J. B. WHARTON *Squad* 21 We picked up two beauties... Oo-la-la—I've learned French—out uv a sleepin' dictionary'—dat's what dey're called. **1965** *Listener* 25 Mar. 461/3 He paints the old China of bound feet,..the endless dinners, the mistress (*sleeping dictionary) as fragile as a butterfly. **1979** M. LINDSAY in C. Allen *Tales from Dark Continent* i. 14 In East Africa..'East African officers as a whole maintained a..stricter code in the matter of sleeping with African women'—sometimes referred to as 'sleeping dictionaries', from their obvious advantages as language instructors—than did their fellow-officers in West Africa. **1856** KANE *Arctic Expl.* I. viii. 89 We had buffalo-robes for our *sleeping-gear. **1908** S. FORD *Side-Stepping with Shorty McCabe* ix. 139 They'd kept his face in a steam box by the hour..made him wear a *sleepin' mask, and done everything but peel him alive. **1944** S. BELLOW *Dangling Man* 79 A black cotton sleeping mask hung around her neck. **1836–7** DICKENS *Sk. Boz, Scenes* xxv, A row of large hooks, ..on each of which was hung the *sleeping-mat of a prisoner. **1965** A. NICOL *Truly Married Woman* 3 He then severely flogged his eldest son..for wetting his sleeping-mat last night. **1979** J. MELVILLE *Wages of Zen* ii. 21 Hanae always folded the sleeping mats up and put them away during the day. **1856** KANE *Arctic Expl.* II. xvi. 168 Two buffalo-robes..forming *sleeping-sacks for the occasion. **1622** T. SCOTT *Belg. Pismire* 12 Salomon the Preacher.. rowseth him vp from that *sleeping-stoole of his. **1897** CAPT.-SURG. HUGHES *Medit. Fever* v. 178 The *sleeping-suit (be it pyjamas or night-dress). **1897** *Outing* XXIX. 335/2 An elk-skin contrivance, miscalled a 'sleeping-suit'.

**c.** In the sense of 'inducing sleep', as ***sleeping cordial***, ***cup***, ***-draught***, ***pill***, ***powder***, ***tablet***, etc. Cf. SLEEPING *ppl. a.* 2.

**1398** TREVISA *Barth. De P.R.* XVII. civ. (Bodl. MS.), Mandragora is a slepinge herbe. **1568** GRAFTON *Chron.* II. 218 By the meane of a sleapyng poyson or drinke that he gaue to his kepers..he escaped. **1592** SHAKS. *Rom. & Jul.* v. iii. 244 Then gaue I her..A sleeping Potion. **1664** LADY HOBART *Let.* 23 Mar. in M. M. Verney *Mem.* (1899) IV. ii. 53 Thay had no way but to give hur a sleping pell, & she slep all night. **1709** E. W. *Donna Rosina* 120 Some sleeping Powders to be administered to Crispin. **1790** J. WOODFORDE *Diary* 17 Sept. (1927) III. 214 Her Child is dead..owing it is supposed to her [having] given him a Sleeping Pill. **1810** CRABBE *Borough* vii. 222 She gave her powerful sweet without remorse, The sleeping cordial. **1819** SCOTT *Ivanhoe* vi, Offer the sleeping cup to his holy man. **1829** —— *Anne of G.* xix, To hand round to the company a sleeping-drink, or pillow-cup. **1838** MRS. CARLYLE *Lett.* I. 97 Any sort of sleeping-draught, which had no opium in it. *c* **1900** H. A. JONES in M. R. Booth *Eng. Plays of 19th Cent.* (1969) II. 414 You'll find a sleeping powder in the second drawer... We must manage to give Lionel a little sleep tonight. **1934** G. B. SHAW *Too True to be Good* I. 42 It must be that new sleeping draught the doctor gave me. **1936** *Time* 19 Oct. 66/2 It was then that she attempted to find independence in an overdose of sleeping powder. **1938** W. S. Maugham *Writer's Notebk.* (1949) 300 He feels the moment can never be excelled and so takes an overdose of sleeping-pills. **1941** C. Milburn *Diary* 4 Oct. (1979) vii. 110 A sleeping tablet last night gave me a good rest. **1973** M. Amis *Rachel Papers* 30 Dozy afternoons slugging on opiate cough mixtures, sleeping-draughts dropped at noon, stolen handfuls of Valium, a sheet of aspirins before breakfast. **1976** H. Wilson *Governance of Britain* iv. 105, I have never had a sleeping pill in No. 10. I have never needed one. **1977** K. O'Hara *Ghost of T. Penry* xv. 148 She'd taken a quadruple dose of sleeping tablets last night.

**d.** Denoting morbid states, as ***sleeping disease, evil.***

(*a*) **1398** Trevisa *Barth. De P.R.* xvii. iii. (Bodl. MS.), Floures isode in oile awakeþ ham þat haue..þe slepinge yuel. **1580** Blundevil *Horsemanship* iv. xix, Of the Sleeping euill. **1639** T. de Gray *Compl. Horsem.* 69 The takings, sleeping-evil, madnesse, and the like.

(*b*) *a* **1586** Sidney *Arcadia* ii. (Sommer) 167 As I haue seene one that was sick of a sleeping disease, could not be made wake, but with pinching of him. **1899** Massee *Plant-Dis.* 328 The disease is indicated by the dull colour of the leaves [of the tomato], which commence to droop; this is quickly followed by a collapse of the stem, hence the name 'sleeping disease'.

**e.** In misc. use, as ***sleeping-halt, hour, partner, posture, stage, -tide, time*** (also *fig.*).

**1456** *Paston Lett.* I. 390 Writan in my slepyng tyme at after none, on Wytsonday. *c* **1560** Bp. Pilkington *Exp. Nehem.* xvi. 21 At noone he must haue his sleeping time. **1590** Shaks. *Mids. N.* iii. ii. 8 While she was in her dull and sleeping hower. **1656** Blount *Glossogr.* s.v. *Dormant*, A Lyon..lying in a sleeping posture. **1707** E. Settle *Siege of Troy* iii. 18 'Tis high sleeping Time, and so let's all home to Bed. **1833** E. B. Browning tr. *Aeschylus' Prometheus Bound* 96 The close and subtle clasping of a chain..Whose links are furnished from the common mine..From work-times, diet-times, and sleeping-times. **1856** Kane *Arctic Expl.* II. xxix. 289 At one of our sleeping-halts upon the rocks. **1887** Morris *Odyss.* iv. 105 When memory maketh loathly my meat and my sleeping tide. **1899** Massee *Plant-Dis.* 328 Shortly after the sleeping stage has been reached. **1903** Farmer & Henley *Slang* VI. 247/1 *Sleeping-partner*... 2. (common).—A bed-fellow. **1926** Maines & Grant *Wise-Crack Dict.* 14/1 *Sleeping time*, one year in Jail. **1959** T. S. Eliot *Elder Statesman* 5 The rhythm that governs the repose of our sleepingtime. **1967** P. D. James *Unnatural Causes* i. vi. 42 Your sleeping partner would provide you with an alibi. **1979** G. Mitchell *Mudflats of Dead* xiv. 144 Camilla wasn't the only predator... People are always changing their sleeping partners.

**sleeping** ('sliːpɪŋ), *ppl. a.* [f. sleep *v.*]

**1. a.** That is asleep; slumbering. Also *absol.*

*a* **1300** *Cursor M.* 21075 And als a slepand aends oft, It bers þe pudre vp o-loft. *a* **1400** *Minor Poems fr. Vernon MS.* xxiii. 1129 Þe geaunt..Þat wel a-wakeþ þe slepynge Of sleep of deþ so long. **1562** Winȝet *Wks.* (S.T.S.) I. 3 Sleuthfull marinaris and sleipand sterismen. **1590** Shaks. *Mids. N.* ii. i. 170 The iuyce of it, on sleeping eye-lids laid. **1605** —— *Macb.* ii. ii. 53 The sleeping, and the dead, Are but as Pictures. **1629** Milton *Hymn Nativity* xxvii, Her sleeping Lord with Handmaid Lamp attending. **1775** Sheridan *Duenna* i. i, My sleeping love shall know Who sings. **1812** Crabbe *Tales* xvi. 467 A sleeping boy the Mother held the while. **1899** *Allbutt's Syst. Med.* VII. 260 Group respiration may frequently be seen in sleeping children.

*Prov.* *c* **1374** Chaucer *Troylus* iii. 764 It is nought good a slepyng hound to wake. **1562** [see dog *sb.* 17 k]. **1597** Shaks. *2 Hen. IV*, i. ii. 174 Since all is wel, keep it so: wake not a sleeping Wolfe. **1623** Wodroephe *Marrowe Fr. Tongue* 505/2 Do not awake the sleeping Cat. **1824** Scott *Redgauntlet* let. xi, Best to let sleeping dogs lie. **1864–86** [see dog *sb.* 17 k].

(*b*) ***Sleeping Beauty*** (occas. ***Princess***), the heroine of a fairy tale (Charles Perrault's *La belle au bois dormant*) who slept for a hundred years, until woken by the kiss of her prince; also (sometimes with small initial) applied allusively and joc. to any sleeping or unconscious person; also *attrib.* and *transf.*

**1729** R. Samber *Perrault's Tales* iv. 32 (*heading*) The sleeping beauty in the wood. **1830** Tennyson (*title*) The sleeping beauty. **1893** S. J. Weyman *Gentleman of France* III. xxviii. 91 The Castle before us..might have been that of the Sleeping Princess, so fairylike it looked. **1907** E. Glyn *Three Weeks* iv. 64 The Austrians..are naturally awake, whereas you English are naturally asleep, and you yourself are the Sleeping Beauty, Paul. **1909** Mrs. H. Ward *Daphne* ii. 40 It had been a Sleeping Beauty story so far. Treasure for the winning—a thorn hedge—and slain lovers! **1936** C. Day Lewis *Friendly Tree* vii. 97 Who could wake the Sleeping Beauty with a kiss of friendship? **1955** E. Bowen *World of Love* vii. 126 Sleeping-beauty briars..swung at her. **1965** J. Porter *Dover Two* ii. 26 A rather smudgy photograph of Curdley's Sleeping Beauty lying motionless in her hospital bed. **1967** V. Nabokov *Speak, Memory* vi. 136 The terra-incognita blanks map makers of old used to call 'sleeping beauties'. **1977** D. Bagley *Enemy* xxiii. 179 You can go in and wake the sleeping beauties. **1979** A. Price *Tomorrow's Ghost* ii. 28 You can be our Sleeping Princess in the Library, and I shall come and wake you with a kiss.

**b.** Occupying a bed or beds in a certain place. ***sleeping attorney*** (see quot. 1809).

**1809** Kendall *Trav.* I. 184 It has been found that a sleeping attorney may be rendered very profitable... His business is to secure a lodging in one of the many-bed-rooms, which at the public inns, happen to be chiefly occupied by a large part of the jury sworn to try the cause. **1876** T. Hardy *Ethelberta* (1890) 32 We've a house full of sleeping company, you understand.

**c.** Of plants: (see sleep *v.* 3 b).

**1757** J. Hill *Sleep of Plants* 3 In what are called the sleeping plants. **1796** Stedman *Surinam* II. xxv. 230 The sleeping plant, so called from its leaves..clapping close together from sun-set to sun-rise.

**d.** In specific names of animals, etc.

**1803** Shaw *Gen. Zool.* IV. 250 Sleeping Gobiomore..: supposed to take its name from the slowness of its movements. **1859** D. Bunce *Trav. with Dr Leichhardt* ix. 94 We disturbed many of the short, knobby-tailed sleeping lizard (*Agama*). **1883** *Harper's Mag.* Jan. 189/1 The eyes of the sleeping monkey (*nyctipithecus*). **1897** G. C. Bateman *Vivarium* 119 The Stump-tailed Lizard (*Trachysaurus rugosus*), also known as the Two-headed Lizard and the Sleeping Lizard, comes from Australia.

**e.** Seen in sleep.

**1781** Gibbon *Decl. & F.* xxx. (1787) III. 139 The mind of Alaric was ill prepared to receive, either in sleeping or waking visions, the impressions of Greek superstition.

**f.** ***sleeping policeman***: see policeman 1 e.

†**2.** Inducing sleep; soporific. *Obs. rare.* Cf. sleeping *vbl. sb.* 2 c.

*c* **1369** Chaucer *Dethe Blaunche* 162 A few wellys..That made a dedly slepynge soun. **1578** Lyte *Dodoens* 447 One is called Solanum somniferum, that is to say Sleeping Nightshade. **1597** Gerarde *Herbal* ii. li. 269 Dwale or sleeping Nightshade hath round blackish stalks.

**3.** Numb: devoid of sensation.

**1562** Turner *Baths* 3 These baths are good for..the unfelinge and slepinge membres. **1818** Hogg *Brownie of Bodsbeck* xii, On pretence of a sleeping leg. **1899** *Allbutt's Syst. Med.* VI. 640 Pressure, not in itself severe, will in time produce the well-known sleeping foot.

**4. a.** Inactive, torpid, quiescent.

**1538** Starkey *England* ii. iii. 208 Thys celestyal doctryne..ys neuer gyuen to idul & slepyng myndys. **1598** J. Davis *Epigr.* ii, Whilst in his sheath his sleeping sword doth bide. **1702** Rowe *Tamerl.* i. i, The magic Numbers rouze our sleeping Passions. **1754** Gray *Pleasure fr. Vicissitude* 6 Till April starts, and calls around The sleeping fragrance from the ground. *a* **1822** Shelley *Fragm. Unf. Drama* 184 Those words in which Passion makes Echo taunt the sleeping strings. **1851** Brimley *Ess.* (1858) 119 As means, he may..use them to move and rouse the sleeping soul.

**b.** ***sleeping table***, an immovable apparatus on which ore is washed.

**1839** Ure *Dict. Arts* 815 The *grilles anglaises* are similar to the sleeping tables used at Idria. **1855** J. R. Leifchild *Cornwall Mines* 207 Then follow the picking, stamping, and washing on a kind of sleeping table.

**c.** ***sleeping rent***, a dead rent (see dead *a.* 30).

**1870** *Law Rep.* 5 *Comm. Pleas* 584 There is no stipulation that the tenant shall pay any sleeping rent or minimum rent, or any rent in the event of no clay being raised during the term.

**5. a.** ***sleeping partner***, a partner in a business who takes no share in the actual working of it.

**1785** in Grose *Dict. Vulg. T.* **1818** Scott *Rob Roy* i, Your father, though his fortune was vested in the house, was only a sleeping partner, as the commercial phrase goes. **1887** W. P. Frith *Autobiogr.* I. xvii. 203 A sleeping partner in a cloth firm at Leeds.

*transf.* **1848** Lowell *Biglow P.* Ser. i. Introd., Associated (though only as sleeping partner) in a book. **1884** Rider Haggard *Dawn* xxxvi, His sole motive in consenting to become, as it were, a sleeping partner in the shameful plot.

**b.** (See quot.)

**1889** 'R. Boldrewood' *Miner's Right* (1899) 66/2 A transfer of a 'sleeping quarter share', that is, a proportion of the property of the claim, involving a sixteenth of the entire profit, without the necessity of representing or paying for the services of an able-bodied miner.

**6.** Quiet, silent; motionless.

**1784** Cowper *Task* i. 763 The moon-beam, sliding softly in between The sleeping leaves. **1794** Mrs. Radcliffe *Myst. Udolpho* xxviii, The lonely murmur of these woods, and the view of this sleeping landscape. **1855** Macaulay *Hist. Eng.* xix. IV. 257 The long lines of painted villas reflected in the sleeping canals. **1872** Black *Adv. Phaeton* xix. 276 The chimneys and slates of the sleeping houses.

Hence †'**sleepingness**, sleepiness. *Obs.*

**1398** Trevisa *Barth. De P.R.* vii. v. (Bodl. MS.), Ʒif..þe woodenes dureþ þre daies with slepingnes,..þere is no hope of rekoueryng.

'**sleepingly**, *adv.* [f. prec.] Sleepily.

**1638** Junius *Paint. Ancients* 237, I doe not use to view the statues and images made by Art sleepingly and slenderly. **1683** Kennett tr. *Erasm. on Folly* (1722) 25 To jog sleepingly through the World in a dumpish, Melancholly Posture cannot properly be said to Live. **1862** S. Wilberforce *Sp. Missions* (1874) 282 Allowing them to go on sleepingly, and comfortably. **1891** *Temple Bar* May 122 The *facchini*..struggled sleepingly upstairs for my luggage.

**sleeping sickness.** [sleeping *vbl. sb.*]

**1.** In general and *fig.* senses.

**1551** R. Robinson tr. *More's Utopia* ii. M.v.[r], Is there annye man so possessed wyth stonyshe insensibilitie, or with the sleping sicknes, that he wyll not graunt health to be acceptable to hym and delectable. **1647** W. Jenkyn (*title*), A Sleeping Sicknes the distemper of the Times. **1904** *Jrnl. R. Microsc. Soc.* Apr. 179 Sleeping Sickness of Silk-worms..is in no wise due to the micro-organisms of the mulberry leaves.

**2.** *Path.* Any of several similar diseases caused by protozoans of the genus *Trypanosoma* and transmitted by flies of the genus *Glossina*, prevalent in tropical Africa, and characterized by the proliferation of the trypanosomes in the blood and changes in the central nervous system leading to apathy, coma, and death. Also *attrib.*

**1875** Gore in *Brit. Med. Jrnl.* 2 Jan. 5/1 The Sleeping Sickness of Western Africa. **1897** Manson in *Allbutt's Syst. Med.* II. 485 Sleeping sickness is a disease of the central nervous system; beri-beri of the peripheral. **1905** [see Gambia]. **1908** W. S. Churchill *My African Journey* v. 96 On April 28th, 1903, Colonel Bruce, whose services had been obtained for the investigation of 'sleeping sickness'.., announced that he considered the disease to be due to a kind of trypanosome, conveyed from one person to another by the bite of a species of tsetse-fly called *Glossina palpalis*. **1926** *Encycl. Brit.* III. 558/1 Sleeping sickness is now treated by compounds of arsenic..; by compounds of antimony..; and by a drug of undisclosed composition called Bayer 205, or Germanin. **1958** L. van der Post *Lost World Kalahari* (1961) vi. 109 A small African outpost on the edge of the sleeping sickness country of Northern Bechuanaland. **1970** Passmore & Robson *Compan. Med. Stud.* II. xix. 7/2 Sleeping sickness in West Africa differs clinically and epidemiologically from the condition in East Africa. In the West, the disease generally runs a chronic course, in the East it is acute.

**3.** = sleepy sickness 2. Now *rare.*

**1918** *Proc. R. Soc. Med.* XII. (Med. Section) p. xvii, The term 'sleeping sickness'..would not be an inappropriate name for this epidemic [*sc.* encephalitis]. **1920** *Lancet* 13 Mar. 620/2 Some popular term for encephalitis lethargica less cumbrous than 'lethargic encephalitis' and free from the objection to 'sleeping sickness'. **1921** *Times* 3 Feb. 7/2 The Registrar-General's returns for the week..show that there were 21 cases of sleeping sickness (*encephalitis lethargica*) notified..in London alone. **1961** L. E. Bollo *Introd. Med. & Med. Terminol.* xiv. 148 The von Economo type of encephalitis (encephalitis lethargica, or sleeping sickness) is said to be of unknown etiology... African sleeping sickness, caused by protozoa of the genus *Trypanosoma*, is discussed later.

†'**sleepish**, *a. Obs.* Also 6 slepy(s)she, -ish(e, sleapish. [f. sleep *sb.* + -ish.] Somewhat sleepy.

**1530** Palsgr. 324/1 Slepysshe, heavy of slepe, *sommeilleux*. **1551** Turner *Herbal* ii. 46 They shal fall into a forgetfull and a slepishe drowsines. **1633** Ford *Love's Sacr.* iv. i, Your sleepish and more than sleepish security. **1675** Traherne *Chr. Ethics* 338 Temperance..puts activity and vigour into it, that it may not be a sleepish but heroick vertue.

**sleepless** ('sliːplɪs), *a.* Also 5 sleples, 6 slepelesse, 6–7 sleeplesse. [f. sleep *sb.* + -less. Cf. (M)Du. *slapeloos* (Kilian *slaeploos*), OHG. *slâflôs* (G. *schlaflos*).]

**1.** Deprived of sleep; unable to sleep.

**1412–20** Lydg. *Chron. Troy* i. 3546 To Medea he hath þe weye take, And sche abood sleples for his sake. **1483** *Cath. Angl.* 344/2 Sleples, *exsompnis*. *a* **1542** Wyatt in *Tottel's Misc.* (Arb.) 80 The body still away slepelesse it weares. *c* **1586** C'tess Pembroke *Ps.* lxxvii. iii, Whole troupes of busy cares..Tooke up their restlesse rest In sleepie sleeplesse eies. **1700** Ken in *Bk. of Praise* 272 When in the night I sleepless lie. **1820** Shelley *Prometh. Unb.* i. 4 Which Thou and I alone..Behold with sleepless eyes. **1848** Thackeray *Van. Fair* xliii, He lay all that night sleepless and yearning to go home. **1888** Allies *Holy See & Wand. of Nations* 83 The monks, called from their never intermitted worship, the Sleepless.

**2.** Yielding no sleep; marked by the absence or want of sleep.

**1633** P. Fletcher *Purple Isl.* i. xxvi, That they may..couch their head In soft, but sleeplesse down. **1662** J. Davies tr. *Olearius' Voy. Amb.* 12 We had a sleepless night of it. **1794** Mrs. Radcliffe *Udolpho* xxxv, She started from a sleepless pillow, to welcome the day. **1815** Byron '*My soul is dark*' ii, It hath been by sorrow nursed, And ach'd in sleepless silence long. **1858** Carlyle *Fredk. Gt.* xvii. vii. (1872) VII. 74 The Old Inn, hospitable though sleepless, stands pleasantly upon the River-brink. **1876** Miss Braddon *J. Haggard's Dau.* II. 38 A sleepless night shed the sober light of reason upon those clouds of sentiment.

**3.** Continually active or operative.

**1792** S. Rogers *Pleas. Mem.* i. 194 Oh mark the sleepless energies of thought. **1820** Shelley *Prometh. Unb.* i. 280, [I] thus devote to sleepless agony This undeclining head. **1848** Gallenga *Italy* I. p. xxv, Thought remained anxious, sleepless, rebellious. **1866** Geo. Eliot *F. Holt* (1868) 8 The quivering nerves of a sleepless memory.

**b.** Unceasing in motion; ever-moving.

**1795–1814** Wordsw. *Excurs.* ix. 212 The sleepless ocean murmurs for all ears. **1812** Byron *Ch. Har.* i. xiv, Winds are rude in Biscay's sleepless bay. *a* **1822** Shelley *To E. Williams* vi, The sleepless billows on the ocean's breast.

**4.** Used punningly: (see quot. and sleepy 1 c).

**1865** *Slang Dict.* 235 *Sleepless-hats*, those of a napless character, better known as wide-awakes.

Hence '**sleeplessly** *adv.*

**1847** in Webster. **1896** *Daily News* 4 Jan. 5/3 He sleeplessly guards his maize during the whole night.

'**sleeplessness.** [f. prec.] The state of being sleepless; *esp.* inability to sleep, insomnia.

**1646** Bp. Hall *Balm of Gilead* (1652) 221 In three years he [Mæcenas] slept not..an hour; which..Lipsius thinks good to mitigate with a favourable construction, as conceiving an impossibility of an absolute sleeplessenesse. **1837** Carlyle *Fr. Rev.* ii. iii. vi, Convulsing with strange pangs the whole sick Body, as in such sleeplessness and sickness the ear will do! **1861** Flor. Nightingale *Notes Nursing* (ed. 2) 53 Sleeplessness in the early night is from excitement generally. **1886** *Manch. Exam.* 8 Feb. 5/4 A correspondent..provides a new remedy for sleeplessness.

'**sleep-out**, *sb.* and *a.* [f. vbl. phr. *to sleep out*: see sleep *v.* 1 k.]

**A.** *sb.* A veranda, porch, or outbuilding providing sleeping accommodation; a sleeping area not in the main building. *Austral.* and *N.Z.*

**1941** *Coast to Coast* 84 'A nice scone and a nice cup of tea and a lay-down in the sleep-out,' Mrs Smith was saying in her warm, motherly voice. 'You'll be fine then.' **1962** A. Seymour *One Day of Year* 7 A multiple set, main areas being the kitchen; the 'lounge'; and Hughie's study, which is a glassed-in sleepout at the side of the house. **1977** *N.Z. Herald* 5 Jan. 2–15/8 (Advt.), Well-established country tearooms with 3-brm attached acom... There is almost an acre of grounds plus a sleepout to go with this bargain. **1979**

*Sunday Mail Mag.* (Brisbane) 29 Apr. 26/3 The sleep-out.. is now back to veranda play space.

**B.** *attrib.* or as *adj.* Of a person: that sleeps away from the premises, non-resident.

**1958** V. P. JOHNS *Servant's Problem* i. 11 It concerned the household in which she was the sleep-out, full-time maid. **1961** in *Webster* s.v., The sleep-out cooks and maids were coming to work.

**'sleep-over,** *sb.* (and *a.*) Chiefly *U.S.* [f. vbl. phr. *to sleep over*: see SLEEP *v.* 1 j.]

**A.** *sb.* **a.** (See quot. 1935.) **b.** An occasion of spending the night at a place other than one's residence. **B.** *attrib.* or as *adj.* Involving spending the night away from one's residence. Of a person: that stays the night.

**1935** *Amer. Speech* X. 236/1 A contributor testifies that in part of Pennsylvania, in college use, a sleep-over is a permission to stay away from church and remain in bed on Sunday morning. **1974** [see SLEEP-IN *a.*]. **1975** [see SLEEP *v.* 1 j]. **1979** *Sunset* (Desert ed.) Apr. 156/2 (*caption*) At night wall hanging unhooks to become a feather-soft mat for sleep-over guests.

**'sleep-walk,** *v.* [Back-formation f. SLEEP-WALKING *vbl. sb.* and *ppl. a.*] *intr.* To walk while asleep; to be in a state resembling that of a sleep-walker. Also *fig.*

**1923** in *Englische Studien* (1935) LXX. 119 The heroine sleep-walks. **1954** *Gramophone* XXXI. 445 She sleep-walks noisily, but with dramatic vigour. **1976** E. O'BRIEN in *New Yorker* 16 Aug. 30/1 Every night Mrs. Reinhardt sleepwalked. **1981** I. MCEWAN *Comfort of Strangers* i. 18 She sleepwalked from moment to moment, and whole months slipped by without memory, without bearing the faintest imprint of her conscious will. **1982** *Daily Tel.* 21 Dec. 4/6 Mr Reagan.. accused Congress of 'sleep-walking' into the future.

**'sleep-walker.** [SLEEP *sb.* 7.] One who walks while asleep; a somnambulist.

**1747** *Gentl. Mag.* XVII. Index, Sleep-walker, strange action of. **1794** *Sporting Mag.* IV. 106 A Sleep-walker and Sleep-talker perambulated and muttered. **1833** HT. MARTINEAU *Charmed Sea* iii. 38 Your life is like the adventure of a sleep-walker. **1871** NAPHEYS *Prev. & Cure Dis.* I. vii. 198 The popular notion that sleep-walkers never hurt themselves is far from true.

So **'sleep-walking** *vbl. sb.* and *ppl. a.*

(*a*) **1797** *Encycl. Brit.* (ed. 3) XVII. 534/2 A lad.. subject to that singular affection or disease called *Somnambulism* or sleep-walking. **1855** EMERSON *Misc.* 90 For they aspire to the highest, and this, in their sleep-walking, they dream is highest. **1899** *Allbutt's Syst. Med.* VIII. 157 Neuroses, such as headaches, night-terrors, sleep-walking or defect of self-control, should be noted.

(*b*) **1842** LYTTON *Zanoni* VI. vi, Sleep-walking yet awake. **1890** *Spectator* 3 May, He seems to let the waking or sleep-walking Prince come in under protest.

**'sleepwort.** *Obs.* or *dial.* (See quots.)

*c*1265 *Voc. Plants* in Wr.-Wülcker 558 *Lactuca*,.. slepwurt. **1597** GERARDE *Herbal* Gen. Table, Suppl., Sleepworte is Lettuce. [**1863** PRIOR *Brit. Pl.*, *Sleepwort*, from its narcotic properties, *Lactuca sativa*.] **1881** *Hardwicke's Science Gossip* XVII. 278 *Pinguicula vulgaris*, 'Sleepweed' or 'Sleepwort'; co. Antrim.

**sleepy** ('sliːpɪ), *a.* Forms: 3–4 slepi, 4–6 slepy, 5–6 slepie, 6 sleapie, 6–7 sleepie, 6– sleepy. [f. SLEEP *sb.* + -Y. Cf. OE. *unslǽpiȝ* sleepless, and NFris. *slîpig*, MDu., MLG. *slāpich* (Du. dial. *slapig, slepig*), OHG. *slâfag, -eg* (MHG. *slâfec, -ic*, obs. G. *schlafig, schläfig*).]

**1. a.** Inclined to sleep; having a difficulty in keeping awake; drowsy, somnolent.

*c*1250 *Gen. & Ex.* 871 He woren drunken and slepi. **1387** TREVISA *Higden* (Rolls) V. 385 þe kyng werþe wonderliche slepy. **1390** GOWER *Conf.* II. 94, I was noght slow ne slepi there. *c*1440 *Gesta Rom.* lxvi. 298 (Addit. MS.), The maiden wexe slepie, and sore vexed, and fille on slepe. **1470–85** MALORY *Arthur* VI. i. 183 For this viij yere I was not so slepy as I am now. *a*1548 HALL *Chron.*, *Edw. IV*, 250 Oh, I am so slepie, that I must make an end. **1587** TURBERV. *Trag. Tales* (1837) 152 She shifted thence with shame Her sleepie husbandes sworde. **1662** J. DAVIES tr. *Olearius' Voy. Amb.* 321 There are some who take of it only once in two or three daies, which makes them sleepy. **1697** DRYDEN *Virg. Georg.* IV. 277 Hollow Murmurs of their Ev'ning Bells, Dismiss the sleepy Swains, and toll 'em to their Cells. **1782** MISS BURNEY *Cecilia* II. v, She soon grew sleepy, and retired to her own room. **1859** MRS. CARLYLE *Lett.* II. 397 Fatigue, which makes an healthy human being sleepy. **1874** J. S. BLACKIE *Self-Culture* 49 Let a man sleep when he is sleepy.

**b.** Given to sleep; lethargic, heavy.

*c*1384 CHAUCER *H. Fame* 75 There slepeth ay this god vnmerie, With his slepy thousande sones. **1398** TREVISA *Barth. De P.R.* VI. xvi. (Bodl. MS.), He is slow, slepie and lusteles and forgendrith alle his lordis nedes. **1504** LADY MARGARET tr. *De Imitatione* IV. vi. 269 So wakynge to fables, so slepy to holy vygyls. **1579** W. WILKINSON *Confut. Fam. Love* Ep. Ded. *iij, Those which are able.. will not, because they are sleepy. **1654** tr. *Scudery's Curia Pol.* 184 Those quiet and sleepy Princes, who have no other thoughts, but for their own defence. **1697** DRYDEN *Virg. Georg.* III. 399 The sleepy Leacher shuts his little Eyes. **1756–7** tr. *Keysler's Trav.* (1760) II. 298 By others, from its sleepy countenance, [[it] is supposed to be designed for the emperor Commodus. **1869** MARTINEAU *Ess.* II. 130 Men are too sleepy to look after it. **1875** JOWETT *Plato* (ed. 2) V. 319 Arithmetic stirs up him who is by nature sleepy and dull.

**c.** *transf.* or *fig.*, in general or specific uses.

For the latter see the quotations in (*b*).

(*a*) **1597** BEARD *Theatre God's Judgem.* (1612) 206 Then his sleepie conscience awaked, and he fell into most horrible despaire. **1685** BAXTER *Paraphr. N.T.* Matt. xxvii. 4 O the stupidity of seared sleepy consciences! **1700** DRYDEN *Cymon & Iphigenia* 29 Love.. oft to virtuous Acts inflames the Mind, Awakes the sleepy Vigour of the Soul. **1807** WORDSW. *White Doe* III. 107 Not loth the sleepy lance to wield, And greet the old paternal shield. **1885** *Times* (weekly ed.) 16 Oct. 4/2 This district was not.. sleepy on the question of political opinion and political action.

(*b*) **1579** LANGHAM *Gard. Health* (1633) 444 The iuyce with Capons grease anointed on, helpeth raw heeles and sleepy galles. **1790** GROSE *Prov. Gloss.* s.v., An apple or pear beginning to rot is said to be sleepy. **1796** *Ibid.* (ed. 3), *Sleepy*, much worn: the cloth of your coat must be extremely sleepy, for it has not had a nap this long time. **1833** LOUDON *Encycl. Archit.* §1975 Where the conduit pipes are of great length.. the water.. is found to lose much of its strength, and become what is technically called sleepy. **1834** MARRYAT *P. Simple* (1863) 372, I expect her to drop every minute, like an over-ripe sleepy pear. **1885** J. LONG *Brit. Dairy-Farm.* 82 Almost every one connected with the dairy knows what 'sleepy' cream is... The whole of the cream assumes the appearance of froth.

**d.** ***sleepy lizard***, one of several Australian lizards of the family Scincidæ, esp. the shingleback, *Trachylosaurus rugosus*, found in the southern part of the country.

**1883** [see BLUE TONGUE, BLUE-TONGUE 2]. **1887** F. McCOY *Zool. Victoria* XIV. 120 Not uncommon about Melbourne, where it is generally called the 'Bluetongued Lizard', or 'Sleepy Lizard'.

**2. a.** Characterized by, appropriate or belonging to, suggestive of, sleep or repose.

*a*1225 *Ancr. R.* 272 þene bimased gost þet in one slepie 3 emeleaste uorȝemeð him suluen. **1390** GOWER *Conf.* II. 93 He routeth with a slepi noise. *Ibid.* III. 48 Of Daniel the slepi dremes. **1577** B. GOOGE *Heresbach's Husb.* IV. (1586) 175 When the sleepie time of the night coms in, they make lesse and lesse noise. **1610** SHAKS. *Temp.* II. i. 211 Surely It is a sleepy Language; and thou speak'st Out of thy sleepe. **1617** MORYSON *Itin.* I. 247 We.. did in this sort passe the sleepy houres in the morning. **1650** VENNER *Censure* 39 If in use of the Water you shall finde a.. sleepy disposition. **1775** GOLDSM. tr. *Scarron's Com. Rom.* I. 287 Rancour began to sleep with more tranquility.., his sleepy faculty not being now disturbed. **1786** MME. D'ARBLAY *Diary* 4 Nov., I did not approach the Queen that night with much of a sleepy composure. **1820** SCOTT *Monast.* Introd. Ep., In the true sleepy tone of a Scottish matron when ten o'clock is going to strike. **1849** JAMES *Woodman* vii, With a sleepy but affectionate look. **1891** BARING-GOULD *In Troubadour Land* xvi. 226 It does a little sleepy trade in salt.

**b.** Of morbid states. See also SLEEPY SICKNESS.

**1623** COCKERAM II, A Sleepie disease, *lethargie*. **1656** W. DU GARD tr. *Comenius' Gate Latin Unl.* 85 Continual [sleep],.. or the sleepie-evil. **1704** *Dict. Rust.* (1726), *Sleepy-evil*, a Distemper in Swine, that takes them in Summer-time. **1707** (*title*), An Exact Relation of the Strange and Uncommon Sleepy Distemper of Dirk Bakker. **1748** HARTLEY *Observ. Man* I. i. §1. 46 During Sleep and sleepy Distempers the Brain is particularly compressed. **1831** W. YOUATT *Horse* 103 Some say that there is a yellowness of the eye.. in the early stage of sleepy or stomach-staggers. **1913** DORLAND *Med. Dict.* (ed. 7) 887/1 *Sleepy staggers, stomach staggers*, a disease of horses, of unknown causation but usually associated with the eating of moldy hay and grain. **1922** *Times Lit. Suppl.* 3 Aug. 511/2 The tomato suffers from the so-called 'Sleepy Disease' manifested in a wilting of the plant.

**c.** Of places. (Common in recent use.)

**1851** MEREDITH *Love in the Valley* xix, Down the sleepy roadway Sometimes pipes a chaffinch. **1868** MISS BRADDON *Dead-Sea Fr.* i, The quiet streets and lonely squares of that sleepy Belgian city.

**3.** Inducing sleep; soporific. Now *rare.*

*c*1386 CHAUCER *Knt.'s T.* 529 His slepy yerde in hond he bar. **1398** TREVISA *Barth. De P.R.* XVII. cxxviii. (Bodl. MS.), Popy hatte Papauere and is a slepye herbe. **1559** W. CUNNINGHAM *Cosmogr. Glasse* 53 Morpheus the God of dreames, with his sleepie rodde. **1598** STOW *Surv.* vii. (1603) 52 Giuing to his keepers a sleepie drinke. **1651** WITTIE tr. *Primrose's Pop. Err.* 391 Those that are poysonous in their whole substance, as sleepy nightshade. **1697** DRYDEN *Virg. Georg.* I. 115 Sleepy Poppies harmful Harvests yield. **1760** *Impostors Detected* IV. vi. II. 209 At length we were forced to have recourse to some sleepy drugs. **1819** SHELLEY *Cenci* V. iii. 123 Come, I will sing you some low, sleepy tune. **1898** CROCKETT *Red Axe* 41 The old clothes.. gave off such a faint, musty, sleepy smell I could scarcely keep awake.

**4.** *Comb.*, as ***sleepy-eyed***, ***-headed*** (also ***-headedness***, ***-headiness***), ***-looking***; **sleepy-bye(s)**, *Sc.* **-baw** *sb.*, a nursery name for sleep; also as *v. intr.*, to go to sleep; **sleepy-head**, a sleepy or lethargic person; a drowsy-head; **Sleepy Hollow, sleepy hollow**, (*a*) a name given to a place with a soporific atmosphere or characterized by torpidity (in quot. 1820, to which some quots. allude, the name of a valley near Tarrytown (Irving's home) in Westchester county, N.Y. State); (*b*) a type of comfortable deep-upholstered armchair; also called ***sleepy-hollow chair***; **sleepy-time** *U.S.*, bedtime.

**1907** N. MUNRO *Daft Days* x. 85 Just you lie down there pet, and *sleepy-baw. **1925** M. BEERBOHM *Observations* 37 Before you go to *sleepy-bye I'll read it to you. **1968** A. DIMENT *Bang Bang Birds* x. 177 'Sleepy byes time, Lex,' and I just felt the prick in my arm before I was blotted out again. **1808** *Sporting Mag.* XXX. 77 The '*sleepy-eyed' beauties of Lely. **1876** GEO. ELIOT *Dan. Der.* xxxv, No sleepy-eyed animal. **1577** tr. *Bullinger's Decades* (1592) 769 These *sleepie-heades haue nothing to alleadge for this their .... imagination of the sleepe of the soul. **1840** DICKENS *Barn. Rudge* xxi, 'Here, sleepy-head,' said Joe, giving him the lantern. 'Carry this.' **1600** *Hosp. Incurable Fooles* 23 Negligent, sluggish, and altogither *sleepie-headed. **1828** SCOTT *F.M. Perth* v, Not to protect thee against this sleepy-headed Henry. **1841** CAPT. HALL *Patchwork* II. xiii. 252 The sleepy-headed manner of doing business in.. Sicily. **1884** G. MOORE *Mummer's Wife* (1887) 24 This charge of sleepyheadedness seemed to discountenance her. **1841** CAPT. HALL *Patchwork* II. xi. 205 The *sleepyheadiness of the Maltese rowers. **1820** W. IRVING *Sk. Bk.* VI. 51 (*heading*) The legend of *Sleepy Hollow. *Ibid.* 53 This sequestered glen has long been known by the name of Sleepy Hollow, and its rustic lads are called the Sleepy Hollow boys. **1834** M. EDGEWORTH *Helen* I. xv. 321 Beauclerc, who had not yet tried the chair, sank into its luxurious depth, and leaning back, asked if it might not be appropriately called the 'Sleepy-hollow'. **1836** *Madrid in 1835: Sk. by Resident Officer* I. v. 94 No friendly arm-chair; none of that somniferous form, not unaptly termed 'sleepy hollow'. **1868** L. M. ALCOTT *Little Women* v. 79 There were.. Sleepy-Hollow chairs, and queer tables. **1897** F. T. BULLEN *Cruise "Cachalot"* xxiv. (1901) 311 The whole place seemed a maritime sleepy hollow, the dwellers in which had lost all interest in life. **1922** JOYCE *Ulysses* 371 Rip van Winkle we played... Then I did Rip van Winkle coming back. She leaned on the sideboard watching. Moorish eyes. Twenty years asleep in Sleepy Hollow. **1924** GALSWORTHY *White Monkey* I. vii. 53 'First time I remember anything of the sort on that Board.' 'Sleepy hollow,' said Soames. **1955** 'A. GILBERT' *Is she Dead Too?* v. 91 There's plenty of work to be had, you don't have to stop in Sleepy Hollow. **1957** M. SWAN *Brit. Guiana* 98 It is a charming little sleepy hollow of a town with long strait streets. **1966** M. M. PEGLER *Dict. Interior Design* (1967) 412 *Sleepy hollow chair*, a mid-19th-century American chair which is upholstered and has a curved back and low, comfortable arms. The seat is usually scooped out. **1976** N. FREELING *Lake Isle* viii. 43 This bastard in Soulay is merely wanting to make a fuss. Sleepy hollow. If he were any good he wouldn't be there. **1981** *London Rev. Bks.* 2–15 July 6/4 The restless forces were never as strong in Britain as the laws of inertia and the politics of Sleepy Hollow. **1842** LOVER *Handy Andy* xxiv, A very *sleepy-looking gossoon entered. **1862** K. STONE *Jrnl.* 19 Aug. in *Brokenburn* (1955) 137 He was satisfied I would not sleep a wink, but at *sleepy time.. we all went to bed and slept soundly. **1918** S. C. BRYANT *Stories to tell Little Ones* p. ix, I have been in the habit of singing them rhymes.. a while before sleepy-time. **1950** O. NASH *Family Reunion* 81 At sleepy-time he beats a path Straight to the bedroom or the bath.

**sleepy sickness.** [SLEEPY *a.*] †**1.** = SLEEPING SICKNESS 2. *Obs.*

**1803** WINTERBOTTOM *Africans Sierra Leone* II. 29 The Africans are very subject to a species of lethargy..; it is called by the Soosoos, Kee Kóllee Kondee, or sleepy sickness. **1903** *Westm. Gaz.* 16 Jan. 7/1 They ran the risk of introducing the 'sleepy sickness' into the Colony.

**2.** Encephalitis lethargica, an often fatal disease widespread between 1916 and 1928, characterized in many of those who survived it by extreme somnolence due to physiological brain damage.

**1922** ASHBY & WRIGHT *Dis. Children* (ed. 6) 389 Encephalitis lethargica. Sleepy sickness. Epidemic stupor. This disease is more common in adults. **1923** *Daily Mail* 26 Feb. 9 Sleepy sickness (encephalitis lethargica) is attacking prominent people in Winnipeg. **1930** A. CHRISTIE *Murder at Vicarage* xiv. 112 There's nothing radically wrong with him. .... He's had Encephalitis Lethargica, sleepy sickness, as it's commonly called. **1962** 'J. BELL' *Crime in our Time* IV. 99 Encephalitis lethargica, or sleepy sickness (not to be confused with trypanosomiasis, sleeping sickness, carried by the tsetse fly). **1973** *Daily Tel.* 27 Jan. 11/1 Survivors of the great sleepy-sickness epidemic, which claimed five million victims between 1916 and 1927, lived on in a kind of somnolence for 40 years till this drug awoke them.

**3.** *Vet.* A disease of pregnant ewes, provoked by imbalance between the degree of nourishment and the stage of pregnancy, and characterized by somnolence and neuro-muscular disturbances; pregnancy toxæmia. Also *Comb.*

**1937** *Vet. Jrnl.* XCIII. 213 In the early stages of sleepy sickness they lie in a perfectly normal recumbent position, but before long.. on their side with legs stretched out. **1950** D. GASCOYNE *Vagrant* 8 Baa, Baa, O sleepy-sickness-rotted sheep, in your nice fold Are none but marketable fleeces. **1964** *N.Z. Jrnl. Agric.* Mar. 546/2 More than 80 per cent of deaths in the ewe flock occur over lambing, when losses due to blood poisoning, bearing trouble, sleepy sickness.. and lambing difficulties occur.

**sleer,** *v. rare.* [Of obscure origin.] *intr.* ? To look askance. Hence **'sleering** *ppl. a.*

The form may be genuine, as mod. dialects have *sleer* to sneer, and *slire, slier*, etc., to look askance. In some instances, however, where editions of 17th and 18th cent. works have *sleer*, the original reading is *fleer*.

**1633** P. FLETCHER *Purple Isl.* VII. xlvi, Ecthros slie, Whose .. sleering eyes still watch and wait to spie When to return still-living injuries. **1680** T. OTWAY *Caius Marius* II. i, But then Marius's Eye agen! how 'twill sparkle, and twinckle, and rowl, and sleer?

**sleer(e,** obs. variants of SLAYER[1].

**sleeresse, sleestere:** see SLAYERESS, -STER.

**sleet** (sliːt), *sb.*[1] Forms: 4 slet(h, 4–6 slete (4 slethe, sclete), 5–7 sleete, 4– sleet (6 *Sc.* sleit); 6 slyte, 8 slite. [Of doubtful origin, but prob. representing OE. (Anglian) *slét (:—*sléatj-*), related to MLG. *slôte* (LG. *slôte, slâte*), MHG. *slôze, slôz* (G. *schlosse*) hail. Norw. dial. *sletta*, Da. *slud*, and Icel. *slydda* have the sense of 'sleet', but it is difficult to associate any of these phonetically with the Eng. word.]

**1. a.** Snow which has been partially thawed by falling through an atmosphere of a temperature a little above freezing-point, usually accompanied by rain or snow.

c1300 *Land of Cokayne* 39 in *E.E.P.* (1862) 157 þer n'is dunnir, slete, no hawle. 13.. *Gaw. & Gr. Knt.* 729 Ner slayn wyth þe slete he sleped in his yrnes. c1385 CHAUCER *L.G.W.* 1220 *Dido*, Doun cam the reyn with hayl & slet so faste. c1460 *Towneley Plays* xiii. 61 Now in snaw, now in slete, When my shone freys to my fete. 1533 BELLENDEN *Livy* II. xxvi. (S.T.S.) I. 236 Incontinent fell sa hevy tempest with slete and snawis out of þe are, þat he was empeschet. 1553-4 *Lett., Doc.*, etc. *Cambridge* (1838) 228 On Sonday frost and som slyte. 1635 SWAN *Spec. M.* v. §2 (1643) 156 We have sometimes sleet; which is snow and rain together. 1697 DRYDEN *Virg. Georg.* III. 564 Perpetual Sleet, and driving Snow, Obscure the Skies. 1704 *Phil. Trans.* XXV. 1695 Some slite in the night. 1784 COWPER *Task* v. 140 Arrowy sleet, Skin-piercing volley, blossom-bruising hail. 1856 STANLEY *Sinai & Pal.* ix. 331 A tremendous storm of sleet and hail gathered from the east. 1875 JOWETT *Plato* (ed. 2) III. 83 The philosopher standing aside in the shower of sleet under a wall.

*transf.* 1666 DRYDEN *Ann. Mirab.* clxxxvi, The midmost Battles,.. Who view, far off, the storm of falling Sleet; And hear their Thunder ratling in the wind. 1671 MILTON *P.R.* III. 324 He saw.. How quick they wheel'd, and.. shot Sharp sleet of arrowie showers against the face Of thir pursuers.

**b.** A storm or shower of sleet. *rare.*

1728-46 THOMSON *Spring* 20 Winter.. bids his driving sleets Deform the day delightless. 1880 W. NEWTON *Serm. for Boys & Girls* (1882) 225 A sleet had fallen the day before and the pavements were very slippery.

**2.** *attrib.*, as ***sleet air***, ***blast***, ***-flake***, ***-gust***, ***-shower***, ***storm***, etc.; ***sleet-bound*** adj.

1782 J. TRUMBULL *M'Fingal* III. 65 He glitter'd to the Western ray Like Sleet-bound trees in wintry skies. 1832 WILSON *Noctes Ambr.* Feb., The Wellington Arms is by no means an uncomfortable howf in a sleet-squash. 1866 WHIPPLE *Character & Char. Men* 34 The sharp sleet air is invigorating. 1877 *Daily News* 27 Dec. 6/1 The Russians are there, out in the sleet blasts. 1888 LEES & CLUTTERBUCK *B.C. 1887* xxiv. (1892) 266 The cold dark clouds.. burst upon us in a furious sleet storm. *Ibid.* xxix. 327 In a blinding sleet-shower. 1928 BLUNDEN *Retreat* 48 Where the lashed sleet-gust foams, buffeting and blinding. 1929 C. DAY LEWIS *Transitional Poem* II. 34 When bullying April bruised mine eyes With sleet-bound appetites and crude Experiments of green.

†**sleet**, *sb.*[2] *Mil. Obs.*$^{-0}$ [? Error for *cleet* CLEAT *sb.*] (See quot.)

1802 JAMES *Milit. Dict.*, *Sleets*, are the parts of a mortar going from the chamber to the trunnions, to strengthen that part. [Hence in later Dicts.]

†**sleet**, *adv. Obs.*$^{-0}$ [Cf. A-SLET *adv.*] Aslant, slanting.

c1440 *Promp. Parv.* 459/1 Sleet, or a-sleet, *oblique*.

**sleet** (sliːt), *v.* Also 4 **slete**, **sleth-**. [f. SLEET *sb.*[1]]

**1.** *intr.* **a.** ***it sleets***, sleet falls.

c1325 *Gloss. W. de Bibbesw.* in Wright *Voc.* 160 *Ore negge, ore cemoie*, sletez. c1340 *Nominale* (Skeat) 585 Hit is slethe for hit slethuth. 1647 HEXHAM I, To Sleete, *sneeuwen*. 1687 MIEGE *Gt. Fr. Dict.* II, To Sleet, *pleuvoir & neiger tout ensemble*. 1755 JOHNSON, *Sleet*, to snow in small particles, intermixed with rain. 1845 DICKENS *Chimes* iv. 142 So it's blowing, and sleeting, and threatening snow. 1902 *Speaker* 7 June 277/1 She's up to some deviltry or other When it storms, or sleets, or snows.

**b.** To fall as, or like, sleet.

1596 LODGE *Marg. Amer.* 15 Or like the snow at once that dries and sleeteth [*rime* fleeteth]. 1955 C. M. KORNBLUTH *Mindworm* 39 Her manicured hand gripped his arm in excitement and terror. Unfelt radiation sleeted through their loins.

**2.** *trans.* **a.** To pour or cast like sleet.

1786 tr. *Beckford's Vathek* (1883) 127 By my formidable art the clouds shall sleet hailstones in the faces of the assailants.

**b.** To drive *away* with sleet.

1891 W. F. MOULTON *Let.* in *Mem.* (1899) 247 Every lingering fragment of inflection would be blown, snowed, sleeted, rained and sunned away.

Hence '**sleeted** *ppl. a.*, beaten upon, or covered with, sleet.

1849 WHITTIER *To Fredrika Bremer* ii, Strong as Winter from his mountains Roaring through the sleeted pines. 1884 *Harper's Mag.* Jan. 173/1 With.. sleeted spars and frozen sails.

**sleetch(y**, variants of SLEECH(Y.

'**sleetiness.** *rare*$^{-0}$. [f. SLEETY *a.*] The fact or condition of being sleety.

1727 BAILEY (vol. II), *Sleetiness*, Raininess and Snowiness. 1847 in WEBSTER.

'**sleeting**, *vbl. sb.* [f. SLEET *v.*] The action of the vb. Also *concr.*, a sleety shower.

1775 ASH *Suppl.*, *Sleeting*,.. the act of falling in sleet. 1841 LEVER *C. O'Malley* cix. 534 A thin sleeting of rain began to fall.

'**sleeting**, *ppl. a.* [f. SLEET *v.*] Falling as sleet; containing sleet; sleety.

1566 PAINTER *Pal. Pleas.* I. 90 By litle and litle he consumed, as sleting snow against the warme sone. 1611 COTGR., *Vent verglas*, a sharpe freezing, or sleeting wind. 1686 GOAD *Celest. Bodies* II. x. 290 There is no Iris ever observed from a Snowy, yea or a Sleeting Cloud. 1778 *Love Feast* 33 Soft as the sleeting Snow. 1907 H. WYNDHAM *Flare of Footlights* xxvii, A sleeting drizzle beat against the panes.

**sleety** ('sliːtɪ), *a.* [f. SLEET *sb.*[1] + -Y[1].]

**1. a.** Of storms, wind, etc.: Laden with, accompanied by, sleet.

1725 RAMSAY *Gentl. Sheph.* III. iii, I've seen with shining fair the morning rise, And soon the sleety clouds mirk a' the skies. 1777 WARTON *Ode 1st of April* 7 The sleety storm returning still, The morning hoar, and evening chill. 1849 WHITTIER *Legend St. Mark* i, The day is closing dark and cold, With roaring blast and sleety showers. 1884 *Harper's Mag.* Apr. 741/2 A cold sleety wind.

**b.** Resembling sleet; sleet-like.

1804 in Sir H. Davy *Rem.* (1858) 93 The sleety rain was still falling. 1846 DICKENS *Cricket on Hearth* i, The water—being.. in that slippy, slushy, sleety sort of state wherein it seems to penetrate through every kind of substance. 1892 H. HUTCHINSON *Fairway Island* 51 The flakes were at first small and sleety.

**c.** Suggestive of, produced by, sleet.

a1821 KEATS *Stanzas* i, The north cannot undo them, With a sleety whistle through them. 1897 CROCKETT *Lads' Love* xxv. 253 The sprinkled sleety grey-green of the water-meadow.

**2.** Of weather or time: Characterized by the presence or prevalence of sleet.

1816 JANE AUSTEN *Emma* II. xvii. 329 The evening of a cold sleety April day. 1826 MISS MITFORD *Village* Ser. III. (1863) 466 It was mid-winter; snowy, foggy, sleety, wet. 1836 E. HOWARD *R. Reefer* ii, That dismal sleety morning. 1876 DAVIS *Polaris Exp.* xxii. 567 At first it snowed and was sleety.

**sleeve** (sliːv), *sb.* Forms: α. 1 **sliefe**, **slife**, **slyf(e**, 5-6 **slyue** (5 **sclyue**, **-ve**). β. 1, 4-5 **slefe**, 6 *Sc.* **sleffe** (5 **scl-**), **sleif**. γ. 3-6 **sleue**, 4 **slieue**, 4, 6-7 **sleeue**, 6 *Sc.* **sleiue**; 4-7 **sleve** (5 **slewe**), 6- **sleeve** (6, 8 **sleave**, 6 *Sc.* **sleive**, **sleyve**, 7 **sleev**). δ. 5 **skleve**, 5-6 **scleve**, 6 *Sc.* **sclewe**. [OE. *slīęfe*, etc. (Anglian *slēfe*) weak fem., and (*slīęf*), *slȳf* str. fem., = EFris. *slêwe*, NFris. *slêv*, *slív* sleeve, related to MDu. *slove*, *sloof* (Kilian *slooue*) covering, Flem. dial. *sloove* band of wood, leather, or metal, etc.]

**1. a.** That part of a coat, shirt, or other garment which covers the arm. In early use freq., and still occas., a separate article of dress which could be worn at will with any body-garment.

See also FORESLEEVE, *hanging sleeve* (HANGING *ppl. a.*).

α. a901 *Laws Ælfred* §66 (Liebermann), Æȝhwelcere wunde beforan feaxe & beforan sliefan and beneoðan cneowe. c960 *Rule St. Benet* lv. 92 Hosa, slyfa, gyrdel, seax. c1000 ÆLFRIC *Hom.* I. 376 He bletsode ðone hlaf, and tobræc, and bewand on his twam slyfum. c1400 *Beryn* 3292 In this thevis sclyve [*rime* a-lyve] The knyff.. was ȝistir-day I-found! c1449 PECOCK *Repr.* II. xiv. 231 A man is not sufficientli clothid.. but if he haue on him his scho, his slyue, his coot. 1526 SKELTON *Magnyf.* 915 His gowne so wyde That he may hyde His dame and his syre Within his slyue.

β. 971 *Blickl. Hom.* 181 Petrus hæfde þonne þone hlaf ȝeseȝnod.. & hine ȝedyde on his twa slefan. c1325 *Metr. Hom.* 111 For qua sa nehe wit hend or slefes Hate molten pic, on thaim it cleuis. c1400 MAUNDEV. (Roxb.) xvii. 77 It has lang slefez and wyde. 1474 *Acc. Ld. High Treas. Scot.* I. 22, ij elne of satyne to lyne the Kingis riding govne scleffis. 1505 *Ibid.* III. 36 For ij elne wellus to be sleffis to ane cote to the King. 1596 DALRYMPLE tr. *Leslie's Hist. Scot.* I. 93 Wyd sarkis, with mony bosumis, and wyde sleifes.

γ. a1225 *Ancr. R.* 56 [He] seið þet heo mei iseon baldeliche holi men; ȝe nomeliche swuche ase he is, uor his wide sleuen. c1300 *Havelok* 1957 Comen her mo þan sixti þeues, With lokene copes, and wide sleues. c1386 CHAUCER *Prol.* 93 Short was his gowne, with sleues longe and wyde. 1452 *Maldon Court Rolls* (Bundle 31, no. 2), A peyr of slevys of blanket, a peyr of furred glovys. a1529 SKELTON *Bouge of Court* 433, I sawe a knyfe hyd in his one sleue. 1592 GREENE *Conny Catch.* III. 18 Which made them.. feel where their pursses were, either in sleeue, hose, or at girdle. 1614 B. JONSON *Bart. Fair* III. i, See you not Goldylocks.. in her yellow gown and green sleeves? 1650 R. STAPYLTON *Strada's Low-C. Wars* I. 7 A Mill of iron.. of such.. smalness, that a Monk could easily hide it in his sleeve. 1712-4 POPE *Rape Lock* i. 147 Some fold the sleeve, whilst others plait the gown. 1768 STERNE *Sent. Journ.* i, 'The coat I have on,' said I, looking at the sleeve, 'will do'. 1805 JANE AUSTEN *Let.* 21 Apr. (1952) 154, I wore my crape sleeves to the Concert, I had them put in on the occasion. 1829 SCOTT *Anne of G.* iii, One sleeve of his vest was dark green. 1860 FAIRHOLT *Costume* (1885) I. 71 Widening their sleeves until they hung, not only over the entire hand, but several inches beyond it. 1873 C. ROBINSON *N.S. Wales* 104 If he is willing to.. take off his coat, turn up his sleeves, and put his shoulder to the wheel of fortune. 1897 *Montgomery Ward Catal.* 297/1 Ladies' Gossamer Rubber Sleeves, 16 inches long. 1967 G. BELLAIRS *Single Ticket to Death* v. 61 He was without jacket and wore black calico detachable sleeves reaching to the elbows of his white shirt.

*Prov.* 1546 HEYWOOD *Prov.* (1867) 17 A broken leeue holdth tharme backe. 1577 HARRISON *England* II. ix. (1877) I. 207 The broken sleeue doth hold the elbow backe. 1625 B. JONSON *Staple of N.* I. ii, A broken sleeue keepes the arme backe.

δ. 1463 *Mann. & Househ. Exp.* (Roxb.) 222 A peyre of breganderys and the sklevys,.. xij. s. 1489 *Acc. Ld. High Treas. Scot.* I. 144 For ane elne of sattin to lyne the sclevis. 1511 *Ibid.* IV. 192 Ane coit with sclewiz. 1544 *Knaresb. Wills* (Surtees) I. 42 My beste paire off scleves.

**b.** Worn as a favour or token, or borne as a heraldic charge (cf. MANCHE[1] 2).

c1374 CHAUCER *Troylus* v. 1043 She made hym were a pencel of here sleue. a1548 HALL *Chron., Hen. VIII*, 63 b, The kyng had on his hed a ladies sleve full of Diamondes. 1596 SPENSER *St. Irel.* Wks. (Globe) 635/2 Knightes in auncient times used to weare theyr mistress or loves sleeve, upon theyr armes. 1603 DRAYTON *Bar. Wars* II. xxiii, A lady's sleeve high-spirited Hastings wore. 1606 SHAKS. *Tr. & Cr.* v. ii. 169 That Sleeue is mine, that heele beare in his Helme. 1859 TENNYSON *Elaine* 602 He wore.. upon his helm A sleeve of scarlet, broider'd with great pearls, Some gentle maiden's gift. 1880 *Encycl. Brit.* XI. 704 Bayard took a lady's sleeve and proclaimed it.. as a prize to be contended for.

**c.** A piece of armour for covering and protecting the arm. *Obs.* exc. *Hist.*

1465 *Paston Lett.* II. 190 The harnys Wyks delyveryd.. to hym..: Inprimis.. a payr slyvys of plate. 1590 SIR J. SMYTH *Disc. Weapons* 46 With sleeues of maile or chained with maile. 1603 *Inventory of Armour Tower Lond.* (Fairh.), Shirts of mail with sleeves. 1660 *Ibid.*, Sleeves of Male with a Velvet Coate to them. 1820 SCOTT *Monast.* xxxv, Armed with cuirass and back-plate, with sleeves of mail, gauntlets and poldroons.

**d.** In University use: A gown having sleeves, or one who wears such a gown.

In quot. 1752 the reference is to the proctorship, and in quot. 1858 to the taking of a degree.

1752 MULSO in *Life G. White* (1901) I. 67, I think you have paid the University a great compliment in accepting of the Sleeves. 1851 THACKERAY *Last Irish Grievance*, And uphold,.. to the world's daytistation, The sleeves that appointed Professor MacCosh. 1858 [J. C. THOMSON] *Almæ Matres* 9 Wait, sweet verdant, till you have put the sleeves on.

**e.** ***Hippocrates' sleeve***: see HIPPOCRATES.

**2.** In figurative or allusive phrases:

**a.** ***to hold***, ***pull***, ***shake***, ***take***, etc., ***by the sleeve***, in order to detain, attract attention, etc.

1390 GOWER *Conf.* II. 391 For thanne is poverte ate gate And takth him evene be the slieve. 1576 GASCOIGNE *Steele Gl.* (Arb.) 67 Let not the Mercer pul thee by the sleeue For sutes of silke, when cloth may serue thy turne. 1592 GREENE *Philomela* Wks. (Grosart) XI. 173 Loue beganne to shake him by the sleeue. 1592 NASHE *Pierce Penilesse* Wks. (Grosart) II. 127 Who can abide a scuruie pedling Poet to pluck a man by the sleeue at euerie third step in Paules Churchyard. 1600 HOLLAND *Livy* x. xvii. 364 Albeit Appius had given him his farewell and pasport, the weale publick & the armie held him still by the sleeve. 1653 GATAKER *Vind. Annot. Jer.* 176 Here I was about to lay down my pen, had not one passage more pulled me by the sleev. 1746 FRANCIS tr. *Hor.*, *Sat.* I. ix. 139, I then began.. To.. pull his Renegado Sleeve, That he would grant me a Reprieve. 1842 TENNYSON *St. Sim. Styl.* 168 Devils pluck'd my sleeve.

**b.** ***to have in*** or ***up one's sleeve***, to have in reserve, at one's disposal, or ready for some need or emergency. Also ***to put up one's sleeve***.

1500-20 DUNBAR *Poems* xxii. 68 Jok.. Can now draw him ane cleik of kirkis, With ane fals cairt in to his sleif. 1577 *F. de Lisle's Legendarie* K vij, He answered that he had contrary Edicts from the King in his sleeue. 1589 PUTTENHAM *Eng. Poesis* III. xxv. (Arb.) 305 To haue a iourney or sicknesse in his sleeue, thereby to shake of other importunities of greater consequence. 1855 TROLLOPE *Warden* xx. 312 Then the bishop brought forward another [plan] which he had in his sleeve. 1890 *Daily News* 19 June 6/1 At the finish Barrett had considerably more up his sleeve than the three lengths with which he finished.

†**c.** ***to hang on***, ***upon***, ***of*** (another's) ***sleeve***, to depend or rely upon for support or assistance. *Obs.*

a1548 HALL *Chron., Hen. VIII*, 69 That he would none of his seruauntes should hang on another mannes sleue, and that he was aswel able to maintein him as the duke of Buckyngham. 1560 DAUS tr. *Sleidane's Comm.* 238 b, I lyke it righte well that you saye howe Themperoure hangeth not of the Bisshop his sleve. 1597 HOOKER *Eccl. Pol.* v. viii. §3 To them which ask why we thus hang our judgment on the Church's sleeve. 1607 HIERON *Wks.* I. 369 You shall see.. a third hanging vpon some lawyers sleeue, to plot and deuise how to perpetuate his estate.

**d.** ***to laugh*** or ***smile in one's sleeve***: see LAUGH *v.* 1 b. Hence in other phrases (see later quots.).

1560 [see LAUGH *v.* 1 b]. 1571 GOLDING *Calvin on Ps.* xxxv. 12 They lawgh in their sleeve, which content themselves with the secret feeling of their owne joy. 1581 J. BELL *Haddon's Answ. Osor.* 259 b, Will they smile in their sleaves at this your folly? or will they laugh openly at it? 1603 DEKKER *Batchelors Banquet* Wks. (Grosart) I. 163 She.. doth not a litle reioyce and smile in her sleeue to see it. 1653 GATAKER *Vind. Annot. Jer.* 36 They laughed, as we use to say, in the sleev at least. 1768-74 TUCKER *Lt. Nat.* (1834) I. 616 A disinterested zeal, which those who recommend it laugh at in their sleeve as a weakness. 1806 BERESFORD *Miseries Hum. Life* VII. xviii, Forcing your lips close together in order to keep it a secret from a dull dog that you are yawning in your sleeve at his stupidity. 1857 TROLLOPE *Barchester T.* l, 'No, not that woman,' said Mr. Harding, enjoying his joke in his sleeve. 1871 L. STEPHEN *Playgr. Eur.* (1894) iv. 91 They had a dim impression that we might be smiling in our sleeves.

**e.** ***to pin.. on***, ***upon***, or ***to one's sleeve***: see PIN *v.* 4 b. Hence † ***to pin one's sleeve upon*** (obs.). Also, †to attach, assign, or attribute (something) to a person.

(*a*) 1575-85 ABP. SANDYS *Serm.* i. 10 How sharply are the Corinthians taken vp by the Apostle, for pinning themselues upon mens sleeues, saying, I am of Paul, and I of Apollos. 1599 [see PIN *v.* 4 b]. 1632 SANDERSON *Serm.* I. 295 We may not.. build our faith upon them.., nor pin our belief upon their sleeves. 1684 N. S. *Crit. Enq. Edit. Bible* 171, Yet am I not such a one as to pin my sleeve so passionately upon St. Jerome as every where to approve his Errors. 1712 M. HENRY *Popery* Wks. 1853 II. 342/1 They require men.. to pin their faith upon the pope's sleeve. 1831 *The Remembrancer* 198 Men who pin their faith on the sleeve of their neighbour. 1873 J. G. HOLLAND *A. Bonnicastle* i. 35, I pinned my faith to my father's sleeve, and believed as fully and as far as he did.

(*b*) 1616 R. C. *Times' Whistle* (1871) 28 Proud Meacock, make the world no more believe Gentility is pind vpon thy sleeve. 1642 MILTON *Apol. Smect.* Wks. 1851 III. 289 What of other mens faults I have pinn'd upon his sleeve, let him shew. 1668 H. MORE *Div. Dial.* II. xxi. (1713) 157 It seems a kind of disparagement, to pin Vertue and Divine Grace upon the sleeves of them that are unwilling to receive it.

**f.** Miscellaneous phrases (see quots.). ***to put the sleeve on*** (someone): (*a*) to beg or borrow money from (someone); (*b*) to arrest (someone): to cause (someone) to be arrested; ***a sleeve***

*across the windpipe*, an assault or severe blow (usu. *fig.*).

*to wear one's heart upon one's sleeve*, see HEART *sb.* 54 f.

**1546** *St. Papers, Hen. VIII*, XI. 110 The other twoo be of so goodde and playne natures,..as the Kinges Highnes might be sure to carry them in his sleve. **1553** T. WILSON *Rhet.* (1580) 183 My maister your father, hath many a tyme and oft, wipte his nose vpon his sleeve: meanyng that his father was a Fishemonger. **1580–3** GREENE *Mamillia* Ep. Ded., Being blamed of Pausanias, for striuing further then his sleeue would stretch. **1589** R. HARVEY *Pl. Perc.* (1590) 22 See how they grid thee in their sleeues already. **1843** LOCKHART *R. Dalton* III. v, Few cut the sleeve by the arm the first trial they make of it. **1860** H. GOUGER *Two Yrs. Impr. Burmah* 212 Our..doctor had crept up the sleeve of the Chief of the prison so far as to draw from him the gift of a bamboo. **1861** GEO. ELIOT *S. Marner* 22 I'd advise you to creep up her sleeve again. **1894** G. DU MAURIER *Trilby* II. 158 But then there's Alice's papa—and that's another pair of sleeves, as we say in France. **1904** H. JAMES *Golden Bowl* I. III. xxiv. 395 'Decide to live—ah yes!—for her child.' 'Oh, bother her child!.. To live..for her father—which is another pair of sleeves!' **1930** D. RUNYON in *Sat. Even. Post* 5 Apr. 72/2 These coppers..know who he is very well indeed and will take great pleasure in putting the old sleeve on him if they only have a few charges against him, which they do not. **1931** *Amer. Speech* VI. 440 *Put the sleeve on*, to borrow; to make a touch from a fellow convict. **1934** H. N. ROSE *Thes. Slang* iii. 29/1 Wait'll I put the sleeve on Joe fer some chewin'. **1937** *Nature* 23 Jan. 130/1 Prof. Furnas's exasperating,..naive volume is altogether another pair of sleeves. **1952** WODEHOUSE *Barmy in Wonderland* i. 13 My wardrobe perished in the holocaust, of course. When you're being given the sleeve across the windpipe by Acts of God, you don't waste time fumbling around for socks and trousers. **1960** WENTWORTH & FLEXNER *Dict. Amer. Slang* 486/1 *Put the sleeve on* (*someone*), 1. To arrest someone; to identify someone to the police for arrest. 2. To stop a friend on the street in order to ask for a loan of money; to ask for a contribution or for money owed. **1972** WODEHOUSE *Pearls, Girls, & Monty Bodkin* ii. 17 Just as if it looked as though all they had to do was collect the bridesmaids, order the cake and sign up the Bishop and assistant clergy, along came the sleeve across the windpipe. Her father refused to give his consent to their union.

**3. a.** [After F. *La Manche.*] The English Channel. *Obs.* exc. as *nonce-use*.

**1574** W. BOURNE *Regiment for Sea* xxii. (1577) 59 b, It is a dangerous place to hit or fal with, to enter into the sleue, comming homewardes out of Spaine or Portugall. **1610** HOLLAND *Camden's Brit.* 79 At Boloigne..a narrow streit [*marg.* called the sleeve] ebbing and flowing. **1626–7** in Birch *Crt. & Times Chas. I* (1848) I. 232 Many others have been likewise taken within the sleeve since the return of Captain Pennington. *a* **1661** HOLYDAY *Juvenal* (1673) 265 To fetch a wind..to bring us home into the Sleeve, our English Channel. **1909** *Daily Chron.* 14 Aug. 4/4 When he learned that a Frenchman had aeroplaned the Sleeve.

†**b.** A channel or strait. *Obs.*

**1614** RALEIGH *Hist. World* II. (1634) 220 If all that part of the Sleeve or Strait [in the Red Sea] had bin by the ebbe of a spring-tyde discovered. *c* **1645** HOWELL *Fam. Lett.* (1650) II. 113, I have already shot divers dangerous gulfs,..while others sail in the sleeve of fortune. **1655** FANSHAWE tr. *Camoens' Lusiad* II. 45 If Antenor with his ship did thred Th' Illyrian-Sleeve.

†**4.** *Mil.* A body *of* troops placed on the flanks of an army, battalion, etc.; a wing or flank. *Obs.*

After F. *manche*, used in this sense in the 16th cent.

**1574** H. S. *Most Briefe Tables* G iij b, It remayneth that wee do intreat howe to make the sleeves of the harkabuzers and winges of the horsemen. **1598** BARRET *Theor. Warres* III. i. 41, I would wish all great sleeues of shot to be deuided into many small troupes. **1604** EDMONDS *Observ. Cæsar's Comm.* 81 A sleeue of archers is auailable against an enemie, aswell in such arrowes as do not hit, as in such as do hit.

**5.** = SLEEVE-FISH. ? *Obs.*

**1611** COTGR., *Casseron*, the Sleeue, or Calamarie. **1655** MOUFET & BENNET *Health's Improv.* (1746) 242 Cuttles, called also Sleeves for their Shape, and Scribes for their inky Humour. **1693** *Phil. Trans.* XVII. 855 The Sleave or Inkfish *Lolligo.* **1722** J. JONES *Oppian's Halieut.* 231 *Τευδίς*, Lolligo, the Sleve, a flying Fish.

†**6.** (See quot.) *Obs.*$^{-1}$

Cf. F. *manche*, a leather or canvas hose used with a ship's pump, etc.

**1613** PURCHAS *Pilgrimage* VIII. iii. 618 Neither can the.. Rockes breake these yeelding Vessels. They haue also (as it were) a Sleeue in the bottome thereof, by which, with a subtile deuise, they conuey the water forth.

**7.** *techn.* **a.** (See quot.)

**1840** *Civil Eng. & Arch. Jrnl.* III. 27/1 This elastic material [in a pump] is surrounded by a sleeve of cloth, which admits sand to pass up and around it.

**b.** A tube, or hollow shaft, fitting over or enclosing a rod, spindle, etc., and designed to protect or strengthen it, or to connect one part with another. *spec.* part of a celt or prehistoric axe.

Also attrib. as *sleeve-axle*, *-coupling*, *-nut* (Knight).

*a* **1864** GESNER *Coal, Petrol.*, etc. (1865) 32 The pump-rods, which are tough wooden rods fitted together by iron sleeves and screws. **1869** RANKINE *Machine & Hand-tools* Pl. I 5, The two worms are united by a hollow shaft or sleeve. **1884** F. J. BRITTEN *Watch & Clockm.* 133 A groove is formed around the sleeve in which is a spring pressing the sleeve upwards. **1929** V. G. CHILDE *Danube in Prehistory* 78 Possibly they were shafted with the aid of horn sleeves. *Ibid.* 107 Axes and adzes hafted in deer-horn sleeves. **1970** BRAY & TRUMP *Dict. Archaeol.* 20/1 *Antler sleeve*, a section of deer antler carved into a mortice at one end to hold a stone axe head.

**c.** *Electr.* A metal cylinder fitted round the full length of the core of an electromagnetic relay to modify the speeds of opening and closing. Cf. SLUG *sb.*[2] 3 c.

**1921** W. AITKEN *Autom. Telephone Systems* I. 45 The copper sleeve and heavy ring on the core of F gives it a greater range of adjustment. **1969** S. F. SMITH *Teleph. & Telegr. A* ii. 45 The skin effect, due mainly to the iron core, tends to confine alternating magnetic fluxes at speech frequencies to the nickel-iron sleeves to give the required impedance.

**d.** *Aeronaut.* = DROGUE 3 (*b*) and (*c*).

**1933** C. K. STEWART *Speech Amer. Airman* (thesis, Univ. Akron) 90 *Sleeve*, a towed target for anti-aircraft guns to practice shooting at. **1933** S. SPENDER *Poems* 45 The airliner..Glides over suburbs and the sleeves set trailing tall To point the wind. **1937** *Times* 12 June 16/4 The target was the usual sleeve, towed behind a Fairey Gordon. **1942** *Tee Emm* (Air Ministry) II. 67 There's the old Henley and there's the sleeve coming up—. They're off!—..A grand salvo after a week's weary waiting.

**e.** A close-fitting protective cover or case, esp. one for a gramophone record; a slip-case. Cf. *record sleeve* s.v. RECORD *sb.* 14.

**1953** *N.Y. Times* 22 Mar. II. 40/6 Another group of buyers is swayed more by the art on the 'sleeve' or jacket than by the quality, or even by the title, of the music. **1954** *Melody Maker* 11 Dec. 15/2 His first LP to be released in this country..reached me without sleeve. **1976** W. GOLDMAN *Magic* III. ii. 119 She lifted the tone arm off, and..put the record back in the sleeve. **1981** *Verbatim* Spring 20/2 This is a man's pocket wallet with some plastic credit card sleeves.

**8. a.** *attrib.* and *Comb.*, as (in sense 1) ***sleeve-band***, ***-hole***, ***knot***, ***-link***, ***-puff***; (sense 7 d) ***sleeve target***; (sense 7 e) ***sleeve artist***, ***design***, ***information***, ***-picture***; ***sleeve-defended***, ***-hidden***, ***-like*** adjs.

**1977** *Times* 18 Apr. (Gram. Suppl.) p. iv/6 Individual *sleeve artists such as Roger Dean or Patrick Woodroffe. **1775** ASH *Dict.*, **Sleeveband*, the band of the sleeve. **1830** HOWITT *Seasons* (1837) 216 The dame..with *sleeve-defended arms, scorns to do less than the best of them. **1977** *Times* 18 Apr. (Gram. Suppl.) p. iv/7 Jazz musicians.. insisted on good *sleeve design. **1886** *Daily News* 8 Apr. 5/3 *Sleeve-hidden aces! **1878** ABNEY *Photogr.* (1881) 223 Below the mask..are two *sleeve-holes with attached sleeves. **1966** *Melody Maker* 23 July 16/5 Bob Houston's review of the John Coltrane album 'Ascension' blindly copies the *sleeve information that Freddie Hubbard plays the first trumpet solo. **1775** ASH, **Sleeveknot*, a knot of ribband worn on the sleeve. **1611** COTGR., *Manche*, a *sleeue-like narrowing of the sea betweene two lands. **1886** PASCOE *Lond. of To-day* xli. (ed. 3) 355 In the way of rings, *sleeve-links, scarf-pins, and the like. **1959** *Times* 10 Jan. 9/5 A disc with an imaginative if punning *sleeve-picture showing wind blowing through barley. **1894** *The Season* X. 38/1 With elegant vest and *sleeve-puffs. **1932** *Aeroplane* 11 May 839 (*caption*), A Fairey IIIF seaplane towing a *sleeve target for gunnery practice. **1955** 'N. SHUTE' *Requiem for Wren* iii. 68 Firing the Oerlikon at a sleeve target towed by an aeroplane. **1979** A. FOX *Threat Warning Red* iii. 27 Sleeve target this afternoon, an AA shoot. **1860** FAIRHOLT *Costume* (1885) II. 369 *Sleeve-weight..; they weighed about two ounces, and were covered with linen, and fastened to the bottom of the large sleeves to make them hang well.

**b.** Special combs., as **sleeve bearing**, a form of bearing in which an axle or shaft turns in a lubricated sleeve; **sleeve-board**, a shaped board on which sleeves are ironed or pressed; **sleeve-cap** *U.S.*, the topmost part of a sleeve; **sleeve-creeper**, one who curries favour by mean or indirect methods (cf. 2 f); **sleeve dog**, a very small Pekinese dog, usually under six pounds in weight; **sleeve gun** *U.S.*, a miniature gun which can be concealed in the clothing; † **sleeve-hand**, the wristband or cuff of a sleeve; † **sleeve-net** (see quot.); **sleeve-note**, an informative or critical note about a gramophone record, printed on the sleeve; **sleeve Pekinese** = *sleeve dog* above; **sleeve-valve**, a kind of valve, employed in certain types of internal-combustion engine, consisting of a hollow cylindrical sleeve fitting closely inside the engine cylinder and moving with the piston in such a way that inlet and exhaust ports are opened and closed at appropriate times; freq. *attrib.*; hence **sleeve-valved** *a.*; **sleeve-waistcoat**, a waistcoat having sleeves.

**1907** W. S. BOULTON *Pract. Coal-Mining* III. 9 The '*sleeve' bearing..is intended to obviate this waste [of oil], and to secure continuously good lubrication. **1967** *Times Rev. Industry* Aug. 22/2 Exhaust silencers, anti-vibration mounts, the substitution of sleeve bearings for ball or roller bearings, [etc.]..are only a few of the attempts made to reduce the noise at source. **1975** *Sci. Amer.* July 50/1 Since many motors, engines and other machines incorporate journal bearings (sometimes designated plain bearings, sleeve bearings, fluid-film bearings or bushings), the annual production of journal bearings is in the billions. **1826** W. E. ANDREWS *Rev. Fox's Bk. Mart.* II. 148 It would have been better for him if he had minded his thimble and *sleeve-board than dabble in theology. **1916** *Daily Colonist* (Victoria, B.C.) 2 July 7/6 (Advt.), Sleeve Boards, regular 75c. Our price 32c. **1969** D. CLARK *Death after Evensong* ii. 31 Trousers, with no fore-and-aft creases.., ironed on a sleeve board. **1964** *McCall's Sewing* xi. 158/1 All set-in sleeves are cut with a *sleeve cap that is larger than the armhole section into which it must fit. **1978** *Detroit Free Press* 2 Apr. 50/1 All too often a knitted sweater is ruined by puckers where the sleeve cap joins the shoulder section. **1809** E. S. BARRETT *Setting Sun* II. 6 Some of them..can discern between a soldier and a *sleeve-creeper. **1890** *Pall Mall G.* 26 Feb. 5/1 The quaint little Japanese terriers, called in their native island *sleeve dogs, because the ladies there carry them hidden in their sleeves. **1931** A. C. DIXEY *Lion Dog of Peking* iv. 12 They were petted and pampered, the smallest—the highly-prized 'sleeve' dogs—being carried in the voluminous sleeves of the long robes worn at Court by both sexes. **1970** P. TAMONY *Americanisms* (typescript) No. 27. 7 The toy or small breeds such as the Pekinese and Shih Tzu had been the sleeve dogs of women at the Imperial Court of China. **1944** R. F. ADAMS *Western Words* 146/1 **Sleeve gun*, a derringer such as a gambler carried up his sleeve. **1971** K. WHEELER *Epitaph for Mister Wynn* xxxii. 396 He..took out a snub-barreled Sharps derringer, a sleeve gun. **1974** E. MCGIRR *Murderous Journey* 153 Have a look at Pout... Sleeve gun and I'd guess an envelope in his breast pocket. *c* **1550** in Leland *Collect.* (1774) IV. 323 A Surcoat of the same [crimson velvet] furred with Mynever pure, the Coller, Skirts, and *Sleeve-hands garnished with Ribbons of Gold. **1611** SHAKS. *Wint. T.* IV. iv. 211 You would thinke a Smocke were a shee-Angell, he so chauntes to the sleeue-hand, and the worke about the square on't. **1611** COTGR., *Manche*, a *sleeue-net, a narrow and long fish-net. **1956** *Gramophone* Oct. 184/2 Each soloist is given his fair share of the spotlight (the *sleeve notes helpfully identify which plays when). **1980** *Early Music* Jan. 85/2 A pity, though, that the programme book's translation of the libretti kept so close to the impenetrable one in the sleeve-notes to the Electrola/Reflexe recording. **1949** I. HARMAN *Pekingese* iv. 37 A Miniature or *Sleeve Pekingese is, officially, any Pekingese which is not more than six pounds in weight. **1978** 'J. MELVILLE' *Axwater* i. 12 A tiny, bright-eyed, button-faced creature appeared..and behind it another even smaller. Two sleeve Pekingese. **1910** *Engineering* 18 Nov. 688/3 Both Messrs. Panhard and Levassor..and Messrs. Milnes Daimler, Limited..showed examples of the Knight *sleeve-valve engine. **1911** *Ibid.* 3 Nov. 590/2 The usual tappet-valves are replaced by a single sleeve-valve. **1958** GIBSON & TUTEUR *Control System Components* xi. 424 A Vickers two-land sleeve valve. **1982** P. DICKINSON *Last House-Party* iv. 49 'This car makes a remarkable amount of smoke.' 'That's the trouble with these sleeve-valve engines.' **1932** *World Today* Feb. 261/2 The news that Daimlers had taken over the Lanchester Company suggested that it might be a *sleeve-valved job. **1824** *Ann. Reg., Chron.* 90 Pittaway had a *sleeve-waistcoat such as he wears now. **1837** CARLYLE *Fr. Rev.* III. II. viii, He ..stands disclosed in a sleeve-waistcoat of white flannel.

**sleeve**, obs. form of SLEAVE *sb.* and *v.*

**sleeve** (sliːv), *v.* Also 5 **slevyn**, 5–6 **sleve**, 6–7 **sleeue**. [f. SLEEVE *sb.*]

**1.** *trans.* **a.** To fit (a garment) with a sleeve or sleeves. Cf. SLEEVED *ppl. a.*

*c* **1440** *Promp. Parv.* 459/1 Sleve garmentys (*K.* slevyn or settyn on sleuys), *manico.* **1598** FLORIO, *Immanicare*,..to sleeue a garment.

**b.** To clothe or cover (the arm, etc.) *with* a sleeve. In quot. *fig.*

**1887** BLACKMORE *Springhaven* III. 61 Although M. Jalais' trees were leafless now, they had sleeved their bent arms with green velvetry of moss.

†**2.** To provide (a body of troops) with a wing or wings. *Obs.*

**1598** BARRET *Theor. Warres* III. i. 41 So should I haue 10 ranks for to sleeue the one flanke of the battallion. **1613** HEYWOOD *Silver Age* II. i, Both our Armies Are cast in forme, well fronted, sleeu'd, & wing'd.

†**b.** *intr.* To draw or line *up* on the flanks or wings. *Obs.*

**1598** BARRET *Theor. Warres* III. i. 40 Hauing passed the straight, to sleeue vp in file. **1623** BINGHAM *Xenophon* 73 He gaue the word, that the following companies should sleeue vp by the first. **1635** BARRIFFE *Mil. Discipl.* lxxx. (1643) 229 The Musquettiers sleeve up file-wise, to the front.

†**3.** In pa. pple.: Pent *up*, confined. *Obs.*$^{-1}$

Used with allusion to SLEEVE *sb.* 3.

**1645** J. BOND *Job in West* 60 It is a Country partly hugg'd in the armes of the Ocean, upon the North; partly sleeved up by the narrow sea, upon the South.

**4.** To fix or fasten *on*, to couple, by means of a sleeve or tube.

**1875** KNIGHT *Dict. Mech.* 1449 The chisels..have weighted pistons sleeved upon them. **1902** *Encycl. Brit.* XXVIII. 97 The motors are sleeved on the axles.

**sleeve-button.** [SLEEVE *sb.*] A button for fastening the loose sides of a wristband or cuff, esp. the cuff of a shirt-sleeve; a sleeve-link.

**1686** *Lond. Gaz.* No. 2203/4 Four Turky Stone Sleeve-Buttons, sett in Gold, and Enamell'd. **1748** *Anson's Voy.* III. ix. 393 His watch,..snuff-box, sleeve-buttons and hat. **1827** SCOTT *Surg. Dau.* vii, You are in a place where a man's life has been taken for the sake of his gold sleeve-buttons. **1848** MARRYAT *Little Savage* (Rtldg.) 167 Having felt great inconvenience for want of sleeve-buttons to hold the wrist-bands of my shirt together. **1880** 'MARK TWAIN' *Tramp Abr.* 245 Cuffs fastened with large oxydised silver sleeve-buttons.

**sleeved** (sliːvd), *ppl. a.* Also 5 **slevid**, 6 **slieved**, **sleued**, *Sc.* **slewit**. [f. SLEEVE *v.* or *sb.* Cf. OE. *ȝesléfed.*] **a.** Fitted or provided with sleeves; having sleeves of a certain kind.

See also *long-*, *short-sleeved*, etc.

*a* **1500** *Chron. London* (1905) 202 Which said ladyes rode vpon..white palfrays in gownys of white Satyn slevid. **1555** WATREMAN *Fardle of Facions* I. iv. 48 Longe garmentes downe to the foote, slieved, and close rounde about. **1570** FOXE *A. & M.* (ed. 2) 1367/1 Then I put on him a sleued coate of mine. *a* **1700** EVELYN *Diary* 11 Jan. 1682, With leather socks.., a rich scymeter, and large calico sleeved shirts. **1823** SOUTHEY *Lett.* (1856) III. 386 A sleeved waistcoat of washing-leather. **1864** BOUTELL *Her. Hist. & Pop.* xiv. 163 The same composition is repeated upon the sleeved jupon of the Earl. **1880** [A. J. MUNBY] *Dorothy* III. 1895 In her russet-grey frock,..Sleeved to the wrists, of course.

**b.** Fitted or covered with a sleeve or sleeves (in sense 7 of the sb.).

**1905** *Engineering Rev.* XIII. 272/1 The Hyatt bearing has ..been successfully applied to sleeved axles, both in small cars and heavy 'buses and lorries. **1970** 'S. HARVESTER' *Moscow Road* i. 13 A stereophonic phonograph and two racks of sleeved discs. **1976** *Gramophone* June 51/3 The pressing is beautifully smooth, and the disc is attractively sleeved; the cover is a water colour of the composer by his son.

**sleeveen** ('sliːviːn, sliː'viːn). *Ir.* and *Newfoundland.* Also **sleiveen, slieveen.** [ad. Ir. *slíghbhín, slíbhín* sly person, trickster.] An untrustworthy or cunning person.

**1834** S. LOVER *Legends & Stories of Ireland* (Ser. 2) 295 How the man was chated by a *sleeveen* vagabone. **1888** W. B. YEATS *Fairy & Folk Tales Irish Peasantry* 220 In trust took he John's lands,—*Sleiveens* were all his race. **1892** J. BARLOW *Irish Idylls* viii. 215 He isn't the *slieveen* to be playin' fast and loose wid your dacint little slip of a girl. **1955** L. E. F. ENGLISH *Historic Newfoundland* 36 *Slieveen*, a deceitful person. *a* **1966** 'M. NA GOPALEEN' *Best of Myles* (1968) 104 A thief, a fly-be-night, a sleeveen and a baucagh-shool. **1973** G. PINSENT *Rowdyman* 42 Mr. Lowe told Will all about his friendship with our father and about how decent a fellow he was, but that Will had 'the looks of a sleeveen about him'. *Ibid.* 53 Well, I took my eyes off him for a half a second and that sleeveen jabbed me in the gut with two hard fingers. **1975** D. O'SULLIVAN in D. Marcus *Best Irish Short Stories* (1977) II. 95 'O, the crabbed, conniving little sleeveen.' 'She's up in London now, dancing in the Harp.'

**sleeve-fish.** [Cf. SLEEVE *sb.* 5.] A fish of the family *Loligo*; esp. the common calamary or squid, *Loligo vulgaris*.

**1611** COTGR., *Taute*, a Calamarie, or sleeue-fish. **1710** SIBBALD *History of Fife* 54, I have found these Crabs, we call Keavies, eating the Slieve-Fish greedily. **1820** T. MITCHELL *Aristoph.* I. 127 On a table or dish, There shall lie a sleeve-fish. **1840** tr. *Cuvier's Animal Kingdom* 340 The Sleeve-fish ..have in the back, instead of a shell, a horny lamina in the shape of a sword or lancet.

**'sleeveful.** *rare*$^{-1}$. In 5 *Sc.* sleiffull. [f. SLEEVE *sb.*] The fill of a sleeve.

*c* **1475** HENRYSON *Poems* (S.T.S.) III. 151 With ane sleiffull of slak, þat growis in the slus.

**sleeveless** ('sliːvlɪs), *a.* [f. SLEEVE *sb.* + -LESS.]

**1.** Of a coat, jacket, or other garment: Having no sleeves; made without sleeves.

*c* **950** *Rule St. Benet* (Schröer) lv. 89 Hæbban hy eac.. scapulare, þæt is ȝehwæde cuȝelan and slyflease. *c* **1000** ÆLFRIC *Voc.* in Wr.-Wülcker 151 *Colobium*, slefleas scrud. *c* **1430** HOCCLEVE *New Cant. T.* 56 Our lady clothid in a garnement Sleuelees, byfore him he sy appeere. **1532-3** *Act 24 Hen. VIII*, c. 13 To weare..in their dublettes and sleuelesse cotes, cloth of golde of tissue. **1562** *Richmond. Wills* (Surtees) 166 One sleveles coote of frees. *a* **1631** DONNE *Sat.* iv. (1633) 338 Sleevelesse his jerkin was, and it had beene Velvet. **1687** SHADWELL *Tenth Sat. Juvenal* 42 The Colour of the Mantle or Sleeveless Gown for the better sort was White. **1799** COWPER *The Salad* 23 Then baring both his arms—a sleeveless coat He girds. **1857** S. OSBORN *Quedah* xxiv. 344 A red sleeveless waistcoat..hung slack round his person. **1880** 'OUIDA' *Moths* I. 65 One of those sleeveless, legless, circus-rider's tunics.

**2.** †**a.** Of words, tales, answers, etc.: Futile, feeble; giving no information or satisfaction; irrelevant, trifling. *Obs.*

Very common *c* 1570–1600, esp. in *sleeveless answer.*

**1387-8** T. USK *Test. of Love* II. viii. (Skeat) l. 77 A wyse man..loketh and mesureth his goodnesse, not by sleuelesse wordes of the people, but by sothfastnesse of conscience. *c* **1440** *Jacob's Well* 181 For summe, in schryfte, schal tarye þe preest wyth sleueles talys, þat no-thyng longyth to schryfte. **1524** in Strype *Eccl. Mem.* (1822) V. 342 His Majesties awnswer unto such a sleveless messeage was [etc.]. **1546** *St. Papers Hen. VIII*, XI. 61 For youe knowe..how long youe laye there, and coulde have no answere butt a sleveles answere. **1579** W. FULKE *Conf. Sanders* 706 Fie vppon this horrible idolatrie which is defended with such a sleueles excuse. **1600** *Look About You* D ij b, You sent Iacke Daw your sonne..To tell a sleueles tale! **1650** MILTON *Eikon.* (ed. 2) vi. 54 With no more but No, a sleevless reason, ..to be sent home frustrat and remediless. **1685** *Refl. Baxter* Pref. A 3 b, He moving a many sleeveless Questions, unseasonably, to ensnare him, and entangle him. *a* **1700** B. E. *Dict. Cant. Crew, Sleeveless story*, a Tale of a Tub, or of a Cock and a Bull.

**b.** Of errands: Ending in, or leading to, nothing; having no adequate result or cause.

Very common *c* 1580–1700; sometimes used of pretended errands on which a person is sent merely to be out of the way for a time.

**1546** HEYWOOD *Prov.* (1867) 14 And one mornyng tymely he tooke in hande, To make to my house, a sleeueles errande. **1577-87** HOLINSHED *Chron.* III. 284 So as all men might thinke that his prince made small account of him, to send him on such a slevelesse errand. **1603** DEKKER *Batchelors Banquet* Wks. (Grosart) I. 214 Shee..had of purpose sent them forth on sleeuelesse arrands. **1663** J. SPENCER *Prodigies* (1665) 232 God never sent an Angel from Heaven upon a sleeveless errand. **1716** M. DAVIES *Athen. Brit.* II. 181 He was employ'd by Pope Alexander the third, upon a sleeveless Errand to convert the Sultan of Iconium. **1785** G. A. BELLAMY *Apol.* (ed. 3) II. 165 He might have conveyed it to me in a letter; and not have brought me to town upon such a sleeveless errand. **1790-** in dial. glossaries (Westm., Yorks., Suffolk, etc.). **1860** WARTER *Sea-board* II. 306 His whole life is but a slieveless [*sic*], useless, errand! **1931** L. STORM *Dragon* xvii. 293 I'd never have the courage like you ..to venture forth on what might be a sleeveless errand. **1948** *Chambers's Jrnl.* 320/2 And, as soon as they were settled in, he had McGilchrist ride openly away, putting it about he was satisfied all the talk of whisky-'stilling was a pack of lies by ill-doing ones willing to give the King's officer a sleeveless errand. **1959** I. & P. OPIE *Lore & Lang. Schoolch.* iv. 58 In some [*sc.* schoolchildren's tricks] he [*sc.* the dupe] is sent on sleeveless errands.

**c.** In general use: Paltry, petty, frivolous; vain or unprofitable. *Obs.* exc. *arch.* or *dial.*

**1550** BALE *Eng. Votaries* II. 106 Whan stryfes..were risen betwen monkes and their bishoppes for sleuelesse matters. **1657** HAWKE *Killing is M.* 18 If we examine his Characters, Marks, and Scutchion of a Tyrant, which he would fasten on his Highness sleeve, we shall find them sleeveless, and altogether impertinent. **1673** KIRKMAN *Unl. Citizen* 208, I was arrested upon sleeveless and idle occasions, undeserved and unlookt for. **1809** MALKIN *Gil Blas* VIII. xi. ¶ 2 You may perceive, I have not entangled you in a sleeveless concern. **1821** SCOTT *Fam. Lett.* (1894) II. xvii. 111 He..had no honourable mode of avoiding the sleeveless quarrel fixed on him. **1867** WAUGH *Tattlin' Matty* ii, He thinks o' nought i' th' world but race-runnin' an' wrostlin',..an' sich like sleeveless wark as that.

†**d.** Of a suit: Made in vain; futile. *Obs.*$^{-1}$

**1600** S. NICHOLSON *Acolastus* II. lxv, My suite was sleeueles, thy regard so colde, As if that I anothers tale had tolde.

**3.** *dial.* Of persons: Devoid of ability or character; shiftless, idle, incompetent.

**1854-** in dial. glossaries (Lanc., Yorks., Northampton).

Hence **'sleevelessness.**

**1882** *Sat. Rev.* 25 Nov. 687/1 The good-natured sleevelessness of Irish landlords. **1890** *Ibid.* 5 July 3/2 His easy-going sleevelessness might have led to the ruin of the whole expedition.

**sleevelet** ('sliːvlɪt). [f. SLEEVE *sb.* + -LET.] A small sleeve. Also, a detachable sleeve used to protect the ordinary one from dirt or wear, or to give additional warmth.

**1889** *John Bull* 2 Mar. 150/1 Even the tiny sleevelets were edged with fur. **1900** *Westm. Gaz.* 28 Sept. 3/2 The narrow little open sleeve, with close-fitting sleevelets.

**sleeven,** var. of SLIVEN *ppl. a.*

**'sleever.** *local, Austral.*, and *N.Z.* (See quots. 1896, 1899.) Also, a measure of drink (usu. of beer) contained in a sleever. Cf. *long-sleever* s.v. LONG *a.*[1] 18.

**1896** *N.B. Daily Mail* 7 Apr. 2 'The sleever,' containing 13 fluid ounces, or 2 3-5ths gills, imperial measure, was another customary Welsh measure. **1899** *N. & Q.* Ser. IX. III. 8/1 A 'sleever' of beer..contains about three-quarters of a pint. **1936** 'R. HYDE' *Passport to Hell* v. 89 Places where the police weren't so quick off the mark if the landlord passed a few sleevers over the counter after six o'clock. **1941** BAKER *Dict. Austral. Slang* 67 *Sleever*, a drink, esp. a large drink. **1970** 'H. CARMICHAEL' *Remote Control* i. 8 'I haven't got a glass with a handle so you'll have to make do with a sleever.'..She brought his beer. **1975** B. MEYRICK *Behind Light* viii. 99 Herby used to nip up to the New Inn, buy a 'sleever' of beer and bring it back.

**sleeve-silk:** see SLEAVE-SILK.

**sleeving** ('sliːvɪŋ), *vbl. sb.* [f. SLEEVE *v.*]

**1.** The action of the vb; the putting or fastening of sleeves to a garment.

**1495-6** *Rec. St. Mary at Hill* (1905) 219 For new slevyng of vj awbis & for parelyng of iij. **1502** *Privy Purse Exp. Eliz. of York* (1830) 22 For upper bodyeng, sleving, and lynyng of a gowne of blake velvet. **1527** *Dunmow Churchw. MS.* 6 For sleuynge of an awbe.

**2.** *Agric.* A piece or ridge of ground on either side of a furrow. ? *Obs.*

**1733** W. ELLIS *Chiltern & Vale Farm.* 56 The Horses.. treading hard on the sleevings of the Stitch, causes the Ground to lie flat. **1759** —— *Pract. Farmer* Gloss. s.v. *Combing*, Tho' a little sharp Ridge, or Sleeving be left, yet in a Manure [? *read* manner], this is neat clean Ploughing.

**3.** A tubular covering for a cylindrical object, esp. of insulating material for an electric cable, etc.; material used for this purpose.

**1923** *Wireless World* 12 May 168/2, ½ lb. No. 20 tinned copper wire and a quantity of insulating sleeving of various colours. **1933** *Electrician* 10 Feb. 185/2 Woven sleevings, stockingettes or circular tapes of cotton or silk are varnished and used extensively for insulating wire connections of windings, radio sets,..etc. **1978** *SLR Camera* Nov. 31/3 Should it prove to be undersize, the best policy will be to use suitable piece of thin-walled aluminium tube (available from model shops) as sleeving.

**sleezy,** variant of SLEAZY *a.*

**sleft,** *ppl. a. rare.* [f. SLEAVE *v.*]

†**1.** Slashed, cut. *Obs.*$^{-1}$

**1627** DRAYTON *Agincourt* cclxxix, Here a sleft shoulder, there a clouen scull.

**2.** *sleft silk*, sleaved silk.

**1752** tr. *Gemelli-Careri's Voy. round World* IV. I. viii. (Churchill), Some being of a cane colour,..others yellow, but soft as any sleft silk.

**slegh,** obs. f. SLY *a.*

**sleȝly,** obs. f. SLYLY *adv.*

**sleght,** obs. f. SLEIGHT.

**sleghte** (*pa. t.*): see SLETCH *v.*

**slehliche,** obs. variant of SLYLY *adv.*

†**sleided** (also sleded), irreg. var. SLEAVED.

**1597** SHAKS. *Lover's Compl.* 48 She..Found yet mo letters sadly pend in blood, With sleided silke..enswath'd. **1608** —— *Pericles* IV. Prol. 21 When they weaude the sleded silke With fingers long, small, white as milke.

**sleigh** (sleɪ), *sb.* Chiefly *U.S.* and *Canada.* Also 8 **slay, sley.** [Originally *U.S.*, ad. Du. *slee*, contracted form of *slede* SLEAD *sb.*]

**1.** A sledge constructed or used as a vehicle for passengers, usually drawn by one or more horses.

**1703** S. SEWALL *Diary* 11 Dec., Corps is brought to town in the governours slay. **1705** *Ibid.* 11 Jan., The governour and his lady essaying to come from Charlestown to Boston in their slay,..his four horses fell in [to the water], and the two horses behind were drown'd. **1721** *New Engl. Courant* 25 Dec., They went to church in a sley. **1768** *Francis Lett.* (1901) I. 81 The Amusements among the Ladies..is riding upon the snow in Sleighs, a kind of open coach upon a sledge, drawn by a pair of horses. **1805** JEFFERSON *Writ.* (1830) IV. 31 The Canadian glows with delight in his sleigh and snow. **1838** STEPHENS *Trav. Russia* 70/1 An enormous sleigh, carved and profusely gilded, and containing a long table with cushioned seats on each side. **1878** LADY BRASSEY *Voy. Sunbeam* 18 At the summit we found basket-work sleighs, each constructed to hold two people, and attended by a couple of men, lashed together.

**2. a.** A sledge or sled employed for the transport of goods over ice or snow.

**1748** in Temple & Sheldon *Hist. of Northfield, Mass.* (1875) 259 The snow coming so soon after the river was froze.., and the river not strong enough to drive up provisions, that I was forced to have it carried upon Indian sleys. **1796** MORSE *Amer. Geogr.* I. 493 Upwards of 1200 sleighs entered the city daily..., loaded with grain of various kinds, boards [etc.]. *a* **1817** T. DWIGHT *Trav. New Eng.*, etc. (1821) II. 208 The produce of these tracts is conveyed to market chiefly in sleighs. **1836** *Backwoods of Canada* 67 No better mode of transport than..through the worst possible roads with a waggon or sleigh.

**b.** *Mil.* (See later quots.)

**1797** NELSON 17 July in Nicolas *Disp.* (1845) II. 414 The Theseus to make a slay for dragging cannon. **1875** *Encycl. Brit.* II. 663 Field artillery..has also been transported by sleighs, as in Canada. The sleigh is a platform placed on runners 16 inches high and 3 feet broad. **1876** VOYLE & STEVENSON *Milit. Dict.* 388/2 The term *sleigh* is also given to the carriage on which heavy guns are moved in store.

**3.** The bone of the upper jaw in a sperm-whale.

**1874** C. M. SCAMMON *Marine Mammals N. Amer.* viii. 75 Next to and above the bone of the upper jaw (which is termed the 'coach' or 'sleigh').

**4.** *attrib.* and *Comb.*, as *sleigh-dog, -man, -robe, -runner*, etc.; *sleigh-driving*; **sleigh bed** *N. Amer.*, a type of bed resembling a sleigh, having head- and footboards curving outwards; a French bed; **sleigh-cutter** (see CUTTER *sb.*[2] 3).

**1902** F. C. MORSE *Furnit. of Olden Time* iii. 77 Plainer bedsteads in this [French bed] style were made, veneered with mahogany, and they are sometimes called *sleigh beds, on account of their shape. **1950** W. BIRD *Nova Scotia* iii. 87 Those who spend the night in the ancient bedrooms, perhaps sleeping on the great 'sleigh bed' that remains in one. **1976** *National Observer* (U.S.) 14 Feb. 4/4 (Advt.), Antique Marketry Furniture, Ca. 1790, Dresser w/mirror, highboy, desk, two sleigh beds. **1846** J. TAYLOR *Upper Canada* 33 *Sleigh-cutters are a simple but elegant carriage, without wheels. **1806** PIKE *Sources Mississ.* (1810) 72 My *sleigh dogs brought me ahead of all by one o'clock. **1884** S. E. DAWSON *Handbk. Canada* 121 *Sleigh-driving, tobogganing, and skating are the pastimes of winter. **1884** *Chambers's Jrnl.* 5 Jan. 11/1 The *sleighman seats himself on one side of the sledge. **1747** *Boston Gaz.* 22 Dec., A pair of handsome *slay runners. **1824** LONGF. in *Life* (1891) I. iii. 37 There was very little snow left beneath the sleigh-runners.

**sleigh** (sleɪ), *v.* Also 8 **slay.** [f. the sb.] *intr.* To travel or ride in a sleigh. Also with *it*.

**1728-9** S. SEWALL *Letter-bk.* II. 264 They waited there for convenient snow to slay it to Salem. **1868** DICKENS *Lett.* (1880) II. 375, I have been sleighing about to that extent, that I am sick of the sound of a sleigh-bell.

Hence **'sleigher,** one who rides in or drives a sleigh.

**1830** SOUTHEY in *Q. Rev.* XLII. 81 As much to the delight of the sleighers as to the annoyance..of those who make their way on foot. **1874** *Daily News* 19 Jan. 5/5 The sleighers and the occupants of the carriages.

**sleigh-bell.** [SLEIGH *sb.*] **a.** One of a number of small bells (see quot. 1859) attached to a sleigh or to the harness of a horse drawing it.

*c* **1780** in *Amer. Poems* (1793) I. 208 Mind and have the sleigh-bells sent. **1849** LONGF. *Kavanagh* xxviii, The chiming sleigh-bells, beating as swift and merrily as the hearts of children. **1859** BARTLETT *Dict. Amer.* 414 *Sleigh-bell*, a small hollow ball, made of bell-metal, having a slit in it that passes half round its circumference, and containing a small, solid ball of a size not to escape. **1873** B. HARTE *Fiddletown* 50 It was the sound of sleigh-bells.

**b.** Used for orchestral purposes.

**1895** *Army & Navy Stores List* 1672 Sleigh Bells... Set of 12 on handle for Band or Orchestral use. **1898** *Eng. Mechanic* 8 July 481 'Sleigh-bells' are generally strung on a wire in ring-form, and fitted with a handle.

**c.** *sleigh-bell duck*, the American black scoter.

**1888** G. TRUMBULL *Names of Birds* 107 In the vicinity of Rangely Lake, Me., this bird is the Sleigh-bell Duck.

**sleighing** ('sleɪɪŋ), *vbl. sb.* [f. SLEIGH *sb.* or *v.*] Riding in or driving a sleigh, esp. as a pastime; also, the state of the ground when this is possible.

**1780** HAMILTON *Wks.* (1886) VIII. 33 When the sleighing arrives, it will be an affair of two days up and two days down. *a* **1817** T. DWIGHT *Trav. New Eng.*, etc. (1821) II. 403 The inhabitants are rarely furnished with good sleighing. **1842** DICKENS *Amer. Notes* (1850) 15/2 The weather being unusually mild.., there was no sleighing. **1886** *Manch. Exam.* 8 Jan. 6/1 Some of the gentry in the West End have taken to sleighing.

*attrib.* **1775** A. Burnaby *Trav.* 50 In the winter..it is usual to make what they call sleighing parties, or to go upon it in sledges. **1870** *Daily News* 22 Apr., Five pounds for what in Canada are known as 'sleighing rights'.

**sleiȝly**, obs. f. SLYLY *adv.*

**'sleigh-ride**, *sb.* Also **sleighride, sleigh ride.**

**1.** A ride in a sleigh. Also *fig.*

**1770** J. Hiltzheimer *Diary* (1893) 2 Apr. 20 Took a sleigh ride, the 'five mile round', with wife, sister, and son Tommy. **1828** H. J. Finn et al. *Whimwhams* 22 Such worthy gentlemen happen to remember..a winter's breakfast at a country inn, after a sleigh-ride of ten miles for an appetite. **1849** Longf. *Kavanagh* xii, Last week we had a sleigh-ride, with six white horses. **1902** W. D. Hulbert *Forest Neighbors* (1903) 181 Not even a sleigh-ride on a winter's night can set the live blood dancing as it will dance and tingle up there above the clouds. **1956** E. B. White *Let.* 14 Jan. (1976) 412, I am cheered up when I see our political giants discovering that the lil ole writing game isn't quite the sleighride they like to think it is.

**2.** *U.S. slang.* The action of taking a narcotic drug, usu. cocaine; the euphoria resulting from taking a narcotic drug. Usu. in phr. ***to take*** (***go on***) ***a sleigh ride*** and varr. Cf. SNOW *sb.*[1] 5 d.

**1925** *Flynn's* 4 Apr. 818/2 *Sleigh-ride*, a jab of morphine from a hypodermic syringe, or the resulting state of intoxication. **1928** M. C. Sharpe *Chicago May* xxxi. 286 *Taking a sleigh ride*, getting morphine. **1938** D. Castle *Do your Own Time* xxix. 251 'He took to going on sleigh rides.' 'No! Where the hell did he get the snow?' **1942** *Detective Fiction* Apr. 56/2 Julio is very fond of his hop. Anything from the weed to a sniff of snow. Suppose he gets on a big sleigh ride and talks out of turn. **1963** 'D. Shannon' *Death of Busybody* iv. 52 It was just some dope out on a sleigh-ride.

**3.** *U.S. slang.* An implausible or false story; a hoax, a deliberate deception. Freq. in phr. ***to take*** (someone) ***for a sleigh ride***, to mislead (someone). Cf. RIDE *sb.*[1] 1 f (*a*).

**1931** G. Irwin *Amer. Tramp & Underworld Slang* 172 An absolutely impossible or unlikely idea or action, or..the cheating or fleecing of a victim... 'We gave him a sleigh ride'—we cheated him by a false story or by sharp practice. **1942** Berrey & Van den Bark *Amer. Thes. Slang* §202/2 Incredible story, *sleigh ride.* **1950** *Sun* (Baltimore) 13 Mar. 1/1 House Republicans, charging that the taxpayers are being taken for a 'bureaucratic sleighride'. **1960** Wentworth & Flexner *Dict. Amer. Slang* 486/2 *Sleighride*, an instance of being cheated, believing a lie, or being taken advantage of. Almost always in the expression 'taken for a sleighride'.

Hence as *v. intr.*, (*a*) to ride in a sleigh; (*b*) to take a narcotic drug. Also **'sleigh-rider; 'sleigh-riding** *vbl. sb.*

**1807–8** W. Irving *Salmag.* (1824) 7 He recollects perfectly the time when young ladies used to go a sleigh-riding..without their mammas. **1833** *Knickerbocker* I. 207 Arrived at the Plains, the sleigh riders stopped at a tavern. **1845** Judd *Margaret* III. (1851) 377 In winter, we sleigh-ride, coast, skate, snow-ball. **1883** *Wheelman* (Boston, Mass.) I. 434, I was making my first trial of it [*sc.* a bicycle] in the snow, among the sleigh-riders. **1915** G. Bronson-Howard *God's Man* VI. iii. 376 Whadda you been doing?—sleigh-riding? Stick to the long bamboo, Charley—that snow's awful bad for the imagination. *Ibid.* VII. i. 409 Petty's kind had been profitable 'sleigh-riders' when he provided 'snow' on Seventh Avenue. **1929** *Detective Fiction Weekly* 13 Apr. 599/1 He's a sleigh rider. You know, sniffs coke. Made a fortune writing papers for booze hustlers and has spent every dime of it on snow. **1934** C. de Lenoir *Hundredth Man* i. 13 Sniffing heroin or cocaine is 'sleigh-riding'. **1949** *Summit Valley Times* (Argo, Illinois) 1 Dec. 4/3 Santa, who now reigns the Christmas card realm, in 1919 managed to sleighride onto only a handful of cards for children. **1977** H. Waugh *Secret Room of Morgate House* (1978) xxxiv. 164 Between times they sleighrode, and even walked. **1982** J. Adair *Founding Fathers* xii. 267 The New Englanders adopted..skating and sleigh-riding from their Dutch neighbours.

**sleight** (slaɪt), *sb.*[1] Forms: α. 3 **sleahþe**, 4 **sleiȝþe**, 4–5 **sleȝþe** (**sleghþe**); 4 **slyhþe, slyȝth, sliȝth**; also 3 **sleþþe**, 4 **sliþe, slythe, sleiþe, sleyþe**, 4–5 **sleithe, sleyth(e**. β. 4–5 **sleȝt, sleghte**, 4–7 **sleght**; 4 **sleyhte, sleihte**, 4–5 **sleyȝte, sleiȝt**, 4–6 **sleyghte, sleighte**, 4–7 **sleyght**, 4– **sleight** (5 **slieght**, 6 **slaight**); also 4–7 **sleyte**, 5 **sleyt**, 6 **sleite**. γ. 4 **slyȝt, sliȝt, slyghte**, 5–6 **slyght** (6 **slyht**), 4–8 **slight**; *Sc.* 5–6 **slycht, slicht** (6 **slichte**). [Early ME. *slēȝþ*, ad. ON. *slǿgð* (Icel. *slægð*, Norw. *sløgd*; MSw. *slögdh*, Sw. *slöjd* SLOYD *sb.*), f. *slǿg-r* SLY *a.*

For the change of the final *-þ* or *-th* to *t* cf. HEIGHT. The three leading types of ME. and later forms are illustrated under some of the senses below, and the following are instances of the chief variations from each of these:—

α. *c* **1275** Lay. 23345 Mid sleþþe he mot slakie loþe his bendes. **1387** Trevisa *Higden* (Rolls) I. 177 þey..fiteþ wiþ sleiþe and wiþ cauteles. *Ibid.* IV. 317 Naso..techeþ sliþe of love craft. *a* **1400** *Gloss.* in *Rel. Ant.* I. 6 *Calliditas*, a queyntyse or a slythe. *c* **1400** *Pilgr. Sowle* (Caxton) II. xlv. (1859) 51 By falshede, sleyth, and by extorcion. *c* **1440** *Promp. Parv.* 458/2 Sleythe, *astucia.*

β. *c* **1330** R. Brunne *Chron. Wace* (Rolls) 7151 Knyghtes þat conne of sleytes. *c* **1385** Chaucer *L.G.W.* 1650 *Hypsipyle & Medea*, Thour the sleyte of hire enchauntement. *c* **1400** *Apol. Loll.* 111 þis þout is sterid to him bi sleyt of þe fend. **14..** *Promp. Parv.* 64/1 (K.), Cavtele, or sleyte,..*cautela.* **1559** *Mirr. Mag.*, *Warwick* viii, Tooke the towne by sleyte. **1577** G. Harvey *Letter-bk.* (Camden) 56 To marke withall Ulisses Sleites. **1621** Quarles *Esther* ii, Who playes a happy game with crafty sleyte.

γ. **1375** Barbour *Bruce* v. 488 He thoucht to virk with slicht. **1456** Sir G. Haye *Law Arms* (S.T.S.) 177 With subtilitee or slycht. **1535** Stewart *Cron. Scot.* II. 160 Gif that he culd be slicht or ȝit ingyne. **1596** Dalrymple tr. *Leslie's Hist. Scot.* I. 295 Be sum slichte and quyet craft.]

**1.** Craft or cunning employed so as to deceive; deceitful, subtle, or wily dealing or policy; artifice, strategy, trickery. Now *rare* or *Obs.*

In very common use down to the 17th cent., and frequently contrasted with *strength, might,* or *force.*

α. *c* **1275** Lay. 17210 Hit was isaid wile, þat betere his sleahþe [*v.r.* liste] þane vuele strengþe. *c* **1330** R. Brunne *Chron. Wace* (Rolls) 4610 þe Bretons wist hit wel ynow, Bot of þer sleigþe lystneþ now. **1340–70** *Alex. & Dind.* 301 To faren in þe feld & fonde wiþ slyhþe For to refe þe brod of briddus of heuene. *a* **1400** *Sir Degrev.* 791 As wymmen conn mychel slyȝth.

β. *c* **1330** R. Brunne *Chron. Wace* (Rolls) 8800 Strengþe ys god wyþ trauaille; þer strengþe ne may, sleyght wil availle; Sleyght & connyng doþ many a chare. *c* **1385** Chaucer *L.G.W.* 931 *Dido.* Whan troye brought was to distruccioun By grekis sleyghte. *c* **1440** *York Myst.* xxii. 88 Sen thy fadir may þe fende be sotill sleghte. **1483** Caxton *Gold. Leg.* 377/2 How they myght by sleyght and deceyte..falle on good crysten men. **1555** Eden *Decades* (Arb.) 81 His kynsefolkes..shoulde haue taken eyther by sleyghte or force as many of owre men. **1582** Stanyhurst *Æneis* II. (Arb.) 45 Thear sleight and stratagems had beene discoouered easlye. **1622** Bacon *Hen. VII*, 103 By which Kind of Sleight rather then Stratageme the Towne of Dam was taken. **1650** Clarke *Eccl. Hist.* (1654) I. 44 The Devil striving against him with all the might and sleight that could be invented. **1841** Emerson *Lect.*, *Conservative* Wks. (Bohn) II. 270 Every interest did by right, or might, or sleight, get represented.

γ. *a* **1400** *Rom. Rose* 3158 It preveth wonder welle, Thy slight and tresoun every deelle. *c* **1400** *Laud Troy Bk.* 13036 'Now,' seyde he, 'kythe ȝoure slyght! Let se now ȝoure qwayntyse'. **1578** Timme *Calvin on Gen.* 297 Satan used his subtle slight to discredit the miracles wrought by God. **1596** Drayton *Legends* iv. 395 Much wrought they with their power, much with their slight. **1652** Urquhart *Jewel* Wks. (1834) 212 Who by hook and crook,..slight and might, having feathered their neste to some purpose. **1699** Temple *Hist. Eng.* 565 He endeavoured to ward this Blow, by Slight rather than Force. **1712–4** Pope *Rape Lock* II. 103 Some dire disaster, or by force, or slight.

†**2.** Prudence; wisdom, knowledge. *Obs.*

*a* **1300** *E.E. Psalter* civ. 20 He lered his princes als him-self reght, And his aldemen teched sleght. *c* **1340** Hampole *Pr. Consc.* 7697 þat wate he best thurgh wytt and sleght, What space þat way contened of heght. *c* **1400** tr. *Secreta Secret.*, *Gov. Lordsh.* 55 Of his [a king's] purueyance and his sleghte.

**3.** Skill, skilfulness, cleverness, or dexterity in doing or making something, in handling a tool or weapon, etc. Now *rare.*

β. **1390** Gower *Conf.* I. 127 With gret sleihte Of werkmanschipe it was begrave. *c* **1400** Maundev. (Roxb.) xxix. 131 þe whilk was made thurgh sleight and wirking of men. **1470–85** Malory *Arthur* XIX. ix. 788 He..put his ryght hand and his suerd to that stroke, and soo putte it on syde with grete sleyghte. **1567** Drant *Horace, Ep.* F viij, Tryflinge things, and things in dede of very slender sleight. **1581** Pettie tr. *Guazzo's Civ. Conv.* I. (1586) 4 b, And as it is not possible without great labour and sleight to take awaie the false imagination [etc.]. *a* **1668** Lassels *Voy. Italy* (1670) I. 215 To it they go, with great nimbleness, sleight, and discretion. **1726** De Foe *Hist. Devil* II. iv, He manages with a sleight particular to himself. **1753–4** Richardson *Grandison* (1781) II. iv. 68 With what a sleight..he pushed down my drawn sword. **1825** Scott *Betrothed* xix, I have already given you a proof of sleight which has alarmed even your experience. *c* **1855** Mrs. Moodie in Borthwick *Brit. Amer. Reader* (1860) 185 The squaw with a peculiar sleight threw her papoose over her shoulder.

γ. **13..** *E.E. Allit. P.* B. 1289 Deuised he þe vesselment, þe vestures clene, Wyth slyȝt of his ciences, his souerayn to loue. *c* **1400** *Destr. Troy* 10673 Mony wondit þat wegh.., And mony slogh..with slight of his bowe. *c* **1460** *Towneley Myst.* iii. 137 On the syde a doore with slyght be-neyth shal thou take. **1555** Eden *Decades* (Arb.) 350 Suche as are donne by the slight & arte of man. **1681** Chetham *Angler's Vade-m.* xi. §1 (1689) 111 People stand and wonder at the slight, and strength, by which they see Salmons leap. **1786** Burns *To a Haggis* iii, His knife see Rustic-labour dight, An' cut you up wi' ready slight. **1821** Joanna Baillie *Metr. Leg.*, *Wallace* xxx, As house-wife's slight, so finely true, The lengthen'd thread from distaff drew.

**b.** Const. *in* or *at* (something).

**1535** Stewart *Cron. Scot.* I. 250 The Romanis..in battell sic prattik had and slycht. *c* **1611** Chapman *Iliad* II. 637 Thaumaciæ,..and Olison the cold, Duke Philoctetes gouerned, in darts of finest sleight. **1655** Fuller *Ch. Hist.* III. 102 As these Western men do bear away the Bell for might and sleight in wrastling. **1687** A. Lovell tr. *Thevenot's Travels* I. 174 They have a wonderful slight in stealing. **1707** J. Stevens tr. *Quevedo's Com. Wks.* (1709) 204 Not knowing the Slight he had at packing the Cards. **1803** *Ann. Rev.* I. 31 Docility to instruction, sleight in the mechanic arts. **1896** *Dial. Notes* (Amer.) I. 424 She had a good slight at hoein'.

**4.** The precise art or method, the special knack or trick, *of* (doing) something. Now *dial.* †Also with other constructions.

*a* **1300** *Cursor M.* 6662 A tabernacle all for to dight, þarof he sceud þam þe slight.

**1547** Heywood *Four P's* (Copland) B iij b, Ye knowe it is no whit my sleyghte To be a iudge in matters of wayghte. **1600** Holland *Livy* XXVIII. xxxvii. 697 The Balears..do exceed and surpasse others in the cast and slight thereof. **1607** Middleton *Michaelmas Term* II. ii, 'Tis the slight, To be remember'd when you're out of sight. **1642** Rogers *Naaman* 368 Get once the slight of it (as we say) and then halfe the worke is at an end. *a* **1680** Butler *Rem.* (1759) I. 210 As Scriveners take more Pains to learn the slight Of making Knots, than all the Hands they write. **1861** Barr *Poems* 10 (E.D.D.), Weel doon, my lass!.. My word! Ye hae the slight o't. **1882** *Jamieson's Sc. Dict.* s.v. *Slicht*, I hae the slicht o't noo.

**b.** *spec.* Skill in jugglery or conjuring; sleight of hand.

**1664** Butler *Hud.* II. iii. 4 Lookers-on feel most delight, That least perceive a Juglers slight. **1850** S. Dobell *Roman* ii. *Poet. Wks.* (1875) 22 The juggler's sleight, That with facility of motion cheats The eye. **1870** Morris *Earthly Par.* III. IV. 25 Soon he 'gan to use his magic sleight: Into a lithe leopard, and a hugging bear He turned him.

**5.** Adroitness, activity, smartness, nimbleness *of* mind, body, etc.

In later use after or influenced by SLEIGHT OF HAND.

*c* **1385** Chaucer *L.G.W.* 2084 *Ariadne*, Sende you grace and sleyght of hert also Yow to defende. **1387** Trevisa *Higden* (Rolls) IV. 167 He chastede þe Schytes þat myȝte nouȝt be overcome toforehonde by sleyþe of witte. **1398** —— *Barth. De P.R.* XIII. xxix. (Tollem. MS.), Also fische ben diuerse in scharpnesse of felynge and in sliþe [1495 sleyghte] of wit. *a* **1680** Butler *Rem.* (1759) II. 206 He has a foolish Slight of Wit, that catches at Words only, and lets the Sense go. **1744** Fielding *Tumble-down Dick* Wks. 1784 III. 402 Gin's genius all these things reveals, Thou shalt perform, by slight of heels. **1829** Macaulay *Misc. Writ.* (1860) I. 353 A new sleight of tongue to make fools clap. **1865** *Reader* No. 123. 506/2 Hawking all his old wares, performing his sleight-of-mind.

*Comb.* **1809–10** Coleridge *Friend* (1818) III. 114 Mere empty disputants, sleight-of-word Jugglers.

**6.** A cunning trick; an artful device or design; a piece of subtle dealing or policy, intended to deceive or mislead; an artifice, ruse, stratagem, or wile. Now *rare.*

Common in the 16th and 17th cent.

β. *c* **1340** Hampole *Pr. Consc.* 1181 Pride and pompe and covatyse, And vayn sleghtes, and qwayntyse. *c* **1380** Wyclif *Sel. Wks.* III. 293 þei bryngen up newe sleiȝtis of covetise. *c* **1400** Love *Bonavent. Mirr.* (1908) 142 Ȝif thou wilt knowe the sleiȝtes of the deuel and be not begiled with his false suggestiouns. *c* **1440** *Jacob's Well* 153 God takyth an othe after þe symple vnderstondyng, & noȝt after wyles & sleyȝtes. **1545** Ascham *Toxoph.* (Arb.) 34 As Leo..in his boke of sleightes of warre telleth. **1594** Plat *Jewell-ho.* II. 15 This is a prettie sleight to deceaue the Purueyor. **1606** Dekker *Seven Sins* II. (Arb.) 19 He resolues therefore to make his entrance, not by the sword, but by some sleyght. **1652** Needham tr. *Selden's Mare Cl.* 230 The manner of guarding the Sea and the subtile sleights they made use of for that purpose. **1713** Swift *Upon Himself* Misc. (1735) V. 57 His watchful Friends preserve him by a Sleight. **1759** Franklin *Ess.* Wks. 1840 III. 354 We are plain people, unpractised in the sleights and artifices of controversy. **1822** Hazlitt *Table-t.* Ser. II. i. (1869) 13 A rare fellow..of infinite sleights and evasions. **1875** E. White *Life in Christ* v. xxviii. (1878) 463 The feminine sleights of forgetting or over-laying the daily remembrance of the terrible fact.

γ. **1577** Harrison *England* II. vi. (1877) I. 161 Such slights also have the alewives for the utterance of this drinke. **1594** Nashe *Unfort. Trav.* Wks. (Grosart) V. 53 We haue found out a slight to hammer it to anie heresie whatsoeuer. **1623** Middleton *More Dissemblers* IV. i, Let your slights be fine, facetious. **1663** Butler *Hud.* I. ii. 747 All thy tricks and slights to cheat, And sell thy Carrion for good Meat. **1760–72** H. Brooke *Fool of Qual.* (1809) III. 68 A variety of slights, deceits, impostures,..and depredations.

**b.** A feat of jugglery or legerdemain; a trick or action performed with great dexterity, esp. so quickly as to deceive the eye.

**1596** Spenser *F.Q.* V. ix. 13 For he in slights and iugling feates did flow, And of legierdemayne the mysteries did know. **1609** Bible (Douay) *Exod.* vii. *comm.*, Other strange thinges done by enchanters..are not in deede true miracles, but..sleights, by quicknes and nimblenes of hand, called legier-demain. **1699** Garth *Dispens.* III. 33 That Jugler which another's Slight will show, But teaches how the World his own may know. **1733** W. Ellis *Chiltern & Vale Farm.* 145 Taking the largest Buds,..with a very quick Slight before the Sap is dry, put them into a little Incision ..in the Bark. **1770** Goldsm. *Des. Vill.* 22 Sleights of art and feats of strength went round. **1801** Strutt *Sports & Past.* III. iii. 158 The sleight of casting up a certain number of sharp instruments into the air, and catching them alternately in their fall. **1857** H. Reid *Lect. Brit. Poets* iii. 108 A curious and elaborate representation of the sleights of alchemy. **1872** *Routledge's Ev. Boy's Ann.* 532 The various sleights [in card-tricks] above described.

†**c.** A design or pattern. *Obs.*[−1]

**1590** Spenser *F.Q.* I. vii. 30 Thereby his mortall blade full comely hong In yuory sheath, ycaru'd with curious slights.

†**sleight**, *sb.*[2] *Obs.* Forms: 1 **sliht, slyht, -slæht**, 1, 3 **sleht**, 3 **sleȝht, sleþt**, 4 **sleȝte, sleiȝt**. [OE. *slyht*, etc. = *slieht* (:—**sleahti*), from the stem of *sléan* (:—**sleahan*) SLAY *v.*[1] Cf. SLAUGHT *sb.*] Slaughter.

*c* **893** K. Ælfred *Oros.* v. xi. 238 Æȝþer ȝe on þeoda forherȝiunge, ȝe on cyninga slihtum, ȝe on hungre. *a* **1000** in Assmann *Ags. Hom.* xv. 177 Sume ic slæpende beswac,.. sume mid slehte & sume on some. *c* **1205** Lay. 2544 Bitweonen him aræs..sleȝht [*c* **1275** sleþt] & muchel seorwa. *Ibid.* 3995 Swiðe heo was sari for sorehfulle þan slehte. *c* **1315** Shoreham III. 245 Ofte þe mannes sleȝte aryst, Were man hyȝt weneþ wel lyte. **1330** *Arth. & Merl.* 6654 (Kölbing), þer was miche sleiȝt of man.

**sleight** (sleɪt), *sb.*[3] *dial.* Also 7 **slaight**, 9 **slait, slate.** [Of obscure origin.] A pasture, esp. one for sheep; chiefly in comb. ***sheep-sleight.***

**1670** Aubrey *Introd. Surv. N. Wilts* in *Misc.* (1714) 32 Anciently the Leghs (now corruptly call'd Slaights), i.e. pastures, were noble, large Grounds. **1813** Davis *Agric. Wilts.* Gloss. s.v. *Sleighting*, A sheep-down is frequently called a sheep-sleight. **1825-** in south-western glossaries, etc. **1854** *Jrnl. R. Agric. Soc.* XV. II. 438 Much benefit is obtained by chalking those sheep sleights retained as permanent pastures.

†**sleight**, *a. Obs.* Forms: 5 sleyghte, 6 sleyght, slight, 6–7 sleight. [f. SLEIGHT *sb.*[1]]

**1.** Marked or characterized by subtle craft, cunning, or strategy; artful, crafty, wily.

**1495** *Trevisa's Barth. De P.R.* XIII. xxvi. 461 Some [fish] ben wonderly sleyghte [*Bodl. MS.* slyȝe] and wyly to scape. *a* **1513** FABYAN *Chron.* VI. cxlix. (1811) 136 Gryffon hauynge suspeccion to yᵉ Saxons,.. leste they wolde betraye hym,.. made for that tyme, a sleyght agrement. **1547** *The Bk. of Marchauntes* b v b, In their practyke they be sowple and sleight. **1583** STOCKER *Civ. Warres Lowe C.* III. 113 The Enemy..went on with all the cunning and slight meanes that possibly coulde bee deuised.

**2.** Skilful, skilled; expert, clever.

*a* **1513** FABYAN *Chron.* (1811) 3 To remytte to theym that ben sleyght And sharpe in lecture, and haue kept theyr studyes.

**3.** Of juggling, etc.: Dexterous, deceptive.

**1533** MORE *Answ. Poysoned Bk.* Wks. 1098/2 Their false and abhominable blasphemous lyes vpon Chrystes woordes, ..their sleyght iuggelyng ouer the bread. *c* **1555** HARPSFIELD *Divorce Hen. VIII* (Camden) 81 Besides a crafty sleight legerdemaine, there concur two notable untruths. **1567** DRANT *Horace, Ep.* A viij, Who..at his hands coulde gayne A tallant by collusion and sleight ligerdemayne. **1634** MILTON *Comus* 155 (Cambr. MS.), Thus I herle My powder'd spells into the spungie air, Of power to cheat the eye with sleight illusion.

**4.** *Comb.*, as ***sleight-eared, -handed***.

**1567** DRANT *Horace, Ep.* To Rdr. *iiij, Or if oure reader were not rather sleight earde, then cleareeyed. **1648** J. BEAUMONT *Psyche* IX. clxx, There lay..quick mutations, Sleight-handed Tricks, importunate Courtesies.

**sleight**, *v.* Now *dial.* [f. SLEIGHT *sb.*[1]]

†**a.** *intr.* To deal guilefully. *Obs.* **b.** *trans.* To deceive, beguile, cheat.

**1530** PALSGR. 721/1, I sleyght with one, I deale craftelye or subtelly with hym. *Ibid.*, Truste hym nat, he sleyghteth with every bodye he dealeth with. **1876** ROBINSON *Whitby Gloss.* 176/2 *Slyted*, or *Sleighted*, cheated.

**sleight**, obs. form of SLIGHT *sb.*, *a.*, and *v.*

†'**sleighter.** *Obs. rare.* In 4 sleiȝster, 6 slayhter. [f. SLEIGHT *sb.*[2], after SLAUGHTER *sb.*]

= SLAUGHTER *sb.* Also in comb. ***sleighter-house.***

*c* **1330** *Arth. & Merlin* 1879 (Kölbing), Þo Angys al þis sleiȝster seiȝe, Wiþ al his miȝt anon he fleiȝe. **1585** *Shuttleworth's Acc.* (Chetham Soc.) 25 A grete roppe for the wyndlas in the slayhter housse.

†'**sleightful**, *a. Obs. rare.* Also 4 slyhtful, 5–6 *Sc.* slichtfull, etc. [f. SLEIGHT *sb.*[1]] Full of, characterized by, craft or artifice; crafty, cunning.

**1380** *Lay Folks Catech.* (Lamb. MS.) 1220 Þey be mysdoers, sotel, and slyhtful dysseyuers. **1500–20** DUNBAR *Poems* lxvi. 7 The sweit abayd, the slichtfull trane, For to consider is ane pane. **1613–6** W. BROWNE *Brit. Past.* II. iv, Wilde beasts forsooke their dens on woody hils, And sleightfull otters left the purling rils.

Hence †'**sleightfully** *adv. Obs. rare.*

*c* **1375** *Sc. Leg. Saints* xxix. (*Placidas*) 241 Þe fals feynd ..þat slichtfully begylyt þe. *Ibid.* xxxii. (*Justin*) 119 To dissawe men slichfully.

†'**sleightily**, *adv. Obs. rare.* Also slyghtyly. [f. SLEIGHTY *a.*] Craftily, cunningly.

**1549** COVERDALE, etc. *Erasm. Par. Eph.* Prol. C iij, Yᵉ false doctours,..which slyghtyly bryng in pernicious sectes amonge the people. **1553** BALE *Gardiner's De Vera Obed.* Pref. A v, Which coulde so advisedly saye yea than,..and so sleightily recante and saye naye now.

†'**sleightly**, *a. Obs. rare.* [f. SLEIGHT *sb.*[1] + -LY[1].] Crafty, cunning, subtle.

*c* **1402** LYDG. *Compl. Bl. Kt.* 255 And tonges false, through hir sleightly wile, Han gon a werre that will not stinted be. **1533** FRITH *Baptism* Wks. (1572) 97 Perceyue you not yet that they would keepe you in darcknes because you shoulde not espye theyr priuy practice and sleightly conueyaunce.

†'**sleightly**, *adv. Obs.* Also 5 sleght-, 5–6 sleyght-, 5 slyght-, 5–6 slyth-, *Sc.* slicht-, 6, 8 slightly, etc. [irreg. f. SLEIGHT *sb.*[1] + -LY[2].]

**1.** With craft, cunning, or artifice; craftily, subtly.

*c* **1330** R. BRUNNE *Chron. Wace* (Rolls) 7809 To come sleightly he scholde fonde, & litel folk wyþ hym brynge to londe. *a* **1400–50** *Alexander* 2870 (D.), Þen slode he slyghtly away when he fra slepe rysys. **1549** COVERDALE, etc. *Erasm. Par. Coloss.* 6 Beware therfore, lest any man..falsly and sleyghtly deceyue you of that reward. **1570** FOXE *A. & M.* 946/1 So subtlely & sleightly these Catholicque prelates did vse their inquisitions. **1604** T. WRIGHT *Passions* III. iii. 91 If thy enemies would bee reuenged of thee, no fitter meanes they might sleightly use, than [etc.] **1626** in Rushw. *Hist. Coll.* (1659) I. 281 Certainly the Earl hath not been sleightly deceived.

**2.** With ready skill, dexterity, or adroitness; by sleight of hand; adroitly, dexterously.

*c* **1511** *1st Eng. Bk. Amer.* (Arb.) Introd. 29/1 They doo all there thynges all sleyghtly. *a* **1548** HALL *Chron., Hen. VIII*, 50 This spere was massy tymber & yet for al that he.. slightely avoyded it to hys great honour. **1581** PETTIE tr. *Guazzo's Civ. Conv.* III. (1586) 126 Prouided it be done so slightly, and so discreetlie, that the artificial dealing be not seene. **1611** BIBLE *Transl. Pref.* ¶13 The father of their Church, who gladly would heale the soare of the daughter of his people softly and sleightly.

†'**sleightness.** *Obs. rare.* In 6 sleyght-, slight-. [f. SLEIGHT *sb.*[1] + -NESS.] Craftiness, adroitness, or subtlety of dealing or policy.

**1526** *Pilgr. Pref.* (W. de W. 1531) 90 b, Fraude, disceyte or sleyghtnes, periury,..with suche other. **1561** T. HOBY tr. *Castiglione's Courtyer* IV. (1577) V vij, As occasion serueth wyth slightnesse to enter in fauour with hym. *Ibid.*, Aristotle so well knew the nature of Alexander, and with slightnesse framed himselfe so wel therafter.

**sleight of hand.** Also sleight-of-hand. [SLEIGHT *sb.*[1]]

**1.** Dexterity or skill in using the hand or hands for any purpose; expertness in manipulation or manual action.

[*c* **1400** *Destr. Troy.* 10306 Achilles..flange at the knight, [and] Slough hym full slawthly with sleght of his hond. *c* **1425** *Non-Cycle Myst. Plays* 24 Of hand to have such slight, To make ship less or mare.] *c* **1460** *Towneley Myst.* xxiii. 157 Let now se who dos the best with any slegthe of hande. **1700** T. BROWN tr. *Fresny's Amusem.* viii. Wks. 1709 III. 70 There's nothing to be learn'd there [at gaming-houses], unless it be Slight of Hand,..sometimes at the Expence of all our Money. **1760** JOHNSON *Idler* No. 90 ¶3 By slight of hand, or nimbleness of foot, all these wonders can be performed. **1825** MᶜCULLOCH *Pol. Econ.* II. ii. 87 A peculiar play of the muscles, or sleight of hand, is necessary to perform the simplest operation in the..most expeditious manner. **1862** *Fraser's Mag.* July 75 A power not fitful or got forth by any sleight-of-hand, but resolutely worked for.

*transf.* and *fig.* **1700** T. BROWN tr. *Fresny's Amusem.* 50 Here Fools by Slight of Hand, are converted into Wits. **1829** CARLYLE *Misc.* (1840) II. 56 Were the public once to penetrate into this his [a playwright's] sleight of hand, it were all over with him.

**b.** In reference to jugglery, conjuring, or performances of a similar kind.

**1622** FLETCHER *Beggar's Bush* III. i, Will ye see any feats of activity, Some Sleight of hand, Legerdemain? **1690** *Lond. Gaz.* No. 2539/4 William Bradshaw..pretending to slight of Hand and swallowing Knives. **1770** LANGHORNE *Plutarch* (1879) I. 395/2 Some of them were forced to get their bread by showing tricks of sleight of hand. **1853** C. BRONTË *Villette* xxii, You know my skill in sleight of hand: I might practise as a conjuror if I liked.

**2.** With *a* and pl. A dexterous trick or feat; a piece of nimble juggling or conjuring.

*c* **1605** ? ROWLEY *Birth Merlin* IV. i, I must keep some other company if you have these sleights of hand. **1699** R. L'ESTRANGE *Erasm. Colloq.* (1725) 22 While they pretend to lay one gift upon the altar, by a marvellous slight of hand they'll steal away another. **1717** tr. *Frezier's Voy.* 166 The Experiments that have been seen made..are fraudulent Sleights of Hand. **1851** LONGF. *Gold. Leg.* II. *Vill. Ch.*, To make a murderer out of a prince, A sleight of hand I learned long since! **1856** MRS. BROWNING *Aur. Leigh* I. 421 Fine sleights of hand And unimagined fingering.

**3.** *attrib.* and *Comb.* **a.** In sense 'using or employing sleight of hand', as ***sleight-of-hand man, professor***, etc.

**1760** GROSE *Voy. E. Indies* 185 The jugglers, or slight-of-hand-men greatly excel whatever I have seen or heard of them in Europe. **1801** *Sporting Mag.* XVII. 209 The exhibitions of a slight-of-hand professor. **1875** *Chambers's Jrnl.* XII. 66 A sleight-of-hand gentleman is selling purses with half-crowns in them for one shilling each.

**b.** In sense 'performed by sleight of hand, artifice, etc.', as ***sleight-of-hand arrangement, juggling, trick***, etc.

**1818** SCOTT *Rob Roy* xix, One of those slight-of-hand arrangements which still sometimes took place in that once lawless district. **1826** DISRAELI *Viv. Grey* III. viii, You are a juggler; and the deceptions of your sleight-of-hand tricks depend upon instantaneous motions. **1828** MOIR *Mansie Wauch* vii, A punch and puppie-show business, and other slight-of-hand work. **1867** RUSKIN *Time & Tide* vi. §26 Then there was some fairly good sleight-of-hand juggling of little interest.

Hence *ellipt.* **sleight-hand.** Also *attrib.*

**1792** WOLCOT (P. Pindar) *Odes* Wks. 1816 II. 390 Sweet are of slight-hand Barrington the tales. **1839** RAYSON *Poems* 62 'Tis whuspert by sleet-han' he's meade lots o' money.

**sleighty** ('slaɪtɪ), *a.* Now *rare.* Forms: 5 sleȝty, sleihty, sleiȝty, -ti, *Sc.* slichty, 5–6 sleyghty (6 -ye, -ie), 6 sleighthy, slightie, 5–7, 9 sleighty (6 -tie). [f. SLEIGHT *sb.*[1] + -Y. Freq. in Lydgate and from *c* 1530 to *c* 1580.]

**1.** Possessed of, making use of, sleight or craft.

*c* **1375** *Sc. Leg. Saints* ii. (*Paul*) 257 Schow wes vode, þat lente to hym a clath sa gud, þat wes sa slichty a creatour. **1412–20** LYDG. *Chron. Troy* II. 1869 Sche is so sleiȝty with hir gynny snare. *c* **1430** —— *Min. Poems* (Percy Soc.) 158 The sleihty fox smal polayl doth oppresse. **1530** PALSGR. 629 Put your sonne to hym, he wyl make hym as sleyghty as an other. **1556** OLDE *Antichrist* 172 b, These toyes..haue the subtil sleighty Marchauntes beaten in to the eares..of the common simple sorte. **1594** WEST *2nd Pt. Symbol.* § 171 Judglers and sleightie curers of diseases. **1615** W. LAWSON *Country Housew. Gard.* (1626) 56 You might sit in your Mount, and angle a peckled Trout, or sleighty Eele.

**2.** Characterized by, of the nature of, sleight or dexterity; crafty, subtle.

**1412–20** LYDG. *Chron. Troy* I. 1947 Þis Medea..From hir fader his tresour hath berafte þoruȝ þe werchyng of hir sleiȝty gyle. *a* **1470** HARDING *Chron.* LXVII. viii, By subteltye and his sleyghty gyn. **1532–3** *Act 24 Hen. VIII*, c. 2 Dyers ..have used & exercised a false sleyghtie & deceyvable waye in dyeng. **1588** J. HARVEY *Disc. Probl.* 69 To..carry away the commons with od rumors, by flimflams, wily cranks, and sleightie knacks. **1600** W. WATSON *Decacordon* (1602) 82 It seemeth impossible for Antichrist to inuent a more sleighty, plausible and colourable deuice. **1631** WEEVER *Anc. Funeral Mon.* 534 Who did vse some sleightie tricks for his owne disports. **1676** CARLETON *Epist. Admon. & Adv.* 6 Learn not the sleighty words and cunning evasions of the deceitful spirits of this world. **1888** DOUGHTY *Arabia Deserta* I. 74 Property, all of his own strong and sleighty getting.

**sleih**, obs. f. SLY *a.*

**sleihschupe**: see SLYSHIP *Obs.*

**sleit**, obs. f. SLIGHT *v.*

**sleiveen**, var. SLEEVEEN.

**slely**, obs. f. SLYLY *adv.*

**slem.** *rare.* Now *dial.* [Cf. Sw. *slem* (MSw. *slemm-*, etc.), G. dial. *schlemm* (G. *schlamm*).] Slime.

*c* **1450** *Mirk's Festial* 294 Mankynde was makyd of slem of þe erth. *a* **1904** in *Eng. Dial. Dict.* s.v., They sow rice in t' slem o' t' Nile.

†**sleme.** *Obs. rare*[−1]. Weariness.

*a* **1300** *E.E. Ps.* cxviii. 28 For sleme [L. *prae taedio*] sleped saule myne.

**slench** (slɛntʃ), *v.* Now *dial.* Also 9 slensh, slinch; *pa. t.* 4 sleynt, 5 slent. [repr. OE. **slęncan*, causative form from *slincan* SLINK *v.*] *intr.* To slink, sneak.

*c* **1330** *Amis & Amil.* 2279 For sorwe he sleynt oway biside, And wepe with reweful chere. **1401** *Pol. Poems* (Rolls) II. 112 Moche mawgre mote thou have thus to frayn a frere, that slily wolde have slent aweye. **1781** J. HUTTON *Tour To Caves* (ed. 2) Gloss. 96 *Slench*, to hunt privately for stealing food as dogs do. **1869-** in northern dial. glossaries.

†**slend**, *v. Obs. rare.* Also 5 sclend. [Of obscure origin.] *trans.* To slice or cut; to split.

**13..** *Sir Beues* (A.) 248 Þre hondred heuedes of a slende Wiþ is brond. *c* **1400** *Lanfranc's Cirurg.* 128 If þat þe brayn panne be so myche I-slend [*v.r.* y-sclend] þat þe part þat is broke, entre vndir þe partie þat is hool. *c* **1580** JEFFERIES *Bugbears* III. iii, Fyrst slend thys square sticke length-wyse in to two.

‖**slendang** ('slɛndæŋ). Also selendang. [a. Javanese *slénḍang*, Indonesian *seléndang*.] In Indonesia, a long scarf or stole worn by women.

**1885** H. O. FORBES *Naturalist's Wanderings Eastern Archipelago* III. ii. 147 Above this the body is girt with a silk *slendang*, half concealing the breasts. **1911** B. MIALL tr. *Cabaton's Java* v. 125 An indispensable article of the feminine toilet is the *slendang*: a scarf in *batik*, often ornamented with fringes. **1937** M. COVARRUBIAS *Island of Bali* iii. 48 It is necessary to be properly dressed to pay or to receive a visit. The breasts of men and women should be covered by a special breast-cloth, a *saput* for men and a *selendang* for women. **1941** *Lincoln* (Nebraska) *Sunday Jrnl. & Star* 12 Oct. D-6/1 Maria Montez, in 'White Savage', will wear a scant bit of cloth called a *slendang*, something like a sarong, only more so, or less so! **1963** J. KIRKUP *Tropic Temper* 168 The men approach the women and claim their selendangs or long gauzy stoles which are used most effectively in the dance movements. **1964** LANGEWIS & WAGNER *Decorative Art in Indonesian Textiles* 27 In a certain *batik* cloth, the *slendang*, a centrally placed undecorated area always appears in the form of an elongated rhomboid.

**slender** ('slɛndə(r)), *a.* (and *adv.*). Forms: α. 4–6 slendre, 5– slender (5 -yr, 6 -ar, slindir). β. 4, 6 sclendre, 5–7 sclender; 5 sklendire, 5–6 -re, 6 -ir, -ur, 5–6, 9 *dial.*, sklender; 6 scl-, sklinder. [Of obscure origin.

An AF. source appears the most probable, but Palsgrave (1530) seems to be the only evidence for a F. *esclendre*. Kilian's 'Slinder, *vet.* Tenuis, exilis' is not otherwise known, and his citation of 'Ang. *slender*' makes the entry of doubtful value.]

**I. 1.** Of persons (or animals), their bodies, etc.: Not stout or fleshy; slim, spare. (Freq. implying gracefulness of form, esp. in later use.)

α. **13..** *Coer de L.* 3530 He is fat, and thertoo tendre, And my men are lene and slendre. **1402** HOCCLEVE *Letter of Cupid* 171 Wheither his shap be outher thikke or slender. **1495** *Trevisa's Barth. De P.R.* IV. x. 95 Colerik men be generally in the body longe and slendre. *a* **1548** HALL *Chron., Edw. IV*, 34 Kyng Henry was of a stature goodly, of body slender. **1601** HOLLAND *Pliny* I. 350 Females vsually in euery kind haue less and slenderer feet than males. **1687** A. LOVELL tr. *Thevenot's Trav.* I. 132 You rub and grate your Back against the aforesaid Stone, unless you be a very slender Man. **1774** GOLDSM. *Nat. Hist.* (1776) III. 389 Having the body longer and more slender, the nose smaller. **1804** ABERNETHY *Surg. Obs.* 210 A German..of a sickly aspect and slender make. **1852** MRS. STOWE *Uncle Tom's C.* xxxiii. 300 She's slender; but these yer slender gals will bear half killin' to get their own way! **1871** *Figure Training* 46 That most elegant female charm, a slender waist.

β. *c* **1386** CHAUCER *Prol.* 587 The Reue was a sclendre colerik man. *c* **1400** MAUNDEV. 291 Thei han a blak Hed.. and the Body is sclender. *c* **1450** *Merlin* xiv. 227 Her flessh whitter than snowe, and was not to fatte ne to sklender. **1509** HAWES *Past. Pleas.* xxx. (Percy Soc.) 146 Her armes sclender and of goodly body. **1538** STARKEY *England* II. i. 152 Though thys body be weke, sklendur, and lakkyth natural strenghth. **1565** COOPER *Thesaurus* s.v. *Digitus*, *Exiles digiti*, sclender [fingers].

**b.** Denoting weakness or absence of robustness. †Also *transf.* of age, etc.: Tender, immature.

*a* **1500** *Abraham* 126 in *Brome Bk.* 54 To folow ȝow I am full fayn, All thow I be slendyr. **1549** COVERDALE, etc. *Erasm. Par. John* 44 So much the more diligently you preache him to them that be of slenderer age. **1718** HICKES & NELSON *J. Kettlewell* I. xxvii. 50 Concerning his First Book..are these Two Things Remarkable,..First at what a Slender Age..it was written. **1798** M. CUTLER in *Life*, etc.

(1888) II. 7 His nerves are excitable, and constitution rather slender. **1848** WEBSTER *Lett.* (1902) 604 Not that we suppose Julia is very sick, but she is slender.

**2.** Of things: Small in diameter or width in proportion to length; long and thin; attenuated.

*α.* *a* **1513** FABYAN *Chron.* v. lxxxiii. (1811) 60 Hengyste.. caused the sayd beests skyn to be cut into a small and slender thonge. **1590** GREENE *Orl. Fur.* Wks. (Rtldg.) 95/1 Seek not ..To..slice the slender fillets of my life. **1615** G. SANDYS *Trav.* 245 About the bottome of the bay, where the City is slender, and free from concourse of people. **1673** [R. LEIGH] *Transp. Reh.* 126, J being the tallest slendrest letter of the alphabet. **1723** CHAMBERS tr. *Le Clerc's Archit.* I. 69 Roundness makes it appear slenderer than it really is. **1788** FRANKLIN *Autobiog.* Wks. 1840 I. 190 The slender line, nearly four miles long, which your army must make. **1810** SCOTT *Lady of L.* I. xxvi, The lighter pine-trees, over-head, Their slender length for rafters spread. **1876** SMILES *Sc. Natur.* iv. (ed. 4) 69 They squeaked like mice, and hung to ..the slenderest twigs.

*β.* **1521** FISHER *Serm. agst. Luther* ii. Wks. (1876) 324 Faythe withouten hope is a sklender beme & of a lytle power. **1563** SHUTE *Archit.* F j b, The higher they stand, the lesser or sklenderer they muste be.

**3. a.** Having little thickness or solidity in proportion to extent of surface; slight or slim in size or structure.

**1444** *Pol. Poems* (Rolls) II. 219 Hows of this snayl, the wallys wer nat stronge, A slender shelle. *a* **1548** HALL *Chron., Hen. VI*, 27 b, One [cannon] beyng weake and slender, brake in peces, and..slewe the kyng. **1581** MULCASTER *Positions* xxxix. (1887) 194 Vnder a sclender veale of counterfeat liberalitie. **1655** M. CARTER *Honor Rediv.* Ep. Ded., That I have preferred so slender a Volume to Your Honorable Patronage [etc.]. **1665** *Phil. Trans.* I. 44 Striking through the slender partition of the Coal-wall. **1715** tr. *Pancirollus' Rerum Mem.* I. II. vii. 83 They were wont to slice their Marble into slender Pieces. **1836** W. IRVING *Astoria* III. 123 They launched forth in their canoes, but soon found that the river had not depth sufficient even for such slender barks. **1871** R. ELLIS *Catullus* lxii. 43 If a slender nail hath nipt his bloom. **1875** MANNING *Mission Holy Ghost* Pref. p. vii, Nearly ten years ago I dedicated to you a very slender book.

†**b.** Of a thin consistency. *Obs. rare.*

**1528** PAYNELL *Salerne's Regim.* F iij b, Wattrishe wine.. whose liquor is as sklender as water. **1635** SWAN *Spec. M.* v. §2 (1643) 130 The aire and water are clean, thin, and slender.

**c.** Of vowels: Narrow, close.

**1755** JOHNSON *Dict.*, Gram., *A* has three sounds, the slender, open, and broad. **1821** O'REILLY *Irish Dict.* 1/2 The rule of writing a slender with a slender, and a broad with a broad vowel. **1828** WALKER *Pron. Dict.* 19/1 The slender *a*, or that heard in *lane.* **1889** *Cent. Dict.* s.v. *Broad.*

**4.** Of small extent, size, or capacity.

**1610** HOLLAND *Camden's Brit.* 463 Bretenham a very slender little towne. **1614** J. NORDEN *Labyrinth Man's Life* L iij b, Of slender sparke ariseth mighty flame. **1669** BOYLE *Contn. New Exper.* I. (1682) 4 If the Reciever be fitly stopt, and slender enough..to let out the air at the first exuction. **1827** HOOD *Wee Man* ii, A slender space will serve my case, For I am small and thin. **1871** R. ELLIS *Catullus* lxiv. 81 When a plague..Spent that slender city.

**II.** †**5. a.** Moderate or deficient in power or strength. *Obs.*

*a* **1400** *Apol. Loll.* 45, I wot not þat I seid it, and mannis mynd is sclendre. **1559** MORWYNG *Evonym.* 249 The fire must be made very light and sclender, and encresed by litle and litle. **1587** TURBERV. *Trag. Tales* (1837) 174 And eke the winde so slender was To cause the ship to steare. **1657** AUSTEN *Fruit Trees* II. 49 The inclinations..are then but very weake and slender.

†**b.** Deficient in energy or vigour; lax. *Obs.*

**1577** HARRISON *England* II. i. (1877) I. 19 The slender demeanours of such negligent ministers. **1598** MANWOOD *Lawes Forest* ii. (1615) 33 The slender and negligent execution of the Forest Lawes.

**6. a.** Of arguments, etc.: Lacking in cogency or conclusiveness; unconvincing.

*a* **1533** FRITH *Disput. Purgat.* Prol. B j, Manye of his probacions are so slender, that they maye well be improued. **1538** STARKEY *England* I. ii. 27 Where as my resonys schal appere to you sklender and weke. **1638** JUNIUS *Paint. Ancients* 15 This is a poore and slender argument. **1639** FULLER *Holy War* III. xxii, The proofs were as slender as the crimes gross. **1759** B. MARTIN *Nat. Hist.* I. Wilts. 101 Though the Reasons alledged..be slender enough.

**b.** Having a slight foundation, ground, or justification.

**1562** WINȜET *Wks.* (S.T.S.) I. 52 Breuelie considering.. thair titill to this thair supreme auctorite, I fand it..sclinder and licht. **1599** THYNNE *Animadv.* (1875) 15 This ys a slender coniecture; for, as honorable howses..haue borne as meane armes as Chaucer. **1762–71** H. WALPOLE *Vertue's Anecd. Paint.* (1786) IV. 73 England has very slender pretensions to this original and engaging painter. **1849** MACAULAY *Hist. Eng.* vi. II. 154 To the applause of the sincere friends of the Established Church Rochester had, indeed, very slender claims. **1886** PASCOE *Lond. of To-day* xxxv. (ed. 3) 311 Some claim (generally of the slenderest kind).

**7.** Slight, small, insignificant, trifling.

Used in a variety of contexts, some of which are here distinguished by separate groups of quotations. In some cases the sense approximates to that of 8.

(*a*) **1530** PALSGR. 697/1 My wytte is to sklender to talke of so wayghty a mater. **1574** A. L. tr. *Calvin, Four Sermons* D viij, We haue not yet comprehended all, for our capacitie is to sclendre. **1687** MIÈGE *Gt. Fr. Dict.* II. s.v., He has but slender Parts. **1738** tr. *Guazzo's Art Convers.* 92, I shall have a special Regard to..those of a slender sense... I shall think I am speaking to Persons of weak Capacities. **1761** HUME *Hist. Eng.* II. xxxvi. 285 The duke..knew the slender capacity of Suffolk. **1849** MACAULAY *Hist. Eng.* ix. II. 496 A young man of slender abilities, loose principles, and violent temper. **1879** GEO. ELIOT *Theo. Such* i. 8 Attainable by the slenderest talent.

(*b*) **1536** CROMWELL in Merriman *Life & Lett.* (1902) II. 36 Their commencement of the same in such slendre and sleight sorte..hathe brought them furthe almost as slendre an answer. **1565** COOPER *Thesaurus* s.v. *Tenuiter*, To reason ..in a sklender style. **1641** 'SMECTYMNUUS' *Vind. Answ.* §6. 77 But what a slender answer is this. **1813** SCOTT *Rokeby* I. vi, Full slender answer deigned he To Oswald's anxious courtesy.

(*c*) **1542** UDALL *Erasm. Apoph.* 230 To receive nothyng but as though it had been a large and high benefite, wer it in deede never so slendre. **1581** PETTIE *Guazzo's Civ. Conv.* I. (1586) A 5 b, You will stand your Countrie but in slender stead..if you bee no schollers. **1634** W. TIRWHYT tr. *Balzac's Lett.* 15 Princes are too poor, and their power too slender to afford them their full merit. **1670** COTTON *Espernon* III. XI. 572 The Wound..was not to be clos'd by so slender a Remedy. **1779** J. MOORE *View of France* (1789) I. ii. 11 They generally afford but a slender entertainment. **1809** MALKIN *Gil Blas* I. xi. ¶6 The anticipation of my slenderest wishes was his..study. **1837** PALGRAVE *Merch. & Friar* (1844) Ded. p. i, A production possessing such slender attractions. *a* **1866** GROTE *Ethical Fragm.* iv. (1876) 96 A child feels that he has not the slenderest power of acting upon the fears of others.

(*d*) **1686** J. SCOTT *Christian Life* I. II. iii. 87 The Slenderest probability will Sway their Understanding to vote [etc.]. *a* **1704** T. BROWN *Ess. Late Politicks* Wks. 1711 IV. 102 The slender Prospect we have of Success in the War against France. **1856** KINGSLEY *Misc.* (1860) I. 80 Proof of what slender grounds there are for calling Raleigh 'suspected'. **1875** JOWETT *Plato* (ed. 2) V. 56 Their only hope, however slender, was in victory.

†**b.** Of persons in respect of station or capacity.

**1548** UDALL *Erasm. Par. Luke* ii. 32 Be thei neuer so slender or lowe of degree. **1571** GOLDING *Calvin on Ps.* lxxii. 4 Not without cause dooth God take more charge of the slenderer sorte, whiche are moste subjecte too wrong and violence. **1651** *Rec. Communion* §7 The abler sort of people, for the good example of the slender ones.

**8.** Small or limited in amount, number, range, etc.

**1564** HAWARD *Eutrop.* II. 12 Although their wealth and substaunce was as yet but very sclender. **1587** TURBERV. *Trag. Tales* 83 b, A iewell of no slender price. **1633** T. STAFFORD *Pac. Hib.* (1821) 146 This Armie is but very slender. **1660** F. BROOKE tr. *Le Blanc's Trav.* 373 In the plains then it never rains, all they ever have is a dew, which is so slender it never wets at all. **1748** *Anson's Voy.* II. iii. 150 Their stock of provisions..was extremely slender. **1752** HUME *Ess. & Treat.* (1777) I. 283 The land is rich, but coarse,..and produces slender crops. **1825** LAMB *Elia* II. *Barbara S——*, Her slender earnings were the sole support of the family. **1852** THACKERAY *Esmond* II. iii, Taking the young gentleman's slender baggage.

**b.** Of sounds: Weak, lacking in fullness.

**1784** COWPER *Task* VI. 78 The redbreast warbles still, but is content With slender notes, and more than half suppress'd. **1820** HAZLITT *Lect. Dram. Lit.* 48 A very callow brood, chirping their slender notes. **1858** HAWTHORNE *Fr. & It. Note-bks.* (1872) II. 170 It gave one little slender squeak. **1859** —— *Marble Faun* iv, Hilda with her slender scream.

**9.** †**a.** Of poor quality; meagre; lacking 'body'. *Obs. rare.*

**1577** B. GOOGE *Heresbach's Husb.* I. (1586) 22 A slendar and leuell ground, subiect to the water, would be fyrst plowed in the ende of August. *Ibid.* 45 The Pastures that lyes by the Lakes of Dumone..are but sclender.

**b.** Poorly supplied. *rare*$^{-1}$.

*c* **1700** PHILIPS (J.), The good Ostorius often deign'd To grace my slender table.

**10.** As *adv.* In a slender manner; slightly. *rare.*

**1581** MULCASTER *Positions* iv. (1887) 20, I could wishe the wittier child, the lesse vpon the spurre,..or the sklenderer kept at it. **1743** *Lond. & C. Brewer* II. (ed. 2) 88 Pale Malt has certainly most of the Grain in it, as being slenderest dry'd, and is therefore most nourishing.

**III. 11.** In specific uses, chiefly in the names of animals, fishes, plants, etc. (see quots.).

Shaw (1802–4) also gives *Slender Cæcilia, Fistularia, Hydrus, Snake, Sparus.* Rennie (1832) has *Slender Gold Tongue* and *Treble Bar* as moth-names; also *Livid, Nebulous, Rufous* (etc.) *Slender.*

(*a*) **1829** GRIFFITH tr. *Cuvier* VIII. 583 *Slender Bill Tern, *Sterna Tenuirostris.* **1859** STAINTON *Brit. Butterfl. & M.* II. 1 Their ample wings, compared to the size of their bodies, have procured for them [*sc.* the *Geometrina*] the designation of *Slender-bodies, by contrast with the *Noctuina* and *Bombycina*, termed Stout-bodied moths. **1896** H. O. FORBES *Hand-bk. Primates* I. 208 The *Slender Capuchin. *Cebus flavus.* **1894–5** LYDEKKER *Roy. Nat. Hist.* III. 60 The *slender dolphin is a spotted species from the Atlantic and the Cape of Good Hope. **1836** YARRELL *Brit. Fishes* I. 260 The *Slender Goby, *gobius gracilis.* **1834** MCMURTRIE *Cuvier's Anim. Kingd.* 50 The Lazy Monkeys ..The second species is called the *Slender Loris, *Lemur gracilis.* **1880** *Cassell's Nat. Hist.* I. 247 The Slender Loris is very common in the lower country of the south and east of Ceylon. **1893** LYDEKKER *Roy. Nat. Hist.* I. 231 The Slender Loris..is the sole species of the genus to which it belongs. *Ibid.* 469 In South Africa..we have also a much smaller species, the *slender mungoose. **1865** COUCH *Brit. Fishes* IV. 216 *Slender Salmon, *Salmo gracilis.* **1893** LYDEKKER *Roy. Nat. Hist.* I. 153 The *Slender Sapajou (*Cebus pallidus*) ..inhabiting Bolivia. **1896** *Ibid.* V. 491 The earliest allies of the herring tribe seem to be the extinct *slender-scales (*Leptolepidæ*).

(*b*) **1855** MISS PRATT *Flower. Pl.* V. 291 Thread Rush, or Slender Rush. *Ibid.* 297 Slender Spreading Rush. **1859** —— *Brit. Grasses* 23 Slender Cotton-grass. *Ibid.* 56 Slender Fox-tail. **1889** MAIDEN *Useful Pl.* 71 *Agrostis scabra*, Slender Bent Grass. *Ibid.* 95 *Oplismenus setarius*, Slender Panic Grass.

**12.** *Comb.* **a.** Parasynthetic, as *slender-finned, -flowered, -footed*, etc., frequently in the specific names of animals, plants, etc.

**1803** SHAW *Gen. Zool.* IV. II. 306 *Slender-finned Flounder. **1796** WITHERING *Brit. Pl.* (ed. 3) III. 699 *Slender-flowered Thistle. **1826** KIRBY & SP. *Entomol.* III. xxxii. 335 The *slender-footed *Cicindelidæ.* **1896** H. WOODWARD *Guide Fossil Reptiles Brit. Mus.* 6 The old type of long and *slender-jawed Teleosaurs. **1851** MANTELL *Petrifactions* ii. §2. 82 Numerous *slender-jointed simple tentacula. **1793** MARTYN *Lang. Bot.* s.v., A *slender-leaved plant. **1889** 'R. BOLDREWOOD' *Miner's Right* (1899) 130/1 The foliage of the slender-leaved eucalypti showed a tinge of softer green. **1737** BRACKEN *Farriery Impr.* (1756) I. 320 Colts that are *slender legg'd. **1663** COWLEY *Pindarique Odes, To Mr. Hobs* iv, The Caspian, And *slender-limb'd Mediterranean. **1894** *Pop. Sc. Monthly* XLIV. 500 These slender-limbed..Caucasians are..temperate. **1831** GRIFFITH tr. *Cuvier* IX. 104 The *slender-muzzled Crocodile. **1882** *Contemp. Rev.* Aug. 310 The *slender-nosed rhinoceros. **1872** TENNYSON *Gareth & Lynette* 3 A *slender-shafted Pine Lost footing, fell, and so was whirl'd away. **1822** *Hortus Anglicus* II. 115 *Slender-spiked Phryma. *Ibid.* 401 *Slender stalked Star Wort. **1858** HAWTHORNE *Fr. & Ital. Note-bks.* (1872) I. 4 *Slender-stemmed trees. **1882** VINES tr. *Sachs' Bot.* 936 In the genus *Vicia*..all the slender-stemmed species have leaf-tendrils. **1832** RENNIE *Butterfl. & M.* 278/1 *Slender-striped Rufous. **1827** GRIFFITH tr. *Cuvier* V. 82 Pouched Bat and *Slender-tailed Bat. *Ibid.* 126 *note*, The *Slender-toed Weasel. **1711** *Lond. Gaz.* No. 4891/4 A fair, clear skin'd Woman,..and *slender Waisted. **1848** BUCKLEY *Iliad* 425 Slender-waisted women. **1647** J. TRAPP *Comm. Acts* i. 18 Papias..was..a *slender-witted man.

**b.** Adverbial, as *slender-growing, -twined.*

**1616** J. HAYWARD *Sanct. Troub. Soul* I. vii. (1620) 105 The slender-twined thred of this life. **1901** *Gard. Chron.* 16 Mar. 173/1 Cytisus filipes, a slender-growing species with tiny white flowers.

**'slender,** *v.* [f. prec.] **a.** *trans.* To attenuate.

**1559** MORWYNG *Evonym.* 343 Thou maiest gather that whiche oyl strengtheneth, digesteth, and sclendereth. **1965** H. PORTER *Cats of Venice* 81 These shape-gripping *cheong sams* had slendered them to elegance.

**b.** *intr.* To become narrower, to narrow. Also with *down.*

**1871** G. M. HOPKINS *Poems* (1967) 13 And slendering to his burning rim Into the flat blue mist the sun Drops out and all our day is done. **1955** E. BOWEN *World of Love* iii. 55 Her strong forearms, which slendered down..to the wrists.

**slender-beaked,** *a.* [SLENDER *a.* 12 a.] Having a slender beak.

**1824** STEPHENS in *Shaw's Gen. Zool.* XII. I. 158 Slender-beaked Sandpiper. **1827** GRIFFITH tr. *Cuvier* V. 382 *Delphinus Rostratus* (Slender-beaked Dolphin). **1859** MISS PRATT *Brit. Grasses* 41 Slender-beaked Bottle Sedge. **1882** *Cassell's Nat. Hist.* VI. 197 The Slender-beaked Spider Crab (*Stenorhynchus tenuirostris*). **1896** LYDEKKER *Roy. Nat. Hist.* V. 513 The slender-beaked sturgeon (*Psephurus gladius*).

**slender-billed,** *a.* [SLENDER *a.* 12 a.] Having a slender bill; tenuirostral.

**1769** G. WHITE *Selborne* xxvi, It ought, no doubt, to have gone..among your slender-billed small birds. **1801** LATHAM *Gen. Synop Birds* Suppl. II. 165 Slender-billed creeper... Bill..very slender and moderately curved. **1839** AUDUBON *Ornith. Biog.* V. 251 Slender-billed Guillemot, *Uria Townsendi.* *Ibid.* 333 Slender-billed Fulmar, *Procellaria Tenuirostris.* **1872** COUES *N. Amer. Birds* 83 Slender-billed Nuthatch. *Ibid.* 332 Slender-billed Shearwater. **1895** LYDEKKER *Roy. Nat. Hist.* IV. 109 The slender-billed cockatoos.

**slender-bodied,** *a.* [SLENDER *a.* 12 a.] Having a slender body.

**1611** COTGR., *Carpion*, a kind of long-headed, slender-bodied,..white-bellied Trout. **1687** *Lond. Gaz.* No. 2298/3 A tall Man..and slender Bodied. *c* **1706** GARDINER tr. *Rapin, Of Gardens* II. 80 The tall slender body'd Pine. **1835–6** *Todd's Cycl. Anat.* I. 531/1 Some of the small slender-bodied subulate species [of calamaries]. **1859** STAINTON *Brit. Butterfl. & M.* Title-p., Vol. II. (Comprising the slender-bodied and small moths.) **1963** *Times* 4 Feb. 13/2 Dresses..with a slender-bodied look.

**slenderish** ('slɛndərɪʃ), *a.* [f. SLENDER *a.* + -ISH[1].] Rather slender.

**1894** CROCKETT *Raiders* vi. 61 Silver Sand was a slenderish man, of middle height.

**slenderize** ('slɛndəraɪz), *v.* Also **slenderise.** [f. SLENDER *a.* + -IZE.] **a.** *intr.* To make oneself slender, to slim. **b.** *trans.* To make (something) slender, to make (the figure) appear slender. Also *absol.*

**1923** *Weekly Dispatch* 4 Feb. 15/5 A slight figure will be more essential than ever. 'You must slenderise,' said one, coining a useful word. **1923** *Daily Mail* 21 Mar. 6/1 (Advt.), Corsets for slenderising full figures. **1946** *Sun* (Baltimore) 10 May 12/1 He brought it down to within a few inches of the ground, slenderized the column on which it hangs in merry-go-round fashion. **1964** *McCall's Sewing* I. 11/1 Lines for the 'Viking' type are a problem. You'll want those which slenderise without adding height. **1976** *National Observer* (U.S.) 13 Mar. 11/5 (Advt.), Starting age 6 yrs. Slenderize. Charm... Clover Lodge [establishment for overweight girls].

Hence **'slenderizer; 'slenderizing** *ppl. a.* and *vbl. sb.*

**1927** *Daily Express* 9 Sept. 5/5 There is the high straight line that is suited to the office frock, and the graceful slenderising V-cut accentuated by removable front of deep ivory crêpe-de-chine. **1928** *Sunday Express* 29 Apr. 15/4 Chefs are searching their brains for the slenderising sweet that will tempt both men and women diners. **1932** *Woman & Beauty* Apr. 87/1 (Advt.), Slenderizing. Free book tells how you can become slim. **1935** *Amer. Speech* X. 192/2 Black velvet, we find, is the best *slenderizer.* **1958** *People* 4 May 7/1 (Advt.), A most flattering and slenderising style.

**1969** *Daily Tel.* 18 Apr. 17 The skirt does a slenderising job where most women want to look slim. **1970** *Globe & Mail* (Toronto) 25 Sept. 10/2 (Advt.), The jacket is a little longer. It continues the slenderizing effect of the waist. **1978** *Detroit Free Press* 5 Mar. B12/1, I made a slenderizing lunch of cottage cheese and grapefruit sections.

**slenderly** (ˈslɛndəlɪ), *adv.* Also 5-6 sklenderly, 6 -lye, -lie, -urly, sclenderly; 6 slenderlye, 6-7 -lie. [f. SLENDER *a.* + -LY².]

**1.** In a slight degree; to a slight or small extent; scantily, meagrely, poorly.

α. *a* **1513** FABYAN *Chron.* VII. (1811) 614 The whiche persone.. shewyd to hym that the castell of Coruyle was but sklenderly manned. **1526** *Pilgr. Perf.* (W. de W. 1531) 274 We haue touched the vertues and the exercyse of yᵉ same but diminutely, breuely and sclenderly. **1577** B. GOOGE *Heresbach's Husb.* I. (1586) 36 Couer it how sclenderly you wyll, it careth not.

β. **1558** WARDE tr. *Alexis' Secr.* 44 b, Take.. sixe cloues lightly or slenderlye beaten. **1587** TURBERV. *Trag. Tales* (1837) 111 He to mercy movde, To see the poore diseasde soule so slenderly belovde. **1620** VENNER *Via Recta* vii. 108 That.. which is but slenderly perceiued of the gustatiue sense. **1674** BOYLE *Excell. Theol.* II. iv. 174 How many others we are but slenderly acquainted with. **1707** MORTIMER *Husb.* (1721) II. 118 It is better to water a Plant seldom and thoroughly, than often and slenderly. **1748** *Anson's Voy.* III. viii. 382 The prisoners.. observed how slenderly she was manned. **1821** LAMB *Elia* I. *Grace before Meat*, The slender, but not slenderly acknowledged, refection of the poor and humble man. **1855** THACKERAY *Newcomes* xlvii, My brothers and sisters will be but slenderly portioned. **1867** F. FRANCIS *Angling* x. (1880) 355 The flies are.. slenderly dressed.

†**2. a.** Feebly, ineffectively. *Obs.*

*a* **1533** FRITH *Disput. Purg.* B ij b, I wyll declare vnto you what solucyons he maketh to these seauen weake reasons,.. for he auoydeth them so slenderlye, that [etc.]. **1577** HANMER *Anc. Eccl. Hist., Socrat.* II. x. (1619) 257 He maintained their opinion very slenderly.

†**b.** Slackly, perfunctorily. *Obs.*

**1545** BRINKLOW *Compl.* 5 b, This [praying] must be done ernestly,.. not slenderly. **1560** DAUS tr. *Sleidane's Comm.* 370 The request of Duke Moris was coldlye and slenderlye preferred unto them. **1603** KNOLLES *Hist. Turkes* (1621) 781 To see him deale so slenderly in a matter of so great importance.

†**c.** Ungraciously, coldly; slightingly. *Obs.*

**1598** YONG *Diana* 66 If by chaunce he sent her anie thing by any of his other seruants, it was so slenderly accepted, that he thought it best to send none vnto her but my selfe. **1624** CAPT. SMITH *Virginia* Wks. (Arb.) II. 587 Seeing.. how slenderly heretofore both had beene regarded.

†**d.** Easily; for little return. *Obs.*⁻¹

**1677** GILPIN *Demonol.* (1867) 375 We must learn this skill, not too easily to give up our hopes, or to be prodigal of our interest in Christ, so as to part with it slenderly.

**3.** In a slender or slim fashion; delicately.

**1591** SPENSER *Virgil's Gnat* 3 We.., like a cobweb weauing slenderly, Haue onely playde. **1844** HOOD *Bridge of Sighs* ii, Fashion'd so slenderly, Young, and so fair! **1885** *Cent. Mag.* Nov. 60 He was a youngish, slenderly made man, with a distinctly good bearing. **1894** H. NISBET *Bush Girl's Rom.* 28 A slenderly-built, red-nosed and dyspeptic patrician he was.

**slenderness** (ˈslɛndənɪs). Also 6 sklendurnes, sclendernesse; 6-7 slendernes(se. [f. SLENDER *a.* + -NESS.]

**1.** The quality of being slender in form or physical condition; slimness, spareness. Also in fig. context.

**1538** STARKEY *England* I. iii. 72 In thys polytyke body, ther ys a certayn sklendurnes, debylyte, and wekenes therof. *Ibid.* II. i. 152 A syngular remedy for the sklendurnes of our polytyke body. **1580** HOLLYBAND *Treas. Fr. Tong, Menuiseté*, thinnesse, slendernesse. **1597** A. M. tr. *Guillemeau's Fr. Chirurg.* 46/2 The legges, hippes and armes are thinner belowe then above; we must therefore on such slendernes apply some compresses. **1626** BACON *Sylva* §116 As for Small Whistles, or Shepheards Oaten Pipes, they give a Sound, because of their extreame Slendernesse. **1686** PLOT *Staffordsh.* 389 According to the bigness and slenderness of the neck. **1713** DERHAM *Phys.-Theol.* 191 Its extraordinary Length and Slenderness is very useful to some. **1851** RUSKIN *Stones Ven.* I. viii. §11 *note*, When shafts are used in the upper stories of buildings,.. no such relative limits exist either to slenderness or solidity.

**2. a.** Pettiness, smallness, slightness, etc.

**1542** BRINKLOW *Compl.* ii. (1874) 26 The court of the Marshyalsee, I can neyther thynck, speake, nor write, the slendernesse.. of that court. **1555** EDEN *Decades* (Arb.) 50 The sclendernesse of theyr capacitie. **1570-6** LAMBARDE *Peramb. Kent* (1826) 303 The yeerely value is but small, the slendernesse wherof [etc.]. **1607** TOPSELL *Serpents* (1658) 813 Mark well the slendernesse of this comparison. **1646** J. GREGORY *Notes on Script.* 133 The Coarsenesse of the Raiment,.. the slendernesse of the dyet. **1743** *Phil. Trans.* XLII. 320, I.. have presumed, on the Slenderness of our Acquaintance, to send thee an Account thereof. **1818** HALLAM *Mid. Ages* (1872) I. 112 Even if we should often doubt particular facts from slenderness of proof. **1870** *Pall Mall G.* 7 Nov. 3 A friend.. knowing the slenderness of my purse.

†**b.** Limited knowledge or intellect. *Obs.*

**1612** WOODALL *Surgeon's Mate* Ep. Salut., Better documents then my slendernesse can unfold. **1651** *Rec. Communion* §2 Their slownesse and slendernesse.. was very great.

**3.** *attrib.* **slenderness ratio** *Engin.*, the ratio of the effective length of a column or pillar to its least radius of gyration (formerly, to its least diameter).

**1905** M. MERRIMAN *Mechanics of Materials* (ed. 10) ix. 191 The ratio $l/r$ is called the 'slenderness ratio' of the column. **1931** *Engineering* 9 Jan. 61/3 Experiments on eccentrically-loaded steel columns... The slenderness ratios ranged from 50 to 150. **1976** R. F. WARNER et al. *Reinforced Concrete* xiii. 308 The effective strength of the column section.. is divided by a reduction factor R... R is given as $R = 1{\cdot}2 - 0{\cdot}01(l/r)$ in which $l/r$ is the maximum slenderness ratio for the column, for bending in any plane.

†**slenderwise**, *adv. Obs.*⁻¹ [f. SLENDER *a.* + -WISE.] In a slender or attenuated manner.

**1541** COPLAND *Guydon's Quest. Chirurg.* F iij b, The thre fyrste be longe and byg,.. and brede sklenderwyse as a tayle.

†**sleng**, *v. Obs.* Also *pa. t.* and *pa. pple.* sleynt. [a. ON. **slengja* (Norw. and Icel. *slengja*, Sw. *slänga* Da. *slænge*), = ONorw. and Icel. *sløngja*, *sløngva*, f. *slangw-* pret. stem of *slyngva* SLING *v.*¹] *trans.* To sling, throw, cast.

*a* **1300** *Havelok* 1923 Summe leye in dikes slenget. *c* **1330** *Amis & Amil.* 2073 He.. hent him in his honden tvain, And sleynt him in the lake. **14..** *Pol., Rel., & L. Poems* (1903) 276 Crist on croys was sleynt; To hys fader he made a pleynt.

Hence †ˈ**slenger**, a slinger. *Obs.*⁻¹

*a* **1400-50** *Alexander* 2219 (D.), Hym-self with slengers & slyke he somned a menȝe.

†**slenk.** *Obs.*⁻¹ ? A side-blow.

The other MSS. have *slynge* and *slyuyng*.

*c* **1400** *Anturs of Arth.* xlviii. (Douce MS.), He atteled withe a slenke haf slayne him in sliȝte.

†ˈ**slenker**, *v. Obs.*⁻¹ [ad. G. *schlenkern* (LG. *slenkern*).] *trans.* To dangle, swing.

**1658** A. FOX *Würtz' Surg.* v. 363 Children.. carryed onely in the arm, and slencker'd up and down by lazy Maids, are easily hurt in that manner.

**slent**, *sb.*¹ Now *dial.* Also 4 slente. [a. ON. **slent* (Norw. *slent* a side-slip *paa slent* aslant; Sw. *slänt* slope, slant, *på slänt* aslant), related to **slenta* SLENT *v.*¹ (whence sense 3). See also SKLENT *sb.* and SLANT *sb.*¹]

**1.** A slope or declivity. = SLANT *sb.*¹ 1.

**13..** *E.E. Allit. P.* A. 141 By-ȝonde þe broke by slente oþer slade, I hoped þat mote merked wore. *a* **1825** FORBY *Voc. E. Anglia* 307 *Slent*, a gentle slope in the surface of the ground.

**2.** *on (the) slent*, aslant. Cf. SLANT *sb.*¹ 3.

**13..** *Cursor M.* 6200 (Gött.), God þaim bad drau inermare Egain on slent þar þai ware. **1894** HESLOP *Northumbld. Gloss.* s.v., 'It's on the slent'—aslope.

†**3.** A sly hit or sarcasm. *Obs.* = SLANT *sb.*¹ 5.

*c* **1557** ABP. PARKER *Ps.* cxix. 42 Fynd thus I maye to answere right and dul blasphemers slents. **1579** NORTH *Plut., Antonius* 982 b, When Cleopatra found Antonius ieasts and slents to be but grosse and souldier like, in plaine manner she gaue it him finely. **1612** *Ibid., Epaminondas* 1110 He was as pleasant a man to giue a fine slent in discourse, as could be possible to be found.

†**slent**, *sb.*² *Obs.* [a. ON. **slent* (Norw. *slett*), f. **slenta* (ON. *sletta*) to dash, throw, etc.]

**1.** A splash or sprinkling.

**13..** *St. Erkenwolde* 331 in Horstm. *Altengl. Leg.* (1881), þe fyrst slent [of water] þat on me slode slekkyd al my tene.

**2.** *Naut.* = SLANT *sb.*²

**1596** RALEIGH *Discov. Guiana* 53 Towards the euening [we] had a slent of a northerly winde that blew very strong. **1622** R. HAWKINS *Voy. S. Sea* (1847) 81 Advising them that with the first calme or slent of wind, they should come off. **1628** SIR K. DIGBY *Voy. Medit.* (Camden) 43 This day the wind and sea were verie high,.. but att the euening a slent of calme came.

**slent**, *v.*¹ Now *dial.* Also 4 slinte, 5 sclente. [a. ON. **slenta* (Norw. *slenta*, older Da. *slente*; cf. MSw. and Sw. *slinta*) to slant, slope, slip. See also SKLENT *v.*]

**1.** *intr.* To slip, fall, or glide obliquely; to strike or lie aslant.

**13..** *Sir Beues* 2539 Ascopard.. Smot after Beues a dent gret, And wiþ is o fot a slintte And fel wiþ is owene dentte [**14..** *Camb. MS. Ff. ii. 38* A fote yn to þe erthe hyt sclente]. **1470-85** MALORY *Arthur* XVII. i. 689 The stroke was soo grete that it slented doune to the erthe. **1655** GURNALL *Chr. in Arm.* II. 337 Though God takes his aim at man, and levels his arrows primarily at his very heart; yet as they go, they slent upon the creature. **1854** MISS BAKER *Northampt. Gloss., Slent*, to slant, to slope.

†**2.** To make sly hits or gibes. *Obs.*

Cf. Brockett (1829), '*Slant*, to utter sly jokes'.

**1567** FENTON *Trag. Disc.* 141 b, Slenting at their sortes of devises in woing. **1579** NORTH *Plutarch* 744 b, One Proteas, a pleasaunt conceited man, and that could slent finely.

**3.** *trans.* To cause to slant; to turn aside.

**1639** FULLER *Holy War* IV. xxiv. (1647) 210 Nimblenesse was also very advantageous to break and slent the downright rushings of a stronger vessel.

Hence ˈ**slenting** *vbl. sb.*

**13..** *Gaw. & Gr. Knt.* 1160 Þer myȝt mon se, as þay slypte, slentyng of arwes.

†**slent**, *v.*² In 4 slente, slinte. [Of obscure origin.] *trans.* To strike *out*; to aim or deliver (a blow); to cast, throw.

**13..** *Sir Beues* 813 Wiþ is swerd out a slinte Twei toskes at þe ferste dent. *c* **1380** *Sir Ferumb.* 1615 Roland ȝerne him gan defende wyþ durendale is brond, And sturne strokes til hymen he slente. *Ibid.* 3313 Grete slabbes of styl & yre to þe walles þo wern y-slente.

**slent**, *v.*³ Now *dial.* [Of obscure origin.]

**1.** *trans.* To split or cleave; to rend.

**1605** SYLVESTER *Du Bartas* II. iii. 1. *Vocation* 857 With a steel Dart..[thou] Art 'twixt thy Cuirace and thy Saddle slent. *a* **1618** —— *Job Triumphant* III. 295 On Cliffs of Adamant hee laies his hands;.. Slents them wᵗʰ sledges. *c* **1645** HOWELL *Lett.* IV. xix, If one do well observe the quality of the Cliffs on both shores, his eyes will judge.. that they were slented and shiver'd asunder by some act of violence. **1851** *Dorset Gloss., Slent*, to tear; to rend. **1897** T. HARDY *Wessex Poems, Valenciennes* vii, A shell was slent to shards anighst my ears.

*absol.* **1591** SYLVESTER *Du Bartas* II. i. 813 Whose two-hand Sword, at every veny, slent, Not through a single Souldier's feeble bones, But keenly slyces through whole Troops at once.

†**2.** *intr.* To burst or split. *Obs. rare.*

**1608** SYLVESTER *Du Bartas* II. iv. III. *Schisme* 188 Th' unsacred Altar sudden slent in twain. *a* **1618** —— *Job Triumphant* IV. 52 My brest is like a Wine-Butt.. Ready to burst, or Bottles like to slent.

**slenter**, var. SCHLENTER, *sb.* and *a.*

ˈ**slenting**, *ppl. a.* Also 7 slinting. [f. SLENT *v.*¹] Oblique, indirect.

**1642** FULLER *Holy & Prof. St.* II. v. 66 Generally writing ingeniously, using sometimes slenting, seldome down-right railing. *a* **1661** —— *Worthies, London* II. (1662) 217 This if literally true, deserved a down-right (and not only so slenting a) mention. **1662** GURNALL *Chr. in Arm.* XIX. xi. §2 (1669) 510/1 So by a slinting blow they hit God himself in contemning his Ambassador.

†ˈ**slentwise**, *adv. Obs. rare*⁻¹. [f. SLENT *sb.*¹ or *v.*¹] In a slanting manner.

**1579** FENTON *Guicciard.* xv. (1599) 692 The hurt was light, being but a blow slentwise.

†**slep**, *v. Obs. rare.* [a. ON. (also Icel., Norw., MSw.) *sleppa.*] *intr.* To slip.

? *a* **1400** *Morte Arth.* 3854 His hand sleppid and slode o-slante one þe mayles. *a* **1420** *Anturs of Arth.* xlviii. (Thornton MS.), The swerde sleppis on slante, and one the mayle slydys.

†**slepe**, *v. Obs.*⁻¹ [a. MDu. *slepen*, = MLG. *slepen*, MHG. *sleifen.*] *trans.* To drag.

**1481** CAXTON *Reynard* (Arb.) 27 They slepid hym and drewe hym ouer stones and ouer blockes wythout the village.

**slepe(r**, obs. f. SLEEP(ER.

**slep(e)ry, sleprie**, obs. ff. SLEEPERY.

**slepyr**, obs. f. SLIPPER.

**slerg**, *v. Sc.* [More commonly written *slairg* (see the *Eng. Dial. Dict.*). Cf. G. dial. *schlargen*, *schlergen* to smear, mess.] *trans.* To slabber.

*a* **1758** RAMSAY *Daft Bargain* 22 Rab.. slerg'd the rest o't in his gab.

**slester**, variant of SLAISTER *Sc.*

†**slet**, *v. Obs.* In 3 sclette, 4 slette. [app. a. ON. *sletta* to slap, etc.] **a.** *trans.* To flatten, lay flat. **b.** *intr.* To fall flat.

*c* **1225** *Ancr. R.* 212 Heo sleateð [*MS. C.* scletteð] adun boa two hore earen. **13..** *K. Alis.* 2262 (W.), Heore hors hedlyng mette, That heo to grounde y-swowe sletten.

†**sletch**, obs. var. of SLEECH *sb.* or SLITCH.

**1743** MAXWELL *Sel. Trans.* 44 Sea-sletch, Clay and Lime. *Ibid.* 125 Indeed they chuse to have Mud with the Sand, and this they call *Sletch*.

**sletch** (slɛtʃ), *v. rare.* Now *dial.* Also 5 slech; *pa. t.* sleghte. [repr. OE. *slæccan* (also *á-*, *ȝeslæccan*), f. *slæc* SLACK *a.* Cf. OS. *slekkian* to weaken, Norw. *slekkja* to slacken (a cord, etc.).]

†**1.** *trans.* To render slack or relaxed; to assuage, mitigate. *Obs. rare.*

? *a* **1400** *Morte Arth.* 2675 Lordes lenande lowe on lemand scheldes,.. And some was sleghte one slepe with slaughte of þe pople. *a* **1500** *Tale of Basyn* 47 in Hazl. *E.P.P.* III. 46 [Go] To the parson thi broder, that is so rich a wrech, And pray hym of thi sorow sum del he wold slech.

**2.** *intr.* To abate, slacken, stop. *dial.*

**1847** in HALLIWELL (I. Wight). **1881** *Isle of Wight Gloss.* s.v., It raained aal day without sletchun.

**sleuce**, obs. form of SLUICE *sb.*

**sleugh**, variant of SLEW *sb.*¹

**sleughi**, var. SALUKI.

†**sleuth**, *sb.*¹ *Obs.* Forms: 1 slæwð, slæwþ, 2 slewðe, 4 sleawþe, 4-5 slewthe, 4-6 slewth; 1 sleuð, 3-4 sleuþe, 4 sleuȝþe, sleauþe, 4-6 sleuthe (5 scl-), 4-6 sleuth, 7 slouth. [OE. *slǽwð*, f. *sláw* SLOW *a.* + -TH¹. In later use chiefly northern and Sc.]

**1.** Sloth; laziness.

*c* **888** K. ÆLFRED *Boeth.* xviii. §3 For heora slæwðd & for ȝimeleste & eac for recceleste. *c* **1000** ÆLFRIC in Assmann *Ags. Hom.* i. 224 We ne maȝon mid slæwðe.. þa ecan myrhðe mid Gode ȝeearnian. *c* **1175** *Lamb. Hom.* 103 *Desidia*, þet is slewðe on englisc. **1297** R. GLOUC. (Rolls) 7508 Þet folc.. turnde to sleuþe & to prute & to lecherie. **1340** *Ayenb.* 32 Efterward comþ sleuþe. *Ibid.*, Efter sleauþe is uoryetinge. **1387** TREVISA *Higden* (Rolls) I. 355 Þey.. ȝeueþ hem alle to idelnesse and to sleuþe. **1422** tr. *Secreta Secret., Priv. Priv.* 228 A grete vysage and broode tokenyth slewthe in manere, as Oxeen and Assis. *c* **1450** *St. Cuthbert* (Surtees) 1749 Why er we þus in sleuth sett? **1513** DOUGLAS *Æneid* x. vi. 46 Than na delay of sleuth, nor feir, ne bost, Wyththeld Turnus. **1529** RASTELL *Pastyme* (1811) 77 Slewth, gloteny, and other pleasurs. **1557** PAYNELL *Jugurtha* 92 There was neuer man whiche obtayned..euerlastyng name by cowardise or sleuth. *c* **1600** MONTGOMERIE *Cherrie & Slae* 1560 Then let us remuve, And sleip nae mair in sleuth. **1629** SIR W. MURE *True Crucifix* 3113 Wks. (S.T.S.) I. 294 Not in the Bed of slouth Reposing.

**b.** As a 'proper term' (cf. SLOTH *sb.*[1] 3).

**1486** *Bk. St. Albans* f vj, A Sleuth of Beeris.

**2.** Slowness, slow movement. *rare*$^{-1}$.

**1387** TREVISA *Higden* (Rolls) III. 207 By þe sleuþe of þe manere of tunes.

**sleuth** (sluːθ), *sb.*[2] Forms: 3-4 sloþ, 4-5 sloth, 4 slotht, slog(t)h; 5 *Sc.* sloith, slouth, sluth(e, 5 *Sc.*, 9 sleuth. [In sense 1 a. ON. (and Icel.) *slóð* (Norw. *slod, slo*) track, trail. In sense 2 ellipt. for SLEUTH-HOUND.]

† **1. a.** The track or trail of a person or animal; a definite track or path. Also *fig. Obs.*

*c* **1200** ORMIN 1194 ȝiff þu..follȝhesst aȝȝ clænnessess sloþ, & læresst me to follȝhenn. *a* **1300** *Cursor M.* 1254 In þat way sal þou find forsoth þi moders and mine our bather slogh [*v.r.* sloth]. *Ibid.* 1285, etc. **1375** BARBOUR *Bruce* VII. 44 Iohne of Lorn Persauit the hund the sleuth had lorn. **1429** in *Cal. Doc. rel. Scot.* (1888) IV. 404 Gif onny man..makking lauchful sluthe as the trewis wil, be slayne. *c* **1470** HENRY *Wallace* V. 137 The sloith stoppyt, at Fawdoun still scho [*sc.* the dog] stude.

**b.** *attrib.*, as ***sleuth-dog***, etc.

*c* **1470** HENRY *Wallace* V. 96 Bot this sloth brache [*v.r.* sluth ratche]..On Wallace fute folowit so felloune fast. **1802** SURTEES *Fray Suport* ix. in Scott *Minstrelsy*, Lang Aicky..Wi' his sleuth-dog sits in his watch right sure. **1822** SCOTT *Peveril* xli, The sleuth-dog, which, eager, fierce, and clamorous in pursuit of his prey, desists from it so soon as blood is sprinkled upon his path.

**2. a.** A bloodhound. Hence ***sleuth-like*** adj. **b.** orig. *U.S.* A detective. Also *transf.*

**1872** *N.Y. Fireside Compan.* 13 May 4/3 The name of the story is *Sleuth, the Detective* and a more remarkable and thrilling story has seldom ever been written. **1876** *N. Amer. Rev.* CXXIII. 371 The quiet, untiring sluth-like assiduity with which Mr. Silden was ferreting out their wrong-doings. **1904** 'O. HENRY' *Cabbages & Kings* iv. 73 Goodwin followed at increased speed, but without any of the artful tactics that are so dear to the heart of the sleuth. **1907** *Black Cat* June 11 The sleuths whose protection he had invoked. **1908** *Westm. Gaz.* 28 Aug. 2/3 The 'sleuth' that tracks down the murderer. **1949** *Manch. Guardian Weekly* 22 Dec. 2/3 A school of newspaper sleuths who attributed every declaration of American foreign policy to the hidden hand of George Kennan. **1958** 'J. BYROM' *Or be he Dead* v. 69, I gather you have Miss Canning as your assistant sleuth. **1979** *Oxf. Jrnl.* 16 Nov. 1 (*caption*) Amateur sleuths Gordon Murray and Jane Lawton... Their investigations launched a top-level probe into an Oxford business.

† **sleuth**, *a.*[1] *Sc. Obs. rare.* Also 7 slueth. [irreg. f. SLEUTH *sb.*[1]] Slothful, slow.

**1567** *Gude & Godlie B.* (S.T.S.) 180 Wald thay na mair Impugne the treuth, Syne in thair office be nocht sleuth [1621 slueth]. **1570** *Satir. Poems Reform.* x. 92 Quhen pleisit God to send ȝow Scottis þe treuth, The same to further at Leith he was not sleuth.

**sleuth**, *a.*[2] *rare*$^{-1}$. [Inferred from SLEUTH-HOUND.] Persistent, dogged.

**1864** BLACKMORE *Clara Vaughan* vii, A treacherous, blue, three-cornered blade,..sleuth as hate, and tenacious as death.

† **sleuth**, *v.*[1] Also 3 sleuhþen, 5 slewthyn; 5-6 slewth, 6 *Sc.* sleucht, sluthe. [f. SLEUTH *sb.*[1] In later use only *Sc.*]

**1.** *intr.* To be slothful. *rare.*

*c* **1300** *Moral Ode* [37] in *Anglia* I. 9 Ne solde no man don a first, ne sleuhþen wel to donne. *c* **1440** *Promp. Parv.* 459/1 Slewthyn, or sluggon, *torpeo, torpesco.*

**2.** *trans.* To delay, put off, neglect.

*c* **1430** *Pilgr. Lyf Manhode* II. xc. (1869) 108, I slewthede it, and dide no more ther too;..and wel ofte bi me hath be many a good werk slewthed. **1450** *Paston Lett.* I. 175 That thys be not slewthed, for taryeng drawth perell. **1513** DOUGLAS *Æneid* XI. ix. 62 Mony was him self he accusit, That he sa lang had slewthit and refusit To ressaue glaidly the Troiane Enee. **1534** *St. Papers Hen. VIII*, V. 12 We do nocht sleucht nor contenow no manor thing yat concernis the King. *a* **1578** LINDESAY (Pitscottie) *Chron. Scot.* (S.T.S.) I. 135 Sieing all was sluthit, thair was no mischeif could befall our king bot was deliuerit wnto ws.

**b.** To waste in sloth.

**1585** JAS. I *Ess. Poesie* (Arb.) 74 Men sould be warr, To sleuth the tyme that flees fra them so farr.

Hence **'sleuthing** *vbl. sb.*

*c* **1450** *Godstow Reg.* 78 With-out tariinge or slewthynge, al so sone as hyt myht lawfully be done. *a* **1585** MONTGOMERIE *Cherrie & Slae* 542 Persauis thou not quhat pretious tyme thy slewthing dois oreschute?

**sleuth** (sluːθ), *v.*[2] [f. SLEUTH *sb.*[2] 2.]

**a.** *trans.* To track (a person); to investigate (something or someone). Also with *out* (in quot. 1939: to detect or expose).

**1905** *Review of Rev.* Sept. 254 Berton..has been sleuthed by the detectives. **1909** GUNTER *Prince Karl* 269 You sleuth her to Buffalo and it will get you a raise in salary. **1939** [see RECORD *sb.* 5 g]. **1949** *Sun* (Baltimore) 16 Nov. 14/3 Men who qualify for the tremendous job of sleuthing a single big industry like steel or coal—and determining the facts to make wage, hour and pension recommendations. **1956** A. CHRISTIE *Dead Man's Folly* xviii. 240 'Who hired you to sleuth me?'..'You are in error,' replied Poirot. 'I have not been sleuthing you.' **1968** P. DICKINSON *Skin Deep* v. 108 It had been something private he'd sleuthed out, something secret. **1979** *Amer. Speech 1978* LIII. 285 Ten years ago, sleuthing a clue from Lenneberg, I wrote..'The use of tools may be much older than language'.

**b.** *intr.* To act as a detective; to conduct an investigation. Also with *around.*

**1912** L. J. VANCE *Destroying Angel* xx. 276 So I went sleuthing; traced you through the canal to Peconic. **1930** 'SAPPER' *Finger of Fate* 99 My poor friend..labours under the delusion that he is a detective. He goes about with magnifying glasses, and sleuths. **1975** *High Times* Dec. 31/2 If you sleuth around—beginning at the roach-infested gringo palace, the Hotel Astorial—you can get directions to the mushroom fields overlooking San José. **1980** E. DEWHURST *Drink This* ii. 28 He had been sleuthing, unconsciously..all the time he had thought he was relaxing.

Hence **'sleuthing** *vbl. sb.*

**1900** ADE *More Fables* 193 He called himself a Reformer, and he did all his Sleuthing in the line of Duty. **1924** *Weekly Westm. Gaz.* 13 Sept. 580/2 One always knew all about his theories and his sleuthing. **1946** *Reader's Digest* Sept. 76/1 Izzy knew nothing of sleuthing procedure; he simply knocked on the door. **1958** T. F. T. PLUCKNETT *Early Eng. Legal Lit.* v. 83 Teasing as these references are, they seem too obscure and divergent to permit any plausible conclusion as to the authorship of *Brevia Placitata*, in spite of the very clever sleuthing of Mr Turner. **1979** *Dædalus* Summer 111 It is possible, through conscientious sleuthing, to decode the secondary associations of symbols.

† **'sleuthful**, *a. Obs.* Also *Sc.* 5 slouth-, 6 slewth-, 7 slueth-. [f. SLEUTH *sb.*[1] In later use only *Sc.*] Slothful.

*c* **1400** tr. *Secreta Secret., Gov. Lordsh.* 104 Man ys..wayk and sleuthfull as Bere. *Ibid.* 115 Sleuthful, and vnobeyssant. *c* **1470** HENRY *Wallace* VII. 348 In thair brawnys sone slaid the sleuthfull sleip. **1533** BELLENDEN *Livy* I. Prol. (S.T.S.) I. 9 How sleuthfull war þe maneris of romanis, quhen morall disciplynis began to failȝe. **1596** DALRYMPLE tr. *Leslie's Hist. Scot.* I. 286 Mony of þair kinsmen and freindis, this law walde fettir, ydle, sueir, and sleuthfull. *c* **1614** SIR W. MURE *Dido & Æneas* Wks. (S.T.S.) I. 78 None sluethfull in the citty do remaine.

Hence † **'sleuthfully** *adv.*, † **sleuthfulness.**

*c* **1470** HENRY *Wallace* I. 3 Our antecessowris..We lat ourslide, throw werray sleuthfulness. *Ibid.* III. 234 Our slouthfully our keparis leit him pass. **1520** *Peebles Burgh Rec.* (1872) 50 Gyf it happynis..that the saidis landis faill throuch neclegens, wantonnes, or slewthfulness of the chaplane. **1565** *Reg. Privy Council Scot.* I. 430 The samyn wes sleuthfullie left furth of the procurationis.

**sleuth-hound** ('sluːθhaʊnd). Forms: 5 sloith-, slewth-, sleuth-, 5-6 sluth(e)-, 7 slwth-hund; 5 slwthound, 6 sleuthound; 7 slugh-, 7 (9) sluth-, 8 slothe, slooth, 7, 9- sleuth-hound (9 sleugh-). [f. SLEUTH *sb.*[2] Originally northern and Sc.]

**1.** A species of bloodhound, formerly employed in Scotland for pursuing game or tracking fugitives. Now *Hist.* or *arch.*

**1375** BARBOUR *Bruce* VI. 484 A sleuthhund had he thar. *Ibid.* VII. 40 The sleuth-hund maid stynting thar. *c* **1470** HENRY *Wallace* V. 135 Thair sloith hund the graith gait till him ȝeid. **1483** *Cath. Angl.* 345/2 A Sluthe hunde, *sapifur, oderinsecus.* **1536** BELLENDEN *Cron. Scot.* (1821) I. p. xlii, He that denyis entres to the sleuthound..sal be haldin participant with the crime and thift committit. **1596** DALRYMPLE tr. *Leslie's Hist. Scot.* I. 7 Throuch thir woddis the gretter parte of the nobilitie hes thair maist recreatione in hunting with the sluthe-hundes. **1607** TOPSELL *Four-f. Beasts* 149 The second kind is called in Scotland a Sluth-hound. **1610** HOLLAND *Camden's Brit.* II. 18 Tracing them..by their footing..as quick senting Slugh-hounds doe lead them. **1674** N. COX *Gentl. Recreat.* I. (1677) 29 The Blood-hound differeth nothing in quality from the Scotish Sluth-hound. **1777** LIGHTFOOT *Flora Scot.* I. 7 Slough or slothe hounds. **1828** SCOTT *Tales Grandfather* Ser. I. I. viii, These bloodhounds, or sleuth-hounds,..were used for the purpose of pursuing great criminals. **1849** C. BRONTE *Shirley* II. xi. 259 These persons Moore hunted like any sleuth-hound. **1885** MISS BRADDON *Wyllard's Weird* iii, If I were a criminal, I would as soon have a sleuthhound on my track as Joseph Distin.

*attrib.* **1870** LOWELL *Study Wind.* 123 The remarkable feature of Mr. Carlyle's criticism..is the sleuth-hound instinct with which he presses on to the matter of his theme.

**2.** *transf.* A keen investigator or pursuer; a tracker; *U.S.* a detective.

[**1849** A. B. REACH *Clement Lorimer* xiii. 130 There is an awful mystery which the sleuth hounds of the law may trace—a mystery of suspicion, perhaps a mystery of crime.] **1856** FROUDE *Hist. Eng.* II. 316 Cromwell..had his sleuth-hounds abroad, whose scent was not easily baffled. **1857** MRS. GASKELL *C. Bronte* (1860) 9 The West Riding men are sleuth-hounds in pursuit of money. **1890** 'R. BOLDREWOOD' *Col. Reformer* (1891) 209 The inspector and I followed..our sable sleuth-hounds. **1902** WODEHOUSE *Pothunters* iv. 66 Jim's respect for the abilities of our national sleuth-hounds was greater than Tony's, and a good deal greater than that of most people. **1929** *Bookman* Nov. 264/1 'What is it, Fra Diavolo?' he asked... 'A peeler, fellow, a sleuth-hound.' **1948** *Amer. Speech* XXIII. 306/2 The hunt for it would be engrossing to a literary sleuth-hound.

† **'sleuthy**, *a. Obs.*$^{-1}$ [f. SLEUTH *sb.*[1]] Slothful.

*a* **1400** in *Sel. Wks. Wyclif* (1871) III. 34 For defaute of good teching, not of God, but of sleuþi prestis.

**sleuuol**: see SLEWFUL *a.*

**sleve**, obs. form of SLEEVE *sb.* and *v.*

† **sleve**, *sb. Obs.*$^{-1}$ (Meaning unknown.)

**1523** FITZHERB. *Husb.* §5 Or he shall lode his corne, he muste haue a wayne, a copyoke, a payre of sleues, a wayne-rope, and a pykforke.

† **sleve**, *v. Obs. rare.* Also 5 slefe, *Sc.* slewe. [OE. *slēfan*, of uncertain relationship. Cf. SLIVE *v.*[2]]

**1.** *trans.* To cause to slip (*on, down, over*, or *into* something).

? *a* **950** *Guthlac* (1909) xvi. 153 Guðlac hine sylfne unȝyrede, and þæt reaf..he hit slefde on þone..man. **14..** *Master of Game* (MS. Douce 335) xxxiv. lf. 62 b, Thanne shold the hunter slefe doun the skyn as fer as he may. *c* **1470** HENRY *Wallace* VII. 207 A rynnand cord thai slewyt our his hed. **1513** DOUGLAS *Æneid* VI. iv. 25 Sum slevit knyffis in the beistis throtis.

**2.** *intr.* With *over.* To slip past.

*a* **1510** DOUGLAS *K. Hart* II. 187 ȝe did greit miss..That sleuthfullie suld lat ȝour tyme our sleif, And come thus lait.

**slew** (sluː), *sb.*[1] Also slue, sleugh. [Variant spellings of *sloo*, ME. *slō*: see SLOUGH *sb.*[1]]

**1. a.** *U.S.* and *Canada.* A marshy or reedy pool, pond, small lake, backwater, or inlet.

α. **1708** S. SEWALL *Diary* 18 Dec., Got home well in my slay, had much adoe to avoid Slews. **1867** F. N. LUDLOW *Fleeing to Tarshish* 112 It's in my heart to believe we could get the Lord's charriat out of this slew. **1888** *Home Missionary* (N.Y.) Dec. 380 We came to a 'slew' full of water... The horse..sank deeper and deeper, until he came to a standstill in the middle of the 'slew'.

β. **1870** J. ORTON *Andes & Amazons* (1876) xvi. 239 Beside a slue of sluggish black water. **1902** *Blackwood's Mag.* April 504/1 In the first 'slue' we crossed.

γ. **1891** E. ROPER *By Track & Trail* vi. 80 At length we came to a very pretty sleugh, a pond of perhaps ten acres, surrounded by growing rushes and short willow bushes. **1894** C. L. JOHNSTONE *Canada* 47 The frog makes its voice heard in the ponds, or 'sleughs', as they are called out here.

**b.** More generally, an expanse or mass of water. *rare.*

**1915** D. H. LAWRENCE *Rainbow* ix. 227 Tilly, an old woman now, came in saying that the labourers who had been suppering up said the yard and everywhere was just a slew of water. **1941** *Penguin New Writing* II. 20 Great slews of water flushed along the deck.

**2.** *Coal-mining.* (See quot.)

**1883** GRESLEY *Gloss. Coal-m.* 225 *Slew*,..a basin or natural swamp in a coal seam, often running several hundred yards in length.

**slew** (sluː), *sb.*[2] Also slue, slieu. [f. SLEW *v.*]

**1.** The act of turning, or causing to turn, without change of place; a turn, a twist; the position to which a thing has been turned.

*c* **1860** H. STUART *Seaman's Catech.* 49 The man in the crosstrees..keeps the yard on the right slue, that is with the jackstay up. **1879** STEVENSON *Trav. Cevennes* 22 The pack, the basket, and the pilot-coat would take an ugly slew to one side or the other. **1893** ALSTON & WALKER *Seamanship* (ed. 3) 241 The new sail has been swayed up, carefully kept on the right slue.

**2.** = SLEWING *vbl. sb.* 2. Usu. *attrib.*

**1958** J. G. TRUXAL *Control Engineers' Handbk.* III. 6 (*table*) Slew rate. **1981** *Popular Hi-Fi* Mar. 78/2 Measurements of slew rate do appear to be relevant to the performance of an amplifier.

**slew** (sluː), *sb.*[3] *colloq.* (orig. *U.S.*). Also slue. [ad. Ir. *slua(gh)*, crowd, multitude.] A very large number *of*, a great amount *of*. Also in pl.

**1839** D. P. THOMPSON *Green Mountain Boys* II. x. 145 He has cut out a road, and drawn up a whole slew of cannon clean to the top of Mount Defiance. **1858** *Harper's Mag.* May 767/2 By gracious! three thousand dollars is a 'tarnal slue of money. **1897** R. E. ROBINSON *Uncle Lisha's Outing* i. 2 I've seen slews on 'em [*sc.* ducks] on the ma'shes. **1937** *Sun* (Baltimore) 13 Nov. 8/1 This fable furnishes an excuse for a whole slue of low-comedy gags and wheezes. **1958** *Listener* 19 June 1015/2, I got up and checked with another inspector. There seemed to be slews of them lounging around. **1970** *Guardian* 9 Apr. 3/2 The offer has brought in 'piles of letters'... In addition..he has received a 'slew of calls' from other bankers asking about the offer. **1978** J. CARROLL *Mortal Friends* IV. vi. 458 Should I ask a slew of questions just to draw his gaze my way? **1982** *Radio Times* 11-17 Sept. 86/2 Roger Dennhardt had served three years of a 13-year sentence for armed robbery when..he offered to give evidence for the Crown against a slew of former associates.

**slew** (sluː), *sb.*[4] *Basketry.* [Orig. uncertain: perh. a new sense of SLEW *sb.*[2]] A filling made of two or more strands worked together. Hence **slew** *v.*[2]; **'slewing** *vbl. sb.*[1]

**1902** P. N. HASLUCK *Basket Work* 50 Next fill in by working two rods together; this process is known by basket-makers as slewing. *Ibid.* 53 Start slewing with one rod, add another a few stakes farther on. **1907** [see FITCH *sb.*[3]]. **1912** T. OKEY *Art of Basket-Making* vi. 27 The slath being now finished he slews up the bottom to its required size. *Ibid.* vii. 59 Any small modification..may be made, during the slewing up of the bottom. **1953** A. G. KNOCK *Willow Basket-Work* 47 The upsetting, which is begun with tops, consists of four rounds of three-rod waling, and the siding is a three-rod slew. **1960** E. LEGG *Country Baskets* 79 It was made of coarse brown willows in the familiar slew beloved of the worker anxious to turn out as many baskets as he could. **1964** H. HODGES *Artifacts* x. 146 Both slewing and randing require an odd number of stakes.

**slew** (sluː), *v.* Also slue. [Origin unknown; first recorded as a nautical word and with the spelling *slue*, which is still freq. employed.]

**1.** *trans.* To turn (a thing) round upon its own axis, or without shifting it from its place; also loosely, to swing round:

**a.** *Naut.* and *Mil.*

α. **1769** FALCONER *Dict. Marine* (1780), *To Slue*, is to turn any cylindrical or conical piece of timber about it's axis, without removing it. **1841** DANA *Seaman's Manual* 56 Slue the boom with the block up. *c* **1860** H. STUART *Seaman's Catech.* 21 To slue up the other reefs. **1882** NARES *Seamanship* (ed. 6) 183 Slue the mast round.

β. **1859** GRIFFITHS *Artill. Man.* (1862) 110 To slew a gun, or mortar,..is to turn it on its axis without moving it from the spot on which it rests. This is called slewing the trunnions. **1879** *Man. Artill. Exerc.* 451 The trunnions may be slewed, to bring them horizontal or vertical [etc.]. *Ibid.* 452 To slew a Gun end for end.

**b.** In general use.

α. *c* **1825** J. CHOYCE *Log of a Jack Tar* (1891) 79, I'll slue your toplights or you'll not see the road to heaven. **1833** MARRYAT *P. Simple* vi, Now, my lads,..we must slue (the part that breeches cover) more forward. **1884** E. F. KNIGHT *Cruise Falcon* (1887) 23 A roller caught us and slued the boat round.

β. **1849** DE QUINCEY in *Blackw. Mag.* LXVI. 749 He slewed him round on the pivot of his hind legs. **1893** 'Q.' (Quiller Couch) *Delectable Duchy* 120 The old woman.. slewed her head painfully round and stared at him.

**c.** *refl.*

**1834** M. SCOTT *Cruise Midge* xiii, I gradually slewed myself, so as to lie more on my side. **1852** READE *Peg. Woff.* (1853) 212 Mr. Vane..slewed himself round in his chair into a most awkward position. **1872** G. MACDONALD *W. Cumbermede* I. xiii. 219, I..caught hold of one of the small pillars which supported the roof, and slewed myself in.

**d.** *fig.* To beat, to outwit, to trick; also in phr. ***to get slewed***, to lose one's bearings in the bush, to be 'bushed'. *Austral.* and *N.Z.*

**1813** V. PYKE *Wild Will Enderby* (ed. 2) I. xi. 62 The general impression seemed to be that Jack Ketch had been 'slued' (*anglice*, robbed of his dues) by the trio. **1890** 'R. BOLDREWOOD' *Col. Reformer* (1891) 106, I was as right as ninepence, and then to be slewed that way, and all for the want of a strap or two. **1929** K. S. PRICHARD *Coonardoo* xvii. 167 We separated, followin' tracks, and I managed to get slewed. **1944** *Living off Land* iv. 65 Many a bushman has become bushed before now, while even a good bushman may get slewed for a few hours in strange and difficult country.

**e.** To intoxicate (cf. SLEWED *ppl. a.*).

**1888** CHURCHWARD *Blackbirding* 209 An awful chap to drink, but it took a tremendous lot to slue him.

**2.** *intr.* To turn about; to swing *round*. Also with *over*. More recently, of motor vehicles, to skid uncontrollably (*across* a surface); to slide and turn out of the proper course, to 'career'.

α. **1823** W. SCORESBY *Jrnl. Whale Fish.* 301 The floe.. began to 'slue' or revolve. **1840** R. H. DANA *Bef. the Mast* xxv. 83 The martingale had slued away off to leeward. **1883** *Cassell's Fam. Mag.* Dec. 59/2 The two front skates, or runners, are made to slue round at the will of the driver.

β. **1840** R. H. DANA *Bef. Mast* xxv, They slewed round and were hove up. **1863** W. C. BALDWIN *Afr. Hunting* vi. 171 The giraffe..slewed round like a vessel in full sail. **1873** G. C. DAVIES *Mountain & Mere* xvi. 136 He was just within shot when his boat slewed round broadside to the waves. **1914** KIPLING *Diversities of Creatures* (1917) 389 'We overtake on the right as a rule in England.' 'Thanks!' Mr Lingnam slued over. **1943** *Sun* (Baltimore) 8 Sept. 3/2 The ..luxury train..slewed crazily over four tracks when its locomotive boiler blew up. **1965** M. BRADBURY *Stepping Westward* viii. 380 On one sharp bend the car slewed across the road and angled round again just short of the edge of a deep ravine. **1982** B. CHATWIN *On Black Hill* xx. 97 The car slewed off down the yard.

**3.** Of a control mechanism or electronic device: to undergo slewing (SLEWING *vbl. sb.*[2] 2).

**1958** GIBSON & TUTEUR *Control System Components* v. 237 A servo using this circuit tends to have relatively poor synchronizing characteristics when slewing, i.e., when large and rapid changes of the input are made. **1962** L. A. STOCKDALE *Servomechanisms* vii. 112 The slewing time may form part of the servo specification, i.e. the servo to slew through 90° in the minimum time.

**slewce**, obs. form of SLUICE.

**slewed** (slu:d), *ppl. a.* Also *dial.* sluy'd. [f. SLEW *v.*] Intoxicated.

**1801** A. ELLICOTT in C. V. Mathews *Andrew Ellicott* (1908) 201 He was two thirds slewed (as the Rahway people call being in liquor). **1834** M. SCOTT *Cruise Midge* xviii, Poor Hause,..who was by this time pretty well slewed. **1844** DICKENS *Mart. Chuz.* xxviii, He came into our place one night..rather slued, but not much. **1849** G. CUPPLES *Green Hand* i. (1856) 2 We'll all save our grog, and get slewed as soon as may be. **1885** RUNCIMAN *Skippers & Shellbacks* 250 I'll get drunk too or anyway half slewed. **1886** [see BOILED *ppl. a.* c]. **1935** H. H. FINLAYSON *Red Centre* xiii. 129 When questioned closely he admitted rather sheepishly that he was 'sleued'. **1975** D. LODGE *Changing Places* iii. 106, I was somewhat slewed by this time and kept calling him Sparrow.

**slew-eyed**, *a.* [f. SLEW *v.*] Squint-eyed.

**1807–8** W. IRVING *Salmag.* (1811) I. 67 Another Caliban! —Vernon slew-eyed—people of Brunswick, of course, all squint.

**slew-foot.** *U.S. slang.* Also slough-, slue-foot, etc. [f. SLEW *v.*] A person who walks with his feet turned out; a clumsy person. Also *transf.* Hence **slew-foot** *v.*; **slew-footed** *ppl. a.*

**1896** BOGERT & O'BRIEN *Slew Foot Sal* (song) 3 I'll tell you of a lady, her name is Slew Foot Sal,..She's heavy and she weighs five-thirty-three. **1922** F. SCOTT FITZGERALD *Beautiful & Damned* I. iii. 122 A man in a striped blue suit, walking slue-footed in white-spatted feet. **1945** L. SAXON et al. *Gumbo Ya-Ya* xxiii. 496 She is hoping that her galloping, slue-foot, light-brown, lazy husband..will soon find a job. **1950** R. STARNES *Another Mug for Bier* xx. 130 Haggis [*sc.* an Airedale] shrugged and slough-footed away. **1961** J. B. PRIESTLEY *Saturn over Water* iv. 53 Leaving your work to go slewfooting in South America.

†**'slewful**, *a. Obs.* Also 4 sleu-, sleauuol, sleawol. [app. f. SLEU(TH) + -FUL.] Slothful. Hence †**'slewfully** *adv. Obs.*[−1]

**1340** *Ayenb.* 32 Huanne he is sleuuol. *Ibid.*, Huo þet ys sleauuol, ofte uoryet. *Ibid.*, Hit nis no wonder þaȝ he hit do sleuuolliche. **1398** TREVISA *Barth. De P.R.* v. iii. (Tollem. MS.), Bestis þat haue to gret brayne ben ful slewful.

**slewing** *vbl. sb.*[1]: see SLEW *sb.*[4]

**slewing**, *vbl. sb.*[2] [f. SLEW *v.*]

**1.** *gen.* In senses of the verb.

**1875** KNIGHT *Dict. Mech.* 2207 *Slewing*, in serving land artillery, turning the piece on the spot where it stands, equivalent to *training* on shipboard. **1892** *Pall Mall G.* 27 July 5/2 The railway disaster..was brought about by the slewing of the up line.

**2.** *spec.* The response of a control mechanism or electronic device to a sudden large increase in input, esp. one that causes the device to respond at its maximum rate (the ***slewing rate*** or ***speed***). Usu. *attrib.*

**1958** O. J. M. SMITH *Feedback Control Systems* vii. 201 The infrequent large-magnitude changes of the average input to a servo produce slewing of the output at maximum velocity. **1962** R. N. CLARK *Introd. Automatic Control Systems* vii. 270 The large signal (or slewing speed) response characteristics of a system. **1975** G. J. KING *Audio Handbk.* ii. 47 The maximum frequency at which full power can be obtained is a function of the amplifier's slewing rate, which is different from rise time.

**slew-rope.** *Naut.* Also slue-. [f. SLEW *v.*] A rope used in slewing an object.

**1867** SMYTH *Sailor's Word-bk.*, *Slue-Rope*, a rope peculiarly applied for turning a spar or other object in a required direction. **1882** NARES *Seamanship* (ed. 6) 64 Put two slue-ropes round the masts.

**slewth**, var. SLEUTH.

**sley**, var. SLAY *sb.*[1]; obs. f. SLAY *v.*, SLEIGH *sb.*, SLY *a.*

**sleyar**, obs. Sc. var. SLAYER[1].

**sleyh**, obs. f. SLY *a.*

**sleyre**, var. SKLEIR *Obs.*

**sleythe**, obs. f. SLEIGHT *sb.*[1]

**sli**, var. SLIKE *a.* (such), SLY *a.*

†**slibber-sauce.** *Obs.* Also 7 sliber-. [? f. older Flem. *slibber* (Kilian), slime, ooze, = MDu. *slibbe*, Du. *slib*; LG. *slibb(e*: cf. SLIBBERY *a.* The relation to SIBBER-SAUCE and SLABBER-SAUCE is not clear.]

**1.** A compound or concoction of a messy, repulsive, or nauseous character, used esp. for medicinal purposes.

**1527** TINDALE *Parab. Wicked Mammon* Wks. 65/1 His stomacke..longyng after slibbersause and swashe, at which a whole stomacke is readye to cast hys gorge. **1579** LYLY *Euphues* (Arb.) 116, I loath almost to thincke on..all their slibber sawces, whiche bring quesinesse to the stomacke. **1601** HOLLAND *Pliny* I. 423 Oftentimes also they make sliber-sauces of it selfe without any other mixture. *a* **1656** USSHER *Ann.* (1658) 288 [He] was but a weak spirited man, ..by such slibber-sauces, and drugs as Olympias had procured to be given him.

**2.** A preparation of this kind used as a cosmetic.

**1581** G. PETTIE tr. *Guazzo's Civ. Conv.* III. (1586) 137 There are no sortes of ointments and slibber sauces, which they will not proue, to make their haire of the braueest coulour. **1583** STUBBES *Anat. Abus.* 55 To color their faces with such slibbersawces. **1627** HAKEWILL *Apol.* (1630) 413 For the face they used so much slibber-sauce, such dawbing and painting [etc.]. **1633** HART *Diet of Diseased* I. xxii. 98 Our gentlewomen..dirt-dawb their faces with their severall slibber-sauces and paints.

Hence †**slibber-sauced** *a. Obs.*

**1601** BP. W. BARLOW *Defence* 147 Without any slibber-sauced ceremonies.

†**slibber-slabber.** *Obs.* Also 7 -slobber. [Cf. prec. and SLABBER *v.*]

**1.** = SLIBBER-SAUCE 1. Also *attrib.*

**1566** STUDLEY *Medea* 111, The bryde..with slibber slabber sosse of chauntments shalbe tryde. **1591** R. TURNBULL *St. James* 184 We haue no children, and..we seek by some slibber slabber, or other deuice, to obtain them. **1603** FLORIO *Montaigne* (1632) 437 There is no poore Woman so simple..whose slibber-slabbers and drenches we doe not employ.

**2.** = SLIBBER-SAUCE 2.

**1622** MABBE tr. *Aleman's Guzman d'Alf.* I. 12 The vsing of Complexions, and such like slibber-slabbers. **1631** —— *Celestina* VI. 79 Only a little faire Fountaine-water ..(without any other slibber-slabbers). **1668** R. L'ESTRANGE *Visions of Quevedo* 222 To see them..with their Menstruous Slibber slobbers, dawbing one another.

†**'slibbery**, *a. Obs. rare.* Also 3 slibbri. [ad. LG. (also Du. and Flem.) *slibberig.*] Smooth and slippery; lubric.

*c* **1225** *Ancr. R.* 74 þe tunge is sliddri [*v.r.* slibbri], uor heo waded ine wete. **1658** A. FOX *Würtz' Surg.* III. v. 230 There is a moisture in joints, called by Surgeons a Gluten, because it maketh the joints slibberie.

**slicche**, obs. form of SLITCH.

**slice** (slaɪs), *sb.*[1] Forms: α. 4 sclyce, 5 sclice; 4, 7 sclise, 5 sclys(e, 6 *Sc.* sclyise; 5–6 sklyce, sklyse (6 -ss), 5, 7 sklice, 6–7 sklise. β. 5–7 slyce (6 slyese), 6 slise, 5– slice. [ad. OF. *esclice*, *esclisse* (mod.F. *éclisse*) splinter, shiver, small piece (of wood, etc.), vbl. sb. f. *esclicer*: see SLICE *v.*[1]]

**I.** †**1.** A fragment, a shiver, a splinter. *Obs.*

**13..** *K. Alis.* 3833 (Laud MS.), Hij braken speres alto slice [*v.r.* sclyces]. *c* **1425** WYNTOUN *Cron.* VIII. xxxi. 5153 A sklysse of þe schaft, þat brak, In til his hande a wounde can mak. **1577–87** HOLINSHED *Chron.*, *Hist. Scotl.* I. 278/1 This worthie prince James the second was slaine by the slice of a great peece of artillerie, which by ouercharging chanced to breake. **1596** DALRYMPLE tr. *Leslie's Hist. Scot.* II. 102 At last in Paris, standing besyd a singular combatt, [the duke] is slane with a sklyse of a speir.

**2. a.** A relatively thin, flat, broad piece cut from anything. Freq. const. *of* or *from*.

*c* **1420** *Liber Cocorum* (1862) 48 In hom þou cast With sklices of bacon. **15..** *Christ's Kirk* 133 in *Bann. MS.* 286 Fra his thowme thay dang a sklyss. **1613** PURCHAS *Pilgrimage* (1614) 752 If it be a wound hee healeth it after the same manner, applying a round slice of Beauers stones. **1700** DRYDEN *Ovid's Met.*, *Baucis & Phil.* 65 High o'er the hearth a chine of bacon hung; Good old Philemon seiz'd it.., Then cut a slice. **1728** CHAMBERS *Cycl.* s.v. *Veneering*, The Wood intended for Veneering, is first saw'd out into Slices, or Leaves about a Line thick. **1811** KNOX & JEBB *Corr.* II. 42 Having..taken a slice off my right thumb, whilst pruning a rose tree. **1859** W. S. COLEMAN *Woodland, Heaths & H.* (1866) 10 A transverse slice from the trunk of an immense tree. **1888** RUTLEY *Rock-Forming Min.* 37 A parallel-faced slice of a uniaxial crystal is cut.

*ellipt.* *a* **1764** LLOYD *Dial. betw. Author & Friend* Wks. (1810) 109/1 Whether the Grecians took a slice Four times a-day, or only twice. ? **1780** COWPER *Love World reproved* 36 Each thinks his neighbour makes too free, Yet likes a slice as well as he.

*fig.* **1796** *Grose's Dict. Vulgar T.* (ed. 3), *To take a slice*, to intrigue, particularly with a married woman. **1818** SCOTT *Rob Roy* vi, We hae nae slices o' the spare rib here..except auld Martha.

**b.** *Geol.* A relatively thin, broad mass of rock situated between two approximately parallel thrust faults, esp. when these make a small angle with the horizontal. Also ***thrust slice***.

**1914** PEACH & HORNE *Guide Geol. Model Assynt Mts.* 18 The slices of strata thus repeated have been driven westwards by major thrusts along planes which truncate the overlying reversed faults. **1942** M. P. BILLINGS *Structural Geol.* xvii. 327 Surrounding the basin is a zone..of outwardly-driven thrust slices. In still another zone.. rootless slices and isolated blocks of various slices are common. **1957** *Q. Jrnl. Geol. Soc.* CXIII. 59 They occur.. as infolds, and slices brought up along the Strathconon tear-fault. **1969** BENNISON & WRIGHT *Geol. Hist. Brit. Isles* iii. 46 In it [*sc.* the Laxfordian orogeny] are found fragments of earlier orogenic belts brought up as thrust slices.

**c.** *Electronics.* A small, thin slab of semiconducting material on which circuit elements have been formed.

**1964** *Proc. IEEE* LII. 1713 (*heading*) Evolution of the concept of a computer on a slice. **1975** *Sci. Amer.* May 36/2 National Semiconductor..introduced a four-bit PMOS slice that could be used as a modular unit in the design of machines ranging from four to 32 bits.

**3.** *transf.* **a.** A portion, share, piece, part, etc.

**1550** CROWLEY *Information & Petit.* Wks. 171 None can be buried but they wyl haue a slyese. **1622** FLETCHER *Span. Cur.* III. ii, A short slice of a Reading serves us, Sir. **1689** BURNET *Trav.* II. (1730) 89 A Slice of the Alps came down upon it, and buried it quite. **1743** WALPOLE *Corr.* (1820) I. lxxx. 284 Your brother slipped a slice of paper into a letter which he sent me. **1857** HUGHES *Tom Brown* I. i, A fellow.. who has spent a good slice of his life here. **1876** HOLLAND *Seven Oaks* xxiv. 332 A heavy slice of his ready money had been practically swept out of existence. **1893** PEEL *Spen Valley* 55 A considerable slice of that side of the township.

**b.** ***slice of life*** [tr. F. *tranche de la vie*, a term orig. applied to French Naturalist literature: see quot. 1890], a realistic and detailed portrayal in drama, narrative, painting, etc., of incidents typical of everyday life. Freq. (usu. with hyphens) *attrib.*

[**1890** J. JULLIEN in *Art et Critique* 9 Aug. 500/2 Ce n'est donc qu'une tranche de la vie que nous pouvons mettre à la scène.] **1895** G. B. SHAW in *Sat. Rev.* 19 Oct. 503/1 The substitution of a homogeneous slice of life for the old theatrical sandwich of sentiment and comic relief. **1914** H. JAMES in *Times Lit. Suppl.* 19 Mar. 134/4 The Orgreaves.. come..as near squaring aesthetically with the famous formula of the 'slice of life' as any example that could be adduced. **1938** R. G. COLLINGWOOD *Princ. Art* p. v, We have..a new drama, taking the place of the old 'slice of life' entertainment, in which the author's chief business was to represent everyday doings of ordinary people as the audience believed them to behave. **1954** M. EWER *Heart Untouched* ix. 154 This is a costume picture, not a slice-of-life drama. **1962** *Listener* 14 June 1028/2 The pure landscape, the still life, the 'slice of life', the painting for painting's sake, is a late development. **1976** *National Observer* (U.S.) 4 Dec. 20/3 Mrs McFarland is one of the just-folks who appeared in one of those slice-of-life commercials. **1981** *Daily Tel.* 19 Feb. 13/1 Yet another indigestible slice of life about 'a warm, winning, and wise and wonderful Jewish family'.

**II.** †**4. a.** A spatula used for stirring and mixing compounds. *Obs.*

*c* **1400** *Lanfranc's Cirurg.* 347 Meue hem wiþ a sclise longe, for þe more þat þei ben stirid togidere þe bettir it wole be. *a* **1425** tr. *Arderne's Treat. Fistula*, etc. 31 Moue þam all wayse wiþ a sklyse þat þai cleue not to þe panne. **1558** WARDE tr. *Alexis' Secr.* (1568) 62 b, Sturrynge them with a broade skylse of woode. 1580 BLUNDEVIL *Horsemanship* IV. xxxiv. 16 b, Stirre them continuallie with a flat sticke, or slice, vntill they be throughlie mingled..together. 1601 HOLLAND *Pliny* II. 520 Calcin it ouer the fire in a pan, stirring and mixing it together with little slices or pot-stickes. 1686 W. HARRIS tr. *Lemery's Course Chem.* (ed. 3) 220 Dry it by a small fire of Sand, stirring it with an Ivory or Wooden slice.

†b. (See quots.) *Obs.*

1611 COTGR., *Espatule*, a (Chirurgions, or Apothecaries) little slice. 1627 HAKEWILL *Apol.* I. i. §5 The Pellican hath a beake broade and flat, much like the slice of Apothecaries and Surgions, with which they spread their plaisters.

5. One or other of several flattish utensils (sometimes perforated) used for various purposes in cookery, etc. (see quots., and cf. *egg-*, *fish-slice*).

α. 1459 *Paston Lett.* I. 490 Item, j. fryeyng panne, j. sclyse. 1548 ELYOT, *Spatha*,..also an instrument of the kytchen to turne meate that is fried, a sklise. 1611 COTGR., *Friquette*, a lingell, smalle sklice, little scummer.

β. *a* 1529 SKELTON *E. Rumming* 409 A fryinge pan, and a slyce. 1605 PLAT *Delightes for Ladies* liv, You must also haue a brasen slice to scrape away the sugar from the hanging bason. 1688 HOLME *Armoury* III. 317/1 A Slice..to cut Dough into pieces, called a Beater, a Break. *Ibid.* 396/1 A long piece of Wood cut after the manner of a Slice which Deary-women use about their Butter. 1814 tr. *Klaproth's Trav. Cauc.* 131 An iron pot.., together with a large perforated iron slice. 1858 SIMMONDS *Dict. Trade, Slice*,..a spatula for serving cooked fish. *a* 1887 *Cassell's Dict. Cookery* 201 Take the eggs out carefully with a small slice.

6. A form of fire-shovel; also, an instrument for clearing the bars of a furnace when choked with clinkers.

α. 1465 *Priory of Finchale* (Surtees) 299, j quarell mell, j bochyng axs, j sclys. 1555 *Ludlow Churchw. Acc.* (Camden) 60 Paid for a sklyce to cary fyer to the churche. 1601 HOLLAND *Pliny* XXXIII. viii, Lay a peece of silver ore upon a sclise, plate, or firepan of yron red hot.

β. 1612 in *Antiquary* Jan. (1906) 28 In the Kytchin..a fire slyce, two fire shovells [etc.]. 1677 MOXON *Mech. Exerc.* i. 8 You must with the Slice clap the Coals upon the outside close together. 1750 BLANCKLEY *Naval Expos.* 153 Slices are used by the Smiths to clear and keep their Fire together. 1835 HAWTHORNE *Tales & Sk., Old Wom. T.* (1879) 178 It was a sort of iron shovel (by housewifes termed a 'slice'), such as is used in clearing the oven. 1879 *Spons' Encycl. Manuf.* I. 291 The workman with his 'slice' then spreads the charge over the bed, so as to thoroughly expose every portion to the action of the flames.

7. A flattish instrument, implement, etc., of various kinds (see quots.).

1483 *Cath. Angl.* 322/2 A Sclice, *vertinella, est forceps medici, spatula.* 1541 *Extr. Aberdeen Reg.* (1844) I. 176 Ane stuffin sclyise, with ane yeirning sclyise. 1580 BLUNDEVIL *Horsemanship* IV. cx. 51 Then with a flat slice of iron, loosen the skin within from the flesh. 1611 BIBLE *Lev.* ii. 5 A meate offering baken in a panne [*marg.* on a flat plate *or* slice]. 1665 PEPYS *Diary* 16 Mar., Two large silver candlesticks and snuffers, with a slice to keep them upon. 1707 MORTIMER *Husb.* (1721) II. 126 Then with a slice, without digging, you may force off all the under Slips. 1712 *Lond. Gaz.* No. 4960/3 A sliver Slice to fold Paper. 1875 KNIGHT *Dict. Mech.* 2207/2 *Slice*..2. (*Nautical.*) *a.* A bar with a chisel or spear-shaped end, used for stripping off sheathing or planking. *b.* A spade-shaped tool used in flensing whales. 1879 *Cassell's Techn. Educ.* IV. 112/1 One of the workmen detaches the adhering crystals [of lead] by means of a long iron bar shaped at the end like a chisel, called a slice.

8. *Printing.* a. An ink-knife (cf. *ink-slice*).

1683 MOXON *Mech. Exerc., Printing* x. ¶11 The Slice is a little thin Iron Shovel about three or four Inches broad, and five Inches long; it hath a Handle to it. 1688 HOLME *Armoury* III. xxi. (Roxb.) 257/2 He beareth Argent, a Printers Slice, Sable. 1808 STOWER *Printer's Gramm.* 336 The Brayer and Slice. 1888 JACOBI *Printers' Vocab.* 126 *Slice*, a flat wide iron knife used for lifting ink out of the can.

b. The sliding bottom of a slice-galley.

1683 MOXON *Mech. Exerc., Printing* v, The three Sides of the Frame..stand about three fifth parts of the height of the Letter above the superficies of the Slice. *Ibid.* xxii. ¶6 He..draws the Slice with the Page upon it, out of the Galley. 1875 KNIGHT *Dict. Mech.* 936/1 The galley sometimes has a groove to admit a false bottom, called a *galley-slice*.

9. *Ship-building.* (See quot. 1846.)

1791 *1st Rep. Comm. Woods & Forests* (1792) App. XXIX. 143 The old Method..of launching Ships on a Curve Line, with short Bulgeways, and Slices under each end of them. 1846 A. YOUNG *Naut. Dict.* 285 *Slices*, in shipbuilding, tapered pieces of wood driven between the bilgeways, etc., preparatory to launching a vessel. 1884 *J. Peake's Naval Archit.* (ed. 5) 233 Large wedges called slices..are placed inside and outside of the bilgeways.

10. *attrib.*, as slice-bar, -galley (see quots.).

1846 A. YOUNG *Naut. Dict.* 285 A slice or *slice bar also means a bar of iron with a sharp end, used to strip off sheathing, ceiling, etc. 1874 RAYMOND *Statist. Mines & Mining* 40 The straight grate-bars also clog with this coal, and the fireman has to use his slice bar liberally. 1875 KNIGHT *Dict. Mech., Slice-bar*, a hooked poker for removing slag and cinders from grate-bars of furnaces. *Ibid.*, **Slice-galley*, a galley having a movable false bottom or slice. 1896 DE VINNE *Moxon's Mech. Exerc., Printing* 407 Each compositor to make up his matter on a slice-galley.

**slice** (slaɪs), *sb.*[2] [f. SLICE *v.*[1]]

1. A sharp cut, a slash. *rare.*

1611 COTGR., *Taillure*,..a slice, cut, slit, slash, &c.

2. *Golf* and *Tennis.* A slicing stroke. Cf. SLICE *v.*[1] 5.

1886 HUTCHINSON *Hints Golf* 27 The cut, or slice, is put on the ball by stretching the arms to their full length..as the club is raised [etc.]. 1890 —— *Golf* (Badm.) 204 It is not this slice, but the slice from above downwards, which causes both the high loft and the back spin with its dead fall. 1969 *New Yorker* 14 June 47/3 He hits a slice so hard and with such sharp placement, close to the sideline, that the ball jumps cleanly past Graebner's racquet for a service ace. 1971 LAVER & COLLINS *Educ. Tennis Player* xi. 144 My slice (a left-hander's) will move to a right-hander's backhand, and that's convenient.

**slice** (slaɪs), *v.*[1] Forms: α. 5 sklyce, 5, *Sc.* 9 sklice, 6 sclyce, 7 sklise. β. 6 slyse, slies-, 6–7 slyce, slise, 6– slice. [ad. OF. *esclicer, esclisser*, etc. (mod.F. *éclisser*), to reduce to splinters or pieces, ad. OHG. *slîzan*: see SLITE *v.* In later use perh. partly from SLICE *sb.*[1]]

1. a. *trans.* To cut into slices; to cut into or through with a sharp instrument.

*c* 1420 *Liber Cocorum* (1862) 43 Take befe and sklice hit fayre and thynne. *Ibid.*, þenne take þy rost, and sklyce hit clene. 1551 TURNER *Herbal* I. (1568) 150 The roote is sliced and layd up as Scilla is. 1593 NASHE *Christ's T.* Wks. (Grosart) IV. 112 Loe there goes the woman shall they say, that hath slyced & eaten her owne sonne. 1634 SIR T. HERBERT *Trav.* 124 He would haue sliced his body into as many parts as there be dayes in a yeare. 1648 WINYARD *Midsummer-Moon* 1 Dido, with his hide, might have had ground enough for her Carthage without slicing it into leashes. 1747–96 MRS. GLASSE *Cookery* v. 76 Slice a French roll thin, peel and slice a very large onion, pare and slice three or four turnips. 1769 MRS. RAFFALD *Eng. Housekpr.* (1778) 259 Slice a penny loaf as thin as possible. 1836–9 *Todd's Cycl. Anat.* II. 503/1 The coagulum is first to be sliced in thin pieces with a sharp knife. 1867 J. HOGG *Microsc.* I. iii. 213 Cells..may be made of vulcanite by slicing tubing made of this material. 1897 G. ALLEN *Typewriter Girl* xix. 205 Shops where red water-melons, sliced open,..adorn the slabs.

b. *transf.* and *fig.*

*c* 1500 *Little Gest of Robin Hood* ccxcii, Thryes Robyn shot about, And alway slist the wand. 1594 NASHE *Dido* 1181 Abourd, abourd,..And slice the Sea with sable coloured ships. 1601 WEEVER *Mirr. Mart.* E iij, Ship slice the sea. 1605 SYLVESTER *Du Bartas* II. iii. III. *Law* 343 Through their skin With scourges slyc't, must their bare bones be seen. 1690 T. BURNET *Theory Earth* IV. v. 162 Ambitious Princes and Tyrants, that slice the Earth amongst them. 1860 W. H. RUSSELL *Diary India* I. 55 Our sharp bow sliced the blue depths.

*Comb.* 1591 SYLVESTER *Du Bartas* I. iii. 564 The winding Rivers bordered all their banks With slice-Sea [= sea-slicing] Aldars.

c. In colloq. phr. ***no matter how*** (or ***whichever way***, etc.) ***you slice it***: however you look at it. orig. and chiefly *U.S.*

1936 C. SANDBURG *People, Yes* 160 No matter how thick or how thin you slice it it's still baloney. 1941 WODEHOUSE *Berlin Broadcasts* in *Performing Flea* (1961) I. 261 Slice it where you like, it is still a German prison camp. 1968 J. SANGSTER *Touchfeather* xvii. 198 Whichever way you sliced it, I had absolutely nothing on Roger Gerastan except what I had guessed. 1979 'A. HAILEY' *Overload* III. xii. 257 Whichever way you slice it,..Cameron Clarke has done our cause a lot of harm.

2. a. To cut *out* or *off* in the form of a slice or slices; to remove with a clean cut.

*c* 1550 H. RHODES *Bk. Nurture* in *Babees Bk.* 76 Of bread, slyce out fayre morsels to put into your pottage. 1582 STANYHURST *Æneis* I. (Arb.) 24 Soom doe slise owt collops on spits yeet quirilye trembling. 1607 HEYWOOD *Wom. Killed w. Kindn.* (1617) H ij, Heere's a knife, To saue mine honor, shal slice out my life. *c* 1645 HOWELL *Lett.* I. I. xix, They then slic'd off his Ears. 1755 SMOLLETT *Quix.* I. IV. iii. (1803) II. 39 That ferocious adversary of yours, whose proud head I hope to slice off. 1860 TYNDALL *Glac.* I. xvi. 111 One side of the pyramid had been sliced off. 1885 *Manch. Weekly Times* Suppl. 20 June 4/3 To lay the leather face downward..and slice away the back of it with a sharp ..knife. 1892 ZANGWILL *Bow Myst.* 44 A door panel sliced out and replaced was also put forward.

*fig.* 1608 ARMIN *Nest Ninn.* (1880) 51 Not sparing any price to please appetite, though the edge of it slice from the bosome of good old Abraham, very heauen it selfe. 1629 Z. BOYD *Last Battell* 1016 By years, dayes, and houres, our life is Continuallie cut and sklised away. 1874 SAYCE *Compar. Philol.* ii. 76 One would slice off a letter at the end of a word.

b. To remove by means of a slice.

1683 MOXON *Mech. Exerc. Printing* xxiv. ¶11 He Slices the whole mass of Inck into the farthermost corner of the Inck-block. 1884 C. G. W. LOCK *Workshop Rec.* Ser. III. 354/2 A workman keeps stirring the lead, and 'slicing', or freeing from the sides, the portions setting on them.

3. a. *intr.* To cut cleanly or easily. Also *transf.*

1605 SYLVESTER *Du Bartas* II. iii. III. *Law* 537 Boats do slide, where Ploughs did slice of late. 1634 SIR T. HERBERT *Trav.* (1638) 334 A Cuttan; an Indian sword which slices easily. 1853 DICKENS *Bleak Ho.* x, He stands..snipping and slicing at sheepskin. 1910 *Blackw. Mag.* Apr. 540/1 He watched the saw slice to the heart of a mighty spruce.

b. To use a slice or fire-shovel.

1893 *Westm. Gaz.* 22 Feb. 8/2 They throw coal on and slice and rake until the ship shakes beneath them.

4. *trans.* To make (a way) by slicing.

1872 TENNYSON *Gareth & Lynette* 499 Knights, who sliced a red life-bubbling way Thro' twenty folds of twisted dragon.

5. *Golf.* To hit (the ball) in such a manner that it flies or curves off to the right. Also *absol.* Also in other sports, to make a sharp stroke across a ball rather than straight on it, causing it to be propelled forward at an angle (on purpose or unintentionally); in *Lawn Tennis*, etc., to impart spin or swing in this manner. Cf. CHOP *v.*[1] 7 d, e.

1890 HUTCHINSON *Golf* (Badm.) 104 It is..advisable in such circumstances..to play to slice the ball. *Ibid.* 178 We slice when instead of sweeping along the line of fire, we draw the club towards ourselves across it. 1894 *Times* 28 Apr. 13/3 Approaching the fifth Mr. Laidlay sliced his drive. 1905 H. A. VACHELL *Hill* xii. 255 Scaife has been transformed into a tremendous human machine, inexorably cutting and slicing, pulling and drawing. 1954 J. B. G. THOMAS *On Tour* 68 Birt, normally the safest of place kickers, made his mark, only for the ball to be sliced towards the corner flag. 1969 *New Yorker* 14 June 61/2 He'll slice. He'll lob. 1976 J. SNOW *Cricket Rebel* 63 Alan Smith.. started to hit out boldly, slicing the ball repeatedly over and through the covers.

†**slice**, *v.*[2] *Hawking. Obs.* Also 5 sclise, sklyse, 6 slyse. [ad. OF. *esclicier, esclisser*, etc. (mod.F. *éclisser*), to squirt, splash.]

1. *intr.* Of birds: To mute, so that the fæces are ejected to some distance. Also *transf.*

*c* 1450 *Bk. Hawking* in *Reliq. Antiq.* I. 296 Ye schull say that your hawke mutith and not sclisith. 1486 *Bk. St. Albans, Hawking* a vj b, Ye shall say yowre hawke mutessith or mutith and not sklysith. 1575 [see MUTE *v.*[1]]. 1600 SURFLET *Countrie Farme* VII. xliii. 706 Porkes flesh giuen them warme with a little Aloes, maketh the bird loose and to slice out readily. 1651 FULLER *Abel Rediv., Cranmer* 226 As the Herneshaw when unable by maine strength to grapple with the Hawke, doth Slice upon her. 1710 *Acc. Last Distemper Tom Whigg* I. 5 The Criminal had sliced immoderately on the Sign of the Old Bishop's Head in Lambeth.

2. *trans.* To eject in muting.

1628 WITHER *Brit. Rememb.* 3 Our Herneshawes, slicing backward filth on those, Whose worths they dare not openly oppose.

**sliceable** (ˈslaɪsəb(ə)l), *a.* [f. SLICE *v.*[1] + -ABLE.] That can be sliced or divided.

1976 *Evening Post* (Nottingham) 16 Dec. 11/2 Other useful buys here for Christmas catering are..1 litre packs Walls sliceable vanilla ice cream. 1978 *Aslib Proc.* XXX. 33 On-line data bases..are tools which are infinitely sliceable into subsets.

**sliced** (slaɪst), *ppl. a.* [f. SLICE *v.*[1]]

1. a. Cut into slices; cut cleanly.

1589 in Hall *Eliz. Age* (1886) 218/1 For slist bief, vj *d.* 1591 MARKHAM *Sir R. Grinuile* cxxxiii, Streaming diuine blood from his sliced side. 1599 B. JONSON *Cynthia's Rev.* III. i, A dish of slic'd caviare, or so. 1675 HAN. WOOLLEY *Gentlew. Comp.* 137 Sliced Dates and good big pieces of Marrow..with sliced Lemon. 1771 SMOLLETT *Humph. Cl.* I. 29 May, Devouring sliced beef. 1806 *Culina* 71 Put the meat into an earthen pot with plenty of sliced turnips. 1842 J. AITON *Domest. Econ.* (1857) 111 Add half a pound of sliced soap. 1883 H. DRUMMOND *Nat. Law in Spir. W.* (1884) 372 The sliced specimen of some..stone.

*fig.* 1642 MILTON *Apol. Smect.* Wks. 1851 III. 313 The schisme of a slic't prayer.

b. Of food: sold already cut into slices, esp. ***sliced bread***. Also in colloq. phr. ***the best*** (or ***greatest***, etc.) ***thing since sliced bread***: an expression of enthusiastic appreciation, esp. of a new invention or discovery.

1958 J. MORTIMER *What shall we tell Caroline?* ii. 109 The trouble with living here, the butter gets as hard as the rock of Gibraltar. It blasts great holes in your sliced bread. 1963 L. DEIGHTON *Horse under Water* xxxi. 124 They prodded.. their product... Sliced, sterilized and Cellophane-wrapped; a loaf. 1969 R. JAFFE *Fame Game* (1970) v. 106 You're the greatest thing since sliced bread. 1970 *Guardian* 28 Feb. 10/1 The biggest thing since sliced bread is now in the shops. It is called part-baked bread. 1972 WODEHOUSE *Pearls, Girls, & Monty Bodkin* xii. 183 Bodkin regards you as the best thing that's happened since sliced bread. 1973 J. THOMSON *Death Cap* ii. 34 Mrs King asked me to..buy half a pound of sliced ham and I cut the sandwiches. 1976 *National Observer* (U.S.) 21 Aug. 6/3 They're the best thing since sliced bread and they're selling like wildfire here,' says Dan Wagner, proprietor of the Georgetown Cycle Shop. 1981 *Austral. Forest Industries Jrnl.* Suppl. (Plywood & Veneer) Oct. 35 (*heading*) Sheathing—the greatest thing since sliced bread!

2. Having a slice cut or taken off.

1874 HEATH *Croquet Player* 25 Cylindrical Heads... Sliced Mallets. *Ibid.*, The majority of good players play with sliced mallets.

3. *Golf* and *Tennis.* (See SLICE *v.*[1] 5.)

1890 HUTCHINSON *Golf* (Badm.) 104 All sliced balls start away high. 1901 *Scotsman* 9 Sept. 4/7 In bents off a sliced drive, Herd again dropped two holes behind. 1971 LAVER & COLLINS *Educ. Tennis Player* xi. 144 Most of the time I used a sliced serve, and that seems to be the common delivery.

**slicer** (ˈslaɪsə(r)). Also 6 sclycer. [f. SLICE *v.*[1]]

1. An implement or instrument specially adapted or used for slicing.

Also in combs., as *bread-*, *turnip-*, *vegetable-slicer*.

1530 PALSGR. 267/2 Sclycer, *tournoyre.* 1575 TURBERV. *Falconrie* 299 Take up the hawe handsomely and cut it with a little slicer. 1850 HOLTZAPFFEL *Turning* III. 1098 Slitting Mill or the Slicer, is a very thin sheet-iron disk, the edge of which is charged with diamond powder. 1875 KNIGHT *Dict. Mech.* 2208/1 The slicer is firmly clamped, like a circular saw, between two flanges on its spindle. 1891 T. HARDY *Tess* xlvi. (1900) 114/2 They were at some distance from the man who turned the slicer. 1907 *Yesterday's Shopping* (1969) 215/2 The Sterling Slicer. Slices any kind of vegetable or fruit evenly. 1956 F. S. ATKINSON in D. L. Linton *Sheffield* xiv. 269 Intensive efforts are being made to replace the hand-loading of coal on to conveyors by mechanical power-loaders and, in seams over 3 ft. 3 in. considerable success is being achieved with Meco Moore Loaders..and Huwood Slicers. 1971 [see PLOUGH, PLOW *sb.*[1] 5 i].

2. One who slices.

1598 FLORIO, *Tagliuzzatore*, a slicer, a cutter. 1709 *Tatler* No. 71 ¶8 When a Witling stands at a Coffee-house Door, and sneers at those who pass by,..he is no longer Surnamed a Slicer, but a Man of Fire is the Word. 1778 *Ann. Reg., Projects* 124/2 This man, who is called the slicer,..pricks it with the slicing knife. 1864 SALA in *Daily Telegr.* 16 July, Young ladies..employed in the bureau as press feeders, stampers, slicers, trimmers. 1881 *Academy* 8 Jan. 30 A grand Zoologist and not a mere hardener and slicer of microscopic stuff.

‖**slich** (small ore): see SLICK *sb.*[2]

**slicht**, Sc. form of SLEIGHT *sb.*[1], SLIGHT *a.*

**slicing** (ˈslaɪsɪŋ), *vbl. sb.*[1] [f. SLICE *v.*[1]] The action of the verb in various senses.

**1580** HOLLYBAND *Tres. Fr. Tong, Decoupure*, a cutting, or slycing. **1611** COTGR., *Hachement*, a hacking, shredding, slicing. **1763** MILLS *Pract. Husb.* IV. 214 Grafting in the Rind, or Shoulder-grafting, likewise called slicing and packing. **1848** THACKERAY *Van. Fair* iv, Amelia went away, perhaps to superintend the slicing of the pine-apple. **1899** *Westm. Gaz.* 22 Dec. 2/1, I am convinced that this habit of following after is responsible for much of the slicing and pulling [in golf].

*attrib.* **1778** [see SLICER 2]. **1820** SCORESBY *Acc. Arc. Regions* II. 175 A man..sliced it..and then pushed it into an adjoining receptacle, called a 'slicing cooler'. **1833** *Wauldby Farm Rep.* 102 in *Husb.* III. (L.U.K.), A roller with slicing-knives attached to it. **1844** H. STEPHENS *Bk. Farm* II. 78 The slicing-wheel..is a disc of cast-iron. **1875** KNIGHT *Dict. Mech.* 2208/1 Slicing-machine. (Pottery.)

†ˈ**slicing**, *vbl. sb.*[2] *Obs.* [f. SLICE *v.*[2]] Muting.

**1596** HARINGTON *Metam. Ajax* 31 Doe not you sometime ..talke both of putting a heron to the mount, and then of his slicing?

**slicing** (ˈslaɪsɪŋ), *ppl. a.* [f. SLICE *v.*[1]] Cutting easily or cleanly.

**1578** H. WOTTON *Courtly Controv.* 10 What Slicing blade doth cut my gale. **1590** MARLOWE *1st Pt. Tamburl.* v. ii, There sits imperious Death, Keeping his circuit by the slicing edge. **1634** SIR T. HERBERT *Trav.* (1638) 190 Three Coosel-bashes..with their slicing Semiters whipt off their heads. **1641** BAKER *Chron., Edw. VI* (1643) 72 The rest were ..well furnished with..slicing swords broad and thin. **1896** CROCKETT *Grey Man* v. 35 A fragment of a leather rein..cut across with a clean, slicing cut.

Hence ˈ**slicingly** *adv. rare.*

**1598** FLORIO, *Sminutamente*, mincingly, slicingly.

**slick** (slɪk), *sb.*[1] [f. SLICK *a.* or *v.*]

**1.** †**a.** A cosmetic, an unguent. *Obs.*

**1626** tr. *Boccalini's New-found Politick* 233 My face..is done ouer with Ladies licks, slicks, and other painting stuffe of the Levant.

**b.** *Carpentry.* (See quot.)

**1875** KNIGHT *Dict. Mech.* 2208 *Slick*, a wide-bitted chisel, used by framers in paring the sides of mortises and tenons.

**c.** An implement used for slicking; a slicker.

**1883** *Archæol. Cant.* XV. 103, I have..discovered..some elegant slicks or scrapers of peculiar form. *Ibid.*, When trimmed on one side only, such a flake [of flint] was used as a scraper or slick.

†**2.** *Card-playing.* (See quot. 1674.) *Obs.*

**1674** COTTON *Compl. Gamester* (1680) 94 The Slick is when before-hand the Gamester takes a Pack of Cards, and with a slick-stone smooths all the Putt-Cards. **1711** PUCKLE *The Club* (1817) 23 The bent, the slick, the breef, the spur.

**3. a.** orig. *U.S.* A smooth place or streak on the surface of water, usually caused by the presence of some oily or greasy substance. (Cf. SLEEK *sb.*[3]) *spec.* A floating mass of oil. Also *transf.*

**1849** D. WEBSTER *Priv. Corr.* II. 333 You have seen on the surface of the sea, those smooth places, which fishermen and sailors call 'slicks'. **1857** THOREAU *Maine W.* (1894) 228, I emptied the melted pork..into the lake, making what sailors call a 'slick'. **1888** GOODE *Amer. Fishes* 210 They..leave in their track similar 'slicks' of oil and blood. [**1889**, etc: see *oil slick* s.v. OIL *sb.*[1] 6 e.] **1938** *Daily Progress* (Charlottesville, Va.) 30 July 1/8 The slick..caused by oil from the 'Hawaii Clipper'. **1950** *Jrnl. Marine Res.* IX. 69 Artificial slicks form in harbor waters contaminated with refuse and oil. **1973** *Daily Tel.* (Colour Suppl.) 9 Mar. 12/2 You can see the mouse-run quite clearly because of the slick of oil which all rodents leave behind on walls and floors if they regularly move along a particular route. **1982** H. INNES *Black Tide* II. i. 28 The slick now stretched in a great smooth, brown, greasy layer right across the bay.

**b.** *Mining.* (See quot.)

**1883** GRESLEY *Gloss. Coal-m.* 225 *Slicks*, smooth partings or mere planes of division in strata.

**c.** A place on the hair or fur of an animal which has been made sleek by licking or the like.

**1891** in *Cent. Dict.*

**4.** A dash or stroke.

**1881** E. COXON *Basil Plant* II. 226 'Isn't it wonderful?' said one, 'painted with just two slicks of the brush'.

**5.** *U.S.* A wild, unbranded horse, cow, or other range animal; a maverick.

**1890** *Stock Grower & Farmer* 12 July 6/3 Seven of them were branded, the remainder were 'slicks', or horses which had run wild from birth. **1934** in J. A. & A. Lomax *Amer. Ballads* xvi. 411 No maverick or slick will be tallied In that great book of life in His home. **1965** G. SHEPHERD *West of Yesterday* xiv. 127 By picking up slicks or unbranded cattle on the way—gathered a nice little herd.

**6.** *U.S.* An expensive or 'glossy' magazine (opp. *pulp magazine* s.v. PULP *sb.* 5 c).

**1934** *Writer* Mar. 73/2 Perhaps he [*sc.* the author] gets an offer for two hundred dollars from one of the 'slicks'. **1952** S. KAUFFMANN *Philanderer* (1953) iv. 65 We're going to change one of our present magazines—from a confession to a woman's slick. **1958** *Manch. Guardian* 26 Sept. 4/3 Jack Finney's stories, which have been popular in the better American slicks, point the trend all the more for not all being science fiction. **1977** *Transatlantic Rev.* LX. 57 One will keep on about 'the slicks' he wants to write for.

**7. a.** A smooth tyre used on various kinds of racing vehicle.

**1959** *Wall St. Jrnl.* (Eastern ed.) 11 Aug. 1/4 Both Goodyear Tire & Rubber Co. and General Tire & Rubber Co. have jumped into the business..developing and building 'slicks'—smooth racing tires—for the little vehicles. **1965** *Daily Mail* 2 Oct. 5/7 The slicks (smooth, £20-a-piece racing tyres) burst into smoke and then into flame. **1978** 'D. RUTHERFORD' *Collision Course* 56 Everybody had fitted 'slicks', the smooth treadless tyres used on dry roads.

**b.** (See quots.)

**1969** I. KEMP *Brit. G.I. in Vietnam* iii. 45 The 'slicks'—small Huey helicopters—would fly the troops to the battle zone, while the larger Chinooks brought in their heavy equipment. **1974** N. MEYER *Target Practice* (1975) v. 61 We were lifted by choppers called 'Hueys' (or 'slicks', because they land on runners instead of wheels).

**8.** *U.S. slang.* A clever or smart person; a cheat or swindler. Cf. SLICKER 3; SLICKSTER.

**1959** N. MAILER *Advts. for Myself* (1961) I. 28 To try a major novel about the last war in Europe without a sense of the past is to fail in the worst way—as an over-ambitious and opportunistic slick. **1970** R. D. ABRAHAMS *Positively Black* iv. 88 These stories commonly turn on some way in which the 'slick' manages to trick the white storekeeper 'Mr. Charlie' into giving him respect and service. **1971** E. BULLINS in W. King *Black Short Story Anthol.* (1972) 76 Dandy's mother had a civil-service job in the city, and the city slick Dandy was from Philly. **1973** [see RUN *v.* 52 h].

**9.** Special Comb.: **slick-licker** *Canad. colloq.*, an apparatus for removing oil floating as a slick.

**1970** *Globe & Mail* (Toronto) 7 May 4 (*caption*) Slick-lickers—barges in Nova Scotia's Chedabucto Bay designed to suck in oil off the water's surface from the wrecked tanker Arrow and transfer it to 45-gallon drums. **1972** *Daily Colonist* (Victoria, B.C.) 12 Feb. 9/5 The federal transport department has placed a $150,000 order for 22 slicklicker machines... The machine..picks up oil from water surfaces by using an endless belt that has been treated chemically. **1975** *Lamp* (Exxon Corporation) Winter 24/1 Imperial Oil Limited, Exxon Corporation's Canadian affiliate, is employing a 'slicklicker' to counter the menace of oil spills on water.

**slick**, *sb.*[2] *rare.* [ad. G. *schlich*, related to *schleich* SLIKE *sb.*] Finely pounded ore. Also *attrib.*

The form *slich* occurs in E. Browne *Trav. Germ.* etc. (1677) 135, and hence appears in *Chambers's Cycl.* Suppl. (1753) and some later works of reference.

**1683** PETTUS *Fleta Min.* II. iii. 113 Of Gold Slicks. Further, know also that when the Gold Oars and Gold Slicks are cleansed for to quicken [etc.]. **1892** *Pall Mall G.* 8 Aug. 7/2 There were produced in Russia..in 1881, 2,382 poods (of 36 lb.) of slick-gold.

**slick** (slɪk), *a.* Now chiefly *dial.* and *U.S.* Forms: α. 4–6 **slyke** (5 **slyk**), **slike.** β. 6 **slycke**, 6–7 **slicke**, 6– **slick.** [ME. *slīke* (developing into *slick* and SLEEK *a.*), prob. representing an OE. **slice*, related to the vb. *slician* (see SLICK *v.*) and perhaps cognate with MFlem. *sleec*, *sleic* (see SLEEK *sb.*[1])

An apparent OE. *slīc* given in Dictionaries is the result of a misreading: see Napier *Contrib. O.E. Lexicogr.* 57–58. *Slykker* in Palsgr. 324/1 is prob. a misprint for *slykke*.]

**1.** Of skin, hair, etc.: Smooth, glossy, sleek. Also, of a surface: slippery (chiefly *U.S.*).

α. **13..** *Cursor M.* 28026 (Cott. Galba), When ȝe to sight haue made ȝow slike þan say ȝe men will ȝow biswike. ?*a* **1366** CHAUCER *Rom. Rose* 542 Hir flesh tendre as is a chike, With bent browis, smothe and slyke. *c* **1386** —— *Wife's Prol.* 351 If the Cattes skyn be slyk and gay, She wol nat dwelle in house half a day. *c* **1440** *Promp. Parv.* 459/1 Slyke, or smothe, *lenis.* *a* **1470** H. PARKER *Dives & P.* x. vi. (W. de W. 1496) 379/2 The basynet..is clene fur-busshed from ruste, and made slyke and smothe that shot may soone glyde of. **1582** STANYHURST *Æneis* II. (Arb.) 59 Lyke the.. adder..His tayle smoog thirling, slyke breast to Titan vpheauing. **1594** NASHE *Unfort. Trav.* Wks. (Grosart) V. 88 A skin as slike and soft as the backe of a swan.

β. **1549** CHALONER *Erasm. on Folly* B j, This other with the slicke skinne and fayre fedde bodie is called Delicacie. **1593** G. HARVEY *Pierce's Super.* Wks. (Grosart) II. 59 A deft conceite, a slicke forhead, a smugg countenaunce. **1639** T. DE GRAY *Expert Farrier* 8 Her hayre more slicke and close to her skin. **1653** GATAKER *Vind. Annot. Jer.* 137 A prone and plain path..not slick and smooth onely, but even steep and slipperie. **1707** J. STEVENS tr. *Quevedo's Com. Wks.* (1709) 335 He is all slick with Grease without. **1725** *Fam. Dict.* s.v. *Peach-Tree*, Those Peaches which are not slick, ought to be but indifferently hairy. **1841** HARTSHORNE *Salop. Ant.* Gloss., *Slick*,..smooth, shining. **1880** 'MARK TWAIN' *Tramp Abr.* xiii. 101 It struck that hard, slick, carpetless floor. **1901** A. H. RICE *Mrs. Wiggs of Cabbage Patch* xi. 143 When the floor was dry and the candle sprinkled over it, Australia and Europena were detailed to slide upon it until it became slick. **1936** M. MITCHELL *Gone with Wind* xxxv. 590 The horse..plodded off, picking its way carefully down the slick road. **1979** C. FREEMAN *Portraits* (1980) vi. 31 The streets were covered with a white blanket of snow and ice so slick it was almost impossible for him to walk. **1981** *Railway Mag.* Mar. 115/3 No. 765 [*sc.* a steam locomotive] was true to her breed, losing her footing temporarily on the slick rails as she fought for adhesion.

*transf.* **1679** *The Confinement* 49 More soft than a slick Gale, From Mountains top blown o're the flowry vale.

**2. a.** Of animals, etc.: Sleek in hair or skin; plump; well-conditioned. Now *rare.*

*c* **1440** *Pallad. on Husb.* I. 689 In dayes thries x, let make hem [*sc.* chickens] slyke And faat ynough. **1599** T. M[OUFET] *Silkwormes* 74 How a louer wise Delighteth more to touch Astarte slick Then Hecuba. *c* **1611** CHAPMAN *Iliad* II. 680 The brauest mares..Both slicke and daintie. **1698** FRYER *Acc. E. India & P.* 99 Meal of Garavance, which fattens all their Beasts of War, and makes them slick and fine. **1740** SOMERVILLE *Hobbinol* III. 287 As the slick Lev'ret skims before the Pack. **1841** CATLIN *N. Amer. Ind.* (1844) I. 27 All of them selected as the fattest and slickest of the herd.

**b.** Of range animals: unbranded, wild. *U.S.*

**1955** R. HOBSON *Nothing too Good* xvii. 181 The pounding of slick horses hitting across the range. **1973** R. SYMONS *Where Wagon Led* I. iii. 39 Then brand everything that's 'slick'—provided you know they're off your own mares.

**3.** Smooth; plausible; = SLEEK *a.* 3. (Of persons or things personified.) See also sense 4 below.

For a doubtful example see *Havelok* 1157.

**1599** JONSON *Cynthia's Rev.* I. i, Slick flattery and she Are twin-born sisters. *a* **1600** *Nobody & Someb.* in Simpson *Sch. Shaks.* (1878) 355 Smoth spaniel, soothing grome, Slicke, oyly knave, egregious parasite! **1640** RAWLINS *Rebellion* IV. i, Whilst slick Favonius plays the fawning slave. **1848** LOWELL *Biglow P.* Ser. I. iv. Wks. (1884) 226 To the people they're ollers ez slick er molasses. **1876** HOLLAND *Seven Oaks* xx. 282, I hate a slick man. **1936** AUDEN & ISHERWOOD *Ascent of F6* (1937) I. i. 17 Evening. A slick and unctuous Time Has sold us yet another shop-soiled day.

**4.** Adroit, deft, quick, smart; skilful in action or execution. Also (merging with sense 3), glibly clever, having easy assurance. (Of persons.)

**1807** *Lancaster* (Pa.) *Jrnl.* 16 Oct. 3/1 You are getting too slick. What a charming thing it is to see men under good discipline. **1818** H. B. FEARON *Sketches Amer.* 5, I have been *slick* in going to the stand right away. **1830** GALT *Lawrie T.* IV. ii. (1849) 148, I ain't..slick at the gruelling of sick folks. **1893** J. MᶜCARTHY *Red Diamonds* I. 43, I had been a pretty slick voyager in my time. **1921** E. O'NEILL *Diff'rent* I, in *Emperor Jones* 213 Jim Benson's one o' them slick jokers, same's Jack; can't keep their mouths shet or mind their own business. **1951** [see REGISTER *v.* 3 c]. **1953** R. LEHMANN *Echoing Grove* 155 Give her a pen and she cannot be trusted not to express herself in clichés, like a schoolgirl with a smear of the popular slick journalist. **1966** 'J. HACKSTON' *Father clears Out* 98 The rest of our local colour was made up of a community of slick, quick-off-the-mark jumpers.

**5.** First-class, excellent; neat, in good order; smart, efficient, that operates smoothly; superficially attractive, glibly clever. (Of things, actions, etc.)

**1833** *Jamestown* (N.Y.) *Jrnl.* 25 Sept. 2/1 Of all the inventions I've hearn on of Mr. Van Buren's, this is about the slickest. **1837** *Baltimore Commercial Transcript* 4 Sept. 2/3 Prudence guessed strawberries and cream were slick. Jonathan thought they wa'nt so slick as Pru's lips. **1860** J. G. HOLLAND *Miss Gilbert's Career* viii. 131, I love to see a young man that keeps things slick around him. **1866** in BROGDEN *Prov. Lincs.* **1891** *Fur, Fin & Feather* Mar. 169 They reckons to make mighty slick work in cleaning everything up on the way back. **1901** W. CHURCHILL *Crisis* I. xii. 104 'You'd die laughing, Lige, to hear how he did it.' 'Some *slickness*, I'll gamble,' grunted Captain Lige. 'Well, I reckon 'twas slick.' **1904** W. H. SMITH *Promoters* i. 19 I've seen the thing done a hundred times, with a slick word every time. **1905** *MᶜClure's Mag.* June 121/1 'They certainly gave us a slick time,' said the lad. 'Why our dinner cost nine dollars! **1920** E. O'NEILL *Beyond Horizon* I. ii. 35 'He'll make this one of the slickest, best-payin' farms in the state.' .. 'Seems to me it's a pretty slick place right now.' **1921** GALSWORTHY *To Let* 286 He could not go on staying here, walled in and sheltered, with everything so slick and comfortable. **1927** *New Republic* 12 Oct. 218/2 His dialogue is of that slick and well oiled kind that you may meet in good vaudeville or in the Saturday Evening Post. **1931** E. F. BENSON *Mapp & Lucia* i. 18 Let us practise that scene where I knight you. We must get it very slick. **1933** E. O'NEILL *Ah, Wilderness!* III. i. 95 How was that for a slick way of getting rid of him? **1940** M. V. HUGHES *London Family between Wars* xii. 157 America.., with its slick, fervid haste and its terrifying efficiency. **1958** *Woman* 22 Feb. 23/3 That's what 'Six-Five Special' does to you!.. We must admit that it's about the slickest light show on TV today. **1972** E. H. GOMBRICH *Story of Art* (ed. 12) xxvi. 439 He had more and more become convinced that art was in danger of becoming slick and superficial. **1978** *Electronics & Power* Nov./Dec. 824/1 When that [*sc.* the robbing of banks] became difficult we went for the cash in transit, until the professionals got their drill so slick that the game was not worth the candle. **1978** *Lancashire Life* Oct. 155/2 The Accord four-door I drove had a slick, finger-light, five-speed manual gearbox with a well chosen set of ratios. **1979** *Church Times* 6 July 16/5, I will scrap Series Three And invent something slicker. How grand to be free—A real alive Vicar!

**6. a.** *Comb.*, as ***slick-faced***, ***-haired***, ***-tongued***;

**1598** MARLOWE & CHAPMAN *Hero & Leander* III. 343 Slick-tongde fame, patcht vp with voyces rude. *c* **1611** CHAPMAN *Iliad* XI. 343 You slick-hair'd louer: you that hunt and feere at wenches so. *c* **1680** COTTON *Morning Quatrains* xvii, The slick-faced school-boy satchel takes. **1879–** in *Eng. Dial. Dict.* (Slick-faced, -tongued). **1914** *World's Work* XXVII. 447/1 Any 'slick-ear' (steer not marked on the ears or branded) found on the range about which inquiry was made was promptly assigned to his ownership, and 'slick-ears' eventually became known as 'mavericks'. **1958** 'W. HENRY' *Seven Men at Mimbres Springs* vii. 74 I'd clean forgot the slick-ear son of a bitch! **1966** H. MARRIOTT *Cariboo Cowboy* iv. 48 Sometimes the cow would die for some reason or another and the calf would be left without a mother, in which case it grew up an orphan calf or a 'slick-ear'.

**b. slick-paper** *U.S.*, a kind of glossy paper used esp. for printing popular magazines (cf. SLICK *sb.*[1] 6); usu. *attrib.*; hence **slick magazine, story.**

**1930** D. WILHELM *Writing for Profit* iv. 102 There are between 100 and 125 pulp-paper magazines alone beside all the illustrated and 'slick paper' magazines! **1936** *Amer. Mercury* XXXVII. 286/2 Occasionally I have put aside two weeks..in which to attempt a slick magazine story. **1949** H. E. NEAL *Writing & Selling Fact & Fiction* ii. 17 The average slick story is divisible into six parts. **1976** *National Observer* (U.S.) 23 Oct. 22/5 They will come again next year with.. their suitcases stuffed with slick-paper brochures full of self-praise. **1980** *TWA Ambassador* Oct. 82/3 Two distinct genres of regional business publications are trying to serve this market: the tabloid and the slick magazine.

**slick** (slɪk), *adv.* Orig. *U.S.* [f. SLICK *a.*]

**1.** Smartly, cleverly; easily; quickly.

**1825** LONGF. in *Life* (1891) I. v. 59 They manage things there so slick that the college saves annually three thousand dollars! **1836** HALIBURTON *Clockm.* (1862) 11 A woman's tongue goes so slick of itself..that it's no easy matter to put a spring stop on it. **1882** MISS BRADDON *Mt.-Royal* II. iv. 55 I'll just take a hurried look round and be back again slick.

**2.** As an intensive: Right, clean; completely.

**1818** H. B. FEARON *Sk. Amer.* 123 Did she die slick right away? **1832** MACAULAY in *Trevelyan* 6 July, A Yankee has written to me... I guess I must answer him slick right away. **1840** THACKERAY *Shabby Genteel Story* iii, I was right slick up over head and ears in love with her at once. **1900** POLLOK & THOM *Sports Burma* vi. 210, I..imagined they had bolted slick away.

**slick** (slɪk), *v.* Forms: *α.* (1 -slician,) 3-4 sliken, 4 slyken; 4-6 slike, slyke. *β.* 6 slycke, slicke, 6- slick. [OE. *-slician* (in *niȝslicod*): cf. SLEEK *v.* It is not clear how this is related to Icel. *slíkja*, Norw. *slikja*, to be, or to make, sleek.]

**1. a.** *trans.* To render smooth or glossy; to polish; to smooth with a slicker.

*α.* [*a* **900** *O.E. Martyrol.* 17 Nov. 206 Heo glytenode..swa scynende sunne oððe niȝslicod hrægel.] *a* **1225** *Leg. St. Kath.* 1660 Istenet [is] euch strete mid deorewurðe stanes,.. isliket & ismaket as eni gles smeðest. *c* **1325** *Gloss. W. de Bibbesw.* in Wright *Voc.* 172 *Ke ele lusche*, [that she] slike. *c* **1340** *Nominale* (Skeat) 158 W[oman] oft with slikeston slikyth. **1591** HORSEY *Trav.* (Hakl.) 234 Silkes, silver and gold, the threed sliked flat, to illustrat the bewty therof.

*β.* **1558** WARDE tr. *Alexis' Secr.* (1568) 90 b, Take a cloute or linnen cloth wete in water, wherwith you shall slycke and make smoth the said tables. **1601** HOLLAND *Pliny* XVII. xxvi, To slick, polish, and smooth them again with the pumy stone. **1657** R. LIGON *Barbadoes* 75 Parchment dyed green, and slickt with a slick-stone. **1674** COTTON *Compl. Gamester* (1680) 85 Some have a way to slick with a Slickstone all the Honours very smooth. **1728** E. SMITH *Compl. Housew.* (1750) 180 Make it up into a paste; slick white paper, roll your paste out [etc.]. **1839** URE *Dict. Arts* 379 It is next slicked with a good grit-stone, to take out the wrinkles. **1852** C. MORFIT *Tanning & Currying* (1853) 347 It [the leather] is then pared, slicked, and beaten out flat. **1875** KNIGHT *Dict. Mech.* 2208/1 Slickers..are used to slick down the curved surfaces of molds after withdrawal of the pattern.

**b.** *transf.* To polish up, make elegant or fine. Also with *off*, *up*.

Sometimes with derogatory overtones.

**1340** *Ayenb.* 99 He ne heþ none hede of longe ryote of tales y-slyked ne y-rymed. *Ibid.* 212 Wordes afaited and y-sliked ueleuold. **1582** STANYHURST *Æneis* Ded. (Arb.) 4 With woordes so fitlye coucht, wyth verses so smoothlye slyckte. **1638** QUARLES *Elegies* iii, No farr-fetch'd Metaphor shall smooth or slick My ruffled straine. **1831** [see BETTER *a.* 4 b (*b*)]. **1848** LOWELL *Biglow P.* Ser. I. i, The parson kind o' slicked off sum o' the last varses. **1863** *Harper's Mag.* 55/1 He got into Peter's way by attempting..to 'slick up' the barn. **1953** R. LEHMANN *Echoing Grove* 187 Stop slicking it up into cheap melodrama. **1973** E.-J. BAHR *Nice Neighbourhood* iii. 25 I'm going to get her all slicked up in her new outfit from Aunt Joan and show her off.

**c.** With *away* or *out*: To remove by smoothing or polishing.

**1639** T. DE GRAY *Expert Farrier* 116 This clyster.. slicketh away all slimy substance. **1882** *Encycl. Brit.* XIV. 386/2 The superfluous moisture and the superficial bloom are now slicked out [with the slicker].

**d.** *intr.* To smarten or tidy *up*. *U.S.*

**1841** *Knickerbocker* XVII. 41 In a little while he recovered his self-possession, or, to make use of one of his own expressions 'he slicked up'. **1887** M. E. WILKINS *Humble Romance* 395 I'm going to slick up here a little for you while I stay... He watched her..as she flew about putting things to rights. **1948** *Family Circle* June 96/2 It's always serious when they slick up for a girl!

†**2. a.** To make specious or plausible. Also *absol.*, to use specious language. *Obs.*

*c* **1250** *Owl & Night.* 841 Alle þine wordes beoþ isliked,.. þat alle..weneþ þat þu segge soþ. **1390** GOWER *Conf.* II. 351 For so wel can ther noman slyke. *Ibid.* 365 He can so wel hise wordes slyke To putte awey suspecioun.

†**b.** To flatter, treat pleasantly. *Obs.*

*c* **1250** *Long Life* 43 in *O.E. Misc.* 158 Ȝef þe world wið weole þe slikeð þat is for to do þe wo.

**3.** To make (the skin, hair, etc.) sleek or glossy, esp. by some special treatment.

*a* **1300** *Cursor M.* 28026 Yee leuedis..Quen yee yow-self sua slight and slike, Yee sai þat men you wille besuike. **1377** LANGL. *P. Pl.* B. II. 98 To sitten and soupen..Tyl sleuth and slepe slyken his sides. **1555** WATREMAN *Fardle of Facions* II. viii. 181 No face painted, no skinned slicked, no countrefeicte countenaunce. *c* **1570** [JEFFERIES] *Bugbears* I. iii, He is coombed and slicked and wasshed. **1593** MUNDAY *Def. Contraries* 21 Oftentimes they..rub, slick, chafe and washe themselues, only to seeme faire. **1611** BEAUM. & FL. *Kt. Burning Pestle* II. iii, A gentle Squire..Who will our Palfries slick with wisps of straw. **1620-6** QUARLES *Feast for Wormes* 1089 He..Stayes not to bathe his weather-beaten ioynts, Nor smooth'd his countenance, nor slick't his skinne. **1838** HOLLOWAY *Prov. Dict.*, *To slick*, to comb, or make sleek, the hair. **1841** CATLIN *N. Amer. Ind.* (1844) I. xiii. 98 Slicks down his long hair, and rubs his oiled limbs to a polish.

*absol.* **1576** GASCOIGNE *Steele Gl.* Epil., They neuer stande content,..But paint and slicke til fayrest face be foule.

**4.** *colloq.* (See quot.)

**1860** *Slang Dict.* 218 *Slick*,..as a verb,..has the force of 'to despatch rapidly', turn off, get done with a thing.

**slicked** (slɪkt), *ppl. a.* [f. SLICK *v.*] **a.** In various senses of the vb. Also with *back*, *down*.

**1594** O. B. *Quest. Profit. Concern.* M j b, These Boare pigs and Beare whelpes,..for all their slickt coates and smooth tongues, vnderstand not what courteous behauiour and gentle deeds meane. **1629** Z. BOYD *Last Battell* 952 A slicked tongue and a slacke hand keepe other companie. **1674** COTTON *Compl. Gamester* (1680) 85 The rest..will slip off from the slickt Card. **1704** *Lond. Gaz.* No. 4067/8 Lost.., a yellow coloured slick'd Greyhound Bitch. **1921** E. O'NEILL *Diff'rent* I, in *Emperor Jones* 215 His hair [is] wet and slicked in a part. **1937** A. CHRISTIE *Murder in Mews* 163 It was the good-looking young man with the slicked-back hair who had spoken. **1949** E. DE MAUNY *Huntsman in his Career* II. 128 There was dandruff on the collar from his slicked-back, fair hair. **1964** *Economist* 20 June 1365/2 Mr McNamara's slicked-down patent leather hair. **1975** B. GARFIELD *Death Sentence* (1976) xi. 57 Latins, with slicked hair. **1976** N. THORNBURG *Cutter & Bone* iv. 86 He had a distinctly Arabic look about him, slicked-down black hair. **1977** *Listener* 17 Nov. 653/2 People with slicked-back hair.. jitter-bugging round the radio.

**b.** With *up*: dressed up, smart, elegant; also *fig.*, made more sophisticated. orig. *U.S.*

**1836** HALIBURTON *Clockm.* (1862) 133 Now this grand house has only two rooms down stairs, that are altogether slicked up and finished off complete. **1867** *Atlantic Monthly* Jan. 109/2 Is this my farm?... It looks more slicked up than ever it used to. **1928** J. GALSWORTHY *Swan Song* I. xi. 81 Montpellier Square..was all slicked up since he was last there... Builders and decorators must have done well lately. **1957** R. HOGGART *Uses of Literacy* xi. 276 The new-style popular publications..are pallid but slicked-up extensions even of nineteenth-century sensationalism. **1979** *Tucson Mag.* Apr. 34/1 In the same wave came..the new City Hall and the slicked-up El Presidio Park.

**'slicken**, *v. rare.* [f. SLICK *a.* + -EN[5].] *trans.* To make smooth or polished.

**1621** BURTON *Anat. Mel.* 442 The Eban stone which Goldsmiths vse to slicken their gold with. **1688** HOLME *Armoury* III. 15 A Band..Starched, Slickened and Smoothed by the care of the Landress. *Ibid.* 292 A Shooemakers polishing stick..is that wherewith they polish and slicken their Leather. **1893-4** HESLOP *Northumbld. Gloss.*, *Slickened*, polished. Used to describe the appearance found on the planes of bedding where a fault in the strata has occurred.

**slickens** ('slɪkɪns). *U.S.* [? f. SLICK *sb.*[2]] (See quots.)

**1882** *Cent. Mag.* XXV. 337 It is the lighter soils of the hydraulic mines and the pulverized matter from the quartz-mills of the mining region which constitute 'slickens'. **1894** *New York Tribune* 1 Feb. 1/3 All of this [500 acres] will be covered with 'slickens', washings from the mines in the mountains, and thus be rendered valueless.

**slickenside** ('slɪk(ə)nsaɪd). Also -sides. [f. dial. *slicken*, var. of SLICK *a.* + SIDE *sb.*[1]]

**1.** *Min.* A specular variety of galena found in Derbyshire.

**1768** METTAM in Whitehurst *Formation of Earth* (1778) 188, I send you, by the bearer, two specimens of our slickensides, containing all the variety of minerals where the explosions happen. **1789** J. PILKINGTON *Derbyshire* I. 195 Slickenside with a smooth surface on each side... The crackling and explosions caused by scraping these slickensides with a pick-ax are well known. **1810** MILLAR *J. Williams' Min. Kingdom* II. App. 448 Slickenside, which is a variety of galena, or sulphuret of lead, is also a product of these [Derbyshire] mines. **1850** ANSTED *Elem. Geol., Min.* etc. Gloss., *Slickensides*,..one of the ores of lead found in Derbyshire.

**2.** *Geol.* A polished (and sometimes striated) surface on the wall of a mineral lode, or on a line of fracture in a rock-mass; a smooth glistening surface produced by pressure and friction.

**1822** CONYBEARE & PHILLIPS *Geol. Eng. & Wales* 401 These planes, when separated, are the slickensides of the mineralogist. **1859** R. HUNT *Guide Mus. Pract. Geol.* (ed. 2) 164 The *Slickensides* evidently point to some sliding or grinding motion in the mass constituting the lode. **1880** *Nature* XXI. 459 A kind of universal slickenside, consequent upon the crushing of a rock consisting of thin laminæ of different texture.

*attrib.* **1839** MURCHISON *Silur. Syst.* I. xxxiv. 462 The direction of these joints (many of which have slickenside surfaces). **1884** *Nature* 13 Nov. 35 Parallel with the slickenside-lines. **1888** PRESTWICH *Geol.* II. 134 Extreme lateral pressure, the result of which is the formation of slickenside surfaces, often strongly striated.

Hence **'slickensided** *ppl. a.* and *pa. pple.*; **'slickensiding** *vbl. sb.*

**1875** DAWSON *Dawn of Life* ii. 32 This graphite is composed of contorted and slickensided laminæ. **1883** *Science* I. 191/2 A roof of slickensided 'soapstone'. **1884** *Geol. Mag.* 553 The dissolution being unequal, caused bosses to be left standing up, which were then 'slickensided' by the downward movement of the chalk. *Ibid.* 552 This movement would be..amply sufficient to account for the slickensiding observed.

**slicker** ('slɪkə(r)). [f. SLICK *a.* or *v.*]

**1. a.** A tool used for scraping or smoothing leather. (Cf. SLEEKER.)

**1851-3** TOMLINSON *Cycl. Arts & Manuf.* (1867) II. 34/1 The cylinder drags the hide under the governor, which acts similarly to a slicker. **1860** —— *Arts & Manuf.* Ser. II. *Leather* 20 It is..well rubbed with a smooth lump of glass called a 'slicker'. **1885** *Harper's Mag.* Jan. 277 The hides are 'whitened' by scraping them with a whitening slicker.

**b.** A tool used for smoothing the surfaces of moulds in founding.

**1875** KNIGHT *Dict. Mech.* 2208/1.

**2.** orig. and chiefly *U.S.* A waterproof overcoat; *spec.* a loose-fitting oilskin outer garment, usu. of a bright yellow or orange colour.

**1884** *Harper's Mag.* July 300/1 Carry..a rubber pillow, and a 'slicker'. **1888** *Home Missionary* (N.Y.) May 14, I put on my thick overcoat, then a duster, and over them my slicker. **1910** C. E. MULFORD *Hopalong Cassidy* xx. 126 After throwing his saddle on his horse he went back to the house to get his 'slicker', a yellow water-proof coat. **1953** M. PEAKE *Mr Pye* xxii. 176 Tintagieu..now wore a black oilskin slicker. **1971** *N.Z. Listener* 19 Apr. 56/5 One was a nuggety bloke in a sou'-wester, oilskin slicker, and bowyangs. **1978** R. LUDLUM *Holcroft Covenant* iii. 43 Police and maintenance crews were everywhere, distinguished from one another by the contrasting black and orange of their slickers.

**3.** = *city slicker* s.v. CITY 9. orig. and chiefly *U.S.*

**1900** 'J. FLYNT' *Notes Itinerant Policeman* iii. 62 Pick-pockets!.. You just bring the slickers in. **1932** J. T. FARRELL *Young Lonigan* vi. 230 Swan, the slicker, who wore a tout's gray checked suit with narrow-cuffed trousers [etc.]. **1936** *Sat. Morning Advertiser* (Durant, Okla.) 14 Mar. 1/3 (*heading*) 'Slicker' insurance agents better be a bit wary now. **1946** WODEHOUSE *Money in Bank* xii. 106 I'm going to put it across that slicker..if it's the last thing I do. **1978** *Morecambe Guardian* 14 Mar. 15/4 He becomes a sort of Midnight Cowboy, lost and confused by the slickers around him.

**4.** *U.S.* = SILVER-FISH 2.

**1902** L. O. HOWARD *Insect Bk.* 380 (Order *Thysanura.*) The insects of this order are usually of very small size... They comprise the little insects known as springtails, bristletails, fishmoths or slickers. **1962** METCALF & FLINT *Destructive & Useful Insects* (ed. 4) xix. 905 The silverfish or slicker..is uniform, silvery or greenish gray.

Hence as *vb. trans.*, to cheat; to defeat by being 'slick'.

**1935** H. DAVIS *Honey in Horn* xxii. 376 His entertainment had mostly been swindling and slickering them. **1971** LAVER & COLLINS *Educ. Tennis Player* xiii. 157 It happens all the time, an older, less powerful team who understand the principles of doubles slickering a couple of youths who might be considerably superior in singles. **1974** *Tel.* (Brisbane) 4 Sept. 30/4, I thrive on guys who try to slicker me. **1979** *Globe & Mail* (Toronto) 16 May 41/8 What was it Charlie had said about being slickered?

**slickered** ('slɪkəd), *a.* *U.S.* [f. SLICKER *sb.*[2] + -ED[2].] Wearing a slicker.

**1972** C. L. COOPER *Black* 151, I could see..slickered cops smoking on duty. **1975** *New Yorker* 10 Mar. 29/1 About twelve horses on the track, a few running hard, their slickered riders standing tall in the stirrups.

**slicking** ('slɪkɪŋ), *vbl. sb.* [f. SLICK *v.*]

**1. a.** The action of making sleek or smooth, etc.

**1495** *Act 11 Hen. VII*, c. 27 By crafty sliking they make the same Fustions to appere to the comen people fyne, hole and sounde. **1600** ABBOT *Jonah* 592 Are there not which take more care of their slicking and of their platting, then of the Kingdom of Heaven? **1636** *Lyly's Euphues* F iij, I loath almost to thinke on..the sliking of their faces. **1875** KNIGHT *Dict. Mech.* 2192/1 The size is flour-paste,..and the operation on the rope is called *snugging*, *slicking*, or *finishing*.

*attrib.* **1588** CHURCHYARD in Nichols *Progr. Q. Eliz.* (1823) II. 595 As it were rubde and smoothde with slicking-stone. **1841** HARTSHORNE *Salop. Ant.* Gloss., A shoemaker talks about slicking the soles of his shoes with a slicking stick. **1896** *Archæol. Jrnl.* LIII. 46 Thumb-flints, or slicking-knives, also occur.

**b.** *spec.* In hat-making: (see quot.).

**1875** KNIGHT *Dict. Mech.* 2208/2 *Slicking*,..the attaching of the fur nap to the felt body.

**2.** With *up*: the action of making (oneself, a place, etc.) neat and tidy. *U.S. colloq.*

**1855** *Trans. Mich. Agric. Soc.* VI. 495 The farm needs a good deal of slicking up to make the general appearance equal to what nature has done for the land. **1907** *Springfield* (Mass.) *Weekly Republ.* 9 May 1 Denver has been having her period of spring slicking up.

**3.** *Mining.* In *pl.* Narrow veins of ore.

**1843** J. Y. WATSON *Compend. Brit. Mining* 81.

**slickly** ('slɪklɪ), *adv.* Also 6 slickely. [f. SLICK *a.* + -LY[2].]

**1.** Sleekly, smoothly. *rare.*

**1596** SHAKS. *Tam. Shr.* IV. i. 93 Let their heads bee slickely comb'd. **1973** *Daily Tel.* 11 Jan. 17/1 Walter Albini likes to see his male models with their hair oiled slickly down like George Raft's.

**2.** Cleverly, deftly.

**1893** *Daily News* 14 Apr. 2/2 Look..how slickly they are painted, with what knowledge and skill. **1927** *Daily Tel.* 16 Aug. 12/5 The play..needs to be more slickly produced and better acted in order to be made convincing. **1978** K. ROYCE *Satan Touch* vi. 99 Slickly he turned his hand down to indicate the chair.

**slickness** ('slɪknɪs). [f. SLICK *a.* + -NESS.]

**1.** Smoothness. *rare.*

**1667** *Phil. Trans.* II. 482 Some of which [stones, *Calculi*] were so bestow'd as to slide upon others, and had thereby worn their flats to a wonderfull slikness. **1976** *Billings* (Montana) *Gaz.* 28 June 3-A/1 It's a three-quarter ton pickup with skid-trailer, painted the bright orange of the Montana Highway Department. It tests the slickness of the road surface.

**2.** Smartness.

**1872** *Daily News* 5 Aug., I know not whether the uniform ..gives him a greater appearance of what in the North is called 'slickness'.

**3.** Dexterity, cleverness. Now freq. *derog.*

**1895** *Daily News* 5 June 7/2 A mere sketch, it is true, but with all his slickness and deftness of execution. **1899** *Ibid.* 22 Apr. 9/4 The slickness of the painting..is quite admirable. **1927** *Music & Letters* July 321 Pure artistry may decline to a mere slickness and facility. **1967** E. SHORT *Embroidery & Fabric Collage* iv. 112 Anything cheap, shoddy, shallow or clever to a degree of slickness, is out of place.

**slickster** ('slɪkstə(r)). *U.S. slang.* [f. SLICK *sb.*[1] + -STER.] A swindler.

**1965** C. BROWN *Manchild in Promised Land* xiv. 332 All the Muslims now felt as though 125th Street was theirs. It used to belong to the hustlers and the slicksters. **1973** [see RUN *v.* 52 h].

**ˈslickstone.** Now *rare.* Also 4, 6 slike-, 5 slyk-, 6 slycke-. [f. SLICK *v.* Cf. ON. *slikisteinn* (Norw. *slikjestein*).] = SLEEKSTONE.

*c* **1325** *Gloss. W. de Bibbesw.* in Wright *Voc.* 172 A slikestone. *c* **1340** *Nominale* (Skeat) 158 W[oman] oft with slikeston slikyth. **14..** *Lat.-Eng. Voc.* in Wr.-Wülcker 563 *Amethon*, a slykston. *Ibid.* 593 *Litatorium*, a slykston. **1530** PALSGR. 271 Slyckestone, *lisse a papier.* **1594** NASHE *Unfort. Trav.* 15 Their shooes shined as bright as a slike-stone. **1657** R. LIGON *Barbadoes* 75 Shining as parchment dyed green, and slickt with a slick-stone. **1674** COTTON *Compl. Gamester* (1680) 85 Some have a way to slick with a Slick-stone all the Honours very smooth. *c* **1711** PETIVER *Gazophyl.* x. §96 A large smooth shining Gowry, which is used for a Polish or Slick-stone. **1771** MRS. HAYWOOD *New Present for Maid* 267 Smooth them [ribands] with a glass slick-stone. **1812** J. SMYTH *Pract. Customs* (1821) 242 Slick Stones, the 100—£0 8*s.* 0*d.* **1893–4** HESLOP *Northumbld. Gloss.* s.v., Slickstones were sometimes made with a stalk or handle. **1895** *Stand. Dict.*, *Slickstone*,.. Archeol., a pre-historic stone implement used in preparing skins.

**slick-worm.** *Sc.* (See quot. and cf. SLECK *sb.*)

**1796** *Statist. Acc. Scotland* XVII. 469 This brook has a rich muddy bottom, in which there is plenty of slick-worm (a species of food which the trout peculiarly delight in).

**slid,** *sb.* Now *rare.* Also 6 slidd, slydd-. [Obscurely related to SLED *sb.* or SLIDE *v.*] A device by which something may be slid along the ground; a sled or sledge; a skid.

**1513** *Life Henry V* (Kingsford) 111 A slidd laden with greate stakes and with other greate peeces of greene wood. **1519** HORMAN *Vulgaria* 244 b, This house may be remoued with trocles, & slyddis. **1657** R. LIGON *Barbadoes* 112 If they pave the waies, between the Canes, for the Slids and Assinigoes to passe. **1788** *Trans. Soc. Arts* VI. 203 The advantages of the high wheels, and troughs or slids, over common wheels. *Ibid.* 207 The troughs or slids which accompany the Carriage, are to be placed under the wheels. **1904** *Dundee Advertiser* 15 Aug. 6 The hay 'slipes' or 'slids' for shifting the coles or ricks to the shed.

**b.** ? A load sufficient for a sled.

**1887** *Archit. Soc. Dict.* s.v., Thirty-four pollards produced a slid, and an average slid produced 13 faggots, or about 7½ slids to a hundred faggots.

**slid,** *a. Sc.* Also 6 slide, slyd(e. [Related to SLIDE *v.*]

**1.** Slippery.

**1501** DOUGLAS *Pal. Hon.* III. ii, Ane passage.. Hewin in the roche of slid hard marbell stone. **1513** —— *Æneid* VII. vii. 29 Full slyde scho slyppis hir membris our allquhayr. **17..** RAMSAY *Betty & Kate* iii, On a slid stane, or smoother slate. **1737** —— *Sc. Prov.* (1750) 37 He has a slid grip that has an eel by the tail. **1808** JAMIESON, *Slid ice*, ice that is glib. **1850** STRUTHERS *Poet. Wks.* II. 239 The brawling burn We ploutered aft, slid eels to snare. **1899–** in *Eng. Dial. Dict.*

**2.** *fig.* **a.** Mutable, changeable, uncertain.

**1501** DOUGLAS *Pal. Hon.* I. lv, The slide inconstant destenie or chance. *Ibid.* III. lxxviii, This warldis glorie, Maist inconstant, maist slid and transitorie.

**b.** Smooth, polished, sleek, sly.

**1719** RAMSAY *Ep. J. Arbuckle* 50 Something sae auld-farran, Sae slid, sae unconstrain'd and darin. **1721** —— *Poems* Gloss. s.v., He's a slid lown. **1725** —— *Gentle Sheph.* I. i, Ye have sae saft a voice, and slid a tongue. **1896** in *Eng. Dial. Dict.*

**slid,** *ppl. a.* [f. SLIDE *v.*] Uttered with a kind of sliding tone.

**1898** KIPLING *Day's Work* 320 It was the unreproducible slid *r*, as he said this was his 'fy-ist' visit to England, that told me he was a New Yorker.

**'Slid,** *int. Obs.* exc. *arch.* Also 7 slydd. [abbrev. of *God's lid* (eyelid): see GOD *sb.* 14 a.] A form of oath, common in the 17th century.

**1598** SHAKS. *Merry W.* III. iv. 24 Ile make a shaft or a bolt on't, slid, tis but venturing. **1606** *Sir G. Goosecappe* I. ii, Slydd there's not one of them truely emphaticall. **1650** COWLEY *Guardian* II. ii, Here's company; 'slid I'll fight then. **1689** *Dial. betw. Timothy & Titus* 6 Slid! this is insufferable. **1855** KINGSLEY *Westw. Ho!* iii, 'Slid, it seems half a life that I've been away.

**slidable,** var. SLIDEABLE.

**slidage** (ˈslaɪdɪdʒ). *Canadian.* [f. SLIDE *v.*] The payment for the right of using a log slide.

**1884** *Law Rep.* 9 *App. Cases* 411 A promise to pay slidage for the use and occupation of such works.. could not be enforced.

**ˈslidden,** *ppl. a. rare.* [See SLIDE *v.* A. 3 b.] That has slipped or slid down.

**1827** HODGSON *Northumberland* I. II. 165 *note*, The celebrated figure.. cut in high relief upon a huge block of 'slidden' sandstone rock.

**ˈslidder,** *sb. dial.* [Cf. SLIDDER *a.* and *v.*] A trench or hollow running down a hill; a steep slope.

For other uses see the *Eng. Dial. Dict.*

*a* **1793** G. WHITE *Selborne, Obs. on Veget.* (1853) 301 One of the slidders, or trenches, down the middle of the Hanger .. is still called strawberry-slidder. **1842** *Dumfries Herald* Oct., Tearing and wearing his corduroys, up trees and down *slidders*, to very reasonable tatters. **1876** *Whitby Gloss.*, *Slidder*,.. a track down the hill side for the water.

† **ˈslidder,** *a.* and *adv. Obs.* Forms: α. 1–2 slidor, 2–6 slider (4 -ere, 5 -ur, -re), 4–5 slidir, 5–6 slyder (4 -ir, 5 -yr, -ere); 4 sledyr, 4–5 sleder; 1 sliddor, 5– slidder (6 -yr, slydder, -ir). β. 5 sclidere, -yr, sclydyr, sklyder. [OE. *slidor*, f. *slĭd-* weak grade of *slīdan* SLIDE *v.*]

**A.** *adj.* **1.** Slippery; on which one readily slips. Also as quasi-*sb.* (quot. 1501).

*a* **1000** *Runic Poem* 29 Is byþ oferceald, unȝemetum slidor. *c* **1280** in Horstm. *Altengl. Leg.* (1875) 168 Þe oþer was þat heo [a bridge] was so slider, þat me ne scholde þer on noȝt gon. *c* **1303** R. BRUNNE *Handl. Synne* 5260 Þe plank þat on þe brygge was, was as sledyr as any glas. **1387** TREVISA *Higden* (Rolls) I. 63 Somme may nouȝt clymbe on þe hilles, þe wey is so slider. *c* **1440** *Promp. Parv.* 459/1 Slydyr (or swypyr as a wey), *lubricus.* **1483** *Cath. Angl.* 322/2 Sclidere (*A.* Sclydyr), *labilis.* **1501** DOUGLAS *Pal. Hon.* III. lv, Thay na grippis thair micht hald for slidder. **1526** SKELTON *Magnyf.* 1840, I trowe it be a frost, for the way is slydder. **1570** *Satir. Poems Reform.* xxi. 31 Clyde banks.. thay sall find slidder, Quhen kindlit is Gods ire.

**b.** *fig.* or in fig. context.

*c* **1000** *Ags. Ps.* (Thorpe) xxxiv. 7 Syn heora weȝas þystre and slidore. *c* **1250** *Owl & Night.* 956 Þu schalt falle, þi wey is slider. *c* **1400** *26 Pol. Poems* 22 He wol the lede in wayes slidre. **1533** J. HEYWOOD *Mery Play* 296 The way to heven is very slydder.

**c.** *fig.* From which one may easily slip or fall; uncertain, mutable.

*c* **1480** HENRYSON *Fables, Wolf & Wether* xxii, Bewar in welth, for hall benkis ar richt slidder. **1552** LYNDESAY *Monarche* 4977 Sen ȝe.. Hes causit me for to consydder Quhow warldlye Pompe and glore bene slydder. *a* **1578** LINDESAY (Pitscottie) *Chron. Scot.* (S.T.S.) I. 151 Oft tymes thay find that seit most slidder That they haue keipit in the kingis menoritie.

**2.** Inclined to slip or fall. *rare.*

**1388** WYCLIF *Lam.* iv. 18 Oure steppis weren slidir in the weie of oure stretis. *a* **1500** in *Ratis Raving* 103 Men suld considyr That womenis honore is tendyr & slydder.

**3.** Of a smooth or slippery nature.

**1388** WYCLIF *Prov.* xxvi. 28 A slidir mouth worchith fallyngis. **1398** TREVISA *Barth. De P.R.* v. xxxviii. (Bodl. MS.), Ȝif he were slider and smoþe within by sliderness mete schuld passe oute. *Ibid.* XI. ii. (Tollem. MS.), Eyer [air] is of slider kynde, and þerfore he entreþ and comeþ in to dennes of þe erþe. **1686** G. STUART *Joco-ser. Disc.* 20 My Tongue is grown sae slip and slidder.

**B.** *adv.* In a sliding or unstable manner.

*a* **1400** *Minor Poems fr. Vernon MS.* lii. 149 Mony folk slod to helle slider. *c* **1400** *26 Pol. Poems* iv. 7 And hem-self stoden so slydere. *c* **1430** *Hymns Virgin* (1867) 49 In heuen blis ȝe stooden full slidir.

**slidder** (ˈslɪdə(r)), *v.* Now *dial.* Forms: 1 slid(e)rian, 5 slideren, slyder(yn), slydre, slidre; 3 sliddren, 7– slidder, 9 *Sc.* scl-, sklidder. [OE. *slid(e)rian*, = MDu. *slid(e)ren*, *slidderen*, LG. *sliddern*, G. *schlittern*, a frequentative from *slĭd-*, the weak grade of *slīdan* SLIDE *v.*]

**1.** *intr.* To slide, to slip.

For variations of sense see the *Eng. Dial. Dict.*

*c* **897** K. ÆLFRED *Gregory's Past. C.* xxxviii. 276 (Cotton MS.), Ðonne hie on moniȝfaldum wordum slidriað. *c* **1000** *Ags. Ps.* (Thorpe) xvii. 35 Mine fet ne slideredon. *Ibid.* xxxvii. 16 Ðif hy ȝeseon þæt mine fet slidrien. **14..** *Langland's P. Pl.* A. v. 113 (Univ. Coll. MS.), I mai it not trowe þat he ne schulde slideren þeron, so was [it] þred bare. **1426** LYDG. *De Guil. Pilgr.* 7119 Yiff they slydre, or falle doun, Thys Emperesse.. doth hem releue. *c* **1430** *Syr Gener.* (Roxb.) 4152 So hard thei smote than to-gedre, Out of here sadils thei gan to slidre. *c* **1440** *Promp. Parv.* 459 Slyderyn (*K.* slidyn). **1697** DRYDEN *Æneid* II. 751 With that he dragg'd the trembling Sire, Slidd'ring through clotter'd Blood, and holy Mire. **1720** POPE *Iliad* XXI. 267 His feet, upborn, scarce the strong flood divide, Slidd'ring, and stagg'ring. **1806** BERESFORD *Miseries Hum. Life* II. ix, Feeling your foot slidder over the back of a toad. **1851** G. H. KINGSLEY *Sport & Trav.* (1900) 508 Angular pieces of stone .. 'sliddering' down by the ton. **1879** *Trans. Dev. Assoc.* XI. 516 These tiny animals.. creep and slidder under stones.

**2.** *trans.* To make slippery or smooth.

**1398** TREVISA *Barth. De P.R.* XIX. lxxi. (1495) 903 Yf mylke is tomoche corrupte it slydereth the roughnesse of the stomak. **1891** in *Eng. Dial. Dict.*

Hence **ˈsliddering** *vbl. sb.* Also *attrib.*

*a* **1225** *Ancr. R.* 252 Vondunge is sliddrunge. **1866** MARK LEMON *Wait for the End* v. 54 Those were the dancing days of Old England, putting to shame our shambling, hopping, sliddering times.

† **ˈslidderness.** *Obs.* [f. SLIDDER *a.*] Slipperiness, smoothness. Also *fig.*

**971** *Blickl. Gl.* (Ps. xxxiv. 6), Slidornis, *lubricum.* *c* **1380** WYCLIF *Sel. Wks.* II. 4 Many men felden doun for slidirnesse of þis weie. **1398** TREVISA *Barth. De P.R.* v. xxxviii. (Bodl. MS.), Ȝif he were slider and smoþe within, by slidernes mete schuld passe oute. *c* **1400** *Comm. Luke* i. 15 (MS. Bodl. 43), He is seid a perfit man whiche.. feliþ not þe slidirnesse or leccherie of ȝong wexinge age. *c* **1475** HENRYSON *Orph. & Eur.* 305 For slyddrenes skant mycht he hald his feit. **1483** *Cath. Angl.* 323/1 A Sclidyrnes, *labilitas.*

**ˈsliddery,** *a.* Now *dial.* Forms: 3 slid(d)ri, 5 slydrye, 6 slyddry, -rie, 6–7 slidrie, 8 slidd'ry, 8–9 sliddry; 3–5 slideri, 4 -ery, slydery, sledery (6 *Sc.* -erie), 5, 7 (9) slidderie, 9 sliddery. [f. SLIDDER *v.* + -Y. Cf. MDu. *sliderich.*]

**1.** Slippery; on which one may readily slip.

*a* **1225** *Ancr. R.* 252 To wel we hit wuteð hu þe wei of þisse worlde is sliddri. *c* **1280** in Horstm. *Altengl. Leg.* (1875) 221 Bi a luytel bosk he tok his hondlyng, And set his feet on a slidri bas. *c* **1325** *Gloss. W. de Bibbesw.* in Wright *Voc.* 160 [The way is] slidery. **1382** WYCLIF *Jer.* xxxviii. 22 Thei han drenchid thee doun in the myre, and in the sledery thing thi feet. *c* **1480** HENRYSON *Fables, Preach. Swallow* xxxi, Slonkis and slaik maid sliddérie with the sleit. **1489** CAXTON *Faytes of A.* II. xxxix. 163 They can unuthe stande upon theyre fete so slydrye it is. **1513** DOUGLAS *Æneid* x. vi. 42 Slyddry glar so from wallis went That oft thar feyt was smyttyn vp on loft. *a* **1724** in Ramsay *Tea-table Misc.* (1876) II. 219 Is not this warld a slidd'ry ball? And thinks men strange to catch a fall? **1827** J. WILSON *Noctes Ambr.* Wks. 1855 II. 9 Slimy and sliddery as the sea-weed. **1874** HISLOP *Sc. Anecd.* 147 The floor was as sliddery as ice.

**b.** Uncertain, unstable, changeable, fleeting. (Cf. SLIDDER *a.* 1 c.)

*a* **1400** *Minor Poems fr. Vernon MS.* xxiii. 980 Þe eȝen of vr inward þouht Lyft vp from slideri þinge. **1567** *Gude & Godlie B.* (S.T.S.) 102 Full slyddrie is the sait that thay on sit. **1596** DALRYMPLE tr. *Leslie's Hist. Scot.* I. 292 Quhair may be seine how vnconstant and slidrie was the end of that battell. *c* **1610** SIR W. MURE *Sonn.* x. Wks. (S.T.S.) I. 56 Quhose othe & promeis ar a slidrie ground To build wpon, to make a man assuird. **1640** *Canterburians Self-Convict.* 32 A full peace in tearmes so generall, so ambiguous, so slidderie. **1786** BURNS *Farewell Brethren St. James's Lodge* i, Tho' I to foreign lands must hie, Pursuing Fortune's slidd'ry ba'. **1818** SCOTT *Br. Lamm.* xv, It will be present service.. which, in these sliddery times, will be expected by a man like the Marquis.

**2.** Inclined or prone to slip. *rare*$^{-1}$.

**1382** WYCLIF *Lam.* iv. 18 Thei maden slidery oure steppis in the weie of oure stretes.

**3.** Of a smooth or slippery nature. Also *fig.*, sly, deceitful.

*a* **1225** *Ancr. R.* 74 Þe tunge is sliddri, uor heo wadeð ine wete. **1382** WYCLIF *Prov.* xxvi. 28 The slideri mouth werchith fallingis. **1551** ABP. HAMILTON *Catech.* 76 Thai ar lyk to ane slederie eil. **1791** LEARMONT *Poems* 45 Unless some slidd'ry means he us'd. **1816** G. MUIR *Clydesdale Minstrelsy* 8 (E.D.D.), Lawyers fam'd for slidd'ry gabs. **1868** W. SHELLEY *Flowers* 181 Some gleg-gabbit slidderie lier.

† **ˈsliddy,** *a. Obs.* = SLIDDERY *a.* 1.

**1623** WODROEPHE *Marrow Fr. Tongue* 107/2 It is sliddy (*glissant*) wether. *Il verglace.* It freeseth after a rayne, it is sliddy.

**slide** (slaɪd), *sb.* Also 6 *Sc.* slyde. [f. SLIDE *v.*]

**I. 1. a.** The act or fact of sliding; an instance of this; also, the manner in which a thing slides.

**1596** FITZ-GEFFREY *Sir F. Drake* (1881) 81 As some travel-tired passenger.. Sits downe to view the sight-reviving slide, The wanton bubling-waters gentle glide. **1609** DEKKER *Gull's Horn Bk.* Wks. (Grosart) II. 231 You may publish your suit.. with the slide of your cloake from the one shoulder. **1726** SHELVOCKE *Voy. round World* 58 My third Lieutenant broke his leg by a slide on the deck. **1860** TYNDALL *Glac.* I. xi. 78 The edge of the precipice, to which less than a quarter of a minute's slide would carry us. **1878** B. TAYLOR *Pr. Deukalion* III. i, The bubble and slide of the rill Is heard.

**b.** *fig.* in various applications.

**1570** *Satir. Poems Reform.* xvi. 23 Sen he hes maid sa mony slydis Trow ȝe he can be trew? **1607–12** BACON *Ess.*, *Nobility* (Arb.) 196 Kinges, that have able Men of theire Nobilitye, shall finde ease in ymploying them, and a better slyde in theire busines. **1625** *Ibid.*, *Fortune* 381 Like Homers Verses, that haue a Slide, and Easinesse, more then the Verses of other Poets. **1833** T. HOOK *Parson's Dau.* III. vii, Thence, by a graceful slide down the family-tree, her ladyship traced out the consanguinity.

**c.** *Music.* A kind of grace (see quots.); also = PORTAMENTO.

**1818** BUSBY *Gram. Mus.* 152 The *Slide*, a grace in very frequent use. It generally consists of two notes gradually ascending or descending to the note it is intended to ornament; and to which it is attached by a curve. **1881** *Grove's Dict. Music* III. 534 *Slide*,.. an ornament frequently met with in both vocal and instrumental music, although its English name has fallen into disuse. It consists of a rapid diatonic progression of three notes, either ascending or descending, of which the principal note, or note to be ornamented, is the third, and the other two are grace-notes. **1908** *Grove's Dict. Mus.* (ed. 2) IV. 482/1 To violinists the 'slide' is one of the principal vehicles of expression, at the same time a means of passing from one note to another at a distance. **1913** F. THISTLETON *Mod. Violin Technique* xv. 74 The slide is one of the principal mediums of expression on the violin. **1938** L. TERTIS *Beauty of Tone in String Playing* 14 The celerity with which this is done is the secret of discreet natural portamento... There must be no drawling, languishing, or lingering in the action of the slide.

**d.** *fig.* A rapid decline; a downturn. Also in phr. *on the slide.*

**1884** GLADSTONE in *Spectator* 16 Feb. 220/1 When I saw his mind shaken and, so to speak, on the slide. **1931** *Economist* 14 Mar. 569/2 Unsatisfactory traffics, and the passing of the B.A. Great Western dividend, accentuated the 'slide' of prices. **1969** N. COHN *Pop from Beginning* ix. 86 He began to flag. By early 1964, he was definitely on the slide. **1981** *Times* 5 May 18/1 A 20 per cent slide in profits at the half-way stage.

**e.** *Baseball.* A plunging or sliding approach made to a base along the ground.

**1886** H. CHADWICK *Art of Batting* 68 A slide in time saves an out. **1934** *Baseball Mag.* Apr. 497/2 Chapman has a natural talent as a base stealer... He knows how.. to make a perfect slide. **1944** E. ALLEN *Major League Baseball* xv. 204 There are four types of slides: the hook slide, the bent leg slide, the feet first slide and the head first slide. **1972** J. MOSEDALE *Football* iii. 32 He stretched it into a triple with a daring slide [contextually in Baseball].

**f.** *Surfing.* A ride across the face of a wave (see quot. 1963); a wave suitable for this.

**1935** D. KAHANAMOKU in T. Blake *Hawaiian Surfboard* i. 32 (*caption*) A fine illustration of the slide. The wave is coming on while the rider is sliding left across the face of the swell. **1946** J. A. BALL *Scrapbk. of Surfriding* 57 (*caption*) Tom Blake streaking along on a long belly slide. **1963** J. POLLARD *Austral. Surfrider* ii. 20/1 A 'slide' can be either 'left' or 'right', angling down the wave to one side or the other. **1968** *Surfer Mag.* Jan. 47/3 Ten-foot waves that peel off in good right and left slides.

**g.** *Curling.* A delivery in which a curler slides some distance forward in launching his stone.

**1950** K. WATSON *Curling* i. 42 By delivering the stone at the end of a long slide, a player could be more accurate in delivery. **1962, 1969** [see *long slide* s.v. LONG *a.*[1] A. 18].

**h.** *Jazz.* = GLISSANDO.

**1959** 'F. NEWTON' *Jazz Scene* 289 Technical terms either duplicate existing, but unfamiliar, ones—e.g. *slide, smear,* for glissando..or they describe things for which no proper academic equivalent exists. **1973** *Black World* Nov. 48/1 Performance practices require a 'slur' and/or 'slide' when moving from tone to tone.

**2. a.** An earth-slip, a landslip, an avalanche; a place on a hill-side, etc., where this has happened.

**1664** *Maldon Borough Deeds* (Bundle 151 fol. 1), [To] amend and restore all such slides, decayes, or breaches, of and in the calcway. **1829** SCOTT *Anne of G.* ii, He..was led ..to believe that this rock marked the farthest extent of the slip or slide of earth. **1860** O. W. HOLMES *Elsie V.* xxxi, It proved to be not so much a slide as the breaking off and falling of a vast line of cliff. **1900** *Jrnl. Sch. Geog.* (U.S.) Apr. 157 Immediately following this tremendous slide came a crowd of people rushing in every direction.

**b.** A sliding mass or stretch *of* water.

**1869** BLACKMORE *Lorna D.* vii, I stood at the foot of a long pale slide of water.

**3.** *Mining.* **a.** A fracture in a lode resulting in the dislocation or displacement of a portion of it; a vein of clay, etc., marking such dislocation.

**1778** W. PRYCE *Min. Cornub.* 82 That fracture which we call a slide or heave. *Ibid.* 83 The slide or heave of the Lode manifests the greater subsidence of the Strata. **1839** URE *Dict. Arts* 316 Clay veins; of which there are two sets, the more ancient, called *Cross-Fluckans*; and the more modern, called *Slides.* **1865** J. T. F. TURNER *Slate Quarries* 23 Walls of hardah..are dreaded, because they are generally accompanied by slides, which dip precipitously from east to west. **1890** *Melbourne Argus* 16 June 6/1 Every main reef is cut by a slide dipping from west to east.

**b.** Matter dislodged by an earth-slip.

**1841** WHITTIER *To a Friend* iv, Loose rock and frozen slide Hung on the mountain-side. **1874** RAYMOND *Statist. Mines & Mining* 296 The shaft passes 45 feet through 'slide', and then 155 feet on the vein.

**c.** *Geol.* A fault formed at and associated with a fold.

**1910** E. B. BAILEY in *Q. Jrnl. Geol. Soc.* LXVI. 593 'Fold-fault' itself is too cumbrous for constant repetition, and accordingly 'slide' has been introduced to take its place. **1934** —— in *Ibid.* XC. 467 'Fold-fault' is an old word for a fault formed in close causal connexion with folding... I employed the word 'slip' in this sense, but on Lapworth's suggestion exchanged it for 'slide'. Now that reversed and unreversed limbs are often distinguishable through the help of current-bedding, the word 'slide' is less necessary, since it can often conveniently be replaced by 'thrust' or 'lag'. The following are helpful though incomplete definitions:—A thrust is a slide replacing an inverted limb, actual or ideal. A lag is a slide replacing a normal limb. **1969** BENNISON & WRIGHT *Geol. Hist. Brit. Isles* iii. 55 An important structural break, the Iltay Boundary Slide, separates two contrasted sedimentary successions both in Scotland and northern Ireland.

**4. a.** A kind of sledge. (Cf. SLID *sb.*)

**1685-90** COAD *Wonderful Provid.* (1849) 10 Reply was made that I was not able to go or ride; at which he ordered them to bring me on a slide. **1764** *Museum Rust.* II. 362 We frequently procure a slide, to be drawn by one horse, made of two poles about ten feet long. **1861** SMILES *Lives Engineers* I. 193 The slide or sledge is seen in the fields. **1896** *Pilgrim Missionary* (Boston) Sept. 10, I..borrowed a mule and a slide, and hauled to the house some planks and pickets.

**b.** A runner on which a gun is mounted.

**1830** MARRYAT *King's Own* xxx, Their guns..were fixed on slides,..to enable them to be fired over the bows. **1833** —— *P. Simple* (1863) 248 They all carried guns mounted upon slides, which ran fore and aft between the men.

**II. 5.** A sliding part of some mechanism; a device which slides or may be slid; *N.Z.*, a serving hatch (see j); *Mus.*, on wind instruments; also a slide guitar or the playing of it (see k).

In various technical uses: cf. SLIDER *sb.* 4. Ash (1775) gives the general definition, 'a part of an instrument or machine to be pulled in and out'. A few out of the many special applications are here illustrated.

**a.** *c* **1608** *Sarum Churchw. Acc.* (Swayne, 1896) 158 For the fifth bell..a Rope Slide and other Implementes.

**b.** *c* **1800** BUSBY *Dict. Mus.* s.v. *Trumpet*, By the aid of a newly invented *slide* many other notes which the common trumpet cannot sound are now produced. **1872** H. C. BANISTER *Text-bk. Music* (1899) 228 The Trombone is a brass instrument with slides shortening or lengthening its tube.

**c.** **1805** R. W. DICKSON *Pract. Agric.* I. 46 Air should likewise be pretty freely admitted..by means of slides or other contrivances. **1855** LARDNER *Mus. Sci. & Art* V. 25 The methods of opening and closing the passages by means of lids slipping over them called slides. **1857** DICKENS *Dorrit* I. xxii, These instructions Mr. Chivery..called through a little slide in the outer door.

**d.** **1852** SEIDEL *Organ* 57 The slides are ledges of good dry oak, about two or two and a half inches wide, and one third of an inch thick.

**e.** **1858** SIMMONDS *Dict. Trade, Slide*,..part of a forcing-pump.

**f.** **1869** RANKINE *Machine & Hard-tools* Pl. H 10, This lathe has..a self-acting slide..for boring out..short lengths. **1893** SPON *Mechanic's Own Book* (ed. 4) 536, *a* is a slide which fits the lathe-bed very accurately, but will yet slide freely upon it.

**g.** **1877** *Encycl. Brit.* VI. 490 The 'slide', or lock, receding from the spindles during the twisting of the threads, and returning to the spindle again during the winding on of the yarn.

**h.** **1879** THOMSON & TAIT *Nat. Phil.* I. I. 194 Attached to the framework let there be, close to the circumference of each cylinder, a slide or guide-rod to guide a moveable point, moved by the hand of an operator.

**i.** **1884** BRITTEN *Watch & Clockm.* 92 In full plate lever watches the slide is jewelled and supports the bottom pivot of the balance staff.

**j.** **1949** J. R. COLE *It was so Late* 92, I was standing by the slide in the lounge one night. **1955** *Numbers* I. IV. 14 Charlie ordered for them both and Kate dragged back to the slide.

**k.** **1968** *Down Beat* 31 Oct. 18/1 He had quite a lot of advantages on his guitar for that time. Played slide a lot. **1976** A. BAINES *Brass Instruments* iv. 94 (*heading*) Renaissance slides. **1976** *Rolling Stone* 22 Apr. 16/5 After some initially slavish imitations of Muddy and Elmore, slide became better integrated into rock. **1977** J. WAINWRIGHT *Do Nothin' till you hear from Me* viii. 129 Walter Green—trombonist... As a slide-player he is average.

**6.** A kind of tongueless buckle or ring used as a fastener, clasp, or brooch; a small perforated object sliding on a cord, etc. Now *spec.* a clasp for fastening in the hair.

**1779** *Ann. Reg.* 203 A gold slide, set with diamonds. **1824** JANE TAYLOR *Contrib. of Q.Q.* (1828) II. 149 If a slide broke in her frock,..instead of re-placing..she would exclaim—'there's that tiresome slide gone'. **1897** *Army & Navy Stores List* 271 Tortoiseshell slides for the hair, 1/0. **1932** L. GOLDING *Magnolia Street* III. ix. 593 That slide which has just slid out of her hair on to the parquet floor. **1952** M. LASKI *Village* ii. 33 Her soft brown hair caught back with a slide. **1981** J. B. HILTON *Playground of Death* ii. 10 There wasn't a grip, clip or slide on the market that would keep my mam's hair up.

**7. a.** A slip of glass or other material on which an object is mounted or placed to facilitate its examination by a microscope.

**1837** GORING & PRITCHARD *Microgr.* 14 That part of the old compound microscopes which used to carry the slide of object-glasses. **1895** G. E. DAVIS *Pract. Micros.* (ed. 3) 375 Objects are generally mounted upon glass slides, or 'slips', as they are sometimes called.

**b.** A picture prepared for use in a magic lantern or stereoscope (now chiefly *Hist.*); a photographic transparency for use in a slide projector.

**1819** M. EDGEWORTH *Let.* 17 Apr. (1971) 199 You know him and his magic lantern of good things. Some new figures on the slides. **1846** DICKENS *Cricket on Hearth* i, He had even lost money..by getting up goblin slides for magic lanterns. **1858** *Edinb. Rev.* July 207 His history..passes before us like a series of slides in a magic lantern. **1890** ATKINSON *Ganot's Physics* 598 A stereoscope..which will give us, with the ordinary stereoscopic slides, a reversed picture. **1940** P. E. BOUCHER *Fundamentals of Photogr.* (1941) xiii. 200 Valuable slides..which are to be subjected to considerable use should be mounted in glass. **1978** M. J. LANGFORD *Step by Step Guide to Photogr.* 176 Before presentation, your slides must be inserted in holders ready for projection.

**c.** *Photogr.* A flat case or receptacle within which plates are placed for the purpose of being inserted in a camera. Freq. ***dark slide.***

**1856** *Orr's Circ. Sci., Pract. Chem.* 184 It is best to let the water dry off previously to the plate being placed in the slide. **1876** ABNEY *Instruct. Photogr.* 166 The sensitized plate in the dark slide. **1878** —— *Treat. Photogr.* 216 The slide is divided into two parts, hinged so as to fold one against the other.

**8.** *Rowing.* A sliding seat.

**1875** STONEHENGE *Brit. Rur. Sports* (ed. 12) 643/1 A well-known amateur who..had never used the slide. **1894** LEHMANN in *Daily News* 6 Feb. 3/5 In 1871 a crew of professionals used a seat that slid on the thwarts, and beat a crew that was generally held to be superior, and from that moment slides, as we now know them, came into general use.

**III. 9.** A smooth surface, esp. of ice, for sliding on, or formed by being slid on; a slippery place.

**1687** MIÉGE *Gt. Fr. Dict.* II, *Slide*, a frozen place slid upon. **1837** DICKENS *Pickw.* xxix, Mr. Pickwick..took another run and went slowly and gravely down the slide. **1856** THACKERAY *Lett.* Wks. 1901 X. p. xxvii, A poor old gentleman slipped down and broke his thigh on a slide. **1899** B. CAPES *Lady of Darkness* xi. 91 A perfect little slide of grease that had formed on the boards below.

**10. a.** An inclined plane for the transit of heavy goods, esp. timber. Chiefly *Amer.*

**1832** BABBAGE *Econ. Manuf.* xxviii. (ed. 3) 282 The mines of Bolanos..are supplied with timber from the adjacent mountains by a slide similar to that of Alpnach. **1878** *Lumberman's Gaz.* 16 Mar., The logs are then placed in the trough of the slide and very easily drawn by horses to their destination. **1886** B. HARTE *Snowbound* 127 A slide was a rude incline for the transit of heavy goods that could not be carried down a trail.

**b.** *Amer.* A sloping channel constructed to facilitate the passage of logs down stream; a chute.

**1858** in SIMMONDS *Dict. Trade.* **1880** *Lumberman's Gaz.* 7 Jan. 28 The government constructs 'slides' for the passage of timber around shoals or rapids where there are no canals. **1884** S. E. DAWSON *Hdbk. Canada* 20 The streams for floating timber to market have been opened up by slides, booms, and dams.

**c.** The bottom of a gold-washing cradle.

**1855** W. HOWITT *Land, Labour & Gold* I. 206 We take the fine gravel out of the slide of the cradle. **1864** J. ROGERS *New Rush* II. 27 The heavier gold remaining on the slide.

**d.** A structure with a smooth sloping surface used as a toy or piece of playground equipment down which children slide, or as an entertainment at a fairground. Cf. CHUTE *sb.*[1] 3 c.

**1890** *Century Mag. Advertising Suppl.* Dec. 70 Wood's parlor toboggan slide. The most satisfactory toy yet invented for children. **1924** *Ladies' Home Jrnl.* Nov. 126/1 This kiddies' slide is more fun than the old cellar door! **1954** R. DAHL *Someone like You* 210 All week the swings and the see-saws and the high slide with steps going up to it stood deserted. **1975** I. STARSMORE *English Fairs* iv. 92 (*caption*) The Portable Slide. Height 29 ft... The three 100 ft. lanes guide 'passengers' down the slide. **1979** 'J. LE CARRÉ' *Smiley's People* (1980) xxi. 257 There was a children's slide in the garden.

**11. a.** A device of the nature of a bed, rail, groove, etc., on or in which a thing may slide.

**1846** HOLTZAPFFEL *Turning* II. 897 The work to be continually moved to and fro upon the slide or railway, a distance equal to its own length. **1851** GREENWELL *Coal-trade Terms, Northumb. & Durh.* 48 *Slides*, upright rails, of wood or metal, fixed in a shaft, for the purpose of steadying the cages, which have corresponding grooves attached to them. **1869** RANKINE *Machine & Hand-tools* Pl. F 11, The hammer-head is of cast iron, and works in slides, which are firmly rivetted into the frames.

**b.** *U.S. slang.* (See quot. 1932.)

**1932** *Even. Sun* (Baltimore) 9 Dec. 31/5 *Slide*, a trouser's [*sic*] pocket. **1967** 'I. SLIM' *Pimp: Story of my Life* (1969) iii. 68 How would you like a half a 'G' in your 'slide'?

**12.** The track of an otter.

**1842** J. E. DEKAY *Zool. N.Y.* I. 40 The steel trap is placed ..at the bottom of one of their slides. **1894** LYDEKKER *Roy. Nat. Hist.* II. 95 These otters are usually caught in steel traps, which are set beneath the water where one of the 'slides' or tracks of the animals leads to the margin.

**slide**, obs. variant of SLID *a.*

**slide** (slaɪd), *v.* Pa. t. slid. Pa. pple. slid (slided, slidden). Forms: (see below). [OE. *slídan*, = NFris. *slîde* (*slîre*), *sklid*, older LG. *slîden* (*slijden*), MHG. *slîten*: for related forms see SLIDDER *v.* and SLEAD *sb.*]

**A.** Inflexional forms.

In OE. the conjugation is more fully represented in the compound *áslidan* (*-slád, -slidon, -sliden*). In early ME. the short pret. stem appears in the subj. *slĭde* in the *S. Eng. Leg.* I. 212/427.

**1. a.** *Inf.* (and *Pres.*, etc.) 1 slídan, 3 sliden, 4 slyden, 5 slidyn; 3- slide (4 slid), 4-7 slyd(e, 5-6 sclyde.

*a* **950** *Gunthlac* v. (1909) 123 Of þære lyfte slidan. *a* **1225** *Ancr. R.* 252 ȝif eni uoð on uorte sliden. *c* **1250** *Owl & Night.* 1390 Flesches lustes hi makeþ slide. *c* **1330** R. BRUNNE *Chron. Wace* (Rolls) 8150 Þ at makes þy werk slyden o slep. **13..** *Cursor M.* 894 Þou sal slid apon þi brest. *c* **1400** *Destr. Troy* 789 He shulde slyde forth sleghly. **1435** MISYN *Fire of Love* 7 Sclyde doune & comforth me. **1538** BALE *Brefe Comedy* in *Harl. Misc.* (Malh.) I. 206 Slouthfulnesse shall slyde. **1559** W. CUNNINGHAM *Cosmogr. Glasse* 94 Let not this slide out of your memory. **1617** SIR W. MURE *Misc.* xxi. 99 Heir silver brooks doe slyd.

**b.** *3rd sing. Pres. Ind.* (1 -slit), 3-4 slit, slyt, 5 slitte.

*a* **1225** *Ancr. R.* 252 He slit & falleð sone. *a* **1310** in Wright *Lyric P.* xxxix. 110 Hit is muche wonder that he nadoun slyt. *c* **1386** CHAUCER *Can. Yeom. Prol.* 129 It slit awey so faste.

**2.** *Pa. t.* α. (1 -slád); *north.* and *Sc.* 4-5 slad, 5, 8- slade; 4-5 slayd (5 slayde), 4- slaid, 9 slaed, etc.

**13..** *Cursor M.* 23222 (Edinb.), þoh a firin fel..þar into slad. **1375** BARBOUR *Bruce* III. 701 The schippys our the wawys slayd. *c* **1450** *St. Cuthbert* (Surtees) 5456 þa waters sone away slade. **1533** BELLENDEN *Livy* (S.T.S.) I. 120 Ane serpent slaid..out of ane pillare. **1591** JAS. I *Poet. Exerc., Chorus Venetvs*, Our enemies feet they slaid. **1721** RAMSAY *Lucky Spence* xiv, I slade away wi' little din. **1785** BURNS *Death & Dr. Hornbook* xxvi, The wife slade cannie to her bed.

β. 4-5 slood (slod), 4-7 slode; 9 *dial.* slod.

**13..** *Gaw. & Gr. Knt.* 1182 In slomeryng he slode. **1387** TREVISA *Higden* (Rolls) VII. 237 He slood wiþ his oon foot. **1470-85** MALORY *Arthur* IX. xviii. 365 His swerd slode adoune. **1523** LD. BERNERS *Froiss.* I. cclxx. 403 He slode and fell downe. **1698** FRYER *Acc. E. India & P.* 257 We slode step by step.

γ. 5-6 slydde, 6-7 slidde, 6- slid.

*c* **1450** *Myrr. our Ladye* 198 All thynges that slydde vnto them. **1590** SPENSER *F.Q.* III. iv. 32 Whiles..they softly slid. **1598** JONSON *Ev. Man in Hum.* IV. iv, I slidde downe..into the streete. **1676-7** MARVELL *Corr.* cclxxxiii. Wks. (Grosart) II. 515 This slid over.

δ. 6 slyded, 5- slided.

*c* **1489** CAXTON *Sonnes of Aymon* xiv. 345 The swerde slided vpon the helme. *c* **1580** J. HOOKER *Life Sir P. Carew* in *Archæol.* XXVIII. 121 His foote slyded or slipped. **1681** RYCAUT tr. *Gracian's Critick* 187 Others slided along with a good Air. *a* **1774** GOLDSM. *Surv. Exp. Philos.* (1776) I. 269 A number of parts..which slided. **1826** HOOD *Last Man* 20 Then down the rope..I slided.

**3.** *Pa. pple.* α. 3 islide, 4 islyde, 5 (y)slide.

*c* **1250** *Owl & Night.* 686 Hit nis of horte islide. **13..** in *E.E.P.* (1862) 132 Hou sone þat hit is forþ islyde. *a* **1420** BIBLE *Prov.* xxiv. 10 Thou that hast slide [*v.r.* yslide].

β. (1 -sliden), 4-5, 7 sliden (4 -un, 5 -on), 4-5 slyden (5 -yn); 4 *Sc.* sclyddyn, 5 *Sc.* slyddin, 6 slydden, 6- slidden (9 *dial.* sledden).

**1375** BARBOUR *Bruce* XVII. 126 Sum ar slyddin our the wall. **1382** WYCLIF *Lam.* iii. 53 Slyden is in to a grene my lyf. **1392** in Fraser *The Lennox* (1874) II. 48 Throw errour sclyddyn. *c* **1450** tr. *De Imitatione* III. lx, Sliden & viciat by þe first man. **1579** W. WILKINSON *Confut. Fam. Love* 9 The truth whence ye haue slydden. **1622** MALYNES *Anc. Law-Merch.* 14 Now changed and slidden backe. *a* **1697** AUBREY *Surrey* IV. 148 A great Part..is slidden down into the Grounds below. **1881** E. COXON *Basil Plant* I. 64 So easily had he slidden back into his old habits.

γ. 6 slyded, -yd, 7- slided.

**1535** COVERDALE *2 Sam.* xxii. 37 Myne ankles haue not slyded. **1644** DIGBY *Nat. Bodies* xxxv. §7. 301 Other spirits which..would haue slided downe more leisurely. **1776** SEMPLE *Building in Water* 36 This Block must be slided over to *c.* **1824** LANDOR *Imag. Conv., Chesterf. & Chatham*, We have slided into Cicero's language.

δ. 7- slid.

*a* **1700** EVELYN *Diary* (Chandos Classics) 188 He had slid and fall'n. *a* **1751** BOLINGBROKE *Ess.* I. vii. Wks. 1754 III. 489 They have not only slid imperceptibly. **1860** TYNDALL *Glac.* I. xiv. 95 Before I had slid a dozen yards.

B. Signification.

I. *intr.* **1. a.** To pass from one place or point to another with a smooth and continuous movement, *esp.* through the air or water or along a surface.

*a* **950** *Guthlac* v. (1909) 123 Ða comon semninga twegen deoflu to him of þære lyfte slidan. **1375** BARBOUR *Bruce* III. 701 The schippys our the wawys slayd. **1382** WYCLIF *2 Sam.* xxii. 11 He..slood vpon the pennys of the wynd. *c* **1400** *Destr. Troy* 12690 [þai] Letyn sailes doune slide sleghli & faire. *a* **1547** SURREY *Æneid* II. 302 Thus slided through our toun The subtil tree. *a* **1599** SPENSER *F.Q.* VII. vii. 43 Two fishes..Which through the flood before did softly slyde And swim away. **1629** QUARLES *Arg. & Parthenia* III. 2 April's gentle showers are slidden downe, To close the wind-chapt earth. **1667** MILTON *P.L.* VIII. 302 He took me rais'd,..over Fields and Waters, as in Aire Smooth sliding without step. **1712** ADDISON *Spectator* No. 369 ¶9 The Gods..slide o'er the Surface of the Earth by an uniform Swimming of the whole Body. **1789** J. WILLIAMS *Min. Kingd.* I. 214 The vestige of the coal is sure to slide down the slope of the ground. **1824** LANDOR *Imag. Conv., Gen. Kleber & French Officers* Wks. 1853 I. 43/1 The officer slided with extended arms from his resting-place. **1843** HOLTZAPFFEL *Turning* I. 401 The metal could be made to slide upon itself without puckering. **1871** TYNDALL *Fragm. Sci.* (1879) I. xii. 364 Whitish-green spots..over which the pencil usually slid as if the spots were greasy.

**b.** To move in this manner while standing more or less erect upon a surface, *esp.* that of ice.

Formerly used of skating, now distinguished from it.

*c* **1340** *Nominale* (Skeat) 164 M[an] sliduth vp-on hyse. **1530** PALSGR. 721/1, I have sene one in Hollande slyde as faste upon the yse as a bote dothe in the water whan it is rowed. **1585** T. WASHINGTON tr. *Nicholay's Voy.* II. xxi. 58 b, [He] mounteth vpon your backe, and so with his feet slydeth vp and downe vpon you. **1617** MORYSON *Itin.* III. 34 The Virgins in Holland,..hand in hand with young men, slide upon the yce farre from their Fathers house. **1681** DRYDEN *Span. Friar* III. ii, As Boys [fear] to venture on the unknown Ice, That crackles underneath 'em while they slide. **1715** DESAGULIERS *Fires Impr.* 38 Those that Slide, Scate, or use any other violent Exercise in frosty Weather. **1776** JOHNSON in *Boswell* (Oxf. ed.) I. 41, I answered I had been sliding in Christ-Church meadow. **1855** MACAULAY *Hist. Eng.* xvii. IV. 4 Many thousands came sliding or skating along the frozen canals. **1883** *Harper's Mag.* Dec. 93/1 'Do you slide?' 'I never have slidden much.'

**c.** To slip *off* something.

**1623** BINGHAM *Xenophon* 68 The Souldiers..vpon whom the Snow fell, and slid not off, became miserably distressed. **1756** C. LUCAS *Ess. Waters* III. 300 A..white precipitate subsides to the bottom, and slides off the glass.

**d.** *Baseball.* To perform a slide (sense 1 e).

**1891** *Harper's Weekly* 23 May 391/4 His base running, in spite of his care about sliding, is of the old-time quality that has already won two championships for Yale. **1904** J. J. McGRAW *Science of Baseball* 67 He shouldn't slide unless his pants are properly padded. **1932** *Baseball Mag.* Oct. 501/2, George Watkins, quick to grasp Dazzy's slight slip, turned on a full burst of speed and slid across home plate with the only run of the game. **1977** *Rolling Stone* 30 June 76/2 Do you always think about baseball players when you're making love?.. I couldn't figure out why you kept yelling, 'Slide!'

**e.** *Surfing.* To ride across the face of a wave.

**1931** *Country Life in Amer.* Jan. 57 If the wave proves exceptionally steep, keep to the stern of the board and then, after you 'catch' the wave, head the board at an angle to it. This will enable you to 'slide' with the wave. **1959** J. BLOOMFIELD *Know-How in Surf* iii. 27 The gradually breaking crest enables the body to slide down its front at an angle of approximately 45 degrees.

**f.** *Curling.* To move forwards while delivering the stone.

**1936** F. B. TALBOT *Mr Besom starts Curling* xiii. 34 Many good players slide out of the hack *as* they deliver the stone. **1950** K. WATSON *Curling* i. 1 Whether you slide or do not slide, that follow-through is essentially the smooth delivery of the stone.

**2.** Of streams, etc.: To glide, flow. Now *rare.*

**1390** GOWER *Conf.* II. 266 A wounde upon his side Sche made, that therout mai slyde The blod withinne. *a* **1425** *Cursor M.* 11984 (Trin.), Ihesu soone in þat tide lett þe watir rynne & slide. **1513** DOUGLAS *Æneid* v. xiii. 71 The flude Tibir throw Lawrent feildis slidis. *c* **1586** C'TESS PEMBROKE *Ps.* XLVI. ii, A river streaming joy, With purling murmur safelie slides. **1633** P. FLETCHER *Pisc. Eclogs* I. v, Where Thames and Isis heire By lowly Æton slides. **1668** CULPEPPER & COLE *Barthol. Anat.* I. xiii. 32 To suck out the wheyish Blood which slides along that way. **1738** *Common Sense* II. 176 It has neither rushed down the Rock, nor slided thro' the Plain. **1746** W. MASON *On the Cam* Poems 1830 II. II. 49 Without a rill the even tide Slided silently away. **1819** WIFFEN *Aonian Hours* 90 Ever from his lid a tear would slide. **1833** TENNYSON *Eleanore* 109 As waves that up a quiet cove Rolling slide.

**3.** Of reptiles, etc.: To glide, crawl. Now *rare.*

*a* **1300** *Cursor M.* 894 þou worm,..þou sal slid apon þi brest. *c* **1375** *Sc. Leg. Saints* xxxix. (*Cosmo & D.*) 261 As þe serpent had entre in at his mouth,..one þe sammyne wise it slad oute. *a* **1400** in Horstm. *Altengl. Leg.* (1878) 222 Neddre,..vppe þi breste þou schalt slyden. **1530** PALSGR. 721/1 It is a wondrouse thyng to se an adder or a snake slyde so faste as they do and have no fete. **1561** T. NORTON *Calvin's Inst.* I. xiii. 44 These slippery snakes doe slide away. **1607** TOPSELL *Serpents* (1658) 601 He espyed the Snake to slide up into the bed-straw. **1687** A. LOVELL tr. *Thevenot's Trav.* II. 39 These thieves slide cunningly along upon their bellies like Snakes. **1856** [see SLIDING *ppl. a.* 3].

**4. a.** To move, go, proceed unperceived, quietly, or stealthily; to steal, creep, slink, or slip *away*, *into* or *out of* a place, etc.

**1382** WYCLIF *1 Kings* xx. 39 Keep this man; the which if were slyden aweye, thi lijf shal be for the lijf of hym. *a* **1400-50** *Alexander* 4456 Quen ȝe ere slide hyne. *c* **1470** HENRY *Wallace* VIII. 1333 Slely he slayd throuch strenthis off Scotland. **1530** PALSGR. 721/2 Who wolde ever have thought it, that he shulde have slydden out at this narow hole. **1590** SPENSER *F.Q.* I. i. 54 So slyding softly forth, she turnd as to her ease. **1602** MARSTON *Ant. & Mel.* III. Wks. 1856 I. 33 Then, noble spirit, slide, in strange disguise, Unto some gratious Prince. **1697** DRYDEN *Virg. Georg.* IV. 594 The slipp'ry God will..attempt to slide away. **1742** RICHARDSON *Pamela* III. 365 You observe how he slid away ..as soon as I open'd my Door. **1760-72** H. BROOKE *Fool of Qual.* (1809) I. 126 Slouching my hat, I slid out of doors. **1829** LYTTON *Devereux* II. iii, Steele slid into a seat near my own. **1889** D. C. MURRAY *Dang. Catspaw* 7 An officer of the court slid to the door of the judge's apartments.

*fig.* *c* **1375** *Sc. Leg. Saints* xxxviii. (*Adrian*) 212 Hou þu had grace criste for to kene,..and þu fra hym þis [= thus] slad! **1594** KYD *Cornelia* III. i, He slides More swiftly from mee then the Ocean glydes.

**b.** *colloq.* To make off. Orig. *U.S.*

**1859** BARTLETT *Dict. Amer.* 415 *To slide*, to go, be gone, be off. **1873** B. HARTE *Fiddletown*, etc. 85 She led William where he was covered by seventeen Modocs, and—slid! **1904** [see BUSY *sb.*[2]]. **1932** E. WALLACE *When Gangs came to London* xxvii. 269 There's only one word that any sensible man can read in this situation, and that word is—slide!

**II. 5. a.** To pass away, pass by, so as to disappear, be forgotten or neglected, etc. Now *rare.*

*c* **1250** *Owl & Night.* 686 For Alured seyde of olde quide & yet hit nis of horte islide. **13..** in *E.E.P.* (1862) 132 Knowe þis worldly honoure Hou sone þat hit is forþ islyde. *c* **1374** CHAUCER *Troylus* v. 769 Bothe Troylus and Troye toun Shal knotteles thorugh out here herte slyde. *c* **1400** *Destr. Troy* 4032 Frostes were faren,..The slippond slete slidon of the ground. **1503** S. HAWES *Examp. Virt.* XIV. ccxcviii, That his redolent buddes shall not slyde But euer encrease. **1577** HANMER *Anc. Eccl. Hist.* (1663) 60 Thus this slander slided away with the time. **1607** TOPSELL *Four-f. Beasts* (1658) 391 Presently the black hairs will fall and slide away, and in some short time there will come white. **1824** LAMB *Elia* II, *Capt. Jackson*, Alack, how good men, and the good turns they do us, slide out of memory.

**b.** With *let* (or *allow*). In later use freq., to let (something) take its own course.

*c* **1386** CHAUCER *Clerk's T.* 26 In his lust present was al his thought,..Wel ny alle othere cures leet he slyde. *a* **1400** *Minor Poems from Vernon MS.* I. 492 [Let him] put his wylle in gode þewes, And alle wikked let slyde. *c* **1440** CAPGR. *Life St. Kath.* I. 935 ȝe wyl not lete þis mater slyde, parde. *a* **1586** SIDNEY *Arcadia* II. (1590) 107 With a calm carelessness, letting each thing slide. **1596** SHAKS. *Tam. Shr.* Ind. i. 6 Therefore..let the world slide. **1611** COTGR. s.v. *Chargé*, To take no thought, passe the time merrily, let the world slide. *a* **1859** in Bartlett *Dict. Amer.* (ed. 2) 241 If California was going to cost the Union so much, it would be better to let California slide. **1885** *Manch. Exam.* 3 June 5/1 The question at issue was not allowed to slide. **1897** *Field* 6 Feb. 166/1 The supine way we English have of letting things slide.

**c.** Of time: To pass, slip *away*, go *by*, imperceptibly or without being profitably employed.

*c* **1374** CHAUCER *Troylus* v. 351 So sholdestow endure, and laten slyde The tyme. **1390** GOWER *Conf.* II. 3 Thus have I lete time slyde For Slowthe. **1592** J. DAVIES *Immort. Soul* xxx. x, Since our Life so fast away doth slide. *c* **1600** MONTGOMERIE *Cherrie & Slae* 824 The season With slowthing slyds away. **1620** T. GRANGER *Div. Logike* 147 Time slides away like the running streame. **1716-8** LADY M. W. MONTAGU *Lett.* I. xii. 44, I need not..tell you how agreeably time slides away with me. **1734** FIELDING *Old Man taught Wisdom* Wks. 1784 III. 119 How happily must my old age slide away. **1860** HAWTHORNE *Marble Faun* (1879) II. vii. 76 Let the warm day slide by. **1897** WATTS-DUNTON *Aylwin* I. iv, In this manner about six weeks slid away.

**6.** †**a.** To fall *asleep*, etc. *Obs.*

*c* **1330** R. BRUNNE *Chron. Wace* (Rolls) 8150 By-neþe þe erþe..Is a water rennyng dep, þat makes þy werk slyden o slep. **13..** *E.E. Allit. P.* A. 59, I slode vpon a slepyng slaȝte. *c* **1400** *Destr. Troy* Prol. 6 Off aunters [that] ben olde..And slydyn vppon slepe by slomeryng of Age. *c* **1470** HENRY *Wallace* VII. 68 Apon a sleip he slaid full sodandly. **1513** DOUGLAS *Æneid* VII. Prol. 111 On slummyr I slaid full sad.

**b.** To pass easily or gradually *into* some condition, practice, etc. †Also in early use with *to.*

In some contexts there is connexion with sense 9.

**1398** TREVISA *Barth. De P.R.* II. iv. (1495) 31 Aungels neuer slyde to vice nother to synne. *c* **1450** tr. *De Imitatione* I. xxv. 38 He þat eschuiþ not smale defautes, litel & litel shal slide in to gretter. **1503** HAWES *Examp. Virt.* I. ix, That ye to fraylte shall not slyde. **1579** W. WILKINSON *Confut. Fam. Love* 79 b, When they shall here any of the Familie slide into any of these affirmations. **1754** YOUNG *Centaur* ii. Wks. 1757 IV. 137 Thus, looking out for some shadow of excuse, we naturally slide into groundless doubts. **1766** FORDYCE *Serm. Yng. Wm.* (1767) I. vi. 230 She will.., when her province is enlarged, slide into the duties of it with readiness. **1802** MRS. J. WEST *Infidel Father* II. 128 Even Lord Glanville, while he made his bow, so far slided into equivoque [etc.]. **1847** HELPS *Friends in C.* I. iii. 36 When an honourable man ..slides into some dishonourable action. **1871** CARLYLE in *Mrs. Carlyle's Lett.* I. 144, I had slid into something of correspondence with Lockhart.

**c.** To pass by easy or gradual change or transformation into some other form or character.

*a* **1500** *Sir Cawline* xxii. in Child *Ball.* II. 59/1 The timber these two children bore Soe soone in sunder slode. **1731** POPE *Ep. Burlington* 66 Parts answ'ring parts shall slide into a whole. **1763** J. BROWN *Poet. & Music* vii. 143 The Narrative..did easily slide into dramatic Representation. **1847** HELPS *Friends in C.* I. vi. 96 The great danger..of representative government, is lest it should slide down from representative government to delegate government. **1862** MERIVALE *Rom. Emp.* (1865) VIII. lxiv. 99 Rhetorical amplifications slid swiftly into direct mis-statements. **1876** FREEMAN *Norm. Conq.* V. xxiv. 503 It was an easy step for the patron to slide into the beneficiary.

**7. a.** To move, pass, make way, etc., in an easy or unobtrusive manner.

*c* **1374** CHAUCER *Boeth.* III. pr. xii. (1868) 106 The deuyne substaunce..ne slydeþ nat in to outerest foreine þinges. *c* **1386** —— *Can. Yeom. Prol.* 129 That science is so fer vs beforn, We mowen nat..It ouer-take, it slit awey so faste. *a* **1400** *Minor Poems fr. Vernon MS.* lii. 149 Mony folk slod to helle slider. *c* **1450** *Myrr. Our Ladye* 198 Righte so the holy goste vouched safe to slyde in to the hartes of the prophetes. **1577** *F. de Lisle's Legend.* C ij b, Seeking..to slyde in among the princes, and beare the like port as they. **1591** SYLVESTER *Du Bartas* I. vii. 255 The Fall Of Eden's old Prince; whose luxurious pride Made on his seed his sin for ever slide. **1622** MALYNES *Anc. Law-Merch.* 14 The which places of the Sunne are now changed and slide backe in the Iulian Kalender. **1697** COLLIER *Ess.* (1702) II. 183 A good Conscience..makes him slide into the Grave by a more gentle and insensible Motion. **1748** RICHARDSON *Clarissa* (1811) I. i. 2 So desirous..of sliding through life to the end of it unnoted. **1792** MARY WOLLSTONECR. *Vind. Rights Wom.* 8, I shall try to avoid that flowery diction which has slided from essays into novels. **1820** HAZLITT *Lect. Dram. Lit.* 136 The poet's verse slides into the current of our blood. **1858** HOLMES *Aut. Breakf.-t.* iii. 25 All lecturers..have ruts and grooves in their minds, into which their conversation is perpetually sliding.

**b.** Of speech or music, or with reference to these; *spec.* (see quot. 1875).

**1553** T. WILSON *Rhet.* (1580) 3 Euery Orater should earnestly labour to file his tongue, that his woordes maie slide with ease. **1864** BROWNING *Abt Vogler* xii, I feel for the common chord again Sliding by semitones. **1875** STAINER & BARRETT *Dict. Mus. Terms* s.v., To slide is to pass from one note to another without any cessation of sound, or distinction between the intervals.

**c.** Of the eye or sight: To pass quickly from one object to another.

**1756** BURKE *Subl. & B.* III. xv, The deceitful maze, through which the unsteady eye slides giddily. **1784** COWPER *Task* I. 511 The weary sight..slides off, Fastidious, seeking less familiar scenes.

**III. 8. a.** To slip; to lose one's foothold.

*a* **1225** *Ancr. R.* 252 þer on geð him one in one sliddrie weie, he slit & falleð sone. *c* **1290** *S. Eng. Leg.* I. 212 Heo was so slider, þat man ne miȝte þare-oppe gon bote he slide and felle a-doun. **1375** BARBOUR *Bruce* x. 596 For hapnyt ony to slyde or fall, He suld be soyne to-fruschit all. **1485** CAXTON *Paris & V.* 18 Hys hors slode and thenne geffroy overthrewe to the erthe. **1530** PALSGR. 721/2 He slydde and bothe his fete folded underneth him. *a* **1548** HALL *Chron., Hen. VIII*, 213 To the entent that the horses should not slide on the Pavement. *a* **1700** EVELYN *Diary* (Chandos Classics) 187 Capt. Wray's horse..slid downe a frightfull precipice. **1763-5** CHURCHILL *The Times* Poems 1767 II. 19 So sure, they walk on ice, and never slide. **1819** SHELLEY *Cenci* III. i. 12, I see a woman..motionless, whilst I Slide giddily as the world reels.

*fig.* **1388** WYCLIF *Lam.* iii. 53 My lijf slood in to a lake. **1390** GOWER *Conf.* III. 241 He makth a treigne, Into the which if that he slyde, Him were betre go besyde. **1624** MASSINGER *Renegado* v. vii, Tho' the descent Were steep as hell, I know I cannot slide. **1668** BP. HOPKINS *Serm.* (1685) 45 We are apt to slide off from the smoother part of our lives, as flies from glass. **1795** BURKE *Regic. Peace* iv. Wks. 1907 VI. 399 It is not possible that the downhill should not be slid into.

**b.** Of the foot: To slip. Also *fig.*

**1340** *Ayenb.* 149 Huanne þe on uot slyt, þe oþer him helpþ. **1382** WYCLIF *Deut.* xxxii. 35, Y shal ȝeeld to hem in tyme, that the foot of hem slyde. **1483** CAXTON *Gold. Leg.* 147 b/1 Hys foot slode so that he fyl in to the Ryuer. **1535** COVERDALE *2 Sam.* xxii. 37 Thou hast enlarged my goinge vnder me, and myne ankles haue not slyded. **1590** SPENSER *F.Q.* I. xi. 45 His nigh forwearied feeble feet did slide, And downe he fell. **1831** SCOTT *Cast. Dang.* xx, His foot sliding in the blood of the young victim.

**c.** In general use: To slip. Also with advs. and preps.

**1388** WYCLIF *Deut.* xix. 5 The yrun slidith fro the helue, ..and sleeth his freend. *c* **1400** *Anturs Arth.* 617 The swerde sleppis on slante, and one the mayle slydys. **1470-85** MALORY *Arthur* I. xvi. 58 The swerd slode doune by the hauberk behynde his back. **1610** BARROUGH *Physick* II. xii. (1639) 90 Their temples be slidden downe, their eyes be hollow. **1680** MOXON *Mech. Exerc.* XIII. 228 Its point will not describe a Circle on the greatest Extuberances of the Globe, but will slide off it. **1748** JOHNSON *Vis. Theodore* Wks. 1796 II. 399 The declivities grew more precipitous, and the sand slided from beneath my feet. **1834** W. GODWIN *Lives Necromancers* 340 Just as he thought he had caught him by the hand, the miserable wretch slided from between his fingers. **1859** TENNYSON *Merlin & V.* 737 The snake of gold slid from her hair.

*fig.* **1820** SCOTT *Monast.* xxii, Muttering these last words, which slid from him, as it were unawares.

**9.** *fig.* To lapse morally; to commit some fault; to err or go wrong.

*a* **1000** *Salomon* 378 Ðonne he ȝeong færeð, hafað wilde mod,..slideð ȝeneahhe [etc.]. *c* **1250** *Owl & Night.* 1390 Nis wunder nou þah he abide, Vor fleysses lustes hi makeþ slide. **1382** WYCLIF *Ecclus.* xix. 16 Ther is that slideth in his tunge, but not of inwit. **1436** *Pol. Poems* (Rolls) II. 182 When grace shynethe sone are wee slydynge. *c* **1540** COVERDALE tr. *Calvin's Treat. Sacrament* C ij, The rule, whyche yf we folowe, we shall neyther slyde nor erre. *a* **1591** H. SMITH *Wks.* (1867) II. 266 The strong and just God, that consumed Nineveh slidden back. **1606** CARPENTER *Solomon's Solace* vi.

23 No man so wise but he may by an occasion slide. **1738** Wesley *Ps.* v. 5 Lead me in all thy righteous Ways, Nor suffer me to slide. **1779** Cowper *Olney Hymns* xli, I find myself a learner yet, Unskilful, weak, and apt to slide. **1868** Edmeston in *Sacred Poetry* 143 The Saviour suffers when his children slide.

**10.** *Sc.* (See quot.)

*a* **1814** Ramsay *Scotl. & Scotsmen 18th c.* (1888) II. 68 It was imagined they would *slide—i.e.*, 'lose beef and tallow'—by the change of food.

**IV.** *trans.* **11.** To cause to move with a smooth, gliding motion; to push over a level surface.

*c* **1537** J. London in Ellis *Orig. Lett.* Ser. iii. III. 132 Then must they putt in to the trowgh a peckke of oots, and when they wer oons slydyd vndre the Awter [etc.]. **1669** Sturmy *Mariner's Mag.* ii. xvi. 93 Then slide your Sight-Vane a little higher towards V. **1683** Moxon *Printing* x. iv. 43 The Tennants of the Till being slid in through the Cutting-in aforesaid. *Ibid.* xv. i, They may be slid forwards so far. **1793** Smeaton *Edystone L.* §225 *note*, We slid the stones to their respective places. **1815** J. Smith *Panorama Sci. & Art* I. 80 The cheeks must be of such a height, that the cutter-frames can be slidden along upon them. **1843** Holtzapffel *Turning* I. 211 The right hand being slided towards the head in the act of lifting the hammer. **1877** W. R. Cooper *Egypt. Obelisks* viii. (1878) 35 The obelisk was slid off from the deck of the galley, on to a low cart.

*fig.* **1779** Sheridan *Critic* i. i, Haven't we the signors and signoras calling here, sliding their smooth semibreves? **1815** Scott *Guy M.* xxxvii, Sliding his whisper from between his lips, which were as little unclosed as possible. **1844** Kinglake *Eothen* viii. (1878) 109 Madly sliding his splendid army, like a weaver's shuttle, from his right hand to his left.

**12.** With *in* or *into*: To introduce quietly or dexterously; to slip (something) *into* one's hand, etc.

**1627** Donne *Serm.* v. (1640) 51 Slide wee in this note by the way. **1677** Miège i. s.v. *Glisser*, To slide his hand into ones pocket. **1713** Steele *Englishm.* No. 8. 50 He was..to slide the Letter into her Hand, but let no Body see. *a* **1748** Watts (J.), Little tricks of sophistry by sliding in, or leaving out, such words as entirely change the question, should be abandoned by all fair disputants. **1818** Scott *Br. Lamm.* xviii, Sliding into the butler's hand the remuneration, which ..was always given by a departing guest. **1841** Dickens *Barn. Rudge* xlviii, Gashford slid his cold insidious palm into his master's grasp. **1871** R. H. Hutton *Ess.* (1877) I. 44 He slides in immediately a very favourite maxim of the religious know-nothing school.

**13.** To move over, traverse, descend, etc., in a sliding manner.

**1621** Speght in Farr *Sel. Poet. Jas. I*, 200 Like a ship that ..slides the sea. **1635** Quarles *Embl.* iv. iii, The idle vessell slides the watry lay. **1770** Foote *Lame Lover* i, Frederick Foretop and I were carelessly sliding the Ranelagh round. **1773** —— *Bankrupt* i. I flatter'd myself with [the prospect of] gently sliding the down-hill of life.

**14.** With *away*: To spend in sliding.

**1827** Clare *Sheph. Cal.* 3 Or seeking bright glib ice to play And slide the wintry hours away.

**slide-**, the verbal stem or the sb. in combs. (sometimes not hyphened): **a.** With names of apparatus, implements, parts of machines, etc., characterized by a sliding action, as ***slide-bar, -block, -bolt, -car, cornet, trombone, trumpet, whistle***, etc. **slide fastener** chiefly *U.S.*, a zip-fastener; **slide-wire** *Electr.*, a resistance wire along which a contact slides in a Wheatstone bridge or similar device.

For technical descriptions of some of these, and of two or three others, see Knight *Dict. Mech.*

*c* **1886** Kipling *Railway Folk* 63 A *slide bar about red hot. **1869** Rankine *Machine & Hand-tools* Pl. F9, An inclined groove is formed in the tup, in which a *slide block is fitted. **1841** Browning *Pippa Passes* 225 Push the lattice ..; of course The *slide-bolt catches. **1763** *Museum Rust.* I. 94 These loads are carried in baskets fixed on *slide-cars. **1861-2** *Ulster Jrnl. Archæol.* IX. 145 Some time after..what were called slide-cars were used, that is, carts without wheels. **1844** H. Stephens *Bk. Farm* II. 291 The *slide-clutch, with a slide-rib, being now placed on the shaft. **1926** Whiteman & McBride *Jazz* ix. 206 The jazz band has introduced some little known instruments such as..the *slide cornet and the czimbalon. **1946** Mezzrow & Wolfe *Really Blues* (1957) i. 12 He showed up in the band room with a slide cornet. **1853** Ure *Dict. Arts* I. 228, *g* is the charcoal-meter, with a *slide door. **1879** Stevenson *Ess. Trav., Amateur Emigrant* (1905) 23 Through the open slide-door we had a glimpse of a grey night sea. **1875** Martin *Winding Mach.* 84 It is of very great importance not to multiply..such things as slide-valves and *slide-faces. **1934** *Newsweek* 21 July 29/2 The Prince of Wales uses a *slide fastener on his trousers. **1944** *Sun* (Baltimore) 16 Sept. 7/4 The B. F. Goodrich Company announced today development of a 'zipped lip' construction that makes a metal slide fastener watertight and airtight. **1971** N. Marsh *Tied up in Tinsel* vi. 135 'Let's have a look at the robe.'.. A slide fastener ran right down the back. **1844** H. Stephens *Bk. Farm* II. 293 A *slide-frame in which two leading pulleys, mounted in a case, are fitted to slide in the vertical direction. **1874** J. W. Long *Amer. Wild-fowl.* vi. 106 The draught is regulated commonly by *slide-gates, but various methods may be employed. **1884** F. J. Britten *Watch & Clockm.* 241 [The] *Slide Guage..[is] a measuring instrument consisting of one fixed and one sliding jaw. **1869** Rankine *Machinery & Millwork* 571 In this machine the tool-holder..slides vertically in a guiding groove in the *slide-head. **1881** Raymond *Mining Gloss.*, **Slide-joint*, a connection acting in rod-boring, like the jars in rope-boring. **1885** C. G. W. Lock *Workshop Rec.* Ser. iv. 239/2 There are two kinds of plough in use..termed respectively 'bolt knife' and '*slide knife'. **1833** Holland *Manuf. Metal* II. 142 An ingenious contrivance, known as the *slide-lathe. **1846** Holtzapffel *Turning* II. 528 The slide-lathe, and..the planing-machine and many other most invaluable tools. **1791** *Selby Bridge Act* 34 The *slide leaf or leaves of the said bridge. **1846** Holtzapffel *Turning* II. 634 The back-stay is fixed to the *slide plate. **1844** *Slide-rib [see *slide-clutch*]. **1825** J. Nicholson *Operat. Mechanic* 446, *h*, the *slide rod, on which the knife *f* is fixed. **1876** Preece & Sivewright *Telegraphy* 172 The slide rod being removed, the iron pole is fixed in its place. **1846** Holtzapffel *Turning* II. 633 The nut of the *slide screw..is made with two tails. **1825** J. Nicholson *Operat. Mechanic* 324 For turning faces of wheels, hollow work, &c. where great accuracy is wanted, Mr. Maudslay has contrived a curious apparatus, which he calls a *slide-tool. **1891** C. R. Day *Descr. Catal. Musical Instruments, R. Military Exhib.* x. 180 *Slide trombone... In this instrument, as should always be the case, the taper of the bell is carried right through the tuning slides. **1934** *Hound & Horn* July-Sept. 595 The harpsichord seems a very complicated instrument to compare alongside the single-noted valve trumpet, or a slide trombone. **1977** 'E. Crispin' *Glimpses of Moon* xiii. 269 How we could brighten our Church Fêtes up, short of breaking all the Ten Commandments simultaneously to a fanfare of slide-trombones. **1885** G. B. Shaw in *Mag. of Music* II. 112/1 These *slide trumpets are not the instruments Bach wrote for. **1888** *Encycl. Brit.* XXIII. 594/1 The slide trumpet is mentioned by T. E. Altenburg [1795], who compares it, and with reason, to the alto trombone. *Ibid.*, The slide trumpet is still used in England in a somewhat modified form. **1939** *Sears, Roebuck Catal.* Fall-Winter 914/3 *Slide whistle. Professional model... Has full chromatic scale of two octaves. **1976** *Gramophone* Feb. 1355/2 The flight grows slower to reveal gentle tones of slide-whistles, zither and harp. **1885** J. Dredge *Electric Illumination* II. i. 53 The *Slide-Wire, or Metre Bridge..is a modification of the bridge due to Kirchoff, and is especially useful for the measurement of low resistances. **1922** Glazebrook *Dict. Appl. Physics* II. 714/2 The first bridge to employ a slide wire was devised by Fleeming Jenkin in 1862 and was used to intercompare the standard coils made for the British Association Committee on Electrical Standards. **1964** *Oceanogr. & Marine Biol.* II. 359 The depth element is a Bourdon tube coupled to a slide-wire potentiometer. **1969** A. Brodgesell in B. G. Lipták *Instrument Engineers' Handbk.* I. ix. 942 Potentiometric displacement sensors consist of a slide wire and wiper. The slide wire is powered by a constant voltage representing full scale travel.

**b.** Denoting something along which objects may slide or be slid, as ***slide-ladder, -way***.

**1793** Smeaton *Edystone L.* §226 The slide-ladder, which was very strongly lashed down to eye-bolts. **1825** J. Nicholson *Operat. Mechanic* 12 The slide-ladder used by brewers in loading and unloading their carts. **1856** Olmsted *Slave States* 550 The boat came to the shore at the foot of a plank slide-way. **1883** *Scotsman* 11 July 5/2 The ways were new, and made of oak and pine, with guide-battens on the inner edges of the slideways.

**c.** Misc., as ***slide-blowing*** adj.; ***slide carrier, -centerer, changer, -coupler, -maker, projector; slide-movement, -principle, show, viewer; slide-in*** adj.; **slide area** *U.S.*, an area in which landslips or avalanches are likely to happen; **slide-back** *Electronics*, the alteration of the grid bias of a thermionic valve which is necessary to restore the anode current to zero after the application of a signal voltage to the grid; apparatus to measure this alteration, freq. as an indirect measure of the signal voltage; also **slide-back voltmeter; slide guitar**, a style of guitar-playing characterized by a glissando effect produced by moving an object along the strings; a guitar used for this; **slide-rock**, talus rock; **slide-tape** *attrib. phr.*, involving photographic slides shown in a predetermined sequence to the accompaniment of a synchronized commentary recorded on magnetic tape.

In most of these *slide-* represents the sb. in senses 5 and 7.

**1959** *Sunday Times* 7 June 16/6 The '*slide area' itself is that part of the Californian coast which is physically slipping, dropping and sliding towards the sea. **1970** *Wall St. Jrnl.* (Eastern ed.) 19 May 1/4 The Kildares live in what is euphemistically called here a 'slide area'. **1925** *Year-bk. Wireless Telegr.* 847 When a control room is some distance from the transmitter it is usual to install a valve voltmeter with a *slideback which either measures the voltage across the output of the main amplifier or indicates when a certain voltage is exceeded. **1931** *B.B.C. Year-bk. 1932* 356 The 'slide-back'..consisted of a valve or similar device so biassed that no indication occurred until there was present and superimposed upon the bias a voltage greater than, and opposing in phase, the biassing voltage. **1938** H. A. Brown *Radio-Frequency Electr. Measurements* (ed. 2) vi. 279 Peak, or slide-back, voltmeters are coming more and more into use. **1948** A. L. Albert *Radio Fundamentals* ix. 354 There is an error involved with this slide-back voltmeter, but with large signals..the error is small. **1965** *Wireless World* July 19 (Advt.), Slide-back measurement of time and amplitude by means of directly-calibrated shift controls. **1890** Bauerman *Metallurgy Iron* 178 The so-called *slide-blowing engines, where the flap valves are replaced by a slide similar to that used in steam engines. **1953** A. Pearlman *Rollei Manual* xxiii. 357 Sticky exudations may foul the *slide carrier of the projector. **1971** *Sci. Amer.* Sept. 224/2 An adequate beam can be formed by making a pinhole aperture in the slide carrier of a 35-millimeter projector. **1895** G. E. Davis *Pract. Micros.* (ed. 3) 376 In mounting objects, a *slide-centerer should be employed. **1959** *IRE Trans. Mil. Electronics* III. 97/1 Like a projection *slide changer, we can observe one slide while discarding the slide already observed and replacing it with a new one. **1962** *Which?* Mar. 69/1 We did not test fully automatic projectors, but 6 had semi-automatic slide changers built in. **1881** C. A. Edwards *Organs* 109 In this instrument is an arrangement called the '*Slide Coupler'. **1968** P. Oliver *Screening Blues* i. 35 Another..version was recorded in 1937 by Black Ace (B. K. Turner) who accompanied himself with brilliant *slide guitar playing. **1969** *Rolling Stone* 22 Apr. 16/5 W. C. Handy first heard the blues and a slide guitar in 1903 when he happened upon an itinerant black musician in ..Mississippi. **1976** *Morecambe Guardian* 7 Dec. 23/2 And inevitably those ubiquitous sessioners, Klaus Voorman (bass)..and Jesse Ed Davies (slide guitar), have played a major part. **1977** McKnight & Tobler *Bob Marley* ix. 111 The Wailers version is decorated by an ethereal slide guitar solo. **1987** *Washington Post* 1 Mar. f6/4 Olney also turns in some burning, bluesy slide guitar. **1973** G. Davey *Fun with Hi-Fi* v. 35 The BSR MacDonald playing deck which I use has *slide-in facilities for fitting the cartridge of one's choice. **1977** *Gramophone* Apr. 1629/2 The head-shell has a slide-in cartridge carrier. **1889** *Anthony's Photogr. Bulletin* II. 356, I would suggest to *slide-makers a more extended use for their work. **1846** Holtzapffel *Turning* II. 471 The employment of the two, or the three *slide movements, to which method Mr. Nasmyth has judiciously applied the term 'Slide Principle'. **1846** *Slide principle [see *slide movement* above]. **1956** E. S. Bomback *Retina Manual* xxi. 222 (*caption*) The Leitz Prado 150-watt *slide projector. **1979** P. Niesewand *Member of Club* ii. 17 Two slide projectors were being positioned... 'Remember, when the lights go out, we'll be showing some slides.' **1901** *Yearbk. U.S. Dept. Agric. 1900* 195 In the mountains we often find the hillside slopes covered with broken rock of various sizes. This we call *slide rock. **1974** Flint & Skinner *Physical Geol.* vii. 121/2 Weathering converts the sliderock into fine-grained regolith which, with its pores of extremely small diameter, can hold much more moisture than sliderock and thus acquire both vegetation and soil. **1956** E. S. Bomback *Retina Manual* xxi. 222 The color *slide show has quite a lot in common with the motion picture film. **1978** *Peace News* 25 Aug. 18/3 On their last visit to Britain four years ago they did a slide show and a question and answer session. **1971** *Publishers' Weekly* 22 Mar. 20/2 The final part of the program..consisted of a *slide-tape commentary. **1977** J. Hedgecoe *Photographer's Handbk.* 305 Sound for slide-tape presentations can be prepared from studio recordings using a microphone direct. **1960** *Which?* Oct. 228/2 *A slide viewer should give a good *optical performance*.

**ˈslideable**, *a.* Also slidable. [f. slide *v.*]

**a.** Liable to slide or alter. *rare*$^{-1}$.

**1662** Chandler tr. *Van Helmont's Oriat.*, It desired a more stable and quiet Inn, than that which should be slideable every hour.

**b.** That may be slid.

**1888** *Engineer* LXV. 538/4 A screw mounted in a bearing slidable in a right line. **1925** A. W. Judge *Carburettors & Carburation* iv. 63 M is a slidable clip. **1969** *Jane's Freight Containers 1968–69* 408/2 The bogie will be slidable along the full length of the chassis.

Hence ˈ**slidably** *adv.*

**1907** F. W. Lanchester *Aerodynamics* 348 A square plane of thin brass, mounted 'slidably' on anti-friction rollers. **1954** *Patents for Inventions. Abridgments of Specifications* Group xxxiv. 23/1 The spiders 8 of which are also slidably mounted on the shafts.

**ˈslideableness.** [Cf. prec.] Fitness for sliding.

**1886** Miss Broughton *Doctor Cupid* II. 159 The glassy slideableness of the turnpike road.

†**slide-groat.** *Obs.* [f. slide *v.* + groat.] Shove-groat, shovelboard.

**1552** *Nottingham Rec.* IV. 102 Dyce, slyde grote,..or any other maner of game. **1586** Hooker *Giraldus' Hist. Irel.* in *Holinshed* II. 86/2 On a night, when the lieutenant and he for their disport were plaieng at slidegrote, or shoofle-boord. **1605** Armin *Foole upon F.* (1880) 21 All alone he playd at slide groate, as his manner was: peeces or counters he had none. **1635** *Maldon Borough Deeds* (Bundle 124 No. 9), [He] continued there about three quarters of an hour, and plaied two games at slidegroat.

**slider** (ˈslaɪdə(r)). [f. slide *v.* + -er[1].]

**1. a.** One who slides; †a skater.

**1530** Palsgr. 225/2 Glydar, a slyder. **1598** Florio, *Sbrisciatore*,..a slider vpon the yse. *a* **1700** Evelyn *Diary* 1 Dec. 1662, The strange and wonderful dexterity of the sliders on the new Canal. *a* **1851** Moir *Poet. Wks.* (1852) II. 386 The ring of the slider's heel. **1853** Dickens *Bleak Ho.* iii, The skaters and sliders had brushed the snow away.

*transf.* **1860** Tyndall *Glac.* ii. xiii. 297 The rocks of Britain bear to this day the traces of these mighty sliders [*sc.* glaciers].

**b.** *Rowing.* One who uses a sliding seat.

**1880** *Daily News* 22 Nov. 5/3 Hanlan, the Canadian,..is a great slider.

**c.** *U.S.* The red-bellied terrapin. Also *attrib.*

**1877** *Scribner's Monthly* Nov. 11/1 'Sliders', the common river turtles of almost all the rivers of the region, grow to a much larger size. **1883** *Science* I. 149/2 The heart of the 'slider' terrapin. **1884** Goode *Nat. Hist. Aquat. Anim.* 155 The 'Red-bellied Terrapin', *Pseudemys rugosa*,..is also known under the names 'Potter', 'Red-fender', and 'Slider'.

**d.** *Baseball.* A fast pitch that breaks or slides away from its original path.

**1936** *Sun* (Baltimore) 14 Aug. 12/6 It looks like what some of the modern pitchers call 'a slider'. **1980** *Washington Post* 1 Aug. d3/3 The human body isn't meant to throw the slider.

**2.** A beam or plank on which something heavy may be slid; also *dial.*, a sledge.

**1582** Stanyhurst *Æneis* ii. (Arb.) 51 Thee wheels weer prop with a number Of beams and sliders. **1805** R. Sutcliff *Jrnl.* 6 Jan. in *Trav. N. Amer.* (1811) iv. 67 They make use of a boat that has two sliders, one on each side the keel. **1886** Elworthy *W. Somerset Word-bk.* 680 In the Hill country.. the hay is always carried in upon *slitters* or *sliders*. **1900** *Engineering Mag.* XIX. 679 Two lines of 'sliders', consisting of heavy oak plank,..are placed..on each side of the keel, and one line of sliders under the keel.

**3.** *Mining.* (See quot. 1828.)

**1653** Manlove *Customs Lead-Mines* 257 (E.D.S.), Bunnings, Polings, Stemples, Forks, and Slyder. **1746** Hooson *Miner's Dict.* s.v., Sliders are cut of such a Length as the Miner designs the Square of his Shaft to be. *Ibid.* s.v. *Squarewood*, This consisteth of two Sliders and two Forks. **1828** Carr *Craven Gloss.*, *Sliders and forks*, timbers for the support of shafts and sumps in mines.

**4. a.** A thing or part which slides or may be slid; *esp.* a sliding part or device in some mechanical apparatus.

**1681** GREW *Musæum* IV. ii. 366 A Slider, with a thin Plate-Spring, which plays against the said Teeth. **1692** *Capt. Smith's Seaman's Gram.* II. xxiv. 130 A small Line must be drawn quite thro' the Slider. **1733** TULL *Horse-Hoeing Husb.* xxii. 339 (Dubl.), To fix in this Wreath from coming off, we make use of the Slider. **1763** *Museum Rust.* I. 78 The aperture in the floor of the third cell is shut by means of the slider. **1790** *Phil. Trans.* LXXXI. 27 The front of this vessel is a plate of glass, and the back a tin-plate slider. **1834–6** *Encycl. Metrop.* (1845) VIII. 751/1 In a groove under the dovetail is a slider L, moved by a wire K. **1839** URE *Dict. Arts* 983 Betwixt these guides, friction-roller sliders are placed,.. to which sliders the corves are suspended. **1884** *Law Times* LXXVIII. 8/1 An upright rod, up and down which worked a slider which contained the cartridge.

*fig.* **1825** HAZLITT *Spirit of Age* 64 He has only to draw the sliders of his imagination, and a thousand subjects expand before him.

**b.** *Organ-building.* (See quot. 1875.)

**1781** *Encycl. Brit.* (ed. 2) VIII. 5747/2 R, R, are the rollers, to move the sliders, by help of the arms *cf, cf.* **1855** HOPKINS *Organ* 43 The pallets and sliders of the several sound-boards. **1875** STAINER & BARRETT *Dict. Mus. Terms* s.v. *Organ*, We now apply the word slide or slider only to that strip of wood which, passing under a row of pipes from right to left, admits the air to a particular row of pipes or stops. **1881** C. A. EDWARDS *Organs* 56 The sliders are long pieces of wood, usually made of mahogany.

**c.** *Locksmithing.* A tumbler that moves horizontally.

**1796** *Repertory Arts* V. 227 In these notches are placed six sliders or small bars. **1833** HOLLAND *Manuf. Metal* II. 268 The form of these levers, sliders, or other movables.. may be varied without end. **1879** *Cassell's Techn. Educ.* IV. 242/2 In these slits are inserted little pieces of steel, called sliders.

**d.** Part of a guillotine. Also *fig.*

**1795** BURKE *Regic. Peace* Wks. VIII. 109 Fitting to their size the slider of his guillotine! **1798** *Loves of Triangles* in *Anti-Jacobin* (1799) 141 To the pois'd plank tie fast the monster's back, Close the nice slider, ope the expectant sack. [**1903** MORLEY *Gladstone* x. ii. (1905) II. 618 The report next fell under what Burke calls the accursed slider.]

**e.** *Bell-ringing.* (See quot. 1901.)

**1871** [see STAY *sb.*[2] 2 h]. **1901** H. E. BULWER *Gloss. Techn. Terms Bells & Ringing* 4 *Slider*, usually a bar of wood pivoted at one end on one of the lower members of the 'frame', and extending across the bottom of the 'bell-pit' so that its free end may move to and fro on a bed provided for it on the opposite side of the 'pit'. **1931** E. MORRIS *Hist. & Art Change Ringing* i. 15 For many years.. bells were rung without stay or slider as we now know them. *Ibid.*, Stedman .. mentions what would be the fore-runner of the stay and slider adjustment. **1974** J. CAMP *Bell Ringing* ii. 30 *(caption)* The stay has pushed the slider to the limit of its movement and the bell cannot turn any further.

**f.** A sliding electrical contact, forming part of a variable resistance or the like, or serving as a control on electrical equipment.

**1872** *Jrnl. Soc. Electr. Engineers* I. 202 The slider *n* is moved on the compensating wire so as to destroy the deflection of the galvonometer. **1923** *Popular Wireless* 13 Oct. Suppl. 1 Suppose we have a coil consisting of 500 turns of No. 22 wire,.. fitted with a slider, and we wish to know approximately where to put the slider to receive the Dutch concerts. **1965** *Wireless World* Sept. 432/1 The base.. is taken to the slider of a potentiometer connected across the output terminals of the power supply. **1975** *Hi-Fi Answers* Feb. 76/3 Set the input level sliders to about three-quarters of full travel and route the signal back through the amplifier by means of the tape monitor button. **1978** *Gramophone* Aug. 392/3 The latest in Bang and Olufsen's range of Beomaster tuner-amplifiers is.. distinguished by its.. absence of switches and knobs—all functions being handled by sliders, press-keys, and wheels.

**5. a.** A device for holding, and inserting in a microscope, the glass or other plates with the objects to be studied. ? *Obs.*

**1702** *Phil. Trans.* XXIII. 1357 The Sliders with the plain and concave Glass plates for Objects [are] very convenient. **1740** *Ibid.* XLI. 515 Making use of fine transparent Muscovy Talc or Isinglass, placed in Sliders, to inclose Objects in. **1822** IMISON *Sci. & Art* I. 280 You may change the objects in your sliders for what others you think proper. **1855** LARDNER *Mus. Sci. & Art* VI. 94 The wings.. of this gnat.. make very beautiful objects when mounted under thin glass in sliders.

**b.** A lantern-slide. ? *Obs.*

**1793** W. & S. JONES *Catal. Optical* (etc.) *Instr.* 3 Small magic lanthorns, with twelve sliders complete. **1823** *New Monthly Mag.* VII. 246 A second face coming across us, like the sliders of a magic lantern. *c***1865** *Wylde's Circ. Sci.* I. 64/1 One of these sliders will give a picture upon the white screen.

†**6.** A sliding ring, loop, or similar device, used to fasten an article of dress, the hair, a long purse, etc. *Obs.*

The sense in quot. 1699 is uncertain.

**1699** J. DICKENSON *Jrnl. Trav.* 64 The Governour.. gave us a Shirt and Sliders, a Hat, and a pair of Silk-Stockins. **1742** A. MONRO in *Med. Ess. Edinb.* V. 455 Till the Slip-ring or Slider is thrust towards the End of the Handles. **1782** [T. VAUGHAN] *Fashionable Follies* II. ccxiv. 138 A purse, with brilliant sliders, and a pair of very fine shoe buckles. **1810** S. GREEN *Reformist* I. 81 Drawing the sliders of his weighty purse,.. he threw down two guineas.

**7. a.** A stand or holder for a bottle or decanter, intended to be slid along the table; a coaster.

**1770** tr. *Mme. du Bocage's Lett.* I. 67 Litte round vessels called sliders, of the same [Indian] wood, serve to hold the bottles. **1895** 'SARAH TYTLER' *Macdonald Lass* ix. 123 There are the sliders and the cruet, and father's tankard. **1905** *Daily Chron.* 1 Sept. 6/6 Two chased and pierced decanter sliders.

**b.** Ice-cream served in a sandwich form between two wafers. *colloq.*

**1915** J. J. BELL *Wee Macgregor Enlists* ii, Come on oot wi' me an' I'll stan' ye a dizzen sliders. **1935** L. MACNEICE *Poems* 63 Ice cream in sliders Bought in dusty streets. **1967** R. MACKAY *House & Day* 75 'I'll have a slider too.'.. The woman took a wafer.. and covered it with the thin yellow ice-cream... She put a second wafer on the top.

**8.** *attrib.* and *Comb.*, as ***slider bridge, clutch, control, -crank, -holder, potentiometer, -pump, switch, tube.***

**1919** S. F. WALKER *Electr. Mining Machinery* xxiii. 186 Use of the *slider bridge in connection with the loop test for finding a fault to earth in a cable. **1972** *World of Wild Wheels* (Custom Car) 57/2 One of the latest innovations being tried in the States.. is the *slider clutch. **1978** *Detroit Free Press* 16 Apr. F14/1 (Advt.), Enderle fuel injection, 2 spd Lenco, new slider clutch, Airheart disc brks. **1973** *Wireless World* Oct. 72 (Advt.), Top quality *slider controls. **1884** COTTERILL *Appl. Mech.* 113 Mechanisms derived from the *slider-crank chain. **1797** *Encycl. Brit.* (ed. 3) XI. 713/2 The *slider-holder should be removed when you are going to view opaque objects. **1837** GORING & PRITCHARD *Microg.* 13 The slider-holder.. must be very small. **1972** *Wireless World* Jan. 88/2 (Advt.), New *slider potentiometers. As used on only the most exclusive of Audio Amplifiers and Mixers. **1875** KNIGHT *Dict. Mech.*, **Slider-pump*, a form of Rotary Pump. **1970** *Wireless World* July 87/2 (Advt.), *Slider switches. Double pole, double throw. **1823** J. BADCOCK *Dom. Amusem.* 51 A.. lens fastened to the *slider tube.

**'slide-rest.** Also slide rest. [f. SLIDE *v.*] An appliance for holding tools in turning, enabling the tools to be variously held in relation to the material worked on.

**1839** URE *Dict. Arts* 268 The pieces of wood.. are placed upon the slide-rest of the.. machine. **1869** RANKINE *Machine & Hand-tools* Pl. H 4 The slide rest, which carries the cutting tools, is provided with as many holders as there are tools required. **1879** *Cassell's Techn. Educ.* II. 62/1 The slide-rest is really an iron hand which holds the tool and enables it to be turned towards the work, or from it.

*attrib.* **1843** *Penny Cycl.* XXV. 426/1 Slide-rest screw. **1859** *Handbk. Turning* 93 Diminish their size by moving the slide rest screw backwards half a turn.

**'slide-rule.** Also slide rule. [f. SLIDE *v.*] A sliding rule. *spec.* A device whereby multiplication and division, and sometimes other mathematical operations, may be performed with speed but limited accuracy, consisting essentially of two rules marked with logarithmic scales and capable of being slid along one another, and usually also a transparent cursor marked with a line crossing the scales, so that a required result may be obtained by inspection after proper movement of these. Also *fig.*

This, not *sliding rule*, is now the usual name.

**1663** PEPYS *Diary* 14 Apr., I walked to Greenwich, studying the slide rule for measuring of timber. **1838** *Civil Eng. & Arch. Jrnl.* I. 122/1 To assist in facilitating the use of the slide rule among working mechanics. **1876** *Handbk. Scientif. Appar.* 30 The slide rule,—an apparatus for effecting multiplications and divisions by means of a logarithmic scale. **1890** *Engineering News* 20 Dec. 543 In France the slide rule is seen on the desk of almost every manufacturer, miller or engineer. **1930** *Engineering* 31 Jan. 131/3 A special form of slide rule.. for the purpose of simplifying calculations relating to structures of reinforced concrete. **1958** *Times Lit. Suppl.* 10 Jan. 19/1 They bring out their slide-rule at the sight of a signature, and then, by nice calculation, decide whether there has been any sense in the prose equations which precede it. **1974** *Encycl. Brit. Macropædia* XI. 653/2 The first known slide rule in which the slide worked between parts of a fixed stock was made by Robert Bissaker of Great Britain in 1654. *Ibid.*, Amédée Mannheim, an officer of the French artillery, invented in 1859 what may be considered the first of the modern slide rules... This rule.. brought into general use a cursor. **1976** NICHOLS & ARMSTRONG *Workers Divided* 68 Workers were incensed by the efforts of a new manager to run their plant flat out all the time: 'You have to have a real feel for the plant not just be all slide-rule like him.'

*attrib.* **1891** *Anthony's Photogr. Bulletin* IV. 209 The system of circular slide rule calculators. **1958** *Listener* 11 Sept. 375/1 Towards the end of the war many of the operations of war, especially those concerned with aircraft, were kept under close scientific scrutiny and control. This was the era of the so-called slide-rule strategy.

†**'slide-thrift.** *Obs.* [f. SLIDE *v.*, after SLIDE-GROAT.]

**1.** Shovelboard, slide-groat.

**1541** *Act 33 Hen. VIII*, c. 9 § 1 New and craftie games and plaies, as.. slide thrift, otherwise called shoue groat. **1630** J. TAYLOR (Water P.) *Wks.* III. 79 Some of the Townesmen were.. bowling: some at slide-thrift, or shouel-board.

**2.** A spendthrift.

*a***1591** H. SMITH *Wks.* (1866) I. 327 So you depart from our sermons like a slide-thrift's purse, which will hold no money.

Hence †**'slidethrifter**, one who plays at shovel-board. *Obs.*

**1579** RICE *Invective agst. Vices* D ij b, Neither.. Slide-thrifters, Scailers, nor Darters.

**'slide-valve.** Also slide valve. [f. SLIDE *v.*] A valve having a sliding plate for opening and closing an orifice; *spec.* one which does this alternately and regularly.

**1802** *Specif. M. Murray's Patent* No. 2632, My new invention.. consists in application of one slide valve. **1846** A. YOUNG *Naut. Dict.* 298 On one side of the cylinder is this casing which.. confines the slide-valves. **1892** LOW *Machine Draw.* 74 Slide valves are generally made of brass, bronze, or cast iron.

*attrib.* **1844** H. STEPHENS *Bk. Farm* II. 311 The other eccentric moves the slide-valve-rod. **1846** A. YOUNG *Naut. Dict.* 298 Slide-valve Casing.

†‖**Slidikins**, *int. Obs.* [f. 'SLID *int.* Cf. 'SBODIKINS.] A form of minced oath.

**1694** CONGREVE *Double-Dealer* II. i, Slidikins, can't I govern you? What did I marry you for? **1710** SWIFT *Lett.* (1767) III. 25 Slidikins, I have been the best boy in Christendom. *c***1755** MURPHY *Apprentice* II. ii, Slidikins, this is a letter from the unfortunate young fellow.

**sliding** ('slaɪdɪŋ), *vbl. sb.* [f. SLIDE *v.*]

**1.** The action of the verb in various senses (chiefly intransitive).

(*a*) *c***1325** *Prose Ps.* lv. 13 þou deliuered.. myn fete fram slydynge. **1382** WYCLIF *Ecclus.* xx. 20 The slidyng of the false tunge [is] as he that is falling in the pament. *c***1460** *Contin. Brut* II. 460 The stretes were strawed thurghout for slidyng of theire horses. **1495** *Trevisa's Barth. De P.R.* VII. l. 263 The wombe is greuyd with slidynge and slippernesse. **1561** NORTON & SACKVILLE *Gorboduc* II. i, So slow a slidynge of his aged yeres. **1581** SIDNEY *Apol. Poet.* (Arb.) 70 The Dutch.. [is so full of] Consonants, that they cannot yeeld the sweet slyding, fit for a Verse. **1605** MARSTON *Dutch Courtezan* II. i, Lying, malice, envie, are held but slidyngs. **1683** MOXON *Printing* x. ix, Extuberancies of Nail-heads would hinder the free sliding of the Quoins. **1801** STRUTT *Sports & Past.* II. ii. 78 Sliding is but little practised, except by children. **1860** TYNDALL *Glac.* II. xxviii. 395 A sliding of the particles of ice past each other. **1882** *Standard* 9 Dec. 2/8 The crew rapidly fell to pieces, the sliding being short, the time bad.

(*b*) **1651** N. BACON *Disc. Govt. Eng.* II. xv. (1739) 82 This way of the Parliament tended to a tacite sliding him out of the Government of the Kingdom.

**2.** *attrib.* **a.** In sense 'on which sliding is performed', as ***sliding-place, -surface, -way.***

**1611** COTGR., *Babouïn*,.. a frozen place, whereon boyes vse to slide; a sliding place. **1648** HEXHAM II, *Een glijdbaen*, a Sliding path. **1792** BELKNAP *Hist. New-Hampshire* III. 157 On the top of the dam.. [beavers] always leave a sluice or passage..; and when the stream is large, they leave two or three, which the hunters call sliding-places. **1839** R. S. ROBINSON *Naut. Steam Eng.* 48 The exterior of the valve slightly projects.. in a line with the sliding surfaces. **1875** KNIGHT *Dict. Mech.* 2210/2 The sliding-ways are the inclined planes down which the vessel slides, and are made of planks 3 or 4 inches wide, laid on blocks of wood.

**b.** In sense 'of the nature of, connected with, sliding', as ***sliding contact, motion, principle.***

**1690** LOCKE *Essay Hum. Und.* II. xxiii. 144 All parts of Bodies must be easily separable by such a lateral sliding motion. **1815** J. SMITH *Panorama Sci. & Art* II. 664 The lights.. should be of the usual sliding construction. **1843** HOLTZAPFFEL *Turning* I. 378 A very considerable amount of the sliding motion of the metal would be called into play. **1869** RANKINE *Mach. & Millwork* 114 The acting surfaces of a pair of pieces in sliding contact. **1875** KNIGHT *Dict. Mech.* 2210/2 The gages used by carpenters and artificers generally are on the sliding principle.

**sliding** ('slaɪdɪŋ), *ppl. a.* [f. SLIDE *v.*]

**I. 1.** *fig.* **a.** That slides or slips away; transitory; unstable, inconstant; passing.

*a***900** *O.E. Martyrol.* 22 Aug. 150 Ne do ic þæt, forðon þe þeos mennisce tyddernes bið swa slidende swa þæt glæs. *a***1000** *Saxon Leechd.* I. p. lviii, Fleoȝ þu wesan ealdor slidendes pleȝan. *c***1374** CHAUCER *Boeth.* I. met. v. (1868) 22 Whi suffrest þou þat slidyng fortune turneþ to grete vtter chaungynges of þinges. *c***1386** —— *Can. Yeom. Prol. & T.* 179 That slidynge science hath me maad so bare, That I haue no good. **1500–20** DUNBAR *Poems* lxvi. 5 The slydand joy, the glaidness schort. **1597** DANIEL *Civ. Wars* II. xxx, The sliding faith of those That cannot long their resolution hold. **1628** FELTHAM *Resolves* II. ix, We dye with doing that, for which only, our sliding life was granted. **1697** DRYDEN *Virg. Past.* III. 62 His Name who made the Sphere, And shew'd the Seasons of the sliding Year. **1765** [E. THOMPSON] *Meretriciad* 11 Erase thy vices with the sliding day.

†**b.** Of persons: Slippery, unreliable; apt to fall or transgress. *Obs.*

*c***1435** *Chron. London* (Kingsford, 1905) 45 A man, the which is nat slyding in his tunge. *c***1450** tr. *De Imitatione* I. iv. 6 þei knowiþ mannys infirmite redy to euel & sliding ynow in wordes. *Ibid.* III. xxii. 90, I am so slidyng & so weike to wiþstonde passions.

**2.** Slippery; steeply sloping. *rare.*

*c***1325** *Gloss. W. de Bibbesw.* in Wright *Voc.* 160 *Le chimyn trop lidaunt*, slidery (sclidinde). **1608** TOPSELL *Serpents* (1658) 704 By fertil vale of Pelethun his sliding road. **1616** W. BROWNE *Brit. Past.* II. iii, A hill, whose sliding sides A goodly flocke, like winter's cov'ring, hides.

**3. a.** That moves by sliding or slipping; flowing, gliding, etc.

*c***1374** CHAUCER *Boeth.* v. metr. ii. (1868) 152 þe flowynge ordre of þe slidyng water. ?*a***1400** *Morte Arth.* 2976 The slydande spere of his hande sleppes! **1483** *Cath. Angl.* 323/1 Sclydynge, *labens.* **1500–20** DUNBAR *Poems* lxxvi. 3 Quhat is this lyfe bot.. A slyding quheill ws lent to seik remeid. **1562** PILKINGTON *Exposit. Abdyas* Pref. 8 Safelye slips away the slyding shippe. **1604** B. JONSON *Entertainm.* Wks. (1616) 882 The many falls Of sweete, and seuerall sliding rills. **1634** MILTON *Comus* 892 By the rushy-fringed bank.. My sliding Chariot stayes. **1784** COWPER *Task* IV. 126 Thy throne A sliding car, indebted to no wheels. **1825** J. NICHOLSON *Operat. Mech.* 664 The laws which regulate the friction of rolling and sliding bodies. **1856** BRYANT *Prairies* 107 Sliding reptiles of the ground, Startlingly beautiful.

**b.** Accompanied by a sliding movement.

**1796** *Hist. Ned Evans* I. 198 Lord Rivers advancing to Edward with a sliding bow. **1818** SCOTT *Br. Lamm.* xxii, Craigengelt.. made a sliding bow to the Marquis. **1838** LYTTON *Alice* v. vi, Mrs. Merton, with a sliding bow, had already quitted the room. **1948** *Assoc. Football* ('Know the Game' Series) 31/2 A sliding tackle done fairly is not dangerous.., especially when clear contact is made with the ball, and should therefore not be penalised. **1974** *Liverpool Echo* (Football ed.) 12 Oct. 1/2 Foggon went racing through again, but Boersma took the ball off him with a splendid sliding tackle.

**4.** Of language or music: Flowing easily.

**1627** DRAYTON *Agincourt* 207 Dainty Sands that hath to English done, Smooth sliding Quid. **1678** L'ESTRANGE *Seneca's Mor.* (1702) 376 His Speech was rather Easie, and Sliding, than Quick. **1844** MRS. BROWNING *Drama of Exile* 560, I think that they With sliding voices lean from heavenly towers. **1875** STAINER & BARRETT *Dict. Mus. Terms*, *Sliding relish*, a grace in old harpsichord music. **1876** LOWELL *Among my Books* Ser. II. 156 His attempts to naturalize the sliding rhymes of Sannazzaro in English.

**II.** In special uses.

**5.** Of a knot: Made so as to slip along a cord; running.

**1591** PERCIVALL *Sp. Dict.*, *Corrediza*, a sliding knot. **1597** A. M. tr. *Guillemeau's Fr. Chirurg.* 34 b/2 We must tye the endes of the threde together, and with a slidinge knott binde the same together. **1622** MABBE tr. *Aleman's Guzman d'Alf.* I. 253, I..knit a sliding knot vpon the instep of one of his feete. **1818** *Encycl. Metrop.* (1845) III. 26/1 If one or many of the fixed knots..be replaced by sliding knots, or moveable rings.

**6. a.** Designating parts of apparatus or machinery which slide, or are characterized by some sliding device, as ***sliding-bar***, ***-collar***, ***-joint***, etc.; ***sliding contact***, a connection in an electric circuit that can be slid along a length of resistance wire; see also s.v. SLIDING *vbl. sb.* 2 b; ***sliding valve*** = SLIDE-VALVE.

**1778** [W. H. MARSHALL] *Minutes Agric.*, *Digest* 54 *note*, The *Sliding bar..ought to be set at such a depth, as..to have a collection of mould before it. **1889** *Anthony's Photogr. Bulletin* II. 293 By means of the sliding-bar..this instrument can be adapted to reduce from negatives of almost any size. **1849** *Mech. Mag.* Apr. 314 The *sliding carriage in or upon which is to be placed any log..intended to be cut. **1680** MOXON *Mech. Exerc.* xiv. 239 The Neck of the *Sliding Collar. **1825** J. NICHOLSON *Operat. Mechanic* 125 The balls will fall towards each other, and let down the sliding collar. **1872** *Jrnl. Soc. Telegr. Engineers* I. 208 The wire with *sliding contact was apt to wear if much used. **1926** R. W. HUTCHINSON *Wireless* 77 Sliding contacts can be moved to and fro along two brass sliding rails. **1971** B. SCHARF *Engin. & its Language* xxi. 307 In order to vary the value of one of the known resistances a rheostat may be used, or two of the known resistances may be replaced by a single wire of known resistance with a sliding contact. **1883** GRESLEY *Gloss. Coal-m.* 225 **Sliding Joint*, a boring rod made in two portions, one sliding within the other. **1869** RANKINE *Machine & Hand-tools* Pl. L 2 The spindle is keyed by a *sliding key. **1711** *Lond. Gaz.* No. 4855/4 A Silver Jewel Watch,..the *sliding Piece on the Dyal-plate. **1839** *Penny Cycl.* XV. 175/1 Instead of fixing the wire to the telescope tube, it is stretched across a sliding-piece. **1825** J. NICHOLSON *Operat. Mechanic* 325 The nuts of the screws.. are not screwed fast to the *sliding plates. **1832** BABBAGE *Econ. Manuf.* x. 49 The same process by the aid of the lathe and the *sliding-rest. **1833** HOLLAND *Manuf. Metal* II. 44 Some very handsome pruning instruments of the *sliding-shears description. **1846** HOLTZAPFFEL *Turning* II. 862 Small wires and other pieces are also held in a species of pliers,..called pin-tongs, or *sliding-tongs. **1909** *Westm. Gaz.* 11 Nov. 5/1 The new Daimler engine may be said to have brought us to the end of the first stage of the *sliding-valve principle. **1838** *Civil Eng. & Arch. Jrnl.* I. 350/2 The method of reading the figures of the stave itself, instead of the *sliding vane.

**b.** Designating doors, lids, panels, etc., which are opened or shut by sliding.

**1715** DESAGULIERS *Fires Impr.* 96 There must be *sliding Boards, or Doors. **1839** URE *Dict. Arts* 983 At the pit mouth, where shutters or sliding boards must be used. **1829** in Willis & Clark *Cambridge* (1886) III. 104 They must all admit of communication..by *sliding Double Doors. **1887** *Times* 14 Oct. 3/6 A short tramcar,..having a sliding door at each end. **1833** LOUDON *Encycl. Archit.* Gloss., **Sliding hatches*, covers or shutters fitted in grooves. **1894** DOYLE *Memoirs Sherlock Holmes* 100 A small wooden box, with a *sliding lid. *a* **1817** JANE AUSTEN *Northanger Abbey* (1818) II. v. 76 Have you a stout heart?—Nerves fit for *sliding pannels and tapestry? **1832** BREWSTER *Nat. Magic* xi. 275 The chess-player may be introduced into the chest through the sliding panel. **1862** *Chambers's Encycl.* III. 93/1 Later in the reign, the royal carriages had sliding panels. **1929** *Motor World* 29 Mar. 199/1 One or other of the various types of sun-saloons (folding or *sliding roof) may be offered at an extra charge. **1959** *Observer* 1 Mar. 21/6 Although many will welcome the sliding roof, the handle is rather prominent. **1766** T. H. CROKER et al. *Compl. Dict. Arts & Sciences* II., s.v. *Madder* col. 4, The *sliding-shutters are pulled down. **1842** FRANCIS *Dict. Arts*, *Sluice*,..a description of sliding shutter made in a lock or flood-gate. **1889** WELCH *Text Bk. Naval Archit.* xii. 131 The air can enter into the various compartments through sliding shutters or *louvres*. **1724** in *Maryland Hist. Mag.* (1911) VI. 1 Two *sliding windows..with good frame shutters. **1880** *Dict. Leading Techn. & Trade Terms Archit. Design & Building Construction* 207/1 Another form of opening and closing window is one used in domestic structures of a humble character, and termed a 'sliding', sometimes a 'rolling window'. **1976** H. MACINNES *Agent in Place* xxv. 260 A stretch of sliding windows opening onto a balcony.

**7.** *Naut.*, etc. **a.** ***sliding keel***, an extra deep keel which slides vertically through the bottom of a vessel. Also *attrib.*

**1797** *Encycl. Brit.* (ed. 3) XVII. 376/1 Captain Schank's vessel with three sliding keels beat the other vessel. **1802** *Naval Chron.* VII. 40 The idea of sliding keels is taken from the *balza* of South America. *c* **1850** *Rudim. Nav.* (Weale) 148 *Sliding keels*, an invention of.. Captain Schank, of the Royal Navy, to prevent vessels being driven to leeward by a side wind. **1876** T. HARDY *Ethelberta* (1890) 251 'That one you saw was a cutter..,' he replied. 'Built on the sliding-keel principle.'

**b.** In various uses (see quots.).

For *sliding-gunter* (*Naut.*) see GUNTER 2.

**1818** SCOTT *Br. Lamm.* xxxi, As bold a smuggler as ever ran out a sliding bowsprit. **1846** A. YOUNG *Naut. Dict.* 34 The planks fitted under the bottom of the ship to descend with her upon the bilge-ways, are termed sliding planks, sliding baulks, or bilge coads.

**c.** ***sliding seat***, a seat in an outrigger which moves backwards and forwards with the action of the rower; also, a seat which can be slid out beyond the gunwale of a yacht.

**1874** *Ann. Reg.*, *Chron.* 36 The sliding seats, which were used for the first time in this race, must be pronounced a complete success. **1884** *St. James' Gaz.* 29 Mar. 6/1 University crews have rowed the course on sliding seats. **1895** *Outing* XXVI. 463 'Sliding-seats' began to get longer and longer, until the champion sailed, not in his boat, but stretched entirely outside of it.

**8. a.** ***sliding rule***, a mathematical gauging or measuring instrument consisting of two graduated parts, one of which slides upon the other, and so arranged that when brought into proper juxtaposition the required result may be obtained by inspection. Now usu. SLIDE-RULE, q.v.

**1663** PEPYS *Diary* 15 Apr., Reading of my book of Timber measure, comparing it with my new Sliding Rule. **1684** T. EVERARD (*title*), Stereometry made easie, or the description and use of a new gauging rod or sliding-rule. **1701** MOXON *Math. Instr.* 19 Sliding Rules, for gauging and measuring; ingeniously contrived and applied. **1798** *Nicholson's Jrnl.* I. 450 On the Advantage of inverting the Slider in many operations on the Common Sliding Rule. **1832** BREWSTER *Nat. Magic* xi. 294 The figures..were not exhibited to the eye as in sliding rules and similar instruments. **1895** *Daily News* 20 Nov. 9/4 A small sliding rule gives the value of any required number of shares at the above fractions at any necessary numerator.

†**b.** So ***sliding gauge***, ***Gunter*** (see quots.). *Obs.*

**1683** MOXON *Printing* XII. iv, The Sliding Gage is..a Tool commonly used by Mathematical Instrument-Makers... Its Use is to measure and set off Distances between the Sholder and the Tooth, and to mark it off from the end, or else from the edge of your Work. **1701** —— *Math. Instr.* 18 Sliding Gunter, made of Box, with a middle piece that slides between 2 pieces, with Lines to answer Proportions by inspection: chiefly used by Mariners. **1727–41** [see GUNTER 1 b].

**9.** ***sliding scale***: **a.** A sliding rule.

**1706** PHILLIPS (ed. Kersey), *Sliding-Rules* or *Scales*, are Mathematical Instruments [etc.]. **1788** *Phil. Trans.* LXXVIII. 126 A small thermometer with a sliding scale. **1875** KNIGHT *Dict. Mech.* 2210/2 *Sliding-scale*, a rule with a sliding member.

**b.** A scale or standard (of payments, wages, etc.) which rises or falls in proportion to, or conversely to, the rise or fall of some other standard.

**1842** C. GUEST *Jrnl.* 14 Feb. (1950) vii. 129 His opinion that in times of scarcity the fixed duty he proposes would have to give way, which is exactly the argument the Tories use when advocating the sliding scale. **1843** CARLYLE *Past & Pres.* II. iii, Neither do we ascertain what kind of Corn-bill he passed, or wisely-adjusted Sliding-scale. **1869** ROGERS *Hist. Glean.* I. 183 The agricultural interest suffered ...and we owed the latest sliding-scale to their importunities. **1883** GRESLEY *Gloss. Coal-m.* 226 *Sliding Scale*, a mode of regulating the amount of wages in mining districts by taking as a basis for calculation the market value of coal or iron.

*attrib.* **1868** ROGERS *Pol. Econ.* xiv. (1876) 192 During the existence of the sliding-scale system of duties. **1882** *Daily News* 3 June 6/4 The leaping prizes..are arranged on a sliding-scale principle.

**10. a.** ***sliding hernia*** (Med.) (see quot. 1958).

**1910** SPENCER & GASK *Pract. Surg.* xvii. 995 Retro-peritoneal hernia... The cæcum or sigmoid flexure may slide up and down behind the peritoneum, 'Sliding hernia', 'Hernie par glissement'. **1936** COLE & ELMAN *Textbk. Gen. Surg.* xxv. 753 Sliding hernias descend so readily that a truss is rarely satisfactory in maintaining reduction. **1958** D. L. B. FARLEY in L. Oliver *Basic Surg.* xiii. 198 Hernia 'en glissade' ('sliding' hernia) refers to herniation of a viscus such as the cæcum or bladder which has an extraperitoneal surface. **1974** R. M. KIRK et al. *Surgery* vi. 78 Sliding hernia. If the lower oesophagus and cardia straighten out and slide into the chest, the competence of the cardiac sphincter may be impaired so that gastric contents reflux into the oesophagus.

**b.** ***sliding filament*** (Physiol.), used *attrib.* to designate the model of the action of striated muscle in which contraction results from filaments of actin and of myosin sliding past one another.

**1957** *Jrnl. Biophys. & Biochem. Cytol.* III. 640 The results which have been described above give full support to the 'sliding filament model' of striated muscle. **1973** *Times* 14 Aug. 14/7 This..provided the main basis for the 'sliding filament' theory of muscle contraction, now universally accepted.

**11.** ***sliding parity*** (Econ.) = *crawling peg* s.v. CRAWLING *ppl. a.* b.

**1966** *Economist* 25 June 1440/2 A tiny minority advocates completely free exchange markets... Possibly a majority favours continued official intervention to set limits to market fluctuations... But an increasing minority favours a compromise system, variously called the crawling peg..or ..the sliding parity. **1970** *Times* 9 Feb. 20/1 It sets out to demolish the arguments of those who are..downright hostile to the introduction of the so called sliding parity or crawling peg.

**ˈslidingly**, *adv.* [f. SLIDING *ppl. a.*] In a sliding manner; with a smooth, gliding movement.

**1644** DIGBY *Nat. Bodies* xiv. §7. 120 They come slidingly one ouer an other. **1870** LOWELL *Among my Bks.* Ser. I. (1873) 23 What a slidingly musical use he makes of the sibilants.

**ˈslidingness.** *rare*$^{-1}$. [f. as prec.] Sliding quality; easy movement or flow.

*a* **1586** SIDNEY *Arcadia* II. (1622) 200 In Tragedies..he had learned, besides a slidingnes of language, acquaintance with many passions.

**ˈslidness.** *Sc. rare.* [f. SLID *a.*] Smoothness.

*a* **1758** RAMSAY *To Duncan Forbes* iii, Enjoy..and judge the wit And slidness of a sang.

**slie**, obs. f. SLY *a.*

**slieghly**, obs. f. SLYLY.

**slieveen**, var. SLEEVEEN.

**'Slife** (slaɪf), *int.* *Obs.* exc. *arch.* An abbreviation of *God's life* (see GOD *sb.* 14 a) used as a petty oath or exclamation.

*a* **1634** CHAPMAN *Rev. Hon.* III. ii, 'Slife, a prince, And such a hopeful one, to lose his eyes is cruelty prodigious. **1693** CONGREVE *Old Bach.* I. i, Hold hold, 'slife that's the wrong. **1740–1** RICHARDSON *Pamela* III. 324 'Slife—I'll thresh my Jades..when I come home. **1777** SHERIDAN *Sch. Scand.* IV. iii, Behind the screen! 'Slife, let's unveil her! **1828** CARR *Craven Gloss.*, *Slife*, an exclamation. **1860** WHYTE MELVILLE *Holmby Ho.* vii, 'Slife, Frank,..you've the devil's luck and your own too.

†**sliffe.** *Obs.*$^{-1}$ [Of obscure origin; perh. an error for SLUDE.] ? Mica.

**1664** POWER *Exp. Philos.* I. 24 It was clear and diaphanous like a thin film of Sliffe or Muscovy-glass.

**slift**$^1$. Now *dial.* or *Obs.* [Related to SLIVE *v.*$^1$; cf. *rift* and *rive.*] (See quot. 1823, and cf. SLEAVING.)

**1657** REEVE *God's Plea* 252 These slifts, which have been taken from you, are grown up to a wonderful height. **1823** E. MOOR *Suffolk Wds.* 361 *Slift*, a slip off a growing plant or shrub, rent, not cut off.

**slift**$^2$. *E. Angl.* [Of obscure origin.] The fleshy part of a leg of beef.

*a* **1825** FORBY *Voc. E. Anglia* 307 The grand round of beef is the upper and under slift together. **1869** *N. & Q.* 4th Ser. IV. 33 A sirloin of beef, roast ribs of beef, and a boiled slift of beef. **1897** RYE *Norfolk Songs*, etc. 70 Nor is slift of beef preferred by Norwichers to sirloin.

**slifter** (ˈslɪftə(r)). Now *dial.* [Related to SLIFT$^1$ and SLIVE *v.*$^1$ Cf. also obs. or dial. G. *schlifter* gully, watercourse.]

**1.** A cleft or crack; a crevice.

**1607** TOPSELL *Four-f. Beasts* (1658) 21 The chapping, clefts, or slifters, in the body, which come by cold. *Ibid.* 536 There are also certain slifters or clifts in the hoofs of Horses, which are cured in one nights space. **1611** COTGR., *Fente*, a cleft, rift, slifter, chinke. *c* **1746** J. COLLIER (Tim Bobbin) *View Lanc. Dial.* (1775) 21 Oth Leawp-hoyles, on th' Slifters ith Leath Woughs. *a* **1800** in PEGGE *Suppl. Grose.* **1828** in CARR *Craven Gloss.* **1874** WAUGH *Chimney Corner* (1879) 170 There isn't a slifter, nor a ginnel, nor a gorse-bush.

†**2.** A splinter. *Obs.*

**1606** G. W[OODCOCK] *Lives Emperors* in *Hist. Ivstine* Ll 5, Henry the French king was slaine by the slifter of a speare broke vpon him.

Hence **ˈsliftered** *ppl. a.*, riven asunder, cloven.

**1602** MARSTON *Ant. & Mel.* I, Straight chops a wave, and in his sliftred panch Downe fals our ship. **1866** WAUGH *Lanc. Songs* (1870) 50 He toots abeawt, i' th slifter't cleawd To find a bit o' sky.

**sligh**, **sliȝ(e**, obs. ff. SLY *a.*

**slight**, obs. f. SLEIGHT *sb.*$^1$ and *a.*

**slight** (slaɪt), *sb.* Also 6–7 **sleight.** [f. SLIGHT *a.* and *v.*]

†**1.** A very small amount or weight; a small matter, a trifle. *Obs.*

**1549–62** STERNHOLD & H. *Ps.* lxii. 9 The sonnes of men deceitfull are, on ballaunce but a sleight. **1601** SIR W. CORNWALLIS *Ess.* II. xxix. (1631) 35 No lawes being so excellent as those that..being slights produce the weightiest and best effects. **1647** H. MORE *Poems* 130 The same sleights By turns do urge them both in their descents and heights. **1678** MOXON *Mech. Exerc.* IV. 66 Yet it is but a sleight to those Practice hath inur'd the Hand to.

†**b.** In phr. ***to make a*** (etc.) ***slight*** (*of*). Cf. SLIGHT *a.* 5 d. *Obs.*

*c* **1619** R. JONES *Serm. Resurrection* (1659) 11 His Disciples were..such tall fellows with their weapons, that they made it but a sleight either to withstand or assault a whole multitude. **1704** J. PITTS *Acc. Moham.* ix. (1738) 190 He made a slight of that. **1730** BURDON *Pocket Farrier* 38 There is a Lameness..; Our Farriers make great Slight of it.

**2.** Display of contemptuous indifference or disregard; supercilious treatment or reception of a person, etc.; small respect *for* one.

**1701** PENN in *Pennsylv. Hist. Soc. Mem.* IX. 48 Pray don't hurt him by an appearance of neglect, less of slight. **1740–1** RICHARDSON *Pamela* IV. 268, I don't care that such a Proposal should be received with undue Slight. **1841** D'ISRAELI *Amen. Lit.* (1867) 359 The subjects he has written on..incurred the slight of the cavillers of his day. **1867** HOWELLS *Ital. Journ.* 250 Treating him with good-natured slight. **1897** —— *Landlord at Lion's Head* 374 He knew too well his mother's slight for Whitwell to suppose that he could have influenced her.

**3.** An instance of slighting or being slighted.

**1719** D'URFEY *Pills* (1872) V. 57 This Slight bred sad domestic Strife. **1780** *Mirror* No. 91, We see daily examples of men.. who meet with slights where they demand respect. **1825** SCOTT *Jrnl.* 23 Dec., He was kindly treated, but.. suspected slights.. where no such thing was meant. **1856** FROUDE *Hist. Eng.* (1858) I. iii. 267 They revenged the studied slight which had been passed by Henry on themselves. **1875** JOWETT *Plato* (ed. 2) IV. 123 He could hardly have passed upon them a more unmeaning slight.

**slight** (slaɪt), *a.* and *adv.* Forms: α. 4 **sliȝt, slyȝt,** 4– **slight** (6 **slighte**), 7 **slite**; *Sc.* 6 **slycht, slichte,** 6– **slicht.** β. 4 **sleȝt,** 5 **sleiȝte**; 4–5 **sleght,** 4–7 **sleight.** [ME. (orig. northern) *slight, sleght,* ad. OScand. **sleht-* (ON. *sléttr,* Icel. *sléttur,* Norw. *slett*; Sw. *slät,* Da. *slet*), = OE. **sliht* (only in *eorðslihtes* adv.), OFris. *sliucht* (WFris. *sljucht*), OS. *sliht,* MDu. and MLG. *slecht, slicht* (Du. *slecht,* LG. *slicht, slecht*), OHG. and MHG. *sleht* (G. *schlecht, schlicht*), Goth. *slaihts*; the relations of the stem are uncertain.]

**A.** *adj.* **1.** Smooth; glossy; sleek. *Obs.* exc. *dial.*

*a* **1300** *Cursor M.* 4562 Me thoght.. þai i com in a medu slight. *c* **1400** *Destr. Troy* 3063 The slote of hir slegh brest sleght for to showe, As any cristall clere. **1483** *Cath. Angl.* 344/1 A Sleght stone, *lamina, licinitorium.* **1530** PALSGR. 324/1 Sleight or smothe, *alis.* **1535** COVERDALE *1 Sam.* xvii. 40 He.. chose fyue slighte stones out of the ryuer. **1596** HARINGTON *Metam. Ajax* 4 The contentments;.. if we catch them they proue but like Eeles, sleight and slipperie. **1615** MARKHAM *Eng. Housew.* 33 Vpon the same place rubbe a sleight stone, and then with it sleight all the swelling. **1866** EDMONDSTON *Shetl. & Orkn. Gloss.* 108 *Slight,* smooth, unruffled, applied to the sea. **1868** ATKINSON *Cleveland Gloss.* 465. **1892** M. C. F. MORRIS *Yorksh. Folk-Talk* 372.

*fig.* *a* **1300** *Cursor M.* 26582 Noght wit wordes fayr and slight Agh þou for to plane þi plight.

**2.** Slender, slim, thin; of a small and slender form or build.

**13..** *E.E. Allit. P.* A. 190 Þat gracios gay.. So smoþe, so smal, so seme[ly] slyȝt. *c* **1400** *Rom. Rose* 7257 Beggers.. With sleight [*MS.* sleight] and pale faces lene. **1578** LYTE *Dodoens* 28 The roote is sleight or single. **1683** *Brit. Spec.* 46 They had only little Skiffs, the Keels and Footstocks whereof were made of slight Timber. **1810** SCOTT *Lady of L.* I. xviii, E'en the slight hare-bell raised its head. **1849** C. BRONTE *Shirley* xxviii, Some fine slight fingers have a wondrous knack at pulverizing a man's brittle pride. **1877** MRS. FORRESTER *Mignon* I. 10 A slight dark girl is singing an old English Ballad.

**b.** ***slight falcon*** = FALCON-GENTLE.

**1591** FLETCHER *Russe Commw.* (Hakl.) 14 They have.. great store of hawkes, the eagle, the gerfaulcon, the slight-faulcon, the goshawke. **1615** LATHAM *Falconry* (1633) 17 Although the Faulcons gentle, or slight Faulcons, are by nature all of one kind. **1725** *Fam. Dict.* s.v. *Hawk,* The Long-wing'd, which last Hawks are the Faulcon or Slight-Faulcon. **1828** SEBRIGHT *Obs. Hawking* 3 The slight falcon.. and the goshawk.. are the two species generally used in falconry.

**3.** Of light, thin, or poor texture or material; not good, strong, or substantial; rather flimsy or weak.

**1393–4** *Rolls of Parlt.* III. 322/2 [Dont les Leyns cressantz es ditz Countees sont unes maneres des Leyns appellez] sleght wolle. **1497** *Naval Acc. Hen. VII* (1896) 242, xxxv boltes of Sleght Canvas price of euery bolte x$^s$. **1505** *Acc. Ld. High Treas. Scot.* III. 80 Ane cheseb of rede chamlot to the Gray Freris of Air, with cors of slicht gold. **1558** in Feuillerat *Revels Q. Eliz.* (1908) 17 Howe many maskes, and whether riche or slite. **1594** NASHE *Unfort. Trav.* 18 He that could make a garment slightest and thinnest carried it away. **1601** R. JOHNSON *Kingd. & Commw.* 145 The soile of the countrey for the most parte is of a sleight sandie moulde. **1663** GERBIER *Counsel* 91 For which price, but very slight work hath been furnished. **1790** BRUCE *Source Nile* I. 105 This slight structure of private buildings seems to be the reason so few ruins are found. **1807** G. CHALMERS *Caledonia* I. ii. I. 69 Their infantry were.. armed.. with slight shields, short spears, and handy daggers.

**b.** Lacking in solid or substantial qualities.

**1585** T. WASHINGTON tr. *Nicholay's Voy.* III. xi. 90 b, The Turks do content themselues with slight meates and easily dressed. **1597** MORLEY *Introd. Mus.* 180 The slightest kind of musick.. are the vinate or drincking songes. **1603** DRAYTON *Odes* i. 86 To those that with despight Shall terme these Numbers slight Tell them their Judgement's blind. **1653** H. MORE *Antid. Ath.* III. xi. §3 Slight Rhetorications, no sound Arguments. *a* **1715** BURNET *Own Time* III. (1724) I. 414 He has published many books,.. but all full of faults; for he was a slight and superficial man. **1736** BUTLER *Anal.* II. v. Wks. 1874 I. 211 This may be but a slight ground to raise a positive opinion upon. **1823** SCOTT *Quentin D.* Introd., Every species of author-craft, slighter than that which compounds a folio volume of law or of divinity. **1886** *Manch. Exam.* 3 Nov. 3/3 Fiction is represented by a good but rather slight story.

†**c.** Foolish, unwise. *Obs.*$^{-1}$

**1663** BUTLER *Hud.* I. i. 775 But no Beast ever was so slight, For Man, as for his God, to fight.

**4.** Of persons: †**a.** Of little worth or account; mean, low; humble in position. *Obs.*

*c* **1460** *Towneley Myst.* xvi. 235 Hard I neuer.. that a knafe so sleght Shuld com.. and refe me my right. **1586** LUPTON *Notable Things* (1675) 271 It would be a disparagement to him and to her to marry such a sleight fellow. **1588** *Reg. Privy Council Scot.* IV. 268 Ane grite nowmer of slicht men and invyous personis. **1651** WELDON *Crt. K. Chas. I,* 206 Otherwise it had been impossible so many grave Judges should have been over-ruled by such a slight and triviall fellow. *a* **1700** EVELYN *Diary* 8 Apr. 1685, Very meane and slight persons (some of them gentlemen's servants, clearkes, and persons neither of reputation nor interest).

†**b.** Unworthy of confidence or trust. *Obs.*$^{-1}$

**1607** TOURNEUR *Rev. Trag.* IV. i, He that knows great men's secrets, and proves slight, That man ne'er lives to see his beard turn white.

†**c.** Loose in morals. *Obs.*$^{-1}$

**1685** *Caldwell Papers* (Maitl. Cl.) I. 159, I having.. been suspicious of her being a slight person, would goe into no room with her.

**5.** Small in amount, quantity, degree, etc.

**1530** PALSGR. Introd. p. xvi, For the same cause, they gyve somtyme unto theyr consonantes but a sleight and remisshe sounde. **1588** LAMBARDE *Eirenarcha* III. iv. 368 By a sleight view and rehearsall of the most part. **1601** BP. W. BARLOW *Serm. Paul's Cross* 48 That sleight feares make women shrike. **1663** S. PATRICK *Parab. Pilgrim* x. (1687) 58 If he knew that he conceived so much joy from such slight appearances and shadows of comfort. **1726** GAY in *Swift's Wks.* (1841) II. 591, I have been very much out of order with a slight fever. **1746** FRANCIS tr. *Horace, Epist.* II. i. 14 Their Toils could raise But slight Returns of Gratitude and Praise. **1815** J. SMITH *Panorama Sci. & Art* II. 111 The effect is very slight, and at thirty feet it would probably be altogether imperceptible. **1857** MILLER *Elem. Chem., Org.* ix. 581 It has also a slight, peculiar, but not unpleasant odour. **1871** C. DAVIES *Metric Syst.* III. 177 A slight attention will give thirds, sixths, and twelfths.

**b.** Unimportant, trifling.

*a* **1548** HALL *Chron., Edw. V,* 17, I doubt not some man wyl thynke this woman to be to slight to be written of emong graue and weyghtie matters. *Ibid., Hen. VIII,* 18 The lordes of Englande.. made report to their capitain accordyng, whiche thought it verie sleight. *a* **1656** BP. HALL *Rem. Wks.* (1660) 146 Are we furious upon every sleight occasion? **1697** DRYDEN *Virg. Georg.* IV. 8 Slight is the Subject, but the Praise not small. **1828** SCOTT *F.M. Perth* xiii, I do no injustice.. when I say he is too slight to be weighed with the Douglas. **1847** TENNYSON *Princ.* IV. 109 O for such, my friend, We hold them slight. **1848** DICKENS *Dombey* xxxvi, Therefore I am glad to take this slight occasion—this trifling occasion,.. to say that I attach no importance to them in the least.

**c.** Used emphatically in the superlative.

**1599** SHAKS. *Much Ado* II. i. 272, I will goe on the slightest arrand now to the Antypodes that you can deuise to send me on. **1750** *Student* I. 57 The cautious father.. was upon the watch.. on every the slightest occasion. **1790** BURKE *Fr. Rev.* 244 Those loose theories to which none of them would chuse to trust the slightest of his private concerns. **1825** BENTHAM *Offic. Apt. Maximized, Indications* (1830) 43 Of the extortion.. not any the slightest intimation. **1848** THACKERAY *Van. Fair* lxv, He never had had the slightest liking for her. **1879** R. K. DOUGLAS *Confucianism* iii. 72 The Sage.. pursues the heavenly way without the slightest deflection.

**d.** ***to make slight of,*** to regard or treat as of little importance or consequence.

**1606** G. W[OODCOCK] *Hist. Ivstine* IX. 39 But they.. made slight of his defiance and hostile forces. *a* **1632** T. TAYLOR *God's Judgem.* II. iii. (1642) 40 Though men make slite of these.. butcheries. **1740** tr. *De Mouhy's Fort. Country Maid* (1741) I. 53, I was startled, but my Governess and her Niece made slight of it. **1796** J. MOSER *Hermit of Caucasus* II. 58 He at first made slight of his indisposition.

**e.** Wanting in fullness or heartiness.

**1660** F. BROOKE tr. *Le Blanc's Trav.* 237 The King.. asking him what he was, received but a slight answer. **1706** HEARNE *Collect.* 27 Jan., Y$^e$ Duke.. receiv'd them after a slight manner. **1864** TENNYSON *Aylmer's F.* 238 Slight was his answer 'Well—I care not for it'.

**f.** Performed with little exertion.

**1667** MILTON *P.L.* IV. 181 He.. in contempt, At one slight bound high overleap'd all bound Of Hill or highest Wall.

†**6.** Slighting, contemptuous. *Obs. rare.*

**1632** MASSINGER & FIELD *Fatal Dowry* II. ii, Recant your stern contempt and slight neglect Of the whole court and him. **1688** *Col. Rec. Pennsylv.* I. 245 Saying you may command the Judges,.. and other slight and scornfull Expressions he vsed.

**7.** *Comb.,* as ***slight-billed, -bottomed, -limbed,*** etc.; also ***slight-seeming.***

**1660** BRETT *Threnodia* viii, Slight-bottom'd Passion's quickly spent. *a* **1697** AUBREY *Brief Lives* (1898) II. 241 Sir John [Suckling] was but a slight timberd man, and of midling stature. **1703** *Lond. Gaz.* No. 3942/4 A black slight Limb'd Mare,.. narrow Ey'd. **1803** BEDDOES *Hygëia* IX. 196 How essential it is to check even slight-seeming nervous disorders in their commencement. **1847** TENNYSON *Princ.* VII. 249 If she be small, slight-natured, miserable, How shall men grow? **1895** LYDEKKER *Roy. Nat. Hist.* IV. 117 The slight-billed parraquet,.. the sole representative of its genus.

**B.** *adv.* **1.** Poorly, slightly; contemptuously.

**1606** SHAKS. *Ant. & Cl.* I. i. 56 Is Cæsar with Anthonius priz'd so slight? **1671** MILTON *P.R.* III. 109 Think not so slight of glory. *a* **1716** BLACKALL *Wks.* (1723) I. 313 In this corrupt Age.. perhaps Oaths are thought much slighter of than ever they were in former Times.

**2.** Slimly, slenderly. Chiefly in *Comb.*

**1667** PRIMATT *City & Co. Builder* 69 A plain Balconie,.. made very slight, may not be worth above three pence half penny the pound. **1800** *Asiatic Ann. Reg.* IV. 19/1 The Hindûs of the lower provinces are a slight made people. **1837** CARLYLE *Fr. Rev.* I. IV. iv, That other, his slight-built comrade, and craft-brother.

**3.** Slightly; to a small extent.

**1671** MILTON *Samson* 1229 Come nearer, part not hence so slight inform'd. **1727–46** THOMSON *Summer* 1590 The neck slight-shaded, and the swelling breast.

**slight** (slaɪt), *v.* Forms: α. 4– **slight,** 7 **slyght,** 8– *Sc.* **slicht**; 4, 7 **slite.** β. 5 **sleght,** 7 **sleight, slaight.** [In sense 1 f. SLIGHT *a.* 1, or a. OScand. **slehta* (ON. and Icel. *slétta,* Norw. *sletta,* Sw. *slätta,* Da. *slette*). In sense 2 ad. Du. *slechten,* LG. *slichten,* or G. *schlichten* to level. In senses 3–4 f. SLIGHT *a.* 5.]

†**1.** *trans.* To make smooth or level. *Obs.*

*a* **1300** *Cursor M.* 28026 Leuedis,.. Quen yee yow-self sua slight and slike, Yee sai þat men you wille besuike. **1483** *Cath. Angl.* 344/1 To Sleght, *lucibrucinare.* **1580** HOLLYBAND *Treas. Fr. Tong, Calendrer vne toile,* to slighte a webbe, or linnen. **1613** MARKHAM *Eng. Husb.* I. I. ix. (1635) 51 You must not at any time sleight or smooth your Corne, but after a shower of Raine. **1620** —— *Farew. Husb.* (1625) 50 After your ground is sowne and harrowed, you shall then clotte it, sleight it, and smooth it.

**2.** To level with the ground; to raze (a fortification, etc.). *Obs.* exc. *Hist.* (common *c* 1640–80).

**1640–4** in Rushw. *Hist. Coll.* III. (1692) I. 368 That the works may be slighted, and the places dismantled. **1667** TEMPLE *Let. to Ld. Holles* Wks. 1720 II. 37 When the Works were about half slighted,.. came seven or eight hundred French Horse. **1698** T. FROGER *Voy.* 28 A Council was held to determine, whether the Fort should be kept or slighted. **1974** *Country Life* 28 Mar. 747/3 In March 1645–46, Parliament gave orders that Corfe [Castle] should be slighted. **1976** E. N. LUTTWAK *Grand Strategy of Roman Empire* ii. 57 It was standard practice to slight the defenses once the site was left. **1977** *Brit. Med. Jrnl.* 24 Dec. 1619/1 Mrs Barbara Castle shattered the political confidence of consultants as effectively as Henry II slighted his opponents' strongholds.

*fig.* **1646** H. LAWRENCE *Comm. Angels* 187 Till you have overcome your enemie and sleighted his workes. **1676** CUDWORTH *Serm. 1 Cor. xv.* 71 Christ our Lord.. slighted and dismantled that mighty Garrison.

**3. a.** To treat with indifference or disrespect; to pay little or no attention or heed to; to disregard, disdain, ignore.

α. **1597** SHAKS. *2 Hen. IV,* v. ii. 94 Heare your owne dignity so much prophan'd, See your most dreadfull Lawes so loosely slighted. **1619** DRAYTON *Odes* xii. 22 The time I knew She slighted you, When I was in her fauour. **1655** FULLER *Ch. Hist.* II. 131 The Count slighted his Excommunication, conceiving his Head too high for Church-Censures to reach it. **1727** A. HAMILTON *New Acc. E. Indies* II. l. 225 He.. told me, that he had taken much Pains to serve me, but that I slighted his Service. **1780** COWPER *Progr. Error* 419 We slight the precious kernel of the stone, And toil to polish its rough coat alone. **1847** EMERSON *Repr. Men, Napoleon,* He delighted in the conversation of men of science,.. but the men of letters he slighted. **1865** DICKENS *Our Mut. Friend* III. iv, The confidences of lovely women are not to be slighted.

β. **1612** WOODALL *Surg. Mate* Wks. (1653) 84 Like him which in hast sleighted his good friends. **1652** NEEDHAM tr. *Selden's Mare Cl.* 120 Neither is that to bee sleighted here which wee find in the letters of David. **1673** CAVE *Prim. Chr.* III. iv. 333 Do my Souldiers think thus to Sleight my Royal Orders?

†**b.** To put *off* disdainfully. *Obs.*

**1601** SHAKS. *Jul. C.* IV. iii. 5 Wherein my Letters, praying on his side,.. was slighted off. **1627** S. WARD *Life of Faith* 66 Many gulls and gallants we may heare sometimes slight off death with a iest, when they thinke it out of hearing.

†**c.** To throw contemptuously. *Obs.*$^{-1}$

**1598** SHAKS. *Merry W.* III. v. 8 The rogues slighted me into the riuer with as little remorse, as they would haue drown'de a blinde bitches Puppies.

†**d.** *intr.* with *at.* To be indifferent. *Obs.*$^{-1}$

**1618** WITHER *Juvenilia* (1633) 538 When to bar me ought He sees it fit, He doth infuse a Mind to sleight at it.

**4.** To gloss or pass (a thing) *over* carelessly or with indifference. ? *Obs.*

**1620** R. WALLER in *Lismore Papers* (1887) Ser. II. II. 248 Though I coniectured the busynes yet I sleighted it ouer with a kinde of pretended ignorance. **1652** NEEDHAM tr. *Selden's Mare Cl.* 470 This his Majestie takes for an high point of his Soveraigntie, and will not have it slighted over in any fashion whatsoever. **1656** PHILLIPS *Purch. Pattern* 144 But this must not alwayes be so slighted over, lest you run into great errour. **1824** SCOTT *Redgauntlet* ch. x, I lodge a complaint before you as a magistrate, and you will find it serious to slight it over.

**5.** *dial.* To do (work) carelessly or negligently.

**1854** [see SLIPSTRING 2].

†**'Slight,** *int. Obs.* An abbreviation of *God's light* (see GOD *sb.* 14 a), used as a petty oath or exclamation.

**1598** B. JONSON *Ev. Man out of Hum.* II. ii, 'Slight, an it had come but four days sooner. **1605** CHAPMAN *All Fools* Plays 1873 I. 119 Slight hence, the olde knight comes. **1668** SEDLEY *Mulb. Gard.* II. ii, 'Slight here's Sir John.

**slighted** (ˈslaɪtɪd), *ppl. a.* [f. SLIGHT *v.*]

**1.** Treated with indifference or disdain.

**1619** A. NEWMAN *Pleas. Vis.* 33 The slighted outcast, he did lye. **1665** BOYLE *Occas. Refl.* III. vi. (1848) 44 By the meanest Creatures, and slighted'st object. **1719** YOUNG *Busiris* I. i, The slighted altars tremble. **1784** COWPER *Task* VI. 51 Not to understand a treasure's worth Till time has stol'n away the slighted good. **1848** DICKENS *Dombey* ix, His breast was full of interest for the slighted child. **1870** BRUCE *Life of Gideon* ii. 43 You will.. fall into the.. hands of a slighted and therefore grievously insulted God.

†**2.** Levelled, razed. *Obs.*

**1636** DENHAM *Poems, Virg. Æneis* II. 28 All through th' unguarded Gates with joy resort To see the slighted Camp, the vacant Port. **1716** POPE *Iliad* VIII. 218 High o'er their slighted trench our steeds shall bound.

**'slighten,** *v. rare.* Also 7 **sleighten.** [f. SLIGHT *a.* or *v.*] **1.** *trans.* = SLIGHT *v.* 3.

**1605** B. JONSON *Sejanus* v, It is an odious wisdome to blaspheme, Much more to slighten, or deny their powers. **1633** FORD *'Tis Pity* IV. ii, She, as 'tis said, Slightens his love, and he abandons hers. **1646** FEATLY *Dippers Dipt* 37 The custome of our Mother the Church.. is no way to be slightned [1645 sleighted] or rejected.

**2.** To make smaller or more slight.
**1954** P. Toynbee *Friends Apart* vii. 90 Dysentery.. had thinned his face and slightened his broad body.
Hence **'slightening** *ppl. a.*
**1916** A. Quiller-Couch *Art of Reading* (1920) i. 14 God forbid that anyone should hint a slightening word of what our sons and brothers are doing just now.

**slighter** ('slaɪtə(r)). Also 7 **sleighter.** [f. slight *v.* + -er[1].] One who slights or disdains.
**1646** Saltmarshe *Groans for Liberty* 29 Sermon sleighters. **1651** Baxter *Saints' R.* (ed. 2) iv. 65 Unworthy sleighters of Christ and glory. *a* **1661** Fuller *Worthies* (1840) III. 151 Italians (the admirers only of themselves and the slighters-general of all other nations). **1747** Doddridge *Mem. Col. Gardiner* (1808) 72 The miserable condition of those that are slighters of pardoning grace. **1846** Trench *Mirac.* 67 The breaker through and slighter of the apparitions of sense.

†**'slightfully,** *adv.* *Obs.*[−1] [f. slight *sb.*] Slightingly.
**1627** W. Sclater *Exp. 2 Thess.* (1629) 169 And why so slightfully regard we euidences or authorities brought to auouch doctrines as being *de fide?*

†**'slightily,** *adv. Obs. rare.* [f. slighty *a.*]
**a.** Carelessly. **b.** Slightingly; disdainfully.
**1679** Penn *Addr. Protestants* i. 6 Sin gives the deadliest of all Wounds to Mankind; I grieve to say it, but 'tis too true; there is no Wound so slightily healed. **1740** *Col. Rec. Pennsylv.* IV. 459 We make no Doubt, however slightily he may treat us [etc.].

†**'slightiness.** *Obs. rare.* [f. as prec.] Carelessness, indifference.
**1662** Newcome *Diary* (Chetham Soc.) 111 A sudden crosse had God brought on mee.. for my sleightyness and neglect of meditation. **1678** *Young Man's Calling* 19 Neglect and slightiness in the means of our salvation.

**'slighting,** *vbl. sb.* [f. slight *v.* + -ing[1].]
†**1.** The action of levelling (ground). *Obs.*
**1613** Markham *Eng. Husb.* i. i. ix. (1635) 50 A Rouler.. is for this purpose of sleighting and smoothing of grounds of great use and profit. **1615** —— *Eng. Housew.* ii. v. (1668) 130 So fine a mould as you can possibly break with your harrows, clotting beetles, or sleighting.
**2.** The action of razing or demolishing. *Obs.* exc. *Hist.*
**1640** *Kirkcudbright War-Committee's Minute Bk.* (1855) 66 In obedience of the warrand.. for sleighting of the hows of the Threive. *c* **1645** Tullie *Siege of Carlisle* (1840) 14 Daily skirmishes.. and now and then the sleighting of a work. **1707** in Picton *L'pool Munic. Rec.* (1886) II. 39 The immediate slighting the said castle and demolishing.. the outworks thereof. **1936** *Times Lit. Suppl.* 6 June 479/4 In spite of Cromwellian 'slighting' and the quarrying of local builders and road-makers, so much.. still remains. **1977** H. R. Loyn *Vikings in Britain* v. 95 Evidence of possible slighting of fortifications at Cricklade and Cadbury, may well indicate the confidence of the new régime at least in Wessex under Cnut and Earl Godwin.
**3.** The action of treating with disdain, disregard, or indifference.
**1622** Fletcher *Beggar's Bush* iii. iv, Yet will ye love me? Tell me but how I have deserv'd your slighting? **1659** C. Noble *Mod. Answ. Immod. Queries* 6 To charge him with neglects and slightings and disregardings to his friends. **1711** *Brit. Apollo* No. 15. 2/1 She has return'd to her former Reservedness and.. slighting of me. **1859** Helps *Friends in C.* Ser. ii. II. v. 104 Prone to believe he is the subject of any intentional slighting.
**4.** The action of glossing *over.* ? *Obs.*
**1617** Hieron *Wks.* II. 325 My silence, my conniuence, my slighting ouer of these things.

**'slighting,** *ppl. a.* [f. as prec. + -ing[2].]
**1.** Conveying or implying a slight; of a contemptuous or disdainful character.
**1632** B. Jonson *Magn. Lady* i. i, To hear yourself.. glanced at In a few slighting terms. **1641** Baker *Chron., John* 96 In this slighting humour he returnes into England. **1691** Wood *Ath. Oxon.* II. 405 [It] was generally looked upon as a scornful slighting and very unfair way. **1825** Scott *Betrothed* xviii, The Constable felt the full effect of this slighting reception. **1892** *Athenæum* 21 May 658/2 A slighting allusion to one of his literary productions.
**2.** Acting contemptuously or disdainfully.
**1684** *Roxb. Ball.* (1886) VI. 85 Never did a slighting Lover So much cruelty discover As this Tyrant doth to me. *a* **1697** Aubrey *Lives* (1898) I. 277 A squeamish, disobliging, slighting, insolent, proud fellow.

**slightingly** ('slaɪtɪŋlɪ), *adv.* [f. prec. + -ly[2].] In a slighting manner; contemptuously, disdainfully; with little regard or respect.
**1636** Davenant *Wits* Wks. (1673) 208 You speak slightingly of it, As if 'twere a poor thing. **1654** *Nicholas Papers* (Camden) II. 51 Ormond replied, 'perhaps his Lordship had a faculty to make any thing good', and slitingly neglected him. **1740–1** Richardson *Pamela* II. 291 Hush! said he: I will not bear to hear her spoken slightingly of! **1790** Beatson *Naval & Milit. Mem.* I. 42 By failing in this hazardous exploit, which he had treated so slightingly. **1831–3** E. Burton *Eccl. Hist.* xvi. (1845) 359 The passages.. might lead us to think slightingly of his candour. **1881** Saintsbury *Dryden* iii. 65 Dryden speaks slightingly of these University prologues.
So **'slightingness,** disdainfulness. *rare*[−1].
**1683** Cave *Ecclesiastici, Greg. Naz.* 328 The Emperor quickly discern'd the slightingness of his carriage.

**slightish** ('slaɪtɪʃ), *a.* [f. slight *a.* + -ish[1].] Somewhat slight, slender, or small.
**1761** *Ann. Reg., Useful Projects* 128/2 She.. only complained of a slightish pain and heaviness in her head. **1866** Carlyle *Remin.* (1881) I. 269 Charles himself was a swart, slightish, insipid-looking man. **1881** Watson in *Jrnl. Linn. Soc., Zool.* XV. 265 *Operculum* testaceous, scored with slightish radiating lines.

**slightly** ('slaɪtlɪ), *adv.* Also 6 **slyghtly, sleyghtly, sleightlie,** 6–7 **-ly.** [f. slight *a.* + -ly[2]. Cf. MDu. and MLG. *slechte-, slichtelik(e,* MHG. *slehtlîch(e,* G. *schlechtlich.*]
**1.** Slimly, slenderly; flimsily, unsubstantially.
**1521** *Coventry Leet-bk.* 673 That they put sufficient stuf in them.., and that they make them not slyghtly. **1529** *Act 21 Hen. VIII,* c. 12 §1 Traces, halters and other tacle ben by the said persons sleyghtly and deceyvably made. **1549–50** *Act 3 & 4 Edw. VI,* c. 2 §1 The same Clothes soe sleightlie and subtillye made. **1602** Shaks. *Ham.* iv. vii. 22 So that my Arrowes Too slightly timbred for so loud a Winde, Would haue reuerted. **1635–56** Cowley *Davideis* ii. 325 That fatal net, Which though but slightly wrought, was firmly set. **1724** Swift *Drapier's Lett.* Wks. 1755 V. ii. 148 To raise the prices.. and manufacture the said goods more slightly and fraudulently than before. **1745** Pococke *Descr. East* II. i. 197 A well of good water, from which the city is supplied by an aqueduct very slightly built. **1847** C. Bronte *J. Eyre* xi, She was quite a child,.. slightly built.
**b.** Loosely, slackly.
**1599** Shaks. *Much Ado* i. i. 289 The guardes are but slightly basted on. **1667** Milton *P.L.* iv. 967 The facil gates of hell too slightly barrd. **1821** Scott *Kenilw.* v, The flower had been stuck so slightly into the cap.
**2.** Without much care or attention; carelessly; lightly.
*a* **1557** Mrs. Basset *Let.* in *More's Wks.* 1435/1 For the instruction of my conscience in the matter, I haue not sleightly looked, but by many yeres studied & aduisedly considred. **1594** Kyd *Cornelia* i, [Fortune] slightly sowes that sildom taketh roote. **1617** Moryson *Itin.* i. 197, I slightly passe over the places described in my former passage those waies. **1679** Moxon *Mech. Exerc.* vii. 120 He that knows how to work curiously, may when he lists work slightly. **1773** Goldsm. *Stoops to Conq.* iii, I know they are too valuable to be so slightly kept. **1843** Bethune *Sc. Fireside Stor.* 36 Affection may try to.. pass slightly over the darker evidence against him.
**b.** Without much interest, insistence, or heartiness; indifferently.
**1599** Drayton *Idea* viii, I say I loue, you slightly aunswer I? **1709** Swift *Vind. Bickerstaff* Wks. 1757 II. i. 174 There is one objection.. which I have sometimes met with, though indeed very slightly offered. **1779** Johnson *L.P., Mallet,* When Mallet entered one day, Pope asked him slightly what there was new. **1833** Ht. Martineau *Loom & Lugger* i. v. 78 Mrs. Draper slightly returned the farewell of her visitors.
**c.** With slight exertion or effort. *rare.*
**1613** Shaks. *Hen. VIII,* ii. iv. 112 You haue by Fortune.. Gone slightly o're lowe steppes. **1760–72** H. Brooke *Fool of Qual.* (1809) IV. 58 He catched at the upmost bar with his left hand, and, throwing himself slightly over, opened the gate.
**3.** Easily, readily; weakly.
**1594** Kyd *Cornelia* ii, He that retyres not at the threats of death, Is not, as are the vulgar, slightly fraied. **1596** Shaks. *Merch. V.* v. i. 167 You were too blame,.. To part so slightly with your wiues first gift. *c* **1605** Rowley *Birth of Merlin* iv. i, Is it the weakest part I found in thee To doubt of me so slightly? **1646** J. Whitaker *Uzziah* 4, I should wrong goodnesse.., if I should sleightly give that title to unknown persons. **1825** Scott *Betrothed* xix, She has.. advisers, who may not.. recommend to her to sit down slightly with this injury.
**4.** With little respect or ceremony; disparagingly, slightingly. Now *rare.*
**1599** B. Jonson *Cynthia's Rev.* iii. ii, I'le censure it slightly, and ridiculously. **1623** in Foster *Eng. Factories Ind.* (1908) II. 244 The sending of the young Prince and ould gentlleman so slightly from the Kinge is by some conjectered to bee a ploott. **1654** *Nicholas Papers* (Camden) II. 136 Walter Montague doth proceed to speeke very slitly of the Kings commands. *a* **1779** Warburton *Wks.* (1811) IX. 260 Learned Men, who have affected to think slightly of the Religion of their Country. **1825** Scott *Betrothed* xv, I am not to be treated as an ordinary person, who may be received with negligence, and treated slightly with impunity. **1892** Lumsden *Sheep-head* 289 The country lass they'll slightly pass, An she were dirt.
**5.** In a slight or small degree; to a slight extent.
**1594** Kyd *Cornelia* v. 331 O radiant Sunne that slightly guildst our dayes. **1663** Cowley *Verses & Ess., Liberty,* I do but slightly touch upon all these particulars of the slavery of Greatness. **1794** Mrs. Radcliffe *Myst. Udolpho* xxxviii, He bade her good morning, and, bowing slightly to the count, disappeared. **1818** Scott *Hrt. Midl.* xxxvi, As the Duke tapped slightly at it, a person.. unlocked the door. **1837** Carlyle *Fr. Rev.* iii. ii. vi, He had breakfasted but slightly. **1863** Lyell *Antiq. Man* 17 Sometimes worn down to the surface of the mud, sometimes projecting slightly above it.
**b.** Used to qualify a following pple. or adj.
**1592** Kyd *Sp. Trag.* iii. xiii. 70 My cause, but slightly knowne, May mooue the harts of warlike Myrmydons. *a* **1700** Evelyn *Diary* 3 June 1666, The Duke of Albemarle was slightly wounded. **1732** Berkeley *Alciphr.* ii. §8 Those who are even slightly read in our philosophy. **1747** Wesley *Prim. Physick* (1762) 108 A slice of Apple slightly boiled. **1791** *Gentl. Mag.* 22/1 A servant maid, who from her childhood had been slightly deaf. **1835** J. Duncan *Beetles* (Nat. Lib.) 126 The outer edge of the elytra is slightly sinuated at the apex. **1855** Macaulay *Hist. Eng.* xix. IV. 371 To William he was already slightly known. **1884** *Cent. Mag.* Jan. 419/2 After a heavy rain the stream was.. slightly darker in hue.
**c.** Forming attributive collocations with pples. or adjs., and frequently hyphened.
**1800** Shaw *Gen. Zool.* I. i. 245 Slightly hairy Trichechus. **1804** *Ibid.* V. i. 48 Slightly gilded Salmon. **1829** W. Ellis *Polynesian Res.* I. ii. 55 Resembling.. the white of a slightly boiled egg. **1833** Lyell *Princ. Geol.* III. 311 Slightly-worn and angular flints. **1837** J. T. Smith tr. *Vicat's Mortars* 26 A large disengagement of hot slightly-caustic vapour. **1892** Greener *Breech-Loader* 54 Slightly-used guns of their cheaper qualities.

**slightness** ('slaɪtnɪs). [f. as prec. + -ness.] The character or quality of being slight, in various senses of the word.
**1.** Lack of substance, strength, thoroughness, etc.
**1607** Shaks. *Cor.* iii. i. 148 It must omit Reall Necessities, and giue way the while To vnstable Slightnesse. **1691** T. H[ale] *Acc. New Invent.* 104 The service and firmness of the Cast-Lead, and the sleightness and the charge of the other. **1727** Bailey (vol. II), *Sleaziness* (of Cloth), Slightness of Workmanship. **1788** Sir J. Reynolds *Disc.* xiv. (1842) 254 The slightness which we see in his [Gainsborough's] best works cannot always be imputed to negligence. **1817** Jas. Mill *Brit. India* I. ii. iv. 163 It is treated with a negligence and slightness due to a matter of subordinate importance. **1856** Ruskin *Mod. Paint.* II. iii. i. x. §3 It is.. easy to know the slightness of earnest haste from the slightness of blunt feeling, indolence, or affectation.
**2.** Smallness in amount, degree, etc.
**1747** tr. *Astruc's Fevers* 206 A mild fever, through the slightness of the inflammation. **1846** Hawthorne *Mosses fr. Manse* ii. xii. (1864) 254 Glancing with imperceptible slightness at the artist's small and slender frame. **1884** *Manch. Exam.* 13 Dec. 5/2 The slightness of the change is duly appreciated elsewhere. **1889** *Law Rep. 14 P.D.* 109 The absence or slightness of the evidence.
**3.** Slimness, slenderness.
**1797–1805** S. & Ht. Lee *Canterb. T.* V. 128 He had a fixed redness in his face, and had lost the slightness of his person.

†**slightually** ('slaɪtjuːəlɪ), *adv. Obs. U.S. joc.* [f. slight(ly *adv.* + act)ually *adv.*] Actually slightly.
**1859** E. H. N. Patterson *Jrnl.* 29 Mar. in L. Hafen *Overland Routes to Gold Fields* (1942) 79 The weather has been beautiful, although last night was 'slightually' frosty. **1873** 'Mark Twain' *Gilded Age* xxix. 266 The Hooverville *Patriot and Clarion* had this 'item':—Slightually Overboard.

**slighty** ('slaɪtɪ), *a. Obs.* exc. *dial.* Also 7 **sleighty.** [f. slight *a.* + -y.]
†**1.** Superficial; lacking in thoroughness. *Obs.*
**1619** J. Dyke *Caveat* (1620) 19 If so slighty and easie a performance will discharge it. **1650** Baxter *Saint's R.* iii. viii. (1654) 156 The neglect or slighty performance of that great duty. **1671** Eachard *Obs. Answ. Cont. Clergy* 129 Where any thing is advised or commanded after this slothful and slighty way.
†**b.** Of persons: Negligent, careless. *Obs.*
**1655** Gurnall *Chr. Compl. Arm.* vii. 200/1 Till this be done, thou wilt be but sluggish and slighty in thy endeavours for faith. **1661** Newcome *Diary* (Chetham Soc.) 8, I was slighty in secret prayer this morninge.
†**2.** Slighting, contemptuous; light. *Obs.*
**1642** J. Ball *Answ. Canne* i. 118 In his other writings.. he is insolent, censorious, scornfull and slighty. **1674** N. Fairfax *Bulk & Selv.* To Rdr., Should I say I had slighty thoughts of it [etc.].
**3.** Slight, unimportant, trivial; also, unsubstantial, slender, weak.
**1669** Gurnall *Chr. in Arm.* xxiv. §4. 317/2 Thou mayst not think thou goest upon a slighty errand. **1679** Mansell *Narr. Popish Plot* Addr. c 2, Nor does it argue more of Wisdom, to rear such a Massive.. Structure.. upon so slender and sleighty a Foundation. **1713** M. Henry *Wks.* (1855) I. 132/1 To neglect them or make but a short and slighty business of them. *a* **1825** Forby *Voc. E. Anglia* 307 *Slighty,* slim, weak. **1841** Hartshorne *Salop. Ant.* Gloss., *Slighty,* slight, feeble, insufficient, unenduring. **1882** in *W. Worc. Gloss.*

†**sligo.** *slang. Obs.*[−1] (See quot. and tip *v.*)
**1775** S. J. Pratt *Liberal Opin.* lxxii. (1783) III. 34, I tips Slappim the sligo, and nudges the elbow of Trugge, as much as to say, Soho!.. I have him in view.

**slike,** *sb. Sc.* and *north.* Now *rare* or *Obs.* Forms: 5, 8 **slyk (5 slyik),** 5–6 **slyke;** 5–6, 9 **slike (6 slik);** 9 **sleyk.** [? OE. **slíc,* = Fris. *slyk,* MDu. *slijc, sliec* (Du. *slijk*), MLG. *slîk, slyk* (LG. *slîk*), OHG. *slîch* (G. dial. *schleich*): see slitch and cf. slick *sb.*[2]] Mud, slime, sludge.
**1375** Barbour *Bruce* xiii. 352 Bannokburne, that sa cummyrsum was Of slyk, and depnes for till pas. *c* **1425** Wyntoun *Cron.* iv. iii. 263 Slyk and claye mycht þan be seyn Qwhar wattyr deip befor had beyn. *c* **1500** Kennedie *Passion of Christ* 230 In cauld and hunger rynand throw slik and clay. **1513** *Acc. Ld. High Treas. Scot.* IV. 525 To bere the tymer furth of the slyke that came up fra the Margret. **1513** Douglas *Æneid* i. viii. 83 Drivin to land By force of storme, the slyke thai ws deny. **1704** in *Ess. Witchcraft* (1820) 143 William was desired to bring some slyk. **1812** W. Hall *Local Hist. Fens* 11 Seeing rudds run by shoals 'bout the side of Gill sike, Being dreadfully venom'd by rolling in slike. **1870** Robson *Evangeline* 356 An' in the sleyk poor Feely stuck.

†**slike,** *a. Obs.* Chiefly *north.* Also 4–5 **slyk, slyke, slic,** 4 **slik, sli.** [a. ON. *slík-r* (Norw. and Sw. *slik,* Da. *slig*), for earlier **swa-likr,* = Goth. *swa-leiks* 'so-like': see such *a.*] Such. Also with numerals (cf. sic *a.* 1 b).
*a* **1300** *Cursor M.* 6786 To cumlinges do yee right na suike, For quilum war yee seluen slike. *Ibid.* 7472 Ilk dai he come in place, And batail bede wit sli manace. **13..** *Gosp. Nicod.* 1092 (Harl. MS.), To spek of his pouste, yhe may meruaile slyke fyue. *c* **1386** Chaucer *Reeve's T.* 253 Wha herkned euere slyk a ferly thyng? **1446** in *Rep. Hist. MSS. Comm.* (1900) XLVI. 527 Slike distress was never seen within the said town. **1483** *Cath. Angl.* 344/2 Slyke, *huius modi.*
Hence †**slikins,** of such a kind. *Obs.*[−1]
*a* **1300** *Cursor M.* 12010 Ioseph sun Slikins maistris do was won Bifor þe folk of israel.

**slike**, obs. form of SLICK *a.*

†**slike**, *v. Obs.*[−1] [Cf. MLG. and LG. *slîken* (NFris. *slīke*), OHG. *slîhhan* (MHG. *slîchen*, G. *schleichen*) to slide, glide, creep, etc.] *intr.* To slide, glance.

*c* **1400** *Anturs of Arth.* xlviii, The squrd slippus on slonte, and on the mayle slikes.

**slily**: see SLYLY *adv.*

**slim**, *sb.* [f. SLIM *a.*] †**1.** A lanky, lazy, worthless, or despicable person. *Obs.*

**1548** ELYOT *Longurio, -onis*, a longe slymme. **1589** WARNER *Alb. Eng.* VI. xxxi. (1602) 153 Lesse mannerd, and worse gated than this Saturns-Eue-made Slim God neuer made. **1611** COTGR., *Couille*,..a heartlesse, faint-hearted, or white-liuered slimme. *Ibid.*, *Longue eschine*, a luske, slimme, longbacke, or slowbacke.

**2.** A course of slimming, a diet; usu. in phr. ***sponsored slim***.

**1977** *Gay News* 7–20 Apr. 8/1 Barrie announced his intention to go on a sponsored 'slim'. People were asked to sign pledge forms to give a certain amount of money for every pound Barrie would lose between Cambridge and Oxford. **1977** *Navy News* Aug. 30/6 Bill Skilliter went on a sponsored slim and lost 3st.

**slim** (slɪm), *a.* [a. Du. or LG. (also Fris.) *slim*, repr. MDu. *slim(p*, *slem(p*, MLG. *slim(m*, *slym(m*, *slem*, = MHG. *slim*, *slimm-* (G. *schlimm*), OHG. **slimb* crooked, perverse, bad, mean, etc.]

**1. a.** Slender, (gracefully) thin.

Said of persons (or animals), less freq. of things.

(*a*) **1657** G. THORNLEY *Daphnis & Chloe* 61 He's small and slim, and so will slip and steal away. **1692** R. L'ESTRANGE *Fables* I. lv. 55 A Slim, Thin-Gutted Fox made a Hard Shift to wriggle his Body into a Hen-Roost. **1712** STEELE *Spect.* No. 266, I was jogged on the Elbow..by a slim young Girl of..Seventeen. **1753** HOGARTH *Anal. Beauty* xi. 83 Imagine the slim figure of a Mercury, every where neatly formed for the utmost light agility. **1843** JAMES *Forest Days* ii, A man somewhat above the middle size, of a slim and graceful figure. **1859** DARWIN *Orig. Spec.* iv. (1860) 90 The swiftest and slimmest wolves would have the best chance of surviving.

(*b*) **1824** DIBDIN *Library Comp.* 564 Who possess the interminable slim quartos. **1827** HOOD *Tim Turpin* 38 With a cudgel in his hand—It was not light or slim. **1886** MRS. EWING *Mary's Meadow* 69, I put them into a slim glass on my table.

*transf.* **1876** LOWELL *Among my Bks.* Ser. II. 241 An organ ..capable equally of the trumpet's ardors or the slim delicacy of the flute.

**b.** Small, slight; of little substance; poor.

*a* **1677** BARROW *Serm.* Wks. 1716 I. 326 If this be all they are good for, it is..a very slim benefit they afford. **1717** KILLINGBECK *Serm.* 376 Now how vain and slim are all these, if compared with the Solid..Encouragement which our Religion offers. **1862** MAURY in Corbin *Life* (1888) 214 The chances of your getting this [letter] are slim. **1877** G. FRASER *Wigtown* 370 They seemed to have rather slim faith in the stability of the structure.

**c.** *dial.* Of fabrics: Flimsy, thin.

**1813** PICKEN *Poems* I. 123 To weer slim trash o' silk. **1880** WATT *Poet. Sk.* 39 (E.D.D.), His claes were the slimmest that ever ye saw.

**d.** Meagre, scanty, sparse.

**1852** BRISTED *Five Yrs. Eng. Univ.* (ed. 2) 130 We had a very slim audience, not more than a dozen. **1892** *Nation* 1 Sept. 156 Various reasons are given for the slim attendance.

**e.** Delicate; not robust.

**1877** S. O. JEWETT *Deephaven* (1893) 205 She's had slim health of late years.

**f.** Of clothes: cut on slender lines; designed to give an appearance of slimness.

**1884** [see *scoop-shovel bonnet* s.v. SCOOP *sb.*[1] 7]. **1970/71** *Kay's Catal.* Autumn-Winter 145/1 Crimplene Skirt elegantly slim with a raised stripe effect. **1979** *Daily Tel.* 4 June 17/3 (Advt.), One of the most handsome and utterly wearable of this spring's suits is the linen-y slim one in a soft lilac-grey.

†**2.** Of jests: Sly, malicious. *Obs. rare.*

**1668** H. MORE *Div. Dial.* I. xxx. (1713) 65 He does indeed say so, but by way of a slim jear to their ignorance. **1681** GLANVILL *Sadducismus* I. (1682) 161 It cannot be said by any man in his wits, unless by way of sport or some slim jest.

**3.** Of persons, their actions, etc.: Sly, cunning, crafty, wily, artful.

In recent use adopted from S. African Dutch.

**1674** RAY *N.C. Words* 43 *Slim*... It's a word generally used in the same sence with Sly. **1703** THORESBY *Lett. to Ray* s.v., A slim customer. **1768** ROSS *Rock & Wee Pickle Tow* 67 She was never ca'd chancy, but canny an' slim. **1848** LOWELL *Biglow P.* Ser. I. ix, I wish I may be cust, Ef Bellers wuzn't slim enough to say he wouldn't trust! **1899** *Times* 26 Oct. 5/2 The issue of the proclamation by the Boers..is regarded..as a 'slim' (crafty) move on the enemy's part.

**4.** *Comb.* **a.** Parasynthetic, etc., as ***slim-ankled***, ***-built***, ***-faced***, ***-footed***, ***-leaved***, ***-legged***, ***-muzzled***, ***-pointed***, ***-sandalled***, ***-shanked***, ***-tailed***, ***-textured***, ***-waisted***, etc.

**1824** DIBDIN *Library Comp.* (1825) 729 Out of 333 slim-waisted quartos and octavos. **1834** WRANGHAM *Homerics* 11 Him..Pitying, slim-ancled Ino spied. **1838** POE *Narr. A. G. Pym* xix. 160 Slim-legged hogs. **1862** G. M. HOPKINS *Poems* (1967) 10 And spread Slim-pointed seagull plumes. **1866** —— *Jrnls. & Papers* (1959) 142 After six a very slim-textured and pale causeway of mare's tail cloud running N.E. and S.W. **1868** MORRIS *Earthly Par.* (1870) I. I. 371 The slim-leaved trees against the evening sky. **1870** *Ibid.* III. IV. 16 Close by that a slim-trunked tree did grow. **1872** HARDY *Under Greenwood Tree* I. I. ii. 22 The slim-faced martel had knocked 'em down to me because I nodded to en in my friendly way. **1873** HOWELLS *Chance Acquaintance* i. (1883) 22 Villages,..each clustering about its slim-spired church. **1880** 'MARK TWAIN' *Tramp Abr.* x. 95 A long, slim-legged boy, he was, encased in quite a short shirt. *Ibid.* 96 Into the midst of this peaceful scene burst that slim-shanked boy in the brief shirt. **1885** BLACK *White Heather* i, A slim-built built and yet muscular young man. **1912** W. DE LA MARE *Child's Day* 14 But there, Ann dear, You'd rather be A slim-tailed mermaid In the sea. **1914** D. H. LAWRENCE *Prussian Officer & Other Stories* 20 His slim-legged, beautiful horse. **1922** JOYCE *Ulysses* 530 Milly Bloom, fairhaired, greenvested, slimsandalled.., breaks from the arms of her lover. **1923** D. H. LAWRENCE *Birds, Beasts & Flowers* 61 Cyclamens putting their ears back. Long, pensive, slim-muzzled greyhound buds. **1927** —— *Mornings in Mexico* 83 Donkeys, mules, on they come..great bundles bouncing against the sides of the slim-footed animals. **1978** W. F. BUCKLEY *Stained Glass* 225 Himmelfarb..grinned at his long-legged, slim-faced, lightly freckled assistant. **1981** A. SEWART *Close your Eyes & Sleep* vi. 57 He was slim-waisted and muscular looking.

**b. slim-cake**, a kind of plain cake used in Ireland; **slim hole** *Oil Industry*, a drill hole of smaller diameter than normal; usu. *attrib.* (with hyphen); **slim volume**, a book of verse by a little-known poet (freq. mildly *derog.*); hence **slim vol** *colloq. abbrev.*

**1847** *Paddiana* (1848) I. 219 His share of the *slim-cake alone would have furnished him with indigestion for a month. **1894** *Blackw. Mag.* Sept. 318 Where we found tea and Irish slim-cakes provided for us. **1953** *World Oil* June 112/3 Analysis of areas favorable and unfavorable to *slim hole drilling may have been influenced by the performance of available bits in the various types of formations encountered. **1959** *Wall St. Jrnl.* (Eastern ed.) 20 July 15/3 'Slim-hole' drilling..employs conventional equipment—but less of it. The idea is to substitute small pipe and other tinier tools to do a job historically done by larger, more costly units. **1972** L. M. HARRIS *Introd. Deepwater Floating Drilling Operations* iii. 16 Some companies use slim-hole designs and special-clearance couplings on casings. **1975** A. P. SZILAS *Production & Transport of Oil & Gas* iv. 345 (*caption*) Bottom-hole arrangements for the sucker-rod pumping of slim holes. **1920** E. WALLACE *Daffodil Mystery* iii. 23 Thornton Lyne was a store-keeper, a Bachelor of Arts, ..and the author of a *slim volume. **1953** R. LEHMANN *Echoing Grove* 242 The accent, I gather, is on culture—lots of slim vols in the house now. **1979** *Church Times* 1 June 5/3 Friends will..welcome a slim volume of his poems that has come out.

**slim**, *v.* [f. SLIM *a.*]

**1.** *trans.* With *away*: To waste (time) in idling. Chiefly *dial.*

**1812** THOM *Amusem.* 35 (E.D.D.), Bids them mind their meat and wark, And not to slim their time away.

**2.** To scamp (work). Also with *over*. Chiefly *dial.*

**1808** JAMIESON s.v., In the very same sense we say, *To slim o'er*, to do one's work in a careless and insufficient way. **1847** MRS. CARLYLE *Lett.* I. 393 Postie had also helped to beat the carpets, considering that Eaves was rather slimming them. **1854** MISS BAKER *Northampt. Gloss.* s.v., A shoemaker, who brought his apprentice up before the magistrates, complained that 'he slimmed his work so, he could put up with it no longer'.

**3. a.** To make slim or slender. Chiefly *dial.*

**1862** MRS. NORTON *Lady of La Garaye* I. 115 The rich purple of her velvet vest Slims the young waist, and rounds the graceful breast.

**b.** *fig.* To reduce in size or extent. Freq. const. *down.*

**1963** *Richmond* (Va.) *Times-Dispatch* 16 Dec. 19/1 He set out to slim the budget. **1971** *Daily Tel.* 16 Aug. 11/6, I have slimmed down my holding of Westland Aircraft..by selling 1,250 at 46½p. **1976** A. WHITE *Long Silence* xix. 169 We'd been able to slim our plan down considerably, to make do with the minimum of men. **1980** *Daily Tel.* 18 Jan. 1/8 Sir Charles Villiers, British Steel's chairman, ended weeks of speculation over the future of two plants..when he said both works would be slimmed.

**4.** *intr.* To try to reduce one's weight by dieting; to become slim. Also with *down*. Also *fig.*

**1930** *Punch* 2 Apr. 366/2 The hostess ate hardly any. She is slimming. **1937** L. C. DOUGLAS *Forgive us our Trespasses* xiii. 254 As the minutes slimmed down to four, three, two, Dinny found his heart beating rapidly. **1963** 'E. MCBAIN' *Ten Plus One* xii. 158, I was too fat... But the funny part was, once I slimmed down, I didn't want to be an actor any more. **1975** G. HOWELL *In Vogue* 1/2 'Dressing on a war income' was a regular feature [in British *Vogue*],.. recommending that women should slim in order to use less fabric.

Hence **'slimmed-down** *ppl. a.*; also **'slim-down** (usu. *attrib.*).

**1978** *Detroit Free Press* 5 Mar. B14/5 Other corporations are impressed by their strong cash positions, their slimmed-down lease structures and their good earnings. **1978** *N.Y. Times Mag.* 23 July 23/2 Frye-boot chic was swept aside as big-top looks became slimdown looks. **1980** *Daily Tel.* 4 Nov. 1/2 There may be a repeat of the late-1979 confrontation over the British Leyland slimdown and efficiency programme. **1981** *Times* 7 Aug. 20/3 Mercantile House continued to advance in its slimmed-down form.

**slime** (slaɪm), *sb.* Forms: 1, 3 slim, 3–5 slym, 5 slyym, 3–7 slyme; 5– slime. [Common Teut.: OE. *slím*, = Fris. *slym*, *slīm*, *slim*, MDu. *slijm*, *slym-* (Du. *slijm*), MLG. *slym*, *slim* (LG. *slîm*), MHG. *slîm* (G. *schleim*), ON. *slím* (MSw., Norw., Da. *slim*, †*sliim*). The stem is prob. related to that of L. *limus*.]

**1. a.** Soft glutinous mud; alluvial ooze; viscous matter deposited or collected on stones, etc.

*a* **1000** in Wr.-Wülcker 195 *Borbus, cena*, slim. *c* **1050** *Ibid.* 439 *Limus*, slim. *c* **1150** *Cant. Ps.* lxvii. 2 Afestnod ic æm on ..slim dipæ. *c* **1290** *S. Eng. Leg.* I. 338 Anonriȝt þe se wende aȝein, with watur and with slyme. *a* **1300** *E.E. Ps.* lxviii. 2, I am festened in slime [that] depe esse. **1387** TREVISA *Higden* (Rolls) I. 133 Nilus..bycause of slym þat renneþ þerwith.. makeþ þe londe fatte. **1422** tr. *Secreta Secret., Priv. Priv.* 191 God wold not fourm woman of the Slyme as he dud man. *c* **1440** *Pallad. on Husb.* I. 762 See slyme..and slyme of flood, With other donge ymynged, is right good. **1568** WITHALS *Dict.* 7 b/1 Slime or mudde in water, *dicitur limus.* **1590** SPENSER *F.Q.* I. i. 21 As when old father Nilus gins to swell..His fattie waues do fertile slime outwell. **1602** MARSTON *Antonio's Rev.* IV. iii, Let him feed on slime That smeares the dungeon cheeke. **1697** DRYDEN *Virg. Georg.* IV. 414 The teeming Tide..Makes green the Soil with Slime, and black prolific Sands. **1756–7** tr. *Keysler's Trav.* (1760) IV. 432 The struggling of the fish, in order to extricate itself at first from the slime. **1774** GOLDSM. *Nat. Hist.* (1776) VI. 24 An oily slime, found in the bottoms of ditches and of weedy pools. **1867** AUGUSTA WILSON *Vashti* xxxiii, A greenish slime overspread the lower portions of the wall, and coated the uneven pavement. **1894** S. WEYMAN *Lady Rotha* xxiii, The clinging slime and the reek of the marsh.

**b.** Applied to bitumen.

**1530** TINDALE *Prol. to Five Bks. Moses* Wks. 6/2 That slyme was a fatnesse that issued out of the earth, like vnto tarre; and thou mayst call it cement, if thou wilte. **1535** COVERDALE *Gen.* xi. 3 They toke bryck for stone, & slyme for morter. **1601** HOLLAND *Pliny* VII. xv, The very clammie slime Bitumen. **1667** MILTON *P.L.* x. 298 The rest his look Bound with Gorgonian rigor..And with Asphaltic slime. **1764** HARMER *Observ.* iii. §vii. 97 Norden describes the Ægyptian..architecture as differing from the Roman, being of mud and slime. **1853** LAYARD *Nineveh & Babylon* 202 To bring fresh slime to the surface, the Arabs threw large stones into the springs.

**2. a.** A viscous substance or fluid of animal or vegetable origin; mucus, semen, etc.

*a* **1225** *Ancr. R.* 276 Nert tu icumen of ful slim? *c* **1290** *S. Eng. Leg.* I. 191 þare feol out of eiþer eiȝe Fuylþe ase þei it were slym. *a* **1400** *Minor Poems fr. Vernon MS.* 334 þei coruen hit of me & wosch awei mi slym. **1426** LYDG. *De Guil. Pilgr.* 9115 A lyknesse off ordure, And a statue off slyym vnclene. **1530** PALSGR. 271/1 Slyme of fysshe, *lymon.* **1578** LYTE *Dodoens* 291 The Decoction of Betonie..doth clense and scoure the breast and lunges from flegme and slyme. **1610** HOLLAND *Camden's Brit.* 434 Tenches..with their glutinous slime. **1617** HIERON *Wks.* II. 219 Like that slime which the snaile leaues when it creepes. **1693** EVELYN *De la Quint. Compl. Gard.* II. 195 Too frequent Rains infect them with Slime and Snivel. **1774** GOLDSM. *Nat. Hist.* (1776) VIII. 167 The earth-worm..takes hold by the slime of the fore part of its body. **1796** WITHERING *Brit. Pl.* (ed. 3) IV. 110 Branches shaped like a worm, filled with slime containing granulations. **1822–7** GOOD *Study Med.* (1829) I. 227 The discharge thrown up consists of acrid slime and porraceous bile. **1884** BOWER & SCOTT *De Bary's Phaner.* 180 The masses of starch containing slime..have not yet been discovered in the plants in question.

**b.** Applied to star-jelly (see JELLY *sb.*[1] 2 b).

**1471** RIPLEY *Comp. Alch.* in Ashm. *Theatr. Chem. Brit.* (1652) 191 The Slyme of Sterrs that falleth to the grownde. **1642** H. MORE *Song of Soul* II. i. i. 2 Like to a Meteor, whose materiall Is low unwieldy earth, base unctuous slime. **1656** COWLEY *Misc.*, *Reason* ii, So Stars appear to drop to us from skie,..But when they fall..What but a sordid Slime is found?

**3.** *fig.* **a.** Applied disparagingly to the human body, to man in general, or to single persons.

*c* **1315** SHOREHAM IV. 112 þat doþ þat mannes body ybered Nys bote a lyte slym. *c* **1340** HAMPOLE *Pr. Consc.* 565 Saynt Bernard says..þat 'man here es nathyng elles Bot a foule slyme'. *c* **1450** *Mirk's Festial* 2 He ys not but a wryche and slyme of erth. **1504** ATKYNSON tr. *De Imitatione* III. xiv. 209 Lerne, thou erth & slyme, to humble the. **1590** SPENSER *F.Q.* II. x. 50 What time th' eternall Lord in fleshly slime Enwombed was. **1602** MARSTON *Antonio's Rev.* V. v, *Ant.* Scum of the mud of hell! *Alb.* Slime of all filth! **1652** BENLOWES *Theoph.* V. xv. 63 Dares mortal Slime..expresse What ev'n Celestials do confesse Is inexpressible?

**b.** Applied to what is morally filthy or otherwise disgusting.

**1575–85** SANDYS *Serm.* 156 Now that Christ hath cleansed vs from our sinne, let vs not swinelike returne to wallowe in that slime againe. **1593** NASHE *Strange Newes* K j, Art, like yong grasse.., was glad to peepe vp through any slime of corruption. **1616** R. C. *Times' Whistle* (1871) 70 Drunkennesse, whose putrefactious slime Darkens the splendour of our common wealth. **1822** HAZLITT *Table-t.* Ser. II. iii. (1869) 66 It is varnished over with the slime of servility. **1898** G. MEREDITH *Odes Fr. Hist.* 15 What raised This wallower in old slime to noblest heights.

**4. a.** *Mining.* Finely crushed or powdered metallic ore in the form of mud.

**1758** BORLASE *Nat. Hist. Cornw.* 180 Thus the slimes are finished, and brought to as great a degree of purity as the size of the tin..will permit. **1778** PRYCE *Min. Cornub.* 226 Leavings of Tin..consist of slime and tails. **1839** URE *Dict. Arts* 751 The metallic slime being first floated in the water of the trough, then flows out and is deposited in the tank. **1855** J. R. L[EIFCHILD] *Cornw. Mines* 205 The ore, on issuing forth, deposits its *rough* in the first basin, and its *slimes* in the following basins. **1874** RAYMOND *Statist. Mines & Mining* 415 By slimes or slums I do not mean to include any slimes whatever from the pan-tailings. *Ibid.*, The slimes here spoken of..have never been worked at all.

**b.** Also ***anode slime***. The deposit of insoluble material formed at the anode in the electrolytic refining of copper and some other metals; = *anode mud* s.v. ANODE c.

**1902** J. MCCRAE tr. *Arrhenius' Text-bk. Electrochem.* xvi. 276 The other impurities, such as gold, silver,..and lead, remain undissolved, or form insoluble compounds..and falling from the anode, collect in the so-called anode slime. **1935** W. A. KOEHLER *Princ. & Applic. Electrochem.* II. xxiii. 170 A large part of the silver produced is obtained from the slimes which are a by-product from the electrorefining of baser metals, especially from the refining of copper, lead, nickel, and zinc. **1954** M. C. SNEED et al. *Comprehensive Inorg. Chem.* II. ii. 128 Copper refinery slime is a dirty-black mixture of very finely divided copper and metallic and nonmetallic anode impurities. **1969** H. T. EVANS tr. *Hägg's Gen. & Inorg. Chem.* xxxvi. 749 Silver and gold by-products of the production of copper are collected in the anode slime during copper electrolysis.

**5.** *techn.* (See quot.)

**1839** URE *Dict. Arts* 1164 The thin stuff, called *slimes*, upon the surface of the starch, is removed by a tray of a peculiar form.

**6.** *attrib.* and *Comb.* **a.** In sense 1, as ***slime-bank, -bath, lagoon; slime-browned***, etc.

**1597** MARLOWE *Ovid's Elegies* III. v, Floud with reede-growne slime bankes. **1756** tr. *Keysler's Trav.* (1760) III. 421 Here is also..a muddy bath. [*marg.*] Slime bath. **1776** MICKLE tr. *Camoens' Lusiad* IX. 370 Each joyful sailor..with firm tugs the rollers from the brine, Reluctant dragg'd, the slime-brown'd anchors raise. **1861** DICKENS *Gt. Expect.* xxviii, I saw the boat..waiting for them at the slime-washed stairs. **1877** RUSKIN *St. Mark's Rest* I. ii. 23 The crocodile, ..slime-begotten of old. **1897** MARY KINGSLEY *W. Africa* 338 More specimens of those awful slime lagoons.

**b.** In sense 2, as ***slime-gland, -pore, -track; slime-secreting*** adj.

*a* **1656** BP. HALL *Rem. Wks.* (1660) 24 As the snail cannot but leave a slime-track behind it. **1883** *Science* I. 433/2 A terminal slime-gland accentuated by a short deep groove. **1896** LYDEKKER *Roy. Nat. Hist.* V. 570 A ciliated slime-secreting band. *Ibid.* VI. 344 The hinder end of the foot..terminating in a conspicuous mucus or slime-pore.

**c.** In sense 4, as ***slime-ore, -table, -tin, -yard; slimes dam*** (S. Afr.); ***slime-coated*** adj., ***-separator, -silvered*** adj., etc.

**1778** PRYCE *Min. Cornub.* 238 It still retains much dirt and mud, whence it is called Slime Ore. *Ibid.*, It may be trunked ..the same as slime Tin. **1874** RAYMOND *Statist. Mines & Mining* 414 The shaking collects the floured and slime-coated quicksilver. *Ibid.* 415 In such cases it is necessary to build slime-yards outside the mill. **1875** KNIGHT *Dict. Mech.* 2210/2 Slime-separator. **1927** JOYCE *On Beach at Fontana* in *Pomes Penyeach*, A senile sea numbers each single Slimesilvered stone. **1956** *Archit. Rev.* CXX. 48/3 There are three main varieties of dump, the sand dumps.., the rock dumps.., and the slimes dams, 50 to 100 feet high, covering wide areas, flat-topped. **1971** *Sunday Times* (Johannesburg) (Mag. Section) 28 Mar. 11/5 That square outline you see at the corner of what looks like a Witwatersrand slimes dam is, in fact, the remains of a Roman army camp.

**7.** Special combs.: **slime-eel** (see quots.); **slime-flux**, a slimy excretion on trees; **slime-fungi**, = MYXOMYCETES; **slime-head**, a fish of the sub-family *Berycoidea*; **slime-moulds**, = *slime-fungi*; **slime-sponge** (see quot.).

**1860** WRAXALL *Life in Sea* v. 129 The *Slime Eel (*Myxine glutinosa*) bears a great likeness to the Lamprey. **1884** GOODE *Nat. Hist. Aquat. Anim.* 681 The 'Slime Eel'..is found on the Atlantic coast north of Cape Cod. **1897** W. G. SMITH tr. *Tubeuf's Dis. Plants* 141 According to Ludwig, species of Endomyces have much to do with the *slime-flux of trees. *Ibid.* 523 The vegetative body of the *Slime-fungi consists of naked protoplasm without a firm membrane. **1896** LYDEKKER *Roy. Nat. Hist.* V. 353 The Berycoids or *Slime-Heads. *Ibid.*, The slime-heads..are all marine fishes, with a practically cosmopolitan distribution. **1880** BESSEY *Botany* 170 Even in the lowest plants, the *Slime Moulds..will contract into rounded masses. **1899** *Nature* 21 Dec. 173/2 We do not think that the adoption of the name 'slime moulds' is a happy one. **1883** W. S. KENT in *Fisheries Bahamas* 38 The skeletonless *Slime-sponge (*Halisarca Dujardinii*) more usually resembles..dabs of red-currant jelly scattered upon the surface of the rocks or seaweeds.

**slime** (slaɪm), *v.*[1] [f. SLIME *sb.* Cf. Fris. *slymje*, LG. *slîmen*, G. *schleimen* to give out slime, clean from slime, etc.]

**1.** *trans.* To smear or cover with slime.

**1628** FELTHAM *Resolves* II. xxi, Like the Crocodile, he slimes thy way, to make thee fall. **1682** DRYDEN & LEE *Duke of Guise* III. i, Daubing the Inside of the Court like Snails, Sliming our Walls, and pricking out your Hornes. **1807** J. BARLOW *Columb.* VIII. 415 Your lawless Mississippi, now who slimes And drowns and desolates his waste of climes. **1859** LANG *Wand. India* 264 The snake..commenced, with his forked tongue,..to slime his victim all over. **1872** TENNYSON *Last Tourn.* 471 The knights..sank his head in mire, and slimed themselves.

*fig.* **1860** TENNYSON *Sea Dreams* 189 Gifts of grace he forged, And snake-like slimed his victim ere he gorged. **1897** BLACKMORE in *Blackw. Mag.* Sept. 369 The trivial wormcasts of rank and money which cannot even slime the scythe of death.

**2. a.** To make (one's way) in a slimy fashion. **b.** *intr.* To crawl slimily; to become slimy.

**1842** *Tait's Mag.* IX. 374 Stealthily, serpently, he slimed his way Unto the pay-master. **1851** G. H. KINGSLEY *Sport & Trav.* (1900) 533 The happy *insouciance* of a snail 'sliming' up the side of the Parthenon.

**3.** *techn.* To clear (skins, fish, etc.) of slimy matter by scraping.

**1723** J. NOTT *Cook's & Confectioner's Dict.* sig. R5ᵛ, *To fry Lampreys*, Bleed them, preserve their Blood, slime them, and cut them in pieces. **1747** H. GLASSE *Art of Cookery* ix. 86 Slime your Tenches. **1845** G. DODD *Brit. Manuf.* V. 203 The skins are removed to a beam and there 'slimed', that is, scraped on the flesh side to remove a slimy substance which exudes from the pores.

**slime** (slaɪm), *v.*[2] *Harrow slang.* [Of obscure origin.] *intr.* To move in a gliding, stealthy, or sneaking manner.

**1898** HOWSON & WARNER *Harrow School* 282 His 'house-beak' 'slimed' (went round quietly) and 'twug' him. **1905** VACHELL *The Hill* i, When he does come over on our side of the House, he slimes about in carpet slippers.

†**slime,** *v.*[3] *Obs.*⁻¹ (Meaning uncertain.)

*c* **1400** *Destr. Troy* 8096 Hit pleaside hir priuely, playntyde ho noght, Let hit slip from hyr slyly, slymyt þerat.

**slimed,** *ppl. a. rare.* [f. SLIME *sb.* or *v.*[1]] Full of, covered with, slime; slimy.

**1393** LANGL. *P. Pl.* C. VIII. 1 Tho cam sleuthe al by-slobered with two slymed eyen. **1563** A. NEVELL in Googe *Eglogs*, etc. (Arb.) 83 For thou..Dost by thy Snares and slymed Hooks entrap the wounded Harts. **1608** TOPSELL *Serpents* (1658) 785 A certain glutinous kinde of Jelly, or slimed juice. **1940** W. FAULKNER *Hamlet* ii. 201 He..stooped and began to drag away the slimed and rotten branches. **1952** *Chambers's Jrnl.* Feb. 110/1 A dark, dank, and sepulchral sphere of silent stone, where passage succeeded passage in an unending monotony of slimed and moss-grown solitude. **1972** F. WARNER *Lying Figures* IV. 43 Two bodies..still slimed from the womb.

**'slimeless,** *a. rare*⁻¹. [f. SLIME *sb.* + -LESS.] Free from slime or filth.

**1672** *Life & Death of Jas. Arminius & Simon Episc.* I. 22 Those pure and slimeless Fountains.

†**'slimely,** *a. Obs.*⁻¹ Slimy.

**1528** PAYNELL *Salerne's Regim.* O j b, A tenche..is a freshe water fyshe, whose skynne is slyppery and slymely.

**'slime-pit.** Also **slime pit.**

**1.** In or after Biblical use: A pit or hole yielding asphalt or bitumen.

**1530** TINDALE *Prol.* 5 *Bks. Moses* Wks. 6/2 Slyme was their morter, chap. 11. and slyme pittes, chap. 14. **1535** COVERDALE *Gen.* xiv. 10 Yᵗ brode valley had many slyme pyttes. **1611** BIBLE *Gen.* xiv. 10 And the vale of Siddim was full of slime-pits. **1737** WHISTON tr. *Josephus, Antiq.* I. ix, They pitched their camp at the vale called the Slime Pits. **1853** LAYARD *Nineveh & Babylon* 202 In an hour the bitumen was exhausted for the time,..and the..moon again shone over the black slime pits. **1895** SAYCE *Patriarchal Palestine* iv. 178 Here were the 'slime-pits' from which the naphtha was extracted.

**2.** *techn.* A pit or reservoir in which metallic slimes are collected.

**1778** PRYCE *Min. Cornub.* 234 The slimy earthy parts are carried by the water into a slime pit just below. **1839** URE *Dict. Arts* 752 Slime pits or labyrinths, called buddle holes in Derbyshire, are employed to collect that matter. **1882** *U.S. Rep. Prec. Met.* 610 A copper miner..would tell you..what a large proportion would go to enrich the slime pits.

†**'slimikin,** *a. Obs.*⁻¹ [f. SLIM *a.*] Small and slender.

**1745** MRS. DELANY *Life & Corr.* (1861) II. 383 You know I am a little slimikin thing, not unlike a perch or an eel.

**slimily** ('slaɪmɪlɪ), *adv.* [f. SLIMY *a.* + -LY².] In a slimy manner; with accompaniment of slime.

**1606** S. GARDINER *Bk. Angling* 117 They are slippery Eles indeede,..being so slimily and sordidly giuen, as they may not be handled. **1878** BLACK *Macleod of Dare* I. 180 The inside of this glass box was alive with snakes..slimily crawling over each other. **1883** *Cent. Mag.* July 422/2 At length, the long submerged streets..rose slimily out of the retreating waters.

**'slim-in.** Also **slim in.** [f. SLIM *v.* + -IN³.] A course of (usu. sponsored) slimming undertaken by several people in competition with or in support of one another.

**1973** *Inverness Courier* 31 July 5/4 A sponsored 'slim-in'..recently raised £15. **1977** *Cornish Times* 19 Aug. 10/1 The sponsored 'slim in' was won by Mrs V. Humphries.

**sliminess** ('slaɪmɪnɪs). Also 6 **slymy-, slymines.** [f. as SLIMILY *adv.* + -NESS.] The state or quality of being slimy; slimy character or consistency.

**1528** PAYNELL *Salerne's Regiment* O j b, Greatte estates haue them [carps] sodde in wyne, and so the slymynes is done away. **1555** EDEN *Decades* (Arb.) 184 The slymines of the earth and water. **1615** H. CROOKE *Body of Man* 51 This is prooued by..the lentor or sliminesse of their substance. **1662** R. MATHEW *Unl. Alch.* §9. 5 We find it so potent in cleansing all Windiness, Sliminess, Stone or Gravel. **1742** H. BAKER *Microsc.* II. x. 122 The Sliminess of the Eel will immediately foul the Glass. **1812** W. TAYLOR in *Monthly Mag.* XXXIII. 253 The sliminess [of the snail] is considered as the greatest delicacy. **1846** HAWTHORNE *Mosses fr. Manse* I. vii. 139 It impressed the beholder with an association of sliminess.

**'sliming,** *vbl. sb.* [f. SLIME *sb.* or *v.*[1]]

**1.** (See quots.)

**1615** LATHAM *Falconry* Gloss., *Sliming*, is when a Hawke muteth from her longwaies in one intire substance; and doth not drop any part thereof. **1895** ELWORTHY *Evil Eye* 41 [The cobra] then gave [the hawk]..another sliming and soon made a meal of him.

**2.** *Mining.* The reduction of ore to slime (SLIME *sb.* 4).

**1920**, etc. [see *all-sliming vbl. sb.* and *ppl. a.* s.v. ALL 13]. **1965** G. J. WILLIAMS *Econ. Geol. N.Z.* v. 56/1 The fine grinding which was necessary to liberate the gold caused losses in scheelite through sliming.

**'sliming,** *ppl. a. rare.* [f. SLIME *sb.*] Defiling with slime; slimy.

*a* **1400-50** *Alexander* 4456 þus make ȝe vessels in vayne to ȝoure foule corses,..þat ilk slymand slugh, quen ȝe ere slide hyne.

†**'slimish,** *a. Obs.*⁻⁰ Somewhat slimy.

**1648** HEXHAM II. s.v. *Slijmachtigh*, Slimish water.

†**'slimishness.** *Obs. rare.* Sliminess.

**1574** T. N[EWTON] tr. *Gratarolus' Direct. Health* L j, Suche fishes..neuer are embroyned with anye filth or diertie slimishnes. **1597** A. M. tr. *Guillemeau's Fr. Chirurg.* 32/1 Washinge the sayed horseleeches with your handes, from all ther viscositye and slimishnes.

**slim jim** (slɪm dʒɪm). Also **slim Jim, Slim Jim.** [Rhyming combination of SLIM *a.* and the proper name *Jim.*] A very slim or thin person.

**1889** 'MARK TWAIN' *Conn. Yankee* xxxix. 500 Go it, slim Jim!

**2.** *transf.* (See quot. 1925.)

**1916** JOYCE *Portrait of Artist* ii. 104 He had..eaten slim jim out of his cricket cap. **1925** —— *Let.* 31 Oct. (1966) III. 129 This is a kind of sweet meat made of a soft marshmellow jelly which is coated first with pink sugar and then powdered, so far as I remember with cocoanut chips. It is called 'Slim Jim' because it is sold in strips about a foot or a foot and a half in length and an inch in breadth.

**3.** *attrib.* Designating something long and thin or narrow, as ***slim-jim pants, tie***, etc. Also *ellipt.* in pl.

**1916** R. FROST *Mountain Interval* 60 That ought to make you An ideal one-girl farm, And give you a chance to put some strength On your slim-jim arm. **1956** *Amer. Speech* XXXI. 307 *Frontier Pants..slim jims*, long pants, tapered so closely that they must be zipped at the ankles, or must have slits. **1957** [see JEAN 2 b]. **1960** *Guardian* 9 Mar. 6/1 Warm flannelette lined corduroy 'slim jims'. **1962** *Times* 13 Apr. 6/4 Worthing Museum..is asking for a Teddy boy costume, 'with narrow trousers, fancy waist-coat, three-quarter jacket, Slim Jim tie and thick-soled crepe sneakers'. **1962** *Spectator* 27 Apr. 536 The spade ties everyone wore before the slim jims came in. **1973** O. SELA *Portuguese Fragment* (1974) xi. 61 He wore a long sleeved white shirt and slim-jim tie.

**slimline, slim-line** ('slɪmlaɪn), *a.* [f. SLIM *a.* + LINE *sb.*² 14 b.] **a.** Slim, narrow, gracefully thin in style or appearance. Occas. *absol.* as *sb.*

**1949** PENDER & DEL MAR *Electr. Engineers Handbk.* (ed. 4) xv. 33 (*headings*) Technical data on fluorescent lamps...Standard line lamps... Slimline lamps. **1961** *Economist* 28 Oct. 328/3 Stereophonic equipment, slim-line television, the second wireless set. **1964** *N.Y. Post* 21 Oct. 18/2 (Advt.), Elegant long gowns..slinky slim-lines and ultra-feminine bouffants. **1971** *New Scientist* 11 Feb. 323/1 Whenever I switched on the box I seemed to find pontificating doctors: podgy ones telling me to smoke cigars, slimline ones telling me to eat less. **1976** C. EGLETON *State Visit* viii. 82 'What if you wanted to speak to someone outside the airport?' Mostyn pointed to a red slim-line. 'Then I would use that one [*sc.* telephone],' he said. **1978** *Times* 10 Aug. 11/1, I put on my white crepe slimline dress.

**b.** *fig.* Exiguous, economical, stripped of unnecessary elaboration.

**1973** *Listener* 26 July 125/2 This slim-line plot is made the occasion for many a worthy animadversion on man's rape of the surface of the earth. **1975** B. J. ENRIGHT in Barr & Line *Ess. on Information & Libraries* v. 66 A hesitant and doubtful response greeted Maurice Line's forecast of 'lean muscular libraries' to replace 'fat bloated ones of the past'—the 'new slimline library' seemed a somewhat dubious proposition. **1980** *Daily Tel.* 18 Jan. 1/8 The board has decided to concentrate further consultations and discussions with the unions and the work-force on a 'slimline' operation.

**slimly** ('slɪmlɪ), *adv.* [f. SLIM *a.* + -LY².]

**1.** Artfully; cunningly.

**1681** GLANVILL *Saddiucismus* I. 124 This man certainly is either delirant and crazed, or else plays tricks, and slimly and obliquely insinuates that [etc.].

**2. a.** Slenderly; delicately.

**1831** TRELAWNY *Adv. Younger Son* cxiii, A little white-faced, slimly-formed sickly girl. **1865** J. CAMERON *Malayan India* 274 She is not a slimly built vessel,..but is of thorough man-of-war build.

**b.** So as to give an effect or appearance of slimness.

**1970-1** *Kay's Catal.* Autumn-Winter 60/1 A casual classic that's never out of fashion; slimly styled in knitted Courtelle. **1979** *Homes & Gardens* June 103/1 The front [of the skirt] double wraps, so that it fits sleekly and slimly.

**3.** Scantily; sparsely; thinly.

**1801-67** in *Eng. Dial. Dict.* **1886** *Daily News* 13 Dec. (Cassell), The farewell all-night meetings which were held in a small church here were slimly attended.

**slimmer** ('slɪmə(r)). [f. SLIM *v.* 4 + -ER¹.] One who practises slimming.

**1974** *Country Life* 12 Dec. 1845/1 The horrors of a slimmer can be as awful as those of an alcoholic, at least until his stomach shrinks. **1978** J. PUDNEY *Thank Goodness for Cake* 124 It was not designed as a slimmer's diet but I lost weight. **1980** *West Lancs. Evening Gazette* 11 Aug. 10 (Advt.), Slimmers, have you heard that the..new slimming method..is now available?

**slimming** ('slɪmɪŋ), *ppl. a.* [f. SLIM *v.* + -ING².] Producing an appearance of slimness; conducive to slimness.

**1925** *Daily Express* 18 Nov. 6/3 The Lord Chamberlain took out the words 'slimming over the hips', which is a phrase used every day by fashionable costumiers. **1927** *Daily Chron.* 29 Mar. 15/4 Orange juice with a dash of gin in it..is said to be slimming! **1952** *Observer* 14 Sept. 8/6 Youthlines '1980'. The so-slimming girdle in marvellous American Leno. **1980** *Daily Tel.* 13 Oct. 19/3 Slimming Nehru jackets, buttoned close to the throat.

**slimming** ('slɪmɪŋ), *vbl. sb.* [f. SLIM *v.* + -ING¹.]

**a.** The practice of using special means, such as dieting and exercises, to produce slimness of body. Also *fig.*

**1931** GALSWORTHY *Maid-in-Waiting* xi. 101 Perhaps the young of today will nevah grow fat. They do slimming—ah-ha! **1958** *Spectator* 7 Feb. 165/1 If such a drastic slimming is to be enforced on agriculture, there is little doubt that [etc.]. **1974** *Times* 17 Apr. 10/5 A medical view of slimming. **1982** *Daily Tel.* 3 Aug. 13/2 The slimming of prime rates brought investors back in force late in the session.

**b.** *attrib.* (passing into *adj.*)

**1932** *Times* 1 Feb. 9/3 She was a bit exercised about getting too stout and might have been going in for 'slimming' exercises as sometimes ladies did. **1951** M. MCLUHAN *Mech. Bride* (1967) 154/1 The plump wife who went off for a prolonged slimming course. **1979** A. MORICE *Murder in Outline* x. 85 She was taking slimming pills... She was..worried about her weight.

**'slimmish,** *a. rare*$^{-1}$. Somewhat slim.

**1841** D. JERROLD *St. Giles* (1852) I. 314 He's a slimmish chap.

**slimnastics** (slɪm'næstɪks), *sb. pl.* (const. as *sing.*). *U.S.* [Blend of SLIM(MING *vbl. sb.* and GYM)NASTICS.] (See quots. 1970.)

**1967** *New Yorker* 22 Apr. 138/2 The calendar on the Community Center bulletin board lists citizenship classes, pinochle and bridge games,.. 'slimnastics', ceramic classes, and dances of the Teen Club. **1970** M. PEI *Words in Sheep's Clothing* ii. 12 'Slimnastics' (gymnastics that slim you down). **1970** NOTTIDGE & LAMPLUGH *Slimnastics* i. 9 'Slimnastics' is a combination of slimming and gymnastics in a group. **1979** *Honolulu Advertiser* 8 Jan. A-4/3 Women's Slimnastics Classes. **1983** *N.Y. Times* 12 Jan. B 2/5 In a gymnasium, 40 women were exercising in a 'slimnastics' class.

**slimness** ('slɪmnɪs). [f. SLIM *a.* + -NESS.]

**1.** Slenderness; (graceful) thinness.

**1727** in BAILEY (vol. II). **1776** PENNANT *Brit. Zool.* I. 334 The slimness of their bodies, and great length of tail. **1816** KEATS *Ep. to C. Cowden Clarke* 87 To see..morning shadows streaking into slimness Across the lawny fields. **1859** GEO. ELIOT *Adam Bede* I. ii, An effect which was due to the slimness of her figure. **1893** F. F. MOORE *I Forbid Banns* xi, Young ladies, who, with all the insolence of slimness, called her stout.

**2.** Artfulness, wiliness, cunning.

**1899** *Westm. Gaz.* 27 Dec. 1/2 Courage is no good unless it is backed up by what the Boers themselves call 'slimness'. **1900** *Daily Telegr.* 2 Oct. 6/1 A double dose of original slimness.

**'slimskin.** *U.S.* [f. SLIM *a.* + SKIN *sb.*] A sea-elephant in an emaciated state.

**1884** in Goode *Nat. Hist. Aquat. Anim.* 73 The animal.. sometimes becomes very thin, and is then called a 'slimskin'.

**†slimslack.** *Obs.*$^{-1}$ [f. SLIM *a.* + SLACK *a.*] A person mentally or physically defective.

Cf. Forby (1825), '*Slimslacket*, of very thin texture, loose and flaccid'.

**1600** *Hosp. Inc. Fooles* 25 These poore slimslacks, who haue need of internal remedies for the restitution of their disturbed braine.

**slimsy** ('slɪmsɪ), *a. U.S.* Also **slimpsy**. [app. f. SLIM *a.*] Flimsy, frail.

**1845** S. JUDD *Margaret* II. viii, The building is old and slimsy. **1895** *Missionary Herald* (Boston) Dec. 493 These ladies have to stay in that slimsy shed day and night. **1899** *Milwaukee Sentinel* 14 May 4/2 Of the same slimsy material the..claim is constructed.

**slimy** ('slaɪmɪ), *a.* Forms: 4-6, 8 **slymy** (6 sleymy), 6-7 **slymie**; 6 **slimye**, 6-7 **slimie**, 6- **slimy**. [f. SLIME *sb.* + -Y. Cf. MDu. *slimich* (Du. *slijmig*), MHG. *slîmich* (LG. and NFris. *slîmig*, older Da. *slimig*), MHG. *slîmic* (G. *schleimig*).]

**1.** Of the nature or consistency of slime; viscous.

**1398** TREVISA *Barth. De P.R.* VI. xxi. (Bodl. MS.), Slymy water and glewye..staunchep rennyng of blood. **1477** NORTON *Ordin. Alch.* v. in Ashm. (1652) 65 A Calcedonie in Slymy substance. **1539** ELYOT *Cast. Helthe* (1541) 92 The poulse called *Lenticula*, and they that are slymy like malowes. **1562** BULLEIN *Bulwarke, Bk. Compounds* 9 b, This doen, presse forthe the slymie sappe of them. **1650** BULWER *Anthropomet.* 238 They annoint themselves with a certain slimie oyntment. **1697** DRYDEN *Virg. Georg.* III. 441 From their Groins they shed A slimy Juice. **1735** SOMERVILLE *Chase* IV. 370 Th' insinuating Eel, that hides his Head Beneath the slimy Mud. **1774** GOLDSM. *Nat. Hist.* (1776) VII. 25 That slimy substance with which it is so copiously furnished. **1844** MRS. BROWNING *Vis. Poets* lviii, His foot slips in their slimy oil. **1871** T. R. JONES *Anim. Kingd.* (ed. 4) 460 It is concealed by a brownish slimy secretion.

**b.** *techn.* Of ore: In the form of slime.

**1778** PRYCE *Min. Cornub.* 227 Moving the slimy Tin to and fro with a light hand.

**2.** Characterized by the presence of slime; covered with slime.

**1377** LANGL. *P. Pl.* B. v. 392 Þanne come sleuthe al bislabered with two slymy eiʒen. **1551** TURNER *Herbal* (1568) 7 The hole herbe is very sleymy and full of slepery iuice. **1604** E. G[RIMSTONE] *D'Acosta's Hist. Indies* VII. xxvii. 582 The fire..was of the wood of fat and slimy firre-trees. **1664** POWER *Exp. Philos.* I. 36 In this slimy Animal.. are very many rare and excellent Observables. **1798** COLERIDGE *Anc. Mar.* II. x, Yea, slimy things did crawl with legs Upon the slimy sea. **1845** DARWIN *Voy. Nat.* xi. (1879) 239 The stem is round, slimy, and smooth. **1885** BUCHANAN *Annan Water* iii, Down the broken walls clung slimy weeds and mosses.

**b.** *esp.* Of rivers, shores, etc.

**1398** TREVISA *Barth. De P.R.* XIII. v. (Bodl. MS.), [The Nile is] troublye, erþy, slymy, and wosie. *c* **1586** C'TESS PEMBROKE *Ps.* LXXVIII. xx, That rich land, where over Nilus trailes Of his wett robe the slymy seedy train. **1599** NASHE *Lenten Stuff* Wks. (Grosart) V. 211 The Saxons..that had giuen vp the ghost, in those slymie plashie fieldes of Gorlstone. **1613** PURCHAS *Pilgrimage* (1614) 493 A pit of standing water..wherein euery morning they wash themselues, although it be greene, slimie, and stinking. **1650** VENNER *Via Recta* 98 In slimy and muddy rivers. **1818** SHELLEY *Prometh. Unb.* IV. 311 On the slimy shores, And weed-overgrown continents of earth. **1839** FR. A. KEMBLE *Resid. Georgia* (1863) 18 A slimy, poisonous-looking swamp. **1873** G. C. DAVIES *Mount. & Mere* xv. 123 The black slimy sides of the ditch.

**3.** *transf.* and *fig.* Morally defiled or objectionable; vile, disgusting.

**1575** tr. *Luther's Galat.* iii. 1 The slimy Body and the Remnants of Sin remain still in us. **1597** MIDDLETON *Wisd. Solomon* xv. 7 If thou want'st slime, behold thy slimy faults. **1602** *2nd Pt. Ret. fr. Parnass.* I. vi. 482 What slimie bold presumtious groome is he? **1693** DRYDEN, etc. *Juvenal* xiv. (1697) 347 The rest are all by bad Example led, And in their Father's slimy Track they tread. **1796** COLERIDGE *Destiny of Nations* 432 The locust-fiends that crawled And glittered in Corruption's slimy track. **1898** G. B. SHAW *Plays* II. *Man of Destiny* 165 I'll spoil his beauty, the slimy little liar!

**4.** *Comb.*, as *slimy-born*, *-coated*.

**1687** DRYDEN *Hind. & P.* I. 311 A slimy-born and sun-begotten Tribe. **1833** *Ridgemon. Farm Rep.* 139 in *Husb.* III. (L.U.K.), These slimy-coated insects are all abroad in the night.

**sline** (slaɪn). *Coal-mining.* Also **slyne** [Of obscure origin.] (See quots.)

Gresley (1883) also gives 'potholes in the roof'.

**1811** FAREY *Derbyshire* I. 181 The Slines, or lengthway joints which naturally divide the Coal-seams vertically, generally range about ESE and WNW. **1871** *Trans. Amer. Inst. Min. Eng.* I. 304 In some seams the slines, smooth planes of cleavage parallel with the face, are much closer together than in others. **1875** *Ure's Dict. Arts* (ed. 7) I. 815 The smooth clean surface of the coal coinciding with this well-defined set of joints is known as the cleat, face, or slyne.

**sliness,** obs. form of SLYNESS.

**sling** (slɪŋ), *sb.*[1] Forms: *α.* 4- **sling** (4 scling), 4, 6 **slinge**, 4-6 **slyng(e**, 5 **sclyng(e**; 4 **sleng(e**. *β. Sc.* 5 **slong**, 6 **sloung**, 5-6, 9 **slung**. [app. of Continental origin, but the precise source is not clear. The forms in the cognate languages which correspond most closely to the usual *sling* are MLG. *slinge*, OHG. *slinga* (*slinka*, MHG. *slinge*, G. dial. *schlinge*), older Da. *slinge*, *slynghe* (Da. *slynge*); cf. also OF. *eslingue* (*elingue*, mod.Norm. and Pic. *élingue*). The rare ME. *sleng* answers to MLG. *slenge*, OHG. *slenga* (MHG. *slenge*, older or dial. G. *schlenge*, *schlenke*). The Sc. *slung*, †*slong*, resembles the MSw. *slonga* (*slionga*, *sliunga*), Sw. *slunga*, but it is difficult to assume direct connexion.

ON. *slǫngva* (Icel. *slanga*) would normally have given ME. **slang*, but the form might have been modified under the influence of the vb. There is no independent evidence of the Flem. *slinge* 'funda' given by Plantin and Kilian along with the usual *slinger*.]

**1. a.** An implement or weapon for hurling stones or similar missiles by hand with great force or to a distance, consisting of a strap attached to two cords or strings, or to a stick or staff (= STAFF-SLING); the impulse is given by rapid whirling of the sling before discharging it. Also locally, a boy's catapult.

Freq. in allusions to the slaying of Goliath by David (1 Sam. xvii. 40, 49-50).

*α. a* **1300** *Cursor M.* 7528 His arms fra him did he suing, And tok bot a staf and a sling [*Gött.* slenge]. **13..** *Ibid.* 14431 (Gött.), Dauid.. þat sclou golias wid his scling. **1387** TREVISA *Higden* (Rolls) IV. 455 [He] was anon i-smyte wiþ a stoon of a slynge. *c* **1450** *Mirour Saluacioun* (Roxb.) 52 Dauid orthrewe hym sone with his stone and his slyng. **1484** CAXTON *Fables of Æsop* v. ix, Alle the men came to gyder, somme with slynges, and somme with bowes. **1530** PALSGR. 271/2 Slynge made in a shepherdes staffe, *fonde hollette*. **1600** J. PORY tr. *Leo's Africa* 47 In war their weapons are slings, and swordes made of base iron. **1632** LITHGOW *Trav.* VII. 333 Twenty Moores broke out vpon me, with shables and slings. **1697** DRYDEN *Virg. Georg.* I. 415 With Balearick Slings, or Gnossian Bow, To persecute from far the flying Doe. **1737** WHISTON tr. *Josephus, Antiq.* VI. ix. §5 Taking one of the stones,..and fitting it to his sling, he slang it against the Philistine. **1828** W. CLARKE *Boy's Own Bk.* (ed. 2) 25 The sling... Whirl it round several times, let go the shorter thong, and the stone will be shot to a great distance. **1846** GREENER *Sci. Gunnery* 3 Not allowing their children any food until they struck it from the top of a pole with a stone from a sling. **1878** BROWNING *Poets Croisic* 34 Pebble from sling Prostrates a giant.

*β.* **1456** SIR G. HAYE *Law Arms* (S.T.S.) 169 David.. vencust that grete Goulyas, with..his slong and his slung stanis. **1533** BELLENDEN *Livy* I. xvii. (S.T.S.) I. 95, xxx centuries quhilkis war commandit to bere sloungis and casting stanis. **1535** STEWART *Chron. Scot.* II. 19 With bow and slung to cast arrow and stane. **1596** DALRYMPLE tr. *Leslie's Hist. Scot.* I. 145 ʒoung men soulde vse for waepinis a slung with a bow. **1808** in JAMIESON (and still in common use).

**b.** *fig.* or in fig. contexts.

*c* **1315** SHOREHAM VI. 25 Þou ert þe slinge, þy sone þe ston Þat dauy slange golye op-on. **1533** MORE *Answ. Poysoned Bk.* Wks. 1126/1 Yong foolishe Dauid, that hath..with the slyng of hys heresyes slonken [*sic*] hymselfe to the deuill. **1548** UDALL, etc. *Erasm. Par.* Pref. a iij b, Out of the slyng of his Regall autoritee [he] cast the corner stone. **1602** SHAKS. *Ham.* III. i. 58 The Slings and Arrowes of outragious Fortune. **1737** BRACKEN *Farriery Impr.* (1757) II. 123 If he [a horse] would not be a Sap-whistle, he might be a Sling at any time. [**1874** S. COX *Pilgrim Ps.* ii. 42 The slings and arrows of adversity.]

**c.** A machine or implement for hurling large stones or missiles; a ballista.

**1535** COVERDALE *Ezek.* xxvi. 9 His slynges & batelrammes shal he prepare for thy walles. **1609** BIBLE (Douay) *1 Macc.* vi. 51 He placed there..instruments to cast fyre,..and scorpions to shoote arrowes, and slings [L. *fundibula*]. **1682** BUNYAN *Holy War* (1905) 232 The Kings Captains had brought with them several slings, and two or three Battering-Rams. **1736** AINSWORTH *Lat. Dict.* II, *Cestrosphendone*, a sling, an engine of war to throw darts.

**2.** *attrib.* and *Comb.*, as *sling-caster*, *-maker*, *-thrower*; *sling-bullet*, *-cord*; †**sling-bone** (see quot. 1730).

**1535** COVERDALE *Judith* vi. 12 Whan they drew nye vnto the mountaynes, the slynge casters came out agaynst them. **1598** GRENEWEY *Tacitus, Ann.* II. v. (1622) 39 The Captaine ..commaunded the sling-casters and stone-casters to let freely at them. **1609** BIBLE (Douay) *2 Kings* viii. *comm.*, These were archers and sling-throwers of the guard. **1647** HEXHAM I, A Sling-maker, *een slinger-maker*. **1730** BAILEY (fol.), *Ballistæ Os*,..the Sling Bone, the same with *Astragalus*. **1764** J. FERGUSON *Lect.* ii. 13 A pebble moved round in a sling..will fly off the moment it is set at liberty, by slipping one end of the sling-cord. **1890** *Academy* 2 Aug. 94/1 A small haematite weight, resembling a barrel or sling-bullet in shape.

**sling** (slɪŋ), *sb.*[2] Forms: 4 **sleng(e**, **slyngg**, 4-5 **slyng**, 4-6 **slynge**, 7- **sling**. [Perhaps ultimately the same word as prec. The senses correspond to some extent with those of LG. *sling(e*, G. *schlinge*, Sw. *slinga* noose, knot, snare, arm-sling, etc.; also OF. *eslingue* (1322), Sp. and Pg. *eslinga*, Romansch *slinga*. The immediate source of the word in English is not obvious.]

**1. a.** A device for securing or grasping bulky or heavy articles while being hoisted or lowered, usually a belt, rope, or chain formed into a loop and fitted with hooks and tackle (cf. quots. 1627, 1769); a loop of this kind by which heavy objects are lifted, carried, or suspended.

**1323-4** *Ely Sacr. Rolls* (1907) II. 47 In slyngg emendand. 2d. Item in uno corrio equino empt. pro le Slyngg, 1s. 4d. **1338** *Roll* in Nicolas *Hist. Royal Navy* (1847) II. 475 La nief appelle la carake,..un bowespret, ove ii. polyves,..ii. slenges, un trusse. **1485** *Naval Acc. Hen. VII* (1896) 37 Bote and Cokke slyngs, vij. *c* **1515** *Cocke Lorell's B.* 12 Some wounde at yᵉ capstayne..; Some stode at yᵉ slynge. **1551-60** *Invent.* in H. Hall *Eliz. Age* (1886) 153 In the Brewe-house. .. A paier of slynges ijᵈ. **1627** CAPT. SMITH *Seaman's Gram.* v. 21 Slings are made of a rope spliced at either end into it selfe with one eye at either end, so long as to bee sufficient to receiue the caske;..another sort are made much longer for the hoising of ordnances. **1649** in *Archaeologia* X. 401 One outward wine celler..fitted with..one payre of slinges. **1743** *London & C. Brewer* III. (ed. 2) 186 The heavy Burden of a Barrel of Drink on the Slings. **1769** FALCONER *Dict. Marine* (1780), *Slings*,..a rope whose ends are fixed in such a manner to it's other part, as to encircle a cask, bale, or case, and suspend it whilst hoisting or lowering. **1800** *Asiatic Ann. Reg.* IV. 56/1 Slings were then prepared, and Mrs. Harris and the child were lowered into the boat. **1844** *Regul. & Ord. Army* 351 When the horse is deposited in the hold, and released from the slings. **1876** VOYLE & STEVENSON *Milit. Dict.* 389/1 A sling for lifting a gun off its carriage. *Ibid.* 389/2 *Shot Sling*, a sling for carrying heavy shot or shell.

**b.** In mountaineering, rock-climbing, etc., a short length of rope used to provide additional support for the body in abseiling or belaying.

**1920** G. W. YOUNG *Mountain Craft* iv. 194 Not only is the single sling more likely to snap under the rub of the hard ring. **1946** J. E. Q. BARFORD *Climbing in Britain* ii. 24 *Slings*. Most parties doing exposed or difficult rock climbs nowadays carry one or more slings. **1965** A. BLACKSHAW *Mountaineering* II. vii. 204 Most British climbers carry nylon slings... The use of slings has been very highly developed by British mountaineers; mainly, no doubt, because natural running belays have come to be used much more here than elsewhere. **1976** G. MOFFAT *Over Sea to Death* v. 53 She placed her slings, clipped in her rope and, watching it fall, caught her second's eye.

**2.** *Naut.* **a.** (See quots.)

*c* **1625** *Nomenclator Navalis* (MS. Harl. 2301) s.v., There are first slings to sling casks in..; a third sorte is anie Roape or Chaine wherewith wee binde fast the yards [a]loft to the Cross Trees. **1627** CAPT. SMITH *Seaman's Gram.* v. 21. **1867** SMYTH *Sailor's Word-bk.* 632 *Yard-slings*, the rope or chain used to support a yard which does not travel up or down a mast.

**b.** The middle part of a yard (see quot. 1846).

**1670-1** NARBOROUGH *Jrnl.* in *Acc. Sev. Late Voy.* I. 159 Broke our Main Topsail-Yard being rotten in the Slings. **1689** *Lond. Gaz.* No. 2505/3 The *St. Albans* breaking her Fore-yard in the Slings. **1769** FALCONER *Dict. Marine* (1780) s.v. *Yard*, The distance between the slings and the yard-arms..is..divided into quarters. **1797** JERVIS in Nicolas *Disp. Nelson* (1845) II. 335 The Colossus..had her fore and fore-top-sail yards wounded, and they unfortunately broke in the slings. **1830** MARRYAT *King's Own* xvi, The fore-yard of the Frenchman was divided in the slings. **1846** A. YOUNG *Naut. Dict.* 286 *Slings*, that part of a yard encircled by the sling-hoop, which suspends it from the mast, or by which it is hoisted and lowered. *c* **1860** H. STUART *Seaman's Catech.* 76 Topsail yards..are.. strengthened by four battens in the slings and quarters.

**c.** (See quots.)

**1769** FALCONER *Dict. Marine* (1780), *Slings of the Buoy*, the ropes which are fastened about it, and by which it is hung. **1867** SMYTH *Sailor's Word-bk.* 632 *Buoy-slings* are special fittings adopted in order that a buoy may securely ride on the wave.

**3. a.** A leather strap attached to a rifle, etc., enabling it to be carried slung over the shoulder, or on the arm.

**1711** *Milit. & Sea Dict.*, *Slings* are Leather Thongs, made fast to both Ends of the Musket, and serving for the Men to hang them by on their Shoulders. **1802** JAMES *Milit. Dict.* s.v., The sling consists of three straps of leather. **1833** M. SCOTT *Tom Cringle* vii, A short gun..with a sling to be used on a march. **1897** *Army & Navy Stores List* 1632 Brown Leather Golf Sling. **1902** *Encycl. Brit.* XXX. 124 The lance ..is provided with a sling, through which the trooper passes his right arm when the lance is carried slung.

**b.** A strap, band, wire, etc., forming a kind of loop by which something is suspended or hung.

**1771** SMOLLETT *Humph. Cl.* II. 10 July, The leather sling [in a coach]..cracked. **1843** HOLTZAPFFEL *Turning* I. 348 The flask..can be then turned round in the slings..to enable it to be repaired. **1852** SEIDEL *Organ* 49 On the lower end of the palate..there is a sling of iron or metallic wire. **1878** HUXLEY *Physiogr.* xvi. 262 This iron is furnished with a shoulder which carries the iron-wire sling.

**c.** A piece of cloth or other material, formed into a loop and suspended from the neck so as to support an injured arm (or foot).

**1720** DE FOE *Capt. Singleton* vi. (1840) 97 The sling his arm hung in. **1794** MRS. RADCLIFFE *Myst. Udolpho* li, He wears his arm in a sling. **1826** S. COOPER *First Lines Surg.* (ed. 5) 114 The arm is to be kept perfectly quiet in a sling. **1860** MRS. CARLYLE *Lett.* III. 51 He came..with his arm in a sling. **1895** ARNOLD & SONS *Catal. Surg. Instr.* 681 Foot Sling, with strap for neck.

**d.** *to have* (one's) *ass in a sling*, etc.: (see quot. 1960); to be in trouble. Cf. ASS *sb.*[2], arse. *U.S. slang.*

**1960** WENTWORTH & FLEXNER *Dict. Amer. Slang* 10/1 *To have one's ass in a sling*, to be or to appear to be sad, rejected, tired, or defeated. **1976** 'B. SHELBY' *Great Pebble Affair* (1977) 157, I figure there's no money in it for me, but I sure as hell want Rosale's ass in the sling. **1982** S. F. X. DEAN *Such Pretty Toys* (1983) vi. 94 Gonna get my ass in some sling if I miss that plane.

†**4.** A noose or snare. *Obs.*

This is a prominent sense of G. *schlinge*.

*c* **1425** *Cast. Persev.* 1208 in *Macro Plays* 113 *Luxuria.* I may soth synge: 'Mankynde is kawt in my slynge'.

†**5.** ? A quantity (of match) made up in the form of a loop or skein. *Obs.*

**1644** PRYNNE & WALKER *Fiennes's Trial* App. 29 Two Barrells of Musket and Carabine shot, and two slings of Match for the use of the said Tower Harris.

**6.** *techn.* in *Pottery.* (See quot.)

**1851–3** *Tomlinson's Cycl. Arts* (1867) II. 343/2 As the clay issues from the pug-mill it is cut into lengths of about 2 feet with a sling, or wire-knife, consisting of a piece of wire with two handles.

**7.** *attrib.* and *Comb.*, as *sling-bolt*, *-rope*, *-socket*; **sling-back**, used *attrib.* and *absol.* to designate (*a*) a woman's shoe which has an open back and is held on by a strap across the heel; so **sling-backed** *a.*; (*b*) a type of chair characterized by a fabric seat suspended from a rigid frame; **sling-bag**, a bag with a long strap which may be hung from the shoulder; **sling-cart** *Mil.*, a two-wheeled cart to which a cannon is slung in order to be transported; **sling chair** *U.S.*, a sling-back chair (see *sling-back* (*b*) above); **sling-dog, -hoop** (see quots.); **sling-jacket** (see quot. 1900); **sling-life-buoy** (see quot.); **sling-load, sling load**, a load which is lifted in a sling; also (with hyphen) as *v. trans.*; **sling pump** *N. Amer.*, a sling-back shoe (see *sling-back* (*a*) above); **sling-sleeve**, a form of sleeve for mantles, etc., suggestive of a sling for the arm; **sling-wagon**, *Mil.* a wagon for the same purpose as a sling-cart.

In some cases the first element might be taken as the stem of SLING *v.*[2]

**1949** *10 Eventful Years* (Encycl. Brit.) II. 312/2 They were soft suede slippers, little leather *sling-backs, ankle-high boots, and ballet slippers of all colours and materials. **1950** 'S. RANSOME' *Deadly Miss Ashley* ii. 25 Neat black sling-back wedgies on small feet. **1973** 'D. JORDAN' *Nile Green* xxvii. 119, I was sitting on a sling-back chair looking out on the Nile. **1974** *Country Life* 21 Mar. 688/1 A canvas sling-back with a rope wedge sole for £5. **1976** B. BOVA *Multiple Man* iii. 34, I walked across to the Scandinavian sling back that I usually sat in... I eased myself into the slingback chair. **1978** *Vogue* 1 Mar. 131 (*caption*) Sling-back high heels..£37. **1948** 'J. BELL' *Wonderful Mrs Marriott* vii. 86 A pair of toeless *sling-backed wedge-heeled shoes. **1965** M. SPARK *Mandelbaum Gate* vii. 218 Sturdily clutching with one thumb the shoulder strap of her *sling-bag. **1976** *Woman's Weekly* 6 Nov. 11/1 The letter still lay in the bottom of her sling bag. **1875** BEDFORD *Sailor's Pocket Bk.* vi. (ed. 2) 223 Toggle it with a stretcher through the aftermost of the foremost *sling bolts. **1802** JAMES *Milit. Dict.* s.v. *Ropes*, Drags for the gin, for the *sling-cart and waggon. **1859** F. A. GRIFFITHS *Artill. Man.* (1862) 123 *Sling Cart.* This cart is used for moving heavy guns, not exceeding 65 cwt., on hard, level roads, and for 8-inch, and 10-inch mortars. **1879** *Man. Artill. Exerc.* 510 There are two descriptions of sling carts in the service, both of wood, the one..will carry 3½ tons; the other..56 cwt. **1957** *Holiday* Nov. 141/1 The *sling, or Hardoy, chair, a leather suspension from a rigid metal cradle, adapted from a wooden folding chair used by Italian officers in North Africa. **1978** L. BLOCK *Burglar in Closet* ix. 75 Jillian..sat in a sling chair. **1863** A. YOUNG *Naut. Dict.* 130 Two of this latter kind fastened together through the eyes by a rope..are called *Sling-dogs. **1875** KNIGHT *Dict. Mech.*, *Sling-dog*, an iron hook with a fang at one end and an eye at the other for a rope. Used in pairs for hoisting, hauling, rafting, etc. **1846** A. YOUNG *Naut. Dict.* 286 A lower yard is hung by chains, called slings, attached to the *sling-hoop and mast head. **1867** SMYTH *Sailor's Word-bk.*, *Sling-Hoop*, that which suspends the yard from the mast, by which it is hoisted and lowered. **1900** HARDY in *Sphere* 21 Apr. 419/2 In those days the Hussar regiments still wore over the left shoulder that attractive attachment, or frilled half-coat, hanging loosely behind like the wounded wing of a bird, which was called the pelisse, though it was known among the troopers themselves as a '*sling-jacket'. **1908** —— *Dynasts* III. II. I Will the gay sling-jacket glow again beside the muslin gown? **1882** *Encycl. Brit.* XIV. 572/2 The rescuers haul off the hawser, to which is hung the travelling or *sling lifebuoy. **1933** M. LOWRY *Ultramarine* v. 213 The cargo, chests of tea, was hoisted in *slingloads of ten from the piles. **1968** *Globe & Mail* (Toronto) 3 Feb. B1/2 The union was asking for a 22-man basic work gang: extensive sling-load limitations, [etc.]. **1969** *Jane's Freight Containers 1968–69* 8/1 The line of action of the sling load is assumed to be parallel to and not more than 38 mm..from the outer face of the corner fitting. **1969** I. KEMP *Brit. G.I. in Vietnam* x. 176 A Chinook to sling-load our chopper back to Phuoc Vinh. **1941** *Women's Wear Daily* 31 Oct. I. 13/1 The shoe which so many retailers claimed they could not sell, the *sling pump, is due to make another trip, very definitely an evidence that women want them and like them. **1968** *Globe & Mail* (Toronto) 17 Feb. 12 (Advt.), Cool sandal sling pump with adjustable T-strap, low heel. **1325–6** *Ely Sacr. Rolls* (1907) II. 59 In *slyngeropis empt. 1s. **1497** *Naval Acc. Hen. VII* (1896) 91 Slyng Ropes. **1888** *Bow Bells Weekly* 6 Jan. 11/1 Mantles are generally seen either in the mantelet or *sling-sleeve shape. **1896** *Daily News* 10 Oct. 6/3 Sling sleeves are to be seen,.. with some fur capes and coats. **1609** HOLLAND *Amm. Marcell.* 222 Yron hookes, from which there hangeth a *sling-socket of tow or yron. **1802** JAMES *Mil. Dict.* s.v. *Rider*, A four-wheel carriage, such as the..block-carriage, and *sling-waggon. **1875** *Encycl. Brit.* II. 664 The sling waggon is composed of a body and limber, and fitted with windlass arrangement so that guns can be slung up underneath.

**sling** (slɪŋ), *sb.*[3] Also 6 slyng. [f. SLING *v.*[1]]

**1. a.** The act of slinging, throwing, etc.; a cast, fling, or throw.

The first two examples are somewhat doubtful.

**1530** PALSGR. 271/1 Slyng of an horse, *ruade.* **1558** PHAER *Æneid* v. N iij b, And now the right hand stroks, and now the left hand sends the slinges. **1667** MILTON *P.L.* x. 635 At one sling Of thy victorious Arm..Both Sin, and Death,.. Through Chaos [were] hurld. **1849** DE QUINCEY *Eng. Mail Coach* Wks. 1854 IV. 355 With one sling of his victorious arm, he might snatch thee back from ruin. **1850** BLACKIE *Æschylus* I. 58 If with wise sling the merchant fling Into the greedy sea A part to save the whole.

**b.** The swing *of* a gallop. Cf. SLING *v.*[1] 6.

**1852** LEVER *Maurice Tiernay* ix, He took them [*sc.* fences] in the 'sling' of his stretching gallop.

**2.** *slang.* A drink or draught; a 'pull'. *rare.*

**1788** J. MAY *Jrnl. & Lett.* (1873) 26 A case-bottle..filled with Hollands, of which each of us took a sling.

**3.** *Austral.* A gratuity; a bribe. Also *sling back.* Cf. SLING *v.*[1] 9.

**1948** K. S. PRICHARD *Golden Miles* viii. 92 'There's some hungry bastards,' the men said, 'making big money on their ore, never give the poor bugger boggin' for 'em a sling back.' The sling back might be ten bob on pay-day, or no more than a few pots of beer, but was always appreciated. *Ibid.* ix. 102 Sling backs to the shift boss got some men their jobs. **1953** K. TENNANT *Joyful Condemned* xxiv. 232 Say I take twenty per cent of the cop for myself..all the rest goes in slings. **1969** *People* (Austral.) 15 Jan. 21/2 It is not uncommon for a [poker] machine to go into a club with what is known in the trade as 'a sling'..to someone or other of the 'power men'... These 'slings' can range up to $300 a machine sold. **1973** *Nation Rev.* (Melbourne) 31 Aug. 1450/1 The hospital..must have been quite notorious in police circles. As far as I knew, we were exceptional in refusing to pay the customary sling.

†**sling**, *sb.*[4] *Obs.* Also 6 *Sc.* slung. [var. of SLANG *sb.*[1], perh. influenced by SLING *sb.*[1]] A serpentine or culverin.

Southey's use of the word in his *Joan of Arc* v. is merely an echo of Drayton (quot. 1627).

**1566** in J. J. Cartwright *Chapters Hist. Yks.* (1872) 93 Munition or ordinaunce..abord his shipp,..one saker, 2 quarter slings. *a* **1578** LINDESAY (Pitscottie) *Chron. Scot.* (S.T.S.) I. 251 Quarter fallcouns, slingis, pestelent serpitantis and doubill doggis. **1594** *Extr. Aberd. Reg.* (1848) II. 93 Twa peice of artailȝeirie, callit twa half slungis. **1627** DRAYTON *Agincourt* xciv, Their brazen slings send in the wilde-fire balls. **1627** CAPT. SMITH *Seaman's Gram.* xiv. 66 Chambers is a charge made of brasse or iron which we use to put in at the britch of a sling or Murtherer. **1648** HEXHAM II, *Een Slange*, a Culvering, or a Sling.

*attrib.* **1547** in Meyrick *Ancient Armour* (1824) III. 9 Slinge shotte, 20. Demi slinge shotte, 40. **1644** N. DRAKE *Siege of Pontefract* (Surtees) 7 During all this time there was 15 sling-peeses shott. **1736** DRAKE *Eboracum* I. v. 162 Two sling pieces, and one small drake.

**sling** (slɪŋ), *sb.*[5] [Of doubtful origin: cf. SLING *sb.*[3] 2.]

**1.** An American drink composed of brandy, rum, or other spirit, and water, sweetened and flavoured. Cf. GIN-SLING.

**1792** P. FRENEAU in *National Gazette* (Philadelphia) 28 June 280/1 Rum ne'er shall meet my lips..In shape of toddy, punch, grog, sling or dram. **1807** JANSON *Stranger in Amer.* 299 The first craving of an American in the morning is for ardent spirits mixed with sugar, mint, or some other hot herb, and which are called slings. **1836** MARRYAT *Midsh. Easy* (1863) 271 You won't take a glass of sling this fine night with a countryman? **1853** WOLFF *Pictures Sp. Life* 38 Beverages..unequalled even in Paris, or in the land flowing with sling and cobblers. **1871** MRS. STOWE *My Wife & I* ix, When the public call for hot brandy sling.

*attrib.* **1807** J. HARRIOTT *Struggles thro. Life* II. 110 Mr. Miles..served his customers with sling-drams, grog, or cider, himself. **1848** BARTLETT *Dict. Amer.* s.v. *Liquor*, Slingflip.

**2.** The juice of the sugar-cane, as obtained in the manufacture of sugar.

**1826** H. N. COLERIDGE *Six Months W. Indies* (1832) 65 There is so much trash, so much scum, and sling, and molasses, that my nerves have sometimes sunk under it. **1871** KINGSLEY *At Last* xvi, If..care were taken..not to spoil the preserves..by swamping them with sugar or sling. **1885** C. G. W. LOCK *Workshop Rec.* Ser. IV. 163/2 The difficulty is determining the exact moment when the boiling of the 'sling' in the striking-teach must cease.

**sling** (slɪŋ), *v.*[1] Pa. t. and pple. **slung** (slʌŋ). Forms: *Inf.* 4–6 **slynge** (6 **sklynge**), 5–6 **slyng** (5 **sclyng**), 5– **sling.** *Pa. t.* 3–6 **slong** (5 **sclong**), 3–5 **slonge**, 7– **slung**; 4–8 (9 *dial.*) **slang**, 4–6 **slange** (5 **slaunge**); 6–7 (9 *dial.*) **slinged.** *Pa. pple.* 5 **slongyn, -ene, 6 -en**; 5 **slungyn, -in, -en, 7– slung,** 9 *dial.* **slinged.** [prob. ad. ON. *slyngva* (pa. t. *slǫng*, *slungu*, pa. pple. *slungenn*) in the same sense; cf. Norw. *slyngia*, Da. *slynge* (Sw. *slunga*).

A strong verb *slingan* (*slang*, *slung-*) is also found in OHG. (and OE. ?), and is represented by MHG. (M)LG., and MDu. *slingen* (G. *schlingen*), but usually has the sense 'to creep, wind, twist', etc., although the sense 'to throw, sling' appears in MHG. and mod.G. dialects. (Kilian's '*slinghen*, funda jacere' is not otherwise certified as a Flemish use.) OF. *eslinguer*, *eslinder* (mod.Norm. and Pic. *élinguer*) is of Teutonic origin, but its immediate source is not clear.

A weak verb from the stem *slang-* is represented by ON. *slengva*, *-ja* (Icel. and Norw. *slengja*, Sw. *slänga*, Da. *slænge*), and by LG. *slengen*, G. *schlengen*. The ON. form would have given early ME. **sleng*, and this would subsequently have become *sling*.]

**I.** *trans.* **1. a.** To strike, to bring or knock *down*, by means of a sling. *rare.*

*a* **1225** *Juliana* 63 (Bodl. MS.), Þe lutle dauið..slong & ofsloh wið a stan to deaðe þe stronge Golie. **1699** POTTER *Antiq. Greece* III. iv. II. 52 We are told by some..that young Children were not allow'd any Food by their Mothers, 'till they could sling it down from the Beam, where it was plac'd aloft.

**b.** To throw or cast (stones, etc.) by means of a sling. Also *fig.*

*c* **1315** SHOREHAM VI. 26 Þou ert þe slinge, þy sone þe ston Þat dauy slange golye op-on. **1533** MORE *Answ. Poysoned Bk.* Wks. 1126/1 An heauy thing it is to here of hys yong foolishe Dauid, that hath thus..with the slyng of hys heresyes slonken [*sic*] hymselfe to the deuill. **1539** BIBLE *1 Sam.* xvii. 49 Dauid put his hande in his bagge, and toke out a stone, and slange it. **1560** —— (Geneva) *Judges* xx. 16 All these colde sling stones at an heere breadth, and not faile. **1648** *Hunting of Fox* 26 One of which [stones] being sling'd against the face of that uncircumciz'd Philistine, made him measure his length on the earth. **1737** [see SLING *sb.*[1] 1]. **1825** SCOTT *Betrothed* iv, A hail-storm of shafts, javelins, and stones, shot, darted, and slung by the Welsh. **1861** C. READE *Cloister & H.* xliii, The besiegers kept constantly slinging smaller stones on to the platform.

**c.** *absol.* To cast or discharge missiles by means of a sling; to use a sling. Also *fig.*

*c* **1440** *Promp. Parv.* 459/2 Slyngyn, *fundo*, *fundibalo.* **1530** PALSGR. 721/2, I holde the a penye I slynge as farre as thou. **1577** HANMER *Anc. Eccl. Hist.* (1663) 30 They vexed one another, they slinged one at another, but there was none to bridle them. **1623** BINGHAM *Xenophon* 53 The Rhodians slinged further, than the Persians could sling. **1861** READE *Cloister & H.* xliii, The besieged slung at the tower, and struck it often.

**2. a.** To throw, cast, hurl, or fling (a person or thing) in some direction or to some point. Usually const. with preps. or advs.

Common in 14–15th cent. Now chiefly *dial.* or *colloq.*

*c* **1290** *S. Eng. Leg.* I. 355 Þat bodi..into ane diche man it drovȝ, and þare-inne man it slong. *a* **1300** *Cursor M.* 8930 Þar was a stank bot littel fra,..þar-in þe king[es] tre þai slang. *c* **1386** CHAUCER *Manc. T.* 202 To þe crowe he stert.. and out at dore him slong. *c* **1400** *Destr. Troy* 3217 Sum þat were slayne & slungen to ground. *c* **1440** *Gesta Rom.* lxx. (Harl. MS.), That we shulde..take him, and sling him in our ovyn. **1530** PALSGR. 721/2 And thou medell with me, I wyll slynge the in the fyre. *a* **1547** SURREY in *Tottel's Misc.* (Arb.) 4 The adder all her sloughe aweye she slinges. **1596** DALRYMPLE tr. *Leslie's Hist. Scot.* (S.T.S.) I. 196 He slingis the ansinȝie out of his mind. **1684** T. BURNET *Theory Earth* I. xii. 166 How were these great bodies slung thorough the Air from their respective Seas. **1698** FRYER *Acc. E. India & P.* 36 The Platform of the City mounted with Brass Pieces that sling their Shot an incredible way. *c* **1715** RAMSAY *Vision* xix. in *Evergreen* (1761) I. 224 Pan foryets to tune his Reid, And slings it cairless bye. **1835** CROCKETT *Tour Down East* 37 When the captain told them I was [on board], they slung their hats, and gave three cheers. **1880** F. W. BURBRIDGE *Gardens of Sun* xi. 209 The imp took up one of the chocolate cups..and then slung it out at the open door. **1901** *N. & Q.* 9th Ser. VIII. 215/1 A..spud, with which lumps of earth were dug up and slung at straying sheep.

*fig.* *a* **1834** LAMB *Three Graves*, Rivers of blood from dripping traitors spilt, By treachery sling from poverty to guilt. **1959** E. H. CLEMENTS *High Tension* vii. 128 He'd been slung out of the test because he'd hurt his foot. **1977** W. MARSHALL *Thin Air* vi. 69 He was so bloody stupid we slung him out.

†**b.** To cast away. *Obs.*

*c* **1440** *York Myst.* xxxii. 321 As touchyng his money..Þat Judas..has wauyd away,.. Howe saie ȝe þerby? *Anna.* Sir, sen he it slang, we schall it saue. *c* **1450** *St. Cuthbert* (Surtees) 4557 Gude men had grace, schrewes ware slongen, To drery dede doune war þai dongen.

**c.** Of sheep: To cast (a lamb). Cf. SLINK *v.* 3.

So LG. *slengen*, G. *schlingen* (see Grimm).

**1750** [see SLUNG *ppl. a.*[1] 1]. **1794** *Young's Annals Agric.* XXII. 225 Ewes are apt to sling their lambs.

**d.** *absol.* To strike or launch *out* in boxing.

**1812** *Sporting Mag.* XL. 174 He seems to have copied from Crib, as he slings out well with the left hand in retreating.

**3.** In various colloquial or slang uses.

**a.** To utter (words). **b.** To hand round, distribute, dispense. Also in phr. ***to sling hash***, to wait at tables. *U.S.* Cf. *hash-slinger* s.v. HASH *sb.*[1] 6. **c.** ***to sling ink***, to write articles, etc. **d.** ***to sling one's Daniel*** or ***hook***, to make off, clear out. See also HOOK *sb.*[1] 16 b. **e.** To use or relate (some form of speech) to a person; to speak or utter (language, etc.) well or fluently; ***to sling the bull***, to talk glib nonsense (*U.S.*). Cf. sense 3 a above. **f.** (See quots.) **g.** To give up, abandon; also ***to sling in*** or ***up***.

**a.** *c* **1400** *Laud Troy Bk.* 6581 But Eneas be war, he abyes The bolde wordes that [he] dede sclyng.

**b. 1860** *Slang Dict.* 218 *Sling*, to pass from one person to another. **1889** H. O'REILLY *50 Yrs. on Trail* 7 As junior waiter..I could sling dishes around with the best of them. **1876** [see *Calamity Jane* s.v. CALAMITY 3]. **1903** *Daily Chron.* 31 Aug. 3/4, I have a friend in Beira,..who 'slings drinks' in a saloon. I believe he slings them very efficiently. **1906** 'O. HENRY' *Four Million* 106 I'm going back there and ask her to marry me. I guess she won't want to sling hash any more when she sees the pile of dust I've got. **1949** *Life* 24 Oct. 20/2 She..slung hash for a couple of weeks.

**c. 1870** 'ARTEMUS WARD' *Wks.* 305 You ask me, sir, to sling ink for your paper.

**d. 1873** J. GREENWOOD *In Strange Company* 338 [He] swore..that if we did not that instant 'sling our Daniels',.. he would [etc.]. **1874** *Slang Dict.* 295 *Sling your hook*, a polite invitation to move-on. **1897** *Daily News* 1 Sept. 2/2 If you don't sling yer hook this minute, here goes a pewter pot at yer head.

**e. 1874** E. EGGLESTON *Circuit Rider* vii. 72 He was beginning to sling his rude metaphors to the right and left. **1881** MRS. LYNN LINTON *My Love* I. xii. 220, I am awfully sorry if I slung you any slang. **1892** KIPLING *Barrack-Room Ballads* 67 An' 'ow they would admire for to hear us sling the *bat* [= speak the language]. **1904** *Strand Mag.* Mar. 254/1 Maybe you think I am just slinging you a yarn. **1904** G. B. SHAW *Lett. to Granville Barker* (1956) 27 One of them, the stage Irishman,..might be done by, say, Neville Doone, if he can sling the dialect. **1934** T. E. LAWRENCE *Let.* 8 June (1938) 806 In such an eyewash job as this of mine, the power to sling the gab would be very helpful. **1940** A. H. MARCKWARD *Scribner Handbk. Eng.* vii. 212 Undoubtedly the chief reason for the conversational effectiveness of many individuals is their inherent ability to sling it. **1982** *Verbatim* Autumn 14/2 Watch out for..the low-down curs and dirty dogs, who sling the bull and then send you on a wild goose chase.

**f.** *c* **1890** *5 Years' Penal Servitude* ii. 56 'Slinging his hook' is the professional term for picking pockets. *Ibid.* 59 His 'mate' soon finds out who the 'blooming screw' is that 'slung the smash'—i.e. brought in the tobacco.

**g. 1902** H. LAWSON *Children of Bush* 240 Just you sling it [i.e. drink] for a year and then look back... Sling it for good, Joe. **1910** G. B. LANCASTER *Jim of Ranges* ii. 48 I've slung her [*sc.* Queensland] up. Guv her the go, the ole jade. **1911** G. B. SHAW *Blanco Posnet* 384 Stow it, Boozy. Sling it. Cut it. Cheese it. Shut up. **1953** K. TENNANT *Joyful Condemned* xxxii. 309 We both slung in our jobs..and went off after him.

†**4.** To beat or whip (the white of an egg). *Obs.*

*c* **1450** *M.E. Med. Bk.* (Heinrich) 196 [Take] þe whyte of viij. eyren, & slyng hem wel.., & euer styre faste. *Ibid.* 197 [Take] .ix. whytes of eyren, & slyngge hem, & mak hem in gleyr.

**II.** *intr.* **5.** To move with some force or speed; to fly as if thrown by a sling; to fling oneself.

**13..** *K. Alis.* 5538 (Laud MS.), On þe destrer onon he slang, Als arewe of bowe forþ he sprang. *c* **1400** *Laud Troy Bk.* 14252 He let his stede to him flyng Als harde as he myght slyng. *c* **1430** *Hymns Virgin* (1867) 120 Thorowe the strength off þe wynd Into the Welken hitt schall slynge. **1582** STANYHURST *Æneis* (Arb.) 137 From whence, with flownce furye slinging, Stoans, and burlye bulets, lyke tamponds, maynelye be towring. **1790** BEATSON *Naval & Mil. Mem.* I. 214 The ship, for some time, was ungovernable, and slung up in the wind. **1821** CLARE *Vill. Minstr.* I. 65 Thou corner-chair, In which I've oft slung back in deep despair.

**6.** To advance, walk, etc., with long or swinging strides. Chiefly *Sc.* or *north.* and *Austral.*

**1808** in JAMIESON. **1818** J. HOGG *Brownie of Bodsbeck* iii, I slings aye on wi' a gay lang step. **1828** CARR *Craven Gloss.* s.v., 'My horse slings away at a girt rate,' that is, he quits the ground with apparent ease. **1890** 'R. BOLDREWOOD' *Col. Reformer* vi. 48 All day they was very sulky and slinged along, and wouldn't feed. **1893** J. A. BARRY *Steve Brown's Bunyip* 17, I saw the man slinging off into the scrub.

**7.** Of a millstone: To swing from side to side.

**1875** KNIGHT *Dict. Mech.* 1020/1.

**8.** ***to sling off*** (***at***), to jeer (at). *Austral.* and *N.Z. colloq.*

**1911** S. RUDD *Dashwoods* 24, I heard yer both slingin' off. **1916** *Anzac Bk.* 31, I could not understand them slinging off at 'im and 'im thinking they were treatin' 'im like as 'e was one of themselves. **1921** K. S. PRICHARD *Black Opal* xiii. 112 The rest of the men continued nevertheless to 'sling off', as they said, at Bully and Roy O'Mara as they saw fit. **1941** *Coast to Coast* 232 'Why was he so wild?' 'Aw, it was just some chaps'd been slinging off at him,' I said. **1960** N. HILLIARD *Maori Girl* III. vii. 221 The *pakehas* think you're slinging off about them or saying something rude. **1963** J. CANTWELL *No Stranger to Flame* v. 86 'Stop it,' Barry said, flushing. 'Stop slinging off.' **1975** M. R. LIVERANI *Winter Sparrows* II. xv. 232 She glowered at the driver suspiciously. Was he slinging off at her?

**9.** To pay a bribe or gratuity. Occas. with *it.* Cf. SLING *sb.*[3] 3. *Austral.*

**1939** K. TENNANT *Foveaux* II. 172 'I'm slinging it to Hamp,' Bardy said sullenly. **1949** L. GLOSSOP *Lucky Palmer* 5 Clarrie, he ain't gone off in six months. Must sling to the cops. Wonder how much he pays 'em. **1953** T. A. G. HUNGERFORD *Riverslake* vi. 130 'Sling, Stefan!' When the Pole looked at him uncomprehendingly Murdoch whipped a ten-pound note out of the bundle and handed it to the ring-keeper. 'He don't know,' he explained. 'It's the first time he's played.' **1971** F. HARDY *Outcasts of Foolgarah* 56 On first name terms with every shire President so long as they didn't forget to sling when backhanders came in.

**sling** (slɪŋ), *v.*[2] Also 6 slyng. [f. SLING *sb.*[2]]

**1. a.** *trans.* To place in, or secure with, a sling or slings in order to admit of or facilitate hoisting or lowering; to raise up or let down by means of a sling or slings.

**1522** *MS. Acc. St. John's Hosp., Canterb.*, For the dyner of iij men that holp slyng and lyft the cow that broke her legg. *c* **1625** *Nomenclator Navalis* (MS. Harl. 2301), *Sling* is to make faste anie Caske, Ordnance, Yarde, or ye like in a paire of Slings. **1669** STURMY *Mariner's Mag.* v. xii. 81 [He may] have himself [let] down..to the bottom of the Sea.. and sling the Ship, and Guns. **1771** LUCKOMBE *Hist. Print.* 327 He..slings the Stone in two strong pack-threds, placing one towards either end of the Stone. **1803** *Phil. Trans.* XCIII. 322 The ship being in the fore-mentioned state,..I next proceeded to sling her; which was done with two nineteen-inch cables. **1869** RANKINE *Machine & Hand-tools* Pl. O 3, It terminates with the usual hook and swivel for slinging the load.

**b.** With adverbial complement.

**1627** CAPT. SMITH *Seaman's Gram.* xiii. 60 Let vs..sling a man ouer boord to stop the leakes. **1692** DRYDEN *Cleomenes* I. i, Amidst the shouts Of mariners, and busy care to sling His horses soon ashore, he saw not me. **1833** T. HOOK *Parson's Dau.* III. xi, The horses were slung down into the stalls. **1890** DOYLE *White Company* xv, Horse after horse was slung by main force up from the barges.

**2.** *Naut.* To pass chains or lashings round (a sail or yard) to secure it to the mast.

**1626** CAPT. SMITH *Accid. Yng. Seamen* 6 Fore-mast men, to take in the Topsayles,..Furle, and Sling the maine Saile. **1669** STURMY *Mariner's Mag.* I. ii. 19 Sling our Main Yard, with the Chains in the Main-top. **1777** COOK *Voy. S. Pole* III. ii. II. 17 The yard is slung nearly in the middle, or upon an equipoise. **1867** SMYTH *Sailor's Word-bk.* 632. **1875** KNIGHT *Dict. Mech.* 2211/2 To sling the yards for action is to secure them at the slings by iron chains fitted for the purpose.

**3.** To hang or suspend, to fix or fasten (something) about the person in a sling or in a loose manner so as to be carried easily.

Usually const. with preps., as *across*, *from*, or *over* (the shoulders or back); *at*, *by*, (*up*)*on*, *to*, etc. (the side, arm, etc.); *about* or *round* (the neck or person).

**1688** HOLME *Armoury* III. xix. (Roxb.) 153/1 Granadeers haue a care. Sling your musketts. **1791** COWPER *Iliad* I. 55 The God,..with his radiant bow And his full quiver o'er his shoulder slung, Marched in his anger. **1814** S. ROGERS *Jacqueline* I. 41 He slung his old sword by his side. **1833** *Regul. & Instr. Cavalry* I. 169 The lance is slung on the left arm. **1859** JEPHSON *Brittany* vi. 82 A guitar slung round her neck by a blue ribbon. **1885** *Law Rep.* 14 *Q.B.D.* 725 A police constable saw the appellant..with some rabbits slung over his back.

**4. a.** To hang up or suspend, esp. from one point to another; to put up (a hammock). Also in phr. ***to sling one's hammock***, to have a period of time off-duty to get used to a new ship. *Naut.*

**1697** DRYDEN *Virg. Past.* III. 150 From Rivers drive the Kids, and sling your Hook. **1706** E. WARD *Wooden World Dissected* (1708) 97 Sling him up in a Hammock, and he shall lie a whole Night. **1730** A. GORDON *Maffei's Amphith.* 18 These Theatres were not founded in the Ground, but slung, and supported in the Air; that is, they both rested on Hinges and Pivots. **1779** *Mirror* No. 17 The poor little creatures sleep..in a hammock, slung up to the roof. **1824** MISS L. M. HAWKINS *Annaline* II. 213 Attendants [were] slinging their grass woven hammocks. **1853** SIR H. DOUGLAS *Milit. Bridges* (ed. 3) 354 The platform or road-way is slung, by vertical tackles, to points equidistant from each other. **1883** *Law Rep.* 11 *Q.B.D.* 506 The dock owner supplied..an ordinary stage to be slung..outside the ship for the purpose of painting her. **1913** T. T. JEANS *John Graham Sub-Lieutenant R.N.* iii. 58 There was no 'school' till morning, the Padré had a day off 'to sling his hammock'. **1917** 'TAFFRAIL' *Sub* iii. 92 'You'll have to-morrow to sling your hammock and to get used to the ship, youngster,' he went on. **1946** G. HACKWORTH JONES *Sixteen Bells* I. iv. 67 Reggie was hardly given a day to 'sling his hammock' before he was instructed to take over the afternoon watch.

**b.** ***to sling the monkey***, a kind of game played by sailors.

**1838** *Bentley's Miscell.* III. 588 But I say,..did you ever play *sling the monkey*? *Ibid.* 589 I'm bless'd, shipmates, if we didn't sling the monkey in fine style. **1893** SLOANE-STANLEY *Rem. Midshipm. Life* II. iii. 51 Whilst we Middies were playing sling the monkey the ship's company were diverting themselves in a variety of ways. [A full description of the game is given on page 50.]

**5.** *techn.* in *Pottery.* (See quot.)

**1851-3** *Tomlinson's Cycl. Arts* (1867) II. 343/2 If the clay be very foul, or full of stones, it is slung; that is, as the clay issues from the pug-mill it is cut into lengths of about 2 feet with a sling, or wire-knife.

**sling,** *v.*[3] *U.S.* [f. SLING *sb.*[5] I.] *intr.* To drink or take sling.

**1836-8** HALIBURTON *Clockm.* (1862) 444, I ordered a pint o' the best [toddy], and so we slinged. **1867** SMYTH *Sailor's Word-bk.* 632 On the American coast..the custom of *slinging* prevails..extensively, even where intoxication is despised.

**sling-,** the stem of SLING *v.*[1] used in combs., as †**sling-dart**, a military engine for throwing darts; **sling-fruit**, a fruit which forcibly ejects the seeds when ripe; **sling-net**, a casting-net; **sling-snake** *Zool.*, a name given to a genus of snakes belonging to the Colubrine group of the *Colubridæ*; **sling-spear**, a spear hurled with a throwing-stick; **sling-trot**, a loose swinging trot or pace.

**1600** HOLLAND *Livy* XLII. lxv. 1154 Most hurt they had by certaine weapons called Cestrosphendonæ (*sling darts). A new kind of dart this was and lately devised. *a* **1899** OLIVER tr. *Kerner's N.H. Plants* II. 833 The fruits of *Dorycnium* and *Acanthus* may be taken as types of a large group designated by the name of *Sling-fruits. **1589** FLEMING *Virg. Georg.* I. 6 Now one with *slingnet beats vpon the riuer brode and large, Reaching vnto the very depth. **1866** MRS. GASKELL *Wives & Daughters* I. x. 112 He had been out dredging in ponds and ditches, and has his wet sling-net, with its imprisoned treasures..over his shoulder. **1896** LYDEKKER *Roy. Nat. Hist.* V. 205 We mention as a second genus of this group the *sling-snakes, of which there are about twenty known species. **1888** ANDREWS *Temple Mystic* 79 None further the *sling-spear threw. **1853** J. PALLISER *Solitary Rambles & Adventures Hunter in Prairies* vi. 144, I saw my stag begin to fall in the rear of the band, and his pace slacken to a *sling trot. **1860** W. H. RUSSELL *Diary in India* I. xvi. 247 Stewart and I at once started off at a sling trot. **1866** MRS. GASKELL *Wives & Daughters* xxix, The long sling-trot, so well known to the country people as the doctor's pace.

**slinge** (slɪndʒ), *v. dial.* Also **slindge, sleenge.** [Of obscure origin.] *intr.* To slink, skulk, lounge, loaf, etc.

**1747** RELPH *Poems* Gloss., *To slinge*, to go creepingly away, as ashamed. **1828** CARR *Craven Gloss.*, *Slinge*, to skulk, to sneak, to creep about. **1834** LOVER *Leg. Irel.* Ser. II. 232 What are you slindging there for, when it's minding your work you ought to be? **1842** —— *Handy Andy* xiv, Idle blackguards who were slingeing about the place eternally.

**slinger** ('slɪŋə(r)), *sb.*[1] Also 5-6 slynger, -ar(e. [f. SLING *v.*[1] + -ER. Cf. OHG. *sling-*, *slengari*, *-eri*, etc. (MHG. *slingære*, *-er*, G. *schlinger*), MDu. *slinger*, MSw. *sliungare* (Sw. *slungare*); also OF. *eslingour*, *-ur*, etc.]

**1.** One who casts missiles by means of a sling, *esp.* a soldier armed with a sling. Now chiefly *arch.* or *Hist.*

**1382** WYCLIF *2 Kings* iii. 25 The cyte is enuyround of slyngers. *a* **1400** *Octouian* 1599 (W.), Spermen, slyngers, and arblasteres. *c* **1440** *Promp. Parv.* 459/2 Slyngare, *fundibuiarius.* *c* **1550** N. SMYTH tr. *Herodian* III. 33 All the Mauritanyan Slyngers that were in his seruyce. **1610** HOLLAND *Camden's Brit.* 211 The Inhabitants [of Dorset] of all English-men were the cunningest slingers. **1671** MILTON *Samson* 1619 Behind [him] Archers, and Slingers, Cataphracts and Spears. **1737** WHISTON *Josephus, Wars Jews* I. vii. §3 The slingers of stones beat off those that stood above them. **1788** GIBBON *Decl. & F.* l. V. 241 The heights had been occupied by the archers and slingers of the confederates. **1825** SCOTT *Betrothed* iv, Their own archers.. were supported by numerous bodies of darters and slingers. **1870** EMERSON *Soc. & Sol.*, *Work & Days*, The sympathy of eye and hand by which..a practised slinger hits his mark with a stone.

**2.** One who flings or throws. (Cf. *ink-slinger.*)

**1902** *Sat. Rev.* 5 July 12/2 Last year he was a mere slinger, to-day he bowls a capital length. **1920** D. J. KNIGHT in P. F. Warner *Cricket* i. 45 The man [*sc.* fast bowler] who bowls with his arm more or less horizontal—a slinger. **1926** *Variety* 29 Dec. 5/3 The erudite word slingers. *Ibid.*, The slang *slingers.* **1944** E. BLUNDEN *Cricket Country* iv. 52 T. was soon displaced for a less expensive slinger. **1979** *Vole* June 45/2 The slingers of the mid-nineteenth century terrified lesser batsmen.

**3.** Chiefly *Services' slang.* Bread soaked in tea. Usu. *pl.* Also applied *loosely* to other food.

**1882** F. W. P. JAGO *Anc. Lang. & Dial. Cornwall* 267 Slingers. Kettle broth made of boiling water, bread, salt, and pepper, with sometimes a little butter. **1890** BARRÈRE & LELAND *Dict. Slang* II. 256/2 *Slingers*,..bits of bread floating in tea. **1895** KIPLING in *Pall Mall Gaz.* 30 May 2/2 You won't have no mind for slingers, not to-morrow—.. bein' sick! **1925** FRASER & GIBBONS *Soldier & Sailor Words* 261 *Slingers*, tea or coffee with bread soaked in it. Dumplings. **1962** W. GRANVILLE *Dict. Sailors' Slang* 108 *Slingers*, ship's biscuits or bread soaked in cocoa. A snack eaten before *slinging* one's hammock. Supper is very early in the Navy and *slingers* help to fortify the men until breakfast the next day. **1965** 'J. LE CARRÉ' *Looking Glass War* ii. 31 We had the canteen in the old days. Slinger and wadge.

**slinger** ('slɪŋə(r)), *sb.*[2] [f. SLING *v.*[2]] A workman employed in slinging.

**1881** *Daily News* 16 Nov. 7/1 A slinger in the employ of Messrs. Maudslay, the engineers,..who was killed by the fall of a boiler plate which he was..slinging. **1969** *Daily Tel.* 2 Apr. 1/1 The slip was dropped from an overall pocket by a slinger—a man who guides car bodies and other parts into position on the assembly track—and it showed that he was earning as much as the assembly workers themselves. **1974** P. WRIGHT *Lang. Brit. Industry* viii. 69 In heavy electrical engineering, where the crane-driver can see the slinger directing his load, they communicate by shouts. **1982** *Sunday Times* 27 June 3/1 I've been in the ropery 12 years and my husband's been in the yard, as a slinger, for 17 years.

**slinger** ('slɪŋə(r)), *sb.*[3] [f. SLING *sb.*[5]] One who is given to drinking sling.

**1807** JANSON *Stranger in Amer.* 299, I know of no custom more destructive than that which is practised by slingers and eleveners.

†'**slinger,** *v. Sc. Obs.*[−1] [ad. Du. *slingeren* (Fris. *slingerje*) or LG. *slingern* (Da. *slingre*, G.

*schlingern*), frequent. of *slingen*: see SLING *v.*[1]] *intr.* To swing, roll.

**1767** MESTON *Poems* 129 As ships, that bear more sail then ballast, Slinger before the very smallest Unequal blast.

**slinget** ('slɪŋɪt). *dial.* [dim. of *sling* var. of SLANG *sb.*[2]] = SLANG *sb.*[2]

**1790** GROSE *Prov. Gloss., Slinget*, a narrow slip of ground. **1826** *Rep. Comm. Inquiry Charities* (1827) XVII. 832 A slinget of ground. **1839-** in dial. glossaries (Heref., Worc., Glouc., etc.).

**'slingful.** [f. SLING *sb.*[2] 1 + -FUL.] As much as a sling will hold.

**1913** *Cassell's Mag. Fiction & Popular Lit.* June 183/1 A stevedore was killed by a falling slingful of railway sleepers. **1941** E. P. O'DONNELL *Great Big Doorstep* xxii. 313 She heard the donkey engines clanking aboard an approaching ship, and slingfuls of fruit splashing into the water.

**slinging** ('slɪŋɪŋ), *vbl. sb.*[1] [f. SLING *v.*[1] + -ING[1].] The action of the vb. in various senses.

**13..** *K. Alis.* 1616 (Laud MS.), Wiþ gredyng, & wiþ þretyng, And wilde fire slyngyng. *c* **1400** *Destr. Troy* 6006 Myche slaghte in the slade, & slyngyng of horse! *Ibid.* 7693 Gret slaght in þe slade, & slyngyng to ground. **1648** WILKINS *Math. Magic* I. xvii. 120 The mother would not give any meat to her child, till he could hit it with slinging. **1801** STRUTT *Sports & Past.* II. ii. 65 The art of Slinging or casting of stones with a sling, is of high antiquity.

**b.** *attrib.*, as *slinging-cast, -engine, -machine.*

**1657** *North's Plutarch, Add. Lives* 5 Archimedes..caused a slinging Engine to be made of a wonderfull height and greatness. *a* **1693** *Urquhart's Rabelais* III. xii. 93 The.. slinging Casts of the Vulcanian Thunderbolts. **1860** *Chambers's Encycl.* I. 640/1 The *mate-griffon* and *mate-funda*, both slinging-machines. **1861** READE *Cloister & H.* xliii, The besiegers turned two of their slinging engines on this monster.

**'slinging,** *vbl. sb.*[2] [f. SLING *v.*[2]] The act of securing, suspending, lifting, etc. by means of a sling.

*c* **1635** CAPT. N. BOTELER *Dial. Sea Services* (1685) 165 The third sort of Slings, is that which is here mentioned in the slinging of the Yards. **1833** *Regul. & Instr. Cavalry* I. 169 The slinging of the lance on either side..requires much practice. **1844** *Regul. & Ord. Army* 351 Horses are much less liable to be injured by the operation of slinging after having undergone moderate exercise. **1901** *Business Terms, Phrases & Abbrev.* (ed. 2) 109 The buyer must attend to their being put on board, and pay the dues or the charges for slinging, should any be incurred.

*attrib.* **1875** KNIGHT *Dict. Mech.* 2203/2 Hog-slaughtering apparatus consists of scalding-tubs and slinging devices.

**'slinging,** *ppl. a.* [f. SLING *v.*[1] + -ING[2].] Of a trot or pace: Characterized by long swinging strides; loose and swinging.

*c* **1843** M. J. HIGGINS *Ess.* (1875) 65 Off he goes at a slinging trot, clearing every obstacle which presents itself. **1883** *Harper's Mag.* 888/1 The priest walked onward at a long, slinging pace. **1897** W. H. THORNTON *Reminis. W.-Co. Clergyman* i. 1 We boys..started away at a slinging trot.

**'slingshot.** orig. *U.S.* Also sling-shot.

**1. a.** A catapult.

**1849** N. KINGSLEY *Diary* 23 Oct. (1914) 77 Many are getting up sling-shots,..but I hope we shall never have occasion to use them, but we must all do something to pass away the time. **1895** *Outing* XXVII. 51/1 The natives, who now and then throw stones from a sling-shot at the bolder birds. **1901** *Daily Colonist* (Victoria, B.C.) 15 Oct. 5/2 The police have started a crusade against the use of slingshots and air and pea guns by boys. **1966** *Economist* 2 July 28/2 In peasant style, they placed women and children to the fore, and used slingshots with shepherds' accuracy to defend themselves against the detachment of police cavalry. **1977** C. MCCULLOUGH *Thorn Birds* i. 3 She played happily with the whistles and slingshots..her brothers discarded.

**b.** In various *fig.* and *transf.* uses implying propulsion from or as from a catapult (see quots.) Also as quasi-*adv.*

**1951** *Sun* (Baltimore) 10 July 15/3 [In a game of soft-ball] I've never seen a pitcher get away with an illegal pitch in the national or league play... Most of them throw just like I do —straight windmill—and out on the Coast, they throw slingshot. **1964** W. GOLDING *Spire* ix. 159 The weather.. began to squeeze bursts of rain out of the air like slingshot, so that although the men were wet, they were warm with the stinging. **1975** *New Yorker* 30 June 81/1 That's the slingshot there—where the rubber is stretched between bumpers [in a pinball machine]. **1976** J. JAMES *Bridge of Sand* iii. 62 There came immediately on us a great storm of hail. The sling-shots of the Gods rattled on our helmets, bounced off our shields, almost cut our faces. **1976** *6,000 Words* 184 *Slingshot*. n, 1: a maneuver in auto racing in which a drafting car accelerates past the car in front by taking advantage of reserve power 2: a dragster in which the driver sits behind the rear wheels. **1979** 'A. HAILEY' *Overload* III. vii. 222 Harry London's feet hit the floor like slingshots.

**c.** *Astronaut.* A space flight which uses the gravitational pull of a celestial body in order to accelerate sharply and, usu., to change course. Freq. *attrib.* (see sense 3 below.)

**1970** N. ARMSTRONG et al. *First on Moon* viii. 174 The three men on Apollo II had to decide whether to allow themselves to be 'captured' by lunar gravity—or take the slingshot and come home. **1971** *Encyclopedia Science Suppl.* 350 The next flight now scheduled is for 1973, a 'slingshot' that will pass close to Venus on its way to Mercury.

**2.** A weapon consisting of a heavy weight wrapped in a cloth or equivalent and used as a cosh; a blackjack. ? *Obs.*

**1891** H. HERMAN *His Angel* ix. 149 He made a ghastly horrible sling-shot by filling a heavy tumbler with the iron tops screwed off from the fire-irons, and tying the lot in a handkerchief. **1904** *N.Y. Evening Post* 24 June 2/6 The guards..are authorized to carry slingshots... [They] are heavily loaded with lead, and are securely attached to the wrist.

**3.** *attrib.*, as (sense 1 a) ***slingshot crotch***; (sense 1 b) ***slingshot dragster***; (sense 1 c) ***slingshot action, attitude, flight, manœuvre, trajectory.***

**1979** *Guardian* 3 Sept. 11/3 Accelerated and turned by the slingshot action of Saturn's gravitational field, the spacecraft is heading out past Titan on a new trajectory. **1970** N. ARMSTRONG et al. *First on Moon* iv. 83 We've completed our maneuvers to observe the slingshot attitude. **1923** W. S. CATHER *Lost Lady* ii. 16 They had behaved like wild creatures all morning;..cutting sling-shot crotches. **1962** *Engineering* 5 Jan. 5/1 Sydney Allard's immaculately prepared 'slingshot' dragster, with its 480 hp. Roots-blown Chrysler V8 engine. **1971** *Guardian* 16 Dec. 13/5 Designed ..to use the gravitational fields of the planets for 'sling-shot' flights which—using Jupiter as the primary springboard— visit Saturn and Pluto, then Uranus and Neptune. **1970** N. ARMSTRONG et al. *First on Moon* iv. 82 A 'slingshot' maneuver, a trajectory which would take it behind the trailing edge of the moon. **1976** *Sci. News* 18 June 391 The 'slingshot' trajectory between the worlds has carried Pioneer 11 about 16° above the plane of the ecliptic.

Hence **'slingshot** *v. intr.*; **'sling-shooting** *ppl. a.*

**1969** *Daily Progress* (Charlottesville, Va.) 5 July 6/4 'I could stay with him in a draft (the two cars running one behind the other).'.. Yarborough said he purposely gave Baker two chances to slingshot past to learn if he was fast enough. **1975** B. GARFIELD *Death Sentence* xxi. 106 The lights were all gone: stone-throwing and sling-shooting kids routinely used them for target practice. **1980** *Dirt Bike* Oct. 68/1 Ward's body inched forward with increasing speed until he slingshotted at blurring velocity to and beyond the Yamaha.

**'sling(s)man.** [f. SLING *sb.*[1]] A slinger.

**1579-80** NORTH *Plutarch* (1595) 627 Two thousand archers and slingmen. **1605** SYLVESTER *Du Bartas* II. iii. I. *Vocation* 825 A band of Sling-men he anon doth force. **1768** BARETTI *Manners & Customs Italy* II. 241 One of the slingsmen had the insolence to fling a stone where she was. **1895** SIR H. MAXWELL *Duke of Britain* ix. 133 The ordinary spearmen, slingsmen,..bowmen, or mounted troopers.

**'sling-stone.** Also slingstone, sling stone; *Sc.* 5 slong, 8 slung stane. [SLING *sb.*[1] Cf. older G. *slingen-, schlingstein*, ON. *slǫngusteinn*, MSw. *slyngo-, slongasten* (Sw. *slungsten*), older Da. *slynge-, slingesten.*]

**1.** A stone or pebble used as a missile to be cast by a sling.

*c* **1374** CHAUCER *Troylus* II. 941 (Corpus MS.), Who hath ben wel Ibete To-day with swerdes and with slyng stones [*v.r.* slynke stones]. **14..** *Lat.-Eng. Voc.* in Wr.-Wülcker 608 *Risidus*, a slyngeston. **1456** SIR G. HAYE *Law Arms* (S.T.S.) 169 David..vencust that grete Goulyas, with..his slong and his slong stanis. **1535** COVERDALE *Zech.* ix. 15 They shall consume and deuoure, and subdue them with slynge stones. **1682** BUNYAN *Holy War* (1905) 373 The sling-stones were to him and his like Hornets. **1768** ROSS *Helenore* 78 Tho' I'm amo' you cast like a slung stane, I was like ither fouk at hame ye ken. **1865** LUBBOCK *Prehist. Times* 76 That some have really served as slingstones seems to be indicated by their presence in the peatmosses. **1866** LAING *Prehist. Rem. Caithn.* 22 Several round pebbles or slingstones about the size of an apple.

**2.** A stone used as an anchor; a killick.

**1865** J. C. WILCOCKS *Sea-Fisherman* 117 A stone for mooring is termed a sling stone or killick, and should be attached to a piece of half-worn rope.

**slink** (slɪŋk), *sb.* Also 7 slinke, slincke, 8 sclink. [Related to SLINK *v.*]

**I. 1. a.** An abortive or premature calf or other animal. Chiefly *dial.*

**1638** PEACHAM *Valley of Varietie* 32 The Germans loath to eate of a Slinke (or yong Calfe, cut out of the Cowes belly before it be calved). **1706** PHILLIPS (ed. Kersey), *Slink*, a cast Calf. *a* **1800** PEGGE *Suppl. Grose.* **1826-** in dial. glossaries (Yorks., Lancs., Chesh., Derb., Nhp., Wilts., etc.). **1895** *Melbourne Argus* 26 Nov., As to 'slinks' a great scare seemed to have been created, but from a health point of view they were merely indigestible.

†**b.** *transf.* An illegitimate child; a bastard.

**1702** COMBERBACH in Byron & Elms *Life* 391 (Cent.), What did you go to London for but to drop your slink?

**c.** The skin or flesh of a premature calf or other animal. Also *transf.* (quot. 1816).

(*a*) **1741** *Compl. Fam.-Piece* I. i. 57 Take liquid Styrax, spread it thin upon Sclink, or some very fine Kid's Leather. **1858** SIMMONDS *Dict. Trade, Slinks*, the skins of prematurely born lambs, calves, etc.

(*b*) **1808** JAMIESON s.v., When this [flesh] is palmed on an ignorant purchaser for veal, it is called *slink*. **1816** SCOTT *Antiq.* xv, He hasna settled his [butcher's] account wi' my gudeman..for this twalmonth—he's but slink, I doubt.

**2.** *attrib.* **a.** Designating the skins or meat obtained from premature or abortive animals.

Sometimes also applied to inferior, bad, or diseased meat.

(*a*) **1607** T. COCKS *Acc.* 23 May (MS.), For ij payre of slincke skynne gloves ij *s.* viij *d.* **1678** *Lond. Gaz.* No. 1308/4 A Slink skin Purse. **1711** *Act 10 Anne* c. 26 §1 All Slink Calve-skins..dressed..with the Hair on. **1794** in Scott *Statist. Acc. Perth* (1790) 38 A good many small and slink kid, and mort lamb-skins. **1812** J. SMYTH *Pract. Customs* (1821) 108 Slink Foal Skins are always entered, and the Duty charged thereon, as Horse Hides.

(*b*) **1770** P. SKELTON *Wks.* V. 599 Would they indulge in bear bread and slink veal, while their master lives on leeks and cold potatoes? **1820** C. R. MATURIN *Melmoth* I. i. 10 There was the slink-veal flanked with tripe. **1892** *Pall Mall G.* 28 Oct. 4/3 Preston was deluged with 'slink' meat, owing to the laxity of their sanitary system. **1895** *Melbourne Argus* 26 Nov., In some countries unborn calves were sold as 'slink' meat.

**b.** Designating animals of this kind.

**1750** *Student* I. 340 This membrane does not properly appertain to dogs, etc. yet it may be found in slink calves. *a* **1825** FORBY *Voc. E. Anglia* 307 *Slink-calf*, the abortion of a cow. **1858** SIMMONDS *Dict. Trade, Slink-lamb*, one that has been dropped or born prematurely.

**c.** In sense 'trading in or selling slink or diseased meat', as ***slink-butcher.***

**1832** *Examiner* 89/2 On Sunday morning last a number of slink butchers from Manchester fetched it away in a cart. **1886** *St. James' Gaz.* 14 May 4 (Cassell), The protection of our own slink-butchers from any dishonourable competition..with their industry.

**d.** ***slink-weed***, rose-bay, willow-herb. *U.S.*

**1858** THOREAU *Jrnl.* 29 Aug. in *Writings* (1906) XVII. 134 F. says they call the cardinal-flower 'slink-weed', and say that the eating it will cause cows to miscarry. **1889** *Chambers's Encycl.* IV. 401/1 This species [*Epilobium angustifolium*] with several others is common in North America, where it is sometimes called..slink-weed, from a belief that it causes cows to 'slink' or miscarry.

**II. 3. a.** *dial.* or *colloq.* A sneaking, shirking, cowardly fellow; a sneak or skulk.

**1824** MACTAGGART *Gallovid. Encycl.* 398 Tho' ye were an unco slink, I'm sad without ye. **1830** *Examiner* 813/1 He had given Sack a turn because he was such a d——d slink. **1862** *Morning Star* 24 Jan. 6/5 He had been called a skulk, a slink, a moral coward.

*Comb.* **1842** LOVER *Handy Andy* xiv, He's blackguardin' and blastin' away about that quare slink-lookin' chap.

**b.** *dial.* and *U.S.* (See quots.)

**1863** WISE *New Forest* Gloss. s.v., 'A slink of a thing'.. means either a poor, weak, starved creature, or anything which is small and not of good quality. **1891** *Cent. Dict.*, *Slink*,..a thin or poor and bony fish, especially such a mackerel.

**4. a.** A slinking, sneaking, or stealthy pace or tread.

**1853** G. J. CAYLEY *Las Alforjas* I. 151 He decamped, with a sort of half slink, half swagger. **1896** F. A. STEEL *Face Waters* II. i, Those who went forth with the dog's trot might return with the cat's slink.

**b.** A downcast or furtive glance or look. *rare.*

**1863** MRS WHITNEY *Faith Gartney* xxxvi, The boy showed a slink in his eyes, like one used to shoving and rebuff.

**slink** (slɪŋk), *a.*[1] *dial.* [? Related to SLINK *sb.* and *v.*] Lank, lean, poor, ill-conditioned.

**1673** MRS. BEHN *Dutch Lover* III. ii, Do you remember.. when instead of a Periwig, you wore a slink, greasie hair of your own. **1818** SCOTT *Rob Roy* xxvii, It was a slink beast, and wad hae eaten its head aff, standing at Luckie Flyter's at livery. **1823** E. MOOR *Suffolk Words* 361 *Slink*, lank, slender; combined with awkwardness. **1889** *Cent. Dict.* s.v. *Mackerel, Slink mackerel*, a poor thin mackerel taken among schools of fat ones in the fall of the year. **1892** EWING *Poems* 16 (E.D.D.), Their coachman freen', leen, slink and lang.

**slink,** *a.*[2] (or *adv.*). [f. SLINK *v.*] Slinking, furtive, submissive.

**1792** WOLCOT (P. Pindar) *Ode to Ld. Lonsdale* Wks. 1812 III. 45 Juries before the Judges won't look slink. No, No; they fancy they've a right to think.

**slink** (slɪŋk), *v.* Pa. t. and pa. pple. **slunk** (slʌŋk). Forms: 1 slincan, 4 slynke, 6 slynk, slinck-, 7 slinke, 6- slink; 5 sclynk, 6 sclink; 5 slenk. *Pa. t.* 1 scluncon, 6 slo(o)nke, 7 slonk, slunke, 7- slunk, 7, 9 slank, slinked. *Pa. pple.* 7- slunk, 9 *dial.* slunken, slinked. [OE. *slincan* to creep, crawl (of reptiles), = LG. *slinken* (MSw. and Sw. dial. *slinka*), G. *schlinken* (see Grimm). Cf. MDu. and MLG. *slinken* to sink, subside. See also SLENCH *v.*]

**1. a.** *intr.* Of persons or animals: To move, go, walk, etc. in a quiet, stealthy, or sneaking manner. Usu. const. with preps. and advs.

For OE. examples, in the sense 'to creep or crawl', see Bosworth-Toller, s.v. *Slincan*.

α. *c* **1374** CHAUCER *Troylus* III. 1535 He softe into his bed gan for to slynke To slepe longe. *c* **1400** *Beryn* 3334 Som of ȝew shall be riȝt feyn to sclynk a-wey & hyde. **1448** *Paston Lett.* IV. 19 He slenkyd behynd and toke his master on the hepe suyche a stroke that..brake his hepe. **1567** MAPLET *Gr. Forest* 105 She..commeth againe steeling and slinketh into his companie. **1582** STANYHURST *Æneis* I. (Arb.) 25 Antenor was habil, from Grekish coompanye slincking, Too passe through Greceland. **1624** J. GEE *Foot out of Snare* iii. 22 The poor husband is fain to slink away hungry to his rest. **1671** FLAVEL *Fount. of Life* xxiii. 69 The Wretch slinked away from him into the city. **1735** SOMERVILLE *Chase* III. 184 The wily Fox..slinks behind And slily creeps thro' the same beaten Track. **1848** THACKERAY *Van. Fair* xlix, A withered, old, lean man,..slinking about Gray's Inn of mornings chiefly, and dining alone at clubs. **1857** DICKENS *Lett.* (1880) II. 28, I think I should slink into a corner and cry. **1879** FARRAR *St. Paul* (1883) 373 He had to slink into Thessalonica incognito and by night.

β. **1534** MORE *Comf. agst. Trib.* I. Wks. 1162/2 Then left them their gameners and slily slonke awaye. **1587** GOLDING *De Mornay* xxxiii. (1592) 534 When a plague was begunne [Apollonius] gaue warning of it: and when it grew strong, he sloonke away. **1600** HOLLAND *Livy* XLIV. xlv. 1199 The Thracians durst not goe abourd.., but slunke every man away to his own home. **1667** MILTON *P.L.* IV. 602 For Beast and Bird, They to thir grassie Couch, these to thir Nests Were slunk. **1725** DE FOE *Voy. r. World* (1840) 40 Will Jones slunk in among the rest. **1786** HAN. MORE *Florio* II. 183 The din alarm'd the frighten'd deer Who in a corner slunk for fear. **1815** SCOTT *Guy M.* ii, He slunk from college by the most secret paths he could discover. 1883 STEVENSON *Treas. Isl.* xxi, We all slunk back to our places.

*γ.* 1656 S. HOLLAND *Zara* III. v. 198 The Champion therefore, having imbraced Soto, .. slank down into his bed the second time. 1824 LANDOR *Imag. Conv., Southey & Porson* Wks. 1853 I. 17/2 There were some few who slank obliquely from them as they passed. 1856 'C. BEDE' *College Life* 155 Wall-time came, and I slank across the Quad. for my dinner. 1879 FARRAR *St. Paul* II. 145 The false brethren secretly introduced, who slank in to spy out our liberty.

**b.** *transf.* or *fig.* in various contexts.

An OE. example occurs in *Be Domes Dæȝe* 240.

1533 MORE *Debell. of Salem* Wks. 968/1 To hide the trouthe oute of syght, [and] slinke into lurkes lane. 1602 MARSTON *Antonio's Rev.* I. v, Whom fretful gaules of chance .. Makes not his reason slinke. 1657 AUSTEN *Fruit Trees* II. 104 Being by Christ told what to do, he slinks back from Christ. 1664 BUTLER *Hud.* II. iii. 112 When Brass and Pewter hap to stray And Linnen slinks out of the way. 1806 BERESFORD *Miseries Hum. Life* VI. xxxv, Seeing the sun quietly slink behind a mass of black clouds. 1822 HAZLITT *Table-t.* Ser. II. vi. (1869) 136, I should not be pleased to see him slink out of his acknowledged opinion. 1858 HOLLAND *Titcomb's Lett.* viii. 241 Temptations that .. slink from him without attack.

†**c.** To skulk, hide oneself. *Obs. rare.*

*a* 1575 *Pol. Verg. Eng. Hist.* (Camden, No. 36) 71 Catus Decianus .. slinkinge in the middest of this feare, passed into Fraunce.

**2.** *trans.* **a.** To draw quietly; to slip. *rare*$^{-1}$.

1626 in Foster *Eng. Factories India* (1909) III. 137 Perceiveing the President .. more forward then himself, upon faire and equall tearmes which cutt off his advantagious devices, he slonk his head out of the coller, and so the project dying [etc.].

**b.** To avoid, shirk, evade. *rare*$^{-1}$.

1657 G. STARKEY *Nature's Explic.* Ep. Rdr. 30 If I slink the proof of experiment, let me be reputed what they please.

†**c.** To hang (the head). *Obs.*$^{-1}$

1682 DRYDEN & LEE *Dk. Guise* III. i, Yet Spight of all this Factor of the Fiends Cou'd urge, they slunk their Heads like Hinds in Storms.

**d.** To withdraw from. *rare.*

1853 J. G. BALDWIN *Flush Times Alabama* 26 Many a witness .. 'slunk his pitch mightily' when old Kasm put him through on the cross-examination.

**e.** To turn (the eyes) *round* in a stealthy or slinking manner. *rare.*

1923 GALSWORTHY *Captures* 162 Leaning down to our scoundrel and slinking her eyes round at the Countess, she murmured something malicious.

**3. a.** Of animals, esp. cows: To bear or bring forth (young) prematurely or abortively. Cf. CAST *v.* 21, and SLING *v.*[1] 2 c.

1640 GOWER *Ovids Festivalls* IV. 91 Beasts slunk their young with most untimely throws. 1721 MORTIMER *Husb.* II. 222 To prevent a Mare's slinking her Foal. 1794 WASHINGTON *Lett. & Writ.* (1892) XIII. 15, I was told .. that almost all the mares had slunk their foals. 1844 H. STEPHENS *Bk. Farm* II. 438 Over exertion in walking .. may .. make her slip calf,—or to *slink the calf*, as it is usually termed. 1886 *Field* 13 Feb. 205/3 Sometimes all cows in a dairy slink their calves.

*fig.* *a* 1658 CLEVELAND *Char. Diurn. Maker* (1677) 104 He is the Embryo of a History slink'd before Maturity.

*absol.* *a* 1722 LISLE *Husb.* (1757) 282 To let a cow keep company with other cows, after she has slunk her calf, will be apt to make some of the others slink also. 1886 *Field* 16 Jan. 86/2 Swedes have not proved a cheap food when ewes in lamb have 'slinked' after living on them. 1889 [see SLINK *sb.* 2 d].

†**b.** With *away*: To reduce by miscarriage.

1664 PEPYS *Diary* 17 Aug., Lady Castlemayne, who he believes has lately slunk a great belly away.

**slinker** ('slɪŋkə(r)), *sb.*[1] [f. SLINK *v.* 3 + -ER[1].] An animal which slinks or casts its young.

1810 in W. H. Marshall *Rev.* (1818) II. 62 The quantity [of cheese] may be stated at 300 lb. from each cow, 'slinkers' (such as cast their calves) and bad milkers included.

**'slinker**, *sb.*[2] [f. SLINK *v.* + -ER[1].] One who slinks about; a shirker. So as *v. intr.*, to shirk.

1880 G. SMITH *Gipsy Life* ii. 48 When the task-master perceived the 'gang' had begun to 'slinker' he would shout out. 1919 G. W. DEEPING *Second Youth* xxviii. 238 It makes a man so mean, so sly, such a slinker round corners. 1923 —— *Secret Sanctuary* x. 97 He had seen the most inveterate slinker change into a creature of crude and bounding energy when a piece of leather was to be kicked about a field. 1954 J. R. R. TOLKIEN *Two Towers* II. iii. 247 Sam's guess was that the Sméagol and Gollum halves (or what in his own mind he called Slinker and Stinker) had made a truce and a temporary alliance.

**'slinkiness.** [f. SLINK *v.*, or the dial. and colloq. *slinky* sly, stealthy, etc.] Furtiveness or stealthiness of manner or bearing.

1894 A. T. PASK *Eyes Thames* 238 The hereditary paupers can be picked out at a glance. There is a lazy 'slinkiness' about them.

**slinking** ('slɪŋkɪŋ), *vbl. sb.* [f. SLINK *v.*]

**1.** The action of moving quietly or stealthily, etc.; also *attrib.*

1611 COTGR., *Regnarderie*, .. a stealing, slipping, or slinking aside. 1687 MIÉGE *Gt. Fr. Dict.* II. s.v., A Slinking (or stealing) away. 1806 A. DOUGLAS *Poems* 78 I'm no sae foolish as aver, .. That they alike disposed are, To flatt'rin' an' to slinkin'. 1865 DICKENS *Mut. Fr.* I. xiii, As the time so passed, this slinking business became a more and more precarious one.

**2.** The action or fact of bearing prematurely.

1844 H. STEPHENS *Bk. Farm* II. 440 The actual diseases of gestation .. occasion always a tendency to slinking, or the cow slipping her calf. 1886 *Field* 13 Feb. 205/3 Unwholesome water is .. a common cause of slinking amongst animals on the farm.

**'slinking**, *ppl. a.* [f. SLINK *v.* Cf. OE. *slincende* creeping (things).] That slinks; moving, walking, etc. in a furtive or stealthy manner; marked or characterized by stealth or secrecy.

1840 DICKENS *Barn. Rudge* xxxv, His manner was smooth and humble, but very sly and slinking. 1859 W. H. GREGORY *Egypt* I. 176 The mangy, growling, but slinking pariah, the denizen of the dirt-heaps about Fellah villages. 1899 *Allbutt's Syst. Med.* VIII. 148 Such traces of albumin .. I have often found in anæmic, slinking youths.

So **'slinkingly** *adv.*

1830 GALT *Lawrie T.* v. viii, He was slowly and slinkingly moving towards his own house. 1889 GISSING *Nether World* III. ix. 185 He went slinkingly, hurrying round corners, avoiding glances.

**slinky** ('slɪŋkɪ), *a.* [f. SLINK *v.* + -Y[1].] Of a woman, esp. from the manner of her dress: sinuous, slender, gliding; of a garment: close-fitting, as if moulded to the figure. In extended use (with varying degrees of approval): stealthy, dextrous, furtive.

1921 *Ladies' Home Jrnl.* Jan. 8/1 Even now I seem to see in memory a slinky, slant-eyed person with long, slender finger nails, who wears green. 1923 *Glasgow Herald* 21 July 6/5 Jessica was swathed in a slinky gown of flat crepe in a deep blue shade. 1932 D. L. SAYERS *Have his Carcase* xviii. 235 She now selected a slinky garment, composed of what male writers call 'some soft, clinging material'. 1944 R. CHANDLER *Lady in Lake* 116 One of those slinky glittering females. 1951 N. C. HUNTER *Waters of Moon* III. i. 69 Some really classy young man with heaps of money. A Guards officer, for instance, or something rather slinky on the Stock Exchange. 1962 *Times* 28 Dec. 9/5 Miss Ross sings a variety of songs—slinky, torchy, witty. 1973 *Country Life* 8 Mar. 633/2 Slinky dresses that have the finest of straps or are completely strapless. 1980 J. WAINWRIGHT *Eye of Beholder* 18 His missus. The slinky, brittle bint.

Hence **'slinkily** *adv.*

1935 *Amer. Speech* X. 192/2 A long flowing gown trails slinkily on the floor.

**Slinky** ('slɪŋkɪ), *sb.* Also **slinky**. [f. SLINK *v.* + -Y[6].] The proprietary name of a toy consisting of a flexible helical spring which can be made to 'somersault' down steps as an inverted U. Also *Slinky toy*. Also *fig.*

1948 *Trade Marks Jrnl.* 11 Feb. 114/2 Slinky. 654,972. Games (other than ordinary playing cards) toys and sporting articles (except clothing). James Industries Inc.., 4932, Portico St., Germantown, Philadelphia .. —24th Dec. 1946. 1968 *Habitat Xmas Catal.*, Slinky toy—fun for childish adults and grown up children! 1975 *Publishers Weekly* 7 Apr. 83/1 The tangled slinky-toy lives of these three turned-on folk heroes. 1979 *Early Learning 1979–80* (Early Learning Centre) 32/2 Plastic Slinky... Walks down stairs!

**slinte, -ing**, variants of SLENT(ING.

**slinter**, var. SCHLENTER *sb.* and *a.*

**slip** (slɪp), *sb.*[1] Forms: 1 **slipa**, 1, 5 **slype**, 1, 5–6 **slyppe**, 5 **slyp(p**, **slep**, 7– **slip**. [OE. (see sense 1), of doubtful form and obscure origin. Cf. Norw. *slip*, *slipa* slime, as on fish; G. dial. *schlipper* curdled milk.]

†**1.** A soft semi-liquid mass. *Obs.*

Cf. the second element in COWSLIP and OXLIP.

*c* 1000 *Saxon Leechd.* II. 18 Ȝenim sealh & ele, do ahsan, ȝewyrc þonne to slypan. *Ibid.*, Do þonne on þone sl pan. *Ibid.* III. 38 Wyrc slypan of wætere & of axsan, ȝenim finol, wyl on þære slyppan.

**2. a.** Curdled milk. Now *U.S.*

*c* 1425 *26 Pol. Poems* 110 My hert shulde be stedefast, þou hast lopred as mylk, and slep in þouȝ t, Riȝt as chese þou croddest me fast. 1859 BARTLETT *Dict. Amer.* (ed. 2) 416 *Slip*, milk turned with rennet, etc., before the whey separates from the curd.

**b.** *slip cheese, curd*: (see quots. 1784, 1854).

1784 TWAMLEY *Dairying Exemp.* 31 When the whole is in a state of Slip Curd, or Slippery Curd, which is a state all Curd is in, before it becomes solid Curd. 1846 J. BAXTER *Libr. Pract. Agric.* (ed. 4) I. 207 Some dairy-maids now add the slip curd. 1854 MISS BAKER *Northampt. Gloss.*, *Slip-cheese*, soft cheese, plate-cheese: that which is made without crushing out the whey.

†**3.** Mud, slime. *Obs.*

*c* 1440 *Promp. Parv.* 459/2 Slyp (*S.* slype, *P.* slypp), *idem quod* slyme. *a* 1500 *Adrian & Epotys* 167 in *Brome Bk.* 30 Slyppe of þe erthe wos on off thoo, Watyr of the see god toke ther-too.

**4. a.** *techn.* A semi-liquid material, made of finely-ground clay or flint, etc., mixed with water to about the consistency of cream, and used for making, cementing, coating, or decorating pottery, tiles, etc.; also, clay suitable for making this.

1640 in Entick *London* II. 178 Slip, the barrel, .. 1*d.* 1686 PLOT *Staffordsh.* 122 This they call Slip, and is the substance wherewith they paint their wares. *Ibid.*, Red Slip, made of a dirty reddish clay, which gives wares a black colour. 1778 *England's Gaz.* (ed. 2) s.v. *Horsley*, A reddish earth, called slip, with which they paint the vessels made at Wednesbury. 1799 KIRWAN *Geol. Ess.* 299 Under this [is] white slip, that is, potter's clay. 1825 J. NICHOLSON *Operat. Mechanic* 484 The inside is rendered white by a wash of slip, flint, and procelain clay. 1853 URE *Dict. Arts* II. 451 The clay, which is used in a semi liquid state about the consistency of cream and called 'slip'. 1884 C. G. W. LOCK *Workshop Receipts* III. 295/2 Some 'slip', or finely-ground flint used in glazing earthenware.

**b.** *attrib.*, as ***slip-house***, ***-kiln***, ***-room***; ***slip-decoration***, ***-glaze***, ***-inlay***, ***-state***, etc. **slip casting**, the manufacture of ceramic articles by allowing slip to solidify in a porous mould.

1901 W. P. RIX tr. *E. Bourry's Treat. Ceramic Industries* iv. 231 (*heading*) Moulding by *slip casting. 1959 *Jrnl. Iron & Steel Inst.* CXCI. 208/1 A description is given of the technique of slip casting, and its application to the casting of high-temperature materials including ceramics and metallo-ceramics. 1974 F. H. NORTON *Elem. Ceramics* viii. 95 The slip-casting method is much used in ceramic production as it is possible by this means to reproduce very complicated shapes in plaster molds. 1960 R. G. HAGGAR *Conc. Encycl. Cont. Pottery & Porc.* 458/1 Slip decoration consists of applying to the unfired clay surface of the ware, before it has been dried and fired, contrasted coloured slips, either by trailing from a quill, [etc.]. 1973 R. FOURNIER *Illustr. Dict. Pract. Pottery* 211/2 (*caption*) Slip decoration. An English slip-trailed dish—possibly Tickenhall. 1960 *Times* 6 Aug. 9/7 Without the *slip-glaze upper decoration finish. 1832 G. R. PORTER *Porcelain & Gl.* 40 The place where this evaporation is performed is called the *slip-house. 1902 A. BENNETT *Anna of Five Towns* viii. 167 The clay travelled naturally in a circle from the slip-house by the canal to the packing-house by the canal. 1961 M. JONES *Potbank* viii. 30 The maker breaks a lump of clay off the hunk brought from the sliphouse. 1878 *Encycl. Brit.* VIII. 188/2 When the '*slip' inlay has become nearly of the same consistency as the tile itself. 1769 J. WEDGWOOD *Let.* 9 Apr. (1965) 73 The *Slip Kiln is nearly finished. 1825 J. NICHOLSON *Operat. Mechanic* 457 The whole is passed through fine lawn into a reservoir, from whence it is pumped upon the slip-kiln. 1752 *Gentl. Mag.* XXII. 348 The *slip and treading rooms. 1867 BRANDE & COX *Dict. Sci.*, etc. s.v. *Tiles*, The clays .. are passed through lawn sieves in the liquid or **slip* state.

**c.** *Comb.*, as ***slip-decorated***, ***-decorator***, ***-glazing***, ***-maker***, ***-making***, ***-painting***, ***-strainer***, ***-trailer***, ***-trailing***.

1883 L. M. SOLON *Art Eng. Potter* 27 (*heading*) *Slip-decorated ware. 1900 F. LITCHFIELD *Pottery & Porcelain* ii. 25 At Wrotham .. were produced .. quaint, slip-decorated posset-pots, tygs, and dishes. 1979 *Essex Jrnl.* XIV. 20 There were also a number of small sherds of slip-decorated lead-glazed jugs and plates produced at Harlow. 1921 *Dict. Occup. Terms* (1927 § 105 **Slip decorator*, applies a pattern to pottery in the green state by blowing on coloured clay slips. 1960 *Times* 6 Aug. 9/6 The dual colouring .. was obtained by slip-glazing before firing. 1825 J. NICHOLSON *Operat. Mechanic* 459 The *slip-maker carefully attends to the evaporation. 1834–6 *Encycl. Metrop.* (1845) VIII. 450/1 **Slip making.*—In the preparation of the clay for best flint ware [etc.]. 1902 *Encycl. Brit.* XXXI. 874/2 Turning to the decorative side of pottery work, we have in **slip-painting* a method as old as primitive pottery itself. 1964 H. HODGES *Artifacts* i. 33 One particularly elaborate form of slip painting, *feather combing*, involves the use of a brush with multiple points. 1891 *Cent. Dict.*, **Slip-strainer*, .. a strainer of any form through which the slip is passed. 1940 B. LEACH *Potter's Bk.* ii. 33 There are at least half a dozen potteries in Japan where the *slip-trailer is employed. 1960 H. POWELL *Beginner's Bk. Pottery* II. 64 *Slip trailer* .., a small rubber bag with a narrow neck into which is fitted a thin glass tube. 1940 B. LEACH *Potter's Bk.* vi. 147 One glaze can be trailed over another with the same instrument that is used in *slip trailing. 1964 H. HODGES *Artifacts* i. 33 The clay may be applied in a fairly fluid form using for the purpose a container with a nozzle, much as a cake is iced by bakers. This method is called *slip-trailing*. *a* 1977 *Harrison Mayer Ltd. Catal.* 27/1 A range of coloured slips prepared for slip trailing.

**slip** (slɪp), *sb.*[2] Forms: 5–7 **slippe**, 6–7 **slipp**, 6– **slip**; 5 **slyp**, 6 **slyppe**, **sleppe**. [app. a. MDu. or MLG. *slippe* (Du. and Flem. *slip*, LG. *slipp*, *slippe*, G. *schlippe*, *schlipfe*) cut, slit, strip, lappet, skirt, etc. The first sense of the Eng. word, however, is not recorded in any of these languages.]

**I. 1. a.** A twig, sprig, or small shoot taken from a plant, tree, etc., for the purpose of grafting or planting; a scion, cutting.

1495 *Trevisa's Barth. De P.R.* XVII. cxviii. 682 Propago is a yonge braunche of a vyne that spryngith of a slippe. 1530 PALSGR. 271/2 Slyppe of an herbe, *branche*. 1553 T. WILSON *Rhet.* 80 b, Geve me some slippes of that tree that I might set them in some orcharde. 1577 B. GOOGE *Heresbach's Husb.* I. (1586) 38 To be set of the slippes. 1615 W. LAWSON *Country Housew. Gard.* (1626) 39 My fairest Apple-tree was such a Slip. 1697 DRYDEN *Virg. Georg.* II. 38 The Lab'rer cuts Young Slips, and in the Soil securely puts. 1786 ABERCROMBIE *Gard. Assist.* 224 Propagate them by cuttings, or slips of the young shoots. 1844 DICKENS *Mart. Chuz.* xxxvi, Blighted stumps and flourishing young slips. 1872 H. MACMILLAN *True Vine* iii. 116 A slip taken from a tree dying of old age.

**b.** In fig. context. (Common *c* 1600.)

1513 MORE *Rich. III* (1883) 64 Bastard slippes shal neuer take depe roots. 1570–76 LAMBARDE *Peramb. Kent* (1826) 299 This suppressed house .. was some slippe of that tree which one James did first plant in Spaine. 1580 LYLY *Euphues* (Arb.) 368 Beautie was no niggard of hir slippes in this gardein. 1613 DEKKER *Devil's Last Will* Wks. (Grosart) III. 353 Because he is a slip of mine owne grafting, I likewise bequeath to him my best Slippers. 1643 *Myst. of Iniq.* 17 These Southerne plants, being slips of an Italian Stocke, could not endure this Northerne Climate.

**c.** A scion or descendant.

1588 SHAKS. *Titus A.* V. i. 9 Braue slip, sprung from the Great Andronicus. *a* 1639 WOTTON in *Reliq.* (1651) 340 Julia a little before dying, .. together with an infant she bare, .. and she gone without any slip remaining [etc.]. 1764 CHURCHILL *Gotham* II. Poems 1772 III. 114 Any Slip of Stuart's tyrant race. 1810 CRABBE *Borough* XX. 247 He talk'd of bastard slips, and cursed his bed. 1825 T. HOOK *Sayings* Ser. II. *Man of Many Fr.* I. 292 No doubt .. that slip [= daughter] of the country parson, keep's the whip-hand.

1855 THACKERAY *Newcomes* I. 110 Even rosy little slips out of the nursery who cluster round his beloved feet.

**d.** *fig.* An offshoot, outgrowth.

1626 R. BERNARD *Isle of Man* (1627) 214 Covetousness is .. indeed a slip of Thrift. 1831 CARLYLE *Misc. Ess., German Poet.* (1888) III. 238 Some small slip of heathendom.

**2. a.** A young person of either sex, esp. one of small or slender build.

1582 STANYHURST *Æneis* IV. (Arb.) 97 The slip Ascanius .. Shee cols for the father. 1589 NASHE *Martin Marprelate* Wks. (Grosart) I. 163 The good health and wellfare of these two yong Slipps his sonnes. 1821 SCOTT *Kenilw.* xv, We know how that matter fell out, and we have corrected for it the wild slip, young Raleigh. 1841 LEVER *C. O'Malley* xciv, Shusey Dogherty was a good-looking slip. 1879 BROWNING *Ivan Ivanovitch* 139 He was puny, an under-sized slip,—a darling to me, all the same!

**b.** With *of* (introducing descriptive term), esp. in ***a slip of a girl***. (Cf. 8.)

*a*1660 *Contemp. Hist. Irel.* (Ir. Archæol. Soc.) III. 38 This slippe of a boye Sir Walter Dungan. 1821 SCOTT *Kenilw.* ii, Tony hath but a slip of a daughter. 1856 EMERSON *Eng. Traits* xv. Wks. (Bohn) II. 120 Every slip of an Oxonian or Cantabrigian who writes his first leader. 1861 HUGHES *Tom Brown at Oxf.* vi, There was his wife, and the slip of a girl.

**c.** A thin or slender person.

1703 STEELE *Tender Husband* IV. ii, My Lady Shapely has by that thin Slip eight Children. 1888 MISS BRADDON *Fatal Three* I. i, She was a tall slip of a woman.

**3. a.** *dial.* and *N.Z.* A young store-pig.

1832 HT. MARTINEAU *Ireland* ii. 31 His mother .. had a cow, and a slip of a pig. 1886 ELWORTHY *W. Somerset Word-bk.* 679 A store pig of older growth would be described as a 'hard slip'. 1950 *N.Z. Jrnl. Agric.* Dec. 559/1 The usual practice is to buy the pigs as slips. 1977 *Cornish Times* 19 Aug. 1/1 (Advt.), Strong quality Slips and Pigs for slaughter accepted.

**b.** A sole of intermediate size.

1881 *Daily News* 4 Mar. 4/6 Small soles, .. under the name of 'slips', were introduced into the *menus* of Greenwich hotels. 1884 *British Alm. & Comp.* II. 31 Small soles, known in the trade as 'slips' and 'tongues'.

**II. 4.** †**a.** The edge, skirt, or flap of a robe or garment. *Obs. rare.*

*c*1440 *Promp. Parv.* 459/2 Slyp, or skyrte, *lascinia.* 1648 HEXHAM II, *Heft u Slippen op*, take up the Edge or Slip of your Kirtle.

**b.** A light under-waistcoat with the edge showing to form a border to a waistcoat worn with morning dress.

1933 C. ST. J. SPRIGG *Fatality in Fleet St.* viii. 98 Oakley looked like .. a monkey which had surprisingly been trained to wear a morning-coat and grey slip. 1941 H. G. WELLS *You can't be too Careful* III. x. 158 And you looking *lovely* in a silk hat and light grey trousers. You'll have, you know, white slips to your waistcoat.

**5.** A spoon-handle having the top cut off obliquely; a spoon with a handle or stem of this form. (Cf. SLIPPED *ppl. a.*[2] 1.) Now *Hist.*

*c*1530 in Gutch *Coll. Cur.* II. 312 Twoo doson of Sponnes with Slippis un gilte. 1552 *Will G. Hynde* (Somerset Ho.), Sixe silver sponnes callyd slyppes. 1583 in Cripps *Old Eng. Plate* (1901) 281, xij spones called slippes weying xxiiij ownces and a half.

*Comb.* 1580 in Cripps *Old Eng. Plate* (1901) 281 Dosen spones, theis spones being sleppe endyd. 1902 *Westm. Gaz.* 1 May 8/1 A set of James I. slip-top spoons. 1908 MACQUOID *Plate Collector's Guide* 103 Spoons called 'slip-topped' originated in the second half of the sixteenth century.

**6. a.** A long and relatively thin and narrow piece or strip of some material. Freq. with *of.*

1555 EDEN *Decades* (Arb.) 140 Such as were brused they tyed fast with theyr gyrdels with slippes of the barkes of trees. 1575 *Gammer Gurton* I. i, Out at doores I hyed mee, And caught a slyp of bacon, when I saw that none spyed mee. 1645 *Doc. S. Paul's* (Camden) 144, 218 carved narrowe slipps [of wood]. 1665 *Roxb. Ball.* (1887) VI. 437 The burly fat Dutchmen being cut out in slips. 1758 REID tr. *Macquer's Chym.* I. 252 Let .. the joint [be] covered with a slip of canvas smeared with lute. 1793 SMEATON *Edystone L.* §97 It was steadied in that position, by .. two slips of deal. 1823 J. NICHOLSON *Operat. Mechanic* 322 This joint is connected with the nut by means of two steel slips... The other ends of these slips turn .. on pins. 1863 HUXLEY *Man's Place Nat.* ii. 93 One slip of the muscle is attached .. to the tendons of the long flexors. 1888 RUTLEY *Rock-Forming Min.* 25 A glass slip is now placed on the hot plate.

**b.** In special uses (see quots.).

1771 LUCKOMBE *Hist. Print.* 387 We always begin an Index upon an uneven page, and put a Slip or double rule at the Head thereof. 1820 SCORESBY *Acc. Arc. Regions* II. 299 The harpooners .. divide the fat [of the whale] into oblong pieces or 'slips'. 1833 LOUDON *Encycl. Archit.* §82 To put .. jambs, slips (sides of the jambs), and shelves to both the fireplaces. 1875 SIR T. SEATON *Fret Cutting* 8 Slips are pieces of Turkey or other stone about four inches long and one and a quarter wide. 1895 G. E. DAVIS *Pract. Microscopy* (ed. 3) 375 Objects are generally mounted upon glass slides, or 'slips', as they are sometimes called. 1903 G. JACK *Wood Carving* iii. 43 For sharpening the insides of tools, 'slips' are made with rounded edges of different sizes. One slip of 'Washita' stone and one of 'Arcansas'. 1960 C. H. HAYWARD *Cabinet Making for Beginners* (ed. 2) iv. 104 Drawer Making. .. Grooved slips are glued to the sides to hold the bottom.

**c.** An excised piece of this form.

1704–15 *Maryland Laws* vii. (1723) 22 With a Slip cut down the Face of the Tree near the Ground.

**7.** A strip, a narrow piece or stretch, *of* land, ground, etc.

1591 FLETCHER *Russe Commw.* (Hakl.) 7 A little isthmus or narrow slippe of lande. 1682 WHELER *Journ. Greece* I. 6 The long slip of Rocks .. is .. stored with many curious Plants. *a*1700 EVELYN *Diary* 14 Aug. 1668, A lease of a slip of ground out of Brick Close. 1745 P. THOMAS *Jrnl. Anson's Voy.* 67 Acosta .. divides the country into three long narrow Slips. 1775 ROMANS *Hist. Florida* App. 72 The island .. is a narrow slip of sand-hills. 1815 ELPHINSTONE *Acc. Caubul* (1842) II. 48 The slip of barren country between the Indus and the plain of Peshawer. 1846 MCCULLOCH *Acc. Brit. Empire* (1854) I. 525 Cottiers, who pay for their small slips of land by working for the principal lessees.

**8.** An example or specimen *of* something having an elongated or slender form. (Cf. 2 b.)

1730 A. GORDON *Maffei's Amphith.* 303 There is also a small Loop-Hole besides the Slip of the Window. *Ibid.* 312 The Light .. comes from certain Slips of Windows. 1762 *Ann. Reg., Chron.* 132/2 These children were kept to work in a small slip of a room. 1825 T. HOOK *Sayings* Ser. II. *Passion & Princ.* vi, When he found himself ushered into a neat sanded slip of a coffee-room. 1833 HT. MARTINEAU *Briery Creek* iii. 57, I have a slip of a garden, .. and, though it is but a slip, it is of rare mellow mould. 1881 H. JAMES *Portrait of a Lady* xxxvi, Her anxious eyes, her charming lips, her slip of a figure.

**9. a.** A window, apartment, passage, etc., of an elongated form.

1730 A. GORDON *Maffei's Amphith.* 302 A high and narrow Window, or a Slip, as we shall call it. 1886 WILLIS & CLARK *Cambridge* I. 330 A narrow slip about five feet wide, separated from the rest of the room by a transverse partition.

**b.** *U.S.* A narrow, doorless church-pew.

1828–32 in WEBSTER. 1858 *Rev. Statutes Wisconsin* 200 All houses of public worship, .. and the pews or slips and furniture therein. 1878 MRS. STOWE *Poganuc P.* iii. 23 Why, .. if there ain't the minister's boys down in that front slip!

**c.** *pl.* (See quot. 1874.)

1805 SIR R. WILSON in *Life* (1862) I. 345 Those ladies who had not boxes sat in what would be termed in England one shilling slips. 1836–7 DICKENS *Sk. Boz* (1850) 165/2 They thought they couldn't do better than go at half-price to the slips at the City Theatre. 1851 MAYHEW *Lond. Lab.* I. 19/1 When the gallery is well packed, .. on the partition boards, dividing off the slips, lads will pitch themselves, despite the spikes. 1874 *Slang Dict.* 296 *Slips*, the sides of the gallery in a theatre are generally so called.

**10. a.** A piece of paper or parchment, esp. one which is narrow in proportion to its length. Freq. with *of.* Also ***betting slip***: see BETTING *vbl. sb.*[1] 2.

1687 MIÉGE *Gt. Fr. Dict.* II. s.v., It is called Slip in English, from its Shape, it being printed in a long Slip of Paper. 1706 PHILLIPS (ed. Kersey), *Scroll*, a slip or Roll of Parchment, &c. 1724 WODROW *Corr.* (1843) III. 112 If that worthy person will let me know by post or a slip, wherein I can serve him here. 1771 SMOLLETT *Humph. Cl.* (1815) 154 I'll find a slip of sheep-skin that will do his business. 1846 SIR F. MADDEN *Laȝamon* I. Pref. p. xli, After writing near 50,000 slips, it was found impracticable to carry the design [of the glossary] into execution. 1886 *Weekly Notes* 188/2 The registrar made a note of this declaration on a slip of paper.

†**b.** A newspaper (or part of one) printed in the form of a long slip of paper. *Obs.*

1687 [see prec.]. 1692 LUTTRELL *Brief Rel.* (1857) II. 417 It is said in one of the French slips, that they design to land some 1000 men in Scotland in May. 1699 (*title*), The London Slip of News, both foreign and domestick. [Continued as, The London Post.] 1727 BOYER *Dict. Royal* I, *Lardon*, (*supplement de la Gazette de Hollande*) the Slip that comes from Holland with the Gazette.

**c.** *Insurance.* (See quots.)

1816 G. J. BELL *Comm. Laws Scotl.* (1826) I. 603 The policy is preceded by a Slip, which is merely a jotting or short memorandum of the terms, to which the underwriters subscribe their initials. 1880 *Encycl. Brit.* XIII. 184 It is customary for the underwriter to sign a 'slip', or short memorandum of the insurance, until the stamped policy can be completed.

**d.** *Typog.* A proof pulled on a long slip of paper, for revision before the type is made up into pages.

1818 *Blackw. Mag.* III. 250 Bate only the correcting in the slip Never was easier Conductorship. 1832 BABBAGE *Econ. Manuf.* xxi. (ed. 3) 208 The present work was set up in slips. 1878 HUXLEY in *Life* (1903) II. 253, I have received slips up to chap. ix. of Hume. 1880 BRITTEN *Old Country & Farm. Wds.* Introd. p. vii, He has read the extracts in slip.

**11.** A certain quantity *of* yarn, etc. Now *dial.*

1647 HEXHAM I, A Slip of yarne, *een stuck garens.* 1791 *Statist. Acc. Scotl.* II. 308 A stone of the finest [wool] .. will yield 32 slips of yarn, each containing 12 cuts. 1886 *Cheshire Gloss.* 322 *Slip*, .. a hank of silk or yarn before it is wound on the quills or pirn. [Cf. SLIPPING *vbl. sb.*[2] 1.]

†**12.** A slit or cut. *Obs.*[−1]

1688 HOLME *Armoury* III. xv. (Roxb.) 20/2 In the pen there is the nick or slip or slit called the neb.

**III. 13.** *attrib.* **a.** In senses 1–3, as ***slip-graft***, ***-plant***; ***slip-pig***.

1657 R. AUSTEN *Fruit-Trees* I. 136 They have an innate spirit from the seede .., which makes them grow better then slip-plants. 1725 *Fam. Dict.* s.v. *Gardiner*, The Master Shoot of a slip Graft. 1844 in Caroline Fox *Jrnls.* (1882) 187, I have three cows, three slip pigs. 1882 *West. Morn. News* 25 Nov. 1/5 Two large slip pigs.

**b.** In senses 6–10, as ***slip-centre***, ***-room***, ***-window***; ***slip-chase***, ***-galley***, ***proof***, ***-song***, ***-ticket***.

1833 LOUDON *Encycl. Archit.* §249 Twenty-three *slip centres to the arches (a slip of deal cut to the intended line of the soffit of the arch). 1888 JACOBI *Printers' Vocab.* 126 **Slip chases*, long narrow chases made specially for 'heading' work. 1882 J. SOUTHWARD *Pract. Print.* (1884) 1 Newspaper *slip-galleys are made with either zinc or brass bottoms. 1888 JACOBI *Printers' Vocab.* 126 *Slip galley*, a long galley the reverse of a quarto or square galley. 1892 A. OLDFIELD *Pract. Man. Typogr.* iii. 37 Proofs are required in various stages, and have a distinct name in each stage, as follows:—'*slip', or galley proofs [etc.]. 1908 W. S. CHURCHILL *Let.* 8 Sept. in R. S. Churchill *Winston S. Churchill* (1969) II. Compan. II. 839 Messrs Hodder & Stoughton should let me have all the *Strand* articles up to date in slip proof as soon as possible. 1973 S. JENNETT *Making of Books* (ed. 5) I. vi. 99 Paging is a manual operation carried out by compositors... Each man has his share of slip proofs. 1837 DICKENS *Pickw.* xliv, A baldheaded cobbler who rented a small *slip-room in one of the upper galleries [in the Fleet]. 1878 EBSWORTH *Bagford Ball.* 918 Much less rare are the Garlands and *slip-songs which swell the volume to 918 leaves. 1888 BRYCE *Amer. Commw.* III. lxvi. II. 493 A *slip ticket is a list, printed on a long strip of paper, of the persons .. recommended by the same party or political group for the posts to be filled up at any election. 1882 H. C. MERIVALE *Faucit of Balliol* II. I. xxiv. 110 A narrow strip of a chamber opening into the drawing-room only, and like it facing the street through a *slip-window.

**slip** (slɪp), *sb.*[3] Forms: 5 slypp (slepe), 5–6 slyppe, 5–7 slipp(e, 5– slip. [f. (or related to) SLIP *v.*[1] Cf. OHG. and MHG. *slipf* (G. dial. *schlipf*, also *schlipfe*) a sliding, slip, error, etc.]

**I. 1. a.** An artificial slope of stone or other solid material, built or made beside a navigable water to serve as a landing-place.

1467 *Ordin. Worcester* in *Eng. Gilds* 374 That the slippe and the keye, and the pavyment ther, be ouerseyn and repared. *Ibid.* 397 That the keye Slippes, and the pavyment of the grete Slippe, be made in hast. 1475 *Waterf. Arch.* in *10th Rep. Hist. MSS. Comm.* App. V. 312 That no .. man .. putte .. fylth into the ryvere over no key nor slippe of the citie. 1644 PRYNNE & WALKER *Fiennes' Trial* 64 On the Key side next the City, there is a wall of stone .. which no horse can enter, .. unlesse at a slip or two. 1704 in *Pennsylv. Hist. Soc. Mem.* IX. 291, I designed to build a granary on part of that slip that comes down to the dock. 1776 G. SEMPLE *Building under water* 3 They came to the Slip, where one of the Horses broke his Traces and swam out. 1855 LONGF. *Birds of Passage* I. *My lost youth* iii, I remember the black wharves and the slips. 1885 WARREN & CLEVERLY *Wanderings 'Beetle'* 71 We made for a ferry-slip, where the Commander and Doctor landed to forage.

**b.** *Shipbuilding.* An inclined plane, sloping gradually down to the water, on which ships or other vessels are built or repaired.

Hence Sw. *slip*, G. *slip*, *schlipp*, *schlippe*.

1769 FALCONER *Dict. Marine* (1780), *Slip*, a place lying with a gradual descent on the banks of a river convenient for ship building. 1800 COLQUHOUN *Comm. & Pol. Thames* xiii. 371 No Slips, dry Docks, &c. for building or repairing Vessels shall be made. 1850 LONGF. *Building of Ship* 95 'Thus,' said he, 'will we build this ship! Lay square the blocks upon the slip'. 1894 *Times* 1 Mar. 7/5 At Chatham, where the largest of the available building slips is being prepared for the reception of the new vessel.

**c.** A contrivance (patented in 1818) for hauling vessels out of the water in order to repair them.

1830 *Edinburgh Encycl.* XVIII. 256 Slips have also been sent by Mr. Morton to France and Russia. 1880 *Encycl. Brit.* XI. 470 Slips are the contrivance of the late Mr. Thomas Morton of Leith, and consist of a carriage or cradle working on an inclined railway [etc.].

**2.** †**a.** A stairway. *Obs. rare.*

*a*1490 BOTONER *Itin.* (1778) 175 Item at the begynnyng of the bakk, there the fyrst gryse called a slypp, ben twey weyes, the fyrst wey ys the seyd slepe of .. yerdes long. *Ibid.* 218 Longitudo de 'le slip', anglice 'a steyre' de lapidibus .. a summitate viæ desuper le bak usque ad ultimum gradum.

**b.** At Bath: A means of descending into one of the public baths (see quots.).

1778 *Encycl. Brit.* (ed. 2) II. 1053/2 The person intending to bathe .. is carried in a close chair .. to one of the slips which open into the bath. There he descends by steps into the water. 1791 COLLINSON *Hist. Somerset* I. 40 There are slips by which the bathers descend, and adjoining to them are dressing-rooms. 1806 *Guide to Watering Places* 27 Sufficient fires .. to be made in the slips, .. and to be continued the usual hours of bathing.

**c.** *local.* A narrow roadway or passage.

Cf. SLYPE *sb.*, and G. *schlippe* (also *schlupf*, *schlupfe*).

1739 LABELYE *Piers Westm. Bridge* 2 The Slip or Passage commonly call'd by the Name of Mathew's Causeway. 1788 M. CUTLER in *Life*, etc. (1888) I. 427 Came through Dunning's Slip, where the river divides Dunning Mountains, and in a short distance passed through another Slip, which divides Turris Mountain. 1868 *Exeter & Plymouth Gaz.* 13 Mar., The slip or roadway .. down to the Parlor had always been a parish road.

**II. 3. a.** A leash for a dog, etc., so contrived that the animal can readily be released; esp. one used for a couple of greyhounds in coursing, by which they can be let go simultaneously.

1578 BULLEIN *Dial. agst. Pest* (1888) 91 He hath a Lyon in a chaine on the one side, and a Fox in a slippe on the other side. 1592 GREENE *Conny Catch.* II. Wks. (Grosart) X. 93, I looke for a grey-hound that hath broken my slip, and is run into this house. 1607 TOPSELL *Four-f. Beasts* (1658) 366 The lion was given unto him .. who led him up and down the streets in a leam or slip. 1657 G. THORNLEY *Daphnis & Chloe* 69 Bind his hands behind him with a dog-slip. 1704 *Dict. Rust.* (1726) s.v. *Grayhound*, They must also be kept in a Slip, while abroad, till they can see their Course. *a*1774 GOLDSM. tr. *Scarron's Com. Romance* (1775) II. 60 His men walking all the way by his side, like a greyhound in a slip. 1816 *Sporting Mag.* XLVIII. 61 The dogs are now loosed from slips of a better construction than those formerly in use. 1839 *Laws of Coursing* in Youatt *Dog* (1845) App. 260 All courses shall be from slips, by a brace of greyhounds only. 1862 H. H. DIXON *Scott & Sebright* III. 254 Their talk is all of dogs .. and fine young puppies coming forward or lost for ever to the slips.

*transf.* 1864 CARLYLE *Fredk. Gt.* IV. 156 He has never yet sent the Old Dessauer in upon them; always only keeps him on the slip, at Magdeburg.

†**b.** A cord provided with a running knot; a noose. *Obs.*

1687 A. LOVELL tr. *Thevenot's Trav.* III. 41 They use a certain Slip with a running-noose, which they can cast ..

about a Mans Neck, when they are within reach of him. **1691** WOOD *Ath. Oxon.* I. 535 The Students did not forbear to whisper among themselves, that..he sent up his soul to heaven thro a slip about his neck.

†**c.** A cord or string. *Obs.*$^{-0}$

**1687** MIÉGE *Gt. Fr. Dict.* II, A hempen slip, *une corde.* **1727** BOYER *Dict. Royal* II, A Slip, (or Silk-string), *Corde de Soye.*

**d.** *Bookbinding.* (See quots.)

**1875** KNIGHT *Dict. Mech.* 2211/2 *Slip*,..the end of the twine to which the sheets are sewed, serving to attach the book to the boards. **1894** *Amer. Dict. Print. & Bookmaking* 511 *Slip*, a cord used in fastening the back of a book.

**e.** *Naut.* (See quot.)

**1886** *Encycl. Brit.* XXI. 604 *Slips*, ropes with toggles, shackles, and tongues, and various contrivances for letting go quickly.

**4.** †**a.** The neck-opening in a shirt. *Obs.*$^{-0}$

**1648** HEXHAM II, *Hooft-gat*,..the Hole or the Slip of a Shirt through which one puts his head.

**b.** A child's pinafore or frock. Now *dial.*

**1690** C. NESS *Hist. & Myst. O. & N. Test.* I. 417 Sport with them as children do with their slips, or as monkeys with their collars. **1775** S. J. PRATT *Liberal Opin.* lxxvii. (1783) III. 75 Her infants were habited in slips, or robes, evidently made by a maternal hand. **1825-** in northern glossaries (Northumbld., Cumbld., Yks., etc.).

**c.** An article of women's attire, formerly an outer garment, later worn under a gown of lace or similar material. Also *transf.*, an infant's garment of this nature. In twentieth c. use, an underskirt or petticoat dependent from the waist or the shoulders and having no sleeves. Colloq. phr. ***your slip is showing***: see SHOW *v.* 28 g.

**1761** *Ann. Reg., Chron.* 228/2 His..sister the princess,..drest also in a slip with hanging sleeves. **1780** MRS. DELANY *Life & Corr.* Ser. II. II. 527 The coat maker advises girts to be fastened on y$^{e}$ top of the stays,..w$^{ch}$ will not appear, being under her slip. **1816** *Med. Chirurg. Trans.* VII. 480 His daughter was one day dressed in a pink slip. **1824** MISS L. M. HAWKINS *Annaline* I. 206 A damsel arrayed in a green bonnet and yellow slip. **1825** H. WILSON *Mem.* II. 103 What do you call a slip? do you mean a petticoat, or an intrigue? **1858** SIMMONDS *Dict. Trade*, *Slip*,..a woman's muslin or satin under-skirt or petticoat. **1897** *Army & Navy Stores List*, Baby Linen—Infant's Long Slip... American Satin Slip. **1903** M. M. *How to dress & what to Wear* 185 Slips. This term is applicable either to a skirt or a bodice. A skirt slip is made of silk, satin, or even batiste, and is employed for wearing under a thin upper dress... Slips may, or may not, be provided with sleeves. **1904** *Queen* 30 Jan. 178/3 Entire lace gowns hung over chiffon slips made graceful toilettes. **1920** M. S. WOOLMAN *Clothing* ix. 135 Slips or underfrocks with detachable sleeves have also been designed... Many of the slips are made without sewed-in lining. **1944** H. CROOME *You've gone Astray* xv. 158 He glowered at Linda, sitting on the edge of the bed in her slip with one stocking off. **1957** J. BRAINE *Room at Top* xi. 109 She came over in her slip... She was already a different person in the blue silk garment. **1979** R. JAFFE *Class Reunion* (1980) I. vi. 85 In her slip and pants and garter belt and stockings she would lie down.

**d.** A pillow-slip, pillow-case.

**1800** *Naval Chron.* IV. 337 Pillows, and slips. **1977** *New Yorker* 27 June 72/3 What I want is my pillow... The slip is homemade.

**e.** *Upholstery.* A slot-hem in which a wire or the like may be inserted.

**1891** in *Cent. Dict.*

**f.** *pl.* In full ***bathing slips***: bathing-drawers. (No longer in use.)

**1904** *Times* 11 Aug. 10/3 He wore a pair of bathing slips and a broad-brimmed white linen cap. **1927** W. E. COLLINSON *Contemp. Eng.* 62 Bathing togs consisted of a bathing suit and slips, a reduced type of bathing-drawers.

**5.** *pl.* The sidings of a theatrical stage, from which the scenery is slipped on, and where the actors stand before entering.

**1771** C. BURNEY *Present State of Mus. France & Italy* 244 Printed sonnets, in praise of singers and dancers, were thrown from the slips. **1812** J. & H. SMITH *Rej. Addr.*, *Theatr. Alarm-bell* (1873) 152 Soldiers will be stationed in the slips. **1837** THACKERAY *Ravenswing* iv, She nodded to all her friends on the stage, in the slips. **1855** —— *Newcomes* xx, Raddled old women who shudder at the slips.

†**6. a.** A division in a pocket-book. *Obs.*$^{-1}$

**1804** EUGENIA DE ACTON *Tale without Title* I. 69 An elegant pocket-book, the private slip in which was furnished with bank-notes.

†**b.** *slang.* (See quot.) *Obs.*$^{-0}$

**1812** J. H. VAUX *Flash Dict.*, *Slip*, the slash pocket in the skirt of a coat behind.

**7.** A cylindrical iron case, in which wood for making gunpowder is charred.

**1876** VOYLE & STEVENSON *Milit. Dict.* 389/2 In each slip there are two holes, which correspond with similar holes in the retort. *Ibid.*, If of large size, the slip will hold 150 lbs.

**III. 8. a.** ***to give (one) the slip***, or variants of this: To evade or escape from (a person); to elude, steal off or slip away from unperceived.

**1567** in Ellis *Orig. Lett.* Ser. III. III. 326 This sayd Faithfull gave them all the slip, and never appeared afterwards. **1590** NASHE *Pasquil's Apol.* Wks. (Grosart) I. 242 Not satisfied wyth the slippe he hath giuen the Vniuersities and Lawes of learning. **1600** HOLLAND *Livy* XXVII. xliv. 661 Hee..gave him the faire slip, & escaped out of his hands. **1675** HOBBES *Odyssey* (1677) 193 There he found means to give them all the slip. **1728** MORGAN *Algiers* II. iii. 237 Salem gave his imperious Guests the Slip, and retired among his Arabs in the Country. **1773** MME. D'ARBLAY *Early Diary* July, He said he had rode the whole way,..having given the Colbourns the slip. **1817** JAS. MILL *Brit. India* IV. iii. II. 98 One of the principal officers of finance..had given the slip to his guards. **1852** THACKERAY *Esmond* III. iv, [I] thought to put an end to myself, and so give my woes the slip. **1884** G. MOORE *A Mummer's Wife* (1887) 78 [They] discussed how the slip should be given to Mrs. Ede.

*transf.* **1837** P. KEITH *Bot. Lex.* 207 If it is to give us the slip, after a sowing or two more, there will be but little chance left of our ever falling in with it again.

†**b.** Without personal object. *Obs. rare.*

**1596** H. MOUNTAGU in *Buccleuch MSS.* (Hist. MSS. Comm.) I. 231, I perceived two of his charge gave the slip. **1600** HOLLAND *Livy* XXXIX. xli. 1050 Many of them..made not appearance, but gave the slip.

†**c.** With punning allusion to SLIP *sb.*$^{4}$ *Obs.*

**1592** SHAKS. *Rom. & Jul.* II. iv. 50 What counterfeit did I giue you? *Mer.* The slip, sir, the slip, can you not conceiue? **1598** B. JONSON *Ev. Man in Humour* II. v, Let the world thinke me a bad counterfeit, if I cannot giue him the slip, at an instant. *c* **1613** MIDDLETON *No Wit like Woman's* III. i, You have given me a ninepence here, and I'll give you the slip for't.

**d.** An act of evading or escaping; *spec.* in horsemanship (see quot. 1607). *rare.*

**1607** MARKHAM *Caval.* III. (1617) 59 By giuing him slippes in winding and turning seeke to ouertoile him. *Ibid.* 75 If hee come vpon your right hand,..hurle your horse roundly about vpon your left hand: this is cald a slippe. **1669** PEPYS *Diary* 4 Feb., This morning I made a slip from the Office to White Hall.

**9. a.** An act of slipping, sliding, or falling down.

**1596** SPENSER *F.Q.* VI. vii. 48 At aduantage him at last he tooke, When his foote slipt (that slip he dearely rewd). **1611** COTGR. s.v. *Pas*, *Vn faux pas*, a slip, or misse, in footing. *a* **1700** EVELYN *Diary* 7 Feb. 1645, Not without many untoward slipps which did much bruise us. **1719** DE FOE *Crusoe* II. (Globe) 471 By..some Slip of my Foot..I fell down. **1816** *Sporting Mag.* XLVIII. 61 A slip, is losing the foot. **1833** NYREN *Cricket. Tutor* 43 The long stop..is required to cover many slips from the bat, both to the leg and the off-side. **1876** L. STEPHEN *Eng. Thought 18th Cent.* II. 376 A fop who has spoilt his fine clothes by a slip in the kennel. **1888** *Lockwood's Dict. Mech. Engin.* 329 *Slip*, the sliding of riveted joints one over the other to such an extent as to be visible. **1892** A. OLDFIELD *Man. Typog.* iii, Sometimes a page may be inadvertently squabbled in correcting, by a mere slip of the hand. **1950** *Sci. News* XV. 143 The copper-rich oxide layer..acted as a lubricant between billet and container... This particular type of oxide layer seems to favour slip or slide of the metal under it.

*fig.* **1847** TENNYSON *Princ.* v. 191 Bursts of great heart and slips in sensual mire.

**b.** *Prov.* (Cf. CUP *sb.* 12.)

**1850** THACKERAY *Pendennis* lxxii, There's many a slip between the cup and the lip! Who knows what may happen. **1861** TROLLOPE *La Beata* II. xv. 131 There are fewer slips between cup and lip in such matters in continental life. **1870** MORRIS *Earthly Par.* II. III. 39 But yet befell a grievous slip Betwixt that fair cup and the lip.

**c.** The difference between the pitch of a propeller (on a ship or aircraft) and the distance it moves through the ambient medium in one revolution.

**1844** *Civil Eng. & Arch. Jrnl.* VII. 84/1 The amount of 'slip' of the screw in the water..was stated not to exceed 5 per cent. **1877** W. H. WHITE *Man. Nav. Archit.* 525 From 15 to 20 per cent. appears to be a fair average for the slip of paddle-wheels. **1895** *Mod. Steam Eng.* 78 A certain part of the advancing power is lost, which loss is called the *slip* of the screw. **1910** R. W. A. BREWER *Art of Aviation* viii. 110 A certain amount of slip is necessary in order to obtain thrust. **1919** [see PITCH *sb.*$^{2}$ 25 e]. **1946** H. ROUSE *Elem. Mech. Fluids* ix. 293 At peak efficiency the effective pitch of the propeller is somewhat below the geometric pitch, which results in a so-called 'slip' of the blades. **1965** C. N. VAN DEVENTER *Introd. Gen. Aeronautics* viii. 194/1 (*caption*) A comparison of geometric pitch with working pitch and slip.

**d.** An act of slipping or stopping; an intermission.

**1898** *Allbutt's Syst. Med.* V. 941 Recurrent slips unmistakeably indicate dilapidation of the heart.

**e.** The sudden descent of material within a blast furnace. Cf. SLIPPING *vbl. sb.*$^{1}$ 1 c.

**1881** *Encycl. Brit.* XIII. 305/2 A 'slip' (or sudden jerky motion downwards of a mass of material that had previously more or less 'scaffolded'). **1911** *Jrnl. Iron & Steel Inst.* LXXXIII. 587 The causes of accidents peculiar to blast-furnaces, especially explosions, slips, and break-outs. **1948** G. R. BASHFORTH *Manuf. Iron & Steel* I. x. 166 The sudden slip of cold solid material into a hotter zone..may result in serious explosions. **1969** K. R. HALEY in J. H. Strassburger *Blast Furnace* II. xii. 592 A slip..causes wear on the lining.

**f.** Movement relative to a solid surface of the fluid immediately adjacent to it.

**1887** *Encycl. Brit.* XXII. 771/1 While greater surface than is offered by [a swimmer's] hands and feet was always given, with the evident intention of reducing 'slip', much resistance took place at the neutral or negative part of the stroke. **1891** *Phil. Trans. R. Soc.* A. CLXXXI. 560 From equation (i.) it follows that the effect of slip varies inversely as the radius of the tube. **1937** DODGE & THOMPSON *Fluid Mech.* xii. 308 The principal reason..is the fact that the hypothesis of zero slip at the boundary of the solid has been abandoned. **1967** R. S. BRODKEY *Phenomena of Fluid Motions* vii. 91 If slip at the boundary were allowed, the flow rate would become $Q$ = [etc.]. **1979** *Nature* 22 Mar. 350/2 Circumferential slip is essential if a helical object is to develop thrust in a true liquid, that is, if it is to propel itself using viscous forces.

**g.** *Electr. Engin.* The proportion by which the speed of an electric motor falls short of the speed of rotation of the magnetic flux inside it.

**1893** *Jrnl. Inst. Electr. Engineers* XXII. 328 The machine has a frequency of 50 and a slip of 6 per cent. **1936** SAY & PINK *Performance & Design of Alternating Current Machines* xii. 211 On no load the slip is generally less than..1 per cent. **1976** A. R. DANIELS *Introd. Electr. Machines* vii. 122 The rotor is driven at a small slip with respect to the armature rotating m.m.f.

**h.** *Cryst.* The movement of one layer of ions over another in a stressed crystal.

**1899** *Proc. R. Soc.* LXV. 86 The real character of the lines is apparent when the crystalline constitution of each grain is considered. They are not cracks, but *slips* along planes of cleavage or gliding planes. **1932** *Jrnl. Iron & Steel Inst.* CXXVI. 600 These results are in accord with the theory of deformation by slip. **1966** C. R. TOTTLE *Sci. Engin. Materials* iii. 64 In slip, a restricted number of planes are involved, and a restricted number of directions, so that whole areas of the crystal are affected. **1976** M. C. NUTT *Metallurgy & Plastics for Engineers* v. 70 Since metals deform by slip only on certain planes of atoms, it follows that anything that interferes with the slip process hardens the metal.

**i.** The turning of one plate of a clutch relative to the other when they are in contact.

**1902** A. C. HARMSWORTH *Motors & Motor-Driving* vi. 95 On the road also, if a clutch does not act, due to slip, a small dose of water puts matters right at once if the mechanical portions are in order. **1925** *Morris Owner's Man.* 22 The more pressure there is on the foot-board the less pressure is available in the clutch, and consequently there is a danger of slip starting. **1976** C. WEBB *Be your own Car Mechanic* vii. 96 When a clutch is worn it begins to slip. The slip generates heat and can cause the clutch spring or springs to lose their strength.

**j.** *Aeronaut.* A movement of an aircraft that includes a sideways component, esp. downwards towards the centre of curvature of a turn. Cf. SKID *sb.* 4 b.

**1916** GRAHAME-WHITE & HARPER *Learning to Fly* v. 50 The machine being near the ground, it came into contact with the surface of the aerodrome before the 'slip' had time to develop any high rate of speed. **1929** HALL & NILES *One Man's War* 114 Our slip was a slow one. It would be impossible to come out of a fast slip because that was done by putting on the rudder nearest to the direction of the slip. **1930** R. DUNCAN *Stunt Flying* ix. 79 A slip sideways into a landing is invaluable if it is necessary to land in a small area. **1952** [see SKID *sb.* 4 b]. **1965** C. N. VAN DEVENTER *Introd. Gen. Aeronaut.* x. 233/2 Information on slip and turn is nearly always wanted at the same time. **1983** D. STINTON *Design of Aeroplane* xiii. 465 A spiral dive..is marked by increasing airspeed and, usually, no slip or skid.

**10. a.** An error in conduct; *esp.* an instance of moral fault or transgression.

**1601** DENT *Pathw. Heaven* 94 Peters fall, Abrahams slips, Salomons weaknesse, &c. **1659** HAMMOND *On Ps.* CXXX. iv. 650 His pardoning of the frailties and slips of our lives. **1684** BUNYAN *Pilgr.* II. 98 Let Christian's slips before he came hither..be a warning to those that come after. **1711** ADDISON *Spect.* No. 99 ⁋2 A Slip in a Woman's Honour is irrecoverable. **1752** FIELDING *Amelia* IV. v, I hope, notwithstanding this fatal slip, I do not appear to you in the light of a profligate. **1833** MARRYAT *P. Simple* (1863) 306 O'Brien, who then called to mind what a slip of decorum he had been guilty of, immediately rose. **1858** FROUDE *Hist. Eng.* III. 364 Eyes watching for any slip which might betray their antagonists to the powers of the law.

**b.** A mistake or fault in procedure, argument, inference, etc.

**1579** W. WILKINSON *Confut. Fam. Love* 42 Beyng not to..get out of so manifest a slip, he returneth the fault vpon me. **1676** MARVELL *Mr. Smirke* 43 Only out of the affection I have for him, I would wish him to correct here one slip. **1700** *Pennsylv. Arch.* I. 136 Through that unhappy Slip of neglecting the Register, both Ship and Cargoe were condemned before my Arrival. **1790** PALEY *Horæ Paul.* i. Wks. 1825 III. 12 No advertency is sufficient to guard against slips and contradictions. **1821** SCOTT *Kenilw.* v, Since the hour that my policy made so perilous a slip, I cannot look at her without fear. **1885** *Law Reports* 29 Chanc. Div. 527 There must be some error, some slip in the decision.

**c.** A mistake or fault, esp. one of a slight or trivial character, inadvertently made in writing, speaking, etc.; an unintentional error or blunder.

**1620** BRINSLEY *Virg. Eccl.* Direct., Though the slips in this..be very many, the difficultie..may pleade for me. **1639** FULLER *Holy War* II. i, Such slips are incident to the pens of the best authors. **1680** BAXTER *Answ. Stillingfl.* xxxv. 59 It was an ill Slip, to put our *Condemning them*, for *Commending them*. **1712** ADDISON *Spect.* No. 285 ⁋2 A good-natur'd Reader sometimes overlooks a little Slip even in the Grammar or Syntax. **1764** HARMER *Observ.* v. §xiv. 228, I will not however press this, since it seems to be merely a slip of the translators. **1839** HALLAM *Hist. Lit.* III. iv. §159, I have commented upon very few, comparatively, of the slips which occur in his pages on this subject. **1885** *Law Reports* 29 Chanc. Div. 827 An error arising from an accidental slip or omission.

**d.** In the phrases ***a slip of the pen, tongue***, etc.

**1659** COWLEY *Let. to Ormonde* 7 Oct., Hopeing that his Majesty..will pardon the slip of that man's pen in one expression. **1677** R. CARY *Palæol. Chron.* II. I. xx. 153, I am apt to think that the Number..was originally the Transcriber's slip of the Pen. **1725** BAILEY *Erasm. Colloq.* (1733) 334 In Matters so sacred there is Danger in a Slip of the Tongue. **1732** BERKELEY *Alciphr.* vi. §3 Things once committed to writing are secure from slips of memory. **1778** MISS BURNEY *Evelina* xliv, It was a slip of the tongue; I did not intend to say such a thing. **1840** *Penny Cycl.* XVII. 42/1 A casual mistake, a slip of the press. **1849** LD. MAHON in *Croker Papers* (1884) 31 Dec., This second letter..is caused by the foolish slip of memory in my first. **1874** L. STEPHEN *Hours Libr.* (1892) I. vi. 203 A slip of the pen, such as happens to real historians. **1906** H. C. WYLD *Hist. Study of Mother Tongue* iv. 72 He at once perceives the difference [in his pronunciation], and 'corrects' the result as a 'mistake' or a 'slip of the tongue'. **1928** E. O'NEILL *Strange Interlude* VIII. 314 'You said "Navy".'..'Slip of the tongue! I meant Gordon.' **1939** G. B. SHAW *In Good King Charles's Golden Days* I. 13 'What did you call the gentleman, Mr Fox?'..'A slip of the tongue, Mistress Basham.' **1958** J. WAIN

*Contenders* vii. 151 The Canon was still beating down Robert's attempt to explain away that slip of the tongue. **1975** *Economist* 21 June 31/2 Transcripts of the call, accurate to the last slip of the tongue, have been sent to the magazine Stern.

†**11.** An abortion. *Obs.*[-1]

*a* **1657** HARVEY *Opera* (1766) 576 Nostrates *false conceptions* et *slips* nominant.

**12. a.** *Geol.* A slight fault or dislocation caused by the sinking of one section of the strata.

**1789** J. WILLIAMS *Min. Kingd.* I. 9 The coal is thrown either up or down by one of those slips. *Ibid.* 11 In a slip the strata are all cut or broke asunder, frequently in a straight line. **1802-3** tr. *Pallas's Trav.* (1812) I. 13 The projecting heights display, in various slips, precipitated strata of reddish clay. **1855** J. PHILLIPS *Man. Geol.* 203 The district is greatly traversed by faults or 'slips'. **1883** GRESLEY *Gloss. Coal-m.* 226 *Slip*, .. a smooth joint or crack in strata.

**b.** The slipping or subsiding of a mass of earth, etc., from a higher level; the quantity of earth which has thus fallen; = LANDSLIP.

**1838** F. W. SIMMS *Publ. Wks. Gt. Brit.* II. 10 These slips measuring altogether 4383 cube yards. **1845** DARWIN *Voy. Nat.* xiv. (1879) 303 The inhabitants thought that when the rains commenced far greater slips would happen. **1883** *Specif. Alnwick & Cornhill Rlwy.* 22 Should any slips take place in the cutting during the excavation of the material.

**13.** *Coursing.* **a.** The act of letting a dog go in order to pursue a deer, hare, etc.; also, the length of the start given to the hare.

**1602** *2nd Pt. Ret. fr. Parnass.* II. v. (1886) 108 The Buck broke gallantly: my great Swift being disaduantaged in his slip was at the first behinde. **1856** 'STONEHENGE' *Brit. Rur. Sports* 211/1 Length of Slip.—In all cases.. the hare ought to have from 70 to 100 yards' law. *Ibid.* 213/2 An awkward or wilfully-bad slip is also guarded against.

†**b.** A trip or jerk. *Obs.*[-1]

**1615** MARKHAM *Country Contentm.* I. vii. (1668) 43 If after the turn be given, there shall be neither coat, slip, nor wrench extraordinary.

**14.** *Cricket.* **a.** One or other of the fielders who stand behind and on the off-side of the wicket to which the ball is bowled.

For the origin of this use cf. quot. 1833 in sense 9 a.

**1833** NYREN *Yng. Cricketer's Tutor* 44 The situation for the [short] slip is between the wicket-keeper and point of the bat. *Ibid.* 45 The long slip is generally placed between the short slip and point, and near enough to save the run. **1891** W. G. GRACE *Cricket* 216 Box's favourite hit was a smart cut between the slips. **1894** *Times* 25 May 11/2 With the total at 70 Mr. Murdoch played the ball into slip's hands.

**b.** The ground or position occupied or guarded by these players

*sing.* **1816** W. LAMBERT *Cricketer's Guide* (ed. 6) iii. 41 In *backing up*, he [*sc.* point] should take care to give the man at the slip sufficient room. **1833** NYREN *Yng. Cricketer's Tutor* 79 Each usually played in the slip when the other was not present. **1851** LILLYWHITE *Guide Cricketers* 22 A third man in the slip at times is required. **1883** F. M. PEARD *Contrad.* xxi, You should have seen Henderson caught at slip from a 'skyer'.

*plur.* **1850** 'BAT' *Cricket. Man.* 101 His mode of cutting the ball into the slips.. is.. peculiar. **1882** *Daily Telegr.* 19 May, Being caught in the slips when he had put on 29.

**c.** With qualifying words indicating the various positions in the slips, and the fieldsmen stationed there, as †***extra slip***, a man who stands outside second slip; third slip; ***first slip***, the slip fielder who stands immediately to the right of the wicket-keeper (for a right-handed batsman); his position; similarly, ***second*** (***third***, etc.) ***slip***, ranged in a line out from the wicket-keeper; ***leg slip***: see LEG *sb.* 17 b; †***long slip***, a fieldsman placed as first slip, but deeper (or wider) in the field; †***middle slip***, short third man; †***short slip*** = ***first slip*** above. Also COVER-SLIP 1 (*Obs.*).

**1816** W. LAMBERT *Cricketer's Guide* (ed. 6) iii. 41 The Fieldsman that can best be spared is placed between the first Slip and Point. *Ibid.* 43 The Long Slip to cover the Short Slip. This man must stand.. about the same distance from the Wicket as the Long Stop. *Ibid.* 44 This man should stand the same distance, playing between the Point and second slip. **1851** J. PYCROFT *Cricket Field* v. 75 A third man on, and a forward point, .. with slow bowling, or an extra slip with fast, made a very strong field. *Ibid.* x. 193 A third man up, or a middle slip, is at times very killing. *Ibid.* xi. 222 A third slip can hardly be spared. **1892** W. G. GRACE in G. A. Hutchison *Outdoor Games* i. 26 Third man, who is, perhaps, rather a middle-slip, being long-slip placed in close enough to save the run. **1900** P. F. WARNER *Cricket in Many Climes* iii. 45, I was missed at extra slip.. when I had only made a few runs. **1921** —— *My Cricketing Life* xii. 227 Jack was.. a short slip of the same class as Tunnicliffe [, etc.]. **1955** *Times* 4 July 3/3 He swung the ball both ways, supported by a hostile, close-set field, Holliday taking two sharp low catches at first slip. **1976** *Times* 23 July 9/4 After adding 43 with Murray, Rowe was out to a tumbling catch at first slip; when Snow took over from Ward, Murray was well caught at second slip; when Willis came on, Holder gave third slip a catch.

**IV. 15. a.** *attrib.* and *Comb.*, as (sense 1 b) ***slip-dock***; (sense 2 b) ***slip-apartment***; (sense 3) ***slip-steward***; (sense 4 c) ***slip-bodice***, ***-body*** (Sc.), ***-dress*** (U.S.); (sense 12 a) ***slip-cleavage***, ***-dyke***, ***-trouble***, ***-vein***; (sense 14) ***slip-catch***, ***-catcher***, ***-catching***, ***-fielder***, ***-fielding***, ***fieldsman***.

**1791** COLLINSON *Hist. Somerset* I. 40 The hours of bathing are from six to nine.., during which time fires are kept in the *slip apartments. **1897** *Army & Navy Stores List* 1226 Long Cloth *Slip Bodices and Camisoles. **1889** BARRIE *Window in Thrums* viii, When he grew out o' it, she made a *slip-body o't for hersel. **1903** S. L. JESSOP in H. G. Hutchinson *Cricket* v. 119 This range [of hits for practising catches] will include different kinds of chances, from '*slip' catches to catches in the long field. **1977** *World of Cricket Monthly* June 29/3 Raja took his third wicket through a slip-catch. **1920** LYTTELTON & WILSON in P. F. Warner *Cricket* vii. 268 As a *slip catcher he was worthy to rank with R. E. and G. N. Foster. **1963** *Times* 17 Apr. 3/2 Downside are looking for proficient slip-catchers to give the required support to R. F. Thompson, a fast bowler, for whom they have high regard. **1950** W. HAMMOND *Cricketers' School* vi. 64 His *slip-catching is first-rate. **1883** GRESLEY *Gloss. Coal-m.* 226 **Slip cleavage*, the cleat of the coal running in planes parallel with slips. **1875** KNIGHT *Dict. Mech.* 2212/1 **Slip-dock*, .. a dock whose floor slopes toward the water [etc.]. **1964** *Glamour* May 149 Andrea wears a bare blue linen *slip-dress. **1789** J. WILLIAMS *Min. Kingd.* I. 32 There are indeed some dykes which throw the coal, etc. a little off the former level, and these I will, for distinction's sake, call *slip dykes. **1912** P. F. WARNER *Eng. v. Australia* i. 2 The Committee.. invited George Gunn, Woolley, and Mead, *slip-fielders all of them. **1963** *Times* 13 June 3/5 The slip fielder is Titmus. **1906** A. E. KNIGHT *Complete Cricketer* iv. 153 The possibilities of *slip fielding are so very great. **1976** *Times Lit. Suppl.* 16 July 896/5 There are a number of mistakes of fact (the editors' slip-fielding is not infallible). **1906** A. E. KNIGHT *Complete Cricketer* iv. 153 In degree it is true of all fieldsmen, yet it is more true of *slip fieldsmen, that a position in the field is largely what the individual fieldsman cares to make it. **1920** G. L. JESSOP in P. F. Warner *Cricket* iv. 167 The importance of a slip fieldsman is only second to that of a wicket-keeper. **1856** 'STONEHENGE' *Brit. Rur. Sports* 203/2 The *Slip-Steward, if there is one, regulates the proceedings of the dogs at the slips, and sees that the next brace is ready. **1887** MRS. DALY *Digging & Squatting* 133 There was a coursing club, of which my husband was slip-steward. **1883** GRESLEY *Gloss. Coal-m.* 227 *Slip-trouble. **1789** J. WILLIAMS *Min. Kingd.* I. 270 The *slip veins are seldom wider above than below, but are generally narrower.

**b.** Special Combinations. **slip angle**, (*a*) a parameter of a screw propeller (see quots. 1878, 1902); (*b*) *Motoring*, (see quot. 1959[2]); **slip band**, a slip line, or a cluster of such lines; **slip face**, the steepest face of a sand dune, down which sand slips; **slip flow**, in fluid dynamics, a mode of flow of a gas over a surface, the gas in contact with the surface having a definite velocity relative to it; **slip line**, (*a*) a fine line visible on a polished crystalline surface where it is cut by a slip plane; (*b*) a line in a solid whose tangent at any point is one of the shear directions at that point; **slip plane**, a plane along which slip occurs in a crystal; **slip ratio**, the ratio of the slip of a propeller to its pitch.

**1878** W. FROUDE in *Trans. Inst. Naval Architects* XIX. 50 The difference between the direction of the plane itself.. and the direction of its motion through the water.. may be called the *slip angle. **1902** *Encycl. Brit.* XXXII. 587/1 The slip angle (obliquity of surface to the line of its motion) ought always to have the same value (proportional to the square root of the coefficient of friction). **1936**, **1959** [see OVERSTEER *v.*]. **1959** *Manch. Guardian* 27 July 2/3 The slip angle is the difference between the direction in which the wheels are pointing and the actual direction in which the car travels. **1899** EWING & ROSENHAIN in *Proc. R. Soc.* LXV. 87 Rotation of the stage to which the strained specimen is fixed makes the bands on one or another of the grains flash out successively, with kaleidoscopic effect. In what follows we shall speak of these lines as *slip bands. **1976** C. BRADSHAW *Metallurgy for Schools* vi. 60 (*caption*) Photomicrograph showing slip bands formed on the surface of brass strip that has been stretched. **1941** R. A. BAGNOLD *Physics of Blown Sand & Desert Dunes* xiv. 224 The seif dune differs more markedly from the barchan in that its *slip-face, instead of running mainly transverse to the prevailing wind, runs parallel with it. **1976** *Nature* 22 July 284/2 The beetles either burrowed into dune slipfaces when returned or remained active. **1946** HSUE-SHEN TSIEN in *Jrnl. Aeronaut. Sci.* XIII. 654/2 It was found that gas no longer sticks to the surface but slips over the surface with a definite velocity... This type of flow can be called the *slip flow. **1978** *Jrnl. Fluid Mech.* LXXXV. 731 (*heading*) Slip flow past a tangential flat plate at low Reynolds numbers. **1900** *Phil. Trans. R. Soc.* A. CXCIII. 369 In gold or copper, it is very usual to find, on examining a strained specimen that one portion of a grain is covered with simple *slip lines. **1931** NÁDAI & WAHL *Plasticity* xvii. 110 (*caption*) Helical slip lines on polished marble cylinder after compression. **1950** *Sci. News* XV. Plate 16 (*caption*) Slip-lines in pure zinc after exposure to 50 thermal cycles between 30°C and 150°C (× 500). **1973** JOHNSON & MELLOR *Engin. Plasticity* xii. 383 In order to determine the load necessary for a particular plastic forming operation, we must first of all obtain the slip-line field pattern. **1976** M. C. NUTT *Metallurgy & Plastics for Engineers* v. 66 In Fig. 5-2 the intersection of individual slip planes with the polished surface is observed, thus forming slip lines. **1925** *Jrnl. Iron & Steel Inst.* CXII. 87 The authors consider that the lowest value for tensile strength in an iron crystal will be obtained when two *slip planes of the crystal make angles of 45° to the axis of stress. **1975** *Nature* 10 Apr. 489/1 Granular xenoliths.. in which olivine and pyroxene show various strain effects, including undulose extinction.., slip-planes, and subgrain development. **1878** *Trans. Inst. Naval Architects* XIX. 50 The area which will drive the ship with a given *slip ratio, is directly as the ship's resistance and is inversely as the square of her speed. **1902** *Encycl. Brit.* XXXVIII. 587/2 In combining the results from the four propellers great assistance was derived from the discovery that the curves expressing the variation of efficiency with slip-ratio had a close similarity. **1920** A. FAGE *Airscrews* vi. 70 In the writer's opinion the notion of slip is superfluous; and the introduction of a slip-ratio as a performance parameter quite unnecessary.

†**slip**, *sb.*[4] *Obs.* [Of obscure origin; perh. a special use of prec. or of *sb.*[2]] A counterfeit coin.

**1592** GREENE *Disput.* Wks. (Grosart) X. 260 He went and got him a certaine slips, which are counterfeyt peeces of mony being brasse, and couered ouer with siluer, which the common people call slips. **1607** R. C[AREW] tr. *Estienne's World of Wonders* 115 A counterfet peece of gold and a false peece of siluer (which we call a slip). **1612** J. DAVIES (Heref.) *Muse's Sacr.* Wks. (Grosart) II. 5/2 So, their Folly flies abroad the World, like Slips, that shame their Mint. **1624** SANDERSON *Serm.* I. 111 To take a slip for a currant piece, or brass for silver.

*attrib.* **1618** T. ADAMS *Fool & his Sport* Wks. 1861 I. 247 This is the worldling's folly, rather to take a piece of slip-coin in hand than to trust God for the invaluable mass of glory.

*transf.* **1594** NASHE *Unfort. Trav.* 40 Aie me, she was but a counterfet slip. **1598** E. GUILPIN *Skial.* (1878) 43 She, which thee deceaues With copper guilt is but a slip. **1608** MACHIN *Dumb Knight* v. i, An't please your majesty, we have brought you here a slip, a piece of false coin.

**b.** In phr. ***to nail up for a slip***, with reference to the exposure of spurious coin (cf. NAIL *v.* 1 d). Also *transf.*

**1594** LYLY *Mother Bombie* II. i, I shall goe for siluer though, when you shall bee nailed vp for slips. **1602** MARSTON *Antonio's Rev.* I. iii, Your nose is a copper nose, and must be nail'd up for a slip. *a* **1634** AUSTIN *Medit.* (1635) 108 But (here) they Naile him up, for a Slippe (a Brasen Counterfeit;) one, that did but say hee was a King.

**c.** With punning allusion to SLIP *sb.*[3] 8.

**1618** in Foster *Eng. Factories Ind.* (1906) I. 32 Hee was desirous to ride before to showe his horse, which indeed was only to pay them with a slippe, for from that daie to this wee never heard more of him.

†**slip**, *sb.*[5] *Obs.* In 7 **slipp**, 8 **slippe**. [app. a. older Flem. *slip* (Kilian), = MLG. *slip*, G. *schliff*, †*sliff*, related to Flem. and Du. *slijpen* to sharpen, polish, SLIPE *v.*[1]] (See quots.)

**1667** SIR W. PETTY in Sprat *Hist. Roy. Soc.* 296 The Filings of Steel, and such small particles of Edge-tools as are worn away upon the Grindstone, commonly called Slipp, is used to the same purpose in dying of Silks. **1791** HAMILTON tr. *Berthollet's Dyeing* II. II. i. 13 Some dyers.. use.. the powder found in the troughs of cutlers' grindstones. [*Note.*] This is known among our workmen by the name of slippe.

**slip** (slɪp), *v.*[1] Also 4-7 **slyppe**, **slipp**, 5-7 **slippe**; 5 **slipe**, 5-6 **slype**. [prob. ad. MLG. *slippen* (LG., Du., Flem. *slippen*, G. *schlippen*), = OHG. *slipfan* (MHG. *slipfen*, G. dial. *schlipfen*) to slip, slide, glide, etc., related to the ON. strong verb *sleppa* (Norw. and Icel. *sleppa*; in Sw. *slippa* and Da. *slippe* the vowel has been influenced by LG). The stem *slip-* appears in OE. in the adj. *slipor*: see SLIPPER *a.*]

**I.** *Intransitive senses.* (See also LET *v.*[1] 28.)

* **1.** To escape, get away, make off. *rare.*

*a* **1300** *Cursor M.* 4001 If þou wil, sal i slip And fal noght in his hand grip. **13..** *E.E. Allit. P.* B. 1785 Segges slepande were slayne er þay slyppe myȝt. **1572** *Satir. P. Reform.* xxxvi. 64 Lyndsay.. tuik þair geir, and luit thame selfis slip. **1621** ELSING *Lords' Deb.* (Camden) App. 131 A motion that Fowles should be closely keept in, otherwise it is thought hee will slipp. **1866** BROGDEN *Prov. Lincs.*, *Slip*, to run away.

**2.** To pass or go lightly or quietly; to move quickly and softly, without attracting notice; to glide or steal. Used with various advs. and preps.

In some cases the prominent idea is that of escape; more usually it is that of quick, easy motion.

**a.** With *away*, *off*, *out*; *from*, *out of*.

*c* **1450** *St. Cuthbert* (Surtees) 5931 Gif þir theues away slipp, ȝe haue grete los parfay. **1530** PALSGR. 721/2 Who wolde ever have thought that a thefe coulde have slypped out here. **1582** STANYHURST *Æneis* II. (Arb.) 64 Hold you my duitye so sclender, Too slip from Troytowne. **1617** MORYSON *Itin.* I. 44 There is no way to get out of the Church, except they slip out of the doores. **1671** MILTON *P.R.* IV. 216 When slipping from thy Mothers eye thou went'st Alone into the Temple. **1709** PRIOR *Hans Carvel* 24 So in a Morning..[she] Slipt sometimes out to Mrs. Thody's. **1773** *Life N. Frowde* 44, I took that opportunity to slip away. *c* **1810** W. HICKEY *Mem.* (1960) xix. 309, I.. might slip off *sans cérémonie* and proceed to join the Oxfordshire party. **1844** DICKENS *Mart. Chuz.* xlix, Some say he's slipped off, to join his friend abroad. **1878** T. HARDY *Ret. Native* v. viii, So I came downstairs without any noise and slipped out. **1888** BURGON *Lives 12 Gd. Men* II. v. 31 At the end of two or three hours.. most of those present had slipped away for luncheon.

*transf.* **1668** CULPEPPER & COLE *Barthol. Anat.* Man. III. ii. 324 These Nerves slip out of the Marrow about the Saddle of Sphœnoides.

*fig.* **1872** W. D. HOWELLS *Wedding Journ.* 279 You must slip out of it some way.

**b.** With *by*, *past*, *through*, etc. Also in fig. contexts.

**13..** *E.E. Allit. P.* B. 985 þay slypped bi & syȝe hir not þat wern hir samen feres. *a* **1591** H. SMITH *Wks.* (1867) II. 23 In the Spanish inquisition the protestants are examined, but the papists slip by. **1705** COLLIER *Ess. Mor. Subj.* III. *Pain* 16 That they should slip through Torture without Pain. **1748** *Anson's Voy.* II. v. 174 There might be less danger of any of the enemy's ships slipping by unobserved. **1831** SCOTT *Cast. Dang.* xix, Bertram slipped clear of his English friend. **1874** L. STEPHEN *Hours Libr.* (1892) II. x. 347 Some idiot.. who has somehow managed to slip past us in the race of life.

*transf.* **1875** *Daily Tel.* 4 Aug. (Cassell), There is always a certain proportion of Bills which may be said to slip through both Houses.

**c.** With *in*, *into*. Also *fig.*, and in slang use *to slip into*, to give (one) a good blow or beating.

*c* **1400** *Destr. Troy* 4703 þai.. Let sailes doune slide, slippit into botes. **1535** COVERDALE *Joel* ii. 9 They shal clymme vp vpon the houses, & slyppe in at the wyndowes like a thefe. **1592** MARLOWE *Jew of Malta* II. iii, Even now as I came home, he slipt me in. **1697** DRYDEN *Virgil, Life* (1721) I. 61 When People crouded to see him, he would slip into the next Shop..to avoid them. **1712** ARBUTHNOT *John Bull* (1727) 59 He would slip into the cellar, and gauge the casks. **1786** MME. D'ARBLAY *Diary* 25 July, I heard the King's voice. I slipped into my room, but he saw me. **1847** C. BRONTE *Jane Eyre* xxvi, The strangers had slipped in before us. **1867** TROLLOPE *Chron. Barset* I. viii. 65 I'll have a chair for you... You can slip into it and say nothing to nobody. **1888** BRYCE *Amer. Commw.* II. li. 292 If the voters are apathetic and let a bad man slip in.

*transf.* **1643** BROWNE *Relig. Med.* I. §17 When unexpected accidents slip in, and unthought of occurrences intervene. **1824** LANDOR *Imag. Conv.* (1846) II. 93 Curiosity slips in among you before the passions are awake. **1874** H. R. REYNOLDS *John Bapt.* III. §2. 185 Huge assumptions have been allowed to slip into the process of the argument, and to vitiate the proof.

*slang.* **1850** SMEDLEY *F. Fairlegh* (1894) 3 When you know how to use your fists,..slip into him. **1879** F. W. ROBINSON *Coward Conscience* II. xi, If you would oblige us all by slipping into Cabbage with a stick for half a minute.

**d.** With *back*, *home*, *over*, *to*, etc.

**1513** DOUGLAS *Æneid* IX. viii. 31 The weyngit messengeir ..slippand come to thy moder. **1560** DAUS *Sleidane's Comm.* 270 They serued vnwyllyngly, and..forsakyng their enseignes, slyppe home euery man. **1607** TOPSELL *Four-f. Beasts* (1658) 101 If the formost be weary, then slippeth he back to rest his head upon the hindmost. **1664** W. MOUNTAGU in *Buccleuch MSS.* (Hist. MSS. Comm.) I. 315 You will hear of Lord Chamberlain from Kimbolton, who slipped thither last week. *a* **1700** EVELYN *Diary* 3 June 1666, So having been much wearied with my journey, I slipp'd home. **1781** COWPER *Retirem.* 436 Then swift descending ..[he] Slips to his hammock. **1837** CARLYLE *Fr. Rev.* II. IV. vi, [He] privily..slips over to the Townhall to whisper a word. **1863** B. TAYLOR *H. Thurston* i. 17 Mrs. Waldo slipped to the door and peeped in. **1865** J. HATTON *Bitter Sweets* iii, I'll slip up with some bread and milk for you.

*fig.* **1859** TENNYSON *Guinevere* 377 Her memory..Went slipping back upon the golden days.

**3.** †**a.** With *on* or *upon*: To fall or sink into (sleep). Cf. SLIDE *v.* 6 a. *Obs.*

**13..** *E.E. Allit. P.* C. 186 He..Slypped vpon a sloumbe slepe. **13..** *Gaw. & Gr. Knt.* 244 As al were slypped vpon slepe, so slaked hor lotez. *c* **1400** *Destr. Troy* 2378 Sleghly on slepe I slypped be-lyue.

**b.** To enter gradually or inadvertently *into* a theme, digression, opinion, etc.

**1641** J. JACKSON *True Evang. T.* iii. 206, I am not slipt into that Anabaptisticall conceit and tenet..that all warres were utterly unlawfull under the Gospel. **1685** BOYLE *Enq. Notion Nat.* iv. 119, I perceive I have slipped into a somewhat long digression.

**c.** To pass *into* a certain state. Also with *off*.

**1864** TENNYSON *Alymer's Fi.* 6 Which at a touch of light.. Slipt into ashes, and was found no more. **1888** 'J. S. WINTER' *Bootle's Childr.* ii, She began to cry weakly, and at last slipped off into a dead faint.

**4.** To pass *out of*, escape *from*, the mind, memory, etc. Also without const.

*a* **1340** HAMPOLE *Ps.* cxviii. 93 It may noght slip out of my mynde. *c* **1430** HOCCLEVE *Minor Poems* xviii. 46 Let me nat slippe out of thy remembrance. **1567** MAPLET *Gr. Forest* 21 It will neuer let it sincke or slip out of minde. **1606** SHAKS. *Tr. & Cr.* II. iii. 28 If I could haue remembred a guilt counterfeit, thou would'st not haue slipt out of my contemplation. **1676** RAY *Corresp.* (1848) 125 The experiments..were quite slipt out of my memory. **1724** WATTS *Logic* I. v. (1726) 73 The Mind is ready to let many of them slip, unless some Pains and Labour be taken to fix them upon the Memory. **1818** SCOTT *Br. Lamm.* xxix, The idea of her mother's presence seemed to have slipped from the unhappy girl's recollection. **1892** J. TAIT *Mind in Matter* 300 Important truths had slipped out of the consciousness of the Church.

**5.** To break or escape *from* a person, the tongue, lips, etc.

*c* **1400** *Destr. Troy* 3891 Ector..warpit neuer worde of wrang with his mowthe. Ne sagh þat was vnsemond, slipped hym fro. **1500–20** DUNBAR *Poems* liii. 41 Ane blast of wind soun fra hir slippis. **1607** SHAKS. *Timon* I. i. 20 *Pain.* You are rapt sir, in some worke, some Dedication... *Poet.* A thing slipt idlely from me. **1654** tr. *Scudery's Curia Polit.* 39 Hasty rash words slip often from us inconsiderately. **1674** HICKMAN *Quinquart. Hist.* (ed. 2) 215 This last clause sure slipped from him unawares. **1773** *Life N. Frowde* 42 The reply..slipp'd as glibly from my Tongue, as if in reality I had known no other [name]. **1859** TENNYSON *Marriage Geraint* 446, I will not let his name Slip from my lips if I can help it. **1866** G. MACDONALD *Ann. Q. Neighb.* xv, Lest..he should let anything slip that might give a clue to the place or people.

**b.** To leak *out*, become known.

**1848** THACKERAY *Van. Fair* lxiii, When one side or the other had written any particularly spicy despatch, news of it was sure to slip out. **1942** T. BAILEY *Pink Camellia* xxiv. 180, I didn't mean it, darling. It just slipped out. **1979** *Homes & Gardens* June 77/2, I always know if he's worried but he never tells me the details straight out. It sometimes slips out in conversation when the crisis is over and I think, Oh, that's what it was about.

**6.** Of time: To go by quickly or imperceptibly; to pass unmarked; to run. Chiefly with advs., as *along*, *away*, *by*.

**1564–78** BULLEIN *Dial. agst. Pest.* (1888) 19 By little and little tyme doth slip awaie. **1581** PETTIE *Guazzo's Civ. Conv.* I. (1586) 48, I neuer thought how some of that time is slipt away. **1662** J. DAVIES tr. *Olearius' Voy. Amb.* 190 Perceiving the day slipp'd away without any hope of relief. **1730** T. BOSTON *Mem.* x. 312 The season for publishing it is slipt. **1793** JEFFERSON *Writ.* (1859) IV. 93 Time slipped along. **1848** DICKENS *Dombey* xv, As time was slipping by, and he had none to lose, he felt that he must act. **1864** TENNYSON *En. Ard.* 468 Trying his truth..Till half-another year had slipt away.

**7. a.** To pass *over* (a subject or matter) without adequate attention or notice; to neglect, overlook.

**1577** tr. *Bullinger's Decades* (1592) 439 Last of all I will not slip ouer this difference, although it bee of little weight. *a* **1591** H. SMITH *Wks.* (1867) II. 70 That no man's matters should slightly be slipped over. **1676** HALE *Contempl.* II. *Medit. Lord's Pr.* 138 Slipping over it in thy Prayer without a particular animadversion upon it. **1793** SMEATON *Edystone L.* §300 The circumstance might not have been slipped over, without my knowledge.

**b.** To progress or travel *across*, *down*, *over*, a stretch of ground, etc., quickly.

**1864** TENNYSON *En. Ard.* 527 Yet unvext She slipt across the summer of the world. **1874** L. STEPHEN *Hours Libr.* (1892) I. viii. 290 No man seems on the whole to have slipped down the stream of life more smoothly. **1890** 'R. BOLDREWOOD' *Col. Reformer* (1891) 188 A ten-mile stage.. having been slipped over.

**** 8.** Of the foot: = SLIDE *v.* 8 b.

*a* **1340** HAMPOLE *Ps., Comm. Canticles* 520, I sall ȝeld þaim ..in tyme..þat þaire fote slipp. **1535** COVERDALE *Ps.* xvi. 5 Ordre thou my goynges in thy pathes, that my fote steppes slippe not. **1596** SPENSER *F.Q.* VI. vii. 48 His foote slipt (that slip he dearely rewd). **1611** COTGR. s.v. *Glisser*, Better the foot slip then the tongue trip. **1827** WILLIS *Saturday Aft.* 23 My feet slip up on the seedy floor. **1864** *Law Times Rep.* X. 719/2 His foot slipped and he fell into the street.

**b.** To slide or glide, esp. on a smooth or slippery surface; to lose one's foothold; = SLIDE *v.* 8. Also in fig. context.

**1530** PALSGR. 721/2 Syt nat there, I rede you, leste you slyppe downe or you beware. ? *a* **1550** *Freiris Berwik* 582 in *Dunbar's Poems* (1893) 304, I saw him slip..Doun our the stair. *a* **1618** J. DAVIES *Wit's Pilgr.* I. ii, From it (being moist, and slippie) she doth slipp To thy faire Teeth. **1634** SIR T. HERBERT *Trav.* (1638) 59 Suddenly he slipt downe forty steps or degrees. **1779** E. CLARK *Poems* 193 Our wife yence slippit i' this sliddry gate. **1841** THACKERAY *Great Hoggarty Diamond* iii, 'Hadn't you better come into the carriage,.. Mr. Preston?'.. 'Oh, I'm sure I'll slip out, ma'm,' says I. *c* **1850** *Arab. Nts.* (Rtldg.) 581 As this spot was rather steep, and the ground moist.., he slipped down.

*fig.* **1538** STARKEY *England* II. i. 167 He folowyth not the ordynance of God, but..blyndyd wyth ignorance, flythe from hyt and slyppyth from hys owne dygnyte. **1579** GOSSON *Sch. Abuse* (Arb.) 63 He slippeth down presently into a dirtie comparison of a dutch Mule and an english mare.

**c.** To fall into mistake, fault, or error; to err, †to sin. Also with *into* (error, etc.).

(*a*) *c* **1340** HAMPOLE *Psalter* xxxviii. 1 Oure tonge..lightly ..slippis, as we doe when we ga in sklyþer way. **1435** MISYN *Fire of Love* 83 It wer meruayl if he to so grete wrongis suld slype. **1570** T. NORTON tr. *Nowel's Catech.* 64 b, There lieuth no mortall man that doth not oft slippe in doing his dutie. **1603** SHAKS. *Meas. for M.* V. i. 477, I am sorry, one so learned, and so wise,..Should slip so grosselie. **1638** JUNIUS *Paint. Ancients* 34 Great Masters..slip sometimes unawares. **1658** CROMWELL *Sp.* 20 Jan. (Carlyle), Therefore it is that men yet slip, and engage themselves against God. *a* **1702** J. POMFRET *Love Triumphant* 145 The best may slip, and the most cautious fall. **1891** *Pall Mall G.* 17 Jan. 4/2 Either Mr. Goldwin Smith's memory has slipped, or he has been..misreported.

(*b*) **1610** HOLLAND *Camden's Brit.* 504, I may seeme to slip into an errour. **1777** TYRWHITT in *Chatterton's Rowley Poems* App. 321 It might seem invidious to point out living writers..who have slipped into the same mistake.

**d.** orig. *U.S.* With *up*: To fail; to make a mistake. Freq. const. *on*.

**1855** *Jrnl. Discourses* II. 67/2 Some men think the way they are going to be saviors is to get as many wives as they can, and save them; now, they may slip up on that. **1856** B. HARTE *Dow's Flat* iii, He slipped up somehow On each thing thet he struck. **1866** *Weekly New Mexican* 14 July 2/1 The knowledge that he has 'slipped up' and been exposed is more than sufficient punishment for the offense. **1888** *Cent. Mag.* June 279/1 Slip up in my vernacular! How could I? I talked it when I was a boy with the other boys. **1923** C. J. DUTTON *Shadow on Glass* xviii. 247 All of us slipped up. **1940** J. REITH *Diary* 31 Jan. (1975) v. 240, I wish I had been City member instead of Southampton. I slipped up on that. **1959** J. VERNEY *Friday's Tunnel* viii. 80, I couldn't help feeling that Daddy had slipped up pretty badly this time. **1981** A. MORICE *Men in her Death* x. 108 Somewhere along the line I had slipped up.

**e.** Of a person: to fall away from a standard (in behaviour or achievement); to deteriorate; to lose one's command of things. Chiefly as *pres. pple. colloq.*

[**1907** G. B. SHAW *Major Barbara* III. 286 You are fencing, Euripides. You are weakening: your grip is slipping. **1914** 'HIGH JINKS, JR.' *Choice Slang* 18 *Slipping*, failing, 'losing out', 'going under'.] **1930** *Publishers' Weekly* 22 Feb. 933/2, I must be slipping for I turned in a measly 78 on No. 4 in the Lenz-Rendel book. **1949** 'J. TEY' *Brat Farrar* xxvii. 242 I'm behaving very badly to-night, aren't I? I seem to be slipping. **1962** 'E. FERRARS' *Busy Body* ix. 104 He'd been slipping lately, drinking too much and boasting. **1976** H. MACINNES *Agent in Place* xiii. 137 The journalist was the first to know he was slipping; next his editors; and then the public. End of a career.

**9.** To move out of place with an easy sliding motion; to fail to hold or stick; to slide. ***to slip off the hooks***: see HOOK *sb.*[1] 15 e.

**1382** WYCLIF *Deut.* xix. 5 The yren, slipt of fro the haft, smytith his freend. **1530** PALSGR. 721/2, I slyppe, as a thyng dothe that is thought to be tyed and holdeth nat faste, *je me lasche. Ibid.*, I can take no holde upon hym, my handes slyppeth so. **1641** BAKER *Chron.* 173 A Garter..slipping off in a Dance, King Edward stooped and tooke it up. **1669** STURMY *Mariner's Mag.* II. ii. 53 Fasten the Scale of Equal Parts, and the Scale to be made together, so as they may not slip. **1733** W. ELLIS *Chiltern & Vale Farm.* 172 The Bark will be prevented slipping up, as it is very apt to do.., when the Sticks or Cuttings are forced into the Ground of themselves. **1815** J. SMITH *Panorama Sci. & Art* II. 605 It should have grooves crossing each other..to prevent the bones from slipping aside. **1860** TYNDALL *Glac.* I. xxii. 157 My axe slipped out of my hand, and slid..away from me. *Ibid.* II. iv. 249 The snow upon steep mountain-sides frequently slips and rolls down in avalanches. **1867** AUGUSTA WILSON *Vashti* xxix, The sudden movement uncovered the letters, which slipped down and strewed the carpet.

**b.** To enter or fall *into* by slipping or losing hold.

**1679** MOXON *Mech. Exerc.* ix. 157 Lest with the Grain the edge of the Adz should slip too deep into the Board. **1807** P. GASS *Jrnl.* 22 A place where the bank has slipped into the river.

**c.** *intr.* and *trans. Aeronaut.* = SIDE-SLIP *v.* b.

**1911** *Aero* July (Suppl.) 2/2 The extra weight caused the machine to slide down sideways when steeply banked round the end corner. The Blériot slipped downward. **1930** R. DUNCAN *Stunt Flying* iii. 15 Side-slipping..enables the machine to be put down in a far shorter space than would be possible through a normal glide, forward speed being reduced to a minimum by slipping the air-plane sideways down to within a few feet of the ground. **1941** POPE & OTIS *Elem. Aeronaut.* iii. 19 If the banking is insufficient for such a turn, the plane will skid, and if the banking is too great, the plane will slip toward the inside of the curve. **1952** A. Y. BRAMBLE *Air-plane Flight* xiii. 199 Slipping may be used deliberately with useful effect, providing the air-plane is of the type that may be 'slipped'. **1965** [see SKID *v.*[1] 3 c].

**10.** To glide or pass easily *out of* (or *from*) *one's hand* or *grasp*, *through* (or *between*) *one's fingers*, etc., so as to escape or be lost. In later use chiefly *transf.*

**1390** GOWER *Conf.* II. 72 In liknesse of an Eddre he slipte Out of his hond, and forth he skipte. **1555** EDEN *Decades* (Arb.) 100 They slypped owte of their handes. **1622** FLETCHER *Prophetess* III. ii, Hold her fast, She'll slip thorow your fingers like an Eel else. **1668** HOPKINS *Serm. Vanity* (1685) 85 All our treasures are like quicksilver, which strangely slips between our fingers, when we think we hold it fastest. **1746** *Rep. Conduct of Sir J. Cope* 110 How this Person..slip'd out of his Hands. *a* **1770** JORTIN *Serm.* (1771) I. 132 Wealth by various means slips from the possessor's hands. **1807** W. IRVING *Salmagundi* (1824) 125 So, between them, the lady generally slipped through their fingers. **1853** JAMES *Agnes Sorel* (1860) I. 19 To exercise the authority in the land which slips from the grasp of the monarch. **1888** BRYCE *Amer. Commw.* III. xcviii. 379 Not only has the direction of politics slipped in great measure from their hands [etc.]. **1915** W. S. MAUGHAM *Of Human Bondage* xlvii. 236 He was mad to have let such an adventure slip through his fingers. **1970** J. A. T. ROBINSON *Christian Freedom in Permissive Society* p. ix, Try to net it [*sc.* the concept of freedom] in the categories of discursive knowledge,..it slips through your fingers, and you end up ..by concluding that it does not exist.

**b.** Similarly with *away*, or without const.

**1611** COTGR. s.v. *Passer*, Good lucke vnheeded quickly slips away. **1759** ROBERTSON *Hist. Scot.* VII. Wks. 1813 I. 503 Elizabeth did not suffer such a favourable opportunity to slip. **1780** COWPER *Progr. Error* 22 The rhet'ric they display Shines as it runs, but, grasp'd at, slips away.

**c.** ***to slip through the net***: to evade detection or apprehension; to escape someone's vigilance; to be overlooked.

**1902** G. B. SHAW *Mrs. Warren's Profession* p. xviii, Nothing can really shake the confidence of the public in the Lord Chamberlain's department except a remorseless and unbowdlerized narration of the licentious fictions which slip through its net. **1970** *Times* 21 Feb. 7/5 All those in the 'know' in the underworld..maintain that it was a man who was never on trial but who slipped through the net. **1977** M. DRABBLE *Ice Age* I. 67 The real poor..were better off than they would have been in the thirties, for Britain is, after all, a welfare state, and not many slip through its net.

**11.** To allow oneself to drop or fall with an easy, gliding motion; to slide *down*.

**1470–85** MALORY *Arthur* IX. xl. 404 So whanne syr Dynas wente oute on huntynge she slypped doune by a tuell. **1847** TENNYSON *Princ.* VII. 172 Now folds the lily all her sweetness up, And slips into the bosom of the lake. **1867** SMYTH *Sailor's Word-bk.* 633 *To slip by the board*, to slip down by the ship's side.

**12.** Of rivers, etc.: To run smoothly or gently; to flow, glide; to pass *into* the sea.

**1570–6** LAMBARDE *Peramb. Kent* (1826) 189 It..falleth.. to Rotherbridge,..from whence it soon after slippeth into the sea. **1598** MARLOWE *Ovid's Elegies* II. xiii, Swift Nile in his large channell slipping. **1784** COWPER *Task* I. 192 The softer voice..of rills that slip Through the cleft rock. **1864** TENNYSON *En. Ard.* 629 The silent water slipping from the hills. **1885** STEVENSON *Child's Garden, Foreign Lands* iv, To where the grown-up river slips Into the sea among the ships.

*transf.* **1748** THOMSON *Castle Indol.* I. xx, Yet they [*sc.* vibrations] slipt along In silent ease.

**13. a.** To get *out of* or *into* a garment, etc., in an easy or hurried manner.

**1500–20** DUNBAR *Poems* xxxiii. 106 He schewre his feddreme that was schene, And slippit owt of it full clene. **1609** FIELD *Woman is a Weathercock* II. i, Then my lord (like a snake) casts a suit every quarter which I slip into. **1857** LD. DUFFERIN *Lett. High Lat.* (ed. 3) 206 Slipping into a pair of fur boots. **1893** KEITH *'Lisbeth* II. ii, He's slipping into a clean shirt as fast as he can.

**b.** To slide *in* or *into* a socket, etc.

**1815** SCOTT *Let.* in *Lockhart* (1837) III. xii. 401 The thistle..is entirely detached, in working, from the figure, and slips into a socket. **1859** *Handbk. Turning* 75 A groove, in which one end of the tool slide..slips and is firmly fixed ..by a nut underneath.

**14.** To move easily and smoothly.

**1680** MOXON *Mech. Exerc.* x. 179 So oft as the Workman has occasion to oyl the Centers of his Work, to make his Work slip about the easier. **1869** RANKINE *Machine & Hand-tools* Pl. I 3, The cord wheel slipping within its encircling cord.

**b.** To admit of being taken *off*, or put *on*, by a slipping process.

1669 STURMY *Mariner's Mag.* v. xii. 63 Before you paste your Paper on the form, first Tallow him, so will the Canvas and Paper slip off without starting or tearing. 1747–96 MRS. GLASSE *Cookery* xiv. 227 You must boil your beans so that the skin will slip off. 1820 SCOTT *Monast.* x, I am grown somewhat fatter.., and my leathern coat slips not on so soon as it was wont.

**c.** Of bark: To peel off.

1788 DEANE in *M. Cutler's Life*, etc. (1888) I. 388, I have had chairs bottomed with the rind [of basswood], which will slip finely in June. 1878 JEFFERIES *Gamekeeper at Home* 61 When the sap is rising, the bark of the smaller shoots of the lime-tree 'slips' easily.

**II.** *Transitive senses.*

*** **15.** To cause to move with a sliding motion; to draw or pull in this manner.

In quot. 1850 prob. suggested by Du. *slepen*.

1513 DOUGLAS *Æneid* VII. vii. 28 Full slyde scho slyppis hir membris our allquhayr. 1633 HERBERT *Temple, Praise* vi, After thou hadst slipt a drop From thy right eye. 1688 MIÉGE *Gt. Fr. Dict.* I. s.v. *Derober*, To slip beans out of their skins. *a* 1700 EVELYN *Diary* 11 June 1652, It was long before I could slip the cord over my wrists to my thumb. 1733 W. ELLIS *Chiltern & Vale Farm.* 187 Their Bark must never be slip'd up at their putting into the Earth. 1833 HT. MARTINEAU *Manch. Strike* vii. 77 Make every one knock that wants to come in. If they won't obey,..slip the bolt. 1850 R. G. CUMMING *Hunter's Life S. Afr.* (ed. 2) I. 149, I ..despatched men with a span or team of oxen to slip the wildebeest to camp. 1889 GRETTON *Memory's Harkback* 161 One of the men slipped a brand from a bundle of wood.

*fig.* 1795 BURKE *Regic. Peace* iv. (1892) 268 Having therefore slipped the persons, with whom we are to treat, out of view.

**b.** With *off* or *on*. (Cf. 2.) Also *refl.*

1662 BOYLE *Spring of Air* 114 Since..such Surfaces are as easily slipt of, and extended in the end of the depression as in the beginning. 1680 MOXON *Mech. Exerc.* x. 188 On this Crook is slipt the Noose of a Leather Thong. 1707 *Curios. in Husb. & Gard.* 197 A Cinnamon-Tree..bears none but its Bark, which Slips itself off every Year. 1778 MRS. RAFFALD *Eng. Housekeeper* 25 Take the cloth carefully off, and slip it on to your dish. 1837 CARLYLE *Fr. Rev.* II. I. vi, On the President's chair [can] be slipped this cover of velvet. 1885 *Law Reports* 15 *Q. B. Div.* 360 The belts..could be slipped off the drum of the shaft..at pleasure.

**c.** *Sc.* To go or take (one's way) in a quick and quiet manner. With advb. compl.

1818 SCOTT *Hrt. Midl.* xxxviii, If I were to..slip my ways hame again. —— *Rob Roy* xxii, I..came slipping my ways here to see what can be dune anent your affairs.

**d.** *Motoring. to slip (in) the clutch*, to let in, release the clutch (CLUTCH *sb.*[1] 6 a), slightly or momentarily.

1904 A. B. F. YOUNG *Compl. Motorist* 214 When the brake lever is in the 'on' position, it is impossible to start the car by slipping in the clutch until it has been released. 1912 *Motor Man.* 73 The metal clutch..can be 'slipped' to any extent without affecting the surface of the discs. 1965 PRIESTLEY & WISDOM *Good Driving* ix. 63 It is permissible [in reversing] to slip (feather) the clutch a little so as to maintain an even rate of travel. 1972 HILLIER & PITTUCK *Fundamentals of Motor Vehicle Technol.* 20 Most modern engines have a speed range from about 400 revolutions per minute..unless the clutch is partly disconnected or slipped.

**16. a.** To strip or take off (a garment, etc.); to cast (the skin, etc.). Occas. with advs., as *down, off*. Also in fig. context.

1535 LYNDESAY *Satire* 2172 Slip doun ȝour hois. *a* 1591 H. SMITH *Serm.* (1637) 454 As a man slippeth off his clothes, ..so we must slip off all our sins. 1603 DEKKER *Whore Babylon* Wks. 1873 II. 244 The snake slips off his skinne. 1673 *Humours Town* 45 They ought now, like the Serpent, to slip their Skin. 1727 BOYER *Dict. Royal* II, To slip (or pull) off one's Shoes, *tirer ses Souliers*. 1842 TENNYSON *Talking Oak* 188 When that, which breathes within the leaf, Could slip its bark and walk. 1901 J. WATSON *Life Master* ix. 87 He slips his past and puts on a new shape.

**b.** To put *on* (an article of apparel) hastily or carelessly.

1590 LODGE *Rosalind* (1592) H iij, With that she slipt on her peticoat, and start vp. *c* 1660 *Roxb. Ball.* (1886) VI. 213 Come slip on your slippers, and trip down the stairs. 1687 MIÉGE *Gt. Fr. Dict.* II, To slip his Clothes on, *s'habiller*. 1773 *Life N. Frowde* 92, I jumped out of Bed, slipp'd my Coat on, and..called the Chamberlain. 1786 MME. D'ARBLAY *Diary* 17 July, I was obliged to slip on my morning gown,..and run away as fast as possible. 1818 SCOTT *Hrt. Midl.* vii, Porteous might, however, have eluded the fury,..had he thought of slipping on some disguise. 1856 KANE *Arctic Expl.* II. ix. 95 The watch-officer slips on his bear-skin.

**17.** To withdraw (one's head or neck) *out of* or *from* a collar, etc. Also *fig.* (cf. COLLAR *sb.* 8).

1583 GOLDING *Calvin on Deut.* cxxv. 772 Albeit we.. would slippe our heades out of the coler seeking to shift off yᵉ matter. 1594 SHAKS. *Rich. III*, IV. iv. 112 My burthen'd yoke, From which, euen heere I slip my wearied head. 1687 MIÉGE *Gt. Fr. Dict.* II, To slip his Neck out of the Collar.

**18.** To insert or introduce gently or surreptitiously. Const. *in, into*.

1688 MIÉGE *Gt. Fr. Dict.* I. s.v. *Couler*, To slip mony into his pocket. 1713 ARBUTHNOT *John Bull* (1727) 76 He had tried to slip a powder into her drink. 1748 H. ELLIS *Voy. Hudson's Bay* 136 When they want to lay their Child out of their Arms, they slip it into one of their Boots. 1852 MRS. H. B. STOWE *Uncle Tom's C.* xxi. 219 The choicest peach or orange was slipped into his pocket to give to her when he came back. 1888 'J. S. WINTER' *Bootle's Childr.* iii, He took the loose cushion..and slipped it under Lassie's head.

*transf.* 1837 [MISS MAITLAND] *Lett. fr. Madras* (1843) 155 A —— quoted all the old divines, and I slipped in texts. 1900 H. LAWSON *On Track* 55 The time when he slipped three leaden pills into 'Blue Shirt' for winking at a new chum behind his..back.

**b.** *Cards.* To palm (a card); †*absol.*, to cheat in this manner in playing. ***to slip the cut*** (see quot. 1879).

1760 FOOTE *Minor* I. Wks. 1799 I. 239, I am..an adept in their science, can slip, shuffle, cog, or cut with the best of 'em. 1807 *Sporting Mag.* XXIX. 197 Few could more dextrously slip a card or cog a die. 1836 in Curtees *Rep. Cases Eccl. Courts* I. 414 *note*, He..detected him slipping the king, commonly called 'palming', for the purpose of cheating.. him. 1879 *Sporting Exam.* 19 Aug. 262 The usual method of slipping the cut is to pick up with your right hand the cards removed from the top of the pack, and place them in the open palm of your left hand [etc.].

**c.** To give quietly or slyly.

1841 S. HAWKINS *Poems* V. 25 (E.D.D.), The cannie lass whiles..slips me down a bit o' bread. 1865 CARLYLE *Fredk. Gt.* x. v. III. 256 The Custom-house people..were pacified by slipping them a ducat. 1922 E. O'NEILL *Hairy Ape* vii. 78 Man in de Moon, yuh look so wise, gimme de answer, huh? Slip me de inside dope. 1935 [see DUCAT 2 b]. 1936 WODEHOUSE *Laughing Gas* xix. 210 You tell me..and I'll slip you that money you wanted. 1952 'N. SHUTE' *Far Country* ix. 257 Jim must have known the man was a boozer, and he might have thought some of his mates would try to slip him something. 1968 P. H. NEWBY *Something to answer For* iii. 88 If it's money you want, give me a little time, I can slip you a few hundred. 1978 S. BRILL *Teamsters* iv. 133 At one lunch, he testified, he slipped Provenzano $1,500.

**d.** In *slang* phr. ***to slip*** (something) ***over*** (***on***) (someone), to take advantage of someone by trickery, to hoodwink; ***to slip a fast one over on*** (someone) = to pull or put over a fast one (see FAST *a.* 11).

1912 C. MATHEWSON *Pitching in Pinch* iii. 63, I attempted to slip a fast one over on Cooley and got the ball a little too high. 1927 *Daily Tel.* 29 Mar. 10/7 If one only had the nerve and audacity one could 'slip it over' the German every time. 1936 WODEHOUSE *Laughing Gas* v. 63 Can you imagine my lawyer letting them slip that over! 1960 'B. MCCORQUODALE' *Price is Love* iii. 53 It was something he really wanted to know and was trying to slip it over on her unexpectedly.

**19.** To cause to slip or lose hold; *esp.* to undo (a knot) in this way. Also in fig. context.

1606 SHAKS. *Tr. & Cr.* v. ii. 156 The bonds of heauen are slipt, dissolu'd, and loos'd. 1674 FAIRFAX *Bulk & Selv.* 74 Should but any one pin of it be misdriven, or the running of its least wheel slipt or jostled. 1761 STERNE *Tr. Shandy* III. x, Tight, hard knots,..in which there is no quibbling provision made..to get them slipped and undone by. 1818 SCOTT *Rob Roy* iii, The manner in which my father slipt a knot, usually esteemed the strongest which binds society together. 1894 HALL CAINE *Manxman* v. v, 'Kate's knot,' thought Pete... He slipped it, and opened the lid.

**b.** To dislocate (a joint). ***to slip a disc***: to sustain a 'slipped disc' (SLIPPED *ppl. a.*[1] 2).

1727 GAY *Begg. Op.* I. xiii, May my pistols miss fire, and my mare slip her shoulder while I am pursu'd, if I ever forsake thee! 1760 C. JOHNSTON *Chrysal* (1822) II. 45 Who rode against him, and slipped his shoulder. 1842 LOVER *Handy Andy* xxxvii, My horse, I fear, has slipped his shoulder. 1868 *Daily News* 18 July, This boar..slipped its hip last Saturday while it was being washed. 1958 'J. BYROM' *Or be he Dead* v. 68 An unfortunate tramp who had slipped a disk. 1974 G. MITCHELL *Javelin for Jonah* ii. 33 He told Margot to rake the long-jump pit..and she slipped a disc.

**c.** To suffer an accidental slipping or sliding of (one's foot).

1769 *Middlsx. Jrnl.* 15–17 June 4/4 A carpenter..coming down stairs..slipped his foot and got..a desperate fall. 1813 *Examiner* 5 Apr. 215/2 A..man..unfortunately slipped his foot, and fell. 1874 LADY HERBERT tr. *Hübner's Ramble World* II. vi. (1878) 365 He slipped his foot and fell.

**** **20.** †**a.** To allow to pass idly or unprofitably; to waste or lose (time). *Obs.*

1435 MISYN *Fire of Love* 88 Woo be to þame qwhos days ar slippyd & passyd in vanite. 1645 G. DANIEL *Poems* Wks. (Grosart) II. 82 Poor crauling Emmetts! in what busie toyle Wee slip away our Time? 1687 *Hist. Sir John Hawkwood* iv. 7 To slip no time, lest he should be anticeeded, he sits him down.

**b.** To allow (an occasion, opportunity, etc.) to slip or pass by; to neglect or fail to take advantage of.

*c* 1592 MARLOWE *Jew of Malta* v. ii, Slip not thine oportunity. 1597 DANIEL *Civ. Wars* II. xlvii, Here, my sou'raigne, to make longer stay..May slippe th' occasion, and incense their will. 1647 N. WARD *Simp. Cobler* 35 If this market be slipt, things may grow..deare. 1699 BENTLEY *Phalaris* 187 The consciousness of his own guilt made him slip this fair occasion of traducing me. 1721 DE FOE *Mem. Cavalier* (1840) 175 Advantages slipt in war are never recovered. 1781 C. JOHNSTON *Hist. J. Juniper* I. 193 He could not slip the opportunity. 1831 SHENNAN *Tales* 164 (E.D.D.), Then slip not the chance when it is in your power.

†**c.** To fail in keeping (a prescribed time). *Obs.*

1605 SHAKS. *Macb.* II. iii. 52 He did command me to call timely on him, I haue almost slipt the houre. 1707 J. STEVENS tr. *Quevedo's Com. Wks.* (1709) 395, I slipt my Time.

**21.** To pass over, omit in speaking; to avoid mention or consideration of. Also with *over*.

1605 B. JONSON *Volpone* IV. i, I do slippe No action of my life, thus, but I quote it. 1612 WEBSTER *White Devil* IV. i, Some divines you might find foulded there; But that I slip them o're for conscience sake. 1690 *Andros Tracts* II. 63 We had almost slipt the Notice of a Bawl or two these Libellers make about Damnifying their Church. 1748 WASHINGTON *Jrnl.* 25 Mar., Writ. 1889 I. 3 Nothing remarkable on Thursday... So shall slip it. 1850 TENNYSON *In Mem.* cxxii, Like an inconsiderate boy,..I slip the thoughts of life and death.

**b.** To neglect; to omit or fail to prosecute, perform, employ, etc.; to skip, to miss.

1592 *Arden of Feversham* III. ii, Wert not a serious thing we go about, It should be slipt til I had fought with thee. 1620 *Hist. Frier Rush* 22, I pray thee..briefly to make an end of thy enterprise, and slip it not. 1711 SWIFT *Lett.* (1767) III. 259 Our ministers are too negligent of such things: I have never slipt giving them warning. 1721 AMHERST *Terræ-Fil.* No. 10 (1726) 51 Whether it was usual now and then to slip a lecture or so. 1728 RAMSAY *General Mistake* 137 [He] changes, lends, extorses, cheats and grips, And no ae turn of gainfu' us'ry slips.

***** **22.** To elude or evade, esp. in a stealthy manner; to escape from; to give the slip to.

1513 DOUGLAS *Æneid* II. vi. 41 Bot lo! Panthus, slippit the Grekis speris,..Cummis like ane wod man to our ȝet rynning. 1607 TOURNEUR *Rev. Trag.* III. vi, Why was't not my inuention, brother, To slip the Judges. 1669 PENN *No Cross* I. iii. §6 No, not a Thought must slip the Watch. 1702 VANBRUGH *False Friend* v. i, He sees me; 'tis too late to slip him. 1746 H. WALPOLE *Lett.* (1846) II. 107 To prevent the rebels slipping the Duke. 1891 ROBERTS *Adrift Amer.* 198 That very night I slipped him while he was asleep, and got clear away.

**b.** To pass by, get in front of; to outdistance.

1856 H. H. DIXON *Post & Paddock* xiii. 324 He had slipped all the rest of the field. 1896 *Sportsman* 10 July 3/8 The metropolitan crew managed to slip their doughty antagonists at the start.

**c.** With *up*. To defraud or swindle; to disappoint. *Austr. slang.*

1890 *Melbourne Argus* 9 Aug. 4/2, I'd only be slipped up if I trusted to them. 1891 NAT. GOULD *Double Event* 92 It's deuced hard lines..to be slipped up like this.

**d.** To escape from the grasp of (a person).

1898 G. MEREDITH *Odes Fr. Hist.* 62 She swung the sword for centuries: in a day It slipped her.

**23.** To disengage oneself or get loose from (a collar, halter, etc.). Freq. *fig.* (cf. COLLAR *sb.* 8).

1579 W. WILKINSON *Confut. Fam. of Love* 16 He can not slippe the coller with me as erst he did, in leauyng the former sentence. 1594 LYLY *Mother Bombie* II. i, I hope you shall neuer slip string, but hang steddie. 1607 TOPSELL *Four-f. Beasts* (1658) 5 Mammonets..are tied by the hips, that they slip not collar. 1662 J. DAVIES tr. *Olearius' Voy. Amb.* 309 They also fasten them..that, in case they should break or slip their Halters, they may not get away. 1821 SCOTT *Kenilw.* xiii, Hobgoblin..is like to play the devil in the world, if he can once slip the string. 1836 *Uncle Philip's Convers. Whale Fishery* 38 [The whale] must be struck in the proper way or he will slip the harpoon. 1837 CARLYLE *Fr. Rev.* I. VII. x, Rascality has slipped its muzzle. 1890 *Spectator* 28 June, An overworked man who has contrived for a week or two to slip the collar of professional responsibility.

**24.** To escape from (one's memory); to elude (one's notice, knowledge, etc.).

1652 COLLINGES *Caveat for Prophanen.* xxvii. (1653) 112 Reasons..which have slipt my memory. 1709 BAYNARD *Cold Baths* II. 188 Very few..remarkable Passages..of the Ancient..Writers slip your Observation. 1733 W. ELLIS *Chiltern & Vale Farm.* 140 Several good Properties of this Tree having slip'd the Knowledge and Notice of Authors. 1768 STERNE *Sent. Journ.*, *Le Dimanche*, Le Fleur..let as few occasions slip him as his master.

**25.** To pass or escape inadvertently from (the pen, tongue, etc.).

1751 WARBURTON in W. & Hurd *Lett.* (1809) 82 The word Hutcheson slipped my pen before I was aware. 1887 G. MEREDITH *Ball. & Poems* 148 Weak words he has, that slip the nerveless tongue.

****** **26.** To allow to slip (from one's hand, etc.); to loosen one's hold or grasp of; to let go.

*c* 1586 C'TESS PEMBROKE *Ps.* LXXVIII. xi, He slipt the raines to east and southerne wind. 1592 GREENE *Def. Conny Catch.* Wks. (Grosart) XI. 67 Jacke all this while had an eye to the Bitch, and determined at last to slip her haulter. 1684 R. H. *School Recreat.* 59 Caveating or Disengaging. Here you must..slip your Adversaries Sword, when you perceive him about to bind or secure yours. 1764 J. FERGUSON *Lect.* ii. 13 A pebble moved round in a sling..will fly off the moment it is set at liberty, by slipping one end of the sling-cord. 1878 BOSW. SMITH *Carthage* 104 These..slipped the ropes and did battle with their assailants. 1883 *Law Times Rep.* XLIX. 332 The tow-rope of the tug was slipped.

*fig.* 1611 SHAKS. *Cymb.* IV. iii. 22 Wee'l slip you for a season, but our iealousie Do's yet depend.

**b.** To allow to escape; to utter (†or commit) inadvertently. Also with *out*.

*a* 1591 H. SMITH *Wks.* (1867) II. 12 That they may forget themselves at such a time, and step too far, and slip a sin. 1687 MIÉGE *Gt. Fr. Dict.* II, To slip out a Word, *lâcher une parole*. 1723 *Pres. State of Russia* II. 151 But I was drunk, ..and I slipt those Words, trusting to my Servants. 1766 GOLDSM. *Vicar W.* ix, They once or twice mortified us sensibly by slipping out an oath.

**c.** ***to slip one's breath*** or ***wind***, to expire; to die. *colloq.*

*a* 1819 WOLCOT (P. PINDAR) *Wks.* (1830) 69 (Davies), And for their cats that happed to slip their breath, Old maids.. might mourn. 1833 MARRYAT *P. Simple* (1863) 282 He thinks I am slipping my wind now—but I know better. 1856 READE *Never too late to mend* I. x. 180 You give him the right stuff, doctor,..and he won't slip his wind this time.

**d.** To emit, send out (light, etc.). *rare*$^{-1}$.

1873 BROWNING *Red Cott. Nt.-cap* 122 Each pullet-egg Of diamond, slipping flame from fifty slants.

**e.** *Knitting.* (See quots.)

1840 J. GAUGAIN *Lady's Assistant* 13 Slip a stitch having wool in front, then pass the wool to the back under the left pin. 1880 *Plain Hints Needlew.* 14 To decide whether it should be done by knitting 2 loops together, or by slipping a loop (i.e. taking it off without knitting). 1926 E. K. MIDDLETON *New Knitting* 15 To decrease two at a time. Slip one. Knit two together. Draw the slipped stitch over. 1951 E. CLOSE *Knitting* ii. 29 Slip one stitch from the left hand to the right hand needle as if you were about to knit it. **1973** M. STRADAL *Knitting, Crochet & Looping* i. 26 Slip one stitch purlwise, thread over needle and knit together the slipped stitch and the thread-over-needle of previous row.

**f.** To detach (the end carriage or coach) from an express or non-stopping train while running, in order to allow passengers to get out at a certain station.

**1866** *Bradshaw's Railw. Guide* Jan. 39 A carriage slipped at Slough at 10.45 aft. **1884** *G.W.R. Time Tables* July 48 Carriage slipped at Reading at 2.4. **1898** *Daily News* 11 Oct. 8/1 The Great Western..were slipping coaches in 1865.

**27.** To release (a greyhound or other dog, or a hawk) from a leash or slip. Also *fig.*

**1596** SHAKS. *Tam. Shr.* v. ii. 52 Oh sir, Lucentio slipt me like his Gray-hound. *a* **1625** BEAUM. & FL. *Women Pleas'd* II. ii, When they grow ripe for marriage They must be slipt like Hawkes. **1649** G. DANIEL *Trinarch., Hen. IV*, ccxlix, The Age (it seemes)..broke in the Cell; Slipt her Rebellions, like rude Molaes forth. **1668** ETHEREDGE *She wou'd if she cou'd* II. i, Indeed methinks they look as if they never had been slip'd before. **1753** *Chambers' Cycl.* Suppl. s.v. *Coursing*, The mungril greyhound, whose business it is to drive away the deer before the greyhounds are slip'd. **1841** LANE *Arab. Nts.* I. 126 The horsemen are instantly at full speed, having slipped the dogs.

*absol.* **1893** *Times* 18 Dec. 10/3 W. slipped well. **1904** *Field* 6 Feb. 220/2 Wright I have rarely seen slip better.

**b.** With *after, at,* or *upon* (game, etc.).

**1673** HICKERINGILL *Greg. F. Greyb.* 8 He has stood three or four courses already; the first..that was slipt at him made more hast than good speed. **1753** *Chambers' Cycl.* Suppl. s.v. *Coursing*, If a proper deer come out, and it is suspected that the brace or leash of greyhounds slip'd after him, will not be able to kill him. **1816** SCOTT *Fam. Lett.* 21 Dec. (1894) I. 387 Maida is a little lame, but if he gets better I would like to slip him at a fox. **1827** D. JOHNSON *Ind. Field Sports* 177 Grey-hounds were slipped after such as were wounded. **1859** TENNYSON *Elaine* 654 Our falcon yesterday, Who lost the hern we slipt her at. **1903** SIR M. G. GERARD *Leaves fr. Diaries* vii. 213 A friend of mine saw thirteen of these dogs slipped upon a wounded tiger.

*fig.* **1676** ETHEREDGE *Man of Mode* II. i, I am going to slip the boy at a mistress. **1832–4** DE QUINCEY *Cæsars* Wks. 1859 X. 218 The Roman army hungered..to be un-muzzled and slipped upon these false friends.

**c.** To unyoke, release.

**1859** CAPERN *Ball. & Songs* 41 The ploughman slips his weary team.

**28.** *Naut.* To allow (an anchor-cable, etc.) to run out, freq. with a buoy attached, when quitting an anchorage in haste; to drop or disengage (an anchor) in this way.

**1681** *Lond. Gaz.* No. 1643/1 The Tripolines slipped their Anchors and made what haste they could into the Port. **1698** FRYER *Acc. E. India & P.* A4b, Found three anchors slipped in the Bay. **1722** DE FOE *Col. Jack* xviii, She immediately slipped her cable, and put herself under sail. **1790** BEATSON *Naval & Mil. Mem.* I. 173 Few of them lost any time in weighing their anchors, but either cut or slipped them. **1840** R. H. DANA *Bef. Mast* xiv. 35 We made sail, slipped our cable,..and beat about, for four days.

*absol.* **1667** *Lond. Gaz.* No. 203/4 One of them..was forced to come to an Anchor, but the night proving stormy obliged her to slip. **1683** *Ibid.* No. 1787/4 Several other Vessels in this bad Weather slipt, and went to Sea. **1793** SMEATON *Edystone L.* §226 The Weston..was therefore ordered to slip and make her best port. **1840** R. H. DANA *Bef. Mast* xviii, Vessels are obliged to slip and run for their lives on the first sign of a gale.

**b.** *to slip one's cable*, to die.

**1751** SMOLLETT *Per. Pic.* lxxix, I told him [a doctor] as how I could slip my cable without his..assistance. **1868** YATES *Rocks Ahead* Prol. ii, Our poor friend, who has, as it were, slipped his cable before my arrival.

**29.** Of animals: To miscarry with; to drop, bring forth, or cast prematurely. Also *transf.* of persons.

**1665** PEPYS *Diary* 31 Mar., My Lady Castlemaine is sick again; people think slipping her filly. **1757** *Phil. Trans.* L. 536 As appears by the cows with calf not slipping their calves. **1759** R. BROWN *Compl. Farmer* 52 These [dogs] have sometimes caused them [sows] to slip their pigs. **1827** *Sport. Mag.* XXI. 38 My grey mare had slipped a fine horse foal.. and my best cow her calf. **1859** GEO. ELIOT *A. Bede* vi, The cheese may swell, or the cows may slip their calf.

******* **30.** *Shipbuilding.* To place (a boat) on a slip (SLIP *sb.*[3] 1 b) for inspection, repair, etc.

**1950** H. M. DENHAM in *Jrnl. R. Cruising Club 1949* 122, I got Korby slipped (only £4) and put on a coat of anti-fouling. **1964** *Roving Commissions 1903* 207 We crossed to Hermione in the hopes of finding a caique yard which would slip us for a reasonable fee to check up on the bump we received at Finike. **1975** R. BUTLER *Where all Girls are Sweeter* iii. 23 The boat looked new. Short of slipping her she was in prime condition.

**slip** (slɪp), *v.*[2] Also 6 slyppe. [a. MFlem. or MLG. *slippen* (LG. *slippen*, MSw. *slippa*; obs. G. *schlipfen*), to cut, incise, cleave, etc.]

†**1.** *trans.* To cut (a spoon-handle) obliquely at the end. *Obs.*

**1498** *Test. Ebor.* (Surtees) IV. 142, xij coclearia argentea, Slipped in lez stalkes. **1538** *Ibid.* VI. 81, ij spones of sylver slipped at the endes. **1549** *Inv. Edw. VI* in Jackson *Hist. Eng. Plate* (1911) 497 Fourtene Spones well gilt slipped at thendes.

**2.** To part (a slip or cutting) from a stock, stalk, or branch, esp. for the purpose of propagation; to divide (a plant, root, etc.) *into* slips.

**1530** PALSGR. 721/2, I slyppe an herbe a [? *read* or] stryke slyppes of it, or leaves from the stalke. **1597** *2nd Pt. Good Housew. Jewel* B viij, Put these..into an earthen pot with.. Time and rosemary slipped. **1615** W. LAWSON *Country Housew. Garden* (1626) 39 If he be little, slip him, and set him, perhaps he will take. **1669** WORLIDGE *Syst. Agric.* (1681) 157 The Branches also may be slipped and planted. **1731** *Gentl. Mag.* I. 93 Sow scorzonera salsfy, and slip skerrits of the last year's growth. **1786** ABERCROMBIE *Gard. Assist.* 273 Burnet—may be planted and slipped. **1808** *Ann. Reg., Chron.* 67 When the plant had tillered, I took it up, and slipped or divided it into four sets of slips.

*absol.* **1614** BRETON *I would & I would not* xxxviii, I would I were a Gardiner, and had skill To digge and rake, and plant, and sowe, and slippe.

**b.** With *off* or *from.* Also to cut, gather (a flower, etc.).

**1563** HYLL *Art Garden.* (1593) 107 Then do the Gardners slip them off from the greater stalkes. **1577** B. GOOGE *Heresbach's Husb.* II. (1586) 55 The branches being slipped off, and set in the spring. **1663** BP. GRIFFITH *Four Admirable Beasts* 20 We can slip a cluster of Grapes from a Vine. **1687** MIÈGE *Gt. Fr. Dict.* II, To slip off a Flower, *cueillir une Fleur.* **1766** *Compl. Farmer* s.v. *Skirrets*, The side roots should be slipped off with an eye or bud to each. **1790** *Trans. Soc. Arts* VIII. 81, I slipped off several off-sets from the heads of large plants. **1825** *Greenho. Comp.* II. 190 Leaves slipped off and planted in moist moss will root, and become plants.

**c.** In fig. contexts.

**1580** LYLY *Euphues* (Arb.) 367 When ye flower of their youth (being slipped too young) shall fade before they be olde. **1785** PALEY *Mor. Philos.* VI. i. (1818) II. 111 Every branch which was slipped off from the primitive stock.. would..take root, and grow into a separate clan.

†**3.** *Dicing.* (See quot.) *Obs.*

**1711** PUCKLE *The Club* 31 The Doctors, the Fulloms, Loaded Dice.., High-Slipt, Low-Slipt. [*Note.*] Dice with their Edges polish'd off, so as to make them run high... Ditto, so as to make them run low.

**slip,** *v.*[3] *rare*[−1]. [f. SLIP *sb.*[1] 4.] *trans.* To paint or ornament (pottery) with slip.

**1686** PLOT *Staffordsh.* 123 These also being dry, they then Slip or paint them with their several sorts of Slip.

**slip,** *v.*[4] [f. SLIP *sb.*[2]]

**1.** *trans.* To face *with* a slip of some material.

**1885** SPON *Mech. Own Book* 353 The shelves and divisions..are slipped with rosewood on the fore edges. *Ibid.* 373 The proper way is to 'slip' them with good mahogany, at least ¼ in. thick.

**2.** To note or enter upon a slip or slips.

**1895** *Westm. Gaz.* 15 May 7/2 He is sure to be near winning the first event for which he is 'slipped'. **1902** *Athenæum* 23 Aug. 256/1 Miss Betham-Edwards's new story..is being 'slipped' by Dr. Wright..for his 'Dialect Dictionary'.

**slip-.** The stem of SLIP *v.*[1] in combination, as:

**1. a. slip-bend** (see quot.); **slip-buoy,** a buoy attached to a cable when slipping an anchor; **slip-case,** a close-fitting box with one side open into which a book or books are placed for protection, while allowing the spine to remain visible; also, a similar case for gramophone records or photographic equipment; hence **slipcased** *a.*, contained in a box of this kind; **slip-coat,** ? a coat which slips on readily; **slip-cord,** a cord with a slip-knot made on it; **slip-cover** *U.S.* = *loose cover* s.v. LOOSE *a.* 9; hence as *v. trans.*, to cover with a slip-cover; **slip crew** *Aviation*, an aircrew stationed at an intermediate point or carried to take over the operation of an aeroplane on a long-distance flight; **slip edition,** a special (usu. local) edition of a newspaper, carrying news items not included in the main issue; **slip-finger,** *a.*, that has slippery fingers; in quot. *fig.*; **slip gauge** *Engin.*, a Johansson block (see JOHANSSON); **slip-gear,** a gear designed to slip if loaded above a predetermined limit; **slip-gibbet,** a scape-gallows (now *dial.*); †**slip-groat,** = SLIDE-GROAT; †**slip-halter,** = *slip-gibbet*; **slip-hook** (see quots.); **slip-horn,** a slide-trombone; **slip-jig,** some kind of dance; **slip joint,** (*a*) (see quots.); (*b*) a joint in a pipe, one section of which can move telescopically within another, to allow longitudinal expansion and contraction and so prevent damage by temperature changes or jolts; **slip-link** (see quots.); **slip-noose,** a noose which tightens and slackens by means of a slip-knot; **slip ring** *Electr. Engin.*, a ring of conducting material which is attached to and rotates with a shaft, so that electric current may be transferred to a stationary circuit through a fixed brush pressing against it; also *attrib.*; **slip road,** a short (usu. one-way) road giving access to or exit from a main highway, esp. a motorway; an approach road; **slip rope** (see quot.); **slip scraper** *U.S.*, a horse-drawn earth-moving device; **slip-screw, -shackle** (see quots.); **slip sheet** *Printing*, a sheet of paper interleaving newly printed sheets to prevent set-off or smudging; hence **slip-sheet** *v. trans.*, **slip-sheeting** *vbl. sb.*; **slip-shelled** *a.*, ? having the outer covering removed; †**slip-skin** *a.*, slippery, evasive; **slip sole** *Sc.*, **slip spear** (see quots.); †**slip-sprung** *a.*, illegitimately born; **slip-stitch** *sb.* (see quots.); hence ***slip-stitch*** vb., ***slip-stitcher***; †**slip-stocking,** ? a short stocking, a sock; **slip-stopper** (see quots.); **slip thong,** a thong which operates by means of a slip-knot; †**slip-thrift,** shovel-board; a spendthrift; cf. SLIDE-THRIFT; **slip winder** (see quot. 1921); also ***slip winding.***

Various other accidental or trivial combs. of this and the following types appear in recent use.

**1867** SMYTH *Sailor's Word-bk.* 633 **Slip-Bend*, when a man makes a false step, and slips down a hatchway, or overboard. **1798** CAPT. MILLER in Nicolas *Disp. Nelson* (1846) VII. p. clviii, We hove up to our best bower..and got a *slip buoy on the end of our sheet cable. **1930** A. E. NEWTON *This Bk.-Collecting Game* ii. 20 Many collectors, in binding their books or in having *slip cases made for them,..have their novels..in one colour, their poetry in another. **1942** W. STEVENS *Let.* 17 Sept. (1967) 420, I should like the general effect of the binding to be light... There should, of course, be a slip case. **1966** P. J. KAVANAGH *Perfect Stranger* xiii. 187 Why not put all three [volumes] into a slip-case..and sell them as a set? **1977** *Gramophone* May 1738/2 Decca have also made again available this month an integral recording of the five Beethoven Piano Concertos, previously issued in a slip-case but now in a box. **1979** *Amat. Photographer* Feb. 54/3 Both versions are supplied in a gift outfit with flash unit, slip case and wrist chain at a price of about £85. **1969** *Times* 15 Nov. p. iv/6 (Advt.), *Magellan's Voyage*.. 2 volumes *slipcased. **1978** *Amer. N. & Q.* Nov. 44/2 A handsome slip-cased volume..seems to be under-priced. **1562** PHAER *Æneid* IX. Cc ij, You must haue..gay ioly Jerkins, saffron shirts, Your *slipcoats must haue sleeues. **1847** W. C. L. MARTIN *The Ox* 166/1 Let the *slip-cords be applied to the fore-legs, and held by an assistant. **1886** *Home Decoration* 3 Apr. 79/1 The *slip covers for the furniture are of..toile. **1911** [see KLAXON *sb.*]. **1920** *T. Eaton & Co. Catal.* Spring & Summer 395/2 Slip Covers for Ford Cars... Set consists of cover for each seat and back of seats, doors, kicking pad for front seat and complete cover for hood. **1952** S. KAUFFMANN *Philanderer* (1953) iii. 36 Cora had, of course, made all the curtains, slip covers and bedspreads herself. **1965** T. CAPOTE *In Cold Blood* ii. 78 The couch.. that Nancy had slip-covered. **1978** T. GIFFORD *Glendower Legacy* 75 The slipcovers were wearing out at the arm. **1947** *Shell Aviation News* No. 112. 8/3 One of the most important problems is that of aircrew fatigue, and research on this question includes investigation into..provision of '*slip' crews at strategic points, facilities for crew rest in aircraft. **1973** C. EGLETON *Seven Days to Killing* xix. 196 The RAF are not carrying a slip crew on this trip. They would need to rest before the return flight. **1961** 'B. WELLS' *Day Earth caught Fire* iii. 39 This is terrific stuff. We'll have a *slip edition. **1975** T. ALLBEURY *Palomino Blonde* iv. 12 Issues of the *Northumberland Gazette* with slip editions for Morpeth and Berwick. **1848** *Fraser's Mag.* XXXVIII. 428 The empty, tattered Past,..the greased *slipfinger Present. **1919** *Engineering* 11 July 33/3 The minimeter for comparing *slip gauges to an accuracy of one-millionth of an inch is another of the new precision instruments. **1971** B. SCHARF *Engin. & its Language* vii. 47 In order to combine two slip gauges, they are slid together with slight pressure. **1897** E. K. SCOTT *Local Distribution of Electric Power in Workshops* 53 The current at starting a heavy lift can be materially reduced by having a *slip gear or belt, so as to enable the motor to get up speed. **1930** *Engineering* 4 Apr. 431/2 An electric motor fitted with a centrifugal clutch and slip-gear. **1785** GROSE *Dict. Vulgar T.* s.v. *Scapegallows*, A *slip gibbet, one for whom the gallows is said to groan. **1521** in Inderwick *Cal. Inner Temple Rec.* (1896) 63 [None of the society shall play within the Inn at the game called] shoffe boorde [or] *slypgrote. **1659** *Lady Alimony* IV. vi, As I hope for mercy, I am half-persuaded that this *slip-halter has pawned my clothes. **1863** A. YOUNG *Naut. Dict.* 356 **Slip hook*..is 'especially useful on shipboard in securing and slipping towing cables, etc.' **1875** KNIGHT *Dict. Mech.* 2212/1 [The] Slip-hook..may be disengaged or *slipped* by the motion of a trigger, a sliding ring, or otherwise. **1923** G. MCKNIGHT *Eng. Words & their Background* iv. 45 **Sliphorn*, trombone. **1938** D. BAKER *Young Man with Horn* III. i. 120 He doesn't play a valve trombone either, just a regular slip-horn. **1957** *Melody Maker* 4 May 6/2 Wilbur himself was somewhat subdued, using both slip-horn and valve, but what he did was pleasant trombone. **1829** G. GRIFFIN *Collegian* I. ii. 19 Eily was dancing with a strange young gentleman..and..he would not let her go until she had finished the *slip jig. **1895** *Cath. News* 13 July 2/3 He would not let her go until she had finished the slip jig. *a* **1966** 'M. NA GOPALEEN' *Best of Myles* (1968) 284 The lads who believe that in slip-jigs we have a national prophylaxis make life less stark. **1876** PREECE & SIVEWRIGHT *Telegraphy* 234 If the pipes are iron, one of them has to be broken; where this is unavoidable a *slip joint is afterwards employed to protect it—that is to say, two half pipes..are placed one over and the other under the break; they are screwed together and the ends tightly packed. **1930** WALKER & CROCKER *Piping Handbk.* vii. 504 Slip joints are used very extensively in water and saturated-steam lines. **1972** L. M. HARRIS *Introd. Deepwater Floating Drilling Operations* ii. 6 Slip joints compensate for vertical motion in the lower section of the drill string. **1875** KNIGHT *Dict. Mech.* 2212/1 **Slip-link*, a connecting link which allows a certain freedom of motion. **1837** *Slip noose [see LASSO *sb.* 1]. **1847** W. C. L. MARTIN *The Ox* 166/1 It may be necessary to put a slip noose on each fore limb. **1897** G. C. BATEMAN *Vivarium* 225 A properly-contrived slip-noose. **1896** S. P. THOMPSON *Dynamo-Electric Machinery* (ed. 4) iii. 35 There must..be sliding contacts to maintain the coils of the revolving field-magnet part in continuous metallic connexion with the auxiliary exciting circuit. In either case the appropriate device consists of a pair of *slip rings, against each of which a brush presses. **1958** *Times Rev. Industry* Feb. 46/1 Automatic starting of slip-ring electric motors has always presented many problems. **1974** *Physics Bull.* May 204/2 Special emphasis is placed on the study of aluminium as a contact material in place of copper for sliprings and commutators. **1953** *Times* 11 Feb. 3/3 A '*slip-road' a mile and a half long..would draw away from the narrow streets of High Barnet the great number of heavy lorries now passing through this congested centre. **1968** W. GARNER *Deep, Deep Freeze* iii. 36 He took the slip road on to the *Autobahn.* **1979** A. PRICE *Tomorrow's Ghost* ii. 17 He waited to leave the slip-road for the motorway proper. **1750** BLANCKLEY *Naval Expos.* 136 *Slip Ropes for triseing up the Bites of the Cable to the Rails of the Head. **1846** A. YOUNG

*Naut. Dict.* 287 *Slip-rope*, a rope bent to any thing in such a manner that it may be slipped when required. **1909** *Man. Seamanship* (Admiralty) II. III. ix. 177 If there is much strain on the slip rope, it should be eased before letting it go. **1964** Slip rope [see HONDA]. **1934** *Sun* (Baltimore) 9 Nov. 15/3 Ringle, while clearing loose dirt with the aid of a horse and *slip scraper, lost his footing and fell. **1942** W. FAULKNER *Go down, Moses* 113 Throwing dirt..faster than a slip scraper could have done it. **1879** *Cassell's Techn. Educ.* IV. 117/1 A '*slip-screw', viz., one in which the threads do not bite, and the screw turns round in its receptacle. **1867** SMYTH *Sailor's Word-bk.* 633 **Slip-Shackle*, a shackle with a lever-bolt, for letting go suddenly; yet, when ringed, is sufficient to secure the ship. **1917** F. S. HENRY *Printing for School & Shop* xiv. 237 Never use enameled paper for *slipsheets, or the sheets will stick together. **1924** —— *Essent. Printing* x. 149 While an expert feeder can sometimes do his own *slipsheeting, it is customary to have an assistant place the slipsheets as the printed sheets are stacked on the feedboard. **1949** MELCHER & LARRICK *Printing & Promotion Handbk.* 279/2 This slip sheeting assures a clean job of mimeographing where it is necessary to print on non-absorbent paper. **1957** JACKSON & CLEVERDON *Printing* III. 139/2 Clean unprinted newspaper..makes good slip sheets. **1967** V. STRAUSS *Printing Industry* vii. 516/2 In two-sided printing..it may be necessary to 'slip-sheet' the job. (Slip-sheeting means that a sheet of waste paper is inserted after each printed sheet. When the ink is dry the slip sheets are removed.) **1826** HONE *Every-day Bk.* II. 1352 Walnuts *slip-shelled are heaped in a basket. **1641** MILTON *Animadv.* Wks. 1851 III. 205 A pretty *slip-skin conveyance to sift Masse into no Masse, and Popish into not Popish. **1887** *Archit. Soc. Dict.* VII. 90 **Slip Sole*, the term in some parts of Scotland for a step. **1883** GRESLEY *Gloss. Coal-m.* 227 **Slip Spear*, a tool for extracting tubing from a borehole. **1665** MANLEY *Grotius' Low-C. Wars* 21 Altogether forgetful ..that they preferred before him a Bastard, *slip-sprung from an unlawful coition. **1872** *Young Englishwoman* Oct. 558/1 Work 2 *slip-stitches on the first 2 chain. **1882** CAULFEILD & SAWARD *Dict. Needlwk.* 125/1 *Slip Stitch*, a stitch much used in Raised Crochet, both in joining together detached sprays, and in passing from one part of a pattern to another at the back of the work. **1932** D. C. MINTER *Mod. Needlecraft* 92/2 *Single Crochet* (*or Slip-stitch*)..is used for making a very narrow row. **1951** *Good Housek. Home Encycl.* 58/1 Tack, and slip-stitch by hand. **1964** *McCall's Sewing* ii. 32/1 *Slip-stitch*, tiny hand-stitches taken through and under a fold of fabric where the stitching must be invisible. **1897** *Westm. Gaz.* 4 Feb. 3/3 The silk should be turned over on the right side and *slip-stitched. **1896** *Daily Chron.* 7 Aug. 10/7 Ties.—Good *slipstitchers for derbys, outdoors. **1673** HICKERINGILL *Greg. F. Greybeard* 242 Plung'd themselves into perplexities, or into Parson *slip-stockins extravagancies. *a* **1680** BUTLER in D'Urfey *Pills* (1719) III. 334 Slip-stocking Similitudes. **1698** COLLIER *Immor. Stage* ii. 60 This lady's fancy is just slip-stocking-high, and she seems to want sense more than her breakfast. **1831** *Ann. Reg.* LXXIII. 445 The apparatus [for releasing the life-buoy] is kept in place by what is called a *slip-stopper, a sort of catch-bolt, which can be unlocked at pleasure, by merely pulling a trigger. *c* **1860** H. STUART *Seaman's Catech.* 54 The slip stopper..is used for stoppering the cable,..to prevent the cables running out of the hawse-hole. **1799** *Monthly Rev.* XXX. 367 All carry lances, which, when on horseback, by means of a *slip thong, they sling to a rest in the stirrup. **1579** RICE *Invective agst. Vices* B ij b, What to dooe there? To Bowle, or to plaie at Dise, or Cardes, Penipricke, or *slipthrift? **1621** GRANGER *Eccles.* 273 Thus it is in the house of prodigals, drinking slipthrifts, and Belials. **1921** *Dict. Occup. Terms* (1927) §371 **Slip winder*; winds silk threads, for use in lace making, from hanks or cops on to spools or bobbins. **1976** *Evening Post* (Nottingham) 16 Dec. 17/5 (Advt.), Wanted male or female experienced slip winder (cone to spool). **1940** *Chambers's Techn. Dict.* 778/2 **Slip winding* (Textiles), the process of transferring yarn from a hank to flanged bobbins in lace manufacture.

**b.** Applied generally to devices that may be slipped or slid aside, back, in, out, etc., or to things provided with these, as ***slip-bar*** (***-gate***), ***-board***, ***-bottom***, ***coffin***, ***-coupling***, ***-door***, ***-feather***, ***-feathering***, ***gap***, ***ladder***, ***-lid***, ***-panel***, ***-ring***, ***-shave***. Also SLIP-RAIL.

**1805** R. W. DICKSON *Pract. Agric.* I. 143 The **slip-bar-gate* is a form of gate often used. **1726** SWIFT *Gulliver* II. viii, I..ventured to draw back the *slip-board on the roof. **1854** H. MILLER *Sch. & Schm.* (1858) 285 In square wicker-work panniers with *slip-bottoms. **1900** J. J. VERNON *Parish of Hawick 1711–1725*, 167 Interring tramps..by means of 'a *slip coffin', *i.e.*, a coffin which upon being lowered..by ropes attached to it, could be recovered, the body being left in the grave. **1844** H. STEPHENS *Bk. Farm* III. 927 The spindle may be attached to another shaft..by means of a *slip-coupling. **1764** LLOYD *Actor* Poet. Wks. 1774 I. 19 But in stage customs what offends me most Is the *slip-door, and slowly-rising ghost. **1881** *Mechanic* §444. 194 The *slip feather that is to be pressed into the grooves to hold the boards. *Ibid.* 193 The modes..adopted for this juncture of pieces of wood are..known respectively as rebating,.. grooving and *slip feathering [etc.]. **1859** BARTLETT *Dict. Amer.* 167 A **Slip gap* is a place provided in a fence, where the bars may be slipped aside and let down. **1795** HOLCROFT in Kegan Paul *W. Godwin* (1876) I. 149, I fell from a *slip ladder, and broke it fairly in two. **1938** *Shelf Appeal* July 26/2 The *slip-lid tin was evolved rather over fifty years ago. **1979** *Gloss. Packaging Terms* (*B.S.I.*) II. 8 *Slip lid*, a lid that fits over the mouth of the container body. **1864** ELIZ. MURRAY *Ella Norman* I. 161 Jock..rode on, until he came to some *slip panels; these he let down. **1881** A. C. GRANT *Bush Life Queensland* II. xxviii. 107 His step, as he bowled up to the slip-panel, was brisk and energetic. **1742** A. MONRO in *Med. Ess. Edinb.* V. 455 A Spring which keeps the Handles [of a needle-holder] asunder..till the *Slip-ring or Slider is thrust towards the End of the Handles. **1884** KNIGHT *Dict. Mech.* Suppl. 823/2 **Slip Shave*, a point or shave made to slip over the nose of the mold-board.

**c.** In the sense 'detached, or intended to be detached, from a railway train while running', as ***slip-carriage***, ***-coach***, ***-compartment***, ***-portion***. Hence ***slip-guard***, the guard of such a carriage, etc. Also in connection with other vehicles and craft, as **slip-tank**, a fuel tank that may be jettisoned from an aircraft when empty.

**1869** *Echo* 23 Aug., A 'slip' carriage placed in the rear of the train, which is dropped at Hatfield. **1884** *G. W. R. Time Tables* July 33 Slip Coach detached at Bridgewater. **1898** *Daily News* 11 Oct. 8/1 Entering the slip compartment, one finds little to differentiate it from a small guard's van. *Ibid.*, Where the detached slip-portion has collided with the train it has just left. **1920** *Flight* XII. 957/1 Seventeen tanks may be readily slipped overboard to act as ballast. These slip-tanks have no bottom connections, and petrol is drawn from them by means of a semi-rotary pump. **1932** G. GREENE *Stamboul Train* I. i. 8 The party..belonged to the slip-coach for Athens. **1978** *Lancs. Life* Apr. 52/2 The L & Y..brought in slip coaches, notably at Rochdale where two trains from Bradford to Manchester unhitched the back two coaches without stopping.

**2.** In comb. with advs., as **slip-along** *a.*, slipshod; **slip-down** *dial.* (see quot. 1828); **slip-in** *a.*, admitting of a person or thing slipping in, or being slipped in, easily or readily; **slip-on**, something that may be slipped or put on readily, *esp.* (formerly) a great-coat or overall, (*U.S.*) a glove, and now usu. a shoe; also *attrib.* or as *adj.*; **slip-out** *a.*, that one may slip out of in a convenient manner; **slip-over** *a.*, of a garment: made without an opening at the front, and to be slipped on over the head; hence as *sb.* (usu. one word), a sweater or pullover, usu. with a V-neck and no sleeves; **slip-up**, the act of slipping up (see SLIP *v.*[1] 8 d), a failure, mistake, blunder.

**1849** MAITLAND *Reformation Eng.* xx. 559 It would be less worth while to read Fox's *slip-along stories. **1828** CARR *Craven Gloss.*, **Slip-down*, old milk, a little curdled, which readily slips down the throat. **1859** SALA *Gaslight & D.* xxii. 252 He knows all the *slip-in and slip-out public-houses in London. **1906** *Westm. Gaz.* 1 Dec. 18/2 Both slip-in and paste-on mounts, upon which the photographs can be mounted with the minimum of trouble. **1815** [MRS. JOHNSTONE] *Clan-Albyn* xiii. (1853) 66 Hugh flung his *slip-on around him. **1904** *Ladies Field* 14 May 426/1 The 'Slip-on' coat for all weathers. **1920** *T. Eaton & Co. Catal.* Spring & Summer 395/3 Running Board Mat. Fastened with patent slip-on fasteners. **1923** *Ibid.* 214/3 One of the smartest of the new models [of coat]..a double-breasted 'slip-on', with yoke. **1938** [see SCUFF *sb.*[1] 4]. **1949** *Sun* (Baltimore) 8 Sept. 5/1 (Advt.), Wear Right gloves... Shorties and slipons all hand-sewn. **1956** *People* 13 May 3/7 (Advt.), Slip-on Casual. Brown Willow uppers, leather sole. **1959** *Wall St. Jrnl.* 13 Dec. (Eastern ed.) 17/4 'Slim slip-ons', or dressy shoes without laces, will be promoted for men. **1965** *N.Y. Times* 9 Dec. 5 (Advt.), Hand-in-Glove with fashion:..Elbow-deep slipons. **1972** J. BALL *Five Pieces of Jade* xiv. 178 Tibbs..noted the slip-on shoes which ..could be shed within a second or two. **1978** L. CHARTERIS *Saint in Trouble* (1979) I. iii. 33 His eyes..started with the suede slip-ons, journeyed up..the light grey suit. **1982** BARR & YORK *Official Sloane Ranger Handbk.* 33/2 These are smart tough slip-ons, in black or dark blue patent or leather, with a chunky heel and gilt snaffle or chain across the top. **1859** *Slip-out [see *slip-in* above]. **1919–20** *T. Eaton & Co. Catal.* Fall & Winter 153/3 *Slip-over Nightgown. **1923** *Daily Mail* 6 Mar. 1 (Advt.), Elastic bust bodice of special value, slip-over shape. **1936** *Times* 10 Jan. 7/4 Bargains for men include poplin shirts at 9s. 6d. and all wool slip-overs at 10s. **1941** *Picture Post* 3 May 32/1 Pullovers, Slipovers, and Beach Shirts for men and boys. **1945** *Richmond* (Va.) *Times-Dispatch* 9 Jan. 16 (Advt.), All-wool slipover sweater. **1962** *Punch* 26 Sept. p. xvii, Burberrys have..reversible alpaca slip-overs. **1981** *Times* 6 Jan. 12/7 According to numerous shop window displays observed during the current sales, the garment I have always called a pullover is now known as a slipover. **1909** *N.Y. Even. Post* (semi-weekly ed.) 30 Sept. 1 Should there be any *slip-up in the present plans. **1948** 'G. ORWELL' *Let.* 21 Dec. in *Coll. Essays* (1968) IV. 459, I suppose there *may* be some slip-up, but if not my address..will be The Cotswold Sanatorium. **1978** H. JOBSON *To die a Little* ii. 26, I..had a slight feeling of apprehension... Had there been some legal slip-up?

**slip-cheese, -curd**: see SLIP *sb.*[1] 2 b.

**slip-cloth.** Also slip cloth.

**1.** A coat used to protect a coursing-dog while in the slips.

**1856** 'STONEHENGE' *Brit. Rur. Sports* I. III. vii. 200/2 These particular patterns are called 'slip cloths'. [Description follows.]

**2.** A narrow cloth used to protect a table-cloth, table, or side-board.

**1889** 'J. S. WINTER' *Mrs. Bob* (1891) 209 They dine on the table with slip-cloths. **1899** *Daily News* 23 Dec. 6/2 Then on the white slip cloths the dishes can be laid.

**slip-coat.** [Cf. SLIP *sb.*[1] 2 b.] A kind of soft cream-cheese. Chiefly in ***slip-coat cheese***.

*a* **1648** DIGBY *Closet Opened* (1669) 270 My Lady of Middlesex makes excellent slipp-coat cheese of good morning milk, putting cream to it. **1682** HARTMAN *Direct. Cookery* 53 To make slip-coat cheese, as Sir Kenelm's house-keeper made them for him. **1736** BAILEY *Household Dict.* s.v. *Cheese*, To make slip Coat Cheese otherwise call'd Cream Cheese. **1784** TWAMLEY *Dairying Exemp.* 58 The way to make soft Cheese, or slip-coat Cheese. **1858** SIMMONDS *Dict. Trade*, *Slip-coat*, new-made cheese; a small and very rich variety of Yorkshire cheese, not unlike butter but white.

**slipe** (slaɪp), *sb.*[1] *Sc.* and *north.* Also 5 *Sc.* slyp, 6 slype. [app. a. LG. *slîpe* (cf. MSw. *slipa* to drag, draw), var. of the usual *slêpe*, = MHG. *sleife* (G. *schleife*) sledge, train, loop, knot, etc., related to LG. *slîpen* to whet, and *slêpen* to drag (see *Grimm's Wbch.* s.v. *schleifen*).]

For various dialect uses see the *Eng. Dial. Dict.*

**1.** A sledge or drag.

*c* **1470** HENRY *Wallace* IX. 1625 He..Graithyt him a drawcht, on a braid slyp and law. *Ibid.* 1633 To ground the slyp can ga. **1489** *Acc. Ld. High Treas. Scot.* I. 124 Item, to Will, wryth, that past to bryng the bott fra the Blaknes and makyng of hir slyp, iiij li. **1739** SIR J. CLERK in *Mem. W. Stukeley* (Surtees) II. 92 [At Whitehaven] the Coal when brought up to the level of the sea, is putt on slips [? *read* slipes], and conveyed into the cavity of a hill. **1756** MRS. CALDERWOOD *Jrnl.* (1884) 64 A great many things they carry on slipes, for instance barrells. They have slipes of a great length. **1807** *Ann. Reg.* 868 A sledge without poles, moved by drag-ropes, and termed a slipe. **1860** *Eng. & Foreign Mining Gloss.* (ed. 2) 79 *Slipes*, the sledges at the bottom of the skip, used to draw the coals upon. **1880–** in *Eng. Dial. Dict.* (Sc., Irel.).

**b.** Part of a plough (see quots.).

**1616** SURFL. & MARKHAM *Country Farme* V. vi. 532 Then the slipe to keep the plow from wearing. **1831** J. HOLLAND *Manuf. Metal* I. 157 The sole or under plate, and the curved side or slipe, formerly called the earth-board,..are of iron or cast metal. **1877** *N.W. Linc. Gloss.*, *Slipe*, the flat sheet of iron on the land or left side of a plough. **1891** in *Sheffield Gloss.* Suppl.

**c.** *Mining.* (See quots.)

**1860** *Eng. & Foreign Mining Gloss.* (ed. 2) 44 *Slipes*, flat pieces of iron for the corves to slide on. **1881** RAYMOND *Mining Gloss.*, *Slipes*,..sledge-runners, upon which a skip is dragged from the working breast to the tramway.

†**2. a.** ? A flap or lappet. **b.** A noose or halter. *Obs.*

**1540** *Test. Ebor.* (Surtees) VI. 113 My bonnet with slipes. **1587** *Shuttleworth Acc.* (Chetham Soc.) 41 A corde to make slypes for horsies to tye them in, v[d].

**slipe**, *sb.*[2] Now *dial.* (and *U.S.*). Also 6 slype. [Of obscure origin: cf. SLIP *sb.*[2] and SLYPE *sb.*] A slip or slice; a long narrow piece or strip. Also *fig.* (quot. 1597).

**1538** LELAND *Itin.* (1769) VII. 72 A Soyle Champayne on every Syde, in the whiche as in Slypes, were some prety Groves and Woods. **1597** HOOKER *Eccl. Pol.* V. lxxviii. §5 (1611) 420 Deuiding their charge into slipes, and ordaining of vnder-officers. **1624** *Maldon Borough Deeds* (Bundle 108 fol. 3), One kitchin or building (with a little Slipe of ground therunto in Al S[cts.] parish). **1854** in MISS BAKER *Northampt. Gloss.* **1876–** in *Eng. Dial. Dict.* (Cumb., Yks., Bedf., Som.). **1896** *Amer. Dial. Notes* I. 66 (E.D.D.), Cut me a slipe of bacon.

†**slipe**, *sb.*[3] *Obs.*[−1] [? var. of SLIP *sb.*[1]] (See quot.)

**1716** *Phil. Trans.* XXIX. 472 The Cliffs consist of great ragged Sand-Stones till we come to near a Yard..of the Bottom; then we meet with what they call a Slipe, *i.e.* a slippery sort of Clay always wet.

**slipe** (slaɪp), *sb.*[4] [f. SLIPE *v.*[2]] A certain quality of skin-wool.

**1856** *Farmer's Mag.* Nov. 448 Silesian slipes and skins in bundles. **1889** *Daily News* 12 Dec. 2/4 Bales marked with the names of the stations upon which the wool was grown, or the breed of sheep, such as 'Bridgwater Cheviot, Lincoln Slipes', &c.

†**slipe**, *v.*[1] *Obs.* In 4–5 slype. [a. MDu. *slîpen* (Du. *slijpen*) or MLG. *slîpen* (LG. *slîpen*, Sw. *slipa*, Da. *slibe*), = OHG. *slîfan* (G. *schleifen*) to whet, etc.] *trans.* To make smooth, to polish; to whet or sharpen.

**1390** GOWER *Conf.* II. 347 His mouth upon the gras he wypeth, And so with feigned chiere him slypeth. **1390** *Earl Derby's Exped.* (Camden) 46 Pro slypyng gladiorum domini. **1471** RIPLEY *Comp. Alch.* VI. xxvii. in Ashm. (1652) 167 Whych lyke a sworde new slypyd then wyll shyne. **1490** CAXTON *Eneydos* xxviii. 107 A swerde well sharpe slyped, myghte haue broughte the two susters to deth bothe atones.

**slipe**, *v.*[2] Now *dial.* Also 4 slype. [Of obscure origin. For the various dialect uses see the *Eng. Dial. Dict.*]

**1.** *trans.* To strip, peel, skin; to take *off* by peeling or stripping, etc.

? *c* **1390** *Form of Cury* in Warner *Culin. Antiq.* (1791) 5 Take the whyte of lekes, slype hem, and shrede hem small. **1781** J. HUTTON *Tour to Caves* (ed. 2) Gloss. 96 *Slipe*, to strip off the skin or bark of any thing. **1788** W. H. MARSHALL *Yorksh.* II. 353 To *Slipe off*, to draw off superficially; as skin from the body, bark from a tree, &c. **1824–** in dial. glossaries, etc. (Sc. and northern).

**2.** *intr.* To fall *over* softly.

**1786** BURNS *To Auld Mare* xii, Till spritties knowes wad rair't an' risket, Au' slypet owre.

†**slipe**, *v.*[3] *Obs.*[−1] In 5 slype. (Meaning not clear.)

*a* **1500** MEDWALL *Nature* (Brandl) I. 1072 Than shall hys hosen be stryped, Wyth corselettys of fyne veluet slyped Down to the hard kne.

**sliper**, obs. f. SLIPPER *a.*; see also SWORD-SLIPER.

**slip form.** *Engin.* Also slip-form, slipform. [f. SLIP *v.*[1]] A mould open at both ends in which a structure of uniform cross-section is cast by filling it with concrete and continually moving and refilling it as the concrete sets. Freq. *attrib.* with reference to this technique of construction, esp. as ***slipform*** (***concrete***) ***paver***, a machine which continually forms the concrete surface of a road or the like by this technique.

**1958** *Construction Methods & Equipment* Aug. 72/2 Slip-form placing of concrete reduced material and manpower requirements to a fraction of what they might have been with timber forms and scaffolding. *Ibid.* 73/2 The contractor supported slip forms with a number of steel yokes. **1963** *Contractors & Engineers* Jan. 40/4 Slip-form pavers are shorter this year... The early slip-form machines, with 40 to 60 feet of sliding form, amazed many people. **1964** [see FORM *sb.* 18 b]. **1974** *Sci. Amer.* Dec. 145/1 The road itself, that great ribbon of concrete, is being placed by the slip-form paver, which spreads, smooths, levels, cuts the edges squarely and even finishes the surface. **1975** *Offshore* Sept. 147/1 The steel slipform is guided on rails cast into the interior surface of the cylinder wall.

Hence **'slipform** *v. trans.*, to cast by this technique; **'slipformed** *ppl. a.* **'slipforming** *vbl. sb.*

**1968** J. J. WADDELL *Concrete Construction Handbk.* xxxiv. 1 The ultimate approach in incorporating a slipform into building construction is to slipform all vertical concrete. *Ibid.*, Slipforming is a faster method of construction than conventional forming. *Ibid.* 2 Slipformed-concrete. **1975** *Offshore* Sept. 147/1 Tests are complete on the slip-forming of inclined legs for a deepwater concrete platform. **1981** *Times* 12 Mar. 3/6 The contractors are slip forming 2,000 metres of double track. This track-laying method was first used in 1967.

**slip-in**: see SLIP- 2.

**slip-knot** ('slɪpnɒt). Also **slip knot**. [f. SLIP *v.*[1]]
**a.** A knot which may readily be slipped or untied. **b.** A knot so constructed as to slip along the cord or line round which it is made; a running knot; also, a noose.

**1659** TORRIANO, *Cáppio*, a slipknot that may be untied. **1679** MOXON *Mech. Exerc.* VII. 126 They .. fasten the rest of the Line there, upon the Line Rowl with a Slip-knot, that no more Line turn off. **1710** *Managers' Pro & Con* 40 They labour to make the Crown hang upon Her Head, only by that Slipknot of Hereditary Right. **1760** STERNE *Tr. Shandy* III. x, Knots,—by which .. I would not be understood to mean slip-knots. **1827** D. JOHNSON *Ind. Field Sports* 55 Elephants .. are caught in Nepaul .. by *phauns* (nooses made with slip knots). **1847** W. C. L. MARTIN *The Ox* 166/1 By dexterous manipulation, the slip-knot of a cord may be fastened round each leg. **1888** *Archæol. Rev.* Mar. 25 The youngest of these princesses is caught while bathing, by means of a magical slip-knot.
*transf.* **1842** T. MOORE *Jrnl.* Sept. 14 in *Mem. Thomas Moore* (1856) VII. 330 Had already formed a sort of slip-knot with Easthope to dine at his country house, but he had luckily put me off till to-morrow. **1863** COWDEN CLARKE *Shaks. Charac.* v. 135 A free woman of the world,.. retaining her virtue only by a slip-knot. **1888** *Harper's Mag.* July 320/2 Hasty marriages—slip-knots tied by one justice to be undone by another.

**slip-on**: see SLIP- 2.

**slippage** ('slɪpɪdʒ). [f. SLIP *v.*[1] + -AGE.]
**1. a.** The act of slipping or subsiding. **b.** Amount or extent of slip.

**1850** MALLET in *Rep. Brit. Assoc.* I. 61 The sudden slippage under water of large masses of submarine banks of sand or mud. **1898** T. THORNLEY *Draw & Fly Frames* 71 This, of course, is the effect produced by slippage of cone belt alone.

**2.** *Mech.* The difference between the expected and the actual output of a system.

**1905** W. ROGERS *Pumps & Hydraulics* II. 384 Pump slip or slippage represents the difference between the calculated and the actual discharge of a pump. **1936** *Kent's Mech. Engineers' Handbk.* (ed. 11) II. I. 41 Actual Volumetric Efficiency/Indicated Volumetric Efficiency = Slippage Efficiency [of an air compressor]. This is the ratio of the volume of measured air delivered to the apparent volume shown by the indicator diagram.

**3.** *transf.* and *fig.* Falling away from a standard; the measure of this. *spec.* with reference to (*a*) failure to meet a deadline or fulfil a promise, delay; (*b*) loss of public esteem, of a candidate for office in popularity ratings; (*c*) *Econ.*, decline in value.

**1920** in WEBSTER. **1960** *Washington Post* 1 Jan. A16 It is almost as if a deliberate decision had been taken to accept second-place status. This continued slippage also affects starkly the challenges that lie ahead. **1960** *Guardian* 13 May 10/5 The failure (or 'slippage' as delays are now called) of their 400-mile anti-aircraft missile. **1968** *Ibid.* 22 Aug. 9/7 The latest Gallup poll .. shows that Nixon would get 45 per cent of the votes compared with Humphrey's 29 per cent. That is an astonishing slippage for the Vice-President. **1970** *Nature* 13 June 1011/2 ESRO's biggest project .. is the half-ton TD1 astronomy satellite which was to have been launched in spring 1972, although some slippage now seems likely. **1972** *Guardian* 1 Nov. 12/2 British living standards could be eroded by a continued slippage of sterling. **1976** *Times* 20 Apr. 13/3 There is widespread concern among parents that standards of achievement and behaviour in schools have been allowed, if not to collapse, at least to slip. .. This apparent slippage has taken place at the time when the number of comprehensive schools has increased rapidly. **1980** M. LEE *Govt. by Pen* 211 His health had been giving way, and there were signs of mental slippage. **1982** *Sunday Times* 10 Oct. 54/3 Given the traditional slippage that occurs in the timetable on such projects, the company will not know at the outset just when it will have to draw down the cash for each stage payment.

**slipped** (slɪpt), *ppl. a.*[1] [f. SLIP *v.*[1]] **1.** That has been let go, cast off, etc.; that has slipped or slid down.

**1649** G. DANIEL *Trinarch., Hen. V*, ccxxxii, Singlie Slipt Greyhounds chase Whole-Burnish't Herds. **1820** SCOTT *Abbot* x, I will leave them the slipp'd collar in their hands on the first opportunity. **1829** J. PHILLIPS *Geol. Yks.* 98 The bay beyond is overhung by a broken slipped cliff. **1840** J. GAUGAIN *Lady's Assistant* 11 Take in back stitch of three, by slipping off backwards without working the first, .. lift over the first slipped one over the taken-in loop. **1872** *Young Englishwoman* Nov. 607/1 In decreasing .. a stitch may be slipped, the following stitch knitted and the slipped stitch drawn over it. **1926**, etc. [see SLIP *v.*[1] 26 e]. **1958** J. NORBURY *Knitting Adventure* i. 15 Purl slipped stitch from cable needle.

**2.** *slipped disc*, an intervertebral disc that is ruptured or injured, causing pain in the back or (if nerve roots are compressed) in other parts of the body. *colloq.*

**1953** E. SIMON *Past Masters* III. 142 The slipped disk everybody nowadays is suffering from. **1959** *Listener* 10 Sept. 397/3 Achondroplasic breeds [of dogs] are also more apt to develop so-called 'slipped discs'. **1972** J. MINIFIE *Homesteader* x. 79 God help the farmer who 'pulled his back', as they used to say before 'slipped disc' became the fashionable term. **1974** PASSMORE & ROBSON *Compan. Med. Stud.* III. xxv. 56/2 If a load exceeds the ultimate tolerance of a disc .. the nucleus may be forced through the annulus or cause it to bulge locally, a condition known as ruptured or prolapsed or slipped disc.

**slipped** (slɪpt), *ppl. a.*[2] [f. SLIP *v.*[2]]
†**1.** Cut obliquely. *Obs.*

**1618** in Cripps *Old Eng. Plate* (1901) 281 Spoons with slipped ends.

**2.** *Her.* Of plants, etc., used as charges: Represented as torn off from the stem.

**1610** GUILLIM *Heraldry* III. x, The field is Sable, three Lilies slipped. *Ibid.*, He beareth .. three Gilliflowers Slipped. **1797** *Encycl. Brit.* (ed. 3) VIII. 448/1 Gules on a Bend Argent, three Trefoils slipped proper. **1864** BOUTELL *Her. Hist. & Pop.* xi. 70 [Trees are] slipped, when irregularly broken or torn off. **1868** CUSSANS *Heraldry* vi. (1893) 106 The Trefoil is usually blazoned as *Stalked* and *Slipped*... *Slipped*, applied to a plant, is the same as *Erased* to the limb of an animal.

**slipped** (slɪpt), *ppl. a.*[3] [f. SLIP *v.*[3]] Painted or ornamented with slip.

**1914** *Oxf. Univ. Gaz.* 11 Mar. 574 A boar's head in slipped painted ware of Late Hittite date. **1976** *Nature* 15 Apr. 581/2 This pottery includes sophisticated slipped wares.

**slipper** ('slɪpə(r)), *sb.* Also 5 sclypper, 5–6 slyppar, -er; 6 slep(p)er. [f. SLIP *v.*[1] + -ER[1].]
**I. 1. a.** A light and usually heelless covering for the foot, capable of being easily slipped on, and chiefly employed for indoor wear.

**1478** *Paston Lett.* III. 237, ij. schyrtes, and a peyer of sclyppers. **1479** *Ibid.* 240 In the whyche letter was viij *d.* with the whyche I schuld bye a peyer of slyppers. *c* **1496** *Sermo pro Episcopo puerorum* (W. de W.) b iij, Euyll fasshened garmentes & deuyllysshe shoon & slyppers of frens-men. **1509** BARCLAY *Shyp of Folys* (1570) 85 Some with their slippers to and fro doth praunce, Clapping with their heeles in Church and in queare. **1576** FLEMING *Panopl. Epist.* 405 You should .. come tripping to mee in your silcken sleppers. **1607** DEKKER & MARSTON *Northw. Hoe* III. D.'s Wks. 1873 III. 41 What a filthy knaue was the shoo-maker, that made my slippers, what a creaking they keepe. **1687** A. LOVELL tr. *Thevenot's Trav.* I. 30 Their Shoes are of the same colour, and made almost like Slippers. **1716** LADY MONTAGU *Lett.* I. i. 8, I walked almost all over the town .. in my slippers, without receiving one spot of dirt. **1756** tr. *Keysler's Trav.* (1760) I. 444 Within the altar is kept a slipper of his of red velvet, with a very low heel. **1819** BYRON *Juan* II. cxxi, Her small snow feet had slippers, but no stocking. **1859** DICKENS *Tale Two Cities* II. v, He had his slippers on, and a loose bed-gown.

**b.** In phrases, etc. See also *hunt the slipper* s.v. HUNT *v.* 14 b, and LADY'S SLIPPER.

? *c* **1570** [JEFFERIES] *Bugbears* IV. v, I cannot [tell] what you cal being with child: She hath trode her slipper awrie. **1625** BP. MOUNTAGU *App. Cæsar* 42, I am loth to touch here, or to meddle beyond my slipper. [Cf. LAST *sb.*[1] 2 c.] **1767** Shuffle the slipper [see DRAW-GLOVE 1]. **1792** S. ROGERS *Pleas. Mem.* I. 35, 'Twas here we chased the slipper by the sound.

**c.** [After F. *pantouflier*.] The hammerhead shark.

**1796** H. HUNTER tr. *St.-Pierre's Stud. Nat.* (1799) I. 589 The seal, the sea-dog, the shark, the slipper, the thornback.

**d.** *transf.* The lip or labellum of an orchid.

**1902** F. BOYLE *Greenhouse Orchids* 92 Dorsal sepal—that which stands upright above the slipper. **1905** R. HAGGARD *Gardener's Year* Sept. 328 What the bee or other insects do when they enter the slipper of a Cypripedium.

**e.** As an instrument of punishment with which a child (etc.) is disciplined by beating. In phr. *to take a slipper to* (someone).

[**1682**, etc.: implied at SLIPPER *v.*[2] 1]. **1876** [see REAR *sb.*[3] 2 b]. **1924** GALSWORTHY *White Monkey* III. viii. 266 Teach him a sense of other people, as young as possible, with a slipper if necessary. **1932** A. J. WORRALL *Eng. Idioms* ii. 18 He is very impudent in his manner, and I should dearly like to take my slipper to him. **1978** R. MILLS *Comprehensive Educ.* 21 'I haven't done my homework, my History.' 'Ha, ha, it's the slipper for you then.' **1982** *Daily Tel.* 1 Mar. 10/7 The cane and slipper never did the likes of us any harm.

**f.** A temporary shoe for a horse.

**1903** SOMERVILLE & 'ROSS' *All on Irish Shore* iii. 82 He [*sc.* the smith] examined each hoof in succession .. and then, turning to Mr Fennessy, remarked:—'Ye'd laugh if ye were here the day I put a slipper on this one.' **1953** G. BROOKE *Introd. Riding & Stablecraft* vi. 52 You should pull up at a shoeing-smith's, and .. he will tack on what they call a slipper; that is, a shoe that fits well enough, and will see you through the day.

†**2.** *Her.* (See quot. 1610 and cf. FUSIL[1].)

**1610** GUILLIM *Heraldry* IV. vii, This is called a wharrow spindle, where the other are called Slippers that passe thorow the Yarne as this doth. **1680–4** DINGLEY *Hist. fr. Marble* (Camden) II. p. cclxxxvii, Hobye who beareth argent three Fusils upon slippers gules.

†**3.** *Arch.* = PLINTH 1. *Obs. rare.*

**1611** COTGR., *Plinthe*, a Plinth, or Slipper; a flat, and square peece of Masonrie, &c. **1703** [R. NEVE] *City & C. Purchaser* 244 *Slipper*, the same as Plinth. [Also in later Dicts.]

**4. a.** A form of skid used to retard the speed of a vehicle in descending a hill.

**1827** *Sporting Mag.* XX. 267 The 'Nimrod' coach with a skid, or slipper. **1854** MISS BAKER *Northampt. Gloss.*, *Slipper*, a skid-pan. **1876** *Encycl. Brit.* IV. 212 A slipper or 'skid' which can be placed under a wheel.

**b.** *Mining.* (See quots.)

**1883** GRESLEY *Gloss. Coal-m.*, *Skids*, slides or slippers upon which certain coal-cutting machines travel along the faces whilst at work. *Ibid.*, *Slippers*, .. steel or iron guides fixed to the ends and sides of cages, to fit and run upon the conductors.

**c.** A device for conveying electricity from a conductor rail to a tram or train.

**1900** *Engineering Mag.* XIX. 747/2 A slipper is placed on each carriage, so that one end of the train makes a contact before the other runs off.

**d.** *Mech.* Also *slipper block*. A guide block attached to a reciprocating rod, esp. a piston rod or its cross-head, so as to slide with the motion of the rod against a fixed plate and prevent any tendency of the rod to bend.

**1881** N. P. BURGH *Mod. Marine Engin.* (rev. ed.) 72/1 The guide channels .. are the ordinary kind, arranged to receive slipper blocks. **1883** A. E. SEATON *Man. Marine Engin.* viii. 144 To preserve the piston-rod in its true course, a guide is provided, and the piston-rod end fitted with blocks or slippers to work in it. **1952** FOX & MCBIRNIE *Marine Steam Engines & Turbines* ix. 155 A single slipper crosshead is generally made as shown. **1971** *Naval Marine Engin. Practice* (Min. of Defence) (ed. 2) I. vi. 137 A slipper is fitted to the crosshead, and this slipper slides in a vertical guide to maintain straight reciprocating motion against the thrust of the connecting rod. The slipper may be circular .. or in the form of a flat plate.

**e.** *Mech.* A part that is capable of sliding in the direction of its length.

**1903** *Electr. World & Engin.* 21 Nov. 845/2 The buckets of the Riedler turbine resemble those of the well-known Pelton type. The steam jet is divided by a central 'slipper' in two parts. **1930** *Engineering* 25 Apr. 539/3 About half-way along this arm is attached a slipper, D, which is kept in contact with the straight-edge, E, by a weight, F. **1966** *McGraw-Hill Encycl. Sci. & Technol.* XI. 611/2 Sleds are carried on shoes or slippers that grip the railhead in order to prevent derailing.

**5.** 'A kind of apron for children, to be slipped over their other clothes to keep them clean' (Webster, 1828–32).

**1818** L. D. CLARK *Diary* 11 July in *Firelands Pioneer* (1920) XXI. 2314 Made a slipper for Mrs. Caufield's baby.

**II. 6. a.** One who slips; also with *away*.

**1648** HEXHAM II, *Een glipper*, a Stealer away, or a Slipper away. **1860** WORCESTER, *Slipper*, one who, or that which, slips.

**b.** As a fish-name: (see quot.).

**1866** BUCKLAND in *Life* (1885) 171 Curious eel-like fish, with an ugly, pert-looking head, and frill down the back, .. and a spotted and exceedingly slimy body; their local name is 'slippers' because they slip from the hand so easily.

**7. a.** *Coursing.* The person appointed to slip the hounds at the proper moment.

**1825** *Sporting Mag.* XVI. 268 The slipper should be a horse's length in advance of the beaters. **1856** 'STONEHENGE' *Brit. Rural Sports* 209 If a judge or slipper be in any way connected with a dog .. entered in a stake [etc.]. **1885** *Daily News* 19 Feb. 2/7 The first pair of animals handed over to .. the slipper were R. Halliday and Mayflower.

**b.** *Cricket.* One who fields in the slips. *colloq.* Somewhat *rare.*

**1903** D. L. G. JEPHSON in H. G. Hutchinson *Cricket* iv. 102 There were good slips, bad slips, fast-asleep slips, and since his time every variety of 'slipper' has passed across the stage. **1973** *Daily Tel.* 23 July 32/1 If Hayes be sufficiently rated as a slipper, Roope could be spared.

**8.** *dial.* (See quot.)

**1841** HARTSHORNE *Salop Ant.* Gloss., *Slipper*, a mare who casts her foal.

**III. 9.** *attrib.* and *Comb.* (in sense 1), as ***slipper-like*** adj., ***maker***, ***manufacturer***, ***shape***, ***-shaped***, †***-shoe***.

**1568** *MS. Depositions* (Cant. Cath. Libr. 161), With a pair of slipper showes on her feete. **1796** C. MARSHALL *Gardening* xix. (1813) 340 The flower .. is esteemed only for the curiosity of its slipper shape. **1830** LINDLEY *Nat. Syst. Bot.* 275 The central fleshy slipper-like body from within which the stamens proceed. **1847** STEELE *Field Bot.* 164 Lip of cor[olla] slipper-shaped. **1858** SIMMONDS *Dict. Trade*, *Slipper manufacturer*, a maker of carpet shoes, or light thin indoor leather shoes. **1889** *Pall Mall G.* 5 Oct. 7/1 There are slipper makers .. engaged in it.

**10.** Special combs.: **slipper animalcule**, a common infusorian of the genus *Paramecium*; †**slipper barnacle** (?); **slipper-bath**, a partially covered bath shaped somewhat like a slipper; now usu. one of a number of single baths of the modern domestic style installed for hire at public baths; **slipper-brake** = sense 4 a; **slipper chair** *U.S.*, a low-seated, freq. upholstered chair with a high back; **slipper-drag** = sense 4 a; **slipper limpet** (see quot. 1890); **slipper-orchid**, orchis, an orchid of the genus *Cypripedium*; †**slipper-pear** (?); **slipper-plant**

(see quot.); **slipper satin**, a strong, closely woven fabric with a semi-glossy appearance, used for making slippers, dresses, furnishings, etc.; **slipper-shell** (see quot.); **slipperslapper** *nonce-wd.*, a loose, sloppily-fitting slipper (cf. SLIP-SLOP *sb.* 4); **slipper socks, sox** *pl.*, a pair of slippers with socks combined; **slipper spurs**, = *slipper-plant*; **slipperwort**, the calceolaria or campanula.

**1882** *Cassell's Nat. Hist.* VI. 355 They are about four times as long as broad, and their shape has given them the name of *Slipper animalcules. **1891** *Chambers's Encycl.* VII. 754/1 Paramecium, or Slipper Animalcule, an Infusorian very common in pond water or in vegetable infusions. **1767** *Phil. Trans.* LVII. 432 The shelly bases of the..Worm-shell, the Tree Oyster, and the *Slipper Barnicle. **1829** COOPER *Good's Study Med.* I. 388 The occasional use of.. the *slipper-bath and fomentations. **1898** *Daily News* 18 Apr. 10/7 Four large swimming-baths and a large number of private or slipper-baths. **1960** L. WRIGHT *Clean & Decent* xii. 172 Confusion may arise from the fact that single baths of the ordinary modern kind, on hire at Public Baths, are there still called 'Slipper Baths'. Such, no doubt, they originally were; the term has survived the change. **1981** *Times* 25 Feb. 8/5 The council closed down a slipper bath which had been used by pensioners living in bed-sitters. **1884** *Daily News* 2 Sept. 2 He was under the impression.. that the *slipper-brake was attached all right. **1938** *House Beautiful* Jan. 41 *Slipper chair... Typical of the French Regency. Broad proportions, beech frame delicately carved. Circa 1715. **1957** M. MILLAR *Soft Talkers* x. 94 Her mother sat in a slipper chair. **1979** M. MCMULLEN *But Nellie was so Nice* (1981) I. v. 42 He..made himself pleasant to Ursula in her slipper chair. **1883** *Good Words* 186 When we stop to adjust the *slipperdrag before rushing full speed down a break-neck precipice. **1861** *Chambers's Encycl.* II. 528/1 Bonnet Limpets, and *Slipper Limpets. **1890** *Ibid.* VI. 638 The family Acmæidæ..are often called 'slipper-limpets', from the presence of an internal flange on the incipiently spiral shell. **1885** LADY BRASSEY *The Trades* 158 The brown *slipper-orchid, fit *chaussure* for Cinderella or a fairy-queen. **1889** *Chambers's Encycl.* III. 642/2 Cypripedium, or *Slipper-orchis. **1664** EVELYN *Kal. Hort.* (1729) 213 Windsor, Sovereign, Orange, Bergamot, *Slipper-Pear. **1848** CRAIG, **Slipper-plant*, the common name given to plants of the genus Pedilanthus. **1937** M. SHARP *Nutmeg Tree* xxiii. 297 They saw the Disgusted Lady..marvellous in ice-blue *slipper satin. **1970** D. CLARK *Deadly Pattern* v. 104 A gilt-legged Chesterfield upholstered in cream slipper satin. **1858** BAIRD *Cycl. Nat. Sci.* I. 95/1 Of the genus *Crepidula*, or *slipper shell, forty recent species are known. **1922** JOYCE *Ulysses* 86 Slop about in *slipperslappers for fear he'd wake. **1950** *Sears, Roebuck Catal.* Fall/Winter 1324/6 *Slipper socks. **1951** *Ibid.* Fall/Winter 371 (*heading*) Footease slipper socks for every member of the family. **1970** *Guardian* 15 Dec. 9/3 Just tee-shirts with dungarees or jeans—plus slippersox. **1973** *Sunday Advocate-News* (Barbados) 9 Dec. 25/1 Slipper socks and bow ties can be great ways to gift him. **1887** G. NICHOLSON *Dict. Gardening* III. 58 *Pedilanthus*,..*Slipper Spurs. **1819** *Pantologia* II, Calceolaria, *Slipperwort. **1885** G. NICHOLSON *Dict. Gardening* I. 253 *Campanula*,..Bell-flower: Slipper-wort.

**slipper** ('slɪpə(r)), *a. Obs.* exc. *dial.* Forms: 1 slipor, 3 sluper, 1, 4–6 sliper (5 scliper, slipir, 6 -ar), 4–6 slipre, slyper, 5–6 sleper (5 slepyr); 5– slipper (5 slippyr, 6 *Sc.* -ar), 5–6 slypper, 9 *dial.* slepper, zlipper. [OE. *slipor*, = MLG. *slipper* (MSw. *slipper*), G. *schlipfer*, related to SLIP *v.*[1]]

**1.** Having a smooth slippery surface or exterior; readily slipping from one's grasp or out of place, etc. Also *fig.*

*a* **1050** *Liber Scintill.* lxxviii. (1889) 210 Deoful soðlice næddre ys slipor. *c* **1380** WYCLIF *Sel. Wks.* I. 393 Þei ben so slipre and so hard þat Goddis word takiþ not in hem. *c* **1430** *Two Cookery Bks.* 23 Wasshem..wyth Ale & Salt, an do so whele þey ben slepyr [*v.r.* sliper]. **1481** CAXTON *Reynard* (Arb.) 103 Thenne was his body also glat and slyper, that the wulf sholde haue none holde on hym. **1545** RAYNOLD *Byrth Mankynde* 71 The whiche do make the waye slypper, sople, & easy for it to procede, with yᵉ oyles or oyntmentes spoken of before. **1594** CAREW *Huarte's Exam. Wits* (1616) 138 The melancholicke haue euer their mouth full of froath and spittle, through which disposition their tongue is moyst and slipper. **1847** H. BAIRD (N. Hogg) *Poet. Lett.* (1858) 26 Ma staff wis za zlipper.

*fig.* **1591** LODGE *Catharos* vi. 52 Their wordes..are more slipper than oile, but in the ende they are steeled arrowes to destroy.

**b.** Of a hold: Liable to slip.

**1460** in *Pol., Rel., & L. Poems* (1866) 60 He..of his hert also hathe sliper hold. **1523** SKELTON *Garl. Laurel* 501 A slipper holde the taile is of an ele. **1562** J. HEYWOOD *Prov. & Epigr.* (1867) 170 Slyper as an eeles tayle is the holde of it.

**c.** Readily passing through the body.

**1539** ELYOT *Cast. Helthe* 46 Moreouer take hede, that slypper meates be not firste eaten.

**2.** Slippery; difficult to stand upon.

*c* **1290** *S. Eng. Leg.* I. 426 Him þouȝhte he saiȝ a sluper brugge swyþe fayr and heiȝ. *a* **1300** *E.E. Psalter* xxxiv. 7 Mirkenes and sliper be þare wai. *c* **1420** LYDG. *Assembly of Gods* 1074 Howe be hyt, the slepyr grasse made many of hem fall. **1490** CAXTON *Eneydos* vii. 32 Fortune..imposed vnder the feet of the righte chaste quene, thyng slypper & lubrick, for to make hir to ouerthrowe. *c* **1510** BARCLAY *Mirr. Gd. Manners* (1570) Cj, As on a slipper grounde, oft man doth fall or slide. **1553** BRENDE *Q. Curtius* Aa v, Thei were easelie beaten downe, by reason the Rocke hadde so slippar and unstable standing. **1665** BOYLE *Occas. Refl.* I. iv. (1848) 84 Ice is at once the smoothest and slipperest of ways. **1718** S. SEWALL *Diary* 28 Jan., Twas Foggy and slipper and Rain, and the Slay fail'd. **1886** ELWORTHY *W. Somerset Word-bk.* 680 The road's so zlipper's glass.

**3.** Of a shifty, unreliable character; deceitful, insincere: **a.** Of disposition, conduct, actions, etc.

*c* **1000** ÆLFRIC *Hom.* II. 92 Þwyrlice ðing ðe heora hlafordas doð ȝeswencte fram carum, and slipere þurh unstæððiȝnysse. **1382** WYCLIF *Prov.* xxvi. 28 The slideri [*v.r.* slyper] mouth werchith fallingis. *c* **1407** LYDG. *Reson & Sens.* 3295, I..haue espyed eke ful wel, How of slyper conscience Thow yaf a doom. *c* **1450** in *3rd Rep. Roy. Comm. Hist. MSS.* 280 Therfore he hath by slypper eschaunge the lordship and castell of Glaxton. **1547** LATIMER in Foxe *A. & M.* (1563) 1349/2, I haue charitablye monished you in a secret letter of your slipper dealinge, and such like misbehauiour. **1587** GOLDING *De Mornay* xvi. (1592) 262 A thousand sortes of slipper deuices and idle words.

**b.** Of persons.

*c* **1400** *Beryn* 1641 Ther-in dwellid a Burgeyse, þe moste scliper man Of al the town þurh-out. *a* **1540** BARNES *Wks.* (1573) 283/1, I know they bee slipper that I haue to doe wyth, and there is no holde of them. **1575** CHURCHYARD *Chippes* (1817) 189 Thus waiters on, doe nought but friends beguile, And slipper lads, as false and fine as those, For no offence, become most mortall foes. **1604** SHAKS. *Oth.* II. i. 246 A slipper, and subtle knaue, a finder of occasion.

**4.** Of memory: Not retentive; forgetful.

**1432–50** tr. *Higden* (Rolls) I. 5 For schort lyfe..and a slipper memory lete vs to knowe mony thynges. **1509** FISHER 7 *Penit. Ps.* cxliii. Wks. (1876) 240 Many haue so slypper a mynde that can not kepe in memory a thynge shewed vnto them by the space of an houre. **1539** ELYOT *Cast. Helthe* 75 Wherof do happen unstablenesse of wytte and slipper remembraunce.

**5.** Of conditions: On which one cannot depend; having no stability or certainty.

*c* **1430** HOCCLEVE *New Cant. T.* (E.E.T.S.) 14 In thys slypre lyf and peryllous, Staff of comfort & help to man ys she. **1483** CAXTON *Gold. Leg.* 96/1 Thys lyf..is so sleper and fleeyng that whan one weneth to holde it it fleeth away. *a* **1533** BERNERS *Gold Bk. M. Aurel.* (1546) A a v b, Theyr vayne glorie and slypper prosperitee, endured but two daies. **1557** *Tottel's Misc.* (Arb.) 161 For slipper welth will not cuntinue, plesure will weare away. **1598** GRENEWEY *Tacitus, Ann.* I. xv. (1622) 29 The higher he should clime, the slipperer his estate should be.

**6.** Insignificant, trifling. *rare*[−1].

**1567** HARDING in Jewel *Def. Apol.* (1611) 463 These be smal and slipper faults which if they were alone might be winked at.

**7. a.** Easily uttered or pronounced.

**1589** PUTTENHAM *Eng. Poesie* I. iv. (Arb.) 24 The vtterance in prose..is also not so voluble and slipper vpon the tong. *Ibid.* II. xiii. 134 Such letters as be by nature slipper and voluble and smoothly passe from the mouth.

**b.** dial. Fluent, voluble; given to talk.

**1842** H. J. DANIEL *Bride of Scio*, etc. 177 Yer tongue..'s too saucy, and too slepper. **1900** J. H. HARRIS *Our Cove* xi. 150 Wimmen's tongues es too slipper in what doan't consarn 'em.

**8.** Light, wanton. (Cf. SLIPPERY *a.* 5.)

**1581** G. PETTIE tr. *Guazzo's Civ. Conv.* I. (1586) 29 She began to make relation of the slipper prankes of the Dutchesses Gentlewomen, and had neuer done with her reprochfull reportes.

**9.** *Comb.*, as ***slipper-fast, -tongued, -witted***.

**1550** BALE *Image both Ch.* II. xvi. 106 b, The folyshe, fantastycall, and slypper wytted sort. **1569** *Bl. Letter Ball. & Broadsides* (1867) 221 Ye knowe, whyles louers are vnbounde, The knotte is slyper faste a. **1586** HOOKER *Hist. Irel.* in *Holinshed* II. 89/1 The lord Thomas..answered, as one that was somewhat slipper toonged, in this wise.

**†'slipper**, *v.*[1] *Obs. rare.* [ad. MDu. *slipperen* (= obs. or dial. G. *schlippern, schlipfern*), f. *slippen* SLIP *v.*[1]] *intr.* To slip or slide.

**1585** T. WASHINGTON tr. *Nicholay's Voy.* I. xix. 21 b, The shot which can but slippering passe ouer it. **1648** HEXHAM II, *Slibberende*, Slippring. *Ibid.*, *Een slibberinge*, a Slippering, or a Sliding.

**slipper** ('slɪpə(r)), *v.*[2] [f. SLIPPER *sb.* 1.]

**1.** *trans.* To beat or strike with a slipper.

**1682** HEDGES *Diary* 2 Nov. (1887) I. 45 Yᵉ same day [he] was brought forth and Slippered. **1683** *Ibid.* 17 Apr. I. 78 Yᵉ same person who slippered yᵉ Merchant. **1857** HUGHES *Tom Brown* I. vii, Slipper him on the hands! **1893** KIPLING *Many Invent.* 78 That yellow desert-bred girl from Cutch, who.. slippered the young prince across the mouth.

**2.** To provide or cover with slippers.

**1856** MRS. OLIPHANT *Zaidee* I. 9 The small feet which Mrs. Vivian slippers so handsomely.

**3.** *intr.* To walk or shuffle along in slippers.

**1888** MAYNE REID *Child Wife* xxix, The man slippered off towards the office, in the interior of the hotel.

**slipper coal.** [? f. SLIPPER *a.*] A variety of coal (see quot. 1877).

**1712** *Phil. Trans.* XXVII. 541 Coal, less black and shining than the former, called Slipper-Coal. **1877** *Encycl. Brit.* VI. 66 A smaller drift for ventilation..is carried above it in one of the upper beds called the slipper coal. *Ibid.*, The coal is first cut to the top of the slipper coal from below.

**slippered** ('slɪpəd), *ppl. a.* [f. SLIPPER *sb.*]

**1. a.** Wearing or shod with slippers.

**1600** SHAKS. *A. Y. L.* II. vii. 158 The sixt age shifts Into the leane and slipper'd Pantaloone. **1837** DICKENS *Pickw.* xv, Tom sat with his slippered feet on the fender. **1879** SALA *Paris herself again* (1880) I. xv. 228 Her poor old slippered legs disappeared in the darkness.

**b.** *fig. Lit.* and *poet.*

**1851** H. MELVILLE *Moby Dick* II. xvii. 136 The slippered waves whispered together. **1912** R. BROOKE *Coll. Poems* (1970) 68 A vague unpunctual star, A slippered Hesper.

**2.** Associated or connected with the wearing of slippers.

*a* **1817** R. L. EDGEWORTH in *Life* (1826) II. 419 By the assistance and solace afforded to him in his slippered decrepitude. **1856** R. A. VAUGHAN *Mystics* XIII. iii. (1860) II. 268 He leaned back in his arm-chair enjoying slippered ease. **1884** *Harper's Mag.* Feb. 431/1 They heard the colonel's slippered tread.

**3.** Retarded by means of a slipper-brake.

**1905** J. B. FIRTH *Highw. & Byeways Derby.* 380 A road where the slippered wheels..have dug great trenches.

**slipperily** ('slɪpərɪlɪ), *adv.* [f. SLIPPERY *a.* + -LY[2].] In a slippery manner. Chiefly *fig.*

**1603** *Adv. Don Sebastian* in *Harl. Misc.* (Malh.) II. 401 He missed certain papers..which were slipperily conveyed away. *a* **1635** SIBBES *Conf. Christ & Mary* (1656) 36 When we have..dealt slipperily with him. **1681** H. MORE *Expos. Dan.* vi. 196 Many shall joyn themselves to them slipperily, not firmly and sincerely. **1736** in AINSWORTH I. **1845** JANE ROBINSON *Whitehall* xlii. 295 Hoofs clattered slipperily.

**slipperiness** ('slɪpərɪnɪs). Also 6 slippri-, 7 slypperi-, sliperi-, 8 slipperyness. [f. SLIPPERY *a.* + -NESS.]

**1.** The quality or condition of being slippery, in literal senses: **a.** Of substances, or of objects in respect of their surface.

Formerly common of food liable to produce laxity of the bowels, or of the latter in a relaxed state.

**1562** TURNER *Baths* 8 b, The slipperines of the stomack, whych maketh that it can not well holde any meat. **1620** VENNER *Via Recta* vii. 115 They must be taken, by reason of the moysture and slipperinesse of their substance, before meat. **1699** SALMON *Bate's Dispens.* (1713) 614/2 It is a slippery thing, and cleanses and smooths the Passages from the Reins by its slipperiness. **1733** CHEYNE *Eng. Malady* II. ii. (1734) 128 Few..can bear the Slipperiness, and violent Cholicks and Gripes, which it brings on. **1753** *Chambers' Cycl.* Suppl. s.v. *Muræna*, The manner in which its slipperyness makes it roll about, and escape the catcher. **1856** EMERSON *Eng. Traits, Literature*, The Englishman.. takes hold of things by the right end, and there is no slipperiness in his grasp. **1859** *Hdbk. Turning* 25 A little chalk..will give it a firmer hold, and prevent the slipperiness.

**b.** Of the ground or other footing. Also in fig. context.

**1603** KNOLLES *Hist. Turks* (1621) 111 Scarce able to stand by reason of the slipperinesse of the bloud there shed vpon the pauement. **1674** tr. *Scheffer's Lapland* 86 That neither mice nor wild beasts could be able to climb up for slipperiness. **1743** *Lond. & C. Brewer* III. (ed. 2) 186 The great Danger that attends such a wooden Floor in its Slipperiness when wetted. **1754** WASHINGTON *Lett.* Writ. 1889 I. 127 A season in which horses cannot travel over the mountains on account of..slipperiness of the roads. **1836** LADY GRANVILLE *Lett.* (1894) 29 Dec., For years there has not been seen here such snow and slipperiness. **1860** W. WHITE *All round Wrekin* 369 With the steepness and slipperiness of the turf from dry weather. **1872** *Times* 23 Oct., The slipperiness of the political ground upon which they have been trying to keep their footing.

**2. a.** Inclination to babble or talk. *rare.*

**1589** NASHE *Martin Marprelate* Wks. (Grosart) I. 93 It is thought that one Pope or other, mistrusting the slipprines of my tounge, blest me into a stone to stoppe my mouth. **1674** *Govt. Tongue* 108 We do not only fall by the slipperiness of our tongues, but we deliberately discipline and train them to mischief.

**b.** The quality of being unreliable, shifty, insincere, or deceitful.

**1656** J. TRAPP *Expos. Ephes.* iv. 25 Shall we not abhor sleights and slipperiness in contracts and covenants? **1667** FLAVEL *Saint Indeed* (1754) 145 It is the slipperiness of our hearts, in reference to the world, that causes so many slips in our lives. **1681** H. MORE *Expos. Dan.* Pref. p. xc, Our wantonness and slipperiness in matters of Doctrine. **1818** BENTHAM *Ch. Eng. Catech. Exam.* 260 So prudential an indeterminateness and slipperiness. **1863** *Sat. Rev.* 606/1 They are conscious of illusion and slipperiness, of a sort of impostors. **1897** MRS. OLIPHANT *W. Blackwood* II. xxi. 357 Politicians..coming to shake their heads over the slipperiness of Peel.

**3. a.** Instability, uncertainty.

*a* **1618** RALEIGH *Rem.* (1661) 119 The gliding slipperinesse, and running streams of our uncertain life. **1621** DONNE *Serm.* lxx. 710 To note the Slipperinesse of our times. **1656** W. DU GARD tr. *Comenius' Gate Lat. Unl.* 187 Although by reason of the slipperiness of things our circumspection somtimes disappointeth us. **1781** COWPER *Lett.* 21 Aug., I experience as you do, the slipperiness of the present hour and the rapidity with which time escapes me.

**b.** Aptness to slip or go wrong.

**1612** T. TAYLOR *Comm. Titus* ii. 7 Young men for the slipperines of their age, need the benefit of good example.

**c.** Liability to be forgetful.

**1665** HOOKE *Microgr.* Pref., The slipperiness or delusion of our Memory. *a* **1708** BEVERIDGE *Thes. Theol.* (1711) II. 231 Slipperiness in our memories; forgetting God's goodness to us.

**slippering**, *vbl. sb.* [f. SLIPPER *v.*[2] + -ING[1].] Beating with a slipper.

**1851** H. MELVILLE *Moby Dick* I. iv. 41 Beseeching her as a particular favour to give me a good slippering for my misbehaviour. **1919** H. WALPOLE *Jeremy* ii. 33 A slippering from his father or idiotic punishments from the Jampot. **1934** M. V. HUGHES *London Child of Seventies* iv. 35 A threatened 'slippering' of the boys by my father if they are too noisy. **1953** J. CARY *Except the Lord* ix. 32 Beating was a punishment that could be graded from a random cuff.., through a hard smack, to a formal slippering. **1972** *Times* 9 Oct. 13/5 Children..respected striking or slippering as common..in their schools.

**'slipperish**, *a. rare*[−0]. Somewhat slippery.

**1648** HEXHAM II, *Slibberende*, Slippring, or Slipprish.

† **'slipperishness.** *Obs.*$^{-1}$ Slipperiness.
**1597** A. M. tr. *Guillemeau's Fr. Chirurg.* 36/1 In the water streames we may see that the stones, through the slipperishenesse of the water, are carried away.

† **'slipperly,** *adv. Obs.*$^{-1}$ In 5 sliper-. [f. SLIPPER *a.* + -LY$^2$.] Insecurely.
*c* **1412** HOCCLEVE *De Reg. Princ.* 1357 He sliperly stant who þat þow enhauncest.

† **'slipperness.** *Obs.* Also 1 slipor-, 5 sliper-, slipir-, 5–6 slypper-, 6 sleper-. [f. SLIPPER *a.*] Slipperiness, in lit. or fig. senses.
(*a*) *a* **1000** *Durham Hymn.* (Surtees) 36 Beon ut anydde.. slipornysse. **1401** *Pol. Poems* (Rolls) II. 99 Writyng was ordeyned for slipernes of mynde. *c* **1412** HOCCLEVE *De Reg. Princ.* 941, I fynde schal as frendly slipirnesse As tho men now doon, whos frendeschipe is rote. **1533** MORE *Apol.* xlviii. Wks. 925/1 Of a lightnesse of wit and slippernesse of tonge. **1560** DAUS tr. *Sleidane's Comm.* 193 b, The disceiptefullnes, uncertentye, & slyppernes of woordly thynges. **1590** GREENE *Mourning Garment* Wks. (Grosart) IX. 206 All his affects are slippernesse, and the effects full of preiudiciall disparagement.
(*b*) **1398** TREVISA *Barth. De P.R.* VII. l. (Bodl. MS.), Also þe wombe is igreued wiþ slidernes and slipernes. **1495** *Ibid.* XI. ii. (W. de W.) 385 Wynde.. wypyth of slyppernesse and vnclennesse. **1519** HORMAN *Vulg.* 37, I felle with slepernesse of the stayre. **1539** ELIOT *Cast. Helthe* (1541) 24 Gourdes, by reason of the slypperness of their substance, lyghtly passe forth by the bealye. **1609** BIBLE (Douay) *Ps.* xxxiv. 6 Let their way be made darkenesse and slippernes.

† **'slipperous,** *a. Obs. rare.* [Cf. SLIPPER *a.* and SLIPPERY *a.*] Smooth, slippery.
**1585** T. WASHINGTON tr. *Nicholay's Voy.* III. x. 86 The slipperous glyding of the oyle dropping vpon the dead leather.

**slipper-slopper,** *a. dial.* and *colloq. rare.* [Redupl. f. SLIPPER *sb.*] Wearing loose slippers; down-at-heel, sloppy.
**1825** J. JENNINGS *Observations Dial. W. Eng.* 70 *Slipper-slopper*,.. having shoes or slippers down at the heel; loose. **1888** F. T. ELWORTHY *West Somerset Wd.-bk.* 680 Father, be sure you baint gwain out all slipper-slopper like that. **1904** in *Eng. Dial. Dict.* V. 525/1 Slippers trodden down at the heels are said to be slipper-slopper. **1951** J. FRAME *Lagoon* 29 Their shoes were slipper-slopper.
Hence as *v. intr.*, to walk about in loose slippers; also **slipper-slopping** *vbl. sb.*
**1929** R. HUGHES *High Wind in Jamaica* viii. 192 Jonsen slipper-sloppered up and down his side of the deck. **1933** L. A. G. STRONG *Sea Wall* I. i. 13 He was roused from his meditations by a.. slipper-slopping on the stairs.

**slippery** ('slɪpərɪ), *a.* Also 6 slypery, slepery, 6–7 slyppery, slipperie; 7 sliperye. [Alteration of SLIPPER *a.*, possibly after LG. *slipperig* (G. dial. *schlipperig*), = MHG. *slipferic, slipfrig* (G. dial. *schlipferig*).]
**1. a.** Having a smooth, polished, or slimy surface which renders foothold insecure.
**1535** COVERDALE *Ps.* xxxiv. 6 Let their waye be darcke and slippery. **1596** SPENSER *F.Q.* V. v. 43 But foolish Mayd.. Through slipperie footing fell into the brooke. **1623** BINGHAM *Xenophon* 65 The Riuer rough with many great and slipperie stones. **1687** A. LOVELL tr. *Thevenot's Trav.* I. 168 Many steep and slippery places to be climb'd up. **1718** LADY M. W. MONTAGU *Lett.* II. lii. 73 The descent is.. steep and slippery. **1779** FLETCHER *Lett.* Wks. 1795 VII. 226, I.. ride out every day when the slippery roads will permit me. **1819** SCOTT *Ivanhoe* xxxi, Forming a slippery and precarious passage for two men abreast to cross the moat. **1871** L. STEPHEN *Playgr. Eur.* (1894) iii. 79 The rocks were steep and slippery.
**b.** In fig. contexts.
*a* **1586** SIDNEY *Arcadia* III. (1605) 235 The ground he stood vpon being.. slippery through affection, he could not hold himselfe from falling into such an error. **1613** PURCHAS *Pilgrimage* (1614) 631 Bloud is a slippery foundation, and pillage a pill'd wall. **1654** Z. COKE *Logick* Pref., Greatness without goodness is a slippery height. **1707** J. NORRIS *Treat. Humility* x. 396 The more slippery the ground is, the more circumspectly should we walk. **1789** BELSHAM *Ess.* I. vii. 132 [He] will find the ground upon which he stands very unstable and slippery. **1821** BYRON *Sardanap.* II. i. 135 Does it disappoint thee To find there is a slipperier step or two Than what was counted on? **1889** GRETTON *Memory's Harkback* 273 He speedily made his mark, and climbed higher and higher up the slippery tree.
**c.** *slippery slope* fig., a course leading to disaster or destruction.
**1951** J. FLEMING *Man who looked Back* x. 132 You go off down the slippery slope; it'll do you good. **1964** *Daily Tel.* 6 Jan. 12/2 While Western feet thus approach what some fear may be a 'slippery slope' towards recognition of the East, Ulbricht's ground seems as firm as ever it was. **1979** N. LASH *Theology on Dover Beach* iv. 74 It could be argued.. that to give priority to love, to trust, to action, to commitment, is to start down the slippery slope along which rationality, objectivity and—eventually—truth are abandoned.
**2. a.** Of a soft oily or greasy consistency; having a smooth surface, so as to slip or slide easily; slipping readily from any hold or grasp.
**1551** TURNER *Herbal* I. B i, The hole herbe is very sleymy and full of a slepery iuice [*pr.* -nuce]. **1567** MAPLET *Gr. Forest* 84 b, The chiefest that is marked in the Ele is that it is slipperie. **1612** WOODALL *Surg. Mate* Wks. (1653) 151 A good strong Lixivium made with fresh water and ashes till it be slipperie. **1669** STURMY *Mariner's Mag.* V. xiii. 88 The Line.. being rubbed over with soft Sope to make it slippery. **1738** J. KEILL *Anim. Œcon.* Pref. (ed. 2) p. x, The different Junctures of the Bones,.. which are slippery and exceedingly moveable. **1796** WITHERING *Brit. Pl.* (ed. 3) III. 869 Leaf oblong, indented, slippery. **1859** TENNYSON *Elaine* 215 The maiden dreamt That.. this diamond.. was too slippery to be held. **1871** R. ELLIS *Catullus* xc. 6 Melting lapt in flame fatly the slippery caul.
**b.** Of persons: Able to slip away or escape easily; difficult to catch or hold.
**1573** G. HARVEY *Lett. Bk.* (Camden) 126 Mye very mistrisse.. Moughte yit be woon agayne, like a slippery elfe. **1663** COWLEY *Verses & Ess.* (1669) 13 Harvey was with her there, And held this slippery Proteus in a chain. **1697** DRYDEN *Virg. Georg.* IV. 586 The slipp'ry God will try to loose his hold. **1890** 'R. BOLDREWOOD' *Col. Reformer* (1891) 204 Before he could seize him, however, the slippery savage, eluding his grasp, was bounding through the trees.
†**c.** Of the bowels: Lax, loose, open. *Obs.*
**1597** GERARDE *Herbal* 242 By moistning of the belly it maketh it the more slipperie. **1733** G. CHEYNE *Eng. Malady* II. ii. (1734) 129 Cinnabar of Antimony.. seldom keeps the Bowels slippery.
**d.** *slippery elm*, the North American red elm, *Ulmus fulva*, or the inner bark of this, used medicinally; also, a Californian shrub, *Fremontia Californica*, with similar bark. Cf. *red elm* s.v. RED *a.* 17 d.
**1748** D. DRAKE *Let.* 1 Jan. in *Pioneer Life Kentucky* (1870) iv. 73 Of the whole forest the red or slippery elm was the best. **1780** W. FLEMING *Jrnl.* 20 Mar. in N. D. Mereness *Trav. Amer. Colonies* (1916) 640 Bear fat is preserved sweet and pure by putting in a bunch of the Slippery Elem [*sic*] bark into it when rendering. **1810** [see *moose elm* s.v. MOOSE$^1$ b]. **1824** TORREY *Flora U.S.* I. 299 Slippery Elm, Red Elm. **1879** *Encycl. Brit.* VIII. 152 The bark of.. the Slippery or Red Elm of the United States and Canada.
**e.** In names of fishes: (see quots.).
**1876** GOODE *Fishes of Bermudas* 48 The 'Slippery Dick' and the 'Skip-jack' of the fishermen probably belong to this family. **1881** DAY *Fishes Gt. Brit.* I. 318 Whistler or whistle-fish,.. slippery-Jemmy, Dalkey, Dublin Bay. **1884** GOODE *Nat. Hist. Aquat. Anim.* 188 The Slippery Sole—*Glyptocephalus pacificus*.
**3. a.** Of conditions, affairs, etc.: Unstable, uncertain, insecure; that cannot be relied upon as lasting or assured. (Cf. 1 b.)
**1548** UDALL, etc. *Erasm. Par. 1 Peter* 2 Rewardes that are transitory and wage that is slyppery. **1573** G. HARVEY *Lett. Bk.* (Camden) 1 In so slipperi a case as I am, I am enforcid to do as I do. *c* **1617** MORYSON *Itin.* IV. (1903) 13 Were not this high estate of his very slipperye, and subject to sudden destruction. **1632** STRAFFORD in Browning & Forster *Life* (1891) 302 To hold him faste by the sliperye ties of feare and strained professions. **1704** TRAPP *Abra-Mulé* I. i, O slipp'ry State Of Human pleasures. **1790** BURKE *Fr. Rev.* (ed. 2) 341 That their future fidelity in a slippery concern might be established. **1855** BAIN *Senses & Intell.* III. ii. §37 The logical Caution.. is still more requisite in the slippery regions of Analogy. **1872** BAGEHOT *Physics & Politics* (1876) 24 An aggregate of families owning even a slippery allegiance to a single head.
†**b.** Of knowledge: Inexact, imperfect. *Obs.*$^{-1}$
**1584** B. R. tr. *Herodotus* II. 81 b, Not contented with a slippery knowledge, but mooued with desire to learne the truth.
**4. a.** Of persons: Inclined to be fickle or faithless; not to be depended on; shifty, deceitful.
**1555** EDEN *Decades* (Arb.) 100 *note*, Women are slippery cattayle. **1590** GREENE *Never too Late* Wks. (Grosart) VIII. 26 Some of them are as Sapho was, subtile to allure, and slippery to deceiue. **1618** BOLTON *Florus* III. i. 164 That most false and slippery man.. was betrayed into the hands of Sulla. **1679** OATES *Narr. Popish Plot* 10 But the Deponent standing by, said, what if the Duke should prove slippery! **1753** FOOTE *Englishm. in Paris* I. Wks. 1799 I. 35 He's a slippery chap, you know. **1805** SCOTT in *Lockhart* 12 Apr., He is hard and slippery, so settle your bargain fast and firm. **1855** THACKERAY *Newcomes* I. 248 By degrees this slippery penitent was induced to make other confessions. **1879** FROUDE *Cæsar* xxii. 378 The slippery politicians in the capital were on the watch.
**b.** Of actions, etc.: Characterized by shiftiness, deceitfulness, or want of sincerity.
**1579** SPENSER *Sheph. Cal.* Sept. 200 Long time he vsed this slippery pranck. **1598** E. GUILPIN *Skial.* (1878) 43 She Will one day shew thee a touch as slippery. **1664** COTTON *Scarron.* IV. (1715) 83 Th' slippery Trick he meant to play her. **1713** J. WARDER *True Amazons* 142 Not knowing what a slippery Trick you have play'd them. **1861** THACKERAY *Four Georges* iii. (1876) 84 He exercised a slippery perseverance, and a vindictive resolution. **1872** M. CREIGHTON *Hist. Ess.* ii. (1902) 84 Some.. refer all his slippery actions to a sincere desire for the good of Christendom.
**c.** Prov. phr. *as slippery as an eel.* Cf. EEL 1 c.
[*c* **1412** HOCCLEVE *Reg. Princes* (1897) 1985 Mi wit is also slipir as an eel. **1562** [see SLIPPER *a.* 1 b].] **1601** HOLLAND tr. *Pliny's Nat. Hist.* I. IX. xx. 247 All that be long and slipperie as Yeels and Congres. **1622** S. ROWLANDS *Good Newes & Bad Newes* sig. B1$^v$, Fie vpon giddie Fortune, and her wheele, Vnconstant, and as slipperie as an Eele. **1739–40** RICHARDSON *Pamela* (1740) I. 245 You'll find her as slippery as an eel, I'll assure you. **1855** MRS. GASKELL *North & South* I. xvii. 209 He's as slippery as an eel, he is. He's like a cat,—as sleek, and cunning. **1914** T. DREISER *Titan* xxvi. 220, I am morally certain he uses money to get what he is after as freely as a fireman uses water. He's as slippery as an eel. **1980** J. GARDNER *Garden of Weapons* II. i. 128 He's big, but slippery as an eel.
**5.** Licentious, wanton, unchaste; of doubtful morality.
**1586** T. B. *La Primaud. Fr. Acad.* I. (1594) 478 He shall cause hir.. to become slipperie & lascivious. **1592** GREENE *Disput.* 33, I giue thee.. a counterfect coyne, which is good inough for such a slipperie wanton. **1611** SHAKS. *Wint. T.* I. ii. 273 Ha' not you seene Camillo?.. or heard?.. or thought?.. My Wife is slipperie? **1738** tr. *Guazzo's Art Convers.* 54 She began to tell the slippery Pranks of the Dutchess's Gentlewomen. **1871** R. ELLIS *Catullus* lxi. 135 A slippery Love calls lightly, but yet refrain. **1874** BLACKIE *Self-Cult.* 48 Unnecessary and slippery luxuries, such as drink and tobacco.
**6.** Liable or prone to slip; readily giving way. Also of the memory, forgetful.
**1548** UDALL, etc. *Erasm. Par. 1st Ep. Timothy* 14 The vowe of continencie is not to be committed vnto fraile slypperye age. **1555** EDEN *Decades* (Arb.) 63 Leaste I shulde bestowe my slippery yeares in vnprofitable Idlenesse. **1606** SHAKS. *Tr. & Cr.* III. iii. 84 When they fall, as being slippery standers [etc.]. **1653** R. SANDERS *Physiogn.* 107 The party is a vain babler, perfidious, and of a slippery memory. **1664** EVELYN *Sylva* xviii. (1729) 86 This profound fixing of Aquatick-trees being to preserve them steddy.. in their liquid and slippery Foundations.
**7.** Of the tongue: Talking too freely.
**1727** BOYER *Dict. Royal* II, A slippery (or free) Tongue, *une Langue trop-libre, qui dit tout, qui ne cache rien.*
**8.** *look slippery* = *look slippy* s.v. SLIPPY *a.*$^1$ 2. *dial.* or *colloq. rare.*
**1922** JOYCE *Ulysses* 418 Two Ardilauns. Same here. Look slippery.
**9.** Quasi-*adv.* Smartly, closely.
**1828** *Sporting Mag.* XXIII. 19, I found him in the yard, looking pretty slippery after the strappers.
**10.** *Comb.*, as *slippery-bellied, -breeched, -footed, -shod, -tongued*; also *slippery-looking, -sleek*; **slippery-back**, a West Indian skink (*Cent. Dict.*); **slippery hitch** *Naut.*, a knot made fast by catching part of the rope beneath the bight, released at a pull on the free end; also *fig.*; **slippery pole** = *greasy pole* s.v. GREASY *a.* 9 (in quots. *fig.*); **Slippery Sam**, a card-game (cf. *blind-hookey* s.v. BLIND *a.* 16).
**1852** 'NIGHTLARK' *Meanderings Mem.* I. 64 Thou silvery-backed, and *slippery-bellied Eel. **1611** L. BARRY *Ram Alley* IV. i, She is shewing Some *slippery breech'd courtier rare faces In a bay-window. **1903** *Slippery-footed [see HOT-FOOT *v.*]. **1832** *Slippery hitch [see HITCH *sb.* 6 b]. **1903** 'T. COLLINS' *Such is Life* vii. 273 Alf, it appeared, had left the station six or eight weeks before, bound for no-one knew where. Jack's opinion was that in so doing he had made a slippery-hitch. **1944** C. W. ASHLEY *Bk. Knots* i. 19 The *Slippery Hitch* is often found in the sheets and halyards of small boats. **1903** SIR M. G. GERARD *Leaves fr. Diaries* viii. 262 The only approach to these is by a *slippery-looking pathway. **1972** *Village Voice* (N.Y.) 1 June 20/1 The Voice had this wonderfully sobering policy of rejecting your stories right when you thought you had a firm grasp on the *slippery pole. **1977** H. GREENE *FSO-1* xviii. 167 All of these years of clambering up the slippery pole only to find there was no top to it. **1923** L. H. DAWSON *Hoyle's Games Modernized* I. 162 *Slippery Sam is a variation of and by many considered an improvement on Blind Hookey. **1954** A. S. C. ROSS in *Neuphilologische Mitteilungen* LV. 22 Solo whist.. is non-U, though much 'lower' games (e.g. pontoon, nap and even slippery sam) are not necessarily so. **1978** C. STORR *Winter's End* iv. 58 The others were exclaiming and shouting at Racing Demon... They'd changed to Slippery Sam. **1682** O. HEYWOOD *Diaries* (1885) IV. 85 It was a frost and snow, my horse *slippery shod. *a* **1618** SYLVESTER *Map of Man* Wks. (Grosart) II. 97 Though shee simper, though shee smile,.. Shee is alwayes *slippery-sleeke. **1843** BETHUNE *Sc. Peasant's Stor.* 299 By and by evidence began to appear of Jock's being tarry-fingered as well as *slippery-tongued.

† **'slippet$^1$.** *Obs. rare.* [f. SLIP *sb.*$^2$ + -ET$^1$.] A slip or strip.
**1657** W. COLES *Adam in Eden* cccxii, One long hollow Flower,.. with a long piece or slippet, as it were, at one side. **1690** LEYBOURN *Curs. Math.* 180 These five slippets do now contain the whole Multiplication Table of Pythagoras.

**'slippet$^2$.** [f. SLIP *sb.*$^3$] (See quot.)
**1898** *N. & Q.* 9th Ser. I. 407/2 In mining operations.. a slippet is a sand-slide in the bore-hole or excavation... A slippet is a source of danger to workmen, occurring without warning.

**'slippiness.** *rare.* [f. SLIPPY *a.*$^1$] **a.** Slipperiness.
**1821** SCOTT *Kenilw.* xvii, She leaned on him somewhat more than the slippiness of the way necessarily demanded.
**b.** Speed, promptitude, alacrity. *colloq.*
**1974** WODEHOUSE *Aunts aren't Gentlemen* xii. 98, I think I outlined the position.. rather well, making it abundantly clear that.. the cat.. must be restored to its proprietor with all possible slippiness.

**'slipping,** *vbl. sb.*$^1$ [f. SLIP *v.*$^1$]
**1. a.** The action of the verb in intransitive senses. Also with advs. or preps., as *away, into, out, up.*
*a* **1340** HAMPOLE *Ps.* xlix. 21 It likes þe to speke ill, not for slipynge of þi tonge or in chawnce, bot wiþ study. *a* **1548** HALL *Chron., Hen. VII*, 55 b, Other also.. durst not hasard themselues for feare of galtroppes or slippynge into yͤ fyer. **1591** SAVILE *Tacitus, Hist.* I. vii. 23 Many accidentes stayed the purpose; fearefull messages, the slippings away of his friendes [etc.]. **1602** CAREW *Survey Cornwall* II. 127 b, The thankful acknowledgement of many corrected slippings in.. my notes. **1676** WISEMAN *Surg. Treat.* VII. ii. 480 The Ancients called it a Slipping of the Head of a Bone out of its Cavity. **1840** [ETHERIDGE] *Life Adam Clarke* 255 He had met with a serious accident by the slipping of his study ladder. **1860** TYNDALL *Glac.* II. x. 278 The place was watched for some time, but the slipping was not repeated. **1865** KINGSLEY *Herew.* vii, There was the usual splintering of lances and slipping up of horses.
**b.** *spec.* (See quot.) *U.S.*
**1896** HOWELLS *Impress. & Exp.* 9 The 'slippin',' as the sleighing was called,.. lasted from December to April with hardly a break.
**c.** = SLIP *sb.*$^3$ 9 e.

**1912** *Q. Rev.* Jan. 182 The danger attendant on the 'slipping' of a charge in a blast furnace—the descent of hunks of limestone and ore that are hurled into the air when such a 'slip' occurs. **1948** G. R. BASHFORTH *Manuf. Iron & Steel* I. x. 166 Slipping is the aftermath of scaffolding or hanging. *Ibid.*, Slipping or irregular descent of the stock may..occur due to badly designed bosh walls. **1969** K. R. HALEY in J. H. Strassburger *Blast Furnace* II. xii. 592 (*heading*) Hanging and slipping.

**2.** The action of the verb in transitive senses. Also *fig.*

**1571** *Reg. Privy Council Scot.* II. 125 Nane of the saidis partiis salbe interessit throw slipping of the occasioun and tyme of warning. **1865** *Slang Dict.* 235 *Slipping*, a trick of card-sharpers, in performance of which, by dexterous manipulation, they place the cut card on the top, instead of at the bottom of the pack. **1885** *Daily News* 19 Feb. 2/7 The slipping and judging gave entire satisfaction. **1898** *Ibid.* 11 Oct. 8/1 The practice of 'slipping', that is, of mechanically detaching coaches from off express trains. **1925** *Morris Owner's Man.* 22 Persistent slipping of the clutch must not be resorted to. **1959** *Listener* 17 Dec. 1085/3 Such statements as that on page 169..may be regarded as a momentary slipping of the clutch.

**3.** *attrib.*, as ***slipping-apparatus, system.***

**1856** 'STONEHENGE' *Brit. Rur. Sports* I. III. vi. 194 Thus alternately using the slipping system and the horse-exercise. **1895** *Daily News* 7 Sept. 7/5 He was riding in the front van of a first-class coach, in which the slipping apparatus was fitted.

**'slipping,** *vbl. sb.*² [f. SLIP *v.*²]

**1.** A skein or hank of yarn. Cf. SLIP *sb.*² 11. ? *Obs.*

**1541-2** *Inv.* in *Lanc. & Chesh. Wills* (1857) 81, xxv teir of hempe slippingis, xxij canvis slippingis, x flaxen slippingis. **1599** *Nottingham Rec.* IV. 251 Certen slippinges of hardne yarne. **1603** *Shuttleworth Acc.* (Chetham Soc.) 152 Delivered to her xxviij haspes or slippinges of line yearn,.. and v haspes or slippinges of canves yearne. **1615** G. MARKHAM *Eng. Housew.* II. v. (1668) 137 Divide the slipping or skean into divers Leyes, allowing..twenty leyes to every slipping. **1688** HOLME *Armoury* III. 107/1 A *Slipping*, is as much as is wond upon the Reel at a time, which is generally about a pound of Yarn. **1879** MISS JACKSON *Shropshire Word-bk.* 389.

**2.** The action of taking slips from a plant.

**1548** ELYOT, *Frondatio*, a slyppyng of leaues or bowes, loppyng of trees. *c* **1614** CAMPION *2nd Bk. Ayres* Wks. (1909) 144 Thriue faire plants e'er the worse for the slipping? **1707** MORTIMER *Husb.* (1721) II. 133 Calamint is raised by Slipping, or parting of the Roots.

**b.** A cutting of a plant; a slip.

**1638** PEACHAM *Valley of Variety* xii. 103 It was planted like unto our vines, by setting the slippings into the earth. **1908** [MISS FOWLER] *Betw. Trent & Ancholme* 15 Such slippings or cuttings as the receiver might chance 'to grow'.

**'slipping,** *ppl. a.* [f. SLIP *v.*¹] That slips, in senses of the intransitive verb; also *fig.*, transient, passing quickly.

*c* **1400** *Destr. Troy* 4032 The slippond slete [was] slidon of the ground. **1435** MISYN *Fire of Love* 64 þat vaynglory of slippand praysynge þe sawle may not seyk. **1581** T. HOWELL *Deuises* (1879) 258 The slipping ioyes that worldly wights possest. **1636** STRAFFORD *Lett.* (1739) II. 18 To cozen all Strangers by those slipping Conveyances. **1726** SWIFT *Gulliver* II. viii, The slipping-board that I had lately opened. **1839** *Penny Cycl.* XV. 175/2 We should recommend fixing the position micrometer upon a slipping-piece.

†**b.** ***slipping knot,*** = SLIP-KNOT. *Obs.*

*a* **1425** tr. *Arderne's Treat. Fistula*, etc. 29 þat þe þrede.. be so bonden..þat it may be loused without kuttyng, þat is with a lache knotte or slyppyng knotte. **1647** WARD *Simple Cobler* 67 Apron-string tenure is very weak, tyed but of a slipping knot.

Hence **'slippingly** *adv.*

**1830** GALT *Lawrie T.* IX. (1849) 233 Without retiring from the scene he had come slippingly behind us.

**slippy** ('slɪpɪ), *a.*¹ Also 6 slyppie, 6–7 slippie. [f. SLIP *v.*¹ + -Y¹; cf. MHG. *slipfec, -ig*, obs. G. *schlipfig*. Not directly connected with OE. *slipiȝ* viscid.]

**1.** = SLIPPERY *a.*, in various lit. and fig. senses.

(*a*) **1548** UDALL, etc. *Erasm. Par. Luke* xix. 154 It pleased him..to mocke the glory of this worlde, shewing howe vaine it is and howe slippie to trust to. *Ibid. 1 Tim.* iii. 11 Not bablers, or women of slyppie credence. **1828** CARR *Craven Gloss.* s.v., 'A slippy chap,' an unfair dealer, in whom is no confidence or security.

(*b*) *a* **1618** J. DAVIES (Heref.) *Wit's Pilgr.* ii. Wks. (Grosart) II. 6 From it (being moist, and slippie) she doth slipp, To thy faire Teeth. **1658** J. JONES *Ovid's Ibis* 79 Because the waters ebb and flow the sand Is slippy. **1772** J. R. FORSTER *Kalm's Trav.* II. 132 The side of the bark which has been upon the wood..is smooth and slippy. **1836** DICKENS *Sk. Boz* (1837) III. 313 Those slippy, shiny-looking wooden chairs peculiar to places of this description. **1871** TYNDALL *Fragm. Sci.* (1879) I. xi. 352 Turning short, particularly in slippy weather. **1891** MISS DOWIE *Girl in Karp.* 166 The hill was steep, and whortle-berry bushes slippy to the feet.

**2.** *dial.* or *colloq.* Of persons: Nimble, spry; sharp, quick; *esp.* in phr. ***to be*** or ***look slippy.***

**1847** HALLIW., *Slippy*, very quick. *Var. dial.* **1854** MISS BAKER *Northampt. Gloss.* s.v., Come, be slippy. **1885** RUNCIMAN *Skippers & Shellbacks* 212, I don't know what may happen, so you'll have to look slippy. **1889** 'R. BOLDREWOOD' *Robbery under Arms* (1890) 30 Get out the lot we've just branded,..and just slippy. **1915** [see *buck-rabbit* s.v. BUCK *sb.*¹ 3]. **1924** D. MOORE *Fen's First Term* i. 4 There is a hurry... Go and change and look slippy. **1972** WODEHOUSE *Pearls, Girls, & Monty Bodkin* xi. 178 Both of you get out of the car... And make it slippy, because I haven't got all day.

**3.** *Mining.* (See quot.)

**1883** GRESLEY *Gloss. Coal-m.* 227 *Slippy Backs*, vertical planes of cleavage occurring every four or five inches in the seam of coal.

**slippy** ('slɪpɪ), *a.*² [f. SLIP *sb.*² + -Y¹.] Slim; slender.

**1883** *Pall Mall G.* 12 May 4/1 Mdlle. Julie has a slight, slippy figure. **1892** *Daily News* 6 June 2/2 This tall, lithe, slippy figure has much in common with the graceful reeds which bend all round about her.

**'slip-rail.** *Austr.* [SLIP- 1 b.] A fence-rail, forming one of a set which can be slipped out so as to leave an opening. Chiefly *pl.* Also *attrib.*

**1828** CUNNINGHAM *N.S. Wales* II. 171 These patches might..communicate with the fields by means of slip-rail entrances. **1852** MUNDY *Antipodes* (1857) 198 The greater part of our route lay through bush-roads.., through scores of slip-rails—the primitive gate of Australia, and along the bush-ranges. **1885** MRS. PRAED *Austral. Life* 79 Many men rode thro' the slip-rails and turned out their horses.

**slipshod** ('slɪpʃɒd), *a.* Also 6 slippeshood, 7 slip-sho'd, 7- slip-shod. [f. SLIP *v.*¹ + SHOD *ppl. a.*, after SLIP-SHOE.]

**1.** Wearing slippers or very loose shoes, in later use esp. such as are down at the heel. Also *fig.*

*pred.* **1580** LYLY *Euphues* (Arb.) 334 Thinking it.. if one suffer you to treade awry, no shame to goe slipshad [*sic*; **1581** slippeshood]. **1605** SHAKS. *Lear* I. v. 12 Thy wit shall not go slip-shod. **1682** N. O. *Boileau's Lutrin* IV. 220 Another durst not stay to tye his shooes, But slip-sho'd hobbl'd, lest he Breakfast loose. **1747** FRANCIS tr. *Horace, Ep.* II. i. 233 Dossennus slip-shod shambles o'er the Scene. **1781** COWPER *Hope* 75 To rise at noon, sit slipshod and undress'd. **1825** J. NEAL *Bro. Jonathan* II. 340 One of those..who shuffle thro' the serious duties of life—slip-shod. **1851** MELVILLE *Whale* xv. 74 With each foot in a cod's decapitated head and looking very slip-shod.

*attrib.* **1607** MIDDLETON *Your Five Gallants* III. v, Out a' th' house, you slipshod, sham-legged..rascal! **1653** URQUHART *Rabelais* I. liv. 236 Here enter not vile bigots, hypocrites,..Slipshod caffards. **1728** POPE *Dunc.* III. 15 A slip-shod Sibyl led his steps along. **1781** COWPER *Truth* 144 The shiv'ring urchin,..With slip-shod heels. **1838** DICKENS *Nickleby* xxii, At intervals were heard the tread of slipshod feet. **1840** —— *Old C. Shop* xxxiv, Dick..descried a small slipshod girl in a dirty coarse apron and bib. **1887** SIR R. H. ROBERTS *In the Shires* i. 9 A sliphsod stable-helper holds the hired horse by the head.

*transf.* **1861** SALA *Dutch Pictures* vi. 76 All you hear of her [is]..the slipshod scuffling of her shoes about the house.

**b.** Of shoes: Loose or untidy; in bad condition; down at the heel.

**1687** A. LOWELL tr. *Thevenot's Trav.* III. 37 As they do who go with their shoes slipshod. **1824** SCOTT *St. Ronan's* xvii, His feet were thrust into old slip-shod shoes, which served him instead of slippers. **1848** DICKENS *Dombey* vi, The slipshod shoes.

**c.** In shabby condition.

**1818** SCOTT *Hrt. Midl.* i, A sort of appendix to the half-bound and slip-shod volumes of the circulating library.

**2.** *fig.* Slovenly, careless: **a.** Of style or language.

**1815** L. HUNT *Notes Feast Poets* 47 Between the lameness of Cowper and the slip-shod vigour of Churchill. **1831** CROKER *Boswell's Johnson* I. 417 The following slipshod but characteristic epitaph. *a* **1861** CLOUGH *Poems*, etc. (1869) I. 331 The fashionable jargon of the day..seems to have been a sort of slipshod English, continually helped out with the newest French phrases. **1891** *Spectator* 18 Apr., Her style is occasionally slipshod, so much so that in certain passages it is difficult to discover the nominative.

*absol.* **1842** J. STERLING *Ess.* (1848) I. 436 In the latter half of the poem,..the lax shapelessness of structure, the endless slipshod,..become very disagreeable.

**b.** Of statements, arguments, etc., or of writers in respect of these.

**1837** HOWITT *Rur. Life* (1842) 479 You also find..even more slipshod writers just as much in vogue. **1859** KINGSLEY *Misc.* I. 63 This is the sort of slipshod dilemma by which Elizabeth is proved to be wrong. **1877** CONDER *Basis of Faith* iv. 183 The slipshod inaccuracy of those who really know better.

**c.** Of habits, methods, etc.

**1845** DISRAELI *Sybil* (1863) 204 Men..who lead a sort of facile, slipshod existence, doing nothing, yet mightily interested in what others do. **1863** ANSTED *Ionian Isl.* 193 The case is singularly illustrative of the slipshod and unpractical habits of the people. **1880** MISS BRADDON *Just as I am* xi, She reigned supreme in a slip-shod household.

Hence **'slipshoddiness; 'slipshoddy** *a.*; **'slipshodism; 'slipshodness.**

*a* **1849** POE *Marginalia* Wks. 1864 III. 583 The *slipshodiness is so thoroughly in unison with the nonchalant air of the thoughts. **1887** *Jrnl. Education* Dec. 520 The chief fault..was the 'scrappiness' and 'slipshoddiness' of the answers. **1882** *Spectator* 22 Apr. 534 Such *slipshoddy statements may be of little account. **1897** *Naturalist* 269 *Slipshodisms in phrase abound. *a* **1877** BAGEHOT *Lit. Studies & Mem.* (1879) I. p. xlvi, A number of small inaccuracies, harshnesses and *slipshodnesses in style. **1883** *American* VI. 183 A continual confusion, largely due to bad writing, careless proof-reading, and other slipshodness.

**'slip-shoe.** *Obs.* exc. *dial.* Also 6 slippe, 7 slip(p)-shooe. [f. SLIP *v.*¹ + SHOE *sb.* Cf. OE. *slypescó* 'soccus'.] A light or loose shoe; a slipper.

**1555** WATREMAN *Fardle of Facions* II. xi. 250 They vse a maner of slippe shooes, that may lightly be putte of and on. **1592** *Arden of Feversham* v. i, For in his slipshoe did I find some rushes. **1615** G. SANDYS *Trav.* (1637) 63 The rest.. going in yellow or red slip-shooes, picked at the toe. *a* **1697** AUBREY *Lives* (1898) I. 122 He went not out of the College gates,..but was in slip-shoes. **1719** S. SEWALL *Diary* 15 Sept. (1882) III. 228 Going out to call the Fisherman in Slip-shoes, I fell flat upon the pavement. **1762** STERNE *Tr. Shandy* VI. xix, The open shoe. The close shoe. The slip shoe. **1859** BARTLETT *Dict. Amer.* (ed. 2) 416 A loose shoe or slipper is called a slip-shoe in Norfolk [England]. **1886** ELWORTHY *W. Somerset Word-bk.* 680 *Slip-shoes*,..an old loose pair of shoes worn at night after taking off the half bats.

Hence †**slip-shoed** *a.*, slipshod. *Obs.*

**1702** BAYNARD *Cold Baths* II. (1709) 385 A Gentleman.. having strain'd his Ankle..went lame and slip-shoo'd for at least a Year and a half. **1726** G. ROBERTS *Four Yrs. Voy.* 30, I..was Slip-shoe'd, and without Stockings, being just as I turn'd out of my Cabin. **1748** RICHARDSON *Clarissa* (1811) VIII. 156 They were all slip-shoed.

†**slipshot,** *a. Obs.*⁻¹ (Meaning uncertain.)

*a* **1635** CORBET *Poems* (1807) 218 Saturne crawls much like an iron catt, To see the naked moone in a slipshott hatt.

**slip-slap** ('slɪpslæp), *sb.* [f. SLAP *v.*¹, with usual variation of vowel.]

†**1.** ? A slipper. *Obs.*⁻¹

**1669** PENN *No Cross* xvii. §5 (1682) 336 Shoes and Slip-slaps lac'd with Silk or Silver-Lace.

**2.** The repeated flapping sound caused by loosely-worn shoes.

**1890** D. GERARD *Lady Baby* vi, The well-known slip-slap of the lodging-house servant's down-trodden shoes.

**slip-slap,** *v.* [See prec.] **1.** *intr.* To slap repeatedly in rapid succession. *rare*⁻¹.

**1721** MRS. CENTLIVRE *Artifice* 111, I ha' found her Fingers slip-slap, this a-way, and that a-way, like a Flail upon a Wheat-sheaf.

**2.** = SLIP-SLOP *v.* 3. *rare.*

**1926** T. E. LAWRENCE *Seven Pillars* v. lvii. 302 At Cairo my sandalled feet slip-slapped up the quiet Savoy corridors. **1965** 'LAUCHMONEN' *Old Thom's Harvest* v. 58 She slip-slapped in her cut-back slippers to the door.

**slip-slop** ('slɪpslɒp), *sb.* Also 7 (8 *Sc.*) -slap, 9- slipslop. [f. SLOP *sb.*², with variation of vowel. In sense 2 with allusion to the mistakes in language made by Mrs. Slipslop in Fielding's *Joseph Andrews* (1742).]

**1.** A sloppy compound used as a food, beverage, or medicine.

**1675** COTTON *Burlesque upon B.* 49 No, thou shalt feed, instead of these, Or your slip-slap of Curds and Whey, On Nectar and Ambrosia. **1683** TRYON *Way to Health* 241 Such Cordials, and other compounded Slip-slops as the Sick are forced continually to swallow down. **1737** BRACKEN *Farriery Impr.* (1757) II. 151 To run to Apothecaries Shops for this or that whimsical Slip-slop, which may be told him as a Nostrum. **1754** *Connoisseur* No. 19, When the jellies and slip-slops were coming in, the beef was carried off. **1796** MRS. M. ROBINSON *Angelina* I. 148, I hate slip-slops, I never taste tea. **1821** COMBE *Syntax, Search Wife* I. (Chandos) 260 At length the coffee was announc'd,..'And since the meagre slip-slop's made, I think the call should be obey'd'.

**2. a.** A blunder in the use of words, esp. the ludicrous misuse of one word for another; the habit of making mistakes of this nature.

**1788** MME. D'ARBLAY *Diary* 8 Jan., Then he told us a great number of comic slip-slops of the first Lord Baltimore, who made a constant misuse of one word for another. **1826** F. REYNOLDS *Life & Times* II. 220 One of the party (amongst other slipslops) saying instead of *Pasticcios*, he liked *Pistachios*. **1837** J. MORIER *Abel Allnutt* xxxii. 187 Mrs. Goold Woodby would usually exert her talent in slip-slop, by calling the last [*sc.* Curius Dentatus] 'Curious 'tatoes'.

**b.** A person given to making such blunders.

*a* **1791** GROSE *Olio* xxii. 93 These slip-slops are frequently of the rank he has drawn his lady. **1857** LADY CANNING in Hare *Two Noble Lives* (1893) II. 202 What by some old official slip-slop is called Provincial (meaning Provisional) Commander-in-Chief.

**3. a.** Twaddle; loose or trifling talk or writing.

**1811** J. CREEVEY in *C. Papers* (1904) I. vii. 149 No one observation the Regent has made yet out of the commonest slip-slop. **1861** THACKERAY *Four Georges* iv. (1862) 185 Some man..cleaned up the slovenly sentences, and gave the lax maudlin slipslop a sort of consistency. **1886** *Athenæum* 30 Oct. 559/3 In..his history this style is wanting, and is replaced by modern slipslop.

**b.** A tag or phrase.

**1823** BYRON *Juan* XIII. xlvii, '*Cosi viaggino i Ricchi!*' (Excuse a foreign slipslop now and then).

**4. a.** *U.S.* (See quot.)

**1859** BARTLETT *Dict. Amer.* (ed. 2) 416 *Slip-slops*, old shoes turned down at the heel.

**b.** A kind of beach sandal; = FLIP-FLOP *sb.* f. Chiefly *S. Afr.*

**1971** *Studies in English* (Univ. Cape Town) Feb. 29 Beach-thongs, sandles [*sic*] made of rubber..have a great many names here—sloppies, slip-slops, plakkies, etc. **1974** 'G. BLACK' *Golden Cockatrice* iv. 66, I couldn't believe they had my shoe size too, almost relieved to find only a pair of slip-slops. **1976** J. MCCLURE *Rogue Eagle* ii. 31 Knotted blouse, blue jeans and slip-slop sandals.

Hence **'slip-ˌsloppery,** slipslop condition or methods; **'slip-ˌsloppish** *a.*, of the nature of slip-slop; **'slip-ˌsloppism,** = sense 2; **'slip-ˌsloppy** *a.*, wet, sloppy.

**1797** COLERIDGE *Lett.* (1895) 223 'Engages the eye,' applied to a gibbet, strikes me as slipsloppish. **1803** *Lett. Miss Riversdale* III. 228 Slip-sopism [*sic*] is not confined to females, now-a-days, I perceive. **1830** MISS MITFORD *Village* Ser. IV. (1863) 135 A body of excavators (navigators our villagers by an ingenious slip-slopism were pleased to call them). *a* **1845** BARHAM *Ingol. Leg.* Ser. III. *Blasphemer's Warning*, There was no taking refuge too then,..On a slip-sloppy day, in a cab or a '*bus.* **1848** *Illustr. Lond. News* 12 Feb. 88/3 The general slip-sloppery of its warehouses.

**'slip-slop,** *a.* [See prec.]

†**1.** Characterized by, given to, blundering in the use or forms of words. *Obs.*

**1757** MRS. GRIFFITH *Lett. Henry & Frances* (1767) III. 105 Memorandums..become, as Captain H—— expressed it once, by a lucky slip-slop Phrase, Remorandums. **1776** G. COLMAN *Posth. Lett.* (1820) 335 Her dialect is particularly vulgar,..not by murdering words in the slip-slop way, but by a mean twang in the pronunciation. **1809** *Sporting Mag.* XXXIII. 252 A slip-slop Colonel having sent for an architect to construct a mausoleum. **1824** MISS L. M. HAWKINS *Mem.* I. 140 *note,* Is the reply of Quin to a slip-slop milliner at Bath very trite?

**2.** Having no substance or solidity; sloppy, feeble, trifling.

**1814** *Sporting Mag.* XLIV. 84 We may again expect in the slip-slop prints the usual selection of important incidents. **1825** T. HOOK *Sayings* Ser. II. *Man of Many Fr.* II. 2, I.. have abandoned her to the slip-slop attentions of the shame-faced George. **1879** *Chambers's Jrnl.* 6 Sept. 561 A system of swindling..arising out of the loose slip-slop legal procedure.

**b.** Of discourse, writings, style, etc.

**1827** A. W. FONBLANQUE *Eng. under 7 Administr.* (1837) I. 27 Like the slip-slop, wishy-washy..speeches of Lords in the Upper House. **1841** *Blackw. Mag.* L. 635 The abstruse sciences are reduced to slip-slop literature for the young. **1874** S. WILBERFORCE *Ess.* (1874) II. 238 A loose slip-slop style of English composition.

**'slip-slop,** *v.* [Cf. SLIP-SLOP *sb.*]

**1.** *intr.* (See quots. and cf. SLIP-SLOP *sb.* 2.)

*a* **1791** GROSE *Olio* 93 There is a grosser misapplication of words, which, from a character..delineated by Fielding,.. has been called slip-slopping. **1796** *Grose's Dict. Vulgar T.* (ed. 3), *Slipslopping,* misnaming and misapplying any hard word.

**2.** To drink a sloppy beverage.

**1834** BECKFORD *Italy* I. 297 The Capitol..was quite deserted, the world, thank Heaven, being all slip-slopping in coffee houses.

**3.** To slip or move about in a sloppy manner or with a flapping sound. Also used adverbially.

**1870** FARJEON *Grif* I. viii. 167 The dirty broken bluchers in which Grif's feet slip-slopped constantly. **1887** JEFFERIES *Amaryllis* vi, So they paddled along to the fair, slip-slop, in the dust. **1891** HARDY *Tess* (1900) 47/1 At the farther end the great churn could be seen revolving, and its slip-slopping heard.

**slip stone, slipstone** ('slɪpstəʊn). [f. SLIP *sb.*⁵ + STONE *sb.*] A shaped oilstone used for sharpening gouges.

**1927** H. HUBBARD *Colour Block Print Making* 209 *Slip stone,* a thin sharpening stone so shaped as to remove the burr or ragged edge from the inside of a gouge. **1947** J. C. RICH *Materials & Methods of Sculpture* x. 300 With gouges, the sharpening method is generally reversed. Specially shaped slip stones..are employed and the stone is rubbed on the gouge. **1958** J. R. BIGGS *Woodcuts* 36 Remember to have one slip-stone with its smallest curve small enough to sharpen the smallest gouge. **1976** *Billings* (Montana) *Gaz.* 27 June 4-G/5 With a slipstone, the tool is held firm while the sharpener is moved along the edges. With a whetstone, the tool is moved across it to get sharp edges.

**slip-stream** ('slɪpstriːm). Also slip stream, slipstream. [f. SLIP *sb.*³ + STREAM *sb.*] **1. a.** The current of air or water driven backward by a propeller or downward by a rotor.

**1913** A. E. BERRIMAN *Aviation* viii. 79 Each blade deflects air backwards as it moves; the combined effect of both blades operating always in the same region when the machine is standing still produces a concentrated flow of air, which becomes a very pronounced draught. Technically, this draught is called the slip stream. **1919, 1920** [see *air scoop* s.v. AIR *sb.*¹ B. II]. **1935** *Sun* (Baltimore) 19 Jan. 9/2 The slip stream from the propeller cast bits of mud and ice into the air during the take-off. **1963** J. ROWLAND *North to Adventure* ix. 132 Her rudder was one of those absurd little metal plates which are utterly ineffective unless the slipstream from the propeller is impinging directly upon them. **1973** C. BONNINGTON *Next Horizon* xiii. 190 The snow leapt up at me, and I was there, in one piece, with the slip-stream of the helicopter hammering at me.

**b.** Any localized current associated with an object, esp. a moving one.

**1947** in J. A. Carruth *Loch Ness & its Monster* (1950) 31 'We unmistakably sighted,' said Mr. Cottier, 'on the placid surface of the loch a fairly long slip-stream which quickly developed in length.' **1963** *Times* 8 June 5/2 He [*sc.* a cyclist] sat at the back, carried along in the slipstream of his adversaries, and so was the least tired rider when it came to the final sprint. **1973** 'A. HALL' *Tango Briefing* v. 62 The slipstream didn't cool anything: it just circulated the heat. There were gnats already sticking to the windscreen. **1974** M. BABSON *Stalking Lamb* xxv. 183 The candles flared and died..leaving little slipstreams of smoke.

**2.** *fig.* An assisting force considered to draw something along with or in the wake of the principal.

**1957** *Universe* 16 Aug. 4/2 The kaleidoscope of life which has moved with such tremendous upheavals..for the people caught up in its slipstream since 1933. **1961** *Times* 30 June 4/1 Sangster it was..who proved himself the leader, drawing in his slipstream Wilson. **1970** D. MATHEW *Courtiers of Henry VIII* III. vi. 203 They stood in contrast to all the slipstream of the modern State. **1980** *Times* 29 Feb. 1/2 Some of those who were trying to get into the slipstream behind the Labour Party.

Hence as *v. trans.*, to follow closely behind (another vehicle) so that the resistance of the air to one's progress is less; also, to pass after travelling in another's slipstream; also **'slip-streaming** *vbl. sb.*

**1957** S. MOSS *In Track of Speed* ii. 18, I tried for the first time the art of slip-streaming... What you do is to tuck in behind a faster car, so that you are more or less sucked along in the 'partial vacuum'. **1960** *News Chron.* 18 July 5/4, I planned to slip-stream him on the last lap. **1969** *Man* (Austral.) Mar. 43/1 If you are in near-equal machinery, it becomes a case..of slip-streaming an inch behind him and diving out for a pass at the vital moment. **1979** L. PRYOR *Viper* viii. 156, I caught them on the pit straight as they slipstreamed each other on the left side of the road.

**'slip-string.** Now *dial.* Also 6 slypstryng, 7 slipp-string(e, 6–7, 9 slipstring. [f. SLIP *v.*¹ + STRING *sb.*]

**1.** One who deserves to be hanged; a rogue or rascal, a shifty person.

**1546** J. HEYWOOD *Prov.* II. vii. (1562) I iiij, Euery good thyng, Thou lettest euen slyp, lyke a waghalter slypstryng. **1575** GASCOIGNE *Weedes, Supposes* Wks. (1587) 25 If he spie a slipstring by yᵉ way, such another as himselfe, a page, a lakey or a dwarfe. **1594** NASHE *Unfort. Trav.* Wks. (Grosart) V. 85 She not only gaue me the slip, but had welnie made me a slipstring. **1611** COTGR., *Pendardeau,* a little crackrope, young slipstring. **1624** HEYWOOD *Captives* v. iii, Now if thou bee'st wyse drawe thy neck out of the collar, doo, Slipp-stringe, doo. **1828** CARR *Craven Gloss., Slip-string,* a knave, a mean rascal, one whom the gallows groans for.

**2.** *attrib.* Of persons or actions: **a.** Roguish, rascally. **b.** *dial.* (See quot. 1854.)

**1629** DEKKER *Londons Tempe* Dram. Wks. 1873 IV. 123 We are making arrowes for my slip-string sonne. **16..** *MS. Bright* 170 fol. 1 (Halliw.), Such a slippstring trick As never till now befell us heeretofore, Nor shall, I hope, befall us any more. **1824** SCOTT *Redgauntlet* ch. vi, You are a sort of a slip-string gentleman. **1854** MISS BAKER *Northampt. Gloss., Slip-string ways,* careless, slovenly ways; applied almost exclusively to servants who slight their work.

**slip-top(ped:** see SLIP *sb.*² 5.

**slipware, slip-ware** ('slɪpwɛə(r)). [f. SLIP *sb.*¹ + WARE *sb.*³] Pottery coated with slip. Also *fig.* and *attrib.* passing into *adj.*

**1883** L. M. SOLON *Art Eng. Potter* 41 We shall conclude by mentioning another sort of Slip-ware also made now-a-days, the sham 'old Slip', of which we have to confess the possession of several pieces, bought..for genuine specimens. **1929** H. READ *Staffordshire Pottery Figures* 2 The Staffordshire potters, who had already acquired considerable skill in the manipulation of clays in the making of the type of pottery known as slipware. **1935** *Burlington Mag.* Oct. 180/1 A Wrotham slipware dish. **1957** *Listener* 17 Oct. 608/1 My second preference among English pots.. would be slip ware, which seems to be the earliest which can definitely be assigned to Staffordshire. **1968** J. ARNOLD *Shell Bk. Country Crafts* 232 Slip-ware is a porous earthenware on which a creamy clay has been applied on the still damp body, before firing, either by immersion or brush trailing. **1976** 'D. HALLIDAY' *Dolly & Nanny Bird* vii. 92 Two girls in curled hats..and pink slip-ware faces.

**slip-way** ('slɪpweɪ). Also slipway. [f. SLIP- + WAY *sb.*]

**1.** A sloping way leading down into the water; a slip. Also *fig.*

**1840** *Civil Eng. & Arch. Jrnl.* III. 431/1 Two flat-bottomed boats..were brought to the slipway, at the back of the mast-houses. **1862** ANSTED *Channel Isl.* I. iii. 42 Slip-ways and berthing for vessels. **1879** *Cassell's Techn. Educ.* IV. 189/1 Ships are usually built on *slip-ways,* sloping down to the water. **1912** *Flight* 7 Dec. 1133 (*caption*) The machine being launched from the slipway that leads down to the water from the hangar. **1922** *Encycl. Brit.* XXX. 48/1 The management of these [seaplane] stations is very similar to that of an aerodrome, with the exception of slipways up and down which aircraft are moved on leaving and entering the water. **1936** *Sun* (Baltimore) 6 July 9/1 The giant four-motored plane, prototype of the airliner with which Britain is to face the Atlantic voyage, made its first appearance on the slipway at Rochester this week. **1938** G. GREENE *Brighton Rock* I. iii. 46 The coffin slid smoothly down into the fiery sea... The clergyman smiled gently from behind the slipway. **1982** P. CONNON *In Shadow of Eagle's Wing* 28 On the evening of Wednesday, August 3, the hydromonoplane was launched down the slipway into Bowness Bay.

**2.** An inclined roadway leading into a mine.

**1863** *Cambrian Jrnl.* 151 The Austrian mines have circular slip-ways, viz., without steps, of an inclined plane, winding round a newel.

**slirt** (slɜːt), *sb. U.S.* [f. next.] A slight sweep or jerk.

**1870** S. GREEN *Trout Culture* vii. 63 The female diving down at intervals against the gravel, and as she comes up giving it a slirt to one side with her tail.

**slirt** (slɜːt), *v. U.S.* [Of obscure origin: *slirt* 'to squirt water' is recorded as Yorkshire dialect.] *trans.* To sweep or jerk lightly.

*Slirted,* given by Richardson (s.v. *Slur*) in a quot. from Ben Jonson, is an error for *flirted.*

**1870** S. GREEN *Trout Culture* vii. 63 She would slirt with her tail all the stones of proper size to be found near her nest. **1876** *Forest & Stream* 20 July 385/2 Slirting (Seth Green's word) her spawn over the same spot at every turn.

**slish.** *rare*⁻¹. [Jingling alteration of SLASH *sb.*¹] A slit.

**1596** SHAKS. *Tam. Shr.* IV. iii. 90 Heers snip, and nip, and cut, and slish and slash, Like to a Censor in a barbers shoppe.

†**sliss,** *v. Obs. rare.* [ad. Du. and Flem. *slissen.*] *trans.* To slake or slack (lime).

**1599** A. M. tr. *Gabelhouer's Bk. Physicke* 330/2 Take vnslissed lime, slisse him 8 or 9 times with water. *Ibid.* 331/1 Then take of the slissede lime, a little oyle, and both the waters.

**slit** (slɪt), *sb.* Forms: 3–6 slytte, slitte, 6 slyt, 6–7 slitt, 4, 6– slit. [f. SLIT *v.* Cf. OE. *ȝeslit* tearing, biting, = ON. (Icel., Norw., MSw.) *slit* (Da. *slid*), G. *schliss*; OE. *slite,* = MDu. and MLG. *slete* (Du. and LG. *sleet*); also MDu. *slitte, slette* (Du. *slet*) and OHG. *sliz* (G. *schlitz*).]

**1.** A straight and narrow cut or incision; an aperture resembling a cut of this description:

**a.** In clothing; †sometimes in specific senses, as the opening in the front of a shirt, a pocket, etc.

*a* **1250** *Owl & Night.* 1118 If hi mowe i-seo þe sitte, Stones hi doþ in heore slytte. *a* **1300** *Floriz & Bl.* 348 Þu most habbe redi mitte Twenti Marc ine þi slitte. *c* **1330** *Arth. & Merl.* 1406 (Kölbing), Þe king was wondred out of witt & toke þe messanger bi þe slit. **1530** PALSGR. 271/2 Slytte of a womans gowne, *fente, dune robe a femme.* **1563** FOXE *A. & M.* 1076/2 A close hoode, with two holes for his eyes..& a slit for his mouthe to breath at. **1613** PURCHAS *Pilgrimage* (1614) 432 Hee put the sword into the fire,..and so thrust it into the slit of his shirt. **1796** W. MASON *Birth of Fashion* Poems (1830) II. 32 To show her legs (inglorious thought) By well-chose slits in petticoat. **1855** BELL *Wks. Chaucer* VII. 41 *note,* The fashion of..cutting it [*sc.* the dress] in slits so as to show the under-garment or lining.

**b.** In general use.

**1398** TREVISA *Barth. De P.R.* XVII. cii. (Bodl. MS.), Droppinge þat comeþ oute atte kenes & slittes þat beþ made þerein is acounted lasse worþe. *c* **1440** *Pallad. on Husb.* I. 1120 With brymstoon resolute ypitte Aboute in euery chynyng, clift, or slitte. **1523** FITZHERB. *Husb.* §3 The hynder ende of the ploughebeame is put in a longe slyt. **1571** DIGGES *Pantom.* I. xxii. G iij, A thinne plate halfe an ynche broade,..and in the middes a fine slytte. **1668** CULPEPPER & COLE *Barthol. Anat.* IV. ix. 166 A long slit is made in each of them. **1697** DRYDEN *Virg. Georg.* II. 106 Just in that space a narrow Slit we make. **1747–96** MRS. GLASSE *Cookery* v. 57 Take a large leg of lamb, cut a long slit on the back. **1769** *Lloyd's Even. Post* 20–2 Sept. 283/3 Quills thus ..hardened, bear longer Slits, which Slit is always free. **1833** J. HOLLAND *Manuf. Metal* II. 157 When the cutting had once commenced, it was easily continued until a deep slit was produced in the steel. **1856** G. WILSON *Gateways Knowl.* (1859) 12 When Pussy is basking in the sun..she shows..only a narrow slit for a pupil. **1871** B. STEWART *Heat* (ed. 2) §19 The thermometer is inserted through a closely fitting slit in a thick piece of india-rubber.

**c.** A long narrow aperture in a wall; a window of this form. Also *transf.*

**1607** *Fabric Rolls York Minster* (Surtees) 119 To a joyner for a great casement for one of the longe slitts, 3s. 4d. **17..** RAMSAY *Up in the Air* ii, Nae starns keek throw the azure slit. **1859** JEPHSON *Brittany* vi. 70 An aisle pierced by twenty-four mere slits of round-headed windows. **1894** J. MACINTOSH *Ayrshire Nights Entert.* xvii. 304 On the right-hand side is an arrow-slit commanding the outer doorway.

**d.** The vulva. *coarse slang.*

Its currency is restricted in the manner of other coarse terms: see small-type note s.v. FUCK *v.*

**1648** R. HERRICK *Hesperides* 47 Scobble for Whoredome whips his wife; and cryes, He'll slit her nose; but blubb'ring, she replyes, Good Sir, make no more cuts i' th' outward skin, One slit's enough to let Adultry in. **1714** *Cabinet of Love* 18 His tarse, as soon as to my slit applied Up to the hilt into my cunt did slide. **1970** G. GREER *Female Eunuch* 265 The vagina..belittled by terms like..*slit.* **1977** *Rolling Stone* 24 Mar. 41/4 What am I going to call it? Snatch, Twat? Pussy? Puss puss, nice kitty, nice little animal that's so goddam patronizing it's almost as bad as saying 'slit'.

**e.** A narrow, usu. straight aperture in an optical instrument through which a beam of light can be received.

[**1832** *Nat. Philos.* (Libr. Useful Knowl.) II. II. iii. 25/1 Instead of a row of holes, he formed one narrow slit in the shutter... By this means a spectrum of any required breadth may be formed.] **1863** E. ATKINSON tr. *Ganot's Elem. Treat. Physics* VII. iv. 410 A telescope, the eyepiece of which can be regulated by a micrometric screw... The slit is in the focus of the object-glass of the telescope. **1888** *Proc. R. Soc.* XLIII. 130 Huggins's photograph of the spectrum of Comet Wells, taken with a wide slit. **1905** E. C. C. BALY *Spectroscopy* iii. 48 As generally used at the present time the slit is formed between two metal jaws, one of which is fixed while the other is moved by a fine-pitched screw. **1926** *Jrnl. Optical Soc. Amer.* X. 186 If the spectrophotometer has a second collimator, the continuous spectrum may be formed from an incandescent light placed in front of its slit. **1969** D. W. TENQUIST et al. *University Optics* I. xi. 293 (*caption*) Fraunhofer diffraction at a double slit.

**2.** *fig.* A schism, division, split. *rare*⁻¹.

**1390** GOWER *Conf.* I. 15 In holy cherche of such a slitte Is for to rewe unto ous alle.

**3.** *Agric.* A part of a field which has been 'split' in ploughing. *rare.*

**1778** [W. H. MARSHALL] *Minutes Agric.* 25 Oct. 1775, A level field, plowed in gathers and slits with a fixed-wrist plow.

**4.** *Coal-mining.* (See quots.)

**1860** *Eng. & For. Mining Gloss.* (ed. 2) 44 *Slit,* a communication between two adits. **1883** GRESLEY *Gloss. Coal-m.* 227 *Slit,* a short heading put through to connect two other headings.

**5.** *attrib.* and *Comb.*, as *slit-like, -shaped, -ways, -wise*; **slit drum**, a primitive percussion instrument made out of a hollowed log with a longitudinal slit; **slit-eyed** *a.*, having long and narrow eyes; **slit fricative** *Phonetics*, a fricative or spirant sound made by expelling the breath through a narrow aperture; **slit-gong** = *slit drum* above; † **slit-graft**, a graft inserted in a slit in the stock, or intended for this purpose; † **slit-**

**grafting**, grafting performed by means of a slit in the stock; **slit lamp** *Ophthalm.*, a lamp which emits a narrow but intense beam of light, used for examining the interior of the eye; freq. *attrib.*; **slit-limpet** (see quots.); **slit-planting, -setting**, a mode of planting or setting in which mere slits are made in the ground with a spade or similar implement; **slit pocket**, a side pocket in a garment, with a vertical opening; **slit sampler**, a device for studying the bacterial content of the air, having a slit through which it is drawn; **slit setting**: see *slit planting* above; **slit sound, spirant** *Phonetics* = *slit fricative* above; **slit-trench**, a narrow trench made to accommodate and protect a soldier or weapon in battle.

**1933** *Africa* VI. 155 The deep-toned *slit-drum..is assigned by ethnologists..to the matriarchal 'two-class' culture circle. **1957** *New Oxf. Hist. Music* I. ii. 185 The wooden fish, still in use among Taoists and Buddhists, is a slit-drum. **1974** *Encycl. Brit. Macropædia* XIV. 61/2 In Vietnam the slit-drum is both a temple and a watchmen's instrument. On Java slit-drums can be traced to the Hindu-Javanese period (1st–9th century AD). **1894** *Daily News* 18 June 6/3 Bands of *slit-eyed Chinamen. **1899** F. T. BULLEN *Log Sea-waif* 44 That slit-eyed pagan..found me out. **1955** H. A. GLEASON *Introd. Descr. Linguistics* ii. 22 Because of the *slit-like shape of the opening, these sounds are called slit fricatives. **1973** J. C. WELLS *Jamaican Pronunc. in London* 127 This feature is an extension of the..distinction between 'groove' and 'slit' fricatives. **1938** *Jrnl. R. Anthrop. Inst.* LXVIII. 241 Samara returned to the village and after beating the *slit-gong gave vent to his grievance. **1970** *Times* 23 Feb. 10/4 (*caption*) A 'slit gong' which has been accepted by the Queen as a gift... The gong is used in the New Hebrides to convey messages, summon people and sound the alarm. **1706** LONDON & WISE *Retir'd Gard.* I. II. xii. 164, I desire you would tell me how a *Slit-graft should be cut. *Ibid.* 159, I shall only mention Three different Sorts of Grafting, *viz.* Scutcheon-grafting, *Slit-grafting, and Crown-grafting. **1763** MILLS *Pract. Husb.* IV. 213 Cleft-grafting, called also Stock, or Slit-grafting. **1922** *Arch. Ophthalm.* LI. 271 Many new phases of examination of the living eye are made possible by the use of the *slit lamp. **1961** [see GONIOSCOPE]. **1978** *Jrnl. R. Soc. Med.* LXXI. 100 Slit-lamp examination revealed a moderate number of cells in the anterior and posterior vitreous. **1869** G. LAWSON *Dis. Eye* (1874) 137 To draw the opaque lens out of the eye through a *slit-like opening. **1901** E. STEP *Shell Life* 193 The *Slit-limpets (*Fissurellidae*)..have a slit which serves the purpose of an excretory orifice. *Ibid.* 195 Common Slit-limpet (*Emarginata fissura*). **1832** *Planting* 35 in *Husb.* (L.U.K.) III, *Slit planting is the most simple mode, and is practised on soils in their natural state. **1843** J. SMITH *Forest Trees* 64 What is called slit-planting I consider best on shallow ground. **1933** J. E. LIBERTY *Practical Tailoring* ix. 169 *Slit pockets are somewhat similar to trouser pockets and are made with jettings, or welts, but the pocket is not sewn twice. The mouth of the pocket is almost upright and at least 7 in. long for a normal size coat. **1978** M. SICHEL *Costume Reference 8: 1918–1939* 36 Many skirts worn with blouses had pockets at the sides or slit pockets and belts of the same material. **1941** R. B. BOURDILLON et al. in *Jrnl. Hygiene* XLI. 220 The range of concentrations which can be measured accurately with the *slit sampler is from about 1 to 10,000 per cu. ft. **1963** WALTER & ISRAEL *Gen. Path.* xix. 295 The slit-sampler consists of a narrow slit through which air is sucked on to a rotating culture plate beneath it. **1868** *Rep. U.S. Commissioner Agric.* (1869) 253 The injury is less than that of the same kind incident to *slit-setting, by means of a spade. **1890** DOYLE *White Company* xxix, The narrow *slit-shaped openings at either side of the ponderous gate. **1912** *Slit sound [see RILL *sb.*[1] 4]. **1958** *Slit spirant [see RILL *sb.*[1] 4]. **1970** *Publ. Amer. Dial. Soc. 1968* L. 21 The phoneme /θ/ of *thirty, Martha, hearth* is a voiceless dental slit spirant [θ]. **1942** *Slit trench [see FOX-HOLE]. **1944** *Times* 12 May 3/2 At Manus Island the prisoners were made to dig slit trenches for the Japanese. **1971** B. W. ALDISS *Soldier Erect* 162 My slit-trench is the first on the right, next to the cookhouse. Cheerio, Ali, you old robber! **1725** *Fam. Dict.* s.v. *Grafting*, The Azerole or small Medlar may particularly be grafted *Slitwise [**1727** Slit-ways] upon the white Thorn.

**slit** (slɪt), *v.* Pa. t. and pa. pple. slit. Forms: (see below). [ME. *slitte* weak vb., obscurely related to OE. *slítan*: see SLITE *v.*

It is very doubtful whether there is any direct connexion with the ONorthumb. forms *-slitten* for the pa. pple. *-sliten*, and *-slittes, -slitteð, -slittað* for *-slítes*, etc., which belong to the verb (*to*)*slítan*. The ME. weak verb may rather correspond to OHG. *slizzan* (MHG. *slitzen*, G. *schlitzen*):—**slitjan*. The earliest example occurs in the pa. pple. *i-slit*; for slightly later instances see TO-SLIT *v.*]

**1.** *trans.* To cut into, or cut open, by means of a sharp instrument or weapon; to divide or sever by making a long straight cut or fissure; also, to take *off* or *out* in this way.

α. *Inf.* (and *Pres.*) 4–6 **slytte**; 4–5 **slitte** (5 **sclitte, slitt**), 4, 6– **slit.**

*c* **1386** CHAUCER *Frankl. T.* 532 To doon his diligence,.. Or with a swerd þat he wolde slitte his herte. **1530** PALSGR. 721/2 Slytte this stycke in twayne. **1596** SHAKS. *Tam. Shr.* v. i. 134 Ile slit the villaines nose that would haue sent me to the Iaile. **1637** W. CARTWRIGHT *Royal Slave* III. iii, Let's slit this graver weazen. **1687** A. LOVELL tr. *Thevenot's Trav.* II. 114 They slit the Noses of all their Asses, to make them breath more freely. **1747–96** MRS. GLASSE *Cookery* v. 53 Slit them in two, and put the yolk of an egg over. **1867** TROLLOPE *Chron. Barset* II. li. 85, I was going to slit the picture from the top to the bottom. **1869** TOZER *Highl. Turkey* II. 280 To slit the branch of a sapling tree.

β. *Pa. t.* 4 **slitte**, 5 **slytte, slyt**, 4–5, 7– **slit**; also 4–5 **slitted**, 5 **slytted.**

(*a*) **13..** *Sir Beues* 866 Sum vpon þe helm a hitte, In to þe sadel he hem slitte. **1387** TREVISA *Higden* (Rolls) V. 39 þan sche kutte and slitte here cloþes. *c* **1400** *Pilgr. Sowle* (Caxton, 1483) III. ix. 55 Thenne sawe I yet another companye of whiche fowle Sathanas slytte the throtes. *c* **1450** *Merlin* vii. 118 He slyt a-sonder the sadell and the chyne of the horse. **1664** POWER *Exp. Philos.* I. 55 We slit a black Horse's Hair with a Razor, and perceived it to be hollow. **1873** DIXON *Two Queens* I. iv. I. 27 The figure drew a sword and slit Arbues through the elbow.

(*b*) *a* **1300** *E.E. Psalter* xxix. 14 þou slitted mi sek in twa. *c* **1440** *Jacob's Well* 298 þe turmentourys..slytted hym & his herte a-sunder. **1483** CAXTON *Gold. Leg.* 421/1 As hys cook dressyd and slytted it [*sc.* the fish].

γ. *Pa. pple.* 3 **i-slit**, 4 **i-slitte**, 5–6 **slitte**, 5 **slyt(t, sclyt**, 6– **slit** (7 **slitt**); also 7, 9 **slitted.**

The mod. north. dial. *slitten* is perh. a new formation, but may be a survival of the pa. pple. of SLITE *v.*

(*a*) *c* **1205** LAY. 14221 þa al islit wes þe þong, he wes wunder ane long. **1387** TREVISA *Higden* (Rolls) IV. 443 þe bowels were i-slitte and y-turned to seche gold wiþ ynne. *c* **1400** *Beryn* 3204 With that cam þe vomman,—hir tunge was nat sclytt. **1451** CAPGRAVE *Life St. Aug.* 34 This same Innocent..had a greuous sor, whech sor myth not be hol.. with-outen þat it wer slitte. **1555** WATREMAN *Fardle Facions* I. iv. 47 Y[e] skinne beyng pretely slit. **1589** *Pasquil's Ret.* B iij b, Your tongue will be slitte if you take not heede. *a* **1632** T. TAYLOR *God's Judgem.* I. I. ii. (1642) 29 Many.. flying to the Enemy, were taken and slit in pieces. **1687** A. LOVELL tr. *Thevenot's Trav.* I. 29 Their Shirt (which hath sleeves like our Womens Smocks, and is slit in the same manner) comes over their Drawers. **1710** STEELE *Tatler* No. 164 ¶4 Sirrah, you deserve to have your Nose slit. **1823** H. J. BROOKE *Introd. Crystallogr.* 88 Crystals which might be conceived to have been slit in a particular direction. **1884** J. GILMOUR *Mongols* xxiv. 296 The tongue they had slit and hung up to dry.

(*b*) **1602** FULBECKE *Pandects* 79 The nostrils of the adulteresse were slitted. **1900** *Daily Mail* 26 Apr. 4/4 The earth is all slitted with trenches.

**b.** *fig.* To divide, separate, sever.

*a* **1300** *E.E. Ps.* lxxxviii. 24 (Eg.), I sal slit [*Harl.* slitte] fra his face his ille-wiland. **1637** MILTON *Lycidas* 76 Comes the blind Fury with th' abhorred shears, And slits the thin spun life. **1645** —— *Colast.* Wks. 1851 IV. 358 Now hee comes to the Position,..and like an able text man slits it into fowr. **1798** *Poet. Anti-Jacobin* No. 24. 127 'Till deadly Atropos with fatal sheers Slits the thin promise of the expected years.

**2.** *techn.* To cut (iron) into rods or (wood) into thin deals.

**1522-** [see SLITTING *vbl. sb.* 1, and SLITTING-MILL 1]. **1796** MORSE *Amer. Geogr.* I. 410 The slitting-mills in this district, it is said, annually slit 600 tons of iron. **1831** J. HOLLAND *Manuf. Metal* I. 146 The practice of slitting, as it is termed, sheets of metal into light rods. **1873** RICHARDS *Operator's Handbk.* 114 Carriage saws, such as are used for jointing floor boards or slitting very long stuff.

**3.** *Agric.* To 'split' in ploughing.

**1766** *Compl. Farmer* s.v. *Lucern*, In March the same year ..he slit the ridges with the plough.

**slit**, *ppl. a.* [f. prec.]

**1.** Of garments: Rent, torn; slashed.

**1387** TREVISA *Higden* (Rolls) I. 297 Cloþed in slitte cloþis and foule. **1438** *E.E. Wills* (1882) 111 A gowne..with slyt slyues y-furred. *a* **1450** *Knt. de la Tour* (1868) 30 Thei were the furst that brought up this astate that ye use of gret purfiles and slitte cotes. **1706** *Lond. Gaz.* No. 4257/4 A brown Coat, with slit Sleeves. **1711** ADDISON *Spect.* No. 129 ¶10 A Coat with long Pockets, and slit Sleeves.

**2.** Naturally divided or cloven.

**1607** TOPSELL *Four-f. Beasts* (1658) 99 The face of this beast is fleshy,..his ears..are slit. **1664** POWER *Exp. Philos.* I. 2 His feet are slit into claws or talons. **1774** GOLDSM. *Nat. Hist.* (1776) IV. 170 Its tongue..is forked or slit at the end like that of serpents.

**3. a.** Cut with a sharp instrument; divided by slitting.

**1611** COTGR., *Fendu*, the slit, or clouen side of a thing. **1648** HEXHAM II, *Gesliste ooren*, Slit or Cropped eares. **1670** MILTON *Hist. Eng.* VI. Wks. 1851 V. 254 Canute..took the hostages.., and with slit Noses..setting them ashore, departed into Denmarke. **1725** *Fam. Dict.* s.v. *Grafting*, Loam and slit Osier. **1835–6** *Todd's Cycl. Anat.* I. 240/2 Looking along the slit-side of the vessel. **1865** TYLOR *Early Hist. Man.* i. 1 The weights that pull the slit ears in long nooses to the shoulder. **1885** MEREDITH *Diana* i, Poniarded, slit-throat, rope-dependant figures.

**b.** *spec.* Of deals: (see quot. 1842).

**1632** in E. B. Jupp *Carpenters' Co.* (1887) 297 The dividing of..Chambers and other roomes..with slitt or whole deales. **1683** MOXON *Mech. Exerc.*, *Printing* iv, The Bearers are made of Slit-Deal. **1703** STANTON in De Foe *Storm* (1896) 329 We are obliged to make use of slit deals to supply the want of slats and tyles. **1772** T. SIMPSON *Vermin-Killer* 26 Lay a piece of slit deal over the trap. **1842** GWILT *Archit.* Gloss. s.v. *Board*, Fir boards of this sort, one inch and a quarter thick, are called whole deal, and those a full half inch thick, slit deal. **1875** KNIGHT *Dict. Mech.* 2212/2 *Slit-deal Plane*, a tonguing or grooving plane.

**c.** In various special collocations (see quots.). **slit skirt**, a tight skirt slit upward from the hem for ease of movement or sexual allurement.

**1890** 'R. BOLDREWOOD' *Col. Reformer* (1891) 107 Wether, hogget, ewe, weaner, *slit-ear. **1789** *Deb. Congress U.S.* 17 Apr. (1834) I. 167 To lay an impost of seven and a half per cent..upon..*slit or rolled iron. **1843** HOLTZAPFFEL *Turning* I. 188 These rods are also made of larger sizes, when they are called slit iron. **1799** J. ROBERTSON *Agric. Perth* 96 An oblong hole, into which a *slit-nail is put. **1846** HOLTZAPFFEL *Turning* II. 540 The nose-bit,..called also the *slit nose-bit,..is slit up a small distance near the center. **1677** YARRANTON *Eng. Improv.* 47 The third [school] is for Boys painting the Toys and *slit Pictures. **1825** J. NICHOLSON *Operat. Mechanic* 503 A circular rack..that holds the curb or *slit-piece. **1835** URE *Philos. Manuf.* 270 This slit-piece [in a silk-winding engine] is called the cleaner. **1879** *Cassell's Techn. Educ.* II. 319 '*Slit rods,' which are used for nail-making. **1882** *Worc. Exhib. Catal.* iii. 18 Slit rods for making into nails. **1881** *Cassell's Nat. Hist.* V. 216 Genus *Pleurotomaria*, '*Slit-shell'. **1897** WOODWARD in *Concise Knowl. Nat. Hist.* 632 The Pleurotomidae, or slit-shells, have conical, spiral shells with a notch in the outer lip at the periphery. **1913** *Punch* 30 July 101/2 Four young women who last week promenaded Fifth Avenue, New York, in *slit skirts..were surrounded by an enraged mob. **1954** C. G. BRADLEY *Western World Costume* xxi. 342 The hobble skirt of 1914 was worn even on long walking excursions. The slit skirt of the same year brought protests from bishops and ministers. **1976** 'M. DELVING' *China Expert* i. 7 The slit skirt of the *ch'i pao* she always wore. **1662** EVELYN *Chalcogr.* 18 Such as were the *Slit-stones, or Slates which succeeded the stately marbles. **1799** S. FREEMAN *Town Officer* 124 All boards, plank, timber and *slitwork..shall be surveyed.

**4.** *Comb.*, as *slit-eared, -footed, -nosed.*

**1607** TOPSELL *Four-f. Beasts* (1658) 176 Cloven- or slit-footed into many claws. **1850** W. IRVING *Mahomet* xxxv, Al Adha or the slit-eared, the swiftest of his camels. **1880** BROWNING *Dram. Idyls, Muléykeh* 32 You feed young beasts ..of famous breed, Slit-eared, unblemished. **1884** COUES *N. Amer. Birds* 733 *Gaviæ*, Slit-nosed Longwings.

**slitch** (slɪtʃ). *Obs.* exc. *dial.* Forms: 5 **slicche, slycche**, 5–6 **sliche**, 6 **slich, slyche, slytche, slitche**, 7– **slitch**. [app. representing an OE. **slíc* (see SLIKE *sb.*); for the phonetic development cf. *ditch, sitch.*] = SLEECH *sb.* (See also quot. 1794.)

*c* **1400** *Destr. Troy* 5763 The Troiens dong hom doun in the depe sliche. *Ibid.* 13547 Thurgh the slicche and the slyme in þis slogh feble. **1432–50** tr. *Higden* (Rolls) I. 133 Nilus..makethe the londe plentuous thro slycche that hit drawethe with hit. *c* **1585** PILKINGTON *Expos. Nehemiah* ii. 27 b, For the wickednes of Sodom..that pleasant ground.. is now barren, full of filthie mire, slitche, tarre, &c. **1688** *Phil. Trans.* XVII. 985 They may..get admirable Slitch, where-with to Manure all their uplands. **1794** HUTCHINSON *Hist. Cumb.* I. 564 Lime is chiefly used as a manure, with clagg or slitch, as the farmers call it, being the wreck left by the tide on the shore. **1878** in *Cumberld. Gloss.*

**slite** (slaɪt), *sb.* Now *E. Angl. dial.* Also 9 **slight, sleight.** [f. SLITE *v.*, or ad. Du. *slijt* (cf. G. *schleiss*), f. *slijten* (see next).] Impairment through use; wear and tear.

**1614** GENTLEMAN *Way to win Wealth* 36 But the yearely slite and weare of her tackell and war-ropes and nets will cost some eighty pounds. **1879** *Norfolk Archaeol.* VIII. 173, I have a wonderful sleight for shoes with my children. **1895** *E. Angl. Gloss.* 200, *Slite*, wear and tear.

**slite**, *v.* Now *rare* or *Obs.* Also 5 **slytyn**, 5, 9 **slyte.** *Pa. t.* 6, 8–9 *Sc.* **slate, slait.** *Pa. pple.* 5 **slytyn.** [Representing either OE. *slítan* (*slát*, etc.) or ON. *slíta* (Icel. *slíta*, Norw. and Sw. *slita*, Da. *slide*), corresponding to OFris. *slîta* (WFris. *slite*), MDu. *slīten* (Du. *slijten*), OS. *slîtan* (MLG. and LG. *slîten*), OHG. *slîzan* (G. *schleissen*).

Common in OE., but rare in the later language; the mod. dial. pa. pple. *slitten* is now associated with SLIT *v.*]

**1.** *trans.* To slit or split; to cut or rip up.

*c* **1440** *Jacob's Well* 226 þe o feend slyteth wyth a swerd my body, & begynneth at myn heued dounwarde. **1536** BELLENDEN *Chron. Scot.* Proh. (1541) A vij, Duke Hanniball ..Brak doun the wallis, and the montanis slait. **1825** JAMIESON *Suppl.*, *To Slite, Slyte*, to rip up any thing that is sewed. **1841** in R. Chambers *Pop. Rhymes Scot.* (1870) 156, I sewed a pair o' sheets, and I slate them.

**2.** To impair by wear; to wear out. Hence **'sliting** *vbl. sb.* (Cf. SLITE *sb.*)

*c* **1440** *Promp. Parv.* 459/2 Slytyn, or weryn, *attero, vetero. Ibid.*, Slytynge, *veteracio, consumpcio.*

**3.** *Sc.* To whet or sharpen.

**17..** *Gil Morrice* xviii. in Percy *Reliques* III. i, Now he has drawn his trusty brand, And slaited [*read* slait it] on the strae. *a* **1800** in Child *Ballads* IV. 491 Johnny drew forth his good braid glaive, And slate it on the plain. **1825** JAMIESON *Suppl.* s.v. *Slait, Slite* is used in this sense [*sc.* to whet] in Lanarks[hire] and also in Loth[ian].

**slite**, obs. form of SLEET *sb.*

†**slithe**, *v.* *Obs.* Also 5 **slythe**; *pa. t.* **slathe.** [app. an alteration of SLIDE *v.*, on the analogy of SLITHER *v.* or under Scand. influence.] *intr.* To slip, slide. Hence †**'slithing** *vbl. sb.* and *ppl. a.*

*a* **1300** *E.E. Psalter* lv. 13 Mi saule dede toke þou fra, Mi fete fra sliþinge als-swa. *Ibid.* cxiv. 8 He toke..Mi fete fra slithing þer i ga. *c* **1460** *Mirour Saluacioun* (Roxb.) 17 Than sithen be slithing gudes the werld wold vs betrayse. *Ibid.* 46 A stone with out mans hande was kytte And in the feet of the ymage or mawmet doun slathe itte. *c* **1460** *Towneley Myst.* xiii. 122 It is euer in drede and brekyll as glas, And slythys.

**slither** ('slɪðə(r)), *sb.* Also *Sc.* **sclither.** [f. SLITHER *a.* or *v.*]

**1.** *pl.* 'Loose stones lying in great quantities on the side of a rock or hill' (Jamieson). *Sc.*

**1805** J. NICOL *Poems* II. 103 (Jam.), Fir'd wi' hope, he onward dashes, Thro' heather, sclithers, bogs, an' rashes. **1884** SPEEDY *Sport Highl.* xiii. 220 They will often be seen running among the grey stones or 'sclithers'.

**2.** *local.* (See quots.)

**1811** J. FAREY *Derbyshire* I. 145 The Slither, or indestructible rubble of Limestone. *Ibid.*, It slips from beneath the feet of an animal which attempts to cross it, whence the name Slither, or sliding gravel. **1829** *Glover's Hist. Derby* I. 49 Patches of slither are the most barren spots that can be imagined.

**3.** *techn.* (See quot.) Also *fig.*

**1830** *Examiner* 419/2 Slither is, we believe, the technical term..[given] to the cuttings and rubbish put in between the outer and the inner soles of shoes. *Ibid.*, Even the slither of O'Doherty is inserted, while matter of real importance from O'Connell is omitted.

**4. a.** A slipping or sliding. Also *transf.* and *fig.*

**1861** TROLLOPE *Tales of All Countries* 67 Then there was a great slither, and an exclamation, and the noise of a fall. **1897** W. WESTALL *Red Eagle* xxvi, A slither down a slope that would have tried the nerve of a chamois-hunter. **1915** E. WALLACE *Man who bought London* ii. 23 So many people were following closely in that hurried slither to the platform. **1970** *Guardian* 12 Nov. 12/2 If the whole slither into inflation is not to accelerate..some private employers will have to stand firm.

**b.** Something smooth and slippery; a smoothly sliding mass; = SLIVER *sb.*[1] 1.

**1919** E. POUND *Quia Pauper Amavi* 40 If she goes in a gleam of Cos, in a slither of dyed stuff, There is a volume in the matter. **1955** N. NICHOLSON *Lakers* xi. 188 Only after rain, when..the rocks are hung with slithers of water like lace curtains against the black slate. **1966** G. GREENE *Comedians* I. v. 153 Little fenced saucers of earth where a few palm-trees grew and slithers of water gleamed between. **1981** *Daily Tel.* 27 May 15/1 Calvin Klein's newest dress is a slither of silk shaped simply like an overgrown T-shirt.

**slither** ('slɪðə(r)), *a.* Now *dial.* and *rare.* Also 4 **sklıþer**, 5 **slyther**. [Later variant of SLIDDER *a.*] Slippery. Also as *adv.*, smoothly.

*a* **1340** HAMPOLE *Psalter* xxxiv. 7 Þe way of þaim be made merknes and skliþer. *Ibid.* xxxviii. 1 Lightly it slippis, as we doe when we ga in skliþer way. *c* **1489** CAXTON *Blanchardyn* xxiv. 89 The grasse wher vpon he trad was sore weet & slyther. **1892** JANE BARLOW *Bogland* (1893) 54 Whin-ever there's little that ails ye, An' all goes slither as grase.

**slither** ('slɪðə(r)), *v.* Forms: 2 **sleðren** (?), 4 **sliþer**, 5 **slyther**, 8- **slither**; 4 **sklythir**, 9 *Sc.* **sclither**. [Later variant of SLIDDER *v.*, with normal change of *d* to *th*: cf. *gather*, *hither*, etc.]

**1.** *intr.* To slip, slide, glide, esp. on a loose or broken slope or with a clattering noise; †to fall gently. Freq. with *down*.

*c* **1200** *Trin. Coll. Hom.* 99 Þis is þe holi manne þe ure drihten sende alse snow sleðrende. *a* **1340**, *c* **1360** [see the *vbl. sb.*]. *a* **1450** *Mankind* (Brandl) 109 Yf ȝe sey þat I lye, I xall make yow to slyther. **1788** W. H. MARSHALL *Yorksh.* II. 353 To *Slither*,..to slide; as down a rope, a ladder, or the side of a hill. **1825-** in many dial. glossaries. **1861** DODSON in *Peaks, Passes, & Glac.* I. 199 He slithered down the polished surface of the gully, like a tree down a timber shoot. **1880** *19th Cent.* Sept. 455 The way they [Colorado horses] will climb up places, and slither down places.., is marvellous. **1896** BADEN-POWELL *Matabele Campaign* xiv, On these [smooth rocks] the men with their nailed boots slithered and clattered to an awful extent.

*fig.* **1878** HUXLEY in *Life* (1900) I. xxxiii. 502 You go slithering down avalanches of work.

**b.** *trans.* To make or cause to slide.

**1892** *Daily News* 1 Oct. 2/1 It is many a long day since Meg and Margery took a hand each and slithered him down hill. **1897** *Pall Mall Mag.* Mar. 307 She slithered her feet along the ground.

**c.** To make (one's way) by slipping or sliding.

**1888** F. COWPER *Caedwalla* 223 Quite safely the man slithered his way over the mud.

**2.** *intr.* To walk in a sliding manner; to slip along or away.

**1848** A. H. CLOUGH *The Bothie* iv. 30 The streets of the dissolute city, Where dressy girls slithering by upon pavements give sign for accosting. **1857** KINGSLEY *Two Y. Ago* III. 183 Gay girls slithered past him, looked round at him, but in vain. **1894** HALL CAINE *Manxman* 36 Philip slithered softly through the dairy door.

**3.** Of reptiles: To creep, crawl, glide.

**1839** FR. A. KEMBLE *Resid. in Georgia* (1863) 262 How horrid it [a snake] did look, slithering over the road. **1883** *Fortn. Rev.* Apr. 563 Feeling an unpleasantly cold something slithering down my right leg. **1888** J. INGLIS *Tent Life in Tigerland* 29 An odious, repulsive-looking *Säp go* (a species of iguana) slithered noiselessly through a gap.

**4.** Of things: To move in a slipping or sliding manner.

**1869** *Routledge's Ev. Boy's Ann.* 600 The rope had 'slithered' through his hands. **1869** *Echo* 9 Mar., The blades slither on the water, which at times made the boat roll.

Hence **'slithering** *vbl. sb.* and *ppl. a.*

*a* **1340** HAMPOLE *Psalter* cxiv. 8 In þe sensualite ȝit we fele sklythiryngе [*v.r.* scliteryng] and lust. *c* **1360** *E.E. Ps.* lv. 13 (Eg.), Þou toke mi saul dede fra, Mi fete fra sliþeringe als-swa. **1840** M. EDGEWORTH *Let.* 30 Dec. (1971) 573 Not one name when introduced had I been able to make out from Mrs. Hollands slithering pronunciation. **1864** J. C. ATKINSON *Stanton Grange* 219 His [a viper's] quiet, slithering gait. **1885** LADY BRASSEY *The Trades* 241 We continued to descend with a rapidity of 'slithering' and sliding, which might have considerably alarmed a timid Amazon. **1897** *Outing* XXIX. 596/1 His wheel shot past me with a slithering, vertiginous pace.

**'slitherness.** *rare*$^{-1}$. [f. SLITHER *a.*] Slipperiness. In quot. *fig.*

**1491** CAXTON *Vitas Patr.* (W. de W. 1495) I. i. 5 b/2 Wylte thou be now chaste and relygious, Thou whyche haste all thy lyfe lyued in slytherenesse of the worlde?

**slithery** ('slɪðərɪ), *a.* orig. *dial.* Also **slithry**, *Sc.* **sclithery**, **-ie**. [Alteration of SLIDDERY *a.*]

**a.** Slippery, in various senses.

**1825** in JAMIESON s.v. *Sclitherie*. **1861** J. F. HARDY in *Peaks, Passes, & Glac.* I. 390 The rock..in general..was well covered with snow. This in parts was very dry and slithery. **1884** SPEEDY *Sport Highl.* xix. 375 The 'sclithery' rock giving way, we slid down again into the bottom of the 'rut'. **1902** *Daily Chron.* 4 Sept. 3/2 The Jesuit..was mysterious, elusive, not to say slithery. **1922** E. R. EDDISON *Worm* xxvi. 332 With rocks and pits hidden in the heather, and slithery slabs of granite. **1946** M. PEAKE *Titus Groan* 298 His lordship..was gazing at his daughter with a slithery smile upon his mouth that had once been so finely drawn. **1952** L. A. G. STRONG *Darling Tom* i. 12 Against the wall stood four slithery horse-hair chairs. **1975** E. HUXLEY *Gallipot Eyes* (1976) 168 Oaksey Wood is a morass with yellowish water lying deep in slithery tractor ruts.

**b.** *Comb.*, as *slithery-eyed*, *-slobbery* adjs.

**1921** D. H. LAWRENCE *Sea & Sardinia* iii. 123 Give me the old, salty way of love. How I am nauseated with sentiment and nobility, the macaroni slithery-slobbery mess of modern adorations. **1977** *New Yorker* 8 Aug. 11/1 He picks out the very lad:..a twin..identical to the slithery-eyed boy destined to grow up into Marty Feldman.

†**'slithy**, *a.*[1] *Obs.*$^{-1}$ ? var. of SLEATHY *a.*

**1622** W. WHATELY *God's Husb.* II. 116 We make no great matter of the lower degrees of sinne, and so grow slithy, and fashionable, and dead in our confessions.

**slithy** ('slaɪðɪ), *a.*[2] Also †**slythy**. [Presumably a blend of SLIMY *a.* and LITHE *a.*] A word invented by 'Lewis Carroll': 'smooth and active' ('Carroll', 1855, 140) and popularized esp. in phr. *slithy toves* from *Through the Looking-Glass* (1871). Also in subsequent allusive uses.

**1855** 'L. CARROLL' *Rectory Umbrella & Mischmasch* (1932) 139 Twas bryllyg and the slythy [1871: slithy] toves Did gyre and gymble in the wabe. **1920** 'K. MANSFIELD' *Let.* 27 Sept. (1928) II. 48, I watched him [*sc.* a lizard] come forth to-day—*very* slithy—and eat an ant. **1928** A. S. EDDINGTON *Nature of Physical World* xiii. 291 Eight slithy toves gyre and gimble in the oxygen wabe; seven in nitrogen. **1937** G. FRANKAU *More of Us* 2 While the free-versifier gyres and gimbles The slithy tove—with his own 'private symbols'. **1960** H. MARCHAND *Categories* x. 368 Lewis Carroll's *slithy* .., *chortle*.. have become common property. Shakespeare's *glaze* (f. *glare* and *gaze*) has not. **1981** *Time Out* 20–26 Mar. 54/1 Pity the slithy toves of academe.

**'slitless**, *a.* [f. SLIT *sb.*] Of a spectroscope: Made without the usual slit for admitting the light.

**1881** C. A. YOUNG *Sun* 235 By examining the eclipse with a so-called slitless spectroscope. **1885** CLERKE *Pop. Hist. Astron.* 223 Making separate trial of a 'slitless spectroscope' devised for the occasion.

**slit-mill.** *rare.* [f. SLIT *v.* 2.] A slitting-mill.

**1776** ADAM SMITH *W.N.* II. i. (1869) I. 277 The furnace, the forge, the slit-mill are instruments of trade.

**'slitted**, *ppl. a. rare.* = SLIT *ppl. a.* 3.

**1797** MATON *West. Counties Eng.* I. 120 A candle stuck in a piece of slitted stick.

**'slitted**, *a. rare.* [f. SLIT *sb.* + -ED[2].] Having a slit or slits; shaped like a slit.

**1936** B. BROOKER *Think of Earth* I. i. 20 Stale fumes of beer ..were belched at the Canon as he passed the slitted swing doors of the bar. **1947** W. STEVENS *Transport to Summer* 139 A face of stone in an unending red, Red-emerald, red-slitted-blue, a face of slate. **1974** R. ADAMS *Shardik* xxiv. 184 The window-openings, rounded and slitted like key-holes, which lit the spiral stairways.

**slitter** ('slɪtə(r)), *sb.* [f. SLIT *v.* + -ER[1].] One who, or that which, slits; *spec.* as the name of various implements.

**1611** COTGR., *Tailleur*, a cutter, slitter, hewer. **1862** MRS. H. WOOD *Mrs. Hallib.* xxv, The slitters slit the four fingers, and shaped the thumbs and forgits. **1865** BAUERMAN *Catal. Mining Models* 21 Pick (*Slitter*), a double-armed pick,.. used for slitting out the vein. **1875** KNIGHT *Dict. Mech.*, *Slitter*, a machine for shearing up sheet-iron into slips for nail-rods, etc. **1895** G. E. DAVIS *Pract. Microscopy* (ed. 3) 280 The slitter is a thin wrought-iron disc about 11 inches in diameter,..and when used its edge is charged with diamond dust.

†**'slitter**, *v.*[1] *Obs. rare.* Also 4 **slyter**. [A frequentative from SLIT *v.*] *trans.* To cut (a garment) with ornamental slits. Hence **'slittered** *ppl. a.*, wearing clothes so ornamented.

? *a* **1366** CHAUCER *Rom. Rose* 840 Wrought was his robe in straunge gise, And al to-slytered for queyntise. *c* **1380** WYCLIF *Wks.* (1880) 121 Þei wasten hem in..pelure & costelewe cloþis & proude slitterede squyerys & haukis & hondis.

**'slitter**, *v.*[2] Now *dial.* Also 4 **sclıter**. [Obscurely related to SLIDDER *v.* and SLITHER *v.*] *intr.* To slide, slip, glide.

*a* **1400** [see SLITHERING *vbl. sb.*]. **1825-** in dialect use (see *Eng. Dial. Dict.*).

†**slitterkins.** *Obs.*$^{-1}$ [Cf. 'SLIDIKINS.] A form of minced oath.

**1786** *Microcosm* in Sydney *Engl. 18 C.* I. 54 Mincing blasphemy into odsbodikins, slitterkins, and such like.

**slitting** ('slɪtɪŋ), *vbl. sb.* [f. SLIT *v.* + -ING[1].]

**1.** The action of making a slit or slits, or of cutting in this manner. Also with *up*.

*c* **1175** *Lamb. Hom.* 33 Hunger and þurst and chele and feonda bitinga and neddre slittinga. **1398** TREVISA *Barth. De P.R.* XVI. vii. (Bodl. MS.), Auripigmentum..haþ kinde of slittinge and fretinge. **1522** *MS. Acc. St. John's Hosp., Canterb.*, For slyttyng of xliij fote of tymber. **1562** *Act 5 Eliz.* c. 14 §14 Imprisonment, Loss of Ears, slitting and searing of Nose. **1611** COTGR., *Coupement*, a cutting,.. cleauing, slitting. *a* **1712** KING *Art of Love* 713 Zoe..sav'd the slitting of his nose, By timely changing of her cloaths. **1750** *Act 23 Geo. II*, c. 29 §9 No mill or other engine for slitting or rolling of iron. **1879** *St. George's Hosp. Rep.* IX. 761 If phymosis coexists with warts..the slitting-up of the prepuce, or circumcision, is advisable.

**2.** *attrib.*, as *slitting-disk*, *-file*, etc.

In most of these *slitting* might also be taken as the *ppl. a.* For descriptions see Knight *Dict. Mech.*

**1819** *Pantologia* X. s.v., By passing it [*sc.* iron] through the slitting rollers, it is..slit up. *Ibid.*, A slitting machine. **1846** HOLTZAPFFEL *Turning* II. 822 Round files, square, equalling, knife and slitting files. **1875** KNIGHT *Dict. Mech.* 2212/2 [Slitting-file, -gage, -machine, -plane, -roller, etc.]. **1884** F. J. BRITTEN *Watch & Clockm.* 241 A screw slitting file, used principally for cutting the slits in screw heads. **1888** RUTLEY *Rock-Forming Min.* 23 To draw the clamped stone against the edge of the slitting disc.

So **'slitting** *ppl. a.*

**1387** TREVISA *Higden* (Rolls) II. 163 Al þe longage of þe Norþhumbres..is so scharp, slitting, and frotynge and vnschape [etc.].

**'slitting-mill.** [SLITTING *vbl. sb.*]

**1.** *Metall.* A mill or machine by which iron bars or plates are slit into nail-rods, etc.

**1667** PRIMATT *City & C. Builder* 8 A Slitting-Mill, which is for the forming of Iron into some fashion, as into Iron-rods, Nails, and such like things. **1686** PLOT *Staffordsh.* 163 Those they intend to be cut into rodds, are carryed to the slitting Mills. **1711** *Lond. Gaz.* No. 4862/7 Leases of two Forges, Furnace and Slitting Mill. **1792** *Descr. Kentucky* 49 The slitting and rolling mills of Pennsylvania. **1835** URE *Philos. Manuf.* 56 The operations of..the slitting-mill, the flatting-mill, &c.

**2.** *Gem-cutting.* A slicer, slitting-disk.

**1850** HOLTZAPFFEL *Turning* III. 1098 Slitting Mill or the Slicer, is a very thin sheet-iron disk, the edge of which is charged with diamond powder, and lubricated with brick oil.

**3.** A saw-mill for slitting deals.

**1884** KNIGHT *Dict. Mech.* Suppl.

**slitty** ('slɪtɪ), *a.* [f. SLIT *sb.* + -Y[1].] Of the eyes: long and narrow. Also in *Comb.*, as *slitty-eyed*, slit-eyed.

**1908** R. BROUGHTON *Mamma* x. 104 Her slitty eyes, opened so wide as almost to look large. *Ibid.* xxiii. 218 Her slitty eyes dancing with mirth and benevolence. **1926** G. FRANKAU *My Unsentimental Journey* 276 Where the slitty-eyed Chinese are. **1947** M. MORRIS *Township* 9 She was a sturdy young woman.., with..bright, slitty black eyes. **1976** *Listener* 18 Mar. 324/1 The English couple who turned down the Thai baby that was procured for them 'because its eyes are too slitty'.

**slive** (slaɪv), *sb.* Also 6 **sliue**. [f. SLIVE *v.*[1]]

**1.** A piece cut off; a slice. Now *dial.*

**1577** FRAMPTON *Joyful News* III. (1596) 103 This fruit.. being so grated they put it into a sliue of palme. **1668** WILKINS *Real Char.* 37 Shread, snip, slive, slice, collop, cut. *a* **1800** PEGGE *Suppl. Grose* s.v., A slive off a cut loaf will not be missed. **1854-** in dial. glossaries (Yks., Northampt., Leic., Warw.).

†**2.** A cut, a stroke. *Obs. rare.*

**1589** NASHE *Martin Marprelate* Wks. (Grosart) I. 138 You brag you haue giuen M. D. Bancroft such a sliue ouer the shoulders, as the credite of hys Chaplenship shall not recouer. **1747** POCOCKE *Journ. Scot.* (1887) 1 He gave me such a slive as a dog that has done some mischief.

**slive** (slaɪv), *v.*[1] Now *dial.* Forms: 5 **slyvyn**, **slyfe**, 5-6 **slyve**, **slyue**, 6 **sliue**, 6, 8- **slive**. *Pa. pple.* 4 **sleuyne**, 5 **sleuene**, 6-7 **sliuen**, 7 **sleeven**, 7, 9 *dial.* **sliven**, 8-9 *dial.* **sloven**. Also *pa. t.* and *pa. pple.* 6 **slyved**, **sliu'd**, **sliude**, 7 **slıued**, 6- **slived**. [OE. **slīfan* (the pa. t. occurs in the compound *tó-sláf*), app. not represented in the cognate languages.]

**1.** *trans.* To cleave, split, divide.

**13..** in Horstm. *Altengl. Leg.* (1881) 455 Þaire cotis ware al to-reuyne And þaire lymmes in sondir sleuyne. *c* **1440** *Promp. Parv.* 459/2 Slyvyn a-sundyr, *findo*, *effisso*. **1558** PHAER *Æneid* v. 96 With their stemmes yᵉ seas thei sliue. **1589** ? LYLY *Pappe w. Hatchet* E ij, Hee sliues one, has a fling at another. **1600** SURFLET *Countrie Farme* III. xlvii. 520 All trees which through force of winde..shall be clouen..or sliuen must be cured with mire. **1610** HOLLAND *Camden's Brit.* I. 135 They did cut downe a branch..and slived or cleft the same into slips. **1647** HEXHAM I, To Slit, cleave, or slive, *klieven ofte splijten*. **1703** THORESBY *Let. to Ray*, To *Slive*,..to rive. **1790** GROSE *Prov. Gloss.* s.v. *Sloven*, The honours are sloven; i.e. equally divided. Spoken at the game of whist. **1819-** in dial. glossaries, etc. (see *Eng. Dial. Dict.*).

**b.** *absol.* To cut *through* something.

**1558** PHAER *Æneid* v. M iij, The fomy waters through thei sliue.

**2.** To separate or remove by cutting or slicing; to take *off* in this manner.

*a* **1400** *Sir Cleges* 211 A lytyll bowe he gan of slyve, And thowght to schewe yt to his wife. **1530** PALSGR. 722/1, I slyve a gylowfloure or any other floure from his braunche or stalke. **1575** GASCOIGNE *Flowers* Wks. p. lxxi, He sliude the gentle slippe, which could both twist and twind. **1594** WILLOBIE *Avisa* (1880) 139 For hauing sliu'd the gentle slip, his loue was turnd to hate. **1601** HOLLAND *Pliny* XIII. xxxiv, The trees may be replanted of the very truncheons,..slived and divided from the very brain (as it were) of the green tree. **1793** *Trans. Soc. Arts* XI. 76 When the knife has penetrated to about the half [of the potato], the other half should be slived or broken off. **1841** HARTSHORNE *Salop. Ant.* Gloss., *Slive*,..to cut away in slices, strip bark from a tree. **1854** MISS BAKER *Northampt. Gloss.*, *Slive*, to..slice off any thing.

Hence **slived**, **sliven** *ppl. adjs.*

†*slived* or *sliven silk*: see SLEAVED *ppl. a.*

*a* **1548** HALL *Chron.*, *Hen. VIII*, 55 b, Sodainly came oute ..viii wyldemen, all apparayled in grene mosse, made with slyved sylke. **1575** TURBERV. *Faulconrie* 214 They cannot flee or stirre their wings by mean of some broke or slived feathers. **1688** HOLME *Armoury* II. 86/1 A Sliven, Shivered, or Cloven Tree. *Ibid.* III. 99/1 *Gum Work*, is by Gumming of several colours of sleeven Silk together.

**slive** (slaɪv), *v.*[2] Now *dial.* Forms: 5 slyue, 6, 9 slyve, 8- slive. *Pa. t.* 5 slafe, 9 slove (*dial.* sluv, sliv). *Pa. pple.* 5 sliven, 6 sleaven, 9 *dial.* slivven. Also *pa. t.* and *pa. pple.* 5, 9 slived, 6 slyued, 8 sliv'd. [app. a variant of SLEVE *v.* (OE. *sléfan*), with conjugation assimilated to prec.]

**1.** *trans.* To cause to slip *down*, *over*, etc.; to slip *on* (a garment), put *on* hastily or carelessly.

*c* **1410** *Master of Game* (MS. Digby 182) xxxiii, þenne shulde þe hunter slyue [*v.r.* slefe] doune þe skynn as fer as he may. **1494** in *Househ. Ordin.* (1790) 121 With his furred hudd sliven over his head and rolled about his necke. *Ibid.* 130 Yf he weare not his robe, he must have his hoode slived about his necke. **15..** *Bk. of Precedence* in *Q. Eliz. Acad.* 25 Nether may any weare hoodes with a Rowle slyued ouer there heades, or other wayes being of that fashon. **1593** *Rites & Mon. Church of Durham* (Surtees) 79 All the pippes of it was of Sylver to be sleaven on a long speare staffe. **1820** CLARE *Poems* (ed. 3) 145 When, unknown to her parents, Nell slove on her hat. **1828** CARR *Craven Gloss.* s.v., I'll slive my gown on and gang wi the. **1868** in *Cleveland Gloss.*

**b.** To convey furtively or quietly.

**1821** CLARE *Vill. Minstr.* I. 54 Where her long-hoarded groat oft brings the maid, And secret slives it in the sybil's fist. *Ibid.* II. 88 To slive her apron corner to her eyes.

**2.** *intr.* To slide; to slip. *rare.*

*c* **1440** *Alph. Tales* 323 When he was at mes and sulde lifte, as þe vse is, his lyn slevis slafe bakk. **1530** PALSGR. 722/1, I slyve downe, I fall downe sodaynly, *je coule*.

**b.** To slip *off* or away; to move quietly or slyly in some direction; to sneak or hang about; to loiter, idle.

**1707** MRS. CENTLIVRE *Platonick Lady* IV, I know her Gown agen—I minded her when she sliv'd off. **1725** BAILEY *Erasm. Colloq.* 33 What are you sliving about you Drone? **1787** GROSE *Prov. Gloss.*, *To slive*, to sneak. **1820** CLARE *Poems* (ed. 3) 59 Sun bid 'good night', and slove to bed. **1821** —— *Vill. Minstr.* I. 88 The cowboy oft slives down the brook. **1871** PEACOCK *Ralf Skirl.* II. 109 They'll believe he'd slive off into th' west country.

**sliver** ('slɪvə(r), 'slaɪvə(r)), *sb.*[1] Forms: 4 slivere, sleyvere, 6 sleuer, slyuer, 6-8 sliuer, 6- sliver (9 *dial.* slivver). [f. SLIVE *v.*[1]]

**1. a.** A piece cut or split off; a long thin piece or slip; a splinter, shiver, slice. Also *fig.*

*c* **1374** CHAUCER *Troylus* III. 1013 Allas, that he, al hool, or of him slivere, Shuld have his refut in so digne a place. *a* **1533** LD. BERNERS *Huon* xvi. 42 Ther spers brake to ther handes, so that yͤ sleuers flew a hye in yͤ ayer. **1575** TURBERV. *Faulconrie* 308 Which marreth their beakes, so as it is enforced to fall away in slivers and peeces. **1641** MILTON *Reform.* II. Wks. 1851 III. 35 What they can bring us now.. that can cut Tacitus into slivers and steaks, we shall presently hear. **1665** HOOKE *Microgr.* 45 A small sliver of Iron. **1715** tr. *Pancirollus' Rerum Mem.* I. IV. vii. 168 They were wont to cut them [tortoise shells] into certain Slivers, and to cover their Tables or Beds with them. **1747-96** MRS. GLASSE *Cookery* xviii. 291 When it is cold, it will cut in slivers as Dutch beef. **1811** SCOTT in *Lockhart* (1839) III. 353 A sliver of the wood run a third of an inch between my nail and flesh. **1874** MRS. JAY *Holden with Cords* 454 A delicate and difficult surgical operation, to remove pus, sliver of bone, or other foreign matter. **1967** T. KINSELLA *Nightwalker* I. 5 Bone-splinters, slivery slivers of screams. **1978** J. CARROLL *Mortal Friends* III. vi. 327 People on buses and on the streets of Boston traded slivers of information as if they were coins.

**b.** Applied to parts of trees or plants.

**1602** SHAKS. *Ham.* IV. vii. 174 An enuious sliuer broke, When downe the weedy Trophies, and her selfe, Fell in the weeping Brooke. **1656** W. DU GARD tr. *Comenius' Gate Lat. Unl.* 31 Onyon, Garlick, and Leek, and these bulbous herbs have slivers instead of leavs. **1861** LYTTON & FANE *Tannhäuser* 81 A maze of shrubs, Whose emerald slivers fringed the rugged way.

**c.** *U.S.* The side of a small fish sliced off in one piece for use as bait.

**1869** *Maine Acts & Resolves* 24 Any pumice, scraps or other offal arising from the making of oil or slivers for bait. **1880** G. B. GOODE *Hist. Menhaden* 201 (Cent.), The slivers (pronounced *slyvers*) are salted and packed in barrels.

**2.** A continuous ribbon or band of loose, untwisted, parallelized fibres of wool, cotton, flax, or other textile material, ready for drawing, roving, or slubbing.

**1703** *Wakes Colne* (Essex) *Overseers Acc.* (MS.), Paid for woollen sliuers to wrap him in, £o. o. 8. **1738** L. PAUL *Pat. Specif.* No. 562. 2 A strict regard must be had to make the slivers of an equal thickness from end to end. **1805** LUCCOCK *Nature of Wool* 225 It produces.. a sliver more compact than the old wools of either the Leicester or the Lincoln district. **1845** MCCULLOCH *Acc. Brit. Emp.* (1854) I. 675 After passing through the second pair of rollers, the reduced sliver is attached to a spindle and fly. **1894** *Times* 12 Mar. 13/5 The ordinary tow sliver.. is fed into the machine.

*attrib.* **1864** *Riddel & Co. Catal. Mill Furnishings*, Sliver Cans. **1875** KNIGHT *Dict. Mech.* 2213/2 Sliver-box. **1891** R. MARSDEN *Cotton Spinning* (ed. 4) 129 The sliver cans being taken and placed at the back.

**3.** In various technical uses: (see quots.).

a. **1842** *Archæologia* XXIX. 271 *note*, The little wooden instruments called slivers used in yarn spinning in the West of England.

b. **1846** A. YOUNG *Naut. Dict.* 287 *Sliver*, in shipbuilding, any thin piece of wood used as a filling. **1886** *Encycl. Brit.* XXI. 820 Wedges.. called slivers or slices, by which means the ship's weight is brought upon the 'launch' or cradle.

c. **1851** GREENWELL *Coal-trade Terms Northumb. & Durh.* 48 *Sliver*, a thin lath, placed within two grooves, cut lengthways for the purpose, in the edges of two planks intended to be joined together, for the purpose of making the joint airtight. **1883** GRESLEY *Gloss. Coal-m.* 227 *Slivers*, strips of wood or iron fitted in between the edges of boards in wooden bratticing, to make the joints air-tight.

**4.** A slashing cut or stroke.

**1806** J. BERESFORD *Miseries Hum. Life* III. xxxv, Becoming so tired of your own timidity in paring the paper too little, as to spoil all by one rash sliver. **1897** TROTTER *Life J. Nicholson* xx. 249 Nicholson.. clove him.. literally in two. 'Not a bad sliver that!' he remarked.

**5.** *attrib.* in **sliver-edge**, a very fine edge on a piece of timber.

**1874** THEARLE *Naval Archit.* 57 An efficient caulk not being obtainable when the deck plank snapes off to a 'sliver edge'.

**sliver** ('slaɪvə(r)), *sb.*[2] Now *dial.* [f. SLIVE *v.*[2]]

†**1.** *pl.* (Meaning doubtful.) *Obs.*[−1]

**1572** *Wills & Inv. N.C.* (Surtees, 1835) 373 A pair of Buffins with the slyuers to the same, one doblat of white bombasyne.

**2.** *dial.* (See quots.)

**1847** HALLIW., *Sliver*,.. a short slop worn by bankers or navigators. **1866** BROGDEN *Prov. Lincs.*, *Sliver*, a workman's linen jacket, a short blowse. **1908** MISS FOWLER *Betw. Trent & Ancholme* 54 A sliver was an over-all, an' they was made o' Drabette an' Cantoon.

**sliver** ('slɪvə(r), 'slaɪvə(r)), *v.* Also 7 sliuer. [f. SLIVER *sb.*[1]]

**1.** *trans.* To separate or remove as a sliver; to cut, split, or tear into slivers.

**1605** SHAKS. *Lear* IV. ii. 34 She that her selfe will sliuer and disbranch From her materiall sap, perforce must wither. **1605** —— *Macb.* IV. i. 27 Slippes of Yew, Sliuer'd in the Moones Ecclipse. **1654** GAYTON *Pleas. Notes* IV. xxv. 282 They sang aloud, good Lord de-liver us, And suffer not this Don to sliver us. **1706** PHILLIPS (ed. Kersey), *To Sliver*, to cut into Slivers, or thin Slices. **1825** HONE *Every-day Bk.* I. 882 People delight to sliver lettuces into bowls. **1845** S. JUDD *Margaret* I. iii, The floor of the room was warped in every direction, slivered and gaping at the joints. **1885** RUNCIMAN *Skippers & Shellbacks* 213 Down with the other ten or I'll sliver you.

**b.** *intr.* To split, or split off.

**1880** *Scribner's Mag.* May 79/1 The planks being cut across the grain to prevent slivering. **1896** KIPLING *Seven Seas* 64 The splinter slivered free.

**2.** *trans.* To convert (textile fibres) into slivers (see SLIVER *sb.*[1] 2).

**1796** MORSE *Amer. Geogr.* I. 543 Machinery to sliver, rove, and spin flax and hemp into thread. **1805** *Ann. Reg.* 848 Improvements in slivering and preparing hemp, flax [etc.].

Hence **'slivering** *vbl. sb.* Also *attrib.*, as ***slivering-knife***, ***-machine***.

**1875** KNIGHT *Dict. Mech.* 2214 *Slivering-machine* (Wood-working), a machine for cutting splints, slivers, or shreds of wood for various purposes. **1880** G. B. GOODE *Hist. Menhaden* 147 (Cent.), The operation of slivering is shown. *Ibid.* 201 The knife used is of peculiar shape, and is called a 'slivering knife'.

**'sliverly**, *a. dial. rare.* Crafty, deceitful.

**1674** RAY *N.C. Words* 43 (Lincoln), A sliverly fellow, *vir subdolus*, *vafer*. [Hence in Grose, etc.] **1877** *N.W. Linc. Gloss.* 228/2 He's a real down sliverly chap.

**slivery** ('slɪvərɪ), *a.* [f. SLIVER *sb.*[1] 1.] (See quot.)

**1832** *Planting* 91 in *Husb.* (L.U.K.) III, *Slivery*.—Small, straight shoots of large ash, &c., cleft into hoops for the purposes of the cooper.

**'sliving**, *vbl. sb.* Now *dial.* [f. SLIVE *v.*[1]]

**1.** A slash; the action of cutting.

*c* **1400** *Anturs of Arth.* xlviii. (Ireland MS.), He wend with a slyuyng, hade slayn him with slyȝt. *c* **1440** *Promp. Parv.* 459/2 Slyvynge, cuttynge a-wey, *avulsio*, *abscisio*.

**2.** A slip or cutting; a scion; a shoot or branch cut off. (Cf. SLAVING *sb.* and SLEAVING.)

*c* **1400** MAUNDEV. (Roxb.) vii. 26 Men take plantes or slyfynges þeroff and sett þam in oþer placez. *c* **1440** *Promp. Parv.* 459/2 Slyvynge, of a tre or oþer lyke, *fissula*. **1577** B. GOOGE *Heresbach's Husb.* II. (1586) 76 Some are also set of the slips, or sliuinges. **1580** FRAMPTON *Joyful News* (1596) 134 There dooeth come from them [*sc.* buds] many round coddes or slyuinges. **1879** MISS JACKSON *Shropsh. Word-bk.* 390 The term *sliving* is more especially applied to a branch—usually of hedge-row trees—sliced off with the hatchet in 'pleaching' the hedge.

**3.** A slice.

**1796** PEGGE *Derbicisms* Ser. I. 64 (E.D.S.), A great sliving of bread. *a* **1825** FORBY *Voc. E. Anglia* 307 *Sliving*, a slice of flesh.

**sliving** ('slaɪvɪŋ), *ppl. a.* [f. SLIVE *v.*[2] + -ING[2].] Slow-moving, dilatory; sneaking; stealing imperceptibly.

Also in dialect use as a *sb.*, explained by Thoresby (1703) as 'a lazy fellow' and by Hutton (1781) as 'a slovenly clown'.

**1661** K. W. *Conf. Charac. Conceited Coxcombs* (1860) 67 He would prove an unmatchable piece of sliving policy. **1710** MRS. CENTLIVRE *Man's Bewitched* III. i, The sliving baggage will not come to a resolution yet. *a* **1800** PEGGE *Suppl. Grose* s.v., A sliving fellow, one who loiters about with a bad intent. **1821** CLARE *Vill. Minstr.* I. 22 Ere sliving night around his journey threw Her circling curtains. *c* **1909** D. H. LAWRENCE *Collier's Friday Night* (1934) iii. 75 I'm not a fool, if you think so. I can pay you yet, you sliving bitch! **1913** —— *Sons & Lovers* iv. 66 What should go runnin' up my arm but a mouse... They'll get in your pocket an' eat your snap, if you'll let 'em.. the slivin', nibblin' little nuisances.

†**'slivings.** *Obs.*[−1] [f. SLIVE *v.*[2]] Loose or wide breeches.

**1601** T. WRIGHT *Passions* (1604) VI. 332, I have seene Tarleton play the Clowne, and vse no other breeches, than such slops or slivings, as now many Gentlemen weare.

**slivovitz** ('slɪvəvɪts). Also sliwowitz; ‖slivovic(e), slivovitza, sljivovica. [ad. G. *slibowitz*, f. Bulg. *slivovitza*, Serbo-Croat *šljivovica* plum brandy, f. OSl. *sliva* plum; cf. SLOE.] A central and eastern European plum brandy.

α. **1885** *Encycl. Brit.* XVIII. 692/2 Other important articles of commerce are wine, wool, cattle, timber, hides, honey, wax and 'slivovitza', an inferior spirit made from plums. **1938** C. MORGAN *Flashing Stream* I. i. 72 They have a drink called Šljivovica. It's a kind of plum-brandy. **1950** [see *plum brandy* s.v. PLUM *sb.* 6]. **1973** S. JACKMAN *Guns covered with Flowers* vi. 98 They drank two small glasses of sljivovica.

β. **1897** B. STOKER *Dracula* i. 11 There is a flask of slivovitz.. underneath the seat, if you should require it. **1900** 'ODYSSEUS' *Turkey in Europe* viii. 374 The plum-trees [of Northern Servia] that produce the national drink of slivovitz, or plum-brandy. **1940** M. HEALY *Stay me with Flagons* 273 Kirsch and Kirschwasser.. never have appealed to me; and Slivovitz I have never drunk, I think. **1951** F. BROWN *Murder can be Fun* viii. 104 What are you drinking? Me, I like slivovitz. **1960** A. E. BENDER *Dict. Nutrition* 114/2 *Sliwowitz*, plum brandy originating in Yugoslavia. **1960** R. ST. JOHN *Foreign Correspondent* ix. 192 There was a young German in his compartment who had drunk too deeply of Bulgarian slivovitz. **1976** *New Yorker* 22 Mar. 47/1 He sits by the kitchen window of his little flat,.. drinking the slivovitz he smuggles into Sweden each September in carefully emptied beer bottles.

γ. **1958** P. KEMP *No Colours or Crest* viii. 172 A flask of excellent Prizren slivovic. **1961** E. WAUGH *Unconditional Surrender* III. ii. 226 Once, after a jack-pot, he was offered a glass of Slivovic. **1971** *Southerly* XXXI. 17 Here's to scotch, to bourbon, to slivovic, to uyzo.

**slize** (slaɪz), *v.* Now *dial.* Also 5 slyse. [Of obscure origin.] *intr.* To look askance.

*c* **1400** *Laud Troy Bk.* 14043 Troylus eyen be-gan to slyse, The Gregeis sone he gan dispyse. **1825** BRITTON *Beauties Wiltsh.* 378 *Slize*, to look sly. **1883-93** in Hampsh. and Wiltsh. glossaries.

**slo**, obs. form or var. of SLAY *v.*, SLOE, SLOUGH *sb.*[1]

**sloak**, variant of SLOKE[1].

**sloam**, variant of SLOOM.

**sloan** (sləʊn). *Sc. rare.* [Of obscure origin: the form in northern English dialects is *slon*.] A severe snub or reproof; a 'taking-down'.

**1824** SCOTT *St. Ronan's* i, None so likely as Meg to give them what in her country is called a *sloan*. **1828** —— *Hrt. Midl.* Note xix, To have an opportunity of reviling the Judges to their faces, or giving them, in the phrase of his country, 'a sloan'.

**Sloane Ranger** (sləʊn 'reɪndʒə(r)), *sb.* and *adj. phr.* [Blend of *Sloane* Square, London, and *Lone Ranger*, a well-known hero of western stories and films.] (Of, pertaining to, or characteristic of) an upper class and fashionable but conventional young woman in London. Also occas. extended to any member of the class to which such young women belong, and *ellipt.* as ***Sloane***. Hence **'Sloaneness**.

**1975** P. YORK in *Harpers & Queen* Oct. 190/3 The Sloane Rangers.. are the nicest British Girl. *Ibid.* 191/2 The Sloane Rangers always *add tone*. They never put on prole accents, like self-conscious Oxford boys in the sixties. *Ibid.* 191/3 Once a Sloane marries and moves to Kennington and starts learning sociology through the Open University, she is off the rails. *Ibid.*, Sloaneness, some people would say, is a track to be liberated from. *Ibid.* 192/3 Sloane Ranger pet hates.. incense, Norman Mailer. **1978** *Evening Standard* 21 Aug. 13/2 A way of life neither Mayfair, nor West End nor Sloane Ranger, but which is summed up in the words Cafe Society. **1978** D. MACKENZIE *Deep, Dark & Dangerous* i. 55 Emma.. was a hell of a lot different to the succession of Sloane Rangers who had been her predecessors, harpies bent on getting far more than they gave. **1980** S. ALLAN *Dead Giveaway* xv. 154 She wore a cashmere sweater.. a Sloane ranger type. **1981** J. MANN *Funeral Sites* xviii. 111 The all-English Phoebe with her Sloane Ranger voice and manners. **1982** BARR & YORK *Official Sloane Ranger Handbk.* 10/1 Sloane Rangers hesitate to use the term 'breeding' now (of people, not animals) but that's what background means. **1983** *Times* 16 Apr. 3/7 (*headline*) Bogus Sloane Ranger lived like a lord. *Ibid.* 3/8 He even emulated the voice of those known as Sloane Rangers and men about town.

**sloap, sloath**, obs. ff. SLOPE, SLOTH.

**sloat**, variant of SLOTE.

**slob** (slɒb), *sb.*[1] [Mainly a. Irish *slab* (slɒb) mud, SLAB *sb.*[2]; but cf. also SLOBBER *sb.* and Du. *slobbe*, Fris. *slobbe*, *slob* clout, swab, slut.]

Chiefly in Irish use, or with reference to Ireland.

**1. a.** Mud, esp. soft mud on the sea-shore; ooze; muddy land.

**1780** YOUNG *Tour Irel.* II. 75 Under the slob or sea ooze he dug some very fine blue marle. **1828** CROKER *Leg. S. Irel.* II. 188 Being very near plumping into the river.. and being stuck up to the middle.. in the slob. **1879** W. H. DIXON *Royal Windsor* II. xv. 163 Landing on the Essex shore, he hid himself in the slob. **1882** PAYNE-GALLWEY *Fowler in Irel.* 26 When the birds gather on an island of slob.. at about half-tide.

**b.** A stretch of mud or ooze.
**1842** S. C. Hall *Ireland* II. 178 The same master Ned I tended duck-shooting over the slobs. **1860** *Athenæum* 28 Jan. 134 Those vast tracts..were then extensive slobs, covered with water at every tide. **1884** *Macm. Mag.* Sept. 357 Like some fair river which..ends its course amid dull flats and muddy slobs.

**c.** A sloppy mass; a mess.
**1885** *Reports Provinc., Devon* 108 (E.D.D.), That gravel, when wet, will make a slob.

**d.** *Canad.* = *slob-ice*, sense 4 below.
**1878** *North Star* (St. John's, Newfoundland) 30 Mar. 3/1 The bay here was caught over last week, and a string of 'slob' made its appearance across the mouth, but the heavy sea of Thursday broke it all up. **1907** J. G. Millais *Newfoundland* ii. 44 They themselves had hooked seventeen white coats out o' the slob (shore ice). **1920** W. T. Grenfell *Labrador Doctor* ix. 174 This ice is of very different qualities. Now it is 'slob' mixed with snow born on the Newfoundland coast. **1951** *Beaver* Sept. 20 Wind half a gale, temperature away down and slob in harbour and around schooner turning to ice.

**2.** A large soft worm, used in angling.
**1815** *Sporting Mag.* XLV. 96 A gentleman was angling with the maiden slob for trout. **1890** in D. A. Simmons *S. Donegal Gloss.*

**3.** A dull, slow, or untidy person; a careless or negligent workman; a lout, a fat person; one who is gullible or excessively soft-hearted, a fool; a person of little account. *slang.*
**1861** Clington *Frank O'Donnell* 101 A heavy-looking poor slob of a man. **1863** Le Fanu *House by Church-yard* I. v. 65 The Lord Mayor, a fat slob of a fellow. **1887** T. E. Brown *Doctor* 187 The dirty mob Of a cap that was at her —Aw a reglar slob. **1894** *Union Printer* (N.Y.) 21 Apr. 5/3 (Standard Dict.), It is easier for a good man to set 40,000 ems a night than it is for a slob to set 20,000. **1904** 'No. 1500' *Life in Sing Sing* 252/2 *Slob*, a person easy to impose upon; an untidy person. **1904** G. V. Hobart *Jim Hickey* i. 16 You're a warm young guy When you start to buy—You're a slob when you lose the price! **1927** H. V. Morton *In Search of England* x. 185 He was no beauty to look at, but then women seem to like the ugly slobs, don't they? **1938** R. Flannagan *County Court* 36 That praying old slob, Jones, has three boys and every one of 'em has run away. **1950** Wodehouse *Nothing Serious* 29 'The poor old slob,' she murmured. **1953** *If; Worlds of Sci. Fiction* Sept. 40/1 Speaking..as an ordinary slob that doesn't follow rarefied reasoning very well. **1958** S. Ellin *Eighth Circle* ii. xv. 123 A big, fat, gutless, slob. **1959** I. & P. Opie *Lore & Lang. Schoolch.* ix. 168 The unfortunate fat boy..is known as:.. slob, [etc.]. **1960** 'E. McBain' *Heckler* v. 60 There are people.. who always look like slobs... The tendency toward sloppiness first exhibits itself when the subject is still a child. **1966** A. Cavanaugh *Children are Gone* ii. vi. 49 'I'm a slob,' Shirley said. 'I'm not an intellectual.' **1970** R. Price *Gt. Roob Revolution* 7 The hucksters who control the..mass media think they are manipulating what they refer to as 'the slobs'. **1972** T. P. McMahon *Issue of Bishop's Blood* (1973) ii. 17 He's a real slob for his employees. He buys them houses, goes to their bar mitzvahs. **1978** J. Irving *World according to Garp* ix. 184, I think you're an irresponsible slob.

**4.** *attrib.* (in sense 1), as *slob-weir*; **slob ice** orig. *Canad.*, densely-packed, sludgy ice, esp. sea ice; **slob trout**, a brown trout, *Salmo trutta*, which stays in a river estuary instead of going further out to sea.
**1835** E. Wix *Six Months Newfoundland Missionary's Jrnl.* (1836) 16, I crossed through the '*slob ice', which was very thick in Conception Bay, to Port de Grave. **1920** W. T. Grenfell *Labrador Doctor* vi. 132 The slob ice had already made ballicaters and the biting cold of winter so far north had set in with all its vigour. **1955** *Sci. Amer.* Apr. 52/3 On the way to Little America, its first Antarctic port of call, the Atka saw very little of the drifting ice pack that surrounds the continent. It passed through a few 'bergy bits' and pieces of 'slob ice'—melting remnants of the pack. **1965** F. Russell *Secret Islands* vii. 88 The island was isolated because it was surrounded by impassable slob ice. **1907** W. L. Calderwood *Life of Salmon* i. 6 In the West of Ireland we have..the so-called *slob trout. **1930** G. H. Nall *Life Sea Trout* vi. 75 These brown Trout, feeding in brackish and salt water, are numerous, and special names have been given to them, such as 'Slob Trout', and 'Estuarine Trout'. **1960** C. Willock *Angler's Encycl.* 190/1 Slob-trout: sometimes called bull trout, are brown trout that migrate only as far as the estuary. **1851** Newland *The Erne* p. viii, The destruction of the intrusive *slob-weirs.

**slob** (slɒb), *sb.*[2] *rare.* [var. of SLAB *sb.*[1]] A slab of timber.
**1776** G. Semple *Building in Water* 32 You may Spike on the Slob or Plank. **1841** Hartshorne *Salop. Ant.* Gloss., *Slob*, an outside board, 'a shide'.

**slob** (slɒb), *v.* [f. SLOB *sb.*[1]] *trans.* To slop (*out*); to express by slobbering. So **'slobbed** *ppl. a.*
**1887** Parish & Shaw *Dict. Kentish Dial.* 152 *Slobbed*, slopped, spilt. *a* **1918** W. Owen *Poems* (1963) 69 Drooping tongues from jaws that slob their relish. **1946** B. Marshall *George Brown's Schooldays* 56 The master began to slob out the tapioca.

**slobber** ('slɒbə(r)), *sb.* Also 5 slober(e, slobur. [Related to SLOBBER *v.* Cf. SLABBER *sb.*[1] and SLUBBER *sb.*[1]]

**1.** Mud or slime; slush, sleety rain; a sloppy mess or mixture.
*c* **1400** *Destr. Troy* 12529 In the Slober & the sluche slongyn to londe, There he lay. *c* **1440** *Promp. Parv.* 459/2 Slobur, or slobere, *feces immunde. Ibid.*, Slobur, or blobur of fysshe and oþer lyke, *burbulium.* **1841** Carlyle *Let.* in *Atlantic Monthly* LXXXII. 450/2 For a week past there has been nothing but sleet, rime and slobber, the streets half an inch deep with slush. **1879** *Shropshire Gloss.*, *Slobber*, thin, cold rain, mixed with snow; a sloppy sleet. **1887** *S. Cheshire Gloss.* s.v., 'A slobber o' reen an' snow'..is a slight downfall of rain mixed with snow.

**2.** Slaver, slabber. Also *pl.*, a disease in rabbits marked by excessive salivation.
**1755** in Johnson. **1775** Ash, *Slobber*, liquor spilled, slaver. **1889** K. W. Knight *Book of the Rabbit* (ed. 2) 274 That unpleasant and often fatal complaint, slobbers—*i.e.*, running at the mouth. **1902** C. G. Harper *Cambridge Road* 73 Lips running with the thin slobber of the drunkard.

**3.** A jelly-fish.
**1863** J. G. Wood *Illust. Nat. Hist.* 743 We now come to a very large order of acalephs,..familiar under the title of Jelly-fishes, Slobbers, and similar euphonious names.

**'slobber,** *a.* [f. prec. or next.]
**1.** Clumsy, awkward.
**1866** C. Spencer *Mod. Gymnast* 43 This [the short swing, or circle] is designated by the euphonious name of the 'Slobber Swing', as it is rather a clumsy way of doing it.
**2.** Wet and flabby.
**1895** *Daily News* 12 July 6/3 The crushed nose, the slobber lips, all red and wet.

**slobber** ('slɒbə(r)), *v.* Also 5 slober. [Related to SLABBER *v.* and SLUBBER *v.* The vowel corresponds with that of Du. *slobberen* (Fris. *slobberje*) to slap up, to eat or work in a slovenly manner.

There is little evidence for the simple word before the 18th cent., but the compound *by-slober* BESLOBBER occurs in ME. In the *E.E. Allit. P.* C. 186 the form *sloberande* is prob. an error for *slomberande* slumbering. Modern dialects exhibit some minor variations of sense not illustrated here: see the *Eng. Dial. Dict.*]

**1.** *intr.* **a.** To feed in a slabbering or slovenly manner. Now *dial.*
**14..** in Wright *Songs & Carols* (Percy Soc.) 63 Nor bryng us in no dokes flesche, for thei slober in the mer. **1847** in Halliw. **1877–89** in Sheffield and Linc. glossaries.

**b.** To slaver. Cf. SLABBER *v.* 4.
**1733** Swift *Life & Charac. Dean S.* Wks. 1745 VIII. 125 But, why would he, except he slobbered, Offend our patriot, great Sir Robert. **1755** Walpole *Lett.* 29 Sept. (1857) II. 472 As at present there are as many royal hands to kiss as a Japanese idol has, it takes some time to slobber through the whole ceremony. **1826** Scott *Woodst.* xxii, Bevis slobbered and whined for the duck-wing. **1849** Macaulay *Hist. Eng.* i. I. 74 It was no light thing that..royalty should be exhibited to the world stammering, slobbering, shedding unmanly tears. **1893** Earl Dunmore *Pamirs* II. 231 The old gentleman slobbered in a most infantine way.

**c.** *dial.* To blubber, to cry.
**1878** *Cumbld. Gloss.* 89/1 He slobber't an' yool't like a barn. **1893** Cozens-Hardy *Broad Norf.* 35 The terms for crying, such as slobber and blare.

**d.** fig. *to slobber over*, to be over-attentive or over-affectionate towards (someone); to be exaggeratedly enthusiastic about (something).
**1825** Scott *Fam. Let.* 21 Feb. (1894) II. 239 Think how many antiquarian chops have slobbered over the fiery trial. **1892** 'Mark Twain' *Amer. Claim.* xiii. 139 They treat you as a tramp until they find out you're a congressman, and then they slobber all over you. **1914** W. Owen *Let.* 28 Aug. (1967) 282 He received me like a lover. To use an expression of the Rev. H. Wigan's, he quite slobbered over me. **1927** D. L. Sayers *Unnatural Death* iii. xxii. 257 Miss Climpson had little difficulty in reconstructing one of those hateful and passionate 'scenes' of slighted jealousy... 'I do everything for you—you don't care a bit for me..!' And 'Don't be.. ridiculous... Oh, stop it, Vera! I hate being slobbered over.' **1978** P. Theroux *Picture Palace* viii. 50 Even if they had slobbered over every blessed picture in the place they would not have understood.

**2. a.** *trans.* To wet in a dirty or disagreeable manner; to beslaver, befoul. Cf. SLABBER *v.* 1 and 2.
**1709** W. King *Art of Cookery* 29 The Cook that slobbers his Beard with Sack Posset. **1732–8** Swift *Polite Convers.* 210 It is not handsome to see one hold one's Tongue; Besides I should slobber my Fingers. **1835** *Politeness & Good-breeding* 67 Never cram your mouth so full, that..the contents..slobber your own cheeks and chin. **1840** Thackeray *Paris Sk.-bk.* (1872) 241 They all wear pinafores; as if the British female were in the invariable habit of wearing this outer garment, or slobbering her gown without it. **1858** Carlyle *Fredk. Gt.* i. iii. (1872) I. 26 He.. took to investigating one of his shoe-buckles; would.. slobber it about in his mouth.

**b.** To make wet with kissing.
**1724** Swift *Corinna* Wks. 1755 III. ii. 154 She made a song, how little miss Was kiss'd and slobber'd by a lad. **1831** Trelawny *Adv. Younger Son* I. 51 She..slobbered my cheek, and parted from me. **1874** Green *Short Hist.* viii. 474 Whose cheek he slobbered with kisses.

**3.** To utter thickly and indistinctly.
**1860** Forster *Gr. Remonstr.* 98 He not only slobbered his words when he talked, but drank as if he were eating his drink. **1890** *Tablet* 4 Jan. 10 Some person or other with unctuous eloquence slobbering out the shibboleth of civil and religious freedom.

**4. a.** To execute carelessly or in a slovenly way. Usu. with *over*.
**1694** Locke in Ld. King *Life* 204 Our Company of Stationers, having the monopoly here.., slobber them over as they can cheapest. **1838** *Civil Eng. & Arch. Jrnl.* I. 339/1 [Water-colours] exceedingly rough and sketchy, not to say slobbered. **1854** Miss Baker *Northampt. Gloss.* s.v., To do work in a slovenly, untidy manner, is to slobber it over.

**b.** To slur *over*. *rare*$^{-1}$.
*a* **1734** North *Examen* iii. vii. §99 (1740) 581 But see what false disingenuous Dealing here is to slobber over a base Business that will remain an eternal Shame to his Party.

**c.** To deal *out* in a clumsy manner. *rare*$^{-1}$.
**1859** Trollope *Bertrams* xxii, She went on slobbering out the cards, and counting them over and over again.

**d.** To muddle *away* (a thing).
**1889** *Daily Express* (Dublin) 4 Feb. 2/7, I frankly owned that they had slobbered away the money since in an unjustifiable manner.

Hence **'slobbered** *ppl. a.* (also with *on*).
**1811** W. Taylor in *Monthly Rev.* LXV. 142 They did not, however, tolerate any slobbered work. **1862** Scrope *Volcanos* 429 Overflowing waves of slobbered drops of highly viscid lava. **1863** Whyte Melville *Gladiators* 329 Syllables that drop like slobbered wine from the close shaven lip. **1880** *Paper & Print. Trades Jrnl.* xxxi. 37 It was dulled and ruined by the slobbered-on paste.

**'slobber-chops.** [f. prec. Cf. SLABBER-CHOPS.] One who slobbers in eating, etc. Also *dial.*, a variety of pear.
**1667** Davenant & Dryden *Tempest* iii. i, I have Other affairs to dispatch of more importance betwixt Queen Slobber-Chops and my self. **1832** W. Stephenson *Gateshead Local Poems* 66 I'll tell you slobber-chops, You'll find that sooner said than done—perhaps. **1857** Holland *Bay Path* xvii. 192 What do you mean, you little Slobber-chops?

**slobberer** ('slɒbərə(r)). [f. SLOBBER *v.* + -ER[1].]
**1.** One who slobbers.
**1744** Ozell tr. *Brantome's Sp. Rhodom.* 99, I have observed a great many of your gigantic People..to be mere Dolts, Slobberers and Oafs, both by Nature and Art.
**2.** (See quots.)
**1787** W. H. Marshall *E. Norfolk* (1795) II. 388 *Slobberers*, slovenly farmers. **1847** Halliw., *Slobberer*, a jobbing tailor.

**slobberhannes** ('slɒbəhænɪs). [Origin unknown. Perh. ad. Du.: cf. Du. dial. *slabberjan* the name of a game, and Du. *Hannes* Jack.] A card-game for four persons played with only high-ranking cards, in which the object is to lose tricks. Also, a point scored at this game.
**1877** W. B. Dick *Mod. Pocket Hoyle* (ed. 8) 211 *Slobberhannes*... The object of the game is to *avoid* making points, as the player who first gets ten points loses the game. *Ibid.* 212 If a player scores *all* of the three foregoing points, he receives one point extra, which is called 'Slobberhannes'. **1952** J. B. Pick *Phoenix Dict. Games* 276 *Slobberhannes* (4 players). Played with a pack from which all cards below seven have been withdrawn. **1964** A. Wykes *Gambling* vii. 165 *Greek hearts*..and *slobberhannes* are slightly simpler variations on the trick-losing theme.

**slobbering** ('slɒbərɪŋ), *vbl. sb.* [f. SLOBBER *v.* + -ING[1].]
**1.** The action of the verb, in various senses.
**1784** J. Barry *Lect. Art* vi. (1848) 226 Amidst all his [Titian's] dashing and slobbering, there is still remaining [etc.]. **1839** Hood *Literary & Literal* 14 The slobbering of a hungry Ursine Sloth. **1883** Simcox *Latin Literature* iv. ii. II. 36 The expression of such feeling came easy as slobbering. **1899** *Allbutt's Syst. Med.* VII. 736 There is rarely any affection of swallowing, although slobbering is not uncommon.
*attrib.* **1839** Thackeray *Fatal Boots* Aug., The kissing and slobbering scene went on again.
**2.** *slobbering bib*, a slabbering bib.
**1760–72** H. Brooke *Fool of Qual.* (1809) III. 149 [He] advanced without a mask in petticoats, a slobbering bib, and apron. **1792** Young *Trav. France* 9 Giving a babe a blue slobbering bib instead of a white one! **1826** Scott *Woodst.* x, A band as broad as a slobbering bib under his chin.

**slobbering** ('slɒbərɪŋ), *ppl. a.* [f. SLOBBER *v.* + -ING[2].] That slobbers, in senses of the verb; characterized by slavering.
**1607** Tourneur *Rev. Trag.* iii. iv, 'Twill teach you to kiss closer, Not like a slobbering Dutchman. **1782** Mason *Dean & Squire* Wks. (1810) 422/1 When, bless each little slobbering mouth, It had not cut a single tooth. **1787** Beckford in *Italy*, etc. (1834) II. 133 A good-natured, slobbering grey-beard. **1830** [E. Hawkins] *Anglo-Fr. Coinage* 154 The prince is a slobbering idiot. **1855** Smedley *H. Coverdale* xxi, She found the baby in a great state of slobbering splendour. **1874** Green *Short Hist.* viii. 464 His big head, his slobbering tongue.

**'slobberness.** [f. SLOBBER *sb.* or *v.*]
Slovenliness; slovenly writing.
**1880** *Papers Manch. Lit. Club* vi. 193 The influence of this facility on lesser men has simply rendered all this kind of slobberness hateful.

**slobbery** ('slɒbərɪ), *a.* Also 4–6 slobery. [f. SLOBBER *sb.* or *v.* Cf. MDu. *slobberich*, Du. dial. *slobberig.*]
**1.** Characterized by slobber or slobbering; disagreeably wet, slimy, or dirty.
**1398** Trevisa *Barth. De P.R.* xviii. xxvii. (Bodl. MS.), An olde hounde is ofte slowe and slobery. **1541** Hyrde tr. *Vives' Instr. Chr. Wom.* 96 b, Lykewyse no more do I alowe fylthy and slobery rayment. **1599** Shaks. *Hen. V*, iii. v. 13, I will sell my Dukedome To buy a slobbry and a durtie Farme. **1710–11** Swift *Jrnl. to Stella* 22 Jan., The weather had given a little, as you women call it, so it was something slobbery. **1712** *Ibid.* 18 Dec., We have terrible snowy slobbery weather. **1831** Carlyle *Sart. Res.* i. ix, A watery, pulpy, slobbery freshman and new-comer in this Planet. **1848** Walsh *Aristophanes, Clouds* i. i, Slobbery kisses, Profusion, gluttony and Venus'es. **1887** W. P. Frith *Autobiogr.* I. 27 Sucking an orange in a loud slobbery fashion.
**2.** Of a soft, yielding texture.
**1826** J. Wilson *Noct. Ambr.* Wks. 1855 I. 178 You keep rugging at the lang slobbery worsted till it comes aff.
**3.** Slovenly, careless.
**1858** Carlyle *Fredk. Gt.* ix. ii. (1872) II. 406 His continual haste, and slobbery manner of working up those

Hundred and odd volumes of his. **1881** *Leic. Gloss.* s.v., A very slobbery job, John.

**slobby** ('slɒbɪ), *a.* [f. SLOB *sb.*[1] + -Y.] **1.** Muddy.
**1854** MISS BAKER *Northampt. Gloss.*, Slabby or slobby, muddy, sloppy. **1886** *Pall Mall G.* 18 Feb. 5/1 There now only remained the geese, far up on the slobby ooze. **1897** BUTLER *Brit. Birds* IV. 155 The grasses which grow on the slobby foreshores.

**2. a.** Sloppy, sentimental. **b.** Of or pertaining to a slob (SLOB *sb.*[1] 3).
**1913** R. BROOKE *Let.* 3 July (1968) 479, I had a bad fit of home-sickness this morning... I threw up quite a lot of slobby old memories. **1967** *Spectator* 4 Aug. 131/1 To be honest, backbone isn't, as it were, at the forefront of my character. I am pretty slobby within. **1970** W. BURROUGHS JR. *Speed* (1971) v. 108 Vicki told me that I looked like a slobby bum. **1976** W. GOLDMAN *Magic* III. ix. 181 She'd end up stranded some place maybe with..some slobby dummy. **1976** *New Yorker* 9 Feb. 84/3 Peter Boyle's role is small, but ..he does slobby wonders with his scenes as the gently thick Wizard.

**slob-furrowing**, *vbl. sb.* [Cf. SLOB *sb.*[2]] Rib-furrowing; ribbing. Also **slob-furrow** *v.*
**1787** W. H. MARSHALL *E. Norfolk* (1795) I. 142 In slob-furrowing, the flag is turned toward the plowed ground, the coulter passing fifteen or sixteen inches from the last plow-furrow. **1805** R. W. DICKSON *Pract. Agric.* I. 346 There the old grass-fields, when it is proposed to burn the sward, are *rib* or *slob furrowed* about the beginning of winter. *Ibid.* 579 This in some places is termed by farmers *rib-furrowing*, and in others *slob-furrowing*.

**slobgollion** (slɒb'gɒljən). *Whaling slang.* [Origin unknown: cf. SLUMGULLION.] A substance found in sperm-oil (see quot.).
**1851** H. MELVILLE *Moby Dick* III. viii. 65 It is called slobgollion; an appellation original with the whalemen... It is an ineffably oozy, stringy affair, most frequently found in the tubs of sperm, after a profound squeezing, and subsequent decanting.

**slob-land.** Also slob land. [f. SLOB *sb.*[1] I.]
**1.** Muddy ground; *esp.* alluvial land reclaimed from the water.
**1861** *Times* 4 Oct. 7/4 A large acreage of slob land... Slob land varies in character, but here it is a rich marine alluvium. **1881** *Ibid.* 10 Feb. 4/3 He..enclosed from the tide a considerable area of useful slob-land.
**2.** A stretch of ground of this kind.
**1862** *Limerick Chron.* 8 Feb., The people's thoughts.. became fixed on the slob lands of Corkanree. **1890** J. HEALY *Insula Sanctorum* 139 The slob-lands of the harbour have been reclaimed.

**sloch**, Sc. form of SLOUGH *sb.*[2]

**slock** (slɒk), *v.*[1] Chiefly *Sc.* Forms: 4-7, 9 sloke, 6 sloik, 9 sloak; 5 slok, 5, 9 slokk-, 8- slock. [f. ON. *slokinn*, pa. pple. of *sløkkva* (Norw. *sløkka*, Sw. dial. *slökka*) to be extinguished, go out; the stem is related to that of SLACK *a.* Cf. SLOCKEN *v.* and *pa. pple.*]
†**1.** *intr.* **a.** To slacken, cease. *Obs.*[−1]
**13..** *Gaw. & Gr. Kt.* 412 For þou may leng in þy londe, & layt no fyrre, bot slokes.
†**b.** Of fire: To go out. *Obs.*[−1]
**1456** SIR G. HAYE *Law Arms* (S.T.S.) 161 Quhen men takis the brandis fra the grete fyre, it slokis the sonar.
**2.** *trans.* To put out, extinguish, quench (fire, thirst, etc.). Also *fig.*
*c* **1375** *Sc. Leg. Saints* xxi. (*Clement*) 34 Fore be with-drawine of acces Is slokit oft sic wantones. *Ibid.* xlix. (*Tecla*) 85 Slete & snaw..slokit þat fir alsone as men a candel suld haf done. *a* **1500** in *Ratis Raving* (1870) 24 Þow sal finde the froyt thar-of mony ȝere efterwart, and sal slok mekle syne. **1513** DOUGLAS *Æneid* II. xi. 13 Watter to sloik the haly fyr. **1755** in JOHNSON. **1819** TENNANT *Papistry Storm'd* (1827) 100 Untill his hail-life's drowth were slockit. **1842** VEDDER *Poems* 232 The rain in torrents poured, It slockit at ance the witch's fire.
†**b.** To suppress, bring to an end. *Obs.*[−1]
**1456** SIR G. HAYE *Law Arms* (S.T.S.) 126 The autoritee of the grete officer ryale slokis as than, and gerris cess, the autoritee of the smallare officer.
†**c.** To slake (lime). *Obs.*
**1655** in A. Laing *Lindores Abbey & Burgh of Newburgh* (1876) 238 He was slokin ye lym and mixing it with sand.

**slock** (slɒk), *v.*[2] Now only *south-western dial.* Also 5-7 slocke, 9 sloke. [? ad. AF. *esloker, *esloquer*, OF. *eslochier*, etc. (see Godef.), to move, shake, stir.]
**1.** *trans.* To entice away; to draw or lead *away* by some allurement.
Also *dial.*, to convey clandestinely, to pilfer.
**1483** in *Eng. Gilds* (1870) 336 That none of the said crafte slocke ony manis prentise. **1604** BABINGTON *Notes Exod.* xxi. 5 To slocke away (as wee speake) a mans seruant..was a grieuous sinne with God. **1886** ELWORTHY *W. Somerset Word-bk.* s.v., The chillern..be all a-slocked away wi' prizes..and that to the meetin-house. **1897** HOCKING in *Christian World* Xmas No. 3 They're trying to slock (entice) away others who do come.
**2.** To entice, allure, lead on, tempt.
**1594** CAREW *Tasso* (1881) 10 What so may slocke or pricke a courage stout. *Ibid.* 113 In vaine she sought to slocke, or with mortall Sweetnings t'enroll him in Cupidos pay. **1850** *Beck's Florist* 50 The bright sun of February..*slocks* (in Cornish vernacular) the young and eager buds to unfold their premature growth.

**slock-dolager:** see SOCK-DOLAGER.

**slocken** ('slɒk(ə)n), *v. north.* and *Sc.* Forms: 4-9 sloken, 4-6 slokyn, 5-6 (9) slokin (6 -yne); 4, 6 slokkin, 4 (9) slokken, 6 slo(c)kne, 6- slocken (9 -an, -in). [a. ON. *slokna* (Norw. *slokna*, *slokkna*, Sw. *slockna*, older Da. *slogne*, *slugne*), f. *slokinn*, pa. pple. of *sløkkva*: see SLOCK *v.*[1]]
**1.** *trans.* To quench, extinguish, put *out* (fire, flame, etc.). Also in fig. context.
*a* **1300** *Cursor M.* 28641 Als þe water it slokkens glede. *c* **1340** HAMPOLE *Prose Treat.* (1866) 3 Sothely na thynge slokyns sa fell flawmes, dystroyes ill thoghtes [etc.]. *c* **1375** *Sc. Leg. Saints* vi. (*Thomas*) 593 Vndyr þam sprange vpe a well & sloknyt sone..þai brynnand platis. *c* **1450** *St. Cuthbert* (Surtees) 287 Þan þai, wenand a fyre to slokyn, þai fand þe house no thyng bryn. **1536** BELLENDEN *Cron. Scot.* (1821) I. 20 To rais amang us ane flame that sall nevir be sloknit. ? *a* **1550** *Freiris Berwik* 219 in *Dunbar's Poems* (1893) 292 Be bissy als, and slokkin out the fyre. **1588** A. KING tr. *Canisius' Catech.* 171 Watter slokins out burning fyr. **1781** J. HUTTON *Tour to Caves* (ed. 2) Gloss. 96 *Slocken*, to quench. *c* **1817** HOGG *Tales & Sk.* V. 276 It is not customary to sloken one fire by kindling another. **1825** BROCKETT *N.C. Gloss.*, *Slocken*,..to quench.
**2.** To suppress, put down, do away with, destroy, stamp *out*. Also with adjectival compl.
*a* **1300** *Cursor M.* 18360 Lauerd.., sua þou slockens al vr sin. *a* **1340** HAMPOLE *Psalter* lxxii. 14 When he..slokens þe temptacioun wiþ sorowe of pyne. *c* **1425** *St. Mary of Oignies* II. iii. in *Anglia* VIII. 158/6 Þe whiche good man..was casten downe and slokenyd nere for sorowe. **1508** DUNBAR *Tua Mariit Wemen* 522 And kindill agane his curage thocht it wer cald sloknyt. **1560** ROLLAND *Seven Sages* 7 Ane meik answer slokins Melancolie. **1596** DALRYMPLE tr. *Leslie's Hist. Scot.* II. 352 The Quene with litle labour slokned out this seditioune.
**3.** To quench or allay (thirst).
*a* **1340** HAMPOLE *Psalter* cxlii. 7 Slokyn my threst. **1423** JAS. I *Kingis Q.* 69 My drye thrist with teris sall I slokin. **1535** COVERDALE *Wisd.* xi. 4 Their thirst [was] slockened out of yᵉ harde stone. **1584** HUDSON *Judith* III. (1613) 37 That bottell sweet..serued.. not to slocken thirst. *a* **1585** MONTGOMERIE *Cherrie & Slae* 444 Ʒone Slae..May satisfie to slokkin Thy drouth now. **1786** BURNS *Dining w. Ld. Daer* ii, When mighty Squireships..Their hydra-drouth did sloken. **1824** SCOTT *Redgauntlet* ch. xiii, Get the blue bowl; ..that will sloken all their drouth.
*absol.* **1684** *Yorks. Dial.* 161 (E.D.S.), Heve you ought that will slocken weel?
**b.** To slake the thirst of (a person, etc.).
**1718** RAMSAY *Christ's Kirk Gr.* III. xiv, Wasted was baith cash and tick, Sae ill were they to slocken. **1795** H. MACNEILL *Scotland's Skaith* I. xxvii, Slockned now, refresh'd and talking. **1858** E. B. RAMSAY *Scot. Life & Char.* ii, It weets the sod, it slockens the yowes. **1871** C. GIBBON *Lack of Gold* xx, Here's a cappy full of water, see if that'll sloken you.
**4.** To sate or satisfy (desire). *rare.*
**1508** DUNBAR *Tua Mariit Wemen* 283, I had a lufsummar leid, my lust for to slokyn. **1596** DALRYMPLE tr. *Leslie's Hist. Scot.* I. 151 Thay could nocht al..slokne his vnquencheable ..appetite.
**5.** To soak, wet, or moisten; to slake (lime).
**1487, 1609** [see the *vbl. sb.*]. **1621** SANDERSON *Serm.* I. 173 The rain that falleth upon the earth, whether it moisten it kindly,..or whether it choak or slocken and drown it. **1821** SCOTT *Pirate* v, I could never away with raw oatmeal, slockened with water, in all my life.
**6.** *intr.* To go out, be extinguished.
**1535** STEWART *Cron. Scot.* III. 407 Ony fyre that he culd bring thairtill, It sloknit ay ilk tyme of the awin will.
Hence **'slockening** *vbl. sb.*
*c* **1440** *Promp. Parv.* 460/1 Sloknynge, or qwenchynge, ..*extinctio*. **1487-8** *Durh. Acc. Rolls* (Surtees) 651 Et eidem pro le Sloknyng ejusdem [limekiln] et portacione dicti calcis, vj s. viij d. **1596** DALRYMPLE tr. *Leslie's Hist. Scot.* I. 115 The slokning out of a certane commoune flame of burneng. **1609** *Churchw. Acc. Pittington*, etc. (Surtees) 61 Item payed for slokening of the lime, v s. **1829** HOGG *Shepherd's Cal.* vi, I hae muckle need o' a slockening.

†**'slocken**, *pa. pple. Obs.* Also 5 slokyn. [a. ON. *slokinn*: see SLOCK *v.*[1]] Extinguished; soaked, immersed.
*c* **1400** *York Manual* (Surtees Soc.) p. xvii, Be thare lantern slokyn fro yᵉ blys that euer schall last. **1643** A. TUCKNEY *Balm of Gilead* 21 That she which hath suckled you with her milk, may not be slocken in her own blood. **1647** H. MORE *Minor Poems, Cupid's Conflict* lvi. Wks. (Grosart) 173/1 Back she returns.., Drown'd, chok'd or slocken by her cruell nurse. **1653** —— *Conject. Cabbal.* (1713) 224 When it is..slocken and drowned in sensuality and intemperance.

†**'slocker:** see SLOCKSTER (quot. 1706).

**'slocking-stone.** *Cornish dial.* [f. SLOCK *v.*[2]] (See quots.)
**1778** PRYCE *Min. Cornub.* Gloss. s.v., *Slocking-Stone*, a tempting, inducing, or rich stone of Ore. *Ibid.*, There have been..instances of Miners who have deceived their employers by bringing them Slocking-Stones from other Mines. **1864** MRS. LLOYD *Ladies of Polcarrow* 89 These deceptive specimens are called 'slocking-stones' by the mining community. **1880** *E. Cornw. Gloss.* s.v. *Slock*, Slocking stones are tempting, selected stones shown, to induce strangers to adventure in a mine.

**'slockster.** Now *dial.* [f. SLOCK *v.*[2] + -STER.]
†**a.** (See quots.) *Obs.* **b.** *dial.* A pilferer.
Cotgrave is prob. the only source of the later quots.
**1611** COTGR., *Plagiaire*,..a stealer, or suborner of mens children, or seruants,..(in which sence we tearme him a Slockster). **1647** HEXHAM I, A Slockster that by alluring causeth servants to forsake their maisters. **1677** in MIÉGE. **1706** PHILLIPS (ed. Kersey), *Slocker* or *Slockster*,..one that entices away other Mens Servants; a Kid-napper.

**slod(e**, obs. or dial. pa. t. SLIDE *v.*

**slodge** (slɒdʒ), *v. dial.* [? Imitative.] *intr.* To trail or drag the feet in walking; to walk slouchingly.
**1829** COOPER *Good's Study Med.* I. 554 He slodged and reeled about as he walked. **1877** in *Holderness Gloss.* **1902** C. G. HARPER *Cambridge Road* 295 The slodger slodges among the dykes.

**slodger** ('slɒdʒə(r)). *dial.* [? f. prec.] An inhabitant of the Fen district. Also *fen-slodger*.
**1827** HONE *Table-bk.* 139 His ancestors..were all 'fen slodgers'. **1856** P. THOMPSON *Hist. Boston* 644 The Fen-men..were..known as Slodgers or Fen-Slodgers. **1893** BARING-GOULD *Cheap Jack Zita* I. 74 The tract over which the ancestral slodger..had exercised more or less questionable rights.

**sloe** (sləʊ). Forms: α. 1 slah (slach-), slaȝ (slaȝh-), 1, 5 sla, 3-7 slo, 4-6 sloo, 6 sloa, 6- sloe (9 *dial.* sloo, slue, slew). β. *pl.* 1 slan, 4 slon, 5 sloon, 5-6 sloen, 7 slone, slane. γ. 6-7 slow(e. δ. 6- *Sc.* and *north.* slae, 9 *north.* sla(a, slaigh, slay, slea, slee, etc. [OE. *slá(h)*, etc., = Fris. *slé*, MDu. *slee*, *slie* (Du. *slee*, Flem. *slei*, *sleie*), *sleeu* (Kilian *sleeuwe*), MLG. *slee* (LG. *slê*, *slî*), OHG. *slêha* (MHG. *slêhe*, G. *schlehe*, †*schlee*), perh. related to OSlav. and Russ. *sliva*, Lith. *slýwas* plum.
The original plural in *-n* (OE. *slán*, ME. *slōn*) is recorded down to the 17th cent., and is the source of the sing. forms now current in southern dialects (see *Eng. Dial. Dict.* s.v. *Slone*). A similar transference appears in MDu. *sleen* (Flem. *sleen*, *slene*), MLG. *slên*, *slein* (LG. *slên*, *slein*, *slîn*, also *slôn*, whence probably Da. *slaaen*, Sw. *slân*).]
**1. a.** The fruit of the blackthorn (*Prunus spinosa*), a small ovate or globose drupe of a black or dark-purple colour and sharp sour taste.
α. *c* **725** *Corpus Gloss.* B 75, *Bellicum*, slaȝ. *a* **1000** *Voc.* in Wr.-Wülcker 196 *Brumela*, *bellicum*, *vel* sla. *c* **1000** *Saxon Leechd.* II. 32 Ðenim onwære slah..& wring þurh clað on þæt eaȝe. *c* **1340** *Nominale* (Skeat) 679 Appul, pere, and slo. ? *c* **1366** CHAUCER *Rom. Rose* 928 Blak as bery, or any slo. *c* **1440** *Promp. Parv.* 459/2 Slo, frute, *prunum*, *vel spinum*. **1483** *Cath. Angl.* 342/2 A Sla, *spinum*, *mespilum*. **1558** PHAER *Æneid* III. H iv, For hunger, sloes hath ben my food. **1582** STANYHURST *Æneis* III. (Arb.) 91 My self I dieted with sloas. **1620** VENNER *Via Recta* vii. 118 The iuyce of them, especially of Sloes,..is of excellent efficacy. **1697** DRYDEN *Virg. Georg.* IV. 215 He knew to..tame to Plumbs, the Sourness of the Sloes. **1713** STEELE *Englishm.* No. 7. 47 He will swallow, with Transport, what was squeezed from the Sloe. **1774** PENNANT *Tours Scotl.* 214 Sloes are the only fruits of the island. **1842** *Dumfries Herald* Oct., Sloes..are almost always plentiful. **1885** TENNYSON *The Flight* iv, The blackthorn-blossom fades and falls and leaves the bitter sloe.
β. *a* **1000** *Voc.* in Wr.-Wülcker 269 *Moros*, slan. **13..** *K. Alis.* 4983 (Laud MS.), Oþer mete þai ne habben Bot hawen, hepen, slon, & crabben. **14..** *Ms. Harl. 3388* in Cockayne *Saxon Leechd.* III. 345/1 *Succus prunellarum immaturarum*, grene slane wose. *c* **1450** *M.E. Med. Bk.* (Heinrich) 86 Take and gedre þe a good quantite of sloon, þat bene rype. **1573** BARET *Alv.* (1580) F iij, Haw-bearies, sloen, gooseberries and such like. **1601** HOLLAND *Pliny* II. 169 Bulleis, Skegs, and Slone (which are the berries, as it were, or fruit of the wild Plum tree). **1633** HART *Diet of Diseased* I. xvi. 63 Plummes..are of two sorts, either wilde, called sloes or slane [etc.].
γ. **1589** GREENE *Menaphon* (Arb.) 86 Slowes blacke as ieat. **1604** DRAYTON *Owle* 702 The Hip, the Haw, the Slow, the Bramble-berrie. **1657** R. LIGON *Barbadoes* (1673) 11 As far ..as the best Abricot is beyond the worst Slow or Crab.
δ. *a* **1585** MONTGOMERIE *Cherrie & Slae* 322, I saw..A bush of bitter Slaes. [See also SLOCKEN *v.* 3.]. **1786** BURNS *Holy Fair* iii, Their visage wither'd, lang an' thin, An' sour as ony slaes! *a* **1802** *Cospatrick* xx. in Scott *Minstrelsy*, To the grene wood I maun gae, To pu' the red rose and the slae. **1828** CARR *Craven Gloss.*, *Slaa*, sloe. **1837** R. NICOLL *Poems* (1843) 75 To feast on the bramble-berries brown An' gather the glossy slaes. **1838** HOLLOWAY *Prov. Dict.*, *Slaigh*, the fruit of the black-thorn.
**b.** As the type of something having little or no value. (So OF. *parnele*, = F. *prunelle*.)
*c* **1250** *Orison our Lady* 28 in *O.E. Misc.* 160 Þis liues blisse nis wurð a slo. *a* **1300** *Havelok* 2051 Of hem ne yeue ich nouht a slo. **13..** *Guy Warw.* (A.) 141 Þer nas man in al þis londe..þat bireft him worþ of a slo [*C.* sloo]. *c* **1412** HOCCLEVE *De Reg. Princ.* 1120 Þou schalt do so, And by desir of good, nat sette a slo. *c* **1450** LOVELICH *Merlin* 7152 Al availled hit hem not a slo.
**c.** *transf.* The apple *of* one's eye.
**1884** *Graphic* Xmas No. 13/2, I loved him..like the sloe of my eye.
**2. a.** The blackthorn, *Prunus spinosa*.
**1753** *Chambers' Cycl.* Suppl. s.v. *Sloe-worm*, That of the sloe is of a greyish hue, and its spines longer. **1791** BURNS *Lament Mary Queen of Scots* iii, The hawthorn's budding in the glen, And milk-white is the slae. **1796** WITHERING *Brit. Plants* (ed. 3) IV. 51 [This lichen is] whitest on the sloe. **1841** *Penny Cycl.* XIX. 68/2 Of the Plum genus, thus restricted, there is in common use the Garden Plum,..the Bullace,..and the Sloe. **1882** *Garden* 15 Apr. 247/1 We are grateful to the Sloe for the way which it adorns hedgerow, rock, or copse..in spring with its fearless bloom.
**b.** *U.S.* (See quots.)
**1846-50** A. WOOD *Class-bk. Bot.* 303 *Viburnum prunifolium*, Black Haw, Sloe. **1882** F. B. HOUGH *Elem. Forestry* 269 Haw: Sloe: Arrow-Wood (Genus *Viburnum*). **1898** L. H. BAILEY *Evol. Native Fruits* 224 The black sloe of the southern states, *Prunus umbellata*, attains a height of twelve to twenty feet.

**3.** *attrib.* and *Comb.*, as ***sloe-black***, ***-blue***, ***-bush***, ***-eye***, ***-eyed***, ***-feeder***, ***gin***, ***-juice***, ***-leaf***, ***-stem***, ***-worm***.

**1735** SOMERVILLE *Chase* I. 241 His large *Sloe-black Eyes Melt in soft Blandishments. **1882** BLACK *Shandon Bells* i, Those soft, large, sloe-black eyes. **1799** M. UNDERWOOD *Dis. Childr.* (ed. 4) II. 183 A *sloe-blue or leaden colour of the lips. **1562** TURNER *Herbal* II. (1568) 104 Our *slobush or blak thorn is one kynde. **1894** E. CLODD *FitzGerald's Grave* 8 The hedges, in their tangle of sweetbriar and sloe-bush and bramble. **1957** V. J. KEHOE *Technique Film & T.V. Make-Up* ix. 107 (*caption*) Effect of *sloe eye after applying latex to outer ends of lashes and eyelid and pressing them together. **1977** N. MARSH *Last Ditch* ii. 37 His sloe eyes looked out of a pale face. **1867** AUGUSTA WILSON *Vashti* xii, This *sloe-eyed, peony-faced girl. **1894** D. C. MURRAY *Making of a Novelist* 133 Hook-nosed, sloe-eyed and greasy of complexion. **1855** *Zoologist* XIII. 4846 It is probable that many other *sloe-feeders will be found also to occur on the plum. **1895** *Outing* XXVII. 194 Sampling some of his famous *sloe gin. **1798** O'KEEFFE *Wild Oats* I. i, Poison yourself wiıh *sloe-juice. **1846** MRS. GORE *Eng. Charact.* (1852) 140 His evening paper and sloe-juice negus. **1825** T. HOOK *Sayings* Ser. II. *Passion & Princ.* vi, A small amount of dried *sloe-leaves. **1708** PHILLIPS *Cyder* I. 19 The *Sloe-Stem bearing Sylvan Plums austere. **1753** *Chambers's Cycl.* Suppl., **Sloe-worm*, . . the name of an insect found on the leaves of sloe, or black-thorn, and sometimes on those of the garden-plum.

**sloe**, obs. variant of SLAY *v.*

**'sloe-thorn.** Forms: (see quots.); also 9 *north.* **slaa-**, *Sc.* **slae-**. [f. SLOE *sb.* + THORN *sb.* Cf. MDu. and Du. *sleedorn*, MLG. and MHG. *slêdorn*, G. *schleh-*, †*schlee-*, †*schleh(e)ndorn*, Da. *slaaentorn*.] The blackthorn. Cf. SLOE 2.

*c* **725** *Corpus Gloss.* N 119 *Nigra spina*, slaȝhðorn. *Ibid.* S 474 *Spina nigra*, slahðorn. *c* **1000** *Saxon Leechd.* II. 86 Wice, ac, slahþorn, bircean, elebeam. *c* **1325** *Gloss. W. de Bibbesw.* in Wright *Voc.* 163 *Le fourder*, slo-thorne. *c* **1450** *MS. Sloane 4* fol. 80 The kanker y[t] bredyth yn the Slo-thorne. **1615** BRATHWAIT *Strappado*, etc. (1878) 290 Sad Philomela . . sung with a pricking slothorne at her brest. **1825** SCOTT *Betrothed* xxiii, Small eminences . . overgrown with hazel, sloethorn, and other dwarf shrubs. **1854** H. MILLER *Sch. & Schm.* (1858) 404 A dreary moor, bristling with furze and sloe-thorn.

*attrib.* *c* **1000** *Saxon Leechd.* II. 98 Nim þonne apuldor rinde, . . slahþorn rinde, & wir rinde. **1804** GRAHAME *Sabbath* (1808) 62 He hid beneath the milk-white sloe-thorn spray. **1815** SCOTT *Guy M.* iii, She . . had in her hand a goodly sloethorn cudgel.

**'sloe-tree.** Forms: (see quots.); also 9 *Sc.* and *north.* **slae-**. [f. SLOE *sb.* + TREE *sb.*] = prec.

*c* **1340** *Nominale* (Skeat) 655 Slotre, birche, and ellertre. **1382** WYCLIF *Dan.* xiii. 54 Vndir a sloo tree. **14..** *Lat.-Eng. Voc.* in Wr.-Wülcker 613 *Spinus*, a Slotre. **1483** *Cath. Angl.* 343/1 A Sla tre, *spinus, mespila*. **1548** TURNER *Names Herbes* (E.D.S.) 65 Prunus syluestris is called in english a slo tree, or a sle tree. **1589** FLEMING *Virg. Georg.* IV. 61 Slo trees bearing damsons now. **1598** FLORIO. *Prugno*, . . a plum tree, damzon tree or slow tree. **1647** HEXHAM I. (Trees), A Sloe tree, *een wilde Pruymen boom*. **1706** PHILLIPS (ed. Kersey), *Spinus*, the Sloe-tree, or Bullace-tree. **1777** JACOB *Catal. Plants* 90 *Prunus spinosa*, the Black Thorn, or Sloe Tree. **1842** TENNYSON *Amphion* 44 Poussetting with a sloe-tree. **1882** 'OUIDA' *In Maremma* I. 117 Under their thickets of the prickly sloe-tree.

**sloe-worm(e**, obs. forms of SLOW-WORM.

**sloff**, *v.* Now *dial.* [Imitative.] *intr.* (See quot. 1841.) Hence **'sloffing** *vbl. sb.*

*c* **1440** *Promp. Parv.* 459 Sloffynge, or on-gentyll etynge, *voracio, devoracio, lurcacitas*. **1841** HARTSHORNE *Salop. Ant.* Gloss., *Sloff*, to eat greedily, dirtily, or slovenly.

**slog** (slɒg), *sb. colloq.* [f. the vb.]

**1.** Hard, steady work; a spell of this.

**1888** JACOBI *Printers' Vocab.* 127 When a person is working hurriedly he is said to have a 'slog on'. **1903** McNEILL *Egregious English* 172 That one way amounts to sheer mechanism and slog.

**2.** A vigorous blow; a hard hit at cricket.

**1846** *Swell's Night Guide* 76 And she felt inclined to mug her rival, only she thought it would be no bottle, cos her rival could go in a buster at a slog. **1865** *Lilly-white's Cricketers' Compan.* 139 Too fond of losing his wicket for a 'slog'. **1895** *Daily News* 5 Feb. 3/5 Ford sent a ball straight into point's hands. Peel tried a blind slog. **1897** H. W. BLEAKLEY *Short Innings* vi. 94 Sixey made a mighty slog, but failed to strike the ball.

**slog** (slɒg), *v. colloq.* [Of obscure origin. Cf. SLUG *v.*[4]]

**1. a.** *trans.* To hit or strike hard; to drive with blows. Also *fig.*, to assail violently.

**1824** *Session Papers Central Criminal Court* 21 Sept. 535/1 One of them said, 'Go back and slog him.' **1853** 'C. BEDE' *Verdant Green* xi. 106 His whole person [had been] put in chancery, stung, bruised, fibbed, . . slogged, and otherwise ill-treated. **1884** 'R. BOLDREWOOD' *Melb. Memories* iv. 32 We slogged the tired cattle round the fence. **1891** *Spectator* 10 Oct. 487/1 They love snubbing their friends and 'slogging' their enemies.

**b.** *Cricket.* To obtain (runs) by hard hitting.

**1897** H. W. BLEAKLEY *Short Innings* iii. 49 Mr. Dolly slogged sixes and fours until he had made about eighty.

**2.** *intr.* To walk heavily or doggedly.

Halliwell's '*Slog*, to lag behind' probably belongs to SLUG *v.*

**1872** CALVERLEY *Fly Leaves* (1903) 119 Then *abiit* . . off slogs boy. **1876** *Mid-Yorksh. Gloss.*, *Slog*, to walk with burdened feet, as through snow, or puddle. **1907** *Westm. Gaz.* 2 Oct. 2/1 Overtaking the guns, we 'slogged' on with them for a mile or more.

**3. a.** To deal heavy blows, to work hard (*at* something), to labour *away*, etc.

**1846** *Swell's Night Guide* 37 Most of them can slog, that is to say, . . fight. **1888** *Daily News* 22 May 5/2, I slogged at it, day in and day out. **1894** HESLOP *Northumberland Gloss.* s.v., They slogged away at the anchor shank. **1903** *19th Cent.* Mar. 392 They have no incentives to slog and slave.

**b.** *Cricket.* To hit, or attempt to hit, the ball hard and with abandon.

**1869** *Baily's Mag.* July 21 Not only did he 'slog', in the true sense of the word, which we take to be hitting blindly and high in the air, but [etc.]. **1904** F. C. HOLLAND *Cricket* 36 You should go to the nets, not to slog, but to play. **1935** J. C. MASTERMAN *Fate cannot harm Me* viii. 167 At the fifth ball the Admiral slogged with even crookeder bat and even more mighty effort; he missed it, and all three stumps were spreadeagled. **1980** *Cricketer International* Feb. 11/1 The incredible thing is that he never had to slog once to make his runs.

**slogan** ('sləʊgən). Forms: *α.* 6 **slogorne**, 6–7 **sloggorne**, **sluggorn(e**, 8 **slugorn**, **slogurn**; 6 **sloghorne**, 6, 8 **slughorne**, 7, 9 **slughorn**. *β.* 8 **slughon**, 7– **slogan**, 9 **slogen**. [ad. Gael. *sluagh-ghairm*, f. *sluagh* host + *gairm* cry, shout.]

**1. a.** A war-cry or battle cry; *spec.* one of those formerly employed by Scottish Highlanders or Borderers, or by the native Irish, usually consisting of a personal surname or the name of a gathering-place.

*α.* **1513** DOUGLAS *Æneid* VII. xi. 87 The slogorne, ensenȝe, or the wache cry. **1536** BELLENDEN *Cron. Scot.* (1821) I. 59 That nane of thaim name thair capitane with ony uthir sloggorne, bot with the auld name of that tribe. *a* **1572** KNOX *Hist. Ref.* Wks. 1846 I. 87 Great was the noyse . . that was heard, whill that everie man calles his awin sloghorne. *a* **1578** LINDESAY (Pitscottie) *Chron. Scot.* (S.T.S.) II. 263 Thay hard ane slughorne cryand on the gait in this maner 'ane hammiltowne', 'ane hammiltowne'. **1680** MACKENZIE *Sci. Her.* 97 Not unlike these Motto's are our Slughorns, which are called *Cris de guerre* in France. **1683** MARTINE *Reliq. Divi S. Andreæ* (1797) 3 They . . go about begging, and use still to recite the sluggornes of most of the true ancient surnames of Scotland, from old experience and observation. **1723** W. BUCHANAN *Acc. Fam. Buchanan* 165 The isle of Clareinch was the slogurn or call of war, proper to the family of Buchanan. **1851** M. A. DENHAM *Slogans N. Eng.* 1 Occasionally, as in Scotland, the name of the rendezvous was used as a Slughorn.

*β.* **1680** MACKENZIE *Sci. Her.* 97 The Name of Hume have for their Slughorn (or Slogan, as our Southern Shires terme it) a *Hume, a Hume*. **1805** SCOTT *Last Minstrel* IV. xxvii, To heaven the Border slogan rung, . . The English war-cry answer'd wide. **1861** GOLDW. SMITH *Irish Hist.* 67 An Act . . was passed to abolish the words Crom-a-boo and Butler-a-boo, the Slogans of these two clans. **1879** DIXON *Windsor* III. 3 Edward had struck the Genoese, . . Monmouth the French to one great Slogan, that of St. George of England.

**b.** *transf.* The distinctive note, phrase, cry, etc. of any person or body of persons.

**1704** in Maidment *Scott. Pasquils* (1868) 384 Your slughons are falsehood and plunder. *a* **1859** MACAULAY *Hist. Eng.* xxv. V. 301 The popular slogans on both sides were indefatigably repeated. **1880** MRS. WHITNEY *Odd or Even?* xiv, 'Duty, God, immortality'—the very slogan of the pulpit. **1887** A. LANG *Bks. & Bookmen* 114 Printers and authors had their emblems and their private literary slogans. **1922** *Times* 20 June 7/4 'Post early.' New P.O. slogan on letters. **1928** *Publishers' Weekly* 9 June 2386 As an advertising man, Mr. Calkins believes the slogan 'a cent a copy to sell the art of reading', a great and revolutionary one. **1951** H. ARENDT *Burden of Our Time* I. ii. 38 Antisemitic slogans were highly effective in mobilizing large strata of the population. **1958** P. H. GIBBS *Curtains of Yesterday* xix. 157 On the other side [of an ancient gateway] with big letters deeply carved was the new slogan of Lenin's Russia. 'Religion is the Opium of the People.' **1968** V. S. PRITCHETT *Cab at Door* ix. 163 All sects have their jargon and Father, eager as an advertising man is for slogans, had picked them all up and lived by them. **1971** H. MACMILLAN *Riding the Storm* xv. 478 The somewhat disingenuous slogan of 'ban the bomb'. **1972** F. FITZGERALD *Fire in Lake* viii. 277 Thousands of soldiers and civil servants marched with the dock workers shouting anti-government and occasionally anti-American slogans. **1980** R. SCRUTON *Meaning of Conservatism* iii. 59 One particular slogan will later occupy our attention—'equality of opportunity'.

**2.** *attrib.* and *Comb.*, as ***slogan-cry***, ***song***, ***yell***; ***slogan-shouter***, ***-shouting*** vbl. sb. and ppl. adj.; ***slogan-like*** adj.

**1849** AYTOUN *Lays Scottish Cavaliers* (ed. 2) 46 That day through high Dunedin's streets, Had pealed the *slogan-cry. **1936** WIRTH & SHILS tr. *Mannheim's Ideology & Utopia* I. 36 Two *slogan-like concepts 'ideology and utopia'. **1975** *Language for Life* (Dept. Educ. & Sci.) xiii. 199 Public debate . . has often been conducted through a series of slogan-like headings: progressive, formal, integration, basics, and several more. **1940** G. CUNNINGHAM *Jrnl.* 14 Dec. in N. Mitchell *Sir G. Cunningham* (1968) iv. 83 Heard from Peshawar that *slogan shouters had been told to go home. **1968** N. MITCHELL *Ibid.*, On the 12th, the slogan shouters sent notices to the Deputy Commissioner where and when they would shout their slogans on 14th December. **1940** G. CUNNINGHAM *Jrnl.* 24 Dec. in *Ibid.* 84 *Slogan shouting by Satyagrahis has stopped as Gandhi has declared a holiday for Christmas. **1972** J. BIGGS-DAVISON *Africa—Hope Deferred* x. 98 These are but a few of the problems facing independent Africa that can no longer be concealed by an excess of slogan-shouting. **1976** M. ZIA-UD-DIN *Memoirs* 63 Wherever it stopped there were large crowds of slogan-shouting Muslims. **1978** *Jrnl. R. Soc. Arts* CXXVI. 696/2 *Medical Inspection* destroys the 'nobility' of war more readily than 1,000 slogan-shouting demonstrators. *c* **1860** J. R. RANDALL *Maryland* vi, Come . . And ring thy dauntless *slogan song, Maryland! **1808** SCOTT *Marmion* V. iv, Nor harp, nor pipe, his ear could please Like the loud *slogan yell.

Hence **'sloganed** *a.*, marked with a slogan.

**1966** 'G. DOUGLAS' *Odd Woman Out* ix. 60 This tall girl . . in jeans and a sloganed sweater. **1978** *Church Times* 1 Sept. 15/2 With . . leather waistcoats or sloganed T-shirts. **1979** *Sci. Amer.* Apr. 30/1 A graffiti remover which was developed by the organic chemistry section in response to a government campaign to clean-up the much-sloganed areas of Belfast and Londonderry.

**sloganeer** (sləʊgə'nɪə(r)). orig. *U.S.* [f. SLOGAN + -EER.] One who devises or who uses slogans.

**1922** R. CONNELL in *Sat. Even. Post* (U.S.) 29 Apr. 100/2 (*heading*) Once a sloganeer. **1935** *Sat. Rev. Lit.* 11 May 30/3 The day may come when a West Coast sloganeer will proudly proclaim, 'If it isn't at San Marino, it isn't a book.' **1963** D. OGILVY *Confessions Advertising Man* vii. 127 Posters are for sloganeers. **1971** *N.Z. Listener* 31 May 5 'Sloganeers'—young, sometimes older people, who do not analyse a problem but pick up a current catchcry. **1978** *Times* 7 Aug. 12/4 Questions are a favourite device of envelope sloganeers. 'Is he to be our next President?' asked one.

Hence as *v. intr.*, to express oneself in slogans (now usu. in a political context); **sloga'neering** *vbl. sb.* and *ppl. a.*

**1941** H. S. JOHNSON *Hell-Bent for War* ii. 37 In this modern sloganeering day, . . the constant repetition of a lie has become the . . weapon of the totalitarian propagandist. *Ibid.* iv. 85 We are . . getting all ready to do it all over again with hardly a variation in timing sequence or superficial sloganeering. **1944** *Sun* (Baltimore) 18 Mar. 6/6 To speak of the German dead in terms of carpets is not to exaggerate or 'sloganeer'. **1949** *Ibid.* 13 Oct. 18/3 Eastern Germany's tireless Communists, still a bit breathless from the ten-day marathon of sloganeering over the new 'East German Republic', [etc.]. **1967** *Philos. Rev.* LXXVI. 105 An area where superficiality and sloganeering too often hold sway. **1970** K. MILLETT *Sexual Politics* III. v. 265 What she does 'become' is only a nonentity, utterly incorporated into Birkin, his single follower, proselytizing and sloganeering. **1978** *New Statesman* 27 Oct. 556/3 The islanders have learnt to deploy the bullying sloganeering and empty hard sell of 'Westminster' politics. **1981** *Encounter* Apr. 48/2 To distinguish truth from sloganeering licence and exaggeration.

**sloganize** ('sləʊgənaɪz), *v.* [f. SLOGAN + -IZE.]

**1.** *trans.* **a.** To make (something) the subject of a slogan; to express in a slogan.

**1929** *Bull. Amer. Library Assoc.* Apr. 70 Infected with the economy virus sloganized by recent high national executives. **1941** AUDEN *New Year Let.* II. 39 Round a provincial régime that sloganized the Rights of Man. **1949** *Archit. Rev.* CV. 96/2 To sloganize the present trend in Sweden: 'Personal, organic creation in a harmonious democracy'—which should be vague enough to please everybody. **1981** *R. United Services Inst. Jrnl.* June 7/1 If you try to sloganise it I think it is quite dangerous.

**b.** To influence by means of slogans.

**1954** *ADA World* Feb. 1M/1 Of all the economic prescriptions that have been written in Washington in the past 25 years, none is stranger or more dangerous than the current attempt to sloganize the country out of an economic decline.

**2.** *intr.* To compose slogans, to utter slogans.

**1960** *Encounter* June 38/1 Mao's ability to sloganise and reduce complex matters to simple formulas has been one of his key assets. **1975** *Daily Tel.* 24 June 11/2 The conspirators met in a pub and sloganised about tyrants.

Hence **'sloganized** *ppl. a.*, expressed in the form of a slogan or slogans; **'sloganizer**, one who uses slogans; **'sloganizing** *vbl. sb.* and *ppl. a.*

**1940** *New Statesman* 2 Mar. 274/1 Snappy presentation and slick sloganising. **1965** *Ibid.* 29 Oct. 660/3 This could become mere sententiousness, the jingling or sloganising final flourish in a poem like 'Waiting'. **1970** *Times* 31 Mar. (Austral. Suppl.) p. ii/7 Throughout the 1950s and early 1960s Mr. (later Sir) Robert Menzies encapsulated this *weltanschauung* in the sloganized search for 'great and powerful friends'. **1974** *Daily Tel.* 27 June 18 The cliché-ridden sloganisers of the extreme Left. **1975** R. LEWIS *M. Thatcher* v. 42 The manifesto gave an easy sloganised summary of the 'action' to which the Party was committing itself. **1981** *Times Lit. Suppl.* 15 May 548/1 The success of 'All You Need is Love' . . encouraged the Beatles to try their hand at sloganizing.

**slogardie**, etc., obs. variants of SLUGGARDY.

**slog-dollager**: see SOCK-DOLAGER.

**slogger** ('slɒgə(r)), *sb.* [f. SLOG *v.* + -ER[1].]

†**1.** *Cambridge slang.* (See quots.) *Obs.*

**1852** J. F. BATEMAN *Aquatic Notes* 47 In this year [1844] so many boats appeared that it was determined that only twenty-eight should row on the regular race-days, and the rest on alternate days; the first boat in these trial or 'slogger' races being entitled to row last on the regular race-days. **1860** *Slang Dict.* 218 *Sloggers*, i.e., slow-goers, the second division of race-boats at Cambridge.

**2.** *colloq.* **a.** One who delivers heavy blows; a pugilist, prize-fighter; a heavy blow. Also *fig.*

**1829** P. EGAN *Boxiana* 2nd Ser. II. 19 He got away from a *slogger*, but immediately commenced an exchange of blows. **1846** *Swell's Night Guide* 75 No one dares to dispute the ability of the boshman; 'cos he's . . a numming slogger. **1857** HUGHES *Tom Brown* II. v, He was called Slogger Williams, from the force with which it was supposed he could hit. **1866** *Reader* 28 July, He is the patron and often the familiar friend of the pet 'Slogger' of the day. **1886** *Pall Mall G.* 4 Nov. 2/1 Sir William Harcourt was the slogger of the fight.

**b.** One who slogs at cricket.

**1850** *County Herald* 31 Aug. 7/3 Who went in a slogger, scoring two's and three's, till the scorers called game. **1864** *Slang Dict.* 235 A hard hitter at cricket is termed a Slogger. **1884** *Lillywhite's Cricket Ann.* 11 A rough and ready slogger.

**c.** A person or machine that works hard or with effort, often with a suggestion of ponderousness or lack of sparkle.

**1928** G. B. SHAW *Intelligent Woman's Guide* xlix. 208 The employers, to find out how much work can be got out of a man, pick out an exceptionally quick and indefatigable man called a slogger. **1968** J. SANGSTER *Touchfeather* xiii. 138 Bill was a bloody genius... Harvey's a slogger. It takes him a year to arrive where Bill could in twenty-four hours. **1977** *Drive* Mar.–Apr. 56/2 The Manta's 1.9 engine is a solid, reliable slogger in the General Motors tradition.

**3.** *Rogues' slang.* A heavy weight on a string; a slung-shot.

**1892** *Daily News* 12 Apr. 7/1 The prisoner..said if he did not go away he would fetch his 'sloggers' to him. **1904** *Times* 8 Jan. 10/5 Striking him about the head with an instrument called a 'slogger'.

**slogger** ('slɒgə(r)), *v. dial.* [Of obscure origin: cf. LOGGER *v.*] *intr.* To hang loosely; to go about untidily, etc.

**1888** etc. in *Eng. Dial. Dict.*

**sloggering** ('slɒgərɪŋ), *ppl. a.* [f. SLOGGER *v.*]

**1.** That hangs loosely; going about untidily, etc.

**1825** BROCKETT *N.C. Gloss.*, *Sloggering*, loose, untidy. **1853** R. S. SURTEES *Sponge's Sp. Tour* iii. 8 Sloggering, baggy-breeched, slangey-gaitered fellows. **1898** LD. E. HAMILTON *Mawkin* xvii. 228 Perse with his great sloggering frame, and low beast-like face.

**2.** [Perh. a different word.] (See quot. 1977.) *rare*⁻¹.

**1876** G. M. HOPKINS *Wr. Deutschland* in *Poems* (1967) 57 The inboard seas run swirling and hawling; The rash smart sloggering brine Blinds her. **1977** J. MILROY *Lang. G. M. Hopkins* 245 *Sloggering*..: Certainly imit., belonging to phonaesthetic series (*slither*, etc.), a derivative (*slog*, etc.), and a blend... Complex associations suggest the meaning: 'dashing (against the ship) repeatedly and drawing back with a sucking gurgling noise'.

**slogging** ('slɒgɪŋ), *vbl. sb.* [f. SLOG *v.* + -ING[1].] The action of the verb; vigorous striking; hard hitting. Also *attrib.*

**1857** *Bell's Life* 31 May 6/4 Nor ought we to omit notice of Reynolds's 15 by a kind of paralytic slogging, which *sometimes* tells. **1859** *Slang Dict.* 95 *Slogging*, a good beating. **1864** *Daily Telegr.* 16 May, For a long time to come ..their hitting [at cricket] will be 'slogging'. **1871** *Daily News* 23 Jan., The *status quo* of steady slogging at the forts and batteries of junction is steadily maintained. **1895** *Month* Mar. 432 All sporting men remember the hard slogging of the 'Cleresly Chicken'. **1934** [see RUN *sb.*[1] 2 a]. **1958** F. C. AVIS *Boxing Ref. Dict.* 103 *Slogging match*, a contest in which both men hit each other heavily and very often.

**slogging** ('slɒgɪŋ), *ppl. a.* [f. SLOG *v.* + -ING[2].] Hitting or striking hard. Also *fig.*

**1871** *Daily News* 12 Jan., To tempt our batteries forward, till..the time has come when slogging blows can be dealt. **1882** *Cornhill Mag.* May 535 His slogging style of controversy. **1895** *Forum* Apr. 235 As what may be called a 'slogging' debater, he has perhaps no fellow in Parliament.

**sloggy**, obs. variant of SLUGGY.

**slogh(t)e**, obs. forms of SLOUGH *sb.*[1]

**'slogster.** [f. SLOG *v.*] A slogger.

**1881** CLARK RUSSELL *Ocean Free-Lance* I. vi. 269 With no more hesitation..than the slogster Mendoza exhibited when he stepped into the ring.

**slog-wood.** (See quot.)

**1864** GRISEBACH *Flora Brit. W. Ind.* 787/2 Slog-wood, *Hufelandia pendula.*

**sloh**, obs. form of SLOUGH *sb.*[1]

**sloid, slöjd**: see SLOYD.

‖**sloka** ('sləʊkə). Also 8 sloca. [Skr. *śloka* sound, noise, call, hymn, stanza, etc.] A couplet or distich of Sanskrit verse, each line containing sixteen syllables.

**1800** *Asiatic Ann. Reg.* I. 80/1 Divine authority revealed to Menu the sacred principles in a hundred thousand slocas, or verses. **1842** W. C. TAYLOR *Anc. Hist.* xviii. (ed. 3) 571 The great Hindoo epic..which contains one hundred thousand slokas, or distichs. **1895** R. W. FRAZER *Silent Gods* (1896) 56 The wide Brâhman street..which once echoed with the sacred sound of the Sanskrit sloka.

**slokan.** *Anglo-Irish.* Also 8 slukane, 9 slocaun, sloukawn. [ad. Ir. *sleabhacán*: see next and SLAWK.] = next.

**1758** [see SLAWK I]. **1858** SIMMONDS *Dict. Trade*, *Slokan*, *Sloke*, names for the edible sea-weed..also called laver. **1866** *Treas. Bot.* 1065/1 *Sloak*, *Sloke*, or *Sloukawn*.

**sloke**[1] (sləʊk). Also 9 sloak. [var. of SLAWK.] = SLAWK I and 2.

**1777** LIGHTFOOT *Flora Scotica* II. 967 *Ulva umbilicalis*.. Navel Laver, *Anglis.* Sloke or Slake, *Scotis.* Upon the sea rocks frequent. *Ibid.* 970 *Ulva Lactuca*,..Lettuce-Laver, or Oyster-Green, *Anglis.* Green Sloke, *Scotis.* **1845** GOSSE *Ocean* i. (1849) 41 Mr. Drummond informs us that *P[orphyra] laciniata*, called Sloke in Ireland, is gathered during the winter months only. **1851** *Art Jrnl. Illustr. Catal.*, *Veg. World* II. p. iv, The so-called Irish moss, which is the *Chondrus crispus*, and the *Ulva* or sloke, both British plants. **1876** *Mid-Yorkshire Gloss.* s.v., A farmyard pond will be alluded to as being 'all slime and sloak'.

*Comb.* **1907** D. S. SHORTER *Collected Poems* 6 He saw one gleam of foam-white arms, Of sea-green eyes, of sloak brown hair.

**sloke**[2]. Also shloke. Anglicized form of SLOKA.

**1788** *Asiatick Researches* I. 127 Thus speak the following *Slokes* from the *Dhormo Onoosaason.* **1841** R. N. CUST in *Haileybury Observer* III. 21 The history of the coward, of which this is the first sloke. **1881** E. ARNOLD *Indian Poetry* 2 Dhoyi holds the listener still With his shlokes of subtle skill.

**slom(b)er**, etc., obs. forms of SLUMBER.

**slommack**, *dial.*: see SLAMMAKIN.

**slommacking**, etc., varr. SLAMMAKIN *a.*

**slon(e**, obs. inf. and pa. pple. SLAY *v.*; obs. pl. or dial. ff. SLOE.

**slong**: see SLING *sb.*[1] and *v.*[1]

**slonk** (slɒŋk), *sb. Sc.* and *north. dial.* [Of doubtful origin: cf. Da. dial. *slånk*, *slunk* a hollow or depression in the ground, and MLG. *-slunc*, LG. *slunk*, G. dial. *schlunk*, *schlonk* gullet, gorge, abyss.] (See later quots. and cf. SLUNK *sb.*)

The *Eng. Dial. Dict.* also records the word from Kent.

*c* **1470** HENRY *Wallace* III. 4 Baith erbe and froyte, busk and bewis, braid Haboundandlye in euery slonk and slaid. **1513** DOUGLAS *Æneid* XI. xi. 84 In dern sladis and mony scroggy slonk. **1563** WINȜET tr. *Vincent. Lirin.* ii. Wks. (S.T.S.) II. 19 Sa grete dangerous slonkis of sindry errouris. ? **16..** *Lindesay's* (Pitscottie) *Chron. Scot.* (1728) 90 She standing in a slonk [*v.r.* slake] bringing home water. **1728** RAMSAY *Poems* Gloss., *Slonk*, a Mire, Ditch, or Slough. **1880** *Antrim & Down Gloss.*, *Slonk*,..a ditch; a deep, wet hollow in a road. **1894** HESLOP *Northumbld. Gloss.*, *Slonk*, a depression in the ground, like a 'swallow hole'.

**slonk**, *v. rare.* [Of obscure origin: cf. Du. *slokken* to swallow, and the G. forms cited under prec.] *trans.* To swallow greedily.

Caxton may have read *slont ende at* in place of *stont ende at* in the Dutch original.

**1481** CAXTON *Reynard* (Arb.) 55 The false keytyf ete and slonked her in so hungerly that he lefte neyther flessh ne bone. [**1897** F. S. ELLIS *Reynard* 131 A cynic grin His face bore while he slonked her in.]

**sloo**, obs. f. SLAY *v.*; obs. or dial. f. SLOUGH *sb.*[1]

† **'Slood**, variant of 'SLUD. *Obs.*

**1599** B. JONSON *Cynthia's Rev.* IV. iii, S'lood what have you to doe? **1606** CHAPMAN *Gentl. Usher* II. i, Slood me thinks a man Should not of meere necessitie be an Asse.

**sloom** (slu:m), *sb.*[1] Now *north. dial.* and *Sc.* Forms: 1 sluma, 3 slume, 4 sloumbe, 8–9 sloum, 9 slowm, sloom, slum; 8–9 slome, 9 sloam; 8–9 slaum, 9 slawm, etc. [OE. *slúma*, related to SLOOM *v.*[1] Cf. Fris. *slûm*, *slom(me*, older Da. *slum* slumber, doze.] A gentle sleep or slumber; a light doze. Also *attrib.*

In the *Destr. Troy* 13281 *slym* is prob. an error for *slum.*

*a* **1000** *Guthlac* 314 (Gr.), þæt hine æreste elne binoman slæpa sluman. *c* **1050** *Be Domes D.* 240 Se earma flyhð uncræftiȝa slæp, sleac mid sluman. **13..** *E.E. Allit. P.* C. 186 He..Slypped vpon a sloumbe slepe, & sloberande he routes. *Ibid.* 466 He slydez on a sloumbe slep, sloghe vnder leues. **1781** J. HUTTON *Tour to Caves* (ed. 2) Gloss. 96 *Sloum*, or *slaum*, a gentle sleep, or slumber. **1785** —— *Bran New Wark* 150 A third [will be] nodding his head in an easy slome. **1829-** in northern dial. glossaries. **1863** ROBSON *Bards of Tyne* 359 When weary wi' weepin I sink to a slum. **1868** W. SHELLEY *Flowers by Wayside* 256 Whyles when I'm in a quiet sloom my Willie's hame to me.

**sloom**, *sb.*[2] *local.* Also slum(b, sloam. [Of obscure origin: the variant forms indicate an original *slūm-*.] (See quots.)

**1803** PLYMLEY *Agric. Shropshire* 54 *Slumbs*, black-slaty earth, and a heaving measure. *Ibid.* 56 Top-coal and pound stone. Slums. Foot-coal. **1842** BRANDE *Dict. Sci.*, etc. 1123/1 *Sloam*, layers of clay between those of coal. **1883** GRESLEY *Gloss. Coal-m.* 227 *Sloom*, a softish earthy clay or shale often underlying a bed of coal. *Ibid.* 228 *Slum*, *Slums*, *Slumbs.* 1. A blackish, slippery, indurated clay. 2. A soft clayey or shaley bed of coal.

**sloom** (slu:m), *v.*[1] Now *north. dial.* and *Sc.* Forms: 3 slume(n, slumme, slomme, 5, 9 slowm, 8–9 sloum, 9 sloom, slum, sloam, etc. [ME. *slūmen*, *slummen*, = Fris. *slûmje*, *slomje*, MDu. *slūmen* (*sluymen*), MLG. *slûmen*, *slomen*, *slommen*, MHG. *slummen*, obs. G. *schlummen*, older Da. *slumme* (*slome*): cf. SLUMBER *v.*] *intr.* To slumber; to doze.

*c* **1205** LAY. 17995 Merlin gon to slume swulc he wolde slæpen. *Ibid.* 32058 þa gon he to slepen, þa gon he to slumme. *a* **1400-50** *Alexander* 5174 Ser Telomew..Fand him slowmand on slepe & sleely him rayses. **1768** ROSS *Helenore* 58 Whiles slouming, whiles starting wi' her fright. **1819** TENNANT *Papistry Storm'd* (1827) 124 To tell th' unpillow'd crowds that lie Souffin' and sloomin' round. **1828-** in northern dial. glossaries. **1860** ROBSON *Song Solomon* vii. 9 Garrin' the lips o' a' thae that slum to speak. **1868** W. SHELLEY *Flowers by Wayside* 54, I laid me down And sloomed aneth the Roden Tree.

**sloom** (slum), *v.*[2] *Sc.* [app. of Scand. origin: cf. Norw. *sluma* to run up into long weak straw, and see next.] Of grain, grass, etc.: To become laid or lodged through being soft and heavy in growth; to begin to decay on this account. Hence **sloomed** *ppl. a.* (see quot. 1824).

**1765** A. DICKSON *Treat. Agric.* (ed. 2) 440 A strong crop of pease, or any other kind of corn laid down, and what is commonly called *slooming.* **1824** *Farmer's Mag.* Aug. 329 Those places where the weight and softness of the grass has flattened it with the earth... No other spot..offered as much verdure at this time as these seemingly *sloomed* places. **1875** *N. & Q.* Ser. v. III. 147 Ulster Words... 'Sloam', applied to corn crops when the stalks are too luxuriant in growth.

**'sloomy**, *a. dial.* Also 7 sloumie, 9 slowmy, sloamy, slaumy. [f. SLOOM *v.*[2]]

**1. a.** Of grain: Not properly filled.

**1641** BEST *Farm. Bks.* (Surtees) 54 The stemme will bee stronge and steare, and the barley itselfe sloumie and not pubble. **1808** JAMIESON, *Sloomy corn*, a phrase used with respect to grain, when it is not well filled.

**b.** Of corn, etc.: Laid or lodged through being soft and heavy; beginning to rot.

**1825** in JAMIESON *Suppl.* **1877-86** in Cheshire and Cumberld. glossaries.

**2.** Sluggish, dull, spiritless. Also as *adv.*

**1820** CLARE *Poems* (ed. 3) 127 O'er pathless plains, at early hours, The sleepy rustic sloomy goes. **1821** —— *Vill. Minstr.* II. 103 They then, like school-boys that at truant play, In sloomy fear lounge on their homeward way. **1851** STERNBERG *Northampt. Dial.*, *Sloomy*, dull and gloomy. **1880** TENNYSON *Northern Cobbler* vii, An' Sally wur sloomy an' draggle tääil'd.

**sloon**, obs. pa. pple. SLAY *v.*; obs. pl. SLOE.

**sloop** (slu:p), *sb.*[1] Also 7 slope, sloope. [ad. Du. *sloep*, = Fris. and LG. *slûp*, Da., Sw., Norw. *slup*, G. *schlup*; also older Du. *sloepe* (Kilian), LG. *slupe*, Da. *sluppe*, G. *schlupe*. The history of the Du. and LG. word is obscure, but it appears more probable that it is an adoption of F. *chaloupe* or Sp. *chalupa* than that it is the source of these. (F. has also *sloop* or *sloupe* from Eng. or Du.) Cf. CHALOUPE, SHALLOOP, and SHALLOP.]

**1. a.** A small, one-masted, fore-and-aft rigged vessel, differing from a cutter in having a jib-stay and standing bowsprit.

**1629** in Foster *Eng. Factories India* (1909) III. 315 They keepe allways some 5 or 6 sloopes and junks trading..from porte to porte. **1677** W. HUBBARD *Narrative* II. 45 Some persons that belonged to a Sloop and a Shallop..were over desirous to save some of their Provision. **1719** W. WOOD *Surv. Trade* 285 The Trade from that Island to New Spain, is carry'd on generally by Sloops. **1775** JOHNSON *West. Isl.* Wks. X. 486 Sloops are loaded with the concreted ashes. **1830** MARRYAT *King's Own* ix, The vessels..are generally small luggers or sloops, from forty to sixty tons burthen. **1885** RUNCIMAN *Skippers & Shellbacks* 98 The little old sloops were generally family concerns.

**b.** A relatively small ship-of-war, carrying guns on the upper deck only. Also in full ***sloop-of-war***.

(*a*) **1676** *Lond. Gaz.* No. 1130/4 St. Ann of Ostend, Burthen 16 Tuns,..a square stern'd open Sloop, with 2 Guns, and 20 Men. **1707** *Ibid.* No. 4379/3 Her Majesty's Ship Somerset, with..the Weesel Sloop, and Isabella Yacht, is sail'd for the River. **1761** *Ann. Reg.* 190 A short view of the whole royal navy..; 68 sloops, from 8 to 14 [guns] besides swivels. **1844** H. H. WILSON *Brit. India* III. 96 A flotilla of sloops and gun-brigs was attached to it. **1875** KNIGHT *Dict. Mech.* 2214 War-vessels of 2000 tons and upward,..carrying 12 to 22 heavy guns, are now termed sloops.

(*b*) **1769** FALCONER *Dict. Marine* (1780) Hh 3, The sloops of war carry from 18 to 8 cannon. **1790** BEATSON *Nav. & Mil. Mem.* II. 255 A number of frigates and sloops of war. **1836** MARRYAT *Midship. Easy* vii, He had succeeded in obtaining his appointment to a sloop of war.

† **2.** A large open boat; a long-boat. *Obs.*

**1631** J. TAYLOR *Turne of Fortune's Wheele* (Halliw.) 22 In Zealand where our forces all were broake, Sloops, punts, and lighters, seventy-eight confounded. **1699** *Laws Nevis* xxvii. (1740) 21 If any Person..steal..any fishing or other Boat, Canoe, Shallop, Sloop, Bark-log, or any other Vessel. **1719** DE FOE *Crusoe* II. (Globe) 518 Five Sloops or Boats,.. full of Men... We..could see the Boats at a Distance, being five large Long-Boats.

**3.** *attrib.* and *Comb.*, as ***sloop-broker***, ***load***, ***-man***, ***-model***, ***-rig***, ***-rigged***.

**1676** T. GLOVER *Acct. of Virginia* in *Phil. Trans. R. Soc.* XI. 625 The sloop man dropped his grap-line. **1722** DE FOE *Moll Flanders* (Bohn) 281 A sloop load of..hogs and stores. **1737** *Calendar Virginia State Papers* (1875) I. 229 Paid a Sloop man for 2 gals of rum. **1769** Sloop-rigged [see RIGGED *ppl. a.*[1] 1 b]. **1840** *Evid. Hull Docks Comm.* 69 What is the nature of your business as a sloop-broker? **1849** G. CUPPLES *Green Hand* ii. (1856) 22 The saucy *Iris*—as perfect a sloop-model..as ever was eased off the ways of Chatham. **1862** *Zoologist* XX. 8087, I saw three of them which a sloopman had towed behind his vessel. **1893** *Outing* XXII. 146/1 The sloop-rig—jib and mainsail—is better than a single sail. **1894** N. BROOKS *Tales of Maine Coast* 33 The 'Whisper' was a sloop-rigged craft.

**sloop** (slu:p), *sb.*[2] *Canada.* [Of obscure origin.] A simple form of drag used in lumbering. Hence **sloop** *v. trans.*, to draw on a sloop.

**1891-** in American Dicts.

**sloor**, obs. form of SLUR *sb.*

**sloosh** (slu:ʃ), *sb. dial.* and *colloq.* [Echoic: cf. SLOSH *sb.*, SLUSH *sb.*[2] But perhaps partly a variant of SLUICE *sb.*] A pouring of water; a wash; a noise of, or as of, heavily splashing or rushing water.

**1919** *Athenæum* 11 July 582/2 Among the brand-new slang one may discern some that had an onomatopœic or at any rate an imitative origin; for instance 'sloosh', a wash. **1920** *Blackw. Mag.* Apr. 500/2 There was the sloosh of bilge-water. **1926** W. DE LA MARE *Connoisseur* 187 Mr. Thripp.. not only tidied up his own and Tilda's bedroom.. but even gave a sloosh to the bath. **1973** C. BONINGTON *Next Horizon* v. 88 He got about half-way up, and suddenly there was a sloosh, and he came shooting down the steep snow. **1981** P. THEROUX *Mosquito Coast* xiv. 173 The only sounds were the flap and splash.. and the sloosh of water in the culverts.

**sloosh** (sluːʃ), *v. dial.* and *colloq.* [Echoic: cf. SLOSH *v.*[1], SLUSH *v.* But perhaps partly a variant of SLUICE *v.*] **1.** *trans.* **a.** To wash with a copious supply of water; to pour water or other liquid copiously over.

**1912** W. DE LA MARE *Child's Day* 10 Elizabeth Ann.. stands slooshing herself With that 'normous sponge. **1933** G. MURRAY tr. *Acharnians* in *Aristophanes* i. 27 Niagara'd me and slooshed me, till—almost—In so much sewage I gave up the ghost.

**b.** To pour with a rush, to dash (water).

**1952** L. A. G. STRONG *Darling Tom* 129 The butcher's boy in his blue Sunday suit had got the gardener's wheeled tank from the park, and was slooshing water down the area.

**2.** *intr.* To make a heavy splashing or rushing noise; to flow or pour with a rush.

**1914** [see CLICKY *a.*]. **1920** *Blackw. Mag.* Apr. 502/2 The slooshing bilge-water. **1971** C. BONINGTON *Annapurna South Face* xii. 153 Tom knocked it [*sc.* the primus stove] over, sending the liquid slooshing over the tent floor. *Ibid.* xiii. 167 Instant porridge.. a hot, palatable food that simply slooshed down the throat. **1981** P. THEROUX *Mosquito Coast* xxvi. 345 She gazed at the torrent of water slooshing downstream.

So **'slooshy** *v. trans.* = SLOOSH *v.* 1 a.

**1907** W. DE MORGAN *Alice-for-Short* xlix. 531 But Cook was turning cataracts of water into her sink, to slooshy it well out after a real good wash-up.

**sloot**, var. SLUIT.

**sloothering** ('sluːðərɪŋ), *vbl. sb. Anglo-Ir.* Also sluthering. [Perh. ad. Ir. *lúdar* fawning, flattery with prosthetic *s-* (A. J. Bliss).] Cajoling, wheedling. Hence as *ppl. a.*

**1892** J. BARLOW *Irish Idylls* viii. 215 There do be girls will get round a man wid their sloothterin'. **1896** G. B. SHAW in *Sat. Rev.* 1 Feb. 123/1 Boucicault had a charming brogue: not even the speech of the eminent journalist.. is more musical in sound or irresistible in insinuation—'sloothering' would be the right word, were it current here—than his. **1901** J. BARLOW *From Land of Shamrock* 79 Coaxing and sluthering, reinforced by a couple of.. florins. **1919** G. B. SHAW *O'Flaherty V.C.* 188 You foul-mouthed, dirty minded, lying, sloothering old sow. **1922** JOYCE *Ulysses* 756 He used to amuse me the things he said with the half sloothering smile on him.

**slop** (slɒp), *sb.*[1] Also 4–7 sloppe, 4, 6 slope, 7 slopp. [Of obscure history. Sense 2 corresponds to MDu. *slop*, OIcel. *sloppr*, and appears earlier in the OE. compound *oferslop* (MDu. *overslop*, OIcel. *yfirsloppr*): see OVERSLOP. The relation of the other senses to this is not clear.]

†**1.** A charmed bag employed to steal milk from cows. *Obs. rare.*

**1303** R. BRUNNE *Handl. Synne* 522 Þere was a wycche, and made a bagge... Þys wycche here charme began to sey, Þe slop ros up, and ȝede þe weye. *Ibid.* 537 Þe sloppe lay stylle, as hyt ded wore.

**2. a.** An outer garment, as a loose jacket, tunic, cassock, mantle, gown, or smock-frock.

For modern examples cf. the *Eng. Dial. Dict.* s.v. *Slop* sb.[2] 1.

*c* **1386** CHAUCER *Pars. T.* ¶422 The.. scantnesse of clothyng as been thise kutted sloppes or haynselyns. *c* **1440** *York Myst.* xxxi. 77 Se þat my sloppe be wele sittande. *c* **1440** *Promp. Parv.* 460/1 Sloppe, garment, *mutatorium*. *c* **1489** CAXTON *Sonnes of Aymon* xxi. 466 Gyve me a newe sloppe and a large hode. **1523** LD. BERNERS *Froiss.* I. clxxvi. 213 He armed hymselfe with secrete armour, and dyd on a sloppe aboue, and a cloke aboue that. *a* **1548** HALL *Chron., Hen. VIII*, 55b, The mantels had great capes like to the Portingal slopys. *a* **1618** SYLVESTER *Hymn of Alms* 195 Wks. (Grosart) II. 210 To see some painted face, Or Fire-new Fashion in a Sleeve or slop. *a* **1668** DAVENANT *News fr. Plymouth* IV. i, I will embrace thy long loose slopp and kiss Thy drivell'd Beard. **1825** KNAPP & BALDWIN *Newgate Cal.* III. 448/2 A slop or shirt over it. **1841** BORROW *Zincali* I. i, He was dressed in a coarse waggoner's slop. **1881** YOUNG *Ev. Man his own Mechanic* 12 The clothes of the amateur.. should be protected at least by a loose 'slop' or jacket of canvas.

†**b.** *spec.* (See quot.) *Obs.*[−1]

**15..** *Bk. of Precedence* in *Q. Eliz. Acad.* 28 A slope is a morning Cassock for Ladyes and gentile wemen, not open before.

†**c.** (See quot.) *Obs.*[−0]

**1688** HOLME *Armoury* II. 395/2 A Womans face proper, with a Slop on her head..; the attire.. makes me judge it to be rather some kind of Slop or Maunch for the head... Some term this a French Hood pendant.

†**3.** *pl.* Some kind of foot-wear. *Obs. rare.*

**1480** *Wardr. Acc. Edw. IV* (1830) 118 A paire of sloppes of blac leder, v d. **1483** in *Antiq. Rep.* (1807) I. 42, ij pair of shoon, ij pair of slops, and viij paire of botews of Spaynysh leder.

**4. a.** *pl.* Wide baggy breeches or hose, of the kind commonly worn in the 16th and early 17th cent.; loose trousers, esp. those worn by sailors. Now chiefly *dial.*

In the Geneva, Bishops', and Douay Bibles *sloppes* is employed in rendering Isa. iii. 20, where the AV. has 'the ornaments of the legges' and the RV. 'the ankle chains'. For some particulars relating to the history of the garment, see Fairholt *Costume* I. 237, 263, etc., and cf. the *Eng. Dial. Dict.* s.v. *Slop* sb.[2] 3.

**1481–90** *Howard Househ. Bks.* (Roxb.) 518 For the same Magnus a whyt cote, a payre sloppes. **1530** PALSGR. 271/2 Sloppes, hosyn, *brayes a marinier*. **1558** in Feuillerat *Revels Q. Eliz.* (1908) 19, viii paire of Sloppes parted, the one legge of the said blewe clothe of golde and the other of greene clothe of Silver. *a* **1586** SIDNEY *Arcadia* (1622) 60 He had nothing vpon him but a paire of sloppes, and vpon his bodie a Goate-skinne. **1608** WILLET *Hexapla Exod.* 656 The two sloppes or breeches were tied and knit together about the middle. **1656** W. DU GARD tr. *Commenius' Gate Lat. Unl.* 109 Below the girdle are the breeches, that is, either slops,.. or trusses somwhat strait. **1706** PHILLIPS (ed. Kersey), *Slops*, a wide sort of Breeches worn by Seamen. **1820** SCOTT *Monast.* xvi, Two pair black silk slops, with hanging garters of carnation silk. **1842** BARHAM *Ingol. Leg.* Ser. II. *Dead Drummer* (1905) 338 He would give an occasional hitch, Sailor-like to his 'slops'.

*transf.* **1598** B. JONSON *Ev. Man in Hum.* IV. ii, Sirrha, you ballad-singer, and slops, your fellow there, get you out.

†**b.** *sing.* in the same sense, or denoting only one leg of the garment. *Obs.*

**1562** J. HEYWOOD *Prov. & Epigr.* (1867) 193 The man.. Werth on eche legge, one male, for his sloppes are, Eche one sloppe one male. **1565** in Ellis *Orig. Lett.* Ser. II. II. 306 A lyning of Cotton stytched to the Sloppe over & besydes the lynnen lynyng straytt to the legg. **1580–3** GREENE *Mamillia* I. Wks. (Grosart) II. 19 Their narrow shoulders must haue a quilted Dublet of a large sise:.. their crooked legges, a side sloppe. **1602** MARSTON *Ant. & Mel.* v. Wks. 1856 I. 61 When I see.. another wallowe in a greate sloppe, I mistrust the proportion of his thigh. **1630** J. TAYLOR (Water P.) *Wks.* II. 175/1 His gay slop hath no sooner kist the Cushions, but.. he hath neuer left Roaring, row, row, row. **1652** *News Lowe-Co.* 2 The French Trunck sometimes doth him house, The Dutch Slopp, and the Irish Trouse.

†**c.** The loose or wide part of a pair of breeches of this kind. *Obs. rare.*

**1592** R. GREENE *Conny Catch.* II. 5 So quaintly and artificially made, that it may bee put in yᵉ slop of a mans hose. **1592** —— *Upst. Courtier* (1871) 10 A plain pair of Cloth-Breeches.., straight to the thigh,.. without a slop.

**5. a.** *pl.* Ready-made clothing and other furnishings supplied to seamen from the ship's stores; hence, ready-made, cheap, or inferior garments generally.

**1663** PEPYS *Diary* 16 Mar., Advising upon the business of Slopps, wherein the seaman is so much abused by the pursers. **1764** COMM. BYRON *Voy.* in *Hawkesworth* I. 9 The men.. who had contrived to sell not only all their warm clothes, but their bedding,.. now applied in great distress for slops. **1799** NELSON 16 Feb. in Nicolas *Disp.* (1845) III. 267 Slops are not to be purchased here but at an enormous price. **1847** L. HUNT *Men, Women, & B.* I. ii. 22 A young sailor, with a face innocent of everything but a pride in his slops. **1878** BESANT & RICE *By Celia's Arbour* xxx, He used to sell his slops for brandy, and cobble his old garments with the brown canvas of the sandbags.

*fig.* **1791** WOLCOT (P. Pindar) *Rights of Kings* Proemium, That a Monarch's wife yclept a Queen May not.. be a downright Slop, Form'd of the coarsest rags of Nature's shop? **1802–12** BENTHAM *Ration. Judic. Evid.* (1827) IV. 348 In the Roman law, the clergy had been used to see a sort of warehouse, in which slops of all sorts were to be had ready-made.

**b.** *sing.* in collective use, or denoting a single garment of this kind.

**1798** WOLCOT (P. Pindar) *Tales of the Hoy* Wks. 1812 IV. 385 When the Men of Slop The Jew and Gentile turn towards their shop In alleys dark. **1887** BESANT *The World went* x. 84 He wore a common sailor's petticoat or slop.

**6.** Used as a term of contempt. *rare.*

**1599** NASHE *Lenten Stuff* Wks. (Grosart) V. 240 Not a slop of a ropehaler they send forth to the Queenes ships, but hee is first broken to the Sea in the Herring mans Skiffe or Cock-boate.

**7.** *attrib.* and *Comb.* **a.** In senses 2 and 4, as *slop-frock*, †*-hose* [cf. MDu. *slophose*], *-pouch*.

**1530** PALSGR. 251 Payre of sloppe hoses. **1565** R. ONSLOW in Ellis *Orig. Lett.* Ser. II. II. 306 A sloppe-hose not cutte in panes. **1821** SCOTT *Kenilw.* iv, This purse has all that is left of as round a sum as a man would wish to carry in his slop-pouch. **1821** CLARE *Vill. Minstr.* II. 68 With slop-frock suiting to the ploughman's taste. **1837** *Lincoln Herald* 17 Jan. 2/2 John Cowley, indicted for stealing at Binbrook, one slop frock and one hat. **1851** STERNBERG *Northampt. Dial.*, *Slop frock*, a smock-frock.

**b.** In combs. relating to seamen's slops, or to cheap ready-made garments, as *slop-boat*, *-book*, *-chest*, *-clothes*, *-clothing*, etc.

**1823** SYD. SMITH *Wks.* (1859) II. 21/2 A large stock of rum was immediately laid in from the circumambient *slop-boats. **1755** *Abstr. Act* in *M.P.'s Let. on R.N.* 14 Five.. Pay-books shall be.. made out.., and a *Slop-book. **1867** SMYTH *Sailor's Word-bk.* 633 *Slop-Book*, a register of the slop clothing, soap, and tobacco, issued to the men; also of the religious books supplied. **1840** R. H. DANA *Bef. Mast* xxix. 102 Having begun the voyage with very few clothes, he had taken up the greater part of his wages in the *slop-chest. **1874** *Law Times' Rep.* XXXI. 20/2 They had each received ..6 dollars from the slop chest on the voyage. **1699** LUTTRELL *Brief Rel.* (1857) IV. 493 The deduction of 12*d.* in the pound by the paymaster for *slop cloaths.. is without warrant. **1745** *Proj. Manning of Navy* 11 Sea-mens Wages are not Half consum'd in.. Slop-Cloths. **1802** D. COLLINS *Acct. Eng. Colony in New S. Wales* II. xiii. 131 For want of *slop clothing and bedding, indeed, they were much distressed. **1819** J. H. VAUX *Mem.* II. 109 After putting on each a suit of coarse slop-clothing, we were ironed and sent below. **1834** *Tait's Mag.* I. 416/1 One pound sterling is paid ..as the price of his bedding and slop-clothing. **1884** *Spectator* 737/2 Their cheapness is due to the fact that they are really '*slop goods'—goods, that is, produced at a price which cannot give the worker a decent maintenance. *c* **1645** in *Archaeologia* LII. 134 A *slopmaker for Seamen neare Billingsgate. **1897** G. ALLEN *Type-writer Girl* xvi. 170, I told him of my work among the East-End slop-makers! **1799** *Hull Advertiser* 12 Oct. 2/4, I, John Brown, of Kingston-upon-Hull, *Slopman. **1812** *Examiner* 4 May 280/2 F. Richmond,.. taylor and slopman. **1819** SHELLEY *Peter Bell* II. iv, He did appear Like a *slop-merchant from Wapping. **1851** MAYHEW *Lond. Lab.* III. 231/1, I could not meet with one woman 'working a *slop-needle'. *c* **1850** *Rudim. Navig.* (Weale) 149 **Slop-room*, the place appointed for the purser to keep the ship's slops in. *c* **1860** H. STUART *Seaman's Catech.* 62 Slops and marine necessaries in the slop-room. **1802** *Naval Chron.* VII. 447 The *Resolve* *slop ship was laid up in ordinary. **1813** SOUTHEY *Nelson* I. 74 His vessel was kept at the Nore.., serving as a slop and receiving ship. **1851** MAYHEW *Lond. Lab.* III. 231/1 Working for *slop shirt-makers, &c., upon the coarser sorts of work. **1851** *Ibid.* II. 23/1 The garret-master buys lasts to do the *slop-snobbing cheap. **1861** DICKENS *Gt. Expect.* xl, He was at present dressed in a seafaring *slop suit. **1894** A. MORRISON *Mean Streets* 132 His mother had had no *slop-waistcoat finishing to do for three or four days. **1714** *Lond. Gaz.* No. 5272/9 Anne Lee, of Gosport.., *Slop-woman. **1867** SMYTH *Sailor's Word-bk* 633 A short *slop wrapper, formerly called a *sliving*.

**c. slop-builder**, a jerry-builder; **slop-built**, jerry-built; loosely-made; **slop-chit** *Naut.*, a note offered at a ship's stores in exchange for clothing; also *transf.*, an expense sheet.

**1835** *Edinb. Rev.* LX. 343 The temptation to construct what are called slop-built ships.. is therefore quite irresistible. **1869** *Latest News* 5 Sept. 7 They were only contract built edifices by 'slop builders'. **1903** W. CRAIG *Adv. Austral. Goldfields* 39 He was slop-built. **1946** 'TACKLINE' *You met such Nice Girls in Wrens* I. 11 Sailors come in at different times with what we call Slop-Chits, but which are really nothing but shopping lists. So the slop-chits are the things they want, such as shoes and socks and caps and things. **1969** S. HYLAND *Top Bloody Secret* II. 123 Superb autobahn all the way, and a reasonably fast car on his slopchit, made Karlsruhe almost one of the nearer suburbs.

**slop** (slɒp), *sb.*[2] Also 8 (9 *dial.*) slap. [prob. representing an OE. **sloppe* (cf. *cúsloppe*, var. of *cúslyppe* COWSLIP), related to *slyppe* SLIP *sb.*[1], and to *slúpan* to slip.]

**1.** †**a.** A muddy place; a mud-hole. *Obs.*[−1]

?*a* **1400** *Morte Arth.* 3923 He.. Slippes in in the sloppes o-slante to the girdylle.

**b.** ? A splash of mud or slush.

**1731** *Gentl. Mag.* I. 332 To walk through Rag Fair in dirty weather,.. a jostle in one place, a slip in another, a slop in a third.

**c.** Liquid mud; slush.

**1796** MORSE *Amer. Geogr.* I. 605 The inhabitants have to walk in almost perpetual slop. **1851** MAYHEW *Lond. Lab.* II. 207/1 In wet weather the dirt swept or scraped to one side is so liquified that it is known as 'slop'. **1891** *Pall Mall G.* 13 Jan. 1/2 Every one.. viewed the accumulating slop.. with a pious faith in its restoration in a few days.

**2. a.** An act of spilling or splashing; a quantity of liquid spilled or splashed.

**1727** BOYER *Dict. Royal* I, *Faire un Gâchis*, to make a slap, to wet a Room. **1782** MME. D'ARBLAY *Diary* 28 Dec., When she came there happened to be a great slop on the table. **1796** —— *Camilla* IV. 116 Don't mind it, I beg,.. a little slop's soon wiped up. **1836** [MISS MAITLAND] *Lett. fr. Madras* (1843) 15 On the other side of it there was an immense slop oozing out from something. **1874** MRS. WHITNEY *We Girls* vi. 121 There never was a slop on the stove, or a teaspoonful of anything spilled.

**b.** *Naut.* A choppy sea, chop.

**1956** *Sun* (Baltimore) 21 Nov. 23/6 Mostly southerlies, they pick up to twenty knots and kick up a good slop. **1974** F. MOWAT *Boat who wouldn't Float* xi. 120 A slop was banging against her bows, giving her life and motion. **1977** *Austral. Sailing* Jan. 65/1 The Tornados and Hobie 16s revelled in the slop.

**3. a.** Liquid or semi-liquid food of a weak, unappetizing kind; applied contemptuously to invalids' spoon-food, tea, etc. Now usually *pl.*

*sing.* **1657** G. STARKEY *Helmont's Vind.* 174 It is not every ridiculous slop that is a Medicine. **1786** MME. D'ARBLAY *Diary* 14 Aug., [She] exclaimed, 'Oh dear, you've got no tea!' Then pouring out a dish of slop, added [etc.]. **1801** tr. *Gabrielli's Mysterious Husb.* III. 59 The old woman.. went down to prepare the slop. **1897** *Allbutt's Syst. Med.* III. 498 Full of slop as he is, the patient burns with thirst.

*pl.* *c* **1672** WOOD *Life*, etc. (O.H.S.) I. 177 Much physick and slops being taken in the winter following. **1741** RICHARDSON *Pamela* III. 332 He physicked himself out of his Life—He would be always taking Slops. **1798** *Monthly Mag.* Mar. 183 Tea, and thin chocolate, and such like enervating slops. **1829** COBBETT *Adv. to Youth* xxxi, Experience has taught me that those slops [tea, coffee, etc.] are injurious to health. **1863** MRS. CARLYLE *Lett.* III. 158 The cold first came into my tongue, swelling it... I had to live on slops.

**b.** *colloq.* (orig. *U.S.*). Sentimentality, affected sensibility.

**1866** 'MARK TWAIN' *Lett. from Hawaii* (1967) 33 You can go on writing that slop about balmy breezes and fragrant flowers, and all that sort of truck. **1917** E. POUND *Let.* Mar. (1971) 108, I would suggest that a series of this sort [*sc.* essays on French poets] by me, Eliot, and De Bosschère would at least keep out a certain amount of *slop* from the prose section. **1924** GALSWORTHY *White Monkey* I. xiii. 106 Sentiment being 'slop', and championship mere condescension. **1927** *Sunday Express* 24 July 4 'Seventh Heaven', the swamp of sentiment into which the critics were invited to plunge a few days ago. Personally I should describe it as the sublimity of slop. **1942** BERREY & VAN DEN BARK *Amer. Thes. Slang* §265/1 *Sentimentality*,.. slop.

**c.** *U.S.* and *Austral. slang.* Beer. Usu. *pl.*

**1904** 'No. 1500' *Life in Sing Sing* 252/2 *Slop*, beer. **1919** *Dial. Notes* V. 42 *Slops*, beer. **1949** L. GLASSOP *Lucky*

*Palmer* I. 5 Keep your shirt on. There's no harm in having a jug of slops, now is there? **1953** T. A. G. HUNGERFORD *Riverslake* x. 197 His wife and both of his kids got burned to death when his house went up... They reckon that's what sent him onto the slops in the first place. **1963** *Australasian Post* 14 Mar. 51/2 Bung me and me mate over a droppa slops, will yer love?

**4. a.** Refuse liquid of any kind; rinsings of tea, coffee, or other beverages; the dirty water, etc., of a household. Usu. *pl.*

**1815** SCOTT *Guy M.* lii, He..threw the slops..into the sugar-dish instead of the slop-basin. **1848** CLOUGH *Bothie* ii, The removal of slops to be ornamentally treated. **1882** LADY BLOOMFIELD *Remin.* (1883) I. xi. 336 The slops had never been emptied, so the rooms were anything but odoriferous.

**b.** *U.S. dial.* and *colloq.* Kitchen refuse or swill fed to cattle or pigs. Usu. *pl.*

**1805** R. PARKINSON *Tour in America* I. 39 It was natural for me to inquire, what they kept their cows and horses on during the winter. They told me—their horses on blades, and their cows on slops. **1912** T. DREISER *Financier* xii. 127 A slop-man,..who could come with a great wagon filled with barrels and haul away the slops from your back door, was absolutely essential. **1961** *Publ. Amer. Dial. Soc.* XXXVI. 7 *Slop*, food for pigs.

**c.** *fig.* Nonsense, rubbish; insolence.

**1952** B. MALAMUD *Natural* 214 Roy tore it up and told the usher to take no more slop from him. **1978** J. IRVING *World according to Garp* vi. 120 'Sometimes I feel it is my responsibility to say no,' the editor was quoted as saying, 'even if I know people *do* want to read this slop.'

**5.** *Pottery.* = SLIP *sb.*[1] 4.

**1844** *Civil Eng. & Arch. Jrnl.* VII. 154/1 The halves of the mould are then put together, and the slop intended for the ground poured in.

**6.** A dance (see quot. 1962).

**1962** *Punch* 16 May 761/1 In the Slop the partners face each other and perform rhythmic movements with feet stationary, the arms swinging pendulum-like in front of the body. **1966** T. PYNCHON *Crying of Lot 49* v. 131 Each couple on the floor danced whatever was in the fellow's head: tango, two-step, bossa nova, slop. **1969** N. COHN *Pop from Beginning* ix. 84 There was the Hully Gully,..the Slop and ..the Frug.

**7.** *attrib.* and *Comb.*, as (senses 1 c and 4) ***slop-barrel, -bowl, -bucket, -can, -dirt, -pail, -tank, -tub***, etc.; (sense 3) ***slop-diet, -fed*** adj.; (sense 5) ***slop-clay***; also **slop-moulding** (see quots.); **slop-stone** *dial.*, a stone slab used as a surface for washing; **slop-wash** (see quot.).

**1831** J. M. PECK *Guide for Emigrants* 172 With..a dairy and *slop barrel..pork may be raised from the sow. **1856** KANE *Arctic Expl.* II. vii. 84 Emptying..some twelve to fifteen bucketfuls from the slop-barrel. **1810** *Columbian Centinel* 25 Aug. 4/2 For sale at Davis & Brown's Silver Ware and Jewellry Store..Sugar Basons,..*Slop-Bowls. **1861** TROLLOPE *Orley Farm* (1862) I. xi. 85 A small pile of buttered toast on the slop-bowl, kept warm by hot water below. **1884** *Harper's Mag.* Jan. 233/2 Sugar-bowl,..and slop-bowl. **1856** KANE *Arctic Expl.* II. vii. 83, I am thankful that I am here, able to empty a *slop-bucket. **1926** *Scribner's Mag.* Aug. 204/1 A strange black dog..supporting himself by raiding the *slop-cans of Nigger Town. **1851** MAYHEW *Lond. Lab.* II. 268/2 The expense of *slop-cartage. **1825** J. NICHOLSON *Operatic Mechanic* 459 When the proper proportions of *slop clay and flint have been well blunged together, the liquid is pumped out of the reservoir on the top of the slip-kiln. **1829** COOPER *Good's Study Med.* II. 58 Pale thin men, relaxed by sedentary habits and a spare *slop diet. **1896** *Allbutt's Syst. Med.* I. 399 In severer febrile attacks a slop-diet is advisable. **1851** MAYHEW *Lond. Lab.* (1864) II. 210/1 When in combination with a greater quantity of water, so that it is rendered almost liquid, it is known as '*slop-dirt'. **1871** NAPHEYS *Prev. & Cure Dis.* I. ii. 56 *Slop-fed unhealthy cows. **1875** KNIGHT *Dict. Mech.*, *Slop-hopper, the basin of a water-closet or sink. **1884** *Cent. Mag.* Dec. 261/2 The slop-hopper is generally a receptacle for rags and rubbish. **1855** MOTLEY *Corr.* (1889) I. vi. 178 Celestial *slop-jars, heaps of clean towels, etc. **1843** *Civil Eng. & Arch. Jrnl.* VI. 348/1 '*Slop-moulding,' in which process the mould is dipped into water previous to its receiving the clay. **1875** KNIGHT *Dict. Mech.* 2215 Slop-molding.. requires several molds; pallet-molding only one. **1854** B. P. SHILLABER *Life & Sayings Mrs. Partington* 212 My boy knows very well how to manage it when the *slop-pail is within reach. **1860** F. NIGHTINGALE *Notes on Nursing* 14 A slop-pail should never be brought into a sick room. **1864** CARLYLE *Fredk. Gt.* XVI. v. (1872) VI. 172 Of Hanbury's News-Letters from Foreign Courts, four or five..are like the contents of a slop-pail. **1884** *Health Exhib. Catal.* 60/2 Tip-up Lavatory, Urinal, or *Slop-sink combined. **1882** NODAL & MILNER *Gloss. Lancs. Dial.* 245 **Slopstone*, a place for washing. **1911** A. BENNETT *Card* viii. 197 A gas range and a marble slopstone with two taps. **1978** *Lancashire Life* Oct. 83/2 Ah want thad slop-stooan scrubbin'. **1968** *New Scientist* 25 Jan. 196/2 One of the ship's tanks is selected to serve as a *slop tank... The tanks to be cleaned are washed in turn and washings are pumped continuously into the top of the slop tank. **1979** F. FORSYTH *Devil's Alternative* ix. 223 She had sixty giant tanks, or holds... One of these was the slop tank, to be used for..gathering the slops from her fifty crude-carrying cargo tanks. **1867** 'MARK TWAIN' *Celebrated Jumping Frog* 169 You will proceed toward the window and sit down in that *slop-tub. *a* **1825** FORBY *Voc. E. Anglia* 307 **Slop-wash*, an occasional and hasty washing of small linen.

**slop** (slɒp), *sb.*[3] *E. Anglian dial.* [Of obscure origin.] Growing underwood.

**1784** CULLUM *Hist. Hawsted* 173 *Slop*, the underwood in a wood. *a* **1800** PEGGE *Suppl. Grose*, *Slop*, under-wood when growing. Norf. and Suffolk. **1804** *Survey Gestingthorpe* (Essex) 6 (E.D.D.), The slop of the respective occupiers pay tithe per acre when cut in the said grounds. **1902** CORNISH *Naturalist Thames* 90 Four acres of low slop, brambles, shoots, and blackthorns.

**slop** (slɒp), *sb.*[4] *slang.* [Modification of *ecilop*, back-slang for *police*.] A policeman.

**1859** in *Slang Dict.* 95. **1868** *Morning Star* 4 June, I saw the b—— slops by the public-house. **1879** F. W. ROBINSON *Coward Conscience* II. xxi, You'd better cut—the slops are after you.

**slop** (slɒp), *v.*[1] [f. SLOP *sb.*[1]] *trans.* To provide with slops or cheap ready-made clothing.

**1803** *Naval Chron.* X. 257 After being furnished and slopped with new cloaths, previous to their being sent on board.

**slop** (slɒp), *v.*[2] Also 6, 8 (9 *dial.*) slap. [f. SLOP *sb.*[2]]

**1. a.** *trans.* To spill or splash (liquid); to dash or lay *on* carelessly. Also with *over*.

**1557** TUSSER *100 Points Husb.* (1878) 229 Their milke slapt in corners, their creame al to sost. **1805** R. W. DICKSON *Pract. Agric.* I. 61 As hogs are apt to slop over and spill a part of their food. **1854** MISS BAKER *Northampt. Gloss.* s.v., If you don't mind you'll slop half your beer out of the mug. **1859** H. KINGSLEY *G. Hamlyn* III. 21 Now and then she would slop tons of water on her deck. **1894** *Brit. Jrnl. Photog.* XLI. 8 It must only be just moistened, not slopped on.

**b.** To wash or tumble (one) out of some place.

**1839** HOOD *Storm at Hastings* xxiii, Mrs. Snell Was slopp'd out of her seat. **1889** JEROME *Three Men in Boat* 18 You get fooling about with the boat, and slop me overboard.

**c.** *Prison slang.* To empty the contents of (esp. a chamber-pot). Usu. *absol.*

**1955** [implied at SLOPPING *vbl. sb.* b]. **1957** *Listener* 28 Nov. 893/3 He watched the prisoners 'slopping out', working, and attending classes. **1963** T. & P. MORRIS *Pentonville* v. 104 The next two hours are given over to getting washed, shaved, breakfasted and 'slopped out'. **1967** *Guardian* 2 June 6/1 Along the landing from his cell is a single recess for 'slopping out' chamber pots and wash-basins. **1973** *Times* 20 Dec. 2/3 At Brixton..they queue at communal lavatories to slop out their pots. **1978** 'A. GARVE' *Counterstroke* I. xvi. 67 Prisoners rise at 6.30 a.m. Slop out. Clean their cells.

**2.** To lap *up* greedily or noisily; to gobble *up*. Now *dial.*

**1575** *Gammer Gurton* II. i, Thy mylk slopt up, thy bacon filtched. **1611** J. DAVIES (Heref.) *Scourge of Folly* cvi. Wks. (Grosart) II. 20/2 Some foule-mouth'd Readers then..So slop them vp that it would make one spew. **1651** R. CHILD in *Hartlib's Legacy* (1655) 88 They make Meshes for their Cows,..which the Cows will slop up like Hogs. **1746** *Exmoor Scolding* 190 (E.D.S.), Nif et be Loblolly, tha wut slop et oll up. **1886** in ELWORTHY *W. Somerset Word-bk.* 682.

**3. a.** To slobber (one). *rare*$^{-1}$.

**1696** T. SOUTHERNE *Oroonoko* II. i, Such fine folk are not used to be slopt and kiss'd.

**b.** To make wet with spilled liquid.

**1721** BAILEY, *Slop*,..to dash with Water. **1736** AINSWORTH, To slap, or slop a place with wet, *madefacio*. **1806** BERESFORD *Miseries Hum. Life* VI. xv, A large round deal table, well slopped with beer. **1841** HARTSHORNE *Salop. Ant.* Gloss., *Slop*,..to wet or dirty.

**4. a.** *intr.* To prepare or drink any weak liquid.

**1742** FIELDING *J. Andrews* I. xiii, She had just done drinking it [*sc.* tea], and could not be slopping all day. **1771** [see SLOPPING *vbl. sb.*].

**b.** With *up*: to become intoxicated. *U.S. slang.*

**1899** [implied at *slopping-up* s.v. SLOPPING *vbl. sb.* b]. **1916** 'W. SCOTT' *Seventeen Years in Underworld* xi. 64 The illgotten gains are spent 'slopping up' (getting drunk). **1919** *Bookman* (N.Y.) Apr. 208/2 Discuss the effect of the Prohibition Amendment on a white liner. What would be his chances after its passage of procuring sufficient powders to enable him to get slopped up (a) in the State of Maine, (b) in New York City? **1926** J. BLACK *You can't Win* ix. 108 No use takin' a bunch of thirsty bums along and stealin' money for them to slop up in some saloon the next day.

**5. a.** To walk or travel *through* a place in mud or slush. Also with *along* or *on*. Also *fig.*

**1834** BECKFORD *Italy* I. 7 Anybody might slop through the Low Countries that pleased. **1851** NEWLAND *The Erne* 187, I really have no fancy to go slopping through the wet grass and muddy roads for nothing. **1880** 'MARK TWAIN' *Tramp Abr.* ii. 51 Hour after hour we slopped along by the roaring torrent.

**b.** *colloq.* With *about*, *around*, etc.: to wander aimlessly, to move in a slovenly manner; to mess *about*.

**1907** W. DE MORGAN *Alice-for-Short* xlv. 471 Old pictures do slop about the world in a vague way, till some aesthomenous person detects quality in them. **1922** M. ARLEN '*Piracy*' III. xi. 236 When I said that you were too fine and I was too old to slop about Europe in a hole-and-corner way, I meant that this disorderly kind of life is unworthy of you. **1958** X. FIELDING *Corsair Country* i. 22 So many of them slop about in cast-off men's shoes several sizes too big. **1973** *Times* 28 Nov. 13/6 Jimmy always says I mustn't slop about while I'm learning a piece, and I think that's good advice. **1982** *TV Times Mag.* 9–15 Oct. 47/1 At home.. there's nothing she likes better than to 'slop around in anything that's comfy to wear'.

**6. a.** To run or flow *over*; to flow or dash *up*.

**1853** N. HAWTHORNE *Tanglewood. T.* (Chandos) 193 The king's hand trembled so much that a great deal of the wine slopped over. **1883** *Harper's Mag.* Feb. 393/1 A fine wash.. slopping up into the..summer-houses overhanging the river.

**b.** *fig.* With *over*. To run to excess. *U.S.*

**1859** 'ARTEMUS WARD' *Wks.* (1865) 124 Washington.. never slopt over! The prevailin weakness of most public men is to slop over. **1896** *Daily News* 17 Nov. 5/2 The 'Herald' has 'slopped over' this time, but it will steady itself as soon as it gets the facts.

**c.** To pass *over* suddenly.

**1900** G. SWIFT *Somerley* 30 Boys 'slop over' from the good into the bad..in such illogical ways, that there is no setting them down under definite heads.

**7.** *U.S. dial.* and *colloq.* To feed (pigs or cattle) with slops.

**1848** D. DRAKE *Pioneer Life in Kentucky* (1870) 92 To slop the cows..was another [labour]. **1920** C. RUSSELL *Story of Nonpartisan League* 63 An angry representative told them to 'go home and slop the hogs'. **1947** *Time* 27 Jan. 21/2 Did you ever slop a hawg? **1966** R. G. TOEPFER *Witness* iii. 19 First off, he'd better feed the chickens and slop the pigs. **1976** *New Yorker* 17 May 34/1 Your hosts..will be up at dawn to slop their pig.

**8.** The vbl. stem in comb., as **slop-over** *U.S.*, an act or instance of slopping over; also *fig.*

**1908** Z. GALE *Friendship Village* 275, I see 'em all sprinkled along comin' from the funeral—neighbours an' friends an' just folks—an' most of 'em livin' in Friendship peaceful an'—barrin' slopovers—doin' the level best they could. **1952** *Richmond* (Va.) *Times-Dispatch* 5 Jan. 17/4 The ordinary foams used in fire-fighting do the rest of the job. The job is easy because there is no slop-over, frothing or expansion of the hot oil layer. **1977** *Time* 9 May 26/2 My motive in everything I was saying or certainly thinking at the time was not to try to cover up a criminal action but—to be sure that as far as any slip-over—or should I say slop-over, I think, would be a better word—any slop-over in a way that would damage innocent people.

**slop**, obs. var. SLAP *sb.*[2] and *v.*[2] *Sc.*

**slop**, obs. or dial. form of SLOPE *a.* and *v.*[1]

**'slop-basin.** [f. SLOP *sb.*[2] 4.] A basin for holding slops. Also in fig. phrase (cf. TEA-CUP c).

**1778** *Phil. Trans.* LXVIII. 628 A couple of slop-basons full of the grounds of old quass. **1796** MME. D'ARBLAY *Camilla* II. 228 Is it tea? It looks prodigiously as if just imported out of the slop basin. **1829** LYTTON *Disowned* 16 Raising her hand to a shelf on which stood an Indian slop-basin. **1861** DICKENS *Gt. Expect.* xxvii, Splashing it into the slop-basin. **1878** FROUDE *Table-Talk* 159, I have got into Cæsar, and think no more of this storm in a slop-basin.

Hence **slop-basinful.**

**1858** A. MAYHEW *Paved with Gold* II. xvii, A slop-basinful of mustard.

**slop-dash.** *rare*$^{-1}$. = SLIP-SLOP 1.

*c* **1810** MAR. EDGEWORTH *Rose, Thistle, & Shamrock* III. ii, Does he expect tea can be keeping hot for him to the end of time? He'll have nothing but slop-dash.

**slope** (sləʊp), *sb.*[1] Also 7 sloop, 8 sloap. [Aphetically f. ASLOPE *adv.*

The adv. was freq. written and printed as two words, and occurs in contexts which would readily admit of taking *a* as the indefinite article, e.g. **1551** MORE *Utopia* II. (1895) 129 An other ryuere..runneth downe a slope.]

**1. a.** A stretch of rising or falling ground; a portion of the earth's surface marked by a gradual ascent or descent, whether natural or artificial. *spec.* in *pl.*, ski-slopes.

**1626** BACON *Sylva* §537 The growing [of moss] upon Slopes. **1693** EVELYN *De la Quint. Compl. Gard* I. 167 These Banks or Slopes are very useful..for producing Early and Hasting Peas. **1727–46** THOMSON *Summer* 603 Falling fast from gradual slope to slope. **1799** YOUNG *View Agric. Lincoln.* 19 A slope of country..very well wooded. **1809–10** COLERIDGE *Friend* (1865) 88 The very large garden that occupies the whole slope of the hill on which the house stands. **1860** TYNDALL *Glac.* I. ii. 11 My eyes were fixed upon a white slope some thousands of feet above me. **1891** E. PEACOCK *N. Brendon* I. 340 The village stood on a gentle slope. **1924**, etc. [see *nursery slope* s.v. NURSERY 8 c]. **1972** P. A. WHITNEY *Snowfire* (1973) vi. 100 Snow bunny..was a term applied to beginners, usually female, who haunted the slopes. **1976** J. FARRIS *Fury* (1977) xviii. 306 He bought.. clothing for the slopes and for après-ski.

*transf.* **1784** COWPER *Task* IV. 202 The self-complacent actor, when he views..The slope of faces, from the floor to th' roof.

*fig.* **1850** TENNYSON *In Mem.* lxiv, On Fortune's crowning slope. **1887** BESANT *The World went* ii. 14 We are now nearing three score years, and on the downward slope of life.

**b.** An inclined surface of the nature of a bank, *esp.* one artificially constructed, as in fortification or engineering.

**1702** *Milit. & Sea Dict.* (1711) s.v. *Counterscarp*, Counterscarp is properly the *Talus*, or Slope of the Ditch, on the farther side from the Place. **1707** MORTIMER *Husb.* (1721) I. 12 You may lower the Ground on each side with a slope two Foot deep. **1774** *Hull Dock Act* 8 At any time after that the said slope or batter is made. **1811** WELLINGTON in Gurw. *Disp.* (1837) VII. 638 Some time must elapse before a slope will be made in it by battering. **1838** SIMMS *Public Wks. Gt. Brit.* 19 The slopes of the excavation shall be finished as the cutting advances. **1876** VOYLE & STEVENSON *Milit. Dict.* 390/1.

**c.** *Mining.* An inclined roadway.

**1863** *Harper's Mag.* Sept. 459/2 There is an entrance to the mine by means of an inclined plane, called a slope. **1874** RAYMOND *Statist. Mines & Mining* 41 To get down to these [seams] there are at present two slopes and one tunnel... Each of the slopes is furnished with hoisting-engines. **1883** GRESLEY *Gloss. Coal-m.* 227. **1890** *Daily News* 8 Feb. 5/8 A dozen men escaped..in the log slope some distance away from Cook's slope.

**2. a.** Upward or downward inclination; deviation from the horizontal or perpendicular.

**1611** COTGR., *Talus*, a slope, sloping, slopenesse. **1664** EVELYN tr. *Freart's Archit.* iii. 16 Its extraordinary projecture, which is after a sort augmented by the sloops which the Architect has given to the drops which compose the ornament of the nether face. **1704** J. HARRIS *Lex. Techn.* I. s.v. *Talus*, The Talus of a Bastion or Rampart, is the Slope allowed to such a Work. **1759** MILLS tr. *Duhamel's Husb.* II. i. (1762) 125 Where the ground had not slope enough for the water to run off. **1815** ELPHINSTONE *Acc. Caubul* (1842) I.

117 The slope of the countries on each side of the mountains, is pointed out by the direction of the streams. **1863** BARRY *Dockyard Econ.* 139 The frame timbers are then cut by the sawyers to the slope required by the moulds. **1878** HUXLEY *Physiography* 15 The rapidity with which a river flows will depend upon the amount of slope in its bed.

**b.** *Mil.* A position between perpendicular and horizontal.

**1868** *Regul. & Orders Army* §615e, The crowbar is carried at the Slope resting on the right Shoulder. **1887** *Times* (weekly ed.) 28 Oct. 18/4, I..brought the rifle from the 'slope' to the 'port'.

**c.** The tangent of the angle between a line and the horizontal; the ratio of the projection on the *y*-axis of an infinitesimal segment of a graph to its projection on the *x*-axis; the value of the first differential of some quantity, esp. with respect to distance.

**1889** J. A. FLEMING *Alternate Current Transformer* I. iii. 92 We shall call the trigonometrical tangent of the angle PTN, the slope of the tangent at the point P. *Ibid.* 93 The firm line curve is a curve of sines... The dotted line is a curve of sines, whose ordinate QN at any point represents the slope of the tangent at P on the original curve. **1898** *Proc. R. Soc.* LX. 478 If the slope of RR is positive we may say that large values of *x* are on the whole associated with large values of *y*, if it is negative large values of *x* are associated with small values of *y*. **1905** *Physical Rev.* XX. 174 The difference of temperature slope at different parts of the two bars was measured by means of thermoelectric couples. **1933** G. VAN PRAAGH *Introd. Calculus* i. 9 If *y* is a function of *x*, the differential coefficient or derivative of *y* with respect to *x* measures the rate of change of *y* with *x* for some particular value of *x*, $x_1$, and is the slope of the graph of f(*x*) at the point $x_1$. **1959** *Listener* 26 Feb. 371/2 The ball will slow up because of the gravitational 'slope'. **1971** *Physics Bull.* Feb. 86/1 A ln $\sigma$ against $1/T$ plot should, at the temperature of conversion, exhibit a change of slope.

**3. a.** A slant; an inclined surface of any kind.

**1707** MORTIMER *Husbandry* 397 [In] those Boughs that lean from the Head, cut the sloap on the lower side. **1828** STARK *Elem. Nat. Hist.* II. 98 Shell triangular,..cartilage slope rather protruded. **1837** GORING *Microgr.* 91 Two pieces of wood carved out to fill the slope of the upper part of the face. **1928** L. F. H. WHITBY *Med. Bacteriol.* iii. 46 Secondary cultures, or subcultures, are made by picking colonies from the plate and planting them on to slopes. **1951** —— & HYNES *Ibid.* (ed. 5) iii. 24 Slopes are made by allowing the medium to set in test-tubes or bottles tilted about 10° from the horizontal. **1974** R. K. PAWSEY *Techniques with Bacteria* iv. 51 The loop is introduced to the base of the slope and a wavy line made on the slope with the loop gradually rising to the top.

**b.** A desk, or substitute for this, having a sloping top.

**1833** T. HOOK *Love & Pride, The Widow* xi, A small writing-desk, or as it is technically called by cabinet-makers, a slope. **1897** *Army & Navy Stores List* 742 Blotting Desk Slopes.., room under the pad for loose papers.

**4.** *Naut.* (See quot.)

**1867** SMYTH *Sailor's Work-bk.*, *Slope of Wind*, a breeze favouring a long tack near to the required course, and which may be expected to veer to fair.

**5.** *Electronics.* The mutual conductance of a valve (so called because it is numerically equal to the slope of one of the characteristic curves of the valve).

[**1918** *Wireless World* Nov. 458 (*heading*) A thermionic valve slopemeter. *Ibid.*, The effectiveness of a valve as a relay and amplifier depends primarily on the slope of the grid voltage-plate current characteristic.] **1932** *B.B.C. Year-bk.* 395 It is now the common practice of valve manufacturers to give a figure for the mutual conductance (or slope) of each of their products. **1948** C. A. QUARRINGTON *Mod. Practical Radio & Television* (ed. 2) I. x. 78 The measurement of slope may be carried out under any conditions of grid voltage. **1953** A. H. W. BECK *Thermionic Valves* ix. 246 The mutual conductance or slope $= (\partial I_a/\partial V_g)$, *Va* const.

**6.** *U.S. slang.* An oriental; more recently, *spec.* a Vietnamese. (Abusive.) Cf. *slopehead* s.v. SLOPE- a, SLOPY *sb.*, and SLANT *sb.*[1] 10.

**1948** G. H. JOHNSTON *Death takes small Bites* v. 121 He seemed a hell of a lot more concerned with his bunch of flea-bitten slopes and his pots of medicine. **1966** *Publ. Amer. Dial. Soc. 1964* XLII. 45 *Slope* and *slopehead* were the most popular terms applied to all 'indigenous personnel' [in Korea in 1950–1]. **1966** *New Statesman* 25 Mar. 436/3 He confirms the soldiers' contempt for the Vietnamese ('slopes' and 'gooks'). **1969** [see DINK *sb.*[3]]. **1978** R. THOMAS *Chinaman's Chance* iii. 35 All the Chinaman's gotta do is get into Saigon... Once he's in nobody's gonna notice him, because all those slopes look alike.

**7.** Used *attrib.* to designate a quantity defined as a rate of change or derivative instead of as a ratio; chiefly in ***slope resistance***.

**1931** L. B. TURNER *Wireless* vii. 203 In the metallic parts of the circuits..the slope resistance $\partial e/\partial i$ and Ohm's resistance $e/i$ are equal. *Ibid.* viii. 235 It is necessary to allow ..for the very small slope or differential permeability $dB/dH$ of the core. **1971** *Gloss. Electrotechnical Power Terms (B.S.I.)* II. ii. 18 *Slope resistance*, value of forward resistance calculated from the slope of the straight line used when determining the threshold voltage from the forward current/voltage drop characteristics of a diode or thyristor in the on-state.

**slope** (sləʊp), *sb.*[2] *colloq.* [f. SLOPE *v.*[2]] An act of making off, running or slinking away, etc.

**1859** BARTLETT *Dict. Amer.* (ed. 2) 416 *Slope*, a running away, elopement, escape. **1897-** in *Eng. Dial. Dict.* ('to do a slope').

**slope,** obs. var. SLAP *sb.*[2] *Sc.*, SLEEP *sb.*

**slope** (sləʊp), *a.* Now *poet.* Also 6 sloape, 8 slop. [f. as SLOPE *sb.*[1]]

**1.** Sloping, slanting.

**1502** ARNOLDE *Chron.* 64 Thou most..kitt it soo with a slope draught. **1555** W. WATREMAN *Fardle of Facions* App. 315 But se there be none ascence ther vnto by staiers, but onely..by a slope bancque of Turfes. **1594** BLUNDEVIL *Exerc.* III. I. ii. (1636) 295 What is the Zodiaque? It is a broad, oblique, or slope Circle. **1626** BACON *Sylva* §880 There the Water Rowleth, and Moveth,..with a Sloper Rise, and Fall. **1677** MOXON *Mech. Exerc.* iii. 46 The slope Teeth of the Worm wheel will gather into the slope Grooves of the Spindle. **1724** SIR W. HOPE *Vind. Art. Self-defence* 131 Cross his sword..by a slop or squint motion of your sword-hand. **1735** SOMERVILLE *Chase* III. 440 To drain the stagnate Fen, to raise the slope Depending Road. **1811** *Self Instructor* 27 For the slope hands, turn your left side a little towards the desk. **1884** TENNYSON *Becket* II. ii, Holy Church..will not wreck, nor our Archbishop Stagger on the slope decks.

†**2.** Affording no certainty. *Obs. rare.*

**1587** *Mirr. Mag.*, *Forrex* xviii. 6 For hope is sloape, and hold is hard to snatche.

**slope** (sləʊp), *v.*[1] Also 6–8 sloap (7 sloape), 7 sloop-, 8 slop. [f. SLOPE *a.*]

**1.** *intr.* To take, to move or proceed in, an oblique direction.

In some cases with suggestion of sense 2.

**1591** SYLVESTER *Du Bartas* I. v. 538 He..sloaping swiftly overthwart those Seas..Makes double haste to finde some happy strand. **1598** *Ibid.* II. ii. IV. *Columnes* 319 Where Titan's..Chariot sloaps. **1633** *Cal. of State P., E. India & P.* VIII. 380 The houses being so near the waterside that a man coming ashore may presently slope into one and find chapmen. **1798** COLERIDGE *Ball. Dark Ladie* iv, The sun was sloping down the sky. **1825** W. COBBETT *Rur. Rides* (1885) II. 1 Crossing Lord Carnarvon's park,..and sloping away to our right over the downs. **1860** TYNDALL *Glac.* I. ii. 22 The sun was sloping to the west. **1890** CLARK RUSSELL *Marriage at Sea* iv, The [setting] sun that was now sloping into the Atlantic.

**2.** To assume, to have or be in, a sloping or slanting position or direction.

*α.* **1709** DAMPIER *Voy.* III. II. 88 The burning Island.. runs from the Sea a little sloaping towards the Top. **1765** A. DICKSON *Treat. Agric.* (ed. 2) 226 That the first coulter be set almost perpendicular..; that the second slope but a little. **1796** T. TWINING *Trav. India*, etc. (1893) 128 On the left of the fire-place was a sofa, which sloped across the room. **1825** J. NICHOLSON *Operat. Mechanic* 106 The canal..should slope about four inches in the first 200 yards. **1877** A. B. EDWARDS *Up Nile* xviii. 478 The corner where the mountain slopes down to the river.

*β.* **1707** SIR W. HOPE *New Method Fencing* (1714) 11 His Sword's Point must slop towards the middle part of his Adversary's advanced Thigh.

**3.** *trans.* To bring into, to place or put in, a sloping or slanting position; to bend down; to direct downwards or obliquely.

**1605** SHAKS. *Macb.* IV. i. 57 Though Pallaces and Pyramids do slope Their heads to their Foundations. **1638** MILTON *Lycidas* 31 Till the Star..Toward Heav'ns descent had slop'd his westering wheel. **1667** —— *P.L.* I. 223 The flames..slope their pointing spires. **1748** THOMSON *Cast. Indol.* I. lviii, When Dan Sol to slope his wheels began. **1833** ELLIS *Elgin Marbles* I. 14 They come.., sloping their way. **1844** LD. HOUGHTON *Mem. Many Scenes* 104 His spirit of splendour has gone forth, Sloping wide violet rays.

**b.** *spec.* To bring (a weapon) into, or hold (it) in, a sloping position. Also *transf.*

**1625** MARKHAM *Souldiers Accid.* 24 Sloape your Musquet. **1634** MASSINGER *Very Woman* III. i, Face to your left hand;—Feather you hat;—slope your hat;—now charge. **1688** HOLME *Armoury* III. xix. (Roxb.) 147/2 Slope your pike, is to draw the But end of the pike (being shouldred) almost to the ground and the point aloft. **1707** SIR W. HOPE *New Method Fencing* 13 He must, as the thrust is coming home, slop his point to make a cross. **1796** *Cavalry Instr.* (1813) 243 In general swords will be carried with the blade resting on the hollow of the shoulder, and by the word *Slope Swords*. **1807** J. BARLOW *Columb.* VII. 346 Till..the meeting ranks Slope their strong bayonets. **1859** F. A. GRIFFITHS *Artill. Man.* (1862) 34 The leading division will..slope arms.

**4.** To cut, form, or make, with a slope or slant.

**1611** COTGR., *Taluër*, to slope, to set, cut, or make aslope. **1715** DESAGULIERS *Fires Impr.* 122 Let both be bezell'd or sloap'd. **1763** MILLS *Pract. Husb.* IV. 216 The first [way] is, to slope the cion off a full inch, or more. **1797** *Trans. Soc. Arts* XV. 188 The bank and ditch being properly laid out and sloped. **1815** J. SMITH *Panorama Sci. & Art* I. 216 Each side..should be sloped off, to receive the bond of the adjoining work. *a* **1878** SIR G. SCOTT *Lect. Archit.* (1879) I. 249 Mouldings which received much rain..were very much more sloped than in Classic work.

**b.** *absol.* To give a slope to the letters in writing.

**1837** DICKENS *Pickw.* xiv, The lines they used to rule in the copybooks at school, to make the boys slope well.

**slope** (sləʊp), *v.*[2] *colloq.* [Originally *U.S.*; perh. formed by wrong analysis of *let's lope* (see LOPE *v.*), but cf. some of the uses of SLOPE *v.*[1] I.]

**1. a.** *intr.* To make off, depart, decamp.

**1830** *Palladium of Brit. N. Amer.* (Toronto) 29 Aug. 224/1 Bad climate indeed, wonder people dont all *slope*. **1839** MARRYAT *Diary America* Ser. I. II. 232 Here are two real American words:—'Sloping'—for slinking away; 'Splunging', like a porpoise. **1857** *Slang Dict.* 19 *He sloped*, he went off. **1866** MISS BRADDON *The Lady's Mile* i, We may as well slope,..it's nearly 7 o'clock. **1890** 'R. BOLDREWOOD' *Col. Reformer* (1891) 80 You may go straight..to the.. police station as soon as I slope.

**b.** With advs., esp. *off*. Also, to move (*off*, *in*, etc.) in a leisurely manner; to amble (*in*, etc.); to depart surreptitiously, sneak off.

**1851** MAYNE REID *Rifle Rangers* vi. 50 We can't go on to Washington—what can we do but slope home again? **1861** *Sat. Rev.* 22 June 629 If it is pretty lively, they stay; if it is dull, they slope off. **1876** TROLLOPE *Prime Minister* II. xvi. 265 You should have seen the policeman sloping over and putting himself in the way. **1898** G. W. E. RUSSELL *Collect. & Recoll.* xxxiv. 477 Whoever slopes homewards, the Government must stay. **1922** JOYCE *Ulysses* 298 Come in, come on, he won't eat you... So Bloom slopes in with his cod's eye on the dog. **1980** *Private Eye* 26 Sept. 13/1 Anyway, he sloped in for a chinwag with the Boss.

**2.** *trans.* To leave (lodgings) without paying.

In the sense of 'cheat, trick', *slope* is recorded in dialect use from 1828 onwards.

**1908** *Reminis. Stonemason* 100 They had 'sloped' their lodgings.

†**slope,** *v.*[3] *Obs.*[−1] (Meaning obscure.)

**13..** *Minor Poems fr. Vernon MS.* xxxvii. 772 And ȝif þe luste riȝt wel slope, Cum whon he doþ of his Masse-cope.

**slope** (sləʊp), *adv.* [Aphetic for ASLOPE *adv.*] In a sloping or slanting manner or position. (In later use only *poet.*)

*a* **1470** TIPTOFT *Cæsar* v. (1530) 8 Theyr horsys ronne in placys slope steepyng. **1572** MASCALL *Plant. & Graff.* (1592) 73 Ye shall bore slope a hole with an Auger, in the biggest part of the bodie of the Tree. **1577** B. GOOGE *Heresbach's Husb.* III. (1586) 129 Both sortes must be laied slope, that the water may run away. **1653** H. COGAN tr. *Pinto's Trav.* lv. (1663) 217 The Temple..is built all slope fifteen fathom high. **1667** MILTON *P.L.* IV. 591 That bright beam, whose point now raisd Bore him slope downward to the Sun. **1807** J. BARLOW *Columb.* I. 188 Steep before them stood, Slope from the town, a heaven-illumined road. **1820** KEATS *Hyperion* I. 204 Hyperion..Came slope upon the threshold of the west.

**slope-.** In combs., representing either the sb. or adj., or the stem of the vb. **a.** With nouns, as ***slope-block***, ***-board***, ***-desk***, etc. (see quots.); **slope circuit** *Electronics* = *slope filter* below; **slope current,** (*a*) an air current produced when wind is deflected upwards by a hill; (*b*) an ocean current that arises when the surface of the sea slopes as a result of wind action; **slope detection** *Electronics*, the detection of a frequency-modulated signal by means of a slope filter followed by a detector for amplitude-modulated signals; so **slope detector**; **slope filter** *Electronics*, a filter whose response increases or decreases more or less uniformly over the frequency range in which it is used; **slopehead** *U.S. slang* = SLOPE *sb.*[1] 6 (abusive; cf. also SLOPY *sb.*); **slope wash, slopewash** *Geomorphol.*, the downhill movement of soil or rock under the action of gravity assisted by running water not confined to a channel.

**1834–47** J. S. MACAULAY *Field Fortif.* (1860) 206 The *slope-block is a cube of wood, whose side is made equal to the intended difference of level. **1648** HEXHAM II. s.v. *Galm*, The *Slope-board-windowes in a Steeple of Bells, to give them the better sound. **1966** M. SCHWARTZ et al. *Communication Systems & Techniques* v. 230 One side of a resonance curve is used as a '*slope circuit' in a frequency detector. **1978** S. HAYKIN *Communication Systems* iv. 342 Basically, a frequency discriminator consists of a slope circuit followed by an envelope detector. **1931** V. W. PAGÉ *Henley's ABC Gliding & Sailflying* vii. 150 This ascending air current, which is defined as a *slope current, is the source of energy for sailing flight. **1939** REVELLE & SHEPARD in P. D. Trask *Recent Marine Sediments* 277 In the Southern California region..the chief role in the transportation of débris must be played by tidal currents and non-permanent eddying 'slope currents' resulting from wind action. **1968** G. NEUMANN *Ocean Currents* iv. 195 The resulting slope of the sea surface produces horizontal pressure gradients in meridional direction which, in turn, cause slope currents to develop. **1884** YATES *Recoll.* iii, On the edge of his green *slope-desk. **1949** B. GROB *Basic Television* xxi. 433 While *slope detection is seldom used in television receivers for reception of the associated sound signal, the principle is important because it illustrates how an FM signal can be received with an AM system. **1978** D. CAMERON *Audio Technol. Systems* iv. 129 Economy-type FM tuners occasionally use some form of slope detection. **1958** A. W. KEEN *Frequency Modulation* iii. 83 This circuit, with the resonant frequency adjusted above the highest value of the f.m. signal-frequency, or below the lowest, was the first to be used..as an f.m. detector and is known as a '*slope' detector. **1977** F. G. STREMLER *Introd. Communication Systems* vi. 293 Although the slope detector is economical, it has a very limited range and its use is restricted to input signals with small frequency variations. **1805** R. W. DICKSON *Pract. Agric.* I. 389 Machines..for scooping out *slope drains, where necessary, in a field. **1937** *Proc. IRE* XXV. 474 The intermediate-frequency output of a superheterodyne receiver is fed through a limiter to a *slope filter or conversion circuit which converts the frequency modulation into amplitude modulation. **1942** A. HUND *Frequency Modulation* i. 84 For the upper cutoff frequency ..of the slope filter a voltage $2E$ is obtained at the output of this filter. **1966** *Slopehead [see SLOPE *sb.*[1] 6]. **1968** *Listener* 23 May 656/2 At Can Tho, two years ago, I heard American Air Force men sing a ballad about the Vietnamese, whom they then called 'slopeheads' or 'slopes'. **1828** SIEUART *Planter's G.* (ed. 2) 199 No water can stagnate..where the entire bottom of the space..is worked to a uniform level, that is, a *slope-level. **1875** KNIGHT *Dict. Mech.* 2214/2 The slope-level or clinometer is used for determining the angle of embankments, the grade of roads, pitch of roof [etc.]. **1712** J. JAMES tr. *Le Blond's Gardening* 67 The Turf must be laid so that..the *Slope-line be kept without Elbows and Inequalities. **1859** Cayley *Math. Papers* IV. 108 A system of contour lines and steepest or slope lines. **1683** Moxon *Mech. Exerc., Printing* xiii. ⁋3 The *Slope-sholdering of the Counter-Punch. **1669** Sturmy *Mariner's Mag.* II. xvi. 96 This Distance from B to H is the true Length of the *Sloap-side BE. **1870** Morris *Earthly Par.* II. III. 469 A gay-striped tent Just raised upon the slope-side. **1864** Dasent *Jest & Earnest* (1873) I. 38 These *slope-swards are often so large, that it takes more than a day to work them out. **1938** C. F. S. Sharpe *Landslides & Related Phenomena* i. 8 The series can be represented as follows: Stream-flow (much water, small load, low angle), *Slopewash, Sheetflood, Mudflow, Earthflow, Debris-avalanche, Landslide (little water, large load, moderate to high angle). **1966** J. Wyckoff *Rock, Time, & Landscape* iv. 71 As the ravine is cut deeper, its walls are worn back by weathering, mass wasting, and slope wash. **1978** *Nature* 23 Feb. 740/1 Slopewash seems important in sediment transport and fallen sandstone blocks and trees accumulate sediment on their upslope sides.

**b.** Forming parasynthetic adjs., as ***slope-browed, -eared, -roofed, -toothed.***

**1647** R. Stapylton *Juvenal* 129 Thou satest up till midnight; which..None that cards wooll with sloap-tooth'd wyre would do. **1813** J. N. Brewer *Beauties Eng. & Wales* XII. II. 116 It has very ancient church with a slope-roofed tower. **1827** Griffith tr. *Cuvier* II. 153 The slope-eared bat (*vespertilio emarginatus*) is another of the bats of Europe. **1837** Carlyle *Fr. Rev.* III. III. ii, A bald, rude, slope-browed, infuriated visage of the canine species.

**sloped** (sləʊpt), *ppl. a.* Also 7 **sloapt**, 8 **sloap'd**. [f. SLOPE *v.*$^{1}$] Formed with a slope; cut, raised, placed, etc., in a sloping position.

**1683** Moxon *Mech. Exerc., Printing* xxiv. ⁋10 Turning the Ball about by its Handle, [he] presses it hard against the sloapt edge of the Ball-knife. **1693** Evelyn *De la Quint. Compl. Gard.* I. 167, I will make into Sloped Banks the 15 Toises or Fathoms of Augmentation to the South. **1728** Chambers *Cycl.* s.v. *Engrafting*, Almost as long as the sloap'd Part of the Cyon. **1766** *Compl. Farmers* s.v. *Surveying*, An index, which is a large ruler of wood..having a sloped edge. **1842** *Civil Eng. & Arch. Jrnl.* V. 319/1 The sloped work had been destroyed. **1859** Ruskin *Perspective* xviii. 132 Cut a piece of strong white pasteboard.., and dip it in a sloped position into water. **1893** Earl Dunmore *Pamirs* I. 73 Two Kashmiri soldiers..marching along with sloped arms.

†**'slopely**, *adv. Obs.*$^{-1}$ In 6 **sloaply**. [f. SLOPE *a.*] Slopingly; aslope.

**1598** Sylvester *Du Bartas* II. ii. IV. *Columnes* 312 The next, which there beneath it sloaply slides.., is called the Zodiac, the Planet's path.

†**'slopeness.** *Obs.* [f. SLOPE *a.*] The condition of having a slope; sloping form or position.

**1551** Recorde *Pathw. Knowl.* Pref., If he kepe not a.. iuste slopenesse in the sides.., the diche shall be faultie many waies. **1598** Barret *Theor. Warres* Gloss. 251 Pendent, is the bending or slopenesse of the Parapet outward. **1611** Cotgr., *Biseau*,..such a slopenesse, or slope forme, as is in the point of an yron leauer, chizle, &c. **1624** Wotton *Archit.* in *Reliq.* (1651) 269 The Italians are very precise in giving the Cover a gracefull pendence of sloapnesse.

**sloper** ('sləʊpə(r)). *U.S.* [f. SLOPE *sb.*$^{1}$] An inhabitant of the Pacific slope of the United States.

**1892** *Nation* (N.Y.) 14 Apr., All other 'slopers'..can avoid this evil and at the same time contribute to the prosperity of the slope.

**slopeways** ('sləʊpweɪz), *adv.* [f. SLOPE *sb.*$^{1}$ or *a.*] In a sloping manner or position.

**1670** J. Smith *Eng. Improv. Reviv'd* 25 Setting them upright, or slope ways, or flatt. **1681** Chetham *Angler's Vade-m.* iii. §4 (1689) 20 From the inside to the back of the hook slope-ways. **1765** *Museum Rust.* IV. cvi. 459 The beets should be put into the canals slope-ways. **1893** Kipling *Many Invent.* 18 The rigging, which ran criss-cross and slopeways.

**'slopewise**, *adv.* Now *rare* or *Obs.* = prec.

In common use *c* 1530 to 1770.

**1530** Palsgr. 702/1, I shedde, as an hyll dothe slopewyse downwardes to the valley. **1577** B. Googe *Heresbach's Husb.* II. (1586) 84 But Plinie would haue them slope wise. **1657** Austen *Fruit Trees* I. 61, I should rather cut off a convenient height from the ground, slope-wise. **1669** Worlidge *Syst. Agric.* (1681) 244 Prick the Rods sloap-wise against the Wind. **1743** *Phil. Trans.* XLII. 418 It had the Appearance which a Tube, or rather a Cone, would make cut slopewise. **1771** *Encycl. Brit.* II. 211/2 Large iron cards, placed slopewise.

**slopey**: see SLOPY *a.*

†**slopfall.** *Obs.*$^{-0}$ A cord or rope fastened to the front frame of a loom in order to support the weaver when bending to the shuttle.

**1782** *Encycl. Brit.* (ed. 2) IX. 6711/2.

**slopiness.** *rare*$^{-0}$. = SLOPENESS.

**1611** Cotgr., *Talus*,..slopenesse, or slopinesse. **1650** *Cotgrave's Dict.* (ed. 3), *Glacis*,..a sloaping, sloapinesse, gentle bending downewards.

**sloping** ('sləʊpɪŋ), *vbl. sb.* [f. SLOPE *v.*$^{1}$] The fact of being or forming a slope; degree of slope; a sloping surface.

**1611** Cotgr., *Glacis*,..a sloaping, sloapenesse, gentle bending downewards. **1645** N. Stone *Enchiridion Fortif.* 3 On the inward side they gave them [*sc.* the walls] a *Talud* or slooping. **1656** H. Phillips *Purch. Patt.* (1676) 204 If the sloaping of the Tun be not much. **1712** J. James tr. *Le Blond's Gardening* 27 The great Walk in the middle..is supposed to be a gentle Sloping. **1794** Sullivan *View of Nature* II. 145 The different sloping of the ground. **1830** Tennyson *Arab. Nts.* 30 Where all The sloping of the moon-lit sward Was damask-work. **1903** Davidson *O.T. Prophecy* ix. 138 The stair-like sloping to heaven of the land.

**sloping** ('sləʊpɪŋ), *ppl. a.* [f. as prec.] That slopes, in senses of the vb.

**1610** Holland *Camden's Brit.* (1637) 727 Mountaines, whose sloping sides in some places beare good grass. **1642** H. More *Song Soul* III. I. vi, Many thousand sloping sunnes have set. **1687** A. Lovell tr. *Thevenot's Trav.* III. 25 Where there are no Steps there is a sloaping descent to the Bason. **1765** A. Dickson *Agric.* (ed. 2) 211 A curved mold-board with a sloping sheath. **1797** Coleridge *Anc. Mar.* I. xii, With sloping masts and dipping prow.. The ship drove fast. **1822** J. Parkinson *Outl. Oryctol.* 189 The ligament..is inserted in the sloping depression in each valve. **1875** Sir T. Seaton *Fret-Cutting* 94 The extra wood..given by the sloping cut can be pared away afterwards.

**b.** In quasi-adverbial construction.

**1658** tr. *Porta's Nat. Magick* III. xvii. 98 Bore a hole sloaping into the body of a Tree. **1665** *Phil. Trans.* I. 45 These Crucibles are laid sloaping. **1715** Desaguliers *Fires Impr.* 124 In such manner, that it may open sloping within the Funnel. **1748** *Anson's Voy.* II. viii. 218 The course of the water..ran sloping with a rapid but uniform motion. **1838** *Penny Cycl.* XI. 342/1 The stock is cut over, sloping, above a smooth and straight part.

**slopingly** ('sləʊpɪŋlɪ), *adv.* [f. prec.] In a sloping manner or position; obliquely, slantingly.

**1644** Digby *Nat. Bodies* xi. §7. 92 These atomes do not descend alwayse perpendicularly, but sometimes sloapingly. **1675** Han. Woolley *Gentlew. Comp.* 115 Raise the Merry-thought from the breast, and lace it down sloppingly. **1748** *Anson's Voy.* II. x. 241 A great number of mats, which..they place slopingly against the gunwale. **1809** *Ann. Reg.* 346 A regular descent will be made, by cutting away the earth slopingly. **1846** *Blackw. Mag.* LX. 770 The partridge glances slopingly through the trees. **1887** *Cent. Mag.* XXIII. 593 A long straight shaft, cut slopingly through the solid stone.

†**'slopingness.** *Obs. rare.* [f. as prec.] Sloping condition or position.

**1644** Digby *Nat. Bodies* xxx. §6. 266 The litlenesse of the angle and the sloapingnesse of the line. **1727** Bailey (vol. II), *Slopingness*, Slantingness, going diagonally.

**sloppage** ('slɒpɪdʒ). *rare.* [f. SLOP *sb.*$^{2}$ or *v.*$^{2}$] Slops collectively; slopped matter. Also, the action of slopping.

**1884** *Cent. Mag.* Dec. 264/1 Sloppage, leakage, and the tainted air..make this space untidy and in every way objectionable. **1962** J. Onslow *Bowler-Hatted Cowboy* viii. 79, I filled the barrel among the boulders of the creek, and put a few sticks to float in it. These served as baffles and minimized the loss from sloppage.

†**slopped**, *ppl. a.*$^{1}$ *Obs.*$^{-1}$ In 7 **slopt**. [f. SLOP *sb.*$^{1}$ + -ED$^{2}$.] Dressed in slops; wearing wide breeches.

*a* **1601** *Pasquil & Kath.* (1878) I. 125 Nor doe I enuie Poly-phemian puffes, Swizars slopt greatnesse.

**slopped** (slɒpt), *ppl. a.*$^{2}$ [f. SLOP *v.*$^{2}$ + -ED$^{2}$.] Soiled or marked with slops; sloppy.

**1806** J. Beresford *Miseries Hum. Life* IX. i, Coarse, grimed, slopped, scanty table cloth. **1864** M. Eyre *Walks S. France* IX. (1865) 104 The tables..were all dusty, and all slopped.

†**slopper**, *sb.*$^{1}$ *Obs.*$^{-1}$ = SLOP *sb.*$^{1}$ 4.

**1549** *Wills & Inv. N.C.* (Surtees, 1835) 131 It'm I gyue to Robert sawer a payre of frese sloppers.

†**slopper**, *sb.*$^{2}$ *Obs.*$^{-1}$ A scupper.

**1622** R. Hawkins *Obs. Voy. S. Sea* xvii. 40 The *Iesus of Lubecke*..had beene burnt without redemption, if that my Father..had not commaunded her Sloppers to be stopt, and the men to come to the Pumpes.

**slopper** ('slɒpə(r)), *sb.*$^{3}$ [f. SLOP *sb.*$^{1}$ + -ER$^{1}$.] A dealer in slop-clothing.

**1854** *Illustr. Lond. News* 16 Dec. 624/2 The old system of making clothes by the wholesale sloppers.

†**slopper** (also **-are**), obs. variant of SLIPPER *a.*

**1423** Jas. I *Kingis Q.* clxiii, The sudayn weltering Of that Ilk quhele, that sloppare was to hold. *c* **1540** *Boke of fayre Gentylwoman* A iv, Cast up thyne eye and seke howe slopper chaunce Illudeth her men.

**sloppery** ('slɒpərɪ). [f. SLOP *sb.*$^{2}$ + -ERY.] Sloppy matter.

**1832** *Chambers's Edin. Jrnl.* I. 130/1 Their pails, and buckets, and brushes, and all their slopery, are just as rife.. as they were a month earlier. **1858** Carlyle *Fredk. Gt.* VIII. iii. (1872) III. 11 A ragout of old bones full of hairs and slopperies.

**sloppily** ('slɒpɪlɪ), *adv.* [f. SLOPPY *a.* + -LY$^{2}$.] In a sloppy or slovenly manner.

**1898** *Daily News* 11 Oct. 6/4 His broadly but not sloppily touched landscapes. **1909** *Chambers's Jrnl.* Sept. 572/2 The swish of the water licking sloppily against the yacht's side had a very lonesome sound. *a* **1911** D. G. Phillips *Susan Lenox* (1917) II. xv. 354 She regarded his play as mediocre claptrap..fit only for the unthinking, sloppily sentimental crowd. **1942** E. Paul *Narrow St.* xi. 83 In first class, one was slighted by the poverty-stricken employees, and served sloppily in the dining car, if any. **1952** S. Kauffmann *Philanderer* (1953) iii. 39 I've done it six summers now and its all a lot of crudney. Rush around and push shows together sloppily. **1979** *Country Life* 18 Jan. 134/3 The subject..is perilously near the sloppily mawkish.

**sloppiness** ('slɒpɪnɪs). [f. SLOPPY *a.* + -NESS.] The state of being sloppy.

**1727** Bailey (vol. II), *Slabbiness*, Sloppiness, Fulness of Plashes. **1828–32** Webster, *Sloppiness*, wetness of the earth; muddiness. **1862** Miss Yonge *C'tess Kate* xii, The sloppiness of a grey November day. **1884** *St. James's Gaz.* 12 Jan. 6/2 The general sloppiness of the handling [in a painting]. **1928** [see *animal-lover* s.v. ANIMAL *sb.* and *a.* C. 1]. **1939** A. Thirkell *Before Lunch* vii. 187 It had also crossed her mind that Daphne liked young Mr Bond, but.. Daphne was all against what she called sloppiness. **1960** [see SLOB *sb.*$^{1}$ 3]. **1980** *Maledicta* Summer 157 Because of the sloppiness of most original references.. I have spent many years tracking down complete bibliographical data.

**slopping** ('slɒpɪŋ), *vbl. sb.* [f. SLOP *v.*$^{2}$] **a.** The action of the verb in various senses.

**1771** Foote *Maid of B.* I. (1778), When I am got out of one fit, how the devil am I to gather strength to encounter the next? Do you think it is to be done by sipping and slopping? **1881** *Daily Telegr.* 28 Jan., The slopping of the water outside made a strange sound. **1888** *Scribner's Mag.* III 427 It prevents slopping, but on the other hand makes it hard to pour.

**b.** With advbs., as *-out* (see SLOP *v.*$^{2}$ 1 c), *-over*; ***slopping-up*** (N. Amer. slang), a drinking-bout.

**1899** 'J. Flynt' *Tramping* II. iv. 271 The bums intended to have a great 'sloppin'-up' (drinking-bout). **1922** H. Kemp *Tramping on Life* 133 'Slopping up' is what the tramps call a drinking jamboree. **1945** H. Read *Coat of Many Colours* lxii. 304 But there is no slopping-over of *irrelevant* emotion. **1948** *Richmond* (Va.) *Times-Dispatch* 9 Jan. 16/1 This [*sc.* a fulsome speech] is what is known among the hamlets of his native State as 'slopping over', and is considered as serious a breach of etiquette as..beating one's grandmother in public. **1955** *Times* 25 May 6/6 A hospital officer at the prison, said that on May 7 he was unlocking doors for 'slopping out' to be done. **1968** L. Deighton *Only when I Larf* xviii. 232 You can tell a new warder; they just can't stand the smell of the slopping-out each morning. **1976** O. Jacks *Assassination Day* v. 80 A long term in prison.. reviled him, from slopping out to terrible food.

So **'slopping** *ppl. a.*

**1839** Hood *To St. Swithin* vii, Milkmaids, and other slopping benefactors!

**sloppy** ('slɒpɪ), *a.* Also 8 (9 *dial.*) **slappy**. [f. SLOP *sb.*$^{2}$ + -Y$^{1}$.]

**1.** Of ground, etc.: Very wet and splashy; covered with water or thin mud.

**1727** Bailey (vol. II), *Sloppy*,..plashy. **1727** Boyer *Dict. Royal*, *Gacheux*,..slabby, slappy, plashy. **1768–74** Tucker *Lt. Nat.* (1834) I. 207 Notwithstanding some trifling inconveniences of sloppy roads. **1798** Jefferson *Writ.* (1859) IV. 215 It is snowing fast at this time, and the most sloppy walking I ever saw. **1806** Beresford *Miseries Hum. Life* III. ix, Cricket on very sloppy ground. **1837** Dickens *Pickw.* li, The streets were wet and sloppy. **1890** F. W. Robinson *Very Strange Family* 4 A wet, sloppy, windy, October day.

**2.** Of a semi-liquid consistency; watery and disagreeable: **a.** Of snow, etc.

**1794** Gisborne *Walks in Forest* vi. (1796) 98 Sloppy pools In the surrounding pulp lay stagnant. **1830** *Q. Rev.* XLII. 81 You have the varieties of deep and fresh snow, soft and sloppy, or covered with a crackling coat of ice. **1846** *Peter Parley's Ann.* VII. 10 The rain began to fall, the ice to get sloppy. **1860** Tyndall *Glac.* I. iii. 27 A glacier, the ice of which was covered by sloppy snow.

**b.** Of articles of diet.

**1825** J. Neal *Bro. Jonathan* I. 412 Pure indeed!.. Nasty, sloppy stuff. **1828** *Sporting Mag.* XXII. 209 She has lived on sloppy mashes and green meat. **1866** Mrs. Gaskell *Wives & Daughters* xl, Having had to eat sloppy puddings with a fork instead of a spoon.

**3. a.** Splashed or soiled with liquid; wet from slopping; covered with slops; messy.

**1838** Dickens *Nickleby* x, A silver coffee-pot, an egg-shell, and sloppy china for one. **1848** Thackeray *Van. Fair* lxvi, Idlers, playing cards or dominoes on the sloppy, beery tables. **1882** B. M. Croker *Proper Pride* I. viii. 155 Passing a very sloppy cup recklessly towards her.

**b.** *colloq.* Of the sea: choppy.

**1970** *Studies in English* (Univ. of Cape Town) I. 26 Mushy, or sloppy surf, indicates a troubled, choppy water surface which would be difficult to ride. **1977** *Austral. Sailing* Jan. 69/1 However the sloppy Botany Bay conditions plus a series of freakish thunder storms made the series wide open.

**4. a.** Weak, feeble; lacking in firmness or precision; slovenly.

**1825** J. Neal *Bro. Jonathan* I. 73 Each after a fashion of his own—more or less dignified or sloppy, as he is more or less afraid of being caught. **1881** *Academy* 15 Oct. 289 Too prone to indulge in sloppy English. **1897** *Bookman* Jan. 123/2 Seventeen sloppy and scandalously inaccurate pages.

**b.** *colloq.* Weakly sentimental.

**1883** 'Mark Twain' *Life on Miss.* xlviii. 482 The sloppy twaddle in the way of answers, furnished by Manchester. **1919** J. C. Snaith *Love Lane* xxxi. 163 The Corporal stopped suddenly, took Melia in his arms and kissed her. It was a sloppy thing to do, unworthy of old married people. **1936** R. Lehmann *Weather in Streets* ii. 53 Kate said with a funny look, as if she were saying something a tiny bit embarrassing, on the sloppy side. **1959** [see DRIP *sb.* 3 c].

**c.** *Comb.*, as ***sloppy-minded, -mindedness.***

**1903** G. B. Shaw *Let.* 15 Sept. (1946) 18 Sloppyminded lunatics. **1965** B. Sweet-Escott *Baker Street Irregular* ii. 43 He had a sharp tongue for the sloppy-minded and the half-baked. **1976** *Listener* 22 July 89/2 This final hymn to sloppy-mindedness.

**5.** Of dress: Loose, slack, ill-fitting.

**1825** Brockett *N.C. Gloss.*, *Sloppy*, loose, wide. **1852** Maitland *Eight Ess.* 236 Adorned with a sloppy dressing-gown. **1882** *Queen* 7 Oct. (Cassell), It must not be imagined that, to be easy, dress must necessarily be sloppy.

6. Special collocations: **Sloppy Joe, sloppy joe** *colloq.*, (*a*) used *attrib.* and *absol.* to designate a loose-fitting sweater; (*b*) *U.S.*, a kind of hamburger in which the minced-beef filling is made into a kind of meat sauce; (*c*) a slovenly person.

**1942** BERREY & VAN DEN BARK *Amer. Thes. Slang* §87/32 *Sloppy Joe*, a loose cardigan sweater. **1943** *Knitted Outerwear Times* 15 May 1/1 You can't look like Lana Turner in a Sloppy Joe. Well—maybe Lana could. **1944** *Life* 15 May 67/1 (*caption*) Traditional garb of all school girls is 'Sloppy Joe' sweater, single string of pearls, pleated skirt, socks and shoes. **1958** E. HYAMS *Taking it Easy* II. 147 The young men were dressed in fashionable jeans and sloppy joes. **1961** R. E. CHURCH *Burger Cook Bk.* I. 42 *Sloppy Joes* ..ground beef..onions..celery..sweet pickle relish.. brown sugar..Worcestershire sauce..chili sauce..vinegar ..green pepper..hamburger buns. **1961** WEBSTER, *Sloppy joe*.., a man who is negligent of his clothes or personal appearance. **1966** 'L. LANE' *ABZ of Scouse* 99 *Sloppy Joe*, a careless, shiftless person. **1974** *Washington Post* 1 Aug. D-1/2 Bill Myer..sits in the cafeteria..eating sloppy joes. **1980** *Ibid.* 17 Jan. B-5/1 Teen-agers wore a baggier variety [of sweater], often pairing 'sloppy joe' sweater..with pleated skirts.

† **slopsauce**, variant of SLAPSAUCE 1. *Obs.*

**1595** *Locrine* III. iii, You..cockscomb, you slopsauce, lick-fingers, will you not heare?

**'slop-seller.** [f. SLOP *sb.*[1]] A dealer in slop-clothing.

**1665** PEPYS *Diary* 21 Mar., A couple of state-cups..from Burrows the slopseller. **1691** MAYDMAN *Naval Specul.* 129 The Slop-seller, is a Person crept into the Navy, I mean to Monopolize the vending of Cloathing solely. **1758** *M.P.'s Let. on R.N.* 12 The Surgeons, Pursers, and Slopsellers,.. are put to great Trouble. **1760** C. JOHNSTON *Chrysal* I. xii, Encouraging Slop-Sellers to come on board, when the men are paying. **1804** *Naval Chron.* XII. 249 The slop-sellers, and other sharks, at this port. **1838** DICKENS *Nickleby* xxx, Nicholas hurried into a slopseller's hard by, and bought Smike a great-coat. **1882** SERGT. BALLANTINE *Exper.* xxxiv. 331 A little Hebrew slopseller from the Minories.

So **'slop-selling** *vbl. sb.* and *ppl. a.*

**1842** BARHAM *Ingol. Leg.* Ser. II. *Dead Drummer* Wks. (1905) 339 Addressing those slop-selling females afloat. **1848** DICKENS *Dombey* xxxii, One of those convenient slopselling establishments..at the eastern end of London.

**'slop-shop.** [f. SLOP *sb.*[1]] A shop where slop-clothing is sold.

**1723** *Lond. Gaz.* No. 6194/11 John Lees,..Slopshop. **1796** *Modern Gulliver* 175 From the whole stock of a slop-shop, I procured linen sufficient for a pair of trowsers. **1851** MAYHEW *Lond. Lab.* I. 369/1 The old coats and trowsers are wanted for the slop-shops; they are to be 'turned', and made up into new garments. **1879** SALA *Paris herself again* (1880) I. iii. 29 There yet remain slop-shops in the Palais Royal; but they are few in number.

*fig.* **1794** MATHIAS *Purs. Lit.* (1798) 375 When Philosopher Hume..set up a kind of slop-shop of morality in the suburbs of Atheism. **1853** LOWELL *Moosehead Jrnl.* Prose Wks. 1890 I. 39 So we all go to the slop-shop and come out uniformed,..with habits of thinking and doing cut on one pattern.

*attrib.* **1853** KANE *Grinnell Exped.* xl. (1856) 365 Legs in sailor pants of pilot cloth, slop-shop cut. **1884** *Cent. Mag.* XXVIII. 549 Brown and I will back you up in it, and so will the slop-shop man.

**'slop-work.** [f. SLOP *sb.*[1]]

**1.** The making of slop-garments; the articles thus made.

**1849** *Knife & Fork* 34 A charge of illegally pawning slop-work. **1855** DICKENS *Dorrit* I. xviii, The waistcoat of sprigs—mere slop-work, if the truth must be known. **1890** *Spectator* 4 Oct., The girls do not retain the use of their needle..: and the slop-work is so cheap.

*attrib.* **1885** *Queen* 26 Sept. (Cassell), Worse done than if sent to the worst slop-work shop in the East-end.

**2.** Work cheaply and imperfectly done.

**1861** SMILES *Lives Engineers* II. 216 He would not risk his reputation..on slop-work. **1870** J. B. BROWN *Eccl. Truth* 267 The starvation wages on which it [capital] can get its slop-work done.

So **'slop-worker**, one who does slop-work; **'slop-working** *vbl. sb.*

**1850** C. KINGSLEY *Cheap Clothes & Nasty* 22 It served as a blanket to the fever-stricken slopworker. *Ibid.* 26 Fresh victims are being driven by penury into the slop-working trade. **1851** MAYHEW *Lond. Lab.* (1864) II. 342/2 The slop-workers..will make nine such sized mantles in a week. **1859** GEO. ELIOT in Cross *Life* (1885) II. 133 The little sleeping slop-worker who had pricked her tiny finger so. **1890** *Spectator* 4 Oct. 438/2 That slop-workers should be trained to sew, does not enter into their programme.

**slopy** ('sləʊpɪ), *a.* and *sb.* Also **slopey**. [f. SLOPE *sb.*[1] or *v.*[1] + -Y[1].] **A.** *adj.* Sloping.

**1740** RICHARDSON *Pamela* I. 229 When they see the dead Corpse of the unhappy Pamela dragg'd out to these slopy Banks. **1793** G. WHITE *Selborne, Invitation to S.*, Here Nature hangs her slopy woods to sight. **1860** TROLLOPE *Framley P.* xxxvi, A green slopy bank of land. **1866** *Amer. Newsp.* in *Sat. Rev.* 14 July 40/1 The tender meetings on the slopy swards of the park.

**B.** *sb. U.S. slang.* An oriental, a Chinese. (Abusive.) Cf. SLOPE *sb.*[1] 6, *slopehead* s.v. SLOPE-a.

**1948** G. H. JOHNSTON *Death takes small Bites* v. 107 'And you'll find it mighty hard, son, to convince Petroleum Developments that the fields aren't as important as a bunch of flea-bitten slopeys!' 'Well, go on.' 'Okay—as long as you understand that oil's a pretty important commodity—and Chinese ain't.' **1962** E. SNOW *Red China Today* (1963) xii. 85 One might assume that contempt for American imperialism would by now have produced Chinese equivalents of insulting American epithets such as slopeys, slant-eyes and chinks.

**slore**, obs. or dial. form of SLUR *sb.*[1]

**slorm**, var. SLAUM *v.*

**slorp** (slɔːp), *v. dial.* and *Sc.* [Cf. Du. and MLG. *slorpen* in the same sense. See also SLURP *v.*] *intr.* and *trans.* To drink, sup, or eat greedily, noisily, or coarsely.

**1802** in SIBBALD *Chron. Sc. Poet.* IV. Gloss. **1808** in JAMIESON. **1825-** in northern and western dial. glossaries. [See *Eng. Dial. Dict.* for other senses.]

**slorry, slory**, dial. and obs. ff. SLURRY *v.*

**slosh** (slɒʃ), *sb.* [Cf. next and SLUSH *sb.*[1]]

**1.** Slush, sludge.

**1814** SOUTHEY *Lett.* (1856) II. 342 Now that it is converted into good wholesome *slosh*, I resume my morning walks. **1851** *Illustr. Lond. News* 27 Sept. 395/2 High fur-trimmed boots, the very things for American sloughs and slosh. **1887** ASHBY STERRY *Lazy Minstr.* (1892) 50, I care not a feather for slime or for slosh!

**2. a.** Watery, weak, or unappetizing drink; watery, sodden, or unappetizing food.

**1819** 'R. RABELAIS THE YOUNGER' *Abeillard & Heloisa* 198 A pow'rful dose of slosh administer'd by way of emetic. **1861** F. W. ROBINSON *No Church* viii, 'Beer, brandy, rum, gin, anything but slosh,' he muttered, as Mary placed a cup of tea at his side. **1899** 'A. RAINE' *Berwen Banks* 156 Ay don't want her cup o' tea! Never could bear the slosh. **1923** BLUNDEN *Christ's Hospital* 201 *Slosh*, boiled rice. **1959** I. & P. OPIE *Lore & Lang. Schoolch.* ix. 163 Any kind of milk pudding is 'slosh' or 'baby pudding'. **1980** *Telegraph* (Brisbane) 16 Jan. 2/3 Honesty in advertising. A sign outside a Noosa Heads fast food shop 'American Slosh'.

**b.** Weak and trifling work or writing.

**1894** G. B. SHAW *Let.* 2 June (1965) I. 440 The assumption that society likes the sort of loyal, constitutional, jingo, pietistic slosh it has to pretend to like. **1896** *Q. Rev.* July 194 Rossetti in confounding all previous schools under the term 'slosh' is as much out of court as Ruskin in ignoring Dutch painting. **1915** E. M. FORSTER *Let.* 2 Aug. in P. N. Furbank *E. M. Forster* (1977) II. i. 19 He [*sc.* Rupert Brooke] was essentially hard: his hatred of slosh went rather too deep.

**3.** A quantity of some liquid.

**1888** *Cornh. Mag.* Oct. 375 Corn-cake washed down with a generous slosh of whisky.

**4.** A blow, an act of striking.

**1936** WODEHOUSE *Laughing Gas* x. 107, I recalled that I had noticed her hand quiver once or twice, as if itching for the slosh. **1977** *Daily Mirror* 12 Apr. 20/5 (*caption*) I'll give you such a slosh when I get up from here.

**5.** A game played on a billiard table with six coloured balls and one white, with which each player tries to pocket the coloured balls in a certain order.

**1938** [see HYPOMANIC *sb.*]. **1951** G. FRANKAU *Oliver Trenton* xxiii. 180 His brother-in-law was teaching her to play slosh. **1961** E. WAUGH *Unconditional Surrender* I. iv. 60 Guy spent the remaining hours of his fortieth birthday at Bellamy's playing 'slosh'. **1976** *Daily Tel.* 29 Apr. 18 The equipment was suitable not only for billiards but also for 'slosh'.

**slosh** (slɒʃ), *v.*[1] [f. prec. or imitative.]

**1.** *intr.* To splash about in mud or wet.

**1844** KINGLAKE *Eothen* ii, Then on we went, dripping and sloshing. **1847** LORD HADDO *Mem.* (1866) I. 16 We..slosh through the moor to a shepherd's house. **1894** SIR J. D. ASTLEY *50 Yrs. Life* I. 286, I then slipped, slid, and sloshed down into Balaclava.

**2.** *U.S.* To move aimlessly; to hang or loaf about.

**1854** in BARTLETT (1859). **1864** *Daily Telegr.* 29 Aug., I am the rather loafing about Canada. I am 'sloshing around', as the Louisiana negroes..are said to 'slosh'. **1879** TOURGEE *Fool's Errand* vi. 26, I was just sorter sloshin' around loose-like.

**3. a.** To make a splashing sound.

**1888**, etc. [implied at SLOSHING *vbl. sb.*[1]]

**b.** Of liquid: to splash; to flow in streams.

*a* **1953** E. O'NEILL *Touch of Poet* (1957) I. 35 When he attempts to raise the glass to his lips the water sloshes over his hand. **1969** L. MICHAELS *Going Places* 59, I might, as I toppled, blood sloshing through my lips, beg forgiveness. **1977** 'J. LE CARRÉ' *Honourable Schoolboy* i. 29 The rain poured off them..sloshing in red rivulets round their ankles.

**4.** *trans.* **a.** To pour or dash (liquid); to splash, throw, pour, or swallow carelessly. Also *fig.* Usu. with advbs. *colloq.*

**1875** *Chicago Tribune* 3 Sept. 2/5 The Ring-paid scribblers and papers will slosh on the usual amount of whitewash. **1885** *Century Mag.* Nov. 63/2 If mining records was ever kep' as they'd ought to be, and not sloshed round so public like. **1899** G. B. SHAW *Let.* 26 Apr. (1972) II. 85, I dipped into the book.., and sloshed down a heap of words. .. But it is a scandalously poor job of a review. **1926** E. FERBER *Show Boat* x. 221 Often he sloshed down whole gallons of river water before she came. **1936** M. MITCHELL *Gone with Wind* liv. 934 He picked up the decanter and sloshed a glassful, untidily. **1945** *Everybody's Digest* Aug. 86 He sloshed on his sombrero and went outta there, heatin' his axles. *a* **1953** E. O'NEILL *Touch of Poet* (1957) III. 100 He sloshes whiskey from the decanter into both their glasses. **1960** J. STROUD *Shorn Lamb* xxii. 239 It had..attic bedrooms and Harry used to go up there and slosh paint about. **1964** L. DEIGHTON *Funeral in Berlin* xv. 91 He laughed a deep, manly laugh and sloshed down some beer. **1978** 'J. LYMINGTON' *Waking of Stone* vi. 149 She sloshed out porridge into plates.

**b.** To pour or dash liquid upon, to douse. *colloq.*

**1912** G. W. DEEPING *Sincerity* ii. 18, I can't stand these counter-bouncing little beasts like Threadgold. He's only fit to slosh people with treacle and water. **1917** H. GARLAND *Son of Border* xxviii. 371, I generally managed to slosh myself with cold water from the well. **1979** *Amer. Poetry Rev.* Mar./Apr. 26/2 Rain began to pelt the cars and slosh the yard and spatter down the flowers.

**5.** *colloq.* To hit, to strike; to crush, to defeat. Also *fig.* Cf. SLASH *v.* 2 b.

**1890** KIPLING *Barrack-Room Ballads* (1892) 11 We sloshed you with Martinis, an' it wasn't 'ardly fair; But for all the odds agin' you, Fuzzy-Wuz, you broke the square. **1904** E. NESBIT *Phoenix & Carpet* v. 94, I say, slosh 'em.. and get clear off with the swag. **1914** C. MACKENZIE *Sinister Street* II. IV. ii. 881, I wouldn't half slosh his jaw in, if I was a man. **1918** R. P. FLEMING *Let.* in D. Hart-Davis *Peter Fleming* (1974) ii. 33, I saw one [adder] coiled up asleep in some bushes, and picked it up by the tail..and we took it into the open and sloshed it. **1921** A. S. M. HUTCHINSON *If Winter Comes* II. vii. 138 These Balkan chaps set to, to slosh Turkey. **1933** *Punch* 18 Oct. 421/1 'I wish to contradict the rumour that I wish to slosh Sir Stafford Cripps,' says Mr. Ernest Bevin. **1967** N. FREELING *Strike out where not Applicable* 75 Somebody sloshed him, if I may be allowed the word. *a* **1974** R. CROSSMAN *Diaries* (1975) I. 399 Characteristically enough, at the end the committee chairman who had been wildest in his wrath moved the vote of thanks and said, 'Well, we have to have a good go sometimes at sloshing our Labour Minister.' **1977** 'J. GASH' *Judas Pair* x. 118 I've sloshed her..sometimes when she'd got me mad.

† **slosh**, *v.*[2] *Obs. rare.* In 6 **sloss(h)e**. [Imitative: cf. prec. and SLOFF *v.*] *trans.* To lap up or swallow greedily.

**1548** UDALL, etc. *Erasm. Par. 2 Ep. Peter* II. 19 The dogge slosseth vp agayn that he hath once caste vp. **1553** BALE *Gardiner's De Vera Obed.* B iiij, Yᵉ bishop of Rome..will easyly content himselfe, specially whan there is one morsell or other layde to him to slosshe.

**sloshed** (slɒʃt), *ppl. a. slang.* [f. SLOSH *v.*[1] + -ED[1].] Drunk, tipsy. Also *absol.*

**1946** *Word Study* May 3/1 Synonyms for *drunk* now current in England..*tiddley, oiled* or *well oiled, sloshed.* **1952** 'R. GORDON' *Doctor in House* xi. 120 Tony, you're sloshed already. **1966** L. SOUTHWORTH *Felon in Disguise* viii. 118 The D.S.O. was due to an overdose of Italian vino. I was too sloshed to care. **1978** R. LUDLUM *Holcroft Covenant* iii. 41 They drank a *great* deal... They appeared quite sloshed. **1979** *Logophile* III. II. 17/1 It started as a pub game, played for the amusement of the slightly sloshed.

**sloshing** ('slɒʃɪŋ), *vbl. sb.* [f. SLOSH *v.*[1]]

**1.** Splashing; the sound made by a moving liquid when it comes into contact with a solid object.

**1888** F. COWPER *Caedwalla* 54 They could just hear the sloshing sound made by his feet as he got into the mud. **1894** *Times* 12 Apr. 13/3 She next heard a 'sloshing' of water. *Ibid.*, All the time that she was listening she heard the 'sloshing' of water.

**2.** = HIDING *vbl. sb.*[2]

**1931** T. R. G. LYELL *Slang, Phrase & Idiom* 693 He ran up against a gang of roughs in the street last night, and they gave him an awful sloshing!

**slosh-wheel.** (See quot.)

**1875** KNIGHT *Dict. Mech.* 2610/2 *Trammel-wheel.* Sometimes called a *slosh-wheel.*

**sloshy** ('slɒʃɪ), *a.* [f. SLOSH *sb.*] Slushy; sloppy, sentimental.

**1797** B. HAWKINS *Let.* 22 Feb. in *Coll. Georgia Hist. Soc.* (1916) IX. 88 Flat piney sloshy land. **1828** CARR *Craven Gloss.*, *Sloshy*, in a state of slosh. **1862** G. H. KINGSLEY *Sp. & Trav.* (1900) 379 London the foggy, with its dirty, sloshy, melting snow. **1879** MISS BRADDON *Cloven Foot* xiii. 118 The sound of a footstep on the sloshy gravel walk. **1913** A. LUNN *Harrovians* ii. 35 Because..if they had form games some sloshy old chaw [*Note*, i.e. Old Harrovian, a term of affection] would write to the papers. **1920** *Glasgow Herald* 30 Apr. 9 They are living not merely upon vegetables, but sloshy vegetables. **1924** E. F. BENSON *David of King's* vii. 136 'Positively his last appearance,' said David. 'Rather theatrical, but not sloshy.' **1933** *Daily Mirror* 26 Oct. 12/4 'Sloshy talk' is simply the perpetration of such phrases as 'too, too marvellous' and 'utterly divine'. **1949** [see BOOB *sb.* 4]. **1957** D. PIPER *English Face* x. 244 Broader, indeed sloshy, effects were needed by an emulator of Reynolds, Daniel Gardner. **1978** C. STORR *Winter's End* ii. 37 You thought it was like in those rotten stories... I've read enough sloshy stuff in my time.

Hence **'sloshiness.**

**1894** *Amateur Gardening* 4 Feb. 391 The drainage of such a path will be imperfect, hence 'sloshiness' in wet weather.

**slot** (slɒt), *sb.*[1] Chiefly *north.* and *Sc.* Also (4) 5-6 **slotte**, 5-7 (9) **slott**, and SLOTE *sb.* [a. MDu. or MLG. *slot* (so Du. and LG.), = OHG. *sloz* (G. *schloss*) door-bolt, lock, from the weak grade of the stem **slūt-, sliut-* to close (MDu. *sluten*, Du. *sluiten*; OHG. *sliozan*, G. *schliessen*).]

**1.** A bar or bolt used to secure a door, window, etc., when closed. Now *dial.*

*a* **1300** *E.E. Ps.* cvi. 16 He forgnod yhates,..And slottes irened brake he pare. *c* **1340** *Nominale* (Skeat) 471 *Sere, veroil et cerrure*, Barre, slot and stapul. **1391** *Mem. Ripon* (Surtees) III. 108 In iij slottes ferri pro camp'is (?) figend. 3*d.* **1424-5** *Durh. Acc. Rolls* (Surtees) 272, j fenestra in domo carbonum, cum j slott, j stapill. *c* **1440** *Promp. Parv.* 460/1 Slot, or schytyl of a dore, *verolium.* **1515** *Acc. Ld. High Treas. Scot.* V. 13 Expensis..on lokkis, irne slottis, bandis of irne..for reparing and dichting of the palice. **1570** LEVINS *Manip.* 176 Yᵉ Slot of a doore, *pessulus.* **1651** *Depos.*

*York Castle* (Surtees) 49 Who assaulted his house, attempting to break in by opening two slotts or boults. **1663** in *Scottish N. & Q.* (1902) July 2 [They] did bring..ane number of yrons, bolts or slotts and caused put the samen vpon the doores. **1695** KENNETT *Paroch. Antiq.* Gloss. s.v. *Slade*, In Northumberland the *slot* of a door is the bolt. **1825–** in many northern dialect glossaries. **1855** AINSLIE *Land Burns* (1892) 243 Our cadger..slippit in, Syne cannilie shot the muckle door slot. **1874** J. CRAWFORD *Mem. Alloa* 76 He drew the slot, an'..In..the stranger passed.

**b.** A bolt forming part of the mechanism of a lock.

**1890** W. A. WALLACE *Only a Sister?* 325, I did my best to put back the slot of one of the locks.

**2.** A metal rod; a flat wooden bar, esp. one forming a cross-piece.

**1399** *Mem. Ripon* (Surtees) III. 133 In slot de ferro empto pro prædicto baner, 4*d.* *c* **1400** in Nicolas *Hist. Royal Navy* (1847) II. 444 Slot of iron [for the guns]. **1497** *Acc. Ld. High Treas. Scot.* I. 334, iij serpentinis gunnis..; with ilkane tua chameris, thair mykkis and thair slottis. **1542** *Extr. Aberd. Reg.* (1844) I. 185 Menzes and..Nicholsoune to be maisteris of the artillierie, and to provyd boolis, slottis, and all vder munitionis requirit thairto.

**1788** W. H. MARSHALL *Yorksh.* II. 353 *Slot*, any broad, flat wooden bar. **1833** LOUDON *Encycl. Archit.* §1316 A bridge [in a cider-press]..is suspended at each end by two slots (cross bars) playing on a rim. **1853** SIR H. DOUGLAS *Milit. Bridges* (ed. 3) 336 Bridges formed of four or six rough trees, secured at their crossings by the cross-pieces (slots in carpentry). **1892** *Daily Telegr.* 17 June 4/8 He noticed that the 'slot' worked from the next box was down.

**b.** *spec.* One of the cross-bars connecting the bulls of a harrow.

Occurs much earlier as *slote*: see SLOTE *sb.* 2.

**1799** *Hull Advertiser* 15 June 2/2 Timber. For sale,.. harrow bulls and slots. **1808** in JAMIESON. **1844** H. STEPHENS *Bk. Farm* II. 527 Four longitudinal bars,..with four lighter transverse bars, or *slots*. **1846** J. BAXTER *Libr. Pract. Agric.* (ed. 4) II. 359 The 'slots' or cross-pieces of thin ash.

**slot** (slɒt), *sb.*[2] Also 5–6 slote, 5, 8–9 slott. [ad. OF. *esclot* in sense 1 (see examples in Godefroy, wrongly explained), of obscure origin.]

**1.** The slight depression or hollow running down the middle of the breast. Now *Sc.* and *rare.*

**13..** *Gaw. & Gr. Knt.* 1330 Syþen þay slyt þe slot, sesed þe erber. *Ibid.* 1593 Þe mon..Set sadly þe scharp in þe slot euen, Hit hym vp to þe hult, þat þe hert schyndered. ? *a* **1400** *Morte Arth.* 2254 O-slante doune fro þe slote he slyttes at ones! *c* **1400** *Destr. Troy* 3063 The slote of hir slegh brest [was] sleght for to showe. **1741** *Compl. Fam. Piece* I. i. 43 If a Child..has Pain in the Back, or Slot of the Breast. **1808** JAMIESON, *Slot of the breast*, the pit of the stomach; where the breast-bone slopes away on each side, leaving a hollow. *a* **1904** in *Eng. Dial. Dict.*

**2. a.** An elongated narrow depression or perforation made in the thickness of a piece of timber, etc., usually for the reception of some other part or piece, whether fixed or movable.

*slot hole* occurs earlier (1485) in this sense: see 7.

**1523** FITZHERB. *Husb.* §4 At the ploughe-tayle, where be two wedges, that be called slote-wedges: the one is in the slote above the beame, the other in the saide slote, vnder the plough-beame. **1577** HARRISON *England* II. xi. (1877) I. 227 A square blocke of wood.., which dooth ride vp and downe in a slot, rabet, or regall betweene two pieces of timber. **1747** HOOSON *Miner's Dict.* S iv, Formerly the Fork[s] were used to be Tennerd, and the Sills made with Slotts to put them in. **1825** J. NICHOLSON *Operat. Mechanic* 435 The catch-box has a slot, fitting a feather on the spindle. **1850** CHUBB *Locks & Keys* 33 A brass guard, in which there was a slot for a pin to slide in. **1881** YOUNG *Every Man his own Mechanic* 76 Mortising machines and others for boring and making slots in timber.

**b.** The opening in a slot-machine for the reception of a coin. Also *fig.* Also (*slang*), a slot-machine.

**1888** *Pall Mall G.* 25 Sept. 5/1 'Drop a penny into the slot' and you can..obtain a cigarette. **1893** *Times* 28 Apr. 9/3 The Chancellor..has had recourse to the latest automatic invention, and has put a penny in the slot. **1950** R. BISSELL *Stretch on River* xiii. 135 The slots are going night and day. **1978** M. PUZO *Fools Die* xviii. 197 The slots usually brought in a profit of about a hundred thousand dollars a week.

**c.** The middle of the semi-circular or horseshoe-shaped desk at which a newspaper's sub-editors work, occupied by the chief sub-editor. *U.S. slang.*

**1917** H. GRANT *Two Sides of Atlantic* iii. 44 The man who 'sits in the slot' (the chief-sub.), will know for a certainty that the decision of 'Bill' to invade Windy City will automatically entail the departure of all who 'hunt' with Bill. **1923** [see RIM *sb.*[1] 3 c]. **1970** R. K. KENT *Lang. Journalism* 123 *Slot*, the middle of the horseshoe-shaped copy desk where the news editor or copy editor (sometimes called *slotman*) sits. To be *in the slot* is to be in charge of the copy desk.

**d.** *Aeronaut.* A linear gap in an aerofoil, running parallel to its leading edge, which allows the passage of air from the lower to the upper surface and so increases the lift. Cf. SLAT *sb.*[1] 4 d.

**1920** *Flight* XII. 1124/1 It has already been mentioned that the slot separating the false from the main leading edge is contracted towards the upper surface. **1936** *Discovery* Mar. 73/2 The Weick and Hammond have..a control which is a combination of slot and aileron. This is intended to obviate the need of a rudder. **1960** C. H. GIBBS-SMITH *Aeroplane* II. 221 Ingenious as the machine undoubtedly was,..there is no visible trace of any slots, or of any wires or other gear attached to, or passing anywhere near, the wings that could be associated with slots.

**e.** The vulva. *coarse slang.* Cf. SLIT *sb.* 1 d.

**1942** BERREY & VAN DEN BARK *Amer. Thes. Slang* §121/38 *Female pudendum*..shape, slot, snatch, tail. **1977** MILLER & SWIFT *Words & Women* vii. 117 No such positive connotations attach to prick, but even this word does not convey the absolute scorn of slit, slot, snatch, and gash.

**f.** A marked-out parking space. Chiefly *U.S.*

**1944** R. CHANDLER *Lady in Lake* xiii. 74, I..parked in one of the diagonal slots at the side of the Prescott Hotel. **1968** A. DIMENT *Great Spy Race* iii. 35, I shunted my car into a small slot near the fire station. **1978** R. LUDLUM *Holcroft Covenant* xvii. 195 Holcroft backed the car out of its slot, then drove through the entrance posts onto the country road.

**g.** A prison cell; also, = CELL *sb.*[1] 4 b. *Austral. slang.*

**1947** *Pix* 20 Sept. 15 *Peter* or *slot*, cell. **1969** *Sydney Sunday Tel.* 21 Dec. 14/4 'I'd hate to try and tot up the number of hooks and badges (rank and good conduct insignia) that little lot's whipped away since the ship came out.'..'And what about the slot (cells) they've dished out. It must run into years!' **1976** *Cleo* Aug. 33 Some of the old heads are in the slot, he says. The slot is jail.

**3.** (See quots.)

**1590** COKAINE *Treat. Hunting* D j, Diuers Buckes haue sundrie slots in their palmes: some haue slots on both sides: other some are plaine palmed. **1900** POLLOCK & THOM *Sports Burma* 373 The slots or divisions of the hoofs now showed very deep and distinctly in the soft earth.

**4.** *dial.* (See quots. 1796 and 1882.) Also *attrib.*, as ***slot-hem***.

**1796** F. LEIGHTON *MS. Letter*, To the Yorkshire words add *Slot*, meaning the open hem in which the strings run of a purse, work-bag, night cap, &c. **1828–** in dialect glossaries (Yks., Lanc., Linc.). **1844** H. STEPHENS *Bk. Farm* II. 508 A couple of tapes drawn tight in a slot-hem. **1882** CAULFEILD & SAWARD *Dict. Needlwk.* 452/2 *Slot*, an inelegant term, employed in the eastern counties of England to denote a casing formed either by a double Running, or by a Hem, for the reception of a ribbon or tape, to be used as a Running-string.

**5. a.** *Sc.* (See quot.)

This sense is also recorded for Norw. *slot* (Ross), and may represent a different word.

**1808** JAMIESON, *The slot of a hill*, a hollow in a hill, or between two ridges.

**b.** *Austral.* and *N.Z.* A crevasse.

**1959** *Tararua* XIII. 46 *Slot*, for a crevasse, sometimes used by climbers, is not necessary and is merely slang. **1968** K. WEATHERLY *Roo Shooter* 58 This was the roughest bit of country yet—short, miserable, scrubby trees and stringy bushes; broken country, high slots and hollows full of water.

**6.** *fig.* **a.** A position in a list, hierarchy, system, or scheme; a position to be filled; a category; a place or division in a timetable, esp. in broadcasting.

**1942** BERREY & VAN DEN BARK *Amer. Thes. Slang* §672/10 Rank or rating in league, division, percentage ladder, slot. **1947** AUDEN *Nones* (1952) 64 Among those staring blemishes that mark War's havockíng slot. **1956** *Sat. Rev.* (U.S.) 2 June 50/2 No management slot is harder to fill today than the research director's post. **1956** W. H. WHYTE *Organization Man* II. viii. 104 Sales work..is about the only slot they would qualify for if they took English or history. **1964** *Economist* 25 Jan. 327/2 There is a 'slot' in the market for a medium-range supersonic airliner. *Ibid.* 20 June 1369/3 The 'slots' once gained, were never given up [by regional TV stations]. **1966** *Listener* 6 Oct. 518/1 It seems perverse that when the Monday evening 'slot' has been extended to as much as two hours for lesser fry, it should be made to stand at ninety minutes for *The Merchant of Venice* (Home Service, September 26). **1967** *Ibid.* 6 Apr. 467/3 'Theology, during the great controversies of the mid-nineteenth century, was anti-scientific.'.. (Try fitting Newman or even Kingsley into that slot!) **1969** *Times* 21 Nov. 23/5 How serious is the situation at Heathrow?.. There are no spare 'slots' into which landing and taking-off airliners can be fitted. **1970** *Daily Tel.* 3 Sept. 13/2 The third Radio London slot each day will be from 6.45 a.m. to 9 a.m., a blend of news, music, personalities and information called 'Rush Hour'. **1972** *Business Week* 18 Mar. 81/1 Although he held a top slot at SNIA, he was lured away for the even bigger job at Alitalia. **1973** C. BONNINGTON *Next Horizon* xxii. 298 An Italian millionaire..had permission for an autumn reconnaissance in 1972 to be followed by a spring attempt in 1973. Owing to sickness he gave up his autumn slot. **1974** *Guardian* 26 Mar. 14/1 Welland's script was accepted by the BBC for its 'Play For Today' slot. **1976** *National Observer* (U.S.) 24 Apr. 19A/3 Stanford has 10,009 applications for 1,450 freshman slots next fall. **1976** A. DAVIS *Television: First Forty Years* viii. 86 Suitable slots are normally of 90 to 120 minutes, with time for commercials to be taken out of this, but films are rarely obliging enough to run to exactly the length required. **1977** *Film & Television Technician* Mar. 6/4 The British programme-makers are actually pushing the Americans out of the number one slot in key Western Europe and Scandinavian countries. **1977** *Times* 25 Aug. 1/8 The importance of taking a flight 'slot' when it comes up. **1978** M. PUZO *Fools Die* xii. 131 After six months of free-lance work he offered me a magazine editor slot. **1980** *Jrnl. R. Soc. Arts* July 529/2 Many place Kokoschka in the slot 'Expressionist'.

**b.** *spec.* in *Linguistics* (see quot. 1960). Also *attrib.* and *Comb.*

**1957** K. L. PIKE in *General Linguistics* Spring 36 The characteristics of a grammeme which in many instances are perhaps most readily recognized in current descriptions of a grammemic system are the functional slot with its class filler. **1959** [see DIAPHONEME]. **1959** W. H. MITTINS in Quirk & Smith *Teaching of English* iv. 116 Some teachers..seek to achieve a kind of concentration and continuity by methodically working through batteries of vocabulary exercises in slot-filling..and the like. **1960** ELSON & PICKETT *Beginning Morphology-Syntax* ii. 16 A *slot* is a grammatical position or function (e.g. subject) which is *filled* by a list of mutually substitutable items (e.g. nouns). The tagmeme is the unit of grammatical arrangement involved in or resulting from this slot-class correlation. *Ibid.* 37 Make a chart with the slot names.., listing fillers below each slot name. *Ibid.* iii. 40 As a filler class they can only be united by some such term as 'subject slot fillers'. **1962** W. A. STEWART in F. A. Rice *Study of Role of Second Languages in Asia, Africa, & Latin Amer.* 21 Under various conditions, the same language may occupy more than one functional slot. **1964** E. BACH *Introd. Transformational Gram.* iii. 44 But the basic points of the slot-symbol and class-symbol description and the lack of context-sensitive rules remain untouched. **1964** *Language* XL. 314 American slot-and-filler grammatical description. **1965** *Word Study* Feb. 3/1 Word groups filling noun slots and verb slots comprise the chief building blocks of utterances. **1970** B. M. H. STRANG *Hist. English* 25 When, through cross-cultural experience, speakers of one language are conscious of an 'empty slot' in their language which is filled in another language.., they may..fill the gap by borrowing the filler. **1972** *Archivum Linguisticum* III. 22 The lexical co-occurrence restrictions which hold between the fillers of predicate and subject slots are different from the restrictions which hold between the fillers of predicate and instrument slots. **1972** *Computers & Humanities* VII. 14 Some recent publications include ..'Computerized Japanese Haiku', which describes how the poems are created by slot-filling. **1972** M. L. SAMUELS *Linguistic Evolution* 65 A new slot-filler may arise from borrowing or creation, or the 'pull' of the empty slot may hasten a new process of extension in another existing word. **1981** *Word 1980* XXXI. 230 He makes use of the slot-and-filler infrastructure, characteristic of tagmemics.

**7.** *attrib.* (in sense 2), as ***slot-arm, -bar, -bearing, hole***, etc.; ***slot-wedge*** (see 2 a, quot. 1523).

**1879** *Cassell's Techn. Educ.* IV. 392/2 As the *slot-arm [in a lathe] oscillates, it gives a reciprocating motion to the shaping slide. **1844** H. STEPHENS *Bk. Farm* II. 331 The *slot-bar..is for the purpose of adjusting the length of the fourth foot of the machine to any inequalities of the barn-floor. **1869** RANKINE *Machine & Hand-tools* Pl. J 2, The bottom of the slot bar is arranged with a capped bearing. **1839** URE *Dict. Arts* 1109 The spindles with their bobbins revolve in two *slot-bearings. **1869** RANKINE *Machine & Hand-tools* Pl. J 2, These carriages and *slot heads are quite independent of each other in all their motions. **1485** *Nottingham Rec.* III. 244 For boryng of ij. *slott holes in a bote stake. **1869** RANKINE *Machine & Hand-tools* Pl. H 9, The tools are fixed..in square slot holes. **1867** SMYTH *Sailor's Word-bk.*, **Slot-hoop*, the same as truss-hoops. **1869** RANKINE *Mach. & Millwork* 167 The axis..of the *slot-lever. **1888** *Lockwood's Dict. Mech. Eng. Terms* 285 The *slot link..of an engine, which, through the medium of the eccentrics, alters the valve for forward or backward motion. **1835** URE *Philos. Manuf.* 119 The *slot-piece *b* adjusts the roller *a*, and a similar slot-piece..adjusts the roller *b*. **1891** *Daily News* 28 Dec. 3/1 In the concrete..are embedded at intervals cast iron tube frames, to which the *slot rails are bolted. **1892** Low *Machine Draw.* 108 What is the object of the *slotway in the upper part of the ram?

**8. a.** *Comb.*, as ***slot-borer, -boring, -drilling, -headed***.

**1869** RANKINE *Mach. & Millwork* 169 Crank and Slot-headed Sliding Rod. **1875** KNIGHT *Dict. Mech.* 2215 Slot-drilling Machine. **1884** *Ibid.* Suppl. 823/2 *Slot Borer*, a tool used for opening the cut in connection with slotting machines. *Ibid.*, Slot-boring Machine.

**b.** Special combs., as **slot aerial, antenna**, an aerial in the form of one or more slots in a metal surface; **slot-back**, *N. Amer. Football*, (the position of) a back who stands behind a gap in the forward line; **slot car**, a miniature racing car, powered by electricity, which travels in a slot in a track; **slot-machine**, a machine which is operated by inserting a coin in a slot; also *fig.* and *attrib.*; **slot man** *U.S. slang*, a newspaper's chief sub-editor, a news editor; **slot-meter**, a meter which is operated by inserting a coin in a slot; **slot racer** = *slot car*; so **slot-race** *v. intr.*, **slot-racing** *vbl. sb.*; **slot radiator** = *slot aerial*; **slot seam**, a clothing seam reinforced underneath; also, = *channel seam* s.v. CHANNEL *sb.*[1] 12; **slot television**, a coin-operated television; **slot winding** *Electr. Engin.*, an armature winding in which the conductors are laid in slots or grooves in the core; so **slot-wound** *a.*

**1946** *Jrnl. Inst. Electr. Engineers* XCIII. IIIA. 626/1 It would appear that *slot aerials are capable of making a contribution to the problem of designing a radiating element that produces circular polarization in all directions of radiation. **1956** *B.B.C. Handbk. 1957* 56 To keep staff up to date, training supplements on such items as slot aerials, television lighting, frequency modulation, and other developments are issued. **1946** *Jrnl. Inst. Electr. Engineers* XCIII. IIIA. 749/2 In spite of the length of the *slot antenna, this load can be treated as lumped at the position of the centre of the slot. **1975** D. G. FINK *Electronics Engineers' Handbk.* XVIII. 43 Very low profile slot antennas utilizing shallow cavities fed by coaxial cables have been designed for aircraft use. **1959** *Washington Post* 21 Nov. A14/4 He helped develop Elroy (Crazy-legs) Hirsch into a *slotback with the Los Angeles Rams. **1970** *Globe & Mail* (Toronto) 28 Sept. 18/2 Slotback Dick Smith took a 12-yard pass from Sonny Wade in the second quarter for one Montreal touchdown. **1974** *Anderson* (S. Carolina) *Independent* 24 Apr. 5B/1 At slot back..Rut Livingston..has the makings of a great player. **1966** *Maclean's Mag.* 22 Jan. 9A The track on which *slot cars race is a tabletop affair. **1971** *Publishers' Weekly* 27 Sept. 129/3 (Advt.), *The New Zealand Boys' Book of Crafts, Pets, Sports and Hobbies* by Anthony Harvey and Peter Snell provides information on..model-making, rugby, sailing, slot cars, and wood-carving. **1891** *Brooklyn Daily Eagle* Index July–Dec. 155/2 *Slot machine. **1892** *Pall Mall G.* 2 June 1/3 An ostrich's stomach is not filled with mechanism like a slot machine's. *a* **1910** 'O. HENRY' *Rolling Stones* (1912) 196 Mac McGowan was to..drop his silver talent into the slit of the slot-machine of fame and fortune that gives up reputation and dough. **1929** *Sun* (Baltimore) 15 Nov. 1/6 'Spike' O'Donnell,.. beer baron and bootlegger,.. is acting as his own lawyer in the 'slot machine' trial. **1933** C. Day Lewis *Magnetic Mountain* 12 Eating chocolate creams from the slot-machines. **1957** *Observer* 1 Sept. 13/4 At Las Vegas the plane empties of passengers who, with cold passion, play the slot-machines in the concourse until ten minutes later, when it is time to go. **1978** J. Wainwright *Jury People* lxiv. 216 A slot-machine arcade. One of these pin-table places. **1928** *Amer. Speech* IV. 134 Presiding over the copy readers is the 'head of the desk' or '*slot man'. His chief duty is to judge the amount of space to be given any 'story' or news article and to designate the size of the 'headline' or 'head'. **1972** Slot man [see revise *sb.* 3]. **1899** *Westm. Gaz.* 10 Aug. 2/2 A reduction of 2d. per thousand to those using the *slot meter. **1966** *Daily Progress* (Charlottesville, Va.) 4 Feb. 13 (*caption*) J. P. Evans.. and Ed Johnson get ready to put their *slot racers through a gruelling five-lap race. **1965** *Wall St. Jrnl.* 27 Aug. 22 A rapidly growing number of Americans.. have caught the *slot-racing bug. **1967** J. Symons *Man who killed Himself* I. vi. 69, I haven't joined a slot racing club... I like slot racing on my own. **1946** *Jrnl. Inst. Electr. Engineers* XCIII. IIIA. 748/2 When *slot radiators which were very loosely coupled to the guide had to be measured, standing-wave measurements of single slots became unreliable. **1967** *IEEE Trans. Antennas & Propagation* XV. 826/1 If the boundaries of the dielectric cover are kept within the local reactive fields of the slot, the primary effect upon the radiation is a change in the impedance of the slot radiator. **1918** E. & M. Wallbank *Dress Cutting & Making* x. 69 *Slot Seam, in which both edges are overlapped on to a wrap piece or 'slot'. **1968** J. Ironside *Fashion Alphabet* 99 *Channel Seam* (*slot seam*): to make a channel or slot seam, the seam turnings should be basted together. An additional strip of fabric should be laid under the basted seam and should then be machined approximately half-inch or so away from the basted seam line. **1958** *Kinematograph Weekly* (Studio Rev.) 29 May p. iv/3 If *slot television gets a real hold on the public, commercial cinema.. is doomed. **1977** *Grimsby Even. Tel.* 26 May 3/8 (Advt.), Slot television, bargains galore. **1900** *Jrnl. Brit. Inst. Electr. Engineers* XXIX. 802 A hole-winding produces a somewhat smoother pole than a *slot-winding. **1968** Fink & Carroll *Standard Handbk. Electr. Engineers* (ed. 10) vi. 10 Fractional slot windings, where the number of slots per phase per pole is not an integer, have unequal coil groups. **1931** L. B. Turner *Wireless* xiv. 471 The calculation of E.M.F. in a *slot-wound dynamo.

**slot** (slɒt), *sb.*[3] Also 6 slotte. [ad. AF. and OF. *esclot* (pl. *escloz*, *esclos*) hoof-print of a horse, etc., by Godefroy identified with *esclot*, *esclop* wooden shoe, but more prob. ad. ON. *slóð* track, sleuth *sb.*[2]]

**1.** The track or trail of an animal, esp. a deer, as shown by the marks of the foot; sometimes misapplied to the scent of an animal; hence generally, track, trace, or trail.

**1575** Turberv. *Venerie* 26 Take your Bloudhoundes and with them finde out the view or Slotte of the Harte or Bucke. **1579** Gosson *Sch. Abuse* (Arb.) 35 To dogge them a little,.. and so discouer by slotte where the Deare taketh soyle. **1612** Drayton *Poly-olb.* xiii. 115 The Huntsman by his Slot, or breaking earth, perceaves.. Where he hath gone to lodge. **1637** B. Jonson *Sad Shepherd* I. ii, By his slot,.. His frayings, fewmets, he doth promise sport. **1663** Killigrew *Parson's Wedding* v. iv, If he had had as much hoof as horn, you might have hunted the beast by his slot. **1735** Somerville *Chase* III. 472 See here his Slot; up yon green Hill he climbs. **1777** Lightfoot *Flora Scotica* I. 7 They were called.. slothe hounds, from their following the slot or track of men or cattle. **1801** Southey *Thalaba* II. xxiii, The Deer Hath left his slot beside the way. **1865** Boner *Transylv.* 154 The slot of the bear is quite like that of a human being. **1888** Doughty *Arabia Deserta* I. 161 We found in the sand where an hyena had lately passed: Sâlih asked if I knew the slot.

*fig.* **1645** Milton *Colast.* Wks. 1851 IV. 372 This odious fool.. leavs the noysom stench of his rude slot behind him. **1820** Scott *Monast.* ix, We know Norman a true bloodhound, who will never quit the slot. **1864** *Daily Telegr.* 10 Oct., The Emperor, who rarely quits the slot of an idea. **1884** *19th Cent.* Oct. 558 The most viciously virtuous reviewer that ever gave tongue on the slot of an imaginary scandal.

**2.** A deer's foot.

**1876** *World* I. No. 121. 15 As to what is the correct name of a deer's foot,.. I never heard it called anything but 'slot'. **1901** *Westm. Gaz.* 3 Sept. 2/2 Another spoil of the chase of the wild red deer is the foot or 'slot', as it is called, and these slots may be found serving as bell-pulls, or even as door-knockers and ink-stands.

**3.** *Comb.*, as **slotwise** adv.

**1865** Swinburne *Poems & Ball.*, *Laus Veneris* 255 And tracking ever slot-wise the warm scent. **1890** 'R. Boldrewood' *Colonial Reformer* (1891) 126 Following the track (slotwise) at dawn of day.

†**slot**, *sb.*[4] *Obs. rare.* In 5 sclot(t. [Of obscure origin.] A muddy place; mud.

Perh. a var. of sloth *sb.*[2]; the same vocab. has *paytt* for 'path'. Halliwell's '*Slot*, wet sticky clay. *Linc.*' (copied by Brogden) is of very doubtful genuineness.

*c* **1475** *Pict. Voc.* in Wr.-Wülcker 797 *Hic linus* [= *limus*], a sclott. *Ibid.* 798 *Hoc volutabrum*, a selot [*sic*].

†**slot**, *sb.*[5] *Obs.*$^{-1}$ [a. Du. or LG. *slot* (G. *schloss*): see slot *sb.*[1]] A castle.

**1578** Riche *Allarme to England* To Rdr., Thou paydst for building of a slot, that wrought thine owne decay.

**slot** (slɒt), *v.*[1] Now *dial.* [f. slot *sb.*[1] 1.]

**1.** *trans.* To bolt (a door).

The entry in Johnson (1755) 'To *Slot*, v.a. (*slughen*, Dutch), to strike or clash hard' is prob. an echo (through Bailey) of Skinner, who connects the word with Du. *sluyten*.

**1563** Winȝet *Wks.* (S.T.S.) I. 139 Ȝour scoleris.. hes in thare imaginatioun cloisit vp, slotit, and neidnalit the samin ȝettis of our hæretage. **1671** Skinner *Etymol.* s.v., To Slot a door, *vox agro Linc. usitatissima*, (*i.e.*) *januam claudere.* [**1674** Ray *N.C. Words* 43 To *Slot* a door, Lincoln, i.e. to shut it. **1787** Grose *Prov. Gloss.*, *To slot a door*, to shut it hastily, or in a passion.] **1811** H. Macneill *Bygane Times* 18 Whan they see The door, tho' slotted, budge a wee. **1825–** in dialect glossarie (Nhb., Yks., Linc., Shropsh.).

**b.** (See quot.)

**1695** Kennett *Par. Antiq.* Gloss. s.v. *Slade*, In the South to *slot* a lock is to thrust it back.

**2.** To secure (a lock) by shooting a bolt.

**1904** A. Griffiths *50 Yrs. Public Service* xxi. 318 He found that his skeleton-key would open the lock, even when 'on the double' or slotted.

**slot** (slɒt), *v.*[2] [f. slot *sb.*[2]]

†**1.** *trans.* To pierce through the 'slot'. *Obs.*$^{-1}$

? *a* **1400** *Morte Arth.* 3853 He schokkes owtte a schorte knyfe.., And scholde haue slottede hyme in, bot no slytte happenede.

**2. a.** To cut a slot or slots in; to furnish with a slot. Also with *out*.

**1747** Hooson *Miner's Dict.* Q iij, The Sliders are Slotted at both Ends to receive the Forks. **1869** Rankine *Mach. & Hand-tools* Pl. J 2, This machine is intended to slot the sides of connecting rods. *Ibid.* J 4, The tool holder, X, is provided with a circular motion.. for slotting out curves. **1892** Low *Machine Draw.* 54 After it is turned, planed, and bored it is slotted across.

**b.** *Coal-mining.* To hole.

**1883** Gresley *Gloss. Coal-m.* 227.

**3.** To drop (a coin) through a slot in a slot-machine.

**1888** *Pall Mall G.* 25 Sept. 5/1 All the would-be purchasers who have carelessly slotted their pence.

**4.** To thread (material etc.) *with* (ribbon).

**1922** Joyce *Ulysses* 344 She had four dinky sets,.. each set slotted with different coloured ribbons. **1975** G. Howell *In Vogue* 243 The flowerpot hat.. in coffee cream satin slotted with a brown ribbon.

**5.** *intr.* **a.** To admit of being threaded through a hole or slot.

**1928** *Daily Express* 9 Jan. 13 The unique collar slots through the buckle.

**b.** *fig.* To fit *in* or *into*; to take up a position *in* a space or slot (slot *sb.*[2] 6).

**1940** H. G. Wells *Babes in Darkling Wood* I. i. 40 We are not the people we were yesterday. We slot into the new order. **1965** *New Statesman* 7 May 715/1 Personally I never knew yet quite what I was nor where I slotted in; I suppose I was ready for total identification somewhere, but never where I happened to be. **1966** 'A. Hall' *9th Directive* xx. 187, I.. watched the police-car slot in between us and the car ahead; then it pulled out and one lost it. **1971** *Daily Tel.* 9 June 2/4 Initially the trains will operate at a maximum 125 mph to 'slot in' with new-type conventional diesels. **1976** *Times* 15 Apr. 27/1 The French company augments its range in Britain with the GTL, which slots in between the 956cc TL and the high-performance TS. **1976** *Ilkeston Advertiser* 10 Dec. 19/1 They produced a great team display with new boy Henshaw slotting in well. **1980** S. Brett *Dead Side of Mike* xiii. 149 There are quite a few details which haven't slotted into position yet, but.. the outline's right.

**6.** *trans.* **a.** To fit (something) *in* or *into* a position, space, or slot (slot *sb.*[2] 6).

**1966** A. Battersby *Math. in Management* viii. 211 Certain complex calculations.. are available in a form which can be readily 'slotted in' to bigger programs. **1968** *Listener* 4 Jan. 27/1 The television slotting system.. separates programmes into categories... But slotting also creates a climate in which surprise is unwelcome... Slotted into one of the arts programme times the Beatles' film would hardly have raised a whisper. **1970** O. Norton *Dead on Prediction* i. 14, I.. managed to slot the Mini into the corner of the temporary car park. **1971** *Country Life* 8 Apr. 801/1 The richly Italianate facade of the Finsbury Bank for Savings.. was slotted into the terrace in 1840. **1972** M. Williams *Inside Number 10* xiii. 339 The National Agent went to great pains to slot this function into the election tour. **1973** *Scotsman* 13 Feb. 8/4 Steady progress up the scale leads to a salary of £3638. It is inconceivable that the Bishop of Bath and Wells.. would be slotted in at the minimum. **1977** C. Dexter *Silent World N. Quinn* viii. 71 He slotted the book back into its shelf. **1977** *Irish Times* 8 June 8/4 Why, for instance, wasn't Sile de Valera slotted into this constituency once Vivion de Valera stood down?

**b.** *spec.* in *Football.* To kick (the ball, a pass) accurately through a narrow space, esp. *in* or *into* the goal; to score (a goal) in this way. Also *absol.*

**1970** F. C. Avis *Soccer Dict.* (ed. 3) 86 *Slot in*, to pass, or to score a goal, by the very skilful placing of the ball through a narrow gap between players. **1974** *Observer* 1 Sept. 18/4 Boersma hardly needed to leave the ground to slot his.. header into the net. **1975** *Liverpool Echo* (Football ed.) 1 Feb. 1/4 United took the lead through Jones who slotted home. **1975** *Evening News* (Edinburgh) (Sports Final ed.) 15 Mar. 10/2 McDowell slotted the ball into the net. **1977** *Wandsworth Borough News* 7 Oct. 10/1 He beat Newton, centre-half Robinson and goalkeeper Stevenson before slotting the ball in. **1978** *Cornish Guardian* 27 Apr. 5/3 The home team were showing good touches and Hargreaves slotted in a third goal after Barker had sent a good shot screaming goalwards.

**slot** (slɒt), *v.*[3] [f. slot *sb.*[3]] *trans.* To trace by the slot; to follow the track of (a stag, etc.).

**1582** Stanyhurst *Æneis* I. (Arb.) 23 Three stags sturdye wer vnder Neere the seacost gating, theym slot thee clusterus heerdflock. **1725** *Fam. Dict.* s.v. *Hart*, If the Way is too hard to slot, be sure to try far enough back. **1838** *Sporting Mag.* Aug. 342 The hounds could own no such thing, neither could the knowing ones 'slot' the animal. **1884** *Longman's Mag.* IV. 489 The ground may be so wet.. that it is impossible to 'slot' a deer.

**slote** (sləʊt), *sb.* Also 5 sloot, 7 sclote; 8– sloat. [var. of slot *sb.*[1]]

†**1.** A door-bolt. *Obs.* = slot *sb.*[1] 1.

*c* **1440** *Promp. Parv.* 460/1 Sloot, or schytyl of speryynge, *pessulum.* **1515** *Acc. Ld. High Treas. Scotl.* V. 11 Ane grete slote to monsure Sanct Romanis chalmour. **1614** *Churchw. Acc. Pittington*, etc. (Surtees) 170 For makinge two holes in stones for the sclotes goinge in our church dore. **1633** Rutherford *Lett.* (1862) I. 105, I have gotten now.. the gate to open the slote and shut the bar of His door. **1721** Ramsay *Poems* Gloss., *Slote*, a Bar or Bolt for a Door.

**2.** A bar; a cross-bar; also in special senses (see quots. and cf. slot *sb.*[1] 2).

α. **1485** *Fabric Rolls York Minster* (Surtees) 87 Les tyers et slotes pro eisdem altaribus, 4l. 17s. 4d. **1523** Fitzherb. *Husb.* §15 [The] harowe-bulles.. haue slotes of wode put through theym lyke lathes,.. and the formest slote must be bygger than the other. **1674** Ray *N.C. Words* 43 The *Slote* of a ladder or gate, the flat step or bar. **1688** Holme *Armoury* III. 339/2 The Slotes are the vnder peeces which keepe the bottom of the Cart together. *Ibid.* 340/1 The several parts of a Wagon... The Slotes [are] the cross pieces which hold the Shafts together. **1841** Hartshorne *Salop. Ant.* Gloss., *Slote*, a kind of bolt for bottoms or sides of wagons, 'tumbrels', or harrows. **1879–87** in Shropshire and Cheshire glossaries.

β. **1704** *Dict. Rust.* s.v. *Cart*, The Sloats are the under pieces which keep the bottom of the Cart together. **1750** W. Ellis *Mod. Husb.* III. v. 78 The Sloats of a Gate or Hurdle. **1853** Wayland *Mem. Judson* II. 340 The openings in the sloats above the windows. **1858** Simmonds *Dict. Trade*, *Sloat*, a piece of wood used as a stretcher, as the bar of a chair, the sloats of a cart.

**3.** A trap-door in a theatre stage.

**1853** *Punch* XXIV. 128/2 The working of various mysterious engines of machinery, called 'sloats' and 'scrutopieces'. **1858** in Simmonds *Dict. Trade.*

Hence **'sloted** *ppl. a.*, furnished with slots or cross-bars; having (so many) slots.

**1523** Fitzherb. *Husb.* §15 The horse-harrowe is made of fyue bulles,.. not soo moche as the other, but they be lyke sloted and tinded. **1750** W. Ellis *Mod. Husb.* IV. iv. 65 (E.D.S.), The open five-sloted hurdle.

**slote**, var. sluit.

**sloth** (sləʊθ), *sb.*[1] Forms: α. 2 slauðe, 3–5 slauþe, 5 slaw(e)th(e, slauth (6 slaughte). β. 3 slouhðe, 4 slouȝte, slougthe, 5 sloughe, slought. γ. 4–5 slouþe, 4–6 slouthe, 4–6 slouth; 4 s(c)lowþe, 4–5 slowthe, 5, 7 slowth. δ. 6–8 sloath. ε. 5 slothe, 6– sloth. [Early ME. *slāwð(e*, *slōwð(e*, directly formed on *slāw*, *slōw* slow *a.* in place of OE. *slǣwð* sleuth *sb.*[1]]

**1.** Physical or mental inactivity; disinclination to action, exertion, or labour; sluggishness, idleness, indolence, laziness.

α. *c* **1175** *Lamb. Hom.* 19 þe licome luuað muchele slauðe and muchele etinge. *c* **1205** Lay. 27039 Stið imodede men & swifte, slauþe bidæled. **13..** *E.E. Allit. P.* B 178 For fele fautez may a freke forfete his blysse,.. þen for slauþe one. *a* **1400–50** *Alexander* 4293 Surfet, surquidry, & slawth.

β. *a* **1225** *Ancr. R.* 144 Heo wule scheken of hire slep of vuel slouhðe. *c* **1380** Wyclif *Wks.* (1880) 200 Oure owene necligence & slouȝte. **1437** *Libel Eng. Policy* in *Pol. Poems* (Rolls) II. 187 Nowe here be ware.. That for sloughe and for rach[l]eshede [etc.]. *c* **1489** Caxton *Sonnes of Aymon* iv. 117 Me semeth that.. slougthe is amonge vs.

γ. **1340–70** *Alex. & Dind.* 344 We nolle sclepe in no sclowþe til we hem sclain haue. **1390** Gower *Conf.* I. 15 Ofte is sen that mochel slowthe, Whan men ben drunken of the cuppe, Doth mochel harm. *a* **1450** *Knt. de la Tour* (1868) 42 Another ensaumple.. of hem that for slouthe lessethe her masse. *c* **1535** Elyot *Educ. Children* Bj, For Slouth destroyeth the power of nature. **1597** Hooker *Eccl. Pol.* v. lxxii. §17 Slouth and fulnesse in peaceable times at home.

δ. *a* **1618** Sylvester *Paradox agst. Libertie* 225 Wks. (Grosart) II. 57 Not one of them will brook his Son in sloath to lurk. **1628** Prynne *Censure Cozens* 42 Their sloath and lasinesse is so great. **1697** Dryden *Virg. Georg.* I. 190 Himself did.. Arts ordain; Nor suffer'd Sloath to rust his active Reign.

ε. **1575–85** Sandys *Serm.* xvii. 298 To withdraw men.. from sloth. **1606** Dekker *Seven Deadly Sins* Wks. (Grosart) II. 50 This nastie, and loathsome sin of Sloth. **1648** Wilkins *Math. Magick* I. ii. 8 These arts.. admit not either of sloth or wearinesse. **1700** Rowe *Amb. Step-Moth.* I. i, Sloth and folly Shiver and shrink at sight of toil and hazard. **1790** Burke *Fr. Rev.* 247 The same lazy but restless disposition, which loves sloth and hates quiet. **1847** Yeowell *Anc. Brit. Church* vii. 64 Ease has a natural tendency to engender sloth. **1867** Freeman *Norm. Conq.* (1877) I. v. 366 Deposed by his subjects on account of his sloth and luxury.

**b.** Personified.

**1362** Langl. *P. Pl.* A. II. 69 In al þe seruyse of Slouþe I sese hem to-gedere. **1390** Gower *Conf.* II. 9 Bot Slowthe mai no profit winne, Bot he mai singe [etc.]. *c* **1425** *Cast. Persev.* 898 in *Macro Plays*, Lechery, Slawth, & Glotonye, to mans flesch ȝe are fendis Fre. **1609** Dekker *Warres* Wks. (Grosart) IV. 115 Sloth, by reason that he is troubled with the gout, busies himselfe little with State matters. **1769** Gray *Ode Installat.* 4 Dreaming Sloth of pallid hue.

**c.** *Comb.*, as ***sloth-jaundiced***, ***-loved***, ***-promoting***, ***-shunning*** adjs.

**1591** Sylvester *Du Bartas* I. vi. 868 What can be hard to a sloath-shunning Spirit? **1598** *Ibid.* II. ii. II. *Babylon* 530 Down in my sloath-lov'd bed again I shrink. **1754** 'J. Love' *Cricket* I. 64 Of sloth-promoting sports, forewarn'd, beware! **1794** Coleridge *Lines on Friend* Poems (1907) 27 Energic reason and a shaping mind... Sloth-jaundiced all!

**2.** Slowness; tardiness.

*c* **1380** Wyclif *Wks.* (1880) 313 þus many men for sich slowþe of sharp reprouyng synnen meche. *c* **1386** Chaucer *2nd Nun's T.* 258 If it so be thou wolt with-outen slouthe Bileue aright. **1451** Capgrave *Life St. Aug.* 21 Augustin began to accuse him-self sor..of þe slauth of his returne to God. **1628** Ford *Lover's Mel.* v. i, Wherefore drop thy words in such a sloth? **1729** Shelvocke *Artillery* v. 379 [To] fill all his..Fuzes or Trains of Communication with a Composition whose Sloth he has been assured of. **1815** Jefferson *Writ.* (1830) IV. 265 From sloth of proceedings, an embargo was permitted to run through the winter.

**3.** As a 'proper term', by later writers taken to mean: A company *of* bears (or erroneously, boars).

*c* **1452** in *Trans. Philol. Soc.* (1909) III. 52 A Slouthe of Beerys. *Ibid.* 53 A slothe of bayris. *c* **1470** *Hors, Shepe, & G.* (Roxb.) 31 A slouth of beres. [Cf. sleuth *sb.*[1] 1 b.] **1616** Bullokar *Eng. Exp.*, *Slowth*, a heard or company of wild Boares together. **1688** Holme *Armoury* II. 132/1 The Proper terms given to Beasts when they are in Companyes. .. Beares, a Slowth. **1801** Strutt *Sports & Past.* 17 A sloth of bears.

**4.** An edentate arboreal mammal of a sluggish nature, inhabiting tropical parts of Central and South America.

Two genera of sloths are recognized, viz. *Bradypus*, with three toes on the fore-feet, and *Cholœpus* with only two.

**1613** Purchas *Pilgrimage* 704 *note*, The Spaniards call it.. the light dog. The Portugals Sloth. The Indians, Hay. **1681** Grew *Musæum* I. II. i. 11 The Sloath... An Animal of so slow a motion, that he will be three or four days, at least, in climbing up and coming down a Tree. **1699** Wafer *Voy.* (1729) 401 The Sloath. Is a very slow-paced Animal, taking a whole Day in going fifty Paces. **1774** Goldsm. *Nat. Hist.* (1776) IV. 343 Of the sloth there are two different kinds, distinguished from each other by their claws. **1834** McMurtrie *Cuvier's Anim. Kingd.* 93 The Sloths have cylindrical molars, and sharp canini longer than those molars. **1894-5** Lydekker *Roy. Nat. Hist.* III. 207 Sloths are mainly nocturnal; and in their usual attitude they hang suspended back downwards.

*fig.* **1826** Hood *Last Man* 160, I..never was one of the sloths. **1852** H. Rogers *Eclipse of Faith* (1864) 140 Man has been gradually crawling up, a very Sloth in 'progress', from the lowest Fetichism and Polytheism.

**b.** Applied, usually with distinguishing epithets, to other animals, as the sloth-bear, the koala or koolah, the slow lori or lemur, and the mylodon or megatherium.

See also *ground sloth* s.v. ground *sb.* 18b.

(*a*) **1790** Shaw *Naturalist's Misc.* II. pl. 58 The Ursine Bradypus, or Ursiform Sloth. **1793** Pennant *Synop. Quadr.* (ed. 3) II. 243 Ursiform Sloth with a long and strong nose, truncated at the end. **1800** Shaw *Gen. Zool.* I. I. 160 The Ursine Sloth is about the size of a Bear. **1827** Griffith *Cuvier's Anim. Kingd.* II. 238 The *Ursus Labiatus*, placed erroneously by Pennant and others among the Sloths, under the name of the Ursine Sloth.

(*b*) **1813-27** [see koala]. *a* **1862** J. G. Wood *Illustr. Nat. Hist.* I. 468 The name of Australian Sloth..has been applied to it [the Koala, *Phascolarctos cinereus*] because it is able to cling with its feet to the branches after the manner of the sloths.

(*c*) **1827** Griffith *Cuvier's Anim. Kingd.* I. 229 The Slow Loris, or Sloth of Bengal (*Lemur tardigradus*, L.). **1903** Lydekker *Mostly Mammals* 314 The name 'sloth' is not infrequently misapplied by travellers to the slow-lemurs of India and the Malay countries, or to their cousins the galagos of Africa.

(*d*) **1842** Owen (*title*), Description of the Skeleton of an Extinct Gigantic Sloth, *Mylodon robustus*. *Ibid.* 147 The osseous frame-work of the gigantic extinct Sloths.

**c.** A species of Protozoa (see quot.).

**1859** P. H. Gosse *Evenings Microscope* (1877) 392 Two more species of this extensive genus [*Euglena*]..have received the appellations of the Pear (*E. pyrum*) and the Sloth (*E. deses*.)

**5.** Special combs.: **sloth-animalcule** (see quots.); **sloth-bear**, an Indian species of bear (*Melursus labiatus* or *ursinus*); **sloth-monkey**, the slow loris or lemur; **sloth-tree**, the South American trumpet-tree (*Cecropia peltata*), whose leaves are eaten by the sloth.

**1871** *Carpenter's Zool.* II. 230 A number of minute creatures, well known to microscopic observers as *Sloth or Bear-Animalcules. **1889** Geddes & Thomson *Evolution of Sex* vi. §5. 72 The degenerate water-bears or sloth-animalcules (*Tardigrada*). **1835** *Penny Cycl.* IV. 90/2 Labiated Bear, or *Sloth Bear. *a* **1862** J. G. Wood *Illustr. Nat. Hist.* I. 407 The Aswail, or Sloth Bear. **1894** Lydekker *Roy. Nat. Hist.* II. 26 The sloth-bear may be regarded as one of the most characteristic..mammals of India. **1891** *Cent. Dict.* s.v., *Sloth-monkey. **1905** A. R. Wallace *My Life* I. xx. 324 The two species of Sloth-monkeys (*pithecia*) are found. **1885** Lady Brassey *Trades* 29 Among them was the *sloth tree (*Cecropia*), all arms and legs.

† **sloth**, *sb.*[2] *Obs.* Also slothe. [app. an alteration of *slogh* slough *sb.*[1] The examples are E. Anglian.] A miry or muddy place; a slough.

*c* **1440** *Promp. Parv.* 460/1 Slothe, where fowle water stondythe, *lacuna. Ibid.*, Slothe, where swyne or oþer bestys han dwellyd, *volutabrum.* **1447** Bokenham *Seyntys* (Roxb.) 125 But thi goddys..Or ben of bras..Or ellys of stonys wych in a sloth to laye Wer bettyr to skepyn from the foul weye.

† **sloth**, *a. Obs. rare.* Also 5 slouth(e, slought. [f. sloth *sb.*[1] Cf. sleuth *a.*[1]] Slothful, slow.

**1412-20** Lydg. *Chron. Troy* I. 3646 Of þe future slouth and necligent. *c* **1450** *Cov. Myst.* (Shaks. Soc.) 367 A! ȝe fonnys and slought of herte For to beleve in holy Scrypture. **1549** Latimer *2nd Serm. bef. Edw. VI* (Arb.) 48 God is a good God,..and very sloth to reuenge hys blasphemie. **1605** Sylvester *Du Bartas* II. iii. III. *Law* 138 What? are ye growne so sloth?

**sloth** (sləʊθ), *v.* Now *rare.* Forms: α. 5 slawth. β. 4-5 slowth (5 slowȝth), 4-6 slouthe, 7- sloth. [f. sloth *sb.*[1] Cf. sleuth *v.*[1]]

† **1.** *trans.* To allow to slip through slothfulness or delay; to neglect. *Obs.*

**1390** Gower *Conf.* II. 2 Som time he slowtheth in a day That he nevere after gete mai. **1455** *Rolls of Parlt.* V. 286/2 Diverses matiers..have be slowthed and throwen into grete ..omission. **1477** Earl Rivers (Caxton) *Dictes* 22 Slouthe nor delay not that thou must nedely execute. **1500** *Will of Catelyn* (Somerset Ho.) My tithes necligently forgoten or slowthed. **1708** M. Bruce *Lect.* 13, I do not bid you cast away your Callings nor Sloth them neither.

† **b.** To waste, pass *away* (time) in idleness.

**1523** *State P., Hen. VIII*, VI. 171 Whiche thinges must nedes geve the more occasion to thEmperour not to slouthe any time that may be taken for avauncement of this enterprise. **1676** Bunyan *Strait Gate* 69 The most of professors are for imbezzeling, mispending and slothing away their time.

**2.** *intr.* To be or become indolent or lazy.

**1390** Gower *Conf.* II. 116 Yit ne wol he noght travaile.., Bot slowtheth under such a drede. *c* **1440** *Jacob's Well* 281 þat þou schalt noȝt dullyn and slawthyn in þi labour of þi prayers. **1888** Doughty *Arabia Deserta* I. 279 Strenuous solitary men, whose unquiet mettle moves them from slothing in the tent's shadow to prowl as the wolf in the wilderness.

Hence '**slothing** *vbl. sb.*

*c* **1690** Jas. Fraser in Wodrow *Sel. Biogr.* (1847) II. 239 Mispending of time, excess in lawful comforts, slothing of private duties.

**slothful** ('sləʊθfʊl), *a.* (and *sb.*). Forms: α. 5 slouthe-, 5-7 slouth-, 6 slought-; 5 slowt-, 6 slowth-. β. 6 slothe-, 6- sloth-, 7-8 sloath-. Also 5-7 -full. [f. sloth *sb.*[1] Cf. sleuthful *a.*]

**1.** Of persons, etc.: Full of sloth; indisposed to exertion; inactive, indolent, lazy, sluggish.

α. *c* **1400** *Pilgr. Sowle* (Caxton, 1483) III. viii. 55 Sloutheful haue they ben aboute theyr owne hele. **1484** Caxton *Fables of Æsop* v. xiii, I am so slouthfull that I maye not ete. **1552** Latimer *Serm. Lord's Prayer* vii. 56 God tempteth us for exercyse sake, that we should not be slouthfull. **1582** N.T. (Rhem.) *Matt.* xxv. 26 Naughtie and sloughtful seruant. **1590** Spenser *F.Q.* II. vi. 18 The slouthfull waue of that great griesly lake.

β. **1530** Palsgr. 324/2 Slowe or slothfull, *lente, tardif.* **1555** Eden *Decades* (Arb.) 194 Least the residue shulde waxe slothefull with Idlenes. **1606** Dekker *Seven Sins* IV. (Arb.) 33 Hee is the true Slothfull man that does no good. **1656** Stanley *Hist. Philos.* III. II. 119 Admit not a sloathfull person unto your doctrines. **1717** Pope *Iliad* x. 74 Still, with your Voice, the sloathful Soldiers raise. **1752** Hume *Ess. & Treat.* (1777) I. 290 A nation..cannot maintain..its fleets and armies from the industry of such slothful members. **1828** Scott *F.M. Perth* viii, You shall not find Patrick Charteris slothful in a matter of this importance. **1876** B. Martin *Messiah's Kingd.* VI. ii. 301 The church has been slothful.

**b.** *absol.* (chiefly as *pl.*).

**1630** B. Jonson *Disc.* Wks. (Rtldg.) 752/2 He is grown to active men an example, to the slothful a spur. **1678** Bunyan *Pilgr.* Introd., It will make the sloathful active be. **1781** *Scot. Paraphrases* XII. v, Ye indolent and slothful rise.

**c.** As *sb.* A lazy person, a sluggard.

**1648** Herrick *Hesp., Dissw. fr. Idlenesse*, Toiles, or Manicles Set on purpose to enthrall Men, but Slothfulls most of all.

**2.** Of habits, etc.: Characterized by sloth or disinclination to exertion.

*c* **1400** *Pol., Rel., & L.P.* (1866) 5 Fy on slowtfull contenewaunce. **1539** *Act 31 Hen. VIII*, c. 9 The slouthfull and ungodly lief wch hathe bene used emonges all those sorte wch have borne the name of religious folke. **1587** *Mirr. Mag., Mempricius* vi. 1 Then wickedly I fell to slouthfull ease. *a* **1700** Evelyn *Diary* 29 Mar. 1689, The slothfull, sickly temper of the new King. **1808** Scott *Marm.* v. iv, His peaceful day was slothful ease. **1846** McCulloch *Acc. Brit. Emp.* (1854) I. 303 They have also been obliged to lay aside their slothful habits.

**slothfully** ('sləʊθfʊlɪ), *adv.* Also 6 slought-, 6-7 slouth-, 7 sloath-. [f. prec.] In a slothful manner; lazily, sluggishly.

**1529** S. Fish *Supplic. Beggers* (1871) 3 Is it any merueille that the taxes..haue bin so sloughtfully, ye painfully leuied? **1560** Daus tr. *Sleidane's Comm.* 44 He hath hitherto wrought slouthfullye. **1591** Percivall *Sp. Dict.*, *Perezosamente*, slothfully. **1741** Bp. Berkeley in Fraser *Life* (1871) viii. 274 If I tamely and slothfully gave myself up to be ridden..by the Pope. **1871** R. Ellis *Catullus* lxi. 194 Not too slothfully tarrying, Thou art here.

**slothfulness** ('sləʊθfʊlnɪs). Also 6 slought-, 6-7 slouth-, sloath-. [f. slothful *a.* + -ness.] The state or character of being slothful; sluggishness, laziness.

**1526** *Pilgr. Perf.* (W. de W. 1531) 131 All slouthfulnes, all negligence. **1555** Eden *Decades* (Arb.) 55 Inexcusable slothfulnesse and negligence. **1638** Junius *Paint. Ancients* 24 Such occasions as may serve for an excuse of slouthfulnesse. **1689** tr. *Buchanan's De Jure Regni apud Scotos* 61 [They] prefer a quiet sloathfulness to honest hazards. **1736** Ainsworth I. s.v., The refusing of labour is a proof of slothfulness and laziness. **1878** Spurgeon *Treas. David* cviii. Introd., To use the same words continually.. would show great slothfulness.

† '**sloth-head.** *Obs.*[−1] In 4 sloghþhede. [f. sloth *sb.*[1]] Slothfulness.

**1303** R. Brunne *Handl. Synne* 5075 ȝyt ys þyr an vnkynde sloghþhede, þat a man vnneþ..wyl wurschep God derwrþly.

† '**slothly**, *adv. Obs.*[−1] In 5 slowthlyche. [f. sloth *a.* + -ly[2].] Sluggishly, lazily.

*c* **1410** *Master of Game* (MS. Digby 182) xiii, Other manere of rennynge houndes þer bee þe whiche hunteth somdele more slowthlyche and heuylich.

'**slot-hound.** [f. slot *sb.*[3]] A sleuth-hound.

**1537** *St. Papers, Hen. VIII* (1836) V. 97 Diverse of his tenauntes pursewed the trade with a slott hownd. **1819** Scott *Ivanhoe* xxviii, The misfortunes which track my foot-steps like slot-hounds. **1839** J. Snowe *Rhine* I. 352 The wrath of the archbishop, which still tracked them like a slot-hound. **1864** Carlyle *Fredk. Gt.* XVI. xiii. (1872) VI. 298 The slot-hounds [being] uncoupled and put on his trail, poor Cameron was unearthed.

† **slot-staff.** *Sc. Obs.*[−1] [? f. slot *sb.*[1] 2.] Some form of staff used as a weapon.

**1561** *Burgh Recs. Prestwick* (Maitl. Club) 66 Ane slot staf, or ane pow ax, suerd and buklar.

**slotted** ('slɒtɪd), *ppl. a.* [f. slot *sb.*[2] 2 or *v.*[2]]

**1.** Having a slot or slots. *spec.* in *Aeronaut.*: cf. slot *sb.*[2] 2 d. Also, ***slotted armature*** (Electr. Engin.), an armature having slots or grooves to contain the conductors; a slot-wound armature; ***slotted line***, a length of coaxial cable or wave guide having a slot running lengthwise in its outer conductor to receive a probe for investigating standing waves.

**1849** *Mech. Mag.* Oct. 327 A pin..which takes into a slotted piece which slides up and down in a curved groove. **1869** Rankine *Mach. & Hand-tools* Pl. I 4, The reversing lever..is carried..through the slotted lever. **1881** A. G. Bell *Sound by Radiant Energy* 11 The beam of light is interrupted by its passage through the two slotted disks. **1902** *Encycl. Brit.* XXVII. 582/2 These wires lie side by side in the smooth-core armature with one layer, or one on the top of the other if there are two layers, as is usually the case in slotted armatures. **1921** *Jrnl. R. Aeronaut. Soc.* XXV. 274 (*heading*) Flap experiments with slotted wings. *Ibid.* 275 (*caption*) Slotted aerofoil with flap. **1926** *Ibid.* XXX. 357 With a combination of slotted aileron and forward aerofoil, complete lateral control at the stall has been obtained. **1935** C. G. Burge *Compl. Bk. Aviation* 240/1 The Handley-Page Slotted Wing is one of the best-known devices for preventing this stalling, at least within the normal range of angles which an aeroplane is likely to reach. **1947** E. A. Yunker et al. in H. J. Reich *Very High-Frequency Techniques* II. xxiv. 592 A notched coaxial cable is a cheap and easily made substitute for a slotted line and is satisfactory for measurements not requiring great accuracy. **1966** *McGraw-Hill Encycl. Sci. & Technol.* VII. 44/2 A commercial slotted line for measuring impedances at the lower microwave frequencies is shown. **1973** J. D. Edwards *Electr. Machines* ii. 53 The basic machine equations are the same for a slotted armature as for a smooth cylindrical armature, provided that the total pole flux..is unchanged. **1977** *R.A.F. Yearbk.* 31/2 On rolling or overshooting, the lifting power of the wing with full slotted flaps is an experience to behold.

**2.** Threaded through a hole or slot.

**1932** *Woman & Beauty* Apr. 27 A slotted scarf gives a great many opportunities for freshening up an everyday frock.

'**slotter**, *sb.* [f. slot *v.*[2]] One who makes slots; also, a slotting-machine.

**1881** *Instr. Census Clerks* (1885) 42 Engine and Machine Making:..Slotter. Screwer. **1891** *Pall Mall G.* 24 Nov. 7/2 Planers, slotters, turners, smiths, and men engaged in skilled work.

**slotter** ('slɒtə(r)), *v.* Now *dial.* Also 4-5 sloter(yn). [Of obscure origin: cf. Du. *slodderen*, LG. *sluddern*, G. *schlottern*, some senses of which come near to those of the English word.]

**1.** *trans.* To make foul or dirty; also, to spill or splash about, to slop.

The sb. *slotter* spilled liquor, a filthy mess, etc., is also recorded in dialect use from 1787 (Grose) onwards.

*c* **1340** Hampole *Pr. Consc.* 2367 þan aght þe saul of synful with-in Be ful foule þat es alle slotered in syn. *c* **1430** *Syr Gener.* (Roxb.) 7066 'Abide,' she seid, 'so mot I thee, More slotered thei most be'. *c* **1440** *Promp. Parv.* 460/1 Sloteron, or defowlyn, *maculo, deturpo.* **1825-** in dialect glossaries, etc. (Sc. and South-western).

**2.** *intr.* To be slothful or slovenly. *Sc.*

**1553** *Douglas's Æneid* IV. Prol. 164 Thou auld hasard leichoure,..That slotteris [*Small's ed.* flotteris] furth euer-mare in sluggardry. **1808** Jamieson, *Slotterin, slutterin*, acting in a slovenly manner; Loth[ian].

Hence † '**slotterbug**, a dirty or filthy person.

*c* **1440** *Promp. Parv.* 460 Sloturburgge [*other texts* slotyrbugge], *cenulentus, maurus, obcenus.*

'**slottery**, *a. Sc.* and *dial.* Also *Sc.* slottry. [f. slotter *v.*]

Todd (1818) gives *slottery* from Urry's ed. of Chaucer (*Knt.'s T.* 2025), but the correct reading is *flotery*.

**1.** *Sc.* Sluggish, slothful.

**1513** Douglas *Æneid* VI. iv. 87 The slottry Sleip, Deidis cusing of kynd. **1808** Jamieson, *Slottry*, slumbering, drowsy, inactive; Loth[ian].

**2.** *dial.* Of weather, etc.: Wet, dirty.

**1790** Grose *Prov. Gloss.*, *Slottery weather*, foul, wet weather. **1866** G. W. Thornbury *Greatheart* II. 244 The roads [round Boscastle, Cornwall] are slottery.

'**slotting**, *sb. rare.* = slot *sb.*[3] 1.

**1909** B. Grohman *Master of Game* 262 All of which may lead his slotting to be mistaken for the tracks of a hind.

**slotting** ('slɒtɪŋ), *vbl. sb.* [f. SLOT *v.*²]

†**1.** *Sc.* The practice, on the part of butchers, of 'scoring' flesh. *Obs.*

**1647** *Extr. Burgh Recs. Stirling* 193 The actis and ordinances..anent slotting and spuilyeing of flesche.

**2. a.** The action of making or cutting a slot or slots.

**1844** H. STEPHENS *Bk. Farm* II. 689 There is no slotting, as in the common harrow, but the bulls and bars are simply crossed. **1879** *Organ Voicing* 20 When fairly voiced, the slotting may be commenced.

**b.** *attrib.*, as ***slotting auger, bar, machine(ry.***

**1841** *Civil Eng. & Arch. Jrnl.* IV. 234/1 Improvements in slotting machines. *Ibid.*, The fourth part is an improvement in the slotting bar. **1863** *Q. Rev.* CXIV. 298 The planing, slotting, or turning machinery of these factories. **1869** RANKINE *Mach. & Hand-tools* Pl. P 17, The ordinary turning, planing, and slotting tools. **1875** KNIGHT *Dict. Mech.* 185/1 The Slotting Auger cuts laterally.

**3.** *Coal-mining.* (See quot.)

**1883** GRESLEY *Gloss. Coal-m.* 227 *Slottings*, coal cut away in the process of holing.

**4. a.** The action of threading through a hole or slot. Also, ornamentation with threading.

**1923** *Daily Mail* 18 June 1 Filet lace and hem stitching, finished ribbon slotting at low waist line.

**b.** The action or condition of fitting in a slot (SLOT *sb.*² 6). Also *attrib.*

**1959** *Washington Post* 26 Dec. A19/1 Ratings have climbed despite the show's unhappy time slotting between 'Laramie' and 'Bronco', without a big show preceding it on the network. **1968** [see SLOT *v.*² 6].

**slottysshe**, obs. form of SLUTTISH *a.*

**slouch** (slaʊtʃ), *sb.* Forms: 6 slouche, sloutche, 7 slowch(e, 7– slouch (8 *dial.* zlouch). [Of obscure origin: cf. SLOUK, and dial. *slotch* in the same sense. Senses 3 and 4 are from the vb.]

**1. a.** An awkward, slovenly, or ungainly man; a lubber, lout, clown; also, a lazy, idle fellow.

Freq. in 16th and 17th c. as a term of disparagement without precise significance.

**1515** BARCLAY *Cyt. & Uplondyshman* Prol., A lordes stomake and a beggers pouche Full yll accordeth, suche was this comely slouche. *c* **1566** *Merie Tales of Skelton* in S.'s Wks. (1843) I. p. lxv, A cobler..which was a tall man and a greate slouen, otherwyse named a slouche. **1608** SYLVESTER *Du Bartas* II. iv. IV. *Decay* 1077 The louzie Couch Of some base Ruffon, or some beastly Slouch. **1642** H. MORE *Song of Soul* I. iii. 8 A foul great stooping slouch with heavie eyes, And hanging lip. **1709** *Brit Apollo* No. 61. 3/2 A Capacious Pouch, Which look'd like Tail at Rump of Slouch. **1714** GAY *Sheph. Week* I. 39 Begin thy Carrols then, thou vaunting Slouch. **1785** GROSE *Dict. Vulgar T.*, *Slouch*,..a negligent slovenly fellow. **1808** J. STAGG *Misc. Poems* 143 Ye'd luok but silly slouches. **1881–** in dial. glossaries (I. of W., Berks., Lancs.). **1884** STEVENSON *Lett.* (1901) I. 342, I recognise myself, compared with you, to be a lout and slouch of the first water.

**b.** orig. *U.S. slang.* A poor, indifferent, or inefficient thing, place, person, etc. Chiefly in the negative phrase ***no slouch of*** (something); also const. *at* or with qualifying phr.

(*a*) **1796** A. BARTON *Disappointment* III. i. 73 He's no slouch of a fellow. **1840** C. F. HOFFMAN *Greyslaer* II. II. x. 23 You are no slouch of a woodsman to carry a yearling of such a heft as that. **1869** 'MARK TWAIN' *Innoc. Abr.* iv. 27 It ..became a most lamentable 'slouch of a journal'. **1879** TOURGEE *Fool's Errand* 308 The mare..was no slouch, either. **1888** LEES & CLUTTERBUCK *B.C. 1887* xxxiii. (1892) 366 We came to Spokane Falls, which seemed to be 'no slouch of a city'. **1924** GALSWORTHY *White Monkey* III. x. 281 'No slouch of a miracle!' he thought, 'modern town life!'

(*b*) **1874** J. W. LONG *Amer. Wild-fowl.* viii. 139, I guess you a'n't much of a 'slouch' at shooting. **1898** F. T. BULLEN *Cruise 'Cachalot'* x. 107 He was no 'slouch' at the business either. **1956** *People* 13 May 4/5 But Tony, no slouch when it comes to showmanship, helped it along by wearing..a rose brocade dinner jacket. **1961** *Coast to Coast 1959–60* 42 Speaking of Bradman, Mr Stulpnagel, they say you were no mean slouch with the bat yourself. **1967** G. F. FIENNES *I tried to run a Railway* ii. 7 He, Happy, himself no slouch at basic English, was revolted by George's language. **1978** R. HOLLES *Spawn* v. 42 He was making his pile... He's certainly no slouch in the business world.

**2.** *ellipt.* A slouch hat or bonnet.

**1714–28** in *N. & Q.* 5th Ser. XI. 247/1 Paid 20s. for a ribbon and slouch for Molly. *c* **1754** GARRICK *Epil. Fielding's Fathers*, The high-cocked, half-cocked quaker, and the slouch, Have at ye all! **1867** F. H. LUDLOW *Fleeing to Tarshish* 189 With his long grey hair streaming from under his slouch. **1891** E. KINGLAKE *Australian* 107 His hat is either small, round and hard, or a black slouch.

**3. a.** A stooping, or bending forward of the head and shoulders, in walking; a loose, ungainly carriage or bearing; a walk or gait characterized by this.

**1725** SWIFT *Corr.* Wks. 1841 II. 579 He hath a sort of a slouch in his walk! **1771** MACKENZIE *Man of Feeling* xi, He was known by the slouch in his gait, and the length of his stride. **1835** MARRYAT *J. Faithful* iii, The slouch in the back is taken out, their heavy walk is changed to a firm..tread. **1865** DICKENS *Mut. Fr.* I. xii, Making himself more round-shouldered..by the sullen and persistent slouch. **1885** J. RUNCIMAN *Skippers & Shellbacks* 258 The slight slouch that most of our men cultivated.

**b.** Const. *of* (the shoulders, etc.).

**1825** HONE *Every-day Bk.* I. 881 The carter..plods with double slouch of shoulder. **1892** STEVENSON *Across Plains* v. 176 The very slouch of the fellows' shoulders tells their story.

**4.** The fact or condition of slouching or hanging down loosely.

**1851** MAYNE REID *Scalp Hunt.* ix, Fierce glances lower under the slouch of broad sombreros.

**slouch**, obs. Sc. f. SLOUGH *sb.*²

**slouch**, *a. rare.* [f. the sb. or v., or back-formation from combs. like *slouch-eared.*]

†**1.** Drooping or hanging loosely; slouching.

**1688** HOLME *Armoury* III. 207/1 Temptation or Sathan.. is drawn with a Dragons head and Wings, to the middle like a Man with slouch hanging Breasts. **1709** *Lond. Gaz.* No. 4540/8 A..Bay Gelding,..hath large slouch Ears. **1829** WIDOWSON *Pres. St. Van Diemen's Land* 142 A very large head, Roman nose, slouch ears.

**2.** *dial.* Clownish, loutish; slovenly. Also *Comb.*

**1837** THORNBER *Hist. Blackpool* 110. **1886** *Spectator* 1587 An educated loafer, the aimless, shiftless, slouch-souled dependant.

**3.** Slouched. (Cf. SLOUCH HAT.)

**1812** E. WEETON *Let.* 15 June (1969) II. 34, I had on a small slouch straw hat, a grey stuff jacket, and petticoat. **1844** LOUISA S. COSTELLO *Béarn & Pyrenees* I. x. 179 All the bathers..were in cloaks and slouch bonnets.

**slouch** (slaʊtʃ), *v.* [app. f. the sb., or the ppl. a. (SLOUCHING), which is found earlier. Cf. dial. *slotch* in sense 1.]

For dialect forms and senses, see the *Eng. Dial. Dict.*

**1.** *intr.* To move or walk with a slouch or in a loose and stooping attitude. Const. with advs. or preps.

**1754** FIELDING *J. Wild* I. xiv, They with lank ears and tails slouch sullenly on. **1768–74** TUCKER *Lt. Nat.* (1834) I. 151 The circumstance of slouching through mire. *a* **1845** BARHAM *Ingold. Leg.* Ser. III. *Jarvis's Wig* (1905) 502 In a few minutes his tiny figure was seen 'slouching' up the ascent. **1862** SALA *Seven Sons* II. vii. 179 He slouched to and fro on his beat in the dockyard. **1886** JEROME *Idle Thoughts* 42 A genuine idler..is not a man who slouches about with his hands in his pockets.

*fig.* **1880** *Times* 30 Aug. 4/3 They slouched through their lives with a look of cheerful ignorance on their faces.

**b.** To carry oneself with a slouch or stoop; to droop the head and shoulders.

**1755** JOHNSON, *Slouch*, to have a downcast clownish look. **1785** GROSE *Dict. Vulgar T.*, *To slouch*, to hang down one's head. **1884** *Cambridge Rev.* 10 Dec. 131 He slouched over his oar very badly at the finish. **1900** ELINOR GLYN *Visits Elizabeth* (1906) 54, I am going to be like her, and not like the women at Nazeby (who all slouched).

**c.** Of a hat: To hang down, droop.

**1818** SCOTT *Hrt. Midl.* xliii, Even the old hat looked smarter;..instead of slouching backward or forward on the Laird's head [etc.]. **1845** BROWNING *Flight of Duchess* x, What signified hats if they had no rims on, Each slouching before and behind like the scallop?

**2.** *trans.* To put on, or pull down, (one's hat) in such a way that it partly conceals the face.

**1760–72** H. BROOKE *Fool of Qual.* (1809) I. 126 Slouching my hat, I slid out of doors. **1815** SCOTT *Guy M.* xxvi, The villains wore their hats much slouched. **1818** —— *Br. Lamm.* ix, His hat was unlooped and slouched. [**1828–32** in WEBSTER; hence in later Dicts.]

**b.** Const. *over* (the face, brow, etc.).

**1806** SURR *Winter in London* I. 165 Slouching his hat over his face, he motioned Edward..to depart. **1858** LYTTON *What will He do?* II. xiv, He wore a large hat of foreign make, slouched deep over his brow. **1870** MORRIS *Earthly Paradise* III. IV. 41 [He] slouched down his hat Yet farther o'er his brows.

**3. a.** To go or make (one's way) in a slouching manner. In quot. *fig.*

**1861** GEO. ELIOT *S. Marner* 58 Having slouched their way through life with a consciousness of being in the vicinity of their 'betters'.

**b.** To stoop or bend (the shoulders).

**1865** KINGSLEY *Herew.* II. xi. 170 The Wake slouched his shoulders, and looked as mean a churl as ever.

**c.** To make (a bow) with a slouch or stoop.

**1897** MEREDITH *Amazing Marriage* viii, Woodseer passed him, slouching a bow.

**slouch-eared**, *a.* Now *rare* or *Obs.* [app. f. SLOUCH *sb.*] Having loose hanging ears.

**1556** OLDE *Antichrist* 11 That men maye se what a slowche eared asse his is. **1580** HOLLYBAND *Treas. Fr. Tong*, *Qui a les Oreilles lasches & pendantes*, hanging eares, or slouch eared. **1607** BREWER *Lingua* III. vi, There was an old..slouch-eard slaue that looking himselfe by chance in a Glasse died for pure hate. **1793** PENNANT *Quadr.* (ed. 3) II. 313 Slouch-eared Bat with large pendulous ears, pointed at the ends. **1855** *Trans. Mich. Agric. Soc.* VI. 511 The original English breed [of hogs]—those long-legged,..slouch-eared, big-headed..animals.

**slouched** (slaʊtʃt), *ppl. a.* [f. SLOUCH *v.*]

**1.** ***slouched hat***, a slouch hat. Also, one worn in such a manner that the brim hangs over the face.

**1779** *Mirror* No. 47 ¶4 Dressed in a short coat, and an old slouched hat with a tarnished gold binding. **1785** GROSE *Dict. Vulgar T.*, *A slouched hat*, a hat whose brims are let down. **1818** SCOTT *Hrt. Midl.* vi, Others in large loose-bodied great-coats, and slouched hats. **1840** R. H. DANA *Bef. Mast* xiii, Every common ruffian-looking fellow, with a slouched hat. **1870** MORRIS *Earthly Par.* III. IV. 34 His hair falls down From 'neath a wide slouched hat of brown.

**2.** Slouching, slouchy.

**1858** *Chambers's Jrnl.* IX. 106 Men..standing in groups, in slouched attitudes, and slouchingly attired.

**sloucher** ('slaʊtʃə(r)). [f. SLOUCH *v.*] One who slouches, or walks with a slouching gait; a slouch; *spec.* in *Horse-racing*, a jockey who intentionally rides slowly in the early stages of a race.

**1881** JEFFERIES *Wood Magic* II. iv. 102 The sloucher took up his quart, and said that he saw 'no call' to hurry. **1897** *Daily News* 21 Dec. 8/3 Well-dressed gentlemen are seen alongside the sloucher, with neck hidden in a shawl.

**slouch hat.** [Cf. SLOUCHED *ppl. a.*] A hat of soft or unstiffened felt or other material, esp. one having a broad brim which hangs or lops down over the face.

**1837** CARLYLE *Fr. Rev.* I. IV. iii, A grand controversy which there was, as to 'slouch-hats or slouched-hats'. **1843** LE FEVRE *Life Trav. Phys.* I. I. i. 11 A celebrated doctor who wore a slouch hat. **1891** MRS. CLIFFORD *Love-Lett. Worldly Woman* vii. 92, I prefer..thick muddy shoes and a slouch hat to a slim umbrella and a frock-coat.

So **slouch-hatted** *a.*, wearing or having a slouch hat.

**1826** SCOTT *Woodst.* v, A slouch-hatted, long-cloaked, sour-faced fanatic. **1837** CARLYLE *Fr. Rev.* I. v. i, Much may remain unfixed..in the Slouch-hatted heads, in the French Nation's head. **1897** *Westm. Gaz.* 1 Oct. 5/3 A group of slouch-hatted warriors.

**'slouchily**, *adv.* [f. SLOUCHY *a.*] In a slouchy or slovenly manner.

**1890** SARA J. DUNCAN *Social Departure* 79 Wearing their European jackets still a little slouchily. **1891** *Daily News* 14 Oct. 5/5 Two..slouchily dressed policemen.

**'slouchiness.** [f. SLOUCHY *a.*] The state or condition of being slouchy or slovenly.

**1891** in *Cent. Dict.* **1897** *Amer. Ann. Deaf* Sept. 334 Certain personal habits of our pupils,..slouchiness when sitting or standing.

**slouching** ('slaʊtʃɪŋ), *vbl. sb.* [f. SLOUCH *v.*] Ungainly walking, lounging or loafing, etc.

*a* **1764** LLOYD *Dial.* 285 As some take stiffness for a grace, ..And others, for familiar air Mistake the slouching of a bear. **1891** SCRIVENER *Our Fields & Cities* 80 The men you see standing in groups..are branded lazy fellows, who prefer slouching to any other condition.

**slouching** ('slaʊtʃɪŋ), *ppl. a.* [f. as prec.]

**1.** Hanging down, drooping; heavy. *rare.*

**1611** COTGR., *Oreilles lasches*, slowching, or hanging eares. **1655** tr. *Com. Hist. Francion* III. 76 A famisht Norman..fell into such a passion against the Pastry-man,..that he flung all the Crust of the Pye at his slouching Chops. **1886** *Westm. Rev.* CXXV. 85 He had..rather rough-hewn slouching features.

**2.** Of persons: Having an awkward, stooping, slip-shod carriage or gait; walking or moving with a slouch.

**1668** H. MORE *Div. Dial.* II. xxi. (1713) 157 The forcing of a rich, beautiful and vertuous Bride upon some poor slouching Clown. **1845** DICKENS *Chimes* iii. 126 A slouching, moody, drunken sloven. **1868** HELPS *Realmah* vii. (1876) 146 It did not..enable him to perceive a timid, slouching figure. **1874** BURNAND *My Time* xi. 95 A slouching young man..touched his hat to me.

**3.** Of a hat: Having a brim which hangs over the face. Also *transf.* of other garments, etc.: Hanging down in a loose untidy manner; slovenly.

**1691** tr. *Emilianne's Frauds Rom. Monks* (ed. 3) 406, I go to the Lawyers..with my great Slouching-Hat. **1719** D'URFEY *Pills* I. 354 Next then the slouching Sledo, and our huge Button, And now our Coats, flanck broad, like Shoulder Mutton. **1840** DICKENS *Barn. Rudge* xxxiv, Enveloped from head to foot in an old, frowsy, slouching horse-cloth. **1842** BORROW *Bible in Spain* xxiii, They wear the sombrero, or broad slouching hat of Spain. **1878** BRET HARTE *Man on Beach* 115 His thought was not always clothed in the best language, and often appeared in the slouching, slangy undress of the place and period.

**4.** Marked or characterized by a slouch or clumsy stooping carriage or bearing.

*a* **1773** CHESTERFIELD (Todd), The awkward, negligent, clumsy, and slouching manner of a booby. **1774** in Burke *Corr.* (1844) I. 513 Formerly they had a slouching, slovenly air. Now every peasant..is erect and soldier-like. **1838** DICKENS *Nickleby* xliv, The man..lingered with slouching steps by the wayside. **1888** F. HUME *Mme. Midas* I. Prol., He was followed by the dumb man with bent head and slouching gait.

Hence **'slouchingly** *adv.*, in a slouching or slovenly manner.

**1858** *Chambers's Jrnl.* IX. 106 Men lounging about..in slouched attitudes, and slouchingly attired. **1889** MARY E. CARTER *Mrs. Severn* II. II. ii. 141 Man and dog advanced slouchingly.

**slouchy** ('slaʊtʃɪ), *a.* [f. SLOUCH *sb.* and *v.* + -Y.] Slouching, in various senses; slovenly, untidy. Freq. in recent *U.S.* usage.

*a* **1693** *Urquhart's Rabelais* III. xvii. 141 What meaneth this..wagging of her slouchy Chaps? **1864** I. TAYLOR in *Good Words* 227 The ample auburn locks are in part huddled up within a broad-bordered slouchy cap. **1868** M. H. SMITH *Sunshine & Shadow N. York* 283 His dress slouchy and countrified, his oratory uninviting. **1882** *Cent. Mag.* XXV. 176 Looking like a slouchy country bumpkin.

**slough** (slaʊ), *sb.*¹ Forms: α. 1, 3–4 sloh, 1 sloȝ(h, 5 slogh, 4–5 sloghe (5 sloghte); 4 slowh, slowȝ (5 -e); 4 slouhe, slouȝ(e, 4– slough (6 -e), 5 sclough, 9 *Sc.* slouch. β. 4, 6–7 slowe, 4–8 slow. γ. 1, 3, 5 slo, 4–5, 9 *dial.* sloo. (See also SLEW *sb.*¹)

[OE. *slóh* (*slóȝ*, *sló*), of doubtful origin; perhaps ultimately related to SLONK.]

**1. a.** A piece of soft, miry, or muddy ground; *esp.* a place or hole in a road or way filled with wet mud or mire and impassable by heavy vehicles, horses, etc.

α. **c 900** tr. *Baeda's Hist.* v. vi. (1890) 400 þæt hors.. sume sloh on þæm wæȝe mid swiðþran ræse oferhleop. **a 1023** WULFSTAN *Hom.* xlvi. (1883) 239 Ðeah se man nime ænne stan and lecȝe on ful sloh. **1390** GOWER *Conf.* I. 142 Of the welles brinke Or of the pet or of the slowh. **c 1400** *Destr. Troy* 13547 Wanto the lond, Thurgh the slicche and the slyme in þis slogh feble. **a 1425** *Cursor M.* 15826 (Trin.), Forþ þei ihesus drowȝe And lugged him.. ouer hilles, dale, & slowȝe. **1483** *Cath. Angl.* 345/1 A Sloghte, *tesquum, vel tesqua, volutabrum.* **c 1500** *God Speed the Plough* 14 By downe and by dale and many a slough. **1577** HARRISON *Descr. Brit.* xix. in *Holinshed* I. 114 Manie a slough [would] proue hard ground that yet is deepe and hollow. **1670** MILTON *Hist. Eng.* II. Wks. 1851 V. 78 Many a time enclos'd in the midst of sloughs and quagmires. **1678** BUNYAN *Pilgr.* I. 9 They drew near to a very Miry Slough... The name of the Slow was Dispond. **1732** SWIFT *Corr.* Wks. 1841 II. 682 Every meadow a slough, and every hill a mixture of rock, heath, and marsh. **1784** COWPER *Task* III. 5 One who.., having long in miry ways been foil'd.., from slough to slough Plunging [etc.]. **1827** SCOTT *Chron. Canongate* iii, An old-fashioned road, which, preferring ascents to sloughs, was led in a straight line. **1869** BLACKMORE *Lorna D.* ii, The sloughs were exceedingly murky.

*transf.* **1856** KANE *Arctic Expl.* I. xvi. 187 And then piloted my dogs out of their slough. **1890** E. H. BARKER *Wayfaring in France* 27 Sand sloughs into which they may step unawares.

β. **13..** *K. Alis.* 6075 (W.), Into theo mores they heom drowe, To quede paththes, to quede slowe. **c 1386** CHAUCER *Manciple's Prol.* 64 (Hengwrt MS.), He hath also to do moore than ynow To kepen hym and his capil out of the Slow. **1537** *Bury Wills* (Camden) 132 Mendyng the fowle slowys betwene thys my howse and Reuyttes gate. **1642** ROGERS *Naaman* 558 To lie as a beast in a slow. **1678** [see above]. **1710** *Acc. Distemper Tom Whigg* II. 44 Breaking his Horse's Back as he plung'd into a Slow.

γ. **a 1000** in Birch *Sax. Chartul.* I. 530 Of þan slo to þan lytlan beorhe. *Ibid.* II. 41 In readan sloe. **c 1250** [see b]. **a 1300** *Assump. Virg.* 507 Cast we it in a foule sloo. **c 1386** CHAUCER *Friar's T.* 267 Now is my cart out of the sloo parde! **c 1425** *Castle Persev.* 2242 in *Macro Plays*, Lete slynge hem in a fowle slo. **1426** LYDG. *De Guil. Pilgr.* 13597 By brookys and by sloos fowle, A-mong the clay they hym dyffoule. [**1891** *Hartland Gloss.* s.v. *Slough*, A bye-road at H. is called *Sloo Road*, and an adjoining field *Sloo Park*.]

**b.** *fig.* A state or condition (esp. of moral degradation) in which a person, etc., sinks or has sunk.

**c 1250** *Owl & Night.* 1394 Vor mony wymmon haueþ mysdo þat aryst vp of þe slo. **c 1340** HAMPOLE *Psalter* xxix. 3 Wha sa gifis þaim til lustis of fleysse.., þai light in þe sloghe, and þai ere enmys of Jesu crist. **1415** HOCCLEVE *Sir J. Oldcastle* 105 Ryse vp, a manly knyght, out of the slow Of heresie. **c 1425** *Castle Persev.* 2757 in *Macro Plays*, þus hast þou gotyn, in synful slo, of þyne neygboris, be extorcyon. **1593** Q. ELIZ. *Boeth.* IV. pr. iii. 81 See you not in what a great slowe [L. *cœno*] wicked thinges be wrapt in. **1632** *Star Chamber Cases* (Camden) 105 For this man Carrier when he talks of religion he is in a slowe. **1742** YOUNG *Nt. Th.* VI. 222 Ambition, av'rice; the two daemons these, Which goad thro' ev'ry slough our human herd. **1768–74** TUCKER *Lt. Nat.* (1834) II. 149 To take the adventurous leaps of folly, or plunge into the sloughs of vice. **1823** ROSCOE tr. *Sismondi's Lit. Europe* (1846) I. viii. 257 A disgusting slough swallows up those, who abandon themselves to choleric passions. **1850** HT. MARTINEAU *Hist. Peace* IV. ix. (1877) III. 35 The clergy sank into a deeper slough of popular hatred. **1888** H. MORTEN *Hospital Life* 22 It had.. lifted her out of the miserable slough in which marriage had landed her.

**c.** *Slough of Despond*, after Bunyan's use (see 1 a and DESPOND *sb.*).

**1776** TWINING in *Country Clergyman of the 18th C.* (1882) 31, I remember slumping all on a sudden into the slough of despond, and closing my letter in the dumps. **1818** SCOTT *Hrt. Midl.* i, The miry Slough of Despond, which yawns for insolvent debtors. **1839** FR. A. KEMBLE *Resid. Georgia* (1863) 12 If one individual.. were to raise himself out of such a slough of despond. **1884** HAWEIS *My Musical Life* I. 137 Musical criticism has been in the same Slough of Despond.

**2.** The matter of which a slough is composed; soft mud or mire. ? *Obs.*

**a 1225** *Leg. Kath.* 1662 Euch strete.. bute sloh & slec, eauer iliche sumerlich. **1393** LANGL. *P. Pl.* C. XIII. 179 Bote yf þe sed þat sowen is in þe sloh sterue, Shal neuere spir springen vp. **a 1425** *Cursor M.* 1964 (Trin.), Also ȝe ete of no flesshe elles þat in slouȝe & erþe dwelles. **1732** SWIFT *Epist. Corr.* Wks. 1841 II. 682 You can't ride half a mile.. without being in slough to your saddle-skirts. **1774** GOLDSM. *Nat. Hist.* I. iv. (1862) II. 261 Covered over with weeds, slough, and all the filth of the sea. **1776** G. SEMPLE *Building in Water* 71 A Hole, which was immediately filled up with Slough.

**3.** A ditch, dike, or drain; also, a cart rut. ? *Obs.*

**1532** HERVET *Xenophon's Treat. Househ.* (1768) 67 Thinke you than that we do not make the dyches and sloughes in the fieldes for a good cause? **1598** FLORIO, *Carreggista*, the rut or slough of a cart wheele. **1640** G. ABBOTT *Job Paraph.* 169 By his labour and skill he cuts out passages and sloughs in the hard stony rocks. **1685** *Phil. Trans.* XV. 956 In the Bog, observe which way the little Sloughs run; be sure to cut their drains across them.

**4.** *N. Amer.* (slu:). = SLEW *sb.*[1] Also, a side channel of a river, or a natural channel that is only sporadically filled with water.

**1714** *Rep. Record Commissioners* (Boston Registry Dept.) (1877) III. 217 Between his old house & the Slough or Small Bridge. **a 1817** T. DWIGHT *Trav. New Eng.* etc. (1821) II. 142 The slough will be covered with a causey; and the marsh by draining be converted into a meadow. **1858** W. P. BLAKE *Rep. Geol. Reconnaissance in California* i. 10 There lay outstretched the broad and green Tulares—great swamps or lowlands overgrown with rushes and threaded by the sinuous channels and sloughs of the river. **1859** *Brit. Colonist* (Victoria, B.C.) 17 Dec. 3/2 At Old Langley, the slough is entirely frozen up. **1874** J. W. LONG *Amer. Wild-fowl.* viii. 128 Mallards breed in small numbers in the various swamps and sloughs of the Western country. **1888** GOODE *Amer. Fishes* 109 Oftentimes the current cuts out a deep 'slough', or sluice, within reach of high water mark... It forms a space of smooth water between the outer and inner breakers. **1888** D. M. GORDON *Mountain & Prairie* 143 At the same time there are many sloughs, or 'slews' so-called, where part of the river flows by some devious and half-hidden course. **1891** C. ROBERTS *Adrift Amer.* 29, I went over head and ears into a slough, a long narrow stretch of water formed by a depression in the prairie. **1913** THOMAS & WATT *Improvement of Rivers* (ed. 2) I. i. 30 In valleys with narrow bottom lands the result is a slough or drain close to the hills which returns the water to the main channel further down, one slough succeeding another along the valley. **1924** M. H. MASON *Arctic Forests* 225 There was an Indian toboggan trail on the long slough, past Jenny Island up to the eight-mile point. **1932** C. R. LONGWELL et al. *Textbk. Geol.* I. iii. 60 Most [short cuts].. are abandoned as the flood subsides and are left as sloughs, which are slowly undercut as the meander shifts downstream. **1939** W. HÄNTZSCHEL in P. D. Trask *Recent Marine Sediments* III. 202 The sloughs (Priele) on the tidal flats are comparable to rivers and brooks. *Ibid.*, Where the range in tides in Jade Bay is as high as 3·6 meters, the sloughs are deeply incised. **1962** W. STEGNER *Wolf Willow* I. i. 8 In deep sloughs tules have rooted, and every such pond is dignified with mating mallards. **1970** LEOPOLD & WOLMAN in G. H. Dury *Rivers & River Terraces* vii. 199 Opposite the gravel island is a slough aligned with a grassed depression. Both features undoubtedly carry water during flood flow. **1974** P. GZOWSKI *Bk. about this Country* 20, I remember seeing a bunch of geese sitting in a little slough. **1976** *Prof. Paper U.S. Geol. Survey* No. 929. 150/2 The ecological model is designed to relate the wildlife in the Shark River Slough to the availability of food and water.

**5.** *attrib.*, as ***slough-cake***, ***-water***, etc. Also **slough bass**, a black bass of the genus *Micropterus*; **slough grass**, one of several coarse grasses of swampy ground, esp. a species of the genus *Muhlenbergia*; **slough hay** *Canad.*, (hay made from) slough grass.

**1877** C. HALLOCK *Sportsman's Gaz.* 276 Locally they are termed perch.. *slough bass, etc. **1881** J. A. HENSHALL *Bk. Black Bass* 142 Slough Bass. **1888** GOODE *Amer. Fishes* 56 'Marsh Bass,'.. 'Slough Bass,'.. are other names applied to one or both species [of black bass]. **1869** BLACKMORE *Lorna D.* ii, The great blunderbuss.. was choked with a dollop of *slough-cake. **1860** *Trans. Ill. Agric. Soc.* IV. 488 Then [I] make a band of whatever material I have at hand, (*slough grass is preferable). **1880** BESSEY *Botany* 455 *Muhlenbergia glomerata* and *M. Mexicana* constitute the 'Fine Slough Grass' of the Mississippi valley prairies. **1907** L. H. BAILEY *Cycl. Amer. Agric.* II. 454/1 In wet and swampy places, slough-grass (*Spartina*) furnishes a supply of coarse hay. **1980** *Country Life* 13 Nov. 1819/3 The hay is made of wild slough grass. **1934** G. BETTANY *Valley of Lost Gold* 264 In the tall *slough hay beside them orange lilies raised their heads waist high. **1948** T. ONRAET *Sixty Below* 135, I have often seen them kneeling on their forelegs to feed in comfort on short willows and slough hay. **1955** *Sentinel-Courier* (Pilot Mound, Manitoba) 31 Mar. 4/1 (Advt.), For sale—Baled slough hay, wire tied. **1968** S. E. ROBERTS *Of Us & Oxen* ii. 14 This 'slough hay' is said to be less nutritious than the 'upland hay' cut from buffalo grass. **1874** J. W. LONG *Amer. Wild-fowl.* ix. 150 Lager-beer.. is much better to drink than *slough-water.

**slough** (slʌf), *sb.*[2] Forms: 4 slohu, slouh, 5 sloȝ, 4, 7 slow; 4–5 slughe, 4 slught, 5, 7 slugh; 5 slouȝe, 6–7 sloughe, 6 slougth, 6– slough, 8 sluf, 9 *dial.* sluff; *Sc.* 6 slouch(t, slowch, sluich, 9 sloch. [ME. type *sloh*, *sloȝ*, of uncertain origin, perh. related to LG. *sluwe*, *slu* husk, peel, shell.]

**1.** The outer or scarf skin periodically cast or shed by a snake, adder, or similar reptile; also generally, the skin of a serpent, eel, etc.

**a 1300** *Cursor M.* 745 þis nedder forth þat he ne blan Bot in hijs slught [*v.rr.* slohu, slouȝe] was self satan. **a 1400–50** *Alexander* 5085 Fellis of fischis.. with lions on lyue & lamprays sloȝis. **1483** *Cath. Angl.* 345/2 Slughes of eddyrs. **1513** DOUGLAS *Æneid* II. viii. 60 Lyke to the eddir.. [that has] Now slippit hir sloucht with schynyng skyn new brerd. **1593** SHAKS. *2 Hen. VI*, III. i. 229 As the Snake, roll'd in a flowring Banke, With shining checker'd slough. **1608** TOPSELL *Serpents* (1653) 810 The slow of the viper cureth the ring-worm. **1681** GREW *Musæum* I. III. 49 The Slough of an English Viper. **1713** DERHAM *Physico-Theol.* IX. i. 438 Although he missed seeing the Serpents Yet he saw great numbers of their *Exuviæ*, or Slufs. **1774** GOLDSM. *Nat. Hist.* IV. 99 If the old slough be then viewed, every scale will be distinctly seen. **1851** CARPENTER *Man. Phys.* (ed. 2) 138 The continuity is well seen in the cast skin or *slough* of the Snake. **1897** G. C. BATEMAN *Vivarium* 182 A slough when perfect is an exact copy of the exterior of the Snake from which it came.

**b.** The skin of a caterpillar, locust, etc. cast in the course of transformation, as from the nymphal to the imago stage.

**1681** GREW *Musæum* I. VII. iii. 176 A very large Aurelia and Slough of a Silk-Worme. **1818** KIRBY & SP. *Introd. Entom.* xvi. (ed. 2) II. 16 The moisture that remained upon them [i.e. locusts] after casting their sloughs.

**c.** *fig.* A feature, quality, etc. which is thrown off.

**1583** GOLDING *Calvin on Deut.* cxxi. 744 Vnlesse she.. haue put her old bringing vp quite out of her minde, yea and euen cast her slough as they say. **1602** MARSTON *Ant. & Mel.* I. Wks. 1856 I. 9 Can man by no meanes creepe out of himselfe, And leave the slough of viperous griefe behinde? **1774** BURKE *Sp. Amer. Taxation* Wks. I. 175 Are we to give them.. the slough of slavery, which we are not able to work off, to serve them for their freedom? **1797** GODWIN *Enquirer* I. xiv. 121 He casts the slough of sedentary confinement. **1818** HALLAM *Mid. Ages* (1872) I. 131 The barbarians.. had early cast off the slough of their rude manners. **1868** TENNYSON *Lucretius* 177 The mountain there has cast his cloudy slough.

**d.** Apparel, clothing.

**1808** SCOTT *Marmion* VI. vii, For now that sable slough is shed,.. I scarcely know me in the glass. **1820** —— *Monast.* xviii, I did but wait to cast my riding slough. **1821** —— *Kenilw.* xxx, While those.. get rid of their slough, and doff their riding-suits.

**2.** A skin, caul, or membrane, enclosing or covering the body or some part of it.

**13..** *Hampole's Pr. Consc.* 520 Bot a rym [*v.rr.* slow, slouh] þat es ful wlatsome,.. þat es noght bot a blody skyn þat he [man] byfor was lapped in. **a 1400–50** *Alexander* 4456 þus make ȝe vessels in vayne to ȝoure foule corses,.. þat ilk slymand slugh. **c 1460** *Towneley Myst.* xiii. 385, I was flayd with a swevyn, My hart out of sloghe. **1486** *Bk. St. Albans*, *Hunting* f iij b, Than shall ye slyt the slough ther as the hert lith. **1599** JAS. I *Dæmonol.* 125 As to their [werwolves] having and hiding of their hard and schelly sluiches. **1599** ROLLOCK *Serm.* Wks. 1849 I. 385 Na creature.. can tak aff the slouch of thy hart to let thee see.

**b.** An enclosing or covering layer, coat, or sheath of some kind.

**1610** HOLLAND *Camden's Brit.* 556 By reason that under the upper crust of the earth there is limestone which supplyeth a batling fruitfull slugh, or humour. **1610** FLETCHER *Faithf. Sheph.* III. i, No slough of falling Star did ever hit Upon this bank. **? c 1730** RAMSAY *Horace to Virgil* 12 With heart hool'd in three sloughs of brass.

**c.** *dial.* The outer skin of certain fruits; a husk.

**c 1660** in *Select Biogr.* (Wodrow Soc.) I. 265 Such a crosse is mine, and the sweet kirnell of the blessing under the sour slough that is without. **1691** RAY *N.C. Words* (ed. 2) 65 A *Slough*, a Husk; it is pronounced *sluffe*. **1855** [ROBINSON] *Whitby Gloss.*, *Sluffs*, the skins of all such fruit as gooseberries and currants are called sluffs or sloughs. **1869–** in dial. glossaries (Yks., Lancs., Linc.); also in Sc. use.

**3.** *Path.* A layer or mass of dead tissue or flesh formed on the surface of a wound, sore, or inflammation; a sphacelus.

**1513** DOUGLAS *Æneid* II. x. 83 The clud.. That on ȝour mortale ene.. Lyke to ane wattery slowch standis dyme about. **1612** WOODALL *Surgeon's Mate* Wks. (1653) 409 The first eskers or Cadaverous sloughes being removed. **1676** WISEMAN *Surg. Treat.* I. xxi. 98 The matter of the Humour .. may be arsenical, as appears by the Sloughs we sometimes find made in a night. **1797** *Encycl. Brit.* (ed. 3) XVIII. 97/2 Gun shot wounds are commonly covered from the beginning with deep sloughs. **1835–6** *Todd's Cycl. Anat.* I. 61/2 The inflammation.. producing.. sloughs of the adipose tissue. **1877** F. T. ROBERTS *Handbk. Med.* (ed. 3) I. 49 A slough is formed, which becomes isolated from the living textures and undergoes a process of separation.

*fig.* **1842** TENNYSON *St. Simeon Stylites* 2 From scalp to sole one slough and crust of sin.

*Comb.* **1857** LD. DUFFERIN *Let. High Lat.* 116 Crumpled shreds and shards of slough-like incrustations. **1897** *Allbutt's Syst. Med.* II. 488 The discharge appears so to cling to the sore surface as to form a thick slough-like yellow pellicle.

† **slough**, *sb.*[3] *Obs.*[−1] (See quot.)

**1647** J. CLEVELAND *Poems, King's Disguise* 33 The false scabberd of a Princes tough Metall, and three-pil'd darknesse, like the slough Of an imprisoned flame. [*Note.*] A damp, in Cole-pits usuall.

**slough** (slʌf), *sb.*[4] Also sluff. [app. f. SLOUGH *v.*[2]] (See quots.)

**1838** *Civil Eng. & Arch. Jrnl.* I. 144/2 Preventing those sloughs, or slipping at the foot of the materials, which may be observed on most large embankments. **1839** MURCHISON *Silurian Syst.* I. xxix. 376 The cliff vein.. terminates in what the miners here [Pembroke] call a 'slough', i.e., it is bent suddenly downwards, accompanied on each side by the usual measures. **1908** *Daily Chron.* 16 Dec. 1/2 Two seconds afterwards the sluff came down in hundreds of tons.

**slough** (slaʊ), *sb.*[5] Also 9 sloo, sloe. [Corresponds to Norw. *slo*, Icel. *sló* (whence the Shetland form *sloe*), but the currency of the word in southwestern dialect is remarkable.] (See quots.)

**1721** BAILEY, *Slough*,.. the spungy or porous Substance in the Inside of the Horns of Oxen or Cows. **1844** BARNES *Poems Rural Life* Gloss., *Sloo of a horn*, the inner bony prominence from the skull, or quick part of a cow's horn, which bleeds when broken. **1883** R. HALDANE *Workshop Rec.* Ser. II. 300/2 Dry materials:.. Horn 'sloughs' (the pith or core of horns). **1890** in *Gloucester Gloss.* 142.

**slough** (slaʊ), *v.*[1] [f. SLOUGH *sb.*[1]] **a.** *trans.* In passive: To be swallowed (*up*) in a slough.

**1861** in *Daily Colonist* (Victoria, B.C.) (1911) 16 Apr. 1/6 Several of the wagons while conveying passengers and freight from the steamer on Sunday night became sloughed and the passengers were compelled to 'foot it' to town. **1904** ELEANOR ORMEROD *Econ. Entomologist* v. 38 Another time somebody.. got nearly sloughed up in one of the great marsh ditches.

**b.** *slang.* To imprison, to lock (*up*). Usu. in passive.

**1848** *Ladies' Repository* Oct. 317/1 *Slough*, to lock. **1894** 'J. FLYNT' in *Century Mag.* Feb. 518/2 I've boozed around this town.. for seven years, and I've not been sloughed up yet. **1926** J. BLACK *You can't Win* vii. 87 They'll.. haul us over to Martinez.. an' slough us in the county jail. **1935** A. J. POLLOCK *Underworld Speaks* 108/2 *Sloughed*, arrested.

**slough** (slʌf), *v.*[2] [f. SLOUGH *sb.*[2]]

**1. a.** *intr.* Of diseased skin, tissue, etc.: To come *away* or *off*, to be shed, as a slough.

**1720** QUINCY tr. *Hodges' Loimologia* 138 Those which went no further than the skin, would oftentimes slough off. **1787** *Med. Comm.* II. 160 A large portion of the integuments ..sloughed away. **1813** J. THOMSON *Lect. Inflamm.* 269 The injured part of the artery sloughed off with the ligature. **1847** W. C. L. MARTIN *Ox* 160/2 The diseased part.. sloughs away, and new and healthy skin is reproduced.

*transf.* and *fig.* **1857** GOSSE *Omphalos* vii. 131 Every one of these scars indicates where a leaf has grown..and whence, after death and decay, it at length sloughed away. **1886** *Boston Jrnl.* 7 Aug. 1/9 The situation improved up to the time the eight-hour agitation began, when trade sloughed off and became dull.

**b.** To become covered or encrusted with a slough; to form or develop necrosed tissue.

**1787** *Med. Comm.* II. 160 It was evident that some part of the urethra had also sloughed. **1804** ABERNETHY *Surg. Obs.* 54 The exposed tumour inflamed and sloughed progressively, till it entirely came away. **1846** BRITTAN tr. *Malgaigne's Man. Oper. Surg.* 319 The columna..sloughed from the fourth day, and was removed with the scissors. **1880** MACCORMAC *Antiseptic Surg.* 14 In the other case of protracted recovery, a large portion of skin sloughed.

*fig.* **1861** LYTTON & FANE *Tannhäuser* 49 [To] seek from gross hearts, slough'd in sin, Approval of pure Love to win.

**2.** *trans.* To eat *away*, to throw *off*, by the formation of a slough or sloughs.

**1762** R. GUY *Pract. Obs. Cancers* 48 Four large Ulcers were sloughing the Breast away. **1844** H. STEPHENS *Bk. Farm* II. 612 The portion of the vertebra which has been cut through will have to be sloughed off before the wound can heal.

**3. a.** Of a serpent or similar reptile: To cast or shed (the skin) as a slough; to exuviate.

**1845** [see b.]. **1854** MARY HOWITT *Pict. Cal. Seasons* 427 About the middle of the month [September] the common snake sloughs or casts its skin. **1870** GILLMORE tr. *Figuier's Reptiles & Birds* i. 13 Reptiles..slough their old covering, or in other words cast their skin.

*absol.* **1875** TENNYSON *Q. Mary* III. iii, The serpent that hath slough'd will slough again. **1897** G. C. BATEMAN *Vivarium* 231 Young Snakes slough more frequently than their older relatives do.

**b.** *fig.* To cast off, drop, discard, give up, get rid of (something). Also with *off*.

(*a*) **1845** DE QUINCEY *Susp. de Prof.* I. in *Blackw. Mag.* LVII. 283, I saw a ewe suddenly put off and abjure her own nature, in a service of love—yes, slough it as completely, as ever serpent sloughed his skin. **1851** D. JERROLD *St. Giles* xxii. 226 With such change, he cannot but slough much of the bad reputation..fixed upon him. **1876** MEREDITH *Beauch. Career* II. xvi. 287 Nevil will slough his craze.

(*b*) **1848** MILNES *Life, Lett.*, etc. *Keats* I. 23 The wonder is rather that he sloughed off so fast, so many of his offending peculiarities. **1860** MAURY *Phys. Geogr.* (ed. 8) ii. §112 Why does the Gulf Stream slough off and cast upon its outer edge, sea-weed, drift-wood [etc.]? **1873** T. HARDY *Pair of Blue Eyes* II. 3 She could slough off a sadness and replace it by a hope.

**4.** To take *off* in grinding.

**1844** H. STEPHENS *Bk. Farm* II. 353 The small bran..is only generated after the large bran has been sloughed off.

**5.** *intr.* Of soil, rock, etc.: to fall *away* or slide *down* into an adjoining hole or depression.

**1897** W. STARLING *Floods of Mississippi* i. 14/1 Water leaking through the old bank infiltrates the new earth and it sloughs away bodily. **1942** W. FAULKNER *Go down, Moses* 30 As though the whole mound had stooped roaring down at him—the entire overhang sloughed. **1955** HENNES & EKSE *Fund. Transportation Engin.* ii. 30 The processes of weathering tend to loosen surface material and cause it to slough and drift down any slope greater than the angle of repose of the dry loose material. **1957** A. C. CLARKE *Deep Range* v. 54 Sometimes, in deep ocean waters far from the eternal rain of silt which sloughs down from the edges of the continents, it was possible to see as much as two hundred feet. **1974** P. L. MOORE et al. *Drilling Practices Manual* iii. 46 Shale sloughs into the hole.

Hence **sloughed** (slʌft), *ppl. a.*

**1857** GOSSE *Omphalos* ix. 248 *note*, 'The rattle is cast annually' with the sloughed skin. **1897** W. STARLING *Floods of Mississippi* i. 14/1 A good thick dressing of brush is laid on the sloughed mass.

**slough-dog, -hound.** *Sc.* and *north.* [See SLEUTH *sb.*[2]] = SLEUTH-HOUND I.

**1774** PENNANT *Tour Scotl. in 1772* 68 The inhabitants of the marches were obliged to keep such a number of slough dogs, or what we call blood-hounds. *a* **1784** *Hobbie Noble* xv. in Child *Ballads* IV. 3 Aft has he beat your slough-hounds back. **1842** JEFFERSON *Allerdale Ward* 23 The dogs appointed to be kept for defence were called slough dogs. **1843** *M. A. Richardson's Historian's Table-bk., Leg. Div.* I. 159 The slough dogs of the Borderers.

**sloughful(nesse**, varr. SLOWFUL(NESS *Obs.*

**sloughi**, var. SALUKI.

**'sloughiness.** *rare*[−1]. [f. SLOUGHY *a.*[2]] The condition of being sloughy.

**1788** *Med. Comm.* II. 178 Its [*sc.* erysipelas] termination ..is never in suppuration, but in..sloughiness, or gangrene.

**sloughing** ('slʌfɪŋ), *vbl. sb.* [f. SLOUGH *v.*[2]]

**1. a.** *Path.* The process of forming a slough.

**1800** *Med. Jrnl.* IV. 548 On a subsidence of the swelling, there was a sloughing. **1826** S. COOPER *First Lines Surg.* (ed. 5) 52 When sloughing and ulceration have actually taken place, some surgeons apply lint. **1879** *St. George's Hosp. Rep.* IX. 289 After first week there was some sloughing about amputation wound.

**b.** *attrib.* in *sloughing process, state.*

**1802** *Med. Jrnl.* VIII. 454 Their gangrenous sloughs once removed, and the sloughing process..corrected. **1813** J. THOMSON *Lect. Inflam.* 473 The sloughing and gangrenous states.

**2.** The action or process of casting a slough; exuviation. Also *attrib.*

**1835** URE *Philos. Manuf.* 238 When the sloughing process begins for shifting their skins. **1857** GOSSE *Omphalos* viii. 216 A great many periodical sloughings of the crust [of a crab] must have occurred. **1897** G. C. BATEMAN *Vivarium* 180 The sloughing of a Snake is a very interesting operation to watch.

*fig.* **1865** PUSEY *Truth Eng. Ch.* 194 The sloughing-off of the imperfection ingrown as it were with the soul.

**3.** The collapse of soil or rock into a hole or down a bank.

**1897** W. STARLING *Floods of Mississippi* i. 14/1 There is no incident..more alarming..than the sloughing or slipping of the inside slope of a levee. **1948** TERZAGHI & PECK *Soil Mech. in Engin. Pract.* viii. 336 To prevent sloughing of the toes of the slopes, the small quantity of water that flows through the gaps between the wells is removed. **1957** *Nature* 13 July 100 (*heading*) Vernal sloughing of sludge deposits in a sewage effluent channel. **1972** L. M. HARRIS *Introd. Deepwater Floating Drilling Operations* vi. 90 On completion of drilling, the hole is normally filled with gel-water mud to prevent sloughing and fill.

**'sloughing,** *ppl. a.* [f. as prec.]

**1.** *Path.* Developing or forming a slough or sloughs.

**1813** J. THOMSON *Lect. Inflam.* 649 The too-long-continued use of stimulating remedies in sloughing burns. **1845** BUDD *Dis. Liver* 71 The sloughing ulceration in acute dysentery. **1896** *Allbutt's Syst. Med.* I. 434 Charcoal poultices..usually ordered for sloughing wounds.

*Comb.* **1869** LAWSON *Dis. Eye* (1874) 30 In the majority of cases..a sloughing looking ulcer is left.

**2.** Of soil or rock: collapsing, sliding.

**1974** P. L. MOORE et al. *Drilling Practices Manual* iii. 46 It has been common practice to reduce water-loss when sloughing shale becomes a problem.

**sloughishnesse**, obs. form of SLUGGISHNESS.

**sloughtful(ly**, obs. forms of SLOTHFUL(LY.

**sloughy** ('slaʊɪ), *a.*[1] [f. SLOUGH *sb.*[1] + -Y[1].] Of the nature of, resembling, slough or soft mud; abounding in or full of slough; miry, muddy.

**1724** SWIFT *Drapier's Lett.* vii. Wks. 1755 V. II. 152 Low ground, with a thin green sward, and sloughy underneath. **1776** G. SEMPLE *Building in Water* 71 That they may not lean either to the one Side or the other in that sloughy Ground. **1813** J. C. HOBHOUSE *Journey* (ed. 2) 102 The path very bad and sloughy. **1872** S. MOSTYN *Perplexity* I. ii. 45 He will..kneel in sloughy banks. **1890** STANLEY *Darkest Africa* II. xxii. 57 Belts of sloughy mud, disparted by small streams.

**sloughy** ('slʌfɪ), *a.*[2] Also 5 **slughy.** [f. SLOUGH *sb.*[2] + -Y[1].]

**1.** Consisting or formed of slough or cast skin. *rare.*

**1483** *Cath. Angl.* 345/2 Slughy, *squamosus.* **1695** BLACKMORE *Pr. Arth.* x. 71 The sloughy Spoils from his sleek Back depos'd.

**2.** *Path.* Of the nature of, resembling, a slough; marked or characterized by the presence of a slough or sloughs.

*c* **1720** GIBSON *Farrier's Guide* II. iv. (1738) 12 A disease proceeding..from some viscid sloughy matter. **1775** *Phil. Trans.* LXVI. 436 The wound..made but an indifferent appearance; the edges of it were very sloughy. **1804** ABERNETHY *Surg. Obs.* 232 The whole surface..was found in a sloughy and putrid state. **1879** *St. George's Hosp. Rep.* IX. 329 During the following three days, the stump assumed a sloughy condition.

*Comb.* **1839–47** *Todd's Cycl. Anat.* III. 55/1 A large sloughy-looking opening. **1879** *St. George's Hosp. Rep.* IX. 339 A ragged excavated sore, having a white sloughy-looking base.

**slougi**, var. SALUKI.

**slougish**, obs. form of SLUGGISH *a.*

**slouk.** *dial.* and *rare.* [Cf. Norw. *slōk*, Icel. *slókr*, in the same sense.] An idle, lazy fellow.

A verb, *slouk* to slouch, occurs in *S.W. Linc. Gloss.* (1886).

**1570** LEVINS *Manip.* 217 A Slouke, *iners, ignarus.* **1867** J. POOLE *Gloss. Wexford* 68 Slouk, an idle, heedless person.

**slounge,** *v.* *Sc.* and *north. dial.* Also 7– **slunge,** 9 **sloonge.** [Cf. LOUNGE *v.*] *intr.* To move, or hang about, in a lazy or slouching manner.

The sb. *slounge* or *slunge*, a slouching fellow, idler, etc., is also current: see the *Eng. Dial. Dict.*

*c* **1680** F. SEMPILL *Banishm. Poverty* in *Poems Sempills* (1849) 54 The morn I ventur'd up the Wynd, And slung'd in at the Nether-bow. **1788** JAMES MACAULAY *Poems* 131 (E.D.D.), Thou lazy, slounging, donart sot. **1808** J. STAGG *Misc. Poems* 143 Ye'd luok but silly slouches,..heame wi' empty pouches, To slounge this day. **1808** in JAMIESON. *c* **1860–** in dialect glossaries, etc. (N. Irel., Yks.).

**slour,** *v.* *Cant.* (See quots.)

**1812** J. H. VAUX *Flash Dict.*, *Slour*, to lock, secure, or fasten; to *slour up* is also to button up; as one's coat, pocket, &c. **1834** AINSWORTH *Rookwood* III. v, No slour'd hoxter my snipes could stay. **1859** *Slang Dict.* 95 Slour'd hoxter, an inside pocket buttoned up.

**slouse** (slaʊz), *v.* *dial.* Also **slouze.** [perh. suggested by *sluice* and *souse.*] *trans.* To wash with a copious supply of water.

**1726** in *Evesham Jrnl.* 8 Mar. 1902 (E.D.D.), Slousing ye pavement. **1909** *Westm. Gaz.* 28 Aug. 2/3 After a big catch, especially of herrings, they [*sc.* the nets] are also given a slouzing.

**sloush** (slaʊʃ), *v.* *dial.* [Cf. prec. and SLUSH *v.*] *trans.* To slush or sluice (something) in washing; to dash or throw (water) *over.*

**1889** JEROME *Three Men in Boat* vii. 102 You..slosh the things about in the water. **1900** *Longman's Mag.* Nov. 63 You'ld put the clothes in a trough..and then slosh the water over them. *Ibid.*, Slosh them again.

**slouth**, obs. form of SLOTH.

**Slovak** ('sləʊvæk, formerly 'slɒvɑːk, slə'vɑːk), *sb.* and *a.* Also **Slovac(k.** [a. Slovak and Czech *Slovák* (pl. *Slováci*), Pol. *Słowak*, Russ. *Slovak*, G. *Slowake* (pl. *Slowaken*), f. the stem *Slov-*: see SLOVENE.]

**A.** *sb.* **1.** A person belonging to a Slavonic race dwelling in Slovakia, formerly part of Hungary, now the Slovak Socialist Republic and part of Czechoslovakia.

**1829** *Encycl. Metrop.* (1845) XX. 397/1 The Walachians ..multiply in Eastern as the Slovacs do in Western Hungary. **1842** *Penny Cycl.* XXII. 125/2 This literary movement was shared by the Slovaks of Hungary. **1887** *Encycl. Brit.* XXII. 153/2 For a long time the Slovaks employed Chekh in all their published writings.

**2.** The language or dialect spoken by this people.

**1862** LATHAM *Elem. Comp. Philol.* 628 The Slovak, with a minimum amount of literary culture. **1887** *Encycl. Brit.* XXII. 150/2 Slovenish exhibits an older form of Slavonic than Servian, just as Slovak is earlier than Bohemian.

**B.** *adj.* Of or belonging to the Slovaks, or their language; Slovakian.

**1887** *Encycl. Brit.* XXII. 153/2 The first Slovak grammar was published..at Presburg in 1790. **1905** *Contemp. Rev.* Apr. 584 The Slovak nation in Hungary numbers more than 2,000,000.

Hence **Slovakian** (sləʊ'vækɪən, formerly slə'veɪkɪən), *a.* and *sb.*; **Slovakish** (slə'veɪkɪʃ), *a.* and *sb.* (*obs.*).

**1829** *Encycl. Metrop.* (1845) XX. 397/1 The Russniacs.. mix but little with their Slovachian neighbours. *Ibid.*, The dialect spoken by the Slovachians. **1850** 'TALVI' *Hist. View Lang. Lit. Slavic Nations* III. i. 217 A voluminous Slovakish dictionary. *Ibid.* 219 Books written in Slovakish. **1881** *Encycl. Brit.* XII. 365 Hungarian was used in 7024 [schools],..Slovakian in 1901. **1883** *Nation* (N.Y.) XXXVI. 546 The annexation of the Slovakish territory of Hungary. **1883** MORFILL *Slavonic Lit.* i. 9 The dialect, Ugro-Slovenish.., shows some connexion with Slovakish.

**slovan** ('sləʊvən). *Mining.* [? Cornish.] The end or termination of an adit, lode, etc.

**1778** W. PRYCE *Min. Cornub.* 133 An open trench, like the tail or low slovan of an adit. **1886** J. W. ANDERSON *Prospector's Handbk.* 124 *Slovan*, the 'cropping out' of a lode or strata.

**slove**, obs. or dial. pa. t. of SLIVE *v.*

**sloven** ('slʌv(ə)n), *sb.* and *a.* Forms: 5 **sloveyn,** 6 **slovayne, sloueyne, slovein;** 6 **slouyn, -in, slovyn, slooven,** 6–7 **slouen,** 6– **sloven.** [Of doubtful origin; perh. an AF. formation on Flem. *sloef* dirty, squalid, shabby (see Kilian), or Du. *slof* careless, negligent.]

**A.** *sb.* †**1.** A person of low character or manners; a knave, rascal. *Obs.*

*c* **1450** *Cov. Myst.* xxiii. (Shaks. Soc.) 218 Com forth, thou sloveyn! com forthe, thou scolde! **1515** BARCLAY *Egloges* ii. (1570) B iij b, If thou one manchet dare handle or els touche, ..Then shall some slouen thee dashe on the eare. **1530** PALSGR. 271/2 Slovyn, a knave, a rybaude, *ribauldeau.* **1548** UDALL, etc. *Erasm. Par. Mark* iii. 29 He wandered up and downe with a sort of rascal slouens, and vile felowes folowing him at the heles. *c* **1680** *Delect. Hist. of Poor Robin* v, How poor Robin served one of his Companions a sloven's trick.

†**2.** A person of slothful or indolent habits or way of life; a lazy, idle fellow. *Obs.*

**1523** SKELTON *Garl. Laurel* 191 Some sluggyssh slouyns, that slepe day and nyght. **1530** PALSGR. 271/2 Sloven or luske, *bovcanier.* **1576** FLEMING *Panopl. Epist.* 355 Let vs abhorre to resemble that slouthfull slouen, who..differed nothing from a dead carkasse.

*attrib.* **1532** MORE *Confut. Tindale* Wks. 574/2 Not a litle child, but a great slouen slouche.

**3. a.** One who is careless or negligent in respect of dress, personal appearance, or cleanliness; an untidy or dirty person.

**1530** PALSGR. 424 Thou shalte be but a slovayne and thou were clothed in clothe of golde. **1553** T. WILSON *Rhet.* (1580) 164, I can call them by none other name but slovens, that maie have good geare, and neither can nor yet will once weare it clenly. **1621** BURTON *Anat. Mel.* I. ii. II. v. (1651) 83 Madrit,..a pleasant site; but the inhabitants are slovens, and the streets uncleanly kept. **1690** C. NESSE *Hist. & Myst. O. & N. Test.* I. 77 Good meat may be disowned for being dress'd up by some nasty sloven. **1700** T. BROWN tr. *Fresny's Amusem.* vii. Wks. 1709 III. I. 63 Marriage..often melts down a Beau into an errant Sloven. **1796** BURKE *Regicide Peace* Wks. II. 365 The committee for foreign affairs were such slovens, and stunk so abominably, that [etc.]. **1825** SIR J. BOWRING *Autobiog. Recoll.* (1877) 319 She came in—a dirty sloven, her hair tangled, a common cotton gown on. *c* **1850** MACAULAY *Biog.* (1860) 88 Being frequently under the necessity of wearing shabby coats,..he [Johnson] became a confirmed sloven.

†**b.** Used allusively in *Sloven's Hall, Inn, press. Obs.*

*c* **1515** *Cocke Lorell's B.* 5 Patrycke peuysshe, a conynge dyrte dauber, Worshypfull wardayn of slouens In. **1594** NASHE *Terrors of Night* Wks. (Grosart) III. 258 They haue beene layd vp in slouens presse, and with miscarriage and misgouernment are so fretted and galled [etc.]. **1600** —— *Summer's Last Will* 682 That pride is not my sinne, Slouens Hall where I was borne, by my record.

**4.** One who works, etc. in a careless, perfunctory, or slipshod manner; a writer who is careless in style or composition.

**1771** GOLDSM. *Haunch of Venison* 113 The baker..that negligent sloven Had shut out the pasty on shutting his oven. **1799** A. YOUNG *View Agric. Linc.* 138 There are some slovens remaining, who either hoe but little, or..execute it in a very insufficient manner. **1815** W. H. IRELAND *Scribbleomania* 24 He that in Blank-Verse a sloven can be, Must slur every flight of divine Poesy. **1846** LANDOR *Imag. Conv.* I. 224 It must be conceded that we moderns are but slovens in composition. **1884** J. PARKER *Apost. Life* II. 306 The painter who desires..to reach perfection will excel the sloven who never knew the compulsion of a pure ambition.

**5.** *Canad.* (See quots. 1895, 1941.) Also called ***sloven-wagon***.

**1895** *Dialect Notes* I. 381 *Sloven*, a low truck wagon. **1907** *Canad. Mag.* XXIX. 442/1 It is called a 'sloven-waggon' (doubtless for some good reason). **1941** H. MACLENNAN *Barometer Rising* 11 Grinding on the cobble-stones behind a pair of plunging Clydesdales came one of Halifax's most typical vehicles, a low-slung dray with a high driver's box, known as a sloven. **1964** *Atlantic Advocate* Aug. 79 As evening approached the horses were hitched to a long, low wagon, known in our country as a 'sloven', and the apples were hauled to the house.

**6.** *Forestry.* (See quot. 1957.)

**1946** F. SARGESON *That Summer* 175 The stumps still had the sloven sticking up. **1953** H. L. EDLIN *Forester's Handbk.* xiii. 201 Only when the crown of the tree strikes the ground will the last link be broken; the 'hinge' will then break, the tree pulling an irregular splinter of wood out of the stump below it. This splinter, or sloven, is then sawn off. **1957** *Brit. Commonwealth Forest Terminol.* II. 178 *Sloven*, the torn splintered portion of timber left on a stump or the end of a butt, where the key finally broke when the tree fell.

**B.** *adj.* Slovenly. Also *U.S.*, uncultivated; untrained.

**1815** *Sporting Mag.* XLVI. 54 This sloven way of touching the component parts of a landscape. **1821** CLARE *Vill. Minstr.* II. 73 In sloven garb appears each bawling boy. **1856** EMERSON *Eng. Traits, Stonehenge*, There, in that great sloven continent, in high Alleghany pastures,..still sleeps and murmurs..the great mother [Nature]. **1882–3** SCHAFF *Encycl. Relig. Knowl.* I. 156 The sloven imagination of people who received no religious instruction.

**sloven** (ˈslʌv(ə)n), *v. rare.* [f. SLOVEN *sb.*]

†**1.** *intr.* To be slothful or indolent. *Obs. rare.*

**1560** PILKINGTON *Aggeus* E viij b, Is it tyme for you to lye slouenyng in your couches night and day, and Gods house vnbuylded? *Ibid.* F iiij b, The sluggarde..is a slouen styll and lyes slouenynge in hys bed, takyng no paynes to doo good.

†**2.** *refl.* To dress in a slovenly or untidy manner. *Obs.*⁻¹

*a* **1591** H. SMITH *Serm.* (1622) 37 They care not how they slouen themselues, so their Wiues jet like Peacockes.

**3.** *trans.* To expend, to treat, in a slovenly or careless manner. *rare.*

**1824** C. WELLS *Joseph & Brethren* I. i, I cannot bear To see thy dotage sloven'd on a child. **1863** COWDEN CLARKE *Shaks. Char.* xix. 487 No one, I should think, would be so hardy as to maintain..that Shakespeare slovened his insignificant characters in order to throw his principals into high relief.

Hence ˈ**slovened** *ppl. a.*, done in a slovenly manner; †ˈ**slovening** *ppl. a.*, idle; indolent (*obs.*).

**1549** COVERDALE, etc. *Erasm. Par. Jude* II. 23 Doe not they sinne after like sorte, which being deluded with slouening dreames of false pleasures [etc.]. *Ibid., James* II. 38 Your golde and your siluer is marred with rust in the custody of a nygarde & slouening heyre. **1937** 'G. ORWELL' *Road to Wigan Pier* I. i. 17 It was not only the dirt.., but the feeling..of having got down into some subterranean place where people go creeping round and round..in an endless muddle of slovened jobs and mean grievances.

**Slovene** (ˈsləʊviːn, sləʊˈviːn), *sb.* and *a.* [a. G. *Slovene* (*Slowene*), pl. *Slovenen*, ad. Styrian, etc. *Slovenec*, pl. *Slovenci*; the name is a survival of the old native designation of the Slavs, which appears in OSlav. as *Slověne*, and is supposed to be derived from the stem of *slovo* word, *sloviti* to speak.]

**A.** *sb.* **1.** A member of the southern Slavonic group of peoples, dwelling in southern Austria and in Slovenia (formerly part of Austria, now a constituent republic of Yugoslavia); formerly also called *Wend* (WEND *sb.* 2).

**1883** MORFILL *Slavonic Lit.* x. 248 The Slovenes belong to the eastern..branch of the great Slavonic family. **1887** *Encycl. Brit.* XXII. 147/2 The Slovenes have preserved an old form of the family name.

**2.** The language of the Slovenes.

**1911** *Encycl. Brit.* XXV. 245/2 Except for a few 15th-century prayers and formulæ we do not find any more specimens of Slovene until the Reformation. **1960** O. MANNING *Great Fortune* III. 174 David smiled down modestly. 'My Slovene is a little rusty,' he said. **1972** W. B. LOCKWOOD *Panorama Indo-Europ. Lang.* ix. 161 Slovene is the official language of the Constituent Republic of Slovenia. **1980** *English World-Wide* I. 256 Of the remaining essays not involving English, most are on minority languages, such as..the individual cases of Slovene in Southern Austria.

**B.** *adj.* Slovenian; Slovenish.

**1902** *Q. Rev.* July 169 The equalisation, in all public offices, of the Czech and Slovene languages with the German.

**Slovenian** (sləʊˈviːnɪən), *a.* and *sb.* [f. prec. + -IAN.] **a.** *adj.* Belonging or pertaining to the Slovenes. **b.** *sb.* The language of the Slovenes. Also, a Slovene.

**1844** *Proc. Philol. Soc.* I. 273 The corresponding tense of the Slovenian dialect. **1862** LATHAM *Elem. Comp. Philol.* 628 The Illyrian or Slovenian of Carinthia and Carniola, closely akin to the western dialects of the Servian group. **1885** [see CROATIAN *sb.* and *a.*]. **1902** [see sense a above]. **1902** *Encycl. Brit.* XXVI. 16 Of late years attempts have been made to turn the Slovenian national movement into this direction, and to attract the Slovenians also towards the Orthodox non-Austrian Slavs. **1922** M. S. STANOYEVICH *Early Jugoslav Lit.* viii. 69 The works of Croatian and Slovenian authors..hardly contributed anything towards progress in linguistics science and literature. **1955** [see MACEDONIAN *sb.*[1] c]. **1960** O. MANNING *Great Fortune* I. 5 When they woke the next morning they were on the Slovenian plain. **1978** *Language* LIV. 451 The beginner thus has to look in the glossary if he wishes to ascertain whether the forms cited in these examples are younger or older Old Slavonic, Old Slovenian, or 15th-century Russian spellings.

**Slovenish** (sləʊˈviːnɪʃ), *a.*[1] and *sb.* [f. SLOVENE *sb.* + -ISH.] = SLOVENIAN *a.* and *sb.*

**1883** MORFILL *Slavonic Lit.* i. 8 The geographical extent of the territory over which..Slovenish and its dialects are spoken. *Ibid.* ii. 35 To this day..the name Windish is frequently given by the Germans to what would be more correctly called the Slovenish language.

ˈ**slovenish,** *a.*[2] *rare*⁻¹. [f. SLOVEN *sb.* + -ISH.] Of or pertaining to slovens.

**1648** J. BEAUMONT *Psyche* XII. clxxxvi, To be betray'd To slovenish Altars, and to clownish Rites, By fained Zeal's irreverent Deceits.

ˈ**slovenlike,** *a.* and *adv.* [f. SLOVEN *sb.*] = SLOVENLY *a.* and *adv.*

**1800** in *Spirit Public Jrnls.* IV. 252 To give myself a slovenlike appearance. **1821** SCOTT *Kenilw.* xxxviii, I will have a look into this letter, however, which he hath sealed so slovenlike.

**slovenliness** (ˈslʌv(ə)nlɪnɪs). [f. SLOVENLY *a.*] The quality or state of being slovenly or untidy; *esp.* habitual neglect or carelessness with regard to dress, personal appearance, or cleanliness.

**1611** COTGR., *Grobianisme*, grobianisme, slouenlinesse. **1617** MORYSON *Itin.* III. 46 Old Writers reproch..the Suevians with Slovenlinesse. **1651** HOBBES *Govt. & Soc.* x. §1. 148 Out of it, there is a Dominion of Passions, war, fear, poverty, slovinlinesse... In it, the Dominion of reason, peace, security, riches, decency. **1796** MORSE *Amer. Geogr.* II. 612 In eating, their slovenliness is shocking. **1837** LOCKHART *Scott* I. v. 147 He rallied Walter..on the slovenliness of his dress. **1882** MISS BRADDON *Mt. Royal* I. ii. 68 No slovenliness claiming to be excused as artistic disorder.

**b.** Carelessness or negligence in work, style, etc.; an instance of this.

**1641** BP. HALL *Def. Humble Remonstr.* §16 Whether the multitudes of Sects, and professed slovenlynesse in Gods service,..have not bin guilty of the increase of profanenesse amongst us. **1693** EVELYN *De la Quint. Compl. Gard.* II. 178 Negligence, Slovinglyness, &c. which we are to look upon as the Monsters of Kitchen Gardens. **1767** YOUNG *Farmer's Lett. to People* 291 Bad management..through slovenliness, idleness, or other obstructions to any profitable husbandry. *a* **1834** COLERIDGE *Table T.* (1836) 247 When he gets..into a sentence of five or six lines long, nothing can exceed the slovenliness of the English. **1884** *Spectator* 4 Oct. 1324/2 Certain inconsistencies of matter and slovenlinesses of manner which are of little consequence.

**slovenly** (ˈslʌv(ə)nlɪ), *a.* Also 6 slouin-, slouing-, 7 slovin-, 7–8 slovingly. [f. SLOVEN *sb.* + -LY[1].]

†**1.** Low, base, rascally; lewd. *Obs. rare.*

*a* **1515** *Cocke Lorell's B.* 3 Cocke dyde set them there as knaues sholde be, Amonge the slouenly sorte. **1579** GOSSON *Sch. Abuse* (Arb.) 40 Neither with Amorous gesture wounding the eye: nor with slouenly talke hurting the eares of the chast hearers.

**2.** Of persons:

**a.** Habitually or naturally careless in dress or personal appearance; untidy.

**1583** STUBBES *Anat. Abus.* II. (1882) 65 He that is borne vnder Capricornus shall be a slouenly, ill sauoured, and vncleane fellowe. **1617** MORYSON *Itin.* III. 44 The Germanes ..are..more slovenly in their apparrell, in their Stoves and all manner of linnen. **1682** S. PORDAGE *Medal Rev.* Ep. p. 3 The one being a much slovenlier Beast than the other. **1704** N. N. tr. *Boccalini's Advts. fr. Parnass.* II. 22 These Slovingly Fellows all over daub'd with Blood. **1822** W. IRVING *Braceb. Hall* xxii, A thin, elderly man, rather threadbare and slovenly. **1831** SCOTT *Castle Dang.* i, Do you suffer your youthful pupils to be indeed so slovenly and so saucy?

**b.** Careless or negligent in work of any kind.

**1781** COWPER *Table Talk* 682 Churchill.., Surly and slovenly, and bold and coarse, Too proud for art, and trusting in mere force. **1818** SCOTT *Hrt. Midl.* xxx, The ground was partly cultivated, and partly left in its natural state, according as the fancy of the slovenly agriculturists had decided. **1826** *Art of Brewing* (ed. 2) 29 Some slovenly and covetous brewers adopt the following dangerous and unfrugal practice.

**3.** Of dress, appearance, habits, etc.: Marked or characterized by untidiness or want of attention to neatness and cleanliness.

In older use occas., 'nasty, disgusting'.

*a* **1568** ASCHAM *Scholem.* (Arb.) 54 Yet som warlike signe must be vsed, either a slouinglie busking, or an ouerstaring frounced hed. **1602** MARSTON *Ant. & Mel.* Induct., As slovenly as the yeasty breast of an ale-knight. **1682** DRYDEN *Medal* 285 A heav'n, like Bedlam, slovenly and sad. **1784** COWPER *Task* II. 456 This..offends me more Than in a churchman slovenly neglect And rustic coarseness would. **1809** PINKNEY *Trav. France* 78 Railings..which are generally in a condition to give the country not only a naked but a slovenly appearance. **1834** *Brit. Husb.* I. 111 (L.U.K.), Although the common class of Irish farmers are generally accused of slovenly habits. **1861** GEO. ELIOT *Silas M.* 58 His person showed marks of habitual neglect; his dress was slovenly.

**4.** Marked or characterized by want of neatness, care, precision, or thoroughness. (Frequent with *manner* or *way*.)

**1621–3** MIDDLETON & ROWLEY *Changeling* II. ii, Hunger and pleasure, they'll command sometimes Slovenly dishes. **1693** DRYDEN *Ded. Juvenal* Ess. (Ker) II. 93 There is still a vast difference betwixt the slovenly butchering of a man, and the fineness of a stroke that separates the head from the body. **1774** BRYANT *Mythol.* I. 416 Inventing the most slovenly legend that ever was devised. **1777** MME. D'ARBLAY *Early Diary* July, You must suppose it spoke in a very slow and slovenly voice. **1804** *Med. Jrnl.* XII. 58 Many such proofs..shew great carelessness and the slovenly want of attention that seems so generally to prevail. **1819** SCOTT *Bl. Dwarf* ii, This slovenly and imperfect mode of cultivation left much time upon his own hands. **1875** WHITNEY *Life Lang.* viii. 148 Careless or slovenly handling of language.

**5.** *Comb.*, as ***slovenly-dressed, -minded*** adjs.

**1880** *Daily News* 26 Mar. 5/4 What Mr. Lowe would call a rather slovenly-minded person. **1886** W. J. TUCKER *E. Europe* 236 The 'cafetier'..was peremptorily addressing a sleek, slovenly-dressed waiter.

ˈ**slovenly,** *adv.* Also 7 slovingly. [f. SLOVEN *sb.* + -LY[2].] In a careless, negligent, or untidy manner.

**1576** FLEMING *Panopl. Epist.* 311 Let not your gowne sitt vppon your backe too nicely, nor yet weare it too slouenly. **1598** MARSTON *Sco. Villanie* I. ii. 177 Lewd Precisians Who ..take the symbole vp, As slouenly, as carelesse Courtiers slup Their mutton gruell. **1659** GAUDEN *Slight Healers* (1660) 77 They will heal their hurts very slovenly, slowly, and ill-favouredly. **1713** SWIFT *Frenzy of J. Denny* Wks. 1755 III. I. 139, I..hang my clothes on somewhat slovenly. **1796** MORSE *Amer. Geogr.* II. 614 The churches are full of pictures slovenly painted on parchment. **1870** ROCK *Text. Fabr.* Introd. II. 100 Every part was done in the feather-stitch, slovenly put down.

†ˈ**slovenness.** *Obs.* [f. SLOVEN *sb.* + -NESS.] Slovenliness.

**1630** *R. Johnson's Kingd. & Commw.* 88 The Gentlemen are proud of nothing but slovennesse, unbeseeming familiarity, and disorder. **1642** FULLER *Holy & Prof. St.* III. vi. 165 Yet 'tis more pardonable to be proud even of cleanly rags, then..of affected slovennesse. **1786** *New London Mag.* May 230 Sloth and slovenness are said to be often the cause of scurvy.

**slovenry** (ˈslʌv(ə)nrɪ). Also 6 sloovenry, 6–7 slovenrie. [f. SLOVEN *sb.* + -RY.] The quality or condition of being slovenly; neglect of neatness or cleanliness; slovenliness, carelessness, negligence.

Common *c* 1600–1650; now *rare*.

**1542** UDALL *Erasm. Apoph.* 74 Persones yt dooe glorie & braggue of their niggyshe sloovenry. **1586** HOOKER *Hist. Irel.* in *Holinshed* II. 86/2 The onelie meane..whereby hir husband his countrie was reclamed from sluttishnesse and slouenrie. **1648** J. BEAUMONT *Psyche* I. clxii, Never did Slovenry more misbecome Nor more confute its nasty self than here. **1681** RYCAUT tr. *Gracian's Critick* 198 It is a barbarous Slovenry after we have blown our Nose, to look on the Snot in our Handkerchief.

**1847** *Blackw. Mag.* LXII. 662 It has a little dash of slovenry. **1895** *Sotheran's Catal.* Jan. 11 This first edition of the two novels is curiously mis-titled through the publisher's slovenry.

**Slovincian** (slɒˈvɪnsɪən). Also **Slovintian, Slovinzian.** [f. F. *Slovince*, ad. G. *Slowinze*, f. Kashubian *Słovinsći* + -IAN.] An extinct dialect of Kashubian.

**1883** *Trans. Philol. Soc. 1880–1* 373 With regard to Baltic Slavonic, represented by its only surviving dialects, Slovintian and Cassubian, I shall treat it as an independent language. **1934, 1935** [see KASHUBE]. **1939** L. H. GRAY *Foundations of Lang.* 355 Polish (closely connected with Kashubian and Slovincian). **1965** G. Y. SHEVELOV *Prehist. Slavic* i. 1 Slovincian was still extant in the early twentieth century in the district of Slupsk, now in north-western Poland. **1972** W. B. LOCKWOOD *Panorama Indo-Europ. Lang.* 158 Due west of the present Kashubian area lies the district of Slupsk (Stolp), where autochthonous Slavonic survived until the end of the last century, when it was entirely supplanted by German; here the dialects were locally termed Slovinzian. **1974** [see POMERANIAN *a.*].

**slow** (sləʊ), *sb.* Also 1 slawa, 4–5 slowe. [f. SLOW *a.* or *v.*]

In the *Rom. Rose* 4751 it is very doubtful whether *a slowe* can be taken to mean 'a moth'; it is more probable that it is due to some misunderstanding or misreading. In *Leg. Holy Rood* (1871) 214 the sense of *with-oute slow* is not clear, perh. 'without delay'.

**1.** A slow or slow-going person; a sluggard.

*c* **897** K. ÆLFRED tr. *Gregory's Past. C.* xxviii. 190 Ðu slawa, ga ðe to æmethylle. **1382** WYCLIF *Prov.* xx. 4 For cold the slowe wolde not eren. *Ibid.* xxiv. 33 Hou longe, slowe, thou slepist? *c* **1450** in *MS. Douce* 52 lf. 21 Lothe to bedde and lothe fro bedde, men schall know þe slow. **1861** PYCROFT *Agony Point* (1862) 191 Only one year before, he would have numbered with 'the old fogies' and the slows.

**2. a.** A slow-paced horse.

**1826** *Sporting Mag.* XVIII. 213 Our 'slows' are certainly quicker than most of that genus whom I have observed in other countries. **1832** SIR G. C. LEWIS *Lett.* 17 Lest Gilbert should think that the Hereford horses have a monopoly of the slows.

**b.** A slow train.

**1956** *Railway Mag.* Mar. 163/2 There is a daily slow, stopping at all stations between Damascus and Deraa. **1976** P. LOVESEY *Swing, swing Together* xiii. 55 We can take a train... We can catch a slow to Oxford.

**c.** A slow tune in popular music.

**1956** B. BURNS in S. Traill *Play that Music* ii. 34 His style is hot and aggressive—pushing the beat in fast numbers and rhapsodic in slows. **1977** J. WAINWRIGHT *Do Nothin' till you hear from Me* xi. 184 In that set of standard slows, this ten-piece [band] of mine was like Ellington's piano.

**3.** *Cricket.* **a.** A slowly-bowled ball. **b.** A slow bowler.

**1854** F. LILLYWHITE *Guide to Cricketers* 84 [He] is a good bat, and can bowl 'slows' well. **1862** *Sporting Life* 14 June, Some of the slows seemed to puzzle him sorely. **1881** *Standard* 14 June 3/8 This was due to the condition of the wicket, on which the fast bowling bumped and the slows popped about a great deal. **1895** *Strand Mag.* Aug. 141, I have met some capital bowlers in the past. I should class them in two sections, the slows..and the fasts.

**4. a.** *pl.* (See quot.) *U.S.*

**1855** DUNGLISON *Med. Lex.* (ed. 12) 564/1 *Milk Sickness*, Sick stomach, Swamp sickness, Tires, Slows... A disease occasionally observed in..Alabama, Indiana, and Kentucky, which affects both man and cattle, but chiefly the latter. *Ibid.* 792/2 *Slows*, Milk-sickness.

**b.** ***the slows*** (colloq.), an imaginary disease or ailment accounting for slowness.

**1843** *Ainsworth's Mag.* IV. 124 If somewhat troubled with 'the slows', not a hound but was as true as the sun. **1843** J. C. SHAIRP *Let.* 25 Sept. in W. A. Knight *Principal Shairp* (1888) vi. 71 This..makes good my summer's work. 'The Slows' are my bane, but I must be courageous and face what remains... If I could but secure a *second*, I should be happy. **1927** *Daily Express* 13 Dec. 16/2 Rimell's mare, How Nice, had a fit of the slows, for she was always in the next division from start to finish. **1970** D. FRANCIS *Rat Race* viii. 102 They might as well send him [*sc.* a racehorse] to the knackers. Got the slows right and proper, that one has.

**5.** [f. the vb.] ***slow-up***, an act or instance of slowing a train, etc. See also SLOW-DOWN.

**1891** *Cent. Dict.*, *Slow-up*, the act of slackening speed. **1899** *Westm. Gaz.* 25 Aug. 4/1 Including two slow-ups, an average speed of 50.9 sec. per mile was maintained.

**slow**, obs. variant of SLOUGH *sb.*[1]

**slow** (sləʊ), *a.* Forms: α. (Chiefly *north.* and *Sc.*) 1, 3– **slaw**, 1, 4–6 **slawe**, 3, 6 **slau**, 9 **sla**. β. 2– **slow** (5 sclow), 4–6 **slowe**, 3–4, 7 **slou**; 6 **slo**, **sloo**. γ. 3 **slovȝ**, 3–4 **slouȝ**, 4 **slouȝe**, 5 **slowȝ**, **slough(e**; 4 **slouh**, 4–5 **slowh**, 5 **sclowh**; 4 **sloȝ**, **sloghe**. [Common Teutonic: OE. *sláw* (:—OTeut. *slaiwaz*), = MDu. and Du. *sleeuw*, *slee*, OS. *sleu* (MLG. and LG. *slê*), OHG. *slêo* (MHG. *slê*, *slêw-*, G. dial *schleh*, *schlehe*), ON. *slǽr*, *sljár*, *sljór* (Norw. *sljo*, *sljø*, etc.; Sw. *slö*, Da. *sløv*), blunt, dull, etc. The stem is perh. the same as in L. *lævus*, Gr. λαιός left.]

**I. 1.** Not quick or clever in apprehending or understanding a thing; obtuse, dull: **a.** Of persons. Also with *in* or *of*.

*c* **888** K. ÆLFRED *Boeth.* xxxvii. §4 þone sænan þe bið swa slaw [L. *stupidus*] þu scealt hatan assa ma þonne man. **1387** TREVISA *Higden* (Rolls) V. 255 (MS. γ), Constatyn..was slouȝ and dol of wyt. *c* **1475** *Promp. Parv.* (K.), Slaw, dulle of wyt, *ebes.* **1611** COTGR., *Pucelle nicette*, a slow, dull, simple, foolish, or nice girle. **1825** SCOTT *Betrothed* xiii, My nephew..hath a fancy like a minstrel. Myself am but slow in imagining such devices. **1858** DICKENS *Lett.* (1880) II. 73, I thought them a dull and slow audience. **1875** JOWETT *Plato* (ed. 2) III. 228, I am slow of understanding.

**b.** Of the mind, etc.

*a* **1100** *Ags. Hymns* (Surtees) 37 Mod..ðæt slawe, *Mens..torpida.* **1398** TREVISA *Barth. De P.R.* v. xii. (Bodl. MS.), It is a token of dulnes and of slowe witte and vndirstonding. **1422** tr. *Secreta Secret., Priv. Priv.* 231 Tho that..haue moisti flesh and lytill hette, bene..of slow vndyrstondynge. **1651** HOBBES *Leviath.* I. viii. 32 A slow Imagination maketh that Defect..which is commonly called Dulnesse. **1727** BOYER *Dict. Royal* II, A slow (heavy or dull) Wit, *un Esprit lent ou pesant.* **1849** MACAULAY *Hist. Eng.* vi. II. 11 Such reasoning had no effect on the slow understanding and immperious temper of James.

**2. a.** Naturally disinclined to be active or to exert oneself; constitutionally inert or sluggish; lacking in promptness or energy.

α. *c* **897** [see sense 15]. *c* **1000** *Ags. Gosp.* Matt. xxv. 26 þu yfela ðeow & slawa. *a* **1023** WULFSTAN *Hom.* (1883) 72 Se ðe wære full slaw, weorðe se unslaw. *c* **1200** *Trin. Coll. Hom.* 183 To gode þu ware slau and let, and to euele spac and hwat. *c* **1425** *Castle Persev.* 1033 in *Macro Plays*, He is provd, wrathful, & Envyous; Glotons, slaw, & lecherous. **1483** *Cath. Angl.* 343/1 To be Slawe,..*pigrare, pigrescere.* **1533** BELLENDEN *Livy* I. xii. (S.T.S.) I. 74 þai held þe king of Romanis for ane slaw and effemynate prince. *c* **1600** MONTGOMERIE *Cherrie & Slae* 943 Nothing he saw In age, but anger, slack and slaw.

β. *c* **1200** *Trin. Coll. Hom.* 7 Longe we habben lein on ure fule synnes..alse slou man doð on swete slape. *c* **1250** *Ten Abuses* 5 in *O.E. Misc.* 184 Proest þat is wilde, Bischop slou. *a* **1310** in Wright *Lyric P.* xxxix. 110 He is the sloweste mon that ever wes y-boren. **1388** WYCLIF *Prov.* xx. 4 A slow man nolde ere for coold; therfor he schal begge in somer. *c* **1440** *Gesta Rom.* lvi. 239 (Harl. MS.), He that is the sloweste of yow, or most slewthe is in, shall have my kyngdom aftir my discese. **1538** STARKEY *England* I. iii. 79 Lyke as in a dropcy the body ys vnweldy, vnlusty, and slo, no thyng quyke to moue. **1588** SHAKS. *L.L.L.* III. i. 60 Is not Lead a mettall heauie, dull, and slow? **1824** [see SLOWISH *a.*]. **1831** *Society* I. 321 A clever hint to show slow personages what is expected from them.

γ. *a* **1225** *Ancr. R.* 258 Hwo mei beon, uor scheome, slummi & sluggi & slouh, þet bihalt hwu swuðe bisi ure Louerd was on eorðe? *c* **1290** *S. Eng. Leg.* I. 319 Ho-so hath of þe watere mest, he schal beo..gret slepare and slovȝ þar-to. *c* **1386** CHAUCER *Melib.* ¶51 (Corpus MS.), And he þat is ydel & slowh, can neuer fynde couenable tyme for to doon his profyte.

**b.** Characterized by, of the nature of, sloth or sluggishness.

*c* **1384** CHAUCER *H. Fame* III. 1778 Ye maisty Swyne, ye ydel wrechhes, Ful of roten, slowe techches. **1390** GOWER *Conf.* II. 92 Ther ben othre vices slowe, Whiche unto love don gret lette. *a* **1586** SIDNEY *Astr. & Stella* Sonn. xcvi, Slow heauinesse in both holds one degree.

**c.** Having a dull edge; blunt. Now *dial.*

This sense is prominent in the cognate languages.

*c* **1440** *Promp. Parv.* 458/1 Slaw, or dul of egge, *ebes, obtusus.* *a* **1904** in *Eng. Dial. Dict.* s.v., T' knife is slow.

**d.** *Med.* Torpid; sluggish.

**1896** *Daily News* 26 May 6/4 In the case of one's having a slow liver..the jerking might, perhaps, be of some service. **1899** *Allbutt's Syst. Med.* VII. 259 Producing a high blood-pressure..and a slow heart.

**3. a.** Not quick, ready, prompt, or willing *to* do something.

*c* **1200** ORMIN 9885 Stunnt & stidiȝ, dill & slaw To sekenn sawless seollþe. **1297** R. GLOUC. (Rolls) 9327 He is..Slou to fiȝte & quic to fle, & þat nis no manhede. *c* **1340** HAMPOLE *Pr. Consc.* 188 To listen and lere þai er ful slaw. **1390** GOWER *Conf.* III. 110 He schal be..slouh and lustles to travaile In thing which elles myhte availe. **1565** COOPER *Thesaurus* s.v. *Piger*, Slow to write: loth to take the paynes to write. **1592** SHAKS. *Rom. & Jul.* IV. i. 3, I am nothing slow to slack his hast. **1697** DRYDEN *Virg. Past.* I. 37 Freedom..came at length, tho' slow to come. **1781** COWPER *To Protestant Lady* 20 How slow to learn the dictates of his love. **1815** SCOTT *Guy M.* xxi, As some have not been slow to tell their lords. **1885** *Manch. Exam.* 15 May 5/3 They will not be slow to return him like for like.

**b.** With *in*.

**1382** WYCLIF *Rom.* xii. 11 Not slow in bisynesse, feruent in spirit. **1432–50** tr. *Higden* (Rolls) III. 151 When the peple was slawe þer in [etc.]. **1526** *Pilgr. Perf.* (W. de W. 1531) 158 Not slowe in commynge therto, nor sluggysshe therin. **1594** KYD *Cornelia* I. 166 The wrath of heauen..is slow In punishing the euils we haue done. **1736** AINSWORTH *Lat. Dict.* I. s.v., He is naturally slow in speech, and very dull. **1831** SCOTT *Ct. Rob.* iv, These men, quick in malice, though slow in perilous service. **1866** G. MACDONALD *Ann. Q. Neighb.* xxx. (1878) 517 The people were very slow in dispersing.

**c.** With *of*.

**1382** WYCLIF *Luke* xxiv. 25 A! foolis, and slowe of herte for to bileue. **1555** HARPESFELD in Bonner *Hom.* 30 b, Fooles and sloo of belefe. **1590** SHAKS. *Mids. N.* I. ii. 69 Pray you.., giue it me, for I am slow of studie. **1611** BIBLE *Exod.* iv. 10, I am slow of speach, and of a slow tongue. **1730** BAILEY (fol.), *Tardiloquious*, slow of Speech.

**4.** Tardy or dilatory in action; displaying a lack of promptitude or energy under particular circumstances; spending a comparatively long time in the performance of some act; doing something in a slow or deliberate manner. ***slow learner***: spec. in *Educ.* (see quot. 1981).

*c* **1340** HAMPOLE *Pr. Consc.* 1464 Now er we smert, now er we slawe. **1387** TREVISA *Higden* (Rolls) III. 149 But þe peple was slowȝ, and þerfore Daniel prayed to God þat [etc.]. ? *a* **1400** *Arthur* 365 He was not sclowh, But to þe hulle hym drowh. **1482** *Cely Papers* (Camden) 128 Hyt wyllbe whel done for goude detturs ar sclow payars. **1533** BELLENDEN *Livy* IV. xii. (S.T.S.) II. 90 3e ar full of mynassing in tyme of pece, and richt slaw in tyme of batall. **1596** DALRYMPLE tr. *Leslie's Hist. Scot.* II. 451 Quhen he tariet lang in Paris, and in cuming furth was ouer slawe. **1648** MILTON *Ps.* lxxxv. 55 Then will he come, and not be slow; His footsteps cannot err. **1697** DRYDEN *Virg. Georg.* III. 736 The Victim Ox..Sunk of himself,..Preventing the slow Sacrificer's Hand. *a* **1722** SIR J. LAUDER *Decis.* (1759) I. 14 Ordinarily Mr. Gideon was in the rear of all their [witches'] dances, and beat up those that were slow. **1784** COWPER *Task* III. 505 Experience, slow preceptress, teaching oft The way to glory by miscarriage foul. **1822** LAMB *Elia* II. *Thoughts on Bks. & Reading*, Seldom-readers are slow readers. **1833** NYREN *Yng. Cricketer's Man.* (1902) 122 He was a slow bowler, and a pretty good one. **1938** *High Points* Apr. 33/1 The problem of the slow learner continues to grow involved as increased numbers flow into high school. **1945** 'O. MALET' *My Bird Sings* II. ii. 121 Your sister does not benefit so swiftly by her education... She is a slow learner. **1946** P. BOTTOME *Lifeline* xvi. 144 She wanted everything... I'm exactly the opposite in love. I'm a slow starter. I want little. **1963** *Times* 25 May 9/4 Here is comfort for the slow-starter who begins at the bottom. **1975** *Times* 26 Apr. 7/4, I was 24 and I'd run away from home... I was kind of a slow starter. **1977** *Wandsworth Borough News* 7 Oct. 28/2 (Advt.), Tutorials: 'A' and 'O' level, most subjects; public examinations; slow learners welcome. **1981** D. ROWNTREE *Dict. Education* 286 *Slow learner.* A term often used rather loosely of any child whose attainments have always fallen noticeably behind those of other children of the same age, without any implication as to what might be thought to be the cause..or whether the child might be enabled to speed up or catch up. Sometimes, however, the term is used to indicate children who are not only expected to remain slow learners but also to be unable ever to learn as much as others. Some people would even restrict the term to pupils who are educationally subnormal.

**5. a.** Not readily stirred or moved *to* something (esp. anger, revenge, etc.); not too ready, willing, or susceptible. Also with infin.

**1382** WYCLIF *James* i. 19 Slowe to wraththe. **1422** tr. *Secreta Secret., Priv. Priv.* I. xxix. 189 Be ryghtfull to al men, Slow to be wroth, Redy to mercy. **1567** *Gude & Godlie Ball.* 115 Mercyfull is he, Slaw to reuenge, and to forgiue reddie. **1593** NASHE *Christ's T.* (1613) 166 There is a certaine kind of good sloth, as to be slowe to anger, slowe to iudgement, slowe to reuenge. *c* **1600** SHAKS. *Sonn.* xciv, Vnmooued, could, and to temptation slow. **1648** MILTON *Ps.* lxxxvi. 55 Thou Lord art..Slow to be angry. **1784** COWPER *Task* VI. 547 Heav'n, tho' slow to wrath, Is never with impunity defied. **1866** G. MACDONALD *Ann. Q. Neighb.* xii. (1878) 234 A clergyman of all men should be slow to take offence.

**b.** Without const., or with *in*.

**1639** S. DU VERGER tr. *Camus' Admir. Events* 55 So is it with slow, heavy, and timorous humors, they must have time to increase their choller. **1818** SCOTT *Br. Lamm.* xxix, We know that maiden's ears must be slow in receiving a gentleman's language.

**c.** Inattentive *to* something.

**1667** MILTON *P.L.* III. 193 To prayer, repentance, and obedience due,..Mine eare shall not be slow. **1746** FRANCIS tr. *Horace, Art Poet.* 236 Rough to Reproof, and slow to future Cares.

**6. a.** Of things, actions, etc.: Marked or characterized by slowness or tardiness. Of music: solemn, tragic. ***slow handclap***: see HANDCLAP c.

*c* **1290** *S. Eng. Leg.* I. 319 Ho-so hath of þe eorþe mest, he is..Of slouȝ wreche and Aruȝ mouth. **1382** WYCLIF *Exod.* iv. 10, Y am of more latsum and of more slow tonge. **1390** GOWER *Conf.* II. 44 Al hire mod was overtorned, Which ferst sche hadde of slow manere. **1430–40** LYDG. *Bochas* I. xiii. (1554) 23 Slowe credence Hath in some be founde full noyous. **1535** COVERDALE *Exod.* iv. 10 For I haue a slowe speach, & a slowe tunge. **1593** SHAKS. *3 Hen. VI*, IV. viii. 40, I haue not..posted off their suites with slow delayes. **1611** —— *Cymb.* I. i. 64 That..the search [should be] so slow That could not trace them. **1681** DRYDEN *Abs. & Achit.* 697 Few words he said, but..those..More slow than Hybla drops, and far more sweet. **1754** GRAY *Poesy* 36 Slow melting strains their Queen's approach declare. **1781** COWPER *Charity* 471 With slow deliberation he unties His glitt'ring purse. **1797** GODWIN *Enquirer* II. xii. 462 The style ..of *Tom Jones*..is feeble, costive, and slow. **1810** CRABBE *Borough* xix. 3 The like slow speech was his. **1814** BYRON *Corsair* Ep. Ded., The stanza of Spenser is perhaps too slow and dignified for narrative. **1826** F. REYNOLDS *Life & Times* II. 144 The curtain to the new piece having risen, the heroine entered to slow music. **1884** *Encycl. Brit.* XVII. 96 The first movement..is succeeded generally by one in a slow tempo. **1895** *World* 4 Dec. 27/1, I could see the conductor of the orchestra waiting eagerly for the word 'mother'—the cue for the slow music—and I was, oh! so thankful when it came. **1926** G. B. SHAW *Translations & Tomfooleries* 78 You were not found..with the limelight streaming on your white face, and the band playing slow music.

**b.** *Med.* Of the pulse: Below the average rapidity.

**1728** CHAMBERS *Cycl.* s.v. *Pulse*, A slow Pulse denotes.. That the Contractions of the Heart are slow. **1818–20** E. THOMPSON tr. *Cullen's Nosologia* 214 First with lassitude,.. afterwards with slow pulse. **1899** *Allbutt's Syst. Med.* VII. 635 A slow pulse, slowness of cerebration.

**c.** Of trade, business, etc.: Slack; not brisk.

**1887** *Daily News* 7 Feb. 2/5 Good sound samples not plentiful,..and the trade slow all round. **1903** *Times* 1 Dec. 35 Business in flannel was slow.

**7. a.** Of a fire: That burns gently or slowly; gentle. Also *transf.* of heat.

**1604** E. G[RIMSTONE] *D'Acosta's Hist. Indies* II. vii. 96 Gold and silver, which wee refine with quicke-silver, the fire being small and slow. **1662** J. DAVIES tr. *Olearius' Voy. Amb.* 64 Being rather a moderate slow heat than an excessive scorching. **1769** MRS. RAFFALD *Eng. Housekpr.* (1778) 26 Let it stew on a slow fire. **1811** A. T. THOMSON *Lond. Disp.* (1818) 670 Distilling the charge..by a slow and gradually increased heat. **1840** R. H. DANA *Bef. Mast* xxix. 98 We.. made a slow fire of charcoal, birch bark, brimstone, and other matters.

*fig.* **1893** *Outing* XXII. 118/1 The slow-fire of restlessness, doubt and curiosity.

**b.** Of an oven: of such a temperature that it cooks slowly.

**1747** H. GLASSE *Art of Cookery* ix. 113 Bake it in a slow oven, with crust as above. **1846** A. SOYER *Gastronomic Regenerator* 571 Place them in a slow oven to bake. **1917** F. KLICKMANN *Between Larch-Woods & Weir* xiii. 242 She had told Dick to put the patties into a slow oven for ten or twelve minutes before eating. **1973** *Times* 1 Dec. 11 Place the casserole in a slow oven.

**c.** ***slow burn*** fig.: (*a*) (see BURN *sb.*[3] 1 d); (*b*) *Theatr.*, delayed response or slow reaction to a joke; also *attrib.*

**1975** *Daily Tel.* 10 Feb. 12 For some of her jokes in public Margaret Thatcher relies..on what professional comedians call the 'slow burn'. **1975** D. LODGE *Changing Places* i. 22 The realization..strikes him, like a slow-burn gag in a movie-comedy.

**8.** *colloq.* **a.** Slow-going; behind the times; out of fashion; not smart or up-to-date.

**1827** *Sporting Mag.* XXI. 29 Long courtships are stupid things, and voted slow. **1842** C. J. APPERLEY *Life Sportsman* ii, John Hawkes and myself always ride in leathers, though people say 'it looks slow'. **1857** HUGHES *Tom Brown* I. iv, Slow place, sir; slow place; off the main road.

**b.** Dull or tedious in character; tiresome; apt to bore one.

**1841** LEVER *C. O'Malley* xxix, How very slow, all this! thought I. **1848** *Punch* XV. 19 All books are slow,..all domestic, all quiet enjoyments are slow. **1887** SMILES *Life & Labour* 332 It must..be admitted that angling is a very 'slow' amusement to persons of active habits.

**c.** Of persons: Having no briskness or animation; dull, lifeless, insipid; humdrum.

**1841** LEVER *C. O'Malley* xxix, Slow fellows, like them, must find any place stupid. **1849** ALB. SMITH *Pottleton Legacy* (1854) 281 He was a good creature, but too 'slow'.

**d.** ***slow poke, slowpoke*** (colloq., chiefly *U.S.*) = SLOW-COACH; also *attrib.* or as *adj.*, slow, idle. Cf. POKE *sb.*[3] 3.

**1848** BARTLETT *Dict. Americanisms* 255 'What a slow *poke* you are!' A woman's word. **1877** F. ROSS et al. *Gloss. Words used in Holderness* 128/2 *Slaw-pooak*.., a dunce; a driveller. **1920** G. ADE *Hand-Made Fables* 226 He placed the Experiences of an ordinary slow-poke year into one Week. **1935** J. T. FARRELL *Judgment Day* xvi. 367 Slackers, slow-pokes, easy-going, unambitious fellows, I neither want, nor can tolerate. **1959** *Guardian* 31 Aug. 2/3 'Slowpokes'—unnecessarily slow drivers—cause other road users to take additional risks. **1971** W. H. MCNEILL in A. Bullock *Twentieth Century* 54/1 What could a slow-poke airplane do against intercontinental missiles? **1981** S. RUSHDIE *Midnight's Children* I. 112 Come on, slowpoke, you don't want to be late.

**II. 9. a.** Taking or requiring a comparatively long time; tardy in progress, growth, etc.; very gradual. ***slow pass***: spec. in *Bridge* (see quot. 1934); ***slow-scan*** (Television), scanning at a much slower rate than in ordinary television, so that the resulting signal has a much smaller bandwidth and can be transmitted more cheaply; usu. *attrib.*

*c* **1230** *Hali Meid.* 37 His waxunge se lat, & se slaw his þrifti. **1565** COOPER *Thesaurus, Exitus segnis*, slow death. **1574** W. BOURNE *Regiment for Sea* xxii. (1577) 60 These markes be very yare..: and those markes very slowe and asketh some distance in sayling. **1604** SHAKS. *Ham.* I. ii. 58 (Q²), Hath my Lord wroung from me my slowe leaue. **1667** MILTON *P.L.* x. 692 These changes in the Heav'ns, though slow, produc'd Like change on Sea and Land. **1781** GIBBON *Decl. & F.* xix. (1787) II. 156 He had recourse to the slower but more certain operations of a regular siege. **1816** SCOTT *Old Mort.* xxxii, The bridge was long and narrow, which rendered the manœuvre slow as well as dangerous. **1859** DARWIN *Orig. Spec.* iv. (1860) 108 Variation.. is apparently always a very slow process. **1876** J. PARKER *Paraclete* I. x. 154 Intellectual illumination is sudden, but intellectual education is always slow. **1934** *Amer. Speech* IX. 11/1 A *slow pass* is a pass preceded by a long period of thought, and since it conveys the impression that some strength is held without paying the regular price of a bid, is regarded as unethical. **1955** *Sun* (Baltimore) (B ed.) 7 Dec. 3/4 The so-called slow-scan system paints a picture every two seconds and requires only 8,000 cycles. *Ibid.* 3/5 Slow scan cannot handle objects in motion. **1960** *Guardian* 20 Apr. 4/1 The National Broadcasting Company will show short excerpts to American audiences at breakfast-time by using the 'slowscan' process and transmitting film by cable to Montreal. **1970** N. ARMSTRONG et al. *First on Moon* v. 110 TV was tried on Gordon Cooper's Mercury flight, using a slow-scan black and white camera. **1973** *Times* 2 June 10/6 It was agreed when North South protested the score that East's pass over Three Spades was a 'slow pass'. **1975** D. G. FINK *Electronics Engineers' Handbk.* xi. 62 Slow-scan tubes are useful for remotely located cameras requiring a data link to the monitor wherein the band-width reduction significantly lowers the data-link cost.

**b.** With various complements implied, as (slow) in growing, coming in, rising, going off, etc. ***slow bell*** (*Naut.*, *N. Amer.*), a bell signalling that a ship should proceed slowly; chiefly in prepositional phrases, at a reduced speed; also *fig.*; ***slow puncture***, a puncture from which the air escapes gradually.

**1594** SHAKS. *Rich. III*, II. iv. 15, I would not grow so fast, Because sweet Flowres are slow, and Weeds make hast. **1775** DE LOLME *Eng. Const.* Advt. p. xiii, These profits I indeed thought to be but scanty and slow. **1798** LANDOR *Gebir* III. 251 Some Sowed the slow olive for a race unborn. **1857** EMERSON *Poems* 67 Slow structures, stone by stone, Built in an age. **1861** DICKENS *Uncomm. Trav.* iv, Held out at arm's length at frequent intervals and soundingly slapped, like a slow lot at a sale. **1901** *Daily Colonist* (Victoria, B.C.) 5 Nov. 3/2 Early in the evening she [*sc.* S.S. City of Seattle] had run among a number of small icebergs and she was coming down the channel under a slow bell. **1944** *Amer. Speech* XIX. 108 Another of the best [phrases], used especially in declining a drink or an extra job of work, is 'Not me, thanks; *I'm taking it on the slow bell*.' **1946** *Seafarers' Log* 19 Apr. 3/4 There will be no slow bell on the organizing drive. **1958** *Wall St. Jrnl.* 17 Dec. 26/2 We were at slow-bell for much of '58 because of the recession. **1958** E. NEWBY *Short Walk in Hindu Kush* xviii. 217 Our airbeds had slow punctures and the ground was hard. **1968** C. P. BRACKEN *Roman Ring* xv. 147 He had left the Fiat at a garage outside Rome to have a slow puncture repaired. **1974** A. MORICE *Death of Heavenly Twin* xii. 124 I've got a flat tyre. It's probably a slow puncture.

**10. a.** Of fevers, etc.: Not rapidly developing into a serious form; not acute.

*c* **1290** *S. Eng. Leg.* I. 76 A slouȝ feuere him cam on, þat ne nam him nouȝt ful strongue. **1596** DALRYMPLE tr. *Leslie's Hist. Scot.* I. 5 That sair seiknes..cam nevir till ws, nochtthelesse, continual caldes, albeit slawe. **1725** N. ROBINSON *Th. Physick* 291 Of the Cure of slow Fevers, attended with Hectic Heats. **1776** GIBBON *Decl. & F.* xiii. (1782) I. 467 He soon contracted a slow illness. **1822–7** GOOD *Study Med.* (1829) II. 237 The first variety..has.. been commonly distinguished by the name of low or slow nervous fever. **1897** *Allbutt's Syst. Med.* III. 82 A dull slow swelling appears in the menaced joints.

**b.** Not rapid in operation or effect.

**1611** SHAKS. *Cymb.* I. v. 10 These most poysonous Compounds, Which are the moouers of a languishing death: But though slow, deadly. **1794** MRS. RADCLIFFE *Myst. Udolpho* lv, A slow poison was administered. **1796** BURKE *Corr.* (1844) IV. 401 The work will be new, and slow in its operation, but it is certain in its effect. **1867** BLOXAM *Chem.* 418 Touch-paper or slow port-fire, which consists of paper soaked in a weak solution of saltpetre and dried.

**c.** *Photogr.* Of a plate, etc.: That takes or receives impressions with comparative slowness; not quickly affected by light, and therefore requiring a longer exposure. Also of other photographic items: necessitating longer exposures (e.g., in the case of a lens, because its aperture is small).

**1889** *Anthony's Photogr. Bulletin* II. 161 With a slow plate it is better..to leave the trees alone. **1890** ABNEY *Photogr.* (ed. 6) 125 Plates prepared with it are slow and give thin images. **1902** *Encycl. Brit.* XXXI. 695/1 Owing to the small working aperture it [*sc.* a lens] seems slow, but it is not so for the definition and flatness of field obtained. **1915** D. GRANT *Manual of Photogr.* 74 'Slow' papers give plucky results from flat negatives. **1957** E. S. BOMBACK *Photogr. in Colour* x. 107 The use of slow contact printing paper..may result in negative or partially negative images in the print. **1973** *Sci. Amer.* Dec. 39/3 Telescopes such as the 100-inch reflector on Mount Wilson, which has a focal ratio of *f*/5, are quite 'slow', that is, they require long exposure times.

**d.** *Med.* ***slow (virus) disease*** or ***infection***, any of various progressive diseases caused by a virus or virus-like organism that multiplies slowly in the host organism and having incubation periods of months or years; hence (by a false analysis) ***slow virus***.

**1954** B. SIGURDSSON in *Brit. Vet. Jrnl.* CX. 350 If the word chronic is taken to mean not only protracted, but also something which lingers on, has an irregular and unpredictable course and may end in any one of several different ways, then the expression should not be used about the diseases I have discussed here; these infections should perhaps rather be called *slow* infections. *Ibid.* 352 It seems as if an important group of slow virus infections is gradually coming to light. **1967** *New England Jrnl. Med.* CCLXXVI. 392/1 (*heading*) Slow-virus infections of the nervous system. **1971** *Jrnl. Virol.* VII. 301 Progressive pneumonia virus, the causative agent of slow, pulmonary disease of Montana sheep, was shown to be antigenically related to two other slow viruses of sheep, visna and maedi. **1976** R. H. KIMBERLIN *Slow Virus Diseases of Animals & Man* i. 5 One major distinguishing feature of slow diseases..was this: once clinical signs of disease have appeared the disease then follows a regular progressive course which always ends in serious illness and usually death. **1977** *Sci. Amer.* May 140/2 A dozen fatal diseases of the human central nervous system stand suspect of slow-virus origin.

**11. a.** Of time: Passing slowly or heavily. Also *transf.* of a dial.

**1565** COOPER *Thesaurus, Anni segnes*, slow yeres passyng away in idlenesse. **1593** SHAKS. *Rich. II*, I. iii. 150 The slye slow houres shall not determinate The datelesse limit of thy deere exile. **1611** SIR W. MURE *Misc. Poems* Wks. (S.T.S.) I. 17 The too slou day To steil away. **1792** S. ROGERS *Pleas. Mem.* I. 102 When the slow dial gave a pause to care. **1818** SHELLEY *Julian* 489 As slow years pass, a funereal train. **1842** [see HOUR 2].

**b.** ***slow time***, a rate of marching in which only 75 paces, of 30 inches each, are taken in a minute.

**1802** in JAMES *Milit. Dict.* **1837** CARLYLE *Fr. Rev.* II. I. xii, There is wheeling and sweeping, to slow, to quick and double-quick time. **1876** VOYLE & STEVENSON *Milit. Dict.* 390/1 The instruction given in manual and firing exercises is performed in slow time.

**12. a.** Of clocks, etc.: Indicating a time in retard of the true or standard time; behind in time. Also of the sun: Behind mean time.

**1696** W. DERHAM *Artificial Clockmaker* (1759) 158 By the Table, you see how many Minutes, and Seconds, the Dial is too fast, or too slow. **1742** R. LONG *Astronomy* II. III. xii. 509 In the common equation tables it is sometimes said the clock is too fast or too slow. **1855** LARDNER *Mus. Sci. & Art* V. 135 From the 25th December to the 15th April the sun is always slow. **1886** J. MERRIFIELD *Naut. Astron.* 165 The chronometer..is..fast when it shows a later time, and slow when it shows an earlier time than the true Greenwich mean time.

**b.** Of local time: Less advanced than the standard to which it is referred.

**1894** *Amer. Ann. Photogr.* 22 The local time of a place 3° 56 West of the [Eastern Standard] meridian..would be 15 m. 44 sec. slow.

**III. 13. a.** Moving, flowing, etc., in a slow or sluggish manner; taking a long time to go a comparatively short distance; having a relatively low speed or velocity. ***slow-pitch*** (***softball***) *U.S.*, a type of softball in which each pitch must travel in an arc of a specified minimum height; ***slow wheel*** spec., a type of potter's wheel turned at a slow speed.

*c* **1400** MAUNDEV. xv. (1839) 162 Saturne is sloughe and litille mevynge. **1423** JAS I *Kingis Q.* clv, The slawe ase, the druggare beste of pyne. **1565** COOPER *Thes., Segnipes*, slow of foote: goyng slowly. **1590** SHAKS. *Com. Err.* I. i. 117 [They] would haue reft the Fishers of their prey, Had not their barke beene very slow of saile. **1605** —— *Macb.* I. iv. 17 Swiftest Wing of Recompence is slow, To ouertake thee. **1667** MILTON *P.L.* IV. 173 Satan had journied on, pensive and slow. **1764** GOLDSM. *Trav.* 293 The slow canal, the yellow-blossom'd vale. **1774** —— *Nat. Hist.* (1776) VII. 180 The viper, that is but a slow, feeble bodied animal, makes way in a heavy undulating manner. **1852** THACKERAY *Esmond* I. vi, In those days letters were slow of travelling. **1871** PRINCESS ALICE *Mem.* (1884) 274 The train..is the slowest I was ever in in my life. **1946** W. B. HONEY *Art of Potter* II. ii. 12 A device was introduced for rotating the pot while it was being built, on a horizontal pivoted table or disc ..; this 'slow wheel' presumably led to the invention of the fully developed potter's wheel. **1964** H. HODGES *Artifacts* i. 28 Many archaeologists are in the habit of distinguishing between a *slow wheel*, that is to say a device in which the movement of the wheel-head is either intermittent or relatively slow, and a fast wheel. **1971** *Canadian Antiques Collector* Apr. 16/1 Most frequently Ipswich ware is formed on a 'slow wheel' which is in principle a freely-revolving turntable. Both pot and wheel were revolved by hand. **1971** *N.Y. Times* 6 June 95/5 With the opening of the annual Long Beach Slow Pitch Softball League..policemen and addicts met for the first time in friendly competition. **1976** *Billings* (Montana) *Gaz.* 2 July 1-c/1 Softball fans will have a chance to glimpse some of the top men's slowpitch teams in the northwest during the Town & Country-Corner Pocket Men's Slowpitch Softball Tournament.

**b.** ***slow lemur, loris, monkey***: (see quots.).

**1800** SHAW *Gen. Zool.* I. I. 81 Slow Lemur, *Lemur Tardigradus*. **1833** *Zool. Soc. Trans.* I. 69 Future observers of these *slow monkeys*, as M. F. Cuvier denominates them. **1882** *Encycl. Brit.* XIV. 443 *N*[*ycticebus*] *tardigradus*, the common slow lemur or loris.

**c.** Nuclear Physics. ***slow neutron***, a neutron with little kinetic energy, esp. as a result of being slowed down by a moderator; freq. = *thermal neutron*; also *attrib.*; so ***slow reactor***, a reactor in which fission is produced primarily by moderated neutrons; a thermal reactor.

**1934** *Chem. Abstr.* XXVIII. 2263 The slow neutrons are probably emitted from Be when an excitation of a Be nucleus by α-particles occurs without capture. **1938** R. W. LAWSON tr. *Hevesy & Paneth's Manual of Radio-activity* (ed. 2) x. 112 These slow neutrons are produced by allowing fast neutrons, such as those emitted by a radon-beryllium source, to pass through water, paraffin wax, or other substances containing hydrogen. **1945** H. D. SMYTH *Gen. Acct. Devel. Atomic Energy Mil. Purposes* ii. 23 For a slow-neutron chain reaction using a moderator and unseparated uranium it was almost certain that tons of metal and of moderator would be required. **1949** *Atomics* Sept. 45/2 The so-called 'slow neutron reactor'. These reactors take advantage of the fact that neutrons produce fission in uranium more easily as they go slower. **1958** *Chambers's Techn. Dict.* Add. 1014/1 Slow reactor. **1964** M. GOWING *Britain & Atomic Energy 1939–1945* iv. 115 Bombs were discussed in terms of slow neutron chain reactions. **1973** *Daily Tel.* 12 Oct. 8/5 Fast reactors, cooled by sodium instead of carbon dioxide, as in slow reactors now used, can provide more heat more rapidly.

**14. a.** Of pace, movement, etc.: Leisurely; not quick, fast, or hurried. *spec.* (i) ***slow motion***, (*a*) motion of slower speed than normal; also *attrib.*; (*b*) *Cinemat.*, the technique of shooting a film at a faster speed than normal so that when it is projected the action will appear to be slowed down; also *transf.*, and *attrib.*; (ii) of a ballroom dance: with steps at walking-pace.

**1422** tr. *Secreta Secret., Priv. Priv.* 235 Whoso hath the Paas large and slow, he is..wel spedynge in al his dedys. **1513** DOUGLAS *Æneid* XII. vii. 7 With steppis slaw furth stalkand all in feyr. **1533** BELLENDEN *Livy* I. xi. (S.T.S.) I. 64 Mecius..fled with slaw passage to þe montanis. **1613** SHAKS. *Hen. VIII*, I. i. 132 To climbe steepe hilles Requires slow pace at first. **1667** MILTON *P.L.* XII. 648 With wandring steps and slow. **1774** GOLDSM. *Nat. Hist.* (1824) III. 192 The motion of this serpent is slow. **1797–1805** S. & HT. LEE *Canterb. T.* I. 301 That journey itself became visibly slower and slower. **1801** J. STRUTT *Sports & Pastimes* III. ii. 130 At a show in the country, about forty years ago, which was contrived in such a manner, that the whole group descended and ascended with a slow motion to the sound of music. **1827** SCOTT *Surg. Dau.* xiii, He understood it was the purpose..to proceed by slow marches and frequent halts. **1833** *Reg. & Instr. Cavalry* I. 16 This is the slowest step at which troops are to move. **1834** *Mechanics' Mag.* 4 Oct. 16/2 The gear was changed from the quick to the slow motion. **1860** TYNDALL *Glac.* I. vii. 52 Hence the slow motion of these glaciers. **1878** ABNEY *Photogr.* 305 To enable the operator to grasp the slow-motion focussing-screw. **1903** *Work* 4 July 341/2 Next make the ball and vertical slow-motion screw. **1924** *Spectator* 3 May 720/1 Its deliberation becomes a separate quality, akin to the slow motion of the cinema. **1928** *'H.M.V.' Catal.* 76/2 Slow F[ox]-T[rot]. **1929** E. WILSON *I thought of Daisy* ii. 102 A slow-motion diving picture of champion woman swimmers. **1938** W. S. CHURCHILL *Let.* 9 June in M. Gilbert *W. S. Churchill* (1976) V. xlvi. 946 In all my experience of public offices..I have never seen anything like the slow-motion picture which the work of this Committee has presented. **1943** J. B. PRIESTLEY *Daylight on Saturday* xi. 70 The sound of their slow-motion patter..just gets your goat. **1949** A. CHUJOY *Dance Encycl.* 76/2 *Baston*, a form of slow waltz..in which the couples turn in circles in several directions. **1949** A. WILSON *Wrong Set* 56 She was almost lying in Bruce's arms as he carried her through the slow foxtrot. **1956** J. BALDWIN *Giovanni's Room* I. ii. 57 Like those figures in slow motion one sometimes sees on the screen. **1962** F. I. ORDWAY et al. *Basic Astronautics* vii. 316 This test is accomplished by firing the model engine in a wind tunnel and observing the flow of the exhaust gases with the aid of slow motion cameras. **1962** J. BRAINE *Life at Top* ii. 54 They were taking their partners for a waltz now, a slow waltz, an old waltz from the days of Carroll Gibbons and the Orpheans. **1966** 'M. HALLIDAY' *Wicked as Devil* ix. 79 The floor was crowded for a slow foxtrot. **1973** *Listener* 23 Aug. 244/1 Time on Friday moved very slowly. Everything seemed to be as if in a slow motion film. **1976** *Listener* 29 July 105/2 Going to the dancing class to practise the slow waltz and the tango.

**b.** Characterized by slowness of motion, progress, etc. (In later quots. after Pope.)

**1709** POPE *Ess. Crit.* 357 A needless Alexandrine..That, like a wounded snake, drags its slow length along. **1788** GIBBON *Decl. & F.* IV. 192 The slow length of a sickly and desponding host was heavily dragged along the Flaminian way. **1856** *N. Brit. Rev.* XXVI. 269 Three, four, and five years did cases drag their slow length along. **1868** J. S. MILL *Eng. & Irel.* 36 This great undertaking must not drag its slow length through generations.

**c.** Causing or tending to cause slowness of movement or speed; retarding, heavy.

**1868** *J. Lillywhite's Cricketers' Compan.* 61 The wickets were in excellent order, though somewhat 'slow' for Gravesend. **1873** BENNETT & CAVENDISH *Billiards* 77 On a slow table a No. 2 is required. **1881** *Chicago Times* 4 June, With..time allowance for 'slow' track. **1904** *Field* 6 Feb.

202/3 A system..lacking directness on a slow and heavy turf.

**d.** Of a railway track: Utilized for traffic of low speed. Of a lane of a dual carriageway or motorway: intended for vehicles which are not overtaking; also *fig.*

1898 *Daily News* 1 Mar. 5/5 In passing from the slow to the main line the engine fouled the points. 1967 'M. Carrel' *Dark Edge of Violence* ix. 80 The police car..dropped back and sulked along in the slow-lane. 1969 R. Petrie *Despatch of Dove* III. 146 He'd put himself in a silly position, in the slow lane without the chance of a turn-off. 1972 B. Everitt *Cold Front* v. 38 'Are we conversing or making love?'.. 'Let's go into the slow lane for a minute. What are you doing between leaving Medicom and joining the Grand Old Man?' 1977 R. Rendell *Judgement in Stone* xix. 151 Joan's driving had become erratic, and her jerky zigzagging from slow lane to fast was a frightening experience.

**IV. 15.** *absol.* as *pl.* Those who are slow in any sense. (Cf. slow *sb.* 1.)

*c* 897 K. Ælfred *Gregory's Past C.* xxxix. 280 Ða slawan sint to manianne ðæt hie ne forielden ðone timan for hiera slæwðe. *a* 1225 *Ancr. R.* 258 Aȝean slowe & slepares is swuðe openlich his earlich ariste from deað to liue. 1390 Gower *Conf.* II. 13, I am al beknowe That I have ben on of tho slowe. *Ibid.* 44 Thus sche was on of the slowe As of such hertes besinesse. 1605 Shaks. *Macb.* III. i. 96 The valued file Distinguishes the swift, the slow, the subtle. 1860 Hughes *Tom Brown at Oxf.* xiv, The fastest of the fast and the slowest of the slow.

**V. 16.** *Comb.* **a.** Parasynthetic, as ***slow-blooded, -gaited, -hearted, -minded, -motioned***, etc. Also ***slow-heartedness, -mindedness.***

1884 W. C. Smith *Kildrostan* 91 It is a quakerish thing.., Tame and *slow-blooded. 1608 H. Clapham *Errour Left Hand* A 5 To helpe the *slowe conceited. 1744 Akenside *Ode on Leaving Holland* 23 The *slow-eyed fathers of the land. 1588 Shaks. *L.L.L.* III. i. 56 He is verie *slow gated. 1863 Mrs. Gaskell *Sylvia's Lovers* I. ix. 187 She.. sauntered back behind the patient slow-gaited creatures. 1581 Mulcaster *Positions* xlii. (1887) 257 If the maister be verie sharp witted..and the boy *slowheaded. 1690 Norris *Beatitudes* (1692) 28 To convince the *slow-hearted and distrustful World. *a* 1680 Charnock *Attrib. God* (1834) I. 743 The frequent rebukes of their *slow-heartedness. 1705 S. Dale *Pharmacologia Suppl.* 332 *De Blatta*,..the *slow leg'd Beetle. 1695 *Lond. Gaz.* No. 3136/4 A very strong bay Mare, 8 years old,..*slow mettled. 1930 D. H. Lawrence *A Propos of Lady Chatterley's Lover* 9 The evocative power of the so-called obscene words..perhaps are [*sic*] still too strong for *slow-minded, half-evoked lower natures to-day. 1935 Kipling *Two Forewords* 16 The seller..berated, for their *slow-mindedness, men who, but for being too much urged to buy, would have bought. 1856 'Mark Twain' *Let.* 10 June (1917) I. 33 They are either excessively *slow motioned or very lazy. 1951 N. G. Annan *Leslie Stephen* x. 285 Progress for him was an incalculable and slow-motioned operation. 1530 Tindale *Exod.* iv. 10, I am *slowe mouthed and slowe tongued. 1882 Blackmore *Christowell* xxi, Persons..slow-mouthed at making, or taking, a joke. 1682 *Lond. Gaz.* No. 1731/4 A thin Melancholy Man,..*slow Speeched. 1592 Nashe *P. Penilesse* Wks. (Grosart) II. 60 Prooue it when you will, you *slowe spirited Saturnists. 1820 Keats *Lamia* I. 365 One came near,..*Slow-stepp'd. 1530 *Slow-tongued [see *slow-mouthed*]. 1836 J. H. Newman *Lyra Apost.* (1849) 123 And slow-tongued Moses rule by eloquence of deed! 1596 Shaks. *Tam. Shr.* II. i. 208 Oh *slow wing'd Turtle, shal a buzard take thee? 1897 *Outing* XXX. 354/2, I watched the slow-winged clouds floating far above. 1571 Golding *Calvin on Ps.* viii. 8 There is no man so dull and *slowe-witted. 1909 *Expositor* Aug. 174 The more slow-witted and less versatile Romans.

**b.** With verbs, as ***slow-clap, -foot, -handclap*** (see handclap c), ***-march, -steam, -time, -waltz.***

1960 *Slow-clap [see out-score *v.*]. 1979 *Guardian* 26 Oct. 2/1 Mrs Thatcher was also slow-clapped and heckled.. during her speech. 1590 Spenser *F.Q.* I. iii. 10 At last she has A damzell spyde *slow footing her before. 1885 W. B. Yeats in *Dublin Univ. Rev.* May 82/2, I see the night, Deep-eyed, slow-footing down the empty glade. 1760 *Lett. to Hon. Brigadier General* 9 Lord George *slow-marched the Cavalry at the Battle of Minden. 1927 T. E. Lawrence *Let.* 19 May (1938) 516 These long dreary slow-marching books are invaluable friends in Drigh Road. 1977 *Times* 30 July 2/3 The RAF colour squadron slow-marched the old colour.. off the parade ground. 1975 *Petroleum Economist* Sept. 356/3, 22 per cent of the active fleet..was estimated to be *slow-steaming in July. *Ibid.* 341/2 Due to slow-steaming, fuel consumption..fell. 1977 *Living with Tanker Surplus* (Shell Internat. Petroleum Co.) 5 The financial rewards for slow-steaming small vessels are greater than for large vessels, because a small ship consumes relatively more bunkers per tonne of cargo. 1898 *Engineering Mag.* XVI. 105 A resolute attempt to *slow-time the machinery. 1976 'P. B. Yuill' *Hazell & Menacing Jester* viii. 81 He recovered a bit as I was *slow-waltzing him to the stairs.

**c.** With adjs., as ***slow-sudden, -sure, -syruppy.***

1742 Young *Nt. Th.* I. 384 Beware, Lorenzo! a slow-sudden death. 1837 Carlyle *Fr. Rev.* II. v. viii, An epigrammatic slow-sure Manuel. 1863 Grosart *Small Sins* (ed. 2) 70 If man would but mark the slow-sure advance of the very least sin! 1922 Joyce *Ulysses* 261 Neatly she poured slowsyruppy sole.

**d.** With sbs., as ***slow-beat, -burn*** (see sense 7 c), ***-combustion, -contact, -gait, -growth, -neutron*** (see sense 13 c), ***-pitch*** (see sense 13 a), ***-poke*** (see sense 8 d), ***-scan*** (see sense 9 a), ***-speed, -tempo; slow-release*** adj., (*a*) *Electr.*, applied to a relay in which the delay between a de-energizing signal and the opening of the contacts is intentionally increased; (*b*) characterized by the slow release of an active substance (as by a pharmaceutical preparation); ***slow-wave*** adj., *spec.* applied to the commonest form of non-REM sleep, in which brain waves having a frequency of ½ to 3 hertz, lower than that of alpha or beta waves, are detectable.

1965 *Economist* 4 Sept. 857/2 Egypt's slow-beat socialism is not so agreeable to Moscow as was Algeria's hot rhythm under Mr Ben Bella. 1977 J. Wainwright *Do Nothin' till you hear from Me* viii. 125 He can blow a beautiful slow-beat chorus. 1885 Spon *Mech. Own Bk.* (1893) 663 Improved Economic Slow Combustion Hot Air Stove. 1907 Hodges *Elem. Photogr.* (ed. 6) 101 Gas-light or Slow-contact Papers. 1940 C. Day Lewis tr. *Virgil's Georgics* II. 41 Waggonloads drawn home by the slow-gait oxen. 1965 H. I. Ansoff *Corporate Strategy* vi. 109 The electronics industry ranges from high growth in technologically sophisticated areas, such as optical electronics, to slow-growth consumer oriented product-markets, such as radio and television. 1970 *Globe & Mail* (Toronto) 26 Sept. B2/2 Ontario Development Corp. has granted loans totalling more than $1-million to 10 companies planning to set up plants in slow-growth areas of the province. 1928 *Jrnl. Inst. Electr. Engineers* LXVI. 342/2 The No. 2 armature is especially suitable for slow-release relays. 1961 *Lancet* 29 July 230/1 Possibly the diminished efficacy of penicillin in the treatment of uncomplicated gonorrhœa may be due to the wide use of slow-release preparations giving a prolonged, though low, blood concentration. 1969 S. F. Smith *Teleph. & Telegr. A* ii. 43 One particularly useful way of obtaining a slow release feature without making the relay slow to operate is to connect a permanent shunt across the operating coil of the relay. 1974 *Nature* 25 Jan. 199/2 The efficiency of slow-release nitrogen was investigated as an initial and maintenance fertiliser treatment. 1958 *Newnes Compl. Amat. Photogr.* 33 An older box camera with a slow-speed shutter can be speeded up very simply. 1971 *Engineering* Apr. 20/1 In the case of slow-speed engines, machining can often be confined to pin and journal diameters and web faces. 1980 *Redbook* Oct. G12/2 Slow-speed film lets you get good pictures even on a sun-drenched sandy beach or glistening ski slope. 1962 D. Francis *Dead Cert* vi. 55 We swayed lazily round the floor to some dreamy slow-tempo music. 1978 T. Williamson *Technicians of Death* viii. 60 The invisible disc jockey began to play a slow-tempo number. 1963 G. Troup *Masers & Lasers* (ed. 2) iv. 71 There are three kinds of structures suitable for slow-wave propagation in the paramagnetic maser. 1967 *Physiol. Rev.* XLVII. 118 Slow wave sleep. 1968 *Brit. Med. Bull.* XXIV. 257/1 There is a reduction in the amplitude of the evoked response during rapid eye-movement sleep as compared with slow-wave sleep. 1974 W. P. Koella in van Praag & Meinardi *Brain & Sleep* 9 Stages 1 to 4 are referred to as NREM-sleep; the term 'slow-wave-sleep' should be reserved for stages 3 and 4 which are characterized by the 'slow' delta-waves.

**slow** (sləʊ), *adv.* Also 6 slaw(e, slau. [f. slow *a.*]

**1. a.** In a slow or tardy manner; slowly.

*a* 1500 *Adrian & Epotys* 22 in *Brome Bk.* 25 Than seyd þe Emprore, note slawe, 'Arte thow wysse wysdam to teche?' 1513 Douglas *Æneid* VIII. vii. 105 The mychty God of fyr..als tyte, And no slawer,..Furth of his bed startis. 1590 Shaks. *Mids. N.* I. i. 3 But oh, me thinkes, how slow This old Moon wanes. 1632 Milton *Penseroso* 76, I hear the far-off Curfeu sound,..Swinging slow with sullen roar. 1680 Moxon *Mech. Exerc.* xii. 209 In large and heavy Work the Tread comes slow and heavily down. 1733 W. Ellis *Chiltern & Vale Farm.* 109 It grew so slow, as provoked him to take it up. 1762 Sir W. Jones *Arcadia* Poems (1777) 103 Slow he approach'd; then wav'd his awful hand. 1812 Byron *Ch. Har.* II. xli, As the stately vessel glided slow Beneath the shadow. 1848 Thackeray *Van. Fair* viii, We drove very slow for the last two stages on the road. 1858 *Edin. Rev.* July 207 The narrative moves slow.

**b.** ***slow back***: a direction to a golfer when the club is swung back from the ball in making a stroke.

1886 H. G. Hutchinson *Hints on Golf* 17 Golfers have gone so far as to instruct their caddies to say to them, 'Slow back,' so as to keep them in mind of this precept each time they addressed themselves to drive the ball. 1909 P. A. Vaile *Mod. Golf* viii. 136 Gather speed as you go up, but do not get up much speed on the upward swing, for if you do you have to waste energy fighting it at the top of the swing. This is the reason for 'slow back'. 1922 Wodehouse *Clicking of Cuthbert* iii. 73 Slow back—keep the head.

**2.** *Comb.* **a.** With pres. pples. and ppl. adjs., as ***slow-burning, -circling, -creeping***, etc. *spec.* ***slow-reacting substance*** (Physiol.), any of various substances that are produced in the body in response to various stimuli and cause slower and longer lasting contraction of smooth muscle than does histamine; *spec.* one released in anaphylaxis; abbrev. SRS (see S 4 a); ***slow-releasing*** = *slow-release* adj. (*a*) s.v. slow *a.* 16 d.

Combinations of this type are extremely common from *c* 1725; many examples from 18th century poetry are collected by Jodrell.

1591 Sylvester *Du Bartas* I. ii. 186 Then Slow-growing Babes should instantly be Men. 1630 Milton *Shaks.* 9 Whilst to th' shame of slow-endeavouring art, Thy easie numbers flow. 1697 Dryden *Virg. Georg.* III. 843 The slow creeping Evil eats his way. *Ibid.* IV. 689 Baleful Styx..With Nine slow circling Streams. *a* 1716 Blackall *Wks.* (1723) I. 223 Being Burnt alive in a slowburning Fire. 1779 Warner in Jesse *Selwyn & Contemp.* (1844) IV. 301, I shall..come in a steel-springed slow-driving hack on Friday. 1833 Rennie *Alph. Angling* 59 The pike,..which likes to prowl about in slow-running, weedy waters. 1859 Darwin *Orig. Spec.* iv. (1860) 103 The case of slow-breeding animals. 1876 'Mark Twain' *Tom Sawyer* xxxi. 237 The slow-dragging ages. 1891 Roberts *Adrift Amer.* 237 The big slow-sailing turkey buzzards. 1894 Kipling *Jungle Bk.* 95 Asleep in the arms of the slow-swinging seas. 1904 —— *Traffics & Discoveries* 368 Warn them of seas that slip our yoke Of slow conspiring stars. 1904 H. G. Wells *Food of Gods* II. i. 142 They were children—slow-growing children of a new race. 1910 J. Poole *Pract. Telephone Handbk.* (ed. 4) xi. 169 A slow-acting relay. 1912 W. de la Mare *Listeners* 24 Whose feathers..Gleam with slow-gathering drops of dew. 1915 D. H. Lawrence *Rainbow* i. 1 They were fresh, blond, slow-speaking people. 1916 A. Huxley *Burning Wheel* 22 The chime Of bells slow-dying. 1920 E. Sitwell *Wooden Pegasus* 101 A slow-leaking tap. 1921 D. H. Lawrence *Tortoises* 10 You..set forward. slow-dragging, on your four-pinned toes. 1921 R. Graves *Pier glass* 44 Slow-rising smoke and nothing wrong! 1923 T. E. Herbert *Telephony* xiii. 334 The special feature of the slow releasing relay..is the extension of the core on which is placed a solid copper collar. 1924 R. Campbell *Flaming Terrapin* iii. 43 The death-cry and the agony supreme Of the slow-drowning world. 1925 Slow-running [see *idling passage*]. 1925 F. Scott Fitzgerald *Great Gatsby* iii. 59 But I am slow-thinking. 1927 T. Wilder *Bridge of San Luis Rey* II. 38 That city of large girdled Women..slow-moving and slow-smiling, a city of crystal air. 1930 E. Pound *XXX Cantos* v. 20 A Knight with slow-lifting eyelids. 1930 Blunden *Poems* 315 At last slow-mending From the hacked wounds of our proud error's field. 1931 A. Huxley *Cicadas* 33 Death in the Scorpion hunts him up the sky..round the vault of time, round the slow-curving year. 1932 W. Faulkner *Light in August* i. 23 The slowspitting and squatting men. 1932 Auden *Orators* II. 75 O charged-to-the-full-in-secret slow-beating heart. 1939 Kellaway & Trethewie in *Austral. Jrnl. Exper. Biol.* XVII. 227 The perfusate was also tested for the presence of the substance described by Feldberg and Kellaway (1938) which, after a latent interval, causes contraction of the gut followed by slow relaxation and by characteristic after-changes in the excitability of the muscle. This substance we have called S.R.S. (slow reacting substance). 1947 Crowther & Whiddington *Science at War* 160 The slow-sinking depth charges may be evaded by the submarine. 1948 R. Graves *Coll. Poems, 1914–1947* 240 Under your Milky Way And slow-revolving Bear. 1954 J. R. R. Tolkien *Fellowship of Ring* 212 A long slow-climbing slope. 1954 A. G. L. Hellyer *Encycl. Garden Work* 18/2 Basic slag is a relatively slow-acting fertilizer. *a* 1957 R. Campbell tr. *Rimbaud's Drunken Boat* in *Coll. Poems* (1960) III. 18 Where with slow-pulsing and delirious fires,.. ferments the crimson bitterness of love. 1958 J. W. Freebody *Telegraphy* iv. 85/1 For slow operating or slow releasing relays three lengths of slug are employed. 1958 *Pharmacol. Rev.* X. 419 Two entirely different groups of slow reacting substances have been established; one.. consists of polypeptides, the other one of lipid-soluble acids. 1964 L. MacNeice *Astrol.* ii. 66 With slow-running planets the *transits* are the things to look for. 1970 Passmore & Robson *Compan. Med. Stud.* II. xxiv. 3/2 Histamine, the slow reacting substance (SRS-A) and bradykinin may be the most important agents involved in the pathogenesis of human bronchial asthma. 1975 *New Phytologist* LXXIV. 367 In alpine regions of Africa, there are trends from erect pachycaul plants towards stout slow-growing plant forms.

**b.** With pa. pples., as ***slow-breathed, -developed***, etc.; ***slow-drawn, -run, -spoken.***

1727–46 Thomson *Summer* 1646 Yonder slow-extinguish'd clouds. 1798 Miss H. M. Williams *Tour Switz.* I. 21 Responsive to the solemn, slow-breathed chant. 1821 Scott *Kenilw.* xli, Some slow-spoken, long-breathed brother of the congregation? 1849 Rock *Ch. Our Fathers* II. 495 The sullen splash of slow-drawn oars. 1891 *Daily News* 14 Feb. 3/4 In a slow-run race he was defeated by Sheridan. 1896 Kipling *Seven Seas* 53 To the grist of the slow-ground ages. *Ibid.* 65 Each man drew his watchful breath slow taken 'tween the teeth. 1910 W. de la Mare *Three Mulla-Mulgars* xi. 153 Between his slow-drawled, shakety notes of deep and shrill Nod listened for the least stir in the forest. 1914 Kipling *For All We have & Are* 3 Comfort, content, delight, The ages' slow-bought gain. 1916 A. Huxley *Burning Wheel* 39 While on the windy down-land..The slow-driven sun beheld us. 1944 Blunden *Shells by Stream* 43 Your eyes..Enfold the slow-bloomed scenes. 1949 —— *After Bombing* 34 All other lightning Might be as honey or kind balms slow-melted.

**slow**, obs. form of pa. t. of slay *v.*[1]

**slow** (sləʊ), *v.* Also 6 slowe. [f. slow *a.* Cf. OE. *slāwian* to be or become slow, and the compound *forslāwian* forslow *v.*]

**I.** *trans.* †**1.** To lose (time) by delay; to put off. *Obs.*$^{-1}$

? 1522 in Ellis *Orig. Lett.* Ser. II. I. 223 Assoone as God shall sende weder any thing mete for men to goo to the see, I shall slowe no tyme.

†**2.** To be slack or tardy in performing (business). *Obs.*$^{-1}$

1586 Hooker *Hist. Irel.* in *Holinshed* II. 142/2 The lord deputie, not slacking, nor slowing his businesse, followed out of hand the foresaid rebels.

**3. a.** To delay, check, retard; to make slower in some respect. Also with *down.*

1557 N.T. (Genevan) *Luke* xii. 45 My master sloweth his commyng. 1578 Banister *Hist. Man* v. 67 The meat is left destitute of concoction, and distribution therof in the body slowed. 1624 T. Heywood *Gunaik.* II. 117 Their speed may bee slackned though not stay'd, and their pace slowed though not quite stopt. 1645 in Carte *Ormonde* (1735) III. 399, I doubt..that this will be neglected, or so far slowed that the season will be lost. 1867 Dk. Argyll *Reign of Law* iii. 146 A bird can, of course, allow itself to fall backwards by merely slowing the action of its wings. 1875 H. C. Wood *Therap.* (1879) 138 Digitalis is capable of slowing the beat of the isolated heart of the frog. 1896 *Allbutt's Syst. Med.* I. 123 The arterial current becomes therefore relatively slowed. 1971 *Engineering* Apr. 34/1 Most neutron radiography has been carried out using slowed-down thermal neutrons. 1976 'J. Ross' *I know what it's like to Die* xxiv. 151 A creeping slowed-down vision with a dreamlike clarity.

**b.** To reduce the working rate or speed of (an engine); to ease. Also with *down.*

1839 R. S. Robinson *Naut. Steam Eng.* 138 The engine should always, except in case of absolute necessity, be *slowed* or eased, before it is stopped. 1859 *Merc. Mar. Mag.* (1860) VII. 46 By slowing her engines, she can stop and take soundings. **1890** Clark Russell *Marriage at Sea* xiv, The engines were 'slowed down',..and a minute later the revolutions of the propeller ceased.

**c.** To cause (a vessel, vehicle, or train) gradually to slacken in speed. Also with *down* or *up*.

**1864** Webster s.v., To slow a steamer. **1889** *Boy's Own Paper* 16 Nov. 103/1 The ship was now slowed, for we could not cross the bar that night. **1899** *Expositor* Jan. 55 We do not want men..to..slow the advancing chariot by hanging on listlessly behind.

**II.** *intr.* **4. a.** To slacken in speed; to move or go more slowly.

**1594** R. Carew *Tasso* (1881) 33 To the King she came, Nor for he angry seemes, one step she slowes. *a* **1653** G. Daniel *Idyll* v. 118 The world Slow'th, Readie to take the Fillup of a Hand Must cure her Dropsie. **1870** *Daily News* 28 Dec., They came on very steadily for about a quarter of a mile, then they slowed, and finally halted. **1894** *Law Times' Rep.* LXXI. 102/2 The *Diana* also..slowed, so as to permit the tug to pass her.

**b.** With advs., as *down, up*.

**1881** *Cent. Mag.* XXIII. 184 Slowing up, the..Cunarder ..drew towards us. **1885** W. D. Howells *Silas Lapham* (1891) I. 61 He brought the mare down to a walk, and then slowed up almost to a stop. **1891** *Cornhill Mag.* Jan. 15 He slowed down into a shambling walk.

**c.** Of a railway train: To move with slackening speed *into* a station, etc.

**1877** Black *Green Past.* xxi, He caught sight of her just as the train was slowing into the station. **1881** *Times* 28 Feb. 11/4 A Watford up train..was slowing into Dalston, where it was to stop.

†**5.** To suffer delay; to be deferred. *Obs.*[−1]

**1602** Dolman *La Primaud. Fr. Acad.* (1618) III. 750 The wicked..may thinke that their condemnation sloweth.

**6.** To become slower, less active or vigorous, etc. Also with *down*.

**1879** *Lumberman's Gaz.* 23 Aug., The chances were that the boom company would be obliged to slow down for a few days. **1891** S. Mostyn *Curatica* 161 The oscillation quickened—to slow again, however. **1904** *Field* 6 Feb. 202/3 The game slowed down a little after Hobbins had scored once more.

Hence **'slowing** *ppl. a.*

**1890** Humphry *Old Age* 5 A smaller supply of fuel.., not enough to choke the slowing fires.

†**'slowback.** *Obs.* [f. slow *a.* + back *sb.*[1]]

**1.** A slothful or sluggish person; a sluggard.

**1577** tr. *Bullinger's Decades* (1592) 266 For God doeth not assist slouthfull persons and idle slow backes. **1609** Holland *Amm. Marcell.* xvii. ii. 93 Rayling at him as a slow-backe and coward. *a* **1639** W. Whateley *Prototypes* i. xix. (1640) 234 Slow-backs, whose hand is no sooner from under the Governours eye, but that it is also off from the work.

**2.** *transf.* A drone-bee.

**1601** Holland *Pliny* I. 314 They [*sc.* bees] mark and note the slow-backs, they chastise them anon.

**3.** *attrib.* or as *adj.* Laggard; sluggish.

**1619** W. Sclater *Exp. 1 Thess.* (1630) 256 How much adoe haue we..to hale on our slow-back Nature to perfection. *Ibid.* 572 God be mercifull to this declining Age, this slow-backe, or rather backsliding generation.

**slow-bellied,** *a. rare.* [Cf. next.]

†**1.** Sluggish; indolent. *Obs.*

**1570–6** Lambarde *Peramb. Kent* (1826) 281 Marke..the grosse iugling that these slowe bellyed Syres used to delude the world withall. **1602** F. Hering *Anat.* 4 Slowbellyed Monkes, who haue made escape from their Cloysters.

**2.** That moves or crawls slowly.

**1662** Stillingfl. *Orig. Sacræ* iii. iv. §4 The unknown kind of Serpents in Brasil, the slow-bellied creature of the Indies [etc.].

**slow-belly.** [f. slow *a.*] A lazy, idle, or indolent person; a sluggard, laggard. Chiefly *pl.*

After Gr. γαστέρες ἀργαί, in the line attributed to Epimenides and quoted in the Epistle to Titus. Tindale's rendering is followed by Coverdale, etc.; but the Rheims version has 'slothful bellies', and the R.V. 'idle gluttons'.

[**1526** Tindale *Titus* i. 12 The Cretayns are..evyll beastes, and slowe belies.] **1607** Hieron *Wks.* I. 271 The maintenance of a sort of slow-bellies, whose seruice to Gods church was altogether vnprofitable. **1656** Baxter *Reformed Pastor* 248 To be a Bishop or Pastor is not..as idle slow-bellies to live to our fleshly delight and ease. **1698** Fryer *Acc. E. India & P.* 170 He derides and tells him he is no slowbelly, to desire to expire lazily on a Bed. **1865** *Athenæum* 20 May 681/2 They are no longer slow-bellies, for in many places they had eaten up all that could be called food. **1899** Kipling *Stalky* 27 Such boys,..evil-speakers, liars, slow-bellies—yea, incipient drunkards.

*attrib.* **1647** Trapp *Marrow Gd. Authors* in *Comm. Ep.* 619 'Rebuke them sharply,'..saith S. Paul of those slow-belly Cretians.

**slowche,** obs. form of slouch *sb.*

**'slow-coach.** Also slowcoach, slow coach. [f. slow *a.*] One who acts, works, or moves slowly; a slow, idle, or indolent person.

**1837** Dickens *Pickw.* xxxiv, What does this allusion to the slow coach mean?.. It may be a reference to Pickwick himself, who has..been a criminally slow coach during the whole of this transaction. **1837** Marryat *P. Keene* xii, He's not very quick in temper, or anything else; he's what we call a slow coach. **1886** Jerome *Idle Thoughts* 42 There are plenty of lazy people and plenty of slow-coaches, but a genuine idler is a rarity.

Hence **'slow-coaching, 'slow-coachish** *adjs.*

**1844** Thackeray *Crit. Rev.* Wks. 1886 XXIII. 209 A venerable bald-headed gentleman, with a most benignant tho' slow-coachish look. **1855** Smedley *H. Coverdale* i. 3 None of your old slow-coaching days for me; life's not long enough for dreaming.

†**slowde.** *Obs.*[−1] (Meaning uncertain.)

? *a* **1400** *Morte Arth.* 3719 Thane was it slyke a slowde in slakkes fulle hugge.

**slow-down.** Also slowdown. [f. slow *v.* + down *adv.*] The action or process of slowing down; an instance of slowing down; *spec.* (*a*) *U.S.*, a form of industrial protest in which employees work at a deliberately slow pace; (*b*) an economic recession, a decline in productivity or demand. Also *attrib.*

**1897** *Pall Mall Mag.* Sept. 77 Each slow-down caused delay of one minute. **1937** *Daily Progress* (Charlottesville, Va.) 16 Apr. 1/5 An official of the U.A.W.A. said the objective of workers in a slow-down was to 'try to see how little they can do without actually stopping work entirely'. **1939** *Sun* (Baltimore) 10 Jan. 16/3 The slow-down strike was called off late today. **1942** J. Steinbeck *Moon is Down* v. 70 'I think I fixed the mine for a while.' 'What's your trouble?'..'Oh, the usual thing with me—the slow-down and a wrecked dump car.' **1944** *Sun* (Baltimore) 28 Oct. 12/1 Low-quoted stocks..came out in blocks running to 33,000 shares and propped volume, although slowdowns were plentiful. **1950** *Ibid.* 7 Feb. 7/4 Helmstedt, Germany, checkpoint for the Russians' off-again, on-again 'slowdown' of Berlin-bound highway traffic. **1953** *Encounter* Nov. 70/1 In dozens of factories there were slow-downs..or sit-down strikes. **1957** *Economist* 28 Dec. 1132/1 At least 5,000 employees in lead-zinc mines and smelters..have lost their jobs this year... The slow-down extends even to the largest and most diversified producers. **1969** *Nature* 19 Apr. 218/2 The search will now be on for further eccentric behaviour in ..the Crab Nebula pulsar which has the shortest period and the fastest slowdown rate of all. **1969** *Guardian* 2 Oct. 12/1 Has the Government any plans to protect Britain from a slowdown? **1973** *Nature* 3 Aug. 260/1 The observed evolutionary slowdown in higher primates may simply be the consequence of progressive prolongation of their generation time. **1977** *New Yorker* 24 Oct. 79/2 The mess-hall workers staged a work slowdown. **1977** J. W. Kendrick *Understanding Productivity* iv. 35 The factors explaining the 1966–69 slowdown also help to explain why productivity advance recovered..during the final complete subperiod. **1978** *Sci. Amer.* July 28/2 Energy is required, for example, to accelerate the vehicle from traffic stops and slowdowns, to climb hills and to overcome the rolling resistance of the tires. **1980** A. Coppel *Hastings Conspiracy* xxviii. 184 The switchboard operators are starting a slow-down over wages. **1981** *Washington Star* 14 Jan. F4/2 The University of the District of Columbia barely overcame the visitors' slow-down tactics and escaped with a bizarre 28–27 victory last night at D.C. Armory.

**slow drag.** Also slow-drag. [f. slow *a.* + drag *sb.*] A slow blues rhythm; a piece of music in this rhythm; a dance characterized by dragging of the feet, performed to this rhythm. Also *attrib.* Hence **slow-drag** *v. intr.*, to dance the slow drag.

**1911** S. Joplin *Treemonisha* (music score) xxvii. 215 Directions for the Slow Drag. 1. The Slow Drag must begin on the first beat of each measure. 2. When moving forward, drag the left foot; when moving backward, drag the right foot, [etc.]. **1924** *Etude* Aug. 527/1 An exceedingly popular jazz is the slow drag. **1926** A. Niles in W. C. Handy *Blues* ii. 9 The songs were woven of the same stuff as the other overlapping items..the over-and-overs, slow-drags, pats, and stomps. **1935** Z. N. Hurston *Mules & Men* i. ix. 185 The piano was throbbing like a stringed drum and the couples slow-dragging about the floor were urging the player on to new lows. **1941** W. C. Handy *Father of Blues* (1957) vi. 76 It was not easy for me to concede that a simple slow-drag and repeat could be rhythm itself. **1949** B. A. Botkin *Treas. S. Folklore* v. i. 745 This is one of the best-known of the slow-drag work songs sung by Negro prisoners in South Texas. **1968** P. Oliver *Screening Blues* iii. 94 The shuffle of the 'slow drag' would have been effective at the medium tempo of the tune. **1970** —— *Savannah Syncopators* 57 On occasions..'slow-dragging' couples may be seen to be shuffling in a manner reminiscent, perhaps, of the 'shout'. **1976** A. Murray *Stomping Blues* vi. 83 There is Bessie Smith's slow-drag version..recorded in 1925. **1980** *Amer. Speech* LV. 210 They slow-dragged to low-down blues.

**'slower,** *sb. rare.* [f. slow *v.*] That which checks or impedes; a retarding influence. Also with *down*.

*a* **1610** Babington *Wks.* (1622) 82 Making Gods mercy a spurre to his..diligence, and not a slower of him as no doubt many would. **1947** Crowther & Whiddington *Science at War* 144 The most suitable substance for use as a slower-down was heavy water. **1961** P. Frankau *Pen to Paper* 64, I know also that one fatal slower of the pace can be found in the adjectives.

**'slower,** *v. rare.* [f. slow *a.*, perh. after lower *v.*] *trans.* = slow *v.* 3 c.

**1881** M. Reynolds *Engine-Driving Life* 17 To take the bulk of the momentum out of the train with the brake, and then to slower the train under control to the platform.

**'slow-foot,** *a.* [f. slow *a.*] Slow-footed; slow-paced. Also *transf.*

**1642** H. More *Song of Soul* i. ii. 57 The slow-foot beasts on which we rode. **1870** Morris *Earthly Par.* II. iii. 479 Telling the wondrous ways of slowfoot time. **1891** —— *Poems by the Way* 114 The slow-foot hope of the poor.

**slow-footed,** *a.* [f. slow *a.*] Slow of foot; that walks or goes slowly; slow-moving, slow-paced. Also *transf.*

**1642** H. More *Song of Soul* i. ii. 148 Although full loth I were Slow-footed eld the journey should command. **1711** Shaftesb. *Charact.* (1737) II. 301 Ask not merely, why man is..slower-footed than the beasts. **1775** Adair *Hist. Amer. Ind.* 133 He who feeds on venison is..swifter..than the man who lives on..the slow-footed tame cattle. **1873** Morley *Rousseau* II. 135 A man who handles sets of complex facts is necessarily slow-footed. **1892** Rider Haggard *Nada* 271 The pace of a regiment is the pace of its slowest-footed soldier.

†**'slowful,** *a. Obs.* Also 5 sloweful(l, slouful, 5–6 slowfull, 6 slowghfull, sloughful, *Sc.* sclawful. [f. slow *a.*, perh. after slothful *a.* (cf. slewful *a.*).]

**1.** Slack, slow, sluggish.

**14..** in *Alexander* (1886) 279, I..pray you..be most obeyssiant to hym þat..shall not be slowefull to kepe & defende you. **1483** Caxton *Gold. Leg.* 427 b/1 He was neuer founde sloweful ne neglygente. **1526** *Pilgr. Perf.* (W. de W. 1531) 53 The dull and slowfull asse. **1539** in Strype *Ann. Ref.* I. 561 The slowghfull and ungodly lyff which hath bene usid among all those sects.

**2.** Showing or marked by ingratitude; thankless, ungrateful. Also const. *of*.

**1484** Caxton *Fables of Æsop* [vi.] xi, None ought to be slowful of the good whiche he receyueth of other. —— *Fables of Poge* iv, The studye of the huntynge and hawkynge is a slouful cure.

†**'slowfulness.** *Obs.* [f. prec. + -ness.]

**1.** Sloth; slowness.

**1482** *Monk of Evesham* (Arb.) 78 By cause he fille fro the loue of god..vnto the coolde of worldly slowfulnes. **1525** Ld. Berners *Froiss.* II. lxxx. [lxxvi.] 239 They be lytel worth, for we haue sene suche slowfulnes in them that we haue no grete trust to them. **1552** Latimer *Serm. Linc.* ii. 71 What shall be their reward for their sloughfulnesse?

**2.** Ingratitude; thanklessness.

**1484** Caxton *Fables of Æsop* [vi.] xi, None ought to forgete the benyfyce whiche he hath receyued of some other, for slowfulnesse is a grete synne.

**'slow-going,** *a.* [f. slow *adv.*]

**1.** Indisposed to be active or enterprising; inclined to take things easy.

**1798** *Sporting Mag.* XI. 57 His Majesty, with a profusion of slow-going gentry. **1833** T. Hook *Parson's Dau.* i. ii, This love at first sight has often been a subject of ridicule amongst slow-going people. **1859** Helps *Friends in C.* Ser. ii. I. v. 205 Was his one of those slow-going intellects we sometimes.. read of? **1866** *Daily Telegr.* 16 Jan. 7/4 The Dutch are a slow-going people.

**2.** That moves or goes (comparatively) slowly.

**1836** *Penny Cycl.* VI. 190/1 The load of a *heavy* or slow-going camel. **1894** *Outing* XXIV. 382/1 The wild and unusual gesticulations of that slow-going old pacer had broken the harness.

**slowh(e,** etc., obs. ff. pa. t. of slay *v.*[1]

**slow-hound** ('sləʊhaʊnd). [prob. a variant of slough-hound, with first element assimilated to slow *a.*] A sleuth-hound.

*slow hound* is given by Skinner (1671) as an explanation of '*Slouth* or *Sleuthound*', but is is not clear whether he knew it to be really in use.

**1796** Lauderdale *Poems* 97 (E.D.D.), Slow-hound, pointer, tarrier, colley. **1816** Scott *Antiq.* iii, He had the scent of a slow-hound, sir, and the snap of a bull-dog. **1856** Miss Manning *Tasso & Leonora* 141 He had tracked it out like a slow-hound. **1865** Kingsley *Herew.* II. iv. 68 It was the contrast between the slow-hound and the grey-hound.

**'slowing,** *vbl. sb.* [f. slow *v.*] The action of becoming or making slow(er); an instance of this. Also with advs.

**1875** H. C. Wood *Therap.* (1879) 326 This slowing of the circulation. **1879** Proctor *Flowers Sky* iv. (1883) 15 The gradual slowing of the earth's rate of turning on her axis. **1884** *Nature* 26 June 212/1 The pulse showed slowings after the exhibition of ergotin. **1889** Skrine *Mem. Thring* 53 Slowing-down would not have improved its action. **1900** [see control *sb.* 3 c]. **1960** E. Delavenay *Introd. to Machine Translation* 82 This means a slowing-up in the matching of input words with words stored in the dictionary. **1965** J. Pollitt *Depression & its Treatment* vi. 82 In the elderly, particularly those in the senium, the effects of retardation are added to the existing slowing-up process associated with aging.

**slowish** ('sləʊɪʃ), *a.* [f. slow *a.* + -ish[1].] Somewhat slow or dull.

**1824** Miss Mitford *Village* Ser. i. (1863) 176 George Harris..Slowish—slow but sure. **1851** Carlyle *J. Sterling* iii. i, The cabman, sensible that his pace was slowish, took to whipping. **1885** *Field* 3 Oct. 486/1 A slowish kind of sport, all things taken into consideration.

**slowly** ('sləʊlɪ), *adv.* Forms: *α.* (latterly *north.* and *Sc.*) 1 slawlice, slaulice, -lece, 2 slawliche; 4–5, 9 slawly, 6 slawlie, slaulie. *β.* 4–5 slowliche, 5 -lich; 4–5 slowli, 5 slouly, 5–6 slowely, 7 slowlye, 6– slowly. [f. slow *a.* + -ly[2]. Cf. MDu. *sleulijch*, ON. *slǽ-*, *sljá-*, *sljóliga* (MSw. *sliolica*).]

†**1.** In a remiss or negligent manner; sluggishly; slackly. *Obs.*

*c* **897** K. Ælfred *Gregory's Past. C.* xxviii. 190 Ðæt hie to slawlice ðara ne ȝiemen þe him befæste sien. *a* **950** in *Anglia* X. 143 Ne dyde he þat naht slaulice ac he hine eallum middan ȝeardas ehtum onȝerede. *c* **1200** *Trin. Coll. Hom.* 11 Ðe þridde is þat man..slawliche ariseð and late to chireche goð. *c* **1380** Wyclif *Wks.* (1880) 314 Hely þe heyȝ prest was dampned, for he reproued hise sones but to softliche & slowliche. **1526** *Pilgr. Perf.* (W. de W. 1531) 155 b, Perfeccyon, whiche they slowly & weykly or fayntly desyre. **1563** Winȝet tr. *Vincent. Lirinensis* xxviii. Wks. (S.T.S.) II.

60 That afore wes precheit slawlie, the samin thing eftir to be precheit mair feruentlie.

**2.** Not quickly, rapidly, or hastily: **a.** Of processes, operations, etc.

*c* **1340** HAMPOLE *Pr. Consc.* 3193 Þai brin mar slawly als hay brynnes. **1398** TREVISA *Barth. De P.R.* v. xxiii. (Bodl. MS.), Moche ayer is slowlich ymeued. **1435** MISYN *Fire of Love* 81 Now qwhykliar, now slawlyer, it warmes. **1528** PAYNELL *Salerne's Regiment* G iv, The grape that hath the thynnest huske descendeth sonest from y[e] stomake: and the thycker huske the slowelyer. **1595** SPENSER *Epithalamion* 280 How slowly do the houres theyr numbers spend? How slowly does sad Time his feathers moue? **1650** R. STAPYLTON *Strada's Low C. Wars* VI. 12 The businesse with the Prince of Orange went slowlyer on. **1688** *Col. Rec. Pennsylv.* I. 237 Violent Courses..will Slowly and meanly Commend y[e] policy of their Authors. **1761** GRAY *Odin* 26 From out the hollow ground Slowly breath'd a sullen sound. **1837** P. KEITH *Bot. Lex.* 280 If it volatilizes..slowly, its evaporation is protracted. **1860** TYNDALL *Glac.* II. xviii. 326 Crevasses, on their first formation, are..narrow rents, which widen very slowly.

**b.** Of movement, advance, etc.

**1382** WYCLIF *Acts* xxvii. 7 Whanne many dayes we seiliden slowli. **1587** A. FLEMING *Contin. Holinshed* III. 982/1 The armie went on, but so much the slowlier, bicause the waie was somewhat narrow. **1628** HOBBES *Thucydides* (1822) 78 They marched the slowlier for the rain which had fallen the same night. **1667** MILTON *P.L.* IV. 541 The setting Sun Slowly descended. **1712** *Spect.* No. 316 ¶4 Indolence is a Stream which flows slowly on. **1794** MRS. RADCLIFFE *Myst. Udolpho* xlviii, Presently he sees him come slowly down the avenue. **1837** CARLYLE *Fr. Rev.* II. IV. v, They ride slowly Eastward. **1863** KINGLAKE *Crimea* (1877) II. xix. 306 The English war-fleet..moved slowly out of the bay.

**c.** Of personal actions.

*c* **1430** *Pilgr. Lyf Manhode* II. cli. 136. I..aroos ayen. Slowliche it was: for j was feeble. *c* **1440** *Jacob's Well* 126 Þe more þat god smyteth hem.., þe slawlyere [they] gon to goddys seruyse. **1573** J. TYRIE *Refutation*, etc. (S.T.S.) 8 Quhou slaulie he ansueris thairto. **1595** SHAKS. *John* IV. ii. 269, I coniure thee but slowly: run more fast. **1802** WORDSW. *Resolution & Indep.* 86 A gentle answer did the old Man make, In courteous speech which forth he slowly drew. **1818** SHELLEY *Rosalind* 1171 Slowly now he turned to me.

**3.** *Comb.* **a.** With ppl. adjs., as ***slowly-acting***, ***-churning***, ***-dripping***, etc.

*c* **1742** GRAY *Ignorance* 3 Rushy Camus' slowly-winding flood. **1744** MASON *Musæus* Poems (1764) 10 All these slowly dripping rills, That tinkling wander o'er the pebbled floor. **1829** *Chapters Phys. Sci.* 181 The meandering brook, or the slowly-flowing river. **1860** TYNDALL *Glac.* I. viii. 59 We can prove the effects to be due to slowly-acting causes. **1876** GEO. ELIOT *Dan. Der.* xv, The slowly-churning chances of his mind. **1921** D. H. LAWRENCE *Tortoises* 33 That mud-hovel of his slowly-rambling spouse. **1926** J. S. HUXLEY *Essays in Pop. Science* 195 They [*sc.* frogs in Arctic zones] would be so slowly-working that their growth would be prolonged over an uneconomic number of seasons. **1931** R. CAMPBELL *Georgiad* ii. 47 A blush began to dawn As rosy as a slowly-cooking prawn. **1937** *Discovery* July 196/1 Long strings of slowly-moving camels. **1951** S. SPENDER tr. *Rilke's Life of Virgin Mary* 15 And if the gleam from distant flambeaux plays On slowly-nearing ceremonial dresses. **1965** PHILLIPS & WILLIAMS *Inorg. Chem.* I. viii. 292 Now in many of these inter-combinations $dA/dx$ is a slowly-varying function, sometimes over relatively small ranges but often over very wide ranges of composition. **1967** *Oceanography & Marine Biol.* V. 468 On soft substrata two biocoenoses may be recognized, namely, one on beaches..with quickly-drying wracks and a second where slowly-drying wracks are present.

**b.** Misc., as ***slowly-dittied***, ***-painful***, ***successive***.

**1744** MASON *Musæus* Poems (1764) 3 Till with harmonious teen Ye sooth his shade, and slowly-dittied air. **1842** TENNYSON *St. Simeon Stylites* 56 More slowly-painful to subdue this home Of sin. **1845** PARNELL *Chem. Anal.* 278 So as to allow the gas to escape in slowly successive bubbles.

**slow match.** Also **slow-match.** [f. SLOW *a.*] A rope-match made so as to burn very slowly (see MATCH *sb.*[2] 2).

**1802** JAMES *Milit. Dict.* s.v. *Match*, Slow match is made of hemp or tow, spun on the wheel like cord, but very slack; and is composed of three twists. **1828** J. M. SPEARMAN *Brit. Gunner* (ed. 2) 275 During the Siege of Gibraltar, slow-match was made there in the following manner. **1871** KINGSLEY *At Last* i, [She] ignored the very existence of a mere Negro like Jamaica Joe, as she sat by her cigars, and slow-match.

*attrib.* **1887** G. NICHOLSON *Dict. Gardening* III. 442 Slow-match tree. A common name for *Careya arborea.* ['The bark..is said to be used in some parts of India as a slow match for firelocks'—*Treas. Bot.* s.v. *Careya.*]

**slow-moving,** *a.* [SLOW *adv.*] That moves or goes slowly; slow-going.

*predic.* **1720** POPE *Iliad* XXII. 494 Be this the song, slow-moving toward the shore. **1784** COWPER *Task* I. 160 Thence with what pleasure have we just discern'd The distant plough slow moving. **1856** AYTOUN *Bothwell* II. xxvii. 75 Overhead a meteor came, Slow-moving, tinging..The murky clouds.

*attrib.* **1784** COWPER *Task* VI. 697 The statesman of the day, A pompous and slow-moving pageant, comes. **1836–9** *Todd's Cycl. Anat.* II. 54/2 The arteries of the limbs in several slow-moving animals. **1890** 'R. BOLDREWOOD' *Col. Reformer* (1891) 308 Large droves of patient, slow-moving cattle arrived.

**b.** *transf.* Making slow progress; advancing or acting slowly.

**1644** MILTON *Areopagitica* (Arb.) 76 The slow-moving Reformation we labour under. **1878** MORLEY *Carlyle* 160 Our slow-moving and unimaginative public. **1899** MACKAIL *W. Morris* II. 237 At last the slow-moving arm of authority came down upon it.

**slowness** ('sləʊnɪs). Forms: α. *Sc.* and *north.* 4 **slau-**, 4–6 **slawnes** (5 **slawe-**), 5 **slawnesse**, 9 **slawness**. β. 4 **slogh(e)-**, 5 **slouȝnes**; 5–7 **slownes**, **-nesse**, 7– **slowness**. [f. SLOW *a.*]

†**1.** Sloth, indolence, sluggishness. *Obs.*

α. *a* **1300** *Cursor M.* 10110 Slaunes, and wreth, and pride. *a* **1340** HAMPOLE *Psalter* iii. 5, I ristid me first in synful lyfe and in slawnes. **1435** MISYN *Fire of Love* 88 Qwher lufe kelys not, nor vnto slawnes may not bowe. *c* **1600** A. HUME *Chr. Precepts* Poems (S.T.S.) 81 Thou knawes what hurt and grief thy slawnes and slouthfulnes hes wrought thee.

β. **1303** R. BRUNNE *Handl. Synne* 4237 Now shul we speke of sloghnes; Among þe toþer ful wyk hyt ys. **1414** BRAMPTON *Penit. Ps.* (Percy Soc.) 62 Slownes is a cursid thing; For it is evere weri of weel doyng. **1736** AINSWORTH *Lat. Dict.* I. s.v., He reflected upon him by reason of his slowness and sluggishness.

**2.** Dullness of intellect or comprehension; lack of acuteness, promptitude, or readiness.

**1495** *Trevisa's Barth. De P.R.* (W. de W.) v. x. 115 Yf the forehede be tomoche, it tokenyth slownes that draweth to foly. **1601** SHAKS. *All's Well* I. iii. 10 The complaints I haue heard of you I do not all beleeue, 'tis my slownesse that I doe not. **1651** *Rec. Communion* §2 Their slownesse and slendernesse..was very great. **1755** JOHNSON, *Dulness*, stupidity;..slowness of apprehension. **1822** LAMB *Elia* I. *Old Actors*, In expressing slowness of apprehension, this actor surpassed all others. **1897** MISS KINGSLEY *W. Africa* 527 The acknowledged slowness of men in putting two and two together.

†**b.** Bluntness of edge. *Obs.*$^{-0}$

*c* **1440** *Promp. Parv.* 458/2 Slawnesse, or dulnesse of egge, *ebetudo, obtusitas.*

**c.** Lack of animation; dullness, tediousness.

**1887** *Cassell's Encycl. Dict.* s.v., The slowness of an entertainment.

**3.** The quality of being slow in respect of action, progress, or accomplishment.

**1398** TREVISA *Barth. De P.R.* v. xxiii. (Bodl. MS.), Þe heuynes of voice folowith þe slownes þereof. *Ibid.* xxxvii, For slouȝnes of breeþ tokeneþ defaute of þe vertu of out putting. **1526** *Pilgr. Perf.* (W. de W. 1531) 246 b, A pronite or redynesse to all vyce, and a slownesse to all goodnes. **1566** *Reg. Privy Council Scot.* I. 441 The greit delay and slawnes of justice within this realme. **1611** BIBLE *Transl. Pref.* ¶14 Fearing no reproch for slownesse, nor coueting praise for expedition. **1656** EARL MONM. tr. *Boccalini's Advts. fr. Parnass.* I. lii. (1674) 67 Slowness could not consist with swiftness. **1731** *Swift's Corr.* (1766) II. 149 The slowness of my answers does not come from the emptiness of my heart. **1788** FRANKLIN *Autobiog.* Wks. 1840 I. 171 From the slowness I saw at first in the working I could scarcely believe that the work was done. **1857** MILLER *Elem. Chem., Org.* i. 30 The oxidating influence of which can be applied with sufficient slowness and regularity. **1879** BARTLETT *Egypt to Pal.* xxvii. 541 Another lamented the slowness of the work.

*fig.* *a* **1742** BENTLEY *Serm.* (J.), Because of the hardness and slowness of their hearts.

**4.** The quality of being slow in motion.

*c* **1440** *Promp. Parv.* 458 Slawnesse, of mewynge, *morositas, tarditas.* **1611** SHAKS. *Cymb.* III. v. 168 This Fooles speede Be crost with slownesse. **1653** W. RAMESEY *Astrol. Restored* 56 All Planets give unto him their light..by reason of his slowness. **1728** CHAMBERS *Cycl.* s.v. *Pulse*, A Slowness of the Influxes of the nervous Juice from the Brain into the *Villi* of the Heart. **1794** MRS. RADCLIFFE *Myst Udolpho* vi, The extreme slowness of his pace made St. Aubert look again from the window to hasten him. **1860** TYNDALL *Glac.* I. xxii. 158, I had descended with extreme slowness and caution for some time. **1886** W. J. TUCKER *E. Europe* 164 This beats any funeral procession for slowness.

**b.** A soft or heavy condition of ground or turf which does not permit of swift riding or running or of good play.

**1881** *Chicago Times* 4 June, Three well known and distinguished horsemen..are to adjudge the 'slowness' of the track. **1899** *Oakham School Mag.* 29 The slowness of the ground quite precluded that possibility.

**slow-paced,** *a.* [SLOW *a.*]

**1.** Having a slow pace, gait, or motion: **a.** Of persons or animals. ***slow-paced lemur*** or ***loris***, the slow lemur.

**1594** KYD *Cornelia* III. i, The sleepie Waine-man softly droue His slow-pac'd Teeme. *c* **1605** WALLINGTON *Optick Glasse* 40 Heare what the poet affirmes in an epigram vpon a slowpac'd lurdaine. **1664** H. POWER *Exp. Philos.* I. 36 This Slimy Animal (the slow-paced Engine of Nature) The great Black Snail. **1737** POPE *Hor. Epist.* I. i. 16 *note*, Like the sober and slow-paced Animal generally employed to mount the Lord Mayor. **1784** COWPER *Task* v. 32 Patient of the slow-pac'd swain's delay. **1800** SHAW *Gen. Zool.* I. I. 81 *Lemur Tardigradus*, Slow-paced Lemur. **1870** BRYANT *Iliad* VI. I. 203 Achilles the swift-footed slew them all Among their slow-paced bullocks.

*fig.* and *transf.* **1648** J. BEAUMONT *Psyche* XIV. xli, The Judge may know Whether his Sentence more by Passion's haste, Than slow-pac'd Reason's Rules he has not past. **1681–6** J. SCOTT *Chr. Life* (1747) III. 503 Our slow-pac'd Natures cannot travel from one to the other.

**b.** Of inanimate objects.

**1617** DRUMM. OF HAWTH. *Forth Feasting* Wks. (1711) 37/2 Some few Years And Revolutions of the slow-pac'd Spheres. **1713** SWIFT *Elegy on Partridge* Wks. 1755 III. II. 80 That slow-pac'd sign Bootes.

**2.** Of time, etc.: Slow in coming or passing; tardy, lingering.

**1629** MASSINGER *Roman Actor* v. ii, How slow-paced are these minutes! **1667** MILTON *P.L.* x. 963 This days Death denounc't,..Will prove no sudden, but a slow-pac't evill. *a* **1700** KEN *Edmund* Poet. Wks. 1721 II. 262 Each slow-pac'd Minute seems to be a Year. **1743** FRANCIS tr. *Hor., Odes* IV. vii. 14 Yet Summer dies in Autumn's fruitful Reign, And slow-pac'd Winter soon returns again. **1878** B. TAYLOR *Pr. Deukalion* II. iii. 70 Slow-paced is Fate.

**slow-worm** ('sləʊwɜːm). Forms: α. 1 **slawerm**, **-wyrm**, 5 **-worme**, 9 *north. dial.* **slaa-**, **slea(a)-worm**, *Sc.* **slayworm**. β. 2 **slowurm**, 5 **-wurme**, **-werme**, 6 **-worme**, 6, 9 **-worm**; 6 **slooworme**; 6 **sloewourme**, 7 **-worme**, 7, 9 **-worm**. γ. 6 **slowe worme**, 6–7 **slow-worme**, 7–9 **slow worm**, **slowworm**, 7– **slow-worm**. [OE. *slá-wyrm*; the obscure first element appears also in MSw. *slā* (Sw. *slå*, dial. *slo*; also in comb. *ormslå*), Norw. *slo* (and *ormslo*), *sløa*, *sleva*, etc., a slow-worm. Association with the adj. *slow* is not apparent before the 16th cent.]

**1.** A small harmless scincoid lizard, *Anguis fragilis*, native to most parts of Europe; the blindworm.

In early glossaries, etc., the word is used to render various Latin names of serpents and lizards. Shaw (1802) used *slow-worm* as a generic name for the *Angues*.

α. *a* **900** *Kentish Glosses* in Wr.-Wülcker 80 *Regulus*, slawerm. *a* **1050** *Liber Scintill.* xxviii. (1889) 105 Snacas & ealswa slawyrm [L. *regulus*] attru hit tosend oþþe ongytt. *a* **1100** in Napier *O.E. Glosses* 50/1856 *Spalangii, musci uenenosi*, þære scortan næddran, slawyrmes. **1483** *Cath. Angl.* 343/2 A Slaworme, *secula.* **1821** *Ayr & Wigton Courier* 22 Mar. (Jam.), Tho' slayworms and adders be coiled by thy rills. **1828** CARR *Craven Gloss.*, *Slaa-worm*, a blind worm. **1878** *Cumbld. Gloss* 88/2 *Slea worm*,..the so-called blind worm, slo-worm.

β. **11..** *Voc.* in Wr.-Wülcker 544 *Stellio*, slowurm. **14..** *Ibid.* 571 *Cecula*, a Slowerme. *c* **1475** *Ibid.* 766 *Hic calus*, a slowurme. **1530** PALSGR. 271/2 Sloo worme. **1581** DERRICKE *Image Irel.* (1883) 35 Behold you not the Slo-worme there, with Vipers generation? **1655** MOUFET & BENNET *Health's Improv.* (1746) 176 The Stork delighteth in Newts, Water-snakes, Adders, and Sloe-worms. **1823** E. MOOR *Suffolk Words* 365 *Slow worm*, or *Sloe-worm*,..the blind worm. **1878** [see α].

γ. **1558** W. WARDE tr. *Alexis' Secr.* 30 b, A certayne litle Serpent called a Slowe worme. **1589** GREENE *Menaphon* (Arb.) 86 Thine eyes are like the slowwormes in the night. **1646** SIR T. BROWNE *Pseud. Ep.* 153 So are slow-Wormes accounted blinde,..although their eyes be evident. **1681** GREW *Musæum* I. III. 48 The greater Slow-worm,..Called also the Blind-worm. **1762** *Phil. Trans.* LII. 475 As to the slow-worm, I have had two fair trials, to conclude, that his bite is quite harmless. **1791** BURNS *Let.* in Wks. (Globe) 495 When I matriculate in the herald's office, I intend that my supporters shall be two sloths, my crest a slow-worm. **1864** TENNYSON *Aylmer's F.* 852 Where the two contrived their daughter's good,..The slow-worm creeps..and all is open field. **1897** G. C. BATEMAN *Vivarium* 114 The Slow-worm has made itself famous by being the first to reveal to science the mysterious pineal, or median, eye.

*transf.* *a* **1548** HALL *Chron., Hen. IV*, 23 Avoidyng the slowe worme and deadely Dormouse called Idlenes. **1596** NASHE *Saffron Walden* Wks. (Grosart) III. 62 Was euer.. Ledgerdemaine a slow-worme, or Viuacitie a lasie-bones?

**2.** Used to render L. *scytale* in its original or modern application.

**1611** COTGR., *Scytale*, the Scytall; a dangerous Sloe-worme. **1668** CHARLETON *Onomast.* 31 *Scytale*,..the slow Worm. **1802** SHAW *Gen. Zool.* III. II. 590 Seban Slow-worm, *Scytalæ Americanæ*,..a small species, figured and slightly described in the work of Seba.

**3.** (See quot.)

**1897** G. C. BATEMAN *Vivarium* 129 The Spotted Slow-worm (*Acontias meleagris*).—The general shape of this Lizard is not unlike that of the Common Slow-worm (*Anguis fragilis*), hence its English name.

†**sloy.** *Obs.*$^{-1}$ An opprobrious epithet for a woman.

**1596** WARNER *Alb. Eng.* XI. lxii. (1597) 288 How tedious were a Shroe, a Sloy, a Wanton, or a Foole.

**sloyd** (slɔɪd), *sb.* Also **slöijd**, **slöjd**, **slojd**, **sloid.** [ad. Sw. *slöjd*, corresponding to ON. *slœgð*, whence SLEIGHT *sb.*[1]] A system of manual instruction or training in elementary woodwork, etc., originally developed and taught in Sweden.

The verb *sloyd* (*slöjd*, etc.), and the sbs. *sloyder*, *sloydist*, have also been occasionally employed.

α. **1884** [see FAD *sb.*[2] 1]. **1885** *Pract. Teacher* Oct. 357/2 Slöjd. A Short Description of a System of Handiwork taught in many Elementary Schools in Sweden. **1888** *Encycl. Brit.* XXIII. 107/2 In Sweden 'slojd', or elementary woodwork,..is taught with considerable success to children of both sexes.

β. **1886** *Pall Mall G.* 21 Sept. 14/1 'Sloyd'..aims at establishing handicraft as one of the subjects generally taught in schools. **1893** *Athenæum* 8 Apr. 437/3 Sloyd..is by no means the same as carpentry; tools, objects, methods, are different in the two pursuits.

*attrib.* **1885** *Pract. Teacher* Oct. 358/2 [We] spent a week in Stockholm, visiting nearly every Slöjd school there. **1886** *Pall Mall G.* 21 Sept. 14/1 The kindergarten system of Fröbel may be regarded as the precursor of the Sloyd movement.

**slub** (slʌb), *sb.*[1] Now chiefly *dial.* Also 7 **slubb(e.** [? ad. MDu. *slubbe* in the same sense.] Thick sludgy mud; mire, ooze. Also *attrib.*

**1577–87** HOLINSHED *Chron.* IV. 853 His wall..consisting onlie of slub and beach shoveled together. **1593** NORDEN *Spec. Brit., Cornw.* (1728) 6 The lande..fortefies it selfe with heaped mountes of sande, slub, and pibble stones. **1610** W. FOLKINGHAM *Art of Survey* I. x. 24 Ouer-flowing them with Fords or Land-flouds, affording a fatte and slimie substance or slubbe. *a* **1676** HALE *De Jure Maris* I. iv. in *Hargrave's Law Tracts* (1787) I. 17 The exaggeration of sand and slubb, which in process of time grow firm land. **1823** [see SLUBBY *a.*]. **1892** MRS. OWEN & D. JORDAN *Within an Hour of London* (ed. 2) 162 To the stranger, the slub looks like a level flat. *Ibid.*, The 'gripes' and gullies of the slub ooze.ays (Normal)*Ibid.* 163 If he is on the slub flats, .. his situation is not to be envied.

**slub** (slʌb), *sb.*[2] [Of obscure origin.] **1.** A lump on a thread.

**1825** J. NICHOLSON *Operat. Mechanic* 395 Taking out the slubs .. left in the silk by the negligence of the foreign reeler. **1897** *Leeds Merc. Suppl.* 23 Oct. (E.D.D.), Pike thi slubs off.

**2.** A yarn containing thickened parts, or slubs, at intervals; a fabric woven from such a yarn. Also *attrib.*, having an irregular effect given by a warp of uneven thickness.

**1928** *Daily Express* 14 Aug. 4 Slub reps, artificial silk velour, chenille combined with artificial silk .. are shown. **1940** *Chambers's Techn. Dict.* 779/1 *Slub yarns*, fancy yarns with thickened parts at frequent intervals. **1946** *Daily Progress* (Charlottesville, Va.) 30 Apr. 12/7 Solid color blue slub-weave and white striped blue chambray. **1957** *Textile Terms & Defs.* (Textile Inst.) (ed. 3) 42 Spun slubs may be produced by an intermittent acceleration of one pair of rollers during spinning. **1958** *Observer* 24 Aug. 7/7 Structured skirt fabrics come from Manchester as well as from Switzerland, but there they go by the general, somewhat unfeminine designation of 'slubs'. **1974** *News & Reporter* (Chester, S. Carolina) 24 Apr. 6-A (Advt.), Textured rayon with interesting slub highlights. **1979** *Radio Times* 5-11 May 14/1 In his choice of clothes—slub silk tie, silk pocket handkerchief, hound's-tooth jacket with turn-back cuffs—as in his choice of claret he declares himself a man of some style.

Hence **slubbed** *a.*, of fabrics: containing slubs.

**1961** *Harper's Bazaar* June 55 Three piece in white slubbed rayon. **1980** M. DRABBLE *Middle Ground* 171 Her vast off-white, gold-tasselled, slubbed-silk settee.

**slub** (slʌb), *sb.*[3] Also **slubb.** [f. SLUB *v.*[2]] A slubbing of cotton or wool; a roving.

**1851** *Art Jrnl. Illustr. Catal.* p. v**/2 By the revolution of the spindle and flyer the cotton slub receives its twist. **1868** *Chambers's Encycl.* X. 265/1 The spindles upon which these slubbs or slubbings are wound.

**slub** (slʌb), *v.*[1] *dial.* [f. SLUB *sb.*[1]] *trans.* To cover or plaster with mud.

**1823** E. MOOR *Suffolk Words* 365 Walls raised from the ooze of rivers require to be slubb'd over. **1886** JEFFERIES *Field & Hedgerow* (1889) 187 Those who try to go through get 'slubbed' up to their knees.

**slub** (slʌb), *v.*[2] Also **slubb.** [Of obscure origin; the vbl. sb. is found earlier.] *trans.* To draw out and twist (wool, cotton, etc.) after carding, so as to prepare it for spinning. Also *absol.* Hence **slubbed** *ppl. a.*

**1834** *New Monthly Mag.* XLI. 527 Machinery for roving and slubbing cotton and wool. **1844** G. DODD *Textile Manuf.* iii. 107 The 'slubbed' wool is taken from the mill to the house of the clothier, there to be spun. **1864** A. JEFFREY *Hist. Roxburghshire* IV. 116 The manufacturers were forced to get two women from Leeds to teach them to slubb and spin.

**slubber** ('slʌbə(r)), *sb.*[1] *dial.* [Cf. SLUB *sb.*[1] and SLOBBER *sb.*] Mire, mud; ooze, slime.

**1570** LEVINS *Manip.* 76/42 Slubber, *limus.* **1823** E. MOOR *Suffolk Words* 365 *Slub, Slubber*, mire, mud, the thick puddle on roads. **1828** CARR *Craven Gloss.*, *Slubber*, any gelatinous substance. **1890** HARTLEY *Clock Alm.* 29 (E.D.D.), He mud as weel ha' tried to climb up a hill side o' slubber.

**slubber** ('slʌbə(r)), *sb.*[2] [f. SLUB *v.*[2]]

**1.** One who manipulates a slubbing-machine.

**1835** URE *Philos. Manuf.* 8 Slubbing is a handicraft operation, depending on the skill of the slubber. **1843** *Penny Cycl.* XXVII. 552/1 The workman or 'slubber' .. elongates the 'carding' into 'slubbing'. **1891** *Leeds Mercury* 14 Dec. 2/4 If he wanted to borrow, he would apply to his weavers and not his slubbers.

**2.** A slubbing-machine.

**1897** *Traill's Social Eng.* VI. 73 In the preparing frames, known as slubbers or rovers, the bobbins were necessarily large and weighty.

**slubber** ('slʌbə(r)), *v.* Now chiefly *dial.* Also 6 sloubber. [Probably of Du. or LG. origin: cf. MDu. *overslubberen* to wade through mud, LG. *slubbern* (hence Da. *slubre*), G. *schlubbern*, *schluppern* to gobble, to scamp in working, etc.]

**1. a.** *trans.* To stain, smear, daub, soil.

**1530** PALSGR. 324/2 Sloubberde with wepyng, *esplouré*. *Ibid.* 722/1 Fye, howe you have slubbred your geare for one dayes wearyng. **1577** HANMER *Anc. Eccl. Hist.* (1663) 182 They were .. so slubbered and darkned with a black colour, that they became unprofitable for publick sight. **1603** H. CROSSE *Vertues Commw.* (1878) 75 That face that is slubbred & starched with so many ointments & drugs. **1639** HORN & ROB. *Gate Lang. Unl.* lxviii. §739 Let him not slubber (soile) or slurry his books, but use them cleanlily. **1682** T. FLATMAN *Heraclitus Ridens* No. 55 (1713) II. 95 Thou couldst not think that Glass wanted new-foiling, .. and thou hast slubber'd it only to cover the foul *Plagium.* **1854** MISS BAKER *Northampt. Gloss.*, *Slubber*, to smear, or obscure with dirt.

**b.** *fig.* To sully (renown, etc.).

**1600** HEYWOOD *2nd Pt. Edw. IV*, Wks. 1874 I. 185 Going about to slubber our renowne. *a* **1625** FLETCHER *Hum. Lieutenant* IV. i, If it be an honest end, That end's the full reward and thanks but slubbers it. **1641** MILTON *Reform. Eng.* II. Wks. 1851 III. 33 There is no art that hath bin .. more soyl'd and slubber'd with aphorisming pedantry then the art of policie.

**c.** To obscure, darken. *rare*$^{-1}$.

**1605** *1st Part Ieronimo* II. iv, The euening to[o] begins to slubber day.

**d.** *intr.* To become indistinct. *rare*$^{-1}$.

**1665** REA *Flora* 53 It is a little apt to run, that is, in one or two hot days the colours to slubber and run one into the other.

**2.** With advs. **a.** With *up*, = sense 1. *rare*$^{-1}$.

*a* **1586** SIDNEY *Arcadia* (1622) 7 Each place handsome .., not so daintie as not to be trode on, nor yet slubbered vp with good fellowship.

**b.** To wear *out* by dirty handling. *rare*$^{-1}$.

**1621** S. WARD *Life Faith* 97 Wilt thou dye before thou hast liued, as Boyes slubber out bookes before they learne their Lesson?

**c.** To daub *over* so as to cover or conceal. Chiefly *fig.*, to gloss *over*.

**1646** EARL MONM. tr. *Biondi's Civil Wars* VIII. 150 Richard had much adoe to colour over his Cruelties, which not being to be Denied, hee slubber'd them over, not naming them. **1653** A. WILSON *Jas. I*, 63 The Court-trick to daub and slubber over things that may be perspicuous. **1654** VILVAIN *Theorem. Theol.* i. 11 A lepry .. which may be sullied or slubbered over with palliativ salvs. *a* **1797** WALPOLE *Mem. Geo. II* (1822) I. 238 The blemishes which these varnishers have slubbered over.

**3. a.** With *up*: To perform, make, concoct, deal with, etc., in a hurried and careless manner.

**1550** LEVER *Serm.* (Arb.) 65 He minisheth Gods sacraments, he slubbers vp his seruice. **1589** NASHE *Anat. Absurd.* 20 That some stitcher, Weauer, .. or Fidler, hath suffled or slubberd vp a few ragged Rimes. **1602** CAREW *Surv. Cornw.* II. 127 b, Many a bad mariage bargaine is there yerely slubbred vp. **1610** J. DOVE *Advt. Seminaries* 2 It doth appear they slubber up many things negligently, and performe them loosely. *a* **1625** BEAUM. & FL. *Captain* V. v, If a marriage should be thus slubberd up in a play.

**b.** So without *up*.

**1596** SHAKS. *Merch. V.* II. viii. 39 Slubber not businesse for my sake Bassanio. *a* **1659** BP. BROWNRIG *Serm.* (1674) II. xviii. 226 Matters of less moment .. may be slubbered and slighted. **1664** JER. TAYLOR *Dissuas. Popery* I. i. §3 The Council of Trent .. slubber'd the whole matter both in the question of Indulgences and Purgatory. **1806** J. BERESFORD *Miseries Hum. Life* IX. i, Knife and fork slubbered through the general knife-cloth. **1827** HOOD *Legend of Navarre* xvi, Her servants stow'd him, (I am asham'd to think how he was slubber'd,) Stuck bolt upright within a corner cupboard!

**4.** To run or skim *over* hurriedly and in a careless or slovenly manner. Also with *through*.

In very common use in the 17th century.

**1592** *Consp. Pretended Reform.* Pref. p. iii, Matters .. are so sleightly and ignorantly slubbered ouer by such Preachers. **1649** BLITHE *Eng. Improv. Impr.* 80, I dare say, one Acre of Corne thus throughly husbanded, may be worth two Acres, nay three, slubbered over. **1670** BAXTER *Heav. Medit.* 23 Which may be lost by hasty breaking off, and slubbering over so great a business. *a* **1716** BLACKALL *Wks.* (1723) I. 194, I am encumbred with much Business, so that sometimes I forget, and at other times am forc'd to slubber over my Prayers. **1767** S. PATERSON *Another Trav.* I. 166 Anxiety to have the business slubbered over as fast as possible. **1941** AUDEN *New Year Let.* I. 24 Time and again have slubbered through With slip and slapdash what I do.

**5.** To gobble *up* slobberingly.

**1640** BRATHWAIT *Lanc. Lovers* iv, Slubber up a sillibub.

**6.** *intr.* To be lubberly; to slabber or slobber.

*c* **1820** HOGG *Tales, Basil Lee* (1866) 239/2 When I see a young chap lying slubberin' an' sleepin' a' the day in a heather bush. **1825** J. WILSON *Noct. Ambr.* Wks. 1855 I. 3 The bloated kings .. Shall slubber and snore.

**slubberdegullion** (ˌslʌbədɪ'gʌljən). [f. SLUBBER *v.*, with fanciful addition; cf. SLABBERDEGULLION.] A slobbering or dirty fellow; a worthless sloven.

*a* **1616** BEAUM. & FL. *Custom of Country* I. ii, Yes they are knit; but must this slubberdegullion Have her maiden-head now? **1630** J. TAYLOR (Water P.) *Laugh & be fat* Wks. II. 78 Contaminous, pestiferous, .. slubberdegullions. **1663** BUTLER *Hud.* I. iii. 886 Although thou hast deserv'd, Base Slubberdegullion, to be serv'd As thou did'st vow to deal with me. *a* **1700** B. E. *Dict. Cant. Crew*, *Slubberdegullion*, a slovenly, dirty, nasty Fellow. [Hence in later Dicts.] **1866** G. W. THORNBURY *Greatheart* III. 92 Do you take us for green hands, you sluberdegullion? **1891** FORD *Thistledown* xvi, This slubberdegullion o' a maister. **1905** R. GARNETT *Shaks.* 55 Aroint thee, .. vagabond, wretch, base Slubberdegullion!

**slubbered** ('slʌbəd), *ppl. a.* [f. SLUBBER *v.*]

**1.** Soiled, smeared; dirty; sullied.

**1588** CHURCHYARD *Sparke of Frendship*, etc. D iiij, All slubbred things must needes be washt anue. **1606** DEKKER *Seven Deadly Sins* Wks. (Grosart) II. 33 Wyping their slubberd cheekes with wispes of cleane Strawe. **1642** HOWELL *Twelve Treat.* (1661) 83, I see Religion in torn ragged weeds, and with slubber'd eyes sitting upon weeping-Crosse.

*fig.* **1619** FLETCHER *False One* II. iii, Pompey I overthrew: what did that get me? The slubber'd Name of an authoriz'd Enemy.

**2.** Hastily put together; hurriedly gone through; done or performed carelessly, etc.

**1602** *2nd Pt. Return fr. Parnass.* Prol. 22 What we present I must needes confesse is but slubbered inuention. **1669** FLAMSTEED in Rigaud *Corr. Sci. Men* (1841) II. 77 These .. induced me to apply myself, with these not slubbered supplications, to your Honour. **1690** C. NESSE *Hist. O. & N. Test.* I. 77 Neither will the King of Heaven accept of thy slight and slubberd services.

**'slubberer.** [f. SLUBBER *v.*] One who works hastily and carelessly. Also with *over*.

**1580** HOLLYBAND *Treas. Fr. Tong*, *Brouilleur*, .. a tumbler togither, a slubberer. *a* **1591** H. SMITH *Wks.* (1866) I. 444 The physician which doth but almost cure, is but a slubberer. **1611** COTGR., *Boiffeur*, a bungler vp, or slubberer ouer, of things in hast. **1638** A. READ *Chirurg.* ix. 62 By want of this [neatness] a slubberer and sloven is discerned from a cleanly workman. **1649** BLITHE *Eng. Improv. Impr.* (1653) 42 Idle Practitioners and Slothfull impatient Slubberers.

**'slubbering,** *vbl. sb.* [f. SLUBBER *v.*] The action of the vb., in various senses.

**1582** BATMAN *Barth. De P.R.* VI. xii. 74 A servant woman is .. put to office and worke of travaile, toylyng, and slubbering. *a* **1591** H. SMITH *Serm.* (1637) 143 By their slubbering of the Word (for want of study and meditation). **1604** E. G[RIMSTONE] *D'Acosta's Hist. Indies* IV. xi. 238 To paint the face and bodies of themselves and their idolls .., which they call slubbering. **1638** *Penit. Conf.* iii. (1657) 21 A careless debasing and slubbering of the body.

**'slubbering,** *ppl. a.* [f. SLUBBER *v.*] That slubbers; working in a dirty or slovenly manner; showing haste and carelessness.

*a* **1591** H. SMITH *Serm.* (1886) I. 314 The Jews abhorred the sacrifice for the slubbering priests. **1594** *Zepheria* ii, My slubbring pencil casts too grosse a matter. **1642** MILTON *Apol. Smect.* Wks. 1851 III. 325 Who ingrosse many pluralities under a non-resident and slubbring dispatch of soules. **1681** H. MORE *Expos. Daniel* Pref. 17 His Expositions are .. so dilute, shallow and slubbering. **1731** FIELDING *Grub St. Op.* III. x, Go, and like a slub'ring Bess howl, Whilst at your griefs I'm quaffing. **1818** *Sporting Mag.* II. 89 A sort of scumming, smearing, slubbering way of sketching. **1854** MISS BAKER *Northampt. Gloss.* s.v., A [slovenly] servant is called 'a slubbering thing'.

Hence **'slubberingly** *adv.*

**1622** DRAYTON *Poly-olb.* xxi. 168 Such as .. slubberingly patch up some slight and shallow rhime. **1657** J. SERGEANT *Schism Dispach't* 284 The Verse .. which he brings to testify his tenet expressely, but, by omitting it slubberingly, bids it say nothing.

† **'slubberly,** *a. Obs. rare.* [f. SLUBBER *v.*] Dirty, foul; muddled.

**1540** HYRDE tr. *Vives' Instr. Chr. Wom.* (1592) P vij, For it were better for thee to eat brown bred .. then cause thy husband to fall unto any slubberlie work, or stinking occupation. **1673** HICKERINGILL *Greg. F. Greybeard* 268 Brother Wild had now made his brains as foul and slubberly with his Guzling as are the fore-skirts of his doublet.

**slubbery** ('slʌbərɪ), *a.* [f. SLUBBER *v.*] Lacking in neatness; slovenly.

**1880** *Daily News* 20 Mar. 5/5 Whether the clumsy 'slubbery' style of Cambridge is more telling than the regular .. form in which the Oxford men row.

**'slubbing,** *vbl. sb.* Also 8 **slobbing.** [Of obscure origin.]

**1.** A process of drawing and twisting by which cotton or wool slivers are prepared for spinning.

**1779** R. PEELE *Pat. Specif.* No 1212. 1 My Invention of a Method for the .. Slobbing, Roving and Spinning of Cotton, Silk, Worsted and Woollen. **1825** J. NICHOLSON *Operat. Mech.* 386 A machine called the billy, or roving-billy, the operation of which is called roving or slubbing. **1835** URE *Philos. Manuf.* 8 There is a process between carding and spinning the wool, called slubbing. **1876** I. WATTS in *Brit. Manuf. Indust.* V. 135 The operation which follows the drawing is that of slubbing, where the sliver has a certain amount of twist imparted to it.

**2.** One of the loosely-compacted threads obtained by this process.

**1786** J. ROYDS *Pat. Specif.* No. 1564. 2 This machine being for the purpose of passing at once two or more slubbings betwixt the rollers. **1835** URE *Philos. Manuf.* 171 It .. thus forms what is called a slubbing or roving—a soft thread to be thereafter spun, on the mule-jenny, into yarn fit for the loom. **1884** W. S. B. McLAREN *Spinning* (ed. 2) 123 The slubbing should be strong enough to pull out easily when stretched by the hands.

**3.** *collect.* Cotton or wool which has been slubbed.

**1836** *Bingham's New Cases* II. 451 Manufacturers .. took their wool .. to the mill for the purpose of being .. made into slubbing. **1891** R. MARSDEN *Cotton Spinning* (ed. 4) 162 Two strands of slubbing are put up, and by a draught of two are united into one.

**4.** *attrib.*, chiefly with names of apparatus, as ***slubbing-billy***, ***-frame***, ***-jenny***, ***-machine***; also ***slubbing-thread***, ***-waste***.

**1795** *Edinb. Advertiser* 6 Jan. 15/3 One slubbing jeanny, with one mule jeanny. **1835** URE *Philos. Manuf.* 9 The long wooden rod from his slubbing-frame. *Ibid.* 171 The Slubbing Machine, or Billy, performs the next operation. *Ibid.* 175 It might be supposed that the slubbing threads would be apt to coil round the spindles. **1891** R. MARSDEN *Cotton Spinning* (ed. 4) 221 The slubbing billy .. in a modified and improved form .. still exists in the woollen trade. **1894** *Times* 17 Aug. 9/5 Slubbing waste, roving waste, .. and all waste or rags composed wholly or in part of wool.

**slubby** ('slʌbɪ), *a. dial.* [f. SLUB *sb.*[1]] Muddy; sticky or slippery with mud.

**1570** LEVINS *Manip.* 107/13 Slubbie, *lubricus.* **1823** E. MOOR *Suffolk Words* 365 Wet, poachy ground, recently trodden by cattle, is said to be slubby, or all of a slub. **1886** JEFFERIES *Field & Hedgerow* (1889) 187 The lanes and the gateways in the fields they say are slubby enough in November.

**sluce,** obs. form of SLUICE *sb.* and *v.*

† **sluch.** *Sc. Obs.* Also **slucht.** [Of obscure origin.] A suit (of clothes).

**1582** *Records of Elgin* (1903) I. 165 Item thre schillingis four penneis for ane sluch of clais to Johne Innes. **1598** *Extr. Burgh Rec. Aberd.* (1848) II. 163 To Alex[r]. Checkum, .. fyve pundis to help to by him a slucht of blew.

**sluchched:** see SLUTCH *v.*

**slucy,** obs. form of SLUICY *a.*

†**'Slud**, *int. Obs.* App. a variant of 'SBLOOD. (Cf. 'SLOOD.)

**1601** B. JONSON *Cynthia's Revels* IV. i, 'Slud, I never saw him till this morning. **1608** TOURNEUR *Rev. Trag.* V. iii, 'Slud, 'tis all false! **1749** FIELDING *Tom Jones* XVII. iii, Slud! then.. I tell you I have power, and I will fulfil it.

†**'sludden.** *Obs.*$^{-0}$ A sleuth-hound.

**1570** LEVINS *Manip.* 61 A Sludden, *pedisequus, sanguisecus, canis.*

**sludder** ('slʌdə(r)), *sb. dial.* [Cf. LG. *sleuder* lather, G. dial. *schluder* slush, mud, etc.] (See quot. 1796.) Hence **'sludder** *v. intr.*, to wallow.

**1796** W. H. MARSHALL *Yorksh.* (ed. 2) II. 345 *Sludder*, or *Sluther*, loose, broken, slippery, pappy matter; as curds and whey, loose fat, mud, &c. **1874** WOOD *Nat. Hist.* 144 Transfixing them as they lay 'sluddering' on the mud or sand.

†**slude.** *Obs. rare.* [ad. Russ. *slyúda* (locally *slúda*, *slud*; Czech *slída*) mica.] Russian mica in thin transparent plates.

**1591** FLETCHER *Russe Commw.* (Hakl.) 13 In the province of Corelia.. there groweth a soft rocke which they call *slude*. This they cut into pieces,.. and so use it for glasse-lanthorns and such like. **1613** M. RIDLEY *Magn. Bodies* 45 This needle and semicircle would be covered with some glasse and slude, as dials use to be covered. **1662** *Irel., Statues at Large* (1765) II. 407 Muscovy glass or slude the pound, 2ˢ.

**sludge** ('slʌdʒ), *sb.* Also 8 **sluge.** [var. of SLUTCH *sb.*]

**1. a.** Mud, mire, or ooze, covering the surface of the ground or forming a deposit at the bottom of rivers, etc. Cf. SLUDGE *v.* 6.

**1649** BLITHE *Eng. Improv. Impr.* (1653) 143 A Mud, or Sludg, that lyeth frequently in deep Rivers, which is very soft. **1707** MORTIMER *Husb.* (1721) II. 70 In that Water I put the Earth.., so as to make it a meer soft Sludge or Mud. **1745** *Beverley Beck Act* ii. 2 Choaked and warped up by the sludge and soil brought in by the tides. **1782** *Phil. Trans.* LXXII. 364 When we saw it, the moist filth, or sludge, at bottom.. was two or three inches deep. **1822** SCOTT *Nigel* iii, The natural scent of the ooze and sludge left by the reflux of the tide. **1875** SMILES *Boy's Voy. r. World* xi. 113 A wide stretch of ground was covered by a thick deposit of sludge. **1946** L. D. STAMP *Britain's Struct. & Scenery* iii. 20 In tundra lands the sub-soil remains permanently frozen whilst the surface thaws in summer and, where there are steep slopes, masses of sludge slide downhill. **1959** G. H. DURY *Face of Earth* xv. 181 The loess records cold, very dry climate. The underlying sludge was formed in a preceding episode of moister conditions when the topsoil thawed annually.

**b.** *Naut.* Ice imperfectly formed, or broken up into minute pieces (cf. quots.).

**1817** SCORESBY in *Ann. Reg., Chron.* 534 The first appearance of ice whilst in the state of detached crystals, is called by the sailors sludge. **1820** —— *Acc. Arctic Reg.* I. 227 Sludge consists of a stratum of detached ice-crystals, or of snow, or of the smaller fragments of brash-ice floating on the surface of the sea. **1885** *Encycl. Brit.* XIX. 328 The ice first forms in thin, irregular flakes called 'sludge', and when this is compact enough to hold snow it is known as 'brash'.

**c.** The colour of sludge. Also *attrib.*

**1962** *Sunday Express* 4 Feb. 19/2 Pyjama stripes—navy, 'sludge' or 'smog' on white. **1977** *Vogue* Feb. 90/1 From a commanding frilly and deep sludge dress, Merle Park changes into her working clothes.

**2. a.** Any earthy or slimy matter or deposit; a mixture of some finely powdered substance and water. *spec.* Such material formed as waste in various industrial and mechanical processes.

**1702** SAVERY *Miners' Friend* 60 Sluge or Fine Dirt.. will do my Engine no Injury. **1840** HODGSON *Hist. Northumb.* III. II. 319/2 That sort of ammoniacal sleck or sludge which comes from kitchens. **1883** HALDANE *Workshop Rec.* Ser. II. 53/2 They [sulphites] act well with salt water, giving a soft sludge, which should be readily removed by the blow-pipe. **1920** CROSS & BEVAN *Paper-Making* 144 It constitutes a 'sludge', practically devoid of useful felting properties. **1933** *Charlottesville* (Va.) *Daily Progress* 22 May 6/5 The death of five men in a drainage vat at the Hess and Drucker Tannery was being investigated... The fifth was a would-be rescuer, who plunged into the tank of sludge. **1965** *New Statesman* 19 Nov. 809/4 (Advt.), Industrial Chemist required by Company dealing in sludges & effluents of all kinds. **1974** J. DYSON *Prime Minister's Boat is Missing* xxx. 180 The sludge of crude oil in the bottom of tanks.

**b.** *Metall.* Finely crushed ore mixed with water; metalliferous slime.

**1757** tr. *Henckel's Pyritologia* 341 All these cobalds or pyrites must previously be parted from the barren minerals, by stamping and washing, and made into a pure sludge. **1778** PRYCE *Min. Cornub.* 226 Some have concluded, that Tin in the state of sludge or slime, by length of time, must grow and increase. **1839** URE *Dict. Arts* 752 It is impossible to prevent some of the finely attenuated portions of the galena called sludge, floating in the water. **1898** *Daily News* 5 July 9/5 Further tenders have just been accepted for a quantity of sludges valued at over 1,000*l.*

**c.** The precipitate in sewage tanks.

**1877** J. B. DENTON *Sanit. Engineering* 266 The third gradation of the solid matter in sewage known as 'sludge'. **1887** *Times* 26 Aug. 9/4 The sediment or sludge left at the bottom of the precipitation tanks.

**d.** A loose sediment that forms in boilers and other vessels in which water is habitually heated.

**1839** R. S. ROBINSON *Naut. Steam Eng.* 123 To prevent any sludge, &c. from issuing out at the mouth of the pipe, and falling on the decks of the vessel. **1912** R. B. DOLE in Rogers & Aubert *Industr. Chem.* iii. 47 If magnesium and sulphates are comparatively low or if suspended matter is comparatively high the scale is soft and bulky and may be in the form of sludge that can be blown or washed from the boiler. **1937** E. PULL *Boiler-House Practice* xv. 147 Every opportunity should be taken to remove accumulations of grease, scale, sludge and soot. **1955** KIRK & OTHMER *Encycl. Chem. Technol.* XIV. 940 This led to the system.. of maintaining at all times in the boiler water a small but sufficient excess of phosphate ion so that all calcium ion entering with the feed water would be precipitated as a loose sludge of calcium phosphate rather than as a hard scale.

**e.** The mixture of water or mud fluid with cuttings that is produced in rock drilling.

**1871** [see SLUDGER]. **1911** DANA & SAUNDERS *Rock Drilling* ii. 21 The shales will often form a sludge containing such proportions of large and small particles as to cake on the bit. **1933** R. S. LEWIS *Elements Mining* xiv. 422 Where much sludge is made it is very important to have the water return with sufficient velocity to lift the heaviest particles in the sludge. **1963** *Gloss. Mining Terms (B.S.I.)* III. 13 *Sludge*, rock cuttings produced by the drill bit.

**f.** A dark viscous liquid or semi-solid mass deposited when a petroleum distillate is mixed with strong sulphuric acid during refining. Also called *sludge acid* (see sense 4), *acid sludge*.

**1885** *Encycl. Brit.* XVIII. 719/1 The acid 'sludge', consisting of the oil of vitriol combined with the impurities of the oil and forming a black tarry liquid, settles to the bottom.. and is drawn off. **1938** OLIVER & SPANGLER in A. E. Dunstan et al. *Sci. Petroleum* IV. 2765/1 At refineries on the sea coast acid sludge was frequently discharged into the ocean. **1954** KIRK & OTHMER *Encycl. Chem. Technol.* XIII. 493 Most refineries hydrolyze the light nonlube sludges, effecting an incomplete separation of acid tars from the weak impure acid. **1965** O. T. FASULLO *Sulfuric Acid* v. 127 The tendency of sludges to evolve sulfur dioxide.., in addition to the enormous quantity in which sludges are necessarily produced by the petroleum industry, makes these materials worthy subjects for the application of pollution control measures.

**g.** = SLIME *sb.* 4 b.

**1900** *Jrnl. Brit. Inst. Electr. Engin.* XXIX. 274 In copper refining with high current densities less anode sludge is formed. **1948** T. C. ELLIOTT *Electric Accumulator Man.* iii. 26 The piling up of sludge.. and the creation of possible short circuits through the growths clinging to the tubes.. must be avoided. **1977** BRODD & KORDESCH tr. *Bode's Lead-Acid Batteries* iii. 222 A Pb content of more than 5% is supposed to cause difficulties during the formation of positive plates (swelling or warping or extensive sludge formation).

**h.** A thick, semi-solid deposit that tends to form in oil when it is heated, exposed to the air, or mixed with another kind of oil.

**1920** *Whittaker's Electr. Engineer's Pocket-bk.* (ed. 4) 245 When the transformer is examined, it is found that the windings and core are covered with a reddish-brown flocculent deposit or sludge. **1927** *Jrnl. Soc. Chem. Industry* 8 Apr. 135T/2 The sludge deposits which are sometimes found in hollow crankpins.. are due evidently to decomposition products of the oil being thrown out by centrifugal action. **1941** D. F. MINER *Insulation Electr. Apparatus* iv. 81 The purification of oil used in circuit breakers and transformers consists principally in the removal of water, carbon, and sludge. **1973** G. ZWICK *Everyman's Guide Car Maintenance* (1974) vi. 153 If the motorist has consistently been using a high grade heavy duty oil, the chances are that the interior of the engine is clean, with a bare minimum of sludge and other residues.

**i.** *Med.* (A quantity of) sludged blood. Cf. SLUDGING *vbl. sb.* 4.

**1947** *Science* 7 Nov. 436/2 Many human patients have various degrees of unexplainable edema... These can now be examined for sludges. **1972** H. I. BICHER *Blood Cell Aggregation* ii. 27 All of this provides strong additional support for considering sludge as.. a possible antecedent to thrombosis.

**3.** *local.* (See quot.)

**1839** SIR G. C. LEWIS *Gloss. Heref., Sludge*,.. a wet or muddy place.

**4.** *attrib.*, as *sludge-door*, *-hole*, *-ice*, etc. (see quots.); *sludge brown*, *green*, *grey* sbs. and adjs.; *sludge-coloured* adj.; **sludge acid** = sense 2 f above.

**1885** *American* IX. 222 Around New York *sludge acid.. is doing deadly work among the bivalves. **1891** *Cent. Dict.*, *Sludge acid*, acid which has been used for the purification of petroleum. **1938** OLIVER & SPANGLER in A. E. Dunstan et al. *Sci. Petroleum* IV. 2766/2 Formerly it was possible to use some of this weak separated sludge acid for the manufacture of superphosphate fertilizer, but the objections.. to the presence of evil-smelling hydro-carbon derivatives in superphosphate has practically stopped this. **1965** O. T. FASULLO *Sulfuric Acid* v. 127 Heavy sludges are generally mixed with lighter sludge acids to produce a blend with a middle-range viscosity. **1977** D. CLARK *Gimmel Flask* v. 82, I thought this sort of *sludge brown varnish paint went out with Queen Victoria. **1962** A. LEJEUNE *Duel in Shadows* vii. 91 An Englishman in a *sludge-coloured raincoat. **1979** S. GAINHAM in G. Hardinge *Winter's Crimes* XI. 69 The woman in sludge-coloured tweed. **1855** OGILVIE *Suppl.*, **Sludge-doors*, in boilers, closed openings by which the matter deposited at the bottom.. can be taken out. **1971** *Vogue* 1 Oct. 127 *Sludge green knit tights. **1972** *Guardian* 8 Feb. 11/2 Cheesecloth smock shirt.. natural, yellow, sludge green, red or blue. **1976** *Times* 3 Feb. 9/7 Single breasted coat.. sludge green with maroon overcheck. **1977** *Listener* 22-29 Dec. 855/4 He's a moray eel, a *sludge-grey reptilian lurker. **1846** A. YOUNG *Naut. Dict.* 313 There are also *sludge-holes at the ends of the water passages between the flues, by which the deposit can be raked out. **1853** KANE *Grinnell Exped.* xxxi. (1856) 268 Suddenly a seal rose close by him in the *sludge-ice. **1896** *Durh. Arch. Trans.* (1901) 26 A circular tank or cistern provided with an outflow or '*sludge'-pipe at the bottom. **1887** *Archit. Soc. Dict.* VII. s.v., **Sludge pit*, a cesspool. **1883** GRESLEY *Gloss. Coal-m.* 227 **Sludge pump*, a short iron pipe or tube.. with which the boremeal is extracted from a borehole. **1889** *Pall Mall G.* 31 July 6/1 It will then.. be pumped through pipes extending along a jetty into the *sludge ships, for conveyance and discharge into the German Ocean. **1869** BLACKMORE *Lorna D.* xliv, Here and there the ice was fibred with the trail of *sludge-weed, slanting from the side.

**sludge** (slʌdʒ), *v.* [f. the sb.]

**I. 1.** *trans.* To convert into sludge.

**1757** tr. *Henckel's Pyritologia* 42 A native metal may lie.. in so light and tender a form.. as that the noble metal cannot be sludged, but be carried away by the stream. **1950** *Brit. Birds* XLIII. 383 The bird was on a pool used for sludging boiler ash, which has been constructed within the last two years. **1978** *Sci. Amer.* Jan. 85 (Advt.), In industry, chromic acid and oil-water emulsions usually live only once. They do their job; then they get discharged, sludged, trucked away, and buried.

**2.** To stop up, fill the crevices of (an embankment), with liquid mud.

**1875** KNIGHT *Dict. Mech.* 2217.

**3.** To clear from sludge or mud.

**1890** *Eastern Morning News* (Hull) 26 Sept. 1/4 For mowing the sides and bottom of Newland Beck,.. also to sludge same.

**4.** *intr.* To form or deposit sludge.

**1941** D. F. MINER *Insulation Electr. Apparatus* iv. 80 Transformer oil that has begun to sludge will continue to do so after it has been purified by means of the centrifuge or filter press. **1977** BRODD & KORDESCH tr. *Bode's Lead-Acid Batteries* iii. 271 Those plates that have been formed at 40°C with 1·06 kg/liter (acid concentration) and 74 A/m² (current density) are the last to sludge.

**II. 5.** *intr.* To trudge, to tramp; to labour. Cf. SLUTCH *v.* 3.

**1908** M. & J. FINDLATER *Crossriggs* xxiii. 170 She had got to sludge back to the station in the rain, and then go home and give a cheerful account of her day. **1913** D. H. LAWRENCE *Love Poems & Others* 44 A widow o forty-five As has sludged like a horse all her life. **1954** *New Statesman* 3 Apr. 432/3 'Well, goodnight,' he said, sludging away.

**III. 6.** *intr.* To move slowly by solifluction.

**1938** *Geol. Mag.* LXXV. 254 Only the upper 800 feet is precipitous, the lower 600 feet.. consisting of vegetated scree down which recent waste is sludging. **1940** C. F. C. HAWKES *Prehistoric Foundations of Europe* ii. 7 Seasonal thawing will cause surface deposits to sludge over more deeply frozen subsoil: this phenomenon is called solifluxion. **1959** G. H. DURY *Face of Earth* xv. 177 Sludging downslope, rock-waste tends to mask the break between high and low ground. **1964** *New Scientist* 8 Oct. 105/2 Half frozen material sludges rapidly downhill in the spring thaw.

Hence **sludged** *ppl. a.*

**1941** D. F. MINER *Insulation Electr. Apparatus* iv. 80 No method is yet available that will.. bring sludged oil back to its original condition. **1947** *Science* 7 Nov. 435/2 The resistance of sludged blood to its own passage through the bottlenecks of the circulatory system forcibly reduces the rates of blood flow through all the open vessels of the body. **1972** H. I. BICHER *Blood Cell Aggregation* ii. 35 Ischemic changes in the myocardium as a result of sludged blood.

**sludger** ('slʌdʒə(r)). [f. SLUDGE *v.*] An appliance for removing the sludge from a bore-hole, or for boring in quicksand.

**1839** URE *Dict. Arts* 966 The sludger, for bringing up the mud. **1851** GREENWELL *Coal-trade Terms Northumb. & Durham* 9 Sludgers.. are used when a bore-hole is so wet that the borings would.. be washed out of the cylinder. **1871** W. MORGANS *Mining Tools* 134 A sludger which is fitted with an inside piston.. in order to suck the sludge into the cylinder.

**sludging** ('slʌdʒɪŋ), *vbl. sb.* [f. SLUDGE *sb.* or *v.* + -ING¹.] **1.** The action of filling up crevices in dried clay by means of free-flowing mud; also, the mud so used.

**1852** J. WIGGINS *Embanking* 19 As these spits contract in drying, the crevices outside are therefore filled with mud, which is called 'sludging'. *a* **1877** KNIGHT *Dict. Mech.* III. 2217/1 *Sludging*, stopping the crevices incident to the contraction of clay piled in embankments, by mud sufficiently fluid to run freely. **1940** *Chambers's Techn. Dict.* 342/1 The crevices left when the clay has dried out are filled with sludging.

**2.** The formation or deposition of sludge, esp. in oil.

**1922** GLAZEBROOK *Dict. Appl. Physics* II. 928/1 Various schemes and devices are used to prevent sludging, such as.. by using a float on the oil surface. **1931** HOFFERT & CLAXTON *Motor Benzole* vi. 143 The difference in the solubilities of the resinous substances in different types of wash oils, also accounts for the sludging that usually occurs when such oils are mixed. **1969** *Practical Motorist* Jan. 557/1 Most modern engine oils incorporate additives which are designed to reduce sludging. **1973** *Times* 1 June 11/5 No black sludge will be able to form in your central heating system. How horrid. I never knew sludging was going on behind those pipes.

**3.** = SOLIFLUCTION.

**1946** *Amer. Jrnl. Sci.* CCXLIV. 626 The down-slope movement of the fine-grained components is presumed to be largely a flow as mud and is called by English writers 'sludging'. **1959** G. H. DURY *Face of Earth* xv. 177 Widespread sludging is mainly responsible for the featureless aspect of many Arctic landscapes. **1964** *New Scientist* 8 Oct. 105/3 He also showed.. that the much-discussed movement by freeze-thaw sludging (solifluction) is quantitatively of very little significance [in a Lappland valley]. **1975** J. G. EVANS *Environment Early Man Brit. Isles* i. 7 The Upper Gravel.. was most likely formed by downhill sludging under conditions of impeded drainage.

**4.** *Med.* The aggregation of blood cells into jelly-like masses in such a way as to impede circulation.

**1950** *Amer. Jrnl. Med. Sci.* CCXIX. 538/2 We have.. found a close correlation between the blood sedimentation rate and the degree of sludging in the capillaries. **1976** *Path. Ann.* XI. 3 This hemorrhage is sustained for up to 24 hours until the deeper intact capillaries adopt a ballooned appearance due to stasis and sludging of red cells.

**sludgy** (ˈslʌdʒɪ), *a.* [f. SLUDGE *sb.* + -Y.]

**1.** Muddy, miry, oozy.

**1782** W. GILPIN *Obs. on Wye* (1789) 53 Sludgy shores too appeared on each side. **1805** FORSYTH *Beauties Scotl.* II. 220 A rich sludgy mixture of fine earth and clay. **1844** H. STEPHENS *Bk. Farm* I. 560 The man should remove any wet sludgy matter from the bottom of the drain with a scoop. **1878** *Cassell's Techn. Educ.* III. 326 The whole coming off in a sludgy mess, and leaving the paper quite bare.

**2.** Consisting of newly formed particles of ice; full of sludge-ice.

**1853** KANE *Grinnell Exped.* xxxviii. (1856) 348 No sludgy streams of pancake. **1856** —— *Arctic Expl.* I. xxxi. 423 The rise and fall of the sludgy water.

**3.** Of the colour of sludge.

**1975** *Country Life* 18 Dec. 1770/2 'Workwear', made in sludgy colours and materials. **1978** *Daily Tel.* 6 Dec. 17/4 All colours are sludgy at the fashionable end of the market at present... Pinks, yellows and purples are just unsaleable.

†**sluds.** *Obs.*$^{-0}$ (See quot.)

**1753** *Chambers' Cycl.* Suppl., *Sluds*, a term used by the miners in Cornwall for half-roasted ores. [Hence in some later Dicts.]

**slue,** freq. variant of SLEW *v.* and *sb.*$^2$

**slue,** obs. pa. t. SLAY *v.*$^1$

**sluff** (slʌf), *v. U.S.* var. SLOUGH *v.*$^2$ 3.

For other uses see *Engl. Dial. Dict.* s.v. *Slough* sb.$^1$ and vb.$^1$.

**1934** *Amer. Ballads & Folk Songs* i. 24 And sluffed their coin for 'dago red'. **1959** T. REESE *Bridge Player's Dict.* 206 *Sluff*, to discard; to throw a card, other than a trump, of a suit different from the one led. **1964** *N.Y. Times Mag.* 6 Dec. 20 Its water-repellent finish sluffs off snow. **1966** J. DOS PASSOS *Best Times* (1968) ii. 56, I had sluffed off Harvard indifference, but Harvard snobbery still hung on. **1972** *New York* 8 May 43/3 His [*sc.* a dog's] shedding mechanism, which now goes about building up and sluffing off the coat. **1972** *Village Voice* (N.Y.) 1 June 50/4 When I consulted a urologist he complained that he was sick of other doctors sluffing the problem off on him all the time. **1976** *National Skat & Sheepshead Q.* Mar. 5 The picker sluffed off the club king. **1978** *Detroit Free Press* 2 Apr. 19C/3 East is now squeezed in the red suits—he must either give up a trick to the jack of hearts or sluff two diamonds, which sets up declarer's third diamond. **1980** *Amer. Speech* LV. 210 Black jazzmen returned to the linguistic roots of their art which had been sidetracked and sluffed off in the *bebop/bop* movement of the 1940s.

**sluff,** obs. or dial. form of SLOUGH *sb.*$^2$

†**ˈsluffer,** *v. Obs.*$^{-1}$ [Imitative. Cf. SLOFF *v.*] *trans.* To gobble *up* noisily.

*a* **1529** SKELTON *Agst. Garnesche* iii. 32 Ye slvfferd vp sowse In my lady Brewsys howse.

**slug** (slʌg), *sb.*$^1$ Also 5–7 slugg(e. [Related to SLUG *v.*$^1$: cf. Norw. dial. *slugg* a large heavy body, *sluggje* a heavy slow person.]

**1. a.** A slow, lazy fellow; a sluggard. †Also personified, slothfulness.

*c* **1425** *Castle Persev.* 2341 in *Macro Plays*, A, good men! be-war now all of Slugge & Slawthe, þe fowle þefe! *a* **1500** *Pol., Rel., & L. Poems* (1866) 32 The slugge lokyth to be holpe of god that commawndyth men to waake in the worlde. **1575** TURBERV. *Faulconrie* 159 Do this as often as she useth to fishe or to play the base slugge on that fashion. **1615** *Curry-Combe for a Coxe-Combe* i. 14 Hee that is lumpish at his meales, will proue but a slug in his more serious affaires. **1686** GOAD *Celest. Bodies* II. viii. 256 Nature is a Slugg, and doth nothing at the sight of a Whip. **1778** *Learning at a Loss* II. 149 My Uncle you know is a devilish Slugg in Conversation at best. **1812** TENNANT *Anster Fair* III. x, For who like arrant slugs can keep their heads In contact with their pillows now unstirr'd. **1888** DOUGHTY *Arabia Deserta* I. 90 A loiterer at his labour and a slug in the morning.

**b.** A contemptible person; a fat person.

In some instances the influence of sense 4a is probable.

**1931** A. HUXLEY *Let.* 25 Sept. (1969) 355, I am making notes for a short study..and tho' this cannot be specifically a retort to Murry it will in effect try to undo some of the mischief that that slug has undoubtedly done. **1940** G. & S. LORIMER *First Love Farewell* iv. 133 'He didn't love me and I felt pretty bad about it!' 'The complete and utter slug!' **1959** I. & P. OPIE *Lore & Lang. Schoolch.* ix. 168 The unfortunate fat boy..is known as..slug. **1966** 'J. HACKSTON' *Father clears Out* 104 No more big slugs turning up, the rush lost its enthusiasm.

†**2.** A slow-sailing vessel. *Obs.*

*a* **1548** HALL *Chron., Hen. IV*, 26 b, His shippe was but a slugge. **1624** *Cal. State P., Col.* 260 [The Rose,] being a slug, will never make a good man-of-war. **1666** *Lond. Gaz.* No. 59/4 All the rest of our ships, besides the heavy sluggs .., are come in to the Gunfleet. **1687** *Phil. Trans.* XVI. 456 They will certainly be Sluggs, not near so good Sailers as Ships made of Timber fell'd later in the Year. *a* **1734** NORTH *Lives* (1826) III. 92 The characters of the several vessels.., some windwardly, some not stay well, some slugs.

*fig.* **1622** C. FITZ-GEFFRY *Elisha* 37 Flie Boates for their owne profit, very Sluggs for the Republique. **1659** GAUDEN *Tears Church* 381 Presbytery..soon grew a slug, when once the North-Wind ceased to fill its sailes.

**3. a.** An animal, vehicle, etc., of a slow-moving or sluggish character; (see also quot. 1727).

**1618** LATHAM *Falconry* (1633) 7 The slower flying Hawke or slugge doth winne what she gets most by her policie. **1650** FULLER *Pisgah* II. viii. 177 Massie iron [chariots] (such would have been slugs in fight). **1727** BOYER *Dict. Royal* s.v. *Garde-boutique*, A Commodity that grows a Slug, a Commodity that sticks by one. **1778** [W. H. MARSHALL] *Minutes Agric.* 4 Dec. 1775, He has not worked harder than the rest of the [ox-] team,..for he was always a slug. **1806** BERESFORD *Miseries Hum. Life* VI. *Stage Coaches* ii. Travelling..in a stage-coach—I beg pardon—in a '*Slug*'. **1863** W. C. BALDWIN *Afr. Hunting* vii. 276 Manelle, my other nag, is an incorrigible slug. **1894** MRS. DYAN *Man's Keeping* (1899) 171 When not excited, an Arab horse is a slug.

†**b.** A relaxed or weak bow. *Obs.* (Cf. SLUG *v.*$^1$ 4, quot. 1600.)

**1614–25** BOYS *Wks.* (1629) 487 Cupid shoots in a slugge, and hits none but the sluggish.

**4. a.** A slow-moving slimy gasteropod or land-snail (of the type represented by the families *Limacidæ* and *Arionidæ*), in which the shell is rudimentary or entirely absent.

**1704** PETIVER *Gazophyl.* ii. §xvii, This resembles our small Slug, and like it, is whitish below, but brownish above. **1725** *Fam. Dict.* s.v. *Mushroom*, Garden Snails, the large black Dew Snails, and others without Shells call'd Slugs. **1803** *Med. Jrnl.* IX. 358 Moles..are carnivorous animals, preying on the slug, the great enemy of horticulture. **1844** EMERSON *New. Eng. Ref.* Wks. (Bohn) I. 259 A society for the protection of ground-worms, slugs, and mosquitos. **1873** MISS BROUGHTON *Nancy* II. 206, I feel as if a slug had crawled over me.

**b.** With distinguishing epithets.

**1780** *Encycl. Brit.* (ed. 2) VI. 4235/2 The black slug, the white slug, the reddish slug, the ash-coloured slug, &c. **1807** A. YOUNG *Agric. Essex* (1813) II. 93 The depredations of the white slug or snail. **1839** *Penny Cycl.* XIII. 486/2 This section consists of the Grey Slugs. *Ibid.*, The supposed virtues of a decoction..of Red Slugs. **1858** BAIRD *Cycl. Nat. Sci.* s.v. *Limax*, The variegated slug. **1870** ROLLESTON *Anim. Life* 187 Cellar Slug (*Limax flavus*). **1887** *Encycl. Brit.* XXII. 187/2 The larger black slugs are species of Arion.

**c.** (See quot.)

**1863** WOODWARD in *Intellect. Obs.* Nov. 229 Every collector of fossils has heard of the 'Fairy-loaves'..and 'Slugs' (palatal teeth of *Ptychodus*, etc.).

**5. a.** A slug-worm; a caterpillar or larva resembling a slug (see quots. 1868 and 1892).

**1799** W. D. PECK *Nat. Hist. Slug Worm* 13 The viscous coat of the Slugs seems to be their sufficient defence in the larva state. **1862** T. W. HARRIS *Insects Inj. Veget.* 517 Others have dark-colored slimy skin, which has caused them to be called slugs, or slug-worms. **1868** *Q. Rev.* CXXIV. 466 The caterpillars of two moths of the genus *Agrotis* are often called slugs. **1892** *Chambers's Encycl.* IX. 512/1 The name Slug is often applied by gardeners to the larvae of saw-flies (*Tenthredinidae*).

**b.** A sea-slug.

**1855** KINGSLEY *Glaucus* (1878) 114 A group of milk-white slugs (*Cucumaria hynumanni*), from two to six inches long. **1860** WRAXALL *Life in Sea* viii. 188 A protecting apparatus, into which the slugs can withdraw their soft bodies on the approach of danger. **1865** MRS. L. L. CLARKE *Common Seaweeds* i. 23 On the green *Ulva* creeps the lovely little slug ..called *Acteon viridis*.

**6.** *attrib.* and *Comb.*, as ***slug-eaten***, ***-eater***, ***-killer***, ***-like***, etc.; †**slug-beetle** (?); **slug caterpillar**, a caterpillar of the genus *Limacodes*; **slug-fly**, the fly of the slug-worm; **slug pellet**, a pellet of bait containing a poison to kill slugs; **slug-snail**, = sense 4.

*c* **1711** PETIVER *Gazophyl.* x. §92 Black Pounc'd Madras *Slug-beetle. **1862** T. W. HARRIS *Insects Inj. Veget.* 420 The most common of these *slug-caterpillars, in Massachusetts, live on walnut-trees. **1867** *Gard. Chron.* 7 Sept. 937 A large portion was *slug-eaten. **1890** *Science-Gossip* XXV. 149/2 Thrushes are..great *slug-eaters. **1799** W. D. PECK *Nat. Hist. Slug Worm* 11 The *Tenthredo Cerasi* or Saw-fly of the Cherry-tree has the greatest affinity to the *Slug-fly. **1862** T. W. HARRIS *Insects Inj. Veget.* 529 This slug-fly is of a glossy black color. **1883** *Sutton's Cult. Veget. & Fl.* 281 Lime, salt, soot, and nitrate of soda, are certain *Slug Killers. **1826** KIRBY & SP. *Entomol.* xxx. III. 140 The larvæ of Haworth's genus,..remarkable for their *slug-like shape and appearance. **1877** HUXLEY & MARTIN *Elem. Biol.* 23 Another common form progresses rapidly with a slug-like movement. **1960** *Do it Yourself Gardening Ann.* 100/3 The most effective way of controlling slugs and snails is to use a metaldehyde-bait mixture... The easiest way to do this is to use a proprietary brand of *slug pellets. **1976** L. THOMAS *Dangerous Davies* xvi. 188 A large tin of garden slug pellets. **1867** *Gard. Chron.* 7 Sept. 937 The *slug-pest is this year in full vigour. **1687** MIÉGE *Gt. Fr. Dict.* II, *Slug-snail, *un Limaçon*. **1706** PHILLIPS (ed. Kersey), *Slug* or *Slug-Snail*, a Dew-snail that has no Shell. **1812** SIR J. SINCLAIR *Syst. Husb. Scot.* I. 211 The frequent ploughings..effectually prevent the depredations of the slug-snail.

**slug** (slʌg), *sb.*$^2$ Also 7–8 slugg(e, 7 sluge. [Perhaps the same word as prec.]

**1. a.** A piece of lead or other metal for firing from a gun; a roughly-formed bullet.

**1622** *MS. Sessions Roll, Durham*, Unum tormentum anglice a gun oneratum cum quadam plumbea machina vocata *a Slugg*. **1645** in Rushw. *Hist. Collect.* IV. I. 58 They were pelted with Granadoes and Slugs of hot Iron. **1726** SHELVOCKE *Voy. r. World* 263 All our small shot was expended, which oblig'd us to fall astern to make some slugs. **1753** HANWAY *Trav.* (1762) I. III. xxxvi. 163 One of the pieces went off, and carried two slugs through the top. **1803** WITTMAN *Trav. Turkey* 201 The wounded man was brought off; and the balls and slugs afterwards extracted. **1855** MACAULAY *Hist. Eng.* xiii. III. 375 Cutting lead from the roof of the Marquess's house and shaping it into slugs. **1879** STANLEY *Through Dark Cont.* XXIV. (1889) 440 We.. replied with shot, slugs, and bullets.

*fig.* *a* **1677** BARROW *Serm.* Wks. 1700 I. 356 Discharging sluggs against our neighbours reputation.

**b.** *slang.* Some kind of strong drink (*obs.*); a dram; a drink. Now chiefly *U.S.*

**1756** W. TOLDERVY *Hist. Two Orphans* (1765) II. 112 Gunpowder, slug, wild-fire, knock-me-down. **1762** SMOLLETT *Sir L. Greaves* xvii, He ordered the waiter..to.. bring along-side a short allowance of brandy or grog, that he might cant a slug into his bread-room. **1785** GROSE *Dict. Vulgar T.* s.v., *To fire a slug*, to drink a dram. **1895** in *Funk's Stand. Dict.* **1916** H. L. WILSON *Somewhere in Red Gap* vi. 245 Even the new Episcopalian minister..took a slug of rye and said it was undeniably delightful. **1940** R. CHANDLER *Farewell, my Lovely* v. 34, I poured her a slug that would have made me float over a wall. **1958** C. WILLIAMS *Man in Motion* (1959) i. 6 Pouring another cup of coffee, I dropped a slug of bourbon in it. **1973** C. BONINGTON *Next Horizon* xv. 216 The scene was Hogarthian—with a soldier lying flat in the gutter,..a mother giving her eighteen-month babe a slug of the fire-water, to stop it crying. **1978** L. HEREN *Growing up on The Times* v. 182 Their simple niceness was almost as good as a slug of scotch and a cigarette which I.. could not enjoy in their company.

**c.** A compact mass of liquid regarded as retaining its identity as it travels.

**1947** I. THOMAS *Injection Molding of Plastics* vi. 353 If the reservoir were omitted the cold slug of material would enter the cavity and possibly cause smudge or flow marks in the molded article. **1967** *Guardian* 13 Feb. 14/6 In each pipe will be methane gas plus liquid oil called the 'slug'... Once ashore the gas and slug have to be separated and cleaned. **1971** *Nature* 21 May 181/1 A rapid intravenous injection leads to a 'slug' of relatively undispersed drug traversing the arteries on the first circuit. **1975** *Petroleum Rev.* XXIX. 315/3 A collection of liquid, known as a 'slug', can amount to several hundred thousand gallons and will travel along the pipeline at a speed of up to 10 miles per hour. **1979** *Nature* 8 Feb. 441/1 The velocity of the ejected slug of [volcanic] debris.

†**2.** A heavy gun or cannon. *Obs.*$^{-0}$

**1677** in MIÉGE *Fr. Dict.* II. (Hence in some later Dicts.)

**3. a.** A heavy piece of crude metal, usually rounded in form; a nugget (of gold).

**1849** *Picayune* (New Orleans) 6 June 1/6 The gold from that stream is generally in large pieces, more generally termed slugs or coarse, but very fine gold, if you please. **1855** *Golden Era* (San Francisco) 21 Jan. 2/7 We took out one slug weighing 60 ounces of pure gold, in the shape of an ox's tongue. *a* **1891** *Elect. Rev.* (Amer.) XVI. viii. 2 (Cent.), 'That is platinum, and it is worth about $150.' It was an insignificant looking slug. **1894** *Westm. Gaz.* 5 May 7/1 Rumours were current..as to the finding of a 17lb. 'slug' of gold at Kurnalpi.

**b.** *Pottery.* (See quot.)

**1880** JANVIER *Pract. Keramics* xii. 132 The coarser sorts [of stoneware] are..piled up, only separated by 'slugs'— rolls or pieces of sandy clay.

**c.** *Electr.* A metal cylinder fitted round the end of the core of an electromagnetic relay to modify the speeds of opening and closing. Cf. SLEEVE *sb.* 7c.

**1928** *Jrnl. Inst. Electr. Engineers* LXVI. 346/1 A thick copper cylinder—or 'slug'—placed over part of the core, or a thin cylinder—or 'sleeve'—placed over the whole of the core, will provide a closed path of very low resistance in which currents of considerable magnitude may flow. **1943** A. L. ALBERT *Fund. Telephony* ix. 199 The amount of time delay can be regulated by the size and location of the copper slug. **1969** M. L. GAYFORD *Mod. Relay Techniques* iii. 60 A slug at the armature end slows down both operation and release. A slug at the rear or heel end has little effect on the operate time but produces suitable delay on release.

**d.** *Nucl. Engin.* A rod or bar of nuclear fuel.

**1945** H. D. SMYTH *Gen. Acct. Devel. Atomic Energy Mil. Purposes* vii. 69 The uranium would react chemically with the water,..probably to the point of disintegrating the uranium slugs. **1952** [see PLUTONIUM 2 b]. *a* **1958** K. EDWARDS in 'E. Crispin' *Best SF 3* (1958) 34 The uranium slugs were short and the aluminium cans that held them in the centre of the pile..were long. **1967** J. T. LONG *Engin. Nuclear Fuel Reprocessing* xi. 838 The slugs were cooled by natural convection of water in a finned tank. **1973** *Trans. Amer. Nuclear Soc.* XVII. 508/2 A charge of fuel particles, a preformed matrix slug, and a top punch are inserted.

**e.** *Electr.* An adjustable magnetic core used to vary the inductance of a coil containing it. Chiefly in ***slug tuning*** (so ***slug-tuned*** adj.).

**1957** *Practical Wireless* XXXIII. 566/1 Now adjust trimmers or slugs of discriminator transformer to obtain a symmetrical pattern. **1959** R. L. SHRADER *Electronic Communication* xiv. 390 A few receiver RF amplifiers..use slug tuning, having a mechanical means of pulling the slug into the desired position in the coil by a dial on the front of the equipment. **1960** *Practical Wireless* XXXVI. 416/2 Coil L2 is also heavily damped and variable tuning is hardly worthwhile; it is accordingly slug-tuned to the centre of the three transmissions to be received. **1979** A. A. LIFF *Color & Black & White Television Theory & Servicing* iv. 108 The individually tuned circuits in the oscillator section are all slug tuned.

**4. a.** A hatter's or tailor's heating-iron.

**1858** SIMMONDS *Dict. Trade.*

**b.** *Printing.* A metal bar used as a division (see earlier quots.), or one produced by a Linotype machine for printing from. Orig. *U.S.*

Hence *slug-machine*, a Linotype machine.

**1871** RINGWALT *Amer. Encycl. Printing* 416 *Slugs.*— Pieces of metal of various lengths and thicknesses, but always thicker than leads, which they resemble in other respects. **1875** KNIGHT *Dict. Mech.* 2217/2 Slugs are used to fill out a short page or between display lines. **1888** JACOBI *Printers' Vocab.* 127 *Slugs*, numbered divisions of metal between different takes of copy. **1896** *Linotype Co.'s Specimen Bk.*, The Linotype produces and assembles, side by side, metal bars or slugs.

**c.** *U.S.* A heavy gold piece privately coined in California in 1849, subsequently prohibited.

**1851** *Oregon Statesman* 23 Sept. 2/6 He accordingly 'pungled down' two of Moffat's $50 slugs, and of course, cut the black, there being no red spots in the pack. **1872** S. POWERS *Afoot & Alone* 303 A shining 'slug', fresh from the San Francisco mint, [was] laid scrupulously in the place. **1890** *San Francisco Bulletin* 10 May (Cent.), An interesting reminder of early days in California, in the shape of a round fifty-dollar slug. **1892** *Blackw. Mag.* Apr. 554 A small hillock of gold in 10 and 50 dollar slugs.

**d.** A thick boot-rivet or sprig.

**1892** [see SLUGGER[3]].

**e.** *U.S. slang.* A dollar; a counterfeit coin; a token.

**1887** *Lantern* (New Orleans) 4 June 5/2 She'd sooner put up her ten slugs and go back to the pipe. **1913** *Dial. Notes* IV. 28 *Slug*,..round piece of metal for slot machines. **1934** J. T. FARRELL *Young Manhood of Studs Lonigan* xvii. 259 He bought a slug from the cashier in the Chain drugstore at Prairie and walked back to the telephone booths.

**f.** *Journalism.* = *slug-line*, sense 7 below.

**1925** G. M. HYDE *Newspaper Editing* (ed. 2) ii. 89 Use expressions that will not offend readers..if the slugs slip into print... 'Kill widow'..may be misunderstood. **1927** *Amer. Speech* II. 240/2 'Slug'..is a brief title..placed above a story for the guidance of the copy-reader and the printer. **1949** T. F. BARNHART *Weekly Newspaper Writing & Editing* xxii. 224/2 In many newspaper plants some other term is substituted for guidelines, such as catch-lines, slugs and slug-lines. **1979** 'A. HAILEY' *Overload* IV. vii. 324 The newspaper put a copyright slug over her story.

**5.** The core of an ox-horn (cf. SLOUGH *sb.*[5]); a stunted horn.

**1842** S. C. HALL *Ireland* II. 395 The slug or core on which the horn is moulded. **1878** SIR B. T. B. GIBBS in *Rep. Paris Exhib.* II. 347 There shall be no horns, slugs, abortive horns. *Ibid.*, Occasionally some have small 'slugs' or stumps which are not affixed to the skull.

**6.** *Engin.* A unit of mass equal to 32·1740 lb., being the mass of a body which accelerates at one foot per second per second when acted on by one pound force.

**1902** A. M. WORTHINGTON *Dynamics of Rotation* (ed.4) p. viii, I have ventured to give the name of a 'slug' to the British Engineer's Unit of Mass, *i.e.*, to the mass in which an acceleration of one foot-per-sec.-per-sec. is produced by a force of one pound. **1923** A. R. LOW in W. L. Marsh *Rep. Internat. Air Congr.* 62 The 'slug' of 32·2 pounds avoirdupois mass, which has actually been imposed on British aeronautics by the Advisory Committee. **1936** F. W. LANCHESTER *Theory of Dimensions & its Application for Engineers* v. 37 Even amongst the advocates of Perry's system.., the slug has never taken shape except on paper; it has, and has had no real material existence. **1944** N. A. V. PIERCY *Compl. Course Elem. Aerodynamics* iv. 86 At 15° C. and 760 mm. pressure, ρ [*sc.* the density of air].. = 0·00238 slug per cubic foot. **1973** *Nature* 20 July 184/3 The statement that the unit of mass in the British system is the slug is several years out of date.

**7.** *attrib.* and *Comb.*, as ***slug-bullet, -cartridge, -gun, -shot; slug-loaded*** adj.; **slug-line** *Journalism*, an identifying title, usu. occupying one slug, accompanying a news story in draft and galleys; **slug-setting** *Printing*, the method of setting an entire line of type on a single slug; so **slug-set** *a.*

**1665** PEPYS *Diary* 4 Feb., This message he sent in a *slugg-bullett, being writ in cypher, and wrapped up in lead. **1901** H. SEEBOHM *Birds of Siberia* xxi. 222, I put a *slug-cartridge into my gun. **1940** *Illustr. London News* CXCVI. 53 (*caption*) Their training includes the use of tear-gas, while they are armed with '*slug-guns', ·303 rifles and staves. **1973** M. AMIS *Rachel Papers* 218 The youth, handsomely reading Tennyson on summer evenings, or trying to kill birds with feeble, rusted slug-guns. **1930** K. E. OLSON *Typogr. & Mechanics of Newspaper* xi. 360 Sometimes the printer forgets to remove the *slugline when he places a story in its column, and this would appear above the story unless caught in the final check. **1976** J. MCCLURE *Rogue Eagle* ii. 27 He tapped out the name of his freelance agency and the slug-line. **1873** *Routledge's Young Gentlem. Mag.* May 355 To make use of the *slug-loaded pistols first. **1963** *Slug-setting [see FILMSET *v.*]. **1970** *Times Lit. Suppl.* 9 Apr. 387/2 It is an instance of their attention to quality that even novels are 'Monotype' set, whereas most publishers use slug-setting. **1975** J. BUTCHER *Copy-Editing* ii. 7 Slugsetting is unsuitable for complex tables, though Monotype may be used for tables in a slugset book. **1873** *Routledge's Young Gentlem. Mag.* May 356 The *slug-shot had entered his arm.

**slug** (slʌg), *sb.*[3] *north.* and *U.S.* [f. SLUG *v.*[3]]

**1.** A heavy or hard blow; a beating.

**1830** T. WILSON *Pitman's Pay* III. xxxvii, We'll spend wor hin'most plack, Te gi'e them iv'ry yen a slug. **1891** in *Cent. Dict.* **1894** HESLOP *Northumbld. Gloss.* 659 A *slug* or a *sluggin* is a dire beating.

**2.** *attrib.* and *Comb.*, as **slug-fest** [FEST] *U.S. slang*, a hard-hitting contest, *spec.* in boxing and baseball; **slug-nutty** *a.* (*U.S. slang*), punch-drunk; hence **slug-nuttiness**.

**1916** *Nebraska State Jrnl.* 27 July 3/1 (*heading*) Denver wins in slugfest. **1933** G. TUNNEY *Man must Fight* 14 If Dempsey would gamble with me in a slug-fest I would beat him to the punch every time. **1943** *Amer. Speech* XVIII. 105 A good inning at bat..is a..*slug-fest.* **1969** *Daily Colonist* (Victoria, B.C.) 21 Mar. 1/4 A meeting between Canadian MPs and a high French government official turned into a verbal slugfest as the Canadians raked the Gaullist government for its policies towards Quebec and Ottawa. **1976** M. MACHLIN *Pipeline* x. 116 For a while it looked as though there was going to be a real slugfest. **1979** *Arizona Daily Star* 1 Apr. B5/4 'Back to Basics' is today's biggest educational debate topic. But so far, it has generated a mostly muddled, emotional slugfest. *Ibid.* 8 Apr. C1/2 Powers gave up four runs on seven hits, a contrast from the 33-hit slugfest of Friday night. **1943** *Gen* 16 Jan. 30/1 Though no medical man, I know enough about slug-nuttiness to tell you..how it comes about. **1933** 'P. CAIN' *Fast One* vi. 196 He shook his head sadly without looking up. 'Slug-nutty.' **1936** J. STEINBECK *In Dubious Battle* ii. 16 Don't mind Joy. He's slug-nutty. He's been smacked over the head too much. **1950** E. HEMINGWAY *Across River & into Trees* iv. 26 He's been beat up so much he's slug-nutty.

†**slug**, *a. Obs.* [Cf. SLUG *sb.*[1] and *v.*[1]]

**1.** Slow, sluggish, inactive.

*c* **1440** *Promp. Parv.* 460/1 Slugge, *deses, segnis.* **1589** A. FLEMING *Virg. Georg.* I Thou Tityr slug in shade Dost teach the woods to sound so shrill. **1626** SHIRLEY *Brothers* V. iii, *Carlos.* Will none deliver me? *Lu.* They are somewhat slug. **1635** QUARLES *Embl.* I. xiii, Lord, when we leave the world and come to thee, How dull, how slug we are.

**2.** Of vessels: Slow-sailing.

*c* **1626** *Dick of Devon* V. i. in Bullen *Old Pl.* II. 86 Slug shipps can keepe no pace. **1666** *Lond. Gaz.* No. 59/1 The *St. Paul*, and two other Slug Ships, that seemed unserviceable.

**slug** (slʌg), *v.*[1] Now somewhat *rare.* Also 4 **sluggyn, 6 slogge, sloug, 6–7 slugg(e.** [Perh. of Scand. origin: cf. Sw. dial. *slogga* to be slow or sluggish, and the Norw. forms cited under SLUG *sb.*[1] Earlier evidence for the occurrence of the stem in English appears in FORSLUG *v.* (*c* 1315) and SLUGGY *a.* (*a* 1225).]

**1.** *intr.* To be lazy, slow, or inert; to lie idly or lazily. Also with *it.*

*c* **1425** *St. Mary of Oignies* II. v. in *Anglia* VIII. 166/21 She..slugged neuer wiþ slouþe; she defayled in trauayle neuere or seldom. *c* **1440** *Promp. Parv.* 460/2 Sluggyn, *desidio, torpeo, pigritor.* **1530** PALSGR. 722/1 Whye slogge you nowe more than you have be wont to do? *c* **1560** INGELEND *Disobedient Child* (Percy Soc.) 50, I would most commonly slugge in my bed, Untyll it were verye farre forth daye. **1591** SYLVESTER *Du Bartas* I. vii. 340 The Soldier, slugging long at home in Peace, His wonted courage quickly doth decrease. **1625** BP. SANDERSON *Serm.* I. 129 Men account him no wiser than he should be, that sluggeth in his own business, or goeth heartlesly about it. *a* **1677** BARROW *Serm.* (1686) III. xxii. 256 When he mispendeth an hour, or sluggeth on his bed. **1702** C. MATHER *Magn. Christi* III. II. iii. (1852) 374 He complained, 'I lie slugging a bed, when others are at work'. **1869** *Fortn. Rev.* Feb. 157 How often do I slug in bed on the long bright summer mornings.

**b.** *fig.* or in fig. context.

**1549** COVERDALE, etc. *Erasm. Par. Jas.* 31 Of like sorte doubtles shall the profession of faith..bee vnauayleable, but lyeth slugging like as it were deade. **1567–9** JEWEL *Def. Apol.* (1611) 557 If they, whiles the Pope and his Prelats slug and sleep,..do bridle the Priests sensuality. **1607** J. CARPENTER *Pl. Mans Plough* 207 These ungodly..slug on the waves of this world, slumber as in the darke night. *a* **1646** J. BURROUGHS *Exp. Hosea* ix. (1652) 312 The Lord offereth deliverance and we lie slugging on our beds.

**c.** To withdraw through laziness. *rare*[−1].

**1642** ROGERS *Naaman* 45 The Lord..suffered him not to slug out of the worke, till he had finished it.

**2.** To move slowly; to loiter or delay.

**1565** T. STAPLETON *Fortr. Faith* 84 Their destruction sluggeth not. **1646** W. PRICE *Man's Delinquencie* 14 Like a Bowle, he began to slugge toward the end of the Alley. **1692** L'ESTRANGE *Fables* (1694) 362 There were two men together on a journey. One of them went slugging on... T'other jogg'd merrily away. **1812** TENNANT *Anster Fair* II. xlii, Others..ride, Slugging on their slow-gaited asses stout.

**3.** *trans.* To pass (time) in inactivity or idleness. Also with *out.*

*a* **1548** HALL *Chron., Hen. VI*, 177 Wherfore losyng no tyme nor sluggyng one houre he sayled from Deuelyne to Chester. **1621** R. BOLTON *Statutes Irel.* 313 Who losing no time, nor slugging one houre, hath so actually followed the warre that [etc.]. **1888** DOUGHTY *Arabia Deserta* I. 224 How may your lubbers slug out these long days till evening?

**4.** To relax or slacken; to make inert or sluggish.

**1600** HOLLAND *Livy* XXXVII. xli. 968 Moreouer, the dropping weather slugged their bowes, softned their slings. **1641** MILTON *Reform. Eng.* 4 It is still episcopacy that.. worsens and slugs the most learned and seeming religious of our ministers. **1678** CUDWORTH *Intell. Syst.* I. iv. §18. 321 Contending..that it..would weaken and enervate Mans natural Faculties, by slugging them.

**5.** To hinder, retard, delay.

**1605** BACON *Adv. Learn.* II. vii. §7 They are..but Remoraes and hindrances to stay and slugge the Shippe from furder sayling. **1650** TRAPP *Comm. Num.* xiv. 24 When a bowl runs down-hill, every rub quickens it; whereas if up-hill, it would slug it. **1665** HOOKE *Microgr.* 69 Several of these Rays..will be slugged or stopped by the tinging particles. **1876** ROBINSON *Whitby Gloss.* 176/2 *Slug*, to hinder; to retard progress.

**slug** (slʌg), *v.*[2] [f. SLUG *sb.*[2]]

**1.** *trans.* To load (a gun) with slugs.

**1831** *Examiner* 273/2 They would scarcely applaud.. Tyburn Jack for slugging the blunderbuss up to its expansive muzzle. **1864** in WEBSTER.

**2.** *trans.* and *intr.* Of a bullet: (see quot.).

**1875** KNIGHT *Dict. Mech.* 2217/2 The bullet, when forced to assume the sectional shape of the bore in the act of firing, is said to *slug* or to be *slugged.*

**3.** *Journalism. trans.* To mark with a slug-line; with compl.: to give as a slug-line or other heading.

**1925** G. M. HYDE *Newspaper Editing* (ed. 2) ii. 27 What the copywriter does..may be summarized... 'Slugs' story for record and make-up. **1928** *Amer. Speech* IV. 135 The hardened deskman merely grins, squeezes the gist of a column story into ten words and 'slugs' the article to designate the 'head' that is to accompany it. **1940** N. MACNEIL *Without Fear or Favor* v. 74 The foreign editor.. may slug his stories by correspondent. **1953** B. WESTLEY *News Editing* xii. 197 When they moved a story about the possible use of bacteriological warfare.., the United Press slugged it: 'Germs'. **1974** J. BANNING *How I fooled World* xix. 77 The [news] story, slugged 'Television', ran something like this. **1976** *Daily Tel.* 13 Oct. 6/7 Members of the National Union of Journalists..called..for all relevant copy to be marked, or 'slugged', 'Not for Preston'. *Ibid.*, There was a previous precedent for slugging copy in an outside dispute.

**slug** (slʌg), *v.*[3] Chiefly *north.* and *U.S.* [Cf. SLOG *v.*] **1. a.** *trans.* To strike (also, to drive, throw, etc.) heavily or violently; to slog.

**1862** in ROBINSON *Dial. Leeds* 413. **1869** *Echo* 8 Mar., He has several times been told by unionists on strike that he would be 'slugged' if he went on as he was going. **1883** *The Bread-Winners* (1884) 213 'Who's afraid of half-a-dozen cops?' said a burly ruffian, who carried a slung-shot... 'We'll slug 'em this time!' **1890** GUNTER *Miss Nobody* i. (1891) 11 They mean..to slug him, crush the wind out of his body, and leave him battered and bruised.

**b.** *fig.* To treat roughly; to drug; to exploit; to overcharge; to force *out* of; to churn *out.*

**1925** A. S. M. HUTCHINSON *One Increasing Purpose* I. xviii. 112, I know..that really you were court-martialled and hoofed out... But what the facts were, *why* you were slugged, *how* they found out your hideous goings-on, I never could discover. **1938** J. STEINBECK *Long Valley* 116, I guess the doctor slugged me pretty hard... I feel all right now, only a little dopey. **1941** S. J. BAKER *Dict. Austral. Slang* 68 *Get slugged*, to be charged excessively. **1946** K. S. PRICHARD *Roaring Nineties* 326 Alf knew the mine-owners were slugging the prospectors and alluvial diggers. **1962** 'K. ORVIS' *Damned & Destroyed* vi. 46 She had..slugged herself insensible with a terrific overdose of heroin. **1974** P. DE VRIES *Glory of Hummingbird* ii. 14 The thankless task of slugging contributions out of the congregation. **1976** *Australasian Express* 11 June 26/2 Canberra: Big cars will be slugged for extra insurance if a report to the Government is adopted. **1977** *New Yorker* 19 Sept. 96/2 I've been slugging out so many notes of American music I'm turning into a piece of apple pie.

**c.** *to slug it out*: to fight it out; to stick it out.

**1943** *Time* 10 May 98/3 Twice it screens exciting action: once when the sub slugs it out with a disguised German raider. **1952** M. LOWRY *Let.* 11 Jan. (1967) 286 Somehow we slugged it out, without having to abandon the house. **1970** *Listener* 23 July 127/3 It decided not to slug it out directly with *News at Ten.* **1973** *Black World* Mar. 58, I saw the two shadows boxing on the side of the brick building... It was Bernie and Bennie Speakes, twins about 10, slugging it out in the alley. **1978** *Detroit Free Press* 16 Apr. 14C/1 They'll slug it out, week by week, blow by blow, for all the world to see.

**2.** *intr.* To slog. Also with *along, away.*

**1943** *Fortune* Feb. 122/1 Guns slugging at close range. **1943** *Newsweek* 9 Aug. 27/1 This found them..still slugging along at a point between the coastal villages of Tetere and Zovi. **1944** *Reader's Digest* Nov. 62/1 But always he was slugging away at novel writing on the side. **1959** *Times* 9 Mar. 3/1 In the second [half], largely an affair of forwards slugging away with barely diminished vigour, the Navy's packing became untidy.

**slug** (slʌg), *v.*[4] [f. SLUG *sb.*[1] 4.] *intr.* To hunt for slugs.

**1887** BARING-GOULD *Golden Feather* iv, She went with him to see the garden and help to 'slug'.

**slug-a-bed** (ˈslʌgəbɛd). Also 7, 9 **sluggabed**, 9 **slugabed.** [f. SLUG *v.*[1] 1 + ABED *adv.*] One who lies long in bed through laziness.

**1592** SHAKS. *Rom. & Jul.* IV. v. 2 Why Lambe, why Lady, fie you sluggabed. **1648** HERRICK *Hesp.*, *Corinna's going a Maying*, Get up, sweet Slug-a-bed, and see The Dew-bespangling Herbe and Tree. **1692** L'ESTRANGE *Fables* ccciii. (1694) 367 But these People are Hearing Causes too, with our Slug-a-bed in the Apologue. **1785** GROSE *Dict. Vulgar T.*, *Slug-a-bed*, a drone, one that cannot rise in the morning. *a* **1849** H. COLERIDGE *Ess.* (1851) I. 90 Thomson, who was a notorious slug-a-bed, is peculiarly eloquent on the subject of early rising. **1897** W. HURTON *Doomed Ship* xxii, I found Oriana, as usual, up before me, for I always was a sad slug-a-bed.

*attrib.* **1683** TRYON *Way to Health* 289 Many ordinary Country People..have nothing the trouble at such times as our fine lazy sluggabed-Dames. **1897** F. THOMPSON *New Poems* 42 Even the slug-abed snail upon the thorn.

**sluggard** (ˈslʌgəd), *sb.* and *a.* Forms: *α.* 5–6 **slogard(e, 5–6 sloggarde.** *β.* 5 **sluggarde,** 6 **slougarde, slugerd,** 6– **sluggard;** *Sc.* 5, 7 **sluggart,** 6 **slug(g)ird.** [f. SLUG *v.*[1] + -ARD.]

**A.** *sb.* **a.** One who is naturally or habitually slow, lazy, or idle; one who is disinclined for work or exertion of any kind; a slothful or indolent person.

*α.* **1398** TREVISA *Barth. De P.R.* IX. viii. (Bodl. MS.), Also scharpenes of winter makeþ men slogardes and slowe to worching. ? *a* **1500** *Chester Pl.* VIII. 297 Such dotards never shall, ne no sleeping slogard, make my right title cease! *a* **1548** HALL *Chron., Edw. IV*, 249 b, If thei be slogardes and geuen to slothe.

*β.* **1423** JAS. I *Kingis Q.* lviii, Sluggart, for schame! lo here thy goldin houre. **1500–20** DUNBAR *Poems* xlvi. 86 Luve makis sluggirdis fresche and weill besene. **1549** COVERDALE *Erasm. Par. 1 Cor.* 27, I runne not lyke a slougarde, as they are wonte to doe which hasten to no certayn marke at al. **1576** FLEMING *Panopl. Epist.* 251 Least your delayes gett you the report of a sluggarde or idle lubber. **1617** MORYSON *Itin.* III. 4 But it is the part of an industrious man, to act their affaires in the world, tho sluggards lie by the fire. **1663** S. PATRICK *Parab. Pilgr.* (1687) 358 This is the effect of the Sermon which that Excellent Man made to Drones and Sluggards. **1738** WESLEY '*Let us go forth, 'tis God commands*' ii, If any now to Work refuse, Let not the Sluggard eat. **1819** COBBETT *Eng. Gram.* viii. (1847) 72 Read it early, while your mind is clear, and while sluggards are snoring. **1877** LADY BARKER *Housek. S. Africa* iv, Our garden is precisely in the condition of the sluggard, gate and all.

*transf.* **1856** DOVE *Logic Chr. Faith* III. iii. 143 Even light ..is but a sluggard when compared to thought.

*Comb.* **1706** A. PHILIPS *Past.* iv. (1710) 16 He that late lies down, as late will rise, And, Sluggard-like, till Noon-day snoring lyes. **1892** J. LUMSDEN *Sheep-head & Trotters* 301 Harvest, however, came at length, lagging on a-pace, sweet and sluggard-wise. **1910** W. DE MORGAN *Affair of Dishonour* vii. 87 That he should, simply from an idle indulgence of laziness, lie sluggard-wise till near mid-day.

†**b.** *spec.* A sloth. *Obs. rare.*

See also POTTO 1, quot. 1705.

**1668** CHARLETON *Onomast.* 16 *Ai, sive Ignavus*, the Sluggard. **1796** H. HUNTER tr. *St.-Pierre's Stud. Nat.* (1799) I. 294 The sluggard, or sloth, likewise has hands.

**B.** *adj.* Sluggish, slothful, lazy.

**1593** SHAKS. *Rich. II*, III. ii. 84 Awake thou sluggard Maiestie, thou sleepest. **1593** —— *Lucr.* 1278 The more to blame my sluggard negligence. **1700** DRYDEN *Pal. & Arc.* I. 177 For sprightly May commands our Youth to keep The Vigils of her Night, and breaks their sluggard Sleep. **1867** R. PALMER *Life P. Howard* 25 The still more dreadful lukewarmness that hag-rode the sluggard orders. **1874** WILBERFORCE *Essays* II. 113 The old sluggard slumberers of the last generation.

Hence **'sluggarding** *vbl. sb.*, the practice of playing the sluggard.

**1864** CARLYLE *Fredk. Gt.* XV. xiv. (1873) VI. 112 By slumbering and sluggarding over their money tills.

†**sluggardise.** *Obs.* [f. SLUGGARD *sb.* + -ISE[2].] Slothfulness, laziness.

**1532** HERVET *Xenophon Treat. Househ.* (1768) 5 Slouthfulnes, sluggardise, lacke of stomacke and quickenesse. **1555** [WATREMAN] *Fardle Facions* App. 345 Banishyng sluggardise, and kieping your mindes in continuall exercise. **1606** *Choice, Chance & Change* (1881) 51 Mistris, quoth I, shall the seruant be in bed after his Mis? that wer to much sluggardise.

**'sluggardish,** *a. rare*[−1]. [f. SLUGGARD *a.*] Somewhat slothful.

**1649** SCLATER *Comm. Malachy* (1650) 166 If those sluggardish fooles amongst us..would consider this.

**sluggardize** ('slʌgədaɪz), *v.* [f. SLUGGARD *sb.* + -IZE.]

**1.** *trans.* To make idle or lazy.

**1591** SHAKS. *Two Gentl.* I. i. 7 Liuing dully sluggardiz'd at home. **1798** *Monthly Mag.* Feb. 92 To continue..dully sluggardized in that dismal torpor.

**2.** *intr.* To play the sluggard.

**1837** LOFFT *Self-formation* II. 230 An enervating lethargic spirit, that kept my soul abed, idly sluggardizing.

**sluggardly** ('slʌgədlɪ), *a.* [f. SLUGGARD *sb.* + -LY[1].] Lazy, indolent, slothful.

**1865** CARLYLE *Fredk. Gt.* XX. iii. (1872) IX. 53 Astonishment at unjust fortune, or at his own sluggardly cunctations. **1877** *Tinsley's Mag.* XXI. 609, I feel bitterly ashamed of selfish sluggardly humanity. **1884** *Manch. Exam.* 25 Feb. 5/2 The sluggardly and inefficient way in which the Irish railway companies..do their business.

**sluggardness** ('slʌgədnɪs). [f. as prec. + -NESS.] Slothfulness, laziness.

**1398** TREVISA *Barth. De P.R.* VIII. xxix. (Bodl. MS.), [Light] wakeþ men of slepe of slogardnes and of slewthe. **1538** ELYOT, *Secordia*,..sluggardnesse, vnaptnesse. **1550** HOOPER *Serm. Jonas* vi. 162 b, To put awaye the slugerdnes of hys people. **1866** ROSE *Virgil* 59 He chaseth sluggardness forth from his reign. **1891** *Daily News* 26 Jan. 6/2 A duet in which jolly Friar Tuck..twits the Black Knight upon his sluggardness.

**'sluggardry.** *rare.* = next.

**1513** DOUGLAS *Æneid* IV. Prol. 164 Thow ald hasart lychour..That flotteris furth euermair in sluggardry. **1925** V. WOOLF *Common Reader* 79 The extremes of passion are not for the novelist;..he must tame his swiftness to sluggardry. **1935** W. DE LA MARE *Early One Morning* 145 Unusual discomfort of mind or body may slow down the wheels of existence to a sluggardry almost beyond endurance.

†**'sluggardy.** *Obs.* Forms: α. 5 sloggardye, 5–6 **slogardy(e**, 5–7 **slogardie.** β. 5 **slugardie**, 4, 6–7 **sluggardie** (6 **-dye**), 6 **slouggardie**, 5– **sluggardy.** [f. SLUGGARD *sb.* + -Y.] Slothfulness, indolence, laziness.

α. *c* **1386** CHAUCER *Knt.'s T.* 184 (Camb. MS.), For may wele haue no slogardye on nyȝt. **1426** LYDG. *De Guil. Pilgr.* 10223 Slowh and ful off slogardye. *c* **1470** HENRY *Wallace* v. 658 'Der schyr,' he said, 'ye leiff in slogardy'. **1509** HAWES *Past. Pleas.* 23 The bryttel fleshe, nourisher of vyces, Under the shadowe of evyll slogardy, Must neede haunte the carnall delices. **1545** *Primer Hen. VIII*, 70 Thee to praise and magnifie Of night we leave the slogardie. **1616** J. LANE *Contn. Sqr.'s T.* x. 558 Truith without Justice is slogardie.

β. **1390** GOWER *Conf.* II. 92 [He] seith that for no Druerie He wol noght leve his sluggardie. **1495** *Trevisa's Barth. De P.R.* VIII. xxix. 342 [Light] wakyth men of slepe and sluggardy. **1539** ELYOT *Cast. Helthe* (1541) 92 In the preservation of helth, sluggardy is the greattest mischiefe. **1542** UDALL *Erasm. Apoph.* 87 b, The same much auailleth ..to quicken the slouggardie of others. **1601** CHESTER *Love's Mart.*, etc. (1878) 54 The foule staine of beastly sluggardie. **1606** HOLLAND *Suetonius* 155 The olde infamous note of sluggardie and foolishnesse.

**slugged** (slʌgd), *a.*[1] Now *rare.* Also 5 **slughed, sluggid, sluggyd.** [f. SLUG *sb.*[1] or *v.*[1]] Sluggish.

*c* **1430** *Pilgr. Lyf Manhode* II. liii. (1869) 96 Thou hast noon so gret lettinge..as of that he is so slugged. **1445** in *Anglia* XXVIII. 269 Where sluggid Idilnes myght not vprise. *c* **1450** [see SLUGGISH *a.* 2].

**1847** *Tait's Mag.* XIV. 728 His intelligence, usually slugged and lazy,..acts with..rapidity.

Hence †**sluggedly** *adv.*; †**sluggedness.** *Obs.*

*c* **1425** *St. Mary of Oignies* II. ii. in *Anglia* VIII. 151/39 As a prikke, lest she shulde be slowe þurgh sluggednesse. *c* **1440** *Promp Parv.* 460/2 Sluggydnesse, *torpor, segnicies, ignavia.* *c* **1450** Sluggedly [see SLUGGISHLY]. *a* **1500** *Polit., Relig., & L. Poems* (1866) 32 Sluggednes & myshappe be seldome dyssevyrde.

**slugged** (slʌgd), *a.*[2] [f. SLUG *sb.*[2] + -ED[2].] Having a slug or slugs.

**1906** *Daily Colonist* (Victoria, B.C.) 5 Jan. 9/1 (Advt.), Boys' Calf Boots, double soles, slugged bottoms, sizes 1 to 5. **1922** *Daily Mail* 10 Nov. 4 Boys' unlined slugged soles Derbys. **1928** *Jrnl. Inst. Electr. Engineers* LXVI. 341/1 The release of slugged relays is complicated by saturation. **1958** J. W. FREEBODY *Telegraphy* iv. 84/1 The actual release lag of a slugged relay depends also on the spring tension.

†**'slugger**[1]. *Obs.* [f. SLUG *v.*[1]] A sluggard.

**1539** TAVERNER *Erasm. Prov.* (1552) 40 With sluggers or unhardye persons, it is alwayes holy daye. *c* **1560** BP. COX in *Abp. Parker's Corresp.* (Parker Soc.) 130 Satan is no slugger, nor Judas no sleeper.

**slugger**[2] ('slʌgə(r)). orig. and chiefly *U.S.* [f. SLUG *v.*[3]]

**1.** = SLOGGER *sb.* 2. Also in *Baseball*, a hard-hitting batter.

**1877** [see COON *sb.* 4 b]. **1883** *Chicago Tribune* 3 July 6/5 Poor Burns fell an easy victim to the Cleveland sluggers. **1884** *Harper's Mag.* Jan. 300/1 Let the young disciple beware of those teachers [of boxing] who are known as 'sluggers'. **1894** G. MEREDITH *Let.* 19 Feb. (1970) III. 1155 Harrison is a controversial slugger. I did not expect he would descend to the use of street missiles. Your answer hit the right tone. **1895** *Daily News* 6 Mar. 6/4 The champion slugger at football. **1946** *Sun* (Baltimore) 27 May 15 (*caption*) Charlie Keller, the Yankee's slugger, is shown being caught in a rundown. **1952** *Manch. Guardian Weekly* 16 Oct. 2/1 Their team includes Mr. Gromyko and the notorious slugger Vyshinsky. **1967** *Boston Sunday Herald* 26 Mar. II. 3/1 Tony has the build of a slugger... Maybe some club will make an offer for him, giving a dependable pitcher in return. **1970** *Daily Tel.* (Colour Suppl.) 9 Oct. 27/3 No amateur karate exponent stands a halfway chance against an old-fashioned slugger and kicker who has real experience of street brawls. **1972** J. MOSEDALE *Football* vii. 100 One of the National League's most powerful sluggers as a Cincinnati Red. **1977** *Times of Zambia* 7 Sept. 10/7 The new holder of baseball's all-time Home Run record, Japanese slugger Sadaharu Oh.

**2.** A flat-surfaced boss, knob, or projection on a roll for crushing ore. Also *attrib.*

**1903** R. H. RICHARDS *Ore Dressing* I. 105 These sluggers and knobs are cast upon segments. *Ibid.*, The slugger roll has 16 knob segments and two slugger segments.

**3.** Usu. *pl.* Ear-to-chin whiskers. Also called ***slugger whiskers.*** *U.S. slang.*

**1898** F. P. DUNNE *Mr. Dooley in Peace & War* 211 Ganderbilk he was there, too, standin' out on th' steps in th' cold, combin' his whiskers... He wears a pair iv sluggers.. with his fingers. **1900** G. ADE *More Fables* 118 The mild old Gentleman with the straw-colored Sluggers..came near. **1960** WENTWORTH & FLEXNER *Dict. Amer. Slang* 489/2 *Slugger*.., an ear-to-ear chin beard, as worn by a stage Irishman. **1960** B. KEATON *My Wonderful World of Slapstick* i. 12 A fright wig, slugger whiskers, fancy vest.

**'slugger**[3]. [f. SLUG *sb.*[2]] **1.** (See quot.)

**1892** *Labour Commiss. Gloss.*, *Slugger*, a machine which makes and drives into the bottoms of boots very thick rivets or sprigs called slugs, muds, or studs, to make the soles wear longer.

**2.** One who attaches the top piece of the heel of a shoe to the seat.

**1911** *Rep. Labour & Soc. Cond. Germany* (Tariff Reform League) III. VI–VII. 30 The average wages paid in the district were:.. Sole layer 20s. to 32s. Slugger 30s. to 35s. **1921** *Dict. Occup. Terms* (1927) §414 *Slugger*,..operates, by means of a lever, slugging machine, which attaches top piece of heel to seat.

†**'slugginess.** *Obs. rare.* [f. SLUGGY *a.*] Sluggishness, slothfulness.

*c* **1440** *Jacob's Well* 111 He was wery for trauayle, &, for sluggynes & slewthe, thouȝte to haue esyd hym wyth schortere travayle. *Ibid.* 114 3if it be omytted for heuynes & sluggynesse. **1596** LODGE *Wits Miserie* P j b, Let this persuade you to cast off your sugginesse.

**slugging** ('slʌgɪŋ), *vbl. sb.*[1] [f. SLUG *v.*[1]] The fact or practice of playing the sluggard.

**1532** MORE *Confut. Tindale* Wks. 686/1 If rebellion be no pride,..nor slugging a bed no slouth. **1542** UDALL *Erasm. Apoph.* 15 b, By vacaunt tyme of leasure he mened not slouggyng, loiteryng or slouthful idlenes. **1576** FLEMING *Panopl. Epist.* 343 Nowe, after their long sleepe and slugging, they are awaked. **1633** T. ADAMS *Exp. 2 Pet.* iii. 3 The sluggard quits himself from pragmatical meddling, the busy-body from lazy slugging.

**slugging** ('slʌgɪŋ), *vbl. sb.*[2] *north.* and *U.S.* [f. SLUG *v.*[3]] Slogging; hard hitting; a beating. Also *attrib.* and *fig.*

**1862** C. C. ROBINSON *Dial. Leeds* 413 Gi'e him a good slugging lad! **1884** *Science* IV. 473 Even pugilism would have no charm if it were mere slugging. **1890** GUNTER *Miss Nobody* i. (1891) 13 The slugging and scrimmaging..had been something awful. **1942** BERREY & VAN DEN BARK *Amer. Thes. Slang* §675/3 *Game with many hits*..slugging match. **1956** A. H. COMPTON *Atomic Quest* 315 The war would become a heavy slugging match. **1959** *Economist* 30 May 819/1 The abortive Shawwaf revolt in Mosul set off a slugging match between Cairo and Baghdad. **1974** *Sumter* (S. Carolina) *Daily Item* 23 Apr. 7A/5 His slugging percentage? A whopping .860. **1978** J. CARROLL *Mortal Friends* III. vi. 339 A month's worth of slugging along a coastline through a series of towns.

**slugging** ('slʌgɪŋ), *ppl. a.* [f. SLUG *v.*[1]] Slothful, sluggish.

*c* **1430** *Pilgr. Lyf Manhode* II. lv. (1869) 97 Yit j seye thee that slough thou shalt fynde him and sluggingе. **1597** DRAYTON *Heroical Ep.* 27 b, Nor durst his slugging Hulks approch the strand. **1611** COTGR. s.v. *Dormir*, The slugging or sleepie Cat at length awakes.

Hence **'sluggingly** *adv.*

**1653** URQUHART *Rabelais* I. v. 27 After the procession, they went sluggingly into the fratry room.

**sluggish** ('slʌgɪʃ), *a.* Forms: 5 **slugis(sh, -ys(s)h, sluggyssh, -us(s(h, -isshe**, 6 **-ysshe, -ysh(e, -ysch, -ische** (5 **-esch**, 6 **-essh**), 6– **sluggish**; 6 **slogish, slo(u)ggysshe, slouggish**, 7 **slouggish.** [f. SLUG *sb.*[1] or *v.*[1] + -ISH.]

**1. a.** Of persons: Indisposed to action or exertion; inclined to be slow or slothful; not easily moved to activity.

*c* **1440** *Alph. Tales* 20 Fro thens furth, he was neuer slugissh to rise & go vnto Goddis serves. **1489** CAXTON *Faytes of A.* I. vii. 18 Ne be he not slouthful, sluggyssh, ne slepy. **1535** COVERDALE *Prov.* vi. 9 How longe wilt thou slepe, thou slogish man? **1581** MARBECK *Bk. Notes* 1146 They were sluggish and sought not that which was for the edification of the people. **1632** LITHGOW *Trav.* x. 429 The Turke, and the Irish-man, are the least industrious, and most sluggish liuers vnder the Sunne. **1678** WANLEY *Wonders Lit. World* v. i. §90. 467/2 He was sluggish and careless. **1780** JOHNSON *Let. to Mrs. Porter* 8 Apr., I am indeed but a sluggish correspondent. **1807** CHALMERS *Caledonia* I. Pref. p. vii, The scholars of Scotland remained sluggish, and silent. **1872** BAGEHOT *Physics & Pol.* (1876) 37 A sluggish Englishman will often catch the American look in a few years.

*absol.* **1614–25** [see SLUG *sb.*[1] 3 b].

**b.** Of animals; also *spec.* (see quot. 1884).

[**1827** D. JOHNSON *Ind. Field Sports* 214 There is one kind of snake in India of a sluggish nature.] **1842** COMBE *Digestion* 27 Compared with the torpid and sluggish reptile, the active..quadruped requires..a much larger quantity of nutriment. **1884** *Encycl. Brit.* XVII. 241/1 The sluggish puff-adder (*Clotho arietans*) is common and very dangerous.

**2.** Of the mind, disposition, etc.: Characterized by or exhibiting lack of vigour, alertness, or energy; slow in apprehension or decision; dull.

*c* **1450** tr. *De Imitatione* III. iii, Dedly mennes hertes waxe sluggussh [*v.r.* slugged]. **1538** STARKEY *England* II. iii. (1878) 214 For sluggysch myndys lyue in cornarys and content themselfys wyth pryuate lyfe. **1560** PILKINGTON *Expos. Ageeus* (1562) 88 That the mynde be not made sluggish by cromminge in meate. **1631** GOUGE *God's Arrows* v. §10. 419 They..manifested thereby a luskish, sluggish disposition. **1663** S. PATRICK *Parab. Pilgr.* (1687) 31 This will prepare you..to throw out the sluggish humour which is in all our natures. **1750** JOHNSON *Rambler* No. 56. ¶5 Men, whose perceptions are languid and sluggish. **1825** SCOTT *Betrothed* iii, Ill policy it is to plant such sluggish natures in our borders. **1871** L. STEPHEN *Playgr. Eur.* ix. (1894) 207 Sluggish imaginations require strong stimulants.

**3. a.** Of conditions, etc.: Characterized by want of, or disinclination to, action or exertion.

**1561** HOLLYBUSH *Hom. Apoth.* 4 b, A slouggish or slepery disease. **1570** *Satir. Poems Reform.* xi. 111 Remuif all sluggische slewth away. **1632** LITHGOW *Trav.* x. 446 This sluggish and idle husbandry. **1670** MILTON *Hist. Eng.* VI. Wks. 1851 V. 244 Ethelred, whom no adversity could awake from his soft and sluggish life. **1788** REYNOLDS *Disc.* 250 Either a vain confidence, or a sluggish despair. **1798** EDGEWORTH *Pract. Educ.* (1811) I. 116 It is of consequence to distinguish between slow and sluggish attention. **1838** PRESCOTT *Ferd. & Is.* (1846) III. 25 A life of sluggish inaction. **1873** HAMERTON *Intell. Life* I. iii. 21 Each of us has a little cleverness and a great deal of sluggish stupidity.

**b.** [Rendering of Russ. *stértaya* (*shizofreniya*), worn, hackneyed (schizophrenia).] Applied to an alleged type of schizophrenia ascribed to political or religious dissidents confined in state psychiatric hospitals in the U.S.S.R.

**1977** *Science News* 10 Sept. 165 'Even if one should accept the diagnosis of sluggish schizophrenia in these and similar cases,' Chodoff said, 'one must wonder why a disease without delusions, hallucinations or agitated behavior should require injections of chloropromazine (an antischizophrenic drug) for its treatment.' **1978** *Nature* 4 May 6/2 Yet, when committed, Shikhanovich was diagnosed as a 'psychopath with the possibility of the onset of sluggish schizophrenia' (the latter 'disease', of course, being unknown to non-Soviet diagnosis). **1980** *Prisoners of Conscience in USSR* (Amnesty Internat.) (ed. 2) 184 Schizophrenia, often in its 'sluggish' form, has been the diagnosis most commonly made of dissenters.

**4. a.** Of things: Not readily stirring or moving; slow to stir, act, or make progress in any way.

**1640** WILKINS *New Planet* ix. (1707) 250 Matter is of it self a dull and sluggish thing. **1692** BENTLEY *Boyle Lect.* vi. 213 This poor Atom, sluggish and unactive as it is, doth involve Necessity of Existence. **1764** CHURCHILL *The Ghost* Poems I. 329 The sluggish Oars suspended hung. **1785** CANNING *Poet. Wks.* (1827) 4 Pale ivy throws its sluggish arms around. **1805** R. W. DICKSON *Pract. Agric.* I. 420 A very sluggish species of land is formed. **1849** MACAULAY *Hist. Eng.* iii. I. 406 Bacon had sown the good seed in a sluggish soil and an ungenial season. **1897** *Daily News* 1 Apr. 2/6 Yarns are sluggish, and..the tendency in some directions favours buyers.

**b.** *Med.* Of the pulse, liver, etc.

**1843** R. J. GRAVES *Syst. Clin. Med.* ix. 100 Sluggish and dilated, or else extremely contracted pupils. **1845** BUDD *Dis. Liver* 172 Pulse..sluggish, exceedingly compressible. *Ibid.* 317 The bowels are sluggish. **1897** *Allbutt's Syst. Med.* IV. 25 A symptom of 'sluggish liver'.

**c.** *Med.* Slow in responding to treatment.

**1899** *Allbutt's Syst. Med.* VIII. 519 An effect similar to that of nitrate of silver in sluggish ulcers.

**5. a.** Moving, flowing, etc., very slowly or tardily; slow in movement.

**1611** SHAKS. *Cymb.* IV. ii. 205 To shew what Coast thy sluggish c[r]are Might'st easilest harbour in. **1665** HOOKE *Microgr.* 33 These Glass Drops..being exceedingly hot, and thereby of a kind of sluggish fluid Consistence. **1791** GILPIN *Forest Scenery* II. 147 The river dwindles into a sluggish, little, bull-rush stream. **1812** BYRON *Ch. Har.* II. xx, To waste on sluggish hulks the sweetest breeze! **1842** BISCHOFF *Woollen Manuf.* II. 166 Germany being a flat country, and the rivers..sluggish. **1878** HUXLEY *Physiogr.* 192 A hot mud which rolls down the hill in a sluggish stream.

*fig.* **1891** *19th Cent.* Dec. 858 The currents of public life..are sluggish and slow in Germany.

**b.** Of motion, etc.: Very slow or tardy.

**1648** WILKINS *Math. Magic* I. xx. 141 That orb being the lowest of all, and consequently of a dull and sluggish motion. **1796** MME. D'ARBLAY *Camilla* v. ii, His wry looks and sluggish pace always proclaimed his ill will to the task. **1826** SAMOUELLE *Direct. Collect. Insects & Crust.* 38 The former have a sluggish flight. **1835** J. DUNCAN *Beetles* (Nat. Lib.) 252 Its motions are so sluggish, that it may be said to drag itself along rather than walk. **1849** MACAULAY *Hist. Eng.* iii. I. 379 Their velocity is..contrasted with the sluggish pace of the continental posts.

**6.** *Comb.*, as ***sluggish-minded***, ***-moving*** adjs.

**1851** HELPS *Comp. Solit.* iii. (1854) 34 The most sluggish-minded man craves amusement. **1899** CROCKETT *Black Douglas* 68 The broad sluggish-moving river.

**sluggishly** ('slʌgɪʃlɪ), *adv.* [f. prec. + -LY[2].] In a sluggish or torpid manner; lazily, slowly.

*c* **1450** tr. *De Imitatione* III. xxi, þe eselier þou shalt bere it, made redy þerto nat sluggisly [*v.r.* sluggedly] in herte & by use. **1565** COOPER *Thesaurus*, *Somniculose*, dreamingly: negligently: sluggishly. *c* **1650** Z. BOYD in *Zion's Flowers* (1855) Introd. 52 Who, sluggishlie gapeing and stretching himself, lyeth lusking on the downe. **1674** R. GODFREY *Inj. & Ab. Physic* 189 To do my Work sluggishly by halfs. **1784** REYNOLDS *Disc.* xii. (1842) 201 To go sluggishly about a prescribed task. **1832** R. & J. LANDER *Exped. Niger* III. xvii. 45 Our men at first paddled sluggishly. **1866** R. M. FERGUSON *Electr.* (1870) 33 Hence the compass-needle..oscillates more sluggishly.

**sluggishness** ('slʌgɪʃnɪs). [f. as prec. + -NESS.] The character or quality of being sluggish, torpid, or slow: **a.** Of persons (or animals).

*c* **1440** *Alph. Tales* 20 A monk..tempyd with sleuthe & slugisnes. *c* **1450** tr. *De Imitatione* I. xviii, O þe sluggussnes & þe negligence of oure tyme, þat we..are wery to lyue for sluggussnes and werynes! **1539** ELYOT *Cast. Helthe* 48 b, Sluggyshenes dulleth the body. **1577** B. GOOGE *Heresbach's Husb.* I. (1586) 2 b, We loose the healthfullest and sweetest time with sluggishnesse. **1617** MORYSON *Itin.* III. 160 Hay, whereof they make little for sluggishnesse. **1657** R. LIGON *Barbadoes* (1673) 41 Nor can this be called slothfulness or sluggishness in them,..but a decay of their spirits. **1790** BURKE *Fr. Rev.* 127 Thanks to the cold sluggishness of our national character, we still bear the stamp of our forefathers. **1841** SPALDING *Italy & It. Isl.* II. 187 The time was one neither of sluggishness nor of performance, but of active and earnest preparation. **1875** H. G. WOOD *Therap.* (1879) 156 The first symptom manifested is sluggishness, as shown by a disposition to be quiet.

*personif.* *a* **1610** HEALEY *Cebes* (1636) 129 To defie desperation the daughter of sluggishnesse.

**b.** Of things, their motion, etc.

**1715** tr. *Gregory's Astron.* (1726) I. 135 Lest this Motion should languish by degrees on account of the sluggishness of Matter. **1804** *Med. Jrnl.* XII. 525 The part [has] put on that degree of sluggishness and livid hue, as to require a very different mode of treatment. **1856** KANE *Arctic Explor.* I. xxiv. 322 The sluggishness of the compass..in the Arctic seas. **1879** HARLAN *Eyesight* ii. 24 A sluggishness in the flow of the blood.

†'**sluggy**, *a.*[1] *Obs.* Also 3 sluggi, 5 sloggy. [See SLUG *v.*[1], and cf. Norw. *sluggjen* slow, backward.] Sluggish, indolent.

*a* **1225** *Ancr. R.* 258 Hwo mei beon, uor scheome, slummi & sluggi & slouh, þet bihalt hwu swuðe bisi ure Louerd was on eorðe? *a* **1386** CHAUCER *Pars. T.* ¶706 Thanne cometh Sompnolence, that is sloggy slombrynge. **1408** tr. *Vegetius De re milit.* (MS. Digby 233) lf. 184 b/1 It most be vsed & asayed byfore in ȝouþe or þe body be made sleutheful & sloggy by age. *c* **1440** *Jacob's Well* 289 þat þou schalt noȝt be wery, heuy, ne sluggy ne fayle þer-in. *a* **1533** LD. BERNERS *Golden Bk. M. Aurel.* (1546) Cc j b, The more I slept, the more sluggy I was. **1608** TOURNEUR *Rev. Trag.* IV. ii, As if sleep had caught him, Which claimes most interest in such sluggy men.

**sluggy** ('slʌgɪ), *a.*[2] [f. SLUG *sb.*[1] 4.] Abounding in slugs, or shell-less snails.

**1882** *Gard. Chron.* XVII. 25 They let the slugs in that very sluggy year, 1879, abound around them. **1884** *Blackw. Mag.* Nov. 636, I not only gave them 'cawed' mutton, but also 'sluggy' cabbage.

**slug-horn**[1]. [Erroneous use of *slughorn*, the earlier form of SLOGAN.] A trumpet.

*a* **1770** CHATTERTON *Battle of Hastings* II. 99 Some caught a slughorne, and an onsett wounde. **1855** BROWNING *Childe Roland* xxxiv, Dauntless the slug-horn to my lips I set, And blew.

**slug-horn**[2]. [Cf. SLUG *sb.*[2] 5.] (See quots.)

*a* **1825** FORBY *Voc. E. Anglia* 308 *Slug-horn*, a short and ill-formed horn of an animal of the ox kind, turned downwards, and appearing to have been stunted in its growth. **1878** SIR B. T. B. GIBBS in *Rep. Paris Exhib.* II. 346 A 'slug' horn..gives an indication of the original blood.

Hence '**slug-horned** *a.*

**1899** RIDER HAGGARD in *Longman's Mag.* June 136 Six of these..not polled, but 'slug-horned', that is, with horns about the size and shape of a large sausage.

†'**slugly**, *adv. Obs.*[−1] [f. SLUG *a.*] Sluggishly; lazily.

**1436** *Libel Eng. Policy* in *Pol. Poems* (Rolls) II. 203 God yeve us grace..slugly not to slepe In shame of synne.

†'**slugness**. *Obs. rare.* [f. SLUG *a.*] Slothfulness; indolence.

*c* **1440** *Jacob's Well* 111 As þe feend wryteth & noumbryth þi slauthe, slugnes, & ydelnes. *Ibid.* 116, etc. *a* **1500** *Promp. Parv.* (K.) 460/2 Slugnes, *torpor, segnicies, ignavia*.

†'**slugplum**. *Obs.* [f. SLUG *a.*; *plum* is perh. = PLUMB *sb.*] A sluggard.

**1593** G. HARVEY *Pierce's Superer.* Wks. (Grosart) II. 283 Was..Viuacitie a lasie-bones, or Entelechy a slugplum? *Ibid.* 323 Though my Pen be a slugplum.

†'**slugring**, *ppl. a. Obs.*[−1] [? f. **slugger* vb., f. SLUG *a.* or *v.*] Sluggish.

**1566** STUDLEY *Medea* iv, Made Morpheus locke thy sleepy liddes and shut thy slugring eyne.

**slug-worm**. [f. SLUG *a.* or *sb.*[1] 4.] One or other of the slug-like and slimy larvae of certain saw-flies (esp. those formerly classed in the genus *Selandria*).

**1799** W. D. PECK (*title*), Natural History of the Slug Worm. **1815** KIRBY & SP. *Entomol.* vi. (1818) I. 198 In North America a second species nearly related to it, known there by the name of the *slug-worm*, has become prevalent. **1890** E. A. ORMEROD *Injurious Insects* (ed. 2) 324 The Slug-worms feed on the upper surface of the leaves of the Pear and Cherry.

*attrib.* **1862** T. W. HARRIS *Insects Inj. Veget.* 525 The slug-worm saw-fly.

**sluice** (slu:s), *sb.* Forms: α. 4–7 scluse, 5–7 scluce, 6 sklus. β. 6 sleuss, sleuse, slewse, slowese. γ. 6 *Sc.* slus, 6–7 sluse, 6–8 sluce. δ. 6 sluyce, 7– sluice. [ad. OF. *escluse* (*-clusse*, *-clouse*, etc.; mod.F. *écluse*), = Sp. and Pg. *esclusa*, late and med.L. *exclusa* (also *sclusa*, etc.), fem. sing. of L. *exclūsus*, pa. pple. of *exclūdere* to shut out, EXCLUDE *v.*

OF. is also the source of MDu. *sluse*, *sluyse*, *sluus* (Du. *sluis*, WFris. *slûs*), MLG. *sluse*, *sluze* (LG. *slüse*, *slüs*, G. *schleuse*), Da. *sluse*, Sw. *slus*. For the English forms which represent the late L. *clūsa* see CLOW *sb.*[1]

The spelling with *ui* (cf. *juice*) did not come into general use until the 18th century.]

**1. a.** A structure of wood or masonry, a dam or embankment, for impounding the water of river, canal, etc., provided with an adjustable gate or gates by which the volume of water is regulated or controlled. Also, rarely, the body of water so impounded or controlled.

*falling sluice*: see FALLING *ppl. a.* 5 b.

α. **1340** *Ayenb.* 255 Zome uolk..byeþ ase þe melle wyþoute scluse þet alne-way went be þe yernynge of þe wetere. **1449** *Rolls of Parlt.* V. 149/1 Geteys, Keyes, Scluces, Bankes, and other reparations. *c* **1480** *Reg. Oseney Abbey* (1907) 76 To an scluse to be maade, or locke if þey will. **1558** *Galway Arch.* in *10th Rep. Hist. MSS. Comm.* App. V. 388 The sklus or dame, besyde the said myll. **1583** STOCKER *Civ. Wars Lowe C.* III. 107 Some of these souldiers ..chose rather to leape from the scluse into the water. **1609** HOLLAND *Amm. Marcell.* XXIV. i. 241 The scluces or floudgates made of stone worke, to let out or restraine the waters. **1665** MANLEY *Grotius' Low-C. Wars* 245 Being brought within a Lock of the River or Scluse, near the Castle.

β. **1533** *MS. Rawl. D.* 776 fol. 175 Makyng of Certayne new slewssis vnder the kynges new whalke. **1541–2** *Act 33 Hen. VIII*, c. 33 The maintenance..of other Clowes, sloweses, gettiez, gutters, goottes. **1582** in *Archæologia* XXVIII. 20 A sufficiente sleuss shalbe made for the water-course. **1667** PRIMATT *City & C. Builder* 9 Whether the water be kept up by Art, in slewces.

γ. **1538** ELYOT, *Emissarium*, a sluse [**1548** sluce]. **1568** *Bannatyne MS.* (Hunter. Club) 403 Ane sleiffull of slak that growis in the slus. **1577** B. GOOGE *Heresbach's Husb.* IV. (1586) 172 b, Some greate streame..which by Fludde or Sluse, may let in alwaies fresh water. **1611** CORYAT *Crudities* 157 The fresh and salt water would meete,..were it not kept asunder by a sluce. **1648** J. RAYMOND *Il Merc. Ital.* 183 We went through nine..Machines not much unlike our Sluses, to keep up and let down the water. **1695** PRIOR *Ode after Queen's Death* xxiii, As Waters from her Sluces, flow'd Unbounded Sorrow from her Eyes.

δ. **1596** LAMBARDE *Peramb. Kent* (ed. 2) 148 A Pent and Sluyce hath been made, which both open the mouth, and scowre the bottome of the hauen. **1611** COTGR., *Escluse*, a Sluice, Floud-gate, or Water-gate. **1699** GARTH *Dispens.* I. (1700) 3 While from each Sluice, a briny Torrent pours. **1745** P. THOMAS *Jrnl. Anson's Voy.* 189 It was necessary to set a great Number of Sluices to work. **1785** J. PHILLIPS *Treat. Inland Nav.* p. ix, When the water is..like to over-flow.., they take care to open the sluices to convey it away. **1839** STONEHOUSE *Isle of Axholme* 78 A sluice was erected at Misterton to prevent the tides from flowing beyond that point. **1879** H. PHILLIPS *Addit. Notes Coins* 3 The citizens were prepared to open the sluices and dykes in order..to flood the country.

*transf.* **1794** S. WILLIAMS *Vermont* 97 The beavers always leave sluices, or passages near the middle, for the redundant waters to pass off.

**b.** *fig.* or in fig. contexts. (Common in 17th cent.)

*sing.* **1340** *Ayenb.* 255 Ac þe wise zetteþ þe scluse of discrecion uor to of healde þet weter of fole wordes. **1586** T. B. *La Primaud. Fr. Acad.* I. (1594) 268 The number of them being verie small, who would not willinglie make (as we say) a sluce to their consciences. **1642** MILTON *Apol. Smect.* Wks. 1851 III. 288 His margent, which is the sluce most commonly, that feeds the drouth of his text. **1693** CONGREVE *Old Bach.* v. iv, She's the very sluce to her Lady's secrets. **1778** MISS BURNEY *Evelina* lxxiv, I have..drained every sluice of compassion. **1800** WEEMS *Washington* x. (1877) 120 On receiving the ball which opened in his breast the crimson sluice of life. *a* **1850** CALHOUN *Wks.* (1874) IV. 63 If the sluice of expenditures was stopped in one place, it was sure to burst through another.

*pl.* **1578** TIMME *Calvin on Gen.* 32 If so be the sluses or floodgates of heaven were not shut. **1654** WHITLOCK *Zootomia* 402 Heare him..reckoning up the many Sluces of his Treasury. **1672** CROWNE *Chas. VIII*, I, To my window streight I did repair, And setting wide those sluces of the air [etc.]. **1718** POPE *Odyss.* VIII. 581 So from the sluices of Ulysses' eyes Fast fell the tears. **1754** YOUNG *Centaur* I. Wks. 1757 IV. 111 Thus the sluices are set open for all sensuality..and studied arts of excess, to pour in un-controuled. **1850** MERIVALE *Rom. Emp.* (1865) I. iii. 119 The execution of Lentulus and his associates would reopen the sluices of bloodshed.

**c.** A paddle or slide in a gate or barrier by which water is held back. Also *fig.*

**1616** *Pasquil & Kath.* III. 287 Haue I drawne the sluce Of life vp? and..set my prisoned soule at large? **1791** W. JESSOP *1st Rep. Navig. Thames* 12 A Bar of Sand or Gravel, which is most easily to be removed by drawing the Sluices of the Lock. **1857** P. COLQUHOUN *Compl. Oarsman's Guide* 32 The sluices, otherwise called the paddles, are slides travelling in a slot or groove in the gate.

**d.** A device by which the flow of water, esp. into or out of some receptacle, is regulated; a valve, pipe, etc., by which water may be let in or run off.

**1617** MORYSON *Itin.* III. 137 The medicinall Baths..are shut up certaine howers of the day, that not man should enter them till by their sluces they be purged of all filth. *c* **1710** CELIA FIENNES *Diary* (1888) 5 About 2 yards off the doore is severall pipes..that with a sluce spoutts water up. **1798** J. HUTTON *Course Math.* (1806) II. 344 To determine the Time of emptying a Vessel of Water by a Sluice in the Bottom of it. **1833** LOUDON *Encycl. Archit.* §1243 The cast-iron trough for the water is marked *b*, and the sluice, also of iron, *c*. **1879** *Cassell's Techn. Educ.* I. 79/2 Water was admitted by sluices into the caisson, which then sank.

**2.** A channel, drain, or small stream, *esp.* one carrying off overflow or surplus water.

**1538** LELAND *Itin.* (1768) II. 66 Ther goith a sluse out of this Bath, and servid in Tymes past, with Water derivid out of it, 2 places in Bath Priorie. **1594** R. ASHLEY tr. *Loys le Roy* 38 b, Towards the South it is enuironed with the scluses of Nilus. **1634** SIR T. HERBERT *Trav.* (1638) 8 A meare or fluxe of the Sea,..swelling in 100 armes or sluces. **1725** DE FOE *Voy. r. World* (1840) 289 The little streams and sluices of water. **1848** BOKER *Calaynos* I. i, Ere it flows Past the foul sluices that Seville outpours. **1888** [see SLOUGH *sb.*[1] 4].

*transf.* *c* **1645** HOWELL *Lett.* (1650) II. 3 While wee have sluces of warm bloud running through our veins. **1669** W. SIMPSON *Hydrol. Chym.* 172 By those secret sluces or chanels in the air.

†**3.** A gap, breach, opening, or hole; a gash or wound. *Obs.*

**1648** GAGE *West Ind.* xi. 40 He made a sluce, or breach of halfe a league of length. **1651** BIGGS *New Disp.* 187 ¶250 Unlesse it were repelled out at another sluice or *exit*. **1664** POWER *Exp. Philos.* I. 39 The Lamprey hath seven holes or cavities..and no gills at all—these holes or sluces do indeed supply the defect of gills. **1752** FIELDING *Amelia* I. ii, Certain open sluices on his own head, sufficiently showed whence all the scarlet stream had issued.

†**4.** A drawbridge. *Obs. rare.*

*a* **1634** CHAPMAN *Alphonsus* III. i, Some run unto the Walls, some draw up the Sluce, Some speedily let the Perculless down. **1642** *Lanc. Tracts Civil War* (Chetham Soc.) 22 The King swore he would..take the towne..; but Sir John Hotham drawing up the sluce, his Majesty retreated.

**5.** In gold-washing: An artificial channel or flume, usually consisting of a long sloping trough, or series of troughs, fitted with riffles, or grooves, into which a current of water is directed in order to separate the particles of gold from the auriferous earth.

**1851** *San Francisco Picayune* 14 Oct. 2/4 In the neighbourhood of Rough and Ready, a sluice of fourteen miles in length has been constructed. **1862** B. TAYLOR *Home & Abroad* Ser. II. 144 The sand [is swept] into a long sluice. Here it is still further agitated by means of riffles [etc.]. **1872** RAYMOND *Statist. Mines & Min.* 70 The gold-saving method is the simplest— amalgamation in battery, copper-plate, riffle-boxes, and a tail sluice. **1882** *U.S. Rep. Prec. Metals* 629 The sluices are several hundred and sometimes several thousand feet in length.

**6.** *attrib.* and *Comb.* **a.** With names of things, as ***sluice-block***, ***-cock***, ***-door***, ***-house***, ***-valve***, ***-work***; **sluice-fork**, a fork used to break up lumps of gravel in a gold-miner's sluice-box; **sluice-head** orig. *U.S.*, a supply or head of water sufficient for flushing out a sluice; also *fig.*

**1882** *U.S. Rep. Prec. Metals* 101 They overhauled and refitted the flume, putting in new sluice-blocks. **1837** *Civil Eng. & Arch. Jrnl.* I. 27/1 Certain improvements in the construction of Sluice Cocks for Water-works. **1852** WIGGINS *Embanking* 87 Some difficulty may exist as to keeping open the sluice doors. **1856** *San Francisco Call* 16 Dec. 4/2 As he went—took it *puss*'nal—it commenced raining 'sluice-forks'. **1874** A. BATHGATE *Colonial Experiences* viii. 92 The large stones..lifted out by hand..while the smaller ones are sometimes taken out with a long handled long pronged sluice-fork. **1909** H. THOMPSON in A. E. Currie *Centennial Treasury of Otago Verse* (1949) 59 Slinging stones out with his sluice-fork—what a pleasant little game. **1855** *Golden Era* (San Francisco) 4 Mar. 1/6 At Eureka there are only twelve sluiceheads of water running. **1863** V. PYKE in *App. Jrnls. House Reps. N.Z.* D. VI. 15 Head races..represent about 200 sluice heads. **1901** E. DYSON in *Austral. Short Stories* (1951) 58 Mrs. Mooney..wept sluice-heads... She had been replenishing the fountain of tears with whisky. **1906** *Daily Colonist* (Victoria, B.C.) 6 Jan. 12/3

Although little opened, the springs now have a flow of two sluice-heads. 1935 G. L. MEREDITH *Adventuring in Maoriland in Seventies* xiii. 145 The one we went to is just a boiling spring, running about five 'sluice-heads' of boiling water. 1829 HOOD *Epping Hunt* iv, In a sluice-house box He took his pipe and pot. 1889 WELCH *Text Bk. Naval Archit.* xi. 127 The water being conducted.. through vertical sluice valves. 1819 *Pantologia* s.v., The level of the sluice-work.

**b.** With agent-nouns, etc., as ***sluice-keeper***, ***-maker***, ***-master***; also ***sluice-employing*** adj.

*a* 1725 LD. WHITWORTH *Acc. Russia in 1710* in Dodsley *Fug. Pieces* (1761) II. 214 Contrary to the Opinion of all the Ship-Carpenters and Sluice-makers. 1779 *Phil. Trans.* LXIX. 622 Many sluice masters.. are accustomed to shut their gates next the sea a little after half flood. 1842 *Penny Cycl.* XXII. 142/1 Many self-acting sluices have been contrived.. to save the expense of a sluice-keeper. 1890 'R. BOLDREWOOD' *Miner's Right* (1899) 118/2 The dams and water-races of the sluice-employing miner.

**sluice** (sluːs), *v.* Forms: 6–7 sluce, 6–7 (9) sluse, 7 sluyce, 8– sluice. [f. the sb. Cf. OF. *escluser*, MDu. *slusen*, to shut in by, to provide with, a sluice.]

**1.** *trans.* To let *out*, to cause to flow *out*, by the opening of a sluice. Freq. *fig.*

1593 SHAKS. *Rich. II*, I. i. 103 [I say] that he did plot the Duke of Glousters death,.. And.. like a Traitor Coward, Sluc'd out his innocent soule through streames of blood. 1599 *Warning Faire Women* D ij b, Then stand close George, and with a luckie arme, Sluce out his life. *a* 1641 BP. MOUNTAGU *Acts & Mon.* (1642) 26 Every drop of it.. sluced out from every part of his body. 1660 W. SECKER *Nonsuch Prof.* 6 You cannot.. imagine that I should sluce out a bitter stream from so sweet a spring. 1838 *Civil Eng. & Arch. Jrnl.* I. 257/1 It is proposed that this quantity of water shall be sluiced out through the great embankment.

*refl.* 1850 CLOUGH *Dipsychus* II. iv. 105, I must sluice out myself into canals, And lose all force in ducts.

**b.** To let out or draw *from* some source or place in this manner. Usu. in pa. pple. Freq. *fig.*

1593 NASHE *Christ's T.* Wks. (Grosart) IV. 170 More relishsome.. then the nectarized *Aqua cælestis* of water-mingled blood, sluced from Christs side. 1630 J. TAYLOR (Water P.) *Wks.* I. 2 The vnpolluted blood from him was sluc'de. 1667 MILTON *P.L.* I. 702 Veins of liquid fire Sluc'd from the Lake. 1805–6 CARY *Dante, Inf.* VII. 106 A well That boiling pours itself down to a foss Sluiced from its source. 1830 TENNYSON *Arab. Nts.* 26 A broad canal From the main river sluiced.

**c.** To lead or draw *off* by, or as by, a sluice.

1753–4 RICHARDSON *Grandison* (1781) I. xv. 89 When a stream is sluiced off into several channels, there is the less fear that it will overflow its banks. 1790 W. TAYLOR in Robberds *Mem.* (1843) I. 68 The National Assembly,.. whose pure streams.. will soon be sluiced off into the other realms of Europe. 1846 HAWTHORNE *Mosses* II. vii, He will not survive it above a month, unless his accumulations be sluiced off in some other way. 1869 *Contemp. Rev.* XI. 170 By what other means.. could so many members of the human family have been sluiced off.. into those stagnant pools?

**2.** To draw off or let out water from (a pond, lake, etc.) by means of a sluice or sluices. Freq. *fig.* and *transf.*

1594 NASHE *Unfort. Trav.* Wks. (Grosart) V. 119 If by rain.. those ponds were so full they need to be sluste or let out. 1697 CONGREVE *Mourning Bride* V. iii, I'll sluce this Heart, The Source of Woe, and let the Torrent loose. 1807 J. BARLOW *Columb.* I. 678 Led by this arm thy sons shall hither come,.. Nor sluice their lakes, nor form their soils in vain. 1819 SCOTT *Fam. Lett.* (1894) II. 39 My veins have been sluiced so often that they give me pain in writing. 1892 *Harper's Mag.* Oct. 799/2 A project for sluicing the universities, called university extension.

**b.** Const. *into* (one or more streams, channels, etc.) or *in*. Also *fig.*

1596 WARNER *Alb. Eng.* XII. lxxv. (1602) 310 The once ship-bearing Ley by Alfred slu'ste in Three. 1642 HOWELL *For. Trav.* (Arb.) 45 Germany.. is like a great River sluced into sundry Channels. 1681 DRYDEN *Span. Friar* I. i, Let Honour Call for my Bloud; and sluce it into streams. 1855 SINGLETON *Virgil* I. 119 Where.. the Tuscan tide Into th' Avernian friths is sluiced. 1856 HAWTHORNE *Eng. Note-bks.* (1879) II. 34 Avenues by which the commonplace world is sluiced in among the Highlands.

**c.** To drain of blood, to kill. *rare*⁻¹.

1749 SMOLLETT *Regicide* IV. ii, To sluice them in th' unguarded hour of rest! Infernal sacrifice!

**3.** To cast, fling, or pour (something) as if through a sluice.

1610–11 J. DAVIES (Heref.) *Paper's Compl.* 20 Wks. (Grosart) II. 75 What a dewce Meanst thou such filth in my white face to sluce? 1793 SOUTHEY *Lett.* (1856) I. 17 The ground spouts up water,.. and.. you get completely sluiced for curiosity and amusement. *a* 1803 C. L. LEWES *Mem.* (1805) I. 26 He was (at the moment I sluiced him) either dosing or fast asleep. 1846 THACKERAY *Cornhill to Cairo* xii. Wks. 1900 V. 686 Water so fresh.. never sluiced parched throats before. 1861 HUGHES *Tom Brown at Oxf.* xiii, His neck and face, which he had been sluicing with cold water.

**b.** *Lumbering.* To send or float (logs) down a sluice-way.

1877 *Lumberman's Gaz.* 17 Nov. 309 The Chippewa will sluice down on the river mills at least 400,000,000 feet of logs. 1879 *Ibid.* 15 Oct., The last of the logs.. will probably be sluiced through the dam some time this week.

**4.** To throw or pour water over (a person or thing); to swill with water, esp. in order to clean or wash; to flush or scour with a rush of water. Also, to fill with water.

(*a*) 1755 H. WALPOLE *Lett.* 19 Oct. (1840) III. 161, I have told you what I think ought to sluice my public eye; and your private eye too will moisten, when I tell you [etc.] 1793 SOUTHEY *Lett.* (1856) I. 17 The ground spouts up water,.. and.. you get completely sluiced for curiosity and amusement. *a* 1803 C. L. LEWES *Mem.* (1805) I. 26 He was (at the moment I sluiced him) either dosing or fast asleep. 1846 THACKERAY *Cornhill to Cairo* xii. Wks. 1900 V. 686 Water so fresh.. never sluiced parched throats before. 1861 HUGHES *Tom Brown at Oxf.* xiii, His neck and face, which he had been sluicing with cold water.

(*b*) 1798 CAPT. MILLER in Nicolas *Disp. Nelson* (1846) VII. p. clvii, I had the Ship completely sluiced, as one of our precautionary measures against fire. 1831 *Lincoln Herald* 28 Oct. 2/4 On slusing Grimsby dock.. the body.. was found in the mud. 1853 SURTEES *Sponge's Sp. Tour* (1893) 211 Jack Horsehide, who, as usual, was sluicing the flags with water. 1862 SALA *Seven Sons* II. vii. 195 To scrub the pannikins, and sluice out the tubs with water.

**b.** *slang.* (See quots.)

1796 *Grose's Dict. Vulgar T.* (ed. 3), *Sluice your Gob*, take a hearty drink. 1865 *Slang Dict.* 236 *Sluicing one's bolt*, drinking.

**c.** *U.S.* and *Austr.* To wash (auriferous ore) in a gold-miner's sluice. Also with *out*.

1859 [see SLUICING *vbl. sb.* b]. 1877 RAYMOND *Statist. Mines & Min.* 350 In sluicing out the ore now on hand. 1890 *Goldfields of Victoria* 7 The area of ground sluiced is much in excess of previous quarters.

**5.** *intr.* To flow or pour *out* or down as through a sluice. Also *fig.*

1593 NASHE *Christ's T.* (1613) 61 The siluer gates of the Temple.. were.. but slimy flood-gates for thicke iellied gore to sluce out by. 1834 LANDOR *Exam. Shaks.* Wks. 1853 II. 292/1, I fear me, for once, all his wisdom would sluice out in vain. 1855 A. W. COLE *Legends in Verse* 3 The rain on the windows kept.. Sluicing and dashing.

Hence **sluiced** (sluːst), **'sluicing** *ppl. adjs.*

1607 WALKINGTON *Optic Glass* 156 The other with a double-sluced eye Did sacrifice his teares. 1848 DICKENS *Dombey* xxxii, This here sluicing night is hard lines to a man as lives on his condition.

**sluice-box.** [SLUICE *sb.* 5.] One of the long troughs of which a gold-washing sluice is composed; a riffle-box.

1857 *Hutching's Mag.* July 7/1 A continuous line of these troughs or 'sluice boxes', the smaller and lower end of each, inserted for three or four inches into the larger end of the next one below, form the 'sluice'. 1864 *Richmond-Atkinson Papers* (1960) II. ii. 110 You will not be quite out of the rattle of the shovel, long tom, and sluice box, for we are very golden just now. 1874 RAYMOND *Statist. Mines & Min.* 17 The long tunnel becomes a sluice-way, through the whole length of which sluice-boxes are laid at once. 1879 ATCHERLEY *Trip to Boërland* 114 A long square trough, termed a 'sluice-box', about a foot in width and 20 feet long. 1882 *U.S. Rep. Prec. Metals* 642 Below this tank, and running down the bed of the ravine, are the sluice boxes.

**sluice-gate.** [SLUICE *sb.*] The gate of a sluice, the part which can be opened or shut to let out or retain the water; also, the upper gate of a lock.

1781 *Chambers' Cycl.* s.v. *Lock*, Lock is.. a kind of canal inclosed between two gates; the upper called by workmen the sluice-gate. 1802 BLOOMFIELD *Rural T.* 41 To raise the sluice-gates early every morn. 1865 DICKENS *Mut. Fr.* I. xiv, Not a sluice gate, or a painted scale upon a post or wall, showed the depth of water. 1893 *Archaeologia* LIII. 540 A singularly constructed sluice-gate in the city wall.

**b.** *fig.* or in figurative contexts.

1815 *Sporting Mag.* XLVI. 153 Those who opened the sluice-gates of their wrath against Mr. Wynne's Bill. 1846 MRS. GORE *Eng. Charact.* (1852) 137 The.. sinews of the war of life lie at his disposal. At his nod, the sluice-gates close or open which control the fate of a country. 1897 MISS KINGSLEY *W. Africa* 4 Having opened upon myself the sluice gates of advice, I rapidly became distracted.

**sluicer** ('sluːsə(r)). [f. SLUICE *v.*] **a.** One who attends to a sluice; a sluice-keeper. **b.** *U.S.* and *Austr.* A gold-miner who works at a sluice.

1873 *Daily News* 4 Oct., This money.. was what I earned at Daylesford... I was a sluicer. 1890 *Goldfields of Victoria* 22 The puddlers and sluicers are gradually decreasing in number. 1893 *Scribner's Mag.* June 715 Sluicer's boot, with calks.

**sluice-way.** [f. SLUICE *sb.*] A channel or waterway fed or controlled by means of a sluice or sluices. Also in *Lumbering* (see quot. 1851).

1779 W. MCKENDRY *Jrnl.* 8 Aug. in *Proc. Mass. Hist. Soc.* (1886) II. 461 The sluce way was broke up and the water filld. the river immediately. 1851 *Harper's Mag.* III. 517 For taking logs down mountain sides.. we construct what are called dry sluice-ways. 1856 EMERSON *Eng. Traits, Ability*, A mill is built, a banking-house is opened, and men come in, as water in a sluice-way. 1874 [see SLUICE-BOX]. 1879 *Lumberman's Gaz.* 16 July 5 The bark is thrust into sluice-ways to the chains and carried by them outside.

*fig.* 1858 E. D. PROCTOR *Beecher's Life Th.* (1860) 114 A drain or sluiceway by which the heavenly stream of God's favour escapes from them.

**sluich**, obs. Sc. form of SLOUGH *sb.*²

**sluicing** ('sluːsɪŋ), *vbl. sb.* [f. SLUICE *v.* + -ING¹.] The action of the verb, in various senses.

1840 THACKERAY *Catherine* viii, They wanted a sluicing. 1874 RAYMOND *Statist. Mines & Min.* 327 The all-important drawback is the lack of water for sluicing, or even for simple washing. 1889 *Anthony's Photogr. Bulletin* II. 373 A good sluicing of the eyes in cold water every morning will be found beneficial.

**b.** *attrib.*, as ***sluicing claim***, ***company***.

1859 CORNWALLIS *New World* I. 328 The St. Andrew's Mining and Sluicing Company. 1882 *U.S. Rep. Prec. Metals* 105 The Fox Creek and Boulder Creek sluicing claims have uniformly done well. 1890 'R. BOLDREWOOD' *Col. Reformer* (1891) 293 A great sluicing claim, where the water.. spouted clear and strong over heaps of auriferous earth.

**sluicy** ('sluːsɪ), *a.* Chiefly *poet.* Also 7 slucy. [f. SLUICE *sb.* + -Y¹.]

**1.** Of rain, etc.: Falling or pouring copiously or in streams, as if from a sluice; streaming, drenching.

1697 DRYDEN *Virg. Georg.* I. 437 Oft whole sheets descend of slucy Rain. 1715 POPE *Iliad* V. 122 While Jove descends in sluicy sheets of rain. 1813 T. BUSBY *Lucretius* II. V. 443 Rapid rivers, swelled by sluicy showers. 1863 *Pilgr. over Prairies* I. 148 The deluges of rain that in compact, sluicy sheets now descended.

**2.** Resembling a sluice; acting like a sluice. *rare.*

*a* 1703 POMFRET *Last Epiphany* iii, Such were the boding Times, Ere Ruin blasted from the sluicy Sky. 1706–7 FARQUHAR *Beaux' Strat.* IV. i, That hospitable Seat of Life.. open'd all its sluicy gates to take the Stranger in.

**3.** Of sand: Wet, soaking.

1818 KEATS *Endym.* I. 946 'Tis the grot.. where her tender hands She dabbles, on the cool and sluicy sands.

**sluit** (sluːt), *S. African.* Also slote, sloot, sloet. [(Cape) Du. *sloot* ditch, = LG. *sloot*, OFris. *slât* (WFris. *sleat*).] A channel, ditch, or gully, usually one formed by heavy rain and dry during the greater part of the year.

α. 1863 W. C. BALDWIN *Afr. Hunting* 30 On coming into a mud sluit.. the sudden check of the wagon threw me off. 1882 *Times of Natal* 8 June, About 3,900 yards of the sluits remain uncovered. 1896 BADEN-POWELL *Matabele Campaign* xvii, One evening I heard the old brute moving in the sluit, close to the camp.

β. 1818 C. I. LATROBE *Jrnl. Visit to S. Afr.* x. 187 It has.. water in abundance, brought by a *slote*, or canal, from a considerable distance. 1852 C. BARTER *Dorp & Veld* iv. 33 Going one dark night to a friend's house, and keeping in the middle of the road to avoid the 'sloots', I stumbled over.. a large black ox. 1862 L. DUFF GORDON *Let.* 29 Dec. in F. Galton *Vacation Tourists* (1864) 157 There is no water but what runs down the streets in the sloot, a paved channel, which brings the water from the mountain and supplies the houses and gardens. 1889 FR. OATES *Matabele-Land* 198 In crossing a small 'sloot' one of the wheels gave way. 1897 ANNA HOWARTH *Jan* xxiv, Beds of wild yellow marigolds glorified every little hollow and sloet.

**slukane**, variant of SLOKAN.

**slum** (slʌm), *sb.*¹ [Of cant origin, and in all senses except 2–4 only in slang or canting use.]

**I.** † **1.** A room. *Obs.*

1812 J. H. VAUX *Flash Dict.*, *Slum*, a room. 1823 BEE *Dict. Turf.* s.v., Thus we may have 'the little slum',.. 'the back slum', and a slum in front. 1824 *Hist. Gaming* 28 Regaling.. in the back parlour (*vulgo* slum) of an extremely low-bred Irish widow.

**2. a.** A street, alley, court, etc., situated in a crowded district of a town or city and inhabited by people of a low class or by the very poor; a number of these streets or courts forming a thickly populated neighbourhood or district where the houses and the conditions of life are of a squalid and wretched character. Chiefly *pl.*, and freq. in the phrase ***back slum(s)***. Also *rarely*, a house materially unfit for human habitation.

(*a*) 1825 WESTMACOTT *Eng. Spy* II. 32 The back slums lying in the rear of Broad St. 1851 DICKENS *Lett.* (1880) I. 251 When the back slums are going to be invaded. 1871 L. STEPHEN *Playgr. Eur.* (1894) ix. 203 The unspeakable ugliness of a back slum in London. 1880 R. S. WATSON *Visit Wazan* iv. 72 The back slums are not more inviting than those of many European towns.

(*b*) 1845 *Athenæum* 18 Jan. 75 In the thick of the once renowned 'slums' of St. Giles's. 1860 *All Year Round* No. 74. 570 An obscure cabaret—say pothouse—lying in a slum. 1889 JEROME *Idle Thoughts* 117 A little mite sitting on a doorstep in a Soho slum. 1894 SALA *London up to Date* vi. 79 Large tracts of indescribably dirty, profligate, and felonious slums. 1955 *Times* 25 Aug. 5/5 Nowadays people who live in so-called slum houses (a 'slum', as officially defined means a house materially unfit for habitation), set a good standard of cleanliness. 1972 *Observer* 31 Dec. 8/2 He had inherited nearly two million slums.

*fig.* 1870 LOWELL *Among my Bks.* Ser. I. (1873) 84 The slums and stews of the debauched brain.

**b.** *Theatr.* (See quot.)

1886 *Stage Gossip* 69 Such lowly edifices of the drama as wooden buildings of humble erection and booths are frequently designated 'slums'.

**3.** Representation of slum life or conditions.

1885 *Pall Mall G.* 7 Apr. 10/1, I should like to know who would stand five acts of 'slum'.

**4. a.** *attrib.* and *Comb.*, as ***slum area***, ***-burrow***, ***-dweller***, ***-literature***, ***-people***, ***property***, ***street***, etc.; ***slum-bred*** adj.

Many combs. of these types occur in recent newspaper usage. (N.E.D.)

1863 B. JERROLD *Signals of Distress* 7 It is a genuine bit of slum-literature. 1878 GORDON *Jrnl.* in Hill *G. in C. Africa* (1881) 326 These slum people liked their visitor. 1887 *Contemp. Rev.* Dec. 772 That class rarely stray.. from their slum-burrows and dens. 1891 *Contemp. Rev.* Oct. 548 Tens of millions will be exposed to the physical and mental blight of the 'submerged' slum-dweller. 1898 E. HOWARD *To-morrow* xiv. 147 What will become of this slum property?.. These wretched slums will be pulled down. 1924 *Glasgow Herald* 8 Mar. 7 The slum problem is fundamentally not one of stone and lime or cubic space, but of mental and social outlook. 1928 GALSWORTHY *Swan Song* I. vii. 57 Slum-dwellers were such good sorts! 1932 L. GOLDING *Magnolia St.* III. vi. 537 A tribe of inconceivable people who lived in a slum street in a dark English town. 1935 C. S. FORESTER *Afr. Queen* iv. 86 His slum-bred father and mother. 1939 C.

DAY LEWIS *Child of Misfortune* II. ii. 151 The Church..held slum-property, helped to exploit innocent native tribes and ruined their morals and physique. **1940** 'G. ORWELL' *Inside Whale* 20 Low wages and the growth and shift of population had brought into existence a huge, dangerous slum-proletariat. **1959** I. & P. OPIE *Lore & Lang. Schoolch.* xviii. 389 A row of crowded slum houses with front doors cheek by jowl. **1959** J. CARY *Captive & Free* ix. 41 The mid-town terraces which can and have so easily become slum tenements. **1960** 'F. NEWTON' *Jazz Scene* vi. 100 The penalties of the isolated, community-less life of the slum-bred entertainer. **1968** *Globe & Mail* (Toronto) 13 Feb. 27/1 Maple Leafs can muddle into the slum area of fifth place and there are few hoots of derision. *a* **1974** R. CROSSMAN *Diaries* (1975) I. 182 The town itself has some 30,000 or 40,000 inhabitants..who don't want Birmingham slum dwellers dumped on them as overspill. **1979** G. ST. AUBYN *Edward VII* viii. 379 She insisted on being shown his slum property in the East End of London. **1980** J. MELVILLE *Chrysanthemum Chain* 135 Walker made his way out and into the shabby slum street.

**b.** Special Combinations: **slum clearance**, the evacuation and demolition of slums, usu. accompanied by the rehousing of the inhabitants; freq. *attrib.*; also **slum clearer, clearing** *ppl. a.*; **slumland**, the slums; **slum landlord**, one who lets slum property to tenants, esp. one who allows his property to fall into disrepair; hence **slum landlordism**, the practice of letting slum property; **slumlord** *U.S.* = *slum landlord* above; hence **slumlordship**; **slum-sister**, a woman devoted to charitable and educative work in the slums.

[**1900** A. SMITH *Housing Question* iii. 60 The clearance of slums should not be taken to make room for housing schemes.] **1907** E. R. DEWSNUP *Housing Problem in Eng.* xi. 227 Local Authorities..have hesitated to shoulder the financial burden that would result from any general application of the powers of slum clearance placed at their disposal by statute law. **1930** T. E. LAWRENCE *Let.* 19 Jan. (1938) 678 The area it occupied turned into a public garden, in pursuance of the slum-clearance scheme. **1936** T. S. ELIOT *Essays Ancient & Modern* 132 We recognize that possibility in every work of slum-clearance and housing reform. **1953** E. SMITH *Guide to English Traditions & Public Life* 133 The necessity of slum-clearance had to be faced. **1961** L. MUMFORD *City in History* viii. 220 Such systematic slum clearance projects as Nero's great fire naturally increased the housing shortage. **1979** *Punch* 28 Nov. 1032/3 Ms Greer..does not establish much that is positive; but she has performed a monumental work of intellectual slum-clearance. **1934** 'R. CROMPTON' *William—the Gangster* viii. 177 They were all lofty and spacious enough to satisfy the most determined and particular of slum clearers. **1977** *Listener* 28 Apr. 531/1 If the developer had to pay over a slice to the slum-clearing authorities, this would allow them to rehouse the slum-dwellers. **1893** *Graphic* 25 Mar. 298/3 The appearance of respectability..deprives him of the glamour of slumland. **1929** S. LESLIE *Anglo-Catholic* i. 10 He felt at home in the East End and refreshed..when he lay back at night and sniffed the indefinable steam of slumland. **1978** D. MURPHY *Place Apart* vi. 110, I..cycled back to slumland to spend the rest of the day with Catholic families. **1893** G. B. SHAW *Widowers' Houses* III. vii. 84 The worst slum landlord in London. **1931** W. HOLTBY *Poor Caroline* iii. 97 There was so much to be done..slum landlords to be confronted. **1972** C. DRUMMOND *Death at Bar* vii. 179 A slum landlord who augmented his meagre rents in strange and unlawful ways. **1892** *Black & White* 17 Dec. 698/1 As a discussion, with open doors, of the pros and cons of slum-landlordism..Mr Shaw's *Widowers' Houses* is..a very considerable piece of work. **1967** *Sunday Times* 30 Apr. 11/1 Slum landlordism..has not been seriously curtailed. **1953** *Chicago Daily News* 12 Sept. 3/7 Reporters..found that slumlords frequently twist Illinois' trust laws into blinds for escaping detection. **1957** *N.Y. Times Mag.* 12 May 36/3 The landlord had bitterly protested..that he was not a 'slumlord' and avowed that he was ready to put the building in condition *if* he could get a guarantee that it would stay that way. **1978** S. WILSON *Dealer's Move* vii. 121 A big place in Surrey—it belonged to one of the king slum-lords. **1966** *Atlantic Monthly* Nov. 128 Within the chivalric order of slumlordship he is a very minor vassal. **1890** *Guardian* 31 Dec. 2096/1 This 'slum-sister' gathers children for instruction on Sunday afternoons.

**II.** †**5. a.** Nonsensical talk or writing; gammon, blarney. Also, gipsy jargon or cant. *Obs.*

**1812** P. EGAN *Boxiana* I. 122 The flowing harangue of some dusty cove..lavish with his slum on the beauties possessed by some distinguished pugilist. **1820** in *Grose's Dict. Vulgar T.* (1823) s.v., And thus, without more slum, began..To settle..The rigs of this here tip-top nation. **1822** J. WILSON *Noctes Ambros.* iv, He may have written some pretty things, but he is taken now to slum, scissorsing, namby pamby, and is quite spoiled. **1823** BEE *Dict. Turf* s.v., The gipsey language, or cant, is slum. *Ibid.*, Loose, ridiculous talk, is 'all slum'. 'None of your slum,' is said by a girl to a blarneying chap.

**b.** *up to slum*, knowing, wideawake; not to be 'taken in' or 'done'.

**1857–9** in *Slang Dict.*

**c.** 'An insinuation, a discreditable inuendo.'

**1865** *Slang Dict.* 236.

**6.** A begging-letter.

**1851** MAYHEW *Lond. Lab.* I. 224 A slum's a paper fake. *Ibid.* 311 Of these documents there are two sorts, 'slums' (letters) and 'fakements' (petitions).

**7.** 'A chest or package' (*Slang Dict.* 1859).

**8.** *N. Amer.* **a.** Cheap or imitation jewellery. Also as *adj. Criminals' slang.*

**1914** JACKSON & HELLYER *Vocab. Criminal Slang* 77 *Slum*, jewelry of any description, but lately reduced in scope of meaning to include only the less valuable kinds of jewelry... 'He's got a bale of slum for sloughings.' **1924** G. C. HENDERSON *Keys to Crookdom* 418 *Slum*, plated jewelry. **1931** *Amer. Speech* VII. 102 Nail the stones but blow the slum. **1946** S. S. JACOBS in *Mag. Digest* Aug. 89/2 A guy buys a slum ring for ten cents. **1955** *Publ. Amer. Dialect Soc.* xxiv. 122 Any kind of jewelry, usually exclusive of watches, was—and still is—referred to as *slum*. **1962** 'K. ORVIS' *Damned & Destroyed* vii. 53 Jewellery... Top stuff. No slum.

**b.** Cheap prizes at a fair, carnival, etc.

**1929** *Sat. Even. Post* 19 Oct. 26/2 Business Opportunities hammer at every door in the advertising columns of this trade paper. Slum, 1008 pieces for tie pins, collar pins, brooches, cigarette holders, rings, $695 the lot. **1956** H. GOLD *Man who was not with It* (1965) i. 5 The slum prizes dripped from their hands, taffy, teddy-bears, streamers of paper.

Hence **'slumism** [-ISM], the existence of slums; the deprivations and other ills associated with or characteristic of life in the slums.

**1967** *Britannica Bk. of Year 1966* 804/2 *Slumism*, the existence of highly congested urban residential areas characterized by deteriorated unsanitary buildings, poverty, and social disorganization. **1967** *Harper's Mag.* Feb. 83 We must show the same unhesitating commitment to fighting slumism, poverty, ignorance, prejudice, and unemployment that we show to fighting Communism. **1971** L. CHESTER *Martin Luther King* xi. 262 We are victims of slumism!

**slum** (slʌm), *sb.*² *U.S.* [? ad. G. *schlamm* in the same sense.] = SLIME *sb.* 4.

**1874** RAYMOND *Statist. Mines & Min.* 350 The discharge near the top carries off light particles and slums. **1877** *Ibid.* 97 This material..is like the slum or tailings from a mill.

**slum**, *sb.*³ *slang.* [App. abbrev. of SLUMGULLION.] **1.** = SLUMGULLION 2 c.

**1847** J. MITCHELL *Reminisc. College* 117 Though the son of Vulcan found the pork and cabbage harmless, I am sure that slum would have been a match for him. **1865** 'MARK TWAIN' *Notebook* 28 Jan. (1935) i. 6 Chili-beans and dish-water three times today as usual and some kind of 'slum' which the Frenchman called 'hash'. **1898** E. H. BLATCHFORD *Let.* 17 July (1920) 37 Beef stew, commonly known as slum. **1918** *Stars & Stripes* 5 Apr. 4 Everyone knows that there are at least three different kinds of slum —the watered kind, the more solid variety and the occasional special sort that wears a pie-crust. The Marines describe these three types in sea-lingo: 'slum with the tide in', 'slum with the tide out', and 'slum with an overcoat'. **1972** J. M. MINIFIE *Homesteader* xx. 182 There would be white table-cloths and sparkling glass and silver, instead of a mess-tin of slum on a dirty table in barracks.

**2.** Special Combinations. **slum burner**, an army cook; **slum gun**, a field-kitchen.

**1930** *Our Army* Aug. 33 The..cook..is a 'slum-burner'. **1943** M. HARGROVE *See here, Private Hargrove* xlii. 118 Oscar of the Waldorf, in the Army, would still be..a *slum-burner*. **1917** R. BATCHELDER *Watching & Waiting on Border* vii. 90 The regiment owned a field-kitchen, or 'slum-gun', a bulky vehicle in which food might be prepared on the march. **1947** D. RUNYON *Poems for Men* 213 Our slum-gun busted down.

**slum**, variant of SLOOM *sb.*¹ and *sb.*²

**slum** (slʌm), *v.* [Cf. SLUM *sb.*¹]

**1.** *trans. Cant.* (See quots.)

**1859** *Slang Dict.* 96 *Slum the gorger*, to cheat on the sly, to be an eye servant. **1874** *Ibid.* 297 *Slum*, to hide, to pass to a confederate.

**2. a.** To do (work) hurriedly and carelessly.

**1865** *Daily Telegr.* 25 Aug., The builders were not men to 'slum' or 'scamp' their work.

**b.** *intr.* (See quot. 1965.) Also *trans.*, to shear (a sheep, etc.) in this manner. *Austral. Sheep-shearing.*

**1965** J. S. GUNN *Terminol. Shearing Industry* II. 24 A shearer slums if he works as fast as he can, and perhaps carelessly, while the pen is full, and thus takes a large proportion of the easy sheep. **1966** J. CARTER *People of Inland* (1967) xvii. 165 Then at shearing time, these same 'guns' can slum pen after pen of fine, clean sheep, because the opportunity to set a new record has presented itself.

**3.** *intr.* **a.** To go into, or frequent, slums for discreditable purposes; 'to saunter about, with a suspicion, perhaps, of immoral pursuits'.

*a* **1860** in Oxford use. **1865** *Slang Dict.* (as Cambridge Univ. slang).

**b.** 'To keep to back streets to avoid observation' (Barrère and Leland, 1897).

**4. a.** To visit slums for charitable or philanthropic purposes, or out of curiosity, esp. as a fashionable pursuit. Also with *it*. Freq. in phr. *to go slumming* (see SLUMMING *vbl. sb.* 2).

**1884** *Referee* 22 June (Cassell), A wealthy lady went slumming through the Dials the other day. **1884** *Boston* (Mass.) *Jrnl.* 1 Oct. 2/3 A party of young fashionable people of New York thought they would go a slumming. **1887** *Good Words* 238 He had taken tea hundreds of times in workmen's houses; he had 'slummed' so far back as 1846. **1899** W. JAMES *Let.* 8 Feb. (1920) II. 88 Kipling knows perfectly well that our camps in the tropics are not college settlements or our armies bands of philanthropists, slumming it.

**b.** To accept, temporarily and voluntarily, a standard (of living, travel, etc.) lower than that to which one is accustomed; to mix with one's inferiors. Freq. as *pres. pple.* and with *it*. Also *fig.*

**1928** E. WALLACE *Gunner* xxiii. 192 'What are you doing down here?' 'Slumming,' said Gunner Hayes coolly. 'I like now and again to establish contact with the underworld.' **1944** N. COWARD *Middle East Diary* 95 We quite enjoyed slumming it in the ordinary pullman. **1946** R. G. COLLINGWOOD *Idea of Hist.* IV. 145 It is necessary to go slumming among the most unsavoury relics of third-rate historical work. **1951** E. COXHEAD *One Green Bottle* ii. 57 He isn't quite a professor yet. She's just slumming till he becomes one. **1959** *Ann. Reg. 1958* 192 Mr Rockefeller, as he slummed it in New York in the battle with his fellow millionaire the Democratic Mr Harriman. **1978** P. PORTER *Cost of Seriousness* 35 On its dorsal, a monster is drumming Messages for the new world—each wraith Is a spirit of old Europe slumming. **1981** *Birds* Autumn 68/1 It [*sc.* a brambling] was quite unabashed by the proximity of the feeding area to the back door and was happily 'slumming it' with the resident sparrows, chaffinches and greenfinches.

**slumber** ('slʌmbə(r)), *sb.* Forms: α. 5 slomur, -owre, 6 slommer, 5–6 *Sc.* slummer (9 *dial.*), -ir. β. 5–6 slomber (5 -bre, -bir), 6 sloumber, 6– slumber. [f. SLUMBER *v.* Cf. Fris. *slommer*, *slûmer*, Du. *sluimer*, LG. *slümer*, late MHG. *slummer* (G. *schlummer*), Da. and Sw. *slummer*.]

**1. a.** Sleep, repose. Chiefly *poet.*

? *a* **1400** *Morte Arth.* 3221 He..fore slewthe of slomowre one a slepe fallis. **1530** PALSGR. 271/2 Slommer, *somme, somneil.* **1582** STANYHURST *Æneis* III. (Arb.) 75 With slumber is holden Eche liuing creature. **1599** SHAKS. *Hen. V*, III. ii. 123 Ere theise eyes of mine take themselues to slomber. **1634** MILTON *Comus* 1001 Young Adonis.. Waxing well of his deep wound In slumber soft. **1697** DRYDEN *Virg. Georg.* IV. 583 His Eyes with heavy Slumber overcast. **1754** GRAY *Poesy* 23 Quench'd in dark clouds of slumber. **1848** LYTTON *Harold* VII. iv, There was no further thought of slumber that night. **1871** R. ELLIS *Catullus* lxiv. 122 When her eyes lay bound in slumber's shadowy prison.

**b.** With possessive pronouns.

*c* **1386** CHAUCER *Miller's T.* 630 This carpenter out of hese slombir sterte. *c* **1402** LYDG. *Compl. Bl. Knt.* 16 With a sigh I gan for to abreyde Out of my slombre. **1500–20** DUNBAR *Poems* xiv. 1 Devysing in my slummer, How that this realme [etc.]. **1616** W. BROWNE *Brit. Past.* II. v, Let this her slumber..Make her beleeve our love was but a dreame! **1849** JAMES *Woodman* ix, The next instant, her slumber was broken.

**2.** A period or occasion of sleep or repose; freq., a light or short sleep.

α. *c* **1400** *Destr. Troy* 13285 Thai have no dainty of drynk, ..But derkon euon down on a depe slomur. *c* **1470** HENRY *Wallace* VII. 71 In that slummir, cummand him thocht he saw Ane agit man. **1500–20** DUNBAR *Poems* xxxv. 9 For weirines on me ane slummer soft Come. *a* **1599** A. HUME *Poems* (S.T.S.) v. 91 He makes the physicke take effect, the slummers soft he geifis.

β. **1509** HAWES *Past. Pleas.* I. (Percy Soc.) 7 Thus as I satte in a deadly slomber, Of a great horne I harde a royal blast. **1550** CROWLEY *Epigr.* 1178 He fell in a sloumber. **1611** TOURNEUR *Ath. Trag.* v. i, No, my Lord. Nor sleepe nor wake. But in a slumber troublesome to both. **1661** DRYDEN *Panegyrick Coronation* 42 Officious slumbers haste your eyes to close. **1725** N. ROBINSON *Th. Physick* 319 If he takes none the first Night, his Slumbers may be more compos'd the following. **1791** MRS. RADCLIFFE *Rom. Forest* i, Madame La Motte found her sunk in a disturbed slumber. **1836** THIRLWALL *Greece* xi. II. 27 His youth..passed away in a preternatural slumber. **1841** SPALDING *Italy & It. Isl.* I. 304 The Mons Vultur, which sheltered Horace's infant slumbers.

**3.** *fig.* A state or condition of repose, rest, inactivity, or quiescence.

**1552** LYNDESAY *Monarche* 6300 Dreid nocht to dee; for deith is bot ane slummer. **1579** W. WILKINSON *Confut. Fam. Love* 17 b, Your imagination is but the shadow of a slumber. **1605** G. POWEL *Refut. Ep. Puritan-Papist* 85 It was by reason of impunitie and slumber of Iustice. **1781** GIBBON *Decl. & F.* xxix. (1787) III. 132 The son of Theodosius passed the slumber of his life, a captive in his palace. **1797** GODWIN *Enquirer* I. vi. 37 The human mind awoke from a slumber. **1822** SHELLEY tr. *Calderon's Mag. Prodig.* I. 239 Thou canst not Restore it [a sword] to the slumber of the scabbard. **1845** MAURICE *Mor. Philos.* in *Encycl. Metrop.* (1847) II. 650/1 Those who teach that the powers of man woke at once from a deep slumber just at the beginning of the XVth Century.

**4.** *attrib.* and *Comb.*, as ***slumber-bed***, ***-land***, etc.; ***slumber-bound***, ***-closing***, ***-wrapt*** adjs.; **slumber cap**, a light, close-fitting cap of lace, ribbon, etc., worn in bed to keep the hair tidy; **slumbercoach** *U.S.*, a railway car which provides economical private sleeping accommodation; **slumber net**, a slumber cap made of net; **slumber party** *U.S.*, a party for youngsters (esp. girls) who stay on to sleep overnight; **slumber room** *U.S.*, a room in which a corpse is laid out by an undertaker until the funeral takes place; **slumberwear**, night-clothes.

*c* **1445** LYDG. *Nightingale* 57 Oute of thy *slombre-bed of slouth & sleep. **1820** SHELLEY *Two Spirits* 30 Look from thy dull earth, *slumber-bound. *c* **1840** MRS. BROWNING *Isobel's Child* ix, The little mouth so slumber-bound. **1928** *Sunday Dispatch* 8 July 16 Shingle caps or *slumber caps for the seaside..in Nottingham lace, bound with pink, blue or any coloured satin ribbon. **1971** 'A. GILBERT' *Tenant for Tomb* iii. 47 She rolled up the plaits under..a slumber cap, an affair of bright blue silk and lace and a ribbon bow. **1798** SOTHEBY tr. *Wieland's Oberon* (1826) I. 162 Strive to unbolt their *slumber-closing eye. **1958** *Washington Post* 26 June C19/3 B & O charges regular coach fare plus $6 service charge for a single room..for its *slumbercoaches, which are operated on only one train, the Baltimore-Washington-Chicago Columbian. **1979** *United States 1980/81* (Penguin Travel Guides) 19 Long-distance trains offer sleeping accommodations..slumbercoaches, private rooms,.. roomettes. **1882** SWINBURNE *Tristr. of Lyonesse* vi. 109 The great good wizard..Takes his strange rest at heart of *slumberland. **1887** *Illustr. Lond. News* 20 Aug. 217 We are half way to Slumberland. **1930** J. RHYS *After leaving Mr Mackenzie* II. xiii. 217 Out of the second door emerged a lady in a pink dressing-gown, with her hair hidden by a *slumber-net. **1950** A. WILSON *Such Darling Dodos* 79 The artifice of the black waved hair..beneath the neat mesh of the slumber net. **1966** *Olney Amsden & Sons Ltd. Price List* 23 Hair and slumber nets. [**1942** BERREY & VAN DEN BARK *Amer. Thes. Slang* §251/1 *Sleep*,..*slumber party.] **1949** *Senior Prom* Nov. 22/2 For a girls' party you might have a brunch, lunch, dinner,..or slumber party. **1954** *Life* 26 Apr. 186/2 Because it was to be a slumber party, the 19 girls ..came carrying pillows, blankets and floppy animals—but no one really expecting to get much sleep. **1974** A. LURIE *War between Tates* ix. 181 'I'm invited to Elsie's slumber party.' 'Oh? And what is a slumber party?' 'Don't you even know that? You have a party, and then you sleep overnight.' **1936** *Slumber-room [see *funeral-home* s.v. FUNERAL *sb.* 6]. **1963** J. MITFORD *Amer. Way of Death* iv. 61 The slumber rooms are elusively reminiscent of some other feature of American life... 'So then you've got a slumber room tied up for three days or more,' he said... 'How much would it cost you to stay in a good motel for three days?'.. Motels for the dead! That's it, of course. **1979** *Sun-Times* (Chicago) 28 Sept. 4 Would it be considered improper to take a photograph of a deceased friend or relative in the slumber room during viewing hours? **1909** *Punch* 24 Mar. 206/3 The famous house so long consecrated to the habiliments of Morpheus, or '*slumberwear', as of late we have been taught to call them. **1961** L. P. HARTLEY *Two for River* iv. 74 If he called her now she would probably be in bed, and come down in her nightgown or her pyjamas, or whatever slumberwear she favoured, and that would never do. **1838** ELIZA COOK *Sailing Song* i. 6 The *slumber-wrapt might of the waves.

**slumber** ('slʌmbə(r)), *v.* Forms: α. 3 slumeren, 4 slomyr, 5 -yre, -eron, 5–6 slom(m)er, 6 *Sc.* slummer. β. 4–6 slombre, 5 sloumbre, 6 slomber; 4– slumber. [ME. *slūmeren*, etc., f. *slūmen* SLOOM *v.*[1] or *slūme* SLOOM *sb.*[1], corresponding to Fris. *slûmerje*, MDu. *slum-*, *sloem-*, *sluymeren* (Du. *sluimeren*), MLG. *slômeren* (LG. *slommern*, *slümern*), late MHG. *slum(m)ern*, *slommern* (G. *schlummern*); Da. *slumre*, Sw. *slumra* are of G. origin. The development of the *b* between *m* and *r* is in accordance with English phonetic tendencies.]

**1.** *intr.* To sleep, *esp.* to sleep lightly; to doze or drowse.

α. *c* **1220** *Bestiary* 576 in *O.E. Misc.* 18 Sipmen..slumeren and slepen, and to late waken. *a* **1340** HAMPOLE *Psalter* lxxv. 6 Þai slomyrd þat steghe horsis. *c* **1400** *Destr. Troy* 8428 As þis burde was in bed.., slomeryng a while, Sho was affrayet full foule. *c* **1440** *Promp. Parv.* 460/1 Slomeron, *dormito, nictitor.* **1561** WINȜET *Tract.* Wks. (S.T.S.) I. 6 He nother slepis nor slummeris quha behaldis al ȝour doingis.

β. **1362** LANGL. *P. Pl.* A. Prol. 10 As I lay..and lokede on þe watres, I slumberde in a slepyng. *c* **1400** *Rom. Rose* 4005 He slombred, and a nappe he toke. *c* **1485** *Digby Myst.* (1882) I. 302 To sle and morder yong children þat in þer cradell slumber. **1530** PALSGR. 722/1 He dothe nat slepe nowe, he dothe but slomber. **1599** THYNNE *Animadv.* (1875) 56 He neyther slombrethe nor slepethe, but alwayes watchethe. **1605** B. JONSON *Volpone* I. i, *Corb.* Does he sleep well? *Mos.* No wink, sir, all this night, Nor yesterday; but slumbers. **1681** DRYDEN *Abs. & Achit.* 447 Like a Lion, Slumb'ring in the way, Or Sleep dissembling, while he waits his Prey. **1746** FRANCIS tr. *Horace, Art Poet.* 488, I..hold it for a Fault..If honest Homer slumber o'er his Muse. **1818** SCOTT *Br. Lamm.* xxxv, He ate without refreshment, and slumbered without repose. **1878** BROWNING *La Saisiaz* Introd. ii, Soul that canst soar! Body may slumber.

*transf.* **1825** T. HOOK *Sayings* Ser. II. *Man of Many Fr.* I. 320 Her..tooth-brush and nail-brush slumbered together in one small tray.

**b.** *fig.* To lie at rest in death or the grave.

**1588** SHAKS. *Titus A.* II. iv. 15 That I may slumber in eternall sleepe. ? **1809** SHELLEY *Death, a Dial.* 6 Say, victim of grief, wilt thou slumber with me? **1837** CARLYLE *Fr. Rev.* I. I. ii, The Dead all slumbering round it. **1851** LONGF. *Gold. Leg.* (1856) 58 Underneath this mouldering tomb.. Slumbers a great lord of the village.

**2.** *fig.* To live in a state of inactivity or negligence; to remain or be sunk *in* sin, sloth, etc.; to be dilatory or tardy *in* doing something.

*c* **1380** WYCLIF *Wks.* (1880) 395 For siche occupacions and chargis maken prestis slepynge & slumbrynge in synne. *c* **1400** *Rom. Rose* 2576 Whyl thou so slomrest in that thought, That is so swete and delitable. *a* **1400** *Relig. Pieces fr. Thornton MS.* 58 Tho sawles..slomers noghte no slepis noghte in þe slowthe of fleschly lustes. **1515** BARCLAY *Ecloges* iv. (1570) C iij b, In sloth thou slombrest as buried were thy song. **1601** SHAKS. *All's Well* III. vi. 78 *Ber.* But you must not now slumber in it. *Par.* Ile about it this euening. **1751** JOHNSON *Rambler* No. 161 ¶3, I have always thought it unworthy of a wise man to slumber in total inactivity. **1788** GIBBON *Decl. & F.* li. V. 366 The successors of Alaric had slumbered in a long peace. **1848** GALLENGA *Italy* (1851) 459 That fatal security which had..allowed the Lombards to slumber on the mere fame of their exploits.

**3.** Of things, faculties, etc.: To be dormant, inoperative, or quiescent.

**1582** N.T. (Rhem.) *2 Peter* ii. 3 And their perdition [1611 their damnation] slumbereth not. **1667** MILTON *P.L.* IV. 24 Now conscience wakes despair That slumberd. **1727** DE FOE *Hist. Appar.* iii. (1840) 23 As the Scripture says in another case, his damnation slumbereth not. **1799** CAMPBELL *Pleas. Hope* I. 460 The might that slumbers in a peasant's arm. **1818** SCOTT *Rob Roy* v, As my kinsman's politeness seems to be still slumbering. **1845** S. AUSTIN *Ranke's Hist. Ref.* II. 383 We see the lowering tempest which slumbered behind this appearance of confidence.

**b.** To be calm, peaceful, or still.

**1764** GOLDSM. *Trav.* 312 Dull as their lakes that slumber in the storm. **1818** SCOTT *Rob Roy* xxxiii, The clouds of mist which might otherwise have slumbered till morning on the valley. **1830** TENNYSON *Arab. Nts.* 79 The garden-bowers and grots Slumber'd.

**c.** To flow, move *along*, sleepily or peacefully.

**1868** HAWTHORNE *Amer. Note-bks.* (1879) II. 69 The stream..slumbers along.

†**4.** *trans.* To cause to sleep; to render inactive or inoperative; to dull or deaden. *Obs.*

*c* **1532** DU WES *Introd. Fr.* in *Palsgr.* 922 O fortune, sorowe increasyng, and slombryng all delyces. **1547** *Bk. of Marchantes* b vj, They haue so slombred, blinded, and abeasted the poore worlde. **1622** DONNE *Serm.* 24 Feb. (1626) 22 To smother sinne from the eye of the world, or to slumber the eye of our owne conscience from the sight of sinne. **1642** WOTTON *Dk. Buck'm.* in *Reliq.* (1672) 232 To honest a deed after it was done, or to slumber his conscience in the doing.

†**b.** To render still, calm, or quiet; to muffle (a drum), silence (a noise). *Obs.*

**1622** DONNE *Serm.* 15 Sept. 4 This Song of Deborah were enough..to slumber any storme, to becalme any tempest. **1647** FARINGDON *Serm.* i. 18 This is it, which alone is able to slumber this noise.

**5.** To pass, spend, or waste (time) in sleep or slumber. Const. *away*, *out*, *through*; rarely without adverb.

**1749** FIELDING *Tom Jones* VIII. ix, She had slumbered away the day in order to sit up all night. **1750** JOHNSON *Rambler* No. 33 ¶9 Rest..reposed herself in alcoves, and slumbered away the winter upon beds of down. **1820** SCOTT *Monast.* vi, He would in other times have slumbered out his term of preferment with as much credit as any other 'purple Abbot'. **1854** J. S. C. ABBOTT *Napoleon* (1855) II. i. 31 They slumbered away their remaining years in idleness.

**b.** To drive *away*, get rid of, by slumbering.

**1829** H. BLUNT *Hist. S. Peter* (1832) 169 These reflections ..had been slumbered fruitlessly away.

Hence **'slumbered** *ppl. a.*, wrapt in slumber; unconscious. *rare.*

**1590** SPENSER *F.Q.* I. vii. 15 Then vp he tooke the slombred senceless corse.

**slumberer** ('slʌmbərə(r)). Also 4 slomerer, slomrer, 5 slummerare; 4 slombrer. [f. SLUMBER *v.* + -ER[1]. Cf. Du. *sluimeraar*, G. *schlumm(e)rer*, Da. *slumrer*, Sw. *slumrare*.] One who sleeps or slumbers; one who is asleep; a slothful or indolent person.

*c* **1380** WYCLIF *Eng. Wks.* (1880) 395 Bischoppis, persones and vikers, þat ben slepers & slombreris in lustis of þe fleysch. *c* **1394** *P. Pl. Crede* 91 Swiche slomerers [*v.r.* slomrers] in slepe slauþe is her ende. *c* **1440** *Promp. Parv.* 460/2 Slummerare, *dormitator, dormitatrix.* *a* **1631** DONNE *Progr. Soul* xv, As a slumberer stretching on his bed. **1817** SHELLEY *Rev. Islam* I. xxiv. 3 Such mysterious dream As makes the slumberer's cheek with wonder pale. **1871** MEREDITH *H. Richmond* (1886) 2 A hard rider, deep drinker and heavy slumberer.

**'slumberful**, *a.* [f. SLUMBER *sb.* + -FUL I.] Marked by slumber.

**1844** MRS. BROWNING *Drama Exile* Wks. (1904) 134 Your bodies shall lie smooth in death, and straight and slumberful. *a* **1849** MANGAN *Poems* (1859) 203 In slumberful stupor.

**slumbering** ('slʌmbərıŋ), *vbl. sb.* [f. SLUMBER *v.* Cf. MDu. *slumer-*, *sluymeringhe* (Du. *sluimering*), MHG. *slommeringe*, *slummerunge* (G. *schlummerung*), Sw. *slumring*).]

**1.** The state, condition, or fact of being in a slumber; sleeping; sleep.

**13..** *Gaw. & Gr. Kt.* 1182 As in slomeryng he slode, sleȝly he herde A littel dyn at his dor. *c* **1386** CHAUCER *Pars. T.* ¶705 Thanne cometh Sompnolence, that is, sloggy slombrynge, which maketh a man be heuy and dul, in body and in soule. *c* **1450** LOVELICH *Merlin* 12364 He ne slepte.. tyl that lady was fallen in Slombring. *c* **1491** *Chast. Goddes Chyld.* 42 Whan nede drew hem to slombryng or slepe. **1523** SKELTON *Garl. Laurel* 30 Whylis I stode musynge.., In slumbrynge I fell and halfe in a slepe. **1592** KYD *Span. Trag.* III. xv, For in vnquiet quietnes is faind, And slumbring is a common worldly wile. **1651** HOBBES *Leviath.* III. xxxii. 196 A man..not having well observed his own slumbering. **1864** [see SLUGGARDING *vbl. sb.*].

**b.** An instance or occasion of this; a slumber or slumberous condition; a sleep.

*c* **1374** CHAUCER *Troylus* II. 67 Ever lay Pandare a bedde, half in a slomeringe. *Ibid.* v. 246 Whan he fil in any slomeringes. *c* **1440** *Gesta Rom.* lxx. 324 (Harl. MS.), þer com vpon him such a slombring, that..he most nedis slepe. **1470–85** MALORY *Arthur* v. iv. 165 As the kyng laye in his caban in the shyp he fyll in a slomerynge. **1611** BIBLE *Job* xxxiii. 15 In slumbrings vpon the bed.

**2.** *attrib.*, as *slumbering bed*, *cup*, *posture*, etc.

**1535** COVERDALE *Isaiah* li. 17 Thou that hast..sucked out the slombringe cuppe to the botome. **1581** DERRICKE *Image Irel.* II. E iv b, And other some to stiffle quight in slumbryng bedde that lyes. **1595** BARNFIELD *Cassandra* xxxii, Heerewith awaking from her slumbring sleepe. **1825** SCOTT *Talism.* xv, Rising from his slumbering posture.

**'slumbering**, *ppl. a.* [f. as prec.]

**1.** That slumbers or is asleep; dozing.

**1390** GOWER *Conf.* II. 103 With mochel wo..His slombrende yhen he upcaste. *c* **1742** GRAY *Ignorance* 16 Dost thou..Still stretch..The massy sceptre o'er thy slumb'ring line? **1807** CRABBE *Par. Reg.* III. 830 Th' expecting people view'd their slumbering priest. **1817** BYRON *Manfred* II. iv, I have..Startled the slumbering birds from the hush'd boughs. **1895** SIR H. MAXWELL *Duke of Britain* i. 4 We stroll through the slumbering camp.

**b.** Marked or characterized by slumber; idle, indolent; drowsy.

**1538** STARKEY *England* I. i. 5 For the mayntenaunce of theyr idul and slomeryng lyfe. **1737** *Gentl. Mag.* VII. 567/1 Sprightly I start, and free from slumb'ring yawn, Leave the soft bed. **1784** COWPER *Task* II. 774 Her, whose winking eye And slumb'ring oscitancy mars the brood.

**2.** Quiet, peaceful; calm, still, motionless.

**1632** MILTON *L'Allegro* 54 Oft list'ning how the Hounds and horn Chearly rouse the slumbring morn. *c* **1635** —— *Arcades* 57 Ere the odorous breath of morn Awakes the slumbring leaves. **1794** MRS. RADCLIFFE *Myst. Udolpho* xliii, When..slumbering ocean faint and fainter glows. **1849** RUSKIN *Seven Lamps* vi. §xx. 182 An influence from the silent sky and slumbering fields. **1890** 'R. BOLDREWOOD' *Col. Reformer* (1891) 161 At no great distance lay the slumbering sea-lake.

**3.** Dormant, inoperative, quiescent; torpid.

**1703** ROWE *Ulysses* II. i, And thou Revenge! Shoot all thy Fires, and wake my slumb'ring Rage. **1794** MRS. RADCLIFFE *Myst. Udolpho* xxviii, When Montoni absolutely refused it, her slumbering mind was roused. **1818** BYRON *Corsair* I. xi, The slumbering venom of the folded snake. **1845** S. AUSTIN *Ranke's Hist. Ref.* II. 223 In Franconia the slumbering fires of discontent burst forth. **1878** HUXLEY *Physiogr.* 195 Its shape led hardly any one to suspect that the mountain was a slumbering volcano.

Hence **'slumberingly** *adv.*, in a slumbering manner; **'slumberingness**. *rare*$^{-0}$.

**1647** HEXHAM I, Slumberingly, *sluymachtighlick.* **1648** *Ibid.* II, *Vaeckerigheydt*, Sleepienesse, Slumbringnesse. **1847** WEBSTER, *Slumberingly.* [Hence in later Dicts.]

**'slumberless** ('slʌmbəlıs), *a.* [f. SLUMBER *sb.* + -LESS.] Obtaining or yielding no slumber; sleepless.

**1820** SHELLEY *Prometh. Unb.* I. i. 563 The present is spread Like a pillow of thorns for thy slumberless head. **1884** *Cent. Mag.* XXIX. 88 The overstraining and almost slumberless labor of the last days and nights.

†**'slumberness**. *Obs.* [f. SLUMBER *sb.*] Sleepiness, somnolence; sloth, indolence.

*c* **1440** in *Roy's Rede me* (Arb.) 164 Parsones, vicaries, þat ben slepers in lustes of þe fleshe and in slomebernes. **1495** *Trevisa's Barth. De P.R.* (W. de W.) VII. xxxii. 246 Of quakinge of the herte kynde heete fayllyth and therof bredeth slombrenesse and slouthe.

**slumberous** ('slʌmbərəs), **'slumbrous**, *a.* Also 5 slombrous, 8–9 slumb'rous. [f. SLUMBER *sb.* + -OUS. The older form is *slumbrous* (cf. *wondrous*), but that with the *e* is the one given by Johnson (1755) and has been the commoner spelling during the 19th cent.]

**1.** Inclined to slumber or sleep; unduly given to slumber; somnolent, lethargic.

**1495** *Trevisa's Barth. De P.R.* XIX. xiii. 872 In theym whyche doon slepe tomoche, and in slombrous men, the body is pale and dyscoloured. **1733** P. WHITEHEAD *State Dunces* 82 At length a slumbrous Briton clos'd his Eyes. **1826** SCOTT *Jrnl.* 9 July, Rather slumbrous to-day from having sat up till twelve last night. **1861** DICKENS *Gt. Expect.* vi, My sister clutched me, as a slumberous offence to the company's eyesight, and assisted me up to bed. **1895** ZANGWILL *Master* III. xi, Behind a casement a slumbrous old crone snuffed herself.

**b.** Of the eyes, or eyelids: Heavy or drooping with slumber or sleep.

**1828** LANDOR *Wks.* (1876) II. 121 Her eyes, slumberous with content. **1845** LONGF. *Belfry of Bruges, Carillon* v, He ..finds his slumbrous eyes Wet with..tears. **1887** HALL CAINE *Son of Hagar* I. viii, The man lifted his slumbrous eyelids.

**2.** Bringing or inducing sleep; soporific.

α. **1667** MILTON *P.L.* IV. 615 The timely dew of sleep Now falling with soft slumbrous weight inclines Our eye-lids. **1725** POPE *Odyss.* II. 444 Ev'ry eye with slumbrous chains she bound. **1751** CAMBRIDGE *Scribleriad* v. 30 The senseless chief the slumbrous potion quaft. **1810** SCOTT *Lady of L.* I. xxxii, While our slumbrous spells assail ye. **1842** TENNYSON *Day Dream, Sleeping Beauty* i, The slumbrous light is rich and warm. **1887** BOWEN *Æneid* IV. 486 Over them moist sweet honeys and slumbrous poppies to pour.

β. **1839** LONGF. *Voices of Night* Prel. iv, A slumberous sound, a sound that brings The feelings of a dream. **1850** B. TAYLOR *Eldorado* viii. 52 Scarcely a leaf stirred in the slumberous air; and giving way to the delicate languor [etc.]. **1877** BLACK *Green Past.* xxxvii, The continuous, monotonous murmur of sound was soothing, slumberous, dreamlike.

**3.** Moving very slightly or slowly; lying quiescent or at rest; calm, still, peaceful.

**1765** BEATTIE *Judgm. Paris* cxv, Faint heaves the slumberous wave. **1794** W. BLAKE *Songs Experience* Introd. 15 Morn Rises from the slumbrous mass. **1833** TENNYSON *Lotos Eaters* 13 Some [streams] thro'..shadows broke, Rolling a slumbrous sheet of foam below. **1858** G. MACDONALD *Phantastes* xvii, Across a shining, slumberous landscape. **1898** G. F. R. HENDERSON *Stonewall Jackson* I. 390 The buzzards sailing lazily above the slumberous woods.

**4.** Appropriate to, characterized by, suggestive of, slumber or sleep.

**1818** WORDSW. *Pilgrim's Dream* 18 The murmur of a neighbouring stream Induced a soft and slumbrous dream. **1826** SCOTT *Jrnl.* 12 Mar., I was interrupted by a slumberous feeling which made me obliged to stop once or twice. **1853** KANE *Grinnell Exped.* viii. (1856) 59 There was something about them [icebergs] so slumberous and so pure. **1889** *Spectator* 9 Nov. 632/1 The slumberous condition in which the mental faculties grow torpid.

**5.** *transf.* Marked or characterized by inactivity, indolence, or sluggishness.

α. **1809** IRVING *Knickerb.* (1861) 100 The tempestuous times..which overhang the slumbrous administration of the renowned Wouter Van Twiller. **1885** *Contemp. Rev.* July 13 The slumbrous reign which gradually became intolerable to the commonalty.

β. **1876** MISS BRADDON *J. Haggard's Dau.* I. 7 The great Anglican revival has doubtless awakened that slumberous old parish-church into new life and vigour. **1889** *Times* 17 Jan. 9/4 The British plantations would have remained..as slumberous as they have been in the past.

**b.** Of places, etc.: Quiet, sleepy, tranquil.

**1863** HAWTHORNE *Old Home* (1879) 130 She liked the old slumberous town. **1869** *Daily News* 23 Jan., In slumbrous country towns or quiet country houses people go to bed early and get up early. **1883** *American* VI. 282 This quiet corner of a sleepy town in a slumberous land.

**'slumberously,** *adv.* [f. prec.] In a slumberous, drowsy, or sleepy manner; quietly, tranquilly, indolently, etc.

*α.* **1819** SHELLEY *Peter Bell 3rd* VII. xv. 2 A printer's boy, ..Fell slumbrously upon one side. **1826** SCOTT *Jrnl.* 1 July, I wrote a page or two last night slumbrously.

*β.* **1816** L. HUNT *Rimini* III. 490 She was used to leave her cares Without, and slumberously enjoy the airs. **1827** N. P. WILLIS *Widow of Nain* 13 Upon his spear the soldier lean'd ..And slumberously dozed on. **1898** BODLEY *France* III. i. II. 40 As a rule the rural municipalities slumberously perform their useful functions.

**'slumberousness.** [f. as prec.] Sleepiness, drowsiness.

**1842** MRS. BROWNING *Grk. Chr. Poets* (1863) 95 A slumberousness without a dream. **1863** SALA in *Temple Bar* VIII. 72, I have carried my slumberousness about with me.

**slumbersome** ('slʌmbəsəm), *a.* [f. SLUMBER *sb.* + -SOME.] Slumberous, sleepy.

**1884** *Bath Jrnl.* 19 Apr. 8/1 Who could persuade it to be lulled into slumbersome silence. **1892** *Black & White* 27 Aug. 255/2 My inventive genius was slumbersome.

**slumbery** ('slʌmbərɪ), *a.* Now *rare* or *Obs.* Also 4, 6 **slombry,** 6 **slombre,** 6, 7 **slumbry;** 5 **slomry.** [f. SLUMBER *sb.* + -Y. Cf. Fris. *slomm-, slûmerich,* MDu. *slumerich* (Du. *sluimerig*), G. *schlummerig,* Sw. *slumrig.*] Slumberous, sleepy; of the nature of slumber.

*c* **1386** CHAUCER *Pars. T.* ¶724 Thanne wexeth he slough and slombry. *c* **1450** in Aungier *Syon* (1840) 252 If any.. sluggeschly slepe, or be slomry, in any conuentual acte. **1530** PALSGR. 324/1 Slombrye, slepysshe, *pesant.* **1578** PHAER *Æneid* VI. Q iij b, On the ground himself he spred.. and groueling lay with slumbry head. **1590** SPENSER *F.Q.* III. vi. 26 That..shadie couert, whereas lay Faire Crysogone in slombry traunce. **1605** SHAKS. *Macb.* v. i. 12 In this slumbry agitation, besides her walking,..what..haue you heard her say? **1616** DRUMM. OF HAWTH. *Poems* B j b, Lampe of Heauens Christall Hall,..who makes the vglie Night At thine Approach flie to her slumbrie Bowrs. **1818** KEATS *Endym.* II. 406 Tenderly unclos'd, By tenderest pressure, a faint damask mouth To slumbery pout.

**slumbrous,** variant of SLUMBEROUS *a.*

**slumdom** ('slʌmdəm). [f. SLUM *sb.* + -DOM.] Slums collectively; the inhabitants of the slums. Also, the condition or character of slums or slum-dwellers.

**1882** *Church Rev.* XXII. 187 We have wandered through slumdom. **1890** *Pall Mall G.* 16 July 2/1 To reform our prison system, to plant out slumdom in the country. **1896** *Night & Day* Feb. 2/3 Lodging houses in the deeps of London slumdom. **1927** G. B. SHAW in *Yorks. Even. News* 30 Nov. 9/2 Civilisation means 'Respect my life and property and I will respect yours.' Slumdom means 'Disregard my life and property and I will disregard yours.' **1962** *Economist* 18 Aug. 593/1 Another 60,000 old houses slip into slumdom. **1973** *Daily Tel.* 7 Nov. 13/1 A pre-war, cottage-type housing estate that is slipping into slumdom as fast as the downward slope will take it.

**slum'gullion.** *slang.* (chiefly *U.S.*). [Probably a fanciful formation.]

**1.** (See quot. 1874.)

**1872** 'MARK TWAIN' *Roughing It* iv. 44 He poured for us a beverage which he called '*Slumgullion*'. **1874** *Slang Dict.* 297 *Slumgullion,* any cheap, nasty, washy beverage.

**2. a.** 'Offal or refuse of fish of any kind; also, the watery refuse, mixed with blood and oil, which drains from blubber' (*Cent. Dict.* 1891). *U.S.*

**b.** A muddy deposit in a mining sluice. Also *transf. U.S.*

**1887** B. HARTE *Millionaire & Devil's Ford* 146 We preach at them for playing in the slumgullion, and getting themselves splashed. **1894** —— in *My First Book* 264 A quantity of slumgullion which really belongs to the sluices of a placer mining camp. **1906** C. DE L. CANFIELD *Diary of Forty-Niner* 27 The mud we were sending down the stream buried them under slumgullion. **1948** O. WESTON *Mother Lode Album* 82 The miners..insisted on calling it 'Slumgullion', because when it rained the knee-deep adobe mud was no small problem.

**c.** A kind of watery hash or stew. Chiefly *U.S.*

**1902** J. LONDON *Daughter of Snows* 45 'What do you happen to call it?' 'Slumgullion,' she responded curtly, and thereafter the meal went on in silence. **1904** E. ROBINS *Magnetic North* iv. 59 'Mix 'em with cold potaters in a salad.' 'No, make slumgullion,' commanded O'Flynn. **1932** J. DOS PASSOS *1919* 17 Bedbugs in the bunks in the stinking focastle, slumgullion for grub. **1959** A. SILLITOE *Loneliness* 7 The first thing a long-distance cross-country runner would do..would be to run as far away from the place as he could get on a bellyful of Borstal slumgullion. **1976** T. WALKER *Spatsizi* x. 115 For want of a better word we called it slumgullion.

**slumgum** ('slʌmgʌm). *U.S.* Also **slum gum.** [f. SLUM *sb.*[2] + GUM *sb.*[2]] The residual wax, propolis, and other impurities that remain when the honey and most of the wax are extracted from honeycombs by warming them.

**1890** *Gleanings Bee Culture* XVIII. 704/2 The cappings are laid on this perforated tin, and, when they melt, the wax and honey run through into the chamber below, leaving what Californians call the 'slumgum' on the tin above. **1917** *Rep. Iowa State Apiarist* 36 A third of the weight of this slumgum is wax and should be saved. **1946** R. A. GROUT *Hive & Honeybee* xxii. 544 Slumgum is the material remaining after some rendering treatment has been performed on comb material. It may be more or less rich in beeswax and is usually dark brown or almost black in color. **1980** *Bee Craft* LXII. 154/2 The water..had to heat to the extractor temperature and this allowed the dross or slum gum to coagulate on the under surface of the straining cloth.

**slumless** ('slʌmlɪs), *a.* [f. SLUM *sb.*[1] + -LESS.] Containing no slums.

**1924** *Glasgow Herald* 8 Mar. 7 The difference between almost slumless Düsseldorf and slummy Glasgow is not altogether in municipal policy or school education. **1946** P. BOTTOME *Lifeline* xxx. 235 Berlin..bustling, self-determined, ordered, slumless. **1966** *Guardian* 16 May 15/3 Any big-city mayor..can successfully achieve a relatively slumless city.

**slummer** ('slʌmə(r)). [f. SLUM *sb.*[1] and *v.*[1]]

**1.** One who visits the slums, esp. from charitable or philanthropic motives.

**1887** *Pall Mall G.* 29 Sept. 3/2 The risk of giving a violent shock to literary slummers. **1889** J. HATTON *J. L. Toole* i. 20 'Slumming' is a modern fashion, but both Irving and Toole were always slummers. **1894** SALA *London up to Date* 2 The writer who is ambitious to become an efficient 'slummer'.

**2.** An inhabitant of the slums.

**1888** *Pall Mall G.* 18 Oct. 3 Gaffs, those penny places of amusement partronized by slummers. **1889** *The Voice* (N.Y.) 7 Mar., Had this wanton insult..come from some shirtless slummer it would have signified little.

**'slummery.** *rare.* [f. SLUM *sb.*[1]] Slums collectively; slumdom.

**1892** LD. ROSEBERY in *Daily News* 16 Dec. 2/4 Cleaning out the Augean stables of slummery.

**'slumminess.** [f. SLUMMY *a.* + -NESS.] The state of being slummy.

**1888** BLACK *Adv. Houseboat* xxiv, We had encountered next to nothing of the slumminess that is supposed to be characteristic of canals. **1926** A. HUXLEY *Two or Three Graces* 176 It was a slummy street... It was not hard to know where respectable slumminess ended and gay Bohemianism began. **1961** *Guardian* 29 Mar. 9/3 Being overcrowded does not necessarily imply slumminess.

**slumming** ('slʌmɪŋ), *vbl. sb.* [f. SLUM *v.*[1]]

**1.** *slang.* (See quots.)

**1839** *Slang Dict.* 34 *Slumming,* passing bad money. **1888** JACOBI *Printers' Vocab.* 127 *Slumming,* a slang term used to describe the secreting of type or sorts.

**2. a.** The visitation of slums, esp. for charitable or philanthropic purposes.

**1884** *Chr. World* 22 May 391/3, I am not one of those who have taken to 'slumming' as an amusement. **1894** D. C. MURRAY *Making of Novelist* 87 Slumming had not become the fashion at that time of day.

**b.** *attrib.*, as ***slumming expedition, party.***

**1884** *Boston* (Mass.) *Jrnl.* 1 Oct. 2/3 The slumming party engaged in conversation audibly. **1888** *Cath. Press* 18 Aug. 272/3 The Isle of Dogs has recently been the scene of some new slumming expeditions for the ladies.

**c.** *fig.* with defining adj. Cf. sense 4 b of the vb.

**1933** DYLAN THOMAS *Let.* (1966) 70 Few understand the works of Cummings, And few James Joyce's mental slummings. **1958** [see DEMOTIC *a.* 2]. **1977** M. DRABBLE *Ice Age* I. 35 She accused Anthony of hypocrisy, of intellectual slumming, of *folie de grandeur,* of brain fever.

So **'slumming** *ppl. a.*

**1884** *Pall Mall G.* 17 Mar. 6 One of my recently acquired slumming friends. **1892** *Tablet* 30 July 171 Sir Rufus..is an admirable foil to a slumming Marquis.

**'slummock,** *v.* Also **slummuck.** [var. of the common dial. *slommack, slammack*: see the *Eng. Dial. Dict.*]

**1.** *trans.* To eat up greedily.

**1854** P. B. ST. JOHN *Amy Moss* 64 They must be in force. They've slummucked the pigs and the cow-beef, and left no mark.

**2.** *intr.* To move about awkwardly or clumsily. Also *transf.* of speech.

**1883** A. E. T. WATSON *Racecourse & Covert Side* 291 Don't let his head go too loose, or else he'll slummock all over the place. **1893** KIPLING *Many Invent.* 234 His speech, which up to that time had been distinct,..began to slur, and slide, and slummock.

**'slummock,** *sb. dial.* and *colloq.* [Var. of dial. *slammock*: see *Eng. Dial. Dict.* and SLUMMOCK *v.*] A dirty, untidy, or slovenly person; a slut. Freq. as a disrespectful term of address. Cf. SLAMMAKIN *sb.* 2.

19th.-cent. dial. examples in *Eng. Dial. Dict.* s.v. *Slammock* sb.

**1932** 'L. G. GIBBON' *Sunset Song* 186 Chris found herself dancing with Mistress Mutch, the great, easy-going slummock. **1953** L. HILL tr. *Anouilh's Waltz of Toreadors* in J. C. Trewin *Plays of Year* VIII. 444 A slummock, a girl who hasn't even washed! **1966** M. KELLY *Dead Corse* i. 10 'You are the greatest slummock,' she said. 'How can you bear to lie on an unmade bed?' **1974** P. FLOWER *Odd Job* ix. 59 He wiped Norah's table-top... Norah was a slummock.

**slummocker** ('slʌməkə(r)). *dial.* Also **slummicker.** [Of obscure ulterior etym.: see SLAMMAKIN *sb.* and *a.*; SLUMMOCK *v.* This form is not recorded in dialect dicts.] = SLAMMAKIN *sb.* 2; an awkward or careless person.

**1905** G. B. SHAW *Let.* 13 Aug. in A. T. Schwab *James Gibbons Huneker* (1963) xiii. 167 You will never be anything but a clever slummocker in America. **1905** —— *Let.* 16 Sept. in J. G. Huneker *Steeplejack* (1920) II. 258 The reason I call you a slummocker and heap insults on you, is that you are very useful to me in America, and quite friendly; consequently, you must be educated or you will compromise me. **1940** C. STEAD *Man who loved Children* (1941) ix. 376, I have to let that great big slummicker wash the dishes and smash every glass and plate in the house.

**slummocking:** see SLAMMAKIN *a.*

**'slummocky,** *a. dial.* and *colloq.* Also (rarely) **slammocky, slommachy, slummacky, slummucky.** [Cf. SLUMMOCK *v.*, and see the *Eng. Dial. Dict.* s.v. *Slammocky.*] Slovenly, untidy. Hence **'slummockiness.**

? **1861** MRS. GASKELL *Let.* 28 Feb. (1966) 643 A tall, gentlemanly, slammocky-as-to-figure man. **1897** MISS KINGSLEY *W. Africa* 120 This tidy, carefully minute way, so entirely different from the slummacky African methods of doing things. **1899** —— *W. African Stud.* i. 23 It had too its varying moods of tidiness, now neat and dandy coiled, now dishevelled and slummocky. **1914** KIPLING in *Nash's Mag.* June 278/1 The rough-ironed table-linen,..the slummocky set-out of victuals at meals. **1926** W. DE LA MARE *Connoisseur* 65 A help from the village—precious little good *she* was. Slummocky—and *stupid!* **1947** M. PENN *Manchester Fourteen Miles* iii. 34 Grandma Winstanley was..a slattern. .. Lizzie couldn't abide her slummockiness. **1953** J. CARY *Except the Lord* xxxviii. 169 Girls after a few months service would return on holiday not only in smart clothes but with quite new scorn for what they called our slummucky ways. **1962** J. CANNAN *All is Discovered* ii. 29 'An attractive woman?' 'No, sir. A slummacky sort. More like a gyppo.' **1973** P. WHITE *Eye of Storm* viii. 376 Her hands had been coarsened by menial grind, her body made slommacky by childbearing. **1974** H. R. F. KEATING *Underside* xix. 187 The doom-laden slummockiness of his bohemian days.

**slummy** ('slʌmɪ), *a.*[1] [f. SLUM *sb.*[1] + -Y.]

**1.** Given to frequenting the slums.

*a* **1860** in Oxford use. (Cf. SLUM *v.* 3 a.)

**2.** Of the nature of a slum; abounding in or possessing slums. Also *absol.*

**1873** C. M. DAVIES *Unorth. Lond.* I. 352 Out of Goldsmith's Row, which is slummy,..turns a court which is slummier still. **1885** M. PATTISON *Mem.* I. 14 Oxford, not then overbuilt and slummy, looked..charming. **1892** *Spectator* 5 Mar. 332/1 Where the street verges on the slummy.

**b.** Dealing with the slums or slum-life.

**1906** *Pall Mall G.* 5 Mar. 4 The slummy novel, probably, is no longer fashionable.

**3.** Slovenly, careless.

**1881** in *Pall Mall G.* 8 Sept. (1886) 13/2 It was to draw and to paint most carefully, and to avoid slummy, sloppy work,..that we banded ourselves together.

†**'slummy,** *a.*[2] *Obs.*[−1] [f. ME. *slumme,* var. of *slume* SLOOM *v.*[1]] Drowsy; inclined to slumber.

*a* **1225** *Ancr. R.* 258 Hwo mei beon, uor scheome, slummi & sluggi & slouh.

**slummy** ('slʌmɪ), *sb. colloq.* Also **slummie.** [f. SLUM *sb.*[1] + -Y[6].] A slum-dweller.

**1934** P. O'MARA (*title*) Autobiography of a Liverpool Irish slummy. **1964** A. PRIOR *Z Cars Again* xvi. 158 The remains of many meals stood on..a newspaper... It was a typical slummie's house. **1973** 'J. PATRICK' *Glasgow Gang Observed* xii. 111 Big Fry..tauntingly called out: 'We're the slummies!'

**slump** (slʌmp), *sb.*[1] *Sc.* [a. LG. *slump* heap, mass, quantity (*im slump köpen* to buy in the lump), = Du. *slomp,* Fris. *slompe.* The LG. word is also the source of Da., Sw., and Norw. *slump.*]

**1.** A large quantity or number; chiefly in phrases ***by*** or ***in (the) slump,*** rarely ***in a slump,*** as a whole, not separately or individually, collectively; in the lump.

(*a*) **1795** *Statist. Acc. Scotl.* XV. 344 The brae farms, and the pasture land, are let by slump; it is impossible to say what they rent per acre. **1808** JAMIESON s.v., Coft by slump. **1851** H. STEPHENS *Bk. Farm* (ed. 2) II. 742 The grain is.. paid in slump or advance at the middle of the year's engagement.

(*b*) **1814** SCOTT *Diary* 10 Aug., Marriages and baptisms are performed, as one of the Isles-men told me, *by the slump.* **1827** *Blackw. Mag.* XXI. 893 We would not give General Holt..for all the Greek chiefs in a slump. **1866** BLACKIE *Homer & Iliad* I. 29 There is a tendency to fling away honest old traditions in the slump.

**2.** *attrib.* and *Comb.*, as †**slump number,** a large or round number; †**slump reckoning,** a reckoning in round numbers; **slump sum,** a lump sum; **slump work,** = *lump work* (LUMP *sb.*[1] 9).

**1718** WODROW *Corr.* (1843) II. 397 At a slump reckoning of 900 ministers at 1000 merks per piece. **1721** —— *Hist. Suff. Ch. Scot.* (1830) III. 341 The slump number he has taken..from the Scots Mist. **1808** JAMIESON s.v., *Slump wark,* work taken in the lump. **1844** H. STEPHENS *Bk. Farm* III. 1052 In hiring,..it is not unusual to give a slump sum for the harvest. **1862** BEVERIDGE *Hist. India* V. iv. II. 334 From this transaction alone a slump sum of fifty lacs..had been obtained. **1877** DAWSON *Orig. of World* viii. 189 Creation was not a sort of slump-work to be perfected by the operation of a law of developement.

**slump** (slʌmp), *sb.*[2] [f. SLUMP *v.*[2]]

**1.** *Stock Exchange.* A heavy fall or sudden decline in the price or value of commodities or securities.

**1888** *Boston* (Mass.) *Jrnl.* 22 Dec. 4/2 There was another slump in oil on the Consolidated Exchange to-day... Opening at 89⅜,..the price dropped to 87⅞. **1895** *Tablet* 19 Oct. 623 In a single week there has been a slump to the extent of twenty-two million sterling. **1895** *Daily News* 20 Nov. 8/3 The Glasgow Commercial Exchanges to-day took a gloomy view, and prices fell with a slump.

**2.** *transf.* **a.** A sudden or heavy decline or falling off; a collapse. *spec.* in *Econ.*, a sharp or sudden decline in trade or business, usu. accompanied by widespread unemployment; freq. with reference to a particular instance, esp. the Great Depression of 1929 and subsequent years.

**1888** Howells *A. Kilburn* xxv, What a slump!—what a slump! That blessed short-legged little seraph has spoilt the best sport that ever was. **1896** *Westm. Budget* 3 Jan. 3/1 There is clearly no 'slump' in the matrimonial market. **1897** *Leeds Mercury* 10 July 11/4 It..became apparent that a slump in the demand for cycles had set in. **1922** H. A. Silverman *Substance of Economics* xv. 231 Industries grew to depend increasingly on one another... It became inevitable..that a 'boom' or a 'slump' in one branch should synchronize with similar conditions elsewhere. **1930** *Engineering* 10 Jan. 42/2 To discover opportunities for employment on such jobs during industrial slumps. **1936** J. M. Keynes *Gen. Theory Employment, Interest & Money* iv. xvi. 218 In the succeeding 'slump' the stock of capital may fall for a time below the level which will yield a marginal efficiency of zero. **1936** N. Streatfeild *Ballet Shoes* vi. 89 'Well, I can't go back to Kuala Lumpur.' 'Why?' 'A thing called a slump.' **1952** *Granta* 15 Nov. 12/1 We wanted to fight Fascism, War and the Slump. **1953** M. Scott *Breakfast at Six* iii. 24 Bought all this land—got it cheap in slump time. **1957** I. Cross *God Boy* (1958) iii. 27 Then there was the slump..and then I never did get a chance with that hotel in Wellington. **1976** *Economist* 16 Oct. 13/2 A record rise in mortgage charges during a building slump.

**b.** *Geomorphol.* A landslide in which soil, sediment, or the like slides a short distance with some degree of cohesion and usu. a slight backward rotation owing to the concavity of the surface of separation from the parent mass; movement of this kind; also, a mass of material that has so fallen.

**1905** Chamberlin & Salisbury *Geology* I. iv. 218 (*heading*) Creep, slumps, and landslides. **1949** F. J. Pettijohn *Sedimentary Rocks* iv. 145 A structure of similar appearance..is reported from some limestones and dolomites. The cause of the folding may be due to subaqueous slump. **1954** W. D. Thornbury *Princ. Geomorphol.* v. 104 Mantle rock..is moved downslope by creep, slump, other types of mass-wasting, and by sheet-wash. **1963** D. W. & E. E. Humphries tr. *Termier's Erosion & Sedimentation* vii. 166 Water-laid phenomena (slumps, low-angle cross bedding) are observed, and suggest that eolian sands have been blown into a shallow sea. **1964** V. J. Chapman *Coastal Veget.* i. 2 A large scale change induced by a major cliff-fall or slump. **1970** W. H. Matthews *Geol. made Simple* (rev. ed.) viii. 117 Slump is a common occurrence along the banks of streams. **1978** A. L. Bloom *Geomorphology* viii. 178 An elaborate engineering technology has been developed to predict the surface of rupture beneath a slump in order to drill into it and drain the water from the vicinity.

**c.** *Engin.* The height through which the top of a mass of fresh concrete sinks when the mould containing it is removed, as in the slump test (see sense 4 below).

**1920** D. A. Abrams *Design of Concrete Mixes* (Bull. No. 1, Structural Materials Res. Lab., Lewis Inst., Chicago) 13 Normal consistency..requires the use of such a quantity of mixing water as will cause a slump of ½ to 1 in. in a freshly molded 6 × 12-in. cylinder of about 1:4 mix. **1934** S. C. Hollister in L. C. Urquhart *Civil Engin. Handbk.* vii. 562 Concrete for buildings ranges from 4 to 6 in. slump. **1977** D. E. Branson *Deformation of Concrete Structures* i. 48 Creep correction factors... May be marginal but normally can be neglected for slumps up to 4 in.

**3.** *gen.* A slumping movement or fall.

**1850** S. Judd *Richard Edney* i. 12 Move carefully! It is a slip, or a slump, all the way through. **1867** 'T. Lackland' *Homespun* i. 90 A..black snake..slid down with a slump..into the water. **1900** S. Hale *Let.* 29 Apr. (1919) 361, I let my huge bulk down with a slump.

**4.** *attrib.*, as (sense 2 b) *slump bed*, *bedding*, *block*, *series*, *sheet*, *structure*; **slump test** *Engin.*, a test of the consistency of fresh concrete in which the slump is measured following the removal of a mould of specified size and shape (usu. the frustum of a cone).

**1974** *Sedimentology* XXI. 2 Exposures of banks and slump beds extend along the whole of the coast. **1949** F. J. Pettijohn *Sedimentary Rocks* iv. 145 The disturbance is restricted to layers a mere inch or two thick. Such deformation is usually due to subaqueous slump or gliding and has been termed 'slump' or 'glide bedding'. **1964** *Gloss. Mining Terms* (*B.S.I.*) v. 13 *Slump bedding*, disturbed strata interbedded between undisturbed strata, caused by flow of newly deposited sediment. **1969** D. J. Easterbrook *Princ. Geomorphol.* xi. 228 During movement of a slump block, secondary slumps may develop and produce a stair-step-like series of parallel slump blocks. **1978** A. L. Bloom *Geomorphology* viii. 178 Vegetation or even houses may be carried intact on the surface of a large slump block. **1937** O. T. Jones in *Q. Jrnl. Geol. Soc.* XCIII. 272 In view of the fact that a thick mass..may have been formed by successive sliding or slumping of sediments, it is proposed to speak of it as a slump series, and where it is reasonably certain that a mass is the result of a single episode, that mass is referred to as a slump sheet. A slump series is or may be..made up of several slump sheets separated by a greater or lesser thickness of normal mudstones. **1976** *Jrnl. Geol. Soc.* CXXXII. 125 Sequence 4, in the upper part of the slump sheet, is most complexly deformed, showing closed and contorted folds. **1963** *Geol. Mag.* C. 205 The slump structures which characterize the Torridonian red sandstones of North-West Scotland. **1975** J. L. Wilson *Carbonate Facies Geol. Hist.* viii. 238 The limestone..has graded beds, lamination, microbreccias and slump structure. **1920** F. L. Roman in *Engin. & Contracting* 3 Mar. 241/1 Cone No. 1..was far better than a cylinder for determining the consistency of concrete by means of a 'slump' test. **1975** *Concrete Inspection Procedures* (Portland Cement Assoc.) iv. 41 A slump test is made at the start of the operation each day and whenever the appearance of concrete indicates a change in consistency.

**slump** (slʌmp), *v.*[1] Chiefly *Sc.* [f. slump *sb.*[1]]

**1.** *trans.* To lump; to put, place, regard, deal with, etc., as one quantity, mass, or group. Freq. *to slump together*.

(*a*) **1822** W. J. Napier *Pract. Store-farming* 147 No farmer ever gives in an offer, first, for the value of the pasture, and then, for the landlord's improvements. He may say that he slumps them all together. **1856** Ferrier *Inst. Metaph.* 61 The inconceivable as here laid down, is thus slumped together..with the absolutely inconceivable. **1873** J. Geikie *Gt. Ice Age* i. 4 The deposits, which were at one time slumped together,..are really the records of a long series of changes.

(*b*) **1827** Scott *Jrnl.* 14 Jan., I have let my cash run ahead since I came from the Continent.—I must slump the matter as I can. **1828** Steuart *Planter's G.* (1848) I. 314 He slumps the whole under one head. **1890** Cochran-Patrick *Evid. Mining Royalties Commiss.* No. 7613, Copper, lead, tin,.. are mentioned by name, and the others are slumped.

**2.** *intr.* To club *together* in paying.

**1849** G. Cupples *Green Hand* ii. (1856) 25 Slump together for the other guinea, will ye?

Hence **'slumping** *vbl. sb.*

**1822** W. J. Napier *Pract. Store-farming* 147 This 'slumping'..will never serve to pay to the landlord that identical interest [etc.]. **1850** *Chambers's Jrnl.* 23 Mar. 191/2 The *slumping* of the whole loss into the arbitrary..sum of five pounds. **1873** J. C. Maxwell in L. Campbell *Life* (1882) 439 The slumping together of multitudes of cases.

**slump** (slʌmp), *v.*[2] Chiefly *dial.* and *U.S.*, esp. in earlier use. [Probably imitative: cf. plump *v.*[1] Norw. has *slumpa* in sense 1, as well as in that of Sw. *slumpa*, Da. *slumpe*, from LG. *slumpen*, G. *schlumpen* to come about, happen by accident.]

**1. a.** *intr.* To fall or sink *in* or *into* a bog, swamp, muddy place, etc.; to fall *in* water with a dull splashing sound. Also in fig. context.

*a* **1677** Barrow *Serm.* (1686) III. 191 [The young men] walk upon a bottomless quag into which unawares they may slump. **1684** I. Mather *Remark. Provid.* (1846) 28 Being in this swamp that was miry, I slumpt in and fell down. **1776** T. Twining in *Country Clergyman of the 18th C.* (1882) 31, I remember slumping on a sudden into the slough of despond, and closing my letter in the dumps. *a* **1828** Bewick *Mem.* (1862) 116 Thinking the bog she had to pass through, might be frozen hard enough to bear her, she 'slumped' deep into it. **1835** *New Monthly Mag.* XLIII. 159 We dreaded to meet even a single sleigh, lest in turning out, the horses should 'slump' beyond their depth, in the untrodden drifts. **1872** Coues *N. Amer. Birds* 52 This enables the birds to run lightly over the floating leaves of aquatic plants, by so much increase of breadth of support that they do not slump in. *fig.* **1835** Gilchrist *Bards Tyne* 416 (E.D.D.), Newcassel hes fairly slump't into disgrace.

**b.** Const. *through*, *beneath*, etc. Also *fig.*

**1856** Lowell *Lett.* I. 296 No danger of her slumping through the clouds. **1871** —— *Study Wind.* (1886) 44 The man may slump through,..where the boy would have skimmed the surface. **1884** *Harper's Mag.* Aug. 337/1 But one awful night Kampen..simply 'slumped', as they say in the far west, beneath the waters and mud that ingulphed it.

**2. a.** Of the wind: To fall, drop.

**1855** *Trans. Philol. Soc.* 36 (Norfolk words), The wind slumped. **1894** *Outing* XXIV. 376/2 The breeze had been gradually dying for an hour, and now it bid fair..to slump entirely at midnight.

**b.** To slide *off* heavily; to plump down; to fall or collapse clumsily or heavily. *spec.* in *Geomorphol.* of soil, sediment, etc.: to fall in a slump (sense 2 b).

**1884** Burroughs *Pepacton* 217 Its body slumps off, and rolls and spills down the hill. **1889** 'Mark Twain' *Yankee at Crt. K. Arthur* v, Clarence had slumped to his knees before I had half finished. **1905** Chamberlin & Salisbury *Geology* I. iv. 220 Where a stream's banks are high.. considerable masses sometimes slump from the bank. **1920** *Engin. & Contracting* 3 Mar. 241/1 Large voids or stone pockets tend to cause the concrete specimen to slump on one side rather than vertically. **1937** *Q. Jrnl. Geol. Soc.* XCIII. 276 Sediments accumulating on a sub-aqueous slope would slide or slump if the weight increased beyond a certain amount. **1978** Friedman & Sanders *Princ. Sedimentol.* xii. 400/1 Strata that slumped and were deformed may be.. overlain by turbidites.

**c.** Of stocks, values, etc.: To fall heavily or suddenly. Also with †*off*. (Cf. slump *sb.*[2] 1.)

**1888** in Farmer *Americanisms* (1889) 495/2 'How's North-western this morning, Uncle Zeke?' asked Dick... 'Slumped off six points, hang it!' scowling viciously over his paper. **1896** *Daily News* 9 Dec. 10/7 The market again slumped down on further indications of a heavy crop movement. **1898** *Ibid.* 8 Mar. 3/6 Prices slumped from 2 to 5 points generally.

**d.** *transf.* and *fig.*

**1925** *Sunday Times* 20 Sept. 12/6 Where one's sympathy slumps and all one's optimism fails is in face of two depressing facts. **1970** *Daily Tel.* 16 May 12 Better pay and conditions are essential if police morale is not to go on slumping. **1977** *Cork Examiner* 6 June 7/1 The over-night leader..slumped to an 80 in his second round for 150.

**3.** To move or walk in a clumsy, heavy, or laborious manner. Also *fig.*

**1854** Lowell *Jrnl. Italy* Prose Wks. 1890 I. 115 He.. paces the deck..much as one of those yellow hummocks goes slumping up and down his cage. **1887** —— *Old Eng. Dramatists* (1892) 18 In such collections as Dodsley's 'Old Plays', where we slump along through the loose sand.

**4.** *trans.* **a.** To throw *down* heavily; to slam.

**1836** Haliburton *Clockm.* (1862) 126 She slumped down her nittin, and clawed off her spectacles. **1853** G. J. Cayley *Las Alforjas* I. 233 Some shivering adorer, who stands in the night air till John has slumped the tight door into the panel.

**b.** *local.* (See quots.)

**1874** C. J. Palmer *Perlust. Gt. Yarmouth* II. 260 *note*, The suitor who lost his cause was said to be 'slumped'. *Ibid.*, 'Slumped agin', was shouted derisively to one who had been a second time unsuccessful.

**c.** To cause to depreciate suddenly.

**1899** *Church Times* 13 Oct. 421/1 Suppose some 'bear' determines to 'slump' the market.

Hence **slumped**, **'slumping** *ppl. adjs.*

**1899** *Church Times* 13 Oct. 421/1 The vicious operations of the slumping bear and the tossing bull. **1937** *Q. Jrnl. Geol. Soc.* XCIII. 277 Local after-slides..added low ridges on the surface of the major slumped mass. **1965** G. J. Williams *Econ. Geol. N.Z.* iii. 31/2 There is a good deal of glacial debris and slumped ground under the thick forest. **1976** J. E. Sanders et al. *Physical Geol.* vii. 244 A slumped mass usually does not travel very far nor spectacularly fast.

**slumper** ('slʌmpə(r)), *v. rare.* [Probably imitative: cf. prec. 3, and G. *schlumpern* to go about in a slovenly or slipshod condition.] *intr.* To move or travel heavily or with difficulty on account of miry or muddy roads; to flounder *through* or *along*.

**1829** G. Robertson *Rural Recoll.* 38 In wet weather they became mere *lairs*, (sloughs,) in which the carts or carriages had to slumper through in a half-swimming state. **1894** Smiles *J. Wedgwood* x. 92 The lanes were scarcely sufficient for the slumpering along of packhorses, let alone for carts.

**slumpflation** (slʌmp'fleɪʃən). *Econ.* [Portmanteau blend of slump *sb.*[2] + in)flation 6: cf. stagflation.] A state of economic depression in which decreasing output and employment in industry are accompanied by increasing inflation.

**1974** W. Rees-Mogg *Reigning Error* iv. 75 So-called stagflation and slumpflation are the inevitable reflection of the progressive divergence between a rising nominal and a falling real supply of money. **1976** *Economic Jrnl.* LXXXVI. 171 Chronic slumpflation has given rise to much agonising reappraisal of doctrines that were hardening into orthodoxies. **1980** *Economist* 23 Feb. 13/1 The government can get less slumpflation in British industry only by making life easier for the employers' wage negotiators. **1981** J. Sutherland *Bestsellers* xix. 201 Portugal wallows in the slumpflation that will eventually lead to fascism.

**slumping** ('slʌmpɪŋ), *vbl. sb.*[2] *Geomorphol.* [f. slump *v.*[2] + -ing[1].] The fall of soil, sediment, or the like in a slump (slump *sb.*[2] 3 b).

**1907** R. D. Salisbury *Physiography* vi. 106 Slumping is very common on slopes composed of unconsolidated material, such as clay or accumulations of loose rock. **1944** A. Holmes *Princ. Physical Geol.* x. 148 Similar conditions favour landslides on a bigger scale, wherever slumping (Fig. 63) or sliding (Fig. 64) can occur on the sides of undercut slopes, precipices, and cliffs. **1979** *Geogr. Mag.* July 668/3 Many sub-circular pans on the Essex marshes may be formed by the blocking-off by slumping and vegetation overgrowth of the large number of creek heads which appear rounded in outline.

**'slumpy,** *a.*[1] *Sc.* [f. slump *sb.*[1]] Taking things in the lump; rough, general.

**1864** R. Reid *Old Glasgow* 35 Here nothing is said about square yards..; but half-acres, or thereby, are set forth in a fine slumpy manner.

**slumpy** ('slʌmpɪ), *a.*[2] Also **slumpey**. [f. dial. *slump* a marshy or muddy place; cf. LG. *schlump* in the same sense.] Marshy, swampy, muddy, boggy.

**1823** E. Moor *Suffolk Words* 366 Such a meadow is said to be slumpy. **1853** G. Johnston *Nat. Hist. E. Bord.* I. 250 A large extent of rushy ground, either dry and hard, or slumpy and wet. **1883** E. H. Rollins *New Eng. Bygones* 79 The slumpy drifts had to be cut down beforehand to make the roads passable.

**slumscape** ('slʌmskeɪp). [f. slum *sb.*[1], after landscape, etc.: cf. scape *sb.*[3]] Slum scenery, or a picture of this.

**1947** Wyndham Lewis *Let.* Apr. (1963) 405 Down another [road] moved a great slumscape painter. **1967** *N.Y. Times* 4 May 41/5 They walked slowly through the scarred and dreary slumscape.

**'slumward(s,** *adv.* [f. slum *sb.*[1] 2.] In the direction of the slums.

**1892** *Pall Mall G.* 12 Oct. 2/2 It was the Congregationalists..who set much of the current of assistance slumward in recent years. **1897** F. T. Bullen *Cruise 'Cachalot'* 318 Draggled branches borne slumwards by tramping urchins.

†**'slunchin,** obs. variant of luncheon 1.

**1622** Mabbe tr. *Aleman's Guzman d'Alf.* ii. 274 For our last course..we had a thinne slice of cheese,..alleaging that those thicker slunchins would dull our wits.

**slung** (slʌŋ), *ppl. a.*[1] [f. sling *v.*[1]]

†**1.** Of an animal: Dropped or cast prematurely. Cf. slunk *ppl. a.*

**1750** tr. *Leonardus' Mirr. Stones* 82 It should be wrapt in the skin of a calf, or a slung hart, and bound to the left arm.

**2.** Thrown by means of a sling.

For Sc. *slung stane* see SLING-STONE.

**1893** HUXLEY *Evol. & Ethics* 3 It may be likened to the ascent and descent of a slung stone.

**slung** (slʌŋ), *ppl. a.*² [f. SLING *v.*²] Placed in, hung or suspended by, a sling or slings.

**1773** J. JACOB *Obs. Wheel-Carriages* 84 Of the method of hanging coaches, and other slung vehicles. **1868** *U.S. Rep. Munit. War* 242 To fire a slung rocket..from a ship against a ship would not be very difficult. **1891** *Daily News* 31 Oct. 5/7 Her great, open fireplace, with its slung kettle.

**slunge,** variant of SLOUNGE *v. dial.*

**slung-shot.** *U.S.* [f. *slung*, pa. pple. of SLING *v.*²] A shot, piece of metal, stone, etc., fastened to a strap or thong, and used as a weapon (cf. quot. 1848).

**1848** BARTLETT *Dict. Amer., Slung-shot*, an offensive weapon formed of two leaden or iron bullets fastened together by a piece of rope five or six inches long. **1858** O. W. HOLMES *Aut. Breakf.-t.* (1883) 27 A slung-shot could not have brought her down better. **1883** A. K. GREEN (Mrs. Rohlfs) *Hand & Ring* i, The man..having evidently been hit on the head by a slung-shot.

**slunk** (slʌŋk), *sb. Sc.* [var. of SLONK *sb.*] A muddy or marshy place; a miry hollow.

**1665** J. FRASER *Polichron.* (S.H.S.) 346 Not adverting to a slunk or breach in the sea bank, his horse tumbled. **1727** P. WALKER in *Biogr. Presbyt.* (1827) II. 18 Lying in the Dear-slunk, in Midst of a great flow Moss. **1819** W. TENNANT *Papistry Storm'd* (1827) 88 Amang the harbour's sludge and mud; They row'd [= rolled] thegither in the slunk. **1892** in *Eng. Dial. Dict.* (Antrim).

**slunk,** *v. Sc. rare.* [Cf. prec.] *intr.* To wade in mud or mire.

**17..** RAMSAY *To W. Starrat* 28 Feckfu' folk can..slunk thro' moors, and never fash their mind.

**slunk** (slʌŋk), *ppl. a.* [f. SLINK *v.* 3.] Of calves: Cast prematurely. Cf. SLUNG *ppl. a.*¹ 1.

**1837** WHITTOCK *Bk. Trades* (1842) 371 Drum-heads are made..from abortives, or at least very young sucking calves called 'slunk' by the workmen.

**'slunker.** *U.S.* (See quot.)

**1903** GOODE & GILL *Amer. Fishes* 527 These spent females [*sc.* sturgeons] are called 'slunkers', and are of little value.

**slup,** *v.* [In early use, cf. SLOP *v.*² 2, and G. dial. *schluppen* to suck. Modern examples may represent an echoic form. Cf. SLURP *v.*] *trans.* To sup, swallow. Hence **slup** *sb.*, the noise of slupping; **'slupping** *ppl. a.* and *vbl. sb.*

**1598** MARSTON *Sco. Villanie* I. ii. C 3, Lewd Precisians.. take the simbole vp As slouenly, as carelesse Courtiers slup Their mutton gruell. **1947** *Time* 7 Apr. 74/2 A julep-slupping burlesque of a Southern politico. **1949** *Daily Progress* (Charlottesville, Va.) 2 Mar. 10 (*caption*) Put a muffler on that soup sluppin'. **1949** H. HORNSBY *Lonesome Valley* 11 The mule slupped the clear water. **1952** J. STEINBECK *East of Eden* 23 There was no talk at supper. The quiet was disturbed only by the slup of soup and gnash of chewing. **1971** G. EWART *Gavin Ewart Show* I. 28, I am a bottle of wine..slup me rough and homely and I'll taste fine.

**slur** (slɜː(r)), *sb.*¹ Now *dial.* Also 5 sloor, 5, 9 slore, 7 slurre. [Of obscure origin. Cf. MDu. *slore* (Du. *sloor, sloerie*) a sluttish woman.] Thin or fluid mud. Cf. SLURRY *sb.* Also *fig.*

*c* **1440** *Promp. Parv.* 460/1 Sloor [*v.r.* slore], or sowr.., *cenum, limus.* *a* **1614** D. DYKE *Myst. Selfe-Deceiving* (1614) 382 Yet it [work] may not be foule, being soyled, and slubbered with the slurre of a rotten heart. *a* **1825** FORBY *Voc. E. Anglia* 308 *Slur*,..loose, thin, almost fluid mud. **1829** BROCKETT *N.C. Gloss.* (ed. 2), *Slore*, dirt, sump. **1878** MILLER & SKERTCHLY *Fenland* iv. 131 *Slur*—thin washy mud.

**slur** (slɜː(r)), *sb.*² Also 7 slurr. [f. SLUR *v.*²]

**1.** †**a.** A gliding movement in dancing. *Obs.*

**1598** MARSTON *Sco. Villanie* III. x. H 3, In discoursing of the gracefull slur: Who euer heard spruce skipping Curio Ere prate of ought, but of the whirle on toe. **1667** DRYDEN *Secret Love* v, I can..walk with a courant slurr, and at every step peck down my Head. **1673** WYCHERLEY *Gent. Dancing-Master* IV. i, One, two, three, and a slur.

**b.** *dial.* A slide; a sliding course.

**1854-** in Lanc. and Northampt. dialect.

†**2.** A method of cheating at dice (see SLUR *v.*² 1). *Obs.*

*a* **1643** W. CARTWRIGHT *Ordinary* II. iii, Your hollowed thumb join'd with your wriggled box, The slur, and such like are not to be talk'd of. **1662** J. WILSON *Cheats* IV. i, Did not I..teach you, your Top, your Palm, and your Slur?.. And generally, instructed you from Prick-penny, to Long Lawrence? *a* **1680** BUTLER *Rem.* (1759) I. 143 Rooking Gamesters..venture all their Bets Upon the Slurs, and cunning Tricks of ablest Cheats.

**3.** A sliding piece of mechanism in a knitting-machine, serving to depress the sinkers. Also *attrib.*, as *slur-bar, -cock*, etc.

**1796** *Trans. Soc. Arts* XIV. 279 To move the catches from the end of the jacks, and let them fall, the slur..passes behind them. *Ibid.* 280 The slur is composed of two pieces screwed together. **1834-6** *Encycl. Metrop.* (1845) VIII. 747/2 A straight iron bar,..called the slur bar, is extended beneath all the jacks, and upon this a piece of metal, called the slur, travels with rollers to reduce the friction. **1875** KNIGHT *Dict. Mech.* 1237/2 The sinkers..are at the same time depressed, one after another, by the cam or slur above them. **1927** T. WOODHOUSE *Artificial Silk* ix. 98 The jack sinkers..are operated directly or indirectly by means of the cam of a 'slur-cock'. **1962** *Engineering* 15 June 771/1 Straight bar knitting machines..depend largely for their successful operation upon the motion given by a linear cam known as the 'slurcock'.

**slur** (slɜː(r)), *sb.*³ Also 7 slurr(e. [f. SLUR *v.*¹]

**1. a.** A deliberate slight; an expression or suggestion of disparagement or reproof.

**1609** [BP. W. BARLOW] *Answ. Nameless Cath.* 287 The Count..would bee inraged at this Slur and mockage. **1660** H. MORE *Myst. Godl.* VII. xvi. 346 Which is a scurvy slur to these Astrologers. **1666** PEPYS *Diary* 4 Nov., My Lord Generall is become mighty low in all people's opinion, and ..hath received several slurs from the King. **1862** MERIVALE *Rom. Emp.* lvi. (1865) VII. 105 Vitellius seems to have felt this officious zeal as a slur on his own torpidity. **1888** BRYCE *Amer. Commw.* I. xix. 25 A district would think it a slur to be told that it ought to look beyond its own borders for a representative.

**b.** A mark, stain, or blot; a discredit (incurred by or cast upon a person, etc.). Const. *to* or *upon*.

**1662** GLANVILL *Lux Orient.* viii. 85 It would have been a slurre to the divine goodnesse not to have given being to such creatures. *a* **1716** SOUTH *Serm.* (J.), No one can rely upon such an one..without a slur to his reputation. **1722** DE FOE *Moll Flanders* (1840) 101 Not to get the least slur upon my reputation. **1820** BYRON *Mar. Fal.* I. ii, Who..on the honour of..my wife..Left a base slur to pass from mouth to mouth. *a* **1862** BUCKLE *Civiliz.* (1869) III. iii. 148 Whose revolting predilections are not only a slur upon the age which tolerated them, but a disgrace.

**c.** In the phrases *to cast, put, throw* (etc.) *a slur on* or *upon* (a person or thing).

**1654** *Nicholas Papers* (Camden) II. 151 Some say there was never such a slur put upon the Jesuits. **1655** FULLER *Ch. Hist.* VII. 404 It would cast a slurre on the credit of such Bishops. **1726** DE FOE *Hist. Devil* (1840) I. xi. 155 Provoked at the slur that was put upon him. **1785** B. HARRISON in Sparks *Corr. Amer. Rev.* (1853) IV. 90 They..would sensibly feel any slur cast on your reputation. **1855** MACAULAY *Hist. Eng.* xviii. IV. 239 Tourville would not consent to put such a slur on his profession. **1877** E. R. CONDER *Basis Faith* iii. 96 To cast an intolerable slur and disgrace upon human intellect.

†**2.** A fault, mistake, blunder. *Obs.*

**1662** H. MORE *Antid. Ath.* II. xii. §14 That Nature should implant in Man such a strong propension.., is such a Slur committed by her as there can be in no wise excogitated any Excuse. **1675** TRAHERNE *Chr. Ethics* 167 That desire, which makes to the perfection of all goodness, must infinitely avoid every slur and miscarriage as unclean.

**3.** *Printing.* (See quots.)

**1771** LUCKOMBE *Hist. Print.* 501 *Slur*, when the impression of the sheets appear smeared. **1882** SOUTHWARD *Pract. Print.* (1884) 427 The letters may print double—this is caused by a 'slur'. **1888** JACOBI *Printers' Vocab.* 127 *Slur*, when a printed sheet is blurred or smeared—also called a 'shake'.

**4.** *Mus.* A curved line placed over or under two or more notes of different degrees to show that they are to be played or sung smoothly and connectedly.

**1801** BUSBY *Dict. Mus., Slur*, a character..drawn over or under the heads of those notes which are meant..to be blended by a kind of smooth, gliding progression. **1848** RIMBAULT *Pianoforte* 63 The chief marks of expression are the Slur, the Tie, and the Dash or Point. **1875** STAINER & BARRETT *Dict. Mus. Terms* s.v., In violin music a slur directs that the notes under it are to be played with one bow.

*attrib.* **1818** BUSBY *Gram. Mus.* 148 A manner commixed of that indicated by the Slur Curve, and that implied by the Staccato Dash.

**5.** A slurred utterance or sound.

**1861** READE *Cloister & H.* I. 60 There were none of.. those whining slurs, which are now sold so dear by Italian songsters. **1894** SWEET *Anglo-Sax. Reader* (ed. 7) p. lxxxvi, Two short syllables..constituting a slur,..which must be uttered very rapidly. **1898** G. MEREDITH *Poems* 111 He [the lark] drops the silver chain of sound..In chirrup, whistle, slur and shake All intervolved.

**6.** The act or habit of slurring, or doing hurriedly and imperfectly. Also *Comb.*

**1882** BLACKMORE *Christowell* xxii, As every one who does good work, in this age of slur, gets overworked immediately. **1884** JEFFERIES *Life of the Fields* (1893) 234 Country people have not yet got into the habit which may be called slur-reading.

**7.** A blurred atmosphere.

**1880** BLACKMORE *Mary Anerley* II. xv. 272 After the fog and the slur of the day, to see the sky at all was joyful.

**slur** (slɜː(r)), *v.*¹ [f. SLUR *sb.*¹]

**1.** *trans.* To smear, stain, smirch, sully. Also *fig.* Now *dial.*

**1602** MARSTON *Antonio's Rev.* III. ii, Her cheekes not yet slurd ouer with the paint Of borrowed crimsone. **1614** LATHAM *Falconry* (1633) 47 A piece of Flannell or Cotten,.. foule and slurred. **1658** OWEN *On Temptat.* viii. Wks. 1852 IV. 145 Its beauty would be slurred, its good things reviled. **1716** HEARNE *Collect.* (O.H.S.) V. 239 This Gent. hath many good Qualities, tho' they were all slurr'd by his complying with the Rebells in opposition to K. James. **1815** W. H. IRELAND *Scribbleomania* 187 Pennant,..Whose pages, though slurr'd with the dear *egomet*, Demand from a public warm gratitude's debt. **1833** I. TAYLOR *Fanat.* ii. 46 The most pernicious and virulent heart has no power of ejecting its venom upon a fair surface;—it must slur whatever it means to poison. **1854-** in dialect glossaries (Northampt., Derby, Yks.).

**b.** *Printing.* To smudge or blur.

**1683** MOXON *Mech. Exerc., Printing* xiii. ¶4 The Broad Sholdering..receiving the Ink..slurs the Printed Paper. *Ibid.* xxiv. ¶15 The Plattin..shoves the Sheet upon the Face of the Letter, and sometimes Slurs, and sometimes Doubles it. **1870** *Eng. Mech.* 11 Feb. 534/3, I do not find the proof slurred.

**c.** *U.S.* To coat or cover (a wall) with plaster or rough-cast.

**1885** *Harper's Mag.* Mar. 531/1 The rear wall is slurred, and from it three windows open into a garden.

**2.** To disparage, depreciate, calumniate, asperse.

**1660** H. MORE *Myst. Godl.* IV. i, Coming into the World on purpose to slight and slur that which is of the greatest esteem..with the Natural Man. *a* **1677** BARROW *Serm.* Wks. 1716 I. 35 It is an aggravation of impiety..that it slurs (as it were) and defames God. **1707** HUMFREY *De Justif. Baxteriana* 4 That you appear to slur, what I and Mr. B. have wrote, by terming it Arminianism. **1770** BURKE *Corr.* (1844) I. 231 The idea of a triennial parliament, which the jury of London..thought proper to fasten upon him in order to slur us. **1805** SCOTT *Let.* 10 Feb. in *3rd Rep. Hist. MSS. Commiss.* 431/2 Hardly anything was so likely to be of advantage to the Lancastrians as to slur the descent of the house of York. **1867** J. B. ROSE *Virgil's Æneid* 322 Think not I blame or slur your bravery.

**3.** To pass over lightly, without proper mention or consideration.

**1660** H. MORE *Myst. Godl.* V. xvii. 203 By slurring the main Scope of the Apocalypse, and pretending [etc.]. **1678** CUDWORTH *Intellect. Syst.* 684 Triumphing to see the cause of theism thus betrayed by its professed friends.., and the grand argument for the same totally slurred by them. **1781** COWPER *Hope* 555 Beneath well-sounding Greek I slur a name a poet must not speak. *c* **1850** KINGSLEY *Misc.* (1859) I. 19 Biographers have slurred a few facts in their hurry to carry out their theory of favourites. **1871** FARRAR *Witn. Hist.* i. 8 To silence a doubt, or slur a difference.

**b.** Freq. with *over*. Also with ref. to utterance.

**1725** SWIFT *Let. to Stopford* 26 Nov., Your other correspondents tell me that Mr. G...lost 200*l.* in money, which to me you slur over. **1775** SHERIDAN *Art Reading* 212 The little word, as, which is always slurred over. **1815** W. H. IRELAND *Scribbleomania* 216 The very laconic manner in which the great Sir Noodle slurs over the above topics of literature. **1889** JESSOPP *Coming of Friars* vii. 330 Carlyle has gone far to spoil the story by slurring it over.

**c.** To disguise, conceal. *rare*⁻¹.

**1826** LAMB *Elia* II. *Conf. Drunkard*, Those juggling compositions, which..slur a great deal of brandy or other poison under less and less water continually, until they come ..to none at all.

†**4.** To put *off with* something trivial or unsatisfactory. *Obs.*

**1749** *Power of Numbers in Poet. Comp.* 28 Whilst the longest Syllable or the most emphatical Word shall be slur'd off with a Crotchet or a Quaver. **1751** J. BROWN *Shaftesb. Charac.* 157 Thus, we see how dextrously he puts the change upon the unwary reader; and..slurs him off with an accidental consequence.

**5.** *Mus.* To sing or play (notes) in a smooth and connected manner; to mark with a slur.

**1746** [see SLURRED *ppl. a.*]. **1782** [see sense 6]. **1873** H. C. BANISTER *Music* 256 Exception would be made to this..in the case of a series of notes included in one phrase, especially if slurred. **1881** *Grove's Dict. Mus.* III. 536/2. The notes included within its limits are said to be slurred.

**6.** To render confused or indistinct; to blur.

**1782** SIR J. REYNOLDS *Notes Mason's tr. Dufresnoy* lvi, The parts [of the human figure] never appearing uncertain or confused, or, as a Musician would say, slurred. **1889** J. M. ROBERTSON *Ess. Crit. Method* 120 Lax imagination slurs and confuses the lineaments of living character.

**b.** *intr.* To become indistinct through imperfect articulation.

**1893** KIPLING *Many Invent.* 234 His speech, which up to that time had been distinct, began to slur.

**7.** To go through hurriedly and carelessly. Also *intr.* with *through*.

**1857** HUGHES *Tom Brown* I. ix, They only slurred through their fagging. **1894** BLACKMORE *Perlycross* 13 Having slurred his early dinner with his usual zest.

**slur** (slɜː(r)), *v.*² Also 7-8 slurr, 9 *dial.* slir. [? Related to LG. *slurrn* (G. *schlurren, schlorren*) to drag the feet, to shuffle: cf. MLG. *slûren* (LG. *sluren*), MDu. *sloren* (Du. *sleuren*), to drag, trail.]

†**1.** *trans.* To slip or slide (a die) out of the box so that it does not turn. *Obs.*

**1594** NASHE *Unfort. Trav.* 3 If he slur a die. **1660** HARRINGTON *Pres. Pop. Govt.* I. xi. (1700) 292 A man that has read my Writings..cannot chuse but see how he slurs his Dice. **1674** COTTON *Compl. Gamester* (1680) 11 On a smooth table..it is usual for some to slur a Dye two yards or more without turning. *c* **1700** PRIOR *Cupid & Ganymede* 32 The usual Trick: Seven, slur a Six; Eleven: A Nick.

†**b.** In fig. uses or contexts. *Obs.*

*a* **1680** BUTLER *Charact.* (1908) 90 He [the quibbler] commonly slurs every fourth or fifth Word, and seldom fails to throw Doublets. **1681** T. FLATMAN *Heraclitus Ridens* No. 19 (1713) I. 128 But then, Sir, by the by, does he slur in upon them his State Enthusiasms. **1685** F. SPENCE tr. *Varilla's Ho. Medici* 304 Piero de Medici thought Bentivoglio had talk't thus..to slur upon him a Bravade.

†**2.** To cheat or cozen. *Obs.*

**1664** BUTLER *Hud.* II. ii. 192 What was the Publick Faith found out for, But to slur men of what they fought for? **1679** *Hist. of Jetzer* 30 The Fathers design'd to put a trick upon him, but in the event they would be slurred themselves. **1731** FIELDING *Lottery* Epil., This too may turn me off tomorrow morning. If that should happen, I were finely slur'd.

**3.** *intr.* To slide, slide about. Now *dial.*

**1617** ASSHETON *Jrnl.* (Chetham Soc.) 62 To Portfield: ther paid up and made merrie. Tables slurring almost all night. **1675** TEONGE *Diary* (1825) 78 Severall tumbles wee had, wee and our plates, and our knives slurrd oft together. **1796-** in many dialect glossaries, etc.

**4.** To drag, move heavily.
**1889** *Cent. Mag.* June 250 Her soft, heavy footsteps slurred on the stairway as though her strength were failing.

**slurb** (slɜːb). orig. *U.S.* [App. f. *sl-* (as in *sloppy, sleazy*, etc.: see quot. 1962) + URB(AN *a.*, though later re-analysed as if from SL(UM *sb.*$^1$ + SUB)URB.] An area of unplanned suburban development.
**1962** WOOD & HELLER *California going, Going...* 10 The character and quality of such urban sprawl is readily recognizable... These are the qualities of most of our new urban areas—of our *slurbs*—our sloppy, sleazy, slovenly, slipshod semi-cities. **1966** *Guardian* 22 Apr. 12/3 About 35 miles west of London there is a new town that no one knows about. It is in Berkshire, between Reading and Sandhurst, and it includes Wokingham and Crowthorne. It is what Californians, who have plenty of them, call a 'slurb'—an amorphous and intermittent spread of houses. **1967** *Economist* 8 July 120/2 The pattern which has turned Los Angeles into an 'un-community', into 'twenty suburbs in search of a city', into the archetypal 'slurb'. **1979** B. WARD *Progress for Small Planet* xxi. 235 The basic concept of 'urban villages' (the Chelseas, the Trasteveres, the Greenwich villages)..often allow a vitality and an attractiveness which the world's concrete suburban deserts, slurbs, and sprawls so demonstrably lack.

†**'slurbow.** *Obs.* Also 6-7 -bowe, 7 -bo. [The first element is obscure.] A species of cross-bow commonly used for discharging fire-arrows, perh. one having a barrel attached to the stock. Also *attrib.*
**1588** *Cal. State Papers, 1581-90* (Dom. Ser.) 562 For slurr bows 20;..for 20 dozen of firework arrows for the said slurr bows. **1599** in *Archaeologia* (1800) XIII. 399 Crossbowe arrowes 500 decaied. Slurbowe arrowes with fierwoorkes 184, inde 19 without fierwoorks. **1615** R. COCKS *Diary* (Hakl. Soc.) I. 75 He desired to have the slurbo to take a sample by to make an other. **1622** R. HAWKINS *Voy. S. Sea* liii. 127 The brasse Balles of Artificiall fire, to be shott with slur-bowes.

†**slurf.** *Obs. rare.* ? Error for SCURF *sb.*$^1$
**1674-7** J. MOLINES *Anat. Obs.* (1896) 13 A little excoriation..as though there was a slurfe. *Ibid.*, To pull off the slurfe.

†**slurg,** *v. Obs. rare.* [Cf. G. dial. *schlurgen* to go about in a slovenly manner.] *intr.* To lie sleepily or sluggishly.
**1557** PHAER *Æneid* VI. Q iij b, Æneas toke the place, while thus the porter slurging was. **1562** *Ibid.* IX. Aa iv b, They themselues in wynes and sleepe Resolued, slurg on grounde.

**slurp,** *v.* Also 9 *dial.* slurrup. [= Du. *slurpen* (Norw. *slurpa*), G. *schlurfen, schlürfen*: cf. SLORP *v.*] **1. a.** *trans.* To drink or eat greedily or noisily. (See also quot. 1976). Also with *down, up.*
**1648** HEXHAM II, *Zuypen, Slorpen, ofte gulsigh drincken*, to Sup, or Slurpe, or to Drinke too much. *a* **1825** FORBY *Voc. E. Anglia* 308 *Slurrup*, to swallow any liquid greedily and with a noise of the lips or in the throat. **1917** *Dialect Notes* IV. 329 *Slurp, v.t.* and *i.*..to eat liquid food with audible inhalation of air. **1947** *Richmond* (Va.) *Times-Dispatch* 30 Dec. 15/1 The stars just whirl in.., slurp a cup of coffee and zoom out again. **1952** C. ARMSTRONG *Black-Eyed Stranger* ii. 10 'You know—' Baby slurped food, 'If you want to live you got to eat.' **1962** R. LOWELL *Imitations* 39 They are slurping their dinners quite happily. **1974** P. CAVE *Mama* (new ed.) xiii. 107 The Angels obediently slurped down the remainder of their teas and rose to their feet noisily. **1976** *Daily Tel.* 21 Jan. 15/5 After about seven years of 'slurping' (the correct professional word) tea in the tasting room he [*sc.* a tea-taster]..has prospects of becoming a buyer or blender.
**b.** *transf.* and *fig.*
**1968** *Punch* 11 Dec. 858/1 The idiocies of British holiday habits, which tend to waver between 'slurping up the kilometres' and getting away from it all amid insanitary *souks*. **1973** M. AMIS *Rachel Papers* 15 Mrs Bladderby had an even wreckier mother, who..had, moreover, during a recent outing, got her left leg slurped into a dreadful piece of agricultural machinery.
**2.** *intr.* **a.** To make a sucking noise in drinking or eating.
**1917** [see sense 1 a above]. **1961** B. CRUMP *Hang on a Minute, Mate* 108, I had my head inside the can slurping happily away. **1975** A. A. THOMPSON *Message from Absolom* iv. 24 The Americans ate hungrily. At the other table, the Elberts slurped audibly.
**b.** *transf.* and *fig.*
**1958** J. KEROUAC *On Road* vii. 155 He..stuck his finger in Marylou's dress, slurped up her knee. **1963** [see MATIÈRE]. **1971** B. W. ALDISS *Soldier Erect* 24 On bed immediately... Fanny swimming with juice, slurps when touched. Marvellous tits, delicious underarms. **1976** P. CAVE *High Flying Birds* iv. 51 With a couple of pints of champagne slurping around her insides, she found it increasingly difficult to wrap her tongue round the hard Anglo-Saxon consonants.
Hence **'slurping** *ppl. a.* and *vbl. sb.*
**1960** W. SHEED *Middle Class Educ.* (1961) 31 The slurping roar of the undergraduates. **1976** *Daily Tel.* 21 Jan. 15/5 Mr Ronald Calvert, chief taster for Ridgways,..wonders if women are daunted by a job entailing the 'slurping' of 200 to 400 mouthfuls of tea on an average working day. **1980** *Sunday Express* 27 July 16 No one would want them to endanger their striped pants by sitting next to spotty Coca-cola slurping children.

**slurp** (slɜːp), *sb.* and *int.* [f. the vb.]
**A.** *sb.* A slurping sip or lick; the noise of slurping.
**1949** H. HORNSBY *Lonesome Valley* xxi. 270 The second cow..slammed her nose against her side and swiped at flies with her tongue. Almost before the slobbery slurp was over with the cow trotted after the other. **1959** A. BAILEY *Making Progress* 142 The slurps and gulps of the Danes moodily drinking their beer. **1960** I. CROSS *Backward Sex* 140 He..took a huge slurp of tea. **1977** D. CLARK *Gimmel Flask* iv. 79 Green took a slurp of his coffee, grimaced at the taste.
**B.** *int.* An interjection imitating the sound of a slurp.
**1966** L. COHEN *Beautiful Losers* I. 16 It is recorded that she prayed incessantly. Glog, glog, dear God..slurp, flark, glamph, hiccup, jerk. **1967** W. H. CANAWAY *Mules of Borgo San Marco* iv. 51 She dipped her spoon in the soup, sipped, and said, 'Perfect!' '*Slurp*,' said Major Widdicombe. **1970** *Private Eye* 22 May 16 Leetle Germaine eez at votre service!!! (slurp!).

**slurred** (slɜːd), *ppl. a.* [f. SLUR *v.*$^1$] Run together, rendered indistinct, blurred, etc.
**1746** TANSUR *New Mus. Gram.* 99 Ty'd or slur'd Notes. **1827** TATE *Grk. Metres* in *Theatre of Greeks* (ed. 2) 446 It may justify our adoption of slurred Anapest and slurred Dactyl, as terms not inappropriate for that purpose. **1843** RUSKIN *Mod. Paint.* I. II. IV. ii. §16 It is quite a mistake to suppose that slurred or melting lines are characteristic of distant large objects. **1883** S. C. HALL *Retrospect* I. 5 They are faded and gone—pieces of slurred paper, nothing more.

**slurring** ('slɜːrɪŋ), *vbl. sb.*$^1$ [f. as prec.] The action of SLUR *v.*$^1$ in various senses.
**1661** R. BURNEY *Chas. II. Presented* 32 A King most properly commands Free Subjects, without the violation of their priviledges, or slurring of the Leaves of Magna Charta. **1683** MOXON *Mech. Exerc., Printing* xxiv. ¶ 19 This is rather slurring than Doubling.., but when it is real Doubling, it happens generally on the whole Sheet. **1811** BUSBY *Dict. Mus.* (ed. 3), *Slurring*, performing in a smooth gliding style. **1866** G. STEPHENS *Runic Mon.* I. 22 In Old-North English this slurring was still more prevalent. **1871** LOWELL *Study Wind.* (1886) 243 Slurrings-over and runnings-together of syllables.

**'slurring,** *vbl. sb.*$^2$ [f. SLUR *v.*$^2$] The action of SLUR *v.*$^2$ in various senses.
**1668** HEAD & KIRKMAN *Eng. Rogue* IV. xvi. 226 Slurring, is when you throw your Dice so smoothly on the Table that they turn not. **1673** HEAD *Cant. Acad.* 17 Three parts of every nights dream is spent..in topping, slurring, palming. **1675** TEONGE *Diary* (1825) 78 It could not stand on the table for the ship's tossing..; som securing themselves from slurring by setting their feete against the table.
*attrib.* **1674** COTTON *Compl. Gamester* (1680) 85 That is done by lying a fore-finger on the top indifferent hard, and giving a slurring jerk to the rest.

**'slurring,** *ppl. a.* [f. SLUR *v.*$^1$]
**1.** Of utterance: Indistinct.
**1848** KEIGHTLEY *Notes to Horace* Introd., Hence..their rapid slurring pronunciation, as is shown by the metre of their comic poets. **1865** DICKENS *Mut. Fr.* II. i, 'Yes', said Headstone in a slurring way. **1897** *Allbutt's Syst. Med.* II. 903 My speech was slurring, my gait ataxic.
**2.** Careless, hurried.
**1880** 'MARK TWAIN' *Tramp Abr.* 279, I never allow myself to do things..in a slurring, slipshod way.
**3.** Slighting; depreciatory.
**1892** GUNTER *Miss Dividends* (1893) 227 This decidedly slurring description of the belle of Newport's last season makes the girl think every one despises her.

**slurry** ('slʌrɪ), *sb.* Also 5 slory, 9 slorry. [Related to SLUR *sb.*$^1$]
**1. a.** Thin sloppy mud or cement. Also in extended use, any fluid mixture of a pulverized solid with a liquid (usu. water), freq. used as a convenient form in which to handle solids in bulk.
*c* **1440** *Promp. Parv.* 203/2 Gore, or slory, *limus, tessequa.* **1878** F. S. WILLIAMS *Midl. Railw.* 492 A nearly semi-fluid mass of 'slurry', which settles down like glue to the bottom of the wagon. **1886** *Cycl. Tour. Club Gaz.* IV. 187/2 The sand..should be watered until it..can be worked up into slurry with brooms. **1901** *Longm. Mag.* Sept. 396 Its sluggish streak of creeping slurry miscalled a creek. **1935** *Discovery* Apr. 119/1 The strata are pounded into a 'slurry' by the constant rising and falling of the heavy drilling tools. **1948** *Chambers's Jrnl.* July 388/1 The idea here is to break up the turf bank face by means of high-pressure jets, like firemen's hoses, into slurry. **1955** *Sci. News Let.* 20 Aug. 115/2 The U.S.-designed power plant..uses..thorium oxide slurry in heavy water in another part of the device, called a homogenous reactor. **1961** *Aeroplane* CI. 342/3 Whatever form of contaminant is selected, it is first mixed with kerosene to form a 'slurry', so representing the normal state in which it would pass through a filter in service. **1975** *Nature* 30 Oct. 818/1 In a second experiment, another batch of about 3 ml of the packed cell slurry was resuspended in the culture medium.
**b.** *spec.* A mixture of water and fine particles of coal, produced esp. as a by-product of the washing of coal; such material in dried form, used as fuel.
**1913** *Trans. Inst. Mining Engineers* XLV. 429 Where the moisture percentage is not over 5, the small dust measuring less than 1 cubic millimetre (which is the cause of all the slurry trouble) can be just as efficiently treated by dry-percussive screening as by any other method. **1930** *Ibid.* LXXVIII. 27 It cannot be claimed that slurry is a suitable fuel for pulverizing. **1955** *Times* 4 July 15/5 They [*sc.* the N.C.B.] have been using a new type of mechanical stoker, which is fully automatic, to burn slurry—fine particles of coal and soluble shale which is rejected from washeries. **1976** 'R. LEWIS' *Witness my Death* v. 180 That tip up there, it's full of water. The slurry is drifting down.
**c.** *spec.* A mixture of manure or farmyard waste and water; manure in fluid form.
**1965** *Punch* 22 Dec. 932/2 In a modern fattening house..the manure from several hundred swine falls through slatted floors into tanks beneath the building where a daily dose of water soon turns it into a forbidding quantity of evil-smelling slurry. **1970** R. JEFFRIES *Dead Man's Bluff* i. 5 He went through from the dairy into the herringbone parlour and stared..at the two days' accumulation of slurry. **1971** *Farmers Weekly* 19 Mar. 48/4 It takes one man about six minutes a day to clear away the slurry and a bit longer to put out the hay.
**2.** In technical use: (see quots.).
**a. 1825** J. NICHOLSON *Operat. Mechanic* 462 (Pottery), The thrower..forms the inside of the vessel.., and smoothes it by removing the *slurry*, or inequalities. **1832** G. R. PORTER *Porcelain & Glass* 46 By the assistance of one of these [instruments] the inside is smoothed and any inequalities, technically called *slurry*, are removed.
**b. 1841** HARTSHORNE *Salop. Ant.* Gloss., *Slorry, Slurry*, the levigated matter which forms under a grindstone.
**3.** *attrib.*, as ***slurry disposal, pipeline, pit, pump, refiner, tank, tanker***; **slurry seal** (see quot. 1967).
**1970** R. JEFFRIES *Dead Man's Bluff* i. 5 He stared angrily at..the slurry disposal unit. **1969** *Daily Colonist* (Victoria, B.C.) 13 Dec. 9/3 Kaiser..was contemplating a slurry pipeline to the coast as an alternative to rail. **1976** *Cumberland News* 3 Dec. 13/4 There was a slurry pit also under a byre, made of slate. **1940** KRISTAL & ANNETT *Pumps* 338/2 (Index), Slurry pumps. **1976** *Cumberland News* 3 Dec. 34/3 (Advt.), Alfa Laval slurry pumps. **1916** *Trans. Inst. Mining Engineers* LI. 272 With the combination of this slurry-refiner and the elevated settling-tank.., it has been found possible to work a washery, year in and year out, without any outlet whatever. **1967** *Gloss. Highway Engin. Terms* (*B.S.I.*) 30 *Slurry seal*, a mixture of binder, fine aggregate and mineral filler with water added to produce a material of slurry consistency. **1974** *Globe & Mail* (Toronto) 7 Feb. 5/6 Slurry seal is a tar-like chemical substance that is spread on city streets to preserve them. It is cheaper than asphalt. **1936** *Economist* 25 Apr. 213/2 Property account has been increased to £12,557 by the addition of the slurry tanks and quartz deposit. **1971** *Farmers Weekly* (*Extra*) 19 Mar. 5/1 (Advt.), We know we have the best slurry tanker.

**slurry** ('slʌrɪ), *v.* Now *dial.* Forms: 5 slory, 6 slorye, 7 slorie; 6, 9 *dial.* slorry, 7 slourry; 6-7 slurrie, 7, 9 slurry. [Cf. prec. and SLUR *v.*$^1$] *trans.* To dirty, soil, smear, daub, etc.
*c* **1440** *Promp. Parv.* 460/1 Sloryyd, *cenosus, cenolentus, lutulentus.* **1552** HULOET, Slorye or make fowle, *sordido.* **1555** BRADFORD in Coverdale *Lett. Martyrs* (1564) 252 Though you lye in the darke, slorryed wyth the bishoppes blacke cole dust, yet [etc.]. **1591** R. TURNBULL *S. James* 231 b, Malicious persons, who..soyle, slurrie, and file the garmentes of our neighbours. **1603** HOLLAND *Plutarch's Mor.* 195 As they that soile and slourry writing tables when they be faire scoured and clensed. **1635** J. SWAN *Spec. M.* vi. (1643) 293 Amiantus..being put into the fire, is not hurt nor slurried. **1647** HEXHAM I, To Slorie, or make foule. **1828** CARR *Craven Gloss.*, *Slurry*, to daub, to dirty. **1841** HARTSHORNE *Salop. Ant.* Gloss., *Slorry*, to plaster, daub over.
*fig.* **1647** TRAPP *Marrow Gd. Authors* in *Comm. Ep.* 717 Divinity..that had been shamefully obscured and slurried with needlesse and endlesse doubts. **1678** CUDWORTH *Intell. Syst.* I. iv. 191 All the Great..things of this world, are slurried and disgraced, comparatively with the Life of Christ. **1736** AINSWORTH I. s.v. *Slur*, To slur, slurry, or cast a slur on one's reputation.
Hence **'slurrying** *vbl. sb.*
**1600** ABBOT *Jonah* 363 The slurrying which was used toward him,..hath made him shine the brighter. **1611** COTGR., *Souillement*, a soyling, slurrying, durtying.

**slurry** ('slɜːrɪ), *a.* [f. SLUR *v.*$^1$ + -Y$^1$.] Blurred, indistinct: now usu. of speech. Also **'slurrily** *adv.*
**1937** *Daily Express* 12 Feb. 5/3 This is the way to detect a forgery— look for notes that are rather blurred or 'slurry'. **1969** 'H. CALVIN' *Chosen Instrument* ii. 22 'We want nothing, we need nothing,' the fat boy said slurrily. **1977** J. MCCLURE *Sunday Hangman* xv. 174 'Why leave the bodies everywhere?' Willie demanded, driven..to speak his mind, if a little slurrily.

**slush** (slʌʃ), *sb.*$^1$ Also 8-9 *dial.* sluss. [Of doubtful origin: cf. SLUDGE and SLUTCH (both from the 17th cent.) and the more recent SLOSH.
The late appearance of the word makes it doubtful whether there is any connexion with such forms as older Da. *slus* sleet, mud, or Norw. *slusk* slops, sloppy ground or weather.]
**1. a.** The watery substance resulting from the partial melting of snow or ice.
**1641** BEST *Farm. Bks.* (Surtees) 76 This speedy thowe caused a wonderfull slush. **1806** BERESFORD *Miseries Hum. Life* II. v, The ice proving treacherous and bedding you in slush to the hip. **1862** *Macm. Mag.* Apr. 456 Whenever there was a temporary thaw, this mass of ice and snow became a pond of slush. **1876** DAVIS *Polaris Exp.* v. 118 A great deal of snow fell during the day, forming slush upon the surface of the water.
**b.** Liquid mud or mire.
**1772** *Hartford Merc.* Suppl. 18 Sept. 2/2 The new inclosures, which formerly were almost covered with water and slush. **1791** *Gentl. Mag.* LXI. I. 126 There is another term also in use..in that county [Norfolk], namely, *sluss* or *slush*, to express the mire of the highway in its most liquid state. **1815** W. H. IRELAND *Scribbleomania* 13, I mean dirty puddle,..slush from the ditch that's in rear of the mountain. **1860** WYNTER *Curios. Civiliz.* III. 106 The wart hog,..which wallows up to its eyes in slush and mire. **1878** BROWNING *Poets Croisic* 12 They reared.., mid the slush and ooze Of yon low islet.., a temple.
*fig.* **1853** W. JERDAN *Autobiog.* III. xviii. 282 His literary career was..through the usual mud and slush of its miry obstacles. **1875** TENNYSON *Q. Mary* II. ii, Your rights and charters hobnail'd into slush.

**2. a.** *Naut.* The refuse fat or grease obtained from meat boiled on board ship.

**1756** *Gentl. Mag.* XXVI. 419 He..used much slush (the rancid fat of pork) among his victuals. **1757** W. THOMPSON *R.N. Adv.* 21 Tars whose Stomachs are not very squeamish, and who can bear to paddle their Fingers in stinking Slush. **1812** J. HENRY *Camp. agst. Quebec* 143 A great quantity of liquid fat which the men called slush. **1856** KANE *Arctic Expl.* I. xxviii. 364 With a copper lamp, a cooking-basin, and a liberal supply of slush for fuel.

*fig.* **1833** CARLYLE *Cagliostro* in *Misc. Ess.* (1888) V. 78 Wheresoever..a slush of so-called vicious enjoyment [is] to be swallowed. **1898** *Chr. Herald* (N.Y.) 23 Feb. 144/4 That the people of this country demand moral slush instead of healthy and intellectual food.

**b.** Food, esp. of a watery consistency. *slang.*

[**1898**: see sense 2 a *fig.*] **1941** J. SMILEY *Hash House Lingo* 51 *Slush*, hash. **1955** J. THOMAS *No Banners* ix. 79 It was years since he had tasted anything but jail slush. **1962** W. GRANVILLE *Dict. Sailors' Slang* 108/2 *Slush*, any 'sloppy' food: e.g., soup or stew.

**3. a.** (See quot. and cf. SLUTCH *sb.* 2.)

**1843** HOLTZAPFFEL *Turning* I. 191 The top is covered.. with the waste or slush from the grindstone trough.

**b.** A mixture of grease and other materials used for lubricating.

**1847** in WEBSTER.

**c.** A mixture of white lead and lime, used for painting parts of machinery to preserve them from oxidation.

**1864** in WEBSTER.

**4. a.** Rubbishy discourse or literature. Also *gen.*, nonsense, drivel; sentimental rubbish. Also as *int.*

**1869** 'MARK TWAIN' *Innoc. Abr.* x. 91 He'll..grind out about four reams of the awfullest slush. **1896** *Daily News* 23 Jan. 6/1 Two stout volumes of what the American editor would have called 'delirious slush'. **1906** *Dialect Notes* III. 156 O, slush! What nonsense. **1919** C. E. VAN LOAN *Score by Innings* 332 A woman reporter..took one look at Conley ..and tore off a whole page of slush. **1937** PARTRIDGE *Dict. Slang* 786/1 As = sickly sentiment, *slush* is familiar S.E. **1944** [see *blush-making* adj. s.v. BLUSH *sb.* C.]. **1949** [see KITSCH]. **1953** F. SCOTT FITZGERALD *Tender is Night* I. ix. 51, I mean, would I have been the sort of girl you might have —oh, slush, you know what I mean. **1961** *Observer* 26 Nov. 27/4 The ending is purest slush, and there are some cheap dramatics in the camera work. **1970** R. K. KENT *Lang. Journalism* 124 *Slush*,..cheaply sentimental copy; trash; drivel.

**b.** Counterfeit paper money. *slang.*

**1924** E. WALLACE *Room 13* i. 11 Young Legge's..the biggest printer of slush in the world! And it's not ord'nary slush. Experts..can't tell 'em from real Bank of England stuff. **1933** D. HUME *Crime Unlimited* vii. 64 We've been handling slush lately—ten bobs and quids. Where they were printed doesn't matter to you.

**5.** *dial.* **a.** A slovenly or dirty person; a slut.

**1825** BROCKETT *N.C. Gloss.*, *Slush*, a reproachful term for a dirty person. **1836** *Wilson's Tales Borders* II. 163 Dinna speak o' the slush to me..; for he's a speeritless hash.

**b.** A drudge.

**1825** in JAMIESON *Suppl.* c **1861**- in *Eng. Dial. Dict.* **1883** MISS BRADDON *Gold. Calf* xxi. 235 He told her she was cook, slush, and bottle-washer.

**6.** *attrib.*, as (sense 1) ***slush-ice***; (sense 2) ***slush-bucket*** (also *transf.*), ***-lamp***, ***-light***, ***-tub***; (sense 4) ***slush melodrama***, ***novel***; **slush casting**, a method of making hollow castings in which molten metal is poured into a mould and then poured out again after a layer of metal has solidified on the inner surface of the mould; a casting produced by this method; also **slush-cast** *v.*; **slush-money** orig. *U.S.*, money paid out from a SLUSH FUND b; **slush moulding**, a process identical to the slush casting of metal but carried out with plastic or latex; so **slush mould**, a mould for use in slush moulding; **slush-moulded** *ppl. a.*; **slush oil** *U.S.*, crude oil found in association with certain shales or sandstones (? *obs.*); **slush pit** (see quots.); **slush pump**, (*a*) a pump used to circulate mud through a rotary drilling column; (*b*) *U.S. slang*, a trombone.

**1785** GROSE *Dict. Vulgar T.*, **Slush bucket*, a foul feeder, one that eats much greasy food. **1867** SMYTH *Sailor's Word-bk.* 634 *Slush-Bucket*, a bucket kept in the tops, to grease the masts, sheets, &c. **1934** WEBSTER, *Slush-cast, *v.t.* & *i.* **1965** E. TUNIS *Colonial Craftsmen* iv. 75/2 Feet and knobs were cast solid, but spouts and handles were slush cast, a system used also for such things as sand shakers and nursing bottles whose inner surfaces wouldn't be visible. **1930** M. STERN *Die-Casting Pract.* i. 16 The thickness of a *slush casting depends upon the length of time that the metal is left in the mold. **1934** CHARNOCK & PARTINGTON *Mech. Technol.* (ed. 2) xxxv. 485 Slush casting is a method of producing light hollow castings without the use of cores. **1936** H. L. CAMPBELL *Metal Castings* iii. 53 Slush castings are produced by pouring the low-melting alloys of lead, antimony, and zinc into metal molds and, after a short interval, slushing out the metal which remains in a liquid state. **1963** JONES & SCHUBERT *Engin. Encycl.* (ed. 3) 1161 The process known as slush-casting is employed extensively in the production of ornamental objects made of spelter or zinc. **1867** SMYTH *Sailor's Word-bk.* 634 **Slush-Ice*, the first layer which forms when the surface is freezing. **1871** C. L. MONEY *Knocking about N.Z.* vi. 77 An old volume of 'Household Words' to spell over at my little fire in the evenings by the light of my *slush-lamp. **1883** KEIGHLEY *Who are You?* 45 The slush-lamp shone with a smoky light. **1893** J. A. BARRY *Steve Brown's Bunyip* 41 A tin which he had just taken from over the big slush lamp. **1887** S. SAMUELS *Forecastle to Cabin* vi. 76 This thump, we found out afterwards, was caused by a handspike; the jar from it put the *slush light out. **1972** *People* (Austral.) 13 Feb. 12/2 They..lit their earth-floored bunkhouses at night with slushlights made from treacle-tins filled with fat. **1916** 'B. M. BOWER' *Phantom Herd* vii. 112 You want those stories worked up in a lot of darned, sickly *slush melodramas. **1842** J. F. COOPER *Wing-and-Wing* II. 20 They were only put there yesterday..a little *slush-money did it all. **1976** *National Observer* (U.S.) 24 Jan. 3/3 There have been a series of well-founded reports..that the multinational corporations have been shoveling slush money into Christian Democrat coffers. **1957** V. J. KEHOE *Technique Film & Television Make-up* xii. 148 It [*sc.* dental stone] has low absorption qualities so is not suitable for *slush molds. **1965** E. TUNIS *Colonial Craftsmen* iv. 75/2 The slush mold's two halves shaped only the outside of the article. The caster poured hot metal into it, sluiced it around carefully, and then poured it out again. **1954** N. J. RAKAS *Plastics Engin. Handbk.* x. 314 The physical qualities of *slush-molded plastisol are such that it is possible to do exceptionally accurate work. **1943** SIMONDS & ELLIS *Handbk. Plastics* 971 **Slush molding*, a process for molding hollow castings with accelerated thermoplastic phenolic resins. **1957** V. J. KEHOE *Technique Film & Television Make-up* xii. 154 Slush molding requires the use of a fillered latex as the unfillered variety will not build-up on itself in a plaster mold. **1963** H. R. CLAUSER *Encycl. Engin. Materials & Processes* 491/2 Vinyl foam products such as armrests.. are manufactured by first forming a tough vinyl skin by spraying, slush molding or rotational molding. The interior then is formed by casting..a vinyl plastisol foam within the pregelled skin. **1977** *Listener* 3 Mar. 284/4 Communications —meaning journalism, detective fiction, *slush novels, and film-making. **1880** J. F. CARLL *Geol. Oil Regions of Warren* [etc.] *Counties* 254 The measures above the Warren and Bradford 'Third sands' have produced considerable 'shale or *slush oil', which may perhaps be attributed to a fissured condition of these rocks. **1884** *U.S. Tenth Census* X. 13 The first well sunk to the Bradford sands was drilled..2 miles northeast of Bradford. 'Slush oil' was found at a depth of 751 feet, and in November, 1871, producing sand was struck at 1,110 feet. **1931** *Sun* (Baltimore) 29 Apr. 1/4 Four lay in the *slush pit, an earthen depression intended to catch drilling refuse. **1975** L. CROOK *Oil Terms* 105 *Slush pit*, pit used for storing drilling mud. **1913** *Oil & Gas Man's Mag.* VIII. 822/2 Two *slush pumps are usually installed with each drilling outfit—one pump to operate and the other one to act as a relay. **1921**, etc. [see *mud-laden fluid* s.v. MUD *sb.*[1] 5]. **1937** *Amer. Speech* XII. 48/2 *Slushpump*, a trombone. **1938** [see *gob-stick* s.v. GOB *sb.*[2] b]. **1943** *N.Y. Times* 9 May II. 5/4 That man with the Slush Pump was a fine sender. **1949** *Our Industry* (Anglo-Iranian Oil Co. Ltd.) (ed. 2) ii. 37 The circuit of this mud-laden fluid..commences at the slush pumps. **1962** J. WAIN *Strike Father Dead* 141, I could see at once why he preferred the valve trombone to the ordinary slush-pump. **1974** *BP Shield Internat.* Oct. 19/3 There's always a lot of work we can do in the sheltered places —like maintaining the slush-pump. **1977** J. WAINWRIGHT *Do Nothin' till you hear from Me* x. 176 Get Walt to help on the slushpump try-outs. Walt stays first trombone. **1836** E. HOWARD *R. Reefer* xl, D–n you, and your *slush-tub too! **1858** SIMMONDS, *Slush-tub*, a vessel for holding grease.

**slush** (slʌʃ), *sb.*[2] [Imitative, or f. SLUSH *v.*]

**1.** A heavy splashing sound. Also ***slush-slush***.

[**1848** *Life in Normandy* (1863) I. 111 Slush, slush, went the two wheels into two holes.] **1880** BLACKMORE *Mary Anerley* I. xviii. 311 The hollow of the rocks received the first billow with a thump and a slush. **1900** H. SUTCLIFFE *Shameless Wayne* xxvii, The faint *slush-slush* of horse-hoofs striking sodden earth.

**2.** A copious wash; a sluicing.

**1902** ALICE TERTON *Lights & Shad. Hospital* viii. 118 A stable bucket I could give myself a good slush in.

**slush** (slʌʃ), *v.* [Partly f. SLUSH *sb.*[1] and partly imitative; the senses belonging to the two sources are not clearly separable.

An early use of the word is given by Thoresby (1703), '*To slush through work*, to do much, but slimly, carelessly'.]

**I.** *trans.* **1.** To splash or soak with slush or mud.

**1807** SIR R. WILSON *Priv. Diary* (1862) II. viii. 262 We were quite slushed in the mire. **1819** 'R. RABELAIS THE YOUNGER' *Abeillard & H.* 122 Feeling his garments and himself slush'd. **1873** DIXON *Two Queens* I. VI. viii. 355 All slushed and soiled with the November rain.

**2. a.** *Naut.* To grease (a mast) with slush. Also with *down*.

**1823** J. F. COOPER *Pioneers* xv, I larnt how a topmast should be slushed. **1840** R. H. DANA *Bef. Mast* ii, The officer..ordered me to slush the mainmast. **1910** *Blackw. Mag.* Aug. 170/1 He ordered him aloft with a bucket of grease to 'slush down' the mast.

**b.** To paint (machinery) with a mixture of white lead and lime.

**1864** in WEBSTER.

**c.** To fill *up* or cover by dashing on mortar and cement.

**1875** KNIGHT *Dict. Mech.* 2219 *Slushed-up*, the joints and intervals between the bricks and courses filled with mortar. **1902** R. STURGIS *Dict. Archit. & Building* s.v., Slushed work permits bricks to be laid dry..in the interior of a wall, and makes inferior work.

**3. a.** To wash with a copious supply, or with dashing on, of water; to sluice.

**1854** MISS BAKER *Northampt. Gloss.*, *Slush*, to wash with much water without rubbing. 'Slush it in the river.' **1865** DICKENS *Mut. Fr.* II. xvi, So he were there skilfully rubbed down and slushed and sluiced, and polished and clothed.

**b.** To dash (water) *over* one.

**1889** 'Q.' [QUILLER COUCH] *Splendid Spur* 213 Stand thee so, an' slush the water over me.

**II.** *intr.* **4.** Of pigs: To eat greedily and noisily.

**1833** M. SCOTT *Tom Cringle* xii. (1859) 289 Like so many pigs slushing at the same trough.

**5.** To go or walk through mud, etc., with a dull splashing sound. Also with cognate object, and *fig.*

**1853** MOSSMAN & BANISTER *Australia visited & Revisited* iv. 45 The dirty work, mud, and slushing in water..are so contrary to the habits of the many, that few can stand the training. **1855** [ROBINSON] *Whitby Gloss.*, *To Slush on*, to proceed or persevere in one's course of life, as the saying is, 'through thick and thin'. **1888** F. COWPER *Caedwalla* 214 The raft..slushed its way through the water. **1904** *Field* 6 Feb. 223/2 As for horses, they slushed in and slushed out of the wet compound.

**6.** To descend or degenerate *into* something.

**1882** *Good Words* 99 Conversation which..by and by *slushed* into unexpected and not very profitable discussion about legitimate and illegitimate children.

**7.** To rush (*down*) with a splashing sound.

**1883** STEVENSON *Lett.* (1901) I. 272 The filthy gutter slushes. **1889** TENNYSON *Owd Roa* xxi, The snaw slushin' down fro' the bank to the beck.

**8.** To dash *at* something in heavy splashes.

**1900** STRAIN *Elmslie's Drag-net* 227 Slushed at by the waves, buffeted by the wind, she battled her way across the road.

**slusher** (ˈslʌʃə(r)). [f. prec.] **1.** *Austr.* The cook's assistant on a station during shearing time.

**1890** *Melbourne Argus* 20 Sept. 13/6.

**2.** *Mining.* A mechanical device for loading or packing broken material in which a bucket is drawn to and fro through a pile of the material by ropes wound round a drum at each end of its length of travel.

**1923** *Mine & Quarry* July 1267/1 The contractor..has what is practically the double drum slusher in the ordinary drag line excavator and also in his back-filling machine. **1946** *Trans. Inst. Mining Engineers* CVI. 115 Four scours, totalling 1,200 yds., have been driven with the slusher. **1976** *Times Lit. Suppl.* 8 Oct. 1281/2 Diamonds... To mine them you need, among other things,..a double drum slusher.

**slush fund.** orig. and chiefly *U.S.* [SLUSH *sb.*[1] 2.]

**a.** In the Navy: money collected from the sale of slush, etc., and used to buy luxuries for the crew. Also, a similar fund in the Army.

**1839** W. MCNALLY *Evils & Abuses in Naval & Merchant Service* xvii. 162 The sailors in the navy are allowed salt beef. .. From this provision, when cooked..nearly all the fat boils off; this is carefully skimmed..and put into empty beef or pork barrels, and sold, and the money so received is called the *slush fund*. **1884** *Naval Encycl.* 759/2 *Slush-fund*, money obtained from the sale of slush. It is to be used for premiums for target firing, etc., and not for ship's purposes. **1963** T. PYNCHON *V.* i. 14 Pappy ended up borrowing 500 for 700 from Mac the cook's slush fund.

**b.** *transf.* A fund used to supplement the salaries of government employees; a fund used to bribe, or influence the action of, a person or group of persons, *spec.* for political ends; a fund used to support a favoured political candidate.

**1874** *Congr. Record* 17 Apr. 3166/1 We have had this 'slush-fund' since 1866... It was divided among these officers to increase their salaries. **1894** *Ibid.* 16 Jan. 904/1 [Cleveland] was not elected in 1888..because of pious John Wanamaker and his $400,000 of campaign slush funds. **1924** *Glasgow Herald* 16 Feb. 10 A huge fund alleged to have been deposited in a Washington bank to the credit of a widely-known citizen very intimate with men prominent in public life... The name given to the mysterious fund is the 'slush fund'... 'Slush', in the American acceptance of the word, means illicit commission, bribery, corruption, and graft. **1931** *Economist* 10 Oct. 658/1 How candidate-deputies will react against this suppression of what has usually, in the past, been regarded as an electoral 'slush' fund remains to be seen. **1962** *Guardian* 15 Mar. 9/6 Eisenhower's running mate was accused of being the beneficiary of a 'slush fund' subscribed by wealthy backers. **1977** *Whitaker's Almanack 1978* 567/2 The Prime Minister on May 23 commissioned Mr. Dell, the Trade Secretary, to review Government policy and commercial practices in the light of the 'slush fund' allegations. **1980** *Washington Post* 1 Feb. A1/1 The company had a secret $600,000 slush fund for entertaining Pentagon officials.

**ˈslushiness.** [f. SLUSHY *a.*] The quality of being slushy.

**1904** *Westm. Gaz.* 11 Apr. 2/2 Water-colour drawings that cherish inordinate ambitions almost invariably fall into either dryness or slushiness.

**ˈslushing,** *vbl. sb.* [f. SLUSH *v.* or *sb.*[1] + -ING[1].] The action of the vb. *spec.* in *Mining*, the action or process of moving or scraping broken ore into a dump or on to a wagon or chute.

**1864** CARLYLE *Fredk. Gt.* IV. 363 Moony workings, and slushings hither and thither..in the muddy tide-currents. **1923** *Mine & Quarry* July 1267/1 The scraping or slushing of one into chutes or raises or into mine cars is only one of the many uses for the portable double drum hoists. **1946** *Trans. Inst. Mining Engineers* CVI. 116 Both for hand-filling and slushing one haulage-hand was engaged in getting the tubs away from the contractor. **1966** S. D. WOODRUFF *Methods of Working Coal & Metal Mines* III. B. ii. 287 As soon as a cut was completed the tramming, or slushing, floor was filled with waste before another cut was started.

**ˈslushing,** *ppl. a.* [f. SLUSH *v.* or *sb.*[1] + -ING[2].] That slushes or splashes. *spec.* pertaining to or designating a viscous oil or grease used to protect bright metal surfaces, when paint or other fixed coatings cannot be used.

**1863** MRS. GASKELL *Sylvia's Lovers* x, Philip went.. through keen black east wind, or driving snow, or slushing thaw. **1920** *Technologic Papers Bureau of Standards* (U.S.) No. 176. 4 Slushing oils or slushing compounds are of a varied nature, sometimes being straight mineral greases.. sometimes mixtures of mineral and animal greases..finely divided mineral matter, and volatile solvents. **1939** BURNS & SCHUH *Protective Coatings for Metals* xvi. 381 The successful use of slushing compounds depends to a considerable extent upon proper cleaning of the metal surface beforehand. **1975** *Chem. Abstr.* LXXXIII. 13232 A slushing oil was prepd. from a mixt. of a metal mahogany or naphthalene sulphonate, a $C_{15-60}$ fatty acid, a cosolvent, and mineral oil.

**slushy** ('slʌʃɪ), *sb.* Also **slushey, slushie.** [f. SLUSH *sb.*[1] or *v.*]

a. A ship's cook; *spec.* as a nickname. Also in more gen. application: a cook; any unskilled kitchen or domestic help. **b.** = SLUSHER I.

**1859** in *Slang Dict.* 96. **1876** F. W. H. SYMONDSON *Two Years abaft Mast* xiii. 261 An unexpected roll of the ship sent both pig and cook sliding... There was 'Slushy' sometimes over, sometimes under the pig. **1887** HALL CAINE *Deemster* x, The cook, better known as the slushy. **1900** H. LAWSON *On Track* 135 As the shearers' 'slushy' hates the shearers' cook. **1904** *Bulletin* (Sydney) 15 Sept. 39/1 Terms as usual, 4s. per man per week, the cook to find his own slushy. **1919** W. H. DOWNING *Digger Dial.* 46 *Slushey*, a mess orderly. **1936** A. RUSSELL *Gone Nomad* iii. 14, I had to take my turn at butchering the ration sheep and as 'slushy' to 'Doughboy' Terry, the cook. **1936** [see POISONER b]. **1953** 'CADDIE' *Sydney Barmaid* 25 Nellie, a wisp of a girl who was slushie at Mrs Murphy's boarding-house. Slushie was the name given to anyone who worked at a camp boarding-house. **1959** H. P. TRITTON *Time means Tucker* 25/2 Having over 100 men to cook for, he selected two off-siders, sometimes called 'slushies', and started his duties immediately. **1967** C. DRUMMOND *Death at Furlong Post* xii. 153 'You could get a job as a slushy in any restaurant,' he pronounced, 'good short-order cookery.' **1970** K. GILES *Death in Church* iv. 85 A grey-headed woman was crying in a corner—'The part-time slushy,' said Perman.

**slushy** ('slʌʃɪ), *a.* [f. SLUSH *sb.*[1]]

**1.** Covered with, consisting of, having the character of, slush (in senses 1 a and 1 b).

(*a*) **1791** W. BARTRAM *Carolina* 178 They bury themselves in the slushy bottoms of rivers and ponds. *a* **1825** FORBY *Voc. E. Anglia* 309 *Slushy*, miry. **1861** MISS BEAUFORT *Egypt. Sepul. & Syrian Shrines* I. 220 We..continued our road on the soft slushy sand along the edge of the wave. **1884** *Good Words* 156 Stepping through the sedges, regardless of the slushy footing.

(*b*) **1825** JAMIESON *Suppl.* s.v., *Slushie*, abounding with snow in a state of liquefaction; as, 'The streets are very slushie.' **1857** B. TAYLOR *North. Trav.* xvii. 174 Mud under foot, alternating with slushy snow. **1878** JEFFERIES *Gamekeeper at H.* 42 The snow slips and comes down in slushy, icy fragments.

**b.** Marked by the prevalence of slush.

**1848** THACKERAY *Contrib. to 'Punch'* Wks. 1886 XXIV. 203 [He] came over ten miles to Squattleborough in the most slushy weather, and delivered four lectures. **1871** M. COLLINS *Marq. & Merch.* I. x. 304 There are slushy splashy raw comfortless mornings in..winter.

**2.** Weak, washy.

**1839** McDOWALL *Poems* 117 (E.D.D.), Can slushy tea ere be compared Wi' cogs o' brose? **1844** J. T. HEWLETT *Parsons & W.* xxv, Something stronger and better than water or slushy tea.

**b.** *fig.* Rubbishy, trivial.

**1889** *Voice* (N.Y.) 15 Aug., That is a slushy sentiment. **1894** *Times* 3 Jan. 7/5 A large portion of the British public is steeped in a sloppy and slushy sentimentalism.

**3.** Thick, indistinct.

**1861** DICKENS *Gt. Expect.* III. 250 He spoke in a slushy voice.

**sluss,** dial. form of SLUSH *sb.*[1]

**slut** (slʌt), *sb.* Also 5 **slotte,** *north.* **slute,** 5–6 **slutte,** 7 **slutt.** [Of doubtful origin: cf. G. (now dial.) *schlutt, schlutte, schlutz*, in sense 1. Forms having some resemblance in sound and sense also occur in the Scand. languages, as Da. *slatte* (? from LG.), Norw. *slott*, Sw. dial. *slåta*, but connexion is very doubtful.]

**1. a.** A woman of dirty, slovenly, or untidy habits or appearance; a foul slattern.

**1402** HOCCLEVE *Letter of Cupid* 237 The foulest slutte of al a tovne. *c* **1440** *Pallad. on Husb.* IV. 273 Ful ferd is hit for touching of vnclene Wymmen—and slottes y suppose hit mene. **1483** *Cath. Angl.* 345/2 A Slute, *vbi* foule. **1530** PALSGR. 271/2 Slutte, *souilliart, uilotiere.* **1581** PETTIE *Guazzo's Civ. Conv.* III. (1586) 137 b, I haue noted often those dames which are so curious in their attire, to be verie sluttes in their houses. **1621** BURTON *Anat. Mel.* To Rdr. 24 Women are all day a dressing, to pleasure other men abroad, and go like sluts at home. **1715** HEARNE *Collect.* (O.H.S.) V. 98 Nor was she a Woman of any Beauty, but was a nasty Slut. *a* **1763** SHENSTONE *Odes* Wks. (1765) 190 She's ugly, she's old,..And a slut, and a scold. **1848** KINGSLEY *Saint's Trag.* II. viii, Almshouses For sluts whose husbands died. **1883** S. C. HALL *Retrospect* II. 249 She looked the part of a ragged, slatternly, dirty slut.

*fig.* **1602** MARSTON *Ant. & Mel.* II. Wks. 1856 I. 26 Would'st thou have us sluts and never Shift the vestur of our thoughts? **1642** FULLER *Holy & Prof. St.* II. xii, Did Rome herein look upon the dust behind her own doores, she would have but little cause to call her neighbour slut.

**b.** A kitchen-maid; a drudge. *rare.*

*c* **1450** *St. Cuthbert* (Surtees) 133 The quene her toke to make a slutte, And to vile services her putt. **1855** J. D. BURN *Autobiogr. Beggar Boy* (1859) 68, I lived with him..for nearly six months, and acted the part of cook, slut, butler, page, footman, and *valet de chambre.*

†**c.** A troublesome or awkward creature. *Obs.*$^{-1}$

*c* **1460** J. RUSSELL *Bk. Nurture* in *Babees Bk.* (1868) 158 Crabbe is a slutt to kerve & a wrawd wight.

**2. a.** A woman of a low or loose character; a bold or impudent girl; a hussy, jade.

*c* **1450** *Cov. Myst.* (Shaks. Soc.) 218 Com forth, thou sloveyn! com forthe, thou slutte! *c* **1515** *Cocke Lorell's B.* 11 Sluttes, drabbes, and counseyll whystelers. **1577–82** BRETON *Flourish upon Fancie* Wks. (Grosart) I. 6/2 To haunt the Tauernes late,..And swap ech slut vpon the lippes, that in the darke he meetes. **1621** BURTON *Anat. Mel.* I. ii. IV. i. (1651) 143 A peevish drunken flurt, a waspish cholerick slut. **1698** FRYER *Acc. E. India & P.* 375 Disputes of their Religion, in which he found the crafty Slut would involve him. **1742** FIELDING *J. Andrews* II. iv, I never knew any of these forward sluts come to good. **1777** SHERIDAN *Trip to Scarborough* IV. i, These lords have a power of wealth indeed, yet, as I've heard say, they give it all to their sluts and their trulls. **1839** DICKENS *Nickleby* xviii, Never let anybody who is a friend of mine speak to her; a slut, a hussy. **1848** —— *Dombey* xliv, Does that bold-faced slut intend to take her warning, or does she not? **1881** BESANT & RICE *Chapl. of Fl.* I. xii, My lord shall marry this extravagant slut.

*fig.* **1602** KYD *Sp. Trag.* III. xii *a*, Night is a murderous slut, That would not haue her treasons to be seene.

**b.** In playful use, or without serious imputation of bad qualities.

**1664** PEPYS *Diary* 21 Feb., Our little girl Susan is a most admirable slut, and pleases us mightily. **1678** BUNYAN *Pilgr.* I. 112 As the Mother cries out against her Child in her lap, when she calleth it Slut and naughty Girl, and then falls to hugging and kissing it. **1710–1** SWIFT *Lett.* (1767) III. 79 Ah! you're a wheedling slut, you be so. **1740–2** RICHARDSON *Pamela* III. 207 Well did the dear Slut describe the Passion I struggled with. **1846** LANDOR *Imag. Conv.* I. 233 Nanny, thou art a sweet slut. **1884** GORDON *Jrnls.* (1885) 115 Why the black sluts would stone me if they thought I meditated such action.

*transf.* **1862** THACKERAY *Philip* xiii, You see I gave my cousin this dog,..and the little slut remembers me.

**3.** A female dog; a bitch. Also *attrib.*, as *slut-pup.* ? orig. *U.S.*

**1821** J. FOWLER *Jrnl.* 13 Nov. (1898) 42 A large Slut Which belongs to the Party atacted the Bare. **1845** G. LAW in *Youatt's Dog* (ed. Lewis, 1858) iii. 88 The dog-pup..and the slut-pup. *Ibid.* 89 The dog was of a dingy red colour, and the slut black. **1853** W. IRVING in *Reader* No. 57. 131/3 My little terrier slut Ginger..having five little Gingers toddling at her heels. **1893** J. INGLIS *Oor Ain Folk* (1894) 10, Sluts were not so frequently used for shepherding purposes as dogs, being less tractable.

**4. a.** A piece of rag dipped in lard or fat and used as a light.

**1609** C. BUTLER *Fem. Mon.* (1634) 151 Matches are made of linen rags and Brimstone, after the manner that maids make Sluts. **1852** *Blackw. Mag.* Mar. 363 Writing by the light of what Irish Jenny called 'sluts'—twisted rags, dipped in lard, and stuck in a bottle. **1886** L. M'LOUTH in *Library Mag.* Aug. (1887) 64 Sometimes..there were for additional light, lard 'sluts', or tallow 'dips'.

**b.** The guttering of a candle.

*a* **1864** GESNER *Coal, Petrol.*, etc. (1865) 92 The melted material overflows, and bears with it the name of 'slut'.

**5.** Special collocations, as †**slut's corner,** a corner left uncleaned by a sluttish person; also *fig.*; **slut-, slut's-hole,** a place or receptacle for rubbish; also *fig.*; †**slut's-pennies,** hard pieces in a loaf due to imperfect kneading of the dough; **slut's wool,** the fluff or dust left on the floor, etc., by a sluttish servant or person.

**1573** TUSSER *Husb.* (1878) 167 Sluts corners auoided shall further thy health. **1583** GOLDING *Calvin on Deut.* cxxxiii. 814 Our house shalbe swept, & we will good heed yt no sluts corner be left. **1608** TOPSELL *Serpents* (1658) 779 Rubbing, brushing, spunging, making clean sluts-corners. **1710** SWIFT *On a Broomstick* Wks. 1755 II. I. 181 He sets up to be ..a remover of grievances, rakes into every slut's corner of nature [etc.] **1750** W. ELLIS *Country Housew. Comp.* 21 There is often what we call slutts-pennies among the bread, that will appear and eat like kernels. **1862** *Sat. Rev.* 15 Mar. 298 There are a good many slut-holes in London to rake out. **1862** *Edin. Rev.* Apr. 410 Upstairs there is 'slut's wool' under the beds. **1893** *Westm. Rev.* Jan. 17 She would also.. see that floors were scrubbed, and corners clear of 'slut's-wool', and spiders well kept down.

†**slut,** *a. Obs. rare.* Also 6 *Sc.* **slute, slutt.** [f. prec.] Sluttish, untidy.

**1500–20** DUNBAR *Poems* xxvi. 71 Mony slute daw and slepy duddroun. **1596** DALRYMPLE tr. *Leslie's Hist. Scot.* I. 290 The foullest slutt husies and seruandis. **1638** BRATHWAIT *Barnabees Jrnl.* II. (1818) 53 An hostesse none more slutter.

**slut** (slʌt), *v.* Also 7 *Sc.* **slute.** [f. SLUT *sb.*]

†**1.** *trans.* To render sluttish. *Obs.*

*a* **1618** SYLVESTER *Tobacco Battered* 585 Wks. (Grosart) II. 272 Don Tobacco's damnable Infection, Slutting the Body, slaving the Affection. **1645** Z. BOYD *Holy Songs* in *Zion's Flowers* (1855) App. 12/1 Words..Which slute the body, and als slave the affection.

**2.** *intr.* To act as a drudge. Also, to behave like a slovenly woman or a woman of loose morals. Also with *about.*

**1829** *Examiner* 18/1 The Professional morality..rendered it a point of pride to stop short of 'slutting for all work' for the attorneys. **1913** A. LUNN *Harrovians* ii. 37 They groise their horrid eyes off and get out of fagging in a term or two, while we poor devils have to slut about 'on boy' for three years. **1948** G. GREENE *Heart of Matter* II. III. i. 200 Perhaps I'd have slutted with Bagster or killed myself. **1955** D. BARTON *Glorious Life* 199 In winter she had less of the Cinderella look that slutting about in summer cottons imposed on her.

**slutch** (slʌtʃ), *sb.* [Of uncertain origin: cf. SLUDGE *sb.* and SLUSH *sb.*[1]

It is doubtful whether *sluche* in the *Destr. Troy* 12529 is an early example of this, as the form in other passages of the poem is *slic(c)he* SLITCH; but cf. SLUTCH *v.* 1.]

**1.** Mud, mire, slush. Now *dial.*

Cf. also *sea-slutch* (SEA 18 e) and *star-slutch.*

**1669** *Phil. Trans.* IV. 1062 A blackish Slutch mixt with the Sand, which infects the whole Spring. **1776** G. SEMPLE *Building in Water* 73 All that soft Slutch would be thrown out, and a firm Stone-work put in the Place of it. **1777** PENNANT *Brit. Zool.* (ed. 2) IV. 66 Discovered by an aperture in the slutch. **1800** W. CHAPMAN *Facts & Rem. rel. Witham & Welland* 49 A great portion of rich slimy mud or slutch. **1854** MISS BAKER *Northampt. Gloss.*, *Slutch*, mud. **1897** RHOSCOMYL *White Rose Arno* 92 Mucked up fro' heel to hat wi' slutch (mud) as thou art.

**2.** = SLUSH *sb.*[1] 3 a.

**1889** W. MARCROFT *Ups & Downs* 58, I gave orders..that the grinding slutch must be wheeled out before breakfast time each morning.

**slutch** (slʌtʃ), *v.* Now *dial.* Also 4 **sluchche.** [Cf. prec.]

**1.** *trans.* To cover or soil with mud; to bemire. Hence **slutched** *ppl. a.*

**13..** *E.E. Allit. P.* C. 341 Þenne he swepe to þe sonde in sluchched cloþes. **1868** WAUGH *Sneck Bant* i, He was 'welly (well-nigh) slutched up to th' neck' with peat mire.

**2.** To clean out by removing mud.

**1690** in Picton *L'pool Munic. Rec.* (1883) I. 288 It is order'd in Councel yt no allowance be given him to slutch ye frosse lake. **1735** *Cheshire Farm Acct.* in *Sheaf* (1879) I. 330 By lading and slutching. **1886** HOLLAND *Cheshire Gloss.* 324 To 'slutch a pit' is to clean out the mud from a pond.

**3.** *intr.* To wade about *in* mud, etc.

*c* **1861–** in dialect use (Lanc., Yks.).

**slutchy** ('slʌtʃɪ), *a.* [f. SLUTCH *sb.* + -Y.] Muddy, slushy.

**1701** in Picton *L'pool Munic. Rec.* (1883) I. 291 Pan-tiles ..requiring a blew slutchy clay. **1777** PENNANT *Brit. Zool.* (ed. 2) IV. 66 Lodged under slutchy ground, near low-water mark. *a* **1890** WAUGH *Heather* (1892) Ser. II. 95 The highway was full of slutchy ruts.

**sluth(e:** see SLEUTH *sb.*[2] and *v.*[1]

**sluther** ('slʌðə(r)), *v. dial.* [var. of SLITHER *v.*] *intr.* To slide, slip.

**1796** PEGGE *Derbicisms* Ser. II. 122 *Slither*, or *Sluther*, to slide; to slip. **1854** MISS BAKER *Northampt. Gloss.* s.v., Sluther down the hill. **1888** DALBY *Mayroyd* II. 165 He.. wriggled his body, and was about to 'sluther' down.

**sluthering,** var. SLOOTHERING *vbl. sb.*

†'**slutly,** *adv. Obs.*$^{-0}$ [f. SLUT *sb.* or *a.*] Sluttishly, foully.

*c* **1460** *Promp. Parv.* (Winch.), Slutly, *cenulente.*

So †'**slutness,** sluttishness, foulness. *Obs.*$^{-0}$

*a* **1500** *Promp. Parv.* (K.), Sluthnes, *cenositas.*

†'**sluttered,** *ppl. a. Obs.*$^{-1}$ [Cf. next.] Befouled, dirtied.

**1589** NASHE *Anat. Absurd.* B ij b, That those that neuer tasted of any thing saue the excrements of Artes..shoulde preferre their sluttered sutes, before other mens glittering gorgious array.

**sluttery** ('slʌtərɪ). Now *rare.* [f. SLUT *sb.*]

**1.** Sluttishness, filthiness, dirtiness, untidiness.

*a* **1586** SIDNEY *Arcadia* III. (1590) 389 Yet let not sluttery, The sinke of filth, be counted huswifery. **1594** *Mirr. Policy* (1599) 153 Cleannesse..is the thing that bringeth her into most estimation: as contrariwise slutterie and filthinesse breeds her most hatred. **1627** DRAYTON *Nimphidia* ix, These make our Girles their sluttery rue, By pinching them both blacke and blue. **1661** PEPYS *Diary* 22 Dec., I took occasion ..to fall out with my wife and my mayde for their sluttery. **1698** FRYER *Acc. E. India & P.* 200 They are not to be taxed ..with Sloth or Sluttery in respect of their Bodies. **1814** SCOTT *Diary* in *Lockhart* (1839) IV. 235 They are a long lived race, notwithstanding utter and inconceivable dirt and sluttery. **1818** MARY CARLYLE in Froude *Life C.* (1882) I. v. 58 It shall be my earnest desire never to imitate the abominable slutteries of Mrs. Maclarty.

†**b.** *concr.* Dirt, filth, impurity. *Obs.*

**1607** J. DAVIES *Summa Totalis* F 4*, We can but immure Those Sp'rituall Guifts with Fleshes sluttery. **1644** HAMMOND *Serm.* ix. Wks. 1684 IV. 530 All the debaucheries in the world could no more vitiate them, than the..gold by the sluttery it may be mixt with. **1656** EARL MONM. tr. *Boccalini's Advts. fr. Parnass.* II. xiv. (1674) 158 How..any man should be so sullied with the sluttery of uncleanness, as that he dare publish those obscenities.

†**c.** A slut. *Obs.*$^{-1}$

*a* **1652** BROME *City Wit* IV. ii, You hurden smock'd sweaty sluttery, that couldst love a fellow that wore worsted stockins footed, and fed in Cooks shops.

†**2.** Work appropriate to a slut; drudgery. *Obs.*$^{-1}$

**1615** J. STEPHENS *Satyr. Ess.* 266 She is a receiver to all professions, and acquainted by experience with cookery or sluttery.

†**3.** Vile or criminal conduct. *Obs.*$^{-1}$

*a* **1656** USSHER *Ann.* (1658) 357 She..poisoned him,..and to cover this sluttery of hers, she caused one Artemon, who was very like him, to lie in his bed.

**4.** An untidy room; a work-room.

**1841** *Tait's Mag.* VIII. 150 There is a little store-room.. —I may have that for my sluttery, I dare say.

**'sluttikin.** *rare*⁻¹. [f. SLUT *sb.*] A little slut.
1711 SWIFT *Jrnl. Stella* 29 Aug., But what care you who is privy-seal, saucy sluttikins?

**sluttily, -ness:** see SLUTTY *a.*

**sluttish** ('slʌtɪʃ), *a.* Forms: 5 slottisch, 6 -ysshe, slottish; 5 sluttissh, 6 sluttys(s)h(e, -ishe, 6- sluttish. [f. SLUT *sb.* + -ISH.]
**1.** Of persons: Dirty and untidy in dress and habits, esp. to an extent which is repulsive or disgusting. Now *spec.* of women.
(*a*) *c* 1386 CHAUCER *Can. Yeom. Prol.* 83 Why is thy lord so sluttissh, I the preye, And is of power bettre clooth to beye? 1525 LD. BERNERS *Froiss.* II. xxxi. 92 Then he shewed them..the nature of the Spanyardes, howe they are sluttysshe and lousy. 1597 BEARD *Theatre God's Judgem.* (1612) 513 A woman gaily attired,..before whom marched an euill fauoured sluttish vsher. 1632 LITHGOW *Trav.* I. 26 They of the vulgar kind are both ignorant, sluttish and greedy. 1698 FRYER *Acc. E. India & P.* 269 Their Rusticks are truly..Sluttish and Slothful.
(*b*) 1592 *Arden of Feversham* IV. iv, If well attyred, thou thinks I will be gadding; If homely, I seeme sluttish in thine eye. 1600 J. PORY tr. *Leo's Africa* II. 107 Their women are most forlorne and sluttish. 1635 BRERETON *Trav.* (Chetham Soc.) 97 We observed the sluttish women, washing their clothes in a great tub with their feet. 1709 *Tatler* No. 75 ¶9 Jenny's only Imperfection is an Admiration of her Parts, which inclines her to be a little, but a very little, sluttish. 1758 JOHNSON *Idler* No. 15 ¶4 The..maid..is as lazy and sluttish as her mistress. 1822 W. IRVING *Bracebr. Hall* (1845) 276 Venting their direful wrath..upon the sluttish dairy-maid. 1850 KINGSLEY *A. Locke* i, The coarse men and sluttish women.
*fig.* *c* 1600 SHAKS. *Sonn.* lv, Vnswept stone, besmeer'd with sluttish time. 1673 [R. LEIGH] *Transp. Reh.* 140 This gallant..espouses the sluttish mother church of Geneva.
†**b.** Of a low or lewd character. *Obs.*
1575 *Gamm. Gurton* III. iii, Stand to it, thou dastard,..Ise teche the, a sluttish toye! 1606 SHAKS. *Tr. & Cr.* IV. v. 62 Set them downe, For sluttish spoyles of opportunitie; And daughters of the game.
**2.** Of things: Unclean, dirty, grimy; untidy.
1549 COVERDALE, etc. *Erasm. Par. 2 Tim.* 23 In sluttishe clothes, with a countrefaicte grauitie of countenaunce,.. they conueye them selues in to other mens houses. 1553 *Respublica* III. vi. 853 Suche hongrye doggs will slabbe vp sluttishe puddinges. 1599 DAVIES *Immort. Soul* Introd. xxxiii. (1714) 9 The Man loves least at Home to be, That hath a sluttish House. 1617 MORYSON *Itin.* III. 180 Their wives..are attired in a sluttish gowne. 1665 SIR T. HERBERT *Trav.* (1677) 311 Some boil the cream in a raw skin, so as it is commonly very sluttish, full of hairs and unsalted. 1678 CUDWORTH *Intell. Syst.* 798 This Foul and Gross Body of ours..remaining still Nasty, Sluttish and Ruinous within. 1824 SCOTT *St. Ronan's* xvii, Two or three miserable tubs with suds, or such like sluttish contents.
**3.** Appropriate to, characteristic of, a slut or sluts: †**a.** Low, despicable, immoral, lewd. *Obs.*
1561 T. HOBY tr. *Castiglione's Courtyer* 22 Not to vse sluttish and Ruffianlike pranckes with anye man. 1587 TURBERV. *Trag. Tales* (1837) 123 Both God and man such sluttysh sutes detest, The lawfull love is ever counted best. 1694 CROWNE *Married Beau* IV. 44 Who play'd this sluttish trick with these gentlemen?
**b.** Partaking of, marked or characterized by, gross slovenliness or untidiness.
*a* 1601 *Pasquil & Kath.* (1878) I. 82 In hot pursuit Of cold abhorred sluttish niggardise. 1625 N. CARPENTER *Geogr. Del.* II. xiv. (1635) 245 The sluttish carelesnesse of the one, and the cleanly neatnesse of the other. 1664 PEPYS *Diary* 7 Aug., The ill, improvident, disquiett, and sluttish manner that my father and mother and Pall live in the country. 1718 PRIOR *Epitaph* 28 Sluttish plenty deck'd her table. 1727 *Fam. Dict.* s.v. *Clear-Starching*, Some stir the Starch about with a Candle,..but this is rejected as a sluttish way. 1824 W. IRVING *Tales Trav.* II. 21 The same air of departed gentility and sluttish housekeeping. 1843 CARLYLE *Misc.* (1857) IV. 269 A drowsy life, of ease and sluttish abundance.

**sluttishly** ('slʌtɪʃlɪ), *adv.* Also 5 sluttisshly, -ysshly, 6 -ishely, -yshely. [f. prec.] In a sluttish manner; untidily, dirtily; carelessly.
*c* 1490 CAXTON *Rule St. Benet* (1902) 129 Who so euer neclygently or sluttisshly entretyth ony thyng of the place, anone be they rebukyd & punysshid. 1539 ELYOT *Cast. Helthe* (1541) 14 Moch people in smal roume living unclenly and sluttishely. 1542 UDALL *Erasm. Apoph.* (1877) 160 Mustie or sluttishely kept loues of bread. 1606 DEKKER *Seven Sins* IV. (Arb.) 34 It is all sluttishly ouergrowne with Mosse on the out-side. 1661 K. W. *Charac. Conceited Coxcombs* (1860) 78 So that she is finely sluttish and sluttishly fine. ? *a* 1729 in Chappell *Pop. Mus.* II. 649 Whether decently clothed or sluttishly dress'd. 1771 MRS. HAYWOOD *New Present for Maid* 254 Without leaving any [dust] sluttishly in corners. 1976 J. COOPER *Harriet* xiii. 106 They had a nice, relaxed eveing..sluttishly eating curry off their knees.

**sluttishness** ('slʌtɪʃnɪs). Also 5 slwttisnes, 6 scluttishnes. [f. as prec. + -NESS.] The character or state of being sluttish; dirtiness; gross slovenliness or untidiness.
1483 *Cath. Angl.* 345/2 Slwttisnes; *vbi* fowlnes. *c* 1530 *Crt. of Love* lxviii, That thou eschewe With sluttishnesse thyself for to offend. 1549 COVERDALE, etc. *Erasm. Par. 1 Peter* 2 Which can neither be corrupted with death,..ne yet fade away by age or sluttishnes. 1600 BRETON *Pasquil's Fooles Cap* xxxviii, Shee that is giuen to Ease and Sluttishnesse, And trifles out the time in Trompery. *a* 1659 BP. BROWNRIG *Serm.* (1674) I. xxx. 382 Christ compares an Hypocrite to a piece of sluttishness. 1748 SMOLLETT *Rod. Rand.* xxxviii. (1804) 251 She neglects her person even to a degree of sluttishness. 1776 *Euphrosyne* I. 18 My study is, I must confess The sacred shrine of sluttishness.
*fig.* 1568 TURNER *Herbal* III. 80 The scluttishnes, filthines, and foulnes of the soule. 1637 PRESTON *Mount Ebal* (1638) 42 Suffer not any sluttishnesse..to rest in your hearts. 1893 *Daily News* 12 Dec. 6/7 That sluttishness of financial prosperity which has been denied to art in all ages.

**'slutty,** *a.* Now *dial.* [f. SLUT *sb.* + -Y.] Dirty, foul; slovenly.
*a* 1400 in Horstman *Hampole's Wks.* (1895) I. 303 If þou gafe a gret lorde drynke in a slutty coppe & foule. *c* 1440 *Promp. Parv.* 460/2 Slutty, *cenulentus.* 1897 G. FORD *Larramys* 101 You'm a slutty, poor varmer,..sure 'nough.
Hence †**'sluttily** *adv.*; **'sluttiness.**
*c* 1440 *Promp. Parv.* 460/2 Sluttyly,..*cenulente.* 1451 CAPGRAVE *Life St. Aug.* 46 In summe men we lakkyn þe grete cost of aray, and with summe ar we wroth her sluttynesse.

**sly** (slaɪ), *a.*, *adv.*, and *sb.* Forms: α. 3 sleh, 4 sleȝ, sleeȝ, 4-5 sleȝe, slegh(e, 5 scleȝ, sclegh; 3-4 sleyh, 4 sleih; 3 sleiȝh, 3-4 sleiȝe, 4 sleiȝ, 5 scleyȝ; 4 sleigh(e, sleygh(e. β. 3-5 sley, 4-5 sleye, 5 scley; 4, *Sc.* 5-6 sle, 5, *Sc.* 7-9 slee. γ. 4 slyh(e, sliȝ, 4- 5 sliȝe, slyȝ(e, 4-5 slygh, 4-6 slyghe, 4-7 sligh. δ. 4-5 sli, 5 sclie, 5-8 slie; 4-7 slye, 4- sly. [ME. *slēȝ*, ad. ON. *slœg-r* (Icel. *slægur*, Norw. *sløg*; MSw. *slögh*, older Da. *sløff*) clever, cunning, originally 'able to strike', f. *slóg-* pret. stem of *slá* to strike. The later development into northern *slee*, midland and southern *sligh*, *sly*, is normal. The corresponding abstract noun is SLEIGHT *sb.*[1]]
**A.** *adj.* **1. a.** Of persons: Skilful, clever, dexterous, or expert in doing something; possessing practical skill or ability; skilled, knowing, wise. (Also occas. of animals.) *Obs.* exc. *north. dial.*
α. *c* 1200 ORMIN 13498 Her wass wiss Filippe sleh & ȝæp & haȝherr hunnte. *c* 1275 *Five Joys Virgin* 32 in *O.E. Misc.* 88 þer þe schulen engles grete, for þu ert boþe hende and sleyh. *c* 1290 *S. Eng. Leg.* I. 378 A carpenter..ich am, quoynte and sleiȝh. *c* 1340 HAMPOLE *Pr. Consc.* 7570 Als clerkes says, þat er wise and sleghe. *c* 1350 *Lybeaus Disc.* 351 As a noble knyght, As werrour queynte and sclegh. *c* 1420 *Liber Cocorum* (1862) 19 Be sleȝe and powre in water þerfore.
β. *a* 1300 *Havelok* 1084 Hwere mithe i finden ani so hey So Hauelok is, or so sley? 1375 BARBOUR *Bruce* XVI. 335 He gert get vrichtis that ves sle. 14.. in *Vicary's Anat.* (1888) App. IX. 228 Apone the nose..Schall thowe lete blode, if thowe be sle. 1807 STAGG *Misc. Poems* (1808) 93 When Seymie..was as slee as onny Danniel. *c* 1859 T. MOORE *Song Sol.* vii. 1 A slee warkman.
γ. 13.. *Sir Beues* 579 þe king him louede also is broþer, And þe maide, þat was so sliȝ. *c* 1380 WYCLIF *Sel. Wks.* III. 10 He is makir of my kynde, as a sliȝ werkman. *a* 1425 tr. *Arderne's Treat. Fistula*, etc. 2 God..hath hid many thingis fro wise men and sliȝe whiche he vouchesaf aftirward for to shewe to symple men. *c* 1430 *Syr Gener.* (Roxb.) 5333 Generides was hardie and sligh, And saw hem flee, and drogh him nigh.
δ. *a* 1300 *Cursor M.* 8695 þe king, þat was sa sli a clerc. *c* 1320 *Cast. Love* (1849) 78 So slye and crafty they shull byn alle, That they shull do all thyng that in here hert doth falle. 1495 *Trevisa's Barth. De P.R.* XVIII. liii. 812 Amptes ben full lytyll and ben neuerthelesse more slye [*Bodl. MS.* sliȝe] and besy than many grete beestys. 1600 FAIRFAX *Tasso* X. xli. 187 You..(whom grauer age And long experience hath made wise and slie). 1865 *Danby Gloss.* s.v., He war a desput sly chap wha fost thow't o' thae sun-pict'rs.
†**b.** Const. *in* or *of* (also *at*, *on*) something. *Obs.*
(*a*) *a* 1300 *Cursor M.* 27280 In spiring loke þe preist be sli, Noght ouerbald bot als on drei. *c* 1340 HAMPOLE *Pr. Consc.* 2662 þarfor þou man in þi werk be slyghe. *c* 1400 *Rowland & O.* 690 þe gentill Grauntere In Batayle þat was so sleghe. 1513 DOUGLAS *Æneid* V. v. 76 Of Creit..born was sche, And in the craft of Mynerve wondir sle.
(*b*) *a* 1300 *Cursor M.* 7251 For he was sle on [*Gött.* sly of] harpingleu. 1375 BARBOUR *Bruce* XIV. 938 He send for masonis..That sleast wes of that misteir. 1393 LANGL. *P. Pl.* C. XXIII. 163 This sleuthe was sleyh of werre and a slynge made. *c* 1470 HENRY *Wallace* I. 375 Off that labour as than he was nocht sle. 1500-20 DUNBAR *Poems* l. 30 Gy of Gysburne, na Allan Bell,..At schot war nevir so slie.
†**c.** With infinitive. *Obs.*
*a* 1300 *Cursor M.* 27290 þat þe preist be slei To gar þe man him-seluen wrei. *c* 1400 *Laud Troy Bk.* 11112 He..asked hem..'Whether thei were alle so sly To saue Ector withoute poudre'. *c* 1450 *Bk. Curtasye* 300 in *Babees Bk.*, With woso men..The falle to go, loke þou be slegh To aske his nome. 1513 DOUGLAS *Æneid* VI. xv. 2 The peple..Bene..moir sle To forge and carve lyflyk staturis of bras.
†**2.** Marked or characterized by skill or dexterity; showing skilfulness or ingenuity; cleverly or finely made. *Obs.*
1297 R. GLOUC. (Rolls) 7187 Louerd he sede þat ech þing madest quointe & sley. *c* 1330 R. BRUNNE *Chron. Wace* (Rolls) 2258 Atte laste he wolde fleye, Feþer-hames he made hym sleye. 1398 TREVISA *Barth. De P.R.* XVIII. i. (Bodl. MS.), Here [i.e. ants, bees, etc.] workes beþ sliȝe and sotel. *c* 1440 *Pallad. on Husb.* v. 154 Wher the swarmes dwelle, is craft tespie... Se heer the craft, and truly hit is sligh. *c* 1470 *Gol. & Gaw.* 883 Thai hynt of his harnese, to helyn his wound; Lechis war noght to lait, with sawis sa sle. 1513 DOUGLAS *Æneid* I. Prol. 108 Reid oftair than anis, Weill at ane blenk slee poetry nocht tane ys. 1590 SPENSER *F.Q.* II. ix. 46 Lids deuiz'd of substance sly, That readily they shut and open might. 1721 RAMSAY *Elegy on Patie Birnie* i, In sonnet slee the man I sing.
**3. a.** Of persons: Adept or skilful in artifice or craft; using cunning or insidious means or methods; deceitful, guileful, wily, underhand.
α, β. *a* 1200 *St. Marher.* 12 þu hauest grimliche ibroht mi broðer to grunde, þen slehest deouel of helle. *c* 1275 LAY. 14366 þe worse was þare wel neh, þat to soche game his wel sleh. *c* 1375 *Cursor M.* 731 (Fairf.), þat wyly deuel was ful sley. *a* 1450 MYRC 1401 Wayte þat þow be slegh & fel. *c* 1470 HENRY *Wallace* V. 740 He was full sle, and ek had mony cast. 1535 W. STEWART *Cron. Scot.* I. 281 Ane subtill man and of ingyne richt hie, In all his tyme he wes baith fals and slie. 1724 RAMSAY *Tea-Table Misc.* (1733) I. 85 Little did her auld minny ken What thir slee twa togither were say'n. 1825 BROCKETT *N.C. Gloss.*, *Slee*, sly, cunning.
γ, δ. *c* 1386 CHAUCER *Friar's T.* 24 He hadde a Somonour redy to his hond, A slyer boye was noon in Engelond. 1390 GOWER *Conf.* II. 235, Thei ben slyhe in such a wise That thei be sleihte..Of Fals witnesse bringen inne [etc.]. *c* 1420 *Chron. Vilod.* 381 þus Danes weren fulle fals and slyȝe. *c* 1450 *Pol. Poems* (Rolls) II. 230 The traytours wene they bene so sly, That no mane can hem aspy. 1530 PALSGR. 324/1 Slye, crafty, subtyll, *cautelleux.* *Ibid.*, Slye, wylye, *fyn.* 1579 W. WILKINSON *Confut. Fam. Love* Ep. Ded. *ij b, The subtle assaultes of so slye and cruell enemyes. 1642 ROGERS *Naaman* 16 A master having a slie servant, oft drunken and carelesse. 1676 DRYDEN *Aurengz.* I. i, Some slie Court-Devil has seduc'd your Mind. 1775 SHERIDAN *Rivals* II. i, He was, indeed, a little inquisitive; but I was sly, sir; devilish sly! 1865 *Sat. Rev.* 11 Feb. 162/2 He is slyer, less easy to fix with the responsibility of his actions. 1874 MOTLEY *John of Barneveld* I. ii. 131 Smoothest and sliest of diplomatists.
**b.** Of animals, etc. *to run sly* (see quot. 1845).
1640 SIR W. MURE *Wks.* (S.T.S.) II. 6 This slie fox, hunted from hole to hole. 1667 MILTON *P.L.* IX. 613 So talk'd the spirited sly Snake. 1756 tr. *Keysler's Trav.* (1760) I. 119 Whatever might be his fidelity to the duke, he [a wolf] was very sly and malicious to others. 1776- [see SLY-GOOSE]. 1807 CRABBE *Par. Reg.* II. 29 A sly old fish, too cunning for the hook. 1845 YOUATT *Dog* ii. 38 The Scotch greyhound.., instead of depending on his speed alone,..has recourse to occasional artifices in order to intercept the hare, in sporting language, he runs sly.
**c.** Of looks: Expressive of slyness.
1821 SCOTT *Kenilw.* xxxii, Varney has a sly countenance, and a smooth tongue. 1848 DICKENS *Dombey* xiv, The grim sly faces in the squares and diamonds of the floor-cloth.. peeped out at him with less wicked eyes.
**4. a.** Of actions, things, etc.: Marked or characterized by, displaying or indicating, artifice, craft or cunning; of an insidious or wily nature.
*c* 1380 WYCLIF *Wks.* (1880) 321 Freris bildyng..is comuneliche makid bi slyh robbyngis of þe fend. *c* 1386 CHAUCER *Nun's Priest's T.* 395 A colfox, ful of sly Iniquitee. *c* 1440 CAPGRAVE *Life St. Kath.* IV. 808 Wherfore I thenke a slyere weye to renne, That hir purpos shal not thus encrees. *a* 1548 HALL *Chron.*, *Hen. VI*, 153 By this pratye cautele and slyghe imposture, was the towne..taken. *a* 1586 SIDNEY *Ps.* XXXV. iii, Let their sly witts unwares destruction gett. 1603 KNOLLES *Hist. Turks* (1621) 98 Still disappointing all the slie designes of the Popes. 1671 MILTON *P.R.* II. 115 Satan with slye preface to return Had left him. *a* 1755 WATTS (J.), Envy ..works in a sly and imperceptible manner. 1781 COWPER *Conversation* 744 A mere mask of sly grimace. 1833 HT. MARTINEAU *Berkeley* I. iv. 78 The buyers and sellers will make any kind of sly and circuitous bargain. 1855 MACAULAY *Hist. Eng.* xvii. IV. 69 The Celt found many opportunities of taking a sly revenge.
†**b.** Of words, etc.: Full of duplicity or wile; subtle; disingenuous. *Obs.*
1387 TREVISA *Higden* (Rolls) VII. 371 Wily and sly silogismes. *c* 1400 *Cursor M.* 27998 (Cotton Galba), If þou euer..wowid hir with wordes sleghe. *c* 1440 *Jacob's Well* 150 Thruȝ slye woordys & fayre to make a man wene þat he hath vertu.. whan he hath non. 1567 *Gude & Godlie Ball.* 150 Tak gude keip To thame that cumis to the..With subtell Sermonis slie. 1675 BAXTER *Cath. Theol.* II. v. 88 A sly equivocation, turning the question from the *potentia operata* to the *potentia operans.* 1829 LYTTON *Devereux* II. v, He knows not what sly conclusions may be drawn from his premises.
**5. a.** Marked or characterized by secrecy or stealth; working, moving, etc., in a stealthy or underhand manner. Also of places: Quiet, secret.
*c* 1440 *Promp. Parv.* 472/1 Stalkynge, or soft and sly goynge, *serptura.* 1593 SHAKS. *Rich. II*, I. iii. 150 The slye slow houres shall not determinate The datelesse limit of thy deere exile. 1608 TOPSELL *Serpents* (1658) 699 Slie poyson takes the marrow, and eating fire Burning the bowels warm till all consumed. 1641 MILTON *Ch. Govt.* II. iii, That severe assise of surveying and controuling the privatest and sliest manners of all men. *a* 1764 LLOYD *Poet. Professors* Poet. Wks. 1774 I. 35 At some sly corner in the Strand. 1766 GOLDSM. *Vicar W.* vi, I therefore approached my chair by sly degrees to the fire. 1807 J. BARLOW *Columb.* VII. 184 With..the sly watchword whisper'd from the tongue. 1821 SCOTT *Kenilw.* xix, Thou canst give a friend a sly place at a mask or a revel now. 1895 A. FORBES *Mem. War & Peace* 102 One of a 'sly patrol' which I was accompanying one July morning.
**b.** *slang.* Illicit, illegal; esp. *Austral.* in ***sly grog*** (***seller***, etc.).
1829 H. WIDOWSON *Present State of Van Diemen's Land* iv. 24 To these [inns] also, I believe, I may add a like number of 'sly grog shops', as they are called. 1840 T. P. MACQUEEN *Australia* 23 Increased powers ought to be given the magistrates and police to prevent the nuisances usually termed sly grog shops. 1844 *Port Phillip Patriot* 11 July 2/5 An information..against a party for sly grog selling. 1851 MAYHEW *Lond. Lab.* I. 294/2 A sly trade's always the best for paying, and for selling too. 1858 MCCOMBIE *Hist. Victoria* x. 127 Convicts, who erected huts, and became 'sly grog' sellers. 1875 *Melbourne Spectator* 21 Aug. 190/1 Several vendors of sly-grog were fined. 1936 F. CLUNE *Roaming round Darling* xxiv. 265 What a promotion—a sly-grogger to king of the Toko blacks! 1941 BAKER *Dict. Austral. Slang* 68 *Sly-groggery*, a sly-grog shop. 1959 M. SCOTT *White Elephant* xiii. 137 It's a sly-grogging hole and ..I didn't go there. 1969 W. DICK *Naked Prodigal* 64 We were on our way to the sly grog joint to buy a dozen bottles.
**6.** Playfully mischievous or malicious; roguish; waggish.
1764 GRAY *J. T.* 1 When sly Jemmy Twitcher had smugg'd up his face. 1785 BURNS *1st Ep. to J. Lapraik* xiv, A spunk o' Allan's glee, Or Ferguson's, the bauld an' slee.

**1800** Mrs. Hervey *Mourtray Fam.* I. 156 Looking, with a sly wink, at Emma. **1805** N. Nicholls *Corr. w. Gray* (1843) 45 The sly, delicate, and exquisitely elegant pleasantry of La Fontaine. **1833** Tennyson *Miller's Daughter* 133 And so it was—half-sly, half-shy, You would, and would not, little one.

**7.** In special collocations, as **sly bread, -bream, -cake, silurus** (see quots.); also †**sly-cap**, a sly or cunning person; **slypuss** [puss 3 b], a cunning or deceitful girl, a minx; so **slypussness**.

**1681** Otway *Soldier's Fort.* iv. i, Ah, villain! Ah, sly-cap! have I caught you? **1836** Yarrell *Brit. Fishes* I. 403 The Sly Silurus, *Silurus glanis.* **1854** Owen in *Orr's Circ. Sci., Org. Nat.* I. 181 The sly-bream (*Sparus insidiator* of Pallas). **1855** [Robinson] *Whitby Gloss., Sly-cakes*, tea-cakes plain and uninviting on the outside, but when eaten are found full of currants and richness within. They are also called Cheats. *a* **1887** *Cassell's Dict. Cookery* s.v., Sly Bread, or Bread Fritters (an economical..sweet dish). **1908** W. De Morgan *Somehow Good* ix. 79 Laetitia, whose speech..appeared to impute insight, or penetration, or sly-pussness..to her young friend. **1942** [see nitwitted *a.*].

**8.** *Comb.*, as *sly-eyed, -looking, -tongued.*

**1967** G. Kelly in *Coast to Coast 1965–6* 97 He hated blonde women—sly-eyed, breasts..undulating above her..tunic. **1795** P. Freneau *Poems* (1902) II. 341 A youngster was order'd to hold himself ready, A sly looking lad that was 'prentice to Snip. **1945** 'G. Orwell' *Animal Farm* vi. 47 He was a sly-looking little man. *c* **1730** Ramsay *Fables, Fox & Rat* 30 Dragon, lord chief treasurer, must pay To sly-tongu'd Fleechy.

**B.** *adv.* In a sly, skilful, or cunning manner; slyly. Also *Comb.*, as *sly-couched, dealing.* Now *rare* or *poet.*

*a* **1300** *Cursor M.* 8420 Þow do him for to foster slei, To be lered him-self to lede. **1370–80** *Visions St. Paul* 125 in *O.E. Misc.* 226 Þe Aungel seide to him ful sleih, 'Þei vsuden Ocur and vsuri'. *a* **1400** *Rom. Rose* 7449 For semblant was so slye wrought, That falsnesse he ne espyed nought. **1628** Feltham *Resolves* i. xxxv, Satan began first hesitations, and his sly-couch'd Oratory. *a* **1802** *Katharine Jaffray* vii. in Child *Ball.* IV. 220/2 Up then spak Lord Faughanwood, An he spak very slee. **1931** H. Belloc *Sonnets & Verse* 80 Wine, bright avenger of sly-dealing wrong.

**C.** *absol.* or as *sb.* **1.** *pl.* Skilful or crafty persons. †Also *sing.*, one who is skilled or cunning.

**1297** R. Glouc. (Rolls) 7405 A monek he sende him in message, & dude as þe sley. *a* **1320** *Sir Tristr.* 271 And euer he dede as þe sleiȝe. *Ibid.* 379 O lond þai sett þat sleiȝe. *c* **1400** *Pride of Life* in *Non-Cycle Myst. Plays* 94 Þou spekis noȝt as þe sleye. *c* **1470** Henry *Wallace* x. 382 On the fyllat full sternly straik that sle.

**2.** *on* (*upon, under,* or *by*) *the sly*, in a secret, clandestine, or covert manner; without publicity or openness; secretly, covertly, stealthily.

(*a*) **1812** J. H. Vaux *Flash Dict.* s.v., Any business transacted, or intimation given, privately, or under the rose, is said to be done *upon the sly.* **1866** Reade *G. Gaunt* (ed. 2) III. 102 A certain farmer's man, who wired hares upon the sly.

(*b*) **1818** Keats *Let.* 18 Dec. (1958) II. 13 It might have been a good joke to pour on the sly bottle after bottle into a washing tub and roar for more. **1825** *Sporting Mag.* XVI. 330 We should find them ever on the 'sly', as it is called. **1851** Mayhew *Lond. Lab.* I. 387/1 They sold it..to ladies that liked a drop on the sly. **1888** Bryce *Amer. Commw.* III. xc. 234 Prominent politicians came to seek favours from him on the sly.

(*c*) **1840** Longf. *Span. Student* iii. v, As soon as you see the planets are out, in with you, and be busy with the ten commandments, under the sly.

(*d*) **1859** Geo. Eliot *A. Bede* vii, Mrs. Poyser..continually gazed at Hetty's charms by the sly. **1861** *Rom. Dull Life* xxx. 218 It seems to me disgraceful to do things by the sly, that you dare not have known.

**sly** (slaɪ), *v. Sc.* and *U.S.* [f. sly *a.*] *intr.* To move, go, etc., in a sly or stealthy manner; to slip unobserved; to slink.

For other Scottish dial. senses, see *Jamieson's Dict.* s.v. *Slee* and *Sly.*

**1825** Jamieson *Suppl.*, To *Sly*, to go or approach silently and slily. **1845** S. Judd *Margaret* i. xi. (1871) 64 She would creep from her room and sly into the street. **1888** *The Advance* (Chicago) 6 Dec., Nobody noticed Caddie slying along to the desk where the teacher had laid the switch.

†**sly**, var. of *sli* slike *a.*, such. *Obs.*

*c* **1375** *Cursor M.* 12052 (Fairf.), Quy dos þou, sone, on sly manere.

**sly**, obs. form of slay *v.*

†**sly-band**, variant of slee-band *Obs.*

**1762** Mills *Pract. Husb.* I. 256 This [Rotherham] plough, of which AB is the beam,..NP the bridle, S the sly-band.

**sly-boot(s.** *colloq.* Also slyboot(s. [f. sly *a.* + boots[1] 3.] A sly, cunning, or crafty person; one who does things on the sly. Freq. in mild or jocular use, and usually in plural form.

*pl. a* **1700** B. E. *Dict. Cant. Crew, Sly-boots*, a seeming Silly, but subtil Fellow. **1701** Cibber *Love Makes a Man* ii. i, Look, look,—look, o' Sly-boots; what, she knows nothing of the Matter! **1774** Goldsm. *Retaliation* 28 That sly-boots was cursedly cunning to hide 'em. **1833** T. Hook *Parson's Dau.* iii. ii, Had there been any body to watch the venerable sly-boots. **1897** Rhoscomyl *White Rose Arno* 49 But, Ithel, you are a slyboots too; pretending to read for the law! *transf.* **1838** Emerson *Address Literary Ethics* Wks. (Bohn) II. 212 Truth is such a flyaway, such a slyboots. **1894** Hall Caine *Manxman* iii. xxi, 'Oh, but the sun is an old sly-boots', she answered. *sing.* ? **1730** Swift *Dan Jackson's Reply* Wks. 1755 IV. i. 256, I much suspect you mean the latter, Ah sly-boot! **1810** *Splendid Follies* I. 97 Yes you do,..you young slyboot, only you won't understand.

**sly-goose.** *Orkney.* Also slygoose. [f. sly *a.* + goose *sb.*] The sheldrake, *Tadorna cornuta* or *T. vulpanser.*

**1776** Pennant *Brit. Zool.* (ed. 2) II. 500 From this instinctive cunning..the natives of the Orknies to this day call them [sheldrakes] the *sly goose.* **1793** *Statist. Acc. Scotl., Orkney* VII. 546 The dunter or eider duck, the sly goose, the awk. **1822** Hibbert *Desc. Shetl. Isl.* 408 The shieldrake, or slygoose, builds in these rabbit burrows.

**sly-grog:** see sly *a.* 5 b.

**slyish** ('slaɪɪʃ), *a.* [f. sly *a.* + -ish.] Somewhat or rather sly; roguish.

**1828** *Mirror* X. 348/2 This chap was a slyish young dog. **1886** Stevenson *Dr. Jekyll & Mr. Hyde* 31 A..smooth-faced man of fifty, with something of a slyish cast perhaps.

**slyly, slily** ('slaɪlɪ), *adv.* Forms: α. 3 slah-, 4 slehliche, sleȝlych; 4–5 sleȝ- (4 sleeȝ-, 5 sleȝe-), 5 sleghly, -li; 4 sleiȝli, 5 -ly; 5–6 sleighely. β. 4–5 slely (5 scle-), 6 slelie; 4 sleyli, -ly; sleili, 5 -ly, 6 -lye, *Sc.* slealie, -lye, 5–6 *Sc.* 8– sleely. γ. 4 slyh-, slihly, 4–5 sliȝli (4–5 -lich), 5 slyȝly, 6 slygh(e)-, slighly. δ. 4 slilich, 4– slily (6 slilye, 7 sliely). ε. 4 slylich, 4– slyly (5 slyely). [f. sly *a.* + -ly[2]. Cf. ON. *slœgliga*, MSw. *slögeliga.*]

**1.** †**a.** Cleverly, skilfully, dexterously; wisely. *Obs.* **b.** Cunningly, artfully; covertly, secretly, stealthily, quietly.

α. *c* **1205** Lay. 8586 He ferde ut of Doure..in to ane muchele slæde & slahliche his folc hudde. ? *c* **1370** Chaucer *Troylus* v. 83 He ful soft and sleighely gan hire seye, 'Now hold youre day'. *c* **1380** *Sir Ferumb.* 3509 Þan þay be-speken how he myȝt Sleȝlych a-scape out of þe syȝt. **1393** Langl. *P. Pl.* C. vii. 107 For to slee hym slehliche slehthes ich by-þenke. *c* **1400** *Destr. Troy* 12690 [Þai] letyn sailes doune slide sleghli & faire. *a* **1425** tr. *Arderne's Treat. Fistula*, etc. 4 Answere he sleiȝly to thingis y-asked, that he be noȝt y-take in his wordes.

β. *a* **1300** *Cursor M.* 9404 In paradis he did him rest, And sleili slepe apon him kest. **1375** Barbour *Bruce* xix. 538 On the ferrer syd Toward thame slely can he ryd. *c* **1400** *Laud Troy Bk.* 913 The lady rauȝte A fair ymage and him by-tauȝte, And bad him sclely with him bere. *c* **1440** *Gesta Rom.* lxxi. 390 (Addit. MS.), Was neuer soule so slely wonne and sauyd. **1513** Douglas *Æneid* i. vi. 77 Slelie with ane knyfe, Or he was war, [he] reft Sicheus the lyfe. **1584** *Leg. Bp. St. Androis* 909 Maister Jhone Dowglass weill can tell, How slealie he deceavit him sell. **1722** Ramsay *Three Bonnets* iv. 5 [She] sleely, when he did appear, About his success 'gan to speer.

γ. *c* **1350** *Will. Palerne* (Roxb.) 29 He slod sliȝli a doun a slepe ful harde. **1390** Gower *Conf.* I. 130 So slihly cam it noght aboute That thei ne ben discoevered oute. **1412–20** Lydg. *Chron. Troy* iv. 4507 Lo, how þe serpent of discord can glyde Ful slyȝly in. *c* **1449** Pecock *Repr.* ii. ix. 194 The feend hath deceyued sliȝli and wijlily men..whiche han worschipid ymagis. *a* **1470** H. Parker *Dives & Pauper* (W. de W. 1496) i. lxiv. 108/2 How pryuely and how slyghely they may begyle her euen crysten. **1580** Sir H. Cobham in *Cal. State Papers, For., Eliz.* 143 [There are ways and means used] slieghly.

δ. **13..** *Cursor M.* 11231 (Gött.), Bot sliliker he come and ȝede. **1387** Trevisa *Higden* (Rolls) II. 41 Me may nouȝt seile by þis swolwe but slily at þe ful see. **1393** Langl. *P. Pl.* C. xii. 266 Dauid þe douhty þat deuynede how vrye Mighte slilokeste be slayn. **1594** Shaks. *Rich. III*, iv. iv. 3 Heere in these Confines slily haue I lurkt. **1676** Hubbard *Happiness of People* 58 Yet doth this sin slily insinuate it self into the heart of the forwardest Professors. **1728** Morgan *Hist. Algiers* II. iv. 273 The Letter dropped under the Bank on which he sate rowing,..but a Spanish Renegado..took it up slily. **1760–72** H. Brooke *Fool of Qual.* (1809) I. 78 They slily crouded behind the door,..ready to issue, in an instant. **1833** Ht. Martineau *Charmed Sea* vii. 111 But would they not be slily kept for money? **1869** Swinburne *Ess. & Stud.* (1875) 205 The Chorus, secretly reassured and slily hopeful. *transf.* **1651** Davenant *Gondibert* iii. ii. 17 Beneath that shade Two Rivers slily steal. **1686** J. Moyle *Abstract Sea Chyrurg.* x. 113 A Catarrh is a Rhume that has taken a habit of trickling slily down the *Aspera arteria.*

ε. *c* **1385** Chaucer *L.G.W.* 2045 *Ariadne*, So slyly & so wel I shal me gye. **1387** Trevisa *Higden* (Rolls) I. 91 Þey feyneþ for to flee..þat þey mowe þe slyloker here enemyes wynne and slee. *a* **1450** Myrc 554 Thenne moste þou slyly Aske of hem [etc.]. **1474** Caxton *Chesse* iv. ii. (1883) 168 Hit is necessarye that he goo temperatly and slyly. **1509** Barclay *Shyp of Folys* (1570) 190 Death dayly stealeth slyly on thee. **1593** Shaks. *3 Hen. VI*, i. i. 3 While we pursu'd the Horsmen of yᵉ North, He slyly stole away. **1624** Gataker *Transubst.* 185 Which he slyly passeth by, and maketh not a word of. **1738** J. Fisher *Value of Divine Truth* (1803) 10 These set themselves in opposition to all Confessions, whether more openly or more slyly. **1812** Crabbe *Tales* xiii. 297 So we can slyly our amusements take. **1848** Mrs. Jameson *Sacr. & Leg. Art* (1850) 87 A boy is slyly appropriating the money which the apostle has thrown down. **1878** *Masque of Poets* 32 Fate follows faster And snares us slyly from behind.

**2.** In a playfully mischievous or malicious manner; with a touch of malice or ridicule; roguishly, waggishly.

**1837** Dickens *Pickw.* xxxi, The clerk winked slily at Mr. Pickwick. **1873** M. Collins *Sq. Silchester's Whim* I. iii. 42 'It might tempt some people', said Mrs. Silchester slyly.

†**3.** Used for slightly *adv.* 4. (Perh. an error.)

**1582** Stanyhurst *Æneis* iv. (Arb.) 103 Why the Lauin regions, and stock, he so slilye reputeth? *Ibid.* 104 You buyld a cittye, youre owne state slilye regarding.

**slyne**, variant of sline *sb.*

**slyness** ('slaɪnɪs). Also 4 slegh-, 5 sleey-, 8–9 *Sc.* slee-, 7 sliness(e. [f. sly *a.* + -ness.] The quality or state of being sly (†or wise).

**1357** *Lay Folks Catech.* 424 The fift vertu..[is] slegh[t]e or sleghness [L. *prudencia*]. **1382** Wyclif *Ecclus.* xix. 22 Ther is certeyn sleeynesse, and it is wicke. *c* **1440** *Promp. Parv.* 459 Slyenesse, *idem quod* sleythe. **1530** Palsgr. 271 Slynesse, *finesse.* **1603** Knolles *Hist. Turks* (1621) 1110 Most good men detesting the lightnes of the one, the ambition of the other, and the slinesse of the third. *c* **1718** Swift *Sheridan's Submission* iv, Then, with wonted wile and slyness, They left me in the lurch. **1791** A. Wilson *Poems & Lit. Prose* (1876) II. 23 In Allan's verse sage sleeness we admire. **1822** Hazlitt *Table-t.* I. iv. 86 The eye turned round to look at you without turning the head indicates generally slyness or suspicion. **1885** *Manch. Exam.* 22 Sept. 5/3 There is a certain slyness and caution about him.

**b.** A sly or covert allusion. *rare.*

**1823** Moore *Fables* ii. 106 And satires at the Court they levelled, And small lampoons, so full of slynesses.

†**slyp.** *Obs.*[-1] (Meaning uncertain.)

**13..** *E.E. Allit. P.* B. 1264 He..brestes vp þe ȝates, [they] Slouen alle at a slyp þat serued þer-inne.

**slype** (slaɪp), *sb. Arch.* [Perhaps a special sense of slipe *sb.*[2], but cf. WFlem. *slipe, slijpe* a secret path.] A covered way or passage, esp. one lying between the transept of a cathedral or monastic church and the chapter-house, and commonly leading out from the cloister.

**1860** M. E. C. Walcott *Cathedrals in U.K.* (ed. 2) 261 The slype is the passage on the south-west side of the nave. **1861** G. G. Scott *Westm. Abbey* 37 It occupies a space which is very frequent in abbeys, intervening between the transept and the entrance to the chapter-house, and often called by the expressive name of 'the slype'. **1865** *Ecclesiologist* XXV. 207 The Slype was the passage which led to the cemetery lying usually between the transept and chapter house. **1884** *19th Cent.* Jan. 104 Where the transept ended there usually came a narrow passage called a slype. **1888** *Daily News* 6 Sept. 6/5 The stones form part of the vaulting of the slype or corridor leading to the old burial ground of the monks.

*attrib.* **1896** *Westm. Gaz.* 11 Sept. 3/1 Examples of twelfth-century work..may be seen on the slype door of the south transept of St. Alban's Abbey.

**slype** (slaɪp), *v. Basket-making.* Also slipe. [Prob. var. slipe *v.*[2]] *trans.* To cut away one side of (a rod or cane) with a long slanting cut, so that it comes to a point. Hence **slype** *sb.*; **slyped** *ppl. a.*; **'slyping** *vbl. sb.*

**1910** *Encycl. Brit.* III. 482/2 If the bottom is made on a hoop the butts of the stakes are 'sliped', *i.e.* cut away with a long cut of the shop-knife, and turned tightly round the hoop; they are then said to be 'scallomed' on. **1912** T. Okey *Introd. Art of Basket-making* vii. 68 Having prepared the stuff, slype six bottom-sticks. *Ibid.* 154 *Slype*, a long cut. **1953** A. G. Knock *Willow Basket-Work* 27 The blackberry basket,..requires a bow of stout rod fitted across the basket..by inserting its slyped ends down into the siding. **1959** D. Wright *Baskets & Basketry* vi. 136 *Slype*, a slanting or flat cut. **1960** E. Legg *Country Baskets* 52 The liners are duly slyped before insertion... Slyping is done whenever you need to shape a rod or cane to fit it snugly and securely against another.

**slyper:** see sword-sliper.

†**slyre.** *Sc. Obs.* [ad. LG. *sleier, slijer*, G. *schleier* fine linen, veil.] A fine kind of linen or lawn. Also *slyre-lawn.*

**1621** *Sc. Acts, Jas. VI* (1816) IV. 626/1 That no persoun..weare vpoun þair bodies tifneis, Cobwebe, Lanes, or Slyires. **1661** *Ibid., Chas. II* (1820) VII. 254 Slyreland [= -lawn] ilk hundreth ells, three ounces.

†**'slyship.** *Obs.*[-1] In 4 sleihschupe, -schipe. [f. sly *a.* + -ship.] Skill, cleverness.

*c* **1320** *Cast. Love* 801 Foure vertues cardinals þer beoþ: þat is, strengþe and sleihschupe [*v.r.* sleihschipe], Rihtfulnesse and worschupe.

**slyte**, obs. form of sleet *sb.*[1]; var. of slite *v.*

**slyther(nesse**, obs. forms of slither(ness.

**smack** (smæk), *sb.*[1] Forms: 1 smæc, 3–4 smac (*Orm.* smacc), 4–6 smak (6 smake), 5–6 smakke, 4–7 smacke, 6– smack. [OE. *smæc*, = OFris. *smek*, MDu. *smac*, MLG. *smak* (LG. *smakk, schmakk*; also Sw. *smak*, Da. *smag*), OHG. and MHG. *smac, smach* (G. dial. *schmack*; cf. G. *geschmack*). Slightly different in formation are OFris. *smaka* (WFris. *smaek*), MDu. *smake* (Kilian *smaeck*; Du. *smaak*), MLG. *smake* (LG. *smâk, schmaak*). See also smatch *sb.*[1]]

**I. 1.** A taste or flavour; the distinctive or peculiar taste of something, or a special flavour distinguishable from this.

*a* **1000** in Wr.-Wülcker 225 *Dulcis sapor, i. dulcis odor*, swete smæc. *c* **1050** *Ibid.* 455 *Nectar*,..þone swetan smæc. *c* **1200** Ormin 1653 Forr witt and skill iss wel inoh þurrh salltess smacc bitacnedd. *Ibid.* 14294 Swa summ þeȝȝ waterr wærenn, Off wikke smacc. **1340** *Ayenb.* 112 Þet is kynges mete huerinne byeþ ech manyere lykinges and alle guode smackes. *a* **1400** *Stockh. Medical MS.* ii. 608 in *Anglia* XVIII. 322 Of henbane arn spycys iij..Alle wyll sauour an hidhows smak. *c* **1475** Henryson *Poems* (S.T.S.) III. 152 It wilbe þe softar and sweittar of þe smak. *a* **1530** *Proverbs* in *Songs, Carols*, etc. (E.E.T.S.) 128 Thowgh peper be blak, it hath a good smak. **1578** Lyte *Dodoens* II. lxxxv. 263 The leaues..are of a very strong and pleasant sauour, and good smacke or taste. **1606** J. Carpenter *Solomon's Solace* xxviii. 118 Those vessels will long retaine and yeeld the smack of that liquor which was in them first steeped. **1675** Evelyn *Terra* (1729) 29 Every plant has a smack of the Root. **1710** T. Fuller *Pharm. Extemp.* 1 Midling Ale..that hath no burnt, musty, or otherwise ill smack. **1761** Churchill *Rosciad* Wks. 1763 I. 24 And Boniface, disgrac'd, betrays the smack..of Falstaff's sack. **1823** J. Badcock *Dom. Amusem.* 21 It possesses a dull, acidulous, offensive smack, and an empyreumatic smell. **1873** Browning *Red Cott. Nt.-cap* 245 And now, for perfume, pour Distilment rare,.. Till beverage obtained the fancied smack.

**b.** *fig.* or in fig. context.

**1340** *Ayenb.* 177 Efterward me ssel lete þane smak of zenne. **1593** in *Lyly's Wks.* (1902) III. 451 Experience bids me..champe the bridle of a bitter smacke. **1690** Dryden *Amphitryon* I. i, He's constant to a handsome family; he knows when they have a good smack with them. **1850** Thackeray *Pendennis* xli, There are works of all tastes and smacks.

†**c.** Pleasant or agreeable taste or relish. *Obs.*

**1573** Tusser *Husb.* (1878) 132 Least Doue and the cadow, there finding a smack, with ill stormie weather doo perish thy stack. **1600** Tourneur *Trans. Metam.* xxix. 202 If this sweet sinne still feedes him with her smacke.

†**2.** Scent, odour, smell. *Obs.*

*a* **1000** [see sense 1]. *c* **1250** *Owl & Night.* 823 Þenne is þes hundes smel fordo; he not þurh þe meynde smak hweþer he schal vorþ þe abak. **1549** E. Allen *Par. Rev.* 19 A cat of y$^{e}$ mountayne.., whiche with her smacke and savour, draweth many beastes unto her.

**3.** *transf.* A trace, tinge, or suggestion *of* something specified.

Common *c* 1570–1680, and in mod. use.

**1539** Cromwell in Merriman *Life & Lett.* (1902) II. 173 To powre in som smak of the pure lernying of Cristes doctrine amonges them. **1577** B. Googe *Heresbach's Husb.* III. (1586) 138b, Whatsoeuer commeth of an olde stocke, hath lightly a smack of his olde parentes imperfection. **1602** *2nd Pt. Return fr. Parnass.* II. vi, Good faith, the boy begins to haue an elegant smack of my stile. **1639** Fuller *Holy War* IV. viii. (1840) 191 The others were suspected to have a smack of the imperial faction. **1688** Holme *Armoury* III. 233/1 The Orcadians..use the Gothish Language, which they derive from the Norwegians,..of whose qualities they still have a smack.

**1845** S. Austin *Ranke's Hist. Reform.* II. 75 Graceful poems—not the less attractive for a slight smack of the workshop. **1874** Burnand *My Time* xxix. 280 A smack of real earnestness in his tone.

†**b.** A slight or superficial knowledge; a smattering. Chiefly in phr. ***to have a smack of, at,*** or ***in*** something. *Obs.*

(*a*) **1551** Robinson tr. *More's Utopia* (1895) 9 If it be one that hath a lytell smacke of learnynge. **1581** Mulcaster *Positions* xxxvii. (1887) 144 Bycause they haue some petie smake of their booke. *c* **1618** Moryson *Itin.* IV. 229 Hauing gott a smacke of the grownds of our lawe. **1685–90** J. Cood *Wonderful Provid.* (1849) 104 A very young man..who had got a smack of the Latin tongue. **1791** Mrs. Radcliffe *Rom. Forest* (1820) I. 66, I learned a smack of boxing of that Englishman.

(*b*) **1579** Lyly *Euphues* (Arb.) 151 Whereby he may.. haue in al sciences a smacke, whereby he may readily dispute of any thing. **1602** *2nd Pt. Return fr. Parnass.* III. i, He hath also a smacke in poetry. **1679** M. Mason *Tickler Tickled* 2 For Padge hath a Smack at Latin, but let them English it that will.

**c.** A mere tasting, a small quantity, *of* liquor; a mouthful. Also *fig.*

**1693** Dryden *Persius* iv. 69 He 'says the wimble, often draws it back, And deals to thirsty servants but a smack. **1759** Garrick *High Life below Stairs* II, He has had a smack of every sort of wine. **1766** Anstey *New Bath Guide* (ed. 2) 135 May I venture to give Her a Smack of my Muse? **1824** W. Irving *Tales Trav.* I. 18 A relish of the Marquis's well-known kitchen, and a smack of his superior Champagne and Burgundy. **1865** J. Hatton *Bitter Sweets* iii, We'll just have one smack of the liquor before you're off to Helswick.

**d.** A touch or suggestion *of* something having a characteristic odour or taste.

**1848** Dickens *Dombey* vii, There was a smack of stabling in the air of Princess's Place. **1886** Stevenson *Silverado Sq.* 34 A rough smack of resin was in the air. **1889** Doyle *Micah Clarke* 320 A gentle breeze, sweet with the smack of the country.

**II.** †**4. a.** The sense or faculty of taste. *Obs.*

So OFris. *smek*, G. (*ge*)*schmack*, etc.

*a* **1200** *Vices & Virtues* 17 Ʒesihthe, ȝeherhþe, smac, and smell, and tactþe.

†**b.** *fig.* Delight or enjoyment; inclination, relish. Chiefly in phrases. *Obs.*

**1340** *Ayenb.* 33 He..to-ualþ ine þa slacnesse þet he ne heþ smak, ne deuocion, wel to done. **1551** Robinson tr. *More's Utopia* II. (1895) 254 So quyckelye they haue taken a smacke in couetesenes. **1580** Lyly *Euphues* (Arb.) 426 Philautus had taken such a smacke in the good entertainment. **1609** *Ev. Woman in Hum.* II. i, I haue no appetite at all to live in the countrie.., now, as they say, I have got a smacke on the Cittie. **1620** Shelton *Quix.* III. xi. I. 231 She hath a very great Smack of Courtship, and plays with every one.

**smack** (smæk), *sb.*[2] Also 6 **smacke.** [Related to SMACK *v.*[2] Cf. MDu. *smack* (Kilian *smacke*; Du. and Fris. *smak*), LG. *smacke*, G. dial. *schmacke*; also Da. *smæk*, Sw. *smäck*.]

**1. a.** A sharp noise or sound made by separating the lips quickly, esp. in kissing, and in tasting or anticipating food or liquor.

**1570** Levins *Manip.* 5 Y$^{e}$ smacke of a kisse, *suauium*. **1596** Shaks. *Tam. Shrew* III. ii. 180 Hee..kist her lips with such a clamorous smacke, that at the parting all the Church did eccho. **1679** Dryden *Limberham* I. i, She has a notable Smack with her! I believe Zeal first taught the Art of Kissing close. **1712** Steele *Spect.* No. 508 ⁋3 Tasting the Wine with a judicious Smack. **1739** R. Bull tr. *Dedekindus' Grobianus* 142 The Dogs may lick it with a sav'ry Smack. **1838** D. Jerrold *Men of Character* (1851) 10 She..gave me such a salute, a team two fields away went gallop off at the smack. **1878** Browning *Poets Croisic* 116 With smack of lip, and long-drawn sigh through teeth Close clenched o'er satisfaction.

**b.** A loud or sounding kiss.

**1604** T. M. *Black Bk.* in *Middleton's Wks.* (Bullen) VIII. 24 The slave..bussed the bawd for joy: when presently I left them in the midst of their wicked smack. **1651** J. Cleveland *Poems* 2 Love prints her Signets in her smacks, Those Ruddy drops of squeezing wax. **1729** Gay *Polly* II. ix, Come, noble captain, take one hearty smack upon her lips, and then steer off. **1786** Mrs. A. M. Bennett *Juvenile Indiscr.* I. 97 Giving the females first a warm smack round. **1815** Scott *Guy M.* xxiv, 'Whisht! whisht! gudewife,' said her husband, with a smack that had much more affection than ceremony in it.

*transf.* **1809** Malkin *Gil Blas* II. viii. ⁋3 Bestowing such hearty smacks upon the bottle, as to empty it very shortly.

**2.** The crack *of* a whip, lash, etc.

**1781** Cowper *Expost.* 519 Thy soldiery..Were train'd beneath his lash, and knew the smack. **1803** tr. *P. Le Brun's Mons. Botte* II. 10 Five or six smacks of a whip roused their attention. **1825** *Sporting Mag.* XVII. 36 Old coachmen.. like a smack of the whip. **1901** *Daily Express* 28 Feb. 6/7 At the first swishing smack of the lash.

**3. a.** A sounding blow delivered with the flat of the hand or something having a flat surface; a slap.

Also *fig.* ***a smack in the face***, a sharp rebuff; ***a smack in the eye***.

*c* **1746** J. Collier (Tim Bobbin) *View Lanc. Dial.* (1775) 58 Th' bigger rascot should ha' th' bigger smacks on moor on um. **1789** Wolcot (P. Pindar) *Ep. to falling Minis.* Wks. 1812 II. 127 Just now and then a gentle smack To inform his Royal Colt what Being rode him. **1827** G. Higgins *Celtic Druids* 128 A naughty or saucy boy, at school, often gets a smack on the face. **1886** Stevenson *Kidnapped* iii, He jumped up..and hit me a smack upon the shoulder. **1895** A. W. Pinero *Second Mrs. Tanqueray* III. 105 One gets so many smacks in the face through interfering in matrimonial squabbles. **1930** A. P. Herbert *Water Gipsies* viii. 84 'I'm leaving here.' 'Leaving us, Mr. Bryan?' Jane thought 'Oh, Lord, another smack in the face!' **1941** Baker *Dict. Austral. Slang* 68 *Smack in the eye, a*, a disappointment, a refusal, a rebuff. **1949** E. Coxhead *Wind in West* vii. 191 Well, but it was a nice smack in the face! To keep him, with all his experience..so completely in the dark. **1958** I. Cross *God Boy* xii. 98, I could tell that what he said was supposed to be a smack in the eye for me.

**b.** A vigorous or powerful hit with a cricket-bat.

**1875** *Lillywhite's Cricketers' Ann.* 26 Two tremendous 'smacks' over the chains sent the crowd into raptures.

**c.** *colloq.* A slap or go *at* something.

**1889** *Pall Mall G.* 30 Dec. 2/2, I am longing to have a smack at these Matabeles.

†**4.** (See quot.) *Obs.*$^{-1}$

**1798** Jane Austen *Lett.* (1884) I. 169 The ball on Thursday was a very small one indeed, hardly so large as an Oxford Smack.

**5.** *Comb.*, as **smackwarm** *nonce-wd.* (see quot.).

**1922** Joyce *Ulysses* 262 She let free..her nipped elastic garter smackwarm against her smackable woman's warmhosed thigh.

**smack** (smæk), *sb.*[3] *Naut.* Also 7 **smacke.** [prob. a. Du. *smak*, earlier *smacke* (Kilian), = LG. *smakke*, *smak* (Da. *smakke*, Sw. *smacke*), G. *schmack*(*e*. The source, and the relation to F. *semaque*, Sp. *esmaque*, Pg. *sumaca*, are uncertain.]

**1.** A single-masted sailing-vessel, fore-and-aft rigged like a sloop or cutter, and usually of light burden, chiefly employed as a coaster or for fishing, and formerly as a tender to a ship of war.

**1611** [see 2]. **1684** E. Chamberlayne *Pres. St. Eng.* II. (ed. 12) 245 The Gravesend Smack. **1689** *Lond. Gaz.* No. 2468/4 Yesterday came in here a Ketch and a small Smack from the Fleet. **1696** *Phil. Trans.* XIX. 350 Plenty of large Soals, taken in Troul-Nets, the Smacks being under Sail trailing them along. **1740** Woodroofe in Hanway *Trav.* (1762) I. II. xvii. 74 They had..on the stocks..five smacks of one hundred and eighty tons. **1750** Blanckley *Naval Expos.* 150 Smacks are necessary Transporting Vessels, with one Mast and half Spreet-sail. **1801** Nelson 4 Aug. in Nicolas *Disp.* (1845) IV. 440 Pray send one of the Smacks to Hosely Bay with my letter to Sir Edward Berry. **1827** O. W. Roberts *Voy. Centr. Amer.* 169 A small smack of about fifteen tons burden. **1877** Black *Green Past.* xxix, Not dangerously for ourselves, but for the anchored schooners and smacks.

**b.** *U.S.* A fishing-vessel having a well in which fish may be kept alive.

*a* **1891** *Fisherman's Memorial Bk.* 70 (Cent.), Many of them were made into smacks, so-called, which was done by building a water-tight compartment amidships, and boring holes in the bottom to admit salt-water, and thus the fish were kept alive.

**2.** *attrib.*, as ***smack commander, -master, -owner***; ***smack-load***; ***smack-sail, vessel***, etc.; **smack-boat** *U.S.*, = sense 1 b (*Cent. Dict.*).

**1611** Cotgr., *Catepleure*,..a smacke, or mizzen sayle. **1683** Hedges *Diary* 25 Aug. I. 105, 2 Sloops of about 25 Ton apiece, with Smack Sailes. **1688** Sir C. Shovel in *Naval Chron.* VI. 32, I may have..some other smack vessell. **1737** J. Chamberlayne *St. Gt. Brit.* (ed. 33) II. 67 A Smack Commander. **1750** Blanckley *Naval Expos.* 149 Shoulder of Mutton, Square, Lugg, and Smack Sails. **1871** *Daily News* 22 Sept., The principal ship-owners and smack-owners of the port of Ipswich. **1885** *Manch. Exam.* 4 Feb. 4/7 Three Yarmouth smackmasters charged with piracy on the high seas. **1888** Goode *Amer. Fishes* 94 In the year 1831 ..a smack-load of Scuppaugs arrived in Boston.

**smack** (smæk), *sb.*[4] *slang* (orig. *U.S.*). [Prob. alteration of SCHMECK.] A drug, *spec.* heroin.

**1942** Berrey & Van den Bark *Amer. Thes. Slang* §509/8 *Smack*,..a small packet of drugs. **1960** R. G. Reisner *Jazz Titans* 164 *Smack*, heroin. **1964** *N.Y. Times Mag.* 23 Aug. 64/2 Cocaine..referred to as..*smack*. **1968** *Sunday Truth* (Brisbane) 6 Oct. 36/3 When I first came here you were a big swinger if you turned on with pot. Now they're going straight on to smack (another slang word for heroin). **1969** *Oz* May 36/1 In the paper today it said that Jimmy Hendrix got busted for smack. **1976** R. Condon *Whisper of Axe* II. vii. 208 She began by having the smack pushers recruit from 53 street gangs. **1980** P. Kinsley *Vatchman Switch* xii. 91 You're dealing and..I'm going to prove it. You're into opium and smack.

**smack** (smæk), *v.*[1] Also 4, 6–7 **smacke**, 4–5 **smakke.** [f. SMACK *sb.*[1] Cf. MHG. *smacken* (G. *schmacken*), NFris. *smak*, Icel. *smakka* (from G.). For variant forms see SMAKE *v.* and SMATCH *v.*]

**1.** *trans.* Of persons: To perceive by the sense of taste. †Also *fig.*, to experience; to suspect.

**1340** *Ayenb.* 93 Huo þet hedde wel ytasted and ysmacked þe ilke zuetnesse þet god yefþ to his urendes. *Ibid.* 106 Huanne þe man onderuangþ þise yefþe he..smackeþ and uelþ þe zuetnesse of god. *a* **1550** *Image Hypocr.* I. 48 in *Skelton's Wks.* (1843) II. 414/1 We..Must sey that white is blacke, Or elles they sey we smacke, And smell we wote not what. **1591** Greene *Conny Catch.* I. Wks. (Grosart) X. 17 If he smack the setter, and smels a rat by his clawing,..then away goes the setter. **1648** Hexham II, *Smaecken ende Proeven*, to Tast, or to Smack a proofe of wine, &c. **1827** Carlyle *Germ. Rom.* I. 175 He soon smacked the taste of physic hidden in this sweetness.

**2.** *intr.* Of food, liquor, etc.: To taste (well or ill); to have a (specified) taste or flavour; to taste or savour *of* something.

**1398** Trevisa *Barth. De P.R.* VII. lxix. (Bodl. MS.), Som bitter þinges..þat smakkeþ [1495 smackyth] of aloye. **1530** Palsgr. 722/1 This veneson smacketh to moche of the pepper. **1573** Barret *Alv.* s.v., [It] Smacketh like pepper. **1648** Hexham II, *Smaeckelick*, that Smacks, Savours, or Tasts well. **1755** Smollett *Quix.* (1803) IV. 271 Your fingers smack of vinegar! **1846** *Edin. Rev.* LXXXIV. 175 The best Xeres that ever smacked of the skin. **1860** Tyndall *Glac.* I. xi. 73 Tea..had been left a whole night in contact with its leaves, and smacked strongly of tannin.

*fig.* **1596** Shaks. *Merch. V.* II. ii. 18 Indeede my Father did something smack, something grow too; he had a kinde of taste. [**1813** Scott *Let.* in *Lockhart* (1837) III. ii. 64 Our little friend..is, notwithstanding his many excellent qualities, a little on the score of old Gobbo—doth somewhat smack—somewhat grow to.]

**b.** *fig.* To partake or savour *of*, to be strongly suggestive or reminiscent *of*, something.

Very common in the 19th cent.

**1595** Shaks. *John* I. i. 208 He is but a bastard to the time That doth not smacke of obseruation, And so am I whether I smacke or no. **1603** —— *Meas. for M.* II. ii. 5 All Sects, all Ages smack of this vice. **1657** W. Morice *Coena quasi Κοινὴ* v. 60 An argument smacking more of the Beast than rational Creature. **1748** Thomson *Castle Indol.* I. vi. 53 Whate'er smacked of 'noyance, or unrest, Was far far off expelled. **1778** Han. More *Florio* I. 177 A mass of knowledge, Which smacks of toil, and smells of college. **1858** J. B. Norton *Topics* 147 On the other hand, however, this scheme smacks of centralization. **1892** G. S. Layard *C. Keene* iii. 65 It was part of his nature to love everything that smacked of antiquity.

**c.** With adjectival complement.

**1847** Disraeli *Tancred* VI. v, He always calls her a moon or a star; that smacks nocturnal and somewhat sombre.

†**3.** To have a trial *at* something. *Obs.*

*a* **1653** G. Daniel *Idyll.* v. 69 He smacks at everie Science; and præscribes Rules as he had Quarter'd 'em, into Tribes.

**smack** (smæk), *v.*[2] Also 6–7 **smacke.** [Corresponds to MDu. and MLG. *smacken* (Du. and LG. *smakken*, Fris. *smakke*), G. dial. *schmacken*, prob. of imitative origin.]

**1. a.** *trans.* To open or separate (the lips) in such a way as to produce a sharp sound; to do this in connexion with eating or drinking, esp. as a sign of keen relish or anticipation.

**1557** Seager *Sch. Vertue* in *Babees Bk.* 344 Not smackynge thy lyppes As comonly do hogges. **1736** Ainsworth I, To smack one's lips, *labiis strepitum edere*. **1826** Disraeli *V. Grey* VI. i, As he smacked his lips after dashing off his glass. **1861** Hughes *Tom Brown at Oxf.* xli, Tom..smacked his lips over the long-necked glass. **1872** Darwin *Emotions* viii. 214 The Australians smacked and clacked their mouths at the sight of his horses.

**b.** *intr.* or *absol.* Also with *at*.

**1608** Sylvester *Du Bartas* II. iv. III. *Schisme* 744 The King..Dreams of the dainties he hath had yer-while, Smacks, swallows, grindes both with his teeth and jaws. **1675** Han. Woolley *Gentlew. Comp.* 71 Do not smack like a Pig, nor make any other noise which shall prove ungrateful to the company. **1760–2** Goldsm. *Cit. W.* lxxi, She had praised detestable custard, and smacked at wretched wine. *a* **1764** Lloyd *Fam. Ep. to Friend* 280 Wks. (1790) 280 In vain I taste, and sip and smack, I find no favour of the Sack. **1840** Thackeray *Shabby-genteel Story* iii, *Mr. Gann.* (Smacks.) 'A fine fruity wine as ever I tasted.'

*fig.* *a* **1677** Barrow *Serm.* (1687) I. xvii. 248 He that pleasingly relisheth and smacketh at it, or expresseth a delightfull complacence therein,..is a sharer in the guilt.

**c.** *trans.* To taste (wine or liquor) with keen relish or satisfaction.

Perh. influenced by or confused with SMACK *v.*[1]

**1822** W. IRVING *Braceb. Hall* vii. (1877) 65 Said the general..as he smacked a glass of rich burgundy. **1848** THACKERAY *Van. Fair* xxi, George,..filling himself a glass of wine, smacked it. **1850** —— *Pendennis* viii, 'But of course', added the Major, smacking the wine [etc.].

**2. a.** To kiss noisily or loudly. Now *Obs.* or *dial.*

**1570** LEVINS *Manip.* 5/28 To smacke, kisse, *suauiare.* **1570-6** LAMBARDE *Peramb. Kent* (1826) 288 Abusing the lips ..in smacking and kissing the upper leather of an olde shoe, reserved for a Relique. **1586** WARNER *Alb. Eng.* I. II. x. 73 God blesse thee Mouse the Bridegroome sayd, and smakt her on the lips. *a* **1658** CLEVELAND *Old Man Courting* 49 Wks. (1687), Come smack me then my pretty Dear. **1746** FRANCIS tr. *Hor., Sat.* II. v. 134 Your prudent honourable Spouse, It seems, was faithful to her nuptial Vows. But had she..smack'd Her Cully [etc.]. **1807-8** W. IRVING *Salmag.* (1824) 368 Smacking the lips of all fair ladies the which he did meet. **1825** BROCKETT *N.C. Gloss., Smack*, to kiss with a noise.

†**b.** ***to smack calf-skin*** (see quot. 1785). *slang.*

**1785** GROSE *Dict. Vulgar T.* s.v., To smack calves skin, to kiss the book, i.e. to take an oath. *a* **1791** —— *Olio* (1796) 231 But smacking calf-skin to an alibi, I..brought her off. **1818** SCOTT *Hrt. Midl.* xx, Why, I have smacked calf-skin fifty times in England for a keg of brandy.

**3.** To crack (a whip, thong, etc.).

*a* **1700** [implied in *smacking-cove*: see SMACKING *ppl. a.* 1]. **1728** YOUNG *Love of Fame* v. 126 As she guides it [a horse] thro' th' admiring throng, With what an air she smacks the silken thong. **1780** *Mirror* No. 84, The noise of somebody below, who hooted and hollow'd, smacked his whip. **1826** W. ROBINSON in J. A. Heraud *Voy. & Mem. Midshipm.* xi. (1837) 194 The whip is of very great length..; it requires both hands to smack it. **1843** LEFEVRE *Life Trav. Phys.* I. ix. I. 197 The four postilions smacked their whips in concert.

*absol.* **1812** COMBE *Syntax, Picturesque* XXII. 208 The coachman smack'd, and off they bounc'd.

**4.** To bring, put, or throw *down* with a smack or slap; to clap (the hands) *together*; to slam (a door) *to*. Also *fig.*

**1801** tr. *Gabrielli's Mysterious Husb.* II. 200 The attending servant having smacked to the door, they drove off in a moment. **1834** DE QUINCEY *Autob. Sk.* Wks. 1853 I. 73, I smacked my little kingdom of Gombroon down into the tropics. **1857** HUGHES *Tom Brown* I. iv, Says the guard, smacking his hand down on his knee. **1871** MEREDITH *H. Richmond* v. (1889) 44 He smacked his hands together.

**5. a.** To strike (a person, part of the body, etc.) with the open hand or with something having a flat surface; to slap. Also *spec.* to chastise (a child) in this manner and *fig.*

**1835** DICKENS *Seven Dials* in *Bell's Life* 27 Sept. 1/1 Mrs. A. smacks Mrs. B.'s child for 'making faces'. **1840** THACKERAY *Shabby-genteel Story* ii, The unfeeling girl.. never offered to smack her mamma's hands,..or to restore her with a glass of water. **1856** F. E. PAGET *Owlet of Owlst.* 167 Won't she smack you all over? **1881** BESANT & RICE *Chapl. of Fl.* I. iv, He smacked his leg with his hand, and burst out laughing. **1892** G. B. SHAW *Let.* 12 Aug. (1965) I. 359 Smacking Bebel & Singer in the eye for their *dénigrement* of our programme. **1918** E. POUND *Let.* 1 Jan. (1971) 127, I liked your comment p. 89, Nov. no. Naturally pleased to see the folk song idea smacked again. **1976** *Evening Post* (Nottingham) 14 Dec. 18/9 It appeared to have been put there by her two-year-old son, who had been smacked for moving things about the house.

**b.** To hit (a ball) vigorously with a cricket-bat. Also *absol.*

**1882** *Daily Telegr.* 24 June, Steel supplemented this by smacking the same bowler to the on for a quartette. **1894** GALE *Cricket Songs* 59 The Champion smacked, and the Terror's reign Could not bring his wicket under.

**c.** ***to smack it about*** (see quot. 1962). *Naut. slang.*

**1914** 'BARTIMEUS' *Naval Occasions* i. 5 Better man your boat from the boom and shove straight off. Smack it about! **1915** —— *Tall Ship* iv. 71 It's three o'clock now, so I advise you to smack it about and clean if you're going ashore. **1962** W. GRANVILLE *Dict. Sailors' Slang* 108/2 *Smack it about!*, naval exhortation to the hands to 'get a move on';..from the smacking of paint brushes about the ship's hull by the side party.

**6.** *intr.* To make or give out a sharp smacking sound; to crack.

**1890** *Fishing Gaz.* 13 Dec. 321/2 Eels are smacking all round in the star-lit water. **1892** LUMSDEN *Sheep-head* 38 The crowd gart muskets smack there.

**7.** Used with adverbial force. **a.** With, or as with, a smack; suddenly and violently; slap. Also with *down, through*, etc.

**1782** COWPER *John Gilpin* 41 Smack went the whip, round went the wheels. **1799** GEO. [IV] in *Paget Papers* (1896) I. 150 He..tumbled..smack on his face. **1806** H. SIDDONS *Maid, Wife, & Widow* II. 101 Smack comes a ball from the enemy and carries away his head. **1836** T. HOOK *G. Gurney* I. 239 So away I went—smack bang into a quaker's shop to buy myself a pair of gloves. **1863** W. C. BALDWIN *Afr. Hunting* v. 141 As I ducked under on the lower side he came smack through.

**b.** Completely, entirely; directly.

**1828** WHEWELL in Todhunter *Acc. Writ.* (1876) II. 90 We have got a decision which is smack against us. **1857** MRS. MATHEWS *Tea-Table T.* II. 128 The wind being smack in their teeth the greater part of the voyage. **1864** TYTLER *Hist. Scot.* III. 387 [Cardan] made the bishop smack whole in twenty-four hours.

**8.** In *Comb.*, as **smack-bottom**, a childish expression for a smack on the bottom given in chastisement.

**1970** P. LAURIE *Scotland Yard* iii. 89 'Put them down, Pop, or you'll get a smack-bottom.'.. The old man has gone back to babyhood. **1978** K. AMIS *Jake's Thing* xvii. 182 What he needs is a damn good smack-bottom and being told not to be so boring.

**smackable** ('smækəb(ə)l), *a. rare.* [f. SMACK *v.*[2] + -ABLE.] That may be smacked.

**1922** [see *smackwarm* s.v. SMACK *sb.*[2] 5].

**smack-dab,** *adv. U.S. dial.* and *colloq.* Also **smack dab.** [f. SMACK *v.*[2] 7 + DAB *adv.*] Exactly, precisely; with a smack. Cf. SLAP-DAB *adv.*

**1892** *Dialect Notes* I. 232 He hit him smack dab in the mouth. **1893** H. A. SHANDS *Some Peculiarities of Speech in Mississippi* 75 *Smack-dab*, a term used by all classes, but more especially by the uneducated, to mean *exactly, precisely*; as, 'I hit him *smack-dab* in the face'. **1934** D. RUNYON in *Collier's* 3 Mar. 8/2 The old King tumbles smack-dab into the street. **1949** H. HORNSBY *Lonesome Valley* 16 He gave a little hop and landed smack-dab in the water. **1953** *Sun* (Baltimore) 30 Apr. (ed. B) 19/6 An April rain fell today where no man..would have dared tread last night—smack dab between the bristling New York Yankees and St. Louis Browns. **1967** *Boston Globe* 18 May 27/2 The university trustees apparently want to put it [*sc.* a university] smack-dab into Copley sq. **1970** N. ARMSTRONG et al. *First on Moon* xiii. 321 Here was the LM..right smack dab where it should have been. **1979** *United States 1980/81* (Penguin Travel Guides) 395 Whether you want to be..smack-dab downtown,..or conveniently near Lambert Field Airport, quality hotels are available.

**'smacker,** *sb.*[1] *rare*$^{-0}$. [f. SMACK *v.*[1]] One who takes, or has, a smack or taste.

**1648** HEXHAM II, *Een Smaecker*, a Taster, a Smacker, or a Savourer.

**'smacker** ('smækə(r)), *sb.*[2] [f. SMACK *v.*[2]]

**1.** One who, or that which, smacks or gives a smack; one who kisses loudly.

**1611** COTGR., *Baiseur*, a kisser, smoutcher, smacker. **1860** WORCESTER, *Smacker*, one who, or that which, smacks.

**2.** A smack.

**1775** ASH, *Smacker*, a loud kiss; a smart sounding blow. **1847-** in *Eng. Dial. Dict.*

**3.** *slang* (orig. *U.S.*). A coin or note of money; *spec.* a dollar; a pound.

**1920** *Chicago Herald & Examiner* 2 Jan. 14/2 Along comes Earl Gray and knocks off the U.S. treasury for 13,000,000 smackers. **1924** WODEHOUSE *Bill the Conqueror* xvi. 261, I asked him to lend me a hundred smackers. **1928** [see GRAFT *sb.*[5] a]. **1935** C. W. T. CRAIG *Paraguayan Interlude* xxvi. 302 'I will give you a thousand beautiful smackers for your church.'.. Mac took out a thousand peso bill and handed it to me. **1937** C. W. PARMENTER *Kings of Beacon Hill* I. x. 70 Easy to touch, too, whether for a cigarette or a hundred smackers. **1946** F. SARGESON *That Summer* 86, I gave him a couple of smackers. **1953** R. LEHMANN *Echoing Grove* 205 Could I touch you for a smacker? I'm stony broke. **1968** *Landfall* XXII. 42, I wouldn't mind a few smackers. Enough for a case of whisky. **1979** 'L. BLACK' *Penny Murder* i. 5 'Gone at twelve thousand pounds.'.. Twelve thousand smackers for a tray of old coins. Whew!

†**'smacker,** *sb.*[3] *Obs.*$^{-1}$ In 6 smaker. [Cf. next.] Smack, taste, savour. In quot. *fig.*

**1549** LATIMER *5th Serm. bef. Edw. VI*, P vj, They felte y[e] smaker of thys worlde, a perillous thing.

†**'smacker,** *v. Obs.*$^{-0}$ [f. SMACK *v.*[2] Cf. G. dial. *schmackern.*] To kiss; to smack the lips.

**1598** FLORIO, *Baciare*, to kisse, to smacker. *Ibid., Biassciare*, to smack or smacker in chawing.

†**'smackering,** *vbl. sb.*[1] *Obs.* Also 6 smak-. [perh. an alteration of SMATTERING *vbl. sb.*, after SMACK *sb.*[1] or *v.*[1]; but cf. SMACKER *sb.*[3]]

**1.** A slight or superficial knowledge *in* or *of* something; a smattering.

**1579** TOMSON *Calvin's Serm. Tim.* 286/1 When a man beginneth to haue some taste and smakering in any matter whatsoeuer, he thinketh himselfe a greate doctour. **1586** T. B. *La Primaud. Fr. Acad.* (1589) 3 After he had indifferently taught his schollers the Latine toong, and some smackering of the Greeke. **1622** MABBE tr. *Aleman's Guzman d' Alf.* II. 268, I haue some little smackering also in the Liberall Arts. **1644** BULWER *Chiron.* 112 As the Satyrist scoffes at those who had a smackering of the Greeke Tongue.

**2.** An inclination *towards*, a hankering or longing *after* or *for*, a person or thing.

*a* **1586** SIDNEY *Arcadia* II. (Sommer) 106 Mopsa (who already had had a certaine smackring towardes me). **1633** FORD *Love's Sacr.* II. i, The duke has a smackering towards you. **1662** COKAINE *Trag. Ovid* V. iii, I must confess I have some smackering that way. **1687** MIÈGE *Gt. Fr. Dict.* II, To have a smackering after a Thing. **1727** BAILEY (vol. II) s.v., To have a Smackering for a Thing, to long for it.

†**'smackering,** *vbl. sb.*[2] *Obs.*$^{-0}$ [f. SMACKER *v.*] (See quots.)

**1598** FLORIO, *Bacio*, a kisse, a smackering. *Ibid., Bichiacco*, a smack or smackring with the toong. *Bichiacchie*, iestes, toyes,..flim-flam tales, smackrings.

**smackeroo** (ˌsmækə'ruː). *slang* (orig. and chiefly *U.S.*). [f. SMACKER *sb.*[2]: see -EROO.] Used in senses of SMACKER *sb.*[2]: a coin or note of money; a kiss; a blow. Also as *int.*

*Amer. Speech* (1942) XVII. 14/1 gives citations of *smackeroo* 'dollar' used on U.S. radio programmes in 1940 and 1941.

**1942** BERREY & VAN DEN BARK *Amer. Thes. Slang* §29/2 *Something excellent*..smackeroo. *Ibid.* §559/16 *Silver dollar* ..smacker,..smackeroo. *Ibid.* §702/1 *Blow*..smackeroo. **1951** P. BRANCH *Lion in Cellar* ix. 102 She grimps up the ladder... And what happens?.. *Smackeroo!* **1961** S. PRICE *Just for Record* viii. 71, I got out the crisp crackling smackeroos and counted out two hundred of them. **1964** C. CHAPLIN *Autobiogr.* xvii. 300 You're getting the Legion of Honour, kid... That's the wrong colour—that's what they give to school-teachers; you don't get the smackeroos on the cheek for that one. **1977** 'E. V. CUNNINGHAM' *One-Penny Orange* (1978) vii. 90 The price is eight thousand pounds, and the pound was five dollars then, so that makes it forty thousand smackeroos.

**'smackful.** [f. SMACK *sb.*[3]] As much or as many as a (fishing-) smack can hold or carry.

**1890** *Pall Mall G.* 25 June 2/1 When he went to Bremen with a smackful of fish.

**'smacking,** *sb.* [f. SMACK *sb.*[3], after *shipping.*] *attrib.* Owning or employing smacks.

**1887** *Standard* 16 Mar. 3/4 Members of large smacking firms.

**smacking** ('smækɪŋ), *vbl. sb.*[1] [f. SMACK *v.*[1]] The action of tasting; a taste, etc.

**1648** HEXHAM II, *Een Proevinge*, a Proving, a Tasting, or a Smacking. **1847** TENNYSON *Princ.* Prol. 89 Strange was the sight and smacking of the time.

**smacking** ('smækɪŋ), *vbl. sb.*[2] [f. SMACK *v.*[2]] The action of the vb. in various senses; kissing, or the sound made by this.

**1628** EARLE *Microcosm.* (Arb.) 41 His smacking of a Gentle-woman is somewhat too sauory. **1632** J. HAYWARD tr. *Biondi's Eromena* 22 He heard..the smacking of their kisses. **1668** DRYDEN *Even. Love* Prol. 10 Like the faint smackings of an after-Kiss. **1841** HOOD *Tale of a Trumpet* 492 Smacking of vulgar lips. **1870** R. BROUGH *Marston Lynch* ii. 10 A little hard smacking occasionally would be no bad discipline.

*attrib.* **1897** *Allbutt's Syst. Med.* II. 689 From time to time it makes a peculiar smacking noise with its lips.

**'smacking,** *ppl. a.* [f. as prec.]

**1.** That smacks, in senses of the vb.

**1592** R. D. *Hypnerotomachia* 94 b, My minde still fixed upon delightfull pleasures and their smacking kisses. **1598** FLORIO, *Baciózzo*, a smacking kisse. *a* **1700** B. E. *Dict. Cant. Crew, Smacking-cove*, a Coachman. *a* **1704** T. BROWN *Lett. to Gentl. & Ladies* Wks. 1709 III. II. 91 Thou hast the daintiest of smacking Lips in the Universe. **1715** POPE *2nd Ep. to Miss Blount* 26 Some Squire..Who..presents you birds, Then gives a smacking buss, and cries,—'No words!' **1896** A. MORRISON *Child Jago* 131 Leary's great fists shot into his face with smacking reports.

**2.** Of a breeze: Blowing strongly or vigorously; spanking.

**1820** W. IRVING *Sketch Bk.* (1859) 6 The wind was blowing a smacking breeze, and we were going at a great rate. **1840** R. H. DANA *Bef. Mast* xxvii, We had a smacking breeze for several hours.

**3.** *dial.* Exceptionally or unusually large or fine.

**1888** *Berks. Gloss.* 150 Ther' be zome smackin' big apples on our tree. **1892** P. H. EMERSON *Son of Fens* 175 You've got some smacking load on there.

Hence **'smackingly** *adv.*

**1598** FLORIO, *Basciuccare*, to kisse smackingly. **1611** COTGR., *Suçoter*, to sucke gently, and smackingly.

†**smackly,** *adv. Obs.*$^{-1}$ [irreg. f. SMACK *sb.*[2] + -LY[2].] With a smack or loud kiss.

**1582** STANYHURST *Æneis* I. (Arb.) 40 Queene Dido shal col the, and smacklye bebasse thee.

**'smacksman.** [SMACK *sb.*[3]] One of the crew of a smack, esp. of a fishing-smack; the owner of a smack.

**1883** *St. James's Gaz.* 21 Dec. 6/1 As the object of the smacksman is to clear his ship and start again. **1890** CLARK RUSSELL *Marriage at Sea* vi, A smacksman who has fished in the North Sea in winter.

**smack-smooth,** *a.* and *adv.* Chiefly *dial.* or *colloq.* Also **smack smooth.** [f. SMACK *v.*[2] 7 + SMOOTH *a.*]

**1.** *adj.* Perfectly smooth, level, or even with the surface. Now *dial.*

**1755** SMOLLETT *Quix.* IV. 29 Their faces smack-smooth as if they had been clean shaven. **1798** *Spirit Public Jrnls.* (1799) II. 29 In fine, the bleeding trunk, smack smooth, with the head only remaining to the body, was immersed in the styptic. **1867** SMYTH *Sailor's Word-bk.* 634 *Smack-smooth*, level with the surface; said of a mast which has gone by the board. **1877** *N.W. Linc. Gloss.* 229/1 Why, it's as smack-smooth as a gress-plat.

**b.** *U.S.* (See quot.)

**1848** BARTLETT *Dict. Amer.* 409 *Smack smooth*, at the West, a term applied to land which is thoroughly cleared.

**2.** As complement or *adv.* So as to leave a smooth or level surface.

**1788** DIBDIN *Poor Jack* i, Though the tempest top gallant mast smack smooth shall smite. **1833** T. HOOK *Parson's Dau.* I. i, My master..hated trees; down he had them smack, smooth. **1837** MARRYAT *Dog-Fiend* xxix, A hurricane swept us smack smooth fore and aft.

**b.** *fig.* Smoothly; without any impediment or obstruction.

**1802** H. MARTIN *Helen of Glenross* I. 188 A tour in former times was pleasant enough; went on smack smooth, except a rough road, now and then an Alps, or a Pyrenees.

**c.** *dial.* In a reckless or random manner; recklessly.

**1847-** in Lincolnshire dial.

**smad,** *v. Sc. rare.* [Cf. LG. *smaddern* (G. dial. *schmaddern*) to befoul, f. *smadder* (*schmadder*) mud, filth.] *trans.* To cover with dirt or grime; to stain, discolour.

Jamieson (1808) also gives *Smad* 'a stain of any kind'.

*c* **1450** HOLLAND *Howlat* 825 The barde, smaddit lyke a smaik smorit in a smedy, Ran fast to the dure, and gaif a gret rair. **1808** in JAMIESON.

**smahan** ('smæhən, ‖'smahan). *Anglo-Ir.* [ad. Ir. *smeathán*.] A drop (to drink); a taste or nip.

**1914** JOYCE *Dubliners* 117 Pony up, boys. We'll have just one little smahan more. **1961** 'F. O'BRIEN' *Hard Life* iii. 21 That reminds me—I think I deserve a smahan. Where's my crock?

**smaik.** *Sc.* Now *arch.* Also 6 **smaike, smayk, smaick, smak(e.** [perh. ad. MDu. or MLG. *smēker*, *smeiker* (= OHG. *smeichâri*, G. †*schmeicher*), f. *smēken*, *smeiken* to flatter.] A low, mean, or contemptible fellow; a rascal, rogue.

*c* **1450** [see SMAD *v.*]. **1513** DOUGLAS *Æneid* VIII. Prol. 133 Quod I, Smak, lat me sleip; sym skynnar the hing. **1546** *St. Papers Hen. VIII* (1836) V. 571 Quhen I wret to ȝour Lordschip to do for Salmond, I knew nocht þat smaikis falset. **1584** J. CARMICHAEL *Lett.* in *Misc. Wodrow Soc.* (1844) 438 Triumphing over the ministers, and calling them lownes, smaicks, seditious knaves. **1815** SCOTT *Guy M.* xxvi, He was nane o' the smaiks that had been on their quarters on the moss. **1828** —— *F.M. Perth* viii, I thought that smaik's name had been Robert. **1897** PRYDE *Queer Folk* 55 Low-born smaik,..to scandaleese his betters!

*attrib.* **1508** DUNBAR *Tua mariit wemen* 113 Quhen the smy on me smyrkis, with his smake [*v.r.* smaik] smolet. **1525** *Aberdeen Reg.* XV. 613 (Jam.), Smaik carll, I sell lay vpoun thi lyppis.

† **smaikry.** *Sc. Obs. rare.* [f. prec.] Mean or contemptible conduct; roguery, trickery.

**1573** *Satir. Poems Reform.* xxxix. 189 Thair febill smaikrie I think ill to tell, With luik lyke Lyounes, and sa lytill done. **1583** *Leg. Bp. St. Androis* 199 When Holie-glass is deid and rotten, His smaikrie sall nocht be forgett.

**smake,** obs. form of SMACK *sb.*[1]

† **smake,** *v. Obs.* [ME. *smaken* (f. *smak* SMACK *sb.*[1]), = OFris. *smakia* (EFris. *smake*), MDu. and Du., MLG. and LG. *smaken* (hence Sw. *smaka*, Da. *smage*); later supplanted by SMACK *v.*[1]]

**1.** *trans.* To perceive by scent or smell.

*c* **1220** *Bestiary* 4 in *O.E. Misc.*, Ðe leun stant on hille, and he man hunten here, Oðer ðurȝ hise nese smel Smake ðat he neȝȝe [etc.].

**2.** *intr.* To smell, give out a (sweet) smell or odour. Also *fig.*, to be redolent *of* something.

*c* **1250** *Gen. & Ex.* 2443 Iosep dede hise lich..riche-like smeren, And spice-like swete smaken. *c* **1315** SHOREHAM I. 1313 The bysschop..seyþ, 'tak and by-come redere Of word þat of god smakeþ [L. *redolet*]. *c* **1440** *Promp. Parv.* 460/2 Smakyn, or smellyn, *odoro*.

**3.** *trans.* To taste, or taste of (something). In quots. *fig.*

*c* **1315** SHOREHAM I. 1600 He hedde y-brout forþe hys bearm-team Wyþ-oute senne i-smaked. *c* **1380** WYCLIF *Sel. Wks.* (1880) III. 411 Suche beggynge moste smake synne, ouþer in hym þat begges, or in hym þat first schulde helpe hym.

**4.** *intr.* To have a (certain) taste.

**14..** LANGL. *P. Pl.* A. v. 207 (MS. U.), Þe hungriest hound..Ne durst lape of þat laueyne so vnloveli it smakith.

**smaker:** see SMACKER *sb.*[3] *Obs.*

**Smal'caldian,** *a.* [-IAN.] = next.

**1679** NESS *Antichrist* 185 The slaughter of the witnesses.. fulfilled in the Smalcaldian war. **1882-3** SCHAFF *Encycl. Relig. Knowl.* I. 323 During the Smalcaldian War the city sustained a long siege with great heroism.

**Smal'caldic,** *a.* [ad. mod.L. *Smalcaldic-us*, f. *Smalcaldia*, ad. G. *Schmalkalden*, a town of Thuringia.] Of or pertaining to Schmalkalden in connexion with the early history of Protestantism.

**1668** H. MORE *Div. Dial.* IV. xxxvii. (1713) 395 The condition..of the Reformation in Germany before the Smalcaldick War. **1716** M. DAVIES *Athen. Brit.* II. 36 Cromwell..joyning his Master's Interest with that of the Protestant Smalcaldick League in Germany. **1882-3** SCHAFF *Encycl. Relig. Knowl.* II. 1575 After the end of the Smalcaldic war. **1902** GAIRDNER *Hist. Eng. Ch. 16th C.* xii. 237 The princes and cities of the Smalcaldic League.. agreed to support each other..in defence of the Augsburg Confession.

† **small,** *sb.*[1] *Obs. rare.* [OE. *smæll* (= MIcel. *smell-r*, Norw. *smell*, Sw. *smäll*, Da. *smæld*, also †*smald*), related to **smellan* str. vb. (cf. Icel. *smella*, etc.) and *smyllan* wk. vb., of imitative origin.] A smack or blow; an onset, shock.

*c* **950** *Lindisf. Gosp.* John xviii. 22 An astod ðara ðeȝna salde dynt *vel* smæll mið honde uutearde ðæm hælende. *c* **1205** LAY. 27052 At þan uorme smællen Romanisce veollen: fiftene hundred folden to grunden.

**small** (smɔːl), *a.* and *sb.*[2] Forms: 1 smæl, 1, 3 smel, 1, 3-7 smal; 3-7 smale, 5 *Sc.* smaill; 5 smalle, 5- small; 6 smaul(e, 5-6 *Sc.* smaw, 8-9 *Sc.* sma', sma. [Common Teutonic: OE. *smæl*, = OFris. *smel* (WFris. *smel*, NFris. *smēl*), MDu. (Du.), OS. (MLG., LG.), OHG. (MHG.) *smal* (G. *schmal*), ON. *smal-r* (rare; Norw., Sw., and Da. *smal*, are perh. mainly from LG.), Goth. *smal-s*; connexion with ON. and Icel. *smá-r* (Norw. and Da. *smaa*, Sw. *små*) small, OHG. *smâhi* (MHG. *smæhe*) insignificant, is doubtful, and relationship to forms outside of Teut. (as OSlav. *malŭ*) somewhat uncertain. In the later Continental languages the prevailing sense is that of 'slender', 'narrow'.

The form *smale*, representing OE. disyllabic forms, is common in ME. and occurs as late as the 17th cent.]

**A.** *adj.*

**I. 1. a.** Of relatively little girth or circumference in comparison with length; not thick, stout, or fleshy; slender, thin. Now *dial.* exc. of the waist.

*c* **725** *Corpus Gloss.* G 155 *Gracilis*, smel. *c* **888** K. ÆLFRED *Boeth.* xxix. §1 Him..ne hangað nacod sweord ofer ðæm heafde be smale þræde. *c* **1000** *Sax. Leechd.* (Rolls) II. 122 Wiþ þam smalan wyrme. *c* **1200** *Trin. Coll. Hom.* 207 Smiten of smale longe ȝerden. *c* **1250** *Owl & Night.* 73 Þi body is scort, þi swere is smal. *a* **1310** in Wright *Lyric P.* vi. 28 With middel smal ant wel y-make. *c* **1386** CHAUCER *Miller's T.* 48 Fair was the yonge wyf, and therwithal As eny wesil hir body gent and smal. *c* **1440** *Promp. Parv.* 460/2 Smalle, as a wande, *gracilis*. **1490** CAXTON *Eneydos* xxix. 113 Dydo..[had] handes soupple and thynne, with long fyngers and smalle. **1530** PALSGR. 324/2 Small, lyke a fyne threde or a heare, *delye*. Small as a woman in the waste or a wande, *gresle*. **1590** SIR J. SMYTH *Disc. Weapons* 4 Rapier blades being so narrow, and of so small substance. **1621** BURTON *Anat. Mel.* I. i. II. vi. (1651) 22 A like skin..struck upon by certaine smal instruments like drum sticks. **1683** MOXON *Printing* xi. ¶23 They..prick the Oynion fast upon the end of a small long Stick. **1712** *Lond. Gaz.* No. 5022/2 An Allowance shall be made..in consideration of wast in reducing the same ['big wire'] to small Wire. **1779** *Mirror* No. 25, Now that small waists have come into fashion again. **1818** MOORE *Fudge Fam. Paris* i, Like an hour-glass, exceedingly small in the waist. **1870** J. HARTLEY *Budget* 119 (E.D.D.), He wor soa small he luk'd like a walkin' clooas prop.

**b.** *spec.* Applied to the more slender portions of the intestines; esp. ***small gut(s)***.

*c* **1000** ÆLFRIC *Gloss.* in Wr.-Wülcker 159 *Ilia*, smæleþearmas. *c* **1275** *XI Pains of Hell* 152 in *O.E. Misc.*, Ne beo þe þarm ne so smel, Eft heo werpeþ al in al. **1486** [see GUT *sb.* 2]. **1548** ELYOT s.v. *Lactes*, Some saye that they bee caules, wherein the small bowelles dooe lye. After other, the small guttes, by the whiche the meate passeth. **1621** BURTON *Anat. Mel.* I. i. II. iv, The guts, or *intestina*,..are divided into small and great, by reason of their site and substance, slender or thicker. *a* **1625** [*Comb.*; see GUT *sb.* 2 e]. **1668** DRYDEN *Even. Love* II. i, I'll give them leave to make fiddle-strings of my small-guts. **1767** [see INTESTINE *sb.*]. **1836-48** B. D. WALSH *Aristoph., Knights* IV. i, Slices too Of the small-guts, the belly and the paunch. **1885** HUXLEY *Elem. Physiol.* vi. 161 The rest of the small intestines is no wider than the duodenum.

†**c.** Of persons, etc.: Slender, slim; graceful. Chiefly in ***gent(le) and small***. *Obs.*

*c* **1250** *Owl & Night.* 204 Þeyh..leof hym w[e]re Nihtingale, And oþer wyhte gent & smale. *a* **1300** *Cursor M.* 13138 His broþer doghter, gent and smal. *c* **1420** *Sir Amadace* (Camden) liv, The lordes and the lades small That comon wer of gentyll blode. **15..** *Batayle of Egyngecourte* 28 in Hazl. *E.P.P.* II. 94 Grete well, he sayd, your comely kynge, That is bothe gentyll and small. **1591** SHAKS. *Two Gentl.* II. iii. 23 My sister..is as white as a lilly, and as small as a wand.

**2.** Having little breadth or width in proportion to length; narrow. Now *rare*.

**847** *Charter* in *O.E. Texts* 434 Fram smalan cumbes heafde to græwanstane. *c* **893** K. ÆLFRED *Oros.* I. i. 18 He sæde ðæt Norðmanna land wære swyðe lang and swyðe smæl. *Ibid.*, Norðeweard he cwæð, þær hit smalost wære, þæt hit mihte beon þreora mila brad to þæm more. *a* **1000** in Birch *Cartul. Sax.* II. 600 Andlangan þes smalan paðes. *c* **1205** LAY. 5867 Scradieð eower sceldes al of þe smal enden. *c* **1386** CHAUCER *Prol.* 329 Girt with a ceint of silk, with barres smale. **1387** TREVISA *Higden* (Rolls) I. 165 Dido.. kutte þe hyde into a þong þat was ful long and ful smal. **1424** *Mem. Ripon* (Surtees) III. 152 Item pro ij payr smale bandis ad ostia in campanili, 6*d*. **1473** *Acc. Ld. High Treas. Scot.* I. 16, viij elne of smale rybbanis for the King. **1610** HOLLAND *Camden's Brit.* 183 Cornwall..waxeth smaller and smaller in manner of an horne. *c* **1710** CELIA FIENNES *Diary* (1888) 252 Ye rest is filled with haire, Jewells and gold, and white small Ribon. **1803** PLYMLEY *Agric. Shropshire* 339 The small cloth is about one-eighth of a yard narrower than the other.

**II. 3. a.** Of limited size; of comparatively restricted dimensions; not large in comparison with other things, esp. of the same kind.

Also used to qualify such words as *dimensions*, *size*. Phr. ***small is beautiful***: expressing a belief that small-scale institutions, systems, etc., are more desirable than large-scale ones; also as *adj. phr.*

*α. c* **888** K. ÆLFRED *Boeth.* xvi. §2 Ða smalan wyrmas ðe ðone mon æȝðer ȝe innan ȝe utan wyrdað. *a* **1225** *Juliana* 154 An angel myd a naked swerd..hew it al to smale peces. *c* **1290** *S. Eng. Leg.* I. 63/329 Wilde foules, smale and grete. *a* **1300** *Cursor M.* 375 Þe light wit sterns, gret and smale. *c* **1386** CHAUCER *Sir Thopas* 49 Ther spryngen herbes grete and smale. *c* **1400** MAUNDEV. (Roxb.) xxii. 100 Þai hafe twa smale holes in steed of eghen. **1488** *Cal. Anc. Rec. Dublin* (1889) 494 A dyche of smale thornes and breres. *c* **1510** BARCLAY *Mirr. Gd. Manners* (1570) F. iij, The rauen neuer shall sing..like other birdes smale. **1562** A. SCOTT *Poems* (S.T.S.) i. 220 Smaill sweit smaragde. **1578** *Nottingham Rec.* IV. 52 An ironmonger of smale made wares, videlicet, of nayles, horse shues [etc.].

*β. c* **1000** *Saxon Leechd.* II. 180 Flæsc..lytelra wuhta, smælra fuȝla. *c* **1290** *S. Eng. Leg.* I. 319 Ho-so hath of fuyre mest, he is smal and red. *c* **1375** *Sc. Leg. Saints* xl. (*Ninian*) 1445 [It was] smallare sum part..þane þe todire leg had bene. *c* **1391** CHAUCER *Astrolabe* I. §21 Euery smal deuysioun in a signe. *c* **1420** *Liber Cocorum* (1862) 14 Take peions and hew hom in morselle smalle. **1445** in *Anglia* XXVIII. 271 In noon smal boke thei may be writen. **1530** PALSGR. 324/2 Small as a massyfe thing is of quantite, *petit*. **1560** ROLLAND *Seven Sages* 26 Ane proper sterne he saw, That was richt cleir perfite and wonder smaw. **1600** J. PORY tr. *Leo's Africa* VII. 290 Abundance of cattell here are both great and small. **1657** AUSTEN *Fruit Trees* I. 63 Whereas young trees of a smaler sise may be removed with all their Roots. **1737** [S. BERINGTON] *Mem. G. di Lucca* (1738) 174 Their Horses, as I observed before, are but small. **1751** D. JEFFERIES *Treat. Diamonds* (ed. 2) 20 Small Stones (which means Stones under the weight of a carat). **1815** J. SMITH *Panorama Sci. & Art* II. 140 The top of the small cylinder, should have a communication with the bottom of the larger cylinder. **1848** THACKERAY *Van. Fair* xxxvi, A very small comfortable house in Curzon Street. **1868** LOCKYER *Elem. Astron.* §627 The smaller bodies attract the larger ones.

*Phr.* **1973** E. F. SCHUMACHER (*title*) Small is beautiful. **1975** *Country Life* 25 Dec. 1784/1 Adapting Schumacher's phrase, we decide that not only small but piecemeal is beautiful. **1976** *Seed* V. v. 6/3 Included are articles on self-sufficiency, 'small-is-beautiful' politics and agriculture and nutrition. **1977** D. JAMES *Spy at Evening* xxiv. 193 Small Is Beautiful—but big pays more. **1978** *Times* 23 Mar. 16/3 Mr. St John-Stevas..has proclaimed that 'small is beautiful'. There will be 'no more of those monster schools'. **1979** *Jrnl. R. Soc. Arts* July 468/1 It is worth mentioning another and different pressure upon the nature and shape of the hospital: and that is the vague but pervasive notion that 'small is beautiful'.

**b.** Of places, countries, etc. Also in phr. (***it's a***) ***small world*** and varr.: a comment on an unexpected meeting with an acquaintance or other similar coincidence.

*a* **1000** in Birch *Cartul. Sax.* III. 210 Þat lond at Silham.. and alle þe smale londe þat þere to bereth. **1382** WYCLIF *Luke* xiv. 21 Go out soone in to grete stretis and smale streetis of the citee. *c* **1386** CHAUCER *Clerk's T.* 427 To thee, that born art of a smal village. **1582** N. LICHEFIELD tr. *Castanheda's Conq. E. Ind.* I. v. 13 All of them [*sc.* islands] being but little or small. **1611** BIBLE *Numb.* xxxii. 41 Iair.. tooke the small townes. **1630** *R. Johnson's Kingd. & Commw.* 373 This small City is neighbour to two others. **1846** MCCULLOCH *Acc. Brit. Empire* (1854) I. 166 Rutland, the smallest of the English counties. **1869** A. R. WALLACE *Malay Archip.* (1902) xix. 221 A small country like Holland ..having possession of a very small island.

*Phr.* **1895** A. W. PINERO *Second Mrs. Tanqueray* III. 147 Mr. Ardale and I have met in London... They say the world's very small, don't they. **1959** M. GILBERT *Blood & Judgement* i. 17 He was in the pub tonight... It's a small world, isn't it? **1967** R. RENDELL *Wolf to Slaughter* iii. 21 'Small world,' he said... 'That bloke was in here yesterday.' **1973** 'H. CARMICHAEL' *Too Late for Tears* v. 69, I might've guessed even if I hadn't seen..you at the inquest in Aylesbury. Small world, isn't it? **1979** S. BARLAY *Crash Course* I. 13 'How did you know?'..'It's a small world.'

**c.** Of children, etc.: Not fully grown or developed; young. Also, of a sibling: younger.

*small boy* has become fairly common in modern colloquial use, but is felt to differ in connotation from *little boy*, usually by suggesting greater activity and independence, also *small girl*.

*c* **1250** *Gen. & Ex.* 656 Of his kin bi his liue dai;..wel fowre and .xx. ðhusent men,..wið-uten wif-kin and childre smale. **14..** W. PARIS *Cristine* 141 (Horstm. 1878), What hathe Cristyne, my doughter smalle, Done with oure goddes? **1484** CAXTON *Fables Æsop* v. x, He fond a sowe, and her smal pygges with her. **1786** G. WASHINGTON *Diary* 5 July (1925) III. 86 That Cowpers Jack and Day, with some small boys and girls,..were assisting the farmer. **1796** H. MCNEILL *Waes o' War* III. v, Monster! wha could leave neglected Three sma' infants and a wife. **1821** J. F. COOPER *Spy* I. i. 14 A small boy was directed to guide him to his room. **1841** THACKERAY *Gt. Hoggarty Diamond* ix, There was a garden that certain *small people* might play in when they came. **1876** C. M. YONGE *Three Brides* II. xv. 292 He still looked on the tall, young man as the small brother to be patronized, and protected. **1891** L. T. MEADE *Sweet Girl Graduate* xxii. 182 Three small girls were making themselves busy with holly and ivy. **1896** *Westm. Gaz.* 12 Dec. 1/3 To the great delight of various small boys. **1903** *Daily Chron.* 5 Jan. 6/7 In some cases the parents may threaten to leave our employ unless we give work to their small children. **1923** E. E. CUMMINGS *Let.* 28 July (1969) 99 What happens to my 'small' 'sister'..is not among the interests of my own completely erratic..existence. **1936** N. STREATFEILD *Ballet Shoes* iv. 58 About twenty small girls.. were learning tap-dancing. **1949** 'J. TEY' *Brat Farrar* xii. 100 If he had ever had a small sister he would have liked her to be just like Jane. **1973** M. MACKINTOSH *King & Two Queens* i. 14 'Go away, small girl,' Frances commanded. **1977** A. WILSON *Strange Ride R. Kipling* i. 23 The strength of Rudyard's love for his small sister.

**d.** Of words: Short, simple. †Also of language: Simple, plain.

*c* **1250** *Gen. & Ex.* 18 Ðan man hem telled soðe tale Wid londes speche and wordes smale. **1679** V. ALSOP *Melius Inq.* I. iii. 135 As if we were not as much obliged to tell the People their duty as God our wants in small English. **1821** BYRON *Sardanap.* I. ii. 511 Your first small words are taught you from her lips.

**e.** *local.* Of a river, water, etc.: Low, shallow.

**1791** W. H. MARSHALL *W. England* (1796) II. 258 Some days ago..the water was unusually low—provincially and not improperly 'small'. **1886** in Elworthy *W. Somerset Word-bk.* s.v., I an't a zeed our water zo smaal, not's years.

**4. a.** Used with collective nouns, denoting the limited size of the individual things, pieces, etc. ***small print***: freq. applied to the detailed information or conditions qualifying the principal text of a document, and printed in a smaller type; also *attrib.* and *fig.* Cf. *fine print* (FINE *a.* 7 i).

**1398** TREVISA *Barth. De P.R.* XVIII. i. (Bodl. MS.), Bestes þat eteþ smal gras and herbes. **1479** in *Eng. Gilds* (1870) 425 All smalwodde to be dischargid at the Bak. **1535** COVERDALE *2 Sam.* xxiii. 11 A pece of londe full of small corne. *c* **1588** in J. Morris *Troubles Our Forefathers* Ser. II. (1875) 310 A very large narration.., which contained six-and-fifty sheets of paper written..in a very small letter. **1683** TRYON *Way* *to Health* iv. (1697) 83 No Baker can preserve the pure white Colour in his fine small Bread, if he be not quick about it. **1698** FRYER *Acc. E. India & P.* 50 A small Print might easily be read by it. **1778** *Eng. Gazetteer* (ed. 2) s.v. *Lenton*, Round ore, small ore, and smithum. **1785** T. JEFFERSON *Notes on State of Virginia* xxii. 323 A large octavo volume of small print. **1856** [see PRINT *sb.* 8]. **1879** *London Society* Christmas No. 64/1 A brilliant little flirt.. who condescended to waste on me a good deal of small artillery. **1893** SPON *Mechanic's Own Book* (ed. 4) 330 Smaller wood is got from the branches of trees. **1902** OWEN WISTER *Virginians* xxiv, The quaking-asps.. are in small leaf. **1944** BLUNDEN *Cricket Country* xvi. 161 What all these curious titles [of games said by Rabelais to have been played by Gargantua] meant in practice may be left to the small print of the commentaries. **1970** 'W. HAGGARD' *Hardliners* xi. 126 His contract had been terminated under some small-print clause he hadn't much studied. **1971** *Daily Tel.* 2 Nov. 14 Some interest attaches therefore to the 'small print' of the Queen's speech and how far it avoids firm undertakings on some of the more controversial measures. **1972** A. PRICE *Col. Butler's Wolf* xii. 136 There was nothing in the small print about having to like the men one served with. **1974** *Times* 17 Aug. 12/5 The collapse will.. strengthen Government moves to reform the 'small print' [holiday] booking conditions. **1979** *Sunday Times* (Colour Suppl.) 18 Nov. 35/2 The Prince of Wales reckoned he got the better of the PM in one or two exchanges on the small print of recent Cabinet memoranda.

**b.** Of money: Of little size and low value; consisting of coins of low denomination. ***small change***: see CHANGE *sb.* 7.

**1561** AWDELAY *Frat. Vacab.* (1869) 55 Thou hast shewed vs none but small money. **1624** GATAKER *Good Wife* II. 9 The Kings Almoner may cast small siluer about. **1727** A. HAMILTON *New Acc. E. Indies* I. xxi. 249 Paid in small Money to discharge the Accounts of the Shoemaker, Taylor [etc.]. *a* **1894** STEVENSON *St. Ives* (1902) ix. 65 Here are four pounds of it in.. notes, and the balance in small silver.

*fig.* **1879** MEREDITH *Egoist* xxxiii, If we are not to be beloved, spare us the small coin of compliment on character.

**c.** Of a family: Consisting of young children. ***small help*** (see quot. 1903).

**1829** BROCKETT *N.C. Gloss.* (ed. 2) s.v., In our Northern phraseology, a small family means a family of young children, however numerous. **1895** *Edin. Rev.* Apr. 422 For the sake of her unborn babe and her large small family. **1903** *Daily Chron.* 5 Jan. 6/7 One official of a mill-owning company.. admits that 'small help'—*anglice* 'child labour'—is a great mistake.

**5.** Little in amount or quantity: **a.** Of material things, or properties naturally connected with these, as number, quantity, etc.

**1297** R. GLOUC. (Rolls) 5394 Ac is gode moder ofte smale ȝiftes him tok. *a* **1300** *Cursor M.* 972 Qui sal þi parte be sa smal? *c* **1386** CHAUCER *Friar's T.* 128 My wages been ful streite and ful smale. *c* **1450** *Merlin* xv. 257 Thei ete soche vitaile as thei hadde, but it was full smalle. *c* **1470** HENRY *Wallace* VIII. 1340 His wynnyng was in Scotland bot full smaw. *a* **1530** J. HEYWOOD *Play of the Wether* 1116 (Brandl), This nomber is smale, there lacketh twayne of ten. **1577** B. GOOGE *Heresb. Husb.* (1586) 146 Seeing that.. the profit of the Milke is not smal. **1593** SHAKS. *2 Hen. VI*, IV. x. 20 This small inheritance my Father left me. **1626** in *Rep. Hist. MSS. Comm., Var. Coll.* (1907) IV. 171 The necessitie of useing some smale quantitie of bay salt therein. **1632** LITHGOW *Trav.* VII. 323 [I did] in all my trauells prosecute the like course of a small diet,.. often too small against my will. *a* **1700** EVELYN *Diary* 13 July 1684, Some small sprinkling of raine. **1779** *Mirror* No. 12, I am a plain country-gentleman, with a small fortune and a large family. **1809** *Med. Jrnl.* XXI. 25 This should certainly be the smallest dose I would use in this disease. **1849** MACAULAY *Hist. Eng.* iii. I. 287 The revenue of England, under Charles the Second, was small. **1890** WORMELL & WALMSLEY *Electr. Serv. Man* 139 The comparatively small currents passing through a single incandescent lamp.

**b.** Of immaterial things, as actions, faculties, feelings, etc.

The exact sense varies to some extent with the sb., and in some cases the reference is rather to effect, force, or capacity than to amount.

*a* **1300** *Cursor M.* 16946 Alle þe pines o þis werld to tell þai war ful small [*v.r.* to his ner but smalle]. **1390** GOWER *Conf.* I. 6 My wittes ben to smale To tellen every man his tale. **1523** LD. BERNERS tr. *Froissart* I. xcvi. 118 They.. fledde to the market place, but they kept but a small order. **1559** *Mirr. Mag., Dk. Suffolk* vi, My travayle was not smal. **1611** BIBLE *2 Kings* xix. 26 [They] were of small power. **1697** J. LEWIS *Mem. Dk. Glocester* (1789) 33 His appetite was but small, considering how active he was. **1726** SWIFT *Gulliver* II. viii, I had gotten a small cold. **1774** GOLDSM. *Nat. Hist.* (1776) VII. 262 They consider the loss of them as but a small misfortune. **1810** CRABBE *Borough* xviii. 80 His spirits low, and his exertions small. **1855** MACAULAY *Hist. Eng.* xviii. IV. 170 As culpable as her small faculties enabled her to be.

**c.** Denoted by a number which is among the least of a series; of low numerical value or ordinal rank; low. *spec.* of playing-cards.

**1391** CHAUCER *Astrol.* II. §21 For so gret a latitude or for so smal a latitude is the table compowned. **1669** STURMY *Mariner's Mag.* VI. iii. 112 Small Latitudes, or Countreys betwixt the Tropicks. **1672** WYCHERLEY *Love in a Wood* I. ii, Like the small cards..; when the play begins, you should be put out as useless. **1748** HOYLE *Games* (1778) 94 Three small Clubs or Spades, Queen and two small Hearts, King and one small Diamond. Play a small Trump. **1863** *Hoyle's Games* ii. 23 Having only a few small trumps, make them when you can. **1910** W. DALTON *'Saturday' Bridge* iii. 63 Suppose that he holds ace, king, and three small diamonds, and ace, knave, and two small hearts. **1973** *Country Life* 10 May 1331/2 The declarer.. led a small Spade to dummy.

**6. a.** Only a little or slight amount or degree of (something); not much; hardly any.

*c* **1386** CHAUCER *Prioress' T.* 84, I kan but smal grammeere. *c* **1449** PECOCK *Repr.* IV. iv. 442 It schulde not bicome me or eny man, having ful smal witt and discrecioun [etc.]. **1526** *Pilgr. Perf.* (W. de W. 1531) 2 Some may be excellently lerned, & yet haue but small felyng of these thynges. **1577** GOOGE *Heresbach's Husb.* I. (1586) 35 b, It wil also grow wel yenough.. in any ground with small labour. **1649** DRUMM. OF HAWTH. *Hist. Jas. V*, Wks. (1711) 97 But small confidence could be long among reconciled enemies. *a* **1693** ASHMOLE *Antiq. Berksh.* (1719) I. 151 The small need the Lady had of Physick. **1719** DE FOE *Crusoe* II. (Globe) 328 They had indeed small Hope of their Lives. **1786** BURNS *Holy Fair* xxv, Sma' need has he to say a grace. **1819** SCOTT *Ivanhoe* v, You do but small credit to your fame, Sir Prior! **1857** BUCKLE *Civiliz.* I. x. 619 They had paid small attention to the etiquette of courts. **1874** MOTLEY *John of Barneveld* I. i. 28 He had small love for the pleasures of the table.

**b.** ***no small***, great, considerable, marked; much, a good deal of. Cf. NO *a.* 2 b.

**1548** HALL *Chron., Rich. III*, 50 b, He tooke there newes as a matter of no small momente. **1560** DAUS tr. *Sleidane's Comm.* 52 The plucking downe of Images, hath procured us no smale displeasure. **1639** S. DU VERGER tr. *Camus' Admir. Events* a j b, This variety being no small attractive. **1697** J. LEWIS *Mem. Dk. Glocester* (1789) 49 To the no small joy of the Prince and Princess. *a* **1770** JORTIN *Serm.* (1771) II. xi. 217 It is no small impertinence to take hold of the attention of others. **1779** *Mirror* No. 62. 211 There, to my no small surprise, I found the Dean. **1843** MACAULAY *Ess.* III. 552 There was.. no small curiosity to know how he would acquit himself.

**c.** Used in the superlative for emphasis: The least; the slightest.

**1596** SHAKS. *1 Hen. IV*, III. ii. 159, I will dye a hundred thousand Deaths Ere breake the smallest parcell of this Vow. **1604** —— *Oth.* III. iii. 188 Not from mine owne weake merites will I draw The smallest feare, or doubt of her reuolt. **1716–8** LADY M. W. MONTAGU *Lett.* I. xxxi. 104, I never can forget the smallest of your.. Commands. **1797–1805** S. & HT. LEE *Canterb. T.* I. 382 He risked.. life, if he betrayed the smallest suspicion. *a* **1828** BENTHAM *Wks.* (1843) I. 240 In the most direct terms, and without any the smallest doubt, disguise, or reserve. **1891** *Law Times* XCI. 2/2 The court, without the smallest hesitation, made absolute the rule for a *habeas corpus*.

**d.** ***in the smallest***, in the least. *rare.*

**1603** SHAKS. *Meas. for M.* IV. ii. 179, I may make my case as Claudio's, to crosse this in the smallest. **1827** CARLYLE *Germ. Rom.* III. 276 The best wives will complain of their husbands to a stranger, without in the smallest liking them the less on that account. **1864** —— *Fredk. Gt.* IV. 35 Not molesting Prince Karl in the smallest.

**7.** Of no great length; short, brief: **a.** Of time.

**1430–40** LYDG. *Bochas* VIII. v. (1558), But a small season last his prosperite. *a* **1548** HALL *Chron., Edw. IV*, 32 The duke of Somersets battayl.. wer wythin a smal season, shamefully dyscomfited. **1585** T. WASHINGTON tr. *Nicholay's Voy.* I. xv. 16 b, Within this small time I indeuoured.. to see.. the things most notable. **1611** BIBLE *Isaiah* liv. 7 For a small moment haue I forsaken thee, but with great mercies will I gather thee. **1632** LITHGOW *Trav.* III. 91 Within a small time he found the Captaines promise and performance different. **1707** *Curios. in Husb. & Gard.* 25 Their Fragility and small Duration. **1745** P. THOMAS *Jrnl. Anson's Voy.* 27 The small Stay we made here.. lost us at least 60 or 70.. able Men. **1815** SCOTT *Guy M.* xlii, A letter to compose, about which he wasted no small time. **1874** W. S. JEVONS *Princ. Sci.* xiii. (1900) 299 The duration of the spark was immeasurably small.

**b.** Of journeys, distance, etc.

*c* **1450** LOVELICH *Merlin* 10137 (E.E.T.S.), Smale jornes they gonne to ryde The contre to serchen jn that tyde. **1579** NORTH *Plutarch, Cæsar* (1612) 729 The souldiers.. by small iourneys came at length vnto the citie. **1615** W. LAWSON *Country Housew. Garden* (1626) 23, I suppose twenty yards distance is small enough betwixt tree and tree. **1766** GOLDSM. *Vicar W.* v, At a small distance from the house. **1885** W. K. CLIFFORD *Common Sense Exact Sci.* iii. (1892) 96 Instead of counting feet we count inches, which are smaller than feet.

*transf.* *a* **1859** MACAULAY *Hist. Eng.* xxiv. V. 229 The flesh of wild animals and the green fat of the turtle.. went but a small way.

**8.** Composed or consisting of, containing, few individuals or members; numerically little or weak. †Also of years: Few.

*c* **1470** HENRY *Wallace* v. 807 Our power is to smaw;.. To few we ar agayne yon fellone staill. *a* **1569** KINGESMYLL *Man's Est.* xi. (1580) 69 Where thei found that sillie Shepherde with his smal flocke. **1594** PARSONS *Confer. Success.* I. 189 He being a child of so smale yeares. **1611** BIBLE *2 Chron.* xxiv. 24 The armie of the Syrians came with a small companie of men. **1681** DRYDEN *Abs. & Achit.* 914 A small but faithful Band Of Worthies. **1724** DE FOE *Mem. Cavalier* vi. (1894) 80 A small party of the musketeers followed me. **1788** GIBBON *Decl. & F.* l. V. 185 The right of peace and war is now confined to a small, and the actual exercise to a much smaller, list of respectable potentates. **1802** JAMES *Milit. Dict.* s.v. *Guard*, Quarter Guard is a small guard commanded by a subaltern officer. **1874** *Treas. Bot.* Suppl. 1342/2 A small group of plants from New Grenada and Peru. **1889** A. R. WALLACE *Darwinism* 80 Species of large genera vary more than species of small genera.

**9. a.** Constituting a lower standard (of weight, size, etc.) than another having the same designation. **b.** Falling somewhat short of the proper or usual standard.

**1554** HASSE in *Hakluyt's Voy.* (1886) III. 94 They divide the small pound into 48 parts. **1640** in Entick *London* (1776) II. 166 Catling, the great gross, qt. 12 small gross of knots. **1660** *Act 12 Chas. II*, c, 4 Schedule s.v. *Bosses*, Bosses for Bridles the small groce, cont. 12 dozen. **1698** FROGER *Voy.* 47 The island of St. Ann,.. from which they are distant two small leagues. **1705** tr. *Bosman's Guinea* 11, I have travelled above three small days Voyage upon it. **1753** R. CLAYTON in Maundrell *Journ. Jerus.* 18 After an ascent of a small half hour we came to a most delicious fountain of cold water. **1834** *Lowndes' Bibliogr. Man.* I. 84 Austin's Urania.. London, 1629. small 8vo. **1886** ELWORTHY *W. Somerset Word-bk.* s.v. *Long-hundred*, A hundred of five score is called a small-hundred. **1888** JACOBI *Printers' Vocab.* 127 *Small post*, a size of writing paper, $16\frac{1}{2} \times 13\frac{1}{2}$ inches.

**c.** Introducing a repetition of the initial letter of a word to show that it has general rather than specific reference or that it is a less serious variety of the thing denoted. Cf. CAPITAL *a.* 5 b, BIG *a.* 3 h.

**1952** *Observer* 18 May 7/6 Back to liberalism-with-a-small-l they trail. **1960** *Times* 22 Oct. 8/1 A newspaper that is serious, lively, and radical with a small r. **1968** *Globe & Mail Mag.* (Toronto) 13 Jan. 2/4 A general mood of small-c conservatism in the country. **1971** 'A. GARVE' *Late Bill Smith* v. 139 They were both ardently liberal with a small 'l'. **1974** W. GARNER *Big enough Wreath* xii. 165 You're not out of trouble but I'm just beginning to spell it with a small t. **1979** L. MEYER *False Front* ii. 14 They came from different sides of the track, but that wouldn't have been enough to stop a small 'd' democrat like Winston.

**III. 10. a.** Composed of fine or minute particles, drops, etc. In later use chiefly of rain.

*c* **897** K. ÆLFRED *Gregory's Past. C.* lvii. 437 Swiðe lytle beoð ða dropan ðæs smalan renes, ac hi wyrceað ðeah swiðe micel flod. *c* **1000** *Sax. Leechd.* (Rolls) I. 240 ðenim of ðysse wyrte.. swyþe smæl dust. *Ibid.* II. 86 ðenim þonne smæl beren mela. *c* **1175** *Lamb. Hom.* 85 þe ilke þe foleȝeð þes fleisces lust, Alse deð þet smalchef þe winde. **1382** WYCLIF *Exod.* xxx. 36 Whanne thow hast pownede alle.. into moost smal powdre. *c* **1410** *Master of Game* (MS. Digby 182) xii, Boyle mastyke and sence in smale poudre. *Ibid.*, Take water and smale salte. **1574** *Reg. Privy Council Scot.* II. 406 The exhorbitant derth of small salt within this realme. **1583–** [see SALT *sb.*[1] 1 b]. *a* **1586** SIDNEY *Ps.* XVIII. xi, I bett these folkes as small as dust. *a* **1649** WINTHROP *New Eng.* (1853) I. 209 The Rebecka,.. two days before, was frozen twenty miles up the river; but a small rain falling set her free. **1676** WOOD *Jrnl.* in *Acc. Sev. Late Voy.* I. (1694) 177 Thick Fogs with small Rain. **1727** A. HAMILTON *New Acc. E. Indies* I. xxii. 262 A small Rain happened to fall that damped my Powder. **1823** SCOTT *Quentin D.* i, Heaven, who works by the tempest as well as by the soft small rain.

**b.** Fine, as opposed to coarse, in various applications.

*a* **1000** in Thorpe *Dipl. Angl.* 158 Tu hund greates hlafes and þridde smales. *c* **1050** *Voc.* in Wr.-Wülcker 357 *Artocobus*, smæl hlaf. **13..** *E.E. Allit. P.* B. 226 As smylt mele vnder smal siue smokes for-þikke. **1450–80** tr. *Secreta Secret.* liii. 32 Some metes are smale, and some metes are grete, and some are mene. **1742** *Lond. & Co. Brewer* I. (ed. 4) 72 If high dried, a gross Grinding is best, otherwise a smaller may be done. **1856** MORTON *Cycl. Agric.* I. 193 This is to be done by sieves just smaller in the mesh than the size of the grain. **1891** *Hartland Gloss.*, *Small-sieve*, a fine-meshed wooden sieve used in Rewing.

†**c.** Of air: Thin, rarefied. *Obs.*[−1]

**1495** *Trevisa's Barth. De P.R.* XIV. xlv. 483 The ayre is.. more smalle and clere than in ualleyes.

**11.** Of cloth, yarn, garments, etc.: Fine in texture or structure. *Obs.* exc. *dial.*

In the case of cloth it is sometimes difficult to decide whether examples belong to this sense or to 2.

*c* **900** tr. *Baeda* IV. xxv. 354 Ða fæmnan.. swa oft swa hio æmtan habbað, þæt hio smaelo hræȝel weofað and wyrcað. *c* **1200** *Trin. Coll. Hom.* 163 His alter cloð [is] great and sole, and hire chemise smal and hwit. **1473** *Acc. Ld. High Treas. Scot.* I. 13, xiij elne of smale Hollande clath for iij sarkis and a curche. **1488** *Ibid.* 150 For viij elne of small braide clayth to be sarkis to the King. **1536** BELLENDEN *Cron. Scot.* (1821) I. p. xxxvi, In the vale of Esk is sa quhit and small wol, that it hes na compair in Albion. **1585** T. WASHINGTON tr. *Nicholay's Voy.* IV. xi. 123 b, They bring.. smal clothes of diuers sorts and colours.. from.. Cambaye and Ormmus. **1637** *Bury Wills* (Camden) 169 There is some sixe and thirtie grosse of small yarne. **1901** in *Eng. Dial. Dict.*, *Small weft*, a very fine sort of yarn. Lanc[ashire].

**12.** Of low alcoholic strength; light, weak: **a.** Of specific liquors, as ale, wine, etc., or diluted forms of these. See also SMALL BEER.

*c* **1440** *Promp. Parv.* 460/2 Smal wyne, *villum*. **1467** in *Eng. Gilds* 382, iij. galons of smale ale for j.d. **1500–20** DUNBAR *Poems* xxv. 13 O! ȝe heremeitis.., That.. drynkis no wyn confortatiue, Bot aill and that is thyn and small. **1526** *Pilgr. Perf.* (W. de W. 1531) 53 b, Theyr vynes brynge forth but temperate and small wynes, as reed, claret, and whyte. **1605** *London Prodigal* I. ii, Let me haue sacke for vs old men: For these girles and knaues small wines are best. **1664** DRYDEN *Rival Ladies* Ep. Ded., It being at best, like small Wines, to be drunk out upon the Place. **1707** MORTIMER *Husb.* (1721) II. 336 If your Fruit be unripe, or your Cyder small. **1732** ARBUTHNOT *Rules of Diet* in *Aliments*, etc. 270 Small Ale without Hops. **1789** BUCHAN *Domest. Med.* (1790) 149 His drink may be small negus,.. and sometimes a little weak punch. **1827** GOOD *Study Med.* (1829) I. 170 The drink [should] be small brandy and water. **1864** *Daily Telegr.* 17 Mar., Customers, who had contrived to make themselves uncommonly merry with pots of the smallest ale. **1879** STEVENSON *Trav. Cevennes* 33 The wine is of the smallest.

**b.** Of drinks, beverages, or liquors in general, sometimes applied to such as are non-alcoholic.

In quot. 1471 said of water in contrast to spirit.

**1471** RIPLEY *Comp. Alch.* I. xi. in Ashm. (1652) 131 The better therefore shall be Solucyon, Then yf thou dyd it wyth Water small. **1544** PHAER *Regim. Lyfe* (1560) I vj, To abstayne from all kyndes of wyne, & to use himselfe to small drinke. **1626** BACON *Nat. Hist.* §394 By Making Drinks, Stronger, or Smaller with the same Quantity of Mault. **1675** E. WILSON *Spadacrene Dunelm.* 86 Stronger Stomachs must be content with smaller Beverages, and Wine diluted. **1705** *Lond. Gaz.* No. 4108/3, 16 Tuns, and 2 Hogsheads of Small Beveridge and Anjue Wine. **1748** RICHARDSON *Clarissa* (1811) VI. 372 Cheated by a stronger liquor for a smaller. *a* **1800** in *Good's Study Med.* (1829) V. 573 Encouraging the eruption, by taking small warm liquors, as tea, coffee, wine-whey, broth, and nourishing meats.

**c.** In general use: Weak, thin. *rare.*

**1676** WISEMAN *Surg. Treat.* 488 His drink was *decoct. sarsæ* [sarsaparilla], but so small, as it was little better than water. **1747** WESLEY *Prim. Physick* (1762) 68 The leaves of it boiled in small Broth.

**13. a.** Of sound or the voice: Gentle, low, soft: of little power or strength; not loud, harsh, or rough.

*c* **1250** *Gen. & Exod.* 4056 Luuelike and wið speche smale, To wenden hem fro godes aȝe. *c* **1386** CHAUCER *Prol.* 688 A voys he hadde as smal as hath a goot. —— *Miller's T.* 174 He syngeth in his voys gentil and smal. **1483** CAXTON *Gold. Leg.* 28/1 After the stroke of the fyre descended a swete sowne of ayer softe and smalle. **1565** COOPER *Thesaurus, Vox tenuata*, a small voyce. **1611** BIBLE 1 *Kings* xix. 12 After the fire, a still small voice. **1697** POTTER *Antiq. Greece* II. xviii. (1715) 351 They proposed their Question in a small whispering Voice. **1750** GRAY *Elegy* 73 In still small accents whisp'ring from the Ground. **1753** MISS COLLIER *Art Torment.* II. ii. (1811) 129 Throw a languidness into your countenance; let your voice grow small. **1842** LOVER *Handy Andy* xxxviii, So still was it, that he could hear the small crumbling sound of the dying embers as they decomposed. **1880** MISS BROUGHTON *Sec. Thoughts* I. xii, 'Thank you,' she says, in a small voice.

**b.** Of vowels: Narrow, close; *spec.* in Gaelic phonology of the vowels *e* and *i*, and of certain consonants when in contact with these.

**1599** MINSHEU *Sp. Gram.* 6, E..in Spanish..must neuer be so small as the English ee, as fee, wee. **1707** LHUYD *Archæol. Brit.* 299 That as the Vowels are divided into Broad and Small; so the Diphthongs and Triphthongs ending in *a*, *o*, or *u*, are Broad; and those in *e* or *i* Small. **1736** AINSWORTH *Lat. Dict.* II. s.v. *I*, The next small vowel *e*. **1801** A. STEWART *Elem. Galic Gram.* 20 They [*l*, *n*, *r*] have the small sound when..they are preceded or followed by a small vowel. **1830** MACLEOD & DEWAR *Gael. Dict.* s.v. *Leathan*, Upon the same principle, the rule 'Caol ri caol' regulates the small vowels.

**14.** Of wind: Light, slight, gentle.

**1542** *Lament. & Piteous Treat.* in *Harl. Misc.* (Malh.) I. 235 A smal and softe wynde. **1671** tr. *Frejus' Voy. Mauritania* 9 We held on our course..with a small West-wind. **1698** FROGER *Voy.* 154 We had a small gale that was favourable enough. **1748** *Anson's Voy.* II. iv. 162 A small breeze springing up from the W.N.W. **1802** M. CUTLER in *Life*, etc. (1888) II. 108 Small wind, nearly ahead.

**15.** Of the pulse: Beating weakly.

**1755** *Phil. Trans.* XLIX. 50 The pulse small, the mouth and tongue foul. **1797** *Monthly Mag.* III. 230 A quick and small pulse. **1834** *Good's Study Med.* (ed. 4) I. 544 If a pulse be exceeding hard, and at the same time small, then it has been called a wiry pulse. **1897** *Allbutt's Syst. Med.* III. 849 The pulse is small, rapid, and thready.

**IV. 16. a.** Of persons: Low or inferior in rank or position; of little importance, authority, or influence; common, ordinary. Now *rare*.

In early use with ref. to military importance.

*c* **1205** LAY. 436 Al þat smale mon-kun he dude ȝeond þea muntes. *Ibid.* 21803 His smale uolc he setten alle bi weste siden. *c* **1375** BARBOUR *Bruce* IX. 569 His small folk gert he ilk deill Vith-draw thame till a strate neir by. **1422** tr. *Secreta Secret., Priv. Priv.* I. ii. 128 To deme..euynly betwene grete men and Smale, ryche and Power. *c* **1489** CAXTON *Sonnes of Aymon* viii. 187 All the small people had ben all dead for hungre. **1517** in *10th Rep. Hist. MSS. Comm.* App. V. 397 That every tope man paye xl.*s.* and every small man xx.*s.* **1561** WINȜET *Wks.* (S.T.S.) I. 6 The smallaste ane that sall perise throw ȝour negligence. **1613** SHAKS. *Hen. VIII*, v. i. 129 Your Enemies are many, and not small. **1833** T. HOOK *Parson's Dau.* III. vii, At dinner, some of the smaller neighbours were invited. **1863** MISS MULOCK *Mistr. & Maid* xxii, She was altogether a very great lady, and Hilary..felt an exceedingly small person beside her.

**b.** Having but little land, capital, etc.; dealing, doing business, etc., on a small scale. *spec.*, ***the small man***, the typical small businessman.

**1746** FRANCIS tr. *Horace, Epist.* I. vii. 99 Philip next Morn our honest Pedlar found, Dealing his Iron Merchandise around To his small Chaps. **1835** C. F. HOFFMAN *Winter in West* I. 79 They were chiefly plain people, small farmers and graziers. **1849** MACAULAY *Hist. Eng.* ix. II. 480 Two beasts, such as the small yeomen of that time were in the habit of riding. **1850** C. KINGSLEY *Alton Locke* II. xi. 154 In helping to pass the Reform Bill, [they had] only helped to give power to the two very classes who crushed them—the great labour kings, and the small shopkeepers. **1887** HINDLEY *Hist. Catnach Press* 257 From a small beginner in the world, Catnach was soon able to see his way clear to amass a fortune. **1926** CHESTERTON *Outl. Sanity* IV. iii. 170 If the small man found his small mechanical plant helped to the preservation of his small property, his claim would be very considerable. **1931** V. WOOLF *Waves* 255 How comforting it is to watch the lights coming out in the bedrooms of small shopkeepers on the other side of the river. **1935** M. EGAN *Dominant Sex* I. 27 In these days of trusts and combines the small man hardly stands an earthly. **1947** MCCALLUM & READMAN *Brit. Gen. Election 1945* iii. 63 The Conservatives ..professed that they were not in favour of the growth of monopoly, and that they were anxious to curb it for the sake of the 'small man'. **1948** KOESTLER in *Partisan Rev.* XV. 38 The petite bourgeoisie—the store-keeper, artisan, small businessman, white-collar worker. **1960** A. CLARKE *Horse-Eaters* 9 Thousands Bred yearly will fatten Small farmers. **1973** *Sat. Rev. Soc.* (U.S.) Mar. 58/1, I was a small farmer ..and there's no way you can do it today. You need technology and you need efficiency..and you can't afford.. it if you're down there on a small farm. **1974** *Times* 12 Nov. 14/2 The Smaller Businesses Association..set up to champion the interests of the small business man. **1976** R. BARNARD *Little Local Murder* ix. 106 'Aven't you 'eard 'ow difficult things are for the small shopkeeper?

**17. a.** Of minor rank, note, or importance, in respect of some specified office, function, etc.

**1338** R. BRUNNE *Chron.* (1810) 27 Þe smale kynges of þe lond all were þei comen. **1382** WYCLIF *Prol. Bible* i. 1 Alle these xij smale prophetis ben o book. **1456** SIR G. HAYE *Law Arms* (S.T.S.) 126 The autoritee of the grete officer..gerris cess the autoritee of the smallare officer. *a* **1578** LINDESAY (Pitscottie) *Chron. Scot.* (S.T.S.) II. 57 The haill bischopis, pryouris, and wther small preistis. **1588** *Reg. Privy Council Scot.* IV. 311 The small barronis and freehaldaris of this realme. **1610** B. JONSON *Alch.* I. ii, A speciall gentle, That.. Consorts with the small poets of the time. **1763** CHURCHILL *Ghost* III. 860 Confine thy rage to weaker slaves, Laugh at small Fools, and lash small Knaves. **1765** GRAY *Shaks.* 6 Fumbling baronets and poets small. **1826** DISRAELI *V. Grey* II. xii, A small author, and smaller wit. **1855** MACAULAY *Hist. Eng.* xix. IV. 260 All their confederates, from Cæsar.. down to the smallest Margrave.

**b.** That is (such) to a small or limited extent, degree, etc.

Sometimes used to suggest the converse of the noun.

**1523** LD. BERNERS tr. *Froissart* I. cccxxxii. 519 He was but a small gentylman,..for a very gentylman wyll neuer set his mynde on so euyll an entent. **1567** ALLEN *Def. Priesthood* 207 Where there is nowe putte no difference betwixte small offendours and moste greuouse sinners. **1634** SIR T. HERBERT *Trav.* 71 Zenall Chawn..(our small friend, at our being in his Citie). **1653** H. COGAN *Scarlet Gown* 125 They were but small friends to Pamphilio, and as such, they shewed themselves obstinate against his elections.

**c.** With negative, in emphatic use.

**1551** T. WILSON *Logike* (1580) 83, I remember of an other, and that no small birde, whiche was better learned then wise. **1657–61** HEYLIN *Hist. Ref.* I. ii. §4. 38 This Master Cook..was apt enough to think himself no small fool at a joynt of Divinity. **1784** *Unfortunate Sensibility* II. 72 The master of the inn..was no small body, for he was the owner of the vessel we came in.

**18.** Of things, etc.: Of little or minor consequence, interest, or importance; trifling, trivial, unimportant.

With quot. 1483 cf. Cotgrave's '*Menues pensées*,..idle, priuate, or prettie thoughts.'

*c* **1340** HAMPOLE *Pr. Consc.* 5702 Noght anly of gret dedes of elde, Bot of smale dedes of þair youthe. *c* **1374** CHAUCER *Boeth.* II. pr. vii. (1868) 59 Ȝe seken ȝoure gerdouns of þe smale wordes of strange folke. **1451** CAPGRAVE *Life St. Aug.* (1910) 8 Thus lerned he þe smale sciensis, as spellyng, reding and constrewyng. **1483** CAXTON *G. de la Tour* m j b, She shalle euer be in melancholye and in smalle thoughtes. **1500–20** DUNBAR *Poems* lvi. 2 Think that small partis makis grit seruice. **1568** GRAFTON *Chron.* II. 8 He..conferred the same vnto the Normanes and that for very small and light causes. **1624** DONNE *Devot.* Wks. 1839 III. 552 We have heard of Death upon small occasions and by scornful Instruments. **1651** HOBBES *Leviath.* (1839) 85 How a man should..pick his teeth before company, and such other points of the *small morals*. **1734** FIELDING *Intrig. Chambermaid* I. iv, She sent me, Sir, of [= on] a small message to you. **1837** CARLYLE *Fr. Rev.* I. I. iii, And then walk majestically out again, to embroidery, small-scandal, prayers, and vacancy. **1893** *Academy* 13 May 412/1 The fact..accounts, no doubt, for certain small recurrent defects in it.

**19.** Not prominent or notable; humble, modest; unpretentious. In later use chiefly in the phrase ***in a small way***.

*c* **1386** CHAUCER *Merch. T.* 381 Al were it so she were of smal degree, Suffiseth hym hir yowthe and hir beautee. **1548** HALL *Chron., Hen. V*, 65 Therfore I over passyng small names and muche doyng, wil returne [etc.]. **1611** BIBLE *Job* viii. 7 Though thy beginning was small, yet thy latter end should greatly increase. **1809** *European Mag.* LV. 19 An emporium no less respectable in a small way. **1815** JANE AUSTEN *Emma* iii, She lived with her single daughter in a very small way. **1872** T. HARDY *Under Greenw. Tree* Pref., A composer in a small way.

**20. a.** Base, low; mean, ungenerous.

**1824** SYD. SMITH *Wks.* (1859) II. 52 The pitiful propensity..to vent their small spite at their [the American] character. **1874** GREEN *Short Hist.* 755 The smaller passions, the meaner impulses of the world around him. **1890** *Spectator* Oct. 468/1 That is trickery, not statesmanship; and..it is small trickery too.

**b.** Incapable of large views or great actions; small-minded, mean-souled.

**1837** CARLYLE *Fr. Rev.* I. IV. iv, A man unfit for Revolutions? Whose small soul..could by no chance ferment into virulent *alegar*? **1871** SMILES *Charact.* iii. (1876) 84 Small men may be envious of their fellows, but really great men..love each other. **1881** J. F. CLARKE *Self-Culture* 258 Among the flippant and the frivolous, we also become small and empty.

**c.** As complement with *feel* and *look*: Humiliated, mortified, injured in self-respect. Cf. sense 16 a.

**1784** E. SHERIDAN *Jrnl.* 6 Oct. (1960) 31 Linley came to see my Father, he received him very kindly but poor L. look'd very small. **1840** MRS. TROLLOPE *Widow Married* xix, I should feel a little small at being seen in such a place. **1863** T. TAYLOR *Ticket-of-Leave Man* IV. i. 74 You've no right to be..coming after a chap, to make him look small this way. **1894** A. ROBERTSON *Nuggets* 190, I felt very small, for the scoundrel had been within my grasp, and I had let him slip.

**V. 21. a.** Special collocations.

***small ad***, ***small advertisement***, a small advertisement in a newspaper, usu. in a separate section devoted to such and printed with lack of display; ***Small-Back***, Death, imagined as a skeleton; ***small balls***, a variety of ironstone; ***small body***, in Printing (see quot.); ***small-bourgeois*** adj. = PETIT BOURGEOIS; so ***small bourgeoisie***; ***small capitals***, in Printing, capital letters differing little in size from the lower-case letters of the same fount; ***small caps*** = ***small capitals***; ***small cattle***, cattle below the size of oxen, as calves or sheep; ***small chisel*** (see quot.); ***small chop*** [CHOP *sb.*[6]] (W. Afr. colloq.), small items of food; ***small circle***, in spherical trigonometry (see quot.); ***small end***, in a piston engine, the end of a connecting rod nearer to the piston; also *attrib.*; ***smallest room*** (colloq.), the lavatory of a particular building (cf. *small room* below); † ***small figures***, Arabic numerals; ***small folk***, = ***small people***; ***small-for-dates***, (of a new-born baby) smaller than would be expected in view of the time since its conception; ***small fortune***: see FORTUNE *sb.* 6; ***small fruit*** (N. Amer.) (see quot. 1892); ***smallgoods*** (Austral.), sausages, bacon, etc.; ***small-hand*** (see HAND *sb.* 16); ***small hand-paper*** (see quot.); ***small helm***, Naut. (see quots.); ***small-holder***, one who owns or works a small-holding; ***small holding***, (*a*) a holding smaller than an ordinary farm; also *spec.* (see quot.); (*b*) the practice or occupation of working a small-holding; † ***small meat***, ? meat sold in small quantities; ***small paper***, in *Printing*, paper of the ordinary size, as distinct from *large paper* (LARGE *a.* 8 b); ***small part***, a minor part or character in a play; ***small people***, in local use, the fairies; ***small-pipe(s)***, a Northumbrian bellows-filled bagpipe; † ***small play***, play for low stakes; ***small room*** (colloq.), a lavatory (cf. *smallest room* above); ***small round***, ***sail(s***, Naut. (see quots.); ***small screen***, television; also *attrib.*; ***small seed*** (see quot. 1950); ***small slam***: see SLAM *sb.*[2] 2 b; ***small stores*** (Naut.), (*a*) items for personal use or consumption on a sea-voyage; (*b*) *U.S.* articles of regulation issue clothing; a shop selling these; also *attrib.* (in *sing.* or *pl.*); ***small stuff*** (see quots.); † ***small-world***, = MICROCOSM. See also DEBT *sb.* 4 f, HOUR 3 b, PICA[1] 2, POTATO 5 a, RAISIN 2 b, TITHE, TRUNK, etc., and SMALL ARM(S, BEER, -CLOTHES, etc.

**1922** *Small ad [see AD]. **1961** 'F. O'BRIEN' *Hard Life* vi. 45, I put a small ad. in one of the papers. **1969** *Sunday Times* 2 Mar. 8/3 To recruit models, they ran a string of small-ads asking: 'Are you really ugly?' **1978** J. WAINWRIGHT *Ripple of Murders* 11 A small ad. in the Personal Column..will read, 'J. D. Message received.' **1919** *Times* 6 Nov. 2 *Small Advertisement order form. **1937** M. ALLINGHAM *Dancers in Mourning* xxiii. 285 Uncle William put down *The Times*. He had been looking at the small advertisements. **1823** SCOTT *Quentin D.* xxxvii, Men have queer fancies when old *Small-Back is griping them; but Small-Back must lead down the dance with us all in our time. **1793** A. YOUNG *Agric. Sussex* 13 A marl sets on, in the different depths of which the iron-stone comes on regularly in all the various sorts as follows: 1. **Small balls*, provincially *twelve foots*, because so many feet distant from the first to the last bed. **1683** MOXON *Mech. Exerc., Printing* 20 Long-Primer and downwards are accounted *small Bodies. **1930** A. BENNETT *Imperial Palace* lv. 414 Customers of the *small bourgeois class. **1974** N. FREELING *Dressing of Diamond* 134 A very small-bourgeois existence, with a canary. **1970** F. C. WEFFORT in I. L. Horowitz *Masses in Lat. Amer.* xi. 398 They did not feel so much like members of a decadent *small bourgeoisie, but rather like operators with a stable position moving toward the better. **1770** LUCKOMBE *Hist. Print.* 250 *Small Capitals are mostly used to denote, that a more particular stress and emphasis is intended by the Author. **1888** JACOBI *Printers' Vocab.* 127 *Small capitals*, the smaller capitals laid in the upper case, distinct from the full capitals. **1856** GEO. ELIOT in *Westm. Rev.* Oct. 454 She informs us, with all the lucidity of italics and *small caps, that '*function*, not *form*,..weakly engrossed her'. **1967** *Style Man.* (U.S. Govt. Printing Off.) (rev. ed.) iii. 31 In matter set in caps and small caps.. capitalize all principal words. **1593** *Benefits Observ. Fish-days*, The number of Beefes aforesaid,..and other *small Cattel, as Calues, Sheepe, and Lambes innumerable. **1875** KNIGHT *Dict. Mech.* 2219 **Small-chisel*, a burin or graver used by engravers. **1963** M. LAURENCE in R. Weaver *Canad. Short Stories* (1968) 2nd Ser. 140, I use the shallow ones to put groundnuts in..for *small-chop with drinks. **1971** J. SPENCER *Eng. Lang. W. Afr.* 11 Pidgin words, known and used by almost everyone,..who has lived in the coastal areas of West Africa..*chop* n and v, 'food' and 'eat', and its recent extensions in phrases such as *small chop*, 'cocktail eats', *chop box*,..etc. **1873** PRYDE *Pract. Math.* 365 Circles, whose planes pass through the centre of the sphere, are called great circles; and all others, *small circles. **1850** T. TREDGOLD *Steam Engine* (ed. 3) I. IX. 7 Into these guide-blocks are fixed the cross-heads, forming the bearings for the *small ends of the connecting rods. **1908** *Autocar Handbk.* (ed. 2) ii. 38 The gudgeon pin end of the connecting rod is called the small end, and the other end the big end. **1922** *Encycl. Brit.* XXX. 36/2 The ordinary small-end bronze bush system with gudgeon pins fixed in the piston was used. **1948** A. W. JUDGE *Mod. Motor Engineer* (ed. 4) I. ix. 208 After a considerable period of running..the small-end brush may wear oval, due to the more or less vertical thrust of the connecting rod. **1971** B. SCHARF *Engin. & its Language* xii. 122 Connecting rods... They comprise a big end..and a small end through which the gudgeon pin..passes. **1930** *Smallest room [see GEOGRAPHY 1 d]. **1933** P. GODFREY *Back-Stage* xvi. 202 The smallest room in the house invariably has prohibitory notices of a stern and intimate character. **1960** *Guardian* 29 Apr. 12/6 Soon she had become unable..to take herself into her 'smallest room' in the midget backyard. **1973** 'H. CARMICHAEL' *Candles for Dead* xii. 150 At a guess, I'd say he's probably in the smallest room. **1711** HEARNE *Collect.* (O.H.S.) III. 110 He makes *small Figures to be as old as A.D. 1050. **1865** R. HUNT *Pop. Rom. W. Eng.* (1896) 118 The gardens of the Small People, or, as they are called by the natives, *Small Folk. **1965** *Clinics in Developmental Med.* XIX. 1 Not all '*small for dates' babies should necessarily be regarded as suffering from pathological growth retardation. **1978** *Nature* 30 Mar. 404/1 During the past twenty years it has become accepted that some babies are born small not because they are premature but because their growth has been retarded in the uterus. These so-called small-for-dates babies..are at greater than normal risk at birth. **1822** J. C. LOUDON *Encycl. Gardening* III. 537 This operation [*sc.* gathering] in the case of *small fruits, as the gooseberry, strawberry, &c. is generally performed by the under gardeners. **1892** A. A. CROZIER *Dict. Bot. Terms* 164/2 Small fruits, a horticultural term for certain low-growing perennial, fruit-bearing plants and their product, including the strawberry, raspberry, blackberry, gooseberry, currant, huckleberry, and cranberry. **1926** *Daily Colonist* (Victoria, B.C.) 11 July 12/3 Small fruit continue to show prominence, but some varieties are becoming scarce. **1950** *Sci. Monthly* Apr. 212 The story of the evolution of the groups from which our small fruits have been derived is shrouded in the mists of the geological past. **1969** *Northern Territory News* (Focus '69) 22 (Advt.), It sells the best cuts of meat—beef, lamb, veal and pork—as well as *smallgoods. **1973** *Bulletin* (Sydney) 25 Aug. 20/3 What are the smallgoods manufacturers putting in their sausages now that mutton, the backbone of their industry, has ceased to be cheap and plentiful? **1821** *Small hand [see NARY *a.*]. **1847** DICKENS *Dombey* (1848) xiv. 134 He would be expected to inform Doctor and Mrs. Blimber, in superfine small-hand, that Mr. P. Dombey would be happy to have the honour of waiting on them. **1860** W. COLLINS *Woman in White* xi, The handwriting..was..in the cramped, conventional, copybook character, technically termed 'small hand'. **1888** JACOBI *Printers' Vocab.* 127 *Small hand paper, a common machine-made paper, generally straw-coloured, used for post wrappers and such purposes. **1867** SMYTH *Sailor's Word-bk.* 634 **Small-Helm.* One of the principal results of sound seamanship is the proper trim of the vessel and the sail carried; by which means the action of the rudder is reduced to a minimum. **1886** *Encycl. Brit.* XXI. 604 *Small helm*, when the sails are well balanced and the rudder but little used. **1837** LOCKHART *Scott* IV. i. 16 The property all about his original farm had been in the hands of various *small holders (Scotticé *cock-lairds*). **1915** H. R. HAGGARD in *Times* 15 Mar. 3/2 The wives and daughters of smallholders will help their menfolk because they are labouring for themselves. **1977** *Times* 18 Aug. 14/6 A smallholder living in a hut on the duneland plantation. **1892** *Act.* 55–56 *Vict.* c. 31 §1 The expression '*small holding'.. shall mean land acquired by a council..which exceeds one acre and either does not exceed fifty acres, or..is of an annual value..not exceeding fifty pounds. **1927** S. L. BENSUSAN *Latter-Day Rural Engl.* viii. 73 Smallholding thrives in Lincolnshire. **1742** *De Foe's Tour Gt. Britain* (ed. 3) I. 24 [Ipswich] has five Market-days weekly; Tuesday and Thursday for *small Meat; Wednesday and Friday for Fish. **1708** *Small paper [see 22]. **1936** W. M. SALE *S. Richardson* 31 It was not until the autumn of 1742 that he began to see the need for publishing his second small paper edition. **1798** O'KEEFFE *Wild Oats* IV. i, Drill the servants that I've given the *small parts to. **1865** R. HUNT *Pop. Rom. W. Eng.* Ser. I. 65 The *Small People are believed by some to be the spirits of people who inhabited Cornwall many thousands of years ago. **1855** in Wright *Eng. Dial. Dict.* (1904) V. 548/1 The torch was lit on point of spear—And *small pipes they did sound. **1927** *Observer* 30 Oct. 8 A humble performer on the Northumbrian small-pipes. **1967** A. L. LLOYD *Folk Song in Eng.* vi. 333 The silvery-toned Northumbrian small-pipes struggling to be heard above the full shrill singing. **1975** S. MARCUSE *Mus. Instruments* 482/1 The mid-18th c., when the characteristic feature of the small-pipe was developed: its chanter was stopped. **1629** H. BURTON *Babel no Bethel* 7 [He] is willing rather to play *small play, then to giue out. **1858** QUEEN VICTORIA *Let.* 7 Feb. in R. Fulford *Dearest Child* (1964) 35 Has the railway carriage got a *small room to it? **1979** D. SANDERS *Queen sends for Mrs. Chadwick* 134 Where..was the nearest small room to the Queen's drawing-room, where the President would be received? **1863** A. YOUNG *Naut. Dict.* 358 **Small round*, that end of the shank of an anchor which is next the stock. **1669** STURMY *Mariner's Mag.* I. ii. 16 Take in your Main and Main-top-sail, Steering-sails [etc.]... Thus you have all the *small Sails in. **1867** SMYTH *Sailor's Word-bk.* 634 *Small-Sails*, topgallant-studding-sails and the kites. **1886** *Encycl. Brit.* XXI. 604 *Small sail*, and *snug sail*, low and reduced, ready for bad weather. **1956** *B.B.C. Handbk. 1957* 79 This unit.. provides the means for young writers to become acquainted with the requirements of the *small screen. **1963** 'E. CRISPIN' *Best SF Five* 9 The success of the *Quatermass* series has given science fiction a limited yet tolerably regular share in the hotchpotch purveyed by the small screen. **1966** *Guardian* 29 Mar. 10/3 Both sides have studiously kept their small-screen liabilities out of the studios. **1971** *Oxford Times* 26 Nov. 31/4 The stars and the characters they portray are as in the small-screen version. **1980** *Times Lit. Suppl.* 31 Oct. 1229/4 Jonathan Miller had little success in finding the play's natural rhythms and adapting them to the small screen. **1840** W. DEANS *Let.* 30 Oct. in J. Deans *Pioneers Canterbury* (1939) 29, I..have got in about two acres of potatoes and..numerous *small seeds. **1950** *N.Z. Jrnl. Agric.* Apr. 359/1 Small seeds [grown in a Canterbury district] include perennial and Italian rye-grass, cocksfoot, crested dogs-tail, and clover. **1814** G. COGGESHALL *Jrnl.* 24 Mar. in *Voyages* (1851) 55 We took on board six casks of fresh water, some fresh provisions, and sundry small stores. **1877** *Nautical Mag.* XLVI. 195 Small stores as coffee, tea, or sugar was called by the 'geordies'. **1927** *U.S. Navy Bluejackets' Man.* 379 The storekeeper who issues this clothing will make out a small-store slip in duplicate. **1938** *Ibid.* 20 Besides the small stores where you can get all your clothing at very cheap prices, your station will have the following shops. **1950** *Ibid.* 124 The storekeeper who issues this clothing makes out a small-stores slip, in duplicate. **1966** NOEL & BUSH *Naval Terms Dict.* 93 *Clothing and small stores*, standard articles of uniform for officers and enlisted men with such related articles as buttons, brushes, etc. **1867** SMYTH *Sailor's Word-bk.* 634 **Small Stuff*, the term for spun-yarn, marline, and the smallest kinds of rope, even for yarns. **1897** *Daily News* 18 June 5/2 The scarcity of spoons, forks, and knives,..called 'small stuff' in the catering business. **1612** J. DAVIES (Heref.) *Muse's Sacr.* Wks. (Grosart) II. 64/1 Whose soule did animate thy *small-world too To be the soule of all that here I doe.

**b.** In the specific or popular names of plants, as ***small basil***, ***bugloss***, ***chaffweed***, etc.

A large number of other examples occur in Lyte (1578) and Miss Pratt *Flowering Pl.* (1855).

**1578** LYTE *Dodoens* 240 Busshe Basill, or *small Basill gentle. **1855** MISS PRATT *Flowering Pl.* IV. 245 *Small Chaffweed, or Bastard Pimpernel. **1796** WITHERING *Brit. Pl.* (ed. 3) II. 264 *Small Currants. **1548** TURNER *Names Herbes* 15 The third kinde [of Aristolochia] is called Clematites & it may be called in english *small Hertworte. **1796** WITHERING *Brit. Pl.* (ed. 3) II. 287 *Tordylium officinale* .., Small Hartwort. *Ibid.*, Fine-leaved Bastard Parsley. *Small Hensfoot. **1597** GERARDE *Herbal* 478 The Pinke is called..in English Pinkes, and *Smal Honesties. **14..** *Lat.-Eng. Voc.* in Wr.-Wülcker 612 *Solatrum i. morella*, *smalmorell. **1573** TUSSER *Husb.* (1878) 75 Set chestnut and walnut, set filbeard and *smalnut. **1842–59** *Small-reed [see REED *sb.*[1] 5]. **1900** *G. Nicholson's Dict. Gard.* Suppl., *Calamagrostis.* Smallreed. This genus..was formerly included under *Arundo.* **1855** MISS PRATT *Flowering Pl.* III. 158 *Small Woodruff, or Squinancy-wort.

**c.** In names of fishes, birds, insects, etc.

Further examples may be found in special works, as Shaw *Gen. Zool.* (1801–11), Rennie *Butterfl. & Moths* (1832), etc.

**1754** CATESBY *Carolina* I. 80 The *small Bittern. **1846** *Proc. Berw. Nat. Club* II. 171 The *Small Copper [Butterfly] again made its appearance. **1840** F. D. BENNETT *Whaling Voy.* II. 72 That curious fish, the *Leptocephalus*, or '*small-head'. **1884** GOODE *Nat. Hist. Aquat. Anim.* 550 '*Small Herring', 'Anchovies,' 'Skarp Herring.' **1787** BEST *Angling* (ed. 2) 104 The Palmers. 6. The *small Red Spinners. 6. **1734** ALBIN *Nat. Hist. Birds* II. 67 The *small Water-Hen.

**22. a.** With sbs. forming combs. used attributively, as ***small-angle***, ***-band***, ***-boat***, ***-bore*** (also *fig.*), ***-boy***, ***-budget***, ***-calibre***, ***-city***, ***-claims***, ***-college***, ***-debt***, ***-drink***, ***-end*** (see sense 21 a), ***-farm***, ***-fry***, ***-gauge***, ***-girl***, ***-grain***, ***-group***, ***-letter***, ***-master***, ***-note***, ***-paper***, ***-part***, ***pattern***, ***-plane***, ***-power***, ***-print*** (see sense 4 a), ***-sample***, ***-screen*** (see sense 21 a), ***-shop***, ***-signal***, ***-size***, ***-step***, ***-store***(*s*) (see sense 21 a), ***-tooth***, ***-type***; **small-cell** *Path.*, used *attrib.* to designate various tumours of uncertain origin composed of small cells, esp. an oat-cell carcinoma of the bronchus; **small-scale** *a.*, operating or executed on a small scale; drawn to a small scale; of small size or extent; **small-yield** *a.* = *low-yield* adj. s.v. LOW *a.* 23.

Combs. of this type are very numerous in recent newspaper usage. (N.E.D.)

**1960** *Proc. R. Soc.* A. CCLIV. 242 (*heading*) The *small-angle scattering of photons. **1979** *Jrnl. R. Soc. Arts* Jan. 106/2 *Small-angle x-ray scattering*, which is another versatile structural tool for phase transformations, defects and voids, supported catalysts, polymers and various biological materials. **1941** *Jazz Information* Nov. 25/2 They are the best jazz recordings of the New Orleans *small-band type. **1977** *New Yorker* 12 Sept. 122/2 Hampton was enough of a sensation to be asked by Victor in 1937 to lead a series of small-band recordings. **1897** *Outing* XXX. 333/1 The annals of *small-boat sailing. **1898** W. S. CHURCHILL in *Morning Post* 7 Oct. 5/7 The Dervish gunboat *Bordaine*.. returned from its quest with nearly a hundred men wounded by the *small-bore bullets of a civilised force which was in occupation. **1900** *Congress. Rec.* 14 Feb. 1804/2 No small-bore, two-by-four, radical politicians can hurt that great court. **1932** *Sun* (Baltimore) 15 Nov. 10/2 The thing to do is to sweep this ghastly mess out of doors, once and for all. It will not be easy to do—if small-bore statesmanship is to continue to rule us. **1976** *R.A.F. News* 11–24 May 19 (*caption*) Brawdy's small bore rifle team pictured with..the Nobel Challenge Cup. **1861** *Harper's Mag.* June 133/1 We sometimes sell skates: and buying a lot at auction last fall, we thought to monopolize all the *small-boy trade by posting a flaming placard announcing that we sold skates at twenty cents a pair. **1937** M. ALLINGHAM *Dancers in Mourning* xiii. 178 He was..handsome in the downy, small boy fashion of his kind. **1973** J. STRANGER *Walk Lonely Road* xiii. 92 He grinned at her, and she grinned her small-boy grin back at him. **1961** *Times* 31 July 14/7 Hardly anyone in Hollywood makes *small-budget pictures any more. **1979** 'P. O'CONNOR' *Into Strong City* xxxiv. 122 Someone in London ..would rush out a small-budget film into which they would cram every Scottish actor and actress. **1896** *Spectator* 31 Oct. 589/1 If it be suitable, the *small-calibre bullet will do much more damage. **1929** CLUTE & SMITH in *Arch. Surg.* XVIII. 11 In the fourth and last group..we have another debatable form of tumor. For the purposes of classification, we have designated it as the *small cell carcinoma. This is the type of tumor which is sometimes called lymphosarcoma, as it is made up of small round cells, poorly differentiated..with a prominent nucleus and an almost negligible amount of cytoplasm. **1966** WRIGHT & SYMMERS *Systemic Path.* I. v. 265/1 In the earlier days of histopathology, although lymphocytic and lymphoblastic types of lymphosarcoma were recognized, various tumours were frequently confused with them, including..small-cell anaplastic carcinomas (for example, of the thyroid and bronchus). **1976** *Path. Ann.* XI. 319 In the differential diagnosis of acute leukemia the following should be considered: small cell epithelial tumors (eg, oat cell carcinoma, carcinoid, islet cell tumor), neuroblastoma, [etc.]. **1977** V. COLEMAN *Paper Doctors* xiii. 139 Surgery for small-cell cancer of the bronchus. **1964** S. M. MILLER in I. L. Horowitz *New Sociology* 292 The small-town and *small-city poor suffer from the demise of local industry. **1977** *Sat. Rev.* (U.S.) 5 Mar. 12/2 This array of small-city labor disputes. **1961** WEBSTER, *Small-claims court. **1972** M. KAYE *Lively Game of Death* vii. 38, I simply threatened him with Small Claims Court... The maximum claim there is five hundred dollars. **1978** *Listener* 3 Aug. 159/3 The London Small Claims Court..is being run on an experimental basis and only handles claims up to £350. **1840** THACKERAY *Shabby-genteel Story* viii, Tufthunt was a *small-college man of no family. **1838** W. BELL *Dict. Law Scot.* 919 The statute 39 and 40 Geo. III. c. 46, commonly called the *Small Debt Act. *Ibid.* 923 A case..remitted..to the small debt court. **1659** R. WILDE *Poems* (1870) 1 Our *small-drink times Must be contented, and take up with rhymes. **1960** *Farmer & Stockbreeder* 16 Feb. 60/3 This pinpoints the need for a cheaper *small-farm tank of from 80 to 125 gallons capacity. **1970** S. L. BARRACLOUGH in I. L. Horowitz *Masses in Lat. Amer.* iv. 112 If any group has been systematically discriminated against, it is the small-farm producers and landless workers. **1874** 'MARK TWAIN' in *Altantic Monthly* Nov. 592/2 Dey wa'n't no *small-fry officers, mine you; dey was de biggest dey is. **1897** MARY KINGSLEY *W. Africa* 544 Alarm, excitement, fear, fright, and all those small-fry emotions. **1957** R. FRANKENBERG *Village on Border* 10 The *small-gauge railway. *a* **1976** A. CHRISTIE *Autobiogr.* (1977) VI. i. 296 An expedition in a small-gauge train. **1980** 'A. SKINNER' *Mind's Eye* v. 73 'Thank you,' she said with careful, *small-girl politeness. **1840** J. BUEL *Farmer's Comp.* 197 The *small-grain crops are the greatest exhausters of the fertility of the soil. **1951** in Rohrer & Sherif *Soc. Psychol. at Crossroads* 333 The very few *small-group studies made in recent years. **1955** KEEPNEWS & GRAUER *Pictorial Hist. Jazz* xi. 117 Alternating big-band work with prolific small-group recording activity. **1964** I. L. HOROWITZ *New Sociology* 25 Even at the level..of small-group research, time must be recorded. **1972** G. LITTLE in G. W. Turner *Good Austral. Eng.* vii. 135 The pupils sit in groups face to face, and pursue a variety of small-group activities. **1974** *Melody Maker* 13 Apr. 50/7 A lovely example of small-group jazz by players who have worked together. **1979** in W. G. Lawrence *Exploring Indiv. & Organiz. Boundaries* vi. 91 The students were told that they would participate in a small group experience. **1771** LUCKOMBE *Hist. Print.* 261 Of these *Small-letter Sorts, some are lodged in the Upper-case. **1945** E. JOHNSTON *Writing & Illuminat. & Lettering* xv. 263 More time and material than a Small-letter MS. entails. **1950** *Language* XXVI. 13 Small-letter vowels. **1851** MAYHEW *Lond. Labour* II. 331/2 The last mentioned of the several modes..is the '*small-master system'. **1823** W. COBBETT *Rural Rides* (1885) I. 387 The injury recently done to about forty thousand poor families..by the *Small-note Bill. **1708** HEARNE *Collect.* 8 Apr., 3 *small-paper Livys. **1904** MRS. ALEC TWEEDIE *Behind Footlights* xi. 204 Those in the rank of 'principals', or '*small-part ladies'. **1836** DUBOURG *Violin* ix. (1878) 270 Lorenzio Guadagnini.. copied the *small-pattern fiddles of his master. **1964** G. LYALL *Most Dangerous Game* vi. 42 He was the only other pilot doing *small-plane charter work in Lapland that year. **1956** *Nature* 18 Feb. 322/2 Specifications for two light-weight *small-power sprayers. *Ibid.* 28 Jan. 160/1 Techniques of *small-sample loading employing micro-pipettes. **1968** *Brit. Med. Bull.* XXIV. 220/2 The calculations in the program have been written for the particular needs of the medical research worker; thus 'small sample' statistical theory is well represented. **1852** C. W. H[OSKINS] *Talpa* 151 It is very fine..to connect one's own *small-scale improvements, after this fashion. **1887** [see SCALE *sb.*[3] 11 a]. **1935** *Discovery* Mar. 78/1 The small-scale structure of the ice will be examined. **1951** R. FIRTH *Elem. Social Organization* ii. 43 These are small-scale units..the members of which are in close personal contact in daily life. **1954** M. RICKERT *Painting in Britain: Middle Ages* v. 131 Softer, finer vellum, more suitable for the small-scale miniatures. **1960** *Farmer & Stockbreeder* 16 Feb. 75/3 The disadvantages of small-scale farming heavily outweighed the advantages. **1964** W. L. GOODMAN *Hist. Woodworking Tools* 56 The difficulties of showing detail in small-scale carvings. **1979** *N. & Q.* Feb. 16/2 Orrery was very much the literary dilettante and small-scale Mæcenas. **1937** *Discovery* Feb. 45/1 Flicker, 'rain' and a rather dim appearance make the demonstration noticeably inferior in quality to that obtained with the *small screen receivers now on the market. **1868** G. MEREDITH *Let.* Oct. (1970) I. 376 Eleven a.m. plates of *small-shop ham, thick cut, grisly with brine: four smashed eggs on it. **1967** KARCH & BUBER *Offset Processes* ii. 9 The graphic arts is a small-shop industry. Only about 1,000 plants employ more than 100 employees, and the average is 17. **1949** *Bell Syst. Techn. Jrnl.* XXVIII. 401 An explicit calculation of the transient phenomena outside the range of *small-signal theory. **1877** RAYMOND *Statist. Mines & Mining* 44 *Small-size garnets are found..in this claim. **1962** SIMPSON & RICHARDS *Physical Princ. Junction Transistors* xv. 372 The equivalent circuits..may be used in the determination of the transient response of video amplifiers by estimating their time of response to a *small-step input of current or voltage. **1687** MIÉGE *Gt. Fr. Dict.* II, A *small tooth Comb. **1732** *Acc. of Workhouses* 40 Their heads combed with small tooth combs every morning. **1858** SIMMONDS *Dict. Trade*, *Small-tooth comb*, a comb of ivory or bone with small teeth on each side. **1962** R. WILLIAMS *Communications* iii. 58 Regular columns of close print, with *small-type headlines. **1976** *Amer. Speech 1974* XLIX. 267 Good lexicography keeps open a variety of approaches to defining, which include..exploiting small-type notes for added comment. **1959** *N.Y. Times* 19 Mar. 16/1 The three Project Argus detonations involved relatively *small yield nuclear devices. **1963** *Listener* 7 Feb. 251/2 The introduction of compact, mobile 'small yield' weapons into service with American forces in Europe.

**b.** In combs. of the type ***small-boyhood***, ***-boyish***, ***-colleger***, etc.

**1841** ROSCOE *Swift's Gulliver* I. iv. *note*, Papists and protestants are the big-endians and small-endians. **1852** BRISTED *Five Yrs. Eng. Univ.* (ed. 2) 127 The idea of a Small-Colleger beating all Trinity was deemed preposterous. **1864** J. C. ATKINSON *Stanton Grange* 40 Tom subsided into small-boyhood again. **1882** W. JAMES *Let.* 9 Nov. (1920) I. 214 Baginsky's torrent of words was even more overwhelming than Munk's. I never felt quite so helpless and small-boyish before. **1895** K. GRAHAME *Golden Age* 96 This dreary pastime found way into his small-boyish being.

**c.** Forming verbs, as **small-hoe**, to clean with a small hoe; **small-gang**, *slang*, to mob.

**1786** ABERCROMBIE *Gard. Assist.* 139 Salsafy, scorzonera, skirrets—small-hoe, and thin six inches distance. **1851** MAYHEW *Lond. Lab.* I. 420/2 They 'small-ganged' me; and afterwards I went seven days to prison. **1892** P. H. EMERSON *Son of Fens* 162, I see 'em kind o' looking and talking low; so, think I, they're going to small-gang me.

**23. a.** In parasynthetic combs., as ***small-bodied***, ***-boned***, ***-brained***, etc. Also ***small-mindedness***.

Only a few of the earlier or more important examples of this type are here given.

**1685** *Lond. Gaz.* No. 2019/8 A brown bay Nag,..full Haunched, and *small Bodied. **1812** CRABBE *Tales* iii. 50 He soon display'd his skill In *small-boned Lambs. **1835–6** *Todd's Cycl. Anat.* I. 566/1 The *small-brained and cold-blooded classes of Vertebrata. **1873** T. H. GREEN *Introd. Path.* (ed. 2) 170 The groups of epithelial elements are always surrounded by a *small-celled ('indifferent') tissue, the small-celled growth preceding the epithelial invasion. **1633** *Gerarde's Herbal* 1437 Flowers..which turn into *small cornered bladders of winter cherries. **1733** W. ELLIS *Chiltern & Vale Farm.* 330 The Crop becomes hopper, *small ear'd, and will not yield like the large one. **1771** LUCKOMBE *Hist. Print.* 226 The same Letter..being adjudged too *small-faced for..Small Pica. *a* **1930** D. H. LAWRENCE *Etruscan Places* (1932) 143 A small-faced, weedy sort of youth. **1967** KARCH & BUBER *Offset Processes* iv. 78 Sizes range from a small-faced six point to a 13-point full point sized capital letter font. *c* **1550** CHEKE *Matt.* vi, How much moor, ye *smalfaithed men, wil he cloth yow? *a* **1734** NORTH *Lives* (1826) I. 71 The leading counsel in a *small-fee'd case. **1603** BRETON *Mad World my Masters* Wks. (Grosart) II. 8/1 A..faire-handed, *small-footed, straight-bodied..gentlewoman. **1707** MORTIMER *Husb.* (1721) I. 105 The *small-grained Sand is esteemed the best. **1851** GLENNY *Hdbk. Fl. Gard.* 21 They grow exceedingly well, especially all the *smaller-habited kinds. **1851** H. MELVILLE *Moby Dick* I. xli. 303 The White Steed of the Prairies; a magnificent milk-white charger, large-eyed, *small-headed, bluff-chested. **1931** W. FAULKNER *Sanctuary* xvii. 159 The thick small-headed shape of him would be clinging to the bars, gorilla-like. **1847** HELPS *Friends in C.* I. v. 85 *Small-minded people carry their narrow notions and their acidity into their benevolence. **1886** BESANT *Childr. Gibeon* II. xv, That kind of *smallmindedness was impossible. **1796** KIRWAN *Elem. Min.* (ed. 2) I. 293 A fine *small-pored white enamel. **1670** EACHARD *Cont. Clergy* 98 We must have a great care of comparing our *small-preferr'd clergy with those but of the like fortune in the church of Rome. **1956** P. A. LARKIN *Less Deceived* 40 Nor the shelves stuffed with *small-printed books for the Sabbath. **1951** C. W. MILLS *White Collar* I. iii. 34 The ideology suitable for a nation of small capitalists persists, as if that *small-propertied world were still a going concern. **1542** RECORDE *Gr. Artes* Pref., In those *small reasoned persons [is] a certaine kind of reverence toward wisdome and reason. **1780** *Phil. Trans.* LXX. App. p. xxxvii, I have never succeeded in killing any rabbit (even the *smallest-sized one) with it. **1899** *Allbutt's Syst. Med.* VIII. 854 Bodin has found on the horse a microsporon closely allied to the *small-spored fungus described by Sabouraud. **1964** M. HYNES *Med. Bacteriol.* (ed. 8) xxvii. 418 (*caption*) Ringworm of hair—Small-spored ectothrix. **1830** M. DONOVAN *Domest. Econ.* II. 107 The flesh is inferior to that of the *small-tailed sheep. **1640** GATAKER *Whitgift* in *Fuller's Abel Rediv.* (1867) II. 203 He was a man of middle stature,..*small-timbered. **1802** *Phil. Trans.* XCII. 350 Each row looks somewhat like a *small-toothed comb. **1891** T. HARDY *Let.* 4 Mar. (1978) I. 230 My own occupation at present is that of correcting a bundle of miserably *small-typed proofs. **1902** M. BEERBOHM in *Sat. Rev.* 15 Nov. 612/2 The authentic 'star'..is a no greater person than small-typed, smuggled-in 'J. M. Barrie'. **1930** W. DE LA MARE *Poems for Children* 35 The *small-windowed moonlit house. **1976** *Times* 21 Aug. 12/3 One-storeyed, small-windowed cottages.

**b.** Freq. in the specific names of animals, birds, plants, etc.

**1884** COUES *N. Amer. Birds* 290 *Mniotilta varia borealis*, *Small-billed Creeper. **1827** GRIFFITH tr. *Cuvier* V. 178 *Phoca Leptonyx* (*Small-clawed Seal). **1752** HILL *Hist. Anim.* 168 The *small-eared, very thin Pecten. **1789** PILKINGTON *View Derbyshire* I. 439 *Malva parviflora*, *small-flowered, or dwarf Mallow. **1796** WITHERING *Brit. Pl.* (ed. 3) II. 507 Small-flowered Crowfoot. **1822** *Hortus Angl.* II. 86 *Leonurus Marrubiastrum.* Small-flowered Motherwort. **1894** LYDEKKER *Roy. Nat. Hist.* II. 293 The *small-horned gazelle (*Gazella leptoceros*) of the Sudan. *c* **1880** *Cassell's Nat. Hist.* II. 241 The *Small-nailed Seal (*Phoca leptonyx*). **1803** SHAW *Gen. Zool.* IV. II. 514 *Small-Scaled Labrus, *Labrus Microlepidotus.* **1831** GRIFFITH tr. *Cuvier* IX. Syn. 63 Small scaled Zonurus, *Zonurus Microlepidotus.* **1836** YARRELL *Brit. Fishes* II. 367 The *Small-spotted Dog-fish. **1766** *Compl. Farm.* s.v. *Radish* 6. I 1/1 The *small topped,..the scarlet, and the long topped striped radish.

**B.** *absol.* or as *sb.*[2]

**1. a.** Persons or animals of small size or stature; little ones, children. (Now only with *the.*)

*c* **1220** *Bestiary* 515 in *O.E. Misc.*, Ðe smale he wile ðus biswiken, ðe grete maiȝ he noȝt bigripen. *a* **1300** *E.E. Psalter* xvi. 16 Þar leuinges to þair smale left þai. **1388** WYCLIF *Matt.* xviii. 6 Who so sclaundrith oon of these smale, that bileuen in me. *c* **1430** *Syr Tryam.* 1556 'A lytulle lower, Syr,' seyde hee, 'And let us smalle go wyth thee'.

**b.** A child, a little one.

**1907** W. DE MORGAN *Alice-for-Short* xxx. 300 How much can you remember of all that time, Alice? You were only a small, you know. *Ibid.*, I wasn't such a small as all that. **1947** *Forum* (Johannesburg) 5 Apr. 37/1 In a dozen other ways the prefects are the right-hand men of their Housemasters and me, and many a small owes a very great debt indeed to them. **1968** *Guardian* 1 Apr. 7/3 Leave two smalls to the tender mercies of a baby sitter? **1981** P. DICKINSON *Seventh Raven* vi. 75 After each performance there's always a dozen smalls wandering miserably around.

**2.** Persons of low or inferior rank or position, or of little ability or attainment. Chiefly in phr. ***great and small***, or ***small and great.***

**13..** *E.E. Psalter* cxviii. 130 Schirenes of þi speche lightes wit, Vnderstanding to litel [*Egerton MS.* smale] giues it. **13..** *Cursor M.* 6014 (Gött.), Þair king þai banned, gret and small. *a* **1400** *Minor Poems fr. Vernon MS.* xxiii. 1152 Heil þou..Kyng of gret and smalle. *c* **1440** *Ipomydon* 96 All spake of hym, bothe grete and smalle. **1535** COVERDALE *Ps.* cxiii. 12 Yee he blesseth all them that feare the Lorde, both small & greate. **1597** I. T. *Serm. Paules Crosse* 29 The cause of the smalle, as well as the greate. **1654** WHITLOCK *Zootomia* 97 Quacking Mountebanks are admitted in the Bed-chambers of great and small. **1781** COWPER *Truth* 375 Envy, ye great, the dull, unletter'd small.

**3.** †**a.** Little, not much. Also with *of. Obs.*

**1390** GOWER *Conf.* II. 279 Touchende Usure I have al herd, Hou thou of love hast wonne smale. *a* **1425** *Cursor M.* 18246 (Trin.), Now is oure kyngdome fordone al Of monkynde gete we ful smal. **1444** LYDG. in *Pol. Poems* (Rolls) II. 215 To thynke mochyl, and seyn but smal. **1588** SHAKS. *L.L.L.* I. i. 86 Small haue continuall plodders euer wonne. **1596** SPENSER *F.Q.* VI. ix. 20 Hauing small, yet doe I not complaine Of want. **1640** *King & Poor North. Man* 144 in Hazl. *E.P.P.* IV. 298 Let me in, Ise give thee a good single penny. I see thou wilt ha small, ere thou't doe for nought.

*Comb.* **1588** SHAKS. *L.L.L.* I. i. 253 There did I see..that vnletered small knowing soule.

†**b.** ***by small and small***, by degrees; gradually, slowly. *Obs.*

**1558** PHAER *Æneid* I. C ij b, He..by smal and smal doth make The Queene forget her husband dead. *Ibid.* VI. 128 By small and small to landward than I swamme. **1593** SHAKS. *Rich. II*, III. ii. 198, I play the Torturer, by small and small To lengthen out the worst, that must be spoken.

**4.** †**a.** *in* or *to small*, in fragments. *Obs.*

*a* **1400-50** *Alexander* 1309 Quen it was smeten in small.. Ilka gobet his gate glidis fra othire. *a* **1450** MYRC *Par. Pr.* 256 Leste to smale þey done hyt breke.

**b.** *in small* (rarely *the small*), on a small scale; in little. In early use in reference to painting, etc.: In miniature.

(*a*) **1611** TOURNEUR *Ath. Trag.* I. ii, You have giuen me her picture in small. *a* **1700** EVELYN *Diary* 22 Oct. 1644, The Labours of Hercules in massy silver, and many incomparable pictures in small. *a* **1716** SOUTH *Serm.* (1823) III. 259 His soul; that noble copy and resemblance of its Maker, in small indeed, but [etc.]. **1762-71** H. WALPOLE *Vertue's Anecd. Paint.* (1786) II. 132 Vandyck actually made the design, but..it was executed only in small by Ph. Frutiers.

(*b*) **1765** *Museum Rust.* IV. lxii. 273 Let him beware of trying experiments from books, except in small. **1793** SMEATON *Edystone L.* §219 *note*, I have made trial of this method, both in small and in large. **1847** H. BUSHNELL *Chr. Nurture* (1861) II. v. 316 We are infants too, men and women in the small. **1855** BROWNING *Old Pictures in Florence* xxi, Where the strong and the weak..Repeat in large what they practised in small.

†**5. a.** With *a* and pl. A small quantity or amount; a little piece, a morsel. *Obs.*

**1373-4** CHAUCER *Compl. to his Lady* 113 And ye lete me thus sterve, Yit have ye wonne ther-on but a smal. **1566** DRANT *Horace, Sat., Wail. Jeremiah* v. L j b, That we might haue a smal of bred, our carcas to contente. **1567** —— *Horace, Ep.* I. x. E j, For that he will not knowe to vse and lyue vpon a small. **1624** SANDERSON *Serm.* I. 243 Can there be greater unthankfulness, than to grudge Him a small, who hath given us all?

**b.** In or after proverbial use. (Also without plural ending.) ? *Obs.*

**1303** R. BRUNNE *Handl. Synne* 2366 Many smale makeþ a grete. *c* **1386** CHAUCER *Pars. T.* §362 The prouerbe seith that manye smale maken a greet. **1542** HEYWOOD *Prov.* (1867) 30. **1553** *Respublica* I. i. 109 Yet manye a smale makith a greate. **1602** CAREW *Cornwall* 68 b, The stock, which by many smalls, groweth to a meetly greatnes. **1632** LITHGOW *Trav.* VII. 305 All which are but as Suburbs to the new Caire, that of many smalles make vp a Countrey, rather then a City. **1737** RAMSAY *Sc. Prov.* (1750) 73 Mony sma's make a great.

**c.** *in* (or *by*) *smalls*, in small amounts, portions, or sums. *Sc.*

**1529** *Extr. Burgh Rec. Edinb.* (1871) 8 At na personis.. regrait nor by meill to sell the samyn agane in smallis. **1584** *Reg. Privy Council Scot.* III. 649 His haill vicarage is bot tuelf pundis or thairby, pait to him in smallis, in iiis and iiiis in sum placis. **1637-50** ROW *Hist. Kirk* (Wodrow Soc.) 287 Fifty merks (whilk he confessed..he had at sundrie tymes stollen out of the boxe in smalls). **1825** J. WILSON *Noct. Ambr.* Wks. 1855 I. 114 God's blessings are aye God's blessings, though they come in sma's and driblets. **1865** *Glasgow Her.* in *Pall Mall G.* 3 Aug. 10/1 Some speculating genius who saw a chance of turning a dishonest penny by retailing it in smalls.

**6.** The small, slender, or narrow part *of* something: **a.** Of the leg.

**1489** in *Ann. Reg.* (1772) *Antiq.* 151 After that a Gounne had borne away his foote by the small of the legge. **1523** FITZHERB. *Husb.* §15 They be two yardes longe, and as moche as the small of a mannes legge. *a* **1586** SIDNEY *Arcadia* (1622) 459 A long coate of white veluet, reaching to the small of his legge. **1623** MARKHAM *Cheap Husb.* (ed. 3) 47 The smals of his fore-legs, vnder his knees, and for the smals of his hinder legges somewhat below the spauin ioynts. **1697** DAMPIER *Voy.* I. 32 A piece of Cotton Cloath about the small of their Leg, from the Ankle to the Calf. **1726** SWIFT *Gulliver* I. i, His Excellency, having mounted on the small of my right leg.

*ellipt.* **1588** SHAKS. *L.L.L.* v. ii. 645 *Lon.* His legge is too big for Hector. *Boy.* More Calfe certaine. *Dum.* No, he is best indued in the small. **1630** DRAYTON *Muses Elizium* Nymphall i. 107 A swelling Calfe, a Small so fine, An Ankle, round and leane. **1715** *Lond. Gaz.* No. 5328/4 Large Legs, the Small pretty big.

**b.** Of the back (†or belly).

? **1536** LATIMER in *Lett. Suppress. Monast.* (Camden) 148, I am in a fayntt werynesse over all my body, butt cheffly in the small of my backe. **1607** TOPSELL *Four-f. Beasts* (1658) 51 The marrow of a Bul beaten and drunk, cureth the pain in the smal of the belly. **1710** STEELE *Tatler* No. 215 ¶7 Our best Customers show but little above the Small of their Backs. **1803** *Med. Jrnl.* X. 528 Severe pain in the head and small of the back. **1884** HUNTER & WHYTE *Ducats & Dau.* xviii, His eyes fixed on the small of the coachman's back.

**c.** Of a whale (= the part of the tail in front of the flukes).

**1725** *Phil. Trans.* XXXIII. 256 With those Fins they clasp about her Small, and so hold themselves on. **1845** GOSSE *Ocean* v. (1849) 230 The head gradually sinks, the 'small' is projected from the water, and presently the 'flukes' of the tail are raised high in the air. **1903** *Strand Mag.* Nov. 536/1 His blubber..being..nine inches [thick] on the belly and six inches on the 'small'.

**d.** Of things (see quots.).

*c* **1475** *Pict. Voc.* in Wr.-Wülcker 779 *Hic stilus*, a smal of a pelyr. **1687** MIÈGE *Gt. Fr. Dict.* II, The Small of the Sword, *le foible de l' Epée.* **1847** *Infantry Man.* (1854) 22 The right hand grasps the small of the butt. **1867** SMYTH *Sailor's Word-bk.*, *Small*,..that part of the anchor-shank which is immediately under the stock. **1893** F. C. SELOUS *Trav. S.E. Africa* 133 Holding the small of the stock in my right hand, and the barrel in my left.

**7.** ***the small***, that which is trifling, petty, or unimportant.

*a* **1225** *Ancr. R.* 314 Al so schal þe þet schriueð him, efter þe greate, schuuen ut þet smele. **1796** H. HUNTER tr. *St.-Pierre's Stud. Nat.* (1799) II. 54 These pretended plans of universality,..which make her descend into the infinitely small. **1836** EMERSON *Nature* 67 To magnify the small, to micrify the great.

**8.** Small coal; slack. In recent use also *pl.*, varieties of small coal. Also *Comb.*

**1851** MAYHEW *Lond. Lab.* II. 83/2 Frequently they mix them up with 'the small' of north country coals of better quality. **1851** GREENWELL *Coal-trade Terms, Northumb. & Durham* 48 *Small Leader*, a lad employed to put away small, to a stow-board, from the hewer working by separation in a narrow place. **1898** *Daily News* 21 Mar. 3/6 Not for some years have best steam smalls been in such demand.

**9.** *pl.* **a.** Small clothes; formerly, breeches; now underclothes.

**1837** DICKENS *Pickw.* xvi, A difficult process it is to bow in green velvet smalls. **1848** THACKERAY *Van. Fair* lvi, Her footman, in large plush smalls and waistcoat. **1886** JEROME *Idle Th.* 133 An eager, bright-eyed boy, with..dandy shoes and tight-fitting smalls. **1943** N. COWARD *Middle East Diary* (1944) 80 Their mothers stood nearby washing out a few 'smalls' in the shallows. **1951** *People* 3 June 4/6 Most of those who do send out to the laundry still wash smalls and personal linen themselves. **1973** *Guardian* 12 Mar. 10/2 Not many Americans..can have a clear idea of what to use the bidet for, apart from soaking the smalls.

**b.** Parcels or consignments of comparatively little weight (see quots.). Also *attrib.*

**1889** *Manch. Exam.* 4 May, The word 'smalls'..is used to represent the thousands of small parcels which are daily forwarded from the warehouses of Manchester and other large cities to shopkeepers throughout the kingdom. *Ibid.*, A firm whose 'smalls' traffic is very extensive. **1890** *Times* 4 Dec. 11/2 Then with regard to 'smalls', or quantities of less than 3 cwt.;..hitherto in Birmingham 'smalls' had been defined to be quantities less than 2 cwt.

**c.** Small kinds of bread; fancy bread, rolls, etc. 'Freq. in advertisements.' *N.E.D.*

**1892** *Glasgow Her.* 22 Apr. 2/1 Baker..; one well up in smalls and pastry.

**d.** In miscellaneous uses (see quots.).

**1883** *Good Words* July 443/1 Small broken rice, known as 'smalls'. **1884** *Pall Mall G.* 13 Dec. 9/1 He saw him have several halves of whisky—'smalls' they were called there. *a* **1891** *Engineer* LXX. 126 (Cent.), The ore..is tipped from trucks on to a grating of iron bars about 2½ in. apart; the 'mine smalls' pass through. **1895** J. W. ANDERSON *Prospector's Handbk.* (ed. 6) 166 *Smalls*—Small-sized pieces of ore and gangue. **1919** H. ETHERIDGE *Dict. Typewriting* 125 May be in either capitals and smalls or all capitals. **1947** M. MORRIS in 'B. James' *Austral. Short Stories* (1963) 344 Make it another small... All round. **1976** *Wymondham & Attleborough Express* 10 Dec. 21/2 Mediums [*sc.* eggs] from 46p to 43p per dozen with only smalls below this rate.

**e.** Small advertisements.

**1942** *New Statesman* 11 July 25/3 The members of staff usually responsible for selecting 'smalls' and rejecting those that are undesirable. **1959** *Times* 2 Dec. 9/4 The Press figure does not take into account the booming Classified advertising revenue, or 'Smalls'.

**10.** *pl.* At Oxford: The colloquial term for the examination officially called Responsions.

The evidence is not sufficient to show whether the name is due to the old expressions *in parvisiis* or *in parviso* (see PARVIS 2), through association with *parvis* abl. pl. of *parvus* small; cf. however the use of *parvis disputationibus* in the Laudian Statutes, App., III. §9, p. 271.

**1852** BRISTED *Five Yrs. Eng. Univ.* (ed. 2) 92 The Little Go (at Oxford the Smalls). **1861** HUGHES *Tom Brown at Oxf.* x, I ought to be going up for smalls myself next term. **1880** MRS. LYNN LINTON *Rebel of Family* ii, He had been 'ploughed' for 'smalls' and everything else.

**11.** ***the smalls***, in theatrical use (see quot. 1891).

**1891** *Ardrossan Her.* 11 Sept. 4 Having travelled much through the smalls (a theatrical term applied to towns not boasting a regularly built and properly appointed theatre). **1907** H. WYNDHAM *Flare of Footlights* xxx, Wanted..Smart Young Gent to tour the smalls.

**12.** ***small and early***, a small evening party not intended to continue to a late hour.

[**1865** DICKENS *Mut. Fr.* xi, For the clearing off of these worthies, Mrs. Podsnap added a small and early evening to the dinner.] **1880** LD. BEACONSFIELD *Endymion* lxxvii, Well, there are not many dinners among them, to be sure... Small and earlies. How I hate a 'small and early!' **1888** H. JAMES *Partial Portr.* 360 To the afternoon tea, to the fashionable 'squash', to the late and suffocating 'small and early'.

**small** (smɔːl), *adv.* Forms: 1, 4-5 smale, 5 smalle, 4-7 smal, 5- small. [f. SMALL *a.*]

**1.** Into small pieces or morsels.

In some examples perh. the adj. used predicatively.

*c* **888** K. ÆLFRED *Boeth.* xiii, Þeah ðu hi smale todæle swa dust. **1381** in Knighton *Chron.* (Rolls) 138 Iakke Mylner.. hath grounden smal smal. *c* **1430** *Two Cookery-bks.* 6 Þan choppe hem smale. *Ibid.* 10 Tese it smal an bray it in a morter. **1578** LYTE *Dodoens* 278 The floures are blewe,.. with five little leaves underneath them, very small cut and jagged. **1650** TRAPP *Comm. Levit.* xvi. 12 This incens smal-beaten might figure Christ in his Agonie. **1653** WALTON *Angler* I. iii. (1896) 57 Bruise or cut very small into your butter, a little Time. **1759** R. BROWN *Compl. Farm.* 81 Geese will..fatten well on carrots cut small. **1815** J. SMITH *Panorama Sci. & Art* II. 811 A quarter of an ounce avoirdupoise of the finest white soap, grated small.

†**2. a.** To a small extent or degree; little, not much; slightly. *Obs.*

*c* **1375** *Sc. Leg. Saints* i. (*Peter*) 411, I dred rycht small þine angelis. *c* **1386** CHAUCER *Wife's Prol.* 592, I wepte but smal.

1456 SIR G. HAYE *Law Arms* (S.T.S.) 11 He trompit nocht small, quhen he send his Apostlis our all the warld to ger schawe the cristyn faith. 1560 ROLLAND *Seven Sages* Prol. ii, I knew small quhat hir mater did mene. 1593 SHAKS. *Lucr.* 1273 If thou dost weep.., it small avails my mood. 1637 STRAFFORD *Lett.* (1739) II. 83 But in Truth, this moves me very small.

†**b.** Const. *to* one's gain or profit. *Obs.*

1582 A. MUNDAY *Eng. Rom. Life* 61 Promising..hee would informe the Pope of it, which should bee but small to their profite. 1587 HOLINSHED *Chron.* (1808) III. 94 The Frenchmen..sometimes made issues foorth, but small to their gaine.

**3. a.** Quietly, gently; in a small or low voice.

13.. *K. Alis.* 7239 (Laud MS.), Alisaunder gynneþ leighȝe smale. 1590 SHAKS. *Mids. N.* I. ii. 49 That's all one, you shall play it in a Maske, and you may speake as small as you will. 1598 —— *Merry W.* I. i. 49 She has browne haire, and speakes small like a woman. 1887 STEVENSON *Mem. & Portraits* viii, The reposing toiler, thoughtfully smoking, talking small, as if in honour of the stillness.

†**b.** Slyly; wantonly. *Obs.*$^{-1}$

*c*1450 *Knt. de la Tour* (1868) 16 She helde not her astate .., for she loked smal and wynked ofte.., and euer loked ouer the shuldre.

**4.** *to sing small*: †**a.** (See quot.) *Obs.*$^{-0}$

1623 COCKERAM I, *Minurize*, to sing small, to faine in singing.

**b.** *colloq.* To adopt a humble tone or manner; to use less assertive language, or to qualify or withdraw a previous statement; to say nothing, to be silent or dumb.

See also the *Eng. Dial. Dict.* for dialect usage.

1753–4 RICHARDSON *Grandison* (1812) I. 120, I must myself sing small in her company; I will never meet at hard-edge with her. 1785 GROSE *Dict. Vulgar T.*, *Sing small*, to be humbled, confounded, or abashed, to have little or nothing to say for one's self. 1840 BARHAM *Ingol. Leg.* Ser. II. *Row in Omnibus*, Fiddle-de-dee's at the top of the tree, And Doldrum and Fal-de-ral-tit sing small! 1880 GLADSTONE in Morley *Life* VIII. vii. (1905) II. 354 Sir R. Peel endorsed the remonstrance and I had to sing small.

**5.** In a fine or small manner; on a small scale, etc. Also in ***small-drawn***, ***-set*** adjs.

1637 RUTHERFORD *Lett.* (1862) I. 197 It would be no art.. to spin small, and make hypocrisy a goodly web, and to go through the market as a saint among men. 1703 *Lond. Gaz.* No. 3944/4 Also John Simonds, a small-set Fellow. 1820 KEATS *Lamia* II. 47 Her open eyes, Where he was mirror'd small in paradise. *a*1918 W. OWEN *Poems* (1920) 13 And terror's first constriction over, Their hearts remain small drawn.

**6.** *Naut.* Close to the wind.

1848 J. F. COOPER *Oak-Openings* II. xiv. 203 All the difficulty was reduced to steering so 'small', as seamen term it, as to prevent one or the other of the lugs from jibing. 1911 J. BARTEN *Compl. Naut. Pocket Dict.* 192 Steer small.

**small** (smɔːl), *v. rare.* Also 5 smalyn, smale. [f. SMALL *a.* Cf. OE. *smaliȝan* (rare), MDu. *smalen* (*smallen*), MLG. *smalen*, *smelen*, MHG. *smaln* (G. dial. *schmalen*) and *smeln* (G. *schmälen*), older Da. *smale, smalle.*]

**1.** *trans.* To make small; to lessen, reduce. *rare.*

*c*1400 *Lanfranc's Cirurg.* 85 Smale þe lippis of woundis þat ben greate. *c*1440 *Promp. Parv.* 460/2 Smalyn, or make lesse, *minoro.* 1611 COTGR., *Apointi*,..sharpened, or smalled, at the point. 1962 'K. ORVIS' *Damned & Destroyed* xiv. 95 Welch smalled his hands against his desk.

**2.** *intr.* To become small; to diminish, grow less. Hence **'smalling** *ppl. a.*

*a*1618 SYLVESTER *Woodman's Bear* liv, I saw,.. Smalling down by measure's law, Her straight comely shapen back. 1665 HOOKE *Microgr.* 36 By sucking at the smalling Pipe, more of the Air..may be suck'd out. 1899 T. HARDY *Departure* Poems (1902) 7 The broad bottoms rip the bearing brine—All smalling slowly to the gray sea line.

**smallage** ('smɔːlɪdʒ). Forms: α. 3 smal, 4 smale ache, 5–6 smalache, 5–7 -ach, 6–7 smallach(e. β. 5 smalege, -edge, 6–7 smalledge, 7 -adge, 6– smallage. [f. SMALL *a.* 21 b + ACHE *sb.*$^2$] One or other of several varieties of celery or parsley; *esp.* wild celery or water parsley, *Apium graveolens.* Now *rare.*

α. *c*1290 *St. Cuthbert* 52 in *S. Eng. Leg.* I. 360 'Nim,' he seide, 'þe milk of one kov.., Iuys of smal-Ache do þar-to'. *a*1387 *Sinon. Barthol.* (Anecd. Oxon.) 11 *Apium simpliciter*, ..smale ache. *c*1400 *Lanfranc's Cirurg.* 94 Leie on þis confeccioun maad of flour of wheete & hony & ius of smalache. *c*1450 *M.E. Med. Bk.* (Heinrich) 101 Take smalache, reed fenel, rewe, verueyne [etc.]. 1545 RAYNOLD *Byrth Mankynde* 134 The decoction of rosemarye,.. alexander, smallach, &c. 1578 LYTE *Dodoens* 606 Smallache hath shyning leaues of a darke greene colour. 1603 HOLLAND *Plutarch* 719 Afterwards when these [Isthmian] Games were accounted, they translated thither..the chaplet of Smallach.

β. 14.. *Nom.* in Wr.-Wülcker 711 *Hoc apium*, smalege. 1530 PALSGR. 271/2 Smallage an herbe, *ache.* 1562 TURNER *Herbal* (1568) 40 Smallage hath suche a strong savor,..that no man can..eat it with hys meate. 1636 W. DENNY in *Ann. Dubrensia* (1877) 13 Each three yeeres Victor was with Smallage crown'd, Whose pendant leaves, his head enshadow'd round. 1685 TEMPLE *Ess. Gardens* Wks. 1720 I. 178 The Plants he mentions, are the *Apium*, which tho' commonly interpreted *Parsly*, yet comprehends all Sorts of Smallage, whereof Sellery is one. 1712 *Pomet's Hist. Drugs* I. 2 The large Smallage, which the Gardiners falsly call Macedonian-Parsley. 1785 MARTYN *Rousseau's Bot.* xvii. (1794) 236 Our wild Smallage,..which is common by ditches and brooks, cannot be rendered esculent by culture. 1822–7 GOOD *Study Med.* (1829) I. 248 The *cicuta virosa*, or water-hemlock, the leaves of which have been mistaken for smallage. 1876 *Encycl. Brit.* V. 290/2 Celery,..a biennial plant..which, in its native condition, is known in England as smallage.

*attrib.* *c*1550 H. LLOYD *Treas. Health* g iv, Smalladge rote hanged aboute thy necke doth alay the tooth ache. *a*1648 DIGBY *Closet Opened* (1677) 130 Smallage Gruel. 1658 ROWLAND tr. *Moufet's Theat. Ins.* 1063 Give in Wine the decoction..of the Cyprus Nut, Smallage-seed. 1853 SOYER *Pantroph.* 141 When it is cooked, add pepper and smallage seed.

**'small-arm.** Also small arm. [Back-formation from SMALL-ARMS, at first in attrib. use.]

**1.** *attrib.* **a.** Using or provided with small-arms.

1805 E. P. *Let.* in Polwhele *Trad. & Recoll.* (1826) II. 577, I acted both in the capacity of a commanding officer,.. small-arm-man, and powder-boy. 1833 M. SCOTT *Tom Cringle* xv, Fire, small arm men, and take good aim. 1892 BRIGHTON *Sir P. Wallis* 67 The Chesapeake had attached much importance to her small-arm force.

**b.** Intended or adapted for small-arms.

1807 *Ann. Reg., Hist. Europe* 219/2 Small-arm ammunition. 1876 VOYLE & STEVENSON *Milit. Dict.* 390/2 Small-arm Cartridge.

**2.** A fire-arm which may be carried in the hand.

1875 KNIGHT *Dict. Mech.* 2219/2 *Small-arm*, a term including muskets, rifles, carbines, and pistols. 1881 GREENER *Gun* 113 Owing to the introduction..of the Snider breech-loader, which prevented the general use of the Whitworth small-arm in military circles.

Hence **'small-armed** *a.*, provided with small-arms; **'small-ˌarmoury**, an armoury for small-arms.

1766 ENTICK *London* IV. 340 Two..rooms, one of which is a small-armoury for the sea-service. 1806 A. DUNCAN *Nelson* 50 Their force consisted of 80 marines, and 180 small-armed seamen. 1812 *Examiner* 31 Aug. 553/1 To disperse some small armed men collected on the shore.

**'small-arms.** [f. SMALL *a.* + ARM *sb.*$^2$ 2.] Fire-arms capable of being carried in the hand, as contrasted with ordnance.

1710 *Lond. Gaz.* No. 2702/2 Powder, small Ball, and small Arms. 1748 *Anson's Voy.* III. viii. 379 Her topmen..made prodigious havock with their small arms. 1817 *Parl. Deb.* 756 During the war no less than three millions of small arms had been manufactured there for the use of the Allies. 1879 *Cassell's Techn. Educ.* III. 267/2 The fire of modern small-arms has become so infinitely more deadly.

*attrib.* 1858 BRIGHT *Sp., Reform* 10 Dec., The Government small-arms establishment at Enfield. 1905 H. NEWMAN in E. Candler *Unveiling of Lhasa* x. 192 Then followed several hours of cannonading and small-arms fire.

**small beer.** [SMALL *a.* 12 a.]

**1.** Beer of a weak, poor, or inferior quality.

1568 GRAFTON *Chron.* II. 359 For drinke, they had none but small Ale or Beere. 1592 NASHE *Four Lett. Conf.* Wks. (Grosart) II. 242 His Poetry more spiritlesse than small beere. 1636 MASSINGER *Gt. Dk. Florence* II. ii, Such as eat store of beef..may preserve their healths With that thin composition called small beer. 1690 J. MACKENZIE *Siege Londonderry* 56/2 That every Soldier..shall be allowed a quart of small Beer *per diem.* 1721 AMHERST *Terræ Fil.* (1726) App. 317, I think there ought to be something allow'd besides small-beer and apple-dumplings. 1770 MASSIE *Tax upon Malt* 6 The Quantity of small Beer annually brewed for Sale in England and Wales, is about Two Millions Three Hundred Thousand Barrels. 1822 IMISON *Sci. & Art* II. 168 The liquor in this state is pretty nearly of the colour of small beer. 1840 BARHAM *Ingol. Leg.* Ser. II. *Bl. Mousquetaire* 535 The Black Mousquetaire was as dead as Small beer!

**2.** *transf.* **a.** Trivial occupations, affairs, etc.; matters or persons of little or no consequence or importance; trifles.

[1604 SHAKS. *Oth.* II. i. 161 To suckle Fooles, and chronicle small Beere. 1710 ADDISON *Whig Examiner* No. 4 ¶5 As rational Writings have been represented by Wine; I shall represent those Kinds of Writings we are now speaking of, by Small Beer.] 1777 J. ADAMS *Wks.* (1854) IX. 464 The torment of hearing eternally reflections upon my constituents, that they are..smallbeer,..is what I will not endure. 1844 THACKERAY *B. Lyndon* xiv, All the news of sport, assize, and quarter-sessions were detailed by this worthy chronicler of small-beer. 1883 *Fortn. Rev.* Sept. 379 A twice-told tale, or a chronicle of small beer.

†**b.** (See quot.) *Obs.*$^{-1}$

1789 T. WRIGHT *Meth. Watering Meadows* (1790) 23 Our farmers..call even the second running [of the water] by the significant name of small-beer.

**c.** ***to think small beer of***, or variants of this: To have a poor or low opinion of (oneself or others). Chiefly with negatives. *colloq.*

1825 C. WESTMACOTT *English Spy* I. 32 He was not thought small beer of. 1855 THACKERAY *Newcomes* xxxix, She thinks small beer of painters, J. J.—well, we don't think small beer of ourselves, my noble friend. 1873 *Punch* 18 Jan. 30/2 Is it consistent for..a teetotaller to think no small beer of himself?

**3.** *attrib.* **a.** In sense 1, as ***small-beer allowance***, ***-firkin***, ***wort***, ***yeast.***

1743 *Lond. & Co. Brewer* II. (ed. 2) 157 The small-beer-firkin being 9 Gallons. 1746 W. THOMPSON *R.N. Adv.* (1757) 47 The Fleet sailed without Small Beer Allowance. 1801 *Med. Jrnl.* V. 275, I recommended them to procure some small-beer yeast. 1815 J. SMITH *Panorama Sci. & Art* II. 741 Litmus blue is prepared by boiling litmus in small-beer wort.

**b.** In fig. uses (cf. sense 2), as ***small-beer air***, ***character***, ***chronicle***, etc.

1648 G. DANIEL *Eclog* iii. 262 Eudæmon, still..in Small-beer ayre [you] Flutter with feeble wings. 1682 MRS. BEHN *City Heiress* 29 That..Puritanical, Phanatical, Small-beer face of thine. 1721 AMHERST *Terræ Fil.* (1726) App. 318 A lad may..chop logic as glibly in a college, where they eat and drink like christians, as in any small-beer hall whatsoever. 1789 GOUVR. MORRIS in Sparks *Life & Writ.* (1832) II. 92 If the reigning prince were not the small-beer character that he is. 1824 *Westm. Rev.* July 181 The second volume [of *Redgauntlet*] contains a diary, or small-beer journal. 1861 THACKERAY *Round. Papers, Small-beer Chronicle*, In the House of Commons what small-beer orators try to pass for strong?

**4.** *Comb.* (sense 1), as ***small-beer brewer***, ***drawer***, ***-drinker.***

1638 T. WHITAKER *Blood of Grape* 31 When as water or small-beere-drinkers looke like Apes rather then men. 1721 AMHERST *Terræ Fil.* No. 25 (1726) 132 Under pain of having his said lucubrations burnt..by the hands of the small-beer drawer. 1743 *Lond. & Co. Brewer* II. (ed. 2) 159 Two considerable Small-Beer Brewers.

**small-clothes.** Also smallclothes. [SMALL *a.* 3.]

**1.** Breeches; knee-breeches. (Cf. SMALL *sb.* 9 a.)

1796 J. HUNTER *Trav.* 297 The immensity of their breeches, (for, in spite of the fashionable phrase, it would certainly be a perversion of terms to call them small-clothes). 1812 W. COMBE *Syntax, Picturesque* xx, One who was in full fashion drest,..His small-clothes sat so close and tight. 1841 THACKERAY *Gt. Hoggarty Diamond* iii, Two great footmen, with red whiskers and yellow plush smallclothes. 1883 J. HAWTHORNE *Dust* I. 84 He leaned back in his chair, with one hand in the pocket of his small-clothes.

**2.** *transf.* One who wears breeches.

1825 COLERIDGE *Lett., Convers.*, etc. II. 210 An audience of respectable smallclothes and petticoats.

**small coal.** Also small-coal. [SMALL *a.* 4.]

**1.** Charcoal. *Obs.* exc. *Hist.*

1638 FORD *Fancies* v. i, Your suds and pan of small-coal. 1646 SIR T. BROWNE *Pseud. Ep.* 88 Smal-coale is commonly known unto all, and for this use is made of Sallow, Willow, Alder, Hasell, and the like. 1705 *Lond. Gaz.* No. 4094/3 The Bran and Smallcoal made at their Office on Tower-hill. 1728 CHAMBERS *Cycl.* s.v. *Coal*, An Artificial Fuel made.. by half burning the Branches and Roots of Trees; properly call'd *Charcoal*, and *Smallcoal.*

**2.** Coal of small size; slack.

1665 DUDLEY *Mettall. Martis* (1854) 8 Knowing that if there could be any use made of the Smal-coale.., then would they be drawn out of the Pits. 1677 *Phil. Trans.* XII. 898 The Men..hid themselves as well as they could in the loose sleck or small Cole. 1755 JOHNSON, *Slack*, small coal; coal broken in small parts. 1843 HOLTZAPFFEL *Turning* I. 205 Small-coal is thrown..into the hollow fire to replace that which is burned. 1891 *Weekly Notes* 136/2 The small coal was mainly produced by the friction of the blocks while being brought to the surface.

**3.** *attrib.*, as ***small-coal man***, ***question***, ***trade***, etc.

1673 R. HEAD *Canting Acad.* 129 He lookt like a Small-Coal-man. 1715 HEARNE *Collect.* (O.H.S.) V. 103 Thomas Britton..set up the Small-coal Trade. 1847 THACKERAY *Curate's Walk* Wks. 1900 VI. 552 The Curate was very deep in conversation with a small-coalman. 1898 *Daily News* 6 May 2/7 At the same time there was a vehement dispute on the small coal question.

**small-craft.** [See CRAFT *sb.* 9 a.] In attrib. use, as ***small-craft man***, ***vessel***, etc. Also *transf.*

1693 DRYDEN, etc. *Juvenal* iii. (1697) 51 He..whom t'other Day A small-craft Vessel hither did convey. 1711 SHAFTESB. *Charac.* (1737) III. 97 We essay-writers are of the small-craft or galley-kind. 1832 CARLYLE *Remin.* (1881) I. 33 On board some small-craft man of war. 1856 OLMSTED *Slave States* 143 Captain Jerry had the habit, which small-craft men are apt to get, of consulting aloud with himself.

**small-eyed**, *a.* [SMALL *a.* 23.] Having small eyes. Also *transf.* of spectacles.

1630 DRAYTON *Noah's Flood* 481 The small-ey'd slow-worm held of many blind. 1686 *Lond. Gaz.* No. 2176/4 A black Negro Man,..small in the Waste, small Ey'd. 1801 SHAW *Gen. Zool.* II. II. 502 Small Eyed Cachalot, *Physeter Microps.* 1836 YARRELL *Brit. Fishes* II. 433 The Small-eyed Ray, *raia microcellata.* 1840 DICKENS *B. Rudge* iv, Sim..was an old-fashioned,..sharp-nosed, small-eyed little fellow. 1898 *Westm. Gaz.* 5 Oct. 9/3 Small-eyed spectacles made at the suggestion of Sir Isaac Newton.

**small fry**: see FRY *sb.*$^1$ 4.

**small-headed**, *a.* [SMALL *a.* 23.] Having a small head.

1611 COTGR., *Saupe*, a small-headed,..vnwholesome sea-fish. 1752 HILL *Hist. Anim.* 113 The great, thick, small-headed Testudo. 1775 *Phil. Trans.* LXVII. 13 A tall small-headed tree. 1812 A. WILSON *Amer. Ornith.* VI. 62 Small-headed Flycatcher, *Muscicapa minuta.* 1836 YARRELL *Brit. Fishes* II. 221 *Pleuronectes microcephalus*, Small-headed Dab. 1854 H. MILLER *Sch. & Schm.* (1858) 320 A tall, large-bodied, small-headed man.

**smalling**, *ppl. a.*: see SMALL *v.*

**smallish** ('smɔːlɪʃ), *a.* [f. SMALL *a.*] Somewhat small; rather little.

?*a*1366 CHAUCER *Rom. Rose* 826 His shuldres of a large brede, And smalish in the girdilstede. 1611 COTGR., *Menuët*, smallish. 1763 COLE in *Collect. Topogr. & Gen.* (1837) IV. 48 The 4th coffin has nothing on yᵉ plate, and is a smallish one. 1764 H. WALPOLE *Let. to G. Montagu* 24 Dec., I send you a decent smallish muff, that you may put in your pocket. 1820 SCORESBY *Acc. Arctic Reg.* II. 440 The pieces of ice were fortunately of smallish dimensions. 1858 CARLYLE *Fredk. Gt.* I. v. (1872) I. 42 Small troubles, the antagonism to which is apt to become itself of smallish character. 1890 'R. BOLDREWOOD' *Col. Reformer* (1891) 385 These cattle are smallish and weak.

**small-leaved**, *a.* Also small-leafed. [SMALL *a.*] Having small leaves.

**1699** M. LISTER *Journey to Paris* 209 The Tree most in use here, was the small-leaved Horne-Beam. **1731** P. MILLER *Gardeners Dict.* s.v. Tilia, The small-leav'd Lime-tree. **1827** GRIFFITH tr. *Cuvier* V. 80 *Rhinopoma Microphylla* (Small-leaved Rhinopome Bat). **1884** W. C. SMITH *Kildrostan* 50 Graceful tufts Of small-leaved ferns. **1889** MAIDEN *Useful Pl.* 561 *Laportea photiniphylla*... Small-leaved Nettle. *Ibid.* 466 *Eucalyptus hæmastoma*... In the extreme south a variety sometimes goes by the name of 'Rough', or 'Small-leaved Stringybark'. **1962** R. PAGE *Educ. Gardener* v. 159 The small-leaved elm *Ulmus pumila*.. seems resistant to elm-disease. **1967** *Coast to Coast 1965–6* 209 The dunes gave way to the.. hardy small-leafed bushes. **1979** P. THEROUX *Old Patagonian Express* xxi. 322 These sparse, small-leaved thorn bushes create the illusion of green.

**small-mouth**, *a.* [SMALL *a.* 22.] Of bass: Small-mouthed.

**1884** GOODE *Nat. Hist. Aquat. Anim.* 401 The Big-mouth Black Bass,.. and the Small-mouth Black Bass, *micropterus dolomiei.* **1909** *Daily Chron.* 22 Sept. 1/6 Bass of the small mouth variety live better in fresh water.

**b.** *ellipt.* as *sb.*

**1884** GOODE *Nat. Hist. Aquat. Anim.* 401 The Small-mouth shares with the Large-mouth in the Southern States the names 'Jumper', 'Perch', and 'Trout'. *Ibid.* 402 The Small-mouths found their way into the Hudson in 1825 or soon after.

**small-mouthed**, *a.* [SMALL *a.* 23.] Having a small mouth; *spec.* of certain fishes (see later quots.).

**1523** FITZHERB. *Husb.* §78 The .ix. propertyes of an asse. The fyrste is to be small-mouthed. **1611** COTGR., *Derbro*, a kind of small-mouthed.. Sea-fish. **1803** SHAW *Gen. Zool.* IV. II. 445 Small-mouthed Sparus, *Sparus Microstomus.* **1839** YARRELL *Suppl. Brit. Fishes* 36 The Small-mouthed Wrasse, *Crenilabrus exoletus.* **1882** JORDAN & GILBERT *Syn. Fishes N. Amer.* 485 *Micropterus dolomiei*, Small-mouthed Black Bass.

**smallness** ('smɔːlnɪs). Also 4–7 smal-, 6–7 smale-, 7 smalle-; 4–7 -nesse, 5–7 -nes (5 -nez). [f. SMALL *a.*]

†**1.** Slimness; slenderness. *Obs.*

**1387** TREVISA *Higden* (Rolls) II. 181 Whan þe lymes beeþ.. as they schulde be in schappe,.. quantite, and gretnesse and smalnesse. *a* **1425** tr. *Arderne's Treat. Fistula*, etc. 60 If þe pacient of emoroidez be of malencolious complexion, þise bene toknez:—smalnez of body [etc.]. **1483** *Cath. Angl.* 346 A Smalnes, *gracilitas.* **1565** COOPER *Thesaurus, Exilitas*, sclendernesse: thinnesse. *Foliorum exilitas*,.. the smalnesse. **1623** COCKERAM II, Smalnes, *tenuitie.* **1733** TULL *Horse-Hoeing Husb.* i. (Dubl.) 7 The Roots, tho' very weak and slender, are easily supported.., notwithstanding their Length, Smallness and Flexibility. **1761** HUME *Hist. Eng.* I. xiii. 336 Notwithstanding the great length and smallness of his legs.

**2.** The fact or quality of being small, in various senses: **a.** In size or extent.

**1398** TREVISA *Barth. De P.R.* XVII. i. (Bodl. MS.), Treen beþ diuers.. in gretenes and in smalnes and in strengþe. **1512** *Act 4 Hen. VIII*, c. 19 §14 Nott regardyng the.. greatnesse or smalnes of the same penyes. **1577** B. GOOGE *Heresbach's Husb.* I. (1586) 31 Not vnlyke the Beechemast both in colour and fourme, differing onely in the smalenesse. **1630** *R. Johnson's Kingd. & Commw.* 425 The Sea Oxe differeth nothing from the Land Oxe, save in smalnesse of stature. **1669** WORLIDGE *Syst. Agric.* (1681) 212 According to the height you raise the Water, may you proportion the greatness or smallness of your Engine. **1719** DE FOE *Crusoe* I. (Globe) 138 The Smallness of my Boat. **1792** A. YOUNG *Trav. France* 399 The great evil is the smallness of farms. **1802** DIBDIN *Edit. Classics* Advt., The smallness and closeness of the type. **1840** LARDNER *Geom.* 221 Proportional to the smallness of the pieces into which the sphere is divided. **1884** G. F. BRAITHWAITE *Salmonidæ Westm.* ii. 7 They are easily distinguished.. by the smallness of their scales.

**b.** In capacity, ability, etc.

**1435** MISYN *Fire of Love* 96 Þe smalnes certan of my mynde can-not opyn itt. **1557** NORTH *Gueuara's Diall Pr.* Author's Prol., That.. the smalnes of my eloquence.. shold be lytle regarded. **1594** T. B. *La Primaud. Fr. Acad.* II. 291 God.. abaseth himselfe to our smallnesse. **1662** J. BARGRAVE *Pope Alex. VII* (1867) 9 The embassadors.. being the apter to bear with the smallness of his sufficiency.

**c.** In strength, quality, or vigour.

**1565** COOPER *Thesaurus* s.v. *Exilitas*, The smalnesse of a womans voyce. **1620** VENNER *Via Recta* ii. 39 There is great difference to be found in Beere, according to the strength and smalnesse of it. **1661** R. LOVELL *Hist. Anim. & Min.* Isagoge e v b, Sadnesse doth by degrees dissolve the spirits, .. and cause.. palenesse, and smallenesse of pulse. **1755** in JOHNSON. **1828–32** WEBSTER s.v., The smallness of a female voice. **1847** W. C. L. MARTIN *The Ox* 133/1 Let not the smallness of the pulse deter from bleeding.

**d.** In amount, quantity, etc.

**1649** E. REYNOLDS *Hosea* iii. 12 The greatnes of his work for us to the smalnes of ours unto him. **1677** YARRANTON *Eng. Improv.* 107 By reason of the.. smallness of the Rains .. most Rivers are much wanting in Water. **1770** LANGHORNE *Plutarch* (1851) I. 241/1 They never considered the smallness of his supplies. **1794** S. WILLIAMS *Hist. Vermont* 299 Encouraged by the smallness of the taxes. **1849** MACAULAY *Hist. Eng.* x. II. 554 The smallness of the booty disappointed the plunderers. **1885** *Manch. Exam.* 6 Apr. 4/6 The smallness of the work achieved.

**e.** In respect of numbers.

**1781** GIBBON *Decl. & F.* xxix. (1787) III. 127 Such was the smallness of their establishments, or the difficulty of recruiting. **1801** *Farmer's Mag.* Nov. 469 A large growth of grass,.. owing to the comparative smallness of stock kept, remains.. to be consumed. **1890** *Spectator* 3 May, The smallness of his party—on his biggest expedition he only had five men..—may partly account for this.

**3.** Littleness of mind; meanness, pettiness.

**1813** *Examiner* 31 May 350/1 There is a stiff smallness about his mind. **1869** BLACKMORE *Lorna D.* xiii, That was honest enough, and no smallness of me there. **1883** *Good Words* 196 Not one of his children but tried to conquer self and smallness when he was by.

**4.** With pl. A small part, portion, etc. *rare.*

**1832** L. HUNT *Poems* (1860) 269 Compound of lovely smallnesses.

**small-pock.** Now *rare* or *Obs.* Also **small pock.** [SMALL *a.* 3.] One of the pustules which appear on the skin in the disease of smallpox; the disease itself. Also *attrib.*

**14..**, **1530** [see POCK *sb.* 2β]. **1736** AINSWORTH *Lat. Dict.* II, *Pustula*,.. a small pock. **1797** *Phil. Trans.* LXXXVII. 207 The upper part.. was a little concave, like the head of a turned small-pock. **1800** *Med. Jrnl.* IV. 339 Master T——, the first subject mentioned with Small-pock, died on the 27th. **1825** *Q. Rev.* XXXIII. 238 Valli diluted the pestilential matter with small-pock matter.

**small-pox** ('smɔːlpɒks), *sb.* Forms: α. 6–7 **small pockes** (6 pokkes, 7 pocks), 7–9 **small-pocks.** β. 7 **small poxe**, 7– **small pox, small-pox**, 8– **smallpox.** [f. SMALL *a.* + POX *sb.*, earlier *pocks* (POCK *sb.* 2 α). Long written as two words, the adj. being employed to distinguish the disease from the pox proper, or *great pox.*]

**1.** The pox or pustules on the skin which form the most characteristic feature of the acute contagious disease sometimes called variola; hence commonly, the disease itself. **a.** With *the.*

It is only in certain contexts that the two senses can be clearly distinguished. In later use, when denoting the disease, the word is construed as a singular.

α. **1518** PACE in *Lett. & Papers Hen. VIII* (1864) II. II. 1333 They do die in these parts [Wallingford].. of the small pokkes and mezils. **1547** BOORDE *Brev. Health* ccxvi. 74 There be many sodein sickenesses, as the pestilence,.. the small pockes, the crampe. **1608** DOD & CLEAVER *Expos. Prov.* xi–xii. 81 They are as willing that the small pockes should deforme theyr faire faces. **1676** *Phil. Trans.* XI. 569 The third Epidemical Constitution.. was that of the Small-pocks. **1788** *Med. Comm.* II. 183 The small-pocks are often confluent upon the face and head, whilst they are distinct every where else.

β. **1623** HART *Arraignm. Ur.* iii. 46 Small wheales like the small poxe. **1634** BRERETON *Trav.* (Chetham Soc.) 39 Prince Maurice.. hath lately been much disfigured by the small-pox. *c* **1672** WOOD *Life* (O.H.S.) I. 45 This yeare he had the small pox so much that he was for a time blinded with them. **1764** REID *Let.* Wks. 1863 I. 40/2 The street we live in.. was infested with the smallpox, which were very mortal. **1789** MRS. PIOZZI *Journ. France* II. 306 The small-pox was not to be named in his presence. **1843** ABDY *Water Cure* 180 Thirty or more of the boys.. fell sick of the small-pox. **1891** C. ROBERTS *Adrift Amer.* 87 The small-pox was making fearful havoc with the country.

**b.** Without article.

α. **1565** COOPER *Thesaurus, Pustulæ*, Small pockes. **1804** *Med. Jrnl.* XII. 335 The disorder of small pocks or measles.

β. **1676** J. COOKE *Marrow Chirurg.* IV. ii. ix. (1685) 213 Custom tells us, that those large Pustles.. are called Small-Pox. **1784** *New Spectator* No. xvii. 3 A young man of some little education, pitted with small pox. **1842** *Penny Cycl.* XXII. 143/1 Small-pox according to its severity, is distinguished by authors into two varieties, the *distinct* and the *confluent.* **1877** F. T. ROBERTS *Handbk. Med.* (ed. 3) I. 149 Small-Pox is very easily conveyed from one individual to another by inoculation, contact and infection. **1889** G. GRESSWELL *Dis. Ox* 311 'Small pox in Sheep'.. is known scientifically under the name of *Variola ovina.*

**2. a.** *attrib.*, as *smallpox case, epidemic*, etc.

**1775** ASH s.v., Smallpox hospital. **1834** *Cycl. Pract. Med.* III. 736/1 The pestilential vapour of small-pox pustules. *Ibid.* 744/1 Medical men who visit small-pox patients. **1867** AUGUSTA WILSON *Vashti* xxxi, Are you aware that.. this building is assigned to small-pox cases? **1898** RIDER HAGGARD *Dr. Therne* 2 The appalling smallpox epidemic.

**b.** *smallpox cowry, shell* (see quots.).

**1796** NEMNICH *Polyglot.-Lex.* V. 896 Small-pox shell, *Cypraea caurica.* **1837** *Penny Cycl.* VIII. 257/1 *Cypræa pustulata*, Lam., commonly called by collectors the Small-pox Cowry.

**c.** *Comb.*, as *smallpox-pitted* adj.; also *fig.*

**1897** 'MARK TWAIN' *Following Equator* xlix. 465 Saharas of sand, smallpox-pitted with footprints. **1926** D. H. LAWRENCE *Plumed Serpent* v. 92 The pug-faced Mexican in charge, and his small-pox-pitted assistant.

Hence **'smallpox** *v.*; **'smallpoxed** *a.*, marked by or suffering from smallpox; also *fig.*

**1774** *Westm. Mag.* II. 281 A man must have a daring front to attack these small-poxed Muses. **1862** *Sat. Rev.* 5 July 9 The present of 300 smallpoxed prisoners. **1897** GUNTER *S. Turnbull* xvi. 196 'What do you say to taking a tour of the hospitals?' 'Gad! Do you wish to smallpox me?' growls Philip, angrily. **1901** 'MARK TWAIN' *Let.* 28 July (1917) II. 711 Water, small-poxed with rain-splashes. **1952** *Landfall* Mar. 28 The smallpoxed plaster walls of the railway station that the English had shelled from the sea.

**small shot:** see SHOT *sb.*

**small-sword.** [SMALL *a.* 2.] A kind of light sword, tapering gradually from the hilt to the point, and esp. used in fencing.

**1687** [see below]. **1707** HOPE *New Method Fencing* p. ix, A sufficient Guard and Defence, against all the Thrusts of the Small-Sword. **1777** SHERIDAN *Sch. Scand.* v. ii, Isn't it a wound with a small-sword? **1836** MARRYAT *Midsh. Easy* xxii, He accepted the challenge, but having no knowledge of the small-sword, refused to fight unless with pistols. **1852** THACKERAY *Esmond* I. v, Father Holt was an expert practitioner with the small-sword.

**b.** *attrib.*, as *small-sword exercise, logic, man*, etc.

**1687** HOPE (*title*), The Scots Fencing-Master, or Compleat Small-Sword-Man. **1779** SHERIDAN *Critic* II. ii, The *pro* and *con* goes as smart as hits in a fencing-match. It is, indeed, a sort of small-sword logic. **1803** *Ann. Reg., Chron.* 525/2 If he would take a foil and indulge him with a lesson in the small-sword exercise. *a* **1814** *Manœuvring* IV. iii. in *New Brit. Theatre* II. 117 All this sparring and small-sword play of wit.

**small-talk**, *sb.* Also **small talk.** [SMALL *a.* 18.] Light talk or conversation; chit-chat, gossip. Also *attrib.*

**1751** CHESTERF. *Let.* 20 June, A sort of chit-chat, or *small-talk*, which is the general run of conversation.. in most mixed companies. **1762** LADY S. LENNOX in *Life & Lett.* (1901) I. 122, I have wrote a great deal of *small talk*, as Mercadie calls it. **1810** CRABBE *Borough* iii. 70 As your tea you sip, While the town small-talk flows from lip to lip. **1885** PAYN *Talk of Town* I. 18 The mere offer.. may lead to volumes of small-talk. **1905** A. BENNETT *Tales of Five Towns* I. 22 'Will Harry be late at the works to-night again?' she asked in her colder, small-talk manner, which committed her to nothing. **1977** *Gay News* 7–20 Apr. 16/3 He will begin in a very small talk kind of way about anything and before long he builds up a kind of empathy between him and the other person.

Hence **small-talk** *v. intr.*, to engage in small-talk; **small-talkable** *a.*, **-talker, -talking.**

**1782** G. K. (*title*), The Festival of Wit; or, [the] Small Talker. **1786** COLMAN in *European Mag.* IX. 370 Small wit, small plot—and last—not least, small-talking. **1848** CLOUGH *Bothie* v. 116 Thou in the palace, its author, art dining, small-talking and dancing. **1860** W. COLLINS *Wom. in White* I. vi, A flirtable, danceable, small-talkable creature of the male sex.

**small time, small-time**, *sb.* and *a.* (*phr.*) orig. and chiefly *U.S.* [SMALL *a.*] **A.** *sb. Theatr.* (See quot. 1926.) Also *transf.*

**1910** *Variety* 30 Apr. 9/4 Acts on the 'small time' of any merit or quality will not play in the houses calling for 'five shows daily'. **1917** WODEHOUSE *Man with Two Left Feet* 38 He's booked me in the small time at thirty-five dollars a week. **1926** *Amer. Speech* I. 436/2 *Small time*, the lower salaried circuits or where acts must work three or more times a day. **1960** B. KEATON *My Wonderful World of Slapstick* v. 88 Rather than play the small time, other big-time acts preferred not to work. **1977** B. LANGLEY *Death Stalk* ix. 103 Small-time hoodlums looked very much alike. Perhaps it was that streak.. of uniformity which kept them in the small-time.

**B.** *adj.* Of or pertaining to second-rate vaudeville; *gen.* operating on a small scale, second-rate, unimportant, insignificant.

**1910** *Variety* 30 Apr. 9/4 The Hartford Opera House has been taken under a five-year lease by S. Z. Poli who will operate it as a 'small time' vaudeville house. **1921** A. G. EMPEY *Madonna of Hills* iii. 24 She had been given a 'tryout' before a booking agency, and had made good to the extent of working in 'small time' vaudeville. **1934** *Punch* 7 Mar. 280/2 He lumbered, mined and starved in Canada; he became an itinerant 'small-time' wrestler and pugilist all over the United States. **1938** WODEHOUSE *Code of Woosters* xiii. 278 Sidney Carton.. was small-time stuff compared with you, Bertie. **1940** R. CHANDLER *Farewell, my Lovely* xxxii. 244 You think I'm a small time private dick trying to push ten times his own weight. **1949** 'J. TEY' *Brat Farrar* xv. 139 Timber.. was a deliberate and intelligent rogue.. There was nothing small-time about Timber. **1961** *John o' London's* 5 Jan. 22/2 A gang of big-time smugglers want to eliminate the small-time hero. **1968** P. OLIVER *Screening Blues* iv. 130 The words [of a blues song] were gauche but revealing of the anxieties of the small-time player. **1976** P. R. WHITE *Planning for Public Transport* x. 204 Many economists expert in the finer points of judging small-time savings, or the effect of taxation in determining net resource costs, have only the haziest idea of costs. **1977** I. SHAW *Beggarman, Thief* III. viii. 307 Do you intend to be a small-time tennis pro.. all your life?

Hence **small-timer**, (*a*) a small-time theatre (*rare*); (*b*) a small-time operator, an insignificant person.

**1910** *Variety* 30 Apr. 9/4 S. Z. Poli.. will operate it as a 'small time' vaudeville house, under the booking direction of J. J. Clancy, and in conjunction with the other Poli 'small timers'. **1935** A. J. POLLOCK *Underworld Speaks* 109/1 *Small timer*, a person who doesn't amount to much; a piker. **1950** *Sport* 24–30 Mar. 21/4 The small-timer is now not only demanding protection from the Guild but a rightful place in boxing affairs. **1959** R. SIMONS *Houseboat Killings* viii. 90 She was a small timer when I met 'er... Then she got so 'igh and mighty she wouldn't speak to me. **1976** 'TREVANIAN' *Main* (1977) x. 189 A couple of small-timers.. who make their money by 'laundering' men for the American organized-crime market.

**small-town**, *a.* Also **small town.** [SMALL *a.*] Of, pertaining to, or characteristic of a small town; unsophisticated, provincial.

**1824** *Blackw. Mag.* June 659/2 Nothing can be better than Miss Austin's [*sic*] sketches of that sober, orderly, small-town, parsonage, sort of society in which she herself had spent her life. **1859** *Bentley's Q. Rev.* July 437 If 'George Eliot' proves to be.. a very young man, son of a small town tradesman [etc.]. **1881** *Harper's Mag.* Jan. 223/2 Cosmopolitans, they do not sink into the ruts of small-town life. **1930** R. MACAULAY *Staying with Relations* xvii. 254 It looked even a little more decayed and small-town than the Miramar. **1937** J. M. MURRY *Necessity of Pacifism* iii. 47 Their natural mode of feeling is still small-town and parochial. **1949** KOESTLER *Promise & Fulfilment* I. ii. 14 The Jews had.. only a homogeneous lower-middle-class of Eastern European small-town origin. **1959** *Times* 30 Sept. 13/4 A lawyer who is by no means so simple and small-town as he makes himself out to be. **1964** R. MILIBAND in I. L. Horowitz *New Sociology* 80 A rural, small-town, one-man-one-gun America. **1969** A. LURIE *Real People* 105 Not a slick professional show like Saratoga; but very amateurish, small-town. **1975** *Verbatim* May 12/1 Can a small-town girl from Kansas and Indiana make good as a reporter in the wilds of Greater Boston? **1980** *Times Lit. Suppl.* 19 Sept. 1047/4 Pinning her characters.. in small-town Oregon.., she uncovers the hidden principles and ambitions of little men and women as they battle against the smothering ordinariness of suburban life.

So **small-towner**, an inhabitant of a small town, one who comes from a small town; **small-townish, small-towny** *adjs.*, characteristic or suggestive of a small town.

**1920** S. LEWIS *Main Street* xxix. 353 It's dreadfully tabby and small-towny. **1931** H. CONCANNON *St. Patrick* xiv. 189 The smooth paths of a smug small-townish officialdom. **1945** *Sun* (Baltimore) 17 Apr. 1/2 A friendly, small-townish man of the Middle West, called suddenly to the presidency ..by the death of Franklin D. Roosevelt, [etc.]. **1969** *Listener* 5 July 3/2 The small-towners gratefully seized upon this idealised portrait, using it as psychological support and insulation from the cold reality of their dependence on the mass society. **1974** Small-townish [see OREGONIAN *a.*].

† **'smallum**, *adv. Obs.*$^{-0}$ [f. SMALL *a.* Cf. LITLUM *adv.*] In small pieces or quantities.

*Smallums*, 'small quantities', 'small sums', occurs in modern north. dial. use.

**1483** *Cath. Angl.* 346/1 Smallum,.. *minutim*.

**small-ware(s.** [SMALL *a.* 3.] (See quot. 1839.) Chiefly in pl.

**1617** MINSHEU *Ductor*, An Habberdasher of small wares. .. In London also called a Millenier. **1630-** [see HABERDASHER *b*]. *a* **1704** T. BROWN *Decl. Advs.* Wks. 1730 I. 40 Achilles.. fell.. into a great huff with Alexander Magnus, haberdasher of small-wares. **1719** D'URFEY *Pills* (1872) IV. 216 A spruce Haberdasher first spoke me fair, But I would have nothing to do with small-ware. **1839** URE *Dict. Arts* 1141 *Small Wares*, is the name given in this country to textile articles of the tape kind, narrow bindings of cotton, linen, silk, or woollen fabric; plaited sash cord, braid, &c. **1884** *B'ham Daily Post* 24 Jan. 3/4 Hosiery, Haberdashery, Smallwares, Wools, &c.

*fig.* **1720** SWIFT *Adv. to Young Poet* Wks. 1841 II. 299 Every one knows Grub-street is a market for small ware in wit.

**b.** *attrib.*, as ***small-ware dealer, merchant, shop***.

**1834** *Picture of Liverpool* 73 Smallware dealer. **1848** MRS. GASKELL *Mary Barton* xiv, I.. set up a small-ware shop. **1858** SIMMONDS *Dict. Trade*, *Smallware-dealer*, *Smallware-merchant*, a shop-keeper who keeps small wares; a merchant who supplies them.

**smally** ('smɔːlı), *a.* [f. SMALL *a.* + -Y.]

† **1.** Of liquor: Weak, small, thin. *Obs.*$^{-1}$

**1577** GOOGE *Heresbach's Husb.* II. 88 b, They make a drinke called Cyder, and a smaly drinke beside with water.

**2.** Of persons or animals: Puny, little; smallish. *Sc.* and *north dial.*

**1808** in JAMIESON. **1820** *Glenfergus* II. 267 On the swaird before the mansion, two smally dry haired ponies were feeding. **1855** [ROBINSON] *Whitby Gloss.* s.v., A poor smally creature. **1866** *Cornh. Mag.* Mar. 359 But Jane was our only daughter,.. a wee, smally bit thing.

**'smally**, *adv.* Now *rare* Forms: 4 **smalliche**, 5–7 **smally**, 6 **smallye, -ie, smaly**. [f. SMALL *a.* + -LY$^2$. In very common use *c* 1525–1650.]

**1.** In or into small or minute pieces, fragments, etc.; finely, minutely.

**1340** *Ayenb.* 111 Þet me ssel recordi zueteliche and smalliche be little stechches alle þe guodnesses of oure lhorde. *c* **1475** *Cath. Angl.* 346/1 Smally, *minutim*. **1578** LYTE *Dodoens* 301 His leaves are not so smally cut. **1598** FLORIO, *Piouelicare*, to drizle, to mizle, or raine smallie. **1610** MARKHAM *Masterp.* II. lii. 299 Water wherein.. the hearb of arsmanarck hath bin wel sod in, and smally chopt. **1662** CHANDLER *Van Helmont's Oriat.* To Rdr., Gold and Silver, how smally soever they may be divided.

**2.** By a small number; sparsely, scantily.

*a* **1513** FABYAN *Chron.* v. (1811) 111 This swerdman.. fand yᵉ kyng smally accompanyed. **1548** HALL *Chron.*, *Hen. VI* (1809) 196 Besieged the citie of Arques,.. whiche was smally defended and sone gotten. **1604** E. G[RIMSTONE] *D'Acosta's Hist. Indies* I. ix. 32 Although it bee in a climate more commodious.., yet is it smally peopled and inhabited.

**3. a.** In only a slight or small degree; to a small or limited extent; not much, very little. Freq. preceded by *but*.

(*a*) **1523** LD. BERNERS *Froissart* I. ccxxxviii. 343 This courtesy.. dyde the prince to the kynge, the whiche after was but smally rewarded. **1553** BRENDE *Q. Curtius* III. 39 The hurt of his shoulder, whereof the skin was but smally perished. **1622** FOTHERBY *Atheom.* I. ii. 11 Which you doe but smally credite. **1656** EARL MONM. tr. *Boccalini's Advts. fr. Parnass.* I. xxv. 42 Seneca quitted the Audience with this but smally satisfactory resolution.

(*b*) **1532** in J. H. Blunt *Ref. Ch. Eng.* (1868) I. 221 We think this answer.. will smally please you. **1549** CHALONER *Erasm. on Folly* Q iij b, In case ye smally beleve myne, marke, I praie you, his owne woordes. *a* **1603** T. CARTWRIGHT *Confut. Rhem. N.T.* (1618) 541 It is needlesse, or at least smally to the purpose. **1670** EACHARD *Cont. Clergy* 109, I cannot prove.. that a man smally beneficed must of necessity be dissolute.

**b.** With verbs of considering, regarding, etc. Very common from *c* 1550 to *c* 1630.

**1532** in Strype *Eccl. Mem.* (1721) I. 213 All such acts made for reformation.. be smally regarded. **1562** MOUNTGOMERY in *Archæologia* XLVII. 220 Ower natiue Inglishe sowldior, ..whome wee smallie consider. **1609** R. BARNERD *Faithf. Sheph.* 16 They smally account of our translations. **1634** W. TIRWHYT tr. *Balzac's Lett.* (vol. I) 303 Smally valuing either Gold, or Pearles as I doe.

**c.** ***not smally***, greatly, very much.

**1562** LEGH *Armory* (1597) A iv b, Rome eke was not smally inriched by her Orator. **1578** J. JONES *Preserv. Body & Soul* I. xxx. 60 Not a little auayleable to his.. immortall glory, not smally beneficial to yᵉ Romane Empire. **1610** R. TOFTE *Honour's Acad.* 2 Not smally fortunate did he thinke himselfe.

**4.** In small form or compass; slenderly.

**1613** DEKKER *Strange Horse-Race* Wks. (Grosart) III. 336 As that nut-shell held all Homers Iliads smally written in a peece of Vellum. **1630** *Tom Thumbe* in Hazl. *E.P.P.* II. 179 His shirt.. Both light and soft for those his limbes that were so smally bred. **1946** B. MARSHALL *George Brown's Schooldays* xxx. 128 Abinger moved smally in between them.

**5.** Of a sound: with low volume.

**1958** T. H. WHITE *Once & Future King* II. ii. 224 All these noises came up to the two on the tower smally, as though they were listening through the wrong end of a megaphone. **1964** F. O'ROURKE *Mule for Marquesa* 55 Hoover said, 'Good luck,' and his words died smally in the thud of seats hitting saddles.

**smalm**, dial. var. SMARM *v.*

**smalmy**, var. SMARMY *a.*

**smalt** (smɔːlt), *sb.* (and *a.*). Also 6, 8 **smalte**, 7 **smault(e**. [a. F. *smalt* (cf. Du. *smalt*, G. *schmalte*), ad. It. *smalto* SMALTO.]

**1. a.** A species of glass, usually coloured a deep blue by oxide of cobalt, etc., and after cooling finely pulverized for use as a pigment or colouring matter.

**1558** W. WARDE tr. *Alexis' Secr.* I. VI. 118 b, Take white smalte well beaten in poulder. **1573** *Art of Limming* p. iiij, Smalte or florrey being tempered in a shell with gumme water maketh a blewe. **1612** PEACHAM *Gentl. Exerc.* 83 The principale blewes.. are Blew bice, Smalt. **1618** *Patent Specif.* (1856) No. 7. 1 And shall also make the same Smaulte as good.. as the Smault heretofore brought from beyond the Seas. **1688** HOLME *Armoury* III. 149/2 *Smalt*, some call it blew Starch; because much used by Landresses in their Starch to make it blew. **1763** W. LEWIS *Phil. Comm. Arts* 325 Being strewed upon oil paintings for a sparkling black in the same way as smalt is strewed for blue. **1791** E. DARWIN *Bot. Gard.* I. Notes 52 The Saxon mines have till very lately almost exclusively supplied the rest of Europe with.. zaffre and smalt. **1839** URE *Dict. Arts* 302 The.. nickel.. must not be suffered to become oxidized, lest it should spoil the colour of the smalt. **1862** MILLER *Elem. Chem.*, *Org.* ii. §3 (ed. 2) 102 The starch is washed, mixed with a little smalt, to give it the blue tinge preferred in the market. **1879** *Cassell's Techn. Educ.* IV. 225/2 The beauty of the blue colour, upon which the value of smalt depends.

**b.** *pl.* Various kinds of this. *rare.*

**1598** R. HAYDOCKE tr. *Lomatius* III. 106 Azures and smaltes shaddow those skiecolours, which are made of them and white mixed together.

**2.** A deep blue colour like that of smalt.

**1881** *Spectator* 2 July 860 Red and yellow, and emerald-green and smalt, all figure together on the same ribbon or dress piece. **1904** *19th Cent.* July 136 The cruder smalts and chromes and dead gold of old illuminators.

**3.** A piece of coloured glass. Cf. SMALTO.

**1864** *Chambers's Encycl.* VI. 581/2 The pieces of glass of every shade of colour are technically called *smalts*; they are generally opaque. **1887** SIR G. W. COX *Cycl. Comm. Things* (ed. 6) 391 Roman Mosaics are pictures composed of little pieces of coloured glass called *smalti* or smalts. *Ibid.*, The smalts are made in long slender rods of many thousands of different colours and shades.

**4. a.** *attrib.* and *Comb.*, as ***smalt-blue*** adj., ***furnace, -glass, -maker***, etc.; **smalt-blue**, powder blue.

**1681** GREW *Musæum* IV. III. 376 A piece of Smalt-Glass. **1753** *Chambers' Cycl.* Suppl. s.v., The necessity of having expert workmen for the smalt-making. *Ibid.*, Intelligent persons are necessary in the smalt-works. **1796** KIRWAN *Elem. Min.* (ed. 2) I. 27 Smalt blue,.. paler than the preceding [azure blue]. **1834** MRS. SOMERVILLE *Connex. Phys. Sci.* xx. 174 A smalt-blue finger glass. **1839** URE *Dict. Arts* 302 A round smalt furnace. **1855** J. R. L[EIFCHILD] *Cornw. Mines* 216 An ore of cobalt,.. from which the beautiful blue glass and smalt-blue are made. **1921** *Dict. Occup. Terms* (1927) §143 *Smalt maker*, places powdered mixture of cobalt oxide, silica (pure sand) and potassium carbonate into a wheeled fireclay crucible [etc.]. **1923** *Chambers's Jrnl.* 15 Dec. 36/1 The supreme obstacle confronting the smalt-makers.

**b.** As *adj.* Of the colour of smalt; deep blue.

**1880** MRS. C. READE *Brown Hand & W.* I. 2 A courtyard roofed in by the smalt heaven of Italy.

Hence **'smalter**, one who prepares smalt.

**1923** *Chambers's Jrnl.* 15 Dec. 36/1 The Venetian glassmakers.. were content to purchase their requirements from the 'smalters' of Germany.

**smaltine** ('smɔːltaın). *Min.* [f. SMALT *sb.* + -INE$^5$.] Tin-white cobalt.

**1837** DANA *Min.* 402 Smaltine usually occurs in veins, accompanying other ores of cobalt and ores of silver and copper. **1877** *Encycl. Brit.* VI. 81 Smaltine or speiss cobalt, an arsenide of the isomorphous bases, cobalt, nickel, and iron.

**'smaltite.** *Min.* [f. SMALT + -ITE$^1$ 2 b.] = prec.

**1868** DANA *Min.* 71 *Cobaltite*.. and smaltite afford the greater part of the smalt of commerce. **1875** *Encycl. Brit.* II. 635/1 The ores employed in the metallurgy of arsenic are.. arsenical pyrites, smaltite, and cobaltite.

‖ **'smalto.** Also *pl.* **smalti** (8 **smalte**). [It. (cf. med.L. *smaltum*, from 9th cent.), of Teutonic origin and related to SMELT *v.* Cf. AMEL *sb.*] Coloured glass or enamel used for mosaic work, etc.; a small cube or piece of this.

**1705** ADDISON *Italy* 377 Old Roman Mosaic, compos'd of little Pieces of Clay half vitrify'd, and prepar'd at the Glass-Houses, which the Italians call *Smalte*. **1859** GULLICK & TIMBS *Paint.* 80 These *smalti* are vitrified but opaque, partaking of the nature of stone and glass, or enamels. **1880** 'OUIDA' *Moths* I. 14 Buttons of repoussé work, or ancient smalto. **1896** *Daily News* 27 Mar. 2/1 The work of producing the 'smalto', or choice opaque glass of various colours.

**smalts** (smɔːlts). [app. the plural of SMALT taken as a sing.] = SMALT *sb.* 1.

**1610** FOLKINGHAM *Art Surv.* II. vi. 57 Pasture would be put into a deeper Greene made of the mixture of Azure and Smalts with Pincke. **1669** STURMY *Mar. Mag.* VII. xxxiv. 49 With Blew Smalts strew very thick the Border while it is wet. **1800** HENRY *Epit. Chem.* (1808) 257 The substance termed smalts, used as a colouring substance. **1812** J. SMYTH *Pract. Customs* (1821) 64 The calx of Cobalt has the property, that it can be melted into a blue glass, called smalts. **1877** *Encycl. Brit.* VI. 82/2 The principal use of smalts is for bluing paper.

**smaragd** ('smærægd). Now *rare*. Forms: α. 3–8 **smaragde**, 4– **smaragd** (6–7 **smarag**). β. 6 **smaradg**, 6–7 **smaradge**. [α. OF. *smaragde* (more commonly *esmaragde*, *esmeraude*, *-alde*: see EMERALD), or ad. L. *smaragdus* SMARAGDUS. Cf. MDu. and Du. *smaragd*, MHG. *smaragt* (G. *smaragd*, †*schmaragd*).] A precious stone of a bright green colour; an emerald.

α. *a* **1272** *Luue Ron* 174 in *O.E. Misc.*, Smaragde, Beril, and crisopace. **13..** *K. Alis.* 5683 (Bodl. MS.), Safyres, Smaragdes, & Margarites. **1387** TREVISA *Higden* (Rolls) I. 135 In þe whiche londe beeþ.. smaragdes, and oþer precious stones. *c* **1400** MAUNDEV. (Roxb.) vii. 25 Þare þai fynd.. þe fairest smaragdes þat er ower whare. **1445** in *Anglia* XXVIII. 265 Habergeownys also with smaragdis grene, & helmys with iacinte clere. **1555** EDEN *Decades* (Arb.) 158 The Smaragde is the trew emerode. **1580–3** GREENE *Mamillia* Wks. (Grosart) II. 43 What is more pleasaunt to the sight, then a Smaragde, yet what lesse profitable, if it be not vsed? **1638** JUNIUS *Paint. Ancients* 178 The famous sealing-ring of Polycrates was a Smaragde. **1686** PLOT *Staffordsh.* 55 Borax or green Earth.. is the better, by how much the nearer it comes to the colour of a true Smaragd. **1728** CHAMBERS *Cycl.* s.v., The Oriental Smaragds are.. the hardest, and their Splendor the most vigorous. **1847** THACKERAY *Novels by Eminent Hands*, *Codlingsby* III. xxiv, Ruby, amethyst, and smaragd. **1885** R. F. BURTON *Arab. Nts.* (1887) III. 41 Its skirts were set with the greenest smaragds.

*transf.* **1562** A. SCOTT *Poems* (S.T.S.) i. 220 Cherie maist chaist,.. Smaill sweit smaragde, smelling but smit of smot.

β. **1567** MAPLET *Gr. Forest* 20 The Smaradge hath his name of his excellent and fresh greene colour. **1608** TOPSELL *Serpents* 804 It is also said that, if a viper do behold a good smaradge, her eyes will melt. **1635** SWAN *Spec. M.* (1670) 259 The Emerald is a precious stone of a green colour, something like unto the Smaradge. **1688** HOLME *Armoury* II. 41/1 The Smaradge, is of an excellent fresh green, far passing any Leaf.

**sma'ragdian**, *a. rare.* [f. SMARAGD + -IAN.] (See quot. and SMARAGDINE *a.* 2.)

**1673** *Two Strange & Wonderful Prophets*, etc. Title-p., A New Prophecy lately discovered, written on a Smaragdian Table, by a Learned Rosy Crusian.

**smaragdine** (smə'rægdın, -aın), *sb.* and *a.* Also 5 **smaragdin, -yn(e, -en, -an, -one**, 6 **smaradine**. [ad. L. *smaragdin-us* of emerald, a. Gr. σμαράγδιν-ος, f. σμάραγδος: see SMARAGDUS. Cf. OF. *smaragdine* sb., mod.F. *smaragdin*, *-ine* adj.]

**A.** *sb.* = SMARAGD.

This use is due to a misunderstanding of the Vulgate text of *Rev.* iv. 3 'similis visioni smaragdinæ', which in turn is an inaccurate rendering of the Gr. ὅμοιος ὁράσει σμαραγδίνῳ.

**1382** WYCLIF *Rev.* iv. 3 The reynbowe was in the cumpas of the seete, lijk to the siȝt of smaragdyn. **1390** GOWER *Conf.* III. 112 Ther sitten fyve Stones mo: The smaragdine is on of tho. *c* **1400** *Destr. Troy* 924 Þis stone full of strenght,.. smaragden hit hat. **1423** JAS. I. *Kingis Q.* clv, Off bestis sawe I mony diuerse kynd:.. The pantere, like vnto the smaragdyne. **1584** R. W. *Three Ladies of Lond.* D iv, Besides I haue Diamondes, Rubyes, Emerodes,.. Smaradines,.. and almost of all kinde of precious stones.

**B.** *adj.* **1.** Of or belonging to, consisting of, a smaragd; resembling that of a smaragd; of an emerald green.

**1591** LODGE *Catharos* F j b, He putteth a Smaragdine stone in his nest, against venemous beastes of the mountaines. **1611** H. BROUGHTON *Req. Agreement* 56 Now what meaneth this: A Rainbow was about the throne, in sight Smaragdine. **1651** FRENCH *Distill.* v. 170 If gold and silver together, a Smaragdine colour. **1826** KIRBY & SP. *Entomol.* IV. xlvi. 283 Smaragdine (*Smaragdinus*), the green splendour of the emerald. **1839–48** BAILEY *Festus* 29/1 The spiritual sun, The Heavenly Earth smaragdine,.. still exist. **1855** —— *Mystic*, etc. 91 That smaragdine mirror (their chief toy Which all the angels wrought).

*Comb.* **1651** FRENCH *Distill.* v. 168 A smaragdine-greene. **1842** W. HOWITT *Life Germany* 349 Lakes and floods of the most lovely smaragdine-coloured waters.

**2.** ***smaragdine table***, a mediæval Latin work on alchemy, *Tabula Smaragdina* (publ. 1541), attributed to the Egyptian Hermes Trismegistus.

**1597** tr. *Hortulanus* (J. de Garlandia), A brief Commentarie upon the Smaragdine Table of Hermes of Alchemy. **1652** H. P. (*title*), Five Treatises of the Philosophers Stone... To which is added the Smaragdine Table. **1712** STEELE *Spect.* No. 426 ¶6, I shall never forget the venerable Air of his Countenance, when he let me into the profound Mysteries of the Smaragdine Table of Hermes.

**smaragdite** (smə'rægdaɪt). *Min.* [a. F. *smaragdite* (Saussure, 1796), f. Gr. σμάραγδ-ος SMARAGD + -ITE[1] 2 b. Cf. Gr. σμαραγδίτης (λίθος).] A brilliant grass-green or emerald-green variety of amphibole or hornblende.

In early use occasionally identified with diallage, to which it bears some resemblance.

**1804** *Edin. Rev.* III. 306 The triple identity of the smaragdite, or diallage, the schiller spath, and the labrador horn-blende. **1823** W. PHILLIPS *Min.* (ed. 3) 71 Smaragdite is of a brilliant or emerald green colour, and of a silky or pearly lustre. **1873** *Proc. Amer. Phil. Soc.* XIII. 373 The grains of smaragdite are very indistinct in form.

‖**smaragdus** (smə'rægdəs). Now *rare.* [L., a. Gr. σμάραγδος, first recorded in Herodotus; the form μάραγδος also occurs in poets. The word is probably foreign to Greek, and connected with Skr. *marakata, marakta* emerald.] = SMARAGD.

**1382** WYCLIF *Rev.* xxi. 19 The first foundement, iaspis;.. the fourthe, smaragdus. *c* **1400** *Three Kings Cologne* 45 In þis hille is founde a preciouse stone þat is cleped þere smaragdus; and þis stoon.. is kitte out of þis hille. **1486** *Bk. St. Albans, Her.* a ij b, The secunde stone is cald Smaragdus, a grauely stone signifiyng vert in armys. **1553** EDEN *Treat. New Ind.* (Arb.) 23 The precyous stone called Smaragdus (which is ye true Emerode). **1592** LODGE *Euphues Shadow* B iij, Who so liueth in Passan, must beare the stone Smaragdus with the Griphon against the stinging of Serpents. **1681** GREW *Musæum* III. I. iv. 287 The Smaragdus, growing together with a pale Amethyst in one Matrix. **1748** J. HILL *Hist. Fossils* 596 The Gem, call'd by the antients Smaragdus, or the Emerald, was evidently the same with that we now know by that name. **1875** EMERSON *Lett. & Soc. Aims* viii. 196 Color, taste, and smell, smaragdus, sugar, and musk.

†**smarald.** *Obs.*[−1] [var. of SMARAGD, after Fr. forms in *-alde.*] A smaragd; an emerald.

**1599** R. LINCHE *Fount. Anc. Fiction* K iij, His shoes are made of the greene Smarald.

**smarm** (smɑːm), *v. colloq.* (orig. *dial.*) Also 9 **sma(a)m, smalm, smawm.** [Of obscure origin.]

**1.** *dial.* To smear, bedaub.

**1847** HALLIW., *Smawm*, to smear. *Dorset.* **1890** JESSOP *Trials Country Parson* iv. 160 Mummies smalmed over with tawdry pigments.

**b.** To make smooth with an oily or greasy substance; to smooth or slick *down.* Also *fig.*

**1937** KIPLING *Something of Myself* viii. 211 The Provincial Press has been syndicated, standardized, and smarmed down out of individuality. **1953** *Chambers's Jrnl.* June 356/1, I remembered in time the need to attach a canvas, oil-filled bag to the sea-anchor, so that the thin trickle of oil would smalm the crippling seas. **1953** *Landfall* June 126 He twitted me about my orange brogues, my smarmed-down hair, my nervous attempts at wit. **1977** M. KENYON *Rapist* i. 5 The rapist looked in the looking-glass at the smarmed hair.

**c.** To treat in a wheedling, flattering way.

**1902** *Little Folks* Mar. 221/2 You can go and smarm him over if you want to.

**2. a.** *intr.* To behave in a fulsomely flattering or toadying manner, to suck *up to* a person. Also const. *about, over.*

**1911** O. ONIONS *Widdershins* ix. 265 It had been the usual thing.. twenty years ago—smarming about Art and the Arts. **1920** 'O. DOUGLAS' *Penny Plain* xx. 218 The people you try to help will smarm to your face and black-guard you behind your back. **1924** H. DE SELINCOURT *Cricket Match* v. 184 Loving her to tease him.. and not sort of smalm over him like some chaps' maters did. **1928** A. P. HERBERT *Trials of Topsy* xxiii. 138, I will *not* spend week-ends *smarming* about in your *ulcerated* town. **1942** G. R. GILBERT *Free to Laugh and Dance* vi. 29 The.. children of his two previous marriages were indignant but they couldn't do anything about it, they all hanging round and smarming up to the old man, and his marrying again in spite of them. **1950** J. CANNAN *Murder Included* vi. 108 Murder was the last thing that a toady like that doctor would look for in the family he smarmed over. **1960** F. RAPHAEL *Limits of Love* III. vi. 343 Dulles and Eden were smarming up to Nasser.

**b.** *to smarm one's way*, to make one's way by flattery or toadying.

**1940** G. D. H. & M. COLE *Counterpoint Murder* i. 15, I am going to report you to Mr. Marston. So it's no use you thinking you can smarm your way out of it. **1975** *Times Lit. Suppl.* 20 June 692/4 He is as convincing an uncaught villain as any in crime fiction; cautious and false, smarming his way into the upper reaches of such a society as only such a man would seek to crawl into.

Hence **smarmed** *ppl. a.*; **'smarming** *vbl. sb.* and *ppl. a.*

**1950** J. CANNAN *Murder Included* ii. 22 Bunny strove to use tact and courtesy: Elizabeth accused her of 'smarming'. **1953** Smarmed [see SMARM *v.* 1 b]. **1957** L. DURRELL *Justine* II. 143 He is a complete *parvenu* of course and rose on.. judicious smarming of powerful people. **1970** E. BERCKMAN *She asked for It* ix. 108 It's wonderful how greedy people are for these smarming little compliments. **1974** D. GRAY *Dead Give Away* iii. 31 He hated her smarming ways. **1977** Smarmed [see SMARM *v.* 1 b].

**smarm** (smɑːm), *sb. colloq.* Also **smalm.** [f. the vb.] An unctuous bearing; fulsome flattery; flattering or toadying behaviour.

**1937** H. C. BAILEY *Clunk's Claimant* xiii. 84 That smarm of holiness.. was pretty near the ruddy limit. **1962** M. URQUHART *Frail on North Circular* xiii. 72 'That's a nice new hair-do, Lil.'.. 'Don't come your smarm with me.' **1966** C. FENN *Pyramid of Night* iii. 60 The manager escorted her right to the door. There was no doubt that this kind of smarm was cute. **1969** B. COBB *Scandal at Scotland Yard* xvi. 154 He was ready to turn on the smarm with the 'Kiss and be friends again' talk. **1978** *Guardian Weekly* 19 Feb. 22/1 'George' did this, 'George' did that, all the way through. 'George' is the victim of bonhomie and smarm.

**smarm**: see SMALM *v.*

**smarmy** ('smɑːmɪ), *a.* (and *sb.*). *colloq.* Also **smalmy.** [f. SMARM *v.* or *sb.* + -Y[1].]

**A.** *adj.* **a.** Smooth and sleek. **b.** Ingratiating, obsequious; smug, unctuous.

**1909** C. HAMILTON *Plain Brown* i. 4 A tall, slight, smarmy-headed man. **1924** 'L. BROCK' *Deductions Col. Gore* iv. 51 Don't you be taken in by that smarmy swine. **1928** K. CLARK *Gothic Revival* ix. 236 If he [*sc.* Gilbert Scott] saved a few cathedrals from ruins, we must, I suppose, look more kindly on their smalmy surfaces. **1929** ST. J. ERVINE *First Mrs. Fraser* II. 49 *Janet.* But, Ninian dear, you shouldn't have said anything. *Ninian.* He was looking so smarmy and self-satisfied that I had to. **1930** *London Mercury* Aug. 380 Our forefathers rejected 'smarmy' overtures with 'Fair words butter no parsnips'. **1955** H. SPRING *These Lovers fled Away* 133 Uriah Heep's sort of smarmy humbleness. **1962** S. RAVEN *Close of Play* I. vi. 77 He's a smarmy, ingratiating swine. **1976** J. B. HILTON *Gamekeeper's Gallows* viii. 66 She used to.. tell her how grateful she was. Not smarmy, like; genuine. **1979** R. JAFFE *Class Reunion* I. ix. 98 He always treated her as if she were a little bit better than he was; an attitude that was smarmy in other men.

**B.** *absol.* as *sb.* A smarmy person. *rare.*

**1957** T. GUNN *Sense of Movement* 22 You understand.. the speculative man or passionate You know the smarmies, but side-step the grease.

Hence **'smarmily** *adv.*; **'smarminess.**

**1934** H. NICOLSON *Let.* 17 Nov. (1966) 189 There is something about the smarminess of Americans which makes me see red. **1958** 'A. BRIDGE' *Portuguese Escape* 184 The art of making himself agreeable in his current surroundings, whatever they were; but.. he rather over-did it.. 'smarminess' described his conversation with painful accuracy. **1968** J. PORTER *Dover goes to Pott* i. 15 Dover, sycophant and snob that he was, smarmily agreed. **1974** 'D. KYLE' *Raft of Swords* II. xii. 129 With deliberate smarminess, Gawthorpe thanked him. **1982** *Sunday Express* 30 May 6/8 It is smarmily hypocritical.

**smart** (smɑːt), *sb.*[1] Forms: 3 **smi(e)rte,** 3–6 **smerte** (4 **-tte**), 4–6, 9 *Sc.* **smert,** 7 *Sc.* **smairt;** 5–6 **smarte,** 5– **smart.** [ME. *smierte, smerte,* app.:—OE. **smiertu*, f. *smeart* SMART *a.* Cf. Fris. *smert*, MDu. and MLG. *smerte, smarte* (Du. and LG. *smart*, Da. *smerte*, Sw. *smärta*), OHG. *smerza* fem., also *smerzo* masc. (MHG. *smerze, smerz*, G. *schmerz* masc.).]

**1.** Sharp physical pain, esp. such as is caused by a stroke, sting, or wound. Also with *a* and pl.

*a* **1200** *Moral Ode* 114 Wa se seið þet he bo hal him solf wat best his smirte [*Trin.* smierte, *Eg.* smerte]. *c* **1320** *Cast. Love* 1153 For vre woke þou3tes he þolede smerte. **1398** TREVISA *Barth. De P.R.* v. xxx. (Bodl. MS.), Þe touche of senewes haþ no feeling of soore and of smerte. *c* **1440** *Generydes* 6242 For eny wo or smerte.. I wist hym neuer onkynde. *c* **1491** *Chastysing Goddes Chyldern* 15 It felt no smerte sharply tyll the rodde came. **1526** *Pilgr. Perf.* (W. de W. 1531) 204 b, Yf he had pretended to suffre payne, and had feled no smarte. **1585** T. WASHINGTON tr. *Nicholay's Voy.* II. vi. 36 She procureth present death wyth-out any smart. **1641** J. JACKSON *True Evang. T.* I. 46 He.. inflicted both corporall smart and pecuniary mulcts upon them. **1681** BAXTER *Apol. Nonconf. Min.* 58 We knew it by our smarts, being sure to be whipt. **1718** POPE *Iliad* XI. 574 Raging with intolerable smart, He writhes his body. **1792** COWPER *Stanzas Bill Mortality* iv, Strange world, that costs it so much smart. **1870** BRYANT *Iliad* I. XI. 374 Patroclus.. applied a root Of bitter flavor to assuage the smart.

**b.** Const. *of.* Also in fig. context.

**1570** LEVINS *Manip.* 33/29 Yᵉ Smart of a wound, *æstus.* **1596** BP. W. BARLOW *Three Serm.* iii. 142 Euen the Prophets.. haue felt the smart of hunger. *a* **1604** HANMER *Chron. Irel.* (1633) 32 Ireland.. felt little smart of the Romane sword. **1726** SWIFT *Gulliver* I. i, When I felt the smart of their arrows upon my face. **1886** R. F. BURTON *Arab. Nts.* (abr. ed.) I. 262 For the smart of the stick I confessed, 'It was I who stole it'.

**c.** Degree of smarting or painfulness.

**1888** BERNARD *Fr. World to Cloister* v. 114 The discipline,.. at its highest possible smart, never equalled.. the sting of such a caning.

**2.** Mental pain or suffering; grief, sorrow, affliction; sometimes, suffering of the nature of punishment or retribution.

**1303** R. BRUNNE *Handl. Synne* 3964 3yf þou.. felyst weyl yn þy herte Of a lytyl sorow or smerte. **1412–20** LYDG. *Chron. Troy* IV. 2204 Alweye contunyng in his smerte For þe loue of feire Polycene. *c* **1430** *Syr Gener.* (Roxb.) 1632 To tel you hou I caght this smert, And al myn evel how it began. *c* **1532** DU WES *Introd. Fr.* in *Palsgr.* 921 A man doutfull.. is sone converted and tourned in smerte. **1590** SPENSER *F.Q.* I. I. 54 Ne let vaine feares procure your needlesse smart, Where cause is none. **1647** COWLEY *Mistr., Loves Visibility* v, The very Eye betrays our inward smart. **1679** BUNYAN *Fear of God* Wks. 1855 I. 460 Sorrow is the effect of smart, and smart the effect of faith. **1766** GRAY in *Corr. G. & Nicholls* (1843) 63 Time.. will cure the smart, and in some hearts soon blot out all the traces of sorrow. **1808** H. MORE *Cœlebs* II. 333 Examine your own heart;.. it will be a salutary smart. **1872** BLACKIE *Lays Highl.* 3, I love the oaks of Derry, And to leave them gives me smart.

**b.** Const. *of.*

*c* **1500** *Lancelot* 1051 So prikith hyme the smart Of hevynes, that stood vnto his hart. *a* **1591** H. SMITH *Wks.* (1867) II. 186 He came when man had sinned, and had felt the smart of sin. **1631** GOUGE *God's Arrows* III. §58. 298 No marvell then that they.. be made sensibly to feele the smart of their folly. **1702** *Eng. Theophr.* 141 All parties blame persecution when they feel the smart on't. **1827** HALLAM *Const. Hist.* (1876) I. i. 21 Some were sent to prison for hasty words, to which the smart of injury excited them. **1849** ROBERTSON *Serm.* Ser. I. ix. (1855) 147 There is a diseased sensitiveness which shrinks from the smart of acknowledgment.

†**c.** *pl.* Loss, damage; adversity. *Obs.*

**1552** in Strype *Ann. Ref.* (1824) VI. 486 Yf chance should fal.. that a ship should be lost, the halls might easily bear the smarts therof. **1591** SAVILE *Tacitus, Hist.* II. lxiv. 90 Neither did shee.. participate any thing els of hir sonnes estate, saue onely the smarts of hir house when it fell.

**3.** *ellipt.* = SMART MONEY.

**1802** JAMES *Milit. Dict.*, *Smarts*, the different sums which are received by recruiting parties under the head of *Smart money*, are frequently so called. **1887** *Jamieson's Sc. Dict.* Suppl. 321/1 He listed.., but paid the smert and wan hame.

**4.** *attrib.* **a. smart-ticket** (see quot. 1846).

**1801** NELSON 11 Oct. in Nicolas *Disp.* (1845) IV. 504, I will send to the Gannet for Smart Tickets. **1816** A. C. HUTCHISON *Pract. Obs. Surg.* (1826) 184 Making a pretext of being ruptured in the service, and thereby obtaining smart-tickets, which will entitle them to pensions for life. **1846** A. YOUNG *Naut. Dict.* 288 *Smart-ticket*, a certificate granted by the surgeon.. in favour of any person who has been wounded or hurt in the service, in order that he may receive a single gratuity, or a pension from Greenwich Hospital.

**b.** *U.S.* **smart-grass,** = SMARTWEED.

**1845** S. JUDD *Margaret* II. i, May-weed, smart-grass, and Indian tobacco.

**smart** (smɑːt), *sb.*[2] [f. SMART *a.*]

**1.** One who affects smartness in dress, manners, or talk. (Common in 18th cent.; now *Hist.*)

**1712** STEELE *Spect.* No. 442 ¶3 All Beaux, Rakes, Smarts,.. and all Sorts of Wits. **1721** AMHERST *Terræ Fil.* No. 46 (1726) 254, I have given great offence to a large body of fine gentlemen there, call'd Smarts. **1753** *Scots Mag.* Oct. 491/2, I put on a sword, supped every night at a tavern,.. and was universally confessed to be improved into a Smart. **1821** SCOTT *Pirate* xiv, The word passed through among the young Templars, and the wits, and the smarts. **1859** GREEN *Oxf. Stud.* ii. (O.H.S.) 47 The smart of the day [18th cent.] rises late in an age of early risers.

**2.** Smartness in talk or writing.

**1845** TENNYSON in *Life* (1897) I. 228, I said something that offended him; and.. he.. told me that I was 'affecting the smart'. **1899** *Westm. Gaz.* 25 Oct. 3/2 This needless introduction of the presumably 'smart' would ruin the art of any novel.

**3.** Usu. *pl.* Intelligence, cleverness, acumen; wits. *U.S. slang.*

**1970** *It* 27 Feb.–13 Mar. 14/4 Now Abbie's a very brilliant cat. He's very far out, very freaked out, but he's still got some smarts. **1970** *New Yorker* 28 Nov. 126/3, I knew I had the smarts—the business smarts—even then. **1972** H. KEMELMAN *Monday Rabbi took Off* xlv. 263 The whole story is a little weak.. I mean, this kid of yours has the normal amount of smarts. **1977** *N.Y. Times* 9 Oct. 26 Mrs. Maynard said that Mr. Miller.. 'doesn't have enough smart to run a union as big as the United Mine Workers'. **1979** *Sunday Star* (Toronto) 6 May B7/4 You know—streetwise, lots of smart, lots of quick, playing pinochle with vice cops. **1981** *Guardian Weekly* 26 July 15/4 They complain that the level of intelligence is low and that the soldiers have neither the smarts nor the education to work the complicated weapons of modern warfare.

**smart** (smɑːt), *a.* Forms: 1–2 **smeart,** 3 **smært,** 3–5 **smerte** (5 **smyrte**), 4–5 **smert** (5 **-tt**); 3– **smart** (4 **-tt**), 4–6 **smarte.** [OE. *smeart*, related to *smeortan* SMART *v.* Not represented in the cognate languages.]

**I.** †**1. a.** Of a whip, rod, etc.: Inflicting or causing pain; sharp, biting, stinging. *Obs.*

*a* **1023** WULFSTAN *Hom.* (1883) 295 Ic wylle swingan eow mid þam smeartestum swipum. *a* **1175** *Cott. Hom.* 243 Þu ahst to habben.. Stede and twei sporen and ane smearte 3erd. *a* **1300** *Cursor M.* 15785 Wit maces and wit neues smert vn-rekenli on him [they] ran. *c* **1325** *Chron. Eng.* 929 He was yschote With an arewe kene ant smert. *c* **1440** *Pallad. on Husb.* I. 940 The Greek seith eek that if a cloude arise Of bresis smert [L. *locustarum*], men must in house hem hide. **1447** BOKENHAM *Seyntys* (Roxb.) 47 Whan he on ye crosse.. Heng nakyd fastnyd wyth nayles smerte. **1593** SHAKS. *2 Hen. VI*, III. ii. 325 Their softest Touch, as smart as Lyzards stings. **1671** FLAVEL *Fount. Life* xvi. (1836) 143 Sometimes he spares their outward, and afflicts their inner man, which is a much smarter rod.

†**b.** Sharp or rough to the touch. *Obs.*

*c* **1400** *Destr. Troy* 924 Þis stone.., Be it smethe owþer smert, smaragden hit hat.

†**c.** Severe or hard *on* or *upon* one. *Obs.*

**1549–62** STERNHOLD & H. *Ps.* xxxii. 4 Thy hand on me so grievous was and smart. **1648** BP. HALL *Breathings Devout Soul* (1851) 164 When thy hand hath been smart and heavy upon me.

**2.** Of blows, strokes, etc.: Sufficiently hard or severe to cause pain. (In later use approximating to sense 5.) Also in fig. contexts.

*c* **1200** *Trin. Coll. Hom.* 207 Þenne me hine pined mid.. smerte smiten of smale longe 3erden. *c* **1205** LAY. 21364 [They] uppen Colgrime smiten mid swiðe smærte biten. *a* **1300** *Cursor M.* 25543 Iesu.. Sufferd.. Dintes sare and smert. **13..** *Sir Beues* 2883 Beues þanne wiþ strokes smerte Smot þe dragoun to þe herte. *c* **1400** *Rule St. Benet* 22 Yef any be tane ofte in faute,.. wyd smerte beting sal sho be chastyd. *c* **1435** *Torr. Portugal* 2572 Smert boffettes they yeldyd there. **1602** SHAKS. *Ham.* III. i. 50 How smart a lash that speech doth giue my Conscience? **1658** SIR T. BROWNE *Hydriot.* iv. (1736) 45 The smartest Strokes of Affliction leave but short Smart upon us. **1764** REID *Inquiry* v. §6 Suppose him first to be pricked with a pin—this will, no doubt, give a smart sensation. **1841** LANE *Arab. Nts.* (Rtldg.) 12 Take a good-sized stick, and give her a smart thrashing. **1859** GEO. ELIOT *A. Bede* xxx, When a man's got his limbs whole, he can bear a smart cut or two.

†**3.** Of pain, sorrow, wounds, etc.: Sharp, keen, painful, severe. *Obs.*

*a* **1300** *Cursor M.* 58 Wyt chaunce of ded, or chaunce of hert, þat soft began has endyng smart. *c* **1369** CHAUCER *Dethe Blaunche* 507 Hym thought hys sorwes were so smerte. *c* **1420** *Chron. Vilod.* 1787 Of goddus Passion..& of his wo & of his woundys hard and smert. *c* **1485** *Digby Myst.* (1882) IV. 192 The sorow of your harte Makes my passion mor bitter & mor smarte. **1513** DOUGLAS *Æneid* V. xii. 63 The fadir Eneas, smyt with this smart cais. **1678** *Lively Oracles* III. §5. 264 That long train of smart calamities which succeeded his sin. **1688** BUNYAN *Jerus. Sinner Saved* (1886) 64 The gospel..threateneth them with the heaviest and smartest judgments.

**4. a.** Of words, etc.: Sharp, severe; cutting, acrimonious. Now *rare.*

*a* **1300** *Cursor M.* 3034 Abraham..thoght þis wordes war to smert. **13..** *Ibid.* 12084 (Gött.), Thoru bolning of his hert, To ioseph spac he wordes ouer smart. **1625–8** tr. *Camden's Hist. Eliz.* III. (1688) 269 A Book which was written..against the Marriage in a smart and stinging Style. **1639** FULLER *Holy War* II. xxiv, He would often give a smart jest, which would make the place both blush and bleed where it lighted. **1726** SWIFT *Gulliver* II. iii, He seldom failed of a smart word or two upon my littleness. **1751** *Narr. H.M.S. 'Wager'* 128 This smart Remonstrance touch'd the Lieutenant to the very Heart. **1825** *Gentl. Mag.* XCV. I. 397 'To start' is to apply a smart word to an idle or forgetful person. **1842** LOVER *Handy Andy* xviii, The crowd ceased its noise when the two Squires were seen engaged in exchanging smart words.

†**b.** Sharp in criticism or comment *upon* one.

**1692** WASHINGTON tr. *Milton's Def. People Eng.* iii. Wks. 1851 VIII. 75 The Lawyer, whoever he be, that you are so smart upon, was not so much out of the way. **1699** BENTLEY *Phal.* 390 He fansied, he was very smart upon me; but as it generally happens with him, he lashes himself.

**5.** Brisk or vigorous; having a certain degree of intensity, force, strength, or quickness: **a.** Of natural forces or processes.

**13..** *K. Alis.* 1184 (Bodl. MS.), To mouþe he sett his Olyfaunt, He bloweþ smert & loude sounes. *c* **1340** HAMPOLE *Pr. Consc.* 3257 Thai er dungen..With smert stormes als of wynd and rayn. *c* **1386** CHAUCER *Can. Yeom. Prol. & T.* 215 What sholde I tellen..of the esy fir, and smart also, Which that was maad? *a* **1400–50** *Alexander* 1309 Quen it was smeten in small with þe smert wazes. **1672** SIR T. BROWNE *Lett. Friend.* xii. 136 Sepulchral fires and smart flames. **1692** RAY *Disc.* II. ii. (1732) 107 A smart and continued Rain. **1711** SWIFT *Jrnl. to Stella* 31 Jan., We are here in as smart a frost for the time as I have seen. **1726** T. SMITH *Jrnl.* (1849) 265 This has been a very smart, close winter. **1800** *Med. Jrnl.* V. 31 They..had a smart fever for three days, and then an eruption. **1808** *Ibid.* XIX. 106 Leaving for him two smart purges of calomel and jalap. **1829** *Chapters Phys. Sci.* 463 It demonstrates its presence both by a sudden flash and a smart report. **1875** *Ure's Dict. Arts* III. 1055 The assistant must look to the oil, and bring it to a smart simmer.

**b.** Of liquor, with reference to its effect on the palate.

**1648** J. BEAUMONT *Psyche* IX. lxxxi, A flood, to which.. smart Gall is dropping Myrrh. **1664** POWER *Exp. Philos.* I. 33 Both in the keenest and smartest, as well as in the weakest and most watrish Vineger. **1710** T. FULLER *Pharm. Extemp.* 3 The smarter and staler [ale is], the more it openeth and detergeth. **1760–2** GOLDSM. *Cit. W.* lv. (Globe) 177/1 It will eat best with some smart bottled beer. **1818** KEATS *Lett.* Wks. 1889 III. 166 We have now begun upon whisky,..very smart stuff it is.

**c.** Of encounters, attacks, etc.

*a* **1700** EVELYN *Diary* 2 July 1685, There was a smart skirmish. **1716** CHURCH *Philip's War* (1865) I. 125 In the Evening they heard a smart firing at a distance from them. **1791** GOUVR. MORRIS in Sparks *Life & Writ.* (1832) II. 137 A good smart action would be useful rather than pernicious. **1813** *Sporting Mag.* XLII. 68 Cooper planted a smart hit on his adversary's neck. **1844** H. H. WILSON *Brit. Ind.* II. 51 A smart affair with the enemy took place. **1885** *Manch. Exam.* 21 Mar. 6/2 A smart passage at arms between his Grace and Lord Bramwell.

**6. a.** Pretty steep. Now *dial.* or *colloq.*

*a* **1668** LASSELS *Voy. Italy* (1698) I. 44, I went up a smart hill called Mount Aurigo. *a* **1904** in *Eng. Dial. Dict.*

**b.** Sharp, abrupt, clearly outlined. *rare.*

**1753** HOGARTH *Anal. Beauty* xiii. 182 These objects which ..come forwardest to the view, must have large, strong, and smart oppositions. **1784** J. BARRY *Lect. Art* v. (1848) 187 The cast and manner of their several foldings, some more smart and frequently interrupted, others more flowing. **1870** G. M. HOPKINS *Jrnls. & Papers* (1959) 201 The day had been very bright and clear, distances smart.

**7. a.** Considerable (in number, amount, extent, etc.). Chiefly *dial.* and *U.S.*

Bartlett *Dict. Amer.* (1848) 313 gives various quotations, including three for *a smart chance* in the sense of 'a good deal, a large quantity', etc.

**1778** S. FOOTE *Devil upon Two Sticks* II. 44 in *Wks.* IV, [Scot loq.] Ah! for the mater of that, it is a praty smart little income. **1839** SIR G. C. LEWIS *Gloss. Heref.* s.v., 'A smart few' means a considerable number. **1855** THACKERAY *Newcomes* lxxx, Madame..left a smart legacy to the.. children. **1882** *Mrs. Raven's Temptation* I. 276 Hope you will get a smart fee with it.

**b.** So ***right smart***; also as *sb.*, a good deal. *U.S.*

**1842** J. S. BUCKINGHAM *Slave States of America* II. 327, I asked here, whether the people made much maple-sugar in this neighbourhood; when the gentleman..answered, 'Yes, they do, I reckon, right smart.' **1856** MRS. STOWE *Dred* II. xvi. 162, I sold right smart of eggs des yere summer. **1857** OLMSTED *Texas* 301 A 'right smart chunk of bacon'. **1863** S. L. *J. Life in South* I. vii. 91 We have read right smart of that book. **1879** TOURGEE *Fool's Errand* (1880) 88 Directing the work, and, Yankee-like, 'doing right smart of it' himself, as they say here. **1932** W. FAULKNER *Light in August* i. 25 There is a right smart of folks in Jefferson I don't know. **1938** M. K. RAWLINGS *Yearling* vi. 54 'Howdy, Mr. Forrester. Proud to see you. How's your health?' 'Howdy, sir. I'm right smart tol'able, seein' as how I be near about done for.' **1949** L. NORDYKE *Cattle Empire* 81 Heard a right smart about you, Pincham.

**II. 8.** Pert, forward, impudent. *Obs. rare* exc. *predic.* in *to be* or *get smart* (U.S.).

**13..** *K. Alis.* 4160 (Bodl. MS.), Darrie was wel sore anoyede..And seide, 'of tale þou art smart'. *c* **1449** PECOCK *Repr.* I. i. 5 In this trowing and holding thei ben so kete and so smert and so wantoun. **1607** TOPSELL *Four-f. Beasts* (1658) 114 The curst, sharp, smart,..implacable and wanton-rowling-eyed Women. **1933** E. O'NEILL *Ah, Wilderness* II. 60 *Tommy*... Uncle Sid's soused again. *Mrs. Miller*... You be quiet! Did I ever! You're getting too smart! **1955** W. C. GAULT *Ring around Rosa* v. 59 Don't get smart, Callahan. **1956** B. HOLIDAY *Lady sings Blues* (1973) i. 4 This time Cousin Ida beat me for being smart with her.

**9. a.** Of persons: Quick, active; prompt.

*a* **1300** *Cursor M.* 7168 Sampson, þat was selcuth smert, Vte o þair handes son he stert. *c* **1380** *Sir Ferumb.* 5575 Þe Sarzyn, þat was fers & smert, howel oppon þe helm he gert. *a* **1500** *How good wife taught her daughter* 194 in *Q. Eliz. Acad.* 50 When þi seruantes haue do þer werke, To pay þer hyre loke þou be smerte. **1530** PALSGR. 324/2 Smarte, swyfte, *soudayn.* **1655** FULLER *Ch. Hist.* IV. iii. §1 This year began the smart and active Councel of Basil. **1687** tr. *Sallust* (1692) 96 All the while Catiline, with the most active and smartest of his followers kept still in the head of his Men. **1847** C. BRONTË *J. Eyre* iv, Bessie Lee..was smart in all she did. **1899** F. T. BULLEN *Log of Sea-waif* 342 We were mighty smart getting under way.

**b.** *transf.* Of things.

*a* **1325** tr. *Stat. Westm.* II c. 26 (MS. Rawl. B. 520 lf. 20 b), þer nis no writ..ware þoru þe plaintifs habbez smarttere riȝt þane þoru þe writ of nouele disseisine. **1658** SIR T. BROWNE *Hydriot.* Introd., Water hath proved the smartest Grave; which in Forty Days swallowed almost Mankind.

**c.** Healthy, well. *U.S.*

**1788** J. MAY *Jrnl.* 31 Aug. (1873) 116 Didn't feel smart enough to go to meeting. **1832** J. J. STRANG *Diary* 23 Aug. in M. M. Quaife *Kingdom of St. James* (1930) 205 This commenced the sickest day I ever suffered since my remembrance but now (evening) I am again smart for a sick person. **1956** B. HOLIDAY *Lady sings Blues* (1973) i. 1 By the time she worked her way out of hock in the hospital and took me home to her folks, I was so big and smart I could sit up in a carriage.

**10. a.** Clever, capable, adept; quick at devising, learning, looking after oneself or one's own interests, etc. In later use chiefly *U.S.*

**1628** LE GRYS *Barclay's Arg.* 81 For he a smart young man, and of great iudgement,..held vp the Kings side. *a* **1656** USSHER *Ann.* VI. (1658) 525 Being.. loath to engage in fight with Fimbria, who was both a smart fellow, and a Conqueror to boot. **1709** STEELE *Tatler* No. 26 ⁋5 [He] is what we most justly call, a Smart Fellow. **1786** M. CUTLER in *Life, Jrnls.*, etc. (1888) I. 189 Those of my subscribers who are smart, able men, I have told shall have an equal chance with other proprietors. **1844** MRS. HOUSTON *Yacht Voy. Texas* II. 215 The Opossum is held in great respect by the Yankees, as a particularly 'smart' animal. **1888** BRYCE *Amer. Commw.* (1890) II. lxv. 484 In America every smart man is expected to be able to do anything he turns his hand to.

**b.** Marked by special skill or dexterity.

**1895** *Daily News* 17 May 3/7 Chatterton being out to a very smart catch at mid-on.

**c.** Of a device: capable of some independent and seemingly intelligent action. Cf. *smart bomb* in sense 15 below.

**1972** *Proc. IEEE* LX. 1282/1 The term 'smart terminal' is used here to identify an interactive terminal in which part of the processing is accomplished by a small computer or processor contained within the terminal itself. **1977** *Sci. Amer.* Sept. 188/1 When smart traffic signals become ubiquitous and are linked to a control center, the traffic cop at the intersection will become obsolete. **1980** *Economist* 15 Mar. 84/3 Tomorrow's vehicles are likely to have a series of 'smart' transducers attached to the engine, gear-box, brakes, etc, all sending coded messages via a common wire to the dashboard. **1982** *Times* 1 June 15/5 Smart sensors ensure a direct hit on a target.

**11. a.** Clever in talk or argument; capable of making witty remarks; good at repartee.

**1639** MASSINGER *Unnatural Combat* IV. ii, A smart quean! **1695** J. EDWARDS *Perfect. Script.* 514 The younger Vossius is a smart advocate for the Septuagint. **1727** POPE, etc. *Art of Sinking* 109 It is by virtue of this style that..Tully is as short and smart as Seneca. **1753** MISS COLLIER *Art of Torment.* (1811) 194 This, I have been told, is what they call being smart in company. **1778** MISS BURNEY *Evelina* lxiv, You're so smart there's no speaking to you. **1895** *19th Cent.* Aug. 324 He is decidedly smarter as an all-round talker.

**b.** Of sayings, etc.: Clever, pointed; witty.

**1656** EARL MONM. tr. *Boccalini's Advts. fr. Parnass.* I. lv. (1674) 71 We find some Histories..abounding in smart Politick Precepts. **1673** *S'too him Bayes* 19, I acknowledge this Expression to be nice and smart. **1734** tr. *Rollin's Anc. Hist.* (1827) VI. xv. 2 Cicero, who ascribes this saying to Timæus, declares it a very smart one. **1752** JOHNSON *Rambler* No. 194 ⁋11 He mistakes the question, that he may return a smart answer. **1824** DIBDIN *Libr. Comp.* 539 A short, but smart notice of him. **1865** DICKENS *Mut. Fr.* I. x, She has a reputation for giving smart accounts of things. **1874** L. STEPHEN *Hours Libr.* (1892) II. vi. 188 Mandeville ..passes off his smart sayings upon the public as serious.

**12. a.** Alert and brisk; esp. combining briskness with neatness or trimness of appearance.

**1602** MARSTON *Ant. & Mel.* III. Wks. 1856 I. 37, I.. Strook a faire wench with a smart speaking eye. **1683** WOOD *Life* 9 Sept., The smart lads of the city march'd downe the streets with cudgells in their hands. **1784** COWPER *Task* IV. 648 He hates the field,..And sighs for the smart comrades he has left. **1827** O. W. ROBERTS *Voy. Centr. Amer.* 80 Sufficient [room] for a smart vessel to work in or out. **1865** KINGSLEY *Herew.* v, To a tight smart Viking's son. **1884** *Pall Mall G.* 29 Aug. 1/2 The Egyptian soldier is..smart, clean, and cheap.

**b.** Neatly and trimly dressed.

**1789** MRS. PIOZZI *Journ. France* II. 204 We observed.. how the town was become neater, the ordinary people smarter. **1806** BERESFORD *Miseries Hum. Life* II. xxiii, Walking out to dinner, clean and smart. **1848** DICKENS *Dombey* ix, He became a little smarter in his dress. **1888** *Poor Nellie* 127 Adela had noticed how smart he looked.

**c.** Of dress, etc.: Neat and trim; stylish.

(*a*) **1716** DARRELL *Gentl. Instr.* (ed. 3) III. i. 476 Nothing would please his Worship, but Smart Shoes, Smart Hats, and Smart Cravats... The truth is he had been bred up with the Groom, and transplanted the Stable-dialect into the Dressing-room. **1754** FIELDING *J. Wild* I. x, A blue plush coat,..a smart sleeve, and a cape. **1823** SCOTT *Quentin D.* ii, The smart blue bonnet..was already recognized as the Scottish head-gear. **1859** W. COLLINS *Q. of Hearts* (1875) 23 The man..had a collection of smart little boots and shoes. (*b*) **1823** CT. DE SOLIGNY *Lett. Eng.* II. lxviii, Looking out on the smart shops, the nicely paved streets. **1851** HAWTHORNE *Twice-t. Tales* I. xvi. 252 There, in a smart chaise, a dashingly dressed gentleman and lady. **1894** SIR J. ASTLEY *Fifty Yrs. Life* I. 94 We put up at a very smart hotel. (*c*) **1864** D. G. MITCHELL *Sev. Stor.* 3 One of them..is bound in smart red leather. **1888** *Poor Nellie* 8, I will make a cover for them,..a smart one of blue velvet.

**13.** Fashionable, elegant, esp. in a very high degree. (Common in recent use, from *c* 1882.)

The reappearance of the word in this sense was the subject of much comment and criticism in newspapers, etc., from about 1885, and the phrases ***smart people, smart society, the smart set***, etc., have been commonly used as a general designation for the extremely fashionable portion of society (sometimes with implication of being a little 'fast').

**1718** *Freethinker* No. 158 A Cluster of smart Men, in tawdry Dresses, with little Rapiers. **1793** ANNA SEWARD *Lett.* (1811) III. 275 This beach..covered with smart people, and with equipages. **1845** M. J. HIGGINS *Ess.* (1875) 24 They..got my wife invited to several very smart balls. **1881** MALLOCK *Romance 19th Cent.* I. 97, I have seen plenty of smart society. *Ibid.* II. 254 Many smart people were shy of Mrs. Crane. **1885** E. W. HAMILTON *Diary* 20 May (1972) II. 867 Dined at Brook House... This is a house at which one meets the 'grand set' as distinct from the 'smart set'—two totally different sections of the best London Society. **1900** *Smart Set* Apr. 137 The Smart Set of London has for the last ten or fifteen years..been the chief influence of our English playwrights, plays and players. **1937** K. BLIXEN *Out of Africa* I. i. 12 Our Quasi Smart Set of the Colony. **1949** P. HASTINGS *Cases in Court* v. 265 Mrs Barney's family were well-known in Mayfair and both Mrs Barney and the dead man were notorious members of the so-called young 'smart set'. **1974** P. DICKINSON *Poison Oracle* ii. 66 Dinah [*sc.* an ape]..had indeed left the slums to join the evolutionary smart set, Man. **1981** V. GLENDINNING *E. Sitwell* ix. 131 Edith's interest in the intrigues of the smart set was minimal.

**14.** *Comb.*, as ***smart-looking, -suited, -tongued, -witted.***

**1601** B. JONSON *Poetaster* IV. v, A good smart-tongued Goddesse. **1770** 'P. PENNYLESS' *Sentimental Lucubrations* ii. 31 A smart-looking waiter came up to me. *a* **1859** in Bartlett *Dict. Amer.* (ed. 2) s.v., A powerful smart looking chunk of a pony. **1897** *Daily News* 28 Sept. 2/1 That friendly, but smart-witted Power. **1922** JOYCE *Ulysses* 249 James's wax smartsuited freshcheeked models.

**15.** Special collocations: **smart bomb**, a powered missile which is guided to its target by an optical system; **smart money** *U.S.*, money bet or invested by persons with expert knowledge; *transf.* knowledgeable persons; **smart mouth** *U.S. slang*, one who is good at repartee, one who gives cheek; so **smart-mouth** *v. trans.* to be cheeky to, to be witty at the expense of; **smart-mouthed** *a.*

**1972** *Guardian* 29 June 4/2 Three out of four [missions] have been using 'smart' bombs. **1975** *N.Y. Times* 8 Sept. 2/4 Since 1973 the Israeli Air Force has been furnished with a variety of 'smart bombs' guided by laser beams of television. **1982** *Sunday Tel.* 9 May 17/5 The American 'smart' bomb, which homes on a laser beam shone on to the target by a spotter aircraft. **1926** *Amer. Mercury* Dec. 464/2 In referring to money wagered by persons with good tips or information, the term used is *smart* money. **1930** W. R. BURNETT *Iron Man* I. 5 'Well,' said Regan, 'all the smart money's on the black boy.' **1947** *Sun* (Baltimore) 6 Aug. 10/5 Bookmakers and layoff men are gamblers and many times they add personal wages to 'smart money'. **1977** H. FAST *Immigrants* II. 87 Germany has declared war on Russia, and the smart money says that this is only the beginning. **1981** *Times* 7 Nov. 6/8 Mr Weinberger..is close to the President..much closer than Mr Haig has ever been. In a battle for Mr Reagan's ear, all the smart money would be on Mr Weinberger. **1968** *Sun Mag.* (Baltimore) 13 Oct. 19/1, I was a smart mouth, a troublemaker in school. **1976** R. B. PARKER *Promised Land* (1977) xii. 65 Don't smart-mouth me, man. You wising off at me? **1978** J. L. HENSLEY *Killing in Gold* (1979) viii. 97 He..beat up three kids..when one of them smart-mouthed him. **1976** *Publishers Weekly* 19 Apr. 82/3 Smart-mouthed film critic for *Gotham* magazine. **1978** J. IRVING *World according to Garp* xii. 229 Some smart-mouthed motorist..will..ask.., 'What are you in training for?'

**smart** (smɑːt), *adv.* Forms: 3–4 smerte, 4–5 smert; 4 smarte, 4– smart. [f. SMART *a.*] = SMARTLY, in various senses. (Common in 14th c.)

*a* **1300** *Havelok* 215 Þe king..dede him sore swinge, And wit hondes smerte dinge. *c* **1330** R. BRUNNE *Chron. Wace* (Rolls) 1643 Þey..smyten to-gyder al so smert. **1377** LANGL. *P. Pl.* B. XI. 426 Þere smit no þinge so smerte ne smelleth so soure. *a* **1400–50** *Alexander* 5515 Þan made he smythis to gaa smert & smethe him a chaiere. **1422** tr. *Secreta Secret., Priv. Priv.* 180 Thes newely come me shale moche more Smertre assayle. **1697** DRYDEN *Virg. Georg.* I. 541 The Stars shine smarter. **1771** T. HULL *Sir W. Harrington* (1797) I. 141 Dressed as smart as my close mourning would permit me. **1794** NELSON 19 July in Nicolas *Disp.* (1845) I. 449 The Enemy have fired smart since daylight. **1852** MRS. STOWE *Uncle Tom's C.* ii. 10 He'd ..put him to hoeing and digging, and 'see if he'd step about so smart'. **1886** *Pall Mall G.* 29 Nov. 3/1 It is better for tenants to be compelled to pay up smart than to allow them to heap up a great burden of arrears.

*Comb.* **1632** J. HAYWARD tr. *Biondi's Eromena* A iv b, Fenced..with sharp-pointed brambles and smart-stinging briers. **1752-3** A. MURPHY *Gray's Inn Jrnl.* No. 22, A laced Coat, and smart-cocked Hat. **1851** MAYHEW *Lond. Labour* I. 379 Smart-dressing servant-maids, perhaps, are my best customers. **1884** PAE *Eustace* 97 We want a smart-built craft like yon.

**smart** (smɑːt), *v.* Forms: 1 -smeortan, 3 smeorte(n, 4 smurte; 2-5 smerten (5 -yn), 2-5 smerte, 4-5 smert, 7 *Sc.* smairt; 5-6 smarte, 5- smart. *Pa. t.* 2 smeart, 3 smart, 3-4 smert, 4 smurte; *pl.* smo(u)rte, smerte. [OE. *smeortan* str. vb., = Fris. *smerte*, MDu. *smerten, smarten* (Du. *smarten*), MLG. and LG. *smerten* (hence Da. *smerte*, Sw. *smärta*), OHG. *smerzan* str. vb. (MHG. *smerzen* str., G. *schmerzen* wk.); the ablaut-stem *smert-, smart-, smurt-* is perh. the same as that of Gr. *σμερδνός, σμερδαλέος* terrible, and L. *mordēre* to bite. Cf. SMART *a.*]

**1.** *intr.* Of wounds, etc.: To be a source of sharp pain; to be acutely painful.

[*c* **893** K. ÆLFRED *Oros.* I. vii. 36 Gnættas comon..mid fyrsmeortendum bitum.] *c* **1175** *Lamb. Hom.* 83 Win makeð wunde smerte. *a* **1225** *Ancr. R.* 238 þeo hwule þet ȝichinge ilest, hit þuncheð god for to gniden: auh þerefter me iveleð hit bitterliche smeorten. *a* **1300** *Havelok* 2647 þe dint bigan ful sore to smerte. *c* **1340** HAMPOLE *Pr. Consc.* 1317 Yhit es happe of welthe to drede mare þan chaunce of angre, þat smertes sare. *c* **1400** *Sowdone Bab.* 1544 Here woundis sore did smerte. *c* **1430** *Hymns Virgin* (1867) 126 Sche answerd me schortly with wordys þat smartyd. *a* **1548** HALL *Chron., Edw. IV*, 228 b, Besyde this angre ther came the next daye another corsey that smarted a littell sorer. **1594** NASHE *Unfort. Trav.* Wks. (Grosart) V. 168 They basted him with a mixture..which smarted to the very soule of him. **1848** DICKENS *Dombey* xlv, He saw that this..rankled and smarted in her haughty breast, like a poisoned arrow.

†**b.** To be heavy or hard *upon* one. *Obs.*

**1601** CORNWALLIS *Ess.* II. xxxvi. (1631) 122 This smarted doubly upon the taxed people.

**2.** With dative: To cause pain, be painful, to (a person, etc.).

†**a.** Impersonally (*him, her*, etc., *smarts*). *Obs.*

*c* **1200** *Trin. Coll. Hom.* 21 Swo þat hire ne oc ne ne smeart. *c* **1290** *S. Eng. Leg.* I. 206 He criede anon to ihesu crist, þo him smert so sore. **13..** *Guy Warw.* (A.) 433 Sore me meneþ, for me smert, Miche care is in mine hert. **1362** LANGL. *P. Pl.* A. III. 161 For þe pore may haue no pouwer to playne, þauȝ hem smerte. *c* **1412** HOCCLEVE *De Reg. Princ.* 1025, I dar wel seyn it smerteth hym ful sore In euery veyne and place of his body.

**b.** With sbs., passing into *trans.*: To affect with pain or smarting.

*a* **1225** *Ancr. R.* 326 Nis þing i þisse worlde þet smeorteð him so sore ase him doð swuch beatunge. *c* **1310** in Wright *Lyric P.* xxv. 70 Thi suete body to-toren y se, Hit maketh heorte to smerte me. *c* **1374** CHAUCER *Boeth.* II. pr. iv. (1868) 39 þis is a þing þat gretly smertiþ me whan it remembreþ me. *c* **1400** *Pilgr. Sowle* (Caxton, 1483) IV. xx. 65 So sore as this martirdom smertith me. *c* **1430** *Syr Gener.* (Roxb.) 6075 Mi woundes smert me so sore With you may I fight nomore. **1558** PHAER *Æneid* II. 30 Than pardon we for pity gaue, this wayling smartes us so. *a* **1568** A. SCOTT *Poems* (S.T.S.) xxxiv. 50 Thay swoun to se ȝow smartit. *a* **1653** ADAMS *Serm.* Wks. 1862 II. 195 A goad that pricks the skin and smarts the flesh—affliction. **1787** *Minor* III. viii. 188 My wound..still continued to smart me. **1844** H. STEPHENS *Bk. Farm* II. 505 It is better that the effluvium be so strong as to smart the eyes. **1884** J. BURROUGHS *Locusts & Wild H.* 109 There was not enough moisture in the air to take the sting out of the smoke, and it smarted the nose.

**3.** *intr.* To feel sharp pain or distress; to suffer acutely or severely. Freq. with preps., as *at, beneath, by, from, under.*

*c* **1200** *Trin. Coll. Hom.* 207 þenne wile his heorte aken and smerten. *c* **1290** *S. Eng. Leg.* I. 322 þe bodie..þat in strong Anguysche deth smeorte [*v.r.* smurte]. **13..** *Sir Beues* 631 þo his bodi be-gan to smerte, He gan plokken vp is hertte. **1398** TREVISA *Barth. De P.R.* VII. xv. (Bodl. MS.), Smoke þat dymmeþ þe yȝen and [maketh them] smerte. **1421-2** HOCCLEVE *Dialog* 650 Smertith the fool for lak of good auys. **1496** *Coventry Leet Bk.* 575 Which I dought not I shall haue ayen or Lammasse day, or ells iij or iiij of þe best of yowe shall smart. **1530** PALSGR. 722/1 If thou ytche, care nat, but if thou smarte, beware. *a* **1568** A. SCOTT *Poems* (S.T.S.) xxiv. 17, I speik expart, suppois I smart. **1609** BP. HALL *Passion Serm.* (1627) 432 Thou strikest: Christ Iesus smarteth, and will reuenge. **1670** COTTON *Life of Espernon* II. VIII. 371 Countreys that yet smarted with the last years War. **1781** BURNS *Stanzas Prosp. Death* 9, I..justly smart beneath his sin-avenging rod. **1849** MACAULAY *Hist. Eng.* vii. II. 200 The just indignation of the public was inflamed by many who were smarting from his ridicule. **1885** HORNADAY *2 Yrs. Jungle* xxiii. 268 The salt perspiration ran into my eyes and caused them to smart.

**b.** To bear the penalty, to suffer severely, *for* some offence, misdemeanour, etc.

**1548** SOMERSET *Epist. to Scots* A vij b, If you doo then..smart for it, whom can you blame, but youre awne eleccion? **1579** W. FULKE *Conf. Sanders* 585 Balthasar abused the holy vessels, he smarted for it. **1634** HEYWOOD *Maidenh. well lost* I. Wks. 1874 IV. 104, I shall ne're smart for't, what is't to me? **1687** A. LOVELL tr. *Thevenot's Trav.* I. 78 Away, I say, else I'll make you smart for it. **1748** RICHARDSON *Clarissa* (1811) I. xxxii. 243 Offences against warning ought to be smarted for. **1837** DICKENS *Pickw.* ii, 'You shall smart for this,' gasped Mr. Pickwick. **1884** *Sat. Rev.* 5 July 5/2 He has done us a wrong, and should be made to smart for it.

†**4.** *trans.* To atone for (an offence) by suffering. *Obs.*$^{-1}$

*a* **1400** *Rom. Rose* 7057 He shal in prisoun dye; But if he wol..smerten that that he hath do.

**smart alec** (ˈsmɑːt ˌælɪk). *colloq.* (orig. *U.S.*). Also **aleck, alick**, hyphenated, and with capital initial(s). [f. SMART *a.* + *Alec*, dim. of personal name *Alexander*.] A would-be clever person; a 'know-all'; occas., a man who is ostentatiously smart in dress or manner. Also *attrib.* or as *adj.*

**1865** *Carson* (Nevada) *Appeal* 17 Oct. 2/3 Halloa, old smart Aleck—how is the complimentary vote for Ashley? **1873** J. H. BEADLE *Undevel. West* vii. 140, I had the pleasure of seeing at least a score of 'smart Alecks' relieved of their surplus cash. **1887** F. FRANCIS *Saddle & Mocassin* 312 You may talk about..your Smart Alicks, and your Joe-dandies and daisies. **1902** [see RUN *v.* 64 h]. **1904** W. N. HARBEN *Georgians* ix. 92 Thar was a smart Alec of a feller from Little Dogtrot over in the mountains. **1934** C. STEAD *Seven Poor Men of Sydney* vi. 184 Rawson, from the Trades Hall, ready, assured, blatant, a political opportunist, whom Joseph called a 'real smart-alec'. **1934** H. G. WELLS *Exper. Autobiog.* I. v. 276 Nowhere was there protection from those Smart Alecs, the primary poison of the whole process, who piled up the rents. **1941** B. SCHULBERG *What makes Sammy Run?* xii. 221 He's a smart-aleck. I can see already he thinks he knows more than I do. **1942** C. BARRETT *On Wallaby* x. 202 One smart Alick came to..offer his services in return for a large tin of pineapple slices. **1956** C. V. WEDGWOOD *Lit. & Historian* 9 The imitators of Lytton Strachey managed by their smart-aleck antics to obscure for a long decade what was really valuable in the new approach to biography. **1964** L. NKOSI *Rhythm of Violence* II. ii. 33 I'm bored with their smart-aleck talk! **1976** T. STOPPARD *Dirty Linen* 40 Smart alec-paragraphs about innocent tripe-and-onions with tittian voluptuaries? **1979** L. MEYNELL *Hooky & Villainous Chauffeur* vii. 99 Smart alec, aren't you? Smart and smug like all you intellectual lot.

Hence **smart-alec(k)ism**, smart-aleckry; an instance of this; **smart-aleckry**, behaviour characteristic of a smart alec, ostentatious or smug cleverness; **smart-alecky** *a.*, characteristic of a smart alec, ostentatiously or smugly clever.

**1905** *Dialect Notes* III. II. 157 *Smart Elecky*, impertinent, impudent. 'He's too *Smart Elecky* for me.' **1926** G. J. NATHAN *House of Satan* 6 Ripples of smart-aleckry. **1929** J. B. PRIESTLEY *Good Companions* III. v. 579, I wouldn't have minded so much if he hadn't been so Smart Alecky about it. **1934** *Sun* (Baltimore) 28 Aug. 8/7 The futility of those modern writers who mistake smart aleckism for sophistication and vulgarity for art. **1938** *Scrutiny* VI. IV. 400 His [*sc.* Fauré's] supreme disregard of public opinion is difficult to parallel in an age in which composers seek consolation for their lack of popular appreciation in the formation of cliques and the cultivation of a pert smart-alecism. **1958** *Spectator* 5 Sept. 306/2 *Brouhaha* remains a hodgepodge of smartaleckry aimed..at the intellectual teddy-boy set. **1962** *Listener* 21 June 1091/3 A sophisticated bit of smart-aleckism like the 'nine-minute opera' *Introductions and Goodbyes*. **1965** *New Statesman* 30 Apr. 690/1 The last thing the Hansons go in for is the shrug of the shoulders or the smart-alecism—unless it's at the expense of psychoanalysing critics who..suggest that Tchaikovsky was ..rather odd. **1976** *National Observer* (U.S.) 10 July 8/3 She now writes regularly for New York magazine, though her cautious, measured manner of speaking doesn't seem to fit that magazine's usually brash, smart-alecky tone. **1981** *Times Lit. Suppl.* 6 Mar. 247/5 The various lists in the book have an air of Christmas competition-setting smart-aleckry.

**smart-arse, -ass** (ˈsmɑːtɑːs, -æs), *a.* and *sb.* *slang.* Also as one word without hyphen and as two words. [f. SMART *a.* + ARSE *sb.*, ASS *sb.*[2]] = SMART ALEC.

Only the form with *-ass* is current in the U.S.

**1962** J. D. MACDONALD *Girl, Gold Watch & Everything* ix. 118 Some smart-ass crowd set up all the confusion so as they could clean out them stores. **1965** W. DICK *Bunch of Ratbags* 245 Anyhow, where else could we go, do you know, smartarse? **1970** B. OAKLEY *Salute to Great McCarthy* 28 That smart arse from the city. **1972** D. DELMAN *Week to Kill* 115 But you've got a smart-ass answer for that, haven't you? **1972** P. MARKS *Collector's Choice* ii. 102 You're too pretty to be such a smart-ass. Just watch your step. **1973** *Guardian* 24 Feb. 8/5 A picture of a rose..needn't be just beautiful, or decorative, or a matter of smart-arse graphics. **1975** *Time Out* 9 May 13/2 When I'm hyping a film, as I'm doing now, I try not to get too smartass and articulate. **1977** *Private Eye* 1 Apr. 23/4 (Advt.), Get it together to put down pseuds, poseurs and general smartasses. **1981** J. BARNETT *Firing Squad* x. 92 He had indulged in reckless speculation... He was just as much a smart-arse as the Farnham D.I.

So **'smart-ass** *v. trans.*, to say in a smart-alecky manner; *intr.* and *trans.*, to behave in a smart-alecky manner (towards). **'smart-arsed, -assed** *adjs.*, smart-alecky.

**1960** P. BLONDAL *Candle to light Sun* 191 A lot of smart-assed novelists would have you believe they're dirt-coat. **1962** A. SEYMOUR *One Day of Year* 49 Going round with smart-arsed little sheilas from the North Shore. It's all wrong, son. **1970** E. TIDYMAN *Shaft* (1971) vii. 95 'You can complain to the union,' he had smart-assed Persons, 'but twelve-fifty an hour is only my rate for living. I get a lot more for dying.' **1971** R. THOMAS *Backup Men* iv. 31 Is that supposed to be a smartassed answer? **1976** R. B. PARKER *Promised Land* xix. 115 Don't smart-ass with me, Johnny, or you'll be looking very close at the floor. **1977** J. WAINWRIGHT *Day of Peppercorn Kill* 68 No smart-arsed lawyer's going to shift *my* evidence. **1978** F. ROSS *Sleeping Dogs* 152 'I guess it's something to do with the generation gap, sir.' 'Don't smart-ass me!' **1979** *Globe & Mail* (Toronto) 15 Sept. 42/1 It is tempting to be smart-assed when reviewing a Richard Rohmer novel.

**smarten** (ˈsmɑːt(ə)n), *v.* [f. SMART *a.* In U.S. colloq. the form *smart* is also employed.]

**1.** *trans.* To make smart or spruce; to improve in appearance. Usually with *up*.

**1815** JANE AUSTEN *Emma* x, The vicarage..had been very much smartened up by the present proprietor. **1833** SIR F. B. HEAD *Bubbles fr. Brunnen* 127 The..fashion of smartening up us old people with the teeth and hair of the dead. **1876** MISS BRADDON *J. Haggard's Dau.* (1876) II. 54 We must think of smartening the old rooms a little bit.

*refl.* **1857** KINGSLEY *Two Y. Ago* III. 201 Tom..smartened himself as best he could, went up to the great house, and found Miss Mary. **1887** 'MARK RUTHERFORD' *Revol. Tanner's Lane* xvi, When the 'things were washed up', servant and mistress began to smarten themselves.

*absol.* **1861** HUGHES *Tom Brown at Oxf.* xxvi, He has smartened up, and wears as good a coat as I do. **1881** T. G. BOWLES *Flotsam & J.* (1883) 246 We are now running into Gibraltar bay, and smartening up to go ashore.

**2.** To brighten *up*, make livelier. Also *intr.*

**1864** *Realm* 15 June 8 The dialogue has been smartened up. **1899** CROCKETT *Kit Kennedy* 372 The clerk smartened up noticeably at the entrance of the pretty girl.

**3.** With *up*. To accelerate.

**1888** *Times* 30 June 17/1 The 10.30 p.m. is smartened up 70 minutes.

Hence **'smartened** *ppl. a.*; **'smartening** *vbl. sb.*

**1864** *Gentl. Mag.* II. 222 The recent 'smartening up' of the front of the George Hotel. **1873** MISS BRADDON *Str. & Pilgr.* III. xiv, The people dancing in smartened morning-dress.

†**'smartful,** *a.* *Obs.* [f. SMART *sb.*[1]] Painful, distressing.

**1556** J. HEYWOOD *Spider & Fly* lxvii. 12 What naturall father can se [this]..Without his hart smarting, in most smartfull smart. **1600** ABBOT *Jonah* 595 He maketh the wildernesse tedious and bitter and smartfull to us. **1660** *Plea for Ministers in Sequestration* 4 Their smartful experience speaks it enough.

†**'smarthead.** *Obs.*$^{-1}$ [f. SMART *a.*] Severity.

**1338** R. BRUNNE *Chron.* (1810) 306 þorgh smerthed of þe law he did þam justise.

†**'smarthole.** *Obs.*$^{-0}$ [f. SMART *v.* + HOLE *sb.* 8.] Smartweed.

*c* **1440** *Promp. Parv.* 108/1 Culrache, smerthole, herbe, *persiccaria*.

**smart-hoop.** [perh. f. SMART *sb.*[1] or *a.*; but cf. also older Da. *smert, smært*, Sw. *smärt* slender, slim.] (See quot.)

**1832** *Planting* 90 in *Husb.* III. (L.U.K.), *Smart-hoops.*—Shoots of the hazel, six feet in length; they are cleft for hoops, and are used..for salmon kits, small tubs, and other purposes of the cooper. [Cf. Peacock *Lonsd. Gloss.* (1869) 77/1 *Smarts*, small rods cut down in coppice woods.]

*Comb.* **1881** *Instr. Census Clerks* (1885) 82 Smart Hoop Maker, Bender, Shaver.

**smartie**, var. SMARTY

**smarting** (ˈsmɑːtɪŋ), *vbl. sb.* [f. SMART *v.*] The fact or sensation of feeling a sharp pain, such as is caused by a wound, sore, burn, or the like.

*c* **1175** *Lamb. Hom.* 83 Win makeð wunde smerte. Ah þe smertinge clenseð þe wunde. *a* **1225** *Ancr. R.* 294 ȝif þi sulf ..one smerte discepline, & drauh..þet swete likunge into smeortunge. *a* **1300** *Cursor M.* 29101 Oft for þam smerting sendis he. **1398** TREVISA *Barth. De P.R.* v. xxviii. (Bodl. MS.), Furste he makeþ icching and tekeling, & after þat greete ache and smerting. *a* **1425** tr. *Arderne's Treat. Fistula*, etc. 27 þis enoyntment doþe away alle smertyng and fleyng. **1526** *Pilgr. Perf.* (W. de W. 1531) 207 Not hauyng there ony sensible payne or smartyng. **1599** T. M[OUFET] *Silkwormes* 6 Wounds how to cure, and smartings to allay. **1605** ARMIN *Foole upon F.* (1880) 23 In an enuious spleene smarting ripe, [he] runnes after him. **1715** DESAGULIERS *Fires Impr.* 41 It causes a smarting also in Animals. **1815** *Hist. J. De Castro* I. 22 Nothing will cure this crack-brain'd coxcomb but a good smarting. **1879** *St. George's Hosp. Rep.* IX. 742 He suffers bad smarting and itching.

**smarting** (ˈsmɑːtɪŋ), *ppl. a.* [f. as prec.]

**1.** Causing to smart; painful; sharp, acute.

**1548** ELYOT, *Aestus ulceris*, the smartyng peyne of a sore, or byle. **1575** FENTON *Gold. Ep.* (1577) 63 They crucified him vnder a most smarting and infamous death. **1633** P. FLETCHER *Elisa* I. xi, Some fault..Hath forc't thee frown, and use thy smarting rod. **1725** POPE *Odyss.* xv. 207 He..flung Athwart the fiery steeds the smarting thong. **1818** SCOTT *Hrt. Midl.* xviii, The old man winced, as one whose smarting sore is suddenly galled. **1879** *St. George's Hosp. Rep.* IX. 741 She complains of excess of perspiration,..and much of smarting pain.

**2.** Feeling sharp pain. Also *fig.*

**1754** DODSLEY *Agric.* II. 266 Since oft Its cruel twigs compel the smarting youth To dread the hateful seat. **1865** DICKENS *Mut. Fr.* III. i, With smarting eyes and irritated lungs. **1882** *Daily News* 3 Jan. 3/3 A financial crash would at once be laid at its door by the smarting holders of worthless security.

**smartingly** (ˈsmɑːtɪŋlɪ), *adv.* [f. prec. + -LY[2].] Painfully.

*c* **1555** HARPSFIELD *Divorce Hen. VIII* (Camden) 200 Miseries..which..we have smartingly felt. **1648** HEXHAM II, *Smertelick*, Smartingly, or Painfully. **1822** *Blackw. Mag.* XII. 667 A covenanting slug still stuck smartingly in his shoulder. **1861** DICKENS *Gt. Expect.* iv, I got so smartingly touched up by these moral goads. **1891** G. MEREDITH *One of our Conquerors* II. iii. 41 Those unaccustomed musical tones ..were so smartingly persuasive.

**smartish** ('smɑːtɪʃ), *a.* and *adv.* [f. SMART *a.* + -ISH.
Hexham (1648) has '*Smertigh*, Smartish, or Full of Paine', perh. f. the sb.]

**A.** *adj.* **1.** Somewhat smart, in various senses.
**1740** RICHARDSON *Pamela* (1824) I. xx. 32 Two pairs of ordinary blue worsted hose, that make a smartish appearance, with white clocks. **1748** —— *Clarissa* (1811) IV. 173 Prettier entertainment.. than sitting with a too smartish daughter. **1807** JANE AUSTEN *Lett.* (1884) I. 328, I flatter myself I have constructed a smartish letter, considering my want of materials. **1843** MARRYAT *M. Violet* xxvii, The most rascally, but *smartish* trick in the world. **1860** WHYTE-MELVILLE *Mkt. Harborough* 107 It takes a smartish nag.. to win a steeple-chase.
*Comb.* *c* **1816** MRS. SHERWOOD *Stories Ch. Catech.* xii. 102 A smartish looking woman went up to their door and knocked. **1852** C. W. H[OSKINS] *Talpa* 131 Dobson said he seemed smartish like.

**2.** Considerable in amount, degree, extent, etc.
**1799** R. WARNER *Walk* (1800) 65 What with smartish work,.. I began to find my legs give out. **1833** T. HOOK *Parson's Dau.* II. xiii, The housemaid.. had a smartish bilious attack. **1858** HUGHES *Scour. White Horse* 18 Pretty nigh ever since King Alfred's time, which I reckon is a smartish time ago.

**B.** *adv.* Somewhat smartly.
**1877** *Coursing Calendar Autumn 1876* 5 Vicar-of-Bray.. won a smartish-run trial with his extra pace. **1896** G. F. NORTHALL *Warwickshire Word-book* 218 *Smartish, adj.* and *adv.*, fairly well. 'How are you?' 'Smartish, thank you.' 'I'm getting on smartish now.' **1973** W. H. CANAWAY *Harry doing Good* II. iii. 155 You nipped off.. a bit smartish, didn't you? **1979** N. FREELING *Widow* xiii. 79 Whip out smartish to the Italian grocer.

**'smartism.** [f. SMART *a.*] Smartness in talk; a smart saying.
**1830** *Fraser's Mag.* I. 236 Talking endless smartisms of wearisome wit. **1834** *Oxf. Univ. Mag.* I. 39 The self-complacent smartism of the satirist.

† **'smartle,** *v.* *Obs.*$^{-0}$ (See quot.)
**1674** RAY *N.C. Words*, To *Smartle* away, to wast[e] away. [Hence in Kersey, Grose, Brockett, etc.]

**'smartless,** *a. rare.* [f. SMART *sb.*[1]] Free from smart.
**1593** R. BARNES *Parthenopil* Sonn. xlvii, Whether he rest at ease, in joys and smartless. *a* **1618** SYLVESTER *Trag. Hen. Gt.* 607 Wks. (Grosart) II. 244 Hee must be heart-less that is smart-less found.

**smartly** ('smɑːtlɪ), *adv.* Also 3-4 smert(e)liche (4 *comp.* -loker), 4 smartliche, 4-5 smertli, 4-6 smertly, etc. [f. SMART *a.* + -LY[2].]

**1.** Vigorously, forcibly; sharply (in respect of physical action).
*a* **1225** *Leg. Kath.* 1990 Almihti godd.. smit se smertliche herto, þat alle þeos fowr hweoles tohwiðerin to stucchen. **13..** *Guy Warw.* (A.) 3485 Asaileþ hem smerteliche. **13..** *E.E. Allit. P.* B. 711 Hem to smyte.. smartly I þenk. *c* **1400** *Laud Troy Bk.* 6217 Many of Troye in his defence At that tyme ful smartly stryues. **1616** W. BROWNE *Brit. Past.* II. iii, Thrice had the golden Sun his hote steedes.. smartly lasht Out of the baulmy east. **1673** *Essex Papers* (Camden) I. 146 We went to supper, were very merry, and drank smartly. **1705** HICKERINGILL *Priest-cr* II. viii. 80 Thus the Nurse.. Kisses the Wanton.. when it ought.. to be Smartly Whipt. **1796** MORSE *Amer. Geogr.* I. 761 A breeze.. which blows smartly from the land. **1867** F. FRANCIS *Angling* xiv. (1880) 487 The fish played smartly for a minute. **1883** HUXLEY *Pract. Biol.* 8 Pressing smartly with the handle of a mounted needle.

**b.** Sharply (in respect of treatment, language, etc.); severely; curtly.
*a* **1300** *Cursor M.* 21496 Me war leuer.. þan dempt sua smertli to be. *c* **1449** PECOCK *Repr.* I. ix. 47 Of this same mater it is quikli and smertli spoken in a litil book therto.. maad. *a* **1661** FULLER *Worthies* (1662) II. 165, I admired much that a man of his age, could write, so smartly, so solidly, so significantly. **1695** LD. PRESTON *Boeth.* II. 84 He answered smartly [L. *mordaciter*] again, I had indeed believed it, if thou couldst still have held thy Tongue. **1709** STRYPE *Ann. Ref.* I. xxxvii. 382 Haddow smartly answered, this was too impudent an hyperbole. *Ibid.* 390 He treated his adversary now more smartly than he had done before. **1809** PINKNEY *Trav. France* 258 Mrs. Younge replied very smartly to some questions of her husband. **1841** THACKERAY *Gt. Hoggarty Diam.* x, I let him one day know pretty smartly, that I was.. a considerable shareholder in the Company.

**c.** Sharply (in respect of feeling); keenly; also, heavily, largely.
**1677** in *Lauderdale Papers* (1885) III. 96 Therfor the fynes to be exacted wold be such as may be smartlie felt by the transgressors. **1800** *Asiatic Ann. Reg.* 255/2 The air proved here as cold.., and having no shelter from trees, was the more smartly felt. **1884** *Manch. Exam.* 22 May 5/2 Foreigners will not be allowed to share in this advantage without paying pretty smartly for the privilege.

**2.** Promptly, quickly, briskly (and trimly).
*a* **1300** *Cursor M.* 17810 Quen þat þai herd þis word be said, Ful smertli þai þam þider graid. *c* **1340** HAMPOLE *Pr. Consc.* 3323 Þarfor þai swippe þurgh purgatory Als a foul þat flyes smertly. *c* **1400** *Pilgr. Sowle* (Caxton) I. xxxiii. (1859) 37 That bylle whan it was leyd in the balaunce peysed so sore, that smartely that other syde aroos. *c* **1450** *Merlin* xx. 324 Thei ronne to armes hastely, and peyned hem harde to be smartly armed and soone. ? *a* **1550** *Freiris Berwik* 563 in *Dunbar's Poems* (1893) 303 Vpoun his feit he stude, And throw the myre full smertly than he ȝude. **1711** BUDGELL *Spect.* No. 161 ⁋3 A Trip which was given him so smartly that I could scarce discern it. **1833** *Reg. & Instr. Cavalry* I. 112 Come smartly to the position of 'Attention'. **1849** DICKENS *Barn. Rudge* xxxv, The horsemen wheeled smartly round. **1872** *Routledge's Ev. Boy's Ann.* Apr. 281 They walked smartly past the door.

**3.** Cleverly, neatly; wittily.
**1673** *Remarques Humours Town* 46 He replied handsomely and smartly. **1680** H. MORE *Apocal. Apoc.* 204 And Tertullian himself, briefly and smartly [says] *Omnis Spiritus ales est.* **1748** RICHARDSON *Clarissa* (1759) II. 115 Smartly put, Betty. **1859** HAWTHORNE *Transformation* ii, What old man.. could have turned a silly compliment more smartly than that!

**4.** Handsomely, elegantly, fashionably.
**1836** MARRYAT *J. Faithful* xxxvi, He expended all his earnings on dressing himself smartly, and making presents to her. **1840** THACKERAY *Shabby-genteel Story* i, Upon this.. the two managed to live pretty smartly, and to maintain an honourable reputation. **1891** *Leeds Mercury* 27 Apr. 4/7 The guests dressed very smartly, and the wedding was a really pretty one.
*Comb.* **1838** DICKENS *O. Twist* xxii, Dressed in a smartly-cut snuff-coloured coat. **1859** REEVE *Brittany* 236 Two smartly dressed girls came to the door.

**'smart-money.** [f. SMART *sb.*[1]]

**1.** A sum of money paid to sailors, soldiers, workmen, etc., as compensation for disablement or injuries received while on duty or at work.
**1693** *Lond. Gaz.* No. 2836/3 Smart-Money to such Seamen as have been Wounded in Their Majesties Service. **1696** LUTTRELL *Brief Rel.* (1857) IV. 28 No seaman.. not registred shall have any smart money. **1758** J. BLAKE *Mar. Syst.* 62 To say nothing of smart-money, those in the navy are entitled to short allowance money. **1809** LANGFORD *Introd. Trade* 112 Also to all such pensions, salaries, smart-money,.. which.. may be due. **1840** HOOD *Up Rhine* 262, I do hope.. that the King of Prussia will double that poor fellow's smart-money. **1860** *Eng. & For. Mining Gloss.* (ed. 2) 63 *Smart money*, money paid weekly by the owners to persons who have received an injury in the work.

**b.** Any compensation made for injury or the like; also *spec.* in *U.S. law* (see quot. 1851).
**1749** FIELDING *Tom Jones* III. viii, Mr. Allworthy gave Tom Jones a little horse, as a kind of smart-money for the punishment. **1851** A. M. BURRILL *New Law Dict.* II. 936 *Smart-Money*... Damages beyond the value of a thing sued for, given by a jury in cases of gross misconduct or cruelty on the part of a defendant. **1890** HALL CAINE *Bondman* II. i, He.. sent Adam Fairbrother an instant warning, with half-a-year's salary for smart money.

**2.** Money paid to obtain the discharge of a recruit who has enlisted in the army.
**1760** *Cautions & Advices to Officers of Army* 144 This Sum the Officer generally divides among his Recruiting Party,.. and the more there are who pay this Smart-money, as they call it, the more they share. **1778** *Ann. Reg.* 196 The law.. gives a certain time for those who are inlisted to get off, upon returning the inlisting money and what is called the smart money. **1844** *Queen's Regul. & Ord. Army* 390 When Recruits are set at liberty by a magistrate, on the payment of smart-money. **1894** *Daily Telegr.* 11 Jan. 5/7 When a young man he enlisted, but his father paid the smart money,.. and secured his release.

**b.** Money paid on account of cancelling or not fulfilling a bargain or agreement, or in order to free oneself from some disadvantage, recover some lapsed privilege, etc.
**1818** SCOTT *Rob Roy* xxvii, He accomplished the exchange ..; nor did I hear further of his having paid any smart-money for breach of bargain.

†**3.** (See quot. and cf. GARNISH *sb.* 5.) *Obs.*
**1856** DE QUINCEY *Conf.* Wks. 1862 I. 151, I have always looked upon this fine of five or seven shillings (for wax that you do not absolutely need) as a sort of inaugural *honorarium* entrance-money, what in jails used to be known as *smart* money.

**smartness** ('smɑːtnɪs). Also 4 smartnes, 5 smertnesse. [f. SMART *a.* + -NESS.]

**1.** Pain, smarting. *rare.*
*c* **1412** HOCCLEVE *De Reg. Princ.* 2226 Disceyt, and.. inward fikilnesse, Bulteth out schame, and causeþ gret smartnesse. **1855** BAIN *Senses & Intell.* II. ii. §7 (1864) 184 A sensation of smartness is produced.

**2.** That which induces pain or distress; sharp discipline; severity (*of* something).
**1303** R. BRUNNE *Handl. Synne* 4966 To chastyse hem wyþ fyn awe And with þe smartnes of þe lawe. **1653** BINNING *Serm.* (1845) 561 If you find not the Smartness of the Gospel ..ye are yet in your Sins. **1666** *Phil. Trans.* I. 359 They [waters] had a rough smartness, as if they carried Sand or Gravel into the Eye. **1706** Z. CRADOCK *Serm. Charity* (1740) 17 Mov'd by the smartness of a present calamity.

**3.** Vivacity and wit in conversation or writing.
**1656** *Artif. Handsom.* 111 Those sharp, Satyricall, and popular invectives.. To which your Ladyship hath given as much (or more) edge and smartnesse, as ever I found from any. **1664** DRYDEN *Rival Ladies* Ep. Ded., The sudden smartness of the answer. **1711** STEELE *Spect.* No. 132 ⁋2 The Quaker, who happened to be a Man of Smartness, answered. **1751** JOHNSON *Rambler* No. 174 ⁋8 With no other hope than that of gaining the reputation of smartness and waggery. **1827** HALLAM *Const. Hist.* (1876) II. viii. 39 His letters to Strafford display some smartness, but no great capacity. **1886** *Manch. Exam.* 27 Jan. 3/2 He has been led astray by that passion for smartness which is the bane of contemporary criticism.

**4.** Trimness or fashionableness in dress, etc.
**1752-3** A. MURPHY *Gray's Inn Jrnl.* No. 17, The more humble, whose Genius does not exceed the Smartness of a Cut Bob. **1801** tr. *Gabrielli's Mysterious Husb.* IV. 164 She ..had an air of smartness which rather prepossessed the Prince's household in her favour. **1866** ROGERS *Agric. & Prices* I. xxii. 578 Several of the complaints refer to undue smartness in dress. **1892** MALLOCK in *N. Amer. Rev.* July 29 Smartness.. represents the perfection of superficial living, and it has a natural.. influence over persons of a certain temperament.

**5. a.** Briskness, activity, alertness.
**1867** MACGREGOR *Voy. Alone* (1868) 34 Hasty smartness is slowest. **1873** *Daily News* 27 Aug., Their thorough efficiency and soldierly smartness in a cavalry soldier's best work.

**b.** *Mil.* Neatness of dress and person combined with brisk orderly bearing.
**1861** *Times* 24 Sept., A want of the.. soldierly spirit which begets attention to personal smartness. **1886** *Pall Mall G.* 19 Oct. 4/3 Keep your person and accoutrements always neat, and acquire that quality.. 'smartness'.

**6.** Extreme cleverness or shrewdness, esp. for one's own advantage. Chiefly *U.S.*
**1800** M. EDGEWORTH *Little Merchants* in *Parent's Assistant* (ed. 3) III. 111 His son's *smartness* was no longer useful in making bargains. **1819** M. WILMOT *Let.* 8 Dec. (1935) 34 We have got ourselves settled in.. with fewer plagues than almost any family of strangers could boast. This we owe.. to Willys smartness in his quiet way. **1842** DICKENS *Amer. Notes* (1850) 171/1 This smartness has done more in a few years to impair the public credit.. than dull honesty.. could have effected in a century. **1843** MARRYAT *M. Violet* xxxvi, I was perfectly *au fait* to all the tricks of Arkansas' smartness. **1890** *Spectator* 26 Apr., Mr. Blaine.. instructed his supporters in the Press and on the platform to proclaim the 'smartness' of his scheme.

**'smartweed.** Chiefly *dial.* and *U.S.* [f. SMART *sb.*[1] or *a.*] A name given to various species of *Polygonum*, esp. the arsesmart or water-pepper (*Polygonum Hydropiper*).
**1787** W. H. MARSHALL *E. Norfolk* (1795) II. 388 *Smart-weed*, biting and pale-flowered persicarias; arsmart. **1848** *Amer. Jrnl. Med. Sci.* XVI. 247 The Smart-weed as a Remedy for Mercurial Salivation. **1883** E. H. ROLLINS *New Eng. Bygones* 50 About my grandfather's gate smart-weed and dock-weed and plantain grew profusely. *Ibid.* 181 The smart-weed bed underneath them was always hunted by eager children.

**smarty** ('smɑːtɪ), *sb.* and *a.* orig. *U.S.* Also smartie. [f. SMART *a.* II.] **A.** *sb.* A would-be smart or witty person; a smartly-dressed person; a member of a smart set.
**1861** *Calif. Mag.* Aug. 39/2 'Juvenile smartys' are interesting, even to a vagabond. **1876** 'MARK TWAIN' *Tom Sawyer* i. 22 Smarty! You think you're *some*, now. *Ibid.* xviii. 156 That Saint Louis smarty that thinks he dresses so fine. **1880** —— *Tramp Abr.* xxiii. 198 The village smarties recognized a treasure in Nicodemus, right away—a butt to play jokes on. **1902** OWEN WISTER *Virginians* xxvii, 'He is a smarty,' said he, once or twice. **1929** D. H. LAWRENCE *Pansies* 89 But it is hard to be tolerant with the smarties. **1932** AUDEN *Orators* II. 44 Poops and smarties, Who pilfer always but are never whipped. **1933** R. STRACHEY *Many Happy Returns* II. 123 A gala night at the 'Shadwell Palace', dancing those Limehouse blues with her smartie. **1956** L. McINTOSH *Oxford Folly* viii. 118 It's amazing how easy it is for anyone like me, with no background, to pose as an Oxford smartie. **1957** M. MILLAR *Soft Talkers* xxi. 204 'Do you happen to know how much it was?' 'No, and neither do you, smartie.' **1962** A. BOURNE *Doctor's Creed* ii. 46 The worst payers were what we used to call the 'West End Smarties', flimsy young women who would appear from nowhere with no doctor's letter or tangible recommendations.

**B.** *adj.* **a.** Smart-alecky; ostentatiously smart.
**1883** 'MARK TWAIN' *Life on Mississippi* xxxiii. 370 The barkeeper.. was gay and smarty and talky. **1940** *Horizon* Feb. 68 Another line of attack is to concede that the first number is interesting, but to add that it is middlebrow and 'smarty'. **1948** M. ALLINGHAM *More Work for Undertaker* vi. 83 He was full of smarty ideas and had no manners. **1960** D. POTTER *Glittering Coffin* vi. 96 A smarty gossip column. **1967** G. KELLY in *Coast to Coast 1965-6* 104 The local smarty boys, the privileged class.

**b.** Special Combs. (also written *smarti-*), as **smarty-boots,** (orig. *U.S.*) **-pants** *colloq.*, an overly clever person, a know-all, a smart alec; also *attrib.* or as *adj.*
**1962** *Times* 7 June 16/3 The phoney-ness of a smarti-boots Ivy League undergraduate. **1962** *John o' London's* 22 Nov. 467/1 A cold, well-bred English smarty-boots. **1965** J. PORTER *Dover Two* xiii. 166 He was grateful that smartie-boots MacGregor had overlooked the obvious, too. **1970** *Sunday Times* (Colour Suppl.) 6 Dec. 31/3 His self-confidence and satisfaction in his own life got under people's skin.. phrases like 'Smartie Boots' were attached to him. **1979** *Guardian* 12 Nov. 13/7, I am not trying to be wilfully iconoclastic or smarty-boots when I say that.. Picasso simply is not the greatest painter of the 20th century. **1941** B. SCHULBERG *What makes Sammy Run?* iv. 57 One of those Vassar smarty-pants. **1953** M. DICKENS *No More Meadows* vi. 266 [Amer. loq.] He jumped right in with his slick talk. .. That smarty pants. **1967** N. MARSH *Death at Dolphin* viii. 199 Hawkins, Mr. Smartypants, has a little chat. **1969** *Punch* 26 Mar. 465/3 *Cage Me a Leacock* (BBC-2) owed everything—though not, I hope, the smarty-pants title—to Braden's enormous enthusiasm for his subject. **1976** *Listener* 24 June 815/2 Technologically outclassed and outsold by pinstriped smartipants from foreign business schools. **1981** *Times Lit. Suppl.* 13 Feb. 158/3 The smarty-pants youthfulness is very period.

**smash** (smæʃ), *sb.*[1] [f. SMASH *v.*[1]]

**1. a.** *dial.* or *colloq.* A hard or heavy blow. (In earliest quots. *fig.*)
**1725** E. WIGAN *Let.* 25 Sept. in N. D. Mereness *Trav. Amer. Colonies* (1916) 156 They design to keep out look-outs every way and be ready to give them a Smash in their Towns. **1779** T. TWINING in R. Twining *Recr. & Stud.* (1882) 68 This last American smash of Sir George Collier's. **1780** *Ibid.* 79, I want nothing but one good smash at the French fleet. **1816** G. MUIR *Minstrelsy* 24 (E.D.D.), Their shoon wi' tackets Were ca'd as fu' as cobler's smash Cou'd get them thacket. **1886** WILLOCK *Rosetty Ends* (1887) 21 Seizin' a hoe.. he made a smash at the beast. **1898** *Daily News* 24 Nov. 7/3 Sharkey came back with his right, delivering several smashes on Corbett's wind.

**b.** *Lawn-Tennis.* A hard and fast overhand volley. Also in Badminton, Table Tennis, etc.

**1882** *Daily Telegr.* 18 July 2 Fourth game: Won by E. Renshaw, after some grand play, 'smashes' being frequent. **1894** *Outing* XXIV. 297/2 One of Hovey's smashes brought an end to the situation. **1950** *Badminton* ('Know the Game' Ser.) 30/1 The smash is perhaps the most vulnerable stroke in the game. **1981** G. MACBETH *Kind of Treason* xvi. 156 'Fourteen-fifteen,' said Yoshida, serving again. He'd lost the point..by a wasted smash.

**2.** †**a.** *slang.* Mashed turnips. *Obs.*

**1785** GROSE *Dict. Vulgar T.* s.v., Leg of mutton and smash. **1799** *Sporting Mag.* XIII. 360 W. S. Green,..for a wager of a leg of mutton and smash, drank three pints of Cogniac brandy in half an hour.

**b.** A shivered or broken-up condition. Chiefly in phrases ***to break, knock*** etc., or ***go, to smash.*** Also used *fig.* (cf. 4a).

(*a*) **1798** CHARLOTTE SMITH *Yng. Philos.* III. 124 She *rayally* thought her *carridge* would have been broke to smash. **1807–8** IRVING *Salmag.* (1824) 203 He determined to do the thing genteelly, to go to smash like a hero, and dashed into the limits in high style. **1830** GALT *Lawrie T.* II. iv. (1849) 54 It beats Shedry and Abendy to immortal smash. **1840** MARRYAT *Poor Jack* v, [It] had..knocked his figure-head all to smash. **1874** HUXLEY in *Life* (1900) I. xxviii. 413 The..arrangements all went to smash.

(*b*) **1857** HUGHES *Tom Brown* II. ii, The door panels were in a normal state of smash. **1883** STEVENSON *Treasure Isl.* v, You cannot imagine a house in such a state of smash.

**3. a.** A loud sound of breaking or crushing; a severe or extensive crushing, shivering, or breaking of anything, esp. accompanied by a crashing sound; a violent collision or impact.

**1808** JAMIESON, *Smash*,..the sound of breaking, a crash. **1833** M. SCOTT *Tom Cringle* i, I could distinctly hear a heavy *smash* as the large and ponderous blocks..struck the doomed sailor. **1841** [see *railroad line* s.v. RAILROAD *sb.* 3a]. **1853** LOWELL *Moosehead Jrnl.* Prose Wks. 1890 I. 4 The last great railroad smash. **1863** GEO. ELIOT *Romola* xiv, One of the dim floating lights disappeared with a smash from a stone. **1876** BRISTOWE *Th. & Pract. Med.* (1878) 113 A smash of the leg. **1909** *Westm. Gaz.* 27 Apr. 4/2 If the brakes fail to hold it is impossible to avoid a bad smash. **1957** M. SPARK *Comforters* viii. 196 If I hadn't had the smash I'd have got you last autumn.

**b.** *Geol.* (See quot.)

**1902** *Encycl. Brit.* XXXIII. 775 The Lower Chalk formation..contains many ruptures and dislocations, 'smashes' as they are now commonly called.

**4. a.** Commercial failure; stoppage through insolvency; bankruptcy. (Cf. CRASH *sb.*[1] 2b.)

**1839** LOCKHART *Ballantyne-humbug* 114 He was careful enough to give his wife £250 on the very morning of the smash! **1858** O. W. HOLMES *Aut. Breakf.-t.* x, A commercial smash kills a hundred men's houses for them. **1867** TROLLOPE *Chron. Barset* I. xxxix. 341 There is no saying what day a smash may come.

**b.** A crushing defeat or overthrow.

**1888** *Spectator* 30 June 878 A smash of Sir E. Watkin by an instinctive vote of the House. **1896** BADEN-POWELL *Matabele Campaign* v, It was a final smash to the enemy in the north.

**c.** A break-up of some kind; a revolution.

**1890** *Spectator* 2 Aug., The 'smash' at Buenos Ayres, which has been expected for the last six weeks,..took place last Saturday.

**5. a.** An American beverage made of spirit, ice, water, sugar, and flavoured with mint.

**1850** [see *brandy-smash* s.v. BRANDY *sb.* 2]. **1859** F. FOWLER *Southern Lights* 52 *A Smash*, ice, brandy, and water. **1861** *Times* 10 July, Thirsty souls, who have hastened on board..for a julep, a smash, or a cocktail. **1871** [see *corpse reviver* s.v. CORPSE *sb.* 6]. **1909** [see *brandy-smash* s.v. BRANDY *sb.* 2]. **1958** A. L. SIMON *Dict. Wines, Spirits & Liqueurs* 147/2 *Smashes*, mixed iced drinks always with a spirit foundation and some mint flavouring. **1973** WODEHOUSE *Bachelors Anonymous* xiii. 170 What more likely than that he should have fetched up in Hollywood, made a packet, perished of a surfeit of brandy smashes, and left that packet to that nephew.

**b.** An alcoholic drink, esp. wine. *N. Amer. slang.*

**1959** *Maclean's Mag.* 15 Aug. 28/2 So I had a couple of smashes and marched in. **1966** *Globe & Mail* (Toronto) 15 Mar. 35/8 Every time you wanted a smash the check girl would hand the coat to you over the counter, so you could get your mickey without actually taking the coat out. **1975** *Amer. Speech 1972* XLVII. 153 Let's get in the wind and belt some smash.

**6.** A great success; a film, person, play, song, etc., which enjoys popular success; a hit (HIT *sb.* 4). Also *attrib.*, esp. in **smash hit.**

**1923** *Variety* 11 Oct. 16 (*heading*) 'Rosie O'Reilly' and 'The Fool', Loop's Two Smash Hits. **1930** *Times Lit. Suppl.* 16 Oct. 841/1 An entirely strange girl; whom anyone would have admitted to be a 'smash'. **1931** *Daily Express* 21 Sept. 9/3 The magnates who had contracted to buy the picture indulged in fits of doubt concerning its prospects as a box-office 'smash'. **1935** *Amer. Speech* X. 193/2 Terminology from other fields aids the fashion editor... The sports writer is also responsible for the *smash hit* dinner dress. **1935** WODEHOUSE *Blandings Castle* xii. 305 Our whole programme is built around it. We are relying on it to be our big smash. **1948** W. S. MAUGHAM *Colonel's Lady* in *Quartet* 201 The English publisher said to him: 'We've not had a success like this with a book of verse for twenty years.'.. The American publisher said to him: 'It's swell. It'll be a smash hit in America.' **1949** R. CHANDLER *Let.* 23 Apr. (1981) 174 You can't make me into a smash best seller. **1956** B. HOLIDAY *Lady sings Blues* (1973) xix. 158 *Holiday on Broadway* was a sellout, and the first performance made us think we had a smash. **1961** *Amer. Speech* XXXVI. 110 It was a smash commercial success. **1969** R. LOWELL *Notebk. 1967–68* 71 Eliot dead, you [*sc.* Ezra Pound] saying, 'And who is left to understand my jokes? My old Brother in the acts..and besides, he was a smash of a poet.' **1973** *Black World* Apr. 18/2 All smash Broadway musical hits. **1975** D. FRANCIS *High Stakes* 232 The oddly mixed party proved a smash-hit success. **1978** *Times* 1 Nov. 13/1 [His] aim..has been to expand a truthful little ethnic comedy into a popular smash.

**smash,** *sb.*[2] *slang.* [Of doubtful origin: not clearly connected with prec.]

**1. a.** Counterfeit coin. Also in comb. ***smash-feeder*** (see quot. 1860).

**1795** POTTER *Dict. Cant, Smash*,..bad coin. **1839** *Slang Dict.* 34 *Smashfeeder*, a silver spoon. **1860** *Ibid.* 219 *Smash-feeder*, a Britannia metal spoon,—the best imitation shillings are made from this metal.

**b.** Loose change.

**1821** D. HAGGART *Life* 13 M'Guire got L.7 of smash; I got a L.10 banknote. **1953** W. BURROUGHS *Junkie* (1972) ii. 22 Soon I was buying his drinks and meals, and he was hitting me for 'smash' (change) at regular intervals. **1953** K. TENNANT *Joyful Condemned* iii. 21 Giving her his smash on pay-night so's she can blow it. **1965** *Australasian Post* 4 Mar. 47 Russell goes on to point out that all loose change is sometimes known as 'smash'.

**2.** (See SLING *v.*[1] 3f.)

**smash** (smæʃ), *v.*[1] [Probably imitative: cf. Norw. dial. *smaska* to crush, *slaa i smask* to knock to smash (Ross).]

**I.** *trans.* †**1.** *slang.* (See quot.) *Obs.*

*a* **1700** B. E. *Dict. Cant. Crew, Smash*, to kick down Stairs.

**2. a.** To break (anything) in pieces violently; to dash to pieces; to crush, shatter, or shiver.

**1778** FOOTE *Tailors* II. iii, While others shall assault each house of call, Smash all their slates, and plunder every box. **1786** in R. Twining *Recr. & Stud.* (1882) 139 To have his legs and arms smashed. **1815** SCOTT *Guy M.* xxxiii, The first person he met was Frank Kennedy, all smashed and gory. **1820** SHELLEY *Vis. Sea* 145 Some hideous engine whose brazen teeth smash The thin winds and soft waves into thunder. **1851** G. H. KINGSLEY *Sport & Trav.* (1900) 530 The bottle is smashed, smashed to atoms! **1885** HORNADAY *2 Yrs. Jungle* xviii. 198 Nearly every bamboo..had been pulled down and smashed to splinters.

**b.** In imprecations, with or without object expressed.

**1819** MIDFORD in *Coll. Songs* 47 Smash! Jemmy, let us buss, we'll off, And see Newcassel Races. **1825** BROCKETT *N.C. Gloss.*, *Smash*, a kind of oath among the pitmen near Newcastle. **1833** M. SCOTT *Tom Cringle* viii, Smash my eyes, man, but them barrels be full of pimento. **1894** CLEGG *David's Loom* 181 Smash me! I won't be guilty of bragging.

**c.** *Bookbinding.* To flatten or compress (the sheets of a book) before binding.

**1875** [implied in *smashing machine*].

**3. a.** To dash or fling (anything) with noise and violence; to batter; to cause to strike hard.

*c* **1800** *The Earl o' Bran'* xxviii. in Child *Ball.* IV. 444/2 An he smashed them doun a' bane by bane. **1822** AINSLIE *Land of Burns* 200, I reft at the rock.., an wou'd hae geen a warl' to be able to lift it, an smash't it in amang them. **1852** MRS. STOWE *Uncle Tom's C.* viii. 55 If you give me one word out of your head, I'll smash your face in. **1864** BP. WILBERFORCE in *Life* (1882) III. v. 137 My mare..smashed my head on the gravel. **1872** SPURGEON *Treas. David* lviii. 6 It is asked that their grinders may be smashed in, broken off, or dashed out.

**b.** *Lawn-Tennis.* To strike (the ball) violently and swiftly in an overhand volley. Also *absol.* and in Badminton, Squash Rackets, etc.

**1882** *Daily Telegr.* 18 July 2 W. 'smashing' a ball into the net, left the game and sett in his brother's favour by six games to two. **1890** *St. Nicholas* Sept. 921 He told them.. when to 'smash' a ball. **1965** *Badminton* ('Know the Game' Ser.) (ed. 2) 31/1 The man should take the shuttle as early as possible, playing drives when the shuttle is too low to smash. **1968** *Squash Rackets* ('Know the Game' Ser.) 43/1 You cannot smash a good high lob as you can at lawn tennis. *Ibid.* 44/2 A lob that was too high above the player's head has been smashed on to the tin.

**4. a.** To defeat utterly; to crush completely; to overcome, overwhelm, or destroy.

**1813** SIR R. WILSON *Priv. Diary* (1862) II. 443 It is difficult to smash above one hundred and eighty thousand men resting on fortified bulwarks. **1845** DISRAELI *Sybil* (1863) 226, I am told..that the police were regularly smashed. **1865** *Examiner* 18 Mar. 162 Suddenly to set aside the spirit and substance thereof for the purposes..of 'smashing' a particular bill is an act of suicidal wrong. **1884** *Western Daily Press* 28 May 8/5 To join in a British expedition to 'smash' the Mahdi.

**b.** To render insolvent or bankrupt.

**1857** BORROW *Rom. Rye* xli, My father did his best to smash the Bank of England by passing forged notes, and I did my best to assist him. **1858** O. W. HOLMES *Aut. Breakf.-t.* ix, Folks rich once,—smashed up.

**II.** *intr.* **5.** To move rapidly with shattering effect; to dash or smite violently; to crash.

**1835** MONTEATH *Dunblane Trad.* (1887) 122 Headlong he over hillocks rush'd, And wet through bogs and mosses smash'd. **1842** LOVER *Handy Andy* xiii, You may smash away as hard as you can. **1852** MRS. STOWE *Uncle Tom's C.* xxxv. 314 Picking up the silver dollar, he sent it smashing through the window-pane out into the darkness. **1898** SIR W. CROOKES *Addr. Brit. Assoc.* 25 The quick moving molecules, smashing on to the surface, have their energy reduced.

**6.** *colloq.* To fail financially; to be ruined; to become insolvent or bankrupt. Also with *up*.

**1839** HOOD *My Son & Heir* xix, A Glazier?—what if he should smash! **1862** SALA *Seven Sons* III. vii. 142 A firm that had smashed for so tremendous an amount. **1876** BESANT & RICE *Golden Butterfly* (1877) 211 The Republic..cannot hope to pay its dividends—Must smash up, in short.

**7.** To break or fly in pieces, esp. as the result of a blow or impact.

**1904** W. W. JACOBS *Dialstone Lane* ii. 27 The pipe fell from the listener's fingers and smashed unheeded on the floor.

**III. 8. a.** Used adverbially, as in ***to go*** (also ***run***) ***smash.***

**1818** [see GO *v.* B. 10]. **1823** *Spirit Public Jrnls.* (1824) 204 The last went smash through the shop window into the street. **1842** LOVER *Handy Andy* vi, Here the hens flew against the dresser, and smash went the plates and dishes. **1849** T. T. JOHNSON *Sights Gold Region* xxii. 211 The afternoon of our 'first day out' was signalized by running smash into a big sycamore tree. **1888** VEITCH *Dean's Dau.* I. i. 25, I saw the great egg go smash against her head.

**b.** ***to play smash***: to come to grief; to wreak havoc ***with***. *dial.* and *U.S. colloq.*

**1841** *Spirit of Times* 2 Jan. 523/2 Bill Spence got drunk and played smash with all the arrangements. **1842** D. VEDDER *Poems* 84 Slates an' tiles, frae aff the houses, On the causey crown played smash. **1887** *Courier-Journal* (Louisville, Kentucky) 17 Jan. 1/7 (*caption*) Plays Smash With a Passenger Train on the Fitchburg Railroad. **1903** W. N. HARBEN *Abner Daniel* ii. 11 Yore pa's as bull-headed as a young steer, an' he's already played smash anyway. **1912** *Dialect Notes* III. VIII. 585 *Play smash*,..a euphemism for *play hell* or *play the devil*. **1915** *Ibid.* IV. III. 187 *Play smash*, ..to make a great blunder; do a thing wholly wrong.

**smash,** *v.*[2] *Cant.* [Cf. SMASH *sb.*[2]]

**1.** *trans.* To pass (counterfeit money).

**1801** *Sporting Mag.* XIX. 88/1 He had never seen any [forged notes] that were better done; he had *smashed* several. **1811** in *Lexicon-Balatronicum.* **1851** *Household Words* 25 Jan. 423, I [a bad shilling] remained to be 'smashed' (passed) by my master. **1898** A. M. BINSTEAD *Pink 'Un & Pelican* x. 229 The small tradesman, afraid to smash his notes at a bureau, had them still intact when the police called upon him. **1905** —— *Mop Fair* ii. 28 The imaginary 'bailiff' who spoke about the handcuffs is well known in the neighbourhood..while the counterfeit 'tipstaff' who smashed the cheque is a dog-fighting publican.

**2.** (See quot.)

**1812** J. H. VAUX *Flash Dict.*, To *smash* a guinea, note, or other money, is, in a common sense, to procure, or give, change for it.

**smashable** ('smæʃəb(ə)l), *a.* [f. SMASH *v.*[1] + -ABLE.] Capable of being smashed.

**1884** YATES Recoll. iv, The complete smash of everything smashable. **1888** LEES & CLUTTERBUCK *B.C. 1887* iii. (1892) 31 He..smashed all the smashable furniture.

**smash-and-grab.** Also **smash and grab, smash'n-grab.** [f. SMASH *v.*[1], GRAB *v.*] Used *attrib.* to designate a type of robbery in which the thief smashes a shop-window and grabs the goods there displayed. Also *transf.* and *fig.*, and *absol.* Hence **smash-and-grabber; smash and grabbing** *vbl. sb.*

**1927** J. C. GOODWIN *Crook Pie* ii. 52 'Smash and Grab' raids seem to be the order of the day. **1928** *Daily Tel.* 9 Oct. 12/2 Three men in a motor-car were concerned in a smash-and-grab raid... One of them threw a stone through the window. They then seized all the cameras available and returned to the car, which was driven away before a chase could be started. **1932** [see SCREWER 2]. **1933** BLUNDEN *Charles Lamb* vii. 206 A literature of the smash-and-grab type..seems to have some chance of superseding the thorough, persuasive, modulated and interwoven style. **1937** A. L. ROWSE *Sir Richard Grenville* v. 106 A smash-and-grab run upon the Isthmus of Panama. **1938** [see PICK-UP *sb.* a(vi)]. **1939** T. S. ELIOT *Old Possum's Practical Cats* 23 They were..remarkably smart at a smash-and-grab. **1944** G. B. SHAW *Everybody's Political What's What?* xxvi. 232 Monstrous world wars and smash-and-grab revolutions. **1951** M. MCLUHAN *Mech. Bride* (1967) 145/2 A commercial society dedicated to the smash and grab and one-man fury of enterprise. **1960** *Observer* 24 Jan. 5/1 A sausage team always had to work three-handed... One to do the smash and grabbing. **1965** H. I. ANSOFF *Corporate Strategy* (1968) iii. 39 In reaction to the public outrages at the 'smash'n-grab imperialism' of the nineteenth century, business has acquired a sense of social responsibility. **1970** *Oxf. Times* 23 Oct. 1/6 A smash and grab raid was carried out on the shop of Horns..shortly before midnight. **1973** W. M. DUNCAN *Big Timer* iv. 29 They tell me there was a smash-and-grab at Shader's, miss. **1978** *Daily Mail* 25 Jan. 12/2 Robbery with violence..used to be a 'snatch' or a 'smash-and-grab'.

**smashdom** ('smæʃdəm). [f. SMASH *sb.*[1] + -DOM.] The state of being (financially) smashed.

**1859** SALA *Twice r. Clock* (1861) 201 It was indeed the great knell of universal railway smashdom.

**smashed** (smæʃt), *ppl. a.* [f. SMASH *v.*[1] + -ED[1].] **1.** Crushed; broken to pieces. Also *fig.* and ***smashed-down, -up.***

**1819** SHELLEY *Peter Bell 3rd.* I. xv, Smashed glass—and nothing more! **1857** JANET HAMILTON *Lessons fr. Gt. Biogr.* (1859) 289 A pile of smashed pillars and scorched timbers. **1897** MARY KINGSLEY *W. Africa* 251 A mass of slimy gray abomination on a bit of plantain leaf—smashed snail. **1909** J. R. WARE *Passing Eng.* 227/1 *Smashed* (Navy), reduced in rank. **1915** J. WEBSTER *Dear Enemy* 325 Our poor smashed-up doctor. **1918** W. S. CHURCHILL in M. Gilbert *Winston S. Churchill* (1977) IV. Compan. I. 365 Ought we to build our lives & policy & the future arrangement of the world on the unreal basis of a smashed-up Russia & an invincible Germany. **1935** A. J. POLLOCK *Underworld Speaks* 109/1 *Smashed*, to have lost all material possessions. **1938** E. BLUNDEN in *Times Lit. Suppl.* 8 Oct. 633/2 Nor the dead in smashed-down den. **1982** J. HANSEN *Gravedigger* iii. 24 No abandoned or smashed-up Rollses.

**2.** Intoxicated, drunk; under the influence of drugs; 'stoned'. *slang* (orig. *U.S.*).

**1962** J. D. MacDonald *Key to Suite* (1968) viii. 139 Are you figuring on getting smashed? **1968** *New Scientist* 26 Sept. 679/2 The males rapidly acquired a taste for the stuff [*sc.* alcohol], bent their elbows with great application, and soon became smashed. **1968** A. Young in A. Chapman *New Black Voices* (1972) 147 Turns out he was half-smashed and half-drunk because he'd smoked some dope when he got up that morning, then on the way to school he'd met up with Wine, so the two of them did up a fifth of Nature Boy, a brand of sweet wine. **1973** D. Laing *Freaks* 20 He would get smashed on two and a half pints of Worthington E from the wood, and fall about misquoting the poetry of the beat generation. **1977** *New Society* 27 Jan. 185/3 If you're smashed out of your skull all the time on peyote, then even the bizarre patronage of Marlon Brando must seem tolerable.

**smasher**[1] ('smæʃə(r)). [f. smash *v.*[1]]

**1.** *slang.* **a.** Anything uncommon, extraordinary, or unusual, *esp.* unusually large or excellent.

**1794** *Gentl. Mag.* LXIV. i. 216/1 *Smasher*..signifies any thing larger than common. *a* **1800** in Pegge *Suppl. Grose.* **1853** Moodie *Life Clearings* 106 If you make it twelve and a half cents, you'll have a *smasher* [= a full house]. **1894** *Daily News* 11 Sept. 5/1 Lord Rosebery's colt, who, if not the 'smasher' which his precipitate admirers declared him to be.., is above the average of high-class three-year-olds.

**b.** A very pretty or attractive woman; an attractive man.

**1948** Partridge *Dict. Forces' Slang* 173 To a Scotsman an attactive girl was 'a wee smasher'. **1949** J. R. Cole *It was so Late* 61 'Yes. No kidding,' Don said. 'But she was easier to look at than anything around here. She was a smasher—straight she was!' **1957** A. Wilson *Bit off Map & Other Stories* 74 When the jeunes filles met Rodney, Jackie..put her head on one side and said, 'I say, isn't he a smasher!' **1963** *Security Gazette* V. i. 13/2 The applicant for a shorthand typist's job—she was a smasher. **1977** C. McCullough *Thorn Birds* xviii. 458 In a long black wig, tan body paint and my few scraps of metal I look a smasher.

**2.** *colloq.* **a.** A severe or crushing reply, article, review, etc.

**1828** *Blackw. Mag.* XXIV. 189 His reply..was a complete smasher. **1849** Thackeray *Pendennis* xxxi, He's a tremendous hand at a smasher. **1864** *Reader* No. 100. 674/1 The Edinburgh Review had 'come down a smasher on Robert Browning'.

**b.** A bad or damaging fall; a heavy blow.

**1829** P. Egan *Boxiana* 2nd Ser. II. 706 Tom, by the effect of this *smasher*, lost his equilibrium. **1875** Buckland *Log-Book* 4 The horses will come a terrific smasher. **1897** *Daily News* 1 June 8/2 Before I could consider,.. I had fetched him the smasher.

**3.** An appliance or machine which smashes or crushes; *spec.* a bookbinder's compressing-machine; a form of embossing-press.

**1822** W. James *Naval Hist.* (1826) I. 47 Its destructive effects..induced its ingenious inventor to give it the name of smasher. **1876** *Encycl. Brit.* IV. 44 The folded sheets are sometimes condensed in another American machine called 'The Smasher'. **1882** J. B. Nicholson *Art Bookbinding* 44 A powerful embossing press, technically called a smasher.

**4.** One who smashes.

**1884** *Pall Mall G.* 4 July 1/2 Every day the smashing is postponed..the more likely will it be that the Mahdi will be the smasher and we the smashed. **1921** [see *double-faulter* s.v. double *a.* C. 3]. **1928** B. Nuthall *Learning Lawn Tennis* vii. 114, I am not an expert smasher myself.

**5.** *attrib.* in ***smasher hat***, a slouched hat. Also *ellipt.*

**1891** E. Glanville *Fossicker* xviii. 156 The Dutchmen stared at him from under the brims of their felt 'smashers'. **1892** J. R. Couper *Mixed Humanity* i. 4 A wide-awake, called in South Africa a 'smasher'. **1894** C. H. W. Donaldson *With Wilson in Matabeleland* ix. 189 Brown cord jackets and 'smasher' hats, bandoliers and rifles. **1899** G. H. Russell *Under the Sjambok* x. 107 The men..are content to put a piece of crape round the arm and smasher hat.

**smasher**[2] ('smæʃə(r)). *slang.* [f. smash *sb.*[2] or *v.*[2]]

**1.** One who passes or utters counterfeit coin or forged notes.

**1795** Potter *Dict. Cant*, *Smasher*, a passer of counterfeit coin. **1796** Colquhoun *Police Metropolis* 107 The Dealer.. for the most part disposes of it to the utterers, vulgarly called Smashers. **1836** *Lincoln Herald* 20 Dec. 4/2 Several individuals have been imposed upon by the smashers. **1857** Borrow *Romany Rye* xli, When I said that my father was a smasher, I meant one who passes forged notes. **1895** *Westm. Gaz.* 18 Sept. 3/1 Most frequently the single-handed 'smasher' contents himself in passing one coin in an evening.

*fig.* **1872** *Punch* 2 Mar. 97/1 Some smashers have lately been trying to pass the base word 'cablegram'.

**2.** A counterfeit coin. *rare*[−1].

**1851** Mayhew *Lond. Lab.* (1864) II. 488/2 Every bit of it, every coin,..was bad—all smashers.

**3.** A receiver of stolen property. *rare.*

**1929** C. Humphreys *Gt. Pearl Robbery* i. 60 The goods might be disposed of to a 'smasher', that is, a receiver of stolen property.

**smasheroo** (ˌsmæʃə'ruː). *slang* (orig. and chiefly *U.S.*). [f. smash *sb.*[1] + -eroo.] A great success.

**1948** *Life* 26 Jan. 47/2 The press snickeringly reported Virginia's coming-out party, a smasheroo, right down to the 500 bottles of ginger beer, the spots left on the furniture. **1960** S. Kauffmann *If it be Love* iii. iv. 211 A smasheroo. All seven reviews were great. **1962** *John o' London's* 11 Jan. 43/3 In the historical hokum-pokum bracket there's been one real smasheroo, *El Cid.* **1967** *Punch* 29 Nov. 822/2 A smasheroo musical will bring its creators vastly more. The most spectacular example of this in recent years is *Hello, Dolly!* **1975** *New Yorker* 17 Mar. 92/1 Is one going to make the burning a big Broadway smasheroo of a scene?

**smashery** ('smæʃərɪ). [f. smash *v.*[1]] A smashing or destruction; a state of smash.

**1830** Galt *Lawrie T.* iii. i. (1849) 84 Having a smashery among his crockery ware. **1849** E. Forbes in Wilson & Geikie *Life* xiii. 465 It is the most singular mince-meat smashery of about eight feet of shales and chert-bands. **1854** Lever *Dodd Family Abroad* xxxii, The smaller details are, a universal smashery, with occasional vestiges of that part of the creation consigned to hair-dressers..and milliners.

**smashing** ('smæʃɪŋ), *vbl. sb.*[1] [f. smash *v.*[1]]

**1.** The action of smash *v.*[1] in various senses.

**1821** Galt *Ann. Parish* xxii, There was such a smashing of the poor weans, as had not been known for an age. **1842** De Quincey *Marquess Wellesley* Wks. 1858 VIII. 28 The last great political act of Lord Wellesley was the smashing of the Peel ministry in 1834. **1886** *Law Times* LXXX. 285/1 Mere smashing of windows was held not to be a felonious demolition. **1902** 'Linesman' *Words Eyewitness* 285 That they..endure smashing after smashing, is..as admirable as it is marvellous.

**2.** *attrib.*, as ***smashing branch***, ***capacity***, ***power***; **smashing-machine**, a heavy press used by bookbinders (Knight *Dict. Mech.* 1875); **smashing-press**, an embossing-press (*Ibid.* Suppl. 1884).

**1849** *Punch* XVII. 214 A Bankrupt..to superintend the smashing branch. **1889** *Pall Mall G.* 19 Feb. 2/3 The smashing capacity even of a lion is..limited. **1892** Greener *Breech-Loader* 152 The increased range and smashing power of the large shot.

**'smashing**, *vbl. sb.*[2] [f. smash *v.*[2]] (See quot. 1812.)

**1812** J. H. Vaux *Flash Dict.*, *Smashing*, uttering counterfeit money; *smashing of queer screens*, signifies uttering forged bank notes. **1891** M. Williams *Later Leaves* xii. 144 When once a man commences smashing or passing, he never gives up the practice.

**smashing** ('smæʃɪŋ), *ppl. a.*[1] [f. smash *v.*[1]]

**1.** That smashes, in various senses.

**1833** M. Scott *Tom Cringle* i, A heavy smashing thump against our bows. **1841** Lever *C. O'Malley* xcii, A smashing volley was poured into the squadron. **1853** W. Irving *Life & Lett.* (1864) IV. 124 Thackeray..said the Bostonians had published a smashing criticism on him. **1884** *Pall Mall G.* 23 Oct. 1/2 [To] deal them a smashing blow by an appeal to the country.

**2.** *colloq.* Very good; greatly pleasing; excellent; sensational.

*a* **1911** D. G. Phillips *Susan Lenox* (1917) II. vi. 164 When you get dressed up a bit..you'll do a smashing business. **1914** W. Owen *Let.* 27 Dec. (1967) 310, I come in hungry to find a 'smashin' dinner. **1922** [see crack *sb.* 1 d]. **1944** M. Paneth *Branch Street* 8 When the children came.. to play in the house they thought it 'smashing'. **1948** *Mind* LVII. 418 The fact is, the verification principle is a metaphysical proposition—a 'smashing' one if I may be permitted the expression. **1959** *Times Lit. Suppl.* 2 Oct. 564/2 It is not her fault that the publishers, in big letters on the jacket, promise 'as smashing a last sentence as we can recall!' That promise is not fulfilled. The final twist is surprisingly unsurprising. **1977** *Chem. in Brit.* XIII. 118/2 This is a smashing book for anyone interested in surface chemistry and physics to have available on his bookshelf.

Hence **'smashingly** *adv.*, in a smashing manner.

**1884** *Pall Mall G.* 19 Mar. 2/1 A man..who is too keen to pause unless he is hit smashingly. **1923** *Daily Mail* 8 Sept. 6/6 Her volleying is splendid, And smashingly she serves. **1956** 'C. Blackstock' *Dewey Death* iv. 75 He was so smashingly handsome. **1970** *Daily Tel.* 21 July 13/4 The Férand evening midis of white organdie, smashingly printed with swirls of grey and cocoa.

**'smashing**, *ppl. a.*[2] [f. smash *v.*[2]]

**a.** Counterfeit, forged. **b.** Engaged in 'smashing'.

**1857** Borrow *Romany Rye* xli, My father had paid for the horses with his smashing notes. **1899** *Pall Mall G.* 15 May 7/3, 98 per cent. of the 'smashing' fraternity make silver and not gold money.

**'smash-up.** Also (*U.S.*) **smashup.** [f. smash *sb.*[1] or *v.*[1]] **a.** A complete smash. Also *fig.*

**1858** Holland *Titcomb's Lett.* viii. 74 Follow it, and see how long it will be before you come to a stump and a smash-up. **1890** S. W. Baker *Wild Beasts* I. 16 A hollow bullet.. is intended..to secure an expansion and smash-up of the lead upon impact with the animal. **1892** *Cath. News* 27 Feb. 5/5 May this smash-up of his facts remain as a warning to him. **1940** W. Empson *Gathering Storm* 67 Politicians, etc., living now, who made a smash-up of international affairs. **1974** [see *military police* s.v. military *a.* 3 b]. **1978** H. Wouk *War & Remembrance* xxxix. 399 Historians tend to miss the awful simultaneity of the fourfold smashup.

**b.** *spec.* A collision, esp. of road or rail vehicles; a crash. Chiefly *U.S.*

**1856** M. J. Holmes *'Lena Rivers* 36 The old lady, sure of a *smash-up* this time, had attempted to rise. **1875** H. W. Shaw *Josh Billings' Farmer's Allminax* 13 Got the orfull smash up on the rale rode. **1923** M. B. Watts *Luther Nichols* 354 There had been..a smash up; a delivery-wagon..had run head-on into that there stone. **1931** *Kansas City Times* 3 Oct. e/6 What could run more typically true to form than a smashup when that bee got up a motorist's pants leg a short time ago? **1978** J. Irving *World according to Garp* xii. 236 They all drive so fast... If it weren't for you, I sometimes think they'd be having their smashups right in my living room.

**smatch** (smætʃ), *sb.*[1] Forms: 2 **smecch**, 3 **smech**; 4, 6–7 **smach**, 5–6 **smache**, **smatche**, 6– **smatch**. [ME. *smech*, *smach*, app. an alteration of OE. *smæc* smack *sb.*[1], under the influence of smatch *v.*]

**1.** Taste, smack, flavour; †also, the sense of taste.

*a* **1200** *St. Marher.* 9 On his hehe hokede neose þreaste smeorðrinde smoke ut smecche forcuðest. *a* **1225** *Ancr. R.* 94 þis smech and tis cnowunge kumeð of gostliche sihðe. *Ibid.* 276 Bitweonen smech muðes and neoses smel. **13..** *E.E. Allit. P.* B. 461 He hade þe smelle of þe smach & smoltes þeder sone, Fallez on þe foule flesch [etc.]. **1563** Langham *Gard. Health* (1633) 536 Those that be distilled in mettall, haue some smatch of the mettall. **1581** J. Bell *Haddon's Answ. Osor.* A vj, But it is not errour forthwith that hath somewhat a bitter smatch, and is unsavory to every queysie stomacke. **1600** Surflet *Countrie Farme* v. xx. 713 The meal of the corne of Champagne, craueth a newer made leauen,..because it hath a smatch of the earth. **1681** Grew *Musæum* iv. i. 353 These Salts have also some-what of a Nitrous Tast, but mixed with a smatch of a Vitriolick. *a* **1764** R. Lloyd *Author's Apol.* 92 Whosoe'er, though slightly, sips, Their grateful flavour with his lips, Will find it leave a smatch behind. **1853** Surtees *Sponge's Sp. Tour* xxv. 148 We had a bottle with a queer smatch the other night. **1892** *Pall Mall G.* 29 Mar. 7/3 Not the least smatch or bad taste has ever been imparted to the liquor.

*fig.* **1583** Golding *Calvin on Deut.* cxxi. 746, I haue yet.. this smatch of my wicked bringing up..remayning in mee.

**b.** A mere tasting. *rare.*

*c* **1456** Pecock *Bk. Faith* (1909) 205 Whiche bokis, if ȝe wolen rede diligentli..and not forto take an hasti smel or smatche in hem. **1571** Golding *Calvin on Ps.* lxxi. xviii, If God should withdraw his grace, when men have tasted but a little smatch of it. **1755** T. H. Croker *Orl. Fur.* xxxiii. iii, The monsters..Which did his victuals spoil,..Nor suffer'd him to taste, or have a smatch.

**2.** A slight indication, suggestion, or tincture *of* some quality, etc.

*c* **1525** *Tale of the basyn* 25 in Hazl. *E.P.P.* III. 45 A wyfe that has an yvell tach, Ther of the husbond shalle haue a smache. **1548** Udall, etc. *Erasm. Par. Luke* Pref. 6 He hath in sundry woordes and phrases sum smatche of his natiue countrey phrases, that he was borne in. **1628** Earle *Microcosm.* (Arb.) 44 Hee passes the more plausibly because all men haue a smatch of his humour. **1669** Holder *Elem. Speech* 59 Some Nations may be found to have a peculiar Guttural or Nasal smatch in their Language. **1727** *Philip Quarll* 174 A Smatch of that Respect he has forfeited by his fatal Transgression. **1760–72** H. Brooke *Fool of Qual.* (1809) I. 56 Has not your Pegasus some smatch of the qualities of the famous Rosinante? **1788** Cowper *Let.* Wks. 1836 VI. 155 In the style of the lady's note to you, I can easily perceive a smatch of her character. **1808** Lamb *Charac. Dram. Writ.* 531 She speaks the dialect of despair; her tongue has a smatch of Tartarus. **1855** [Robinson] *Whitby Gloss.* s.v., He has gotten a smatch of London in his talk. **1889** *Archaeol. Æliana* XIII. 313 A smatch of the old lawless spirit of their ancestors.

**b.** A slight touch *of* illness, pain, etc.

**1647** Lilly *Chr. Astrol.* xliv. 243 Not that moment when first the Patient felt a Smatch of it. **1772–84** *Cook's Voy.* (1790) I. 143 It was resolved to give him a smatch of the cat-o'-nine-tails. **1865** Banks *Wakefield Words* 65 'Hez he gotten t'feaver?' 'Noa, bud he's a smatch on it.'

**3.** A slight knowledge, a smattering, *of* something. †Also, a slight turn or trial *at* a thing.

**1571** Golding *Calvin on Ps.* xl. iv, As yit we comprehend it not perfectly, but onely have a little smatch of it. **1628** Earle *Microcosm.* (Arb.) 26 If he haue leasure to be idle.. he ha's a smatch at Alcumy. **1703** De Foe *Reformat. Manners* Misc. 102 A little smatch of Modern Blasphemy. **1719** —— *Crusoe* ii. (Globe) 549 They have..a Smatch of the Knowledge of the Mathematicks. **1780** Cowper *Progr. Error* 365 We give some Latin, and a smatch of Greek. **1825** A. Headley in J. Raine *Mem. J. Hodgson* (1858) II. 66 If you can get Joe Fenwick to give him a smatch of the value of the land it will be of great service to him.

† **smatch**, *sb.*[2] *Obs.* Also 6 **smatche**. [Of obscure origin.] The wheatear, *Saxicola œnanthe*.

Turner appears to be the only real authority for the name, and the statement in quot. 1753 is very doubtful.

**1544** Turner *Avium Hist.* C vj, *Κυανός*, *Cæruleo*, Anglicé, a clotburd, a smatche, an arlyng, a steinchek. **1655** Moufet & Bennet *Health's Impr.* 100 The Clotbird (called sometimes a Smatch, or an Arling) is as big almost as a Thrush. **1668** Charleton *Onomast.* 88 *Cæruleo*, the Clot-bird, Smatch, or Stone-Check. **1753** *Chambers' Cycl.* Suppl., *Smatch*, in zoology, a name by which the common œnanthe is called in many parts of England.

† **smatch**, *v.* *Obs.* Forms: *α.* 1 **-smeccan**, 3 **smecchen**, **smechen**; *pa. t.* **smeihte**, *pa. pple.* **i-smeiht**, **i-smecched**. *β.* 1 **smæccan**, 4 **smache**, 5–6 **smacche**, 4, 6 **smatche**, 4, 6–7 **smatch** (7 **smach**); *pa. t.* 3 **smachte**, 4–5 **smauȝt(e**; *pa. pple.* 3 **i-smaht**, **i-smauht**. [OE. *(ȝe)smeccan* and *smæccan*, f. *smæc* smack *sb.*[1] Cf. OFris. *smekka*, *smetsa* (WFris. *smeitsje*), MLG. and LG. *smecken*, OHG. *smecchen* (G. *schmecken*). Finally supplanted by the later smack *v.*[1]]

**1.** *intr.* To have a (specified) flavour or taste; to smack (in some way).

*c* **1000** Ælfric *Gram.* (Z.) xxviii. 166 *Sapio*, ic wat oððe ic smæcce. *a* **1225** *Leg. Kath.* 1526 Mi swete lif, se swoteliche he smecheð me & smealleð. **13..** *E.E. Allit. P.* B. 955 Al in smolderande smoke smachande ful ille. **1377** Langl. *P. Pl.* B. v. 363 Is non so hungri hounde..Durst lape of þe leuynges, so vnlouely þei smauȝte [*C.* smauhte]. **1682** Hickeringill *Black Non-Conf.* Wks. 1716 II. 152 Revenge ..to a polluted Palate..relishes and smach's more sweet.. than Muscadine and Eggs.

**b.** *fig.* To smack *of* something.

*c* **1380** Wyclif *Wks.* (1880) 393 þe whiche smachen of symony and extorcion. *c* **1380** —— *Sel. Wks.* II. 226 Many men wenen þat al þes newe sectis..smatchen sumwhat of heresie. **1565** JEWEL *Reply Harding* (1611) 327 This terme, All, heere smatcheth of spight. **1578** BANISTER *Hist. Man* I. 22 Allowing his description therin to retain and smatche of veritie. *a***1604** HANMER *Chron. Ireland* (1809) 15 The Hebrewes by reason of their peregrination and captivities do smach of the Chaldees, Syriack and Arabick tongues. **1613** DAY *Festivals* viii. (1615) 242 The new Cask will ever smatch of that wherewith it hath beene seasoned.

**c.** *trans.* To smack of (something).

*c***1380** WYCLIF *Sel. Wks.* I. 27 So eche secte smatchiþ many synnes. *Ibid.* 28 Al þes þree sectis mote nedis smatche errour. **1402** *Pol. Poems* (Rolls) II. 64 Sith alle that is not groundid smacchith grete synne. **1589** PUTTENHAM *Eng. Poesie* II. xiv. (Arb.) 140 They smatch more the schoole of common players than of any delicate Poet Lyricke or Elegiacke. *Ibid.* III. xix. 243 Such as smatch morall doctrine and teach..good behauiour.

**2.** *trans.* To taste, feel the taste of. Also *fig.*

*a***1225** *Ancr. R.* 94 Hit is a derne healewi þet no mon ne icnoweð þet naueð hit ismecched. *Ibid.* 106 He smeihte galle on his tunge, uorto leren ancren þet heo ne gruchie neuermore uor none mete. *a***1240** *Ureisun* in *O.E. Hom.* I. 189 Al þet ich abbe..mid muþ ispekin oþer ismaht. *c***1400** *Beryn* 3122 He held it nat al foly þat Geffrey did clatir,.. For parcell of his wisdom to-fore he had smaught.

Hence †ˈ**smatching** *vbl. sb. Obs.*

*a***1225** *Ancr. R.* 64 Spellunge & smecchunge beoð ine muðe boðe, ase sihðe is iðen eien. *c***1230** *Hali Meid.* 13 Hire fif wittes, sihðe & heringe, smecchunge & smealunge & euch limes felunge.

†ˈ**smatchcock.** *Obs. rare.* [Of obscure origin.] **a.** A collop. **b.** A spitchcock.

**14..** *Lat.-Eng. Voc.* in Wr.-Wülcker 584 *Frixa*, a colhoppe, or a smachecok. **1746** *Moufet & Bennet's Health's Impr.* 276 Either to broil them [*sc.* lampreys] as Smatchcocks [1655 Spitchcocks], or to bake them.

**smatchet** (ˈsmætʃɪt). *Sc.* Forms: α. 6 **smachart**, 6, 9 **smatcher, -ert**, 9 **-art, -ard**. β. 7 **smatched**, 9 **smatchet (-it)**. [Of obscure origin.] An insignificant contemptible person; a chit.

α. *c***1582** MONTGOMERIE *Flyting* (Tull.) 623 For schismes, and Symonie, þat smachart [*Harl.* smatched] wes schameit. **1583** *Leg. Bp. St. Androis* 996 Bot ay the mair this smatcher gettis, The closser garris he keip the yettis. **1846** W. CROSS *Disruption* xxxii, Some other smatchert they call Duncanson it seems is coming. **1878** 'SAXON' *Galloway Gossip* 98 (E.D.D.), A sort of misleer't kind of a smatchart.

β. **16..** *Montgomerie's Flyting* (Harl.) 473 Where that smatched hade sucked, so sair it was to shed it. **1834** *Tait's Mag.* I. 428/1 These Oxford smatchets too, singing through their noses, in mockery of the Dissenters! **1871** W. ALEXANDER *Johnny Gibb* (1873) 118 Impident smatchet that he is.

†ˈ**smatchless,** *a. Obs.*$^{-1}$ In 3 **smechleas.** [f. *smech* SMATCH *sb.*$^1$] Devoid of savour.

*a***1225** *Ancr. R.* 138 Al ure deden, & al þet we wurcheð wiðuten salt, þet is, wisdom, al þuncheð God smechleas.

**S-matrix**: see S II. 11.

**smatter** (ˈsmætə(r)), *sb.* [f. the vb.]

**1.** Superficial knowledge; a smattering.

**1668** WILKINS *Real Char.* 205 Unskilfulness, bungling,.. slubber, smatter. **1690** TEMPLE *Ess. Learning* Wks. 1720 I. 297 Other Sciences..were in a manner extinguish'd.., excepting only a Smatter of Judicial Astrology. **1787** W. TAYLOR *Scots Poems* 6 An' than jog on wi' rhymin smatter To toom my noddle. **1881** THOMPSON *Proc. U.S. Superintendents' Conv.* 35 The mistake lies in the substitution of smatter for knowledge. **1883** ADAMS *College Fetich* 27 That worthless smatter of the classics.

**2.** *pl.* Scraps, trifles, fragments; small sums. *Sc.*

**1766** A. NICOL *Poems* 76 He can pray, and tell long scrifts of Greek, And broken smatters of the Hebrew speak. **1808** in JAMIESON.

**smatter** (ˈsmætə(r)), *v.* Forms: 4 **smatre**, 4–6 **smater**, 6 **smatyr**, 5– **smatter**. [Of uncertain origin. Similar forms occur in Sw. *smattra* to patter, crackle, rattle, etc., G. *schmettern* to dash, resound, etc., but real connexion is very doubtful. In dialects there is also a verb *smatter* to smash: see the *Eng. Dial. Dict.*]

**1.** †**a.** *trans.* To dirty, smirch, pollute, defile. *Obs.*

The sense in the Chaucer passage is not quite certain.

**13..** in *Reliq. Antiq.* I. 240 Swarte smekyd smethes smateryd with smoke. *c***1386** CHAUCER *Pars. T.* ¶857 Yet wol they Kisse..and smatre [*v.r.* smater] hem. **1575–6** *Durham Deposit.* (Surtees) 278 They of St. Margaret's wolde not smatter ther own church yard with thoise that then died in the plage. **1600** W. WATSON *Decacordon* (1602) 110 To say the Iesuits are all smattred with Atheisme, I will not. *Ibid.* 245 More odious stuffe then I haue handled, or am willing to smatter my pen withall.

**b.** *U.S.* To splash, splatter. Also *intr.*

**1893** *N. & Q.* 15 July 45 In the daily reports of the interesting Lizzie Borden murder trial, recently held in Massachusetts, I notice the peculiar use of the words *smatter, smattering*, and *smattered* in reference to splashes of blood. **1958** S. A. GRAU *Hard Blue Sky* III. 125 The first heavy drops fell and smattered in the dust. **1974** D. RICHARDS *Coming of Winter* v. 144 The man had on a long grey coat, smattered with mud.

†**2. a.** *intr.* To talk ignorantly or superficially, to prate or chatter, *of* something. *Obs.*

*c***1440** LOVELICH *Merlin* 3167 Where-offen with sorwe smateryth he of ony thing that to vs longeth for to be? *c***1522** SKELTON *Why nat to Court?* 711 For I abhore to smatter Of one so deuyllysshe a matter. But I wyll make further relacion. **1571** R. EDWARDS *Damon & Pithias* in Hazl. *Dodsley* IV. 41 Damon smatters as well as he, of crafty philosophy. **1733** SWIFT *On Poetry* 51 Of State-Affairs you cannot smatter, Are aukward when you try to flatter.

†**b.** Without const. *Obs.*

*c***1475** in Wright *Songs & Carols* (Percy Soc.) 89 Trow ye that they lyst to smatter, Ore ageynst ther husbondes to clatter? **1523** SKELTON *Garl. Laurel* 1194 How Cownterfet Cowntenaunce..With Crafty Conueyaunce dothe smater and flater. **1592** SHAKS. *Rom. & Jul.* III. v. 172 Good Prudence, smatter with your gossip, go. *a***1661** HOLYDAY *Juvenal* (1673) 263 Such rules..your nurses teach children, when they can scarce smatter. **1691** E. TAYLOR *Behmen's Theos. Phil.* 204 No Tongue or Pen can more than smatter, at the recital of the love-inspired Words.

**3. a.** To have a slight or superficial knowledge or practice *of*; to dabble, to be a smatterer (*in* or *at* something).

**1530** PALSGR. 722/2, I smatter of a thyng, I have lytell knowledge in it. *Ibid.*, He smattereth a lytell of the lawe. **1547** BOORDE *Brev. Health* Pref. 2 Fooles and incipient persons..wyl enterpryse to smatter and to meddle to mynyster medecynes. **1573** L. LLOYD *Marrow of Hist.* (1653) 218 If a man can but smatter in six or seven languages he is noted to be a rare fellow. **1805** G. M$^c$INDOE *Poems* 151 That's no' to hinder me to smatter..At making rhyme. **1827** HOOD *Craniology* 39 Just as in making broth they smatter By bobbing twenty things in water. **1882** *Harper's Mag.* LXV. 595, I never knew you to smatter.

**b.** To go *through* in a superficial manner.

**1881** MAHAFFY *Rep. Irish Schools* 26 The system makes it far more lucrative to smatter through all these things than to learn the great subjects.

**4.** *trans.* To talk or utter without proper knowledge or proficiency.

**1609** B. JONSON *Sil. Woman* IV. ii, The barber smatters Latin, I remember. **1663** BUTLER *Hud.* I. i. 185 In proper terms, such as men smatter When they throw out and miss the matter. **1708** *Brit. Apollo* No. 68. 3/1 So harsh and so mean are the Lines that you smatter. **1819** *Metropolis* II. 253 A man..who could at least smatter a little French. **1860** THACKERAY *Lovel* i, He smattered words in not a few foreign languages.

**5.** To dabble in (a subject); to study or learn superficially.

**1883** *American* XXVI. 281 Then I smatter botany some. **1885** STEVENSON *Dynamiter* Wks. 1907 VI. 191, I have smattered law, smattered letters, smattered geography, smattered mathematics.

**smatterer** (ˈsmætərə(r)). Also 6 **smaterar, smatrer**, 6–7 **smaterer.** [f. SMATTER *v.*] One who has only a slight or superficial knowledge *of* (now rare) or *in* a matter; a dabbler. Also used without const.

(*a*) **1519** HORMAN *Vulgaria* 41 b, Smaterars or bunglers of physyke. *Ibid.* 92 b, He is a smaterar of grammar. **1577** tr. *Bullinger's Decades* (1592) 844 The captious smatterers of Rhetorique. **1810** D. STEWART *Philos. Ess.* 162 A degree of celebrity among the smatterers of science.

(*b*) **1529** MORE *Dyaloge* III. Wks. 244/2 Some proude smaterer in learning. **1576** FLEMING *Panopl. Epist.* 342 A man..would thinke that in versifying he is but a smatterer. **1621** BURTON *Anat. Mel.* II. iii. i, Smatterers in other mens matters. **1654** WHITLOCK *Zootomia* 104 More mischiefe cometh from such Smatterers in Physick, than those more ignorant. **1711** ADDISON *Spect.* No. 58 ¶13 For the Benefit of our modern Smatterers in Poetry. *a***1763** W. KING *Lit. & Polit. Anecd.* (1819) 150 A bare smatterer in the Latin tongue. **1818** HALLAM *Mid. Ages* (1872) III. 283 Chilperic ..was a smatterer in several kinds of literature. **1893** JESSOPP *Stud. Recluse* Pref. p. ix, A clergyman with a cure of souls..must give up all hopes of being anything but a smatterer in science.

(*c*) **1586** W. WEBBE *Eng. Poetrie* (Arb.) 20 Noble Poetry, pittifullie mangled and defaced, by rude smatterers. **1599** H. BUTTES *Dyets drie Dinner* D ij, Such hurt..ensueth by.. medling with medlers or common smatterers. **1637** GILLESPIE *Eng.-Pop. Cerem.* III. viii. 138 Every smatterer among them hath this much in his mouth. *a***1680** BUTLER *Rem.* (1759) I. 213 As Smatterers prove more arrogant and pert, The less they truly understand an Art. **1748** SMOLLETT *Rod. Random* (1812) I. 257 No smatterer could read as I had done. **1805** D'ISRAELI in Smiles *Mem. J. Murray* (1891) I. ii. 48 Could you secure the numerous Smatterers of this age, you will have an enviable body of subscribers. **1882** *Manch. Guard.* 5 Sept. 6 Once off a very special line of his own Dr. Richardson is, we fear, no better than a smatterer.

ˈ**smattering,** *vbl. sb.* [f. SMATTER *v.*]

**1. a.** A slight or superficial knowledge *in* or *of* something. Also without const.

(*a*) **1538** STARKEY *England* I. i. 17 Such haue only a lytyl smateryng in gud lernyng. **1631** BRATHWAIT *Whimzies, Almanack-maker* 14 Wherein, trust me, hee ha's a pretty smattering. **1704** F. FULLER *Med. Gymn.* (1711) 55 Known to every one who has but the least smattering in Distillations. **1806** BERESFORD *Miseries Hum. Life* IV. i, Your utter incapability of ever arriving at the slightest smattering in any of the infernal dialects. **1856** *N. Brit. Rev.* XXVI. 255 It is the only alternative to a superficial smattering in all things.

(*b*) **1589** GREENE *Menaphon* (Arb.) 10 Euerie priuate Scholler..beganne to vaunt their smattering of Latine. **1631** WEEVER *Anc. Funeral Mon.* 785 Onely a little smattering of learning he had. **1742** RICHARDSON *Pamela* IV. 43, I propose to give you a Smattering of the French and Italian. **1836** MARRYAT *Japhet* iv, I soon obtained a very fair smattering of my profession. **1874** L. STEPHEN *Hours Libr.* (1892) II. ii. 33 He had..given his son the chance of acquiring a smattering of 'scholarship'.

(*c*) **1581** MULCASTER *Positions* xxxix. (1887) 219 It were a great deale better that they had no learning at all and knew their owne ignorance, than any little smattering, vnperfit in his kinde. **1612** BRINSLEY *Ludus Lit.* 108 They who haue had but a smattering, or some little beginning. **1693** EVELYN *De la Quint. Compl. Gard.* I. 3 That dangerous and so much fear'd station, which is call'd Smattering. **1865** RUSKIN *Sesame* 161 There is a wide difference between elementary knowledge and superficial knowledge—between a firm beginning, and a feeble smattering.

†**b.** A slight trace or symptom. *Obs.*$^{-1}$

**1763** *Phil. Trans.* LIII. 197 The patient, at the usual time for the return of his fit, felt some smattering of his distemper.

**c.** A small amount or number.

**1973** *Nation Rev.* (Melbourne) 31 Aug. 1442/6 The news that *does* appear—other than a smattering of inconsequential rubbish—is..thinly disguised opinion. *Ibid.* 1464/2 There were 10,000 men (and a smattering of women) of letters in the UK. **1975** D. NOBBS *Death of Reginald Perrin* 154 There was a surprised pause, then a smattering of applause, which grew slowly into a tolerable ovation.

**2.** The action of discoursing or studying in a superficial manner. *rare.*

**1649** MILTON *Observ. Articles Peace* Wks. 1851 IV. 564 The changing forsooth of Monarchy into Anarchy, sounds so like the smattering of some raw Politician. **1692** BENTLEY *Boyle Lect.* ii. 70, I would advise them to leave off this dabbling and smattering in Philosophy.

ˈ**smattering,** *ppl. a.* [f. SMATTER *v.*]

†**1.** ? Ready for smacking or kissing. *Obs.*$^{-1}$

*a***1450** *Mankind* (Brandl) 597, I wyll..geett me a lemman wyth a smattrynge face.

†**2.** Given to prating or talking. *Obs.*$^{-1}$

**1526** SKELTON *Magnyf.* 2121, I warne you beware of to moche lyberte;..[of being] To flatterynge, to smatterynge, ..To claterynge, to chaterynge [etc.].

**3.** Dabbling; imperfectly learned.

**1581** MULCASTER *Positions* xli. (1887) 236 Simple coniectures of some smattering writers concerning the matter of his traine. **1609** HOLLAND *Amm. Marcell.* 93 A bookish smattering Grecian. **1683** KENNETT tr. *Erasm. on Folly* 140, I, who am but a smattering Novice in Divinity.

**4.** Slight, superficial, imperfect.

*c***1589** *Theses Martinianae* 31, I haue a prety smattering gift in this Pistle-making. **1604** F. HERING *Mod. Defence* 32 Hauing attained any little smattering knowledge. **1686** tr. *Chardin's Coronat. Solyman* 124 Writers of Travels, who understood not the Eastern Languages or at least had but a smattering understanding of 'em. **1818** MOORE *Fudge Fam. Paris* ix. 481 My French..Is, on the whole, but weak and smattering. **1873** HAMERTON *Intell. Life* XI. ii. 406 That smattering acquaintance with questions of religion, politics, and literature which the world calls 'well-informed'.

Hence ˈ**smatteringly** *adv.*

**1849** MAURY in Corbin *Life* (1888) 52 To see how smatteringly they are taught, look at the great majority of middle-aged women. **1864** TENNYSON *Aylmer's F.* 433 As we task ourselves To learn a language known but smatteringly.

ˈ**smatter of fact.** Also **smatterer fact, smatter fact**, etc. Repr. colloq. pronunc. of phr. *as a matter of fact*. Cf. FACT 6 a.

**1922** S. LEWIS *Babbitt* iv. 44 Besides, smatter fact, I'll tell you confidentially. *Ibid.* vi. 85 Smatter of fact, there's a whole lot of valuable time lost even at the U., studying poetry and French and subjects that never brought in anybody a cent. **1957** V. S. NAIPAUL *Mystic Masseur* iii. 39 But, smatterer fact, I don't like the idea. **1968** A. CLARKE *Darkened Room* v. 59 Oh, I don't mind... 'Smatter o' fact.. I like it. **1972** 'J. & E. BONETT' *No Time to Kill* vi. 67 'Smatter of fact, my real name's Gladys, but..I took to Carmen..'Sides, now I've picked up the lingo, a lot of 'em tell me what good English I speak. **1978** D. BLOODWORTH *Crosstalk* vi. 45 S'matter of a fact, that one's a cinch.

ˈ**smattery,** *sb.* [f. SMATTER *sb.* or *v.*] Smattering; superficial knowledge.

**1892** *Sat. Rev.* 16 Jan. 77/2 Freedom from sciolism and 'smattery'.

ˈ**smattery,** *a.* [f. SMATTER *sb.*] Superficial; of a smattering character.

**1895** *Westm. Gaz.* 14 Feb. 2/2 A small library of the popular literature of the subjects, some of which was as smattery as Madame herself.

**smaw**, obs. Sc. variant of SMALL *a.*

**smay** (smeɪ), *v.* Now *dial.* [Aphetic for DISMAY *v.*$^1$ or ESMAY *v.*] *intr.* To shrink, to flinch; to feel disinclined, etc. Hence ˈ**smaying** *vbl. sb.*

**1632** HOLLAND *Cyrupædia* 8 But Cyrus,..not smaying at all,..readily came upon him againe with a reply. **1667** P. HENRY *Diaries & Lett.* (1882) 205 He was of a strong healthy constitution, not smaying for cold in school, like other children, as his master hath told me. **1678** BP. CROFT *Second Call* 30 Men in Duels..receive deadly wounds one after another without any smaying, as if they felt them not. **1841–** in Cheshire and Shropshire glossaries.

**smaze** (smeɪz). [Blend of SMOKE *sb.* and HAZE *sb.*] A mixture of smoke and haze.

**1953** *Daily Progress* (Charlottesville, Va.) 21 Nov. 1/6 (*caption*) Manhattan skyscrapers look like misty dream-castles as a combination of smoke and haze drifts around them. Called 'smog' by most people, the smoke-haze combination might more aptly be termed 'smaze'. **1953** *N.Y. Times* 22 Nov. 1/1 From smaze and smog, the city got down to an old-fashioned ocean fog yesterday. **1958** *Manch. Guardian* 22 Nov. 4/4 Over seven million domestic chimneys emit at low level smoky particles and tarry substances which cause the urban 'haze' (or 'smaze') in industrial areas. **1960** *Daily Tel.* 16 Nov. 1/8 A Weather Bureau official described the condition as a kind of smog-like haze. 'Call it smaze,' he said. **1968** *Courier-Mail* (Brisbane) 3 July 3/7 That smoky, cloudy, dirty stuff that's been hanging around blurring the buildings of Brisbane these last few mornings is not *smog*, it's *smaze*.

†ˈ**smazky,** *a. Obs.*$^{-1}$ (Meaning obscure.)

**1599** MIDDLETON *Micro-cynicon* A 5, Auant,..Ile anger thee inough, And fold thy firy-eyes in thy smazkie snufe.

**smeach**, variant of SMEECH *sb.*

**smear** (smɪə(r)), *sb.* Forms: 1 **smeoru, -o, smeru, -o, -a,** 3–5 **smere** (4 **smer**), 7 **smeer,** 6–7 **smeare,** 8– **smear** (9 *techn.* **smeir**). [In sense 1 common Teutonic: OE. *smeoru, smeru*, etc., = OFris. *smere* (EFris. *smiri, smēr*, NFris. *smēr, smör*, WFris. *smoar*), MDu. *smere, smeer* (Du. *smeer*), and *smare, smaer*, OS. *smero* (MLG. *smere, smer*), OHG. *smero, smer* (MHG. *smer*, G. *schmer*) fat, grease, ON. *smjǫr* (Icel. *smjer*, Sw. *smör*, Da. and Norw. *smør*) butter:—OTeut. **smerwa* neut. The stem *smer-*, with different suffix, is represented in Goth. by *smairþr* neut., fat. Cognate forms outside of Teut. are Lith. *smarsas* fat, OIr. *smir* (Gael. *smior*) marrow, and perh. Gr. *μύρον* ointment. The later senses are mainly, if not entirely, f. the vb., like G. *schmiere*.

In OE. the *w* of the stem appears regularly in the genitive and dative *smeor(u)wes, -we, smer(e)wes, -we*, etc.]

†**1. a.** Fat, grease, lard; ointment. *Obs.*

*c* **725** *Corpus Gl.* U 257 *Unguentum*, smeoru. *c* **825** *Vesp. Ps.* xvi. 10 Smeoru his [hie] bilucun. *c* **1000** *Sax. Leechd.* I. 74 Cnuciȝe wið eald smeoru. *Ibid.* II. 68 Heorotes smera oþþe gate oþ þe gose. *c* **1200** ORMIN 13244 Nohht þurrh nan eorþliȝ smere, acc all þurrh Haliȝ Gastess sallfe. *c* **1250** *Gen. & Ex.* 1573 In heuene deu, and erðes smere, [Esau] Gatte him bliscing. *c* **1330** *Arth. & Merl.* 1306 (Kölbing), Newe schon þat man haþ bouȝt, .. And smere, to smere hem al about. **1398** TREVISA *Barth. De P.R.* IV. vii. (Tollem. MS.), þe fatnesse þerof .. is mad white and turnid in to talowe and smere. **1447** BOKENHAM *Lyvys Seyntys* (Roxb.) 78 Full of pyke rosen oyle and smere. *c* **1450** *M.E. Med. Bk.* (Heinrich) 201 Tak þe crotyng of a goot, & old smere of a red swyn. **1611** COTGR., *Oing*, (Hogs) grease, or seame; smeare. **1648** HEXHAM II, *Smeeren*, .. to Rub with Grease or Smeare.

†**b.** A 'company' *of* curriers. *Obs.*

*c* **1476** in *Hors, Shepe, & Ghoos* (Roxb.) 4 iv b, A Smere of coryers. **1486** *Bk. St. Albans* f vj b, A Smere of Coryouris.

†**2.** Smeared or dirty condition. *Obs.*$^{-1}$

**1600** *Hosp. Incurable Fooles* 79 Neither was he like a tinker in any thing, but only the smeare and collour of his beard.

**3. a.** A mark, smudge, or stain made by smearing, or suggestive of this; a layer or patch of some substance applied by smearing.

**1611** COTGRAVE, *Macheure*, a blacke .. smeare. **1793** HOLCROFT tr. *Lavater's Physiogr.* xliv. 225, I see through his disguise, as I should the hand of a great master through the smear of varnish. **1859** REEVE *Brittany* 50 As the figures were moving, no trace of them is seen [in the stereograph], except a light smear along the shops. **1865** DICKENS *Mut. Fr.* I. iii, Roof, and walls, and floor, alike abounding in old smears of flour, red-lead, and damp. **1888** RUTLEY *Rock-forming Min.* 25 The smears of balsam being ultimately cleaned off with a piece of rag or silk moistened with benzol.

*fig.* **1858** CARLYLE *Fredk. Gt.* VIII. iv. (1872) III. 20 Here is the unprecise but indubitable fact, as the Prussian Dryasdust has left us his smear of it.

**b.** A small quantity of some substance prepared for microscopical investigation by being smeared upon a slide, *esp.* a sample of human or other cells obtained without surgery; ***vaginal smear***, a smear of cells obtained from the vagina, studied to detect cervical cancer of the womb.

**1903** *Med. Record* 7 Feb. 209 Gonococci were demonstrated .. by smears only. **1904** *Brit. Med. Jrnl.* Sept. 599 A smear from the red marrow in the case appeared identical in character with the picture of the blood film. **1917** STOCKARD & PAPANICOLAOU in *Amer. Jrnl. Anat.* XXII. 227 In order to examine the vagina [of a guinea-pig] thoroughly we have introduced a small nasal speculum which facilitates clear view of the interior and a smear is made of any fluid that may be present. *Ibid.*, A study of the vaginal smears from guinea-pigs. **1920** *Proc. Nat. Conf. Social Work 1919* 58 Dr. Knight's plan of requiring a smear [for the detection of venereal disease] from every female child coming under their care would seem a wise precaution. **1925** *Jrnl. Amer. Med. Assoc.* 8 May 1422/2 The guinea-pig is a particularly suitable animal for such an investigation, on account of the regularity of its estrual cycle. The use of vaginal smear examinations makes it possible to detect the return of estrus in a very exact way. **1928** G. N. PAPANICOLAOU in *3rd Race Betterment Conf.* 530 In a case of benign tumor everything you find in a vaginal smear is more or less normal... In contrast to this, in .. cases .. of malignant tumors, there are some definite characteristic changes. **1943** —— *Diagnosis Uterine Cancer* vi. 34 Vaginal smears made after the operation continued to show the carcinoma cells in considerable numbers. **1958** Cervical smear [see PAPANICOLAOU]. **1966** *Listener* 4 Aug. 151/1 Cervical smear centres for the early diagnosis of womb cancer .. have .. been outstandingly successful. **1969**, etc. [see PAP *sb.*[4]]. **1975** *Nature* 9 Oct. 480/1 The presence of sperm cells in vaginal smears taken [from rats] the following morning was taken as positive indication of pregnancy.

**c.** A slanderous or defamatory remark; an attempt to defame by slander. *colloq.* (orig. *U.S.*).

**1943** *Sun* (Baltimore) 22 Oct. 8/3 'This is an outright smear,' Stromberg asserted. **1953** E. SIMON *Past Masters* IV. v. 256 Our only hope is to get some sort of official enquiry .. to scotch all the smears. **1958** *Spectator* 15 Aug. 225/2, I would have expected from Mr. Lehmann not that implied smear but approving pats on both our heads. **1959** *Listener* 25 June 1115/1, I became aware of a gentle campaign of smear. **1977** E. AMBLER *Send no More Roses* x. 246 There *is* the smear, and I'm the subject of it.

†**4.** *slang.* A painter; a plasterer. *Obs.*

*c* **1700** *Street Robberies Consider'd*, *Smeer*, a painter. **1725** *New Cant. Dict.*, *Smear*, a Painter, a Plaisterer, &c. **1785** GROSE *Dict. Vulgar T.*, *Smear*, a plaisterer.

**5. a.** An application for smearing sheep.

**1802** C. FINDLATER *Agric. Surv. Peebles* 190 *note*, He proposes a smear composed of butter, train oil, and turpentine. **1870** G. ARMATAGE *Every Man his own Cattle Doctor* 559 Arsenical dips and mercurial smears.

**b.** A product in the making of sugar.

**1843** G. R. PORTER *Sugar Cane* (ed. 2) 220 The wet heads are cut off and put into a large mould; these are called bastard heading or smear.

**c.** *Fishing.* (See quot.)

**1848** JOHNS *Week at Lizard* 241 Pollack are often attracted round the boat by what the fishermen call 'smear', that is, offal of fish and bilge-water, which they occasionally throw overboard.

**d.** *Pottery.* A mixture used for glazing.

**1875** KNIGHT *Dict. Mech.* 2220/1 *Smeir*, a semi-glaze on pottery; common salt added to an earthenware glaze. **1884** C. G. W. LOCK *Workshop Receipts* Ser. III. 221/1 'Smears' and 'flows' are glazes applied by volatilization. **1897** [see *semi-glaze*, SEMI- 7 j].

**6.** In *Jazz*, a short glissando; a slurring or sliding effect produced by a brass instrument, esp. a trombone.

**1926** [see PORTAMENTO]. **1944** *New Yorker* 1 July 29/2 Someone may advocate extending a note or cutting it off. The sax section may want to put an additional smear on it. **1959** M. T. WILLIAMS *Art of Jazz* (1960) iv. 36 Those devices that gave .. the illusion of smear and roughness to his tone.

**7.** *attrib.* and *Comb.*, as (sense 1) † ***smear-gavel*** (see GAVEL *sb.*[1]), ***-monger***; (sense 3 c) ***smear document***, ***interview***, ***job***, ***journalism***, ***merchant***, ***-monger***, ***process***, ***sheet***, ***story***; (sense 4 b) ***smear preparation***; **smear campaign**, a plan to discredit someone or something, or to destroy a reputation, by means of smears; † **smear-dock**, *Sc.* **-docken**, English Mercury; † **smear-gelt** (see quot.); **smear-glaze**, = 5 d; hence ***smear-glazed*** adj.; † **smear-nep**, bryony; **smear-shading**, a method of shading used in glass-painting; so ***smear-shadow***; **smear tactics**, the tactics used in a smear campaign; **smear test**, a test for cancer of the womb made by microscopic examination of a smear (see sense 3 b); **smear-word**, a word which in spite of its literal meaning is used to imply something derogatory.

**1938** *Sun* (Baltimore) 7 May 1/5 He called the Lobby Committee 'a snooping committee' which was engaged in 'a smear campaign', a campaign of 'terror and intimidation' against newspapers and magazines which dare to criticize activities of the New Deal. **1978** N. FREELING *Night Lords* vii. 31 We'll get accused of a smear campaign against Rolls-Royce cars. *c* **1325** *Gloss. W. de Bibbesw.* in Wright *Voc.* 162 *Mercurial*, smerowo[r]t (smerdocke). **1775** TIPPERMALLUCH *Receipts* 12 (Jam.), Rub the person over with the juice of Allgood (called in Latin Bonus Henricus, others call it the Smear-docken). **1940** *Sun* (Baltimore) 18 Oct. 22/6 This was the pamphlet attacked by Republicans as a 'smear document'. **1977** M. WALKER *National Front* vii. 183 Tyndall denied responsibility for the smear document. **13..** *Eng. Gilds* (1870) 359 Euerych sellere of grece and of smere and of talwȝ shal .. to þe kynge a peny, in þe name of smergauel. **1785** GROSE *Dict. Vulgar T.*, *Smear gelt*, a bribe. **1893** E. A. BARBER *Pottery & Porcelain of United States* vi. 82 Glaze, which in the kiln would vaporize and form a slight deposit on the ware, technically known as '*smear*' glaze. **1971** L. A. BOGER *Dict. World Pottery & Porcelain* 320/1 Smear glaze was a development following salt glaze and is frequently mistaken for it. **1963** *Times* 26 Jan. 11/7 The delicately smear-glazed porcelain more usually associated with small Victorian statuary and so suggestive of marble that it was known as parian ware. **1960** *New Statesman* 23 Jan. 96/1 But the elaborate smear interviews and paragraphs in Sydney were nobody's mistake, but just the boys obeying orders. **1970** E. AMBLER *Intercom Conspiracy* iii. 73 It was a smear job hashed up to discredit one or another of his clients' competitors. **1967** *Punch* 8 Feb. 190/2 This touched the muddiest depths of smear journalism, full of cheap sneers and nasty innuendo. **1963** *Times* 15 May 9/2 The finding on this point was a bitter disappointment to the smear merchants. **1297** *Placita coram Rege* m. 11 (1897) 65 Johannes le Smeremongere. **1304** in *Cal. Pat. Rolls 32 Edw. I*, 284 Ralph le Smermonger. **1967** *Punch* 8 Feb. 190/2, I read with great satisfaction the editorial .. on the smearmongers of the Press and other vehicles of opinion. *a* **1387** *Sinon. Barthol.* (Anecd. Oxon.) 43 *Viticella*, smernepe. **1904** *Brit. Med. Jrnl.* Sept. 602 Smear preparations were also made in order that the form of the individual cells might be more closely studied. **1958** *Times* 26 Feb. 9/5 Mr Gaitskell's intention was, I imagine, to minimize the value of the report and rob it of its influence .., another application of the now well-known 'smear' process. **1847** WINSTON *Hints Glass Painting* (1867) 284 A stipple shadow is .. always more transparent than a smear shadow of equal depth. **1848** —— *Glass Painting* (1865) 80 The first and oldest kind of shading may be called Smear shading, and the second Stipple shading. **1951** *Observer* 16 Dec. 7/4 He is instructed to dismiss five people .. accused by a smear-sheet of Communist sympathies. **1947** *New Statesman* 22 Nov. 404/3 The Garry Allighan affair has done great harm in confirming in the minds of thoughtless people the smear stories about politicians that are put about by people who are not thoughtless. **1955** 'E. C. R. LORAC' *Ask Policeman* v. 56 They didn't want the Sunday papers to write up Rosetta Towers as a smear story. **1945** *West Va. Rev.* Nov. 40/1 In recent years there has developed in his country a group of press agents who have adopted 'smear' tactics. **1974** *Times* 14 Feb. 22/3 In the old days they used to be called smear tactics but this year .. mini-Watergates. **1950** *Consumer Rep.* XV. 367/1 The smear test for uterine cancer is done by scraping tissue .. from the rear of the vagina. **1977** *Spare Rib* May 19/1 Yearly smear tests are important as they give early warning of a disease which takes 15 years to develop. **1938** I. GOLDBERG *Wonder of Words* xv. 298 The term *Bolshevik* .. becomes so encrusted with non-political significance that it loses any sharpness of outline .. and grows into what has been called 'a smear-word'—a word that takes on whatever emotional color the speaker may .. desire. **1961** *Twentieth Cent.* Jan. 87 'Philology', that smear-word among students everywhere.

**smear** (smɪə(r)), *v.* Forms: α. 1 **smirian** (**smiran**), 3 **smirien**, 4 **smyrie**. *Pa. t.* 1, 3 **smirede** (1 **-ide**), 4 **smired, smyrede**. *Pa. pple.* 3 **i-smiret**. β. 1 **smyrian** (**-iȝan**), 1–3 **smurien**. *Pa. pple.* 3 **i-smured**. γ. 1 **smerian**, 3 **smeorie**, 4 **smerie**; 3 **smeren**, 4–6 **smere** (4 **smer**), 6–7 **smeere**, *Sc.* **smeir**, 7 **smeer**; 6–7 **smeare**, 6– **smear**. *Pa. t.* 1–4 **smerede**, 3–4 **smered** (5 **-yd**), 4 **smerd**. *Pa. pple.* 2–3 **i-**, 2–4 **y-smered** (4 **-smerd**), 3, 6 **smered** (*Sc.* 6 **smerit, smeiret**). [Common Teutonic: OE. *smir-, smyr-, smerian* (also *smir-, smerwan*), f. *smeoru, smeru* SMEAR *sb.*, = OFris. **smera* (EFris. *smēre, smüri*, NFris. *smēr, smerri, smöre*, WFris. *smarre, †smerre*), MDu. *smeren, smieren, smaren* (Du. *smeren*), MLG. *smeren* (*schmärn, schmirn*), OHG. *smirwan* (MHG. *smirwen, smirn*, G. *schmieren, †schmeren*), ON. *smyrva, -ja* (MSw. *smyrja, smöria*, Sw. *smörja*; MDa. *smørie*, Da. *smøre*).]

**1.** *trans.* To anoint with oil, chrism, etc., as a symbolic ceremony. In later use only with contemptuous force.

*c* **825** *Vesp. Ps.* lxxxviii. 21 In ele halȝum minum ic smirede hine. *c* **1250** *Gen. & Exod.* 2457 Cristene folc .. ben smered ðor quiles he liuen, Wið crisme and olie. **1297** R. GLOUC. (Rolls) 9377 Vr lige louerd þat yeled is, & ismered to Ihesu Crist. *a* **1300** *Cursor M.* 7377 Vn-to king þou sal him smer. **1340** *Ayenb.* 93 Of þise oyle byeþ ysmered þo þet god heþ ymad kynges and lhordes of þe wordle. **1550** CROWLEY *Inform. & Petit.* Sel. Wks. (1872) 154 So long as ydle bealies may come to the bishope and be smered for money. **1823** SCOTT *Quentin D.* xxx, What will be left to the descendant .. of Charlemagne, .. save to be smeared with oil at Rheims, and to eat their dinner under a high canopy?

*fig.* *c* **825** *Vesp. Ps.* xliv. 8 Smirede ðec god .. mid ele blisse. *a* **1200** *Vices & Virt.* 33 For ði haueð ðin lauerd ismered þe mid ða ele of blisse.

**2. a.** To anoint, to rub or daub (a part of the body) with oil, grease, or some similar preparation. Said also of the oil, etc. In later use with suggestion of sense 4.

*c* **825** *Vesp. Ps.* cxl. 5 Ele .. synfulles ne smireð heafud min. **971** *Blickling Hom.* 69 Maria ȝenam an pund deorwyrþre smerenesse, & smerede þæs Hælendes fet. *c* **1000** *Ags. Gosp.* Matt. vi. 17 Þonne ðu fæste, smyra þin heafod, and þweah þine ansyne. *c* **1175** *Lamb. Hom.* 53 Alswa doð monie of þas wimmen heo smurieð heom mid blanchet, þet is þes deofles sape. *c* **1305** *Judas Iscariot* 126 in *E.E.P.* (1862) 110 Wiþ þis swete oignement heo smired oure louerd þer. *c* **1315** SHOREHAM I. 374 For oyle smereþ þane champion, Þat me ne schel him festne. **1697** DRYDEN *Virg. Georg.* II. 775 The Groom .. stript for Wrestling, smears his Limbs with Oyl. **1717** PRIOR *Alma* II. 454 The Indian Fair Is nicely smear'd with Fat of Bear. **1772–84** *Cook's Voy.* (1790) I. 33 Their .. foreheads .. being generally smeared with brown and red paints. **1865** LIVINGSTONE *Zambesi* xi. 231 Their foreheads were smeared with white flour. **1885** CLODD *Myths* I. vi. 105 They smear themselves with black paint in memory of that tradition.

*fig.* **971** *Blickling Hom.* 73 Ȝif we nu willaþ ure saula smerian mid mildheortnesse ele. *a* **1225** *Ancr. R.* 244 Beoden smurieð him mid swete oluhnunge, auh teares prikieð him.

†**b.** To prepare (a dead body) with unguents before burial. *Obs.*

*c* **950** *Lindisf. Gosp.* Mark xiv. 8 [Hia] forecuom to smiriane [*Rushw.* smiranne, *Cp.* smyrianne, *Hatt.* smeriene] lichoma min on bebyrȝennise. *c* **1055** *Byrhtferth's Handboc* in *Anglia* VIII. 299 Mid þam man smyrað ricra manna lic. *a* **1225** *Ancr. R.* 372 Nicodemus brohte smuriles uorte smurien mide ure Louerd. *c* **1250** *Gen. & Ex.* 2442 Iosep dede hise lich .. Wassen, and riche-like smeren.

**3. a.** To anoint medicinally; to treat (a wound, etc.) with a copious application of some thick or greasy medicament.

*c* **950** *Lindisf. Gosp.* John ix. 11 Monn .. lam worhte & smiride eȝo mino. *c* **1000** *Sax. Leechd.* III. 114 Smure þæt sar ȝelomelice mid. *c* **1175** *Lamb. Hom.* 79 An helendis Mon .. wesch his wunden mid wine and smerede mid oli. *a* **1225** *Leg. Kath.* 1600 Þe engles wið smirles of aromaz smireden hire wunden. *a* **1290** *S. Eng. Leg.* I. 277 He let is heued of-smyte, and smeorie [*Harl.* smyrede] him with is blod. *a* **1300** *Cursor M.* 13547 Wit þis vn-to þe erth he spitt, .. And smerd þar-wit his oþer ei. **14..** *Sir Beues* 3857 + 16 (MS. C.), [He] smeryd hur with oyntment. **1807** *Med. Jrnl.* XVII. 446 Mischief must extend, although the injured parts be smeared with turpentine. **1843** R. J. GRAVES *Syst. Clin. Med.* xxvi. 331 We were in the habit of smearing it [*sc.* the skin] with zinc ointment for several days successively. **1863** W. C. BALDWIN *Afr. Hunting* vii. 269 We smear him with grease and gunpowder in lieu of sulphur.

*fig.* *a* **1290** *S. Eng. Leg.* I. 7 And bringue with him þe eoyle of milce .. to smeorie þare-with and bringe of pine þine fader and alle his.

**b.** To rub (sheep) with a mixture fitted to keep wet out of the fleece and prevent disease or vermin.

*c* **1395** *Plowman's Tale* III. i. (Thynne, 1542), Ne Christes apostels were never so bold No such lordshippes to hem enbrace; But smeren hir sheep and kepe hir fold. **1561** A. SCOTT *Poems* (S.T.S.) i. 94 Sic sanctitude was Sathanis sorcereis, Christis sillie scheip and sobir flok to smeir. **1684** [see SMEARED *ppl. a.* 2]. **1796** *Statist. Acc. Scotl.* XVIII. 570 In .. November the whole stock is smeared; a practice which .. is found to be .. beneficial. **1844** H. STEPHENS *Bk. Farm* III. 1115 When the skin of sheep is covered with such substances they are said to be *smeared*. **1884** L. F. ALLEN *New Amer. Farm Bk.* 439 Smearing, or salving sheep, is a custom little practiced in this country.

**4. a.** To spread, daub, cover thickly or in patches, *with* some unctuous, greasy, sticky, or dirty substance. Sometimes said of the substance. Also rarely with *in*.

(*a*) **971** *Blickling Hom.* 73 þæt næfre ne afulaþ þæt mid hire ȝesmered biþ. *c* **1200** ORMIN 994 Bulltedd bræd..smeredd wel wiþþ elesæw. *c* **1330** *Arth. & Merl.* 599 (Kölbing), Were ȝour werk ysmerd þer wiþ, Euer it wold stond in griþ. **1340** *Ayenb.* 60 Hy smerieþ þane way of helle mid hony. *a* **1450** *Knt. de la Tour* (1868) 68 The fende alweye wolde smere her in the face with the brennynge piche, grese, oyle, lede, and terre. *a* **1529** SKELTON *E. Rummyng* 88 Her shone smered wyth talowe. **1555** EDEN *Decades* (Arb.) 196 These they smere or annoint with the pytche of molten Bitumen. **1614** GORGES *Lucan* IV. 161 All their bits were smeared ore With dusty dryed frothy gore. **1667** MILTON *P.L.* XI. 727 A Vessel of huge bulk..Smeard round with Pitch. **1744** BERKELEY *Siris* §9 Stems of trees, smeared over with tar, are preserved thereby from being hurt by..goats. **1774** GOLDSM. *Nat. Hist.* (1776) IV. 123 The unctuous substance with which it is smeared. **1818** SCOTT *Br. Lamm.* xxxiv, The fatal weapon was found in the chamber, smeared with blood. **1877** BLACK *Green Past.* i, I don't suppose he smears his hands with treacle.

(*b*) **1592** *Arden of Feversham* V. i, Sweete Arden, smeard in bloode and filthy gore. **1607** SHAKS. *Cor.* I. vi. 69 If any such be heere..that loue this painting Wherein you see me smear'd. **1807** J. BARLOW *Columb.* V. 204 His troops..smear their paths in blood.

**b.** Without const.

*a* **1225** *Ancr. R.* 378 He strecchеð him touward us ase þing þet is ismured. **13..** *Seuyn Sages* 1151 (W.), In ech [hole] he pelt a dosele, And smerede the holes al aboute. **1398** TREVISA *Barth. De P.R.* V. xxvi. (Bodl. MS.), Men vseth to smere þe iointe of an Elephant to dry þe better. **1531** TINDALE *Exp. 1 John* (1537) 82 One..had nede of greace to grease shues or smeere bootes. **1602** MARSTON *Antonio's Rev.* IV. iii, Let him feed on slime That smeares the dungeon cheeke. **1634** SIR T. HERBERT *Trav.* (1638) 302 Other Temples have other Pagods;..some of them are painted or smeered black; others red. **1763** CHURCHILL *Proph. Fam.* Poems 1767 I. 90 Slugs, pinched with hunger, smear'd the slimy wall. **1805–6** CARY *Dante, Inf.* XXI. 8 Tenacious pitch, to smear Their unsound vessels. **1900** *Daily News* 4 June 6/2 The youngsters were smeared to the eyes.

**c.** *fig.* (*a*) Chiefly const. *with*, and usually implying something base or discreditable; (*b*) (without const.), to attempt to discredit (a reputation, etc.) (*colloq.*, orig. *U.S.*).

**1549** COVERDALE, etc. *Erasm. Par. Jas.* II. 37 Why are you smeared with the vaine pleasures of this world? **1596** DALRYMPLE tr. *Leslie's Hist. Scot.* (S.T.S.) I. 296 Sche smeiris baith his mynd and eires with thir wordes. **1598** BARKCLEY *Felic. Man* (1631) 171 Happi's the man..whom glory does not smeere With lying drosse. **1602** MARSTON *Antonio's Rev.* II. iii, If the least soyle of lust smeers my pure love. **1652** BENLOWES *Theoph.* XIII. lvii. 243 After Nights soot smears Heav'n, day gilds its face. **1847** HELPS *Friends in C.* I. iv. 63 People smearing each other over the stupid flattery. **1879** 'E. GARRETT' *Ho. by Works* II. 165 She would not smear his memory by any falsehoods now. **1936** W. IRWIN *Propaganda & News* xxii. 292 When the Republicans began calling this line of attack the 'smear Hoover' campaign, Michelson..faced the microphone with a masterpiece of ingenious invective. **1945** G. ENDORE *Methinks the Lady* xi. 268 You had plenty of time..to hold up the jury while you smeared the science of psychoanalysis. **1948** *Manch. Guardian Weekly* 23 Sept. 9 He is afraid of being smeared. **1951** *Here & Now* (N.Z.) May 23/2 Mary Jane Keeny has been a target for the red-baiters who from time to time try to smear the UN as a Communist-dominated organisation. **1966** *Listener* 30 June 934/2 What the successors are trying to do seems to me not so much to prove particular corruption as to smear the previous regime. **1978** G. MCDONALD *Fletch's Fortune* (1979) xix. 130 Is the campaign against me going to continue? Are the March newspapers going to continue to smear me?

**d.** *techn.* To glaze (pottery) by a process of evaporation.

**1839** URE *Dict. Arts* 1019 The operation called *smearing*, consists in giving an external lustre to the unglazed semi-vitrified ware. **1893** *Handbk. Brit. Pottery & Porc.* (Mus. Pract. Geol.) 58 Certain compositions may also be placed in the bottom of the closed saggers, and by their evaporation the ware in them may be smeared or semi-glazed.

**e.** In Southern Africa, to coat over (the floor of a hut, etc.) with a mixture of cow-dung and water.

**1839** W. C. HARRIS *Wild Sports S. Afr.* xvii. 143 The space was smeared with a mixture of mud and cow-dung, resembling that used in all parts of India for similar purposes. **1878**, **1880** [see DAGGA[2]]. **1893** BLENNERHASSETT & SLEEMAN *Adv. Mashonaland* ii. 32 We were unsuited physically for such work as 'daghering' huts or 'smearing floors'.

**5.** To lay *on* in a thick or greasy layer.

*a* **1300** *Cursor M.* 6077 þis lamb blod..On aider post þer hus to smer. **1595** DUNCAN *App. Etym.* (E.D.S.), *Illino, illinio*, to smeir on. **1847** WINSTON *Hints Glass Painting* (1867) 284 A coat of enamel brown smeared smoothly and evenly on the glass. **1888** RUTLEY *Rock-forming Min.* 23 The [slab] of lead or cast-iron, on which rather, but not very, coarse emery is smeared with water. **1899** *Allbutt's Syst. Med.* VII. 550 If some of the exudation from the brain be smeared on these media.

**6. a.** To rub *out* with a smear or smudge; to rub or draw in a smeary manner.

**1840** DICKENS *Old C. Shop* iii, If he did by accident form a letter properly, he immediately smeared it out again with his arm. **1848** —— *Dombey* iii, You go a smearing your wet face against the expensive mourning that Mrs. Richards is a wearing for your ma. **1854** W. COLLINS *Hide & Seek* III. viii. 231 They seemed to get smeared out of my head—like we used to smear old sums off our slates at school. **1865** DICKENS *Mut. Fr.* IV. xv, Smearing his sleeve across his mouth. **1920** 'K. MANSFIELD' *Bliss & Other Stories* 73 And then there is the waiter... When he is not smearing over the table or flicking at a dead fly or two, he stands with one hand on the back of a chair. **1964** W. GOLDING *Spire* ii. 37 One delver relaxed, and smeared a hand over his sweaty face. *Ibid.* viii. 155 He peered in [a metal sheet] closer and closer until his breath dimmed his own image and he had to smear it off with his sleeve.

**b.** To thrash or kill; to wipe out or destroy by bombing. *slang.*

**1935** A. J. POLLOCK *Underworld Speaks* 109/1 *Smear*, to kill. **1941** BAKER *Dict. Austral. Slang* 68 *To smear someone*, to thrash a person in a bout of fisticuffs. **1944** *Amer. Speech* XIX. 187 He [*sc.* S. J. Baker] gives examples of Australian argot, of which several follow:..*smear*, to murder, [etc.]. **1957** P. FRANK *Seven Days to Never* ix. 245 We can smear every base, every industrial complex, once and for all. **1958** P. BRYANT *Two Hours to Doom* 43 The report on the..Russian I.C.B.M. site had removed his..doubt..whether his bombers could smear it before the missiles were fired off.

**smear-case.** *U.S.* Also **smearcase.** [ad. G. *schmierkäse* (Du. *smeerkaas*), f. *schmieren* to smear + *käse* cheese.] (See quot. 1848.)

**1829** A. ROYALL *Pennsylvania* I. 471 A dish, common amongst the Germans,..is curds and cream. It is very palatable, and called by the Germans *smearcase*. **1848** BARTLETT *Dict. Amer.* 314 *Smear-case*, a preparation of milk made to be spread on bread, whence its name; otherwise called Cottage-cheese. **1893** *Atlantic Monthly* Feb. 231/1 The man held a knife-load of smear-case in front of his mouth. **1934** *Sun* (Baltimore) 21 July 4/7 Under the seat in the old wagon two jars of smearcase. **1978** *Amer. Speech* LIII. 201 The 'miscellaneous' category includes..*clabber cheese* (but more commonly *cottage cheese, Dutch cheese, smear-case*).

**smear-dab.** [? f. SMEAR *sb.* or *v.*: see quot. 1882.] A variety of dab, also called lemon or smooth dab.

**1769** PENNANT *Brit. Zool.* III. 189 The Smear-Dab, *Rhombus lævis. Ibid.*, We found one of this species at a fish-monger's in London last winter, where it is known by the name of the smear-dab. **1836** YARRELL *Brit. Fishes* II. 221 *Platessa microcephalus*, Smear Dab. **1864** COUCH *Brit. Fishes* III. 188 The Smear Dab in comparison with the Common Dab is a larger and thicker fish. **1882** DAY *Fishes Gt. Brit.* II. 29 Smear-dab, due to its being frequently covered with slime.

**smeared** (smɪəd), *ppl. a.* [f. SMEAR *v.* + -ED[1].]

**1.** In contemptuous use: Anointed.

**1550** BALE *Apol.* 17 The popes Smered presthod. **1554** HILARIE *Resurr. Masse* A viij, My smered Chaplens..I make them to be called Syrs euery one. **1583** STUBBES *Anat. Abus.* (1882) II. 70 Being a greasie priest, and smered prelate.

**2. a.** Dirtied or soiled by smearing; bedaubed.

**1584–7** GREENE *Carde of Fancie* Wks. (Grosart) IV. 62 Pasiphæ preferred a Bull before a King, and Venus a smeered Smith before Mars the God of battaile. **1621** G. SANDYS *Ovid's Met.* v. (1626) 92 Nor could he fall; but..Hung by the hand against the smeared post. **1684** SYMSON *Descr. Galloway* (1823) 72 The most part of their laid-wool, call'd in other parts smear'd wool, is..so called, because..they melt butter and tar together, and therewith they..smear their sheep. **1795** in Robertson *Agric. Perth* (1799) 533 The smeared kind at 7s. or 8s. per stone; and their white wool from 8s. to 10s. **1840** BARRET *Water Colour Painting* 16 While the smeared part is being cleaned with India-rubber. **1865** DICKENS *Mut. Fr.* II. xv, Holding out his smeared hand.

**b.** *smeared dagger*, a species of moth.

**1883** W. SAUNDERS *Insects Inj. Fruits* 325 The Smeared Dagger, *Apatella oblinita*... This peculiarity being partly obliterated in this species, it has received the common name of the 'smeared dagger'.

**3. a.** Laid on in a smearing manner.

**1820** KEATS *Isabella* li, The smeared loam With tears, as chilly as a dripping well, She drench'd away.

**b.** *smeared out*: spread out, distributed; averaged over a volume of space or a period of time.

**1931** *Nature* 8 Aug. 211/1 It can be represented..by supposing each electron to move in the field of the nucleus and the other electrons, representing it by the 'smeared out' continuous distribution which the solution of the wave equation gives, and then taking the electron atmosphere to be the sum of these distributions. **1977** *New Scientist* 21 Apr. 120/2 By measuring their extinction properties at a single wavelength we could show that the smeared-out density of dust grains is a few per cent of the density of all matter in interstellar space. **1979** *Nature* 18 Jan. 188/1 This behaviour..will be completely smeared out at experimental temperatures. **1979** *Sci. Amer.* Nov. 128/1 A wave function ..often describes the electron as if it were smeared out over a large region of space.

**smearer** (ˈsmɪərə(r)). [f. SMEAR *v.* + -ER[1].] One who smears.

**1632** SHERWOOD, A smearer, *patrouilleur*. **1881** *Instruct. Census Clerks* (1885) 78 Fur Dyeing... Smearer. Grounder. **1884** *United Presbyt. Mag.* Apr. 156 He was to maintain the smearers of the sheep. **1955** E. POUND *Classic Anthol.* II. 117 Take therefore, I say, these smearers And fellow travellers, chuck 'em To wolves and tigers. **1960** *Guardian* 7 Oct. 9/2 A common trick is for a smearer to..tell..drinkers that a candidate is a teetotaller.

**ˈsmeariness.** [f. SMEARY *a.* + -NESS.] The condition or character of being smeared or smeary.

**1866** COCKAYNE *Sax. Leechd.* III. 345/1 Neither of these plants [smearwort and smeardock] have any smeariness about them. **1901** *Daily Chron.* 14 June 7/5 There is a general smeariness, a want of proper and thorough cleaning.

**smearing** (ˈsmɪərɪŋ), *vbl. sb.* [f. SMEAR *v.* + -ING[1].] **1.** The action or process of anointing, daubing, etc., with some unctuous substance; a substance used for this purpose; a layer of ointment, paint, etc., smeared on.

*c* **1000** in Assmann *Ags. Hom.* xvi. 36 Æniȝ þing..on smyrunge oððe on wyrtum..þæt ðu myhtest myne wunde myd ȝehælan. *c* **1000** *Sax. Leechd.* II. 174 Balzaman smiring wiþ eallum untrumnessum. **1340** *Ayenb.* 148 He ssel þerto do þe smeringes and þe plastres of zuete waringges. **1398** TREVISA *Barth. De P.R.* V. xxvi. (Bodl. MS), Þe cure is resting and smering by somme vnguementes. **1611** COTGR., *Linition*, a smearing, annointing,..rubbing. **1668** WILKINS *Real Char.* 247 Smearing, daubing. *c* **1790** IMISON *School Arts* II. 54 Lay a piece of clean paper upon it, to prevent smearing. **1805** R. W. DICKSON *Pract. Agric.* II. 1154 They are collected together,..in order to undergo the operation of smearing or salving. **1853** KANE *Grinnell Exped.* xxxvi. (1856) 326 A smearing of red sealing-wax. **1893** *Handbk. Brit. Pottery & Porc.* (Mus. Pract. Geol.) 58 Smearing..is produced by the evaporation, or volatilisation, of certain glazes in closed saggers. **1893** [see DAGGA[2]]. **1948** E. ROSENTHAL *African Switzerland* iii. 34 Smearing..is a Basuto custom. You may have noticed that all the native huts are covered on the outside with a layer of mud, and this again is worked into all kinds of pretty and complicated patterns. That is smearing.

*attrib.* **1814** SCOTT *Wav.* xlv, The hovel..seemed to be intended for what is called, in the pastoral counties of Scotland, a *smearing-house*. **1844** H. STEPHENS *Bk. Farm* III. 1117 The sheep should be laid on the smearing-stool. **1875** *Encycl. Brit.* I. 397 The smearing material is a salve composed of tar and butter. **1940** G. SELDES *Witch Hunt* p. xiii, But surely there ought to be some resort to the American spirit of fair play in combating underhanded smearing campaigns.

**2.** In *Jazz*, the production of a smear or glissando.

**1934** S. R. NELSON *All about Jazz* ii. 61 The subtle slurring and smearing of to-day would have astonished some of the early players. **1952** B. ULANOV *Hist. Jazz in Amer.* (1958) vi. 66 Filhe..contrasted his low-register looping and smearing with Bab Frank.

**smearing** (ˈsmɪərɪŋ), *ppl. a.* [f. SMEAR *v.* + -ING[2].] **a.** In *Jazz*, pertaining to a smear or slurring effect. **b.** Slanderous.

**1958** P. GAMMOND *Decca Bk. of Jazz* iv. 57 The smearing, broad glissandi of Christian's trombone. *a* **1974** R. CROSSMAN *Diaries* (1976) II. 627 We also have to overcome something else—the stream of anti-government propaganda, smearing, snarky, derisive, which comes out of Fleet Street.

**ˈsmearless,** *a.* [f. SMEAR *sb.*] Free from smears; not smeary.

**1885** SPON *Mech. Own Book* (1893) 461 The surface..is smearless, hard, and brilliant.

†**smearwort.** *Obs.* Forms: 1 smeoru-, smerowyrt, 4 smerowo(r)t, 5 smerw(o)rt, smerewourt. [OE. *smeoruwyrt* (see SMEAR *sb.* and WORT *sb.*), = MDu. *smere-, smeerworte* (Du. *smeerwortel*), MHG. *smerwurz* (G. *schmeerwurz, schmerwurz*).] One or more plants of doubtful identity (see quots.).

*c* **725** *Corpus Gloss.* U 98 *Ueneria*, smeoruwyrt. *c* **1000** *Sax. Leechd.* I. 114 Ðeos wyrt þe man aristolochiam, & oðrum naman smerowyrt nemneð. *c* **1325** [see SMEAR *sb.* 7]. **14..** *Lat.-Eng. Voc.* in Wr.-Wülcker 565 *Aristologia*, Smerwort. *Ibid.* 596 *Mintuosa*, Smerwort. *a* **1400–50** *Stockholm Med. MS.* fol. 203 Mercurie or papwourtz or þe more smerewourt: *mercurialis*. *c* **1450** *Alphita* (Anecd. Oxon.) 193 *Unctuosa*,..selhele *uel* smerwrt.

**smeary** (ˈsmɪərɪ), *a.* Also 6 smery, smearye, 6–7 smeerie, smearie. [f. SMEAR *sb.* or *v.* Cf. NFris. *smēri, smörig*, WFris. *smoarrich, smoarch*, MDu. *smerich* (Du. *smerig*), MLG. *smerich* (LG. *smerig*, G. dial. *schmêrig*, G. *schmierig*), MSw. *smörug* (Sw. *smörjig*), MDa. *smørugh, -ig*.]

**1.** Marked or characterized by smears; showing smears or dirty marks; bedaubed, begrimed.

*a* **1529** SKELTON *Ware the Hawke* 324 Masyd, wytles, smery smyth, Hampar with your hammer vpon thy styth. **1582** STANYHURST *Æneis* III. (Arb.) 78 You shal be so gaunted in hunger, That youre smeary tabils you wyl most greedelye swallow. **1625** PURCHAS *Pilgrims* II. 1769 The said place being all black, smeerie, and foule therewith. **1844** THACKERAY in *Fraser's Mag.* XXIX. 710 The Wilkie-like pictures of Mr. Fraser, with their peculiar smeary manner. **1861** DICKENS *Gt. Expect.* xliii, A smeary newspaper long out of date. **1883** D. C. MURRAY *Hearts* I. 226 A crying woman whose eyes were actually growing smeary whilst she wept.

**2.** Tending to smear or soil; of a greasy or unctuous nature.

**1582** STANYHURST *Æneis* Ded. (Arb.) 9 That bast theyre papers with smearie larde sauoring al too geather of thee frying pan. **1597** A. M. tr. *Guillemeau's Fr. Chirurg.* 35 b/1 Her sweat is fattye, axungiouse, and smearye. **1683** MOXON *Mech. Exerc., Printing* xi. ¶23 Trane-Oyl..[makes the ink] dull, smeary and unpleasant to the Eye. **1708** ROWE *Royal Convert* III, A smeary foam works o'er my grinding jaws. **1718** —— *Lucan's Pharasalia* III. 1015 The smeary Wax the bright'ning Blaze supplies. **1757** tr. *Henckel's Pyritologia* 317 If again exposed to the air, it becomes smeary, moist, and fluid. **1816** W. SMITH *Strata Identified* 9 Mouldering when dry; smeary when wet. **1899** *Allbutt's Syst. Med.* VIII. 252 A good housekeeper who does not like to set her butter on the table in a smeary state, keeps it in summer on ice.

†**smeat,** *a. Obs.* [OE. *smǽte*, of obscure origin.] Of gold: Refined, pure.

*c* **725** *Corpus Gloss.* O 24 *Obrizum*, smaetegold. *a* **900** *O.E. Martyrol.* 27 Dec. 8 Hie wurdan sona to þam golde þe man hateð *abritsum*, þæt is smæte gold. *a* **1122** *O.E. Chron.* (Laud MS.) an. 1070, þe kynehelm..eall of smeate golde. *a* **1200** *St. Marher.* 11 Guldene ȝerde alre gold smeatest. *a* **1225** *Leg. Kath.* 1655 Glistinde & gleaminde, as hit were seoluer oðer gold smeate.

**smeath** (smiːθ). *local.* Also 7 **smieth,** 7, 9 **smethe,** 9 **smeeth.** [Obscurely related to SMEE.]

**1.** The smee. Also ***smeeth duck***.

**1622** DRAYTON *Poly-olb.* xxv. 67 The gossander..With whom the widgeon goes, the golden-eye, the smeath. **1634** BRERETON *Trav.* (Chetham Soc.) 17 Two pellstarts, two smeathes, two shovelars. *Ibid.* 23 Smeathes he keeps in a hut ..covered with a net. **1674** JOSSELYN *Voy. New Engl.* 101 But of Ducks there be many more sorts, as..Puets, Plovers, Smethes, Wilmotes [etc.]. **1893** COZENS-HARDY *Broad Norf.* 47 *Smee*—Widgeon, Smeeth Duck.

**2.** *U.S.* In New Jersey: The pintail duck.

**1888** G. TRUMBULL *Names & Portr. Birds* 38 Others refer to it as Smethe.

†**Smec(k,** abbrev. forms of *Smectymnuus*: see SMECTYMNUAN.

**1663** BUTLER *Hud.* I. iii. 1166 The Handkerchief about the neck Canonical Crabat of Smeck. **1664** *Ibid.* II. ii. 524 Remember how..We..New-modell'd th' Army, and Cashier'd All that to Legion Smec adher'd.

**smec(c)he,** obs. forms of SMATCH *v.*

**smech(e,** obs. forms of SMEECH *sb.*

**smeck,** var. SCHMECK.

**'smectic,** *a.* (and *sb.*) [ad. L. *smēcticus* (Pliny), ad. Gr. σμηκτικός, f. σμήχειν to wipe, cleanse; cf. SMEGMA.] **1.** Cleansing, abstersive, detergent. *rare.*

**1675** EVELYN *Terra* (1676) 40 Smooth to the touch, as the most Smectic Earths and Marles themselves. **1686** PLOT *Staffordsh.* 124 The Smectic and Figuline Earths. **1858** MAYNE *Expos. Lex., Smecticus*, cleaning;..smectic.

**2.** *Physical Chem.* Applied to (the state of) a mesophase (a liquid crystal) in which the molecules all have the same orientation and are arranged in well-defined planes. Also as *sb.*, a smectic substance. Cf. NEMATIC *a.* [ad. F. *smectique* (G. Friedel 1922, in *Ann. de Physique* XVIII. 276).]

**1923** [see NEMATIC *a.*]. **1936** *Mineral. Abstr.* VI. 237 In addition to the fuller's earths and smectic clays the series includes montmorillonite, confolensite, [etc.]. **1940** GLASSTONE *Text-bk. Physical Chem.* vii. 505 In the smectic state normal liquid flow does not occur: the movement is of a gliding nature, in one plane. **1971** *New Scientist* 14 Jan. 63/2 Once the smectic mesophase had formed, the continuous or 'closed' bimolecular sheets would isolate the aqueous compartments from their neighbours. **1974** *Nature* 25 Jan. 178/3 As yet uncategorised smectics probably exist, for example, the smectic phase of 4′-n-octyl-4-cyanobiphenyl described by Gray.

‖**'smectis.** *rare.* [ad. Gr. σμηκτίς, a kind of fuller's earth.] (See quots. and next.)

**1706** PHILLIPS (ed. Kersey), *Smectis*,..Fullers-Earth. **1783** *Phil. Trans.* LXXIII. 227 It feels like hard soap, or rather like that kind of stone which the mineralogists call *Smectis.* **1794** SULLIVAN *View Nature* II, How is a clay to be distinguished from the smectis or soap-rock? **1905** *Oban Advertiser* 19 Aug. 3 By different authors, the 'lapis nephriticus' has been considered as an agate, a jasper, a gypsum, and a smectis.

**smectite** ('smɛktaɪt). *Min.* [See prec. and -ITE[1] 2 b.] **a.** A kind of fuller's earth. Now *Obs.* exc. *Hist.*

**1811** J. PINKERTON *Petral.* I. 278 [Iconite contains] a combination which nearly corresponds with the smectite of Cimolus. **1868** WATTS *Dict. Chem., Smectite*, a term.. applied..more particularly to an argillaceous mineral from Cilly in Lower Styria,..and another from Condé in France. **1932** *Amer. Mineralogist* XVII. 198 It seems hardly worth while to retain the two names smectite and montmorillonite for what appears to be the same mineral... It seems in the best interests of science to continue the name montmorillonite, and to drop that of smectite. **1942** *Ibid.* XXVII. 810 The differential thermal curve for the smectite sample..is like that of montmorillonite... This is in agreement with Kerr's..conclusion [*prec. quot.*] that smectite is not a valid species because of its similarity to montmorillonite.

**b.** = MONTMORILLONOID. So ***smectite group*** = ***montmorillonite group*** s.v. MONTMORILLONITE b.

**1955** G. BROWN in *Clay Minerals Bull.* II. 296 *Smectites* is the name proposed for the minerals at present variously known as montmorillonoids, montmorins, minerals of the montmorillonite group and frequently even montmorillonites. Smectites are defined as minerals composed of 2:1 or triphormic layers, which, when the readily exchangeable cations are replaced by $Na^+$ and the material is saturated with glycerol, give a basal spacing of 18Å approximately. **1957** R. GREENE-KELLY in R. C. Mackenzie *Differential Thermal Investigation of Clays* v. 140 By far the most abundant dioctahedral smectite is montmorillonite. **1966** [see MONTMORILLONITE a]. **1975** *Amer. Mineralogist* LX. 66/1 The significant chemical and physical properties of smectites often depend on the nature of the interlayer exchange ions. **1979** *Sci. Amer.* Apr. 78/1 (*caption*) Smectite group of clay minerals, formerly called the montmorillonite group, has extremely fine-grained, irregular and thin-layered crystals.

†**Smectymnist,** obs. variant of next.

**1648** E. SYMMONS *Vind. Chas. I* Pref., He then, and the Smectymnists since, and Pim after them, took great pains.

**Smectymnuan** (smɛk'tɪmnjuːən), *sb.* and *a.* [f. *Smectymnuus* (-*vvs*), a fictitious name made out of the initials of the five authors of *An Answer to a Book*, etc. (1641).

The writers thus indicated were Stephen Marshall, Edmund Calamy, Thomas Young, Matthew Newcomen, and William Spurstow. The book was written as a reply from the Presbyterian side to Bishop Hall's *Humble Remonstrance.*]

**A.** *sb.* One or other of the authors of the work published under the name of Smectymnuus; also, one who accepted the views of these writers.

**1646** BP. MAXWELL *Burden Issachar* 56 A sufficient evidence, to evince this truth against the Smectymnuans. **1656** BLOUNT *Glossogr.* s.v., From thence they and their Followers were called Smectymnuans. **1733** NEAL *Hist. Purit.* II. 400 The Smectymnuans admit that our blessed Saviour taught his disciples a form of prayer. **1874** MASSON *Milton* I. p. xxx, There were other pamphlets, of retort and rejoinder, between Hall and the Smectymnuans, in all of which Milton advised and assisted the five Smectymnuans.

**B.** *adj.* Pertaining to, connected with, or characteristic of the Smectymnuans.

**1673** S. PARKER *Reproof Reh. Transp.* 182 How little.. sufficiently appears..by the great Smectymnuan labours. **1678** *Pol. Ballads* (Wilkins, 1860) I. 205, I would as soon turn back to mass..As buckle to Smectymnuan laws. **1882–3** SCHAFF *Encycl. Relig. Knowl.* II. 1417 He was one of the chiefs in the Smectymnuan Controversy with Bishop Hall in 1641. **1883** *Encycl. Brit.* XVI. 329/1 The famous Smectymnuan pamphlet in reply to Hall was mainly Young's.

**smeddum** ('smɛdəm). Forms: 1 **smeodoma, -uma** (**smetuma** ?), **smed(e)ma, smidema,** 8 **smedim, smeadum,** 8–9 **smeddum** (9 **-am**). [OE., of obscure origin.]

**1.** A fine powder; *esp.* fine flour. (For other late examples see SMITHAM.)

*c* **725** *Corpus Gloss.* P 497 *Polenta*, smeodoma. *a* **900** *Leiden Gloss.* 74 *Simila*, smetuma. *c* **1000** *Sax. Leechd.* I. 258 Ðemin ðas wyrte butan wyrttruman, cnuca mid smedman. *Ibid.* II. 132 Ðenim acrinde, & driȝe, & wirc to smedman. **1808** JAMIESON, *Smeddum*, the powder or finest part of ground malt; also called *malt smeddum.*

**b.** A powder used for medical purposes, or as a vermin-killer.

**1786** BURNS *To a Louse* v, O for some rank, mercurial rozet, Or fell, red smeddum. **1828** *Examiner* 35/1 We cannot touch precious ointment without scenting of smeddam.

**c.** *Mining.* = SMITHAM 2.

**1853** URE *Dict. Arts* (ed. 4) II. 37 'Undressed smeddum,' being what has passed through the sieve of the hotching-tub. *Ibid.*, 'Smeddum,' after being dressed or cleared from all foreign substances.

**2.** *Sc.* Spirit, pith, 'go'; alertness of mind and vigour in action; energy.

**1790** D. MORISON *Poems* 4 He has nae smeadum. **1791** LEARMONT *Poems* 215 A guidly band Did smedim shaw on ilka strand. **1821** GALT *Ann. Parish* xxx, Lacking somewhat of that birr and smeddum that is the juice and flavour of books of that sort. **1837** R. NICOLL *Poems* (1843) 129, I was fairly tongue-tied; For I had na the smeddum to chide her. **1897** CROCKETT *Lads' Love* iii, He had been harmlessly expending all the pith and smeddum of his blows upon a.. bolster.

**smedy,** obs. Sc. variant of SMITHY *sb.*

**smee**[1] (smiː). *dial.* and *U.S.* [Prob. a later form of SMEATH. It is not clear how either form is related to early mod.Du. *smeente* (Du. *smient*), LG. *smênt* widgeon, G. *schmi-*, *schmü-*, *schmeiente* a small wild duck.]

**1.** A name variously assigned to the smew, widgeon, pochard, and scaup-duck.

**1668** CHARLETON *Onomast.* 100 *Boscas Mergens*, the Diving Widgeon; *in Norfolcia*, the Smee. **1889** H. SAUNDERS *Brit. Birds* 463 The Smew, or Smee—sometimes called Nun ..is the smallest member of the genus. **1893** [see SMEATH 1].

**b.** ***smee-duck***, a pochard.

**1862** JOHNS *Brit. Birds* 516 On some parts of the coast of Norfolk I found that they are included with the Wigeon under the common name of 'Smee-Duck'.

**2.** *U.S.* In New Jersey: = SMEATH 2.

**1888** G. TRUMBULL *Names & Portr. Birds* 38.

**Smee**[2] (smiː). The name of Alfred *Smee* (1818–1877), English surgeon and experimenter, used *attrib.* and in the possessive to designate an obsolete type of primary cell or battery he invented (*Phil. Mag.* (1840) XVI. 315), consisting of zinc and platinum (or platinized silver) electrodes in dilute sulphuric acid.

**1852** F. S. WILLIAMS *Iron Roads* 314 Great inconvenience arose from the spilling of the acid solution used in Smee's batteries. **1873** F. JENKIN *Electr. & Magnetism* xv. 215 The Smee battery is better than the copper zinc battery. **1950** G. W. VINAL *Primary Batteries* i. 16 Smee's cell of 1840 avoided..the difficulty experienced with polarization in other single-fluid batteries. *Ibid.*, The electromotive force of the Smee cell was low, about 0·5 volt, which was its principal disadvantage.

**smeech** (smiːtʃ), *sb.* Now *dial.* Forms: 1–2 **smec,** 2–4 **smech,** 3–4 **smeche,** 9 **smeech, smeach.** [OE. *sméc*, variant of *smíc*, *smýc* (see SMITCH *sb.*), from the stem of *sméocan* SMEEK *v.* For the equivalent northern forms see SMEEK *sb.*] Smoke; dense or thick vapour, etc. Also in fig. context.

Also in mod. south-western dial. 'fine dust', 'stench', etc.: see the *Eng. Dial. Dict.*

*c* **825** *Vesp. Hymns* xii. 11 Clæne ȝeleafa coelende slepes smec ȝemetȝie. *c* **888** K. ÆLFRED *Boeth.* xxvii. §3 Hi losiað swa swa sceadu oððe smec. *c* **1000** *Ags. Ps.* (Thorpe) ci. 3 Daȝas mine ȝedroren syndan, smece ȝelice. *a* **1200** *Moral Ode* in *O.E. Hom.* I. 177 Eure þer is vuel smech, þusternesse and eie. *c* **1250** *Old Kent. Serm.* in *O.E. Misc.* 28 We mowe sigge þet stor signefieth þe herte, and se smech luue of gode. *c* **1315** SHOREHAM III. 192 Þou ert a sot, and myȝt do bet, Ans so siȝst yn þe smeche. **1340** *Ayenb.* 66 Al alsuo huanne me alyȝt þet uer, lhapþ þet smech efter þe layt.

**1847** HALLIW., *Smeech*,..obscurity in the air, arising from smoke, fog, or dust. *South and West.* **1875** M. G. PEARSE *D. Quorm* 38 A faggot o' green furse 'pon the fire..fillin' the house with smeach and smoke. **1886** ELWORTHY *W. Somerset Word-bk.* 684 Your bakehouse chimley do make such a smeech.

**smeech,** *v.* Now *dial.* Also 9 **smeetch, smeechy.** [f. prec.]

**1.** *trans.* To blacken or soil with smoke. ? *Obs.*

**1611** COTGR., *Patrouiller*, to smeech, begrime,.. besmeere.

**2.** *intr.* To send off smoke, vapour, or the like; to smoke.

**1837–** in south-western dialects.

**3.** *trans.* To perfume or scent.

**1897** F. T. JANE *Lordship* xxvii, The hawthorn smeetched the air all round.

Hence **'smeecher; smeeching** *vbl. sb.*

**1611** COTGR., *Patrouilleur*, a smeecher, begrimer, besmearer. *Ibid.*, *Patrouillement*, a smeeching, begriming, besmearing. **1907** *Sci. Amer.* Suppl. 5 Oct. 210 (Cent. Dict. Suppl.), While the kiln is in operation, the escape of the arsenic fumes can be detected here and there in the form of little jets, which the workmen describe as 'smeeching'.

**smeek,** *sb.* Latterly *Sc.* and †*north.* Forms: α. 2–5 **smeke,** 3 **smec,** 4 **smek,** 5–6 **smeik,** 5, 8– **smeek.** β. 2–4 **smike,** 5 **smyk(e.** [The more northern forms representing OE. *sméc* and *smíc*, *smýc*: see SMEECH *sb.* and SMITCH *sb.*[1]]

**1.** Smoke arising from burning or smouldering matter; reek. Also in fig. context.

Also in mod. Sc. use, 'a strong or foul smell'.

α. *c* **1200** ORMIN 1088 Þær wass swa mikell smec Off recless att tatt allterr. *c* **1250** *Moral Ode* 9 in *E.E.P.* (1862) 22 Ne myht ic isen be-fore me for smeke ne for myste. *c* **1325** *Metr. Hom.* 104 Rekeles..gifs smek that smelles wele, And fer men mai the smek fele. **1382** WYCLIF *Exod.* xix. 18 The smeek steyde vp of it as of a furneys. **1412–20** LYDG. *Chron. Troy* I. 191 But inwarde brent of hate..The hoote fyre, & ȝit ther was no smeke. *c* **1440** *Pallad. on Husb.* VII. 69 Yf the smeke Perpetuel vppon their dwellyng reke. *c* **1590** MONTGOMERIE *Sonn.* xxv. 2, I grein to sie the sillie smiddy smeik. *a* **1774** FERGUSSON *Farmer's Ingle* Poems (1845) 35 Heathery truffs the chimney fill And gar their thickening smeek salute the lift. **1785** BURNS *Vision* iii, The spewing reek, That fill'd, wi' hoast-provoking smeek, The auld clay biggin. **1874** W. ALLAN *Hame-Spun Lilts* 160 Wi' smeek, I thocht they'd baith been smored.

β. *a* **1200** *Moral Ode* in *O.E. Hom.* I. 161 Ne michte ich seon bi-fore me for smike ne for miste. *a* **1300** *Cursor M.* 2742 Þe smike it reches to þe scki. *c* **1440** *Pallad. on Husb.* XI. 362 Let vessel hit, & sette hit vp in smyke. *c* **1460** *Promp. Parv.* (Winch.) 459 Smore with smyk, *fumigo.*

**b.** In *pl.* Also in fig. context.

*a* **1200** *Vices & Virt.* 129 Hwanene cumeð manies kennes smekes of unþolemodnesse. *c* **1400** *Sc. Trojan War* II. 856 With quhilk birnyng now it reikis, As wele apperis by þe smeikis. *c* **1420** *Avow. Arth.* xv, So nyȝe discumford was hee, For smelle other smekis.

**2.** *attrib.* and *Comb.*, as ***smeek-house***; ***-like*** adj.

*a* **1200** *Vices & Virt.* 129 Ðe þu wunest on ðe smec-huse of ðine likame. *a* **1400** *Stockh. Med. MS.* ii. 951 in *Anglia* XVIII. 330 Dun-red is his flour, þe erbe smek lik in colour.

**smeek,** *v.* Latterly *Sc.* and †*north.* Forms: 1 **smeocan,** 2 **smeken,** 5 **smekyn;** 3–4 **smeke,** 9 **smeak, smeik,** 9– **smeek.** [OE. *sméocan* str. vb. (pa. t. *sméac*), = MDu. *smieken* (rare), G. dial. *smiechen*, related by ablaut to OE. *smocian* SMOKE *v.* and to MDu. *smōken*, G. *schmauchen.* Perh. also partly repr. OE. *smécan*, *smícan*: cf. prec.]

**1.** *intr.* To emit smoke; to reek; to send out or give off steam or vapour. Also in fig. context.

*a* **1000** *Gloss.* in Wr.-Wülcker 244 *Fumigabunt*, smeocaþ. *c* **1000** ÆLFRIC *Exod.* xix. 18 Eall Sinai munt smeac [L. *fumabat*]. *c* **1000** *Sax. Leechd.* I. 338 Heortes mearh ȝebærned oð þæt hyt smeoce. *c* **1325** *Prose Ps.* ciii. 32 Þe which toucheþ þe mounteyns, and hij shul smoken [*v.r.* smeke]. **1412–20** LYDG. *Chron. Troy* I. 4380 For hatred olde to brenne can nat lete With newe flawme..; ȝif it nat smeke, it is þe more to drede. *c* **1440** *Promp. Parv.* 460/2 Smekyn, or smokyn, *fumo, fumigo. Ibid.*, Smekyn, or smokyn as hote lycure, *vaporo.*

**2.** *trans.* To apply smoke or fumes to, esp. in order to cleanse, cure, dry, etc.; to fumigate.

*c* **1000** *Sax. Leechd.* I. 352 Wið cyrnla sare, smeoc þone man mid gate hærum. *c* **1375** *Sc. Leg. Saints* xlix. (*Thecla*) 111 Þe fire þat ves dycht to bryne me, to brule & smeke. **1808** JAMIESON, *Smeik, Smeek*, to dry by smoke. **1815** *Pennecuik's Tweeddale* 90 *note*, Smeeking our heads o'er the fire a' winter. **1882** *Jamieson's Sc. Dict.* IV. 303/1 *To smeek fish*, i.e. to cure them. *Ibid.* 303/2 To smeek yarn, to smeek the room.

**b.** To suffocate (bees), to drive out (an animal), by means of smoke.

**1816** SCOTT *Bl. Dwarf* xviii, Elshie's skeps o' bees.. shall ne'er be smeekit by ony o' huz. **1821** —— *Pirate* xxxv, My bees were as dead as if they had been smeaked. **1882** J. WALKER *Jaunt to Auld Reekie* 219 Smeek in his hole the snoozing badger.

†**3.** To scent with incense; to cense. *Obs.*⁻¹

**1382** WYCLIF *Ecclus.* xxiv. 21 And as torax, and galban, and vngula,.. I smekede my dwelling; and as balsame not mengd is my smel.

Hence **smeeked**, **'smeeking** *ppl. adjs.*

*c* **1000** *Ags. Gosp.* Matt. xii. 20 Smeocende [*Hatt.* smekende] flex he ne adwæscþ. **13..** in *Reliq. Antiq.* I. 240 Swarte smekyd smethes smateryd with smoke.

**'smeeky**, *a. Sc.* Also 6 smeikie, 9 smeekie. [f. SMEEK *sb.* + -Y.] Emitting, full of, filled with, smoke; smoky.

*c* **1590** MONTGOMERIE *Sonn.* xxx. 13 The smeikie smeithis cairs not his passit trauel. **1811** A. SCOTT *Poems* 144 (Jam.), Thro' smeekie flame they him addrest. *a* **1837** R. NICOLL *Poems* (1843) 96 (E.D.D.), The smeeky hames o' our toun.

**smeetch**, dial. variant of SMEECH *v.*

**smeeth** (smiːθ, smiːð), *a.* and *sb. Obs.* exc. *dial.* Forms: 1 **smoeðe**, 1–3 **smeðe**, 2–4 **smeþe**, 4–5 **smethe, smeth** (4 **smith**), 9 *dial.* **smeeth, smeath, smeede, smee.** [OE. *smœ́ðe, sméðe* (:—**smōþi-*), related to *smóð* SMOOTH *a.*, which is rare in OE. but from *c* 1400 has almost entirely supplanted *smeeth.*]

**A.** *adj.* Smooth; free from roughness.

*c* **725** *Corpus Gloss.* P 511 *Politis*, smoeðum. *c* **825** *Vesp. Hymns* xii. 7 Ðec stefn smoeðu hlydeð. *c* **950** *Lindisf. Gosp.* John xix. 23 Cyrtil unruh *vel* smoeðe. *c* **1000** *Ags. Gosp.* Luke iii. 5 Unȝerydu [beoð] on smeðe weȝas. *c* **1200** *Trin. Coll. Hom.* 219 þat he [a rod] he riht and smal and long and smeþe. *a* **1225** *Ancr. R.* 2 þe on riwleð þe heorte, þe makeð hire efne & smeðe. *a* **1300** *Cursor M.* 3490 þe first was born was rogh as hare, þe toþer child was smeth and bare. **1398** TREVISA *Barth. De P.R.* v. xxxv. (Bodl. MS.), þe flessch of þe lunges is nassche and smeþe. *c* **1420** *Liber Cocorum* (1862) 47 Thou hit sethe With otene grotes, þat ben so smethe. **1808** JAMIESON s.v., *Smeeth in the mou*, a phrase applied to a horse that has lost mark of mouth. **1878** DICKINSON *Cumbld. Gloss.* 89/2 *Smeeth, Smee*, smooth. **1894** HESLOP *Northumbld. Gloss.* 661 *Smeede, Smeeth*, smooth... This often occurs in place-names.

**B.** *sb.* A level space. *E. Anglian dial.*

*c* **1440** *Promp. Parv.* 460/2 Smethe, or smothe,.. *planicies.* *a* **1825** FORBY *Voc. E. Anglia*, *Smeath*, an open level of considerable extent. [*Rye* (1895) *adds*, commonly pronounced and printed *Smee.*] **1893** COZENS-HARDY *Broad Norf.* 70 *Smeaa*—used for marshland, as 'Down by the carnser and over the smeaa'.

**smeeth** (smiːð), *v. Obs.* exc. *dial.* Forms: 1 **smeðian, smeðan,** 2 **smeþien,** 3 **smeðen,** 4–5 **smeþe,** 4–6 **smethe,** 8 **smeath,** 9 **smeeth.** [OE. *smeðian* and *sméðan*, f. *smeðe* SMEETH *a.*] *trans.* To make smooth. Also *absol.*

*c* **1000** *Sax. Leechd.* II. 210 Ærest him is to sellanne þæt þone innoð stille & smeþe. *a* **1100** in Napier *O.E. Glosses* 47/2 *Salebrosos complanans anfractus*, woȝe smeþiende hylcas. *c* **1175** *Lamb. Hom.* 31 He wile seggen and foxliche smeþien mid worde, Nabbe ic nawiht þer-of. *a* **1225** *Ancr. R.* 4 Rihten hire & smeðen hire is of euch religiun.. al þe strengðe. *c* **1230** *Hali Meid.* 27 Ah Ichulle scheawen hit al wið falschipe ismeðet. **1398** TREVISA *Barth. De P.R.* XVII. lvii. (Bodl. MS.), Enula.. haþ vertu to plane and to smethe ..and to comforte senewes. *Ibid.* XIX. xlv, Bitter þinges.. bi ..drynes.. beþ made smeþinge & softinge. **1788** W. H. MARSHALL *Yorks.* II. 353. **1829** BROCKETT *N.C. Gloss.* (ed. 2), *Smeeth*, to smooth. **1886** HOLLAND *Chester Gloss.*, *Smeeth*, to iron linen. **1894** HESLOP *Northumbld. Gloss.* 661 *Smeeth* (the *th* as in *seethe*), to smooth.

**'smeethly**, *adv.* ? *Obs.* Also 3 **smeðeliche,** 4 **smeþelyche, -lich, -ly,** 4 **smetheliche,** 5 *Sc.* **smeth(e)ly.** [f. SMEETH *a.* + -LY².] Smoothly.

*a* **1225** *Leg. Kath.* 356 þeos meiden.. smirkinde smeðeliche ȝef him þullich onswere. **13..** *Gaw. & Gr. Kt.* 1789 Smeþely con he smyle. **1387** TREVISA *Higden* (Rolls) VII. 259 þe kyng excused hym self smeþeliche. *c* **1425** WYNTOUN *Cron.* VIII. 5072 (Wemyss), And he, as bourdand, said smethly: 'Man, will þov haif of me iusting' [etc.]. **1808** in JAMIESON.

**'smeethness.** ? *Obs.* Also 1 **smeðnysse,** **smeþnys,** 4 **smeþe-,** 4–5 **smethenes.** [f. SMEETH *a.*] Smoothness.

*c* **1000** ÆLFRIC *Hom.* I. 26 He forȝeaf.. hreoflium smeðnysse. *c* **1050** *Suppl. Ælfric's Voc.* in Wr.-Wülcker 177 *Planities*, smeþnys. **1388** WYCLIF *1 Kings* vi. 18 And al the hows.. hadde hise smethenessis, and hise ioynyngis maad suteli. **1398** TREVISA *Barth. De P.R.* v. xxvii. (Bodl. MS.), þe same bones.. meue þe more spedefullich by smeþenes and softenes. *c* **1470** *Promp. Parv.* (K.) 460/2 Smethenes, *planicies.* **1825** JAMIESON *Suppl.*, *Smeethness*, smoothness, Clydes[dale].

‖**smegma** ('smɛgmə). *Phys.* [L. *smēgma*, a. Gr. σμῆγμα a detergent, soap, or unguent, f. σμήχειν: cf. SMECTIC *a.*] A sebaceous secretion, *esp.* that found under the prepuce.

Phillips (ed. Kersey), Bailey, etc., give '*Smegma*, soap, or any thing that scours; a wash-ball', but there is no evidence that the word was ever current in English in these senses.

**1819** *Pantologia* X, *Smegma*,.. soap; any concrete substance resembling it, as the hardened matter often found, in the morning, on the lachrymal caruncle. **1876** DUHRING *Dis. Skin* 108 In the newly-born infant, the smegma serves a valuable physiological function. **1899** tr. *Jaksch's Clin. Diagnosis* viii. (ed. 4) 407 The microbe of smegma readily loses its colour under the action of that substance.

†**smeg'matic**, *sb.* and *a. Obs.* Also 7 **smegmatick**(e. [ad. mod.L. *smegmatic-us*, f. Gr. σμῆγμα, σμήγματ-: see prec.]

**A.** *sb.* Anything that cleanses; a cleanser, a detergent.

**1623** COCKERAM I, *Smegmaticke*, any thing hauing the power to cleanse and scoure as Sope doth. **1695** J. EDWARDS *Perfect. Script.* 192 Smegmaticks, munditiers, cleansers, adorners, are useful.

**B.** *adj.* Detergent; abstersive.

**1656** BLOUNT *Glossogr.*, *Smegmatic*, that hath the power or strength to scoure or cleanse, as soap. **1658** PHILLIPS, *Smegmatick*, belonging to Soap, of a scouring faculty. **1675** EVELYN *Terra* (1676) 23 Bolus's, Rubrics, and Okers, Figuline, Stiptic, Smegmatic, &c. **1710** T. FULLER *Pharm. Extemp.* 344 Smegmatic Pills.

†**smeigh**, *a. Obs.*⁻¹ [Early ME. *smēgh*, related to OE. *sméaȝan* to consider.] Clever, cunning. Hence †**'smeighly** *adv.*; †**'smeighness,** wisdom, skill.

*c* **1200** *Trin. Coll. Hom.* 195 Ðe man.. þat is smegh oðer man to bicharren, and to bi-swiken. *Ibid.* 71 Gif it was erfeð to forðen, and smeihliche bicharede. *Ibid.* 205 þat clene.. kinde þat god haueð þer-on broht þureh his smehnesse.

†**smeke**, *v. Obs. rare.* [a. MDu. or MLG. *smêken* (OHG. *smeichan*, G. *schmeichen*, etc.).] *intr.* To flatter, fawn. Hence †**'smeking** *vbl. sb.*

*c* **1440** *Promp. Parv.* 460/2 Smekynge, or mevyn wythe plesaunte tokenys. *Ibid.* 476/1 Styryn, or mevyn wythe plesaunte tokenys, þat ys clepyd smekynge, *blandior.* **1481** CAXTON *Reynard* (Arb.) 91 They flatre and smeke, and plese the prynce for theyr synguler auayl.

**smelite** ('smiːlaɪt). *Min.* [f. Gr. σμήλη soap + -ITE¹ 2 b. Named by E. F. Glocker, 1845.] = KAOLINITE.

**1850** ANSTED *Elem. Geol., Min.*, etc. 188 The following are, also, hydrous silicates of alumina—Pholerite,.. Gröppite, and Smelite. **1868** WATTS *Dict. Chem.*, *Smelite*, an aluminic silicate from Telkebanya in Hungary.

**smell** (smɛl), *sb.* Forms: α. 2–7 **smel** (3 **smeal,** 4 **smeol**), 3–6 **smelle,** 4– **smell.** β. 2–4 **smul,** 4 **smil,** **smyl,** 5–6 **smyll.** [Related to SMELL *v.* The OE. equivalent is *stenc* STENCH.]

**1.** The sense of which the nose is the organ; the faculty of smelling. Now usually in ***sense, organ***, etc., ***of smell.***

(*a*) *c* **1200** *Trin Coll. Hom.* 183 Hie.. binimeð þe eien here sene,.. muð here smel. *a* **1225** *Ancr. R.* 104 Smel of neose is þe ueorðe of þe vif wittes. **1567** MAPLET *Gr. Forest* 106 He is not onely of most swift pace, but also of smell. **1599** DAVIES *Immort. Soul* XVII. i. (1714) 72 In the Nostrils she doth use the Smell. **1617** MORYSON *Itin.* III. 35 He who hath a quicke smell, is troubled with more stinkes, then he is refreshed with sweet odours. **1697** DRYDEN *Virg. Georg.* IV. 44 Wild Thyme and Sav'ry.. Sweet to the Taste, and fragrant to the Smell. **1712–3** SWIFT *Jrnl. to Stella* 3 Jan., I have no smell yet, but my cold something better. **1774** GOLDSM. *Nat. Hist.* (1776) III. 317 He stops to examine, by his smell,.. the emanations that may come either from his enemy or his prey. **1805** A. DUNCAN *Mar. Chron.* III. 145 A certain brackish flavor, offensive both to the taste and smell. **1899** *Allbutt's Syst. Med.* VII. 324 Smell was impaired on the side of the lesion.

(*b*) **1710** J. CLARKE tr. *Rohault's Nat. Philos.* (1729) I. 179 The Power of exciting the Sensation of Smell in us. **1851** CARPENTER *Man. Phys.* (ed. 2) 549 The lower Mammalia, in which the organ of smell is highly developed. **1872** HUXLEY *Physiol.* viii. 194 The organ of the sense of smell is the delicate mucous membrane which lines a part of the nasal cavities. **1900** POLLOK & THOM *Sports Burma* ii. 40 Elephants have a very keen sense of smell.

**2. a.** That property of things which affects the olfactory organ, whether agreeably or otherwise; odour, perfume, aroma; stench, stink.

α. *a* **1175** *Lamb. Hom.* 53 þurh þe sweote smel of þe chese he bicherreð monie mus to þe stoke. *c* **1220** *Bestiary* 747 in *O.E. Misc.*, Ut of his ðrote cumeð a smel. *a* **1225** *Leg. Kath.* 1588 Swiðe swote smeal com anan þrefter. *a* **1300** *Cursor M.* 1014 Flours þar es wit suete smelles. *c* **1380** WYCLIF *Sel. Wks.* II. 114 þe hous was fillid of smel of þe oynement. *c* **1400** MAUNDEV. (Roxb.) xviii. 84 þe water chaungez diuersely his sauour and his smell. *c* **1440** *Alph. Tales* 96 Sownd of watir rynyng, & syngyng of burdis, and gude smell of flowris. **1508** DUNBAR *Tua Mariit Wemen* 33 Fragrant, all full of fresche odour fynest of smell. **1579** LYLY *Euphues* (Arb.) 90 Muske though it be sweet in ye smel, is sowre in the smacke. **1617** MORYSON *Itin.* I. 5 The streets are broad, but very filthy and full of ill smels. **1667** MILTON *P.L.* v. 379 The Silvan Lodge.. that like Pomona's Arbour smil'd With flourets dec't and fragrant smells. **1747** *Tricks of Town laid open* (ed. 3) 19 He's distinguishable from the rest of his Species, both by his Smell, Garb, Shape and Aspect. **1774** GOLDSM. *Nat. Hist.* (1776) II. 184 As smells are often rendered agreeable by habit, so also tastes may be. **1847** HELPS *Friends in C.* I. iii. 33 There was such a rich smell of pines. **1885** *Law Times* LXXIX. 74/2 There was a nasty smell about the premises.

β. *c* **1200** *Trin. Coll. Hom.* 99 On þe holi fleis bileueð þe shap and hiu and smul of ouelete, and on þe holi blod hew and smul of win. *c* **1290** *S. Eng. Leg.* I. 8 A suote smul þare cam of heom þat smelde in-to al þat lond. **1297** R. GLOUC. (Rolls) 1009 Hii deieþ þoru smul of þe lond. **1387** TREVISA *Higden* (Rolls) IV. 137 þe smyl þerof slouȝ boþe bestes and foules. **1475** *Bk. Noblesse* (Roxb.) 70 The herbers of so soote smyllis.

**b.** An aromatic substance, or the use of this. *rare.*

*a* **1533** LD. BERNERS *Golden Bk. M. Aurel.* (1535) Dd ij b, The vices that they brought [from Asia] to Rome:.. The patritiens bearyng Measques, the Plebeyens usynge smelles. **1697** *Phil. Trans.* XIX. 480 All Methods of Cure in the Paroxysm [of apoplexy], are ridiculous and useless, except Smells, and Blooding in the Jugular.

**3.** *fig.* **a.** A trace, suggestion, or tinge *of* something. Also without article, or with adj. Hence, the special, indefinable, or subtle character of the object, event, etc., described.

*c* **1475** HENRYSON *Orpheus & Eurydice* 25 Off forebearis thay tuke tarage and smell. **1542** UDALL *Erasm. Apoph.* 140 This saiyng hath scacely any smelle or sauour of Diogenes, although he beareth the name of it. **1576** FLEMING *Panopl. Epist.* 151 To haue a smack and smel of auncient Latium. **1617** HIERON *Wks.* 129 There is with Thee not so much as any smell or shadow of iniustice. *a* **1688** BUNYAN *Saints' Privilege* Wks. 1855 I. 669 Without the least smell or tang of imperfection. **1702** S. SEWALL *Diary* (1882) III. 398 Mrs. Thacher.. troubled at her Marriage to Mr. Kemp,.. some smell of Relation between them. **1882** *Nature* XXVI. 59 The methods have a German 'smell'. **1948** 'N. SHUTE' *No Highway* ii. 38 Fifteen years in the aircraft industry... One gets to know the smell of things like this. **1974** J. THOMSON *Long Revenge* iii. 40 The smell of the case had come back to him.. and he had the feeling that there was a great deal more to it.

**b.** That quality by which anything is felt or suspected to be near at hand.

**1691** J. NORRIS *Pract. Disc.* 36 They.. won't so much as come within the Smell of Danger. **1865** KINGSLEY *Herew.* xxx, My spirit likes the smell of gold as well as yours. **1973** *Times* 19 Dec. 14/7 Things are looking up: there is a smell of success in the air. **1981** *Listener* 2 July 3/1 There's a smell of success: people really think they can shift governments.

**4.** An act of smelling; a sniff. Also *fig.*

*c* **1560** INGELEND *Disobedient Child* (Percy Soc.) 16 He hath of knaverye tooke such a smell. *Ibid.* 45 After that I had taken a smell Of their good wyll and fervent love. **1706** E. WARD *Wooden World Diss.* (1708) 16 So many hundred poor Souls, that would reckon it a Blessing to have but one savory Smell at his Flesh-pots. **1817** SCOTT *Let.* in Lockhart (1837) IV. ii. 66 What do you think Constable would give for a smell of it? **1878** J. S. CAMPION *On Frontier* (ed. 2) 25 The winner gets a drink and the losers a smell at the cork of the bottle.

**5.** *attrib.*, as ***smell-reach, -sense***; **smell fox**, the wood anemone, *Anemone nemorosa*; **smell-trap**, a trap to intercept and carry off bad smells.

*a* **1652** BROME *Mad Couple well matched* IV. i, Out of the smell-reach of your Lord's perfum'd gloves. **1851** KINGSLEY *Yeast* vi, Among high art and painted glass, spade farms, and model smell-traps. **1887** *Pall Mall G.* 10 Aug. 5/1 A guardian affected by anosmia, or absence of the smell-sense. **1892** C. M. YONGE *Old Woman's Outlook in Hampshire Village* 49 The beloved *Anemone nemorosa*—the wind-flower —or, as the village children unpoetically call it, 'smell foxes'. **1898** —— *John Keble's Parishes* xv. 172 Smellfox, anemone. **1931** M. GRIEVE *Mod. Herbal* I. 34 Anemone (Wood).. Synonyms. Crowfoot, Windflower, Smell Fox.

**smell** (smɛl), *v.* Forms: α. 3–5 **smellen** (5 **-yn**), 3 **smeallen;** 2–6 **smelle,** 4–7 **smel,** 4– **smell.** *Pa. t.* 4–6 **smelde** (4 **smeld**), 5– **smelled** (6 *Sc.* **smellit**), 6– **smelt.** *Pa. pple.* 3 **i-smelled,** 3, 6– **smelled,** 5 **-id,** 7– **smelt.** β. 2–4 **smullen,** 4 **smille,** 4–5 **smylle.** *Pa. t.* 4 **smulde, smilde.** [Early ME. *smellen* and *smüllen*, no doubt of OE. origin, but not recorded, and not represented in any of the cognate languages.

In the pa. t. and pa. pple. both *smelled* and *smelt* are in use, but the latter is now the more frequent of the two in British English.]

**I.** *trans.* **1. a.** To have perception of (an object, odour, etc.) by means of the olfactory sense.

***to smell powder***: see POWDER *sb.*¹ 3 b.

*c* **1175** *Lamb. Hom.* 153 Hwenne þe nose bið open to smelle unlofne breð. *a* **1240** *Ureisun* in *O.E. Hom.* I. 189 Of al þet ich abbe.. wið neose ismelled. *a* **1300** *Cursor M.* 23456 (Edin.), In þis lif hauis man gret liking.. Swet speceri to thef and smel. *c* **1350** *Leg. Rood* (1871) 57 Anon þer com so swete a smul.. þat al hit smulde wiþ gret Ioye þat in þe cuntre weren þere. *c* **1489** CAXTON *Sonnes of Aymon* xvi. 372 Whan mawgis had passed over the water bayard smelled hym & began to crye. **1509** HAWES *Past. Pleas.* XXIV. (Percy Soc.) 109 The nose, also, every ayre doth smel. **1589** NASHE *M. Marprelate* Wks. (Grosart) I. 80 As good a Hound for his sent to smell a feast as euer man sawe. **1611** BIBLE *Tobit* viii. 3 The which smell, when the euill spirit had smelled, hee fled into.. Egypt. **1691** tr. *Emilianne's Observ. Journ. Naples* 89 The Mole, it seems,.. no sooner had smelt the Oar, but crept into another Hole near to it. **1779** G. KEATE *Sketches fr. Nat.* (ed. 2) II. 209 Paris may be smelt five miles before you arrive at it. **1784** COWPER *Tiroc.* 830 Civeted fellows, smelt ere they are seen. **1833** M. SCOTT *Tom Cringle* iii, A boy, who had seldom smelt powder fired in anger before. **1860** DICKENS *Uncomm. Trav.* xvii, I can smell the heavy resinous incense as I pass the church.

**b.** To inhale the odour or scent of (a thing); to sniff at; to examine in this way.

**1830** G. CRUIKSHANK *Gentl. in Black* i. (1831) 5 'Confound this head-ache.'.. 'Pshaw! pshaw! smell this bottle,' said the stranger. **1845** *Encycl. Metrop.* XXV. 241/1 To smell each other's head or neck is the only mode of salutation practised. **1886** C. E. PASCOE *Lond. of To-day* xl. (ed. 3) 343 They import from Paris.. flowers so natural that one is tempted to smell them.

**2. a.** To perceive as if by smell; *esp.* to detect, discern, or discover by natural shrewdness, sagacity, or instinct; to suspect, to have an inkling of, to divine.

***to smell the ground***, of ships: see GROUND *sb.* 2 b.

*c* **1380** WYCLIF *Wks.* (1880) 216 Men schullen in spirit smelle þe swettenesse & þe holynesse of iesu crist & his lif. **1382** —— *Job* xxxix. 25 Aferr he smellith bataile. *a* **1548**

HALL *Chron., Hen. VI*, 136 b, He secretly smelled, that some men priuely disdained his aduancement. *a* **1553** UDALL *Royster D.* II. iii, If I beginne first, he will smell all my purpose. **1635** PAGITT *Christianogr.* II. vi. (1636) 61 Lest the Lay people should smell their Idolatrie. **1668** PEPYS *Diary* 30 Aug., Lord Brouncker,..I perceive, and the rest, do smell that it comes from me, but dare not find fault with me. **1712** ARBUTHNOT *John Bull* (1727) 56 We were overjoyed.. not smelling what was at bottom of the plot. **1798** WOLCOT (P. Pindar) *Tales of the Hoy* Wks. 1812 IV. 408 The people never smelt the cheat. **1837** CARLYLE *Fr. Rev.* I. III. vii, A victorious Parlement smells new danger. **1885** A. B. ELLIS *W. African Isl.* xi. 267 The reverend father at once smelt a miracle.

**b.** ***to smell a rat***: see RAT *sb.*[1] 2 a.

**3.** To search or find *out* by, or as by, the sense of smell. Chiefly *fig.*

**1538** BALE *Three Laws* III, And hast thou so longe dyssembled thus with me. *Infidelitas.* Yea, for aduauntage, to smell out your subtylyte. **1579** E. K. *Gloss. to Spenser's Sheph. Cal.* June 25 They woulde..smell out the vntruth. **1629** WADSWORTH *Pilgr.* viii. 84 Smelling vs out to be English, [they] made vs rise out of our beds. **1688** PENTON *Guardian's Instruction* (1897) 29 Humility and want of Learning (which Children are apt to smell out). **1756** MRS. CALDERWOOD *Jrnl.* (1884) 339 The Scots folks have an excellent nose to smell out their Countryfolks. **1811** *Sporting Mag.* XXXVII. 76 To smell out a little bargain. **1821** SCOTT *Kenilw.* xxvii, I never smell out a secret, but I try to be either at the right or the wrong end of it. **1892** RIDER HAGGARD *Nada* 12 A rich man..had lost some cattle, and came with gifts to Noma, praying him to smell them out.

**4.** To distinguish (one thing *from* another) by the smell. Chiefly *fig.*

**1582** in Scoones *Four C. Eng. Lett.* 39, I know your L. will soone smell deuises from simplicity, trueth from trecherie. *a* **1592** GREENE *Jas. IV*, I. ii, I can smell a knave from a rat. **1829** LANDOR *Imag. Conv.* Wks. 1853 II. 7/2 The judges there can smell silver from gold through a Russia-leather portmanteau.

**5.** To find or make (one's way) by the sense of smell. Also *fig.*

**1605** SHAKS. *Lear* III. vii. 93 Go thrust him out at gates, and let him smell His way to Douer. **1838** T. MITCHELL *Clouds of Aristoph.* 82 He and his school were provided with noses, which smelt their way into sources of knowledge.

**II.** *intr.* **6. a.** To exercise, employ, make use of, the sense of smell in relation to a specified object. Const. *at*, *of* (now *U.S.*), †*on*, or *to* (†*unto*).

The const. *to* is by far the most frequent down to the 19th cent., during which *at* has become usual.

(*a*) *c* **1200** *Trin. Coll. Hom.* 35 Mid þe nose þarto te smullen. ? *a* **1366** CHAUCER *Rom. Rose* 1669 To pulle a rose of al that route..And smellen to it wher I wente. **1477** NORTON *Ordin. Alch.* v. in Ashmole (1652) 71 It is not wholesome to smell to some Cole. **1545** RAYNOLD *Byrth Mankynde* 132 Let the chyld smell to rue, and to asafetida. **1586** B. YOUNG *Guazzo's Civ. Conv.* IV. 191 b, Lord William,..in taking of the Cup, did smell to the wine. **1607** MARKHAM *Caval.* II. (1617) 32 This Saddle when you first present to the Horse, let him smell to it. **1670** J. SMITH *Eng. Improv. Reviv'd* 213 The Root smelled unto is good for the same purpose. **1757** W. THOMPSON *R.N. Adv.* 20 Dogs.. would not even smell to it. **1803** BEDDOES *Hygëia* IX. 99 The patient drank tea..and smelt to a tuberose. **1890** O. CRAWFURD *Round the Calendar* 147 Their flowers can be plucked or smelled to without bending the back.

(*b*) **1530** PALSGR. 722/2 Smell at my coller, and you shall parceyve whether it be I that stynke or nat. **1644** DIGBY *Nat. Bodies* xxxviii. §5. 333 If the smell do please it, the beast will alwayes be smelling at it. **1704** N. N. tr. *Boccalini's Advts. fr. Parnass.* III. 280 He bid some of his Priests..smell at the French-men's Hands. **1743** FRANCIS tr. *Hor., Odes* v. vi. 10 But You..at Crusts are smelling. **1836** LANDOR *Pericles & Aspasia* cxxxi. Wks. 1853 II. 406/2 She smells at it and turns away. **1863** READE *Hard Cash* III. 115 She smelt at her salts, and soon recovered that weakness.

(*c*) **1624** QUARLES *Sion's Sonn.* xv. 4 When I smelt of my returned hand. **1815** MRS. INCHBALD *Child of Nature* I. iii, Here—smell of this bottle—it will do you good. **1852** MRS. STOWE *Uncle Tom's C.* xv. 130 She recommended to him to smell of hartshorn. **1852** G. W. CURTIS *Lotos-eating* 3, I have not yet done..smelling of all the flowers. **1912** F. J. HASKIN *Amer. Govt.* 276 He took out the cork, smelled of it, and then replaced it. **1919** E. O'NEILL *Moon of Caribbees* 30 His foot hits a bottle. He stoops down and picks it up and smells of it.

(*d*) **1626** J. YATES *Ibis ad Cæsarem* II. 77 Error is the weed we so much smell on. **1684** BUNYAN *Pilg.* II. 25 Fetch something, and give it Mercie to smell on, thereby to stay her fainting. **1707** MORTIMER *Husb.* (1721) I. 207 To which hole they bring the Mare for the Horse to smell on. **1784** *New Spectator* No. 3. 3 Having examined and smelled on the leaves, she was satisfied.

†**b.** *fig.* To take or get a slight touch or taste *of*, to pay some slight attention *to*, a thing. *Obs.*

(*a*) **1553** T. WILSON *Rhet.* (1580) 165 The unlearned or foolishe phantasticall, that smelles but of learnyng. **1583** STOCKER *Civ. Warres Lowe C.* II. 46 b, Not without his great domage, which hee shall both feele, and smell of againe. **1600** ? WEBSTER *Weakest goeth to Wall* G iij b, And dogs keepe out of the Chauncell, ye shall smell of the whip else.

(*b*) *c* **1580** J. HOOKER *Life Sir P. Carew* in *Archæologia* XXVIII. 98 He in noe wise coulde frame the younge Peter to smell to a bo[o]cke. **1653** GAUDEN *Hierasp.* 152 Were there never so sweet..flowers gathered,..these supercilious novellers will not vouchsafe to smell to them.

**7.** Without const. To possess or exercise the sense of smell; to be able to perceive odours, or to be engaged in doing this. Also *fig.*

*a* **1300** *E.E. Psalter* cxiii. 6 Nese-thirles þai haue, and smel sal noght. *a* **1325** *Prose Psalter* cxv. 6 Hij ne shul nouȝt smullen. **1390** GOWER *Conf.* II. 87 Ere and yhe and nase and mouth, Wherof a man mai hiere and se And smelle and taste in his degre. *a* **1500** *Adrian & Epotys* 68 in *Brome Bk.* 27 The joy [of heaven] may no tonge telle, Tyll domys day thow he woll smell. **1579** LYLY *Euphues* (Arb.) 153 Doth not the Lyon for strength..excell Man? Doth not..the Vulter smel better. **1607** SHAKS. *Timon* IV. iii. 160 Downe with the Nose ..Of him, that his particular to foresee, Smels from the generall weale. **1667** MILTON *P.L.* v. 411 Every lower facultie Of sense, whereby they hear, see, smell, touch, taste. **1726** SWIFT *Gulliver* II. i, Two rats..ran smelling backwards and forwards on the bed. **1824** LADY GRANVILLE *Lett.* (1894) I. 283 We walked and smelt for half an hour. **1898** *Daily News* 23 July 6/2 It will be the object of this Committee..to go smelling in Shoreditch.

**III. 8. a.** *intr.* To give out, send forth, or exhale an odour; to have a smell, scent, etc.

*c* **1175** *Lamb. Hom.* 53 He..bret hine [the cheese] for þon þet he scolde swote smelle. *c* **1220** *Bestiary* 751 in *O.E. Misc.*, Al ðat eure smelleð swete. *a* **1225** *Leg. Kath.* 1526 Mi swete lif, se swoteliche he smecheð me & smealleð. *c* **1310** in Wright *Lyric P.* xxx. 88 Hire erbes smulleth suete. *c* **1386** CHAUCER *Miller's T.* 505 He cheweth greyn and lycorys To smellen sweete. *c* **1440** *Pallad. on Husb.* XII. 514 Chaunge hit ofte vntil hit better smylle. **1484** CAXTON *Fables of Æsop* III. xx, Hit smelleth lyke bame. **1530** PALSGR. 722/2 Take away this fysshe, it smelleth nat very well. **1562** TURNER *Herbal* II. (1568) 126 Sage is a long bushe,..smellinge wounderfully. **1610** SHAKS. *Temp.* II. ii. 26 Hee smels like a fish. **1667** MILTON *P.L.* VII. 319 Herbs of every leaf, that..made gay Her bosom smelling sweet. **1726** SWIFT *Gulliver* IV. viii, I observed the young animal's flesh to smell very rank. **1806** *Med. Jrnl.* XV. 486 The whole matter smelt very sour as it was dug. **1842** PARNELL *Chem. Anal.* (1845) 294 A combustible gas, smelling like bisulphuret of carbon. **1885** HORNADAY *2 Yrs. Jungle* xxvi. 304 It smelled like sulphuretted hydrogen.

**b.** *spec.* To give out an offensive odour; to stink.

*c* **1375** *Cursor M.* 14322 (Fairf.), He smellis, for iiij. dayes ar gane syn he was lokin vnder a stane. **1584** COGAN *Haven Health* 263 When the Waters and feelds smoke and smell. **1608** D. T. *Ess. Pol. & Mor.* 80 Beeing told that his breath did smell. **1684** *Contempl. State Man* I. iv. (1699) 35 If he reach old Age..his Breath smells.

**c.** *fig.* Also in phr. ***not to smell right***, to have an air of being not quite in order.

**1377** LANGL. *P. Pl.* B. XI. 426 þere smit no þinge so smerte, ne smelleth so soure, As shame. **1579–80** NORTH *Plutarch, Artaxerxes* (1896) VI. 112 Me thinketh this smelleth like a lye. **1602** SHAKS. *Ham.* III. iii. 36 Oh my offence is ranke, it smels to heauen. **1820** SHELLEY *Prometh. Unb.* I. 339 The hope of torturing him smells like a heap Of corpses, to a death-bird after battle. [*a* **1862** BUCKLE *Civiliz.* (1869) III. iii. 157 That corrupt and tyrannical dynasty whose offences smelt to heaven.] **1939** 'N. BLAKE' *Smiler with Knife* x. 154 It doesn't sound like Fascism. It doesn't smell like Fascism. **1950** 'J. TEY' *To love & be Wise* xvii. 219 It's..the whole set-up... It doesn't smell right. **1969** *Sunday Times* (Colour Suppl.) 21 Dec. 11/1 Jock could not have been nicer... As a matter of fact he has been so nice that it smells bad. **1974** J. THOMSON *Long Revenge* iii. 33 Finch was inclined towards accepting the case... And yet.. he hesitated... It still did not smell right to him.

**d.** To give rise to suspicion; to have an air of dishonesty or fraud.

**1939** *Sun* (Baltimore) 12 Dec. 3/3 What 'smelled' about the..case appeared to have been saved by committee counsel for later inquiry. **1950** *Austral. Police Jrnl.* Apr. 118 *It smells*, it is something to be wary about; highly suspicious. **1970** G. F. NEWMAN *Sir, You Bastard* ii. 78 Things.. wouldn't always get past the sharp-eyed QC. If a case smelt, he would smell it. **1973** 'H. HOWARD' *Highway to Murder* viii. 103 There's a wrong slant to this affair. I can't put my finger on it—but it smells.

**9. a.** To exhale or emit the odour *of*, to have the smell *of*, something. Also rarely *on* (now *dial.*).

(*a*) **1526** [cf. b]. **1560** BIBLE (Geneva) *Ps.* xlv. 8 All thy garments smell of myrrhe and aloes, and cassia. **1599** DAVIES *Immort. Soul* XVII. ii. (1714) 72 They smell best, that do of nothing smell. **1662** J. DAVIES tr. *Mandelslo's Trav.* 94 They gave him a bottle that smelt of Oyle. **1711** W. KING tr. *Naude's Ref. Politics* iii. 109 The answer of a peasant to King Henry, that The pouch will always smell of the herring. **1796** KIRWAN *Elem. Min.* (ed. 2) II. 443 Calcined until it no longer smelled of arsenic. **1848** DICKENS *Dombey* xxxi, One of the..men already smells of sherry. **1855** TENNYSON *Maud* I. VI. vi, That oil'd and curl'd Assyrian Bull Smelling of musk and of insolence.

(*b*) **1567** DRANT *Horace, Ep.* I. xix. F vij, All nighte to sprall and stryue with wyne, all day on it to smell [L. *putēre*]. **1758** BINNELL *Descr. Thames* 179 Its observable that he is thought by some to feed on Water-Thyme, and that he smells on it, at his first being taken out of the Water.

**b.** To have or exhibit a touch, tinge, or suggestion *of* something.

**1526** *Pilgr. Perf.* (W. de W. 1531) 77 b, Not for.. promocyon or other profyte,..for all these smelleth of ypocrisy. **1576** FLEMING *Panopl. Epist.* 3 *marg.*, He supposeth that both their victories will smell of crueltie. **1649** MILTON *Eikon.* xxvi. Wks. 1851 III. 503 Praises in an enemy are superfluous, or smell of craft. **1671** J. DAVIES *Sibylls* II. xxiv. 137 That the Relation of his Adventures smell (as much as may be) of a Romance. **1741** BERKELEY *Wks.* (1871) IV. 270 Most modern writings smell of the age. **1756** LAW *Lett. Important Subj.* 115 Such a free way of speaking..of my own books may have been suspected of smelling too much of self-esteem. **1837** CARLYLE *Fr. Rev.* III. I. i, Some..seem to hint afar off at something which smells of Agrarian law. **1887** *Spectator* 17 Sept. 1241 Proposals smelling of confiscation.

**c.** Of literary work, in the phrases ***to smell of the candle, lamp, oil***, etc., to show signs of being laboured and artificial.

**1542** UDALL *Erasm. Apoph.* 333 Pythias obiected..that his argumentes of rhetorike smelled all of the candle. **1579** [see LAMP *sb.*[1] 1 b]. **1616** HIERON *Wks.* I. 586 It is an honour to a sermon, when (as the saying is) it shall smell of the candle. **1625** B. JONSON *Staple of N.* Prol. (for the Court), A work not smelling of the lamp. **1650, 1675** [see OIL *sb.*[1] 3 d]. **1732, 1768** [see LAMP *sb.*[1] 1 b]. **1839** HALLAM *Hist. Lit.* III. vii. §17 Even his letters to his sister, smell too much of the lamp. **1871** LOWELL *Study Windows* (1886) 282 His sentences..smell of the library. **1887** [see LAMP *sb.*[1] 1 b]. **1927** GALSWORTHY *Castles in Spain* 154 At times he wrote stories unworthy of him. At times his work smelled of the lamp. **1953** G. S. FRASER *Modern Writer & his World* III. iv. 254 This desire of his..to be 'complex' and to bring in a wide range of cultural references at all costs does make his work sometimes smell a little of the lamp.

**10.** *trans.* To have or emit a smell of (something).

*c* **1586** C'TESS PEMBROKE *Ps.* XLV. iv, Mirrh, Aloes, Cassia, all thy robes doe smell. **1598** SHAKS. *Merry W.* III. ii. 70 He smels April and May. **1603** —— *Meas. for M.* III. ii. 194 She smelt browne-bread and Garlicke. **1854** THACKERAY *Wolves & the Lamb* Wks. 1899 XII. 16 There's..crumbs on your cheek, and you smell sherry, sir!

**11.** *colloq.* To cause to smell; to fill or affect with an (offensive) odour. Also with *out*.

**1887** *Aberd. Evening Express* 5 Sept. 2/6 Parts [of a whale] which are still in such a condition that they would smell the whole museum. **1978** *Lancashire Life* Oct. 83/3 Ah must 'a' smelt the class-room a'et When a' them odours mingled. **1979** 'J. ROSS' *Rattling of Old Bones* ii. 17 How..can you have a dead body smelling out the house and not know it?

**smellable** (ˈsmɛləb(ə)l), *a.* [f. SMELL *v.* + -ABLE.] Capable of being smelt.

*c* **1449** PECOCK *Repr.* II. v. 162 Marie Magdalen..vsid the oynement as a seable and a smelleable rememoratijf signe. *Ibid.*, Smelleable signes as encensis. **1843** *Commissioner* 104 It seemed as if he was being pelted with everything eatable, drinkable,..smellable, thinkable, that the world ever produced. **1881** GRANT ALLEN *Evolutionist at Large* 12 [Ants] probably think of most things as smellable only.

**ˈsmellage.** *U.S.* ? *local.* [Alteration of SMALLAGE.] Officinal lovage, *Levisticum officinale*, of the family Umbelliferæ.

**1836** A. H. LINCOLN *Familiar Lect. Bot.* (ed. 5) 110 [*Ligusticum*] *levisticum* (smellage,) leaves many..Medicinal. **1889** R. T. COOKE *Steadfast* iii. 43 A nosegay of lavender, damask roses, smellage, old man, clove pinks [etc.].

**smelled**, *a. rare.* [f. SMELL *sb.*] With qualifying terms: Scented; smelling.

**1617** *Extr. Aberd. Burgh Rec.* (1848) II. 350 Weele washine and weele smellit naprie. **1725** SLOANE *Jamaica* II. 52 A red ungratefully smell'd moist pulp or paste.

**smeller** (ˈsmɛlə(r)). Also 6–7 smellar. [f. SMELL *v.* + -ER.]

**1. a.** One who has or exercises the sense of smell; one who smells *out*, etc.

**1519** HORMAN *Vulgaria* 45 They that haue nostrellis strayght forth be good smellars. **1526** *Pilgr. Perf.* (W. de W. 1531) 258 The smellers or felers therof hath thought them selfe rauysshed as yf they had ben in paradyse. **1562** J. HEYWOOD *Prov. & Epigr.* (1867) 171 The smeller of smellers then, thou art euyn he. **1658** tr. *Porta's Nat. Magick* VIII. i. 218 Adding a little Musk, to gain an easier reception of the Smeller. **1662** STILLINGFL. *Orig. Sacræ* III. i. §12 The first smellers out of so great a design. **1888** H. W. PARKER *Spirit of Beauty* (1891) 92 Calderwood shows how the sensationalists would evolve a whole philosophy of mind and morals from a smell, and that, too, without a smeller.

**b.** *slang.* 'A prying fellow; one who tries to smell out something; a sneaking spy' (*Cent. Dict.*).

**2.** †**a.** *Cant.* A garden. *Obs.*[−0]

**1610** ROWLANDS *Mart. Mark-all* E iv, Smellar, a garden; not Smelling cheate, for thats a Nosegay.

**b.** One who has a smell; a stinker.

*a* **1625** FLETCHER *Nice Valour* IV. i, Such nasty smellers, That..They might have cudgell'd me with their very stink.

**3.** A feeler; a slender tactile organ, hair, etc.; *esp.* one of the whiskers of a cat.

**1665** HOOKE *Microgr.* 180 Of the Eyes and Head of a Grey Drone-Fly... As concerning the horns.., the feelers or smellers.., the Proboscis [etc.]. **1738** *Gentl. Mag.* VIII. 378/2 Smellers, or kind of Whiskers, at his Nostrils. **1785** GROSE *Dict. Vulgar T.*, *Smellers*, a cat's whiskers. **1840** *Peter Parley's Ann.* I. 266 Mosette felt her smellers crackle close to her nose. **1899** *Daily News* 18 Apr. 8/2 A black tom cat. .. White chest, white hind legs, and white smellers.

**4.** *slang.* **a.** The nose; *pl.* the nostrils.

*a* **1700** B. E. *Dict. Cant. Crew.* **1822** *Blackw. Mag.* II. 594 Here was..a hit on the wind—a douss on the smeller. **1853** 'C. BEDE' *Verdant Green* I. xvi, Come on..and let me have a rap at your smellers. **1894** *Nation* 29 Nov. 399/3 He would rather not have to draw his claret and close his peepers and mash his smeller and break his breadbasket.

**b.** A blow on the nose. Also *transf.*

**1824** *Spirit Publ. Jrnls.* (1825) 38 He swore he would tip me a smeller. **1864** *Daily Telegr.* 3 Sept., The Metacomet, which was hitting out wildly,..delivered to the Hartford a 'smeller' intended for the rebel ram. **1872** *Punch* 6 Apr. 150/2 What in low fighting slang is called a smeller.

**5.** *fig.* Anything remarkable for exceptional violence, severity, strength, etc. **a.** = SNORTER[1] 2 b. **b.** *slang.* A heavy fall; usu. in phr. ***to come a smeller***. Cf. STINKER 6 c.

**1898** KIPLING *Fleet in Being* v. 55 Good old gales—regular smellers. **1923** J. MANCHON *Le Slang* 278 *Smeller*, (2) to come a smeller, ramasser une pelle. **1934** WODEHOUSE *Right Ho, Jeeves* ix. 92 A man's brain whizzes along for years exceeding the speed limit, and then something suddenly goes wrong with the steering gear and it skids and comes a smeller in the ditch.

**ˈsmell-feast.** Also 6 smellefyeste, smelle-, smel-feast(e. [f. SMELL *v.* (or *sb.*) + FEAST *sb.*]

**1.** One who scents out where feasting is to be had; one who comes uninvited to share in a feast; a parasite, a greedy sponger. Now *arch.* (very common *c* 1540–1700).

**1519** HORMAN *Vulgaria* 77 Smellefyestes, lyckedysshes, and franchars come vncalled. **1542** UDALL *Erasm Apoph.* 199 Parasites, wer called suche smellefeastes as would seeke to bee free geastes at riche mennes tables. **1602** F. HERING *Anat.* 13 Our Smell-feast will be sure to haunt the Houses and Tables of Rich and great Men. **1664** H. MORE *Myst. Iniq.* 21 Like so many smell-feasts they hankered near the Altars to enjoy the nidorous fumes. **1692** L'ESTRANGE *Fables* (1694) 33 The Fly is an intruder and a common Smell-feast that spunges upon other people's trenchers. **1708** O. DYKES *Refl. upon Eng. Prov.* 163 The Flatteries of Sicophants and Smell-Feasts. **1869** BROWNING *Ring & Book* VIII. 39 The Smell-feasts rouse them at the hint There's cookery in a certain dwelling-place. **1884** DILLWYN *Jill* II. ix. 135 That smell-feast of a Sue meanwhile had profited by the commotion.

**b.** *attrib.* Parasitic, sponging.

**1566** DRANT *Horace, Sat.* I. vii. Fij, I am a smelfeaste belly-god, idle and full of slouthe. **1609** HOLLAND *Amm. Marcell.* 339 These smel-feast-parasites in comedies. **1642** FULLER *Holy & Prof. St.* IV. xx. 343 These smell-feast birds ..came to feed on their carcases. **1772** NUGENT *Hist. Friar Gerund* II. 67 Some smell-feast friars of different communities.

**2.** 'A feast at which the guests are supposed to feed upon the odors only of the viands' (Webster, 1864).

**smellfungus** (smɛl'fʌŋgəs). Also 8 **smelfungus.** Pl. **-fungi** (-'fʌndʒaɪ). [The name by which Sterne designated Smollett on account of the captious tone of the latter's *Travels through France and Italy* (1766).] A discontented person; a grumbler, faultfinder. Also *attrib.*

[**1768** STERNE *Sent. Journ., In the Street, Calais,* The learned Smelfungus travelled from Boulogne to Paris,.. but he set out with the spleen and jaundice, and every object he pass'd by was discoloured or distorted.] **1807-8** W. IRVING *Salmag.* (1824) 15 Let the grumbling smellfungi..rail at the extravagance of the age. **1842** MRS. F. TROLLOPE *Visit Italy* II. xxiii. 380 Smellfungus people, who love to torment themselves.

**smellie** ('smɛlɪ). [f. SMELL *v.* + -IE, after TALKIE.] A (hypothetical) cinema or television film in which smell is synchronized with the picture. Usu. pl. Cf. FEELY.

**1929** A. P. HERBERT in *Punch* 8 May 508/3 These early smellies made a great sensation, particularly *Fish,* a strong story written 'around the life of a San Francisco fishwife of homicidal tendencies'. **1949** *Sun* (Baltimore) 12 Apr. 6/6 (*cartoon caption*) Soviet Smellies present 'Uncle Joe's Pipe'. **1958** *Spectator* 20 June 801/3 We had an Esther Williams picture and I wanted to advertise it as a smellie, with an ozonair machine in the foyer... The circuit wouldn't wear it, though. **1977** *Time* 11 Apr. 33/2 Another treat in the works: smellies—a futuristic device attached to the [T.V.] set will emit aromas into the living room.

**smelliness** ('smɛlɪnɪs). [f. SMELLY *a.* + -NESS.] The condition of being smelly.

**1892** *Critic* Mar. 139 The chronic smelliness of undrained China.

**smelling** ('smɛlɪŋ), *vbl. sb.* [f. SMELL *v.*]

**1. a.** The sense of smell. Cf. SMELL *sb.* 1.

*c* **1175** *Lamb. Hom.* 75 Hore loking, hore blawing, hore smelling, heore feling wes al iattret. *c* **1230** *Hali Meid.* 13 Sihðe & heringe, smecchunge & smeallunge. *a* **1300** *Cursor M.* 17017 Hering, sight, smelling and fele. **1382** WYCLIF *1 Cor.* xii. 17 If al the body be heeringe, where is smellinge. **1426** AUDELAY *Poems* 7 Thi heryng, thi seyng,..thi smellyng, here be iij [senses]. *c* **1450** *St. Cuthbert* (Surtees) 1444 It was odour wondir swete, þat þar with his smellyng mete. *a* **1533** LD. BERNERS *Gold. Bk. M. Aurel.* (1546) I ij b, He had a good and a quycke smellyng. **1592** WYRLEY *Armory, Ld. Chandos* 95 Sweet is fresh aire to lost prisoners smelling. **1633** BP. HALL *Occas. Med.* §93 Smelling, is one of the meanest, and least useful of the senses. **1638** R. BAKER tr. *Balzac's Lett.* (vol. III) 101, I have lost as well my smelling as my taste. **1710** *Brit. Apollo* No. 72. 3/1 He lost his Smelling. **1774** GOLDSM. *Nat. Hist.* (1776) III. 105 His senses of smelling and hearing are in no less perfection.

**b.** The act or fact of smelling. Also with *out.*

**1509** HAWES *Past. Pleas.* XXIV. (Percy Soc.) 109 Whan that the nose therof hath smellinge. **1565** COOPER *Thesaurus* s.v. *Odor,* The smellyng..of a thyng. **1611** COTGR., *Halenement,* ..a smelling, or searching out. **1709** *Tatler* No. 66 ¶15 They cannot ever after come to the Use of their Teeth, or get smelling of a Crust. **1869** SPENCER *Princ. Psychol.* III. iv. I. (1872) 304 Smelling obviously implies the contact of dispersed particles with a specially modified part of the organism. **1893** *Daily News* 20 Sept. 5/4 A smelling-out case by witch doctors. **1899** RIDER HAGGARD *Swallow* ix, She never took part in the 'smelling-out' of human beings for witchcraft.

†**2.** Odour, scent, smell. *Obs.*

**13..** *K. Alis.* 2573 (Laud MS.), Swete is þe smellyng of þe flore. *c* **1386** CHAUCER *Can. Yeom. Prol.* 337 (Harl.), Lo, þus by smellyng and by þredbare array If þat men list, þis folk þey knowe may. *c* **1480** J. WATTON *Spec. Christiani* 46 b, Ther of come swete smellyng; Sweter felt neuer man here lyuyng. **1483** *Cath. Angl.* 346/1 A Smellynge, *odor.* **1611** COTGR., *Senteur,* sent, odor, smelling, sauor.

**3.** *attrib.* †**a.** *smelling cheat* (see quots.). *Cant.*

**1567** HARMAN *Caveat* 84 A smelling chete, a garden or orchard. **1610** [see SMELLER 2 a].

**b.** *smelling-hair, -organ,* etc. (cf. SMELLER 3).

**1596** NASHE *Saffron Walden* Ep. Ded., Almost as slender ..as a Catts smelling haires. **1871** DARWIN *Desc. Man* II. ix. 328 Thread-like bodies, which are believed to act as smelling-organs. **1872** —— *Orig. Spec.* (ed. 6) ii. 33 The other has antennæ much more abundantly furnished with smelling-hairs.

**c.** *smelling-bottle,* a phial or small bottle for containing smelling-salts or perfume ready for use.

**1722** DEFOE *Memoirs of Plague* 239 In a Word, the whole Church was like a smelling Bottle. **1771** SMOLLETT *Humph. Cl.* (1815) 259 My sister began to..use her smelling-bottle. **1827** SCOTT *Surg. Dau.* Concl., When tea had been carried round, handkerchiefs and smelling bottles prepared [etc.]. **1842** MRS. CARLYLE *Lett.* I. 150 He..bought me a very nice smelling-bottle. **1871** M. COLLINS *Marq. & Merch.* III. xii. 285 Ethel's smelling-bottle revived one or two..ladies. **1936** W. FAULKNER *Absalom, Absalom!* vi. 195 Clytie..stood impassive beside the wagon that last day, following the second ceremonial to the grave with the silk cushion and the parasol and the smelling-bottle.

**d.** *smelling-salts,* a preparation of carbonate of ammonia and scent for smelling, used as a restorative in cases of faintness or headache.

**1840** DICKENS *Old C. Shop* xlvi, Vinegar, hartshorn, and smelling-salts. **1892** MRS. CLIFFORD *Aunt Anne* I. 35 She thought he was ill, and..offered him some smelling-salts.

**smelling** ('smɛlɪŋ), *ppl. a.* [f. SMELL *v.*]

**1.** Giving out a smell or odour. Chiefly with qualifying term (see also SWEET-SMELLING).

**13..** *Cursor M.* 3695 (Gött.), Quen he had felt his smelland clath.., 'þis voice,' he said, 'þat i here, Is of Iacob'. **13..** in *Reliq. Antiq.* I. 40, I lilie of the valeyes, that is most white chast love and moste smelȝene. *c* **1400** MAUNDEV. (1839) ii. 11 Therfore thei made that pece [of the cross]..of Cypres; For it is welle smellynge. **1483** *Cath. Angl.* 346/1 Smellynge, *odorabilis, odorifer.* **1530** PALSGR. 324/2 Smellyng, that maye sone be smelled, *odoratif.* **1585** T. WASHINGTON tr. *Nicholay's Voy.* III. ix. 84 b, A..viall ful of sweete and smelling water. **1591** FLORIO *2nd Frutes* Ep. Ded., Some..pronosticate of faire, of foule and of smelling weather. **1611** COTGR., *Regnard,* a long-tailed, and ranke-smelling fish. **1848** DICKENS *Dombey* viii, It was not, naturally, a fresh-smelling house. **1888** 'J. S. WINTER' *Bootle's Childr.* x, A particularly nasty smelling ferret.

**2.** Having the sense of smell, or the faculty of perceiving by smell. *rare.*

**1598** MARSTON *Pygmal.* IV. 150 But Grillus subtile-smelling swinish snout Must sent,..and needes will finde it out. **1607** TOPSELL *Four-f. Beasts* (1658) 121 Unto all these smelling Dogs I may also adde the water Spagnel.

**smell-less** ('smɛllɪs), *a.* [f. SMELL *sb.* + -LESS.]

**1.** Giving out no smell; scentless.

**1612** *Two Noble Kinsmen* I. i, Dazies smel-lesse, yet most quaint. **1683** SALMON *Doron Med.* II. 516 An almost colourless, smell-less, tast-less Liquor. **1855** J. F. W. JOHNSTON *Chem. Common Life* I. xiii. 331 The nearly smell-less juice acquires a fetid..odour. **1882** *Nature* XXVI. 187 Methyl alcohol, in a state of purity, is smell-less.

**2.** Having no sense of smell.

**1873** MIVART *Elem. Anat.* 113 They may..abort altogether, as is the case in the probably smell-less Porpoises.

**smellsip** ('smɛlsɪp), *v. nonce-wd.* [f. SMELL *v.* + SIP *v.*] *trans.* To smell and sip almost simultaneously.

**1922** JOYCE *Ulysses* 170 He smellsipped the cordial juice and..set his wineglass delicately down.

**'smell-smock.** [f. SMELL *v.* + SMOCK *sb.* 1.]

†**1.** A licentious man. *Obs.*

In early use employed suggestively as a surname.

**1550** BALE *Image Both Ch.* II. xi, Ser Saunder smell smock, our parish priest. **1562** PILKINGTON *Expos. Abdyas* 98 So can our belligoddes, the Popes Sir Jhon smell smocke, smel a feast in all parishes nere him. **1607** MIDDLETON *Fam. Love* II. iii, To prevent this smell-smock, I'll to my friend. **1634** HEYWOOD *Maidenh. well lost* II. Wks. 1874 IV. 125, I thinke you'le proue little better then a smell-smocke, That can finde out a pretty wench in such a Corner. **1673** R. HEAD *Cant. Acad.* 147 These attractions..drew on a number of Smell-smocks, which courted her.

**2.** *dial.* As a plant-name, applied to (*a*) the cuckoo-flower, (*b*) the wood-anemone, and (*c*) the wood-sorrel.

**1876-** in dialect glossaries, etc. (cf. Britten & Holland *Plant Names* and the *Eng. Dial. Dict.*).

**smelly** ('smɛlɪ), *a.* [f. SMELL *sb.* + -Y.]

**a.** Emitting a bad smell or smells; stinking. Also *fig.*

**1862** H. MARRYAT *Year in Sweden* II. 398 Down the centre runs a straight canal 'awful smelly'. **1863** KINGSLEY *Water-Bab.* 192 They can't abide anything smelly or foul. **1879** HARE *Story Life* (1900) V. xx. 219 It was a crowded, rolling, smelly steamer.

**b.** Suspicious. *rare.*

**1923** J. MANCHON *Le Slang* 278 *Smelly,*..louche, véreux. **1944** [see RIDE *v.* 9 c]. **1970** G. F. NEWMAN *Sir, You Bastard* viii. 227 Seems a bit smelly, Terry. I should blow him out.

**smelt** (smɛlt), *sb.*[1] [OE. *smelt,* = obs. G. *schmelt, schmelz* (Gesner), Da. *smelt* (from *c* 1600): cf. Du. *smelt,* Flem. *smelte,* G. *schmelte* sand-eel, also Norw. *smelta* a small species of cod or whiting. Relationship to OE. *smolt, smylte* is very doubtful.]

**1.** A small fish, *Osmerus eperlanus,* allied to the salmon, and emitting a peculiar odour; the sparling or spirling.

*c* **725** *Corpus Gl.* S 72 *Sardas,* smeltas. **1328-9** *Exch. K.R. Memoranda* m. 125 Quoad capcionem piscis qui vocatur smelt. *c* **1358** in *Eng. Hist. Rev.* XXIV. 742 Item in smelt ij[d]. **1421** *Contin. Brut* 447 Gurnard rosted... Smelt ffryed. *c* **1440** *Promp. Parv.* 460/2 Smelte, fysche. **1530** PALSGR. 271/2 Smelte, a fysshe, *esp[er]lang.* **1558** *Act 1 Eliz.* c. 17 §4 Places where Smelts, Loches,..Gudgions or Eels, have been used to be taken. **1602** R. CAREW *Surv. Cornw.* 30 Of round fish there are Brit, Sprat,..Smelts, &c. **1655** MOUFET & BENNET *Health's Impr.* (1746) 282 Smelts are so called because they smell so sweet. **1767** *Phil. Trans.* LVII. 285 The smelt are a very small sort of fish,..used for garnish to those that are larger. **1769** PENNANT *Brit. Zool.* III. 264 The smelt inhabits the seas of the northern parts of Europe. **1825** S. & SARAH ADAMS *Compl. Servant* 86 Smelts, when fresh, have a fine bright appearance,..and a fragrant smell, like a cucumber. **1896** LYDEKKER *Roy. Nat. Hist.* V. 503 The beautiful and delicately flavoured little fish known as smelts are represented by three species.

*fig.* **1791** BOSWELL *Johnson* (Oxf. ed.) II. 567 Sir, you were a Cod surrounded by smelts. Is not this enough for you?

**b.** A fish of a related species, esp. *Osmerus mordax* of the American coast.

**1836** W. IRVING *Astoria* III. 189 A daughter of the one-eyed potentate Comcomly, who held sway over the fishing tribe of the Chinooks, and had long supplied the factory with smelts and sturgeons. **1839** YARRELL *Brit. Fishes* Suppl. II. 16 The Hebridal Smelt. **1868** *U.S. Rep. Commiss. Agric.* (1869) 330 Spawn..of the white fish,..the Belgrade smelt, and the wall-eyed pike. **1883** SIR A. SHAW *Newfoundland Fisheries* 7 The American 'smelt' swarms on all parts of the coast.

**c.** Applied to various other small fishes, in the south of England freq. to the atherine or sand-smelt.

**1776** PENNANT *Brit. Zool.* (ed. 4) III. 287 Atherine... This species is very common in the sea near Southampton, where it is called a Smelt. **1886** *Encycl. Brit.* XXI. 224/1 *Retropinna* contains but one species, *R. richardsonii,* which is known as the New Zealand Smelt. **1898** MORRIS *Austral Eng.* 421 *Smelt,* name given, in Melbourne, to the fish *Clupea vittata. Ibid.,* The *Derwent Smelt* is a Tasmanian fish, *Haplochiton sealii.*

†**2. a.** *transf.* A simpleton. *Obs.*

In quot. 1607 there is allusion to 2 b.

**1599** B. JONSON *Cynthia's Rev.* II. iii, What's he, Mercurie? *Mer.* A notable smelt. **1607** DEKKER & WEBSTER *Westw. Hoe* IV. ii, To see how plaine-dealing women can pull downe men: Moll, you'le helpe vs to catch Smelts too? *a* **1625** FLETCHER *Love's Pilgr.* v. ii, Talk what you will, this is a very smelt.

†**b.** Used allusively in the phrase *westward for smelts* (see quots.). *Obs.*

**1607** DEKKER & WEBSTER *Westw. Hoe* II. ii, But wenches, with what pullies shall wee slide..out of our husbandes suspicion, being gone Westward for smelts all night. **1608** *Great Frost* in Arber *Eng. Garner* (1895) I. 85 Say, have none gone 'westward for smelts', as your proverbial phrase is? **1619** (*title*), Westward for Smelts: or, The Waterman's Fare of mad-merry Western Wenches.

**3.** *north. dial.* A smolt. See SMOLT *sb.*[1] 1.

*a* **1633** COKE *On Litt.* II. xlvii. (1642) 478 Yong Salmons, or Salmon peals, or Salmon Smelts. *a* **1672** WILLUGHBY *Hist. Pisc.* IV. iv. 189 Nostratibus in fluvio Ribble agri Eboracensis Salmones primo ætatis anno *Smelts* dicuntur; secundo *Sprods.* **1677, 1769** [see SMOLT *sb.*[1] 1 β]. **1825** BROCKETT *N.C. Gloss., Smelts,* the fry of the salmon; generally called salmon-smelts. **1842** *Proc. Berw. Nat. Club* II. 4 He took Smelts of the Salmon with their silvery sides.

**4.** *attrib.,* as *smelt-boat, family, fishery, -fishing, -leap, net.*

**1384-5** *Cal. Lett. Bk. 'H' Lond.* (1907) 255 [Eight nets called] smelt net [of unlawful mesh]. **1620** MIDDLETON *Chaste Maid* IV. iii, She would not stay for oars; but took a smelt-boat. **1630** in Binnell *Descr. Thames* (1758) 78 That no Peter-man do fish with any Hagan or Smelt Net below London Bridge. *Ibid.* 79 No Fisherman..shall lay down in the River..any Smelt-Leaps before St. Paul's Day yearly. **1795** COLE *Yng. Angler's Comp.* Title-p., The Best Method of Smelt-Fishing. **1884** GOODE *Nat. Hist. Aquat. Anim.* 543 The Smelt Family, *Microstomidæ.* **1888** —— *Amer. Fishes* 492 The smelt fishery is increasing yearly in importance.

†**smelt,** *sb.*[2] *slang. Obs.* [Of obscure origin.] A half-guinea.

**1635** SHIRLEY *Lady of Pleasure* v. i, He..pays the rooks That went their smelts a piece upon his hand. **1688** SHADWELL *Sq. Alsatia* I, Pr'ythee, noble Squire, equipp me with a couple of Meggs, or two couple of Smelts. [**1822** SCOTT *Nigel* xxiii, That noble Master Grahame, whom you call Green, has got the *decuses* and the *smelts.*]

†**smelt,** *a. Obs.*[−1] [? a. ON. *smelt-r* enamelled.] ? Enamelled, polished.

*c* **1400** *Destr. Troy* 1667 A tabill..all of triet yuer, Bourdurt about all with bright Aumbur, þat smelt is & smethe.

**smelt** (smɛlt), *v.* [prob. ad. MDu. or MLG. *smelten* (*smilten*), whence also MSw. and Sw. *smälta,* Norw. *smelta,* Da. *smelte,* = OHG. and MHG. *smelzen* (G. *schmelzen*), a weak trans. verb corresponding to a strong intr. (of the type *smeltan, smalt*) found in the same languages. The stem appears to be a variation of that of MELT *v.*[1]] *trans.* To fuse or melt (ore, etc.) in order to extract the metal; to obtain or produce (metal) by this process.

**1543** in *Mem. Fountains Abbey* (Surtees) 403 For smelting one pece leade. **1602-3** *Shuttleworths' Acc.* (Chetham) 149 To Henry Orrell, bellfounder of Wyggan, for smeltinge the lead ashes, xx[s]. **1686** PLOT *Staffordsh.* 165 Which they Smelted..not far off, where they had Mills, &c. for the purpose. **1729** *Phil. Trans.* XXXVI. 32 This slag is afterwards smelted again with Cowke only. **1812** BRACKENRIDGE *Views of Louisiana* (1814) 148 The floats have no tiff, and are the most easily smelted. **1849** MACAULAY *Hist. Eng.* iii. I. 317 It was not then the practice to employ coal for smelting the ore. **1873** SPON *Workshop Rec.* Ser. I. 10/1 The best plan of smelting brass is to melt the copper in a black-lead crucible first.

*absol.* **1831** [see *smelt-furnace* below].

*fig.* **1850** CARLYLE *Latter-d. Pamph.* viii. (1872) 277 Who will smelt..these scandalous bewildering rubbish-mountains. **1874** H. R. REYNOLDS *John Bapt.* iv. §6. 272 God..will scorch and smelt the true metal in the furnace.

**smelt-**, the stem of SMELT *v.* in combination, as **smelt-furnace**, **-house** [Du. *smelthuis*, G. *schmelzhaus*], **-mill**, places where smelting is carried on.

**1684** *Phil. Trans.* XVII. 741 When the Smelt-Houses were up at Keswick,..this Work was left good. **1771** *Ann. Reg.* 90 Destroying the wear of Mr. Smith's smelt-mill. **1831** CARLYLE *Sart. Res.* I. vi, Those jingling sheet-iron Aprons, wherein your otherwise half-naked Vulcans hammer and smelt in their smelt-furnace. **1860** *Indenture*, The cottage, shop, and buildings formerly a smelthouse.

**smelted** (ˈsmɛltɪd), *ppl. a.* [f. SMELT *v.* + -ED[1].] Fused, melted.

**1750** tr. *Leonardus' Mirr. Stones* 44 This deception is made..chiefly from smelted glass. **1794** SULLIVAN *View Nature* II. 142 The fusion and fluidity of smelted lavas. **1895** *Daily News* 20 Nov. 9/5 The quantity of stone crushed ..has yielded 1,632 ounces of smelted gold.

**smelter** (ˈsmɛltə(r)), *sb.*[1] [f. SMELT *v.* + -ER[1]. Cf. Du. *smelter*, MSw. and Sw. *smältare*, G. *schmelzer*.]

**1.** One who smelts; a workman engaged in smelting; also, an owner of smelting-works.

**1455** in *Mem. Fountains Abbey* (Surtees) 364 [Nicholas Bucke employed by the abbot as a] smeltar [at his lead mines]. **1582** in *Trans. Jewish Hist. Soc.* (1903) IV. 93 All manner of Charges of fireworke and smeltars wages. **1778** W. PRYCE *Min. Cornub.* 68 The smelter having taken to himself perhaps one part more for his expence. **1812** BRACKENRIDGE *Views Louisiana* (1814) 149 The miners usually..dispose of their ore to the smelters. **1848** MILL *Pol. Econ.* I. ii. §1 (1876) 19 The miners and smelters who extracted or prepared the iron. **1891** *Daily News* 6 July 2/6 Manufacturers and smelters are not disposed to accept forward contracts at the current rates.

**b.** *smelter's fume* (see quot.).

**1875** KNIGHT *Dict. Mech.* 2220/1 *Smelter's Fume*, the metallic fume resulting from the smelting of lead, the sublimation of zinc from ore, mercury from cinnabar, etc.

**2.** Smelting-works; a smeltery. Orig. *U.S.*

**1877** RAYMOND *Statist. Mines & Mining* 235 Several smelters are in course of construction to reduce these ores to ingots at home. **1890** *Pall Mall G.* 12 July 3/2 On completion of eight additional smelters and other works.

**3.** *attrib.*, as ***smelter-man***, ***returns***.

**1896** *Columbus* (Ohio) *Disp.* 4 Sept., The millionaire smelterman. **1898** LIEBOLD *Woman Proposes* 68 We tax the gross output of the mines based on the mill and smelter returns.

**smelter** (ˈsmɛltə(r)), *sb.*[2] [f. SMELT *sb.*[1] + -ER[1].] One who fishes for smelts; a smelt-catcher.

**1845** *Zoologist* III. 1080 A smelter may be deemed the personification of patience. **1883** G. C. DAVIES *Norf. Broads* iii. 23 The smelter passes the night in his boat.

**smeltery** (ˈsmɛltərɪ). [f. SMELT *v.* + -ERY. Cf. Du. *smelterij*, G. *schmelzerei*.] A place where ores are smelted.

**1814** in Cleland *Rise & Progr. Glasgow* (1820) 267 Brass founderies and lead smelteries. **1888** *Harper's Mag.* Sept. 592 The product of the smeltery in 1886 had a money value of $1,105,190·76. **1893** C. G. LELAND *Mem.* II. 57 The slag or débris of an iron smeltery.

**smelting** (ˈsmɛltɪŋ), *vbl. sb.* [f. SMELT *v.*]

**1.** The action of the verb SMELT.

**1531-2** *Durh. Househ. Bk.* (Surtees) 78 Et Nicholao Kyrchus et socio pro smeltynge 110 ma. petr. plumbi 6s. 6d. **1582** in *Trans. Jewish Hist. Soc.* (1903) IV. 94 Takeinge the said vitriall or Coppris from the ure before it Come in to the first smeltinge. **1665** HOOKE *Microgr.* Pref., Smelting.. seems capable of being improv'd. *a* **1691** BOYLE *Wks.* (1772) V. 741 What Tools are used in smelting, their Figures, use, &c. **1729** *Phil. Trans.* XXXVI. 32 The Dross of the Ore on smelting is called Slag. **1797** *Encycl. Brit.* (ed. 3) XII. 86/2 In the smelting of copper ores, quartz is used. **1851** D. WILSON *Preh. Ann.* II. III. ii. 85 Smelting and working of iron with fires of wood. **1879** *Cassell's Techn. Educ.* I. 26/1 The smelting, conducted in large blast furnaces, disengages the metal from the oxygen and earths of the ores.

*fig.* **1882** FROUDE *Carlyle* II. 130 The incompleteness of the smelting shows all the more the actual condition of his [Carlyle's] mind.

**b.** A process or product of smelting.

**1872** *Daily News* 12 Oct., The sulphur smoke of the smeltings kills vegetation.

**2.** *attrib.*, as ***smelting bellows***, ***fire***, ***-furnace***, ***-hearth***, ***-house***, ***mill***, etc.

**1610** HOLLAND *Camden's Brit.* 767 Minerall men, who have their smelting house by Derwent side. **1664** OLDENBURG in *Boyle's Wks.* (1772) VI. 150 It is like the smelting miln-smoke. **1667** in Pettus *Fodinæ Reg.* (1670) 35 Five Pair of large Smelting Bellows. **1706** PHILLIPS (ed. Kersey) s.v. *Smelt*, A..Furnace..call'd, The smelting-Furnace. **1778** W. PRYCE *Min. Cornub.* 68 It has been carried to the smelting-house, as it came out of the earth. **1815** J. SMITH *Panorama Sci. & Art* II. 819 The mixture is calcined over a smelting fire. **1836** *Penny Cycl.* VI. 106/2 In the time of the Romans smelting works were carried on in the neighbourhood. **1877** RAYMOND *Statist. Mines & Mining* 339 What are known as smelting-ores in this district are the richer grades carrying usually 300 ounces of silver and upwards per ton. **1890** W. J. GORDON *Foundry* 100 The air driven into the smelting-hearth was cold.

**smere**, obs. form of SMEAR *sb.* and *v.*

†**smere**, *adv. Obs.* Also 4 **smare**. [Representing OE. *smǣre*, found only in *gálsmǣre* given to laughing. Cf. OHG. *smierôn* (MHG. *smieren*, obs. G. *schmieren*, LG. *smeren*) to smile.] ***to laugh smere***, to laugh lightly, merrily, or contemptuously.

*c* **1275** LAY. 14981 þane king hit þohte game inoh, for hire speche he smere loh. *c* **1290** *Childhood Jesus* 984 in Horstmann *Altengl. Leg.* (1875) 34 His Moder..gret Joye hadde and louȝ smere a non. **13..** *S. Eng. Leg.* (MS. Bodl. 779) in Herrig *Archiv* LXXXII. 409/22 Sysin þo for gladnesse gan to leyȝe wel smere. *c* **1380** *Ferumb.* 386 Þe Sarzyn gan to lawe smere, & to Olyuer sayde þan [etc.].

†**smeˈriglio.** *Obs.*[−1] [a. It. *smeriglio* a merlin.] A certain piece of ordnance.

**1688** HOLME *Armoury* III. xviii. (Roxb.) 137/2 The Rabbenett or Rabnett or smeriglio is 300 weight.

**smerk(e**, **smerky**, obs. ff. SMIRK, SMIRKY.

†**smerl**, *sb. Obs.* Also 4 **smerle**, **smerel**. [Back-formation from SMERLES, taken as a plural: cf. RIDDLE *sb.*[1]] Ointment.

*a* **1300** *Cursor M.* 7334 Þis saul haue þai mad þair king, Wit smerl and als wit coruning. *Ibid.* 11503 A smerl o selcuth bitturnes. *a* **1300** *E.E. Psalter* cxxxii. 2 Als þe smerle in heued onon Falles in berde..of Aaron.

Hence †**smerl** *v. trans.*, to anoint. Also †**ˈsmerling** *vbl. sb. Obs.*

*a* **1300** *Cursor M.* 7328 He sal be smerld þair king to be. *Ibid.* 9338 Quen he þat haliest es cumen, Your smerling sal fra yow be nummen.

**smerle** (smɜːl). [a. Flem. *smerle*, prob. a special application of older *smerle* (now *smerlijn*) merlin.] A variety of the domestic pigeon.

**1869** TEGETMEIER *Pigeons* IV. 47 We had a pair of Smerles, or Short-faced Antwerp cocks. **1879** L. WRIGHT *Pigeon Keeper* 210 A really Belgian pigeon called the Smerle.

†**smerles.** *Obs.* Forms: 1 **smyrels**, 3 **smuriles**, **smirles**; 3-4 **smerieles**, **smerles** (4 **-lis**). [OE. *smyrels*, f. *smyrian* to SMEAR *v.* Cf. MSw. *smyr-*, *smörilse* (Sw. *smörjelse*), MDa. *smørielse* (Da. *smørelse*).] Ointment.

In Small's *Metr. Hom.* 17 the form *smersles* may either be an error for *smerles*, or the pl. of *smersel*, = ON. and Icel. *smyrsl*.

*a* **1000** *Canons Edgar* 66 in Thorpe *Laws* II. 258 We læraþ þæt preosta ȝehwilc æȝðer hæbbe ȝe fulluht-ele ȝe seocum smyrels. *c* **1000** ÆLFRIC *Hom.* II. 508 He ȝehælde an mæden, mid halwendum smyrelse ȝehalȝodes eles. *c* **1200** *Trin. Coll. Hom.* 145 [Mary Magdalene] nam ane box..and hine fulde mid derewurðe smerieles. *a* **1225** *Leg. Kath.* 1599 Þe engles wið smirles of aromaz smireden hire wunden. *a* **1300** *Cursor M.* 14003 A bost sco has o smerles nummen. *c* **1325** *Metr. Hom.* 97 The thrid gift thai him tok Was a smerlis, als sais the boc. **1340** *Ayenb.* 187 He ne may naȝt þolye þane guode smel of þe ilke smerieles.

†**ˈsmerlin.** *Obs.* [ad. G. *schmerling*. Cf. Da. *smer-*, Sw. *smärling*.] A loach or groundling.

[**1617** MORYSON *Itin.* III. 81 They have one most delicate kinde, called Smerling, which in Prussen I did eate.] **1668** CHARLETON *Onomast.* 157 *Cobites Aculeata*,..the Smerlin. [Hence in Ainsworth (1736) and later Dicts.]

**SMERSH**, **Smersh** (smɜːʃ). [Russ. abbrev. of *smert' shpionam*, lit. 'death to spies'.] The popular name of the Russian counter-espionage organization, originating during the war of 1939–45, which is responsible for maintaining security within the Soviet armed and intelligence services.

**1953** I. FLEMING *Casino Royale* xxvii. 217 He would take on SMERSH and hunt it down. Without SMERSH, without this cold weapon of death and revenge, the M.W.D. would be just another bunch of civil servant spies. **1955** H. HODGKINSON *Doubletalk* 1 Still to be met with are.. SMERSH (*smert shpionam*: death to spies), the war-time name for the Soviet Army Counter-espionage organisation. **1961** D. MOORE *Highway of Fear* iv. 27 Faster!.. The Smersh zombies..are right behind you. **1967** E. GRIERSON *Crime of One's Own* ix. 73 All this nonsense of Calvert being some type from SMERSH—and Mason's the Man from Uncle, I suppose? **1977** *Times Lit. Suppl.* 29 Apr. 534/3 Missing..from..the *Great Soviet Encyclopedia*..are two Abakumovs, Andrei Ivanovich..and Viktor Semenovich, head of Smersh during the Second World War and Minister for State Security after it.

**smert**, obs. or dial. variant of SMART.

**smetana** (ˈsmɛtənə). Also with Fr. spelling **smitane** (smitan). [a. Russ. *smetána* sour cream, f. *smetat'* to sweep together, collect.] Sour cream. Freq. *attrib.* as *smetana* (or *smitane*) *sauce*, a sauce made with sour cream and seasonings, usu. served with meat.

**1909** M. RONALD *Century Cook Bk.* (rev. ed.) 606 Smetana sauce... Pour a cup of thick sour cream into the pan, let it just brown, and then pour over steaks. **1938** *Zionist Rev.* 11 Aug. 13/1 For supper there is bread and *smetana*. **1939** A. L. SIMON *Conc. Encycl. Gastron.* I. 48/1 *Smitane*, Sauce. Sour cream and onions. **1963** I. FLEMING *On H.M. Secret Service* (1964) xxiii. 242 Rehrücken mit Sahne. That's saddle of roebuck with a smitane sauce. **1968** A. TACK *Spy who wasn't Exchanged* xii. 91 He ordered a sour milk and cream mixture called *Smetana*. **1978** *Chicago* June 242/2 Our favorites are the eggy cheese blintzes..Lithuanian schnitzel with smetana (sour cream) sauce, veal cordon bleu, etc. **1979** N. FREELING *Widow* xiv. 83 Any sort of sauce you like except tomato. Smitane maybe.

**S meter**: see S II. 10.

†**smeth.** *Obs.*[−0] (See quot.)

**1656** BLOUNT *Glossogr.*, *Smeth* or *Smoothery*, a medicine or physical Ointment to take away hair.

**smeth(e**, obs. forms of SMEETH *a.* and *v.*

**smeuse** (smjuːs, smjuːz), *sb.* Also **smeuce**, **smewse**, **-ss**, **smu(i)ce**, **smuse**, etc. [Alteration of MEUSE *sb.*] A hole in a hedge, wall, etc.: see MEUSE *sb.* and cf. SMOOT *sb.*[1]

A common dialect form, esp. in N. Midland counties.

**1819** in C. W. Hatfield *Hist. Notices Doncaster* (1866) I. 70 By the aid of his dark lantern he knew every smeuce in Wharncliffe or Tankersley parks. **1871** PEACOCK *Ralf Skirl* I. 255 There was a smuice through the hedge just again' where I was stan'in'. **1883** PENNELL-ELMHIRST *Cream of Leicestersh.* 304 There was only one hole—and that a mere smeuse—in the next blackthorn wall.

Hence **smeuse** *v.* = MEUSE *v.*

**1851** R. HILL in Gosse *Nat. Jamaica* 388 The terrier.. smuicing it under the brushwood. **1862** WHYTE MELVILLE *Inside Bar* x, The hounds threw their tongues merrily enough, when they were 'smeusing' through a fence.

**smew** (smjuː). [Origin and relation to SMEE uncertain.] A saw-billed duck (*Mergus* or *Mergellus albellus*) belonging to the merganser group; the white nun. The female is known as the ***red-headed smew***.

**1674** DENT in *Ray's Lett.* (1718) 21 A Pocker, a Smew, three Sheldins. **1678** RAY tr. *Willughby's Ornith.* 338. **1709** *Phil. Trans.* XXVI. 466 *Mergus major cirratus*, the Smew, or White Nun. **1768** PENNANT *Brit. Zool.* II. 439 Red-headed Smew. The head is slightly crested, and of a rust colour. **1785** LATHAM *Gen. Synop. Birds* III. II. 429 The Smew is seen in England only in winter. **1838** AUDUBON *Ornith.* IV. 350 The Smew is a bird of extremely rare occurrence in the United States. **1891** *Nature* 4 June 106/2 Last January a friend showed me a smew..shot on the Dee, near Chester.

*attrib.* **1829** GRIFFITH tr. *Cuvier* VIII. 626 Smew Merganser, *Mergus Albellus*.

**smewk**, obs. form of SMOOK, smoke.

**smiche**, obs. or dial. form of SMITCH *sb.*

†**smick**, *v. Obs. rare.* [prob. a jingling modification of SMACK *v.*[2] Cf. SMICK-SMACK.] *trans.* and *intr.* ? To kiss.

**1572** *Schole ho. Women* 132 in Hazl. *E.P.P.* IV. 110 Haue you once turned your eye and back, An other she wil haue to smick and smack. **1685-8** in *Bagford Ballads* (1876) 68 You smack, you smick, you wash, you lick, you smirk, you swear, you grin.

†**ˈsmicker**, *a. Obs.* Forms: 1 **smicer**, 3 *Orm.* **smikerr**, 6-7 **smicker**. [OE. *smicer*: cf. OHG. *smehhar*, *smechar* (MHG. *smecker*) elegant, delicate.]

**1.** Beautiful, elegant, fair, handsome. In later use only of persons.

*c* **725** *Corpus Gl.* (Hessels) E 141 *Elegans*, smicre. *a* **1000** in Cockayne *The Shrine* (1864) 163 Þat he maȝe windan maniȝne smicerne wæn & maniȝ ænlic hus settan. *a* **1000** in Thorpe *Dipl. Angl. Sax.* (1865) 536 Hio..bit þæt hi findon betweox him twa smicere scencingcuppan into beodern for hi. *c* **1200** ORMIN 13679 Þurrh whatt he fell..Inntill niþ hellepine, & warrþ till atell defell þær Off shene & smikerr enngell. **1590** TARLTON *News Purg.* (1844) 114 The Smith seeing what a smicker wench the Coblers wife was,.. sorrowed at the good fortune of the Cobler, that he had so faire a wife. **1590** LODGE *Euphues* (1592) P iv b, A smicker boy, a lyther Swaine, heigh ho a smicker Swaine: That in his Loue was wanton faine, with smiling looks straight came vnto her.

*absol.* **1639** J. SMYTH in *Glouc. Gloss.* (1890) 201 Smoke will to the smicker: meaninge, If many gossips sit against a smokey chimney the smoke will bend to the fairest.

**2.** Of looks: Smirking, gay.

**1589** PEELE *Eclogue Gratulatory* 4 Why bin thy looks so smicker and so proud?

**3.** Loose or lax; wanton.

**1606** FORD *Fame's Memorial* xxx, Reguardfull of his honor he forsooke The smicker vse of court-humanity.

**ˈsmicker**, *v.* Now only *Sc.* Also 9 **smikker**. [app. f. prec.]

†**1.** *intr.* To look amorously or wantonly *at* or *after* a person. *Obs.*

**1668** DRYDEN *Even. Love* III. i, Must you be smickering after Wenches, while I am in Calamity? **1668** DAVENANT *Man's the Master* II. i, No, no, I see I may make love long enough before you smicker at me.

**2.** *Sc.* To smile or smirk.

**1802** SIBBALD *Chron. Scot. Poetry* Gloss., *Smikker*, to smile in a seducing manner. **1819** TENNANT *Papistry Storm'd* (1827) 70 At him, my grandsher, and the Vicar,.. The god o' gaups did laugh and smikker. **1888** DELDAY in Edwards *Mod. Sc. Poets* 12th Ser. 41 To pass the time and have a chat, And see them sweetly smicker.

Hence †**ˈsmickering** *vbl. sb.*, an amorous inclination. *Obs.*

**1699** DRYDEN *Let. to Mrs. Steward* 28 Sept., We had a young doctour, who rode by our coach, and seem'd to have a smickering to our young lady of Pilton.

**ˈsmickering**, *ppl. a. rare*[−1]. That smirks or smickers.

**1930** W. DE LA MARE *Poems for Children* 17 All turned their heads with a smickering smile.

**smicket** ('smɪkɛt). Now *dial.* Also 7-8 **smickit.** [app. dim. of SMOCK *sb.*] A woman's smock or chemise; a small smock.

In use during the 19th cent in many dialects.

*c* **1685** *Adv. to Maidens Lond.* ii. in *Bagford Ballads* (1878) 935 Susan and Joan they will have a Top-Knot, although they have never a Smicket. *c* **1690** in *Roxb. Ball.* (1883) IV. 439 Stripping of all their Cloaths, their Gowns, their Petticoats, Shoes and Hose, Their fine white smickits then stripping. **1718** OZELL tr. *Tournefort's Voy.* I. 219 Over this Smicket they wear a large smock. *Ibid.*, Thus are their richest Smickets no better than a penitential Shirt. **1772** BRYDGES *Hom. Trav.* (1797) I. 337 His dear Nelly, who had scarce An undarn'd smicket. **1815** W. H. IRELAND *Scribbleom.* 141 Misses.. Who, drench'd, ne'er catch cold, though without change of smickets. **1820** COMBE *Syntax, Consol.* v. II. 199 The white smickets wave below, While.. The petticoats appear'd as banners. **1897** E. PHILLPOTTS *Lying Prophets* 177, I found the whole fortune hid beneath her smickets.

†**'smickly,** *adv.* *Obs.*[-1] [Cf. SMICKER *a.*] Elegantly, finely.

**1624** FORD *Sun's Darling* II. i, *Ray.* What's he that looks so smickly? *Fol.* One that loves mutton so well, he always carries capers about him.

**smick-smack,** *sb.* and *a.* [Cf. SMICK *v.* and SMACK *sb.*[2]]

†**A.** *sb.* A smacking noise; a smacking or frequent kissing. *Obs.*

*c* **1550** *Lusty Iuventus* in Hazl. *Dodsley* II. 85 What a hurly-burly is here! Smick smack, and all this gear! **1677** MIÉGE *Fr. Dict.* II. s.v. *Smack*, Smick-smack, *baisotement.*

**B.** *adj.* Elegant, first-rate. *rare*[-1].

**1802** *Spirit Publ. Jrnls.* VI. 186 The Bacchanalian glees were loudly applauded, and the smick smack repast went off with its usual *eclat.*

**smiddie, -dy,** north. and Sc. varr. SMITHY *sb.*

**'smiddum.** *Mining.* [varr. of SMEDDUM.] = SMITHAM 2. Also *attrib.*

**1821** W. FORSTER *Section Strata* (ed. 2) 341 The Ore, that collects at the bottom of the Tub, is called *Smiddum.* **1858** SIMMONDS *Dict. Trade, Smiddum-tails*, in mining, the sludge or slimy portion deposited in washing ore. **1892** HESLOP *Northumb. Gloss., Smiddum*, small particles of lead ore [etc.].

**smidge** (smɪdʒ). [Origin unknown, perh. f. SMITCH *sb.*[2]: cf. next.] A tiny amount. Orig. and chiefly *U.S.*

**1905** *Dialect Notes* III. 65 *Smidge, smitch*, n., smallest piece, tiniest particle. **1934** *Sun* (Baltimore) 21 Sept. 1/6 Every last smidge of his record will be investigated. **1965** AUDEN *About House* (1966) 17 Surrender my smidge Of nitrogen to the World Fund. **1967** 'E. QUEEN' *Face to Face* xli. 184 Do you suppose I might have a smidge of that, Inspector? It looks so good, and I haven't had any breakfast. **1973** *Observer* 28 Oct. 48/4 Inviting us to buy their mail-order course for a smidge under £13. **1976** *Washington Post* 15 June A7/2 A Democratic Party that can't even afford..a smidge of debate.

**smidgen** ('smɪdʒɪn). orig. and chiefly *U.S.* Also **smidgeon, smidgin, smitchin,** etc. [Origin unknown, perh. f. SMITCH *sb.*[2] + *-en, -in*, repr. dial. pronunc. of -ING[1]: cf. prec.] A tiny amount, a trace; a very small person or thing.

**1845** C. M. KIRKLAND *Western Clearings* 71 They wouldn't have left a smitchin o' honey. **1878** J. H. BEADLE *Western Wilds* 611 Not a smidgeon left—just bodaciously chawed up and spit out. **1886** *Trans. Amer. Philol. Assoc.* XVII. 43 *Smidgen*, 'a small bit, a grain', as 'a *smidgen* of meal', is common in East Tennessee. **1913** [see CLIP *sb.*[2] 4]. **1930** *Va. Quarterly Rev.* 6 Apr. 249 He can testify perhaps ..that he has had a bait, a snack, or a mere smidgen of them. **1952** J. STEINBECK *East of Eden* xxiii. 289 You little, silly, half-pint, smidgin of a wife. **1954** R. MILLAR *Waiting for Gillian* in *Plays of the Year* X. 346 There's a smidgin of Gordon's in the whisky decanter. **1960** WODEHOUSE *Jeeves in Offing* iv. 45 'No will of her own?' 'Not a smidgeon.' **1968** *Globe & Mail* (Toronto) 17 Feb. 37 (Advt.), Whether you're nine months or ninety years old, plump or twiggy, tall as a tree or small as a smidgeon. **1971** *N.Z. Listener* 18 Oct. 11/5 It's an unknown quantity often combined with just a smidgen of skill. **1973** *People's Jrnl.* (Inverness & Northern Counties ed.) 15 Dec. 4/5 My family would eat mince pies to a band playing so long as there's at least a smidgeon of rum butter to wipe over the top crust. **1982** R. CONQUEST in *Times Lit. Suppl.* 17 Dec. 1385/4 Any writer allowing the merest smidgin of Soviet reality into his work was headed straight for Magadan.

**smie,** dial. variant of SMY (fish).

**smifligate, -ation,** variants of SPIFLICATE *v.*, SPIFLICATION.

**1839** DICKENS *Nickleby* xxvii, Mr. Pyke threatened with many oaths to 'smifligate' a very old man. *Ibid.*, Conjecturing..that smifligation and bloodshed must be one and the same thing.

**smift.** *Mining.* [Of obscure origin.] A kind of fuse or slow match used in blasting.

**1839** URE *Dict. Arts* 836 Paper rubbed over with gun-powder or grease, for the smifts or fuses. *Ibid.*, A paper smift ..is then fixed to the top of the rush-tube. **1871** W. MORGANS *Mining Tools* 137 A 'smift', which is variously made of either a bit of touch-wood, touch-paper, greased candle-wick or paper,..is attached by a bit of grease or clay to the outside end of the train.

**smig.** Also **smigg.** [Of obscure origin.] (See quot. *a* 1880.) Also attrib., as ***smig bait, herring.***

**1879** *Standard* 17 July 3/7 The mackerel were so intent upon chasing shoals of smigg, that numbers of them were stranded on the beach. *a* **1880** BUCKLAND *Nat. Hist. Brit. Fishes* 281 If a basket of whitebait be examined in April there will be found a large number of minute fish 1 in. to 1½ in. long, perfectly transparent, with a large eye and no scales visible, the body being covered with a few black spots. These are called 'smig herring'. *Ibid.* 282 The spratty stuff and the 'smig' bait comes up the river first.

**'smiggins.** *Cant.* (See quots.)

**1825** KNAPP & BALDWIN *Newgate Cal.* III. 489/1 The Water in which the beef was boiled is thickened with barley, and forms a mess called smiggins. **1828** P. CUNNINGHAM *N.S. Wales* (ed. 3) II. 63 Descanting upon the sorrows of sour *smiggins* (cold-meat hash). **1839** *Slang Dict.* 34 *Smiggins*, nickname for a soup given on board the hulks.

**'smiggot.** *rare*[-1]. *Devon.* A particle, atom.

**1823** *New Monthly Mag.* VIII. 502 Deuce a smiggott of aught wonderful saw we.

**smight,** obs. form of SMITE *v.*

**smil,** obs. form of SMELL *sb.*

**smilacin** ('smaɪləsɪn). *Chem.* [a. F. *smilacin*, f. *smilac-*, stem of SMILAX + -IN[1].] Parillin.

**1836** BRANDE *Chemistry* (ed. 4) 1047 The parillin and smilacin of Palotta and Folchi, I have not been able to identify. **1838** THOMSON *Chem. Org. Bodies* 137 Smilacin is obtained from the root of the Smilax sarsaparilla. **1871** GARROD *Mat. Med.* (ed. 3) 336 Sarsaparilla contains..a peculiar principle occurring as a white powder, *Smilacin*, of which little is known.

**smilacina** (smaɪlə'saɪnə). [mod.L. (R. L. Desfontaines 1807, in *Ann. Mus. Hist. Nat.* IX. 51), f. *smilac-*, SMILAX + -INA[2].] A perennial herb of the genus so called, belonging to the family Liliaceæ, native to North America or temperate parts of Asia, and bearing terminal clusters of small white flowers; also called false Solomon's seal.

**1808** *Curtis's Bot. Mag.* XXIX. 1155 (*heading*) Oval-Leaved Smilacina. **1890** *Harper's Mag.* Apr. 709/1 The little smilacina lifts its spike of tiny, fragrant blossoms. **1970** B. MILES *Bluebells & Bittersweet* viii. 141/3 Though perhaps not as well known [as Solomon's seal], smilacina wants the same situation.

**smilax** ('smaɪlæks). *Bot.* [a. L. *smīlax* (Pliny), a. Gr. σμῖλαξ bindweed, etc.]

**1.** A large genus of liliaceous plants typical of the order *Smilaceæ*, or a species of this genus, the tuberous rootstocks of which constitute the sarsaparilla of commerce.

In earlier writers, as Morwyng (1559) and Turner (1562), *smilax* is used in other senses of the L. and Gr. word, after passages in Pliny or Dioscorides.

**1601** HOLLAND *Pliny* II. 190 Some haue said that Smilax is of 2 sorts: the one..climbing trees, & tufted in the head with clusters..of berries. *c* **1610** FAIRFAX *Eclogues* IV. xv, Bay, Smilax, Myrtle.. Grew there. **1671** SALMON *Syn. Med.* III. xxii. 432 Smilax,..Bindweed; it opens the belly, dissolves hard swellings. **1710** W. KING *Heathen Gods & Heroes* xxvii. (1722) 134 The Ivy, the Smilax, or Ropeweed, ..were the Vegetables that he [Bacchus] delighted in. **1817** J. BRADBURY *Trav. Amer.* 30 There was also an abundance of small prickly vines entwined among the bushes, of a species of smilax. **1839** AUDUBON *Ornith. Biog.* I. 302 The Green Briar, or Round-leaved Smilax,..is common along fences. **1874** COUES *Birds N.W.* 162 The ravines overgrown with smilax and brambles.

*attrib.* **1899** F. V. KIRBY *Sport E.C. Africa* xi. 124 A mass of thorny shrubs woven into an almost solid block by a growth of convolvulus creepers and of the twining smilax yam.

**2.** A climbing species of asparagus, *Myrsiphylium asparagoides*, much used for decorative purposes.

**1870** *Daily News* 13 June, The sprays of smilax, the roses and violets, bloomed from baskets in the windows. **1887** *The Lady* 20 Jan. 38/3 A large square of pink plush was outlined against the white damask, with a broad, graceful border of smilax.

**smile** (smaɪl), *sb.*[1] Also 6 **smyle,** 7 *Sc.* **smyl.** [f. SMILE *v.* Cf. MHG. *smiel*, Da., Sw., Norw. *smil* (NFris, *smiil*, from Da.).]

**1. a.** An act of smiling; a slight and more or less involuntary movement of the countenance expressive of pleasure, amusement, affection, etc., or of amused contempt, disdain, incredulity, or similar emotion. Also in phr. (*to be*) *all smiles*, i.e. wreathed in smiles.

**1562** HEYWOOD *Prov. & Epigr.* (1867) 78 Better is the last smyle, than the fyrst laughter. **1591** NASHE *Pref. Sidney's Astr. & Stella* in G. G. Smith *Eliz. Crit. Ess.* II. 228, I will leaue you to..offer your smiles on the Aulters of Venus. **1621** QUARLES *Div. Poems, Esther* (1638) 105 Where are thy maiden-smiles, thy blushing cheeke? **1667** MILTON *P.L.* IX. 239 This sweet intercourse Of looks and smiles. **1717** LADY M. W. MONTAGU *Lett.* II. xliv. 20 Every smile is waited for with impatience and envied by those who cannot obtain it. **1794** MRS. RADCLIFFE *Myst. Udolpho* vii, St. Aubert gave him a friendly smile for his compliment. **1842** BORROW *Bible in Spain* xiii, The duke was all smiles and courtesy. **1875** GRINDON *Life* xiv. 173 There are more smiles in the world than there are tears. **1916** G. B. SHAW *Pygmalion* III. 154 Higgins:..Dont be nervous about it. Pitch it in strong. Clara (all smiles): I will. Good-bye.

**b.** *transf.* and *fig.*

**1589** GREENE *Menaphon* (Arb.) 23 To see if the Continent were as full of smiles, as the seas were of fauours. **1613** SHAKS. *Hen. VIII*, II. iv. 187 Me thought I stood not in the smile of Heauen. **1727** DYER *Grongar Hill* 82 Transient is the smile of Fate. **1757** GRAY *Bard* 82 Fell Thirst and Famine scowl A baleful smile. **1814** SCOTT *Lord of Isles* v. vi, The sun.. Now tinged them with a parting smile. **1831** —— *Cast. Dang.* xi, A knight, who..was poor in worldly goods, and in the smiles of fortune. **1859** TENNYSON *Marriage of Geraint* 350 Turn, Fortune, turn thy wheel with smile or frown.

**c.** Const. *of* (some quality, feeling, etc.).

**1779** *Mirror* No. 64, I discovered a smile of satisfaction in the countenances of most of the guests. **1794** MRS. RADCLIFFE *Myst. Udolpho* xxxvi, Where he was surrounded with plenty, elegance, and smiles of welcome. **1816** SCOTT *Old Mort.* xxx, At this moment another smile of deep meaning passed between Dalzell and Claverhouse. **1848** THACKERAY *Van. Fair* xx, Beyond the first smile of recognition. **1859** *Habits of Gd. Society* vii. 246, I never yet saw a smile of pity or sympathy on his face.

**2.** *colloq.* A drink, *esp.* of whisky. orig. *U.S.*

**1839** *Spirit of Times* 24 Aug. 294/3 We all agreed to take another smile. **1859** BARTLETT *Dict. Amer.* (ed. 2) 420 *Smile*, a drink, dram. **188.** G. H. KINGSLEY *Sport & Trav.* (1900) vi. 186 You just take a 'smile' of the real, old, blue-grass Bourbon. **1889** JEROME *Three Men in Boat* ii, Harris.. proposed that we should go out and have a smile.

**3. a.** *Comb.*, as ***smile-covering, -frowning, -peopled, -tuned, -wreathed*** adjs.; ***smile-maker.***

*a* **1618** SYLVESTER *Sonn.* i. Wks. (Grosart) II. 50 Eyes cloudy-clear, smile-frowning, stormy-calm. **1676** WYCHERLEY *Pl. Dealer* II. i, I cou'd not sit to a vain young Smile-maker tho' he flatter'd me. **1817** SHELLEY *Rev. Islam* II. xxxiv, The tranquil strength which cradled lay In her smile-peopled rest. **1825** HOOK *Sayings* Ser. II. *Sutherl.* I. 123 A consequent smile-covering frown from the young lady. *c* **1845** MRS. BROWNING *An Island* xxv, Yea, soon, no consonant unsmooth Our smile-tuned lips shall reach. **1895** in *Westm. Gaz.* 12 June 7/3 His sparkling eyes and smile-wreathed face telling of the zest with which the novelty was enjoyed.

**b.** *attrib.*, as ***smile-line, -wrinkle.***

**1921** W. DE LA MARE *Memoirs of Midget* xxiv. 158, I looked at his long, fair eyelashes and the smile-line on his cheek. **1977** *New Yorker* 19 Sept. 58/3 Firkusny is a tall, lithe, trim man with gray hair, blue eyes, and smile lines in his face which soften an almost austere handsomeness. *a* **1930** D. H. LAWRENCE *Phoenix II* (1968) III. 254 The smile-wrinkles on the fresh, pleased face, they give odd quivers.

**smile,** *sb.*[2] *dial.* Also **smale.** [Representing OE. *smyȝel* 'cuniculus' (only in glosses), related to *smúȝan* to creep.] (See quot.)

**1823** E. MOOR *Suffolk Words, Smile*, the same, I believe, or nearly, as Smale; the form or fourm, or seat of a hare.

**smile** (smaɪl), *v.* Forms: α. 4-5 **smylle,** 4-6 **smyle,** *Sc.* 5-6 **smyll,** 7 **smill,** 4- **smile.** β. 6-7 **smoyle,** 7, 9 *dial.* **smoile.** [ME. *smilen*, = OHG. *smîlan* (in pres. pple. *smîlenter*; MHG. *smielen*), also Da. *smile* (hence NFris. *smile*), Norw. and Sw. *smila*; these are prob. adoptions from a MLG. **smîlen*, which may also have been the source of the English word.]

**I.** *intr.* **1. a.** Of persons: To give to the features or face a look expressive of pleasure or amusement, or of amused disdain, scorn, etc.

*to smile in one's sleeve*: see SLEEVE *sb.* 2 d.

α. *a* **1300** *Cursor M.* 2731 'Thar þe noght in hethyng smylle.' Sco said, 'for soth smild i noght'. **1338** R. BRUNNE *Chron.* (1810) 185 Philip held him stille, & bigan to smyle. **1390** GOWER *Conf.* II. 14 For with a goodly lok sche smyleth. *c* **1440** *Alph. Tales* cccl. 241 So þis Cardinall smylid, & commendid hym for his gude tale. *c* **1475** *Rauf Coilȝear* 711 The King preuilie smylit, Quhen he saw that bald. **1530** PALSGR. 722/2, I smyle, I make a countenaunce towarde laughyng and laughe nat outryght, *je me soubzris.* **1560** DAUS tr. *Sleidane's Comm.* 128 b, He..began to smile, & contempne theyr answere. **1601** SHAKS. *Jul. C.* IV. i. 50 Some that smile, haue in their hearts I feare Millions of Mischeefes. **1670** CLARENDON *Hist. Reb.* XIII. §4 They.. reprehended him very sharply if he smiled on those days. **1711** STEELE *Spect.* No. 2 ¶5 He can smile when one speaks to him, and laughs easily. **1754** SHEBBEARE *Matrimony* (1766) II. 107 She hung at Sir William's arm, Smiling in his Face. **1848** THACKERAY *Van. Fair* lvi, He..would smile when George came down late for breakfast. **1898** J. ARCH *Story Life* xv. 357 Chamberlain was smiling all over his face.

β. **1599** BRETON *Mamillia* Wks. (Grosart) II. 49/1 And,.. like an olde horses neyghing, would he be smoyling. **1614** —— *I would & I would not* lxxix, I would I were an honest Countrey-Wench, That only could make Curtsey, smoile, and blush. **1864** TENNYSON *N. Farmer* I. xiv, Loook 'ow quoloty smoiles when they seeäs ma a passin' boy.

**b.** *transf.* and *fig.*

**1594** *1st Pt. Contention* viii, In that I intreat you to vse her well. The world may smile againe and I may liue, To do you fauour if you do it her. **1596** SHAKS. *Two Gentl.* I. ii. 63 When inward ioy enforc'd my heart to smile. **1667** MILTON *P.L.* IX. 480 Then let me not let pass Occasion which now smiles; behold alone The woman [etc.]. **1747** GRAY *Fav. Cat* 28 Malignant Fate sat by, and smil'd. **1794** MRS. RADCLIFFE *Myst. Udolpho* xxxii, Thy soothing strains the pensive heart beguile, And bid the visions of the future smile. *a* **1822** SHELLEY *Mutability* (2) 1 The flower that smiles to-day To-morrow dies. **1825** HOOK *Sayings* Ser. II. *Sutherl.* I. 110 Now indeed was the crisis of his fate at hand, every thing smiled.

**c.** In the slang phrase ***I should smile***, used to ridicule an idea (chiefly *U.S.*). Also in phr. ***to come up smiling***: see COME *v.* 74 b.

**1883** C. H. HOYT *Bunch of Keys* III, in *Five Plays* (1944) 48 'Single room?' 'Well, I should smile.' **1889** 'MARK TWAIN' *Conn. Yank.* ix. 113 They actually wanted *me* to put in! Well, I should smile. **1891** *Youth's Companion* 138 Sing for nothing? Well I should smile!

**d.** Of eyes: to express pleasure, amusement, etc.

**1759** C. Wesley in J. & C. Wesley *Funeral Hymns* 2nd Ser. 37 Those laughing eyes shall smile no more. *a* **1889** G. M. Hopkins *Poems* (1967) 37 And May has come, hair-bound in flowers, With eyes that smile thro' the tears of the hours. **1938** Dylan Thomas in *Seven* Winter 17 She wept in her pain and made mouths, Talked and tore though her eyes smiled. **1940** W. Faulkner *Hamlet* iv. i. 289 His face changed—something fleeting, quizzical, but not smiling, his eyes did not smile.

**2. a.** To look *on*, *upon*, *at*, or *to* a person with a smile or pleasant expression. Also with *advbs.*, as *back*, *down*, *over*, *up*.

**1390** Gower *Conf.* II. 228 Achilles..upon himself to smyle Began, when he was so besein. *c* **1440** *Bone Florence* 1790 He at them can smyle. **1558** Phaer *Æneid* I. A iiij, The maker of the Gods and men to her all swetely smyles. **1581** Pettie *Guazzo's Civ. Conv.* II. (1586) 73 b, To smile upon euerie man, is rather a signe of a vaine minde, then of a cheerefull countenance. **1676** Hobbes *Iliad* (1677) 15 His mother on him smil'd. **1711** Addison *Spect.* No. 69 ¶2 Sir Andrew, who often smiles upon me as he sees me bustling in the Crowd. **1749** Smollett *Gil Blas* xii. xiii. (1782) IV. 268 At these words of my god-daughter, I smiled to her father. **1794** Mrs. Radcliffe *Myst. Udolpho* lii, Ludovico smiled at Annette, and bowed to Emily. **1845** [see rank *sb.*[1] 3 b]. **1847** Marryat *Childr. N. Forest* viii, Edward..smiled upon the little girl. **1860** A. J. Evans *Beulah* xx. 177 He smiled down into her tearful face. **1866** Mrs. C. J. Newby *Common Sense* II. 88 The cheerful rallying tone awoke something of the old pride in him, and he smiled up. **1889** R. L. Stevenson *Master of Ballantrae* iv. 111 How was he to smile back on the deceiver? **1896** Mrs. Steel *Face Waters* ii. iii, They had smiled on little Sonny Seymour as he passed them. **1905** E. M. Albanesi *Brown Eyes of Mary* iii. 38 She smiled up at him from under the white sunshade. **1908** *Smart Set* June 89/1 The girl pushed aside the screen and smiled over at her. **1949** A. Miller *Death of Salesman* 132 He's a man way out there in the blue, riding on a smile and a shoeshine. And when they start not smiling back—that's an earthquake. **1952** E. O'Neill *Moon for Misbegotten* i. 40 She smiles down at Jim, her face softening.

*transf.* **1610** Holland *Camden's Brit.* 499 In the Spring time, the medowes arraied with pleasant flowers smile upon the beholders. **1667** Milton *P.L.* v. 124 When fair Morning first smiles on the world. **1821** Shelley *Adonais* xxxii. 8 On the withering flower The killing sun smiles brightly.

**b.** To look *on* or *upon* one with favour, approval, or encouragement. Freq. *fig.*

*c* **1400** *Rom. Rose* 4355 It is of Love, as of Fortune,.. Which whylom wol on folke smyle, And gloumbe on hem another whyle. **1508** Dunbar *Gold. Targe* 218 Fair Calling did oft apon me smyle, And Cherising me fed wyth wordis fair. **1594** Shaks. *Rich. III*, v. v. 20 Smile Heauen vpon this faire Coniunction, That long haue frown'd vpon their Enmity. **1638** Sir T. Herbert *Trav.* (ed. 2) 220 Yet was it [i.e. a palace] able to smile upon Alexander, when hee extracted thence to pay his Soldats. *c* **1657** Sir W. Mure *Hist. Ho. Rowallane* Wks. (S.T.S.) II. 250 At yᵗ time the Court seemed to smill vpon him. **1709–10** Steele in *Lett. Lit. Men* (Camden) 345 My Lord Hallifax has smiled upon his labours. **1748** Gray *Alliance* 16 If equal Justice with unclouded Face Smile not indulgent on the rising Race. **1833** Ht. Martineau *Tale of Tyne* iii. 60 It is the duty of government to smile on undertakings which favour the industry of the people. **1878** Bosw. Smith *Carthage* 281 Circumstances..seemed to smile on the project.

**c.** To show by the features one's amusement (or pleasure) *at* something.

*c* **1375** *Sc. Leg. Saints* xviii. (*Mary Egypt*) 509 3one 3onge man..at myn fule speke smylit in hy. *c* **1385** Chaucer *L.G.W.* 2123 *Ariadne*, This lady smylith at his stedefastnesse. *c* **1470** Henry *Wallace* xi. 1384 Than Wallace smyld a litill at his langage. **1596** Shaks. *Tam. Shr.* v. ii. 3 Time it is when raging warre is done, To smile at scapes and perils ouerblowne. **1623** Camden *Rem.* (1636) 245 Our first finest Poets may smile at the verses of that time as succeeding ages..will haply smile at theirs. **1681** Dryden *Abs. & Achit.* 912 While he withdrawn at their mad Labour smiles. **1719** De Foe *Crusoe* ii. (Globe) 356 The Spaniard only smil'd at that, and made him no Answer. **1817** Shelley *Rev. Islam* ii. xxxix, Wherefore dost thou smile At what I say? **1879** Mrs. A. E. James *Ind. Househ. Managem.* 60 Though they may smile inwardly at your ways,..they will never allow the smile to be outwardly seen.

**3.** Of physical features, things, etc.: To have or present an agreeable or pleasing aspect.

Common in 18th cent. poetry.

**1594** Kyd *Cornelia* iv. ii, O Faire Sunne, that gentlie smiles From the Orient-pearled Iles. **1667** Milton *P.L.* iv. 165 Cheard with the grateful smell old Ocean smiles. **1703** Rowe *Fair Penitent* ii. i, A better Order of succeeding Days Come smiling forward, white and lucky all. **1769** Sir W. Jones *Palace Fortune* Poems (1777) 26 Each meadow blossom'd, and each valley smil'd. **1805** Wordsw. *Elegiac Stanzas* 19 A sea that could not cease to smile. **1878** Bosw. Smith *Carthage* 11 A country smiling with cornfields and gardens.

**4.** Of wine, beer, etc.: To sparkle. ? *Obs.*

*a* **1700** B. E. *Dict. Cant. Crew* s.v. *Mantles*, When Drink is brisk and smiles. **1721** Mortimer *Husb.* (ed. 2) II. 325 It flushes violently out of the Cock..and then stops on a sudden, and pearls and smiles in a Glass like any bottled Beer. **1828** in Carr *Craven Gloss.*

**5.** (*U.S.*) *slang.* To drink; to have or take a drink.

**1858** [see smiling *vbl. sb.* 2]. **1865** J. C. Hotten in 'Artemus Ward' *His Book* 18 *note*, 'Let us take a tod' was formerly a common phrase. Recently, however, 'To Kiss the Baby' and to 'Smile' have taken its place. **1870** *Daily News* 7 Feb., This 'gentleman'..asked me to 'smile'. I had learned by experience that this is the slang phrase for 'taking a drink'.

**II.** *trans.* **6. a.** To bring or convert into a specified condition by smiling. Const. *in*, *into*, *out of*, etc.

**1588** Shaks. *L.L.L.* v. ii. 465 Som Dick That smiles his checke [= cheek] in yeares. **1601** —— *Twel. N.* iii. ii. 84 He does smile his face into more lynes, then is in the new Mappe. **1608** —— *Pericles* v. i. 139 Thou doest looke like patience..smiling extremitie out of act. **1728** Young *Love of Fame* i. 46 What author shall we find..The courtly Roman's smiling path to tread, And sharply smile prevailing folly dead?

**b.** To dismiss, get rid of, drive *away* (something) with a smile or smiles; to while *away* (time), dry *up* (tears), in or by smiling. Also with *down*, *out*.

**1760–72** H. Brooke *Fool of Qual.* (1809) III. 142 The great ones of thy court have audaciously smiled away the gloom and horrors of guilt. **1792** S. Rogers *Pleas. Mem.* ii. 78 When sober Judgment has his throne resigned She smiles away the chaos of the mind. **1803** Visct. Strangford *Poems of Camoens* Sonn. xx. (1810) 106 Those charming eyes, within whose starry sphere Love whilom sat, and smil'd the hours away. *c* **1850** Mrs. Browning *Hector & Andromache* 102 She received him straight To her bosom's fragrance—smiling up her tears. **1860** G. Meredith *Evan Harrington* xi. 111 'Another!' the hostess instantly smiled down the inhospitable outcry. **1885** 'L. Malet' *Col. Enderby's Wife* i. iii, A woman's reputation must not be smiled away.

*transf.* **1827** Hood *Hero & Leander* xxviii, The drowsy world shone brighten'd in reply; And smiling off her fogs, his slanting beam [etc.]. **1936** R. Campbell *Mithraic Emblems* 52 It is the blossom in our blood With folded petals smiling out the sere, Brown, shuffled slippers of the limping year.

†**7.** To treat with contempt or disdain; to deride, laugh at. *Obs.*⁻¹

**1605** Shaks. *Lear* ii. ii. 88 A plague vpon your Epilepticke visage, Smoile you my speeches, as I were a Foole?

**8. a.** To answer or repeat by smiling.

**1621** G. Sandys *Ovid's Met.* iii. (1632) 91 Thou smil'st my smiles: when I a teare let fall, Thou shedd'st an other.

**b.** To exhibit, indicate, or express by smiling; to grant, bestow, etc., with a smile; with direct speech as obj., to say with a smile. Also *fig.* and with *in* (quot. 1860).

**1646** J. Hall *Poems* 29 Yet it is midnight still with me, Nay worse, unless that kinder she Smile Day. **1803** W. R. Spencer *Year of Sorrow* 46 Thy Susan..Smiled no sweet sunshine on thy closing day. **1814** Byron *Lara* ii. xvii, He ..sadly smiles his thanks to that dark page. **1853** Kane *Grinnell Exped.* xlvi. (1856) 423 They cannot be said to smile a welcome upon the navigator. **1860** Lever *One of Them* iii, 'The very remark I was about to make, my Lord,' smiled in Mrs. Morris. **1880** *Daily Telegr.* 21 Feb., She smiled disbelief. **1886** 'M. Gray' *Silence of Dean Maitland* III. ii. 35 'This is alarming,' smiled the dean. **1902** H. James *Wings of Dove* xv. 231 'He won't..make up his mind about me.' 'Well,' Milly smiled, 'give him time.' **1936** W. Holtby *South Riding* iii. iii. 175 'Well, Dolly, I hope you're looking after these young men,' smiled Carne shyly. **1976** H. MacInnes *Agent in Place* xix. 208 'Not for me,' Georges smiled.

**c.** With cognate object: To give (a smile, esp. one of a specified kind).

**1837** Dickens *Pickw.* xxiii, Mr. Weller junior smiled a filial smile. **1862** Miss Braddon *Lady Audley* xl, She smiled the queerest smile. **1868** Helps *Realmah* ii. (1876) 21 The Caliph smiled a grim smile.

Hence **'smileable** *a.*, at which one may smile; **smiled** *ppl. a.*, spoken or given with a smile; also with *out*.

**1830** *Blackw. Mag.* XXVIII. 893 All speak,..or smile, of all the speakable..and smileable little interesting affairs. **1850** W. C. Bennett *Baby May* Poems 12 Tiny scorns of smiled reprovings That have more of love than lovings. **1892** C. E. Norton *Dante's Parad.* i. 5, I was divested of my first doubt by these brief little smiled-out words.

**'smileful**, *a.* [f. smile *sb.*] Full of smiles; smiling.

**1609** Armin *Maids of More-Clacke* E iv, Be smilefull, and expresse no griefe in sithes. **1850** in Ogilvie. **1895** *Advance* (Chicago) 1 Aug. 157/1 The epoch is signalized with garlands and high festival, with assemblies tearful and smileful.

Hence **'smilefulness**.

**1887** F. Wilson *Alma Murray as Juliet* 13 The flickering smilefulness with which she uttered the lines.

**smileless** ('smaɪllɪs), *a.* [f. smile *sb.*]

**1.** Of persons, the features, expression, etc.: Exhibiting no smile; never smiling; grave, severe.

**1719** Lady Wardlaw *Hardyknute* xxxiv, With smyless luke, and visage wan, The wounded Knight replied. **1837** Wordsw. *Night thought* 11 Ingrates who wear a smileless face The whole year through. **1838** Lytton *Alice* xi. i, Pale, wan,..smileless, she was the ghost of her former self. **1882** C. D. Warner *W. Irving* x. 295 The smileless prig has begun to weary even the popular fancy. **1892** G. Hake *Mem.* xxxv. 115 That free, smileless expression.

**b.** Of words, etc.: Uttered without a smile.

**1810** S. Green *Reformist* I. 208 She either replied not at all, or only answered her by a smileless monosyllable. **1877** *Daily News* 30 Nov., It is a fearfully impressive thing to listen to his smileless, unaltering harangues.

**2.** Devoid of brightness or cheerfulness; dark, dull, cheerless.

**1858** Lytton *What will he do?* vi. ix, And so the old man, whose life had been so smileless, died smiling. **1858** O. W. Holmes *Aut. Breakfast-t.* iv, That smileless eternity to which they look forward. *a* **1873** Lytton *Pausanias* 60 The very moonlight upon these waters, cold and smileless.

Hence **'smilelessly** *adv.*; **'smilelessness**.

**1844** J. T. Hewlett *Parsons & W.* xxvi, Not only smileless herself, but the cause of smilelessness in others. **1869** Aldrich *Story Bad Boy* 68 At seven o'clock my grandfather comes smilelessly down stairs.

**smiler** ('smaɪlə(r)). [f. smile *v.*]

**1.** One who smiles.

*c* **1386** Chaucer *Knt.'s T.* 1141 Ther saugh I..The smyler with the knyfe vnder the cloke. **1668** Dryden *Even. Love* Epil. 5 Where a lot of Smilers lent an Ear To one that talk'd. **1694** *Poet Buffoon'd* 1 Much like the Losers and the Winners, One Smiler and two hundred Grinners. **1742** Young *Nt. Th.* i. 315 Know, smiler! at thy peril art thou pleas'd. **1795** Aikin *Even. Home* xxix. (Dove) 507 Through her pale and emaciated features, he saw something of his little smiler. **1855** Smedley *H. Coverdale* i, A..pleasant smile it was too.., making the smiler look particularly handsome. **1876** T. Hardy *Ethelberta* (1890) 279 Noticing that a few Gallic smilers were gathering round.

**b.** As a moth-name: (see quot.).

**1832** Rennie *Consp. Butterfl. & Moths* 77 The Smiler (*Polia Polymita*).

**2.** *slang.* A kind of shandy-gaff.

**1892** *Daily News* 16 Nov. 2/3 A singular mixture of beer and lemonade known in Manchester as a smiler. **1900** *Ibid.* 30 Apr. 5/1 To take these generous liquors in the diluted forms of 'shandy-gaff' or 'smiler'.

**Smilesian** ('smaɪlzɪən), *a.* Also **Smilesean**. [f. the name of Samuel *Smiles* + -ian.] Of, pertaining to, or characteristic of Samuel Smiles (1812–1904), author of *Self-Help* (1859) and other works for those who wish to 'improve' themselves by personal effort and initiative, or his thought and writings. Also occas. **Samuel-'Smilesian.**

**1889** G. B. Shaw *Fabian Essays in Socialism* 23 With all its [*sc.* private property's] energy, its Smilesian 'self-help', its merchant-princely enterprise,..what has it heaped up, over and above the pittance of its slaves? **1928** A. Huxley *Point Counter Point* xvii. 298 Most Smilesian souls must smell rather nasty, I should think. **1929** —— *Do what you Will* 151 There are..occasions—and this is what..the Samuel-Smilesian morality refuses to admit—when a man ought to permit himself to be subdued to things. **1968** *Punch* 29 May 792/2 It was up to the individual in a Samuel Smilesian way to restore his own fortunes through personal effort. **1969** G. M. Brown *Orkney Tapestry* ii. 53 Religion was Smilesian —heaven looked with favour on those who strove to improve themselves—unto him that hath shall be given. **1981** J. S. Bratton *Impact of Victorian Children's Fiction* ii. 45 In the year after the Great Exhibition, a thrusting optimistic appeal to Smilesean self-confidence..was certainly the shape of things to come.

**smilesmirk** ('smaɪlsmɜːk), *v.* *nonce-wd.* [f. smile *v.* + smirk *v.*] *intr.* To smile in a smirking manner.

**1922** Joyce *Ulysses* 262 She smilesmirked supercilious.

**'smilet.** *rare.* Also 6 smylet. [f. smile *sb.*] A little or slight smile.

**1592** Fraunce *C'tess Pembroke's Ivychurch* ii. ii, I..knew her face to be framyng Now with a smylet's allure, and now to repell with a frownyng. **1605** Shaks. *Lear* iv. iii. 21 Those happy smilets, That play'd on her ripe lip. **1845** J. J. Hooper *Taking Census* in *Some Adventures Capt. Simon Suggs* 175 The wrinkles on Mr. Kuncker's face formed themselves into fifty little smilets. **1906** E. Phillpotts *Portreeve* 8 Her pretty mouth was sunny with smilets.

**smiley** ('smaɪlɪ), *a.* Also **smily**. [f. smile *sb.*]

**1. a.** Inclined to smile; readily smiling.

**1848** Lowell *Biglow P.* Ser. i. *The Courtin'* x, All kind o' smily round the lips An' teary round the lashes. **1873** Leland *Egypt. Sketch Bk.* 120 How they contrived to be so laughy and smiley on pumpkin-seeds and cold water I cannot conjecture. **1969** D. Francis *Enquiry* vii. 97 It's your eyes... Dark and sort of smiley and sad. **1976** H. Kemelman *Wednesday Rabbi got Wet* iii. 21 A short man.. with a round head and smiley face.

**b.** Smiling; cheerful.

**1970** *Sunday Times* 8 Feb. 15/2 If the instruction wasn't nice and smiley, it'd upset me. **1972** *Times* 1 Dec. 20/2 China —new from France with the smiley face in black on yellow. **1976** R. B. Parker *Promised Land* (1977) vii. 35, I..said goodby with smily pleasant overtones in my voice.

**2.** Caused by or causing a smile.

**1974** *Times* 22 Jan. 11/5 For smiley lines which are too deep, just paint out the start of them with a highlight. **1977** *Rolling Stone* 13 Jan. 52/2 To the extent that he includes these fast, cheerful numbers and smiley oddities such as Cole Porter's 'True Love' and the impenetrable fable 'Crackerbox Palace', Harrison seems hoping to achieve fresh popularity.

**smiling** ('smaɪlɪŋ), *vbl. sb.* [f. smile *v.*]

**1.** The action of the verb; an instance of this, a smile. Also *transf.* and *fig.*

*c* **1375** *Sc. Leg. Saints* xli. (*Agnes*) 129 Scho..at his vordis mad smylyng in manere of scornyng. *c* **1386** Chaucer *Prol.* 119 A Nonne..That of hir smylyng was ful symple and coy. *c* **1440** *Promp. Parv.* 461/1 Smylynge, *subrisus.* **1508** Dunbar *Tua Mariit Wemen* 230, I turne it in a tender luke, ..And him behaldis hamely, with hertly smyling. **1553** Bale *Vocacyon* 27 They flonge vp their cappes..with smylinges and laughinges most dissolutely. **1642** Fuller *Holy & Prof. St.* iii. vii. 167 The beere will be sower for the Suns smiling on it. **17..** Ramsay *Marriage of Lord G.* vi. Wks. 1877 II. 218 I'll study thy delight..And..Fix throughout life a constant smiling. **1771** *Junius Lett.* xlix. (1788) 268 May the gift of smiling never depart from him! **1812** Cary *Dante, Parad.* iii. 24 Wonder not thou..at this my smiling.

*attrib.* *a* **1500** *Chaucer's Dreme* in Speght (1598) 359/1 That smiling signe Was token that the hart encline Would to requests reasonable.

**2.** *U.S.* Drinking, tippling.
**1858** in Bartlett *Dict. Amer.* (1859) 420 There are many more fast boys about—some devoted to the sex—some to horses—some to 'smiling'. **1864** *Reader* 7 Apr. 451/3 Tobacco-chewing..and smiling (the new Yankee phrase for liquoring-up).

**smiling** ('smaılıŋ), *ppl. a.* [f. as prec.]
**1. a.** That smiles; covered with or wearing a smile or smiles.
*a* **1300** *Cursor M.* 11509 Ful suetlik wit smiland chere, [He] biheild þaa giftes riche and dere. **1514** Barclay *Cyt. & Uplondyshman* (Percy Soc.) 12 Anone came our Lorde.. And her saluted, with swete and smylynge chere. **1585** T. Washington tr. *Nicholay's Voy.* i. xx. 24 b, A smiling and dissembling countenance. **1602** Shaks. *Ham.* i. v. 106 Oh Villaine, Villaine, smiling, damned Villaine! **1663** S. Patrick *Parable Pilgr.* xxvii, He thought he saw a Man coming to him with a very smiling aspect. **1770** Goldsm. *Des. Vill.* 222 That house..Where grey-beard mirth and smiling toil retired. **1812** Combe *Syntax, Picturesque* xx. 12 His hat a smiling face o'erspread. **1820** Scott *Monast.* xxi, I can judge of the dark purpose, though it is hid under the smiling brow. **1840** Thackeray *Cox's Diary* June, One of the meekest, smilingest little men I ever saw.
**b.** *transf.* or *fig.*
**1576** Gascoigne *Philomene* Wks. 1910 II. 182 But smyling lucke, bewitcht This peerelesse Prince to thinke, That [etc.]. **1692** Norris *Curs. Refl.* 22 These indeed are pretty smiling sentences. ?**1713** Parnell *On Q. Anne's Peace* Posth. Wks. (1758) 260 Here smiling Safety.. Securely walks, and chearful Plenty there. **1796** Burney *Mem. Metastasio* III. 154 Your own talents,..and smiling time of life, render your election certain. **1837** Lockhart *Scott* IV. i. 17 By..representing every thing in the most smiling colours.
**2.** Characterized by smiles or a smiling manner; accompanied by a smile or smiles. Also *fig.*
**1803** Jane Porter *Thaddeus*, Her smiling tears spoke more than her lips. **1842** Browning *Incident French Camp* iii, Then off there flung in smiling joy, And held himself erect By just his horse's mane, a boy. **1901** G. Douglas *Ho. Green Shutters* 207 The cunning old pryer went on, with a smiling suavity in his voice.
**3.** *transf.* Of physical features, etc.: Looking bright or cheerful; pleasant, agreeable to the sight.
**1725** Pope *Odyss.* x. 108 Smiling calmness silver'd o'er the deep. **1742** Gray *West* 1 In vain to me the smileing Mornings shine. **1750** —— *Elegy* 63 To scatter plenty o'er a smiling land. **1805** Wordsw. *Elegiac Stanzas* 38 Not for a moment could I now behold A smiling sea. **1842** Borrow *Bible in Spain* xvi, The grand..desert of Andalusia, once a smiling garden. **1879** *Edinb. Rev.* CL. 436 The hill above is populous with smiling villas.
**4.** Of beer, etc.: Sparkling. ? *Obs.*
**1725** *Fam. Dict.* s.v. *Bottling of beer*, Scum off the same again, and while it is in a smiling Condition, put three Spoonfuls to each Bottle.
**5.** *Comb.*, as *smiling-featured, -lipped, -sweet.*
**1598** Sylvester *Du Bartas* ii. ii. iv. *Columnes* 710 Those eyes so smiling-sweet. **1827** Pollok *Course T.* (1854) 207 Ye smiling-featured daughters of the sun! **1936** C. S. Lewis in *Oxford Mag.* 14 May 575/2 The smiling-lipped Assyrian, cruel-bearded king.

**'smilingly**, *adv.* [f. prec.] In a smiling manner; with a smile or smiles.
*c* **1500** *Three Kings' Sons* 138 Than seide he smylyngly [etc.]. **1590** Greene *Never too late* (1600) 38 She began thus smilingly to assault him. **1624** in Ellis *Orig. Lett.* Ser. i. III. 174 Nay then, smilingly quoth I, your Majestie will [etc.]. **1698** Fryer *Acc. E. India & P.* 18 His Feet,..he often pulling up into his Cott or Couch, would smilingly cross them. **1760–72** H. Brooke *Fool of Qual.* (1809) IV. 117 He smilingly shook hands with all the domestics. **1828** Moore *Swiss Air* i, He Into his bark leaped smilingly. **1883** *Contemp. Rev.* XLIII. 40 The Queen looks smilingly around her as of old.
**b.** *transf.* Pleasantly, agreeably, cheerfully.
**1806** Wordsw. *Horn Egremont Castle* 70 Bold Hubert lives in glee: Months and years went smilingly. **1846** H. G. Robinson *Odes of Horace* ii. vi, Most smilingly on me that nook, Beyond all others, seems to look. **1858** Lytton *What will He do?* i. iv, How smilingly the stream flows on.

**'smilingness.** [f. as prec.] A smiling condition or expression.
**1816** Byron *Ch. Har.* iii. xvi, The very knowledge that he lived in vain..Had made Despair a smilingness assume. **1835** *New Monthly Mag.* XLIII. 73 The kindness of the eye, the smilingness of the lip, are no more there.

†**smilt**, *a. Obs.*$^{-1}$ In 4 smylt. ? Fine.
**13..** *E.E. Allit. P.* B. 226 As smylt mele vnder smal siue smokes for-þikke.

†**smilt**, *v. Obs.*$^{-1}$ [? Cf. dial. *smilt* the milt of a fish.] *intr.* (See quot.)
**1721** Mortimer *Husb.* (ed. 2) I. 341 Many Corns will smilt, or have their Pulp turn'd into a substance like thick Cream.

**smily**, var. smiley *a.*

**S-mine.** Also S mine. [Abbrev. and anglicization of G. *schützenmine*, lit. 'infantryman mine'.] Used, esp. in the war of 1939–45, to designate a variety of enemy anti-personnel mine.
**1944** J. H. Fullarton *Troop Target* 206 The enemy had sown elaborate mine fields—heavy Teller mines and deadly anti-personnel S mines. **1945** [see *anti-personnel* s.v. anti-$^1$ 4 (iii)]. **1972** *Daily Tel.* (Colour Suppl.) 1 Sept. 16/2 In the last war the Germans devised a series of anti-personnel devices, including the S-mine & the 'butterfly-bomb'. **1977** C. McCullough *Thorn Birds* xv. 351 Sometimes a man would step on an unexploded S-mine.

**smirch** (smɜːtʃ), *sb.* Also 7 smyrch. [f. next.]
**1.** A dirty mark or smear; a stain; a smudge; also, that which smirches or dirties.
*a* **1688** Bunyan *Saints' Privilege & Profit* Wks. 1855 I. 647 That men might see their smyrches when they came to wash. *a* **1688** —— *Water of Life* (1838) 430 Crystal..is without those spots and streaks and smirches that are in other precious stones. **1850** Allingham *Poems, Wayside Well* viii, Sheltered cool and free from smirch In thy cavelet shady. **1863** J. Thomson *Sunday at Hampstead* i. v, Away from the smoke and the smirch. **1890** Doyle *White Company* iv, The fellow was but a brown smirch upon the yellow road.
**2.** *fig.* A moral stain or flaw; a blot or blemish; a fault or defect.
**1862** T. A. Trollope *Marietta* iii, One who had blemished the fair escutcheon of the family by a smirch of heresy. **1877** L. Morris *Epic of Hades* iii. 241 Before the soil And smirch of sadder knowledge..Sully its primal whiteness. **1897** *Outing* XXIX. 559/2 That strange insensibility to the sufferings of animals which draws such an ugly smirch across the whole Latin race.

**smirch** (smɜːtʃ), *v.* Also 5–6 smorch, 7 smerch, smyrch. [app. ad. OF. *esmorcher* to torment, torture (as by the application of hot metal), with slight transference of sense.]
**1.** *trans.* Of things: To make dirty, soil, sully, or discolour (something) by contact or touch.
**1495** *Trevisa's Barth. De P.R.* xvi. lxxx. 579 Leed hathe a manere nesshnes, and smorcheth his honde that towchyth it. **1572** Bossewell *Armorie* ii. 77 The stalke therof broken, smorcheth them that touche it all with yealow. **1615** G. Sandys *Trav.* 268 Chaos and ragg'd stone Smircht with blacke Pumice, there reioyce, ore-growne with mournfull Cypresse. **1791** Cowper *Odyss.* xix. 12 [Weapons] smirch'd and sullied by the breath of fire. **1791** —— *Iliad* xxiii. 338 A cauldron of four measures, never smirch'd By smoke or flame. **1805–6** Cary *Dante, Inf.* xv. 26 His parch'd looks.. smirch'd with fire. **1834** Taylor *Philip van Artevelde* i. v, Twinkles the re-illuminated star, And all is out of sight that smirched the ray. **1844** Hood *Workho. Clock* 28 Dingy with smoke..And smirch'd besides with vicious soil. **1894** Sala *London up to date* i. vii, The rain beats down on the smoke, and the smoke on the fog; and all three..smirch your face and hands.
**b.** To tan (the face). *rare*$^{-1}$.
**1828** Scott *F.M. Perth* x, The sun was high, It smirch'd her cheek, it dimm'd her eye.
**2.** Of persons (or animals): To stain, smear, or befoul (the face, person, etc.) *with* or by means of something dirty or having staining properties. Also *refl.* and with adjectival complement.
**1600** Shaks. *A.Y.L.* i. iii. 114 Ile put my selfe in poore and meane attire, And with a kinde of vmber smirch my face. **1615** G. Sandys *Trav.* 215 By chance his dog..smerched his lips with the tincture. **1853** Arnold *Sohrab & Rustum* 711 He seiz'd..the dust which lay around, And threw it on his head, and smirch'd his hair. **1865** Kingsley *Herew.* II. xi. 166, I will go..and smirch myself brown with walnut-leaves.
**3.** *transf.* To cast discredit or disgrace upon (a person, his honour, etc.); to bring into ill-repute; to taint or tarnish. Said of actions, etc., or of persons.
(*a*) **1820** Scott *Monast.* xxv, In public opinion, their names will be smirched and sullied with a stain which his tardy efforts cannot entirely efface. **1878** Jefferies *Gamekeeper at H.* 216 Their infamy spreads abroad, smirching the whole class to which they belong. **1887** T. A. Trollope *What I remember* II. x. 173 Those lower thoughts as well as lower passions which smirch the human soul.
(*b*) **1856** Aytoun *Bothwell* i. xv, They durst not so have wronged their blood, And smirched their fair renown. **1870** Dixon *Tower* II. xxxi. 319 No man's name..had yet been smirched by Carr. **1885–94** R. Bridges *Eros & Psyche* Mar. xix, He changeth dynasties, and on the head Of duteous heroes..Smircheth the laurel that can never die.
Hence **'smircher**; **'smirching** *vbl. sb.*
**1495** *Trevisa's Barth. De P.R.* viii. xvii. 327 He [*sc.* the moon] semyth not wemmyd wyth noo species and smorchynge. **1862** T. A. Trollope *Marietta* ii, Unrevealed smirchings of noble names. **1888** *Scottish Leader* 11 July 4 There will soon not be a place left in his character on which the amateur smircher may operate.

**smirched** (smɜːtʃt), *ppl. a.* [f. prec.] Marked, soiled, made dirty, etc., with a smirch or stain.
**1599** Shaks. *Hen. V*, iii. iii. 17 Impious Warre,..with his smyrcht complexion. **1599** —— *Much Ado* iii. iii. 145 The smircht worm-eaten tapestrie. **1746** Smollett *Advice* 72 From the smirch'd scullion to th' embroider'd Peer. **1833** M. Scott *Cruise Midge* (1859) 489 He hung motionless across the rope like a smirched and half burnt fleece. **1863** Woolner *My Beautiful Lady* 157 Here a smirched artisan who merely bolts The plates of iron fortress.

**'smirchless**, *adv.* [f. smirch *sb.*] Without leaving a smirch or stain.
**1848** Herschel *Ess.* (1857) 739 The thrice royal robe of ermined proof Whence stain glides smirchless, shame ashamed flies.

**'smirchy**, *a.* [f. as prec.] Marked with a smirch or smirches.
**1889** Wright *Chalice of Carden* xxvii, [His] smirchy countenance was irrigated with watercourses of tears.

†**'smiring.** *Obs. rare.* [ad. G. *schmiering.*] A variety of sandpiper.
**1655** Moufet & Bennet *Health's Impr.* 99 *Ochropodes.* Smirings live in watrish Copses with worms, and are a fine and delicate meat.

**'smiris.** ? *Obs.* Also 7 smyris. [a. Gr. σμίρις or σμύρις.] = emery *sb.* 1.
**1610–** [see emery *sb.* 1]. **1661** Lovell *Hist. Anim. & Min.* Isagoge e 8 b, All may have Sculpture by the powder of smiris, except the adamant. **1677** Plot *Oxfordsh.* 74 The best sort of Smiris serves for several uses. **1778** W. Pryce *Min. Cornub.* 65 Those which are mistaken by many for distinct sorts of Fossils, are the Hæmatites, or Bloodstone; ..the Smiris, or Emery. **1803** *Phil. Trans.* XCIII. 82 It is not..improbable, that some other substance has been occasionally denoted by the term smiris, emeril, or emery.

**smirk** (smɜːk), *sb.* [f. smirk *v.*]
**1.** An affected or simpering smile; a silly, conceited, smiling look.
*c* **1560** Ingelend *Disobedient Child* in Hazl. *Dodsley* II. 297 How many smirks and dulsome kisses! **1599** B. Jonson *Cynthia's Rev.* v. iii. *Palinode*, From Spanish shrugs, French faces, smirks, irpes, and all affected humours. **1675** Wycherley *Country Wife* iv. i, He has the canonical smirk, and the filthy clammy palm of a chaplain. **1718** Lady M. W. Montagu *Lett.* II. liv. 81 A jolly face, and a stupid smirk in his countenance. **1782** Miss Burney *Cecilia* v. i, He was regarding her with a facetious smirk. **1814** Scott *Wav.* lxi, Fortunately the bride, all smirk and blush, had just entered the room. **1882** Miss Braddon *Mt.-Royal* III. viii. 164 'It is a poet's privilege to worship the beautiful, Leo,' said the Baron, with a self-satisfied smirk.
†**2.** *slang.* (See quot.) *Obs.*$^{-0}$
*a* **1700** B. E. *Dict. Cant. Crew*, *Smirk*, a finical, spruce Fellow.

**smirk** (smɜːk), *a.* and *adv.* Also 6 smyrke, 6–7 smirke. [app. f. smirk *v.*; but perh. partly suggested by smicker *a.*]
**A.** *adj.* **1.** Neat, trim, spruce in dress or appearance; pleasant, agreeable. Also *U.S.*, smug. Now chiefly *dial.*
*a* **1530** Heywood *Love* (Brandl) 349, I am at one poynt with women all, The smotest, the smyrkest, the smallest [etc.]. **1579** Spenser *Sheph. Cal.* Feb. 72 Seest, howe brag yond Bullocke beares, So smirke, so smoothe, his pricked eares? **1598** Florio, *Trisciato*, smooth, vp-straight, smug, smirke, handsomlie drest vp. **1614** J. Davies (Heref.) *Ecl. betw. Yng. Willie & Old W.* 159 Thy past'rall Minstralsy Beating the aire, atweene resounding Hils, Draw to thee Bonibels as smirke, as hy. **1648** Herrick *Hesp.*, *Nuptial Song Sir C. Crew* vii, The smirk Butler thinks it Sin, in's Nap'rie, not to express his wit. **1791** J. Learmont *Poems* 43 Shaws whilk road is best to follow Fu' sweet an' smirk. **1847** Halliw., *Smirk*, neat; trim. *Oxon.* **1873** 'Ouida' *Pascarèl* II. 246 Italy cannot be trim and smirk in modern wise and modern gear.
†**2.** Of mental faculties: Quick, ready, smart.
**1607** Walkington *Opt. Gl.* xii. 67 A nimble dextericall, smirke, prægnant, extemporary invention. *Ibid.* 82 A smirke, quick, & dextericall wit.
†**3.** Eager, ardent. *Obs.*$^{-1}$
**1674** N. Fairfax *Bulk & Selv.* 129 According as the begetter is hotter and smirker, or cold and listlesser.
†**B.** *adv.* Smirkingly. *Obs.*$^{-1}$
**1556** Heywood *Spider & Fly* xii. 13 Wherat the spider, smirke, and smothlie smiled.

**smirk** (smɜːk), *v.* Forms: 1 smearcian, 1–2 smercian, 6–7 smerk(e; 3– smirk, 5 smyrke, 6 *Sc.* smyrk, 7 smirke, 8–9 *dial.* smurk, etc. [OE. *smearcian, smercian*, app. not represented in any of the cognate languages.]
**1.** *intr.* To smile; in later use, to smile in an affected, self-satisfied, or silly manner; to simper.
*c* **888** K. Ælfred *Boeth.* xxxix. §4 Ða ongon he smearcian & cwæð to me. *Ibid.* xxxiv. §10 Ða smearcode he & cwæð. **971** *Blickling Hom.* 189 Þa Neron þæt ȝehyrde, þa smercode he. *a* **1023** Wulfstan *Hom.* (1883) 140 Þonne þu smercodest and hloȝe, þonne weop ic biterlice. *a* **1225** *Leg. Kath.* 356 Þeos meiden lette lutel of al þet he seide, & smirkinde smeðeliche ȝef him þullich onswere.
*a* **1500** in *Ratis Raving*, etc. (1870) 108 [Let her] kep her [self] in kirk To kek abak, to lauch, or smyrke. **1577–82** Breton *Toyes Idle Head* Wks. (Grosart) I. 37/1 But who so smirking smiles with merry cheare, That countenance shewes that some good newes is neare. **1601** Holland *Pliny* II. 500 A sober Matron weeping, and a light Courtesan smirking. **1604** *Friar Bacon's Proph.* 131 in Hazl. *E.P.P.* IV. 273 He would smirke and she would smile. **1706** Phillips (ed. Kersey), To *Smirk*, to smile, or look pleasant. **1747** Relph *Poems* Gloss., *To Smurk*, to smile. **1796** Mme. D'Arblay *Camilla* IV. 327 The young perfumer came, smirking and scraping, into the room. **1833** Tennyson *The Goose* 20 The parson smirk'd and nodded. **1862** Sala *Seven Sons* I. iii. 51 The little man comes smirking and bowing up to her. **1883** Stevenson *Silverado Sq.* 63 He had a projecting under-lip, with which he continually smiled, or rather smirked.
**b.** Const. *at, on,* or *upon* a person, etc.
*a* **1500** in *Ratis Raving*, etc. (1870) 86 With mekil langag but mesure, Smyrkand one euery creature. **1523** Skelton *Garl. Laurel* 762 He wyll set men a feightynge and syt hymselfe styll, And smerke, lyke a smythy kur, at sperkes of steile. **1567** Drant *Horace, Ep.* A iij, The cheares of men as theie will smerke on those that vse to smyle. **1707** *Refl. upon Ridicule* 207 An Old Dotard smirking upon a Young and Handsome Woman. **1839** Dickens *Nickleby* iii, Gentlemen smirking at each other out of blue and brown skies. **1880** W. H. Dixon *Windsor* III. xiv. 130 Dick smirked at Alice.
*transf.* **1846** Landor *Imag. Conv.* I. 121 Any vices or follies..rather than those that..smirk on us in silks and satins at our churches.

†**2.** *trans.* To trim up, to make neat or spruce.
**1596** NASHE *Saffron Walden* Ep. Ded. cij b, Will it please you to bee cosmologized and smirkt?

**3.** To utter with a smirk. *rare*⁻¹.
**1879** BROWNING *Martin Relph* 129 Till the first knave smirked 'You brag Yourself a friend of the king's?'

Hence **'smirker**, one who smirks.
**1756** COWPER *Connoisseur* No. 138 ¶4 The Smirkers and Smilers, who so prettily set off their faces..by a *je-ne-sçai-quoi* between a grin and a dimple.

**'smirkily**, *adv.* [f. SMIRKY *a.* + -LY².] = SMIRKINGLY *adv.*
*a* **1974** R. CROSSMAN *Diaries* (1975) I. 135 There they were today looking at Jennie rather smugly and smirkily. **1978** *Guardian Weekly* 5 Feb. 18/3 Cryptic allusions..to padlocks and fetters, which most recent biographers have smirkily interpreted as meaning that he was a masochist.

**smirking** ('smɜːkɪŋ), *ppl. a.* [f. SMIRK *v.*]
**1.** That smirks or smiles affectedly; simpering. Said of persons, or their features.
*c* **1000** ÆLFRIC *Hom.* I. 430 Hine befran ða Decius mid smerciȝendum muðe. *c* **1510** BARCLAY *Mirr. Gd. Manners* (1570) Ev, Their smerking paynted chin. **1593** HARVEY *Pierce's Super.* Wks. (Grosart) II. 7 Some smirking minions are fine fellowes in their owne heades. **1606** DRAYTON *Pastorals, Eglog* ix, I met a smerking bony lasse, They call her Daffadill. **1673** *Humours Town* 39 This is the wondrous Mystery,—that Smirkin Monsieur wears so many badges of the Ladies Favours. **1753** MISS COLLIER *Art Torment.* II. iii. (1811) 156 It is easy to guess, my dear, by your smirking countenance, who is expected to-day. **1825** HOOK *Sayings* Ser. II. *Sutherl.* I. 123 Grace, whose back was turned towards the smirking group, did not perceive this evolution. **1868** MISS BRADDON *Dead-Sea Fruit* vi, A smirking young man pounced immediately upon the stranger.
**2.** Accompanied or characterized by, associated with, a smirk; affected.
**1577–82** BRETON *Toyes Idle Head* Wks. (Grosart) I. 37/1 The smyrking looke declares a merry minde. **1592** GREENE *Disput.* Address p. ii, What amorous glaunces, what smirking Oeyliades. **1676** ETHEREDGE *Man of Mode* II. i, He ever had a notable smerking way with him. **1728** YOUNG *Love of Fame* v. 513 Her grizzled locks assume a smirking grace. **1820** W. IRVING *Sketch Bk.* I. 160 The smirking commonplace of his countenance. *a* **1845** BARHAM *Ingol. Leg.* Ser. III. *Ho. Warming* (1905) 477 With a sort of smirking, self-satisfied air.
†**3.** Of wine, etc.: Sparkling. *Obs.*
**1648** HERRICK *Hesp., The Hock-Cart*, If smirking Wine be wanting here, There's that, which drowns all care, stout Beere.

**'smirkingly**, *adv.* [f. prec.] In a smirking manner; with a smirk.
**1567** DRANT *Horace, Ep.* I. vi. Dij, Thou thy selfe moste smerkinglye..Saye father, brother, to eche one. **1748** RICHARDSON *Clarissa* (1811) V. 147 Hanging smirkingly upon all I said. **1773** BERRIDGE *Wks.* (1864) 89 It would do you good to see how smirkingly they go to church in summer. **1856** W. WHITE *Through Tyrol* xiii. 273 The bridegroom..looked as smirkingly jovial as could be expected.

**'smirkish**, *a. rare.* [f. SMIRK *a.* or *sb.*] Smiling, pleasant; somewhat smirky or simpering.
**1674** N. FAIRFAX *Bulk & Selv.* Ep. Ded., Tickled into such a laughing briskness, and fudged up into such a smirkish liveliness. **1834** BECKFORD *Italy* II. 368 The fair Naiads, comfortably fat, and most invitingly smirkish.

**'smirkle**, *v. Sc.* Also 6 smyrkle, 9 smerkle. [f. SMIRK *v.* + -LE 3.] *intr.* To smirk or smile. Hence **'smirkling** *ppl. a.*
The sb. *smirkle* is also illustrated by Jamieson (1825).
?*c* **1590** *Knox's Hist. Ref.* IV. (Wodrow) II. 409 As this wes said, Ledingtoun smyleit [*MS. G.* smyrklit], and spak secreitlie to the Quene in hir eare. **1597** MONTGOMERIE *Cherrie & Slae* 925 (Waldegrave), Experience then smyrkling smyld. **18..** *Lord Dunwaters* iii. in Child *Ballads* IV. 117 He gave a smirkling smile. **1819** TENNANT *Papistry Storm'd* (1827) 19 The friskier for the flytin', they Gaffaw and smirkle in their play. **1839** CHALMERS *Mem.* (1851) IV. 74 The minister I saw smiling and smerkling, in his own characteristic way, at the more ludicrous passages.

†**'smirkly**, *adv. Obs.*⁻¹ [f. SMIRK *a.* + -LY².] Smirkingly.
*a* **1586** SIDNEY *Arcadia* II. (1622) 258 Venus was glad to heare Such proffer made, which she well shewed with smiling cheare... And smirkly thus gan say [etc.].

**smirky** ('smɜːkɪ), *a. Sc.* and *U.S.* Also 8–9 **smerky.** [f. SMIRK *sb.* or *a.* + -Y.] Smart, neat, smiling; simpering; of the nature of a smirk.
**17..** RAMSAY *To Duncan Forbes* v. Wks. 1877 II. 318 How smirky look'd the little wight. **1835** *Fraser's Mag.* XI. 229 A very haughty dame among her fellow-servants of her own sex, but rather smirky and sly with the men. **1848** [A. B. LONGSTREET] *Georgia Scenes* 197, I overtook a swarthy, bright-eyed, smerky little fellow. **1880** 'MARK TWAIN' *Tramp Abr.* ii. 92 He introduced himself, smiling a smirky smile borrowed from the courtiers of the stage.

**smirles**, var. of SMERLES, ointment, *Obs.*

**Smirnoff** ('smɜːnɒf). The proprietary name of a brand of vodka.
**1948** *Official Gaz.* (U.S. Patent Office) 26 Apr. 1008/1 *Smirnoff*..for vodka and kummel. Claims use since 1914. **1959** *Trade Marks Jrnl.* 15 Apr. 411/2 Smirnoff... Vodka. W. & A. Gilbey Limited. **1961** *Twining Bros.* (Oxford) *Wine List* Autumn 15 *Vodka etc.* Smirnoff 65.5° 39/4. **1965** 'M. FALLON' *Keys of Hell* v. 50 One of the bottles contained Smirnoff, his favourite vodka. **1977** *New Yorker* 3 Oct. 46/2, I got out the Smirnoff,..and finished it off.

**smirr**, Sc. variant of SMUR.

**'smirtle**, *sb. Sc.* [f. next.] A smirk.
**1813** W. BEATTIE *Poems* (1871) 9 Ilka face a smirtle put on.

**'smirtle**, *v. Sc.* Also 7 smirtell, 8–9 smurtle. [var. of SMIRKLE *v.*] *intr.* To smirk or smile. Also *transf.*
**1651** CALDERWOOD *Hist. Kirk* (1843) II. 240 Lethington smirtelled, and rounded in her eare. **1722** W. HAMILTON *Wallace* I. iii, Then Wallace did revive, And leugh, and smirtl'd at them in his sleeve. **1768** ROSS *Helenore*, etc. 144 Now I think I may be cocky, Since fortune has smurtl'd on me. **1806** JAMIESON *Pop. Ballads* I. 296 'Hech!' quo' Will,..And smurtled at Dory Maclean.

**smish.** *Cant.* [App. a later form of MISH *sb.*] (See quots.)
**1807** H. TUFTS in E. Pearson *Autobiogr. of Criminal* (1930) II. iv. 292 *Smish*, a shirt. **1812** J. H. VAUX *Flash Dict., Smish*, a shirt. **1864** *Slang Dict.* 237 *Smish*, a shirt or chemise.

**smit** (smɪt), *sb.*¹ Forms: 1 smitte, 4, 7–8 smitt, 5 *Sc.* smyt(e, 5– smit. [OE. *smitte* (related to *smittian* SMIT *v.*¹), = MDu. *smitte*, MLG. and LG. *smitte* (hence MDa. and Da. *smitte*, MSw. and Sw. *smitta*), MHG. *smitze* (G. *schmitze*). Cf. MDu. *smit*, LG. *smit* (MSw. *smit*, Sw. dial. *smitt*), OHG. *smiz*, *bismiz* (MHG. *smitz*, G. *schmitz*); also MDu. and MLG. *smette*, MDu., Du., Fris., LG., and Sw. *smet*, OHG. *bismez*. All of these forms have the senses 'spot, stain, smear', etc. In later use the word is northern and Sc.]
†**1.** A sullying spot or stain; a taint or blemish. Freq. *fig.* of moral taint. *Obs.*
*c* **1030** *Rule St. Benet* (Logeman) 4 Se ðe ingæþ butan smittan, swylce wyrcð rihtwisnesse. *a* **1100** in Napier *O.E. Glosses* 93/2 *Inluuiem, i. inmunditiam*, wom, smittan. *a* **1300** *Cursor M.* 9462 þat sin..nan of left, wit-vten smitt, þat euer was vnder heuen born. *c* **1375** *Sc. Leg. Saints* ii. (*Paul*) 867 Blowmand bewte but wane or smyt of sawle and body to-giddir knyt. *c* **1425** WYNTOUN *Cron.* IX. 1858 Bot qwhat at sal be put in wryte Off falssit sal ber nakyn smyte. *a* **1500** in *Ratis Raving*, etc. (1870) 92 For lesing is sa foul a smyt, That quhay sa euer be taynt with It [etc.]. **1562** A. SCOTT *Poems* (S.T.S.) i. 220 Smaill sweit smaragde, smelling but smit of smot.
†**2.** Smut in grain. *Obs.*⁻⁰
**1585** HIGINS tr. *Junius' Nomenclator* 144/2 The smit, blasting, or burned blacknes of the eares of corne.
†**3.** (See quot. and SMUT *sb.* 3.) *Obs.*⁻¹
**1670** W. SIMPSON *Hydrol. Ess.* 65 Those unripe mines which the cole-miners often..find and call Smitts, as being an imperfect cole.
**4.** A soft reddish earth or clayey ore, esp. used for marking sheep. ? *Obs.*
*a* **1728** WOODWARD *Fossils* 2 The softer Ruddle, or, as 'tis call'd in the North, *Smitt.* **1789** J. WILLIAMS *Min. Kingd.* I. 440 Kidney ore is found in small masses blended in a red, staining, soft clay or earth, called smit, which is also an iron ore. **1794** HUTCHINSON *Hist. Cumb.* I. Catal. 52 The reddle, called by the country people clayey iron ore, rud, and smit.
**b.** A mark of ownership put upon sheep.
**1828** CARR *Craven Gloss., Smit*, a sheep mark. **1886** *Pall Mall G.* 9 Aug. 4/1 A 'Shepherds' Guide' setting forth the tar marks, smits, and ear-slits peculiar to the sheep of each farm in the township.
**5.** A particle of soot; a smut, black spot.
*a* **1825** in JAMIESON *Suppl.* s.v. *Smut.* **1862** C. C. ROBINSON *Dial. Leeds* 413 'Smitted' clothes, or rather the 'smits' themselves, are the plague of the housewife on the washing day.
**6.** Infection; contagion.
**1829–** in northern and Sc. dialect glossaries, etc.

†**smit**, *sb.*² *north. Obs.* In 4 smitt(e, smite, 5 smyte. [Possibly related to next and to SMITE *v.*, and orig. denoting a small piece struck off: cf. Norw. *smitt* (Ross) and G. *schmitzen* in the same sense. In the later quots. the rime-words indicate the form *smīte*: the common mod. dial. *smite* does not quite correspond to this.] A very small piece or portion; a little bit.
*a* **1300** *Cursor M.* 18735 Left he noght þar-of a smitt, Of all þe lagh, þat he ne held it. *a* **1325** in Horstm. *Altengl. Leg.* (1878) 146 Ich comand þe..þat þi fader liif be write, & min also, eueri smite. *c* **1425** *Seven Sages* (P.) 1959 The Emperour..wende hit were al gospel That the clerkys dyden hym to wite, And al was fals every smyte.

**smit**, *sb.*³ Now *dial.* Also 5 smytt. [Related to SMITE *v.* Cf. MLG. *smit*, G. *schmiss*, *schmitz*, in the same sense.] A blow; a stroke; also, the sound of striking. Cf. SMITE *sb.*¹ 1.
*c* **1430** *Sir Tryam.* 1565 Tryamowre on the hedd he hytt, He had gevyn hym an evylle smytt, But his swerde braste. *a* **1803** *Lord William* ii. in Scott *Minstrelsy*, She heard a smit o bridle reins. **1895** *Longman's Mag.* Oct. 641, I have got the death smit.

**smit** (smɪt), *v.* Latterly *north. dial.* and *Sc.* Also 4–5 smyt. *Pa. t.* 1 smittode, 5 smytted, *Sc.* smyt(t)it, 7– smitted. *Pa. pple.* 1 smittud, 4 smetted, smyttid, 5 -ed, 5– smitted; *Sc.* 5 smyttit, smitit, 5–6 smittit; 3 i-smitte, 9 smit, smitten. [OE. *smittian* (f. the weak grade of *smītan* SMITE *v.*), = MDu. and MLG. *smitten* (hence MDa. and Da. *smitte*, MSw., Sw., and Norw. *smitta*), OHG. (*pi*)*smizzan* (MHG. *smitzen*, G. *schmitzen*). Cf. also MDu., Du., and LG. *smetten*, Fris. *smette*.]
**1.** *trans.* To stain or mark in some way; to colour or tinge; to smut. Also in fig. context.
*a* **1000** *Gloss.* in Wr.-Wülcker 244 *Funestauere, maculauere*, smittodan. *c* **1205** LAY. 17701 Iblæcched he hæfede his licame, swulc ismitte of cole. *c* **1375** *Sc. Leg. Saints* ii. (*Paul*) 272 Of his hals firste milk out ran, þe knychtis clathis þat smyttit þan. **1398** TREVISA *Barth. De P.R.* v. iii. (Tollem. MS.), The brayne haþ but litell of blood leste he were infecte and smetted [**1495** smytted] with þe coloure þerof. **1456** SIR G. HAYE *Law Arms* (S.T.S.) 28 Thai ar all smyttit with that ilke myrknes, of the quhilk the sternis was blekkit. **1876** ROBINSON *Whitby Gloss.* 177/1 *Smitted*,..dotted all over; specked on the surface.
†**b.** To contaminate, taint, or infect with sin, guilt, etc. *Obs.*
*a* **1300** *E.E. Psalter* cv. 36 Dropen es þe land in blodes swa; And smitted in werkes of þa. *c* **1380** WYCLIF *Sel. Wks.* I. 198 He was not smyttid wiþ pryde ne wiþ coveityse. *c* **1425** WYNTOUN *Cron.* III. iii. 616 Bot Memprís Smyttit wes with [*v.r.* of] mony vice. *a* **1500** in *Ratis Raving*, etc. (1870) 3 The trespas that Adam and Eue commytyt,..quhar-throw al mankynde was smitit. **1562** A. SCOTT *Poems* (S.T.S.) i. 157 Giff thow persave sum senȝeour it hes smittit, Solist þame softlie nocht to perseveir.
*absol.* *a* **1500** in *Ratis Raving*, etc. (1870) 92 For lesing is sa foul a smyt,..It smytis sa sare it partis neuer.
**c.** To tarnish or sully; to bring into disgrace or discredit.
*c* **1386** CHAUCER *Troylus* v. 1545 As regnes shal ben flitted Fro folk to folk, or whan they shal ben smitted. *c* **1425** WYNTOUN *Cron.* VIII. v. 854 (Cott.), His litil leaute neuirþeles He smyttit þar in his processe. **1786** BURNS *Farewell to J. Kennedy* 3 If e'er Detraction shore to smit you, May nane believe him!
**d.** To mark (sheep) with smit or ruddle.
**1828** CARR *Craven Gloss., Smit*, to mark sheep. **1895** ELLWOOD *Lakeland & Icel.* 56 Lambs are so smitted when first put upon the fell, and sheep at clipping time.
**2.** Of contagious diseases, etc.: To infect, affect by contagion. Also in fig. context. Freq. in pa. pple. with *with*.
*a* **1100** in Napier *O.E. Gloss.* 120/2 *Caccabatus morbo*, smittud mid adle. *c* **1375** *Sc. Leg. Saints* xxix. (*Placidas*) 521 þane amesit sum thing his care, quhen his seknes smytit hym sare. **1427** *Sc. Acts, Jas. I* (1814) II. 16/1 Item at þe bischoppis..inquire diligently in þare visitatiounis..gif ony be smyttit with lippir. *a* **1500** *Ratis Raving* I. 178 Thir thingis..Wyll smyt men that are hail & fere. **1585** R. PARSONS *Chr. Exerc.* Ep. Ded. 3 The readers of them that are before smitted with that kinde of infection. **1788** W. H. MARSHALL *Yorksh.* II. 353 To *Smit*, to infect. **1829–** in dialect glossaries, etc. (see *Eng. Dial. Dict.*).
**b.** Of persons or animals: To convey or communicate a disease to (another); to infect.
**1877–** in dialect glossaries, etc.

**smitane:** see SMETANA.

**smitch**, *sb.*¹ Now *dial.* Forms: 1–2 smic, smyc, 3 smyche, 3, 9 smiche, 9– smitch. [OE. *smic*, *smýc*, var. of *sméc* (see SMEECH *sb.* and SMEEK *sb.*), with development of form as in *díc* ditch.] Smoke arising from burning or smouldering matter; also *dial.*, grime, dirt, dust, smut, etc.
*c* **893** K. ÆLFRED *Oros.* III. xi. 142 Swelce se bitresta smic upp astiȝe. *c* **1000** ÆLFRIC *Gen.* xix. 28 Abraham..ȝeseah, hu þa ysla up fluȝon mid þam smice. *a* **1100** in Napier *O.E. Glosses* 108/1 *Ut fumus euanescens*,..swaswa ȝewitende smyc. *c* **1250** *Hymn* in *Trin. Coll. Hom.* App. 258 He vs bouchte..of bitter helle fur & of þe fule smiche. *c* **1275** *Sinners Beware* 95 in *O.E. Misc.*, Heo schule..in helle smyche Acoryen hit ful wraþe.
**1847** HALLIW., *Smitch*, dirt, but generally applied to smoke or dust. *West.* **1880** *W. Cornwall Gloss.* 52/2 *Smitch*, the smell or smoke arising from anything burnt in frying.

**smitch** (smɪtʃ), *sb.*² (and *adv.*) *Sc.* and *U.S.* [Of doubtful origin: cf. SMIT *sb.*²] A particle, bit. Also used adverbially (*rare*).
*Smitchel* is also used in the same sense in *U.S.*
*c* **1840** J. RAMSAY *Eglinton Park Meeting* xxxv, Every smitch o't was a kin' o' red. **1884** *Advance* (Chicago) 10 July, A little smitch of an island. **1963** M. MCCARTHY *Group* viii. 177 Neat but not gaudy, in a plain skirt and shirtwaist,..an old cameo brooch..—general effect a smitch Victorian.

**smitch** (smɪtʃ), *v.* Now *dial.* [f. SMITCH *sb.*¹] *trans.* To affect with smoke or smut.
**1621** G. SANDYS *Ovid's Met.* v. (1626) 101 That soile.. Now barren grew... Now, too much drouth annoys; now, lodging showres: Stars smitch, winds blast. **1878** E. W. L. DAVIES *Mem. J. Russell* 71 The country-people..left their milk-pans on the fire till the cream was 'smitched', or perhaps burned.

**smitchy** ('smɪtʃɪ), *a. colloq. rare.* [f. SMITCH *sb.*² + -Y¹.] Tiny.
**1888** KIPLING *Plain Tales from Hills* 245 The Copper that takes you up is an old friend that tuk you up before, when you was a little, smitchy boy.

**smite** (smaɪt), *sb.*¹ Also 4–5 smyt-, 5 smete. [f. SMITE *v.* But the ME. examples represent *smīte*, of similar formation to *bīte* BIT *sb.*¹]
**1. a.** A stroke or heavy blow with a weapon, the hand, etc., or the sound made by this. Now chiefly *rhet.* (Cf. SMIT *sb.*³)
*c* **1200** *Trin. Coll. Hom.* 207 þenne me hine pined mid hunger,..and smerte smiten of smale longe ȝerden. **1297** R. GLOUC. (Rolls) 9013 þo þe smite [*v.r.* smytyn] of lance was ido to þe suerd hii nome. *c* **1330** *Arth. & Merl.* 9774 (Kölbing), It carf so wel, men miȝt delite, þat witeþ þe

geaunce of þis smite. **1340** *Ayenb.* 140 Ase zone ase he y-hyerþ þane smite of þe lodes-manne. **14..** *Sir Beues* (S.) 4145 + 16 þat þou3t Beues a good smyte [*v.r.* smete]. **1819** TENNANT *Papistry Storm'd* (1827) 205 The Mainkirk rang wi' slaps and smites. **1828–32** in WEBSTER.

**b.** *Cricket.* A hard hit made by a batsman.

**1888** R. H. LYTTELTON in Steel & Lyttelton *Cricket* ii. 39 There is one hit in particular that in these days is very seldom seen—that is, the smite to long-leg with a horizontal bat. **1898** G. GIFFEN *With Bat & Ball* ii. 19 Since Trott hit one over [the boundary] at square leg, Jack Lyons and Tom Garrett have effected a similar smite. **1905** VACHELL *The Hill* xii, We used to think you a slogger, but you never came anywhere near that smite of Scaife's.

**2. †a.** A slight indication or intimation *of* something. *Obs.* (Cf. CAST *sb.* 9.)

**1640** G. HIM in N. Wallington *Notices Reign Chas. I* (1869) I. 128, I might say more, but this I do to give you a smite of our condition.

**b.** A small or least amount; a particle. *U.S.* and *dial.*

**1843** 'R. CARLTON' *New Purchase* I. xix. 175 Not a smite of noise, only my breathing and a sort of pittin-pattin sound of my heart. *a* **1852** F. M. WHITCHER *Widow Bedott P.* (1856) v. 50 But it dident do a smite o' good. **1913** [see REAM *sb.*[3] d].

**†smite**, *sb.*[2] *Sc. Obs.* In 5–6 smyte. [ad. MDu. *smiete* or MLG. *smîte* (Du. *smijt*, LG. *smîte*, Norw. *smit*, *smitt*, G. *schmeite*, *schmiete*), of obscure origin.] A rope attached to one of the lower corners of a sail.

**1494** *Acc. Ld. High Treas. Scot.* I. 253 Item, fra Will Forstar, tua smytis and ane peis of auld toll [= tow, rope], xviij *s.* **1512** *Ibid.* IV. 304 Tua smytis of gret 3arne of viij[c] xlv pund wecht.

**smite**, *dial.* a particle: see SMIT *sb.*[2]

**smite** (smaɪt), *v.* Forms: (see below). [OE. *smítan* (*smát*, *smiton*, *smiten*), = OFris. *smîta* (WFris. *smite*, EFris. *smite*, *smît*, NFris. *smit*) to throw, MDu. *smiten* (Du. *smijten*) to throw, strike, MLG. and LG. *smîten* to throw, OHG. *smîzan* to smear (also *bismîzan* to smear, sully, *ûzsmîzan* to cast out; MHG. *smîzen*, G. *schmeissen* to throw, strike, smear, excrete), Goth. *bi-*, *gasmeitan* to smear. In the Scand. languages represented by MSw. and Sw. *smita* (*smeta*), Norw. *smita*, Da. *smide*, which are prob. from MLG. The development of the various senses is not quite clear, but that of throwing is perh. the original one.

The compound *besmítan* is common in OE., and FORSMITE occurs in ME.]

A. Illustration of Forms.

**1. a.** *Inf.* (and *Pres. stem*) 1 -smítan, 3 smiten (-enn), 3–4 smyten, 5 smytyn; 3– smite (4 *north.* smete), 4–6 smyte (5 smyit), 5–6 *Sc.* smyt, 5, 7 smytt, 5 smyght, 6–7 smight; 4 smit, *north.* smett, smitt(e.

*c* **1000** *Saxon Leechd.* III. 14 Smite mon ðа sealfe..on þæt heafod. *c* **1160** *Hatton Gosp.* Matt. v. 39 Ʒif hwa þe smite on þin swiðre wænge. *c* **1200** ORMIN 14677 To smitenn itt to dæde. *c* **1200** *Trin. Coll. Hom.* 61 He wile smite mid..swuerde. *c* **1250** *Owl & Night.* 78 Al þat þu myht..smyten. *a* **1300** *Cursor M.* 5656 He sagh an egypcien..Smit a juu. *Ibid.* 15798, I wil noght þat þou smete. **1382** WYCLIF *Gen.* viii. 21, I shal smyte no more. *c* **1440** *Promp. Parv.* 461/1 Smytyn, *ferio, percutio. Ibid.*, Smyte fyyr, *fugillo.* *c* **1450** *MS. Douce* 55 fol. 3, Smytt it in feyre pecys. **1535** COVERDALE *1 Kings* xx. 35, I praye the smite me. **1539** BIBLE (Cranmer) *John* xviii. 23 Why smyttest thou me? **1570** LEVINS *Manip.* 151 To smyte, *percutere, ferire.* **1596** SPENSER *F.Q.* IV. iv. 21 For him likewise he quickly downe did smight. *c* **1635** SIR W. MURE *Ps.* cxli. 5 Wks. (S.T.S.) II. 218 Me let the righteouse smytt. **1641** HINDE *J. Bruen* 18 Smighting their consciences. **1663** S. PATRICK *Parab. Pilgrim* xxxi. (1687) 379 To have a Dead Palsie smite your loyns.

**b.** *3rd pers. sing.* 2–4 smit, 4–5 smyt, 5 smytt(e.

*a* **1200** *Vices & Virt.* 13 Se ðe smit under ðа eare. *c* **1340** *Nominale* (Skeat) 188 Man with hamur smyt on the anfelde. **1390** GOWER *Conf.* I. 40 Whan..the spore The horse side smit to sore, It grieveth ofte. *c* **1400** MAUNDEV. (1839) v. 45 This Ryvere comethe rennynge..; and aftre it smytt unto Londe.

**2.** *Pa. t.* **a.** *Sing.* (latterly also *pl.*) α. 1–2 smát, 3–6 smat (3 smæt), 4–6 smate. (After 1300 *north.* and *Sc.*)

*c* **725** *Corpus Gloss.* I. 352 *Inpingit*, smat, ʒemaercode. *c* **1160** *Hatton Gosp.* Matt. xxvi. 68 Hwæt ys se þe þe smat. *c* **1205** LAY. 20317 Me hine smæt mid smærte 3erden. *a* **1300** *Cursor M.* 20957 A jugelur wit blindnes he smat [*v.r.* smate]. *c* **1440** *Alph. Tales* 516 With his spere he smate hym thrugh. **1513** DOUGLAS *Æneid* IX. xii, Quhou Turnus the big Pandarus smat [*v.r.* smate] down.

β. 3–7 smot, 4 smoth, 5 smotte, 6 smott; 4– smote (also 4–5 *pl.* smoten), 4–5 smoot, smoote (also 5 *pl.* smooten), 5 smoitte, 6 *Sc.* smoit, 7 smoat(e.

*c* **1250** *Gen. & Ex.* 2925 Oc Moyses wirm hem alle smot. *a* **1300** *Havelok* 2654 Ubbe..smoth Godrich. *a* **1325** *Prose Ps.* lxviii. 31 Hym þat tou smote. *c* **1340** *Ayenb.* 48 Þeruore smot god..onam. *c* **1380** WYCLIF *Sel. Wks.* II. 415 Petir..smoot of Malcus eere. *c* **1400** *Sowdone Bab.* 1796 Thay..smoten down right al a-boute. *c* **1450** *Merlin* xv. 237 Anoon thei smote to-geder fercely. **1490** CAXTON *Eneydos* lvi. 152 She smotte grete strokes. **1535** COVERDALE *1 Sam.* xxiv. 5 It smote him..in his hert. **1590** SPENSER *F.Q.* III. i. 28 She..downe him smot. **1604** SHAKS. *Oth.* v. ii. 356, I..smoate him, thus. **1642** D. ROGERS *Naaman* 30 The Lord smot him with the plague. **1714** YOUNG *Force Relig.* Wks. 1752 I. 87 She smote her lovely breast.

γ. *2nd pers.* 1–3 smite, 3–4 smete. *3rd pers.* 4 smite, 5 smete.

*c* **1150** *Canterbury Ps.* iii. 8 Þu ofsloʒe *vel* smite. *c* **1205** LAY. 8157 Þu me smite [*c* **1275** smete]. *a* **1325** *Prose Ps.* iii. 7 Þou smete alle þat were o3ains me. **13..** *Guy Warw.* (A.) 942 Gij o3ain to him smite [*rime* hete]. **14..** *Ibid.* (C.) 1196 He..smete in a grete swowne.

δ. 3–5 smette, 5 smet; 3 smatte, 4 smat.

These would normally represent an OE. **smǽtte*, pa. t. of **smǽtan*, corresponding to MHG. *smeizen.*

*c* **1250** *Gen. & Ex.* 2684 He bi-loc hem & smette a-mong. *a* **1300** *K. Horn* 607 Þe sarazins he smatte þat his blod hatte. *c* **1330** R. BRUNNE *Chron. Wace* (Rolls) 8540 Hengist ageyn anoþer smat [*rime* sat]. *Ibid.* 16371 Þey smette to-gedere so bitterlyke. **1412–20** LYDG. *Chron. Troy* I. 4187 Lamedoun ..smet A riche cercle from his basenet. **1470** *Maldon Court Rolls* (Bundle 47, No. 4), Turned that other ende of the forke and smette hym.

ε. 6 smytt, smitt, 6–7 smit.

**1561** MACHYN *Diary* (Camden) 259 [It] smytt downe serten grett stones. **1590** SPENSER *F.Q.* I. ii. 18 Vpon his crest With rigour..he smitt. **1614** GORGES *Lucan* III. 115 The rowers one another smit. **1684** BUNYAN *Pilgr.* II. 110 Great-heart..smit the head..from his shoulders.

**b.** *Pl.* α. 1 smiton, 3–5 smiten, smyten, 4 smyton, 5 -yn; 3–4 smite, 4–5 smyte; 3–4 smitte(n, 4 smytte(n.

*c* **725** *Corpus Gloss.* F 387 *Funestauere*, smiton. *c* **1205** LAY. 5183 Heo smiten to-gædere. *Ibid.* 30097 Mid longe sweorden heo smitten. *c* **1275** *Passion our Lord* 388 in *O.E. Misc.* 48 Hi..smyten [him] vnder þat ere. **1382** WYCLIF *Gen.* xiv. 5 The kingis..smytyn Raphaym. **1481** CAXTON *Reynard* xxxii. (Arb.) 86 His seruauntis..smyten and bete the asse.

β. 3–5 smete, 4–5 smeten, 5 smetin, -on.

*c* **1275** LAY. 5183 Hii smete to-gaderes. **13..** *Coer de L.* 3988 They schotte to hem, and hard smeten. **14..** *Guy Warw.* (C.) 2897 On þer helmes þey smete. **1481** CAXTON *Reynard* xii. (Arb.) 27 They smeton, beten, and wounded hym.

**c.** *Weak forms.* 5 smit-, smytide, 9 smited.

**1388** WYCLIF *2 Kings* ix. 27 Thei smytiden hym. **1858** KINGSLEY *The Red King* 54 Tyrrel he smited..that day.

**3.** *Pa. pple.* α. 4 y-, 5 i-smyten; 4–6 smyten (4–5 -yn, 5 -on, -un); 3–5 smiten (4 -in, -on).

*c* **1250** *Gen. & Ex.* 3690 Ðor wurð 3he..wið lepre smiten. *a* **1340** HAMPOLE *Psalter* iii. 7 Þou has smyten all contrariand til me. *c* **1380** WYCLIF *Wks.* (1880) 378 Ysmyten wiþ goddis vengance. **1382** —— *Gen.* xli. 6 Smytun with meldew. **1390** GOWER *Conf.* III. 249 He..The Princes hefdes..Hath smiten of. *c* **1450** *Merlin* xv. 239 Than were the saisnes.. harde I-smyten. **1483** CAXTON *G. de la Tour* a vj, A crysten man had his hede smyten of.

β. 3 hii-, 3–4 y-, 3–5 i-smite; 4 i-, 4–5 y-smyte; 4 (6 *arch.*) smite; 4–5 (6 *arch.*) smyte.

*c* **1275** LAY. 10855 Hii-smite he was in fihte. **1297** R. GLOUC. (Rolls) 6186 Þer were duntes ari3t ismite. *c* **1330** *Arth. & Merl.* 8047 (Kölbing), Mani paien to deþ [were] ysmite. *c* **1369** CHAUCER *Dethe Blaunche* 1323 As hyt hadde smyte oures twelve. **1387** TREVISA *Higden* (Rolls) IV. 123 He was i-smyte wiþ a palsy. **14..** *26 Pol. Poems* xxvi. 117 Nowe hathe age y-smyte me. *c* **1450** *Contin. Brut* 366 Þat boþe her hedis schulde be smyte of. **1513** DOUGLAS *Æneid* II. vii. 17 Sum Greikis victouris war smyte [*v.r.* smite] deid.

γ. 4–5 i-smeten; 4–5 smeten, -yn, 5 -on.

**1387** TREVISA *Higden* (Rolls) VII. 477 He was i-smeten wiþ þe vice of pride. **1389** in *Eng. Gilds* (1870) 91 After prime be smeten. **14..** *26 Pol. Poems* xxvi. 173 Now hathe age smetyn..My thryd feder. **1485** CAXTON *Chas. Gt.* 44 Roulland..hade smeton hys vncle.

δ. 4 i-, 5 y-smete; 4–5 smete, 5 smet.

**1303** R. BRUNNE *Handl. Synne* 11920 A lymme..smete yn pallesye. **13..** *Coer de L.* 4956 How the batayle was i-smete. **1387** TREVISA *Higden* (Rolls) VI. 369 Þe enemyes..were i-smete wiþ blyndenesse. **14..** in *Babees Bk.* 35 With thys bytel be he smete. *c* **1440** *Promp. Parv.* 460/2 Smet, or smytyn, *percussus.*

ε. 4, 6– smitten, 5–6 smytten (5 -yn, 6 -yne, smyttin).

*a* **1400** *Cursor M.* 7603 Saul has smitten a thusand. *a* **1483** in *Househ. Ord.* (1790) 59 That the messes be smyttyn [etc.]. **1489** CAXTON *Faytes of A.* IV. iv. 238 To make theyre hedes to be smytten of. **1551** BIBLE *Isaiah* l. 2 Was my hande cleane smitten of? **1556** *Chron. Grey Friars* (Camden) 65 Hys hond was smyttyne of. **1631** GOUGE *God's Arrows* III. §84. 340 By Saul they were..smitten.

ζ. 5–6 smytte, 5 i-smyt, 5–6 smyt(t; 4, 6– smit.

*a* **1400** *Minor Poems fr. Vernon MS.* xliii. 144 Al for my misdede Was he so felli smit! **1423** JAS. I. *Kingis Q.* lviii, Artow seke, or smyt with Ielousye? *c* **1425** *R. Gloucester's Chron.* 5254 (Digby MS.), Heueden þet were of smytte. *a* **1536** *Songs, Carols*, etc. (E.E.T.S.) 123, I hope this gonne was well smytt. **1667** MILTON *P.L.* III. 29 Smit with the love of sacred song.

η. 6–7 smot, 6–9 smote; 7 smotten.

**1590** SPENSER *F.Q.* III. ii. 46 Till thou in open field adowne be smot. **1597** BEARD *Theatre God's Judgm.* (1612) 309 To be smote with the edge of the sword. **1607** HIERON *Wks.* I. 473 Elah, smotten and killed while he was drinking. **1768–74** TUCKER *Lt. Nat.* (1834) II. 523 Turning the right cheek to him that has smote the left. **1813** T. BUSBY *Lucretius* II. VI. 676 What cities have they smote!

B. Signification.

**I.** *trans.* **†1.** To pollute, blemish. *Obs.*[−1]

*c* **725** *Corpus Gloss.* F 387 *Funestauere*, smiton.

**†2.** To smear (a substance) *on* something. *Obs.*

*c* **1000** ÆLFRIC *Exod.* xii. 7 Nymon of his blode and smiton on æʒðer ʒedyre.

**II. 3. a.** To administer a blow to (a person, etc.) with the hand, a stick, or the like; to strike or hit; to beat or buffet; to slap or smack. Now *rhet.* and *rare.*

*c* **1160** *Hatton Gosp.* Matt. v. 39 Ʒyf hwa þe smite on þin swiðre wænge. *a* **1300** *K. Horn* 503 He smot him a litel wi3t & bed him beon a god kni3t. **1382** WYCLIF *Matt.* xxvi. 67 Thanne thei spitten in to his face, and smyten hym with buffetis. *c* **1440** *Gesta Rom.* i. 3 He makith sorowe nowe.. For he smot nor þe ymage [with the arrow]. **1500–20** DUNBAR *Poems* lxxii. 29 Dispituouslie syne [they] did him smyt. *a* **1608** DEE *Relat. Spirits* (1659) I. 82 He smit the round Table with his rod. **1675** J. OWEN *Indwelling Sin* xii. (1732) 147 The Case was the same with Asa in his Anger, when he smote the Prophet. **1718** *Free-thinker* No. 109 The Fairy..smote him on the Shoulder with a Golden Wand. **1791** COWPER *Iliad* IX. 708 Oft would she smite the earth. **1841** DICKENS *Barn. Rudge* viii, Half pausing for an instant now and then to smite his pocket. *Ibid.* xxxix, He smote Mr. Tappertit on the back.

*fig. a* **1225** *Ancr. R.* 324 Smit him anonriht mid te 3erde of tunge schrifte. **1390** GOWER *Conf.* I. 310 To smyte hem with the same rodd With which I am of love smite. **1611** BIBLE *Jer.* xviii. 18 Come and let vs smite him with the tongue. [Also in earlier versions.] **1785** GROSE *Dict. Vulgar T.*, *To smite one's tutor*, to get money from him.

**b.** To strike with the foot (†or spur). Also said of the foot. Now *rhet.* or *poet.*

**13..** *Guy Warw.* (A.) 4059 Mani he smot of fot & fest. **13..** *Sir Beues* (A.) 3398 Sire Morice of Mounclere His stede smot [*v.r.* prekyd] a3enes Sabere. **1821** JOANNA BAILLIE *Metr. Leg.*, *Wallace* xxxvii, And proudly smote the ground with firmer tread. **1829** CARLYLE *Misc.* (1857) II. 110 Happy that the virago's foot did not even smite him. **1842** TENNYSON *Morte d'Arth.* 190 Juts of slippery crag that rang Sharp-smitten with the dint of armed heels.

**c.** To strike or touch (a harp, etc.) so as to produce musical sounds. Now *poet.*

*c* **1384** CHAUCER *H. Fame* II. 777 Eke whan men harpe strynges smyte,..Loo with the stroke the ayre to-breketh. **1486** *Bk. St. Albans* d j b, Then smyte youre tabur, and cry huff, huff, huff and make the fowle to spryng. **1784** COWPER *Task* v. 682 Ah, tinkling cymbal,..Smitten in vain! such music cannot charm [etc.]. **1842** TENNYSON *Locksley Hall* 34 Love took up the harp of Life, and..Smote the chord of Self. **1847** —— *Princ.* IV. 38 A maid, Of those beside her, smote her harp, and sang.

**†d.** *Naut.* (See quot.) *Obs.*[−0]

*a* **1625** *Nomenclator Navalis* (Harl. MS. 2301) s.v. *Smitting*, This Line is called a Smitting Line. Soe they smite the missen, that is pull the Roape that the Saile maie come downe. [Hence in Harris and later Dicts.]

**e.** *Cricket.* To hit with great force; to defeat by hard hitting.

**1891** W. G. GRACE *Cricket* iv. 127 Mr. I. D. Walker.. smote them to the tune of 90. **1904** F. C. HOLLAND *Cricket* 28 After you have smitten him [*sc.* the bowler of yorkers] full-pitch two or three times, he will soon stop bothering you in this way. **1982** P. TINNISWOOD *More Tales from Long Room* vii. 87 My next sermon will take as its text: 'And, lo, Harry Halliday was a plump man, yet many a six did he smite for Yorkshire.'

**4.** Of the Deity, in or after Biblical use: To visit with death, destruction, or overthrow; to afflict or punish in some signal manner. (Cf. 8 b.)

*c* **1150** *Canterbury Ps.* iii. 8 Forðæn þu ofsloʒe *vel* smite ealle wiðerʒiende me. *a* **1300** *E.E. Psalter* civ. 34 He smate al firstkinned in land of þa. **1390** GOWER *Conf.* I. 189 The hond of hevene him smot In tokne of that he was forswore. *c* **1440** *Jacob's Well* 126 Þe more þat god smyteth hem wyth his wreche. **1535** COVERDALE *1 Sam.* xxv. 38 The Lorde smote him, so y[t] he dyed. **1611** BIBLE *Ps.* lxix. 26 Let none dwell in their tents. For they persecute him whom thou hast smitten. *a* **1737** ABP. WAKE (J.), Let us not mistake God's goodness, nor imagine, because he smites us, that we are forsaken by him. **1784** COWPER *Task* VI. 464 The Governor of all..has interpos'd, Not seldom, his avenging arm, to smite Th' injurious trampler upon nature's law. **1843** WHITTIER *C. Southwick* 142 The Lord shall smite the proud, and lay His hand upon the strong.

**5. a.** To strike with a weapon, etc., so as to inflict serious injury or death; also, to strike hard with a cutting tool. Now *rhet.* or *poet.*

Freq. const. *through*, *upon*, etc. (a certain part). ***to smite.. hip and thigh***: see HIP *sb.*[1] 2 d.

*c* **1205** LAY. 6503 Þe king droh his sweord,..and þet deor he smat a-nan uppe þat hæued-bæn. **1297** R. GLOUC. (Rolls) 4473 Lucye þe senatour was mid a spere þoru ysmite. *a* **1300** *Cursor M.* 6671 Qua smites man in wil to sla, He sal him-self be slan alsua. **1375** BARBOUR *Bruce* VI. 136 He smat the first sa rygorusly Vith his spere,..Till he doun to the erd hym bare. *c* **1400** MAUNDEV. (Roxb.) xi. 43 In þat place sawe Dauid þe aungell smytand þe folk with a swerde. *c* **1450** *Contin. Brut* 423 There this persone smote this ffrere Randulf, and sloue hym. **1513** DOUGLAS *Æneid* VI. iii. 46 Smyte with the ax did rair the aikis hie. **1596** SPENSER *F.Q.* IV. ix. 29 Ne yeelded foote,..But being doubly smitten likewise doubly smit. **1641** G. SANDYS *Paraphr. Song of Solom.* v. ii, The Watch..In this pursuit the Afflicted found: Smot, wounded [etc.]. **1676** HOBBES *Iliad* IV. 427 He smote was with a Spear into the Brain. **1842** TENNYSON *Morte D'Arth.* 25, I am so deeply smitten thro' the helm That without help I cannot last till morn. **1844** MRS. BROWNING *Drama Exile* 64 This the sword..That smote upon the forehead, Lucifer The angel.

*refl. c* **1385** CHAUCER *L.G.W.* 915 *Thisbe*, To the herte sche hire self smot. **1514** in Ellis *Orig. Lett.* Ser. I. I. 103 The said Ranalde, with a small knyff that he had secrett, smott hym self.

*fig. c* **1386** CHAUCER *Clerk's T.* 66 Deeth menaceth euery age and smyt. **1590** SPENSER *F.Q.* III. ii. 35 That blinded God, which hath ye blindly smit, Another arrow hath. **1813** T. BUSBY *Lucret.* I. III. 1250 Great Homer lives no more, Smote, like the rest, by Time's relentless power. **1847** TENNYSON *Princ.* III. 176 From my breast the involuntary sigh Brake, as she smote me with the light of eyes.

**b.** With compl. *to death* (cf. DEATH *sb.* 12) or *dead.* Also in fig. context.

*c* **1200** ORMIN 14677 Abraham..hoff þe swerd..To smitenn itt [*sc.* Isaac] to dæde. *c* **1330** *Arth. & Merl.* 8047 (Kölbing), Mani paien to deþ [were] ysmite Wiþ swerdes of stiel. **1377** LANGL. *P. Pl.* B. III. 322 What smyth þat ony [weapon] smytheth be smyte þerwith to dethe. **1513** DOUGLAS *Æneid* v. ix. 91 In the skyis [he] smate hir deid. **1819** SHELLEY *Lines Castlereagh Admin.* ii, The abortion with which she travaileth Is Liberty, smitten to death. **1871** R. ELLIS *Catullus* lxviii. 113 When those monster birds..his arrow Smote to the death.

**c.** In or after Biblical use: To strike, or strike down, in battle; to kill, slay.

*a* **1300** *Cursor M.* 3971 þat quils esau smat an o þe tua þe toþer party suld scape him fra. **1382** WYCLIF *Josh.* vii. 5 The whiche..ben smyten of the men of the cytee of Hay. **1560** BIBLE (Geneva) *Josh.* x. 19 Followe after your enemies, and smite all the hindemost. **1597** BEARD *Theatre God's Judgem.* (1612) 309 He caused..the Citie of the Priests to be smote with the edge of the sword. **1631** GOUGE *God's Arrows* III. §84. 340 By Saul they were once, and again smitten: and finally by David they were utterly vanquished. **1754** YOUNG *Centaur* II. Wks. 1757 IV. 136 Not Babylon alone has been smitten at a banquet, and perished in its joys.

†**6.** Of birds or animals: To strike with beak, claw, horn, hoof, etc. *Obs.*

*c* **1205** LAY. 20172 Hauekes hine [the crane] smiteð. *c* **1250** *Owl & Night.* 78 Al þat þu myht myd clyure smyten. *c* **1374** CHAUCER *Boeth.* III. met. vii. (1868) 80 þe bee..styngeþ þe hertes of hem þat ben ysmyte. **1382** WYCLIF *Exod.* xxi. 28 If an oxe with the horn smyte a man. **14..** *Lat. & Eng. Prov.* (MS. Douce 52) fol. 16 While þe hors kykys war that he the ne smyte.

**7. a.** Of hail, lightning, flame, etc.: To strike and injure; to destroy, blast.

**1382** WYCLIF *Exod.* ix. 25 The hawle smoot..alle that weren in feeldes,..and al erbe of the feelde smoote the hawle. **1387** TREVISA *Higden* (Rolls) III. 63 Romulus was i-smyte wiþ liȝtnynge. *c* **1400** *Rom. Rose* 3755 Whan the flawme of the verry brond..Had Bialacoil with hete smete. **1480** *Robt. Devyll* 343 in Hazl. *E.P.P.* I. 233 A man had ben as good as haue be smytten with thonder, As to haue a stroke of hys hand. **1535** COVERDALE *Exod.* ix. 31 Thus the flax and the barlye were smytten. *c* **1630** MILTON *Arcades* 52, I..heal ..what the cross dire-looking Planet smites. **1760** STERNE *Serm.* III. 136 The hopeful youth..; some cruel distemper lays him prostrate upon the earth, smit and shrivelled up with a malignant blast. **1813** T. BUSBY *Lucret.* II. VI. 676 Eruptive winds, what cities have they smote! **1820** SHELLEY *Vis. Sea* 61 Six the thunder has smitten, And they lie black as mummies.

**b.** To beat or dash against (something).

*c* **1440** *Jacob's Well* 248 þe more grauel & sonde is smet & betyn wyth flodys of þe se, þe more salt & bytter it is. **1624** QUARLES *Job Militant* III. 43 Which [wind] with a full-mouth Blast Hath smote the House. **1805** WORDSW. *Prelude* I. 440 With the din Smitten, the precipices rang aloud. **1839** LONGF. *Hyperion* ii. 6 The storm-wind smites the wall of the mountain cliff.

**c.** Of sunlight, etc.: To beat or shine strongly upon. Also in fig. context.

**1588** SHAKS. *L.L.L.* IV. iii. 28 As thy eye beames, when their fresh rayse haue smot The night of the dew [etc.]. **1667** MILTON *P.L.* IV. 244 Where the morning Sun first warmly smote The open field. **1788** ANNA SEWARD *Lett.* (1811) II. 107 On an open plain smote by the summer's sun. **1832** TENNYSON *Œnone* 54 Far up the solitary morning smote The streaks of virgin snow. **1884** W. C. SMITH *Kildrostan* 43 A broad beam of the garish light Smote with a glory her golden hair.

**8. a.** Of diseases, distempers, etc.: To attack, affect suddenly or grievously. Freq. in pa. pple., and const. *by* or *with* (a malady, etc.).

*c* **1250** *Gen. & Ex.* 3690 Ðor wurð ȝhe ðanne wið lepre smiten. **1303** R. BRUNNE *Handl. Synne* 11920 A lymme þat ys..smete yn pallesye. **1387** TREVISA *Higden* (Rolls) V. 123 Constantyn was i-smyte wiþ a strong meselrie. *c* **1425** *Cursor M.* 11817 (Trin.), þe palesy smoot his oon side. **1663** S. PATRICK *Parab. Pilgr.* xxxi. (1687) 379 You may as well desire..to have a Dead Palsie smite your loyns. **1868** FREEMAN *Norm. Conq.* (1877) II. 446 Abbot Mannig..had been smitten by paralysis.

*transf.* **1796** H. HUNTER tr. *St.-Pierre's Stud. Nat.* (1799) II. 179 A province considered even at Petersburg as smitten with sterility. **1837** CARLYLE *Fr. Rev.* I. I. i, A France smitten..with plague after plague.

**b.** Of personal agents, or of the Deity (cf. 4).

*a* **1300** *Cursor M.* 20957 A jugelur wit blindnes he smat. *c* **1440** *Jacob's Well* 126 þey se noȝt how god smyt hem in here body, wyth sykenes & tribulacyoun. **1535** COVERDALE *Zech.* xiv. 12 This shalbe the plage, wherwith yᵉ Lorde wil smyte all people. **1642** D. ROGERS *Naaman* 30 He forgat himselfe, till the Lord smot him with the plague.

**9.** To infect, imbue, impress, strike suddenly or strongly *with* some feeling or sentiment. Chiefly in pa. pple.

*a* **1300** *Cursor M.* 15643 Wit strang dred he smiton was. **1390** GOWER *Conf.* II. 136 Withoute good discrecioun This king with avarice is smite. **1423** JAS. I. *Kingis Q.* lviii, Artow seke, or smyt with Ielousye? **1535** COVERDALE *Job* xxi. 6, I am afrayed, and my flesh is smytten with feare. **1622** FLETCHER *Prophetess* III. i, 'Twas I that..smote ye all with terrour. **1671** MILTON *P.R.* IV. 562 But Satan smitten with amazement fell. **1718** POPE *Iliad* I. 354 Smit with love of honourable deeds. **1829** HOOD *E. Aram* 50 The Usher took six hasty strides, As smit with sudden pain. **1849** MACAULAY *Hist. Eng.* i. I. 7 Tyrants, who, when at the height of greatness, were smitten with remorse.

**10. a.** Of the heart, conscience, etc.: To discompose or disquiet (one); to affect painfully.

**1382** WYCLIF *2 Sam.* xxiv. 10 The herte of Dauid smoot hym, aftir that the puple is noumbred. **1611** BIBLE *1 Sam.* xxiv. 5 Dauids heart smote him, because he had cut off Sauls skirt. *a* **1700** EVELYN *Diary* 5 May 1659, My heart smote me for it. **1805–6** CARY *Dante's Inf.* XIX. 121 Meanwhile, as thus I sung, he, whether wrath Or conscience smote him, violent upsprang. **1886** 'H. CONWAY' *Living or Dead* II. v, I said good-bye with a coldness for which my heart smote me.

**b.** To distress or perturb (a person, the mind, conscience, etc.).

*c* **1470** HENRY *Wallace* XI. 1366 Thi febyll wordis sall nocht my conscience smyt. **1535** COVERDALE *1 Sam.* xxiv. 5 It smote him afterwarde in his hert, because he had cut of the typpe of Sauls garment. **1606** SHAKS. *Ant. & Cl.* v. ii. 104 A greefe that smites [*pr.* suites] My very heart at roote. **1817** SHELLEY *Rev. Islam* VII. xxii, Her flight..smote my lonesome heart more than all misery.

**11. a.** To strike or impress (the mind, etc.) favourably or attractively. Chiefly in pa. pple. and const. *with*.

**1663** S. PATRICK *Parab. Pilgr.* (1687) 158 They note the pretty stories,..and here and there a small sentence which smites their fancy. **1728** POPE *Dunc.* III. 229 See now, what Dulness and her sons admire! See what the charms, that smite the simple heart. **1784** COWPER *Task* v. 560 Smit with the beauty of so fair a scene. **1847** H. MILLER *Test. Rocks* (1857) 3 Smit by the singular ingenuity of the philosophic infidel. **1875** JOWETT *Plato* (ed. 2) V. 191 Plato is smitten with some features of government which he finds in Egypt.

**b.** To inspire or inflame with love; to enamour. Chiefly in pa. pple. and const. *with* or *by*.

**1663** PEPYS *Diary* 1 Jan., Lord Chesterfield..is..put away from Court upon the score of his lady's having smitten the Duke of Yorke. **1677** MIÈGE *Fr. Dict.* II. s.v., To smite a man, or cause him to fall in love with her. **1687** —— *Gt. Fr. Dict.* II. s.v., To be smitten with a Woman, to be passionately in love with her. **1711** STEELE *Spect.* No. 80 ¶3 Phillis one Day..smote the Heart of a gay West-Indian. **1755** *Mem. Capt. P. Drake* II. xiv. 243 He soon gave me to understand he was smitten with the Landlady. **1848** THACKERAY *Van. Fair* xvii, Young Lieutenant Spatterdash ..was evidently and quickly smitten by Mrs. Crawley. **1871** B. TAYLOR *Faust.* I. iii. (1875) II. 32 Hath one of you a girl with whom he's smitten?

**12.** Of thoughts: To strike or occur suddenly to (a person).

**1870** W. M. BAKER *New Timothy* 104 (Cent.), A sudden thought smote her.

**III. 13. a.** To strike or cut *off* (the head, a limb, etc.) with a slashing blow. (Common in ME.)

*c* **1205** LAY. 9204 He lette smiten him of þæt hæfde. *c* **1275** *Passion our Lord* 198 in *O.E. Misc.* 43 Seynte peter..smot of Malkes ere. *c* **1385** CHAUCER *L.G.W.* 1817 *Lucrece*, Men myghte smyte of hire arm or hed. *c* **1450** *Merlin* xiv. 222 He and Frelent were besy to smyte of his heed. **1568** GRAFTON *Chron.* II. 674 He..commaunded his heade there to be smitten off. *a* **1618** RALEIGH *Mahomet* (1637) 203 With his own hands cut his throat and smoat off his head.

**b.** To strike or knock, to drive or force with a blow or stroke, *away*, *back*, *from*, *off*, *out*, *over*, etc. (Common in ME.) Also *transf.*

*a* **1300** *Cursor M.* 6705 Qua smites vte his thains eie. **1382** WYCLIF *Matt.* x. 14 Smytith awey the dust fro ȝoure feet. *c* **1384** CHAUCER *H. Fame* I. 438 How he lost hys steris-man, Which that the stere..Smote ouer borde. **14..** *26 Pol. Poems* xxvi. 73 Now hathe age y-smete me fro My pryncipall feder of Iolyte. **1470–85** MALORY *Arth.* III. vi. 106 Syre gauayne smote hym of his hors. **1535** COVERDALE *Susanna* i. 25 Then ranne there one to the orcharde dore, & smote it open. **1559** MACHYN *Diary* (Camden) 207 Hytt brust in pesses, and on pesse..smott on of ys leg[s] a-way. **1601** HOLLAND *Pliny* II. 393 Repressing or smiting backe the swelling incident to wounds. **1684** [see A. 2 a. ϵ].

**14. a.** To knock, beat, or strike *down* (†*adown*), *to the earth* or *ground*. (Common in ME.)

*c* **1290** *S. Eng. Leg.* I. 316 Hov is þat hit..smit a-doun wel grete treon? *a* **1300** *K. Horn* 639 Hi gonne me assaille,..I smot hem alle to grunde. *a* **1400** *Lybeaus Disc.* 1185 Thre stedes heoddes doun ryght, He smot at strokes thre. *c* **1470** HENRY *Wallace* XI. 172 To ground he smat him quhar he stud. **1530** PALSGR. 723/1 This wynde hath smytten downe almost all my corne. **1590** SPENSER *F.Q.* III. i. 28 With that her mortall speare She mightily auentred towards one, And downe him smot. **1611** BIBLE *Judges* xx. 39 Surely they are smitten downe before vs. **1858** SEARS *Athan.* II. xii. 250 He ..smote him blind to the earth beneath the blaze.

*fig.* *c* **1330** in *Pol. Songs* (Camden) 339 That is muchel reuthe to wite, That alle manere godnesse is thus adoun i-smite. **1535** COVERDALE *Ps.* cxlii[i]. 3 For the enemie.. smyteth my life downe to the grounde. **1871** FREEMAN *Norm. Conq.* (1876) IV. 249 The last hopes of the House of Godwine had been smitten to the ground.

†**b.** With *down*. To droop or lower (one's head or countenance). *Obs.*

*c* **1305** in Wright *Pol. Songs* (Camden) 193 When the Kyng of Fraunce y-herde this tydynge, He smot doun is heved. *c* **1374** CHAUCER *Troylus* II. 540 With that he smot his heed adoun anone, And gan to motre. **1582** STANYHURST *Æneis* III. (Arb.) 80 Downe she smote her visadge.

**15. a.** To hew, cut, chop, or break in pieces, fragments, etc. Const. with preps., as *a*, *in*, *on*, *to*. Also in fig. context. (Common in ME.)

*a* **1320** *Sir Tristrem* 495 þe chine he smot atvo. *c* **1375** *Cursor M.* 21593 (Fairf.), In foure pecis þai hit smate. **1390** GOWER *Conf.* I. 109 A firy thonder sodeinly He sende, and him to pouldre smot. *c* **1440** *Gesta Rom.* xxxii. 126 Smite the gurdill [of lechery] in thre, *scil.* in prayer, fastyng, and almesdede. **1530** PALSGR. 723/1 He hath smytten his harnayes al to peces. **1611** BIBLE *Ecclus.* xxxvi. 10 Smite in sunder the heads of the rulers.

**b.** To bring *into* a certain condition by, or as by, striking. Also with adj. compl. *rare.*

**1338** R. BRUNNE *Chron.* (1810) 46 þei were a partie smyten in to elde. **1644** MILTON *Areop.* (Arb.) 67 If we look not wisely on the Sun it self, it smites us into darknes. **1837** CARLYLE *Fr. Rev.* III. III. vii, Rabidity smites others rabid.

†**16. a.** To strike (fire) from a stone or other hard substance. Cf. SLAY *v.*[1] 2. *Obs.*

*c* **1290** *S. Eng. Leg.* I. 237 He brouȝte a fuyr-Ire ant a ston, þare-with to smite me fuyr. *c* **1440** *Gesta Rom.* lxvi. 298 Whan þe nyȝt com, þe maide..smot fire at a stone. **1616** B. JONSON *Barriers* Wks. 966 When in a day of honour fire was smit. **1671** J. WEBSTER *Metallogr.* vii. 115 He nameth four of other colours, forth of which fire is smitten.

†**b.** To let out (blood) by lancing. *Obs.*[−1]

**1523** FITZHERB. *Husb.* §58 Take a bloud-yren, and set it streight vppon the vayne, and smyte him blourde on bothe sydes.

**17. a.** To strike, deal, or give (a blow, stroke, etc.).

**1297** R. GLOUC. (Rolls) 4441 Vewe duntes hii smite. *c* **1320** *Cast. Love* 1148 Grete boffetes among me him smot. **1390** GOWER *Conf.* II. 72 Thei smyten strokes bot a fewe. *c* **1450** *Merlin* xxiii. 424 Merlin..drough that wey.. smytinge grete strokes from oke to oke. **1490** CAXTON *Eneydos* lvi. 152 She smotte grete strokes with her swerde. **1851** HAWTHORNE *Snow Image*, etc. (1879) 84 A terrible blow shall be smitten.

†**b.** To engage in or fight (a battle). *Obs.*

**1297** R. GLOUC. (Rolls) 269 Hii smite þer an bataile hard an strong inou. **1338** R. BRUNNE *Chron.* (1810) 14 Under Elendoune þe bataile was smyten. *a* **1470** HARDING *Chron.* CXVII. i. 6 Syxe batayles agayne King Knout he smote. **1600** HOLLAND *Livy* XL. l. 1091 [He] smit a brave and fortunate battaile with the Vaccei. **1631** WEEVER *Anc. Funeral Mon.* 317 This battell was smitten in the yeare of Grace 457.

†**c.** To make or produce (a wound, etc.) by smiting. *Obs.*

*a* **1400** *Stockh. Medical MS.* i. 298 in *Anglia* XVIII. 302 ȝif a gret wounde..be..with a wepyn wyckydly smetyn. **1470–85** MALORY *Arth.* II. xviii. 97 They hadde eyther smyten other seuen grete woundes. **1535** COVERDALE *1 Sam.* xix. 8 Dauid wente forth..and smote a greate slaughter, so that they fled before him. **1581** MUNDAY *Brief Discourse* in Arb. *Garner* VIII. 215 *note*, Drawing his dagger, he smit a great hole in it.

**18. a.** To drive, hammer, knock, strike (a thing) with some degree of force *against*, *into*, *on*, etc., something else.

*a* **1300** *Cursor M.* 6261 In þe see his wand he smat. *c* **1330** R. BRUNNE *Chron. Wace* (Rolls) 4422 Nemny bar þe scheld o sker, & Iulius smot his swerd ouer fer. *a* **1400–50** *Alexander* 3678 Smeten was smaragdans in-to þe smeth werkis. **1502** ARNOLDE *Chron.* 165 Make pinnys of wylowe and smyte them faste in. **1593** SHAKS. *Lucr.* 176 His falchion on a flint he softly smiteth. **1611** BIBLE *Judges* iv. 21 Then Iael..went softly vnto him, and smote the naile into his temples. **1670** PETTUS *Fodinæ Reg.* 41 Then the Smiter of Irons..smites them upon the Monie. **1837** CARLYLE *Fr. Rev.* I. IV. ii, Large clubs, which they smite angrily against the pavement! *Ibid.* II. I. xii, Each smiting heartily his palm into his fellow's.

**b.** To strike, dash, or clap *together* (†*samen*) or *against* each other.

*a* **1300** *Cursor M.* 11998 Iesus samen [*Trin.* togider] his handes smat. **1398** TREVISA *Barth. De P.R.* XIX. cxlii. (1495) 946 Cymbales..ben smytte togider and sowneth and ryngeth. **1535** COVERDALE *Ecclus.* xiii. 2 Yf yᵉ one be smytten agaynst the other, it shal be broken. **1611** BIBLE *Numb.* xxiv. 10 Hee smote his hands together. **1671** J. WEBSTER *Metallogr.* vi. 102 Which rubbed hard or smitten together forcibly,..give sparks of fire. **1842** TENNYSON *Morte d' Arth.* 86 But when he saw the wonder of the hilt,..he smote His palms together.

†**c.** *refl.* (Cf. sense 24.) *Obs.*

*c* **1205** LAY. 25605 þes drake and beore..smiten heom to-gaderen mid feondliche ræsen. **1297** R. GLOUC. (Rolls) 8323 Hii bisegede vaste the toun, so þat the þridde day þe cristine ost smot him out. **1390** GOWER *Conf.* I. 120 So that ayein a Roche of Ston..He smot himself til he was ded. **1490** CAXTON *Eneydos* lx. 158 [They] ranne soone to fetche theyr armures. And thenne Turnus smote hym selfe in to the troians.

†**d.** In pa. pple. Stuck (*full*) *of*, studded or set thickly (with). *Obs.*

*a* **1400–50** *Alexander* 5424 With corouns on hede, As it smytten ware all..of smaragdens fine. *c* **1460** *Contin. Brut* 518 His brigantines smytten ful of gylted nayles.

†**19. a.** To make or contract (an agreement, etc.).

*c* **1325** *Lei le Freine* 322 Treuthe [was] plight. Allas! that he no hadde y-wite, Er the forward were y-smite. **1382** WYCLIF *Gen.* xxi. 27 Bothe thei smyten a boond of pees. **1596** H. CLAPHAM *Brief Bible* I. 31 Iehovah appeareth and smiteth a Covenant with him.

†**b.** To strike or coin (money). *Obs.*

**1338** R. BRUNNE *Chron.* (1810) 238 Edward did smyte rounde peny, halfpeny, ferthyng. **1390** GOWER *Conf.* II. 138 Er gold was smite In Coign. **1423** *Rolls of Parlt.* IV. 258/1 That the Maister of the Mynte do smyte..half nobles. **1535** COVERDALE *1 Macc.* xv. 6, I geue the leaue to smyte money of thine owne.

†**c.** To hew or cut (a step). *Obs. rare.*

*a* **1400–50** *Alexander* 3342 Of a Smeth smaragdane Smyten was þe toþir [step].

†**d.** To cut off (a helping of meat). *Obs. rare.*

*a* **1483** *Liber Niger* in *Househ. Ord.* (1790) 59 That the messes..be smyttyn in a suffycyaunt and according manner.

†**20. a.** To strike (an hour); to announce or notify by sounding a bell. *Obs.* (Cf. 21 c.)

*c* **1369** CHAUCER *Dethe Blaunche* 1323 In the castell ther was a belle, As hyt hadde smyte oures twelve Therewyth I a-wooke my selve. **1389** in *Eng. Gilds* (1870) 60 Ho-so komys aftyr prime be smytyn, he xal pay..j.*d.* *c* **1450** in Aungier *Syon* (1840) 373 Whylst..the president smytethe allign [*sc.* all in], the couente schal stonde in the freytour.

†**b.** To discharge (a cannon). *Obs. rare.*

*c* **1450–75** in Halliw. *E. Eng. Misc.* (Warton Cl.) 52 That gonne was welle smet, Thoȝ it had be with a stonne.

**IV.** *absol.* or *intr.* **21. a.** To deal or give a blow or blows; to strike, deliver strokes. Also with advs., as *on*, *out*. †Of a horse: To kick or fling.

*c* **1200** *Trin. Coll. Hom.* 61 Bute we turnen to gode..he wile smite mid bredlinge swuerde. *c* **1290** *S. Eng. Leg.* I. 316 No wonder þei it smite harde. **13..** *Sir Beues* (A.) 404 A lokeþ, as a wolde smite Wiþ is bat. **1382** WYCLIF *1 Esdras* iv. 8 If he seie to smyten, thei smite. **14..** *Guy Warw.* 10248 Mases of yron..for to smyte wele. *c* **1470** HENRY *Wallace* III. 363 'Smyt on,' he said, 'I defy thine actioune'. **1530** PALSGR. 723/1 You smyte to harde. **1535** COVERDALE *Luke*

xxii. 49 Lorde, shal we smyte with the swerde? **1600** SURFLET *Countrie Farme* 178 If he see that he beginne not to smite and snort,.. he shall leade him by the reines out of the stable. **1667** MILTON *P.L.* VI. 250 Satan.. Saw where the Sword of Michael smote. **1837** CARLYLE *Fr. Rev.* I. VI. iii, Louis.. clutched the tongs, and even smote with them. **1890** DOYLE *White Company* vii, There was one, indeed,.. who smote out like a true man.

*fig.* *c* **1400** *Beryn* 1456 Yeur wyff woll sikirliche.. smyte with hir tunge. **1624** QUARLES *Sion's Elegies* II. xix, That God that smit, oh, mooue that God to heale.

**b.** To strike *with* a hammer in doing smith-work; now *spec.* to strike with the sledge.

**1388** WYCLIF *Isaiah* xli. 7 A smyth of metal smytynge with an hamer. **1560** BIBLE (Geneva) *Ibid.*, So the worke-man comforted the founder, & he that smote with the hammer, him that smote by course. **1881** T. HARDY *Laodicean* I. iv, The husband used to smite for Jimmy More the blacksmith. **1888** ELWORTHY *W. Somerset Word-bk.* 685 The smith *hammers*, the assistant *smites*.

†**c.** Of a clock: To strike, chime. *Obs.*

**1448–9** in Willis & Clark *Cambridge* (1886) I. 383 He wold .. neuer go to werke till the clocke smyte. **1470–85** MALORY *Arthur* XIV. xii. 681 Thenne he herde a clok smyte on his ryght hand. *c* **1550** COVERDALE *Order of Church in Denmark* in tr. *Calvin's Treat. Sacrament* E iij b, Whan the clocke smyteth (which is comenly .vii. in Sommer, & .viii. in wynter).

**22. a.** To strike, deliver a blow or stroke, etc., *at, on,* or *upon* (also †*to*) something.

*c* **1205** LAY. 23963 Frolle.. a-dun riht sloh, and smat an Arðures sceld. *c* **1290** *S. Eng. Leg.* I. 231 He gan i-mete þis luþere fisch, and smot to him faste. **13..** *Sir Beues* (A.) 1043 So harde þe smitest vpon me kroun. **1387–8** T. USK *Test. Love* III. vii. (Skeat) l. 99 So ofte must men on the oke smyte, til the happy dent have entred. **1412–20** LYDG. *Chron. Troy* III. 1204 [Menelaus] smette at him with his scharpe swerde Vp-on þe hede. *c* **1450** *Merlin* xxxi. 624 Ye shull smyte vpon hem of that other partye. **1535** COVERDALE *Jer.* xxxi. 19, I shall smyte vpon my thee. **1611** BIBLE *Exod.* vii. 17, I will smite with the rod.. vpon the waters which are in the riuer.

*transf.* **1842** TENNYSON *Locksley Hall* 33 Love took up the harp of Life, and smote on all the chords with might.

**b.** Of things, in lit. or fig. uses.

**1412–20** LYDG. *Chron. Troy* II. 5075 On hillis hiȝe gan his bemys smyte. **1667** MILTON *P.L.* I. 298 The torrid Clime Smote on him sore besides. **1837** WHITTIER *Fountain* 88 Iron clang and hammer's ringing Smote upon his ear. **1852** MRS. STOWE *Uncle Tom's C.* iii. 15 The words smote heavily on Eliza's heart.

†**23. a.** To come *together* (or *samen*) in conflict.

*c* **1205** LAY. 5183 Heo smiten to-gædere; helmes þere gullen. *c* **1250** *Gen. & Ex.* 2109 Ðe ranc he hauen ðo ouer-cumen, To-samen it smiten. **1382** WYCLIF *1 Esdras* ii. 22 Kingis and cites smitende togidere. **14..** *Guy Warw.* 1893 Now þey smyten faste samen: I wot, ther was lytull gamen. **1470–85** MALORY *Arthur* IV. xviii. 142 [They] smote to gyders with her swerdes that her sheldes flewe in cantels. **1590** SPENSER *F.Q.* I. v. 8 As when a Gryfon.. A Dragon fiers encountreth..: With hideous horrour both together smight.

**b.** To come *together* with some degree of force; to strike or dash *on* or *against* something.

*c* **1275** LAY. 1788 þe sipes smiten o þan strond. *c* **1290** *S. Eng. Leg.* I. 69 And euere þat watur bi-hinden him smot to-gadere þere. **1398** TREVISA *Barth. De P. R.* V. xxvii. (Bodl. MS.), By hardenes of boones þat smyteþ and meueþ togedres. **1535** COVERDALE *Dan.* v. 6 His knees smote one agaynst the other. **1611** BIBLE *Nahum* ii. 10 The heart melteth, and the knees smite together. **1817** SHELLEY *Rev. Islam* IV. i, The old man took the oars, and soon the bark Smote on the beach.

†**24.** To shoot or move rapidly; to dart, rush.

*c* **1220** *Bestiary* 507 in *O.E. Misc.*, Vt of his ðrote it smit an onde. *a* **1225** *Ancr. R.* 94 Ase swifte.. ase is þe sunne gleam, þet smit from east into þe west. **13..** *K. Alis.* 494 (Laud MS.), þe lyoun smoot in to þe Est. **1481** CAXTON *Godfrey* cxxx. 194 Thyse thre smote in emong the .xxx. turkes.

**25. a.** To strike, to pass or penetrate, *in, into,* or *through* something.

*c* **1290** *S. Eng. Leg.* I. 316 ȝwane þe wynd and þat fuyr smiteth þoruȝ þe watur-cloude. *c* **1386** CHAUCER *Knt.'s T.* 362 The deeth he feeleth thurgh his herte smyte. **1393** LANGL. *P. Pl.* C. XX. 323 þe smoke and þe smorþre þat smyt in oure eyen. *c* **1400** *Ywaine & Gaw.* 377 In my face the levening smate. *a* **1425** *Cursor M.* 11824 (Trin.), þe fester smoot þourȝe his body. **1535** COVERDALE *1 Sam.* xix. 10 The iauelynge smote in the wall. *a* **1652** J. SMITH *Sel. Disc.* vi. 187 From whence the objects of dread and admiration.. smite and insinuate themselves into their senses. **1869** TENNYSON *Coming Arthur* 57 But Arthur.. Felt the light of her eyes into his life Smite on the sudden.

†**b.** To give pain *to* one's heart. *Obs.*

*a* **1300** *K. Horn* 1481 Hit smot to hornes herte So bitere þat hit smerte. *c* **1450** *Coventry Myst.* 81 ȝour swemynge smytyht to myn hert depe.

†**c.** To occur suddenly to one. *Obs.*

*c* **1440** *Alph. Tales* 20 It smate in his mynd þat it was bod ane illusion of þe devull.

†**26.** To change, pass, fall, *into* something. *Obs.*

*c* **1305** *St. Dunstan* 74 in *E.E.P.* (1862) 36 Treoflinge heo smot her and þer in anoþer tale sone. **13..** *Gaw. & Gr. Knt.* 1763 With smoþe smylyng & smolt þay smeten in-to merþe. **14..** *Guy Warw.* (C.) 1196 To þe erthe he felle downe And smete in a grete swowne.

**smiter** (ˈsmaɪtə(r)). Also 3 smitar, 4 smitter, 4–7 smyter, 5 -ere. [f. SMITE *v.* + -ER[1]. So Fris. *smiter*, Du. *smijter*, G. *schmeisser*, etc.]

**1. a.** One who smites, strikes, or buffets; a beater, striker.

*a* **1225** *Ancr. R.* 156 Heo wule.. aȝein þe smitare beoden uorð hire cheoken. *a* **1300** *Cursor M.* 6685 þe smiter sal quite his lechyng, And þe scath of his liging. **1382** WYCLIF *Isaiah* l. 6 My bodi I ȝaf to the smyteres, and my chekes to the pulleris. **1495** *Trevisa's Barth. De P.R.* XVIII. lxv. 280 Whan a lyon is wounded he.. resyth on the smyter. **1535** COVERDALE *Isaiah* xxvii. 7 Smyteth he not his smyter, as euel as he is smytten himself? —— *Lam.* iii. 30 He offreth his cheke to the smyter. **1608** A. WILLET *Hexapla Exod.* 477 The smiter was to be apprehended. **1664** J. TOMBES (*title*), Saints no Smiters; or, Smiters Civil Powers not the Work of Saints. **1813** BYRON *Corsair* III. viii, Therefore came I.. To smite the smiter with the scimitar. **1870** JEBB *Sophocles' Electra* (ed. 2) p. vi, Pelops, smiter of horses.

*fig.* **1869** FREEMAN *Norm. Conq.* (1876) II. 118 Lanfranc shone forth as the irresistible smiter of heresy.

†**b.** [After L. *percussor*.] An executioner. *Obs.*

*a* **1380** *Virg. Antioch* 253 in Horstm. *Altengl. Leg.* (1878) 30 A smiter ȝif þer beo to day, Me to sle, nou icomen in [etc.]. *c* **1430** *Life St. Kath.* (1884) 61 The batayl of my stryf fulfylled, I abyde the swerd of the smyter. *c* **1440** CAPGR. *St. Kath.* v. 1885 The mayde leyde foorth hir nekke fayr & white, And thus she seyde on-to the smytere thoo.

**c.** One who applies a thing by striking. *rare*[−1].

**1670** PETTUS *Fodinæ Reg.* 41 Then the Smiter of Irons, after they be graved, smites them upon the Monie.

**d.** *dial.* (See quot.)

**1823** E. MOOR *Suffolk Words, Smiter*, one who does any thing with energy; or in a striking manner.

**e.** *Cricket.* A hard-hitting batsman.

**1897** W. J. FORD in K. S. Ranjitsinhji *Jubilee Bk. Cricket* vii. 267 A little mercy should be shown to the muscular if unscientific 'smiter'. **1897** D. MOFFAT *Crickety Cricket* 25 Stoddart the smiter has carried his bat For a grandly made three-figure score. **1944** E. BLUNDEN *Cricket Country* iv. 53 Poor Charles could not solve the problem of getting this smiter caught in the deep field.

**2.** †**a.** A weapon with which one smites; a sword, a scimitar. *Obs.*

Partly, if not entirely, suggested by *simiter* 'scimitar'.

**1591** LYLY *Endym.* I. iii, It is my Simiter; which I by construction often studying to bee compendious, call my Smyter. **1593** NASHE *Four Lett. Conf.* Wks. (Grosart) II. 202 Put vp thy smiter, O gentle Peter. **1633** B. JONSON *Tale Tub* IV. iii, Put thy smiter up, and hear; I dare not tell the truth to a drawn sword. **1648** *Leg. Capt. Jones* 2 His fatall Smiter thrice aloft he shakes.

**b.** *Cant.* An arm. *rare*[−0].

*a* **1700** B. E. *Dict. Cant. Crew.* [Hence in Bailey, Grose, etc.]

**3.** A variety of fancy pigeon (see quot. 1778).

**1668** CHARLETON *Onomast.* 76 *Gyratices*,.. Clappers, & Smiters. **1676** WILLUGHBY *Ornith.* II. xv. 132 *Percussores, Anglicè* Smiters. **1678** RAY tr. *Willughby* 182 Smiters.. do not only shake their Wings as they fly: But also.. clap them so strongly, that [etc.]... Our Country-men distinguish between *Tumblers* and *Smiters*. **1778** G. WHITE *Selborne* lxxxiv, Pigeons, and particularly the sort called smiters, have a way of clashing their wings, the one against the other, over their backs, with a loud snap. *c* **1800** D. GIRTON *Pigeon Fancyer* 107 The smiter.. nearly resembles the tumbler, the size excepted, it being a much larger bird. **1854** MEALL *Moubray's Poultry* 277 *Smiter*.—This sub-variety, if it ever existed as distinct, has now entirely disappeared.

*attrib.* **1783** LATHAM *Gen. Synop. Birds* II. II. 614 Smiter Pigeon, *Le Pigeon batteur*.

**smith** (smɪθ), *sb.* Forms: 1–3 smið, 4 smiþ, 3– smith, 5 (7) smithe; 2 smyð, 3–4 smyþ, 4–7 smyth (5 smyȝt), 5–6 smythe; 4–5 smeth, 6 *Sc.* smeith. [Common Teut.: OE. *smið*, = OFris. *smeth*, *smid* (WFris. and EFris. *smid*, NFris. *smet*, *smer*, *smas*), MDu. *smit* (*smet*), *smid* (Du. *smid*), MLG. (and LG.) *smid*, *smed*, OHG. *smid*, *smit* (MHG. *smit*, *smid-*, G. *schmied*, †*schmid*), ON. *smiðr* (Icel. *smiður*, Norw. *smid*; MSw. *smiþer*, *smidher*, etc., Sw. and Da. *smed*); Goth. *smiþa* (in *aizasmiþa* coppersmith) differs in declension. The relations of the stem are doubtful. The original sense was app. craftsman, skilled worker, in metal, wood, or other material, and this general use still remains in Icelandic.]

**1.** One who works in iron or other metals; *esp.* a blacksmith or farrier; a forger, hammerman.

Also freq. as a second element in combs., as *black-, copper-, gold-, gun-, iron-, lock-, silver-, tin-, whitesmith*.

In the early examples referring to Joseph, the word does not mean 'carpenter', but is simply used to render L. *faber*.

*Beowulf* 1452 Swa hine fyrndagum worhte wæpna smið. *c* **950** *Lindisf. Gosp.* Matt. xiii. 55 Ah ne ðis is smiðes *vel* wyrihta sunu? *c* **1000** ÆLFRIC *Gramm.* xxxvi. 216 ðyf ðu cweðst *hic cudo*,.. ðonne byð hit nama, smið. *a* **1200** *Vices & Virt.* 51 He wes buhsum ane deadliche manne, Iosepe ðe smiðe. *c* **1275** *Passion our Lord* 59 in *O.E. Misc.*, Hi seyden, he is a smyþes sune, ne beo we noht his frend. *a* **1300** *Cursor M.* 23238 Als it war dintes on a steþi þat smythes smittes in a smeþey. **1390** GOWER *Conf.* II. 159 He was a Smith With Jupiter, which in his forge Diverse thinges made him forge. *c* **1450** *Merlin* xxiii. 427 The Emperour.. sente to seche a smyth to bynde hym in chaynes and feteres. **1484** CAXTON *Fables of Æsop* III. xii, The forge of a smythe. **1530** PALSGR. 187 A farrer or a smythe that shoeth horses. **1595** SHAKS. *John* IV. ii. 193, I saw a Smith stand with his hammer (thus) The whilst his Iron did on the Anuile coole. **1657** BAXTER *Call to Unconverted* (1666) 187 Like the Smiths dog, that is brought by custom to sleep under the noise of the hammers. **1704** T. FULLER *Med. Gymn.* (1711) 49 By incessantly following his Blow, the Smith can bring Heat into his Bar of Iron. **1784** COWPER *Task* v. 219 The first smith was the first murd'rer's son. **1851** D. WILSON *Preh. Ann.* (1863) II. III. ii. 83 The excellence of the ancient Celtic smiths.

*fig.* **1642** FULLER *Holy & Prof. St.* IV. i. 237 True, every man is, *fortunæ suæ faber*, the Smith to beat out his own fortunes. **1687** DRYDEN *Hind & Panther* III. 1268 The Doves repented, tho' too late Become the Smiths of their own Foolish Fate.

**2. a.** In special collocations, as **smith's coal, craft, dust, water, work** (see quots., sense 3, SMITHY *sb.* 4, and SMITH-WORK).

**1578** LYTE *Dodoens* 175 It groweth.. whereas there hath bene myning for Iron and *Smithes cole. **1881** YOUNG *Every Man own Mechanic* 649 The fuel used is fine coal generally called 'Smith's coal' or 'slack'. **1387** TREVISA *Higden* (Rolls) II. 229 Tubalcain fonde first *smythes craft and grauynge. **1561** T. NORTON *Calvin's Inst.* IV. 69 A man may say they haue practised smithes craft all their lyfe. **1614** RALEIGH *Hist. of World* I. I. vi. §4 Tubal and Tubalcain (inuentors of pastorage, smiths-craft, and musick). **1568–9** *Sarum Churchw. Accs.* (Swayne, 1896) 283 Sande and *smythes dust, 2d. **1712** J. JAMES tr. *Le Blond's Gardening* 33 Smiths-Dust is either the Scales beaten off at the Anvil, or Iron Filings. **1544** PHAER *Regim. Lyfe* (1560) H iij b, Julep of roses with a litle of *smiths water. **1565** COOPER *Thesaurus, Ferraria aqua*, smithes water in the cole trough wher in they quench yron. **1626** BACON *Sylva* §84 Smiths water or other Metalline water. **1714** *French Bk. Rates* 331 Iron-Axels, Hinges, Axes, and such like *Smiths Work. **1879** *Cassell's Techn. Educ.* III. 381 Most of the smith's work is taken by weight.

†**b.** *smith's balm* (see quot.). *Obs. rare.*

**1597** GERARDE *Herbal* 561 Smithes Bawme, or carpenters Bawme, is most singular to heale vp green wounds..: Dioscorides and Pliny [call].. this kind of Bawme.. Iron woort.

**3.** *attrib.*, as *smith-shop* (chiefly *U.S.*: also *smith's shop*), *-tool*; also †**smith-coal**, smithy-coal; †**smith-man**, an iron-smelter; **smith ore** (see quot.); †**smith-water**, smithy water; †**smith-wife**, a female smith.

**1521** *Maldon Liber B.* fol. 58 (MS.), Due naves onerate cum *Smythcoll. **1645–52** BOATE *Ireland's Nat. Hist.* (1860) 124 In the place where this Mine standeth, do lie little Smith-coals above the ground. **1408** in *Eng. Hist. Rev.* XIV. 519 In stipendio Johannis Gylle, *smythman alias blomer. **1883** GRESLEY *Gloss. Coal-m.* 228 *Smith Ore,.. a rich brown hæmatite iron ore. **1651** *Early Rec. Dedham, Mass.* (1892) III. 179 Whensoever the said shopp shall be no longer vsed for a *smithes shopp.., then it shall be remoued out of the high way. **1710** *Rec. Early Hist. Boston* (1884) XI. 105 Ordered that complaint be made.. against Enoch Greenliefe for making a Smith Shop in his buildings. **1743** W. ELLIS *Mod. Husbandman* Oct. xxii. 236 The Ploughman here has seldom Occasion to go to a Smith's Shop. **1755** *New Hampsh. Probate Rec.* (1916) III. 705 The Corner where Geo. Warrens Smith Shop Stands. *a* **1816** B. HAWKINS *Sk. Creek Country* (1848) 30 At the public establishment there is a smith's shop. **1882** *Econ. Geol. Illinois* III. 150 The coal.. is.. used in an adjoining smith-shop. **1899** *Daily News* 17 Nov. 5/2 At last there came a deputation from the boiler-shop and smith-shop. **1837** CARLYLE *Fr. Rev.* II. I. i, He sends for his *smith-tools. **1541** COPLAND *Guydon's Form.* R iv, [To] be put with *smyth water.. tyll it be thycke. **14..** *Nom.* in Wr.-Wülcker 692 *Hec fabrissa*, a *smyth wyfe.

**smith** (smɪθ), *v.* Forms: *α.* 1 smiðian, 3 smiðien, smiþien; 3 smiðie, 4 smythye, 5 -ie; 4–5 smith-, smyth-, 5 smyþ-, 7– smith. *β.* 1 smeoðian, 3 smeoðien, 4–6 smeth-, 5 smeþ-, smethe. [Common Teut.: OE. *smiðian*, *smeoðian*, = OFris. **smithia* (WFris. *smeije*, EFris. *smithi*, NFris. *smēde*, *smēre*), MDu. and Du. *smeden*, MLG. *smeden* (LG. *smêden*, *smeen*), OHG. *smidôn* (MHG. *smiden*, G. *schmieden*, †*schmeden*), ON. and Icel. *smiða* (Norw. and Sw. *smida*, Da. *smede*), Goth. *gasmiþōn*, f. the stem of *smiþ-* SMITH *sb.*

There is little evidence for the word from the 15th to the 19th cent., and the modern instances may be derived anew from the sb.]

**1.** *trans.* To make, construct, or fashion (a weapon, iron implement, etc.) by forging; to forge or smithy.

*c* **1000** ÆLFRIC *Saints' Lives* III. 126 He.. het him smiðian on smætum golde anre culfran anlicynsse. *a* **1100** in Napier *O.E. Glosses* 14/2 *Fabricata*, smeoþud. *c* **1205** LAY. 1563 Wa wrðe auer þene smið þa þe mid honden smeoðede [*c* **1275** smiþede]. *a* **1225** *Ancr. R.* 52 Ofte a ful hawur smið smeoðið a ful woc knif. *c* **1386** CHAUCER *Miller's T.* 576 (Ellesm.), A smyth.. That in his forge smythed plough harneys. *a* **1400–50** *Alexander* 5515 þan made he smythis to.. smethe him a chaiere. **1483** *Cath. Angl.* 346/1 To smethe, *fabricare, cudere*. **1647** HEXHAM I, To Smith, *smeden*. **1833** KEIGHTLEY *Fairy Mythol.* I. 258 Sigurd took the very best sword That the Dwarfs had ever smithed.

*fig.* *a* **1225** *Ancr. R.* 284 Al þes world is Goddes smiððe, uorte smeoðien his icorene.

**b.** To fashion articles out of (iron, etc.); to forge or hammer *into* an implement. *rare.*

*c* **1340** *Nominale* (Skeat) 136 *Homme forge fer et quiuere*, Man smethuth Irun and copur. **1377** LANGL. *P. Pl.* B. III. 305 Alle þat bereth baslarde.. Shal be demed to þe deth but if he do it smythye In-to sikul or to sithe.

**c.** To deal with by heating and hammering; to hammer or beat (a blade, etc.) on an anvil.

*c* **1400** *Vis. Tundale* (Wagner) 1077 Hem tought, þai were not smethed [*v.r.* smyþyd] inowe, But throwe a fire efte hem drowe. **1831** HOLLAND *Manuf. Metal* I. 281 The whole [penknife blade] is then smithed, or smartly hammered after it has ceased to be soft. **1846** HOLTZAPFFEL *Turning* II. 683 The blade.. is smithed or hammered, so as to make the saw quite flat. **1851–4** *Tomlinson's Cycl. Useful Arts* (1867) I. 483/1 After forging, the blade is smithed, or beaten on an anvil.

**2.** *intr.* To work at the forge; to practise smith-work. Also *fig.*

*c* **1205** LAY. 30743 Brien enne smið funde, þe wel cuðe smiðie. *a* **1340** *E.E. Ps.* cxxviii. 3 Ouer mi bak smithed sinful ai. *a* **1340** HAMPOLE *Psalter* cxxviii. 3 Abouen my bak synful smythid. **1893** *Month* Feb. 198 Others sail-making, carpentering, smithing [etc.].

Hence **smithed** *ppl. a.*

**1542-3** *Act 34 & 35 Hen. VIII*, c. 6 Pinnes..shalbe double headed,..wel smithed, the shanke wel shauen.

**smitham** ('smɪðəm). Forms: 7 **smithom**, 8-9 **smithum**, 9 **smithem**, 7-8 (9) **smytham**, 8-9 **smitham**. [var. of SMEDDUM, in sense 2 perh. associated with SMITH *sb.* or *v.*]

**1.** The finest particles or dust of ground malt. Also *attrib.* Now *dial.*

**1620** MARKHAM *Farew. to Husb.* (1625) 61 Your Malt-dust which is the sprout, come, smytham, and other excrements of the malt. **1649** BLITHE *Eng. Improver Impr.* (1652) 127 That so it may receive part of Smithom-Meale. **1883** *Almondbury Gloss.* 123 *Smithum*, the smallest of malt.

**2.** *Mining.* The finest part of lead ore, usu. obtained by passing through a sieve, and afterwards ground to powder.

**1653** MANLOVE *Customs Lead Mines* 274 Trunks and Sparks of oar. Sole of the Rake, Smytham, and many more. **1681** T. HOUGHTON *Compl. Miner* Gloss., *Smytham* is Lead Ore stamp'd and pounded down [etc.]. **1747** HOOSON *Miner's Dict.* s.v. *Buddle*, They must have clear Water enough, otherwise the Smytham will look bad. **1778** PRYCE *Min. Cornub.* 244 To separate and cleanse the Ore, which they call Smitham. **1839** URE *Dict. Arts* 751 The sediment called *smitham* is taken out, and piled up in heaps. **1865** METEYARD *J. Wedgwood* I. 125 After the vessels are painted, they lead them with a sort of lead ore they call 'Smithum'.

**3.** *Coal-mining.* (See quots.)

**1883** GRESLEY *Gloss. Coal-m.* 228 *Smithem* or *Smytham.* 1. Fine slack. 2. Clay or shale between two beds of coal. **1891** *Sheffield Gloss.* Suppl. 53 *Smithum*, small coal, slack.

**Smith & Wesson** ('wɛsən). [The names of Horace *Smith* (1808-93) and Daniel B. *Wesson* (1825-1906), founders of a firm of gunsmiths in Springfield, Mass.] The proprietary name of a make of firearm, esp. a type of cartridge revolver.

**1860** *Charleston* (S. Carolina) *Mercury* 6 Nov. 3/3 (Advt.), Smith & Wesson's seven shooters. **1865** [see REMINGTON]. **1881** G. W. ROMSPERT *Western Echo* 115 The second ball from my Smith & Wesson stretched him struggling upon the earth with a bullet through his lungs. **1893** *Official Gaz.* (U.S. Patent Office) 16 May 1058/1 Revolving firearms. Smith & Wesson, Springfield, Mass... Essential feature, the word and character *Smith & Wesson.* Used since 1857. **1928** *Trade Marks Jrnl.* 14 Nov. 1822/1 Smith and Wesson. 482,778. Revolvers and Pistols. Smith and Wesson Inc. **1957** J. E. PARSONS *Smith & Wesson Revolvers* i. 13 The Smith & Wesson revolver had arrived as a de luxe presentation item. **1964** E. S. GARDNER *Case of Phantom Fortune* (1970) xix. 192, I show you a Smith and Wesson revolver. **1981** *Daily Tel.* 18 June 18/5 They prefer to throw truncheons rather than draw a 0.38 Smith & Wesson.

**'smithcraft.** Also 9 **smith-craft.** [f. SMITH *sb.* Cf. OE. *smiðcræft.*] The work, craft, or art of a smith.

In Johnson's quotation from Raleigh the genuine reading is *smiths-craft* (see SMITH *sb.* 2).

**1755** in JOHNSON. **1860** *Artist & Craftsman* 425 If your locks want..picking to pieces, my old smithcraft may stand us in some stead. **1889** P. A. BRUCE *Plantation Negro* 233 It is in smithcraft alone that he would have a wide..field.

†**smithe.** *Obs.* Forms: 1 **smiþþe, smiðþe**, 1, 3 **smiððe**, 3 **smiðe**, 4 **smyþþe, smyþe**; 1 **smeðe**, 5 **smeþe**. [OE. *smiþþe, smiððe* (:—**smiþjōn*, f. the stem of SMITH *sb.* or *v.*), = OFris. *smithe, smitha*, MDu. and Flem. *smisse, smesse* (Du. *smidse*), OHG. *smiththa, smidda*; also OFris. *smitte, -a* (Fris. *smitte*), MDu. *smitte, smit*, OHG. *smitta, -e, -i* (MHG. *smitte*, G. dial. *schmitte*), and MLG. *smede* (LG. *smede, smê*), OHG. *smida* (obs. G. *smide, schmide*, now *schmiede*). Some of these forms are due to the influence of the word for *smith.* For the Scand. forms see SMITHY *sb.*] = SMITHY *sb.* 1.

*a* **900** tr. *Baeda's Hist.* v. xv. (1890) 442 He..ȝewunade in his smiðþan dæȝes & nihtæs sittan & licgan. *c* **1000** ÆLFRIC *Hom.* I. 64 Gað to smiððan, and fandiað þises goldes. *c* **1030** *Rule St. Benet* (Logeman) 23 Smeðe þær we ealle þas ðinc ȝeornlice wyrcean. *a* **1225** *Ancr. R.* 88 Vrom mulne & from cheping, from smiðe,..me tiðinge bringeð. *c* **1305** *St. Dunstan* 60 in *E.E.P.* 36 A priuei smyþþe bi his celle he gan him biseo.

*fig.* *a* **1225** *Ancr. R.* 284 Al þes world is Goddes smiððe, uorte smeoðien his icorene.

**'smither,** *sb. rare.* Also 5 **smyther.** [f. SMITH *v.* + -ER[1].] A smith or smithier; a hammerman.

**1435** *Coventry Leet Bk.* 185 The Jorneymen..of all oþer Craftes..except hakmen and smythers wurche in hur own houses and nott in hur masters housz. **1881** *Instruct. Census Clerks* 45 Cutlery:..Blade Smither. *Ibid.*, File Making: Forger. Heater. Striker. Smither. **1976** *Star* (Sheffield) 3 Dec. 19/4 (Advt.), Retired Smither required for part-time light Machine Knife Smithing work.

†**'smither,** *a. Obs.*[−1] ? Agile, active.

Perhaps an error for *swyper* SWIPPER *a.*

*c* **1420** *Anturs of Arth.* xlii. 543 (Ireland MS.), Gauan was smyther and smerte, Owte of his steroppus he sterte.

**smithereen** (smɪðə'ri:n), *v.* [f. SMITHEREENS *sb. pl.*] *trans.* To smash or blow up into tiny fragments. Hence **smithe'reening** *ppl. a.*

**1927** H. CRANE in *Transition* Dec. 136 Lo, Lord, Thou ridest! Lord, Lord, Thy swifting heart Naught stayeth, naught now bideth But's smithereened apart! **1959** *Listener* 5 Mar. 429/2 A bomb in a suit-case timed shortly to do its smithereening work. **1964** *Economist* 16 May 699/2 Dum-dum bullets or smithereening explosives. **1973** *N.Y. News* 21 Aug. 53/1 He'd like to smithereen the crystal ball.

**smithereens** (smɪðə'ri:nz), *sb. pl. colloq.* and *dial.* [var. of next, with Irish diminutive ending, and either adopted from, or the source of, mod.Ir. *smidirin.*] Small fragments; atoms. Usually in phrases ***to knock, split, blow*** (etc.) ***to*** or ***into, to go to, smithereens.*** Also *fig.*

**1829** G. GRIFFIN *Collegians* II. xxii. 157 A body would tink it hardly safe to stand here under 'em, in dread dey'd come tumblin' down, may be, an' make *smiddereens* of him, bless de mark! **1841** S. C. HALL *Ireland* I. 68 The harness that was broke into smithereens. *Ibid.* III. 303 The sun.. split it into smithereens. **1861** CLARA F. BROMLEY *Woman's Wand.* 189 A celestial worthy..whose prowess and exploits ..seem to have beaten Saint George and the dragon quite to smithereens. **1883** BLACK *Shandon Bells* xxxiii, He'd have knocked the whole town to smithereens. **1922** JOYCE *Ulysses* 372 Crew and cargo in smithereens. **1927** D. H. LAWRENCE *Mornings in Mexico* 16 The sun went bang, with smithereens of birds bursting in all directions. **1933** *Sun* (Baltimore) 22 Dec. 22/6 A substantial charge of dynamite—enough, in fact, to blast the bridge to smithereens. **1961** J. I. PACKER *Evangelism & Sovereignty of God* ii. 31 Books like Deuteronomy and Isaiah and John's Gospel and Romans smash it [*sc.* a man-centred outlook] to smithereens. **1976** *Time* 27 Dec. 36/3 The result is another kind of supernova, a fantastic explosion that blows the star to smithereens, dispersing into space most of the remaining elements that it had manufactured during its lifetime.

**'smithers,** *sb. pl. colloq.* and *dial.* [Of obscure origin; cf. prec.] = SMITHEREENS.

**1847** HALLIW., *Smithers*, fragments; atoms. *Linc.* **1847** FITZGERALD *Lett.* (1889) I. 171 One brother is a rascal—another a spend-thrift..—the family all gone to smithers. **1857** MRS. CARLYLE *Lett.* II. 341 Having one's nerves 'all gone to smithers'. **1865** DICKENS *Mut. Fr.* IV. xiii, Blowed us into shivers and smithers.

**smithery** ('smɪθərɪ). [f. SMITH *sb.* + -ERY. Cf. Fris. *smidterij, smitterij*, Du. *smederij*, G. *schmiederei.*]

**1.** The trade, occupation, or art of a smith; smithcraft, smithing, smith-work.

**1625** A. GILL *Sacr. Philos.* II. xxiv. 188 All the objects of Smithery, locks, guns, swords, and the like. *a* **1661** FULLER *Worthies, Somerset.* III. (1662) 21 More I have not to say of Dunstan, save that..his skill in Smithery was so great [etc.]. **1705** tr. *Bosman's Guinea* 128 Their chief Handicraft, with which they are acquainted, being the Smithery. **1728** CHAMBERS *Cycl.* s.v. *Lock*, The Lock is reckon'd the Masterpiece in Smithery. **1841** FARADAY in Bence Jones *Life* (1870) II. 146, I love a smith's shop and anything relating to smithery. **1850** K. H. DIGBY *Compitum* III. 201 Different labours, such as..masonry, carpentry, smithery, and saddlery.

*attrib.* **1655** FULLER *Ch. Hist.* II. 128 Leave we him at the Furnace in Smithery-work.

**b.** In fig. uses.

**1796** BURKE *Let. to Noble Lord* Wks. II. 271 The din of all this smithery may some time or other possibly wake this noble duke. **1831** DE QUINCEY *Whiggism in Relat. to Lit.* Wks. 1859 VI. 33 From all this sonorous smithery of harsh words..nothing adequate emerged.

**2.** The forge or workshop of a smith; a smithy; *esp.* in British Admiralty dockyards, the building in which the smith-work is done.

**1755** in JOHNSON. **1861** *Times* 24 May 7/8 The ironworks at Chatham consisted of a mere wreck of a smithery. **1871** *Daily News* 5 Sept., An extensive range of black sheds near the sawmills in the Royal Arsenal..are about to be removed, and replaced by a large smithery.

**Smithfield**[1] ('smɪθfi:ld). [The name of a locality in London (orig. *Smethefield*, f. *smethe* smooth), long celebrated as a market for cattle and horses, subsequently the central meat-market.]

**1.** A cattle- or meat-market. *rare.*

**1647** R. STAPYLTON *Juvenal* 154 Hercules, to whom the Romans dedicated two temples, one of them in the Roman Smithfield or *Forum Boarium.* **1900** *N. & Q.* Ser. IX. VI. 389/2 In a Welsh paper I have just read that a certain lady ..has offered to provide 'a free library and a Smithfield' for the town of Newton.

†**2.** ***Smithfield bargain***, a sharp or roguish bargain, one 'whereby the purchaser is taken in' (Grose); also *transf.*, a marriage of interest, in which money is the chief consideration. *Obs.*

**1662** J. WILSON *Cheats* v. v, Is not this better, than a Smithfield bargain? **1710** *Brit. Apollo* No. 77. 3/2 Sure Apollo will not encourage Smith-field Bargains. **1753** RICHARDSON *Grandison* VI. x, The hearts of us women..are pleaded with to rise against the notions of bargain and sale. Smithfield bargains you Londoners call them. **1775** SHERIDAN *Rivals* v. i, To find myself made a mere Smithfield bargain of at last!

†**b.** So ***Smithfield match.*** *Obs.*[−1]

**1742** FIELDING *J. Andrews* II. vi, He resolved never to marry his daughter on a Smithfield match; that whoever had love for her to take her, would, when he died, find her share of his fortune in his coffers.

**Smithfield**[2] ('smɪθfi:ld). *U.S.* The name of a town in Virginia, used *attrib.* to designate a type of ham cured by a special process which originated there.

Properly applied only to hams cured within the corporate limits of Smithfield.

**1908** *Sat. Even. Post* 31 Oct. 25/2 Next to singing a hymn, nothing gives him so much pleasure as a Smithfield ham. **1947** R. BEROLZHEIMER *U.S. Regional Cookbk.* 188 *Smithfield ham*... The hogs fatten rapidly by foraging in the peanut fields after the crop is harvested, special care is taken in curing and smoking. **1973** M. R. CROWELL *Greener Pastures* 113 Smithfield ham is truly worth it all. **1977** *Times* 15 Oct. 13/5 Seek out a Virginian friend..and sip mint juleps..until the Smithfield ham and spoon-bread are ready.

**Smithian** ('smɪθɪən), *a.* [f. the surname *Smith* (see defs.).]

**1.** Devised or suggested by William Smith (1769-1839), the founder of stratigraphical geology.

**1819** *Phil. Mag.* LIV. 133 A stratigraphical or Smithian arrangement of the fossil shells.

**2.** Of or pertaining to, accepting or holding the principles of, Adam Smith.

The sbs. *Smithianism, Smithism*, have also been recently employed.

**1885** *Encycl. Brit.* XIX. 365/2 The successive rise and reign of three doctrines—the mercantile, the physiocratic, and the Smithian. **1891** W. S. LILY *Shibboleths* 198 The whole Smithian school of political economists.

**smithiantha** (smɪθɪ'ænθə). [mod.L. (P. Magnus in C. E. O. Kuntze *Revisio Generum Plantarum* (1891) II. 977), f. the name of Matilda *Smith* (1854-1926), botanical artist + Gr. ἄνθος flower (with fem. ending to conform with the gender of names it superseded).] A small, perennial, rhizomatous herb of the genus so called, belonging to the family Gesneriaceæ, native to Mexico, and bearing hairy, cordate, variegated leaves and clusters of red, yellow, or orange bell-shaped flowers; = GESNERA

**1961** *Times* 27 Sept. 6/6 Colourful smithianthas, better known under their familiar name of gesneria. **1979** A. HUXLEY *Success with House Plants* 364/3 Smithianthas grow best in medium light.

**smithier** ('smɪðɪə(r)). Now *arch.* and *rare.* Also 5 **smythier(e.** [f. SMITH *v.* + -ER, or in early use f. SMITH *v.* + -IER.] A smith. Also *fig.*

*c* **1430** *Pilgr. Lyf Manhode* II. cxlviii. (1869) 134 Dame justice, the smythiere of vertues, and the forgeresse. **1435** *Coventry Leet Bk.* 182 Then the Cardwirdrawers and the myddelmen most nedes bye the wire..of the smythiers. *Ibid.*, And then the smythier, lest he lost his Custemers, wolde make true goode. **1876** MORRIS *Sigurd* II. (1898) 89 And there was I, I Regin, the smithier of the snare.

**smithing** ('smɪθɪŋ), *vbl. sb.* [f. SMITH *v.*] The action of the verb SMITH; the art or process of fashioning or forging metals; forging.

**1435** *Coventry Leet Bk.* 181 He..may..do myche harme ..in the smethyng, yif he be nechgent & mysrule his Iron, that he wirkithe. *Ibid.* 184. **1483** *Cath. Angl.* 346/1 A Smethynge, *fabricatura.* **1677** MOXON *Mech. Exerc.* Pref., I intend to begin with Smithing, which comprehends not only the Black-Smiths Trade, but takes in all Trades which use either Forge or File. **1831** HOLLAND *Manuf. Metal* I. 89 In the forging of the blades just named, there is a final hammer process called smithing. **1843** HOLTZAPFFEL *Turning* I. 227 *note*, Wheels for railways display many curious examples of smithing.

*attrib.* **1714** J. WYETT *Suppl. to Ellwoods's Life* (1765) 400 Not to use his own smithing Metaphors of *clinching* and *rivetting.* **1889** E. MATHESON *Aid Book Engin.* (ed. 2) 722 Hydraulic smithing-machines.

**smithite** ('smɪθaɪt). *Min.* [f. the name of G. F. Herbert *Smith* (1872-1953), English mineralogist + -ITE[1].] A sulpharsenite of silver, $AgAsS_2$, found as red tabular monoclinic crystals.

**1905** *Nature* 13 Apr. 574/2 Further crystallographic and chemical details were given of the three new red minerals from the Binnenthal originally described by R. H. Solly, and named by him Smithite (after G. F. Herbert Smith), Hutchinsonite (after A. Hutchinson), and Trechmannite after C. O. Trechmann). **1905** R. H. SOLLY in *Mineral. Mag.* XIV. 74 Smithite is associated with hutchinsonite, sartorite, and rathite in the white dolomite of the Lengenbach. **1938** *Econ. Geol.* XXXIII. 155 Proustite occurs..in magnificent eutectic relationships with smithite. **1968** I. KOSTOV *Mineral.* 173 Pyrostilpnite, aramayoite, and smithite have perfect pinacoidal cleavage... Smithite is very soft, the other minerals have a hardness between 2 and 3.

**'smithsonite.** *Min.* [Named by Beudant (1832), after James *Smithson* (1765-1829), who had distinguished it from calamine.]

**1.** Silicate of zinc.

*c* **1835** *Encycl. Metrop.* (1845) VI. 520/1 *Smithsonite.* Electric Calamine. *Ibid.* 527/1 *Smithsonite.* Silicate of Zinc. **1878** GURNEY *Crystallog.* 55 Smithsonite..is zinc silicate crystallised with one equivalent of water.

**2.** *U.S.* Carbonate of zinc.

For the difference between the English and the U.S. use of the word, see note on CALAMINE.

**1856** DANA *Rudim. Treat. Min.* 86 Carbonate of Zinc (Calamine, Smithsonite). **1896** CHESTER *Dict. Min.* 251 *Smithsonite*,..found in drusy incrustations or in botryoidal or stalactitic forms.

**Smith-Trager** (smɪθ'treɪgə(r)). *Linguistics.* = TRAGER-SMITH.

**1959** *Canadian Jrnl. Linguistics* V. I. 8 The Smith-Trager schema for plotting the English phonemes and the diaphonemic relations between idiolects and dialects is a case in point. **1964** W. S. ALLEN in D. Abercrombie et al. *Daniel Jones* 9 This should not be taken to imply an acceptance of the 4-term (Smith-Trager) stress system.

**ˈsmith-work.** [SMITH *sb.* Cf. MDu. *smedewerck* (Du. *smeedwerk*), MHG. *smidewerc* (G. *schmiedewerk*).] Work performed or done by a smith; also, the work or occupation of a smith.
**1720** in *Jrnl. Derbysh. Archæol. Soc.* (1905) XXVII. 215 For smith worke, [£]o 3 2. **1837** CARLYLE *Fr. Rev.* I. II. i, He . . determines on a little smith-work; and so . . is learning to make locks. **1869** RANKINE *Mach. & Hand-tools* App. 56 The fitness of bar iron for shipbuilding and smith-work is tested by bending and punching it cold.

**smithy** (ˈsmɪðɪ), *sb.* Forms: *α.* 4 **smiþi,** 5 **smyþi;** 5 **smythie,** 5–6 **-y,** 6 **-ye, smithee,** 6–7 **smithie,** 7– **smithy;** 4 **smeþi, smethi, smeþey,** 5–7 **smethey,** 5–6 **smethy,** 7 **smethie.** *β. Sc.* and *north. dial.* 6–7 **smydy,** 8 **smidy;** 5–6 **smyddy,** 6–9 **smiddie,** 6– **smiddy;** 5 **smede, smedye,** 6 **smedie,** 5–7 **smedy,** 6 **smeddy.** [ad. ON. *smiðja* (Icel. *smiðja*, Norw. *smidja*; MSw. *smidhia, smidia*, Sw. *smedja*, Da. *smedie*), = OE. *smiððe*: see SMITHE *sb.*]
**1.** The workshop of a smith; a blacksmith's shop; = FORGE *sb.* 2. Also occas., a portable forge.
*α. c* **1300** *Cursor M.* 23238 (Edin.), Als it war dintes of a stiþi þat smiþis smitis in þair smiþi [*Cott.* smeþey, *Gött.* smethi]. *c* **1440** *Promp. Parv.* 461/1 Smythy, *fabricia*. **1496** *Acc. Ld. High Treas. Scot.* I. 289 Item, for bering of xxx waw of irn fra the marchant buthis to Thom Barkaris smythy, xlv d. **1546** *Yorks. Chantry Surv.* (Surtees) 247 One cotage or smythye and a garthyne. **1562** *Wills & Inv. N.C.* (Surtees, 1835) 207 The Smethey. One pair of bellowes [etc.]. **1601** HOLLAND *Pliny* II. 512 In the smithies where brasse is made and wrought. **1700** DRYDEN *Ovid's Met.* XII. 390 His blazing Locks . . hiss'd, like red hot Iron within the Smithy drown'd. **1771** SMOLLETT *Humph. Cl.* 10 July, Finding the tools of the defunct, together with some coals, in the smithy. **1849** MACAULAY *Hist. Eng.* ix. II. 486 It proved to be a moveable smithy, furnished with all tools and materials necessary for repairing arms and carriages. **1875** JOWETT *Plato* (ed. 2) I. 229 Not when I pass a smithy; for then the iron bars make a tremendous noise.
*fig.* **1865** *Sat. Rev.* 12 Aug. 204/1 The extent to which rivals in Paris, Liege, or Elberfield, were likely to supplant the great British smithy [Birmingham]. **1866** KINGSLEY *Herew.* vii, They hammered at each other in the devil's smithy.
*β. c* **1425** WYNTOUN *Cron.* I. v. 228 Quhar men war wirkand at a smedye [*v.r.* smyddy]. **1497** *Acc. Ld. High Treas. Scot.* I. 328 For tua laid of colis, in Melros, to the smyddy. **1500–20** DUNBAR *Poems* xxxiii. 56 For smowking of the smydy. **1580** *Reg. Privy Council Scot.* III. 320 Item, in the smiddie, ane irne studie [etc.]. **1665** BRATHWAIT *Comment. Two Tales* 50 Those antient Verses . . That Scholar well deserves a Widdie, Who makes his Study of a Smiddie. **1786** BURNS *Twa Dogs* 19 At Kirk or Market, Mill or Smiddie. **1826** J. WILSON *Noct. Ambr.* Wks. 1855 I. 122 Like . . a vice in a smiddy. **1899** CROCKETT *Kit Kennedy* 243 Kit had trysted with the orra-man to meet him at the smiddy.
†**b.** = BLOOMERY[1]. *Obs. rare*$^{-1}$.
**1565** in West *Antiq. Furness* (1774) App. IX, The queen's majestie's woods . . are like to fall into great decay . . by reason of certain iron smithies there lately erected and demised.
**2.** Smithcraft; smith-work. *rare.*
**1804** W. TAYLOR in *Crit. Rev.* III. 541 Important inventions; as that of clothing, of fire, of smithy, of foundery. **1855** J. R. LEIFCHILD *Cornwall* 178 Details of the Expenses, . . Smithy, Carpentry, and Sawing, £1,701 19 0.
**3.** *attrib.*, as ***smithy ashes, bellows, cur, dust, -fire, vice, work,*** etc.
**1469–70** *Durh. MS. Rolls* (Surtees) 642 Le Smethyhouse infra Abbathiam. **1495** *Naval Accs. Hen. VII* (1896) 158 Smythy Bellowes. ij payer. **1523** SKELTON *Garl. Laurel* 762 Lyke a smythy kur. **1556** *Knaresborough Wills* (Surtees) I. 73 My smithie geare. **1611** COTGR., *Escume de Mareschal*, the refuse, or drosse of yron; smithie dust. **1669** *Records Baron Crt. Stitchill* (S.H.S.) 54 For smydy werke, one pund eight shillings. **1677** *Churchw. Acc. Pittington*, etc. (Surtees) 241 Item for smiddy ashes, 1s. *a* **1837** NICOLL *Poems, The Smith* i, His grip was like a smiddy vice. **1837** CARLYLE *Fr. Rev.* III. v. vi, Smithy-fires . . for the manufacture of arms.
**4.** Special combs.: **smithy-coals,** a kind of small coal used by smiths; **smithy-coom** (see quot. 1855); †**smithy-craft,** smith-craft, smith-work; **smithy-dander,** a forge cinder; **smithy lime,** a limestone layer of Aldstone Moor in Cumbria; †**smithy-man,** an iron-smith; †**smithy-miln,** a smithy in which the work is partly performed by water power; **smithy-slack, slag,** the shale or iron dust of a forge; †**smithy-water,** the water in which a smith cools his heated irons.
**1482** in *Charters*, etc. *Edinb.* (1871) 169 Of ilk chaldir of *smethy colis vi d. **1789** J. WILLIAMS *Min. Kingd.* I. 157 The smithy coal of Balmule and Rosebank. **1611** *Churchw. Acc. Pittington*, etc. (Surtees) 161 Paide for beringe sand and *smethie come to the same lyme, xij d. **1855** ROBINSON *Whitby Gloss.*, *Smithycome* or *Smitticome*, the smith's iron dust or sweepings mixed with hot pitch as an impervious composition for the tops of wooden sheds. **1513** DOUGLAS *Æneid* VIII. vii. 107 The mychty God of fyr . . to his *smyddy craft and forge hym spedis. **1828** SCOTT *F.M. Perth* iii, You cannot suppose that Harry Gow cares the value of a *smithy-dander for such a cub as yonder cat-a-mountain? **1833–4** J. PHILLIPS *Geol.* in *Encycl. Metrop.* (1845) VI. 585/2 *Smiddy lime. *a* **1400** *Isumbras* 410 A *smethymane thus was he there . . And blewe thaire belyes bloo. **1533–4** *Durh. Househ. Bk.* (Surtees) 329 Cristofero Willey, le smedyman. **1523** FITZHERB. *Surv.* 9 b, Cutlersmylnes, *smethymylnes & all suche other. **1831** HOLLAND *Manuf. Metal* I. 194 This larger mass being generally . . imbedded in *smithy-slack. **1837** J. T. SMITH tr. *Vicat's Mortars* 1 Another looked upon *smithy slag and iron-dross as the finest ingredients. *c* **1530** LD. BERNERS *Arth. Lyt. Bryt.* (1814) 43 [The water] was blacker than *smythy water.

**smithy** (ˈsmɪðɪ), *v.* Also 3 **smiðien,** 5 **smyþ-, smyth-.** [f. SMITHY *sb.* With the early examples cf. SMITH *v.*]
**1. a.** *trans.* To make or fashion by smithing; to forge or smith. Also *fig.*
*c* **1205** LAY. 30749 Þe smið gon to smiðeȝe ane pic swiðe long. *c* **1386** CHAUCER *Miller's T.* 576 (Lansd.), A smyþe . . þat in his forge smyþeieþ plouhe hernays.
**1839** BYWATER *Sheffield Dial.* 33, 1st. He moods t' blade. . . 3rd. Then he smithies it. **1892** BROOKE *E.E. Lit.* II. 27 A famous coat of mail that Weland the great forgeman had smithied. **1910** J. MASEFIELD *Ballads & Poems* 66 Until this case, this clogging mould, Be smithied all to kingly gold. **1929** A. CLARKE *Pilgrimage* 19 Smithied in gloom the low day Had glowed upon the axle.
**b.** To weld *together* by forging.
**1868** G. STEPHENS *Runic Mon.* I. 185 In others only every other ring is riveted, the alternate ones being smithied together.
**2.** *intr.* To practise smithing.
**1733** L. THEOBALD in *Works of Shakespeare* VII. 96 To *smithy*, is, to perform the Work and Office of a Smith. **1866** DASENT *Gisli* 11 Gisli sat in the hall and smithied.
Hence **ˈsmithied** *ppl. a.*, **ˈsmithying** *vbl. sb.*
*c* **1449** PECOCK *Repr.* II. xviii. 256 An hamer forto make a knyf in smythiyng. **1868** G. STEPHENS *Runic Mon.* I. 185 Each clincht ring grasps four smithied and . . each smithied grasps four riveted. **1886** P. ROBINSON *Teetotum Trees* 142 To do a bit of smithying up at the forge. **1934** E. BLUNDEN *Challenge to Death* 336 History's smithying should not disappear Without reverberation.

**smiting** (ˈsmaɪtɪŋ), *vbl. sb.* [f. SMITE *v.*]
**1.** The action of the verb; beating, striking. Also *fig.*
*c* **1330** *Arth. & Merl.* 8874 (Kölbing), Wiþ smiteing & wiþ skirminge. **1382** WYCLIF *1 Macc.* xv. 6 Y suffre thee for to make smytyng, or printe, of thin own money. *a* **1425** tr. *Arderne's Treat. Fistula*, etc. 51 Þe skyn was noȝt cleuen alsone after þe smytyng. *c* **1491** CAXTON *Chast. Goddes Chyld.* 74 Say thries this verse with smyting on the brest. **1560** BIBLE (Geneva) *1 Kings* xx. 37 The man smote him, and in smiting wounded him. **1660** J. TAYLOR *Worthy Comm.* i. iii. 55 It was not that smiting that beat the Syrians. **1694** J. KETTLEWELL *Comp. Penitent* 111 Father, let thy smiteing reclaim and amend me. **1820** SCOTT *Monast.* xxxv, It is but the smiting of an Egyptian when all is said out. **1842** MANNING *Serm.* ii. (1848) 29 Who does not feel within the smiting of conscience. **1887** *Athenæum* 26 Mar. 417/3 It is not everybody . . who could take such friendly smiting in this spirit.
*attrib.* **1653** R. SANDERS *Physiogn.* 188 The inflammation and smiting pain of the head.
**b.** With *a* and pl. An instance of this.
*c* **1380** WYCLIF *Last Age Ch.* (1840) 32 Smyttingis to-gidere of folkis and hurtlynge to-gidere of rewmes. *a* **1483** *Cath. Angl.* 346/2 A Smytyng, *iccio, percussio.* **1615** HIERON *Wks.* I. 598 No doubt our hearts would smite vs herein, . . and happy should such secret smitings be. **1656** *Artif. Handsom.* 131 Least they be . . severe beyond Gods smitings. **1837** CARLYLE *Fr. Rev.* II. III. v, Accelerated . . by smitings, twitchings,—spurnings. **1860** PATMORE *Faithful for Ever* I. vii, In smitings as of silver bars.
**2.** *smiting-line* (see quots.).
*a* **1625** *Nomenclator Navalis* (Harl. MS. 2301) s.v., [The] Smitting-line is a small Roape which is made fast to the Missen yard arms. **1627** CAPT. SMITH *Seaman's Gram.* v. 22 The missen hath but one [furling-line] called the smiting line. **1867** SMYTH *Sailor's Word-bk.*, *Smiting-Line*, a line by which a yarn-stoppered sail is loosed, without sending men aloft. If well executed, marks the seaman.

**smiting** (ˈsmaɪtɪŋ), *ppl. a.* Also 4 **smytende.** [f. SMITE *v.*] That smites, strikes, or beats.
**1382** WYCLIF *Prov.* xix. 29 Greithid ben to scorneres domes; and smytende hameres to the bodies of foolis. **1648** G. DANIEL *Eclog.* v. 57 Dire, as the Smiting Haile to newean'd Lambs. **1840** CARLYLE *Heroes* iii. (1906) 93 One smiting word; and then there is silence. **1869** T. T. LYNCH *Church & St.* 10 The smiting strength of the lightning of God.

†**ˈsmittable,** *a. Sc. Obs.* In 5 **smytable.** [f. SMIT *v.*] Capable of being infected.
*a* **1500** in *Ratis Raving*, etc. (1870) 108 It kepis thaim oft tymis fra ill. Fore ful women are so smytable, And till al wykit wycis able.

**smitten** (ˈsmɪt(ə)n), *ppl. a.* [See SMITE *v.* A. 3 ε.] That has been smit; beaten, struck. Also *absol.* with *down.*
*c* **1250** *Gen. & Ex.* 3867 Ut of ðe smiten ston Ynoȝ hem sulde water gon. *a* **1340** HAMPOLE *Psalter* cxlv. 7 Lord vprightys þe smytyn down. **1742** YOUNG *Nt. Th.* IX. 202 Sudden as the spark From smitten steel. **1859** G. MEREDITH *R. Feverel* xxx, Her voice just vibrating . . like a smitten vase. **1888** H. JAMES *Reverberator* II. v. 122 A violation of sanctities, . . a burning of smitten faces.

**ˈsmitting,** *ppl. a.* Now *north. dial.* and *Sc.* [f. SMIT *v.*] Infectious; contagious.
**1562** TURNER *Baths* 2 If he be sieke in a smitting or infective disease. **1595** DUNCAN *App. Etym.* (E.D.S.), *Contagio*, an infection or smitting-sicknes. **1671** SKINNER *Etymol. Ling. Angl.* Xxx b/1 Smiting, *pro* Contagious, Infectious, *vox agro Linc. usitatissima.* **1788** W. H. MARSHALL *Yorksh.* II. 353 *Smitting*, infectious; catching, as a disease. **1858–61** RAMSAY *Remin.* v. (1870) 118 Gantin' may be *smittin'*. **1892** M. C. F. MORRIS *Yorks. Folk-Talk* 73 But she did not think the complaint was smitting.

**ˈsmittle,** *a. north. dial.* and *Sc.* Also 6 **smittel(l,** 9 **smittal.** [f. SMIT *v.* + -LE I. Cf. MSw. *smittol* in the same sense.] Infectious; contagious. Esp. of diseases, etc.
*smittle* has also dialect currency as sb. and vb.; the latter is given by Ray (1674). The adj. *smittlish* is also recorded by Grose (1787) and others.
**1583** *Leg. Bp. St. Androis* 760 Thair wald this halie bischope byde, Saying, forsuith, it was not smittell. **1720** RAMSAY *Rise & Fall of Stocks* 38 The covetous infatuation Was smittle out o'er all the nation. **1781** in J. HUTTON *Tour to Caves* (ed. 2) Gloss. 96. **1811–** in dialect glossaries, etc. **1859** H. KINGSLEY *G. Hamlyn* xxxvi, Get thy saddles off, lad, and come in; 'tis a smittle night for rheumatics.

**smoak, -ing, -y:** see SMOKE, etc.

†**smoch,** *a. Sc. Obs.*$^{-1}$ (Meaning uncertain.)
**1508** DUNBAR *Flyting* 364 Thou wald be fayn to gnaw . . smoch banis behynd doggis bakkis.

**smock** (smɒk), *sb.* Forms: 1, 3 **smoc,** 3–5 **smok,** 4– **smock,** 5–6 **smokk;** 4–8 **smocke,** 5–6 **smokke;** 5–7 **smoke,** 6 **smoake.** [OE. *smoc*, = ON. *smokkr* (once, and perh. from OE.), OHG. *smoccho* (once); cf. also NFris. *smok* woman's shift (Helgoland, perh. from E.), neck-ruff (Sylt). The stem is probably related to that of OE. *smúȝan* to creep, ON. *smjúga* to creep into, put on, a garment.
The sense of ON. *smokkr* is however not certain; it may be some special application of the later Icel. *smokkr*, Norw. *smokk*, sheath, sheath-formed case or receptacle, finger-stall, etc.]
**1. a.** A woman's undergarment; a shift or chemise. Now *arch.* or *dial.* (common down to 18th cent.).
For the use as a plant-name see LADY-SMOCK.
*a* **1000** in Wr.-Wülcker 210 *Colobium*.., loþa, hom, *uel* smoc, mentel. *c* **1000** ÆLFRIC *Gloss.* Ibid. 125 *Colobium*, smoc, *uel* syrc. *c* **1200** *Trin. Coll. Hom.* 163 Hire chemise [is] smal and hwit, . . and hire smoc hwit. *c* **1290** *S. Eng. Leg.* I. 182 Are hire smok were of i-nome. *a* **1320** *Sir Tristrem* 1788 Ȝour smock was solwy to sen, Bi mark þo ȝe schuld ly. *c* **1386** CHAUCER *Miller's T.* 52 Whit was hir smok, and browdid al byfore And eek byhynde on hir coler aboute. *c* **1425** LYDG. *Assembly of Gods* 377 A smokke was her wede, garnysshyd curyously. **1483** CAXTON *Gold. Leg.* 371/1 He . . wold not relece hir obedyence tyl that she was despoyled to hir smocke. **1559** W. CUNNINGHAM *Cosmogr. Glasse* 173 Their shirtes and smokes are saffroned. **1591** GREENE *Farew. Follie* Wks. (Grosart) IX. 316 Shee . . standing in hir smocke by the bed side. **1650** BULWER *Anthropomet.* 200 The women . . weare but three cubits of cloth in their smocks. **1674** tr. *Scheffer's Lapland* xvii. 89 The use of smocks is no more known among women than the use of shirts among men. **1735** POPE *Ep. Lady* 24 Agrees as ill . . As Sappho's di'monds with her dirty smock. **1837** BARHAM *Ingol. Leg.* Ser. I. *Look at the Clock*, You may sell my chemise (Mrs. P. was too well-bred to mention her smock). **1865** KINGSLEY *Herew.* xv, I would sooner have her in her smock than any other woman with a dower.
*Prov.* **1461** *Paston Lett.* I. 542 Nere is my kyrtyl, but nerre is my smok. **1639** J. CLARKE *Parœmiologia* 254 Neare is my petticoat, but nearer is my smock.
*transf.* **1677** GREW *Anat. Pl., Anat. Seeds* (1682) 201 This sticks not to the midle Coat, . . but commonly, remains entire, after those are stripp'd off, being as it were, the Smock of the Seed.
**b.** Offered (formerly) as a prize in races to be run by women or girls.
**1722** MRS. BRADSHAW in *C'tess Suffolk's Lett.* (1824) I. 98 The Colonel gave a smock for the young wenches to run for. **1740** SOMERVILLE *Hobbinol* I. 225 See here this Prize, this rich lac'd Smock behold. **1812** in Holland *Cheshire Gloss.* (1886) 325 A race for a good Holland smock by ladies of all ages. **1859** HUGHES *Scour. White Horse* v. 91, I see, Sir, that 'smocks to be run for by ladies' is left out.
†**c.** Used allusively to denote a woman or womankind. *Obs.*
**1591** GREENE *Conny Catch.* I. Wks. (Grosart) X. 60 The Collier . . said he would be tried by the verdit of the smock. **1612** *Pasquil's Night-cap* (1877) 7 If his sweet worship . . Scrape fauour with some female-wedded smocke. **1693** SHADWELL *Volunteers* III. i, Thou wert a pretty Fellow, to rebel all thy Life-time against Princes, and trail a Pike under a Smock-Rampant at last!
**2. a.** = SMOCK-FROCK I.
**1831** CARLYLE *Sartor Res.* I. iv, The broad button of Birmingham spelter in a Clown's smock. **1882** SERGT. BALLANTINE *Exper.* 16 A man . . clad in one of the ordinary white smocks worn by labourers.
**b.** A loose garment worn by artists over their other clothes to keep them clean; a woman's or child's loose dress or blouse resembling a smock-frock in shape.
**1907** *Yesterday's Shopping* (1969) 790/1 Girls' cashmere smock. In cream, sky, cardinal. **1938** N. MARSH *Artists in Crime* (1941) xiii. 192 He found . . an evening dress in close proximity to a painting-smock. *Ibid.* 193 He was amused to find that even the Seacliff painting-bags and smock smelt of Worth. **1969** R. T. WILCOX *Dict. Costume* 326/2 The smock is now much worn as a coverall by professional people at work, especially artists. **1971** [see MATERNITY 3 b].
**c.** In full ***camouflage smock,*** a loose outer tunic of coarse material dyed brown and green and worn by troops as camouflage.
**1964** L. DEIGHTON *Funeral in Berlin* xxxii. 171 They wore camouflage smocks and steel helmets. . . They were front-line troops, not Waffen S.S. **1974** C. RYAN *Bridge too Far* IV. vii. 295 The only thing I could do for most of them was to take off their smocks and cover their faces. **1978** M. WALKER *Infiltrator* xxi. 224 He tossed me an assault rifle and . . a camouflage smock.
**3. a.** *attrib.* and *Comb.*, as ***smock-dowry, dress, jacket, -linen, -petticoat, -shirt, -skirt, -sleeve;***

also **smock-like** adj.; **smock-ravelled** *dial.*, perplexed.

**1611** MIDDLETON & DEKKER *Roaring Girl* v. ii, A wench with her smock-dowry, no portion with her but her lips and arms. **1980** J. HONE *Flowers of Forest* I. 28 The woman in the pale smock dress. **1976** *Bridgwater Mercury* 21 Dec. 3/2 (Advt.), Half price smock jackets. **1603** J. DAVIES (Heref.) *An Extasie* Wks. (Grosart) I. 90/2 Her nether smockes or smock-like Petticotes. **1880** L. HIGGIN *Handbk. Embroidery* ii. 12 *Smock Linen* is a strong even green cloth.. an excellent ground for working screens. **1882** CAULFEILD & SAWARD *Dict. Needlwk.* 452/2 *Smock linen*, the linen of which our peasants' Smockfrocks are made, which is a strong even green linen, employed also for articles designed for embroidery. **1627** *Lismore Papers* (1886) II. 222, 2 smock petticoats of worsted for my mother and my wife. **1904** in *Eng. Dial. Dict.*, Smock-ravelled. **1913** D. H. LAWRENCE *Let.* 15 Sept. (1962), I feel a bit smock-ravelled—don't know where the east is, nor the north and west. **1883** *Cent. Mag.* Nov. 74/2 Blue smock-shirts have it all to themselves. **1972** *Guardian* 8 Feb. 11/6 A smock shirt is less voluminous than a smock, but has..smock details: the neck is round or square, there is usually a yoke, and often pleated or pin-tucked fronts. **1630** J. TAYLOR (Water P.) *Wks.* II. 165 From the loftie Quoyfe to the lowly.. Smockeskirt. **1596** SPENSER *State Irel.* Wks. (Globe) 635/2 The deepe smock sleeve hanging to the grounde. **1870** A. J. MUNBY *Diary* 25 June in D. Hudson *Munby* (1972) 288 A stout fair girl.. who looked well in her cotton hoodbonnet and red neckerchief, and smocksleeves.

**b.** In allusive terms, usually suggestive of loose conduct or immorality in, or in relation to, women, as ***smock-agent***, ***-council***, ***-employment***, ***-fair***, etc.

Examples are very common in 17th cent. dramatists.

**1632** MASSINGER *Maid Hon.* II. ii, I hope, sir, You are not .. employed by him As a *smock-agent to me. *a* **1652** BROME *City Wit* III. i, I'll be hang'd if this Doctor be not of her *smock-councell. **1624** MASSINGER *Renegado* II. i, 'Tis but procuring; A *smocke emploiment. *a* **1652** BROME *Novella* III. i, What make you here i' th' *Smock-Faire, precious Mistris? **1611** L. BARRY *Ram Alley* IV. i, A knight, and never heard of *smock-fees? **1681** DRYDEN *Sp. Friar* II. i, Now Plague and Pox on his *Smock-Loyalty! **1640** SHIRLEY *Imposture* v. iii, I was the agent 'twixt them: he was pleased To choose me his *smock-officer. **1632** B. JONSON *Magn. Lady* IV. ii, Keep these women-matters, *Smock-secrets to ourselves. **1705** HICKERINGILL *Priest-cr.* II. Pref. A 3 b, Great Kindred, *Smock-Simony, and Whores, have advanc'd many a Sot to the Holy-Chair. **1598** MARSTON *Sco. Villanie* I. ii. 175 Lust fired, Attended only with his *smock-sworne Page. **1582** STANYHURST *Æneis* IV. (Arb.) 102 This *smocktoy Paris.. with falling woommanish hearelocks. **1611** B. JONSON *Catiline* IV. v, There are of us can be as exquisite traitors, As e'er a male-conspirator of you all. *Cethegus.* Ay, at *smock-treason, matron. *a* **1625** FLETCHER *Elder Brother* III. ii, These *Smock-vermine, how eagerly they leap at old mens kisses.

**smock,** *a.* [prob. an attributive or elliptic use of prec.] (See quots.)

**1849** D. J. BROWNE *Amer. Poultry Yd.* (1855) 290 In 1823, he [a game-cock] was milk-white, or 'smock', as the English term it. **1854** MEALL *Moubray's Poultry* 111 [Sub-varieties of Game-Fowl.] White, or Smock (vulgar).

**smock** (smɒk), *v.* [f. the sb.]

†**1.** *trans.* To render effeminate or womanish.

**1614** SYLVESTER *Bethulia's Rescue* III. 28 Here would the Mede show.. that no pomp.. Had ever power his Manly mind to smock.

†**2.** *intr.* To consort with women. *Obs. rare.*

**1719** D'URFEY *Pills* IV. 126 Then we all agree; To.. Smock and Knock it, Under the Green-wood Tree. **1731–8** SWIFT *Polite Conv.* 176 You don't smoke, I warrant you, but you smock.

**3.** *trans.* To dress in a smock.

**1847** TENNYSON *Princ.* IV. 228 This is proper to the clown, Tho' smock'd, or furr'd and purpled.

**4.** *Needlework.* To gather by means of sewing done in lines crossing each other diagonally, after a pattern common on smock-frocks.

**1888** *Pall Mall G.* 30 May 11/1 Her gown is of Liberty silk,.. smocked here and gathered there. **1963** N. STREATFEILD *Vicarage Family* iii. 27 Louise.. was still small enough for smocks and her mother smocked beautifully. **1980** *Daily Tel.* 24 Apr. 14/5 His mother brought him up alone on a war pension plus what she could make by smocking children's clothes.

**'smockage.** *nonce-wd.* [Allusively f. SMOCK *sb.*, after *socage.*] (See quot.)

**1612** CHAPMAN *Widowes T.* I. Wks. 1873 III. 21 Thou shalt hold thy Tenement to thee and thine eares for euer in free smockage, as of the manner of Panderage.

**smocked** (smɒkt), *ppl. a.* [f. SMOCK *sb.* or *v.*]

**1.** Of persons: Provided with, clothed in, a smock. (Cf. *hurden-smocked* s.v. HARDEN *sb.* b.)

**1897** G. ALLEN *Type-writer Girl* xviii. 195 While the smocked milkman still stood.. in the meadows.

**2.** Of a garment: Gathered and worked after the fashion of a smock-frock.

**1890** *Daily News* 8 Jan. 7/6 The New Smocked Yoke Jersey. **1918** E. A. ARCHER *Needlecraft* x. 112, I am sure you will not be contented till Sally Ann has a smocked dress. **1934** A. M. MIALL *Compl. Needlecraft* 92 Smocked garments readily stretch as a child grows.

**smocker** ('smɒkə(r)). [f. SMOCK *sb.* or *v.*]

†**1.** One who consorts with women. *Obs.*

**1708** MOTTEUX *Rabelais* V. (1737) 217 Leachers, Shakers, Smockers. **1756** *Gentl. Mag.* XXVI. 605/2 Henry.. had formerly been a Cocker, Smocker, and Foxhunter.

**2.** One who smocks blouses or the like.

**1892** *Star* 13 May 4/8 Smockers.—Experienced workers wanted at once.

**smock-face.** Now *rare.* [f. SMOCK *sb.*] A pale and smooth or effeminate face; a person having a face of this description.

**1605** CHAPMAN *All Fools* v. i, [Fortune gives] Some wealth without wit, some nor wit nor wealth, But good smocke-faces. **1696** VANBRUGH *Relapse* 1st Prol., Perhaps there's not a smock-face here to-day But's bold as Cæsar to attack—a play. **1786** J. A. D. *Pogonologia* 51 You pretty fellows of the present day,.. and all you with smock-faces and weak nerves. **1820** W. TOOKE *Lucian* I. 398 Who does that smock-face belong to there? **1846** LANDOR *Imag. Conv.* I. 354 Who could have expected it from that smock-face! **1874** *Slang Dict.* 298 *Smock-face*, a white delicate face,—a face without whiskers.

**'smock-faced,** *a.* Now *rare.* [Cf. prec.] Having a pale smooth face; effeminate-looking.

**1693** DRYDEN *Juvenal* x. (1726) 158 But your Endymion, your smooth, smock-fac'd Boy,.. shall a beauteous Dame enjoy. **1706** ESTCOURT *Fair Example* II. i, A smock fac'd Rogue, with.. a great deal of Impudence. **1797** MRS. A. M. BENNETT *Beggar Girl* (1813) I. 49 That poor smock-faced thing of a doctor. **1821** SCOTT *Kenilw.* xiii, A little old smock-faced man,.. soft-haired as well as beardless, appeared. **1855** A. BYWATER *Shevvild Ann.* 24 (E.D.D.), Working men look rayther too smock-faced for beards. **1866** BROGDEN *Prov. Lincs.*, *Smock-faced*, pale. **1923** E. SITWELL *Bucolic Comedies* 16 Forlorn the smock-faced sheep sit.

*transf.* **1684** OTWAY *Atheist* I. i, With a hundred smiling smock-fac'd guineas.

**'smock-frock,** *sb.* [SMOCK *sb.*]

**1.** A loose-fitting garment of coarse linen or the like, worn by farm-labourers over or instead of a coat and usually reaching to mid-leg or lower.

*a* **1800** PEGGE *Suppl. Grose*, *Smock-frock*, a coarse linen shirt worn over the coat by waggoners, &c., called in the South a Gaberdine. **1805** *Ann. Reg.*, *Chron.* 420/2 He pulled off his jacket or smock-frock. **1840** DICKENS *Old C. Shop* xix, Men had lounged about all night in smock-frocks, and leather-leggings. **1883** T. HARDY in *Longm. Mag.* July 258 The genuine white smock-frock.. and the whity-brown one .. are rarely seen now afield.

*Comb.* **1891** *Catholic News* 29 Aug. 8/4 It is smockfrock-like in shape, with a hole for the neck.

**2.** A man wearing a smock-frock.

**1858** THACKERAY *Virginians* I. xv. 112 The smock-frocks did not seem to heed, and clamped out of church quite unconcerned. **1898** J. ARCH *Story Life* ii. 31 Regular pitched battles they were of smock frock against cloth coat, in which smock frock held his own right well.

Hence **'smock-frock** *v. intr.* (with *it*), to wear a smock-frock; **'smock-frocked** *a.*, wearing a smock-frock.

**1808** COBBETT *Political Reg.* XIV. 20 Aug. 257 Among the smock-frocked politicians. **1840** HOOD *Ye Tourists & Travellers* 6 Play dominoes, smoke, wear a cap and smock-frock it. **1885** *Eng. Illustr. Mag.* Aug. 739/1 The stolid smock-frocked peasantry.

**'smocking,** *vbl. sb.* [f. SMOCK *v.* 4.] The action of gathering and working a garment after the fashion of a smock-frock; the ornamental pattern so formed.

**1888** *Bow Bells* 9 Mar., This was.. shaped by means of the 'honeycombing' or 'smocking'. **1890** *Daily News* 27 Nov. 2/4 Smocking is still largely used for the yokes. **1916** *T. Eaton & Co. Catal.* Spring & Summer 23/1 Shoulder yoke with neat smocking trims both sides of the front. **1934** A. M. MIALL *Compl. Needlecraft* 92 Smocking is a special favourite for children's clothes. **1961** A. LILEY *Craft of Embroidery* IV. 174 Smocking generally takes up three times as much fabric as the final width required. **1964** *McCall's Sewing* xiii. 242/1 The same smocking stitches can be used in both types of smocking. **1976** P. CLABBURN *Needleworker's Dict.* 245/2 (*caption*) Smocking: detail of a child's dress, English, 1930.

**'smockless,** *a.* Also 5 **smocles.** [f. SMOCK *sb.* + -LESS.] Having no smock or chemise.

*c* **1386** CHAUCER *Clerk's T.* 819, I hope it be not youre entente That I smocles out of your paleys wente. **1873** STEPHENS *Black Gin* 16 Lo, by the 'humpy' door a smockless Venus!

**'smock-mill.** [f. SMOCK *sb.*, with reference to the shape.] A windmill having a revolving top.

**1802** *Hull Advertiser* 18 Dec. 3/2. **1825** J. NICHOLSON *Operat. Mechanic* 124 The other method of bringing the windshaft and sails into.. position.. is by what is called the smock-mill. **1838–** in dialect glossaries and technical dictionaries. **1888** *Encycl. Brit.* XXIV. 599 The post mill was succeeded by the tower, smock, or frock mill.

**'smock-race.** Also **smock race.** [SMOCK *sb.* 1 b.] A race in which a smock was offered as a prize to be run for by women or girls.

**1707** *Lond. Gaz.* No. 4356/4 The next Day will be a Smock Race run for by Maids in the same Park. **1766** GOLDSM. *Vic. W.* x, I don't like to see my daughters.. red with walking, and looking for all the world as if they had been winners at a smock-race. **1805** *Sporting Mag.* XXV. 304 A smock-race and a jingling-match were to take place. **1825** BROCKETT *N.C. Gloss.* s.v., There used to be frequently, in my recollection, smock races among the young country wenches in the North.

So **'smock-racing** *vbl. sb.*

**1790** J. WOODFORDE *Diary* 24 May (1927) III. 192 Smock-racing at the Heart this Aft. being Whit-Monday. **1878** LECKY *England in 18th C.* iv. I. 566 Among other amusements, smock-racing by women was kept up there [Pall Mall] till 1733.

†**'smockster.** *Obs.*[-1] [f. SMOCK *sb.*] A go-between, a bawd.

**1607** MIDDLETON *Your Five Gallants* v. ii, You're a hired smockster; here's her letter, In which we are certified that you're a bawd.

**smock windmill.** = SMOCK-MILL.

**1795** *Lond. Chron.* 11 Aug. 143 To be Sold, all the Working Geer of a capital Smock Windmill. **1833** LOUDON *Encycl. Archit.* §1259 Another kind of vertical windmill is called a smock, or tower windmill.

†**smod.** *Obs.*[-1] [Cf. SMAD *v.*] Stain, filth.

**13..** *E.E. Allit. P.* B. 711 Hem to smyte for þat smod smartly I þenk þat wyȝes schal be by hem war, worlde with-outen ende.

**smog** (smɒg). [Blend of SMOKE *sb.* and FOG *sb.*[2]]

**1. a.** Fog intensified by smoke. Cf. ***photochemical smog*** s.v. PHOTOCHEMICAL *a.*

**1905** *Daily Graphic* 26 July 10/2 In the engineering section of the Congress Dr. H. A. des Vœux, hon. treasurer of the Coal Smoke Abatement Society, read a paper on 'Fog and Smoke'. He said it required no science to see that there was something produced in great cities which was not found in the country, and that was smoky fog, or what was known as 'smog'. **1905** *Globe* 27 July 3/5 The other day at a meeting of the Public Health Congress Dr. Des Vœux did a public service in coining a new word for the London fog, which was referred to as 'smog', a compound of 'smoke' and 'fog'. **1938** *Daily Progress* (Charlottesville, Va.) 12 May 7 In the opinion of many medical authorities, 'smog' is the principal reason why Pittsburgh has the highest pneumonia death rate in the United States. **1950** *Economist* 25 Feb. 432/2 Smog is a problem, far from completely understood as yet, of air contamination not by smoke, but by the fumes and gases —sulphur compounds, chlorine and so on—given off by modern industrial processes such as oil refining, chemical manufacturing and metallurgy. **1955** *Sci. Amer.* May 63/3 At first it was thought that smoke, dust, sulfur dioxide and hydrofluoric acid were responsible for the smog [in Los Angeles], but soon it became clear that these known pollutants, in the concentrations measured on smoggy days, could not cause the physiological effects observed... It was then that A. J. Haagen-Smit.. suggested that peroxides and ozonides of hydrocarbons were responsible for smog. **1961** L. MUMFORD *City in History* xv. 479 Nor have they eliminated the unburned hydrocarbons which help produce the smog that blankets such a motor-ridden conurbation as Los Angeles. **1975** D. LODGE *Changing Places* ii. 71 It was difficult to tell whether the sediment thickening the atmosphere was rain or sleet or smog.

**b.** *fig.* A state or condition of obscurity or confusion; something designed to confuse or obscure.

**1954** *Ann. Reg. 1953* I. 54 Lord Reading.. described it [*sc.* the Russian Note] in the House of Lords as 18 pages of 'somewhat dismal and turgid "smog"'. **1976** *Billings* (Montana) *Gaz.* 30 June 1-A/1 When the political smog clears, Billings city government somehow continues to function. **1978** D. BLOODWORTH *Crosstalk* xxiv. 191 He hoped.. Zoe's gift might pierce the gathering smog? Because things were getting tough, and the Russians were.. accusing the Maoists of trying to flood Moscow with narcotics.

**2.** *attrib.* and *Comb.*, as ***smog-bank***, ***-burner***, ***mask***, ***producer***; ***smog-bound***, ***-free***, ***-producing*** adjs.

**1975** *Country Life* 16 Jan. 130/2 Take a commuter jet from Los Angeles to San Francisco... You rise above the smog-bank. **1970** *New Scientist* 1 Jan. 8/3 Smogbound, noise-deafened, misanthropic Londoners.. might be taking their high blood pressure with them. **1961** *Engineering* 27 Jan. 175/3 The smog-burner is a mechanical rather than a chemical or catalytic device. **1959** *News Chron.* 19 June 4/3 The six-bedroom houses hardly get dirty in California's smog-free climate. **1981** *Times* 6 Aug. 7/7 Smog-free sunsets over the Indian Ocean. **1954** *Ann. Reg. 1953* IV. 391 The year 1953 might well be remembered as the one in which 'smog' masks first appeared. **1979** *Listener* 5 July 6/1 Visiting journalists [to Tokyo].. were amazed to find they didn't have to wear smog-masks. **1951** *Sun* (Baltimore) (B ed.) 31 Dec. 14/2 More than a dozen Baltimore firms have been definitely albeit informally tagged as smog producers. **1970** *New Scientist* 13 Aug. 324/1 Efforts to curb auto-pollution concern the directly poisonous or smog-producing colourless emissions of carbon monoxide, unburnt hydrocarbons and nitrogen oxides.

Hence as *v. trans. N. Amer. colloq.*, (*a*) with *out*, *up*: to cover or envelop in smog; (*b*) with *in*: to confine or imprison because of smog; (freq. *pass.*); **smogged** *ppl. a.*

**1966** P. TAMONY *Americanisms* (typescript) No. 14. 2 The era of the motor-car smogged up greenery. **1970** *Globe & Mail* (Toronto) 28 Sept. 4/1 Mr. Lewis was 'smogged in' at Sudbury.. and was unable to arrive in time for the Ottawa meeting. **1974** *Science News* 24–31 Aug. 136 Conventional geodesy depends on clear lines of sight, and in the Los Angeles basin these are often smogged out. **1982** *Chr. Sci. Monitor* (Mid-Western ed.) 8 Dec. 12 Yet you can't do it because they have to meet the same pollution standards they do in heavily smogged areas.

**smogger** ('smɒgə(r)). [Origin unknown.] (See quots.).

**1958** F. JENNINGS *Men of Lanes* 217 Veteran tramps have their road-sign language, by which they communicate with each other... Vagabonds call it 'smogger', and it is said to have been introduced into England by gipsies in the time of Henry VIII. **1975** *Indexer* IX. 131/2 Supposing, for example, you see a chalk mark (a 'smogger') made by a tramp on your gate-post, consisting of two large and slightly overlapping circles, you could identify this as meaning 'tell a pathetic story', but if the sign consisted of three small circles in a line, it would mean 'money usually given here'.

**smoggy** ('smɒgɪ), *a.* [f. SMOG + -Y¹.] Characterized by the presence of smog. Hence '**smoggily** *adv.*

**1905** *Daily News* 26 July 9 Observations had proved that, even in the most 'smoggy' periods, there was far less of the evil element in the early hours of the morning. **1948** *Smog Problem in Los Angeles County* 17/1 Smoggy days are usually days of high temperature. **1965** P. WYLIE *They Both were Naked* II. vi. 291 When the fourth day was smoggily born in the black-smudged, yellow opacity that was air I ordered coffee. **1978** P. NIESEWAND *Underground Connection* 25 A smoggy wind blew across the crowded platform as a train thundered in.

**smogless** ('smɒglɪs), *a.* [f. SMOG + -LESS.] Free from smog; characterized by the absence of smog.

**1948** G. MARX *Let.* 27 July (1967) 192 On a smogless day our gleaming skulls can be seen as far east as Cedar Rapids. **1960** *Spectator* 30 Sept. 501/1 In an attempt to bring the smogless society a little closer, the Minister asked..the official black areas to submit their plans for smoke control. **1971** *Nature* 19 Feb. 549/1, I measured the atmospheric extinction in three wavelengths on 31 clear, smogless nights at the Mount Wilson Observatory.

**smogue**: see SMUG.

†'**smoiliness.** *Obs.*⁻¹ (See quot.)

**1530** PALSGR. 271/2 Smoylynesse, fylthynesse, *honnievr.*

**smokable** ('sməʊkəb(ə)l), *a.* and *sb.* Also smokeable. [f. SMOKE *v.* + -ABLE.]

**A.** *adj.* **1.** That may be smoked; fit or suitable for smoking.

**1839** R. M. MARTIN *Stat. Colonies Brit. Emp.* 366 The smokeable extract which each quantity of opium contains. **1872** LEVER *Ld. Kilgobbin* lii, You'll..find it smokeable. **1879** SALA *Paris Herself Again* iv, Very smokable little weeds.

**2.** Able to be ridiculed. Cf. SMOKE *v.* 9. *rare.*

**1818** KEATS *Let.* 31 Dec. (1958) II. 19 The Dress Maker, the blue Stocking and the most charming sentimentalist.. are equally smokeable.

**B.** *sb. pl.* Things which may be smoked. Also in *sing.*

**1849** *Fraser's Mag.* XL. 2 Bills of fare of the various eatables, drinkables, and smokables, of which the author partook. **1890** *Yacht Racing Calendar* 185 It is exasperating ..to have one's drinkables and smokeables sealed up. **1897** 'MARK TWAIN' *Autobiogr.* (1924) I. 98 There are people who strictly deprive themselves of each and every eatable, drinkable and smokable which has in any way acquired a shady reputation.

**smoke** (sməʊk), *sb.* Forms: 1 smoca (smocca), 2- smoke, 5 smokke, 6-7 smok; 6 *Sc.* smoik, 6-8 smoake, 6-9 smoak. [OE. *smoca*, f. the weak grade of the stem represented by OE. *sméocan* SMEEK *v.* To a different grade (*smauk-*) belong MDu. *smoock* (Du. *smook*), MLG. (and LG.) *smôk*, *smōk* (hence Da. *smøg*), MHG. *smouch* (G. *schmauch*). See also SMOOK *sb.*]

**I. 1. a.** The visible volatile product given off by burning or smouldering substances.

α. *c* **1000** *Lambeth Ps.* xvii. 9 Astah smoca on yrre his. *c* **1000** in Cockayne *Narrat.* (1861) 43 Ut æt his nosu eode micel smocca. *a* **1154** *O.E. Chron.* an. 1137, Me henged up bi the fet & smoked heom mid ful smoke. *a* **1200** *St. Marher.* 9 On his hehe hokede neose þreaste smeorðrinde smoke ut. *c* **1290** *St. Brendan* 491 in *S. Eng. Leg.* I. 233 Strong was þe stunch and þe smoke. *c* **1340** HAMPOLE *Pr. Consc.* 4727 Þat es blode and fire and brethe of smoke. *c* **1400** *Destr. Troy* 9512 The smoke of þe smert loghys..waivet in the welkyn. *c* **1440** *Promp. Parv.* 461/1 Smoke, reke, *idem quod* Reke. *a* **1548** HALL *Chron., Hen. VIII*, 100 In the smoke of the gunnes let us entre the gate. **1600** J. PORY tr. *Leo's Africa* III. 133 It cannot be spoiled either by smoke, or too much heat. **1718** PRIOR *Solomon* III. 522 As smoke that rises from the kindling fires Is seen this moment, and the next expires. **1774** GOLDSM. *Nat. Hist.* (1776) III. 156 A large fire..filling the whole place with smoke. **1829** LYTTON *Devereux* I. viii, Don Diego, inhaling the fragrant weed,..replied to the request of his petitioner by smoke. **1888** F. HUME *Mme. Midas* I. v, The smoke was pouring out thick and black from the tall red chimney.

β. **1591** GREENE *Farew. to Follie* Wks. (Grosart) IX. 343 [He] was tied to a post and choaked with smoake. **1660** BOYLE *New Exper.* xxx. (1682) 113 Filled the Reciever with smoak. **1787** WINTER *Syst. Husb.* 47 Soot may be rather deemed the smoak itself. **1810** VINCE *Astron.* xvii. 159 He compared them to smoak and clouds.

†**b.** *ellipt.* The fumes of incense. Also *fig. Obs.*

*c* **1450** *Myrr. Our Lady* 327 Mercifull virgyn,..rodde of smoke, but swete smellynge. *a* **1627** SIR J. BEAUMONT *Poems, The Epiphany* 35 Who lift to God for vs the holy smoke Of feruent pray'rs.

**c.** The fact of smoke coming out into a room instead of passing up the chimney.

**1715** DESAGULIERS *Fires Impr.* 69 We shall..shew of what service the..passage of Air behind the Back is, for hind'ring Smoke. *Ibid.* 72 When you wou'd prevent Smoke.

**d.** *the* (*big, great*) *smoke*, a colloquial name for London. Also, any large city or town (chiefly *Austral.*).

**1848** H. W. HAYGARTH *Recoll. Bush Life in Australia* 6 As he gradually leaves behind him the 'big smoke' (as the aborigines picturesquely call the town), the accommodations become more and more scanty. **1864** *Slang Dict.* 237 Country-people when going to the Metropolis say they are on their way to the Smoke. **1893** J. A. BARRY *Steve Brown's Bunyip* 21 You want to get away amongst the spielers and forties of the big smoke? **1897** F. T. BULLEN *Cruise 'Cachalot'* xxv. (1901) 330, I desired to know what brought him so far from the 'big smoke'. **1903** FARMER & HENLEY *Slang* VI. 270 *The Smoke* = any large city: spec. London: also *The Great Smoke.* **1971** *Sunday Australian* 8 Aug. 5/3 The unhappy pilgrimage from bush to big smoke.

**e.** *transf.* The pollen of the yew when scattered in a cloud.

**1868** LADY TENNYSON in *Life Tennyson* (1897) II. ii. 53 There has been a great deal of smoke in the yew-trees this year. **1869** TENNYSON *Holy Grail* 15 A gustful April morn That puff'd the swaying branches into smoke.

**f.** A shade of grey.

**1882** *Cassell's Family Mag.* Apr. 314/2 Charming colouring.., smoke, bright blues and drabs. **1923** *Daily Mail* 13 Feb. 13 (Advt.), Wool hose..in..It. grey, shoe grey, smoke, mole. **1971** [see KASHA¹ 2]. **1978** *Hot Car* June 98 (Advt.), All Portholes are supplied *domed* either in clear, blue, green, smoke, bronze or black perspex.

**2. a.** With *a* and pl. A volume, cloud, or column of smoke. In Amer. and Austr. use *spec.* one serving as a signal, sign of an encampment, etc. Also, a particular kind of smoke.

*sing.* **1388** WYCLIF *Rev.* ix. 2 A smoke of the pit stiede vp. *c* **1440** *Jacob's Well* 67 þe feend, as a smoke, vanysched awey. **1594** R. WILSON *Coblers Prophesie* G j b, From one part let a smoke arise. **1695** WOODWARD *Nat. Hist. Earth* IV. (1723) 228 Being succeeded by a Smoak, which..resembles fired Gun-powder. **1719** DE FOE *Crusoe* I. 209, I was afraid of making a Smoak about my Habitation. **1796** WITHERING *Brit. Pl.* (ed. 3) IV. 361 On being touched throwing up the seeds in form of a smoke. **1802** BARRINGTON *New South Wales* vii. 224 Mr. Bass discovered a smoke that they had made to draw his attention. **1919** *Jrnl. Amer. Chem. Soc.* XLI. 312 The rate of disappearance of a finely divided smoke of a given concentration was greater than for a coarser smoke. **1950** *Thorpe's Dict. Appl. Chem.* (ed. 4) X. 787/1 Determining the particle size of a smoke.

*pl.* **1426** LYDG. *De Guil. Pilgr.* 21585 A-mong the smokys blake, Ther he gan hys bed to make. **1523** LD. BERNERS *Froiss.* I. cclxxxi. 421 They can nat..put you out of your realme by their smokes. **1620** MARKHAM *Farew. Husb.* II. xvii. (1668) 76 In seed time make great smoaks in your Cornfields. **1697** DAMPIER *Voy.* (1699) 252 We..leave them a sign to know where we are by making one or more great Smoaks. **1748** *Anson's Voy.* II. xiii. 271 The enemy..were.. incamped in the woods about us; for we could see their smokes. **1841** CATLIN *N. Amer. Ind.* (1844) II. xli. 55 Their smokes were seen in various directions. **1890** *Melbourne Argus* 26 July 4/4 By-and-by answers came from smokes away in the bush. **1972** *Combustion Sci. & Technol.* VI. 55/1 Carbon smokes are generated by combustion.

**b.** The smoke arising from a particular hearth or fire-place; hence, a hearth, fire-place, house. Now *rare.*

**1591** SYLVESTER *Du Bartas* I. iii. 1097 Leading all his life at home in Peace, Alwayes in sight of his own smoak. **1610** in *Council Bk. Youghal Corp.* (1878) 11 A scavenger..shall be paid yearly out of every smoak, 4*d.* at Michalmas and Easter. *a* **1687** PETTY *Polit. Arith.* ii. (1691) 42 In Ireland wherein are..near 300 Thousand Smokes or Hearths. **1792** *Stat. Acc. Scotl.* IV. 316 For 6 miles in a well inhabited extent,..there was not a *smoke* remaining. **1883** *Good Words* XXIV. 717 There are [on Minglay] in all thirty houses, or 'smokes', as they are called.

**c.** † (*a*) *N. Amer.* = SMUDGE *sb.*² 2. *Obs.* (*b*) (See quot. 1961.)

**1689** H. KELSEY *Jrnl.* 29 June (1929) 26 Abundance of Musketers & at night could not gett wood Enough for to make a smoke to Clear yᵐ. **1765** R. ROGERS *Conc. Account N. Amer.* 140 It is difficult to sleep without a smoak in your bed-chamber, to expell [mosquitoes]. **1860** H. Y. HIND *Assiniboine* in *Canad. Red River Exped.* I. xiii. 286 At each camping place we were obliged to make 'smokes' to drive away these tormentors [*sc.* mosquitoes]. **1961** *Amateur Gardening* 4 Nov. Suppl. 47/2 Many of the modern insecticides and fungicides are sold in the form of small containers which when ignited give off clouds of vapour carrying fine chemical into all parts of the green-house. These devices are known simply as 'smokes'.

**3. a.** Fume or vapour caused by the action of heat on moisture.

**1398** TREVISA *Barth. De P.R.* V. xxxiii. (Bodl. MS.), Þat þe lunges mowe open and close þe hoote smoke of þe herte. **1422** tr. *Secreta Secret., Priv. Priv.* 218 Dronknesse makyth for-yetynge..by reyson that the grete smokkes gone vp to the brayn. **1562** TURNER *Baths* 9 They that woulde use the smooke or vaperouse ayer of this water. **1584** LYLY *Alex. & Camp.* II. i, Steeds..whose breathes dimmed the sun with smoake. **1621** BURTON *Anat. Mel.* II. ii. II. (1651) 239 To purge the heart and brain from ill smoakes and vapours that offend them. *a* **1693** *Urquhart's Rabelais* III. xxxvii. 311 Demanding payment for the Smoak of his Roast-meat. **1888** 'R. BOLDREWOOD' *Robbery under Arms* xi. 136 You ought to have sense enough not to knock smoke out of fresh horses before we begin.

**b.** A mist, fog, or miasma (see later quots.).

**1648** HEXHAM II, *Een Roock der aerden*, a Smoake, a Mist, or Dampe, rising out of the earth. **1788** FALCONBRIDGE *African Slave T.* 51 Together with what they call *the smokes* (a noxious vapour, arising from the swamps about the latter end of autumn). **1867** SMYTH *Sailor's Word-bk.* 635 *Smokes*, dense exhalations, mixed with the finer particles of sand, on the Calabar shores and borders of the Great Zahara desert, which prevail in autumn. **1897** MISS KINGSLEY *W. Africa* 94 Those thick wool-like mists called smokes, which hang about the whole Bight from November till May.

**4.** In proverbial, figurative, or allusive uses:

**a.** In miscellaneous applications or phrases.

**1390** GOWER *Conf.* I. 211 Whan every thing was fulli spoke, Of sorwe and queint was al the smoke. **1526** *State Papers Hen. VIII*, VI. 542 Of whom..I have lernyd many strange thinges, wherof I smelt a smoke at Calays. **1580** LYLY *Euphues* (Arb.) 287, I perceiue..where the least smoake is, there to be the greatest fire. **1602** MARSTON *Ant. & Mel.* I. Wks. 1856 I. 13 His eyes looke as if they had bene hung In the smoake of his nose. **1670** G. H. tr. *Hist. Cardinals* I. I. 20, I..took my leave, as perceiving him fuller of smoak than of meat. **17..** in *N. & Q.* 3rd Ser. XII. 163/2 Never out of the smoke of your own chimney. **1774** *Westm. Mag.* II. 109 Their *summum bonum* lies in drinking themselves dead-drunk,..playing smoak with the girls. **1854** MISS BAKER *Northampt. Gloss.* s.v., If a lent horse has been over-ridden, it is commonly remarked, 'He played smoke with that horse, he has been good for nothing since'. **1870** LOWELL *Study Wind.* 228 The first lesson of literature, no less than of life, is the learning how to burn your own smoke.

**b.** In the proverbs ***there is no fire without smoke***, and ***no smoke without fire***, or variants of these: (see FIRE *sb.* 1 h).

*c* **1450** *MS. Douce* 52 lf. 20 Where no fyre is no smoke. **1546-** [see FIRE *sb.* 1 h]. **1650** HUBBERT *Pill to purge Formality* 133 There is no fire but there will be some smoak. **1654** GATAKER *Disc. Apol.* 11 There is seldom anie smoak, but where there is some fire. **1705** WYCHERLEY in *Pope's Lett.* (1735) I. 14 You must allow there is no Smoak but there is some Fire. **1820** COLERIDGE *Lett., Conv.*, etc. I. 118 They ..then exclaim: There is no smoke without some fire.

†**c.** ***out of the smoke into the fire***, etc., out of a small danger into a great one. *Obs.* (Cf. L. *de fumo in flammam*, Ammianus.)

**1547** J. HARRISON *Exhort. Scottes* f iv b, Leaste by fleynge the smoke, we fall into the fyre. **1600** SHAKS. *A.Y.L.* I. ii. 299 Thus must I from the smoake into the smother. **1609** HOLLAND *Amm. Marcell.* XIV. ii. 25 Hee..went just as the old proverbe saith, out of the smoke into the light fire.

**d.** Used to designate anything having no real value or substance, or a mere shadow *of* something.

**1548** tr. *Papius' Conc. Apothecaries* in Recorde *Urinal Phys.* (1651) 243 That the selfe-conceited..may learne to.. brag and vaunt forth their vanities and smokes. **1559** *Mirr. Mag.* (1563) I v, Our kyngdomes are but cares,..our power a smouldring smoke. **1601-3** DANIEL *C'tess Cumberland* 35 The all-guiding Prouidence..mocks this smoake of wit. **1621** J. TAYLOR (Water P.) *Superbiæ Flagellum* D 3 Their Pride is..A smoake, a bubble. **1705** WYCHERLEY in *Pope's Lett.* (1735) I. 14 If Compliment be the Smoak only of Friendship. **1749** SMOLLETT *Gil Blas* x. i, Preferring the smoke of public applause to the real advantages which my friendship prepared for him. **1806** *Sporting Mag.* XXVIII. 279 In his opinion it was all smoke. **1875** JOWETT *Plato* (ed. 2) III. 122 The ambitious man will think knowledge which is without honour all smoke and nonsense.

**e.** Denoting a clouding or obscuring medium or influence. *spec.* in *Espionage*, false information to distract opponents.

**1565** COOPER *Thesaurus* s.v. *Fuligo*, To speake obscurely: to cast a darke smoke or miste before their eies. **1581** J. BELL *Haddon's Answ. Osorius* 273 b, Why shamed he not to blind the eyes of the people with such smoakes? **1594** T. B. tr. *De la Primaud. Fr. Acad.* II. 333 Their eies dimmed with some smoake of honours. **1603** J. DAVIES (Heref.) *Microcosmos* Wks. (Grosart) I. 78/1 The Eyes that..smoke of praise Doe dimme, are feeble-sighted. *a* **1677** BARROW *Serm.* Wks. 1716 I. 167 Truth will not be discerned through the smoak of wrathful expressions. [**1859** G. W. MATSELL *Vocabulum* 82 *Smoke*, humbug; any thing said to conceal the true sentiment of the talker; to cover the intent.] **1864** TENNYSON *Aylmer's F.* 672 Thro' the smoke, The blight of low desires. **1873** FARRAR *Silence & V.* Ser. I. 22 Reading them.. through the lurid smoke of sectarian hate. **1966** 'A. HALL' *9th Directive* xxi. 200 'No go. I got myself cornered. One dead.'..'Do you need any smoke out?' **1977** 'J. LE CARRÉ' *Honourable Schoolboy* iv. 91 For smoke..Molly chose a dozen other R's.

**f.** Denoting fraudulent dealing in the fulfilment of bargains or promises; esp. ***to sell smoke*** (after L. *fumum vendere*), to act dishonestly, to swindle.

**1589** GREENE *Menaphon* Wks. (Grosart) VI. 106 You get but a handfull of smoake to the bargaine. **1599** NASHE *Lenten Stuff* Wks. (Grosart) V. 306 That for your selling smoake you may be courtiers. **1655** tr. *Sorel's Com. Hist. Francion* IV. 24, I abandoned their conversation, because I found they were but sellers of smoak. **1692** WASHINGTON tr. *Milton's Def. People* Pref., To relieve the necessities of Nature..by selling of Smoke, as thou dost.

**g.** ***to come to, end in, vanish into, smoke***, to come to nothing, be unrealized, be without result.

**1604** E. GRIMSTONE *Siege Ostend* 184 Their subtill deuises are come to smoake. **1617** MORYSON *Itin.* II. 44 The ill successe of the Queenes affaires (whose..Royall Army they had seene vanish into smoke). **1683** TEMPLE *Mem.* Wks. 1720 I. 470 Thus ended in Smoke the whole Negotiation. **1704** *Collect. Voy. & Trav.* III. 699/2 His Designs vanished into Smoke. **1771** SMOLLETT *Humph. Cl.* (1815) 168, I take it for granted, this whole affair will end in smoke. **1853** MRS. CARLYLE in *New Lett. & Mem.* II. 68 One might let him scheme and talk, hoping it might all end in smoke.

**h.** ***like smoke***, very quickly, rapidly.

**1833** M. SCOTT *Tom Cringle* x, Sail was made, and..she began to snore through it like smoke. **1840** MARRYAT *Poor Jack* vi, Away we all went like smoke. **1853** DICKENS *Bleak Ho.* xi, His brandy-balls go off like smoke. **1860** WHYTE MELVILLE *Market Harb.* 86 The hounds are running like smoke!

**i.** ***to watch someone's smoke*** (*slang*, orig. *U.S.*), to watch someone go, to observe someone's actions; chiefly imp. in phr. ***watch my smoke.***

**1905** G. W. PECK *Peck's Bad Boy with Circus* ix. 114 The elephant..winked at the other elephants, as much as to say: 'Watch my smoke'. **1921** R. D. PAINE *Comrades Rolling Ocean* i. 10 Suspend judgement and watch my smoke. That's all I ask. **1927** WODEHOUSE *Meet Mr Mulliner* iii. 82 'You are a curate, eh?' 'At present. But,' said Augustine, tapping his companion on the chest, 'just watch my smoke.' **1928** C. SANDBURG *Good Morning, America* 18 Let's go. Watch our smoke. Excuse our dust. **1947** WODEHOUSE *Full Moon* ii. 27 Look at Henry the Eighth... And Solomon. Once they started marrying, there was no holding them— you just sat back and watched their smoke.

**j.** ***in(to) smoke*** (slang, chiefly *Austral.*), in(to) hiding.

**1924** C. J. DENNIS *Rose of Spadgers* 72 'Jist now,' says Brannigan, 'Spike Wegg's in smoke. Oh, jist concerns a cove 'e tried to croak.' **1938** P. J. SMITH *Con Man* ix. 179 Denman advised Naysmith to remain 'in smoke'—an expression meaning to hide himself—and play golf until Denman had stood his trial alone for the offence in Glasgow. **1943** K. TENNANT *Ride on Stranger* xvii. 203 The New Zealand delegate returned anonymously, slipped ashore and 'went into smoke' like some famous criminal. **1967** K. S. PRICHARD *Subtle Flame* 252 Meanwhile Tony's got to be kept in smoke?

**k.** ***to go up in smoke***, to be consumed by fire; to be destroyed completely; also *fig.*, to lose one's temper.

**1933** [see GO *v.* 94 h]. **1939** 'N. BLAKE' *Smiler with Knife* 94 Oh, glory no! He'd go up in smoke. **1946** [see INTERIMSETHIK]. **1955** [see HIGHBROW, HIGH-BROW *sb.*].

**5. a.** (*a*) Tobacco. Now *rare* or *Obs.*

**1612** WOODALL *Surg. Mate* Wks. (1653) 20* A small Gallon of Sack, and a pipe of the best smoake. **1616** R. C. *Times' Whistle* (1871) 71 Every skull And skip-iacke now will have his pipe of smoke And whiff it. **1649** J. TAYLOR (Water P.) *Wand. West* 19 They gave me smoake and drinke in Plimouth. **1853** 'C. BEDE' *Verdant Green* I. vii, That if Mr. Larkyns was no smoker himself, he at least kept a bountiful supply of 'smoke' for his friends.

(*b*) Opium; (*c*) marijuana.

**1884** KIPLING *Plain Tales from Hills* (1888) 238 The coffin is gone—gone to China again—with the old man and a couple of *tolahs* of Smoke inside, in case he should want 'em on the way. **1946** C. MCCULLERS *Member of Wedding* iii. 192 Made crazy one night by a marihuana cigarette, by something called smoke or snow. **1956** S. LONGSTREET *Real Jazz Old & New* xiii. 104 He mixed.. with studs shying a toy of opium. But there isn't much record that he went for tea-sticks or the smoke himself. **1963** H. PARKHURST *Undertow* (1964) v. 84 To her 'smoke' and the 'kicks' were the things that seemed to count. **1977** *Rolling Stone* 16 June 76/2 He wondered aloud if there were 'smoke' in the house, prompting people in the front rows to toss lit joints upon the stage.

**b.** A cigar or cigarette; a marijuana cigarette. Also *fig.*

**1882** BESANT *All Sorts* 112 The twopenny smoke, to which we cling, though it is made of medicated cabbage. **1893** C. G. LELAND *Mem.* I. 158 She was,.. as we used to say at college of certain unpopular people, a 'bad smoke'. **1967** [see JOINT *sb.* 14 c]. **1980** 'D. KAVANAGH' *Duffy* iii. 52 He'd known who handled smokes, who handled snort and who handled smack.

**6.** [f. the vb.] A spell of smoking tobacco, etc. ***to have*** (or ***take***) ***a smoke***, to smoke a pipe, cigarette, or cigar.

**1835** A. B. LONGSTREET *Georgia Scenes* 213 *Mrs. B.* [to *Mrs. S.*]. Well, let's light our pipes, and take a short smoke, and go to bed. **1837** W. IRVING *Adv. Capt. Bonneville* II. 286 A crowd of visiters awaited their appearance, all eager for a smoke and a talk. **1860** W. H. RUSSELL *My Diary in India* II. iii. 53 Here.. were to be seen a few soldiers,.. lounging about, taking an early morning smoke. **1887** *Lantern* (New Orleans) May, in *Amer. Speech* (1948) XXIII. 247/2 A book-keeper for a large firm here begged an acquaintance for twenty-five cents to go and have a smoke with. **1890** 'R. BOLDREWOOD' *Col. Reformer* (1891) 241 It was considered reasonable to devote half an hour to rest.. and a smoke for the stockmen. **1922** JOYCE *Ulysses* 112 Ideal spot to have a quiet smoke and read the *Church Times*. **1926** J. BLACK *You can't Win* xi. 141, I.. found my way into the hop joints. Curiosity was my only excuse for my first 'smoke'. **1978** O. WHITE *Silent Reach* xix. 206 Can't say I blame you. Have another smoke?

**7. a.** ***Cape smoke***, a cheap kind of brandy drunk in South Africa.

**1849** E. E. NAPIER *Exc. S. Afr.* II. 9 A young Hottentot, .. as fond of 'Cape Smoke'.. as any of his tribe. **1880** GILLMORE *On Duty* 366 He produced a bottle of smoke (Cape brandy). **1893** *Edin. Rev.* Apr. 297 'Cape Smoke' is the most poisonous of all alcoholic drinks.

**b.** Cheap whisky; a concoction based on raw alcohol, etc., used as a substitute for whisky. *N. Amer.*

**1904** 'O. HENRY' *Cabbages & Kings* iii. 52 Brandy, anisada, Scotch 'smoke' and various wines. **1928** *Daily Tel.* 9 Oct. 11/3 Twelve additional deaths today are attributed to week-end 'jags', which have been traced to 'speak-easies' in the New York east-end, where the liquor is known as 'smoke'. **1940** *Sun* (Baltimore) 14 Nov. 8/2 Judge Eugene O'Dunne yesterday ruled that the sale of denatured alcohol diluted with water and known as 'smoke'—comes within the effect of the liquor laws. **1950** [see *rubby-dub* s.v. RUBBY]. **1959** *Washington Post* 18 Aug. A3/4 It was the smoke that made Heaton a loner and junk peddler in the demolition jungles of the Southwest area. **1980** *Amer. Speech 1977* LII. 117 Blends of anti-freeze and water, sometimes including methyl alcohol, solvent or paint remover, cleaning fluid, canned heat, or other alcohol mixtures: *smoke*.

**8. a.** A Persian cat of a deep cinder-colour, with a white under-coat. Also, a short-haired cat with similar blue-grey or black colouring.

Also in combs., as *smoke-breeder*, *-fancier*, etc.

**1893** *Westm. Gaz.* 17 Oct. 4/3 Miss Brigden's cat should not be overlooked among the 'smokes'. **1933** E. BUCKWORTH-HERNE-SOAME *Cats* xviii. 99 A smoke is one of the most handsome cats living. **1958** *Listener* 28 Aug. 298/2 With two exceptions, the Chinchilla and smoke, short-hairs have the same variety of colour as do long-hairs. **1972** ING & POND *Champion Cats of World* 79/1 The first Smokes were bred by chance. *Ibid.* 99/2 Black and Blue Smoke. Except that the fur is short rather than long, the standard is the same as.. the long-haired varieties. **1976** *Southern Even. Echo* (Southampton) 11 Nov. (Advts. Suppl.) 14/3 Pedigree long-haired male kittens, black and blue smokes.

**b.** An abusive and offensive term for a Black. *U.S. slang.*

**1913** J. T. FOOTE *Blister Jones* viii. 242 'Who you callin' a smoke?' says Snowball, startin' fur Micky. **1932** J. T. FARRELL *Young Lonigan* i. 21 He had bashed the living moses out of that smoke who pulled a razor on him over in Carter playground. **1940** R. CHANDLER *Farewell, my Lovely* iii. 24 There was five smokes carved Harlem sunsets on each other. **1970** L. SANDERS *Anderson Tapes* xxxiii. 109 Five men. One's a smoke.

**II.** *attrib.* and *Comb.* **9. a.** Attrib., in the sense of 'consisting of smoke', as ***smoke-atmosphere***, ***-barrage***, ***-burst***, ***-cloud***, ***-column***, ***-devil***, ***-drift***, ***-dust***, ***-fog***, ***-pall***, ***-palm***, ***-plume***, ***-puff***, ***-ring***, ***-tower***, ***-trail***, ***-tube***, ***-vapour***, ***-whiff***, ***-wreath***, etc.

**1837** CARLYLE *Fr. Rev.* I. IV. iv, It will burn.. its whole *smoke-atmosphere too. **1923** KIPLING *Irish Guards in Great War* I. 317 A Guards Battalion.. came up.. under cover of what looked like a *smoke-barrage. **1852** M. ARNOLD *Empedocles* II. 417 Through the black, rushing *smoke-bursts, Thick breaks the red flame. **1837** CARLYLE *Fr. Rev.* II. I. iii, From yonder White Haven rise his *smoke-clouds. **1932** BLUNDEN *Fall in Ghosts* 10 The youth scurried away to the problem of preventing that *smoke-column from the cookers. **1919** J. MASEFIELD *Battle of Somme* 5 The No Man's Land, into which our men advanced, was a strip of earth without life, made smoky, dusty, and dim by explosions which came out of the air upon it, and left black, curling, slowly fading, dust and *smoke-devils behind them. **1884** *Athenæum* 6 Dec. 739/1 Bars of light and shade belonging to the mist and *smoke-drift of London. **1970** R. LOWELL *Notebook* 247 *Smoke-dust the Chinese draftsman made eternal. **1933** *Gloss. Aeronaut. Terms (B.S.I.)* XIV. 88 **Smoke fog*, fog due to particles of smoke in the atmosphere. A thick haze. **1918** G. FRANKAU *Poetical Wks.* xx. 153 Southward, gray skies with *smoke-pall overcast. **1940** W. FAULKNER *Hamlet* III. 159 He actually heard the cow's voice .. from beyond the smokepall on the other hill. **1864** LOWELL *Fireside Trav.* 8 Nor did the *smoke-palm of Vesuvius stand more erect and fair. **1920** *Glasgow Herald* 3 July 6 We may even be deprived of some of these interesting *smoke-plumes that float proudly and unafraid over public works. **1978** *Sci. Amer.* May 162/1 There are two basic types of smoke plume: the momentum jet.. and the buoyant plume. **1897** W. S. CHURCHILL in *Daily Tel.* 9 Nov. 7/6 The mountain battery.. came into action and began shelling the summits, from which the *smoke-puffs were most frequent and continuous. **1890** SIR R. S. BALL *Star-Land* 335 We can make many experiments with *smoke-rings. **1909** F. BARCLAY *Rosary* xxiv. 257 'And this pleases you?' inquired the doctor, blowing smoke rings into the air. **1959** I. & P. OPIE *Lore & Lang. Schoolch.* xi. 220 A 14-year-old girl, Newbridge, Monmouthshire, writes: 'If you see a smoke ring coming from an engine you can wish once, and if you see two smoke rings you can wish twice.' **1971** *Wall St. Jrnl.* 22 July W.1/5 The industry tries all sorts of promotions from a cigar smoke ring blowing contest at Palisades Amusement Park.. to cigar and cognac tasting sessions. **1813** HOGG *Queen's Wake* II. Wks. (1876) 19 His stature, on the mighty plan Of *smoke-tower o'er the burning pile. **1933** *O.E.D.* (Suppl.) s.v. Sky *sb.*[1] 9, *Smoke-trails made by aircraft. **1979** 'P. O'CONNOR' *Into Strong City* xxxviii. 142 A puffer making its way up the Clyde. A smoke trail. The sea calm. **1837** CARLYLE *Fr. Rev.* I. I. ii, Thou seest the *Smoke-vapour. **1598** MARSTON *Sco. Villanie* III. ix. 219 Belch impious blasphemies,.. Snuffe vp *smoak-whiffs. **1808** SCOTT *Marm.* IV. xxx, The *smoke-wreaths.. That round her sable turrets flow. **1913** D. H. LAWRENCE *Love Poems & Others* 36 To-day a thicket of sunshine with blue smoke-wreaths. **1939** R. CAMPBELL *Flowering Rifle* VI. 138 Through rolling smoke-wreaths, there, like ant-hills rise The kopjes in the nitre-breathing skies.

**b.** Used for, or promoting, the escape of smoke, as ***smoke-flue***, ***-funnel***, ***-hood***, ***-pipe***, ***-vent***, etc.

**1840** *Cottager's Manual* 7 in *Husb.* III. (L.U.K.), Vertical strata of gravel.. alternating with *smoke-flues. **1799** G. SMITH *Laboratory* 143 A sort of funnel, like a *smoke funnel to an oven. **1969** 'M. RENAULT' *Fire from Heaven* (1972) v. 199 King Archelaos had hung a *smoke-hood over the hearth. **1853** URE *Dict. Arts* (ed. 4) II. 105 The *smoke-pipe of a subsidiary fire. **1856** KANE *Arctic Explor.* I. xxxi. 424 The *smoke-tubes of the stove. **1912** J. L. M. MYRES *Dawn of Hist.* viii. 185 In Crete the climate is mild enough.. for portable braziers to suffice, and this release from anxiety for *smoke-vents encouraged the architects to daring experiments. **1936** Smoke-vent [see *smoke-blackening*, sense 9 c below].

**c.** Due to, or caused by, smoke, as ***smoke-blackening***, ***-blackness***, ***-burn***, ***-mark***, ***-nuisance***, ***-smell***, etc.

**1841** *Civil Eng. & Arch. Jrnl.* IV. 386 Smoke nuisance in large towns. **1874** RUSKIN *Fors Clav.* xxxix. 56 Golden light and song.. are better than smoke-blackness. **1876** T. HARDY *Ethelberta* (1890) 81 Sniffing extraordinary smoke-smells which she discovered in all nooks and crannies of the rooms. **1876** 'MARK TWAIN' *Tom Sawyer* xxxi. 23 Holding their candles aloft and reading the tangled web-work of names.. with which the rocky walls [of the cave] had been frescoed (in candle smoke)... They made a smoke-mark for future guidance. **1936** *Discovery* Feb. 55/2 The semi-conical apartment at the east end was evidently a fire-chamber, as traces of smoke-blackening were found on stones that had fallen from the roof and had once surrounded a smoke-vent. **1971** S. HILL *Strange Meeting* ii. 141 He had very pale, almost white eyelashes, and a curious mark, like a smoke burn, across his forehead.

**d.** With names of colours, as ***smoke-blue***, ***-brown***, ***-grey***, etc. (used as sbs. or adjs.).

*London smoke*: see LONDON.

**1807** AIKIN *Dict. Chem. & Min.* II. 98/1 Its colour is ash or smoak-grey. **1839** URE *Dict. Arts* 388 Their ordinary tint verges upon yellow, or smoke-yellow. *a* **1847** ELIZA COOK *Birds* iii, There the smoke-brown Sparrow sits. **1901** CLIVE HOLLAND *Mousmé* 284 Overhung with smoke-blue mosquito curtains. **1903** [see sense 9 e]. **1924** [see HARRIS]. **1976** *Billings* (Montana) *Gaz.* 30 June 9-D/3 (Advt.), For sale 1976 Corvette... Red w/smoke gray interior.

**e.** Having the colour of smoke; of a brownish or bluish grey colour. ***smoke quartz***, smoky quartz.

**1872** E. HULL *Build. & Ornament. Stones* 175 *Smoke quartz*. This is a clouded variety [of rock crystal], with a brownish tint. **1884** *Western Daily Press* 11 Apr. 7/6 There are jackets of the finest cloth, geranium-red, electric-blue, smoke,.. and brown. **1899** *Westm. Gaz.* 21 Sept. 3/2 The smoke fox, a blue-grey colouring which is really dyed. **1903** F. SIMPSON *Bk. Cat* xiv. 185 Perfect smoke cats.. should be black, shading to smoke grey.

**10.** *Comb.* **a.** Objective, with pres. pples., adjs., agent-nouns, or nouns of action, as ***smoke-belching***, ***-burner***, ***-burning***, ***-chaser***, ***-consumer***, ***-consuming***, ***-consumption***, ***-consumptive***, ***-control***, ***-detecting***, ***-detection***, ***-detector***, ***-discharger***, ***-generator***.

Many of these have been in common use from *c* 1840.

(*a*) **1596** FITZ-GEFFREY *Sir F. Drake* (1881) 96 O let our smoak-exhalinge breaths enfold A mightie cloud of sighes. **1612** SELDEN *Illustr. Drayton's Poly-olb.* xi. l. 139 Those foggie mists of error, and smoake-selling imposture. **1842** *Civil Eng. & Arch. Jrnl.* V. 42 This.. furnace operates not upon the smoke-preventive, but upon the smoke-consumptive principle. *Ibid.* 131 The.. furnace is in reality a smoke-burning and not a smoke-preventing. *Ibid.*, Some new smoke-consuming theory. **1891** MORRIS *News Nowhere* 7 The soap-works with their smoke-vomiting chimneys were gone. **1962** *Flight International* LXXXI. 190/2 The Pyrene Co Ltd have contributed smoke-detecting.. equipment to the D.H.121 Trident. **1963** BIRD & HUTTON-STOTT *Veteran Motor Car* 81 They were extremely refined, ..smoke-belching, costly,.. and slow. **1974** Smoke-belching [see SAMLOR].

(*b*) **1604** JAS. I *Counterbl. to Tobacco* (Arb.) 111 Of so many smoke-buyers, as are at this present in this kingdome, I neuer read nor heard. **1838** *Civil Eng. & Arch. Jrnl.* I. 168 The adaptation of the patent smoke-consumer to a locomotive engine. *Ibid.* 344 The only effectual smoke-burner I have ever seen. **1851** *Catal. Grt. Exhib.* I. 328/1 Smoke condenser. **1891** *Cent. Dict.*, *Smoke-washer*, a device for purifying smoke by washing as it passes through a chimney-flue. **1933** *Gloss. Aeronaut. Terms (B.S.I.)* XIII. 3 *Smoke generator*, a pyrotechnic device, placed on the ground, emitting smoke for indicating wind direction. **1935** L. LUARD *Conquering Seas* xii. 153 Shot thirty-five miles east of Cape. Towed for three hours. Double bag. Fish hard and golden. Worked edge of Strunda four days. Good living. Shifted to avoid smoke-chasers.—Trial shoot in 45 fathoms. Nowt. **1942** *Sun* (Baltimore) 14 May 4/2 Lookouts, smoke-chasers, firemen and organized stand-by crews to prevent, detect and fight forest fires. *a* **1944** K. DOUGLAS *Alamein to Zem Zem* (1946) 16 There were also two smoke dischargers to be operated by me. Stacked round the sides of the turret were the six-pounder shells. **1957** *Practical Wireless* XXXIII. 683/2 Such devices as.. a smoke detector and fire indicator. **1961** W. VAUGHAN-THOMAS *Anzio* ix. 211 The smoke generators, manned by cheerful coloured troops, tried to blot out observation and protect the shipping from sneak raiders. **1978** *N.Y. Times* 30 Mar. B16/5 (Advt.), 117 West 58th St... Completely remodeled Prewar Bldg—featuring—.. smoke detectors—ceramic tile kitch & bath. **1979** P. ALEXANDER *Show me Hero* xx. 210 Kemp threw a canister of tear-gas... Quinn threw a smoke-discharger.

(*c*) **1842** *Civil Eng. & Arch. Jrnl.* V. 42/1 An incarnation (so to speak) of the principles of smoke-prevention. **1851** *Catal. Grt. Exhib.* I. p. xcix, Apparatus for effecting Smoke-consumption. **1882** (*title*), Official Report of the Smoke-Abatement Committee. **1936** *Discovery* May 146/2 Other uses [of light-sensitive cells] were for.. smoke detection in factory chimneys. **1956** *Ann. Reg. 1955* 4 Densely populated areas designated for smoke-control. **1967** *Economist* 30 Dec. 1277/1 The real trouble is still the old one: too few smoke control orders in the Black Areas.

**b.** Instrumental, with past pples., as ***smoke-begotten***, ***-bleared***, etc.

**1872** C. W. KING *Antique Gems & Rings* 148 *Smoke-begotten theories of modern German sciolists. **1912** W. DE LA MARE *Listeners* 81 Vainly 'gainst that thin wall The trumpets call, Or with loud hum The *smoke-bemuffled drum. **1890** A. CONAN DOYLE *Firm of Girdlestone* xiv. 111 Puffing at his weed and staring up at the *smoke-blackened ceiling. **1976** M. MACHLIN *Pipeline* lvi. 567 The small smoke-blackened figure walked slowly toward the forepeak of the Globtik Alamo. **1837** CARLYLE *Fr. Rev.* I. v. vi, A.. dwarfish individual, of *smoke-bleared aspect. **1720** *Mem. W. Stukeley* (Surtees) I. 157 Their painted or rather *smoak-bound hides. **1919** KIPLING *Years Between* 42 Witness thy portrait, *smoke-defiled. **1817** *Jrnl. Salem Mechanic* 19 Oct. in *Essex Inst. Hist. Coll.* (1866) VIII. 234, I have not seen a handsome woman since I left Salem; they are here [*sc.* Pittsburgh] all *smoke-dyed. **1822** LAMB *Elia* I. *Distant Correspondents*, Elms,.. [with] smoke-dyed barks, the theme of jesting ruralists. **1748** THOMSON *Cast. Indol.* I. lxx, The *smoke enrolled Their oracles break forth. **1920** *Evening Star* (Washington) 14 June 1/2 Harry Daugherty.. predicted that about 2.11 a.m., 'in a *smoke-filled room', on a certain night during the republican national convention, the next nominee would be chosen. **1965** G. MCINNES *Road to Gundagai* v. 77 These damp and smokefilled holes. **1979** *Now!* 21–27 Sept. 74/3 Presidential candidates are not selected by political pros in smoke-filled rooms these days. **1856** FROUDE *Hist. Eng.* (1862) I. 463 Those streets.. so black and *smoke-grimed. **1903** *Work* 21 Mar. 105/1 Incrustations due to the *smoke-laden atmosphere. **1975** *Economist* 6 Sept. 20/1 If you've ever tried to make clearheaded decisions in a stuffy, smoke-laden conference room, you'll appreciate what we mean. **1963** *Times* 25 May 8/4 A fire officer said: 'When we arrived ammunition was exploding everywhere. Our job was made even more difficult because the building was completely *smoke-logged.' **1976** *Southern Even. Echo* (Southampton) 13 Nov. 16/2 Firemen had to wear breathing equipment to get into the smoke-logged electrical input room on the first floor. **1922** JOYCE *Ulysses* 583 Two shafts of light fall on the *smokepalled altarstone. **1818** SCOTT *Hrt. Midl.* xlii, The daily passage of so many *smoke-pennoned steam-boats. **1893** KIPLING *Seven Seas* (1896) 97 To the *smoke-reddened eyes of Loben. **1888** —— *Departmental Ditties*

(1890) 81 Anger and pain and terror Stamped on the *smoke-scorched skin. **1879** _19th Cent._ No. 31. 401 The swarming bustle of our *smoke-smothered towns. **1833** TENNYSON in _Life_ (1897) I. 130 They are so *smoke-sodden. **1959** C. DEVLIN _Sermons & Devotional Writings of G. M. Hopkins_ 5 In this *smoke-sodden little town he [_sc._ Hopkins] came up against people who needed him desperately. **1849** _Chambers's Edin. Jrnl._ 24 Nov. 327/2 *Smoke-stained walls. **1965** J. A. MICHENER _Source_ (1966) 71 Along the smoke-stained walls hung spears and clubs, animal skins drying for later use and baskets containing grain. **1602** CAREW _Cornw._ 72 Hanging me thus vp, to be *smoke-starued ouer your chimnies. **1632** LITHGOW _Trav._ x. 429 There Fabrickes are ..of *smoke-torne straw..and Raine-dropping watles. **1951** L. MACNEICE tr. _Goethe's Faust_ II. 193 Yon *smoke-warmed garment.

**c.** With adjs., as _**smoke-dim**_, _**-foul**_, _**-like**_, _**-proof**_, _**-tight**_.

**1840** R. H. DANA _Bef. Mast._ xxviii. 98 We calked and pasted, and, so far as we could, made the ship smoke-tight. **1849** THOREAU _Week Concord Riv._ (1894) 4 Skirted..with alder-swamps and smoke-like maples. **1888** G. M. HOPKINS _Let._ 1 May (1938) 145, I..dislike any town..for its bad and smokefoul air. **1901** _Westm. Gaz._ 24 Dec. 7/2 One of the firemen donned a smoke-proof suit and helmet. **1937** 'G. ORWELL' _Road to Wigan Pier_ iv. 71 You walk through the smoke-dim slums of Manchester.

**11.** Special combs.: **smoke alarm**, a device that automatically gives a warning of the presence of smoke; **smoke-arch** _U.S._, the smoke-box of a locomotive (Webster, 1864); **smoke-bell**, **-board** (see quots.); **smoke-boat** _Naut. slang_, a steamship; **smoke-bomb**, a bomb which produces a smoke-screen; **smoke bush** = _smoke plant_; **smoke candle** (see quot. 1962); **smoke canister**, a canister whose contents can be ignited to produce smoke; **smoke concert** _N.Z._, a concert at which smoking is allowed; **smokefall** [after NIGHTFALL] _rare_$^{-1}$, 'the moment when the wind drops and smoke that had ascended descends' (Dame Helen Gardner); **smoke-glass**, an eyepiece or spectacle of smoked glass; **smoke goggles**, goggles that protect the eyes against smoke; **smoke grenade**, a grenade that emits a cloud of smoke on impact; **smoke-head**, (_a_) the head of a column of smoke; (_b_) _Naut._, a funnel; **smoke helmet**, (_a_) a helmet used by firemen, enabling the wearer to see and breathe freely in the midst of smoke; also, a similar helmet used by others; (_b_) a form of respirator used for counteracting poison gas, etc., in the war of 1914–18; †**smoke-hen**, a hen accustomed to perch in the smoke; **smoke-hound** _U.S. slang_, an alcoholic who drinks smoke (see sense 7 b above); **smoke joint** [JOINT _sb._ 14] _U.S. slang_, a bar selling inferior liquor; **smoke-loft**, a loft in which the smoking of bacon, etc., is done; **smoke-mantle**, part of a furnace for roasting tin-ores; †**smoke-merchant**, a tobacconist; **smoke-meter**, an instrument for measuring the density or the composition of smoke; †**smoke-money**, money paid by householders as a due or tax (see quots. and cf. _smoke-penny_); **smoke night**, an evening meeting accompanied by smoking; **smoke-pence**, **-penny** (see quots. and _smoke-money_); **smoke Persian**, a long-haired smoke-coloured cat (cf. sense 8); **smoke plant**, the Venetian sumach, _Cotinus coggygria_, which has a feathery inflorescence suggestive of smoke; **smoke point**, (_a_) the lowest temperature at which an oil or fat gives off smoke; (_b_) the height of the tallest flame with which a particular sample of kerosene will burn; **smoke-pole** _slang_, a firearm; **smoke pot**, a tin containing substances that produce smoke or a similar opaque vapour; **smoke-proof**, an impression taken from a smoked type-punch, etc.; **smoke respirator** (see quots.); **smoke rocket**, a rocket that emits smoke; **smoke-sail** (see quot. 1846); †**smoke-seller** (see SMOKE _sb._ 4 f); also, a tobacconist; **smoke shell** _Mil._, a projectile that generates a dense cloud of smoke after it is fired; **smoke-shop** now _U.S._, (_a_) a tobacconist's shop, †formerly one in which accommodation for smoking was provided; also, a place where people gather to smoke and talk; (_b_) a bar, esp. one selling inferior or cheap liquor; **smoke-signal**, a column of smoke used as a signal (cf. sense 2 a); also _transf._ and _fig._; †**smoke-silver**, silver paid as smoke-money; **smoke-stick** _slang_, = _smoke-pole_ above; **smoke-talk** _U.S._, a social meeting accompanied by smoking; **smoke test**, a method of testing the state of drains and pipes by means of smoke; **smoke-tree**, = _smoke-plant_; (also the American species _Rhus cotinoides_); **smoke tunnel**, a wind tunnel into which smoke can be introduced to make the airflow visible; **smoke-wagon** _U.S. slang_, a firearm; **smoke-wood** (see quot.); **smoke-writing** = SKY-WRITING _vbl. sb._

**1936** _Discovery_ Nov. 359/2 A *smoke alarm apparatus for the small industrial chimney is also provided. **1977** _Chicago Tribune_ 2 Oct. XII. 17/9 (Advt.), Full basement, low assoc. fee, central humidifier and smoke alarm. **1875** KNIGHT _Dict. Mech._ 2223/2 *_Smoke-bell_, a glass bell suspended over a gas-light, to intercept the smoke. **1850** OGILVIE, *_Smoke-board_, a board hung in front of a fire-place, to keep the smoke from emerging into the apartment. **1867** G. E. CLARK _Seven Years of Sailor's Life_ xii. 116 Capen and de missis go munyana in de big *smoke boat. **1901** _Rudder_ Jan. 9/2 The magnificent steam yacht Mayflower passed us close aboard. We had a fine contempt for any and all 'smoke boats', but the sweetness of her lines..compelled admiration. **1929** F. BOWEN _Sea Slang_ 127 _Smoke boat_, the old sailing ship man's term of contempt for a steamer. **1917** A. G. EMPEY _Over Top_ 308 *_Smoke bomb_, a shell which, in exploding, emits a dense white smoke, hiding the operations of troops. **1931** V. BRUCE _Bluebird's Flight_ iii. 29 Throwing over a smoke bomb, I descended on a nice hard piece of ground. **1973** 'I. DRUMMOND' _Jaws of Watchdog_ xv. 205 A little smoke-bomb. I put it through a window... Then I went in through another window. **1902** L. H. BAILEY _Cycl. Amer. Hort._ IV. 1529/1 _Rhus..Cotinus_, Linn. *Smoke Bush. Venice Sumach..fl[ower]s purple, in ample loose panicles. **1940** [see _partridge vine_ s.v. PARTRIDGE 5]. **1977** _Weekly Times_ (Melbourne) 19 Jan. 29/4 The other sample is from the smoke bush. **1932** C. GILSON _Wild Metal_ III. i. 248 We had been provided with *smoke-candles; and when we had cleared the Boche out of his trenches, the wind changed and the smoke masked our own fire. **1950** _Times_ 13 May 4/5 The pilot started to descend in order to round the turning point at not more than 300 ft. for recognition purposes. The point was near a golf course..where white strips had been laid out and smoke candles were fired as the Meteor approached. **1962** _Ordnance Technical Terminol._ (U.S. Army Ordnance School, AD 660 112) 282/1 _Smoke candle_, munition which produces smoke by vaporizing a smoke producing oil. **1973** 'I. DRUMMOND' _Jaws of Watchdog_ x. 135 The *smoke-canisters were not of a recognized pattern..used by any NATO army. **1974** H. MACINNES _Climb to Lost World_ ix. 148 We had smoke canisters all ready, in case we heard a plane. **1888** J. D. WICKHAM _Casual Ramblings_ 42 They had a *smoke concert with a Salvation Army accompaniment till a clock was 'ayont the twal'. **1935** A. MULGAN _Pilgrim's Way in N.Z._ xiv. 90 'A man should go on to the football field,' declared a representative forward at a 'smoke' concert, 'prepared to meet his God.' **1936** T. S. ELIOT _Coll. Poems 1909–1935_ 188 But only in time can..The moment in the draughty church at *smokefall Be remembered. **1769** _Phil. Trans._ LIX. 334 These two observers looked directly at the Sun, having their instruments armed with *smoke-glasses. **1889** _Anthony's Photogr. Bulletin_ II. 373 A pair of light-tinted smoke glasses will afford great relief. **1962** _Flight International_ LXXXII. 487/2 Stowage provision is made for *smoke goggles at each duty station. **1976** B. JACKSON _Flameout_ iv. 59 Fumes and smoke..surged forward into the flight deck. The crew put on smoke goggles. _a_ **1944** K. DOUGLAS _Alamein to Zem Zem_ (1946) 16 Stacked round the sides of the turret were..hand-grenades, *smoke grenades and machine-gun ammunition. **1980** _Globe & Laurel_ July/Aug. 229/2 Twice during the night we were attacked by a small enemy force who ran through our position throwing Chinese crackers and smoke grenades. **1915** KIPLING _France at War_ 11 He pointed to the large deliberate *smoke-heads. **1942** H. BLOOMFIELD _Sailing to Sun_ xvi. 164 There was smoke coming from the smoke-head of the _Owl_. **1900** _Daily Mail_ 24 Apr. 3/2 An officer of the brigade donned a *smoke helmet. **1906** _Royal Mag._ Feb. 338/1 A safety smoke helmet. **1915** D. O. BARNETT _Let._ 10 June 171 We've got a wonderful new respirator issued, a 'smoke helmet' made of cloth.. which is soaked in a solution. **1972** _Police Rev._ 17 Nov. 1491/2 Constables equipped and wearing diving or smoke helmets. **1577** B. GOOGE _Heresbach's Husb._ IV. (1586) 162 b, The cause that the old people made choise in their quitrentes of *smoke Hennes, as of the best. **1932** _Sun_ (Baltimore) 23 Nov. 20/4 If a downpour has just started, the jungles are literally emptied into the stations... They come in by the dozen.., ancient *smoke hounds and middle-aged rovers. **1931** 'D. STIFF' _Milk & Honey Route_ xii. 128 Mark my word, out of the muck hole that was a '*smoke joint' will rise a lily that will outdo the old-time saloon in all those old virtues. **1657** H. CROWCH _Welsh Trav._ 11 Unto the *smoake-loft clim'd he than, and to the bacon crept. **1839** URE _Dict. Arts_ 1246 The *smoke-mantle or chimney-hood, at the end of the furnace. _a_ **1618** *Smoke-merchant [see _smoke-seller_]. **1941** _Jrnl. Soc. Automotive Engineers_ XLVIII. 188/2 The *smokemeter itself is our only means of measuring smoke density precisely. **1961** _Guardian_ 24 Mar. 6/3 In..a letter.. regarding..the control of diesel exhaust smoke..Mr. Marples has indicated that further detailed investigation into the possibilities of using a smokemeter would be worth while. **1662** PETTY _Taxes_ 86 Of all the accumulative excises, that of hearth-money or *smoak-money seems the best. **1778** _England's Gaz._ (ed. 2) s.v. _Brighthelmstone_, The vicar here..claims the old episcopal custom of a penny per head (commonly called Smoak-Money, or the Garden-Penny). **1850** _N. & Q._ 1st Ser. II. 120/2 Smoke Money..under this name is collected every year at Battle in Sussex. **1891** _Melbourne Punch_ 2 June 378/3 The Mutual Store '*Smoke night' was held at the Vienna Cafe on Thursday evening. **1584** R. WILSON _Three Ladies London_ 1, For here were *smoke-pence, Peter-pence, and Paul-pence to be paid. **1631** WEEVER _Anc. Funeral Mon._ 176 Parsons, and Impropriators of Churches, at this day in many places of England, are payed this pennie vnder the name of a *Smoke pennie. **1652** _Answ. Petit. Poor Husbandmen_ 19 The Parishioners do commonly blow away all the tithes due for firewood with a smoak penny. **1850** _N. & Q._ 1st Ser. II. 174/2 Smoke pennies are also yearly levied from most of the inhabitants of the New Forest. **1904** 'SAKI' _Reginald_ 3 You want one of her *smoke Persian kittens. **1973** _Country Life_ 25 Jan. 226/3 My smoke persian was an individualist like Mr. Fearon's cat. **1856** A. GRAY _Man. Bot._ (1860) 76 Sumach... Leaves (simple in R. Cotinus, the *_Smoke-Plant_ of gardens). **1888** _Garden_ 18 Aug. 159/1 The Venetian Sumach, Wig Tree, or Smoke Plant..is one of the most remarkable of late-flowering shrubs. **1948** N. CATCHPOLE _Flowering Shrubs & Small Trees_ 177 Smoke Plant or Burning Bush... The common names relate to the fine, feathery inflorescence. **1933** _Petroleum Handbk._ x. 181 The *smoke point only gives an indication of the burning quality of a kerosine immediately the lamp is lit. **1951** MCMICHAEL & BAILEY in M. B. Jacobs _Chem. & Technol. of Food & Food Products_ II. xxv. 1150 If a fat is to be used for frying..its smoke point, or smoking temperature, is of some importance. **1958** _Jrnl. Home Econ._ L. 778/1 An emulsifier lowers the smoke point of the fat to which it is added. **1975** E. M. GOODGER _Hydrocarbon Fuels_ vii. 134 Two kerosine types of burner fuel are classified as C1 and C2, with minimum smoke-points of 35 and 25 mm, respectively. **1929** M. A. GILL _Underworld Slang_ 11/1 *_Smoke pole_, gun. **1970** _N.Z. Listener_ 21 Sept. 14/5 A long time since he'd fired the old smoke-pole, anyway. **1980** _Hunting Ann. 1981_ 55/1 This requires the hunter to decide in advance whether he wants to hunt with an antique or modern... There is no going out later using a scoped rifle after getting zilched with a smokepole. **1950** _N.Z. Jrnl. Agric._ June 534/3 By taking one or two *smoke pots into a poultry house and seeing where the smoke goes and what happens to it, improvements in ventilation are often suggested. **1965** 'LAUCHMONEN' _Old Thom's Harvest_ x. 135 They all sit down near..their mosquito smoke-pots. **1978** J. GARDNER _Dancing Dodo_ xiii. 92 She would..begin her let down west of Brussels, and start up the smoke pots housed in the starboard nacelles. **1888** _Encycl. Brit._ XXIII. 699 The flame..blackens the letter, and thus enables an impression, called a *_smoke proof_, to be stamped on paper. **1902** DE VINNE _Title-pages_ 79 Pleasing as a new ornament in this style might appear in the smoke-proof, it was sure to be a blotch in the print. **1866** C. F. T. YOUNG _Fires, Fire-Engines_, etc. 44 About the year 1824 one John Roberts..invented a '*smoke-respirator' or hood, by means of which a fireman could enter a burning building or room. **1884** _Health Exhib. Catal._ 60/1 Tyndale's Smoke Respirators are to enable the wearer to enter into most dense and pungent smoke with perfect safety. **1891** A. CONAN DOYLE in _Strand Mag._ July 70/1 'It is nothing very formidable,' he said, taking a long cigar-shaped roll from his pocket. 'It is an ordinary plumber's *smoke rocket, fitted with a cap at either end to make it self-lighting.' **1954** [see _ripple-fired_ adj. s.v. RIPPLE _sb._[3] 7]. **1964** J. S. SCOTT _Dict. Building_ 265 _Smoke Rocket_.., a rocket which gives off a dense, lasting smoke which is directed into a drain under test. **1805** _Naval Chron._ XIII. 379, 90 yards of canvass were puchased to make her *smoke-sail. **1846** A. YOUNG _Naut. Dict._ 288 _Smoke-sail_, a small sail put up for the purpose of preventing the smoke of the galley from going aft to the quarter-deck, when the ship is riding head-to-wind. _a_ **1618** SYLVESTER _Tobacco Battered_ 812 Wks. (Grosart) II. 274 'Let the *Smoak-seller suffocate with Smoak': Which our Smoak-Merchants would no lesse befit. **1649** W. M. _Wandering Jew_ (1857) 25 And when the miserable smoke-sellers die, how are they buried? **1919** P. R. WORRALL _Smoke Tactics_ 27 *Smoke shells may be used as a visible sign to Infantry and Tanks to mark the barrage. **1937** _Times_ 16 Apr. 8/6 The howitzers used smoke shells mixed with their high explosive to give a screen effect. **1966** _McGraw-Hill Encycl. Sci. & Technol._ I. 539/1 The 81-mm and 4·2-in. mortars, capable of lobbing high-explosive or smoke shells onto enemy positions, round out the category of infantry weapons. **1798** _Sporting Mag._ XII. 194 The chit-chat of a Birmingham *smoke shop. **1802** BEDDOES _Hygëia_ VIII. 31 Among..the artisans that croud the smoke-shops. **1937** C. HIMES _Nigger_ in _Black on Black_ (1973) 125 Harold Price.. was just leaving the house for his afternoon tonk session down at the smoke shop at 100th Street and Cedar. **1959** R. M. DORSON _Amer. Folklore_ vii. 267 The enterprising folklorist need not journey into the back hills to scoop up tradition. He can set up his recording machine in the smokeshop or the union grill. **1972** J. WAMBAUGH _Blue Knight_ (1973) i. 19, I walked down to the smoke shop. I picked up half a dozen fifty-cent cigars. **1977** _New Yorker_ 27 June 31/1 Send out to the smoke shop for three cartons of straw-tipped Melachrinos. **1873** S. W. COZZENS _Marvellous Country_ iv. 65 After leaving the Organos Mountains we had noticed Indian *smoke-signals. **1923** _Beaver_ Dec. 108 Another smoke signal was seen curling upward away to the north. **1944** _Living off Land_ iv. 84 A very useful mode of attracting attention is by means of smoke signals. **1962** _Amer. Speech_ XXXVII. 135 _Smoke signals, n._ Sometimes trains were taken on a logging railroad without authority. The men had to keep a sharp lookout for smoke from other trains in order to get onto a side track or to back up quickly: 'We had to watch for smoke signals.' **1978** _Times_ 20 Jan. 4/8 Mr Enoch Powell['s]..delphic remarks certainly got Mrs Thatcher asking herself what smoke signals he intended. **1664** SPELMAN _Gloss._ s.v., By the payment of *Smoke Silver to the Sheriff yearlie. **1698** in _Ho. of Lords MSS._ (1905) III. 257 The duty commonly called Smoak Silver, Peter Pence or Common Fine. **1927** _Flynn's_ 22 Jan. 376/2, I ups and prods him and says, 'Hand it over, er this *smokestick'll do the talking.' **1940** in S. J. Baker _Austral. Lang._ (1945) viii. 153 A rifle is a smoke-stick, a machine-gun is a death-adder. **1893** _Boston_ (Mass.) _Jrnl._ 25 Mar. 2/2 The Association of Railroad and Steamboat Agents..held a *smoke-talk..last evening. **1886** _Encycl. Brit._ XXI. 716 The '*smoke test'.. consists of filling the house-drain, soil-pipes, and waste-pipes with a dense and pungent smoke. **1860** WORCESTER, *_Smoke-tree_. **1887** G. W. COX _Cycl. Common Things_ (ed. 6) 573 The Venetian Sumach of Southern Europe is the common smoke tree or fringe tree of the gardens. **1931** _Flight_ 18 Dec. 1243/2 The type of *smoke tunnel used by Mr. Farren for his demonstrations had cost approximately £65. **1964** P. BRADSHAW _Exper. Fluid Mech._ vi. 151 Smoke tunnels are usually of open-circuit design to prevent the accumulation of smoke in the airstream. **1975** L. J. CLANCY _Aerodynamics_ xiii. 365 The principal requirement of a smoke tunnel is for uniform flow with low turbulence. **1891** J. MAITLAND _Amer. Slang Dict._ 251 *_Smoke-wagon_ (Am.), a revolver. The word is used by the negroes of the Chicago levee. **1926** J. BLACK _You can't Win_ x. 132 I'll have her buy me a pair of 'smoke wagons'. **1950** _Western Folklore_ IX. 138 Familiar epithets for the revolver were equalizer, shootin' iron,..smoke wagon. **1863** PRIOR _Plant-n._, *_Smoke-wood_, from children smoking its porous stalks, _Clematis vitalba_. **1932** _Flight_ 8 July 638 The committee recommend that *smoke-writing should not be prohibited or controlled.

**smoke** (smәʊk), _v._ Forms: 1 **smocian, smokian**, 3 **smokien**, 3–4 **smoken** (5 **smokyn**), 4– **smoke**; 6–7 **smoake**, 6–9 **smoak**. [OE. _smocian_, f. _smoca_ SMOKE _sb._ Cf., with different ablaut-grade, MDu. and Du., MLG. and LG., _smoken_ (WFris. _smoke_), G. _schmauchen_; also the trans.

LG. *smöken* (whence Da. *smøge*), G. *schmäuchen* (†*schmeuchen*):—**smaukjan*. See also SMEEK *v.*]

**I. 1. a.** *intr.* To produce or give forth smoke.

*c* **1000** ÆLFRIC *Gen.* xv. 17 Þa sloh þær micel mist and ferde swilce an ofen eall smociende. *c* **1000** *Lambeth Ps.* ciii. 32 Se þe æthrinð muntas & hiȝ smociað. *c* **1205** LAY. 25734 Þa iseȝen heo..a muchel fur smokien uppen ane hulle. *c* **1290** *S. Eng. Leg.* I. 233/490 Al þe se þare aboute barnde and smokede faste. **1388** WYCLIF *Gen.* xv. 17 A furneis smokynge apperide, and a laumpe of fier. *c* **1440** *Promp. Parv.* 460/2 Smekyn, or smokyn, *fumo, fumigo.* **1530** PALSGR. 723/1 This woode smoketh to moche, it is nat drye ynoughe. **1591** SAVILE tr. *Tacitus, Agricola* 261 The houses fired and smoking farre of. **1647** COWLEY *Mistr., Discovery*, The Gods may give their Altars o're; They'll smoak but seldom any more. **1700** DRYDEN *Ovid's Met., Baucis & Philemon* 52 With Leaves and Barks she feeds her Infant-fire: It smoaks. **1743** DAVIDSON *Æneid* VII. 203 The torch smoaking with grim horrid light. **1815** SCOTT *Guy M.* x, They perceived that she [the ship] grounded, smoked, and, finally, took fire. **1905** F. YOUNG *Sands of Pleasure* II. iii, The cigarette smoked unheeded in her fingers.

**b.** In fig. uses or contexts.

**1535** COVERDALE *Deut.* xxix. 20 His wrath and gelousy shall smoke ouer soch a man. *a* **1548** HALL *Chron., Hen. IV*, 29 b, Where hertes still burne and malice continually smoketh. **1575** GASCOIGNE *Glasse Govt.* III. i, These young gallants are caught without a net..; no man gladder then I, for as long as that chimney smoketh, I..shall not go hungrie to bed. **1639** S. DU VERGER tr. *Camus' Admir. Events* 80 Glory is a perfume fit to smoake no where but before the Altar of vertue. **1677** HUBBARD *Narr.* 48 To cause his jealousie to smoak against those of his own heritage. **1834** DE QUINCEY in *Tait's Mag.* I. 196/1 Ireland was still smoking with the embers of rebellion.

**c.** Of a room, chimney, lamp, etc.: To be smoky, to emit smoke, as the result of imperfect draught or improper burning.

**1663** PEPYS *Diary* 13 Jan., The dining-room smokes unless I keep a good charcoal fire. **1715** DESAGULIERS *Fires Impr.* 31 Every little cranny may be stopp'd up close without fear of the Room smoaking. *c* **1725** POPE *Upon Dk. Marlborough's House at Woodstock* 3 The chimneys..never smoke in any wind. **1807** GASS *Jrnl.* 176 We found our huts smoked; there being no chimnies in them except in the officers' rooms. **1826** SCOTT *Woodst.* xxi, It is best sitting near the fire when the chimney smokes. **1906** H. WALES *Mr. & Mrs. Villiers* xxiii, The lamp had been smoking in his room.

**2. a.** To give off or send up vapour, dust, spray, etc.; *esp.* to steam.

With quot. 1869 cf. SMOKE *sb.* 1 e.

**13..** *E.E. Allit. P.* B. 226 As smylt mele vnder smal siue smokes for-þikke. **1533** J. HEYWOOD *Mery Play* 21 (Brandl), Whan I haue beten her tyll she smoke. **1577** B. GOOGE *Heresbach's Husb.* IV. (1586) 176 Their labour smokes and all of time [= thyme] doth smell, The Hony sweete that in their Coames they lay. **1617** MORYSON *Itin.* III. 97 These often heated meats, which smoaked on the outside, yet were cold on the inside. **1697** DRYDEN *Virg. Georg.* III. 274 The lab'ring Yoke and shining Shares, that make the Furrow smoak. **1732** POPE *Ep. Bathurst* 360 Two puddings smok'd upon the board. **1782** COWPER *J. Gilpin* 127 Which made his horse's flanks to smoke. **1802** PINKERTON *Mod. Geogr.* (1811) 329 The water smokes continually. **1863** W. C. BALDWIN *Afr. Hunting* ii. 57 It rained incessantly the whole night, and we..lay smoking and steaming. **1869** TENNYSON *Holy Grail* 18, I have seen this yew-tree smoke, Spring after spring, for half a hundred years.

**b.** To rise, spread, or move, like smoke.

In later quots. with suggestion of next sense.

**1595** SHAKS. *John* V. iv. 34 This night whose blacke contagious breath Already smoakes [etc.]. **1726–46** THOMSON *Spring* 194 A yellow mist, Far smoaking o'er th'interminable plain. **1781** COWPER *Truth* 238 See where it smokes along the sounding plain, Blown all aslant, a driving, dashing rain. **1821** CLARE *Vill. Minstr.* II. 106 Where the thin clouds smoke along the sky. **1904** J. CONRAD *Nostromo* i, They [clouds]..smoke in stormy trails across the snows of Higuerota.

**c.** To ride, drive, sail, etc., at a rapid pace or great speed. Const. *along* (prep. or adv.).

**1697** DRYDEN *Æneid* VII. 909 Proud of his Steeds he smoaks along the Field. **1725** POPE *Odyss.* III. 615 The coursers..held Their equal pace, and smoak'd along the field. **1735** SOMERVILLE *Chase* II. 232 Then like a foaming Torrent, pouring down Precipitant, we smoke along the Vale. **1827** SCOTT *Chron. Canongate* iii, Smoking along in his travelling chaise-and-four. **1894** *Times* 6 Aug. 5/2 The Vigilant came smoking along in style past Ryde.

**d.** *Austr. slang.* = SLOPE *v.*[2] 1. Also const. *off.*

**1893** in Morris *Austral Eng.* s.v., 'Do not say we were here. Let us smoke.' 'Smoke'..is the slang for the 'push' to get away as fast as possible. **1961** P. WHITE *Riders in Chariot* 415 Dubbo had gone all right. Had taken his tin box, it seemed, and smoked off.

**3.** *fig.* †**a.** To fume, be angry. *Obs.*

*a* **1548** HALL *Chron., Edw. IV*, 212 The Duke..so fumed and smoked at the matter. *a* **1562** G. CAVENDISH *Wolsey* (1893) 47 Evyn so was she commaundyd to avoyde the court ..; whereat she smoked.

**b.** *School slang.* To blush.

**1862** FARRAR *St. Winifred's* iv, 'Why, you're smoking now,' said Henderson, as Walter..began to blush a little.

†**4.** To smart, to suffer severely. *Obs.*

In early use with allusion to actual burning; quot. 1773 partly belongs to sense 2.

*a* **1548** HALL *Chron., Hen. VIII*, 64 b, For feare to bee called heretike, and then they would make hym smoke or beare a faggot. **1595** in *Cath. Rec. Soc. Publ.* V. 352 The farewell was he would make hym smoke for yt before he departed the towne. **1679** DRYDEN *Limberham* v. i, Now I am resolv'd I will go see 'em, or some-body shall smoak for't. **1773** GOLDSM. *Stoops to Conq.* v, No such bad driving; the poor beasts have smoked for it. **1818** A. ROYALL *Let.* 19 Feb. (1830) 104 It's as fair cheatin says I, as I ever seed in my life; and you can make him smoke for it. **1878** J. H. BEADLE *Western Wilds* xxviii. 442 The residents will make him 'smoke' with high taxes on his land.

**II. 5. a.** *trans.* To expose (a person, place, etc.) to the smoke of some curative, purifying, or aromatic substance; to fumigate, esp. as a means of disinfecting.

*c* **1000** *Saxon Leechd.* I. 116 Ðenim þu þas ylcan wyrte, & smoca hit [*sc.* the child] mid. *c* **1400** tr. *Secreta Secret., Gov. Lordsh.* 83 [Let him] after smoke him with ensens couenable to þe tyme. **1530** PALSGR. 723/1, I wyll medyll me with no garmentes that were his tyll they be well smoked. **1546** BALE *Eng. Votaries* I. (1560) 92 b, They are..Censed, Smoked, Perfumed and Worshypped. **1599** SHAKS. *Much Ado* I. iii. 60 As I was smoaking a musty roome. **1665** in Ellis *Orig. Lett.* Ser. II. IV. 32, I smoke your house twice a week. **1772–84** *Cook's Voy.* (1790) IV. 1215 The ship was smoaked between decks with gunpowder. **1796** C. MARSHALL *Gardening* (1813) 398 Orchards, dung, dress, prune, or smoak them. **1840** R. H. DANA *Bef. Mast* xxix, The next day was Sunday, and a good day for smoking ship.

**b.** To expose or subject to smoke, so as to suffocate, stupefy, or make uncomfortable.

It is doubtful whether quots. 1824 and 1825 are based on real knowledge of the phrase they illustrate.

*a* **1154** *O.E. Chron.* an. 1137, Me henged up bi the fet & smoked heom mid ful smoke. **1617** BRATHWAIT *Smoaking Age* 87 That Alexander Severus would have smoaked such sellers of smoake. **1641** J. JACKSON *True Evang. Temper* I. 44 Others inverted..were so smoaked and suffocated to death. **1686** W. HARRIS tr. *Lemery's Course Chym.* (ed. 2) 483 Tabaco kills serpents..if you should smoke them with it. **1712** STEELE *Spect.* No. 358 ¶1 After which they have gone in a Body and smoaked a Cobler. [**1824** SCOTT *Redgauntlet* let. i, Who taught me to smoke a cobbler? **1825** BROCKETT *N.C. Gloss., Smoke-the-Cobbler*, a mischievous pastime among children.] **1900** POLLOK & THOM *Sports Burma* vi. 202 They then smoke the bees until they are stupid.

*fig.* **1595** SHAKS. *John* II. i. 139 Ile smoake your skin-coat and I catch you right. **1601** B. JONSON *Every Man in Hum.* IV. ii, It vanished away like the smoke of tobacco; but I was smoked soundly first. **1680** V. ALSOP *Mischief Imposit.* xii. 98 They formed themselves into separate bodies for Government, and were soundly smok'd for it in the high Commission.

**c.** To fill with, expose to, smoke, esp. so as to blacken, discolour, or render obscure. Also const. *through* (quot. 1846).

**1611** SHAKS. *Cymb.* V. v. 398 Let's quit this ground, And smoake the Temple with our Sacrifices. **1631** A. WILSON *The Swisser* II. i, With some quaint oath in 's mouth, smoaking his nostrills. *a* **1704** T. BROWN *Walk r. Lond.* Wks. 1709 III. III. 64 Others..sat smoaking their Noses, and drinking Burnt-Brandy. **1748** JOHNSON *Van. Human Wishes* 85 The painted face..Smoak'd in kitchens, or in auctions sold. **1800** *Phil. Trans.* XC. 274, I now took two green glasses; but found that they did not intercept light enough. I therefore smoked one of them. **1846** HOLTZAPFFEL *Turning* II. 730 The new piece is laid upon the original, the interstices of which are smoked through with a lamp. **1883** *Cent. Mag.* XXV. 849/1, I copy pictures and he smokes them and sells them as old masters.

**d.** To cure or preserve (bacon, fish, etc.) by exposure to smoke; to smoke-dry.

**1757** WASHINGTON *Lett.* Writ. 1889 I. 413, I have directed the provision..to be smoked, if there are conveniences for doing it. **1767** *Phil. Trans.* LVII. 284 The herring..when salted and smoked. **1836** W. IRVING *Astoria* III. 251 Having no other food, she killed the two horses, and smoked their flesh. **1846** J. BAXTER *Libr. Pract. Agric.* (ed. 4) II. 311 Smoking the bacon is much better than merely drying it.

**6.** †**a.** With *out* or *away*: To convert into smoke. *Obs. rare.*

**1382** WYCLIF *2 Chron.* ii. 4 To brennen encense beforn hym, and to swote thingis to ben out smokid. **1686** tr. *Chardin's Trav. Persia* 154 The three Grains of Incense.. were strew'd upon a few Embers, and smoak'd away.

**b.** To drive *out* or *away* by means of smoke. Also *fig.*, esp. to force *out* into the open (a conspirator); to bring *out* publicly (orig. *U.S.*).

**1593** NASHE *Christ's T.* Wks. (Grosart) IV. 230 In smoaking this..trade out of his starting-holes. **1624** SANDERSON *Serm.* I. 115 The magistrate..that would speedily smoke away these gnats that swarm about the courts of justice. **1720** DE FOE *Capt. Singleton* xv. (1840) 259 William..proposed, that they should..smoke them out. **1829** SCOTT *Anne of G.* xxv, Till we smoke out of his earths the old fox Louis. **1870** MISS BRIDGMAN *R. Lynne* I. iv. 57 He drew out a second cigar, with the..view..of 'smoking her out'. **1914** *Dialect Notes* IV. 164 *Smoke one out, v. phr.*, to find and bring from concealment. 'I'll try and smoke him out again.' **1948** *Times* 28 Feb. 5/7 Speculators were 'smoked out' by a Congressional inquiry. **1959** *Listener* 25 June 1105/2 We were using a food guide, compiled by some daring spy who was determined to smoke out tasty food if it cost him his citizenship. **1977** G. V. HIGGINS *Dreamland* viii. 83, I had done it to smoke them out, and had succeeded.

†**7.** To cause to smoke; to urge at a high speed. *Obs.*[−1]

*a* **1658** CLEVELAND *May Day* ii, Whiles Phœbus..Smoaks his bright Teem along on the Grand Paw.

**8. a.** To get an inkling of, to smell or suspect (a plot, design, etc.). Now *arch.* (in common use *c* 1600–1850).

**1608** CHAPMAN *Byron's Consp.* Wks. 1873 II. 201 Least so he might haue smokt our practises. **1667** DRYDEN & DK. NEWCASTLE *Sir M. Mar-all* I, Sir John, I fear, smokes your design. **1733** FIELDING *Quix. in Eng.* I. viii, Let me tell you, ..I begin to smoke a plot. I begin to apprehend no opposition, and then we're sold, neighbour. **1770** DIBDIN *Deserter* II. i, Oh, Oh, I smoke this business.—Comrade, I'm off, I'm off. **1812** COMBE *Syntax, Picturesque* x. 214 An honest 'Squire, who smok'd the trick, Appear'd well-arm'd with oaken stick. **1837** BARHAM *Ingol. Leg.* Ser. I. *Monstre Balloon* vi, Such a trumpery tale every one of us smokes. **1886** BURTON *Arab. Nts.* (abr. ed.) I. 48 The man, not.. smoking the plot, waxed exceeding wroth.

**b.** *absol.* To have an inkling or idea; to understand. Now *arch.*

**1676** ETHEREDGE *Man of Mode* III. iii, Peace, they smoak. **1688** SHADWELL *Sq. Alsatia* IV, I am sharp, sharp as a needle; I can smoak now, as soon as another. **1757** FOOTE *Author* II, Oh, now I begin to understand..; ecod, I begin to smoke. **1842** BARHAM *Ingol. Leg.* Ser. II. *Lay of St. Medard* xxix, St. Medard paused,—he began to 'smoke'.

**9.** To make fun of, to jest at; to ridicule, banter, or quiz (a person). Now *arch.*

*a* **1700** B. E. *Dict. Cant. Crew, Smoke him, Smoke him again*, to affront a Stranger at his coming in. **1755** *Connoisseur* No. 54 ¶4 The Bucks..sat in another box, to smoke their rusty wigs and brown cassocks. **1772** MME. D'ARBLAY *Early Diary* (1889) I. 159 He..suffered us to laugh at his affectation.., even joining in our mirth and seeming happy to be smoaked. **1818** KEATS *Lett.* (1895) 245 We hated her and smoked her and baited her and I think drove her away. **1859** THACKERAY *Virginians* lxxxix, Our young men were accustomed to smoke her, as the phrase then was.

**10.** To observe, take note of, 'twig'. Now *arch.*

**1715** ADDISON *Drummer* III. i, Thou'rt very smart, my Dear. But see! smoak the Doctor. **1762** FOOTE *Orator* II, Smoke the justice, he is as fast as a church. *c* **1826** J. WILSON *Noct. Ambr.* Wks. 1855 I. 199 Kit, smoke his eyes, how they glare. **1856** 'T. GWYNNE' *Young Singleton* viii, 'Smoke the big-wig Lund!' whispered Fotheringay.

**III. 11.** *intr.* To inhale (and expel again) the fumes of tobacco, or other suitable substance, from a pipe, cigar, or cigarette. More recently, also with reference to marijuana, opium, or other illegal drugs. †Also with *it*.

**1617** BRATHWAIT *Smoaking Age* 174 The sleeping Dormouse..sleepes but all Winter, but this Man i' th' Mist smoakes it all the yeare long: hee proportions his nose [etc.]. **1687** MONTAGUE & PRIOR *Hind & Panth. Transv.* 17 Your Pipe's so foul, that I disdain to smoak. **1721** HEARNE *Collect.* (O.H.S.) VII. 208 Even children were oblig'd to smoak. **1777** DALRYMPLE *Trav. Sp. & Port.* xvii, I declined the favour, but the others smoaked about. **1827** CARLYLE *Germ. Rom.* I. 7 Smoking vehemently on his black stump of a pipe. **1852** THACKERAY *Esmond* II. xi, Mr. Addison was..smoking out of his long pipe, and smiling very placidly. **1895** CONRAD *Almayer's Folly* xii. 267 'And they both smoke,' added Ali. 'Phew! Opium, you mean?' Ali nodded. **1900** POLLOK & THOM *Sports Burma* v. 171 He was..never better pleased than when smoking away at a long Shan pipe. **1957** *Sun* (Baltimore) 12 Jan. 11/2 Asked how he took dope, Harrod replied that he 'smoked, snorted and skin-popped'. **1972** *Guardian* 29 Jan. 9/2 Mr Williams had three previous convictions for possession of cannabis... 'I've said I smoke sometimes.' **1977** 'J. LE CARRÉ' *Honourable Schoolboy* xvi. 381 For a large *divan* secrecy was vital... The safest place to smoke would undoubtedly be upstairs.

**12. a.** *trans.* To use (tobacco, etc.) as material for smoking. Also *fig.*

**1687** A. LOVELL tr. *Thevenot's Trav.* I. 259 Some..have in the mean while smoaked Tobacco, when it was given them. **1716** CHURCH *Philip's War* (1865) I. 28 Capt. Fullers party being troubled with the..lust after Tobacco, must needs strike fire to Smoke it. **1796** MORSE *Amer. Geogr.* II. 85 They also smoke tobacco to excess. **1811** [see HASHISH]. **1840** BARHAM *Ingol. Leg.* Ser. I. *St. Odille* xiv, So put that in your pipe..and smoke it. **1878** STANLEY *Dark Cont.* xviii. (1889) 324 The bandits' custom of smoking banghi (wild hemp). **1946** E. O'NEILL *Iceman Cometh* I. 54 Bejees, Jimmy's started them off smoking the same hop. **1951** *Life* 25 June 21/1, I heard and saw guys who skin pop,..smoke pot, banging and shoot up the main vein in your arm and leg. **1976** *New Yorker* 8 Mar. 98/2 We smoked, sure. At one time, everybody in the platoon had smoked pot except the lieutenant.

**b.** To use (a pipe, cigar, etc.) in the act of smoking; to take (so many whiffs).

**1706–7** FARQUHAR *Beaux' Strat.* I. i, He..smoaks his Pipe Eight and forty Hours together sometimes. **1762** STERNE *Tr. Shandy* VI. vi, My uncle Toby..lighted his pipe, and smoak'd about a dozen whiffs. **1820** W. IRVING *Sketch Bk.* II. 338, I found him..smoking his pipe in the..evening sunshine. **1837** DICKENS *Pickw.* xl, Send down word that he's to spend the change in cigars... I'll smoke 'em. **1902** ELIZ. BANKS *Newspaper Girl* 179, I never saw a woman smoke a cigarette till I came to London.

**c.** With *out* (= to the end, completely).

**1705** tr. *Bosman's Guinea* 306 Which Pipe thus filled they without ceasing can easily smoak out. **1842** BORROW *Bible in Spain* xl, See, I have smoked out your cigar. **1871** M. COLLINS *Marq. & Merch.* II. vii. 216 She smoked one [cigarette] out right seldom.

**13.** To wear *out*, waste (*away*), bring *into* a certain state, etc., by smoking tobacco or some similar substance. Also, to 'rag' by smoking (*U.S.*).

**1604** JAS. I *Counterbl. to Tobacco* (Arb.) 106 If a man smoke himselfe to death with it (and many haue done). **1616** R. C. *Times' Whistle* (1871) 72 He..smokd out all his living at his nose. **1617** BRATHWAIT *Smoaking Age* 195 Sweet Youth, Smoake not thy time; Too precious to abuse. **1688** HOLME *Armoury* III. 294/2 He who smoaks away the chief of his time. **1823** SCOTT *Quentin D.* Introd., I gradually.. smoked myself into a certain degree of acquaintance with [him]. **1844** *N. Brit. Rev.* II. 81 Newton smoked himself into a state of absolute etiolation. **1850** in B. H. Hall *College Words* (1851) 285, I would not have you sacrifice all these advantages for the sake of smoking future Freshmen. **1880** *Harper's Mag.* Nov. 950/1 They hazed and smoked Freshmen. **1893** C. G. LELAND *Mem.* I. 131 To go to their rooms..and smoke them sick or into retreating.

**14.** *intr.* Of a pipe: To draw.

**1883** *Harper's Mag.* July 174/2 These 'church-wardens' smoke freely and softly.

**15.** *trans.* To furnish with tobacco. *rare.*

**1897** 'MARK TWAIN' *Following Equator* xi. 129 He will.. feed you and slake you and smoke you with the best that money can buy.

**IV. 16.** To shoot (a person) with a firearm. *U.S. slang.*

**1926** J. BLACK *You can't Win* xi. 144 Git inside an' stay there or I'll smoke both of youse off. **1942** *Detective Fiction* May 53/1 You chiseling rat. You didn't figure Tommy and those heels could hold *me*, did you? I smoked them just like I'm gonna smoke you, Bugs.

**ˈsmoke-ball.** [SMOKE *sb.* 1.]

**1.** *Mil.* A paper shell filled with a preparation which, when ignited, sends out clouds of smoke.

The ball is fired from a mortar, and the smoke serves to drive men out of mines, conceal manœuvres, etc.

**1753** *Chambers' Cycl.* Suppl. s.v. *Ball*, *Smoak..Balls*, those which..darken a place, to prevent discoveries. **1760** *Ann. Reg., Chron.* 146/1 A smoke-ball burst in General Desagulier's hand, and shattered his arm. **1802** JAMES *Milit. Dict.* s.v. *Ball*, Smoke-balls..continue to smoke from 25 to 30 minutes. **1828** SPEARMAN *Brit. Gunner* (ed. 2) 52 Balls.. are of three descriptions, viz.—lead, light, and smoke-balls. **1859** F. A. GRIFFITHS *Artill. Man.* (1862) 86 The 8 in. Smoke ball burns about 4 minutes.

*fig.* **1796** *Gentl. Mag.* LXVI. II. 1011 When Christianity is assaulted..by the smoke-balls and stink-pots of English vagabonds.

*attrib.* **1809** *Naval Chron.* XXII. 286 Every rocket contains smoak-ball composition.

**2.** A ball used in trap-shooting, which, when struck by a shot, emits a puff of smoke.

**1881** GREENER *Gun* 504 The latest improvement is the American smoke-ball, consisting of two hemispheres of paper placed upon a wooden ball.

**3.** A ball emitting smoke when ignited, used by thieves.

**1899** *Daily News* 21 Mar. 7/2 Raising an alarm of fire by means of smoke balls ignited on the various floors. The smoke balls went beyond their commission and kindled a flame.

**ˈsmoke-black,** *sb.* [SMOKE *sb.* 1.] A form of lamp-black obtained by the combustion of resinous materials.

**1712** tr. *Pomet's Hist. Drugs* I. 204 The black sealing Wax is ting'd or colour'd with Smoak Black. **1841** LANE *Arab. Nts.* I. 130 An inferior kind is the smoke-black produced by burning the shells of almonds. **1858** SIMMONDS *Dict. Trade*, *Smoke-black*, a substance prepared by the combustion of different resinous bodies. **1896** DE VINNE *Moxon's Printing* 412 The crude smoke-black of commerce.

**ˈsmoke-black,** *v.* [SMOKE *sb.* 1.] *trans.* To blacken with smoke.

**1809–10** COLERIDGE *Friend* (Bohn) II. 302 The counterfeit frankincense which smoke-blacks the favourite idol of a Catholic village.

**ˈsmoke-box.** [SMOKE *sb.*]

**1.** A receptacle for smoke. *rare*$^{-1}$.

**1614** W. BARCLAY *Nepenthes* A 8, Not as the English abusers [of tobacco] do, which make a smoke-boxe of their skull.

**2.** *techn.* A chamber in a steam boiler between the flues and the chimney stack; in a locomotive placed at the base of the funnel.

**1846** *Penny Cycl.* Suppl. II. 670/1 That construction of engine in which the cylinders are placed at the bottom of the smoke-box. **1855** LARDNER *Mus. Sci. & Art* VI. 127 The tubes..through which the hot gases..and smoke pass from the fire-box to the smoke-box. **1897** *Pall Mall Mag.* Mar. 354 The exceptional height of the Smoke-box..rendered it necessary to adopt a dwarfed funnel.

*attrib.* **1855** LARDNER *Mus. Sci. & Art* VI. 128 The smoke-box door, opening on hinges at the top. **1878** F. S. WILLIAMS *Midl. Railw.* 652 The smoke-box door did not fit tight.

**smoked** (sməʊkt), *ppl. a.* Also 7 **smoakt, smoak'd,** 8 **smoaked.** [f. SMOKE *v.* + -ED[1].]

**1. a.** Dried or cured by exposure to smoke; impregnated with smoke.

**1603** DEKKER *Wonderf. Yeare* B ij b, For..some smoakt gallant, who at wit repines, To dry Tobacco with my holesome lines. **1648** HEXHAM II, *Een Sore*, a smoakt red Heering. **1700** T. BROWN tr. *Fresny's Amusem.* 117 The best smoak'd Beef in Christendom. **1747** WESLEY *Prim. Physick* (1762) p. xix, Pickled or smoaked or salted Food. **1830** M. DONOVAN *Domest. Econ.* II. 233 Smoked provisions are.. apt to disagree with some persons. **1883** *Fisheries Exhib. Catal.* 370 Smoked Eels,..Smoked Plaice,..Smoked Herrings.

**b.** *smoked sheet*, a form of raw rubber that is preserved for transportation by drying the coagulated latex in a smoky atmosphere.

**1909** *Westm. Gaz.* 26 Oct. 9/2 Buyers..appeared willing to give higher prices for smoked sheet than for crêpe. **1950** *Thorpe's Dict. Appl. Chem.* (ed. 4) 552/1 For the preparation of smoked sheet the strained, diluted latex is poured into rectangular tanks carrying vertical slots at 1½-in. intervals. **1972** P. W. ALLEN *Natural Rubber & Synthetics* iii. 69 The new grading method would free producers from the need to make rubber in those forms such as ribbed smoked sheet which had evolved around the need to fit the traditional grading procedures.

**2.** Obscured, made dark, by smoke.

**1755** B. MARTIN *Mag. Arts & Sci.* 37 This small Telescope, in which I have put a smoaked Glass. **1819** SHELLEY *Œdipus* I. 400 I'll wager you will see them..With pieces of smoked glass. **1885** GOODALL *Physiol. Bot.* (1892) 383 A slowly revolving cylinder covered with smoked paper.

**3.** Tainted or spoiled in taste through contact with smoke.

**1761** COLMAN *Prose on Sev. Occas.* (1787) I. 123 The water is smoaked, the butter rank, the bread heavy. **1857** ELTON *Below Surface* ix, A cup of smoked coffee and a dubious egg.

**4.** Of a smoke-colour. (Cf. SMOKE *sb.* 9 e.)

[**1755**, **1819**: see sense 2 above.] **1827** GRIFFITH tr. *Cuvier* II. 75 *note*, The Smoked Kangaroo, the gray of which is somewhat deeper. **1885** *Encycl. Brit.* XVIII. 447 The shells usually present a dark colour about the edges, like that of 'smoked pearl'. **1892** H. JAMES *Let.* 29 July (1981) III. 391 You all melt away in this hard Swiss light. But I have just bought a tinted (I believe they call it a 'smoked') pince nez, and I am attempting to focus you again. **1898** *Westm. Gaz.* 18 Nov. 3/2 Dark brown fox fur, that which is called 'smoked fox'. **1947** [see *bathy-thermograph* s.v. BATHY-]. **1978** *Lancashire Life* Apr. 141/1 The sun visors..are made of a dark red smoked plastic and slide away completely out of sight. **1979** G. WATSON *Black Jack* xii. 82 A limousine with smoked-glass windows.

**5.** With *-down* or *-out*: Exhausted or consumed by being smoked.

**1859** DICKENS *Tale Two Cities* II. xvi, He put down his smoked-out pipe. **1904** BENSON *Challoners* (1906) 76/2 Martin lit a cigarette from a smoked-down stump.

**ˈsmoke-dried,** *ppl. a.* [SMOKE *sb.* 1.] Dried or cured by exposure to smoke. Also *transf.* and *fig.*

**1653** H. COGAN tr. *Pinto's Trav.* lxiv. (1663) 256 Onyons and some smoak-dried flesh. **1654** H. L'ESTRANGE *Chas. I* (1655) 118 Such a swarthy metamorphosis as neer resembled smoke-dryed Bacon. *a* **1704** T. BROWN *Walk r. London* Wks. 1709 III. III. 3, I made my Smoak-dry'd Infidel shew his Ivory Teeth. **1856** KANE *Arctic Expl.* II. x. 106 Our smoke-dried cabin is a scene worth looking at. **1882** DE WINDT *Equator* 72 The bunch of smoke-dried human heads.

*transf.* and *fig.* **1857** *Chamb. Jrnl.* 17 Jan. 47/1 The smoke-dried trees of our parks. *a* **1941** V. WOOLF *Death of Moth* (1942) 108 The dead weight of smoke-dried culture.

**ˈsmoke-dry,** *v.* [SMOKE *sb.* 1: cf. prec.]

**1.** *trans.* To dry or cure (meat, fish, etc.) by exposure to smoke.

**1704** *Dict. Rust.* s.v. *Chesnut*, It is best to beat the Fruit down from the Tree,..or if you don't, you must Smoke-dry 'em. **1796** STEDMAN *Surinam* II. xx. 111 They even took out the jaw-bones, which they smoke-dried. **1843** BETHUNE *Sc. Fireside Stor.* 62 He even spoke of having an old woman.. hung up in the chimney, and smoke-drying her for three weeks. **1886** *Encycl. Brit.* XX. 174/2 Boiled, smoke-dried, and packed in bags.

**2.** *intr.* To become dried by the action of smoke. In quot. *transf.*

**1855** SMEDLEY *H. Coverdale* ii, You've been smoke-drying in London..till you're out of condition.

Hence **ˈsmoke-drying** *vbl. sb.*

**1812** MISS L. M. HAWKINS *C'tess & Gertr.* I. 265 The discipline of a smoke-drying in one of the closest streets of the city.

**ˈsmoke-farthing.** *Hist.* [SMOKE *sb.* 2 b.] An offering made at Whitsuntide by the householders of a diocese to the cathedral church; also, a hearth-tax (see quot. 1765).

**1444** [see LINCOLN[1] 1]. **1524** *Churchw. Acc. St. Giles, Reading* (ed. Nash) 22 To the Official for smoke farthyngs, iiij[s] j[d]. **1575** in North *St. Martin's, Leicester* 144 For peterpence or smoke farthynges sometyme due to the Anthecriste of roome, xd. **1609** in W. Money *Hist. of Newbury* (1887) 529 P[ai]d for Pentecostalles, otherwise called smoke farthings. **1710** J. HARRIS *Lex. Techn.* II, *Smoke-farthings*, the Pentecostals, or Customary Oblations offered by the Inhabitants within any Diocess, when they made their Processione to the Mother or Cathedral Church. **1765** BLACKSTONE *Comm.* I. 323 As early as the conquest mention is made in domesday book of fumage or fuage, vulgarly called smoke farthings; which were paid by custom to the king for every chimney in the house. **1857** TOULMIN SMITH *Parish* 503 An 'Ale' held at the time of paying the 'Smoke-farthing' or Wax-silver. **1876** [see FUMAGE[1]].

**smoke-ho, -oh.** *colloq.* (chiefly *Austral.*, *N.Z.*, and *Naut.*). Also **smoke-o, smoko.** [f. SMOKE *sb.* 6.: see -O[2].] **1.** A stoppage of work in order to rest and smoke. More generally, a tea-break, a rest period. Also, a cup of tea or a snack taken at work. Also *attrib.*

**1874** L. J. KENNAWAY *Crusts* 124 Sawyers, and stockmen, carpenters, packers, shinglers and loafers, Smoke as they work to assist them, and then knock off for a '*smoke oh!*' **1881** *Adelaide Observer* 31 Dec. 46, I must go to 'smoke O'. **1897** F. T. BULLEN *Cruise 'Cachalot'* viii, This done, it was 'Smoke-oh!' The luxury of that rest and refreshment was something to be grateful for. **1898** DAVITT *Life & Progr. Austral.* lxxvi. 424 There is a 'smoke-ho' time allowed in a few of the prisons. **1900** H. LAWSON *On Track* 133 We go through the day..in runs of about an hour and 20 minutes between smoke-ho's. **1930** V. PALMER *Passage* 247 At smoko, when they took a spell in the middle of loading the boat..the talk was of Lew. **1938** F. WORSLEY *First Voyage* iii. 56 'Five minutes' smoke-oh,' was the mate's reply. **1942** S. CAMPION *Bonaza* i. 21 C'm'on, now, cobbers, we'll go make ourselves smoke-o, eh? Nuthin' like a cuppa. **1953** A. UPFIELD *Murder must Wait* iii. 26 A billy of tea and a slice of brownie..a smoko tea suitable for a half-caste. **1954** T. RONAN *Vision Splendid* 179 If you blokes aren't coming down for your smoko I'll throw it away. **1961** G. FOULSER *Seaman's Voice* ix. 136 It was then 'kaffetid' or smoko as U.K. seamen call it. **1961** P. WHITE *Riders in Chariot* xiii. 456 It was just on smoke-o. The machines were easing... It was now time to relax. **1963** H. C. DE MIERRE *Long Voyage* i. 7 The stevedores broke off for their mid-morning 'smoke-ho'. **1970** D. M. DAVIN *Not Here, Not Now* VI. i. 274 An hour off to eat and then on again from one till three. Another smoko then, and on again till five. **1972** P. NEWTON *Sheep Thief* iii. 27 By 'smoko' time..the three drovers had arrived in from the back. **1978** O. WHITE *Silent Reach* viii. 85 Margan..let the big truck roll to a standstill. 'Smoke-oh,' he announced.

**2.** = *smoke concert* s.v. SMOKE *sb.* 11.

**1918** G. A. TAYLOR *Those were Days* 30 The State Governor was present, and it was a rare incident for that distinguished party to grace an Art Society 'Smoko'. **1957** D. NILAND *Call me when Cross turns Over* vii. 170 He chopped wood for hotels and boarding-houses, and sometimes was roped in as an entertainer at smokos and concerts. **1976** *Australian* 24 Apr. 18 The Leader of the Opposition, Mr Whitlam, worked in his Sydney office and attended a 'smoko' at Wentworthville RSL club last night.

**ˈsmoke-hole.** [SMOKE *sb.* 1.]

**1.** The vent or external orifice of a flue; a hole in the roof of a hut through which the smoke of the fire escapes.

*c* **1340** *Nominale* (Skeat) 479 For smoke a smoke-hole. **1493–4** *Rec. St. Mary at Hill* 201 In expences whane sartayne of þe paryshe yede to Awew þe smoke holys. **1663** GERBIER *Counsel* 22 Cover the top of Chimneyes..; the smoake holes can be..made on the sides. **1825** LOCKHART in *Scott's Fam. Lett.* (1894) II. 298 The smoke-hole..in the roof. **1856** KANE *Arctic Expl.* I. xxx. 406 A smoke-hole passed through the roof. **1891** RIDER HAGGARD *Nada the Lily* xxix. 240 Zinita..had climbed the hut, and now lay there in the dark, her ear upon the smoke-hole, listening to every word.

**b.** = FUMAROLE.

**1899** *Daily News* 18 Nov. 7/2 No lava is flowing, and even the fumarole, or smoke-holes, give forth no sign.

**†2.** *transf.* or *fig.* **a.** An imposture, trick. **b.** A smoking-room. **c.** The mouth of a smoker. *Obs.*

**1580** HOLLYBAND *Treas. Fr. Tong* s.v *Fourbe*, We may easily iudge of this stuffe, or smokehole, or guile. **1673** *Charac. Coffee Ho.* in *Harl. Misc.* (1810) VI. 468 The arch devil, wherewith this smoke-hole is haunted, is the town-wit. *a* **1704** T. BROWN *Walk r. Lond.* Wks. 1709 III. III. 59 Which unsavory Compliment was thus retorted.., viz. Stop your Smoak-hole Nincompoop.

**ˈsmoke-house.** [SMOKE *sb.*]

**†1.** A dwelling-house. *Obs.*$^{-1}$

**1672** PETTY *Pol. Surv. Irel.* (1719) 9 The simple Smoak-houses are..184,000.

**2.** A room in a tannery, heated by smouldering spent tan, where hides are unhaired.

**1797** *Encycl. Brit.* (ed. 3) XVIII. 306/2 The stoutest and heaviest ox hides..are then hung on poles, in a close room called a smoke-house, in which is kept a smouldering fire of wet tan. [So in Ure *Dict. Arts* (1839) 764, *Penny Cycl.* (1842) XXIV. 37.] **1837** HEBERT *Eng. & Mech. Encycl.* II. 60 In some places, the hides were formerly piled wet one upon another..(or otherwise kept warm in what was called a smoke-house).

**3.** A house or room used for curing meat, fish, etc., by means of smoke. Chiefly *N. Amer.*

**1746** in *Lower Norfolk Co. Virginia Antiquary* (1896) I. IV. 110, I..bequeath to my wife Mary the free use & occupation of my dwelling house..with the Kitching, Store house Smoke house, Hen house [etc.]. **1841** A. LANGTON *Let.* 29 May (1904) 282 We intend putting up a smoke-house soon, which is the best way of keeping hung meat. **1860** MAYNE REID *Hunter's Feast* xiv, A part of the bacon furnishes the 'smoke-house' for home consumption during the winter. **1894** *Outing* XXIV. 201/1 A rusty key that probably belonged to some smoke-house of long ago.

*attrib.* **1901** CABLE *Cavalier* liii, The servants were loading the smoke-house meat into a waggon.

**smoke-in** (ˈsməʊkɪn). [-IN[3].] A gathering for the purpose of smoking or otherwise inhaling cannabis.

**1968** *Courier-Mail* (Brisbane) 14 Sept. 7/9 Hashish burnt in a teaspoon held over a gas stove had been inhaled through a metal tube during a 'smoke-in' at a Clayfield flat. **1972** *Guardian* 1 July 1/5 The yippies and the Street People staged a 'smoke-in'.

**ˈsmoke-jack.** [SMOKE *sb.*]

**1.** An apparatus for turning a roasting-spit, fixed in a chimney and set in motion by the current of air passing up this.

**1675** EVELYN *Let.* in Aubrey *Nat. Hist. Surrey* (1719), The Smoke-Jack in my Brother's Kitchen-Chimney; which has been there, I have heard, near a hundred Years. **1754** MRS. DELANY *Life & Corr.* (1861) 301, I think I will have a smoke-jack; the man says he will..keep it in order for nothing. **1777** in *Crts. Europe at Close of Last Cent.* (1841) I. 180 Did you never see a smoke-jack, with a little man in red working away, and seemingly turning the wheel? **1832** BABBAGE *Econ. Manuf.* iv. (ed. 3) 36 The common smoke-jack is an instrument in which the velocity communicated is too great for the purpose required. **1884** JEFFERIES *Red Deer* ix. 172 In how few, even of the most ancient houses, are smoke-jacks still at work!

*attrib.* **1758** FRANKLIN *Lett.* Wks. 1840 VI. 536 This property of chimneys might, by means of smokejack vanes, be applied to some mechanical purposes.

**†b.** *transf.* The head, as the seat of confused ideas. *Obs.*

**1761** STERNE *Tr. Shandy* III. xx, As for my uncle Toby, his smoak-jack had not made a dozen revolutions, before he fell asleep also. **1808** E. S. BARRETT *Miss-led General* 54 That part of the human frame which, in rational mortals, is denominated the Seat of reason; in others, a Smoke-jack.

**2.** *U.S.* A cowl or hood for the end of a railway-carriage stove-pipe (*Cent. Dict.* 1891).

**3.** A cargo-steamer.

**1892** *Daily News* 3 Feb. 5/5 It may do for a 'smoke-jack' to lay off and wait for the fog, but not for a passenger ship with mails.

**4.** A smoke-nuisance inspector.

**1898** *Daily News* 21 Nov. 8/6 The officer who carried out this duty was called a Smoke Jack.

**ˈsmoke-jump,** *v.* *N. Amer.* [f. SMOKE *sb.* + JUMP *v.*] To jump by parachute from an aircraft, in order to extinguish a forest fire. Chiefly as *vbl. sb.*

**1942** *Fire Control Notes* VI. 95 Parachute smoke jumping ..has proved according to all reports, that such a method of attack on small fires is practical. **1949** *Amer. Forests* Oct. 18/3 Smoke jumping is a hazardous occupation. **1958** *Amer. Speech* XXXIII. 180 *Smokejumping* and the verb *to smokejump* appear frequently in newspapers. **1976** *Billings* (Montana) *Gaz.* 11 July 1-D/4 As the blaze spread Friday, the state forestry agency supplied forces, and Missoula sent in two smoke-jumping crews by bus totaling about 40 men.

So **'smoke-jumper** a forest-fire fighter who arrives by parachute.

**1940** *Sci. Amer.* Feb. 97/3 These experiments have proved entirely successful and the 'smoke jumpers' will be of inestimable value in preserving our forests. **1956** PETERSON & FISHER *Wild America* xxxi. 337 Fires are spotted and fought while they are still small. 'Smoke jumpers' parachute from planes to fires in the roadless back country. **1979** *Arizona Daily Star* 5 Aug. A 10/3 The lone survivor..was pulled from the wreckage by smoke jumpers called in to fight a small forest fire touched off by the crash.

**smokeless** ('sməʊklɪs), *a.* [f. SMOKE *sb.* + -LESS.]

**1.** Emitting or producing no smoke.

**1582** T. WATSON *Poems* (Arb.) 134 A Shipwracke of mans life; a Smoaklesse fire. **1732** POPE *Ep. Bathurst* 191 Tenants with sighs the smoakless tow'rs survey. **1795–1814** WORDSW. *Excurs.* VII. 54 The smokeless chimney-top. **1856** KANE *Arctic Expl.* I. xxx. 405 The lamps were cheerful and smokeless. **1868** *Daily News* 2 Sept., It was found that the coals of the Aberdare collieries were comparatively smokeless. **1890** *Nature* 4 Sept., One of the important attributes of a smokeless powder. **1904** *Sci. Amer.* 4 June 446/3 *Smokeless fuel*,..Mr. Weeple employs a simple method of treating such carbonaceous substances as bituminous coal, coal-dust, oil residue, and the like as will produce a fuel that will burn free from 'black smoke' during combustion. **1935** *Economist* 29 June 1479/1 The main product of low-temperature carbonisation is a smokeless solid fuel. **1977** M. RUSSELL *Mr T* xviii. 145 A fireplace..in which smokeless fuel glowed.

**2.** Free from, clear of, smoke. ***smokeless zone***, a district in which the creation of smoke is forbidden by law.

**1631** BRATHWAIT *Whimzies* 53 To leave his smoakelesse house in the country..to riot in the citie. **1802** WORDSW. *Westminster Bridge* 8 All bright and glittering in the smokeless air. **1837** CARLYLE *Fr. Rev.* III. I. ii, The Sun shines; serenely westering, in smokeless mackerel-sky. **1953** *Interim Rep. Comm. Air Pollution* 27 in *Parl. Papers* (Cmd. 9011) VIII. 655 The 'smokeless zone' provision of some local Acts..apply to domestic as well as industrial smoke. **1969** A. E. LINDOP *Sight Unseen* iv. 34 In spite of the fact that we were a smokeless zone I had a comfortable coal fire. **1976** *Daily Record* (Glasgow) 4 Dec. 12/3 It came at a public meeting after Stirling District Council had tried to get a smokeless zone order on the village quashed.

Hence **'smokelessly** *adv.*; **'smokelessness**.

**1877** *Echo* 18 July 1/1 Its Smokelessness, Cleanliness, and Great Economy over all other descriptions [of coal]. *a* **1891** *Engineer* LXIX. 357 (Cent.), The appliances for.. consuming coal smokelessly are already at work.

**smoke-oh**: see SMOKE-HO.

**smoker** ('sməʊkə(r)). [f. SMOKE *v.* + -ER[1]. Cf. Du., Fris., MLG. *smoker*, LG. *smöker* (Da. *smøger*), G. dial. *schmaucher, schmöcher, schmeucher*.]

**1. a.** One who cures fish, bacon, etc., by means of smoke.

**1599** NASHE *Lenten Stuff* Wks. (Grosart) V. 278 Our Herring smoker hauing worn his monsters stale throughout England. **1688** *Lond. Gaz.* No. 2331/4 A Smoaker in Philpot-lane, London. **1699** LUTTRELL *Brief Rel.* (1857) IV. 530 Jeffery Jefferyes, esq. the smoaker. **1831** JANE PORTER *Sir E. Seaward's Narr.* III. 29 Another had been a sausage-maker, or a beef and ham smoker. **1883** F. A. SMITH *Swedish Fisheries* 6 Scotch curers and smokers have, by private enterprise, been sent to Bohuslän.

**b.** One who jests at, or ridicules, others.

**1812** COLMAN *Broad Grins, Two Parsons* lxxxv, These wooden wits, these quizzers, queerers, Smokers.

**2.** Something which emits smoke: †**a.** A war-vessel employed to conceal or assist hostile operations by discharging volumes of smoke. *Obs.*

*a* **1700** B. E. *Dict. Cant. Crew, Smoker*, a Vessel to Blind the Enemies, to make way for the Machine to Play. **1726** SHELVOCKE *Voy. r. World* 321 To bring me away in case I should have occasion to make use of mine as a Fire-ship, or a Smoaker. **1811** *Self Instructor* 587 Vessels of war are..a machine-vessel, a smoaker.

†**b.** *colloq.* A steamer. *Obs. rare.*

**1825** *Sporting Mag.* XVI. 211 We walked four miles early in the morning to the smoker. **1849** H. A. WISE *Los Gringos* xlv. 340, I..took passage in one of them smokers, bigger than a three-decker.

**c.** A smoky chimney, locomotive, etc.

**1883** J. MARTIN *Reminisc. Old Haddington* 29 Dr. Welsh's kitchen chimney was an inveterate smoker. **1897** *Pall Mall Mag.* Sept. 77 Strangers might suppose that American locomotives are inveterate smokers.

**d.** A contrivance for smoking bees.

**1875** J. HUNTER *Man. Bee-keeping* (1884) 150 The simplest smoker of all is a roll of cotton rags.

**e.** A motor vehicle or engine that emits excessive exhaust fumes (see also quot. 1951). *colloq.*

**1951** *Amer. Speech* XXVI. 309/1 *Smoker, n.*, a Diesel-motored truck. **1962** *Daily Tel.* 18 Aug. 13/4 Roadside checks..have resulted in about one diesel lorry in eight being termed a 'smoker' because it is making too much exhaust. **1976** *Globe & Mail* (Toronto) 30 Jan. 1/6 The Ontario Environment Ministry has laid its first pollution charge against the driver of a 'smoker'—a car emitting dense smoke.

**3. a.** One who smokes tobacco, opium, or the like.

**1617** BRATHWAIT *Smoaking Age* 171 Yet of all these, none to me so profest enemies as these smokers of our Age. **1686** PLOT *Staffordsh.* 302 A great smoker, &c., that never spit in his life. **1727** DE FOE *Protestant Monast.* 10 He had been from his Youth a great Smoaker. **1796** MORSE *Amer. Geogr.* II. 86 Both sexes are great smoakers. **1820** BYRON *Juan* III. xxxiv, Afar, a dwarf buffoon stood telling tales To a sedate grey circle of old smokers. **1882** SALA *Amer. Revis.* (1885) 389 The deficient accommodation provided for smokers.

**b.** ***smoker's cough***, a cough caused by excessive smoking. ***smoker's heart, throat***, a diseased condition of the heart or throat caused by excessive smoking. ***smoker's patch***, a smooth, bare white patch on the tongue due to excess in smoking.

**1889** *Buck's Handbk. Med. Sci.* VII. 110 Smoker's Patch. *Ibid.* VIII. 553 Catarrh and hoarseness are so frequent as to give rise to the name 'smoker's throat'. **1906** *Daily Chron.* 16 June 4/4 Nicotine..causing irregular action, and producing the condition known as smoker's heart. [**1907** B. M. CROKER *Company's Servant* i. 7 D'ye hear the cough of him? That's the real Ganja smoker's cough.] **1927** F. HARRIS *My Life & Loves* III. xii. 178 He smoked incessantly though the cigarettes plagued him with smoker's cough. **1942** *R.A.F. Jrnl.* 13 June 17 There was one case of a heavy smoker being sent back to his unit... He had a smoker's cough which betrayed him on night exercises. **1962** *Guardian* 14 Apr. 5/1 His smoker's cough, his overdraft anxiety, his impending divorce. **1967** E. TAYLOR *Second Thursday* i. 9 The old truck burst into life drowning out..the hacking smoker's cough of its owner.

**c.** *U.S.* A grade of tobacco for smoking.

**1880** *U.S. Census, Rep. Culture Tobacco* 15 Class 1. Domestic Cigar Tobacco and Smokers.

**4. a.** A railway carriage or compartment assigned for the use of those travellers who wish to smoke.

**1882** SALA *Amer. Revis.* II. 140 The car known as the 'smoker' is usually relegated to the least eligible part of the train. **1894** *Outing* XXIV. 116/1 We threw our bundles upon the platform of the smoker and climbed up after them.

**b.** A concert at which smoking is permitted.

**1887** *Referee* 9 Jan. 6/3 (Advt.), East Hill Smoking Concert Club.—The first 'smoker' of the above club will be given at the East Hill Hotel, Wandsworth, on Thursday, at 8 o'clock. **1891** *Wheeling* 25 Feb. 401 The Upperthorpe C.C. held a very enjoyable smoker on Thursday evening last. **1894** W. T. VINCENT *Recoll. Fred Leslie* I. xviii. 25 Come down to our concert, A Smoker 'tis called. **1939** JOYCE *Finnegans Wake* 433 Tootling risky *apropos* songs at commercial travellers' smokers. **1961** E. WILLIAMS *George* xx. 319 He was..in the Ouds and last term leading lady in the 'smoker', Oxford for smoking-concert. **1976** W. GOLDMAN *Magic* II. 79 Merlin..brought him along to an Elks' smoker.

**c.** *U.S.* A social gathering of men, sometimes with organized entertainment.

**1899** *N.Y. Jrnl.* 7 Sept. 1/3 Smoker at the Waldorf-Astoria for the sailors of the Olympic. **1911** H. S. HARRISON *Queed* 196 After the bouts or the 'exhibition' of a Saturday, there was always a smoker. **1956** E. N. ROGERS *Queenie's Brood* 42 A smoker was scheduled frequently at which boxing bouts were featured, or a pie race, a wrestling match, [etc.]. **1969** A. R. BOSWORTH *My Love Affair with Navy* xii. 168 Both the tin cans and the subs have long been famed for the smokers they hold ashore.

**5.** *School slang.* One who blushes.

**1866** *Routledge's Every Boy's Ann.* 217 If you happen to blush, he whispers in your ear 'smoker'.

**'smoke-room.** [SMOKE *sb.* or *v.*] A room in a club-house, hotel, or the like, set apart for the accommodation of those who wish to smoke. Also *attrib.*

**1883** *Daily News* 29 Sept. 3/2 A young man..in the smoke-room on the night of sailing from Queenstown. **1891** E. ROPER *By Track & Trail* ix. 125 We smokers left them and took up our quarters in our proper place, the smoke-room. **1906** *Nature* 17 May 53/2 The book is full of smoke-room gossip and snatches of sailors' songs. **1937** [see *lounge bar* s.v. LOUNGE *sb.* 4]. **1945** AUDEN *Coll. Poetry* 134 That caged rebuked question Occasionally let out at clambakes or College reunions, and which the smoke-room story Alone, ironically enough, stands up for.

**smokery** ('sməʊkərɪ). [f. SMOKE *sb.* or *v.* Cf. Fris. *smokerij* smoking.]

**1.** In contemptuous use (see quot.).

**1657** J. WATTS *Dipper Sprinkled* 97 From the publick Ministery or Steeple-houses, (be it so) to private mysteries or smokeries, rather of their Chimney-houses.

**2.** Articles or materials used in smoking.

**1837** *New Monthly Mag.* L. 86 Pipes of all sorts..—all nations and all people were represented in this vast arsenal of smokery.

**3. a.** A place used for smoking; a smoking-room, an opium-den, etc.

**1901** *Daily Chron.* 29 May 5/6 The immorality of the 'smokeries' will probably suffice to close them as disorderly.

**b.** = SMOKE-HOUSE 3. *rare.*

**1794** T. COOPER *America* 132 His *smokery* for bacon, hams, &c. is a room about twelve feet square. **1961** N. FROUD et al. tr. *Montagné's Larousse Gastronomique* 494/1 In modern smokeries, the racks are fitted into the chimney, thus avoiding a great deal of handling.

**smoke-screen** ('sməʊkskriːn). Also **smoke screen, smokescreen.** [f. SMOKE *sb.* + SCREEN *sb.*[1]] **1.** A screen of smoke, *spec.* one produced to conceal military or naval forces or operations, or a stretch of land or sea.

**1915** F. A. TALBOT *Aeroplanes* 172 The 'smoke screen',.. an accepted and extensively practised ruse in naval strategy, and..now adopted by its mosquito colleagues of the air. **1937** [see BLANK *v.* 5 a]. *a* **1944** K. DOUGLAS *Alamein to Zem Zem* (1946) xviii. 107 A straight path would take me behind the..smoke-screen rising and slanting from the carrier. **1977** O. JACKS *Autumn Heroes* xiv. 200 The smoke screen was breaking up patchily to reveal..charred bodies.

**2.** *fig.* Something designed to conceal or mislead; a deliberate distraction or diversion. Also *attrib.*

**1926** R. MACAULAY *Crewe Train* II. iv. 107 The winds, doubtless, were a smoke-screen put up to conceal an advance into some more pithy topic. **1928** *Manch. Guardian Weekly* 7 Sept. 184/3 The 'diplomatic correspondents'..are putting up a smoke-screen of excuse for the Anglo-French naval accord. **1935** A. KENNEDY *Current Eng.* xiii. 567. 'Orismological sesquipedalianism'..has been much employed of late as a form of smoke-screen writing intended to assist advertisers. **1943** H. READ *Politics of Unpolitical* II. 13 The incursions of democracy..are always accompanied by a smoke-screen of righteousness which hides their real nature and dimensions. **1954** *Encounter* Mar. 73/2 Behind the 'scientific' smoke-screen of statistical tables, graphs, codes, and rebarbative language there is a continuous propaganda for more, and more varied, sexual 'outlets' as physiologically good in themselves. **1973** 'H. CARMICHAEL' *Too Late for Tears* viii. 109 Telling you about his other women was just a smokescreen.

Hence **'smoke-screen** *v. trans.* (*a*) to deceive by a smoke-screen; (*b*) to conceal or divert attention from by a smoke-screen; **'smoke-screened** *ppl. a.*, hidden by smoke; **'smoke-screening** *vbl. sb.*, concealment by smoke-screen, the use of smoke-screens.

**1922** O. PARKES *Ships of R. Navy* 147 The sphere of usefulness could be extended to include..smoke screening. **1948** *Nature* 7 Feb. 194/2 Advisory duties at H.Q. Bomber Command..were followed..by duties in connexion with the meteorological aspects of smoke screening. **1950** J. D. MACDONALD *Brass Cupcake* ix. 82 Don't let her smoke-screen you, Chief. **1958** *This Week Mag.* 18 May 35/1 Earlier that day, John Foster Dulles had foxily smokescreened the operation by issuing a statement about summit talks with Russia. **1963** M. ALLINGHAM *China Governess* iii. 47 Some silly little bit..had got him into a scandal which had to be smoke-screened. **1971** N. FREELING *Over High Side* II. 106 He lit it [*sc.* a cigar]... Smoke-screened, he looked back. **1979** I. S. BLACK *Journey to Safe Place* xix. 252 You made a balls of it... Nothing is going to smoke-screen that.

**'smoke-stack.** [SMOKE *sb.*]

**1.** Chiefly *U.S.* **a.** The funnel of a steam-boat.

**1859** *Harper's Mag.* Apr. 606/1 The hoarse breath of the smoke stacks..came from the rosin-fed furnaces. **1862** RUSSELL *Diary North & S.* I. 166 The funnel, *Yankeeicé* smoke stack. **1864** *Daily Telegr.* 30 Aug., The Tennessee.. surrendered, her rudder disabled, her smokestack carried away. **1903** [see *salt-caked* adj. s.v. SALT *sb.*[1] 12 b]. **1942** E. PAUL *Narrow St.* ix. 70 All tugs had smoke-stacks that could be tilted flat when the craft passed under a bridge. **1976** *National Observer* (U.S.) 7 Aug. 7/6 Her smokestacks are lowered..so she can get under some bridges.

**b.** The chimney of a locomotive.

**1875** KNIGHT *Dict. Mech.* 2227/1. **1890** *Daily News* 22 Sept. 5/5 The locomotive's smokestack was just out of the water.

**2.** The chimney of a stove; a chimney-stack.

**1859** *Cairo City* (Illinois) *Gaz.* 8 July 3/1 A number of mischievous boys,..lighting a bunch of fire crackers,.. threw them into the smoke stack. **1871** *Daily News* 9 Feb., Carrying the smoke-stack of a stove through the aperture. **1903** *Westm. Gaz.* 27 Jan. 7/1 The brick smoke-stack of the stoke-house.

**'smoke-up.** *U.S. slang.* [f. SMOKE *v.* + UP *adv.*[1]] An official notice that a student's work is not up to the required standard.

**1927** *Amer. Speech* II. 278/1 [Stanford Univ.] *Smoke up*, official warning of dangerously low standing in history. **1960** *Indiana Daily Student* 23 Nov., Sikes say 56 p.c. of Frosh probably had one Smoke-up.

**smokey**, var. SMOKY *a.* and *sb.*

**Smokey Bear** ('sməʊkɪ bɛə(r)). *U.S. slang.* Also **Smoky Bear**; in sense 2 **Smokey the Bear** and *ellipt.* as **Smok(e)y.** [f. *smokey* var. SMOKY *a.* and *sb.* + BEAR *sb.*[1]: the name of an animal character used in U.S. fire-prevention advertising.] **1.** Used *attrib.* and *absol.* to designate a type of wide-brimmed hat.

**1969** I. KEMP *Brit. G.I. in Vietnam* ii. 23 Sergeants Sullivant, McKane and Rothweiller..wore the round, soft-brimmed hats known by Americans as 'Smokey Bear'—similar to those of the Royal Canadian Mounted Police. **1974** R. M. PIRSIG *Zen & Art of Motorcycle Maintenance* xii. 142 At the park entrance we stop and pay a man in a Smokey Bear hat.

**2.** A state policeman; *collect.* state police.

**1974** *Rolling Stone* 26 Sept. 86 Truckers..keep Don advised for the location of 'Smokies'..so he'll know when to gear the tour bus down from its maximum speed of 82 mph. **1975** *Courier-Mail* (Brisbane) 26 Oct. 36/12 They [*sc.* CB radios] are used by lorry drivers to warn: 'Smokey down the line.' **1975** *High Times* Dec. 67/2 The cab is better outfitted ..with..CB radio (for trackin' those Smokeys in the unwrapped package). **1976** PERKOWSKI & STRAL *Joy of CB* ii. 16 Truckers warned each other of the location of 'Smokey Bears' (the name state troopers were given because their hats resembled that worn by the fabled firefighter). **1976** LIEBERMAN & RHODES *Compl. CB Handbk.* vi. 137 *Smokey the bear*, State Police. **1978** *Weekend* 20–26 Dec. 22 Long distance lorry drivers in Ameria try to avoid smokey bears and tend to drink road tar. Or, in English, avoid state police and drink coffee. **1979** O. McNab *Horror Story* (1980) xviii. 72 That Smoky looking at us? *Ibid.* xix. 79 We've got a Smokey Bear on the side.

**smokie**, obs. var. SMOKY *a.*, *Sc.* var. SMOKY *sb.*

**ˈsmokified**, *ppl. a.* [f. as from *smokify.*] Discoloured or blackened by smoke. Also *transf.*

**1819** *Blackw. Mag.* V. 732 Scrawlings of chalk spread each smokified wall. **1863** B. Savile *Man* ii. 75 Have you heard of the smokified Essays?

**smokily** (ˈsməʊkɪlɪ), *adv.* [f. SMOKY *a.* + -LY².] In a smoky manner; hazily.

**1611** Cotgr., *Fumeusement*, smoakily, fumingly, reekingly. **1755** Johnson, *Smuttily*, blackly; smokily. **1847** Webster, *Smokily*, so as to be full of smoke. **1897** *Westm. Gaz.* 19 May 2/1 Obfuscations that move smokily across the face of truth.

**smokiness** (ˈsməʊkɪnɪs). [f. as prec. + -NESS.] The character or quality of being smoky.

**1587** Golding *De Mornay* xiv. (1592) 222 Our minde..is after a sort troubled..by the smoakiness of the imaginations. **1611** Cotgr., *Fuligine*, soot, sootinesse; smoakinesse. **1656** Blount *Glossogr.*, *Fumidity*, smoakiness. **1727** Bailey (vol. II), *Smokiness*, a being smoky, or infected with Smoke. **1881** *Daily News* 14 Dec. 5/3 The marked characteristic of last night's fog was its smokiness.

**smoking** (ˈsməʊkɪŋ), *vbl. sb.* [f. SMOKE *v.*]

**1.** The action or fact of emitting smoke, giving off steam or vapour, etc.

**1530** Palsgr. 271/2 Smokyng, *fumiere.* **1611** Cotgr., *Fumement*,..a smoaking. **1663** Gerbier *Counsel* 6 To prevent the smoaking of Chimneyes. **1715** *Lond. Gaz.* No. 5392/4 Any smoaking of Chimneys. **1852** Dickens *Bleak Ho.* vi, The smoking and steaming of the heated horses.

**2. a.** The action of inhaling and exhaling smoke from a pipe, cigar, or the like.

**1691** Wood *Ath. Oxon.* II. 709 Given more to bibbing and smoaking than the duty of his Office. **1762** Goldsm. *Beau Nash* 24 Smoaking in the rooms was permitted. **1849** Macaulay *Hist. Eng.* iii. I. 369 Nowhere was the smoking more constant than at Will's.

**b.** *ellipt.* A (railway) smoking-carriage or compartment.

**1889–90** Kipling *Let.* in C. Carrington *Rudyard Kipling* (1955) vi. 140 Went home with him as far as Charing Cross in a 3rd smoking.

**c.** *ellipt.* A smoking-jacket; also (chiefly as a gallicism), a dinner jacket (see DINNER *sb.* 2).

**1922** M. Arlen *Piracy* II. ix. 127 He put on a dress-suit. .. It suited Argentines very well, *le smoking.* But Englishmen were made of sterner stuff. **1934** S. Beckett *More Pricks than Kicks* 77 Cinched beyond reproach in the double-breasted smoking. **1960** R. St. John *Foreign Correspondent* viii. 142, I will make you a 'smoking' of fine English material for twenty thousand lei. **1977** T. Heald *Just Desserts* vii. 171 Guests wore tuxedos if they were American males and black dinner jackets if..European (.. except for the odd Italian in tobacco brown 'smoking').

†**3.** A bantering or quizzing. *Obs.*

**1781** Mme. D'Arblay *Diary* June, What a smoking did Miss Burney give Mr. Crutchley. *Ibid.* Aug., Whether he.. took the opportunity to give us all a smoking.

**4.** The curing of meat, etc., by exposure to smoke.

**1819** in *Pantologia* s.v. **1872** Yeats *Techn. Hist. Comm.* 224 The efficacy of smoking depends on certain chemical products. **1901** Black *Carp. & Build.* vi. 65 The barrel..is covered over at the top, and the smoking proceeds.

**5.** *School slang.* Blushing.

**1862** Farrar *St. Winifred's* iv, Smoking is the name fellows give to blushing.

**6.** *attrib.* **a.** In combs. relating to the curing of provisions by smoke, or the production of smoke for some special purpose, as ***smoking-house***, ***knife***, ***loft***, ***pot***, ***vessel***, ***works***.

**1648** Hexham II, *Een roock-vat*, a Censoir, or smoaking vessell. **1706** Phillips (ed. Kersey), *Thuribulum*, a Censer, or Smoaking-Pot, to burn Incence in. **1736** N. Bailey *Household Dict.* Ll 2 A Smoking Closet for drying Tongues. **1759** R. Brown *Compl. Farmer* 61 Curing bacon..by smoking lofts or closets, adjoining to the funnels of their chimneys. **1791** *Trans. Soc. Arts* IX. 136 The smoking works being erected at the foot, and the tar-funnel higher up the hill. **1805** Lindley *Voy. Brasil* (1808) 260 Flesh..which they salt, and dry in the sun and smoking-houses. **1839** *Mag. Dom. Econ.* IV. 118 The hams..are smoked in smoking-houses. **1883** *Fisheries Exhib. Catal.* 62 New and Improved Smoking Knives for Fishermen.

**b.** In terms denoting things or places used for, or in connexion with, the smoking of tobacco, etc., as ***smoking apparatus***, ***box*** [BOX *sb.*² III], ***-cap***, ***car***, ***-carriage***, ***compartment***, ***-lamp***, ***lounge***, ***-suit***, etc.; **smoking-bean** *U.S.*, the catalpa bean, the pods of which are smoked by boys; **smoking machine**, a device which draws air through a lighted cigarette, etc., so that the smoke may be used for scientific study; **smoking weed**, (*a*) = BEARBERRY a; cf. KINNIKINNIC 2; (*b*) = CANNABIS 1; cf. MARIJUANA, MARIHUANA 2.

**1771** Mackenzie *Man Feeling* xxi, He took from his pocket a particular *smoking apparatus. **1841** Dickens *Old Curiosity Shop* lxxiii. 220 A little cottage at Hampstead.. had in its garden a *smoking-box. **1841** J. Romilly *Diary* 9 Mar. (1967) 211 Dined with Bayne: he..wore an embroidered *smoking cap. **1872** Calverley *Charades* III. ii, Nor work smoking-caps for cousins. **1846** *Amer. Railroad Jrnl.* 380/3 *Smoking Cars—..we mean cars expressly provided for the lovers of the 'weed'. **1931** W. Faulkner *Sanctuary* xix. 202 Horace..went forward into the smoking car. It was full too. **1958** 'E. McBain' *Killer's Payoff* (1960) vi. 59 She boarded the train and went directly to a smoking car. **1862** J. Simmons *Railway Traveller's Handy Book* 83 Some lines have certain *smoking carriages provided. **1871** M. Collins *Marq. & Merch.* III. ii. 67 The..gentlemen were..ensconced in a smoking-carriage. **1891** Peacock *N. Brendon* I. 138 He put on a *smoking coat. **1888** *Amer. Humorist* (London) 5 May 7/1 Came over from New York.. in the *smoking compartment of a parlor car. **1878** H. Smart *Play or Pay* i, Appearing in a radiant *smoking-jacket that matched the cigar-case. **1889** *Cent. Dict.*, **Smoking-lamp*.., a lamp hung up on board of a man-of-war during hours when smoking is permitted, for the men to light their pipes by. **1940** D. Potter *Sailing Sulu Sea* 28 Smoking was prohibited except when the smoking-lamp—a name now almost forgotten—was authorized to be lighted. **1966** J. V. Noel *Naval Terms Dict.* 304 *Smoking-lamp*: If 'lighted', it means that smoking is permitted; if 'out', means smoking prohibited. **1951** E. Paul *Springtime in Paris* iii. 45 He could relax like a tomcat, in an easy chair in the *smoking lounge. **1968** *Globe & Mail* (Toronto) 17 Feb. 6/2 Why should the teachers have a smoking lounge and not the students? **1953** *Life* 21 Dec. 20/1 (*caption*) *Smoking machine puffs on 60 cigarets in front of Dr. Evarts Graham, who, with his collaborator on the mouse cancer research, Dr. Ernest Wynder, perfected the robot. **1963** *Times* 22 Apr. 19/3 A 'smoking machine' is used to demonstrate the amount of chemicals inhaled, including those which cause cancer. **1971** *Nature* 26 Nov. 227/1 Lung explants..were.. exposed in a Filtrona CSM12 smoking machine to puffs of fresh cigarette smoke. **1843** Holtzapffel *Turning* I. 161 Meerschaum, Amber,..are principally used for *smoking-pipes. **1897** *Allbutt's Syst. Med.* II. 885 In competition with the *smoking-shops, there are now shops where injections are to be had at so much the syringeful. **1898** M. Beerbohm *Let.* 12 Jan. (1964) 127, I have a *smoking-suit of purple silk, with dark red facings. **1958** *Listener* 21 Aug. 261/2 Did you know..that women wore smoking suits in the 'twenties? **1884** *Health Exhib. Catal.* 57/2 The *Smoking Temple in the Classic style, with niches and divans in colour. **1796** Morse *Amer. Geogr.* I. 259 Snuff, chewing and *smoaking tobacco. **1880** *U.S. Census, Rep. Culture Tobacco* 15 Other cigar and smoking tobacco. **1857** J. Hector *Jrnl.* 31 Oct. in *Capt. Palliser's Exploration in Brit. N. Amer.* 65 in *Parl. Papers 1863* XXXIX. 441 A gravelly soil supporting a poor growth of grass, but in some parts covered with a dense matting of the *smoking weed.., the bright red berries of which afford food for large coveys of the prairie hens. **1957** C. MacInnes *City of Spades* I. v. 27 I'd seen what plant it was in flower-pots inside there... 'It's smoking weed,' I said.

**c.** In the sense of 'at which smoking takes place or is allowed', as ***smoking-concert***, etc.

**1809** A. Henry *Trav.* 299 In smoking-feasts, or feasts of the pipe, or calumet, held in honour of the spirits. **1886** C. E. Pascoe *London of To-day* vi. (ed. 3) 78 The smoking concert..with its genial Bohemianism. **1895** *Daily News* 4 Feb. 5/3 The annual meeting of the club would be held..as a smoking 'At Home'. **1934** T. S. Eliot *Rock* i. 40 Dance 'alls, picture palaces, swimmin' baths, smokin' concerts, restaurants. **1945** *Daily Mirror* 15 Aug. 7/2 Anyone who could perform well enough for a private party or a smoking concert was roped in. **1971** *Sunday Nation* (Nairobi) 11 Apr. 42/5 The smoking concert will be held on Sunday evening and not on the Saturday as I stated.

**d.** In other senses, as ***smoking-party*** [PARTY *sb.* 8]; **smoking point**, **temperature** = *smoke point* s.v. SMOKE *sb.* 11.

**1898** 'Mark Twain' in *Century Mag.* Nov. 100/1 This smoking-party had been gathered together partly for business. **1923** Kipling *Irish Guards in Great War* I. 206 Leave was possible; smoking-parties made themselves in the big huts. **1915** *Jrnl. Home Econ.* VII. 538 For each case the addition of acid resulted in the lowering of the smoking point. **1931** *Industr. & Engin. Chem.* (Analyt. Ed.) 15 Oct. 348/2 Take the temperature at which the first wisp of smoke is seen rising from the top of the flask as the smoking point. **1915** *Jrnl. Home Econ.* VII. 535 The smoking temperature of a fat may be defined as the temperature at which the fat gives off visible fumes. **1945** *ABC of Cookery* (Ministry of Food) xii. 46 A good frying fat is one that can be heated to a high temperature..before it smokes and burns, that is, it has a high smoking temperature. **1951** Smoking temperature [see *smoke point* s.v. SMOKE *sb.* 11].

**smoking** (ˈsməʊkɪŋ), *ppl. a.* [f. SMOKE *v.*]

**1. a.** Emitting or giving out smoke. Also *fig.*, *spec.* as ***smoking gun***, ***pistol*** (U.S.), a piece of incontrovertible incriminating evidence.

*c* **1374** Chaucer *Boeth.* I. metr. iv. (1868) 12 þe vnstable mountaigne þat hyȝt veseuus, þat wircheþ oute..smokyng fires. **1382** Wyclif *Matt.* xii. 20 He shal nat quenche smokynge flax. *c* **1400** *Pilgr. Sowle* III. vii. (Caxton, 1483) 55 The forneis was al enflammed with smokyng fyre. **1592** Kyd *Sp. Trag.* I. i, Ere Sol had..slakte his smoaking charriot in her floud. **1611** Cotgr., *Fumeau*, a brand, or smoaking sticke. *a* **1700** Evelyn *Diary* 7 Sept. 1666, Clambering over heaps of yet smoking rubbish. **1781** Gibbon *Decl. & F.* xxx. (1787) III. 171 The prospect of the smoking ruins. **1815** Scott *Guy M.* viii, This day have ye quenched seven smoking hearths. **1894** Doyle *S. Holmes* 93 The chaplain stood with a smoking pistol in his hand.

*fig.* **1387** Trevisa *Higden* (Rolls) VII. 331 Lanfrank.. despisede þe smokynge..speche of mysbyleved men. **1587** Greene *Euphues* Wks. (Grosart) VI. 176 Hir heart offred smoaking thoughtes to Venus. **1677** W. Row *Suppl. Life R. Blair* (1848) x. 171 Our smoking desires for a more strict union..did break forth into a vehement flame. **1974** *New Yorker* 21 Oct. 135/1 Some are still searching for what has come to be termed 'the murder weapon'—or 'the smoking gun'—the definitive piece of evidence that the President committed a crime. **1975** *Collier's Year Bk.* 10/2 After the new transcripts were disclosed..members of Congress abandoned Nixon in droves. 'I guess we have found the smoking pistol, haven't we?' asked Representative Barber Conable. **1976** Woodward & Bernstein *Final Days* 269 Buzhardt felt that here was a potential smoking gun. *Ibid.* 271 He had heard the President approve the plan, he had heard him suggest the exact wording. Buzhardt had found the 'smoking pistol'. He had heard the President load it, aim and fire. **1977** *Time* 19 Sept. 24/2 In fact, there may well be no 'smoking gun'—no incontrovertible, black-and-white evidence of wrong-doing by Lance. **1979** *N.Y. Times* 12 Jan. D14 We haven't got a smoking pistol. Unfortunately, everyone is zeroing in on this as a cause, but the case isn't that strong.

**b.** Of a chimney: = SMOKY *a.* 1 b.

**1667** Collins in Rigaud *Corr. Sci. Men* (1841) II. 482, I have been troubled with smoking chimneys. **1693** Evelyn *De la Quint. Compl. Gard.* 77 A House with Smoaking Chimneys. **1728** Chambers *Cycl.* s.v. *Smoak*, There are various Inventions for preventing and curing Smoaking Chimneys.

**2. a.** Giving out steam or vapour, sending up fine dust or spray, etc.

**1593** Shaks. *3 Hen. VI*, II. iii. 21 Their Steeds, That stain'd their Fetlockes in his smoaking blood. **1607** —— *Cor.* I. iv. 11 That we with smoaking swords may march from hence. **1697** Dryden *Virg. Georg.* II. 794 'Tis Time to set at Ease the smoaking Horse. **1716** Pope *Iliad* VII. 382 The victim falls; they strip the smoaking hide. **1784** Cowper *Task* III. 517 The smoaking manure. **1848** Dickens *Dombey* li, They have hot suppers every night,..with smoking drinks upon the board. **1888** Stevenson *Black Arrow* 184 The *Good Hope* continued to tear through the smoking waves.

**b.** quasi-*adv.* in ***smoking-hot***.

**1816** Keatinge *Trav.* (1817) I. 219 The paunch of a goat ..cut out, and applied..smoking hot, to the part. **1842** Lover *Handy Andy* xxi, Where tea and coffee, toast and muffins,..were all smoking-hot together.

**3.** Characterized by, addicted to, the smoking of tobacco. Also *transf.* and *absol.*

**1617** Brathwait (*title*), The Smoaking Age, or The man in the mist: with The life and death of Tobacco. *Ibid.* 174 More guerdon doe I receive of my love from the sleeping Dormouse, than the smoaking Gallants. **1888** G. Trumbull *Birds* 21 [The Widgeon is] known to voyageurs throughout the Fur Countries as Smoking-Duck. [*Note.*] Probably because its note was thought to resemble the puffing sound made while smoking. **1890** *Pall Mall G.* 29 Sept. 3/3 The lazy, the drunken, the smoking, the thriftless.

Hence **ˈsmokingly** *adv.*, smokily.

**1824** Lady Granville *Lett.* (1894) I. 334, I told you she was uncomfortably, smokingly lodged.

**ˈsmoking-room.** [SMOKING *vbl. sb.*] A room in a house, hotel, club, etc., set apart as a place for smoking in.

**1689** Shadwell *Bury Fair* III. i, We'll into my Smoaking-room and sport about a Brimmer. **1754** *Connoisseur* No. 48 ¶3, The Squire gets drunk..in the smoking-room. **1840** Marryat *Poor Jack* xiii, Most of those who prefer smoking collect in..the smoking room. **1890** 'R. Boldrewood' *Col. Reformer* (1891) 147 The same deserted library, the same populous smoking-room.

*attrib.* **1886** *Pall Mall G.* 20 Oct. 4/3 Jotting down short smoking-room stories.

**smokish** (ˈsməʊkɪʃ), *a.* [f. SMOKE *sb.* + -ISH.] Resembling smoke; somewhat smoky.

**1477** Norton *Ordin. Alch.* v. in Ashm. (1652) 69 Odor is a smokish vapour resolved with heate. **1530** Palsgr. 324/2 Smokysshe, *fumeux.* **1630** *R. Johnson's Kingd. & Commw.* 202 Their Water brackish, their Aire foggie and their Fire smokish. **1648** Hexham II, *Roockachtigh*, Smoakish, or Fumie. **1807** W. Irving *Salmag.* (1824) 47 A yellowish, whitish, smokish, dirty-coloured shawl.

Hence **ˈsmokishness.** *rare*⁻⁰.

**1530** Palsgr. 271/2 Smokysshnesse, *fumevseté.*

**smoko**: see SMOKE-HO.

**smoky** (ˈsməʊkɪ), *a.* and *sb.* Also 4, 6–7, 9– (*Sc.*) **smokie**, 7, 9– **smokey** (common in *U.S.*); 6–7 **smoakie**, 6–9 **smoaky**. [f. SMOKE *sb.* + -Y.]

**A.** *adj.* **1. a.** Emitting smoke in considerable volume.

**1310** *St. Brendan* (Bälz) 472 þo seie hi..a lond derk inouȝ Smokie as it smyþes were. *c* **1407** Lydg. *Reson & Sens.* 4122 Than is the fire..Of smoky Ethna the mounteyn. *c* **1440** *Promp. Parv.* 461/1 Smoky, *fumosus.* **1576** Gascoigne *Philomene* Wks. 1910 II. 198 A Swallowe..builds in smoky chimney toppes. **1577** tr. *Bullinger's Decades* (1592) 127 To set up a percher, a taper, or a smoakie torch. **1613** Purchas *Pilgrimage* (1614) 775 They vse smokie fires in their rooms. *c* **1663** Cowley *To Light* xv, In Sympathizing Night he rowls his smoaky Fires. **1726** Gay *Fables* I. xxiii. 11 A wrinkled Hag..Beside a little smoaky flame Sat hov'ring. **1818** Byron *Beppo* xliii, Where reeking London's smoky caldron simmers. **1884** *St. James' Gaz.* 25 July 4/2 Letting off a quantity of the noisiest and smokiest fireworks procurable.

**b.** Of a chimney: Inclined to send out smoke into the room.

**1639** J. Smyth in *Glouc. Gloss.* (1890) 201 If many gossips sit against a smokey chimney the smoke will bend to the fairest. **1785** Franklin (*title*), Observations on Smoky Chimneys. **1844** Emerson *Ess.* II. *Nature*, It..cured the smoky chimney, silenced the creaking door. **1869** E. A. Parkes *Pract. Hygiene* (ed. 3) 141 The down current coming in puffs is one cause of smoky chimneys.

**2.** Of vapour, mist, etc.: Having the character or appearance of smoke; resembling smoke; smoke-like.

*c* **1374** Chaucer *Troylus* III. 628 Every maner womman that was there, Hadde of that smoky reyn a verray fere. **1398** Trevisa *Barth. De P.R.* v. xxxvi. (Bodl. MS.), þe breeste.. putteþ oute smoky vapour þat is ibred in þe hert. **1426** Lydg. *De. Guil. Pilgr.* 11034 Two ful vnkouth skyes..off smoky mystes & vapours. *a* **1542** Wyatt *Ps.* li. 20 There had owt off the sowth A lewk warme wynd browght forth a smoky rayne. **1662** H. Hibbert *Body of Divinity* I. 205 By breathing..the gross and more smoky spirits are exhaled out of the breast. **1743** DAVIDSON *Æneid* VII. 203 The Smoaky Fluid in Foam overflows. **1784** COWPER *Task* v. 105 The light and smoky mist. **1817** J. BRADBURY *Trav. Amer.* 259 The atmosphere..becomes hazy, or what they term smoky. **1853** KANE *Grinnell Exped.* xxix. (1856) 246 The frost-smoke was in smoky banks to the north-west.

**3. a.** Full of, or charged with, smoke; rendered offensive or disagreeable by the presence of smoke.

**1398** TREVISA *Barth. De P.R.* XII. iii. (Bodl. MS.), þerefore here mewes moste be ferre fro smoky places. *c* **1407** LYDG. *Reson & Sens.* 6638 Anoon as he his torche hath queynt, The smoky air..Ran..in lengthe and brede. **1596** SHAKS. *1 Hen. IV*, III. i. 161 O, he is..Worse then a smoakie House. **1608** D. T. *Ess. Pol. & Mor.* 39 To lodge within the inclosure of a smokie roofe. **1700** T. BROWN tr. *Fresny's Amusements* 116 At the Bar..a charming Phillis or two, invite you..into their smoaky Territories. **1749** BERKELEY *Word to the Wise* Wks. III. 440 It takes the peasant from his smoky cabin into the fresh air. **1806** *Med. Jrnl.* XV. 366 Ozanne received them in a smoaky hut. **1869** E. A. PARKES *Pract. Hygiene* (ed. 3) 107 The effect of smoky town atmospheres in producing lung affections. **1891** C. JAMES *Rom. Rigmarole* 18 All through a smoky evening I spent in that inn parlour.

**b.** Blackened or begrimed by smoke.

**1552** ELYOT *Dict.*, *Fumosæ imagines*, olde smoky images. **1588** GREENE *Metamorphosis* Wks. (Grosart) IX. 50 Wilt thou..seeke with the smoky Cyclops to kisse Venus hand? **1634** MILTON *Comus* 324 In lowly sheds With smoky rafters. **1848** DICKENS *Dombey* xxiii, The two trees with the smoky trunks were blighted high up.

**c.** Foggy, misty. Now *rare* exc. in proper names. *U.S.*

**1769** in *Essex Inst. Hist. Coll.* (1877) XIV. 262 This week much smoky. **1824** J. DODDRIDGE *Notes on Virginia* xxxi. 266 The smokey time commenced, and lasted for a considerable number of days. **1825** J. NEAL *Bro. Jonathan* I. 105 See'd him jess now, comin' over the smoky mountain there. **1971** *N.Y. Times Encycl. Almanac 1971* 243/1 In East Tennessee are the Great Smoky and Cumberland Mountains of the Appalachian range.

**4.** *fig.* Having the obscuring, objectionable, or unsubstantial qualities of smoke. *Obs.*

**1533** MORE *Answ. Poysoned Bk.* Wks. 1035/1 The pestilent contagion of al such smoky communicacion. **1581** J. BELL *Haddon's Answ. Osorius* 277 b, Besides vayne crakes of smoky speeches, ye shewe no demonstration of sounde proofe. **1624** SKINNER in Parr *Life Usher* (1686) 358 Other points these devilish Spirits of the Jesuits..by their smoaky Doctrine do resist. **1633** HART *Diet of Diseased* II. xiv. 193 Their smoakie promises not being seconded by answerable events.

**5. a.** Having the flavour or odour of smoke; tasting or smelling of smoke.

**1542** BECON *Potation for Lent* Wks. 1564 I. I. 45 From a smokie pece of Bacon. **1707** FLOYER *Physic. Pulse-Watch* 332 The smoaky Bitters, Cichory, Carduus. **1892** WALSH *Tea* 93 The 'smoky' and 'tarry' flavors possessed by many of them. **1951** E. DAVID *French Country Cooking* 26 The smoky wines of Pouilly-sur-Loire. **1978** *Sunday Times* (Colour Suppl.) 19 Feb. 17/3 *Smoky*, a delicate aroma that is found in several white wines, often originating from the volcanic soil, and also on the bouquet of Madeira as a result of the latter's special *estufado* heat treatment.

**b.** *fig.* Of the sound of a musical instrument or voice.

**1958** G. BOATFIELD in P. Gammond *Decca Bk. Jazz* xxiv. 312 Noone's deceptively easy clarinet and Kelly's smoky trumpet are noteworthy. **1966** *Cavalier Daily* (Univ. of Virginia) 11 Nov. 1 The smooth, smoky sound of the Platters combined with their expressive hand jive will entertain students from 9 to 1 Friday night.

**6. a.** Of the colour of smoke; dark, dusky; *spec.* of a brownish or bluish shade of grey.

**1555** EDEN *Decades* (Arb.) 280 Halfe an houre after the rysynge it appeareth troubeled dymme and smoky. **1598** B. JONSON *Ev. Man in Hum.* I. iii, To conceale such reall ornaments..as a Millaners wife do's her wrought stomacher, with a smokie lawne, or a black cypresse. **1647** HEXHAM I. (Colours), A Smokie colour, *een roock verwe.* **1750** tr. *Leonardus' Mirr. Stones* 38 Blackness is occasion'd by a smoaky and adust terrene. **1796** H. HUNTER tr. *St.-Pierre's Stud. Nat.* (1799) II. 196 The red and smoky colour of their flowers. **1855** BREWSTER *Life Newton* I. vii. 171 A large crystal of quartz of a smoky colour. **1897** *Allbutt's Syst. Med.* IV. 288 If it is present in small quantities only, the urine will be smoky.

**b.** In names of stones, esp. ***smoky quartz***.

**1797** *Encycl. Brit.* (ed. 3) XII. 82/1 Blackish brown, smoky topaz, or *rauch topaz* of the Germans. **1837** DANA *Min.* 340 Smoky quartz is a transparent, or translucent crystalline variety, having a smoky color. **1883** *Encycl. Brit.* XVI. 389 The brown or Smoky Quartz (coloured by a substance containing carbon and nitrogen).

**c.** In names of moths, bats, birds, etc.

**1827** GRIFFITH tr. *Cuvier* V. 63 *Molossus Fumarius* (Smoky Bulldog Bat). **1832** J. RENNIE *Butterfl. & Moths* 87 The Smoky Wainscot. *Ibid.* 142 The Smoky Wave. **1871** *Cassell's Nat. Hist.* I. 320 The Smoky Mastiff Bat is a well-known South American species. **1884** COUES *N. Amer. Birds* 419 *Psilorhinus*, Brown Jays. Smoky Pies.

**7.** Qualifying names of colours.

**1576** FLEMING *Panopl. Epist.* A4 All smokie blacke as Pitch. **1611** COTGR. s.v. *Enfer*, A darke, and smoakie browne. **1629** PARKINSON *Parad.* 182 The three [leaves] that stand upright [are] of a smoakie yellow. **1706** *Lond. Gaz.* No. 4249/4 Lost.., a smoaky gray Horse. **1837** *Penny Cycl.* VII. 26/2 Upper part of the neck smoky red. **1869** [see KENTISH *a.* 3 b]. **1872** COUES *N. Amer. Birds* 194 The belly smoky-gray in some localities. **1934** WEBSTER, *Smoky-blue.* **1934** *Discovery* June 166/2 Plain burnished red ware and smoky grey pottery. **1974** *Men's Wear* 29 Aug. 17/2 Smokey-navy motifs on beige. **1976** H. TRACY *Death in Reserve* xi. 87 A smoky-blue spring evening. **1980** *New Age* (U.S.) Oct. 58 (Advt.), Danish Souperbag..In wilderness rust brown, battleship grey, parrot green, smokey black.

**8.** Steaming, reeking; rising in fine spray.

*c* **1590** MARLOWE *Faustus* 1448 My limbes may issue from your smoaky mouthes. **1594** KYD *Cornelia* v. 323 Fro the wound the smoky blood ran bubling. **1697** DRYDEN *Æneid* v. 185 Lash'd with their Oars, the smoaky Billows rise; Sparkles the briny Main, and the vex'd Ocean fries. **1725** POPE *Odyss.* x. 150 Their oars they seize, And sweep with equal strokes the smoky seas. **1807** J. BARLOW *Columb.* III. 523 [They] then part the smoky flesh, enjoy the feast.

**9.** Addicted to, associated with, the smoking of tobacco.

**1596** NASHE *Saffron Walden* Wks. (Grosart) III. 158 And to approue his Heraldrie, scutchend out the honourable Armes of the smoakie Societie. **1613** PURCHAS *Pilgrimage* (1614) 827 To which opinion, for the excellence of the Tobacco there found, he should happily have the smokie subscriptions of many Humorists. **1806** LAMB in Ainger *Life* (1882) 65 A smoky man must write smoky farces. **1893** *Daily News* 26 Dec. 5/1 The sodden and smokey young men who may be found watching football matches.

†**10.** Quick to suspect or take note; shrewd, sharp, suspicious. *Obs.*

The *Dict. Cant. Crew* (*a* 1700) also gives 'jealous'.

**1688** SHADWELL *Sqr. Alsatia* III. i, They shall find me a smoaky Thief. *Ibid.* IV. iv, I am sharp and smoaky. **1711** STEELE *Spect.* No. 132 ¶3 Thou art, I see, a smoaky old Fellow, and I'll be very orderly the ensuing Part of the Journey. **1765** FOOTE *Commissary* I. (1782) 23 This old brother of ours tho' is smoaky and shrewd, and tho' an odd, a sensible fellow. **1784** R. BAGE *Barham Downs* II. 132 She is what you call a smoky damsel.

**11.** *U.S.* Of horses: Vicious.

**1899** *Scribner's Mag.* XXV. 13/2 Cow-boys often call vicious horses 'smoky' horses.

**12.** *Comb.*, as ***smoky-bearded***, ***-flavoured***, ***-tinted***, ***-voiced***, ***-winged***; ***smoky-looking***, ***-seeming***, ***-tasting***, ***-waving***.

**1598** SYLVESTER *Du Bartas* II. ii. II. *Babylon* 133 Small, smoaky-waving clouds. **1610** B. JONSON *Alchemist* IV. vi, This Doctor, Your sooty, smoakie-bearded compeere. **1611** SPEED *Theat. Gt. Brit.* (1614) 121/1 Certaine thicke and smoky-seeming mists. **1611** COTGR., *Enfumé*,..smoakie-coloured. **1825** T. HOOK *Sayings* Ser. II. *Passion & Princ.* viii. III. 124 The dingy, ill-smelling, smoky-looking coffee-room. **1834** *Tait's Mag.* I. 7/1 The smoky-flavoured Glenlivet toddy. **1862** DANA *Min.* 134 A smoky-tinted quartz crystal. **1925** H. CRANE *Let.* 28 Feb. (1965) 199 Delicious smoky tasting sardines. **1973** J. J. MCKELVEY *Man against Tsetse* ii. 67 He did, however, add entomology to his accomplishments by studying the life cycle of the dark-eyed, smoky-winged tsetse that was causing nagana in Zululand. **1976** *New Yorker* 29 Mar. 6/3 A promising, smoky-voiced jazz and rhythm-and-blues singer.

**B.** *sb.* **1.** *dial.* The hedge-sparrow.

**1889** H. SAUNDERS *Brit. Birds* 85 The Hedge-Sparrow is known by a variety of names, such as..'Smokie', and 'Shuffle-wing'. **1894** in HESLOP *Northumbld. Gloss.*

**2.** *Sc.* A smoked haddock.

**1891** W. GORDON in Edwards *Mod. Sc. Poets* Ser. XIV. 243 Will ye buy ony fish—Bonnie smokies, as cheap as they're clean? **1948** R. DE KERCHOVE *International Maritime Dict.* 690/2 *Scotch haddie* (*U.S.*)... In Great Britain called smokie. **1965** *Arbroath Guide* 3 Apr. 4 The older generation argue that the old time 'smokie' is a haddock freshly caught by line and smoked in the Arbroath way. **1974** *Sunday Tel.* 23 June 15/5 Let us make the distinction between the genuine Arbroath smokie, which gets its colour from the actual smoke when the fish is cured, and the common kipper. **1976** *Daily Record* (Glasgow) 29 Nov., Arbroath's famous 'smokie' industry will be hit by the ban on catching haddock in the North Sea.

**3.** A smoke or smoke-blue cat.

**1898** *Ladies' Field* 6 Aug. 378/2 The two smokies, Cossy and Jetterina.

**4.** See SMOKEY BEAR.

**smolder**, *sb.* and *v.*: see SMOULDER.

**smole** (sməʊl), joc. var. of SMILE *sb.*[1] or *v.* or *smiled* (pa. t. of SMILE *v.*). Now *rare* or *Obs.*

**1858** J. C. THOMSON *Almae Matres* i. 5 Tick, Esquire, rose at our entrance, smole blandly, and mumbled something to the effect that he was glad..to make our acquaintance. **1894** 'MARK TWAIN' in *St. Nicholas* Mar. 400/2 Then he smole a smile that spread around and covered the whole Sahara. **1909** J. R. WARE *Passing Eng.* 227/1 *Smole*.., a grotesque variation of smile. **1937** PARTRIDGE *Dict. Slang* 789/1 (He) smoled a smile (or smole).

†**smolet, -lat.** *Sc. Obs.*[−1] (Meaning uncertain.)

**1508** DUNBAR *Tua mariit wemen* 113 Quhen the smy on me smyrkis, with his smake smolet [*v.r.* smollat].

**smolt** (sməʊlt), *sb.*[1] Orig. *Sc.* and *north.* Forms: α. 6 smolte, 6–7, 9 smolt, 9 smoult. β. 6–7 smowte, 7 smowt, 8–9 smout, 9 smoot. [Of doubtful origin: connexion with SMOLT *a.* is not clear. A later form is *smelt*: see SMELT *sb.*[1] 3.]

**1.** A young salmon in the stage intermediate between the parr and the grilse, when it becomes covered with silvery scales and migrates to the sea for the first time.

α. **1469** *Sc. Acts, Jas. III*, c. 13 (1814) II. 96 All myllaris þat slais Smo[l]tis with crelis or ony vthir maner of way. **1510** *Reg. Magni Sig. Scot.* I. 730 Cum piscationibus, exceptis salmonibus, le keppir, et smolts. *c* **1575** *Balfour's Practicks* (1754) 581 That they tak smoltis or salmond in the miln-dammis. **1609** SKENE *Reg. Maj.* 97 Siclike smolts, sould not be taken..fra the middes of Aprill, to the nativitie of Saint John the Baptist. **1804** A. HUNTER *Georg. Ess.* II. 513 At this period of time they are from four to six inches in length only, being in some places called smoults. **1862** *Act 25 & 26 Vict.* c. 97 §2 'Salmon' shall..include..sea trout, bull trout, smolts, parr, and other migratory fish of the salmon kind. **1881** *Standard* 10 Sept. 2/1 The migratory instinct does not occur till the young fish have become what are called 'smolts'.

*attrib.* **1886** *Encycl. Brit.* XXI. 224 The young salmon, as soon as the smolt stage is reached, migrates down the rivers to the sea.

β. **1533–4** *Act 25 Hen. VIII*, c. 7 The yonge frie, spaume, or broode of any kinde of salmon, called lakspinkes, smowtes, or salmon pele. **1677** JOHNSON in *Ray's Corr.* (1848) 127 In Cumberland, the fishers,..after the first summer, call them free, or frie, as we [in Yorkshire] smowts or smelts, before they come to be lackes. **1769** PENNANT *Brit. Zool.* III. 242 The young [salmon]..gradually increase to the length of four or five inches, and are then termed Smelts or Smouts. **1803** J. WALKER in *Prize Ess. Highland Soc.* II. 351 They are called samlets,..but are generally known among our country people by the name of salmon smouts. **1866** C. W. HATFIELD *Notices Doncaster* I. 99 The young of the salmon..was known only as a smolt or 'smout'.

**b.** *transf.* A small person or thing.

**1808** JAMIESON, *Smolt*, metaph. used to denote a child. **1868** W. SHELLEY *Flowers* 199 Mamma's pet, Smirkin' smout. **1894** HESLOP *Northumbld. Gloss.*, *Smout*.., anything small.

**2.** 'A small trout of the speckled kind' (*Jamieson's Sc. Dict.* 1882 s.v. *Smout*).

†**smolt**, *sb.*[2] *Obs. rare.* Also 5 smolte. [OE. *smolt*, = MLG. and LG. *smolt* (hence MDa., Norw., Icel. *smolt*, Sw. *smult*), MDu. and Du. *smout*, related to MLG. (and LG.) *smalt*, OHG. *smalz* (G. *schmalz*); both stems are ablaut-grades of **smeltan* to melt: see SMELT *v.*] Lard, fat.

In the later quots. perh. after MLG. or MDu.

*a* **1000** in *Anglia* XIII. 404 *Pinguedo*, smolt. *a* **1100** in Napier *O.E. Lex.* 58 þær sculan eac ii fætte swyn up arisan to smolte. **1430** *Maldon Court-Rolls* (Bundle 18, No. 3), 1 barell. de smolte, et dimid. barell. de smolte. **1502** ARNOLDE *Chron.* (1811) 74 Salt smolt, for the barel, iii d.

**smolt** (sməʊlt), *a.* Now only *dial.* Also 6, 9 *dial.* smoult, 6 *Sc.* smowt. [OE. *smolt*, = MDu. *smolt*, *smout* (WFris. *smout* sheltered), Da. *smult*; cf. OS. *smultro* quietly, calmly, MSw. *smultna* (Sw. dial. *smyltna*) to become calm. A commoner form in OE. was *smylte*.]

†**1.** Of weather: Fair, fine, calm. *Obs.*

Halliwell's '*Smoult*, hot; sultry. *Kent.*' is not otherwise certified. In Norfolk dial., *smoultin'* is used to denote the calming down of a stormy sea during the ebb-tide.

*c* **950** *Lindisf. Gosp.* Matt. xvi. 2 [ðe] cueðas, 'smolt bið, read is..heofon'. *c* **1160** *Hatton Gosp.* Matt. xvi. 2 On æfen ȝe cweðeð, 'to-morȝen hit beoð smolt weder'. **1513** DOUGLAS *Æneid* XIII. viii. 30 Makand the hevynnis fayr, cleyr, and scheyne, The weddir smowt, and firmament serene. *a* **1550** *Peblis to Play* vi. in Pinkerton *Sc. Ballads* (1783) II. 4 Mirrie Madinis, think not lang; The wedder is fair and smolt.

†**2.** Pleasant, agreeable, affable. *Obs.*

**13..** *Gaw. & Gr. Knt.* 1763 With smoþe smylyng & smolt þay smeten in-to merþe. **1553** *Respublica* III. iii. 80 (Brandl), *Respub.* This ys Honestee. *People.* A gaye smoult smirking howrecop tis, zo mot I þee!

**3.** Bright, shining; smooth, polished.

**1837** *Wilson's Tales Borders* III. 304/2 He saw their smolt spirits scour awa to heaven like fire flaughts! **1852–** in dial. glossaries (Sussex, Hants.).

**smolt** (sməʊlt), *v.*[1] [f. SMOLT *sb.*[1]] *intr.* Of young salmon: To pass into the smolt stage.

**1855** J. WILSON in *Mem.* (1859) viii. 315 The female parr 'smolt' soon after the completion of the first year.

†**smolt**, *v.*[2] *Obs. rare.* [Of obscure origin.] *intr.* To make off, go, escape, etc.

**13..** *E.E. Allit. P.* B. 461 He hade þe smelle of þe smach & smoltes þeder sone. *Ibid.* 732, I schal forgyue alle þe gylt ..& let hem smolt al unsmyten smoþely atonez.

**smolyaninovite** (smɒljəˈniːnəvaɪt). *Min.* Also smolia-. [ad. Russ. *smolyaninovit* (L. K. Yakhontova 1956, in *Doklady̆ Akad. Nauk SSSR* CIX. 849), f. the name of N. A. *Smolyaninov*: see -ITE[1].] A hydrated arsenate of iron, cobalt, nickel, and other metals found as a yellow oxidation product of cobalt and nickel ores.

**1957** *Chem. Abstr.* LI. 4885 (*heading*) Smolyaninovite, a new mineral. **1977** *Mineral. Mag.* XLI. 388 A specimen purchased by the [British] Museum in 1927..from Schneeberg, Saxony, has been found to carry small amounts of smolyaninovite, constituting a third occurrence of the mineral. **1981** K. FRYE *Encycl. Mineral.* 715/2 *Smolianinovite*, orth.

**smon** (smɒn). *Path.* Also SMON. [Acronym f. the initial letters of *s*ubacute *m*yelo-*o*ptico-*n*europathy.] A disease of the nervous system characterized by recurrent motor, sensory, and visual symptoms, freq. including numbness of the legs.

**1971** *Lancet* 3 Apr. 697/1 The Japanese S.M.O.N. syndrome occurs in patients who have not taken clioquinol or other hydroxyquinolines. **1977** *Arab Times* 31 Oct. 2/3 In June last year, the two firms admitted that the drug quinoform, also called chinoform, had 'a causal relationship' with a disease of the nervous system called smon (subacute myelo-optico-neuropathy), which affects limb movement and can cause blindness. **1979** *Guardian Weekly* 1 Apr. 15/4 Smon (subacute myelo-optico-neuropathy) outbreaks in several communities [in Japan] occurred as early as the 1950s. **1982** *Lancet* 25 Sept. 716/2 They stated that rise and fall in SMON was synchronous with consumption of clioquinol... This is a continuing controversy.

**smooch** (smu:tʃ), *sb.*[1] *U.S.* [Cf. SMOUCH *sb.*[4] and SMUTCH *sb.*] A smutch or smear.

**1825** J. NEAL *Bro. Jonathan* II. 46 Cowhide shoes—newly greased..which left a 'smooch' upon whatever they came near. **1842** MOTLEY *Lett.* (1889) I. 136 The body of the Child is a mere smooch of lamp-black. **1869** MRS. WHITNEY *We Girls* iii. (1873) 58 A smooch of stove-polish across her arm.

**smooch** (smu:tʃ), *sb.*[2] orig. and chiefly *U.S.* [f. SMOOCH *v.*[3] or var. SMOUCH *sb.*[1]] A kiss; a fondling embrace or caress, a cuddle. Also, slow, close dancing; (music suitable for) a dance of this nature. Freq. *attrib.*

**1942** BERREY & VAN DEN BARK *Amer. Thes. Slang* §847/4 *Smooch*, a kiss. *Ibid.* §830/5 *Smoochbuggy*,..an automobile used for 'necking'. **1945** *Tacoma* (Washington) *News Tribune* 27 Oct. 3/3 I'd rather have hootch And a bit of a smooch—The air corps will always do me. **1957** *Time* 2 Sept. 28/3 Ethel Merman and Fernando Lamas..found that their nightly onstage smooch grated too harshly on their star-crossed sensibilities. **1971** *New Scientist* 24 June 730/1 Two Antipodean couples joined their lips in a long-term kiss aimed at beating the standing smooch record. **1973** J. WAINWRIGHT *Pride of Pigs* 43 The smooch classics—*Mood Indigo, Lazy River, Georgia On My Mind*—slow and draggy. **1977** *Record Mirror* 16 Apr. 27/5 Perfect even-tempoed bland MOR until it slows up for a smooch.

**smooch** (smu:tʃ), *v.*[1] Latterly *U.S.* [Cf. SMOOCH *sb.*[1] and SMUTCH *v.*] *trans.* To sully, dirty. Hence **smooched** *ppl. a.*

**1631** HEYWOOD *Fair Maid of West* I. v. i, Must your black face be smooching my Mistresses white lips with a moorian? **1828** WEBSTER s.v. *Smutch*, In New England..*smooch*.. signifies to foul or blacken with something produced by combustion or other like substance. **1835** WILLIS *Pencillings* I. xix. 137 Attracting the attention and courtesies of every smooched petticoat far and near.

**smooch** (smu:tʃ), *v.*[2] *dial.* and *colloq.* [App. an altered form of MOOCH, MOUCH *v.*] **1.** *intr.* To sneak, creep; to wander or prowl *round* (somewhere).

**1904** in *Eng. Dial. Dict.* **1950** R. MOORE *Candlemas Bay* 223 Then he realized his mother would probably send him back for the dish, so he smooched glumly in to retrieve it. **1960** I. JEFFERIES *Dignity & Purity* v. 76 'What are your plans?' 'I'm going to smooch round here, if that's all right.'

**2.** *trans.* To steal.

**1941** J. M. CAIN *Mildred Pierce* xi. 229 Then she..went over to the cash box, and smooched four $10 bills.

**smooch** (smu:tʃ), *v.*[3] orig. *U.S.* [Var. SMOUCH *v.*[1]] *intr.* To kiss; to neck or pet; *spec.* while dancing to a lazy, romantic melody.

**1932** *Amer. Speech* VII. 336 *Smooch*,..to kiss. **1937** *Sat. Even. Post* 20 Feb. 89/2 Once upon a time you 'spooned',.. but now you may 'smooch' or 'perch'. **1952** R. V. WILLIAMS *Hard Way* ii. 19 Maybe she smooched with them. Maybe she didn't. **1959** *Encounter* May 22/1 She would find her mother smooching away with some man. **1964** L. NKOSI *Rhythm of Violence* 41 Mary and Gama are sharing a studio couch on which they are smooching quietly. **1972** 'M. YORKE' *Silent Witness* ii. 39 'I prefer to smooch to subtle melodies,' said Patrick, clasping her closely.

Hence **'smooching** *vbl. sb.* and *ppl. a.*

**1941** J. SMILEY *Hash House Lingo* 51 *Smooching*, employee making love to one of the opposite sex while on duty. **1951** S. J. PERELMAN in *New Yorker* 20 Oct. 29/2 No parenthetical smooching is going to upset her apple-cart. **1962** *John o' London's* 16 Aug. 163/3 When Miss Baxter pokes her head through the window of a smooching couple's car..it's merely funny. **1977** *Time* 8 Aug. 29/2 Stapleton, 46, danced a bit and inspired some affectionate smooching from the guest of honor. **1978** H. JOBSON *To die a Little* iii. 52 We danced on..in a cluster of smooching bodies.

**smoocher** ('smu:tʃə(r)). orig. *U.S.* [f. SMOOCH *v.*[3] + -ER[1].] **a.** One who smooches. **b.** A song or piece of music suitable for accompanying slow, close dancing.

**1946** *Sun* (Baltimore) 18 May 2/6 Seeking out 'necking spots' to catch 'smoochers'. **1976** *Record Mirror* 3 Apr. 19/5 Ella's dreamy reading of the 'How strange the change from major to minor' tune is of course an ace smoocher at any time.

**smoochy** ('smu:tʃɪ), *a.* [f. SMOOCH *v.*[3] or *sb.*[2] + -Y[1].] Amorous, sexy; *spec.* of music: suitable for accompanying slow, close dancing.

**1966** A. E. LINDOP *I start Counting* xvi. 190 Cooings and mewings and smoochy murmurings. **1971** *Woman's Own* 27 Mar. 26/2 He led me to the dance floor... The next smoochy number was played. **1976** G. SIMS *End of Web* xvii. 120 Dated, smoochy music was being played. **1980** I. WATSON *Gardens of Delights* xvii. 111 Partnering the wench in a body-rubbing, smoochy glide.

Hence **'smoochily** *adv.*, **'smoochiness**.

**1976** 'D. HALLIDAY' *Dolly & Nanny Bird* xi. 138 Three or four couples were dancing smoochily at the end of the room. **1977** E. W. HILDICK *Loop* xi. 69 I'm still not sure whether today's callous outspokenness isn't preferable to..sly smoochiness.

**smoodge, smooge** (smu:dʒ), *v.* *Austral.* and *N.Z. colloq.* [Prob. var. SMUDGE *v.*[5]: see *Smudge* v.[1] in *Eng. Dial. Dict.*] *intr.* To act in an ingratiating or fawning manner; to display affection, to behave amorously.

**1906** E. DYSON *Fact'ry 'Ands* v. 54 He would smooge to me when the boss wasn't about, 'n' he said we could run a grand little show on our lonesome. **1916** C. J. DENNIS *Songs Sentimental Bloke* 39 An' there they smooge a treat, wiv pretty words Like two love-birds. **1936** M. FRANKLIN *All that Swagger* xlii. 395 They smoodge around Roger, but they order me about like a rouseabout. **1957** P. WHITE *Voss* v. 110 That is just what ladies do not take to, some big stray tom smoodgin' round their skirts. Ladies like to fall in love. **1969** *Landfall* XXIII. 27 We'd better go in now or he'll thing we're smooging with each other out here. **1973** P. WHITE *Eye of Storm* x. 480 She came smoodging up at her father, and he..kissed her.

So **'smoodger**, a flatterer, a sycophant; **'smoodging** *ppl. a.* and *vbl. sb.*

**1898** *Bulletin* (Sydney) 30 July 32/3 Another undesirable specimen is the 'crawler'. Always carrying yarns to the boss about the other men... He is first cousin to the 'smooger', who is only superficially a white man. **1899** *Ibid.* 7 Jan. 15/1 Lawson..*feels* for the wretch who is out battling, and is kept out by servile, 'smoodging' station lifers. **1916** T. SKEYHILL *Soldier Songs from Anzac* 59 E's a sneakin', smoogin' blighter, An' 'e'll never make a fighter. **1940** F. D. DAVISON *Woman at Mill* 218 He was a mean customer,..a petty bureaucrat, and a smooger, to boot. **1953** D. M. DAVIN in *Landfall* VII. 20 He would be putting his arms around her. 'Smooging won't get you out of it,' she said. **1958** R. STOW *To Islands* i. 19 'Sister,' she sighed lovingly, hiding her face against Helen's neck. 'You old smoodger,' Helen said. **1963** B. PEARSON *Coal Flat* xvii. 304 You do your smooging somewhere else.

**smook** (smuk), *sb.* *Sc.* and *north.* Now *rare.* Also 6 **smooke**; *Sc.* **smowk, smuke, smuik(e, smeuk, smewk.** [prob. ad. older Flem. *smuik* (Kilian *smuyck*): cf. next.] Smoke, reek, vapour.

α. **1500–20** DUNBAR *Poems* xxvi. 120 He smorit thame with smvke [*v.r.* a smuik]. **1549** *Compl. Scot.* vi. 42 The reik, smeuk, and the stink of the gun puldir. **1599** ALEX. HUME *Hymns* v. 8 The altar..is sprinkled be the Iew, He makis a smuike.

β. *a* **1548** HALL *Chron., Hen. VIII*, 41 b, Of the fyer and smolder did ryse suche a smooke. **1570** LEVINS *Manip.* 159/31 Yᵉ Smooke, *fumus.* **1600** FAIRFAX *Tasso* I. xxii, Of glorie vaine to gaine an idle smooke [*rimes* forsook, betooke].

**smook** (smuk), *v.* *Sc.* and *north.* Forms: 6 **smooke,** 9 **smook;** 6 **smowk, smewk** (8 **smuke**), 9 **smuik.** [prob. ad. Flem. *smuiken, smuken* (Kilian *smuycken*, earlier *smuucken*), obscurely related to SMOKE *v.*] *intr.* and *trans.* To smoke, in various senses. Hence **'smooking,** *vbl. sb.* and *ppl. a.*

**1500–20** DUNBAR *Poems* xxxiii. 56 On him come nowthir stole nor fannoun, For smowking of the smydy. *c* **1520** NISBET *N.T., Matt.* xii. 20 He sal..nocht slokin a smewkand brand. **1570** LEVINS *Manip.* 159/34 To Smooke, *fumare.* **1802** R. ANDERSON *Cumbld. Ball.* (*c* 1850) 49 Auld Marget in the fauld she sits, And spins, and sings, and smuiks by fits. **1825** JAMIESON *Suppl., To Smook, Smuik*, to suffocate by means of sulphur; a term applied to the barbarous mode of destroying bees in order to gain their honey.

**smoor** (smur), *sb.* *Sc.* [f. next.] A stifling or suffocating atmosphere, smoke, etc.; smother.

**1894** CROCKETT *Raiders* xiii. 124 Our cave..was full of the white smoor of gunpowder smoke. **1895** —— *Men of Mosshags* 106 In the smoor of the snow.

**smoor** (smur), *v.* *Sc.* and *north. dial.* Forms: 6, 9 **smure,** 6 **smuyr, smuir(e;** 6–7 **smoore,** 6–9 **smoor,** etc. [perh. ad. MDu. or MLG. *smōren* (Du. *smoren*, LG. *smoren, smören*; G. *schmoren*, G. dial. *schmoeren, schmuren*), = OE. *smorian* SMORE *v.* The vowel is not a normal native variant of the *o* of *smorian.*] To smother, in various senses.

**1.** *intr.* To undergo smothering (*lit.* or *fig.*).

*c* **1470** *Gol. & Gaw.* 1204 It war syn, but recure, The knightis honour suld smure, That did me this honoure. **1550** LYNDESAY *Sqr. Meldrum* 45 That his hie honour suld not smure, Considering quhat he did indure. **1791** BURNS *Tam O'Shanter* 90 By this time he was cross the ford, Whare, in the snaw, the chapman smoor'd.

**2.** *trans.* **a.** *fig.* or *transf.* To conceal or hide; to suppress; to deaden, stupefy, etc.

**1513** DOUGLAS *Æneid* XI. Prol. 48 He..nevyr dar vndertak a douchty deyd, Bot doith all curage and all manheid smuyr. **1567** *Satir. Poems Reform.* iv. 188 Hurt not ȝour honouris, the samin to smuire. **1636** *Montgomerie's Cherrie & Slae* (Wreittoun) 261 But ay the more I shoope to smoor'de The bolder it brake out. **1718** RAMSAY *Christ's Kirk Gr.* III. xxiii, They drank, 'Till a' their sense was smoor'd. **1792** BURNS *Duncan Gray cam' here to woo* v, Swelling pity smoored his wrath. **1833** M. SCOTT *Tom Cringle* xii, Ye maun smoor my first born puir conscience atween ye.

**b.** To smother, stifle, suffocate; *esp.* to deprive of life by suffocation.

**1535** COVERDALE *1 Kings* iii. 19 This womans sonne died in the nighte (for she smoored him in the slepe). **1612** WEBSTER *White Devil* v. iv, Ile smoore some of them. **1656** in W. ROSS *Pastoral Wk. in Covenanting Times* (1887) 73 James Tailzor laitlie haid all his horses smoored. **1725** RAMSAY *Gentle Sheph.* I. i, Nine braw nowt were smoor'd. **1787** BURNS *Brigs of Ayr* 33 The bees..Are doom'd by Man, ..The death o' devils, smoor'd wi' brimstone reek. *a* **1800–** in many northern dial. glossaries. **1832** R. SURTEES in G. Taylor *Mem.* (Surtees) 282 Nic. Ward was smoor'd in his father's own draw well. **1881** *Blackw. Mag.* Apr. 530 The sheep had been smoored by scores in the drifts.

**c.** To put out or extinguish (a light or fire). Also in fig. context.

**1721** RAMSAY *Lucky Spence* xv, The quacks wha that fire smoors, And puts nae out. **1808** JAMIESON s.v. *Smore, Smure the candle*, put it out. **1903** *Q. Rev.* July 25 When kindling or 'smooring' a fire.

**smoot,** *sb.*[1] *north. dial.* Forms: 7 **smought, smoute,** 9 **smout,** 8–9 **smoot,** etc. [Of Scand. origin: cf. ON. *smátta*, Norw. dial. *smotta, smott*, Sw. dial. *smott, smutt*, Da. *smutte* narrow passage, hole, etc.] A hole or opening at the foot of a wall, the bottom of a fence or hedge, etc., esp. one allowing the passage of hares, rabbits, or sheep; a narrow passage or entrance in a beehive. (Cf. SMOOT-HOLE.)

**1615** in *Trans. Cumb. & Westm. Archaeol. Soc.* (1906) III. 154 Thomas Langhorne shall make his Smoughts three quarters high and three quarters broad to receive the water which cometh down by the Righouse. **1641** BEST *Farm. Bks.* (Surtees) 62 Then are yow to sette downe the hive on the sieve, leavinge an open smoute for them to goe in just towards the South, and to cover the backside of the hive.. on all sides but onely wheare you make the smoute. **1788** W. H. MARSHALL *Yorksh.* II. 353 *Smoot*, a hare muce; or any small gap or hole in the bottom of a hedge. **1869–** in north. dial. glossaries (in forms *smeut, smeyut, smut(e*, etc.). **1891** J. C. ATKINSON *Moorland Parish* 84 The hare had run through the smout into Nanny's garth. **1893** J. WATSON *Conf. Poacher* 58 I scanned the smoots and gates through which she [a hare] passed.

**smoot,** *sb.*[2] *Printing slang.* In 9 **smout.** [f. SMOOT *v.*[2]] (See quot.)

**1888** JACOBI *Printers' Vocab.* 127 *Smout*, a compositor who seeks odd jobs in various houses.

**smoot** (smu:t), *v.*[1] *north. dial.* [f. SMOOT *sb.*[1] Cf. Da. *smutte* to creep, slink.] *intr.* (See quots.)

**1788** W. H. MARSHALL *Yorksh.* II. 353 To *Smoot*, to creep under or through, as a hare or sheep through a hedge. **1855** [ROBINSON] *Whitby Gloss.* s.v. *Smooting*, A young man is said to smoot after a girl when he dares not appear openly in the courtship.

**smoot** (smu:t), *v.*[2] *Printing slang.* Also **smout.** [Of obscure origin.] *intr.* To do casual work in a printing-house where one is not regularly employed (see quots.). †Also const. *on* (a firm). So **'smooting** *vbl. sb.*

**1683** MOXON *Printing* 360 If a Journey-man Smout more or less on another Printing House. *Ibid.* 390 Workmen when ..out of constant Work, do sometimes accept of a Day or twos Work..at another Printing-house: this By-work they call Smouting. [Hence in Holme and Luckombe.] **1757** FRANKLIN in Lockwood *Amer. Dict. Printing* (1894) 513 If a fat old fellow should come to your printing-house and request a little smouting. **1865** C. KNIGHT *Shadows Old Booksellers* 82 Gent..got no regular employment, but laboured here and there without settlement, upon what was called 'smouting work'. **1892** SOUTHWARD & POWELL *Pract. Printing* (ed. 4) 569 *'Smooting.'*—No member of the [Typographical] Association is permitted to work for any other employer than the one by whom he is engaged.., except in case of accident... Transgression of this rule is called 'smooting'.

**smoot,** obs. form of SMUT *sb.* and *v.*

**smooth** (smu:ð), *sb.* Also 5–6 **smothe.** [f. the adj.]

**1.** †**a.** A level space, = SMEETH *sb.* *Obs.*

*c* **1440** *Promp. Parv.* 460/2 Smethe, or smothe,..*planicies.*

**b.** *U.S.* A meadow; a grass field.

**1845** S. JUDD *Margaret* I. ii, Get some plantain and dandelion on the smooth for greens. **1848** BARTLETT *Dict. Amer.* 314.

**c.** *Naut.* A stretch of comparatively smooth or calm water in a rough sea.

**1840** MARRYAT *Poor Jack* xlii, You will find that two waves will run into one another, and..neutralize each other, so that for a few seconds you have what they call a smooth. **1867** SMYTH *Sailor's Word-bk.*, *Smooth*, a Cornish term applied when the surf abates its fury for a short space. Also, the lee of a ship or of a rock. **1878** D. KEMP *Yacht & Boat Sailing* 245 If there is much sea, a 'smooth' should be watched for, to tack in.

**d.** *Coal-mining.* (See quots.)

**1883** GRESLEY *Gloss. Coal-m.* 228 *Smooth*, the line of face of a stall. *Ibid.*, *Smooths*, planes of cleavage more or less vertical.

**2.** The smooth part or surface *of* something; smoothness.

**1551** BIBLE *Gen.* xxvii. 16 She put yᵉ skynnes vpon his handes, & vpon the smothe of hys necke. **1805** *Spirit Public Jrnls.* IX. 339 Like the silver-wing'd dove was the smooth of her hair. **1880** BROWNING *Dram. Idyls* Ser. II. *Pan & Luna* 13 See how the sluggish jelly..Turns marble to the touch of who would loose The solid smooth.

**b.** Smooth water or ground.

**1667** MILTON *P.L.* VII. 409 On smooth the Seale And bended Dolphins play. **1799, 1821** [see ROUGH *sb.*[1] 2].

**c.** The agreeable or pleasant part, side, or aspect of anything. Used in contrast to *rough.*

**1612–** [see ROUGH *sb.*[1] 6 b].

†**3.** A polite or veiled rebuke or retort. *Obs.*[−1]

**1586** A. DAY *Eng. Secretary* II. (1595) 80 Asteismus, a smooth, as we call it, as when one tels a thing repugnant to the present matter or company, to say, 'I had as lieue he told me it snew'.

**4.** An act of smoothing.

**1848** THACKERAY *Van. Fair* lxv, She..gave one smooth to her hair, and finally let in her visitor.

**5.** An implement for smoothing or reducing the roughness of a surface; a smoother; a smooth file.

**1879** *Cassell's Techn. Educ.* IV. 414/1 When cooled, the roughnesses were taken off with a 'smooth' or scraper, and it was ready to receive the silver. **1881** GREENER *The Gun* 245 The bents are then cut in the tumbler with a small saw, and finished with files and smoothes. **1895** *Model Steam Eng.* 92 'Smooth,' Dead Smooths, the finest of all, complete the various forms of files.

**6. a.** A species of moth (see quot. 1832). **b.** A smooth-coated dog.

**1832** J. Rennie *Butterfl. & Moths* 110 The Smooth (*Cleora teneraria*, Stephens) appears the end of June or beginning of July. **1897** *Westm. Gaz.* 11 May 4/3 He owns a brace of smooths named Dame Fortune and Dona Fortuna.

**smooth** (smuːð), *a.* Forms: 1 **smoð**, 4 **smoþe**, 4–6 **smothe**, 5 **smoth**; 4 **smuth**, 5 **smvythe**; 5 **smowth**, 6 **smooth(e**, 7 **smoath(e**; 6–7 **smoothe**, 6– **smooth**. [OE. *smóð*, found only once (the usual form being *sméðe* SMEETH *a.*), and not clearly represented in any of the cognate languages.]

**1. a.** Having a surface free from projections, irregularities, or inequalities; presenting no roughness or unevenness to the touch or sight.

In the first example the sense is 'unruffled, serene'.

*a* **1050** *Liber Scintill.* i. (1889) 6 Se þe mid soðre lufe full ys mid smyltum mode..& mid smoþestum andwlitum forðstæpþ. **13..** *E.E. Allit. P.* A. 6 So smal, so smoþe her sydez were. ?*a* **1366** Chaucer *Rom. Rose* 542 Hir fleshe tendre as is a chike With bent browis, smothe and slyke. *c* **1440** *Promp. Parv.* 461/1 Smothe, pleyne, *planus. Ibid.*, Smothe, or softe, *lenis. a* **1470** H. Parker *Dives & P.* x. vi. (W. de W. 1496) 379/2 The basynet..is..made slyke and smothe that shot may soone glyde of. **1530** Palsgr. 324/2 Smothe as a borde is that is wel planed, *hony.* **1592** Shaks. *Ven. & Ad.* 143 My smooth moist hand..Would in thy palm dissolve. **1615** G. Sandys *Trav.* 67 Women of elegant beauties, for the most part..cleare, and smooth as the polished ivory. **1682** K. Digby *Chym. Secr.* ii. 171 Cast this Matter upon a smooth stone. **1763** Goldsm. *Misc. Wks.* (1837) II. 493 These inequalities serve the better to grind.. their food, but they grow smoother with age. **1779** *Mirror* No. 11, We are not..to wonder if the smooth enamel of the gentleman has received some little injury from the collision of such coarse materials. **1835** J. Duncan *Beetles* (Nat. Lib.) 148 It is..of a black colour, rather smooth and glossy. **1847** Tennyson *Princ.* v. 70 Brows as pale and smooth As those that mourn..In deathless marble. **1871** R. Ellis *Catullus* lxiv. 48 Smooth ivory glossy from Indies.

*absol.* **1495** *Trevisa's Barth. De P.R.* iii. xxi. (W. de W.) 67 For the vertue of groping the soule knowith..nesshe and hard, smothe and rough.

**b.** Specialized uses in the sciences. (*a*) *Anat.* Applied to those muscles of vertebrates that are neither skeletal (sense b) nor cardiac, such as those forming the gut wall, being capable of sustained but not rapid contraction and generally not under voluntary control; also to the non-striated muscle of invertebrates.

**1860** Busk & Huxley tr. *Kölliker's Man. Human Microsc. Anat.* I. xxxiv. 112 In the *areola* of the nipple, the smooth muscles, which are especially well developed in the female, are disposed circularly in a delicate layer. **1866** [see striated *ppl. a.* 1 d]. **1927** Haldane & Huxley *Animal Biol.* ii. 117 The nervous system controls striped muscle, heart muscle, smooth muscle, and glands. **1959** W. Andrew *Textbk. Compar. Histol.* viii. 335 Alternating with these elastic tissue laminae are the masses of smooth muscle fibers with some collagenous fibers. **1962** *Lancet* 8 Dec. 1192/2 There was swelling of the vessel walls with separation of the smooth-muscle fibres. **1971** N. Garamvölgyi in K. Laki *Contractile Proteins & Muscle* 83 There is a wide variety in the different smooth muscles of invertebrate and vertebrate species. **1982** *Sci. Amer.* June 48/2 It is not known how calcium causes contraction in smooth muscle (most involuntary muscle).

(*b*) *Bacteriol.* Applied to a bacterial phenotype characterized by smooth-looking colonies of regular outline, and by cells having polysaccharide capsules.

[**1920**: see S 4 a.] **1921** [see rough *a.* 1 e]. **1947** *Ann. Rev. Microbiol.* I. 20 The sharply distinct antigenic pattern observed in the smooth colony of encapsulated organisms is not preserved in the rough colony of unencapsulated variants. **1973** Klainer & Geis *Agents of Bacterial Dis.* i. 23 Smooth (S) colonies are convex, round, and slimy and are usually regarded as the 'normal' form.

(*c*) Of a graph, function, or distribution: having no breaks, discontinuities or irregularities.

**1929** *Jrnl. du Conseil* IV. 211 The result was a smooth unimodal curve but very skew. **1933** *Econometrica* I. 242 If the values of a variable extend over a wide range, there will be little likelihood that the distribution will be smooth and unimodal. **1946** M. G. Kendall *Adv. Theory Statistics* II. xxix. 386 The conception of a trend as a 'smooth' or 'regular' movement is equivalent to the supposition that the trend can be represented, at least locally, by a smooth mathematical function. **1959** *Listener* 2 July 14/1 The light-curve is not entirely smooth, as the increase to maximum is steeper than the subsequent drop. **1962** A. Nisbett *Technique Sound Studio* iv. 82 Microphones with a smooth response in the upper middle frequency range have come into general use. **1966** *Rep. Comm. Inquiry Univ. Oxf.* II. 400 Scales A and B bring the total college and university stipend to the same level as far as possible with a smooth college scale.

**c.** In tennis, squash, etc., of one of the two sides of the racket (see quot. 1901): used as a call when the racket is spun to decide the right to serve first or to choose ends. Opp. rough *a.* 1 d.

**1890** J. Marshall in *Tennis, Rackets, Fives* 26 *Smooth*, the front of the racket, which shows no knots. *Spin*, the decision by a racket, thrown spinning up into the air by one player, while the other calls 'rough' or 'smooth'. **1901** *Encycl. Sport* II. 621/2 *Smooth side or racket*, the side from which the twisted gut does not project. **1911** [see rough *a.* 1 d]. **1961** *Times* 4 July 11/4 The vicar's niece, whose professed ignorance of the game [*sc.* lawn tennis] was emphasized by a call of 'heads' when she should have called 'smooth'. **1973** M. Russell *Double Hit* xxv. 186 Nevil spun his racket. 'Smooth,' said Colleano. 'Rough. I'll serve.'

**2. a.** Free from hairs or bristles.

*c* **1386** Chaucer *Prol.* 690 No berd hadde he,..As smothe it was as it were late shaue. **1535** Coverdale *Gen.* xxvii. 11 Beholde, my brother Esau is rough, and I am smooth. **1565** Cooper *Thesaurus*, *Glaber*, smooth without heare. **1774** Goldsm. *Nat. Hist.* (1776) V. 6 On their under side they are thin and smooth, but their upper outer edge is parted into two hairy edges. **1783** *Phil. Trans.* LXXIII. 221 The caterpillar..is of a jetty black, smooth as to a privation of hair, but covered with innumerable wrinkles.

**b.** *Bot.* Of leaves, etc.: 'Free from asperities or hairs, or any sort of unevenness' (Lindley).

**1688** Holme *Armoury* ii. 88/2 Bacchar hath a long smooth leaf. **1776** Lee *Introd. Bot.* 379 *Lævis*, smooth, free from Protuberances or Inequalities. **1796** Withering *Brit. Pl.* (ed. 3) II. 356 Leaves flat and smooth. **1834** *Penny Cycl.* II. 11/2 A perennial plant..having one or two smooth..leaves. **1861** Bentley *Man. Bot.* 593 The Gentian Order... Usually smooth herbs.

**3. a.** Of ground, ways, etc.: Not rugged, rough, or broken; free from obstructions; easy to traverse. Also in fig. contexts.

*c* **1391** Chaucer *Astrol.* ii. §29 Lat thyn Astrelabie kowch adown euene vpon a smothe grond. *c* **1449** Pecock *Repr.* v. viii. 525 Whanne the sitter knowith weel the same ambuler be..redi into stumbling, thouȝ the wey be smothe and euen. **1526** Tindale *Luke* iii. 5 The rought wayes shalbe made smoth. **1644** Milton *Educ.* Wks. 1851 IV. 383 The right path of a vertuous..Education; laborious indeed at the first ascent, but else so smooth,..so full of goodly prospect. **1681** Dryden *Abs. & Achit.* 256 Our Fortune rolls as from a smooth Descent. **1770** Langhorne *Plutarch* (1851) II. 598 The traitor led him by a way that was smooth and easy at first. **1847** James *Woodman* iii, The road was..sandy enough, in all conscience, and not so smooth as it might have been. **1875** Jowett *Plato* (ed. 2) V. 291 Hesiod..says that the road to wickedness is smooth and very short.

†**b.** *to make smooth work of*, to level with the ground, to demolish. *Obs.*[−1]

**1616** J. Lane *Contn. Sqr.'s T.* viii. 433 Biddes battries all, and musketes wholie shoote, and make smoothe worke of th' seaun mountes and the towne.

**4. a.** Of water, the sea, etc.: Not broken or turbulent; free from big waves or roughness; running or flowing evenly, calmly, or gently.

*smooth chance* or *spell*, a stretch of calm water in a rough sea.

*c* **1374** Chaucer *Boeth.* i. metr. ii. (1868) 8 þe causes whennes þe soundyng wyndes moeuen..þe smoþe water of þe see. **14..** Lydgate *Churl & Bird* xxvii, Smothe waters been ofte tyme depe. **1606** Shaks. *Tr. & Cr.* i. iii. 34 The Sea being smooth, How many shallow bauble Boates dare saile Vpon her patient brest! **1667** Milton *P.L.* i. 450 While smooth Adonis from his native Rock Ran purple to the Sea. **1743** Bulkeley & Cummins *Voy. S. Seas* 106 It being smooth Water, she work'd very well. **1754** Gray *Poesy* 8 Now the rich stream of music winds along Deep, majestic, smooth, and strong. **1817** Shelley *Rev. Islam* xii. xix, A river deep, which flies with smooth but arrowy speed. **1840** R. H. Dana *Bef. Mast* v, Seeing what he thought was a 'smooth spell', [he] started to go forward. *Ibid.* xxv, Watching for a 'smooth chance'. **1877** L. Morris *Epic of Hades* ii. 101 Summer sea, Which gently heaved, and surged, and kissed the ledge With smooth warm tides.

**b.** Of a passage, voyage, etc.: Accompanied by or performed in good weather.

Common in recent colloq. use.

**5.** Of wind or weather: Not rough or stormy; agreeable, pleasant. Now *rare.*

*c* **1402** Lydg. *Compl. Bl. Knt.* 57 The eyre attempre, and the smothe wind Of Zepherus, among the blossomes whyte. *c* **1430** —— *Minor Poems* (Percy Soc.) 3 The ayre attempered, the wyndes smowth and playne. **1610** Fletcher *Faithf. Sheph.* i. i, Air..as fresh and sweet, As where smooth Zephyrus plays on the fleet Face of the curled Streams. **1700** S. L. tr. *Fryke's Voy. E. Ind.* 260 We had a smooth Gale of Wind at West.

**6. a.** Of liquids, etc.: Having a uniform or even consistency; free from lumps or knots. †Also of light: Uniform, equable.

*c* **1450** *Two Cookery-bks.* 77 Take vinegre and wyne, & stepe þe brede therein, and drawe hit thorgh a streynour.. til hit be smoth. **1655** Stanley *Hist. Philos.* (1687) 189/2 The fiery light, which being smooth and in some manner thick, they conceived of kin to diurnal light. **1747–96** Mrs. Glasse *Cookery* xiv. 211 Pour it between two vessels, out of one into another, till it is quite smooth. **1846** Soyer *Cookery* 588 Stir in the curdled sauce by degrees until the whole has become very smooth. **1872** Harland *Common Sense in Househ.* 183 Put the flour and salt in a bowl, and add a little at a time of the water or milk, working it very smooth as you go on.

**b.** Of liquor: Soft or pleasing to the taste; free from sharpness or acidity.

**1743** Francis tr. *Hor., Odes* iii. xxi. 12 Corvinus, Guest divine, Bids me draw the smoothest Wine. **1746** *Ibid., Epist.* i. xv. 26 At Sea-port Towns I shall expect to find My Wines of generous and of smoother Kind. **1896** A. Austin *England's Darling* ii. i, More tuns of marsh water, I warrant, than combs of smooth ale.

**7. a.** Of looks, words, etc.: Pleasant, affable, polite; seemingly amiable or friendly; having a show of sincerity or friendliness.

The unfavourable sense is the more usual, as in next.

(*a*) **13..** *Gaw. & Gr. Knt.* 1763 With smoþe smylyng & smolt þay smeten in-to merþe, þat al was blis & bonchef [etc.]. **1606** Dekker *Seven Deadly Sins* v. (Arb.) 36 They knew howe smooth soeuer his lookes were, there was a diuell in his bosome. **1681** Dryden *Abs. & Achit.* 745 Colour'd with a smooth pretence Of specious love and duty. **1703** Rowe *Fair Penit.* ii. i, With such smooth looks, and many a gentle Word The first fair She, beguil'd her easie Lord. **1784** Cowper *Task* vi. 853 Where fashion shall not sanctify abuse, Nor smooth good-breeding..ape the work of love! **1823** Scott *Quentin D.* xii, [Oliver spoke] in his smoothest manner, and in a tone more insinuating than that which he usually employed.

(*b*) **1526** *Pilgr. Perf.* (W. de W. 1531) 97 b, Softe wordes and smothe be to be mynystred to idiottes and fooles. *c* **1590** Greene *Frier Bacon* iii. 22, To sooth me up with such smooth flatterie. **1628** in *Cath. Tract.* (S.T.S.) 272 Knox had withdrawne the harts of the people craftily from the Catholik faith, by his smoath language. **1704** Trapp *Abra-Mulé* iii. i, I..with smooth Words Persuaded him t'intrust me with his Letter. **1754** Washington *Lett.* Writ. (1889) 86, I doubt not but they will indeavour to amuse you with many smooth stories, as they did me. **1820** Byron *Mar. Fal.* iii. i. 58, I cannot shape my tongue To syllable black deeds into smooth names. **1837** Carlyle *Fr. Rev.* i. vii. ix, The General..speaks vaguely some smooth words to the National President.

**b.** Of the tongue, or of persons: Speaking fair or smoothly; using specious or attractive language; plausible, bland, insinuating, flattering.

Usually with implication of insincerity or selfish designs, but occas. in a better sense.

(*a*) *c* **1450** Lydg. *Secrees* 675 Whysperyng tounges,.. Smothe afore folk, to fawnyn and to shyne, And shewe two facys in oon hood. **1570** Levins *Manip.* 230 A Smooth tong, *lingua compta.* **1596** Shaks. *1 Hen. IV*, ii. iv. 79 This Leatherne Ierkin,..Smooth tongue. **1610** Fletcher *Faithf. Sheph.* i. i, A Chastitie, That neither pleasing Age, smooth tongue, or Gold, Could ever break upon. **1837** Carlyle *Fr. Rev.* ii. v. vii, Bertrand-Moleville has a smooth tongue,.. gall in his heart. **1863** Whyte Melville *Gladiators* I. 32 She is not to be won by a smooth tongue and a beardless face.

(*b*) **1592** Timme *Ten Eng. Lepers* E iij b, These kinde of burnished and smooth fellowes do they know not what. **1600** Shaks. *A.Y.L.* v. iv. 46, I haue bin politicke with my friend, smooth with mine enemie. **1653** More *Antid. Ath.* iii. xi. §2 That sly, smooth Physician, and faithful Patron of Witches. **1708** Hearne *Collect.* (O.H.S.) II. 103 A smooth Preacher, and a rank Whigg. **1781** Cowper *Friendship* 23 That man, when smoothest he appears, Is most to be suspected. **1847** Tennyson *Princ.* v. 376, I saw That equal baseness lived in sleeker times With smoother men. **1870** Bryant *Iliad* I. iv. 119 He found the smooth of speech Nestor, the Pylian orator.

*Comb.* **1606** Sylvester *Du Bartas* ii. iv. i. *Tropheis* 584 Those smooth-slie Aspicks, with their poysony sting Murder mine honor.

**c.** Superior, excellent, 'classy'; clever, 'neat'. *colloq.* (orig. *U.S.*).

**1893** W. K. Post *Harvard Stories* 210 'Well, you'll have a rattling good time down there.' 'A smooth time, you mean,' corrected Rattleton. **1900** Ade *Fables in Slang* 43 The Benevolent Lady..derived much Joy from the Knowledge that..People were..remarking..'Say, ain't she the Smooth Article?' **1924** Wodehouse *Bill the Conqueror* iii. 82 How did you come to think of this stunt?.. It was the smoothest trick I ever heard of. **1942** E. B. White *Let.* 31 Jan. (1976) 222 MacLeish looks a little like Doctor Devol, and he is some smooth poet. **1946** Wodehouse *Joy in Morning* xxvi. 237 Smooth work, Uncle Percy... There can't be many fellows about with brains like yours. **1970** C. Major *Dict. Afro-Amer. Slang* 106 *Smooth*, very adept; clever.

**d.** Of manners, dress, etc.: stylish, suave, chic. *colloq.*

Sometimes indistinguishable from senses 7 b and c.

**1922** Wodehouse *Jill the Reckless* xix. 285 'What charming manners Major Selby has. So polished... So smooth!' 'Smooth,' said Mr. Pilkington dourly, 'is right!' **1924** P. Marks *Plastic Age* xi. 99 A 'smooth' boy who prided himself on his conquests. *Ibid.* xvi. 168 These were the 'smooth boys', interested primarily in clothes and 'parties'. **1942** Berrey & Van den Bark *Amer. Thes. Slang* §233/10 *Stylish; 'chic'*...smooth. **1944** *Chicago Tribune* 10 Dec. (Grafic Mag.) 4 Watch those people whom you consider smooth; see how they dress. **1977** [see sharp *a.* 7 b].

**8. a.** Of style or diction: Flowing gently or easily; nicely modulated; not harsh or rugged; polished.

**1589** Puttenham *Eng. Poesie* iii. xix. (Arb.) 207 And our speech is made melodious or harmonicall..by choise of smoothe words. **1665** Boyle *Occas. Refl.* (1848) 342, I some times..tri'd my Pen in a smoother and more florid style. **1697** Dryden *Virg. Past.* ix. 26 Who then shou'd sing the Nymphs, or who rehearse The Waters gliding in a smoother Verse! **1726** Swift *Gulliver* ii. vii, Their style is clear, masculine, and smooth, but not florid. **1795–1814** Wordsw. *Excurs.* vi. 522 Smooth verse, inspired by no unlettered Muse. **1874** Chappell *Hist. Music* I. v. 99 Plato [described the Phrygian mode]..as smooth and fit for prayer.

**b.** Of writers: Having an easy, polished style.

**1670** Milton *Hist. Eng.* i. Wks. 1851 V. 11 Joseph of Exeter, the only smooth Poet of those times. **1805** G. Ellis in Lockhart *Scott* (1837) II. i. 31 Indeed, who is so unequal as Dryden? It may be said that he was not intentionally so —but to be very smooth is very often to be tame.

**9.** Making smooth; producing smoothness.

*a* **1596** *Sir T. More* iv. iii, I haue had A smoothe courte shauing. **1706** Phillips (ed. Kersey), *Smooth Boiling of Sugar*, (among Confectioners) is when the Sugar is Boil'd to such a Degree, that [etc.].

**10.** Free from disturbance or excitement.

**1756** Burke *Subl. & B.* Wks. I. 32 That smooth and voluptuous satisfaction which the assured prospect of pleasure bestows. **1807** Wordsw. *Personal Talk* 48 Hence have I Smooth passions, smooth discourse, and joyous thought. **1837** Carlyle *Fr. Rev.* ii. iv. iii, Majesties' Apartments closed in smooth rest.

**11.** Free from, unaccompanied by, obstruction, interruption, impediment, or difficulty. Also in phr. *to make smooth.*

**1792** Burke *Corr.* (1844) II. 371 If government is perfectly in earnest, every thing ought to be made smooth for them. **1837** Carlyle *Fr. Rev.* ii. iii. iv, Consider too whether he had smooth times of it. **1884** *Manch. Exam.* 21 May 5/3 The progress of the measure through Committee should..be fairly smooth and speedy. **1890** Martineau *Authority in Relig.* i. i. 10 Except where the evolution was smooth and the order eternal.

**12.** Of sounds: Soft, not harsh or grating.

In quot. 1887 used to render L. *tenuis*.

**1836** DUBOURG *Violin* ix. (1878) 267 It is not age, but constant use, that is the means of producing a smooth, clear tone. **1887** COOK *Sievers' OE. Gram.* III, c is the character for the smooth guttural and the smooth palatal.

**13. a.** Special collocations. ***smooth breathing***: see BREATHING *vbl. sb.* 9. ***smooth calf-skin*** (see quot.). ***smooth coat***, a smooth-coated dog. ***smooth-file*** (see quots. 1875); hence ***smooth-file*** v. trans. ***smooth grace***, Mus. (see quot.). ***smooth-head***, Mining (see quot.). ***smooth mouth***, the worn teeth without cusps found in horses more than seven or eight years old; so ***smooth-mouthed*** adj. †***smooth-pate***, a smooth-headed person; *Obs.* ***smooth-plane*** (see quots.). ***smooth-sayer***, U.S., a smooth-tongued or plausible person.

**1746** *Smooth breathing [see BREATHING *vbl. sb.* 9]. **1888** KING & COOKSON *Sound & Inflex. Gr. & Lat.* 172 The prefix *sṃ-* (together) appears as *ἁ-* with a smooth breathing in ἀ-δελφός. **1885** C. G. W. LOCK *Workshop Rec.* Ser. IV. 264/2 Coloured calf-skins may be bought almost as cheaply as '*smooth' calf (uncoloured ones). **1890** *Daily News* 10 Dec. 2/3 This is the best show..ever held by the club, especially of the *smooth coats. **1677** MOXON *Mech. Exerc.* i. 15 The *Smooth file is to take out those cuts or file-stroaks that the fine file made. **1683** *Ibid.*, *Printing* xi. ¶15 These Ribs must be purely Smooth-fil'd and Pollish'd. **1875** KNIGHT *Dict. Mech.* 2227/1 *Smooth-file*, 1. A finishing-file, whose teeth are of a grade of coarseness between the second-cut and the dead-smooth... 2. The rubbing-tool used by the needle-maker in pressing and rolling a pack of wires, cut for needles. **1659** C. SIMPSON *Division Violist* 9 Graces done with the Fingers, are of two sorts: viz. *smooth and shaked. **1883** GRESLEY *Gloss. Coal-m.* 228 **Smooth-heads.* See Bright-heads [backs or slines]. **1940** *Chambers's Techn. Dict.* 560/2 Mouth, *smooth (Vet.). Smooth and polished grinding surface of the molar teeth of horses. **1955** R. HOBSON *Nothing too Good* vi. 51 Between eight and ten years of age..they [*sc.* horses] acquire what we call a smooth mouth. **1974** H. S. THOMAS *Horses* x. 183 At age nine the cusps are gone from the corner incisors. The horse is said to be *smooth-mouthed. **1597** SHAKS. *2 Hen. IV*, I. ii. 43 The horson *smooth-pates doe now weare nothing but high shoes. **1875** KNIGHT *Dict. Mech.* 2227/2 **Smooth-plane*, a smoothing or finishing-plane; the last used of the series of bench-planes. **1884** *Ibid.* Suppl. 825/2 *Smooth Plane*, one the bit of which is set at a relatively more obtuse angle than that of a block plane. **1872** C. D. WARNER *Backlog Studies* 132, I should rather, ten times over, dispense with the flatterers and the *smooth-sayers than the grumblers.

**b.** In the names of animals, esp. fishes and reptiles, as ***smooth anemone***, ***blenny***, ***dab***, ***flounder***, ***hound***, etc. (see quots.); **smooth-head**, a deep-sea fish belonging to the family Alepocephalidæ, resembling a herring with a larger body and dark-coloured skin.

**1858** G. H. LEWES *Sea-side Stud.* i. 16 The common *Smooth Anemone may be had not far from high-water mark in many places. **1769** PENNANT *Brit. Zool.* III. 169 The *Smooth Blenny..on the rocky coasts of Anglesea. **1881** *Cassell's Nat. Hist.* V. 99 The Smooth Blenny (*Blennius pholis*) is commonly known as the Shanny. **1836** YARRELL *Brit. Fishes* II. 221 The Lemon Dab, or *Smooth Dab, is not of such frequent occurrence as the common Rough Dab. **1884** GOODE *Nat. Hist. Aquat. Anim.* 183 The *Smooth Flounder..is very similar in habits and appearance to the Flat Fish. **1931** J. R. NORMAN *Hist. Fishes* viii. 150 A species of *Smooth-head (*Leptoderma*) captured in the Bay of Bengal has been described as having the skin covered all over with a thick, opalescent, and uniformly luminous epidermis. **1969** A. WHEELER *Fishes Brit. Isles & N.-W. Europe* 123 Smooth-heads..are deep-water relatives of the herring family. **1975** *Times* 5 Dec. 12/3 Smooth-head is abundant, but..its flesh has the consistency of custard. **1603** *Smooth hound [see HOUND *sb.*[1] 5]. **1769** PENNANT *Brit. Zool.* III. 91 The Smooth Hound..is called smooth, not that the skin is really so, but because it wants the spines on the back. **1836** YARRELL *Brit. Fishes* I. 9 The *Smooth Perch, *Perca channus*, a fish..frequently occurring on the coast of Cornwall. *Ibid.*, The *Smooth Serranus. *Serranus cabrilla.* **1713** JAGO in *Ray's Syn. Pisc.* 164 *Cataphractus lævis Cornubiensis.* *Smooth Shan. **1836** YARRELL *Brit. Fishes* I. 230 The Shanny, or smooth Shan, *blennius pholis*. *Ibid.* II. 393 *Squalus mustelus*, *Smooth shark. **1880** DAY *Fishes Gt. Brit.* I. 61 It is known as the Sapphirine gurnard ..: sea crow:..*smooth sides. **1802** SHAW *Gen. Zool.* III. II. 515 *Smooth Snake,..*Coronella Austriaca*. **1897** BATEMAN *Vivarium* 273 The Smooth Snake..is by far the most interesting of our three English snakes. **1769** PENNANT *Brit. Zool.* III. 191 The *Smooth Sole..is extremely thin, pellucid, and white. **1881** *Cassell's Nat. Hist.* V. 69 The Scald-fish, or Megrim, or Smooth Sole (*Arnoglossus laterna*).

**c.** In the names of plants or trees, as ***smooth acanthus***, ***archangel***, etc.

**1812** *New Botanic Garden* I. 2 Both the *Smooth and Prickly Acanthus are found to succeed in any common soil. **1822** *Hortus Angl.* II. 88 *Lamium Lævigatum.* *Smooth Archangel. **1790** W. H. MARSHALL *Rur. Econ. Midl.* II. 434 *Smooth Cadlock; *brasica napus*, wild rape. **1887** G. NICHOLSON *Dict. Gard.* III. 446 **Smooth flower*, a popular name for *Leianthus longifolius*, and other species. **1889** MAIDEN *Useful Pl.* 554 *Hedycarya angustifolia*... 'Native Mulberry', '*Smooth Holly'. **1882** F. B. HOUGH *Elem. Forestry* 239 The *Smooth Maple (*Acer glabrum*). **1859** MISS PRATT *Brit. Grasses* 211 *Smooth Rock Spleenwort. **1882** F. B. HOUGH *Elem. Forestry* 297 The *Smooth Sumach (*Rhus glabra*).

**14.** With sbs. used attributively, as ***smooth-face***, ***-tongue***. See also SMOOTH-BORE 2.

**1600** ROWLANDS *Lett. Humours Blood* xii. 18 Therfore for the smooth-face cut he calles. *a* **1700** EVELYN *Diary* 12 Feb. 1686, Lawyers..whereof one was the smooth-tong Solicitor. **1894** *Westm. Gaz.* 12 Apr. 3/3 Some are in handsome smooth-face cloth.

**15. a.** *Comb.* Forming parasynthetic adjs., as ***smooth-bellied***, ***-browed***, ***-cheeked***, ***-chinned***, etc.

Only a few of the earlier or more important examples of this type are given.

**1607** *Lingua* III. ii, And your *smooth-bellied..drones are never without him. **1612** DRAYTON *Poly-olb.* iii. 122 The *smooth-brow'd Plain..doth bid The lark to leave her bow'r. **1633** FORD *'Tis Pity* I. iii, All that *smooth-cheek'd virtue could advise. **1927** V. WOOLF in *Nation & Athenæum* Aug. 661/2 One of those smooth-cheeked, steady-eyed men. **1623** MASSINGER *Dk. Milan* II. i, The *smooth-chinned courtiers are abroad. **1696** *Lond. Gaz.* No. 3243/4 Lost,..a Liver colour and white Spaniel Setting Dog,..*smooth Coated. **1886** C. SCOTT *Sheep-Farm.* 198 Amongst the smooth-coated beauties in the kennel..[is] 'Lady Help'. **1634** MILTON *Comus* 86 His soft Pipe, and *smooth-dittied Song. **1668** WILKINS *Real Charac.* 78 That of *smooth edged leaves: or that whose leaves are..curled or waved about the edges. **1923** D. H. LAWRENCE *Birds, Beasts & Flowers* 41 Fig-trees, weird fig-trees Made of thick, smooth silver..Thick, *smooth-fleshed silver. **1598** JONSON *Ev. Man. in Hum.* v. i, Lets all be *smooth fore headed once agayne. *Ibid.* II. ii, That land..Which to *smooth-fronted peace is most proclive. **1697** DRYDEN *Virg. Georg.* II. 631 Nor Box, nor Limes,..*Smooth-grain'd, and proper for the Turner's Trade. **1963** *Times* 16 May 16/1 Viennese singers are frequently smooth-grained in comparison with their Italian colleagues. **1634** MILTON *Comus* 716 Millions of spinning Worms, That in their green shops weave the *smooth-hair'd silk. **1871** M. LEGRAND *Cambr. Freshman* 30 A smooth-haired terrier. **1930** W. B. YEATS *Wild Apples* 23 And land and strand and all are fair As that *smooth-lined up-tilted boat From which the Foam-Born Queen stept out. **1605** MARSTON *Dutch Courtezan* sig. H^v, But yet when my discourse hath staide your quaking, You will be *smoother lipt. **1862** G. M. HOPKINS *Vision of Mermaids* (1929), Or on the swell Tugg'd the boss'd, smooth-lipp'd, giant, Strombus-shell. **1656** COWLEY *Misc.*, *Elegie upon Anacreon* 21 The *smooth-pac'd Hours of every day Glided numerously away. *a* **1941** V. WOOLF *Captain's Death Bed* (1950) 151 A large, smooth-paced cart horse. **1923** E. SITWELL *Bucolic Comedies* 29 *Smooth-perfumèd stephanotis. **1918** W. DE LA MARE *Motley* 72 The *smooth-plumed bird. **1883** 'MARK TWAIN' *Life on Miss.* xxv. 274 The Devil's Tea Table..a great *smooth-surfaced mass of rock. **1967** M. CLARK in *Coast to Coast* 1965–6 34 Fluffy, bouncy balls and not those smooth-surfaced..ones. **1832** TENNYSON *Œnone* 93 Naked they came to the *smooth-swarded bower. **1834** J. S. KNOWLES *Beggar of Bethnal Green* III. (Rtldg.) I. 380 The *smoothest-temper'd fellow in Christendom.

**b.** In the specific names of birds, fishes, etc.

**1787** LATHAM *Gen. Synop. Birds* Suppl. I. 67 *Smooth-billed Toucan. **1829** GRIFFITH tr. *Cuvier* VII. 467 Smooth-billed Barbican, *Pogonias Levirostris*. **1752** J. HILL *Hist. Anim.* 306 The *smooth-bodied Raia. *Ibid.* 125 The lesser, *smooth-clouded..Cochlea. **1781** LATHAM *Gen. Synop. Birds* I. I. 118 *Smooth-legged Eared Owl,..having the legs bare of feathers. **1752** J. HILL *Hist. Anim.* 154 The yellow, gibbose, *smooth-mouthed Porcellana. **1831** GRIFFITH tr. *Cuvier* IX. Syn. 37 *Smooth-necked Guana, *Iguana Delesatissima*. **1752** J. HILL *Hist. Anim.* 28 The *smooth-nosed Shrimp. **1893** LYDEKKER *Roy. Nat. Hist.* I. 474 The Smooth-nosed Mungooses. **1836** YARRELL *Brit. Fishes* I. 81 The *Smooth-tailed Stickleback, in which the lateral plates extend no farther than the ends of the rays of the pectoral fin. *c* **1880** *Cassell's Nat. Hist.* IV. 91 The second sub-family of the Hirundinidæ.—*Smooth-winged Swallows.

**c.** In the specific names of plants or trees.

**1889** MAIDEN *Useful Pl.* 441 The former [was called] by the colonists 'Rough-barked Bloodwood', and the latter '*Smooth-barked Bloodwood'. *Ibid.* 476 The 'Smooth-barked Ironbark' from Brisbane. *a* **1722** LISLE *Husb.* (1757) 240 *Gramen cristatum*..is in English called *smooth-crested grass. **1887** G. NICHOLSON *Dict. Gard.* III. 35 Buckeye; *Smooth-fruited Horse Chestnut. **1822** *Hortus Angl.* II. 7 Long *Smooth-headed Poppy. **1815** J. SMITH *Panorama Sci. & Art* II. 587 A small species of vetch, called the *smooth-podded tare. **1822** *Hortus Angl.* II. 160 *Biscutella Lævigata.* Smooth podded Buckler Mustard. **1815** J. SMITH *Panorama Sci. & Art* II. 621 *Smooth-stalked meadow-grass thrives best in dry situations. **1854** H. MILLER *Sch. & Schm.* (1858) 398 The prevailing vegetable is the *smooth-stemmed tangle—*Laminaria saccharina*.

**smooth** (smuːð), *adv.* Also 5 smothe. [f. prec.]

**1.** Smoothly, in various senses.

**1422** tr. *Secreta Secret., Priv. Priv.* 177 This worthy lorde began to smothe lagh. **1590** SHAKS. *Mids. N.* I. i. 134 The course of true loue neuer did run smooth. **1593** —— *2 Hen. VI*, III. i. 53 Smooth runnes the Water, where the Brooke is deepe. *c* **1655** MILTON *Sonn.* xx, Time will run On smoother, till Favonius re-inspire The frozen earth. **1746** FRANCIS tr. *Hor., Sat.* I. x. 62 Smooth flow his Lines, and elegant his Style. **1799** NELSON in Nicolas *Disp.* (1845) IV. 41, I well know your conciliating manners will make every thing go smooth.

**2.** *Comb.* **a.** With pa. pples. used attributively or predicatively, as ***smooth-bedded***, ***-combed***, ***-cut***, etc.

**1793** SMEATON *Edystone L.* §148 The third step..*smooth bedded... And the sixth smooth bedded, and all the dove-tails roughed out. **1579** NORTH *Plutarch, Cæsar* (1612) 739 Those fat men and *smooth combed heads. **1818** SCOTT *Rob Roy* xiv, As I paced along the *smooth-cut velvet walks. **1631** WEEVER *Anc. Funeral Mon.* 778 White *smooth hewen Asheler stone. **1598** MARSTON *Sco. Villanie* I. iii. 180 His perfum'd she-goat *smooth-kemb'd and high fed. **1955** E. POUND *Classic Anthol.* I. 49 Double teams matched, *smooth-oiled reins. **1854** tr. *Pereira's Polarized Light* 17 When a beam of light falls on a *smooth-polished surface. **1916** D. H. LAWRENCE *Amores* 102 A new night pouring down shall swirl Us away in an utter sleep, until We are one, *smooth-rounded. **1799** WORDSW. *Poet's Epitaph* 29 One to whose *smooth-rubbed soul can cling Nor form, nor feeling. **1820** KEATS *Eve of St. Agnes* xxxiii, Upon his knees he sank, pale as *smooth-sculptured stone. **1632** MILTON *Penseroso* 66, I walk unseen On the dry *smooth-shaven Green. **1865** KINGSLEY *Herew.* xii, The Flemings..prided themselves on their civilised and smooth-shaven chins. **1958** R. GRAVES *Steps* 249 There are some words carry a curse with them: *Smooth-trodden, abstract, slippery vocables. **1920** A. HUXLEY *Leda* 14 *Smooth-worn silver, polished through the years. **1922** JOYCE *Ulysses* 525 Lifting your billowy flounces on the smooth-worn throne. **1756** DYER *Fleece* IV. 86 Copious webs arrive, *Smooth wov'n, of other than Britannia's Fleece. **1678** J. NORRIS *Misc.* (1699) 37 Who with a *smooth-wrought Pipe shall play the Song.

**b.** With pres. pples., as ***smooth-flowing***, ***-gliding***, ***-going***, ***-rolling***, ***-running***, ***-sliding***, ***-weeping***, etc.

**1837** CARLYLE *Fr. Rev.* I. VI. ii, Parliamentary Eloquence, in bursts, or in plenteous *smooth-flowing floods. **1603** DANIEL *Def. Rhime* G v b, We admire them not for their *smooth-gliding words. **1882** BLACK *Shandon Bells* xvi, The Hansom (..was not quite so *smooth-going as that of Dr. Bude). **1823** HAZLITT *Liber Amoris* III. 156 Thousands of years of *smooth-rolling eternity and balmy, sainted repose. **1917** 'CONTACT' *Airman's Outings* v. 117 The *smooth-running ambulances bring broken soldiers. **1941** J. MASEFIELD *Gautama the Enlightened* 14 The black-bright, smooth-running..typewriting machine. **1977** J. P. ANDERSON in Douglas & Johnson *Existential Sociol.* vi. 186 To make the screening interview a smooth-running interaction, the patient has to be able to talk about the topics the screening worker thinks are important. **1598** SYLVESTER *Du Bartas* II. i. I. *Eden* 117 That never gutter-gorging durty muds Defil'd the chrystall of *smooth-sliding floods. **1637** MILTON *Lycidas* 86 Smooth-sliding Mincius, crown'd with vocall reeds. **1606** SYLVESTER *Du Bartas* II. iv. II. *Magnificence* 682 *Smooth-soothing vows, deep sorrows soon appeas'd. **1753** YOUNG *Brothers* I. i, *Smooth-speaking, insincere, insulting boy! **1944** E. SITWELL *Green Song* 10 The amber blood of the *smooth-weeping tree. **1743** FRANCIS tr. *Hor., Odes* I. ii. 20 Th' uxorious River glides away,..*smooth-winding to the Sea.

**smooth** (smuːð), *v.* Forms: 4 smoþe, 5–6 smothe; 6 smouthe; 5, 7, 9 smoothe, 6– smooth. [f. SMOOTH *a.*, taking the place of the earlier *smēðen* SMEETH *v.* The earliest instance occurs in sense 4 a.]

**I. 1. a.** *trans.* To make (a surface or substance) smooth, even, or level; to remove or reduce the roughness, irregularity, inequality, or unevenness of; to give a smooth or glossy surface to.

*c* **1440** *Pallad. on Husb.* IV. 430 Of the claue Is best an handful greet..Er eyther ende ysmothed is to haue. **1495** *Trevisa's Barth. De P.R.* III. xiv. (W. de W.) 58 This vertue *informatiua* thyrllyth what shall be thirlled, and smotheth what is rough. **1576** FLEMING *Panopl. Epist.* 58 It surpasseth ..all images of the caruer or grauer smothed and fined with his chosen instruments. **1595** SHAKS. *John* IV. ii. 13 To smooth the yce, or adde another hew Vnto the Raine-bow. **1630** DRAYTON *Muses Eliz.* Nymphal vii. 102 Here be fine night Maskes, plastred well within, To supple wrinckles, and to smooth the skin. **1697** DRYDEN *Virg. Georg.* I. 261 Let the weighty Rowler run the round, To smooth the Surface of th' unequal Ground. **1726** SWIFT *Gulliver* I. viii, His Majesty's ship carpenters..helped me in smoothing them after I had done the rough work. **1763** MILLS *Pract. Husb.* IV. 217 The head of the stock being cut off and smoothed. **1823** SCOTT *Quentin D.* Introd., An immense *assiêtte* of spinage, not smoothed into a uniform surface. **1881** H. JAMES *Portr. of Lady* xxxv, Rosier got up, and stood smoothing his hat.

*absol.* **1611** BIBLE *Isaiah* xli. 7 The carpenter encouraged the goldsmith, and he that smootheth with the hammer, him that smote the anuill.

*fig.* **1592** SHAKS. *Rom. & Jul.* III. ii. 97 What tongue shall smooth thy name, When I thy three houres wife haue mangled it. **1850** BLACKIE *Æschylus* I. 200 Time, that smooths All things, hath smoothed the front of my offence.

**b.** To iron (linen, etc.). Now *dial.*

**1617** MORYSON *Itin.* III. 172 They have little skill in washing, starching, or smoothing linnen. **1654** *Nicholas P.* (Camden) II. 58 The girle at that present..being smoothing of Lynnen. **1755** JOHNSON, *Heater*, an iron made hot, and put into a box-iron, to smooth and plait linnen. **1828–** in dial. glossaries and texts (Yks., Lancs., Linc., Derby., etc.).

**c.** To cause (feathers, hair, etc.) to lie smooth and even. Also in fig. context.

**1634** MILTON *Comus* 251 How sweetly did they float upon the wings Of silence,..At every fall smoothing the Raven doune Of darknes till it smil'd. **1784** COWPER *Task* v. 692 To smooth The shag of savage nature. **1859** TENNYSON *Elaine* 345 There to his proud horse Lancelot turn'd, and smooth'd The glossy shoulder. **1879** FROUDE *Cæsar* viii. 81 Sylla himself had to smoothe the ruffled plumes of his aspiring follower.

**d.** *transf.* To reduce to a simple vowel.

**1894** SWEET *Anglo-Sax. Rdr.* (ed. 7) p. xxiv, In Angl. *c*(*x*), *h*, *g*..'smooth' a preceding diphthong.

**e.** To transform or modify (a graph, distribution, or function) so as to make it smooth; to lessen irregularities or fluctuations in (something that can be represented by a graph). Cf. sense 11 c below.

**1889** F. GALTON *Natural Inheritance* vii. 100 These [relations] came out distinctly after I had 'smoothed' the entries. **1898** *Knowledge* 1 Oct. 235/1 Then the thirteen year series of these numbers is smoothed with averages of four. **1934** *Brit. Jrnl. Psychol.* Oct. 249 The theoretical periodogram was..made to conform... It was therefore smoothed per ten units, thus making it resemble a curve of old log. units. **1962** D. F. SHAW *Introd. Electronics* x. 203 The performance of the diode rectifier is improved by the use of a filter circuit to smooth the output. **1979** *Sci. Amer.* May 52/3 This generalization is strictly statistical, because our analysis has smoothed the gas distribution... It does not rule out the existence of isolated patches of vigorous star formation.

**2. a.** To make (a way) easy or plain; to free from obstruction, difficulty, or impediment. Chiefly in fig. contexts.

**1582** STANYHURST *Æneis* III. (Arb.) 83 Thee fats thee passage shal smooth. **1593** SHAKS. *2 Hen. VI*, I. ii. 65, I would remoue these tedious stumbling blockes, And smooth my way vpon their headlesse neckes. **1628** EARLE *Microcosm., Graue Diuine* (Arb.) 24 Hee counts it not profanenesse.. to smooth his way by Aristotle to Schoole-diuinitie. **1695** WOODWARD *Nat. Hist. Earth* I. (1723) 41 The more effectualy to smooth my Way. **1717** POPE *Eloïsa* 322 Thou, Abelard! the last sad office pay, And smooth my passage to the realms of day. **1779** *Mirror* No. 32, A qualification extremely useful for smoothing a man's way through the world. **1865** BURRITT *Walk to Land's End* 99 Intending to smoothe the way to matrimonial happiness. **1882** J. H. BLUNT *Ref. Ch. Eng.* II. 249 His earliest work was to smooth the way for Cardinal Pole's return to England.

**b.** To diminish or clear away (an obstruction, difficulty, etc.).

**1599** SHAKS. *Hen. V*, II. ii. 188 We doubt not now, But euery Rubbe is smoothed on our way. **1867** LADY HERBERT *Cradle L.* v. 147 Those who had so kindly.. smoothed for her all the difficulties of her journey.

**3.** To render (the brow) free from wrinkles, lines, frowns, etc., by natural effort; to invest with, replace by, a calm or placid expression. Also in fig. context.

**1593** SHAKS. *3 Hen. VI*, II. vi. 32 Good fortune bids vs pause, And smooth the frownes of War, with peacefull lookes. **1594** —— *Rich. III*, I. i. 9 Grim-visag'd Warre, hath smooth'd his wrinkled Front. **1602** MARSTON *Ant. & Mel.* III. Wks. 1856 I. 36 How I clap my hands, and smooth my brow! **1671** MILTON *P.R.* II. 164 To.. smooth the rugged'st brow. **1743** FRANCIS tr. *Hor., Odes* III. xxix. 24 Such Scenes have charm'd the Pangs of Care, And smooth'd the clouded Forehead of Despair. **1825** SCOTT *Talism.* ix, The Grand Master,.. on exchanging a glance with the Marquis, smoothed his frowning brow as well as he could. **1895** G. MEREDITH *Odes Fr. Hist.* 28 She smoothed a startled look.

*refl.* **1819** SCOTT *Leg. Montrose* vi, The deep-knit furrows of his brow relaxed and smoothed themselves.

**4. a.** To make smooth, plausible, or specious.

**1340** *Ayenb.* 57 Hit biualþ þet þe speche is grat zenne uor þet hi deþ grat kuead þaȝ hy by uayre and ysmoþed. *c* **1600** ? SHAKS. *Passionate Pilgr.* 306 And when thou comest thy tale to tell, Smooth not thy tongue with filed talk. **1621** T. WILLIAMSON tr. *Goulart's Wise Vieillard* 66 She will deliuer him from the strange woman, which smootheth her words. **1653** MILTON *Ps.* v. 28 An open grave their throat, their tongue they smooth.

**b.** To refine (a person or his manners); to free from rudeness or rusticity. ? *Obs.*

**1644** MILTON *Educ.* Wks. 1851 IV. 391 The solemn and divine harmonies of Musick.. have a great power over dispositions and manners, to smooth and make them gentle from rustick harshness. **1749** CHESTERF. *Lett.* cxcviii. (1792) II. 246, I am very glad that you like good company so well. I already imagine that you are a little smoothed by it. *Ibid.* cxcix. 250 Such a share of them left, as may contribute to smooth and polish you.

**c.** To render smooth to the ear; to polish.

**1667** MILTON *P.L.* v. 626 Harmonie Divine So smooths her charming tones, that Gods own ear Listens delighted. **1697** DRYDEN *Virgil* Note on Æneid IX. 853-4 Both verses are very rough; but of choice; for it had been easy for me to have smoothed them. **1724** L. WELSTED *Epist.*, etc. 43 Great Spencer first.. Smoothed our old Metre, and refined our Lays. **1754** COWPER *Ep. R. Lloyd* 74 Matthew.. with endless pains Smooth'd and refin'd the meanest strains.

**†5. a.** To use smooth, flattering, or complimentary language to (a person). *Obs.* (Cf. 9 a.)

**1591** GREENE *Maiden's Dr.* ix, The poor he smooth'd, the proud he kept in awe. **1592** KYD *Sp. Trag.* II. i, Slie deceits smooth Bel-imperias eares. **1623** CAMDEN *Rem.* (1637) 162 A scholler smoothed him with this foolish allusion. **1670** COTTON *Espernon* III. XI. 572 Some expressions of Civility, and Complement, to smooth him withal, at his departure. **1718** HICKES & NELSON *Kettlewell* I. xxi. 44 He could Smooth or Flatter none upon any Consideration whatsoever.

**†b.** *absol.* To be smooth or plausible in one's language or bearing to others. *Obs.*

**1587** *Mirr. Mag., Sir N. Burdet* iii, Fortunes guyle, Which smirking though at first, she seeme to smoothe and smyle. **1594** SHAKS. *Rich. III*, I. iii. 48 Because I cannot flatter,.. Smile in mens faces, smooth, deceiue, and cogge. *a* **1618** SYLVESTER *Job Triumphant* I. 823 Or, ween you, smoothing, these Deceits to smother?

**†c.** So *to smooth it*. *Obs.*

**1583** BABINGTON *Commandm.* (1590) 427 We must smooth it, and sooth it, and carrie two faces vnder one hoode. **1593** SHAKS. *2 Hen. VI*, II. i. 22 Pernitious Protector, dangerous Peere, That smooth'st it so with King and Common-weale.

**d.** *refl.* To put on smooth ingratiating airs.

**1868** W. CORY *Lett. & Jrnls.* (1897) 251 At the worst, I never smoothed myself for Belial or for Mammon.

**6. a.** To allay, assuage, mitigate the force of (passion, trouble, etc.).

**1589** GREENE *Menaphon* (Arb.) 23 The King thus smoothing the heate of his cares. **1605** SHAKS. *Lear* II. ii. 81 Such smiling rogues as these.. smooth euery passion That in the natures of their Lords rebell. **1667** MILTON *P.L.* IV. 120 Whereof hee soon aware, Each perturbation smooth'd with outward calme, Artificer of fraud.

*absol.* **1837** CARLYLE *Fr. Rev.* II. II. vi, All is dissolution, mutual rancour, gloom and despair: till National Assembly Commissioners.. gradually levelling, strive in all wise ways to smooth and soothe.

**b.** To render (the mind, etc.) calm or tranquil; to soothe.

**1604** EARL STIRLING *Crœsus* v. ii, What could the world afford, or man affect, Which did not smooth my soule. **1633** G. HERBERT *Temple, Nature* iii, O smooth my rugged heart, and there Engrave thy rev'rend law and fear. **1830** TENNYSON *Leonine Elegiacs*, The ancient poetess singeth, that Hesperus all things bringeth, Smoothing the wearied mind. **1859** DICKENS *T. Two Cities* II. v, What has roughened your temper? Put some punch to it and smooth it again.

**7.** To hush up, gloss over, make less conspicuous or offensive.

**1592** KYD *Sp. Trag.* III. x, This that I did was for a policie, To smooth and keepe the murder secret. **1593** SHAKS. *Rich. II*, I. iii. 240 (Q.[1]), Oh had't beene a stranger,.. To smooth his fault I should haue beene more milde. **1697** PRIDEAUX *Life Mahomet* (1716) 125 Which raising a great Noise, and many being offended with him for it, to smooth the matter again, he hath recourse to his old Art.

**8.** *intr.* To become smooth, calm, or tranquil.

**1837** LOCKHART *Scott* lxiv. (1845) 570/1 Mrs. Coutts's brow smoothed, and.. she was as.. easy as ever she was in her life. **1860** *All Year Round* No. 66. 384 Once within the friendly shelter of the pier, the water smoothed rapidly. **1864** J. H. NEWMAN *Apol.* 241, I trust that things are smoothing now.

**II.** With advs. and preps.

**9.** *trans.* With *up*: **†a.** To flatter, encourage.

**1584** B. R. tr. *Herodotus* II. 100b, Hector,.. whome it behoued not to smooth vp his brother in hys filthy leachery. **1593** G. HARVEY *New Lett.* Wks. (Grosart) I. 275 He that neither cockereth himselfe, nor loueth to be lulled, or smoothed-up of freindes. **1652** BP. HALL *Invis. World* III. §5 He smooths us up in the good opinion of our own gracious disposition.

**†b.** To cover or hush up; to conceal. *Obs.*

**1592** GREENE *Def. Conny Catch.* Wks. (Grosart) XI. 92 Al things was smoothed vp so cunningly, yᵗ he suspected nothing lesse then yᵉ reuenge intended against him. *a* **1661** HOLYDAY *Juvenal* (1673) 12 She.. went to her husband with much flattery,.. to smooth-up the matter.

**†c.** To contrive smoothly. *Obs.*⁻¹

**1603** DANIEL *Def. Rhime* G v b, To delight an exterior sense, wee smoothe vp a weake confused sense.

**d.** To polish up, improve.

**1760-2** GOLDSM. *Cit. W.* lii. (Globe) 171 A squire from the country.. desirous of.. smoothing up the rudiments of his rural minuet.

**10.** With *over*: **†a.** To win over, appease. *Obs.*⁻¹

**1608** TOPSELL *Serpents* (1658) 708 For the Dragon being smoothed over with these gifts,.. was contented to forsake the old place.

**b.** To make smooth or smoother in some way, esp. by the removal of a difficulty.

**1611** COTGR., *Calendré*,.. sleeked, or smoothed ouer. **1809** MALKIN *Gil Blas* XIII. vi. ¶ 4 They were politic enough to smooth over the corrugations of their contempt. **1820** BYRON *Mar. Fal.* IV. i. 75 The high moon.. Serenely smoothing o'er the lofty walls Of those tall piles and sea-girt palaces. **1873** BLACK *Pr. Thule* xxv. 418 These minor inconveniences were soon smoothed over.

**c.** To gloss over, minimize.

**1684** BAXTER *Cath. Comm.* 40 By hiding, or smoothing over publick sins. **1827** SCOTT *Surg. Dau.* v, This he smoothed over to his conscience. **1852** MRS. STOWE *Uncle Tom* xxiv. 233 There was something about her that Eva never could make out; and she always smoothed it over with thinking that, after all, it was mamma.

**11.** With *out*: **a.** To take out, remove (a fold or crease) by pressure or rubbing.

**1683** MOXON *Printing* xxiv. ¶ 15 As he comes to a Token-sheet, he.. smooths out the Crease with the back-side of the Nails of his Right Hand. **1815** SCOTT *Guy M.* xxx, He has had a hard task replacing the folios.., smoothing out the creases and dogs-ears. **1847** C. BRONTE *J. Eyre* xxix, The creases left by the wet [were] smoothed out.

**b.** To spread out smoothly or evenly. Also, = sense 1 a.

**1859** JEPHSON *Brittany* ii. 19 Some batter, which she smoothed out with a wooden spoon until it was of about the thickness of a pancake. **1900** *20th Ann. Rep. U.S. Geol. Surv.* II. 196 A belt of country marked by landslide topography which was gradually smoothed out, owing to the decay and erosion of the fallen blocks of basalt.

**c.** = sense 1 e above; also, to lessen (irregularities or fluctuations) in something which can be described by a graph, esp. a time series.

**1933** *Econometrics* I. 238 An elaborately weighted moving function.. prevents the resulting curve from smoothing out fluctuations. **1945** L. A. MAVERICK *Time Series Analysis* p. vii, In smoothing out the monthly cycle.. Wardwell's moving cyclical average of changing length is used. **1957** *Encycl. Brit.* XXIII. 432/1 By the provision of storage facilities at the source and of the main aqueduct service reservoirs, these various fluctuations [in demand] can be smoothed out. **1962** A. NISBETT *Technique Sound Studio* i. 30 At the 'back' [of the microphone] the response is fairly flat—the effect of the pad being to smooth out the peak. **1971** *Sci. Amer.* Oct. 69/1 Tests of nuclear weapons have shown that atmospheric mixing is rapid and that irregularities in composition are smoothed out after a few years. **1978** *Daily Tel.* 6 Jan. 17 The Americans will be very reluctant to do more than smooth out fluctuations in the exchange rate.

**12.** With *down*: **a.** To make smooth by pressing down. Also in fig. context.

**1687** MIÉGE *Gt. Fr. Dict.* II. s.v., To smooth down with the Nail, as Taylors and Seamstresses do. **1768** BURKE *Corr.* (1844) I. 150 However,.. I am to see him to-morrow, and will smooth down the feathers. **1816** SCOTT *Old Mort.* xxxvii, She had an infant in one arm, and with the other she smoothed down her apron. **1847** TENNYSON *Princ.* II. 432 One In this hand held a volume as to read, And smoothed a petted peacock down with that.

**b.** *intr.* To become smooth by settling down.

**1884** *Field* 6 Dec. (Cassell), The falls were smoothing down.

**13.** With *off*, *away*, etc. (See quots.).

**1680** OTWAY *Orphan* II. i, The superstitious States-man has his sneer To smooth a poor man off with that can't bribe him. **1784** COWPER *Tiroc.* 560 Th' indented stick, that loses day by day Notch after notch, till all are smooth'd away. **1819** SHELLEY *Peter Bell 3rd* VII. iii. 5 From his mean front .. Smoothing away the unmeaning furrows. **1837** CARLYLE *Fr. Rev.* II. VI. viii A moment,—which one had to smooth off with oratory. **1893** 'Q.' [QUILLER-COUCH] *Delectable Duchy* 25 Their wives smoothed all intelligence out of their faces as soon as I began to hint at it.

**'smoothable** ('smuːðəb(ə)l), *a. rare.* [f. SMOOTH *v.*] Capable of being smoothed or made smooth.

**1656** W. DU GARD tr. *Comenius' Gate Lang. Unl.* 27 One verie hard, and yet smoothable, Marble.

**†'smooth-boot(s.** *Obs.* [f. SMOOTH *a.* + BOOT *sb.*[3] Cf. SLY-BOOT(S.] One who uses flattering, ingratiating, or plausible language; a bland or smooth-tongued person. Usually in pl. form.

**1599** MINSHEU *Sp. Dict., Halagadór*, a smoothbootes, a flatterer, a faire spoken man, a cunning tongued fellow. *a* **1610** [see SLEEKSTONE 2]. **1691** WOOD *Life* 21 Apr., Dr. Nathaniel Foy bishop of Waterford:.. a smooth boots. **1707** HEARNE *Collect.* (O.H.S.) II. 8 The V.C. (whom some Waggs call a second Smoothboots). **1709** *Ibid.* 175 Old Smoothboots the Vice-Chancellor.

Hence **†smooth-booted** *a.*, flattering, fawning, soft-spoken. *Obs.*

**1706** HEARNE *Collect.* (O.H.S.) I. 231 Just such another smooth-booted Complyer. **1708** *Ibid.* II. 101 Yᵉ last smooth booted, sneaking Oxford Address. **1710** *Ibid.* III. 28 That old smooth-booted, self-interested,.. paultry Lancaster.

**'smooth-bore.** Also **smoothbore, smooth bore.** [f. SMOOTH *a.* + BORE *sb.*[1]]

**1.** A cannon or gun of which the barrel is made with a smooth or unrifled bore.

In quot. 1848 with punning allusion to BORE *sb.*[2]

**1812** *Niles' Weekly Reg.* II. 398/1 It was the best smooth bore he ever shot with in his life. **1834** W. A. CARRUTHERS *Kentuckians in N. Y.* I. 21 Your smooth bores waste a deal of powder and lead. **1848** LOWELL *Fable for Critics* 1229 I divide bores myself, in the manner of rifles Into two great divisions..;—There's your smooth-bore and screw-bore [etc.]. **1859** 'STONEHENGE' *Shot Gun* 306 A ball from a smooth bore (that is, from a barrel not rifled in any way). **1897** *Century Mag.* Aug. 587 A powerful double-turreted monitor, carrying two 18-inch smooth-bores.

*fig.* **1883** PAYN *Thicker than Water* xxiii, One thought expelling another in the narrow smoothbore of her mind.

**2.** *attrib.* **a.** Having a smooth or unrifled bore.

**1799** in *Deb. Congress U.S.* (1851) 7th Congress 2 Sess., App. 1402 One had a rifle, and the other a smooth-bore piece. **1859** *Musketry Instr.* 31 During the passage of the spherical ball through the smooth-bore barrel. **1860** TENNENT *Story Guns* (1864) 228 These trials were made with the old smooth-bore cannon. **1879** *Cassell's Techn. Educ.* I. 65 For many years the arm of the British soldier was a smooth-bore musket.

**b.** Adapted for guns having a smooth bore.

**1859** F. A. GRIFFITHS *Artill. Man.* (1862) 203 Smooth-bore projectiles.

Hence **'smooth-bored** *a.*, = prec. 2 a.

**1859** F. A. GRIFFITHS *Artill. Man.* (1862) 203 Smooth-bored guns. **1890** *Nature* 18 Sept., At short distances.. the smooth-bored guns were reasonably accurate.

**smoothed** (smuːðd), *ppl. a.* [f. SMOOTH *v.*]

**1.** Rendered specious or plausible. *rare.*

**1568** T. HOWELL *Arb. Amitie* (1879) 101 Nor he that files his smoothed speeche. **1575** GASCOIGNE *Weedes* Wks. (1587) 152 Their smoothed toongues are lined all with guile.

**2. a.** Made smooth, even, placid; unruffled, etc.

**1591** SHAKS. *1 Hen. VI*, III. i. 124 The Duke Hath banisht moodie discontented fury, As by his smoothed Browes it doth appeare. **1611** COTGR. s.v. *Perpins*, Stones made iust as thicke as a wall, & shewing their smoothed ends on either side thereof. **1667** MILTON *P.L.* I. 772 They.. on the smoothed Plank.. expatiate. **1713** YOUNG *Last Day* II. 368 How the smooth'd spirit into goodness glides! **1837** CARLYLE *Fr. Rev.* III. v. i, With cheerfully smoothed countenances. **1897** MISS KINGSLEY *W. Africa* 168 Masses of smoothed rock rise up out of the whirling water.

**b.** Of graphs, statistical fluctuations, etc. Cf. SMOOTH *v.* 1 e, 11 c.

**1888** *Proc. R. Soc.* XLV. 140 These smoothed values were obtained by plotting the observed values, after transmuting them as.. described into their respective Q units. **1903** *Science* 17 July 91/2 Smoothed rainfall curve for the British Isles. **1933** *Econometrica* I. 240 The points of inflection should be marked in the smoothed curve, to serve as guides to the desired smoothing line. **1962** D. F. SHAW *Introd. Electronics* x. 204 The advantage of this circuit is that the smoothed d.c. output voltage has a high value and the residual ripple voltage may be reduced to a fraction of 1%. **1964** K. G. LOCKYER *Introd. Critical Path. Anal.* viii. 78 Clearly it is desirable to try to shift some of the earlier over-load into the later under-load. If this could be completely done, then the load would be said to be 'smoothed'.

**†3.** Indulged, pampered. *Obs.*

**1600** BRETON *Pasquil's Fooles Cap* lxxiii, Such smoothed Godsons shew in Wisdomes schoole, A Milk-soppe Babie is more halfe a Foole.

Hence **†'smoothedness**, smoothness. *Obs.*⁻¹

**1573** GOLDING in Baret *Alv.* To Rdr. ix, The natiue propertie Of brode North speech and Sowthren smoothednesse.

**smoothen** ('smuːð(ə)n), *v.* [f. SMOOTH *a.* + -EN[5].]

In frequent use *c* 1820-30, esp. by Landor.

**1.** *trans.* To reduce the force, harshness, or violence of (something); to assuage, mollify, tone down (a passion, etc.).

**1635** R. N. tr. *Camden's Hist. Eliz.* I. 55 The heate of warre..was rather smoothened than any firm peace knit. **1724** WELTON *Chr. Faith & Pract.* 403 The government of our appetites..must needs smoothen and civilize any temper. *c* **1816** FUSELI *Lect. on Art* (1848) 515 The general tone..smoothens the whirlwind that fluctuates on the foreground, and gives an air of temperance to the whole. **1829** LANDOR *Imag. Conv.* Wks. 1853 I. 559/1 For the foundation of civility it is requisite that all malignity be smoothened.

**2.** To make easy or plain; to clear (a way), to free from difficulty, obstruction, etc.; to lighten or lessen (a difficulty).

**1648** HOWELL *Twelve Treat.* (1661) 375 To smoothen and faciliate things, thereby to open a passage, and pave the way to a happy peace. **1795** *Ann. Reg., Hist.* 108 [It] would have smoothened the road to a general pacification. **1829** LANDOR *Imag. Conv.* Wks. 1853 I. 443/1 That I may smoothen the path to arrangements of great advantage to thee. **1857** CANON FLANAGAN *Hist. Ch. in Eng.* II. 42 To smoothen matters to the uttermost Dr. Milner made an ample apology.

**3. a.** To make (a surface, substance, etc.) smooth, level, even, calm, etc.; to free from roughness or inequality.

**1678** MOXON *Mech. Exerc.* iv. 73 [The paring-chisel's] office is..to pare off and smoothen the irregularities the Former [plane] made. **1683** *Ibid., Printing* xiii. ¶3 He goes about to Flat and Smoothen the Face. **1772** J. R. FORSTER tr. *Kalm's Trav.* I. 341 They..scraped off the burnt part of the wood, and smoothened the boat within. **1798** LANDOR *Gebir* Wks. 1853 II. 490/1 There spreads a marble squared And smoothen'd. **1820** W. SCORESBY *Acc. Arctic Reg.* II. 354 The remarkable property of oil in smoothening the surface of the sea. **1890** W. J. GORDON *Foundry* 142 Then we see the furrows smoothened on a stone wheel.

*transf.* **1864** BURTON *Scot Abroad* I. ii. 91 In France..the sharp contour of their name [*sc.* Kennedy] was smoothened into Cenedy. **1868** BROWNING *Ring & Bk.* I. I. 1181 Language that goes as easy as a glove O'er good and evil smoothens both to one.

**b.** Const. *away, back, down, off, out, over.*

**1680** MOXON *Mech. Exer.* xiii. 221 They cut down and smoothen away the Exuberances left by the Sharp-pointed Grooving Tool. **1821** CLARE *Vill. Minstr.* I. 111 Some may ..cut-hedge and lawn adore, Which his shears have smoothen'd o'er. *Ibid.* II. 66 Oft I've seen thy little leg.. Smoothen down thy silken sides. **1879** *Cassell's Techn. Educ.* I. 57 This [pile] is called the 'cast-shadow', and must not have its lower edge smoothened off. **1913** R. KANE *Good Friday to Easter Sunday* iii. 126 She may smoothen back His hair, thick and heavy with crimson moisture. **1945** N. COLLINS *London belongs to Me* II. xx. 189 The sound which it made as he smoothened it out flat.

**4.** *intr.* To become smooth.

**1888** MᶜCARTHY & PRAED *Ladies' Gallery* I. i. 15 His chest expanded, his skin smoothened.

Hence **smoothened** ('smuːð(ə)nd), *ppl. a.*; **smoothening** ('smuːð(ə)nɪŋ), *vbl. sb.* and *ppl. a.*

**1818** *Blackw. Mag.* IV. 45 Every bit of the smoothened, polished..body, thanks a different artist for its ornament. **1841** BROWNING *Pippa Passes* Poems (1905) 176 The soft-rinded smoothening facile chalk That yields your outline to the air's embrace. **1846** LANDOR *Imag. Conv.* Wks. 1853 II. 61/2, I should be sorry to destroy..or even to remove the smoothened plank. **1887** *Amer. Naturalist* XXI. 435 The first step in improvement gained from the chard beets was a smoothening of the root.

**smoother** ('smuːðə(r)). [f. SMOOTH *v.*]

†**1.** One who uses smooth or flattering language; a flatterer. *Obs.*

**1611** COTGR., *Blandisseur*, a blandisher,..smoother, flattering sycophant, or claw-backe. [*a* **1693** *Urquhart's Rabelais* III. iii. 38 My Claw backs, my Smoothers, my Parasites.]

**2.** One who or that which smooths in some respect; a refiner, mollifier, pacifier, etc. Also with *down*.

Freq. in newspaper use at the turn of the century, as in quot. 1902.

**1611** COTGR., *Polisseur*, a polisher..; sleeker, smoother. **1630** LENNARD tr. *Charron's Wisd.* (1670) 473 [Honesty] preserveth the Magistrate free from..bribes, which is the plague, and smoother of truth. **1724** SWIFT *Drapier's Lett.* Wks. 1755 V. II. 71 A seasonable report of some invasion..; which is a great smoother of rubs in publick proceedings. **1767** PERCY *Anc. Eng. Minstrels* in *Reliq.* (ed. 2) I. p. xx, A word which denotes 'Smoothers and Polishers of language'. **1872** BLACK *Adv. Phaeton* xix. 265 A sunset is a wonderful smoother-down of these artificial features in a landscape. **1902** *Westm. Gaz.* 2 July 2/2 Last March Mr. Lehmann.. was very angry with the 'smoothers', as he was pleased to call the peacemakers in the Liberal Party.

**b.** A worker employed in smoothing linen; a calenderer or ironer.

**1776** ADAM SMITH *W.N.* I. i. (1869) I. 7 The bleachers and smoothers of the linen. **1898** *Daily News* 12 July 6/6 Maggie Atkinson, a smoother in Castlereagh Laundry.

**3.** An implement, tool, or machine for smoothing (see quots.).

**1688** HOLME *Armoury* III. 352/1 The third..is termed a *Smoother*, with which all their Leather is *slickened*, as they call it. **1738** CHAMBERS *Cycl.* s.v. *Bookbinding*, The book, being put in the press,..is scraped with a knife called a *scraper*; and after that with another called a *smoother*. **1854** MISS BAKER *Northampt. Gloss.*, *Smoother*, a smoothing iron. **1885** *Trans. Lanc. & Chesh. Antiq. Soc.* III. 256 These [glass] mullers or smoothers were in use for centuries. **1890** W. J. GORDON *Foundry* 154 They [*sc.* pieces of wood] then pass on to the 'smoother', a fixed knife, against which they are driven.

**smoother**, obs. form of SMOTHER *sb.* and *v.*

†**smoothery**: see SMETH. *Obs.*

**smooth-faced**, *a.* [f. SMOOTH *a.* 15.]

**1.** Of persons: Having a face free from hair, wrinkles, etc.; clean-shaven, beardless.

?*c* **1580** in Nichols *Topographer* II. 400 Thomas Myeld in whight armours faire, and smooth-fased. **1591** *Troub. Raigne K. John* xi. 42 A smooth-facte Nunne is all the Abbots wealth. **1621** QUARLES *Esther* iv, Hopefull Princes (ill-aduis'd By young, and smooth-fac'd Councell). **1689** *Lond. Gaz.* No. 2056/4 John Randall,..smooth faced, aged about 20. **1756** C. SMART tr. *Horace, Sat.* I. x. (1826) II. 81 The smooth-faced [L. *pulcher*] Hermogenes. **1856** R. A. VAUGHAN *Hours w. Mystics* (1860) I. 89 No shavelings,.. like the smooth-faced sanctities of the later calendar. **1883** *Standard* 16 May 5/6 Marks of small-pox were so prevalent that it was common to distinguish one free from them as a smooth-faced person.

*transf.* **1594** SHAKS. *Rich. III*, v. v. 33 Let thy Heires.. Enrich the time to come, with Smooth-fac'd Peace, With smiling Plenty.

**b.** *fig.* Having or assuming a bland, ingratiating, or insinuating expression; plausible in manner.

**1595** SHAKS. *John* II. i. 573 He that winnes of all..: That smooth-fac'd Gentleman, tickling commoditie. **1603** J. DAVIES (Heref.) *Humours Heaven* Wks. (Grosart) I. 43/2 Rogh-cast the skin of smooth-fac'd glozing Guile With burning blisters. **1682** CREECH *Lucretius* (1683) 170 Nor could the treacherous smile Of smooth-fac't Wares tempt one poor man to toyl. **1812** SHELLEY *Address* Prose Wks. 1888 I. 228 Take care then of smooth-faced impostors. **1862** SALA *Ship Chandler* ii. 22 How much has that smooth-faced hound given you to stand in with him?

**2.** *fig.* Of words, etc.: Specious, plausible.

**1620–6** QUARLES *Feast for Worms* 415 They whose smooth-fac'd words become the Altar. **1677** GILPIN *Demonol.* (1867) 194 Weak heads cannot see the far end of a smooth-faced doctrine.

**3.** Of things: Having a smooth face or surface.

**1647** H. MORE *Poems* 177 The rough Earth, one smooth-fac'd Round would show. **1648** J. BEAUMONT *Psyche* II. cxxxix, For his rich Ring of smoothfac'd Diamond. **1858** HAWTHORNE *Fr. & It. Note-bks.* (1872) II. 68 Other smooth-faced and stuccoed edifices. **1896** *Daily News* 19 Dec. 6/4 A smooth-faced cloth in a soft tone of heliotrope.

**smooth-headed**, *a.* [f. SMOOTH *a.* 15.] Having a smooth head. Chiefly in the names of animals, plants, etc.

**1752** J. HILL *Hist. Anim.* 326 The variegated-backed, smooth-headed Strix. **1822** *Hortus Angl.* II. 7 *Papaver Dubium.* Long Smooth-headed Poppy. **1831** GRIFFITH tr. *Cuvier* IX. Syn. 65 Smooth-headed Gerrhonote, *Gerrhonotus Leiocephalus.* **1893** LYDEKKER *Roy. Nat. Hist.* I. 156 The Smooth-Headed Sapajou (*Cebus monachus*)..is a species from Rio Janeiro.

**smoothie** ('smuːðɪ), *sb.* and *a.* *colloq.* (orig. *U.S.*). Also **smoothy.** [f. SMOOTH *a.* + -Y[6], -IE.]

**A.** *sb.* A person who is 'smooth' (sense 7); one who is suave or stylish in conduct or appearance: usu. a man. Occas. with unfavourable sense: a slick but shallow or insinuating fellow, a fop.

**1929** *Princeton Alumni Weekly* 24 May 981/3 *Smoothie*.. indicates *savoir faire*, a certain *je ne sais quoi*... Clothes do much to make the *smoothie*. **1932** B. G. DE SYLVA et al. (*song-title*) You're an old smoothie. **1939** R. CHANDLER *Big Sleep* xxv. 213 It might be a smoothie in the detective business trying to get a noseful of somebody else's case. **1943** HUNT & PRINGLE *Service Slang* 60 *Smoothie*, a chap who fancies himself as a ladies' man. **1954** P. FRANKAU *Wreath for Enemy* I. i. 5 Laurent is a smoothy, and I do not see how anybody could be in love with him. **1957** *Listener* 14 Nov. 801/2 A television smoothie. (This last is now gossip-writer's English for a slick commentator or smiling interviewer.) **1958** C. RICE *April Robin Murders* v. 54 This poetic-looking smoothie makes a thing out of marrying women with money. **1960** *Spectator* 8 July 66 The usual smoothie with a pseudo-American accent. **1973** *Guardian* 4 May 31/2 '*They* think there's nothing but muck and pit heaps up here,' say North-easterners, referring to the southern 'smoothies'. **1979** H. JENKINS *Culture Gap* I. iv. 24, I have nothing but contempt for the international art market. It is a racket none the better for being operated by cultivated smoothies.

**B.** *adj.* = SMOOTH *a.* 7.

**1959** I. JEFFERIES *Thirteen Days* iv. 54 Stern..was a real smoothie boy..like what I intended to be when I grew up. **1972** *Times* 7 Sept. 19/1 Max's prime characteristic..is being very tactful without being at all smoothy. **1974** N. FREELING *Dressing of Diamond* 101 Bernard..is good at the smoothie commercial stuff.

ˌ**smoothifiˈcation.** [Cf. next.] A smoothing.

**1799** SOUTHEY in Robberds *Mem. W. Taylor* (1843) I. 291 These [verses] I meant to have returned you with some proffered smoothifications.

ˈ**smoothify**, *v.* [f. SMOOTH *a.* + -(I)FY.] *trans.* To render smooth. In quot. *fig.*

**1694** MOTTEUX *Rabelais* v. xix. (1737) 85 They flatter the Devil here, and *smoothify* his Name.

**smoothing** ('smuːðɪŋ), *vbl. sb.* [f. SMOOTH *v.*]

**1. a.** The action of the verb, in various senses; an instance of this. Also with *out* and *fig.*

**1577** B. GOOGE *Heresbach's Husb.* I. (1586) 33b, The Meale which the people in old tyme dyd vse for the smoothing of their skinnes. **1663** GERBIER *Counsel* d iij, Some of them Bear-like-whelps (by licking and smoothing) have gotten some fashionable like shape. **1676** ROW *Contin. Blair's Autobiog.* xi. (1848) 291 After some smoothings of it, it was approven. **1738** in *6th Rep. Dep. Kpr.* App. II. 120 A new sort of cast metallick Boxes for the smoothing of Linen. **1822** J. PARKINSON *Outl. Oryctol.* 253 Every degree of resolution, from..destroying the finest striæ to the smoothing of ridges. **1885** 'LUCAS MALET' *Col. Enderby's Wife* III. vi, She..slowly settled her mantle into its place, with sundry dainty pattings and smoothings. **1929** *Jrnl. du Conseil* IV. 228 The purpose of the smoothing was to eliminate minor fluctuations of the character of lunar (monthly) cycles which are known to exist in the sardine. **1933** *Econometrica* I. 238 (*heading*) Time series: their analysis by successive smoothings. **1939** *Proc. R. Soc.* A. CLXXI. 81 The smoothing out of the stress distribution becomes less and less effective, and the maximum stress at the stress peaks rises. **1955** L. D. LANDAU in W. Pauli *Niels Bohr* 68 The great difficulties which arise in a physical 'smoothing-out' of particles, as opposed to a purely formal 'smoothing-out'..are well known. **1970** *Nature* 22 Aug. 824/1 The output signal [was] digitally recorded after smoothing with a 1 s time constant electronic filter.

**b.** *Phonology.* (See quot. 1888.)

**1888** SWEET *Eng. Sounds* 22 'Smoothing' or the levelling of the two elements of a diphthong under a monophthong is the result of absorption. **1894** —— *Anglo-Sax. Reader* (ed. 7) p. xxiv, When these smoothings occur in WS and Kt texts they may..be due to Angl. scribes. **1935** *Harvard Univ. Summ. Ph.D. Theses* 288 Under smoothing are included all monophthongizations and monophthong-retaining effects which are due to WG (originally) velar consonants. **1977** *Archivum Linguisticum* VIII. 79 It seems most probable that S[econd] F[ronting] was a rather late change, taking place after *i*-umlaut had occurred although almost certainly before back mutation and smoothing.

**2. a.** *attrib.* in the names of appliances, implements, etc., used in smoothing, as **smoothing-board** (see quot.); **smoothing-box**, a box-iron (now *dial.*); †**smoothing-leather**, a razor-strop; **smoothing-mill, -stone** (see quots.); **smoothing-trowel**, a kind of trowel used in plastering. Also designating devices for reducing ripple in electrical signals, as ***smoothing capacitor, choke, circuit, filter.***

**1688** HOLME *Armoury* III. xx. (Roxb.) 249/1 Four Instruments belonging to the Art of a Lanthorn maker... The second..is called a *Smoothing Board. *a* **1700** EVELYN *Diary* 8 Oct. 1672, A thick piece of yron, such as laundresses use to put in their *smoothing-boxes. **1799** G. SMITH *Laboratory* II. 409 It will be proper to rub the smoothing-box or iron with a little wax. **1959** *Engineering* 20 Feb. 230/2 A small *smoothing capacitor in the reading amplifier prevents the output from falling to zero during the transport of the wiper from one contact to the next. **1941** *P.O. Electr. Engineers Jrnl.* XXXIV. 118/1 With the development of floating battery power supply systems in telephone exchanges and repeater stations, there is a considerable demand for *smoothing chokes. **1940** *Chambers's Techn. Dict.* 780/1 *Smoothing circuit. **1975** G. J. KING *Audio Handbk.* iv. 96 Separate smoothing and filtering circuits are used for the supplies of the preceding stages and for the preamplifier stages of the control section. **1941** *P.O. Electr. Engineers Jrnl.* XXXIV. 118/1 The cost of the complete *smoothing filter may be comparable with that of the associated motor-generator set. **1709** *Phil. Trans.* XXVI. 496, I passed the same Razor over my Strop or *Smoothing-Leather. **1850** HOLTZAPFFEL *Turning* III. 1302 For soft stones the *smoothing mill is sometimes a plain disk of willow wood or mahogany. **1875** KNIGHT *Dict. Mech.* 2227 *Smoothing-mill*, the polishing-mill of the lapidary. *Ibid.*, **Smoothing stone*, a substitute for a smoothing-iron, made of steatite, attached to a plate and handle of metal. **1825** J. NICHOLSON *Operat. Mechanic* 612 This coat is spread with a *smoothing-trowel. **1873** E. SPON *Workshop Rec.* Ser. I. 121/2 The setting is spread with the smoothing trowel.

**b.** ***smoothing-iron***, a flat-iron (also *fig.*); an iron slicker used for smoothing leather.

(*a*) **1627** W. HAWKINS *Apollo Shroving* IV. iii. 63 The lace is so thicke... I know not what can foule it, vnlesse the smoothing-iron cast a rusty colour through the paper. **1755** JOHNSON s.v. *Iron*, A flat iron, box iron, or smoothing iron. **1848** MRS. GASKELL *M. Barton* viii, The smoothing-irons that hung before the fire. **1889** GRETTON *Memory's Harkback* 275, I drew the smoothing-iron over all, by expressing as fully..as I knew how, my admiration of his glorious country.

(*b*) **1852** MORFIT *Tanning & Currying* (1853) 370 The wrinkles in the skin are flattened by means of a mallet or a smoothing iron.

**c.** ***smoothing-plane***, a small fine-set plane used in finishing (see quots.).

**1678** MOXON *Mech. Exerc.* iv. 72 The Fore-Plain is used before the Smoothing-Plain. **1703** [R. NEVE] *City & C. Purchaser* 190 The Smoothing-plane..is a thick Plate of Polish'd-brass, about 9 Inches square, a little turn'd up, on all the 4 edges. **1815** J. SMITH *Panorama Sci. & Art* I. 110 The smoothing-plane is about seven inches in length, it has no tote or handle, and otherwise differs in shape from any of the planes yet mentioned. **1875** SIR T. SEATON *Fret-Cutting* 83 The smoothing-plane must be set very fine, and the upper iron should come quite low down towards the edge.

ˈ**smoothing**, *ppl. a.* [f. as prec.]

**1.** That smooths or makes smooth; having the effect of smoothing.

**1495** *Trevisa's Barth. De P.R.* XIX. xlvii. (W. de W.) 890 Bytter thynges..bi grete drynesse..be made smothyng and softynge. **1650** VENNER *Via Recta* 103 It induceth a smoothing delectation to the gullet. **1857** DICKENS *Dorrit* II. vii, It made her anxious..to be operated upon by that smoothing hand.

†**2.** Plausible, blandishing, flattering. *Obs.*

*a* **1592** GREENE *Jas. IV*, I. i, Princes rather choose a smoothing tongue, Than men of art that can accept the time. **1592** —— *Groat's W. Wit* Wks. (Grosart) XII. 114 He learned likewise with smoothing words to faine. **1593** SHAKS. *Lucr.* 892 Thy secret pleasure turnes to open shame, ..Thy smoothing titles to a ragged name. **1675** OTWAY *Alcibiades* III. i, Fine smoothing Terms to cloke a Passion in.

Hence ˈ**smoothingly** *adv.*

**1854** R. S. SURTEES *Handley Cross* (1898) I. 186 You seem an honest, intelligent sort of man, continued Mr. Bolster smoothingly. **1884** E. FAWCETT *Rutherford* vi, One of his white hands fluttered smoothingly about his yellow beard.

**smoothish** ('smuːðɪʃ), *a.* [f. SMOOTH *a.*]

Somewhat or rather smooth; slightly glabrous.

**1681** GREW *Musæum* II. I. iv. 205 The Skin smoothish. **1796** WITHERING *Brit. Pl.* (ed. 3) II. 103 The smoothish straw, and the creeping root, are obvious distinctions. **1836** T. HOOK *G. Gurney* III. 320 Having made, even in smoothish water, several experiments. **1866** *Treas. Bot.* 920/2 A fast-growing tree, with a smoothish grey bark.

**smooth-leaved**, *a.* [f. SMOOTH *a.* 15.] Of plants: Having smooth leaves. Chiefly in specific names: ***smooth-leaved elm***, a large tree, *Ulmus carpinifolia*, native to Europe, North Africa, and western Asia, and distinguished by smooth leaves with shiny upper surfaces.

**1731** MILLER *Gard. Dict.* s.v. *Acanthus*, The smooth-leav'd Garden Bear's-breech. *Ibid.* s.v. *Ulmus; folio glabro*, The Smooth-leav'd or Witch-Elm. **1751** J. HILL *Hist. Plants* 456 The pinnated smooth-leaved Sorbus. The Quicken-tree. **1811** J. E. SMITH *Eng. Bot.* XXXII. 2248 *(heading)* Smooth-leaved, or Wych Elm. **1825** *Greenho. Comp.* I. 95 A smooth-leaved plant of easy culture. **1840** *Penny Cycl.* XVIII. 172/2 The Smooth-leaved Pine (*Pinus leiophylla*). **1841** *Ibid.* XIX. 485/1 *Rhus glabra* (Smooth-leaved Sumach). **1857** MISS PRATT *Flower. Pl.* V. 108 Smooth-leaved Alpine Willow. **1913** ELWES & HENRY *Trees Gt. Brit. & Ireland* VII. 1887 Smooth-leaved Elm... A tree, with a straight bole, and wide-spreading branches. **1971** *Country Life* 23 Dec. 1772/2 We can be pretty certain that these trees.. are forms of the smooth-leaved elm.

**smoothly** (ˈsmuːðlɪ), *adv.* Forms: 4 **smoþely**, 5–6 **smothely**, 6 **smothly**, 6– **smoothly**, 7 **smoothly**. [f. SMOOTH *a.*]

**1.** In a smooth manner; with smooth, easy, or gentle movement or motion; gently.

**13..** *Gaw. & Gr. Knt.* 407 Þou me smoþely has smyten. **13..** *E.E. Allit. P.* B. 732, I schal.. let him smolt al unsmyten smoþely atonez. *a* **1529** SKELTON *Col. Cloute* 1254 The forecastell of my shyp Shall glyde, and smothely slyp Out of the wawes wod. **1594** KYD *Cornelia* IV. ii, Thine easie streames That glide as smothly as a Parthian shaft. **1612** WOODALL *Surg. Mate* Wks. (1653) 2 To make a Launcet himself which will enter smoothly. **1665** BOYLE *Occas. Refl.* VI. i. (1848) 340 A belief that the toothsome would make the nutritive part go smoothly down. **1722** DE FOE *Col. Jack* (1840) 47, I brushed smoothly, but closely by the man. **1784** COWPER *Task* II. 262 That winds and waters.. May bear us smoothly to the Gallic shore. **1805** WORDSW. *Waggoner* IV. 62 Where, smoothly urged, the vapours sweep Along. **1886** *Manch. Exam.* 8 Jan. 6/1 The sleighs skim along very smoothly and lightly.

*transf.* **1597** DRAYTON *Heroical Ep., Q. Kath. to O. Tudor* 137 The British language.. runnes as smoothly from those lypps of thine, As the pure Thuskan from the Florantine. **1599** SHAKS. *Much Ado* V. ii. 33 Carpet-mongers, whose name yet runne smoothly in the euen rode of a blanke verse.

*Comb.* **1805** WORDSW. *Waggoner* II. 108 A gallant, stately Man-of-war, Fixed on a smoothly-sliding car. **1888** LEES & CLUTTERBUCK *B.C. 1887* xxx, The broad surface of the now smoothly-flowing Kootenay.

**2.** So as to present or leave a smooth, even, or level surface; evenly, regularly.

**1489** CAXTON *Faytes of A.* I. xxiii. 71 A longe trayne of men of armes al clos togyder and renged full smothely. **1641** G. SANDYS *Paraphr. Song Sol.* IV. i, Thy Teeth like Sheep in their return From Chison, washt, and smoothly shorn. **1713** *Guardian* No. 168, Beneath the Shade of flowing Jet The Iv'ry Forehead smoothly set. **1813** J. THOMSON *Lect. Inflam.* 449 A bandage.. should be applied, as smoothly as can be possibly performed. **1877** RAYMOND *Statist. Mines & Mining* 121 The rocks they contain, generally smoothly worn, but not fully rounded, are [etc.].

*Comb.* *c* **1730** SAVAGE *Wks.* (1775) II. 198 Her soft attendants smooth the spotless skin, And, smoothly oval, turn the shapely chin. **1873** TRISTRAM *Moab* v. 71 The wall with its smoothly-sloped facing.

**b.** With clothes of smooth or fine texture.

**1579** GOSSON *Sch. Abuse* (Arb.) 39 They were smoothly appareled, soft lodged, daintely feasted.

**3.** In a bland, mild, or plausible manner; blandly, suavely.

**1523** SKELTON *Garl. Laurel* 504 Some lokyd full smothely, and had a fals quarter. **1592** *Arden of Feversham* III. v, Thou hast.. spoke as smoothly as an orator. **1649** MILTON *Eikon.* 8 Heer he smoothly seeks to wipe off all the envy of his evill Government upon his Substitutes. **1653** H. MORE *Conject. Cabbal.* 226 The Serpent.. looking so smoothly and innocently on't,.. and so deceiving them. **1825** SCOTT *Talism.* vi, Despardieux! This is smoothly said to soothe a sick man. **1845** JAMES *Arrah Neil* iv, Did he speak smoothly and civilly?

**4.** Without impediment, obstruction, or complication; without any trouble or difficulty arising. (Common in 19th cent.)

**1668** CHAS. II in Cartwright *Madame* (1894) 260 Things should go on smoothly. **1777** WATSON *Philip II* (1839) 59 It could not reasonably be expected that the government would proceed smoothly. **1791** BOSWELL *Johnson* an. 1766 (Oxf. ed.) I. 336 Goldsmith.. mentions Luke as a person well known, and superficial readers have passed it over quite smoothly. **1856** MERIVALE *Rom. Emp.* xlii. V. 135 The ceremony passed smoothly without demur or scruple. **1881** LADY HERBERT *Edith* 6 For the first few months all went on smoothly.

**smoothness** (ˈsmuːðnɪs). Also 4 **smoþe-**, 5–6 **smothnesse**. [f. SMOOTH *a.*]

**1.** The quality of being smooth or of having a smooth, level, or even surface; calmness (of water).

*c* **1374** CHAUCER *Boeth.* v. met. 4 (1868) 166 Lettres emprentid in þe smoþenesse or in þe plainesse of þe table of wex. **1495** *Trevisa's Barth. De P.R.* XVII. xx. (W. de W.) 615 Boxe.. for smothnesse of matere.. is able to receyue wrytynge of letters. **1548** ELYOT, *Lævitas*, playnnesse or smothnesse. **1586** MARLOWE *1st Pt. Tamburl.* II. i, His lofty browes in foldes do figure death, And in their smoothnesse, amitie and life. **1656** tr. *Hobbes' Elem. Philos.* (1839) 405 Smoothness, roughness,.. refer to figure, and are therefore common both to touch and sight. *a* **1688** CUDWORTH *Immut. Morality* (1731) 61 Democritus.. makes one of them to consist in Roughness and Ruggedness, the other in Smoothness and Evenness of Parts. **1774** M. MACKENZIE *Maritime Surv.* 86 If the Card of the Compass can be made to stand at Rest in the Boat, either by Art, or the Smoothness of the Sea. **1815** J. SMITH *Panorama Sci. & Art* I. 31 The last degree of smoothness can only be obtained by grinding. **1860** TYNDALL *Glac.* I. xv. 101 The water was of a glassy smoothness.

**b.** *fig.* or in fig. context.

**1593** SHAKS. *Lucr.* 1247 Their [*sc.* women's] smoothness, like a goodly champaign plain, Lays open all the little worms that creep. **1663** S. PATRICK *Parab. Pilgr.* xv. (1687) 124 The roughness of your way, and the asperities of mens manners, must not spoil the smoothness of your soul. **1845** PATTISON *Ess.* (1889) I. 3 A deficiency of moral energy, arising chiefly from the smoothness with which the current of social life runs down.

**c.** The fact of having a smooth or hairless skin.

**1626** BACON *Sylva* §680 The Cause of the Smoothness in Men, is not any Abundance of Heat and Moisture, though that indeed causeth Pilositie.

**d.** A smooth place or part.

**1674** N. FAIRFAX *Bulk. & Selv.* 86 The pieces of a body.. are only clapt together at their little smoothnesses.

**2.** Easy flow, elegance, or polish (of language, diction, etc.).

**1589** PUTTENHAM *Eng. Poesie* II. vii. (Arb.) 93 The smoothnesse of your words and sillables running vpon feete of sundrie quantities. **1602** SHAKS. *Ham.* III. ii. 9 In the verie Torrent.. and (as I may say) the Whirle-winde of Passion, you must acquire and beget a Temperance that may giue it Smoothnesse. **1666** DRYDEN *Pref. Ann. Mirab.* 42, I affected the softness of expression and the smoothness of measure. **1781** COWPER *Table-talk* 513 That verse, whatever fire the fancy warms, Without a creamy smoothness has no charms. **1836** *Random Recoll. Ho. Lords* xvi. 385 His sentiments and arguments flow from his lips with a smoothness and facility .. seldom witnessed. **1885** *Manch. Exam.* 30 Mar. 5/4 The Cabinet, lulled to repose by the smoothness of Lord Clarendon's flowing periods.

**b.** Polish, refinement, ease (of manners, bearing, etc.).

**1832** LYTTON *E. Aram* I. vi, Judge for yourself if I be fit for the smoothness, and confidence, and ease of social intercourse. **1838** —— *Alice* 60 She acquired self-possession and the smoothness of society.

**3.** The quality of being bland, ingratiating, or plausible; assumed or simulated friendliness, civility, or amiability.

**1600** SHAKS. *A.Y.L.* I. iii. 79 She is too subtile for thee, and her smoothnes.., and her patience, Speake to the people. **1611** BEAUM. & FL. *Maid's Trag.* IV, I want smoothness To thank a man for pardoning of a crime I never knew. **1845** JAMES *Arrah Neil* iv, Dry, of Long-soaken, was all smoothness and civility. **1858** W. ARNOT *Laws fr. Heaven* ii. 22 Smoothness is not an equivalent for truth.

**4.** Easiness, facility (of working).

**1893** HODGES *Elem. Photogr.* (1907) 133 Many such devices work with great smoothness and certainty.

**ˈsmoot-hole.** *dial.* Also **smout-**. [f. SMOOT *sb.*[1] Cf. Da. *smuthul.*] (See quots. and SMOOT *sb.*[1])

*a* **1828** BEWICK *Mem.* (1862) 39 The entrance to these last was always by a 'smout hole', or small opening, through which we crept on hands and knees. **1828** CARR *Craven Gloss., Smoot-hole*, a hole in a fence, through which a hare is accustomed to pass. **1893** J. WATSON *Conf. Poacher* 133 A smoot-hole in the fence through which the rabbits run.

**smooth-skinned**, *a.* [f. SMOOTH *a.* 15.] Having a smooth skin.

**1611** TOURNEUR *Ath. Trag.* II. v, I do not like these phlegmatic smooth-skinned, soft-fleshed fellows. **1668** CHARLETON *Onomast.* 128 *Galeus Lævis*,.. the smooth-skinned Dog-fish. **1689** *Lond. Gaz.* No. 2454/4 A smooth skinn'd little Spaniel Bitch. **1798** *Trans. Soc. Arts* XVI. 329 The fruit is of various shapes and sizes,.. some smooth skinned. **1881** *Cassell's Nat. Hist.* V. 41 The Homelyn Ray is a smooth-skinned species.

**smooth-spoken**, *a.* [f. SMOOTH *adv.*] Smooth-tongued, soft-spoken.

**1821** SCOTT *Kenilw.* xxiii, Now, a plague upon all smooth-spoken hosts! **1838** LYTTON *Alice* II. vii, You corroborate my own opinion of that smooth-spoken gentleman. **1854** H. MILLER *Sch. & Schm.* (1858) 255 The landlord, a smooth-spoken, little old man, striving hard to conciliate him.

**ˈsmooth-talk**, *v.* *colloq.* (orig. *U.S.*). [f. SMOOTH *a.*] *trans.* To address or persuade with bland, specious language. Also, to win (one's way) by smooth-talking.

**1950** A. LOMAX *Mister Jelly Roll* (1952) 205 If a cop stopped him he could smooth-talk his way right out of it just like they were relatives. **1956** *Sun* (Baltimore) 2 Mar. 19/6 A Michigan man was accused today of smooth-talking bankers .. into sending him cash by posing over the telephone as a depositor. **1958** J. WAIN *Contenders* 171 She was transferring herself.. as a result of being smooth-talked into it. **1960** *Washington Post* 2 Nov. 3/2 He and his wife had been 'smooth-talked' and later threatened. **1967** 'E. LATHEN' *Murder against Grain* ii. 18, I let him smooth-talk me into doing the Sloan's errands. **1979** F. OLBRICH *Sweet & Deadly* viii. 98 The practised politician smooth-talking his way round an awkward question.

**smooth-tongued**, *a.* [f. SMOOTH *a.* 15.]

**1.** Smooth or plausible in speech; using fair or flattering words; smooth-spoken.

**1592** MARLOWE *Edw. II*, IV. v, Spencer.. Is with that smoothe toongd scholler Baldock gone. **1603–35** BRETON *Mad World my Masters* Wks. (Grosart) II. 8/1 A very artificiall faire, sharpe-witted,.. and, as I after found, smooth-tongued gentlewoman. **1684** OTWAY *Atheist* III. i, What a smooth-tongu'd little Rascal 'tis. **1771** SMOLLETT *Humph. Cl.* (1815) 253 The smooth-tongued rascal found no difficulty to insinuate himself into the place of her heart. **1829** LYTTON *Devereux* I. xiii, Those Jesuits are so smooth-tongued to women. **1864** PUSEY *Daniel* viii. 552 His once smooth-tongued friend, with whom he had taken sweet counsel.

**b.** Of a poet or writer: Polished, refined. *rare*$^{-1}$.

**1658** COKAINE *Poems* 11 Here smooth-tongu'd Drayton was inspired by Mnemosynes's manifold progenie.

**2.** Marked or characterized by, of the nature of, plausibility or speciousness.

**1761** CHURCHILL *Night* 162 Poems 1767 I. 68 By slavish methods must he learn to please, By smooth-tongu'd flatt'ry, that curst court-disease. **1843** BETHUNE *Sc. Fireside Stories* 298 Almost from infancy he had been noted for smooth-tongued falsehood.

Hence **smooth-tonguedness**.

**1737** OZELL *Rabelais* II. 113 The smooth-tonguedness of the Adversary.

**smooting**, *vbl. sb.*: see SMOOT *v.*[2] and SMUTTING.

**smooty**: see SMUTTY.

‖**smørbrød** (ˈsmœrbrød). Also **smorbrodt**. [Norw.: cf. SMØRREBRØD.] A Norwegian open sandwich: also *collect.*

**1933** M. LOWRY *Ultramarine* ii. 96 Nevermore sit in a lunar park in Aalesund, holding each other's hands, or eating smorbrodt. **1980** R. BARNARD *Death in Cold Climate* i. 9 He.. collected on a plate a ham smørbrød and a cheese roll.

**smorch**, obs. variant of SMIRCH *v.*

**smore** (smɔə(r)), *sb.* Now *Sc.* Also 4 **smorre**. [f. SMORE *v.* Cf. Du. and Flem. *smoor*, G. (rare) *schmor.*] Smother, smoke, etc.

**1393** LANGL. *P. Pl.* C. xx. 303 (MS. Cott. Vesp.), Þe smoke and þe smorre þat smyth in oure eyne. *Ibid.* 323. **1866** W. GREGOR *Banffsh. Gloss.* 171 *Smore*, a stifling smoke;.. a close, stifling atmosphere [etc.].

**smore** (smɔə(r)), *v.* Now *Sc.* and *north. dial.* Forms: 1 **smorian**, 4– **smore** (4 **smor**, 6 *Sc.* **smoir**), 7–9 **smoar**; 9 *dial.* **smor(r**, **smur(r**. See also SMOOR *v.* [OE. *smorian*, = WFris. *smoarje*, *smoare*, MDu. and Du. *smoren* (Flem. also *smooren*), MLG. and LG. *smoren* (hence G. *schmoren*), of uncertain relationship. The stem is the base of early ME. *smorðer*, *smorðren* SMOTHER *sb.* and *v.*]

**1.** *trans.* To suffocate, smother.

*c* **725** *Corpus Gloss.* S 558 *St[r]angulat*, wyrgeð, *uel* smorað. *c* **975** *Rushw. Gosp.* Matt. xiii. 7 Sume þonne ȝefetun in þornas & wexon þa þornas & smoradun hiæ. *a* **1300** *Cursor M.* 8670 Mi felaw smord hir barn in bedd. *c* **1340** HAMPOLE *Pr. Consc.* 7601 All suld be smored withouten dout, War ne þa hevens ay moved obout. *c* **1440** *Alph. Tales* 145 As hur fadur was slepand vndernethe a matres, sho smoryd him odead. *a* **1470** HARDING *Chron.* CLXXVIII. xx, Thei smored were by their contrariaunce. **1513** MORE *Rich. III* (1883) 84 Smored and styfled, theyr breath failing, thei gaue vp to God their innocent soules. **1585** JAS. I *Ess. Poesie* (Arb.) 39 A rauing cloude, Which threatnes.. To smore and drowne him. ? *a* **1800** *Lady Diamond* in Child *Ballads* V. 37/2 Bring here to me that bonny boy, And we'll smore him right quietlie. **1808** JAMIESON s.v. *Thow, Smore Thow*,.. a heavy snow, accompanied with a strong wind, which.. threatens to *smore*, smother, or suffocate one.

**b.** To suffocate or smother *in* or *with* smoke, or implying this.

**14..** *Smyth & his Dame* 380 in Hazl. *E.P.P.* III. 215 Whan he had smored her in yᵉ smok. *c* **1450** HOLLAND *Howlat* 825 Lyke a smaik smorit in a smedy. **1500–20** DUNBAR *Poems* xxvi. 120 In the depest pot of hell He smorit thame with smvke. **1584** HUDSON *Du Bartas' Judith* III. 124 Some other vndertooke To fire the gates, or smore the towne with smoke. *c* **1755** R. FORBES *Jrnl. from London* 2 He was like to smore us a' i' the coach wi' the very ewder [of his pipe].

**c.** *intr.* To choke, be suffocated.

*c* **1470** HENRY *Wallace* VII. 452 Sum neuir rais, bot smoryt quhar thai lay. *a* **1586** MONTGOMERIE *Misc. Poems* xlvi. 55, I smore if I conceill, I wrak if I reveill, My hurt. **1808** JAMIESON s.v., 'I was like to smore': I was in danger of being suffocated.

**2.** *fig.* To smother, suppress, keep in obscurity or concealment, put or keep *down*, etc.

*c* **1375** *Sc. Leg. Saints* xl. (*Ninian*) 156 Sa þat þe science lent to þe be nocht tynt na smoryt in þe. *c* **1470** HENRY *Wallace* XI. 1436 Gret harm I thocht his gud deid suld be smord. **1538** CROMWELL in Merriman *Life & Lett.* (1902) II. 164 Yf the same shuld be smored or mysordered after your decease. **1599** JAS. I *Βασιλ. Δωρον* (1603) 47 Vntill yee roote out these barbarous feides, that their effectes may bee .. smoared downe. **1637** GILLESPIE *Eng. Pop. Cerem.* Ep. A iij b, The true life of godlinesse is smoared downe and suppressed by the burthen of these human inventions. **1790** SHIRREFS *Poems* 179 'Till now, I smoar'd my joy within my breast.

†**3.** To smear, bedaub. *Obs.*$^{-0}$

**1530** PALSGR. 723/2 Where have you ben, you have all to smored your face.

†**4.** To cook in a close vessel. Also *intr.* *Obs.*

This sense is prominent in Du., Flem., LG., and G.

**1562** TURNER *Herbal* (1568) 76 They put it [slauke] in a poot, and smore it, as they call it, and then it looketh blake. **1615** MARKHAM *Eng. Housew.* (1660) 67 Set it on a gentle fire, and let it stew, and smoar till the hearbs and onyons be soft.

**5.** *intr.* To smoulder. *rare.*

**1651** H. MORE *Enthus. Tri.* (1712) 17 Melancholy, that lies at first smoaring in the Heart and Blood. **1854** MISS BAKER *Northampt. Gloss.*, *Smore*, to burn without flame. 'The fire smores.'

Hence **'smoring** *vbl. sb.* and *ppl. a.*

*c* **1440** *Promp. Parv.* 461/1 Smorynge, *fumigacio.* **1586** *Rec. Elgin* (Spald. Cl.) II. 6 To prowe the death of hir tua bairnis to have bein without violence and smoiring. **1642** H. MORE *Song of Soul* I. iii. 38 There lyes A little spark.., But smoreing filth so close it doth comprize That it cannot flame out. *Ibid.* II. III. ii. 15 Let fall that smoring mantle. **1647** —— *Exorcismus* ii, Thou fast-bound ball Of smoring darknesse!

**smorgasbord** ('smɔəgəs,bɔəd). Also ‖**smörgåsbord**, *erron.* **smörgosbrod**, etc. [a. Sw., f. *smörgås* (slice of) bread and butter (f. *smör* butter, cogn. w. SMEAR *sb.* + *gås* goose, lump of butter) + *bord* BOARD *sb.*, table: cf. SMØRREBRØD.] **1.** The Swedish hors d'œuvres, typically comprising a cold table of open sandwiches served with an assortment of delicacies; also provided as a separate meal or buffet.

**1893** *Figaro* (Chicago) 26 Jan. 345/1 In every house-hold ..before sitting down to dinner an appetizer, or *smörgosbrod*, is partaken of. **1895** *Baedeker's Norway, Sweden & Denmark* p. xxiii, The Smörgåsbord or Brännvinsbord, where various relishes, bread-and-butter, and liqueurs are served by way of stimulant to the appetite, is peculiar to Sweden. **1926** *Ladies' Home Jrnl.* Nov. 150/2 The 'Smorgesbord', or bountifully supplied relish table, is a Scandinavian institution, though it is said the custom originated in ancient Russia. **1936** *Discovery* Apr. 109/2 Meals, which begin with the smörgåsbord, as in Sweden, are ..excellent and cheap. **1948** 'J. TEY' *Franchise Affair* i. 17 'Sandwiches without tops' the girl called them. 'Smorgasbord'. **1959** *Good Food Guide 1959–60* 314 The first level offers a Swedish—Swedish, not Danish, because hot hors d'œuvres are included—smorgasbord at 8/6. **1968** [see CHUCK WAGGON]. **1975** D. RAMSAY *Descent into Dark* ii. 66 The smorgasbord restaurant Joyce had been fond of. **1978** *New York* 3 Apr. 19 (Advt.), Wine & Dine! Gourmet menu. Smorgasbord..2 bars. Duty-free prices.

**2.** *fig.* A medley, miscellany; a rich variety or selection.

**1948** MENJOU & MUSSELMAN *It took Nine Tailors* xxii. 176 Instead the studio offered me the lead in a piece of *smörgåsbord* called *The Sorrows of Satan*, a novel by Marie Corelli. **1961** *Encounter* Apr. 56/2 The messy smörgasbord of his hysterical whimsical ideas. **1969** T. E. B. HOWARTH *Culture, Anarchy & Public Schools* iii. 55 The smorgasbord system is a form of shorthand to describe the multiplicity of optional 'subjects' pupils in American high schools elect to study. **1978** M. PUZO *Fools Die* xii. 129 Everyday Magazines ..was a group of publications that drowned the American public with information, pseudoinformation, sex and pseudosex... A real smorgasbord.

**'smorning** ('smɔənɪŋ), colloq. or dial. abbrev. of 'this morning'.

**1932** S. GIBBONS *Cold Comfort Farm* xx. 267 She took on something awful about Miss Judith going off 'smorning. **1967** 'G. DOUGLAS' *Death went Hunting* xviii. 155 Well, 'smorning Mr. Bolton comes over to me. **1973** J. MANN *Only Security* xiv. 184, I found her, I did. 'Smorning, when I come rabbiting.

‖**smørrebrød** ('smœrəbrœð). Also **smörrebröd.** [Da., f. *smør* butter + *brød* BREAD *sb.*[1]; cf. SMØRBRØD.] A Danish open sandwich; also *collect.*

**1902** M. THOMAS *Denmark, Past & Present* II. xviii. 133 Your true Dane takes a piece of bread, plasters it with butter, then searches..for the slice of meat or fish he prefers and puts it on the bread and butter... This is called 'smörrebröd' and is the national dish. **1932** G. BRÖCHNER *Wayfarer in Denmark* vi. 76 All Danish cafés..have..a 'Smörrebröds seddel': a long narrow card with a list of the different kinds of Smörrebröd served. **1959** *Good Food Guide 1959–60* 242 It has opened a Scandinavian smörrebröd cold table in its basement. **1975** *tr. Melchior's Sleeper Agent* (1976) III. 247, I will make you some *Smørrebrød*, Rudi, the kind you like.

**smorther,** etc., obs. ff. SMOTHER *sb.* and *v.*

‖**smorzando** (smor'tsando), *adv.* and *sb.* [It., pres. pple. of *smorzare* to extinguish.] (See quot. 1801.) Also **smorzato** (smor'tsato) *adv.* [pa. pple.]

**1800** *Spirit Public Jrnls.* IV. 3 Mesdames Crouch,..De Camp, &c. will warble their dulcet tones, semitones,.. diminuendo's, rallentando's, and smorzando's, in due time and place! **1801** BUSBY *Dict. Mus.*, *Smorzando*, or *Smorzato*, an expression implying that the sounds of the passage over which it is placed are to be gradually diminished in the *legato* style.

**smot,** *sb.*[1] *Sc.* and *dial.* Also 6 **smoit**, 8 **smott**, 6, 9 **smote**. [f. SMOT *v.* Cf. G. dial. *schmotz*, var. of *schmutz*.]

**1.** A spot, stain, mark, blot. Also *fig.*

**1532** *Sc. Acts, Jas. V* (1814) 335/2 Obedient sonnis to..þe auctorite apostolik, without ony manere of smot, violacioune, or defectioune. **1562** WINȜET *Wks.* (S.T.S.) I. 26 That I may be clein fra all smot of blame. *a* **1572** KNOX *Hist. Ref.* Wks. 1846 I. 277 Ever trew and obedient.. without any smote. **1899** 'A. RAINE' *Berwen Banks* 104 The same brown smot on the nother ear, and that's the only smot upon her!

**2.** A distinguishing mark put on sheep; a flock of sheep marked in one way.

*a* **1672** LIVINGSTONE in *Sel. Biog.* (Wodrow Soc.) I. 340 You must have the tarr pigg by your belt, and be ready to give a smott to every one of Christ's sheep as they come in your way. **1808** in JAMIESON. **1857** AITON *Domest. Econ.* 225 No man will break his 'smote', as it is called, but at a loss, even when a fair price is given.

†**smot,** *sb.*[2] *Obs.*[−1] [Irreg. f. *smot(e*, pa. t. of SMITE *v.*] A stroke, blow.

**1566** STUDLEY tr. *Seneca, Agam.* G viij, Thryse aboute to smyte, He staide the smot.

**smot,** *v.* ? *Obs.* In later use *Sc.* [Related to MHG. *smotzen* (? hence Du. *smotsen*), var. of *smutzen* (G. *schmutzen*): see SMUT *v.*] *trans.* To besmirch, defile, befoul. Also *fig.*

Also 'to mark with ruddle, tar, &c.' (Jamieson, 1808).

**1387** TREVISA *Higden* (Rolls) I. 359 Þey be i-smotted wiþ þe schrewednesse and bycomeþ traytours also. *a* **1400** *Apol. Lollards* 18 Þe kirk..forbediþ him comyn feleschip..þat he mend þe raþer, and smot not oþer. **1483** CAXTON *Gold. Leg.* 97/2 The sergeants that sawe hym so black and smotted bete hym wel wyth roddes. **1513** DOUGLAS *Æneid* V. vii. 91 Behald thaim smottit quyte Of his reid blude. *a* **1568** A. SCOTT *Poems* (S.T.S.) xxx. 52 Ladeis suld all thingis eschew That ma thair honor smot.

†**'smoterly,** *a.* *Obs.*[−1] [Cf. SMOTRY *a.* and SMOTTER *v.*] ? Besmirched in reputation.

*c* **1386** CHAUCER *Reeve's T.* 43 And eeck, for she was somdel smoterlich, She was as digne as water in a dich.

**smother** ('smʌðə(r)), *sb.* Forms: *α.* 2 **smorðer**, 3 **smurðre**, 4 **smorþre**, 5 **smorþur, -thour, -ther.** *β.* 3–4 **smoþer**, 6– **smother**, 6–7 **smoother.** *γ.* 5 **smodyr, -er**, 6 **smooder**, 9 *dial.* **smudder.** [Early ME. *smorðer*, f. the stem of OE. *smorian* SMORE *v.*]

**1. a.** Dense, suffocating, or stifling smoke, such as is produced by combustion without flame. (Freq. coupled with *smoke*.)

*α.* *c* **1175** *Lamb. Hom.* 43 Þet þridde [was] fur,..þe siste smorðer. *a* **1225** *Ancr. R.* 272 Þes feones chef þet nis to none þinge nouht bute to helle smurðre. **1393** LANGL. *P. Pl.* C. xx. 303 When smoke and smorþre smyt in hus eyen. *c* **1400** *Destr. Troy* 11796 Hit fest was on fyre, & flappit out onone, Vnto smorther & smoke.

*β, γ.* *a* **1300** *Body & Soul* in *Map's Poems* (Camden) 339 Þe erþe it openede anon, smoke and smoþer op it wal. **13..** *Adultery* 87 in Herrig *Archiv* LXXIX. 420 Smoþer & smoke þer come owte wylde. *a* **1400** *Stockh. Medical MS.* ii. 598 in *Anglia* XVIII. 322 Ȝif vnder nethyn þer hennys sate Of hennebane a smoþer thou make. *a* **1470** H. PARKER *Dives & Pauper* (W. de W. 1496) VI. xxii. 270/2 There shall be brennynge fyre and smoder without ende. *a* **1618** SYLVESTER *Urania* lxxxii, A thick, dark, pitchy Cloud of smoak, That round-about a kindling Fire suppresses With waving smother. **1657** P. HENRY *Diaries & Lett.* (1882) 33 When a fire is first kindled there's a great deale of smoke and smother. **1748** *Anson's Voy.* III. viii. 381 The great smother and smoke of the oakum. **1787** G. WHITE *Selborne* vii, Nothing is to be seen but smother and desolation. **1828** PLANCHE *Descent Danube* i. 25 The distant dome of Saint Paul's rising above the smother of our huge metropolis. **1882** BLACKMORE *Christowell* I, Filled with blue sulphureous fog, and smother of bitumen.

*Prov.* **1600** SHAKS. *A.Y.L.* I. ii. 299 Thus must I from the smoake into the smother. **1890** *Daily News* 25 June 5/1 They had gone from the smoke into the smother.

*fig.* **1565** JEWEL *Reply Harding, Answ. Concl.* (1611) 651 Now the Sonne is vp; your smooder is scattered. **1654** GATAKER *Disc. Apol.* 12 A great smother of foggie fumes, raised by slanderous tongues. **1697** COLLIER *Ess. Mor. Subj.* (1709) II. 2 Why else do they..spend their Taper in Smoak and Smother? **1809** MALKIN *Gil Blas* x. i. (Rtldg.) 337 The mad blockhead was so suffocated by the smother of authorship. **1975** N. NICHOLSON *Wednesday Early Closing* ix. 176 A dull smother of hopelessness hung over the town like the smutch from a smoking rubbish dump.

**b.** A smouldering state or condition; a smouldering or slow-burning fire. Also *fig.*

**1597** J. KING *On Jonas* (1618) 172 It lieth happely in a smother and smoak a long time before it breaketh out. **1625** BACON *Ess., Suspicion* (Arb.) 528 Men should remedy Suspicion, by procuring to know more, and not to keep their Suspicions in Smother. **1893** *Wilts. Gloss.*, *Smother*, a weed and rubbish fire in a garden. **1899** BALDOCK *Cromwell as Soldier* 363 This [liberty] he employed in fanning the smother into flame.

**2. a.** Dense or suffocating dust, fog, etc., filling the air.

**1697** DRYDEN *Æneid* II. 827 Where clouds of dust arise, —Amid that smother, Neptune holds his place. **1806** BERESFORD *Miseries Hum. Life* IV. xlii, Rubbish, flying smother, tumbling bricks, &c. of a half-ruined house. **1845** BROWNING *Flight of Duchess* xi, The Duke..Stood for a while in a sultry smother. **1886** STEVENSON *Dr. Jekyll* 50 Through the muffle and smother of these fallen clouds.

**b.** A confused turmoil or welter of foam or water. Also const. *of.*

**1840** R. H. DANA *Bef. Mast* xviii, We..brought the boat to in a smother of foam. **1888** STEVENSON *Black Arrow* 183 The horror of that great salt smother and welter under my foot here. **1890** CLARK RUSSELL *My Shipmate Louise* II. xx. 108 It made one think..of the smother one falls in with on the edge of the Gulf-Stream.

**c.** A wild profusion *of* flowers, etc.

**1888** *Daily News* 2 July 5/8 The smother of roses along the river fronts.

**d.** A smothered or indistinct noise.

**1904** H. B. M. WATSON *Hurricane Island* i. 7 A smother of sound came to me, as if the swimmer was under water, and his voice stifled.

**e.** *N.Z.* An incident in which sheep are lost by suffocation caused by others falling on top of them, as during a round-up.

**1930** L. G. D. ACLAND *Early Canterbury Runs* 1st Ser. vi. 128 They once had a bad smother there. *Ibid.* Mt. Peel was unlucky with smothers. **1933** —— in *Press* (Christchurch, N.Z.) 2 Dec. 15/7, I believe there was a still worse smother [of sheep] on a station called Roxburgh in Otago. **1949** S. S. CRAWFORD *Sheep & Sheepmen of Canterbury* v. 42 Mt. Peel [station] was unlucky with smothers [of sheep].

**3.** *slang.* (See quots.)

**1851** MAYHEW *Lond. Labour* II. 34 A 'lick-up' is a boot or shoe re-lasted.., and the bottom covered with a 'smother'. *Ibid.*, This 'smother' is obtained from the dust of the room.

**4.** *Rugby Football.* A high tackle in which the player 'smothers' (sense 3 d) his opponent. In full ***smother-tackle.***

**1927** WAKEFIELD & MARSHALL *Rugger* iv. 248 Hoping.. that by the swiftness of your advance you may get him in a smother-tackle, taking both man and ball. **1929** *Illustr. Sporting & Dramatic News* 19 Oct. 183 (*caption*) Getting the ball away from a smother. **1960** E. S. & W. J. HIGHAM *High Speed Rugby* v. 48 *The Smother Tackle.* This tackle is a high tackle and is used when you want to prevent a player from passing or touching down.

**5.** *Comb.*, as ***smother-burned, -dangled.***

**1597** *Pilgr. Parnassus* I. 87 Those Amorettoes that doe spend theire time In comminge of their smother-dangled heyre. **1849** JOHNSTON *Exp. Agric.* 265 Such burned sulphury shales (smother burned) may be tried with advantage.

**smother** ('smʌðə(r)), *v.* Forms: *α.* **smeorðren**, 5 **smorther.** *β.* 3 **smoðren**, 5– **smother**, 6 **smowther**, 6–7 **smouther**, 6–8 **smoother**, 7 **smuther.** *γ.* 6 **smoder**, 6–7, 9 *dial.* **smudder.** [f. SMOTHER *sb.*]

**I.** *trans.* **1. a.** To suffocate with smoke.

*a* **1200–** [see SMOTHERING *ppl. a.* 1]. **1560** DAUS tr. *Sleidane's Comm.* 220 b, They were smothered with smoke and burnt all. **1579** WALSINGHAM in *Victoria Co. Hist., Surrey* (1902) I. 391 A fyre made..by hunters that had earthed a badger, and thought to have smouthered him. **1624** CAPT. SMITH *Virginia* (1629) 85 But the poore Salvage ..was so smoothered with the smoake he had made..that we found him dead. **1719** DE FOE *Crusoe* II. (Globe) 496 The House, which was by this time all of a light Flame, fell in upon them, and they were smothered or burnt together. **1848** BARTLETT *Dict. Amer.* 314 That the inky stream may smother or drive away mosquitoes.

*fig.* **1589** *Pappe w. Hatchet* To Rdr., With the verie smoke the consciences of diuers are smothered. *a* **1704** T. BROWN *Sat. Persius imit.* Wks. 1730 I. 54 By the thick fogs, which from his diet rise, His sense is smothered. **1944** [see BLANKET *sb.* 2 c].

**b.** To suffocate by the prevention of breathing; to deprive of life by suffocation. (Freq. in passive without implication of personal agency.) Also *spec.* of sheep, to suffocate others by falling on top of them, as during a round-up; to cause (sheep) to die in this manner (*N.Z.*).

*a* **1548** HALL *Chron., Hen. VIII*, 55 [Certain criminals] the same Richarde Hun feloniously strangeled and smodered. **1600** E. BLOUNT tr. *Conestaggio* 51 The thirde was smothered in the water. **1665** MANLEY tr. *Grotius' Low C. Wars* 221 They that escaped slaughter..were smother'd in the Mud. **1713** ADDISON *Cato* II. vi, The helpless traveller.. smother'd in the dusty whirlwind dies. **1745** POCOCKE *Descr. East* II. I. vi. 27 Being surrounded, and almost smothered by the crowd. **1819** SHELLEY *Cenci* II. i. 143 How just it were to ..smother me when overcome by wine. **1864** MISS BRADDON *Aurora Floyd* xviii, What does the chap in the play get for his trouble when the blackamoor smothers his wife? **1871** M. A. BARKER *Christmas Cake in Four Quarters* IV. iii. 290, I had to bring 'em [*sc.* the mob of sheep] down uncommon easy, for it was a nasty place, and I didn't want half of 'em to be smothered in the creek. **1930** L. G. D. ACLAND *Early Canterbury Runs* 1st Ser. vi. 128 They once smothered 5000 in the gully. *a* **1948** —— *Ibid.* (1951) 397 Run sheep..are very easy to s[mother] on broken hill ground... They s[mothere]d 1,200 once..at Mount Peel.

*fig.* **1742** YOUNG *Nt. Th.* I. 147 Is it in the flight of three-score years, To..smother souls immortal in the dust? **1781** COWPER *Truth* 316 He begs their flatt'ry,..And, smother'd in't at last, is prais'd to death! ? **1813** SHELLEY *Falsehood & Vice* 50 She smothered Reason's babes in their birth. **1897** MISS KINGSLEY *W. Africa* 472, I therefore used to smother those twins by leading the conversation off.

*absol.* **1817** SHELLEY *Rev. Islam* VI. xlix, I am Pestilence... I flit about, that I may slay and smother.

**c.** Used hyperbolically to denote an effusive welcome, etc., or the gaining of a complete or overwhelming victory.

(*a*) **1676** WYCHERLEY *Pl. Dealer* IV. i, She..smothered me with a thousand tasteless kisses. **1873** HOLLAND *A. Bonnicastle* v. 98 In a moment I was smothered with welcome.

(*b*) **1890** *Pall Mall G.* 1 Dec. 1/3 If there is one club more than another which Notts County would care to smother it is Aston Villa. **1900** *Westm. Gaz.* 30 Mar. 2/2 They have simply smothered every scratch that has rowed against them.

**2.** †**a.** To conceal by keeping silent about; to suppress all mention of, to hush up (a matter, etc.). *Obs.* (Now with *up*: see 6 a.)

**1579** W. WILKINSON *Confut. Fam. Love* 70 b, I lyke not to smother sinnes. **1591** GREENE *Maidens Dr.* ix, Bribes could not make him any wrong to smother. **1642** GAUDEN *3 Serm.* 48 As much as we defalk or smother of an inquired Truth. **1699** BENTLEY *Phalaris* 203 Somebody's artifice in suppressing and smothering what he thinks makes against him. **1704** HEARNE *Ductor Hist.* (1714) I. 344 Great Care has been taken to smoother his Name, but Theopompus..tells us, he was called Erostratus. **1752** YOUNG *Brothers* I. i, [Her story was] Smother'd by the king; And wisely too.

**b.** To cover up, so as to conceal or cause to be forgotten.

*c* **1585** *Faire Em* I. 295 Where neither envious eyes nor thought can pierce, But endless darkness ever smother it. **1613** JACKSON *Creed* II. 357 It was in their hearts, though hid and smothered in the wrinkles of their crooked hearts. **1643** BAKER *Chron., Eliz.* 120 Richard Hooker,..who with too much meeknesse smoothered his great Learning. **1722**

STEELE *Conscious Lovers* I. ii, I am afraid..there's something I don't see yet, something that's smother'd under all this Raillery. **1863** KINGLAKE *Crimea* (1876) I. vii. 100 So he began to turn this way and that, in order that by turmoil he might smother the past.

**c.** To repress, retain from displaying, (feeling, etc.) by the exercise of self-control.

**1591** SHAKS. *1 Hen. VI*, IV. i. 110 Your priuate grudge my Lord of York, will out, Though ne'er so cunningly you smother it. **1593** —— *Lucr.* Argt., Smoothering his passions for the present, [he] departed with the rest. **1624** CAPT. SMITH *Virginia* III. iii. 52 Smothering his distast to avoyd the Saluages suspition. **1662** J. DAVIES tr. *Mandelslo's Trav.* 245 The Gentleman..was a little troubled at it, but smother'd his indignation. **1712** STEELE *Spect.* No. 263 ¶6 Both your Sisters are crying to see the Passion which I smother. **1813** SHELLEY *Q. Mab* III. 43 Smothering the glow of shame. **1847** PRESCOTT *Peru* III. vii. (1850) II. 190 Almagro..had seemed willing to smother his ancient feelings of resentment towards his associate. **1891** E. PEACOCK *N. Brendon* II. 101 She smothered her own grief.

**3. a.** To cover up so as to prevent from having free play or development; to suppress or check in this way.

**1590** SHAKS. *Com. Err.* III. ii. 35 My earthie grosse conceit: Smothred in errors. **1605** —— *Macb.* I. iii. 141 Function is smother'd in surmise. **1650** H. MORE *Observ.* in *Enthus. Tri.*, etc. (1656) 108 You..by your slubbering and barbarous translating..smother the fitnesse of the Sense. **1762** COWPER *To Miss Macartney* 7 Dwells there a wish.. To smother in ignoble rest At once both bliss and woe? **1780** *Mirror* No. 71, These exertions..would soon have been smothered by cold political prudence. **1823** SCOTT *Quentin D.* xxiv, Ridicule..often checks what is absurd, and fully as often smothers that which is noble. **1843** R. J. GRAVES *Lect. Clin. Med.* 371 You may smother the disease while it is merely local. **1882** SERG. BALLANTINE *Exper.* i. 9 Ability.. smothered by pomposity and vulgar pride.

**b.** To prevent (words, etc.) from having full utterance; to render indistinct or silent.

**1601** HOLLAND *Pliny* I. 164 The fore-teeth..yeeld a distinction and varietie in our words,..drawing them out at length, or smuddering and drowning them in the end. **1797–1809** COLERIDGE *Three Graves* IV. xiv, No power Had she the words to smother. **1821** CLARE *Vill. Minstr.* I. 161 Contented she smother'd her sighs on his breast. **1832** BREWSTER *Nat. Magic* vii. 176 Suddenly the voice seemed smothered.

**c.** To stop (a cricket ball) by placing the bat more or less over it. Also in *Assoc. Football* (see quot. 1954).

**1845** N. WANOSTROCHT *Felix on Bat* I. iv. 18 Should it be pitched an inch too far, be sure to get well out at it, and smother it. **1889** *Boy's Own Paper* 4 May 496 How the twists should smothered be Before they reach the middle stump. **1954** F. C. AVIS *Soccer Dict.* 112 *Smother*, to put oneself in the way of an opponent's shot, especially by the goalkeeper advancing from his goal towards the opponent. **1976** *Northumberland Gaz.* 26 Nov., His shot was smothered as the final whistle went.

**d.** *Rugby Football.* To tackle with a bear-like hug embracing the body and arms, preventing one's opponent from releasing the ball or touching it down.

**1920** W. CAMP *Football without a Coach* vii. 132 Unless experience shows that there is a certain definite play to watch or a certain player to smother. **1928** *Sunday Times* 5 Feb. 24/7 He kicked well ahead on the slippery turf, and after Hunt had smothered the full-back, scored.

**4. a.** To deaden or extinguish (fire, etc.) by covering so as to exclude the air; to cause to smoulder. Also *fig.*

*a* **1591** H. SMITH *Serm.* (1637) 727 Many have smothered their light so long that the dampe hath put out the candle. **1627** CAPT. SMITH *Seaman's Gram.* xiii. 61 Smother the fire with wet cloathes. **1657** AUSTEN *Fruit Trees* II. 143 Heat pent up and smoothered for a time. **1758** REID tr. *Macquer's Chym.* I. 141 If care be taken to smother them, so as to prevent their flaming while they burn. **1787** JEFFERSON *Writ.* (1859) II. 322 A fire, which, though smothered of necessity for the present moment, will probably never be quenched but by signal revenge. **1837** CARLYLE *Fr. Rev.* I. IV. iv, A fiery fuliginous mass, which could not be choked and smothered, but would fill all France with smoke. **1856** KANE *Arctic Expl.* I. xxxii. 444, I succeeded in smothering the fire.

**b.** To cook in a close vessel. (Cf. SMORE *v.* 4.)

**1706–7** FARQUHAR *Beaux' Strat.* I. i, They'll eat much better smothered with onions. **1748–** [see SMOTHERED 3].

**5.** To cover up, cover over, densely or thickly by some thing or substance. (Common in recent use.)

**1598** E. GUILPIN *Skial.* (1878) 21 To..shew good legs, spite of slops smothering thies. **1840** R. H. DANA *Bef. Mast* xxxi. 113 In a few minutes the sails [were] smothered and kept in by clewlines and buntlines. **1851** MAYHEW *Lond. Lab.* II. 34/2 When dry and finished, we take what is called a 'soft-heel-ball' and 'smother' it over. **1872** BLACK *Adv. Phaeton* xxi. 297 The small stations we passed were smothered in green foliage.

**6.** With *up*: **a.** To conceal, suppress, hush up (a matter, etc.). Cf. sense 2 a.

**1589** *Pappe w. Hatchet* B iv b, Hee woulde not smoother vp sinne, and deale in hugger mugger against his Conscience. **1649** MILTON *Eikon* ix. Wks. 1851 III. 401 The suspected Poysoning of his Father, not inquir'd into, but smother'd up. **1687** MIÈGE *Gt. Fr. Dict.* II. s.v., The Business was smothered up. **1827** SCOTT *Surgeon's Dau.* Pref., It was thought best to smother it up at the time. **1883** STEVENSON *Treas. Isl.* xiii, He's as anxious as you and I to smother things up.

**b.** To cover up in a close, dense, or suffocating manner, etc.

*c* **1590** GREENE *Fr. Bacon* xiv, A nunne?.. Twere injurie to me, To smother up such bewtie in a cell. **1592** SHAKS. *Ven. & Ad.* 1035 And there [the snail] all smother'd up, in shade doth sit. **1631** GOUGE *God's Arrows* IV. §13. 391 This fire..lay..smothered up. **1644** J. FARY *God's Severity* (1645) 23 The Lords wrath lies long smothered up, but at last it kindles. **1820** KEATS *Hyperion* I. 106, I am smother'd up, And buried from all godlike exercise.

**7.** With *down, out* (see quots.). *rare.*

**1632** LITHGOW *Trav.* VIII. 371 The..ingeniosity of their best styles..is ecclipsed, and smothered downe. **1863** *Gardener's Chron.* 23 May 493 The next year it may be noticed that the wished for crop has been smothered out.

**II.** *intr.* **8.** To be suffocated or stifled; to be prevented from breathing freely by smoke or other means.

*c* **1520** *Everyman* 796 What, sholde I smoder here? **1648** HEXHAM II, *Ick Smoore van den roock*, I Smoother with the smoake, or, I am Choaked with the Vapour. **1871** B. TAYLOR *Faust* v. iv. (1875) II. 283 Ah, the good old father, mother, Doomed among the smoke to smother. **1895** *Cent. Mag.* Aug. 628/2 One opinion was that he would not go into his hole because he was too hot and would smother.

**9. a.** To smoulder; to burn slowly. Now *dial.*

**1600** SURFLET *Countrie Farme* 558 Set on fire a quantitie of haye, after quench it againe by and by,..and whiles it is smoothering and smoaking, spread it vpon a plate of iron. **1667** PEPYS *Diary* 29 July, The fire..lies smothering a great while..before it flames. **1729** G. ADAMS tr. *Sophocles, Antig.* IV. i. II. 56 The Fire shone not from the Sacrifices, but in the Ashes the Flame smothered. **1804** *Naval Chron.* XI. 79 She will burn and smother to the Water's edge. **1825** E. HEWLETT *Cottage Comforts* vi. 42 Let the fire be banked up ..with turves, which will smother on for hours. **1881–** in dialect use (Notts., Leic., Warw.).

**b.** *fig.* or in fig. context.

**1579** L. TOMSON *Calvin's Serm. Tim.* 447/1 He will not haue our sinns couered, and lie smothering so, yᵗ they may not be knowen. **1588** GREENE *Pandosto* (1607) 4 These.. thoughts a long time smothering in his stomacke, began at last to kindle..a secret mistrust. **1621** LADY M. WROTH *Urania* 357 Heere began the harme to smother like wet hay in fire. **1679** MANSELL *Narr. Popish Plot* 5 When their old animosity did yet smoother. **1697** COLLIER *Ess. Mor. Subj.* II. (1709) 65 A Man had better talk to a Post, than let his Thoughts lie Smoking and Smothering in his Head.

**c.** To die *out* in smoulder. *rare*⁻¹.

**1621** T. WILLIAMSON tr. *Goulart's Wise Vieillard* 63 The heate of passions in youth beginning to coole and smoother out in old men.

**10.** Of smoke: To escape slowly.

**1725** DE FOE *Voy. round World* (1840) 262 We saw a smoke indeed *in* the house, rather than coming *out* of it; and the little that did, smothered through a hole in the roof instead of a chimney.

**11.** *Boxing.* (See quot. 1954.)

**1916** [see INFIGHT *v.* 2]. **1954** F. C. AVIS *Boxing Dict.* 103 *Smother*, to prevent, by clever positioning of the arms, the development of an opponent's attack.

Hence **'smotherable** *a.*, that may be smothered.

**1824** *Blackw. Mag.* XVI. 664 A woman who is not over fastidious in all her personal arrangements..is to me the most justifiably smotherable.

**smotheration** (smʌðə'reɪʃən). [Jocularly f. SMOTHER *v.* + -ATION: cf. *botheration.*]

**1.** The action of smothering; the state or condition of being smothered; suffocation.

**1826** J. WILSON in *Blackw. Mag.* XIX. 242 Nor shall we ever forget our horror on being within an ace of smotheration in the cellar. **1840** *New Monthly Mag.* LX. 235 Accidental death, by natural smotheration in the snow. **1882** W. M. WILLIAMS *Sci. in Short Chapters* 360 To return the carbonic acid..to the already suffocated fire can only add smother to smotheration.

**2.** *U.S.* 'A sailor's dish of beef and pork smothered with potatoes' (*Cent. Dict.*).

**smother crop.** [f. SMOTHER *v.*] A crop which is grown to suppress weeds.

**1920** W. E. BRENCHLEY *Weeds on Farm Land* iii. 51 When a smother crop is grown it is of course necessary that the crop seed should be free from weed seed. **1937** A. F. HILL *Econ. Bot.* xv. 336 Barley is also used for hay and pasturage and as a smother crop to kill out weeds. **1973** P. A. COLINVAUX *Introd. Ecol.* xxi. 303 Barley is known as a 'smother crop' because it keeps down weeds in the field. This it does with root secretions, weed killers of its own.

**smothered** ('smʌðəd), *ppl. a.* [f. SMOTHER *v.*]

**1.** Of fire, flame, etc.: Not allowed to burn freely or break out. Also *fig.*

**1594** WILLOBIE *Avisa* xlv. 17 The smothered flame, too closely pent, Burnes more extreame for want of vent. **1697** DRYDEN *Virg. Past.* VIII. 150 Break out ye smother'd Fires, and kindle smother'd Love. **1734** R. ERSKINE *Gospel Sonn.* (1782) 252 My praise is now a smothered fire. **1837** P. KEITH *Bot. Lex.* 217 That the mass..may be still kept burning with a smothered flame.

**2. a.** Suppressed, concealed, restrained, kept down or under in some manner.

**1607** EARL STIRLING *J. Cæsar* III. ii, Whil'st smothred sorrow by a habite smokes. **1645** PAGITT *Heresiogr.* (1661) 75 Their known uncleanness, smother'd mischiefs [etc.]. **1728** ELIZA HEYWOOD tr. *Mme. de Gomez's Belle A.* (1732) II. 229 Angry with himself, that he had so long concealed the smother'd Anguish. **1752** YOUNG *Brothers* I. i, I've partly heard Her smother'd story. **1807** CRABBE *Par. Reg.* II. 552 While smother'd envy rises in the breast. **1856** FROUDE *Hist. Eng.* (1858) I. 222 They must have heard something of the growls of smothered anger.

**b.** *smothered mate* (see quot. 1847). See also MATE *sb.*¹ b.

**1804** *Introd. Hist. & Study of Chess* v. 82 *Smothered mate* is when the king is so surrounded by his own friends that he cannot move out of check for them; and this mate is generally given by the knight. **1822** W. LEWIS *Chess* 24 The Knight is the only piece that can give a smothered mate. **1847** STAUNTON *Chess-Player's Handbk.* 25 *Smothered mate*, a checkmate which is sometimes given by the Knight when the adverse King is hemmed in, or *smothered*, by his own forces.

**3.** Cooked in a close vessel.

**1748** in Omond *Arniston Mem.* (1887) 108 Dinner... Roast goose. Smothered rabbits. **1809** MALKIN *Gil Blas* X. iii. ¶10 A smothered rabbit on one side, and a fricasseed capon on the other. **1877** E. S. DALLAS *Kettner's Book of Table* 369 Smothered Rabbit. This is the name given in England to boiled rabbit. It is smothered with a white onion sauce. **1923** *Mrs. Beeton's Bk. Househ. Managem.* 582 (*heading*) Chicken, Smothered (Poulet étuvé). **1948** *Good Housek. Cookery Bk.* II. 237 *Smothered tongues*... Cook preferably in a double saucepan or in a basin in a steamer. **1975** tr. *Melchior's Sleeper Agent* (1976) III. 290 A juicy steak heaped with smothered onions.

**4.** Of sound: Suppressed, rendered indistinct.

**1810** SOUTHEY *Kehama* XI. x, A sound, like smother'd thunder, Was heard. **1823** W. PRICE *Gram. 3 Oriental Langs.* Pref. p. v, The Persians..seldom give the smothered sound of *u* to the short vowels. **1862** BURTON *Book Hunter* I. 9 It is told in a smothered whisper..to the horrified family.

**5.** Thickly or densely covered up.

**1902** 'LINESMAN' *Words Eyewitness* 89 The red tongue of flame which told that the smothered piece was countering the blow.

Hence **'smotheredly** *adv.*

**1656** DUCHESS OF NEWCASTLE *Nature's Pictures* 117 She perceived his Amorous Humour not to quench, but rather to burn, though smotheredly.

**smotherer** ('smʌðərə(r)). Also 7 smootherer. [f. SMOTHER *v.* + -ER¹.] One who or that which smothers.

**1648** HEXHAM II, *Een Smoorder*, a Smootherer, or a Sweater out. **1687** in MIÈGE *Gt. Fr. Dict.* II. **1897** *Columbus Dispatch* 20 Nov. 4/1 There is but one course..and that is to call upon the smotherers of the protest and petition for an explanation.

**'smother-fire.** [f. SMOTHER *sb.* or *v.*] A smouldering or smoky fire. Also *fig.*

**1625** GILL *Sacr. Philos.* viii. 139 That dampish smother-fire of heresies, which the devill did kindle among his brands. **1905** *Daily News* 27 Jan. 4 If any ashes are to hand from a smother fire this will be found a grand fertiliser for onions.

**'smother-fly.** *dial.* [f. SMOTHER *v.*] A species of aphis.

**1781** G. WHITE *Selborne* xcvii, The people..were surprised by a shower of *aphides*, or smother-flies, which fell in these parts. **1796** W. H. MARSHALL *Rur. Econ. Midl.* (ed. 2) II. 386 The very 'Black bug' 'Negro'—here provincially 'Smother fly'—with which beans are frequently infested. **1851** *B'ham & Midl. Gardeners' Mag.* Dec. 239 The Plum stocks in particular being infested with smother-fly.

**'smotheriness.** [f. SMOTHERY *a.*] The 'state of being smothery' (Webster, 1847).

**smothering** ('smʌðərɪŋ), *vbl. sb.* [f. SMOTHER *v.*]

**a.** The action of the verb, in various senses.

**1602** FULBECKE *1st Pt. Parall.* 83 If any Judge..shall partially demeane himself in the smothering of that fault. **1624** SANDERSON *Serm.* I. 241 All vain boasting of the gifts of God..is a kind of smothering of the receipt. **1857** TOULMIN SMITH *Parish* 382 Any attempt to shut this out.. is but a smothering of the inquiry. **1950** *N.Z. Jrnl. Agric.* July 5/2 It is undesirable to have yards on a very steep slope, as the danger of smothering, particularly with lambs in a large yard, is greatly increased. **1956** G. BOWEN *Wool Away!* (ed. 2) iv. 47 The 'sheepo' must keep an eye on them for smothering, the first sign of which is sheep jumping up in the pen.

**b.** *attrib.*, as *smothering-hole, -pan, -process.*

**1648** HEXHAM II, *Een demp-kuyl*, a smothering-hole. *Ibid.*, *Een Smoor-panne*, a Smoothering-pan. **1834** *Brit. Husb.* I. 376 The smothering process..cannot be so perfectly accomplished.

**smothering** ('smʌðərɪŋ), *ppl. a.* [f. SMOTHER *v.* + -ING².] That smothers, in various senses.

**1. a.** Of smoke, etc.: Stifling, suffocating.

*a* **1200** *St. Marher.* 9 In his ihurnd heauet..preaste smeorðrinde smoke ut, smeeche forcuðest. **1401** *Pol. Poems* (Rolls) II. 54 Ther rose smotheryng smoke, and brese therinne. *Ibid.*, The smorthering smoke is ȝour dymme doctrine. *c* **1475** *Partenay* 3303 The smoky fume smorthering so was, The Abbay it toke. **1575** CHURCHYARD *Chippes* M vj b, A second hell For smothryng smoke, for shot and fiery flame. **1725** POPE *Odyss.* XIV. 340 The whirling ship is..all in clouds of smoth'ring sulphur lost. **1831** SCOTT *Cast. Dang.* xvii, Free from the smothering atmosphere which had before oppressed her like that of a charnel-house. **1863** PRINCESS ALICE *Mem.* (1884) 57 We went..to see the different machines at work, in a crowd close round us and a smothering heat.

**b.** Smouldering; burning slowly.

**1563** FOXE *A. & M.* 1048/1 Greene woode, and other smotheryng rather then burnyng fewel. **1621** G. SANDYS *Ovid's Met.* VIII. (1626) 167 Who stird abroad the glowing coles, that lay In smothering ashes. **1635** QUARLES *Embl.* II. xiv, What fenny trash maintaines the smoth'ring fires Of his desires! **1681** FLAVEL *Method Grace* x. 229 Let not your troubles lye like a secret smothering fire always in your own breasts.

**2.** Covering (or suppressing) completely and overwhelmingly. Also *fig.*

**1586** MARLOWE *1st Pt. Tamburl.* III. i, The spring is hindred by your smoothering host. **1591** HORSEY *Trav.* (Hakl.) 257 The innocent bloud spilt in that smotheringe tyme of tiranie. **1805** R. W. DICKSON *Pract. Agric.* I. 370 If ground can be covered with such smothering crops of the fallow kind. **1851** TRENCH *Poems* (1862) 19 As from beneath the smothering earth The seed strives upward to a birth.

**1899** RODWAY *Guiana Wilds* 113 Fire..covered with green leaves; unable to escape from its smothering burden.

**3.** Characterized by suffocation from smoke, etc.

**1864** *Daily Telegr.* 30 Aug., The Tennessee.. surrendered,..[with] her crew in an exhausted and smothering condition.

Hence **'smotheringly** *adv.*

**1778** *Exmoor Gloss., Smuggle*, to hug violently, smotheringly. **1857** *Chamb. Jrnl.* VIII. 71 Two little arms tight round her neck, smotheringly expressing a wealth of love.

**'smother-kiln.** [f. SMOTHER *sb.* or *v.*] A kiln in which pottery in process of firing is blackened by smoke. Also *attrib.*

**1851** D. WILSON *Preh. Ann.* (1863) II. 13 The rude vessels of the smother kiln. **1865** *Intellect. Obs.* No. 39. 233 What some antiquaries have termed 'smother-kilns'. **1894** *Daily News* 13 Dec. 8/1 Fragments of Upchurch pottery, blackened by process of firing in smother kilns. **1898** *Berks., Bucks. & Oxon. Archæol. Jrnl.* Apr. 12 The coarse 'smother-kiln' ware, probably made in the district.

**'smotherly,** *adv. Obs.*$^{-1}$ (Meaning doubtful.)

*c* **1400** *Rowland & O.* 259 The Sarazyn laughes full smothirly.

**smothery** ('smʌðərɪ), *a.* Also 7 **smoothrie.** [f. SMOTHER *sb.* or *v.* + -Y[1].] Tending to smother.

**1603** HOLLAND *Plutarch's Mor.* 339 Now else should not ..The plough beame hang aloft in smoothrie smoke. **1840** BROWNING *Sordello* III. 717 We and you in smothery chafe, ..stumbled thus far into Zin The Horrid. **1893** *Pall Mall Mag.* I. 781 The softly smothery effect of her manner.

†**'smotry,** *a. Obs. rare.* [f. the stem *smotter-* (see SMOTTER *v.*) + -Y[1].] Smutty, grimy.

*c* **1407** LYDG. *Reson & Sens.* 3791 Vulcanus Was to hir so odious For his smotry, swarte face. **1412–20** —— *Chron. Troy.* II. 5803 Þis smotry smyth, þis swarte Vlcanus.

†**'smotter,** *a. Obs.* [Of obscure origin.] ? Pretty, handsome.

*a* **1500** MEDWALL *Nature* (Brandl) II. 194, I shall shew you the smorterst place [? *read* smotterst face] That euer ye saw wyth eyes. *c* **1515** *Interlude of Four Elements* B vij, We wyll haue bounsynge besse also, And two or thre proper wenchis mo, Ryght feyr and smotter of face.

**'smotter,** *v. Sc. rare.* [f. SMOT *v.* + -ER[5]: cf. SMOTRY *a.* and BESMOTTERED.] *trans.* To bespatter; to soil or stain.

**1513** DOUGLAS *Æneid* VI. v. 13 His smotterit habit, our his schulderis lidder, Hang prevagely [etc.]. **1819** TENNANT *Papistry Storm'd* (1827) 182 Big bluidy draps..Barst out and smotter't a' the stane.

**smouch** (smaʊtʃ), *sb.*[1] Now *dial.* Also 8 *dial.* **smeawtch,** 9 **smoutch.** [Cf. G. *schmutz* (MHG. *smuz*) in the same sense.] A kiss, a buss.

**1578** WHETSTONE *Promos & Cass.* I. IV. vii, Come smack me, I long for a smouch. **1634** HEYWOOD & BROME *Lanc. Witches* II. H.'s Wks. 1874 IV. 194 I'le have one smouch at thy lips. *c* **1746** J. COLLIER (Tim Bobbin) *View Lanc. Dial.* (1775) 66 Let meh ha one smeawtch at parting. *a* **1800** PEGGE *Suppl. Grose, Smouch*, a kiss. North. *a* **1825**- in dial. glossaries (Yorks., Lanc., Chesh., Linc., Northampt., E. Anglia, etc.).

**smouch** (smaʊtʃ), *sb.*[2] Now *rare* or *Obs.* Also **smoutch.** [Alteration of SMOUSE *sb.*]

**1.** A Jew.

**1765** C. JOHNSTON *Chrysal* (1794) III. 60, I hate them [the Inquisitors] mortally ever since I saw them roast some poor Smouches at Lisbon because they would not eat pork. **1785** CUMBERLAND *Observer* No. 38 ⁋2 Smoke the Jew!.. Throw him over, says another, hand over the smoutch! **1826** SCOTT *Jrnl.* I. 137, I took lessons of oil painting..from a little Jew animalcule; a smouch called Burrell. **1842** BARHAM *Ingol. Leg.* Ser. II. *Merch. V.* (1905) 246 You find fault mit ma pargains, and say I'm a Smouch.

**2.** *S. African.* An itinerant trader.

**1849** E. E. NAPIER *Exc. S. Africa* II. 391, I dare say..you have heard that I have turned a regular 'smoutch', the Colonial term for trader.

†**smouch,** *sb.*[3] *Obs.* (See quot.)

**1785** GROSE *Dict. Vulgar T., Smouch*, dried leaves of the ash tree, used by the smugglers for adulterating the black, or bohea teas.

**smouch** (smaʊtʃ), *sb.*[4] [? var. of SMUTCH *sb.* Cf. SMOOCH *sb.*[1] and *v.*[1]] A smudge, a dirty mark.

The vb. *smouch* 'to daub, dirty, stain', is given by Sir G. C. Lewis *Gloss. Heref.* (1839) s.v. *smirch.*

**1873** MISS BROUGHTON *Nancy* III. 192 A huge smouch of black under each of their eyes. **1882** *Harper's Mag.* Aug. 379 They keep carefully away from the smouch of the cigarette trays.

**smouch** (smaʊtʃ), *v.*[1] Also 6 **smowtch,** 6–7 **smoutch.** [Cf. G. dial. *schmutzen* to kiss, to smile.] *intr.* and *trans.* To kiss, buss.

(*a*) **1588** E. D. tr. *Theocritus Six Idillia* A vij, Thinkst thou ..mee to kisse? I haue no will After the Countrie guise to smouch. **1600** HEYWOOD *1st Pt. Edw. IV*, III. i, I had rather than a bend of leather She and I might smouch together. (*b*) **1595** *Eng. Tripe-wife* (1881) 165 Kisse and smowtch the Widdow neuer so much: there is one..must carrie the wench away. **1622** DRAYTON *Poly-olb.* xxi. 71 Chill zmouch thee every morn, before the Sun can rise. **1654** GAYTON *Pleas. Notes* IV. 235 The Knights..did so smouch them, that the lippe-frolicks were heard into the Kitchin. **1811** LADY GRANVILLE *Lett.* (1894) I. 21 The little hideous Duc de Berri smouches us all. *a* **1825**- in dial. glossaries (E. Anglia, Lanc., Cheshire, etc.).

Hence **'smoucher; 'smouching** *vbl. sb.*

**1583** STUBBES *Anat. Abuses* M viij b, What kissing and bussing, what smouching & slabbering one of another. **1611** COTGR., *Baiseur*, a kisser, smoutcher, smacker.

**smouch** (smaʊtʃ), *v.*[2] Now *U.S.* Also **smoutch.** [? f. SMOUCH *sb.*[2]]

**1.** *trans.* To acquire dishonestly; to pilfer.

**1826** COBBETT *Rural Rides* (1830) 514 The far greater part of them are..getting or expecting loaves and fishes... They smouch, or want to smouch, some of the taxes. **1880** 'MARK TWAIN' *Tramp Abr.* xxx. 289 Odds and ends smouched from half-a-dozen learned tongues. **1888** *New Princeton Rev.* V. 49 (Cent.), The rest of it was smouched from House's Atlantic paper.

**2.** *intr.* To deal unfairly or dishonestly.

**1848** BARTLETT *Dict. Amer.* 314 *To Smoutch*, to gouge; to take unfair advantage. Colloquial in New York.

**'smouchy,** *a. rare*$^{-1}$. (Meaning not clear.)

**1803** LAMB *Let. to Manning* 19 Feb., The Tartars, really, are a cold, insipid, smouchy set.

**smought,** obs. form of SMOOT *sb.*[1]

†**smould.** *Obs. rare.* [Of obscure origin.] The sand-eel or launce.

**1605** *Act 3 Jas. I*, c. 12 Every person which..shall fish with any Draw-net or Drag-net..except for the Taking of Smoulds in Norfolk only.

**smoulder** ('sməʊldə(r)), *sb.* Forms: 4–7, 9 *U.S.*, **smolder,** 6, 9 **smoulder.** [Of obscure formation; the first syllable may be related to LG. *smölen, smäulen* (also *smälen, smelen*), Du. *smeulen*, to smoulder, Flem. *smoel, smul* hot.]

Discontinued about (or shortly after) 1600, and revived in the 19th cent.: see the note to the vb.

**1.** Smother; smoky vapour; the result of smouldering or slow combustion.

*c* **1325** *Body & Soul* 435 in *Map's Poems* (Camden) 345 The eorthe openede up anon, Smoke and smolder up ther wel. **1377** LANGL. *P. Pl.* B. XVII. 321 Whan smoke & smolder smyt in his syȝte. *c* **1440** *Pallad. on Husb.* I. 929 The fired nuttis smolder throgh shal fle This grettist hole. *c* **1450** *Merlin* xv. 248 Men myght se the smolder of the fire x myle longe. **1575** GASCOIGNE *Flowers* Wks. 49 The smoulder stops our nose with stench, the fume offends our eies. *a* **1626** BP. ANDREWES *96 Serm., Holy Ghost* xi. (1661) 472 From blood and fire and the smolder of smoke.

**1837** CARLYLE *Fr. Rev.* III. I. viii, Lille too, black with ashes and smoulder. **1851** G. BORROW *Lavengro* III. 355 The smoulder and smoke of that fire-ball have rather bewildered my head. **1862** THORNBURY *Turner* I. 315 That driving smoulder of fire..indicates the mouth of the fatal cave.

**2.** A slow-burning fire or the ashes of this.

*a* **1548** HALL *Chron., Hen. VIII*, 41 b, Of the fyer and smolder did ryse suche a smooke. **1561** DAUS tr. *Bullinger on Apoc.* (1573) 115 b, It ascendeth..as a smoke out of great smolder. **1869** BLACKMORE *Lorna D.* (1889) 398 A barrow-load of the smoulder.

**smoulder** ('sməʊldə(r)), *v.* Forms: 5–7, 9- (now *U.S.*) **smolder** (7 **-ther**), 6 **smoolder, smow(l)der, smoulther,** 6- **smoulder.** [f. prec.]

During the 17th and 18th cents. both sb. and vb. fell into disuse, although poets continued to employ the ppl. adj. *smouldering*, of which Johnson (1755) says 'This word seems a participle; but I know not whether the verb *smoulder* be in use'. The revival of the verb in the 19th cent. was evidently due to Scott.

†**1. a.** *trans.* To smother, suffocate. *Obs.*

**1481** CAXTON *Reynard* xxxiv. (Arb.) 98 Hit stanke that I was almost smoldred therof. **1489** —— *Faytes of A.* I. xxiv. 77 The hete of the sonne was so brennynge hoot that almost hyt smoldred the rommanyns. **1529** RASTELL *Pastyme* (1811) 292 The most commyn opinyon was, that they were smolderyd betwene two fetherbeddes. **1563** GOLDING *Cæsar* (1565) 157 b, Other some..doe smoolder the men wythin them wyth the flame. **1586** WARNER *Alb. Eng.* II. vii. (1589) 24 Some stumbling on the bodies dead are smoldred so and die.

†**b.** To smother, in various fig. uses. *Obs.*

**1571** GOLDING *Calvin on Ps.* li. 12 Although the giftes of the Holy Ghoste were smoldered in him. **1575** *Gammer Gurton* v. ii, How-euer the thing he clockes or smolders. **1603** KNOLLES *Hist. Turks* (1621) 68 Which indignitie..as then..smouldered up in respect of the common cause,.. afterwards brake out againe.

**2. a.** *intr.* To burn and smoke without flame. Also *transf.* (quot. 1851).

**1529** MORE *Suppl. Souls* II. Wks. 321/2 The tone is a light flame sone ended, the tother smowdreth much lenger. **1530** PALSGR. 723/1, I smolder, as wete wood doth. *Ibid.*, This woode burneth nat clere, it dothe but smolder.

**1851** TENNYSON *E. Morris* 147 The light cloud smoulders on the summer crag. **1857** MILLER *Elem. Chem., Orig.* ix. 574 Baryta salt..when burned in open air smoulders like tinder till the naphthalin is consumed. **1859** W. COLLINS *Q. of Hearts* (1875) 55 The floor was smouldering in several places.

**b.** In fig. contexts.

**1575** GASCOIGNE *Flowers* Wks. 88 Nor yet [can] my fancie make such flame, that I may smoulder in the same.

**1814** SCOTT *Lord Isles* II. xxvi, He waked a spark, that, long suppress'd, Had smoulder'd in Lord Ronald's breast. **1855** MACAULAY *Hist. Eng.* xviii. IV. 188 The civil war.., after it had ceased to flame, had continued during some time to smoulder.

**c.** *fig.* To exist or continue in a suppressed state.

**1810** SCOTT *Lady of L.* II. xv, Still..Smoulders in Roderick's breast the feud. **1842** MANNING *Serm.* (1848) I. 3 For wise ends, God suffers this rebellion to smoulder in His Kingdom. **1888** FAGGE *Princ. Med.* I. 185 Intestinal lesions may smoulder on without giving rise to any symptoms.

**d.** To show suppressed anger, hatred, resentment, etc.

**1934** in WEBSTER. **1957** L. DURRELL *Justine* I. 69 She seemed to smoulder like a tar-barrel on the point of explosion. **1983** 'J. GASH' *Sleepers of Erin* iv. 42 Kurak smouldered his way to the Rolls, vibing pure hate in my direction.

†**3.** To be feeble or languid. *Obs.*$^{-1}$

**1578** BANISTER *Hist. Man* IV. 55 It [the midriff] beyng wounded the hart smoldreth, like the lampe that dyeth for lacke of oyle.

Hence **'smouldered** *ppl. a.*

**1796** COLERIDGE *Destiny of Nations* 258 Aside the beacon, up whose smouldered stones The..ivy-trails crept thinly.

**smouldering** ('sməʊldərɪŋ), *vbl. sb.* [f. SMOULDER *v.*] The action of the verb.

**1483** CAXTON *Gold. Leg.* 156/3 They made therin a grete smolderyng of smoke for to dysease hym. **1571** GOLDING *Calvin on Ps.* lxviii. 2 The smooldering itself will compel him to let in the water. **1837** CARLYLE *Fr. Rev.* I. IV. iv, Forty years of that smouldering. **1900** *Westm. Gaz.* 3 Oct. 2/2 Smouldering is often more difficult to deal with than open flame.

**'smouldering,** *ppl. a.* [f. SMOULDER *v.*]

†**1.** Smothering, suffocating, stifling. *Obs.*

**13..** *E.E. Allit. P.* B. 955 Al in smolderande smoke smachande ful ille. **1577** TUSSER *Husb.* (1878) 199 His acts be like the smoldring smoke. **1590** SPENSER *F.Q.* II. v. 3 The smouldring dust did round about him smoke. **1629** MILTON *Hymn Nativ.* xvii, While the red fire, and smouldring clouds out brake. **1697** DRYDEN *Virg. Georg.* III. 740 Clouds of smouldring Smoke forbad the Sacrifice. **1725** POPE *Odyss.* XII. 492 Sulphureous odours rose, and smouldering smoke.

†**2.** Smoky; giving out smoke. *Obs.*

**1577** tr. *Bullinger's Decades* (1592) 210 Least while hee goeth about to auoide the smoulthering cole-pitte hee happe to fall into the scalding lime kill. **1767** JAGO *Edge-Hill* III. 491 From russet Lawns, and smould'ring Furnaces, To trace the Progress of thy steely Arts.

**3.** Burning slowly and without flame.

**1832** HT. MARTINEAU *Weal & Woe* ii. 18 The widow.. applied more fuel to her smouldering fire. **1848** DICKENS *Dombey* xxxiv, When any stray drops of rain fell hissing on the smouldering embers. **1877** BLACK *Green Past.* xlv. (1878) 362 He only stared into the smouldering wood before him.

**b.** In fig. contexts.

**1852** MRS. STOWE *Uncle Tom* xxxv, All the smouldering embers of womanly feeling flashed up. **1856** *N. Brit. Rev.* XXVI. 243 It is not a pleasant duty to rake up the smouldering embers of ancient controversies. **1872** BLACK *Adv. Phaeton* xxv. 343 The smouldering fires of Arthur's wrath.

**c.** *fig.* Existing or continuing in a state of suppression or restraint.

**1818** SCOTT *Rob Roy* xi, I subdued it into a sort of smouldering heart-burning. **1859** GEO. ELIOT *A. Bede* ii, A little smouldering vague anxiety. **1897** *Allbutt's Syst. Med.* III. 56 The continuous smouldering activity of the true rheumatic process.

**d.** Glowing with a dull light.

**1898** DOYLE *Trag. Korosko* iv, Belmont, looking with smouldering eyes at the wretched Mansoor. **1904** BENSON *Challoners* i, The dusky smouldering gold of her hair.

Hence **'smoulderingly** *adv.*; **-ness.**

**1849** LOWELL *Biglow P.* Ser. I. Introd., A smothered smoulderingness of disposition seldom roused to open flame. **1893** F. THOMPSON *Poems* 76 The verge shrivelled inward smoulderingly.

†**'smouldery,** *a. Obs.* Also **smouldry.** [f. SMOULDER *v.* + -Y[1].] = SMOTHERY *a.*

**1590** SPENSER *F.Q.* I. vii. 13 Through smouldry cloud of duskish stincking smoke. **1593** NASHE *Christ's T.* (1613) 185 As Gods hand wee will not take it, but..the hand of close smouldry ayre. **1642** H. MORE *Song of Soul* II. ii. 8 The high arch'd roof of heaven with smouldry smoke they taint.

**smoult** *v.* (dial.): see SMOLT *a.*

**smouse** (smaʊz), *sb.* [ad. Du. *smous* Jew, usurer, supposed to be the same word as G. dial. *schmus* talk, patter, ad. Jewish *schmuoss*, Heb. *sh'mūᵉōth* tales, news, the reference being to the persuasive eloquence of Jewish pedlars. Cf. SMOUCH *sb.*[2]]

†**1.** *slang.* A Jew. *Obs.*

**1705** tr. *Bosman's Guinea* 190 They are as Impertinent and Noisie as the Smouse or German Jews at their Synagogue at Amsterdam. **1761** COLMAN *Genius, Prose on Sev. Occas.* (1787) I. 35 [Earring-] bobs or drops.., which also the insinuating Smouse soon provided for her. **1785** MACKLIN *Man of World* II. 30, I honour the smouse;..it was devilish clever—the Jew distilling the Beeshop's brains.

**2.** *S. African.* An itinerant trader. Also *attrib.*

**1850** R. G. CUMMING *Hunter's Life S. Africa* (1902) 13/2 Here we met a 'smouse', or trader, coming down the country. **1883** OLIVE SCHREINER *Story Afr. Farm* II. iii, A spray of orange-blossom which she had bought from a smouse. **1890** *Eng. Illustr. Mag.* Nov. 112, I..did a little in the 'smouse' line.

Hence **'smousing** *vbl. sb.* Also **'smouser.**

*c* **1876** SIR B. FRERE in J. E. Carlyle *S. Africa & Mission Fields* (1878) 103 This process of smousing, as it is termed in local slang. **1903** E. GLANVILLE *Diamond Seekers* 225 We are smousers (traders), said Amos.

**smouse** (smaʊz), *v.* Also 8 **smouze.** [app. ad. G. *schmausen* (LG. *smûsen*) to feast, to drink or eat luxuriously.] **a.** *intr.* To feast. **b.** *trans.* To eat up, consume, as a delicacy.

**1775** *Election Ball.* 64 Let me, my dear, quaff my Beer, Smouze and carouze. **1840** J. H. FRERE *Aristophanes' Acharnians* Wks. III. 50 Some that require Quickly to be broil'd, devour'd and smoused, On the spot, piping hot.

†**smout**, *ppl. a. Sc. Obs.*$^{-1}$ [ad. MDu. *ghesmouten*, pa. pple. of *smelten* to smelt.] Smelted.

**1595** D. WEDDERBURNE *Compt Buik* (S.H.S.) 30 Ane schip pund gad Iron and..four lib. round wecht smout iron.

**smout**: see SMOLT *sb.* and SMOOT.

**smoutch**, variant of SMOUCH *sb.* and *v.*

**smowk**, obs. form of SMOOK, smoke.

**smowt**, obs. form of SMOLT *sb.* and *a.*

**smuckle(r**, obs. forms of SMUGGLE(R.

**smudge** (smʌdʒ), *sb.*[1] [Related to SMUDGE *v.*[1] Cf. the earlier SMUTCH *sb.*, to which this has the same correspondence as *sludge* to *slutch.*]

**1. a.** A dirty mark or stain, esp. such as is caused by a smear or by trying to rub out a previous mark.

**1768–74** TUCKER *Lt. Nat.* (1834) II. 596 A long sooty smudge upon the lining of my coach. **1846** D. JERROLD *Mrs. Caudle* xviii, And you think I didn't see the smudges of court plaster about her face? **1862** LYTTON *Str. Story* II. 95, I rubbed the circle and the pentacle away,..leaving but an undistinguishable smudge behind. **1874** BURNAND *My Time* vi. 48 Like a smudge from a lead pencil.

*fig.* **1891** HARDY *Tess* (1900) 38/1 The smudge which Tess had set upon that nobility.

**b.** *transf.* A blurred indistinct mass or area.

**1871** MISS MULOCK *Fair France* 3 Mixing earth and sky in one settled 'smudge'. **1885** *Manch. Exam.* 11 June 57 Wales and Scotland [in common maps] are simply smudges of mountains.

**2. a.** A smeary condition, substance, etc.; the result of smearing or dirtying.

**1830** MARRYAT *King's Own* xxvi The master..finds one day that his sextant-case is all of a smudge. **1837** WHITTOCK *Bk. Trades* (1842) 260 The oil, the grease and consequent 'smudge' incur a good portion of uncleanness. **1864** *Soc. Sci. Rev.* 165 The countryman who..declared that it [a picture] was nothing but 'smudge'.

**b.** *techn.* The scum of paint.

**1823** P. NICHOLSON *Pract. Builder* 411 The scum is called smudge, and is used for outside work. **1879** *Cassell's Techn. Educ.* IV. 207/1 Smudge, which consists of the refuse from paint and varnish pots, and therefore contains a number of fatty, oily substances.

**3.** Very small coal; fine slack, coal dust.

**1883** in GRESLEY *Gloss. Coal-m.* 228. **1890** *Pall Mall G.* 4 Oct. 7/2 Small coal, such as smudge and slack, are plentiful.

**4.** *attrib.* and *Comb.*, as ***smudge-faced***, ***pan***, ***-pot***; also **smudge cell** *Med.*, a degenerate leucocyte in a blood film; **smudge-coal**, blind-coal, stone-coal (*Imperial Dict.* 1882).

[**1935** WHITBY & BRITTON *Disorders of Blood* iv. 89 Degenerate lymphocytes usually appear as smudges and are known as 'smear cells'.] **1937** KRACKE & GARVER *Dis. Blood & Atlas Hematol.* vi. 84 It has been stated that smudge forms are degenerating lymphocytes and that basket cells.. are degenerating granulocytes... It seems more probable that the smudge cell is an early stage and the basket cell a later stage of the same process. **1971** W. M. DOUGHERTY *Introd. Hematol.* iii. 70/1 Most often the bare nuclei that we call smudge cells or basket cells are in fact the bare nuclei of the lymphocytes. **1891** H. HERMAN *His Angel* v. 96 A grimy, smudge-faced, half-ragged urchin. **1798** J. CONSTABLE *Let.* 2 Dec. (1964) II. 16, I should be glad of the smudge pan as soon as convenient. **1883** *Fortn. Rev.* 1 Sept. 455 Huge poles ..smeared over by a property-man with a smudge-pot.

**smudge** (smʌdʒ), *sb.*[2] [Related to SMUDGE *v.*[2]]

**1.** A suffocating smoke; *spec.* a smoke made to repel mosquitoes, etc. Now *N.Amer.*

**1767** MASON in *Corresp. w. Gray* (1853) 401, I will sacrifice the first stanza on your critical altar, and let it consume either in flame or smudge as it choose. **1781** J. HUTTON *Tour to Caves* (ed. 2) Gloss. 96 *Smudge*, a suffocating smoke. **1879** BURROUGHS *Locusts & Wild Honey* 125 No smoke or smudge. **1887** E. CUSTER *Tenting on Plains* ii. 77 Eliza..brought old kettles with raw cotton into our room, from which proceeded such smudges and such odors as would soon have wilted a Northern mosquito. **1896** *Pall Mall Mag.* Sept. 63 A small fire of green wood was making a smoke—or 'smudge', to use the Floridan vernacular. **1939** F. P. GROVE *Two Generations* v. 32 If there had been a moon, a person coming over the hills would have seen that smudge as a perfectly level sheet closing the bowl like a lid. **1971** [see REPELLENT *a.* 2 d].

**2. a.** A heap of combustibles ignited and emitting dense smoke, usually made with the object of repelling mosquitoes, etc. Chiefly *N.Amer.*

**1806** A. HENRY in E. Coues *New Light on Early Hist. Greater Northwest* (1897) I. 287 The women closed the openings of the cabins, and made a smudge inside. **1842** MRS. C. M. KIRKLAND *Forest Life* xviii. I. 183, I have had a 'smudge' made in a chafing-dish at my bed-side. **1880** MARY FITZGIBBON *Trip to Manitoba* x. 114 A smudge (a fire of chips mulched with wet hay or green twigs when well started, to create smoke). **1893** EARL DUNMORE *Pamirs* I. 346 We had three or four smudges made, the smoke from which nearly blinded us. **1936** B. BROOKER *Think of Earth* III. vii. 278 'We'll make a smudge,' said Bundy, and..began gathering twigs and handfuls of scorched grass. **1952** *Chambers's Jrnl.* Aug. 503/2 Laddash greeted her, squatting in the smoke of a smudge against the mosquitoes. **1959** [see PUNKY *a.* a].

*attrib.* **1882** *Harper's Mag.* Oct. 724 The most effectual of these is to kindle smudge fires about the vineyard.

**b.** *attrib.*, as ***smudge bonfire***, ***fire***, ***-smoke***, etc.; designating containers for the smouldering fire, as ***smudge box***, ***can***, ***kettle***, ***pot***, etc.

**1846** *Knickerbocker* XXVIII. 241 You make a large 'smudge' fire outside that the smoke may drive these [insects] away. **1860** *Harper's Mag.* Oct. 584/1 Through the smudge-smoke issuing from the half-breeds' quarters we could catch glimpses of dark eyes. **1882** G. C. EGGLESTON *Wreck of Red Bird* 55 'What is a "smudge box", Ned?' 'Simply a shallow box of earth set upon a post, to build a smudge upon.' **1902** S. E. WHITE *Blazed Trail* xx. 148 Thorpe's old tin pail was pressed into service as a smudge-kettle. **1903** *Outing* XLIII. 166/1 Other settlers keep the smudge-pot going and live in smoke. **1909** H. BINDLOSS *Lorimer of Northwest* 3 The dun smoke of a smudge-fire shows that Harry is in prairie fashion protecting our stock. **1923** F. WALDO *Down Mackenzie* 116 One sees the horses after a trip..released for rest, huddling to windward of smudge bonfires, or in default of these standing in a forlorn group together to get in one another's shade. **1944** *Living off Land* ii. 31 Professional beekeepers use a small smoke bellows, but the best substitute is to light a smudge fire and let the smoke drift past the entrance to the hive. **1954** A. M. BEZANSON *Sodbusters invade Peace* 134 A smudge can was my constant companion in or in front of the house. **1965** H. JOHNSON *Bay of Pigs* III. i. 106 While one of the men put up the signs, another lighted the smudge pots. **1978** J. A. MICHENER *Chesapeake* 18 If he kept a smudge-fire going.. he could survive. *Ibid.* 36 The mosquitoes were terrible.. and people stayed close to smudge pots when the sun went down.

**smudge** (smʌdʒ), *sb.*[3] [f. SMUDGE *v.*[4]] A slight sign or indication (*of* laughter, etc.).

**1866** CARLYLE *Remin.* (1881) II. 126 A bright dimpling chuckle sometimes (smudge of laughter, the Scotch call it). **1898** G. A. SMITH *H. Drummond* i. (1899) 3 There was never a glimpse of a phylactery nor a smudge of 'unction'.

†**smudge**, *a. Obs.*$^{-1}$ [Related to SMUDGE *v.*[3] Cf. SMUG *a.*] Smart, trim.

**1596** NASHE *Saffron Walden* Wks. (Grosart) III. 138 A smudge piece of a handsome fellow it hath beene in his dayes, but now he is olde and past his best.

**smudge** (smʌdʒ), *v.*[1] Forms: 5 **smoge**, 6 **smoudge**, 7 **smodge**, **smooge**, 6–7, 9 **smudge**. [Of obscure origin; cf. the later SMUTCH *v.*]

**1. a.** *trans.* To soil, stain, blacken, smirch; to mark with dirty stains or smears.

*c* **1430** *Freemasonry* (1860) 744 Kepe thyn hondes, fayr and wel, From fowle smogynge of thy towel. **1548** ELYOT, *Atratus*, blacked or smudged [1565 *Cooper* smoudged]. **1604** T. M. *Black Bk.* D j b, The Sheetes smudged so durtily. **1609** HEYWOOD *Brit. Troy* v. Epil., The God whose face is Smoog'd with smoke and fiar. **1637** —— *Pleas. Dial.* iv. Wks. 1874 VI. 157 To be smudg'd and grim'd with soot. **1828** CARR *Craven Gloss.*, *Smudged*, begrimed. **1841** J. T. HEWLETT *Parish Clerk* II. 195 His coat..smudged for several inches up the sleeve of the left arm with the wipings of his pens. **1887** DOWDEN *Shelley* I. i. 30 With face and hands smudged and stained by explosive powders and virulent acids.

*fig.* **1602** *How to choose a Good Wife* v. ii, The beauty of the mind, Which neither time can alter..nor the black hand of envy Smudge and disgrace. **1896** *Boston* (Mass.) *Jrnl.* 29 Feb. 5/1 Halifax Chronicle smudged [= charged with libel].

**b.** To rub out or in, to paint or lay on, etc., in a smearing or daubing manner.

**1865** *Slang Dict.* 237 *Smudge*, to smear, obliterate. **1878** [G. N. BANKS] *About some Fellows* 26 [He] made a considerably worse mess trying to smudge it out. **1899** J. G. MILLAIS *Sir J. E. Millais* II. xvii. 213 The critics insisting ..that it was a stuffed bird, just smudged into the picture. **1901** *J. Black's Carp. & Build.* 42 Everybody, even the youngest boy, imagines he can 'smudge' paint.

**c.** *absol.* To make or leave a stain.

**1902** *Longman's Mag.* May 4 The soil here, coloured by old Devon Sandstone, smudges red, not brown.

**2.** To bungle, make a mess of (something).

**1864** WHYTE MELVILLE *Brookes of Bridlemere* xviii, He *smudged* it awfully, but we got over without a fall!

Hence **'smudging** *ppl. a.*, **'smudging** *vbl. sb.*[3] (in quot. *fig.*).

*a* **1861** MRS. BROWNING *Par. Theocritus* Poet. Wks. (1904) 584 One shaggy eyebrow draws its smudging road Straight through my ample front, from ear to ear. **1873** J. BROWN *Let.* 27 Dec. (1912) 288, I always feel insulted by these smudgings and besmearings.

**smudge** (smʌdʒ), *v.*[2] Now *dial.* and *N.Amer.* [Of obscure origin.]

**1.** *trans.* †**a.** To cure (herring) by smoking. *Obs.*$^{-1}$

Halliwell's '*Smudge*, to stifle. *North.*' is not otherwise certified.

**1599** NASHE *Lenten Stuffe* Wks. (Grosart) V. 239 In the craft of catching or taking it, and smudging it (marchant-and chapman-able as it should be), it sets a-worke thousands.

**b.** *N. Amer.* To make a smoky fire in (a tent, etc.); to fill with smoke from a smudge. Also, to cause (a fire) to smoke; to drive (mosquitoes, etc.) *away* by smoke. Now *rare.*

**1860** *Harper's Mag.* Aug. 296/2 The blankets were spread in the tents, the tents smudged or mosquito nets hung. **1866** *Ibid.* Jan. 265/2 The others sat by the fire and 'smudged' it. **1880** D. CURRIE *Lett. of Rusticus* 56/1 Before going to bed we smudged the tent, which made the mosquitoes so drunk that they did not molest us again before morning. **1891** in *Cent. Dict.* **1921** *Daily Colonist* (Victoria, B.C.) 30 Oct. 21/1, I piled on some brush and tried to smudge 'em away.

**c.** Among North American Indians, to smoke (pottery) in order to give it a black shiny finish. See also SMUDGING *vbl. sb.*[2]

**1936** K. M. CHAPMAN *Pottery of Santo Domingo Pueblo* 7 The ware turns light red in firing, though this is often purposely smudged to a more or less dense black after firing is complete.

**2.** *intr.* To smoulder.

**1825** BROCKETT *N.C. Gloss.*, *Smudge*, to burn without a flame, or any appearance of fire, except smoke. **1892** *Whitby Gaz.* 13 May 2 The bed and bed-clothes which burned and smudged for a considerable time before the fire was extinguished.

Hence **'smudging** *vbl. sb.*[2] (*spec.* in sense 1 c of the vb.).

**1846** E. W. FARNHAM *Life in Prairie Land* II. x. 314 This process is more briefly designated by its technical name of '*smudging*'. **1955** BUSHNELL & DIGBY *Anc. Amer. Pottery* iv. 32 In these examples the colour is due rather to smudging with carbon in the fire than to chemical reaction. **1973** A. H. WHITEFORD *North Amer. Indian Arts* 15 Smudging is achieved by smothering the fire with fine damp manure.

†**smudge**, *v.*[3] *Obs. rare.* [Of obscure origin; the sense agrees with that of SMUG *v.*[1] For the form cf. SMUDGE *a.*] *trans.* To make smart or trim; to deck or trick *up.*

**1589** GREENE *Menaphon* (Arb.) 92 Doron smudgde himselfe vp, and iumpde a marriage with..Carmela. **1593** NASHE *Four Lett. Conf.* Wks. (Grosart) II. 279 White wine ..is good for nothing, but to wash sores in, and smudge vp withered beauty with. **1596** —— *Saffron Walden* Wks. (Grosart) III. 135 He..stood..by the glasse,..currying and smudging and pranking himselfe vnmeasurably.

**smudge** (smʌdʒ), *v.*[4] *Sc.* and *north. dial.* Also **smoodge.** [Of obscure origin; connexion with G. dial. *schmutzen* (MHG. *smutzen*) to smile, is very doubtful, but cf. next and SMOUCH *v.*[1]] *intr.* To laugh quietly or to oneself. So **'smudging** *vbl. sb.*[1]

**1789** W. MACLAY *Jrnl.* 11 May (1890) 30 He will..dimple his visage with the most silly kind of half smile which I can not well express in English. The Scotch-Irish have a word that hits it exactly—*smudging.* **1808** JAMIESON, To *Smue*, or *Smudge*, to laugh in one's sleeve, to laugh in a clandestine way. Loth[ian]. **1823** *Blackw. Mag.* Mar. 312 Ye needna smudge and laugh at me now. **1828** MOIR *Mansie Wauch* xvii, Arm-and-arm together, smoodging and laughing like daft. **1861** QUIN *Heather Lintie* (1863) 96 Weel may he smudge within his sleeve At our attempts his snares tae leave.

**smudge** (smʌdʒ), *v.*[5] *rare.* [Cf. SMOUCH *v.*[1]] *trans.* To smouch, to caress.

**1844** J. T. HEWLETT *Parsons & W.* xliv, She smudged them and kissed them so very naturally.

**smudged** (smʌdʒd), *ppl. a.* [f. SMUDGE *v.*[1]] Marked with smudges; smeared, besmirched; applied in a smeary manner.

**1624** HEYWOOD *Gunaik.* IV. 199 To bee seene..with a smodged face. **1658** ROWLAND tr. *Moufet's Theat. Ins.* 1037 Having a black smudged face. **1839** THACKERAY *Major Gahagan* vi, Uncurled wigs, smudged rouge, blear eyes. **1897** *Bookman* Jan. 122/2 A smudged half sheet of paper with bald facts.

Hence **'smudgedly** *adv.*, in a smudged manner.

**1889** *Fabian Ess.* 217 We shall see as in a glass, darkly, or smudgedly,..that confrontation of rich and poor.

**smudgeless** ('smʌdʒlɪs), *a.* [f. SMUDGE *v.*[1] or *sb.*[1] + -LESS.] **a.** That will not smudge or smear. **b.** Without a smudge, clean.

**1913** *Chambers's Jrnl.* Mar. 270/1 So-called indelible and smudgeless inks have been placed upon the market. **1924** W. DEEPING *Three Rooms* xxxvi. 320 She had dealt with the silver, and it lay bright and smudgeless on a sheet of green baize. **1976** *Sci. Amer.* Jan. 15/2 (Advt.), Its built-in silent recorder prepares a permanent cardiotocogram on smudgeless thermal paper.

**smudger** ('smʌdʒə(r)). [f. as SMUDGE *v.*[1] + -ER[1]] One who smudges.

**1884** *Punch* 13 Sept. 129/1 Away with all your 'turps' and tubes, oh, smudgers on the shore. **1887** H. PRATT *Jesus, Bar Rabba*, etc. 311 And the man called the name of his wife *Chavah* (smudger), for she was the stainer of life.

**smudgily** ('smʌdʒɪlɪ), *adv.* [f. SMUDGY *a.*[1]] In a smudgy manner.

**1864** *Athenæum* No. 1891. 121/2 The details..are carelessly, even smudgily, put in. **1887** HISSEY *Holiday on Road* 229 Are we to..ignore the picturesque wholly for.. the smudgily suggestive?

**smudginess** ('smʌdʒɪnɪs). [f. as prec.] The state, character, or quality of being smudgy.

**1864** *Spectator* 31 Dec. 1511 Some of the smudginess that here and there disfigures the *fac-similes.* **1881** *Academy* 13 Aug. 128/2 These reproductions..are pervaded by an unpleasant smudginess.

**smudgy** ('smʌdʒɪ), *a.*[1] [f. SMUDGE *sb.*[1] or *v.*[1]]

**1.** Grimy, dirty; marked with smudges.

**1859** J. R. GREEN *Lett.* (1901) I. 32 Some one..who can paint without having her fingers always smudgy. **1867** MISS BRADDON *Doctor's Wife* i, The young man with the smudgy nose was an author.

*Comb.* **1897** *Outing* XXX. 213/2 As if by magic hundreds of smudgy-faced love-pledges surround you.

**2.** Smeared, smeary; blurred, indistinct.

**1865** *Sat. Rev.* 16 Dec. 675/1 It does not follow that, because an etching is black and smudgy, it has depth and power. **1875** *Zoologist* X. 4485 Dull, smudgy brown..lends security to the brooding bird.

*fig.* **1887** JESSOPP *Arcady* vi. 170 A smudgy surface of dreary, dismal, dull, dead-alivism.

**smudgy** ('smʌdʒɪ), *a.*[2] [f. SMUDGE *sb.*[2] or *v.*[2]]

**1.** *dial.* **a.** Stifling, stuffy. **b.** Thick, foggy.

**1847** HALLIW. s.v., The fire is so large that it makes the room feel quite hot and smudgy. **1871** PEACOCK *Ralf Skirl.* II. 182 If it wasn't so..smudgy we should see 'em.

**2.** Giving out much smoke; smoky.

**1878** *Pop. Sci. Monthly* XIII. 267 If more light was needed, other smudgy lamps were added. **1905** *Blackw. Mag.* Dec. 768/1 He built a fire—a smouldering smudgy fire.

†**smug**, *sb.*[1] *Obs.* [Of obscure origin: cf. SMUGGY *a.*] A blacksmith.

**1600–9** ROWLANDS *Knave of Clubbes* (Percy Soc.) 34 A smug of Vulcan's forging trade. **1629** DEKKER *London's Tempe* 123 Worke, my fine smugges. **1709** E. WARD *Hud. Rediv.* I. 133 'You're an impudent slut,' cries the smug at his bellows.

**smug** (smʌg), *sb.*[2] [f. SMUG *a.*]

*Smug* (and *Sir Smug*) is used as a suggestive personal name by Cowper *Hope* 413 and 438.

**1.** *Univ. slang.* A quiet hard-working student.

**1882** *Daily News* 23 Mar. 4/7 A 'smug' was always unpopular, but all unpopular persons were not smugs. The quiet smug was generally not a rich man. **1884** RADFORD in Birrell *Obiter Dicta* 212 He had many friends at Clement's Inn who were not smugs, nor, indeed, reading men in any sense.

*transf.* **1888** *Pall Mall G.* 17 May 1/1 The Conservative free and easy voters—unlike the Liberal smugs— 'would have their holidays'.

**2.** A smug or self-satisfied person.

**1891** *Sat. Rev.* 13 June 701 The ocean of silly cant which has been poured forth on the occasion by smugs and prigs.

**smug** (smʌg), *a.* Also 6 smogue, smoog, 6–7 smugg(e. [Of doubtful origin; the form is against its being ad. LG. *smuk* (whence Da. *smuk*, Sw. *smukk*, G. *schmuck*) pretty, nice, as the change of *k* to *g* would be very irregular.]

**1.** Of male persons: Trim, neat, spruce, smart; in later use, having a self-satisfied, conceited, or consciously respectable air.

The word has been in very common use from the 16th cent., and the earlier sense shades imperceptibly into the later, so that quotations cannot be separated.

**1551** ROBINSON tr. *More's Utopia* I. (1895) 11 They be so smugge and smoethe, that they haue not so much as one heare of an honest man. **1581** RICH *Farew.* Kj, The Duke.. perceiuyng him to bee a proper smogue yong man, gaue hym entertainment. **1613** HEYWOOD *Brazen Age* II. iv, I was when I was borne A pretty smug knaue. **1669** PEPYS *Diary* 28 Mar., To the Office with Tom, who looks mighty smug upon his marriage. **1706** ESTCOURT *Fair Example* v. i, Thou hast a handsom smug Neighbour that I believe knows her as well. **1740** LADY M. W. MONTAGU *Lett.* I. 124 He is a patrician too, and a smugger gentleman than Livy or any of his heroes. **1812** BYRON *Ch. Har.* I. lxix, Then thy spruce citizen, wash'd artizan, And smug apprentice gulp their weekly air. **1859** THACKERAY *Virgin.* II. 337 A smug officer of the United States Government. **1884** SHARMAN *Hist. Swearing* i. 2 The..smug undertakers of the neighbouring Soho.

**b.** Of women or girls. (Common *c* 1590–1650 in the older sense of the word.)

**1590** GREENE *Never too late* (1600) 98 Nowe Gods blessing on thy heart (quoth Callena) for louing such a smugge lasse. **1627** FELTHAM *Low Count.* (1677) 47 As smug as a Lady that hath newly lockt up her Colours, and laid by her Irons. **1677** OTWAY *Cheats of Scapin* I. i, She is indeed a good smug lass. **1701** STEELE *Grief a la Mode* III. i, Oh, that smug old woman! There's no enduring her affectation of youth.

**2.** Of the face (person, etc.): Smooth, sleek; also, in later use = sense 5.

**1582** STANYHURST *Æneis* II. (Arb.) 59 His tayle smoog [L. *lubrica*] thirling, slyke breast to Titan vpheauing. **1592** LYLY *Midas* IV. i, Cross-gartred Swaines, & Dairie girles, With faces smug, and round as Pearles. **1593** G. HARVEY *Pierce's Super.* Wks. (Grosart) II. 59 A slicke forhead, a smugge countenaunce. **1648** J. BEAUMONT *Psyche* VI. iv, Those dangerous Sirens whose smug maiden face Is ugly mortal Treason's burnish'd Glass. **1712** STEELE *Spectator* No. 428 ¶ 1 The Instrument which is to make your Visage less horrid and your Person more smug. **1790** COWPER *Odyss.* xv. 404 Sleek their heads And smug their countenances. **1852** THACKERAY *Esmond* I. x, It was edifying to behold him, fresh shaved and with smug face, singing out 'Amen!' **1892** MRS. OLIPHANT *Hist. Sk. Q. Anne* v. (1894) 237 Jeremy Bentham, in whose smug countenance Mill divined unspoken offences.

**3.** Of things: Smooth, clean, neat, trim, or tidy; in later use, having an appearance suggestive of complacency or respectability.

**1596** SHAKS. *1 Hen. IV*, III. i. 102 The smug and Siluer Trent. **1603** DEKKER *Wonderful Year* Wks. (Grosart) I. 84 The skie..lookte smug and smoothe, and had not so much as a wart sticking on her face. **1620** MARKHAM *Farew. Husb.* II. xviii. (1668) 88 The Come..falls away and leaves the corn clean and smug of itself. **1777** MME. D'ARBLAY *Early Diary, Journ.*, Putting on clean linnen, a tidy gown, and smug cap. **1841** DE QUINCEY *Rhetoric* (1860) 376 The smug and scanty draperies of his style. **1872** J. HATTON *Memorial Window* II. 262 To them, the smug signboards have been coffin plates.

†**4.** Of language: Smooth, neat. *Obs.*

**1607** WALKINGTON *Opt. Glass* 129 A smug neate stile,.. vernished phrases. **1648** J. BEAUMONT *Psyche* XVII. clxxxviii, His soft smug words tickle your wanton ear. **1682** *Annot. on Glanvill* 184 That trim and smug saying.

**5.** Indicative of, characterized by, complacency or conscious respectability.

**1851** D. JERROLD *St. Giles* xi. 103 Human arrogance,..in the smug belief of its own election,..looks upon its fellow.. as irrevocably lost. **1859** KINGSLEY *Misc.* II. 102 Addressing the audience..in the most smug and self-satisfied tone. **1885** *Athenæum* 30 May 688 A man of smug expediency and polite compromise.

**6.** *Comb.*, as *smug-faced*, *-looking*, *-skinned*.

**1575** GASCOIGNE *Herbs* Wks. 173, I coulde haue brought a noble regiment Of smugskinnde Nunnes into my countrey soyle. **1630** J. TAYLOR (Water P.) *Wks.* II. 252/1 The fourth that entred..Was..a smugfaced furie. **1720** RAMSAY *Wealth* 113 Thrice lucky pimps, or smug-fac'd wanton fair. **1876** MISS BRADDON *J. Haggard's Dau.* II. 2 The smug-faced deacons, in their glossy Sunday coats. **1895** 'IAN MACLAREN' *Beside the Bonnie Brier Bush* i, A trim, smug-looking teacher's house.

**smug** (smʌg), *v.*[1] Now *rare.* Also 7 smugg(e. [f. prec.]

**1. a.** *trans.* To smarten up (oneself or another, one's appearance, etc.); to make trim or gay. Freq. with *up*.

(*a*) **1588** GREENE *Perimedes* To Rdr., To enter parlee with his wif, smugd vp in her best apparrell. **1599** DEKKER *Shoemaker's Holiday* III. iv, Mistress, smug up your looks; on with your best apparel. **1623** MIDDLETON & ROWLEY *Sp. Gipsy* IV. i, Smug up your beetle-brows, none look grimly. **1672** WYCHERLEY *Love in Wood* III. ii, If she has smugged herself up for me, let me prune and flounce my peruke a little for her. **1750** F. COVENTRY *Hist. Pompey* I. ix, Your..master ..has been smugging up his pretty face. **1772** tr. *J. F. de Isla's Friar Gerund* IV. iii. 68 He had smugged himself up, it is evident, with the utmost prolixity. **1888** *Blackw. Mag.* June 788 This worthy tutor, doubtless 'smugged up' in his Sunday suit.

(*b*) **1598** E. GUILPIN *Skial.* (1878) 65, I must craue A little labour to be smug'd, and haue A blessing of Rose-water. **1602** MARSTON *Ant. & Mel.* III. Wks. 1856 I. 37, I have put on good cloathes, and smugd my face. **1654** GAYTON *Pleas. Notes* IV. xvii. 260 But to the Pole annex your Brasen Bason, 'Tis not to smug one then, but to amaze one. **1772** tr. *J. F. de Isla's Friar Gerund* II. v. 362 Our Friar Gerund was so shaved, and combed, and smugged, and spruced, that it was a delight to behold his face. **1841** *Peter Parley's Ann.* II. 234 Poor old Goody Clackett had little thoughts of ever being smugged..to make a guy on the fifth of November. **1841** L. HUNT *Seer* (1864) II. 74 All the thoroughfares in towns near London..have wonderfully plucked up, and *smugged* themselves of late years.

**b.** *absol.* To put on a smart or smug expression.

**1649** G. DANIEL *Trinarch., Hen. V*, ccxcii, The Bloat Face of Rusticitie, Smuggs, looking in A Mirrour. **1719** D'URFEY *Pills* V. 74 You smug, you trick, You toss a twire, a grin.

**2.** To smarten up (a thing); to fit *up* (a room, etc.) neatly or nicely. *rare.*

**1598** FLORIO, *Brandire*, to trick, smug, spruce, or trim vp any thing. **1745** H. WALPOLE *Lett.* (1846) II. 64 The moment I have smugged up a closet or a dressing-room, I have always warning given me, that my lease is out. **1751** *Ibid.* 399 The chapel is very pretty, and smugged up with tiny pews.

**3.** [Perh. a different word: cf. SMUGGLE *v.*[2]] *intr.* To caress, fondle. *dial. rare.*

**1813** E. PICKENS *Poems* I. 176 We'll cuddle baith amang the fug An' while we hug, an' kiss, an' smug, I'll haud thee firm by ilka lug. **1922** JOYCE *Ulysses* 308 Blind to the world up in a shebeen in Bride street after closing time..and hugging and smugging.

Hence **smugged** *ppl. a.* (also *Comb.*); '**smugging** *vbl. sb.*[1]

**1706** HEARNE *Collect.* (O.H.S.) I. 217 Dr. Green was a little spruce smugg'd fac'd..Chaplain. **1719** D'URFEY *Pills* IV. 319 Drapers smugg'd Prentices. **1736** AINSWORTH I, A smugging up, *ornatus nitidus*. **1932** AUDEN *Orators* III. 104 Only hard On smugging, smartness, and self-regard.

**smug** (smʌg), *v.*[2] *slang.* [Of doubtful origin.]

**1.** *trans.* To steal, filch, run away with.

**1825** T. HOOK *Sayings* Ser. II. *Man of Many Friends* I. 320 Some cold cream, which she had *smugged* from Mrs. Abberly. **1834** R. H. FROUDE *Rem.* (1838) I. 386, I have had a horse, which I have been cool enough to smug from the Bishop's stables. **1851** MAYHEW *Lond. Lab.* I. 421/1 After that he used to go 'smugging' (running away with) other people's things. **1887** J. W. HORSLEY *Jottings from Jail* i. 6 We used to go and smug snowy (steal linen) that was hung out to dry.

**2.** *intr.* To copy surreptitiously; to crib.

*a* **1860** ALB. SMITH *Med. Stud.* (1861) 54 Copying out their notes in little, that they may smug from them when locked up in the examination-room.

**3.** *trans.* To hush up (a matter).

**1857** *Morning Chron.* 3 Oct. 8/3 She wanted however a guarantee that the case should be smugged, or, in other words, compromised.

**4.** To arrest, put in prison.

**1896** A. MORRISON *Child Jago* 247 His father had been smugged.

Hence '**smugging** *vbl. sb.*[2] (See quots.)

**1825** HONE *Every-day Bk.* I. 253 When any game was out, ..it was lawful to steal the thing played with; this was called smugging. **1861** MAYHEW *Lond. Lab.* III. 58 Landlord (collaring the bell). Smuggings! pursession is nine points of the law! **1864** *Slang Dict.* 237 *Smuggings*,..shouted out by boys, when snatching the tops, or small play property, of other lads.

**smug-boat.** (See quot.)

**1867** SMYTH *Sailor's Word-bk.*, *Smug-boats*, contraband traders on the coast of China; opium boats.

**smuggery** ('smʌgərɪ). *nonce-wd.* [f. SMUG *a.* + -ERY.] The quality or condition of being smug, or an instance of this; smugness.

**1928** A. HUXLEY *Point Counter Point* xi. 170 Enlargements,..by contrast with our bourgeois and Pecksniffian smuggeries. **1961** G. FRANKAU in P. Frankau *Pen to Paper* 221, I must pray to be redeemed from the sin of Smuggery.

'**smuggish**, *a. rare*[−0]. [f. SMUG *a.*] Somewhat smug or trim. Hence '**smuggishly** *adv.*

**1736** AINSWORTH *Eng.-Lat. Dict.* I. s.v.

**smuggle** ('smʌg(ə)l), *v.*[1] Also 7 **smuckle**, 8 **smugle**. [App. of LG. or Du. origin. The earlier form *smuckle* corresponds to LG. *smukkeln* (G. dial. *schmuckeln*, *schmucheln*) or Du. *smokkelen*, while the slightly later *smuggle* agrees with LG. *smuggeln* (G. *schmuggeln*, Da. *smugle*, Norw. *smugla*, Sw. *smuggla*). The origin of the term, and the precise relationship of the two types, is not clear. Cf. SMUGGLER, which appears earlier.]

**1.** *trans.* To convey (goods) clandestinely into (or out of) a country or district, in order to avoid payment of legal duties, or in contravention of some enactment; to bring *in*, *over*, etc., in this way.

*a* **1687** PETTY *Pol. Arith.* IV. (1691) 84 Two Hundred thousand pounds smuckled by the Merchants. **1687** MIÈGE *Gt. Fr. Dict.* II, To Smuckle. See to Smuggle. **1706** PHILLIPS (ed. Kersey), To *Smuggle Goods*, to run them ashore, or bring them in by stealth, without paying the Custom. **1790** BURKE *Fr. Rev.* 36 In order afterwards to smuggle them back again into this country. **1837** CARLYLE *Fr. Rev.* I. II. v, Weapons, military stores can be smuggled over (if the English do not seize them). **1846** MCCULLOCH *Acc. Brit. Emp.* (1854) II. 397 The means of preventing its being smuggled or the duty evaded.

**b.** *intr.* To practise smuggling.

**1697** DAMPIER *Voy.* (1729) I. 308 The Spaniards can and will Smuggle (as our Seamen call Trading by stealth) as well as any Nation that I know. **1830** MARRYAT *King's Own* xxiii, We don't mean to smuggle any more. **1845** MCCULLOCH *Taxation* II. vi. (1852) 251 The temptation to smuggle was diminished.

†**2.** *to smuggle the coal* (see quot.). *slang. Obs.*

**1687** MIÈGE *Gt. Fr. Dict.* II, *To smuggle the Coal*, to make people believe one has no Money when the Reckoning is to be paid.

**3.** *transf.* **a.** To get possession of by stealth.

**1766** GRAY *Kingsgate* 3 The pious resolution To smuggle a few years. *c* **1790** in Hone *Every-day Bk.* (1827) II. 832, I shall prove the Excise Office to be the greatest smuggle[r] in the nation, for they smuggled the ground from the public.

**b.** To convey, etc., in a stealthy or clandestine manner. Const. with advs. and preps., as *away*, *in*, *into*, *off*, *out of*, *through*, etc.

**1783** W. GORDON *Livy* v. ii. (1823) 400 Among all that number a single Plebeian could not be smuggled in. **1816** SCOTT *Old Mort.* x, She smuggled him out of the garrison through the pantry window. **1853** LYTTON *My Novel* XII. xxxi, I have two private bills I want to smuggle through Parliament. **1872** BLACK *Adv. Phaeton* xiii. 177 On our entrance the document was hastily folded up and smuggled away.

**c.** *intr.* To make *off* stealthily.

**1865** CARLYLE *Fredk. Gt.* (Tauchn.) X. 263 These good people are smuggling off. Let them go in peace.

†'**smuggle**, *v.*[2] *Obs.* [Of obscure origin: cf. SNUGGLE *v.*] *trans.* To cuddle, fondle, caress.

**1679** PRANCE *Narr. Popish Plot* 36 This pretious Saint.. hath been seen to..kiss her many times over, as if it had been part of her Penance to be most filthily smuggled. **1698** FARQUHAR *Love & Bottle* I. i, Oh, the little Lips!—and 'tis the best natur'd little dear.—(Smuggles and kisses it.) **1709** *Brit. Apollo* No. 75. 3/1 He was smugling Blouze. **1719** D'URFEY *Pills* II. 195 He Smuggled her, and Squeez'd her.

*absol.* **1709** E. WARD *Hud. Rediv.* I. 68 You may smuggle and grope.

'**smuggleable**, *a.* [f. SMUGGLE *v.*[1]] Capable of being smuggled.

**1805** SOUTHEY in *Life* (1850) II. 332 Only a box at a time, of such a smuggleable size that a man can easily carry it.

**smuggled** ('smʌg(ə)ld), *ppl. a.* [f. as prec.] Imported, brought in, conveyed, etc., by stealth.

**1706** E. WARD *Wooden World Diss.* (1708) 68 Many a Boat-Load of smuggl'd Ware has he popt forth at his Gun-room Ports. **1810** CRABBE *Borough* xviii. 178 By smuggled news from neighb'ring village told. **1836** MARRYAT *Pirate*, etc. (Rtldg.) 169 [They] handed up all the smuggled goods. **1894** MRS. DYAN *Man's Keeping* (1899) 8 The consciousness of that smuggled paper made her nervous.

**smuggler** ('smʌglə(r)). Also 7 **smuckellor**, **smuckler**. [ad. LG. *smukkeler*, Du. *smokkelaar*, or LG. *smugg(e)ler* (G. *schmuggler*, Sw. *smugglare*): see SMUGGLE *v.*[1]]

**1.** One who smuggles commodities; *esp.* one who makes a trade or practice of smuggling.

**1661** *Proclamation* 9 Aug., A sort of leud people called Smuckellors, never heard of before the late disordered times, who make it their trade..to steal and defraud His Majesty of His Customs. **1670** BLOUNT *Glossogr.* (ed. 3), *Smuglers*, are stealers of Customs; well known upon the Thames. **1740** WESLEY *Wks.* (1872) I. 289 He declared before us all that he was a Smuggler. **1779** *Mirror* No. 62, He had served with *eclat* in the corps established for repressing smugglers of tobacco. **1837** CARLYLE *Fr. Rev.* I. VI. iii, Smugglers of salt go openly in armed bands. **1870** F. R. WILSON *Ch. Lindisf.* 36 It had the reputation..of being the haunt of smugglers.

*transf.* **1790** BURKE *Fr. Rev.* 134 The infectious stuff which is imported by the smugglers of adulterated metaphysics. **1849–50** ALISON *Hist. Europe* VIII. l. §30. 150 An immense annual profit for the behoof of the great Imperial Smuggler in the Tuileries.

**2.** A vessel employed in smuggling.

**1799** *Naval Chron.* II. 443 The *Assistance* Smuggler, from Guernsey. **1836** MARRYAT *Pirate*, etc. (Rtldg.) 164 This vessel.. must be a smuggler. **1894** K. HEWAT *Little Scottish World* i. 12 The casks landed from the smuggler were safely deposited.

**3.** *attrib.* and *Comb.*, as ***smuggler boat, devil, dogger, -hunting.***

**1776** *Ann. Reg.* 135 His majesty's sloop Princess Anne fell in with a smuggler dogger in the frith of Forth. **1815** SCOTT *Guy M.* xlv, Thae smuggler deevils. **1862** THORNBURY *Turner* I. 333 He beat about year after year in all sorts of smuggler boats. **1899** SOMERVILLE & ROSS *Irish R.M.* 202 He had taken up the unprofitable task of smuggler-hunting.

**smugglery** ('smʌglərɪ). [f. SMUGGLE *v.*$^{1}$ Cf. Da. *smugleri*, Sw. *smuggleri*, Du. *smokkelarij*; also LG. *smugg-*, G. *schmuggelei.*] Smuggling.

**1895** *United Service Mag.* 212 This time, as doubtless often before, Mrs. S. succeeds in her smugglery.

**smuggling** ('smʌglɪŋ), *vbl. sb.* [f. SMUGGLE *v.*$^{1}$] Clandestine importation of goods, etc.

**1728** CHAMBERS *Cycl.*, *Smuggling* a cant Term for the Running of Goods. **1769** BLACKSTONE *Comm.* IV. 155 Smuggling, or the offence of importing goods without paying the duties imposed thereon by the laws of the customs and excise. **1845** MCCULLOCH *Taxation* II. ix. (1852) 330 The true way to suppress smuggling is to render it unprofitable. **1894** J. MACINTOSH *Ayrshire Nts. Entert.* vii. 109 The smuggling of tea, tobacco, and brandy formed one of the staple industries of the place.

*attrib.* **1698** LUTTRELL *Brief Rel.* (1857) IV. 409 Mr. David Barrau, committed to Newgate for the smugling trade, has paid his fine. **1748** *Anson's Voy.* I. ix. 85 These smuggling engagements are doubtless very extensive. **1818** SCOTT *Hrt. Midl.* xxxiii, I readily joined Wilson in a perilous smuggling adventure.

**smuggling** ('smʌglɪŋ), *ppl. a.* [f. SMUGGLE *v.*$^{1}$] That smuggles, or is engaged in smuggling:

**a.** Of persons.

**1816** SCOTT *Let.* in *Lockhart* (1837) IV. i. 10 A pirate, or an outlaw, or a smuggling bandit. **1824** —— *Redgauntlet* ch. xxiii, 'Is this the smuggling fellow?' demanded Redgauntlet. **1884** PAE *Eustace* xix. 244 Every smuggling rascal of them has fled to his hole.

**b.** Of vessels.

Perh. properly an attributive use of the *vbl. sb.*

**1813** *Examiner* 22 Feb. 122/2 The prisoner.. was mate of a smuggling cutter. **1815** SCOTT *Guy M.* iii, A smuggling lugger from the Isle of Man. **1836** MARRYAT *Pirate*, etc. (Rtldg.) 174, I.. have sent them in the smuggling vessel.

†**smuggling-ken.** *Cant. Obs.* [Cf. SMUGGLE *v.*$^{2}$] A brothel.

**1725** *New Cant. Dict.* s.v. *Clicketting*, He has pick'd up the Blowse, and they are pik'd into that Smuggling-Ken a Clicketing.

†'**smuggy,** *a. Obs. rare.* Also 6 smoggy. [Cf. SMUG *sb.*$^{1}$] Grimy, smutty.

*c* **1515** *Cocke Lorell's B.* 11 With smoggy colyers, and stynkynge gonge fermers. **1630** J. TAYLOR (Water P.) *Wks.* I. 124/2 Noble Vulcan, a mad smuggy Smith.

**smugly** ('smʌglɪ), *adv.* [f. SMUG *a.*] In a smug, complacent (†smart or trim) manner.

**1575** LANEHAM *Lett.* (1871) 30 Hiz beard smugly shauen. **1598** FLORIO, *Nettamente*, neatly,.. handsomely, smugly. **1656** S. HOLLAND *Zara* (1719) 146 Dragons may now securely sleep, and ugly Deformed Orks seem to look smooth and smugly. **1727** GAY *Begg. Op.* I. iv, Though she be never so ugly, Lillies and roses will quickly appear And her face look wond'rous smuggly. **1840** HOOD *Up Rhine* 207 Instead of looking smugly.. The votaries are all so old and ugly. **1892** *Spectator* 16 Jan. 84/1 Just consider what the smugly respectable man has done for himself.

**smugness** ('smʌgnɪs). [f. SMUG *a.*] The condition or quality of being smug.

**1632** SHERWOOD, Smugnesse, *netteté*. **1677** WYCHERLEY *Pl. Dealer* III. i, She looks like an old Coach new painted; affecting an unseemly Smugness. **1755** H. WALPOLE *Corr.* (1903) III. 341, I like the smugness of the cathedral, and the profusion of the most beautiful Gothic tombs. **1789** MRS. PIOZZI *Journ. France* II. 78 No smugness.. ever crossed the fancy of Schidone. **1836** *Tait's Mag.* III. 491 It has been.. smoothened, and tamed down to smugness, by cultivation, enclosing, and planting. **1883** *Contemp. Rev.* Oct. 602 There is probably no smugness in the world comparable to the complacent smugness of our insular ignorance.

**smuik(e, smuke,** obs. Sc. forms of SMOOK.

†'**smulkin.** *Obs. rare.* [? Irish.] (See quot. 1617.)

**1571** CAMPION *Hist. Irel.* II. v. (1633) 84 Indebted to the Citizens of Divelin.. a thousand poundes, whereof he payde not one smulkin. **1617** MORYSON *Itin.* I. 284 They [*sc.* the Irish] had also brasse farthings, called smulkins, whereof foure made a penny.

†**smult,** *pa. pple. Obs.*$^{-1}$ (Meaning doubtful.)

*c* **1400** *Destr. Troy* 911 With a smorther & a smoke smult through his nase.

**smur** (smɜː(r)), *sb. dial.* and *Sc.* Also smurr, smir(r. [Of obscure origin.]

**1.** Fine rain; drizzle.

**1808** JAMIESON, *Smurr*, a drizzling rain. Ayrs. **1823** E. MOOR *Suffolk Words*, *Smur*, small rain. **1878** *Good Words* 245 Sunday morning, which was grey with mist and 'smur'.

**2.** A drizzle *of* rain, etc.

**1830** GALT *Lawrie T.* VII. iii. (1849) 315 During the afternoon a smur of rain came on. **1872** YOUNG *Lochlomond* (E.D.D.), A cannie smir O' a refreshing simmer shower. **1873** G. C. DAVIES *Mount. & Mere* xix. 176 The morning broke with a little wind and a slight smurr of rain.

**smur** (smɜː(r)), *v. dial.* and *Sc.* Also smurr, smir(r. [Cf. prec.] *intr.* To drizzle.

**1825** JAMIESON *Suppl.*, *It's Smurrin*, it rains slightly. **1838** HOLLOWAY *Prov. Dict.*, *To smur*, to rain lightly and mistily. **1881** FITZGERALD *Lett.* I. 472 It has been what we call down here 'smurring' rather than raining. **1898** N. MUNRO *J. Splendid* 290 Whenever rains are smirring and mists are blowing.

**smurien,** obs. form of SMEAR *v.*

'**smurlin.** *Shetl. dial.* [app. an error for *smurslin* (cf. *smircelin* in the *Eng. Dial. Dict.*), corresponding to Icel. *smyrslingr.*] A species of clam.

**1806** NEILL *Tour Orkney & Shetl.* 93 They have abundance of what are called *culleocks* and *smurlins.* The *smurlin* or *smuthlin* is the Mya truncata, remarkable for a shrivelled leathery process at one end. Both these shell-fish are highly relished by the Shetlanders.

'**smurry,** *a.* [f. SMUR *sb.*] Drizzly.

**1888** BLACK *House-boat* x, The cold hues of green through which we had been sailing on this smurry afternoon.

†**smush,** *a. Sc. Obs.*$^{-1}$ (Meaning uncertain; perhaps a later form of SMOCH *a.*)

**1629** Z. BOYD *Balm of Gilead* 107 He.. seeth him gaping for lyfe lyke a hungry dogge gaping for a smush bone.

**smush** (smʌʃ), *sb.* [Alteration of MUSH *sb.*$^{1}$: cf. SMASH *sb.*$^{1}$] **1.** = MUSH *sb.*$^{1}$ 3 a; a messy pulp. *dial.*

**1825** JAMIESON *Sc. Dict.* (Suppl.) II. 429/1 *Gane to smush*, reduced to a friable or crumbled state, like potatoes too much boiled, &c. **1929** D. H. LAWRENCE *Pansies* 130 Then suddenly the mastodon rose with the wonderful lady And trampled all the listeners to a smush.

**2.** The mouth; = MUSH *sb.*$^{1}$ 3 d. *U.S. slang. rare.*

**1930** [see HAUL *v.* 3 c]. **1935** D. RUNYON in *Hearst's* Jan. 160/2 He grabs Miss Amelia Bodkin in his arms and kisses her kerplump on the smush.

†**smuss,** *v. Obs.*$^{-1}$ [f. MUSS *sb.*$^{1}$; the verb *muss* occurs in Linc. dial. For the prefixed *s-* cf. SMEUSE *sb.* and *v.*] *trans.* To take by force; to grab, seize, or snatch.

**1736** ELIZA STANLEY tr. *Hist. du Prince Titi* 14 He denied himself the Enjoyment of such Knicknacks as were given him, and would scramble for and smuss [F. *grapiller*] those of other Children his Playfellows.

**smut** (smʌt), *sb.* Also 7–8 smutt, 8–9 smoot. [Related to SMUT *v.* Cf. LG. *schmutt*, G. *schmutz*, in sense 1; also MHG. *smuz*, *smutz* fat, grease, G. *schmutz* (Sw. *smuts*, Da. *smuds*) dirt, filth. See also SMOT *sb.*$^{1}$

The adj. *smutty* is recorded earlier in most of the senses, and the sb. may be mainly a back-formation from this.]

**1. a.** A fungous disease affecting various plants, esp. cereals, which are spoiled by the grain being wholly or partly converted into a blackish powder; also, one or other of the fungi (species of *Ustilagineæ*) causing the disease.

**1665** *Phil. Trans.* I. 93 Meldew, Blasting, Smut. **1669** WORLIDGE *Syst. Agric.* (1681) 214 Smut seems to proceed from the same cause. *a* **1722** LISLE *Husb.* (1757) 132 Such grain was apt to carry a smut. **1796** WITHERING *Brit. Pl.* (ed. 3) IV. 388 This is the Smut, so frequently found upon the ears of different sorts of growing corn, and also upon grasses. **1834** *Brit. Husb.* I. 379 (L.U.K.), The practice of steeping seed-wheat.. applies rather to smut, than to rust or mildew. **1875** H. C. WOOD *Therap.* (1879) 555 The Smut of Indian Corn (*Ustilago maidis*) appears to have active medicinal properties.

**b.** A smutted grain. *rare*$^{-1}$.

**1799** *Hull Advertiser* 23 Feb. 1/1 These machines.. do not crush the smuts or bunt in wheat.

**2.** A black mark or stain; a smudge. Also *fig.*

**1664** H. MORE *Myst. Iniq.* 474 That there is not the least smutt of Antichristianism in Episcopacy itself. **1671** WOODHEAD *St. Teresa* II. ii. 12 All that is fair.. in this world, is but a smut with a cole. **1830** 'B. MOUBRAY' *Dom. Poultry*, etc. 163 The smut consists of a black spot on the side of the rabbit's nose. **1861** *Fraser's Mag.* June 772 A black mark on his [*sc.* a rabbit's] nose, which is called a butterfly smut.

**3.** *Coal-mining.* Bad, soft, earthy coal.

**1686** PLOT *Staffordsh.* 146 Above ground they look for a *smut* as they call it, i.e. a friable black earth. **1796** KIRWAN *Elem. Min.* (ed. 2) II. 51 Smut seems also a variety of this species [*sc.* inflammable mineral carbon], but more impure. **1799** —— *Geol. Ess.* 292 The uppermost seam of coal is commonly soft and dusty, it is vulgarly called *smut.* **1806** *Phil. Trans.* XCVI. 346 Smoot and Fire Clay. **1829** GLOVER *Hist. Derby* I. 59 Measures of strata:.. Soft coal or smut 2 ft. 10 in. **1860–** in mining glossaries.

**4. a.** Soot or sooty matter.

**1693** DRYDEN, etc. *Juvenal* vi. (1726) 71 The steam of Lamps still hanging on her cheeks In ropy Smut. **1712** E. COOKE *Voy. S. Sea* 45 Spotted down the Cheeks with white Clay, and some black Streaks of Smut. **1790** BURKE *Let. Noble Lord* Wks. VIII. 97 Our most salutary and most beautiful institutions yield nothing but dust and smut. **1846** LANDOR *Imag. Conv.* II. 91 The furnace is mere smut, and no bellows to blow the embers. **1893** *Scribner's Mag.* June 778/1 The remotest articles of furniture are rife with infinitesimal smut.

**b.** A particle of sooty matter.

**1806** SOUTHEY *Lett.* (1856) I. 375 That cursed composition of smoke, dust, smuts, human breath, and marsh vapour. **1849** LYTTON *Caxtons* XIV. ii, A joyous dance of those monads, called vulgarly *smuts.* **1894** MRS. RITCHIE *Chapters Mem.* viii. 106 A lady sitting with an umbrella in the drizzle of rain and falling smuts from the funnel.

**c.** A very minute insect.

**1899** *Daily News* 28 Dec. 6/4 A trout.. grubs in the weeds, chases larvæ, and revels in almost invisible smuts.

**5.** Indecent or obscene language.

**1698** J. COLLIER *Immor. Stage* i. (1730) 4 The Modern Poets seem to use Smut as the old Ones did Machines, to relieve a fainting Invention. **1707** *Refl. upon Ridicule* 206 'Tis a miserable way of Pleasing, to scatter Smut in all your Stories. **1760–2** GOLDSMITH *Cit. W.* xlix, The gentlemen talked smut, the ladies laughed and were angry. **1821** SCOTT *Kenilw.* ii, Drunken freaks, and drunken quarrels, and smut, and blasphemy. **1858** CARLYLE *Fredk. Gt.* VI. iv. (1872) II. 173 Discourse of a cheerful or of a serious nature,.. and not the least smut permitted. **1886** *Spectator* 4 Dec. 1621 The public must have titles, or smut, or murder, and wishes in its heart always to have two of them together.

†**6.** *slang.* (See quot.) *Obs.*$^{-0}$

**1812** J. H. VAUX *Flash Dict.*, *Smut*, a copper boiler, or furnace.

**7.** *attrib.*, as (sense 1) ***smut bag, corn, fungus, mill, machine, spore,*** etc.; (sense 5) ***smut book, -note; shop,*** etc.; ***smut-hunting*** ppl. adj.; **smut-grass** *U.S.*, a rush-grass (*Sporobolus Indicus*), the spikes of which are usually blackened by a smut; **smut-hound** [cf. HOUND *sb.*$^{1}$ 4 e] *colloq.*, one who seeks to censor or suppress smut (sense 5), esp. in literature.

**1712** ADDISON *Spect.* No. 361 ¶13 He teaches the Smut-note, the Fustian-note, the Stupid-note. **1731** in *6th Rep. Dep. Kpr.* App. II. 119 A new Machine for cleaning Wheat .. is contrived to take away the stains, smut bags, and other trumpery. **1790** *Trans. Soc. Arts* VIII. 32 Wheat, sown too long on the same spot, without changing the seed, will generally become smutt and hen-corn. **1818** *Niles' Reg.* XV. 80/1 *A smutt mill*, for cleaning wheat of smut, is in operation at Plattsburg. **1850** *Mary Wedlake's Priced List Farming Implements* 25 A *Smut Machine*, to clean damaged grain. **1852** *Appleton's Dict. Mach.* II. 588 Smut Machine.. for cleaning all kinds of grain. **1868** *Rep. U.S. Commiss. Agric.* (1869) 37 A few cattle in Massachusetts have died from eating 'smut corn'. **1897** W. G. SMITH tr. *Tubeuf's Dis. Plants* 275 The Ustilagineae or Smut-fungi are distinguished by their dark-coloured or black chlamydospores. *Ibid.* 276 In this way any adherent smut-spores are killed. **1927** H. L. MENCKEN *Let.* 2 Dec. (1961) 305 Of my inventions I am vainest of Bible Belt, booboisie, smut-hound and Boobus americanus. **1928** D. H. LAWRENCE *Let.* 9 Mar. (1962) II. 1042 Mason wrote me rather scared about the censor and smut-hunting authorities. **1930** AUDEN *Poems* 69 Lawrence was brought down by smut-hounds, Blake went dotty as he sang. **1930** *Publishers' Weekly* 31 May 2737/2 The confiscation of dirty picture postals and smut books. **1961** *John o' London's* 28 Sept. 357/3 The bulk of *The High Price of Pornography* is devoted to a survey of the rancid avalanche of smut magazines.. which are pulped out in the States. **1965** E. L. MYLES *Emperor of Peace* I. xiii. 135 He bought.. a two-inch stone burr mill complete with smut mill, cleaner and water wheel. **1967** *Spectator* 1 Dec. 683/1 Eminent men of letters would not be dismissed as fools or smuthounds. **1977** *Zigzag* Apr. 28/3 He said we were turning lunchtime into a 42nd street smut shop.

**smut** (smʌt), *v.* Also 7 smutt, smoot. [Cf. SMOT *v.*, and MHG. *smutzen* (G. *schmutzen*) to smear, dirty.]

**1.** *trans.* To mark with some black or dirty substance; to blacken, smudge.

*α.* **1587** HARMAR tr. *Beza's Serm.* 195 No man can like to be smutted and blatched in his face. **1624** MIDDLETON *Game at Chess* III. i, *W. Pawn.* White quickly soils you know. *B. J. Pawn.*.. Get thee gone then, I shall smut thee. **1668** H. MORE *Div. Dial.* III. iv. (1713) 187 A Company.. whom some unlucky Wag has smutted with his sooty and greazy fingers. **1705** ADDISON *Italy, Pavia* 26 The Inside is so smutted with Dust, and the Smoak of Lamps. **1752** JOHNSON *Rambler* No. 188 ¶12 Contriving to smut the nose of any stranger who was to be initiated into the club. **1836** WHATELY in Miss E. J. Whately *Life* (1866) I. 366 He who wrestles with a chimney-sweeper is sure to be smutted. **1877** *Daily News* 27 Dec. 6/1 The dingy whitewashed walls, smutted by the smoke of the tottering stove.

*β.* **1657** W. MORICE *Coena quasi Κοινὴ* xxxiii. 306 To keep my cloaths from being smooted by a Chimnie-sweeper.

**b.** *fig.* To stain with some fault or imperfection.

*α.* **1601** DENT *Pathw. Heaven* 202 What is the cause why some one sinne doth so blot and smut the most excellent men? **1674** COTTON in *Flatman's Poems* 47 You no prophane, no obscene language use To smut your paper or defile your Muse.

*β.* *a* **1661** FULLER *Worthies* (1840) II. 102 Considering the sottishness of superstition in the age he lived in, he is less smooted therewith than any of his contemporaries.

**2.** To affect (grain) with smut.

**1626** BACON *Sylva* §497 There falleth also Mildew upon Corn and smutteth it. **1812** SIR J. SINCLAIR *Syst. Husb. Scot.* I. 325 Having often observed in his wheat fields, a few ridges alternately clean and smutted. **1841** HOOD *Tale Trumpet* 761 Though the wishes that Witches utter Can.. Smut and mildew the corn on the stalk.

**b.** *intr.* Of grain: To be affected by smut.

**1657** S. PURCHAS *Pol. Flying-Ins.* 143 Corn thus imbibed, and then sown without lime, will not smut. **1677** PLOT *Oxfordsh.* 244 Wheat following the dung Cart on their best Land, is the more liable to smut. **1745** *Gentl. Mag.* 31 Corn managed in this manner is not apt to smut or mildew.

**3.** *trans.* To make obscene.

**1722** WELSTED *Prol. Steele's Consc. Lovers* 11 Another smuts his Scene (a cunning Shaver), Sure of the Rakes and of the Wenches Favour.

**4.** *intr.* Of fish: To rise at, or feed on, smuts.

**1889** *Sat. Rev.* 18 May 612/2 These demonstrations are made by trout bulging, tailing, smutting, or minnowing. **1892** *Field* 4 June 838/2 The fish were smutting or bulging on the shallows.

**ˈsmut-ball.** [f. SMUT *sb.* 1.] A single grain of wheat or other cereal affected by smut or bunt; a cohesive body of smut.

**1750** W. ELLIS *Mod. Husb.* IV. IV. 130 (E.D.S.). *a***1761** S. HALES in Mills *Pract. Husb.* III. 128 The moisture that was equal to the weight of the smut-balls and smut that was washed from the wheat. **1801** *Farmer's Mag.* Apr. 154 The grains were..rubbed between the hands, in such a manner as to break the whole of the smut balls. **1844** H. STEPHENS *Bk. Farm* III. 954 A longitudinal section of a smut-ball taken when the stamens are fully formed within the corolla. **1883** *Good Words* Nov. 736/1 Bunt..is known by various names in different parts of the country, as smut-balls, bladder-brand, stinking-rust, &c.

**smutch** (smʌtʃ), *sb.* Also 6 **smutche**, 7 **smuch**. [Of uncertain origin; related in some way to SMUDGE, which is recorded earlier as a vb. though much later as a sb. More recent forms are SMOOCH *sb.*[1] and SMOUCH *sb.*[4]]

**1.** A black or dirty mark; a stain; a smudge.

**1530** PALSGR. 272/1 Smutche on ones face, *barboyllement*. **1637** Dow *Answ. H. Burton* 125 Though it bee not needfull to wipe off every smutch. **1652** CRASHAW *Wks.* (1904) 360 Those durty smutches, wch their faire fronts wore. **1784** COWPER *Task* IV. 608 The palm is hardly clean—But here and there an ugly smutch appears. **1844** LOWELL *Hunger & Cold* v, He recks not a bloody smutch On his gold. **1879** G. MACDONALD *P. Faber* II. xiii. 256 He in whose eyes even a smutch on her face would have lowered a woman.

**b.** *fig.* A moral stain.

**1648** EARL WESTMORELAND *Otia Sacra* (1879) 15 Our Souls, which before did lye Defil'd through th' smutch of Sin. **1688** BUNYAN *Solomon's Temple* xxxiii, Hence the word of God is compared to a glass,..by which we see..our smutches. **1900** *Westm. Gaz.* 8 Nov. 5/1 The work of cleansing the city from the smutch of Croker and his fellow-ruffians.

**c.** A slight mark or indication; semblance; also, a slight or light touch.

**1776** BURKE *Corr.* (1844) II. 98 Without a shadow, a relish, a smutch, a tinge,..of anger. **1856** MRS. BROWNING *Aur. Leigh* v. 506, I never envied Graham his breadth of style, Which gives you, with a random smutch or two,.. Such delicate perspectives of full life.

**2.** Soot, smut, grime, dirt.

**1790** COWPER *Odyss.* XVIII. 34 Collied with chimney smutch! **1790** —— *Iliad* XVIII. 513 His arms and brawny neck Purified, and his shaggy breast from smutch. **1890** R. BRIDGES *Shorter Poems* III. 13 The soil, the smutch the toil and ache and wear.

**3.** *attrib.*, as ***smutch box***, ***pan***.

**1688** HOLME *Armoury* III. 145/1 Stainshall, of some called a Smuch Box; it is a Tin with a bottom and three sides, in which Oil Pencils are put with their points in Oil to keep them from drying. *c***1896** *Rowney's Price List* 20 Oil Slant and Smutch Pan.

**smutch** (smʌtʃ), *v.* [See prec. and cf. SMOOCH *v.*[1]] *trans.* To blacken, make dirty, smut, smudge. Also in fig. context.

**1611** SHAKS. *Wint. T.* I. ii. 121 Why that's my Bawcock: what? has't smutch'd thy Nose? **1655** GURNALL *Chr. in Arm.* II. 275 It would not do well to have the Collier and Fuller live together; what one cleanseth, the other will crock and smutch. **1690** C. NESS *Hist. O. & N. Test.* I. 20 The brightest ivory, if smutched with the fire, contracteth a filthy blackness. **1790** COWPER *Odyss.* XIII. 536 A cloak And kirtle ..foul And smutch'd with smoke. **1818** KEATS *Endym.* II. 90 As though afraid to smutch Even with mealy gold the waters clear. **1850** BROWNING *Christmas Eve* xiv, Under the foot they could not smutch, Lay all the fleshly and the bestial. **1876** HOLLAND *Seven Oaks* xv. 210 Puppies that might.. fawn before her, but might not smutch her robes with their dirty feet.

**b.** *fig.* To stain, sully, besmirch, etc., morally or otherwise.

**1640** YORKE *Union Hon.* To Rdr., Some, who must quarrell..with my Booke..and smutch it with a scorne of my Profession. *a***1680** BUTLER *Rem.* (1759) II. 134 The Fumes..from his Spleen..have..smutched and sullied his Brain. **1858** MORRIS *Old Love* 158 This love is not so hard to smutch. **1865** J. SKELTON *Campaigner at Home* ix. 264 The passion is always pure. It is never smutched by sensuality.

Hence **ˈsmutching** *vbl. sb.* and *ppl. a.*

**1611** COTGR., *Souillement*, a..slurrying, durtying, smutching. **1648** JENKYN *Blind Guide* i. 3 He is but your scullion to make your integrity shine the brighter by all these reproachfull smutchings. **1871** B. TAYLOR *Faust* III. (1875) II. 182 The black blood's horrible and smutching stains.

**smutched** (ˈsmʌtʃt), *ppl. a.* [f. SMUTCH *v.*]

**1.** Smudged, smutted, stained, sullied.

**1784** COWPER *Task* II. 491 The bow Respectful of the smutch'd artificer. **1848** KEIGHTLEY *Notes to Horace, Sat.* I. ii. 36 The smutched face of the prostitute. **1899** *Macm. Mag.* Nov. 35 A..woman..with a lawless tongue and a smutched reputation.

†**2.** Of corn: Affected by smut. *Obs.*

**1620** MARKHAM *Farew. Husb.* (1625) 108 When it is blacke at both ends, yet full and sound in the middest, and this is called smutcht corne, being disfigured in part, and not in all.

†**ˈsmutchin.** *Obs. rare.* [ad. Ir. *smuiteán*, *smúiteán* powder, fine ashes, soot, = Sc. Gael. *smuidean* a mote, particle of dust.] Snuff.

**1650** HOWELL *Lett.* III. 12 The Spaniards and Irish take it [tobacco] most in powder or smutchin, and it mightily refreshes the brain. *Ibid.*, Their boxes of smutchin.

**ˈsmutchless,** *a.* [f. SMUTCH *sb.*] Unsmirched.

**1853** W. CADENHEAD *Bon-Accord* 177 (E.D.D.), Gar me stain my smutchless name, Wi' lawless pleasures.

**smutchy** (ˈsmʌtʃɪ), *a.* Also 6 **smutchie**. [f. SMUTCH *sb.*] Smudgy, smeary, dirty.

**1579** TWYNE *Phis. agst. Fortune* I. xlii. 60 The woorkemanshyp of a smutchie and filthie woorkeman. **1628** SHIRLEY *Witty Fair One* IV. iv, You are in hope to filch a point from my breeches, Which..you will wear About your smutchy wrist for a bracelet. **1867** LOWELL *Lett.* (1894) I. iv. 423, I have no fear that these smutchy backdoors of hell shall prevail against her. **1883** *Nation* (N.Y.) 20 Dec. 517/1 The illustrations..have that heavy and smutchy effect in the closely shaded parts which is a constant defect in mechanical engraving.

**smutted** (ˈsmʌtɪd), *ppl. a.* [f. SMUT *v.*]

**1.** Begrimed, smirched, dirtied, etc.

**1622** DRAYTON *Poly-olb.* xxv. 34 Whence that infernal Flood, the smutted Acheron Shoves forth her sullen head. **1708** *Phil. Trans.* XXVI. 37 There was left on the Wall a smutted Scar or Trace. **1770** GOLDSM. *Des. Vill.* 27 The swain, mistrustless of his smutted face. **1821** *Blackw. Mag.* IX. 318 Till every smutted feature swell with joy. **1850** P. CROOK *War of Hats* 47 Those heavers, too, of coals, with smutted face.

**2.** Of grain: Affected by smut.

**1766** *Compl. Farmer* s.v. *Smut*, I..have sown smutted wheat..and have not had one smutted ear from the produce. **1801** *Farmer's Mag.* Apr. 155 Some smutted ears, of rather an unusual appearance. **1812** SIR J. SINCLAIR *Syst. Husb. Scot.* I. 339 The Corporation of Bakers at Perth, have a wooden tub for cleaning smutted wheat. **1867** H. MACMILLAN *Bible Teach.* vi. (1870) 118 Myriads of seeds are shed from the smutted ears long before the corn is ripe.

**smutter** (ˈsmʌtə(r)), *sb.* [f. SMUT *v.*]

**1.** One who smuts or stains.

**1611** COTGR., *Barbouilleur*,..a blotter, spotter, smutter, besmearer of.

**2.** A smutting-machine for cleaning grain. Hence ***smutter room***.

**1887** *Daily News* 3 May 6/6 A fire happened at the steam flour mills.., which occasioned the subjoined damage: Smutter room and contents burned out and the roof off.

**3.** A fish that rises at, or feeds on, smuts.

**1889** *Sat. Rev.* 18 May 612/2 'Never take under-sized or ill-conditioned fish' (bulgers and smutters probably).

**smutter** (ˈsmʌtə(r)), *v.* [f. SMUT *sb.* 4 c.] *intr.* = SMUT *v.* 4.

**1899** *Daily News* 28 Dec. 6/4 There are three provoking habits of trout—'bulging',..'tailing',..and 'smuttering' when only a minute not imitable fly is being taken.

**smuttily** (ˈsmʌtɪlɪ), *adv.* [f. SMUTTY *a.*] In a smutty manner; indecently, obscenely.

**1672** MARVELL *Reh. Transp.* (1673) II. 10 Theodorus somewhat smuttily asked him, whether he had seen her without her shift. **1698** J. COLLIER *Immor. Stage* i. (1730) 5 The Poets make Women speak Smuttily. **1710** *Tatler* No. 269 ¶5 It is the same poverty which makes men speak or write smuttily, that forces them to talk vexingly. **1737** *London Mag.* May 261/2, I suppose you do not mean an old Woman, seeing that to talk smuttily to such, would be no great Insult. **1974** P. CAVE *Mama* (new ed.) xiii. 109 'Got some..business, down at the docks, have you?' asked one of the drivers and leered smuttily.

**smuttiness** (ˈsmʌtɪnɪs). Also 7 **smootiness**. [f. SMUTTY *a.*]

**1.** A smutty condition of grain.

*a***1659** SPEED *Adam out of Eden* xiv. 106 It..doth..totally prevent the Smuttiness of Wheat. **1660** SHARROCK *Veget.* 102 The change of seed from grounds of a contrary nature ..is thought to prevent smootiness. **1733** TULL *Horse-Hoeing Husb.* xii. (Dubl.) 143 Smuttiness is when the Grains of Wheat instead of Flour are full of a black stinking Powder. **1764** *Museum Rust.* II. lxviii. 223 Good wheat is so often spoiled by smuttiness and sprouting.

**2.** Indecency, obscenity of language.

**1687** MIÈGE *Gt. Fr. Dict.* II, Smuttiness, *impureté, impudicité*. **1698** J. COLLIER *Immor. Stage* i. (1730) 4 Smuttiness is a Fault in Behaviour as well as in Religion. **1721** AMHERST *Terræ Fil.* No. 26. 135 They begin with satire and funeral lamentation; but end with love, smuttiness, and a song. **1973** *Times* 16 Nov. 5/5 Viewers are also asked.. whether..smuttiness in comedy programmes..is found offensive.

**3.** Sootiness, griminess.

**1881** *Globe* 30 June 2/1 The..kettle cannot..taunt the veriest heathen pot with smuttiness.

**smutting** (ˈsmʌtɪŋ), *vbl. sb.* [f. SMUT *v.*]

**1.** The action of the verb in various senses, or the result of this.

**1621** HAKEWILL *David's Vow* 165 Slander..being..the smutting of a mans good name. *a***1661** FULLER *Worthies, Middlesex* (1662) 189 A help hath been found out against the smooting of Wheat,..I say the smooting of Wheat which makes it a Negro, as Mildew makes it a Dwarfe. **1757** tr. *Henckel's Pyritologia* 171 The smutting or blackness thence arising.

**2.** *attrib.*, in terms relating to the cleaning of grain from smut, as ***smutting device***, ***machine***, ***room***.

**1856** MORTON *Cycl. Agric.* II. 431/2 The screening or smutting machine. **1875** KNIGHT *Dict. Mech.* 2228/1 The outer shell of the conical smutting-device. **1892** *Daily News* 14 Jan. 3/2 The mills consisted of five blocks used as mills, warehouses, smutting rooms, store rooms, and engine and boiler house.

**ˈsmutting,** *ppl. a.* [f. SMUT *v.*]

**1.** Making black or gloomy.

**1626** B. JONSON *Staple of N.* I. vi, This is better farre, then to weare Cypresse, Dull smutting gloues, or melancholy blacks.

**2.** Of fish: Rising at, or feeding on, smuts.

**1899** *19th Cent.* Jan. 122 There is the 'smutting' fish [trout], greedily taking down the tiniest of insects.

**smutty** (ˈsmʌtɪ), *a.* Also 6–7 **smootie**, 7–8 **smooty**, 7 **smuttie**. [f. SMUT *sb.* or *v.* Cf. G. *schmutzig*.]

**1.** Of grain: Affected by smut.

**1597** GERARDE *Herbal* I. l. 70 That corne where it is, is called smootie corne. **1637** REMNANT *Disc. Bees* Title-p., The Causes and Cure of Blasted Wheat,..together with the Causes of Smutty Wheat. **1657** S. PURCHAS *Pol. Flying-Ins.* 142 Usually if one stalk hath the ear smutty, all that arise from the same root are infected. **1733** TULL *Horse-Hoeing Husb.* xii. (Dubl.) 143 The Wheat Plants in the Field, from whence these were taken, brought very few smutty Grains. **1769** REID *Wks.* (1863) I. 49/1, I put some smutty oats in water. **1803** A. HUNTER *Georg. Ess.* I. 182 There was a great deal of smutty wheat that year. **1846** J. BAXTER *Libr. Pract. Agric.* (ed. 4) II. 401 The following experiment was made.. on a smutty sample of wheat.

**2.** Soiled with, full of, characterized by, smut; dirty; blackened.

*c***1645** HOWELL *Lett.* I. IV. v, I pray [you] leave the smutty Ayr of London, and com hither to breathe sweeter. **1665** HOOKE *Microgr.* 3 Like smutty daubings on a matt or uneven floor. *a***1704** *Compl. Servant-Maid* (ed. 7) 119 Though your employment be greasie and smooty. **1716** POPE *Let. to Earl Burlington*, He was a smutty dog yesterday, and cost me near two hours to wash the ink off his face. **1812** SIR W. ELFORD in *Friendships Miss Mitford* (1882) I. iii. 85 On turning the corner, I see my paper is very smutty. **1880** 'VERNON LEE' *Italy* II. iii. 57 A smutty portrait of her dressed in brown brocade.

**3.** Of the colour of smut; dusky; dark.

**1648** EARL WESTMORELAND *Otia Sacra* (1879) 148 The smooty shadows of some one Or others Trophees carv'd in stone. **1658** FRANCK *North. Mem.* (1821) 302 Smooty and discoloured clouds. **1778** W. PRYCE *Min. Cornub.* 91 A smutty black, or black grey Crystal. **1796** KIRWAN *Elem. Min.* (ed. 2) I. 288 It seems of a smutty yellow. **1863** KINGSLEY *Water-Bab.* (1874) 40 Four or five smutty little cubs. **1890** *Spectator* 30 Aug. 274 His once smutty plumage now showing rich colouring of black and white and brown.

**4.** Having the appearance or form of smut.

**1667** MILTON *P.L.* IV. 817 The Smuttie graine With sudden blaze diffus'd, inflames the Aire. **1714** GAY *Trivia* III. 383 The nitrous Store is laid, the smutty Train With running blaze awakes the barrell'd Grain.

**5.** Indecent, immodest, impure, obscene.

**1668** PEPYS *Diary* 20 June, I saw this new play my wife saw yesterday, and do not like it, it being very smutty. *a***1677** BARROW *Serm.* Wks. 1716 I. 146 It is very culpable to be facetious in obscene and smutty matters. **1706** J. H. BROWNE *Pipe of Tobacco* Poems (1768) 124 The smutty tale Of country justice o'er his ale. **1768–74** TUCKER *Lt. Nat.* (1834) II. 124 He..puts the women to the blush with his smutty jokes and rude jeers. **1820** *Blackw. Mag.* VI. 629 Mr. Hunt's smutty story of Rimini. **1851** TH. PARKER in Weiss *Life* (1863) I. 390 He is smutty, and vulgar and low. **1894** *Tablet* 16 June 920 It is only when the details are sensational or smutty that room is found for them in the columns of the great dailies.

**6.** *Comb.*, as ***smutty-face***, ***-faced***, ***-nosed***.

**1675** COTTON *Burlesque upon B.* I. 60 Ha! ha! old *Smutty-face, well said. **1899** F. W. BOURNE *Billy Bray* 99 (E.D.D.), He told the tempter, 'old smutty-face', to do this himself. **1833** HT. MARTINEAU *Tale of Tyne* v. 96 The *smutty-faced crew. **1901** *Dundee Advertiser* 7 June 4 The pride of Mr. Tory's farms are his..'smutty-faced' Dorset Down sheep. **1884** COUES *N. Amer. Birds* 425 *Perisoreus canadensis fumifrons*,..*Smutty-nosed Jay. *Ibid.* 783 *Priofinus melanurus*, Smutty-nosed Shearwater.

†**smy**[1]. *Sc. Obs.* [Of obscure origin.] A knave or rascal.

**1501** DOUGLAS *Pal. Hon.* I. lxiv, Than suddanelie Venus ..Answerit thus, 'Thow subtell smy [etc.]'. **1508** DUNBAR *Tua Mariit Wemen* 113 Quhen the smy on me smyrkis. *a***1585** MONTGOMERIE *Flyting* 648 Sen all is suith that's said of this smy.

**smy**[2]. ? *Obs.* Also **smie**. [Of obscure origin.] A small fish (see quots.).

**1552** ELYOT *Dict.* s.v. *Aphya*, In Essex is a fishe called a Smie, whiche if he be longe kept, will turne to water. **1601** HOLLAND *Pliny* I. 265 The Apuæ, which are the groundlings and Smies, [come] of the fome of the sea set in a heat & chafed after some good shewer. **1611** COTGR., *Melette*, a very small, soft, and fat sea-fish, bred of raine, and water, and called the Smie, or sea-Groundlin. **1668** CHARLETON *Onomast.* 143 *Apua*,..the Spirling, Smy, or Sea-Dace. **1694** MOTTEUX *Rabelais* IV. lx. (1737) 246 Craylings, Smys.

**smyddy,** obs. Sc. variant of SMITHY *sb.*

**smyris,** variant of SMIRIS.

**Smyrna** (ˈsmɜːnə). [A place-name (see def.); L. *Smyrna*, Gr. Σμύρνα.] **a.** The chief port of Asia Minor, situated at the head of the gulf of the same name, used *attrib.* in the names of various things produced in the vicinity of or connected with the city, as ***Smyrna carpet***, ***cotton***, ***earth***, ***fig***, ***kingfisher***, ***opium***, ***rug***, ***runt***, ***wheat*** (see quots.).

**1735** J. MOORE *Columbarium* 44 The Smyrna Runt..is middle siz'd and feather-footed. **1753** *Chambers' Cycl. Suppl.*, *Saponacea terra*,..a kind of native alkali salt, of the nature of the nitre,..called by some Smyrna earth. *Ibid.* s.v. *Wheat*, *Smyrna Wheat*, a peculiar kind of Wheat that has an extremely large ear. **1782** LATHAM *Gen. Synop. Birds* I. II. 615 Smyrna Kingfisher..inhabits the environs of Smyrna. **1840** *Penny Cycl.* XVII. 203/2 The physical characters of the best Smyrna opium. **1877** *Encycl. Brit.* VI. 482/2 One of these [Indian cottons] is cultivated to a considerable extent in the Levant, and is known in the market as Smyrna cotton. **1881** C. C. HARRISON *Woman's Handiwork* III. 165 Curtains of French make, stamped with patterns taken from Turkish or Smyrna rugs. **1897** *Sears, Roebuck Catal.* 12/2 Imported Smyrna Figs, very choice. **1904** W. D. ELLWANGER *Oriental Rug* 153 Smyrna carpets, 97, 98. **1956** S. BEDFORD *Legacy* III. vi. 198 Smyrna figs, grapes in cotton-wool, Turkish delight. **1966** N. FREELING *Dresden Green* I. 16 Two smyrna rugs on the polished wooden floor, that he had made on winter evenings. **1977** 'R. PLAYER' *Month of Mangled Models* vii. 125 They were treading silently on the best Aubusson in Paris although..the little Smyrna carpet in the boudoir was worth three times as much.

**b.** *ellipt.* A Smyrna raisin. Also, a Smyrna carpet.

**1845** G. DODD *Brit. Manuf.* V. 102 The 'Black Smyrnas' [produce] a strong-bodied wine, and the 'Red Smyrnas' and 'Valencias' a rich and full wine. **1904** W. D. ELLWANGER *Oriental Rug* 97 Most other carpets are of Turkish weaving ..and come under the general title of Smyrnas.

**Smyrnæan** (smɜːˈniːən), *sb.* and *a.* Also 9 Smyrnean. [f. L. *Smyrnæ-us* (ad. Gr. *Σμυρναῖος*, f. *Σμύρνα*: see prec.) + -AN.]

**A.** *sb.* An inhabitant or native of (ancient) Smyrna. (Cf. SMYRNIOTE *sb.*)

**1598** GRENEWEY *Tacitus, Ann.* III. xiii. (1622) 83 The Smyrnæans alleaged an oracle of Apollo. **1603** HOLLAND *Plutarch's Mor.* 103 After which sort did the Lacedæmonians..when they had sent corne unto the Smyrnæans. **1807** ROBINSON *Archæol. Græca* III. xix. 308 The Athenians, Smyrnæans, Macedonians. **1840** tr. *Müller's Hist. Lit. Greece* v. §1 Pindar's statements, who in one place called Homer a Smyrnæan by origin. **1904** W. M. RAMSAY *Lett. Seven Ch.* xix. 255 The Smyrnaeans were specially proud of the beauty of their city.

**B.** *adj.* Of or pertaining to Smyrna.

**1807** R. SEMPLE *Observ. Journ. Spain*, etc. II. 204 An old bridge..completes the scenery of this Smyrnean paradise. **1840** tr. *Müller's Hist. Lit. Greece* v. §2 The Smyrnæan river Meles. **1904** W. M. RAMSAY *Lett. Seven Ch.* xx. 278 The Smyrnaean letter is not without similar reference.

ˈ**Smyrnian**, *sb.* and *a. rare.* Also 6 Smir-. [f. SMYRN-A + -IAN.] = SMYRNÆAN *sb.* and *a.*

?**1580** LODGE *Sch. Abuse* A 6, Why seke yᵉ Smirnians to recouer from yᵉ Salaminians the prais of Homer? **1641** MILTON *Prel. Episc.* Wks. 1851 III. 85 The most famous of all the Smyrnian Presbyters. **1718** PRIDEAUX *Connexion O. & N. Test.* II. II. (1799) III. 72 The Smyrnians did the same for Stratonice.

**Smyrniote** (ˈsmɜːnɪət), *sb.* and *a.* Also 7 Smyrneot, 9 Smyrniot. [f. SMYRNA + -(I)OTE.]

**A.** *sb.* An inhabitant or native of Smyrna, esp. in modern times. (Cf. SMYRNÆAN *sb.*)

**1670** COVEL in *Early Voy. Levant* (Hakl. Soc.) 133 The inhabitants of Smyrna..are called Smyrniotes. *a* **1700** KEN *Hymnotheo* Poet. Wks. 1721 III. 292 That Smyrneots may thy glorious Godhead own. **1849** *New Monthly Mag.* Oct. 162 The best lawyers,..if not Germans, are Ionians or Smyrniotes. **1897** *Edin. Rev.* Jan. 111 A Smyrniote of low extraction.

**B.** *adj.* Smyrnæan.

**1867** C. M. YONGE *Pupils of St. John* xii. 191 The strong spirit of contending for the purity of the faith had descended from St. John upon the great Smyrniot bishop. **1869** TOZER *Highl. Turkey* II. 114 The multitude of Smyrniote and Alexandrian merchants. **1881** *Athenæum* 2 July 12/3 The English, French, Italians..form the rest of the Smyrniote community.

†**smyth(e**, ME. variants of SMITE *v.*

*c* **1440** *Eng. Conq. Irel.* 38 Oconnoghur..let smyth of [the] sonnes heed. **1463** *Bury Wills* (Camden) 28 That at twelve of the clokke..he do the chymes smythe. **1483** *Cath. Angl.* 346/2 To smythe fyre, *fugillare. Ibid.*, A Smythynge,..*iccio, percussio.*

**smythite** (ˈsmaɪðaɪt). *Min.* [f. the name of Charles H. *Smyth* (1866–1937), U.S. geologist + -ITE¹.] A sulphide of iron and probably nickel found as opaque bronze-coloured crystals that are strongly magnetic and have a metallic lustre.

**1956** ERD & EVANS in *Jrnl. Amer. Chem. Soc.* LXXVIII. 2017/1 We have found minute, plate-like crystal inclusions in calcite crystals..to be a new iron sulfide... The mineral is named smythite (pronounced smīth'ite) in honor of Professor C. H. Smyth, Jr. **1972** *Amer. Mineralogist* LVII. 1571 Smythite was originally described by Erd *et al.*..as having a rhombohedral structure..and $Fe_3S_4$ composition. These data are in error and smythite is hereby redefined... Nickel is present in all smythites present to date..and it is suggested that smythite is *not* a phase in the Fe-S system but possibly in the Fe-Ni-S system. **1976** *Minerals Sci. & Engin.* VIII. 119/2 There is still considerable doubt about the composition range and thermal stability of natural and synthetic smythite, and even whether it should be included as a phase in the iron-sulphur system.

ˈ**smytrie.** *Sc. rare.* [Cf. Fris. *smite*, used in the same sense.] 'A numerous collection of small individuals.'

**1786** BURNS *Twa Dogs* 76 A smytrie o' wee, duddie weans.

**snaast**, dial. form of SNASTE.

**snab.** *Sc.* [perh. related to NAB *sb.*¹; but cf. MFlem. (1460) *snabbe*, app. point of land, later Flem. *snabbe*, *snab* beak, OFris. *snabba* mouth (Fris. *snabbe* mouth of a purse-net).] A steep place or ascent; a rugged rise or point.

**1797** *Statist. Acc. Scot.* XIX. 554 There is a tradition.. That at the Snabs of Drimmie, it [*sc.* the Tay] sent off a portion of its waters. **1811** A. SCOTT *Poems* 122 (Jam.), Then knees an' elbows like a crab, Spraul up yoursel yon dizzy snab. **1883** J. MARTINE *Reminisc. Haddington* 402 His steady sure-footed cob always took him safe home in a dark night, although he had steep snabs to climb and go down.

**snab**, Sc. variant of SNOB, a shoemaker.

†ˈ**snabble**, *v. slang. Obs.* (See quot.)

**1725** *New Cant. Dict., Snabble*, to rifle, to strip, or plunder. Also to knock down; to cause to reel or stagger by a Blow on the Head. *Snabbled*, is also used sometimes for being apprehended, seized, or taken.

†**snack**, *sb.*¹ *Obs.* Also 1–2 snacc, 3 snak. [Late OE. *snacc*, obscurely related to OHG. *snacga*, *snaga* (G. dial. *snacke*, *schnake*), ON. *snekkja*, etc. Cf. also OF. *esneque*, *esneke*, med.L. (*e*)*snecca*.] A species of ship.

**1052** *O.E. Chron.* (MS. C), þa let Eadward cyng scypian .xl. snacca. *c* **1100** *Ibid.* an. 1066 (MS. D), He for to Scotlande mid .xii. snaccum. **1299** *Stat. & Ordin. Irel.* (Rolls) 216 Quod soluerunt per preceptum Regis pro fretto cuiusdam nauis que vocata fuit le Snack. **1300** *Liber Quotid. Garderobæ*(1787) 275 Johanni Kittey, magistro del snak de la Rye. *Ibid.*, Johanni Manekyn, magistro del snak Sancti Thome.

**snack** (snæk), *sb.*² Also 5 snake, 6 snacke, *Sc.* snak. [f. SNACK *v.* Cf. MDu. *snac*(*k*, WFlem. *snak*, in sense 1.]

**1. a.** A snap, a bite, esp. that of a dog. Now *dial.*

In quot. 1402 *fig.*, with approximation to sense 3.

**1402** HOCCLEVE *Letter of Cupid* 109 She, behinde thy bake, So lyberal ys, she wol no wyght with-sey, But smertly of another take a snake. **1513** DOUGLAS *Æneid* XII. xii. 150 The swipir Tuscan hund..With hys wyd chaftis at hym makis a snak. **1570** LEVINS *Manip.* 5/14 Yᵉ snacke of a dog, *morsus*. **1831** MISS FERRIER *Destiny* xx, The honest man who found a snail in his [broth]. 'Tak ye that snack, my man,' says he, 'for looking sae like a plum-damy'. **1896** LILBURN *Borderer* vi. 39 The bitch overtook the hare and gave a snack at its hinder parts.

**b.** A sharp or snappish remark or jibe.

**1555** tr. *Latimer's Protest.* in Strype *Eccl. Mem.* (1721) III. App. xxxiv. 92, I coulde..not be suffered to declare my faithe befor you..without snakkes, reiagges,..rebukes, and tauntes. **1896** CHANTER *Witch of Withyford* x. 121 She fancied 'twas a snack at the Squire, as he hadn't been near her since the storm.

†**2.** A short time; a snatch. *Obs.*⁻¹

**1513** DOUGLAS *Æneid* VIII. vii. 86 As he had slummerit bot a snak.

**3. a.** A share, portion, part.

**1683** KENNETT tr. *Erasm. on Folly* 112 Because the first, if they are humoured, giue them some snacks out of unjust gain. **1699** E. S——CY *Country Gentl. Vade M.* 98 If any body has any right to a Snack, 'tis this Gentleman, who saw me take it up. **1706** E. WARD *Wooden World Diss.* (1708) 79 It will go plaguy hard, if he miss a Snack of it. **1777** ELIZ. RYVES *Poems* 159 I'll never lose scent of thee, until I have at least had snacks in the reward for apprehending thee. **1855** CARLYLE *Misc.* (1857) IV. 339 None of them without some snack of principality taken from the main lot.

**b.** In phr. *to come* (or *put*) *in for a snack*, etc.

**1693** CHAUNCY *Rej. Williams* 10 But there is another Righteousness..that puts in for a snack, viz. that of the new Law. **1700** EARL BELLOMONT *Let. to Sir J. Stanley* 5 Mar. (Welbeck MSS.), I am told that..I have a right to a third part of them, but if the rest of the Lords come in for snacks, I shall be satisfyed. **1760–72** H. BROOKE *Fool of Qual.* (1809) I. 141 The landlord would take all if we did not come in for snacks.

**c.** *to go snacks* (†or *snack*), to have a share (*in* something), to divide profits.

**1693** DRYDEN, etc. *Juvenal* vii. (1726) 98 If one piece thou take, That must be cantled, and the Judge go snack. **1701** FARQUHAR *Sir H. Wildair* IV. ii, Well, monsieur! 'tis about a thousand pounds; we go snacks. **1748** SMOLLETT *R. Random* (1812) I. 106 A present to the Secretary with whom some of the commissioners went snacks. **1788** COWPER *Pity for poor Africans* 16 While they get riches.., Pray tell me why we may not also go snacks? **1829** CREEVEY in *Creevey P.* (1904) II. viii. 201 To go snacks himself in the acquisition of power and profit. **1862** *Temple Bar* VI. 10 The Princesses..were mean enough to go snacks in the profits.

**4. a.** A mere taste, a small quantity, of liquor.

In quot. 1685 perh. simply in sense 3.

**1685** J. DUNTON *Lett. fr. New-Eng.* (1867) 11 As he was sure to supply us with Drink even without asking, so he would always thrust himself in for a snack, in helping to drink it. **1721** RAMSAY *Lucky Spence* xvi, My malison..On them that drink and dinna pay, But tak a snack and run away. **1848** KINGSLEY *Saint's Trag.* III. ii, And take his snack of brandy for digestion.

**b.** A mere bite or morsel of food, as contrasted with a regular meal; a light or incidental repast.

**1757** *Monitor* No. 90, When once a man has got a snack of their trenchers, he too often retains a hankering after the honey-pot. **1763** FOOTE *Mayor of G.* I. Wks. 1799 I. 174 We have but just time for a snack. **1811** *Ora & Juliet* III. 134, I didn't eat nothing but a bit of a snack at noon, and I am hungry. **1844** ALB. SMITH *Adv. Mr. Ledbury* xli. (1886) 126 Our friends took a slight snack of cold bread and meat. **1874** LISLE CARR *J. Gwynne* I. ii. 46 Just to take a snack of dinner, before going over the outlying parts.

*fig.* **1817** KEATS *Let.* Wks. 1889 III. 75 Having taken a snack or luncheon of literary scraps. **1892** ZANGWILL *Childr. Ghetto* I. 76 He craved more for spiritual snacks between meals than for physical.

**c.** *attrib.*, designating a place at which snacks are sold, as ***snack booth, counter, shop***; in appositive use, as ***snack lunch, meal***; ***snack-sized*** adj. **snack-house**, a restaurant. Cf. SNACK BAR.

**1976** D. HEFFRON *Crusty Crossed* xxii. 147, I sat alone on the sand, watching my sisters parade over to the snack booth with their boyfriends. **1977** W. J. WEATHERBY *Home in Dark* viii. 44 A large woman who served behind the snack counter. **1820** T. CROMWELL *Excurs. Irel.* vii. 2 Partaking of the snack at one or other of the Snack-houses which abound in these villages. **1895** *Amer. Dial. Notes* I. 374 There's a right chance o' snack houses down to Bakervul. **1964** N. MARSH *Dead Water* iii. 85, I..had a snack lunch in the new bar. **1977** W. HILDICK *Loop* ix. 47 After a snack lunch, I walked round to the School House. **1962** *Punch* 28 Nov. 773/1 We are becoming 'increasingly a nation of tea and soft-drink consumers and snack-meal eaters'. **1976** 'K. ROYCE' *Bustillo* xii. 157 Bustillo was eating a snack meal. **1977** *Chicago Tribune* 2 Oct. XII. 18/2 (Advt.), Partial bldg. standing due to fire, selling as is, formerly snack shop, restaurant. **1974** E. AMBLER *Doctor Frigo* III. 153 A snack-sized gobbet of raw flesh.

**5.** *Austral. slang.* Something easy to accomplish, a 'snip'.

**1941** S. J. BAKER *Austral. Slang* 68 *Snack*, a certainty. **1952** T. A. G. HUNGERFORD *Ridge & River* 138 There was nothing to it... It was a snack. **1961** M. CALTHORPE *Dyehouse* 150 In Hughie's day he'd made this a snack. **1970** R. BEILBY *No Medals for Aphrodite* 274 'How could I do that, Harry?' 'Easy. It'll be a snack.'

†**snack**, *sb.*³ *Obs.*⁻⁰ (See quot.)

**1787** GROSE *Prov. Gloss., Snack*, or *Spunk*, a dried fungus, used as tinder.

**snack**, dial. variant of SNECK, latch.

**snack**, *a.* and *adv. Sc.* [? Related to SNACK *v.* Cf. also Norw. dial. *snak* greedy.]

**A.** *adj.* **1.** Quick, alert, clever, smart.

**1710** in RUDDIMAN *Gloss. Douglas' Æneis* s.v. *Snak.* **1719** RAMSAY *First Answ. Hamilton* x, Europe had nane mair snack and snell At verse or prose. **1789** ROSS *Helenore* (ed. 3) 16 By this time Lindy is right well shot out,..And snack and plump. **1791** J. LEARMONT *Poems* 280 Weel I ken ye're snack. **1808** JAMIESON s.v., *Be snack*, be quick, do not lose time.

**2.** Snappish, peevish; greedy.

**1883** *Good Words* 651 It is..the being grasping, or what Scotch people would call 'snack', over every trifle. **1894** *Longm. Mag.* May 9 You needn't be so snack: I can't stop to pick my words when I'm worried.

**B.** *adv.* Quickly, sharply, smartly.

**1739** A. NICOL *Nature without Art* 60 She answered me chastly and snack Why do you impose on me so? **1801** BEATTIE *Poems* 22 (E.D.D.), Trump-about gade on as snack As we'd been lairds. **1828** in Buchan *Ball. N. Scotl.* II. 260 The lassie..ran to the door fu' snack.

**snack** (snæk), *v.* Also 4, 6 snak, 6 snacke. [Of doubtful origin: cf. MDu. or Flem. *snacken* to snap (of a dog), Norw. dial. *snaka* to snatch (of animals). The LG. and Du. *snakken* (G. dial. *schnakken*) to gasp, desire, etc., to talk or chatter, which agree in form, do not correspond in sense. The later senses are partly from SNACK *sb.*²]

**1. a.** *intr.* To bite or snap (esp. *at* a thing). Also *fig.*, esp. to utter or exchange sharp, snapping words or remarks. Chiefly *north.* and *Sc.* Cf. SNAP *v.* 2 a.

**13..** *Peter & Paul* 310 in Horstm. *Altengl. Leg.* (1881) 79 Sone come þare forthe dogges blak, & on Peter gon þai snak. ?**1520** *Dial. Creatures Moralysed* xlvi, Euery of them began to snak at othir & wolde haue torn eche other on smale pecys. **1570** LEVINS *Manip.* 5 To Snacke, byte, *morsitare.* **1635** D. DICKSON *Pract. Writ.* (1845) I. 24 God will not .. Captiously snack at his words. **1895** CROCKETT *Bog-Myrtle* v. ii. 366 He'll no as muckle as snack at a flee that lichts on his nose. **1902** in *Eng. Dial. Dict.* s.v., The pony had never shown any vice..beyond snacking at the collar when put on. **1956** C. P. SNOW *Homecomings* l. 357 They quarrelled and snacked. *Ibid.* 358 The prickles and self-assertiveness which made them snack. **1959** P. H. JOHNSON *Humbler Creation* xii. 85 The usual strung-up celebrations at home, with.. Libby and her mother gently snacking at each other in tones of excessive goodwill. **1960** C. P. SNOW *Affair* viii. 91 Irene and I glanced at each other with discomfort, a discomfort different from just looking on at her husband and my wife snacking.

**b.** *trans.* To snap *up*, seize upon, etc. *Sc.*

**1871** WADDELL *Ps.* lxxviii. 63 His ain youngsters, the lowe snacket up. **1891** BARRIE *Little Minister* xvi, In the tail o' the day ane o' them snacked him up.

**2.** *trans.* To share, divide. ? *Obs.*

**1707** E. WARD *Hud. Rediv.* II. x. 26 Unless they are allow'd to snack The Booty which they jointly take. **1733** *Revolution Politicks* VII. 73 'Tis to be feared, the Guards and the Highwaymen snack'd the Booty. **1745** *Life B. M. Carew* 105 At this Alehouse they tarried some Time, and snack'd the Argot, *i.e.* shared the Money.

*absol.* **1675** WYCHERLEY *Country Wife* III. ii, Who is that that is to be bubbled? Faith! let me snack. *a* **1700** B. E. *Dict. Cant. Crew, Crossbite*, to draw in a Friend, yet snack with the Sharper. **1768** [W. DONALDSON] *Life Sir B. Sapskull* I. iv. 41 If our ministers were as poor and beggarly as the Dutch, they might have snack'd with these illegal executors. **1853** COOPER *Sussex Gloss.* 76 *Snack*, to share or be in partnership with.

**3.** *intr.* To lunch, to take a snack.

**1807** SIR R. C. HOARE *Tour Irel.* 35 At Birr is a good inn, ..where I snacked. [*Note.*] *Snack* is in Ireland synonymous with *lunch* in England. **1894** A. MORRISON *Mean Streets* 90 The snacking women resumed their talk.

Hence ˈ**snacking** *vbl. sb.*

**1959** P. H. JOHNSON *Humbler Creation* v. 30 The meeting petered away as it usually did, into desultory snackings and exchanges of fellowship. **1969** W. CAHN *Out of Cracker Barrel* xxiii. 318 Premium Saltines and Ritz crackers were used as snacks long before snacking came into vogue. **1978** *Radio Times* 18–24 Feb. 67 There are three meals a day, 'more or less regular, with no snacking in between'. **1980** P.

S. POWERS *Obesity* ix. 219 Snacking while watching television is notorious for increasing the total daily calories ingested.

**snack bar.** [f. SNACK *sb.*[2] + BAR *sb.*[1] 28.]

**1.** A bar or counter at which snacks are served to customers; (part of) a restaurant containing such a bar.

**1930** *Punch* 16 Apr. 433 A vegetarian snack-bar. **1937** *Archit. Rev.* Nov. p. lxii *(caption)* A restaurant and snack bar in Regent Street, London. **1943** *Sun* (Baltimore) 14 Oct. 5/1 A 'snack bar', offering sandwiches and soft drinks, is maintained at the Gold street center. **1958** S. HYLAND *Who goes Hang?* xliii, 210 Arthur's highly polished snack-bar. **1965** D. HENDERSON *Heart of Newfoundland* 54 Marty's run a chain of snack bars in different parts of the city. **1978** S. BRILL *Teamsters* vii. 284 Barkett pulled the truck into a gas station snack bar for a coffee break.

**2.** *attrib.* Also *fig.*

**1940** 'G. ORWELL' *Inside Whale* 138 It is a flowing, swelling prose..with rhythms in it, something quite different from the flat cautious statements and snackbar dialects that are now in fashion. **1957** *Observer* 1 Sept. 11/7 Amongst the things most desired are seats bookable by telephone, good coffee and snack-bar service. **1982** J. SCOTT *Uprush of Mayhem* vi. 59 The lunch-time rush for snackbar sandwiches.

**'snackery.** Also **snackerie.** [f. SNACK *sb.*[2] + -ERY.] A snack bar or other public eating-place serving snacks.

**1936** *Amer. Speech* XI. 374/1 *Steve's Snackerie* is the sign over a small café in Lincoln, Nebraska. **1967** *Punch* 30 Aug. 295/2 If we want better pubs, pubs catering for the family, we must..convert them all into decent snackeries, and let them stay open for at least twelve hours a day. **1969** 'R. CRAWFORD' *Cockleburr* I. vi. 55, I..ate a nondescript pizza in a nondescript snackery. **1981** *Nordic Skiing* Jan. 48/3 The ski shop sports rentals, needed accessories, waxing area and snackery.

†**'snacket.** *Obs.*$^{-0}$ [Cf. *snack*, dial. var. SNECK *sb.*] A casement hasp.

**1611** COTGR., *Targette*, a kind of snacket, or haspe, wherewith casemates, &c., are closed. [Hence in Sherwood and some later Dicts.]

**sna'ckette.** *W. Indies.* [f. SNACK *sb.*[2] + -ETTE, after LAUNDERETTE.] A snack bar.

**1973** *Advocate-News* (Barbados) 20 Jan. 3/1 The snackette also offers a take-away service, and customers can make their orders by telephone, and then collect them. **1973** *Trinidad & Tobago Overseas Express* 28 May 11/3 Her husband was returning from a snackette in Marabella. **1974** *Sunday Advocate-News* (Barbados) 3 Mar. 16 (Advt.), Experienced person required to manage and control Snackette and Restaurant.

†**'snackle,** *a. Obs.*$^{-1}$ [prob. a var. of *snaggle* in SNAGGLE-TOOTHED *a.*] ? Snaggy.

?**1567** STUDLEY tr. *Seneca, Hipp.* v. (1581) 74 b, [Let] eke the snackle wheele That whirleth stil enforce my limmes thy swinging swift to feele.

**'snackle,** *v.* [Of obscure origin.] *trans.* To secure, make fast.

**1887** DOYLE *Study in Scarlet* II. vi, This young man here had the bracelets on my wrists, and as neatly snackled as ever I saw in my life.

**'snackly,** *adv. Sc.* [f. SNACK *a.*] Smartly.

**1728** RAMSAY *Robt., Richy, & Sandy* 61 How snackly cou'd he gi'e a fool reproof.

**'snacky,** *a. Sc.* [Cf. SNACK *a.*] Clever, acute, sharp.

**1806** JAMIESON *Pop. Ballards* I. 297 Tam Tod was..Slee, snackie, and wilie, and quirkie. **1866** J. SMITH *Merry Bridal* 3 Snacky Rab, an' pawky Hab.

†**snacot-fish.** *Obs.*$^{-0}$ The garfish.

**1611** COTGR., *Arfie*, a Hornefish, Hornebeake, Snacotfish, Ganefish. *Ibid., Esguille*,..a small fish called a Horne-beake, Snacot-fish,..Piper-fish. [Hence in Beck (1657), Ainsworth (1736), Johnson, etc.]

**snad(e,** obs. forms of SNED *v.*

**snade.** *Cornish dial.* [? Related to SNED *v.* Cf. SNODE *sb.*] A piece cut from the tail of a mackerel for use as bait.

**1901** AFLALO *Sea & Coast Fishing* 134 Matt pushes the 'snade' well down on the bend of the hook, from which it presently dangles [etc.].

**snade,** northern form of SNODE *Obs.*, morsel.

**snaffe,** error for *snaste* SNASTE.

**snaffle** ('snæf(ə)l), *sb.*[1] Also 6–7 **snafle, snaffel** (6 **-ell, -ul**). [Of doubtful origin: connexion with (M)Du. and (M)LG. *snavel* (late OFris. *snavel, snaul*, WFris. *snaffel* mouth), OHG. *snapal* (MHG. *snabel*, G. *schnabel*), beak, bill, mouth, is not clear; but cf. the use of G. *schnabel* for a forked instrument used in training hunting-dogs to keep the head up.]

**1. a.** A simple form of bridle-bit, having less restraining power than one provided with a curb.

**1533** FRITH *Another Bk. agst. Rastell* A vj b, I verye well lyken yow to him that hath a wilde horse to tame,..when he perceueth that he can not holde him with a scottyshe snafle. **1577** B. GOOGE *Heresbach's Husb.* I. (1586) 15 b, Geue a Horse the whip, an Asse the snaffell, and a Foole the rodde. *c* **1618** MORYSON *Itin.* IV. i. (1903) 48 Their bridles are like our snafles but commonly sett with Copper studds guilded. **1686** PLOT *Staffordsh.* 377 They make also great variety of bridles, both Snaffles and Bitts: such as the wheel and joynted Snaffle, the neck-Snaffle [etc.]. **1774** GOLDSM. *Nat. Hist.* (1862) I. 252 They are rid generally in a snaffle, without spurs. **1833** *Reg. & Instr. Cavalry* I. 75 Great care must be taken not to press the horse too suddenly up to the snaffle. **1882** B. D. W. RAMSAY *Rough Recoll.* I. v. 95 Finding [the horse]..would bear no pressure on his mouth, I at last tried him with a plain light snaffle.

**b.** *fig.* or in fig. contexts.

**1542** BRINKLOW *Compl.* xii. (1874) 28 This were a good snafful for the tyrannes and oppressers. **1579** NORTH *Plutarch* (1896) V. 168 Rome also not being used to be brideled with the snaffle of such insolencie. **1639** FULLER *Holy War* III. xxvii. (1840) 167 Being a place of such importance, it would always be a snaffle in the mouth of the Egyptian king. **1679** ALSOP *Melius Inq.* II. v. 264 The Ἄνομος or Lawless person, who has a curb for every mans Conscience, but will not endure a snaffle upon his own. **1813** MOORE *Post-bag* i. 49 His Lordship proposes 'The new Veto-snaffle to bind down their noses'. **1833** T. HOOK *Parson's Dau.* II. vii, Give your own passions the curb, and allow mine the snaffle.

**c.** ***to ride*** (one) ***in, on,*** or ***with the snaffle,*** to rule easily, to guide with a light hand.

**1577** HOLINSHED *Chron., Hist. Scotl.* I. 249, I perceyue this man will neuer obey my commaundements, till he be rydden with a snaffle. **1593** NASHE *Christ's T.* To Rdr., Ile ..ride him with a snaffle vp & down the whole realme. *a* **1668** LASSELS *Voy. Italy* (1670) II. 281 Such a wanton Courser as Naples is not to be ridden with snaffles. **1844** LD. ASHBURTON in *Croker P.* (1884) III. xxiii. 18 As old Hunt said of Manners Sutton as Speaker, he rode them in a snaffle. **1904** BENSON *Challoners* i, The world has begun..to ride life on the snaffle instead of the curb.

**2.** *attrib.* and *Comb.*, as ***snaffle-bit, -bridle, -rein; snaffle-bridled, -mouthed*** adjs.; **snaffle-mouth,** the mouth of a horse which can be managed with a snaffle alone.

**1576** GASCOIGNE *Steele Gl., Philomene* (Arb.) 90 A snaffle Bit or brake, Bebost with gold. **1668** *Lond. Gaz.* No. 272/4 He took away with her a deep skirted Saddle..and a snaffle Bridle. **1814** EARL DUDLEY *Lett.* 7 May (1840) 35 There is no riding the French in a snaffle-bridle. **1856** 'STONEHENGE' *Brit. Rural Sports* 395/1, I have never yet ridden a snaffle-bridled horse comfortably through a run. **1856** LEVER *Martins of Cro' M.* xv, An old worsted bell-rope formed the snaffle-rein of his bridle. **1862** H. H. DIXON *Scott & Sebright* IV. 308 Early in the ensuing year, Becher was again on the snaffle-mouthed Grimaldi. **1875** KNIGHT *Dict. Mech.* 2228/2 Price's bridle-bit..combines the snaffle-bit with a lever-bar. **1910** *Chambers's Jrnl.* 1 Oct. 703/1 A jungle-fowl which..causes my horse to dance a gavotte.., a feat for which his snaffle mouth and indolent disposition eminently unfit him. **1932** J. E. HANCE *School for Horse & Rider* x. 85 From time to time one hears of such and such a horse possessing a 'snaffle mouth'. To be entitled to such a designation the animal would have to be capable of flexing and bending to this form of bit at all paces, and such animals are extremely rare. **1977** *Horse & Hound* 14 Jan. 36/3 (Advt.), Chestnut gelding... Snaffle mouth, quiet in every way.

†**'snaffle,** *sb.*[2] *Cant. Obs.* [perh. the same word as prec., but cf. SNAFFLE *v.*[4]] (See quot.)

*a* **1700** B. E. *Dict. Cant. Crew, Snaffle*, a Highwayman that has got Booty.

**snaffle** ('snæf(ə)l), *v.*[1] [f. SNAFFLE *sb.*[1]]

**1.** *trans.* To put a snaffle on (a horse, etc.); to restrain or guide with a snaffle. Freq. *fig.*

**1559** *Mirr. Mag.* (1563) Liv, For hytherto slye wryters wyly wittes..Have been lyke horses snaffled with the byttes Of fansye, feares or doubtes. **1562** J. HEYWOOD *Prov. & Epigr.* (1867) 139 If thou wylt brydell me, I wyll snafell the. **1581** J. BELL *Haddon's Answ. Osor.* 295 Their arrogaunt insolency, beyng a long tyme reasonably well snafled by the Greeke and Frenche Emperours. **1603** DEKKER & CHETTLE *Grissil* 2622 Asse, Ile haue you snaffled. **1679** BUNYAN *Fear of God* Wks. 1855 I. 478 The guilt and terror that thy sins will snaffle thee with. *a* **1849** MANGAN *Poems* (1859) 279 The animal snaffled by Boileau. **1875** TENNYSON *Q. Mary* v. iii, If you marry Philip, Then I and he will snaffle your 'God's death', And break your paces in.

**2.** *slang.* To arrest; to seize.

**1860** *Slang Dict.* 220 *Snaffled*, arrested, 'pulled up'. **1902** *Essex Weekly News* 24 Jan. 2/6 On one occasion we snaffled a Cape cart in which were two females dressed in male attire.

Hence **'snaffled** *ppl. a.*, bridled.

**1877** BLACKIE *Wise Men* 335 Their powers..discharge Their snaffled wrath at Jove's high beck.

**'snaffle,** *v.*[2] ? *Obs.* [Of obscure origin.] *intr.* To saunter.

**1611** MIDDLETON & DEKKER *Roaring Girl* D.'s Wks. 1873 III. 208, I haue gon snaffling vp and downe by your dore this houre to watch for you. *a* **1743** RELPH *Poems* (1747) 5 Mun I still be..shamefully left snafflen by my sell?

**snaffle** ('snæf(ə)l), *v.*[3] Now *dial.* [Imitative: cf. WFris. *snaffelje* and SNUFFLE *v.*] **a.** *trans.* To utter through the nose. **b.** *intr.* To speak through the nose; to make a snuffling noise.

**1616** HOLYDAY *Persius* I. B 4 If forsooth one clad in purple cloth's Snaffle some mustie stuff through's muffling nose. **1647** CORBET *Poems* (1807) 95 To Saint Denis fast we came To see the sights of Nostre Dame, The man that shews them snaffles. **1826** in Hone *Every-day Bk.* II. 549 A hare-lip.. caused him to speak through the nose, or to *snaffle*, as they term it in Yorkshire. **1869** BLACKMORE *Lorna D.* (1889) 286 Snorting, snaffling, whinnying and neighing.

Hence **'snaffling** *vbl. sb.*

*a* **1668** LASSELS *Voy. Italy* (1698) II. 259 The snaffling through the nose made all the edification that I saw in it.

**snaffle** ('snæf(ə)l), *v.*[4] *dial.* or *slang.* [Of obscure origin; cf. SNAFFLE *sb.*[2]] **1.** *trans.* To steal, purloin.

**1725** *New Cant. Dict., Snaffle*, to steal, to rob, to purloin. *c* **1850** BAGNALL *Songs* 24 (E.D.D.), He cud snaffle the raisins an' currins away. **1897** *Longm. Mag.* Aug. 372 Archy did not 'snaffle' £6000 and invest it in business.

**2.** To appropriate, seize, catch, snatch. Also with *up*.

**1895** KIPLING in *Century Mag.* Dec. 273/2 A year's leave was among the things he had 'snaffled out of the campaign', to use his own words. **1915** D. O. BARNETT *Let.* 7 Aug. 218, I see they've snaffled Warsaw. **1916** 'PETER' *Trench Yarns* 10 A certain airman had engine trouble up aloft and had to come down behind the German lines. Of course they snaffled him. **1928** *Sunday Express* 15 Apr. 11/6, I soon snaffled a double role in a big spectacle. **1959** *Times* 28 May 4/7 Slade threw down Cook's wicket when Meyer tried to snaffle the strike. **1964** M. MCLUHAN *Understanding Media* xxxi. 331 Jack discovered how to extend the TV mosaic image..seemingly snaffling up just anybody from anywhere. *a* **1974** R. CROSSMAN *Diaries* (1975) I. 149 There was a good deal of bleating, but I got my way and was able to snaffle the Statement for myself in the process.

†**'snaffler**[1]. *Cant. Obs.*$^{-0}$ (See quot.)

*c* **1700** *Street Robberies Consider'd, Snafflers*, highwaymen.

**'snaffler**[2]. *dial.* [f. SNAFFLE *v.*[3]] One who talks through the nose.

**1885** *North Star* 1 July 3/2 Like the snarling snafflers such people generally are.

**'snaffles.** ? *Obs.* [Cf. SNAFFLE *v.*[3]] A form of catarrh affecting respiration; the snuffles.

**1822–7** GOOD *Study Med.* (1829) II. 590 Whence in common language it is called emphatically *the distemper*, though vulgarly the *snaffles*,..from the state of the nostrils.

**'snaffling,** *ppl. a.* [f. SNAFFLE *v.*[3]] Snuffling; speaking through the nose.

*a* **1585** MONTGOMERIE *Flyting* 569 Contagious cankers carues his snafling snout. **1620** SHELTON *Quix.* III. vi. I. 164 He stopt his nose very well between his Fingers, and then said with a Snaffling voice. **1651** LILLY *Chas. I* (1774) 211 An obstinate King, wholly led by the nose by these snaffling Priests. *a* **1668** LASSELS *Voy. Italy* (1698) II. 135 The snaffling fellow..will tell you another story of this statue through the nose. **1793** SOUTHEY *Juv. & Minor P., Chapel Bell*, The snuffling, snaffling Fellow's nasal tone. **1805** in 'Geo. Paston' *Side-lights Georgian Period* (1902) 251 Such a little snaffling man, if I may use the expression, I hardly ever heard.

†**'snaffling-lay.** *Cant. Obs.* [Cf. SNAFFLE *sb.*[2] and SNAFFLE *v.*[4]] The trade of highwayman.

**1752** FIELDING *Amelia* I. iii, I thought by your look you had been a clever fellow, and upon the snaffling-lay at least.

**snafu** ('snæfu:), *phr.*, *a.*, and *sb. slang* (chiefly *U.S.*, orig. *U.S. Mil.*). Also **SNAFU.** [Acronym f. the initial letters of *s*ituation *n*ormal: *a*ll *f*ouled (or *f*ucked) *u*p.] **A.** Used acronymically (often with an explanation) as an expression conveying the common soldier's laconic acceptance of the disorder of war and the ineptitude of his superiors.

**1941** *Amer. N. & Q.* Sept. 94/2 *Snafu*, situation normal. **1943** *Amer. Mercury* Nov. 555/2 *Snafu*—politely translated as 'situation normal; all fouled up', to indicate that things are not going too well. **1946** *Amer. Jrnl. Sociol.* Mar. 419 Interestingly, the expression 'snafu', derived from this, 'Situation normal, all f——ed up', is coming into general civilian use. **1966** *Sunday Times* (Colour Suppl.) 4 Dec. 73/4 GI Jargon... *Snafu*, Situation normal, all fouled up. **1975** *Listener* 13 Mar. 349/1 There was a barrack-room mnemonic which fits the ill-starred Dieppe raid: SNAFU, or Situation Normal, All Fouled Up.

**B.** *adj.* Confused, chaotic.

**1942** *Time* 15 June 11/1 Last week U.S. citizens knew that gasoline rationing and rubber requisitioning were snafu. **1950** 'D. DIVINE' *King of Fassarai* (1951) xxviii. 245 Situation Snafu... Send for the Seabees.

**C.** *sb.* Now usu. with *a* and *pl.* A confusion or mix-up; a hitch, mishap; muddle, confused state.

**1943** *Yank* 10 Sept. 9 They worked hard and steadily, with a minimum of snafu. **1945** *Richmond* (Va.) *Times-Dispatch* 11 Dec. 10/7 Corporations struggling with the problems of reconversion, strikes, shortages and snafu in general. **1956** C. W. MILLS *Power Elite* viii. 182 The key to the bureaucratic snafu that has often characterized the navy is that as the ships and the guns and the logistics became more technically complicated, the men who ran them acquired rank less by technical specialty than by seniority. **1958** 'CASTLE' & 'HAILEY' *Flight into Danger* i. 17 It would have to be a big show in Vancouver to justify this snafu. **1963** MRS. L. B. JOHNSON *White House Diary* 28 Dec. (1970) 23 Pretty soon the German plane rolled in, overshooting the red carpet by a few feet, so there was a slight snafu and they had to hop around to get onto it. **1965** *Times Lit. Suppl.* 25 Nov. 1039/1 He must have seen enough 'snafus' to make him sceptical of 'the Brass'. **1976** *Guardian* 20 Oct. 4/8 As that monumental snafu at Domadedovo attests, Aeroflot's shortcomings are also big ones. **1978** W. F. BUCKLEY *Stained Glass* xxi. 206 Singer then rehearsed Blackford in emergency instructions to be followed in the hideous event of a snafu. **1980** B. MASON *Solo* 117 And Holy Moses, *what* a snafu! Why foul up poor, harmless, gormless Glad?

Hence as vb. *U.S. slang*, *(a) trans.* to mess up, to play havoc with; *(b) intr.* to go wrong; also **'snafued** *ppl. a.*

**1943** *Yank* 19 Nov. 9 Then the Army snafued the romance by transferring Kinser to this post. **1944** *Life* 16 Oct. 20/2 It is a symbol of SNAFU.., and a star is rated for each snafued campaign after Guadalcanal. **1953** *Sun*

(Baltimore) 1 Sept. (B ed.) 17/2 Eddie had twice this season snafued a batting order and caused men to be called out for swinging out of turn. **1955** 'J. CHRISTOPHER' *Year of Comet* i. 15 Of course I didn't bring you up here simply to tell you P & M snafued your psychoplan sixteen years ago. **1975** J. GRADY *Shadow of Condor* i. 31 Every now and then something snafus and there is one hell of a mess. **1981** G. MARKSTEIN *Ultimate Issue* 38 My arrangements seemed snafued. I guess the lines got crossed.

**snag** (snæg), *sb.*[1] Also 6–7 **snagge**, 8–9 **snagg**. [prob. of Scand. origin: cf. Norw. dial. *snag* sharp point, projection, stump, spike, etc., also *snage* in the same senses = Icel. *snagi* peg. The stem is also found in OIcel. *snag-hyrndr*, said of an axe having a sharp point. For the retention of *g* in the English word cf. FLAG *sb.*[2]]

**1. a.** A short stump standing out from the trunk, or from a stout branch, of a tree or shrub, esp. one which has been left after cutting or pruning; †also, a fruiting spur.

**1577–87** HOLINSHED *Chron.* (1808) IV. 644 Artificiallie made gates raised of ragged staues, and vpon euerie snag stood a small wax candle burning. **1596** SPENSER *F.Q.* IV. vii. 7 In his hand a tall young oake he bore, Whose knottie snags were sharpned all afore. **1623** CAMDEN *Rem.* (1637) 420 An Ewtree with the Berries, and a great N. hanging upon a snag in the midst of the tree. **1674** JOSSELYN *Voy. New Eng.* 138 They make their.. fire near to a great Tree, upon the snags whereof they hang their kettles. **1731** MILLER *Gard. Dict.* s.v. *Ribes*, These Plants produce their Fruit.. also upon small Snags which come out of the old Wood. **1791** W. BARTRAM *Carolina* 89 Old weather-beaten trees, hoary and barbed, with the long moss hanging from their snags. **1811–** in many dialect glossaries. **1859** DELAMER *Flower Gard.* 167 Above all, do not leave a long snag to die down to the bud. **1898** CARD *Bush Fruits* 363 The top being cut down in spring and the snag removed afterward.

*fig.* **1824** *Blackw. Mag.* XV. 177, I shall make each of these important topics a head, or rather a snag, in my Pastoral Calendar. **1857** *Fraser's Mag.* LVI. 357 A man who has many crotchets.. must be a conglomeration of snags and snarls.

**b.** A trunk or large branch of a tree imbedded in the bottom of a river, lake, etc., with one end directed upwards (and consequently forming an impediment or danger to navigation). orig. *U.S.*

**1807** P. GASS *Jrnl.* 31 About 12 one of the periogues run against a snag which broke a hole in it. **1817–8** COBBETT *Resid. U.S.* (1822) 294 The wheels are made to work in the stern of the boat, so as not to come in contact with the floating trees, snaggs, planters, &c. **1877** H. DIXON *Diana* III. iii, A snag, jammed in the stony bed, throws up a jet of water.

**c.** *fig.* An impediment or obstacle. Also, a disadvantage, a hitch; a defect.

**1830** GALT *Lawrie T.* IV. ix, I guess he's a snag in the Devil's way. **1886** *Pall Mall G.* 4 Aug. 3/1 Our extradition treaty with the United States has run up against its first snag, to use an expression familiar on the Mississippi. **1891** C. ROBERTS *Adrift Amer.* 8, I was continually running against some snag in the shape of an unwritten law. **1903** *N.Y. Times* 20 Oct. 1 A conference lasting three hours took place which was plain sailing until the last moment, when a snag was struck. **1923** WODEHOUSE *Inimitable Jeeves* vi. 66 At this point the scenario struck another snag. **1936** W. H. SAUMAREZ SMITH *Let.* 26 Dec. in *Young Man's Country* (1977) ii. 48 The only snag.. was that Grindlay's had failed to send my tickets to the U.S. Club. **1940** *Economist* 27 Jan. 142/2 Mr Gandhi referred to the 'undoubted snags' in Lord Linlithgow's statement, but a pre-requisite to tackling the 'snags' is a better spirit and some measure of confidence. **1945** C. H. WARD-JACKSON *Piece of Cake* 56 *Snag*, aircraft defect. **1950** J. CANNAN *Murder Included* iii. 39 The house would be all right; the snag would be the skivvies. **1962** *Daily Tel.* 19 Nov. 22/5 (*heading*) Bonn Air Force finds snags in U.S. plane. **1977** B. PYM *Quartet in Autumn* v. 44 There had been a good deal of discussion.. as to whether he should go by coach or by train and the advantages and snags of each method were endlessly weighed up.

**d.** *N. Amer.* A standing dead tree.

**1904** *Dialect Notes* II. 421 There was a big snag with a woodpecker's nest in it south of our house. **1936** *Sun* (Baltimore) 1 Aug. 11/1 Flames.. have turned more than 30,000 acres of once-green forest into charred and smoldering snags. **1946** B. MACDONALD *Egg & I* 94 Incredibly tall, spindly snags leaned threateningly towards me. **1960** M. SHARCOTT *Place of Many Winds* i. 14 The sun touched the hills behind us, lighting the dead white snags that so liberally sprinkled the live spruce. **1975** *Islander* (Victoria, B.C.) 8 June 16/1 Osprey will choose a nest site atop a dead snag from which he can command a view of the habitat around him.

**2. a.** A sharp, angular, or jagged projection.

**1586** BRIGHT *Treat. Melancholy* xxvi. 149 The rowels of the neckbone with their snagges hinder that inclination. **1611** COTGR., *Barbelé*,.. full of snags, snips, iags. **1692** RAY *Disc.* II. ii. (1732) 102 Hailstones.. like great pieces of Ice with several Snags or fangs issuing out of them. **1757** WILKIE *Epigoniad* II. (1769) 28 A ponderous mace.. with snags around Of pointed steel. **1799** E. KING *Mun. Antiqua* I. 105 They [stone arrow-heads].. have snaggs, or as they are called beards on each side. **1817** KIRBY & SPENCE *Entomol.* xxi. (1818) II. 220 The legs, as well as the head, having their little snags and knobs. **1863** BARING-GOULD *Iceland* 103 Blowing snags and splinters [of lava] into cairnlike heaps all around.

**b.** A broken piece or stump of a tooth; a large or unshapely tooth.

**1612** WOODALL *Surg. Mate* Wks. (1653) 11 Crowes bils.. are only used to take hold of any snag of a tooth. **1676** *Poor Robin's Intell.* 4 Apr. 1/2 As old folks when they have but a snag or two left pass for Children. **1717** PRIOR *Alma* II. 428 In China none hold Women sweet, Except their Snags are black as Jett. **1792** WOLCOT (P. Pindar) *Wolves, Bear*, etc. Wks. 1812 III. 74 It is the wish of many a beast, That you consent your teeth may all be pull'd; Damn me, if I would lose my snags, my Lords. **1825–** in many dial. glossaries (esp. of south-western counties). **1829** LANDOR *Imag. Conv.* Wks. 1853 I. 375/2 Their old snags will stick tight in them till they rattle in the coffin.

**c.** A tine or branch of a deer's horn, *spec.* one which is short or imperfectly developed.

**1673** RAY *Journ. Low C.* 27 The Horns have no Brow-Antlers, but only a broad palm with several Snags upon it. **1842** BRANDE *Dict. Arts* s.v. *Deer*, The points between the notches are developed into long branches or *snags*, of which a single antler sometimes sends off as many as fourteen. **1872** NICHOLSON *Palaeont.* 437 This extraordinary.. species .. having horns which have a snag in front.

**3.** *dial.* A rent or tear, such as is made by a sharp projection.

**1854** MISS BAKER *Northampt. Gloss.*, *Snag*, a rent at right angles.

**4.** *attrib.* and *Comb.*, as ***snag-toothed*** adj., **-*voyage***; **snag-boat**, **-pruning**, **-scow** (see quots.).

*a* **1661** HOLYDAY *Juvenal* (1673) 138 What smith then toils so hard? Or who, that wool with snag-tooth'd wire does card? **1823** E. MOOR *Suffolk Words* s.v. *Snags*, That mode of pruning which leaves the snags is called snag-pruning, in distinction from close pruning. **1832** *Reg. Deb. Congress U.S.* (1833) 3 May 2722 The snag boat had been employed in improving the navigation of the Mississippi. **1851** ELIZA COOK *Jrnl.* VI. 100 A snag voyage up the yellow Missouri for some 400 miles, is no joke. **1858** SIMMONDS *Dict. Trade*, *Snag-boat*, a steam-boat fitted with an apparatus for removing snags, or obstructions to navigation in rivers. **1895** ZANGWILL *Master* II. vii, The grotesque snag-toothed hags in the crowd. **1907** C. D. STEWART *Partners of Providence* xiii. 176 The white snag-scow.. did keep the snags pulled out of the mouth of the Missouri anyway.

**snag**, *sb.*[2] Now *dial.* and *rare*. [Of obscure origin: cf. SKEG *sb.*[2], SCAD[2].] A sloe.

**1578** LYTE *Dodoens* 719 The wilde Plummes are the least of al, and are called Slose, Bullies, and Snagges. **1611** COTGR., *Prunelle*, a Sloe, or Snag. **1825** JENNINGS *Obs. Dial. W. Eng.* 70 *Snags*, small sloes. **1901** *Longm. Mag.* Feb. 363 'Twere made o' nought but the snags what grows in the hedges.

*attrib.* **1598** FLORIO, *Spino*, a sloe tree, a black-thorne, a snag tree. **1617** HOLYOKE *Dict. Etymol.*, *Spinus*,.. a blacke thorne, the snagge tree. **1893** *Wiltshire Gloss.* 149 Snag-bush, *Prunus spinosa*, the Sloe.

**snag**, *sb.*[3] *dial.* and *rare*. [Later form or var. of SNEG *sb.* See also SNAG-GREET.] A snail.

**1674** RAY *S. & E. Co. Words* 77 A Snagge, a snail. *Suss.* [Hence in Kersey, Bailey, Grose, etc.] *a* **1700** B. E. *Dict. Cant. Crew*, Snaggs,.. Snails. **1862** LOWER in *Athenæum* 30 Aug. 281 When my occasional gardener talks of the ravages of 'them snags' on a peach-tree.

**snag** (snæg), *sb.*[4] *Austral. colloq.* [Origin unknown: cf. *Snag* vb.[2] and sb.[3] 6 in E.D.D.; *Snag* sb.[1] 2 in S.N.D.] A sausage.

**1941** BAKER *Dict. Austral. Slang* 68 *Snags*, sausages. **1949** R. PARK *Poor Man's Orange* 33 'Let's have sausages.'.. Good old snags. They were always there to be fallen back on. **1972** *Sunday Mail Mag.* (Brisbane) 26 Mar. 13/1 The dog had an uncanny capacity for nicking in to the butcher's shop, snatching a snag and getting out again. **1980** *Bulletin* (Sydney) 6 May 112/3, I make my own snags, my own pies and pasties. The Yanks love them after you've twisted their arms to try them.

**snag** (snæg), *v.*[1] Now *dial.* [perh. related to SNAG *sb.*[1], but the sense has more connexion with NAG *v.*] *intr.* To carp, cavil, sneer, nag. Also const. *at*. Hence **'snagging** *vbl. sb.*[1]

**1554** J. BRADFORD in Coverdale *Lett.* (1564) 326 You are one of hys liuely stones: be contente therefore to be hewen and snagged at. **1642** D. ROGERS *Naaman* 14 How much more then should ye beware of snagging and snarling at Gods secrets. *Ibid.* 291 Let us.. be so farre from snagging or nipping of such, that rather we marke them for peculiar ones. **1806** A. DOUGLAS *Poems* 121 Sic snaggin' an' braggin' An' randy-beggar jaw. **1839** SIR G. C. LEWIS *Gloss. Heref.*, *To snag*, to teaze, to repeat the same thing several times. **1866** BROGDEN *Prov. Lincs.*, *Snag*, to irritate or scold in an 'aggravating' manner.

**snag** (snæg), *v.*[2] [f. SNAG *sb.*[1]]

**1.** *trans.* **a.** In passive: To be caught, pierced, or damaged by a snag. Chiefly *U.S.*, and esp. of river-steamers.

(*a*) **1807** P. GASS *Jrnl.* 229 One of our best horses got snagged to day, and was left here.

(*b*) **1839** DE QUINCEY *Milton v. Southey* Wks. 1862 XI. 196 One does not altogether like being snagged by the Mississippi. **1850** LYELL *2nd Visit U.S.* II. 267, I afterwards learnt, that in the course of her voyage she was snagged. **1864** *Daily Telegr.* 6 Apr., It is no light matter to be 'snagged' on a dark night in Virginia.

(*c*) **1891** C. ROBERTS *Adrift Amer.* 211 Feeling no pull I started to haul my line in, but found I was snagged.

**b.** *fig.* To occupy or block as with a snag; to impede, to inconvenience. Also with *up*.

**1833** *Polit. Examiner* (Shelbyville, Kentucky) 22 June 4/1, I will agree to be shot with a paper wadding if there ar' room enough in the whole clearing for a man of ordinary parts to stand on five minutes at a time, without getting snagged by some tape and cotton yarn dealer in the street. **1863** W. PHILLIPS *Sp.* iii. 38 A great mind, anchored in error, might snag the slow-moving current of society. **1929** HALL & NILES *One Man's War* 131, I decided to try clipping the German's tail with my propeller or snag him in some way. **1962** *Guardian* 19 Dec. 8/3 No place to work and insufficient funds.. had snagged her. **1968** C. BURKE *Elephant across Border* v. 193 He was going to do whatever he could to snag things up.

**2. a.** To cut roughly, or so as to leave snags.

**1811** WILLAN in *Archaeologia* XVII. 158 *Snag*, to hew, or cut rudely with an axe, &c. **1812** HENRY *Camp. agst. Quebec* 24 Blazing the trees and snagging the bushes with our tomahawks. **1840** *Penny Cycl.* XVIII. 216/2 Whether the branches.. should be cut close to the stem at once,.. or whether they should first be *snagged*.

**b.** To tear on or by a sharp projection.

**1854** MISS BAKER *Northampt. Gloss.* II. 258, I have snagged my gown. **1897** *19th Cent.* Feb. 242 My knicker-bockers and stockings were snagged to pieces by these hidden stumbling blocks.

**3.** To clear (a river, etc.) from snags.

**1882** *Law Rep.* 9 *App. Cases* 429, I got much useful information from him when snagging the river. **1889** *New York Times* 21 July (Cent.), Both of these parties.. are engaged in snagging the waterways.

**4.** *N. Amer.* **a.** To catch, get hold of, grab, steal, pick up. *colloq.*

**1895** *Dialect Notes* I. 399 *Snag*, to steal. **1927** *Amer. Speech* II. 278/1 *Snag a pick up*, get a free ride. *Ibid.*, *Snag the current*, get the drift. **1930** D. RUNYON in *Collier's* 1 Feb. 44/2 There is plenty of trouble over Lillian snagging her Peke. **1941** B. APPEL in C. Grayson *New Stories for Men* 32 Red would snag a dollar or two out of me with a promise that I should take it out of his wages. **1946** MEZZROW & WOLFE *Really Blues* xii. 226 You didn't come of age on the welfare, snagging butts out of the gutter. **1962** J. GLENN in *Into Orbit* 221 Two sailors reached over with a shepherd's hook to snag the capsule. **1966** L. J. BRAUN *Cat who could read Backwards* (1967) xiv. 160 I'll get to the club early and snag a quiet table. **1978** J. CARROLL *Mortal Friends* v. i. 503 Colman and Janet did not snag each other with their eyes at the mention of the Ritz.

**b.** *Sport.* To catch or field (a ball); to receive (a pass).

**1942** BERREY & VAN DEN BARK *Amer. Thes. Slang* §679/5 *Field a ball*.. snag the oval. **1968** *Washington Post* 4 July C1/3 (*caption*) Mantle was safe as Ron Hansen's throw, after snagging a line drive by Andy Kosco, was a trifle tardy. **1977** *Time* 30 May 40/2 In their place came players tailored to Big Bill's skills: quick, sure-handed guards to snag his crisp outlet passes and start the fast break rolling.

**c.** *Angling.* To catch (fish), *spec.* with a bare hook; to catch illicitly or improperly.

**1946** *Richmond* (Va.) *Times-Dispatch* 17 Mar. B-11/2 When the herring are in in numbers, you snag a herring about every third or fourth attempt. **1960** *Washington Post* 11 Mar. D5 Unbelievable as it may sound, the herring are so thick at the height of the run that simply jerking a bare hook through the water will snag fish. **1974** *Evening Herald* (Rock Hill, S. Carolina) 18 Apr. 7/1 The largest striper of the first week of the 10 week-long derby went to Sumter's John Benenhaly who also used cut bait to snag a 26 pound, 8 ounce fish. **1979** *Globe & Mail* (Toronto) 7 Feb. 5/6 His six-man patrol is fed up with those who snag fish illegally.

**5.** *intr.* **a.** To strike a snag, to get caught *on* a projection or obstacle.

**1866** *Harper's Mag.* Nov. 810/1 A Mississippi steamer, that snagged and went down on 'Yazoo Bend'. **1929** W. FAULKNER *Sound & Fury* 3 You snagged on that nail again. Cant you never crawl through here without snagging on that nail. **1970** G. F. NEWMAN *Sir, You Bastard* 262 He could neither see the thorn he had snagged on, nor the path by which to pull clear. **1976** M. MACHLIN *Pipeline* lv. 559 The rock itself.. was some seventy-five yards from the ship, which apparently had snagged on an underwater rock projection some hundred feet down.

**b.** Of a fabric: to be rendered imperfect by a pulled thread.

**1970** *Which?* Oct. 300/2 A few brands suffered slightly from pilling.. and several of the Crimplene ones snagged.

**6.** The verb-stem in combinations, as (sense 4 c) ***snag-fishing***, **-*hook***, **-*line***.

**1936** *Sun* (Baltimore) 8 July 8/6 They.. charged all three with using snag lines and snag hooks with intent to do bodily harm to the aforesaid sturgeon. **1952** B. HARWIN *Home is Upriver* viii. 86 He could get an old gasboat somewhere, cheap, some fishhooks and lines enough for snag-fishing. *Ibid.* x. 99 Kip and Lenny fished: snaglines and bushlines. **1960** *Washington Post* 11 Mar. D5 A snag hook is a huge treble hook which can be fished from either a rod or hand. Usually two or three are tied to a strong line (chalk line is a favorite), a singer is attached and the whole shebang is cast into the drink and retrieved in a series of short jerks.

Hence **'snagging** *vbl. sb.*[2]

**1775** in J. J. Henry *Campaign against Quebec* (1812) 53 The paths and carrying places we had sufficiently developed .. by strong blazing and snagging of bushes. **1851** A. O. HALL *Manhattaner in N. Orleans* 179 There may sometimes occur a snagging, or a fire, with perhaps a collision. **1874** *Rep. Vermont Board Agric.* II. 550 The stumps are rotting, and it is nearly ready for the.. work of snagging and bogging. **1880** 'MARK TWAIN' *Tramp Abroad* I. 83 He.. had gone to bed, with his head filled with impending snaggings, and explosions, and conflagrations. **1960** *Washington Post* 11 Mar. D5/1 They're [*sc.* herrings] caught mostly by dipnets and the gentle method known as snagging. **1980** *Outdoor Life* (U.S.) (Northeast ed.) Oct. 56/2 Because Pacific Coast salmon die after spawning, snagging was introduced as a sporting way to harvest huge numbers of fish in a short time.

**snagged** ('snægd), *ppl. a.* [f. SNAG *sb.*[1] or *v.*[2]]

**1. a.** Having projecting points or jagged protuberances; jagged, ragged.

**1658** ROWLAND tr. *Moufet's Theat. Ins.* 964 The edge of the wings like the Bats snagged, and as it were prickly. **1662** H. MORE *Antid. Ath.* II. iii. 49 Howlings and shoutings of poor naked men belabouring one another with snag'd sticks. **1741** *Phil. Trans.* XLI. 563 The Roch, or snagged Wheel, being herein accounted as Part of the great Wheel. **1791** W. BARTRAM *California* 247 Having provided ourselves with a long snagged sapling, called an Indian ladder. **1898** *Westm. Gaz.* 9 Apr. 1/3 By this time his trouser knees were torn in snagged rents.

†**b.** Of teeth: = SNAGGLED *a.* 1. *Obs.*$^{-0}$

**1687** MIÈGE *Gt. Fr. Dict.* II. s.v., A snagged Tooth, that does not stand even.

**2.** Caught or impaled upon a snag. Also *fig.*
**1851** E. C. E. STUART-WORTLEY *Travels in U.S.* 112 In the papers will you often see whole columns, headed, 'Snagged', containing a melancholy list of boats. **1867** A. D. RICHARDSON *Beyond Mississippi* i. 21 A snagged steamer. **1872** C. KING *Sierra Nevada* viii. 174, I made a dash for the snagged mule. **1930** D. RUNYON in *Collier's* 22 Mar. 53/1 Basil is snagged if ever I see a guy snagged, and personally I do not blame him, because Miss Harriet Mackyle may not look like a million, but she has a couple. **1977** *Time* 3 Jan. 34/1 The talks have been snagged for months on how to deal with two new weapons.

**'snagger.** [f. SNAG *v.*[2] 2, 4 c.]
**1.** *dial.* (See quot.)
**1847** HALLIW. s.v. *Snag*, A snagger..is a simple bill-hook without the usual edge on the back. **1877–99** in dial. glossaries (Cumb., Yks.).
**2.** *Austral.* A slow, inexpert, or poor sheep-shearer.
**1887** *Tibb's Popular Songbk.* 11, I found a lot of snaggers Not a shearer in the mob. *a* **1914** *Click go Shears* in R. Ward *Austral. Ballads* (1964) 120 The ringer looks round and is beaten by a blow, And curses the snagger with the bare-bellied yeo. **1945** BAKER *Austral. Lang.* 63 *Snagger*, a shearer who is learning the trade and handling less than fifty sheep a day. **1969** B. HARDY *West of Darling* 106 Since they were slow, inexpert, and rough in their performances, the poorest shearers in the shed were nicknamed 'snaggers'. **1975** *Sunday Mail* (Brisbane) 14 Sept. 6/6 The younger men who have taken the old 'snaggers'' places, stand up on 'the board'..and shear along with the best of them.
**3.** *N. Amer.* One who snags fish; one who catches fish illicitly.
**1946** *Richmond* (Va.) *Times-Dispatch* 17 Mar. B-11/2 Alewives which have been snagged by the many 'snaggers' on the dam. **1976** *Globe & Mail* (Toronto) 20 Oct. 36/3 Among this group were many snaggers, fish hogs using any means to trap the big fish. One man, armed only with a landing net, scooped away at fish in one pool.

**snaggle** ('snæg(ə)l), *sb.* Chiefly *dial.* and *colloq.* [app. f. SNAG *sb.*[1]: cf. SNAGGLE-TOOTH.] **1.** A snaggle-tooth; one who has snaggle-teeth. *rare.*
**1823** M. WILMOT *Let.* 1 Oct. (1935) 197 Blanche [has] become *alas* a snaggle! Those dear little pearls of teeth are going. **1880** COURTNEY & COUCH *Gloss. Words Cornwall* 52/2 What snaggles the cheeld has.
**2.** A tangle; a knotted or projecting mass.
**1904** *Eng. Dial. Dict.* V. 567/1 *Snaggle*,..a knotted, entangled condition. **1968** C. HELMERICKS *Down Wild River North* II. xxii. 336 The girls pitched our tent in the sparse, pristine plant population between rock snaggles. **1978** T. HUGHES in *Times Lit. Suppl.* 14 Apr. 409/1 All eyes watch The weathered, rooty, bushy pile of faces, A snaggle of faces.
**3.** *attrib.*, as ***snaggle-tusk***.
**1922** JOYCE *Ulysses* 424 The famished snaggletusks of an elderly bawd protrude from a doorway.

**'snaggle,** *v. slang.* (See quots.)
**1839** *Slang Dict.* 34 *Snaggling*, driving geese into a corner in a stubble-field. **1864** *Slang Dict.* (Hotten) 238 *Snaggling*, angling after geese with a hook and line, the bait being a worm or snail.

**'snaggled,** *a. U.S.* [Cf. next.]
**1.** Of teeth: Uneven, irregular, projecting. Also *transf.*
**1884** J. G. BOURKE *Snake Dance Moquis* xxxii. 360 His snaggled teeth, projecting tusk-like from an unnecessarily large mouth. **1889** 'C. E. CRADDOCK' *Despot Broomsedge Cove* xxii. 396 He glanced at Jepson with a lively little grin, all his snaggled teeth on parade. **1938** J. STEINBECK *Long Valley* 58 The sharp snaggled edge of the ridge stood out above them. **1942** W. FAULKNER *Go down, Moses* 69 A few snaggled trees of what had been an orchard.
**2.** Knotty, intricate.
**1896** *Advance* (Chicago) 26 Mar. 457/1 Snaggled problems grew plain as light, under the gentle explanations which she could give.

**'snaggle-tooth.** [Cf. next and SNAG-TOOTH.] An irregular or projecting tooth. Also, one with snaggle-teeth.
**1820** M. WILMOT *Let.* 12 Jan. (1935) 51 Catherine has actually lost one of her teeth!.. The poor Cat will be a rare frightful snaggle tooth. **1821** —— *Let.* 17 Mar. 99 Instead of being hideous in the snaggle tooth age..she is..improved. **1825** JENNINGS *Obs. Dial. W. Eng.* 71 *Snaggle-tooth*, a tooth growing irregularly. **1859** *Slang Dict.* 96 *Snaggle teeth*, uneven, and unpleasant looking dental operators. **1897** S. WATSON *Life's Look-out* 67 Every building had its own lurch inwards or outwards, like a mouthful of snaggle teeth. **1906** *Dialect Notes* III. 157 You'll be a snaggle-tooth before you're twenty, if you don't quit eating so much candy. **1909** J. R. WARE *Passing Eng.* 227/2 *Snaggle-tooth*, woman of lower order..who, lifting her upper lip when scolding, shows an irregular row of teeth.

**'snaggle-toothed,** *a.* [app. f. SNAG *sb.*[1]] Having snaggle-teeth. Also *fig.*
**1585** HIGINS tr. *Junius' Nomencl.* 452/1 s.v. *Dento.* **1688** HOLME *Armoury* II. 427/1 *Snaggle*, or *Rake toothed*, is when the teeth stands at a distance, one from the other. **1884** J. C. HARRIS *Nts. Uncle Remus* 105 I'm snaggle-toofed an' double j'inted. **1945** B. MACDONALD *Egg & I* (1946) 85 On grey winter days its snaggle-toothed horizon could be seen plainly. **1954** *Caribbean Quarterly* III. IV. 231 Albert is a bright-eyed, snaggle-toothed little man. **1971** B. W. ALDISS *Soldier Erect* 32 That snaggle-toothed chap in the comic button-up white suit,..—put him in a proper pinstripe and he'd pass for an Eastbourne estate agent! **1977** *Time* 14 Feb. 21/3 Entertainment is provided by..a Hollywood drop-cloth view of snaggle-toothed Mount Kenya.

**snaggly** ('snæglɪ), *a.* Chiefly *dial.* and *colloq.* [f. as SNAGGLE *sb.*: see -Y[1].] Irregular; tangled; ragged.
**1794** W. CLARK *Jrnl.* 4 Aug. in *Mississippi Valley Hist. Rev.* (1914) I. 422 The army was conducted..through intolerable thick woods & the earth covered with Snagley underwoods. **1882** F. W. P. JAGO *Anc. Lang. & Dial. Cornwall* 269 'Snaggly teeth', i.e., very irregular or ill-shaped teeth. **1968** P. S. BEAGLE *Last Unicorn* xiv. 206 Squat, snaggly trees that had never yet bloomed were putting forth flowers in the wary way an army sends out scouts. **1978** R. JANSSON *News Caper* vi. 55 The bullet.. bounced off something metal before it hit her, because the wound is all snaggly.

**†snag-greet.** *Obs.* [app. f. SNAG *sb.*[3] + *greet* GRIT *sb.*[1]] (See quot. and cf. *snail-cod.*)
**1651** R. CHILD in *Hartlib's Legacy* (1655) 34 Snag greet: which is a kind of earth taken out of the Rivers, full of small shels. [Hence in Worlidge (1669) and some later works.]

**snaggy** ('snægɪ), *a.*[1] [f. SNAG *sb.*[1] + -Y.]
**1.** Having snags or sharp protuberances; jagged, knotty; snag-like.
**1581** STUDLEY *Seneca, Medea* 134 Cause yee the snaggy wheele to pawse that rentes the carkas bound. **1590** SPENSER *F.Q.* I. vii. 10 His stalking steps are stayde Vpon a snaggy Oke. **1621** G. SANDYS *Ovid's Met.* ii. (1632) 62 Envie..a snaggy staffe..tooke Wreathed with thornes. **1888** *Harper's Mag.* Apr. 735 A multitude of blackened snaggy shapes protruding above the water. **1895** JANE BARLOW *Lisconnel* ix. 212 His snaggy stick lay at a little distance.
*fig.* **1857** *Fraser's Mag.* LVI. 358 We do not think that your genuine snaggy fellow belongs to any class in particular.
**2.** Of teeth: Suggestive of snags.
**1703** MOTTEUX *Quix.* (1733) III 210 Her Teeth..seem'd to be thin and snaggy.
**3.** Abounding in, full of, snags.
**1806** W. CLARK in Lewis & Clark *Orig. Jrnls. Lewis & Clark Expedition* (1905) V. 380 The Sand bars..confined the [river] to a narrow Snagey Chanel. **1843** 'R. CARLTON' *New Purchase* ix. 58 To learn the nature of 'mash land'—'rooty and snaggy land' [etc.]. **1864** J. K. HOSMER *Color-Guard* xii, We passed into snaggy lakes at last. **1891** *Pall Mall G.* 22 Oct. 2/1 The river is..a turbulent, snaggy stream to navigate.

**'snaggy,** *a.*[2] *Sc.* and *dial.* [Cf. SNAG *v.*[1]] Ill-tempered, peevish, snappish, cross.
**1781** J. HUTTON *Tour to Caves* (ed. 2) Gloss. 96 *Snaggy*, tetchy, peevish. **1806** A. DOUGLAS *Poems* 130 Quo' Maggy fell snaggy, 'Ye lie, you loun, an' joke'. **1823–** in dial. glossaries (Suffolk, E. Anglia, Lincs.). **1898** B. GREGORY *Side Lights* 405 The stalwart President..had become spasmodic, snatchy, and at times snaggy.

**snag-tooth.** [f. SNAG *sb.*[1] Cf. SNAGGLE-TOOTH.] A snag-like tooth.
**1655** COTGRAVE *Wits Interpr.* (1662) 253 How thy snag-teeth stand orderly, Like stakes which strut by th' water side. **1727** in BAILEY (vol. II.). **1890** *Amer. Anthropologist* Oct. 316 Projecting canines or 'snag teeth' are so common in low faces as to be universally remarked.

**snail** (sneɪl), *sb.*[1] Forms: α. 1 **snegl, snegl, snægl, snægl,** 4–7 **snayl,** 5–7 **snayle** (5 **snaylle**); 3, 5– **snail** (6 **snaill**), 5–7 **snaile,** 6–7 **snale.** β. 1 **snél, snǽl,** 5 **snele, snyle,** 9 *dial.* **sneel.** γ. 4 **snawile.** [OE. *snegl, snægl*, etc., = MLG. *sneil* (LG. *snäl, sniel*, etc.), OHG. *snegil* (MHG. *snegel*, G. *schnägel*, now dial. with variants *schnäl, schnel*, etc.), ON. and Icel. *snigill* (Norw. and Sw. *snigel*, Da. *snegl*).]
**1. a.** One or other of the terrestrial or freshwater gasteropods having a well-developed spiral or whorled shell capable of housing the whole body; also formerly (and still *dial.* and *Sc.*) a slug.
The common types of the true snail belong to the genus *Helix* (esp. *H. aspersa* or *hortensis*, the common garden-snail, and *H. pomatia*, the edible snail) or *Clausilia*, of the family *Helicidæ*.
α. *c* **725** *Corpus Gloss.* C 630 *Cocleae*, lytle sneglas. *c* **1000** *Sax. Leechd.* II. 110 Ʒif nǽddre slea man, þone blacan snegl awærc on haliʒ wætre. *c* **1000** ÆLFRIC *Gloss.* in Wr.-Wülcker 121 *Limax*, snægl. *Testudo*, ʒehused snægl. *a* **1250** *Owl & Night.* 87 Snayles Mus and fule wihte Beoþ þine cunde. **13**.. *Coer de L.* 3836 Anon they..gunne to drawen in her hornes, As a snayl among the thornes. *c* **1400** MAUNDEV. (1839) xv. 169 Thei anoynten here Hondes and here Feet with a juyce made of Snayles. **1412–20** LYDG. *Chron. Troy* II. 3313 Wrinkled double, like an hornyd snail. **1542** BOORDE *Dyetary* viii. (1870) 249 Beware that you do not lye in..such chambres as myse, rattes, and snayles resorteth vnto. **1592** SHAKS. *Ven. & Ad.* 1033 As the snail, whose tender horns being hit, Shrinks backward in his shelly cave. **1633** BP. HALL *Occas. Medit.* §29 See there two snails. One hath a house; the other wants it: yet both are snails. **1683** TRYON *Way to Health* 226 If People were sensible of the hurt they do, they would no more eat them, than they would Frogs, Snales. **1727** GAY *Fables* I. xxiv, A snail, Beneath his house, with slimy trail Crawls o'er the grass. **1774** GOLDSM. *Nat. Hist.* (1824) III. 113 The noise which the snail makes in moving the water. **1813** BINGLEY *Anim. Biog.* (ed. 4) III. 467 The garden snail, hedge snail, and grove snail. **1871** T. R. JONES *Anim. Kingd.* (ed. 4) 566 The common Snails..not unfrequently become formidable pests to the horticulturist, from the ravages caused by their voracity.
β. *c* **825** *Epinal Gloss.* 611 *Limax*, snel. [*c* **1000** ÆLFRIC *Gloss.* in Wr.-Wülcker 122 *Chelio*,..sæsnæl.] *c* **1400** MAUNDEV. (Roxb.) xxi. 96 Þer er in þat land so grete snyles þat in þaire schelles three men or foure may be herberd. *c* **1440** *Alph. Tales* 157 He commandid þat þis vglie burth.. sulde be closid in a stone, as a snyle is in hur shell. **1483** *Cath. Angl.* 346/2 A Snele,..*limax.* **1828–** in dial. glossaries (Yorks., Chesh., Linc., Leic.), in form *sneel.*
γ. *c* **1305** *Land Cokayne* 40 in *E.E.P.* (1862) 157 Þe lond is ful of oþer gode... Þer nis dunnir, slete, no hawle, No non vile worme no snawile.
*transf.* **1579** NORTHBROOKE *Dicing* (1843) 58 They were wont, in olde time, to haue paynted snayles in their houses. **1851** PLANCHÉ *Pursuivant of Arms* (1873) 125 Snails are borne by the family of Shelley.
*fig.* **1590** NASHE *M. Marprelate* Wks. (Grosart) I. 245, I wonder how these seelie snayles, creeping but yesterdaie out of shoppes and Graumer-schooles, dare thrust out theyr feeble hornes. **1596** —— *Saffron Walden* Ep. Ded., It shall neuer put foorth his snayles hornes againe.
**†b.** A tortoise or turtle. *Obs.*
**1387** TREVISA *Higden* (Rolls) II. 377 Whan þis snayl was i-roted, þe senewes were i-streyned with ynne þe skyn of þe snayles hous. **1398** —— *Barth. De P.R.* XVIII. cvii. (Bodl. MS.), Þere beþ foure manere [snails], londe snailles & see stronde snailles & venny snailles..[**1495** and ryuer snayles].
**c.** Applied to various animals allied to, or resembling, the snails or slugs. (Cf. SEA-SNAIL.)
**1541** COPLAND *Guydon's Quest. Chirurg.* N iij, The moste dyfference is of blode lettynge, for it draweth the blode deper than the boxynge or the snayles [= leeches]. **1666** J. DAVIES tr. *Rochefort's Caribby Isles* 78 There is a kind of Snailes, called by the French *Soldats* that is Souldiers, because they have no shells proper and peculiar to themselves. **1731** MEDLEY tr. *Kolben's Cape Good-Hope* II. 209 The Nabel-Snail has an upper and an under Shell, like a Muscle. *Ibid.* 208 The Shell of the Sea-Porcupine Snail is ..arm'd on almost every Part with long Prickles. **1783** JUSTAMOND tr. *Raynal's Hist. Indies* IV. 134 On the coast of Guayaquil..are found those snails which yield the purple dye so celebrated by the antients. **1794** *Reports Agric. Survey* Camb. 111 In the first stage of this disease [*sc.* the blood-rot] the liver has not been infected with the snails, or plaice [= liver-fluke]. **1839** *Penny Cycl.* XIII. 337/1 The *Janthina*, or Oceanic Snail. **1865** MRS. L. L. CLARKE *Common Seaweeds* i. 23 As we gather a bunch of seaweed, we shake out dozens of a pretty little snail called Rissoa. **1884** [see *snail-bore* in sense 7].
**2. a.** Used with reference or allusion to the exceptionally slow motion of the snail.
*a* **1000** *Riddles* XLI. 70 (Gr.), Me is snægl swiftra. **1533** J. HEYWOOD *Mery Play* 421 (Brandl), Go and hye the, as fast as a snayle. **1599** PORTER *Angry Women Abington* (Percy Soc.) 105 A man may bee as slowe as a snaile, but as fierce as a lyon. **1617** MORYSON *Itin.* I. 252, I..went forward like a snaile, till despairing of going further I fell vpon the ground. **1652** COLLINGES *Caveat for Prof.* xiii. (1653) 71 Sure..our Saviour *drave snails* as he went, he reckons so long for his journey! **1778** MISS BURNEY *Evelina* lxxv, During our whole ride, I thought the carriage drawn by snails. **1821** COMBE *Syntax, Search Wife* III. (Chandos) 303 He, by degrees, would seldom fail T' adopt the gallop of a snail. **1862** C. C. ROBINSON *Dial. Leeds* 406 As slaw as a sneel. **1881** FREEMAN in Stephens *Life & Letters* (1895) II. 244 Riding..at the pace of a snail.
**b.** ***snail's gallop, pace***, an excessively slow or tardy pace, rate of progress or motion, etc.
*a* **1400–50** *Alexander* 4095 Þan snyȝes þar, out of þat snyth hill as with a snayles pas, A burly best. **1565** COOPER, *Testudineus gradus*, a slowe pase: a snayles pase. **1707–91** [see GALLOP *sb.* 3 c]. **1793** MME. D'ARBLAY *Lett.* 12 Sept., That snail's pace with which business is done by letters. **1816** *Sporting Mag.* XLVII. 32 Every thing short of eight miles per hour is accounted *snail's pace.* **1842** BORROW *Bible in Spain* xvi, The snail's pace at which we were proceeding. **1901** *Scotsman* 5 Nov. 6/8 For a time they were able to get along at a snail's gallop, men leading the horses with torches and lanterns.
**c.** A slow or indolent person; a sluggard.
**1590** SHAKS. *Com. Err.* II. ii. 196 Dromio, thou Dromio, thou snaile, thou slug. *a* **1593** H. SMITH *Serm.* (1866) II. 83 Every snail shall step before thee, and take thy crown from thee. **1641** BROME *Joviall Crew* IV. i. When he comes, he comes apace; he's no snail, I assure you. **1915** *Dialect Notes* IV. 198 We'll have to wait for Edith. She's such a snail. **1959** I. & P. OPIE *Lore & Lang. Schoolch.* xvii. 366 He [*sc.* a latecomer] is a..Snail.
**†3. a.** A structure or formation resembling a snail-shell; a testudo. *Obs.*
**1408** tr. *Vegetius' De Re Milit.* IV. xiv. (MS. Laud 416), The gynne that is clepid the snaile or þe wilk is a frame made of good tymbyr. *c* **1440** *Promp. Parv.* 66/2 Cercle, clepyd the snayle, as of pentys, and other lyke, *spira.* **1610** W. FOLKINGHAM *Art of Survey* 44 Ground-plots are.. externall, as Groves, Arbours, Bowers, Mounts, Mazes, Snailes.
**†b.** *Mil.* A formation resembling the letter **D**; = LIMAÇON 1. *Obs.*
**1579** NORTH *Plutarch* (1895) III. 57 As for the order of their battelles, they knewe not what it ment, nor to cast them selves into a snaill or ringe. **1581** STYWARD *Mart. Discipl.* I. 67 How to bring them into a Ring, an Snaile, or a Snaile, verie profitable for young Souldiers. **1591** *Garrard's Art Warre* 87 This order of a D. otherwise called a snaile.
**4.** *pl.* A species of medick (usually *Medicago scutellata*) having snail-shaped seed-pods.
**1629** PARKINSON *Parad.* 339 *Medica spinosa altera.* Small thorney Buttons, or Snailes. **1730** MILLER *Gard. Dict.* s.v. *Medica Cochleata*, The Snail-Trefoil, commonly call'd in the Seed-shops *Snails.* **1741** *Compl. Fam. Piece* II. iii. 371 Sow these dwarf annual Flowers.., Snails and Catter-pillars. **1846–50** A. WOOD *Class-bk. Bot.* 229 *M. scutellata* (Snails)... This curious plant derives its name from the singular nature of its fruit, which is twisted like the shell of a snail. **1858** R. HOGG *Veget. Kingdom* 269 Some years ago ..some..were admitted into the annual flower borders under the singular names of Snails, Bee-hives,..and similar names suggested by the fancied resemblance of their pods to these animals. **1866** [see *snail-plant* in 7].
**5.** *Mech.* **a.** A flat, spirally curved piece of metal; *esp.* a toothed disc of this shape forming part of the striking mechanism of a clock; a spiral cam.

**1696** W. DERHAM *Artificial Clockm.* (1759) 7 The Snail, or Step-Wheel in Repeating-Clocks. **1764** *Ann. Reg.* I. 79/1 The quarter and half quarter snail. *Ibid.*, The hour snail and star. **1825** J. NICHOLSON *Operat. Mechanic* 38 The collar.. is formed like a snail or camm, which will act upon either of the levers. **1846** HOLTZAPFFEL *Turning* II. 942 The punch being driven through the plate by one revolution of a snail or cam. **1884** F. J. BRITTEN *Watch & Clockm.* 252 Clockmakers generally mark off the snail on the clock itself after the rest of the striking work is planted.

**b.** (See quot.)

**1834–6** *Encycl. Metrop.* (1845) VIII. 280/1 The German snail is an apparatus of nearly the same kind [as the Archimedes' screw]; it consists of a cylinder with its spiral projections detached from the external cylinder or coating within which it revolves.

**6.** *attrib.* and *Comb.* **a.** In sense 1, as ***snail-broth, -culture, -eater, -feast, -garden, snail-trace, -track***, etc.; ***snail-green, -nacreous, -nosed*** adjs.

**1771** MRS. HAYWOOD *New Present for Maid* 41 *Snail Broth. **1875** *Chambers's Jrnl.* XII. 46 Any one desiring a lesson in *snail-culture, may learn all about it in the Tyrol. **1889** *Science-Gossip* XXV. 281/1, I would suggest that conchologists pay some attention to.. these *snail-eaters. **1875** *Chambers's Jrnl.* XII. 46 The Newcastle glassmakers hold an annual *snail-feast. **1895** A. H. COOKE *Molluscs* iv. 119 *Escargotières*, or *snail-gardens, still exist in many parts of Europe. **1931** V. WOOLF *Waves* 25 Louis regards the wall opposite with *snail-green eyes. **1774** GOLDSM. *Nat. Hist.* (1776) VII. 19 Turbinated Shell-Fish of the *Snail Kind. **1883** *Science* I. 492/1 A small open square used as a *snail-market. **1923** D. H. LAWRENCE *Birds, Beasts & Flowers* 60 Cyclamen leaves.. Spurned with mud *Snail-nacreous Low down. **1960** S. PLATH *Colossus* 10 In their jars the *snail-nosed babies moon and glow. **1887** JEFFERIES *Amaryllis* xxxii, My sister, as was in a decline, used to have *snail-oil rubbed into her back. **1861** HULME tr. *Moquin-Tandon* II. III. ii. 85 A *snail paste which enjoyed a certain amount of repute. **1900** *Daily News* 13 Oct. 6/6 Circular lines of fine black braid following each other in what is called the *snail pattern. **1780** *Encycl. Brit.* (ed. 2) VI. 4572/1 With small yellow flowers, succeeded by small, round, *snail-shaped fruit. **1845** LINDLEY *Sch. Bot.* v. (1858) 56 *Medicago orbicularis* (Snails). Legumes unarmed, snail-shaped, orbicular. **1802** BINGLEY *Anim. Biog.* (1805) III. 580 The Romans.. kept these animals in what were called *Cochlearia*, or *Snail Stews. **1966** J. MERRILL *Nights & Days* 42 The brief *snail-trace Of her withdrawal dries upon our faces. **1930** D. H. LAWRENCE *Nettles* 20 All those nasty police-eyes like *snail-tracks smearing the gentle souls that figure in the paint. **1733** W. ELLIS *Chiltern & Vale Farm.* 355 This Slug is a small whitish Insect.. of the *Snail Tribe. **1896** LYDEKKER *Roy. Nat. Hist.* VI. 345 The Snail Tribe,—Family *Helicidæ*. **1682** G. HARTMAN *True Preserver & Rest. Health* 21 Dr. Harvey his excellent *Snail-water against Consumptions and Hectick Feavers. **1712** tr. *Pomet's Hist. Drugs* I. 206 Mix it with Snail-Water, or Bean-Flower-Water, to make a Virgin's Milk, or Wash of.

**b.** Used attrib. to denote: Exceptionally tardy or slow.

**1562** J. HEYWOOD *Prov. & Epigr.* (1867) 163 So may it run, runnyng but a snayle pace. **1828** CARR *Craven Gloss.*, *Snail-gallop*, a very slow motion, like that of a snail. **1845** E. HOLMES *Mozart* 29 The Court delayed to pay them, and their affairs, in German phrase, travelled 'by the snail post'.

**c.** In senses 3 and 5, as ***snail-cam, -mount, -movement, -piece, -work***.

**1591** in *Gentl. Mag.* (1779) XLIX. 81 The 3. and last was a Snaylmount, rising to four circles of green priuie hedges. **1803** *Trans. Soc. Arts* XXI. 399 The snail-piece to raise a weight somewhat similar. **1825** J. NICHOLSON *Operat. Mechanic* 19 The wedge, placed on the internal face of the circle,.. causing.. the obstacle.. to approach nearer to the centre..; this is called the snail movement. **1835** URE *Philos. Manuf.* 149 This traverse movement is effected by an endless screw and toothed-wheel, or snail-work. **1902** W. J. DIBDIN *Public Lighting* 77 Motion was given to the reflecting screen by a fine chain wound upon a snail cam.

**7.** Special combs.: **snail-bore** *U.S.*, a shell-fish (*Urosalpinx cinerea*) which injures oysters by boring; †**snail clover**, (*a*) lucerne; (*b*) sainfoin; †**snail clover-grass**, sainfoin; †**snail-cod**, a kind of fertile mud or sludge obtained from rivers; hence ***snail-codding*** vbl. sb.; †**snail-crawled** *a.*, crawling as slow as a snail; **snail-creep, -creeping** (see quots.); **snail darter** [cf. DARTER 5], a small fresh-water fish, *Percina tanasi*, belonging to the family Percidæ, and found in certain rivers of the U.S.; **snail-eater** *Ornith.*, = OPENBILL; **snail-fish**, a fish related to the lumpsucker; **snail-flower** (see quots.); **snail-house** *dial.*, a snail-shell; **snail-leech**, a species of leech which eats snails; **snail-plant** (see quot. 1866 and sense 4); **snail sea-cucumber** (see quot.); **snail-seeded** *a.*, having seed-pods resembling snails in form; **snail-stone** (see quots. 1611, 1797); **snail trail** *Needlework* (see quots.); †**snail-trefoil**, (*a*) lucerne; (*b*) snail-plant; **snail-wheel** (see quot. 1846 and sense 5).

**1884** GOODE *Nat. Hist. Aquat. Anim.* 696 These small 'Snails', 'Drills', 'Borers', and '*Snail-bores', as they are variously called. **1597** GERARDE *Herbal* II. ccccclxxxv. 1029 Of Medick fodder, or *Snaile Clauer,.. *Trifolium Cochleatum*..: the flowers are very small, and.. turne into round wrinckled knobs, like the water snaile. **1600** SURFLET *Country Farm* v. xviii. 697 There is not.. any pulse.. more pretious for the feeding of beastes then snaile clauer, called in French *Sainct foin*. **1760** J. LEE *Introd. Bot.* 327 Snail Clover, *Medicago*. **1726** *Dict. Rust.*, *Saintfoin*,.. otherwise call'd.. *Snail or Horned Clover-grass. **1649** BLITHE *Eng. Improver* xix. 112 A Mudde or Sludg, that lyeth frequently in deepe Rivers,.. which is very Rich... They Call it *Snayle-Cod, and it hath in it many Snayles and Shells, which is conceived occasioneth the Fatnesse of it. [Hence in later agricultural works.] *Ibid.* xvii. 100 And in thy Tillage are these special Opportunities to Improve it,.. by Liming, Marling,.. Mudding, *Snayle-codding. *a* **1658** CLEVELAND *To T. C.* 13 Wks. (1687), If thou wilt needs to Sea, O must it be In an old Galliasse of sixty three; A *Snail-crawl'd Bottom? **1592** *Will of Kelleway* (Somerset Ho.), One dozen of *snaile creepe worke. **1887** *Archit. Soc. Dict.* VII. 96/2 *Snail creep.* The common form of pointing granite or limestone uncoursed walls. **1792** *Young's Annals Agric.* XVIII. 41 The ends of the beams [of the *Royal William*].. had been gouged in a manner then [in 1719] practised, which was called *snail-creeping*. **1867** SMYTH *Sailor's Word-bk.* 635 *Snail-Creeping*, gouging out the surfaces of timbers in crooked channels, to promote a circulation of air. **1975** *U.S. Federal Reg.* 17 June 25597/2 The Fish and Wildlife Service has evidence on hand that the *snail darter *Percina (Imostoma)* sp. is an endangered species. **1977** *Time* 11 Apr. 17/2 The Mississippi sand-hill crane and the three-inch snail darter of the Little Tennessee River have already halted state and federal bulldozers. **1981** *Science* 15 May 761/3 Populations of snail darters have been found in three new places... If they turn out to be established populations the fish may no longer be an endangered species... The snail darter may be reclassified as a 'threatened'.. species. **1894** NEWTON *Dict. Birds* 655 Shell-eater, Shell-Ibis, and *Snail-eater. **1840** *Cuvier's Anim. Kingd.* 324 There are one or two British species [of *Leparus* or *Liparis*], some of which are called '*Snail-fishes', from their soft and unctuous texture. **1688** HOLME *Armoury* II. 114/2 *Snail Flower, or rather Snail Seed Vessel, is a kind of Pod, in form like a Snail house. **1866** *Treas. Bot.* 1067/2 Snail-flower, *Phaseolus Caracalla*. **1688** *Snail-house [see *snail-flower*]. **1879** MISS JACKSON *Shropsh. Word-bk.* 393 *Snail-housen*, snail-shells. **1865** *Intellect. Obs.* No. 44. 81 The different species of *snail-leech. **1767** J. ABERCROMBIE *Ev. Man own Gardener* (1803) 735/2 *Snail Plant,.. Caterpillar Plant. **1866** *Treas. Bot.* 1067/2 Snail-plant. *Medicago scutellata*, and also *M. Helix*; the pods of these are called snails from their resemblance to those mollusks. **1858** BAIRD *Cycl. Nat. Sci.*, *Psolus phantapus*, the *snail sea cucumber, is a British species. **1858** MAYNE *Expos. Lex.* 1116/1 *Salsola Kali*,.. the *snail-seeded glasswort, or saltwort. **1611** COTGR., *Pierre de Limaçon*, the *Snaile stone; found in the heads of some (dew) Snailes; tis white, somewhat transparent, and rugged. **1681** GREW *Musæum* III. I. i. 262 Divers others Snail-Stones; some of them of a Limy substance, others perfect Flint. **1700** E. LHWYD in Rowlands *Mona Antiqua* (1723) 338 Besides the Snake-Stones,.. the Highlanders have their Snail-Stones, Paddoc-Stones,.. to all which they attribute their several Virtues. **1797** *Encycl. Brit.* (ed. 3) X. 76/2 It is in its [*sc.* the slug's] head and back that the snail-stone is found; which is a small pearled and sandy stone, of the nature of lime stones. **1899** W. G. P. TOWNSEND *Embroidery* vi. 94 **Snail-trail*,.. the same principle as *single coral*, only worked more on the slope. **1948** C. CHRISTOPHER *Compl. Bk. Embroidery Stitches* iii. 64 Snail Trail, or Knot Stitch, makes a series of simple knots connected with each other on the surface of the fabric. **1973** E. WILSON *Embroidery Bk.* (1975) vi. 322 Snail trail worked very close becomes Broad Rope stitch. When worked with the needle at right angles to the thread, instead of slanting, it becomes Coral. **1548** TURNER *Names Herbes* (E.D.S.) 51 Medica.. maye be called in englishe horned Clauer or *snail Trifoly. **1731** MILLER *Gard. Dict.*, *Medica cochleata*, Snail-Trefoil. **1733** W. ELLIS *Chiltern & Vale Farm.* 279 The Plant commonly called La Lucerne is a Medic Clover, or by some called Snail Trefoyl. **1771** R. F. FORSTER *Flora Amer. Sept.* 32 *Medicago virginica*, Snail Trefoil. **1831** M. EDGEWORTH *Let.* 6 May (1971) 535 Inkstands that shut impervious to ink—insured by the *snail wheel tightener. **1846** HOLTZAPFFEL *Turning* II. 891 The snail-wheel of a striking clock.. has an edge formed in twelve steps, arranged spirally, the positions of which determine the number of strokes of the hammer on the bell.

†**snail,** *sb.*[2] *Obs.* [app. an assimilation of *chenille* to prec., perh. through the dial. form *sneel*. Cf. SNAILING *sb.*] = CHENILLE. Also *attrib.*

**1741** LADY POMFRET *Lett.* (1805) III. 216 The dress of the nuns here is all white, with a black silk snail-string about their necks. **1744** MRS. MONTAGU *Lett.* (1906) I. 194, I have brought down a screen to work in snail for the Duchess. **1773** *Ann. Reg.* 124, I'm compass'd now With worms instead of lovely snails.

†**snail,** *sb.*[3] *Obs.*$^{-1}$ (See quot. and SNOUTING[2].)

**1662** *Irish Statutes* (1678) 628 Snouting, alias snayl, or drest towe, the twelve pound, o. 5s. o.

**snail** (sneɪl), *v.* Also 6 **snayle**, 6–7 **snaill**, 7 **snaile**. [f. SNAIL *sb.*[1]]

†**1.** *intr.* Of soldiers: To form into a 'snail' or 'snails'. *Obs.*$^{-1}$

*a* **1548** HALL *Chron., Hen. VIII*, 235 b, All the gonnes seuered themselues into one place,.. and likewise the byllmen, and there rynged and snayled, which was a goodly sight to beholde.

**2. a.** To move, walk, or travel lazily or sluggishly; to go very slowly. Also with *on*.

**1582** STANYHURST *Æneis* IV. (Arb.) 118 Shee trots on snayling, lyk a tooth shaken old hagge. **1748** RICHARDSON *Clarissa* (1811) IV. 124 Draw in your horns, and resolve to snail-on.. in a track we are acquainted with. **1813** SIR R. WILSON *Priv. Diary* (1861) II. 238 The Crown Prince is *snailing* towards the Elbe. **1903** A. ADAMS *Log Cowboy* xviii. 275 The herd was snailing along the North Platte. *Ibid.* xxiii. 365 We snailed on westward at our leisurely gait.

**b.** With *it*.

**1628** FELTHAM *Resolves* I. xciv, You shall finde, that every thing, as farre as the Abilitie will give it Line, does Snaile it after Deitie. *Ibid.* II. xliv, When the grave Vespasian came to snail it, and be leaver'd in the throngs slow march. **1893** W. C. A. BLEW *Brighton* 48 From Clayton Hill the coach *snailed it on* towards Cuckfield.

**c.** To make (one's way) very slowly.

**1936** M. FRANKLIN *All that Swagger* v. 56 Two bullock drays were snailing their way from the Port.

**3. a.** *trans.* To make or construct after the spiral form of a snail-shell. Now *spec.* in clockmaking.

**1591** SYLVESTER *Du Bartas* I. vi. 637 God plac't the Ears.. As in two turrets, on the building's top, Snailing their hollow entries so a-sloap [etc.]. **1885** GLASGOW *Watch & Clock Making* vi. 73 The arbor should be snailed, so that when the spring is wound on to it, it will take a spiral form.

**b.** To finish off with curved eccentric lines.

**1884** F. J. BRITTEN *Watch & Clockm.* 242 Fusee caps, steel keyless watches, &c., are snailed with a copper mill.

**4.** To clear of, keep free from, slugs or snails.

*a* **1661** FULLER *Worthies, Glouc.* I. (1662) 349 Many got great [tobacco] estates thereby, notwithstanding the great.. cost in.. watering, snailing, suckering,.. and rowling it.

Hence '**snailing** *vbl. sb.* (see 3 b).

**1884** F. J. BRITTEN *Watch & Clockm.* 242 Snailing requires a sharp polishing material. **1891** TRIPPLIN & RIGG *Watch-maker's Hdbk.* (ed. 3) 119 A beautiful snailing can be obtained with Arkansas stone mud.

*attrib.* **1884** F. J. BRITTEN *Watch & Clockm.* 242 The snailing mill is fixed in nearly the right position. **1885** GLASGOW *Watch & Clock Making* ix. 119 The snailing roller [is] held in the fingers and prevented from turning.

**snailery** ('sneɪlərɪ). Also 9 **snaillery**. [f. SNAIL *sb.*[1] + -ERY.] A place where (edible) snails are bred or reared.

**1725** in *Archit. Soc. Dict.* (1887) VII. 96/2 [That] a snailery and a place for breeding tortices be made at Kensington for his majesty's service. **1834** W. H. SMYTH *Roman Medals* 210 The luxury and profusion of Roman gastrology were attested by.. their lepories, their lobsteries, and their snaileries. **1874** WOOD *Nat. Hist.* III. 406 There are.. on the Continent several snaileries, where the inmates are abundantly supplied with food.

**snail-horn.** Now *dial.* [SNAIL *sb.*[1]]

**1.** A snail-shell; a snail.

**1672** C. HOOLE tr. *Comenius Vis. World* xxxii, The Snail carrieth about her Snailhorn [*testa*]. **1747** [see b]. **1820** CLARE *Rural Life* (ed. 3) 10 The snail-horn searching, or the mossy nest. **1828–** in dial. glossaries (Yks., Northampt., Leic., Lancs.).

**b.** ***snail-horn stone*** (see quot.).

**1747** HOOSON *Miner's Dict.* Ujb, Snailhorn Stone is a course Stone, having mixt Knotts within it, much like Snail-horns when it is broken, and hard to break.

**2.** (See quot. and next.) ? *Obs.*

**1749** W. ELLIS *Exper. Impr. Sheep* 94 If.. a lamb is gelt at a week or fortnight old, it will cause it to have a thin, short, and what we in Hertfordshire call a Snail-Horn.

So '**snail-horned** *a.* (See quot.) ? *Obs.*

**1787** W. H. MARSHALL *E. Norfolk* (1795) II. 388 *Snail-horned*, having short, down-hanging horns, with blunt points, and somewhat bent, in the usual form of the snail; spoken of cattle.

†**snailing,** *sb. Obs.*$^{-1}$ ? = SNAIL *sb.*[2]

**1688** HOLME *Armoury* III. xiv. (Roxb.) 16/1 The lower Valens.. fringed for state.. either with.. Tufted fring, snailing fring, Gimpe fring.

**snailing,** *ppl. a. rare.* [f. SNAIL *sb.*[1] or *v.*]

Winding spirally, or like the tracks of snails.

**1615** CROOKE *Body of Man* 94 Wherein the snaking and snayling diuarications of the vessels do craule all ouer the belly. *Ibid.* 456 Some of these snailing paths are deeper.

**snailish** ('sneɪlɪʃ), *a.* [f. SNAIL *sb.*[1] + -ISH.]

Somewhat resembling (that of) the snail; slothful, slow, sluggish.

**1581** NUCE tr. *Seneca, Octavia* I. iii, And snaylish age in going soft Unto her thews is not ybounde. **1623** WODROEPHE *Marrow Fr. Tongue* 245/2 O, what snailish heart hast thou! *cœur de limaçon*. **1889** C. EDWARDES *Sardinia* 130 The snailish movements of the dance.

Hence '**snailishly** *adv.*; '**snailishness.**

**1889** *Punch* 1 June 257/2 Your progress may also be snailishly slow. **1905** M. BEERBOHM in *Sat. Rev.* 24 June 835/1 Usually, this pace in elocution does not madden me. But.. I am moved to cry out against this idiotic tradition of snailishness.

**snail-like,** *a.* and *adv.* [f. SNAIL *sb.*[1] + -LIKE.]

**A.** *adj.* **1.** Like or resembling a snail in appearance, habits, etc.

**1607** J. DAVIES (Heref.) *Summa Totalis* Wks. (Grosart) I. 7/1 And though it be.. steepe,.. Yet (Snaile-like) cling to it, and climbing creep, But fall not off it. **1611** COTGR., *Limaceux*,.. Snaile-like. **1665** BRATHWAIT *Comment. Two Tales* (1901) 45 Must I Snayl-like, keep still under roof. **1774** GOLDSM. *Nat. Hist.* (1824) III. 82 Those snail-like animals that receive the name of testaceous fishes. **1881** GRANT ALLEN *Evolutionist at Large* 57 The truest and most snail-like snails. **1901** E. STEP *Shell Life* xix. 347 The snail-like slugs are succeeded by the genus *Helix*.

**2.** Characterized by slowness of progress, etc.; slow, tardy.

**1639** FULLER *Holy War* III. v. (1840) 122 The snail-like siege of Ptolemais, still slowly creeping on. **1831** *Lincoln Herald* 29 July 1/6 The snail-like progress of the English Reform Bill.

**B.** *adv.* With the slow motion characteristic of a snail; tardily, sluggishly.

**1825** SCOTT *Talisman* xxi, The marabout.. glided on gradually and imperceptibly, serpent-like, or rather snail-like. **1898** J. ARCH *Story Life* vii. 162 They would crawl snail-like, to the feet of the squire.

**snail-paced,** *a.* [SNAIL *sb.*[1]]

**1.** Slow, sluggish, or tardy in pace, progress, or motion; slothful, slow-moving. Also *fig.*

**1594** SHAKS. *Rich. III*, IV. iii. 53 Delay leds impotent and Snaile-pac'd Beggery. **1606** —— *Tr. & Cr.* v. v. 18 Goe.. bid the snaile-pac'd Aiax arme for shame. **1646** W. JENKYN

*Remora* 9 Doth that winged speed..deserve a snail-paced Reformation? **1770** ARMSTRONG *Misc.* I. 154 Thus they lash on The snail-pac'd Hyperborean nights. **1862** CHRISTINA ROSSETTI *Goblin Market*, etc. 6 The whisk-tailed merchant bade her taste In tones as smooth as honey,..and the snail-paced even was heard. **1874** J. ROBERTSON in Gordon *Life* xv. (1908) 117 We left here..with a snail-paced horse.

**2.** Marked or characterized by tardiness, slowness, or sluggishness.

**1601** CHESTER *Love's Martyr*, etc. (1878) 123 Snaile-paced gait. **1818** KEATS *Endym.* IV. 25 In very scorn Of our dull, uninspired, snail-paced lives.

†**'Snails,** *int. Obs.* Also 7 **snailes, snayles, 'snayles.** An abbreviation of *God's nails* (see GOD *sb.* 14a), used as a petty oath or exclamation.

**1599** HAYWARD *Hen. IV*, I. 19 Sir Hugh swore, swownes, and snayles, let vs set vpon them. **1605** *London Prodigal* V. i. 222 Snailes, is there such cowardice in that? **1617** MIDDLETON & ROWLEY *Fair Quarrel* V. i, Snailes shees the Phisicians Bronstrops, Trim. [**1821** SCOTT *Kenilw.* xxiv, Nay, 'snails! I think his horse will take the matter in his own hand. **1828** —— *F.M. Perth* xii, 'Snails!..were any neighbour to meet me.., what could they think?]

**snail-shell.** [SNAIL *sb.*[1]]

**1.** The shell or house of a snail; = COCHLEA 3.

**1530** PALSGR. 272/1 Snayle or snayle shell, *lymacon.* **1578** T. N. tr. *Conq. W. India* 311 They entred..with the sound of drummes, snaile-shelles and other instrumentes of Musicke. **1611** COTGR., *Limace*,..any thing that winds or turnes like a Snaile-shell. **1676** *Phil. Trans.* XI. 594 Turn'd helically like a Snail-shell. **1713** PETIVER *Aquat. Anim. Amboinæ* Tab. iv, *Valvata*,..Small waved Snail-shell. **1775** ASH, *Cochlea*,..a genus of shell fish, a snail-shell. **1822** J. PARKINSON *Outl. Oryctol.* 248 The exterior characters of the snail-shells of the present day. **1891** *Science-Gossip* XXVII. 18/1 The lower step..bore witness to the frequent visits of the thrushes, for it was covered with broken snail-shells.

**b.** *attrib.*, as ***snail-shell pattern***; **snail-shell medick,** (*a*) heart-clover; (*b*) snail plant.

**1796** WITHERING *Brit. Plants* (ed. 3) III. 660 *Medicago arabica*,..Snailshell Medick. **1855** MISS PRATT *Flower. Pl.* II. 92 The Snail-shell Medick of the South of Europe (*Medicago scutellata*). **1898** *Daily News* 17 Sept. 6/2 Richly braided in a snail-shell pattern.

†**2.** = COCHLEA 2. *Obs.*[−1]

**1683** *Phil. Trans.* XIII. 261 The Small-bones,..the Snail-shell,..have the same figure and..bulk in Infants which they have in men.

**snail-slow,** *a.* (and *adv.*) [SNAIL *sb.*[1]]

**1.** That is as slow as a snail; very sluggish or tardy in motion, progress, etc. Hence as *adv.*

**1596** SHAKS. *Merch. V.* II. v. 47 The patch is..a huge feeder: Snaile-slow in profit. **1803** *Pic Nic* No. 1 (1806) I. 13 France is..cold and snail-slow in redress or justice. **1812** TENNANT *Anster F.* III. viii, The son, impatient, leaves his snail-slow sire. **1901** E. PHILLPOTTS *Striking Hours* 114 Off goes Squire snail-slow. **1951** W. DE LA MARE *Winged Chariot* 44 Snail-slow moves *everything* for which we wait. **1974** V. CANNING *Painted Tent* x. 203 The time of waiting..had passed snail-slow for Smiler.

**2.** Marked by excessive slowness of progress.

**1900** *Daily News* 12 July 6/2 The era of military reform, which may be said to have begun its snail-slow course in 1870.

**snaily** ('sneɪlɪ), *a.* (and *sb.*) Also 6–7 **snailie,** 7 **snayly,** 9 **snailey.** [f. SNAIL *sb.*[1]]

**1.** Like a snail; resembling that of a snail; snail-like. Also *fig.*

**1596** *Edw. III*, I. i, But I will make you shrinke your snailie hornes. **1611** COTGR., *Limaceux*, Snailie, Snaile-like. **1627** DRAYTON *Agincourt*, etc. 187 These Dialls.., Whose Snayly motion of the moouing hand, (Although it goe) yet seeme to me to stand. **1928** D. H. LAWRENCE *Let.* 17 Mar. (1932) 710 We *must* put salt on the hypocritical and snaily tails, the good public. **1979** *Sci. Amer.* Mar. 27/2 Periwinkles, snaily bivalves and the plants and animals (such as barnacles and algae) that live on other organisms each get a detailed chapter.

**2.** Infested by snails; covered with the slime of snails.

**1870** FURNIVALL in *Boorde's Dyetary* (1870) 249 *marg.*, Don't lie in ratty and snaily rooms. **1882** BLACKMORE *Christowell* xii, The rooks began to caw,..the young lady, reading in a snaily chair, to gaze about.

**3.** *Austr.* **a.** Slightly curled after the manner of a snail-shell; having horns of this description. (Cf. SNAIL-HORN 2.)

**1884** 'R. BOLDREWOOD' *Melb. Mem.* xvii. 123 That black bullock,..him with the snaily horn. **1891** —— *Sydney-side Saxon* viii. 133 There's a snailey Wallanbah bullock I haven't seen this two years.

**b.** As *sb.* A kind of bullock characterized by having such horns.

**1884** 'R. BOLDREWOOD' *Melb. Mem.* ix. 68 Snaileys and poleys, old and young, coarse and fine, they were a mixed herd in every sense.

†**snaip,** *a. Obs.*[−1] (Prob. an error for SNARP *a.*)

*a* **1300** *Cursor M.* 7753 (Cott.), Ful snaip [*v. rr.* snaipe, sharp, scharp] it was þair stur and snell.

**snaip, snair:** see SNAPE, SNARE.

**snake** (sneɪk), *sb.* Forms: 1 **snaca,** 2– **snake,** 6 **snayke, snack.** [OE. *snaca*, = MLG. *snake* (LG. *snake, snaak*): cf. ON. *snákr* (poet.), Sw. *snok*, Da. *snog*, which may be from LG.]

**I. 1. a.** One or other of the limbless vertebrates constituting the reptilian order *Ophidia* (characterized by a greatly elongated body, tapering tail, and smooth scaly integument), some species of which are noted for their venomous properties; an ophidian, a serpent. Also, in popular use, applied to some species of *Lacerta*, and to certain snake-like amphibians.

The various species are freq. distinguished by a prefix denoting colour or marking, habitat, or other characteristic feature, as *black-, carpet-, coach-whip-, coral-, corn-, diamond-, grass-, hooded, rattle-, ribbon-, ringed, tiger-, whip-snake*, etc. (see these words).

*c* **1000** *Ags. Gosp.* Luke x. 19 Ic sealde eow anweald to tredenne ofer næddran & snacan. *a* **1023** WULFSTAN *Hom.* (1883) 192 Sy Dan snaca on weȝe and næddre on pæðe. **1154** *O.E. Chron.* (Laud MS.) an. 1137, Hi dyden heom in quarterne þar nadres & snakes & pades wæron inne. *a* **1200** *Moral Ode* 273 þeor beð naddren and snaken, eueten and frude. *c* **1250** *Gen. & Ex.* 2805 It warp vt of hise hond, And wurð sone an uglike snake. **13..** *K. Alis.* 5972 For hij libben by addren, and snaken. *a* **1340** HAMPOLE *Psalter* xiii. 5 Tricherously þai wroght venome of snakis vndire þe lippes of þa. **1412–20** LYDG. *Chron. Troy* I. 3347 Whos vertu is al venym to distroye,..Of dragoun, serpent, adder & of snake. **1486** *Bk. St. Albans* C ij, Ther be in woddys..wormys calde edders..and also ther be snakys of the same kynde. **1559** W. CUNNINGHAM *Cosmogr. Glasse* 173 Edder, Snack, swift, or such like. **1570** LEVINS *Manip.* 198/16 A Snayke, *anguis.* **1591** SYLVESTER *Du Bartas* I. vi. 202 Th' Esft, Snake, and Dipsas (causing deadly Thirst). **1606** SHAKS. *Ant. & Cl.* II. v. 42 Thou shouldst come like a Furie crown'd with Snakes. **1661** J. CHILDREY *Brit. Bacon.* 73 No Snakes or Adders are to be found about Badminton. **1774** GOLDSM. *Nat. Hist.* (1824) III. 167 That horrible *fætor*, which even the commonest and the most harmless snakes are still found to diffuse. **1817** SHELLEY *Rev. Islam* I. xiii. 236 Then..would the Snake Relax his suffocating grasp. **1847** L. LEICHHARDT *Overland Exped.* i. 16 A carpet snake and a brown snake with yellow belly. **1873** DAWSON *Earth & Man* ix. 217 A peculiarity, seen in some snakes, namely a joint in the middle of the jaw enabling its sides to expand.

*transf.* and *fig.* **1821** SHELLEY *Adonais* xxii, Swift as a Thought by the snake Memory stung. **1847** TENNYSON *Princ.* III. 27 At these words the snake, My secret, seem'd to stir within my breast. **1879** FARRAR *St. Paul* (1883) 753 The Apostle first tramples on the snake of any mere personal annoyance. **1885** *Times* (weekly ed.) 18 Sept. 14/3 There must be snakes of some sort in each earthly Eden.

**b.** A representation, image, or figure of a snake.

**1579–80** in Nichols *Progr. Q. Eliz.* II. 290 An armering of golde,..being a snake with a mean white saphire on the hedd. **1688** [see sense 5]. **1818** R. P. KNIGHT *Symb. Lang.* (1876) 15 The winged disk of the sun is placed between two hooded snakes (or asps). **1859** TENNYSON *Merlin & V.* 737 She hung her head, The snake of gold slid from her hair. **1903** J. E. HARRISON *Study Grk. Relig.* vii. 331 The snakes sculptured on the top round the hollow cup.

**c.** In *pl.* as an exclamation, esp. ***great snakes!***

**1839** *Spirit of Times* 17 Aug. 283/3 Snakes! such a row! **1888** 'R. BOLDREWOOD' *Robbery under Arms* II. xi. 190 So the muchacha went back on yer—snakes alive! I kinder expected it. **1891** *Scribner's Mag.* Sept. 293/1 Why in snakes should anybody want to be a sculptor, if you come to that? **1897** F. T. BULLEN *Cruise 'Cachalot'* i. (1901) 4 Great snakes! why, here's a sailor man for sure. **1922** E. RAYMOND *Tell England* ix. 122, I thought we'd be last for the Swimming Cup. But snakes alive! we'll get in the semi-final. **1927** G. D. H. & M. COLE *Murder at Crome House* xxii. 271 But, snakes, Flint—this is Exeter! **1930** G. B. SHAW *Apple Cart* I. 15 Holy snakes! look at Bill.

**2.** In figurative or allusive uses:

**a.** With reference to the ingratitude or treachery displayed by the snake in Æsop's fable (I. x).

**1593** SHAKS. *2 Hen. VI*, III. i. 343, I feare me, you but warme the starued Snake, Who, cherisht in your breasts, will sting your hearts. **1671** MILTON *Samson* 763 Drawn to wear out miserable days, Entangl'd with a poysnous bosom snake. **1688** SIR S. MORLAND in *Pepys' Diary & Corr.* (1879) VI. 160 To assure me that I was taking a snake into my bosom. **1865** KINGSLEY *Herew.* I. ix. 214 The wild Viking would have crushed the growing snake in his bosom.

**b.** Used to denote some lurking danger, suspicious circumstance or person, etc.; esp. in the phr. ***a snake in the grass*** (after Virgil *Ecl.* III. 93 *Latet anguis in herba*).

**1611** W. BARKSTED *Hiren* (1876) 109 O could this diuell my soule so transforme That I must eate that snake in him did lurke. **1659** HASLERIG in *Burton's Diary* (1828) IV. 337 Consider what a snake lies under this fair Declaration. **1677** YARRANTON *Eng. Impr.* 101 Hold, hold, you drive too fast; there is a snake in the Bush. **1696** [C. LESLIE] (*title*), The Snake in the Grass. **1709** HEARNE *Collect.* (O.H.S.) II. 173 There is a Snake in the grasse, and the designe is mischievous. **1881** EVANS *Leic. Gloss.*, *Sneck-i'-the-gress*, a sneak; a traitor; a treacherous deceiver. **1907** E. GOSSE *Father & Son* xi. 281 He did not scruple to remind the Deity of various objections to a life of pleasure and of the snakes that lie hidden in the grass of evening parties. **1978** J. IRVING *World according to Garp* xiv. 271 We were playing in Dallas, when that snake in the grass..came up on my blind side.

†**c.** *to eat* (or *feed on*) *snakes*, as a means of renewing one's youth or vigour. *Obs.*

**1603** DEKKER *Honest Wh.* Wks. 1873 II. 103, I eate Snakes, my Lord, I eate Snakes. My heart shall neuer haue a wrinkle in it. *a* **1625** FLETCHER *Elder Brother* IV. iv, That you have eat a Snake, and are grown young, game-some, and rampant. *a* **1640** MASSINGER, etc. *Old Law* V. i, He hath left off o' late to feed on snakes; His beard's turn'd white again.

**d.** *to wake snakes*, (*a*) (see quot. 1872); (*b*) to rouse oneself, to look lively; (*c*) see WAKE *v.* 8 c.; ***to have snakes in one's boots, to see snakes***, to have delirium tremens. *U.S. slang.*

**1835** A. B. LONGSTREET *Georgia Scenes* 6 Oh, wake snakes, and walk your chalks! *c* **1859** in Bartlett *Dict. Amer.* (1860) 498 Well, here I be; wake snakes, the day's a-breaking. **1872** DE VERE *Americanisms* 212 The other meaning..makes *waking snakes* equivalent to 'running away quickly'. **1877** J. HABBERTON *Barton Exper.* ix, He's been pretty high on whisky for two or three days,..and they say he's got snakes in his boots now.

**e.** ***snakes in Iceland***: used allusively (see quot. 1758) of something posited only to be dismissed as non-existent.

[**1758** tr. *N. Horrebow's Natural Hist. Iceland* lxxii. 91 No snakes of any kind are to be met with throughout the whole island.] **1791** BOSWELL *Life of Johnson* II. 220 Johnson had said that he could repeat a complete chapter of 'The Natural History of Iceland', from the Danish of *Horrebow*, the whole of which was exactly thus:—'Chap. lxxii. *Concerning Snakes.* There are no snakes to be met with throughout the whole island'. **1906** *Spectator* 5 May 716/1 'The Value of a Public School Education' reminds one of the chapter on the snakes in Iceland... 'So far as the school at large is concerned every Greek and Latin book should be destroyed.' **1978** C. SYKES in R. Buckle *U & Non-U Revisited* 60 And what about hats? Of them it may be said as was said of snakes in *The Natural History of Iceland.*

**f.** ***lower than a snake's belly***: despicable, very low indeed. *Austral. slang.*

**1932** L. MANN *Flesh in Armour* 191 'It was a dirty trick. He knew about me and her.' 'Dirty! Lower than a snake's belly.' **1951** D. CUSACK *Say no to Death* 20 He'd only have to take one look at Jan to be convinced in his honest old heart that his son was lower than a snake's belly. **1965** J. BEEDE *They hosed them Out* 175, I thought, 'if I have to crawl to this illegitimate I'll get lower than a snake's belly.'

**3. a.** Applied to persons, esp. with contemptuous or opprobrious force; in early use freq. ***poor snake***, a poor, needy, or humble person; a drudge.

(*a*) **1590** GREENE *Mourning Garment* Wks. (Grosart) IX. 193 The Gentleman..seeing such a poore snake to hinder his attempt, thought to checke him with a frowne. **1597** TOFTE *Laura* (1880) p. xliii, Then Cupid worke that I (poore Snake in loue) This sdainfull Snake for to be kinde may moue. **1616** R. C. *Times Whistle* (1871) 71 A poore snake, whose best of meanes Is but to live on that he dayly gleanes. **1665** BRATHWAIT *Comment. Two Tales* (1900) 42 These poor Snakes of hers were far from challenging any property in either. **1821** SCOTT *Kenilw.* ix, This Doctor Doboobie had a servant, a poor snake, whom he employed in trimming his furnace,..compounding his drugs [etc.].

(*b*) **1600** SHAKS. *A.Y.L.* IV. iii. 71, I see Loue hath made thee a tame snake. **1643** BAKER *Chron., Hen. III*, 112 The Dragon once appeased or destroyed, these lesser Snakes will soone be trodden downe. **1833** M. SCOTT *Tom Cringle* vii, Don't provoke me to try, you yellow snake, you! **1897** GUNTER *Susan Turnbull* xvi. 193 Do you remember a little toadying snake who used to be at school with us?

**b.** *U.S.* and *Austral. slang.* (See quots.) Cf. *snake charmer*, sense 12 a below.

**1929** *Bookman* (U.S.) July 526/1 A Snake has many jobs. If he's a Hump-brakey he handles the cars rolled onto a series of tracks placed on a slight incline. The engine shoves them 'over the hump' and it is his job to handle the brakes. **1934** *Amer. Speech* IX. 73/2 *Snake*, switchman. His work requires him to crawl around and over cars, and he has a reputation for never hurrying. **1945** BAKER *Austral. Lang.* xiv. 249 There are terms like..*snake-charmers, snakes* or *lizards*, railway platelayers.

**c.** *Austral. Mil. slang.* (See quot. 1945.)

**1945** BAKER *Austral. Lang.* viii. 160 *Snakes*, a sergeant. **1948** [see SNAKE-PIT 2]. **1951** E. LAMBERT *Twenty Thousand Thieves* 314 Baxter reckoned the officers and snakes are pinching our beer.

**4.** Applied to various things resembling a snake in some respect.

†**a.** A long curl or tail attached to a wig. *Obs.* **b.** The long flexible tube of a hookah. **c.** A kind of firework burning with a snake-like movement or having a snaky form. **d.** In various technical uses. **e.** In miscellaneous transf. senses.

**a. 1676** DRYDEN *Ep. Etheredge's Man of Mode* 24 His Sword-knot this, his Crevat this design'd; And this the yard long Snake he twirls behind. **1728** SWIFT *On Five Ladies at Sot's Hole* 34 Misc. 1735 V. 456 We who wear our Wigs With Fan-Tail and with Snake.

**b. 1865** *Reader* No. 123. 508/2 The tube, or 'snake', as it is conventionally called, of a hookah. **1875** in W. Hamilton *Poems Tobacco* (1889) 121 Here's to the hookah with snake of five feet.

**c. 1891** *Chambers's Encycl.* VIII. 509/1 When the lower portion [of the rocket] is burned, the upper..takes fire and sets off its garniture of stars, snakes, and other ornaments.

**d. 1947** *Britannica Bk. of Year* 841/1 *Snake*, nickname of a device used during an advance to destroy wires and detonate mines. **1957** *Daily Progress* (Charlottesville, Va.) 8 Jan. 5/3 A plumber's 'snake' has succeeded where a mixed pack of rats and mongooses failed. *Ibid.*, The snakes are thin flexible cables used to clean or carry wires inside pipes. **1961** W. VAUGHAN-THOMAS *Anzio* ix. 207 The Snake was a 300-foot tube of steel packed with TNT up to about fifty feet from the tank, which first towed the tube into battle and then swung around and pushed it out over a minefield. The crew..exploded the TNT by fire from their machine-guns. **1964** 'E. MCBAIN' *Ax* v. 88 The plumber's snake had caught on one of the cross supports... Hawes reached up and shoved at the snake, coiling it back into the drawer.

**e. 1891** HAGGARD *Nada* xviii, Chaka watched the long black snake of men winding..across the plain. **1894** MRS. DYAN *Man's Keeping* iv. (1899) 40 The floor was strewn with scraps of torn lace, curling snakes of ribbon. **1896** MRS. F. A. STEEL *Face Waters* III. iv, That snake of fire flashing to the powder magazine.

**f.** *Econ.* A narrow range of fluctuation in rates of exchange, agreed to by certain member countries of the EEC (see quot. 1973). Hence ***snake in the tunnel***: this range in relation to a wider range of fluctuation agreed in the foreign exchange markets.

**1972** *Economist* 11 Mar. 87/1 Europe's currencies will try to be held inside the celebrated 'snake' wriggling within the overall 4.5 per cent dollar 'tunnel'. **1972** *Accountant* 12 Oct. 451/2 It would take over the day-to-day running of the so-called 'snake in the tunnel' system of exchange rate margins which Britain opted out of when the £ was floated on June 23rd. **1973** *Business Week* 10 Mar. 37/3 In March 1972, the six charter members of the EEC and the three nations then awaiting membership agreed to keep their currencies trading within a narrower band against one another than they do in trading against the dollar. When set down on graph paper, the snake is the narrow EEC band and the tunnel the wider dollar band. *Ibid.*, A year-old technique that is dubbed, whimsically enough, the 'snake in the tunnel'. **1975** *Sunday Tel.* 11 May 24/4 There may be an agreement on the amount the pound should be devalued.. followed by a return to the European currency arrangement (the 'snake in the tunnel'). **1976** *Times* 14 Aug. 15/1 Finance ministers from the 'snake countries' (Belgium, Denmark, Germany, Luxembourg, The Netherlands, Norway and Sweden). **1979** *Dædalus* Winter 63 But the idea offers an opportunity.. of avoiding the pitfalls of previous efforts that had aimed prematurely at stabilizing exchange rates in a European 'snake'. **1980** T. Barling *Goodbye Piccadilly* viii. 155 An illuminated wallchart showed the present float of the European Money Snake.

†**5.** Some dicing game. *Obs.*$^{-0}$

**1688** Holme *Armoury* III. xvi. (Roxb.) 68/1 A snake board vert; there on a snake depicted, with houses, birds and the like fixed on his back all proper... This is a bord whereon is playd the game of Snake.

**6.** A kind of man-trap used in Ireland. ? *Obs.*

**1835–** in *Eng. Dial. Dict.* **1867** *Chronicle* 13 July 38/1 The 'snakes' in question are iron barbs, theoretically maintained as a terror to trespassers, but hardly existing in fact.

**7.** A species of mediæval war-vessel.

Used as a rendering of OE. *snacc* SNACK *sb.*[1] or ON. *snekkja*.

**1864** Dasent *Jest & Earnest* (1873) I. 275 He was left with only twelve snakes or war-galleys. **1880** Dawkins *Early Man* 396 These boats are to be looked upon as the precursors of the long ships, snakes, and sea-dragons.

**8.** With capital initial. Applied to American Indians of various Shoshone groups, esp. those of Oregon. Freq. *attrib.*, esp. as ***Snake Indian***.

**1791** in *Mass. Hist. Soc. Coll.* (1794) III. 24 The tribes of Indians.. were called.. the Blackfeet tribe, the Snake Indians[, etc.]. **1805** P. Gass *Jrnl.* 22 Oct. (1807) xiv. 154 This.. is the same river whose head waters we saw at the Snake nation. **1821** J. Fowler *Jrnl.* 24 Nov. (1898) 55 Last night on Counting them over find now four Hundred of the following nations—Ietans—Arrapohoes—Kiawa Padduce—Cheans—Snakes. **1831** *Niles' Weekly Reg.* IV. 265/2 They happily fell in with a small party of Snake Indians. **1843** T. Talbot *Jrnl.* 7 Sept. (1931) 45 The trappers prefer Snake Indians and Snake horses before any race of men or horses in the world. **1890** N. P. Langford *Vigilante Days* xiii. 161 [With] a band of Snakes.., we can run off two thousand of the best of those animals. **1920** S. M. Drumm in J. C. Luttig *Jrnl. Expedition Upper Missouri* 166 Snake Indians. This tribe was so generally known by this term as to almost obscure the family name of Shoshoni. **1938** M. Thompson *High Trails Glacier Nat. Park* 53 The Snake warriors got ready for an attack as soon as the moon should come up. **1940** *Places to see in Wyoming* p. xxiv/2 Shoshones were also referred to as Snakes or the Snake People. **1977** [see Paiute *sb.* a].

**II.** *attrib.* and *Comb.* **9. a.** Simple attrib., as ***snake-bite***, ***-broth***, ***family***, ***-poison***, ***-skin***, etc.

**1839** *Penny Cycl.* XIII. 161/1 It is also one of their remedies for *snake-bites, but is no doubt inefficacious. *c* **1880** *Cassell's Nat. Hist.* IV. 323 The population being dense, it is reasonable to expect that great mortality would occur from Snake bites every year. **1894** A. Robertson *Nuggets*, etc. 73 She knows as much about snake-bite as any doctor. **1747** tr. *Astruc's Fevers* 81 Viper or *snake-broth is also powerfully deobstruent. **1885** Hornaday *2 Yrs. Jungle* xxxii. 388 The Dyak proceeded to roast the serpent,.. preparatory to making a *snake curry. *c* **1880** *Cassell's Nat. Hist.* IV. 301 All the species of the *Snake family.. have minute vestiges of hind limbs. **1934** *Discovery* July 207/2 The Pasteur Institute in India, the Snake Institute at Port Elizabeth, South Africa, and the Butantan '*Snake-farm' near São Paulo, Brazil, are the headquarters of snake research and cure. **1979** *United States 1980/81* (Penguin Travel Guides) 34 Traveling by car you can be flexible—making any number of stops at souvenir shops or snake farms. **1774** Goldsm. *Nat. Hist.* (1776) VII. 178 A single meal, with many of the *snake kind, seems to be the adventure of a season. **1976** H. Kemelman *Wednesday Rabbi got Wet* xxxix. 226 As alien and outlandish as snails or *snakemeat or fried termites. **1883** *Science* I. 260/2 It acted like *snake-poison, especially on birds. **1897** *Allbutt's Syst. Med.* II. 810 Snake-poison is a clear limpid fluid of a pale straw to yellow colour. **1874** (*title*), Report on the Effects of Artificial Respiration.. in Indian and Australian *Snake-Poisoning. **1965** R. & D. Morris *Men & Snakes* v. 106 Normally death by snake-poisoning is a prolonged and unpleasant business. **1825** Scott *Talism.* xx, A straight broadsword, with a handle of box-wood, and a sheath covered with *snake-skin. **1897** Mary Kingsley *W. Africa* 270 Each man.. loosened his knife in its snake-skin sheath. **1888** G. Meredith *Poems* (1898) II. 191 The *snake-slough sick of the snaky sin. **1951** Whitby & Hynes *Med. Bacteriol.* (ed. 5) xx. 317 It is possible that other toxins of these soil bacteria are (like the *snake-venoms) primarily digestive ferments rather than aggressive mechanisms. **1805** Southey *Madoc* II. vi. 192 *note*, *Snake worship was common in America. **1883** Monier Williams *Relig. Th. India* I. xii. 319 Many.. believe that snake-worship was the earliest form of religion prevalent among men.

**b.** Attrib., with terms denoting persons or things connected with the catching, selling, exhibition, or worship of snakes, as ***snake-boy***, ***-man***, ***-player***; ***snake-ceremony***, ***-temple***, etc.

**1873** Leland *Egypt. Sketch-Bk.* 60, I did quite a business with that *snake-boy, for I was interested in the study of his ware. **1959** E. Tunis *Indians* ix. 128/1 Nearly all of the rituals had the same purpose: to cajole rain from the gods. The famous *Snake Ceremony had that object. **1958** C. Achebe *Things fall Apart* III. xxi. 159 His father was the priest of the *snake cult. **1965** R. & D. Morris *Men & Snakes* iii. 67 It has been argued that the Egyptian contingent of the Jews in the Exodus may have been *snake cultists and Moses himself a kind of snake shaman. **1836** [Miss Maitland] *Lett. fr. Madras* (1843) 36 Eight cobras and three other snakes.., and the *snake-men singing and playing.. to them. **1859** Sir J. G. Wilkinson in Rawlinson *Herodotus* III. 151 *note*, The *snake-players of the coast of Barbary. **1900** *Outing* June 305/2 Then, like a flash, the *Snake priests dart upon them grabbing in their hands all they can pick up. **1958** C. Achebe *Things fall Apart* III. xxii. 165 One of them was Enoch, the son of the snake-priest who was believed to have killed and eaten the sacred python. **1889** *Cent. Mag.* Aug. 507 The *snake-staff is used to handle snakes. **1902** *Chambers's Jrnl.* Feb. 81/1 Readers of that delightful novel, *The World went very well Then*, will remember Mr Brinjes of the fiery eye and the *snake-stick, who made every negro do his bidding. **1974** H. MacInnes *Climb to Lost World* vi. 97 We were all hypersensitive about the possibility of being stung or bitten, and kept our snake sticks handy. **1891** Miss Gordon-Cumming *2 Yrs. Ceylon* (1892) I. v. 127 There was a very ancient *snake-temple.. near Jaffna.

**c.** Appositive, as ***snake-girdle***, ***-god***, ***-idol***, ***-king***, ***-lock***, etc.

**1606** Sylvester *Du Bartas* II. iv. II. *Magnificence* 912 A Mantle.. round about him ty'd With a Snake-girdle biting off her tail. **1805** Southey *Madoc* II. vi. 192 A temple.. where the Snake-Idol stood. *Ibid.* II. vii. (*heading*), The Snake God. **1863** W. K. Kelly *Curiosities Indo-Europ. Trad. & Folk-Lore* i. 9 The bird, beast, and snake-gods. **1866** Conington *Æneid* VI. 185 Her [Discord's] snake-locks hiss. **1871** Alabaster *Wheel of Law* 136 If a snake-king he will sink into the earth. **1901** *Athenæum* 13 Apr. 475/2 The influence of the snake-woman, gorgeous in beauty and irresistible in allurement. **1925** A. Evans *Ring of Nestor* 15 Besides the well-known Snake Goddess of the Temple Repository at Knossos, a series of other figures have now come to light showing this attribute. **1965** R. & D. Morris *Men & Snakes* ii. 28 The snake god Danh-gbi of Whydah, Dahomey. **1965** R. & D. Morris *Men & Snakes* ii. 49 A similar snake monster, Typhon, who in Greek mythology merges with Typhoeus, was said to be the cause of earthquakes as well as many springs. **1979** *Jrnl. R. Soc. Arts* July 511/2 But in this region they also make paper caskets on bamboo frames which are used in festivals, especially for that of the snake-goddess, Bishahari.

**d.** Used to designate things having the form of a snake, as ***snake-arrow***, ***-bow***, ***-knot***, ***neck***, etc.

**1895** Haddon *Evol. Art* 25 A *snake-arrow which has lost all trace of its saurian ancestry. *c* **1660** Wood *Life* (O.H.S.) I. 300 Lac'd bands and tassell or *snake-bow band-strings. **1968** *New Larousse Encycl. Mythol.* (ed. 2) 484/1 (*caption*) *Snake bracelet from Dahomey. **1979** F. Morton *Nervous Splendour* (1980) ix. 89 He had long wanted to give Martha a gold snake bracelet, a status symbol. *a* **1882** H. Kendall in *Penguin Bk. Austral. Ballads* (1964) 92 A hero.. With a jumper and *snake-buckle belt on. **1971** P. D. James *Shroud for Nightingale* iv. 123 A schoolboy's belt.. clasped with a snake buckle. **1978** M. Dickens *An Open Book* i. 6 Dining room lunch meant putting on a dress instead of the boy's shirt and flannel shorts and snake-buckle belt we wore at Chilworthy. **1944** Blunden *Cricket Country* xi. 122 Wearing a revolver holster on a *snake-hook belt. **1866** G. Stephens *Runic Mon.* I. 327 The intertwining arabesques have everywhere a tendency to the regular *Snake-knot. **1929** D. H. Lawrence *Pansies* 39 In the odd pattern, like *snake-marks on the sand It leaves its trail. **1968** K. Weatherly *Roo Shooter* 16 Two large [kangaroo] does.. came in,.. their tails dragging long snake marks in the dust. **1965** R. & D. Morris *Men & Snakes* ii. 41 A *snake mask set with turquoises, the emblems of the god [*sc.* Quetzalcoatl]. **1865** Kingsley *Herew.* ii, His long *snake neck and cruel visage wreathing about in search of prey. **1625** in *Rymer's Fœdera* (1726) XVIII. 239 One Paire of Goulde Cupps with Covers, haveinge blewe *Snake Rings in the Topp of theire Covers. **1891** M. Williams *Later Leaves* v. 63 A gold snake ring. **1922** Joyce *Ulysses* 715 *The snakespiral springs of the mattress being old.

**10.** Objective and obj. genitive, as ***snake-bearer***, ***-catcher***, ***-charmer***, ***-eater***, ***-worshipper***, etc.; ***snake-charming***, ***-handling***, ***-killing***; ***snake-bearing***, ***snake-devouring***, ***-eating***, ***-handling*** adjs.

**1610** Healey *St. Aug. Citie of God* 383 Æsculapius was.. called.. the *Snake-bearer. **1927** D. H. Lawrence *Mornings in Mexico* 162 The shoulders of the young, *snake-bearing men. **1796** T. Twining *Trav. India*, etc. (1893) 164 The exhibition of the *snake-catchers near Benares. *c* **1880** *Cassell's Nat. Hist.* IV. 306 The Cobras are the favourites of the snake-catchers. **1836** [Miss Maitland] *Lett. fr. Madras* (1843) 36 Those *snake-charmers are most wonderful. **1891** Miss Gordon-Cumming *2 Yrs. Ceylon* (1892) I. v. 129 Professional snake-charmers, who go about with a basket full of these wriggling reptiles for exhibition. **1897** 'Mark Twain' *Foll. Equat.* xlii. 388 The girls went through a performance which represented *snake-charming. **1978** *Amer. Poetry Rev.* Nov./Dec. 25 Adam and eve because they had a snakecharming act. **1621** Quarles *Esther* vii, Enuie did ope her *Snake-deuouring Iawes. **1835** J. Duncan *Beetles* 189 If it enjoyed an inferior degree of veneration to the snake-devouring Ibis [etc.]. **1771** *Phil. Trans.* LXI. 56 This bird [the secretary-bird] was called a *snake-eater, by those who brought it from India. **1872** *Routledge's Ev. Boy's Ann.* 393/1 Such a creature as a snake-eater is man's best friend. *c* **1880** *Cassell's Nat. Hist.* IV. 307 A *snake-eating Snake. **1887** Mrs. Daly *Digging & Squatting* 94 The reptile known as the *Ophiophagus elaps* or snake-eating cobra. **1940** *Sci. News Let.* 17 Aug. 103/2 *Snake-handling religious cultists of Georgia are 'all of a piece' with followers of other cults who go to unusual lengths to show their faith or their access to supernatural powers. The same thing, with or without snake-handling, has been seen in various cultures and various times. **1973** R. L. Fox *Alexander the Great* iii. 45 Snake-handling is a known practice in the wilder sorts of Greek religion. **1895** J. G. Millais *Breath fr. Veldt* (1899) 29 As for his *snake-killing exploits, I think he is a bit of a fraud. **1880** G. C. M. Birdwood *Indust. Arts India* 83 The Nagas are a mythical type of the Scythic race of *snake-worshippers.

**11.** With pa. pples. or (ppl.) adjs., forming parasynthetic, similative, or instrumental combs., as ***snake-bodied***, ***-bred***, ***-drawn***, ***-encircled***, ***-engirdled***, ***-eyed***, ***-green***, ***-haired***, ***-headed***, etc.

Freq. in allusion to the snake-like hair of the Furies.

**1842** *Penny Cycl.* XXII. 47/2 *Snake-bodied Batrachians. **1587** Golding *De Mornay* xvii. (1592) 271 This Diuell.., whom he calleth ὀφιογενῆ or ὀφιόνεον, that is to say *Snakebread or Adderbread. **1876** A. S. Murray *Mythol.* iii. (1877) 42 [Demeter] giving.. to his son, Triptolemos, the seed of barley and her *snake-drawn car. **1765** Goldsm. *New Simile* 32 His hand Fill'd with a *snake-encircled wand. **1873** Symonds *Greek Poets* vii. 227 Hound not Those blood-faced, snake-encircled women on me. **1866** J. B. Rose *Ovid's Met.* 111 Tisiphone.. *snake-engirdled issued forth in air. **1896** Lydekker *Roy. Nat. Hist.* V. 168 *Snake-eyed.. lizards differ from all their kin in having no movable eyelids. **1948** C. S. Lewis in *Punch* 23 June 543/2 Sea-chances brought To her forest-silent And crimson-fruited And *snake-green island Her guests unsought. **1625** K. Long tr. *Barclay's Argenis* v. i. 330 From the barre The *snake-hayrd Sisters dragge the prisoner. **1634** T. Carew *Cœlum Brit.* 19 Thus I charme.. The Snake-heard Gorgon, and fierce Sagittar. **1921** W. de la Mare *Veil* 59 Snake-haired, snow-shouldered, pure as flame and dew,.. Rises the Goddess. **1856** Olmsted *Slave States* 65 These—long, lank, bony, *snake-headed, hairy, wild beasts. **1883** F. Day *Indian Fish* 33 The walking, or snake-headed fishes, *Ophiocephalidæ*, of India. **1976** 'G. Black' *Moon for Killers* i. 7 He looked like a Hollywood top actor of the fifties.. still almost *snake-hipped, with long, thrust-out legs. **1954** G. Barker *Vision of Beasts & Gods* 39 The *snake-locked image of dream Hanging ahead. **1857** Hughes *Tom Brown* I. i, They are a square-headed and *snake-necked generation. *c* **1880** *Cassell's Nat. Hist.* IV. 255 The Snake-necked Tortoises of Monte Video, Buenos Ayres, and Southern Brazil. **1946** R. Graves *Poems 1938–45* 32 By noting that the *snake-tailed chthonian winds Were answerable to fate alone, not Zeus. **1598** Sylvester *Du Bartas* II. i. III. 250 Come *snake-trest Sisters, come ye dismall Elves. **1894** O. Wilde *Sphinx* 28 What snaketressed fury fresh from Hell. **1605** Sylvester *Du Bartas* II. iii. III. *Law* 428 Smiting the Waves with his *Snake-wanded wood. **1682** N. O. *Boileau's Lutrin* I. 85 A corner'd Cap her *Snake-wigg'd Head did cover.

**12. a.** Special combs.: **snake-bit(ten)** *a.*, (*a*) bitten by a snake; (*b*) *U.S.* irremediably doomed to misfortune; †**snake-board** (see sense 5); **snake-boat**, a form of canoe used in the East (see quot. 1882); **snake boot** *N. Amer.*, a boot with a high ankle worn for protection against snake-bites, or a fashion boot resembling this; **snake-box**, (*a*) a box or case for keeping snakes; (*b*) a faro-box fraudulently made so that a slight projection called a snake warns the dealer of the approach of a particular card (*Cent. Dict.*); †**snake-button**, a snake-stone, adder-stone; **snake charmer** *Austral. slang* (see quots.); **snake-doctor**, one who cures snake-bites; **snake eyes**, (*a*) *U.S. slang*, tapioca; (*b*) *N. Amer. slang*, a throw of two ones with a pair of dice; also *fig.*, bad luck; †**snake-foot** *a.* (rendering L. *anguipes*), snake-footed, as a poetic epithet of giants; **snake-headed** *a. slang* (see quot. 1941); **snake hips**, (*a*) very narrow hips; (*b*) the name of a popular dance (see quot. 1970); so **snake-hip** *attrib.*; **snake juice** *slang* (chiefly *Austral.*), whisky; also *loosely*, any alcoholic drink; **snake-line** (see quot.); **snake oil**, a quack remedy or panacea; also *fig.*; freq. *attrib.*, esp. as ***snake-oil salesman***; **snake-piece** (see quot.); **snake-pill**, a pill used as a remedy for snake-bite; **snake poison** *U.S.* and *Austral. slang*, whisky; †**snake-proof** *a.*, proof against snakes; in quot. *fig.*; **snake rail fence** *N. Amer.* = SNAKE-FENCE; **snake room** *Canad.* (see quot. 1912); **snake-spit** *dial.* (see quot.); **snake story**, **yarn**, an incredible tale about a snake, esp. in regard to its great length or size.

**1807** Gass *Jrnl.* 20 One of our people got *snake bitten but not dangerously. **1938** M. K. Rawlings *Yearling* xiv. 149 He sobbed, 'Pa—He's snake-bit.' **1942** W. Faulkner *Go down, Moses* 111 Ah'm snakebit and de pizen cant hawm me. **1957** *Daily Progress* (Charlottesville, Va.) 18 Nov. 14/1 It was another long afternoon Saturday at Scott Stadium for Coach Ben Martin, his assistants and his 'snake-bitten' football players as they fell before South Carolina, 13–0. *Ibid.*, Commenting on the game last Saturday afternoon Martin said: 'We're just snake-bit that's all there is to it.' Snake-bit is a term used by coaches when referring to a team which never seems to have a break in its favor. **1965** Mrs. L. B. Johnson *White House Diary* 10 June (1970) 283 From the first moment of the day we were 'snake-bit'—everything went wrong. **1976** *Columbus* (Montana) *News* (Joliet Suppl.) 17 June 2/3 We managed to get back to the house, not snake-bitten and not smelling *too* much like a skunk. **1882** Annandale *Imperial Dict.*, *Pamban-manche*, a canoe of great length, used on the Malabar coast... Called also Serpent-boat, *Snake-boat. **1900** *Daily News* 14 Feb. 4/4 They have fifteen steam launches and a great number of snake boats at their service. **1965** *Snakeboot [see KINKY *sb.*]. **1972** R. Reid *Canadian Style* (1973) iv. 144 'Say, what is, or are, galoshes?' 'Like rubber snake boots, but they buckle or zip up the front.' **1886** P. Robinson *Teetotum Trees* 92 Very much like the showman's *snake-box in which each reptile had swallowed the one next to it in size. **1699** E. Lhwyd in *Phil. Trans.* XXVIII. 98 The *Snake-button is the same described.. in Camden, by the Name of Adder-beads. **1937** A. W. Upfield *Mr Jelly's Business* 16 'And what are the *Snake Charmers?' 'They are the permanent-way men.' **1969** P. A. Smith *Folklore Austral. Railwaymen* 279 Fettlers are invariably referred to as 'snake charmers'. **1800** *Asiatic Ann. Reg.* 325 A specimen was brought me by a *snake-doctor. **1918** L. E. Ruggles *Navy Explained* 20 Tapioca is '*snake eyes'. **1929** M. A. Gill *Underworld Slang* 11/2 *Snake eyes*, aces up on the dice. **1935** *Jrnl. Abnormal Psychol.* XXX. 364 *Snake eyes*, tapioca. **1964** A. Wykes *Gambling* vi. 134 Modern craps players use..slang for various combinations of two dice: 'snake eyes' for Two, [etc.]. **1972** *Islander* (Victoria, B.C.) 30 July 12/3 But this time Baychimo's annual throw of the dice came up 'snake-eyes', and the ice closed about trapping her forever. **1978** R. Moore *Big Paddle* iv. 88 Cliff..let the dice go... He didn't have to look to know they'd come up snake eyes. **1978** G. Vidal *Kalki* vi. 138 It's like throwing dice. Let's just hope it won't be snake eyes for Jim Kelly. **1598** Chapman *Hero & Leander* vi. 46 To *snake-foote Boreas next she doth remoue. **1920** B. Cronin *Timber Wolves* viii. 137 Anyhow, they's no need to get *snake-headed about it. **1941** S. J. Baker *Dict. Austral. Slang* 68 *Snake-headed*, angry, vindictive. **1932** *Daily Progress* (Charlottesville, Va.) 20 Apr. 4/3 There is a distinct class clash between the Harlem intelligentsia and *snake-hip dancers and chanters of hot-cha-cha and skiddle-de-scow in the black and tan auberges. **1977** *Melody Maker* 26 Mar. 43/2 The biggest sensation of all..was the 'snake-hip' dancer, Bessie Dudley, waggling her bottom, clad in black satin knickers. **1933** *Fortune* Aug. 48/1 Dancers like the gelatinous '*Snake Hips' Tucker. **1956** G. P. Kurath in A. F. C. Wallace *Men & Cultures* (1960) 153 Restraints were shaken off..in an epidemic of angular, foot-twisting gyrations—the Charleston, Snake Hips, Susie-Q, and Truckin'. **1970** C. Major *Dict. Afro-Amer. Slang* 106 *Snake hips*, a Baltimore- and New York-oriented jazz dance. **1977** N. Slater *Crossfire* iii. 62 The fellows..all seem to have snake-hips, painfully tight trousers and platform shoes. **1890** *Pall Mall G.* 3 Sept. 3/2 This whisky, or *snake juice, as bushmen often call the hell-broth prepared for them. **1904** E. S. Emerson *Shanty Entertainment* 70 Then he started them on snake-juice, known as Boot and Blacking Rum. **1965** M. McIntyre *Place of Quiet Waters* xii. 224, I wonder if that snake juice is fit to drink. **1973** R. Robinson *Drift of Things* 290 Broke into Eric's hut, threw the 'pickled' specimens out of the jars, and drank the methylated spirits. That must have been the real 'Snake-Juice'. **1875** Knight *Dict. Mech.* 2229 **Snake-line*, line used in worming a rope. **1927** S. V. Benét *John Brown's Body* 294 Crooked creatures of a thousand dubious trades,..sellers of *snake-oil balm and lucky rings. **1946** E. O'Neill *Iceman Cometh* i. 90 I'll bet he's standing on a street corner in hell right now, making suckers of the damned, telling them there's nothing like snake oil for a bad burn. **1961** *Washington Post* 10 May A4/2 Advertisers who try to 'lubricate the wheels of our economy with snake oil'. **1976** *Listener* 25 Mar. 382/1 Jimmy Savile has always had more *chutzpah* than a wagonload of snake-oil salesmen. **1977** *Rolling Stone* 21 Apr. 66/2 It was, after all, the Jew who was the perennial doubter, the archetypal outsider, longing for redemption while dismissing the claims of would-be redeemers as so much snake oil. **1978** *Times* 21 Jan. 12/7 The pseudo-graphic industry..are snake-oil salesmen deceiving the public. **1867** Smyth *Sailor's Word-bk.*, **Snake-pieces*,..stout props, placed obliquely to the timbers of whalers, to sustain the shock of icebergs. **1800** *Asiatic Ann. Reg.* III. 125/1 So much I can say for the arsenic *snake pills, the only other remedy recommended. **1890** L. C. D'Oyle *Notches* 4 It was variously called for as tangle-foot, *snake-poison,..chain-lightning, or other fancy name, but it was never called for as *whisky*. **1947** K. Tennant *Lost Haven* iv. 66 If Bee-Bonnet ever again wants me to sample his snake poison, I'll pour it on him and set it alight. **1609** Dekker *Gull's Horn-bk.* Wks. (Grosart) II. 203, I am *Snake-proof: and..it is impossible for you to quench..my Alpine-resolution. **1889** B. Harte *Cressy* ii. 38 Mr. McKinstry's '*snake rail' fence was already discernible in the lighter opening of the woods. **1958** H. Symons *Fences* 48 One of the early Canadian fences most popular in the east was the snake rail fence. **1912** J. Sandilands *Western Canad. Dict.* 42/1 **Snake-room*, a side room of a basement where saloon-keepers accommodate doped or drunken people until they recover their senses, presumably a place where they 'see snakes'. **1921** *Daily Colonist* (Victoria, B.C.) 29 Oct. 15/2 'Tommy' was one of a bunch who were swapping stories recently in the snake room. **1975** F. Kennedy *Alberta was my Beat* vi. 73 All adjourned to the 'snake room' in the basement. **1823** E. Moor *Suffolk Words*, **Snake-spit*, small masses of delicately white frothy matter, seen on leaves of weeds or wild flowers..; popularly believed to be the saliva of snakes. **1826** *Virginia Herald* (Fredericksburg) 6 Sept. 3/2 The New-York Spectator will probably class this with the *Snake stories of the day. **1867** *Harper's Mag.* Aug. 281/3 We told snake and fish stories. **1885** Hornaday *2 Yrs. in Jungle* xxvii. 331 All the big snake stories I had heard. **1891** E. Kinglake *Australian* 97 If anyone told a good anecdote with a dash of the *snake yarn about it.

**b.** In the specific or popular names of animals, birds, fishes, etc. (see quots.). **snake doctor** *U.S.* = dragon-fly or hellgrammite; **snake feeder** *U.S.* = prec.

A large number of combs. of this type are given in recent American Dicts., as *snake-blenny*, *-hag* (= lizard), *-mackerel*, etc.

**1881** Day *Fishes Gt. Brit.* I. 330 Snedden... At St. Ives the fishermen term the adult *snake-bait, and the young naked-bait. **1869–73** *Cassell's Bk. Birds* II. 49 About noon the *Snake Buzzard [*Circaëtus gallicus*] appears upon the river banks. **1863** S. L. J. *Life in South* I. vii. 93 The cat-bird, or *snake-charmer. **1869–73** *Cassell's Bk. Birds* IV. 91 The *Snake Cranes (*Dicholophus*) constitute a group of remarkable birds. *a* **1883** G. W. Bagby *Old Virginia Gentleman* (1910) 92 [The water is] full of all manner of nasty and confounded 'mud-kittens', 'snap'n turtles', and *snake doctors. **1948** *Field & Stream* July 42/2 Various stages of the dobson are known as..flip-flaps, snake doctors. **1978** *Amer. Speech* LIII. 201 The flora and fauna terms include..*snake feeder* (listed as the common name for the dragon-fly, *snake doctor* being listed as 'slightly known'). **1668** Charleton *Onomast.* 113 *Hoactzin*,..the *Snake-eater of America. **1829** Griffith tr. *Cuvier* VI. 68 The Snake-Eater, or Secretary (*Serpentarius*). **1803** Shaw *Gen. Zool.* IV. i. 23 *Snake Eel. *Anguilla Serpens.* **1866** *Carpenter's Zoology* II. 75 The *Ophisurus*, or Snake Eel (so called from its strong resemblance to a serpent) of the Mediterranean. **1861** *Trans. Illinois Agric. Soc.* IV. 341 A particular species of dragon-fly, or *snake-feeder, as it is absurdly called in this country. **1904** G. Stratton-Porter *Freckles* xiv. 289 He shifted restlessly, and the movement sent the snake-feeders skimming. **1949** H. Kurath *Word Geogr. Eastern U.S.* 14/1 The line of demarkation over against the Midland snake feeder is remarkably clear and sharp. **1668** Charelton *Onomast.* 42 *Serpentisuga*,..the *Snake-fly. **1817** Kirby & Sp. *Entomol.* xxiii. (1818) II. 309 A kind of snake-fly (*Raphidia Mantispa*, F.) is said to walk upon its knees. **1882** *Cassell's Nat. Hist.* VI. 15 The Snake-flies, or Camel-flies (*Raphidiæ*) form a small genus. **1781** Latham *Gen. Synop. Birds* I. i. 61 Swallow-tailed Falcon..inhabits Carolina in the summer months; where it is called *Snake-hawk. **1863** Russell *Diary North & S.* I. 216 The young gentleman was good enough to bring over a snake hawk he had shot for me. **1816** Keatinge *Trav.* (1817) I. 344 They have a remarkably swift..race of horses, which, from the lankness of their bodies,..are called *snake-horses. **1872** Coues *N. Amer. Birds* 189 *Geococcyx*,..Road Runner. *Snake Killer. **1902** P. Fountain *Mountains & Forests South America* iv. 89 A hawk seen on all parts of the river [Purus] was a beautiful black and white one, known in the States as the *snake-kite, on account of its preying largely on those reptiles. **1802** Shaw *Gen. Zool.* III. i. 305 *Snake-Lizards, with extremely long bodies, and short legs. **1866** *Carpenter's Zoology* I. 564 The Four-toed *Saurophis*, or Snake-Lizard, which is a native of the southern part of Africa. **1863** S. L. J. *Life in South* I. vi. 87 That's a *snake-maid [= dragon-fly]. **1883** J. Curtis *Farm Insects* vii. 201 Linnæus gave them the generic name of Julus; and from the typical species resembling snakes in miniature,..I have applied to them the English appellation of *snake-millipedes. **1900** Davis tr. *Bos' Agric. Zool.* (ed. 2) 195 The Snake Millipedes..or 'False Wireworms'. *c* **1880** *Cassell's Nat. Hist.* IV. 200 The Darters (*Plotus*)..are also called *Snake-necks, from the habit they have of swimming with the body submerged and only the neck exposed above the water. **1713** Petiver *Aquat. Anim. Amboinæ* Tab. 16/32 *Solen Anguinus*,..*Snake pipes. **1804** Shaw *Gen. Zool.* V. ii. 453 *Snake Pipefish,..*Syngnathus Ophidion.* **1883** Day *Fishes Gt. Brit.* II. 261 Ocean pipe-fish and snake pipe-fish. **1868** Darwin *Var. Anim. & Plants* xv. II. 87 Some *snake-rats (*Mus alexandrinus*) escaped in the Zoological Gardens. **1713** Petiver *Aquat. Anim. Amboinæ* Tab. xii, *Serpentulus*,..*Snake-shell. **1800** Shaw *Gen. Zool.* III. i. 72 *Snake Tortoise. *Testudo Serpentina.*

**c.** In the names of plants, etc. (see quots.). **snake-locked anemone** = opelet; **snake plant**, (*a*) (see quot. 1883); (*b*) = *mother-in-law's tongue* s.v. mother-in-law.

Various others occurring in dialect or local use are recorded in the *Eng. Dial. Dict.* and recent American Dicts.

**1846–50** A. Wood *Class-bk. Bot.* 275 *Cereus flagelliformis*,..*Snake Cactus. **1866** *Treas. Bot.* 652/1 *Kunthia*, a genus of palms..of New Grenada, where the natives call it *Cana de la Vibora*, i.e. *Snake Cane, from the resemblance of its stem to a snake. **1882** *Garden* 1 Apr. 219/3 Packets of seed of various plants, including Water Melons and *Snake Cucumbers. **1902** Cornish *Naturalist Thames* 170 The fritillaries, the chequered red or pale '*snake-flowers', are grass-lovers. **1823** Crabb *Technol. Dict.* ii. s.v., *Snake-gourd. **1857** Henfrey *Bot.* §479 The Snake-gourd, *Trichosanthes anguina*, is eaten in India. **1901** Bailey & Miller *Cycl. Amer. Horticult.* II. 874 The long curved forms [of *Lagenaria vulgaris*] are often called snake gourds in this country. **1883** A. K. Green (Mrs. Rohlfs) *Hand & Ring* i, The ground is marshy and covered with *snake grass. **1853** P. H. Gosse *Naturalist's Rambles Devon. Coast* iv. 96 The *Snake-locked Anemone..is by no means common. **1928** Russell & Yonge *Seas* 37 Especially common in the pools is the 'Snake-locked anemone'. **1979** J. D. & J. J. George *Marine Life* 32/1 *Anemonia sulcata*..(snakelocks anemone). A species with many sinuous tentacles. **1845** Lindley *Sch. Bot.* 154 *Lycopodium clavatum* (Clubmoss, *Snakemoss). **1845–50** Mrs. Lincoln *Lect. Bot.* App. 144 *Pogonia ophioglossoides* (*snake-mouth arethusa). **1846** Lindley *Veg. Kingd.* 383 The nut of a Demerara tree, called the *Snake-nut, in consequence of the large embryo, resembling a snake coiled up. **1849** Balfour *Man. Bot.* §807 *Ophiocaryon paradoxum*, is the Snake-nut-tree of Demerara. **1885** C. G. W. Lock *Workshop Rec.* Ser. iv. 277/1 The best variety is known under several names, as those of the *snake osier [etc.]. **1883** W. Robinson *Eng. Flower Garden* (1901) 436 *Arum Dracunculus* (Dragons, *Snake Plant). **1946** M. Free *All about House Plants* xviii. 271 The common Snake-plant..is one of the most inelegant of all plants, with its stiff, 30-inch, upright leaves. **1973** *Daily Colonist* (Victoria, B.C.) 21 Nov. 24/1 He had poured his heart out to a hardy sansevieria, otherwise known as snake plant or mother-in-law's tongues. **1842** *Penny Cycl.* XXIII. 152/2 *Strychnos colubrina*, Snake-wood, or *Snake-poison Nut, is a climbing plant with simple tendrils. **1832** Don *Gen. Syst. Gard. & Bot.* II. 60/1 *Ophispermum Sinense*.., China *Snake-seed. **1866** *Treas. Bot.* 815/2 The fruits [of *Ophiocaryon paradoxum*] are often sent to this country as curiosities, under the name of Snake-nuts or Snake-seeds. **1880** Jefferies *Gt. Estate* 87 The *snake-skin willow, so called because it sheds its bark. **1632** Sherwood, Snake-weede, *snake-wort, *bistorte*.

**13.** In collocations with snake's, chiefly in plant-names (see quots.).

Cf. also the *Eng. Dial. Dict.* and recent American Dicts.

**1866** *Treas. Bot.* 1067/2 *Snake's-beard, *Ophiopogon.* **1597** Gerarde *Herbal* 659 Buglosse..is called..in English vipers Buglosse, *Snakes Buglosse. **1611** Cotgr., *Ail Sauvage*, Wild Garlicke,..Stags Garlicke, *Snakes Garlicke. **1887** G. Nicholson *Dict. Gard.* III. 447 *Snake's-mouth Orchis... *Pogonia ophioglossum.* *c* **1675** R. Cromwell *Let.* in *Eng. Hist. Rev.* (1898) XIII. 93 He hath sent of the *Snakes root of Verginnia..as the best of cordialls. **1879** *Folk-Lore Rec.* II. 81 The..*snake's-spit, or wood-sear of England and Scotland,..is a froth discharged by the young froghoppers. **1863** Prior *Plant-n.* s.v., *Snake's tail, from its cylindrical spikes, *Rottböllia incurvata.* **1866** *Treas. Bot.* 1067/2 Snake's-tail, *Lepturus incurvus. Ibid.*, *Snake's-tongue, *Lygodium.* **1902** Bailey & Miller *Cycl. Amer. Hort.* IV. 1673 Snake's Tongue, *Ophioglossum.*

**snake** (sneɪk), *v.*[1] [f. snake *sb.*]

**I. 1. a.** *trans.* To twist or wind (hair) into the form of a snake. *rare*$^{-1}$.

**1653** J. Hall *Parad.* 114 Who would not be sooner smitten with Tresses curiously snak't.

**b.** *Naut.* (See quot. 1846.)

**1815** Burney *Falconer's Dict. Marine* 487/1 Snaking the Stays, or Ropes on the Quarters, instead of Netting. **1840** Adm. Winnington-Ingram *Hearts of Oak* (1889) 27 Put ratlines on the backstays, snaked the stays, slung the topmasts with chain. **1846** A. Young *Naut. Dict.* 288 *Snake*, to pass small stuff across a seizing at the outer turns by way of finish. To attach lengths of rope between two stays or backstays.

**c.** To move, stretch out, (the head, etc.) after the manner of a snake. Also *refl.*

**1887** D. C. Murray & Herman *Traveller Returns* i, The girl snaking her head hither and thither in the eagerness of her regard. **1890** L. C. D'Oyle *Notches* 60 Then falling down full-length upon the ground he began to crawl, or rather 'snake' himself, up to the brow.

**d.** To cover or decorate *with* spirals or coils.

**1887** *Sporting Life* 22 June 6/5 The portico pillars of the Mansion House were 'snaked' with richly coloured illumination lamps.

**2. a.** *intr.* To move in a creeping, crawling, or stealthy manner suggestive of the movements of a snake.

**1848** in Bartlett *Dict. Amer.* 315 There's some fellows who ..are snaking up to the Grand Jury, on their bellies in the grass, kind of trying to hear what the Jury are talking about. **1848** Lowell *Biglow P.* Ser. i. ix, Pomp he snaked up behin', An' creepin' grad'lly close tu,..grabbed my leg. **1893** Capt. King *Foes in Ambush* 187 Unseen Indians would come skulking, spying, 'snaking' upon their refuge.

*fig.* **1852** Mrs. Stowe *Uncle Tom's C.* viii. 57, I b'lieve.. I could get along and snake through, even if justices were more particular than they is.

**b.** *spec.* (see quots.).

**1875** *Encycl. Brit.* II. 378 An arrow is said to snake when it works itself under the grass. **1876** Voyle & Stevenson *Milit. Dict.* 391/1 Projectiles subject to this influence [i.e. spiral motion of rotation round their original direction] are technically said *to snake*.

**3.** To wind, twist, curve, etc., in a snake-like manner.

**1875** Miss Bird *Sandwich Isl.* xxi. 302 The track..snaked along the narrow tops of spine-like ridges. **1888** Clark Russell *Death Ship* II. 206 The hacked ends of the shrouds snaking out into the hollows and swellings over the side. **1902** A. E. W. Mason *Four Feathers* (1903) 2 A coil of white smoke from a train snaked rapidly in and out amongst the trees.

**4.** *trans.* To make (one's way) in a sinuous or creeping manner.

**1879** Miss Bird *Rocky Mountains* 5 The monster train snaked its way upwards. **1894** D. C. Murray *Making of Novelist* 28 One by one we snaked our way..into the hole.

**II. 5. a.** *U.S.* To drag, pull, or draw; *spec.* in *Lumbering*, to haul (logs) along the ground length-wise by means of chains or ropes.

**1829** T. Flint *George Mason* ii. 21 It was so contrived that ..logs..could be drawn, or, as it is technically phrased, *snaked* into church. **1848** Bartlett *Dict. Amer.* 316 A farmer in clearing land, attaches a chain to a stump or log, whereby to draw it out; this he calls, *snaking it out*. **1878** *Lumberman's Gaz.* 26 Jan., Where the haul is very short, and so close to the streams that the logs are 'snaked' in without being skidded. **1883** *Harper's Mag.* Jan. 206/1 The..cattle snake the log endwise down the hill.

*fig.* **1833** [Seba Smith] *Lett. of J. Downing* (1835) 26 We snaked him out of that scrape as slick as a whistle. **1883** *Philad. Times* No. 2810. 4 Some legal loophole..through which an evasion or extension can be successfully snaked.

**b.** *transf.* To drag or pull forcibly or quickly.

**1856** M. Thomson *Plu-ri-bus-tah* xii. 135 First he pulled the pillow-case off. Then he snaked the stars and stripes off. **1897** F. T. Bullen *Cruise 'Cachalot'* xxvii. (1900) 359 One of the small London tugs..would have snaked those monsters along at the rate of three of four knots an hour. **1899** —— *Log Sea-waif* 341 How we did snake the hatches off.

**6.** *U.S. slang.* To beat, thrash.

*a* **1859** in Bartlett *Dict. Amer.* (ed. 2) 421 Any gal like me ..ought to be able to snake any man of her heft.

**7.** *U.S.* To take *out* surreptitiously.

**1862** Lowell *Biglow P.* Ser. ii. iii, Ef You snake one link out here, one there, how much on 't ud be lef'?

**snake**, *v.*[2] *dial.* and *U.S.* Also **snaik**. [prob. a. ON. *snaka* (Norw. *snaka*, MDa. *snage*) to go snuffing or searching about; cf. G. dial. *schnaken* (*schnacken*) to creep.]

**1.** *intr.* To skulk or sneak.

**1818** Hogg *Brownie of Bodsbeck* vii, Some o' thae beasts that gang snaiken about i' the derk. **1882** *Jamieson's Sc. Dict.*, To *snaik*, to sneak, in walking, working, or speaking. **1894** Hall Caine *Manxman* iv. xvii, Young Ross snaked out of the house same as a cur.

**2.** *trans.* To get or obtain (a thing) furtively or surreptitiously; to steal or pilfer; to cheat (a person) *out of* something. Also, to cheat (someone) at cards.

*a* **1861** T. Winthrop *John Brent* (1862) xvi. 183 They snaked me to the figure of a slug at their cheatin' game. **1881–** in dial. texts and glossaries (Yorks., Lancs., Notts., Somerset). **1886** Kipling *Departmental Ditties* (ed. 2) 36 You will find excuse to snake Three days' 'casual' on the bust. **1921** T. Dreiser *Let.* 2 Jan. (1959) I. 333 Start the ball and if I snake the forty thousand..you get five thousand. **1959** [see shaft *sb.*[2] 10c]. **1977** *Amer. Speech* 1975 L. 66 *Snake*,..steal (one's date) 'Carol tried to snake my date last night'.

**snake-bark** ('sneɪkbɑːk). [f. SNAKE *sb.* + BARK *sb.*[1] 1.] In full, ***snake-bark(ed) maple***. A maple, esp. *Acer pennsylvanicum* from eastern North America or *Acer davidii* from eastern Asia, belonging to a group distinguished by bark streaked with white.

**1838** J. C. LOUDON *Arboretum & Fruticetum Britannicum* I. 407 The striped-barked Maple.. Snake-barked Maple, Moose Wood. **1914** W. J. BEAN *Trees & Shrubs Hardy in Brit. Isles* I. 153 *A. pennsylvanicum*.. Snake-bark Maple... This maple is remarkable chiefly for the exceedingly handsome striping of its younger branches and stem. **1974** A. MITCHELL *Field Guide Trees Brit. Isles* 341 The Snake-barked Maples are a difficult and confused group. *Ibid.* 342 Similar species. *A. distylum*.. although not truly a Snake-bark. **1977** *Harpers & Queen* Nov. 274/4 Suburban gardens.. are now enriched with azaleas,.. snakebark maple, winter-sweet and all sorts of curiosities. **1980** *Amat. Gardening* 25 Oct. 29/1 With the exception of *Acer pennsylvanicum*.. the Snakebarks are native to China or Japan.

'**snake-bird**. Also snakebird, snake bird. [SNAKE *sb.*]

**1.** A bird belonging to the genus *Plotus*, esp. the American species *P. anhinga*, characterized by its long snake-like neck; the darter or water-turkey.

**1791** W. BARTRAM *Carolina* 132 Here is.. in the waters all over Florida, a very curious and handsome bird, the people call the Snake Birds. **1814** A. WILSON *Amer. Ornith.* IX. 79 Black-bellied Darter, or Snake-bird, *Plotus melanogaster*. **1838** AUDUBON *Ornith.* IV. 136 Anhinga or Snake-bird, *Plotus anhinga*. **1883** *Fish. Exhib. Catal.* (ed. 4) 152 The Darter, sometimes known as the snake bird, is not at all uncommon in Bengal. **1895** LYDEKKER *Roy. Nat. Hist.* IV. 280 The darters, snake-birds, or snake-necks, form a group of four species.

**2.** *dial.* The wryneck, *Iynx torquilla*.

**1831** RENNIE *Montagu's Ornith. Dict.* 576 Long Tongue. Emmet Hunter. Snake Bird. **1844** *Zoologist* II. 449 The bird .. proved to be what is here [in Kent] provincially called a 'snake-bird', and only known among the lower orders by that name. **1848** *Ibid.* VI. 2186 The wryneck [in Norfolk] is the 'cuckoo's leader' and 'snake-bird'. **1889** H. SAUNDERS *Brit. Birds* 262 When disturbed, the sitting bird makes a loud hissing,.. which has led to the popular name of 'Snake-bird'.

**snaked** (sneɪkt), *ppl. a.* [f. SNAKE *sb.*] Polished with snakestone.

**1841** *Civil Eng. & Arch. Jrnl.* IV. 185/1 The snaked or finely rubbed [slabs of slate].. when oiled have the appearance of black marble.

'**snake dance**. Also snake-dance. [SNAKE *sb.*]

**1.** Among the Hopi Indians, a religious dance involving the handling of live rattlesnakes. Also, among other American Indian groups, various dances so called from the motion of the dancers or the function of the dance.

**1772** D. TAITT *Jrnl.* 6 Mar. in N. D. MERENESS *Trav. Amer. Colonies* (1916) 517 The women danced the Snake dance, the leader haveing her legs Covered with Turpin shells which is filled with small stones on purpose to make a noise. **1883** *Pall Mall G.* 16 Nov. 12/1 A snake dance of Savages. **1891** *Rep. Bureau Amer. Ethnol.* VIII. 136 Among the Hopi, particularly at Walpi, the snake-dance is renowned. **1901** *Athenæum* 11 May 599/2 He saw snake-dances and fire ceremonies, of which he preserved an accurate report. **1927** D. H. LAWRENCE *Mornings in Mexico* 136 The snake dance (I am told) is held once a year. *Ibid.* 138 Three thousand people came to see the little snake dance this year. **1940** R. CHANDLER *Farewell, my Lovely* xx. 158 I'm no school-marm at the snake dances. **1965** R. & D. MORRIS *Men & Snakes* ii. 38 The snakes used in the famous Hopi Snake Dance are not worshipped, but sent as messengers to the raingods of the underworld. **1970** K. PLATT *Pushbutton Butterfly* ix. 100 A Shoshone snake dance.

**2. a.** A dance performed as a stage entertainment in imitation of the movement of a snake or involving the handling of a snake.

**1895** *N.Y. Dramatic News* 23 Nov. 4 Ida Siddons in her snake dance, two Italian pantomimists [etc.]. **1971** R. RUSSELL tr. *Ahmad's Shore & Wave* vii. 66 'What cabaret girl?' 'The one who does the snake dance.'

**b.** A dance performed by a group of people linked together in a long line and moving about in a zig-zag fashion, as at parties, celebrations, etc. orig. and chiefly *U.S.*

**1911** G. BURGESS *Find Woman* x. 244 So he.. went, reminding them of the [football] score and the snake-dance every time he opened a bottle. **1946** E. B. THOMPSON *Amer. Daughter* 234 A few minutes later [I] was a link in a howling, writhing snake dance that weaved itself in and out of the business section. **1960** *Daily Tel.* 15 July 19/2, 23,000 in Tokyo anti-treaty snake-dance. **1965** G. B. SCHALLER *Year of Gorilla* viii. 206 One grabbed the rump hairs of the first one with both hands, the third animal did the same to the second one, and then all three careened wildly down a slope in snake-dance fashion. **1976** *National Observer* (U.S.) 10 July 11/1 During the rebellious days of the 1960s, college students spurned many traditional campus pleasures, from spring proms and snake dances to the social reassurance offered by membership in fraternities and sororities.

Also (with hyphen) as *v. intr.*; so **snake-dancing** *ppl. a.*; hence **snake-dancer**.

**1922** *Chicago Daily Maroon* 3 Oct. 2/1 The public.. picture.. howling, snakedancing crowds whenever colleges and universities are mentioned. **1931** F. L. ALLEN *Only Yesterday* 17 Eight hundred Barnard College girls snake-danced on Morningside Heights in New York. **1960** *Daily Tel.* 15 July 19/2 They snake-danced through the city with their paper lanterns and red banners and dispersed quietly without incident, police said. **1977** C. MCCULLOUGH *Thorn Birds* v. 93 Princess Houri the Snake Dancer (See Her Fan the Flames of a Cobra's Rage!).

'**snake-fence**. *N. Amer.* [SNAKE *sb.*] A fence made of roughly split rails or poles laid in a zigzag fashion; a worm or zigzag fence; = *snake rail fence* s.v. SNAKE *sb.* 12 a.

**1805** R. PARKINSON *Tour Amer.* I. i. 48 Snake-fences; which are rails laid with the ends of one upon the other, from eight to sixteen in number in one length. **1830** GALT *Lawrie T.* VII. i. (1849) 303 The American regions of stumps and stones, log-houses and snake-fences. **1844** F. MARRYAT *Settlers in Canada* 53 A herd of cattle were grazing on a portion of the cleared land; the other was divided off by a snake-fence.. and was under cultivation. **1864** CHARLOTTE M. YONGE *Trial* II. 173 An untidy desolate-looking region, with a rude snake fence. **1887** I. R. *Ranche Life Montana* 61 They are called 'snake' fences because they don't go straight, but form an angle, where the poles overlap each other. **1904** C. G. D. ROBERTS *Watchers of Trails* 239 The snake fence of split rails which bounded the pasture. **1973** L. RUSSELL *Everyday Life Colonial Canada* ii. 33 In constructing a snake fence the rails of adjacent bays were overlapped at a wide angle... Such a fence was a zig-zag of bays.

'**snake-fish**. [SNAKE *sb.*] One or other of certain fishes (see quots.) having some resemblance to a snake.

**1796** STEDMAN *Surinam* II. xviii. 60 The snake-fish takes its name from its resemblance to that reptile: this is a black eel with a white belly. **1836** YARRELL *Brit. Fishes* I. 195 The red Bandfish, or Red Snakefish, *cepola rubescens*. **1876** GOODE *Fishes of Bermudas* 68 *Synodus Lacerta*,.. Snake-Fish. **1896** LYDEKKER *Roy. Nat. Hist.* V. 438 Snake-fishes. The typical genus *Ophidium*.. has the pelvic fins replaced by a pair of barbel-like filaments. **1899** *Proc. Zool. Soc.* Nov. 985 The two Snake-Fishes (*Polypterus senegalus*) from the River Gambia.

*attrib.* **1884** GOODE *Nat. Hist. Aquat. Anim.* 548 The Snake-fish family, *Synodontidæ*.

'**snake-head**. Also snakehead. [SNAKE *sb.*]

**1. a.** The North American plant *Chelone glabra*.

**1845-50** MRS. LINCOLN *Lect. Bot.* App. 88/2 *Chelone glabra* (snake-head). **1846-50** A. WOOD *Class-bk. Bot.* 400 Snake-head. Salt-rheum Weed... A plant of brooks and wet places,.. with flowers shaped much like the head of a snake.

**b.** The snake's head or common fritillary.

**1884** G. ALLEN *Philistia* I. 146 'Has your brother ever sent you any of the fritillaries?' 'What? snake-heads?'

**2.** *U.S.* (See quots. and cf. SNAKE'S-HEAD 3). Now *Hist.*

**1845** *Yankee* (Boston) 9 Aug. 3/4 Mr. John F. Wall.. was near being killed.. by what is technically called a *snakehead*. **1848** BARTLETT *Dict. Amer.* 315 *Snake-head*,.. the end of an iron rail, which sometimes is thrown up in front of the car wheels, and passes through the cars. **1848-71** W. M. GILLESPIE *Man. Road-making* 305 Most American roads with longitudinal timbers have been laid with plate rails, so thin that their ends sometimes spring up so as to form 'snake-heads'.

**3.** A representation of a snake's head. Also *attrib.*

**1865** KINGSLEY *Herew.* iii, Two ships.. whose long lines and snake-heads.. bore witness to the piratical habits of their owner. **1887** *Archit. Soc. Dict.* VII. 96/2 Snake head Molding.

**4.** A tropical marine or fresh-water carnivorous fish of the family Channidæ, esp. one of the genus *Ophiocephalus*, found in Africa or Asia, usually mottled grey, brown, or black in colour.

**1891** in *Cent. Dict.* **1905** D. S. JORDAN *Guide Study of Fishes* II. xxi. 370 Snake-head mullets.. seem to us nearer the labyrinthine fishes. **1961** E. S. HERALD *Living Fishes of World* 244/2 Snakeheads will live for many hours and sometimes days out of water.

'**snakeless**, *a.* [f. SNAKE *sb.*] Free from, not infested by, snakes.

**1881** TENNYSON *To Virgil* v, Summers of the snakeless meadow. **1893** *Voice* (N.Y.) 2 Feb., In snakeless regions [alcohol is supposed] to bring snakes and in snaky regions to cure their bites.

'**snakelet**. *rare.* [-LET.] A small snake.

**1887** *Pop. Sci. Monthly* XXX. 167 Dozens of young snakelets have been seen crawling into the open jaws.. of certain pythons.

'**snake-like**, *a.* [f. SNAKE *sb.*] Like or resembling a snake or that of a snake; having the characteristic form of a snake; long and slender.

Common in the 19th cent.

**1612** DRAYTON *Poly-olb.* ii. 34 Aloft where Chesil lifts Her ridged snake-like sands, in wrecks and smould'ring drifts. **1824** MISS MITFORD *Village* Ser. I. (1863) 83 My own pet May.. is sliding her snake-like head into my hand. **1839** LEVER *H. Lorrequer* xiii, The long procession wound its snake-like length down the narrow stair. *c* **1880** *Cassell's Nat. Hist.* IV. 301 Many of the smaller Colubrine Snakes resemble some of the Snake-like Lizards.

*fig.* **1821** BYRON *Juan* IV. ix, A long and snake-like life of dull decay. **1839-52** BAILEY *Festus* 99 This is a snakelike world, And always hath its tail within its mouth.

'**snakeling**. [f. SNAKE *sb.* + -LING.] A young snake. (Cf. SNAKELET.)

**1868** J. FERGUSSON *Tree & Serpent Worship* 38 There they laid their eggs and nursed their snakelings. **1894** *Pop. Sci. Monthly* Nov. 78 In these little snakelings the instinct of self-defense was born.

**snakeology** (sneɪ'kɒlədʒɪ). Also **snakology**. [f. SNAKE *sb.* + -OLOGY.] The study of snakes.

**1820** *Sporting Mag.* VII. 27 English snakology and its correlatives. *Ibid.*, His former practical experience in snakology. **1882** HOPLEY *Snakes* xii. 207 Not being specially interested in snakeology.

'**snake-pit**. Also snakepit. [SNAKE *sb.*]

**1.** Among primitive peoples, a large pit containing poisonous snakes into which victims are thrown for execution or as a test of endurance.

**1883** VIGFUSSON & YORK-POWELL *Corpus Poeticum Boreale* II. IX. 346 Anslaug.. gives him a charmed coat, which preserves him even in the snake-pit into which he is cast by Ælla, king of the Northumbrians. **1909** *Saga-Book of Viking Club* VI. I. 73 Ragnarr was captured by King Ella, and cast into a snake pit. **1940-41** *Scandinavian Stud.* XVI. 32 We may say that the theme of the Snake Tower or Snake Pit is foreign to Europe but is a typical Oriental importation. **1961** H. TREECE *Jason* III. xxvii. 224 Medea halted at the edge of the snake-pit... Then she lowered herself to the marble rim of the pit and gently eased down among the little snakes. **1977** A. P. SMYTH *Scandinavian Kings in Brit. Isles 850-880* iii. 36 The account of Ragnarr's invasion of Northumbria and his death in the snake-pit at the hands of King Ælla is found in its most elaborate form in *Ragnars saga*.

**2.** *transf.* and *fig.*

**1941** *Argus* (Melbourne) *Week-End Mag.* 15 Nov. 1/4 *Snake pit*, sergeants' mess. **1948** S. L. ELLIOTT in E. Hanger *Khaki, Bush & Bigotry* (1968) 91 Andy Edwards has been promoted and moved up to the snake pit with you and the other snakes. **1956** A. L. ROWSE *Early Churchills* v. 82 He was a man.. simple and rigid, in that snake-pit of a Court with its twisting.. creatures,.. deceitful and insincere. **1966** B. GLEMSER *Dear Hungarian Friend* ii. 36 He is at the United Nations... That is the only way to survive in the political snakepit. **1969** *N.Y. Review Bks.* 21 Aug. 8/1 The venal and compromising snakepit of American politics. **1976** *Publishers Weekly* 20 Sept. 74/3 All depicted as guilty as hell, conniving, scheming, fighting and feuding. It's a snakepit of a scene. **1977** *Listener* 25 Aug. 245/1 A snake-pit of imperfect chromatic scales.

**3.** *spec.* A mental hospital (after the title of the novel by M. J. Ward: see quot. 1947).

**1947** M. J. WARD (*title*) The snake pit. **1960** *Sunday Express* 15 May 17/4 The snake-pit women's ward. **1968** A. LASKI *Keeper* ii. 22 They had visited him in the snake-pit. **1976** *Courier-Mail* (Brisbane) 30 Apr. 5/1 It's like going back to the days when psychiatric hospitals everywhere were called snakepits.

†**snaker**, *v. Obs. rare.* [Cf. SNAKE *v.*[2] and -ER[5].] *intr.* To approach stealthily; to sneak.

*a* **1225** *Ancr. R.* 290 So sone so þu euer underȝitest þet tes dogge of helle kumeð snakerinde mid his blodie vlien of stinkinde þouhtes, ne lie þu nout stille. *Ibid.* 380 þet te best of helle, hwon he snakereð toward ou uorto biten on ou.

'**snake-root**. Also snake root, snakeroot. [f. SNAKE *sb.*]

**1. a.** The root or rhizome of one or other of several American plants reputed to possess properties antidotal to snake-poison, *esp.* the dried root of *Polygala Senega* and *Aristolochia serpentaria* used largely in medicine; the medicinal preparation obtained from this.

**1635** *Relat. Maryland* iii. 17 An excellent preseruative against Poyson, called by the English, the Snake roote. **1679** MOREAU in Perry *Hist. Coll. Am. Col. Ch.* I. 30, I make bold to send a small quantity of snake root, the best sudorific.. and counter poison that nature.. can afford. **1703** DAMPIER *Voy.* III. I. 72 Drugs of several sorts, *viz.* Sassafras, Snake-root, &c. **1783** *Med. Comment.* I. 143 He was ordered to take a decoction of bark and snakeroot. **1822-7** GOOD *Study Med.* (1829) I. 675 Bark, valerian, snake-root, conium, and the various preparations of the hop. **1866** *Treas. Bot.* 1067/2.

**b.** One or other of these plants.

**1712** *Pomet's Hist. Drugs* I. 26 Snake-Root.. is called by some Dittany, by others Contrayerva of Virginia. **1753** *Chambers' Cycl.* Suppl. *App.*, Snake-root, *aristolochia*,.. a genus of plants, otherwise called birthwort. **1832** GRIFFITH tr. *Cuvier* XIV. 60 The spathes of the snake-root.. are often covered or filled with sylphs. **1846** LINDLEY *Veg. Kingd.* 378 Of these the most celebrated is a North American herb called Snake-root, *Polygala senega*. **1861** G. F. BERKELEY *Eng. Sportsman* xi. 173 Only a flower here and there to be seen [on the prairie], consisting of the snake-root and the wild sun flower.

**c.** Used with specific names, as ***American***, ***black***, ***button***, ***Canada*** or ***Canadian***, ***Red River***, ***Samson's***, ***Seneca***, ***Texan***, ***white***, ***wild snake-root***; **Virginia(n) snake-root**, the root of *Polygala Senega* or *Aristolochia serpentaria*, the medicinal preparation made from this, or either of the plants producing it.

**1857** HENFREY *Bot.* 257 *Polygala Senega*, the *American Snake-root. **1755** JOHNSON s.v. *Ducksfoot*, *Black snake-root, or Mayapple. **1760** J. LEE *Introd. Bot.* 325 Root, Snake, black or wild, of America, *Actæa*. **1812** *New Botanic Gard.* I. 19 [*Actæa Racemosa*] is a native of North America, where it is often distinguished by the title of Black Snake-root. **1858** R. HOGG *Veg. Kingd.* 380 *Sanicula marilandica*, called in the United States Black Snake-root. **1845-50** MRS. LINCOLN *Lect. Bot.* App. 101 *Eryngium aquaticum* (*button snake-root). **1856** A. GRAY *Man. Bot.* 151 *E. yuccæfolium* (Rattlesnake-Master, Button Snake-root). *Ibid.* 184 *Liatris*. Button Snakeroot. **1849** J. H. BALFOUR *Man. Bot.* 491 *Asarum canadense*, Wild Ginger, or *Canada Snake-root, is used as a spice in Canada. **1887** *Encycl. Brit.* XXII. 189 The rhizome of *Asarum canadense*, L., passes under the name of Canadian Snake-root. *Ibid.*, The root of *Aristolochia reticulata*,.. which is known in the United States as *Red

River or Texan Snake-root. **1892** F. P. Foster *Med. Dict.* IV. 2660 *Psoralea eglandulosa.* *Samson's snakeroot. **1845–50** Mrs. Lincoln *Lect. Bot.* 180 We find here Polygala, one species of which is called *Seneca snake-root. **1694** Salmon *Bate's Dispens.* (1713) 258/2 The Sudorifick Tincture, or Tincture of *Virginia Snake-root. **1720** tr. *Hodge's Loimologia* 165 Virginian Snake-Root, when fresh and fragrant is the most efficacious. **1789** W. Buchan *Dom. Med.* (1790) 481 Take of Virginian snake-root in powder, half a drachm. **1841** *Penny Cycl.* XXI. 448/1 A deficiency of saliva..is removed by the Virginian snake-root. **1856** A. Gray *Man. Bot.* 188 *Eupatorium ageratoides* (*White Snake-root).

**2. a.** One or other of several plants so called from a fancied resemblance to a snake in some respect (see quots.).

**1856** Delamer *Fl. Gard.* (1861) 55 The Snake-root, *Arum dracunculus*, or Dragon Arum, is often found in old flower-gardens. **1858** A. Irvine *Handbk. Brit. Plants* Index 832 Snake-root,..*Polygonum Bistorta.* **1895** Oliver tr. *Kerner's Plants* I. 708 The creeping stems of the Snake-root (*Calla palustris*).

**b.** = RAUWOLFIA.

**1955** *Sci. Amer.* Oct. 81/1 Reserpine is an alkaloid extract from the snakeroot plant. **1976** W. A. R. Thomson *Herbs that Heal* ix. 147 The root, popularly known as 'snake-root' because of its long, tapering, crooked nature, contains most of the medicinal properties of the plant.

**snakery** ('sneɪkərɪ). [f. SNAKE *sb.* + -ERY[2].] A snake-house.

**1886** *Voice* (N.Y.) 30 Dec. 2 No man can be a successful snake-killer as long as he owns a snakery. **1888** *Longm. Mag.* Apr. 651 The late king of Oude had built a snakery in the gardens of his palace.

**Snakes and Ladders.** Also with hyphens and small initials. [See below.]

**1.** The name of a board-game for children in which the hazards and advantages are provided by snakes and ladders depicted on the board.

A counter that chances to arrive on a square at the head of a snake must be withdrawn to the snake's tail, while one that arrives at the foot of a ladder can be advanced to its top.

**1907** *Yesterday's Shopping* (1969) 1031/1 *Snakes and Ladders.* An interesting and most exciting game of chance. **1933** N. Streatfeild *Tops & Bottoms* xii. 146 Felicity thought that bringing up Beaty was rather like playing Snakes and Ladders, through no fault of your own stepping on the head of a snake and sliding to the bottom again; in this case, with no ladder in view up which to shoot to regain lost ground. **1946** E. Linklater *Private Angelo* viii. 89 Promotion in war-time was like..a game of snakes-and-ladders. **1964** A. Wykes *Gambling* vi. 128 Backgammon..is the precursor of practically every modern board-and-pieces game in which the moves are decided by dice—even parlor games like *snakes-and-ladders.* **1980** *Daily Tel.* 25 Jan. 15/3 New and more sophisticated versions of snakes and ladders and noughts and crosses will also be provided [on trains].

**2.** *fig.* A series of unpredictable successes and set-backs. Hence ***snake-and-ladder*** adj.

**1930** M. Allingham *Mystery Mile* xxiii. 213 The [fire] engines were still drawn up outside Number Thirty Four. 'Still playing Snakes and Ladders, I see,' said Campion. **1961** *Listener* 31 Aug. 319/2 The artists whose life-work does not find a place in the historical snakes and ladders of *avant-garde* development. **1978** G. Greene *Human Factor* v. iii. 267 After so many years of concealment he was beginning to enjoy this snake-and-ladder game. **1978** G. Sims *Rex Mundi* xix. 117 Snakes and ladders progress, old man—that's all we can hope for. A lucky throw that puts us on the ladder. **1982** *Church Times* 23 July 6/1 Nothing could illustrate more graphically the snake-and-ladder aspect of a political career than the last year of Tony Crosland's life.

**snake's head.** Also snakeshead, snake's-head. [SNAKE *sb.* 13.]

**1.** *attrib.* **a.** ***snake's-head iris***, an iris of the Mediterranean region, *Hermodactylus tuberosus.*

**1739** Miller *Gard. Dict.* II, *Hermodactylus*, the Hermodactyl, commonly called Snakes-head Iris. **1786** Abercrombie *Arr.* in *Gard. Assist.* 59 Tuberous-rooted, or snake's head iris. **1825** *Greenho. Comp.* I. 117 Chalcedonian and Snakeshead Iris. **1882** *Garden* 18 Mar. 176/1 The Snake's-head Iris..is not a new, but a very old, plant.

**b.** ***snake's-head fly*** (see quot.).

**1826** Kirby & Sp. *Entomol.* III. xxxiv. 527 *Raphidia*, the snake's-head fly.

**c.** ***snake's-head fritillary, lily*** (see 2 b).

**1899** *Gardening Illustr.* 29 Apr. 112/1 The beautiful Snake's-head Fritillary..that grows in the Oxfordshire meadows. **1902** Cornish *Naturalist Thames* 180 Butter-burs and wild snake's-head lilies.

**2. a.** *U.S.* = SNAKE-HEAD 1.

**1834** Audubon *Ornith.* II. 150 The Snake's Head [*Chelone glabra*] grows on the banks of rivers and swamps, in the Middle and Southern States. **1866** *Treas. Bot.* 1067.

**b.** The common fritillary, *Fritillaria meleagris*; so called from the fancied resemblance of the bud to the head of a snake.

**1859** Miss Pratt *Flower. Pl.* V. 277 Common Fritillary, or Snake's-head. **1869** Ruskin *Q. of Air* §87 It chequers itself into a snake's head, and secretes in the deep of its bell ..honey-dew. **1897** *B'ham Weekly Post* 17 Apr. 4/7 Snakes-heads, our wild flower is sometimes called, from the shape of the buds.

**3.** *U.S.* (See quots. and SNAKE-HEAD 2.)

**1848** in Bartlett *Dict. Amer.* 315 The road to Petersburg consists of an iron strap laid upon pine timber, and is beautifully diversified with that peculiar half horizontal, vibrating rail, known as 'snake's head'. **1886** *Encycl. Brit.* XX. 223 *n.*, As the ends of the bars became loose and turned upwards they were known as 'snakes' heads'.

**snakeship** ('sneɪkʃɪp). [f. SNAKE *sb.* + -SHIP.] The personality of a snake. (Used as a mock title or humorous designation.)

**1839** F. Barham *Adamus Exul* 14 Thus unknown, My lubricating snakeship will I wind Cunningly onward. **1849** *Zoologist* VII. 2459 Captain Adams, not feeling partial to an encounter with his snakeship, ordered the vessel to be kept off. **1876** E. W. Clark *Life Japan* 90 One of my bearers poked him [a snake] gently with a stick, whereupon his snakeship moved slowly away.

**'snakesman.** *Cant.* Now *Hist.* (See quot. 1785)

**1785** Grose *Dict. Vulgar T.* s.v. *Little, Little snakesman*, a little boy who gets into a house through the sink hole, and then opens the door for his accomplices. **1973** G. Butler *Coffin for Pandora* vii. 153 Perhaps I did train up one or two snakesmen..and perhaps we did work together. **1975** M. Crichton *Great Train Robbery* v. 31 A snakesman was a child adept at wriggling through small spaces.

**'snake-stone.** Also snakestone, snake stone. [f. SNAKE *sb.*]

**1.** An ammonite. Now *dial.*

**1661** J. Childrey *Brit. Bacon.* 77 In this too they agree with the Snake-stones of Keinsham. **1668** Charleton *Onomast.* 267 *Sceleton Serpentis*,..*Ophiomorphites*, Snake-stone. **1696** Aubrey *Nat. Hist. Wilts.* (1847) 45 About two or three miles from the Devises are found in a pitt Snake-stones (*cornua ammonis*) no bigger than a sixpence. **1708** *Phil. Trans.* XXVI. 78 The Sayler or (as 'tis commonly call'd) the Snake-stone. **1758** [see AMMONITE 1]. **1828** G. Young *Geol. Surv. Yorksh. Coast* 138 The well known Whitby snake-stones. **1854–** in dialect glossaries (Yks., Linc., Northants., Leic.).

**2.** A porous or absorbent substance regarded as efficacious in curing snake-bite or as a remedy against poison; a serpent-stone.

**1694** *Phil. Trans.* XVIII. 128, I think they all recovered, to which he applyed the Snake-stones. **1698** Fryer *Acc. E. India & P.* 53 A Factitious Stone (which we call a Snake-stone) is a Counter-poyson to all deadly Bites. **1822** J. Flint *Lett. Amer.* 128 In some parts of the Union, what are called snake-stones are relied on as certain cures for the bite of the reptile, and of mad dogs. **1855** Browning *An Epistle* 17 The vagrant Scholar to his Sage at home Sends..Three samples of true snake-stone. **1903** Sir M. G. Gerard *Leaves fr. Diaries* x. 376 A snake-stone is..a secretion which occasionally forms on the palate of a snake's mouth.

**3.** A small perforated stone (cf. *adder-stone*, ADDER *sb.*[2] 5).

**1700** Lhywd in Rowlands *Mona Antiqua* (1723) 338 Besides the Snake-Stones,..the Highlanders have their Snail-Stones, Paddoc-stones [etc.], to all which they attribute their several Virtues. **1872** J. Evans *Anc. Stone Impl.* 391 In Harris and Lewis the distaff and spindle are still in common use, and yet the original intention of the stone spindle-whorls, which occur there as elsewhere, appears to be unknown. They are called *clach-nathrach*, adder-stones, or snake-stones.

**4.** *techn.* (See later quots.)

**1850** Holtzapffel *Turning* III. 1040 Marks are then made with a piece of snake-stone, blue-stone, or even common slate pencil. **1858** Simmonds *Dict. Trade, Snake-stone*, a kind of hone slate, or whetstone obtained in Scotland, and also known as Ayr stone. **1870** *Eng. Mech.* 7 Jan. 417/3 The snakestone..used by lithographers..is a carbonate of lime, and is found in Germany and in India. The snake stone used by marble polishers is a fine *grit*, and is found at Water of Ayr.

**'snake-weed.** Also snakeweed. [SNAKE *sb.*]

**1.** The plant bistort, *Polygonum bistorta.*

In dial. use the name has also been applied to other species of *Polygonum*, as *P. lapathifolium* and *P. viviparum*; and to the plants *Mercurialis perennis*, dog's mercury, and *Cicuta maculata*, an American hemlock.

**1597** Gerarde *Herbal* II. lxxxi. 323 *Bistorta* is called in English Snakeweede. *Ibid.*, Broade leafed Snakeweede. **1601** R. Chester *Love's Martyr* (1878) 90 Dwarfe gentian, Snakeweed, and Sommer Sauory. **1611** Cotgr., *Bistorte*, Bistort,..Snakeweed. **1707** *Curios. in Husb. & Gard.* 284 Mountebanks..instead of Mandrakes..sell the Roots of Bryony or of Snake-weed. **1760** J. Lee *Introd. Bot.* 327 Snakeweed, *Polygonum.* **1852** Morfit *Tanning & Currying* (1853) 40 Certain annual plants—as the septfoil and bistort, or snake-weed. **1887** *Brit. Med. Jrnl.* Feb. 424 The rhizome of snake-weed..is successfully used by the Lithuanian peasantry as a prophylactic in cases of bite by rabid animals.

**2.** = SNAKE-ROOT 1.

**1631** Winthrop *Hist. New Eng.* (1825) I. 62 He always carried about with him match and a compass, and in summer time snake-weed. **1671** Salmon *Syn. Med.* III. xxii. 392 Snakeweed. The root of the Virginian cures the Plague, poyson, Pox [etc.]. **1725** *Fam. Dict.* s.v. *Fryars-Balsam*, Infuse in it..one Ounce of Virginia Snake-weed cut small. **1855** Dunglison *Dict. Med. Sci.* (ed. 12) 100 *Aristolochia Serpentaria*,..Virginian Snakeroot,..Snake-weed.

**'snakewise,** *adv.* [f. SNAKE *sb.*] In the manner of a snake; with a snake-like movement.

**1874** Lanier *Poems, In Absence* ii, The mottled formulas of Sense Glide snakewise through our dreams of Aftertime. **1894** D. C. Murray *Making of a Novelist* 29 It was so low that we had to go snakewise.

**'snake-wood.** Also snakewood. [SNAKE *sb.*]

**1. a.** A tree or shrub belonging to the genus *Strychnos*, esp. *S. colubrina* of the East Indies; the wood of one or other of these trees used as a remedy for snake-poison. **b.** The East Indian plant *Ophioxylon serpentinum.*

**1598** W. Phillip tr. *Linschoten* I. lxxv. 121/1 Snakewood is most in the Island of Seylon: it is a lowe Tree: the roote thereof being the Snake-woode is of colour white. **1613** Purchas *Pilgrimage* (1614) 507 Snakewood groweth in Seylon, and is good against the stinging of Snakes and other poyson. **1711** *Phil. Trans.* XXVII. 347 The first Figure is of a Wood from India,..*Lignum Colubrinum*, or Snake-Wood. **1835** G. T. Burnett *Outlines Bot.* §4614 *Ophioxylon serpentinum* is one of the snake-woods, which in various parts of India are affirmed to be antidotes to the bites of poisonous reptiles. **1836** J. Gully *Magendie's Formul.* (ed. 2) 6 Nux vomica, the Javanese poison, and the snake-wood all owe their violent action on animals to strychnia [and] brucia. **1861** Bentley *Man. Bot.* 592 The wood of *S[trychnos] colubrina* and *S. ligustrina* is employed in certain parts of Asia as an antidote to the bites of poisonous snakes, hence it is known under the name of *Lignum Colubrinum* or Snake-wood.

**2.** One or other of various trees formerly classed under the genus *Colubrina*, or of the West Indian trees *Cecropia peltata*, the trumpet tree, and *Plumieria rubra*, the red jasmine.

**1832** Don *Gen. Syst. Gard. & Bot.* II. 36/1 *Colubrina ferruginea*... This tree is called *Bois couleuvre* or Snake-wood in Martinique. *Ibid.*, Reclined-branched Snake-wood [and many other species]. **1858** Simmonds *Dict. Trade, Snake-wood*, a name applied both to the *Cecropia peltata*, and the *Plumeria rubra.* **1864** Grisebach *Flora Brit. W. Ind.* 787/2 Snake-wood,..*Colubrina ferruginosa.*

**3.** The wood of the South American timber-tree *Brosimum Aubletii* (or *Piratinera guianensis*), so called from its snake-like markings; letter-wood; also, the tree producing this wood.

**1843** Holtzapffel *Turning* I. 106 Snake-wood is scarce in England, and chiefly used for the most expensive walking-sticks. **1851** *Art Jrnl. Illust. Catal.* II. p. vii/1 The beautiful snake-wood is the timber of a *Brosimum.* **1880** Bessey *Botany* 490 The beautifully mottled and streaked Snakewood, much prized by cabinetmakers, and for making bows.

**snakily** ('sneɪkɪlɪ), *adv.* [f. SNAKY *a.* + -LY[2].] In a snaky or snake-like manner; windingly.

**1870** W. Thornbury *Tour r. Eng.* I. xv. 308 The Orwell ..snakily winding between flat muddy reaches. **1891** G. Meredith *One of our Conq.* III. ix. 179 Foul Furies.. hissing and snakily lashing, hounding her to expulsion.

**snakiness** ('sneɪkɪnɪs). [f. SNAKY *a.*] Snaky character or appearance.

**1842** *Peter Parley's Ann.* III. 143 There was a sort of sleight-of-hand in his face—a snakiness about his jaws. **1881** *Spectator* 19 Feb. 258/2 In the description of Narcissa..her snakiness is expatiated upon to a needless extent.

**snaking** ('sneɪkɪŋ), *vbl. sb.* [f. SNAKE *sb.* or *v.*[1]]

**1.** *Naut.* (See quots. and SNAKE *v.*[1] 1 b.)

**1815** Burney *Falconer's Dict. Marine* 487/1 *Snaking*..is the act of winding small ropes spirally round a large one,.. and is frequently termed Worming. **1867** Smyth *Sailor's Word-bk.* 635 *Snaking*, the passing of small stuff across a seizing, with marline hitches at the outer turns. **1875** Knight *Dict. Mech.* 2229/1 *Snaking*,..stoppers passed alternately from one stay or rope to another throughout their length in a parallel direction.

**2.** A snake-like curl or coil.

**1888** Clark Russell *Death Ship* xli, Heights of the sea.. spouting their prodigious lengths alongside, sometimes tumbling in thunder upon her forward decks, sometimes curling in blown snakings ahead of her.

**3.** *U.S.* The action of dragging *out.*

**1883** *Harper's Mag.* Jan. 206/1 The snaking out of these logs is another source of casualty to the lumberman.

**4.** A rapid oscillation of an aircraft about a vertical axis; a similar motion of a caravan or trailer.

**1945** *Jrnl. R. Aeronaut. Soc.* XLIX. 463/2 There is a possibility of the aeroplane developing an undamped short period oscillation in which rapid movement of the rudder from side to side plays an essential part—the tail wagging the dog. Such an oscillation is known as 'snaking'. **1949** *Aircraft Engin.* Oct. 311/1 Snaking can be cured by sticking on strips to the trailing edge of the rudder. **1966** *Caravanning* ('Know the Game' Ser.) 11 Stabilisers have been devised to overcome any side movement or 'snaking' of the caravan in relation to the direction of the car. **1972** *Nature* 18 Aug. 377/2 Detailed studies of gust effects, and of 'snaking'.

**snaking** ('sneɪkɪŋ), *ppl. a.* [Cf. SNAKE *v.*[1]] Winding, twisting, sinuous.

**1591** Sylvester *Du Bartas* I. vii. 81 The flowry Plains.. Laced about with snaking silver brooks. **1615** Crooke *Body of Man* 94 Wherein the snaking and snayling diuarications of the vessels do craule all ouer the belly. **1906** *Westm. Gaz.* 5 June 2/1 From that height,..the city took an odd look, with its snaking quays and its many domed churches.

**snakish** ('sneɪkɪʃ), *a.* [f. SNAKE *sb.*] Of or pertaining to a snake; snake-like, snaky.

**1532** More *Confut. Tindale* Wks. 512/1 These Heretiques ..whose snakish and serpentine generacions haue..hadde theyr heades troden downe by Godde. **1565** Golding *Ovid's Met.* IV. (1593) 97 Before this snakish shape do whole my body over-run. *Ibid.* 98 On their snakish heads grew crests. **1594** Carew *Tasso* (1881) 26 So gentle seemd a while, the Snakish brood. **1632** Lithgow *Trav.* B j b, The hissing of snakish Papists. **1825** *Examiner* 560/1 The sneaking, snakish, and vile token of displeasure, hissing. **1864** Carlyle *Fredk. Gt.* xv. xi. IV. 168 If you will withdraw your snakish notions, will guarantee Silesia,..he will march home.

Hence **'snakishness.**

**1901** S. Dark *Stage Silhouettes* 18 Mrs. Campbell's subtlety and snakishness as Lady Macbeth.

**snakishly** ('sneɪkɪʃlɪ), *adv.* [f. SNAKISH *a.* + -LY[2].] In the manner of a snake; treacherously, venomously.

**1935** E. R. Eddison *Mistress* xi. 204 The Vicar, regarding him snakishly, drew back his thin lips in a smile. **1963** D. Hughes in Sissons & French *Age of Austerity* iv. 87 Heath

..was accepted..as a quite normal manifestation of that time..which made his vicious sallies into madness..all the more snakishly repellent.

**snaky** ('sneɪkɪ), *a.* Also 6–7 snakie, 7 *Sc.* snaiky, 8 snakey. [f. SNAKE *sb.* + -Y.]

**1. a.** Formed or composed of snakes.

Chiefly in allusions to the serpent hair of the Furies.

**1567** TURBERV. *Epit.*, etc. 64 b, All ye that Ladies are of Lymbo Lake With hissing haire, and Snakie bush bedect. **1595** SPENSER *Sonn.* lxxxv, The Furies fell Theyr snaky heads doe combe. **1602** *2nd Pt. Return fr. Parnass.* IV. ii. 1735 Megæra with her snakie twine. **1633** P. FLETCHER *Purple Isl.* V. lxv, The Furies flung their snakie whips away. **1667** MILTON *P.L.* X. 559 Thicker than the snakie locks That curld Megæra. **1710** ADDISON *Tatler* No. 154 ¶3 The Gorgon with Snakey Hair. **1862** COX *Tales Gods & Heroes* 203 Pegasos, the child of Gorgo with the snaky hair. **1868** MORRIS *Earthly Par.* (1870) I. I. 290 He drew the head out by the snaky hairs.

**b.** ***the snaky sisters***, the Furies.

**1728** RAMSAY *Fables, Miser & Minos* 31 The three-pow'd dog of hell Gowl'd terrible a triple yell; Which rouz'd the snaky Sisters three.

**2.** Entwined with snakes. Said of the caduceus.

**1591** SPENSER *M. Hubberd* 1292 In his hand He tooke Caduceus his snakie wand. **1599** B. JONSON *Cynthia's Rev.* I. i, What? vse the vertue of your snakie tip-staffe there vpon us? **1700** DRYDEN *Ovid, Metamorphoses* I. 928 In his Hand He holds the Virtue of the Snaky Wand. **1735** *Dict. Polygraph.* II. s.v. *Mercury*, A *caduceus*, or snaky staff, *viz.* a slender wand, about which two snakes did annodate.

**3. a.** Of or pertaining to a snake; freq. in allusive use, venomous, guileful, deceitful, treacherous.

*a* **1586** SIDNEY *Arcadia* V. (1605) 455 O snakie ambition, which can wind thy selfe in so many figures. **1596** COLSE *Penelope* (1880) 162 Knowne trueth ne snaky enuies spite, Nor wrath can touch. **1612** CHAPMAN *Rev. Bussy d'Ambois* V. v. 208 Hide, hide thy snaky head! to cloisters fly. **1671** MILTON *P.R.* I. 120 So to the Coast of Jordan he directs His easie steps; girded with snaky wiles. **1729** SAVAGE *Wanderer* III. 125 Can the dove's bosom snakey venom draw? *c* **1840** DE QUINCEY *Murder* Wks. 1862 IV. 65 The oiliness and snaky insinuation of his demeanour. **1865** KINGSLEY *Herew.* vi, His thin Punic lips curved into a snaky smile. **1879** BROWNING *Ivan Ivanovitch* 215 Have at the snaky tongue! That's the right way with wolves! **1933** J. V. ALLEN *Cowboy Lore* IV. 101 If you reckon your mounts are some snakey and raw Just try ridin' herd on a stove that won't draw. **1966** M. & O. MURIE *Wapiti Wilderness* iv. 71 Oh, I believe he's a pretty good horse. He may be a little bit snaky. **1980** [see *shavetail* s.v. SHAVE *v.* 13].

**b.** *Austral.* and *N.Z. slang.* Angry, annoyed.

**1919** W. H. DOWNING *Digger Dialects* 46 *Snaky*,..(1) angry (e.g., to turn snaky); (2) irritable. **1941** K. TENNANT *Battlers* 86 Now lay off, sport... Don't go snaky on the kid. **1943** *Amer. Speech* XVIII. 90 [In New Zealand] *To go crook* is to show anger or annoyance... The verbs *to go snaky, to go maggoty*..have the same implications. **1945** N. MARSH *Died in Wool* vii. 155 There was a hold up... Everyone was snakey. Young Doug says the sheep are dry and I say they're not. **1974** D. WILLIAMSON *Three Plays* 34 What are you snaky about this time? **1981** *Courier-Mail* (Brisbane) 28 Nov. 23/1 They remain very snaky indeed about allegedly non-impartial treatment from players and umpires in Perth.

**4.** Resembling the form of a snake; long and winding or twisting; sinuous, tortuous.

**1596** SHAKS. *Merch. V.* III. ii. 92 Those crisped snakie golden locks Which make such wanton gambols with the winde. *c* **1611** CHAPMAN *Iliad* II. 769 The crooked armes Meander bow'd with his so snakie flood. **1695** BLACKMORE *Pr. Arth.* II. 153 Their watry Train in Snaky Windings slides. **1827** CARLYLE *Misc.* (1840) I. 15 No story proceeds without..voluminous tagrags rolling after it in many a snaky twine. **1869** PHILLIPS *Vesuv.* iv. 126 The black sand lay thick between the snaky ridges of lava. **1887** PALGRAVE *Ulysses* 4 Huge woolly camels..thrust out their shaggy snaky necks.

**5.** ***snaky letter***, a sibilant. *nonce-use.*

**1599** MINSHEU *Sp. Gram.* 8 One of the *Culebrinas létras*, the snakie or hissing letters.

**6.** Of places: Infested with snakes.

**1856** LADY CANNING in Hare *Two Noble Lives* (1893) II. 121 A charming ride round jungly lanes, with..tangles—very snaky, I should fear. **1883** ROLLINS *New Eng. Bygones* 185 The place was said to be snaky.

**7.** Relating to snakes. (Cf. *snake-story*.)

**1882** *Daily News* 18 Jan. 5/5 'Snaky' stories are only fit for that presently-to-vanish corps, the Marines.

**8.** *Comb.*, as ***snaky-footed***, ***-haired***, ***-headed***, etc., ***snaky-sparkling*** adjs.; ***snaky-like*** adv.

**1591** SPENSER *Ruins of Rome* 178 Nor swelling streames of that God [Tiber] snakie-paced. **1596** —— *F.Q.* VII. vi. 18 He on her shoulder laid His snakie-wreathed Mace. **1596** FITZ-GEFFREY *Sir F. Drake* (1881) 96 The snaky-hayred Furies loathsome cell. **1638** JUNIUS *Paint. Ancients* 60 The snaky-headed Furies tearing..and thrusting a hand-full of hissing serpents. **1736** AINSWORTH *Eng.-Lat. Dict.* I, Snaky handed, or snouted (as an elephant), *anguimanus*. Snaky footed (as the fabulous giants), *anguipedes*. **1837** CARLYLE *Fr. Rev.* III. I. iv, May not Murder come; and, with her snaky-sparkling head, illuminate this murk! **1855** SMEDLEY *Occult Sci.* 181 He persuaded that snaky-tailed monster to accompany him. **1871** B. TAYLOR *Faust* (1875) II. II. iii. 134 Her smooth braids, snaky-like, intwine.

**snallygaster** ('snælɪgɑːstə(r), -gæs-). *U.S. dial.* [ad. G. *schnelle geister*, lit. 'quick spirits'.] A mythical monster supposedly found in Maryland. Cf. SNOLLYGOSTER.

**1940** *Maryland* (Writers' Program) 348 Residents of a Negro settlement near the distillery are firm in their belief that the neighborhood has a 'snallygaster'—a fabulous reptilian bird of vast size that preys on poultry and Negro children after nightfall. **1949** *Sun* (Baltimore) 28 July 14/1 (*heading*) Could it have been a snallygaster? **1954** *Sunday Sun* (Baltimore) *Mag.* 31 Oct. (*recto front cover*), Is this, at last, the snallygaster that has been said to terrorize Western Maryland but that most people have considered legendary?

**snam** (snæm), *v. slang.* ? *Obs.* [Origin unknown.] *intr.* To snatch; to steal.

App. recorded only in Dicts.

**1824** J. MACTAGGART *Scottish Gallovidian Encycl.* 429 *Snam*, to snap at any thing greedily. **1874** HOTTEN *Slang Dict.* 298 *Snam*, to snatch, or rob from the person. Mostly used to describe that kind of theft which consists in picking up anything lying about, and making off with it rapidly.

Hence as *sb.*; also **'snammer**, one who snams; a thief.

**1839** H. BRANDON in W. A. Miles *Poverty, Mendicity & Crime* 164/2 *Pudding Snammer*, one who steals from a cook shop. **1887** Snam [see DUB *sb.*[5]]. **1950** PARTRIDGE *Dict. Underworld* 649/1 *On the snam*, engaged in stealing.

**snap** (snæp), *sb.* Also 5–7 snappe, 7 (9) snapp. [Related to SNAP *v.* Cf. Du. *snap*, LG. *snap*, *snapp*, late MHG. *snap* (G. *schnapp* masc.); also *schnappe* fem.) in the same or related senses.]

**I. 1.** A quick or sudden closing of the jaws or teeth in biting, or of scissors in cutting; a bite or cut made in this way. Also *fig.* and in fig. context.

**1495** in *Blackw. Mag.* Apr. (1908) 506/1, 1 bay mare, a snappe in the left ear and in the right ear a ferthyng. **1555** EDEN *Decades* (Arb.) 170 Whiche cutteth a man in sunder.. at one snappe with his teethe. **1592** GREENE *Upst. Courtier* Wks. XI. 247 At euery word a snap with your sissors. **1634** CANNE *Necess. Separ.* (1849) 20 Craving to be put into one of the priests' offices, that he may have a snap at a crust of bread. **1725** DE FOE *Voy. r. World* (Bohn) 299 He took the scissors, and at one snap set them at liberty again. **1816** SCOTT *Antiq.* iii, He had the scent of a slow-hound..and the snap of a bull-dog. **1899** F. V. KIRBY *Sport E.C. Africa* iv. 51 The huge jaws opened once and shut with a vicious snap.

**2.** *slang.* **a.** A share (cf. SNACK *sb.*[2] 3); something worth securing or getting hold of; an odd chance; a good place or job.

**1561** AWDELAY *Frat. Vacab.* (1869) 4 An Vpright man.. may cal them to accompt, & command a share or snap vnto him selfe, of al that they haue gained by their trade in one moneth. *a* **1800** PEGGE *Suppl. Grose* s.v., To go snaps is to go halves in anything. **1864** *Slang Dict.*, *Snapps*, share, portion; any articles or circumstances out of which money may be made. 'Looking out for snapps,' waiting for windfalls or odd jobs. **1893** *Dispatch* (Columbus) 20 Feb., 'A public office is a public trust.' The clerks regard it rather as a public 'snap'. **1897** FLANDRAU *Harvard Episodes* 259 He's on the lookout for snaps.

**b.** *Theat.* A short engagement.

**1882** *Adventures Billy Shakespoke* v. 89, I dropped in to see my old partner..and he proposed that we should try another 'snap' in Lynn. **1885** *Santa Fé Weekly New Mexican* 24 Sept. 4/6 It is the custom, during the summer months, for 'snap' companies to travel through the country and gather shekels. *a* **1891** FREUND *Music & Drama* XIV. xvi. 3 (Cent.), Actors and actresses who have just come in from 'summer snaps' to prepare for the work of the coming season.

**c.** = *soft snap* s.v. SOFT *a.* 29. Chiefly *N. Amer.*

**1877** H. RUEDE *Sod-House Days* 120 It is no snap, for the straw rolls out fast enough to keep them very busy. **1901** *Daily Colonist* (Victoria, B.C.) 27 Oct. 3/4 Formerly porters received as low as $15 a month and this wage in a buffet car was at one time considered a snap, as tips were wont to bring a man's income up to all the way from $100 to $200 a month. **1924** P. MARKS *Plastic Age* xxiv. 287 He had three classes in literature, one in music—partly because it was a 'snap' and partly because he really wanted to know more about music—and his composition course. **1936** V. SHEEAN *Personal Hist.* i. 3 The football players, the social lights, the pretty co-eds, and all the other students who regarded study as an inconvenient detail in college life, rushed to inscribe themselves for 'snap' courses. **1962** A. LURIE *Love & Friendship* iii. 180 The new semester has started, and I have a whole new selection of little 'creative writers' on my hands ...the course is rumored to be a Snap (one thinks of those paper crackers at children's parties). **1967** *Technology Week* XX. 95/2 (Advt.), Blazing a path to the moon is no snap. Neither is charting a career.

**3.** A small piece or portion; a scrap, fragment, or morsel. **a.** In emphatic use, as ***not a snap***, ***every snap***. Now *dial.*

**1610** BEAUM. & FL. *Scornf. Lady* IV. i, Come, come, you would know it;..but not a snap, never long for't, not a snap dear Ladie. **1690** W. WALKER *Idiomat. Anglo-Lat.* 423 They leave not a snap i' th' dish; i.e. eat all up; every bit and snap. **1837** *Wilson's Tales Borders* III. 257 The puir hungry wratches will eat it up, every snap, afore morning. **1875** DICKINSON *Cumbriana* 10 Then he choppt up a drinkin' glass an' eat it ivery snap.

**b.** In general use. ? *Obs.* (freq. in 17th cent.).

**1626** B. JONSON *Staple of N.* I. v, Hee's a nimble Fellow! And alike skil'd in euery liberall Science, As hauing certaine snaps of all. **1642** FULLER *Holy & Prof. St.* V. xiv. 411 He may get some almes of learning, here a snap, there a piece of knowledge, but nothing to purpose. **1698** FRYER *Acc. E. India & P.* 260 Our Burses being but Snaps of Buildings to these famous Buzzars.

**4.** A slight or hasty meal or mouthful; a snack. Now *dial.* or *spec.* (cf. quot. 1883). Also in *Comb.*, as ***snap-time***, ***-tin***.

Not always clearly distinguishable from prec.

**1642** FULLER *Holy & Prof. St.* III. xii. 5 It is one thing to laugh at them *in transitu*, a snap and away, and another to make a set meal in jeering them. **1655** —— *Ch. Hist.* XI. ii. 59 Henry Burton..rather took a snap then made a meal in any University. **1668** R. STEELE *Husbandman's Calling* x. (1672) 251 The Egyptian dogs do taste the waters of Nilus for fear of the crocidiles, a snap and away. **1700** MOTTEUX *Quix.* (1733) II. 55 The Curate's Provision..was but a Snap among so many, for they were all very hungry. **1818** SCOTT *Hrt. Midl.* xxx, First taste a snap of right Hollands. **1858** GEO. ELIOT *Scenes Clerical Life, Janet's Repentance* i, Two hearty meals that might have been mistaken for dinners, if he had not declared them to be 'snaps'. **1883** GRESLEY *Gloss. Coal-m.* 229 *Snap*,..food taken by a collier during his shift. **1913** D. H. LAWRENCE *Sons & Lovers* i. 25 She..put him out a clean scarf and snap-bag. *Ibid.* iv. 65, I went to put my coat on at snap-time. **1935** A. J. CRONIN *Stars look Down* I. ix. 67 'Come on, ye old beggor, and have yer snap,' Tom called out with his mouth full of bread and cheese. **1960** C. DAY LEWIS *Buried Day* vii. 131 The black-faced miners cycling home from work with their snap-tins bumping at their sides. **1980** *Guardian* 11 Nov. 8/3 At 10 o'clock the regular farm hands disappeared to the dutch barn for their 'snap'.

**5. a.** A sudden snatch or catch at something; a quick movement or effort. †***to lie at*** (or ***upon the***) ***snap***, to lie in wait. †***by snaps***, fitfully, spasmodically.

**1631** T. POWELL *Tom of All Trades* 42 A Sea Soldier may now and than chaunce to haue a snapp at a bootie. **1648** HEXHAM II, *Een Luymer, ofte Loerer*, one that Lies upon the Snap, or Leers what one saith. *c* **1660** *Songs & Poems Costume* (Percy Soc.) 152 With sugared words they lye at snap, But I'le be sure to watch 'um. **1692** L'ESTRANGE *Josephus* (1733) 860 Now Apollonius does not carry on his Malice..in a continu'd set Discourse, but now and then by Snaps as the Humour takes him. **1755** JOHNSON, *Snap*,..a catch; a theft. **1823** E. MOOR *Suffolk Words*, *Snap*,..any sharp, quick, short motion. **1882** *Jamieson's Sc. Dict.*, *Snap*, a sudden..grip, or seizure of any kind.

**b.** *Angling.* One or other of different methods of fishing for pike (see quots.).

**1651** T. BARKER *Art of Angling* (1820) 23 There is a way to take a Pike, which is called the taking of a Pike by snap, for which angling you must have a pretty strong rod. *Ibid.* 28 That other fine trick, Which our Artists call Snap, with a Goose or a Duck. **1787** BEST *Angling* (ed. 2) 45 Angling for the pike at the snap is to let him run a little, and then to strike him, the contrary way from whence he runs, with two strong jerks. **1847** T. BROWN *Mod. Farriery* 902 At both troll and snap some persons have two or more swivels to their line.

**c.** ***in a snap***, in a moment, immediately.

So WFris. *yn ien snap*, G. *in einem schnapp*, LG. *mit ên(em) snapp*.

**1768** ROSS *Helenore* 119 An' now the fead [= feud] is softn'd..The face o' things is alter'd in a snap. **1801** *Spirit Public Jrnls.* IX. 381 I'll put you to rights in a snap.

**d.** A card-game, in which the call of 'snap' under certain conditions (esp. when two matching cards are exposed) gives to one player the right to take cards from another. Also *attrib.*, as ***snap-card***.

**1881** *Cassell's Bk. Indoor Amusements* 144 The game of Snap may either be played with the ordinary Whist cards or with special cards prepared for the purpose. **1890** CHAMPLIN & BOSTWICK *Young Folks' Cyclopaedia Games & Sports* 659/1 *Snap*, a game played by any number of persons with 36 cards. **1903** *Cassell's Bk. of In-door Amusem.* 125 Snap..may be played either with the ordinary whist cards, or with a special pack manufactured for the purpose. [Description follows.] **1916** *N. & Q.* 9 Sept. 210/1 Who designed the illustrations that appear on snap cards, and when did they first appear? **1966** J. DERRICK *Teaching English to Immigrants* v. 188 Much pre-reading apparatus can be used for this purpose, such as word-matching cards, snapcards, word lotto, and other sets of apparatus where identifying and matching single words is involved.

**e.** A temporary faro game.

**1845** J. J. HOOPER *Some Adventures Capt. S. Suggs* x. 133 I'll never bet on two pair agin! They're peart at the snap game, theyselves; but they're badly lewed this hitch! **1864** W. B. DICK *Amer. Hoyle* 208 *Snap*, [in Faro] a temporary bank, not a regular or established game. **1938** H. ASBURY *Sucker's Progress* 280 A few of the river gamesters ran Faro snaps when ashore in St. Louis, but most of them concentrated on Poker.

**f.** A U.S. party game in which one of the players chases another round a ring formed by the rest.

**1865** B. L. RIDLEY *Battles & Sk. Army of Tennessee* (1906) 481 Games [in Georgia] soon began—'Thimble', 'Snap', and kissing songs. **1930** *Virginia Jrnl. Educ.* Oct. 73 Social intercourse [in the mountains of Virginia] was very limited. Monthly religious meetings at widely scattered churches, occasional parties at which 'Boston', 'Snap' and 'Shaker's Dance' were played all night long. **1944** G. WILSON *Passing Institutions* 93 Our liveliest game was Snap, a game that used to seem very exciting but now somewhat resembles Drop the Handkerchief.

**g.** *U.S.* and *Canad. Football.* = SNAP-BACK 1 b.

**1922** P. D. HAUGHTON *Football & how to watch It* 30 Watch the offensive ends begin their mad rush downfield at the snap of the ball. **1947** *Richmond* (Va.) *Times-Dispatch* 9 Nov. B7/7 From a single-wing formation to the right, Deuber, the tailback, took the snap and set sail wide around Virginia's left end. **1958** *Edmonton Jrnl.* 7 Aug. 7/2 London kicker Legg fumbled a snap on the third down. **1974** *Plain Dealer* (Cleveland, Ohio) 27 Oct. 2-C/3 Penn State.. converted a fumbled snap into the game's first score only three minutes into the first period.

**6.** A curt or sharp speech or manner of speaking; an angry dispute.

**1648** HEXHAM II, *Een Snap*, a Snap, or a Taunt. **1745** MRS. DELANY *Life & Corr.* (1861) II. 395 The least disapprobation, or snap, from the person I wish to oblige. **1760–2** GOLDSM. *Cit. W.* lxxiv, The moment I ventured to speak I was at once contradicted with a snap. **1859** *Habits of Gd. Society* vii. 245 'Beg your pardon,' answered Tibbs, with a sharp snap, which makes the words sound like 'Don't be a fool!' **1897** W. BEATTY *Secretar* 254 It was while I was watching this game..that we had a bit snap with one another.

**7. a.** A brief and sudden spell *of* cold, winter, etc. orig. *U.S.*

**1740** T. Smith *Jrnl.* (1849) 268 We had..two or three snaps of cold weather, else constantly warm. **1776** *Ibid.* 279 A dismal cold snap of weather. **1885** H. C. McCook *Tenants Old Farm* 114 If there comes a snap of cold. **1899** *Daily Telegr.* 31 Mar. 6/5 She felt the effects of the snap of winter last week.

**b.** A sharp and sudden frost; a short spell of cold weather. Chiefly in ***cold snap*** (very common in recent use).

**1829** Col. Hawker *Diary* (1893) II. 9 A determined 'black snap'.. Harbour all ice. **1830** *Ibid.* 14 The tightest snap on record. **1848** Bartlett *Dict. Amer.* 316 'A cold snap,' i.e. a period of sudden cold weather. A common expression. **1892** W. Pike *Barren Ground N. Canada* 237 The cold snap continued for several days.

**8.** *Mus.* ***Scotch snap***: (see quots. and Scotch *a.* 4).

**1789** Burney *Hist. Mus.* IV. 272 The *Scots snap* seems to have been contagious in that School [the Neapolitan] at this time. **1875** Stainer & Barrett *Dict. Mus. Terms* s.v. *Scotch, Scotch snap*, a peculiarity of the comparatively modern Scotch melodies in which a short note precedes a long one.

**9. a.** = snap-shot *sb.* 1.

**1851** G. H. Kingsley *Sport & Trav.* (1900) 526 Before I had recovered my senses sufficiently to take a desperate snap at him. **1860** W. H. Russell *Diary India* I. xxi. 346 Fellows took snaps at us from balconies, from doors on the roofs of houses.

**b.** = snap-shot *sb.* 2.

**1894** *Amer. Ann. Photogr.* 251 The exposures were mostly 'snaps'. **1899** *St. George's Hosp. Gaz.* VII. 91 An extremely pretty set of Kodak 'snaps' are contributed by Mr. Peck. **1950** *Nat. Geogr. Mag.* Apr. 514/1 We..eventually secured a few satisfactory snaps of the ordinary garden variety of jump. **1977** *Time* 26 Sept. 31/2 They even had a prospectus put together for publishers and included some sample snaps.

**10.** *Wrestling.* A throw made when the hold of one of the wrestlers on the other is broken.

**1868** J. Robinson & S. Gilpin *Wrestling* 57 The stewards were inclined to bring the fall in a 'snap', but the vanquished man very honourably declared himself to be fairly thrown.

**11. a.** Alertness, energy, vigour, 'go'. orig. *U.S.*

**1865** *Harper's Mag.* Jan. 145/2 [They were] good enough people in their way, but had no snap about them. She liked people with snap. **1872** Beecher *Lect. Preaching* x. 185, I like to see a man who has got snap in every part of him. **1885** *Harper's Mag.* Jan. 286/1 There are few..factories which have not 'snap' enough to make a..pair of samples at half a day's notice. **1894** Doyle *Sherlock Holmes* 60 A young, pushing man with plenty of snap about him.

**b.** *transf.* Of writings, etc.

**1870** 'Mark Twain' *Lett. to Publishers* (1967) 49, I should write the book as if *I* went through all these adventures myself—this in order to give it snap and freshness. **1885** G. S. Merriam *S. Bowles* II. 375 The vigorous vernacular, the pithy phrase of the Yankee farmer, gave zest and snap to many a paragraph. **1896** *Peterson's Mag.* Jan. 111/1 A delightful little tale, full of romance, snap, and brightness.

**II.** †**12. a.** *Thieves' Cant.* = cloyer[2] 1. *Obs.*

**1592** Greene *Conny Catch.* Pref. p. iv, When the Foist, the picke pockets (sir reuerence I meane) is cros-bitten by the Snap, and so smoakt for his purchase. *Ibid.* Wks. (Grosart) X. 38 He that bringeth him in, a Nip, He that is halfe with him, the Snap. **1611** Middleton & Dekker *Roaring Girl* D.'s Wks. 1873 III. 220 Then there's a cloyer, or snap, that dogges any new brother in that trade, and snappes, will haue halfe in any booty.

†**b.** A sharper or swindler; a sly or treacherous fellow. *Obs.*

Freq. in 17th c. in *cunning* or *subtle snap.*

**1622** Fletcher *Sp. Curate* II. i, Take heed of a Snap, Sir, ha's a cozening countenance, I do not like his way. **1653** A. Wilson *Jas. I*, 288 Butler being a subtle Snap, wrought so with his companion that he got the possession of it. **1699** R. L'Estrange *Colloq. Erasm.* (1711) 206 There were a great many cunning Snaps that had the Plot in the Wind.

**c.** Applied to persons in somewhat slighting use, but without implication of bad qualities.

**1653** Wharton *Comets* Wks. (1683) 141 Why do I discourage the poor Snap? **1671** Skinner *Etymol. Ling. Angl.*, A merry Snap,..*alacer, lepidus, agilis.* **1676** Wycherley *Pl. Dealer* II. i, Come, lady, pray snap up this young snap at first. **1703** Thoresby *Let. Ray, Snap*, a lad or servant; now mostly used ludicrously.

**d.** *dial.* (See quot. and *snap-dog* s.v. snap-.)

*a* **1796** Pegge *Derbicisms* (E.D.S.) 123 *Snap*, a mongril greyhound with a short tail, excellent at *snapping*, or jumping on a hare.

**e.** *U.S.* A trick, deception, trap; also in phr. ***to give the snap away.***

**1844** *Lexington* (Kentucky) *Observer* 18 Sept. 3/1 Mr Van Buren..with his characteristic politeness *declined to be caught in any such snap.* **1885** *Weekly New Mexican Rev.* 2 July 4/3 He was roped into this snap by Chicago sharpers. **1900** *Congress. Rec.* 15 Feb. 1850/2 Ex-Senator Vilas gave the snap away when he said [etc.]. **1919** E. Hough *Sagebrusher* 501 If that girl's not blind she'll get out and give this snap away.

**III. 13.** †**a.** (See quot.) *Obs.*[−0]

**1611** Cotgr., *Pelican*,..a Snap, or Dog; the toole wherewith Barbers pull out teeth.

**b.** A pistol. *nonce-use.*

**1775** Sheridan *Rivals* IV. i, For your curst sharps and snaps, I never knew any good come of 'em.

**c.** A snap-hook.

**1839** Salter in T. C. Hofland *Brit. Angler's Man.* v. 125 This snap-hook is a double hook, or two single hooks, No. 6, tied back to back, on gimp; to bait this snap, use the baiting-needle. **1856** 'Stonehenge' *Brit. Rural Sports* I. v. iii. 256 The plain snap is made in several ways, as follows.

**d.** A device or implement used for rounding the head of a rivet.

**1869** Rankine *Mach. & Hand-tools* Pl. P. 14, The snap, *c*, has a conical projection at the end, which fits exactly into a corresponding recess in the die. **1890** W. J. Gordon *Foundry* 48 The rivet was inserted from the inside, and held in position by the holder, and the snap outside. **1900** Hasluck *Mod. Eng. Handy-bk.* 124 Rivet with a small hammer, and, for appearance sake, finish with a snap.

*attrib.* **1869** Reed *Shipbuild.* xvii. 329 The snap-point is sometimes formed on snap-headed rivets, and nearly always so in machine riveting. **1874** Thearle *Naval Archit.* 127 This snap tool consists of a hollow cup of steel welded to a punch head for striking upon. **1889** Welch *Text Bk. Naval Archit.* iv. 75 'Snap punch'—a tool provided with a hemispherical hollow at one end.

**e.** In miscellaneous uses (see quots.).

**1875** Knight *Dict. Mech.* 2229/1 *Snap*,..an implement used in making glassware. **1883** Gresley *Gloss. Coal-m.* 229 *Snaps*, a haulage clip. **1888** Addy *Sheffield Gloss., Snaps*, a horizontal vice. **1888** Nicholson *Coal Trade Gloss., Snap*, a small flat pointed pick, used on the screens. **1976** *Eastern Daily Press* (Norwich) 16 Dec. 13/4 The friction strips which make the bang are known as 'snaps' in the industry. **1980** *Daily Tel.* 25 Nov. 15/5 Those who felt inspired to make their own crackers..may have encountered some difficulty in finding the vital bangers, called snaps in the trade.

**14.** †**a.** An ear-ring, fastened with a spring-catch. *Obs.*[−1]

**1748** Richardson *Clarissa* (1811) III. 29 A pair of diamond snaps in her ears.

**b.** A spring-catch, clasp, or fastening, or one closing with a snapping or clicking sound.

*c* **1815** *Houlston's Juvenile Tracts, Cork Jacket* 4 She took off her spectacles, and put them carefully into an old fish skin case with a snap to it. **1859** *Habits of Gd. Society* iv. 179 Rows of pearls, confined by a diamond snap, are beautiful in every [evening] dress. **1903** F. J. Garrard *Watch Repairing* 156 Bottoms and bezels are sometimes jointed to the case band, and sometimes are loose, being merely snapped tight. These circular snaps, as they are called, are much more dust tight than a joint can be.

**c.** *pl.* Hand-cuffs. *slang.*

**1895** J. Caminada *Twenty-Five Years Detective Life* 49, I put the 'snaps' on 'Pudding', and conveyed him..to Livesey Street police station. **1910** [see nipper *sb.*[1] 4 c]. **1958** M. Procter *Man in Ambush* x. 119 We got the snaps on him and locked him up. **1967** —— *Exercise Hoodwink* xxv. 178 Sergeant, we'd better have the snaps on these three.

**d.** *U.S.* A press-stud or snap-fastener. Usu. *pl.*

**1964** *McCall's Sewing* xii. 221/1 Snaps are used to hold fabrics together where there is little strain on the garment. They give a neat flat closure. **1968** J. Updike *Couples* (1970) ii. 160 Frank's delicate hand uncoupled her bra snaps. **1977** *New Yorker* 27 June 72/3 The [pillow]slip is homemade, with snaps at one end.

**IV. 15. a.** A quick, sharp sound or report.

**1611** Cotgr., *Niquet*,..a knicke, clicke, snap with the teeth, or fingers. **1687** Miége *Gr. Fr. Dict.* II. s.v., It gave such a snap, that it made me startle, *cela fit un si grand bruit* [etc.]. *c* **1710** C. Fiennes *Diary* (1888) 153 Set the Coales together with some fire and it shall give a snap and burn up light. **1767** Franklin *Lett.* Wks. 1840 V. 414 In our small experiments, we call this light and sound the electric spark and snap. **1825** Scott *Talism.* iv, A spring bolt,..the snap of which resounded through the place. **1856** Kane *Arctic Expl.* I. xii. 136 With a crack like the snap of a gigantic whip, the ice opened. **1880** Mrs. Riddell *Myst. Palace Gard.* xxx, Edwina shut the book with a snap.

(*b*) ***snap, crackle,*** (***and***) ***pop***, an advertiser's catchphrase representing the lively sound produced by a brand of breakfast cereal when milk is added; used allusively and in *transf.* senses for breakfast cereal or for vigour or energetic behaviour.

**1954** *Daily Mail* 15 Dec. 2/1 (Advt.), With their fascinating 'Snap! Crackle! Pop!' as the milk's poured on, *Rice Krispies* really do seem to be talking. **1959** *Times Lit. Suppl.* 27 Mar. 179/4 In the 1950s the whole of America, Canada, Australia, England and parts of Europe are eating cereals for breakfast—snap, crackle, pop. **1960** *Guardian* 17 Mar. 9/2 Marples..always acting with that zestful snap, crackle, pop that entertains as much as it nourishes. **1962** 'R. Gordon' *Doctor in Swim* xi. 66 Now the poor fellow was as jumpy as a plate of snap-crackle-pop when you pour the milk on. **1962** F. Williams *Amer. Invasion* ii. 20 With every snap, crackle and pop on the breakfast table the American accent carries farther. **1963** *Trade Marks Jrnl.* 1 June 730/2 Snap Crackle Pop. 851,181. Cereal preparations made of rice for food for human consumption. Kellogg Company of Great Britain Limited..Manchester, 3rd July 1963. **1965** *Times Lit. Suppl.* 22 Apr. 315/5 When due allowance has been made for the chapter's snap crackle pop style. **1977** *N.Y. Rev. Bks.* 28 Apr. 11/4 But the few paragraphs of real information are hard to find in the snap, crackle, and pop of gossip and insult. **1979** P. Levi *Head in Soup* vii. 128 Snap, crackle, pop. The telephone went dead.

**b.** In negative phrases denoting complete disregard or indifference.

**1833** S. Smith *Life & Writings J. Downing* 43 As long as I have President Jackson to look to for paymaster, I don't care a snap about sending in any bills. *a* **1852** F. M. Whitcher *Widow Bedott Papers* (1856) xxii. 232 If you don't care a snap for him, what makes you go with him to lecters, and concerts, and sleigh rides? **1859** Farrar *J. Home* ii. 19 Should you care the snap of a finger for the opinion or the acquaintance of a man [etc.]? **1877** Spurgeon *Serm.* XXIII. 60 Never caring a snap of the fingers whether it offended or whether it pleased. **1897** Henty *Irrawaddy* 338, I don't care a snap for the titles.

**16.** The act of snapping or breaking suddenly; a break or fracture.

**1755** Johnson, *Snap*, the act of breaking with a quick motion. **1828–32** Webster, *Snap*, a sudden breaking or rupture of any substance. **1891** C. Roberts *Adrift Amer.* 73 In the majority of cases the snap is so clean that a green hand would most likely pass it by.

**17. a.** *Sc.* and *north. dial.* A small, usually round, cake or biscuit of crisp gingerbread; a ginger-snap.

**1818** Scott *Br. Lamm.* xii, She will gie ye a ginge-bread snap for your pains. **1852** Carlyle in Froude *Life in Lond.* II. 110 The main panes round, and about the size of a biggish snap. **1855** [Robinson] *Whitby Gloss., Snaps*, thin round gingerbread cakes for children.

**b.** *attrib.*, as ***snap-machine, -wife, -woman.***

**1831** R. Shennan *Poems* 42 The auctioneers and snap-wives too, Had staid to try what they could do. **1871** Carlyle in Mrs. Carlyle *Lett.* I. 110 Beggars, ballad-singers, snap-women, &c. **1884** Knight *Dict. Mech.* Suppl. 826/1 *Snap Machine*, a machine for cutting a blanket of dough into snaps.

**18.** *U.S.* (See quots.)

*c* **1770** J. Randolph *Treat. Gardening* in Gardiner & Hepburn *Amer. Gardener* (1818) 275 French beans and snaps are the same. **1842** C. M. Kirkland *Forest Life* II. xli. 165 'Snaps' are green beans. **1848** Bartlett *Dict. Amer.* 316 *Snaps*, young kidney-beans in the pod. **1872** De Vere *Americanisms* 410 Such are the beans, known in England as Kidney-beans or French-beans, while here they are called String-beans..or Snaps, and occasionally Snap-beans.

**snap** (snæp), *a.* *Sc.* [Cf. MDa. *snap* quick, smart.] Quick; smart; sharp.

*Jamieson's Sc. Dict.* (1882) also gives: 'short-tempered, surly'; 'brittle, short-grained, crisp'; these senses may be derived from snap *v.*

**1790** Shirrefs *Poems* 352 She is a lass fu' snap To grant her patronage. *a* **1796** Burns *Poem Pastoral Poetry* ix, Nae snap conceits, but that sweet spell O' witchin' love.

**snap** (snæp), *v.* Also 6 snappe, snoppe, 7 snapp. [app. ad. MDu. or MLG. *snappen* (so mod.Du. and LG.; Fris. *snappe*), = MHG. *snappen* (G. *schnappen*); Da. *snappe*, Sw. *snappa* are also from LG. The stem is prob. based on that of MHG. *snaben*, MLG. *snaven*, of similar meaning; cf. MHG. *snabel*, MLG. *snavel* beak, bill.]

**I. 1. a.** *intr.* Of animals: To make a quick or sudden bite *at* something; to feed *on* in this way.

**1530** Palsgr. 723/2, I snappe at a thyng to catche it with my tethe. *Ibid.*, His horse snapped at myne arme. *c* **1592** Marlowe *Jew of Malta* v. ii, Like the Asse..That labours with a load of bread and wine, And leaues it off to snap on Thistle tops. **1648** Winyard *Midsummer Moon* 2 This makes the mad bandog snap at all hee meets. *a* **1653** Gouge *Comm. Heb.* iii. 13 Fair baits, whereby dangerous hooks are covered over to entice silly fish to snap at them. **1710** Addison *Tatler* No. 120 ¶3 A little Lap-Dog, that barked and snapped at every one. **1832** Irving *Alhambra* II. 261 The seven dogs..snapping at the heels of the terrified friar. **1875** W. S. Hayward *Love agst. World* 14 The fox turns and snaps viciously at his relentless pursuer.

*fig.* **1597** Shaks. *2 Hen. IV*, III. ii. 357 If the young Dace be a Bayt for the old Pike, I see no reason..but I may snap at him.

**b.** Without const.

**1555** Eden *Decades* (Arb.) 236 The hounde..approcheth so neare hym snappynge and grynnynge. **1633** P. Fletcher *Purple Isl.* XI. xxv, A gentle greyhound set around With little curres, which dare his way molest, Snapping behinde. *a* **1692** L'Estrange (J.), All mungrel curs bawl, snarl, and snap. **1858** Holmes *Aut. Breakf.-t.* viii, Settle snapping-turtles snap..before they are out of the egg-shell.

*fig.* **1589** Nashe *Martin Marprelate* Wks. (Grosart) I. 122 The Preachers of the faction..begin to snappe and to turne. **1782** Miss Burney *Cecilia* IX. i, Never mind, my chick,..more to be had; if one won't snap, another will. **1884** *Kendal Mercury* 3 Oct. 5/2 All the newspapers abroad have been set a-barking and snapping, big dogs and little dogs alike.

**2. a.** To utter sharp, tart, or cutting words or remarks; to speak or reply irritably or abruptly. Usu. with *at.*

**1579** L. Tomson *Calvin's Serm. Tim.* 1002/1 By this word, he snappeth at them which haue their eyes so dazeled with these flitting thinges. **1635** Pagitt *Christianogr.* To Rdr., Let him confute the maine plot..and not snap and cavil onely at some particulars in it. **1666** Wood *Life* (O.H.S.) II. 89 Dr. Fell..snapt up and told me 'I should pay [etc.].' **1693** *Ibid.* 13 July, He would not suffer him to speak for snapping and snarling. **1786** tr. *Beckford's Vathek* (1868) 68 He was afraid of being snapped at by Shaban his tutor. **1825** E. Hewlett *Cottage Comforts* xii. 193 They humour the child till they are out of patience with him, and then snap at him. **1865** Trollope *Belton Est.* xxiv. 286 Every now and then speaking a word, and restraining himself from snapping at his rival.

**b.** *trans.* To utter (words) in an angry, sharp, or peevish manner or tone.

**1683** Villiers (Dk. Buckhm.) *Rehearsal* I. i. (ed. 4) 6 Whereupon I presently snapt this upon her; *Non, non, Madam* [etc.]. **1853** Surtees *Sponge's Sp. Tour* (1893) 297 'You *can't* know all about it!' snapped Mr. Sponge. **1884** Browning *Family* 36 The next in age snapped petulant: 'Too rash!' **1897** Rhoscomyl *White Rose Arno* xxviii. 298 He tore into the long reaches behind, panting and snapping curses.

**c.** Similarly with *out.*

**1888** F. Hume *Mme. Midas* I. ii, Slivers was just going to snap out a refusal. **1902** R. Bagot *Donna Diana* viii. 99 She snapped it out, however—the plain, vulgar word *porco.*

**3.** †**a.** *Thieves' cant.* To go shares with a thief or sharper. Cf. snap *sb.* 2. *Obs.*

**1609** Field *Woman's a Weathercock* IV. ii, Thou snapp'st besides with cheats and cutpurses. **1611** [see snap *sb.* 12 a].

**b.** To snatch, to make a quick or eager catch, *at* a thing. Also *fig.*

**1673** Dryden *Marr. à la Mode* I. i, A man in these hard times snaps at them as he does at broad gold. **1691** Wood *Ath. Oxon.* I. 313 Such..are apt to snap at anything to please themselves. **1741** *Chinese Lett.* vi. 34 They delay to take a Revenge,..and when they find an Opportunity, they snap at it greedily. **1778** MME. D'ARBLAY *Diary* 3 Aug., Any bookseller, will snap at what you write. **1827** SCOTT *Jrnl.* 10 July, His resignation was eagerly snapped at. **1898** PR. RANJITSINHJI *With Stoddart's Team* x. (ed. 3) 198 Storer in his eagerness snapped at the ball which otherwise would have landed safely into short slip's hands.

**c.** *to snap short*, to fail to get or obtain.

**1677** W. HUGHES *Man of Sin* II. v. 95 Lay-men may not tast the Cup at all... Their Clergy..will not snap short as the Laity must. **1732–8** SWIFT *Polite Conv.* 109 Snap short makes you look so lean, Miss.

†**d.** *Sc.* To attempt *to* do something. *Obs.*

**1766** A. NICHOL *Poems* 19 If some auld swinger snap to speak Of pink-ey'd queans, he gives a squeek.

†**4. a.** To strike or stab *at* one. *Obs.*[−1]

**1626** B. JONSON *Staple of N.* II. Interm. (1905) 54 I'ld not giue a rush for a Vice, that has not a wooden dagger to snap at euery body he meetes.

†**b.** To pounce *upon* a person or thing. *rare.*

**1648** HEXHAM II, *Een Snap-haen*, a Robber that Snaps upon one in the high way. **1679** PULLER *Moder. Ch. Eng.* (1843) 41 Those who love not to be contained in any good bounds when they read the Bible, choose to do it out of all canonical order, or generally snap upon the chapters fortuitously.

**II. 5. a.** *trans.* To catch, capture, or seize quickly, suddenly, or by surprise.

Common in the 17th c.; now chiefly *dial.*, or spec. in *Cricket*.

**1568** T. HOWELL *Arb. Amitie* (1879) 86 And shall I thus an wofull wretch, be snapt in sugred snare? **1582** STANYHURST *Æneis* II. (Arb.) 46 My coosen was snapt by wycked Vlisses. **1625** FLETCHER & SHIRLEY *Nt. Walker* II, The chest is of some weight, and we may make Such noise ith carriage we may be snap'd. *c* **1645** TULLIE *Siege of Carlisle* (1840) 6 They..failed in snapping Col. Graye's small regement of horse at Stanwick. **1699** BENTLEY *Phal.* 103 The Doctor finds Stesichorus in danger of being snapt in his intended Journey. **1720** DE FOE *Capt. Singleton* x. (1840) 182 We should snap her in the morning. **1798** O'KEEFFE *Wild Oats* v. i, I wish we could snap any straggler to bring before her. **1823** SCOTT *Quentin D.* xxxvi, She is not quite goose enough to fall in love with the fox who has snapped her. **1855** BROWNING *Fra Lippo* 76 As I was stealing back again..You snap me of the sudden. **1872** *Wisden* 23 John Smith stayed with Mr Grace until 63 runs were made, when Pooley snapped him. **1898** PR. RANJITSINHJI *With Stoddart's Team* x. (ed. 3) 195 Iredale also secured an 'egg', Storer snapping him at the wicket.

*transf.* and *fig.* **1580** HOLLYBAND *Treas. Fr. Tong, Prendre au pied levé*, to snappe one in wordes, to take him at aduantage. *a* **1677** BARROW *Serm.* Wks. 1716 II. 104 Alexander was snapt in the flower of his age and glory. **1706** HEARNE *Collect.* (O.H.S.) I. 303 A Daughter who by chance snap'd a Gentleman Commoner..of a considerable Estate. **1859** *Watson's Bards Borders* 73 If disease them didna snap, He wad ha'e plenty tatties.

**b.** To snatch for one's own use; to take to oneself with a quick movement; to steal or purloin in this manner. Also with *away*.

**1624** WOTTON in *Reliq.* (1651) 88 There was near Bayon, an Herd of Goats.., upon which sight the said Sir R. Greham tells the Marquess, he would snap one of the Kids. **1697** DRYDEN *Virg. Past.* III. 24 Did I not see you, Rascal, ..When you lay snug to snap young Damon's Goat? *c* **1756** in W. Wing *Ann. Steeple Aston* (1875) 57 A simple hare, had he but snapt, Or partridge in the wood. **1821** SCOTT *Kenilw.* xx, See that he snap them [gold buttons] not away. **1858** CARLYLE *Fredk. Gt.* II. xiv. (1872) I. 129 Neighbouring potentates..snapped away some convenient bit of territory. **1899** S. MACMANUS *In Chim. Corners* 133 Doesn't one of the king's men snap the shoe off his foot.

**c.** To catch or seize with a quick bite or snap. Also in fig. context.

**1687** MIÈGE *Dict.* II. s.v., An unlucky dog snapt my leg. *a* **1716** SOUTH *Serm.* (1717) IV. 162 He who has escaped in many Battles,..by playing too often at the Mouth of Death, has been snapped by it at last. **1760** JORTIN *Erasmus* II. 153 The Ægyptian dogs, when they drink at the Nile, are said to run all the while, for fear of being snaped by the Crocodiles. **1824** MACTAGGART *Gallovid. Encycl.* 499 Now a trap did snap him:.. A rafter down did fa', Which catch'd a leg. **1863** COWDEN CLARKE *Shaks. Char.* vi. 161 They think it a mere flouting at the gifts of Providence if they do not snap the bait like gudgeons.

**d.** To secure, obtain, take up, quickly or readily.

More frequently with *up*: see 6c.

**1798** O'KEEFFE *Wild Oats* II. iii, Oh, here he is! *Trap.* Snap him at any terms. **1905** *Westm. Gaz.* 15 Feb. 9/1 Recent issues have been readily snapped.

**e.** To secure the passing or giving of (decisions, legislation, etc.) without allowing due time for consideration or discussion.

**1883** GIBSON *Sp. in Parlt.* 14 Aug., To snap legislation.. which they were not gravely asked to pass at the time when it could have been carefully considered. **1885** *Law Rep. 29 Chanc. Div.* 453 He was defeated by the Defendant going to another Court and managing to snap a judgment first. **1901** *Scotsman* 11 Mar. 9/4 They were strong enough..to prevent hasty decisions being snapped behind the backs of the people.

**f.** *U.S.* and *Canad. Football.* To put (the ball) in play by passing it quickly backwards to begin a scrimmage; to make a snap (sense 5g). Also with *back*.

**1887** *Outing* Oct. 70/1 In a scrimmage he places it on the ground, and at a signal from his quarter, snaps the ball back by a downward and backward pressure with his foot. **1920** W. CAMP *Football without Coach* iii. 48 Now let us say the quarter calls the signal..the play would get under way and the center would snap him the ball. **1968** *Globe & Mail* (Toronto) 3 Feb. 37/6 During such periods, when a pass is incomplete or a ball goes into touch, time will not resume until the ball has been snapped on the next play. **1973** *Philadelphia Inquirer* (Today Suppl.) 7 Oct. 42/1 Moss lights up and hunches over his desk, like a linebacker waiting for signals. The ball is snapped; he's off.

**g.** To match (an exposed card in a game of snap); to call out 'snap!' to (an opponent).

**1935** *Encycl. Sports* 568/2 In case a player calls snap when there is nothing to snap on the table, the cards in front of him go to a pool. *Ibid.*, Grimace snap is extremely simple. Instead of snapping each other, the two players are under contract to make each other laugh, to which they may do anything except speak.

**6.** With *up*: **a.** = senses 5, 5b, and 5c.

**1550** COVERDALE *Spir. Perle* x. 84 Whan we liue in ydlenes, in al lust and pleasure, the deuyl snappeth vs vp. **1601** J. WHEELER *Treat. Comm.* 59 The single Merchant.. is many times snapped vp and made a praye to Dunkerkers, and other Sea rouers. **1692** LUTTRELL *Brief Rel.* (1857) II. 427 A yatch..is missing, and 'tis feared is snapt up by some French privateer. **1732** *Tricks of Town* 9 The Dog is instantly snapp'd-up, and convey'd away..to some filthy Cellar or Garret. **1823** SCOTT *Quentin D.* vii, Tristan but pretends to mistake, that he may snap up the kindly Scots that come over to see their kinsfolks. **1865** RUSKIN *Sesame* i. §33 We snap up anything in the way of a scientific bone that has meat on it. **1884** *Spectator* 4 Oct. 1287/2 Merchant-steamers..would be snapped up by the fast cruisers of the enemy.

*fig.* **1809** MALKIN *Gil Blas* IX. vi. (Rtldg.) 320 Then..I snapped up the words out of his mouth. To be sure, my tongue did run at a fine rate against him.

**b.** To secure (a girl) in marriage.

**1842** BARHAM *Ingol. Leg.* Ser. II. *Merch. V.* (1905) 245 Portia..Is not to be snapp'd up like little potatoes. **1865** TROLLOPE *Belton Est.* x. 116 The conquest of Clara would not be too facile. She was a woman of value, not to be snapped up easily. **1889** 'R. BOLDREWOOD' *Robbery under Arms* xxxvi, All the girls about here are getting snapped up quick.

**c.** = sense 5d.

**1873** *Punch* 20 Sept. 118/1 When you see one at that price, don't wait to write, but snap him up—buy him for me. **1887** JESSOPP *Arcady* vii. 196 Every little outlying farm was snapped up and bought by country gentlemen. **1890** 'R. BOLDREWOOD' *Col. Reformer* (1891) 402 Cattle..were snapped up at eight-pounds-ten a head.

**d.** To eat up quickly or hastily.

**1808**- in dial. glossaries (Sc., Lanc., Wilts., Somerset, etc.).

**7.** With *off*: **a.** To bite off (a limb, etc.) sharply and quickly. Also *transf.*, to drink off quickly.

*c* **1590** GREENE *Fr. Bacon* iii. 34 We will to the tavern and snap off a pint of wine or two. **1599** SHAKS. *Much Ado* v. i. 116 Wee had likt to haue had our two noses snapt off with two old men without teeth. **1700** S. L. tr. *Fryke's Voy. E. Ind.* 16 The Carpenter..had his Arm and Shoulder snap'd off. **1774** GOLDSM. *Nat. Hist.* (1776) VI. 241 The shark darted upon him..and snapped off his leg.

**b.** *to snap one's nose*, or *head, off*, to speak or reply to (a person) in a curt, sharp, ungracious, or angry manner.

**1709** [see NOSE *sb.* 9c]. **1742** MRS. DELANY *Life & Corr.* (1861) II. 166 Old G. snapped my nose off for saying I had sent for him. **1861** HUGHES *Tom Brown at Oxf.* xxvii, Do you ever snap people's noses off, or tell them you think them very foolish. **1886** F. ROBINSON *Courting May Smith* I. xiv, If I had not been quite sure he would have snapped my head off. **1950** T. S. ELIOT *Cocktail Party* I. ii. 60 Have you looked in your bag?..Well, don't snap my head off. **1976** J. I. M. STEWART *Memorial Service* i. 12 He adores the place. .. That's why he snaps your head off if you venture to say a good word for it.

**8. a.** To catch or take (one) *up* with an abrupt or sharp remark. Also with *short*.

**1647** HEXHAM I, Snapped him up,..*berispte hem.* **1649** *Nicholas Papers* (Camden) 156 The King grew very chollerick and angry and did snap him up very short. **1691** WOOD *Ath. Oxon.* II. 185 William Earl of Exeter..snapped him up for a begging scholar. **1797** MRS. RADCLIFFE *Italian* xxii, You always snap me up so short at the beginning. *Ibid.* xxiii, I don't much like to be snapped up so. **1848** DICKENS *Dombey* xliv, 'Susan Nipper,' snapping her up particularly short, 'a month's warning from this hour'. **1883** J. PAYN *Thicker than Water* xx, If I am snapped up in this manner, and not permitted to go on,..argument is impossible.

**b.** To interrupt or snub, to cut *short*, in an abrupt or peevish manner. Also with *off*.

**1687** MIÈGE s.v., To snap one, or to speak roughly to him. **1722** DE FOE *Col. Jack* ii. (1840) 30 He snapped me short, Why, says he, how shall I get them to him? **1796** MRS. M. ROBINSON *Angelina* III. 172 To be sure your ladyship did snap and snub her confoundedly. **1837** HOOD *United Family* i, One liking this, one hating that, Each snapping each, like dog and cat. **1899** W. RAYMOND *No Soul above Money* II. i, Never waiting to snap a body off short who had any little favour to ask.

**9. a.** To bring *down* by a quick shot.

**1828** COL. HAWKER *Diary* (1893) I. 342 The only plan was ..to snap down the birds as they rose.

**b.** To take (an instantaneous photograph); to snap-shot.

**1890** *St. Nicholas* Oct. 1034 A hand camera, with which he followed the babies about, 'snapping' them in their best positions. **1892** *Pall Mall G.* 20 Apr. 6/1 The privilege of 'snapping' photographs from the pier.

**c.** *intr.* To take instantaneous photographs.

**1891** *Anthony's Photogr. Bulletin* IV. 202 Perhaps the circus has been in town, and you've snapped on the elephants. *Ibid.*, Why, you were snapping away for dear life. **1894** *Westm. Gaz.* 2 Jan. 7/3 The photographers..were busily at work snapping at everything and anything.

**III. 10.** *trans.* **a.** To close (the jaws, mouth, etc.) suddenly or with a snap.

**1573** TWYNE *Æneid* XII. Nn ij b, He [a dog] snoppes his iawes, and is deceaued [h]is bit by half an inche. **1852** MRS. STOWE *Uncle Tom's C.* viii. 57 Tom, whose great heavy mouth had stood ajar,..now suddenly snapped it together. **1904** *Field* 6 Feb. 208/1 He snapped his beak with a noise like pistol shots.

**b.** To wink or blink (the eyes) quickly or angrily (cf. 14).

**1847** HALLIW. s.v., To snap the eye, i.e. to wink. **1907** W. W. JACOBS *Short Cruises* 205 Mr. Wragg, snapping his eyes nervously, threatened in vain.

**11. a.** To pull the trigger of or fire (a pistol); to strike (a flint, etc.).

**1673** *Justiciary Proc.* (S.H.S.) 131 [They] saw the gun presented and snapped. **1719** DE FOE *Crusoe* I. (Globe) 307, I, snapping an uncharg'd Pistol. **1743** BULKELEY & CUMMINS *Voy. S. Seas* 83 The Lieutenant, bringing a Pair of Pistols to the Carpenter,..did not imagine they were loaded, snapping the first it miss'd Fire. **1847** *Infantry Man.* (1854) 42 He..will be taught to snap caps. **1857** HOLLAND *Bay Path* xxvi. 334, I..drew the old charge, and snapped it two or three times, to let the children see the fire roll.

**b.** Const. *at* a person or thing.

**1798** LD. AUCKLAND *Corr.* (1862) III. 418 He snapped a pocket-pistol at him, which missed him. **1825** HONE *Every-day Bk.* I. 1288 He had the imprudence to snap an unloaded pistol at him. **1852** THACKERAY *Esmond* I. v, The officer, drawing a pistol, snapped it at his lordship.

**c.** To fire off (questions).

**1874** R. TYRWHITT *Sketch Club* 39 They are apt to flash or snap questions at each other as in a French novel.

**12. a.** To cause (something) to make or give out a sharp sound of the nature of a click or crack; to close or fasten, to open or shut, etc., with this sound; to crack (a whip); to jerk *out* with a snap. Also, to switch *off* or *on*, or to shut *to*, with a snapping sound; to cause (fabric, elastic, etc.) to make such a sound.

**1714** MRS. MANLEY *Adv. Rivella* 82 The Man..got up nimbly into his Coach-box, snapt his Whip. **1747** RICHARDSON *Clarissa* xxxi. (1749) I. 198 Many a fan have I caused to be snapped at a sister beauty. **1781** COWPER *Table-T.* 477 Tyranny..Slips the slave's collar on, and snaps the lock. **1853** R. S. SURTEES *Sponge's Sp. Tour* (1893) 153 Snapping his toothpick against the frame of his chair. **1889** *Brit. Jrnl. Photogr.* XXXVI. 605/2 How can any one snap his shutter at the right moment unless he is carefully watching the object. **1893** KIPLING *Many Invent.* 196 Gisborne snapped out the empty shells [from his rifle]. **1911** H. S. HARRISON *Queed* 68 Queed cleverly bethought him to snap on an electric light. **1922** JOYCE *Ulysses* 21 Haines helped himself [to a cigarette] and snapped the case to. **1925** F. SCOTT FITZGERALD *Great Gatsby* viii. 191 About five o'clock it was blue enough outside to snap off the light. **1926** J. MASEFIELD *Odtaa* xvi. 277 He snapped-to the breech of his rifle. **1949** B. A. BOTKIN *Treas. S. Folklore* II. iii. 252 Both Bilbo and Gene Talmadge were famous for their red suspenders, which Talmadge loved to snap. **1962** J. UPDIKE *Centaur* (1963) vi. 178 He laughed and behind me I could hear all the Caucasus laughing and snapping their towels and flipping their silvery genitals. **1979** R. JAFFE *Class Reunion* (1980) II. vii. 248 Ken was dressed, snapping on his wrist-watch. *Ibid.* 254 Ken snapped off the TV with his remote control.

*absol.* **1880** 'MARK TWAIN' *Tramp Abr.* xxiv. 206 She got to snapping the lid of her smelling-bottle,—it made a loud sharp sound, but..she snapped and snapped away.

**b.** To cause (the fingers) to make a sharp noise by striking against the ball of the thumb, esp. as a sign of delight or contempt. Also *fig.*

[**1671** SKINNER *Etymol. Ling. Angl.* X xx j b, To snap with ones fingers,..*digitis concrepare, vel crepitare.* **1721** in BAILEY.] **1742** FIELDING *J. Andrews* I. xvii, He then snapped his fingers,..and took two or three turns about the room in an extacy. **1821** JOANNA BAILLIE *Metr. Leg., Columbus* xlviii. 20 The..Indian..foots the ground like vaunting child, Snapping his thumbs with anticks wild. **1839** T. MITCHELL *Frogs of Aristoph.* 66 *note*, At its conclusion he snaps his fingers in sovereign contempt. **1886** JEROME *Idle Th.* 36 It is not until you have snapped your fingers in Fortune's face.. that she begins to smile upon you.

**c.** *to snap one's fingers at*, to treat with indifference or contempt; to disregard or ignore.

**1806** SCOTT 11 Feb. in *Lockhart*, I hope I shall be very soon able to..snap my fingers at the bar and all its works. **1861** HUGHES *Tom Brown at Oxf.* xli, You'll..be able to snap your fingers at them all. **1886** STEVENSON *Kidnapped* xxiii, The men of his country..would have snapped their fingers at the Court of Session.

**d.** *absol.* To strike *at* with a snapping sound.

**1852** MRS. STOWE *Uncle Tom's C.* iv. 22 He set her on his broad shoulder, and began capering and dancing with her, while Mas'r George snapped at her with his pocket-handkerchief.

**13.** *intr.* **a.** Of things: To make or emit a sharp cracking sound or report; to crack, crackle.

**1673** *Justiciary Proc.* (S.H.S.) 131 He heard not the gun snapp. **1727** BOYER *Dict. Royal* II, To snap, (or to give a snap), *éclater, faire du bruit.* **1768** J. BYRON *Narr. Patagonia* (ed. 2) 74 Cedar..makes a brisk fire, but is..subject to snap and fly. **1789** COLERIDGE *The Nose* iv, Hear ye my entrails how they snap? **1855** BROWNING *Old Pictures in Florence* i, No flash snapped, no dumb thunder rolled. **1884** E. P. ROE *Nat. Ser. Story* ii, My caps only snapped.

**b.** To move or slide *into* place, to close or shut, to fit *home* or *in*, to come *off*, with a snap.

**1793** SMEATON *Edystone L.* §241, I..gave it a violent pull, upon which it snapped into its place. **1875** KNIGHT *Dict. Mech.* 2229/2 *Snap-lock*,..a lock with a spring latch which snaps shut. **1891** KIPLING *Light that Failed* (1900) 217 The studio door snapped behind her. **1892** GREENER *Breech-Loader* 63 They are liable to miss fire if the lever does not snap 'home'. **1967** *Boston Sunday Herald Mag.* 26 Mar. 26/2 (Advt.), Quality absorbent reusable cotton pad snaps in—removes easily for laundering. **1976** *Columbus* (Montana) *News* 1 July 3/3 (Advt.), Safety grilles snap off to clean. 3-speed 20" Fan.

**14. a.** Of the eyelids or eyes: To open and close quickly in an angry manner.

**1870** E. E. HALE *Ten Times One* ii. (Cent. Dict.), How Caroline's eyes snapped and flashed fire! **1899** CAPES *Lady of Darkness* ii, Ned..saw his Madonna jerk erect, her eyelids snapping.

**b.** Of jaws, etc.: To close with a snap.

**1899** F. V. KIRBY *Sport E.C. Africa* iv. 51 The great jaws snapped like the teeth of so many wolf-traps.

**IV. 15.** *intr.* **a.** To break suddenly and (usually) with a sharp noise or report; to give way or part suddenly owing to strain or tension.

Du. *snappen* and Fris. *snappe* have also this sense.

**1602** MARSTON *Ant. & Mel.* I. Wks. 1856 I. 14 What a slender waste he hath! Heele snap in two at every little straine. **a1631** DONNE *Poems, The Storm* (1633) 58 Our tacklings Snapping, like too-high-stretched treble strings. **1799** J. ROBERTSON *Agric. Perth* 236 Scotch oak..is found to snap over when used as ribs to a ship. **1819** MISS MITFORD in L'Estrange *Life* (1870) II. iii. 76 Four or five glasses snapped, one after another. **1850** SCORESBY *Cheever's Whalem. Adv.* xiv. (1858) 198 Another line was taken on board, which immediately snapped. **1897** W. H. THORNTON *Rem. W.-Co. Clergyman* vi. 181 Even strong harness snaps when subjected to a sudden jerk.

**b.** *fig.* or in fig. context.

**1822** SHELLEY *Triumph Life* 158 The fiery band which held Their natures, snaps. **1837** CARLYLE *Fr. Rev.* III. III. i, When the so-called Bonds of Society snap asunder. **1876** MISS YONGE *Womankind* xviii. 137 When your power of arresting mischief snaps. **1896** HOUSMAN *Shropshire Lad* ix, Sharp the link of life will snap. **1927** WODEHOUSE *Meet Mr Mulliner* ix. 310 Something seemed to snap in James. The scales seemed to fall from James's eyes. **1933** E. O'NEILL *Days without End* (1934) I. 49 He knew..she was going to die... He..saw that no miracle would happen... Something snapped in him then. **1970** A. FRY *How a People Die* xxiv. 212 Something snapped. I lost my temper and I chewed that poor guy out from hell to breakfast.

**c.** To be broken *off* with a snap.

**1806** *Med. Jrnl.* XV. 497 Such a violent spasm of the jaw that a piece of one of the incisor teeth snapped off. **1842** LOVER *Handy Andy* xlvii, The butt-ends of the muskets snapped off like tobacco pipes. **1892** STEVENSON *Across Plains* ii. 87 Without a nod of warning, the huge pine-tree snaps off short.

**d.** *colloq.* To change one's behaviour or position quickly, esp. *to snap back*: to recover; *to snap (in)to*: to throw oneself smartly into (an action); *to snap out of*: to desist from (an attitude, etc.), to change a mood, pattern of behaviour, etc., by sudden effort. Freq. as imp. *snap out of it*.

**1918** in F. A. Pottle *Stretchers* (1929) ix. 239 Oh, snap into it! We want to get this done. **1918** [see HIT *v.* 23 e]. **1928** *Sat. Even. Post* 7 Jan. 9/3 Oh, for heaven's sake, Lucia, snap out of it and act like a human being. **1941** N. MARSH *Death & Dancing Footman* (1942) vi. 114 Do snap out of being all Freudian. **1943** K. TENNANT *Ride on Stranger* xviii. 205 Time we were getting a move on... Snap into it, Joe. **1944** *Sun* (Baltimore) 13 Jan. 5/1 If the Government acts quickly.., the aircraft industry will snap back quickly. **1962** J. GLENN in *Into Orbit* 18 We had to demonstrate how well we could undergo all kinds of stress and discomfort and then snap back again. **1967** [see OWNSOME]. **1967** *Boston Sunday Herald* 14 May (This Week Mag.) 15/3 The Senator..spent half an hour persuading a very reluctant repairman to come. 'Why,' asked a guest, 'didn't you just tell him to snap to it?' **1981** M. SPARK *Loitering with Intent* x. 158 We mustn't get morbid. Let's snap out of it.

**16.** *trans.* **a.** To break (something) suddenly and cleanly; to break in two; to cause (a rope, etc.) to part or give way.

**1679** *Trial Lord Cornwallis* 12 My Lord..holding the white Staff..in both hands.., snapt it in two. **1680** MORDEN *Geog. Rect.* (1685) 52 There is the Herb Ossifraga..which snaps the bones of Cattel that tread upon it. **1725** POPE *Odyss.* x. 668 Full endlong from the roof the sleeper fell, And snapped the spinal joint and waked in hell. **1768–74** TUCKER *Lt. Nat.* (1834) II. 638 They found no difficulty in snapping short the single sticks. **1825** J. NICHOLSON *Operat. Mechanic* 33 The shock proceeding from inertia snaps the teeth of the wheels. **1855** TENNYSON *Maud* II. II. iv, The shock Of cataract seas that snap The three decker's oaken spine. **1871** MACDUFF *Mem. of Patmos* xxv. 347 Its moorings are snapped as tow.

*slang.* **1785** GROSE *Dict. Vulgar T.*, *To snap the glaze*, to break shop windows, or shew glasses.

**b.** *fig.* or in fig. context. Also *spec.* in sport, to break a tie or a pattern of performance (*U.S.*).

**1771** FRANKLIN *Autobiog.* Wks. 1840 I. 71 At length a trifle snapped our connexion. **1798** COLERIDGE *Anc. Mar.* VI. x, And now this spell was snapt. **1819** SHELLEY *Cenci* v. i. 82 There arose a Power Which grasped and snapped the threads of my device. **1863** GEO. ELIOT *Romola* II. v, She had been strong enough to snap asunder the bonds she had accepted in blind faith. **1951** *Amer. Speech* XXVI. 230 Michigan snaps Gopher streak. **1967** *Boston Herald* 8 May 16/6 His run-scoring single in the fifth inning climaxed a two-run rally that snapped a 3–3 tie. **1973** *Internat. Herald Tribune* 15 June 15/6 California held on to score a 7–5 home victory over Boston, snapping a four-game losing streak. **1976** *Washington Post* 19 Apr. D3/1 Danny Lawson's goal at 14:53 of the third period snapped a 4–4 tie.

**c.** To break *off* with a snap.

**1808** [see *snapwood* s.v. SNAP-]. **1820** SHELLEY *Sensit. Pl.* III. 109 A northern whirlwind..Shook the boughs..And snapped them off. **1833** T. HOOK *Parson's Dau.* I. vii, A five pound fish..had snapped off the top-joint of his..rod. **1834** *Good's Study Med.* (ed. 4) III. 101 If it be forcibly snapped off, it will shoot out the wider.

**d.** To get (a person) *out of* a certain frame of mind. Cf. sense 15 d above.

**1957** A. GRIMBLE *Return to Islands* iv. 78 Once they had struck their noble attitude officially..nothing but the crack of doom would ever snap them out of it. **1964** M. MCLUHAN *Understanding Media* I. v. 55 The parallel between two media holds us on the frontiers between forms that snap us out of the Narcissus-narcosis. **1968** *Globe & Mail* (Toronto) 13 Jan. 28/5 Brisk way to snap yourself out of the post holiday lethargy is to get out your little or not so little lists and decide to do some entertaining.

**V. 17. a.** Adverbially: With, or as with, a snap; quickly, smartly. Freq. in phr. *to go snap*.

**1583** STUBBES *Anat. Abus.* II. (1882) 50 Then snap go the fingers, ful brauely, god wot. **1598** SHAKS. *Merry W.* IV. v. 3 What wouldst thou haue?..speake, breathe, discusse: breefe, short, quicke, snap. **c1746** J. COLLIER (Tim Bobbin) *View Lanc. Dial.* (1775) 28 On coom snap, on axt meh whot he wantut? **1844** N. PATERSON *Manse Garden* 64 Snap goes the branch, making a very unseemly fracture. **1890** L. C. D'OYLE *Notches* 175 Snap went the noose.

**b.** In phr. *to cry snap*.

In quot. 1782 in allusion to the crying of 'Snap!' in the game *Snip-snap-snorum*.

**1694** JOHNSON *Notes Past. Lett.* I. 13 This is an Argument which cries snap like a Mousetrap, but will catch nothing. **1782** MISS BURNEY *Cecilia* IX. iii, I suppose he'll shilly-shally till somebody else will cry snap, and take her.

**snap** (snæp), *int.* The call in the card-game snap (SNAP *sb.* 5 d); hence as an exclamation used when two similar objects turn up or two similar events take place.

**1890** CHAMPLIN & BOSTWICK *Young Folks' Cycl. Games & Sports* 659/2 When a player turns a card having the same design as one on the top of another player's exposed pile, both must say 'Snap'. **1958** N. F. SIMPSON *Hole* 7 *Cerebro.* He seems to be biding his time at the moment. *Soma.* Snap! **1962** J. BRAINE *Life at Top* v. 88 He passed me his cigarette-case. The cigarettes..bore his initials. I reached for my cigarette-lighter then took out instead one of the books of matches I'd taken away from the Savoy. He looked at the matches and grinned. 'Snap,' he said. **1971** M. RUSSELL *Deadline* viii. 95 'I've read your stuff.' 'Snap.' **1980** J. WAINWRIGHT *Venus Fly-Trap* 39 Daphne, too, was wearing dark glasses... Harry..murmured, 'Snap.'

**snap-.** The stem of SNAP *v.* in combination.

**1. a.** With *sbs.* (also forming derivatives), as **snap action** used *attrib.*, as ***snap action gun*** (see quot. 1884); also to designate switches and relays that make and break contact rapidly, independently of the speed of the actuating mechanism; so ***snap-actioned*** ppl. a.; **snap-apple** (see quot. 1823); †**snap-bag**, = SNAPSACK; **snap-bean** *U.S.* (see SNAP *sb.* 18); **snap-beetle**, a click-beetle (cf. CLICK *sb.*[1] 4); **snap-block** *Naut.* (see quot. 1884); **snap-brim**, used *attrib.* to designate a type of hat for men with a brim which may be arranged in different ways; also *absol.*; hence **snap-brimmed** *a.*; **snap-bug**, = *snap-beetle*; **snap-cap** (see quot. 1876); **snap-dog**, *local*, a lurcher; **snap-dyke** *Sc.* (see quots.); †**snap-fig**, = BECCAFICO; **snap-flask** (see quot. 1875); **snap gauge** *Mech.*, a form of caliper gauge that can be used to check that a component is neither too large nor too small within stated tolerances; **snap-jack**, *dial.* the stitchwort; **snap-plough**, *local* (see quots.); †**snap-rod** (see quot.); **snap-sound** *Path.*, a snapping sound heard in auscultation; **snap-thought** *attrib.*, used for noting ideas as they occur; **snap-tree**, **-weed** (see quots.); **snap-willow**, *local*, the brittle or crack willow, *Salix fragilis*; **snapwood** (see quot.).

Other examples of this type occur in recent use, esp. *dial.* or *U.S.* Similar formations are also employed in Dutch and German.

**1882** *Worc. Exhib. Catal.* III. 56 Top lever *snap action gun. **1884** KNIGHT *Dict. Mech.* Suppl. 826 *Snap Action*, as distinguished from a lever gun; one which as the hinged barrel closes is fastened by a spring catch. **1951** *Chambers's Jrnl.* Oct. 639/2 A snap-action switch..cuts out the power supply at short and timed intervals. **1962** *Newnes Conc. Encycl. Electr. Engin.* 726/1 Many rotary switches are manufactured for d.c. operation with snap-action mechanisms. **1977** R. W. SMEATON *Switchgear & Control Handbk.* III. 4 Snap-action contacts reduce the arcing time. **1875** 'STONEHENGE' *Brit. Rural Sports* I. I. ii. 26 Patents for slight modifications of this *snap-actioned 'central fire'. **1823** E. MOOR *Suffolk Words*, **Snap apple*, a mirth exciting frolic; in which catching..an apple in your mouth, while twirling on a stick suspended on its centre, with a candle at the other end of it, is the jest of the sport. **1870** *Routledge's Ev. Boys' Ann.* Oct. 583 Who's for snap-apple? **1688** HOLME *Armoury* III. xiv. (Roxb.) 17/2 The Port Mantle, of some termed a Bugett, or Snapsack, or *Snapbag. **1770** M. AMBLER *Jrnl.* Sept. in *Virginia Mag. Hist. & Biogr.* (1937) XLV. 156 A Breast of Veal for Dinner *Snap Beans & gooseberry tart. **1870** LANIER *Poems, Nine from Eight* 48 Hit gobbled me up like snap-beans. **1897** *Outing* XXX. 383/2 The supper consisted of fried ham and snap-beans. **1698** PETIVER in *Phil. Trans.* XX. 397 A peculiar species I have seen in England, and call *Snap-Beetles, from their elastick or springing Faculty. **1702** —— *Gazophyl.* i. §10 The Velvet-eyed Virginia Snap-Beetle. **1889** G. NICHOLSON *Dict. Gard.* IV. 213 The names..Click Beetle and Snap Beetle refer to the sound produced in the leap. **1626** CAPT. SMITH *Accid. Yng. Seamen* 15 A *snap blocke is seldom vsed but in heauing of goods and ordnances. **1884** KNIGHT *Dict. Mech.* Suppl. 826/1 *Snap Block*, a block with an opening in the side at which the rope may be laid in the sheave without the trouble of reeving it in. **1928** *Daily Express* 5 July 9/4 The *snap-brim (or turn-down) soft felt hat. **1941** [see BRETON *sb.* and *a.*]. **1969** V. C. CLINTON-BADDELEY *Only Matter of Time* 45 Davie..put on his soft green hat... Why a 'snap brim', by the way? He always wondered. **1972** B. F. CONNERS *Don't embarrass Bureau* (1973) I. 3 The man was wearing a nondescript raincoat and a gray snap-brim hat. **1949** B. A. BOTKIN *Treas. S. Folklore* II. iii. 252 Loud checked suit, flaming necktie, diamond stickpin, and rakish *snap-brimmed felt hat. **1976** *Maclean's Mag.* (Toronto) 15 Nov. 28/1 Al Capone wasn't talking through his snap-brimmed hat. **1834** MᶜMURTRIE *Cuvier's Anim. Kingd.* 350 *Elater noctilucus*..; dusky brown, with a cinereous down... North America is extremely rich in this genus. The insect is usually called a **Snap-bug*. **1844** *Queen's Regul. & Ord. Army* 96 *note*, Muzzle-Stoppers, *Snap-Caps. **1876** VOYLE & STEVENSON *Milit. Dict.* 391/1 *Snap-cap*, a small leather cylinder with a metal top of the size of the hammer of a percussion musket, and fitting closely to the nipple. **1877** *N.W. Linc. Gloss.* 230 **Snap-dog*, a half-bred greyhound. **1891** *Pall Mall G.* 23 Dec. 6/3 Rabbit Coursing Sweepstakes for so many 'snap-dogs'. **1793** *Statist. Acc. Scotland* VI. 104 A kind of stone fence, called *Snap-dykes, peculiar to Carrick and the north parts of Galloway, is admirably fitted for sheep parks; being from 4 to 6 feet in height, strong and firmly locked together at the top. **1812** SIR J. SINCLAIR *Syst. Husb. Scot.* I. 42 Among the various sorts of stone wall usual in Scotland, there is one, known under the name of the Galloway or snap dike. **1603** FLORIO *Montaigne* III. xiii. (1894) 565 The dainty bird beccafico or *snapfig deserveth to bee eaten whole at one morsell. **1875** KNIGHT *Dict. Mech.* 2229/1 **Snap-flask*, a two-part flask having its halves joined together by a butt-hinge at one corner and a latch at the diagonally opposite corner. **1884** C. G. W. LOCK *Workshop Rec.* Ser. III. 252/1 Most malleable castings are..moulded in snap-flasks. **1918** D. T. HAMILTON *Gages, Gaging & Inspection* iii. 67 *Snap gages used in general manufacturing are made in three types; namely, solid, adjustable, and built-up gages. **1964** S. CRAWFORD *Basic Engin. Processes* iv. 298 When using snap gauges for checking external diameters the component should be gauged in a number of positions along and around its surface. **1867** ROCK *Jim & Nell* xlix. (E.D.S.), Whit-zindays, *snap-jacks, goosey-vlops. **1894** WHITBY *Mary Fenwick's Daughter* I. 57 Bird's-eye and snap-jack, ragged robin and hem-lock. **1798** J. MIDDLETON *View Agric. Middlesex* 91 A swing turn-wrest plough..in which the wrest is moved in half the usual time... This farmer calls them *snap ploughs. **1875** W. D. PARISH *Dict. Sussex Dial.* 108 *Snap-plough*, a plough with two wings, so fixed as to snap or move from one side to the other, though only one projects at a time. **1688** HOLME *Armoury* III. 103 A Snapper, or *Snap-Rod, is a strong Pole, peculiar for a Pike. **1898** *Allbutt's Syst. Med.* V. 1021 The *snap sound and the thrill may be observed in some cardiac cycles. **1738** WEDDELL *Voy. Thames* 83 Taking every Opportunity to put down Notes in his *Snap-thought Leger. **c1711** PETIVER *Gazophyl.* x. §91 *Luzone Adhatoda* or *Snap-tree with a Jasmin Flower. **1731** MILLER *Gard. Dict.* s.v. *Adhatoda*, The Willow-leav'd Malabar Nut, commonly call'd, The Snap-tree. **1823** CRABB *Technol. Dict.*, Snap-tree, *Justicia hyssopifolia*. *Ibid.*, *Snapweed, *Impatiens*. **1899** STEP *Romance Wild Fl.* 135 The handsome Jewel-weed, or Snapweed (*Impatiens fulva*). **1880** JEFFERIES *Gt. Estate* 87 The '*snap-willow', which is so brittle that every gale breaks off its feeble twigs. **1808** VANCOUVER *View Agric. Hants.* (1813) xii. §4. 389 A claim..of taking what is called **snap-wood*, that is, all the fallen branches, and such as they can snap off by hand.

**b.** In the names of things or appliances operating, closing, fastening, fitting, etc., with a snap or by means of a catch, as ***snap-bolt***, ***-catch***, ***-gun***, ***-harness***, etc.; **snap-link**, (*a*) (see quot. 1875); (*b*) = KARABINER; **snap-ring**, (*a*) see quot. 1903); (*b*) = KARABINER; **snap switch**, a snap-action switch.

**1875** 'STONEHENGE' *Brit. Rural Sports* I. I. ii. 33 Mr. W. W. Greener's is also a good *snap-bolt. **1897** *Sears, Roebuck Catal.* (1968) 228/3 Gloves... Set in thumbs, and patent *snap buttons. **1976** *National Observer* (U.S.) 23 Oct. 20/2 His pearl snap-button shirt is open, his belt loosened a notch, his head propped up with a bulky, weathered arm. **1880** *Encycl. Brit.* XI. 285/2 The breech is closed sharply on the hinge and is held by a *snap-catch. **1964** *McCall's Sewing* 171/2 (*heading*), Sleeve with *snap closing. **1969** *Sears Catal.* Spring/Summer 16 Band waist, *snap closure. **1976** *National Observer* (U.S.) 10 Apr. 16/3 (Advt.), The waist band and two patch pockets are fitted with permanent and attractive metal snap closures. No buttons to fall off. **1895** *Montgomery Ward Catal.* Spring & Summer 289/3 Men's Genuine Oil Tanned Calfskin Gloves,..one button, patent *snap fastener. **1976** M. MAGUIRE *Scratchproof* xi. 165 My eyes instinctively traced the zipper, buttons and snap fasteners on her suit. **1898** *T. Eaton & Co. Catal.* Spring & Summer 124/3 Men's Klondike sleeping bags,..envelope top, *snap fastenings, riveted corners. **1981** *Sunday Express Mag.* 11 Oct. 17/2 (Advt.), And each of the two key fobs has its own snap fastening. **1644** *Sc. Acts, Chas. I* (1870) VI. 65 Their foote men haveing *snap gunnes and suordis sall have the pay of foote souldiers. **1881** GREENER *Gun* 206 [Mr. Needham's] first snap gun..was so constructed that upon depressing the lever for opening the gun, the hammers were raised to half-cock. **1888** *Daily News* 3 Dec. 3/5 The *snap harness which enables the horses to be harnessed in less than ten seconds. **1956** *Archit. Rev.* CXIX. 213/2 In this case the positive fixing and covering are achieved by a simple *snap-joint incorporated in the edge corrugations. **1968** *Gloss. Terms Mechanized & Hand Sheet Metal Work* (*B.S.I.*) 21 *Snap joint*, the junction between two pieces of sheet or strip, the edges of which are formed so that they can be clipped together to form a rigid joint. **1932** *N. & Q.* 13 Feb. 123/2 Portable Ink-Bottles: these were in quite common use until recent times... I frequently had in a waistcoat pocket, the small square, or oblong leathered covered box, with a *snap-lid. **1875** KNIGHT *Dict. Mech.* 2229/2 **Snap-link*, an open link with a spring, for the purpose of connecting parts of harness, chains, etc. **1946** D. R. BROWER *Man. Ski Mountaineering* (ed. 2) iii. 28 The army aluminium carabiner (snaplink) has equal strength, weighs much less. **1981** L. DEIGHTON *XPD* xxxvii. 294 Never mind all these modern contraptions—pitons, snap links and stirrups. **1913** *Strand Mag.* Nov. 103 (Advt.), Smart, neat, *snap-lock links. Of all Hosiers, Outfitters, etc... *Snap-lock Link Co.* **1971** B. MALAMUD *Tenants* 12 His apartment, stoutly protected by two patent locks plus a strong snap-lock enclosing heavy circular bolts. **1775** G. WHITE *Selborne* lxiii, *Snap mouse-traps baited with tallow or suet. **1886**

*Longm. Mag.* VII. 652 Years ago an immense number of salmon used to be taken by means of these *snap-nets. **1897** *Daily News* 23 Mar. 7/1 *Snap-purses, writing cases, pearl necklets. **1827** CARLYLE *Germ. Rom.* I. 99 A loud humming symphony of *snap-reel and spinning-wheel. **1903** *Sci. Amer.* 14 Feb. 110 These last [= packing rings] are called '*snap rings', from the fact that they are sprung into the piston. **1941** T. A. H. PEACOCKE *Mountaineering* ii. 25 Each climber carries a loop of line... A 'karabiner' (snap-ring) is hung on the loop. **1941** *Engineers' Digest* II. 321/1 Snap rings provide an economical and effective means of facilitating machine assemblies in applications where the loading is not excessive. **1957** *Listener* 28 Nov. 882/2 The less fortunate..of us have to..join the modern school of artificial rock climbers..with their pitons, snap rings, miniature ladders, [etc.]. **1970** K. BALL *Fiat 600, 600D Aubobook* i. 12/2 With a special tool..depress the valve springs, remove the split cotters and snap rings. **1974** *Islander* (Victoria, B.C.) 21 July 11/1 Another day..a *snap shackle on the mizzen staysail broke. **1926** *Gloss. Terms Electr. Engin.* (Brit. Engin. Stand. Assoc.) 159 *Snap switch. **1977** R. W. SMEATON *Switchgear & Control Handbk.* III. 6 (*heading*) Resistance of control-circuit duty contacts and snap switches. **1875** *Zoologist* X. 4662 Rats caught in *snap-traps. **1875** 'STONEHENGE' *Brit. Rural Sports* I. I. ii. 36 The hook in which the *snap-wedge enters to keep the gun closed.

**c.** In combs. relating to or connected with the use of a snap-hook in fishing, as ***snap-angling*** [cf. G. *schnappangel*], ***-fishing***; ***snap-bait***, ***-tackle***.

**1792** OSBALDISTONE *Sportsman* 606 Snap-angling is with two large hooks tied back to back, and one smaller to fix your bait on. **1794** *Sporting Mag.* III. 247 The directions for snap-fishing. **1839** HOFLAND *Brit. Angler's Man.* v. 124, I generally resort to my snap-tackle. **1856** 'STONEHENGE' *Brit. Rural Sports* I. v. iii. 254 Snap-fishing must be practised with the top joints of the rod reduced in length and of greater stiffness. *Ibid.* 257 The Snap-Bait is employed only when the fish are wary and inclined to eject the ordinary kind.

**d.** Formed, taken, performed, etc., hastily or rapidly, as ***snap exposure***, ***-firing***, ***judgement***, etc. Also, **snap freezing**, freezing done by reducing the temperature suddenly to well below freezing point; hence **snap-freeze** *v. trans.*

In this and the next group passing into *adj.*

**1841** *Congress. Globe* X. App. 42/3 This extra session of Congress, called in time of peace to take snap judgments on the American people. **1861** *N. York Tribune* in *Times* 19 Nov., A traveller's snap-judgement formed on the most superficial observation. **1867** *J. Lillywhite's Cricketers' Companion* 13 Get some one to give you difficult catches... You will soon be good at snap-catching. **1876** BLACK *Madcap Violet* xxviii, After..a great deal of snap-firing, the skart was at last stretched on the water. **1888** A. G. STEEL in Steel & Lyttelton *Cricket* iii. 179 The object of short-slip is to pick up snicks which just miss the wicket-keeper, and although he may hold a larger proportion of these quick snap catches when a long way from the wicket, he will get an infinitely greater number when closer in. **1889** *Anthony's Photogr. Bulletin* II. 255 For snap exposures a different course is necessary. **1894** *Amer. Ann. Photogr.* 137 The real necessities for snap photography. **1896** *Congress. Rec.* 27 Feb. 2214/2 When the snap tally was taken, he..went to the clerk. **1898** A. P. ATTERBURY tr. *Sombart's Socialism & Social Movement in 19th Cent.* vi. 137 A snap resolution of a working-men's congress. **1932** 'N. SHUTE' *Lonely Road* xi. 229 This isn't any snap decision on my part. I've been thinking of it for some time. **1933** *Mod. Lang. Notes* XLVIII. 393 In most cases they reflect, not conclusions drawn from research, but snap judgments based on chance observation and personal likes and dislikes. **1940** *Sun* (Baltimore) 23 Sept. 12/2 (*caption*) Charley Gehringer takes a snap throw from Shortstop Dick Bartell. **1954** X. FIELDING *Hide & Seek* v. 67 Unless we were unlucky enough to be held up by a snap Gestapo..check. **1955** *New Biol.* XVIII. 93 Slow cooling is supposed to cause more damage than rapid cooling since it results in the formation of larger ice crystals, and the use of 'snap' or ultra-rapid freezing has been advocated on the grounds that ice crystal formation may be avoided altogether, the system cooling in an amorphous state. **1959** 'A. GILBERT' *Death takes Wife* v. 54, I had to keep this snap appointment. **1959** *Punch* 27 May 704/3 You have to be constantly on the *qui vive* if you are not going to risk being behindhand with the timing of the first drop [of hail], or even missing a snap shower altogether. **1960** Snap-test [see BREATHALYSER]. **1960** V. JENKINS *Lions down Under* xi. 161 There was no doubt about his speed and capacity for 'snap-thinking'. **1965** *Listener* 21 Oct. 637/2 The snap opinions in this programme which I have always respected are those of Patrick Campbell. **1973** *Times* 8 Jan. 3/3 The investigation..will involve snap checks at garages. **1974** HAWKEY & BINGHAM *Wild Card* ix. 95 If he builds a cryogenic tank into the spacecraft, it'll rupture on explosion, spray the tissue with liquid oxygen, snap-freeze it, and provide perfect histological specimens for the investigators. **1974** B. A. NEWTON *Trypanosomiasis & Leishmaniasis* 277 Annear (1956) described a technique for 'snap freezing' *Crithidia oncopelti* on a 'peptone plug'. **1974** 'M. INNES' *Appleby's other Story* viii. 62 One must make no snap judgement. **1974** *Socialist Worker* 26 Oct. 15/1, 2800 teachers in 90 schools staging snap strikes in support of a £15-a-week interim increase. **1976** *Alyn & Deeside Observer* 10 Dec. 16/3 The information arrives at a time which can allow only for a 'snap decision'. **1977** *Times of Zambia* 7 Sept. 2/2 A snap survey of clinics found that medical assistants in the health institutions had not been able to administer prescribed drugs for some time now.

**e.** In Parliamentary usage, as ***snap bill***, ***dissolution***, ***division***, ***election***, ***vote***, one obtained or taken unexpectedly or when comparatively few members are present.

**1879** MCCARTHY *Own Times* xx. II. 96 It was evident that this was only what is called a 'snap' vote. **1883** E. W. HAMILTON *Diary* 19 July (1972) II. 461 The Agricultural Holdings Bill..is on the whole being well received, though the Government were on Tuesday defeated by a snap division on a landlords' amendment. **1884** *Nonconformist* 7 Feb. 129/2 The majority was the result of a 'snap division'. **1892** *Rev. Reviews* V. 3/2 Administrations have tried by a snap dissolution..to capture a fresh majority. **1940** *Sun* (Baltimore) 28 Mar. 12/3 The outcome of the voting in Canada is no surprise. It was a 'snap' election engineered with the greatest skill by Prime Minister W. L. Mackenzie King and the results have fully justified his astute political strategy. **1973** *Times* 8 Dec. 3/8 The strong majority..who do not think the Government should hold a snap general election on this issue are mainly Conservative voters. **1975** J. P. MORGAN *House of Lords & Labour Govt.* viii. 217 The reformers themselves therefore argued that the announcement should be made immediately, and the Lords' reform, including any mention of a snap Bill, indefinitely deferred.

**2.** Forming combinations, esp. with prepositions, used *attrib.* to designate things or appliances operating with a snap (cf. sense 1. b); as ***snap-in***, ***-off***, ***-on***, etc.

**1905–6** *T. Eaton & Co. Catal.* Fall & Winter 158/4 Snap-on Hose Supporters, snaps on to edge of corset. **1939–40** *Army & Navy Stores Catal.* 590 Sports seats... Pigskin covered handle, 'snap-on' ground disc. **1963** *Punch* 17 Apr. 560/3 This is a hygienic, snap-top canisterette. **1967** *Electronics* 6 Mar. 81/1 (Advt.), Printed Circuit Pins (A) may be attached at rates up to 4,000 an hour; snap-in design holds leads in position for easy solder dipping. **1972** *N.Y. Times* 3 Nov. 3/4 (Advt.), 4 snap-close shirts. **1977** *National Observer* (U.S.) 15 Jan. 21/4 Old wine is also served up in snaptop cans in an entertainment called *The Club*, now at the downtown Circle in the Square. **1978** *Detroit Free Press* 16 Apr. (Parade Suppl.) 14/2 (Advt.), Our very special features, such as a new one-piece, snap-in drapery rod. Works like a traverse. No tabs to tear! **1979** *Nature* 29 Mar. p. xxix/2 A unique one-handed operation, using inexpensive snap-on snap-off plastic, disposable tips.

**'snap-back.** Also snapback. [f. SNAP-.]

**1.** *U.S.* and *Canad. Football.* **a.** A centre player; the centre-rusher. ? *Obs.*

**1887** *Outing* Oct. 69/2 He it is who, receiving the ball from the 'center-rusher', or 'snap-back', as he is more commonly called, passes it to some other player for a kick or run. **1893** W. C. CAMP *College Sports* 99 This name [*sc.* center rusher] has since given place almost entirely to 'snap-back'. **1901** *Encycl. Sport* II. 426/1 The influence of the snap-back will at once be realised from the consideration that the moment he puts the ball into play through his legs behind him, he also makes six men besides himself immediately off-side.

**b.** A backward pass from the centre which puts the ball in play to begin a scrimmage.

**1910** [see SCRIMMAGE, SCRUMMAGE *sb.* 4 c (*a*)]. **1947** *Sun* (Baltimore) 8 Nov. 10/3 The first [attempt] fizzled when Wally Wilson fumbled the snapback, while Jones booted wide of the goal posts following the final six pointer.

**2. a.** A recovery of an earlier position or circumstances. **b.** A reaction or retaliation.

**1949** *Sun* (Baltimore) 15 Oct. 13/1 A mild recovery movement in mid-morning cut losses... In the final hour [of trading] there was a snap-back from the lows that gave the whole market a lift. **1961** *Economist* 28 Oct. 370/3 There is little prospect of a swift snapback until the economy shows more signs of strength. **1972** P. TAMONY *Americanisms* (typescript) No. 32. 2 The snap-back of the childish and immature took the form of re-mailings of obscene scrawls. **1979** *Financial Rev.* 11 June 7/1 Behind the upward move of the dollar a pressure cooker effect is building—the kind of pressure that could cause a snap-back and make last year's weakness in the currency look like strength.

**3.** In Boxing, a swift backward movement of the body to evade an opponent's blow.

**1950** J. DEMPSEY *Championship Fighting* xxii. 169 The last and worst type of evasion is the pull-away. Some fighters call it the 'snap-back'. **1952** *Amateur Boxing* ('Know the Game' ser.) 23/1 *Snap back*, a sway backwards—a quick 'snap' back from the hips, sufficient to be out of range of the blow.

**snapdragon** ('snæp,drægən). Also **snap dragon**, **snap-dragon.** [f. SNAP *v.* + DRAGON[1].]

**1. a.** A popular name for one or other of the plants belonging to the genus *Antirrhinum*, esp. *A. majus*, a hardy plant bearing showy flowers, freq. grown in gardens.

**1573** TUSSER *Husb.* (1878) 96 Roses of all sorts... Snap [*pr.* snag] dragons. **1597** GERARDE *Herbal* 438 The flowers [are]..fashioned like..a dragons mouth; from whence the women haue taken the name Snapdragon. **1629** PARKINSON *Parad.* 269 There is some diuersity in the Snapdragons, some being of a larger, and others of a lesser stature and bignesse. **1657** S. PURCHAS *Pol. Flying-Ins.* 93 Those flowers, that..shut hard and close at the top or lips,.. as Toads-flax, Snap-dragon, Fox-gloves. **1705** tr. *Cowley's Plants* Wks. 1711 III. 372 Antirrhinon..takes the Stile Of Lion's Mouth, sometimes of Calf's-Snout vile, By us Snap-Dragon call'd. **1785** MARTYN *Rousseau's Bot.* iv. (1794) 45 Having the two lips not usually open, or gaping, but closed and joined, as you may see in the snap-dragon. **1847** JAMES *Convict* x, Those old walls, time-worn, and lichen-covered, and loaded with snapdragon. **1882** *Garden* 26 Aug. 183/2 Truly the Snap-dragon is one of our finest open-air flowers.

*attrib.* and *Comb.* **1871** KINGSLEY *At Last* xii, This raft supports the little scape of yellow snapdragon-like flowers. **1872** TYNDALL *Fragm. Sci.* (ed. 4) 412 In the path of the bean is interposed this snapdragon light. Alcohol and water are here mixed with a quantity of common salt.

**b.** With distinguishing terms.

**1597** GERARDE *Herbal* 438 The purple Snapdragon hath great and brittle stalks. **1629** PARKINSON *Parad.* 269 Variable Snapdragon... Yellow Snapdragon. *c* **1710** PETIVER *Cat. Ray's Eng. Herbal* xxxv, Small Snap-Dragon. **1731** MILLER *Gard. Dict.* s.v. *Antirrhinum*, The Broad-leav'd Snap-dragon. *Ibid.*, The strip'd Snap-dragon. **1796** WITHERING *Brit. Plants* (ed. 3) III. 549 Ivy-leaved Snap-dragon... Round-leaved Snapdragon. *Ibid.* 550 Creeping Snapdragon [etc.]. **1856** DELAMER *Fl. Garden* (1861) 74 Garden Snapdragon.

**c.** Applied to various other plants having personate flowers (see quots.).

Also *dial.* the foxglove, the columbine, and the common fumitory (*Eng. Dial. Dict.*).

**1753** *Chambers' Cycl.* Suppl. s.v. *Linaria*, The species of toad flax..called by authors the lesser snapdragon... Stone snapdragon. **1760** J. LEE *Introd. Bot.* 327 Snap Dragon of America, *Ruellia*. **1859** MISS PRATT *Flowering Pl.* IV. 125 Lesser Snapdragon. **1864** GRISEBACH *Flora Brit. W. Ind.* 787/2 Snapdragon, *Ruellia tuberosa*. **1866** *Treas. Bot.* 1067/2 Snapdragon,..*Silene Antirrhina*.

**2.** A figure or representation of a dragon, esp. one so constructed as to open and shut the mouth, used in mayoral or civic shows or processions. *Obs.* exc. *Hist.*

**1611** FLORIO, *Mandúco*, a disguised or vglie picture to make children afraid, as wee say, a snap-dragon, a turke, a bug-beare. **1694** ECHARD *Plautus* 234 Antick Figures with wide Mouths, like our Snap-dragons for Mayor's Shows. **1726** in *Hist. Norfolk* (1829) II. 1202 Great preparations are making in this city for the guild on Tuesday next, and the old snap dragon being dead, a young one..will make his first public appearance.

†**3.** ? Burnt brandy. (Cf. next.) *Obs.*

**1676** *Poor Robin's Intell.* 22–29 Aug. 1/1 An old Crony.. with whom he drank Snapdraggon so plentifully [etc.]. **1682** DRYDEN & LEE *Dk. Guise* I. i, I swallow oaths as easy as snap-dragon.

**4.** A game or amusement (usually held at Christmas) consisting of snatching raisins out of a bowl or dish of burning brandy or other spirit and eating them whilst alight; a bowl or quantity of the liquor, etc., used in this game. (Cf. FLAP-DRAGON 1.)

**1704** SWIFT *T. Tub* xi, He bore a strange kind of appetite to snap-dragon, and to the livid snuffs of a burning candle. **1709** STEELE *Tatler* No. 85 ¶2 We got into a dark Corner with a Porringer of Brandy, and threw Raisins into it, then set it on Fire... This fantastical Mirth was called Snap-Dragon. **1792** WOLCOT (P. Pindar) *More Money* Wks. 1812 II. 505 He hates snap-dragon; 'tis a game of danger. **1835** SIR J. ROSS *Narr. 2nd Voy.* xvii. 273 The exhibition of snap-dragon..produced also great surprise. **1847** L. HUNT *Men, Women, & B.* II. xi. 275 The recollections of last night's snap-dragon and blindman's-buff. **1894** *Times* 12 Jan. 9/2 An accident arising from an explosion of methylated spirits used in a snapdragon.

*fig.* **1818** HAZLITT *Eng. Poets* v. (1870) 141 His Muse is, in fact, a giddy wanton flirt, who spends her time in playing at snap-dragon.

**5.** *techn.* (See quots.)

**1833** J. HOLLAND *Manuf. Metal* II. 11 A snap-dragon..is a sort of screw nippers placed in an ordinary vice, and opening horizontally to hold a horn or other scale while being flat filed. **1869** *Our Young Folks* V. 85 This was taken up by a second boy on a 'snap-dragon',—a rod something like a ponty, but with a socket at the end for holding articles of glass,—and carried to a glory-hole. **1875** KNIGHT *Dict. Mech.* 2229/1 *Snap-dragon*, a kind of tongs used by glass-blowers to hold their hot hollow ware.

**snape,** *sb.*[1] *dial.* [f. SNAPE *v.*[1]] **a.** A snub, rebuke, or check. **b.** A check to growth; a change to cold or bad weather.

**1828–** in dial. glossaries and texts (*Eng. Dial. Dict.*).

**snape,** *sb.*[2] *rare.* [f. SNAPE *v.*[2]] A tapering, a bevel; an act of snaping.

**1794** *Rigging & Seamanship* 23 The lower ends [are] haunched away with a snape, resembling the bill of a duck. *Ibid.* 28 The lower ends are..thinned with a duck's-bill snape.

†**snape,** *sb.*[3] *Obs.*[−1] (Meaning uncertain.)

In south-western dial. *snape* denotes a spring or boggy place in a field; it is very doubtful if this can be the same word.

*a* **1400–50** *Alexander* 1560 As blaȝt ere þaire wedis As any snyppand snawe þat in þe snape liȝtis.

**snape** (sneɪp), *v.*[1] Now *dial.* Forms: 4 (9) snaip (4 snaipe), 4–5 snayp- (5 snaypp-), 5– snape, 6 snep, 9 snaap, etc. See also SNEAP *v.* [a. ON. *sneypa* to outrage, dishonour, disgrace (Icel. *sneypa* to chide, snub, Norw. *snøypa* to withdraw, draw in, pinch, etc., MSw. and Sw. *snöpa* to castrate).]

†**1.** *trans.* To be hard upon; to harm, damage, or injure in some way. *Obs.*

**13..** *Gaw. & Gr. Knt.* 2003 Þe snawe snitered ful snart, þat snayped þe wylde. *c* **1400** *Anturs of Arth.* vii, Þe slete and þe snawe, þat snayppede þame so snelle. *a* **1400–50** *Alexander* 3995 Sire Porrus with a proude swerd him on þe pan strikis, So snelle at he snatirs with, nere snaypid him for euire.

**2.** To rebuke or snub (a person, etc.) sharply or severely; to check, restrain, or curb (a child); to call off (a dog). Now *dial.*

*a* **1300** *Cursor M.* 13027 Vte of desert þar he was in, He com to snaip þe king sinn. *Ibid.* 22103 Vr lauerd snaips þir tua tuns, And þus he sais in his sermuns. **1483** *Cath. Angl.* 346/2 To Snape, *corripere*. **1570** LEVINS *Manip.* 26 To Snape, *redarguere*. **1601** [BP. W. BARLOW] *Defence* 201 Durand snaped, about originall sinne, and merite in the workes of grace. **1691** RAY *N.C. Words*, To *snape* or *sneap*, to check [a child]. **1788** W. H. MARSHALL *Yorksh.* II. 353 To *Snape*, to silence, check, or at least threaten, as a barking dog, or a mischievous child. **1811–** freq. in dial. glossaries (Cumb., Durh., Yks., Lancs., Staffs., Shrops., etc.).

**b.** To check or stop (growth); to blight, nip, or mar the growth of (a plant, etc.). Now *dial.*

**1630** CRAVEN *God's Tribunal* (1631) 12 Magistrates, have you laboured to snape the growth of sinne. **1828-** in dial. glossaries (Cumb., Yks., etc.).

3. *dial.* To stint *of* food.

**1847** HALLIW., A step-mother snapes her step-children-in-law of their meat. **1869-** in *Eng. Dial. Dict.*

Hence †'**snaping** *vbl. sb.*, rebuking, snubbing.

*a* **1300** *Cursor M.* 18853 In his snaiping [*Trin.* snybbyng] auful was he. *Ibid.* 24007 Mi spirite for yeild i wend, þair snaiping was sa smert. **1555** *Inst. Gentleman* Cij b, To correcte them in wordes, which manye fonde mothers doo call snepping of a childe, dyscoraging his boldnes.

**snape** (sneɪp), *v.*[2] *techn.* [Possibly the same word as prec.: cf. SNEIPE *v.*]

1. *trans.* To cause or make to taper; *spec.* in *Shipbuilding* (see quot. 1846).

(*a*) **1794** *Rigging & Seamanship* 10 *Snaping*, reducing the ends of any piece to a less substance. *Ibid.* 24 Short fillings are remedied by snaping their ends. **1846** A. YOUNG *Naut. Dict.* 288 *Snape*, or *Flinch*, in shipbuilding, to bevel the end of any thing so as to fay upon an inclined surface. [Hence in Weale, Smyth, etc.] **1869** REED *Shipbuild.* xiii. 144 The butts of the plates were each snaped away with the hammer. (*b*) **1841** HAMILTON *Nugæ Lit.* 354 The handle of a knife is *snaped*. **1888** ADDY *Sheffield Gloss.* s.v., A blacksmith is said to snape a piece of iron to a point when by hammering or some other process he tapers it off to a point.

2. *intr.* To taper (*off*).

**1794** *Rigging & Seamanship* 24 The lower end of the long filling snapes. **1874** THEARLE *Naval Arch.* 57 The deck plank snapes off to a sliver edge.

Hence **snaped** *ppl. a.* (See quot.)

**1875** KNIGHT *Dict. Mech.* 2229/1 *Snaped Timber*, timber cut beveling, so that one face is narrower than the other.

†**snapely**, *adv.* In 5 snaypely. [Cf. ON. *sneypiliga*, MSw. *snöppelica*; but the text is doubtful (cf. SNAPE *v.*[1] 1).] Sharply, severely.

*c* **1420** *Anturs of Arth.* vii. (Ireland MS.), The snyterand snaue, that snaypely [*v.r.* snartly] hom snellus.

†'**snaper**. *Obs.* (Of uncertain meaning.)

*c* **1550** *Pryde & Abuse Women* 200 in Hazl. *E.P.P.* IV. 243 Rubbe a galde horse on thee backe, And he wyll kicke and wynse; And so wyll wanton wylyons When they have anye snaper or twynche.

**snaphance, snaphaunce** ('snæphɑːns, -æ-). Now *Hist.* Forms: α. 6-7 **snaphanse**, 6-7, 9 **snaphance** (6 snapp-), 7 **snaphanch**; 6-7, 9 **snap-hance**; 7 **snap hance, hans**. β. 6-7 **snap-haunse**, 6-7, 9 **snaphaunce**; 7 **snap-haunce**, 7, 9 **-haunch**; 6 **snap haunce**. [Of Continental origin, repr. Du. and Flem. *snaphaan* (in Kilian *snap-haen*), MLG. *snaphân*, LG. *snapphân*, G. *schnapphahn* (†-*han*), f. *snappen*, *schnappen* SNAP *v.* + *haan*, *hahn* cock. It is not quite clear whether the sense is 'snapping cock' or 'cock-snapper' (i.e. cock-stealer). In English the second element may have been confused with the personal name *Hans*; but Heyne (in Grimm's Dict.) cites an early example of G. *schnaphons*.]

†1. An armed robber or marauder; a freebooter or highwayman; a desperate fellow or thief. *Obs.*

α. **1538** TONSTALL *Serm. Palm Sunday* (1539) D viij b, To make this realme a praye to al venturers, al spoylers, al snaphanses, all forlornehopes. **1541** PAYNELL *Catiline* xxiii. 43 Thynkynge..that huge routes of snaphances and hopelostes, from all partes of Italy wolde resorte to hym. **1577-87** HOLINSHED *Chron.* II. 684 He therefore required the prince to rid the realme of those snaphances. β. **1548** UDALL, etc. *Erasm. Par. Mark* v. 37 Euen as thoughe a sorte of snaphaunses set all on mischiefe..would make this peticion. **1609** ARMIN *Maids More-Cl.* (1880) 73 He that shall marry thee, is a matcht y'faith, To English rash, or to a Dutch snap-haunce.

2. An early form of flint-lock used in muskets and pistols (cf. 3); also, the hammer of this.

Freq. contrasted with *firelock* (= wheel-lock), but the distinction is not always observed.

α. **1588** in *Norfolk Archæol.* (1847) I. 16 To Henry Radoe, smyth, for making one of the old pistolls with a snapphance. **1594** LYLY *Mother Bombie* II. i, These old huddles haue such strong purses with locks, when they shut them they go off like a snaphance. **1603** FLORIO *Montaigne* I. xlviii. 157 A pistoll to which belong so many severall partes, as powder, stone, locke, snap-hanse [etc.]. **1660** *Act 12 Chas. II*, c. iv, Daggs with fire lockes or Snaphances. **1680** HARFORD tr. *Gaya* in *Eng. Milit. Discipl.* 22 Upon which, when one intends to fire, he puts down the Snaphaunce, which in stead of a Flint, ought to be provided with a true Mine-stone. β. **1594** BARWICK *Disc. Weapons* 22 A Harquebuze with a snaphaunce. **1607** MARKHAM *Caval.* II. (1617) 120 A pistoll which goes with a Snaphaunce. **1642** SIR E. HARWOOD *Advice* Dj, Whether their Peeces to bee with Fire-locks or Snaphaunces, is questionable.

†b. *transf.* A spring catch or fastening. *Obs.*

**1603** DEKKER *Wonderful Year* Wks. (Grosart) I. 138 A leatherne pouch..that opened and shut with a Snap-hance. *a* **1613** OVERBURY *A Wife*, etc. (1638) 194 His heart goes with the same snaphance his purse doth. **1633** T. ADAMS *Exp. 2 Peter* i. 4 In a countryman's budget, shut up with Snaphance?

¶c. A spring trap. *Obs.*

**1823** SCOTT *Quentin D.* v, There are such traps and snap-haunches as may cost you a limb.

3. A musket, gun, etc., fitted with a lock of this kind, in use in the 16-17th centuries. Now *Hist.*

So Du. and Flem. *snaphaan*, G. †*schnapphahnrohr*.

α. **1590** SIR J. SMYTH *Disc. Weapons* 47 [Not] to strike iust vpon the wheeles being firelockes, or vpon the hammers or steeles, if they be Snap-hances. **1624** CAPT. SMITH *Virginia* III. xii. 93 Three hundred Muskets, Snaphances, and Firelockes. **1651** in H. Cary *Mem. Civ. War* (1832) II. 289 We have left us in store but..two thousand and thirty muskets, whereof thirty snaphancies. **1860** MOTLEY *Netherl.* vi. I. 316 [He] had borne a snap-hance on his shoulder as a volunteer. **1882** *Standard* 10 Feb. 5/3 The seafaring man with his snap-hance, his flint lock, or his steel lance was upon them.

β. *c* **1580** J. HOOKER *Life Sir P. Carew* in *Archaeol.* XXVIII. 139 Sir Peter..hade with hyme a case of excellente snaphaunses. **1591** *Garrard's Art Warre* 129 If the horse men use firelocke peeces, or snap haunces. **1655** MARKHAM *Hunger's Prevention* 44 Tis better it be a fier locke or Snaphaunce then a cocke and tricker. **1656** BLOUNT *Glossogr.*, *Snaphaunse*, a fire-lock, or Gun that strikes fire without the use of a match. **1821** SCOTT *Nigel* xxvii, 'Let me see those pistols.' 'Ye are not so unwise as to meddle with such snap-haunches?' **1840** GRESLEY *Siege of Lichfield* 287 The snaphaunce differed from the modern fire-lock, in the hammer not forming the covering for the pan.

*fig.* **1608** J. DAY *Law Trickes* v. i, A parlous Girle; her wits a meere Snaphaunce, Goes with a fire locke.

†b. A soldier armed with this form of gun.

**1645** N. DRAKE *2nd Siege of Pontefract* (Surtees) 47 Capt. Joshua Walker with..about 20 snaphanches went out through the howses.

†4. *fig.* Ready answer or argument. *Obs.*$^{-1}$

**1598** MARSTON *Sco. Villanie* I. iv. 190 And old crabb'd Scotus..Pay'th me with snaphaunce, quick distinction.

†5. A woman of low character. *Obs.*$^{-1}$

*a* **1625** FLETCHER *Women Pleased* III. ii, 'Faith wholsome women will but spoil ye too, For you are so us'd to snap-haunces.

6. Attrib., as ***snaphance bag, hate, lock, musket, pistol, satirist***.

**1592** NASHE *P. Penilesse* Wks. (Grosart) II. 77 It is your dooing..that these stal-fed cormorants..must bung vp all the welth of the Land in their snap-haunce bags. **1598** E. GUILPIN *Skial.* (1878) 65 The sharp tart veriuice of his snap-haunce hate. **1598** MARSTON *Pygmal. Sat.* ii. Wks. 1856 III. 217, I, that even now lisp'd like an amorist, Am turn'd into a snaphaunce Satyrist. **1643** in *10th Rep. Hist. MSS. Comm.* App. IV. 67 The hundred Snaphance muskets and..other small things. **1688** HOLME *Armoury* III. xviii. (Roxb.) 135/1 A snaphaunch Lock is the generall name for all fire Locks. **1898** *Proc. Soc. Antiquaries* Mar. 107 The President exhibited a snaphaunce pistol of the year 1619.

**snap head**. Also **snap-head**. [f. SNAP *sb.*]

1. A round head to a rivet, bolt, etc.

**1869** REED *Shipbuild.* xvii. 328 The common form of rivet head employed for shipbuilding is that known as 'pair' head; but hemispherical or Snap heads are also used. **1889** WELCH *Text Bk. Naval Archit.* iv. 75 For machine-riveted work, and occasionally for that put together by hand, snap heads and points..are employed.

*attrib.* **1874** THEARLE *Naval Arch.* 128 The snap head rivet, used in machine riveting of beams, boilers, etc.

2. A tool used to shape the head of a rivet.

**1875** KNIGHT *Dict. Mech.* 1947/2 The end is swaged down by striking directly with a riveting-hammer, or a species of die called a snap-head is interposed.

Hence **snap-headed** *ppl. a.*

**1869** REED *Shipbuild.* xvii. 329 The snap-point is sometimes formed on snap-headed rivets.

**snap-hook**. [f. SNAP-.]

1. *Angling*. A device consisting of three or four hooks connected in a special manner.

**1688** HOLME *Armoury* III. xxii. (Roxb.) 277/2 The first is termed a Snap Hooke or a Gorge Hooke. **1741** *Compl. Family Piece* II. ii. 344 Your Snap-hook..should be made thus: Take two Salmon-Hooks..; turn the Hooks back to back, and place the Gimp in the Middle [etc.]. **1820** T. F. SALTER *Troller's Guide* 90 *Snap hooks*, dead or plain, are synonimous terms; meaning all hooks used in Jack fishing that are made without springs. **1839** [see SNAP *sb.* 13 b]. **1856** 'STONEHENGE' *Brit. Rural Sports* I. v. iii. § 10. 256 The snap-hook is either the plain or the spring snap hook. [Description of several varieties follows.]

2. (See quot. 1875.)

**1875** KNIGHT *Dict. Mech.* 2229/1 *Snap-hook*, a hook with a spring mousing by which it is prevented from accidental disengagement. **1889** *Pall Mall G.* 9 July 3/2 A stout leather strap, with a buckle fastening it in front, and snap hooks projecting from each side at the back.

'**snaply**, *a. Sc.* (and *Ir.*). *rare.* [Cf. SNAP *a.*] Sharply, smartly, quickly.

In *Cursor M.* 18228 the Gött. MS. has *snapli*, but the correct reading is no doubt *snarpli* as in the Cott. MS.

**1768** ROSS *Helenore* 43 They shot him in before In a dark hole, an' snaply lock'd the door. **1880** in *Antrim & Down Gloss.* 94.

**snappable** ('snæpəb(ə)l), *a.* [f. SNAP *v.* + -ABLE.] That may be snapped or broken.

**1866** BLACKMORE *C. Nowell* xlvi. (1883) 306 Our life is but a thread at any moment snappable.

†'**snappage**. *Thieves' cant. Obs.* [f. SNAP *sb.* or *v.*] A share in the proceeds of a theft or robbery claimed by a snap or cloyer.

**1602** ROWLANDS *Greenes Ghost* 16 They can no sooner draw a bung but these come in for their tenths, which they generally tearm snapping, or snappage. *Ibid.*, If the cut-purse denie snappage, his cloyer or follower forthwith.. bewrayes him.

**snapped** (snæpt), *ppl. a.* [f. SNAP *v.*] 1. Broken with a snap; also *colloq.*, abrupt, sudden.

**1867** AUGUSTA WILSON *Vashti* xii, Snapped harness, broken carriage, torn flesh, and strained joints. **1893** LELAND *Mem.* II. 293 A lively incident which was to put a snapped end to this humbugging. **1900** *Daily News* 8 Aug. 5/1 A cart..loaded with snapped branches.

2. Designating matching exposed cards which have prompted the call 'snap!' in the game of snap. Cf. SNAP *v.* 5 g.

**1935** *Encycl. Sports, Games & Pastimes* 568/2 The one who calls first obtains all the cards which lie beneath the two snapped ones.

**snapper** ('snæpə(r)), *sb.*[1] [f. SNAP *v.* Cf. Fris., Du., LG. *snapper*, G. *schnapper*.]

†1. *Cant.* ? An accomplice or sharer. (Cf. SNAP *v.* 3 a). *Obs.*

**1532** *Use of Dice Play* (Percy Soc.) 29 This new nurtured novice..is become so good a scholar, that he knoweth readily his flats and barris, and hath been snapper with the old cole at 2 or 3 deep strokes.

2. A thing which snaps or produces a sharp cracking sound: **a.** A pistol. *rare.*

**1577-87** HARRISON *England* II. xvi. (1877) I. 283 The honest traueller is now inforced to ride with a case of dags.., or with some pretie short snapper, whereby he may deale with them further off in his owne defense. **1785** in GROSE *Dict. Vulgar Tongue*.

**b.** *pl.* Bones (see BONE *sb.* 5 b); castanets. ? *Obs.*

**1605** *Entert. of Earl Nottingham* 18 Those six Ladies.. danced a country dance with snappers on their thumbs. **1615** G. SANDYS *Trav.* 172 The instruments [of music] no other than snappers, gingles, and round-bottomd drums. **1699** DAMPIER *Voy.* II. I. 84 They hold them both in the right hand..as our Boys do their Snappers. **1705** tr. *Bosman's Guinea* 268 Like two pieces of Wood stroke against each other, or a pair of Snappers. **1742** C. OWEN *Serpents* III. vi. 239 Whether this Custom be not the Original of Castanets or Snappers in Dancing.

†**c.** *pl.* Prince Rupert's drops. *Obs.*$^{-0}$

**1788** HOWARD *New Roy. Cycl.* II. 1738.

**d.** A cracker-bonbon.

*a* **1845** BARHAM *Ingol. Leg.* Ser. III. *Wedding-day* (1905) 428 Nasty French lucifer snappers with mottoes. **1980** *Times* 22 Dec. 12/8 People write to me of 'snappers' which are available at posh, probably preppy, parties in Boston, and which go pop like crackers.

**e.** *U.S.* A cracker on the end of a whip-lash. Also *fig.*, a sharp or caustic remark.

**1817** J. SANSOM *Sk. Lower Canada* 15 One had proposed to put *a snapper* on the driver's whip. **1841** *Knickerbocker* XVII. 277 All the whips were provided with red snappers. **1882** PENTECOST *Out of Egypt* iii. 60 She brought out the last end of that question like the snapper on the end of a whip. **1890** O. W. HOLMES *Over the Teacups* xii, If I had not put that snapper on the end of my whip-lash, I might have got off without the ill temper which my antithesis provoked. **1903** *N.Y. Even. Post* 29 Sept. 8/2 Senator Carmack..is simply adding a snapper to the lash of his vigorous denunciation of the whole Philippine policy. **1949** B. A. BOTKIN *Treas. S. Folklore* I. v. 117 Showing off his prowess ..he first split a horsefly into pieces, and then tore a bumblebee into shreds with the snapper on the end of his whip.

**f.** *U.S.* A word, sentence, verse, etc., used as a finishing touch or wind-up. Also *attrib.*, as ***snapper ending***.

**1857** J. G. HOLLAND *Bay Path* xiv, You'd 'a said twenty lashes, and she'd got 'em, and Mr. Moxon would 'a said twenty Amens on the end on 'em for a snapper. **1892** CHILD *Pop. Ballads* IV. 393/1 A copy..with the addition of one stanza for a 'snapper'. **1895** 'MARK TWAIN' in *Youth's Companion* 3 Oct. 464/1 The..humorous story finishes with a nub, point, snapper, or whatever you like to call it. **1949** *Newsweek* 19 Dec. 13/3 Then came the snapper: 'No matter by what method we achieve security, we'll not achieve it in a bankrupt economy.' **1962** E. LACY *Freeloaders* ix. 186 This is the end of the story. I hardly think I've been steering you towards a twist, or snapper ending. **1973** *Publishers Weekly* 10 Dec. 31/1 The second story is written as a correspondence between a clerk and an alien, and has an O. Henry snapper at the end. **1976** *New Yorker* 24 May 143/1 The first, a male ensemble with some very good martial-arts-style acrobatics, has a snapper ending that doesn't snap.

**g.** *pl.* Teeth; a set of false teeth. *slang.*

**1924** WODEHOUSE *Leave it to Psmith* i. 36 You see, this fellow understands my snappers. **1958** *Listener* 31 July 154/2 Do your snappers fit snugly?

**h.** A sea-bed sampler that operates by enclosing material between two or more jaws that come together on contact with the bottom. Also ***snapper grab, sampler***.

**1925** *Proc. & Trans. R. Soc. Canada (Math., etc. Sciences)* 3rd Ser. XIX. IV. 51 The 'snapper' is a simple and inexpensive instrument which has long been used in connection with submarine cable laying. **1942** H. U. SVERDRUP et al. *Oceans* x. 344 Bottom samplers used for oceanographic work fall into three general categories: dredges (drag buckets), snappers, and coring tubes. *Ibid.* 345 Snapper samplers of the clamshell type have been widely used for obtaining samples of the superficial layers of the sediments. **1968** R. V. TAIT *Elements Marine Ecol.* iii. 49 For larger samples, various small spring-loaded, snapper grabs have been devised which take a shallow bite out of the sea-floor.

3. **a.** One who snaps *up* or seizes upon a thing quickly.

**1611** SHAKS. *Wint. T.* IV. iii. 26 My Father..was likewise a snapper-vp of vnconsidered trifles. **1823** SCOTT *Quentin D.* xxvi, The possibility of those erratic Countesses of Croye.. falling into the hands of some wild snapper upon the frontiers. **1887** JEFFERIES *Amaryllis* x, From Berlin and Vienna come the eager snappers-up of much considered trifles. **1902** *Westm. Gaz.* 3 Mar. 11/1 The snapper-up of such things should glance at the Mexican Eastern Railway 5 per cent. debentures.

**b.** *U.S. Football.* Also ***snapper-back*** = SNAP-BACK 1 a.

**1887** in P. H. Davis *Football* (1911) 475 Rule 12 altered so as to prohibit interference with the snapper-back until the ball is in motion. **1920** W. CAMP *Football without Coach* 30

That involves a great deal harder work from the center rush or snapper back in getting the ball back to him. **1961** J. S. SALAK *Dict. Amer. Sports* 409 The snapper is the player who snaps the ball. **1974** *Rules of Game* 148/1 The snapper may not slide his hands along the ball before grasping it, nor move his feet or lift a hand until after a snap.

**4. a.** A taker of snapshots; a casual photographer.

**1910** *Chambers's Jrnl.* 13 Aug. 589/1 There is no relief in a protest, for the rampant 'snapper' knows that the law is on his side. **1921** *Ibid.* 30 July 546/1 He who was but a snapper, a presser of a button, and next became a photographic enthusiast. **1977** *Ripped & Torn* vi. 7/2 And thanks a lot to all you budding photographers for the offers of photos, just send 'em in you snappers.

**b.** *slang.* A ticket inspector.

**1938** F. D. SHARPE *Sharpe of Flying Squad* 333 *A snapper*, ticket inspector. **1957** 'N. CULOTTA' *They're a Weird Mob* (1958) x. 142 'E doesn't want yer ticket. The snapper's got yer ticket.

**5.** A snappish person; one who speaks or answers snappishly or roughly.

**1648** HEXHAM II, *Een Versnauwer*, a Snapper, or a Taunter. **1847** HALLIW., *Snappers*, waspish persons that answer crossly or peevishly. **1869** BLACKMORE *Lorna D.* li, What a nasty way you have of telling the very commonest piece of news!.. What man will ever fancy you, you unlucky little snapper? **1908** *Daily Chron.* 17 Aug. 5/7 We are told that though these mischief-makers, these snappers and snarlers, may be few, yet they are very influential.

**6.** †**a.** *Angling.* A snap-hook or snap-rod. *Obs.*

**1688** HOLME *Armoury* III. 103/1 A Snapper, or Snap Rod, is a strong Pole, peculiar for a Pike. *Ibid.* xvi. (Roxb.) 80/1 This is by some termed a cod fish hooke; but by Fishers and Anglers it is termed a Snapper, being made with a loop at the top.

**b.** *local.* (See quot.)

**1892** *Longm. Mag.* Nov. 83 Some of the men were armed with long wooden 'snappers', not unlike blacksmith's tongs, ..thickly set with wire points or projecting nails,..and with these cruel implements they struck at and secured the stupefied fish [= eels].

**7. a.** One or other of various fishes, esp. the West Indian *Lutjanus Blackfordii* or *L. vivanus* or other fish of this group, the N. American rose-fish, *Sebastes marinus*, and the Australian *Pagrus unicolor* (see quots. and b). Cf. SCHNAPPER.

**1697** DAMPIER *Voy.* (1699) 88 Fish, particularly Snappers and Rock-fish, are..plentiful. *Ibid.* 91 The Snapper is a Fish much like a Roach, but a great deal bigger,..the back is of a bright red. **1712** E. COOKE *Voy. S. Sea* 114 Silver Fish, Snappers, Bonito's and very large Craw-fish. **1772–84** *Cook's Voy.* (1790) IV. 1370 There are also snappers, parrot-fish, and a brown spotted rock-fish. *a* **1818** M. G. LEWIS *Jrnl. W. Ind.* (1834) 104 Nothing can be less tempting than the sounds of Jew-fish, hog-fish, mud-fish, snappers,.. and grunts. **1840** F. D. BENNETT *Whaling Voy.* I. 23 They were chiefly of the kinds known as 'rock-cod', 'snappers', or gilt-heads. **1842** W. R. WADE *Journey in Northern Island N.Z.* vii. 180 Some snappers which the lads had caught furnished us with a hearty supper. **1888** GOODE *Amer. Fishes* 73 The Snappers and Grunts are among the most highly colored of the tropical fishes. **1896** [see NANNYGAI]. **1959** A. MCLINTOCK *Descr. Atlas N.Z.* 48 Snapper..is the most important species in the commercial catch. **1977** *Best of Austral. Angler* 9/1 The floating gar system used for tailor is also one of the very best ways to catch snapper from the rocks.

*attrib.* and *Comb.* **1884** GOODE *Nat. Hist. Aquat. Anim.* 395 The Snapper Family—*Pristipomatidæ*. **1888** —— *Amer. Fishes* 76 Snapper-fishing is usually carried on with a bottom bait. *Ibid.*, A trip to the Snapper banks is a favorite summer recreation.

**b.** With distinctive epithets, as ***alligator, bastard, black, brown, grey snapper***, etc. ***red snapper***: see RED *a.* 17 c.

Many different species are mentioned by Goode *Fishes Bermudas* (1876), *Nat. Hist. Aquatic Anim.* (1884), and *American Fishes* (1888).

**1775** ROMANS *Hist. Florida* App. 52 The fish caught here ..are such as..red, grey and black snappers, dog snappers, mutton-fish. **1822–27** GOOD *Study Med.* (1829) I. 241 Fishes of a few other kinds, as..gray-snapper (*coracinus fuscus major*). **1827** O. W. ROBERTS *Voy. Centr. Amer.* 34 They..soon caught plenty of groupers, red and silver snappers. **1833** M. SCOTT *Tom Cringle* xv. (1859) 365 A red snapper for all the world like a gigantic gold fish was hauled on board. **1885** C. F. HOLDER *Marvels Anim. Life* 176 Snappers, red and brown.

**c.** A snapping-turtle.

**1796** [see *mud-turtle* s.v. MUD *sb.*[1] 5 b]. **1872** DE VERE *Americanisms* 388 The Snapping Turtle.., also called simply Snapper, is a ferocious kind, snapping at everything, and inflicting a painful bite. *c* **1880** *Cassell's Nat. Hist.* IV. 255 One of these aquatic Emydes..preys upon small fish, and is called Temminck's Snapper. **1888** *Encycl. Brit.* XXIII. 458 The family of *Chelydridæ* includes freshwater tortoises, which are known under the names of Snappers or Alligator Terrapins.

**d.** A woodpecker (Halliwell, 1847).

**e.** *U.S.* A flysnapper (*Cent. Dict.* 1891).

**8.** *dial.* Something exceptionally large, heavy, etc.

**1874** T. HARDY *Far fr. Mad. Crowd* xv, We get a fine day, and then down comes a snapper [of rain] at night. **1902** *Ardrossan Herald* 3 Jan. 4 That's a snapper o' an orange they've gi'en ye.

**9.** *dial.* **a.** The greater stitchwort, *Stellaria Holostea*. **b.** The bladder campion, *Silene inflata*.

**1882** in FRIEND *Gloss. Dev. Plant-n.* **1886** in BRITTEN & HOLLAND.

**'snapper,** *sb.*[2] *Sc.* [f. SNAPPER *v.*[1]] A stumble or trip. Freq. *fig.*, a slip in conduct; a fault or error; a scrape or difficulty.

*a* **1572** KNOX *Hist. Ref.* Wks. 1846 I. 79 Forresse war runne upon the day to Smallame..and such place nere about, but many snapparis thei gate. **1596** DALRYMPLE tr. *Leslie's Hist. Scot.* (S.T.S.) I. 340 This king dies..throuch the vehement snapper of a Wantount horse. **1629** Z. BOYD *Last Battell* 190, I am not like these sinners which but trip and stumble, and rise again after a snapper. **17..** RAMSAY *Epil. to 'The Drummer'* 8 Men of sense will kindly praise us, And, if we make a little snapper, raise us. *a* **1732** BOSTON *Crook in Lot* (1805) 164 They were only so [over-rash] in applying the time to the promise; a snapper that saints in all ages have made. **1818** SCOTT *Hrt. Midl.* xx, Advocate Langtale has brought folk through waur snappers than a' this.

**'snapper,** *a. Sc.* Also 9 **snappert.** [app. f. SNAP *v.*] Sharp, snappish.

**1673–4** EARL KINCARDIN in *Lauderdale P.* (Camden) III. 30 The K. gave him a snapper ansuer. **1808** JAMIESON *s.v.*, A snappert answer.

**snapper** ('snæpə(r)), *v.*[1] Chiefly (and now only) *north.* and *Sc.* Forms: 4–5 **snaper** (**-ere**, 5 **-ir**, 6 **-yr**), 5 **snap(p)re**, 6 **snappar** (*Sc.* **-ir**), 5– **snapper.** [app. a frequentative from a stem **snap*, corresponding to older and dial. G. *schnappen* to stumble, to limp, related to MHG. *snaben*, MLG. *snaven*, whence MDa. *snave*, MSw. *snava* (Sw. *snafva*), Norw. *snaava*, to stumble, Icel. *snáfa* to sneak, slink.]

**1.** *intr.* To stumble or trip. †Also, to fall through stumbling.

**13..** *Metr. Hom.* (MS. Ashm. 42) fol. 70 b, Full radde he was to snapir rathe, To drowne him & his childir bathe. *a* **1352** MINOT *Poems* (Hall) x. 16 Wight men of þe west neghed þam nerr, And gert þam snaper in þe snare. *c* **1400** *26 Pol. Poems* iv. 90 Many can stomble at a stre; Þey nyl not snapere at a style. *c* **1425** *Thomas of Erceld.* 381 Stedes shall snapre throwght tresoun. **1530** PALSGR. 723/2 My horse dyd nat stumble, he dyd but snapper a lytell. **1597** SKENE *De Verb. Sign.* s.v. *Cathorius*, Quhen ane horse..snappers of fallis with his maister. **1607** MARKHAM *Caval.* II. 134 Or els setting downe his feete vncertainly [he does] both often stumble and snapper. **1650** *Reg. Privy Counc. Scot.* VIII. 233 He snappered and lighted upon ane cart wheele. **1737** BRACKEN *Farriery Impr.* (1756) I. 349 He will not..be so apt to snapper and stumble. **1816** SCOTT *Bl. Dwarf* x, Wouldst thou snapper now and break my neck? **1871** W. ALEXANDER *J. Gibb* (1873) 226 Only Samie's shaltie snappert.

*Prov.* **1641** FERGUSSON *Scot. Prov.* No. 105, A horse may snapper on foure feet. **1721** KELLY *Prov.* 26 A Horse with four Feet may snapper, by a time.

**2.** *fig.* or *transf.* To stumble or make a slip in action or conduct; to fall into error.

*c* **1380** WYCLIF *Sel. Wks.* II. 367 Mannis affecciouns.. shulde stonde stalworþly, lest þe soule snaperide aftir. **1388** —— *Jer.* xviii. 15 My puple hath forȝete me..and snaperiden in her weies. *a* **1500** in *Ratis Raving* 23 The foly of the ful garis hyme snapyr. *a* **1529** SKELTON *Replyc.* Wks. 1843 I. 217 Count ye your selfe good clerkes, And snapper in suche werkes? **1596** DALRYMPLE tr. *Leslie's Hist. Scot.* (S.T.S.) I. 227 He appeiret to snapper, anent the celebratione of the Pasche day.., at quilke stane snappired lykwyse Bischope Aidane. **1731** *Reasons for Presbyterians dissenting* 101 He hath miserably snapper'd upon Hazael for a pattern. **1794** BURNS *'Contented wi' little'* iv, Blind Chance, let her snapper and stoyte on her way.

Hence **'snappering** *ppl. a.*

**1596** DALRYMPLE tr. *Leslie's Hist. Scot.* (S.T.S.) II. 319 To bring..tua bald snapring horsses [L. *summæ pernicitatis equos*] for the flicht.

**'snapper,** *v.*[2] *rare.* Now *dial.* [A frequentative of SNAP *v.* Cf. MLG. *snapperen*, G. *schnappern*, to chatter.]

**1.** *intr.* ? To snap the beak.

**1664** H. MORE *Myst. Iniq.* 333 This Image was made to snapper and chatter something like that Bird [the magpie].

**2.** To snap or crackle; to give out a sharp snapping sound.

**1852–88** in Berkshire glossaries.

**'snappering,** *vbl. sb.*[1] [f. SNAPPER *v.*[1]] Stumbling. Also *attrib.*

**1591** R. BRUCE *Serm.* R ij, I am sory to see, that the maist parte of this countrie shuld mak a snappering stane of that precious corner. **1599** ROLLOCK *Serm.* Wks. 1849 I. 326 When we sall walk in the hevins,..then na snappering neither to this side nor to that.

**'snappering,** *vbl. sb.*[2] [f. SNAPPER *sb.*[1] 6 a.] The action or pastime of fishing for snappers.

**1870** G. H. KINGSLEY *Sport & Trav.* iii. (1900) 57 Sharking and snappering.

†**'snappery.** *nonce-wd.* [f. SNAP *v.*] The action of cutting with a snap.

**1639** *Crabtree Lect.* 57 With thy snippery and snappery thou thinkest to go shear away with all.

**'snappily,** *adv.* [f. SNAPPY *a.*] **1.** Snappishly.

**1890** GUNTER *Miss Nobody* xvii, 'I may and I may not,' he says shortly and snappily. **1898** *Daily News* 24 Aug. 4/7 The 'Post' to-night snappily remarks [etc.].

**2.** Smartly, nattily; crisply, deftly.

**1936** J. T. FARRELL *$1,000 a Week* (1942) 141 He looked unobtrusively at two snappily dressed young fellows on his left. **1947** *People* 22 June 5/1 Another snappily-togged Ascot-bound party of bright young things noisily piling into a glittering £5,000 limousine. **1977** 'A. STUART' *Snap Judgement* 16 A strong, blue-eyed, snappily dressed young man. **1981** E. AGRY *Assault Force* v. 53 Mac reversed the Audi snappily into the nearest driveway.

**snapping** ('snæpɪŋ), *vbl. sb.* [f. SNAP *v.*]

**1.** The action of the vb. in various senses:

**a.** In intransitive senses.

**1583** STUBBES *Anat. Abus.* II. (1882) 50 When they come to the cutting of the haire, what snipping and snapping of the cycers is there. *a* **1734** NORTH *Examen* Pref. (1740) 14 Such Snapping and Quarrelling would not clearly answer his Book. **1812** M. CUTLER in *Life*, etc. (1888) II. 196 The only way to account for the fire is by the snapping of the hemlock wood. **1815** J. SMITH *Panorama Sci. & Art* II. 196 If a person not electrified held his hand near the tube while it was rubbed, the snapping was very sensible. **1891** C. ROBERTS *Adrift Amer.* 47 The snapping and snarling [of wolves], varied by a howl. **1891** *Daily News* 7 Nov. 6/4 In consequence of the snapping of an axle.

**b.** In transitive senses. Also with *up*.

**1646** J. HALL *Horæ Vac.* 113 Hee playes not well at draughts, that onely can avoyd snapping when it comes to a pinch. **1741** *Compl. Family Piece* II. ii. 344 You must remember in Snapping, that you never give a Fish time to run.., but hook and draw him out directly. **1816** SCOTT *Bl. Dwarf* ii, There's me, and my twa brothers,..will be wi' you ..in the snapping of a flint. **1860** GEN. P. THOMPSON *Audi Alt.* cxxxix. III. 115 An abiding arrangement, opening its capacious jaws for the snapping-up of the guilty. **1885** *Law Rep.* 29 *Chanc. Div.* 453 There was no snapping of a judgment in the Irish action.

†**2.** *Thieves' cant.* The proceeds of a theft or robbery; a share of stolen goods claimed by a snap. (Cf. SNAPPAGE.) *Obs.*

**1591** GREENE *Conny Catch.* II. Wks. (Grosart) X. 122 When he hath the window open and spyes any fat snappings worth the Curbing, then streight he sets the Warp to watch. *Ibid.*, Which stolne parcells, they in their Art call snappinges. **1602** [see SNAPPAGE].

**3.** *attrib.*, as ***snapping movement, noise, sound***, etc.; **snapping-point**, the point at which something will snap, or someone's strength or endurance will fail; **snapping time, -tool** (see quots.).

**1815** J. SMITH *Panorama Sci. & Art* II. 193 A sharp pain ..which was accompanied by a snapping noise. **1849** NOAD *Electricity* (ed. 3) 30 A vivid spark will dart between them, accompanied by a sharp snapping sound. **1870** H. A. NICHOLSON *Man. Zool.* (1880) 375 Keeping up a constant snapping movement. **1875** KNIGHT *Dict. Mech.* 2229/2 *Snapping-tool*, a stamping-tool used to force a plate into holes in a die. **1883** GRESLEY *Gloss. Coal-m.* 229 *Snapping Time*, a short period of rest during a shift in which a collier takes his snap. **1933** G. ARTHUR *Septuagenarian's Scrap Bk.* 272 And like all good artists, like Sarah herself, she is a '*traqueuse*' whose head feels hot and hands are cold on a first night, and who, with fever in the veins and nerves strained to snapping-point, will yet perhaps give the most inspired performance of the whole run. **1946** K. TENNANT *Lost Haven* (1947) i. 20 To have not only mud but sticky honeycomb all over her shiny, clean linoleum was the snapping-point. **1982** *India Today* 15 Feb. 125/2 Relations between the Government and the judiciary are stretched to snapping point.

**'snapping,** *ppl. a.* [f. as prec.]

**1.** Sharp, curt, snappish; peevish, petulant.

**1642** MILTON *Apol. Smect.* Wks. 1851 III. 255 His designe was..with quips and snapping adagies to vapour them out. **1718** OCKLEY *Saracens* (Bohn) 177 Omar..grew very angry:..at last he wrote a short snapping sort of a letter. **1746** *Exmoor Scolding* (E.D.S.) 106 Go, ye rearing, snapping, tedious, cutted Snibblenose! **1880** 'OUIDA' *Moths* III. 17 Snapping creatures are thought so sweetly sincere.

**2. a.** That snaps or breaks suddenly.

**1823** LAMB *Elia* II, *Amicus Redivivus*, Marvellous escapes —..by orchard pranks, and snapping twigs. **1899** F. V. KIRBY *Sport E.C. Africa* xx. 218 Our ears were gladdened by the sound of a snapping branch.

**b.** That makes a sharp cracking or snapping noise.

**1891** *Outlook* Dec. 238/1 In the tender light of the rising sun he creeps downstairs, avoiding that squeaking board and that snapping step. **1942** W. FAULKNER *Go down, Moses* 170 They emerged from the narrow, roofless tunnel of snapping and hissing cane, still galloping, onto the open ridge below. **1968** B. HINES *Kestrel for Knave* 132 Every time he tried to escape [from the shower] the three boys bounced him back, stinging him with their snapping towels as he retreated.

**3. a.** That snaps with the jaws or beak.

**1873** G. C. DAVIES *Mount. & Mere* xiv. 116 Such screaming and laughing as they pulled the struggling snapping brutes ashore. **1890** S. W. BAKER *Wild Beasts* II. 29 The force of the snapping jaws would crush any human bone.

**b.** ***snapping-turtle***, one or other of the North American freshwater tortoises of the family *Chelydridæ*, esp. *Chelydra serpentina*, the alligator terrapin. Also ***snapping tortoise***. (Cf. SNAPPER *sb.*[1] 5 c.)

**1784** J. F. D. SMYTH *Tour U.S.A.* I. 338 One kind of them bites very fiercely when incensed..; these are called Snapping Turtles. **1808** T. ASHE *Trav. Amer.* II. 234 The Indians call this by a name which implies the snapping tortoise. **1828** [see SALT RIVER 2 a]. **1840** *Knickerbocker* XVI. 54 The..snapping-tortoises, frogs, squirrels, and such small deer, are their flocks and herds. **1848** BARTLETT *Dict. Amer.* 316 *Snapping-turtle*, a reptile common to all parts of the United States, so named from its propensity to snap at everything within its reach. **1850** LYELL *2nd Visit U.S.* II. 205 On the shore of the lake we caught a tortoise, called here the snapping-turtle. **1884** GOODE *Nat. Hist. Aquat. Anim.* 153 The more northern species, *Chelydra serpentina*, known everywhere throughout the United States as the 'Snapping Turtle'.

c. *snapping beetle* (or *bug*), *snapping mackerel* (see quots.); *snapping shrimp*, a shrimp of the family Alpheidæ, which uses its large chelæ to make a snapping noise; also called the pistol shrimp.

**1868** *Rep. U.S. Comm. Agric.* (1869) 93 These insects [sc. *Elateridæ*] are known in Europe by the common name of 'skip-jacks',..and in America as 'snapping beetles', and erroneously 'snapping bugs'. **1884** GOODE *Nat. Hist. Aquat. Anim.* 433 The Bluefish, *Pomatomus saltatrix*,..[is] in some parts of New England called 'Snapping Mackerel' or 'Snappers'. **1941** STEINBECK & RICKETTS *Sea of Cortez* 194 Sponges and tunicates under which small crabs and snapping shrimps hid themselves. **1964** *Oceanogr. & Marine Biol.* II. 431 The clicking of snapping shrimp..is a form of ambient sound when one is concentrating on the sounds of fish.

**4.** Violent, severe, extreme; usu. as quasi-*adv.*

**1845** *Knickerbocker* XXV. 87 I've got a snapping headache. **1876** *Wide Awake* (Boston, Mass.) July 19/1 The night was snapping cold. **1905** K. D. WIGGIN *Rose o' the River* 93 The snapping cold weather and the depth to which the water was frozen were aiding it.

**snappingly** ('snæpɪŋlɪ), *adv.* [Cf. prec.] With a snap or snaps; snappishly. Also, briskly, smartly. Cf. SNAPPILY *adv.* 2.

**1567** DRANT *Horace, Ep.* B vij, He redeth them so fearse, And doth theire workes so snapingly and snatchingly rehearse. **1884** J. PARKER *Apost. Life* III. 13 When was 'Good-bye' said quite snappingly and briefly and with abruptness? **1896** *Westm. Gaz.* 12 Dec. 1 Numerous dogs of every breed and aggressiveness career snappingly about. **1976** *Gramophone* Dec. 1016/1 The second subject [is] held in a more or less strict tempo but flecked with fine, subliminally caught colours, the mordents now fluttering like spread acciaccaturas, now expressive, now snappingly exact. **1978** *Ibid.* Apr. 1756/2 Bernstein, as one would expect, is ideally alive and snappingly rhythmic at the opening of the last movement's allegro section.

**snappish** ('snæpɪʃ), *a.* Also 6 **snappyshe, -ishe,** 7 **snapish.** [f. SNAP *v.* + -ISH.]

**1.** Of persons: Using, or apt to use, sharp, harsh, or uncivil language; peevish, testy, or ill-natured in speech or reply.

**1542** UDALL *Erasm. Apoph.* 319b, He found his wife coumbresome, crabbed & snappyshe unto hym. **1577** STANYHURST *Descr. Irel.* i. in *Holinshed*, Here percase some snappish carper will..snuffingly snibbe me, for debacing the Irish language. **1626** R. BERNARD *Isle of Man* (1627) 20 Scrupulosity..is an unsociable and snappish fellow. **1672** O. HEYWOOD *Diaries* (1883) III. 119 Clark..was churlish and snappish. **1740** RICHARDSON *Pamela* I. 47 Our Cook.., who is a little snappish and cross sometimes. **1842** BORROW *Bible in Spain* xlii, I found him morose and snappish. **1897** *Allbutt's Syst. Med.* III. 400 [Dyspeptics] are likely to become irritable and snappish.

**b.** Of manner, etc.: Marked or characterized by sharpness or curtness of speech.

**1836** *Random Recoll. Ho. Lords* xiv. 334 The contemptuous and snappish manner in which he spoke to deputations. **1848** DICKENS *Dombey* li, 'Well,' says Mrs Pipchin, in her snappish way, 'he's pretty much as usual'. **1885** *Manch. Even. News* 16 July 2/3 A most femininely snappish tone of voice.

**c.** Of the sea: Somewhat choppy or rough.

**1867** MACGREGOR *Voy. Alone* (1868) 85 When we..met the short, snappish sea in the bay, every wave dashed over me.

**2.** Of words, language, etc.: Sharp, curt, peevish, ungracious.

**1551** ROBINSON tr. *More's Utop.* (1895) 10 Aferd that at euery snappishe worde theire nose shalbe bitten of. **1581** J. BELL *Haddon's Answ. Osor.* 277b, Your crabbed and snappish accusation agaynst Luther. **1603** BRETON *Packet Mad Lett.* I. lxviii, I haue receiued your snappish Letter. **1665** PEPYS *Diary* 22 Dec., Vexed at a snappish answer Madam Williams did give me. *c* **1740** MRS. DELANY *Life & Corr.* (1861) I. 35 No one ever heard him say a snappish or cross thing to me. **1784** COWPER *Task* IV. 198 The smart And snappish dialogue, that flippant wits Call comedy. **1896** H. M. B. REID *Cameronian Apostle* viii. 122 The snappish criticisms recorded in the Presbytery minutes.

†**3.** Bold, forward, impudent. *Obs.*

**1608** TOPSELL *Serpents* (1658) 783 If any wedlock-breakers..dare be so snappish to enter..into anothers house [etc.].

**4.** Of a dog, etc.: Inclined or prone to snap.

*a* **1700** in B.E. *Dict. Cant. Crew.* *a* **1710** POPE *Imit. Eng. Poets, Spenser* 19 The snappish cur..Close at my heel with yelping treble flies. **1727** GAY *Fables* xlvi. 13 A village-cur, of snappish race. **1862** H. H. DIXON *Scott & Sebright* 199 He [a horse] went to Malton, and a very rough snappish customer they thought him.

**b.** *transf.* (Cf. sense 2.)

**1842** LOVER *Handy Andy* xv, The snappish barking of the pets was returned by one hoarse bay from 'Bloodybones'.

**5.** Breaking with a snap; 'short'.

**1833** *New Monthly Mag.* XXXIX. 297 The crust..is exceeding crisp, dry, and snappish.

**'snappishly,** *adv.* [f. prec.] In a snappish manner; in or with sharp, ungracious, or peevish language; curtly, abruptly.

**1548** UDALL, etc. *Erasm. Par. Luke* ii. 39 So did he also at an other time more snappishly make aunswere unto theim. **1602** MIDDLETON *Blurt, Master-Constable* III. iii, You cannot 'scape without a pardon here, if you take us up never so snappishly. **1662** J. DAVIES tr. *Olearius' Voy. Amb.* 266. The other making answer somewhat too snappishly. *c* **1765** FLLOYD *Tartarian T.* (1785) 45/1 'What is that to you!' said the porter very snappishly. **1837** DICKENS *Pickw.* xxxi, He said rather snappishly: 'Who is with me in this case?' **1885** *Manch. Exam.* 12 Aug. 6/1 The hon. member..had been rather snappishly put off.

**'snappishness.** [f. SNAPPISH *a.*] The fact or quality of being snappish; sharpness, curtness, or peevishness of language or speech.

**1598** FLORIO, *Proteruità*, frowardnes,..skittishnes, snappishnes. **1727** BAILEY (vol. II), *Snappishness*, Crossness, Peevishness, Crabbedness in Speech. **1757** RUTTY *Spiritual Diary* (1776) 2nd month, no. 26, Cursed snappishness,..on a bodily indisposition. *a* **1801** WAKEFIELD *Mem.* (1804) I. 25 He threatened with great snappishness to flog me. **1836** HOOK *G. Gurney* III. 174 The cause of my old lady's snappishness to-night. **1876** MISS BRADDON *J. Haggard's Dau.* xi, A little extra snappishness on the part of Judith.

**snappy** ('snæpɪ), *a.* [f. SNAP *v.* + -Y.]

**1. a.** = SNAPPISH *a.* 1.

**1834** in B. Gregory *Side Lights* (1898) 157, I am inclined to be snappy when I am told [etc.]. **1858** E. B. RAMSAY *Scot. Life & Char.* iv, Snappy and disagreeable..in their replies. **1889** JEROME *Three Men in Boat* 155 Harris and George and I were quarrelsome and snappy and ill-tempered.

**b.** = SNAPPISH *a.* 1 b.

**1890** *Star* 13 Oct. 4/1 Hard work..doesn't improve Sir Peter's temper, and consequently he was in a particularly snappy mood to-day. **1892** GUNTER *Miss Dividends* (1893) 16 This request..is given in an off-hand, snappy kind of a way.

**2.** = SNAPPISH *a.* 2.

**1886** *St. James' Gaz.* 25 Sept. 5/1 The Queen's Speech.. might even be called curt and snappy. **1897** W. H. THORNTON *Rem. W. Co. Clergyman* iii. 84 We grew warm, and our conversation snappy.

**3.** *Sc.* (See quot.)

**1825** JAMIESON *Suppl.*, *Snappy*, keen in business, disposed to take the advantage of another, *Ang[us]*.

**4.** = SNAPPISH *a.* 4.

**1881** *Harper's Mag.* LXIII. 496 Sharing the vehicle with a snappy terrier. **1897** *Allbutt's Syst. Med.* II. 701 Dogs inoculated..fell into emaciation, foamed at the mouth and became snappy.

**5.** Of the nature of, producing or emitting, a snap or crack; crackling.

**1878** JEFFERIES *Gamekeeper at H.* 120 Short sharp snappy sounds. **1894** *Outing* June 190/2 The birch..makes a hot, snappy, cheerful fire.

**6.** *colloq.* **a.** Cleverly smart, bright, or pointed (of language, etc.); full of 'go'; brisk.

**1871** 'MARK TWAIN' in *Galaxy* Apr. 615/2, I compressed it into a snappy foot-note at the bottom. **1873** 'SUSAN COOLIDGE' *What Katy did at Sch.* vi. 88 We'll never use the whole name..: we'll say, 'the S.S.U.C.' That sounds brisk and snappy. **1901** *Athenæum* 17 Aug. 209/3 Mere stage back grounds for snappy tales, generally realistic. **1955** *Times* 27 Aug. 8/4 Her clean texture, snappy rhythm, and general strength of tone and purpose all betokened a true grasp of the composer's style. **1977** *N.Z. Herald* 8 Jan. 2-12/4 (Advt.), Painting roofs, for free quotes phone the expert. Snappy service.

**b.** Neat and elegant; smart, 'natty'. ***snappy dresser***, someone who dresses in a stylish or natty manner.

**1881** *Punch* LXXX. 310/3. **1887** W. RYE *Norfolk Broads* 57 The frame of a very 'snappy' little pleasure wherry. **1897** *Outing* XXX. 108/1 A snappy team of grays. **1925** *New Yorker* 9 May 27/1, I always used to be a snappy dresser. **1958** [see DUDE *v.*]. **1977** P. THEROUX *Consul's File* 174 A woman waiting for her lover..whom she would describe as a snappy dresser, a riot, a real card.

**c.** Having a brisk smack or flavour.

**1892** WALSH *Tea* 164 Many..teas are full and round in body, pungent and 'snappy'.

**d.** *U.S.* Designating weather characteristic of a cold snap (SNAP *sb.* 7 a, b).

**1928** J. C. LINCOLN *Silas Bradford's Boy* 149 It was a clear, snappy early winter day. **1951** *Publ. Amer. Dial. Soc.* xv. 60 *Snappy*,..said of crispy cold weather.

**7. a.** Quick, sudden, instantaneous; jerky.

**1872** O. W. HOLMES *Poet at Breakf.-t.* viii. 216 The dry-goodsman's life behind his counter is a succession of sudden, snappy perceptions. **1882** [LEES & CLUTTERBUCK] *Three in Norway* xxiv. (1888) 182 It was almost impossible to get even the snappiest of snap-shots at the agile bird. **1896** MRS. CAFFYN *Quaker Grandmother* 212 To give her a snappy hand-shake.

**b.** Phr. ***to make it snappy***: to make haste, to get a move on.

**1926** G. FRANKAU *My Unsentimental Journey* ii. 31 After that we 'made it snappy' (Anglicè—got a move on). **1945** A. HUXLEY *Let.* 10 Apr. (1969) 520, I wish there had been space in my review to quote you at length on these subjects, But, alas, I had to 'make it snappy'. **1976** J. I. M. STEWART *Young Patullo* ix. 195 Make it snappy. Taxi's waiting.

‖**snaps.** Also **snapps.** [a. Du., Da., or Sw. *snaps.*] = SCHNAPPS.

**1845** [C. H. J. ANDERSON] *Swedish Brothers* 8 A trifling scratch,..which a snaps will soon cure. **1865** *Slang Dict.* 238 *Snapps*, Hollands gin.

**'snapsack.** Now *dial.* Also **snap-sack.** [ad. LG. *snappsack* (hence G. *schnappsack*), f. *snappen* SNAP *v.*] A knapsack.

Common from *c* 1650 to 1700.

**1633** SHIRLEY *Contention* D jb, She cannot eate a Snapsacke, Nor carry baggage. *a* **1656** USSHER *Ann.* (1658) 515 Mithridates sent all the prisoners..home, with provision in their snapsacks. **1670** *Phil. Trans.* V. 2097 A very large Heart,..the figure of which was not Conical, but like a Souldiers *pera* or Snapsack. **1716** CHURCH *Philip's War* (1867) II. 22 He finding..three Snapsacks of Powder, went immediately to the Army. **1725** BAILEY *Erasm. Colloq.* 7 If you put nothing into my Snapsack but Healths, I shall carry them with ease. **1881** *Isle Wight Gloss.* 33 *Snapzack*, a knapsack.

*fig.* **1643** J. P. (*title*), A Spirituall Snapsacke for the Parliament Souldiers, containing cordiall encouragements.

†**'snapsauce.** *Obs. rare.* [f. SNAP *v.* + SAUCE *sb.*] = SLAPSAUCE 1. Also *attrib.*

**1611** COTGR., *Fripe-sauce*, a snap-sauce, licke-dish, lickorous fellow. [**1653** URQUHART *Rabelais* II. xxx, Hector, a Snap-sauce Scullion.]

†**'snapshare.** *Obs.* [f. SNAP *v.* + SHARE *sb.*] A share or portion obtained as an extra emolument.

**1538** COWLEY in Ellis *Orig. Lett.* Ser. II. II. 95 They gayne yerely ij[li] M. markes by their fermes and fees besydes their snap shares. **1548** UDALL, etc. *Erasm. Par. Luke* iii. 32 A porcion of the parties gooddes beyng seased as a forfaict, may come to their snapshare in rewarde of theyr false accusacion. **1553** T. WILSON *Rhet.* 20 A patrone of a benefice wil haue a poore yngrame soule to beare the name of a persone for xx markе, and the patrone hymself wil take up for his snapshare as good as an .c. marke.

**snap-shooter** ('snæpʃuːtə(r)). [f. SNAP-.]

**1.** One who practises or is skilled in snap-shooting.

**1887** *Field* 8 Jan. 41/1, I cannot but believe that our brilliant snap-shooters..are born, not made.

**2.** One who takes snap-shot photographs; a camera suitable for this. Also **snapshooter.**

**1890** *Anthony's Photogr. Bulletin* III. 200 It may become a 'snap shooter', by taking the cork out. **1896** J. ASHBY STERRY *Tale Thames* ii, [It] won't go down in these days of the universal kodak and perpetual snap-shooter. **1904** *Car* X. 240 (*caption*) Mr. W. K. Vanderbilt, Jr.,..is reluctant to pose before a camera, but occasionally falls a victim to wily 'snapshooters'. **1973** C. BONINGTON *Next Horizon* iv. 72, I had always taken a camera with me on my climbs, but had been little more than a holiday snapshooter.

**snap-shooting,** *vbl. sb.* [f. SNAP-.] The practice of taking snap-shots (esp. in senses 1 and 2).

**1872** *Gentl. Mag.* Dec. 664 Snap shooting, as it is termed, is very effective sometimes by experienced gunners. **1883** *Cent. Mag.* Aug. 493 Snap-shooting is generally understood to consist in putting the gun to the shoulder and firing the instant it is in position. **1979** G. MACDONALD *Camera* iv. 57 Snapshooting was..a..haphazard affair... Most snaps were still portraits of family and friends.

**snap-shot** ('snæpʃɒt), *sb.* Also **snap shot, snapshot.** [f. SNAP-.]

**1. a.** A quick or hurried shot taken without deliberate aim, esp. one at a rising bird or quickly moving animal.

**1808** COL. HAWKER *Diary* (1893) I. 11 Almost every pheasant I fired at was a snap shot among the high cover. **1846** GREENER *Sci. Gunnery* 164 Were a bird to spring in a situation where we could get only a snap shot. **1899** F. V. KIRBY *Sport E.C. Africa* iii. 42, I got in a snapshot, tumbling her over like a rabbit.

*fig.* **1865** *Pall Mall G.* 2 Aug. 1 Our courts of law are distinguished from those of other countries by taking snap-shots at justice.

**b.** One who fires such shots; a snap-shooter.

**1845** F. TOLFREY *Sportsman in Canada* II. v. 131 It is capital practice is this snipe-shooting for a youngster; at least it makes a man a good snap-shot. **1887** *Field* 8 Jan. 41/1, I myself am a snap-shot.

**2. a.** An instantaneous photograph, esp. one taken with a hand-camera. Also *transf.* and *fig.*

[**1860** HERSCHEL in *Photogr. News* 11 May 13 The possibility of taking a photograph, as it were by a snap-shot —of securing a picture in a tenth of a second of time.] **1890** *Rev. Reviews* II. 489/2 The annexed snap-shots were taken with a hand camera. **1903** 'O. HENRY' in *Everybody's Mag.* Aug. 194/1 You see a man doing nothing but loafing around making snapshots. **1930** [see HUSTLE *v.* 5]. **1950** G. B. SHAW *Farfetched Fables* iii. 109 What are you doing here?.. Only hiking round the island. May I take a snapshot? **1975** P. FUSSELL *Gt. War & Mod. Memory* i. 10 British and German soldiers..meeting in No Man's Land to exchange cigarets and to take snapshots.

*transf.* and *fig.* **1897** *Daily News* 3 May 8/3 Your Yankee interviewer is a snap-shot incarnate. **1902** A. DOBSON *Richardson* vii. 196 The language of literature seems to tend ..towards the cultus of the short-cut and the snap-shot. **1928** *Observer* 17 June 10/2, I asked President Masaryk..if he could give me a snapshot of the difference between what he found when he came to Prague in 1918, and what he has the satisfaction of seeing now. **1962** M. MCLUHAN *Gutenberg Galaxy* 241 He [*sc.* Montaigne] bred up a great race of self-portrayers by means of the mental snapshot. **1978** P. O'DONNELL *Dragon's Claw* iii. 47 Snapshots of sight and sound, of touch, taste, and smell.

**b.** *Computers.* A record of the contents of some or all of the storage locations in a computer at a particular stage in the execution of a program (see quot. 1963). Freq. *attrib.*

**1963** GREGORY & VAN HORN *Automatic Data-Processing Systems* (ed. 2) xii. 473 Some simplified forms of post-mortem routines give only a storage snapshot, which is a complete copy of all storage locations at the time the processor stopped. A snapshot routine may also list the instruction that caused the program to stop, the current contents of arithmetic units and indexes, and perhaps, several of the most-recently executed jumps thus indicating the path of program control. A differential snap-shot lists the contents of storage locations that have changed from their initial value or from their value in a prior snapshot. **1966** *IFIP-ICC Vocab. Information Processing* 85 When a trace program gives output only on selected instructions, or for selected conditions, it is called a snapshot program. **1973** C. W. GEAR *Introd. Computer Sci.* vi. 244 An alternative is to take a series of snapshots at points in the program section.

**3.** In various sports, a quick shot (of the ball, etc.) at goal.

**1961** *Times* 29 May 4/3 [In Polo.] After Hanut had scored with a lovely snapshot to make it 3-2. **1963** *Globe & Mail* (Toronto) 21 Jan. 16/3 [In Hockey.] Hull responded by taking a quick pass from Balfour and scoring on a quick snap-shot. **1976** *Oadby & Wigston* (Leics.) *Advertiser* 26 Nov. 15/4 [In Football.] Saints hit back and a snapshot by Jim White hit the crossbar.

**4.** *attrib.*, as ***snap-shot photograph(y, system,*** etc.

**1892** GREENER *Breech-Loader* 266 Dr. Carver shoots on the snap-shot system, shooting both barrels in quick succession at the pigeon. **1893** HODGES *Elem. Photogr.* (1907) 15 What is popularly called 'snap-shot' photography. **1894** *Daily News* 26 May 6/1 The book is illustrated with.. interesting views, some of them from snapshot photographs. **1894** [see ENLARGER 1 b]. **1901** MERWIN & WEBSTER *Calumet 'K'* xv. 288 Young men with snap-shot cameras waylaid Bannon. **1967** J. PHILIP et al. *Best of Granta* I. 17 The winning photo in *The Granta* Holiday Snapshot Competition shows a couple kissing on a beach. **1977** R. E. HARRINGTON *Quintain* iii. 24 He searched the terrain, storing quick snapshot impressions. **1977** *N.Y. Rev. Bks.* 23 June 25/3 The crudely chronological order of snapshot-sequences pasted in family albums.

**'snap-shot,** *v.* [f. the sb.] **a.** *intr.* or *absol.* To take snap-shots with a camera. **b.** *trans.* To photograph (a person, etc.) by means of a snap-shot. Also *fig.*

'Freq. in recent newspaper use.' *N.E.D.*

**1894** *Amer. Ann. Photogr.* 63 Many..think it just the thing to commence with a detective camera and snap-shot. **1898** *Pall Mall Mag.* Sept. 29 One of our party desired to 'snap-shot' the scene. **1907** *Outlook* 17 Aug. 206/2 All the peculiar attitude of our race toward dancing was suddenly snapshotted in that absurdity. **1932** *Essays & Stud.* XVII. 84 Thackeray found them [*sc.* the railways] vulgar, but amusing for the opportunities they gave of snapshotting people. **1980** *Daily Tel.* 21 Nov. 15/1 The play snapshots pretty sharply Jimmy's furtive park meetings with his waif.

**c.** To shoot (something) quickly without taking deliberate aim.

**1928** *Daily Express* 6 Dec. 19/3 Mr Blyth...was a fairly deliberate shot, and liked to take his high birds neatly and quietly, but could nevertheless snapshot a woodcock in thick covert with an effortless ease.

Hence **'snap-ˌshotter, -ˌshottist,** one who takes snap-shot photographs; **'snapshotting** *ppl. a.*

**1899** C. G. HARPER *Exeter Road* 211 All trooped back to Amesbury, the *snapshotters disgusted beyond measure. **1978** *Nature* 7 Dec. 647/2 Mr Sankhala also remarks that the *snap-shotting tourist is so preoccupied with shutter speeds, lens apertures and focussing that he fails to see anything around him. **1891** *Scottish Leader* 28 Sept. 6 The Shah of Persia is an enthusiastic *snap-shottist.

**†snap snorum,** obs. f. SNIP-SNAP-SNORUM.

**1622** *MS. Archd. Oxon. c.* 157 fol. 85, Edward Camell for playing at Snape snorum on the Sabaoth day.

**snap-work.** Also snapwork. [f. SNAP-.]

**†1.** *Sc.* A firelock. *Obs.*

**1568** *Satir. Poems Reform.* xlvii. 53 Snapwark, adew, fra dagmen dow nocht stand. **1676** ROW *Contin. Blair's Autobiog.* xi. (1848) 298, 400 men with bows and long Snap works. *a* **1689** W. CLELAND *Poems* (1697) 12 (Jam.), Right well mounted of their gear:—With durk, and snap-work, and snuff-mill. *Ibid.* 34 Some with snapwarks, some with bowes.

*attrib.* **1653** URQUHART *Rabelais* I. lv, The buts and marks for shooting with a snap work-gun [Fr. *l'arquebuse*].

**2.** Snap-shot photography.

**1889** *Photogr. News* XXXIII. 266/2 A very necessary thing in quick snapwork in the streets.

**'snapy,** *a.* Now *dial.* [Cf. note to SNAPE *sb.*[3]] Of land: Wet, marshy, boggy.

**1607** J. CARPENTER *Pl. Mans Plough* 143 The husbandman..brings..into snapy and wet places hotte lime. **1846** in BARNES *Poems Rural Life.* **1883** in Elworthy *W. Somerset Word-bk.* 688 Snapy ground containing small springs, and requiring to be drained.

**snar** (snɑː(r)), *sb. rare.* Now *dial.* [Of doubtful origin: cf. Norw. dial. *snar* a twist or knot.]

**†1.** A knot in wood. *Obs.* (Cf. SNARL *sb.*[1] 4.)

**1611** FLORIO, *Nocchio*, any bosse,..node, snag,..snar, or ruggednesse in any tree or wood.

**2.** A stump or stub. (Cf. *hag-snare* HAG *sb.*[3] 2.)

**1892** M. C. F. MORRIS *Yorks. Folk-talk* 154 A ploughing field with old stumps or snars.

**†snar,** *v. Obs.* [Corresponds to Du., Flem., (M)LG., MHG. *snarren* (G. *schnarren*, Sw. *snarra*, Da. *snærre*, †*snarre*) to rattle, whirr, snarl, etc., prob. of imitative origin.] *intr.* Of dogs, etc.: To snarl or growl.

**1530** PALSGR. 723/2 Take hede of your dogge, alwayes as I come by he snarreth at me. **1553** T. WILSON *Rhet.* 91 b, As uncomely as a dogge dothe when he snarreth. **1596** SPENSER *F.Q.* VI. xii. 27 Tygres, that did seeme to gren, And snar at all, that euer passed by.

**b.** *transf.* or *fig.* Of persons.

**1553** T. WILSON *Rhet.* 91, I maruaile sir what you meane to be euer snarringe at me. **1576** FLEMING tr. *Caius' Dogs* To Rdr. (1880) B 5 b, Such as shall snarr and snatch at the Englishe abrydgement. **1581** RICH *Farew.* (1846) 126, I have written it..not to sette you a snarryng or grudgyng against me.

Hence **†'snarring** *vbl. sb.* and *ppl. a. Obs.*

**1565** COOPER, *Litera aspera*, snarryng. **1576** FLEMING tr. *Caius' Dogs* (1880) 30 This Dogge,..by furious iarring, snarring, and such like meanes, betrayeth the malefactour.

**†snarche,** *v. Obs.* In 3 *pa. t.* **snarchte, snercte.** [app. related to Du. *snerken* to crackle, fry, LG. *snerken* to fry, singe, ON. *snerkja* to sputter, wrinkle, MSw. *snärkia* to wrinkle.] *intr.* To become scorched; to frizzle.

*a* **1200** *St. Marher.* 18 þet te hude snaw hwit swartete as hit snarchte [*v.r.* snercte] ant barst on to bleinen.

**snare** (snɛə(r)), *sb.* Forms: 2 **sneare,** 4- **snare,** 5 **snayr,** 6 **snayre,** 6-7 *Sc.* **snair,** 4 **snarr,** 5-6 **snar.** [In sense 1 a. ON. *snara* (Icel. *snara*, Norw. *snara, snora, snuru*; MSw. and Sw. *snara*, Da. *snare*) noose, snare, = OHG. *snarahha* snare, and related to OHG. and MHG. *snar* (obs. or dial. G. *schnarre*), OS. *snari* (MLG. and LG. *snare, snar*), MDu. *snare, snaer* (Du. *snaar*), string. Sense 2 is probably from the Du. or LG. forms.]

**1. a.** A device for capturing small wild animals or birds, usually consisting of a string with a running noose in which a foot or the head may be caught. Also in fig. context.

*a* **1100** in Napier *O.E. Glosses* (1900) 26/2, *Tenticulam, .i. decipulam*, þelman, snearan, wocie. *a* **1300** *E.E. Psalter* ix. 16 In þis snare whilk þai hid swa Gripen es þe fote of þa. *c* **1325** *Metr. Hom.* 70 Lorde, what thyng sall passe qwyte, And be noght in this snarres tane. **1398** TREVISA *Barth. De P.R.* v. xxiii. (Bodl. MS.), Ofte by swete soune þe fouler bringeþ hem to grenes and snares swetlich. *c* **1440** *Promp. Parv.* 461/2 Snare, *laqueus, pedica.* **1483** *Cath. Angl.* 346/2 A Snare.., *vbi* A gylder. **1535** COVERDALE *Amos* iii. 5 Taketh a man his snare vp from the grounde, afore he catche somwhat? **1570** LEVINS *Manip.* 202/40 A Snayre, *laqueus, pedica.* **1697** DRYDEN *Virg. Georg.* I. 413 The proper time ..For stalking Cranes to set the guileful Snare. **1731** MEDLEY tr. *Kolben's Cape G. Hope* II. 149 Several Snares, made of Horse-Hairs, twisted together, are hung between the Branches. **1774** GOLDSM. *Nat. Hist.* (1776) IV. 167 They either catch them in snares, or take them by surprize. **1847** TENNYSON *Princ.* I. 218 The nightingale, Rapt in her song, and careless of the snare. **1885** HORNADAY *2 Years Jungle* ix. 99 They..set no snares, dig no pitfalls, nor capture game in any way whatever.

**b.** In fig. and allusive uses.

*a* **1300** *Cursor M.* 29532 þat þou mai lightloker þam here, Ar þou be laght in findes snarr. *a* **1340** HAMPOLE *Psalter* cxxiii. 6 þe swetnes of þis life is snare þat þe deuyl gildirs men with. **1412-20** LYDG. *Chron. Troy* I. 3648 Blendid with lust,..Til in þe snare þei ben englued faste. **1451** CAPGRAVE *Life St. Aug.* 12 Faustus, a grete snare of þe deuele, for þis man was þe moost famous heretik of all þe Manicheis. **1538** STARKEY *England* II. i. 156 The daungerys and snarys of the world. **1576** GASCOIGNE *Philomene* Wks. 1910 II. 182 Bewtie was the guileful bayte, which caught their lives in Snare. **1641** MILTON *Reform.* I. Wks. 1851 III. 30 Such commands were no commands, but snares. **1710** LADY M. W. MONTAGU *Lett.* lxvii. 112 Ignorance..exposes them to the snares of any..extreme. **1779** J. MOORE *View Soc. France* (1789) I. i. 5 He who has the vigour to disentangle himself from the snares of deep play. **1825** SCOTT *Betrothed* xxvii, Their very virtues become snares to them. **1844** LD. DENMAN *Judgment O'Connell* 1 Trial by jury itself, instead of being a security to persons who are accused, will be a delusion, a mockery, and a snare. **1866** MARTINEAU *Ess.* I. 235 Dr. Mansel falls, we think, into the same snare.

**†c.** A noose, a halter. *Obs.*[−1]

**1388** WYCLIF *Matt.* xxvii. 5 He passide forth, and ȝede, and hongide hym silf with a snare [L. *laqueo*].

**d.** *Surg.* A device, on the principle of a snare, for removing morbid growths.

**1884** M. MACKENZIE *Dis. Throat & Nose* II. 269 Snares have been used for many years for the removal of polypi. **1897** *Allbutt's Syst. Med.* IV. 690 The larger growths..are best removed by the cold snare. Many advocate the use of the incandescent snare.

**2. a.** One of the strings of gut, rawhide, or (more recently) wire, which are stretched across the lower head of a side-drum.

**1688** HOLME *Armoury* III. xvi. (Roxb.) 61/1 The seuerall parts of a drumme... The Snares, which is made of Bowell strings. **1867** SMYTH *Sailor's Word-bk.*, *Snares*, the cords which pass across the diameter of one hoop at the end of a drum. **1875** STAINER & BARRETT *Dict. Mus. Terms* s.v. *Side-drum*, The lower [surface] having catgut strings called snares, stretched across to check the reverberation.

**b.** *ellipt.* for *snare-drum*, sense 3 b.

**1938** D. BAKER *Young Man with Horn* I. iv. 28 He could, of course, play his snare and..sooner or later he'd have money enough to buy a piano. **1950** A. LOMAX *Mister Jelly Roll* 64, I had a drummer that hit his snares so loud that one night I gave him a couple of fly swatters for a gag. **1960** 'E. MCBAIN' *Give Boys Great Big Hand* xii. 137 The big one is the bass drum, and that round black case is what they call the snare. **1973** J. WAINWRIGHT *Pride of Pigs* 31 The drummer giving his snare a series of flicks with the wire brushes.

**3.** *attrib.* and *Comb.* **a.** In sense 1, as ***snare-cord, -trap, wire; snare-wise*** adv.

*c* **1375** *Sc. Leg. Saints* xii. (*Matthias*) 288 Resone wald þat his throt ware vith a snar cord hangyt ful sare. **1611** COTGR., *Anses*.., th' ends of ropes tyed snare-wise, or made into nooses. **1804** LEWIS & CLARK *Orig. Jrnls. Lewis & Clark Exped.* (1905) VI. 274 Baling Invoice of Sundries for Indian Presents..3 Rolls Ear Wire, 3 do Snare Wire. **1889** *Pall Mall G.* 30 Sept. 6/3 They manufacture a clever snare-trap for the wild geese. **1953** P. PROVENCHER *I live in Woods* iv. 36, I am in no danger because I have my axe, matches, fishing lines and snare-wire. **1964** C. WILLOCK *Enormous Zoo* iv. 56 Snare wire began to make its appearance most frequently... Catching animals with wire snares attached to large logs is understandably popular.

**b.** In sense 2, as ***snare-drum, -head, pin,*** etc.

**1688** HOLME *Armoury* III. xvi. (Roxb.) 61/1 The seuerall parts of a drumme... The Snare head. *Ibid.*, The Snare pin, or Screw. **1704** [E. SMITH] *Athenian Oracle* III. 423 Their drums..received several small shot in the batter heads, which they went through, but immediately struck out again by the Rims, and touch'd not the snare heads. **1873** T. B. ALDRICH *Marjorie Daw* 130 Morning and evening we heard the spiteful roll of their snare-drums. **1875** STAINER & BARRETT *Dict. Mus. Terms* s.v. *Drum*, The lower head has occasionally strings of catgut stretched over its surface, and then it is called a snare drum. **1884** *Harper's Mag.* Sept. 513/2 The little snare-drum trotted bravely along. **1926** E. FERBER *Show Boat* v. 96 A snare drummer who was always called a 'sticks', and the bass drum, known as the bull. **1941** W. C. HANDY *Father of Blues* (1957) i. 5 The youngster would..beat on the strings in the manner of a snare drummer. **1961** A. BAINES *Mus. Instruments* xiv. 335 'Snares'..consist of a number of gut or wire strings stretched across the lower skin or 'snare head'. **1966** *Crescendo* Apr. 30/3 Complete with snare drumming that would make the Dagenham Girl Pipers turn green with envy. **1976** *New Yorker* 8 Mar. 108/3 He would hit the snare directly, or hit the snarehead and the rim.

**snare** (snɛə(r)), *v.* Also 5 **snarre,** 6-7 *Sc.* **snair,** 6 **snayre.** [f. SNARE *sb.* Cf. Norw. *snara*; MSw. *snäria* (Sw. *snärja*), MDa. *snerie, snerge* (Da. *snære*), in similar senses.]

**1. a.** *trans.* To capture (small wild animals, birds, etc.) in a snare; to catch by entangling.

**1388** WYCLIF *Isaiah* xxviii. 13 That thei..falle backward, and be al to-brokun, and be snarid, and be takun. *c* **1440** *Promp. Parv.* 461/2 Snaryn, or snarlyn, *illaqueo.* **1530** PALSGR. 723/2, I snare, I catche in a snare, *je prens au las.* **1548** ELYOT, *Laqueus*, an halter, any thynge that one is snared or intangled in. **1570** LEVINS *Manip.* 202/44 To Snayre, *illaqueare.* **1610** SHAKS. *Temp.* II. ii. 174, I..will.. show thee a Iayes nest, and instruct thee how to snare the nimble Marmazet. **1697** DRYDEN *Virg. Georg.* I. 365 To fire the Brambles, snare the Birds. **1781** COWPER *Retirement* 401 To carve his rustic name upon a tree, To snare the mole. **1832** LYTTON *Eugene A.* III. iii, I should not be surprised if you snared one of Squire Nixon's hares by the way. **1878** BOSW. SMITH *Carthage* 422 The cultivated portions.. swarm with quails, vast numbers of which are snared in nets by the natives.

*absol.* **1807** CRABBE *Par. Reg.* I. 813 He poach'd the wood, and on the warren snared. **1863** [H. W. WHEELWRIGHT] *Spring & Summer in Lapland* 144 Where every one shoots and snares just as he pleases.

**b.** *fig.* To entangle, entrap.

**1401** *Pol. Poems* (Rolls) II. 55 Cauteles and sleiȝtes, ech intrikid in other, to snarre symple soules. *c* **1430** *Life St. Katherine* (Roxb.) 31, I se wel þat þou woldest wyth þy venoms sotyltees snare vs. **1535** COVERDALE *Exod.* x. 7 How longe shall we be snared after this maner? **1567** *Gude & Godlie Ball.* (S.T.S.) 216 Be thow not snairde in Venus snair. **1616** R. C. *Times' Whistle* (1871) 38 Cast downe thy looke, Least prides bait snare thee on the devils hooke. **1642** D. ROGERS *Naaman* 16 Those ten tribes were justly snared by Jeroboams calves. **1810** SCOTT *Lady of Lake* II. xxviii. Themselves in bloody toils were snared. **1864** TENNYSON *Aylmer's F.* 780 Who wove coarse webs to snare her purity.

*refl.* *c* **1550** COVERDALE *Fruitful Lessons* (1593) O iij, Who so goeth about to bind the truth, dooth knitte and snare himselfe with vnlosable bands. **16..** SIR W. MURE *Sonn. to Margareit* iv, Alace!.. To snair myselfe in hope to be reliued. **1642** D. ROGERS *Naaman* 26 Adore it, but snare not thyselfe with it.

**c.** *U.S.* To catch, to win by a small margin.

**1942** BERREY & VAN DEN BARK *Amer. Thes. Slang* §650/6 *Win*...snare a win. *Ibid.* §679/5 *Field a ball; catch*...snare a hit. **1948** *Sun* (Baltimore) 26 Nov. 17/1 Double Brandy.. came from next to last to snare the second money about a half length in front of Brookmeade Stable's Gnu.

**2.** *Surg.* and *Path.* To catch in a loop, *esp.* in order to remove; to cut off with a snare.

**1884** M. MACKENZIE *Dis. Throat & Nose* II. 355 An instrument for snaring nasal polypi. **1897** *Allbutt's Syst. Med.* III. 794 A peritoneal adhesion by which a loop of bowel is snared and acutely strangulated.

Hence **snared** (snɛəd), *ppl. a.*; **'snaring** *vbl. sb.* (also *attrib.*) and *ppl. a.*

*c* **1440** *Promp. Parv.* 461/2 Snarynge, or snarlynge, *illaqueacio.* *a* **1586** SIDNEY *Ps.* XVIII. ii, To my snaring grave to goe. **1591** PERCIVALL *Sp. Dict.*, *Enlazamiento*, intangling, snaring. **1605** EARL STIRLING *Alexandr. Trag.* II. Chor., Then snaring laws did not extend The bounds of Reason. **1640** T. CAREW *Willing Prisoner* ii, Her murdring glances, snaring haires,..so please me. **1837** CARLYLE *Fr. Rev.* I. III. v, Driven mad like the snared lion. **1845** DISRAELI *Sybil* (1863) 160 Meditating the snaring of a hare. **1899** *Allbutt's Syst. Med.* VIII. 899 The artificial snaring of tumours. **1923** *Beaver* Mar. 236/1 Having some snaring twine she killed sufficient rabbits to keep herself and child alive. **1971** A. FRY *Long Journey* iv. 18 The snaring wing, a long brush fence with a few 'escapes'.., each set with a snare. *Ibid.* ix. 52 Three or four men could work together, driving animals.. toward a snaring fence.

**snare,** variant of SNATH(E *v. dial.*

**†'snareful,** *a. Obs.*[−1] [f. SNARE *sb.*] Full of snares; insidious.

*a* **1618** SYLVESTER *Cup of Consolation* 35 Wks. (Grosart) II. 263 All the snarefull Wiles, And cunning Colours of mysterious Guiles.

**'snareless,** *a.* [f. SNARE *sb.*] **a.** Free from snares.

**1823** CAROLINE B. SOUTHEY *Poet. Wks.* (1867) 139 Stopt was the busy mill-wheel now, Snareless the rippling brook.

**b.** Without a snare.

**1978** *Early Music* Jan. 29/1 Drums are often snareless, though the pictorial evidence is that the cylindrical drum almost always had a snare.

**snarer** ('snɛərə(r)). [f. SNARE *v.*] One who sets snares or traps. Also *fig.*

**1597** MIDDLETON *Wisd. Solomon* xvii. 14 Snare without snarer, net without a bait. **1623** —— *More Dissemblers* II. i, He..has broke through the net..And left the snarer here herself entangled. **1807** CRABBE *Par. Reg.* I. 178 Snarers and smugglers here their gains divide. **1885** *Law Times Rep.* LII. 327/1 The proviso did not apply to snarers like Gilham, who captured birds on certain lands.

**snark** (snɑːk), *sb.* [Invented by 'Lewis Carroll' (C. L. Dodgson) in *The Hunting of the Snark* (1876).] An imaginary animal. Also *Comb.*

**1879** *Temple Bar* Nov. 391 Hunting for snarkes is a very pleasant occupation, if you do but make-believe strong enough. **1888** LEES & CLUTTERBUCK *B.C. 1887* xxvi. (1892) 297 There is quite a Snark-hunting ring about it. **1895** K. GRAHAME *Golden Age* 90 Some sinuous and snarklike conflict on the mat.

**snark** (snɑːk), *v. dial.* [Corresponds to MLG. and LG. *snarken* (NFris. *snarke*, Sw. and Norw. *snarka*), MHG. *snarchen* (G. *schnarchen*, †*schnarken*), of imitative origin: cf. SNORK *v.*]

**1.** *intr.* To snore; to snort.

**1866** *N. & Q.* 3rd Ser. X. 248/1, I will not quite compare it [a sound] to a certain kind of snarking or gnashing. **1907** *Westm. Gaz.* 9 Nov. 4/1 All of a sudden she (the mare, I suppose he meant) snarked an' begun to turn round.

**2.** *intr.* and *trans.* To find fault (with), to nag.

**1882** *Jamieson's Sc. Dict.* IV. 314/2 To *Snark*,.. to fret, grumble, or find fault with one. **1904** E. NESBIT *Phœnix & Carpet* x. 185 He remembered how Anthea had refrained from snarking him about tearing the carpet.

**snarky** (ˈsnɑːkɪ), *a. colloq.* [f. SNARK *v.* + -Y[1].] Irritable, short-tempered, 'narky'.

**1906** E. NESBIT *Railway Children* ii. 49 Don't be snarky, Peter. It isn't our fault. **1913** J. VAIZEY *College Girl* xxiv. 326 'Why should you think I am "snarky"?' 'Because—you *are*! You're not a bit sociable and friendly.' **1953** E. COXHEAD *Midlanders* x. 247 I've known you were the soul of kindness, under that snarky way. *a* **1974** R. CROSSMAN *Diaries* (1976) II. 627 We also have to overcome something else—the stream of anti-government propaganda, smearing, snarky, derisive, which comes out of Fleet Street.

Hence **ˈsnarkily** *adv.*; **ˈsnarkiness**; **ˈsnarkish** *a.*

**1912** R. FRY *Let.* 16 Mar. (1972) I. 355 So sorry I seem so snarkish just now. **1960** *Economist* 28 May 859/2 In some of his comments on bureaucracy there is a relapse into snarkiness. **1967** *Listener* 20 July 91/3 Viewers' letters are not just read out. They are commented upon by Kenneth Robinson (usually rather snarkily).

**snarl** (snɑːl), *sb.*[1] Also 4, 7–8 snarle, 9 *dial.* snarrel. [f. SNARE *sb.* or *v.*: see -LE I.]

**1.** A snare, gin; a noose. *Obs.* exc. *dial.* Also *fig.*

*c* **1380** *Metr. Hom.* (Vernon MS.) in Herrig *Archiv* LVII. 247/1 Lord, what þing schal passe quite And in þes snarles not beo tan. **1387** TREVISA *Higden* (Rolls) II. 385 Maydens of Athene were compelled as it were to snarles and grenes. *Ibid.* VI. 27 To brynge þe peple þat was so bygiled þe faster in snarl. **1601** BRETON *Blessed Weeper* xxi, Shame bad me weepe.. to feele how I was feltred in The wretched snarles of wicked nature's knots. **1829** BROCKETT *N.C. Gloss.* (ed. 2), *Snarl*, the snare itself, made of wire. **1893** in *Eng. Dial. Dict.* s.v., They put this snarl or snirrup roond t' gills an' click t' fish oot.

**2. a.** A tangle, knot, ravel, as in the hair.

**1609** *Ev. Woman in Hum.* v. i. in Bullen *O. Pl.* IV, Curle not the snarles that dwell upon these browes. **1611** COTGR., *Grippets*,.. the rufflings, or snarles of ouer-twisted thread. **1741** *Compl. Family-Piece* II. ii. 331 Let your Hair be round, ..twist it neatly without Gaping or Snarles. **1750** GLANDVILLE in W. Ellis *Mod. Husb.* IV. II. 73, I found it [the hairworm] to twist itself all up into a close Snarle. **1836** HALIBURTON *Clockm.* xviii. (1862) 79 To wind off a snarl of ravellins as slick as if it were on a reel. **1854** SUSAN WARNER *Old Helmet* I. 113 The green silk was in a great snarl. **1897** *Outing* XXX. 434/2 The worm.. lying upon the bottom like a snarl of black thread. **1966** J. S. COX *Illustr. Dict. Hairdressing & Wigmaking* 139/2 *Snarl*, a tangle in the hair. **1976** 'TREVANIAN' *Main* (1977) xiii. 243 A young slattern who tugs a snarl out of her hair with her fingers.

**b.** *fig.* or in fig. context. ***traffic snarl*** (U.S. colloq.), a traffic jam.

**1631** QUARLES *Samson* xii, The day's at hand, wherein thou must untie The Riddle's tangled Snarle. **1675** J. SMITH *Chr. Relig. App.* I. 18 Here was.. a snarle in his fortune requiring the aid of a Divine Solution. **1710** S. PALMER *Proverbs* 73 That men and women shou'd be.. in a continu'd snarle, contradiction, hatred, and infinite disorders. **1860** [MRS. M. C. HARRIS] *Rutledge* 111 Dorothy has got her account with the grocer in a great snarl. **1889** *Spectator* 13 Apr., Our children will see how this Irish snarl is unravelled. **1933** E. B. WHITE *Let.* Mar. (1976) 113 At noon I happened to be driving north on Fourth Avenue, and got held up in a traffic snarl. **1950** J. D. MACDONALD *Brass Cupcake* ii. 18, I dove slowly back into the traffic snarl. **1968** S. CHALLIS *Death on Quiet Beach* iii. 30 The traffic was a slow snarl that cost him forty minutes. **1975** *New Yorker* 19 May 99/1 The traffic snarls were impenetrable. **1979** *Arizona Daily Star* 5 Aug. D 3/3 Production snarls kept cars out of the showroom. **1980** R. L. DUNCAN *Brimstone* iv. 65 The congressional reorganization studies.. were resulting in a snarl of immense proportions.

**3.** *U.S.* A swarm, large number.

**1775** in O. E. Winslow *Amer. Broadside Verse* (1930) 141/2, I see another snarl of men. **1825** J. NEAL *Bro. Jonathan* I. 76 There being 'a pootty consid'r'ble snarl o' gals, I guess' the supper was bravely furnished. **1836** W. DUNLAP *Mem. Water Drinker* (1837) II. iii. 24 They swarm like a snarl of bees before hiving. **1855** MRS. WHITCHER *Widow Bedott P.* xxiii, A cheaper minister, and one that hadn't such a snarl o' young ones. **1904** *N.Y. Tribune* 10 Apr. (Suppl.) 7/3 A veritable snarl of street urchins took possession of several benches in Lincoln Park.

**4.** A knot in wood. (Cf. SNARLY *a.*[1] 2.)

**1881-** in dial. glossaries (Leic., Warw.). *a* **1891** *Tribune Book of Sports* 12 (Cent.), Let Italian or Spanish yew be the wood, clear of knots, snarls, and cracks.

**5.** *attrib.* and *Comb.*, as ***snarl-headed*** adj., ***-knot, -preventer.***

**1790** R. TYLER *Contrast* II. ii. (1887) 39 The snarl-headed curs fell a-kicking and cursing of me. **1847** HALLIW., *Snarl-knot*, a very intricate one. **1867** SMYTH *Sailor's Word-bk.*, *Snarl-Knot*, a northern expression for a knot that cannot be drawn loose. **1884** *Illustr. Lond. N.* 27 Sept. 291/1 Mr. Brooks's 'Snarl preventor' is a new form of thread-wire which pounces on snarled threads.

**snarl** (snɑːl), *sb.*[2] [f. SNARL *v.*[2]] An act of snarling; a display of the teeth accompanied by an angry sound. Freq. *fig.*

**1613** SIR E. HOBY (*title*), A Counter Snarle for Ishmael Rabshacheh. **1653** W. RAMESEY *Astrol. Restored* To Rdr. 4, [I] content my self to incur all the Currish Snarls.. of the envious. **1832** W. IRVING *Alhambra* II. 178 With the wary side glance of a cur.. ready for a snap and a snarl. **1855** MACAULAY *Hist. Eng.* xiv. III. 393 A sum.. which he took with the savage snarl of disappointed greediness. **1885** RUSKIN *Pleas. Eng.* 147 The mocking snarl and ruthless blow of the Puritan.

*transf.* **1889** DOYLE *M. Clarke* 189 The blare of trumpets and the long deep snarl of the drums.

**snarl** (snɑːl), *v.*[1] Also 5 snarlyn, 5–7 snarle. [Cf. SNARL *sb.*[1]]

In R. Brunne *Chron. Wace* 4629 (Ropes ryueled, & swerued in lyne) the reading *suarled* cited from the Petyt MS. should prob. be *snarled* in sense 2 or 3; the construction is not quite clear.

**1. a.** *trans.* To catch in a snare or noose; to entangle or secure with a cord, rope, etc.; to strangle. Now *dial.*

**1398** TREVISA *Barth. De P.R.* XVIII. xv. (Bodl. MS.), þee hunter.. knowyþ þat þe beeste is i-snarled and faste yholde. *Ibid.* lxxix, *Sicut orix allaqueatus*, as Orix is isnarled. *c* **1440** *Promp. Parv.* 461/2 Snaryn, or snarlyn, *illaqueo*. *a* **1470** H. PARKER *Dives & Pauper* (W. de W. 1493) IX. vii. G ij b, They [*sc.* sheep] ben so.. snarled amonges brembles and thornes that they may nat go away. **1563** FOXE *A. & M.* 1255/2 He made him priuely to be snarled, and his flesh to be torn. **1565** COOPER, *Laqueus*, an halter: any thyng that one is snarled or tied with. **1602** ROWLANDS *Greenes Ghost* 36 With his necke snarled in an hempen halter. **1648** J. BEAUMONT *Psyche* IX. cclxxv, So may all Rebels find their shameless feet Snarled for evermore in their own Net. **1829** BROCKETT *N.C. Gloss.* (ed. 2), *Snarl*, to insnare; as to snarl hares. **1849-** in dial. glossaries, etc. (Northumb., Durham, Cumb., Leic., etc.).

*refl.* **1530** PALSGR. 723/2 My grayhounde had almost snarled hym selfe to night in his own leesse. **1580** BLUNDEVIL *Horsemanship* IV. 60 b, A Horse.. being laid, and the halter slacke about his feete,.. he snarleth himselfe, so as he is not able to get vp.

**b.** *fig.* To ensnare, entangle, entrap.

**1387** TREVISA *Higden* (Rolls) VII. 431 þe kyng.. snarlede hem wiþ sotil sophyms. *c* **1400** *Pilgr. Sowle* (Caxton) I. i. (1859) 2 That no pylgrym escape, that he ne shal be snarlyd in my trappe. **1447** BOKENHAM *Seyntys* (Roxb.) 192 Wyth þi trecc herous sotylte Us to snarlyn þou besyist þe. **1545** JOYE *Exp. Dan.* viii. S iv, To studye by what engyns mennes myndes might be trapped and snarled. **1593** NASHE *Christ's T.* Wks. (Grosart) IV. 148 Their wealth, they make no other vse of but to snarle and enwrappe men with. **1641** 'SMECTYMNUUS' *Vind. Answ.* xiii. 121 Foreseeing how his owne words would snarle him, if he should grant them all Bishops.

*refl.* *a* **1470** H. PARKER *Dives & Pauper* (W. de W. 1493) IX. vii. G ij b, They snarle themself so in dett & in false richesses. **1551** CRANMER *Answ. Gardiner* 168 You snarle youre selfe into so many and heynouse absurdites. **1597** J. PAYNE *Royal Exch.* 37 Let vs not.. snarle and intangle our selves with over moche toyle and care of the world. *c* **1680** HICKERINGILL *Hist. Whiggism* I. Wks. 1716 I. 37 They lose themselves, and snarl themselves and the Holy Text, so that they never find the right end.

**2. a.** To tangle; to twist together confusedly; to make a tangle of. Now chiefly *dial.* and *U.S.*

*c* **1440** *Promp. Parv.* 439/1 Ruffelyn, or snarlyn, *innodo*. *c* **1440** *Partonope* 2300 Hys swerde is broken; the other tweyn [swords] be Snarled in the sheeldes ryght fast. **1570** LEVINS *Manip.* 32/21 To Snarle, *contrahere*. **1578** LYTE *Dodoens* 97 It bringeth forth many tender branches full of knotty joynts, entangled and snarled, or wrapped one in another. **1606** S. GARDINER *Bk. Angling* 22 The mudde of this place doth pollute the nette, snarle it, and hurte it. *a* **1687** H. MORE *Cont. Remark. St.* (1689) 424 The Daughter had.. her Hair snarled and matted together. *a* **1825** FORBY *Voc. E. Anglia*, *Snarl*, to twist, entangle, and knot together. **1847** PRESCOTT *Peru* (1855) II. 165 Mangrove trees with their complicated roots snarled into formidable coils under the water. **1894** *Outing* XXIII. 404/1 The head tide had snarled the trawls badly.

*absol.* **1890** BYNNER *Begum's Dau.* xxxvii, The begum made bad work of her embroidery in those days; she snarled and knotted, and cut and ravelled.

**b.** *fig.* To render complicated or confused.

**1653** tr. *Przipcovius' Diss. de Pace* 15 You do not comprehend doctrines snarled and entangled with so many knots. **1675** J. SMITH *Chr. Relig. App.* I. 44, I would thus unty these knots with which he snarles this story. **1701** J. NORRIS *Ess. Theory Ideal World* I. 414 'Tis the want of this Distinction.. that has.. so snarl'd and perplex'd this Question. **1901** *Jrnl. Sch. Geogr.* Nov. 340 His starting point ..being different.., everything else must be snarled hopelessly.

**c.** ***to snarl up***: to throw into confusion, to mess up; to entangle, to impede the smooth running of (something). *colloq.*

**1937** C. DAY LEWIS *Starting Point* I. iii. 49 He short-punted ahead, snarling up the defence. **1957** J. F. HORNER *Summary of Scientology* vi. 67 Self-processing tends only to snarl-up the person attempting it. **1960** *Economist* 22 Oct. 317/2 A.. wish to snarl up the relations between the western governments. **1962** *Listener* 5 July 36/2 Private cars are increasing at such a rate.. that the roads will be snarled up. **1976** *Daily Tel.* 22 June 1/3 The Conservatives snarled up Government business by ceasing the pairing of MPs and other co-operation. **1981** *Sunday Express* 25 Oct. (*heading*) 150,000 marchers snarl up London.

**3.** *intr.* To become twisted or entangled; to get into, or form, tangles or knots. Also *fig.* and with *up.*

**1600** HOLLAND *Livy* XXXI. xxxix. 797 Their speares.. snarling within the boughes and branches of trees.. hindered them verie much. **1613** DENNIS *Secr. Angling* I. x, Then twist them finely... But not too hard or slacke,.. Least slacke they snarle, or hard they proue vnsound. **1681** CHETHAM *Angler's Vade-m.* xxx. §5 (1689) 177 Which will cause the wyre to be more tough and not so apt to snarl, or break. **1835** URE *Philos. Manuf.* 226 To cause it to snarl into a knot when left free to turn on itself. **1884** W. S. B. McLAREN *Spinning* 155 The yarn tends to 'snarl' and curl, and cannot be drawn out straight. **1951** *Manch. Guardian Weekly* 19 Apr. 5/3 The traffic clears quickly at times, when it might otherwise snarl—which is the American way of saying it might 'cause an inextricable jam'. **1963** *Listener* 14 Feb. 300/2 The action.. snarls up into an obtrusive expressionism. **1970** G. F. NEWMAN *Sir, You Bastard* viii. 201 Traffic snarled eastwards along Brompton Road at a snail's pace.

**snarl** (snɑːl), *v.*[2] Also 6–8 snarle (7 snarlle). [f. SNAR *v.*: see -LE 3, and cf. GNARL *v.*[1]]

**1.** *intr.* Of dogs, etc.: To make an angry sound accompanied by showing the teeth.

**1589** R. HARVEY *Pl. Perc.* 9 Yf he snarle like a cur at vs, why should not we prouide a Bastinado for him? **1631** QUARLES *Samson* xv, T'one skulks and snarles, the t'other tugges and hales. **1697** DRYDEN *Virg. Georg.* IV. 692 The gaping three-mouth'd Dog forgets to snarl. *a* **1732** BOSTON *Crook in Lot* (1805) 38 A dog snarls at a stone, but looks not at the hand that cast it. **1814** SCOTT *Lord of Isles* III. xxxii, While o'er those caitiffs, where they lie, The wolf shall snarl. **1861** *Morn. Post* 12 Nov., The bear snarled, but crawled on. **1889** RUSKIN *Præterita* III. 48 Their dogs barked and snarled irreconcileably.

*fig.* **1837** CARLYLE *Fr. Rev.* II. I. i, Such Patriotism as snarls dangerously and shows teeth. **1842** TENNYSON *Locksley H.* 106 Nations.. snarling at each other's heels. **1866** B. TAYLOR *Poems, The Test* 414, I hear the angry trumpet snarling.

**2.** Of persons: To quarrel; to grumble viciously; to show strong resentment or ill-feeling.

**1594** SHAKS. *Rich. III*, I. iii. 188 What? were you snarling all before I came,.. And turne you all your hatred now on me? **1612** WOODALL *Surg. Mate* Wks. 1653 Pref. 12 Hee is not ignorant, that a large broode of pregnant wits.. will snarl. **1689** *Muses Farew. to Popery* 28 When Servants snarl, we ought to kick 'em out. **1709** PRIOR *The Ladle* x, Kissing to Day, to Morrow snarling. *a* **1776** in Herd *Anc. & Mod. Sc. Songs* II. 208 The surly auld carl did naething but snarl. **1843** JAMES *Forest Days* ii, Don't let me find you snarling with a gentleman's servants again. **1894** G. M. FENN *In Alpine Valley* i. 6, I should have snarled, written my cheque, and paid.

**b.** Const. *against* or *at* a person or thing.

**1593** NASHE *Four Lett. Conf.* Wks. (Grosart) II. 196 Thy hot-spirited brother Richard.. snarld priuily at Pap-hatchet, Pasquill, and others. **1624** GATAKER *Transubst.* 39 Lest the Heretiques should be snarling at us. *c* **1640** H. BELL *Luther's Colloq. Mens.* (1652) 154 No man giveth a fillip for the Gospel, but all do snarl against it. **1715** CHAPPELOW *Right Way Rich* (1717) 161 Let wicked men snarl and grin at you now. **1881** *Leicester Gloss.* 245 Jane snarls an' snags at Lizzy.

**c.** To give *out* a snarling noise.

**1675** COVEL in *Early Voy. Levant* (Hakl. Soc.) 246 The manner of the Christians buriall here is much the same; all have the *Praeficae* [hired mourners], who sing (or rather howl and snarle out).

**3.** *trans.* To utter in a harsh, rude, or ill-natured manner.

**1693** CONGREVE *Old Bach.* I. iv, Where hast thou been snarling odious truths, and entertaining company.. with discourse of their diseases? **1839** DICKENS *Nickleby* iii, 'Who indeed!' snarled Ralph. **1866** GEO. ELIOT *F. Holt* xlv, When the wicked Tempter is tired of snarling that word failure in a man's cell. **1893** *Times* 18 May 9/4 They would.. confine themselves to snarling complaints.

**4.** To put *down* with snarling.

*a* **1873** LYTTON *K. Chillingley* IV. ix, I can't bear to see a man snarled and sneered down.. by.. rivals.

**5.** *refl.* To bring into a certain condition by snarling.

*a* **1849** SOUTHEY in *Life*, etc. I. v. 306 He has a most critic-like voice, as if he had snarled himself hoarse.

**snarl** (snɑːl), *v.*[3] *techn.* [? f. SNARL *sb.*[1] 4.] *trans.* To raise, or force *up*, into bosses or projections by the use of the snarling-iron.

**1688** [implied in SNARLING *vbl. sb.*[3]]. **1843** HOLTZAPFFEL *Turning* I. 412 If from the shape of the works swage tools.. cannot be employed for raising the projecting parts, they are *snarled-up*. **1851-3** *Tomlinson's Cycl. Usef. Arts* II. 431/1 With them the snarled-up parts are corrected.

**snarled** (snɑːld), *ppl. a.* [f. SNARL *v.*[1]]

†**1.** Ensnared, entrapped. *Obs.*

*c* **1440** *Promp. Parv.* 461/2 Snaryd, or snarlyd, ..*illaqueatus*. **1648** J. BEAUMONT *Psyche* XIV. lxvii, There A snarled Ram untwisted Isaac's fate.

**2. a.** Entangled, twisted, complicated. Also *fig.* Of road traffic: congested (orig. *U.S.*); also with *up.*

*c* **1440** *Promp. Parv.* 439/1 Rufflyd, or snarlyd, *innodatus*. **1571** GOLDING *Calvin on Ps.* xxxvii. 25 Out of the matter itselfe there springeth a difficult and snarled question. **1598** SYLVESTER *Du Bartas* II. i. I. *Eden* 723 Adam's self.. Could scant unwinde the knotty snarled clew. **1648** J. BEAUMONT *Psyche* XVIII. cxliv, Through a thousand snarl'd Meanders, to A goodly Room he soon conducted her. **1667** *Decay Chr.*

*Piety* vii. §3. 259 Whose confus'd snarl'd consciences render it difficult, thus to pull out thred by thred. **1883** W. C. Smith *N. Country Folk* 78 More tangled thrums,.. More snarled hasps. **1884** [see SNARL *sb.*[1] 5]. **1967** N. Marsh *Death at Dolphin* viii. 230 We've caught a snarled-up little job this time. **1973** R. Hill *Ruling Passion* I. vii. 73 Another diversionary tactic. What a snarled-up lot of people they were! **1976** R. Moore *Dubai* i. 8 Fitz pushed his way through the..streets, walking through the snarled traffic. **1980** *Times* 8 July 6/2 One of the worst spots for snarled-up traffic.

b. Mentally confused.

**1881** Cable *Mme. Delphine* viii. 42 The returned rover was a trifle snarled in his top-hamper.

†**'snarler**[1]. *Obs.*⁻¹ [app. f. SNARL *v.*[1]] A species of pedlar or hawker.

**1398** in A. F. Leach *Beverley Town Doc.* (Selden Soc.) 42 Homines mercenarii forinseci, vocati Snarlers et haukers, vagantes per stratas ville.

**snarler**[2] ('snɑːlə(r)). [f. SNARL *v.*[2]]

1. One who snarls; an ill-tempered, grumbling, or fault-finding person.

**1634** Carew *Cœlum Brit.* 7, I shun in vaine the importunity With which this Snarler vexeth all the gods. **1703** Rowe *Ulysses* I. i, 'Tis the Snarler Æthon, A priviledg'd Talker. **1779** *Ann. Reg.* II. 52 The snarlers against Mr. Garrick's management of the theatre. **1821** *Blackw. Mag.* X. 555 A plain good woman, neither blue-stocking nor snarler. **1884** *Contemp. Rev.* Aug. 253 Shakespeare..was much too great to take vengeance or damn the ill-natured snarlers to immortal disgrace.

2. A dog or other animal addicted to snarling.

**1797** *Monthly Mag.* III. 536 Their doors guarded by large and very surly dogs. The women were no great admirers of those snarlers.

**snarler**[3] ('snɑːlə(r)). [f. SNARL *v.*[3]]

1. One who works with a snarling-iron.

**1864** in Webster. **1900** *Daily Mail* 31 Oct., A snarler..is a worker in teapots, and may..be compared with the leaf bumper who bumps up the leaves commonly seen in metal work.

2. A snarling-iron.

**1903** H. Wilson *Silverwork & Jewellery* 59 This causes the point of the snarler to strike against the inner side of the cup.

**'snarley-yow.** *Naut.* [After the name of the dog in Marryat's novel *Snarleyyow, or the Dog-Fiend* (1837).] (See quot.)

**1867** Smyth *Sailor's Word-bk.*, *Snarley-yow*, a discontented, litigious grumbler. An old guard-ship authority who knows when to play the courtier.

**snarling** ('snɑːlɪŋ), *vbl. sb.*[1] [f. SNARL *v.*[1]]

1. The action of snaring, entangling, or twisting. Also *attrib.* in *snarling-net*.

*c* **1440** *Promp. Parv.* 461/2 Snarynge, or snarlynge, *illaqueacio*. **1601** Dent *Pathw. Heaven* 83 This world is..a snarling net, wherein thousands are taken. **1615** Markham *Pleas. Prin.* ii. (1635) 8 Twist your hayres..without eyther snarling, or gaping one from another. **1853** Ure *Dict. Arts* (ed. 4) II. 831 Thus preventing a snarling or damage of the yarn.

2. (See quot.) *rare*⁻¹.

**1750** W. Ellis *Mod. Husb.* III. iii. 88 Some [sheets] are made of the worst sort of hemp, called Snarlings.

**snarling** ('snɑːlɪŋ), *vbl. sb.*[2] [f. SNARL *v.*[2]] The action of the vb., in various senses; the sound produced by this.

**1591** Percivall *Sp. Dict.*, *Gañido*, the snarling of a dogge. **1602** *2nd Pt. Return fr. Parnass.* v. iv, We three vnto the snarling Iland hast, And there our vexed breath in snarling wast. **1632** Lithgow *Trav.* ix. 401 The bussing of Bees, or snarling of Wolues. **1672** Sir T. Browne *Let. Friend* 143 His sober contempt of the world wrought..no laughing or snarling at it. **1806** Sir C. Bell *Anat. Expression* 90 This action of snarling is quite peculiar to the ferocious and carnivorous animals. **1863** Geo. Eliot *Romola* xxii, There was no care that certain snarlings..should be strictly inaudible.

*attrib.* **1806** Sir C. Bell *Anat. Expression* 90 In the carnivorous animal the muscles of the lips are so directed as to raise the lip from the canine teeth... The former I would take the liberty of distinguishing by the name of *Ringentes*, snarling muscles.

**snarling** ('snɑːlɪŋ), *vbl. sb.*[3] [Cf. SNARL *v.*[3]] A method of producing raised work in metal by means of indirect percussion. Chiefly *attrib.* in ***snarling-iron, -tool.***

**1688** Holme *Armoury* III. 259/2 Terms of Art used by the Gold-smiths... *Snarling* is to set or punch it [the metal] out as the shape is drawn. *Ibid.* xxi. (Roxb.) 267/2 He beareth.. three snarling Irons Argent... These snarling Irons haue sharp ends. **1843** Holtzapffel *Turning* I. 412 When the snarling-iron is struck with a hammer..the re-action gives a blow within the vessel. **1877** G. E. Gee *Silversmith's Handbk.* 122, Fig. 32 and 33 represent the snarling-tool.

**snarling** ('snɑːlɪŋ), *ppl. a.* [f. SNARL *v.*[2]]

1. That snarls; given to snarling: a. Of dogs or other animals.

**1595** *Locrine* v. iv, The snarling curres of darkened Tartarus. **1612** Field *Woman is Weathercock* I. i, The snarling dogs were mute. **1675** Marvel *Corr.* Wks. (Grosart) II. 489 Not at all..dejected or much concerned with such snarling curs. **1753** Miss Collier *Art Torment.* I. i. (1811) 28 Little snarling lap-dogs. **1828–32** Webster, *Growler*, a snarling cur.

b. *transf.* Of persons.

**1593** Nashe *Christ's T.* 69 b, Nought but sharpe discipline, is a fitte disputant with snarling Scismatiques. **1635** Barriffe *Mil. Discipl.* lxx. (1643) 187 Snarling Cynicks, I know, will carpe at my curiositie. **1732** Berkeley *Alciphr.* v. §28 A pack of snarling sour bigots. **1841** Thackeray *Gt. Hoggarty Diamond* v, All admired it hugely, except that snarling Scotchman. **1884** *Nonconf. & Indep.* 19 June 594/2 This perpetual worrying, by snarling busybodies,..of the greatest statesman of the age.

2. Of the nature of, accompanied or characterized by, snarling.

**1599** (*title*), Micro-cynicon: Sixe Snarling Satyres. **1633** Bp. Hall *Occas. Med.* (1851) 29, I had justly drawn on.. this snarling importunity. **1667** Temple *Wks.* (1720) II. 44 Such a snarling Peace as that at Breda. **1709** Steele *Tatler* No. 2 ¶9 Long this uncomfortable Life they led, With snarling Meals. **1806** *Med. Jrnl.* XV. 504 That polite language and supreme urbanity which characterize these snarling productions. **1855** J. D. Burn *Autobiogr. Beggar Boy* (1859) 184 It may be supposed that I have made these observations in a snarling temper.

3. Having or producing the sound of a snarl.

**1602** Marston *Antonio's Rev.* Prol., Snarling gusts nibble the juyceles leaves. **1655** Vaughan *Silex Scint.* I. 81 Each snarling blast shot through me. **1820** Keats *Eve St. Agnes* iv, Soon, up aloft, The silver, snarling trumpets 'gan to chide. **1860** Holland *Miss Gilbert's Career* iv. 67 The snarling, grinding din of the gearing was hushed. **1900** St. Barbe *Mod. Spain* 59 The rain drove with an angry, snarling hiss.

Hence **'snarlingly** adv.

**1862** Sala *Acc. Addresses* 35 He..denied, snarlingly, that he was worth a penny. **1865** Carlyle *Fredk. Gt.* xvi. xv. (1872) VI. 313 Whose reflections on it..are stingy, snarlingly contemptuous.

**snarlish** ('snɑːlɪʃ), *a.* [f. SNARL *sb.*[2] or *v.*[2]] Somewhat snarly or ill-tempered.

**1819** *Pantologia* VI. s.v *Menippus*, He wrote some snarlish satires, for which reason writings of that stamp have been sometimes called Menippean. **1848** Mozley *Ess.* (1878) I. 376 This excellent Henry accuses me..of being snarlish and quarrelsome. **1893** Cozens-Hardy *Broad Norf.* 12 A snarlish fellow weak in the head.

**'snarl-up.** *colloq.* [f. vbl. phr. *to snarl up*: see SNARL *v.*[1] 2 c, 3.] A muddle, state of confusion; a mistake; a traffic jam; a blockage. Also *attrib.*

**1960** M. Phillips in *Analog Sci. Fact/Fiction* Nov. 24/1 Both courses..resulted in more snarl-ups. Reports that should have been sent in weeks before arrived too late; reports meant for the eyes of only one man were turned out in triplicate. **1962** J. Braine *Life at Top* xi. 152 There was going to be a huge snarl-up very soon. **1963** *Daily Tel.* 3 June 1/1 On what the AA described as 'snarl-up Sunday' there were queues of up to 19 miles on several major arteries. **1966** *Musical Opinion* Aug. 691/1 The main cause of the brouhaha about electronic instruments is a snarl-up in terminology. **1969** *Daily Tel.* 10 Jan. 1/2 Sixty-three people were injured and more than 100 vehicles smashed up as freezing fog gripped the M1 and M10 yesterday... The AA described it as 'the worst snarl-up since the M1 opened'. **1974** *Financial Times* 15 Mar. 23/7 Small organisation snarl-ups, such as failing to get out the Speakers' Handbook in time. **1977** 'E. Crispin' *Glimpses of Moon* xi. 220 A helicopter..dipped to examine the snarl-up in the lane below.

**'snarly,** *a.*[1] Now *dial.* [f. SNARL *sb.*[1] or *v.*[1]]

1. Tangled, ravelled.

**1647** G. W. *Grand Pluto's Progr. thro. Gt. Brit.* 15 Thy snarly haire, thy cheeks as red As paint that they on signes do spread. **1876** Robinson *Whitby Gloss.* 178/1 *Snarly*, knotty or twisted, as entangled thread.

2. Full of snarls or knots.

**1770** Washington *Writ.* (1889) II. 311 Walnut, cherry, and some other woods that grow snarly and neither tall nor large. **1890** *Gloucester Gloss.* 144 *Snarly*, knotty, cross-grained; of wood.

**snarly** ('snɑːlɪ), *a.*[2] [f. SNARL *sb.*[2] or *v.*[2]] Inclined to snarl; irritable, cross. Also *transf.*

**1798** *Monthly Mag.* VI. 346 My wine's a cure for anguish, My sword for snarly puppies. **1827–** in *Eng. Dial. Dict.* **1838** *Penny Cycl.* XII. 400/2 He [a mad dog] grows sullen and snarly; he..runs about wildly, biting at whatever approaches him. **1869** Mrs. Stowe *Oldtown Folks* xxii, We all know that..the hyena [is] snarly and fretful. **1879** E. M. Cole *Place-names* 31 The weather is said to be 'snarly' when there is a keen cutting wind in Winter.

**snar-noise.** *nonce-word.* [f. SNAR *v.*] A snarling or angry noise.

**1582** Stanyhurst *Æneis* I. (Arb.) 25 Rough the sea floas forward, thee land with snarnoise enhaunting.

†**snarp,** *a. Obs.* [a. ON. *snarp-r* (Norw. *snarp*).] Sharp, keen.

*Snarp* should prob. be read in *Cursor M.* 7753: for the quot. see SNAIP *a.*

*c* **1375** *Sc. Leg. Saints* xxxiii. (*George*) 547 Snarpe [*so MS.*] swerdis scherand in al syde.

Hence **'snarply** *adv.*, sharply.

*a* **1300** *Cursor M.* 18228 And selcut snarpli [*Gött. MS.* snapli, *Laud & Trin. MSS.* sharply] snibbed him.

**snarring:** see SNAR *v.*

†**'snarry,** *a. Obs.*⁻¹ [f. SNAR *v.*] Snarling.

**1582** Stanyhurst *Æneis* III. (Arb.) 84 Whear curs barck bawling, with yolp yalpe snarrye rebounding.

†**snart,** *adv.* and *a. Obs.* [a. ON. *snart* neut. (also as adv.) of *snarr* (Norw., Sw., Da. *snar*) quick, prompt, sharp, etc.] a. *adv.* Sharply, severely. b. *adj.* Severe, strong.

**13..** *Gaw. & Gr. Knt.* 2003 Þe snawe snitered ful snart, Þat snayped þe wylde. *a* **1400–50** *Alexander* 3633 Þire Olifantis..sone was snaypid on þe snowte with þe snart hetis.

Hence †**'snartly** *adv. Obs.*

*c* **1420** *Anturs of Arth.* vii. (Douce MS.), Þe sneterand snawe snartly hem snelles.

**snary** ('snɛərɪ), *a.* [f. SNARE *sb.* + -Y.] Of the nature of, resembling, a snare; ensnaring.

**1592** Daniel *Sonn. Delia* xiv. Wks. (Grosart) I. 45 Those snary locks are those same nets..Wherewith my liberty thou didst surprise. **1697** Dryden *Virg. Georg.* IV. 361 Spiders in the Vault their snary Webs have spred.

**snash** (snaʃ), *sb. Sc.* (and *north. dial.*). [Related to SNASH *v.*] Abuse, impertinence, insolence.

**1786** Burns *Twa Dogs* 96 Poor tenant bodies,..How they maun thole a factor's snash. **1832–53** *Whistle-Binkie* Ser. I. 55 Xantippe's sel', wi' snash sae snell, Was but a lamb compared wi' Betty. **1898** Macmanus *Bend of Road* 102, I doubt if they'd put up with yer *snash* elsewhere.

**snash** (snaʃ), *v. Sc.* [prob. imitative. Cf. WFris. *snasje, snaskje*, Sw. *snaska*, in sense 2; MLG. *snascherie* eating of dainties.]

1. *intr.* To use abusive or impertinent language.

**1802** Galloway *Adm. Crichton*, etc. 77 Until he get ye by degrees To snash and snarl. **1818** W. Muir *Poems* 25 Wae worth them, wha jeering snash.

2. To bite *at* hastily and noisily.

**1856** *Deil's Hallowe'en* 29 (E.D.D.), Ilk deevil, dippin' in his headie, Snashed at the apples unco greedy.

**snaste** (sneɪst), *sb.* Now *dial.* Also 7, 9 **snast**, 9 **snaast, snaist, sneest(e**; 6 **snase**, 9 **snace, snaice, sneeze.** [Of obscure origin: cf. GNAST.] A candle-wick: freq. the burning or burnt part of a wick, a snuff.

**1592** Greene *Upst. Courtier* G iv b, After your weeke or snast [*pr.* snaft] is stiffened, you dip it in filthy drosse. **1596** Nashe *Saffron Walden* Wks. (Grosart) III. 203 His stinking breath, (which smells like the greasie snase of a candle). **1626** Bacon *Sylva* §369 Till some part of the Candle was consumed, and the Dust gathered about the Snast; But then it made the Snaste big, and long, and to burn duskishly. **1646** Sir T. Browne *Pseud. Ep.* 140 In our daies doe men practise to make long-lasting Snasts for lampes. **1691** Ray *N.C. Words, The Snaste*, the burnt Week or Snuffe of a Candle. *a* **1825–** in dial. glossaries, etc. (Northampt., E. Anglia, Essex).

†**snaste,** *v. Obs. rare.* [Cf. prec.] *trans.* To snuff (a candle). Also *fig.*

**1561** Daus tr. *Bullinger on Apoc.* 51 He had the charge.. of seuen candels, for those must he pourge and snaste. *Ibid.*, He..snasteth and pourgeth by faithe, what thinge so euer hath nede to be pourged.

†**snat,** obs. variant of SNOT *sb.*

**1573** Baret *Alv.*, Sneuell, the snat or filth of the noze.

**snatch** (snætʃ), *sb.* Also 4 **snacche, snasche, snache**, 6 **snach, snatche.** [f. SNATCH *v.*]

†1. A hasp, catch, or fastening. *Obs. rare.*

**1341–2** *Ely Sacr. Rolls* (1907) II. 118 In factura..lasches snasches et rening barres pro hostio pro les nouises. **1527–8** *Rec. St. Mary at Hid* 343 Paid for mending of a snach in the morrow mas prestes chist.

†2. A trap, snare, entanglement. *Obs.*

**13..** *K. Alis.* 6559 (Laud MS.), No man ne may hym [*sc.* the unicorn] lacche, Bot by gyle & by snacche. **1568** T. Howell *Arb. Amitie* (1879) 43 By dailie doome these precepts vewe, to scape the bayted snatch. **1581** J. Bell *Haddon's Answ. Osor.* 20 b, You are caught..and so entangled in this snatch, that ye cannot escape. **1620** Shelton *Quix.* III. i, The Chevalier del Febo, being taken in a Gin like unto a Snatch that slipped under his feet. **1655** Baily *Life of Fisher* xxi. 162 They think to take me in a Poppes snatch, but they are deceived.

3. a. A hasty catch or grasp; a sudden grab or snap *at* something. Freq. *fig.*

**1577–87** Holinshed *Chron.* II. 514 At which words George Buchanan giveth a snatch. **1590** Spenser *F.Q.* III. i. 22 Like dastard Curres, that..rome from place to place, To get a snatch, when turned is his face. **1611** Bible *Transl. Pref.* ¶2 Happy is he that is least tossed vpon tongues; for vtterly to escape the snatch of them it is impossible. **1651** N. Bacon *Disc. Govt. Eng.* II. (1739) 175 What was gotten by the snatch was lost by the catch. **1821** Scott *Kenilw.* xx, The fawning wile of the spaniel, the determined snatch of the mastiff. **1873** M. Arnold *Lit. & Dogma* (1876) 226 Here and there he made guesses and snatches at the truth.

b. A catch, check, or hesitancy. *rare*⁻¹.

**1611** Shaks. *Cymb.* IV. ii. 105 The snatches in his voice, And burst of speaking were as his.

c. A sudden twitch or jerk. *rare*⁻¹.

**1822–7** Good *Study Med.* (1829) IV. 477 The movements of his arms were indeed in ungraceful snatches, and the muscles of the neck frequently evinced a like convulsive start.

d. (*a*) An unexpected and quick robbery; an act of forcibly robbing someone; (*b*) *slang* (orig. and chiefly *U.S.*), a kidnapping; also *attrib.*

(*a*) **1866** *Morn. Star* 21 Aug. 3/2 He saw him..walk a few steps in advance of her, then suddenly turn and make 'the snatch' in question. **1885** M. Davitt *Leaves from Prison Diary* I. I. xvi. 152, I did a snatch near St. Paul's. **1939** *Forum* Dec. 275/2 A piece of paper covering the slit was rolled aside in the course of a snatch. **1976** *Southern Even. Echo* (Southampton) 17 Nov. 17/2 Basingstoke police warned women to hang on to their handbags after a sixth attempted snatch in recent weeks. **1980** *West Lancs. Even. Gaz.* 6 June 1 An engineering labourer who was stabbed.. during a wage snatch on Merseyside.

(*b*) **1931** D. Runyon in *Collier's* 26 Sept. 7/2 Harry the Horse and Spanish John and Little Isadore pay no attention whatever to local sentiment and go on the snatch. **1932** E. D. Sullivan *Snatch Racket* p. x, Bootleg millions..have provided the sound support for two hundred standard rackets..in the United States and among them is kidnapping—the 'snatch racket'. **1934** 'D. Hume' *Too Dangerous to Live* xix. 200 Where did this snatch take place, Inspector? **1945** —— *Come back for Body* ii. 21 Their only child..has vanished. It looks like a straightforward snatch. **1950** J. D. MacDonald *Brass Cupcake* ii. 21, I handle it just like a snatch payment. The ransom for Junior. **1980** C. Moorehead *Fortune's Hostages* ii. 26 By 1932 America was in the middle of..the 'snatch racket'. Dozens of children had been seized... Kidnapping was happening everywhere.

**e.** *Weight-lifting.* A lift in which the weight is raised in a single motion from the floor to a position overhead with the arms straight.

**1928**, etc. [see press *sb.*[1] 6c]. **1950** *Sun* (Baltimore) 1 May 15/4 Sheppard lifted 240 in the snatch. **1968** *Globe & Mail* (Toronto) 17 Feb. 11/3 Modern lifters do not perform one-arm lifts. Once, two of them were on the Olympic agenda: the one-arm press and the one-arm snatch. **1976** *All about Games* (Com. Org. des Jeux Olympiques) 81 There are two lifts in modern weight-lifting—the snatch and the clean and jerk.

**f.** Jerkiness in the working of the transmission of a motor vehicle.

**1932** *Motoring Encycl.* 137/1 A little thin oil..will soften the [clutch] surfaces sufficiently to avoid snatch. **1955** *Times* 2 Aug. 10/5 Upward and downward changes were made without any trace of snatch. **1962** *Which? Car Suppl.* Oct. 139/1 The car was in excellent condition, apart from..a little 'snatch' in the transmission.

**4.** *by*, or *in, snatches*, by hasty, unsustained efforts; hurriedly, by fits and starts; intermittently, interruptedly, not continuously. Also rarely *at..snatches*.

(*a*) **1577** B. Googe *Heresbach's Husb.* ii. (1586) 48 By snatches (as it were) and not throughly. **1625** *Commons Deb.* (Camden) 101 What is it..to get or lose a towne by snatches? **1665** Manley *Grotius' Low C. Wars* 507 Hitherto all that was done, was by snatches and intervals, as it were at a breathing. **1733** Pope *Let. to Swift* 28 May, I have begun two or three letters to you by Snatches, and been prevented from finishing them. **1753-4** Richardson *Grandison* (1781) VII. 182 When..she now-and-then could look up, which she did by snatches, as it were. **1837** Lockhart *Scott* (1839) IX. 59 The little that he read of new books..was done by snatches in the course of his meals. **1898** Baring-Gould *Old Eng. Home* xi. 250 He has to take his victuals and his rest by snatches.

(*b*) **1799** J. Robertson *Agric. Perth* 169 The business..must often..be done in snatches, or not done at all. **1850** S. Dobell *Roman* vi. Poet. Wks. (1875) 74 Passing gales in snatches bore me Their evening talk. **1897** Miss Kingsley *W. Africa* 287, I went in again and slept in snatches.

(*c*) **1692** Burnet *Life & Death Rochester* 138 He told me as his strength served him at several snatches.

**5. a.** A brief period, short space (*of* time).

**1563** Foxe *A. & M.* 1187/2, I wene we shall haue a snatch of rebellion euen now. **1573** Tusser *Husb.* li. (1878) 113 Then after a shower to weeding a snatch. **1619** Hieron *Wks.* II. 451 By day is not meant now and then a snatch, or a piece of the forenoone only. **1646** Sir T. Browne *Pseud. Ep.* To Rdr., In this work attempts will exceed performances; it being composed by snatches of time. **1663** Bunyan *Praying in Spirit* Wks. 1855 I. 623 One [vizard] for an appearance before men, and another for a short snatch in a corner. **1825** Lamb *Elia* ii. *Superannuated Man*, The..tedious weeks that must intervene before such another snatch [of holidays] would come. **1893** Stevenson *Catriona* xxix. 339, I was scarce so miserable the next days but what I had many hopeful and happy snatches.

**b.** *esp.* A short spell *of* sleep or slumber.

**1820** L. Hunt *Indicator* xiv, The most relishing snatch of slumber out of bed. **1863** Mrs. Oliphant *Salem Chapel* xxi, Snatches of momentary sleep..had fallen upon her.

**c.** A brief manifestation or display *of* something.

**1880** Jefferies *Gt. Est.* 32 The sunshine broods warm over the mead. It is a delicious snatch of spring. **1885** *Manch. Exam.* 14 July 5/1 Those snatches of fitful energy which mark the movements of the East.

**6. a.** A hasty meal or morsel; a snack.

**1573** Tusser *Husb.* lxxvi. (1878) 168 Call seruants to breakfast by day starre appere, a snatch and to worke. **1611** Beaum. & Fl. *Knt. Burning Pestle* ii. i, Believe me, To sleep without a snatch would mickle grieve me. **1623** Massinger *Dk. Milan* iii. ii, I fear you'll have cold entertainment..; and 'twere discretion To take a snatch by the way. **1694** Motteux *Rabelais* v. vi, After we had pretty well staid our Stomachs with some tight Snatches. **1791** Boswell *Johnson* (1831) II. 490 Our kind host and hostess would not let us go without a snatch as they called it; which was in truth a very good dinner. **1823** E. Moor *Suffolk Words, Snatch*, a mouthful between meals. **1893** Walker *Three Churchmen* vii. 76 He took only a snatch or light refection, returning immediately to his desk.

†**b.** In allusive use (see quots.). *Obs.*

**1592** Greene *Upst. Court.* Wks. (Grosart) XI. 256 Tush! what bawdry is it he wil not suffer, so he may have mony and good chere, and, if he like the wench well, a snatch himselfe. **1611** Cotgr. s.v. *Pain, Prendre vn pain sur la fournée*, to get a snatch at his wench thats readie to be maried. **1621** Burton *Anat. Mel.* iii. ii. v. iii. 648 They had rather go to the stewes, or haue now and then a snatch.., then haue wiues of their owne.

†**c.** A share; a portion seized on. *Obs.*

**1601** Holland *Pliny* I. 368 And not only these haue a share, but also..other seruitors pill and poll, and euery one hath a snatch. *a* **1610** Healey *Theophrastus* (1636) 51 Those which sacrifice and feast he makes great love to, hoping to get a snatch.

**7. a.** A small amount or portion (†taken hurriedly); a mere fragment or disconnected piece.

**1592** Harvey *Four Lett.* iv. 57 A snatch, and away, with..the common sort of studentes, may please a little, but profiteth nothing. **1656** Baxter *Reformed Pastor* 20 It is not now and then an idle snatch or taste of studies that will serve to make a sound Divine. **1673** *Remarques Hum. Town* 124 You will hear..some snatches of occurences, whose beauty you are not able to perceive without the knowledge of the whole. **1732** H. Walpole *Lett.* (1903) I. 1 That little snatch of conversation was so agreeable. **1780** Johnson in *Boswell* (Oxf. ed.) II. 347 Snatches of reading..will not make a Bentley or a Clarke. **1809** Malkin *Gil Blas* ii. vi. ¶5 The barber..had heard some little snatches of my story from Fabricio. **1865** Carlyle *Fredk. Gt.* xiii. iv. (1872) V. 43 We had better give the snatch of Dialogue in primitive authentic form. **1890** Stevenson *Vailima Lett.* (1895) 12, I returned to begin this snatch of a letter before dinner was ready.

**b.** A brief view; a glimpse.

**1816** L. Hunt *Rimini* ii. 133 For leafy was the road, with..distant snatches of blue hills between. **1842** Louisa S. Costello *Auvergne* I. 319 Planted with gigantic trees, from openings between which are charming snatches of country.

**8. a.** A short passage, a few words, *of* a song, etc.; a small portion, a few bars, *of* a melody or tune.

**1602** Shaks. *Ham.* iv. vii. 178 Which time she chaunted snatches of old tunes. **1795-1814** Wordsw. *Excurs.* i. 569 He..whistled many a snatch of merry tunes. **1818** Scott *Hrt. Midl.* xl, Madge was..singing her own wild snatches of songs and obsolete airs. **1837** Carlyle *Fr. Rev.* iii. iii. viii, Not a musical Patriot can blow himself a snatch of melody from the French Horn. **1884** F. M. Crawford *Rom. Singer* I. 10 It was quite natural that he should..begin to sing a snatch of the tenor air to me.

**b.** *ellipt.* in the same senses.

**1823** Lamb *Elia* ii. *New Year's Coming of Age*, Singing..a number of old snatches besides, between drunk and sober. **1847** Alb. Smith *Chr. Tadpole* vii. (1879) 66 Having carolled which snatches, he played a kind of symphony. **1890** Saintsbury *Elizab. Lit.* i. 9 Sometimes..both syntax and prosody..recall the ruder snatches of an earlier time.

†**9.** A quibble; a captious argument. *Obs.*

**1603** Shaks. *Meas. for M.* iv. ii. 6 Come sir, leaue me your snatches, and yeeld mee a direct answere. **1687** R. L'Estrange *Answ. Dissenter* 33 There are several Snatches in This Paper, that are either Founded, or Pretend to be Founded upon the Resolution, and Obligation of Laws.

**10.** That which is obtained in snatches.

**1879** J. D. Long *Æneid* p. v, This, the snatch and pastime of the last year, is not printed because there is want of it.

**11.** *ellipt.* (See quot. 1867 and snatch-block.)

*c* **1850** *Rudim. Navig.* (Weale) 98 The hawser is hauled in through the snatch. **1867** Smyth *Sailor's Word-bk.* 636 *Snatch*, any open lead for a rope: if not furnished with a sheave, it is termed a *dumb snatch*, as on the bows and quarters for hawsers. **1882** Nares *Seamanship* (ed. 6) 180 The snatch for the mast rope must be fitted with a bolt.

**12.** *Mining.* (See quot.)

**1860** *Eng. & For. Mining Gloss.* (ed. 2) 79 *Snatch*, a small chimney at surface,..used to ventilate very limited underground workings by means of one shaft.

**13.** An illicit line used in fishing.

**1899** in *Eng. Dial. Dict.* s.v., Charged with using a snatch for the purpose of catching salmon.

**14.** *dial.* and *slang.* The female pudenda. Also *attrib.* Cf. sense 6b.

**1904** in *Eng. Dial. Dict.* **1955** W. Gaddis *Recognitions* iii. iv. 851 She said, See? and pulled up her dress to show me her..to show there weren't any marks on her...anywhere else on her body.—You mean on her snatch. **1961** J. Heller *Catch-22* xxvii. 303 She..twisted away, fleeing far enough..for Yossarian to lunge forward and grab her by the snatch again. **1969** P. Roth *Portnoy's Complaint* 193 Know what I did when I was fifteen? Sent a lock of my snatch-hair off in an envelope to Marlon Brando. **1971** B. W. Aldiss *Soldier Erect* 128, I was vexed and disappointed that the contact with the *bibi* had been so commercial, so perfunctory—why, I had not even seen or touched her snatch. **1978** J. Updike *Coup* (1979) v. 191 Sooner a black man mate with a lazy shit-smeared sow..than entrust his ebony penis to the snatch of a white devil mare.

**snatch** (snætʃ), *v.* Also 3 snecchen, 4-5 snacche, snache, 6 snach, snatche; 7 *pa. t.* snaught. [Of obscure origin: perhaps related to snack *sb.*[2]]

**1.** *intr.* **a.** To make a sudden snap or bite (*at* something).

*a* **1225** *Ancr. R.* 324 Ase ofte ase þe hund of helle kecched ei god from þe,..smit hine so luðerliche þet him loðie to snecchen eft to þe. **1398** Trevisa *Barth. De P.R.* xviii. xxvi. 788 Whan þei [flies] fleeþ aȝens his face, he [a hounde] snaccheþ after [**1495** snatchyth at] hem wiþ his mouþe. *c* **1400** *Beryn* 651 The dogg lay evir grownyng, redy for to snache. **1568** *Jacob & Esau* ii. ii, *Esau.* If I had thee, I woulde eate thee, to God I vowe... *Ragau.* Fall ye to snatching at folkes: adieu, I am gone. **1595** Shaks. *John* iv. i. 117 And, like a dogge that is compell'd to fight, Snatch at his Master that doth tarre him on. **1718** Bp. Hutchinson *Witchcraft* 6 In that Madness..the Person will Bark, and Snatch at those that are near. **1828** [see snatch- b].

*fig.* **1561** T. Norton *Calvin's Inst.* i. To Rdr., I thinke there is no man, that hath ben snatched at, bitten, & torne in sonder with moe sclaunders than I. **1581** J. Bell *Haddon's Answ. Osor.* 59 b, You come at the length to our Church, the orders whereof you do captiously snatch at.

**b.** To make a sudden catch *at* a thing, in order to secure hold or possession of it. Also *fig.*

**1530** Palsgr. 723/2, I snatche at a thynge hastelye to take it, *je happe apres.* **1590** Shaks. *Mids. N.* iii. ii. 29 Briars and thornes at their apparell snatch. **1604** —— *Oth.* v. ii. 275 This looke of thine will hurle my Soule from Heauen, And Fiends will snatch at it. **1665** Manley *Grotius' Low-C. Wars* 375 The Government..was snatched at on the one side by the Wife..: On the other side, by some Noblemen. **1789** Mme. D'Arblay *Diary* 6 Jan., I had previously entreated my father to snatch at any possible opportunity of expressing his satisfaction. **1829** Scott *Anne of G.* i, All..snatched at bushes and rocks by which to secure themselves. **1831** —— *Cast. Dang.* xix, To snatch at any such occasion as shall be ministered to me. **1882** J. Parker *Apost. Life* I. 93 The Apostles did not snatch at praise for themselves.

**2. a.** *trans.* To seize, to take or lay hold of, suddenly, smartly, or unexpectedly.

*c* **1330** R. Brunne *Chron. Wace* (Rolls) 13889 þe lyon for hunger snacches & sleþ þe best þat he first lacches. **1526** Skelton *Magnyf.* 1170 Snatche a puddyng tyl the rost be redy. **1590** Spenser *F.Q.* i. ii. 17 The Sarazin..Snatcheth his sword, and fiercely to him flies. **1616** J. Lane *Contn. Sqr.'s T.* vii. 262 Algarsife..snaught his swoord, and with a loftie whiff, rann vppon Camball. **1687** A. Lovell tr. *Thevenot's Trav.* ii. 60 He snatches a man, and jumping into the water with him, carries him over to the other side. **1728** Young *Love Fame* i. 47 Will no superior genius snatch the quill, And save me, on the brink, from writing ill? **1837** Carlyle *Fr. Rev.* i. v. iv, All green things are snatched, and made cockades of. **1841** Lane *Arab. Nts.* I. 83 The fisherman hastily snatched the sealed leaden stopper.

*fig.* **1597** Shaks. *2 Hen. IV*, iv. v. 192 It seem'd in mee, But as an Honour snatch'd with boyst'rous hand. **1823** Scott *Quentin D.* i, Those advantages, which..the Duke would have snatched with an armed hand.

**b.** With immaterial object: To take, obtain, acquire, etc., in a hasty or improper manner, or so as to take advantage of a momentary chance.

**1563** Foxe *A. & M.* 1367/1, I could wyshe more faythfull dealyng with Gods woorde, and not to..snatche a part here and another there. **1598** Drayton *Heroical Ep.* viii. 98 My lips haue waited,..And snatch'd his words, ere he could get them forth. **1621** G. Sandys *Ovid's Met.* ii. (1626) 30 What should shee doe? but..snatch a parting kisse? **1667** Milton *P.L.* x. 1025, I fear least Death So snatcht will not exempt us from the paine. **1726** Berkeley *Let.* Wks. 1871 IV. 138, I shall nevertheless snatch the present moment to write you short answers. **1789** Belsham *Ess.* I. xi. 212 Let not..persons..pretend to snatch those graces which are beyond the reach of art. **1829** Lytton *Disowned* 40 Let us snatch what happiness is yet in our power. **1879** *19th Cent.* No. 32. 665 He seeks, at times, to snatch a verdict for his client by ignoring..evidence. **1891** *Labour Commission Gloss.*, *Snatching a victory* by getting an advance in wages. The method employed is to choose a time when the masters are divided in opinion.

†**c.** *refl.* To catch or entangle (oneself). *Obs.*[−1]

**1575** Gascoigne *Flowers*, etc. Wks. 1907 I. 99 His wayting still to snatch himselfe in snare.

**d.** *spec.* (*a*) To steal, esp. by snatching; (*b*) *slang* (orig. and chiefly *U.S.*), to kidnap.

**1765** *Ann. Reg.* i. 215 It was agreed that Matthews and Byfield should that night pick pockets or snatch hats. **1887** G. W. Walling *Recollections N.Y. Chief of Police* xviii. 254 His most brilliant exploit was his 'snatching' of $100,000 from the Royal Insurance Company's office in Broadway in broad daylight. **1919** Wodehouse *Coming of Bill* (1920) i. i. 12 As if she had caught him in the act of endeavouring to snatch her purse. **1932** *Detective Fiction Weekly* 17 Dec. 23/2 It's dollars to doughnuts the kid was snatched up in the park. **1934** *Sun* (Baltimore) 10 Mar. 1/7 Banghart had introduced him to the Touhy mob just before the market speculator was 'snatched'. **1936** *Detective Fiction Weekly* 6 June 12/1 It's one more sweet-running crate. Just about the sweetest I ever snatched. **1973** 'I. Drummond' *Jaws of Watchdog* xii. 156 Why didn't we snatch him in the street and take him away someplace?

**e.** To partake hurriedly of (food, sleep, etc.).

**1803** M. Wilmot *Let.* 6 Aug. in *Russian Jrnls.* (1934) i. 34 We rose with one accord, dress'd, snatch'd a cup of Coffee and got into Mdm R——'s Carriage. **1942** Berrey & Van den Bark *Amer. Thes. Slang* §94/13 *Eat a small or hurried meal*,..snatch a bite. *Ibid.* §251/6 *Take a nap*,..snatch a wink. **1952** M. Steen *Phoenix Rising* i. 27 I'm snatching a sandwich at the club. **1977** M. Kenyon *Rapist* x. 121 He might snatch two hours' sleep..if he swallowed a couple of sleepers.

**f.** *to snatch it* or *one's time*: to resign, to leave a job and take the wages due. *Austral. slang.*

**1941** *Argus* (Melbourne) *Week-End Mag.* 15 Nov. 1/4 *Snatch your time*, resign from the Army, or threaten to leave. **1944** A. Marshall *These are my People* 158 'I suppose you struck some bad bosses in your time?' 'If they're bad, I snatch it.' **1962** T. Ronan *Deep of Sky* 55 What's more, when we pass Silverton I'm snatching my time. **1973** F. Huelin *Keep Moving* 83 What are yous goin' to do? Snatch it or stay?

**3. a.** To seize, catch, or take suddenly *from* or *out of* one's hands, etc.

**1590** Spenser *F.Q.* ii. i. 43 Out of her gored wound the cruell steele He lightly snatcht. **1617** Moryson *Itin.* i. 219 They sent out their boyes to scorne us, who..snatched from us our hats and other things. **1663** S. Patrick *Parab. Pilgr.* xxiii. (1687) 245 She sometimes..threw it abroad among the people; and then again snatched it out of their hands. **1737** [S. Berington] *Mem. G. de Lucca* (1738) 106 He snatch'd it out of my Hands with a prodigious Eagerness. **1812** Cary *Dante, Parad.* iii. 109 [Men] Forth snatch'd me from the pleasant cloister's pale. **1878** M. A. Brown *Nadeschda* 35 He hurries off, with the intent to snatch The savage garland from her locks.

*fig.* **1607** Shaks. *Timon* iv. iii. 441 The Moones an arrant Theefe, And her pale fire, she snatches from the Sunne. **1651** Hobbes *Leviath.* i. viii. 33 Such as they have, that entring into any discourse, are snatched from their purpose. **1781** Cowper *Table-T.* 689 He snatch'd it [the laurel] rudely from the muses' hand. **1825** Scott *Talism.* viii, Nor befits it our fame that a brave adversary be snatched from our weapon by such a disease. **1848** Gallenga *Italy* I. p. xxvi, The sons of the north are snatching from your hands the sceptre of the arts.

*absol.* **1674** N. Fairfax *Bulk & Selv.* To Rdr., While we..snip here and snatch there from some of them.

**b.** With immaterial object. (Cf. 2b.)

**1588** Shaks. *L.L.L.* v. ii. 382 It were a fault to snatch words from my tongue. **1725** Pope *Odyss.* i. 13 Oh, snatch some portion of these acts from fate, Celestial Muse! **1755** Johnson *Let.* 4 Feb. in *Boswell*, Snatch what time you can from the Hall, and the pupils [etc.]. **1795** Coleridge *Sibyl. Leaves, Eolian Harp* 10 How exquisite the scents Snatched from yon bean-field! **1845** James *Arrah Neil* iv, All were anxious to snatch a few hours from the gloomy thoughts that hung over the times. **1871** Freeman *Norm. Conq.* (1876) IV. 116 That a new English host was coming to snatch the victory from the conquerors.

**c.** To remove or avert hastily. Const. *from*.

**1796** Mme. D'Arblay *Camilla* I. 316 She snatched her hands from her face. **1855** Tennyson *Brook* 101 But Katie snatch'd her eyes at once from mine.

**4.** With adverbs: †**a.** With *down*: To devour hastily. *Obs.*$^{-1}$

**1519** Horman *Vulg.* 39b, Beware snatche nat thy meate downe to gredelye.

**b.** To catch, pick, or take *up*, suddenly or smartly.

**1555** Eden *Decades* (Arb.) 173 One of these wylde men.. soodenly snatched vppe a childe of therse. **1592** *Ard. of Feversham* v. i, Chast Diana Would.. Fling down Endimion and snatch him vp. **1638** F. Junius *Paint. Ancients* 112 So were they taught that Art whose instruments they had snatched up. **1698** Fryer *Acc. E. India & P.* 276 The Women.. never are snatch'd up for their Great Fortunes. **1784** Cowper *Task* v. 49 His dog.. snatches up the drifted snow With iv'ry teeth. **1837** Carlyle *Fr. Rev.* I. I. iii, Scarcely.. could they snatch up their 'enormous hoops'. *transf.* **1575** Gascoigne *Certain Notes Instruct.* (Arb.) 33 The light accent is depressed or snatched vp.

**c.** To seize and take *away* suddenly.

**1608** Shaks. *Per.* III. i. 24 Why do you make us love your goodly gifts, And snatch them straight away? **1684** *Contempl. State Man* I. ii. (1699) 15 That which Time spares, is often snatcht away by the covetousness of the Thief. *a* **1770** Jortin *Serm.* (1771) II. xvii. 332 The Devil is here said to snatch the wood away from such persons. **1820** Shelley *Hymn Merc.* xxix, And from the portion.. I will snatch my share away.

**d.** To pull or tear *off* quickly (and roughly).

**1687** A. Lovell tr. *Thevenot's Trav.* I. 33 They snatch it quickly off of the fire, or stir it. **1709** Steele *Tatler* No. 45 ⁋7, I snatched his Hat off his Head. *a* **1763** W. King *Polit. & Lit. Anecd.* (1819) 63 One of Cromwell's soldiers snatched off Sir William Smyth's hat. **1847** Sarah Austin *Ranke's Hist. Ref.* III. 371 Those who were standing near snatched off the wax of the seal.

**5.** To remove quickly *from* sight, etc.; to hide or conceal suddenly.

**1582** Stanyhurst *Æneis* I. (Arb.) 20 Thee clowds snach gloomming from sight of Coompanie Troian Both Light and welken. **1711** Pope *Temple Fame* 354 A sudden cloud strait snatch'd them from my sight. **1835** Lytton *Rienzi* I. xii. 90 The long herbage, and the winding descent, soon snatched her ill-omened apparition from the desolate landscape. **1887** Bowen *Æneid* I. 88 Clouds snatch from the Teucrians' sight Sunlight and sky.

**6. a.** To remove suddenly from this world or life. Used in passive and freq. with *away* and *from*.

**1597** Hooker *Eccl. Pol.* v. xlvi. §1 Rather to bee taken then snatched away from the face of the earth. **1601** Shaks. *All's Well* v. iii. 154, I am a-feard the life of Hellen (Ladie) Was fowly snatcht. **1655** Fuller *Ch. Hist.* IX. 110 William Bradbridge.. was snatcht away with a sudden death. **1694** F. Bragge *Disc. Parables* ix. 335 The covetous rich fool, that trusted in his riches,.. was suddenly snatched from them to give account of his stewardship. **1752** Berkeley *Th. Tar-water* Wks. III. 501 Several who are snatched away by untimely death. **1781** Cowper *Retirem.* 167 They.., unregretted, are soon snatch'd away From scenes of sorrow into glorious day. **1837** Carlyle *Fr. Rev.* II. III. vii, Wailing ..that a Sovereign Man is snatched away. **1888** Burgon *Lives 12 Good Men* I. Pref. p. xiv, He was snatched away while affording.. fresh promise of a truly brilliant Professorial career.

**b.** To cut off *from*, by sudden removal.

**1799** Cowper *Castaway* 63 When, snatch'd from all effectual aid, We perish'd, each alone.

**7.** To save or rescue *from* or *out of* danger, etc., by prompt or vigorous action.

**1601** Shaks. *Twel. N.* III. iv. 394 This youth that you see heere, I snatch'd one halfe out of the iawes of death. **1696** Tate & Brady *Ps.* cxliv. 7 And snatch me from the stormy Rage. **1737** Whiston *Josephus, Antiq.* vi. vi. 169 They snatched him out of the danger he was in. **1791** Burke *Corr.* (1844) III. 215 The men who.. snatch the worst criminals from justice. **1876** Miss Braddon *J. Haggard's Dau.* II. 22 Every soul snatched from darkness and death was a rich harvest. **1893** Matheson *About Holland* 10 A great part of it has been snatched from the sea.

**8.** In miscellaneous uses (see quots.).

**1648** J. Beaumont *Psyche* VII. cxxiv, Through the air they snatch'd their greedy way. **1657** W. Morice *Coena quasi Κοινή* xvi. 256 The Spartan valour, who being struck down by a mortal blow, used to snatch their mouths full of earth [etc.]. **1864** Tennyson *Aylmer's F.* 209 But Edith's eager fancy hurried with him Snatch'd thro' the perilous passes of his life.

**9.** *Naut.* To place (a line) in a snatch-block.

**1769** Falconer *Dict. Marine* (1780) Eee, To snatch the main-bowline, or put it into the snatch-block. **1840** R. H. Dana *Bef. Mast* xxxvi. 136 The line is snatched in a block upon the swifter. **1882** Nares *Seamanship* (ed. 6) 181 Snatch the top-gallant sheets.

**10.** *intr.* Of a mechanism or its control in a motor vehicle, aircraft, etc.: to operate in a jerky or rough manner.

**1932** *Motoring Encyl.* 137/1 When.. fabric disks have settled down and worn smooth, they are sometimes prone to snatch and engage fiercely. **1942** B. J. Ellan *Spitfire* xii. 65 His ailerons were obviously snatching too, as first one wing and then the other would dip violently. **1955** *Times* 12 July 12/6 The car tested was inclined to 'snatch' in the transmission if the speed was allowed to drop too low in top gear.

Hence **'snatching** *ppl. a.*

**1828** Scott *F.M. Perth* vi, Those naked, snatching mountaineers, who are ever doing us wrong.

**snatch-**, the verb-stem used in combs.:

**a.** *Naut.* Denoting devices capable of rapid attachment, or to which a rope can be quickly attached, as ***snatch-cheek***, ***-cleat***, ***-hook***, †***-pulley***, ***-sheave*** (cf. snatch-block).

**1485** *Naval Acc. Hen. VII* (1896) 50 Snache poleis, ij. **1495** *Ibid.* 192 Snache poleyes with oon shever of brasse to yᵉ same. **1842** R. Burn *Fr. Techn. Dict.* 162 *Taquet à gueule*, ..snatch-cleat. **1882** Nares *Seamanship* (ed. 6) 73 A snatch cheek on the after side of the.. yard-arm. *Ibid.* 76 Rove.. through a snatch sheave. **1891** *Cent. Dict.*, *Snatch-cleat*, a curved cleat or chock round which a rope may be led.

**b.** In objective combs., as ***snatch-apple***, †***-cly***, ***-grace***, †***-pasty*** (see quots.).

**1687** Miége *Gt. Fr. Dict.*, A Snatch-pasty, *un Voleur de Pâtez.* **1796** *Grose's Dict. Vulgar T.*, *Snatch cly*, a thief who snatches women's pockets. **1828** Carr *Craven Gloss.*, *Snatch-apple*, an apple suspended by a string, with which children amuse themselves by snatching at it with their teeth. **1884** Browning *Ferishtah* (1885) 65 No scape-grace? Then, rejoice Thou snatch-grace safe in Syria!

**c.** = snap- e.

**1884** E. W. Hamilton *Diary* 15 Mar. (1972) II. 577 A motion.. which.. the Opposition supported in the hope of taking the Government by surprise and putting them in a minority by a snatch division. **1889** *Spectator* 7 Dec., He secured a snatch-vote in favour of a permanent system of arbitration. **1893** *Times* 21 June 9/4 It is impossible to suppose the snatch-division.. has settled the point. **1895** *Westm. Gaz.* 22 June 5/3 What Ministerialists regard as a snatch reverse in Supply.

**d.** Denoting the practice or use of snatching, as ***snatch-thief***; **snatch-back**, the action of taking back; also *attrib.*; (see also quot. 1905); **snatch crop**, a crop grown for quick returns without regard to the future productivity of the soil; also *attrib.* and *fig.*; **snatch squad** *Mil.*, a group of soldiers detailed to seize troublemakers in a crowd; also *transf.*

**1905** *Dialect Notes* III. 94 *Snatchback*, change for the worse in circumstances... 'That's a snatchback for him.' **1949** *New Statesman* 24 Dec. 750/3 The distress caused by the snatch-back is no less tragic than would be suffered by natural parents who were forcibly deprived of their children. **1962** A. Sampson *Anat. of Britain* xxiii. 377 Hire-purchase.. companies.. could be ruthless in enforcing 'snatch-backs' if payments had lapsed. **1965** E. Gundrey *Foot in Door* xvii. 123 'Snatchback' machines, that is ones which had to be returned to dealers by people who failed to keep up their H.P. payments. **1979** H. S. Kent *In on Act* ix. 101 The main objects of the Bill were, first, to make sure that the hire-purchaser knew what he was paying.. secondly, to restrict the seller's rights to 'snatch back' the goods on default... The most dear to Ellen's heart was the ban on the snatch-back. **1937** H. G. Wells *Brynhild* v. 58 Fellows like Blatch can reap a harvest.. at ten per cent... There are too many authors. Blatch is able to live by snatch crops. **1959** *Listener* 30 July 179/2 The heart of the soil.. had been weakened by the greed of the snatch-crop farmers. **1970** *Financial Times* 23 Mar. 1/1 About 150 youths moved out of Bogside.., smashing windows.. and stoning the Army 'snatch squad'. **1976** *Western Mail* (Cardiff) 22 Nov. 1/2 A snatch squad of animal lovers seized 11 beagle pups in a night-time commando-style raid on a top-security breeding centre in West Wales. **1982** *Times* 1 Sept. 3/1 Snatch squads tried ineffectively to combat roaming gangs of pickpockets. **1887** *Courier-Jrnl.* (Louisville, Kentucky) 1 May 13/2 Where the bonnet-buyer is there is the pickpocket and snatch-thief also. **1892** *Boston* (Mass.) *Jrnl.* 3 Nov. 3/7 A snatch thief arrested. **1903** *19th Cent.* Mar. 507 The snatch-thief who relies on his swiftness of foot.

**'snatchable**, *adj.* [f. snatch *v.* + -able.] That may be snatched or seized.

**1896** A. Morrison *Child Jago* 167 Hoping for a temporary absence of the shop-keeper, which might leave something snatchable. **1899** W. James *Talks to Teachers* vi, The child sees a snatchable object in some one's hands.

**'snatch-block.** Also **snatchblock, snatch block.** [snatch- a.] A block having a hole in one side to receive the bight of a rope.

*a* **1625** *Nomenclator Navalis* (MS. Harl. 2301), *Snatch block* is a greate Block with the Sheever in it and a Notch cutt through one of the Cheeks of it by which Notch they reeve anie Roape into it. [Hence in Harris, *Chambers's Cycl.* Suppl., etc.] **1769** Falconer *Dict. Marine* (1780) s.v. *Block*, A snatch-block; a top-block; a voyal-block [etc.]. **1793** *Trans. Soc. Arts* XI. 173 Passing through proper snatch-blocks. **1839** *Civil Eng. & Arch. Jrnl.* II. 97/2 A car.. is suspended to the top round of the ladder by means of a chain passing over a pulley of a snatch block. **1886** R. C. Leslie *Sea Painter's Log* 145 This line, when the boat is launched, passes through.. a snatch-block.

**snatched** (snætʃt), *ppl. a.* [f. snatch *v.*] Hurriedly or hastily obtained or taken.

**1615** G. Sandys *Trav.* I. 84 Full boules Of wine powr'd on; and goblets (gladding soules) Of blacke bloud, and snatcht [L. *rapti*] milke. **1834** Mar. Edgeworth *Helen* (Rtldg.) 129 These snatched moments.. enhanced the enjoyment. **1863** Geo. Eliot *Romola* vi, I remember.. a hastily snatched visit to Athens. **1892** *Pall Mall G.* 25 Jan. 6/3 This is no snatched victory.

**snatcher** ('snætʃə(r)). [f. snatch *v.*]

**1. a.** One who or that which snatches; a thief, a robber. (Also with *at* or *away*.)

**1575** *Mirr. Mag.*, *Tresilian* xi, So catchers and snatchers toyle both night and daye, Not needy but greedy, still prolling for their praye. **1582** Stanyhurst *Æneis* I. (Arb.) 29, I am kind Æneas, from foes thee snatcher of housgods. **1599** Shaks. *Hen. V*, I. ii. 143 We do not meane the coursing snatchers onely, But feare the maine intendment of the Scot. **1611** Cotgr., *Grippeur*, a griper; catcher, snatcher. **1648** Hexham II, *Een Rucker*, a Puller, or a Snatcher away. **1736** Ainsworth *Eng.-Lat. Dict.* I, A snatcher at, *captator.* **1805** Scott *Last Minstr.* IV. iv, Full oft the Tynedale snatchers knock At his lone gate. **1866** *Morn. Star* 21 Aug. 3/2 There having lately been a great many 'snatchers' in the neighbourhood of Whitechapel. **1868** Morris *Earthly Par.* (1870) I. II. 461 The snatchers.. Lurked round the gates of less well-guarded folds.

**b.** A body-snatcher. (See body *sb.* 30.)

**1831** *Ann. Reg.*, *Law Cases*, etc. 321/1 A person in the room.. told him that he must mind what he was at, as they were snatchers. **1884** A. Griffiths *Chron. Newgate* II. vii. 331 The snatchers brought a hamper which contained a body in a sack.

**c.** One who takes fish by 'snatching'.

**1878** *Standard* 21 Oct. (Davies), Some 'snatchers' will use two, three, or even four triangles.

**d.** *slang* (orig. *U.S.*). A kidnapper.

**1932** *Tulsa* (Okla.) *Daily World* 7 Mar. 10/5 'Snatchers' or kidnapers have not been as busy in Tulsa as they have in other cities. **1940** 'D. Hume' *Invitation to Grave* xviii. 235 Mick was reflecting upon the fact that his father's 'snatchers' had entered through this door.

**2.** *pl.* 'A book-name for the Raptores' (*Cassell's Encycl. Dict.* 1887).

**'snatchery.** *nonce-wd.* Snatching.

**1553** *Respublica* v. ix, Thou saiest even trueth, tis a bagg of Rye in dede:.. briberee, snatcherie, catcherie [etc.].

**snatchily** ('snætʃılı), *adv.* [f. snatchy *a.*] By or in snatches.

**1880** Miss Broughton *Sec. Th.* I. xii. 204 The book-case on whose ladder she has so often stood in cramped discomfort, snatchily reading.

**'snatching,** *vbl. sb.* [f. snatch *v.*]

**1.** The action of the verb.

**1526** Skelton *Magnyf.* 1143 *Fan.* Where the Deuyll gate he all these hurtes? *Fol.* By God, for snatchynge of puddynges and wortes. **1589** R. Harvey *Pl. Perc.* (1590) A iij, Soft maisters, faire plaie and no snatching. **1641** J. Jackson *True Evang. T.* I. 73 Our rapacity,.. our snatching, and catching, at far more then is our own. **1846** Trench *Mirac.* ix. (1862) 207 Snatchings on the part of the creature at honours which of right belonged only to the Creator. **1847** Bushnell *Chr. Nurture* II. iii. (1861) 282 The casual snatching and feeding at all hours. **1931** D. Runyon in *Collier's* 26 Sept. 7 (*heading*) The snatching of Bookie Bob. **1955** *Times* 26 July 6/6 As soon as the speed drops to 20 m.p.h., a change to third gear is essential to avoid 'snatching'. **1972** J. Philips *Vanishing Senator* (1973) III. ii. 127 They're all in a state over the snatching of Mrs. Lloyd.

**2.** Twitching.

**1822-7** Good *Study Med.* (1829) IV. 477 The limbs were in a state of constant snatching and trepidation.

**3.** The practice of catching fish by means of hooks which are pulled sharply through the water.

**1878** *Standard* 21 Oct. (Davies), 'Snatching' is a form of illicit piscicapture for which it is impossible to entertain.. sympathy. **1884** Jefferies in *Pall Mall G.* 6 Sept. 1/2 The fish.. are also protected by regulations..; snatching, for instance, is unlawful.

**4.** *techn.* (See quot.)

**1887** *Archit. Soc. Dict.*, *Snatching.* The term for making laths break bond for plastering.

**'snatchingly,** *adv.* [f. *snatching*, pres. pple. of snatch *v.*] In a snatching manner; hurriedly; by snatches.

**1552** Huloet, Bytynge one an other, or as snatchyngelye, *morsicatim.* **1588** Udall *Diotrephes* (Arb.) 8 You seeme to bee so possessed with discontentment that it maketh you to speak (as it were) snatchingly. **1629** H. C. *Disc. Draining Fens* A ij b, The prosecution of this businesse was.. so snatchingly persued, that little fruit came thereof. **1647** Hexham I, Snatchingly, *haestelick, ofte snellick.*

**snatchy** ('snætʃı), *a.* [f. snatch *sb.* or *v.*] Consisting of, characterized by, snatches; irregular; spasmodic.

**1861** *N. Brit. Rev.* May 351 The haste in which so many people live.. tends to foster a shallow and snatchy habit of mind. **1869** Mrs. Whitney *Hitherto* xiv, I like monosyllables. I like brief, snatchy talk. **1886** *Q. Rev.* Apr. 515 Some books lend themselves to a snatchy method of perusal. **1898** [see snaggy *a.*²].

**b.** *spec.* Of rowing.

**1865** *Sk. from Cambridge* 16 The modern style [of rowing] seems short and snatchy; it has not the long majestic sweep of former days. **1893** *Daily News* 14 Mar. 2/6 He does not keep a very even stroke, and to this is largely attributable the 'snatchy' form in the boat.

†**snater**, *v. Obs.*$^{-1}$ [? Error for *snapir* snapper *v.*¹] *intr.* To stumble.

*a* **1400-50** *Alexander* 3995 Sire Porrus with a proude swerd him on þe pan strikis So snelle at he snatirs with.

**snath** (snæθ), *sb.* Chiefly *dial.* and *U.S.* Forms: α. 6 snythe, 9 snithe. β. 7– snathe, 9 snaythe, snaith. γ. 8– sneath, 9 sne(a)the, sneeth. δ. 8– snath. [Variant of snead *sb.*, but all the forms are irregular and difficult to account for.] The pole or shaft of a scythe.

α. **1574** R. Scot *Hop Garden* (1578) 28 Thys helue shoulde boowe somewhat lyke to a Snythe, or to the steale of a Sythe. **1854** Miss Baker *Northampt. Gloss.* s.v. *Snathe, Snithe*, the crooked handle or long shank of a mowing scythe.

β. **1691** Ray *S. & E.C. Words* 114 *A Snathe*, the handle of a Sithe. **1848** Bartlett *Dict. Amer.* 317 Snathe. **1888** Addy *Sheffield Gloss.* 224 Snaith or Snathe. **1899** Dickinson & Prevost *Cumbld. Gloss.* 301/2 Snaythe.

γ. **1704** *Dict. Rust.* (1726) s.v. *Snead, Sneath*, the handle of a Scithe, or the like Tool. **1844** H. Stephens *Bk. Farm* III. 849 The handle, or sned or sneath,.. is made either curved .. or straight. **1866** G. Stephens *Runic Mon.* I. 314 No Sithe could be handled without its pole or shaft or sneath or sned. **1907** 'J. Halsham' *Lonewood Corner* 150 The two 'doles' or grips on the sneath.

δ. **1782** J. SCOTT *Amœb. Ecl.* ii. Poet. Wks. 119 There crooked snaths of flexile sallow make. **1839** *Civil Eng. & Arch. Jrnl.* II. 231/1 An improvement in the Scythe Snath. **1864** WHITTIER *Wreck Rivermouth* 89 O mower, lean on thy bended snath. **1881** *Metal World* No. 22. 343 Suppose the centre of gravity of the snath be..4 in. from the body of the snath.

**snath(e**, *v. dial.* Also 7 sneath, 7, 9 snare, 8 snaze (?). [app. ad. ON. *sneiða* (Norw. *sneida*; MSw. *snetha*) to cut, slice; but the sense is more precisely that of OE. *snǽdan* SNED *v.*] *trans.* To prune or lop (trees, etc.); to remove by lopping. Hence **'snathing** *vbl. sb.*; also *attrib.*

**1485** *Nottingham Rec.* III. 230 For snathing of treez. *Ibid.*, For makyng of a M^lcccc. xl. kyddez of oke of þe seid snathinges. **1609** *Burgery of Sheffield* 312 A payne laid that every person do snath and brush ther hedges. **1641** H. BEST *Farm. Bks.* (Surtees) 121 Yow are to snath off all the small twigges and boughes. *Ibid.*, Hee hayth for this purpose a little broad snathinge axe. **1691** RAY *N.C. Words* 65 To *Snathe* or *snare*, to prune Trees, to cut off the Boughs of Ash or other Timber trees. **1781** J. HUTTON *Tour to Caves* (ed. 2) Gloss. 96 *Snaze*, clip an hedge. **1825** BROCKETT *N.C. Gloss.*, *Snathe*, to prune, to lop. **1866** BROGDEN *Prov. Lincs.*, *Snare*, to cut large boughs off a tree.

†**snat-nosed**, *a. Obs.* [Cf. SNATTED *a.*] Snub-nosed.

**1519** HORMAN *Vulg.* 31 All mooris and men of Ynde be snatte nosed: as be gootis, apis, and beeys. **1542** UDALL *Erasm. Apoph.* 223 Silenus..was an eiuill disfigured apyshe bodye, croumpe shouldreed, shorte necked, snatnosed.

†**'snatted**, *a. Obs.* [Of obscure origin.] Snub.

**13..** *K. Alis.* 6447 (Laud MS.), Hij haue visages euelong, And snatted nosen, þat ben wrong. **1387** TREVISA *Higden* (Rolls) III. 285 ȝe stryveþ for a man wiþ snatted nose. **1398** —— *Barth. De P.R.* XVIII. xcvi. (1495) 842 The ape hight Simea in grewe and hath that name of snattid nose:..for thei ben snattyd in the nose. *c* **1440** *Promp. Parv.* 461/2 Snattyd, or schort nosyd, *simus.*

†**'snatter**, *v. Obs. rare.* [ad. Du. *snateren* (so in MDu., MLG., and MHG.) or LG. *snat(t)ern* (G. *schnattern*, Sw. *snattra*), of imitative origin.] *intr.* To chatter.

**1647** HEXHAM I. (Birds), The Pie snatters, *den Exter snattert.* **1662** R. MATHEW *Unl. Alch.* 189 Many will be angry and snatter at it.

†**snattines**, obs. variant of SNOTTINESS.

**1594** T. B. *La Primaud. Fr. Acad.* II. 377 From hence commeth spettle, snattines of the nose, catharres, & distillations.

†**'snattock.** *Obs.* [Of obscure origin.] A scrap, fragment.

**1654** GAYTON *Pleas. Notes* III. xi. 148 From rags, Snattocks, Snips, irreconcilable and super-annuated Smocks and Shirts. *Ibid.* xiii. 160 The Letter..crumbled into such miserable Snattocks that the Divell could not piece it together.

†**snatty**, obs. variant of SNOTTY *a.*

**1545** ELYOT, *Mucosus*, snatty or sniueled. **1647** HEXHAM I, Sneevelly or snatty, *snotachtigh.*

†**snavel**, *v.*[1] *Sc. Obs.*[−1] In 5 snawil. [Imitative: cf. SNAFFLE *v.*, and Sw. dial. *snavla.*] *intr.* To snuffle.

*c* **1375** *Sc. Leg. Saints* xvi. (*Magdalene*) 459 þe child cane snawil þan, & grape þe modyr pape, for fud to tak.

**snavel** ('snæv(ə)l), *v.*[2] *slang and dial.* (now chiefly *Austral.*). Also snavvle. [Perh. var. SNABBLE *v.* or SNAFFLE *v.*[4]] *trans.* To steal; to appropriate, to grab.

For further material see *Eng. Dial. Dict.* s.v. *Snavel* vb.[2] and sb.[2]

*a* **1790** H. T. POTTER *New Dict. Cant & Flash* (ed. 2, 1795) 54 *Snavel*, to steal when running. **1823** 'J. BEE' *Slang* 162 *Snavel*, to steal, by snatching, probably, or concealing any small property by piece-meal. **1903** 'T. COLLINS' *Such is Life* 18 Well, we had a bunch o' keys at the camp. I had snavelled 'em at the railway station. **1919** W. DOWNING *Digger Dialects* 46 *Snavvle*, take by stealth; steal; capture. **1933** *Bulletin* (Sydney) 4 Oct. 10/1 Could we but snavel *that* We'd incontestably be home and dried In this keen race. **1948** V. PALMER *Golconda* xiii. 100 They're booming the notion o' a new township and snavelling all the land within a mile o' it.

So †**'snaveller**, a thief. *Obs. rare.*

**1781** G. PARKER *View of Society* II. 168 The Snaveller.. coaxes the child up some by-alley,..and grabbles the whole.

**snaw(e, snawy**, Sc. and north. variants of SNOW, SNOWY.

**snawith**: see SNOWISH *a.*

**snax** (snæks), commercial var. *snacks*, pl. of SNACK *sb.*[2]

**1947** I. BROWN *Say the Word* 17 Why does such shop-window spelling, Sox and Snax, irritate me so? **1965** I. FLEMING *Man with Golden Gun* v. 70 A hand-painted sign said '*Snax*'. **1980** 'M. YORKE' *Scent of Fear* vii. 62 She bought sandwiches at Takeaway Snax.

**snayballe**, obs. form of SNOWBALL.

**snaype**, obs. form of SNAPE *v.*[1]

**snazzy** ('snæzɪ), *a. slang* (orig. *U.S.*). [Origin unknown.] Excellent; attractive; classy, stylish, flashy.

**1932** *Amer. Speech* VII. 336 *Snazzy*, agreeable; attractive. **1935** N. ERSINE *Underworld & Prison Slang* 68 That's a snazzy dressup you've got. **1938** W. CHAMBERS *Once too Often* i. 17 It was indeed a very snazzy setup and I wondered how many months he was in arrears with his rent. **1944** R. CHANDLER *Let.* 16 Dec. (1966) 43, I had a very snazzy beginning which they cut out, because it didn't really have anything to do with detective stories. **1946** 'P. QUENTIN' *Puzzle for Friends* iii. 27 Think what a snazzy life you've got. All the money in the world. No worries. No work. **1956** 'J. WYNDHAM' *Seeds of Time* 214 You come here with your ritzy ways and your snazzy talk. **1960** *News Chron.* 30 Sept. 4/5 Rod..takes off his snazzy smoking jacket to rescue his..girl friend. **1968** J. LOCK *Lady Policeman* ix. 82 They've made the plain uniforms look as snazzy as possible with whiter-than-white hat-bands, belts and gaiters. **1971** B. W. ALDISS *Soldier Erect* 115, I see you're all togged up... It's really snazzy you look. **1974** *Early Music* Jan. 24/2, I am convinced that the snazzy rhythms and syncopations that one often hears are wrong. **1978** C. LEOPOLD *Casablack* I A snazzy, loose-fitting pinstripe that was emphatically fashion in..1942.

**snead** (sni:d), **sned** (snɛd). Now *dial.* Forms: α. 1 snæd, 3 snede, 7–9 sneed, 9 sneyd, sneid; 7– snead. β. 9 sned. See also SNATH *sb.* [OE. *snǽd*, of obscure origin and not represented in the cognate languages.] The shaft or pole of a scythe.

α. *c* **1000** ÆLFRIC *Hom.* II. 162 Hwilon eac befeoll an siðe of ðam snæde into anum deopan seaðe. **1235–52** *Rentalia Glastonb.* (Somerset Rec. Soc.) 165 Et [habebit] de herba quantum potest levare cum sidsnede. **1664** EVELYN *Sylva* xii. §2 These Hedges are..kept in order with a Scythe of four foot long..; this is fix'd on a long sneed or streight handle. **1686** PLOT *Staffordsh.* 357 A short strong Sithe.. fitted with a strong Snead. **1813** DAVIS *Agric. Wilts.* in *Archæol. Rev.* (1888), Scythe, or Sive—The handle [is] called the snead. **1825–** in dial. glossaries, etc. (Somerset, Northampt., Chesh., Warwicks.). **1885** *Calendar of Prisoners at Mids. Sessions, Taunton* 30 June, William Chorley..stealing a scythe and snead.

β. **1825–** in dial. glossaries (Northumb., Shropsh., Northampt.). **1844** H. STEPHENS *Bk. Farm* III. 849 The curved sned is usually made of willow. **1901** *Scotsman* 1 Apr. 8/7 He sent his servant..for a scythe sned.

**sneak** (sni:k), *sb.* Also 7 sneake. [app. f. SNEAK *v.*]

By earlier writers used as a suggestive personal name:—**1597** SHAKS. *2 Hen. IV*, II. iv. 12 See if thou canst finde out Sneakes Noyse. **1633** B. JONSON *Tale of Tub* v. viii, Was she..wench to that Sneake-Iohn?

**1. a.** A sneaking, mean-spirited, paltry, or despicable person; one who acts in a shifty, shabby, or underhand manner.

*Jerry Sneak*: see JERRY *sb.*[1] 6.

*a* **1643** W. CARTWRIGHT *Ordinary* IV. v, I'll suffer no such sneaks As you to offend this way. **1668** PEPYS *Diary* 8 Mar., When all is done, he is a sneake; who owns his owing me £10 ..and yet cannot provide to pay me. **1677** W. HUGHES *Man of Sin* II. x. 159 The Devil,..being baffled, packs away, like a silly Sneak as he was.

**1840** THACKERAY *Shabby-genteel Story* iii, We call him tuft-hunter, lickspittle, sneak. **1848** —— *Van. Fair* v, The sneak of an usher jeered at him no longer. **1848** B. D. WALSH tr. *Aristophanes' Knights* II. iii, I knew not..that you had been so long..a sneak and a shuffler. **1874** L. STEPHEN *Hours Libr.* (1892) II. v. 174 A penitent is generally a bit of a sneak.

**b.** One who robs or steals in a sneaking manner, or who enters places clandestinely for that purpose. (See also *area-sneak* s.v. AREA 2 b.)

**1785** GROSE *Dict. Vulgar T.*, *Sneak*, a pilferer. **1839** *Slang Dict.* 34 *Sneaks*, boys who creep into houses, down areas, or into shops, etc. to enter the premises. **1902** *Westm. Gaz.* 30 June 2/3 The genuine poacher—the real article we mean, not the commercial midnight game sneak.

**2.** *Cant.* **a.** The act or practice of stealing in unperceived in order to rob; a robbery effected in this manner. Usu. in phr. ***upon the sneak.*** Also more generally ***on the sneak***, on the sly, by stealth, under concealment.

*a* **1700** B. E. *Dict. Cant. Crew* s.v. *Ken-miller*, *'Tis a bob Ken, Brush upon the Sneak*, 'tis a good House, go in if you will but Tread softly. **1812** J. H. VAUX *Flash Dict.* s.v. *Gammon*, A thief detected in a house which he has entered, upon the sneak, for the purpose of robbing it. *Ibid.*, *Morning-sneak*, going out early to rob private houses or shops by slipping in at the door unperceived [etc.]. *c* **1863** T. TAYLOR *Ticket-of-Leave Man* I. 9 Pottering about on the sneak, flimping or smashing a little when I get the chance. **1930** *Amer. Mercury* XXI. 458/1 You got to work strictly on the sneak. All the spots are hot. **1935** *Sun* (Baltimore) 13 July 9/6 A few of them [*sc.* betting spots] were 'sneaking' with just as many customers as ever... These spots 'on the sneak' usually are located in the upper floors of Loop skyscrapers. **1955** *Publ. Amer. Dial. Soc.* XXIV. 86 If the *road mob* decides to work *on the sneak*, that is, without advance arrangements in any locality, [etc.]. **1982** *Chicago Sun-Times* 6 Aug. 71/1 He does so with all the glee of a schoolkid reading Playboy magazine on the sneak.

**b.** The act of stealing away or running off in a sneaking manner.

**1812** J. H. VAUX *Flash Dict.* s.v., One or more prisoners having escaped..by stealth, without..alarming their keepers, are said to have..*given it to 'em upon the sneak.* **1901** *Wide World Mag.* VI. 478/1 Geronimo and his blood-thirsty cut-throats had 'made a sneak', that is, left their reservation and were on the war-path.

**3.** *Cricket.* A ball bowled so as to roll along the ground; a daisy-cutter.

**1851** J. PYCROFT *Cricket Field* vii. 105 Cowley..put on one Tailor Humphreys to bowl twisting underhand sneaks. **1862** —— *Cricket Tutor* 52 Sneaks jump about and twist with the ground. **1886** —— *Oxford Mem.* II. 93 Once, when good bowling was unsuccessful, they put in Tailor Humphreys to bowl twisting sneaks. **1899** LUBBOCK *Mem. Eton* xviii. 278 A long hop to leg would have been a more suitable ball than a straight sneak.

**4.** *slang.* A soft-soled, noiseless slipper or shoe.

**1862** *Female Life in Prison* I. xvii. 211 The night-officer is generally accustomed to wear a species of India-rubber shoes or goloshes on her feet. These are termed 'sneaks' by the women [of Brixton Prison]. **1883** GREENWOOD *Strange Company* (ed. 2) 321 'Sneaks'..are shoes with canvas tops and indiarubber soles. **1904** A. GRIFFITHS *50 Yrs. Public Service* xiv. 204 His footsteps were..deadened by the 'sneaks', or cloth slippers, worn to conceal his whereabouts.

**5.** *U.S. colloq.* = *sneak preview* s.v. SNEAK- a.

**1941** B. SCHULBERG *What makes Sammy Run?* iv. 60 We'll know better after the sneak... And..when we see whether Mr. and Mrs. Public buy tickets. **1967** *Boston Globe* 5 Apr. 57/1 (*heading*) Sneaks slated at music hall. **1978** E. TIDYMAN *Table Stakes* II. vi. 265 The studio agreed to give the production three previews... The first 'sneak'..took place at a small theater in Redlands.

**sneak** (sni:k), *v.* Also 6 sneke, 7 sneek, sneake. Pa. t. and pple. also (orig. and chiefly *U.S.*) snuck. [Of doubtful origin: the form does not agree with that of early ME. *sníken*, OE. *snícan* to creep, crawl (cf. ON. *sníkja*, Norw. *snikja*, Da. *snige*, in senses similar to 'sneak'), and the historical gap is very great. The stem *sneak-* appears a little earlier in SNEAKISH(LY *a.* and *adv.*]

**I.** *intr.* **1.** To move, go, walk, etc., in a stealthy or slinking manner; to creep or steal furtively, as if ashamed or afraid to be seen; to slink, skulk:

**a.** With advs., as *away*, *down*, *in*, *off*, *out*, etc.

**1596** SHAKS. *1 Hen. IV*, IV. iii. 58 A poore vnminded Outlaw, sneaking home. **1604** DEKKER *Honest Wh.* Wks. 1873 II. 138, I hope he will not sneake away with all the money. **1625** B. JONSON *Staple of N.* II. iv, Where's Madrigall? Is he sneek'd hence? **1709** STEELE *Tatler* No. 9 ¶3 Miss having heard enough, sneaks off for Fear of Discovery. **1740–2** RICHARDSON *Pamela* (1824) I. xix. 31 [The cook] was hot with her work; and I sneaked away. **1844** DICKENS *Mart. Chuz.* xlvii, To avoid people, and sneak on unobserved. **1877** BLACK *Green Past.* i, The two women were sneaking off by themselves. **1887** *Lantern* (New Orleans) 17 Dec. 3/3 He grubbed ten dollars from de bums an den snuck home. **1932** J. T. FARRELL *Young Lonigan* ii. 55 They had all snuck in and were having a good time, making trouble. **1969** *Oz* May 3/1 It was sticking out of a dustbin—the mag I mean..so I snuck off to the park and had a good old read. **1976** S. BRETT *So Much Blood* xvi. 191 At the interval Charles and Frances snuck out to the pub. **1979** *Vassar Q.* Summer 17/3, I have come around the back way and snuck up, as we say in Nebraska, on my subject.

*fig.* and *transf.* **1643** WITHER *Campo-Musæ* 72 That Delusion Which had so hotly charg'd me, sneaked thence. *a* **1661** FULLER *Worthies, Sussex* III. 96 When the Sun ariseth the Moon sneaketh down obscurely. **1857** S. OSBORN *Quedah* xii. 159 Towards dusk a small canoe sneaked out, under the plea of fishing.

**b.** With preps., as *about*, *after*, *from*, *into*, etc.

**1599** SHAKS. *Hen. V*, I. ii. 171 To her vnguarded Nest, the Weazell (Scot) Comes sneaking. **1607** FLETCHER *Woman Hater* v. iv, There are they still poor rogues,..sneaking after cheeses. **1609** ROWLANDS *Dr. Merrie-man* (Hunterian Cl.) 20 The Rusticke..softly sneaking out of doores, About his message goes. **1714** POPE *Let. to Caryll* 25 Sept., I have.. sneaked along the walks with that astonished and diffident air [etc.]. **1749** SMOLLETT *Gil Blas* I. xiii, But I made no reply, and very wisely condescended to sneak into the straw. **1825** T. HOOK *Sayings* Ser. II. *Man of Many Fr.* II. 51 They ..sneaked from my door with every mark of..servile cowardice. **1835** SIR J. ROSS *Narr. 2nd Voy.* ii. 22 Appearing disorderly and dirty, as they..sneaked about the ship. **1879** E. K. BATES *Egypt. Bonds* II. viii. 191 Like truant schoolboys who sneak into the busy schoolroom. **1940** R. CHANDLER *Farewell, my Lovely* vi. 36, I snuck in there and grabbed it. **1958** J. KEROUAC *On Road* II. viii. 159 Four sullen fieldworkers, snuck from their chores to brawl in drinking fields.

*fig.* **1726** DE FOE *Hist. Devil* II. v, Being ashamed, as well as discouraged, they sneaked out of the world as well as they could. **1838** EMERSON *Address, Cambridge* Wks. (Bohn) II. 200 Now man is ashamed of himself; he skulks and sneaks through the world. **1871** BROWNING *Balaustion* 1549 To thee who livest now Through having sneaked past fate apportioned thee.

**c.** Without const. (Freq. used to denote want of courage, independence, or straightforwardness, without reference to place or movement.)

**1665** BOYLE *Occas. Refl.* (1848) 358 As these Russians could not take a better way than that of not sneaking, to avoid the having their Rites and Persons undervalu'd. **1682** N. O. *Boileau's Lutrin* II. 184 For he..scorn'd to stand, and sneak with hands in Pocket. **1699** BENTLEY *Phalaris* xi. 266 He sneak'd like a Cock, that hangs down his wings when he's beaten. **1732** POPE *Ep. Cobham* 154 Tom struts a Soldier,.. Will sneaks a Scriv'ner, an exceeding knave. **1779** JOHNSON *L.P.*, *Pope*, Pope was reduced to sneak and shuffle, sometimes to deny, and sometimes to apologize. **1845** *Nonconformist* V. 133 Law..may allow..them to sneak—but law cannot wipe away the reproach of sneaking. **1861** GEO. ELIOT *Silas M.* ix, If you know where he's sneaking.. you may tell him to spare himself the journey o' coming back home.

*fig.* **1633** G. HERBERT *Temple, Ch. Militant* 121 Thus Sinne in Egypt sneaked for a while. **1692** *Vindication* 15 Vice..always sneaks when bravely born up to. **1765** BEATTIE *Judgm. of Paris* cii, Coward Office..sneaks secure in insolence of state. **1821** CLARE *Vill. Minstr.* II. 83 How blest she'd been,..If, ere want sneak'd for grudg'd support from pride [etc.].

**d.** *U.S. colloq.* To make off quietly.

**1896** G. ADE *Artie* 7 I'd a' sneaked early in the game. **1901** *Scribner's Mag.* Apr. 409/1 When you get over the fence,.. yell fire till the crowd comes, then sneak.

**2.** To cringe or be servile *to* (a person, etc.). *c* **1660** SOUTH *Serm.* (1715) I. 32, I need salute no great Man's Threshold, sneak to none of his Friends or Servants. *a* **1704** T. BROWN *Oxford Scholars* Wks. 1730 I. 10 Pitiful curates and chaplains, that must sneak to the groom and butler. **1796** BURKE *Corr.* (1844) IV. 383 We sneak to the regicides, but we boldly trample on our poor fellow-citizens. **1873** BROWNING *Red. Cott. Nt.-cap.* iv. 257 Why else to me ..Sneak, cap in hand, now bribe me to forsake My maimed Léonce, now bully, cap on head.

*transf.* **1707** HEARNE *Collect.* 30 Sept., Our Bishops sneak to the old Cause.

**3.** *School slang.* To peach, inform, tell tales. **1897** *Daily News* 3 June 7/2 Sneaking, in the ethics of public school boys, is the unpardonable sin. **1902** *Spectator* July 46/2 The boys..usually prefer to suffer rather than 'sneak' of one of their companions.

**II.** *trans.* **4.** To turn or draw *aside*, to put or thrust *in* or *into*, to move or slide *to*, etc., in a stealthy manner.

**1648** J. BEAUMONT *Psyche* I. xlvii, Stout Trees.. From this dire Breath sneak'd their faint heads aside. **1684** OTWAY *Atheist* III. i, Sneak what Ready-mony thou hast into my Hand. **1754** *Connoisseur* No. 32 ¶3, I see a man every minute stealing out a dirty muckender, then sneaking it in again. **1889** *Macm. Mag.* Aug. 253/1, I lay stirless, softly sneaking my right hand to the pistol. **1892** GUNTER *Miss Dividends* (1893) 275 When Lawrence's name comes up for membership, he sneaks in a black-ball, as many another prig ..has done before. **1968** J. M. ULLMAN *Lady on Fire* (1969) xii. 160 You've got a new lead. Maybe something the sister told you after you snuck her out of that hotel. **1971** D. E. WESTLAKE *I gave at Office* (1972) 12 There was some suspicion that a couple of guests had snuck friends in. **1979** R. JAFFE *Class Reunion* I. vii. 69 He wanted to sneak her into his room.

*refl.* **1680** *Advice to Soldier* ii. in *Harl. Misc.* (1753) I. 467, I have seen some of those Gallants..in the Middle of a Sea-fight,..sneak themselves behind the Main-mast.

**b.** To keep out of sight; to hide. *rare*$^{-1}$.

**1701** WAKE *Ration.* 222 (Todd), Some sins dare the world in open defiance, yet this [*sc.* slander] lurks, and sneaks its head.

**c.** To pass *through* in an underhand or stealthy manner.

**1891** *Daily News* 29 Jan. 2/4 Mr. Stephens..objected..to this cruel and unjust Bill being 'sneaked' through Parliament. **1896** *Voice* (N.Y.) 5 Mar. 2/4 A most important measure is being sneaked through the general assembly.

†**5.** To do or act (one's part) in a sneaking or cringing manner. *Obs.*$^{-1}$

**1649** G. DANIEL *Trinarch., Hen. V*, ccxcii, Something hidden lifts the Thought To Noble Actions, when they heare 'em told, And Hee who Sneaks his part, will praise 'em bold.

**6. a.** *Cant.* (See quot.)

**1812** J. H. VAUX *Flash Dict.* s.v., To sneak a place is to rob it upon the sneak. *Ibid.*, One or more persons having escaped from their confinement by stealth, without.. alarming their keepers, are said to have *sneak'd 'em*.

**b.** *colloq.* To steal in a sneaking or stealthy manner; to filch; to take or partake of surreptitiously.

**1883** *Daily News* 14 Sept. 3/7 The various kinds of people who visit public libraries for other than legitimate purposes, such as..those who sneaked umbrellas, and those who stole books. **1889** JEROME *Three Men in Boat* ix. 142 Somebody must have sneaked it, and run off with it. **1900** *Dialect Notes* II. 61 *Sneak*, to appropriate. **1921** E. O'NEILL *Emperor Jones* i. 160 When I sleeps, dey sneaks a sleep, too, and I pretends I never suspicions it. *a* **1953** —— *More Stately Mansions* (1964) II. iii. 136 Each sneaks a suspicious, probing glance at the other. **1955** J. H. O'HARA *Ten North Frederick* (1956) 34, I can sneak us another drink. **1956** M. DUGGAN *Immanuel's Land* 107 The conductor stood on the bucking platform, sneaking a cigarette. **1968** *Globe & Mail* (Toronto) 17 Feb. 6/2 If they did have these smoking areas ..the students wouldn't have to sneak a smoke in the washroom. **1978** J. IRVING *World according to Garp* ii. 30 He was happy to run errands for the patients, deliver messages, sneak food.

**sneak-**, the sb. or verb-stem used in combs., as **sneak-boat** *U.S.*, a boat by which one may readily move or approach unobserved; *esp.* a sneak-box; **sneak-box** *U.S.*, a small, flat, shallow boat used in wild-fowl shooting, and when in use masked with brush or weeds; **sneak-current** *Electr.*, current which escapes or strays owing to leakage or imperfect insulation (1904 in *Cent. Dict.* Suppl.); **sneak-guest**, one who makes public the events of private social gatherings at which he is a guest; **sneak-hunting**, hunting from an unobserved approach; **sneak-pasty** *a.*, insidious, sneaky; **sneak preview** orig. *U.S.*, a showing of a (usually unnamed) cinematic film prior to regular release, to test audience reaction; also *transf.* and *fig.*; hence **sneak-preview** *v. trans.*, (*a*) to show (a film) in a sneak preview; (*b*) to have a sneak preview of (something); **sneak-shooting**, the shooting of wild-fowl from a sneak-boat (*Cent. Dict.*); **sneak-thief** (orig. *U.S.*), one who steals or thieves by sneaking into houses through open or unfastened doors or windows; also, a pickpocket, a snatch-thief; also *attrib.*; hence ***sneak-thief*** vb. trans. (*nonce-wd.*); ***sneak-thiefery, -thievery***; ***sneak-thieving*** vbl. sb.

**1853** *Laws General Assembly of Maryland* 220 Any person or persons [who] shall use any sink boats, *sneak boats or floats,..shall be subject to a fine. **1882** D. KEMP *Yacht Sailing* xvi. (1884) 258 The home of the sneak-boat, or sneak box, or devil's coffin, as the contrivance is indifferently termed, is Barnegat Bay. **1889** BUCKNILL *Submarine Mines* 232 The Howell [torpedo]..is inferior only as an arm for a sneak boat, or for a vessel attempting to run a blockade. **1879** N. H. BISHOP *4 Months in a Sneak-Box* (1880) 1 The comical-looking..Barnegat *sneak-box, or duck-boat. **1884** KNIGHT *Dict. Mech.* Suppl. 826/2 The New Jersey sneak box is from 12' to 14' in length. **1899** K. B. MILLER *Amer. Telephone Practice* xxiii. 275 It frequently happens..that a very small current..will not be sufficient to blow the fuse... These currents are very appropriately termed '*sneak currents'. **1934** A. L. ALBERT *Electr. Commun.* xii. 325 Currents slightly in excess of the normal operating values.. are often called 'sneak' currents. **1930** *Times Lit. Suppl.* 9 Jan. 18/1 Creevey..was in fact (if a very modern term may be forgiven because it is so apt) a '*sneak-guest'. **1958** *Listener* 18 Dec. 1045/1 He [*sc.* Boswell] was regarded in society as something of a 'sneak guest'. **1878** E. B. TUTTLE *Border Tales* 45 By *sneak-hunting, one man can kill a whole band of elk. **1980** *Outdoor Life* (U.S.) (Northeast ed.) Oct. 84/3 Sneak hunting is a difficult and time-consuming sport. **1681** T. FLATMAN *Heraclitus Ridens* No. 15 (1713) I. 101 Some creeping *Sneakpasty Schismatick would have informed against you. **1938** *Daily Progress* (Charlottesville, Va.) 28 Nov. 1/6 A double-barreled, two-blizzard '*sneak' pre-view of the 1938 edition of winter. **1939** *Chambers's Jrnl.* Nov. 858/1 In America, pre-views, frequently called 'sneak pre-views', have always been allowed. **1949** *Sun* (Baltimore) 28 Jan. 13/4 (Advt.), Sneak preview—tonight at 11.40 p.m. Even though the producers say we mustn't tell —we can hint it's..one of the funniest comedies you've ever seen! **1950** *Ibid.* 14 Sept. 16/1 The film was sneak-previewed in Hollywood. **1952** *Art Digest* 15 Sept. 5/1 Sneak Preview. On the theory that our readers like to know in advance about important art events, we summarize..the 1952–53 season. **1960** *Sunday Express* 18 Dec. 9/3 Paris-bound passengers were given a sneak preview of Britain's 'pennyfarthing' airliner, the Vickers Vanguard. **1972** *Guardian* 24 May 13/7 The old-established Oregon primary..served as a sneak preview of the multimillion dollar Californian entertainment. **1975** *New Yorker* 22 Dec. 31/2 Our pal.. delights in opportunities to see things in advance, so he was easily persuaded last week to accept our invitation to sneak-preview the new open-air observation platform twelve feet above the roof. **1980** *Times Lit. Suppl.* 12 Sept. 990/2 This selection brings together poems from all five of her [*sc.* P. Beer's] published collections, plus a satisfying sneak preview of what one hopes will be her sixth. **1859** G. W. MATSELL *Vocabulum* 82 **Sneak-thief*, a fellow who sneaks into areas, basement-doors or windows, or through front doors by means of latch-keys, and entering the various apartments, steals any thing he can carry off. **1866** *Harper's Mag.* Nov. 690/1 A female 'sneak thief' and a 'longshoreman now appear. **1877** TALMAGE *Serm.* 58 The meanest sneak-thief that comes up..at the Tomb Court. *a* **1930** D. H. LAWRENCE *Last Poems* (1932) 100 That is why business seems to me despicable, and most love-affairs, just sneak-thief pocket-picking of dressed-up people. *Ibid.* 242 The jixery perhaps never picked a man's pocket But my god, they sneak-thiefed his very genitals away from him. **1959** M. CUMBERLAND *Murmurs in Rue Morgue* xix. 117 He is the sneak-thief type and the petty blackmailer. **1976** *Liverpool Echo* 6 Dec. 7/9 Wrexham Police to-day warned shoppers to be on the lookout for sneak thieves after a woman shopping in a chemist shop in the town had £200 stolen from her bag. **1923** *Sneak-thiefery [see GANGSTERDOM]. **1963** V. GIELGUD *Goggle-Box Affair* xvii. 177 Nothing else was taken, so it wasn't just *sneak-thievery. **1973** E. BERCKMAN *Victorian Album* 82 So there I was, practising deceit on Christabel and sneak-thievery on Mrs Rumbold. **1884** *Cent. Mag.* Mar. 653/2 The offences are nearly all trivial, most of them being petty larceny and *sneak-thieving.

**b.** In misc. other uses, passing into adj.: that acts or is effected by stealth, deceit, or surprise; unexpected.

**1938** *Sun* (Baltimore) 19 July 8/3 His 'sneak hop' from New York to Ireland terminated successfully. **1943** [see FRINGE *sb.* 2 b]. **1943** *Sun* (Baltimore) 27 Dec. 5/2 A sneak air attack might be attempted by the enemy on Christmas Day. **1944** *Ann. Reg. 1943* I. 21 The soundness of the air defence ..had compelled them to confine themselves largely to 'sneak' raids on coastal towns. **1952** *Sun* (Baltimore) 17 June 4/1 The snail-spread sneak disease, bilharzia. **1955** *Publ. Amer. Dial. Soc.* XXIV. 59 The act of theft from the person by stealth is..referred to as a *sneak job*. **1970** [see LEAD *sb.*$^2$ 5 c]. **1971** 'L. BLACK' *Death has Green Fingers* ii. 18 Horace was a wonderful sneak photographer. **1976** *Evening Post* (Nottingham) 14 Dec. 11/6 A sneak raider stole £740 takings from the Triangle toy shop.

**'sneakaway.** *rare.* [f. SNEAK *v.* 1 a.] One who makes off in a sneaking manner.

**1900** *Westm. Gaz.* 6 June 1/3 Men who know themselves beaten already, but are not the cowards and sneakaways we sometimes make them out to be.

**†'sneakbill.** *Obs.* Also 6 sneke-, sneek-, 7 sneake- (and SNEAKSBILL). [Of obscure origin: cf. SNEAKSBY.] A mean or paltry fellow; a starved or thin-faced person. Also *attrib.*

**1562** J. HEYWOOD *Prov. & Epigr.* (1867) 72 Why will ye ..I shall folow hir will? To make me Iohn drawlache, or such a snekebill. **1577** KENDALL *Floures of Epigr.* 9 Perchaunce thou deemst me in thy minde, Therefore a sneekbill, snudge vnkinde. **1611** COTGR., *Chiche-face*, a chichiface, micher, sneake-bill, wretched fellow. *Ibid.*, *Visage de bec*, a sneake-bill, sharp-nose, chittiface. **1653** URQUHART *Rabelais* I. liv, Here enter not base pinching Usurers,..chichie sneakbil rogues.

**sneak-cup**, app. an error for SNEAK-UP *sb.*

**1596** SHAKS. *1 Hen. IV*, III. iii. 99 *Falst.* How? the Prince is a Iacke, a Sneake-Cuppe. **1673** *S'too him Bayes* 99 You will but cry like Falstaff (when the Prince asked him if he had said he was a Sneak-Cup).

**sneaker** ('sniːkə(r)). [f. SNEAK *v.*]

**1.** A person or animal that sneaks; a sneak.

**1598** FLORIO, *Origlione*, an eauesdropper, a listner,..a sneaker, a lurking knaue. *c* **1613** MIDDLETON *No Wit like Woman's* IV. ii, I thought they were some such sneakers. **1621** BURTON *Anat. Mel.* III. ii. IV. i. (1651) 519 A long lean rawbone, a skeleton, a sneaker. **1715** HEARNE *Collect.* (O.H.S.) V. 66 He being one of the Sneakers and terribly afraid of disobliging the debauched Court of K. George. *a* **1734** NORTH *Examen* III. viii. §37 (1740) 611 The Courtiers that were more used to Sneakers, than to Men of clear Courage. **1800** COLERIDGE *Piccolomini* II. xiv, Not a sneaker among us, thank heaven. **1826** SCOTT *Jrnl.* 7 Mar., We have more sneakers after Ministerial favour than men who love their country. **1865** LIVINGSTONE *Zambesi* vii. 161 He soon departed and we heard no more of the majestic sneaker.

**2.** †**a.** A small bowl (*of* punch). *Obs.* (Common from *c* 1710 to *c* 1740.)

(*a*) *a* **1700** B. E. *Dict. Cant. Crew*, *Sneaker*, (of Punch) a small Bowl. **1726** G. ROBERTS *Four Yrs. Voy.* 71 He would take me on Board the Scooner with him, to treat me with a Sneaker of Punch before parting. **1743** FIELDING *J. Wild* II. iv, He called for a sneaker of punch. **1772** in Jas. Forbes *Oriental Mem.* (1813) IV. 217 He then ordered five sneakers of a mixture which he denominated punch.

(*b*) **1714** *Spect.* No. 616 ¶4, I have just left the Right Worshipful and his Myrmidons about a Sneaker of Five Gallons. **1742** FIELDING *J. Andrews* I. xiii, Mr. Barnabas.. having..drank a bowl of punch.., returned to take the other sneaker; which when he had finished [etc.]. **1775** S. J. PRATT *Liberal Opin.* lxxxviii. (1783) III. 157 A little snug place..where we might take a friendly sneaker together.

**b.** A glass *of* brandy.

**1805** RAMSAY *Scotl. & Scotsmen 18th C.* (1888) II. 293 He had a small sneaker of brandy before retiring to his bedroom. **1821** *Blackw. Mag.* IX. 60 Step to the corner and fetch me a sneaker of brandy.

**3.** *colloq.* (orig. and chiefly *U.S.*) = SNEAK *sb.* 4.

**1895** in *Funk's Stand. Dict.* **1900** G. ADE *More Fables* 193 His Job on this Earth was to put on a pair of Pneumatic Sneakers every Morning and go out and investigate Other People's Affairs. **1914** S. LEWIS *Our Mr. Wrenn* iv. 56 Firm but fearful in his rubber sneakers. **1930** 'S. S. VAN DINE' *Scarab Murder Case* iv. 61 He got relief by wearing white canvas sneakers with rubber soles. **1936** WODEHOUSE *Laughing Gas* xii. 126 You could scarcely expect to turn up in sneakers and a sweater, my good fellow. **1948** J. STEINBECK *Russ. Jrnl.* (1949) 13 She wore canvas sneakers. **1959** *Manch. Guardian* 24 June 7/2 The international uniform of jeans and sandals or sneakers. **1967** A. HENRI in *Penguin Mod. Poets* X. 55 The daughters of Albion..lacing up blue sneakers over brown ankles. **1974** A. LURIE *War between Tates* v. 95 It was Jeffrey who started it; he could not find his left sneaker. **1981** *Sunday Express Mag.* 26 July 16/3 (*caption*) Shades of throwaway chic for pop singer, Graham Bonnet. Old sneakers and a borrowed suit?

**4.** *Cricket.* = SNEAK *sb.* 3.

**1851** J. PYCROFT *Cricket Field* iv. 63 With the primitive fashion of ground bowling, called sneakers, forward play could have no place. **1909** in *Cent. Dict.* Suppl.

Hence **'sneakered** *a.*, clad in sneakers.

**1961** 'E. FENWICK' *Friend of Mary Rose* (1962) iv. 39 He heard..a soft jump—as of sneakered feet. **1976** 'E. MCBAIN' *Guns* (1977) i. 34 He floats on sneakered feet to the back door of the car. **1979** *Listener* 3 May 613/2 Their crew-cut, pony-tailed, sneakered sons and daughters.

**sneaker-snee**, variant of SNICKERSNEE *v.*

**sneakiness** ('sniːkɪnɪs). [f. SNEAKY *a.*] The character or quality of being sneaky.

**1859** BOYD *Recreat. Country Parson* (1862) 63 Sneakiness ..is worse than the most indiscreet honesty. **1865** —— *Crit. Ess.* (1867) 3 His sneakiness as a patriot, his corruption as a judge.

**sneaking** ('sniːkɪŋ), *vbl. sb.* [f. SNEAK *v.*] The action of the vb. in various senses. Also with preps. and advs.

**1649** G. DANIEL *Trinarch., Rich. II*, cxliv, But sneaking smells of Peasant, though they weare Blue Ribbands. **1656** *North's Plutarch* Add. Lives 43 He built a house without his Camp for all strangers.., whereby he prevented their sneaking into his Camp. **1706** HEARNE *Collect.* (O.H.S.) I. 217 By his Sneaking and Cringing. **1772** T. SIMPSON *Vermin-Killer* 20 They appear shy, but that is from your sneaking after them. **1829** CARLYLE *Misc.* (1857) II. 23 An assiduity..which sometimes almost verges towards sneaking. **1895** *Outing* XXVI. 403/2 By hard sneaking it was possible to get within about two hundred and fifty yards.

**sneaking** ('sniːkɪŋ), *ppl. a.* Also 7 **sneeking**. [f. SNEAK *v.*]

**1.** That sneaks; moving, walking, acting, etc., in a furtive or slinking manner. Also *transf.*

**1590** GREENE *Never too late* (1600) 98 Hee is such a sneaking fellowe, that..touch him and he will scrike. **1594** NASHE *Unfort. Trav.* B iij, They will..call him a sneaking Eaues-dropper. **1659** in *Burton's Diary* (1828) IV. 71 Where is then the anarchy, the sneaking oligarchy? **1673** A. WALKER *Leez Lachrymans* 26 He had a great mans mind, not a little sneeking, servile, narrow, soul. **1710** HEARNE *Collect.* (O.H.S.) III. 34 Authoriz'd to be printed by our sneaking Vicechanc[ellor]. **1726** DYER *Country Walk* 75 The sneaking tribe of Flattery. **1824** W. IRVING *T. Trav.* I. 227 Lurking footpads and sneaking pickpockets. **1839** DICKENS *Nickleby* xiii, A nasty, ungrateful, pig-headed, brutish, obstinate, sneaking dog. **1891** C. ROBERTS *Adrift Amer.* 99 Several of these sneaking beasts [coyotes] were prowling round.

*Comb.* **1828** *Lights & Shades* I. 292 The same sneaking-looking animal, whether you meet with it in a palace or a jail.

†**b.** ***sneaking-budge***, one who steals or robs alone; also *erron.* (quots. 1743–51), stealing, pilfering. *Obs.*

*a* **1700** B. E. *Dict. Cant. Crew.* **1743** FIELDING *J. Wild* I. viii, Wild..looked upon borrowing to be as good a way of taking as any, and, as he called it, the genteelest kind of Sneaking-budge. **1751** —— *Amelia* I. iii, I find you are some sneaking-budge rascal.

†**c.** Niggardly, mean, near. *Obs.*

**1696** W. MOUNTAGU *Holland* Pref. 2 We were not Sneaking..but thriftily Liberal. **1749** FIELDING *Tom Jones* x. iii, He had some few blemishes.., yet being a sneaking or a niggardly fellow, was not one of them. **1773** FOOTE *Bankrupt* III, No gentleman can accuse me of being sneaking. Dingey, give him six pence.

*transf.* **1697** TRYON *Way to Health* vi. 116 How many stingy sneaking Names will they call us?

**2.** Marked or characterized by, partaking or suggestive of, sneaking; hence, mean, contemptible.

**1582** STANYHURST *Æneis* III. (Arb.) 84 But Scylla in cabbans with sneaking treacherye lurcketh. **1648** J. BEAUMONT *Psyche* XIII. xxiii, No Conventicle's sneaking Cloisters hid Those Doctrines. **1658** *Verney Mem.* (1907) II. 73 He has an extraordinary sneaking countenance and way with him. **1724** WELTON *Chr. Faith & Pract.* 223 It was, methinks, as sneaking a submission..as it was a false assertion. **1770** FOOTE *Lame Lover* I, An absolute monarch to sink into the sneaking state of being a slave to one of his subjects. **1845** LD. CAMPBELL *Chancellors* lxxiii. (1857) III. 402 They, in a sneaking and paltry manner, pretended that they were not prepared. **1865** DICKENS *Mut. Fr.* I. i, It's worthy of the sneaking spirit that robs a live man.

†**3.** Mean in appearance or amount; petty, paltry, contemptibly poor or small. *Obs.*

**1703** R. NEVE *City & C. Purchaser* 87 Sometimes little sneaking ill-contrived Stair-cases are built in a good comely large Structure. **1733** FIELDING *Quix. Eng.* II. i, For a sneaking fee he pleads the villain's cause. **1779** MME. D'ARBLAY *Diary* 20 Oct., A meaner, more sneaking and pitiful wig..did I never see.

**4.** Of feelings, affection, etc.: Unavowedly cherished or entertained; not openly declared or shown; undemonstrative. Freq. in ***a sneaking kindness***.

**1748** RICHARDSON *Clarissa* (1811) III. 303, I believe I have a sneaking kindness for the sneaking fellow. **1753–4** —— *Grandison* (1812) I. 290 (D.), You..shall reveal to me your sneaking passion, if you have one. **1784** COWPER *Tiroc.* 244 Some sneaking virtue lurks in him, no doubt. **1842** THACKERAY *Miss Tickletoby's Lect.* vii, I can't help having a sneaking regard for him. **1871** L. STEPHEN *Playgr. Eur.* ix. (1894) 204, I have a sneaking..belief in the virtues of the scrambling Briton. **1897** MISS KINGSLEY *W. Africa* 676, I have a sneaking sympathy with these good people.

**'sneakingly**, *adv.* Also 6 snekingly, 7 sneekingly. [f. prec.]

**1.** In a sneaking manner; not openly or boldly.

**1598** FLORIO, *Gatto gatto*, groping, creeping,..sneakingly as a cat. **1599** LINCHE *Anc. Fiction* M iij, The Serpent.. snekingly conueyeth her selfe away. **1633** G. HERBERT *Temple, Ch. Porch* xxi, Doe all things like a man, not sneakingly. **1678** OTWAY *Friendship in F.* IV. i, How sneakingly will he look when he shall find his mistake. **1726** *Brice's Weekly Jrnl.* 17 June 1, I shall not..sneakingly hang my Head, under the smartest Strokes..of Adversity. **1778** MRS. SCOTT in Doran *Lady of last Cent.* (1873) x. 243 If she ever does ill, she will do it sneakingly. **1835** *Tait's Mag.* II. 377 Certain senators, who, having boldly given the lie, give sneakingly the hand of reconciliation. **1873** MISS BROUGHTON *Nancy* I. 80 We hurriedly and sneakingly enter the drawing-room.

†**2.** Meanly; niggardly. *Obs.*

**1695** DE LA PRYME *Diary* (Surtees) 74 He behaved himself the sneakinglyest to him that can be imagined.

**3.** Without open declaration; unavowedly.

**1730** [A. HILL] *Progr. Wit* 7 Unborn to cherish, sneakingly approves, And wants the Soul to spread the Worth, he loves. **1879** BROWNING *Martin Relph* 141 Suppose I had sneakingly loved her myself, My wretched self.

**'sneakingness.** *rare.* [f. as prec.] Sneaking quality; sneakiness.

*c* **1647** BOYLE *Agst. Swearing* Wks. 1772 VI. 16 Such persons are deeply accessary..by a sneakingness, which.. implies a guilt. [**1687** in MIÈGE. **1727** in BAILEY (vol. II).]

**sneakish** ('sniːkɪʃ), *a.* [Cf. SNEAK *sb.* and *v.*]

†**1.** ? Farcical, ludicrous. *Obs.*$^{-1}$

**1570** LEVINS *Manip.* 145 Sneakish, *bardus, mimus.*

**2.** Somewhat sneaky.

**1864** CARLYLE *Fredk. Gt.* IV. 302 The sneakish courtly gentleman. **1897** 'TIVOLI' *Short Innings* xv. 227 Well, it was a beastly, sneakish trick.

Hence **'sneakishness.**

**1895** A. H. S. LANDOR *Corea* 114 It is generally associated with sneakishness, treachery, and perfidy.

**'sneakishly**, *adv. rare.* In 6 sknekyshely. [See SNEAK *v.* This is the earliest example of the stem.] Meanly, despicably. Also, in a sneaking or stealthy manner.

**1560** DAUS tr. *Sleidane's Comm.* 270 b, All men..cried out upon Duke Maurice, whiche serued him so sknekyshely, whome he oughte to haue honoured as his father. **1867** 'T. LACKLAND' *Homespun* I. 55 He begins with throwing a glance at her sneakishly. **1912** *Daily News* 11 May 6 When men come together to profess a creed they come courageously... When they come together in a clique they come sneakishly.

†**sneaks**, *sb. Obs. rare.* = SNEAK *sb.* 1.

**1653** W. RAMESEY *Astrol. Restored* To Rdr. 17 Domineer abroad, be a sneaks at home? **1687** MIÈGE *Gt. Fr. Dict.* II. s.v., A poor Sneaks, or a poor Sneaksby (that is a pitifull Fellow, that scarce dares shew his Head). *a* **1700** B. E. *Dict. Cant. Crew, Peeking Fellow*, a meer Sneaks.

†**'Sneaks**, *int. Obs.*$^{-1}$ An abbrev. of *God's neaks* (see GOD *sb.* 14 b and NEAKES), used as a petty oath. (Cf. 'SNIGS.)

**1602** MARSTON *Antonio's Rev.* IV. ii, S'neaks, and I were worth but three hundred pound a yeare more, I could sweare richly.

†**'sneaksbill.** *Obs. rare.* = SNEAKBILL.

**1602** DEKKER *Satirom.* I iv b, Come Grumboll, thou shalt Mum with vs; come, dogge mee sneakesbill. *a* **1643** CARTWRIGHT *Ordinary* III. ii, A base thin-jaw'd sneaksbill, Thus to work gallants out of all.

**'sneaksby.** Now *rare.* Also 6 **snekesbie**, 7 **sneaksbie**, etc. [Of obscure origin: see -BY 2, and cf. prec. and SNEAKBILL.] A mean-spirited person; a paltry fellow.

**1580** HOLLYBAND *Treas. Fr. Tong, Niez*, an idiote,..a simple soule, a snekesbie. **1611** COTGR., *Coquefredouille*, a meacocke, milkesop, sneaksbie. *a* **1677** BARROW *Serm.* Wks. 1716 III. 274 To be termed..a demure Sneaksby..Men can hardly brook. **1690** DRYDEN *Amphitryon* II. ii. There is no comparison between my master and thee, thou sneaksby. **1785** in GROSE *Dict. Vulgar T.* *a* **1877** COWDEN CLARKE in Rolfe *Shaks. Two Gent.* 28 A woman..will cling to a ruffian, ..but she will despise and shun a pettifogging sneaksby.

**'sneaksman.** *Cant.* [f. SNEAK *sb.* or *v.*] (See quots. 1812, 1859.)

**1812** J. H. VAUX *Flash Dict., Sneaksman*, a man or boy who goes upon the sneak. **1834** AINSWORTH *Rookwood* III. v, There was no such sneaksman..going. **1859** *Slang Dict.* 97 *Sneaksman*, a shoplifter; a petty cowardly thief.

**sneak-up** ('sniːkʌp), *sb.* [f. SNEAK *v.*; see also SNEAK-CUP.] A mean, servile, or cringing person; a sneak; a shirk.

**1596** SHAKS. *1 Hen. IV*, III. iii. 99 (Q.), The prince is a iacke, a sneakeup. **1620** SHELTON *Quix.* II. xlv. 299 You must set other manner of Coltes vpon me then this poore nasty sneake-vp. **1775** ASH, *Sneaksby*, a sneakup. **1798** T. MORTON *Secrets* III. 1 But he is such a Sneakup! Were he a boy of mettle, I would adopt him.

*attrib.* **1851** JERROLD *St. Giles* (1852) I. 305 It's only your sneak-up chaps, that are afraid of the glass, that get into trouble,..and catch rheumatism.

**sneak-up**, *v. pseudo-arch.* Alteration of *snick-up* (see SNICK *v.*$^{1}$), under the influence of prec.

**1855** KINGSLEY *Westw. Ho!* xxx, Here's a fellow..talks about failing..! Blurt for him, sneak-up! say I. *Ibid.*, Marry, sneak-up! say I again.

**sneaky** ('sniːkɪ), *a.* (and *sb.*) [f. SNEAK *sb.*]

**A.** *adj.* **1.** Of persons: Like or resembling a sneak; mean, paltry, sneaking.

**1833** *Christmas Improvement* ii. (1841) 32 She is a nasty sneaky thing, for she is always trying to make us say things that are not true. **1873** MISS BROUGHTON *Nancy* I. 142 'Did you ever see such a fool as I look?' say I, feeling very sneaky.

**2.** Characterized by, partaking of, sneaking.

**1860** G. H. KINGSLEY *Sport & Trav.* (1900) 224 The blue hare..pestering your pointers and setters with his sneaky draws, and foolishly astute meanderings. **1865** BURRITT *Walk Land's End* 333 We attribute a mean, sneaky, hypocritical mind to Mr. Pecksniff. **1868** BOYD *Less. Middle Age* 256 That sneaky way in which some people are able to insinuate evil against their neighbours.

**3.** ***Sneaky Pete, sneaky pete***: a name given to any of various illicit or cheap intoxicating beverages. Also *attrib. slang* (orig. and chiefly *U.S.*).

**1949** *Collier's* 3 Sept. 40/1 A group which was.. discussing the effects of 'sneaky-pete', a generic term for fortified wines. **1951** [see POT *sb.*$^{5}$ 1]. **1955** *Amer. Speech* XXX. 88 *Sneaky pete*, marijuana mixed in wine. **1965** J. S. GUNN *Terminol. Shearing Industry* I. 32 *Sneaky pete*, one of the many vivid names..which shearers and others give to cheap wine. **1971** J. H. JONES in J. H. Clarke *Harlem* 310 He walked around an unconscious Sneaky Pete drinker. **1978** J. GORES *Gone, no Forwarding* (1979) vi. 40 The stranger bought a pint of sneaky pete and he and Sammy went to sit in his short and drink it.

**B.** as *sb.* A small concealed microphone or other device for surveillance or espionage.

**1974** M. COPELAND *Real Spy World* 317 A 'sneaky' differs from the other technical devices in that it is planted inside an intelligence target. **1977** F. WEBB *Go for Out* v. 78 His car had been fitted with a sneaky..searching for a microscopic radio transmitter was pointless. **1978** D. BLOODWORTH *Crosstalk* xxi. 168, I never actually found the mikes or the cameras, but..I just thought I'd get away from all the sneakies.

Hence **'sneakily** *adv.*

**1966** D. VARADAY *Gara-Yaka's Domain* vii. 75 As fast as he drove off one crowd of fluttering birds, another swooped in, nipping sneakily with slashing beaks. **1974** P. CAVE *Mama* (new ed.) ix. 77 Peter the publican was hovering sneakily around with his ears wide open.

**sneap** (sniːp), *sb.* Now *arch.* [f. SNEAP *v.*] A snub or check; a rebuke, reproof.

**1597** SHAKS. *2 Hen. IV*, II. i. 135 My Lord, I will not vndergo this sneape without reply. **1876** WEISS *Wit, Humour*, etc. iv. 149 A charter from Providence to give Falstaff his first sneap of retribution. **1887** *Blackw. Mag.* Sept. 365 He might have spared us this sneap, seeing that his own queen had been enamoured of an ass.

**sneap** (sniːp), *v.* Now *dial.* and *arch.* Also 7 **sneep.** [Later form of *snaip* SNAPE *v.*$^{1}$]

**1.** *trans.* To nip or pinch.

**1588–** [see SNEAPED, SNEAPING *ppl. adjs.*]. **1691** RAY *N.C. Words* 65 Herbs and Fruits sneapt with cold weather.

**2.** To check, repress; to snub, reprove, chide.

**1611** *Sec. Maiden's Trag.* III. i, Nay I am gon, Ime a man quickly sneapt. **1640** BROME *Antipodes* IV. ix, Doe you sneap me too my Lord?.. I had No need to come hither to be sneapt. **1659** MRS. HUTCHINSON *Mem. Col. Hutchinson* (1846) 391 They set him at light,..and made the poor man retire sneaped to his colonel. **1691** RAY *N.C. Words* 65 Children easily sneaped. **1865** S. EVANS *Brother Fabian's MS.* 5 My lord Archbishop sneaps us for our sloth. **1886–** in dial. glossaries, etc. (Lincs., Staffs.).

*fig.* and *transf.* **1623** BP. HALL *Works* (1837) V. 141 That we do enough hate our corruptions; when, at our sharpest, we do but gently sneap them. **1642** H. MORE *Song of Soul* III. iii. 18 Life that's here, When into it the soul doth closely wind, Is often sneep'd by anguish.

Hence **sneaped** *ppl. a.*

**1593** SHAKS. *Lucr.* 333 To ad a more reioysing to the prime, And giue the sneaped birds more cause to sing.

**sneaping** ('sniːpɪŋ), *ppl. a.* [f. SNEAP *v.*] Of the wind, etc.: Checking growth; nipping, biting. Also in fig. context.

**1588** SHAKS. *L.L.L.* I. i. 100 Like an enuious sneaping Frost, That bites the first borne infants of the Spring. **1611** —— *Wint. T.* I. ii. 13 No sneaping Winds at home. **1882** L. CAMPBELL *J. C. Maxwell* 45 His activities were apt..to take odd shapes, as in a healthy plant under a sneaping wind. **1900** *Contemp. Rev.* July 119 Sheltered..from the sneaping winds of ill-usage or mischance.

†**sneap-nose.** *Obs.*$^{-1}$ [f. SNEAP *v.*] One who has a pinched nose. (Cf. SNEIPE *v.*)

**1649** QUARLES *Virgin Widow* II, Must I be thus slighted.. by a Runnagate, a Sneap nose, a thin gut?

**sneath**, dial. var. of SNATH, scythe-pole.

**sneb**, *v.* Now *dial.* Also 5–7 **snebbe.** [var. of SNIB *v.*$^{1}$] *trans.* To reprimand, reprove, or check; to snub. Also *absol.*

In Chaucer *Prol.* 525 (see SNIB *v.*$^{1}$ 1) two or three manuscripts have *snebbe*.

*c* **1440** CAPGRAVE *Life St. Kath.* III. 261 (MS. Arundel), Therfore youre grace wyth pytous voys I pray To punyshe and snebbe youre-self as ye lest. **1579** SPENSER *Sheph. Cal.* Feb. 126 Which made this foolish Brere wexe so bold, That ..he cast him to scold, And snebbe the good Oake, for he was old. *a* **1586** SIDNEY *Arcadia* xxxiii. 22 (Grosart) II. 98 Thou heardst euen now a yong man sneb me sore. **1606** S. GARDINER *Bk. Angling* 157 So was Dauid by Nathan.. snebbed in this sort for his euill example. **1617** COLLINS *Def. Bp. of Ely* II. x. 515 The Nurse her selfe may waken the child ..; chide it and sneb it, as well as giue it the dugge. **1846** W. DRUMMOND *Muckomachy* 18 The man thus snebbit Lost too his tebbit. **1867–** in dial. use (Lancs., Yks.).

**sneck** (snɛk), *sb.*$^{1}$ Chiefly *Sc.* and *north. dial.* Forms: α. 4–5 **snekke**, 5 **snekk**, 5–7, 9 **snek**, 5–6 **sneke**; 6– **sneck**, 7 **snecke**; 7, 9 **snack**; β. 8– **snick.** [Of obscure origin: cf. SNATCH *sb.* 1.]

**1.** The latch of a door or gate; the lever which raises the bar of a latch; †a catch (cf. 2 a).

α. **1324** *Acc. Exch., K.R.* Bd. 165 No. 1 m. 4, Pro xxviij snekkes cum xxviij stapulis ad tenendum trendles ligni pro springaldis tendendis. **1419** *Mem. Ripon* (Surtees) III. 147 Et in j snek ad ostium pulpiti, 1*d.* *c* **1440** *Promp. Parv.* 461/2 Snekke, or latche, *clitorium, pessulum.* *c* **1460** *Towneley Myst.* xiii. 306 *Mak.* Good wyff, open the hek!.. *Vxor.* I may thole the dray the snek. **1530** PALSGR. 272/1 Sneke, latche, *locquet, clicquette.* **1560** *Extr. Burgh Rec. Peebles* (1872) 258 To vphald substantiouslie thair portis in.. stapillis, snekkis and all irne graith necessare. **1600** *Churchw. Acc. Pittington*, etc. (Surtees) 133 For mending the North church gate, and also an iron sneck. **1638** *Ibid.* 302 A snecke for the ministers sette. *c* **1725** in J. J. Vernon *Parish of Hawick* (1900) 80 Paid for 2 Snecks for Quire doore. **1770** BP. FORBES *Jrnl.* (1886) 303 Any one, by Night or by Day, can lift the Sneck and come in. **1781–** in many dial. glossaries and texts (Sc., N. Ir., N. Cy., E. Ang., Derby, Warw., etc.). **1816** SCOTT *Antiq.* xxxiii, The sneck was drawn, and the Countess..entered my dwelling. **1853** G. J. CAYLEY *Las Alforjas* II. 216 Sometimes the demons will undo the sneck of the gate. **1885** RUNCIMAN *Skippers & Shellbacks* 50 The old man lifted the 'sneck' quickly and caught us.

β. **1786** BURNS *The Vision* vii, When click! the string the snick did draw. **1889** A. MUNRO *Siren Casket* 169 He raised the snick Of Allan's cottage door.

**b.** ***to draw a sneck***, to act cunningly or stealthily.

*a* **1500** in *Ratis Raving*, etc. 89 Thar word is fyrst in awdiens, With fenȝeand falsat ay reddy To draw a snek rycht subtely. **1786** BURNS *To G. Hamilton* iii, I ken he weel a Snick can draw, When simple bodies let him.

**c.** ***on the sneck***, latched. So ***off the sneck***.

**1824** SCOTT *St. Ronan's* xxviii, I'se warrant it a twa-handed ghaist, and the door left on the sneck. **1893** STEVENSON *Catriona* xv. 167 The door was on the sneck that day. **1897** CROCKETT *Lads' Love* iv. 43 Then..leave the lang window o' the ben room off the sneck, after the lairds are awa'.

**2.** *techn.* **a.** A catch or device for holding the lever of a spinning-machine.

**1825** J. NICHOLSON *Operat. Mechanic* 426 When in geer they [i.e. levers] are held firm by the sneck. *Ibid.*, The machine is put in motion by raising the main lever into the sneck by hand.

**b.** (See quot.)

**1883** GRESLEY *Gloss. Coal-m.* 229 *Snecks*, appliances for diverting wagons from the main line into a siding.

**3.** *dial.* or *techn.* in various senses (see quots.).

**1810** S. SMITH *Agric. Surv. Galloway* 86 Besides the improvement of locked tops [in stone walls], he invented also snecks or hudds, i.e. spaces built single at short intervals. **1828** CARR *Craven Gloss.*, *Sneck*, a small piece or tongue of land, abutting on or intersecting an adjoining field. **1883** GRESLEY *Gloss. Coal-m.* 229 *Sneck*, a carving [= air-way].

**4.** *attrib.*, as ***sneck-fastening***, ***-lock***; **sneck-band** (see quot. 1828); **sneck-bend**, a form of fish-hook (see quots.); **sneck posset**, a cold reception or greeting; a discharge or dismissal; **sneck-string**, a sneck-band.

The *Eng. Dial. Dict.* contains a number of other examples. **14..** *Nom.* in Wr.-Wülcker 733 *Hec mastiga*, a *snek-bank [? *read* -band]. *Hic gumfus*, a dorbande. **1828** CARR *Craven Gloss.*, *Sneck-band*, the string fastened to the latch, and passed through a hole to the outside of the door. **1855** WAUGH *Life & Local.* 106 The door is still opened from without by a 'sneck-bant'. **1816** BAINBRIDGE *Fly Fisher's Guide* 31 The *Sneckbend, as it is commonly called, diverges from the parallel lines from the bend upwards. **1856** 'STONEHENGE' *Brit. Rural Sports* I. v. ii. 235 Many Scotchmen use what is called the sneckbend, differing slightly from both of the above [hooks], in being made of a more square shape. **1844** H. STEPHENS *Book of Farm* I. 204, 10 Pairs of crooks and bands for feeding-holes. 10 *Sneck-fastenings for ditto. **1570** *Wills & Inv.* (Surtees, 1835) 312, I do geve vnto An Jaxssonn one woode Cheast which haithe a *sneck locke. **1876** J. RICHARDSON *Cumbld. Talk* Ser. II. 65 A *sneck posset I gat. **1885** HALL CAINE *Shadow Crime* 8 He had his own reasons for not quitting Wythburn after he had received his very unequivocal 'sneck posset'. **1758** W. RECKITT *Jrnl.* (1799) 59 They did not so much as pull in their *sneck-string when they went to bed and had neither lock nor bar.

**sneck**, *sb.*[2] *Sc.* [f. SNECK *v.*[2]] A sharp cut; a snick or snip.

**1768** ROSS *Helenore* II. 84 The gully .. may chance to gee's a sneck into the hand. **1814** SCOTT *Wav.* xli, If there's a pair of sheers in the Highlands that has a baulder sneck than her's ain.

**sneck**, *sb.*[3] [Imitative.] A sharp clicking sound. Cf. SNICK *sb.*[3]

**1851** MAYNE REID *Scalp Hunt.* iv, Back went the girth buckles with a 'sneck'. **1861** A. LEIGHTON *Trad. Sc. Life* Ser. II. 116 An industrious house too, wherein the birr of the wheel and the sneck of the reel had sounded.

**sneck** (snɛk), *v.*[1] Chiefly *Sc.* and *north. dial.* Also 5 **snekk-**, 9 **snek**. [f. SNECK *sb.*[1]]

**1.** *trans.* To latch (a door or gate); to close or fasten with or by means of a sneck.

*c* **1440** *Promp. Parv.* 284/2 Latchyn, or snekkyn, *pessulo*. **1560** *Maitl. Club. Misc.* III. 239 The deponar .. fand the dur snecked and vnbarred and sche barred the dur. **1674** RAY *N.C. Words* 43 *Snock* [**1691** *Sneck*] the door: Latch the door. **1768** ROSS *Helenore* 36 Sae out she slips, an' snecks the door behind. **1787-** in dial. glossaries and texts (Sc., N. Cy., Notts., Linc., Warw., etc.). **1868** G. MACDONALD *R. Falconer* I. 175 Sneck the door, laddie. **1889** *Carlisle Patriot* 1 Mar. (E.D.D.), If the gate had been snecked, the cattle could not have got on the line.

**b.** To lock or shut *up*. In quot. *fig.*

**1816** SCOTT *Antiq.* xxix, The secrets of grit folk .. are just like the wild beasts that are shut up in cages. Keep them hard and fast snecked up, and it's a' very weel.

**c.** *intr.* Of a door or gate: To latch, shut.

**1871** MRS. EWING *Brownies*, etc. 107 The gate opened for them and snecked after them. **1889** TENNYSON *Owd Roa* xxxii, I'd clear forgot .. thy chaumber door wouldn't sneck.

**2.** *trans.* (See quot. 1808.) *Sc.*

**1792** *Stat. Acc. Scotl.* II. 534 Farm-houses and Cottages.— .. A very few of them have been stob-thatched, or covered with a deep coat of straw,—and snecked or harled with lime. **1808** JAMIESON, *To sneck* with lime, to make indentations in a wall, filling the blanks with lime; or, in building, to insert a small quantity between the stones in the outer side.

**sneck** (snɛk), *v.*[2] *Sc.* [Origin, and relation to SNICK *v.*[2], uncertain.] *trans.* To cut (*off*).

**1560** ROLLAND *Seven Sages* 103 He tuik hir be the nek, And with ane knife hir heid he did of snek. **1818** SCOTT *Rob Roy* xxxii, Do the folk think I hae another thrapple in my pouch after John Highlandman's sneckit this ane wi' his joctaleg? **1835** CARRICK *Laird Logan* (1854) 156 Mony a ane o' my acquaintances hae gotten the thread o' life sneckit.

**sneck**, *v.*[3] Now *dial.* [Origin obscure.] *trans.* To snatch; to take or seize quickly.

**1607** MIDDLETON *Five Gallants* I. ii, Pursn. Her Chaine of Pearle. *Boy.* I sneckt it away finely. **1873** MURDOCH *Doric Lyre* 43 When rent day comes ye're unca fain To look us up an' sneck the siller.

**sneck-drawer.** Now *Sc.* and *north.* Also 9 **snick-**. [f. SNECK *sb.*[1] + DRAWER *sb.*[1]: cf. *latch-drawer* and DRAW-LATCH.] One who draws or lifts a sneck or latch (in order to enter stealthily); a crafty, flattering, or sly fellow (cf. quot. 1808).

**1402** *Pol. Poems* (Rolls) II. 98 3oure prowde losengerie that rune abowt as snek-drawers. **1806** R. JAMIESON *Pop. Ballads* I. 295 Whan the tittlin ald snick-drawers fell to. **1808** JAMIESON s.v., *An auld sneck-drawer*, one who, from long experience, has acquired a great degree of facility in accomplishing any artful purpose. **1818** SCOTT *Br. Lamm.* xiii, Doited idiot!—that auld clavering sneck-drawer wad gar ye trow the moon is made of green cheese. **1846** CHALMERS in Hanna *Mem.* (1852) IV. xxiv. 457 He was just too much of a sneck-drawer.

So **'sneck-draw**; also **sneck-drawing** *vbl. sb.* and *ppl. a.*, **sneck-drawn** *a.*

**1886** STEVENSON *Kidnapped* xvi, There's many a lying *sneck-draw sits close in kirk. **1894** CROCKETT *Raiders* xxxi, I ken the Maxwell lads and I ken the hill sneck-draws. **1785-6** BURNS *Addr. to Deil* xvi, Ye auld, *snick-drawing dog! **1818** SCOTT *Br. Lamm.* xxi, The old sneck-drawing whigamore her father. *c* **1830** HOGG *Bridal of Polmood* vii, Onye sikkan wylld sneckdrawinge and pawkerye. **1820** T. WILSON *Pitman's Pay* I. liii, If aw din't her bottle fill, Aw's then a skint-flint, *sneck-drawn dog.

**snecke**, obs. form of SNICK *v.*[1]

**snecked** (snɛkt), *ppl. a. Building.* [app. f. SNECK *sb.*[1]] Built of squared stones, but of different sizes and not laid in regular courses.

**1883** *Specif. Alnwick & Cornhill Rlwy.* 48 The abutments, .. foundations and parapets are to be constructed in accordance with the General Specification for Snecked or Fitted Rubble. **1883** *Alnwick Mercury* 17 Nov. 2 The building is of snecked walling.

**'snecket.** [Dim. of SNECK *sb.*[1]] A sneck or sneck-band. Also *transf.*, a noose, halter.

**1611** COTGR., *Loquet d'vne huis*, the latch, or snecket of a doore. **1671** SKINNER *Etymol. Ling. Angl.*, The Sneck or Snecket of a door, *funiculus obicis* [etc. Hence in Ray, Grose, etc.]. **1788** *New London Mag.* 494 Then over his head let the snecket be got, And under one ear be well settled the knot. **1869-** in Cumbld. dial. glossaries.

**sned**, *sb.*: see SNEAD.

**sned**, *v.* Forms: 1 **snædan** (*pa. t.* **snædde, snedde**), 6- **sned**, 7 **snedde, snad, snead**, 8 **snade**. [OE. *snǽdan*, related to *sníðan* SNITHE *v.* For the shortening of the vowel cf. KEP *v.*]

**1. a.** *trans.* To cut or lop off (a branch). Also in fig. context, and with *off*. In later use *Sc.* and *north. dial.*

*a* **800** *Leiden Gloss.* 249 in *O.E. Texts* 117 *Putat*, snædit. *c* **897** K. ÆLFRED *Gregory's Past. C.* xxxiii. 222 Hit bið unnyt ðæt mon hwelces yfles boȝas snæde [etc.]. *c* **975** *Rushw. Gosp.* Matt. xxi. 8 Sume þonne sneddun telgran of treowum & stræȝdun on þæm weȝe. **1513** DOUGLAS *Æneid* XI. i. 14 Ane akin tre, .. The branchis sned and kut abowt alquhair. *a* **1572** KNOX *Hist. Ref.* Wks. 1846 I. 192 Otheris sned the branches of the Papistrie, but he stryckis at the roote. **1637** GILLESPIE *Eng. Pop. Cerem.* III. ii. 26 Whereby they did in some sort snedde the reviving twigs of old superstition. **1645** in *Baillie's Lett. & Jrnls.* (1775) II. 94 Which [writing], although it took not away the root, yet did it sned many of the branches of the evils complained of. **1735** E. ERSKINE *Serm.* Wks. 1871 II. 337 The Lord of the Vineyard sneds the luxuriant branches. **1829** in BROCKETT *N.C. Gloss.* (ed. 2). *c* **1870** W. GRAHAM *Lect. Ephes.* 351 The branch sned off from the vine becomes a sport of the winds.

*transf.* **1786** BURNS *To a Haggis* vii, He .. legs, an' arms, an' heads will sned, Like taps o' thrissle. **1819** TENNANT *Papistry Storm'd* (1827) 199 First his richt ear he clean aff-cleft, And then he sneddit aff his left.

**b.** To prune (a tree); to divest of branches.

**1595** DUNCAN *App. Etym.* (E.D.S.), *Puto, autumno*, .. to sned trees. **1640** RUTHERFORD *Lett.* (1881) II. xxxv. 438 He is only lopping and snedding a fruitful tree. **1686** in *14th Rep. Hist. MSS. Comm.* App. III. 116, I resolve rather to give it over and go home and snad trees at Polwart House. **1710** RUDDIMAN *Gloss. Douglas' Æneis* s.v. *Sneith*, To sned, i.e. to prune timber-trees. **1894** HESLOP *Northumbld. Gloss.* 664 After a tree is cut down it is *snedded*, or divested of all its branches. **1953** H. L. EDLIN *Forester's Handbk.* xiii. 205 As soon as the tree is down it should be lopped or snedded, by cutting the branches away from the trunk. **1971** *Timber Trades Jrnl.* 3 Apr. 58/2 Although the chainsaw has long been used for limbing hardwoods the technique of snedding softwoods with a power saw is relatively new.

**2.** To cut; to form, or sever, by cutting. *Sc.* and *north. dial.*

In ME. this sense occurs in the comb. *to-snēden*.

**1789** BURNS *To Dr. Blacklock* vi, But I'll sned besoms—thraw saugh woodies. **1888** YEATS *Folk Tales* 268 He .. pulled up the fir-tree, .. and having *snedded* it into a walking-stick [etc]. **1889** A. MUNRO *Siren Casket* 239 Heart I've not .. To sned your thread of life.

Hence **'snedded** *ppl. a.*; **'snedder**; **'snedding** *vbl. sb.* (also *attrib.*).

**1584** in *Melvil's Diary* (Wodrow Soc.) 177 The snedders and delvers of the wyneyeard. *c* **1670** J. FRASER *Polichron.* (S.H.S.) 269 The smith .. finding the fresh sneaded branches, makes search under the tree. **1720** T. BOSTON *Fourf. State* (1797) 279 He that would ingraft, must needs use the snedding-knife. **1725** A. JERVISE *Epit.*, etc. (1879) II. 39/1 With spade and Raik, .. The snading ax and pruning knife. **1735** E. ERSKINE *Serm.* Wks. 1871 II. 337 The snedding of the tree contributes to the .. growth of the branches. **1808** JAMIESON, *Sneddins*, the prunings, or twigs, lopped off from trees. **1825** —— *Suppl.*, *Snedder*, a pruner, one who lops off branches.

†**snede.** *Obs.* [OE. *snǽd*, = ON. *sneið*, related to OE. *sníðan* SNITHE *v.*] A small piece, morsel.

*c* **1000** *Saxon Leechd.* II. 268 ðenim rædices .iii. snæda. *c* **1000** ÆLFRIC *Saints' Lives* I. xii. 62 þa hwile ðe se bisceop mæssode and began to etenne he feoll þa æt ðære forman snæde. *c* **1200** *Trin. Coll. Hom.* 181 Enes he [Adam] þar-offe bot, and wearð þar mide acheked, and þureh þat one snede wearð al his ofspring acheked.

**snee** (to cut): see SNICK OR SNEE.

**snee**, variant of SNY (to swarm), *dial.*

**sneeker-snee**, variant of SNICKERSNEE *v.*

**sneer** (snɪə(r)), *sb.* Also 8 **snear**. [f. the vb. Cf. NFris. *sneer* a scornful remark.]

**1.** An act of sneering; a look or expression implying derision, contempt, or scorn; a disdainful or scornful remark or utterance, esp. one of a covert or indirect nature.

**1707** *Refl. upon Ridicule* 107 He is applauded with a Sneer. **1711** HEARNE *Collect.* (O.H.S.) III. 251 He looks upon Atterbury's Complement as a Snear. **1773** GOLDSM. *Stoops to Conq.* III. i, A sneer at my understanding. **1816** J. SCOTT *Vis. Paris* (ed. 5) p. xvii, By making this confession I shall incur the sneers of those .. who have strong prepossessions and few scruples. **1849** MACAULAY *Hist. Eng.* vi. II. 113 Halifax .. answered with a sneer that there was no danger. **1879** H. GEORGE *Progr. & Pov.* II. iii. (1881) 121 Amid the scoffs .. and the sneers that stab like knives.

**b.** Without article: Sneering, scorn.

**1791** LD. AUCKLAND *Corr.* (1861) 396 He speaks even of those who are opposed to his government .. without either sneer or acrimony. **1841** in *Leic. Gloss.* (1881) 246 He could not bear To see her treated with such scorn and sneer.

**2.** *Sc.* A snort.

Jamieson (1825) also gives 'the act of inhalation or inspiration by the nostrils'; 'the act of a horse, when colded, in throwing the mucus from his nostrils'; 'the hiss of an adder'.

**17..** *Lochmaben Harper* in Child *Ballads* IV. 18/1 When she came to the harper's door, There she gave mony a nicher and sneer.

**sneer** (snɪə(r)), *v.* Also 7 **sneare**, 7-8 **snear**. [prob. of imitative origin. The relation to NFris. (Sylt) *sneere* to scorn, is not clear.

Apparent examples of *snere*, *snered*, and *snering* occur about 1300 in the *E.E. Psalter* ii. 4, xxxiv. 16, lxxviii. 4, and lxxix. 7, as renderings of L. *irridebit*, *deriserunt*, and *derisus*; but two of the MSS. have variants *swere*, *swered*, *swering*. The translator was evidently influenced by the OE. glosses *bismerað*, *bismeradon*, *bismerung*, and it is very doubtful whether he was using a word which was really known to him.]

**1.** *intr.* Of a horse: To snort. Now *dial.* †Also *trans.*, to send *out* with snorts.

**1553** *Douglas' Æneid* VII. v. 101 With twa sterne stedis .. At thair neis thyrles the fyre fast furth snering out. **1607** MARKHAM *Caval.* (1617) VI. 12 If .. you doe now and then spirt a little Vinegar into his nostrels, .. it will both make him sneare and neese. **1814** in Hone *Every-day Bk.* II. 1115 The colt .. scampered off sneering, with his tail on his 'riggin'. **1878** DICKINSON *Cumbld. Gloss.* s.v., If a horse sneers efter he coughs he's nut brokken windit.

**b.** *Sc.* Of an animal: To make a twitching movement with the nose.

**1844** H. STEPHENS *Bk. Farm* II. 447 On the extrusion of the calf, the first symptom it shews of life is a few gasps .., and then it opens its eyes, and tries to shake its head, and sneer with its nose.

**2.** To smile scornfully or contemptuously; to express scorn, derision, or disparagement in this way; to speak or write in a manner suggestive or expressive of contempt or disparagement:

**a.** Const. *at* a person or thing.

**1680** H. MORE *Apocal. Apoc.* 357 The Wits of this age that are ready to snear and flear at any such profession. *a* **1744** POPE (J.), I could be content to be a little sneered at in a line. *a* **1763** W. KING *Polit. & Lit. Anecd.* (1819) 20 The French seemed to sneer at this behaviour of the German officers, and looked on them with a kind of contempt. **1814** SCOTT *Wav.* liv, Flora, observing the Lowland ladies sneer at the comparison, produced some reason to shew that it was not altogether so absurd. **1858** MAX MÜLLER *Chips* (1880) III. i. 30 Luther was sneered at because of his little German tracts. **1874** L. STEPHEN *Hours Libr.* (1892) I. x. 361 Walpole sheltered himself behind .. a pension to sneer at the tragi-comedy of life.

**b.** Without const.

**1735** POPE *Prol. Sat.* 202 Damn with faint praise, assent with civil leer, And without sneering, teach the rest to sneer. **1781** COWPER *Conversat.* 182 The fear Lest fops should censure us, and fools should sneer. **1818** SHELLEY *Rosalind* 655 Men wondered, and some sneered to see One sow what he could never reap. **1837** CARLYLE *Fr. Rev.* I. III. iii, Philosophedom sneers aloud, as if its Necker already triumphed. **1855** THACKERAY *Newcomes* i, If authors sneer, it is the critic's business to sneer at them for sneering.

*fig.* **1835** L. HUNT *Poems* (1844) 96 Sneereth the trumpet, and stampeth the drum.

†**3.** To laugh foolishly or smirkingly; to grin.

**1683** WOOD *Life* 17 Feb., They .. stand silent, while their abbettors sneare and grin. **1695** *Ibid.* 23 Mar., With Mr J. Ecc. at the house next the Half-Moon: two snearing and laughing wo[men]: he sneared and laughed with them. **1705** R. BEVERLEY *Virginia* II. xviii. (1722) 121 A Fourth would fondly kiss, and paw his Companions, and snear in their Faces, with a Countenance more antick, than any in a Dutch Droll. **1719** DE FOE *Crusoe* II. (Globe) 558 Our .. Pilot, who had always something or other to say to make us merry, came sneering to me, and told me [etc.].

**b.** *dial.* (See quot.)

*a* **1825** FORBY *Voc. E. Anglia*, *Sneer*, to make wry faces, without intention of expressing contempt or insult.

**c.** *Naut.* (See quot.)

**1867** SMYTH *Sailor's Word-bk.* s.v., To 'make all sneer again' is to carry canvas to such an extent as to strain the ropes and spars to the utmost.

**4.** *trans.* To utter with a sneer or in a sneering tone.

**1693** CONGREVE *Old Bach.* I. iv, I confess I have not been sneering fulsome lyes and nauseous flattery. **1864** TENNYSON *Voyage* 78 'A ship of fools,' he sneer'd and wept. **1904** A. E. GLOVER *1000 Miles of Miracle* x. (1908) 126 He sneered some contemptuous word.

**5.** To speak or write of (a person or thing) with scorn, contempt, or disparagement; to deride or decry. *Obs.* exc. *dial.*

**1707** *Refl. upon Ridicule* 94 When People ridicule and sneer you. **1740-2** RICHARDSON *Pamela* III. 41 Wedlock, which used to be very freely sneered by him. **1755** B. MARTIN *Mag. Arts & Sci.* 64 Blackmore's Banter on the Philosophers .. proved more his own than their Ignorance, when he thus sneers them. *a* **1900** in *Eng. Dial. Dict.* s.v., He sneered me shameful.

**6.** To curl *up* (the lip) in contempt or scorn. *rare.*

**1775** S. J. PRATT *Liberal Opin.* liii. (1783) II. 136 A pennyworth, sir!—cried the steward, (sneering up his upper-lip, till it touched the tip of his nose ..) a pennyworth!

**7.** To affect in a certain way by sneering; to drive or force by means of sneers or scornful speech or manner:

**a.** Const. with preps., as *from, into, out of*.

**1737** Savage *Of Public Spirit* 325 Careless of Whispers meant to wound their Name, Nor sneer'd nor brib'd from Virtue into Shame. **1859** *Habits of Gd. Society* vii. 243 Who contradicts us flatly, and sneers us into insignificance. **1867** Augusta Wilson *Vashti* xviii, The world has not sneered it [feminine constancy] entirely out of existence.

*refl.* **1841** Thackeray *Sec. Funeral Napoleon* iii, It sneaks and bullies and sneers itself into place.

**b.** Const. with advs., as *away* or *down*.

**1816** Scott *Antiq.* xii, But dinna ye sneer awa the lad Lovel. **1838** Lytton *Alice* vi. ii, Proclaimed a sublime genius in the same circles which sneer down Voltaire. **1868** Whyte Melville *White Rose* xlviii, Very likely they were laughing over his infatuation and sneering her fair fame away. **1868** Helps *Realmah* viii. (1876) 237 Sneering can do a great deal: you can sneer down, at any rate for the moment, truth, honour [etc.].

*refl.* **1847** Helps *Friends in C.* i. iv. 68 He mutters to himself sarcastically, sneering himself up as it were to the attack.

**sneerer** ('snɪərə(r)). [f. prec.] One who sneers.

**1713** *Guardian* No. 29, The Sneerers..always indulge their mirth at the expence of their friends, and all their ridicule consists in unseasonable ill-nature. **1770** Langhorne *Plutarch* (1851) II. 795/2 The laughter of these sneerers has cost their country many a tear. **1824** Byron *Def. Transformed* i. ii, Oh, thou everlasting sneerer! Be silent! **1842** Borrow *Bible in Spain* ii, The sneerers and scoffers at religion do not spring from amongst the simple children of nature. **1874** B. Taylor in *Life* (1884) II. 652 The sneerers and cavilers are growing silent one by one.

**'sneerful,** *a.* [f. sneer *sb.*] **a.** Of persons: Given to sneering. **b.** Of words, etc.: Of the nature of a sneer; scornful.

*a* **1763** Shenstone *Economy* iii. Wks. 1764 I. 303 Cell ever squalid! where the sneerful maid Will not fatigue her hand! **1844** Tupper *Heart* xi. 120 Out-swearing and out-threatening our sneerful stock-jobber. **1880** *S. Wales Daily News* No. 2514. 6/6 We had a sneerful and insulting answer.

Hence **'sneerfulness.**

**1873** Leland *Egypt. Sketch-Bk.* 204 Cherishing no feeling of scorn or sneerfulness against them.

**sneering** ('snɪərɪŋ), *vbl. sb.* [f. sneer *v.*] The action of the verb sneer.

**1687** Miége ii, *Sneering*, a kind of ridiculous Laughter. **1847** Hare *Guesses* Ser. i. (ed. 3) 345 Sneering is commonly found along with a bitter, splenetic misanthropy. **1868** [see sneer *v.* 7 b]. **1908** *Edin. Rev.* Oct. 421 The Baron was equal with her in the matter of sneering.

**b.** *attrib.*, as **sneering match**, *E. Angl. dial.* a grinning match (Forby, *a* 1825); **sneering muscle**, a muscle instrumental in producing a sneering expression on the face (*Cent. Dict.* 1891).

**sneering** ('snɪərɪŋ), *ppl. a.* [f. as prec.]

**1.** That sneers; wearing a sneer.

**1681** N. N. *Rome's Follies* 17, I believe the sneering sluts laugh'd at me. **1695** Wood *Life* 23 Mar., Two snearing and laughing wo[men]. **1716** C'tess Cowper *Diary* (1864) 114 Lord Townshend is the sneeringest, fawningest knave that ever was. **1792** Mary Wollstonecr. *Rights Wom.* vii. 285 Thou startest from a dream, only to face a sneering frowning world. **1823** Lamb *Elia* ii. *Poor Relations*, The streets of this sneering and prying metropolis. **1841** Browning *Pippa Passes* Poems (1905) 168 White sneering old reproachful face.

*fig.* **1832** L. Hunt *Poems* 173 The harsh bray The sneering trumpet sends across the fray.

**2.** Of the nature of, marked or characterized by, a sneer; scornful, contemptuous, disparaging.

**1692** L'Estrange *Fables* i. clvi, The Fox in a Snearing Way advis'd him..not to Irritate a Prince against his Subjects. *c* **1695** H. Anderson *Court Convert* 221 You must ..With sneering Praise guild o'er his blackest Crimes. **1771** *Junius Lett.* liv. (1788) 293, I..will not descend to answer the little sneering sophistries of a collegian. **1821** Scott *Kenilw.* xli, His countenance presenting..the habitual expression of sneering sarcasm. **1848** W. H. Kelly tr. *L. Blanc's Hist. Ten Y.* II. 316 They were received with a sneering indifference. **1877** Dowden *Shaks. Primer* vi. 78 Greene's sneering allusion to Shakespere in the 'Groats-worth of Wit'.

**'sneeringly,** *adv.* [f. prec.] In a sneering or scornful manner; with a sneer.

**1711** Hearne *Collect.* (O.H.S.) III. 127 This he spoke sneeringly and by way of derision and Contempt. **1740–2** Richardson *Pamela* II. 227 Well, Child, said she, sneeringly, how dost find thyself? **1813** Byron *Br. Abydos* i. v, Sneeringly these accents fell. **1865** Miss Braddon *H. Dunbar* ii, James Wentworth laughed sneeringly. **1886** W. J. Tucker *E. Europe* 243 'They now rejoice in the aristocratic name of Desewffy,' said he sneeringly.

**'sneerless,** *a.* [f. sneer *sb.*] That does not sneer; free from sneers.

**1884** Birrell *Obiter Dicta* 157 A sneerless Gibbon and an impartial Macaulay.

**'sneery,** *a.* [f. sneer *sb.*] Of a sneering or scornful character.

**1872** Lever *Ld. Kilgobbin* lix, The summary..was acrimonious and sneery. **1919** D. Ashford *Young Visiters* viii. 53 Ethel patted her hair and looked very sneery. **1949** D. Smith *I capture Castle* iii. xv. 289 'Does he believe in it?' 'No, he's always very sneery.' **1967** *Punch* 22 Nov. 776/1 It has taken twenty years to get rid of the amateurs, and the professionals..are having a hard time breaking down the sneery reputation gained. **1977** *N.Y. Rev. Bks.* 9 June 10/4 The sneery attitude toward surgeons that many physicians ..were at one time wont to affect.

**sneesh** (sniːʃ). *Sc.* and *north. dial.* Also 9 sneish; 8–9 **snish.** [? Back-formation from next: but cf. snush *sb.*, of which the Gloucester dial. *snish* is probably a variant. Ir. Gael. has *snaois.*]

**a.** Snuff. **b.** A pinch of snuff.

The verb *sneesh* to snuff, and *sneesher* a snuffer, are also current in mod. Sc. dial. (recorded from 1801–9).

**1786** *Har'st Rig* xix, Led on by Malcolm,.. Wha taks his snish. **1817** [R. D. C. Brown] *Lintoun Green* 57 Whan takan' o' a sneesh. **1874** Hislop *Scot. Anecd.* 6 She did not care one pinch o' snish!

*attrib.* **1825** [see sneeze *sb.* 3].

**'sneeshing.** *Sc.* (*Ir.*) and *north. dial.* Forms: α. 8 snishon, -en, 9 -an (8 snichen, snitian), 8–9 snishin(g. β. 7, 9 sneeshon, 9 -an, 8–9 sneeshin(g, sneeshin', 9 sneechin(g, etc. [Alteration of sneezing *vbl. sb.* 2 b, perhaps after Highland or Irish pronunciation: cf. Sc. Gael. *snaoisean*, Ir. *snaoisín.*]

**1.** Snuff.

α. **1714** R. Smith *Poems* (1853) 12 Thy vile snichen, and thy brose. **1720** Pennecuik *Helicon* 65 A Mill with Snitian, to pepper her Nose. **1724** Ramsay *Tea-t. Misc.* (1733) I. 91 A Mill of good snishing to prie. **1761** in Hull *Select Lett.* (1778) I. 314, I have sent you a little Provision of the best Preston-Pans Snuff,.. with one Bottle of Highland Snishon. **1818** Scott *Br. Lamm.* xii, Bid her fill my mill wi' snishing. **1847** Le Fanu *T. O'Brien* 213 Take a pinch iv the snishin.

β. **1808** Jamieson, *Sneeshin*,.. the vulgar name for snuff. **1816** Scott *Antiq.* xxi, A' the siller I need is just to buy tobacco and sneeshin. **1824** —— *Redgauntlet* ch. vii, Will ye try my sneeshing? **1900** Crockett *Little Anna Mark* xxi, The noblest sneeshan in the worl'.

**2.** A pinch of snuff. Chiefly with negatives, used to denote something of very slight value or significance.

**1686** G. Stuart *Joco-ser. Disc.* 13, I drew my Box, and teuk a sneeshon. **1723** Meston *Knt. of Kirk* Poems (1767) 25 Else they are not worth a snishen. **1787–** in Scottish use (*Eng. Dial. Dict.*).

**3.** *attrib.*, as ***sneeshing-box, -horn, -mill*** or ***-mull.***

**1717** Ramsay *Elegy Lucky Wood* x, To the sma' hours we aft sat still, Nick'd round our toasts and snishing-mill. **1780** W. Forbes *Dominie* i. 79 His fishing-wand, his sneeshing-box. **1786** Burns *Twa Dogs* 133 The luntan pipe, an' sneeshin mill, Are handed round wi' right guid will. **1816** Scott *Antiq.* xxiii, I could take my aith to that sneeshing-mull amang a thousand. **1825** Jamieson *Suppl.*, *Sneeshin-Horn*, a horn used for holding snuff. **1858** Porteous *Souter Johnny* 28 I'm Souter Johnny's sneeshin'-Box.

**sneevel,** Sc. var. snivel *sb.* and *v.*

**sneeze** (sniːz), *sb.* [f. the vb.]

**1.** A powder or preparation for inducing sneezing; snuff. *Obs.* exc. *north. dial.*

**1632** tr. *Bruel's Praxis Med.* 7 A sneeze of bastard Pellitory, Pepper. *c* **1746–** [see b]. *a* **1800** in Pegge *Suppl. Grose.* **1857–** in Lanc. dial. (*Eng. Dial. Dict.*).

**2.** An act of sneezing; a sudden and involuntary expiration of breath through the nose and mouth, accompanied by a characteristic sound.

**1646** Sir T. Browne *Pseud. Ep.* iv. ix. 199 Upon a sneeze of the Emperour of Monomotapa, there passed acclamations successively through the city. **1671** Milton *P.R.* iv. 458 As inconsiderable, And harmless, if not wholsom, as a sneeze To mans less universe. **1839** Dickens *Nickleby* iv, The little boy on the top of the trunk gave a violent sneeze. **1874** Carpenter *Ment. Phys.* i. i. (1879) 17 Whilst the act of coughing can be excited by a mandate of the will,.. we cannot thus execute a true sneeze.

**3.** *attrib.* (sense 1), as ***sneeze-box, -horn, -lurker*** (see quots.); **sneeze gas,** a substance used to incapacitate people by causing them to sneeze when it is inhaled or absorbed through the skin.

*c* **1746** J. Collier (Tim Bobbin) *View Lanc. Dial.* (1775) 40 [Sneeze-horn]. **1825** Brockett *N.C. Gloss.*, *Sneeze-horn* or *Sneesh-horn*, a common sort of snuff-box, made of cow's horn. **1838** Dickens *O. Twist* xliii, To think of.. the Artful Dodger going abroad for a common twopenny-halfpenny sneeze-box! **1864** *Slang Dict.*, *Sneeze-lurker*, one who throws snuff in a person's face and then robs him. **1918** E. S. Farrow *Dict. Mil. Terms* 567 *Sneeze-gas*, a gas which produces paroxysms of sneezing, so that it is difficult to keep on a mask if any of the gas is inhaled. **1966** *McGraw-Hill Encycl. Sci. & Technol.* III. 45/1 Sternutators, sometimes called sneeze gases or vomiting gases, cause physical discomfort.., and general malaise to such an extent that a casualty results.

**sneeze** (sniːz), *v.* Forms: 5 snese, 6–8 sneese (6 scniese), 6– sneeze, 7 sneez. [app. an alteration of fnese *v.*, due to misreading or misprinting it as 'fnese', after the initial combination *fn-* had become unfamiliar.

*Fnese* had app. gone out of use early in the 15th cent., its place being mainly supplied by *nese* neeze *v.* The adoption of *sneeze* was probably assisted by its phonetic appropriateness; it may have been felt as a strengthened form of *neeze*.

In the following places where *sn-* is printed in modern editions the correct reading is *fn-*:—Trevisa *Higden* (Rolls) V. 389; Chaucer *Manciple's Prol.* 62 (Camb. MS. Gg4. 27); *Lanfranc's Cirurg.* 197; Caxton's *Trevisa* (Rolls) V. 389 *footnote*; Caxton *Golden Leg.*, *Litanies* (= fol. xxii/1 of ed. 1483). See also the variants in the quots. below.]

**1. a.** *intr.* To drive or emit air or breath suddenly through the nose and mouth by an involuntary and convulsive or spasmodic action, accompanied by a characteristic sound.

In quot. 1493 = to snort.

**1493** *Festivall* (W. de W.) 108 b, Whan he herde ony man speke of theym anone for grete angre he wolde snese [1483 *Caxton* fnese] at the nose. **1495** *Trevisa's Barth. De P.R.* xvii. xxxviii. 625 Yf it [*sc.* cummin] is.. blowen in to the nosethrilles,.. it makith a man snese [*Bodl. MS.* fnese]. **1540** R. Jonas *Byrth Mankynde* 30 b, Let her be prouoked to sneese with the pouder of eleborus or pepper. **1570** Levins *Manip.* 211 To Sneeze, *sternutare*. **1582** N. Lichefield tr. *Castanheda's Conq. E. Ind.* i. xvii. 44 b, To spit or to scniese. **1601** Holland *Pliny* xxviii. ii. II. 297 If one chaunce to sneese after repast. **1673** Ray *Journ. Low C.* 403 One custom which prevails generally in foreign countreys.. is to salute those that sneez. **1709** Steele *Tatler* No. 35 ¶3 Being unused to Snuff, some Grains from off her upper Lip made him sneeze aloud. **1753** *Scots Mag.* Nov. 544/2 They bowed with a graceful simper to a lady who sneezed. **1849** Lytton *Caxtons* 61 You certainly have caught cold; you sneezed three times together. **1872** Geo. Eliot *Middlem.* lxii, There are conditions under which the most majestic person is obliged to sneeze.

**b.** *refl.* To bring (oneself) *into* a certain state by sneezing.

**1668** R. L'Estrange *Vis. Quev.* vii. (1702) 268 By how much it is more Honorable to Dye upon a Swords-point.. than for a Man to snivel and sneeze himself into another World.

**2.** *colloq.* With *at*: To regard as of little value, worth, or consideration; to despise, disregard, underrate. Chiefly in the negative phrase ***not to be sneezed at.***

(*a*) **1806** Surr *Winter in Lond.* II. 90 It's a sort of thing a young fellow of my expectations ought to sneeze at. **1838** Barham *Ingol. Leg.* Ser. i. *B. Maguire's Acc. Coronation* viii, If any bould traitour.. Sneezes at that, I'd like to see the man! **1902** *Daily Chron.* 12 June 9/3 Supposing this fire had occurred in Hackney,.. it would have been 'sneezed' at, if I may so put it.

(*b*) **1813** Scott 24 Aug. in *Lockhart*, As I am situated, £300 or £400 a-year is not to be sneezed at. **1840** Marryat *Poor Jack* l, She was a prize 'not to be sneezed at'. **1891** N. Gould *Double Event* 82 A thousand pounds.. was not a thing to be sneezed at.

**3.** *trans.* To eject or cast by sneezing.

**1677** Johnson in *Ray's Corr.* (1848) 128 Horsemen are not agreed what that is the foal is said to sneeze, which they call a milt. **1930** R. Campbell *Adamastor* 76 Their horses.. Vast phantom shapes with eyeballs rolling white That sneeze a fiery steam about their knees. **1961** G. Durrell *Whispering Land* viii. 194 Anyway, when I had sneezed some of the dust out of my nose, I clapped dutifully outside the gate.

**4.** To utter with a sneeze. Also with *out*.

The allusion in the first quot. is to Catullus xlv. 9–10.

**1851** Tennyson *E. Morris* 80 Shall not Love to me, As in the Latin song I learnt at school, Sneeze out a full God-bless-you, right and left? **1873** Ld. Houghton *Monogr.* 260 The preacher.. at once *sneezed* out the name *Ker-shaw* several times in various intonations.

Hence **'sneezing** *ppl. a.*

**1642** H. More *Song of Soul* ii. i. i. 22 Swift as the levin from the sneezing skie.

**sneezer** ('sniːzə(r)). [f. sneeze *v.*]

**1.** One who sneezes.

**1648** Hexham ii, *Een Nieser*, a Sneeser. **1684** tr. *Bonet's Merc. Compit.* iii. 65 The Ancients said, that Sneezers.. were indicated by excrementitious humours.. in the Ventricles.. of the Brain. **1801** *Monthly Mag.* XII. 224 He proves from Petronius.. that the custom of blessing sneezers was established among the Romans. **1882** Lubbock *Orig. Civil.* App. 495 A sneeze.. is evidence.. that the sneezer was possessed by some evil-disposed spirit.

**2.** In various slang, colloq., or dial. senses: **a.** A snuff-box. **b.** The nose. **c.** A dram or drink, esp. a stiff one. **d.** A pocket-handkerchief.

The *Eng. Dial. Dict.* gives other purely dial. uses.

**a.** **1725** *New Cant. Dict.*, *Cog a Sneezer*, Beg a.. Snuff-box. **1812** J. H. Vaux *Flash Dict.* **1839** *Slang Dict.* 34.

**b.** **1820** *Sporting Mag.* VI. 271 Hawkins put a tremendous nobber on the tip of Paddy's sneezer.

**c.** **1823** E. Moor *Suffolk Words*, *Sneeser*, or *Sneezer*,.. also ..means a dram. **1841** J. T. Hewlett *Parish Clerk* I. 290 He knew he should get a sneezer of something short for his trouble. **1868** Dickens *Lett.* (1880) II. 363 My New York landlord made me a 'Rocky Mountain sneezer'.

**d.** **1857** *Slang Dict.* 19.

**e.** Something exceptionally good, great, strong, violent, etc., in some respect (cf. quots.).

**1823** E. Moor *Suffolk Words*, *Sneeser*, or *Sneezer*, a severe blow. **1836** Haliburton *Clockm.* i. viii, It's awful to hear a minister swear; and the only match I know for it, is to hear a regular sneezer of a sinner quote Scripture. *Ibid.* xiii, I have one [horse] a proper sneezer, a chap that can go ahead of a rail-road steamer. **1855** F. Francis *Newton Dogvane* (1888) 242 What a fine breeze we have! a regular sneezer. **1867** Smyth *Sailor's Word-bk.*, *Sneezer*, a stiff gale of wind. **1902** *Westm. Gaz.* 22 July 3/1 The ball he bowled Fry with ..was what he would himself describe as a 'sneezer'.

**'sneezeweed.** Also sneeze-weed. [f. sneeze *v.*]

**1.** *U.S.* The plant *Helenium autumnale*, or other species of the same genus.

**1856** A. Gray *Man. Bot.* 224 *Helenium autumnale*, L. (Sneeze-weed). **1857** —— *First Less. Bot.* (1866) 130 In the Sunflower.. it consists of two thin scales..; in the Sneeze-weed, of about five very thin scales. **1885** J. M. Coulter *Bot. Rocky Mt. Region* 196.

**2.** *Austr.* (See quots.)

The two quotations refer to the same plant.

**1877** F. VON MUELLER *Bot. Teachings* 58 The Sneezeweed (*Cotula* or *Centipeda Cunninghamii*). A dwarf, erect,.. odorous herb;..can be converted into snuff. **1889** MAIDEN *Usef. Pl.* 195 *Myriogyne minuta*,..'Sneezeweed' of Southern New South Wales.

**'sneezewood.** Also sneeze-wood. [f. SNEEZE *v.*, probably after Cape Du. *nieshout*.] A South African timber tree, *Ptæroxylon utile*; also, the wood of this tree.

**1834** PRINGLE *Afr. Sk.* vi. 219 A saffron-coloured timber, called sneeze-wood, from the effect of its pungent scent when newly cut. **1854** PAPPE *Silva Capensis* (1862) 5 *Ptæroxylon Utile*... From the fact of its producing violent sneezing when sawn or otherwise worked at, it has received the name of *Sneeze-wood*. **1880** *Silver & Co.'s S. Africa* (ed. 3) 130 Melkhout, Olive-wood, and Sneezewood.

**b.** *attrib.*, as ***sneezewood spade, stump, tree***, etc.

**1877** J. A. CHALMERS *Tiyo Soga* i. 7 The sneezewood spade gave place to the crooked plough-share. *Ibid.* 11 The branches of the sneezewood tree. **1880** BESSEY *Botany* 535 *Ptæroxylon utile*, the Sneezewood Tree of the Cape of Good Hope, furnishes a hard and durable timber. **1887** MISS E. MONEY *Dutch Maiden* (1888) 229 Nodding away on his sneeze-wood stump.

**'sneezewort.** Also 6 sneesewoort, 7 -wort, 8-9 sneeze-wort. [f. SNEEZE *v.*]

**1.** The plant *Achillea Ptarmica*, bastard or wild pellitory, the dried leaves of which are powdered and used as a sternutatory.

**1597** GERARDE *Herbal* 484 The small Sneese woort hath many rounde and brittle braunches... The smell of this plant procureth sneezing. *Ibid.* 607 Sneesewoort is called of some Ptarmica. **1629** PARKINSON *Parad.* 288 We vsually call it double wilde Pelletorie, and some Sneesewort, but *Elleborus albus* is vsually so called. **1712** tr. *Pomet's Hist. Drugs* I. 47 There is also a Pseudopyrethrum which is call'd *Ptarmica* or Sneezewort which grows in Meadows. **1786** ABERCROMBIE *Arr.* in *Gard. Assist.* 48 (*Ptarmica*) or sneezewort double flowered. **1858** R. HOGG *Veget. Kingdom* 455 *Ptarmica vulgaris*, or Sneezewort, is also a native of Great Britain. **1901** *Scotsman* 12 Nov. 8/1 The sneezewort is remarkable for its pungent qualities.

*attrib.* **1855** MISS PRATT *Flower. Pl.* III. 323 Sneeze-wort Yarrow. **1861** S. THOMSON *Wild Fl.* III. (ed. 4) 306 The sneeze-wort yarrow (*Achillea ptarmica*).

**2.** Applied to other plants: **a.** The white hellebore, *Veratrum album* [cf. NEEZE-WORT].

**1629** [see 1]. **1671** SKINNER *Etymol. Ling. Angl.*, *Bot.*, Neese, or Sneese-wort, *Helleborus albus*. **1799** W. TOOKE *View Russ. Emp.* I. 383 Wolf's bane and sneeze-wort [note, *Veratrum*] are taken against almost all accidents.

**b.** ***American, Austrian sneezewort*** (see quots.).

**1611** [see SNEEZING *vbl. sb.* 3 b]. **1760** J. LEE *Introd. Bot.* App. 327 Sneeze-wort, Austrian, *Xeranthemum*. **1846-50** A. WOOD *Class-bk. Bot.* 342 *Helenium autumnale*, American Sneeze-wort.

**sneezing** ('sniːzɪŋ), *vbl. sb.* Also 5 snesynge, 6 sneesyng, 6-8 -ing, 7 *Sc.* sneisin(g, snising, snizing. [f. SNEEZE *v.*]

**1. a.** The action of the verb; an instance of this.

**1495** *Trevisa's Barth. De P.R.* XVII. cxxxi. 688 Powder therof [*sc.* of pepper] makyth snesynge [*Bodl. MS.* fnesinge]. **1545** RAYNOLD *Byrth Mankynde* 67 Farthermore she muste be prouoked to sneesyng. **1580** HOLLYBAND *Treas. Fr. Tong*, *Esternuëment*, a sneesing. **1615** CROOKE *Body of Man* 523 In sternutations or sneezings. **1646** SIR T. BROWNE *Pseud. Ep.* 200 Aristotle hath a Probleme, why sneezing from noone unto midnight was good, but from night to noon unlucky. **1707** FLOYER *Physic. Pulse-Watch* 220 Sneesing promotes the Motion of the Blood, and excites the Pulse. **1770** LANGHORNE *Plutarch* (1851) I. 138/1 A Sneezing was heard from the right. **1818** E. THOMPSON *Cullen's Nosologia* (1820) 203 Contagious inflammatory fever with sneezing. **1844** DICKENS *Mart. Chuz.* xiv, He was taken with a violent fit of sneezing. **1899** *Allbutt's Syst. Med.* VIII. 98 Abnormal visceral or reflex movements, such as.. sneezings, yawnings, or hiccoughings.

*fig.* **1691** BEVERLEY *1000 Yrs. Kingd.* 31 From Time to Time..there have been Sneesings by a Power of God, as I may so express it, of this Prophecy.

**b.** *pl.* Matter emitted in sneezing. *rare*$^{-1}$.

**1607** TOPSELL *Four-f. Beasts* (1658) 431 The sneezings of a Musk-cat is an excellent remedy against the resolution of the sinews or the Palsie.

†**2. a.** A preparation or powder inducing sternutation; an errhine or sternutatory. *Obs.*

**1621** BURTON *Anat. Mel.* II. v. II. iv, Sneesings, masticatories, and nasalls, are generally receiued. **1632** tr. *Bruel's Praxis Med.* 61 A sneezing of pepper, Hellebore. **1653** W. RAMESEY *Astrol. Restored* 119 Of the administration of gargarisms, or sneezings, and such like.

†**b.** Snuff. *Obs.* (Cf. SNEESHING 1.)

**1648** *Dunfermline Kirk Sess. Rec.* (1865) 25 Those that offers and takes snising in the kirk. **1672** *Essex Papers* (Camden Soc.) 7 Who euer sels Ale, Tobacco, Sneezinge Broges, &c. is an Irish Merchant. ? *c* **1680** F. SEMPILL in *Poems Sempills* (1849) 70 A mill of good snizing to prie. **1720** SWIFT *Irish Feast* Wks. 1755 IV. I. 27 Give us a pinch Of your sneezing.

**3.** *attrib.* and *Comb.* **a.** as ***sneezing-coffer, -maker, -mill, -powder, -tobacco***; **sneezing gas** = *sneeze gas* s.v. SNEEZE *sb.* 3.

**1611** COTGR., *Sternutatoire*, a sneezing medicine, or powder. *a* **1616** BEAUM. & FL. *Kt. of Malta* II. iv, Bring a little sneezing powder in your pocket. **1626** BACON *Sylva* §38 Sneezing-powder and other powders or Liquors (which the Physitians call Errhines). **1643** *Dunfermline Kirk Sess. Rec.* (1865) 12 Those who..taks y$^{r}$ sneising tobacco in the most remott..pairt of y$^{e}$ said yle. **1659** in Macgill *Old Ross-sh.* (1909) 377 Walter Denune, sneisin maker. **1681** COLVIL *Whig's Supplic.* II. 134 And there his Sneezing Milne and Box lyes. **1812** J. H. VAUX *Flash Dict.*, *Sneezer* or *Sneezing-Coffer*, a snuff-box. **1918** H. H. TUDOR *Let.* 13 Nov. in M. Gilbert *Winston S. Churchill* (1977) IV. Companion I. 415 The shell you speak of may be sneezing gas, which is not deadly. **1939** H. F. THUILLIER *Gas in Next War* xvi. 145 The General Disarmament Conference of the League of Nations sitting in 1932 sought to divide the known chemical war agents into..two categories [lethal and non-lethal], and to obtain agreement for the use of the non-lethal kind, *i.e.* the lachrimatory (tear gases) and the sternutatory (sneezing gases) in war. **1979** *Guardian* 25 Aug. 12/6 Soup..always tastes the same when you have accidentally emptied the pot of fine grey sneezing powder into it. **1982** *London Mag.* June 31 Once he bought sneezing-powder from the joke-shop in New Oxford Street.

†**b.** ***sneezing-wort***, = SNEEZEWORT. *Obs.*

**1611** COTGR. s.v. *Esternuer*, Sneesingwort, or sneesewort of Austria, wild Pellitorie of Spaine. **1682** WHELER *Journ. Greece* III. 219 With long sharp leaves, with streight Nerves, in shape like Sneezing Woort. **1741** *Compl. Family Piece* II. iii. 397 You have now in Flower the..double Ptarmica or Sneezing-wort.

**c.** ***sneezing brick*** (see quot.).

**1887** *Archit. Soc. Dict.* VII. 97 *Sneezing Brick*, one of the names given to the burnt bricks which case the clamp before burning.

**sneezy** ('sniːzɪ), *a.* [f. SNEEZE *sb.* + -Y.]

**a.** Of persons: Inclined to sneeze. **b.** Of things: Causing one to sneeze; dusty.

**1839** HOOD *Sweep's Compl.* 41, I find my suppress'd voice very uneasy, And comparable to nothing but having your tissue stopt when you are sneezy. **1848** DICKENS *Dombey* lvii, They..have signed their names in one of the old sneezy registers. **1896** *Punch* 7 Mar. 112/1 East winds always make me feel snappy and sneezy.

**sneg,** *sb. Obs.* exc. *dial.* [ME. *snegge*, = MLG. *snigge*, MHG. *snegge*, *snecke*, G. *schnecke*.] A snail. Cf. SNAG *sb.*$^{3}$

**1340** *Ayenb.* 32 Þo anlikneþ þan þet ne dar naȝt guo ine þe peþe uor þane snegge þet sseaweþ him his hornes. **1880-7** in Kentish and Cornish glossaries.

**sneg,** *v. Sc.* [Of osbcure origin: cf. SNECK *v.*$^{2}$] *trans.* To cut.

Jamieson (1808) also gives *sneg* as a sb.

**1718** RAMSAY *Christ's Kirk Gr.* III. xii, [She] sneg'd the raips fow snack, We' er knife that day. **17..** —— *Address of Thanks* xviii, Bring to the warld the luckless wean, And sneg its infant thrapple. **1808-57** in *Eng. Dial. Dict.*

**sneg-stone.** [? f. SNEG *sb.*] (See quot.)

**1815** W. SMITH *Map Strata* Mem. 17 The clay, with some modifications (and in some parts of it beds of Sussex Marble or sneg stone).

**sneipe,** *v. Obs.*$^{-1}$ [perh. identical with SNAPE *v.*$^{1}$ and *v.*$^{2}$] *intr.* ? To become pinched.

*c* **1300** *Old Age* vii. in *E.E.P.* (1862) 149, I snurpe, i snobbe, i sneipe on snovte. [Cf. SNEAP-NOSE.]

†**sneir,** *v. Sc. Obs.*$^{-1}$ [app. repr. OE. *snyrian*, *snyrȝan* to hasten, if not an error for *steir*.] *intr.* To sail.

*a* **1568** A. SCOTT *Poems* (S.T.S.) i. 190 This ȝeir bayth blythnes and abundance bringis, Naveis of schippis out-t[h]roch þe sea to sneir.

**sneith,** *a. Sc.* ? *Obs.* [Of obscure origin.] Smooth, polished. Also *fig.*

**1513** DOUGLAS *Æneid* XI. i. 94 The gapand deidly wound ..Amyd his sneith and fair slekyt breist bane. **1808** A. SCOTT *Poems* 121 This put the dame in perfect wrath; Her words they werena sneith.

†**sneke.** *Obs. rare.* Also 6 snyke. [Of obscure origin.] A cold in the head.

*c* **1440** *Promp. Parv.* 461/2 Sneke, or the poose,..*catarrus*. *c* **1460** *Play Sacram.* 616 All tho y$^{t}$ haue y$^{e}$ poose, y$^{e}$ sneke, or y$^{e}$ tyseke. **1530** PALSGR. 272/1 Sneke, pose, *rime*. **1547** BOORDE *Brev. Health* cccvi. 100 The 306 chapitre doth shewe of the Pose or Snyke.

‖**snekkja** ('snɛkja). Pl. snekkjur, (*erron.*) snekkar. [Icel.: see SNACK *sb.*$^{1}$] An ancient Icelandic or Scandinavian longship.

**1847** N. H. NICOLAS *Hist. R. Navy* I. i. 10 The Scandinavians are said to have possessed small boats with.. twelve seamen, and a longer kind of vessel called 'snekkar' or serpents, chiefly used for war, with twenty rowers. **1889** P. B. DU CHAILLU *Viking Age* II. ix. 137 The *snekkja* was a somewhat smaller long-ship, of which frequent mention is made; but sometimes it must have been as large as a dragon-ship. **1911** *Encycl. Brit.* XXIV. 865/1 The famous *snekkjur* or serpents, said to be represented on the Bayeux tapestry. **1970** FOOTE & WILSON *Viking Achievement* vii. 236 The longship was the real warship, with at least twenty benches. One common sort was called *snekkja*.

**snell** (snɛl), *sb. U.S.* [Of obscure origin.] A short line of gut or horsehair by which a fish-hook is attached to a longer line.

**1846** *Spirit of Times* 9 May 126/2 [The bass] was taken with a jointed rod, with a single gut snell, after half an hour's play. **1859** BARTLETT *Dict. Amer.* (ed. 2) 238 *Leader*, a length of finely twisted hair, gut, or grass, for attaching an angler's hook to the line; a bottom. Called also a Snell. **1883** *Cent. Mag.* July 381/2 Reeling up his line to the snell of the hook. **1894** *Outing* XXIV. 452/2, I..rigged the strongest leader and the heaviest snell and hook in my box.

**snell** (snɛl), *a.* and *adv.* In later use *Sc.* and *north.* Also 1-5 snel, 3 snæll, 4-5 snelle. [Common Teut.: OE. *snel*, *snell*, = OS. (MLG. and LG., MDu. and Du.), OHG. (MHG.) *snel*, *snell-* (G. *schnell*), swift, quick, active, etc., ON. *snjallr* (Icel. *snjallur*, Norw. *snjall*, *snjell*, *snell*; Sw. *snäll*, Da. *snild*); the Scand. languages exhibit a great variety of senses.]

**A.** *adj.* **1. a.** Of persons: Quick in movement or action; prompt, smart, active, strenuous; †good.

In ME. freq. as a general epithet of commendation. In later Sc. use tending towards the sense of 'sharp, keen'.

*Beowulf* 2971 Ne meahte se snella sunu Wonredes ealdum ceorle hondslyht ȝiofan. *a* **1000** *Bi Monna Cræftum* 52 (Gr.), Sum bið ryniȝ,..sum on londe snel, feþespediȝ. *c* **1200** *Trin. Coll. Hom.* 13 Þat man be waker, and liht, and snel,.. and erliche rise. *c* **1250** *Meid. Maregrete* lv, Olibrius heitte þe mai ut of prisun don; Ðe sergaunz were snelle ant broutten hire son. *a* **1300** *Body & Soul* in *Map's Poems* 334 Ȝwere ben thine cokes snelle, that scholden gon greithe thi mete? **1338** R. BRUNNE *Chron.* (1810) 132 Of messengers fulle snelle he sent hider to loke. *c* **1425** *Seven Sag.* (P.) 316 The messangers were ful snelle, Hastilich the way thay nomen. *c* **1450** *Cov. Myst.* xii. (Shaks. Soc.) 121 Byd hym with Mary abyde and dwelle, For it [is] my sone ful snelle That she is with i-wys.

**1720** RAMSAY *Edinb.'s Salut. to Ld. Carnarvon* vi, That in ilk action, wise and snell, You may shaw manly fire. **1721** —— *Elegy Patie Birnie* ix, Jove's nimble son and leckie snell Made the first fiddle of a shell. **1768** ROSS *Helenore* 9 Fu' o' good nature, sharp an' snell with a'. **1817** [R. D. C. BROWN] *Lintoun Green* 91 The Smith, black, bardy, wee, and snell, Served round the nappy ale. **1859** J. BROWN *Rab & Fr.* (1891) 10/2 That horny-handed, snell, peremptory little man. **1889** J. ROBERTSON *Early Relig. Israel* (1892) iii. 57 Amos is a lithe, keen, *snell* man.

*absol.* *a* **1000** *Judith* 199 (Gr.), Þa wearð snelra werod snude ȝeȝearewod. *a* **1250** *Owl & Night.* 526 Þanne erest hit is isene Hwar is þe snelle, hwar þe kene.

**b.** Similarly of animals (or things). ? *Obs.*

*a* **1000** *Phœnix* 123 (Gr.), Se haswa fuȝel..fareð feþrum snell flyhte on lyfte. *a* **1000** *Andreas* 505 On brim snoweð snel under seȝle. *a* **1250** *Owl & Night.* 918 Þu farest so doþ on yde[l] wel þat springeþ bi burne þat is snel. **13..** *Guy Warw.* (A.) 4668 Mi stede þai han, þat is so snelle. *a* **1450** *Le Morte Arth.* 2234 Stedys that were bolde and snelle. **1481** CAXTON *Reynard* xxxix. (Arb.) 106 So subtyl and snelle was the foxe, that many tymes whan the wulf wende wel to be sure of hym, he sterte thenne bytwene his legges. **1596** DALRYMPLE tr. *Leslie's Hist. Scot.* (S.T.S.) I. 25 Thay [*sc.* solan geese] ar sa snell and suift of flicht.

†**c.** Const. *to* (with sb. or inf.). *Obs.*

*c* **1150** *Canterb. Ps.* xiii. 3 [6] Hiræ fet hræþe *vel* snelle to æȝiotæne *vel* to scedende blod. *c* **1275** *Sinners Beware* 41 in *O.E. Misc.* 73 Ne may no tunge telle..of þare pyne of helle; þar-to we beoþ to snelle. **1340-70** *Alex. & Dind.* 437 Hie boldus to bulde be we not snelle. **13..** *Minor Poems fr. Vernon MS.* (1901) 558 To fleo folye be snelle. *c* **1400** *Rowland & O.* 403 To arme hym wele þay were full snelle.

**2.** Keen-witted, clever, sharp, acute, smart.

*c* **1425** *Seven Sages* (P.) 53 The mayster was wys and snel. *c* **1440** *York Myst.* xli. 111 Melachiell, that proffett snell, Hais tolde vs of that babb so bright. *a* **1450** MYRC 121 Teche hem alle to be war and snel, That they conne sey þe wordes wel. **1719** RAMSAY *First Answ. Hamilton* x, Europe had nane mair snack and snell At verse or prose. **1861** J. BROWN *Horæ Subs.* II. 273 He had no want..of quick, snell remark, often witty and full of spirit.

**3.** Severe, sharp, unsparing.

*a* **1425** *Cursor M.* 16628 (Trin.), Sore þei auȝte him drede: þe folke þat were so snelle [*Cott.* fell]. *a* **1560** ROLLAND *Crt. Venus* IV. 184 [To] caus Ladeis to..be haldin..Baith odious, and snell as ane serpent. **1742** R. FORBES *Ajax* (1755) 17 Fa wi' snell words him sair did snib. **1816** SCOTT *Antiq.* xxi, He's snell and dure eneugh in casting up their nonsense to them, as if he had nane o' his ain. **1833** M. SCOTT *Tom Cringle* xii, Conscience is a rough lad,..and I am keen and snell also.

**4.** Of weather; Keen, bitter, severe.

*a* **1300** *Cursor M.* 6018 Þe seuend on-sand þat siþen fell, Was a weder ful selcut snell [*Gött.* fell]. **1375** BARBOUR *Bruce* III. 377 Sa hard anoy thaim then assayit, Off hungir, cauld, with schowris snell. **1513** DOUGLAS *Æneid* VII. Prol. 139 Chiverand for cauld, the sessoun was so snell. **1535** STEWART *Cron. Scot.* I. 342 The snaw so snell ay dryvand with sic drift. **1677** NICOLSON in *Trans. R. Soc. Lit.* (1870) IX. 319 *Snell*, sharp, bitter. **1785** BURNS *To a Mouse* iv, Bleak December's winds ensuin, Baith snell an' keen! **1822** *Blackw. Mag.* XI. 119 The wintry air is snell and keen. **1881** R. BUCHANAN *God & the Man* III. 209 We..passed the snell season without the loss of a single soul aboard.

**5. a.** Grievous, heavy, stinging; rigorous; painful.

*a* **1300** *Cursor M.* 7759 O þis batail þat was sa snell, þe force a-pon þe king it fell. **13..** *Ibid.* 16638 (Gött), Þai gaue him buffetes snell. **14..** *Sir Beues* (E) 4312 + 147 In hys hand a mase ful snel, Þat was maad off good steel. **1755** RAMSAY *To J. Clerk* 88 [He] gave the scarlet whore a box Mair snell than all the pelts of Knox. **1790** A. WILSON *2nd Ep. to Kennedy* Poet. Wks. (*c* 1846) 117 This is the last, the snellest lick, That I'll e'er get frae Fortune's stick. **1824** SCOTT *Redgauntlet* ch. xi, That was a snell law. **1879** J. WHITE *Jottings* 154 (E.D.D.), Bear life's rebuffs, Tho' they're aft unco snell.

**b.** Sharp-tasted; pungent.

**1835** CARRICK *Laird Logan* 172 (E.D.D.), That's just the mustard I mean, an gay snell mustard he is whiles.

**6.** Shrill, clear-sounding.

*c* **1730** *Robin Hood & Bp. of Hereford* vii. in Child *Ballads* III. 198/2 He put his horn in to his mouth, And a snell blast he did blow. *c* **1820** BEATTIE *Arnha'* (1826) 58 Douff like drum, and snell like cymble.

**B.** *adv.* **1.** Quickly, promptly, swiftly.

*a* **1300** *Cursor M.* 14946 Wat yee breþer qui..I weind again sua snell? **13..** *Guy Warw.* (A.) 801 His ost him answerd snelle, 'Of þat turnament y schal ȝou telle'. *c* **1420** *Chron. Vilod.* 556 Hom aȝeyn he come fulle snelle. **1895** CROCKETT *Men of Moss Hags* xlvii, We held fast and snell to the eastward.

**2.** Vigorously, strongly, keenly, etc.

*c* **1330** *Arth. & Merl.* 1322 (Kölbing), Þe messangers bad him þo telle, Whi it was he louȝ so snelle. *c* **1375** *Sc. Leg. Saints* xxix. (*Placidas*) 519 Ȝet wes lewit hym a schele to schrape his scabbis rycht snel. *a* **1400-50** *Alexander* 3995 Sire Porrus..him on þe pan strikis So snelle at he snatirs with. *c* **1470** HENRY *Wallace* II. 250 He saw, As to hys sycht, dede had him swappyt snell. **1728** RAMSAY *Robt., Richy, & Sandy* (1877) II. 5 Ae rough night the blatt'ring winds blew snell. **1773** FERGUSSON *Auld Reekie* 35 Poems 1789 II. 93 Antrin fock may ken how snell Auld Reikie will at morning smell. **1884** R. BUCHANAN *The Lights of Leith* I. i, While the wintry gale..Blew snell thro' sail and shroud.

Hence **'snellness**, sharpness, keenness.

**1915** J. BUCHAN *Salute to Adventurers* i. 15 That bold girl singing a martial ballad to the storm and taking pleasure in the snellness of the air.

**snell**, *v.* *U.S.* [f. SNELL *sb.*] *trans.* To tie or fasten (a hook) to a line. Hence **snelled** *ppl. a.*

**1891** in *Cent. Dict.* **1893** *Outing* XXII. 123/2 Well-made, securely wrapped, double-snelled Aberdeen..are very satisfactory hooks. **1960** *Washington Post* 29 Apr. D9 The somewhat cumbersome assembly of one or more spinner blades ahead of a snelled or long-shanked hook. **1976** *Billings* (Montana) *Gaz.* 28 June 2-D (Advt), Packages of 6 snelled hooks.

**Snellen** ('snɛlən). *Ophthalm.* The name of Hermann *Snellen* (1834-1908), Dutch ophthalmologist, used *attrib.* and in the possessive to designate: (*a*) a scale of similar square-serifed type-faces of different sizes, all subtending the same angle at different rated distances, proposed by him in 1862 (in his *Échelle Typographique*) and used to print test cards which are presented at known distances to ophthalmic patients who are asked to read out as many lines as they can; also, the letters, test cards, etc., associated with this scale; (*b*) a fraction which expresses a patient's visual acuity as the actual reading distance over the rated distance of the smallest Snellen letters read.

**1864** T. LONGMORE *Man. Instructions Defective Vision in Soldiers* ii. 10 The emmetropic eye can read Snellen's types at any of the indicated distances. **1866** H. W. WILLIAMS *Rec. Adv. Ophthalm. Sci.* 29 Two other series have been added as reading tests... Both of these are almost perfectly accurate in their gradations of sizes,—and correspond, the first with the same numbers of Snellen's scale, the second with those of Jaeger's test. **1912** L. LAURANCE *Visual Optics & Sight Testing* iv. 73 The visual acuity, as expressed by a Snellen fraction, varies..with the health of the person. **1934** C. S. PRICE *Improvement of Sight by Natural Methods* ii. 21 The large cards or charts bearing a series of sizes in the types are conveniently known as 'Snellen Charts'. **1960** N. BIER *Correction Subnormal Vision* i. 4 A person with visual acuity of 6/60 Snellen or better should not ordinarily be regarded as blind. **1971** *Jrnl. Gen. Psychol.* LXXXIV. 85 He measured visual acuity, using Snellen letters at 10 meters.

**Snell's law** (snɛlz). *Optics.* [Named after Willebrord van Roijen *Snell* (1591-1626), Dutch astronomer and mathematician, who formulated the law in 1621.] The law which states that for a ray of light passing from one uniform medium to another the sines of the angles of incidence and refraction are always in the same ratio.

**1873** J. TYNDALL *On Light* i. 24 Snell's law of refraction is one of the corner-stones of optical science, and its applications to-day are millionfold. **1935** DAWSON & PORRITT *Rubber* 404/1 Stretched rubber shows double refraction, i.e. a ray of light entering the rubber from air or a vacuum is split up into two rays, one of which..obeys Snell's law of refraction, whilst the other..does not unless it travels in a certain critical direction. **1974** *Nature* 18 Jan. 156/2 Snell's law and a value of 1·67 for the refractive index of the lens were used to determine the angles of refraction at the surfaces of the lens.

**snelly** ('snɛlɪ), *adv.* Also 1 snellice, 4 snellich, -lik. [f. SNELL *a.* Cf. MDu. *snellike*, *-lijc* (Du. *snellijk*), MLG. *snellik(en*, OHG. *snellîcho*, MSw. *sniälle-*, *sniellelika*.] In a snell manner; quickly, smartly, severely, etc.

*a* **1000** *Bi Manna Wyrdum* 82 (Gr.), Sum sceal..snellice snere wræstan. *c* **1305** *Land Cokayne* 163 And euch monke him taketh on, And snellich berith forth har prei. *c* **1325** *Metr. Hom.* (1862) 59 His sawel..bes felaw wit the fend, That snellik sal it scham and schend. **13..** *K. Alis.* 2524 (Laud. MS.), Vche bare xij. oþer xvj. kniȝth, Wel arenged snelly to fiȝth.

**1790** SHIRREF *Poems* p. xix, At first he frown'd, and said, right snelly, It's gryte presumption. *c* **1790** PICKERING in *Burns' Wks.* (ed. Chambers, 1857) IV. 91 The snaw drives snelly through the dale. **1836** M. MACKINTOSH *Cottager's Daughter* 70 The thumbkin was maist snelly screwed. **1881** J. BALLANTINE in *Modern Scot. Poems* III. 30 Snelly the hail smote the skeleton trees.

‖**snelskrif** ('snɛlskrɪf). *S. Afr.* [Afrikaans, f. *snel* rapid + *skrif* writing.] A system of shorthand for the Afrikaans language. Also *attrib.*

**1949** *Cape Argus* 16 Apr. 11/2 (Advt.), Take a rapid course ..in book-keeping, Afrikaans, snelskrif, shorthand, [etc.]. **1952** *Cape Times* 2 Aug. 9/7 Typists who qualify for shorthand and *snelskrif* tests. **1972** *Grocott's Mail* (Grahamstown) 1 Sept. 2 Bilingualism, shorthand, snelskrif, typing..are all essential.

**snepe**, *a.* *rare* [Of obscure origin; *sneep* and *snape* in the same sense are given as current in Linc.] Foolish, silly.

*a* **1250** *Owl & Night.* 225 Hit þincheþ boþe wise & snepe, Nouht þat þu singe, ac þat þu wepe.

**snercte**: see SNARCHE *v.*

†**snese**, *v.* *Obs. rare.* [OE. (*á*)*snǽsan*, f. *snás* spit, skewer. Cf. ON. *sneisa* to spit.] *trans.* To run through with a weapon.

*a* **1225** *Ancr. R.* 212 Hwu þe deoflen schulen..mid helle sweordes alsnesien [*v. rr.* snesen, sneasin] ham þuruhut.

**snet(te**, error in Phillips (1658) and some later Dicts. for SUET.

†**snetched**, *a.* *Obs.*⁻¹ [? Related to SNECK *v.*²] Slaughtered.

**1567** GOLDING *Ovid's Met.* v. (1593) 108 Like a snetched ox Strait tumbling downe against the ground his groveling face he knox.

**sneuel, -ill**, etc., obs. forms of SNIVEL.

†**sneve**, *v.* *Obs.* [Cf. Icel. *snefja* to scent out; Norw. *snev* (also *snevl*, Icel. *snefill*) scent, hint, suspicion.] *trans.* To smell or smell at. Hence **'sneving** *vbl. sb.*

*c* **1200** *Trin. Coll. Hom.* 37 Alse swin þe uulieð and wroteð and sneuieð aure fule. *Ibid.* 183 Hie..binimeð..Eien here sene,..nose here sneuenge, and muð here smel. *Ibid.* 207 He haueð..mid his eȝen bihelden þat he ne sholden..and alse mid nose sneued.

**snevel(l**, etc., obs. forms of SNIVEL.

**'snever**, *a.* *dial.* [ad. ON. *snǽfr* (stem *snǽfr-*, MSw. *snäfr-*, Da. *snæver*; also MSw. *snäfw-*, Sw. *snäf*, Norw. *snæv*, *snøv*) narrow, tight.] Narrow; slender, slight; neat.

**1640** BRATHWAIT *Lanc. Lovers* iv. 18 We han store of goodly Cattell;..peepe here and peepe there, aw the wide dale is but snever to them. **1674** RAY *N.C. Words* 43 A *Snever-spawt*, a slender stripling. **1691** *Ibid.* (ed. 2) 66 *Snever*, slender: an usual Word. **1788** W. H. MARSHALL *Yorksh.* II. 354 *Snevver*, slender and neat. **1855** [ROBINSON] *Whitby Gloss.* s.v., Snever, Sneever.

**snevyll, snevylysshe**, obs. ff. SNIVEL(LISH.

**snew**, *v.* ? *Obs.* Forms: 1 sniwan (sniu-, sniuw-), 3-4 snywe(n, 3 sniuw-, 4 sneuw-, 4-6 snewe. [OE. *sníwan*, = WFris. *snije* (*sneie*, *snīe*), NFris. *snī*, *sneie*, *snaie*, MDu. *sniwen*, *snien*, MLG. *snîghen*, *snygen*, OHG. *snîwan* (MHG. *snîwen*, *snîgen*, *snîen*, G. *schneien*, dial. *schneuen*, *schneiben*, etc.):—**sniȝwan-*, related by ablaut to SNOW *sb.*¹

The evidence for survival in mod. dial. is very slight; it is doubtful whether *snew*, to swarm, is the same word.]

**1.** *intr.* To snow.

*c* **725** *Corpus Gloss.* (Hessels) N 117 *Ninguit*, sniuwið. *c* **900** tr. *Baeda's Hist.* II. xiii, [If] hit rine & sniwe & styrme ute. *a* **1000** *Epist. Alex.* in Cockayne *Narrat. Angl.* (1861) 23 Ða cwom þær micel snaw and swa miclum sniwde swelce micel flys feoll. *a* **1250** *Owl & Night.* 620 His hou [= hue] neuer ne uorlost, Wan hit sniuw [*v.r.* snywe] ne wan hit frost. **13..** *K. Alis.* 6450 (W.), Whan hit snywith [*Laud MS.* snoweþ], other rayneth. *a* **1325** *Orfeo* 245 Þei it comenci to snewe and frese. *a* **1400** *Launfal* 293 Sche was as whyt as.. snow that sneweth yn wynterys day. **1530** PALSGR. 130 *Il neige*, it sneweth. **1746** *Exmoor Scolding* (E.D.S.) 124 Whan [it] sneweth, or blunketh, or doveth, or in scatty Weather. *fig.* *c* **1386** CHAUCER *Prol.* 347 It snewed in his hous of mete and drynke.

**2.** *trans.* To sprinkle like snow.

*c* **1440** *Pallad. on Husb.* XI. 332 On kadis thre Of wyn a certeyn of this flouris snewe.

Hence †**snewed** *ppl. a.*; †**'snewing** *vbl. sb.*

**1300-1400** *R. Gloucester's Chron.* (Rolls) App. xx. 248 Temese was þo ifrore harde..& was swiþe whit aboue of þe snywede snou. *c* **1400** *Laud Troy-bk.* 7318 The wynd sesid the gret blast, The snewyng then no lenger last.

**snew**, obs. or dial. pa. t. of SNOW *v.*

**snib**, *sb.*¹ Latterly *Sc.* Also 5 snybb, 7 snibbe. [f. SNIB *v.*¹ Cf. Da. *snibbe*, Sw. *snybba*, in the same sense.] A check, sharp rebuke, or snub.

*c* **1440** *Alph. Tales* 392 When Hillarion..was giffen alonelie vnto his prayers, he sufferd many snybbis of þe fend. **1587** CHURCHYARD *Worth. Wales* (1876) 61 No sorer snib, nor nothing nips so neere, As feele much want, yet shewe a merrie cheere. *a* **1601** *Pasquil & Kath.* (1878) I. 267 Then may one..Rule all, pay all, take all, without checke or snib. **1681** W. ROBERTSON *Phraseol. Gen.* (1693) 1067 Tart reproofs; Biting and taunting snibs. *c* **1740** SKINNER *Poems* (1809) 128, I thought he might hae gott'n a snib. **1768** ROSS *Helenore* 13 Sick snibs as that, may sair to let us see, 'Tis better for us to be loose an' free.

†**snib**, *sb.*² *Cant.* *Obs.* A petty thief.

**1607** DEKKER *Jests to make you Merrie* Wks. (Grosart) II. 300 Some horse-stealers, some snibs, some foysts. **1823** EGAN *Grose's Dict. Vulgar T.*, *Snib*, a prig. *Scotch cant.*

**snib**, *sb.*³ Chiefly *Sc.* [Of doubtful origin: perh. a. LG. *snibbe* (G. *schnippe*), *snib* (Sw. *snibb*) beak, beak-like point, etc.] A catch or fastening for a door, window, lock, or the like.

**1825** JAMIESON *Suppl.* s.v., The snib is the small bolt placed under the latch, and fastening the door so that it cannot be opened from without. **1869** *N. & Q.* 4th Ser. IV. 467/2 Most doors have both a snib and a sneck. **1891** BARRIE *Little Minister* xxii, An unearthly hand presses the snib of the window, the latch rises.

**snib** (snɪb), *v.*¹ Now *dial.* and *Sc.* Forms: 4-5 snybbyn, snybbe(n, snyb (6 *Sc.*), snybe; 4, 6- snib (4, 6 *Sc.*, snibe), 6 snibb, 6-7 snibbe. See also SNEB *v.* [Of Scand. origin: cf. older Da. *snibbe*, MSw. *snybba*, related to *snubba* SNUB *v.*¹]

**1.** *trans.* To reprove, reprimand, rebuke, check sharply or severely: **a.** A person.

Common in literary use down to *c* 1675.

*a* **1300** *Cursor M.* 18228 Hell hint þan þat gerard grim And selcut snarpli snibbed him. *c* **1386** CHAUCER *Prol.* 525 Hym wolde he snybben sharply for the nonys. *c* **1412** HOCCLEVE *De Reg. Princ.* 2825 But to þe pore, is denyed al grace; He snybbyd is. *c* **1450** CAPGRAVE *Life St. Aug.* 6 Desiryng of him þat he schuld snybbe þe maydenes þat þei schuld not be redy to telle swech tales. **1515** DOUGLAS *Lett.* Wks. 1874 I. p. xxxviii, He is..the instrument of mekyll harm, and I dreyd sall yit be of mayr and he be nocht snybbyt. **1577** STANYHURST *Descr. Irel.* i. in *Holinshed*, Here percase some snappish carper will..snuffingly snibbe me, for debacing the Irish language. **1607** MIDDLETON *Five Gallants* II. iii, You have snibbed the poor fellow too much; he can scarce speak. **1655** FULLER *Ch. Hist.* IX. 139 Hence it was that many Bishops..were checkt and snibt by this great favourite to their no small..discouragement. **1678** BUNYAN *Pilgr.* I. 169 Christian snibbeth his fellow for unadvised speaking. **1742** [see SNELL *a.* 3]. **1836** CARLETON *Fardorougha* vi, If Honor comes to be snibbin' an' makin' little o' me afore them. **1851** W. HAY in *The Lintie o' Moray* 64 No termagant tongue..Dares rattle around us, or scold us, or snib. **1854-** in dial. glossaries (Northampt., Leic., Rutland). [**1888** DOUGHTY *Arabia Deserta* I. 240 In bitterness of a displeasure he will snib his disobedient son with vehement words.]

*absol.* *c* **1440** CAPGRAVE *Life St. Kath.* III. 261 (MS. Rawl.), Therfor ȝour grace..I pray To punch & snybe, ȝourself as ȝe lest.

**b.** A thing, action, conduct, etc.

In later quots. passing into sense 2.

*a* **1300** *Cursor M.* 26233 Spous-brecking, and als hordom, ..þe biscop agh þaa for to snib. **1435** MISYN *Fire of Love* II. ix. 95 If any of slyke þingis ȝee ful seldum wald snyb, to scorne he is laghyd. *a* **1578** LINDESAY (Pitscottie) *Chron. Scot.* (S.T.S.) II. 133, [I] wald snibe the same [conduct] and schaw thame that law of god. **1596** DALRYMPLE tr. *Leslie's Hist. Scot.* (S.T.S.) II. 361 She snibbit the hauiest offences of al men in that cuntrie. **1631** J. DONE *Polydoron* 3 Satyricall Poetry..Snibbing filth in others but retayning it in itselfe. **1648** T. HILL *Dying Saints* Ep. Ded. B iij b, Far bee it from mee to snib the movings of God's Spirit in the weakest..of his saints. **1720** WODROW *Life R. Bruce* (1843) 93 Mr. Bruce wrote..that he was ready to snib the sinister interpretations the people were running to.

**2.** To check by some repressive action.

*c* **1500** *Lancelot* 3387 As at the stok the bere Snybbith the hardy houndis that ar ken, So farith he. **1513** DOUGLAS *Æneid* x. Prol. 15 Wyntyr to snyb the erth wyth frosty schouris. *a* **1607** BRIGHTMAN *Bright. Rediv.* (1647) iv. 117 Though it [hope] moderate the desire.., yet it quenches not, nor snibs the earnestnesse thereof. **1663** R. BLAIR *Autobiog.* (1848) iv. 63 All the corns were thrown down and fully dried, the growing thereon snibbed. **1674** BP. WARD *Serm. 30 Jan.* 13 The seeds of Piety..may be trampled on and kept under, crop'd and snib'd by the bestial part.

**b.** *Sc.* (See quot.)

**1808** JAMIESON, *To Snib a candle*, to snuff it.

**snib**, *v.*² orig. *Sc.* [Cf. SNIB *sb.*³]

**1.** *trans.* To fasten (a door, etc.) by means of a snib or catch; to shut *in* in this way.

**1808** JAMIESON, *To Snib a door*, to fasten it with a small bolt. **1861** RAMSAY *Remin.* Ser. II. 185 Quite a vulgar body, so much so as to ask any one leaving the room to 'snib the door'. **1864** J. BROWN *Horæ Subs.*, *Jeems*, Hurrying them to their appointed place, Jeems snibbed them slowly in. **1869** *N. & Q.* 4th Ser. IV. 467/2 When a door is *snibbed* it cannot be opened from the outside. **1889** A. CONAN DOYLE *Sign of Four* vi. 92 Your ally would..shut the window, snib it on the inside. **1934** R. KNOX *Still Dead* xxii. 269 Trying to shut the door quietly, she left it not quite snibbed properly, so that it came a bit ajar. **1953** A. UPFIELD *Murder must Wait* i. 4 The Yale-type lock was snibbed. **1962** W. H. MURRAY *Maelstrom* v. 73 He snibbed all the ground-floor windows. **1967** I. HAMILTON *Man with Brown Paper Face* ix. 132, I went softly to the main entrance and snibbed it from the inside and put the bolt across. **1971** *Islander* (Victoria, B.C.) 21 Nov. 2/3 The windows were not only unbroken but snibbed shut.

**2.** To catch, secure.

**1813** PICKEN *Poems* I. 59 I'se..reveal to you How..I [*sc.* a rat] maist was snibbit. **1819** R. GALL *Poems* 134 The Dutchmen endeavoured to rin for't, But fand themselves snib'd in a girn.

Hence **'snibbing-bolt**.

**1844** H. STEPHENS *Bk. Farm* I. 218 Fine water-closet latch, with snibbing-bolt and 5-inch joints.

**'snibbing**, *vbl. sb.* [f. SNIB *v.*¹] The action of rebuking, reprimanding, or checking sharply.

*a* **1300** *E.E. Ps.* xvii. 18 Groundes of ertheli werld vn-hiled are For þi snibbing, lauerd myne. *a* **1340** HAMPOLE *Psalter* xv. 7 Alswa oure neris, þat is, oure fleschly delites, makis vs worthi snybynge. *a* **1400** *Minor Poems fr. Vernon MS.* xxiv. 285 From his wraþþe vs schilde, þat we fele not þat harde snibbyng. **1451** CAPGRAVE *Life St. Gilbert* viii. 73 To encrese of religion and snybbyng of vices. **1596** DALRYMPLE tr. *Leslie's Hist. Scot.* (S.T.S.) I. 226 This Columban was scharpe in snibbing of maneris. **1633** T. ADAMS *Exp. 2 Pet.* iii. 1 The man of a pure mind is always of a cheerful look, because there are no secret snibbings within him. **1642** D. ROGERS *Naaman* 94 Others by their snibbing and chiding.. doe blast that bud. **1891** *Rutland Gloss.* 32 Them fox-terriers takes a deal of snibbing.

**'snibble**, *sb.* *Mining.* [Of obscure origin: cf. SNIB *sb.*³] (See quot.)

**1883** GRESLEY *Gloss. Coal-m.* 229 *Snibble*, see *Locker* [a short iron or wooden bar for scotching tram wheels on inclined roads].

Hence **'snibble** *v. trans.*, to scotch.

**1880** J. NICOL *Poems & Songs* 79 Away they go, Though snibbled wheels may slip.

**snibel**, variant of SNIPE-BILL 4.

**snichel**: see SNITCHEL.

**snick**, *sb.*[1] *slang* or *dial.* [Cf. SNICKING *vbl. sb.*] A snack or share. Usu. *pl.*

**1723** DK. WHARTON *True Briton* No. 59, There is no Room for the Encouragement of Industry where the Snicks will hardly pay for a Saturday's Supper. **1888** *Berkshire Gloss.* 151 *Snicks*, shares, halves. **1891** WRENCH *Winchester Word-bk.* (1901) 51 *To go snicks*, = to go snacks.

**snick** (snɪk), *sb.*[2] [f. SNICK *v.*[2]]

**1. a.** A small cut; a nick, a notch.

**1775** ASH, *Snick*,..a small snip or cut as in the hair of a beast. **1828** CARR *Craven Gloss.*, *Snick*, a cut, a hollow, a notch. **1897** *Leeds Merc. Suppl.* 4 Dec. (E.D.D.), Mak' a bit of a snick in 't.

**b.** An act of snipping or slight cutting.

**1898** LD. E. HAMILTON *Mawkin* v. 67 Just a snick of the shears and a dab of walnut juice.

**2.** *Cricket.* A light, glancing blow given to the ball by the batsman, sending it in the direction of the slips or to leg; a ball so hit.

**1857** *Bell's Life* 19 July 7/5 The last jump from 135 to 158 ..included many 'snicks', not hits. **1879** *Sat. Rev.* 5 July 21 Standing at short-leg to stop a snick, he caught Mr. Studd off a leg hit. **1891** W. G. GRACE *Cricket* 258 He [short-slip] has to run after most of the snicks which pass the wicket-keeper.

**snick** (snɪk), *sb.*[3] [f. SNICK *v.*[3] Cf. SNECK *sb.*[3]] A sharp noise; a click.

**1894** DOYLE *Mem. Sherlock Holmes* 241 Suddenly there came from the window a sharp metallic snick. **1899** F. V. KIRBY *Sport E.C. Africa* ii. 23, I pressed the trigger; but only the 'snick' of the striker answered the touch.

**snick**, *sb.*[4] *techn.* [? f. the first element of SNICK-SNARL.] (See quot. and cf. SNICKEY *a.*)

**1875** KNIGHT *Dict. Mech.* 2230/1 *Snick*,..a knot or irregularity on yarn, removed by passing it through a slotted plate.

**Snick** (snɪk), *sb.*[5] *U.S.* Also **SNICK**. [Alt. of *SNCC* (see S 4 a and below).] The Student Non-violent Co-ordinating Committee, an organization of Black Americans campaigning for civil rights and Black power. Also *attrib.*

**1962** *Time* 12 Jan. 15/1 To fight segregation in their own way, young Negroes have organized themselves into a federation called the Student Nonviolent Coordinating Committee ('Snick' for short). **1967** *National Observer* (U.S.) 27 Nov. 1/4 Snick had its origins in the sit-in movements of 1960. *Ibid.*, Snick leaders consider elections a white man's device to deceive Negroes with false promises. **1967** *Telegraph* (Austral.) 5 Aug. 2/1 The white man has been violent towards the Negro for 400 years... If we are violent to him he deserves every bit. SNICK is respected because if we say burn, baby, burn, we'll be the first to strike a match. **1978** L. HEREN *Growing up on The Times* ix. 292 In 1964..white students..met members of the student non-violent coordinating committee. Snick, as it was usually called, was still very much a genuine student movement with religious roots.

**snick**, variant of SNECK *sb.* (latch).

**snick** (snɪk), *v.*[1] *Obs.* exc. *dial.* Also 6 **sneik**, 7 **snecke**. [Of obscure origin.] Used with *go*, or imperatively, and always followed by *up*, in the sense of 'go hang'.

(*a*) **1599** H. PORTER *Angry Wom. Abingt.* (Percy Soc.) 8 And his men be good fellowes, so it is; if they be not, let them goe sneik [*v.r.* snick] vp. **1611** BEAUM. & FL. *Knt. Burning Pestle* III. i, Give him his money George, and let him go snick up. **1631** HEYWOOD *Fair Maid of West* I. Wks. 1874 II. 268 Goe, let your Master snick-up. *a* **1668** DAVENANT *Play-Ho. to be Let* Wks. (1673) 116 He may go snick-up if he hates Nymphidious. [**1821** SCOTT *Kenilw.* xxix, Bidding the steward go snick up, if he came to startle us too soon from our goblets.]

(*b*) **1601** SHAKS. *Twel. N.* II. iii. 101 We did keepe time sir in our Catches. Snecke vp! **1602** MIDDLETON *Blurt, Master-Constable* IV. i, I have been believed of your betters, marry, snick up! **1605** *London Prodigal* v. i, Wherefore to prison? snick vp, I owe you nothing. *a* **1825** FORBY *Voc. E. Anglia*, *Snickup*, begone; away with you! **1883** in *Eng. Dial. Dict.* (West Yks.).

**snick** (snɪk), *v.*[2] Also 8 **snic**. [prob. suggested by SNICK AND SNEE, etc. Connexion with SNECK *v.*[2], or with Norw. and Icel. *snikka*, Sw. dial. *snicka*, to carve, whittle, is very doubtful.]

**1.** *trans.* To cut, snip, clip, nick. Also with *off*, *out*.

*c* **1700** *Street Robberies Consider'd*, *Snic*, to cut. **1825** JAMIESON *Suppl.* s.v. *Sneck*, *Snick*,..to cut with a sudden stroke of a sharp instrument. **1862** H. KINGSLEY *Ravenshoe* lxiii, He began by snicking the corner of her [*sc.* the doll's] foot off with nurse's scissors. **1875** *Ure's Dict. Arts* (ed. 7) I. 422 The third case-maker..quickly snicks out, with a pair of scissors, the superfluous cloth at each of the four corners.

**b.** *intr.* (Cf. SNICK *v.*[3] 2.)

**1863** READE *Hard Cash* III. 22 The heavy scissors were heard snick, snick, snicking all day long.

**2.** *trans.* To strike or hit sharply.

**1880** WEBB *Goethe's Faust* II. v. 130 But we nick 'em and we snick 'em, Wherever they may stick. **1891** MRS. J. A. OWEN *On Surrey Hills* v. 158 He..lets drive, or, as he says, 'snicks him', killing him at once.

**b.** *Cricket.* To strike (the ball) lightly so that it glances off in the slips or to leg; to obtain (so many runs) in this way.

**1871** 'THOMSONBY' *Cricketers in Council* 3 The new trundler then put down a tice..which the Surrey colt snicked cleverly through the slips. **1880** *Daily Telegr.* 23 Sept., Bates drove him finely for 4, and snicked him another 4. **1889** *Pall Mall G.* 8 Aug. 7 [He] snicked the first ball he received for 3.

**3.** *colloq.* To cut or slip across or along (a road) quickly or sharply.

**1883** PENNELL-ELMHIRST *Cream Leicestersh.* 343 The two former jumped an uncompromising piece of timber abreast into the field beyond;..the rest snicked the road for the corner immediately at hand.

**snick** (snɪk), *v.*[3] [Imitative.]

**1. a.** *trans.* To cause to click or sound sharply.

**1828** *Ann. Reg., Chron.* 25/1 They snicked their guns, but I saw no flash. **1900** CROCKETT *Black Douglas* 9 He stood.. drawing it an inch from its sheath and snicking it back again.

**b.** To turn *on*, *off*, *out*, *up*, to push *open*, with a clicking noise.

**1927** *Daily Express* 30 Aug. 3/4 As she snicks open the trellised door. **1927** *Observer* 4 Dec. 12 A Foreman with a lantern..walks down a dark platform snicking on lights. **1959** I. JEFFERIES *Thirteen Days* vi. 75 This corner was all wrong for..firing a pistol round..but I snicked the heat out and exposed an eye. **1973** R. HAYES *Hungarian Game* xxxiv. 207 Hagopian crested the hill and snicked off the ignition. **1977** *Detroit Free Press* 11 Dec. 15-C/1 The electric vacuum system that snicks lamps up with the tap of a toggle on modern cars.

**2. a.** *intr.* To make a sharp, clicking noise. Hence **'snicking** *vbl. sb.*

**1892** KIPLING *Barrack Room Ball.* 76 Ye may hear a breech-bolt snick where never a man is seen. **1893** RAYMOND *Gent. Upcott* xiv, The snicking of the flint and steel sounded hard and vicious.

**b.** To move *back*, to come *open*, with a click.

**1963** C. D. SIMAK *They walked like Men* xiv. 76 The lock snicked back and the door came open. **1972** J. POTTS *Trouble-Maker* (1973) xviii. 146 The back door snicked open.

**snick and snee.** ? *Obs.* Also 7 **snic (snik) and snee, snick and sneer.** [See SNICK OR SNEE.]

**1. a.** *vb.* To thrust and cut. **b.** *adv.* With thrusting and cutting. **c.** *sb.* = SNICK-A-SNEE 1.

*c* **1645** HOWELL *Lett.* I. xli, None must carry a pointed Knife about him; which makes the Hollander, who is us'd to Snick and Snee, to leave his Horn-sheath and Knife a Ship-board when he comes ashore. **1665** MARVELL *Charact. Holland* 96 When, stagg'ring upon some Land, Snick and Sneer, They try, like Statuaries, if they can, Cut out each other's Athos to a Man. **1697** DRYDEN *Virgil* Note on Georg. IV. 660 The monks..were at *snic* and *snee* with their drawn knives. **1802** JAMES *Milit. Dict.*, *Snick and snee*, a combat with knives, such as the Dutch carry.

**2.** *attrib.* (with *knife*), = SNICK-A-SNEE 2.

**1842** BORROW *Bible in Spain* vii, The Spaniard..sprang up like a tiger,..unsheathing instantly a snick and snee knife.

So †**snicking and sneeing** *vbl. sb. Obs.*$^{-1}$

**1674** N. FAIRFAX *Bulk & Selv.* To Rdr., If the humor of huffing be but a little further cocker'd,..snicking and sneeing will be nothing else in the world but writing of Book *a la mode d'Angleterre.*

**snick-a-snee.** ? *Obs.* Also 7 **-sne.** [Cf. prec. and SNICK OR SNEE.]

**1.** A combat with cut-and-thrust knives.

**1673** MRS. BEHN *Dutch Lover* III. iii, There lies my sword, and..I tell you I am as good at Snick-a-sne as the best Don of you all. **1688** B. WILLY *On Dutch War* in Jane Barker *Poet. Recreat.* II. 56 But they'll e'er long come to themselves you'll see When we in earnest are at Snick-a-snee. **1767** S. PATERSON *Another Trav.* II. 115 We may..possibly have a few bouts at snik-a-snee.

**2.** A cut-and-thrust knife. Also *attrib.*

**1760** *Brit. Chron.* 6 Aug. 127 One Turner..with a snick-a-snee stabbed her several times in her body. **1832** MARRYAT *N. Forster* xlix, Flemish seamen, with their long snick-a-snee knives. **1837** —— *Snarleyyow* liv, Jansen stepped forward with his snickasee [*sic*], the rope was divided at once. **1865** in *Slang Dict.* 238.

**snicker** (ˈsnɪkə(r)), *sb.*[1] Also *Sc.* **snicher.** [f. SNICKER *v.*] A smothered laugh; a snigger.

**1836** *Knickerbocker* VI. 562, I was partially 'ware of a general *snicker* through the room. **1857** HOLLAND *Bay Path* iv, That individual..gave utterance to an explosive snicker. **1881** *Daily News* 5 Apr. 6 There's an audible snicker up above. **1888** GUNTER *Mr. Potter* xiv. 175 There comes a cruel silence, broken only by a snicker from Van Cott.

†**'snicker**, *sb.*[2] *slang. Obs.* (See quot.)

**1796** *Grose's Dict. Vulgar T.* (ed. 3), *Snicker*, a glandered horse.

**'snicker**, *sb.*[3] [f. SNICK *v.*[2] The passage is burlesque.] A knife.

**1848** THACKERAY *Van. Fair* vi, If they screak, out with your snickers and slick!

**snicker** (ˈsnɪkə(r)), *v.* Also 9 *Sc.* **snicher.** [Imitative: cf. NICKER *v.* and SNIGGER *v.*[1]]

**1.** *intr.* To laugh in a half-suppressed or smothered manner; to snigger.

**1694** MOTTEUX *Rabelais* IV. lii, While he said this, the Maidens began to snicker at his Elbow, grinning, giggling and twittering among themselves. *a* **1700** B. E. *Dict. Cant. Crew*, *Snickering*, Laughing in his Sleeve or privately. **1796** MRS. M. ROBINSON *Angelina* II. 251 'You may sneer and snicker, and look grand'; cried Sir Edward. **1836** HALIBURTON *Clockm.* Ser. I. vi, The neighbours snickered a good deal, and the Elder felt pretty streaked. **1855** BROWNING *Heretic's Trag.* viii, John, snickering, crook'd his wicked thumb. **1880** J. HAWTHORNE *Ellice Quentin*, etc. I. 255 One or two persons snickered, and others joined in, and almost immediately there was a universal explosion of derisive mirth.

*transf.* and *fig.* **1857** HOLLAND *Bay Path* xii. 144 And the ripples came up, one after another, and whispered and snickered in his ears. **1884** *Harper's Mag.* May 922/1 A squirrel barked and 'snickered'. **1897** *Outing* XXX. 172/1 Every wee water-course seems to snicker gleefully as it romps along.

**2.** Of horses: To neigh, nicker.

**1824** SCOTT *Redgauntlet* let. i, The rascal knows me already, and snickers whenever I cross the threshold of the stable. **1880** *Macm. Mag.* Jan. 217/2 The sturdy colt that hinnied and snickered round his mother in the pasture.

Hence **'snickering** *vbl. sb.* and *ppl. a.*; **'snickeringly** *adv.*, in a snickering manner.

**1775** ASH *Dict.*, *Snickering*, a silly kind of laugh. **1872** HOLLAND *Marble Prophecy* 78 Much as if for a snickering fit or a sneeze. **1878** BROWNING *Poets Croisic* 142 Yes, I'm Macrais, and somebody beside, You snickering monkey! **1885** *Harper's Mag.* Feb. 485/2 They silently—and snickeringly—arose and left the theatre. **1893** *Advance* (Chicago) 9 Nov., There had been..a snickering and chuckling in the further part of the room.

**snicker-snack** (ˌsnɪkəˈsnæk, ˈsnɪkəˌsnæk), *adv.* and *sb.* Also **snickasnack.** [Imit.: cf. SNICK-SNACK *adv.* and *sb.*] (With) a snipping or clicking sound.

**1871** 'L. CARROLL' *Through Looking Glass* i. 22 The vorpal blade went snicker-snack! **1913** C. MACKENZIE *Sinister Street* I. II. xv. 403 Mrs Carthew snipped away, talking in sentences that matched the quick snickasnack of her weapon. **1979** P. WAY *Sunrise* viii. 79 The little man next door was chopping his hedge. The shears were going snicker-snack. *Ibid.* 85 He glanced back at them fiddling with the dominoes... The pattern fell snicker-snack over.

**snickersnee** (ˈsnɪkəsniː), *sb.* Also **snicker-, snikker-snee.** [Alteration of SNICK OR SNEE.]

**1.** = SNICK-A-SNEE 1.

**1727** BOYER *Dict. Royal* II, *Snicker-snee* (the Dutch way of fighting with pointed Knives). **1867** SMYTH *Sailor's Word-bk.*, *Snikker-Snee*, a combat with knives.

**2.** A large knife.

**1775** ASH *Dict.*, *Snickersnee*,..a long kind of knife. **1791** G. HUDDESFORD in *Salmagundi* 86 He pulled out his Snicker-snee With imprecations horrid. **1809** W. IRVING *Knickerb.* (1861) 171 A host more, armed..with swords, hatchets, snicker-snees,..and what not. *a* **1825** FORBY *Voc. E. Anglia*, *Snicker-snee*, a large clasp knife. **1840** THACKERAY *Catherine* xiv, Drawing his snickersnee, he plunged it in the bailiff's chest. **1885** W. S. GILBERT *Mikado* II. 37 As I gnashed my teeth, When from its sheath I drew my snicker-snee.

†**snickersnee**, *v. Obs.* Also 8 **snigger-, sneaker-, sneeker-.** [f. as prec.] *intr.* To fight with knives; to use a knife as a weapon. Hence †**snicker-sneeing** *vbl. sb.* and *ppl. a.*

Cf. the Linc. dial. *snickersneeze*, used in threatening children ('If you do that, I'll snickersneeze you').

**1698** FRYER *Acc. E. India & P.* 119 Boxing among the English; Snicker-Sneeing among the Dutch. **1704** N. N. tr. *Boccalini's Advts. fr. Parnass.* III. 16 But when the Officers came to inforce the Execution of this Decree upon the Dutch, they were ready to fall to Snigger Snee with 'em about it. **1712** ARBUTHNOT *John Bull* IV. vii, He pull'd out a Case-knife, with which he used to sneaker-snee, and threaten'd to cut his own Throat. **1738** [G. SMITH] *Curious Relat.* I. iii. 443 He that acted the Character of the Insolent Sailor, humour'd it to the Life..: He wanted to fight, or Sneeker-snee. **1778** BRYDGES *Homer Trav.* (1797) II. 268 An ugly dream, Wherein a Dutch-built thief did seem To shake a snickersneeing knife.

**snicket** (ˈsnɪkɪt). *north. dial.* [Origin obscure.] A narrow passage between houses, an alley-way.

For further senses of the word see *Eng. Dial. Dict.*

**1898** B. KIRKBY *Lakeland Words* 136 *Snicket*, a narrow passage between buildings. **1947** I. BROWN *Say the Word* 65 We have vennels, gunnels, and snickets in our northern towns. **1957** R. HOGGART *Uses of Literacy* I. ii. 52 Street after regular street of shoddily uniform houses intersected by a dark pattern of ginnels and snickets (alley-ways) and courts. **1968** B. HINES *Kestrel for Knave* 31 He cut down a snicket between two houses, out into the fields. **1981** J. STUBBS *Ironmaster* xx. 276 We are cramming poor people into ginnels and snickets and foetid courts.

**snickety** (ˈsnɪkɪtɪ), *a. rare.* [Origin obscure: cf. PERSNICKETY *a.* (*adv.*).] Fussy, pernickety.

*a* **1960** E. M. FORSTER *Maurice* (1971) IV. xxxix. 186 Maurice hated cricket. It demanded a snickety neatness he could not supply.

**'snickey**, *a. rare*$^{-1}$. [? f. SNICK *sb.*[4]] ? Full of knots or irregularities.

**1845** DISRAELI *Sybil* (1863) 72 'Soul alive, but those Shuffle and Screw are rotten, snickey, bad yarns,' said Mistress Carey.

**'snicking**, *vbl. sb.* [Cf. SNICK *sb.*[1]] The action of getting surreptitiously.

**1673** R. HEAD *Cant. Acad.* 103 She hath half share of her own Gettings besides a little *Snicking* by the by.

**snickle** (ˈsnɪk(ə)l), *sb.* Now *dial.* Also 9 **snikkle.** [Cf. next.] A snare or gin; a noose.

**1681** T. FLATMAN *Heraclitus Ridens* No. 30 (1713) I. 197 This was a way of Man-catching which our Friend Hick ne'er thought on, for a Man to run his own Head into the Snickle. **1688** HOLME *Armoury* III. 104/1 For Pike [fishing], ..Snap, Gorge, Snare or Snickle. **1819** in Hatfield *Hist. Notices Doncaster* (1866) I. 71 Thou hast got a gun this morning, I see, and a pocketful of snickles. **1828** HEBER *Jrnl.* I. 173 The capture of a very beautiful iguana;..one of the boatmen caught it in a snickle. **1862-** in dial. glossaries, etc.

(Yorks., Nhp., Leic.). **1902** CUTCLIFFE HYNE *Thompson's Progress* 183 A fine cock pheasant with..a wire snickle tightly round its neck.

**snickle** (ˈsnɪk(ə)l), *v.* Now *dial.* Also 7 **snickell**. [Of obscure origin.]

In Marlowe *Jew of Malta* IV. v. 1941 the reading is uncertain and the meaning obscure.

**1.** *trans.* To catch with a snickle or noose; to snare. Also with *up*.

**1615** MARKHAM *Pleas. Princ.* vi. (1635) 34 There be some which take great delight to snickell or halter the Pike. **1616** SURFL. & MARKHAM *Country Farme* VII. iii. 648 Some spring-trappes, to snickle or halter either bird or beast. **1674** J. W[RIGHT] *Mock-Thyestes* 128 Seeing his advantage pat, He snickles up the eldest cat. *a* **1800** PEGGE *Suppl. Grose*, *Snickle*, to take a hare in a gin. Derb. **1813** in Hatfield *Hist. Notices Doncaster* (1866) I. 67 [A] game-keeper..was..ill-treated by three men who were snickling hares. **1855** [ROBINSON] *Whitby Gloss.*, *To Snickle*, to snare with a draw-loop as hares are entangled or snickled.

*refl.* **1675** ALSOP *Anti-Sozzo* III. ii. 249, I know no Obligation [that] lies upon me to cut the Rope, as often as he will Snickle himself.

*fig.* **1679** ALSOP *Melius Inq.* II. iii. 248 It seems the Blessed Apostle had not yet learnt to snickle the private Conscience with his publick Authority. **1770** JENNER *Placid Man* VI. v, If I don't see you both fairly snickled before I go, I'll never forgive either of you.

**2.** To draw *out* by means of a noose.

**1865** *Sheffield Indep.* Jan., After..making a new opening into the cave, one hound was 'snickled' out with a noose over his head, after about 24 hours' imprisonment.

†**snick or snee**, *v.* and *sb. Obs.* Also 7 **steake or snye, stick or snee**, 8 **snic or snee**; 7–8 **snick-or-snee**. [orig. ad. Du. *steken* (G. *stechen*) to thrust, stick, and *snijen*, *snijden* (G. *schneiden*) to cut, with subsequent assimilation of the *st-* of the first word to the *sn-* of the second.

In the first quotation the form *snye* indicates a pronunciation of *snijen* similar to that in mod. standard Du.; the later *snee* represents a variant pron. still widely current in Du. and Flem. dialects.]

**1. a.** As *vb.* To thrust or cut in fighting with a knife; to use a knife in this manner.

*a* **1613** ROWLAND *Four Knaves* (Percy Soc.) 31 Let falchion, polax, launce, or halbert try, With Flemings-knives either to steake or snye. **1635** GLAPTHORNE *Hollander* I. i, It is our Countrie Custome onely to Stick or Snee. *a* **1704** T. BROWN *Wks.* (1730) IV. 17 Let the dull-pated Boors Snic or snee at their Punch-Bowls, or slash for their Whores. **1704** D'URFEY *Hell beyond Hell* 55 Fish-wives whom rage does enflame To snick-or-snee at Rotterdam.

**b.** As *sb.* The practice of fighting with cut-and-thrust knives.

**1670** in *14th Rep. Hist. MSS. Comm.* App. IV. 87 [They] fell upon him with knives (one was found afterwards of the Duch fashon, for their snick or snee). **1695** DRYDEN *Parall. Poetry & Paint.* Ess. (Ker) II. 132 The representation of a Dutch kermis, the brutal sport of snick-or-snee. *a* **1704** T. BROWN *Dial. Dead* Wks. 1711 IV. 33 The noble Combats of *Snick* or *Snee*, or some illustrious Sea-fight.

**2.** *transf.* Used to denote one or other of two possible alternatives or courses.

**1675** ALSOP *Anti-Sozzo* 324 Yet that is interpreting Scripture by the sound of words also; so that we are in a Fork, Snick or Snee; and both wayes equally undone. **1680** —— *Mischief Imposit.* viii. 75 The Question now is, Snick or Snee: Turn or Starve: Conform or Hang: Use the Cross or bear the Cross. [**1681** *Reply 'Mischief of Imposit.'* 6 One would guess this man has an aking tooth to be at it again, though with snick or snee, as he calls it.]

**snick-snack** (ˈsnɪk,snæk, ,snɪkˈsnæk), *adv.* and *sb.* Also **snic-snac**. [Imit.: redupl. from SNICK *sb.*[3]] = SNICKER-SNACK *adv.* and *sb.*

**1925** C. DAY LEWIS *Beechen Vigil* 11 Meanders around the rose-beds, gnarled, clay-brown, Old Tom the pruner, snic-snac up and down. **1970** *New Yorker* 28 Nov. 151/1 Big, straight scissors, from Finland..have a nice feel in the hand and a reassuring snick-snack.

ˈ**snick-snarl.** Now *dial.* [f. SNARL *sb.*[1], with obscure first element; cf. the common north. dial. *snock-snarl*.] A tangle, knot, twist. Also *fig.*

**1649** LIGHTFOOT *Battle Wasp's Nest* Wks. I. 383, I could deduce such conclusions from these premises, that would make his opinion..run so on snicksnarles, that..he would find enough to do to unknot it again. **1675** ALSOP *Anti-Sozzo* 277 It were tedious to instance..how they run their Enemies all on Heaps, and perplex their Discourses all into Snicksnarles. **1828** CARR *Craven Gloss.*, *Snick-snarles*, the complication of thread, yarn, &c., the state of its being entangled. **1862** *Oldham Standard* 5 Apr. 2/4 (Cassell), Somebody must unravel the snick-snarls in the hank which somebody else had no more wit than to tangle. **1883** GRESLEY *Gloss. Coal Mining* 145 *Kank*, a twist or snick-snarl in a rope.

†**snick-up**, *sb.*[1] *Obs. rare.* [? f. SNICK *v.*[1]] A hangman's rope; a halter.

**1623** J. TAYLOR (Water P.) *Praise of Hempseed* 15 A Tiburne Hempen caudell well will cure you;..in Sparta it ycleped was Snickvp, which is in English Gallow grasse.

**snick-up**, *sb.*[2] Now *dial.* Also 9 **sniccup**. [Imitative: cf. LG. *snik-up* hiccup, Du. *snik* gasp, sob.] A sneeze, sneezing-fit.

**1692** L'ESTRANGE *Fables* (1694) 397 If there had been but a Snick-up in the case, you'd have cry'd 'The Lord bless ye Sir'. **1879** *N. & Q.* 5th Ser. XII. 45/2 The turkeys in his neighbourhood [Essex] were dying very much this season of the 'snickups'. By this he meant a kind of sneezing fit.

**snick-up**, *v.*: see SNICK *v.*[1]

†**snid.** *slang. Obs.* A sixpence.

**1839** *Slang Dict.* 34.

ˈ**sniddle.** *dial.* Also 5 **snythill**. [prob. f. the stem of OE. *sníðan* to cut: see SNITHE *v.* WFris. has *snyl* (from *snidel) or *snile* in the same sense.] Coarse grass, rushes, or sedge.

*a* **1400–50** *Alexander* 4095 A dryi meere..full of gladen & of gale & of grete redis. þan snyȝes þar, out of þat snyth hill [*read* snythill]..A burly best. **1794** WEDGE *Agric. Chester* 57 Before the cheese is brought into the rooms, the floors are mostly well littered with what the farmers here call 'sniddle'. *a* **1800** PEGGE *Suppl. Grose*, *Sniddle*, long grass; also stubble. Lanc. **1845** *Jrnl. R. Agric. Soc.* VI. I. 119 The floor of the cheese-room is generally covered with..a coarse grass resembling rushes, called 'sniddle'. **1886** HOLLAND *Chesh. Gloss.*, *Sniddle*, any kind of sedge, *Carex*.

**sniddy**, var. SNIDEY *a.*

**snide** (snaɪd), *a.* and *sb. colloq.* (orig. *Cant*). Also **snyde**. [Of obscure origin.]

**A.** *adj.* **1.** Counterfeit, sham, bogus. Also more widely, inferior, worthless.

**1859** G. W. MATSELL *Vocabulum* 83 *Snide stuff*, bad money. **1861** J. CLAY *Prison Chaplain* viii. 537 The observant and experienced E.R. says 'The utterers of "*Snide pewter*" (base silver) are almost all Irish.' **1862** *Cornh. Mag.* Nov. 652 [To] get ready for the trial, and look up the 'snyde witnesses'. **1868** *Temple Bar* XXIV. 538 *Snyde*..means counterfeit or bad. **1887** F. FRANCIS *Saddle & Mocassin* i. 3 These here men don't want none of your..snide outfits, but jest good *bronchos* and a waggon, and strong harness. **1887** *Lantern* (New Orleans) 9 Apr. 2/3 Who runs dat snide hash house. **1893** *Advance* (Chicago) 5 Oct., When stripped of their gay apparel..the most of them were very snide religions. **1894** MASKELYNE *Sharps & Flats* 309 A holdout in the vest is more use than snide jewelry in the pocket. **1899** 'J. FLYNT' *Tramping with Tramps* II. 277 Utica..is sort of a snide place, this time of the year. **1906** E. DYSON *Fact'ry 'Ands* xiv. 180 'Tain't ther liquor wot's snide, it's ther dead hookity hides what it gets chuted into. **1926** [see JUNGLE *sb.* 2 c]. **1973** 'J. PATRICK' *Glasgow Gang Observed* 235 Snide 'boggin': used in phrase 'snide gear', i.e. clothes that are out of fashion, contemptible, inferior.

**2.** Of a person: cunning, sharp.

**1883** E. J. MILLIKEN *Childe Chappie's Pilgrimage* ii. 15 They self-deemed astute and 'snide', Of *nous* bereft, low chaff the bar-queen golden dyed. **1889** *Cent. Dict.* 5730/3 *Snide*,..sharp; characterized by low cunning and sharp practice. **1950** P. TEMPEST *Lag's Lexicon* 193 'He's a "snide" so-and-so' = he's a slippery customer.

**3.** Insinuating, sneering, slyly derogatory.

**1933** *N. & Q.* 14 Oct. 261/2 Our snide way of saying it was cheap, false, and counterfeit. **1939** *Sun* (Baltimore) 15 Apr. 8/1 Snide trick. Any reprehensible bills..enacted in secrecy at a session of the Legislature are bound to come to the surface after the State's lawmakers have left Annapolis. **1943** *Ibid.* 22 Apr. 30/6 It was a horrifying thing..to hear the President..making a snide attack against a group of Americans instead of defending America. **1954** M. DAVENPORT *My Brother's Keeper* 182 She lived in a tenement..and she would fill the whole neighbourhood with snide gossip. **1961** J. HELLER *Catch-22* (1962) x. 103 Ex-P.F.C. Wintergreen was a snide little punk who enjoyed working at cross-purposes. **1978** G. GREENE *Human Factor* VI. ii. 318 Next day when Ivan made his snide references to 'gratitude' he broke furiously out: 'You call this gratitude.' **1981** *Maledicta* V. 123 He..curses a great deal and writes snide letters to careless authors.

**B.** *sb.* **1. a.** Counterfeit jewelry; base coin.

**1885** *Lisbon* (Dakota) *Star* 27 Mar. 5 They pass by the jewels and take 'the snide', for that is all they know. **1887** *Times* 22 Dec. 14/2 Witness caught hold of Clark and said 'Bill, I think you have a little snide (base coin) on you'.

**b.** A base, contemptible person; a swindler, cheat, liar.

**1874** HOTTEN *Slang Dict.* 299 'He's a snide,' though this seems but a contraction of *snide 'un*. **1883** J. HAY *Bread-Winners* xix. 297 'I am right glad I got here to save you from that—' he paused, searching for a word which would be descriptive and yet not improper in the presence of a lady, ..'that snide.' **1919** *Dial. Notes* V. 67 That fellow is a snide, do not trust him. **1935** AUDEN & ISHERWOOD *Dog beneath Skin* II. iii. 99 Young Waters is playing too. He's no snyde at the game. **1972** L. HENDERSON *Cage until Tame* xii. 103 Tolly's not a snide, he's better than most, and he's been bloody unlucky.

**c.** Hypocrisy, pretence; malicious gossip.

**1902** G. H. LORIMER *Lett. Self-made Merchant* vii. 90 Courtesy without condescension,..simplicity without snide. **1966** *New Statesman* 8 Apr. 499/2 She analysed..the nasty state of affairs on the gossip beat. The result was spectacular—some of the popular papers changed the titles of their columns, keyhole snide was banned, [etc.].

**2.** *Comb.*, as ***snide-pitcher***, ***-pitching***; ***snidesman***.

**1862** *Cornh. Mag.* Nov. 649 Every professional thief is considered as belonging to the branch of thieving in which he excels the most, and he is named after it:..a snyde pitcher, a magsman,..as the case may be. **1868** *Temple Bar* XXIV. 538 *Snyde-pitching* is passing bad money. **1896** A. MORRISON *Child Jago* 111 An outer fringe of such dippers—such pickpockets—as could dress well, welshers, and snidesmen.

Hence ˈ**snidely** *adv.*; ˈ**snideness**; ˈ**snidery** = SNIDE *sb.* 1 c; also, an instance of this.

**1942** BERREY & VAN DEN BARK *Amer. Thes. Slang* §317/1 *Treachery*...snideness. **1953** *Britannica Bk. of Year* 639/2 *Snidery*,..hypocrisy, pretence. **1956** D. KARP *All Honorable Men* 39, I drew aside the people from *Time* and asked them if they were going to treat the Institute snidely or soberly. **1961** 'B. WELLS' *Day Earth caught Fire* viii. 119 'If you're right this means no private water at all.' 'Correct,' said Pete snidely. 'Just turn on the taps and hear the rude noise of progress.' **1965** P. WYLIE *They both were Naked* I. ii. 92, I was 'in'...by great good luck and the use of some small snideness. **1967** *Punch* 8 Nov. 697/2 Those sardonic snideries which come too readily to one's lips. **1969** *Daily Tel.* 24 Apr. 21/5 The snidery of the humour may escape those playgoers who cannot look at it with fairly Irish eyes. **1975** *Country Life* 30 Oct. 1160/1, I have often snidely remarked, that the flowers on each spike are not half of them opened before the first are already brown. **1978** A. NOAKES *William Frith* iv. 68 Frith's success with *Derby Day*.. sparked off some ill-tempered snideries.

**Snider** (ˈsnaɪdə(r)). [See def.] ***Snider rifle***, a form of breech-loading rifle invented by Jacob Snider (†1866). Also *ellipt.* for this.

**1868** *U.S. Rep. Munit. War* 32 The Snider rifle..has attracted perhaps as much attention as any breech-loader in Europe or America. **1876** VOYLE & STEVENSON *Milit. Dict.* 27/1 The Snider or converted Enfield rifle cartridge. **1890** KIPLING *Soldiers Three* (1891) 65 The good and virtuous people who hardly know a Martini from a Snider.

**snidey** (ˈsnaɪdɪ), *a. slang.* Also **sniddy, snidy**. [f. SNIDE *a.* + -Y[1].] **a.** Bad, contemptible. **b.** Insinuating, cutting.

**1890** in Barrère & Leland *Dict. Slang* II. 267/2 Since Bill George was nabbed for liftin' them sax things is been very sniddy, so you'll be glad to learn as I have got on a new hook. **1903** FARMER & HENLEY *Slang* VI. 281/1 *Snide*... As *adj.* (also *sniddy* or *snidey*) = bad, wretched, contemptible. **1928** F. HURST *President is Born* xxii. 232 'Fraid! Snidey! Poof! 'Fraid. Poof! Poof! Poof! **1972** *Guardian* 20 Jan. 13/2 Miss Duncan will not allow snidy little one-liners to upset her. **1977** *Sounds* 9 July 33/3 The journalists thought he was being 'Hip' when he was snidey about the Dolls on TV.

Hence ˈ**snidiness**.

**1976** E. DUNPHY *Only a Game?* iii. 98 Because there is glory and money and your career at stake. And that entails backbiting, snidiness, scapegoating and a whole host of other things.

**snidge.** Now Lanc. *dial.* Also 6 **snydge**. [var. of SNUDGE *sb.*] A greedy or miserly person.

**1548** FORREST *Pleas. Poesye* 97 For suche solayne snydges [do thou] caste reformation by forfeture too the poores sustentation. **1855** J. DAVIES in *Trans. Philol. Soc.* 272 *Snidge*, a greedy, sordid person.

**snie**, var. SNYE.

**sniff** (snɪf), *sb.* [f. the vb.]

The phrase ***in a sniff*** 'in a moment' occurs slightly earlier in dial.: see the *Eng. Dial. Dict.*

**1. a.** An act of sniffing; a single inhalation through the nose in order to smell something, usually accompanied by a characteristic short snuffling sound; the sound made in doing this.

**1767** WARTON *Oxford Newsman's V.* 34 Oh, cou'd I but have had one single sup, One single sniff at Charlotte's caudle-cup! **1798** O'KEEFFE *Wild Oats* II. i, Rain over—quite fine—I'll take a sniff of the open air too. **1833** T. HOOK *Parson's Dau.* II. i, Then he made a sort of a sniff with his nose, because he could smell the dinner. **1868** H. SPENCER *Princ. Psychol.* I. vi. (ed. 2) I. 109 When the sniffs have been continued for some time, scarcely any scent can be perceived. **1883** F. M. CRAWFORD *Dr. Claudius* i, [He] was taking his evening sniff of the Neckar breeze.

*transf.* **1860** MAYNE REID *Hunters' Feast* vi, It was a sort of prolonged hiss, that all except Ike believed to be the snort of the black bear. Ike..declared that it was..the 'sniff', as he termed it, of the 'painter' (cougar).

**b.** A smell or scent.

**1844** HOOD *The Turtles* 34 All whiffs, and sniffs, and puffs and snuffs,..That, as we walk upon the river's ridge, Assault the nose.

**c.** Sniffing distance.

**1878** STEVENSON *Inland Voy.* xx. 216 We were within sniff of Paris, it seemed.

**d.** *fig.* A hint, intimation.

**1936** C. DAY LEWIS *Friendly Tree* II. ix. 124, I have been ..wondering if I shall ever get a job... I have just got a sniff of one—experimental work.

**2.** An act of sniffing in order to express or show contempt, disdain, incredulity, or similar feeling.

**1837** CARLYLE *Fr. Rev.* II. III. iii, Lambeth..is met..by nothing but Royalist *brocards*; sniffs, huffs, and open insults. **1840** DICKENS *Barn. Rudge* xli, Miss Miggs gave a great sniff to the same effect. **1884** *Manch. Exam.* 19 Dec. 5/2 A look and a sniff which express as clearly as articulate words a homely rejoinder [etc.]. **1891** 'J. S. WINTER' *Lumley* xii, 'She is downstairs, and I think she's come to stop,' with a sniff of disgust.

**3.** An act (or habit) of clearing the nose by a short inhalation.

**1860** *All Year Round* No. 75. 588 An elderly woman labouring under a chronic sniff. **1883** H. DRUMMOND in G. A. Smith *Life* (1899) viii. 188 The creature..gives vent to a tremendous sniff, as if he had just caught a severe cold in the head.

**4.** *U.S.* A contemptible or insignificant person.

**1890** GUNTER *Miss Nobody* xii, Her mother..cries out, astounded: 'Going to marry that little sniff?'

**5.** *U.S.* A domino game in which the first double played has special significance; the first double played.

**1917** J. HERGESHEIMER *Three Black Pennys* III. xxiv. 289 After dinner, when they were playing sniff. **1930** J. H. APPEL *Business Biogr. J. Wanamaker* xxii. 336 His own favourite game was 'sniff', played with dominoes. **1961** D. C. ARMANINO *Pop. Domino Games* 37 A *singles* may be played off the end of singles, the sides of doubles, and the ends of Sniff. Sniff is the only double on which plays can be made on the ends. **1974** F. BERNDT *Domino Bk.* 33 Sniff is yet another variation of Muggins. *Ibid.*, The first double played is called the Sniff.

**sniff** (snɪf), *v.* Forms: 4–5 **snyff**, 6 **sniffe**, 8– **sniff**. [Imitative: cf. SNIFFLE *v.* and SNUFF *v.*]

**1. a.** *intr.* To draw air through the nose with short or sharp audible inhalations; to clear the nose in this way, esp. when under the influence of emotion.

*c* **1340** *Nominale* (Skeat) 88 Man snyffyth and snyuelith. *c* **1400** *Beryn* 39 She snyffith, sighith, and shooke hire hede, and made rouful chere. *c* **1460** J. RUSSELL *Bk. Nurture* 284 Pike not youre nose.., Snyff nor snitynge hyt to lowd lest youre soueravne hit here. **1575** TURBERV. *Faulconrie* 231 It shall be good..to skowre the head alone, and purge it with some deuise, to force hir snyte and sniffe as men do accustome to sneze. *Ibid.* 232 To discerne this disease of the head, the hawke will sniffe often. **1839** DICKENS *Nickleby* iv, The little boy beyond alternately sniffing and choking, gave no further vent to his emotions. **1885** *Manch. Exam.* 9 May 6/2 The ladies were all weeping wildly,..dozens of men were sniffing suspiciously.

**b.** *spec.* To inhale cocaine, the fumes of glue, etc., through the nose. *slang.*

**1925** *Flynn's* 4 Apr. 819/2 *Sniff*,..to use powdered cocaine as snuff. **1931** E. WALLACE *On Spot* ii. 24 Red, you're..a hop-head... We got no room in this outfit for guys who sniff. **1967** C. DRUMMOND *Death at Furlong Post* v. 62 So they send us a dipso who sniffs! **1970** *New Scientist* 13 Aug. 352/1 These young people generally 'sniffed' from a plastic bag into which they first squirted aeroplane glue, cleaning fluid or whatever. **1975** *Weekend Mag.* (Montreal) 8 Feb. 21 The Whitebear sisters began sniffing almost two years ago, Janice says. 'A friend of ours used to sniff. At first, we didn't know what he was doing, so we asked and then we tried it too.' **1977** J. VAN DE WETERING *Death of Hawker* vii. 73 He's sniffing too... Cocaine powder.

**2. a.** To sniff in smelling; to smell with a sniff or sniffs. Said esp. of animals.

**1788** COWPER *Death of Mrs. Throckmorton's Bulfinch* 40 He [*sc.* a cat]..something in the wind Conjectur'd, sniffing round and round. **1848** DICKENS *Dombey* lv, Some dogs.. that sniffed upon the road. **1874** C. KEENE *Let.* in *Life* (1892) vii. 160 [A] little animal, always sniffing about for mice. **1899** *Allbutt's Syst. Med.* VII. 341 The patient in smelling sniffed with one nostril only.

*fig.* **1865** DICKENS *Mut. Fr.* III. xiv, If he came sneaking and sniffing about the property. **1973** A. MANN *Tiara* ix. 76, I want to..sniff around the Vatican again. **1977** R. PLAYER *Month of Mangled Models* vii. 133 Sniffing around Chelsea and Kelmscott.

**b.** Const. *at.*

**1792** MME. D'ARBLAY *Diary* 27 June, She..sniffed at her flowers with a sort of ecstatic eagerness. **1833** MARRYAT *P. Simple* (1863) 239 After sniffing at it two or three times, I knew it to be otto of roses. **1865** TYLOR *Early Hist. Man.* iii. 45 The Fijians, who used to salute by smelling or sniffing at one another. **1883** OLIVE SCHREINER *Story Afr. Farm* I. i, A curious old ewe came to sniff at him.

**3.** To show or express contempt, disdain, disparagement, incredulity, or similar feeling, by sniffing:

**a.** Const. *at* a person or thing.

**1729** SWIFT *Grand Question* Wks. 1755 IV. I. 109 So then you look'd scornful, and snift at the dean. **1837** CARLYLE *Fr. Rev.* I. VI. iv, Camille Desmoulins, and others, sniffing at him for it. **1864** —— *Fredk. Gt.* XVI. x. (1872) VI. 262 Our Shopkeepers of the Rue St. Honoré would sniff at such a lodging. **1888** *Times* 6 July 9/3 Superior persons..will doubtless sniff at the expression of opinion upon these topics by the House of Lords.

**b.** Without const.

**1837** CARLYLE *Fr. Rev.* I. VI. ii, Dusky D'Espréménil does nothing but sniff and ejaculate. **1871** MRS. WHITNEY *Real Folks* xvii, She did not sniff; she was a great deal too much a lady. **1881** BESANT & RICE *Chapl. Fleet* I. 91 Mrs. Gambitt sniffed disdainfully.

**4. a.** *trans.* To take *up*, draw *in*, (air, etc.) by inhaling through the nostrils.

**1796** MME. D'ARBLAY *Camilla* I. 147 Seeing he was sniffing up the *eau suave* without looking at her. **1822–7** GOOD *Study Med.* (1829) III. 189 Cold water may be sniffed up the nostrils. **1828** LADY GRANVILLE *Lett.* 29 July (1894) II. 29, I sniffed up country air, and felt better and better every mile. **1873** AGNES MATHESON in *Mem. Minister's Wife* (1881) vii. 98, I can sit and sniff in the sea-breezes.

**b.** Without adv.

**1843** SIR C. SCUDAMORE *Med. Visit Grafenberg* 75 Head-bath twice a day; and to sniff water freely several times in the day. **1856** KANE *Arctic Explor.* II. xiii. 138 Dr. Hayes.. came aft and crawled upon deck to sniff the day-light. **1870** R. BROUGH *M. Lynch* x, [He] could sniff the sea breeze through the counting-house window.

**c.** *fig.* or in fig. context.

**1864** DK. MANCHESTER *Crt. & Soc.* I. vii. 106 Sniffing a far-off scent of battle with the restless craving of the war-horse. **1881** BESANT & RICE *Chapl. Fleet* II. x, His turn-up nose seemed so joyfully to sniff the incense of praise.

**5. a.** To smell (a thing).

*a* **1845** HOOD *Town & Country* v, For meadow-buds I get a whiff of Cheshire cheese,—or only sniff The turtle made at Cuff's. **1871** B. TAYLOR *Faust* I. iii. (1875) II. 28 The platter-licker, he sniffs the roasting.

**b.** *fig.* To perceive as if by smell; to sniff or smell out (a plot, etc.); to suspect. Also with *out.*

**1864** C. KNIGHT *Passages Work. Life* I. iii. 175 Lord Sidmouth, as was his wont, had sniffed a plot from afar. **1873** C. M. DAVIES *Unorth. London* (1876) 43 It is not only Rome that sniffs heresy in independent thought or action. **1899** C. SCOTT *Drama of Yesterday* I. xvi. 538, I sniffed more prey. **1946** *Sun* (Baltimore) 12 Aug. 1/2 A pilotless aircraft that is sent into the air to 'sniff out' its own enemy target. **1979** J. BARNETT *Backfire is Hostile!* xi. 111 You should concentrate more on sniffing out the sex fiends than speculating on spies.

**c.** Phr. *to sniff the wind*: see WIND *sb.*[1]

**6.** To regard (something) with contempt or scorn; to sneer at.

**1837** CARLYLE *Fr. Rev.* II. v. viii, Thus some, with up-turned nose, will altogether sniff and disdain Sansculottism.

**7.** To utter with a (scornful) sniff; to express by means of a sniff.

**1859** MEREDITH *R. Feverel* xl, 'Are you cold?' she would ask, smiling charitably. 'I am.'..'You always appear to be,' the bosom sniffed and snapped. **1865** A. SMITH *Summer in Skye* i. 24 Fastidious Edinburgh sniffs disdain. **1870** MRS. RIDDELL *Austin Friars* iv, 'Of course you would forgive anything from her,' sniffed Melinda.

**sniffable** ('snɪfəb(ə)l), *a.* [f. SNIFF *v.* + -ABLE.] That can be sniffed.

**1975** *Weekend Mag.* (Montreal) 8 Feb. 23/1 Stocks of the old sniffable product were being bootlegged by merchants all over Regina. **1977** J. WAMBAUGH *Black Marble* (1978) iv. 36 Lopez boasted that he could..have enough sniffable paint left to get three of his pals loaded.

**'sniffer.** [SNIFF *v.*]

**1. a.** One who sniffs (*lit.* and *fig.*).

**1864** *Realm* 1 June 8 Sniffer and snorter. **1889** *Pall Mall G.* 30 Jan. 3/1 Those who are deaf and those who are sniffers.

**b.** *spec.* One who sniffs a drug or toxic substance. Cf. *glue-sniffer* s.v. GLUE *sb.* 6. orig. *U.S. slang.*

**1920** E. S. BISHOP *Narcotic Drug Problem* iii. 23 The heroin 'sniffer' of idle and curious adolescence. **1928** *Amer. Mercury* Aug. 485/2 The Baron was..a 'sniffer' himself. **1942** J. HENRY *Henry's Famous Cases* iv. 40 Cocaine addicts are known as 'sniffers'. **1968** *Guardian* 22 Mar. 11/1 Doreen was also a 'sniffer'. This is the name given to people who inhale a mixture of ether and methylated spirits and become 'blocked'. **1981** *Daily Tel.* 24 Apr. 3/1 A glue sniffer is under the influence of a drug for the purposes of the 1972 Road Traffic Act, magistrates decided yesterday when a self-confessed 'sniffer' denied being unfit to drive through drink or drugs while in charge of a motorcycle.

**2.** *slang.* The nose.

**1858** [see PILE-DRIVER 2]. **1962** R. COOK *Crust on its Uppers* ii. 34 They'll..look down their sniffers at you.

**3. a.** Any device for detecting gas, radiation, etc. *colloq.*

**1945** *Richmond* (Virginia) *Times-Dispatch* 10 Oct. 2/5 The hydrogen content in copper wire annealing furnaces..is now continuously indicated by a new sensitive apparatus called a sniffer nose. **1946** *Sun* (Baltimore) 21 June 10/3 Louis E. De La Fleur..demonstrated a small hand-borne radio fixer, known as a 'sniffer'. He said that it was so accurate that he had been able..to locate an outlaw transmitter in a New York apartment house where hundreds of legal radios and electrical devices were putting out potential inteference. **1950** *Listener* 5 Jan. 12/1 These tiny Geiger counters first came to public attention last spring in New York... Uranium can turn up anywhere so there is no reason why, if you had a 'sniffer', as they are called, you should not start prospecting here in Great Britain. **1968** *Guardian* 5 Sept. 2/7 Perch a radar sensor on the tail..: insert a diesel fume 'sniffer'. **1972** 'J. LANGE' *Binary* 170 The sniffer..had been developed for use in Vietnam and had been adapted for customs operations... If the sniffer said plastic explosive was behind the door, he had to believe it. **1979** F. POHL *Jem* iii. 26 The car was..an indispensable necessity in what he did for the agency; twice a day, other employees of the agency went over it with electronic sniffers and radio probes to make sure it had been neither bombed nor bugged.

**b.** Usu. *sniffer dog.* A dog trained to detect specific odours, esp. those of drugs or explosives. *colloq.*

**1964** *N.Y. Times Mag.* 23 Aug. 62/3 *Sniffer*, police dog. **1975** A. BEEVOR *Violent Brink* iii. 66 We are using..sniffer dogs at ports and airports so as to increase our chances of catching the explosive coming in. **1977** *Air Mail* Spring 7/1 In the first two months 'sniffer' dogs and handlers trained by the RAF Police Dog Training Flight had helped British Customs and Excise officers detect £125,000 worth of smuggled drugs. **1979** *Daily Tel.* 17 Apr. 1/6 Forty-five 'sniffer' dogs were flown into Yugoslavia from Switzerland and set to work to smell out casualties from debris in towns around Kotor Bay. **1982** *Times* 3 Sept. 10/5 Sniffer-dogs for drugs.

**sniffing** ('snɪfɪŋ), *vbl. sb.* [f. SNIFF *v.*] The action of the vb.; an instance of this, a sniff. Cf. *glue-sniffing* s.v. GLUE *sb.* 6.

**1575** TURBERV. *Faulconrie* 231 You may rubbe..the pallate of your Hawke with the saide powder, and not feede hir after it, vntill such tyme she haue lefte snyting and sniffing. **1842** THACKERAY *Fitz-Boodle's Conf.* Wks. 1869 XXII. 229 People looking and making a strange nasal noise (it is called sniffing). **1872** HUXLEY *Physiol.* iv. 90 Sniffing is a more rapid inspiratory act, in which the mouth is kept shut, and the air made to pass through the nose. **1893** SELOUS *Trav. S.E. Africa* 421 Sometimes these sniffings were very loud. **1968** *Guardian* 22 Mar. 11/2, I asked her what attraction there was in 'sniffing'. **1977** *Lancet* 8 Jan. 84/1 Investigation of the 42 patients..showed that 'sniffing' was a group activity involving mainly adolescents aged 12–19 years, all of whom had a previous history of solvent abuse.

*attrib.* **1899** *Allbutt's Syst. Med.* VII. 870 Obstructive diseases of the nose..occasion sniffing movements of the face. **1975** *Weekend Mag.* (Montreal) 8 Feb. 23/1 In any case, legislation doesn't eliminate the sniffing problem which is nation-wide.

**'sniffing,** *ppl. a.* [f. as prec.] That sniffs, in senses of the vb.; characterized by sniffing.

**1831** CARLYLE *Sart. Res.* I. x, To him thou, with sniffing charity, wilt protrusively proffer thy hand-lamp. **1837** —— *Fr. Rev.* II. I. x, What a humour the once sniffing mocking City of Paris..had got into.

Hence **'sniffingly** *adv.*, with a sniff (esp. of scorn or contempt).

**1873** BAYNE in *Contemp. Rev.* XXI. 411 He glances at Cromwell's speeches jauntily, sniffingly, in a mood of pleasant indifference dashed by cynicism. **1893** K. GRAHAME in *National Observer* 23 Sept. 487/1 Charlotte turned away sniffingly.

**sniffle** ('snɪf(ə)l), *sb.*[1] [f. SNIFFLE *v.*]

**1.** *the sniffles*, the snuffles. Also *U.S. slang*, a fit of low spirits.

**1825** JAMIESON *Suppl.*, *Sniffles*, that difficulty of breathing through the nostrils, which is caused by cold in the head. **1903** A. ADAMS *Log Cowboy* xviii. 279, I hope you won't get the sniffles and tell any [*sc.* gloomy tales].

**2.** An act of sniffling; a slight snivel or snuffle.

**1880** MEREDITH *Trag. Com.* (1881) 195 'You have been a little weak,' the phantom said to her, and she acquiesced with a soft sniffle. **1885** MARTINEAU *Types Eth. Th.* (1886) II. I. v. 174 A curve in the nose, a colour of the hair, a sniffle in the voice.

**'sniffle,** *sb.*[2] *Weaving.* [Origin obscure.] A form of ravel or separator.

**1805** J. AUSTIN in *Trans. Soc. Arts* XXIII. 242 An universal ravel or sniffle, useful at the beaming of all kinds of webs. This machine is of itself complete, and will beam from the coarsest to the finest web.

**sniffle** ('snɪf(ə)l), *v.* Also 9 *dial.* **snifle.** [Imitative: cf. G. (now dial.) *schniffeln*, †*schnifeln*, and see SNIVEL *v.*, SNUFFLE *v.*] *intr.* To snivel or snuffle slightly; to sniff. Also (with *that* and compl.), to say with a sniffle.

The vbl. sb. and ppl. a. are recorded much earlier.

**1819** SCOTT *Leg. Montr.* xiv, So saying, and..sniffling a little to swallow his grief, he turned from the heart-rending spectacle. **1846** LANDOR *Imag. Conv.* Wks. 1853 II. 228/2 He does not sniffle: to my ears he speaks plain English. **1883** L. A. LAMBERT *Notes on Ingersoll* vi. 57 And yet you sniffle that He killed art.

**b.** *transf.* Of a breeze. (Cf. next.)

**1885** RUNCIMAN *Skippers & Shellbacks* 143 About nine it began to sniffle and blow a bit.

**sniffler** ('snɪf(ə)lə(r)). [f. SNIFFLE *v.*]

**1.** A strong, smart, or brisk breeze or wind.

**1768** ROSS *Helenore* 32 Wi weet an wind sae tyte into my teeth,.. I gat na sik a teazle this seven year... I maun na ilka day be coming here, To get sic snifiers [**1789** snifters]. **1833** M. SCOTT *Tom Cringle* viii, At length the sniffler reached us, and the sharp little vessel began to speak. **1891** *Cent. Dict.*, *Sniffler*, a capful of wind.

**2.** One who sniffles.

**1887** W. S. GILBERT *Ruddigore* II, Sniffler, snuffler, wailer, weeper.

**sniffling** ('snɪflɪŋ), *vbl. sb.* [f. SNIFFLE *v.*] Snivelling; snuffling; †canting discourse.

**1653** *Clarke Papers* (Camden) III. 6 This answer not satisfying them they went to the Councell of State with another peticion, where they had much more sniffling but went away free men. **1836** HOWARD *R. Reefer* xiii, You will ..oblige me by not taking snuff.., the sniffling is abominable. **1840** THACKERAY *Catherine* ii, The tip of her nose as red as fire with sniffling and weeping. **1873** B. HARTE *Fiddletown* 13 There now—stop that sniffling.

**'sniffling,** *ppl. a.* Also 7 **sniffeling**, 7–8 **snifling.** [f. SNIFFLE *v.*] That snivels or snuffles; characterized by sniffling.

**1631** WEEVER *Anc. Funeral Mon.* 40 A snifling conuenticle or companie of proud Sectaries. **1654** GAYTON *Pleas. Notes* IV. ii. 181 Notwithstanding his sniffeling example of Amadis Du Gaull, or any other puling Knight. *a* **1796** PEGGE *Derbicisms* (E.D.S.) 123 A *snifling* cold,..a slight running disorder in the nose. **1833** MARRYAT *P. Simple* xlvii, When you were a little spalpeen, with a sniffling nose. **1890** MRS. BARR *Friend Olivia* xiv, A pretty crowd of sniffling, sneaking varlets he has been feeding and pampering!

**sniffly** ('snɪflɪ), *a.* [f. SNIFFLE *v.* + -Y[1].] Sniffling; characterized by sniffling. Also *fig.*

**1927** W. E. COLLINSON *Contemp. Eng.* 59 They vary in intensity from the sniffling or sniffly cold to the church-yard cough! **1929** G. ADE *Let.* 8 Feb. (1973) 139 The warm weather will be welcome. Most of us have sniffly colds. Otherwise we are all right. **1960** *Guardian* 9 Apr. 6/6 We sat there in the bare little room, wet and sniffly with sentiment. **1966** R. H. RIMMER *Harrad Experiment* (1967) 79 Get out your handkerchiefs, wipe your sniffly nose. **1974** [see LUXE 1].

**sniffy** ('snɪfɪ), *a. dial.* and *colloq.* [f. SNIFF *v.*] Prone or inclined to sniff; scornful, contemptuous, disdainful; disagreeable, ill-tempered.

**1871** C. GIBBON *Lack of Gold* xx, Her curt sniffy manner did not alter in the least. **1896** *Westm. Gaz.* 4 Dec. 2/1 When Lothair's sniffy I keep out of his way. **1915** W. S. MAUGHAM *Of Human Bondage* lxxiv. 382 You were rather sniffy about meeting him. **1925** S. BARING-GOULD *Further Reminisc.* iv. 45 Their wives were especially sniffy towards Mrs Jervis. **1965** *Listener* 3 June 834/3 He was catty about Balzac, sniffy about Stendhal, stuffy about Flaubert, and cagey about Baudelaire. **1979** *Jrnl. R. Soc. Arts* July 511/1 Sniffy comments of a patronizing nature about Victorian buildings so regrettably sprinkled throughout earlier books in *The Buildings of England* are carefully avoided.

Hence **'sniffily** *adv.*, **'sniffiness**; **'sniffish** *a.* (*rare*), somewhat sniffy.

**1900** KIPLING *Just So Stories* (1902) 108 'What will happen if I do? said the Jaguar, most sniffily and most cautious. **1927** *Blackw. Mag.* Dec. 834/1, I didn't think sniffiness was usual under the circumstances. **1928** 'M. NEVILLE' *Kiss Proof* xviii. 163 'Oh, if that's the way you feel about it,' Toddles said sniffily. **1933** 'G. ORWELL' *Let.* June (1968) I. 121 There is also a certain sniffish 'I told you so' implication. **1968** M. COLLIS *Somerville & Ross* iii. 45 In her *Irish Memories* (published in 1917) Edith, recalling that time, writes of the sniffyness of her brothers and uncles.

**1973** *Guardian* 30 June 11/3 'He wasn't up to much as a sub-editor,' said one of the older hacks, sniffily. **1981** *Economist* 24 Jan. 22/2 Although for the past two years the United States has been Algeria's largest trading partner, the relationship between the two countries has been marked by a suspicious sniffiness.

**snift,** *sb. techn.* [f. SNIFT *v.*; cf. dial. *snift* a scent, whiff, etc.] (See quot. and SNIFTING *vbl. sb.*)

**1890** *Times* 7 Aug. 10/2 The whole of the 'snift' (which is the waste in bottling aerated waters) is saved by this machine.

**snift** (snɪft), *v.* Now chiefly *dial.* [Imitative: cf. SNIFTER *v.*, and older Da. *snifte, snyfte* (Da. *snøfte*), Sw. *snyfta*, (MSw. *snypta, snöpta*).]

**1.** *intr.* To sniff, in various senses.

The vbl. sb. is recorded much earlier.

**1703** THORESBY *Let. to Ray* (E.D.S.), *Snift*, to draw the wind smartly up the nose. **1744** DESAGULIERS *Exp. Philos.* II. xii. 474 The Air makes a Noise..like a Man snifting with a Cold. **1762** STERNE *Tr. Shandy* VI. v, He shall neither.. hawk, or spit, or snift. **1801** H. F. CARY *Mem.* I. 186 With her mouth and nose drawn up on one side, and snifting through the latter, which..is the highest elevation of her mirth and gladness. **1828-** in dial. glossaries and texts (N. Cy., Yks., Lancs., Leic., Northampt., Warw., etc.). *a* **1845** BARHAM *Ingoldsby Leg.* Ser. III. *Brothers of Birchington* lx, Father Richard..At once began coughing, and snifting, and sneezing. **1893** KIPLING *Many Invent.* 13 More steamers came along snorting and snifting at the buoys.

**b.** *fig.* (With *after* or *at.*)

**1824** LANDOR *Imag. Conv.*, *Bp. Burnet & Humphrey Hardcastle* Wks. 1853 I. 46/2 It now appears that they were still snifting and hankering after their old quarters. **1824** *Spirit Public Jrnls.* (1825) 304 He has seen 'Life', and *dum vivimus vivamus* is a motto not to be snifted at.

**c.** Of an engine, etc.: To blow out air or steam.

**1865** SMILES *Lives Boulton & Watt* 135 The machine snifted at many openings.

**2.** *trans.* To draw *up* by sniffing; to sniff the smell of. *rare.*

**1736** AINSWORTH I, To snift up, *mucum resorbere.* **1796** MME. D'ARBLAY *Camilla* IV. viii, I would sooner snift thy farthing candle once a day, than sustain that nasal cadence ever more.

**snifter** ('snɪftə(r)), *sb.* Chiefly *Sc.* and *north. dial.* [f. the vb.]

Various other dial. senses are recorded in the *Eng. Dial. Dict.* and *Jamieson's Sc. Dict.*

**1.** A strong or rough breeze or wind.

**1789** [see SNIFFLER 1]. **1866-** in northern dial. glossaries. **1886** BRET HARTE *Snowbound* 121 This is no blizzard, but a regular two-days' snifter. **1897** F. T. BULLEN *Cruise 'Cachalot'* 350 There came a 'snifter' from the hills that caught her unprepared, making her reel again.

**2.** *pl.* A bad cold in the head, or the stoppage of the nostrils caused by this; the snuffles. Also, a disease of poultry (see quot. 1844). *Sc.*

**1808** JAMIESON, *Snifters*, a stoppage of the nostrils from cold, which occasions frequent sniffing. **1828** MOIR *Mansie Wauch* xvii, I asked him..about..curing the sturdie, and the snifters. **1837** MRS. CARLYLE *Lett.* I. 71 The blessedness of having a head clear of snifters. **1844** H. STEPHENS *Bk. Farm* II. 260 The only disease [among fowls] I can remember to have seen in winter is what is vulgarly called the *snifters*, that is, a discharge of matter from the nose, which causes a noise in the nose like stifled breathing.

**3.** A sniff. Chiefly *dial.*

*a* **1835** HOGG *Good Man Alloa* xxxiii. Poems (1865) 309 The palfrey dash'd o'er the bounding wave, with snifter and with stenne. **1866-** in Sc., Yks., Lancs. dial. glossaries and texts (*Eng. Dial. Dict.*). **1884** *Good Words* May 324/2 With a snifter of the nostrils he emits a dry, respiratory sound.

**4.** A (small) quantity of intoxicating liquor, a drink, a 'nip'. *colloq.* (orig. *U.S.*).

See note, sense 5 below.

**1844** *Spirit of Times* 20 Apr. 86/2 He swallowed a cool 'snifter' at the nearest cabaret. **1910** G. B. MCCUTCHEON *Rose in Ring* v. 90 You need a snifter of brandy... Joey handed her a drink from his flask. **1924** WODEHOUSE *Ukridge* iii. 56 And now, old horse, you may lead me across the street to the Coal Hole for a short snifter. **1934** *Bulletin* (Sydney) 26 Dec. 41/1 The postboy brought George a telegram, and ..on opening it George smiled and shouted snifters all round. **1942** E. PAUL *Narrow St.* xxvii. 246, I..was on the point of suggesting that he step across to the Café St. Michel for a snifter. **1963** B. PEARSON *Coal Flat* i. 14 Do you want a drink—or would you rather have a bit of a snifter with the boys? **1978** R. V. JONES *Most Secret War* vii. 59 What happened was that he had taken it from his own station to another for a lunch which was preceded, and doubtless followed, by a surfeit of what he termed 'lightning snifters'.

**5.** A glass with a wide body narrowing towards the top, used for brandy, etc. orig. and chiefly *U.S.*

The sense 'the contents of a snifter' is usu. indistinguishable from sense 4 above and may be represented in some examples there.

**1937** G. FRANKAU *More of Us* xvi. 170 And sought that other room to drain a snifter With Herr Staatsschauspielhausmeister Kohn-Goering. **1943** D. BAKER *Trio* 155 She was sitting beside me holding a brandy snifter. **1970** J. HANSEN *Fadeout* i. 4 A bottle of brandy warmed on the hearth... She poured splashes from it into two small snifters. **1978** G. VIDAL *Kalki* x. iii. 241, I drank brandy from a huge Baccarat snifter.

**6. a.** *U.S. slang.* A cocaine addict. Cf. SNIFFER 1 b.

**1925** *Flynn's* 4 Apr. 819/2 *Snifter*, a cocaine fiend. **1929** *Detective Fiction Weekly* 27 Apr. 31/2 A certain cocaine addict, known as Snifter Selton. **1955** *Amer. Speech* XXX. 85 *Snifter*, an addict who inhales cocaine.

**b.** *slang* (orig. *U.S.*). A small quantity of cocaine inhaled through the nose.

**1930** *Detective Fiction Weekly* 5 July 357/1 Well, boys, take me down [to the police station]. Just one snifter of snow and I'm with you. **1934** 'D. HUME' *Too Dangerous to Live* viii. 85 He's been doping for a few months—cocaine. When he was picked up he hadn't had a snifter for nearly twenty-four hours. **1974** J. WAINWRIGHT *Evidence I shall Give* xxi. 99 A snifter when the pain's bad... It ain't for kicks. You're no junkie.

**7.** *U.S. slang.* A portable radio direction-finder. Cf. SNIFFER 3 a.

**1944** *Sci. News Let.* 12 Aug. 103 'The snifter'..is a portable, one-man direction finder that 'smells out' by radio the very room in which an illegal radio transmitter is hidden. **1949** *Life* 5 Dec. 166/2 At the start hunters with radio direction finders, called 'snifters', collect at Brookfield Zoo.

**snifter** ('snɪftə(r)), *v.* [Imitative: cf. SNIFT *v.*]

Other purely dial. senses are recorded in the *Eng. Dial. Dict.*, as, to giggle, to snow slightly, etc.

**1.** *intr.* To sniff, snivel, snuffle.

*c* **1340** *Nominale* (Skeat) 152 Man snyfterith and nose snyt. **1483** *Cath. Angl.* 347/1 To Snyfter, *revmatizare, fleumaticare.* **1611** COTGR., *Brouffer*, to snurt, or snifter with the nose, like a horse. *Ibid.*, *Nifler*, to snifter, or snuffe vp sniuell; to draw it vp by drawing in the wind. **1719** RAMSAY *2nd Answ. Hamilton* xii, Gin I can snifter thro' mundungus. **1825-** in Sc. and north. glossaries and texts (*Eng. Dial. Dict.*). **1835** HOGG *Tales & Sk.* V. 266, I was obliged to.. snifter like a whipped boy. **1853** HICKIE tr. *Aristoph.* (1872) II. 550 He would have lain sniftering if he was a coward.

**2.** *trans.* With *out*: To utter (words) in a snuffling manner. *rare.*

**1880** W. GRANT *Christ our Hope*, etc. p. xx, He is indeed a forcible speaker, sniftering out his words with the quaintest, queerest accent.

Hence **'snifterer; 'sniftering** *ppl. a.*

**1790** A. WILSON *Rabby's Mistake* Poems 1876 II. 41 Nae sniftering dog had he, I wat, To air't him to the lanely spat Whare ony creature lay. *a* **1800** PEGGE *Suppl. Grose*, *Sniftering* fellow; a shuffling sneaking fellow. Lanc. **1855** [ROBINSON] *Whitby Gloss.*, *Snifle*,..to have the habit of puffing in audible successions through the nostrils, as a 'snifterer'.

**'snifting,** *vbl. sb.* [f. SNIFT *v.*] **a.** The action of sniffing; also *attrib.* **b.** (See quot. 1890 and SNIFT *sb.*)

*c* **1430** *Freemasonry* (Halliw. 1840) 36 From spyȝtynge and snyftynge kepe the also. **1755** JOHNSON, *Snuff*,..resentment expressed by snifting. **1849** CRAIG s.v. *Snift*, The snifting noise made by the air in making its escape. **1890** *Star* 5 Nov. 4/1 There is no necessity for what under the ordinary system is called 'snifting'—the process by which the air in the bottles is allowed to escape.

**'snifting,** *ppl. a.* [f. SNIFT *v.*] ***snifting valve***, a valve through which air may be expelled from the cylinder of a condensing steam-engine. So †***snifting clack, pipe***.

(*a*) **1744** DESAGULIERS *Exp. Philos.* II. 474 This is call'd the Snifting Clack, because the Air makes a Noise every time it blows thro' it, like a Man snifting with a Cold. **1812** SMEATON *Rep.* I. 227 The steam, finding a passage at the snifting clack..blows out thereat. [**1873** EVERS *Steam & Steam Eng.* iii. 50 A valve to preserve the vacuum, which valve, from the peculiar noise it made, was called the snifting valve, or snifting clack.]

(*b*) **1759** H. WOOD *Pat. Specif.* No. 739. 2 If the hot air be driven into the cylinder with a force superior to the pressure of the atmosphere, that force will drive out the condensed air through what is now called the snifting pipe.

(*c*) **1822** J. ROBISON *Syst. Mech. Phil.* II. 61 The steam from the boiler will immediately rush in, and..will force the air to issue by the snifting-valve. **1846** A. YOUNG *Naut. Dict.* 302 The tail-valve, or snifting-valve, is at the opposite side of the air-pump from the condenser. **1878** THURSTON *Growth of Steam-Eng.* 138 A snifting-valve, *k*, opens when the engine is blown through.

†**'snifty,** *sb. Sc. Obs.*$^{-1}$ [f. SNIFT *v.* Cf. SNIFF *sb.* 4.] An insignificant person.

**1660** BAILLIE *Lett.* (1842) III. 412 To..be accounted poor feckless snifties, who has no witt nor action to end what he has so magnificentlie begun.

**snifty** ('snɪftɪ), *a. U.S. slang.* [f. SNIFT *v.*]

**1.** Having a pleasant or agreeable smell.

**1891** in *Cent. Dict.*

**2.** *slang* (orig. and chiefly *U.S.*). Haughty, disdainful.

**1889** K. MUNROE *Golden Days* xvii. 188 If you notice me getting anyways snifty..you just bump me down hard. **1902** G. H. LORIMER *Lett. Self-made Merchant* xviii. 268 Clytie said..that spirits were mighty snifty and high-toned. **1909** H. G. WELLS *Tono-Bungay* I. i. 40 'Snifty beast!'..That governess made things impossible. **1942** BERREY & VAN DEN BARK *Amer. Thes. Slang* §301/6 *Arrogant*,..snifty.

**snig** (snɪg), *sb.*[1] Also 5-6 snygge, 6, 8-9 snigg. [Of obscure origin.]

**1.** A young or small eel; a grig. In later use a distinct species of eel (see quots.).

**1483** *Cath. Angl.* 347/1 A Snygge, *vbi a ele.* **1570** LEVINS *Manip.* 118/44 A Snig, *anguillæ genus.* **1586-7** *Shuttleworths' Acc.* (Chetham Soc.) 35 Syxtene snygges, ij$^{s}$ ij$^{d}$. **1601** HOLLAND *Pliny* IX. li, Those scrapings (as it were) which are fretted from them [*sc.* eels], in time come to take life, and prove snigs. **1664** H. POWER *Exp. Philos.* I. 32 Eels in Vinegar..appear like small Silver-Eells, or little Snigs. **1688** HOLME *Armoury* II. 325/1 An Eel, first a Fausen, then a Grigg, or Snigg, then a Scaffling, then a little Eel [etc.]. *c* **1746** COLLIER (Tim Bobbin) *View Lanc. Dial.* (1775) 43, I feel hoose os fat os o Snig. **1781-** in dial. glossaries (N. Cy., Lanc., Chesh., Warw., Wilts., Hants., etc.). **1836** YARRELL *Brit. Fishes* II. 302 The Hampshire Snig differs from our other Eels in its habit of roving and feeding during the day. **1863** H. C. PENNELL *Angler-Naturalist* 400 The Snig, or Medium-nosed Eel (*Anguilla mediorostris*). **1883** G. C. DAVIES *Norfolk Broads* xxxi. (1884) 242 The grig or snig, a yellowish eel with a projecting under-lip.

*fig.* **1581** J. BELL *Haddon's Answ. Osorius* 384 b, This heroycall Gyant..despising and loathing these small snigges of Babish Haddon.

**2.** *attrib.* and *Comb.*, as ***snig-eel, -pie, -pot***, etc.

Other examples are given in the *Eng. Dial. Dict.*

**1836** YARRELL *Brit. Fishes* II. 301 *Anguilla mediorostris*, Snig Eel. **1861** WAUGH *Rambles Lake Cy.* 24 They'd etten so mich snig-pie..that [etc.]. **1865** G. F. BERKELEY *Life & Recoll.* II. 316, I was looking at some snig-pots..in my fishery. **1883** DAY *Fishes Gt. Brit.* II. 242 Sharp-nosed-eel, Dublin-eel, Broad-nosed-eel, Snig-eel.

†**snig,** *sb.*[2] *Obs.*$^{-1}$ [Cf. SNIG *v.*[1], and NIG *sb.*[1]] A covetous or avaricious person.

**1629** GAULE *Holy Madnesse* 322 A Couetous Man..hath more Names, than euer he was christend with. The Best call him no better, than you would call a Wretch;..Cark, Snig, Gripe, Sharke [etc.].

†**snig,** *sb.*[3] *Obs. rare.* [? Dim. of SNAG *sb.*[1]] A slight projection or process.

**1649** J. BULWER *Pathomyot.* II. i. 59 The other [muscle] ariseth from the Snig of the seventh Vertebre of the Neck. *Ibid.*, The knob of the first vertebre of the Neck, which holds Analogy with the Snigs of the other vertebres of the Back.

†**snig,** *v.*[1] *Obs.*$^{-1}$ (Sense not quite clear: cf. SNIG *sb.*[2])

**1642** D. ROGERS *Naaman* 211 Others are so dangerously worldly, snigging and biting, usurers, hard and oppressing.

**snig** (snɪg), *v.*[2] *north. dial., Austral., N.Z.,* and *Canad. local.* [Origin obscure.] *trans.* To drag (a heavy load, esp. timber) by means of ropes and chains. Hence **'snigging** *vbl. sb.*[1] (also *attrib.*).

For further material see *Eng. Dial. Dict.*

**1790** F. GROSE *Provinc. Gloss.* (ed. 2), *Snig*, to drag wood without a cart. **1866** J. T. STATON *Rays fro' th' Loominary* 127 He wur one ut wur brought up to sniggin timber. **1933** L. ACLAND in *Press* (Christchurch, N.Z.) 2 Dec. 15/7 *Snig*, to drag along the ground by horse or bullocks, especially to drag logs or other timber. The stout chain which goes round the log has a ring at one end, and a hook to which the horses' chains are attached. It is called a *snigging chain.* **1946** B. JAMES in Murdoch & Drake-Brockman *Austral. Short Stories* (1951) 251 Peter cut timber on the hills, and snigged it down with the plough horses. **1961** B. CRUMP *Hang on a Minute Mate* 44 They dug their axes into a handy stump and trudged off down the snigging-track. **1968** E. R. BUCKLER *Ox Bells & Fireflies* xv. 221 A group of men have gathered to help another lay a new sill under his barn. 'Hadn't I better hitch up the team and snig her closer the foundation there?' **1969** *Parade* (Austral.) Dec. 17/2 He would get his horse and snig Trompson's body off the claim. **1975** *Sunday Mail* (Brisbane) 1 June 6/2 Bullock teams would snig the logs to the winder.

**snig** (snɪg), *v.*[3] *dial.* and *slang.* [Origin obscure.] intr. and *trans.* To steal.

**1862** C. C. ROBINSON *Dial. Leeds* 415 *Snig*, to steal after a mean fashion, as a man who undertakes any business, or interests himself any way in the property of a person, and is 'snigging' away at it all the time. **1864** J. RAMSBOTTAM *Phases of Distress* 37 They'll pitch an' toss an' swear, An' snig an' snatch owt wheer they con. **1892** KIPLING *Barrack-Room Ballads* 31 If you've ever snigged the washin' from the line.

**snigger** ('snɪgə(r)), *sb.*[1] [f. SNIGGER *v.*[1] Cf. SNICKER *sb.*[1]] An act of sniggering; a slight or half-suppressed laugh; a snicker.

**1823** BEE *Dict. Turf* 162 *Snigger*, ill-suppressed laughter. **1830** *Examiner* 677/2 He appeared to have a constant snigger lurking under his frown. **1855** J. H. NEWMAN *Callista* (1890) 64 Juba..indulged himself from time to time in an inward laugh or snigger. **1882** 'F. ANSTEY' *Vice Versa* vi. 127 Suspecting that the faint sniggers he heard were indulged in at his own expense.

*fig.* **1865** CARLYLE *Fredk. Gt.* xx. v. (1872) IX. 77 Ages.. which have lost their mirth, and become all one snigger of mock-mirth.

**'snigger,** *sb.*[2] *local.* [f. SNIGGER *v.*[2]] A kind of grapple used by salmon poachers.

**1901** *Scotsman* 29 March 7/1 Labourers..poached for salmon on the Don..by means of sniggers.

**snigger** ('snɪgə(r)), *v.*[1] [Imitative: cf. SNICKER *v.*]

**1.** *intr.* To laugh in a half-suppressed, light or covert manner; to snicker.

**1706** PHILLIPS (ed. Kersey), To *Snicker* or *Snigger.* **1728** MORGAN *Hist. Algiers* I. 188 This, and other such Jokes, set most of the Assembly a sniggering. **1771** MME. D'ARBLAY *Early Diary* July, Mr. Featherstone enjoyed it prodigiously, sniggering and joking. **1822** SCOTT *Nigel* iii, So they let me go, and rode a' sniggering, laughing, and rounding in ilk ither's lugs. **1867** CARLYLE *Reminis.* (1881) II. 15 He never laughed loud, and indeed oftener sniggered slightly than laughed in any way. **1887** JESSOPP *Arcady* iv. 112 They snigger and grin sometimes, and then turn away as if ashamed of themselves.

*fig.* **1894** MRS. OLIPHANT *Hist. Sk. Q. Anne* vii. 364 The younger world..still sniggers in its sleeve [etc.].

**b.** Const. *at* or *over.*

**1847** ALB. SMITH *Chr. Tadpole* xxxiii, Fools, sniggering at you because they won't understand what you mean. **1859** THACKERAY *Virginians* lxxviii, She..sniggered over the faults of the self-styled righteous with uncommon satisfaction. **1887** JEFFERIES *Amaryllis* xiv, He kind of sniggered in a foolish way at Amaryllis. **1899** *Q. Rev.* Apr. 487 Norwich has ceased to snigger over the youthful indiscretions of George Borrow.

**c.** *dial.* (See quots.)

**1823** E. MOOR *Suffolk Words, Snigger, Sniggeren*, exulting, boasting, jeering. *a* **1825** FORBY *Voc. E. Anglia, Snigger*, to sneer ill-naturedly.

**2.** *trans.* To utter with a snigger.

**1857** KINGSLEY *Two Y. Ago* I. 96 'Don't you wish yours was, Doctor?' 'Eh, eh, eh,' sniggered Heale. **1905** P. WHITE *Patient Man* xiv, 'Then he has the oddest way of keeping it,' sniggered Mrs. Archie.

**'snigger,** *v.*$^{2}$ *local.* [Of obscure origin: cf. SNIGGLE *v.*$^{1}$] *trans.* To catch (salmon) by means of weighted hooks.

**1886** *Fishing Gaz.* 30 Jan. 58/1 In the way of grappling—or sniggering, as it is more politely termed—i.e., dragging the river with huge grapples and lead attached for the purpose of keeping them to the bottom of the pool. **1898** *Scotsman* 19 Nov. 6 The bailiffs..said they had no doubt, from the position and movements of the accused and his companions.., that they were 'sniggering' salmon.

**sniggerer** ('snɪgərə(r)). [f. SNIGGER *v.*$^{1}$] One who sniggers or laughs covertly.

**1860** DICKENS in *All Year Round* 5 May 87 The sniggerers tempt him to secular thoughts of marbles. **1901** G. DOUGLAS *Ho. w. Green Shutters* 182 Gourlay ceased to care a rap for the sniggerers.

**sniggering** ('snɪgərɪŋ), *vbl. sb.* [f. SNIGGER *v.*$^{1}$] The action of the vb.; half-suppressed laughter.

**1775** ASH *Dict., Sniggering*,..a silly kind of laugh. **1779** MME. D'ARBLAY *Diary* Oct., I..had been obliged to turn my head another way, that my sniggering might not sooner make him see his mistake. **1823** [see SNIGGER *v.*$^{1}$ 1 c]. **1865** *Sat. Rev.* 4 Mar. 245 The sniggering of everybody around one over indecorous inuendos. **1876** FREEMAN in Stephens *Life* (1895) II. viii. 144 The sniggering only shows what a move it was.

**'sniggering,** *ppl. a.* [f. as prec.]

**1.** Of the nature of, accompanied or characterized by, a snigger or sniggers.

**1793** in W. Roberts *Looker-on* No. 54 (1794) II. 312 Hip here, jade, and bring with thee Jokes and sniggering jollity. **1876** *World* V. 21 The writer's innuendoes and sniggering asides..are coarse and disgusting. **1882** BESANT *All Sorts* 44 You saw his sniggerin', sneerin' way with me.

**2.** That sniggers; snickering.

**1815** *Sporting Mag.* XLVI. 68 No doubt there is plenty of gaping and sniggering fools who will say [etc.]. **1860** DICKENS in *All Year Round* 5 May 87/1 The aunt and nephew in this City church are much disturbed by the sniggering boys. **1887** HALL CAINE *Deemster* x, He had almost lifted his hand to fell the sniggering waistrel.

Hence **'sniggeringly** *adv.*

**1886** JEROME *Idle Th.* 111 Glancing round with an imbecile smile, you sniggeringly observe that [etc.].

**'Sniggers,** *int.* ? *Obs.* [Cf. 'SNIGS and NIGS.] A form of minced oath.

**1633** ROWLEY *Match at Midn.* I. i, Sniggers! what does the devil and a saint both in a sign? **1749** SMOLLETT *Gil Blas* I. xvii. ¶3 Odd 'sniggers! this smells strong of intrigues! **1836** HALIBURTON *Clockm.* Ser. I. xxi, I sniggers if you didn't frighten us properly.

**snigger snee,** variant of SNICKERSNEE *v.*

**snigging,** *vbl. sb.*$^{1}$: see SNIG *v.*$^{2}$

**'snigging,** *vbl. sb.*$^{2}$ *techn.* (See quot.)

**1892** *Labour Commission Gloss., Snigging*, term used in the hosiery industry to describe cases in which the thread is partly cut and escapes the notice of the menders.

**sniggle** ('snɪg(ə)l), *sb.*$^{1}$ [f. SNIGGLE *v.*$^{1}$] A baited hook or other device used in sniggling for eels, etc.

**1837** HOOD *Ode to Dr. Hahnemann* iii, When Anhalt-Coethen babies wriggle, Like eels just caught by sniggle. **1848** [W. F. CAMPBELL] *Life in Normandy* (1863) I. 183 There may be one [lobster there] now. I will make the girl try, if she has brought her sniggle with her. *Ibid.* 184 He saw that she had a sniggle stick stuck into the string of her petticoat.

**sniggle** ('snɪg(ə)l), *sb.*$^{2}$ [f. SNIGGLE *v.*$^{2}$] A snigger or snicker.

**1852** MRS. STOWE *Uncle Tom's C.* viii. 54 Marks patronised his joke by a quiet introductory sniggle. **1887** RIDER HAGGARD *Jess* xxxii, A fierce sound—half sniggle, half laugh.

**'sniggle,** *sb.*$^{3}$ *dial.* [Dim. of SNIG *sb.*$^{1}$] A snig or small eel.

**1863** WISE *New Forest* xii. 125 The Avon flows close by, famous for a peculiar eel, locally called the 'sniggle' (*anguilla mediorostris*). **1879–83** in dial. glossaries (Hants., Shrops.).

**sniggle** ('snɪg(ə)l), *v.*$^{1}$ [See SNIGGLING *vbl. sb.*]

Fletcher's *Thierry & Theod.* II. ii. 'I haue snigled him' is cited by Todd and later Dicts. as an early example of this verb; but the correct reading is doubtless 'singled' (cf. SINGLE *v.* 2 and 3).

**1. a.** *intr.* To fish *for* eels by the method known as sniggling.

**1671** SKINNER *Etymol. Ling. Angl.*, To Sniggle, *vox Piscatoribus satis nota.* **1775** ASH, *Sniggle*, to fish for eels by putting a bait to the holes in which they conceal themselves. **1799** G. SMITH *Laboratory* II. 275 How to sniggle for Eels. **1833** *Bowlker's Art of Angling* 96 To sniggle for Eels procure a strong top rod, or a long hazel stick [etc.]. **1867** BURNARD *Happy Thoughts* iii. 17, I ask 'Sniggle for chub?' He..answers, 'No, sniggle for eels'.

**b.** *trans.* To fish for, catch, pull out (an eel or eels) in this way.

**1844** BADHAM *Prose Halieutics* 390 As wily anglers sniggling eels The approved device employ. **1867** F. FRANCIS *Angling* iii. (1880) 89 Sniggling an old eel out of his hole..is not altogether unamusing.

**2.** *trans.* To catch (fish) by means of striking a hook into them.

**1834** MEDWIN *Angler in Wales* II. 197 Charters has since sniggled abundance of trout. **1894** *Sat. Rev.* 6 Jan. 15/1 These noble salmon, netted, speared, sniggled, very likely.

Hence **'sniggled** *ppl. a.*

**1844** TUPPER *Crock of G.* xlvi. 294 He wriggled like a sniggled eel.

**sniggle** ('snɪg(ə)l), *v.*$^{2}$ [Imitative.] *intr.* To snigger or snicker.

**1815** SCOTT *Guy M.* lii, As for the Dominie,..he looked at Lucy—he whimpered—he sniggled—he grinned. **1840** C. BRONTE in Mrs. Gaskell *Life* (1857) I. 215 [The preacher] did not whine; he did not sniggle. **1889** GUNTER *That Frenchman* vi, At which flattery the other sniggles and calls him a wit.

Hence **'sniggling** *ppl. a.*

**1826** SCOTT *Woodst.* xii, Wildrake laughed without ceremony,..and was joined by a sniggling response from behind the cupboard.

**'sniggle,** *v.*$^{3}$ *dial.* or *colloq.* [Of doubtful origin. Cf. Norw. *snygla* to sponge, beg.]

**1.** *intr.* **a.** (See quot. 1837). **b.** To wriggle, crawl, creep stealthily.

**1837** J. F. PALMER *Gloss. Devon Dialogue, To Sniggle*, (at taw) to shuffle the hand forwards in an unfair manner; *Unde* Sniggler. **1881** *Leicestersh. Gloss.* 247 *Sniggle*,..to wriggle away. **1900** FLORA A. STEEL *Hosts of the Lord* xxiii, There's a brute trying to sniggle along the wall.

**2.** *trans.* To get (a thing) *in* surreptitiously.

**1881** *Oxfordsh. Gloss.* 98 *Sniggle in*, to get anything in an underhand manner. **1900** POLLOK & THOM *Sports Burma* vi. 190, I calculated that if I were successful in my application I could sniggle in those two days as well.

**sniggler**$^{1}$ ('snɪglə(r)). [f. SNIGGLE *v.*$^{1}$] One who fishes for or catches eels or salmon by sniggling.

**1840** J. T. HEWLETT *P. Priggins* i, Like an eel in a wall, politely declining a sniggler's offer of a lobworm. **1864** *Q. Rev.* CXV. 186 Towards evening the juvenile sniggler knows that he has the best chance of success. **1890** *Daily News* 6 Nov. 5/1 The truth is that the apparent sportsmen are snigglers, not anglers.

**'sniggler**$^{2}$. [f. SNIGGLE *v.*$^{2}$] A sniggerer.

**1876** ROBINSON *Whitby Gloss., Sniggler*, a derider. **1886** in ELWORTHY *W. Somerset Wordbk.*

**'sniggler**$^{3}$. [f. SNIGGLE *v.*$^{3}$] One who plays in a manner not quite fair or correct.

**1837** [see SNIGGLE *v.*$^{3}$ 1]. **1887** BLACK *Sabina Zembra* i, It has been affirmed..that the pool-players..break out into mild revelry; that derisive cheers overwhelm the 'sniggler'.

**sniggling** ('snɪglɪŋ), *vbl. sb.* [? Related to SNIG *sb.*$^{1}$]

**1.** The action or practice of fishing for eels by means of a baited hook or needle thrust into their holes or haunts.

**1661** WALTON *Angler* xiii. (ed. 3) 193 Because you..know not what *snigling* is, I will now teach it to you..: take a strong small hook tied to a strong line.., and then into one of these holes,..or any place where you think an Eele may hide or shelter her self, there with the help of a short stick put in your Bait. **1669** WORLIDGE *Syst. Agric.* (1681) 260 Eels commonly abscond themselves under stones.., and under Timber, Planks, or such-like.., where you may take them by this way of Snigling. **1740** R. BROOKES *Art of Angling* I. xl. 85 Snigling or Brogling for Eels is another remarkable Method of taking them. **1787** BEST *Angling* (ed. 2) 55 There are two ways to take them in the day time called sniggling and bobbing. **1856** 'STONEHENGE' *Brit. Rural Sports* 258 Sniggling is another mode of taking eels,..and the apparatus consists in a strong needle [etc.]. **1885** *Sat. Rev.* 21 Nov. 673/1 'Sniggling'..is one of the most favourite ways of catching eels.

*attrib.* **1688** HOLME *Armoury* III. 103/1 A Snigleing, or Prokeing Stick, is a forked stick, and a short long Line with a Needle Bated with a Lob Worm. It is only for Eels in their holes. **1867** F. FRANCIS *Angling* iii. (1880) 91 A sniggling stick or rod.

**2.** In salmon-fishing (see quots.).

**1890** *Scottish Leader* 20 Nov. 5 'Sniggling,' means fishing with rod and line and artificial fly, but the hook is made to sink in the water where fish are supposed to be, and the rod so jerked that they are hooked and quickly landed. **1891** *Ibid.* 13 Nov. 4 'Sniggling'..is a mode of fishing by which the hook takes the fish, and not the fish the hook.

**snight,** obs. f. SNITE (the snipe).

**†'Snigs,** *int. Obs.* An abbrev. of *God's nigs* (see GOD *sb.* 14 b and cf. NIGS), used as a minced oath. Cf. 'SNIGGERS.

*a* **1643** CARTWRIGHT *Ordinary* III. ii, 'Snigs, another! *Ibid.* IV. i, 'Snigs, I would fain now hear some fighting news. **1675** COTTON *Burlesque upon B.* 72 S'nigs, well remembred! I'le be gone.

**†snigsnarl,** obs. var. SNICK-SNARL.

**1688** HOLME *Armoury* III. 288/2 The Yarn..is..tied up with a Lay Band, to keep it from ravalling or running into Snigsnarles or Knotted up.

**snik-a-snee,** variant of SNICK-A-SNEE.

**†snike,** *v. Obs.* [OE. *snícan*, prob. related to ON. *sníkja* (Da. *snige*) to sneak.] *intr.* Of reptiles: To creep, crawl.

*c* **897** K. ÆLFRED tr. *Gregory's Past.* 311 On ðinre wambe & on ðinum breostum ðu scealt snican. *c* **1000** *Sax. Leechd.* III. 34 Wyrm com snican. *a* **1240** *Sawles Warde* in *O.E. Hom.* I. 251 þe laðe helle wurmes, tadden ant froggen, þe..snikeð in ant ut.

**snikker-snee,** obs. form of SNICKERSNEE.

**†snilch,** *v. Cant. Obs.* (See quots.)

**1676** COLES, *Snilches*, sees or eyes you. *a* **1700** B. E. *Dict. Cant. Crew, Snilch*, to Eye or See any Body.

**snip** (snɪp), *sb.* Also 6–8 snippe, 6 snypp, 7 snipp. [Related to SNIP *v.*, and in some senses perh. directly of LG. origin: cf. LG. *snip* (G. dial. *schnipf, schnipp*) and *snippe* a small piece, etc., Du. and Fris. *snip* a snappish girl or woman.]

**I. 1. a.** A small piece or slip, esp. of cloth, cut off or out; a shred.

**1558** in Feuillerat *Revels Q. Eliz.* (1908) 27 In to Iagges and Snippes for defacinge of torche bearers. **1606** SYLVESTER *Du Bartas* II. iv. I. *Tropheis* 1103 Her lips two snips of crimsin Sattin are. *c* **1620** MORYSON *Itin.* IV. 489 To weare a litle snipp of yellowe lace vpon the left syde of their Clokes. **1691** T. H[ALE] *Acc. New Invent.* 95 Cut a snip from the thickest and thinnest part. **1756** *Connoisseur* No. 115 ¶7 A snip of hair, or the portrait of a cherry-cheeked gentleman,..are the only remaining proofs of those beauties. **1787** COWPER *Let.* 10 Dec., I thank you for your snip of cloth commonly called a pattern. **1837** CARLYLE *Fr. Rev.* II. VI. viii, Patriotism has torn their red coats into snips. **1849** ALB. SMITH *Pottleton Legacy* (1854) 24 Snips of the metal used in packing tea. **1864** CARLYLE *Fredk. Gt.* IV. 542 A snip of paper.

**b.** *transf.* or *fig.* (Freq. in Fuller.)

**1650** FULLER *Pisgah* 370 No snip, or shred of empty space cut off from the squareness of the Oracle. *a* **1661** —— *Worthies* (1840) III. 391 Yorkshire hath..Lancashire and a snip of Cheshire on the west. **1682** WHELER *Journ. Greece* III. 280 There might be some Mediterranean Snip of Land, running down between Ionia and Lydia.

**†c.** *spec.* Of glass: (see quot.). *Obs.*

**1688** HOLME *Armoury* III. 385/2 A Snip, is the upper halfe, and sometymes a quarter or lesse of a Quarry, Three Snips goes for a quarry.

**2.** A white or light mark, patch, or spot on a horse, esp. on the nose or lip.

Cf. G. dial. *schnippe* a horse with a mark on the nose, *schnipp* a horse or cow with a narrow blaze.

**1562** *Wills & Inv. N.C.* (Surtees, 1835) 202 A younge baye geldinge with a whyte snypp off [= on] ye nose. **1607** MARKHAM *Cavel.* II. (1617) 3 Your redde Sorrell, and your darke Chesnutte, are much graced, if..they be accompanied with any white markes, as..white snippes on the nose. **1679** *Poor Robin's Intelligence* in *Sporting Mag.* XXXIX. 61 Her colour was now coal black, with a star, snip, and one white foot. **1726** *Brice's Weekly Jrnl.* 25 Mar. 3 A Brown Bay Nag, with..a white Snip in one of the hinder Feet. **1799** *Hull Advertiser* 10 Aug. 2/2 A stout handsome chesnut gelding,..a white snip on his nose. **1820–** in Sc. and north. dial. use (Jam. and *Eng. Dial. Dict.*). **1891** E. KINGLAKE *Australian* 118 That brown horse over there with a snip. **1893** M. H. HAYES *Points of Horse* xx. (1897) 222 A white or pink patch on either lip is called a 'snip'.

**3. a.** A small amount, piece, or portion, a little bit (*of* something). ***every snip***, every bit.

(*a*) **1588** SHAKS. *L.L.L.* III. i. 22 Keepe not too long in one tune, but a snip and away. *a* **1641** BP. MOUNTAGU *New Gagg* iii. 42, I like not that the ancient Fathers should be..sent away like school boys with snips. **1749** SMOLLETT *Gil Blas* VII. xii. (1782) III. 89 Let me know what is the business, and I promise you shall get some snips out of the minister. **1833** CARLYLE *Misc.* (1857) III. 185 Picking up a few residuary snips.

(*b*) **1624** J. GEE *New Shreds* Pref. p. ii, Some snips of..their legerdemaine trickes .. here I display. *a* **1668** DAVENANT *Man's the Master* II. i, May not a man see a snip of her face? **1700** DRYDEN *Epilogue Dryden's Benefit* 14 The Poets..Tainted the Stage for some small Snip of Gain. **1831** CARLYLE in *Froude* (1882) II. 179 Sunday morning had a snip of a note from Empson. **1894** BLACKMORE *Perlycross* 50 My hair is such a trouble, I have half a mind sometimes to cut off every snip of it.

**b.** Applied to persons in depreciation or contempt. In later use: A young, slight, or diminutive person.

**1625** MASSINGER *New Way* II. ii, This term-driver, Marrall, This snip of an attorney. **1838** [MISS MAITLAND] *Lett. fr. Madras* (1843) 221 Half the experienced men are kept in subordinate situations, and young raw snips placed over their heads. **1902** *Daily Chron.* 11 Feb. 5/1 Why, this snip is no better than anybody else when he lands here.

**†4. a.** A share or portion; a snack. *Obs.*

**1655** tr. *Sorel's Com. Hist. Francion* I. 13 The Justice of the place..not willing to lose his Snip [etc.]. **1672** WYCHERLEY *Love in a Wood* I. ii, He watches them like a younger brother that is afraid to be mumped of his snip. **1698** FRYER *Acc. E. India & P.* 140 The Governor distributing to the Officers, and they to the Soldiers, every one having their Snips. **1702** STEELE *Funeral* III. ii, Take care of their Young Ladyships; you shall..have a Snip in the Sale of 'em.

**b.** *to go snips* (†or *snip*), to go shares (*with* some one, or *in* something), to share or participate in the profits. Now *dial.*

In very common use *c* 1680–1690, esp. by Hickeringill.

(*a*) **1668** DRYDEN *Even. Love* V. i, Pray, Sir, let me go snip with you in this Lie. **1687** R. L'ESTRANGE *Fairfax' Tasso* Pref. A 2, I recommend it to the Bookseller, for the common benefit, and..I go no snip with the Stationer.

(*b*) **1677** THORESBY *Corr.*, etc. (1830) II. 408 Some of our company went snips with them. **1682** TOPHAM *Rome's Tradit.* 209 The Subtil Old Gentleman..offered him (if he would promote the Trade) to go Snips. **1706** BAYNARD *Cold Baths* II. 202 Those that go Snips with their Apothecaries, are Villains of the first Magnitude. **1725** BAILEY *Erasm. Colloq.* (1733) 322 The Gamester..promises I shall go Snips with him in what he shall win. *a* **1800** PEGGE *Suppl. Grose* s.v. *Snaps.* **1861–** in Sc. and north. dial. use (*Eng. Dial. Dict.*).

**II. 5. a.** A small cut or incision made by, or such as that made by, a pair of scissors; a wound of this nature. Also *dial.*, a small hole or crack.

**1596** SHAKS. *Tam. Shr.* IV. iii. 89 What's this? a sleeue?.. Heers snip, and nip, and cut, and slish and slash. **1600** SURFLET *Countrie Farme* I. xxv. 159 If there by any snips in their skins, you shall apply vnto them melted waxe. **1682** WHELER *Journ. Greece* III. 219 Long sharp leaves.. without snips at the Edges. **1698** J. CRULL *Muscovy* 136 Bonnets, with a little snip open before and behind. **1775** ASH, *Snick*, a small snip or cut as in the hair of a beast. **1867** WAUGH *Tattlin' Matty* ii. 24 Squirtin' wayter into my ear through a snip i' th corner o' th window. **1886** C. SCOTT *Sheep Farm.* 149 The snip and hole are used alternately, to designate.. the exact part of the ear intended to be marked.

**b.** *Pottery.* A small projection on the lip of a vessel, the place for which is prepared by cutting a notch.

**1834-6** BARLOW in *Encycl. Metrop.* (1845) VIII. 455 These manipulations fix on the clay vessels their handles, snips, spouts [etc.]. *Ibid.*, For snips of jugs, &c., a piece is cut out of the upper edge of proper size and shape.

**6. a.** An act of snipping; a single cut or clip *of* scissors, etc.

**1676** WISEMAN *Surg. Treat.* 256, I laid it open by a snip of a pair of Scissors. *c* **1765** FLLOYD *Tartarian T.* (1785) 103/2 Four snips of a pair of scissars will initiate you. **1831** CARLYLE *Sartor Res.* I. v, Every snip of the Scissors has been regulated.. by ever-active Influences. **1886** *Daily Telegr.* 14 Jan. (Cassell), A few snips of the scissors.. and last year's robe will do duty for this.

**b.** A nip, pinch, bite, etc.

**1767** S. PATERSON *Another Trav.* II. 41 He has a snip, or a flip, or a sting, or a fling, at almost every body! **1840** HOOD *Miss Kilmansegg, Education* 509 He got.. Scratches, and pinches, snips, and snaps, As if from a Tigress or Bearess. **1880** BLACKMORE *Mary Anerley* xxxix, The bruising snip a hungry cow makes.

**7.** *slang* or *colloq.* A tailor. Also employed as an allusive personal name for a tailor.

(*a*) **1599** B. JONSON *Ev. Man out of Hum.* IV. v [iv], Well, now, master Snip, let mee see your bill. *a* **1634** RANDOLPH *Muses' Looking Gl.* IV. iii, Sir, here's Snip the Taylor Charg'd with a riot. **1694** MOTTEUX *Rabelais* IV. lii, At Paris.. Snip Groignet the Taylor had turn'd an old Clementinæ into Patterns and Measures. **1824** W. E. ANDREWS *Rev. Fox's Bk. Martyrs* I. 252 Both Snip and Snob were burned for their pains. *a* **1849** H. COLERIDGE *Ess.* (1851) I. 206 Snip can do more—he can make you an impeccable pair of inexpressibles by simply taking the girth of your thumb. **1858** TROLLOPE *Dr. Thorne* II. iii. 56 Well done, Snip; go it again with the wax and thread.

(*b*) **1630** B. JONSON *New Inn* v. i, Hang him, poor snip, a secular shop-wit! He hath nought but his sheers to claim by, and his measures. *a* **1634** RANDOLPH *Muses' Looking Gl.* IV. ii, *Lup.* Where's my wife? *Colax.* Shee's gone with a young Snip, and an old baud. **1785** GROSE *Dict. Vulgar T.*, *Snip*, a taylor. **1808** J. MAYNE *Siller Gun* III. xxi, 'A ring, a ring!' the sutors cried; 'A ring, a ring!' the snips replied. **1853** R. S. SURTEES *Sponge's Sp. Tour* (1893) 26 'Very neat, sir; would look remarkably well on you, sir,' replies the obsequious snip. **1871** MISS BRADDON *R. Godwin* II. i. 6 Shall I give you a line to my snip?

**8.** *pl.* (See quot.) Cf. TINSNIPS.

**1846** HOLTZAPFFEL *Turning* II. 915 Hand shears.. are often called snips, to distinguish them from bench shears. **1940** I. L. IDRIESS *Lightning Ridge* xiii. 88 As the miner's hand gently closed on the snips the jaws came together and bit a chip from the edge of the nobby. **1966** D. F. GALOUYE *Lost Perception* xviii. 188 He fished his snips out of the kit. 'Now we have only to cut the cables.' **1979** *Sunset* Apr. 170/2 The home owner made a pattern first, then used tin snips to cut long pieces of copper trimmings into strips.

**9.** *pl.* Handcuffs. *slang.*

**1891** *Newcastle Even. Chron.* 21 Feb. 3/2 Accused did not offer to go quietly till the police had the 'snips' on him. **1895** A. PATTERSON *Man & Nat.* 141 In a moment the slop.. had the snips (handcuffs) on me.

**10. a.** *slang.* Something easily obtained or won; a sure thing, a certainty.

*a* **1890** *Sporting Life* in Barrère & Leland *Dict. Slang* (1890) II. 268 D. is in glorious form with his wires, and is certain to keep it up next week at the above meetings, for which he knows of several snips. **1894** ASTLEY 50 *Yrs. Life* II. 181 The event looked a dead snip. **1899** *Westm. Gaz.* 24 July 5/3 The half-mile was described by the supporters of the Americans as a 'snip' for their men. **1913** C. MACKENZIE *Sinister St.* I. II. xi. 323 You'll get your Third Fifteen cap for a snip. **1923** E. P. OPPENHEIM *Inevitable Millionaires* xxviii. 285 'You think it will be a good speculation, then?' Stephen observed, a little sadly. 'A dead snip,' Sir Philip assured them. **1945** 'N. SHUTE' *Most Secret* viii. 187 It is a snip; we will get both of them. **1954** WODEHOUSE *Jeeves & Feudal Spirit* ii. 19 Wooster.. is the deadest of snips. He throws a beautiful dart.

**b.** A bargain, a good buy. *slang.*

**1926** H. V. MORTON *Spell of London* 94 She sees a tea-gown with the authentic plainness.. about it that tells her it began life in higher circles. 'Now, that's a snip, miss. Just your style!' **1933** *Camera* Aug. 7 (Advt.), Exchange your present camera for one of these guaranteed 'snips'. **1935** L. A. G. STRONG *Tuesday Afternoon* 20 The smart man comes along, looks in the window, spots the real snip. **1956** 'N. SHUTE' *Beyond Black Stump* ix. 254 Got them for only a couple of quid each, a snip. **1963** *Punch* 30 Jan. 162/1 A snip at forty bucks. **1977** *Times* 29 Oct. 10/6 At a time when Beaujolais prices are soaring it is a snip at £1·90.

**c.** A piece of good fortune. In phr. ***a snip of a*** (thing) to designate something simpler, more excellent, or more pleasing than one could have expected, a 'gift'.

**1932** W. S. MAUGHAM *For Services Rendered* II. 47 It's been a snip for me having this house to come to. Except for all of you I should have had a pretty thin time. **1952** M. TRIPP *Faith is Windsock* xiv. 210 A snip of an op. Cloud over the target thwarted any searchlights, fog kept the fighters down and there was no flak. **1953** DYLAN THOMAS *Under Milk Wood* (1954) 47 Llaregyb this snip of a morning is wildfruit and warm, the streets, fields, sands and waters springing in the young sun.

**III. 11.** *attrib.* and *Comb.*, as *snip-like*, *snip-nosed* adjs.; **snip-bag**, a bag for holding snips of cloth, etc.; †**snip-cabbage**, a tailor; **snip-faced** *a.* (of a horse), marked with a snip; **snip-jack**, a person of little account or worth (cf. quot.); **snip-nose** (see quot. 1753); †**snip-work**, *Glazing* (cf. 1 c above).

**1703** [R. NEVE] *City & C. Purchaser* 154 Ordinary Houses.. are Glazed with Quarries, which is Bevel Work, so likewise is a great deal of Fret, and all Snip-work. **1708** E. WARD *Terræfil.* v. 35 The Gentleman and yonder Snip-Cabbage, his Taylor, [were] Commended for their Ingenuity. **1753** HANWAY *Trav.* (1762) II. XV. iv. 420 This man was from that time called *binnie buride*, or snip-nose. **1814** MOORE *New Cost. Ministers* v, While Y-rm-th, with snip-like and brisk expedition, Cuts up.. a large Cath'lic Petition. **1846** MARRYAT *Privateer's-man* xiv, 'I can do without such snip-jacks as you are.' 'Snip-jacks!'.. replied I, 'if I must say it, we are better born and better bred than you or any of your connections'. **1878** DICKINSON *Cumbld. Gloss.*, *Snip feasst.* **1880** *Plain Hints Needlewk.* 35 Take one yard of 'cheese cloth'.. out of the snip bag. **1880** DAY *Fishes Gt. Brit.* I. 130 *Trachinotus Cumberlandi*,.. the fisherman's name is Snip-nosed-mullet.

**snip** (snɪp), *v.* Also 6 snyppe. [prob. of Du. or LG. origin: cf. Du., Flem., and LG. *snippen*, G. dial. *schnippen*, *schnipfen*, *schniffen*, to snip, snatch, etc.]

†**1.** *trans.* To take (something) quickly or suddenly; to snap or snatch. *Obs.*

**1586** J. HOOKER *Hist. Irel.* in *Holinshed* II. 83/1 One of your horssemen promised me a choise horsse, if I snip one haire from your beard. Well, quoth the earle,.. if thou plucke anie more than one [etc.]. **1633** ROWLEY *Match at Midnight* II. i, Well, and she be snipped by threescore and ten, may she live six-score and eleven. **1720** DE FOE *Capt. Singleton* i. (1840) 7 The captain seldom ordered anything.. but I snipt some of it for my own share.

*absol.* **1592** GREENE *Def. Conny Catch.* Wks. (Grosart) XI. 96 They wil to snip and snap, that al the reuersion goes into hel. **1674** N. FAIRFAX *Bulk & Selv.* To Rdr., While we.. snip here and snatch there from some of them.

**2.** To cut, to cut up or off, by or as by scissors or some similar cutting instrument.

**1593** NORDEN *Spec. Brit.* (Camden) Pref. p. xiv, They have snippers wherwith they snyppe and pare their plates. **1649** G. DANIEL *Trinarch.*, *Rich. II*, xlii, Hee takes the Measure of his Maister's stuffe, And Snips it to a Size.. Convenient for his Fashion. *a* **1687** H. MORE *Cont. Remark. Stories* 420 They would be snipt and slasht full of holes. **1796** *Phil. Trans.* LXXXVI. 445 It was snipt a good deal, and several holes were worn in the middle. **1848** THACKERAY *Van. Fair* xl, He found Becky and her companion.. busy cutting, ripping, snipping, and tearing all sorts of black stuffs. **1871** T. R. JONES *Anim. Kingd.* (ed. 4) 599 If one of these muscular capsules be snipped by means of a pair of very fine scissors.

*fig.* **1628** JACKSON *Creed* VI. Wks. VI. 83 For snipping this secret hypocrisy.. this exercise of the civil sword hath no force or dint. **1674** J. B[RIAN] *Harvest-Home* ii. 5 Th' impartial Fates.. With keenest Scissars snip lifes thread asunder. **1893** *Advance* (Chicago) 11 May, While the 'Higher Criticism' is laboriously snipping the book of Genesis into 'Elohistic' and 'Jehovistic' fragments.

**b.** *absol.* To make a cut or cuts with or as with scissors, etc. Also, of scissors: To cut.

*a* **1680** BUTLER *Rem.* (1759) II. 138 Like a Barber's Scissars, which are always snipping, as well when they do not cut, as when they do. **1827** SCOTT *Jrnl.* 7 Dec., I wish I have not made that article too long, and Lockhart will not snip away. **1848** DICKENS *Dombey* xxix, Miss Tox,.. arming herself with her scissors, began to snip and clip among the leaves. **1872** PROCTOR *Ess. Astron.* xxiv. 312 One can snip round the borders of a region until its size has been reduced.

**c.** To injure by chipping or taking small pieces out of.

**1822-** in north. dial. use (*Eng. Dial. Dict.*). **1884** *L'pool Mercury* 22 Oct. 5/5 The granite pedestal may be snipped; or a thousand other disasters may occur.

**d.** *Cricket.* To hit (the ball) lightly; to snick.

**1890** *Pall Mall G.* 21 Aug. 6/3 Maclaren soon opens his account.., but gently snipping a ball from Streatfeild he is easily caught by Abel in the slips.

**3.** To cut *off* by means of scissors or other sharp instrument. Also *fig.*

**1611** COTGR., *Mordiller*, to nibble, gnaw, fret, snip off. **1624** GATAKER *Transubst.* 214 Hee should have done well.. to have snipt off or concealed at least, the last clause. *a* **1625** FLETCHER *Fair Maid Inn* IV. i, Because I will not afflict you with any large bill Of circumstances, I'll snip off particulars. **1697** DAMPIER *Voy.* (1699) 339 He takes hold of the fore-skin with two sticks and with a pair of Scissars snips it off. **1742** H. BAKER *Microsc.* II. x. 122 A piece of the.. Membrane.. snipped off with a Pair of Scissars. **1826** S. COOPER *First Lines Surgery* (ed. 5) 349 The new opening.. is then to be enlarged by snipping off the flap of the iris. **1846** LANDOR *Imag. Conv.* I. 79 He has snipt off as much as he could pinch from every author of reputation. **1888** FREEMAN in Stephens *Life* (1895) II. x. 380, I simply had my uvula snipped off.

**b.** With *away*, *from*, *out of*, etc.

**1768-74** TUCKER *Lt. Nat.* (1834) I. 101 By snipping away the superfluities of the paper from her figure. **1858** DICKENS *Lett.* (1880) II. 60 He is perpetually snipping pieces out of newspapers. **1896** *Pall Mall Mag.* May 16 A bullet snipped a corner from my hat.

**c.** To cut *out* by snipping. Also *fig.*

**1800** *Asiatic Ann. Reg.* II. 113/2 He next proceeded very accurately to snip out their suspicions into four and twenty parts. **1855** O. W. HOLMES *Poems* 137 Boys.. Who, for a very trifling sum, Will snip one's picture out.

**4.** To snub, check, repress. Now *dial.*

**1601-14** [see SNIPPING *vbl. sb.* 3]. **1647** FULLER *Good Th. Worse T.* 24 If I were curb'd and Snip't in my younger yeares by feare of my parents, from those vicious excrescencies. **1823-** in dial. use (Suffolk, Somerset, Devon).

**5.** Used adverbially to denote either sound or action.

*a* **1661** HOLYDAY *Juvenal* (1673) 189 How many towns he owns, who went snip, snip; As his quick sizzers my young beard did clip!

**snipe** (snaɪp), *sb.* Forms: 4-6 snype, 4, 6 snyppe (7 snippe), 6 sknipe, 7- snipe. [Of doubtful origin: the ME. type *snīpe* corresponds to a Scand. *snīpa* recorded in Icel. *mýrisnípa*, Norw. *myr-*, *strandsnipa*. It is not clear how this is related to MDu. *snippe* (Du. and WFris. *snip*), MLG. and LG. (also older Da.) *snippe*, G. dial. *schnippe*, and MDu. *sneppe* (Du. *snep*), MLG. and LG. *sneppe* (hence Da. *sneppe*, Sw. *snäppa*), OHG. *snepha* (*snepfa*) and *snepho* (G. *schnepfe*, obs. or dial. *schneppe*).]

**1. a.** One or other of the limicoline birds of the genus *Gallinago* (formerly included in the Linnæan genus *Scolopax*), characterized by having a long straight bill, and by frequenting marshy places; esp. *G. cœlestis* or *media*, the common English species.

*c* **1325** *Gloss. W. de Bibbesw.* in Wright *Voc.* 166 *Un oysel ke est dist becaz*, a snype (snyte). *c* **1350** *Wynnere & Wastoure* 349 Barnakes and buturs and many billed snyppes. *c* **1420** *Liber Cocorum* (1862) 35 To wodcok, snype, curlue also, The betore in fere with hom schalle goo. *c* **1440** *Promp. Parv.* 461/2 Snype, or snyte, byrde, *ibex.* **1530** PALSGR. 272/1 Snyppe, a byrde, *cigoigne.* **1551** *Sc. Acts, Mary* (1814) II. 484/1 Item the snype and qualȝie,.. ij d. **1565** COOPER, *Gallinago*, a wodcocke or a snype. *Ibid.*, *Rusticula minor*, a sknipe. **1611** COTGR., *Beccassine*,.. a Snite, or Snipe. **1655** MOUFET & BENNET *Health's Improv.* (1746) 179 Where they perceive a Worm's Hole, as I have seen Snipes to do, there they thrust in their Bill. **1758** JOHNSON *Idler* No. 33 ¶ 16 Went to the common-room, and supped on the snipes with Dr. Dry. **1794** GISBORNE *Walks in Forest* vi. (1796) 104 The snipe flies screaming from the marshy verge. **1827** D. JOHNSON *Ind. Field Sports* 36 The Calcutta market is well supplied with.. snipes. **1865** TENNYSON *On a Mourner* ii, Nature.. greens The swamp, where humm'd the dropping snipe.

**b.** With adjs., denoting species of this bird.

See also *double snipe*, GUTTER-, HALF-, JACK-, MIRE-, WOOD-SNIPE.

*a* **1705** RAY *Syn.* (1713) 193 *Gallinago Maderspatana*,.. the Partridge-Snipe. **1785** PENNANT *Arct. Zool.* II. 471 Finmark Snipe, *Scolopax Gallinaria.* **1813** BINGLEY *Anim. Biogr.* (ed. 4) II. 302 It is stated, that the Common Snipes never frequent woods. **1839** AUDUBON *Ornith. Biogr.* V. 583 Common American Snipe, *Scolopax Wilsoni.* **1843** YARRELL *Brit. Birds* II. 621 *Scolopax grisea*, Brown Snipe. **1866** *Chambers's Encycl.* VIII. 788/1 The Great Snipe, or Solitary Snipe (*Scolopax* or *Gallinago major*),.. abounds in the extensive marshes of continental Europe.

**c.** Applied to various species of birds resembling the snipe. Chiefly with distinguishing epithets.

See also *duck-snipe*, JACK-SNIPE, *painted*, *red-breasted*, *robin snipe*, SEA-SNIPE, *stone-*, *summer-snipe*.

**1785** LATHAM *Gen. Synop. Birds* III. I. 154 *Brown Snipe... The head, neck, and scapulars, of a fine uniform cinereous brown. **1866** *Chambers's Encycl.* VIII. 788/1 The Red-breasted Snipe, or Brown Snipe (*Macrorhamphus griseus*) of North America has been occasionally seen in Britain. **1785** LATHAM *Gen. Synop. Birds* III. I. 155 *Dusky snipe. **1829** GRIFFITH tr. *Cuvier* VIII. 387 Red-shank, or *Gambet Snipe, *Tringa Gambetta.* **1887** *Encycl. Brit.* XXII. 200 The so-called *Pin-tailed Snipe *Gallinago stenura.* **1785** PENNANT *Arct. Zool.* II. 469 *Semi-palmated snipe, with a bill two inches long. **1839** AUDUBON *Ornith. Biogr.* V. 585 Semipalmated Snipe or Willet, *Totanus semipalmatus.* **1785** LATHAM *Gen. Synop. Birds* III. I. 148 *Spotted Snipe.

**d.** Without article, in collective sense.

**1842** LOVER *Handy Andy* l, The delighted pointer would.. dash forward to the well-known 'bottoms' in eager expectancy of ducks and snipe. **1845** J. COULTER *Adv. in Pacific* iii. 29, I have often seen flocks of snipe crossing the bay. **1872** COUES *N. Amer. Birds* 249 In woodcock and true snipe the ear appears below and not behind the eye.

**2.** †**a.** The Egyptian ibis. *Obs.*

**1432-50** tr. *Higden* (Rolls) II. 323 Bryddes callede snypes, odious to serpentes and amiable to men.

**b.** As a moth-name (see quot.).

**1832** J. RENNIE *Butterfl. & Moths* 66 The Snipe (*Xylophasia scolopacina*, Haworth) appears in June.

**3.** As an opprobrious or abusive term.

**1604** SHAKS. *Oth.* I. iii. 391 For I mine owne gain'd knowledge should prophane, If I would time expend with such [a] Snipe. **1730** SWIFT *Panegyric on the Dean* Misc. 1735 V. 133 Sir A——r, since you set the Pattern, No longer calls me Snipe and Slattern. **1896** CROCKETT *Grey Man* xii. 84 The Earl had set a little snipe of a raggetty loon to stir her up.

**4.** *slang.* **a.** *pl.* A pair of scissors.

**1812** J. H. VAUX *Flash Dict.*, *Snipes*, scissors. **1834** AINSWORTH *Rookwood* III. v. (1878) 200 No slour'd hoxter my snipes could stay.

**b.** (See quot.)

**1864** *Slang Dict.* 238 *Snipe*, a long bill or account; also a term for attorneys—a race remarkable for their propensity to long bills.

**c.** *U.S.* The discarded stub of a cigar or cigarette.

**1891** H. CAMPBELL *Darkness & Daylight* iv. 124 The 'Snipe-Shooter' was guilty of smoking cigar-stubs picked out of the gutter, a habit known among the boys as 'snipe-shooting'. **1899** 'J. FLYNT' *Tramping* II. iv. 274 This 'snipe' chewing and smoking is the most popular use of tobacco in trampdom. **1914** 'HIGH JINKS, JR.' *Choice Slang* 18 *Snipe*, a cigar or a cigarette stub. **1939** J. STEINBECK *Grapes of Wrath* x. 129 Winfield was..an inveterate collector and smoker of snipes.

**d.** One of a group of workers, esp. on board ship (see quots.). *U.S.*

**1918** L. E. RUGGLES *Navy Explained* 139 *Snipe*—Firemen in the 'black gang' always refer to each other as 'snipes'. In a gang of snipes below there is generally one dude who is known as the 'king snipe'. He is considered the leading snipe of the watch. **1932** *Santa Fé Mag.* XXVI. II. 34/1 A foreman of a section gang is a *Jerry* or a *king*; a section laborer is a *snipe*. **1951** H. WOUK *Caine Mutiny* xxvi. 289 A big sloppy chowhound named Wagner, a snipe, had made himself a wax impression of the cook's key. **1953** M. DIBNER *Deep Six* xv. 169 A snipe chief wearing a blue shirt and an oil-soiled khaki cap stood legs apart, drinking coffee.

**e.** *Logging.* A sloping surface or bevel cut on the fore end of a log to facilitate dragging.

**1958** W. F. MCCULLOCH *Woods Words* 172 *Snipe*, a bevel hewed on the ride side of the end of a log, making it easier to pull over the skids. **1975** *Islander* (Victoria, B.C.) 2 Mar. 13/1 He took out the long, beautiful 155-foot timbers, 18 inches at the butt and tapered with a four-foot snipe to a four-inch square point.

**5.** *ellipt.* = SNIPE-BILL I.

**1873** *Iron* 1 Feb. 78/2 Planes... Side snipe, per pair, 7/-.

**6.** Also **Snipe**. A type of sloop-rigged sailing boat approximately 15½ ft. long and used for racing; also, the name of this class of boat.

**1931** *Rudder* (U.S.) July 46 Snipe... Designed especially for the *Rudder* by William F. Crosby. *Ibid.* 47/1 Snipe is a design for a small racing sloop. **1941** *Sun* (Baltimore) 20 Aug. 13/6 For the small-boat sailors races have been arranged in the following classes: Snipe, moth, penguin, winabout, Hampton, 20-foot roundbottom, 20-foot (and under) chine built knockabout. **1942** *E. African Ann.* *1941–2* 57/1 There is always some fine sailing to be had.. some craft beating out into the bay or later in the evening some homeward bound 'Snipe' coming in before the wind. **1969** H. HORWOOD *Newfoundland* xix. 149 Holyrood has a small harbour at the mouth of a brook, and a junior sailing club with instructors and racing snipes.

**7.** A long-range shot or attack from a sharp-shooter; the sound of a sniper's bullet. Also *fig.*

**1969** G. MACBETH *War Quartet* 72 The return snipe struck His mouth below the helmet. **1973** E. BULLINS *Theme is Blackness* 6 For paeans of Blackness were videoed throughout Black America, between the stoccado snipe of the assassin's slug. **1977** *Rolling Stone* 13 Jan. 10/1 Rod Stewart..has transcended two years of snipes for his romance with actress Britt Ekland. **1977** *Sunday Times* 3 July 17/5 The difficulty of organising a 'snipe' (assassination by a single gunman) in the tight security of Belfast.

**8.** *attrib.* and *Comb.* **a.** as ***snipe-bog***, ***-dust***, ***-shooter***, ***-shooting***, ***-shot***, etc.; also **snipe-eel**, (*a*) a species of fish belonging to the deep-sea family *Nemichthyidæ*; (*b*) the sea-pike or garfish, *Belone vulgaris*; **snipe-fly** (see quot.); **snipe's-head** (see quots.); †**snipe-knave**, a half-snipe, jack-snipe; **snipe-shell** (see quot. and cf. SNIPE-BILL 2).

**1844** J. T. HEWLETT *Parsons & W.* xi, The road across the marshes and *snipe-bogs. **1851** KINGSLEY *Yeast* viii, Those five miles of heather and snipe-bog. **1861** *Times* 12 July, A creature who carries a smaller charge of *snipe dust in his head. **1882** JORDAN & GILBERT *Syn. Fishes N. Amer.* 365 *Nemichthyidæ*. (The *Snipe-Eels.) **1887** 'J. BICKERDYKE' *Angling in Salt Water* 99 The Garfish,..Snipe Eel, or Sea Needle, is a long, slender fish [etc.]. **1890** *Science-Gossip* XXVI. 6 One of the larger *snipe-flies, the *Empis tesselata*. Notwithstanding the long snipe-like tongue or proboscis of the highly predatory Empis [etc.]. **1887** W. RYE *Norfolk Broads* 13 The finest *snipe ground in England. **1842** *Penny Cycl.* XXII. 54/2 Species with a very long tube and without spines... Example, *Murex Haustellum* (*Snipe's or Woodcock's head of collectors). [Cf. SNIPE-BILL 2.] **1889** *Cent. Dict.*, *Caput gallinaginis*, the snipe's head; the crista urethræ. **1590** *Shuttleworths' Acc.* (Chetham Soc.) 60 Fourtene snypes and five *snype kneves xj[d]. *Ibid.* 61 Seventene snype kneves and foure snypes ix[d]. **1611** COTGR., *Deux pour vn*, a Snipe-knaue; so called, because two of them are worth but one Snipe. **1889** *Loudon's Nat. Hist.* 532 The *Snipe Shell (*Murex haustellus*, or *cornutus*), so called on account of the length of the prominency coming out of the shell. **1833** W. H. MAXWELL *Field Book* 494/2 When these birds are very plenty, the *snipe-shooters never make use of a dog. **1860** *All Year Round* No. 53. 66 The Analogist had the opportunity of studying the snipe-shooter of Albion. **1829** CARLYLE *Misc.* (1857) II. 7 Are not such lies themselves..equal to *snipe-shooting? **1848** THACKERAY *Van. Fair* iii, A fine, lonely, marshy, jungly district, famous for snipe-shooting. **1822** *Sporting Mag.* IX. 174 The best *snipe-shot complained that he had not killed more than sixty of these birds. **1832** BABBAGE *Econ. Manuf.* ii. (ed. 3) 23 A gun loaded with a quantity of sand, equal in weight to a charge of snipe-shot, kicks still more. **1854** BAKER *Rifle & Hound in Ceylon* vi, I had been firing snipe shot at him. **1805** BINGLEY *Anim. Biogr.* (ed. 3) II. 471 The *Snipe Tribe.

**b.** Forming adjs., as ***snipe-beaked***, ***-faced***, ***-nosed***; ***snipe-like*** (also as adv.).

**1812** *Pennant's Brit. Zool.* III. 190 Trumpet Fish ..[*marg.*] Snipe nosed. **1850** JAMES *Old Oak Chest* III. 45 A little snipe-faced man. **1857** J. MILLER *Alcohol* (1858) 55 He who lives thus snipelike by suction. **1872** COUES *N. Amer. Birds* 252 A very snipe-like bird. **1895** LYDEKKER *Roy. Nat. Hist.* IV. 494 Snipe-beaked sandpipers. **1968** M. WOODHOUSE *Rock Baby* xvi. 157, I took the Allen Keys and a small pair of snipe-nosed pliers. **1969** *Gloss. Terms Dentistry* (*B.S.I.*) 48 *Snipe-nosed pliers*, pliers with square nosed flat beaks... Used for bending wire.

**snipe** (snaɪp), *v.* [f. SNIPE *sb.* I.]

**1.** *trans.* To shoot or fire at (men, etc.), one at a time, usu. from cover and at long range; to pick off (a person) in this manner. Also *fig.*

**1782** G. SELWYN *Let.* in *15th Rep. Hist. MSS. Comm.* VI. 621 Now people have been shot by platoons and in corps, the individual will be popped at or sniped, as they call it, from time to time. **1895** *Edin. Rev.* Jan. 14 The Indian soldier has been called on to be 'sniped' by fugitive dacoits. **1900** *Daily News* 30 Apr. 5/4 The other positions were sniped.

**2. a.** *intr.* To fire as in snipe-shooting; to shoot at an enemy in this manner (cf. prec.). Also with *at* and *away*.

**1832** *Oriental Sporting Mag.* May (1882) II. 291/2 They were all found among high cliffs, and we generally sniped at them from a considerable height. **1844** tr. *Mir Hussain Ali's Life Tipu* xiv. 179 The Kuzzaks..remained all night attacking, or sniping and throwing rockets into the English camp. **1897** *Daily News* 4 Sept. 5/4 The enemy sniped away all day without effect. **1901** *Scotsman* 6 Apr. 9/5 Three hundred Boers hung on the rearguard, sniping but refusing battle.

**b.** *fig.* To assault with harsh sly criticism; to rebuke or censure sharply; to make a carping attack *at* (someone).

**1892** [implied at SNIPING *vbl. sb.* 1 b]. **1959** I. & P. OPIE *Lore & Lang. Schoolch.* xvi. 343 Although adult factions may have made peace with each other, their children on the way to school may continue sniping at each other for generations. **1979** 'A. HAILEY' *Overload* I. xiv. 79 The press representatives had eaten and imbibed with gusto, then in published reports, some had sniped at GSP & L for extravagant entertaining at a time of rising utility bills.

**3.** *trans. Logging.* To cut a snipe or bevel on (a log) to ease dragging.

**1870** *Overland Monthly* 5 July 56/1 The fourth man is the 'hook-tender', whose duties are to wait on the team and 'snipe the logs'. **1902** *N.Z. Illustr. Mag.* V. 375 If the weather is favourable, the log is 'sniped' or rounded at one end, an iron grip driven into it, and to this the team is fastened. **1958** W. F. MCCULLOCH *Woods Words* 173 *Snipe*, ..to hew a snipe on the end of a log. *Snipe for the ride*, to put the snipe on the side of the log which would ride on the bottom, saving the work of sniping a bevel around the entire end of the log.

**4.** *trans.* and *intr.* To pilfer, steal; to pick up or obtain (from the roadside, etc.); *spec.* to prospect for gold, as in old diggings. Cf. SNIPER 3. *slang* (chiefly *N. Amer.*).

**1909** R. SERVICE *Ballads of Cheechako* 122, I panned and I panned in the shiny sand, and I sniped on the river bar; But I know, I know, that it's down below that the golden treasures are. **1923** J. MANCHON *Le Slang* 280 *Snipe*, escamoter [*sc.* to steal, filch]. **1932** J. T. FARRELL *Young Lonigan* iv. 169 He walked down to Fifty-seventh St, furtively looked round to see if anyone saw him, and when the coast was clear, he sniped a butt from the street. **1974** F. W. LUDDITT *Campfire Sketches of Cariboo* vi. 27 They.. made small amounts of money sniping for gold. **1977** *New Yorker* 20 June 81/1 He 'sniped' a lot of his gold—just took it from likely spots without settling down to the formalities of a claim.

**ˈsnipe-bill.** Also snipe's bill. [SNIPE *sb.* I.]

**1.** A kind of narrow moulding-plane with a sharp arris, for forming or cutting quirks. Also *attrib.*

**1678** MOXON *Mech. Exerc.* iv. 70 Plains in use among Joyners, called Molding-plains; as, the Round,..the Snipes-Bill. **1728** CHAMBERS *Cycl.* s.v. *Plane*, Moulding-Planes,..as the Round Plane, the Hollow, the OG, the Snipe's Bill, &c. **1842** GWILT *Archit.* Gloss., *Snipe's Bill Plane*, one with a sharp arris for getting out the quirks of mouldings. **1873** *Iron* 1 Feb. 78/2 Planes... Snipe bills, per pair, 5/.

**2.** *Conch.* The snipe-shell or snipe's head.

**1713** PETIVER *Aquat. Anim. Amboinæ* iv, *Haustellum*,.. Snipes-bill.

†**3.** *Naut.* (See quot.) *Obs.*

**1750** BLANCKLEY *Naval Expos.* 154 Snipe Bills are a Sort of Hooks used for fastening the Axle-trees of the Chain Pumps to the Bitts.

**4.** *U.S.* (See quots. Also written *snibel.*)

**1860** WORCESTER, *Snipe-bill*, the bolt which connects the body of a cart with the axle. (Local, U.S.) **1902** *Webster's Suppl.*, *Snipe-bill*, a hinge beneath the body of a dumping cart, consisting of two interlinked eyebolts.

**5.** *attrib.* Resembling the bill of the snipe.

**1795** J. WOLCOT (P. Pindar) *Pindariana* Wks. 1812 IV. 186 Her nose of snipe-bill race Which took a deal of stuff.

**ˈsnipe-fish.** [SNIPE *sb.*]

**1.** Any fish of the genus *Centriscus*; esp. the trumpet-fish, bellows-fish, or sea-snipe, *C. scolopax*.

**1668** CHARLETON *Onomast.* 123 *Scolopax*,..the Snipe-fish. **1681** GREW *Musæum* I. v. i. 101 The figure of his Bill, which is an entire Pipe, shaped almost like that of the Snipe-Fish. **1836** YARRELL *Brit. Fishes* I. 302 *Centriscus scolopax*, Snipe-fish. **1867** *Chambers's Encycl.* IX. 568/1 Trumpet-fish, or Snipe-fish (*Centriscus*), a genus of fishes.. remarkable for the elongated and tubular snout. **1881** DAY *Fishes Gt. Brit.* I. 250 The trumpet, bellows-fish, woodcock or snipe-fish.

**2.** The snipe-eel (*Cent. Dict.* 1891).

**sniper** (ˈsnaɪpə(r)). [f. SNIPE *v.*]

**1.** One who snipes, or shoots from concealment, etc.; a sharp-shooter.

**1824** *E. India Mil. Cal.* II. 541 Several sepoys were killed and wounded by the enemy's snipers. **1897** *Daily News* 30 July 5/2 It is impossible to see the snipers, who generally stalk the sentries from behind stones. **1900** *Daily Telegr.* 27 Feb. 9/3 The artillery keep the Boer snipers down.

**2.** A snipe-shooter.

**1840** E. NAPIER *Scenes & Sp. Foreign Lands* II. v. 140 With his brandy flask by his side, and his well filled bag, the sniper still wanders through his old haunts.

**3.** *U.S.* A prospector for gold or the like.

**1902** *U.S. Geol. Surv., Prof. Paper 10*, 51 Some unsystematic work [searching for gold] was done during the fall of 1901 by snipers, usually working with rockers.

**4.** *Logging.* One who cuts a snipe on a log.

**1905** *Terms Forestry & Logging* (U.S. Dept. Agric. Bureau Forestry) 48 *Sniper*, one who noses logs before they are skidded. **1906** *Log of 'Columbia'* June 8/1 'He ought to be chased out of the woods,' said Jim, the sniper. **1914** *Chambers's Jrnl.* 3 Oct. 696/1 Summoning the sniper for an occasional undersnipe. **1956** R. W. ANDREWS *Glory Days of Logging* 14 These were..snipers who shaped the butt ends, so they [*sc.* logs] wouldn't hang up on the skids.

**5.** *Austral.* (See quot. 1945.)

**1945** BAKER *Austral. Lang.* xiv. 248 A waterfront term of fairly recent origin is *sniper*, a non-union labourer. **1955** J. MORRISON *Black Cargo* 14 It will need only one shout of 'Sniper!' and Lamond will be lucky to get out without being knocked down. **1957** T. NELSON *Hungry Mile* 72 The W.W.F. had preference of work, wharf by wharf. The outsiders (snipers) would stand back at the gate until the W.W.F. men were all used.

**sniperscope** (ˈsnaɪpəskəʊp). [f. SNIPER + -SCOPE.] †**1.** A device incorporating a periscope, whereby a rifle may be fired by a soldier who remains concealed. *Obs.*

**1918** R. H. KNYVETT *Over There* 135 Many of the inventions are forgotten, but some are in use in France today, notably the 'periscope rifle' or 'sniperscope'.

**2.** A small device which converts infra-red radiation to a visible image and may be fixed to a gun so that it can be aimed in the dark.

**1941** *Sun* (Baltimore) 1 Jan. 6/3 The selected few American infantrymen who tried out the 'sniperscope' at Okinawa have already had a glimpse of future warfare. **1954** W. TUCKER *Wild Talent* (1955) xi. 418 'He must have used a rifle. And had good eyesight.' 'He probably had a sniperscope on it.' **1971** F. FORSYTH *Day of Jackal* I. i. 14 A rifle with sniperscope was found at Poinard's flat.

**snipey**, freq. variant of SNIPY *a.*

**ˈsnipiness.** [f. SNIPY *a.* + -NESS.] Undue length and pointedness of the muzzle of an animal, suggestive of a snipe's bill.

**1938** J. W. DAY *Dog in Sport* xv. 204 The jaws should be long and powerful, and quite free from snipiness or exaggeration in length. **1963** B. S. VESEY-FITZGERALD *Cat Owner's Encycl.* 121 The nose is longish, but the cheeks being very prominent do away with any snipiness, which is a bad fault.

**sniping** (ˈsnaɪpɪŋ), *vbl. sb.* [f. SNIPE *v.*]

**1. a.** The action of SNIPE *v.* 1, 2 a.

**1773** *Let. fr. India* in J. W. Fortescue *Hist. Brit. Army* III. 141 [The soldiers..put their hats on the parapet for the enemy to shoot at, and] humorously called it sniping. **1891** *Daily News* 29 Dec. 2/1 The sniping of the outposts against each other. **1898** B. BURLEIGH *Sirdar & Khalifa* x. 162 Our camps upon the right bank of the Atbara were exceptionally open to snipeing by night.

**b.** *fig.* The making of sly critical assaults; sharp fault-finding or carping. Freq. with *at.*

**1892** MRS. H. WARD *David Grieve* I. vi. 128 Hannah's appetite for snipin' returned. **1935** E. POUND *Let.* 7 Feb. (1971) 267 Eng. print so smeared with personal sniping and clique politics that any definition of limitations..is likely to be taken as 'anti-'. **1945** *Sun* (Baltimore) 25 June 1/3 There has been a lot of unfortunate sniping at the project. **1955** *Essays in Criticism* V. 64 Mr. Liddell's 'criticisms' of his essay..are mere sniping and peripheral eroding which say next to nothing about their subject. **1969** H. PERKIN *Key Profession* vi. 229 Hence that perpetual sniping..at the universities for their supposed idleness and inefficiency. **1977** *Time* 4 July 2/3 Your sniping at the U.N. and its jobs-for-the-boys was not premature. **1980** M. FONTEYN *Magic of Dance* 214 Taglioni, tired of petty sniping and endless comparisons favouring her rival, journeyed to St. Petersburg.

**2. a.** Snipe-shooting.

**1875** *Ibis* 15 The doctor..was not accustomed to sniping, and our bag was not so full at the end of the day as it might have been. **1877** HALLOCK *Sportsman's Gaz.* 174 The pleasures of Bay bird shooting should not be spoken of in the same sentence with cocking or sniping.

**b.** *attrib.* Engaged in snipe-shooting.

**1840** E. NAPIER *Scenes & Sp. Foreign Lands* II. v. 142 Frequently the slaughter committed by a sniping party is so great, that..nothing but the brains and trail are eaten, the rest being cast away.

**3.** Prospecting for gold, esp. in old diggings. *N. Amer. slang.*

**1897** M. H. E. HAYNE *Pioneers of Klondyke* 93 There is little 'snipping' [*sic*]—i.e. working old bars—on Forty Mile Creek, but it does not pay much. **1963** *Placer Mining B.C.* 7/1 Chinese miners were particularly adept at sniping... Sniping and bar-combing are..carried out by individuals who would rather do this than work for wages.

**4.** *Austral.* Working as a non-union labourer.

**1951** *Meanjin* (Melbourne) X. 334 You never scabbed, or anything like that? You never did any sniping?

**sniping** (ˈsnaɪpɪŋ), *ppl. a.* [f. SNIPE *v.*] That snipes, or shoots from cover. ***sniping fire***, individual and irregular shooting from a concealed position.

**1821** V. BLACKER *Mahratta War* II. i. 179 But even this advantage was greatly reduced, by their being exposed to a sniping fire from neighbouring walls. **1899** *Daily News* 24

Oct. 5/5, I was.. able to help him out of range of this sniping fire.

**'snipish**, *a. rare.* [f. SNIPE *sb.* + -ISH.] Somewhat resembling the beak of the snipe.
**1834** BECKFORD *Italy* II. 297 A priest or two with enormous spectacles on their thin snipish noses.

**sni'pocracy.** [f. SNIP *sb.* 7 + -(O)CRACY.] The tailoring profession or its leading members.
**1861** G. MEREDITH *Evan Harr.* xiv, By Jove! this comes it strong. Fancy the snipocracy here! **1912** *Nation* 20 Apr. 84/1 The glorified tailor,.. the Marquis of Snipocracy.

**snipped** (snɪpt), *ppl. a.* Also 6 snipte, 7- snipt. [f. SNIP *v.*]
**1.** *Bot.* Irregularly notched or serrated; incised.
**1578** LYTE *Dodoens* 15 The lesser Clote Burre hath grayish leaues,.. iagged or snipte round about the edges. **1601** HOLLAND *Pliny* xxv. vi. II. 220 The leaves.. snipped and cut about the edges ordinarily in five parts. **1682** WHELER *Journ. Greece* I. 67 A fair leaf,.. snipped about the edges with sharp-pointed teeth, like a great saw. **1796** WITHERING *Brit. Pl.* (ed. 3) III. 575 Stem-leaves snipt.
**2.** That has been subjected to snipping; jagged or irregularly cut.
**1601** SHAKS. *All's W.* IV. v. 2 Your sonne was misled with a snipt taffata fellow there. **1611** COTGR., *Passe-poil*, a snipped, or iagged welt of Taffata, &c. in a garment. **1796** *Phil. Trans.* LXXXVI. 446 The snipt edges were hard. **1847** ALB. SMITH *Chr. Tadpole* lviii. (1879) 491 There were no cheerless grates filled up with snipped silver paper.
**3.** Of style: Clipped, disjointed.
**1806** COLERIDGE *Lett.* (1895) 506 Persons who write in a hurry are very liable to contract a sort of snipt, convulsive style.

**snipper** ('snɪpə(r)). [f. SNIP *v.*]
**1.** *pl.* A machine or instrument for snipping or clipping; scissors.
**1593** J. NORDEN *Spec. Brit.* (Camden) Pref. p. xiv, They have snippers wherewith they snyppe and pare their plates, which snippers.. are so artificially placed,.. that by the mocion of the water also the snippers open and shut. **1603** FLORIO *Montaigne* II. ii. (1632) 192 When in Josephus we heare a childe all to rent with bitting snippers. **1647** HEXHAM I, A paire of snippers, *een snip-schaerken*.
**2.** One who snips or clips; *spec.* a tailor.
**1611** COTGR., *Tondeur*, a sheerer,.. barber, vermine-snipper. **1648** HEXHAM II, *Een Knipper*,.. a Snipper. *Ibid.*, *Een snipperaer*, a Snipper or a Cutter off. **1684** DRYDEN tr. *Maimbourg's Hist. League* Postscr. 35 As our Snippers go over once a year into France, to bring back the newest Mode, and to learn to cut and shape it. **1827** *Lancet* 10 Nov. 223/2 For the snippers of broad cloth and calf-skin I had little compassion. **1865** S. EVANS *Brother Fabian's MS.* 156 You'd be delighted to murder the snipper Who measures my waist for a skirt.
**3.** A cattle-dealer on a small scale.
**1869** *Pall Mall G.* 9 Sept. 12 The snippers and provincial jobbers.. furnish the raw material to the Aberdeen dealers and butchers.

†**'snippering**, *vbl. sb. Obs. rare.* [Cf. LG. *snippern* (G. *schnippern*) to snip, cut small.] *pl.* Parings.
**1599** A. M. tr. *Gabelhouer's Bk. Physicke* 143/1 The poulder of combured cobblers snipperinges of oulde shoes. [**1604** R. CAWDREY *Table Alph.*, *Snipperings*, payrings.]

**snipper-snapper.** Now *dial.* [Of fanciful formation: cf. WHIPPER-SNAPPER.] A young insignificant or conceited fellow.
*c* **1590** MARLOWE *Dr. Faustus* xi. 1161 Ile seeke out my Doctor..: O yonder is his snipper snapper. **1600** DEKKER *Shoemaker's Holiday* iv, Quick snipper-snapper, away Firke, Scour thy throat. **1638** FORD *Fancies* I. ii, Thou'rt a prick-ear'd foist,.. a knack, a snipper-snapper! **1677** *Poor Robin's Vision* 12 Having ended his discourse, this seeming gentile snipper-snapper vanisht. **1835** MOORE *Mem.* (1856) VII. 108 Far better worth listening to than many of the young snipper-snappers of his profession. **1854** MISS BAKER *Northampt Gloss.*, *Snipper-snapper*, a small, insignificant, effeminate, self-conceited young man.

†**'snippery.** *nonce-wd.* [f. SNIP *v.*] Snipping.
**1639** [see SNAPPERY].

**snippet** ('snɪpɪt). [f. SNIP *v.* + -ET[1].] A small piece cut off; a small fragment or portion.
**1664** BUTLER *Hud.* II. iii. 824 Witches Simpling, and on Gibbets Cutting from Malefactors snippets. **1862** SALA *Seven Sons* III. 272 [She] used to cut her dress into snippets with a pair of scissors. **1885** LADY BRASSEY *In the Trades* 120 The droll little heaps, and dabs, and snippets in which everything was sold. **1897** F. THOMPSON *New Poems* 135 Snippets and waste From old ancestral wearings.
*attrib.* **1909** *Nation* 30 Oct. 191/1 One of them bears the tell-tale snippet-mark of a leaf-cutter bee.
**b.** In *transf.* or *fig.* uses.
**1880** *Sat. Rev.* 2 Oct. 438/1 The mere sticking on to his dialogue of snippets from Elizabethan phraseology is a vain thing. **1882** F. HARRISON *Choice of Books* (1886) 296 The love of beauty is nothing of dilettantism to be cut into snippets and shreds. **1886** STEVENSON *Prince Otto* II. iv, That is a poor snippet of malicious gossip.
**c.** *spec.* A short passage taken from a literary work; a short scrap of literary matter of any kind.
**1864** *Spectator* 12 Mar., These paragraphs and snippets from the Saturday Review. **1884** *Ibid.* 4 Oct. 1309/2 It is the latest stamp of the true 'classic' to be cut up into snippets for a birthday-book. **1897** *Month* Oct. 435 The text is in fact largely made up of a kind of patchwork of snippets which often amalgamate ill.
*attrib.* **1899** *Daily News* 5 July 8/2 He.. reads nothing but sporting papers and 'snippet weeklies'.

**'snippetiness.** [f. next.] The state or condition of being snippety; scrappiness.
**1878** *Spectator* 16 Feb. 220/2 The defect of Fraser's Magazine.. is snippetiness, a habit of publishing so many articles that they are none of them exhaustive. **1890** *Athenæum* 7 June 730/1 A certain snippetiness of style and arrangement, which is too suggestive of paste and scissors.

**'snippety**, *a.* Also -etty, -ity. [f. SNIPPET.] Of the nature of, suggestive of, a snippet or snippets; composed of snippets or scraps.
**1864** *Spectator* 1406 The snippety style of American reporting. **1865** *Ibid.* 25 Nov. 1307/2 A.. very clever, but somewhat snippety magazine. **1888** *Pall Mall G.* 25 June 1/1 More or less snippetty instalments of our Special Commissioner's Report.

**snipping** ('snɪpɪŋ), *vbl. sb.* [f. SNIP *v.*]
**1.** The action of the verb; cutting, clipping. Also with *off*.
**1583** STUBBES *Anat. Abus.* II. (1882) 50 When they come to the cutting of the haire, what snipping and snapping of the cycers is there. **1611** COTGR., *Retaillement*, a shredding, clipping, snipping. **1648** HEXHAM II, *Een snipperinge*,.. a Snipping off, or a Snip. **1867** MISS BRADDON *Doctor's Wife* xxxvii, She heard the horrible snipping of crape and bombazine going on all day.
*attrib.* **1648** HEXHAM II, *Knip-schaerken*, Snipping Cicers.
**2.** A part or piece snipped or cut off; a clipping, cutting. Usu. in *pl.*
**1611** COTGR., *Retailleures*, shreds, clippings, snippings, parings. **1846** LANDOR *Imag. Conv.*, *Lucian & Timotheus* (1891) I. 321 Give me all the shreds and snippings you can spare me. They will feel like clothes. **1870** PEACOCK *Ralf Skirl.* II. 41 These little snippings of bright coloured raiment.
*fig.* and *transf.* **1862** *Sat. Rev.* 5 July 23 The remaining snippings from our author's book of ethical commonplaces. **1884** *Athenæum* 5 Jan. 21/2 By complete essays or sections, and not by mere snippings here and there.
†**3.** A snibbing, snubbing, or reproving. *Obs.*
**1601** BRETON (*title*), No Whippinge, nor Trippinge: but a kinde friendly Snippinge. **1614** J. TAYLOR (*title*), The Nipping or Snipping of Abvses.

†**'snipping**, *ppl. a. Obs. rare.* In 5 snypp-, 6 snypand. [Of doubtful origin; the verb *snip* is not recorded till much later.] Nipping, biting with cold.
*a* **1400-50** *Alexander* 1560 As blaȝt.. As any snyppand [*v.r.* snappand] snawe þat in þe snape liȝtis. **1513** DOUGLAS *Æneid* VII. Prol. 50 Scharp soppis of sleit, and of the snypand snawe.

**snippy** ('snɪpɪ), *a.* [f. SNIP *v.* Cf. Du. *snippig* (Fris. *snippich*) snappish.]
**1.** *dial.* Parsimonious, mean; covetous.
**1727** BAILEY (vol. II), *Snippy*, parcimonious, niggardly. **1825-** in dial. glossaries, etc. (*Eng. Dial. Dict.*).
**2.** *dial.* and *colloq.* Fault-finding, snappish, sharp; putting on airs, supercilious.
**1848** BARTLETT *Dict. Amer.* 318 *Snippy*, finical; and substantively, a finical person. A woman's word. **1887** GUNTER *Mr. Barnes* xx, So dictatorial!.. And so snippy! **1894** P. L. FORD *Hon. Peter Stirling* xxx. 171 Before I could possibly have said or done anything to offend her, she treated me in the snippiest way. **1896** *Harper's Mag.* June 23/2 She's too snippy for me. **1934** E. CARR *Jrnl.* 12 Feb. in *Hundreds & Thousands* (1966) 95, I don't want to be mean and snippy but I don't think they know. **1952** H. GARNER *Yellow Sweater* 93 There followed an explanation of why her son hadn't been attending school as regular as he should, and how snippy the teacher was getting to be. **1961** *Insurance Salesman* Jan. 47/1 One of our clerks was a snippy, opinionated girl who kept everything unsettled and rubbed everyone the wrong way. **1970** J. POTTS *Affair of Heart* viii. 65, I must say, she was very snippy. Downright rude. **1974** *Times* 28 Feb. 10/6 This irritates Mr Heath... Privately, he is quite snippy about it. **1977** D. RAMSAY *You can't call it Murder* I. 52 Daughter Sarah described as uppity and snippy.
**3.** Scrappy, fragmentary, snippety.
**1886** *Pall Mall G.* 20 May 2/1 Paragraphs and very short articles which may fairly be regarded as 'snippy' bits.

**snip-snap** ('snɪpˌsnæp), *sb.* [f. SNIP *sb.* + SNAP *sb.*, used with imitative effect.]
In Bale *Thre Lawes* (1538) 1474 Hypocrisy addresses Infidelity as 'brother snyp snap'.
†**1.** The action of snipping or clipping with a pair of scissors or the like; an instance of this. Also *fig.*
**1597** G. HARVEY *Trimming T. Nashe* Wks. (Grosart) III. 72 If heere I haue been too prodigall in snip snaps, tell me of it. **1638** FORD *Fancies* V. ii, The fashion of gentry, which is never complete till the snip snap of dexterity hath mowed off the excrements of slovenry.
**2.** Smart remark or reply; sharp repartee.
**1727** POPE, etc. *Art of Sinking* 109 It is by virtue of this style that.. Marcus Aurelius is excellent at snip-snap. **1781** C. JOHNSTON *Hist. J. Juniper* II. 246, I have amused myself with.. playing a game at snip-snap, with Beatrice in Benedick. **1811** MISS MITFORD in L'Estrange *Life* (1870) I. 149 Letters should assimilate to the higher style of conversation, without the snip-snap of fashionable dialogue. **1872** TENNYSON in *Life* (1897) II. iv. 113 *note*, To print the names of the speakers.. over the short snip-snap of their talk.
†**3.** = SNAPPER *sb.*[1] 2 b. *Obs.*$^{-0}$
**1736** AINSWORTH I, A snip snap, or snappers, *crotalum*.

**snip-snap** ('snɪpˌsnæp), *a.* [Cf. prec.]
†**1.** Making a snipping sound; working or acting by snipping or clipping. *Obs.*
**1600** J. LANE *Tom Tel-troth* 120 These snip-snap sheers. **1643** *Mercurius Brit.* No. 28. 211 Barbers and every Snip-snap Jack which can tell the King a faire tale in his eare.
**2.** Of the nature of snip-snap; characterized by snip-snap or smart repartee.
**1673** R. LEIGH *Transp. Reh.* 139 His snip-snap wit, hit for hit, and dash for dash. **1702** MOTTEUX *Prol. to Farquhar's Twin-Rivals*, With volleys of small shot, or snip-snap wit. **1752** A. MURPHY *Gray's Inn Jrnl.* No. 5, Run off from the Point, in a snip-snap Stile, with pert Question and Answer. **1830** H. LEE *Mem. Manager* I. iv. 152 A snip-snap mode of expression. **1861** S. BROOKS *Silver Cord* viii. (1865) 45 It is not a bit of snip-snap impertinence.. that will frighten me. **1884** *Fortn. Rev.* Dec. 785 The snip-snap dialogue about prodigies.
**b.** Of persons: Given to snip-snap. *rare*$^{-1}$.
**1785** [R. GRAVES] *Eugenius* II. xix. 126 He found she.. was not that pert, snip-snap formidable Beatrice, which he at first had some reason to think her.
**3.** Snappish, quarrelsome, irritable. *rare*$^{-1}$.
**1770** C. JENNER *Placid Man* IV. iii. II. 23 In this kind of snip-snap disposition the family arrived in town.

**snip-snap** ('snɪpˌsnæp), *v.* [Cf. SNIP-SNAP *sb.*]
**1.** *intr.* To indulge in snip-snap or smart repartee; to speak in a snappy manner.
**1593** G. HARVEY *Pierce's Super.* Wks. (Grosart) II. 313 If any whosoeuer will needes be offering abuse in fact, or snip-snapping in termes. **1826** MISS MITFORD *Village* Ser. II. (1863) 367, 'I believe.. that you think I have nothing better to do than to read novels.' And so she snip-snaps to the end of the visit. **1845** JUDD *Margaret* I. xvii, Pluck snip-snaps with his wife, cracks on Hash, shows his white teeth to Margaret.
**2.** To snip; to clip with a snipping sound. Hence **snip-snapping** *vbl. sb.*
**1906** *Westm. Gaz.* 14 July 2/2 Scissors join in, with their snip-snapping, as a third bodice is cut out.

**snip-snap**, *adv.* (and *int.*). ? *Obs.* [Cf. prec.] With snip and snap; with a snipping, snapping sound.
**1588** SHAKS. *L.L.L.* V. i. 63 A sweet tutch, a quicke venewe of wit, snip snap, quick & home. **1596** NASHE *Saffron Walden* Ep. Ded., To torment him, and deal as snip snap snappishly with him, as euer he was delt withall. **1602** MIDDLETON *Blurt, Master-Constable* II. i, My sister shoots him off, snip-snap, at her pleasure. **1672** VILLIERS (Dk. Buckhm.) *Rehearsal* III. i. (Arb.) 67 For you shall see 'em come in upon one another snip snap.. as fast as can be. **1793** L. WILLIAMS *Children's Friend* I. 16, I will.. come with my bill-hook, and snip-snap, cut all those briars down to the ground.

**snip-snapper.** *rare*$^{-1}$. [Cf. SNIP-SNAP *v.*] A tailor.
**1626** MIDDLETON *Anything for Quiet Life* II. ii, Not a word more, goodman snipsnapper, for your ears.

**snip-snap-'snorum.** [a. LG. *snipp-snapp-snorum* (also *-snurr*), = G. *schnipp-schnapp-schnorum* (or *-schnurr*), on which see the article in Grimm's Dict.] A round game of cards, played (esp. by the young) in various ways, in which the players on turning up the requisite cards respectively call 'snip', 'snap', and 'snorum'.
In R. Hardie *Hoyle made familiar* (1830) 80 the game is called 'Snip, Snap, Snore 'em', and in describing it the words *snip*, *snap*, and *snore* are employed.
**1755** *Connoisseur* No. 52 ¶6, I saw these strange women place themselves at a huge round table.. to play.. at Pope Joan and Snip-snap-snorum! **1784** *Laura & Augustus* I. 98 The.. enlivening snip-snap snorum; which game they were then playing. **1820** MRS. TRENCH *Rem.* 439 His wife, his children, his garden,.. fill up his day; as snip-snap-snorum does his evening. **1834** SOUTHEY *Doctor* (1837) IV. 72 It had been found convenient to set down the children.. to Pope-Joan, or snip-snap-snorum, which was to them a more amusing because a noisier game. **1887** BESANT *The World Went* xxiv, Bess.. could play All-fours, Put, Snip-snap-snorum.

**snipy** ('snaɪpɪ), *a.* Also snipey, *Sc.* snipie. [f. SNIPE *sb.*]
**1.** Characterized by having a long pointed nose or muzzle suggestive of a snipe's bill. Also *Comb.*
**1825** JAMIESON *Suppl.*, *Snipie-nebbit*, having a nose resembling a snipe's neb or bill. **1884** G. STABLES *Our Friend the Dog* vii, *Snipey*—Applied to the muzzle when peaked like a fox's. **1902** *Fur & Feather* 19 Sept. 232/3 Brindle [cavy] with white blaze,.. rather snipy. **1904** H. COMPTON *20th Century Dog* II. 341 The long-legged, snipy-faced,.. flat-sided specimens.
**2.** Resembling a snipe; snipe-like.
**1888** LEES & CLUTTERBUCK *B.C. 1887* xvii. (1892) 183 In flight they [dowitchers] were not so snipey as the genuine article.
**3.** Frequented by snipe.
**1903** *Blackw. Mag.* Sept. 368/1 The chief characteristics of this essentially snipey tract.

**snirt** (snɜːt), *sb.* Chiefly *north. dial.* and *Sc.* Also 8-9 **snert.** [f. next.] A suppressed laugh; a snicker.
**1781** J. HUTTON *Tour to Caves* (ed. 2) Gloss. 96 *Snert*, an ineffectual effort to stifle a laugh. **1825** in JAMIESON *Suppl.* **1828-** in north. dial. glossaries, etc. (see also *Eng. Dial. Dict.*). **1899** HALL CAINE *Shadow of Crime* xxiv, 'Saucer een,' said Mrs. Garth with a snirt.

**snirt** (snɜːt), *v. north. dial.* and *Sc.* Also 8–9 snert. [Imitative: cf. SNURT *v.*] *intr.* To laugh in a suppressed manner; to snicker.

**1724** RAMSAY in *Evergreen* (1761) II. 15 Now let hir snirt, and fyk her fill. **1791** J. LEARMONT *Poems* 2 They gang by ye wi' sic a huff, An' pridfu' caper, snirt, an' snuff, As gif Death ne'er meant them a cuff. **1829–** in north. dial. glossaries. **1871** BLACK *Daughter of Heth* (1872) 94 The Whaup grew very red in the face and 'snirted' with laughter.

**'snirtle,** *v. Sc.* and *north. dial.* [f. prec. + -LE 3.] *intr.* To laugh in a quiet, suppressed, or restrained manner; to snigger.

**1785** BURNS *Jolly Beggars* xlii, But though his little heart did grieve.., He feigned to snirtle in his sleeve. **1824** MACTAGGART *Gallovid. Encycl.* 112 The Dominie.. fain wad fa' a laughing; He snirtles wi' his neb and snirks. **1887** J. SERVICE *Life Dr. Duguid* iv. 26 Her aul' worl' cracks and stories often mak me snirtle and laugh.

**snish, snishing:** see SNEESH, SNEESHING.

†**snit**[1]. *Obs.*$^{-1}$ In 5 snytte. [Related to SNITE *v.*] The glowing part of the wick of a candle when blown out.

*c* **1420** *Chron. Vilod.* 1277 þis mayde.. blewe ouȝt þe leyȝt anone sodanly—Bot þe weke hulte stylle þe snytte.

**snit**[2]. *slang* (orig. and chiefly *U.S.*). [Of uncertain origin (see quot. 1939[2]).] A state of agitation; a fit of rage or bad temper; a tantrum, sulk. Freq. in phr. ***in a snit.***

**1939** C. BOOTHE *Kiss Boys Good-bye* II. i. 105 'I declare, Mrs. Rand, I cried myself into a snit.' 'A snit?' 'I do deplore it, but when I'm in a snit I'm prone to bull the object of my wrath plumb in the tummy.' **1939** *Sat. Rev. Lit.* 23 Dec. 12/1 The membership could hardly be said to be in a snit,.. as nobody in Georgia seems ever to have heard of either the word or the state of being until Miss Clare Boothe isolated and defined it. **1962** J. POTTS *Evil Wish* x. 136 If you hadn't been in such a snit when I came upstairs I'd have told you so. **1971** *Daily Progress* (Charlottesville, Va.) 21 Jan. 4A/3 If New York solves its problems through gambling, every state in the union is going to follow suit except Nevada, which will probably secede from the nation in a snit. **1975** J. GOULET *Oh's Profit* xxxvii. 208 The President of the United States had bawled him out and left Cambridge College in a fierce snit. **1980** *N.Y. Times* 8 Jan. D 16, I was recently.. put in charge of six other copywriters, two of them men. The men are in a quiet snit.

**snitch,** *sb. slang.* [Of obscure origin.]

†**1.** A fillip (on the nose). *Obs.*

**1676** COLES, *Snitch*,.. a fillip. *a* **1700** B. E. *Dict. Cant. Crew, Snitch*,.. a Filip on the Nose.

**2.** The nose.

*a* **1700** B. E. *Dict. Cant. Crew, Snite his Snitch*, Wipe his Nose, or give him a good Flap on the Face. **1895** RYE *E. Angl. Gloss.* 204 Pull her snitch for her. **1902** *Westm. Gaz.* 3 July 2/1 As the.. egg.. broke on the 'snitch' of the Socialist candidate.

**3.** An informer; one who turns King's or Queen's evidence. In the phr. ***to turn snitch.***

**1785** in GROSE *Dict. Vulgar T.* *c* **1800** in Byron *Juan* XI. xix. Note 14, She'll surely turn snitch for the forty—That her Jack may be regular weight. **1906** *Atlantic Monthly* Nov. 589 He employs that phenomenon of despicability.. in Western parlance called a snitch.. to work up the lawsuit. **1930** *Forum* Dec. 375/1 A police informer in New York, for instance, is a stool or snitch. **1959** I. & P. OPIE *Lore & Lang. Schoolch.* x. 189 The tell tale is.. a sly, a snitch or snitcher (common, especially in the Midlands). **1965** J. WAINWRIGHT *Death in Sleeping City* 142 The 'snitches' and the 'grassers' and the 'stoolpigeons' whispered out of the corner of their mouths, and money changed hands. **1979** S. RIFKIN *McQuaid in August* ix. 97 Lopez was an informant.. a paragon among snitches.

**4.** Phr. ***to have*** (or ***get***) ***a snitch on*** (someone): to have a grudge against or 'down' on; to dislike. *N.Z. slang.*

**1943** J. A. W. BENNETT in *Amer. Speech* XVIII. 90 A person [in New Zealand] complaining of another's ill-will might also say, 'He's got a proper snitch on me'—obviously a variant of 'to snitch upon' (to inform against). **1948** *Landfall* II. 109 These jokers didn't understand the snitch Myers had on you, seemed to think it was right that Myers should always be tormenting you. **1953** O. E. MIDDLETON *Short Stories* 28 He wasn't a man to get a snitch on his neighbours because of a bit of bad luck and it wasn't long before he was his own self again. **1959** G. SLATTER *Gun in my Hand* viii. 91 Got a snitch on me and put me in crook with the boss.

**5.** *Comb.*, as **snitch-rag** *slang*, a handkerchief.

**1940** H. G. WELLS *Babes in Darkling Wood* I. i. 25 Can I borrow your snitch-rag, Gemini?

**snitch** (snɪtʃ), *v.* [Of obscure origin: cf. prec.]

**1. a.** *intr.* To inform *upon* or (now usu.) *on* a person; to peach, turn informer. Also, to reveal or give information *to* (someone). *slang.*

**1801** *Sporting Mag.* XIX. 88 A man who is now in Chester Gaol and has been snitching about me. **1812** J. H. VAUX *Flash Dict.* s.v., To impeach or betray your accomplices, is termed *snitching upon* them. **1839** A. SOMERVILLE *Hist. Brit. Leg.* v. 105 How one of these had frequently threatened to *snitch*—or tell who stole the bridle. **1867** *Crim. Chronol. York Castle* 189 Wright,.. finding that Norburn had been snitching, also made a confession. **1910** 'O. HENRY' *Whirligigs* xiii. 157 Say, don't snitch to the tenants about this, will yer? **1926** J. BLACK *You can't Win* xix. 279 If I get a job some copper will snitch on me to my boss. **1933** *Daily Progress* (Charlottesville, Va.) 26 Jan. 1/8 He did it, he said, because she 'snitched' on him when he played truant from school. **1941** B. SCHULBERG *What makes Sammy Run?* v. 83, I felt a little guilty about snitching on my neighbor. **1957** A. MILLER *View from Bridge* I. 33 The family had an uncle that they were hidin' in the house, and he snitched to the Immigration. **1966** P. MOLONEY *Plea for Mersey* 14 The Captain.. had snitched to the police that his cargo was being pilfered.

**b.** *trans.* To inform or give evidence against (a person or accomplice). *rare*$^{-1}$.

**1801** *Sporting Mag.* XIX. 88 Nadin asked him, how he knew the man had snitched him?

**2.** To catch by means of a noose or loop.

**1900** *Daily News* 13 Oct. 8/2 The pike.. is killed anyhow, 'shot at sight', or snitched with a wire loop, or netted.

**3.** To take surreptitiously, purloin; to steal or 'pinch'. *slang.*

**1904** *N.Y. Times* 6 June 9 They reached Coney Island by snitching rides. **1933** D. L. SAYERS *Murder must Advertise* iii. 46 He first of all snitched people's ideas without telling them, and then didn't give them the credit for it. **1948** L. A. G. STRONG *Trevannion* xvii. 323 You love a girl faithfully for years, and some glib sod comes along at the heel of the hunt and snitches her from you. **1958** [see BOOKSY *a.*]. **1976** M. MACHLIN *Pipeline* xxx. 348 How about that guy who snitched a whole D-9 tractor, brand-new?

Hence **'snitching** *ppl. a.* and *vbl. sb.*

**1812** J. H. VAUX *Flash Dict.* s.v. *Snitch*, An informer, or tale-bearer in general, is called a *snitching* rascal. **1923** W. S. MAUGHAM *Our Betters* III. 172 You really might have left Tony alone. This habit you have of snitching has got you into trouble before. **1933** *Sun* (Baltimore) 24 Aug. 6/7 Not long ago we had the fine stirring story by Neil Swanson 'The Judas Tree', and now comes a snitching of that title by Leslie Ford, who calls his new detective thriller 'The Clue of the Judas Tree'. **1961** B. MALAMUD *New Life* (1962) 298 He had been thinking of discussing with him Bullock's concern with athletes but it was too much like snitching. **1972** J. WAMBAUGH *Blue Knight* (1973) ii. 39 'Okay,' I said, giving him a chance to rationalize his snitching, which all informants have to do when they start out.

†**'snitchel,** *sb. slang. Obs.* [Cf. SNITCH *sb.*] A fillip (on the nose).

**1676** COLES, *Snitchel*, a fillip. *a* **1700** B. E. *Dict. Cant. Crew, Snitchel*, A Filip on the Nose.

Hence †**'snitchel** *v. Obs.*

*a* **1700** B. E. *Dict. Cant. Crew.* s.v. *Gig, Snichel the Gig*, Fillip the Fellow on the Nose.

†**snitch'ems.** *Obs.*$^{-1}$ A card-game.

**1798** *Sporting Mag.* XI. 150 The game of snitch-em's. This game may be ranked among the fairest games on the cards. [Description follows.]

**snitcher** ('snɪtʃə(r)). *slang.* [f. SNITCH *v.*]

†**1.** (See quot.) *Obs.*$^{-1}$

**1761** *Ann. Reg.* II. 51/1 He was a respectable member of.. the Bucks,—Bloods,—Snitchers,—Choice Spirits.

**2.** An informer, peacher; = SNITCH *sb.* 3.

**1827** *Examiner* 796/2 He had committed hundreds of robberies, but would not confess them, as it might implicate other parties, and he scorned to be a snitcher. **1859** in *Slang Dict.* 97. **1862** C. C. ROBINSON *Dial. Leeds* 415 Ah nivver wor a snitcher.

**3.** *pl.* Strings used by policemen in place of handcuffs. *Sc.*

**1864** *Slang Dict.* 238 In Scotland Snitchers mean handcuffs. **1887** SERVICE *Life Dr. Duguid* xxvi. 168 The polisman never had the snitchers in his pooch.

**snite** (snaɪt), *sb.*[1] Now *dial.* Forms: 1, 6– snite, 4–7 (8) snyte, 5 snyghte, snyhte, snyȝt, 6–7 snight. [OE. *snite* (also in comb. *wudusnite*), apparently not represented in any of the cognate languages.]

**1.** = SNIPE *sb.* 1.

Some distinction between *snite* and *snipe* is implied in the following entries in MS. Cott. Nero A. vi. (early 15th cent.):—fol. 165 *v*, Plouer, snytys, snypys, larkys; fol. 177 *r*, Ploueres, snytes, quaylys, snypys.

*c* **725** *Corpus Gloss.* A 138 *Acegia*, snite. *c* **1000** ÆLFRIC *Voc.* in Wr.-Wülcker 132 *Aceta*, snite, *uel* wudecocc. *c* **1325** [see SNIPE *sb.* 1]. **1363** in Riley *Memorials London* (1868) 312 A snyte, 1½d. **1382** WYCLIF *Isaiah* xxxiv. 11 The snyte [L. *ibis*] and the crowe dwelle shul in it. *a* **1400** *Sqr. lowe Degre* 323 With deynty meates that were dere;.. Both storkes and snytes ther were also. *c* **1400** LYDG. *Churl & Bird* in *Minor P.* (Percy Soc.) 192 A downghille doke [is to thee] as deynte as a snyghte. **1515** BARCLAY *Egloges* iv. (1570) C vb/2 A shamfull rable.. presumeth to indite, Though they have scantly the cunning of a snite. **1581** J. BELL *Haddon's Answ. Osorius* 374 Ill may the Snight the Woodcock twight for his long bill. **1604** DRAYTON *Owle* 947 The witlesse Woodcocke, and his Neighbour Snite. **1688** *Phil. Trans.* XVII. 713 These passages are also in the Heads of Snites. **1694** MOTTEUX *Rabelais* IV. lix. (1737) 244 Snytes... Thistle-Finches. **1837–** in Devon and Cornwall glossaries, etc. **1893** BARING-GOULD *Mrs. Curgenven* xlix, Widgeon, nor wild goose, hearn, and snite.

†**b.** Applied to species of birds resembling the snipe. *Obs.*

**1694** *Martens' Voy. Spitzbergen* in *Acc. Sev. Late Voy.* II. 72 This Snite, which is also called the Strand-runner.., is no bigger than a Lark.

†**2.** As a term of abuse. *Obs.* Cf. SNIPE *sb.* 3.

**1653** URQUHART *Rabelais* I. liv, Here enter not vile bigots, hypocrites, Externally devoted Apes, base snites.

**3.** *attrib.*, as †**snyte-knave**, a jack-snipe (cf. *snipe-knave* s.v. SNIPE *sb.* 8).

**1611** COTGR. s.v. *Un, Deux pour vn*, the Snyte-knaue; tearmed so, because two of them are worth but one good Snyte.

†**snite,** *sb.*[2] *Obs.*$^{-1}$ Also snyt. [Cf. WFris. *snjit*, *snitte* a spit or sprinkling of rain.] (See quot.)

*a* **1548** HALL *Chron., Hen. VI*, 186 b, Their fell a small snyt [*Grafton* snite] or snow, which by violence of the wynd was driven into the faces of them.

**snite** (snaɪt), *v.* Now *dial.* and *Sc.* Forms: 1 **snytan,** 5 **snytyn,** 5–7, *dial.* and *Sc.* 9 **snyte** (5 **snyth-**), 5– **snite** (5 **snete**); 6 **snytte,** 7 **snit, snett.** *Pa. t.* 4 **snytte.** *Pa. pple.* 4 **y-snyt,** 7 **snit.** [OE. *snýtan*, = ON. and Icel. *snýta* (Norw. and Sw. *snyta*, Da. *snyde*), OHG. *snûzan* (MHG. *snûtzen*, *sniuzen*, G. *schneuzen*, *schnäuzen*), MLG. *snûten* (LG. *snüten*), Du. *snuiten* (WFris. *snute*): the stem *snūt-* is prob. the same as that of SNOUT *sb.* Cf. also SNOT *sb.*]

**1. a.** *intr.* To clean or wipe the nose; to cast away mucus. **b.** *trans.* To remove by wiping, etc.

*a* **1100** in Napier *Contrib. O.E. Lexicog.* 58 Hræce & snyte bæftan him oððe adun be his sidan. *Ibid.*, Swa hwæt swa man him fram hræce oððe snyte, fortrede hit mid his fotum. *a* **1586** in *Maitland MS.* (Pinkerton, 1786) 185 They snyte, thoch thair na mister be, That ye may thair trim napkyne see. **1598** BP. HALL *Sat.* VI. i, So looks he like a marble toward rain, And wrings and snites, and weeps, and wipes again. **1632** HOLLAND *Cyrupædia* VIII. ii. 181 Hee inured them to this, neither to spit nor snit openly in sight. *a* **1779** GRAHAM *Writ.* (1883) II. 154 A weel blooded hissie.. that.. snites the snotter frae their nose.

**2.** *trans.* To clean or clear (the nose) from mucus, esp. by means of the thumb and finger only; to blow. Also *fig.*, to tweak or pull.

*c* **1305** *St. Dunstan* 85 in *E.E.P.* (1862) 36 Mid his tonge he snytte hire nose, and tuengde hire sore. *Ibid.* 91 As god þe schrewe hadde ibeo atom ysnyt his nose. **1422** tr. *Secreta Secret., Priv. Priv.* 189 Therfor sayth Salamon, whoso ouerharde Snythyth the noos, he draueth blode. *c* **1460** J. RUSSELL *Bk. Nurture* 284 in *Babees Bk.*, Pike not youre nose.., Snyff nor snitynge hyt to lowd. **1530** PALSGR. 724/1 Snytte thy nose, or thou shalte eate no buttered fysshe with me. **1601** HOLLAND *Pliny* XXXV. xi. II. 550 Theodorus drew one snetting his nose. **1632** —— *Cyrupædia* 6 Even yet among the Persians it is held a shamefull thing.. to snit the nose. *a* **1700** B. E. *Dict. Cant. Crew, Snite his Snitch*, Wipe his Nose, or give him a good Flap on the Face. **1701** GREW *Cosmol. Sacra* I. v. 26 Nor would any one be able to snite his Nose, or to Sneeze. **1785** GROSE *Dict. Vulgar T.*, *Snite*, to wipe, or slap. **1804** COUPER *Poetry* II. 61 (E.D.D.), Tibb snyted Madge's muckle nizz Till out the purple sprang. **1828–** in many dial. glossaries, etc. (Cumb., Westm., Lancs., Chesh., Yks., Derby, Linc., Leic., Heref., Glos.).

†**b.** *Falconry.* Of a hawk, etc.: To wipe (the beak or bill) after feeding. *Obs.*

**1486** *Bk. St. Albans, Hawking* a vj, An hawke snytith or sewith hir beke and not wipith hir beke. **1575** TURBERV. *Faulconrie* 289 Let hir tire against the Sunne, snyting and sewing hir beake a little at your discretion.

**3.** To snuff (a candle). ? *Obs.*

Cf. next for evidence of this use in OE.

*c* **1440** *Promp. Parv.* 461/2 Snytyn.. a candyl, *emungo, mungo.* **1483** *Cath. Angl.* 347/1 To Snyte.. a candelle, *mvngere.* ? *a* **1800** in Gordon *Bk. Chron. Keith* (1880) 65 [He could not] snite [the candles and attend to his Psalm Book at the same time.] **1808** in JAMIESON s.v.

†**'snitel(s.** *Obs. rare.* In 1, 4 snytels, 5 -ele. [OE. *snýtels*, f. *snýtan* SNITE *v.*] = next 1.

*c* **1000** ÆLFRIC *Voc.* in Wr.-Wülcker 126 *Emunctorium*, candelsnytels. **1388** WYCLIF *Numb.* iv. 9 The candilstike, with hise lanternes, and tongis, and snytels. *c* **1460** *Promp. Parv.* (Winch.), Snytele of a candel, *munctorium.*

**'sniter.** Also 5, 7 snyter. [f. SNITE *v.*]

**1.** *pl.* A pair of candle-snuffers.

**1382** WYCLIF *Numb.* iv. 9 The candelstik, with the lanterns, and her toonges, and snyters. **1881** *Leicester Gloss.* 247.

**2.** One who wipes or snuffs.

**1611** COTGR., *Moucheur*, a snyter, wiper, snuffer.

**snithe,** *a. north. dial.* Also 9 **snyde.** [Related to next.] = SNITHING *ppl. a.*

**1671** SKINNER *Etymol. Ling. Angl.*, *A Snithe-wind*, vox elegantissima agro Linc. usitatissima. Significat autem Ventum valde Frigidum & Penetrabilem,.. ut nos dicimus, *a Cutting wind.* [Hence in Ray.] **1683** *Yorkshire Dialogue* 39 It is varra Snithe, And Ise flaid, Wife, it will be Frost Belive. **1828–** in north. dial. use (*Eng. Dial. Dict.*). **1884** STREATFEILD *Linc. & Danes* 265 At the fore-end of the year the winds are often hask and snyde.

**snithe,** *v. Obs.* exc. *dial.* [Common Teutonic: OE. *sniðan*, = OFris. *snîtha* (*snida*, *snia*, WFris. *snije*), MDu. *sniden* (Du. *snijden*), OS. *snîdan* (LG. *snîden*), OHG. *snîdan* (MHG. *snîden*, G. *schneiden*), ON. *sniða* (Norw. and Sw. *snida*), Goth. *sneiþan*. The mod. dial. use may be from ON.] *trans.* To cut; †to kill by cutting.

*c* **725** *Corpus Gl.* (Hessels) D 342 *Dolatum*, ȝesniden. *c* **897** K. ÆLFRED *Gregory's Past. C.* 377 Ʒif hwelc god læce bið, ðe wel cann wunda sniðan. *c* **1000** ÆLFRIC *Hom.* II. 40 God.. het niman anes ȝeares lamb æt ælcum hiwisce, and sniðan on Easter-tide. *c* **1200** ORMIN 1338 þe preost.. toc & snaþ þatt oþerr bucc. *Ibid.* 14666 Tacc Ysaac þin wennchell, & sniþ itt, alls itt wære an shep. **1888** ADDY *Sheffield Gloss.* 226 Snithe a piece off with thy knife.

**snithe,** dial. var. SNATH, scythe-pole; obs. f. SNY *v.* to swarm.

**'snithing,** *ppl. a.* Now *dial.* [f. SNITHE *v.*] Of wind, etc.: Nipping, cutting; piercing, sharp. (Cf. SNITHE *a.*)

*a* **1350** *St. Martin* 24 in Horstm. *Altengl. Leg.* (1881) 152 It was cald with wedders wete, Snythand frost with snaw and slete. **1851** STERNBERG *Dial. Northampton* s.v., A snithing wind. **1881** *Leicester Gloss.* 247 *Snithing*,.. applied to weather. 'A bloshing and snithing day.'

**'sniting,** *vbl. sb.* [f. SNITE *v.*]

**1.** The action of the verb; a blowing or wiping of the nose or beak; the snuffing of a candle.

*c* **1000** ÆLFRIC *Voc.* in Wr.-Wülcker 162 *Sternutatio*,.. snytingc, *uel* fneosung. *c* **1440** *Promp. Parv.* 461 Snytynge, of a nose or candyl, *munctura*. *c* **1460** *Vrbanitatis* 19 in *Babees Bk.*, Fro spettyng & snetyng kepe þe also. **1575** TURBERV. *Faulconrie* 306 And ye may perceive this disease by your hawkes often sniting & by making a noyze twice or thryse in hir snyting. **1611** COTGR., *Mouchement*, a snyting, or wiping of the nose. **1656** W. DU GARD tr. *Comenius' Gate Lat. Unl.* 57 The snivel..is detained by the hairs in the nostrils, that it may not flow down before sniting.

†**2.** The snuff of a candle. *Obs.*

*c* **1440** *Promp. Parv.* 461/2 Snytynge, of a candel, *munctorium, emunctorium*. **1483** *Cath. Angl.* 347/1 A Snytynge of a candelle, *licinus, licinum*.

**3.** *Comb.*, as †*sniting hole*; †**sniting instrument,** †**iron,** †**tongs,** candle-snuffers.

**1388** WYCLIF *Exod.* xxxvii. 23 He made also seuene lanternes, with her snytyng tongis. **1398** TREVISA *Barth. De P.R.* v. ii. (Tollemache MS.), þat þe open fumositeis and boystous filþe may be voyded and clensid by open and snytynge holes. *c* **1475** *Promp. Parv.* 461/2 (K.), Snytinge instrument, *munctorium, emunctorium*. **1483** *Cath. Angl.* 347/1 A Snytynge yren, *emvnctorium*.

†**'snitling,** *ppl. a. Obs.*$^{-1}$ ? Trifling.

**1682** H. MORE *Annot. Glanvill's Lux O.* 80 And now for that snitling Dilemma of the eager Opposer of Pre-existence.

**'snitter,** *v.*[1] *Obs.* exc. *dial.* Also 4 sniter-, 5 snyter-, sneter-. [Of obscure origin: cf. SNITE *sb.*[2]] *intr.* Of snow: To fall. Hence **'snittering** *ppl. a.*

**13..** *Gaw. & Gr. Knt.* 2003 þe snawe snitered ful snart, þat snayped þe wylde. *c* **1400** *Anturs of Arth.* vii, Thay ran to the roches,.. For the snyterand [*Douce* sneterand] snaue, that snaypely hom snellus. **1888** ADDY *Sheffield Gloss.* 227 *Snitter*, to snow.

**'snitter,** *v.*[2] *Sc.* and *north. dial.* [Cf. SNICKER *v.*, SNIGGER *v.*[1], SNIRT *v.*, and TITTER *v.*[1]] To laugh in a suppressed, nervous manner (*at* something). Also as *sb.*

**1825** JAMIESON Suppl., *To snuister*, or *snuitter*,..to laugh in a suppressed or clandestine way through the nostrils. *Snuister, snuitter*,..a laugh of this kind. **1892** M. C. F. MORRIS *Yorkshire Folk-Talk* 374 What's ta stannin' theer snitterin' an' laffin' at? **1896** 'G. UMBER' *Ayrshire Idylls* 71 Hoo her words should provoke sae muckle snitterin' an' lauchin'. **1975** *New Society* 31 July 235/2 A prevailing snitter (cross between snigger and titter) greeted the preview of..a new play... There was plenty to snitter at. **1975** W. MCILVANNEY *Docherty* III. v. 270 'Ye micht never be heard o'.' 'Sen' in David Livingstone,' Conn said. Tom snittered. **1977** —— *Laidlaw* xxxviii. 177 Harkness began to laugh. Laidlaw stared at him, then..snittered at himself.

†**'snitting,** *vbl. sb. Obs.*$^{-1}$ (Meaning doubtful.)

**1387** TREVISA *Higden* (Rolls) II. 147 þei beeþ i-cleped Pictes by cause of peyntynge and snittynge of woundes þat beeþ i-sene on hire bodies.

**'snittle,** *sb.* Now *dial.* Also 7 snitle. [Of obscure origin.] A loop with a running knot; a noose, snare; a slip-knot.

**1611** COTGR., *Laqs courant*, a noose, grinne, snitle, running knot. **1642** *Proceedings at Banbury* 7 Till they had all their necks in a snittle. **1862** in C. C. ROBINSON *Dial. Leeds* 415. **1895** RYE *E. Angl. Gloss.* 203 *Snickle, Snittle*, a slip-knot.

**snive,** variant of SNY *v.* to swarm.

**snivel** ('snɪv(ə)l), *sb.* Forms: α. 5 snevel, -yl, 6 -yll, 6–7 -il, 7 -ill; 6 sneuyll, -il, 6–7 -ill; 6 sneeuel, -ill, 9 *Sc.* sneevel, -il. β. 6 snyuell, sniuil, -yll, 6–7 -ell; 7 snivell, -ill, 7- snivel. [f. SNIVEL *v.*]

**1.** Mucus collected in, or issuing from, the nose.

α. **14..** *Parts Body* in Wr.-Wülcker 631 *Pus nasi*, snevel of þe nose. *c* **1440** *Jacob's Well* 247 Wype wyth þi tunge oute of my nase þe snevyl þat hangyth þer-inne. **1530** PALSGR. 272/1 Snevyll whan it hangeth at ones nose, *rovpie, boe*. **1540** —— *Acolastus* I j, He wolde throwe the sneuyll of his nose into it. **1626** BRETON *Pasquil's Madcappe* xi, As sower, As beldam's milke that turned with her sneuill. **1671** W. SALMON *Syn. Med.* I. liv. 136 Without avoiding any thing, except bloody or filthy Matter, like Snevil.

β. **1519** HORMAN *Vulg.* 28b, Thy nose is full of snyuell. **1548** ELYOT, *Mucosus*, snattye,..fulle of sniuyll. **1593** G. HARVEY *Pierce's Super.* Wks. (Grosart) II. 238, I will.. squise thy braine to sniuell, whereof it was curdled. **1621** BURTON *Anat. Mel.* III. ii. vi. iii. (1651) 562 Snot and snivell in her nostrils, spittle in her mouth. **1682** *Eng. Elect. Sheriffs* 46, I will sooner worship the Sun, than..the Snot and Snivel of Loyala's Nose. **1739** R. BULL tr. *Dedekindus' Grobianus* 11 If with your Elbow you wipe off the Snivel, No Man alive shall be esteem'd more civil. **1871** R. ELLIS *Catullus* xxiii. 17 Thee sweat frets not,.. Frets not snivel or oozy rheumy nostril.

**b.** A condition of the nose marked by the accumulation of mucus. Also ***the snivels***.

**1600** SURFLET *Countrey Farme* I. xxviii. 188 For the sniuell, take orpin and brimstone [etc.]. **1844** LOWSON *Mod. Farrier* 209 This affection is termed the snores or snivels. **1877** *Holderness Gloss.* 132/1 *Snivels*, a cold, accompanied by a difficulty of breathing, and a running at the nose.

†**2.** Saliva. *Obs.*$^{-1}$

**1697** *Phil. Trans.* XX. 50 The Snivel or Drivel that comes from the Mouth of a Dog..when mad.

†**3.** (See quot.) *Obs.*

**1693** EVELYN *De la Quint. Compl. Gard.* II. 195 Grounds ..that being colder and stronger or heavier, easily infect them [lettuces] with slimy Snivel [= 'a sort of rotting moisture, hanging about some plants'].

**4.** A slight sniff indicating, or intended to suggest, suppressed emotion.

**1848** DICKENS *Dombey* xxxix, Rob..took up the pieces one by one with a sob and a snivel for each. **1866** GILPIN *Songs Cumbld.* 280 Sae wi' snuffs an' sneevils [he] Rair't out. **1890** *Daily News* 18 Feb. 5/2 A carefully arranged and expressive 'snivel' is regarded as their most valuable acquirement.

**b.** A show or pretence of emotion; hypocritical expression of feeling.

**1878** E. JENKINS *Haverholme* 194 Lords and ladies.. penned elegiacs to his praise in tears and snivel. **1886** *St. James's Gaz.* 9 Feb. (Cassell), The cant and snivel of which we have seen so much of late.

**5.** *attrib.* and *Comb.*, as ***snivel-bottle, -guts, -monger, -nose***.

**1690** DRYDEN *Amphitryon* III. i, A received opinion, snivel-guts. **1778** *Exmoor Scolding* Gloss., *Snibble-nose*, or rather *Snivel-nose*, one who snuffs up the Snot. **1792** WOLCOT (P. Pindar) *Ep. Sir W. Hamilton* Wks. 1812 III. 185 More snivel-bottles, jordens, and old jugs. **1896** A. MORRISON *Child Jago* 149 He preferred the frank rogue before the calculating snivel-monger.

**snivel** ('snɪv(ə)l), *v.* Forms: α. 4 snevele, 5–6 sneuel, 6 -il, snevel(l, -ill, -yll; 9 *dial.* sneavel, *Sc.* sneevil. β. 4 snyvele, 5 -elle, 6 snyuel, 7 sniuel, 7- snivel (9 *dial.* snivvel). [OE. **snyflan* (implied in *snyflung* SNIVELLING *vbl. sb.*), f. *snofl* mucus. Cf. Da. *snøvle* (older *snevle*) to snuffle.]

**1.** *intr.* To run at the nose; to emit mucus from the nose; also, to draw up mucus audibly.

*c* **1325** *Gloss. W. de Bibbesw.* in Wright *Voc.* 173 Ely autre ne pout parler Une parole sanz nasyer, [*glossed*] snevelet, snyvele. *a* **1450** *Langland's P. Pl.* B. v. 135 (MS. Bodl. 814), Now awakiþ wratthe, wiþ two white eiȝen, And sneuelyng wiþ his nose. **1483** *Cath. Angl.* 347/1 To Snyvelle, *naricare*. **1508** KENNEDIE *Flyting w. Dunbar* 550 Out! out! I schout, apon that snowt that snevillis. **1526** SKELTON *Magnyf.* 1865 The snyte snyueled in the snowte and smyled at the game. **1614** B. JONSON *Barth. Fair* II. v, Dos't so, snotty nose? Good Lord! are you sniueling? **1649** QUARLES *Virgin Widow* II, Must I be still yawling, and calling,..whilst y'are.. potting, and piping, and driveling and sniveling! *a* **1722** LISLE *Husb.* (1757) 319 When they are sheared they catch cold, and will be glandered, and snivel very much.

**b.** *trans.* (See quot.) *rare.*

**1530** PALSGR. 723/2, I snevell, I beraye any thynge with snyvell, *je amorue*. Se howe this boye snyvelleth his cote.

**c.** To clear (the nose) by snuffling.

**1835** *Politeness & Gd.-breeding* 104 Never..snivel and snort a wet nose.

**2.** *intr.* To make a sniffing or snuffling sound expressive of real or assumed emotion; to be in, or affect, a tearful state.

**1690** DRYDEN *Prol. to 'Mistakes'*, I left our young Poet sniveling and sobbing behind the Scenes, and cursing somebody that has deceiv'd him. **1712** STEELE *Spect.* No. 364 ¶4 To take a Lad from Grammar and..send him crying and snivelling into foreign Countries. **1791** COWPER *Iliad* II. 329 And whip thee hence Home to thy galley, sniveling like a boy. **1818** SCOTT *Hrt. Midl.* xxiii, What signified his bringing a woman here to snotter and snivel, and bather their Lordships? **1848** THACKERAY *Van. Fair* lxii, Every woman in the house was snivelling at the time. **1882** MISS BRADDON *Mt.-Royal* III. i. 22 Why do you stand there snivelling about him?

**3.** *trans.* **a.** To affect in some way by snivelling; to address in a snivelling manner. *rare.*

**1668** R. L'ESTRANGE *Vis. Quev.* (1702) 268 To snivel and sneeze himself into another World. **1700** CONGREVE *Way of World* I. ix, Let 'em snivel and cry their Hearts out. **1717** *Entertainer* No. 25. 168 Thus they Whine and Snivel the Multitude, to enrich themselves and help forward the Faction.

**b.** To utter with a snivelling or sniffing sound; to shed (tears) snufflingly. Also with *out*.

**1780** COWPER *Progr. Error* 310 Ye novelists, who mar what ye would mend, Sniv'ling and driv'ling folly without end. **1818** SCOTT *Rob Roy* xxx, I heard the former snivel out, in a very subdued tone, 'And ye'll ask her' [etc.]. **1851** THACKERAY *Eng. Hum.* vi. (1876) 328 That fine flower of love..over which Sterne snivelled so many tears. **1865** ALEX. SMITH *Summer in Skye* I. 237 The doctor saluted Flora and snivelled his compliments.

†**snivelard.** *Obs. rare.* In 4–5 sneuel-, 5 snyvelard. [f. SNIVEL *v.*] A sniveller.

**1398** TREVISA *Barth. De P.R.* v. xiii. (Tollemache MS.), The nose is sum tyme let..by bredynge of superfluite..in þe holis of the nose, as it fareþ in sneuelardis. **14..** *Lat.-Eng. Voc.* in Wr.-Wülcker 606 *Pusio*, a sneuelard. *c* **1440** *Promp. Parv.* 461/2 Snyvelard, or he þat spekythe yn the nose, *nasitus*.

**'sniveldom.** *nonce-wd.* [f. SNIVEL *sb.* or *v.*] A slight cold causing one to snivel.

**1767** C'TESS COWPER in *Mrs. Delany's Life & Corr.* Ser. II. I. 91, I caught the first cold I have had this year..; but it was only a 'sniveldom' and is gone off.

**snivelization** (snɪv(ə)laɪ'zeɪʃən). *nonce-wd.* [Melville's factitious blend of SNIVEL *sb.* and CIVILIZATION.] Civilization considered derisively as a cause of anxiety or plaintiveness. Also **'snivelize** *v. trans.*, to reduce (someone) to a state of whimpering civilization; **'snivelized** *ppl. a.*

**1849** H. MELVILLE *Redburn* I. xxi. 200 Ye wouldn't have been to sea here, leadin' this dog's life, if you hadn't been snivelized... Snivelization has been the ruin on ye. *Ibid.*, Snivelized chaps only learns the way to take on 'bout life, and snivel. **1892** 'MARK TWAIN' *Satires & Burlesques* (1967) 169 He was working this character into an elaborate satire on civilization to be called 'Affeland (Snivelization)'. *c* **1938** L. MUMFORD *Report on Honolulu* in *City Development* (1946) x. 106 The restrictions and burdens imposed by what one of Herman Melville's characters derisively called 'snivelization'.

**'snivelled,** *ppl. a.* [f. SNIVEL *sb.* or *v.*] Soiled or foul with snivel.

**1530** TINDALE *Answ. More* (Parker Soc.) 124 That men should shrine his snivelled napkin, and not to believe his preaching. **1576** R. PETERSON *Galateo* (1852) 13 They spare not to snot their sniueld noses vppon them. **1581** G. PETTIE tr. *Guazzo's Civ. Conv.* I. (1586) 43 He woulde through negligence suffer his nose alwaies to be sneueled, and tooke no care to wipe it. **1619** R. WEST *Bk. Demeanor* 46 in *Babees Bk.* 292 To wipe thy snivelled nose Vpon thy cap. **1738** tr. *Guazzo's Art Convers.* 78 He was so negligent, as always to go with a snivell'd nose.

**sniveller** ('snɪv(ə)lə(r)). Also 5 sneveler. [f. SNIVEL *v.*]

**1.** One who snivels or whines. Also in fig. context.

*c* **1450** *Cov. Myst.* (Shaks. Soc.) 396, I schal snarle tho sneveleris wyth rith scharp schouris. **1731** SWIFT *On his Death* Wks. 1755 III. II. 244 [He would] more lament, when I was dead, Than all the sniv'lers round my bed. **1791** WOLCOT (P. Pindar) *Ep. to Ld. Lonsdale* Wks. 1812 III. 13 Despise that thing call'd Meekness; 'tis a sniveller. **1905** *Speaker* 25 Feb. 512/2 Savonarola and his Piagnoni or snivellers..had a fatal influence on art.

**2.** A cold breeze (causing one to snivel).

**1834** COL. HAWKER *Diary* (1893) II. 69 The pinching 'sniveller' was changed to a tempest. **1846** *Ibid.* 271 A chill that I took in a deadly cold 'sniveller'.

†**'snivelliness.** *Obs.*$^{-1}$ [f. SNIVELLY *a.*] A soft glutinous state.

**1622** CHANDLER *Van Helmont's Oriat.* 147 The Eggs of Fishes are at first more hard, and straightway..wax tender into a snivelliness.

**snivelling** ('snɪv(ə)lɪŋ), *vbl. sb.* Also 2 snyflung, 5 -ynge; 5 sneuelyng, 6 -ing, etc. [See SNIVEL *v.*] The action of the vb. in various senses.

*a* **1100** in Napier *Contrib. O.E. Lexicog.* 58 ðif heora æneȝum for unhæle hraca of breoste oððe snyflung of nosa deriȝe. *c* **1430** *Freemasonry* (Halliw. 1840) 711 From spyttynge and snyflynge kepe the also. **1587** MASCALL *Govt. Cattle, Sheepe* (1627) 220 Sheep oftentimes wil haue the glaunders, and a sneuelling at their noses. **1655** MOUFET & BENNET *Health's Improv.* (1746) 380 Spitting, Sniveling and Yawning, are only the Fruits of Fulness or Idleness. **1693** *Apol. Clergy Scot.* 15 They never thought Sniveling necessary to make a great Saint. **1748** SMOLLETT *Rod. Rand.* lxi. (1804) 436 After a good deal of snivelling and sobbing. **1782** COWPER *To the Rev. Mr. Newton* 11 There is nothing but sniv'ling and blowing of noses. **1815** *Hist. J. Decastro* I. 44 Come, John, let us have no more sniv'ling. **1875** EMERSON *Lett. & Social Aims* x. 256 Meantime we hate snivelling.

*attrib.* **1782** ELIZ. BLOWER *G. Bateman* II. 115, I war'nt there was fine sniveling work when ye parted. **1816** GILCHRIST *Philos. Etym.* 52 They only require a gentle grunt through the snivelling organs, to soothe dainty ears with much sweet melody.

**snivelling** ('snɪv(ə)lɪŋ), *ppl. a.* Also 3 snvuelinde, 5 snyvelande; 4 snyvelinge, 5 sneuelyng, snevyllynge, etc. [f. SNIVEL *v.*]

**1.** Of the nose, etc.: Discharging, or full of, snivel. Also of persons, given to snivelling or snuffling.

*c* **1290** *S. Eng. Leg.* I. 319 Snvuelinde nose and wet mouth. **1483** *Cath. Angl.* 347/1 Snyvelande (*A.* Snevyllynge), *naricans, naricus*. **1608** SYLVESTER *Du Bartas* II. iv. IV. *Decay* 175 Stooping as she goes, With driveling mouth, and with a sniveling nose. **1615** *Baud, Ruffe, & Cuffe* (Halliw.) 16 He is a most filthy snivelling fellow..; he will wipe your nose of all, if you put the case to him. **1813** H. & J. SMITH *Rej. Addr.* 72 A snivelling fellow he's call'd by his foes, For he can't raise his paw up to blow his red nose. **1862** *Macm. Mag.* Sept. 380 Another, whom he remembers a little snivelling boy. **1902** *Times* 16 July 13/6 The wonderful picture of leering, chuckling, snivelling senility.

*transf.* **1858** R. S. SURTEES *Ask Mamma* xxiii, The landlady brought a snivelling mould candle into the cheerless.. little inn-parlour.

**b.** Of a cold: Accompanied by snivelling.

**1687** MIÉGE *Gt. Fr. Dict.* II, A snivelling Cold, *un Rûme*.

**2.** Sounding through the nose. *rare.*

**1447** BOKENHAM *Seyntys* (Roxb.) 21 At the laste he thus owt abrayde Wyth a sneuelyng vooys & to hyr sayde. **1816** GILCHRIST *Philos. Etym.* xvii, To see this good, plain dialect superseded by snivelling, flippant, senseless French.

**3.** Displaying emotion or the semblance of it; mean-spirited, weak: **a.** Of persons.

**1647** J. C[LEVELAND] *Char. Lond.-Diurn.* 8 Two of Mars his Petty-toes, such snivelling Cowards, that it is a favour to call them so. **1691** WOOD *Ath. Oxon.* II. 84 The snivling Presbyterians..did not stick to report that he died no better than a Brewers Clerk. **1732** FIELDING *Covent Gard. Trag.* I. vii, Without wine all human kind wou'd be One stupid, sniveling, sneaking, sober fellow. **1790** WOLCOT (P. Pindar) *Advice to Future Laureat* Wks. 1812 II. 343 The little snivelling spirit. **1805** DIBDIN in *Naval Chron.* XIII. 394 The snivlingest scoundrel that ever was seen. **1838** DICKENS *O. Twist* xxvi, Why not have kept him here among the rest, and made a sneaking, snivelling pickpocket of him at once? **1860** EMERSON *Conduct of Life* ii. Wks. (Bohn) II. 335 These Hoosiers and Suckers are really better than the snivelling opposition.

**b.** Of discourse, writings, etc.

**1673** HICKERINGILL *Gregory F. Greybeard* 276 Pickt the peoples pockets with canting long snivelling sermons. **1707**

HEARNE *Collect.* (O.H.S.) II. 19 A poor, sniveling discourse. **1767** STERNE *Tristram Shandy* IX. xii, That snivelling virtue of Meekness. **1771** SMOLLETT *Humph. Cl.* (1815) 4, I have received a snivelling letter from Griffin, offering to make a public submission, and pay costs.

**snivellingly** (ˈsnɪv(ə)lɪŋlɪ), *adv.* [f. SNIVELLING *ppl. a.* + -LY².] In a snivelling or whimpering manner; abjectly.

**1959** *Times* 31 July 9/1 Mary [Queen of Scots] is presented as a creature of radiant perfection surrounded by snivellingly devoted waiting women and surly guards. **1970** N. FLEMING *Czech Point* (1971) i. 9 Beside him I would have appeared a snivellingly puny specimen.

† **ˈsnivellish**, *a. Obs.*⁻⁰ [f. SNIVEL *sb.*]

**1530** PALSGR. 324/2 Snevylysshe, full of snevyll, *morueux*.

† **ˈsnivelly**, *a. Obs.* Also 6 **snevelly, sniuely, -elie,** 6–7 **sniuelly** (7 **-ie**). [f. SNIVEL *sb.*]

**1.** Of the nature of snivel or mucus.

**1576** T. NEWTON tr. *Lemnie's Complex.* (1633) 175 A thicke, filthy, and snevelly Phlegme. **1608** TOPSELL *Serpents* (1658) 620 A foul, stinking, glutinous, and snivelly matter. **1658** ROWLAND tr. *Moufet's Theat. Ins.* 1109 Nothing else but snotty matter..or snivelly flegm.

**2.** Foul with snivel or mucus.

**1580** HOLLYBAND *Treas. Fr. Tong, Morveux*, snotty, sniuelly. **1598** FLORIO, *Moccicoso*, snottie, sniuelie. **1600** SURFLET *Countrie Farme* I. xiii. 89 [The cow's] wide nostrels and sniuely.

**snoach** (snəʊtʃ), *v. dial.* Also 4, 9 **snoche**, 9 **snōtch**. [Imitative.] *intr.* To snuffle; to breathe or speak through the nose, etc. Hence **ˈsnoaching** *vbl. sb.*

**1387** TREVISA *Higden* (Rolls) I. 11, I..schamede and dradde after so noble spekers..to putte forþ my bareyn speche, hosnes and snochynge. **1844** W. BARNES *Poems* Gloss. 350 *Snōtch*, to speak or breathe hardly through the nose. **1881** *Isle of Wight Gloss.* 33 *Snoche*, to speak with a nasal twang. **1886** *W. Somerset Word-bk.* s.v. *Snoachy*.

**snoak**, variant of SNOKE *v.*

**snoar**, obs. form of SNORE *v.*

**snob** (snɒb), *sb.*¹ Also 9 *Sc.* **snab**. [Orig. slang, of obscure origin.]

**1. a.** *dial.* or *colloq.* A shoemaker or cobbler; a cobbler's apprentice.

α. **1781** in Hone *Every-day Bk.* II. 837 Sir William Blase, a snob by trade. **1785** GROSE *Dict. Vulgar T.*, *Snob*, a nick name for a shoemaker. **1819** *Sporting Mag.* IV. 249 Tom Jenkins was known as a cobbler or snob. **1824** W. E. ANDREWS *Rev. Fox's Bk. Mart.* I. 252 Both Snip and Snob were burned for their pains. **1880** *Fraser's Mag.* Nov. 642 Even among the snobs the custom of the trade is against giving credit.

β. **1808** JAMIESON, *Snab*, a cant term for a..cobler's boy. **1813** PICKEN *Poems* II. 132 To flame as an author our Snab was sae bent. **1828** MOIR *Mansie Wauch* xiv, Rory Skirl, the snab, and Geordie Thump, the dyer. **1896** W. HARVEY *Kenneth-crook* 38 (E.D.D.), He had entered the craft in the usual way by being what the villagers called a 'snab'.

**b.** The last sheep to be sheared; hence, the roughest or most difficult sheep to shear; = COBBLER 1 b. *Austral.* and *N.Z. slang.*

**1945** C. E. W. BEAN *On Wool Track* (new ed.) 135 The sheep most difficult to shear, which naturally is left last in the pen, is also called the 'snob'. **1955** G. BOWEN *Wool Away!* 157 *Snob*, the last sheep in the pen. **1971** J. S. GUNN *Distrib. Shearing Terms N.S.W.* 9 As it is the practice to leave rough sheep until last it is only to be expected that *snob* and *cobbler* for both 'rough' and 'last' will occur... *Snob* and *cobbler* meant 'last' before specialising to 'rough'. **1975** L. RYAN *Shearers* i. 49 'Get on to this wrinkled bludger!' he said. It was the last sheep in the pen... 'Real snob, ain't it?'

†**2.** *Cambridge slang.* Any one not a gownsman; a townsman. *Obs.* (Cf. CAD² 4.)

*c* **1796** in Whibley *In Cap & Gown* (1889) 87 Snobs call him Nicholson! Plebeian name. **1828** *Sporting Mag.* XXI. 428 A capital front rank of 'tassells',..all eager for a 'slap at a snob'. **1865** *Sat. Rev.* Sept. 298/2 Happily the annals of Oxford present no instance of a 'snob' murdered in the streets.

**3. a.** A person belonging to the ordinary or lower classes of society; one having no pretensions to rank or gentility.

**1831** *Lincoln Herald* 22 July 3/6 The nobs have lost their dirty seats—the honest snobs have got 'em. **1834** W. H. BROOKFIELD in F. M. Brookfield *Cambridge 'Apostles'* (1906) iv. 66 *Snobs* go early [to the Grand Opera, Paris], buy pit tickets.., and beset comers at a quarter past seven to give them 5½ francs for their tickets. **1841** J. T. HEWLETT *Parish Clerk* III. 165 In the presence of a tail of snobs who accompanied him on his way. **1852** EARP *Gold Col. Austr.* 9 The majority of the colonists are essentially snobs, and they are justly proud of the distinction.

**b.** One who has little or no breeding or good taste; a vulgar or ostentatious person.

**1838** MRS. SHERWOOD *Henry Milner* III. ix. 175 He is a genteel young man—no snob—quite the gentleman. **1843** THACKERAY *Irish Sk. Bk.* Wks. 1879 XVIII. 111 A vulgar man in England..chiefly displays his character of snob by..swaggering and showing off in his coarse dull stupid way. **1859** *Slang Dict.* 97 *Snob*, a low, vulgar..person.

**c.** One who meanly or vulgarly admires and seeks to imitate, or associate with, those of superior rank or wealth; one who wishes to be regarded as a person of social importance.

**1848** THACKERAY *Bk. Snobs* i, I mean by positive [Snobs] such persons as are Snobs everywhere,..being by nature endowed with Snobbishness. **1860** H. MAYHEW *Upper Rhine* iv. i. 183 So necessary..are the professional titles considered by the supreme Snob of an authority from whom we quote. **1863** MISS BRADDON *J. Marchmont's Legacy* I. ii. 42 'What a snob I am,' he thought; 'always bragging of home'. **1882** MRS. RIDDELL *Pr. of Wales's Garden-Party* 127 He was..such a snob, he felt pleased his clerks should hear a butler ask for a situation.

**d.** One who despises those who are considered inferior in rank, attainment, or taste. Freq. in extended sense with defining word that limits its reference to a particular sphere.

Overlaps with sense 3 c.

**1911** G. B. SHAW *Getting Married* 228 All her childish affectations of conscientious scruple and religious impulse have been applauded and deferred to until she has become an ethical snob of the first water. **1925** F. SCOTT FITZGERALD *Great Gatsby* vii. 146 Listen, Tom. If you're such a snob, why did you invite him to lunch? **1931** A. HUXLEY *Music at Night* 121, I have met several adolescent consumption-snobs...these ingenuous young tubercle-snobs. **1935** C. ISHERWOOD *Mr Norris changes Trains* iv. 58, I rather enjoyed playing with the idea that he was, in fact, a dangerous criminal... Nearly every member of my generation is a crime-snob. **1939** [see INTELLECTUAL *a.* 1 b]. **1959** G. FREEMAN *Jack would be Gentleman* iii. 54 God knows, Moyra, I'm not a snob but that sort of person just wouldn't understand. **1960** J. O'HARA *Sermons & Soda-Water* I. 26 He doesn't want to know her any better and neither would my mother. That isn't snobbishness... You're the snob of us two. **1977** T. HEALD *Just Desserts* i. 16 He does..that frightful column in the Chronicle... The wine snob's guide to an early cirrhosis.

**e.** *inverted snob*: see INVERTED *ppl. a.* 9.

**4.** = BLACK-LEG *sb.* 3.

*a* **1859** DE QUINCEY (Webster), Those who work for lower wages during a strike are called snobs, the men who stand out being 'nobs'.

**5. a.** *attrib.*, as *snob ambition, jargon, -land, nature, ore, school, word*, etc.; *snob-free* adj.; **snob appeal**, attractiveness to snobs; **snob-stick**, = sense 4 (cf. KNOBSTICK 2); **snob value**, value as a commodity prized by snobs or as an indication of superiority.

Other examples occur in Thackeray's *Book of Snobs*.

**1866** CARLYLE *Remin.* (1881) II. 189 What of snob ambition there might be in me. **1933** LEAVIS & THOMPSON *Culture & Environment* 15 (*heading*) The snob appeal. **1943** *Scrutiny* XI. 289 There is, of course, the same snob-appeal, and just as Mr. Richards is always introducing a Shakespearean phrase.., so Jeeves is always quoting Pope. **1958** M. DICKENS *Man Overboard* xii. 192 There's a snob appeal about having a retired officer as bursar. **1978** J. PEARSON *Façades* vii. 127 Osbert and Edith [Sitwell]..had inherited..style; their snob appeal was undeniable. **1961** D. L. MUNBY *God & Rich Society* iv. 68 Americans and Scandinavians have a lot to teach us about real social equality and snob-free education. **1952** E. PARTRIDGE *From Sanskrit to Brazil* 59 The most dangerous snob jargon of all is that used by ordinarily well-educated..men and women. **1848** THACKERAY *Bk. Snobs* xxxii, O you pride of all Snobland! O you crawling, truckling..lacqueys and parasites! **1883** *Congregationalist* May 377 The snob nature comes out in strange ways. **1848** THACKERAY *Bk. Snobs* Pref., It is Beautiful..to sink shafts in society and come upon rich veins of Snob-ore. **1953** R. CHANDLER *Let.* 16 Sept. (1981) 351 If your boy won't behave himself..you can send him to one of the New England snob schools like Groton. **1978** M. BIRMINGHAM *Sleep in Ditch* 113 She'd been married, very young, almost the moment she'd left her snob school. **1860** *Slang Dict.* 221 *Snob-stick*, a workman who refuses to join in strikes, or trade unions. **1936** *Proc. Inst. Automobile Engineers* XXX. 762 Generally, if the big luxury car leads with any new refinement sooner or later the lower and lowest-priced cars follow, the new feature acquires from its aristocratic origin what has been aptly termed 'snob-value'. **1955** T. H. PEAR *Eng. Social Differences* 131 The terms of normal psychology have never achieved snob-value. **1969** M. FISH in A. S. C. Ross *What are U?* 78 It was an example of faulty handcraft giving a snob value to a product that could have been made more efficiently by machine. **1935** A. P. HERBERT *What a Word!* iv. 92 'Beginning' is musical and 'commencement' is not. Also, it is a Snob-word.

**b.** Used *predicatively* as *adj.*, fashionable, snobbish, pretentious.

**1958** *Spectator* 14 Feb. 209/3 A little slower than Buchan, a little less naively snob than Dornford Yates. **1970** *Daily Tel.* 9 Apr. 17/2 Champagne we consider too snob, and we're all off hard liquor. We drink wine now as an aperitif.

**snob** (snɒb), *sb.*² [Of obscure origin.] A game of cricket played with a soft ball and a thick stick in lieu of a bat. In full, *snob-cricket*. ? Now *obs.*

**1888** A. LANG in Steel & Lyttelton *Cricket* i. 1 There is a sport known at some schools as 'stump-cricket', 'snob-cricket', or..'Dex'. **1892** *Daily News* 6 May 5/2 They are subject to very dangerous accidents at cricket, and might well confine themselves to 'snob'. **1893** J. W. BAINES in A. G. Bradley et al. *Hist. Marlborough Coll.* xxii. 220 The great thing was 'Snob' cricket, which speedily became a most popular and fashionable pursuit. **1894** *Daily News* 10 May 6/1 Snob, or stump cricket, is indeed an excellent game. **1901** *Blackw. Mag.* Oct. 490/2 The game known as 'snob-cricket', little cricket, 'stump-and-ball', and so forth, might be introduced.

**snob**, *v.*¹ Now *dial.* Also 3–5 **snobbe**. [Imitative.] *intr.* To sob. Hence **ˈsnobbing** *vbl. sb.*

*c* **1300** *Old Age* vii. in *E.E.P.* (1862) 149, I snurpe, i snobbe, i sneipe on snovte. *a* **1380** *St. Ambrose* 940 in Horstm. *Altengl. Leg.* (1878) 23 He wept and snobbed and ofte abreid. **1388** WYCLIF *Lam.* iii. 56 Turne thou not awei thin eere fro my sobbyng [*v.r.* snobbyng] and cries. *c* **1420** *Chron. Vilod.* 1865 He with sore sykyng & snobbyng bothe Vnswered þe monke. *Ibid.* 1986 þus ladyes alle.. snobbedone & sykedone fulle sore. **1608** MIDDLETON *Mad World* III. ii, She cannot hear me for snobbing. **1668** L'ESTRANGE *Vis. Quev.* (1708) 124 There was such Blowing, Snobbing, Sniveling,..that there was no enduring the House. **18..** in *Eng. Dial. Dict.* s.v., She neither sighed, nor snobbed, nor spoke, nor nothing. **1884-** in dial. glossaries (Worc., Glouc.).

† **snob**, *v.*² *Obs.*⁻¹ [? var. of SNUB *v.* Cf. SNOBBERLY *adv.*] *intr.* To gird *at* something.

**1654** GAYTON *Pleas. Notes* III. vi. 107 A few words being spoken to Sancho, snobbing at his Insensiblenesse.

**snobber** (ˈsnɒbə(r)). *colloq.* [f. SNOB *sb.*¹ 1.] A shoemaker, cobbler.

**1900** *Daily News* 15 Aug. 6/4 She takes up with a worthy 'snobber' (shoemaker).

† **ˈsnobberly**, *adv. Obs. rare.* [app. related to SNOB *v.*²] Snubbingly.

*a* **1300** *Cursor M.* 24024 Vn-reufulli þai can him raipe, Ful snoberli [*Edinb.* snubnerlik] him for to snaipe.

**snobbery** (ˈsnɒbərɪ). [f. SNOB *sb.*¹ 3.]

**1.** The class of snobs.

**1833** *Lincoln Herald* 15 Jan. 3/6 In 'talking conversation' with some of the Snobbery of Brummagem. **1887** *Twin Soul* II. xvi. 198 The admiration of all the 'snobbery' of London.

**2. a.** The character or quality of being a snob; snobbishness; vulgar ostentation.

**1843** *Blackw. Mag.* LIII. 232 Snobbery, like murder, will out; and, if you do not happen to be a gentleman born [etc.]. **1853** GEO. ELIOT in Cross *Life* I. 315 They are two capital people, without any snobbery. **1891** *Speaker* 11 July 36/1 A type of snobbery which regards the established religion as a stepping-stone to respectability.

**b.** An instance of this; a snobbish trait.

**1866** *Cornh. Mag.* Nov. 632 Arms sometimes indispensable in mixed societies against the pushing snobberies of vulgar wealth. **1880** *Cope's Tobacco Plant.* Oct. 536/1 Hence youth rivals with youth..in varying vulgarest snobberies with maddest absurdities.

**c.** With defining word: pretension to superior knowledge, taste, etc., in a particular sphere.

**1903** [see INTELLECTUAL *a.* 1 b]. **1937** LD. SAMUEL *Belief & Action* iii. 30 It is a kind of cosmic snobbery to expect us to feel 'humble' in the presence of astronomical dimensions merely because they are big. **1977** *Times* 15 Nov. (Italian Wine Suppl.) p. i/3 It is perhaps another instance of declining wine snobbery when people want to offer a wine that is good but cheap.

**ˈsnobbess.** Also **snobess**. [f. SNOB *sb.*¹ 3.] A female snob.

**1869** *Punch* 14 Aug. 62/2 Reporters in front, snob and snobess behind! **1887** *Truth* 16 June 979 The crowd of snobs and snobesses.

**ˈsnobbiness.** *rare.* [f. SNOBBY *a.*] Snobbishness.

**1851** MILLAIS in J. G. Millais *Life* (1899) I. iv. 142 Revelling in snobbiness at having such distinguished persons at the farm.

**ˈsnobbing**, *vbl. sb.*¹ [f. SNOB *sb.*¹ 1.] The cobbling, or partial making, of boots.

**1880** *Fraser's Mag.* Nov. 643 It has become a custom to endeavour to get the necessary 'snobbing' done between Friday evening and Monday morning. **1900** ANNIE WAKEMAN *Autobiog. Charwoman* viii. 111, I could see meself a-learnin' the easy parts of shoe-makin'—sech as doin' the uppers, called snobbin'.

**ˈsnobbing**, *vbl. sb.*²: see SNOB *v.*¹

**snobbish** (ˈsnɒbɪʃ), *a.* [f. SNOB *sb.*¹ 3.]

**1.** Of, pertaining to, or characteristic of a snob.

**1840** DICKENS *Old C. Shop* lvi, This form of inquiry he held to be of disrespectful and snobbish tendency. **1846** THACKERAY *Snob Papers* Wks. 1886 XXIV. 332, I can conceive nothing more dangerous, insolent—Snobbish, in a word—than such an opposition. **1854** *Illustr. Lond. News* 8 July 7/2 The snobbish display of plush breeches. **1873** HAMERTON *Intell. Life* VII. iii. 242 You will not suspect me of a snobbish desire to pay compliments to royalty.

*absol.* **1848** THACKERAY *Bk. Snobs* Pref., It is Beautiful to study even the Snobbish; to track Snobs through history.

*Comb.* **1891** E. KINGLAKE *Australian* 144 It is doubtless not pleasant for the snobbish-minded man..to remember an origin of the kind.

**2.** Having the character of a snob.

**1849** SAXE *Poems, Proud Miss M'Bride* xv, Depend upon it, my snobbish friend, Your family thread you can't ascend. **1863** W. PHILLIPS *Speeches* xv. 325 Snobbish sons of fathers lately rich. **1885** *Spectator* 30 May 714/2 Julian is..vain, cowardly, snobbish, and untrustworthy.

Hence **ˈsnobbishly** *adv.*

**1848** THACKERAY *Bk. Snobs* iii, It encourages the commoner to be snobbishly mean. **1892** ZANGWILL *Bow Myst.* iv. 51 One whom he seems snobbishly anxious to claim as a friend.

**ˈsnobbishness.** [f. prec.] The character or quality of being snobbish.

**1846** THACKERAY *Snob Papers* Wks. 1886 XXIV. 318 This ..shameful caricature of a man which Snobbishness has set up to worship it. **1859** JEPHSON *Brittany* xvi. 274 So the insolent young sham-aristocrat was punished for his snobbishness. **1881** HUXLEY *Hume* v. 106 One of the most curious peculiarities of the dog mind is its inherent snobbishness.

**ˈsnobbism.** Also **snobism** [cf. SNOBISME.] [f. SNOB *sb.*¹ 3.] The characteristic qualities of a snob; snobbishness. Also, an instance or manifestation of this.

**1845** *Punch* June 254/1 We never saw any living creature in such a high state of snobbism. **1856** GEO. ELIOT *Ess.* (1884) 267 As long as snobbism runs in the blood, why should it not run in our speech? **1869** *Daily News* 2 Sept., All that has been said latterly about the snobbism of our countrymen.. on their travels. **1884** *Contemp. Rev.* Oct. 545 Is there any society.. where such a piece of snobbism could be represented as possible. **1895** [see EGOMANIA]. **1923** J. M. MURRY *Pencillings* 36 Dickens is safe, so safe indeed that within the next twelve months he may become a snobism in his turn... Although I have floundered into most of the artistic snobisms of my time..I have never deserted Mr. Micawber. **1932** P. BALFOUR *Society Racket* i. 48 'Belle's Letters', in which the great social figures..liked to be mentioned and to have their dresses described, is nauseous in its unabashed and luscious snobism. **1940** H. G. WELLS *All aboard for Ararat* iii. 84 Some mysterious process of snobism. **1966** *Punch* 20 July 124/2 It deflates a lot of irritating snobbisms and pomposities. **1972** *Science* 12 May 620/1 A union representative must cope with the inevitable snobbism of the better educated engineer or chemist.

**'snobbite.** *rare*$^{-1}$. In 8 snobite. [f. SNOB *sb.*[1] 2.] A townsman.

*c* **1796** in Whibley *In Cap & Gown* (1889) 87 Plebeian name Which ne'er would hand a Snobite down to fame.

**'snobby,** *a.* [f. SNOB *sb.*[1] 3.] Snobbish.

**1846** MRS. GORE *Eng. Char.* (1852) 128 Thither comes the snobby gig, conveying red-faced individuals. **1858** RAMSAY *Remin. Sc. Life & Char.* 60 If we can't get in with the nobs, ..we will never take up with any society that is decidedly snobby. **1888** *Temple Bar* Aug. 539 Perhaps he was snobby enough to object to my earning money.

**'snobdom.** [f. SNOB *sb.*[1] 3.] The aggregate of snobs; snobs collectively.

**1846** *New Monthly Mag.* Sept. 31 The congress of *mauvais sujets* from all parts of Snobdom, who infest Wiesbaden. **1851** MAYNE REID *Scalp Hunters* xxvi. 196 In savage as in civilized life there is a 'snobdom'. **1873** W. S. MAYO *Never Again* iv. 48 We must go..to England,..where a more rigid tabooism gives a wonderful exaltation to the idols of snobdom.

‖**snobisme** (snobizm). Also *erron.* **snobbisme.** [Fr.] = SNOBBISM.

**1913** E. MARSH in S. Hynes *Edwardian Turn of Mind* (1968) ix. 343, I went with Denis to the Ballet... It's *delicious*, I went thoroughly meaning to dislike it, so it isn't *snobisme* on my part. **1920** A. HUXLEY *Let.* 4 Mar. (1969) 182 What you must go and see in Paris is the Cirque Medrano. .. It's become rather a snobisme to go. **1931** *Punch* 23 Sept. 334 For a womanly yet talented woman of good family, with enough English *snobisme* to relish Society and enough Irish irresponsibility to take its awful procedure lightly. **1958** *Spectator* 18 July 86/2 The one-eyed monster..? Oh dear, must that particular *snobbisme* be perpetuated? **1968** J. M. WHITE *Night-climber* vii. 46 Always marvellous, that English nation, compounded equally of the Bible and *Snobisme*. **1977** T. HEALD *Just Desserts* vii. 145 It was undrinkable... No ludicrous snobisme about it being an English wine, could possibly persuade any normal palate of anything else.

**'snoblet.** *rare*$^{-1}$. [f. SNOB *sb.*[1] 3.] = next.

**1847** ALB. SMITH *Chr. Tadpole* li. (1879) 439 He looked as good a type of the party snoblet, as could be imagined.

**'snobling.** [f. SNOB *sb.*[1] 3.] A little, young, or petty snob. Also *attrib.*

**1848** THACKERAY *Bk. Snobs* xii, You see, dear Snobling, that..he might have been excused from interfering. **1876** *World* V. 13 Every brainless bank-clerk and snobling sub-inspector of constabulary. **1881** CLARK RUSSELL *Ocean Free Lance* II. iii. 149 The contemptuous usage every little snobling..thinks himself privileged to give us.

**snobocracy** (snɒ'bɒkrəsı). [f. SNOB *sb.*[1] 3 + -OCRACY.] The class of snobs, as having some power or exerting some influence. Also **snobo'cratic** *a.*

**1853** J. M. RICHMOND *Let.* 17 July in *Richmond-Atkinson Papers* (1960) I. 129 His impartiality..is not satisfactory to the 'snobocracy', as Jas calls the genteel of this place. **1854** LEVER *Dodd Family Abr.* lxvii, The fun derived from watching the 'snobocracy' I have mentioned. **1858** KINGSLEY *Misc.* (1859) I. 138 Soliciting the votes, not of the people, but of the Snobocracy. **1885** *Manch. Exam.* 7 Apr. 4/4 The Orange flag..would be floating over the houses of the Dublin snobocracy. **1960** *Times Lit. Suppl.* 16 Sept. 589/1 These days of tax-evader farmers and snobocratic huntsmen.

**sno'bographer.** [f. as prec. + -(O)GRAPHER.] A writer on, a describer of, snobs. So **sno'bography**, the description or delineation of snobs; **sno'bologist, sno'bonomer**, a student of, a specialist in, snobs.

**1848** THACKERAY *Bk. Snobs* xxxv, Up that long avenue the *Snobographer walked in solitude. **1868** *Imperial Rev.* Mar. 272, I may mention..that Thackeray, the great Snobographer, hated a Cad much more than he hated a Snob. **1966** *Punch* 29 June 965/3 Auchincloss has surpassed himself in this magnificent comedy of manners... He is *the* post-Freud snobographer. **1848** THACKERAY *Bk. Snobs* xxxviii, In the Country *Snobography my poor friend Ponto has been held up almost exclusively for the public gaze. **1884** *Sat. Rev.* 19 Jan. 76/1 The safer and wiser way in this infancy of the science of snobography is to refrain from the attempt at absolute aphorism. **1888** E. A. PARRY *Lett. Dorothy Osborne* Introd. 158 Both the circumstance and the doggerel should be very instructive to the *snobologist. **1848** THACKERAY *Bk. Snobs* xxiii, Some telescopic philosopher will arise one day, some great *Snobonomer [etc.].

**SNOBOL** ('snəubɒl). *Computers.* [Acronym f. the letters of '*s*tri*n*g-*o*riented sym*bo*lic *l*anguage', after *Cobol*, etc.: cf. STRING *sb.* 15.] A high-level programming language used chiefly in literary research and symbolic computation.

**1964** D. J. FARBER et al. in *Jrnl. Assoc. Computing Machinery* XI. 21 Interest in language translation, program compilation and combinatorial problems has increased... The string-orientated symbolic language SNOBOL has been developed with these problems in mind. **1969** *Computers & Humanities* IV. 74, I..began first to implement a year-long research project on rhythm in the Spanish language, using SNOBOL for text-manipulation and FORTRAN for statistical operations. **1971** *Ibid.* V. 156 SNOBOL IV..is a string manipulation and pattern-matching language and in this area makes both ALGOL and FORTRAN look clumsy... SNOBOL programs are typically shorter in character and line count than a FORTRAN or ALGOL counterpart. **1971** R. A. WISBEY *Computer in Lit. & Ling. Research* 165 The computer used in this study is the IBM 360/91. The language is SNOBOL 4, Version 3, a string manipulation language developed by Bell Telephone Laboratories, Inc.

**Sno-cat** ('snəukæt). orig. *U.S.* Also **sno-cat, Snocat, snocat.** [f. *sno*, an arbitrary respelling of SNOW *sb.*[1] + CAT(ERPILLAR 1 b.] A proprietary name in the U.S. for a type of snowcat (see SNOWCAT).

**1946** *Official Gaz.* (U.S. Patent Office) 10 Sept. 212/1 *Sno-cat.* No claim is made to the exclusive use of the word 'Sno' apart from the mark. For automotive vehicles for traveling over snow. Claims use since Sept. 1, 1941. **1957** *Times* 4 Dec. 11/7 The Snocat..came to the rescue and easily hauled both the Weasels and sledges on to better surfaces. **1958** *Listener* 13 Nov. 793/1 The popular impression that Antarctica is always and only white is matched by the suspicion that a modern expedition in those regions is all sno-cats and telecommunications. **1968** MRS. L. B. JOHNSON *White House Diary* 26 June (1970) 691 We got into a strange vehicle called a 'Sno-Cat', a long cab on caterpillar treads. **1970** *Observer* 20 Dec. 25/1 A wealthy industrialist seriously proposed running a Snocat service along the entire Haute Route. **1977** *New Scientist* 20 Jan. 123 The unloading operation was carried out with heavy cargo sledges towed in relays by snocats on the sea ice and caterpillar tractors on the ice shelf.

**snochynge:** see SNOACH *v.*

**snock.** *dial.* [prob. imitative.] A knock; a smart blow.

**1825** in JENNINGS *Obs. Dial. West Eng.* 71. **1898** T. HARDY *Wessex Poems* 46 Such snocks and slats since war began Never saw raw recruit or veteran.

**snockered** ('snɒkəd), *ppl. a. slang.* Also **snookered.** [Perh. arbitrary alteration of SNOOKERED *ppl. a.*] Drunk, intoxicated. Cf. SCHNOCKERED *ppl. a.*

**1961** S. PRICE *Just for Record* x. 105 You rolled along half-snockered after Sunday lunch. **1969** 'R. STARK' *Dame* xx. 121 'I may be a little high,' she said, 'but I'm not snockered.' **1977** *Amer. Speech* 1975 L. 66 *Snockered adj*, drunk. 'She was snockered; she didn't mean it.' **1980** *Globe & Mail* (Toronto) 4 Oct. 6/6 I'll get a bottle of Jack Daniel's for cocktails. Get them snockered on bourbon and they won't know the difference.

**snod** (snɒd), *a. Sc.* and *north. dial.* Also 7 **snoode** (?). [Of obscure origin: the stem may be the same as that of ON. *snoðinn* bald (Norw. *snoden* bare).]

**1.** Smooth, sleek; even. Also *absol.*

*c* **1480** HENRYSON *Fables, Wolf & Sheep* viii, He wald chais thame baith throw rouch and snod. **1513** DOUGLAS *Æneid* v. xiii. 24 His awin heid warpit with a snod olive, Heich in a schippis forcastell [he] did stand. *a* **1585** POLWART *Flyting w. Montgomerie* 562 Foot-foundred beasts ..Hes not their hair sa snod as other good. **1641** BEST *Farm. Bks.* (Surtees) 4 Howe to choose a good Tuppe. Lett him bee..of a snoode and goode stapple. **1692** A. SYMSON in *Macfarlane's Geogr. Coll.* (S.H.S.) II. 102 The long beards and awnds are separated from the corne; and the corne made, as they terme it, more snod and easie to pass through the mill. **1695** KENNETT *Par. Antiq.* Gloss. s.v. *Snodde*, Wheat ears are said to be *snod* when they have no beard or awns. And a tree is *snod* when the top is cut smooth off. **1781** J. HUTTON *Tour to Caves* (ed. 2) Gloss. 96 *Snod*, smooth. **1790** MRS. WHEELER *Westm. Dial.* (1821) 18 A lile stiff fello, wie a varra snod feace. **1862** C. C. ROBINSON *Dial. Leeds* 416 A snod piece o' cloath—as snod as a bit o' silk!

*Comb.* **1855** WAUGH *Life & Local.* 201 Rough and free as so many snod-backed young modiwarps. **1898** A. OLLIVANT *Owd Bob* xiii. 117 Ye ox-limbed, snod-faced profleegit!

**2.** Of persons: Neat, tidy, trim, smart, spruce.

**1691** RAY *N.C. Words* 66 *Snod*,..neat, handsome. **1719** RAMSAY *To Arbuckle* 71 A black-a-vic'd snod dapper fallow. **1756** MRS. CALDERWOOD *Jrnl.* (1884) 194 The niece was a little, snod, fair lass. **1822** GALT *Provost* xxvi, A tight and snod serving lassie. **1889** BARRIE *Window in Thrums* 14 Here comes the minister himsel', an' very snod he is.

**b.** Of things: Neat, trim, in good order.

**1717** RAMSAY *Elegy Lucky Wood* iv, She..kept her housie snod and bein. **1785** HUTTON *Bran New Wark* 3 The gentleman that treads in black snod pumps. **1819** W. TENNANT *Papistry Storm'd* (1827) 41 His velvet breeks,.. The snoddest pairt o' his attire. **1837** R. P. GILLIES *Recoll. Scott* III. ix. 199, I see ye're admiring how *snod* the library looks there. **1894** CROCKETT *Raiders* xxii. (ed. 3) 195 My clothes were clean brushed and exceedingly neat and snod.

**3.** Comfortable, snug, cosy. Also as quasi-*adv.*

**1695** KENNETT *Par. Antiq.* Gloss. s.v. *Snodde*, To lie snod and snug. **1888** BARRIE *When a Man's Single* (1900) 91/2 'Ay,' he said, with a chuckle, 'but I've a snod bit cornery up there for mysel''.

**snod** (snɒd), *v.* [f. prec.] *trans.* To make smooth, trim, or neat; to tidy, put in order. Also with *down, off, up.*

**1584** HUDSON *Judith* IV. 269 On stake and ryce, hee knits the crooked vines, And snoddes their bowes. *a* **1774** FERGUSSON *Poems* (1789) II. 7 Ye saw yoursel how weel his mailin' thrave, Ay better faugh'd an' snodit than the lave. **1791** J. LEARMONT *Poems* 85 The ploughman cultivates the field, The mower snods the common. **1819** SCOTT *Let.* in *Lockhart* (1837) IV. viii. 251, I have planted a number of shrubs,..and am snodding up the drive of the old farm house. **1865** G. MACDONALD *A. Forbes* xxvi. 115 The.. tallow candles..had..to be *snodded* laboriously.

†**snode.** *Obs.* Also 4 *north.* **snade.** [app. repr. OE. **snād*, unrecorded variant of *snǣd* SNEDE, related to *sníðan* SNITHE *v.*] A piece or bit (of bread or other food); a morsel.

α. *c* **1150** *Voc.* in Wr.-Wülcker 548 *Offa*, snode. *c* **1275** *Passion our Lord* 108 in *O.E. Misc.*, [Judas ate the bread] And þe veond him on bi-com myd þerylke snode. *a* **1300** *E.E. Psalter* cxlvii. 17 He sendes als snodes [L. *frusta panis*, or *buccellas*] his cristal. **1340** *Ayenb.* 111 Þe lecherous..þet ..uorzuelʒþ þane guode snode wyþ-oute chewynge. *Ibid.* 218 Hy..eteþ þe blodi snoden.

β. **13..** *Cursor M.* 15387 (Gött.), Þe morsel laght iudas, wid þat ilk snade..croupe in him sathanas. **13..** *Metr. Hom.* (Vernon MS.) in Herrig *Archiv* LVII. 313 Was neuere Beggere þat þer bade At his hous gete bite or snade.

**snodger** ('snɒdʒə(r)), *a.*, (*adv.*, and *sb.*). *Austral.* and *N.Z. slang.* ? *Obs.* [Of uncertain origin: cf. SNOD *a.* and SNOG *a.*] Excellent, very good, first-rate. Also as *adv.* and *sb.*

**1919** W. H. DOWNING *Digger Dial.* 46 Snodger (adj.), excellent. **1924** C. J. DENNIS *Rose of Spadgers* 40 It was a snodger day!.. The apple trees was white with bloom. All things seemed good to me. **1941** BAKER *N.Z. Slang* vi. 51 Expressions..in constant use by our youngsters..stunner, snorter, snodger, ripsnorter. **1946** *Sunday Sun* (Austral.) 11 Aug. (Suppl.) 15 There they find the con-ships fitted up snodger with bulkheads studded with nails. **1950** *Austral. Police Jrnl.* Apr. 119 If something is a snodger it is 'mighty' in Queensland, it is 'colossal' in N.S.W., and just 'very nice' everywhere else.

**snodly** ('snɒdlı), *adv. Sc.* [f. SNOD *a.* + -LY[2].] Neatly, tidily, trimly.

**1721** RAMSAY *Scribblers Lashed* 75 'Till by degrees it creeps right snodly, On hips and head-dress of the godly. **1791** J. LEARMONT *Poems* 304 Here's something here..will mak life's road to me fu' snodly sleekit. **1823** GALT *R. Gilhaize* lxxii, A clean cambric handkerchief very snodly prined over her breast. **1850** W. HOWSON *Cur. Craven* 118 Shadows flicker On the snodly whitewesh'd wa'. **1904** *Dundee Advertiser* 19 Aug. 6 We took the short road by Burns' Monument and the snodly theekit hoosie at the wayside.

‖**snoek** (snu:k; S.Afr. snʊk), *sb.* Also **snook.** [Du. *snoek* pike: cf. SNOOK[2].] A snake mackerel, *Thyrsites atun*, of the family Gempylidæ, a large marine food fish found in large shoals in colder parts of Southern Hemisphere oceans. Cf. BARRACUDA. Also *attrib.* and *Comb.*

**1797** A. BARNARD *Jrnl.* in *Lives of Lindsays* (1849) 388 The fish called *snook*..when salted and dried, was one of the best fish at the Cape. *a* **1823** J. EWART *Jrnl. Stay Cape Good Hope* (1970) ii. 13 Snoek, a long oily fish which being caught in great quantities and consequently cheap, forms the principal food of the slaves. **1833** *Graham's Town* (Cape Province) *Jrnl.* 14 Feb. 3 Phosphorescent glimmerings of a decayed Snoek. **1853** PAPPE *Edible Fishes C. Good Hope* 24 *Thyrsites Atun.* Cuv. and Val. (Snook; Snoek). **1872** HUTTON & HECTOR *Fishes N. Zealand* s.v. *Thyrsites Atun*, This is, I believe, the fish called snook in Cape Colony. **1880** A. C. L. G. GÜNTHER *Introd. Study of Fishes* 436 In New Zealand it is called 'barracuda' or 'snoek'. **1889** *Science-Gossip* XXV. 50 The unhappy snoek-eaters wander about like so many grown children afflicted with mumps. **1896** BADEN-POWELL *Matabele Campaign* i, Old Cape Town just the same as ever... Malays and snoek fish everywhere. **1913** D. FAIRBRIDGE *That which hath Been* 73 An old Malay fisherman, carrying his baskets of snoek. **1931** *Times Lit. Suppl.* 16 Apr. 301/2 The snoek..is not a pike..but a distant cousin of the mackerel. **1946** L. G. GREEN *So Few are Free* iv. 57 Snoek are caught by each boat's crew at the rate of a thousand to three thousand a day. **1963** S. COOPER in Sissons & French *Age of Austerity* 51 In October 1947.. the hungry British first heard the word 'snoek'. Ten million tins of it from South Africa were to replace Portuguese sardines. **1974** *Stand. Encyl. S. Afr.* X. 28/1 The snoek is also an important food fish in Australia.

**snoek** (snu:k; S.Afr. snʊk), *v. S. Afr.* [f. the sb.] *intr.* To fish for snoek. Hence **'snoeker; 'snoeking** *vbl. sb.*

**1913** W. W. THOMPSON *Sea Fisheries Cape Colony* ii. 50 It is a pretty sight to watch a fleet of fishing boats snoeking under sail. **1937** L. G. GREEN *Great Afr. Mysteries* xii. 137 The total catch by all the snoeking vessels often amounts to a million fish. **1950** *Cape Argus* 28 Oct. (Mag. Section) 3 Fishermen declare that China snoek are caught after the ordinary snoeking season is over. **1952** L. G. GREEN *Lords of Last Frontier* xxi. 299 Snoeking, a trade that has prospered here for forty years, keeps a grand fleet of small craft in commission. **1959** *Cape Times* 5 May 2/7 (*heading*) Snoeker found ringed bird. *Ibid.*, While snoeking at St. Helena Bay, John Mentor..found a dead black sea-duiker.

**snoff.** *Cornish mining.* [A survival of the early form of SNUFF *sb.*[1]] (See quots.)

**1860** *Eng. & For. Mining Gloss.* (ed. 2) 23 *Snoff, or Match*, ..brown paper, or other slowly combustible substance, which is ignited at one end, the other being in contact with the rush or train in blasting. **1881** RAYMOND *Mining Gloss.*, *Snoff*, a short candle-end, put under a fuse to light it. **1891**

J. H. Pearce *Esther Pentreath* I. i, Dick having charged the hole with powder, set fire to the train with a 'snoff' from his candle.

**snoffe**, obs. form of snuff *sb.*[1] and *v.*

**snog** (snɒg), *a.* *north. dial.* and †*Sc.* [app. a. ON. *snǫgg-r* smooth, short-haired, etc. (cf. the etym. note to snug *a.*[1]).] Smooth, sleek; neat, tidy. Hence **'snogly** *adv.*

**1513** Douglas *Æneid* XII. Prol. 186 All snog and slekyt worth thir bestis skynnis. **1615** Crooke *Body of Man* 1111 Thin they are and conuex, that they might lye more snogly vpon the fingers. **1691** Ray *N.C. Words* 66 Snog, neat, handsome: as *snogly gear'd*, handsomely drest. *Ibid.*, *Snog* Malt, smooth with few Combs. **1818** Scott *Hrt. Midl.* xxxii, Thou wouldst be a mettle lass enow, an thou wert snog and snod a bit better. **1855** [Robinson] *Whitby Gloss.*, *Snod and Snog*, smooth and compact.

†**snog**, *v.*[1] *Obs.*$^{-0}$ [Cf. snoggy.] *intr.* To bristle.

**1530** Palsgr. 724/1 I snogge, *je herisonne.*

**snogging** ('snɒgɪŋ), *vbl. sb.* *slang.* [Origin unknown: cf. snug *v.*] Engagement in light, amorous play, esp. kissing and cuddling.

**1945** C. H. Ward-Jackson *It's a Piece of Cake* (ed. 2) 56 *Snogging*, courting, running around with the opposite sex. Comes from India. Thus, 'On my leave I'm going up to the hills for a bit of snogging.' Also used as a verb. **1951** *Sunday Pictorial* 28 Oct. 10/6 Few hounds can get in more than half an hour of 'snogging'—their elegant term for not-too-serious courtship. **1960** N. Epton *Love & English* vi. 341 It is all right..to cuddle. (The current term among teen-agers is 'snogging'.) **1966** P. Willmott *Adolescent Boys* iii. 40, I went upstairs with Jill and we did a bit of snogging on the bed. **1975** *Weekend* 4 Feb. 19/1 If a cinema manager tolerates snogging among his audience he is liable to lose his licence.

Also **snog** *v.*[2] *intr.*, to engage in snogging; **snog** *sb.*, an instance of this; **'snogger, 'snogging** *ppl. a.*

**1945** [see snogging *vbl. sb.*]. **1958** 'J. Brogan' *Cummings Report* xv. 156 He is a..girl-snogging..bounder. **1959** W. Camp *Ruling Passion* xii. 82 Let's pretend we're teenagers and stop for a nice snog. **1962** A. Sampson *Anat. Britain* xxxvi. 574 The cinema has lost its hold—except among unmarried teenagers, two-thirds of whom go at least once a week, perhaps to snog in the doubles. **1965** J. Gaskell *Fabulous Heroine* 94 A most experienced snogger. **1973** M. Amis *Rachel Papers* 21 They were enjoying a kiss—well, more of a snog really. **1981** R. Barnard *Mother's Boys* ii. 20 They had..taken the side way through the little cutting known popularly as 'Snoggers Alley'.

†**'snoggy**, variant of (or error for) snaggy *a.*

**1670** Covel in *Early Voy. Levant* (Hakl. Soc.) 141 They were all short, snoggy trees, much loaded with boughs.

**snogly**, *adv.*: see snog. *a.*

**Snohomish** (snəʊ'həʊmɪʃ), *a.* and *sb.* Also Snow-. [19th-cent. Puget Salish *snuhumš*.]

**A.** *adj.* Of or pertaining to the Snohomish or their language. **B.** *sb.* (A member of) a Salish Indian people of western Washington; also, their language.

**1856** N. D. Hill *Let.* 30 Sept. in *U.S. Congr. House Exec. Doc.* (1857) XXXVII. 77, I received a letter from you appointing me the local agent for the Snohomish, the Snoqualmi, and the Skiquamish tribes of Indians. **1874** *Field & Stream* 20 Aug. 18/3 This assertion was verified afterwards by a Snohomish Indian. **1910** F. W. Hodge *Handbk. Amer. Indians* II. 606/2 Snohomish. A Salish tribe formerly on the s. end of Whidbey id., Puget sd., and on the mainland opposite at the mouth of Snohomish r., Wash. Pop. 350 in 1850. The remnant is now on Tulalip res., Wash., mixed with other broken tribes. **1940** M. W. Smith *Puyallup-Nisqually* 17 In the Puyallup-Nisqually dialect the word means butte or rump but informants thought it might mean something else in the dialects of either the Twana or Snohomish. **1966** *Internat. Jrnl. Amer. Linguistics* XXXII. 350/2 Snowhomish..was spoken in the region around Port Gardner Bay..and along the Snowhomish River. **1977** C. F. & F. M. Voegelin *Classification & Index World's Lang.* 301 Puget Sound Salish = Puget = Toughnowawmish. D[ialect]s Northern Puget Sound (Skagit, Snohomish), Southern Puget Sound (Duwamish, Muckleshoot, Nisqualli, Puyallup, Snoqualmie, Suquamish). 10–20. Washington.

**snoif**, obs. form of snoove *v.* *Sc.*

**snoir(e**, obs. Sc. forms of snore *sb.*

**snoke** (snəʊk), *v.* Chiefly *north.* and *Sc.* Forms: α. 4–5, 9 **snoke** (5 **snokyn**), 6 *Sc.* **snokk-**, 9 **snoak.** β. 6 **snooke**, 7– **snook** (8 *dial.* **snooac**). γ. 7– **snouk**, 8– **snowk.** [prob. of Scand. origin: cf. Norw. dial. *snōka* to snuff, smell.] *intr.* and *trans.* To snuff or smell; to go snuffing or smelling (at); to poke about with the nose. Also *fig.*, to sneak about, to keep watch *over*, etc.

α. *c* **1380** Wyclif *Sel. Wks.* II. 83 Disciplis of Crist wenten into þe citee to bie hem mete; for þei snokiden not fro hous to hous and beggiden mete, as freris doon. *c* **1475** *Promp. Parv.* 462/1 (MS. K.), Snokyn, or smellyn, *nicto.* **1500** *Ortus Vocab.* BB vij, *Nicto*,..to snoke as a honde dos. **1513** Douglas *Æneid* v. ii. 99 The drink, and eik the offerandis gret and small, [the snake] Snokkis [*v.r.* snokis] and likkit. **1831** J. Wilson *Noct. Ambr.* Wks. 1855 III. 98 After smellin an' snokin an' snortin at it for a while. **1834** M. Scott *Cruise Midge* xxi, He lay still, with the beast..poking down its head, and snorting and snoking at him.

β. **1570** Levins *Manip.* 159/35 To Snooke, *olfacere.* **1608** Hieron *Defence* II. 8 Whether he snooketh not as right into Rheames and Rome as maie be [etc.]. **1641** Best *Farm. Bks.* (Surtees) 74 The hogges went snuffinge and snookinge from heape to heape. *a* **1652** Brome *New Acad.* II. i, I must not lose my harmlesse recreations Abroad, to snook over my wife at home. **1687** Miège *Gt. Fr. Dict.* II, To Snook, or ly lurking for a thing. **1722** Wodrow *Hist. Suff. Ch. Scot.* III. viii. II. 449 The Dogs would snook and smell about the Stones under which they were hid, and yet they remained undiscovered. **1788** W. H. Marshall *Yorksh.* II. 354 To *Snooac*, to smell in a snuffing manner. **1834** [Seba Smith] *Lett. J. Downing* (1835) 106 All we've got to do is to open that, and snook among old papers. **1891** R. Ford *Thistledown* ix. 163 That we do not gang..snookin' amang the snaw like mowdiewarts.

γ. **1624** Sanderson *Serm.* I. 241 Like swine under the oaks, we grouze up the acorns, and snouk about for more. **1786** Burns *Twa Dogs* 39 Wi' social nose [the dogs] whyles snuff'd an' snowket. **1861** Quin *Heather Lintie* (1863) 76, I snouk aboot For 'tatty peels and banes o' herrin'. **1894** Crockett *Raiders* xlv. 384 Gin ony o' Agnew's men were gaun snowkin' roond, it micht cause misunderstandings.

Hence **'snoking** *vbl. sb.*

*c* **1440** *Promp. Parv.* 462/1 Snokynge, *olfactus.*

†**snoke-horn.** *Obs.*$^{-1}$ ? A sneaking fellow.

*c* **1460** *Towneley Myst.* ix. 80 Then were my worshyp lorne, If sych a swayn, a snoke horne, Shuld thus be my suffrane.

**'snokey**, *a.* *rare*$^{-1}$. [f. snoke *v.*] Adapted for snuffing or poking.

**1828** *Blackw. Mag.* XXIII. 865 Nuzzling with that snokey nose of his.

**snollygoster** ('snɒlɪgɒstə(r)). *U.S. dial.* and *slang.* [Perh. connected with snallygaster, which is, however, of more recent appearance.] A shrewd, unprincipled person, esp. a politician. Also in other more or less fanciful uses (see quots.).

**1846** *Commonwealth* (Frankfort, Kentucky) 7 Apr. 2/6 Now here I am a rale propelling, double revolving locomotive Snolly Goster, ready to attack anything. **1863** D. Emmett *Black Brigade* 5 We am de snolly-gosters, An' lubs Jim Ribber oysters. **1895** *Columbus* (Ohio) *Dispatch* 28 Oct. 4/3 A Georgia editor kindly explains that 'a snollygoster is a fellow who wants office, regardless of party, platform or principles, and who, whenever he wins, gets there by the sheer force of monumental talknophical assumnacy'. **1912** *Dialect Notes* III. 590 *Snolly-goster*, a shyster. **1915** *Nebraska State Jrnl.* 7 Sept. 6/3 We once knew a miserly old *snollygoster* who used to look in a mirror to see the reflection of a saint. **1952** *N.Y. Herald Tribune* 3 Sept. 17/2 President Truman..said some people like to pray in public so that others will view them as honorable and religious men... 'I wish some of these snollygosters would read the New Testament and perform accordingly.' **1953** *Cavalier Daily* (Univ. of Virginia) 12 Nov. 1/2 Former President Truman may have been making a talknophical assumnacy when he said a snollygoster is what Southerners call a man born out of wedlock. **1972** A. Roudybush *Sybaritic Death* xx. 168 The deaths of a middle-aged tart and an elderly snollygoster are of little moment.

**snomobile**, var. snowmobile.

**snood** (snu:d), *sb.* Forms: 1 snod, 6– (*Sc.* and *north.*) **snude** (9 **sneud**), 7– **snood** (9 **snoud**); *north.* 8 **snead**, 9 **sneiad**; *Sc.* 9 **snid, sneed**, etc. [OE. *snód*, of obscure origin.]

**1. a.** A fillet, band, or ribbon, for confining the hair; latterly, in Scotland (and the north of England), the distinctive hair-band worn by young unmarried women. More recently, a fashionable bag-like or closed woman's hairnet, usu. worn at the back of the head.

*c* **725** *Corpus Gloss.* (Hessels) C 137 *Cappa*, snod. *a* **1000** in Wr.-Wülcker 204 *Cinthium, mitra*, snod. *c* **1000** Ælfric *Hom.* II. 28 Þa lærde hi sum iudeisc man, þæt heo name ænne wernægel..and becnytte to anum hringe mid hire snode. *c* **1150** in Wr.-Wülcker 540 *Uitta*, snod.

**1535** Stewart *Cron. Scot.* I. 377 Ȝone ma nocht saif thair bodie with ane snude. **1643** *Orkney Witch Trial* in *Abbotsford Club Misc.* I. 177 Ȝe said vnto hir that ȝe haid Vrsulla Alexanderis snood, quhilk ȝe haid keipit since ȝe put hir in hir winding sheit. **1677** Nicholson in *Trans. R. Soc. Lit.* (1870) IX. 319 *Snude*, a fillet, or hair lace. **1725** Ramsay *Gentle Sheph.* II. iv, The rashes green..Of which..For thee I plet the flow'ry belt and snood. **1771** Pennant *Tour in Scotl.* (1794) 213 The single women wear only a ribband round their head, which they call a snood. **1810** Scott *Lady of L.* III. v, No hunter's hand her snood untied, Yet ne'er again to braid her hair The virgin snood did Alice wear. **1840** Barham *Ingol. Leg.* Ser. II. *Bloudie Jacke of Shrewsberie* (1905) 322 While her tresses are bound with a snood. **1889** R. Buchanan *Heir of Linne* vii, Her hair was bound up in a simple snood. **1938** *Sun* (Baltimore) 22 Oct. 5/6 (*caption*) New hats in vivid colors... Shakos, pill boxes, turbans, brims, pie plates and snoods. **1939** in C. W. Cunnington *English Women's Clothing* (1952) vii. 262 A spate of hoods and snoods. **1944** M. Laski *Love on Supertax* x. 92 She carefully placed on the top of her head a little forward-tilting black hat whose draped jersey snood just failed to conceal the mass of yellow wrinkles. **1947** E. Jenkins *Young Enthusiasts* 47 They..wore ribbon snoods secured under their buns. **1968** J. Ironside *Fashion Alphabet* 148 A knitted or open-work 'bag' over the back of the hair. Sometimes a snood is attached to a hat.

†**b.** ? A skein. *Obs.*$^{-1}$

**1425** in Kennett *Par. Antiq.* (1695) Gloss. s.v. *Snodde*, In viii snoden de Pakthred.

**2. a.** In sea-fishing: One of a number of short lines, each carrying a baited hook, attached at regular distances along the main line.

*c* **1682** J. Collins *Salt & Fishery* 112 To each of these are fastned 20 Snoods, *alias* Nossels, which are small Lines, with Hooks and Baits at them. **1769** Pennant *Brit. Zool.* (1776) III. 205 The hooks are fastened to the lines upon sneads of twisted horse hair 27 inches in length. **1793** *Statist. Acc. Scotl.* VII. 204 The quantity of line..contains ..720 hooks,..one yard distant from each other, on snoods of horse hair. **1848** *Chambers's Information for People* I. 699 These are long lines, with hooks fastened at regular distances..by shorter and smaller cords called *snoods.* **1883** *Fisheries Exhib. Catal.* 7 Simple Machine, for making Norsels or Snoods of any length.

**b.** *Angling.* A hair or catgut line attaching the hook to the rod line.

**1823** E. Moor *Suffolk Words*, *Snood*, that part of an angler's line to which the hook is affixed. **1832** W. H. Maxwell *Wild Sp. West* I. 263, I..lost time, hooks, and snouds. **1873** W. Graham in *Harp of Perthshire* (1893) 149 My licht thrown snood scarce touched the flood When doun it flew like lichtnin'.

**snood** (snu:d), *v.* [f. prec.]

**1.** *trans.* To bind *up*, fasten *back*, or secure (the hair) with a snood.

**1725** Ramsay *Gentle Sheph.* I. i, Her cockernony snooded up fou sleek. **1793** *Statist. Acc. Scotl.* IX. 325 At home they went bareheaded, with their hair snooded back on the crown of their head, with a woollen string in the form of a garter. **1818** Scott *Hrt. Midl.* xiv, Her hands trembled as she snooded her fair hair beneath the riband. **1837** Carlyle *Fr. Rev.* III. VII. ii, Her sweeping tresses snooded by glittering antique fillet. **1890** *Pall Mall G.* 29 Jan. 6/3 The new fashion of wearing the hair snooded low on the nape of the neck.

*transf.* **1856** S. Dobell *Eng. in Time of War, Home, Wounded* 27 Where The larch is snooding her flowery hair With wreaths of morning shadow.

**2.** *Angling.* To attach (a hook) to a snood.

**1840** Marryat *Poor Jack* vi, He was snooding a hook.

**snooded** ('snu:dɪd), *ppl. a.* [f. snood *sb.* or *v.*] Wearing a snood; bound by a snood.

**1810** Scott *Lady of L.* III. xx, And plaided youth, with jest and jeer, Which snooded maiden would not hear. **1847** Whittier *Barclay of Ury* 81 The snooded daughter.. Smiled on him who bore renown. **1898** R. Buchanan *Father Anthony* xvii, Her hand stole up to her head and touched the snooded folds of the locks.

**snooding** ('snu:dɪŋ). [f. snood *sb.* 2.] The material used for fishing-snoods.

**1815** *Sporting Mag.* XLV. 153 Hempen snooding I always have sold, That will ne'er lose the fish, while the hook have her hold. **1873** G. C. Davies *Mount. & Mere* xix. 176 At short intervals were hooks attached to lengths of snooding. **1884** *Sat. Rev.* 603/1 The amateur, provided with his.. Manchester snooding, his gut trace, and his artificial spinner.

**snoodle** ('snu:d(ə)l), *v.* *dial.* (chiefly *north.*) or nursery. Now *rare.* [See *Eng. Dial. Dict.*: prob. rel. to snudge *v.*[2], snuggle *v.*, etc.] *intr.* To snuggle, nestle. Also *trans.*

**1887** in T. Darlington *Folk-Speech S. Cheshire* 355. **1898** R. Dottie *Rambles & Recoll.* '"R" Dick' 115 Eaur snug, white hostelry snoodlin' i' th' valley. **1904** J. Vaizey *More about Pixie* (1910) i. 9 She snoodled her head along the pillow so as to lean it against the nurse's shoulder. **1908** E. J. Banfield *Confessions of Beachcomber* I. i. 32 Snoodling beside lumps of coral or beneath weather-beaten driftwood, they [*sc.* young birds] afford startling proof of the effect of sympathetic coloration.

†**snook**, *sb.*[1] *north.* and *Sc.* *Obs.* Forms: 3 **snoc, snoke**, 4–5 **snuk(e, snwk**, 7 **snewke.** [Of obscure origin: cf. nook *sb.*[1]] A projecting point or piece of land; a promontory.

*c* **1236** *Newminster Cartul.* (Surtees) 55 In illa parte agri quæ vocatur le Snoc. ? **1297** *Documents Illustr. Hist. Scotl.* (1870) II. 160 In factura pontis castri Berwyci, muri lapidei juxta mare subtus le Snoke. **1375** Barbour *Bruce* I. 188 Fra Weik anent Orknay To Mullyr-snwk in Gallaway. *Ibid.* IV. 556 On Turnberyis nwk [*v.r.* snuke] he may Mak a fyre. *c* **1470** Henry *Wallace* VII. 1044 Furth thai fle Till Dwnottar, a snuk within the se. **1648** Blaeu *Atlas Engl.*, *Map of Insvla Sacra*, The Snewke or Conny warren.

**snook** (snu:k), *sb.*[2] [ad. Du. *snoek* pike: cf. snoek *sb.*] A name given to various fishes, esp. the sergeant-fish, *Elacate canada*, and the robalo, *Centropomus undecimalis.*

**1697** Dampier *Voy.* (1699) 243 The Fish I observed here mostly, were what we call Snooks, neither a Sea fish nor a fresh Water fish, but very numerous in these salt Lakes. **1725** Sloane *Jamaica* II. 288 Snook. It was taken at Passage fort. **1827** O. W. Roberts *Voy. Centr. Amer.* 156 It [Caratasca Lagoon] abounds in various sorts of fish of the finest description, particularly mullet, calapaner, snoak, cavallee, and also manatee. **1858** Simmonds *Dict. Trade*, *Snook*, a common fish, both of the sea and the rivers of the West Indies, the *Centropomus undecimalis.* **1883** *Fisheries Exhib. Catal.* (ed. 4) 170 Model of Fresh-water Fishpot, for taking mullet, snook, &c.

**snook** (snu:k), *sb.*[3] Also snooks. [Of obscure origin.] A derisive gesture, = sight *sb.*[1] 7 c. Chiefly in phr. *to cock a snook* (*at*).

**1791** E. Wynne *Diary* 7 Dec. (1935) I. 90 They *cock snooks* at one on every occasion. **1879** A. J. C. Hare *Story Life* (1900) V. 218 If I put my hands so..(cutting a snooks), they might reproach me very much indeed. **1904** *Times* 24 Sept. 8/3 The young monkey puts his tongue in his cheek and cocks a snook at you. **1906** Drury *Men at Arms* 36 Her Majesty's ship..cocked her jibboom snooks-fashion at her late enemy the sea. **1929** H. S. Walpole *Hans Frost* I. vii. 78 He was like a dirty street boy cocking a snook at Sappho. **1938** E. Ambler *Cause for Alarm* viii. 128 The Rome-Berlin axis..cocked the biggest snook yet at the League of Nations idea. **1959** M. Cumberland *Murmurs in Rue Morgue* v. 38 With his right hand he made the somewhat coarse gesture known as 'cocking a snook'. The thumb and extended fingers, spread in front of the face, made a baffling disguise. **1961** B. Fergusson *Watery Maze* ii. 48 It would be idle to pretend that it was of much importance; it was really only cocking a vulgar snook. **1965** *Listener* 9 Sept. 374/2, I walked past the Thatched House.. where I and other young journalists used to cock snooks at our superiors. **1980** *Times* 29 Feb. 10 East German craft last spring embarked upon a new ploy..to net a Danish torpedo,..cooking a snook at Nato's Baltic muscle.

Hence **'snook-cocking** *vbl. sb.*, **snook-cockingly** *adv.*; **snook-cocker.**

**1950** D. Gascoyne *Vagrant* 57 And not think them impudent snook-cocking. **1958** *Economist* 6 Dec. 880/2 The seven Liberal councillors of Finchley..in snook-cocking protest against the local shortcomings of London Transport's bus service have launched a free private service of their own. **1962** *Spectator* 13 Apr. 478 A snook-cockingly 'blasphemous' film. **1965** E. Gowers *Fowler's Mod. Eng. Usage* (ed. 2) 535/2 Mere snook-cockers of whom it has been said..that their only concern is to 'find someone who is doing something..and fling a few insults at him'. **1978** Cadogan & Craig *Women & Children First* viii. 167 Spike Milligan's snook-cocking record of his war-time experiences.

**snook**, variant of snoke *v.*

**snooker** ('snu:kə(r)), *sb.*[1] *Woolwich slang.* A newly joined cadet.

**1872** *Routledge's Ev. Boy's Ann.* 148/1 These embryo generals..were called by the somewhat sneering terms of 'snookers' or 'last-joined'.

**snooker** ('snu:kə(r)), *sb.*[2] [Of obscure origin.] A game, played with balls on a billiard table, combining pool and pyramids. Also ***snooker('s) pool.***

It is commonly held that the word represents an allusive use of snooker *sb.*[1], a newly joined cadet, first applied to the game by Col. Sir Neville Chamberlain (1856–1944), a subaltern in the Devonshire Regiment stationed at Jubbulpore in central India in 1875, with reference to the rawness of the play of a fellow officer. The story is often repeated, e.g. in *The Times* (1980) 29 Dec. 9.

**1889** Drayson *Pract. Billiards* 110 The game of snooker. **1896** W. Broadfoot *Billiards* xiii. 424 Snooker—or to give it its full title, Snooker's Pool—is a hybrid game, half pool and half pyramids. **1905** Glasfurd *Rifle in Ind. Jungle* 70 The old Doctor and we two, after several games of 'Snookers', had passed into the ante-room.

Hence **'snooker** *v.* (see quots.); also *fig.* (chiefly *pass.*), to place in an impossible position; to balk, 'stymie'; **'snookered** *ppl. a.*, **'snookering** *vbl. sb.*

**1889** Drayson *Pract. Billiards* 111 If each pool ball is covered by a pyramid ball, the player is said to be 'snookered'. **1896** W. Broadfoot *Billiards* xiii. 426 If the striker is by law obliged to play on a red ball or on a coloured ball, but..is unable to do so directly, he is said to be snookered. **1915** *Morning Post* 8 Apr. 5/1 If we had fired the Germans might have sent up a light and then we should have been snookered all right. **1927** C. Mackenzie *Vestal Fire* i. i. 5 One of the recognized amusements of a Sirene dinner-party was to try to snooker Joseph R. Neave over Dante. **1935** *Times* 5 Oct. 5/6 The snookering all through was clever. **1970** K. Giles *Death in Church* iii. 65 In France they might have had a chance..but here they were snookered.

**Snooks** (snu:ks). A proper name or familiar appellation applied to a hypothetical person in a particular case (see quots.); also, any individual person. Cf. *Joe Bloggs* s.v. Joe *sb.*[2] 5 c.

**1860** Hotten *Dict. Slang* (ed. 2) 221 *Snooks*, an imaginary personage often brought forward as the answer to an idle question, or as the perpetrator of a senseless joke. **1919** G. B. Shaw *Inca of Perusalem* in *Heartbreak House* 214 Well, what about Snooks? **1922** Ld. Riddell *Some Things that Matter* ix. 108 '50 per cent of the inhabitants of Bunkumville who use this valuable adjunct to health and personal beauty wear Snooks's Expanders, which are undoubtedly the best.' That may be true, but I omit to mention that only two persons in Bunkumville wear chest expanders, one of whom is Snooks himself. **1959** *Times* 8 Dec. 13/4 The recommended formula goes something like this: 'This is Flaxway 5768. Mr. Snooks is out. If you wish to leave a message, go ahead.'.. Snooks, returning eventually to base, presses a button, and the machine reels off all the messages.

**snookums** ('snu:kəmz). [Nonsense formation: cf. diddums and prec.] A trivial term of endearment, usu. applied to children or lap-dogs.

**1919** *Ladies' Home Jrnl.* May 153/1 Even 'Snookums' knows and appreciates the soothing qualities of Johnson's Toilet and Baby Powder. **1928** *Chambers's Jrnl.* 21 Jan. 128/2 She is now a 'city-lady', with a couple of dear little 'snookums'.

**snool** (snul), *sb. Sc.* and *north. dial.* Also 8– *Sc.* **snule, snuil,** 9 *north.* **snuol.** [Of obscure origin.] A tame, abject, or mean-spirited person.

**1718** Ramsay *Christ's Kirk Gr.* iii. xvi, Ye silly snool, Wae worth ye'r drunken saul. **1791** J. Learmont *Poems* 4 [They] lead ye on like arrant snools, 'Lang error's road. **1815** G. Beattie *John o' Arnha'* (1826) 13 Your snools in love, and cowards in war, Frae maiden grace are banish'd far. **1822** Carlyle *Early Lett.* II. 51 You or any one of us will never be a snool; we have not the blood of snools in our bodies. **1882** J. Walker *Jaunt to Auld Reekie* 87 Crouching snools are kin to gangrel bodies.

**snool** (snul), *v.* [f. prec.]

**1.** *trans.* To keep in subjection; to snub.

**17..** Ramsay *Address of Thanks* iv. Wks. 1877 I. 258 Our dotard dads, snool'd wi' their wives. *a* **1796** Burns *'An' O for ane-and-twenty, Tam!'* ii, They snool me sair, and haud me down. **1830** Galt *Lawrie T.* ix. i. (1849) 406 The arrogance and high hand with which Mr. Bell was attempting to snool us all.

**2.** *intr.* To submit tamely; to cringe; to crawl meekly or humbly.

**1786** Burns *Bard's Epitaph* i, Owre blate to seek, owre proud to snool. **1810** Tannahill *Poems* (1846) 141 Never snool beneath the frown Of any selfish roggie. **1833** Chalmers in Hanna *Mem.* (1851) III. 391 We had to snool back to London the way we came. **1895** 'G. Setoun' *Sunshine* ix. 198 Sandy 'snooled' through life with bovine equanimity.

**snoop** (snu:p), *v.* [ad. Du. *snoepen* (LG. *snôpen*) in sense 1.]

**1.** *intr.* To appropriate and consume dainties in a clandestine manner. *U.S.*

**1848** Bartlett *Dict. Amer.* 318 A servant who goes slyly into a dairy-room and drinks milk from a pan, would be said to be snooping.

**2. a.** To go *around* in a sly or prying manner. Also with other advbs. orig. *U.S.*

In quot. 1832 unusually without following *adv.* or *prep.*

**1832** R. C. Sands *Writings* (1834) II. 291 The world has realms wherein to *snoop*, And I am not a noddy. **1840** C. F. Hoffman *Greyslaer* II. iii. i. 105 Our scouts would make us believe that both he and Bradshawe are snooping about the country among the Tories. **1855** *Knickerbocker* XLVI. 317 The level which the..engineers 'snooped' round and found out, hasn't 'a *parallel*' in all the adjacent region. **1864** Kimball *Was he successful?* 178 Don't come snooping around to find out whether you sometimes go to the theatre. **1876** Besant & Rice *Gold. Butterfly* xx, I see the gells snoopin' around with their eyes as soft as velvet. **1883** *Cent. Mag.* Sept. 744 He had no right to come snoopin' around where I was at work. **1902** H. L. Wilson *Spenders* iii. 26 Work..is something you want to get done; play is something you jest like to be doin'. Snoopin' up these gulches is both of 'em to me. **1931** D. L. Sayers *Five Red Herrings* xviii. 185 It is hardly possible for a local policeman in a country place to snoop about, wheedling information out of the inhabitants. **1943** J. B. Priestley *Daylight on Saturday* xxviii. 220 What are you doing here? Snooping around and then sending in a report in triplicate—eh? **1951** J. Fleming *Man who looked Back* xv. 195 You..have all the fun snooping round and I've got to wait.

**b.** To pry into matters one need not be concerned with. Often const. *on* (a person). *colloq.*

**1921** *Daily Colonist* (Victoria, B.C.) 3 Apr. 9/3 There is the landlady who 'snoops' too much to suit her boarders. **1946** [see ferret *sb.*[1] 1 b]. **1950** *Chicago Daily News* 14 Apr. 18/3 Another thing is that snoopers often get snooped on, in retribution. **1965** M. Spark *Mandelbaum Gate* vii. 254 Has he had any opportunity to snoop? **1975** R. Stout *Family Affair* vi. 55, I wouldn't ask you to snoop on a friend.

**3.** *trans.* To steal, to misappropriate. Also *absol. rare.*

**1924** Galsworthy *White Monkey* i. viii. 57 If we let you snoop copies, all the packers will snoop copies. *Ibid.* iii. viii. 270 Yes, and look at that little snooper himself; he snooped to keep her alive after pneumonia.

Hence **'snooping** *vbl. sb.* and *ppl. a.*

**1936** J. Steinbeck *In Dubious Battle* vii. 109 The health authorities are going to do plenty of snooping. If they can catch us off base, they'll bounce us. **1946** K. Tennant *Lost Haven* (1947) xvii. 288 He was just a snooping tourist. **1952** *Manch. Guardian Weekly* 14 Feb. 13 Whose job it is to engage in political snooping. **1965** D. Francis *Odds Against* iv. 49 All very normal... It was my snooping which seemed unreal. **1974** 'M. Innes' *Appleby's Other Story* xi. 87 'If you want my help—' 'A snooping copper's *help*?' **1977** *Rolling Stone* 13 Jan. 30/2 She collected the results of her snooping in a manila folder.

**snoop** (snu:p), *sb. colloq.* (orig. *U.S.*). [f. the vb.] **1.** = snooper 1; *spec.* one who makes official or other investigation, a detective.

**1891** *Amer. Folk-lore* IV. 160 *Snoop*.—This word I have frequently heard in New England, used both as a verb and as a noun. It implies sneaking, spying, prying around. **1929** *Amer. Speech* V. 152 *Snoop*, one who noses something out. 'That woman is a snoop.' **1942** *New Statesman* 19 Sept. 186/3 *Snoops* are the Service Police, corresponding to the Army's Military Police. **1944** Dylan Thomas *Let.* 21 Sept. (1966) 267 There stinks a snoop in black. I'm thinking it Is Mr. Jones the Cake. **1948** *Time* 3 May 19/3 Every cop,.. stool pigeon and neighborhood snoop in Detroit was working overtime. **1970** A. Sillitoe *Start in Life* vi. 318 His snoops already know I left Beirut. **1978** R. Thomas *Chinaman's Chance* xxxvii. 360 The Congressman seems to have been an awfully fine snoop. But then, he used to be a cop.

**2.** An act of snooping, prying, or investigation; a surreptitious inspection. Freq. with *(a)round.*

**1908** G. H. Lorimer *Jack Spurlock—Prodigal* xi. 274 She couldn't keep her servants, for she was torn with dark doubts of their honesty... Life for her was one long snoop about the house. **1939** 'N. Blake' *Smiler with Knife* xii. 172 Why not have a snoop round in Chilton's study? **1969** M. Pugh *Last Place Left* xxii. 167 'You're going to take this to Brunner's house?' 'Not straight. Once I've had a good snoop round it.' **1972** G. Lyall *Blame Dead* xv. 107, I did a little unpacking and then went for a general snoop.

**'snooper.** [f. snoop *v.*]

**1.** One who pries or peeps; *spec.* one who makes an intrusive official investigation. orig. *U.S.*

**1889** in *Cent. Dict.* **1896** *Westm. Gaz.* 18 Mar. 3/1 Artists sketching whenever they can get a chance, and surrounded by 'snoopers'. **1928** *Chicago Tribune* 11 July 10/4 Prohibition Commissioner Doran has warned dry snoopers to stop gunplay against innocent citizens. **1939** 'N. Blake' *Smiler with Knife* i. 19 What a snooper you are! **1948** *Jrnl. R. Aeronaut. Soc.* LII. 719 The difficulty with this is that the potential user is unlikely to come into the picture in the detail design stage, and the designing firm would probably not, in any case, welcome yet another 'snooper'. **1959** E. H. Clements *High Tension* vi. 103 We should consider ourselves lucky to have a professional snooper as a neighbour. **1965** M. Spark *Mandelbaum Gate* iii. 80 We know Ramdez. He's a snooper for his government. **1978** D. Grylls *Guardians & Angels* iii. 89 The parents..are tip-toeingly attentive... Of course, the adults are not depicted as snoopers.

**2.** A sneak-thief, a misappropriator. *rare.*

**1924** [see snoop *v.* 3]. **1927** 'J. Barbican' *Confessions Rum-Runner* ii. xxiii. 257 You rotten little cross-eyed snooper.

**snooperscope** ('snu:pəskəʊp). [f. snooper + -scope; cf. sniperscope.] A device which converts infra-red radiation to a visible image; esp. a pair of such devices fitted together and worn on the head to provide binocular vision in the dark.

**1946** *Times-Dispatch* (Richmond, Va.) 16 Apr. 2/1 The snooperscope can be used over a special helmet. It weighs from six to seven pounds, and looks like something out of this world. *Ibid.*, The snooperscope had another use. With one on his noggin, a jeep or truck driver could go barrelling down the road to the front without lights. **1955** *Sci. News Let.* 7 May 295/3 A modified snooperscope is being used to 'see' through silicon crystals, spotting imperfections produced in manufacturing transistors, rectifiers and other semi-conducting devices. **1962** *Appl. Physics Lett.* I. 91/2 We looked at the diode output through a 'snooperscope' and above the threshold observed a very intense and narrow beam [of infrared radiation] radiating from the junction region. **1972** J. Mills *Report to Commissioner* 227 Hanson says why not darken the floor and watch the elevator with snooperscopes.

**'snoopery.** orig. *U.S.* [f. snoop *v.* + -ery.] The activity of snooping or prying; surreptitious investigation, *spec.* into another's private affairs.

**1935** *Sun* (Baltimore) 13 Feb. 2/6 C. Jasper Bell (Dem., Mo.) turned the Capitol Hill fight against 'innovations into snoopery' upon another law, the NIRA. Thus, the number of enactments now known to contain provisions making public the private financial affairs of citizens was brought to five. **1964** *Spectator* 13 Mar. 337/1 In time private enterprise snoopery could become a growth industry and major job-supplier for our unemployed. **1972** G. Lyall *Blame Dead* xiv. 104 'He sounds shifty as hell.'.. That.. might help justify David's snoopery. **1981** A. Paton *Towards Mountain* xxii. 187 The rules were simple—no sharing of blankets, the doors to stand open, no boy to sleep in any other dormitory except the one to which he had been assigned. These rules could be evaded, but their evasion was preferable to a reign of snoopery and an encouragement of informers.

**'snoopy,** *a.* [f. snoop *v.* + -y[1].] Inquisitive, excessively curious or prying.

**1895** in *Funk's Stand. Dict.* **1921** S. Ford *Inez & Trilby May* xii. 212 With the cops so snoopy, we can't afford a scene. **1930** P. Macdonald *Link* xi. 216 I'm not snoopy, but I opened my door and listened. **1952** *Chambers's Jrnl.* Feb. 81/2 This was a depot where the Canadian rum-runners met the American bootleggers to exchange Canadian and Scotch whisky for American dollars, and I knew enough about these operations to realise that life did not amount to much when snoopy guys butted in. **1978** J. Wainwright *Jury People* xii. 41 Don't think I was being snoopy—but..I saw you arrive, this morning.

Hence **'snoopiness.**

**1969** L. Hellman *Unfinished Woman* iv. 39 The vicarious, excited snoopiness I knew was mixed with the kindness.

**snoore**, obs. variant of snore *v.*

**snoose** (snu:s, snu:z). *Western N. Amer.* Also **schnoose, snooze.** [ad. Da., Norw., and Sw. *snus* snuff, shortening of Da., Sw. *snustobak*, Norw. *snustobakk* snuff tobacco; cf. snush *sb.*] Chewing snuff, esp. taken by loggers. Also *fig.*

**1912** H. Footner *New Rivers of North* 21 Loud were the lamentations of his foreigners when his 'snooze' gave out, 'snooze' being the local familiarity for snuff. **1925** *Amer. Speech* I. 138/1 He 'fogs-up' on his pipe, or takes a 'rear of snoose'. 'Snoose' is a certain brand of Swedish snuff; it is moist and hot with pepper, and the man who is not used to it will find his gums burning and his head swimming when he tries his first 'rear'; but nearly every logger in this neck of the woods [*sc.* Northwest] has abandoned the old-time American plug for this terrific Nordic concoction. **1942** *Ibid.* XXVII. 221/2 *Give her snoose*, an order to increase power. **1955** R. Hobson *Nothing too Good* xiii. 136 Larkie was a snoose chewer. **1965** *Sun* (Vancouver) 22 Apr. 51/7 (*caption*) Just before ya face the old lady ya shove a wad of schnoose in yer mouth..she'll never smell yer breath. **1977** J. Hodgins *Invention of World* i. 5 He spat snoose out the broken window onto the pavement.

**snoot** (snu:t), *sb.* [dial. var. snout *sb.*[1]]

**1.** = snout *sb.*[1] 2. *dial.* and *slang.*

**1861** J. Barr *Poems* 33 Like harrow teeth they're stickin' out, To catch the dirt below their snoot. **1866** *Galaxy* 1 Oct. 277, I had supposed that such phrases as 'I'll mash your head!' 'I'll bash you on the snoot!' 'I'll mawl yer jaws,' and similar expressive threats, were invented in the New World. **1884** E. W. Nye *Baled Hay* 209 Read our..'Ode to the Busted Snoot of a Shattered Venus de Milo'. **1905** G. H. Lorimer *Old Gorgon Graham* 220 Just as he got good and ready to strike, I pasted him one in the snoot. **1924** Wodehouse *Bill the Conqueror* v. 101 He seethed with generous indignation and even went so far as to state his intention..of busting the fellow one on the snoot. **1938** D. Runyon *Furthermore* v. 86 A bust in the snoot. **1956** D. M.

DAVIN *Sullen Bell* II. iv. 136 At first I was all for poking the bloke in the snoot. **1971** J. AIKEN *Nightly Deadshade* iii. 33 Snell is sticking his long snoot into the middle of things.

**2.** The nose of an aircraft, esp. of adjustable construction (cf. *droop-snoot* s.v. DROOP *sb.* 3). Also, the nose of a car, etc.

**1945**, etc. [see *droop-snoot* s.v. DROOP *sb.* 3]. **1962** *New Scientist* 18 Jan. 135/1 As the flaps are depressed, so the snoot is tilted downwards until at full flaps it is depressed at an angle of 35°. **1977** *Drive* Mar.–Apr. 52/3 Drivers are in a poor position to judge the droop-snoot of the car. **1980** A. COPPEL *Hastings Conspiracy* iv. 32 Through the open door of the flight-deck Brede could see that the snoot had been lowered for better visibility.

**3.** A tubular or conical attachment used to produce a narrow beam from a spotlight.

**1952** *Cinema* 7 Jan. 108/1 (Advt.), Viking Films Ltd... Lighting equipment... Spots... Cans, bashers, overhead banks, snoots, barndoors, diffusers, niggers, etc. **1972** QUICK & LA BAU *Handbk. Film Production* xi. 73 Snoots consist of metal tubes that are mounted on the front of spotlights to control the spread of their beams. **1977** J. HEDGECOE *Photographer's Handbk.* 34 Spotlight accessories include folding barn-doors..and conical snoots..both of which restrict the beam.

**snoot**, *v. U.S.* [f. prec.] **1.** *intr.* = NOSE *v.* 8 b; = SNOUT *v.* 2. (In quot. *fig.*) *U.S. dial. rare.*

**1890** *Dialect Notes* I. 75 *Snoot* (snût), of the human face or nose, apparently the same word as *snout.* A vulgar word in New England. 'I'll bu'st your snoot'; 'hit him on the snoot'. As a verb in 'to snoot round', *i.e.* to nose around, it is reported from *Poughkeepsie*, N.Y.

**2.** *trans.* To snub; to treat scornfully or with disdain. *U.S.*

**1928** E. HATCH *Couple of Quick Ones* IV. 198, I followed him..up the street to where the Wright limousine was snooting the world in general at the kerb. **1939** J. P. MARQUAND *Wickford Point* xi. 124 Don't try to snoot Sue Jaeckel. **1959** V. PACKARD *Status Seekers* iii. 44 Many intellectuals..develop their own ways of snooting. **1977** *Time* 17 Jan. 28/3 Cinderella (Gemma Craven) gets snooted by her Stepsisters and gazes sorrowfully into the flames of the scullery fire.

**snooter** ('snu:tə(r)), *v.* [f. as prec. + -ER[5].] *trans.* To harass, to bedevil; to snub. (Only in P. G. Wodehouse.)

**1923** WODEHOUSE *Inimit. Jeeves* iii. 30 My Aunt Agatha.. wouldn't be on hand to snooter me for at least another six weeks. **1929** —— *Mr. Mulliner Speaking* viii. 286 'As far', replied Mr. Finch, frigidly, 'as a bloke can be said to be all right..who has been..chivvied and snootered and shot in the fleshy part of the leg—.' **1932** —— *Let.* 13 Aug. in *Performing Flea* (1953) 66 Downtrodden young peer, much snootered by aunts, etc., has become engaged to two girls at once.

**snootful** ('snu:tfʊl). [f. SNOOT *sb.* + -FUL.] As much (alcohol, etc.) as one can take; a quantity of alcohol, esp. one sufficient to induce drunkenness. Cf. SKINFUL 3 a.

**1918** R. LARDNER *Real Dope* 43 When somebodys else husband pulls something its O.K. but if their own husband does it he must of had a snoot full. **1935** WODEHOUSE *Luck of Bodkins* xvii. 205 His whole mind was manifestly intent on reaching the smoking-room and getting a snootful. **1953** W. R. BURNETT *Vanity Row* xvi. 117 He was drunk... 'A snootful, eh?' **1969** K. VONNEGUT *Slaughterhouse-Five* ii. 40 Billy didn't usually drink much..but he certainly had a snootful now. **1977** H. GREENE *FSO-1* xi. 103 Kim..had gotten a snootful of the tear gas.

**snootily** ('snu:tɪlɪ), *adv.* [f. SNOOTY *a.* + -LY[2].] In a snooty manner, superciliously.

**1940** 'G. ORWELL' *Let.* 16 Apr. in *Coll. Essays* (1968) II. 22, I get quite a lot of letters..from people snootily pointing out some mistake I've made. **1954** KOESTLER *Invisible Writing* III. xix. 220 And now, when I am down, you snootily refuse to help me with my business. **1961** *Guardian* 29 Mar. 14/3 An old lady..remarked..rather snootily..'It's where you were born that counts.' **1980** I. HUNTER *Malcolm Muggeridge* ii. 36 Vidler was unimpressed by all this and replied somewhat snootily, rejecting all his arguments.

**'snootiness.** [f. as prec. + -NESS.] The character or quality of being snooty; conceitedness, superciliousness.

**1932** J. T. FARRELL *Young Lonigan* iii. 124 She said it served Helen right that she had gotten a crush on a guy like Weary, because Weary would take some of the snootiness out of her. **1942** *R.A.F. Jrnl.* 2 May 22 They in turn mistook our English reserve for 'snootiness'. **1956** S. HOPE *Diggers' Paradise* 155 One or two tourists I met were annoyed about what they described as this 'snootiness'. **1977** *Sunday Times* 15 May 40/1 All these books steer with tact between the contrasting risks of sycophancy and snootiness.

**snooty** ('snu:tɪ), *a.* [f. SNOOT *sb.* + -Y[1].] Supercilious, haughty, conceited; affecting superiority, snobbish; 'highbrow', 'stuck-up'. Occas., irritable, short-tempered.

**1919** A. HUXLEY *Let.* 12 Aug. (1969) 180 A very snooty cousin and a sporty one. **1922** S. LEWIS *Babbitt* xx. 252, I didn't like..the snooty way you talked. **1931** E. LINKLATER *Juan in Amer.* II. xvi. 172 She says you were kinda snooty with her. Tried to high-hat her. **1938** E. BOWEN *Death of Heart* II. vii. 303 Reproaches and rather snooty laughs were exchanged. **1940** in Harrison & Madge *War begins at Home* xiv. 379 They're quite snooty, because you don't buy anything else. **1947** 'A. P. GASKELL' in D. M. Davin *N.Z. Short Stories* (1953) 282, I was lucky to have a girl like Betty who was keen on football. Some of the girls used to go very snooty when the blokes couldn't take them to the Friday-night hops. **1955** E. CADELL *Lark shall Sing* v. 67 One of those snooty little cafés..run by bony gentlewomen. **1959** I. & P. OPIE *Lore & Lang. Schoolch.* x. 178 A short-tempered person is spoken of as being..snappy, snooty (meaning easily irritated), and sharp-edged. **1960** O. MANNING *Great Fortune* II. 142 The English wives were a bit snooty with me. **1980** R. BARNARD *Death in Cold Climate* vi. 60 You know how the English can say 'Really?'—all cold and snooty.

**snoove** (snuv), *v. Sc.* Also 6 **snoif**, 9 **snuive, snuve.** [a. OScand. (east) *snóa (MSw. *snoa*, Sw. *sno*, Da. *snoe*), = ON. and Icel. *snúa* (Fær. *snúgva*, Norw. *snu*). For the development of the vb., cf. the etym. note to RO *sb.*]

**1. a.** *trans.* To twirl, cause to turn. **b.** *intr.* (See quot. 1808.)

**1513** DOUGLAS *Æneid* VIII. vii. 100 To werk the lyne, To snoif the spyndill, and lang thredis twyne. **1722** RAMSAY *Three Bonnets* III. 80 A wife that snooves a spindle. **1808** JAMIESON s.v., A boy's top is said to *snuve*, when it whirls round with great velocity, preserving at the same time an equal motion.

**2.** *intr.* To move or advance steadily, or with a steady pace; to glide. Also *fig.*

**1719** W. HAMILTON *Ep. to Ramsay* III. ii, The pleasure counterpois'd the cumber..And snoovt away like three-hand Ombre. **1786** BURNS *To Auld Mare* xiv, But just thy step a wee thing hastet, Thou snoov't awa. **1830** *Memorabilia Curliana* 106 Come snooving down white ice. **1881** R. BUCHANAN *God & the Man* III. 212 Many a sharp rap did the old ship get [from the ice] as she snooved along.

**snooze** (snu:z), *sb.* Also **snoose.** [Cf. next.]

**1.** *colloq.* A sleep; a nap, a doze.

*a.* **1793** W. ROBERTS *Looker-on* II. 315 That Shuter's self might heave his head From drunken snoozes. **1813** SIR G. JACKSON *Diaries & Lett.* (1873) II. 177, I..had not had my snooze half out, when a courier arrived. **1845** W. H. MAXWELL *Hints Soldier* I. 51, I question whether I could manage to obtain a snooze. **1886** J. R. REES *Pleas. Bk.-Worm* v. 178 With a warm ejaculation on his tongue, the interrupted sleeper returns to his snooze.

*β.* **1812** H. & J. SMITH *Rej. Addr., Tale Drury Lane* 51 Starting from short and broken snoose, Each sought his pond'rous hobnail'd shoes. **1869** *Daily News* 8 Oct., Seals like nothing better than a snoose on the sand.

**2.** *slang.* (See quots.)

**1812** J. H. VAUX *Flash Dict.* s.v., A snooze sometimes means a lodging; as, where can I get a snooze for this darky, instead of saying a bed. **1839** *Slang Dict.* 34 *Snooze*, a bed. **1865** *Ibid.* (Hotten) 239 *Snooze-case*, a pillow-slip.

**3.** *Comb.* **snooze alarm**, an alarm on a bedside clock which may be preset or reset to repeat after a short interval, allowing the sleeper a further nap; **snooze button**, a button on a clock which sets the snooze alarm.

**1973** *Electrical Wholesaler* Sept. 76/1 (Advt.), Snooze alarm clock housed in finely tooled aluminium case. **1976** *Washington Post* 19 Apr. A15/6 (Advt.), Multiband clock radio. Digital Numbers. Wake to Music. Extra Snooze Alarm. **1974** *Sci. Amer.* Oct. 63/2 For years, alarm clocks were dull..even those with snooze buttons and fancy dials.

**snooze** (snu:z), *v. colloq.* [app. a cant or slang word of obscure origin.] *intr.* To sleep; to slumber, to doze.

**1789** G. PARKER *Life's Painter* (*c* 1800) 138 The cull with whom she snooz'd. **1795** POTTER *Dict. Cant* (ed. 2), *Snooze*, to sleep. **1813** MOORE *Diary* VIII. 136 If..I had nothing to do but put on my nightcap and snooze quietly by their side. **1842** MRS. GORE *Fascination* 37 She withdrew, leaving him to snooze beside the fire. **1887** *Pall Mall G.* 20 Sept. 2/3 A swarm of literary drones, who go there to lounge, snooze, and gossip.

**'snoozer.** [f. SNOOZE *v.*] **1. a.** One who snoozes.

**1878** P. ROBINSON *In Ind. Garden* 32 A bird—perhaps the middle one of a long row of closely-packed snoozers. **1887** *Pall Mall G.* 20 Sept. 2/3 The non-workers..may be divided into two classes—the snoozers and the talkers. The snoozer, if he reads at all, is an aimless reader.

**b.** As a vague appellation: a fellow, a chap. *colloq.* (orig. *U.S.*).

**1884** [see BANK *v.*[3] 4 b]. **1891** 'E. PERKINS' *Thirty Years of Wit* 296 I'm the snoozer from the upper trail; I'm the reveler in murder and in gore. **1903** 'O. HENRY' in *Ainslee's* Sept. 116/2 She knows what a wild kind of a snoozer I've been. **1916** *Anzac Book* 99 The chaps of the 16th Battalion Are not easy snoozers to beat. **1923** R. D. PAINE *Comrades of Rolling Ocean* iv. 65 Do you mean to say that the wonderful old snoozer had the grit to cruise out to your country at his age? **1939** JOYCE *Finnegans Wake* 174 They had cornered him about until there was not a snoozer among them but was utterly undeceived. **1946** *Sunday Sun* (Austral.) 20 Oct. (Suppl.) 15 They'd have lamped a snoozer rigged up as an army skipper clop-clopping along on a nag just behind them. **1966** H. MARRIOTT *Cariboo Cowboy* v. 52 Zim was a tough old snoozer. I know that he cut his knee open with an axe and sewed it up with some worsted yarn and his wife's darning needle.

†**2.** A thief who steals from the hotel or house in which he is staying. Cf. SNOOZE *sb.* 2. *slang. Obs.*

**1862** H. MAYHEW *London Labour* Extra vol. 242/1 Some two years ago a robbery was committed by a 'snoozer' or one of those thieves who take up their quarters at hotels for the purpose of robbery. **1882** *Sydney Slang Dict.* 8/1 *Snoozers*, men and women who sleep at hotels and boarding-houses and decamp with other people's effects in the morning. **1889** FARMER *Americanisms* 501/2 *Snooser*, an hotel thief who lives in the place, and thus seeks for opportunities to carry out his depredations.

**'snooziness.** [f. SNOOZY *a.*] The state of being snoozy or sleepy.

**1887** *Temple Bar* Oct. 199, I was just beginning to realise a sense of comfort, and (if I may say so) downy snooziness.

**'snoozing,** *vbl. sb.* [f. SNOOZE *v.*] The fact of dozing or sleeping. Also *attrib.*

**1811** *Lexicon-Balatronicum*, *Snoozing ken*, a brothel. **1851** MELVILLE *Whale* I. xxxix. 274 Grand snoozing tonight, maty. **1867** BRIERLEY *Marlocks* 39 Old Makapenny had made several journeys from his 'snoozing crib' to the door.

**'snoozing,** *ppl. a.* [f. SNOOZE *v.*] Dozing, sleeping, slumbering.

**1836** HOR. SMITH *Tin Trumpet* (1876) 183 What snoozing hum Ascends to thee?—what pæans, what adorings? **1883** STEVENSON *Merry Men, Treas. Franchard* v, The same snoozing, countryfied existence.

**snoozle** ('snu:z(ə)l), *v. colloq.* or *dial.* [Cf. SNOOZE *v.* and NUZZLE *v.*[1]]

**1.** *intr.* To nestle and sleep or doze; to nuzzle.

**1831** *Westm. Rev.* XV. 196 Comfortably snoozling like other birds deep in the fertilizing warmth of their downy boxes. **1862** SALA *Seven Sons* I. vii. 177 The little dog, snoozling on the hearthrug, lifted up his blinking eyes. **1881** G. D. LESLIE *Our River* 12 There were a lot of black Berkshire pigs snoozling in the straw.

**2.** *trans.* To thrust affectionately.

**1847** E. BRONTE *Wuthering Heights* iii, A dog..that snoozled its nose over-forwardly into her face. **1894** 'G. EGERTON' *Discord* 187 The dog..snoozles her snout into the palm of his hand.

Hence **'snoozledom**, the state of nestling and dozing in bed.

**1865** D'ARCY THOMPSON *Odds & Ends* iii. 6 How precious are the last five minutes of snoozledom!

**'snoozy,** *sb. slang.* (See quot.)

**1823** EGAN *Grose's Dict. Vulg. T.*, *Snoozy*, a night-constable.

**snoozy** ('snu:zɪ), *a.* [f. SNOOZE *v.*] Drowsy, sleepy, slumberous.

**1877** C. KEENE in Layard *Life* (1892) ix. 255 This sea air ..makes me snoozy sometimes in the day. **1886** J. R. REES *Pleas. Bk.-Worm* v. 178 [He] sits in a stupid snoozy state.

**snop,** *sb. dial.* [Imitative: cf. next.] A sharp blow or impact; the sound made by this.

**1849** *Boy's Own Bk.* 12 Spans and snops. This is a very simple game; one player first shoots his marble, the second then endeavours to strike or *snop* it, or otherwise to shoot his own within a span of it. **1871–** in south-western dial. glossaries. **1881** JEFFERIES *Wood Magic* II. iv. 110 His body ..rebounded with a snop, and he fell disabled and insensible to the earth.

**snop,** *v. dial.* [Imitative.] *trans.* To strike sharply and smartly; to break in this way. Also *absol.*

**1849** [see SNOP *sb.*]. **1882** JEFFERIES *Bevis* x, I see a man do that once... A' had a gate-hinge snopping um. *a* **1887** —— *Field & Hedgerow* (1889) 141 To stand there swinging that heavy bit of wood all day meant meat and drink..for themselves and families..: but only a few of them could get barns to snop away in.

**Snopes** ('snəʊps). Also **snopes**; *erron. pl.* **Snopes.** The family name of a series of vicious characters in the fiction of William Faulkner (first described in *Sartoris*, 1929), used as a type of an unscrupulous or heartless person.

**1962** *Guardian* 3 Oct. 1/6 There are plenty of snopes waiting to take over and act as though Mr Meredith has never been. **1970** *Times* 10 Apr. 10 In the heated circumstances of the present Mr. Nixon would be joining the yahoos and the snopes. **1977** *Time* 17 Oct. 48/2 His brother, the Snopes in the woodpile, satirizes the theme by assuming the very worst of the American people and braying at them.

**snore** (snɔə(r)), *sb.* Also 6 *Sc.* **snor, snoir(e.** [f. the vb.]

†**1.** A snort; snorting. *Obs. rare.*

*c* **1330** R. BRUNNE *Chron. Wace* (Rolls) 1821 þeyr teþ gnaisted wiþ nose snore, Hurtlede hedes set ful sore; Ilk oþer pulled, ilk oþer schok. **1513** DOUGLAS *Æneid* x. x. 72 For feir thai [*sc.* horses] start abak..And brak away with the cart to the schor, With stendis feyll and mony bray and snor.

**2.** A disease or affection which causes snuffling; the snivels.

*a* **1585** MONTGOMERIE *Flyting w. Polwart* 302 (Tullib.), The snuf, þe snoir, þe scheippisch, the schanker. **1844** W. JAMIE *Muse* 157 (E.D.D.), May he ne'er be subject unto snors. **1844** LOWSON *Mod. Farrier* 209 This affection is termed the snores or snivels.

**3.** An act of snoring; a harsh or noisy respiration through the mouth, or through the mouth and nose, during sleep.

**1605** SHAKS. *Macb.* II. ii. 6 The surfeted Groomes doe mock their charge with Snores. I haue drugg'd their Possets. **1610** —— *Temp.* II. i. 218 Thou do'st snore distinctly, There's meaning in thy snores. **1622** MABBE tr. *Aleman's Guzman d'Alf.* I. 133 The snores and snorts that came from them [a man and his wife]. **1826** F. REYNOLDS *Life & Times* II. 213 Then with a loud snore, he again sank into sleep. **1860** TYNDALL *Glac.* I. ii. 21 The sound rose and fell for several minutes, like a kind of intermittent snore. **1897** MARY KINGSLEY *W. Africa* 418 One of them has an abominable quavering, hysterical, falsetto snore.

**b.** *all of a snore*, filled with the sound of snoring. *rare.*

**1834** BECKFORD *Italy* II. 244 Dark vestibules and guard-chambers (all of a snore with jaded equerries).

**4.** *transf.* A sound resembling that of a snore; a loud roaring or droning noise.

**1709** *Brit. Apollo* No. 41. 3/1 She wak'd from Bag-pipe snore. **1832** DENNISTON *Craignilder* 60 Now dark December's wintry snore Rang through the leafless wood.

**5.** *Mining.* A snore-piece.
**1875** J. H. COLLINS *Met. Mining* 89 The suction pipe *a*, now called the 'wind-bore' or 'snore'.

**snore** (snɔə(r)), *v.* Also 7 snoar, 7–8 snoore. [prob. imitative: cf. SNORK *v.* and SNORT *v.*]
**1. a.** *intr.* Of animals, *esp.* horses: To snort. Now *dial.*
*c* **1400** *Laud Troy Bk.* 7738 The horses snored as it hadde thondred. **1530** PALSGR., 724/1 I snore..as a horse dothe. **1648** HEXHAM II, *Ruchelen*, to Grunt, or to Snoore like Hoggs. **1778** G. WHITE *Selborne* lxxxv, They [owls]..can snore and hiss when they mean to menace. **1786** BURNS *To Auld Mare* viii, How thou wad prance, an' snore, an' scriegh, An' tak the road! **1898** C. SPENCE *Poems* 57 He [a bull]..roared and bored and sniffed and snored.
**b.** *Sc., north. dial.* and *U.S.* Of things, wind, etc.: To make or give out a roaring or droning noise.
**1823** GALT *R. Gilhaize* xiv, I never hear my ain bellows snoring at a gaud o' iron in the fire, but [etc.]. **1842** VEDDER *Poems* 75 A score of rival steamers..Hiss, flap, and snore, like river monsters. **1886** W. ALEXANDER *S. Augustine's Holiday* 135 The wind..Humming and snoring thro' rigging and spar. **1935** W. FAULKNER *As I lay Dying* 40 Beyond the porch Cash's saw snores steadily into the board.
**c.** Of a ship, etc.: To move or cut *through* the water with a roaring sound; to sail or travel quickly. Chiefly *Sc.*
**1830** WILSON in *Blackw. Mag.* XXVII. 540 Our cut-water snores through the swell. **1834** M. SCOTT *Tom Cringle* x, She began to *snore* through it like smoke. **1849** CUPPLES *Green Hand* iii. (1856) 36 The pilot-boat snoring off close-hauled to windward.
**2. a.** To make harsh or noisy sounds in sleep by breathing through the open mouth or through the mouth and nose; to breathe in this manner during sleep. Also *poet.* or *rhet.*, to sleep heavily.
*c* **1440** *Promp. Parv.* 462/1 Snoryn, yn sleep, *sterto.* **1530** PALSGR. 724/1, I wylle nat lye with hym, he snoreth so in his slepe. **1576** FLEMING *Panopl. Epist.* 284 Nature hath not giuen unto men their essence & being..to slugge and snore in the couche of carelessnesse. **1609** HOLLAND *Amm. Marcell.* XXVII. xii. 323 Whiles the centinels by reason of securitie were found asleepe that they snored againe, the citie gate was set open. **1658** A. FOX *Würtz' Surg.* III. ii. 222 Sound peoples sleep is not alike, some snoar in their sleep, others without a noise. **1695** PRIOR *Prol. Dryden's 'Cleomenes'* 20 Most of you snor'd whilst Cleomenes read. **1725** POPE *Odyss.* IX. 440 Then nodding with the fumes of wine, [he] Dropt his huge head, and snoring lay supine. **1784** COWPER *Task* I. 90 The nurse sleeps sweetly, hir'd to watch the sick, Whom snoring she disturbs. **1818** SCOTT *Rob Roy* xxx, [He] tumbled himself into one of the cribs..and soon was heard to snore soundly. **1860** TYNDALL *Glac.* I. xvi. 107 He assured me..that he did not snore, and we lay down side by side. **1900** POLLOK & THOM *Sports Burma* 286 A solitary tusker elephant sound asleep and snoring loudly.
*fig.* **1660** N. INGELO *Bentivolio & Urania* II. (1682) 89 The Soul, having snor'd many hundreds or thousands of years.
**b.** *I snore*, used as a mild expletive. *U.S.*
**1790** *Mass. Spy* 30 Dec. (Thornton), In one village you will hear the phrase 'I snore',—in another, 'I swowgar'. **1836** HALIBURTON *Clockm.* Ser. I. xii, Now its fairly run out, that's a fact, I snore. *Ibid.* xxxvi, You will, I snore.
**3.** *trans.* With *out* or *away*: To spend or pass (time) in snoring.
**1597** SHAKS. *2 Hen. IV*, IV. v. 28 Sleepe with it now, Yet not so sound..As hee whose Brow..Snores out the Watch of Night. *a* **1704** T. BROWN *Walk r. Lond., Tavern* Wks. 1709 III. III. 9 Where she Surfeits upon Sack,..and Snoars away the Remainder of her Life. **1746** FRANCIS tr. *Hor., Sat.* I. iii. 24 He drank the Night away Till rising Dawn, then snor'd out all the Day. **1781** COWPER *Hope* 510 The full-gorg'd savage at his nauseous feast Spent half the darkness, and snor'd out the rest. **1829** SCOTT *Anne of G.* xix, Some..snored away the interval between their own arrival and that of the expected repast.
**4.** To bring into a certain state by snoring (cf. quots.).
**1784** COWPER *Task* I. 97 Sleep Of lazy nurse, who snores the sick man dead. *a* **1793** J. PEARSON *Polit. Dict.* 10 If the House are too sleepy to cough him down, they'll soon snore him down.
**5.** To utter with a snore or with a sound resembling this. Also with cognate object.
**1790** COLERIDGE *Inside the Coach* 22 Till ere the splendid visions close We snore quartettes in ecstasy of nose. **1889** GUNTER *That Frenchman* ii, Maurice..is already asleep and snoring the snores of an exhausted manhood. **1891** *Daily News* 9 Feb. 6/2 Some good people seemed to snore prayer; they were so sleepy.

**snore-,** the stem of the vb. in comb., as *snore-hole, -piece* (see quots.).
**1860** *Eng. & For. Mining Gloss.* (ed. 2) 63 *Snore-holes, the holes in the windbore to admit the water. **1862** SMILES *Engineers* III. 45 The pumps frequently got choked by the sand drawn in at the bottom of the well through the snore-holes, or apertures through which the water is to be raised is admitted. **1883** GRESLEY *Gloss. Coal-m.* 229. **1867** W. W. SMYTH *Coal & Coal-mining* 180 The lowermost portion [of the pump] is the so-called wind-bore, or *snore-piece, where the holes in the bottom..are of such size as to prevent the entry of chips or stones. **1883** GRESLEY *Gloss. Coal-m.* 229 *Snore-piece*, the lowest end of a pump sett through which the water passes.
**b.** With advb. **snore-off** *colloq.* (chiefly *Austral.* and *N.Z.*), a sleep or nap, esp. after drinking.
**1950** *Landfall* June 127, I notice Little Spike's legs sticking out from an empty tallow cask where he is having a snore-off. **1967** K. GILES *Death & Mr Prettyman* vi. 120 He always vowed to cut out these afternoon snore-offs. **1968** D. O'GRADY *Bottle of Sandwiches* 49 He surfaced from his plonk-induced snore-off.

**'snoreless,** *a.* [f. SNORE *sb.*] Of sleep: Unaccompanied by, free from, snoring.
**1830** *Blackw. Mag.* XXVII. 423 The snoreless sleep of the last upper-earth journey. **1845** *Ibid.* LVII. 391 The printer's devil..indulged in snoreless sleep.

**snorer** ('snɔərə(r)). [f. SNORE *v.*]
**1. a.** One who snores.
*c* **1440** *Promp. Parv.* 462/1 Snorare, *stertor.* **1611** COTGR., *Ronfleur*, a snorer, a snorter. **1694** MOTTEUX *Rabelais* xliii. (1737) 174 Old Goodman Æolus, the Snorer. **1751** SMOLLETT *Per. Pickle* (1779) II. lvii. 155 The face of the gaping snorer. **1864** DASENT *Jest & Earnest* (1873) I. 49 Our friend..is not the Club snorer whose feats he recalls so painfully. **1875** EMERSON *Lett. & Social Aims* i. 40 This unwritten play.., composed by the dullest snorer on the floor of the watch-house.
**b.** *slang.* The nose.
**1891** FARMER *Slang* II. 168/1 *Conk*,..the nose... English synonyms..snorer; [etc.]. **1925** O. JESPERSEN *Mankind, Nation & Individual* viii. 156 Lastly we have Slang-words for..the Nose. Danish, *snude*... Engl., a number of expressions:..snorter, snorer. **1959** I. & P. OPIE *Lore & Lang. Schoolch.* ix. 155 Children go in for short sharp words, as in their more usual names for parts of the body:..'snorer', 'snozzle', and 'boko' for nose.
**2.** A stiff breeze or wind.
**1871** *Daily News* 6 Nov., We lay our course famously, running..before a regular snorer—a strong sea on [etc.].

**snoring** ('snɔərɪŋ), *vbl. sb.* [f. SNORE *v.*]
**a.** The action of the vb. Also *transf.*
*c* **1440** *Promp. Parv.* 462/1 Snorynge, *stertura.* **1532** DU WES *Introd. Fr.* in *Palsgr.* 906 The snowring, *le ronfler.* *a* **1616** BEAUMONT *Charme* v. Poems (1640) H iv b, Sable Midnight makes all dumbe, But thy jealous husbands snoring. **1710** STEELE *Tatler* No. 208 ¶6 We have a Member of our Club, that when Sir Jeffery falls asleep, wakens him with Snoring. **1781** R. BURKE in *Burke's Corr.* (1844) II. 404 The meditations of the judge, the snoring of jurors. **1842** LOVER *Handy Andy* xxiv, The dormitory, where..a concert of snoring began to be executed. **1897** WATTS-DUNTON *Aylwin* II. v, It was the snoring of Wynne in a drunken sleep: it filled the entire cottage. **1935** A. J. CRONIN *Stars look Down* I. ix. 69 There was a silence, broken only by the snoring of air through the wind-bore cast of the pump. *Ibid.* 70 The snoring of the pump had stopped. **1951** R. HARGREAVES *This Happy Breed* ix. 102 The obscene snorings of the saxophone.
**b.** *spec.* in *Path.* (see quots.).
**1822–7** GOOD *Study Med.* (1829) I. 537 *Rhonchus Stertor.* Snoring. **1834** J. FORBES *Laennec's Dis. Chest* (ed. 4) 49 We can distinguish five principal kinds of rhonchi:..3. the dry sonorous rhonchus, or snoring.

**'snoring,** *ppl. a.* [f. as prec.]
**1.** That snores. Also *fig.*
**1687** MIÉGE *Gt. Fr. Dict.* I, *Ronfleur*,..a snoring Man. **1714** GAY *Sheph. Week* vi. 36 Cic'ly, brisk maid, steps forth .., And kiss'd with smacking lip the snoring lout. **1809** PINKNEY *Trav. France* 131, I was lying at one end of a dirty room, the other being occupied by the snoring landlord. **1868** GEO. ELIOT *Sp. Gypsy* I. 118 He is of those Who steal the keys from snoring Destiny. **1894** *Outing* XXIV. 119/2 Great rocks which resemble the snouts of snoring humans.
**2.** Of a breeze: Strong, stiff.
**1822** A. CUNNINGHAM *Mariner's Song* ii, But give to me the snoring breeze, And white waves heaving high. **1885** J. RUNCIMAN *Skippers & Shellbacks* 78 A snoring breeze came away from the southward.
**3.** Having the characteristic sound of a snore; loud and harsh.
**1837** CARLYLE *Fr. Rev.* II. IV. iii, Sleeping Paris is now.. silent except for some snoring hum. **1879** *St. George's Hosp. Rep.* IX. 610 On the left side the respiration was loud and 'snoring'... Posteriorly the 'snoring' breathing was audible everywhere. **1898** *Allbutt's Syst. Med.* V. 1018 Most frequently it [a presystolic murmur] is snoring or rolling.
Hence **'snoringly** *adv.*
**1824** *Blackw. Mag.* XV. 593 A set of prosy lines slumber along snoringly.

**snork** (snɔːk), *sb.* [f. the vb.]
**1.** A snort or grunt; a noisy sniff or inhalation. *dial.*
**1814** in Hone *Every-day Bk.* II. 1115 The pig..gave a snork. **1824** MACTAGGART *Gallovid. Encycl.* 430 *Snork*, the snort of an affrighted horse. **1876–99** in Mid-Yks. and Cumbld. glossaries.
**2.** A young pig; a pigling. *dial.*
**1891** 'SON OF MARSHES' in *Blackw. Mag.* Nov. 651 The farm lad who leads a family of snorks from one part of a wood..to another. **1895** —— in *Month* Oct. 248 The little nose-twisting,..curly-tailed, winking, and blinking snorks.
**3.** *Austral.* and *N.Z. slang.* A baby.
**1941** BAKER *Dict. Austral. Slang* 68 *Snork*, a baby. **1941** —— *N.Z. Slang* vi. 57 Other twentieth century New Zealand expressions of varied use include..*snork*, a baby. **1944** L. GLASSOP *We were Rats* 273 Got a scar on his hand, but probably he's had it since he was a little snork. **1956** D. M. DAVIN *Sullen Bell* II. v. 136 What I wasn't expecting was to find her living with the same bloke again and well on the way to having another snork. **1963** B. PEARSON *Coal Flat* x. 194 It's better to knock it on the head at birth, isn't it? Like a snork you don't want. **1970** D. M. DAVIN *Not Here, Not Now* II. vii. 108 Have to give up being on the bum once there's a snork or two to be looked after.

**snork** (snɔːk), *v.* Now *dial.* [prob. ad. MDu. or MLG. *snorken* (still Du. and LG.; hence Da. *snorke*), variant of *snarken* SNARK *v.*]
**1.** *intr.* To snore.
**1531** TINDALE *Exp. 1 John* (1537) 98 We..lye snorkyng lyke sloggardes. **1565** T. STAPLETON *Fortr. Faith* 121 b, Thou shalt not heare there the seruauntes snorke.
**2.** To snort or grunt; to breathe noisily. Said esp. of horses and pigs. Hence **'snorking** *vbl. sb.*
Other dial. senses are recorded in the *Eng. Dial. Dict.*
**1807** HOGG *Pedlar* xxiv. Poems (1865) 66 The horses they snorkit for miles around. **1814** in Hone *Every-day Bk.* II. 1113 The pig ran snorking and grunting after her. **1868–** in Sc. and north. glossaries and texts (*Eng. Dial. Dict.*). **1896** CROCKETT *Grey Man* xii, The old grouting wretch kept up such a snorking.
Hence **'snorker,** = SNORK *sb.* 2.
**1891** 'SON OF MARSHES' *On Surrey Hills* iii. 96 He reckoned it was one o' his young snorkers hed got out.

**snorkel, schnorkel** ('snɔːkəl, 'ʃnɔːkəl). Also ‖Schnorchel ('ʃnɔrçəl), Schnorkel. [ad. G. *schnorchel.*] **1. a.** Usu. in forms **schnorkel, Schnorkel.** An airshaft, invented in the Netherlands and developed in Germany, which was fitted to diesel-engined submarines so that air could reach the engines, allowing them to function, and exhaust gases to be expelled, while the vessel was submerged; also a submarine fitted with such an airshaft. Also *Schnorkel Spirall.*
**1944** *News Chron.* 11 Dec. 4/2 They are the new submarines fitted with what the Germans call the Schnorkel Spirall, the purpose of which is to extend under-water endurance. **1945** *Engineer* 19 Jan. 52/3 We hear that the Germans are fitting their U-boats with what is called the Schnorkel. **1945** *News-Leader* (Richmond, Va.) 12 Mar. 13/3 The 'schnorkel', or stovepipe breather, and the folding kite are chief among the new German gadgets. **1946** [see *breathing-tube* s.v. BREATHING *vbl. sb.* 10]. **1946** *Collier's* 11 May 69/2 The other the Germans called the '*Schnorchel*'. That was a pipe or tube of about periscope height, that extended from the ventilating system of the engines to the surface. **1950** *Sat. Even. Post* 11 Nov. 79 Chief credit for this went to the snorkel, a device which enables subs to breathe under water. Invented by the Dutch, stolen by the Nazis and perfected by the U.S. Navy, the snorkel has revolutionized naval warfare. **1959** *Sunday Times* 8 Feb. 13/4 In the spring of 1944 operational U-boats of the older types began to be equipped with the 'Schnorkel'. **1969** *New Scientist* 28 Aug. 418/1 The invention of the schnorkel reduced the area exposed during recharging to a single pipe extending a few feet above the surface. **1974** L. DEIGHTON *Spy Story* xviii. 192 We came up to periscope depth and let a blow of fresh air through the schnorkel.
**b.** Usu. in form **snorkel.** A short breathing-tube used by underwater swimmers.
**1953** J. Y. COUSTEAU *Silent World* 6 They claimed we drove away fish, damaged nets, looted their seines, and caused mistrals with our schnorkels. **1958** *Oxf. Mail* 17 Apr. 6/7 The American film television series, *Sea Hunt*, claims to be boosting the sport of skin-diving. If that is true there is soon going to be a big demand for snorkels and spear-guns in the Midlands. **1962** *Underwater Swimming* ('Know the Game' ser.) 9/1 By lying on the surface with the face in the water and breathing through the snorkel, the diver can watch the underwater scene continuously. **1968** *T.V. World* 10 Feb. 18/1 It is only when she sees a swimmer's snorkel in her stepfather's room that Mandy realises how the crime could have been committed. **1977** G. DURRELL *Golden Bats & Pink Pigeons* v. 110 We had only masks and no snorkels, and my mask let in water.
**2.** Usu. in form **Snorkel.** A proprietary name for a piece of apparatus used in fighting fires in tall buildings, consisting of a platform which may be elevated and extended.
**1959** *Official Gaz.* (U.S. Patent Office) 27 Oct. TM 140/1 Pitman Manufacturing Company, Grandview, Mo. Filed July 6, 1959. *Snorkel.* For Aerial Platform Apparatus, Particularly Such Apparatus Adapted for Use in Fire Fighting. First use June 11, 1959. **1960** *Amer. City* Jan. 83/2 After re-design and further testing of pilot models, the Pitman Aerial Platform, now known as the Snorkel, was offered in July 1958. **1963** R. I. MCDAVID *Mencken's Amer. Lang.* 258 *Snorkel*... The Chicago Fire Department uses it to designate a piece with an elevated pumping platform, for fighting fires in tall buildings. **1969** *Trade Marks Jrnl.* 26 Nov. 1955/1 *Snorkel* 940,580. Mobile hydraulically operated rotatable and elevatable platforms for use in fire fighting. Simon Engineering Dudley Limited,..Dudley, Worcestershire; Manufacturers. **1973** *Lebende Sprachen* XVIII. 69/2 At Newcastle upon Tyne the Chief Fire Officer has installed a closed circuit television camera on an aerial platform known as a *snorkel.* **1977** *Monitor* (McAllen, Texas) 28 June 1A/9 The fire was declared out at 8 a.m. The Edinburg snorkel was used to wet down all parts under the collapsed roof.
**3.** *attrib.*
**1944** [see sense 1 a above]. **1945** *Illustr. London News* 3 Mar. 229/2 The most recent move in this never-ceasing battle was the introduction..of the 'Schnorkel' apparatus. **1949** *Sun* (Baltimore) 2 Apr. 7/2 (*caption*) First photo of damaged sub... The periscope and snorkel equipment are bent. **1953** J. Y. COUSTEAU *Silent World* 1 My wife, Simone, would swim out on the surface with a schnorkel breathing-tube and watch me through her submerged mask. **1954** E. CLARK *Lady with Spear* xix. 187 He..wasn't a strong swimmer, but he wanted to try a face mask and snorkel tube. **1958** *Times Lit. Suppl.* 9 May 257/4 'There is no tactical requirement for such a fitting,' was the crushing reply to his early suggestion for the designing of a *schnorkel* apparatus. **1962** F. I. ORDWAY et al. *Basic Astronautics* xiii. 510 These devices had snorkel attachments to prevent the entry of water into the systems. **1967** *New Scientist* 9 Mar. 457/1 Modern conventional submarines can proceed at speed for many days with nothing except their 'schnorkel' air-breathing tubes breaking the surface. **1967** O. WYND *Walk Softly, Men Praying* xii. 187 The men..might have got out in snorkel-suits and been picked up by a deep-sea fishing fleet. **1973** *People's Jrnl.* (Inverness) 28 July 10/3 (*caption*) Firemen use the 85ft. snorkel escape ladder to rescue a 'casualty' from the training tower. **1980** P. MOYES *Angel Death* iv. 47 They climbed ashore, with their snorkel masks and fins slung in a string shopping-bag.

Hence as *v. intr.* (also *erron.* **snorkle**), to use a snorkel; to swim underwater using a snorkel; **'snorkeller, 'snorkelling** *vbl. sb.*

**1959** *New Scientist* 26 Mar. 695/2 Pressure variations due to this 'snorkeling' might disturb sensitive instrumentation systems. Mark I could snorkel. **1959** *Elizabethan* June 21/2 But archaeology is really work for trained specialists. You will most likely want to know where to 'snorkel' and fish. **1960** F. M. Roberts *Basic Scuba* ii. 27 Snorkeling through weeds.. might pull the mouthpiece from the diver's lips because the crook gets caught. **1963** *Harper's Bazaar* Jan. 30/2 Many skin divers are content to remain snorkelers, but some want to go deeper and deeper. **1968** J. Updike *Couples* ii. 171 Ken liked to snorkel. **1974** *Country Life* 24 Jan. (Suppl.) 32 Vast golden bays... Each.. an adventure for intrepid snorklers. **1975** D. Marlowe *Nightshade* x. 116 Water sports, shuffleboard, scuba and snorkling. **1977** G. Durrell *Golden Bats & Pink Pigeons* iv. 81 We went snorkling on the reef. **1980** P. Moyes *Angel Death* viii. 104 Henry and Emma swam and snorkelled and sunbathed.

†**'snorkle.** *Obs.*[−1] [Cf. G. *schnörkel* curve, flourish.] ? A wrinkle, crease.

*a* **1340** Hampole *Psalter* cxlvii. 5 Of þaim.. cristis kirtil sall be made, wiþouten spot and snorkil.

†**snorl,** *v. Obs.*[−1] (Meaning uncertain: perh. a misprint for *snarl.*)

**1633** B. Jonson *Tale Tub* ii. ii, Doe you mutter: Sir, snorle this way; That I may heare.

**snort** (snɔːt), *sb.*[1] [f. the vb.]

†**1.** A snore. *Obs. rare.*

**1619** H. Hutton *Follies Anat.* (Percy Soc.) 22 At noon-tide to concoct he takes a snort, His drowsie sences hud-winkt in a cap, Leaning upon his chaire do take a nap. **1622** [see snore *sb.* 3].

**2. a.** An act of snorting; a loud sound made by a horse or other animal in driving breath through the nostrils with some force. Also *transf.*

**1808** Jamieson, *Snocker*, a snort. **1823** Scott *Quentin D.* xxxvi, Wishing.. good-night in a tone resembling the snort of a shy horse. **1828** —— *F.M. Perth* xvii, Inarticulate groans and snorts, like those of a dying boar. **1852** Mrs. Stowe *Uncle Tom's C.* vi, He overturned Sam, and, giving two or three contemptuous snorts,.. was soon prancing away. **1884** W. C. Smith *Kildrostan* i. i. 77 Now and then the snort of steam Sounds from the headland far away.

**b.** A similar sound made by persons in order to express contempt, disdain, or other feeling.

**1865** Dickens *Mut. Fr.* i. x, Medusa.. follows every lively remark made by that dear creature, with an audible snort. **1885** R. Buchanan *Annan Water* vii, The old man uttered a low snort of defiance. **1887** Hall Caine *Son of Hagar* ii. xvi, The lawyer gave a contemptuous snort and turned on his heel.

**3.** *slang* (orig. *U.S.*). **a.** An alcoholic drink; a measure of spirits; a 'snifter'.

**1889** Farmer *Americanisms* 501/2 A *snort* of whiskey is a dram; a nip; a small quantity. **1912** J. Sandilands *Western Canad. Dict. & Phrase-Book* 42/2 The sporting Canadian asks his friends, 'Will you have a snort?' **1925** Wodehouse *Carry on, Jeeves* iv. 80 We were taking a quiet snort in a corner. **1945** J. Steinbeck *Cannery Row* xxix. 189 She.. took out a bottle and a glass and poured herself a snort. **1962** 'R. Gordon' *Doctor in Swim* xii. 75 'How about an—ah—quick snort?' I stared at him. 'But you never drink except at Christmas.' **1966** M. Laurence *Jest of God* xii. 199 Ladies often feel it wouldn't be very nice to drink rye at such a time [as bereavement], but a snort of sherry is usually acceptable. **1981** M. E. Atkins *Palimpsest* viii. 83 We'll have another snort... C'mon, drink up, I'll fill your glass.

**b.** A dose or measure of cocaine or heroin which is taken by inhalation.

**1951** [see *joy-pop* s.v. joy *sb.* 10]. **1959** [see main line 1 c]. **1962** [see horse *sb.* 15]. **1972** H. C. Rae *Shooting Gallery* ii. 73 How did McDowell pick up a big enough snort to do for himself? **1978** G. Vidal *Kalki* iv. 88 'Want a snort?' Bruce produced a cocaine snifter.

**snort** (snɔːt), *sb.*[2] *Naut. slang* (now only *Hist.*). [Anglicized corruption of G. *schnorchel*, after snort *sb.*[1]] = snorkel, schnorkel 1 a. Freq. *attrib.*

**1944** *News Chron.* 11 Dec. 4/2 The first 'snort' U-boats are probably already at sea... 'Snort' is the Navy's nickname for them. **1944** *N.Y. Herald Tribune* 12 Dec. 1/7 (*heading*) 'Snorts' said to enable vessels to stay under 20 days. **1950** *Times* 26 Apr. 6/6 Under the programme 10 existing submarines are to be equipped with the 'Snort' breathing apparatus. **1954** H. M. Burton tr. *Diolé's Under-Water Exploration* v. 69 The chief improvements to the standard type submarine which were introduced during the last war were the work of the Germans. They were responsible, in particular, for the *Schnorchel*, or 'snort'. **1976** *Oxf. Compan. Ships & Sea* 759/1 In the British Navy the schnorkel tube was given the name snort.

Hence as *v.*[2] *intr.*: of a submarine, to travel underwater by means of a snort; **'snorter**[4], a submarine fitted with a snort; **'snorting** *vbl. sb.*[2]

**1953** *John o' London's Weekly* 3 July 602/2 Since the *Andrew* crossed the Atlantic in total submergence, the word snort has acquired a different significance. Said her captain after she had achieved her object: 'All we were told was: "You are going to snort back"—so we snorted.' **1957** *Jane's Fighting Ships 1957–8* 51 On 15 June 1953 *Andrew* completed a 2500 sea miles voyage under water from Bermuda to the English Channel in 15 days, a record for 'snorting' in the Royal Navy. **1962** W. Granville *Dict. Sailor's Slang* 109/1 *Snorter*, submarine fitted with the snorkel device which enables her to keep at sea for a considerable period. **1974** 'M. Hebden' *Pride of Dolphins* iii. ii. 230 'Open Three Main vents. Periscope depth. Stand by to snort.'.. They were snorting slowly back up the Solent. **1979** *Daily Tel.* 3 May 3/3 Since Olympus could reach safety from snorting depth in about a minute, the order to dive was given 45 seconds too late.

**snort** (snɔːt), *v.*[1] Also 6–7 snorte. [prob. imitative: cf. snore *v.* and snork *v.*]

†**1.** *intr.* Of the nose: To turn *up*, as in sniffing.

*a* **1366** Chaucer *Rom. Rose* 157 Hir nose snorted vp for tene, Ful hidous was she forto sene.

†**2. a.** To snore; to sleep heavily or sluggishly. *Obs.*

Common from *c* 1590–1650 in this and the next group.

*c* **1386** Chaucer *Reeve's T.* 243 This Millere hath so wisely bibbed Ale That as an hors he snorteth in his sleepe. —— *Man of Law's T.* 692 He slepeth and he snorteth in his gyse. **1535** Coverdale *Isaiah* lvi. 10 They are slepery: slogish are they, & lie snortinge. **1567** Maplet *Gr. Forest* 96 All winter long he snorteth, and is as he were deade. **1591** Sylvester *Du Bartas* i. i. 809 Their Watch within their Corps de Garde About the fire securely snorted hard. **1602** Marston *Antonio's Rev.* i. i, Strotzo, to bed: snort in securest sleepe. **1648** Gage *West Ind.* 141 Thus do they soundly sleep, and loudly snort after a dayes work. *a* **1680** Charnock *Attrib. God* (1834) II. 534 Some rise out of their.. beds.. at the first,.. others lie snorting longer.

*fig.* **1653** Jer. Taylor *Serm. for Year* 208 The spark of Divinity that dwels within is quenched, and the mind snorts, dead with sleep.

†**b.** In various fig. contexts. *Obs.*

**1581** J. Bell *Haddon's Answ. Osorius* 25 Truly you sleape so soundly, that you snorte agayne. **1583** Stubbes *Anat. Abus.* (1882) ii. 20 Many a one snorteth in palpable ignorance all daies of their life. **1597** J. King *On Jonas* (1618) 14 Haue we not read.. that although themselues slept and snorted in pleasure, yet their damnation slept not? **1630** Dyke *Myst. Self Deceiving* 353 Dauid lay snorting in his owne sin. **1642** *Vind. of the King* 2 The same malignant party.. hath been supinely snorting.

†**c.** *refl.* To convert (oneself) *into* something by idleness. *Obs.*

**1650** J. Hall *Parad.* 15 The King employed the people that way, who else might have sunke into Luxury, or snorted themselves into implacable enemies.

**3. a.** Of a horse: To make a characteristic loud or harsh sound by violently driving the breath through the nostrils, esp. when excited or frightened. Also said of other animals.

*c* **1386** [see 2 above]. **1530** Palsgr. 724/1 This jade snorteth as were a courser of ten pounde. **1577** B. Googe *Heresbach's Husb.* iii. (1586) 116 If farr away There happen a noise,.. he snuffes, and snortes at the same. **1600** Fairfax *Tasso* xx. xxix, He fomes, snorts, neies, and fire and smoake breaths out. **1601** Hakluyt *Galvano's Disc. World* 85 Certaine fishes which make a noyse like vnto hogs, and will snort. **1697** Dryden *Virg. Georg.* iii. 392 The Stallion.. snorts and trembles for the distant Mare. **1735** Somerville *Chase* ii. 162 Snorting they breathe, their shining Hoofs scarce print The grass unbruis'd. **1786** tr. *Beckford's Vathek* (1883) 70 The horses snorted, stamped the ground,.. and plunged about without mercy. **1818** Scott *Br. Lamm.* xxiii, His horse.. suddenly interrupted its steady and composed pace, snorted, reared, and.. refused to proceed. **1825** T. Hook *Sayings* Ser. ii. *Man of Many Fr.* II. 41 The fat poodle snorting and wagging his little lionized tail. **1871** C. Gibbon *Lack of Gold* xxi, The horses were steaming and snorting with exertion.

*fig.* **1891** Baring-Gould *In Troubadour Land* xviii. 252 The Crusaders were snorting for plunder and murder.

**b.** To rush *past* with snorts.

**1899** F. V. Kirby *Sport E.C. Africa* xi. 122, I obtained a glimpse of his dark grey hide as he [a rhinoceros] snorted past.

**4.** *transf.* Of things, esp. in later use of a railway engine: To make or emit a sound resembling or suggestive of a snort.

**1582** Stanyhurst *Æneis* ii. (Arb.) 59 The riuer.. Through the breach owt spurging... It brayeth in snorting. **1822** Shelley *Faust* ii. 50 The giant-snouted crags,.. How they snort, and how they blow! **1879** Sala *Paris herself Again* (1880) II. xxi. 320 The little circular railway puffed and screamed and snorted. **1902** 'Linesman' *Words Eyewitness* 196 The lyddite shells, snorting slowly through the air like a goods train up a gradient.

**5.** Of persons: **a.** To express contempt or indignation by a snorting sound.

**1818** Scott *Hrt. Midl.* xlvi, Duncan.. snorted thrice, and prepared himself to be in a passion. **1827** —— *Two Drovers* i, Ye needna snort, none of you Highlanders. **1889** Gretton *Memory's Harkback* 300 Upon this conclusion, his reverence snorted, and turned upon his heel in dudgeon.

**b.** *dial.* and *U.S.* To laugh loudly or roughly.

**1825** Brockett *N.C. Gloss.*, *Snort*, to laugh outright. **1834** [Seba Smith] *Lett. J. Downing* (1835) 27 We all snorted and snicker'd. **1835** Haliburton *Clockm.* Ser. i. xix, I thought I should have snorted right out two or three times.

**6.** *trans.* **a.** To utter with a snort; to give *out*, drive *away*, etc., by snorting (†or snoring).

*a* **1634** Randolph *Muses Looking-gl.* iv. iii, Your pittifull Worship snorting out pardons To the despairing sinner. **1796** Burke *Reg. Peace* i. (1892) 27 The.. tyrant Carnot shall have snorted away the fumes of the indigested blood of his Sovereign. **1840** Thackeray *Barber Cox* Apr., 'Dat is gut! haw! haw!' snorted the Baron. **1900** Pollok & Thom *Sports Burma* 376 He snorted defiance, challenging us, as it were, to approach nearer.

**b.** To eject or discharge through the nostils with a snort; to spout *out* in this way.

**1818** Keats *Endymion* ii. 885 Fish-semblances, of green and azure hue, Ready to snort their streams. **1853** Kane *Grinnell Exped.* iii. (1856) 28 Great.. wallowing sea-hogs, snorting out fountains of white spray. **1868** Browning *Ring & Bk.* i. 901 The old Triton.. A spray of sparkles snorted from his conch High over the caritellas.

**c.** To clear (the nose) with a snort.

**1835** *Politeness & Gd.-breeding* 104 Never.. snivel and snort a wet nose.

**7.** *slang* (orig. *U.S.*). To inhale (a narcotic drug in powder form, esp. cocaine or heroin). Also *absol.*

**1935** A. J. Pollock *Underworld Speaks* 110/1 *Snort*, to sniff cocaine or heroin. **1958** H. Braddy in *Southern Folklore Q.* Sept. 134 Since ma was a viper And daddy would snort, There wasn't much more I had to be taught. **1967** M. M. Glatt et al. *Drug Scene* iii. 32, I started snorting cocaine through the nose. **1972** M. J. Bosse *Incident at Naha* i. 38 She snorted Methedrine. I saw her do it many times. **1974** M. C. Gerald *Pharmacol.* xv. 291 Cocaine is usually administered intravenously, although some prefer to 'sniff' or 'snort' it. **1980** M. Booth *Bad Track* ii. 46 'Are you snorting?'.. He nodded... He inhaled the cocaine. **1982** *Daily Tel.* 4 Oct. 3/3 Mrs Pulitzer's lawyers claim that she started snorting cocaine after being sucked into the vortex of the 'Palm Beach lifestyle'.

**snort** *v.*[2]: see snort *sb.*[2]

**snorter**[1] ('snɔːtə(r)). [f. snort *v.*]

**1. a.** One who or that which snorts (†or snores); a person who utters a snort in scorn, indignation, etc.; also, a pig.

**1601** Hakluyt *Galvano's Disc. World* 85 Besides these there be certaine fishes which make a noyse like vnto hogs, and will snort, for which cause they be named snorters. **1611** Cotgr., *Ronfleur*, a snorer, a snorter. **1662** J. Chandler *Van Helmont's Oriat.* 213 Surely that thing.. renders the Snorters of the Schooles unexcusable. **1827** in Evans *Leic. Gloss.* s.v., To labourer Tom I give the swine: Snorters collected with great pains. **1894** *Westm. Gaz.* 25 Aug. 1/3 Suppose, then,.. that the Welsh 'snorters' had carried their point.

**b.** *dial.* The wheatear.

**1802** Montagu *Ornith.* s.v. *Wheatear.* **1863** W. Barnes *Dorset Gloss.* 87.

**2.** In various slang or colloq. senses: **a.** *U.S.* 'A dashing, riotous fellow' (Bartlett). **b.** A stiff or strong wind; a gale. **c.** Anything exceptionally remarkable for size, strength, severity, etc. **d.** A blow on the nose (*Slang Dict.* 1874). **e.** The nose itself.

**a. 1846** T. B. Thorpe *Myst. Backwoods* 182, I am a roaring earthquake in a fight,.. a real snorter of the universe. **1872** De Vere *Americanisms* 224 If animal spirits are a little too prominent, and assert themselves with vehemence, they procure for the owner the name of snorter.

**b. 1855** H. A. Murray *Lands Slave & Free* I. vii. 110 My .. regret.. that I could not see her under the high pressure of a good snorter. *a* **1859** in Bartlett *Dict. Amer.* (ed. 2) 424 The skipper said.. we must make all snug, for we're going to have a snorter. **1900** Mrs. Steel *Hosts of the Lord* xix, We had a regular black snorter.

**c. 1859** J. Lang *Wand. India* 399 The Commander-in-Chief.. certainly did put forth 'a snorter of a General Order'. **1886** Mrs. E. Kennard *Girl in the Brown Habit* i, Some of these fences are regular downright snorters. **1888** R. H. Mitchell in Steel & Lyttelton *Cricket* xiii. 380 How different this.. from being compelled to play a real 'snorter' before the breath is fairly recovered after the effort of running several fourers in succession! **1898** G. Giffen *With Bat & Ball* xi. 189, I know of no bowler whom one has to watch so closely [as T. R. McKibben], for you never know when you are going to get a 'snorter' of a break, from one side or the other. **1899** *Daily News* 19 July 5/5 It is a leader of the kind which we used to describe as 'a regular snorter'. **1929** *Morning Post* 11 Mar. 16/4 When in the next Test, at Lord's, McDonald bowled him [*sc.* Hendren] for 0 with a 'snorter'. **1954** J. H. Fingleton *Ashes crown Year* xxiv. 257 May.. now hit another 'snorter' through the covers.

**d. 1829** P. Egan *Boxiana* 2nd Ser. II. 119 The latter got a severe snorter, which not only uncorked the claret, but left a stupifying quality behind it.

**e. 1829** P. Egan *Boxiana* 2nd Ser. II. 353 The snorter of Raines looked red! For why? Jones's mauley had given it a rum tap! **1846** *Swell's Night Guide* 132/2 *Snorter*, the nose. **1925** [see snorer 1 b].

**'snorter**[2]. *Naut.* [Variant or earlier form of snotter *sb.*[2]] **1.** = snotter *sb.*[2] 1.

**1750** Blanckley *Naval Expos.* 154 *Snorters*, the Smiths put them on one End of the Beak Iron, to turn any of their Work with. **1886** *Field* 27 Feb. 251/2 The lower end or heel has been known often to part or jump out of the becket or snorter, which supports it and confines it to the mast.

**2.** = snotter *sb.*[2] 2.

**1950** Bown & Dove *Port Operation & Admin.* iv. 138 The snotter, or snorter, is a length of cordage or S.W.R. with an eye spliced in each end. **1965** R. B. Oram *Cargo Handling* v. 93 Rope snorters are used at Sydney and Brisbane to discharge the pallets and these are left on the cargo at loading.

**'snorter**[3]. *U.S.* (See quot.)

**1859** Bartlett *Dict. Amer.* (ed. 2) 424 *Snorter*, the edge pieces of tortoise-shell, called also toe-nails or nails.

**snorter**[4]: see snort *sb.*[2]

**snorting** ('snɔːtɪŋ), *vbl. sb.*[1] [f. snort *v.*] The action of the vb.

**1575** Gascoigne *Glasse Govt.* Wks. 1910 II. 61 Assone as ever shee is laid she falleth on snorting. **1589** Warner *Alb. Eng.* vi. xxx. 51 Her Lubber now was snorting ripe. **1601** Dent *Pl. Man's Pathw.* 164 The properties of drunkards:.. their staggering, their reeling, their snorting. **1655** Culpepper, etc. *Riverius* vii. i. 147 Asthma is a great and often breathing.. joyned with snorting and wheesing. **1733** Cheyne *Eng. Malady* ii. xiii. (1734) 246 A constant Snorting or Snoring in the Throat and Nostrils. **1849** *Sk. Nat. Hist., Mammalia* III. 15 At each snorting the animal spouted out large streams of blood. **1864** *Reader* 16 Jan. 68 The snorting of a tiger (for the sound this animal makes singularly resembles that of an enormous.. pig). **1884** *Manch. Exam.* 7 Oct. 5/7 The snorting of the postal steamer.

**b.** *spec.* in *Path.*

**1887** *Brit. Med. Jrnl.* 2 Apr. 730/1 Rhinitis with Spasmodic 'Snorting'.

**snorting,** *vbl. sb.*²: see SNORT *sb.*²

**ˈsnorting,** *ppl. a.* [f. as SNORTING *vbl. sb.*¹]

**1.** That snorts; †snoring.

**1573** TUSSER *Husb.* (1878) 17 To raise betimes the lubberlie, both snorting Hob and Margerie. **1598** SYLVESTER *Du Bartas* II. ii. I. *Ark* 553 He wallowes on the ground His shame-lesse snorting trunk, so deeply drown'd In self-oblivion. **1601** HAKLUYT *Galvano's Disc. World* 85 *marg.*, Snorting fishes. **1602** HERING *Anat.* 2 A laizie, drowzie, and slothfull-snorting Thersites. **1767** JAGO *Edge-Hill* III. 110 Oft will his snorting Steed, with Terror struck, His wonted Speed refuse. **1782** COWPER *Gilpin* 83 The snorting beast began to trot. **1848** JOHNS *Week at Lizard* 233 Encountering a shoal of snorting porpoises. **1875** in F. T. Buckland *Log Book* 84 *note*, A steam-ship is not a huge snorting monster trying to run over sailing ships.

**2.** Of the nature of, or resembling, a snort; characterized by snorts.

**1825** JAMIESON *Suppl.* s.v. *Snirt*, A snorting noise from the nostrils. **1833** M. SCOTT *Tom Cringle* xvii, One of the three men..sounded a short snorting note on a..horn. **1842** LOVER *Handy Andy* xxiv, Mrs. Kelly..uttering indignant ejaculations in a sort of snorting manner.

**3.** Of weather or wind: Severe, rough, violent.

**1824** SOUTHEY *Lett.* (1856) III. 450 When I have told you that it is snorting weather. **1888–9** OSBOURNE in G. Balfour *Life Stevenson* (1911) xiii. 196 When..we got our wind, it was a snorting Trade, and we ran into the harbour like a steamboat.

**4.** Exceptionally remarkable for excellence, size, strength, etc. (In quot. as *advb.*) *colloq. rare.*

**1924** GALSWORTHY *White Monkey* II. ix. 195 I've played bridge with him,..—snorting good player.

Hence **ˈsnortingly** *adv.*, in a snorting manner; with a snort.

**1853** KANE *Grinnell Exped.* xx. (1856) 160 They invariably rose after plunging, and looked snortingly around.

**snortle** (ˈsnɔːrt(ə)l), *v.* [f. SNORT *v.* + -LE.]

**1.** *intr.* To snort. Now *dial.*

**1577–82** BRETON *Flourish upon Fancie* Wks. (Grosart) I. 6/2 To wallow almost like a Beare, and snortle like a Hog. **1635** SWAN *Spec. Mundi* viii. §1 (1643) 370 It is supposed that these monsters [i.e. mermen] are very devils..by their howling and snortling under the waters. **1807** BERESFORD *Miseries Hum. Life* xx. II. 244 Where long she lies tumbling, ..And snortling, and grumbling. **1876** ROBINSON *Whitby Gloss.*, *Snortle*, to puff through the nostrils as a person with a cold.

**2.** *refl.* To bring (oneself) into a certain condition by snorting.

**1806** BERESFORD *Miseries Hum. Life* VI. (ed. 3) I. 120 The Monster—when..he has finally pumped, and panted, and snortled himself into tranquillity.

**snorty** (ˈsnɔːrtɪ), *a.* and *adv.* [f. SNORT *v.*]

**A.** *adj.* **1.** Accompanied or characterized by snorting or snoring; given to snorting.

**1582** STANYHURST *Æneis* III. (Arb.) 91 His nodil..droups to the growndward,..vometing with dead sleape snortye the collops. **1828** *Blackw. Mag.* XXIII. 494 What a snout he [the drunkard] turns up to the morning air, inflamed, pimpled, snubby, and snorty.

**2.** *colloq.* or *slang.* Ill-tempered, captious, disagreeable.

**1893** 'KATE WIGGIN' *Cathedral Courtship* 122 She found Mrs. Gooch very snorty, very snorty indeed.

**B.** *adv.* In a snorting manner.

**1892** 'Q.' (QUILLER COUCH) *I saw Three Ships* i, At the word 'whales', let the music go snorty.

**snory** (ˈsnɔərɪ), *a.* [f. SNORE *v.*] Inclined to snore; sleepy, drowsy.

**1837** *Fraser's Mag.* XVI. 266 Sleepy and snory, full of godless slang.

**snot** (snɒt), *sb.* Also 5–6 **snotte**, 6 **snott**. [ME. *snotte* or *snot* (cf. OE. *ȝesnot*), = Fris. *snotte*, *snot*, MDu. *snotte* (Du. *snot*), MLG. (and LG.) *snotte*, *snot* (hence Da. *snot*, †*snaat*, *snøt*), in sense 2; cf. also LG. *snut*, MHG. *snuz* (G. dial. *schnutz*). The stem is related by ablaut to that of SNITE *v.*]

**1.** The snuff of a candle; the burnt part of a candle-wick. Now *north. dial.*

**1388** WYCLIF *Exod.* xxv. 38 Also tongis to do out the snottis. *c* **1420** *Chron. Vilod.* 1281 Þe snotte fast brende, þe clothys cauȝt hete & by-gonne to brenne ful fast. **1829** BROCKETT *N.C. Gloss.* (ed. 2), *Snot*, used by the common people to designate the burnt wick of a candle. **1836** *Wilson's Tales Borders* II. 163 That lang black snot that's hangin' at the candle. **1888–** in dial. glossaries (Northbld., Cumbld., Durh., etc.).

**2.** The mucus of the nose. Now *dial.* or *vulgar.*

Common in the 17th cent.

*c* **1425** *Eng. Voc.* in Wr.-Wülcker 636 *Hic polipus*, snotte. *c* **1440** *Promp. Parv.* 462/1 Snothe, fylthe of the nose (*S.* snotte). **1530** PALSGR. 272/1 Snotte of the nose, *rovpye*. **1561** T. NORTON *Calvin's Inst.* IV. 81 That no man should draw snott oute at hys nosethrilles. **1594** NASHE *Unfort. Trav.* Wks. (Grosart) V. 154 His snot and spittle a hundred tymes he hath put ouer to hys Apothecarie for snowe water. **1621** BURTON *Anat. Mel.* III. ii. VI. iii. (1651) 562 Snot and snivell in her nostrils, spittle in her mouth. **1662** H. STUBBE *Indian Nectar* vii. 126 The Blood is more naturally purg'd..by spittle, and snot, then by any Purges. **1713** DERHAM *Phys.-Theol.* VIII. vi. 421 A great deal of Snot from his Nose. **1774** GOLDSM. *Nat. Hist.* VII. i. (1862) I. 500 From the nose there is always seen issuing a snot. **1808** in JAMIESON s.v. *Snotter.* **1824–** in dial. glossaries (Sc., Cumbld., Yks., Lanc., Linc., Somerset, etc.).

**3.** *dial.* and *slang.* Applied to persons as a term of contempt or opprobrium.

[**1607** DEKKER & MARSTON *Northw. Hoe* I. D.'s Wks. 1873 III. 19 Farewell father Snot.] **1809** DONALDSON *Poems* 171 Ye're a dozen'd, stupid snot. **1825–** in dial. glossaries (Cumbld., Yks., Somerset, etc.). **1875** W. ALEXANDER *Ain Folk* 207 There's Briggies, the aul' snot, at the ga'le [gable] o' the hoose. **1939** JOYCE *Finnegans Wake* 494, I would misdemean to rebuke to the libels of snots from the fleshambles, the canalles. **1952** B. HARWIN *Home is Upriver* xvii. 172 You want that damn' little snot now, hah? A damn' little snot ain't even dry behind the ears. **1974** N. FREELING *Dressing of Diamond* 159 She wasn't going to cry in front of that rotten-toothed snot. **1981** J. MELVILLE *Sort of Samurai* iii. 25 We've let the boy go home on bail... Miserable little snot, but no real harm in him.

**4.** (See quot. and cf. next.)

**1860** *Slang Dict.* 222 *Snots*, small bream, a slimy kind of flat fish. Norwich.

**5.** Attrib., as ***snot-green, -smeared*** adjs.; **snot-fish**, (*a*) the lump-fish, *Cyclopterus lumpus*; (*b*) a species of dace, *Cyprinus* (*Leuciscus*) *dobula* [so G. *schnottfisch*]; **snot-gall**, †(*a*) the nose; (*b*) a Tasmanian fish, *Seriolella brama* (*Cent. Dict.* Suppl. 1909); †**snot-hole**, a nostril; **snotnose** *slang*, a term of contempt applied to a childish, despicable, or conceited person; = SNOTTY-NOSE; **snot-nosed** *a. slang*, foul with nasal mucus; conceited; inexperienced and contemptible; = SNOTTY-NOSED *a.*; **snot-rag** *slang*, a pocket-handkerchief; also *transf.* as a term of opprobrium.

**1648** HEXHAM II, *Het Snot-gat*, the Snot-hole, or Nostrill. **1655** MOUFET & BENNET *Health's Improv.* 156 Lumps are of two sorts,..either of them is deformed, shapeless and ugly, so that my Maides once at Ipswich were afraid to touch it; being flayed they resemble a soft and gellied substance, whereupon the Hollanders call them Snot-fishes. **1668** CHARLETON *Onomast.* 154 Hisce annumeravit Gesnerus *Orbem Britannicum*, sive *Muconem*,..the Snot-fish. **1685** *Poor Robin's Almanack* C vij b, Three Kisses, four Busses, and five licks under the Snot gall. **1886** F. T. ELWORTHY *W. Somerset Word-Bk.* 690 *Snot-rag*.., a pocket-handkerchief. **1916** 'TAFFRAIL' *Pincher Martin* vi. 95 Any schoolboy will tell you what a 'snot rag' is. **1922** Snotgreen [see SCROTUM b]. **1929** T. WOLFE *Look homeward, Angel* xiv. 170, I don't give a good goddam..if you're the President's snotrag. **1939** AUDEN & ISHERWOOD *Journey to War* i. 48 The averted, snot-smeared, animal faces of the very humble. **1941** B. SCHULBERG *What makes Sammy Run?* i. 13 A snot-nosed little office boy. **1941** T. WOLFE *Hills Beyond* ix. 338 How do *you* know whether it's round or flat—a little two-by-fo' snotnose like you that ain't *been* nowhere. **1949** A. MILLER *Death of Salesman* II. 97 That snotnose. Imagine that? **1959** N. MAILER *Advts. for Myself* (1961) 84 One of them said he was going to take my shirt and use it for a snotrag, and they all laughed. **1960** H. LEE *To kill Mockingbird* iii. 34 Ain't no snot-nosed slut of a schoolteacher ever born c'n make me do nothin'! You ain't makin' me go nowhere, missus. **1963** 'E. MCBAIN' *Ten plus One* xi. 143 He was not enjoying this little snotnose..and the college girl talk. **1972** M. WOODHOUSE *Mama Doll* viii. 100 A persuasive manner you picked up at some snot-nosed advertising agency. **1973** J. WAINWRIGHT *High-Class Kill* 241 You are a self-opinionated idiot. You, and every snivelling little snot-rag like you. **1975** T. STOPPARD *Travesties* I. 23 The swiftly-gliding snot-green (mucus mutandis) Limmat River. **1977** H. FAST *Immigrants* I. 72 So don't be young snotnose with me. I like serious boys.

**snot** (snɒt), *v.* Now *north. dial.* and *Sc.* [f. prec. Cf. older Flem. *snotten*, *snutten* (Kilian), G. dial. *schnutzen.*]

**1.** *trans.* To snuff (a candle).

**1388** WYCLIF *Exod.* xxv. 38 Also..where tho thingis, that ben snottid out, ben quenchid, be maad of clenneste gold. **1877** EGGLESTONE *Betty Podkins' Lett.* 7 Noo snot t' candle, Peter. **1888–** in dial. glossaries (Northbld., Durh.).

**2.** To blow or clear (the nose). Also *refl.*

**1576** R. PETERSON *Galateo* (1852) 13 They spare not to snot their sniueld noses vppon them. **1611** FLORIO, *Smozzicare*,..to snot ones nose. **1632** SHERWOOD, To snot (or blow) his nose, *se moucher le nez.* **1653** URQUHART *Rabelais* I. xxi, Then he..sneezed and snotted himself.

**3.** *intr.* To sniff or snivel; to snort.

**1662** *Rump Songs* (1874) II. 199 They cheat us all with their looks, And snivell and snot by roate! **1899** LUMSDEN *Edinb. Poems & Songs* 73 Your faither's gane three hour an' mair, An' still ye snot, an' snotter there.

†**snoter,** *a. Obs.* [OE. *snot(t)or*, *-er*, = OHG. *snottar*, ON. *snotr*, Goth. *snutrs*, in the same sense.] Wise, learned, skilful. Also *absol.*

*c* **950** *Lindisf. Gosp.* Matt. xxiii. 34 Witȝo & snotre menn & uð-uuto. **971** *Blickling Hom.* 107 Ðe ȝeonge ȝe ealde, ȝe snottre ȝe unwise. *c* **1100** *O.E. Chron.* (MS. F.) an. 995, Ðes Ælfric was swyðe ȝewis mann, þet nas nan snotere man on Engla lande. *c* **1200** ORMIN 7087 [The Magi that] unnderrstodenn maniȝwhatt þurrh snoterr gyn bi sterrness.

**snotter** (ˈsnɒtə(r)), *sb.*¹ *Sc.* and *north.* [A derivative from SNOT *sb.*, corresponding to MDu. *snoter*, MLG. *snotter*, G. dial. *schnotter*, *schnodder*: cf. Du. and LG. *snotterig* snotty. Sense 3 is prob. f. SNOT *v.*]

**1.** Snot or nasal mucus. Also used *fig.* to denote something of little or no value, significance, or importance.

Various other dial. senses and attrib. uses are recorded in the *Eng. Dial. Dict.*

*a* **1689** CLELAND *Poems* (1697) 109 (Jam.), Hence I inferr ..No help nor gloss can weigh a snotter. **1720** RAMSAY *Rise & Fall of Stocks* 110 Coachmen, grooms, or pasment trotter, Glitter'd a while, then turn'd to snoter. *a* **1779** D. GRAHAM *Writ.* (1883) II. 154 A weel blooded hissie..that carefully combs the young things' heads,..snites the snotter frae their nose [etc.]. **1808–** in Sc. and north. dial. glossaries. **1836** J. STRUTHERS *Dychmont* II. Wks. 1850 II. 70 Brats in rags, inch thick with snotter.

*attrib.* *a* **1779** ? D. GRAHAM *Yng. Coal-man's Courtship* (1787) 4 His mither..blew her snotter box, primed her nose, kindled her tobacco pipe [etc.].

**2.** *attrib.* and *pl.* (See quots.)

**1781** J. HUTTON *Tour to Caves* (ed. 2) Gloss. 96 *Snotter-gob*, the red part of a turkey's head. **1832** GOODRIDGE *Voy. S. Seas* 30 The parts [of the sea-elephant] we made use of for food, were the heart,..the snotters, (a sort of fleshy skin which hangs over the nose,) and the flippers.

**3.** *slang.* (See quots.)

**1823** BEE *Dict. Turf*, *Snotter*, a ragged, dirty kerchief. **1864** *Slang Dict.* 239 *Snotter*, or *wipe-hauler*, a pick-pocket who commits great depredations upon gentlemen's pocket-handkerchiefs.

**ˈsnotter,** *sb.*² *Naut.* [Of obscure origin: cf. SNORTER².]

**1.** (See quots.)

**1769** FALCONER *Dict. Marine* (1780) s.v. *Sprit*, The lower end of the sprit rests in a sort of wreath or collar called the snotter, which encircles the mast in that place. **1815** BURNEY *Falconer's Dict. Marine* 487/2 *Snotter*,..a short rope spliced together at the ends, and served with spun-yarn, or covered with hide. **1846** A. YOUNG *Naut. Dict.* 288 *Snotter*, a rope going over a yard-arm with an eye forming a becket to bend a tripping-line to, in sending down topgallant and royal yards. **1894** *Outing* XXIV. 149/2 The upper end fits into a cringle or eye in the peak of the sail and the lower end into a snotter on the mast.

**2.** A length of rope with an eye spliced in each end.

**1950** [see SNORTER² 2]. **1956** C. L. SAUERBIER *Marine Cargo Operations* vii. 416 The sling is constructed in the same manner as the fiber rope snotter. **1961** COURSE & ORAM *Gloss. Cargo-Handling Terms* 72 The snotter is stretched out to its full length and the package placed on it centrally. The ends of the snotter are brought over it and one eye rove through the other and placed on the lifting hook.

**ˈsnotter,** *v. Sc.* and *north. dial.* [Cf. SNOTTER *sb.*¹]

The *Eng. Dial. Dict.* contains other dial. uses.

**1.** *intr.* To breathe heavily; to snuffle, snore, or snort.

**1710** RUDDIMAN *Gloss. Virgil* s.v. *Snokis*, Perhaps it may signifie smels or snuffs by sucking in the breath at the nose; which..also we call Snottering, or Snokering, or Sniftering. **1724** RAMSAY *Health* 288 All day he snotters, nods, and yawns. **1776** HERD *Collect. Songs* II. 98 Thou turns sleepy and blind, And snoters and snores far frae me. **1849–** in dial. glossaries and texts.

**2.** To snivel or snuffle in weeping.

**1781** J. HUTTON *Tour to Caves* (ed. 2) Gloss. 96 *Snotter*, to sob or cry. **1818** SCOTT *Hrt. Midl.* xxiii, What signified his bringing a woman here to snotter and snivel, and bather their Lordships? **1825–** in northern dial. glossaries, etc.

†**ˈsnottery.** *Obs. rare.* [f. SNOT *sb.*] Snot; hence, filth, filthiness.

**1598** MARSTON *Sco. Villanie* I. ii, O what dry braine melts not sharp mustard rime, To purge the snottery of our slimie time? **1601** B. JONSON *Poetaster* v. iii, Teach thy incubus to poetize; And throw abroad thy spurious snotteries.

**ˈsnottily,** *adv.* [f. as next.] In a snotty manner.

**1864** in WEBSTER. **1927** *Blackw. Mag.* Dec. 816/2 'Of course I did,' he replied, rather snottily I thought. **1937** J. T. FARRELL *Fellow Countrymen* 180 A man in a hurry bumped into him, and hastening on, snottily suggested that he quit taking up the whole sidewalk. **1973** M. AMIS *Rachel Papers* 59, I had a face looking over my shoulder, no matter how snottily equivocal its expression.

**ˈsnottiness.** [f. SNOTTY *a.*] The state or condition of being snotty.

**1530** PALSGR. 272 Snottynesse, *moruevsetè*. **1728** BAILEY, *Muculency*, snottiness. **1864** in WEBSTER. **1973** *Guardian* 18 June 4/6 The snottiness of the elitist eastern [US] establishment. **1976** *New Society* 19 Aug. 407/3 The snottiness of the French .. Surly waiter .. snapping concierge.

**ˈsnottinger.** *slang.* [f. SNOT *sb.*] (See quot.)

**1864** *Slang Dict.* 239 *Snottinger*, a coarse word for a pocket handkerchief.

†**ˈsnottish,** *a. Obs.*$^{-0}$ [f. SNOT *sb.*] Somewhat snotty.

**1648** HEXHAM II, *Snotachtigh*, snottish.

**ˈsnotty,** *sb. slang.* A midshipman.

**1903** in FARMER & HENLEY. **1904** KIPLING *Traffics & Disc.* 109 He was the second cutter's snotty—*my* snotty—on the Archimandrite. **1916** 'TAFFRAIL' *Pincher Martin* vi. 95 No boat ever left the ship under steam or sail without a 'snotty' in charge. **1943** HUNT & PRINGLE *Service Slang* 61 *Snotty*, midshipman. (So called after the buttons on his sleeve, which are said to be there for a purpose not unconnected with the nickname.) **1974** P. DICKINSON *Poison Oracle* ii. 47 A British Naval Party under the command of a snappily saluting little snotty.

**snotty** (ˈsnɒtɪ), *a.* [f. SNOT *sb.* Cf. MDu. *snottich*, NFris. *snottig*, older Da. *snøttig*, obs. G. *schnutzig*. The variant SNATTY appears earlier.]

The word occurs also as a sb. in dial. use; see the *Eng. Dial. Dict.* and *Jamieson's Sc. Dict.*

**1. a.** Foul with snot or nasal mucus.

Freq. in the 17th cent. of the nose.

**1570** LEVINS *Manip.* 112/9 Snotty, *purulentus*. **1579** FULKE *Refut. Rastel* 797 [They] vsed them..as the Papists did with y^e snottie napkins of Thomas Becket. **1602** *2nd Pt. Return fr. Parnass.* III. iii, *Amoretto.* Her nose is like a beautious maribone. *Page.* Marry a sweete snotty mistres. **1654** GATAKER *Disc. Apol.* 77 A defluxion from his nittie Hed, into his snottie Nose. **1739** R. BULL tr. *Dedekindus' Grobianus* 12 Your snotty Fingers.. Shall well supply the polish'd Mirror's Place. **1752** CHESTERF. *Lett.* (1792) III. cclxxxii. 296 One day his nose was very snotty, upon which I..wiped it for him. **1867** A. DAWSON *Rambling Recoll.* (1868) 11 There was a knot of bare-legged snotty striplings. *prov.* **1611** COTGR. s.v. *Morveux*, Better a snottie nose then none. **1633** G. HERBERT *Jacula Prud.* Wks. (1862) 328 Better a snotty child than his nose wiped off.

**b.** Dirty, mean, paltry, contemptible, etc. Now *dial.* or *slang.*

**1681** RYCAUT tr. *Gracian's Critick* 199 Let the confident Sophister know that he is but a snotty Charlatan. **1681** W. ROBERTSON *Phraseol. Gen.* (1693) 193 He babbles out his snotty slanders. **1712** *Odes of Horace* II. 27/1 Horace is no such snotty author as to have this putid Stuff put upon him. **1828** T. WILSON *Pitman's Pay* (1843) 26 Ye snotty dog, Put in yor tram. **1828-** in dial. glossaries (Northbld., Cumbld., Yks., Wilts., Som., etc.). **1958** J. C. HEROLD *Mistress to Age* (1959) III. xiii. 263 Albertine had slapped the Crown Prince and called him a snotty brat. **1967** P. WELLES *Babyhip* ii. 36 My brother tried to date her, but she rejected him. She told him she didn't admire Catholics. I think that's pretty snotty. We did go to the same Sunday School. **1974** S. ELLIN *Stronghold* 60 'Did it strike you,' Coco asks at his snotty meanest, 'that if we came properly prepared, we could have stopped him from taking off?'

**c.** *dial.* or *slang.* Angry, curt, short-tempered; pert, saucy, impudent; proud, conceited. Now *esp.* supercilious, aloof, 'snooty'.

**1870-** in various dial. glossaries and texts. **1905** JOYCE *Let.* 7 Feb. (1966) II. 80 Are the 'girls' 'snotty' about Nora? **1916** W. OWEN *Let.* 9 Dec. (1967) 417 A snotty, acid, scot, impatient, irritated wretch. **1926** E. HEMINGWAY *Sun also Rises* xviii. 218, I won't eat down-stairs with that German head waiter. He was damned snotty. **1936** J. REITH *Diary* 13 May (1975) ii. 170 This is an insult... I was very snotty and reserved with the prig. **1968** *Globe & Mail Mag.* (Toronto) 13 Jan. 12/3 Francois is not always snotty, thank heaven. **1978** T. GIFFORD *Glendower Legacy* (1979) 39 He..thought for a moment of taking up the possibility of an exchange program with the snotty bastards in Cultural Affairs.

**2.** Consisting of snot; mucous; of the nature of, or resembling, snot; viscous, slimy. ? *Obs.*

**1656** RIDGLEY *Pract. Physick* 88 That snotty white matter is not the fat. **1658** A. FOX *Würtz' Surg.* II. xxii. 137 Cooling Ointments—of Oyls and other snotty and greasie things. **1683** SNAPE *Anat. Horse* III. v. (1686) 111 The snotty Excrements of the Brain. *c* **1720** GIBSON *Farrier's Guide* II. xxviii. (1738) 100 All that snotty matter comes from thence.

**snotty-nose.** Now *rare.* [See prec.]

**a.** One whose nose is dirty with snot; hence, a paltry, mean, or contemptible fellow.

**1602** DEKKER *Honest Whore* I. II. i, Hang him, Mole catcher, it's the dreamingest snotty nose. **1614** B. JONSON *Barth. Fair* II. v, Dos't so, snotty nose? good Lord! are you sniueling? **1712** *Odes of Horace* v. 12/2, I own he is no Snotty-Nose. **1932** L. GOLDING *Magnolia St.* III. i. 495 A little snotty-nose like that..and he's the [boxing] champion from all the world!

**b.** *attrib.* or as *adj.* Snotty-nosed.

**1622** MASSINGER & DEKKER *Virg. Martyr* II. i, Our puling, snotty-nose lady sent me out likewise. **1751** SMOLLETT *Per. Pickle* ii, A snotty-nose boy, whom I myself have ordered to the gun, for stealing eggs.

**'snotty-nosed,** *a.* [Cf. prec.] Having the nose running or dirty with snot; also, mean, paltry, contemptible.

**1610** SELDEN *English Janus* Pref. 25 Let snotty nosed Fellows..approve what I write, or let them flout and fleer. **1712** ARBUTHNOT *John Bull* I. xv, My Husband took him in, a dirty, snotty-nosed Boy. **1721** BAILEY, *Snivelling*, peaking, snotty-nosed, childish. **1886** ELWORTHY *W. Somerset Word-bk.* 690 A snotty-nosed boy. **1894** J. HARTLEY *Clock Alm.* 2 (E.D.D.), Snotty-noased lads 'at aw remember. **1948** *Sun* (Baltimore) 20 Aug. 15/8 It was Walker who once told the Babe on a memorable occasion never to let down 'those snotty-nosed kids' who always loved him. **1971** P. AUDEMARS *Stolen like Magic Away* v. 66 All that love and.. passion—thrown away every day on a bunch of snotty-nosed kids who take it..for granted. **1978** N. J. CRISP *London Deal* vii. 109 There's a snotty nosed young DC from the Yard sitting in his car outside.

**snouch,** *sb.* [f. next.] A jibe, jeer, or scoff.

*c* **1780** in *Gentl. Mag.* (1848) June 616/1 The taunts and snouches which the two English regiments had thrown upon the Virgin Mary's Guards.

**snouch** (snaʊtʃ), *v.* ? *Obs.* Also snoutch. [Of obscure origin.] *trans.* To snub; to treat scornfully. Also *absol.*

**1761** MRS. F. SHERIDAN *S. Biddulph* (1796) III. 156, I am glad of it, said he (very quick); I'll be here to snoutch them. Dear Sir, said I,..you cannot conceive how humbled they are. **1809** *Ann. Reg.* 40 They may pun and epigrammatise, they may sneer, or they may snoutch. **1819** *New Whig Guide* 131 Then at last they might discover 'Tis not well to *snouch* me so.

**snouk,** variant of SNOKE *v.*

**snous** (snaʊs). Also snouse. [ad. Da. or Sw. *snus* snuff.] Powdered tobacco.

**1962** J. ONSLOW *Bowler-Hatted Cowboy* xxi. 204 His lower lip bulged with a wad of 'snouse', or Copenhagen snuff. **1979** *Guardian* 31 Mar. 13/5 The narcotic to which most [Swedish] young people are addicted is..'snous', a concoction of powdered tobacco stuffed under the upper lip.

**snout** (snaʊt), *sb.*[1] Forms: 3-4 snute, 4-6 snoute, 4-7 snowte, 7 snoote; 4- snout (6 snought), 6-7, *Sc.* 8-9 snowt. [ME. *snūt(e,* = WFris. *snût, snute* (NFris. *snüt, snit*), MDu. *snūte, snuut* (Kilian *snuyte*, Du. *snuit*), MLG. *snût(e,* G. *schnauze* (†*schnausze, schnauz*), MSw. and Sw. dial. *snuta*, Da. *snude*, Norw. and Sw. *snut.*

The early history of these forms is somewhat obscure. There is no example of an OE. or ON. *snút* or *snút-*, although the existence of the stem is proved by the verbal derivatives, OE. *snýtan*, ON. *snýta* (see SNITE *v.*), and it is possible that both in English and the Scand. languages the sb. has been adopted from LG. A variation of the stem appears in the synonymous older G. *schnotz(e.*]

**1. a.** The trunk of an elephant. Also *transf.*

*c* **1220** *Bestiary* 669 in *O.E. Misc.*, Rennande cumeð a ȝungling,..his snute him under puteð, and..ðis elp he reisen on stalle. **1387** TREVISA *Higden* (Rolls) V. 159 Þe snowtes of olyfauntes and his hors eren were..ful of gnattes. *a* **1400-50** *Alexander* 3633 Þire Olifantis of ynde..was snaypid on þe snowte with þe snart hetis. **1542** UDALL *Erasm. Apoph.* 196 b, [The elephant] with his snoute tendrely plucked out of his maister's bodye all the said dartes. **1581** MARBECK *Bk. Notes* 72 Also y^e long snout of an Elephant is called an hand or an arme, for that by that instrument he worketh manie things. **1600** J. PORY tr. *Leo's Africa* IX. 337 If the Elephant intendeth to hurt any man, he casteth him on the ground with his long snout or trunk. **1676** WOOD *Life* (O.H.S.) II. 349 Crest unicorne head..between elephants' snowtes. **1753** *Chambers's Cycl.* Suppl. s.v. *Elephant*, The Elephant this author [Linnæus] distinguishes by his snout. **1828-32** WEBSTER, *Trunk*,..the snout or proboscis of an elephant.

**b.** The projecting part of the head of an animal, which includes the nose and mouth (= MUZZLE *sb.*[1] 1); the proboscis or rostrum of an insect; †the beak or bill of a bird, etc.

**13..** *K. Alis.* 6534 (Laud MS.), On his snoute an horne he [the rhinoceros] beres. *c* **1380** WYCLIF *Sel. Wks.* I. 200 Whanne þei bigynen to ȝoule, þei turnen her snowte to hevene ward. **1390** GOWER *Conf.* I. 326 This Leoun..A beste..Hath slain, and with his blodi snoute [etc.]. *c* **1440** *Promp. Parv.* 462/1 Snowte, or bylle, *rostrum.* *c* **1475** HENRYSON *Poems* (S.T.S.) III. 151 With þe snowt of ane selch, ane swelling to swage. **1535** COVERDALE *Prov.* xi. 22 Like a rynge of golde in a swynes snoute. **1570** LEVINS *Manip.* 228 Y^e Snoute of a dog, *rostrum.* *Ibid.*, Y^e Snout of a fish, *rostrum.* **1601** HOLLAND *Pliny* II. 390 Only the little pretty snouts end of a mouse. **1687** A. LOVELL tr. *Thevenot's Trav.* I. 245 They have a long sharp Snout, full of long and sharp Teeth, but no Tongue. **1725** *Fam. Dict.* s.v. *Boar*, In the Choice of this Animal, you must pitch upon one.. having..a thick Head, long Snout. **1753** *Chambers' Cycl.* Suppl. s.v. *Rostrum*, The *rostrum* or snout in fishes varies very much in figure. **1784** COWPER *Task* v. 50 His dog.. snatches up the drifted snow,..or ploughs it with his snout. **1802** SHAW *Gen. Zool.* III. II. 587 Greenish-black Slow-Worm..with elongated snout. **1873** MIVART *Elem. Anat.* ix. 380 An extra median ossicle may be developed in the snout, as e.g. in the mole. **1901** FOUNTAIN *Deserts N. Amer.* ix. 183 The large fleshy snout of the moose.

**2.** Contemptuously: The nose in man, esp. when large or badly shaped; †the face or countenance.

*a* **1300** *K. Horn* 1082 He lokede him abute, Wiþ his colmie snute. *c* **1380** *Sir Ferumb.* 1760 A boȝ adoun on þat tyde and cauȝte hym [the Saracen] by þe snoute. *c* **1400** *Laud Troy Bk.* 7942 Some lefft his hed, and som his snout. **1483** *Cath. Angl.* 347/1 A Snowte, *vbi* A nese. **1508** KENNEDIE *Flyting w. Dunbar* 550 Out! out! I schout, apon that snowt that snevillis. **1548** UDALL, etc. *Erasm. Par. Luke* i. 26 The sturdie holders up of their snoute he hath cast downe. **1592** GREENE *Upst. Courtier* Wks. (Grosart) XI. 242 Betweene the filthy reumicast of his bloudshotten snowt, there appeared smale holes. **1645** MILTON *Colast.* Wks. 1851 IV. 368 But what should a man say more to a snout in this pickle? **1693** DRYDEN, etc. *Juvenal* x. (1697) 250 What Ethiop Lips he has, How foul a Snout, and what a hanging Face! **1708** *Brit. Apollo* No. 38. 2/1 Her Chin and Snout are so firmly united. **1771** SMOLLETT *Humph. Cl.* (1815) 72 A young fellow,..when he first thrusts his snout into the world, is apt to be surprised at many things. **1820** SCOTT *Monast.* xxvi, Sae I said it wad prove since I first saw the false Southron snout of thee.

**†b.** In asseverations or imprecations. *Obs.*

*c* **1330** R. BRUNNE *Chron. Wace* (Rolls) 11935 We schal.. reue hym his regne, maugre his snoute. *c* **1386** CHAUCER *Shipman's T.* 1595 What? evel thedom on his monkes snowte! **14..** *Sir Beues* (MS. C) 1622 + 65 Then seyde the portar, 'Be my snowte, Thys was Befyse, that y lete owte'.

**c.** Phr. *to have a snout on* (someone), to bear ill-will towards someone. *Austral.*

**1941** BAKER *Dict. Austral. Slang* 69 *Snout on, have a*, to bear a grudge against a person. **1949** L. GLASSOP *Lucky Palmer* 212 He's got a snout on the Kid for something. **1966** T. RONAN *Once there was Bagman* 39 The reason you blokes have such a snout on him..is that he's forgotten more Law than you've ever learned.

**3.** The end of a ship's prow; the beak or rostrum of a vessel.

**1387** TREVISA *Higden* (Rolls) III. 237 Schippes of werre wiþ yren snowtes. **1513** DOUGLAS *Æneid* VIII. xii. 2 The weyrly schippis wyth thair snowtis of steyll. *a* **1572** KNOX *Hist. Ref.* Wks. 1846 I. 120 Upon Sounday..ordered thei thare schippis so that a galay or two lade thare snowttis to the craiggis. **1632** J. HAYWARD tr. *Biondi's Eromena* 61 Metaneone..hastened to grapple with the Galley; and.. tearing off her snout,..bruised her all-over. *a* **1668** LASSELS *Voy. Italy* (1698) II. 84 The Rostra or brazen snouts of the ships won from the Antiates. **1853** KANE *Grinnell Exped.* xxiii. (1856) 182 Five black masses [*sc.* ships]..are seen with their snouts shoved into the shore of ice. **1871** R. ELLIS *Catullus* lxiv. 12 Scarcely the forward snout tore up that wintery water.

**4.** A structure, formation, projecting part, etc., resembling or suggestive of a snout; a nozzle or the like. Also with *of.*

*a* **1425** tr. *Arderne's Treat. Fistula*, etc. 9 A snowted nedle ..ow to be no gretter ne lenger in þe snowte þan as it is paynted. *Ibid.* 24 Putte..þe poynt of þe rasour in þe holwnes of þe snowte. **1447** BOKENHAM *Seyntys* (Roxb.) 27 My penne also gynnyth make obstacle,..For I so ofte have maad to penne Hys snowte up on my thombys ende. **1612** WOODALL *Surg. Mate* Wks. (1653) 12 Your glister pot should be made with a snout or lip. **1623** MINSHEU *Sp. Dict.*, *Limon del cárro*, the long snout that goeth between the oxen in a waine. **1687** MIÉGE *Gt. Fr. Dict.* I, *Tuiau de Souflet*, a Bellows-Snout. **1755** JOHNSON, *Snout*,..the nosel or end of any hollow pipe. **1875** KNIGHT *Dict. Mech.* 1535/1 The snout of a pair of bellows or a tuyere. **1902** 'LINESMAN' *Words Eyewitness* 198 The heavy naval ordnance begin to cock their long snouts higher..into the air.

**b.** A projecting point of land, rock, etc.

**1536** BELLENDEN *Cron. Scot.* (1821) I. p. xxviii, Galloway rinnis, with ane gret snout of craggis...in the Irland seis. This snout is callit be the peple, the Mulis Nuk. **1773** FERGUSSON *Poems* II. (1789) 35 The bonny wa'-flowers sprout On yonder Ruin's lofty snout. **1867** N. MACLEOD *Highland Parish, Spirit of Eld* 362 The black raven..sat on a snout of rock above him. **1873** BRUCE in Morley *Gladstone* VI. xi. (1905) II. 47, I see no other rock ahead; but sometimes they project their snouts unexpectedly.

**c.** The front portion or termination of a glacier.

**1841** B. HALL *Patchwork* I. vii. 107 The glacier;..its enormous snout ploughs up the ground before it. **1860** TYNDALL *Glac.* II. xvii. 322 The snout of the glacier abuts against the ground. **1878** HUXLEY *Physiogr.* 161 At the end, or snout, of the glacier, the water issues forth.

**†5.** *slang.* A hogshead. *Obs.*$^{-0}$

**1725** in *New Cant. Dict.* (Hence in Grose.)

**6.** *slang.* A police informer.

**1910** C. E. B. RUSSELL *Young Gaol-Birds* xii. 176 He was in reality a 'snout' or 'nark',..and from time to time had 'given away' many of his comrades. **1938** F. D. SHARPE *Sharpe of Flying Squad* xvii. 189 A 'sneak' or 'snout' is looked upon more or less as a leper in the Under-world. **1954** [see GRASS *sb.*[1] 12]. **1964** *Sunday Mail Mag.* (Brisbane) 5 Apr. 5/5 Then a 'snout' (or informant) called Big Ears made a long trip just to tell me: 'You're in trouble, Monty.' **1977** 'E. CRISPIN' *Glimpses of Moon* xii. 235 His previous arrests had all been..the work probably of some anonymous snout. **1982** *Observer* 15 Aug. 22/6 You may have been 'grassed'..by a 'snout'.

**7.** One or other of various species of moths characterized by having abnormally long palpi projecting in front of the head; esp. the snout-moth, *Hypena proboscidalis.*

**1819** SAMOUELLE *Entomol. Comp.* 424 *Herminia albistrigalis.* The white-line Snout. **1832** J. RENNIE *Butterfl. & Moths* 145 The Snout. *Ibid.* 146 The Small Snout. *Ibid.* 147 White-line Snout... Rib-striped Snout. **1882** *Cassell's Nat. Hist.* VI. 66 The 'Snout' (*Hypena proboscidalis*), a brown Moth, with rather slender body, and very long palpi, resembling a beak.

**8.** *attrib.*, as ***snout-bone, -end, -nose, -piece***; **snout-beetle**, one or other of several species of beetles characterized by having the head prolonged into a rostrum or proboscis; **snout-face**, used as a personal insult; **† snout-flower** (see quot.); **snout-horn**, a rhinoceros (*poet.*); the horn of a rhinoceros or beetle; **snout-moth** (see sense 7); **snout-ring** (see quot.).

**1868** *Rep. U.S. Commiss. Agric.* (1869) 308 The *Curculionidæ*, *snout beetles, or weevils, infest grain, seeds, or fruits. **1889** *Cent. Dict.*, *Otiorhynchidæ*, an important family of rhynchophorous *Coleoptera*, or snout-beetles. **1846** YOUATT *Pig* (1847) 118 Between the supplemental, or *snout-bone, and the proper nasal. **1681** GREW *Musæum* I. II. i. 18 From his *Snout-end to his Tail. **1923** D. H. LAWRENCE *Birds, Beasts & Flowers* 184 But you, you *snout-face, you reject nothing. **1979** *Amer. Poetry Rev.* Mar./Apr. 6/2 And the people In the streets, speechless, saw them passing: The scrawny guy, the bare-foot one, the fellow with The bicycle, The black, Snout-face, that gal in yellow, [etc.]. **1715** *Phil. Trans.* XXIX. 269 *Plantæ Nasifloræ.* *Snout-flowers. **1625** LISLE *Du Bartas, Noe* 28 The *Snout-horne large, The rinde-hide Elephant, the Camel. *c* **1711** PETIVER *Gazophyl.* VII. §70 Sawing thro' the Bark by the Help of their Snout-horn. **1819** SAMOUELLE *Entomol. Comp.* 253 *Snout moth. **1887** *Cassell's Encycl. Dict.* s.v., Snout-moth, *Hypena proboscidalis.* Body slender, wings broad and triangular, colour mainly brown. **1896** LYDEKKER *Roy. Nat. Hist.* VI. 118 The snout-moths (*Hypena*). **1775** ASH, *Silo*,..one that has a *snout nose. **1621** BURTON *Anat. Mel.* III. iii. IV. ii. 702 A modest virgine..to such a faire *snout piece is much to be preferred. **1875** KNIGHT *Dict. Mech.*, *Snout-ring, a ring or staple placed in the nose of a hog to deter him from rooting.

**9.** *Comb.*, as ***snout-bearing, -holy, -horned, -like.***

**1589** [? NASHE] *Almond for Parrat* 4 The painted poison of snout-holy deuotion. **1593** G. HARVEY *Pierce's Super.* Wks. (Grosart) II. 302 That same snowt-horned Rhinoceros. **1883** *Cassell's Encycl. Dict.* s.v. *Curculionidæ*, Sub-tribe Rhynchophora (Snout-bearing Insects). **1909** *Daily Chron.* 18 Jan. 5/3 A very remarkable snout-like head.

**snout** (snaʊt), *sb.*[2] *slang.* [Of obscure origin.]

**1. a.** Tobacco.

**1885** A. GRIFFITHS *Fast & Loose* III. xii. 202 He knows Joe; worked for him, with regard to snout (tobacco); and he's straight—as a rod. **1896** *Westm. Gaz.* 29 May 2/1 Here, mate, give us a bit of the snout. **1904** A. GRIFFITHS *50 Yrs. Public Service* xi. 154 The 'snout'..is introduced in small quantities, and distributed by the prisoners themselves.

**b.** A cigarette.

**1950** P. TEMPEST *Lag's Lexicon* 193 *Snout.* Word used collectively to cover all tobacco, hand-rolled and factory-made cigarettes, cigarette ends, and pipe dottles. **1954** *Evening News* 7 Jan. 2/2 Savage was seen and said: 'You will not find any export snouts here.' **1959** H. HOBSON *Mission House Murder* xxix. 187, I would smoke it slowly and..save the butt—*snouts*, the old lags called them. **1961** R. LONGRIGG *Daughters of Mulberry* 94 'Snout?' said her Ronnie, offering the Rothman's Kingsize. **1966** P. MOLONEY *Plea for Mersey* 54 Goin down the city fer a booze an a snout. **1976** J. O'CONNOR *Eleventh Commandment* vii. 91 If you were wise you chose non-smokers as your friends because they wouldn't shop you to an unscrupulous warder for a couple of snouts.

**2.** *attrib.*, as ***snout ash, baron*** [BARON 2c], ***case, gaff*** [GAFF *sb.*⁴ 3], ***paper***.

**1962** R. COOK *Crust on its Uppers* i. 21 Ever had someone put some snout ash in your rosie? **1950** P. TEMPEST *Lag's Lexicon* 194 Snout-baron. **1964** *Economist* 25 Jan. 317/1 The 'snout barons'—prisoners who make a profit from the shortage of tobacco within prisons. **1962** R. COOK *Crust on its Uppers* iv. 48 'I'm going to give our Brian a fag,' an' he.. brings out this heavy old snout case. **1936** Snout gaff [see GAFF *sb.*⁴ 3]. **1958** *Encounter* Apr. 18/1 He hardly ever spoke to me unless he wanted something, like a smoke or a snout paper.

**snout** (snaʊt), *v.* [f. SNOUT *sb.*[1]]

**1.** *trans.* To finish *off* with a snout.

**1753** *Songs & Poems Costume* (Percy Soc.) 230 Hang a small bugle cap on, as big as a crown, Snout it off with a flower *vulgo dict.* a pompoon.

**2.** *trans.* and *intr.* To root, dig up, or grub, with or as with the snout.

**1857** G. H. KINGSLEY *Sport & Trav.* (1900) 452 He would .. snout and jigger about the stones in a most unsalmon-like manner. **1884** STEVENSON *Lett.* (1899) I. vi. 306 The brutal and licentious public, snouting in Mudie's wash-trough. **1888** *Daily News* 29 Mar. 3/2 Snouting, grubbing, and biting their ditch.. deep enough for great ocean ships to sail through.

**3.** *trans.* To bear ill-will towards; to treat with disfavour, to rebuff. Freq. as pa. pple. and ppl. adj. *Austral. slang.*

**1916** C. J. DENNIS *Moods of Ginger Mick* 11 An' snouted them that snouted 'im, an' never give a dam. **1916** —— *Songs of Sentimental Bloke* 13 The world 'as got me snouted jist a treat. **1944** A. MARSHALL *These are my People* 155, I was sore as a snouted sheila for weeks. **1970** R. BEILBY *No Medals for Aphrodite* 149 That officer happened to have me snouted because I got you across the river, against his orders.

**4.** *intr.* To act as a police informer. *slang.*

**1923** E. WALLACE *Missing Million* xx. 161 The gang found he was snouting. **1930** —— *White Face* xiii. 206 Dr. Marford knows, but he's not the feller that goes snouting on his patients. **1962** D. WARNER *Death of Bogey* II. iii. 71 No one wanted to be seen talking to him in case they were afterwards accused of snouting. Nevertheless, a great many did snout. **1973** 'B. MATHER' *Snowline* x. 116 I've got to live in London when I go back. How long do you think I'd last if word got round that I'd been snouting?

Hence **'snouting** *vbl. sb.* (also *attrib.*).

**1937** PARTRIDGE *Dict. Slang* 795/2 *Snouting*, vbl. n., giving information to the police. **1962** [see sense 4 above]. **1973** J. WAINWRIGHT *Pride of Pigs* 55 Arranging a 'snouting service' with those villains; the lesser hooks being pulled in for the piffling crimes, while the big boys work the blinders without .. being pushed too hard. **1978** F. BRANSTON *Sergeant Ritchie's Conscience* iv. 56 He started on his snouting expedition.

**snouted** ('snaʊtɪd), *ppl. a.* [f. SNOUT *sb.*[1]]

**1.** Of things: Furnished with a snout or distinct terminal part.

*a* **1425** tr. *Arderne's Treat. Fistula*, etc. 9 Anoþer instrument, þat is called 'Acus rostrata', a snowted nedle, for it hath þe tone heued like a snowte. *Ibid.* 32. **1584** B. R. tr. *Herodotus* I. 53 They had.. no beaked or snowted shippes armed with a pyke or stemme of iron. **1605** CAMDEN *Rem.* (1623) 200 Their shooes and patens are snowted and piked more then a finger long crooking vpwards. **1772–84** *Cook's Voy.* (1790) V. 1903 All of them wear a sort of oval snouted cap, made of wood. **1869** in *Eng. Dial. Dict.* s.v., The neat clogs of the factory girls are snouted with brass.

**2.** Of persons or animals: Provided or furnished with a snout, muzzle, or rostrum. In early use predicative with *like*.

Also freq. in combs., as *long-, sharp-, short-snouted*.

*a* **1536** *Songs, Carols*, etc. (E.E.T.S.) 113 Sum [people] be snowted like an ape. **1565** J. PHILLIP *Patient Grissell* 23 (Malone Soc.), A Horse which to my Judgement.. Was snowted like a wodcoke. **1611** COTGR. s.v. *Chenin*, A kind of Badger, that is.. snowted like a dog. **1613** PURCHAS *Pilgrimage* (1614) 503 The Rhinoceros is.. snouted like a Hogge. *a* **1700** EVELYN *Diary* 18 June 1657, A sort of Catt.. snouted much like the Egyptian racoon. **1796** COLERIDGE *Lett.* (1895) 194 [To] feed a couple of snouted and grunting cousins from the refuse. **1802** SHAW *Gen. Zool.* III. II. 587 Snouted Slow-worm. *Anguis Nasuta.* **1804** *Ibid.* V. I. 87 Snouted Salmon. *Salmo Nasus.* **1855** WHITTIER *The Barefoot Boy* 53 For my sport the squirrel played, Plied the snouted mole his spade. **1859** N. P. WILLIS *Convalescent* xxxii. 181, I spied the snouted invader rooting busily in the velvet sward.

**3.** Shaped or fashioned like a snout; snout-like.

**1866** J. B. ROSE tr. *Ovid's Met.* 89 Lycabas.. appeared with gaping jaws and snouted nose. **1872** BLACKIE *Lays Highl.* 100 By this snouted crag will blow Oft a sudden whiff. **1882** *Harper's Mag.* LXV. 89 Adorned a smooth head with a snouted countenance.

**'snouter.** [f. SNOUT *sb.*[1]] (See quot.)

**1875** KNIGHT *Dict. Mech.* 2230/1 *Snouter*, a cutting shears with one curved blade approximating to the shape of a hog's snout, and used for removing at one cut the cartilage wherewith he roots.

†**snout-fair**, *a. Obs.* [f. SNOUT *sb.*[1] Cf. MSw. *snutofagher*, Sw. *snutfager*.] Having a fair countenance; fair-faced, comely, handsome.

Freq. in 16th and early 17th cent., usually with some disparaging suggestion.

**1530** TINDALE *Pract. Prelates* F ij, If he come in to an house, & the wiff be snoutefayre he will rote him self there. **1598** BP. HALL *Sat.* IV. i. 111 Who list excuse? when chaister dames can hyre Some snout-faire stripling to their applesquire. **1616** R. C. *Times' Whistle* (1871) 34, I knowe a snowt-faire, selfe-conceited asse. **1649** QUARLES *Virgin Widow* I, True, She's snout faire; yet by her favour I Would scarce turn tables with her, though I say't.

†**'snouting**[1]. *Obs.*⁻¹ [? f. SNOUT *sb.*[1]] A variety of apple.

**1651** CHILD in Hartlib *Legacy* (1655) 19 In Biscay.. they make Cider of a certain sweet Apple, which hath a little bitterness in it, and is like to our snouting.

†**'snouting**[2]. *Obs.*⁻¹ [app. f. Du. *snuit* tow.] (See quot.)

**1662** *Irish Statutes* (1765) II. 416 Snouting, alias snayl, or drest towe, the twelve pound, [£]0.5ˢ 0.

**'snoutish**, *a.* [f. SNOUT *sb.*[1] + -ISH.] Somewhat resembling a snout.

**1898** G. B. SHAW *Plays* II. *Candida* 88 He is podgy, with a snoutish nose.

**'snoutless**, *a. rare.* [f. SNOUT *sb.*[1]] Destitute or devoid of a snout or point.

**1862** LOWELL *Biglow P.* Ser. II. iv. *Festina Lente*, Here snoutless tails, there tailless snouts: The only gainers were the pouts.

**snouty** ('snaʊtɪ), *a.* [f. SNOUT *sb.*[1]]

**1.** Resembling a snout or muzzle; having a pronounced or prominent snout.

*a* **1685** OTWAY *Compl. Muse* xii, The Nose was ugly, long, and big, Broad, and snowty like a Pig. **1863** HUXLEY *Man's Place in Nature* iii. 147 The skull.. is called 'prognathous'; a term which has been rendered, with more force than elegance, by the Saxon equivalent 'snouty'. **1880** G. MEREDITH *Tragic Com.* iii. (1892) 25 The hairy, hoofy, snouty evil one.

**2.** *colloq.* Overbearing; insolent.

**1858** *Times* 29 Nov., Her manner was so domineering that he could not imagine she was his wife:—her manner was perfectly 'snouty'.

**Snovian** ('snəʊvɪən), *a.* [f. the name of the English writer Charles Percy *Snow* (1905–80), on the model of SHAVIAN *a.* and *sb.*, etc.] Of or pertaining to the writings or ideas of C. P. Snow. Hence **'Snovianism**, the beliefs or theories of C. P. Snow.

**1966** *Listener* 19 May 733/1 This twinkling dancing life and soul of these almost edible pages is also one of the Snovian Olympians. *Ibid.*, Nothing could be more depressing than this total acceptance of the doctrines of Snovianism, even down to the use of the term *mana* and the reluctance to take seriously anyone below the rank of knight bachelor. **1969** *Observer* 17 Aug. 21/2 The attack on scientific rationalism.. first appears in a paper on the Snovian conception of the Two Cultures. **1977** P. JOHNSON *Enemies of Society* xii. 163 The United Kingdom, compared with other.. countries.. had (in 1964) 'the greatest concentration on science and technology in higher education and the biggest proportion of qualified scientists and technologists.. in relation to population and labour-force'—the exact opposite of the conventional Snovian thesis.

**snow** (snəʊ), *sb.*[1] Forms: α. (Latterly *north.* and *Sc.*) 1– snaw, 4–6, 8–9 snawe; 1 snauw, 1–4, 6 snau, 5 snaue; 1, 9 sna, 9 snaa. β. 3– snow (3 snou, snov), 3–7 snowe (5 sknowe), 9 *dial.* sno, snoo. γ. 3–4 snouh, 3 snovȝ, 4 snowh, snowȝ, snoȝ. [Common Teutonic: OE. *snáw*, = OFris. **snê* (WFris. *snie*, EFris. *snē*, *snö*, NFris. *sne*, *sni*, *snīe*), MDu. *sneeu*, *sneu*, *snee* (Du. *sneeuw*, dial. *snee*), OS. *snêu*, *snêw-* (MLG. and LG. *snee*), OHG. *snêo*, *snêw-* (MHG. *snê*, G. *schnee*), ON. *snǽr*, *snjár*, *snjór* (Icel. *snjór*, Norw. *snjo*, *snjø*, *snø*, etc.; MSw. *snyo*, *snyö*, etc., Sw. *snö*; MDa. *snø*, *sne*, Da. *sne*), Goth. *snaiws*:—OTeut. **snaiwaz*. Various grades of the pre-Teut. stem are widely represented in the cognate languages, as Lith. *snĕgas*, OSlav. *snegŭ* (Russ. *snieg'*), OIr. *snechta* (Ir. *sneachd*), L. *niv-is* (*nix*), Gr. *νίφα* (acc.) snow, *νίφει* it snows, etc.]

**I. 1. a.** The partially frozen vapour of the atmosphere falling in flakes characterized by their whiteness and lightness; the fall of these flakes, or the layer formed by them on the surface of the ground.

α. *c* **825** *Vesp. Ps.* cxlvii. 16 Se seleð snaw swe swe wulle. *a* **1000** *Boeth. Metr.* xxix. 63 Swylce hagal & snaw hrusan leccað On wintres tid. *c* **1050** *O.E. Chron.* (MS. C) an. 1046, On þis ylcan ȝeare.. com se stranga winter mid forste & mid snawe. *c* **1175** *Lamb. Hom.* 35 Ic walde fein pinian and sitten on forste and on snawe up et mine chinne. *c* **1205** LAY. 27459 Flan al swa þicke swa þe snau adun ualleð. *a* **1300** *Cursor M.* 22692 A stormi dai.. Bath o frost, and hail, and snau. **1375** BARBOUR *Bruce* IX. 128 This wes eftir the Martymes, Quhen snaw had helit all the land. **1432–50** tr. *Higden* (Rolls) I. 265 Peple.. whiche haue plente of snawe in the tyme of somer. **1549** *Compl. Scot.* vi. 59 The snau is ane congelit rane. **1596** DALRYMPLE tr. *Leslie's Hist. Scot.* I. 31 How deip saeuir be the snawe,.. thay nevir thair heid sett vndir the ruffe of ony hous. **1781** BURNS *Winter* i, The stormy North sends driving forth The blinding sleet and snaw. **1863** QUINN *Heather Lintie* (ed. 2) 196, I.. saw Puir Robin 'midst the driftin snaw.

β. *c* **1200** *Trin. Coll. Hom.* 99 Þis is þe holi manne [= manna] þe ure drihten sende alse snow sleðrende. *c* **1250** *Owl & Night.* 413 Þu singest so doþ hen a snowe. **13..** *Fall & Passion* 13 in *E.E.P.*, Seue daies a seue niȝt as ȝe seeþ þat fallip snowe. **1377** LANGL. *P. Pl.* B. xv. 110 A dongehul, þat were bysnewed with snowe. *c* **1400** *Destr. Troy* 10971 Of cleane white, As the glyssenond glemes þat glenttes on þe sknowe. *c* **1425** *Cast. Persev.* 2642 in *Macro Plays* 156 It [riches] flyet a-wey, as any snowe. **1526** *Pilgr. Perf.* (W. de W. 1531) 140 Let vs stande there in yᵉ rayne or snowe, all thus storuen for colde. **1562** HEYWOOD *Prov. & Epigr.* (1867) 51 Snow is white And lyeth in the dike. **1617** MORYSON *Itin.* I. 179, I could hardly keepe him.. from being drowned in the snow. **1672** PETTY *Pol. Anat.* (1691) 50 The Snow lies not long in the lower ground of Ireland. **1774** GOLDSM. *Nat. Hist.* (1776) I. 372 Some vapours that ascend to great heights, will be frozen into snow. **1813** SIR H. DAVY *Agric. Chem.* (1814) 209 Snow and ice are bad conductors of heat. **1860** TYNDALL *Glac.* I. ii. 19 A vast quantity of snow fell during the night. **1878** HUXLEY *Physiogr.* 155 Snow is white and opaque in consequence of the air entangled among its crystals.

γ. *c* **1250** *Owl & Night.* 430 Hwanne snouh liþ þikke & wide. *c* **1290** *S. Eng. Leg.* I. 209 Þat.. caldore was þane ani ys oþur snovȝ. *c* **1320** *Cast. Love* 722 Þe snowȝ [*v.r.* snowh] þat is sneuwynge. **1382** WYCLIF *Prov.* xxvi. 1 What maner snoȝ in somer, and reyn in rep time [etc.].

**b.** Taken as a type of whiteness or brightness.

See also DRIVEN *ppl. a.* 2.

*c* **825** *Vesp. Ps.* l. 9 Ofer snaw ic biom ȝehwitad. *c* **950** *Lindisf. Gosp.* Matt. xvii. 2 Wedo his ȝeworden weron huita sua sna [*Rushw.* snau]. **971** *Blickling Hom.* 147 Heo hæfde seofon siþum beorhtran saule þonne snaw. *a* **1200** *Vices & Virtues* 83 Ðanne wurð ic.. hwittere ðane ani snaw. **1297** R. GLOUC. (Rolls) 9514 Wite cloþes heo dude hire on, as wo seiþ, ilich þe snowe. *a* **1366** CHAUCER *Rom. Rose* 558 Hir throte, al-so whyt of hewe, As snow on braunche snowed newe. **1423** JAS. I *Kingis Q.* lxvii, Hir faire fresche face, as quhite as ony snawe. *a* **1533** LD. BERNERS *Huon* lxx. 239 He chaunged coloure and waxed as whyte as snowe. **1593** G. FLETCHER *Licia*, etc. (Grosart) 106 So is my sweet, much paler than the snowe. **1634** SIR T. HERBERT *Trav.* 25 The Ocean was as white as snow. **1730–46** THOMSON *Autumn* 916 How, white as hyperborean snow To form the lucid lawn. **1817** SHELLEY *Rev. Islam* I. liv, Some, whose white hair shone Like mountain snow.

**c.** In various fig. or allusive uses.

*a* **1548** HALL *Chron., Edw. IV*, 43 Why you.. so sore laboured and entyced me to passe ouer the Sea, promysynge mountaines of Golde, whiche turned into snowe. **1591** SHAKS. *Two. Gent.* II. vii. 19 Thou wouldst as soone goe kindle fire with snow. **1594** —— *Rich. III*, I. iv. 249 *Cla.* O do not slander him, for he is kinde. [*First Murderer.*] Right, as Snow in Haruest. **1668** DRYDEN *Dram. Poesy* Ess. (ed. Ker) I. 43 He was not only a professed imitator of Horace, but a learned plagiary of all the others; you track him every where in their snow. **1738** *Wesley's Hymns*, *'Come holy Spirit, send down those Beams'* iii, Warm with thy Fire our Hearts of Snow. **1854** MISS BAKER *Northampt. Gloss.* s.v., He looks as cold as snow in harvest. **1860** HUGHES *Tom Brown at Oxf.* xxxiii, When one has been a year at Oxford, there isn't much snow left to soil. **1862** PUSEY in Liddon *Life* (1897) IV. 241 Here.. we seem to be so familiar with our evils as to acquiesce in them, sleeping in the snow, which is death.

**d.** With adjs. of colour, denoting snow tinged by various foreign substances, or the alga, etc., to which the colouring is due.

**1678–** [see RED SNOW 1]. **1842** *Penny Cycl.* XXII. 168/1 A field of green snow. *Ibid.*, Martius arrived at the conclusion .. that the green snow (*Protococcus viridis*) and the red (*P. nivalis*) are one and the same plant. **1898** *Westm. Gaz.* 31 Mar. 7/2 Black snow in the Lake district... On Tuesday,.. it is stated, there was a sharp fall of perfectly black snow. **1909** *Cent. Dict.* Suppl. s.v., Golden snow.

**2. a.** A fall of snow; a snowstorm. Now *rare.*

Not always clearly distinguishable from sense 3.

*c* **888** K. ÆLFRED *Boeth.* xxiii, Norðanwindas & micle renas & snawas. **1408** tr. *Vegetius' De Re Milit.* (MS. Digby 233) 186/2 Sodeyn snowes.. rysyng & encrees of ryuers & flodus. **1489–90** *Plumpton Corr.* (Camden) 90 At my departing I rode.. a full troubleous way in that great snaw. **1562** *Child Marr.* 112 Apon a saturday afore that tyme, beynge a gret snowe. **1588** SHAKS. *L.L.L.* I. i. 106 At Christmas I no more desire a Rose, Then wish a Snow in Mayes new fangled showes. **1694** S. SEWALL *Diary* 16 Mar., A great Snow falls. **1717** *Ibid.* 20 Feb., Another Snow coming on. **1740** T. SMITH *Jrnl.* (1849) 268 We had only two snows and sledding but about three weeks. **1803** MARY CHARLTON *Wife & Mistress* II. 92 Her good man.. walked through a very thick snow, to inform her [etc.]. **1817** SHELLEY *Rev. Islam* IX. xxi, Next come the snows, and rain, And frosts, and storms.

*transf.* **1728** POPE *Dunc.* III. 262 How calm he sits at ease, 'Mid snows of paper and fierce hail of pease. **1855** KINGSLEY *Westw. Ho!* xix, Great white tassels.. tossed in their faces a fragrant snow of blossoms. **1866** B. TAYLOR *Poems, Poet's Jrnl.* 31 The bosom of the lawn Whitened beneath her silent snow of light.

**b.** As marking a period of time; a winter.

**1778** J. CARVER *Trav. N.-Amer.* 250 Those [Indians] in the interior parts.. count their years by winters; or, as they express themselves, by snows. **1825** LONGF. *Burial of Minnisink* iv, Thirty snows had not yet shed Their glory on the warrior's head. **1841** CATLIN *N. Amer. Ind.* (1844) I. xx. 147 The notches he had recorded for the snows (or years) of his life. **1850** TENNYSON *In Mem.* xxii. 4 Thro' four sweet years.., from snow to snow.

**3. a.** An accumulation, mass, expanse, or field, of snow.

*c* **1374** CHAUCER *Troylus* v. 10 The golden-tressed Phebus .. Thryes hadde alle with his bemes shene The snowes molte. **1596** DALRYMPLE tr. *Leslie's Hist. Scot.* I. 5 [There are] mony weitis, deip snawis. **1660** F. BROOKE tr. *Le Blanc's Trav.* 347 There is a large river.., which some Spanish were about to crosse, but could not for snows. **1693** DRYDEN, etc. *Juvenal* vi. (1697) 127 When Winter shuts the Seas, and fleecy Snows Make Houses white. **1705** ADDISON *Italy* 125 This River.. was much increas'd by the melting of the Snows when Cæsar pass'd it. **1748** GRAY *Alliance* 77 O'er Libya's deserts and through Zembla's snows. **1820** SCOTT *Monast.* xxxi, The snows of that Mont Blanc which we saw together. **1854** HOOKER *Himal. Jrnls.* II. xxix. 294 The most conspicuous group of snows seen from Khasia. **1878** Browning *La Saisiaz* 24 Yonder, where the far snows blanch Mute Mont Blanc.

**b.** *pl.* The regions of perpetual snow; the Arctic regions.

**1844** Emerson *Young American* Wks. (Bohn) II. 296 To men legislating for the area betwixt..the snows and the tropics.

**4.** Ellipt. for *snow tyre*, sense 8b below. *N. Amer.*

**1968** *Globe & Mail* (Toronto) 13 Jan. 26/2 (Advt.), 67 Fiat,..special exhaust, snows. **1977** *Detroit Free Press* 11 Dec. 22-D/8 (Advt.), '73 F-350 V8 4spd, dual tanks, PsPb, Ranger, snows.

**II. 5.** Applied to various things or substances having the colour or appearance of snow:

**a.** *Cookery.* A dish or confection resembling snow in appearance, esp. one made by whipping the white of eggs to a creamy consistency.

**1597** *Bk. Cookerie* F b, How to make Snowe. Take a quart of thicke cream, and fiue or sixe whites of eggs [etc.]. **1864** *Englishw. in India* 173 Whip the whites of six eggs to a hard snow. *a* **1887** *Cassell's Dict. Cookery* 375 Lemon snow. *Ibid.* 887 Recipes for the following snows will be found under their respective headings. *Ibid.*, Apple snow may be iced.

**b.** *Chem.* One or other of various substances having a snow-like appearance (see quots.). *spec.* Solid carbon dioxide.

**1802** *Encycl. Brit.* Suppl. I. 240 A white powder, formerly called snow or white flowers of antimony. This is the white oxyd of antimony. **1815** J. Smith *Panorama Sci. & Art* II. 401 Argentine snow, or flowers of antimony. **1841** *Civil Eng. & Arch. Jrnl.* IV. 317/1 A small piece of this carbonic acid snow was placed on the surface of water. **1913** J. Hall-Edwards *Carbon Dioxide Snow* 28 Having prepared our cone, or stick of snow..the first step is to place the patient in a comfortable and easy position. **1931** Dougherty & Kearney *Fire* 243 The 'snow' does not freeze the fire as is sometimes erroneously believed, but blankets or smothers it. **1951** Whitby & Hynes *Med. Bacteriol.* (ed. 5) ii. 20 Many bacteria and viruses..may be preserved by rapid freezing to −70°C, with $Co_2$-snow. **1974** L. E. Long *Geology* i. 19 A frozen 'snow' of methane and ammonia glued the dust particles into globs that eventually grew to about the size of basketballs. **1979** *Nature* 30 Aug. 738/1 Much of the distributed $SO_2$ snow would be expected to fall within a few tens of kilometres of the scarps [on Jupiter's satellite Io].

**c.** *poet.* White marble.

**1848** Bailey *Festus* Proëm (ed. 3) p. vii, Ere new marmoreal floods had spread their couch Of perdurable snow.

**d.** *slang* (orig. *U.S.*). Cocaine; occas. heroin or morphine.

**1914** Jackson & Hellyer *Vocab. Criminal Slang* 78 *Snow*, ..derived from the extremely flocculent nature of cocaine when pulverized. **1915** *Policeman's Monthly* Dec. 17/3 One day, his pal found him depressed and told him to take a little sniff of 'snow', as heroin is known to the vernacular of the criminal. **1925** A. P. Herbert *Laughing Ann* 92 Don't let her know about whisky and 'snow'. **1933** N. Douglas *Looking Back* II. 364 He..walked up and down the room..taking, every now and then, a pinch of cocaine... 'I didn't know you took snow.' **1956** [see jab *v.* e]. **1966** 'A. Hall' *9th Directive* iii. 25 Pangsapa was a narcotics contrabandist and would therefore know people..prepared to kill for a fix of snow. **1967** N. Lucas *C.I.D.* x. 135 Luckier still not to have graduated from pep pills to..'Snow'..—morphine. **1979** P. Driscoll *Pangolin* xx. 151 'Tell me how much this roll will get me.' 'I guess around a hundred twenty grams. That's.. the purest snow you'll ever see.'

**e.** *slang.* (Silver) money.

**1925** Fraser & Gibbons *Soldier & Sailor Words & Phrases* 263 *Snow*, money. Silver. **1936** J. Curtis *Gilt Kid* 173 Count up that snow while I go through the other drawers. **1970** F. McKenna *Gloss. Railwaymen's Talk* 38 *Snow*, small silver i.e. sixpences.

**f.** Spots that appear as a flickering mass filling a television or radar screen, caused by interference or a low signal-to-noise ratio.

**1946** *Proc. IRE* XXXIV. 428/2 These [current] fluctuations give rise to a masking effect, often referred to as 'snow', in the transmitted picture. **1950** Heller & Shulman *Television Servicing* vi. 121 Low signal input may be recognized by the characteristic presence of 'snow' in the received picture. **1977** J. Cheever *Falconer* 209, I took my TV... I had a little snow and asked the repairman to come in. **1978** *Sci. Amer.* Apr. 18/1 The most commonly encountered white noise is the thermal noise produced by the random motions of electrons through an electrical resistance. It causes most of the static in a radio or amplifier and the 'snow' on radar and television screens when there is no input.

**6. a.** The white hair of age. Chiefly in phrases. Also *pl.*

**1638** R. Baker tr. *Balzac's Lett.* (vol. III) 57 If my passions be cooled by the snow of my head, I have then never a white hair [etc.]. **1743** Francis tr. *Hor., Odes* v. xvii. 30 Thy fragrant Odours on my Head More than the Snows of Age have shed. **1757** Duncombe tr. *Horace, Odes* II. xi. 9 Age drops her Snow upon our Heads. **1852** Thackeray *Esmond* I. ii, Attiring herself like summer though her head was covered with snow. **1871** R. Ellis *Catullus* lxiv. 309 Wreaths sat on each hoar crown, whose snows flush'd rosy beneath them.

**b.** *slang.* (See quots.)

**1811** *Lexicon-Balatronicum*, *Snow*, linen hung out to dry or bleach. **1812** J. H. Vaux *Flash Dict.*, *Snow*, clean linen from the washerwoman's hands, whether it be wet or dry. **1859** *Slang Dict.* 97 *Snow*, wet linen.

**c.** White bloom or blossom; spray or foam.

**1859** Geo. Eliot *A. Bede* i, The elder-bushes which were spreading their summer snow close to the open window. **1885** J. H. Dell *Dawning Grey, Songs of the Surges* 97, I stood looking forth o'er the surges,—Looking forth o'er their squadrons of snow. **1900** *Westm. Gaz.* 14 Apr. 2/3 With the May rain still on their petalled snow.

**d.** In some popular names of plants, as ***snow-in-harvest***, ***-in-summer*** (see quots.). Also snow-on-the-mountain.

**1881** *Leicester Gloss.* 247 Snow-in-harvest,..a flower, *Cerastium tomentosum.* **1886** Britten & Holland *Plant Names* 440 Snow-in-harvest,..(2) *Clematis Vitalba*... (3) *Alyssum maritimum.*

**7. a.** The pure white colour of snow; snow-white. Chiefly *poet.*

*a* **1745** Broome in *Fawke's Anacreon, Ode* liii. 33 (1760) 126 The Graces more enchanting show, When rosy Blushes paint their Snow. **1760** Macpherson *Fragm. Anc. Poetry* xiv. 65 The youth with the breast of snow! **1827** Scott *Highl. Widow* v, The daughters of the land were beautiful, with blue eyes and fair hair, and bosoms of snow. **1843** Bethune *Sc. Fireside Stor.* 163 Her eye sae bright and womanly—Her breast o' mountain snaw.

**b.** *pl.* White breasts.

**1803** Visct. Strangford *Poems of Camoens* (1810) 41 Starlight eyes, and heaving snows.

**III. 8.** *attrib.* **a.** In the sense of 'consisting or composed of snow; covered, filled, or mixed with snow; derived from, due to, made in, snow', etc.; as ***snow-bank***, ***-bed***, ***-berg***, ***-blast***, ***block***, ***bridge***, ***-cave***, ***-cloud***, ***cover***, ***-crust***, ***-flurry***, ***-glare***, ***-hut***, ***-light***, ***-patch***, ***-squall***, etc.

Many combs. of this type occur in works specially dealing with Alpine or Arctic regions, as Kane *Arctic Explor.* (1856), Tyndall *Glaciers* (1860), etc.

**1779** E. Parkman *Diary* (1899) 194 *Snow-Banks very high one nigh my saddle-house 6 feet high. **1803** Visct. Strangford *Poems of Camoens* (1810) 106 Like snow-banks scatter'd with the blooms of May. **1845–50** Mrs. Lincoln *Lect. Bot.* xxiv. 139 The Crocus,..not unfrequently blossoming in the neighbourhood of a snow-bank. **1857** M. Arnold *Rugby Chapel* 100 The unseen *snow-beds dislodge Their hanging rain. **1884** *Good Words* Jan. 43/1 We now hastened..across the old snow-beds. **1840** Bremner *Excur. Denmark*, etc. I. 219 Its towers turned into *snow-bergs. **1773** *Cook's Voy.* I. iv. 47 The cold was now become more severe, and the *snow-blasts more frequent. **1889** Gretton *Memory's Harkback* 210 A snow-blast fell upon them, to Devonians almost an unknown thing. **1893** 'Mark Twain' in *Cosmopolitan* Nov. 54/1 My father..built this great mansion of frozen *snow-blocks. **1973** W. S. Avis in *Occasional Papers Dept. English R. Military Coll. Canada* (1978) No. 2. 152 A knife..used primarily in cutting snow blocks for igloo-building. **1982** S. B. Flexner *Listening to America* 22 Alaskan Eskimos often built their igloos out of animal skins, driftwood, etc., using snow-block ones only for temporary or emergency shelters. **1890** *Moose Jaw* (Saskatchewan) *Times* 20 June 1/4 Every observant passenger on the Canadian Pacific Railroad had noticed the *snow bridge on the Illecillewaet, but there are records of ice bridges also. **1921** A. Lunn *Alpine Skiing* vii. 83 On the Grenz glacier a snow-bridge fourteen feet thick, and in the recent Oberaarfoch accident a snow-bridge six feet thick, collapsed beneath men on skis. **1939** [see schrund]. **1979** C. Kilian *Icequake* xiii. 228 The snow bridges seem good and thick, but the quake probably weakened them. **1871** Proctor *Light Sci.* 110 Observing the earth's polar *snow-caps must lead to several important conclusions. **1972** D. Haston *In High Places* ix. 103 On descending they found Mick at the col installed in a *snow-cave that he had dug out. **1981** *Nordic Skiing* Jan. 21/2 You can imagine me huddled in my own hastily dug snow cave waiting out the blizzard. **1879** I. Bird *Lady's Life in Rocky Mountains* x. 168 Looming vaguely through a heavy *snow-cloud. **1899** Crockett *Kit Kennedy* 318 A light haze of snow-cloud obscured the lesser stars. **1871** Whymper *Scrambles Alps* xii. (1900) 246 These *snow-cornices are common on the crests of high mountain ridges. **1919** *Sci. Monthly* IX. 397 A winter *snow-cover prevents deep freezing of the ground. **1956** A. Garnett in D. L. Linton *Sheffield* 48, 1947..was phenomenal for the prolonged and severe cold weather experienced and for the long duration of a snow cover. **1820** Shelley *Liberty* xiii, The cold *Snow-crags by its reply are cloven in sunder. **1824** S. Black *Jrnl.* 24 May (1955) 14 They left the Fort in March on the *snow crust. **1957** G. E. Hutchinson *Treat. Limnol.* I. iii. 214 Teis (1946) examined various snow crusts and firn samples. **1979** R. Fiennes *Hell on Ice* iv. 63 The wind-firm snowcrust. **1866** *Chambers's Encycl.* VIII. 789/1 The different prismatic rays issuing from the minute *snow-crystals. **1856** Kane *Arctic Explor.* I. xxi. 267 The fine impacted *snow-dust of winter. **1879** I. Bird *Lady's Life in Rocky Mountains* ix. 124 The wild flowers are gorgeous.. though..the recent *snow-flurries have finished them. **1936** *Geogr. Jrnl.* LXXXVII. 133 On September 1 came the first snow-flurries of the season. **1797** Coleridge *Anc. Mar.* Marg. Notes 3 A great sea-bird..came through the *snow-fog. **1897** *Outing* XXIX. 368/2 The shadowy forms of birds rapidly vanished in the snow-fog. **1860** M. Reid *Odd People* 394 More likely it is the *snow-glare to which the Laplander, as well as the Esquimaux, is much exposed, that brings about the copious *watering* of the eyes. **1962** L. S. Sasieni *Optical Dispensing* xiii. 326 In snow glare protection is required against the ultra-violet. **1970** R. D. Taring *Daughter of Tibet* xix. 246 Between the smoke and the snow-glare of the day our eyes were red and watering and very sore. **1827** Scott *Diary* 28 May, As ideas..flag and something like a *snow haze covers my whole imagination. **1823** *Lit. Gaz.* 25 Oct. 673/3 A tribe of about fifty Esquimaux who were erecting their *snow-huts. **1882** *Imperial Dict.*, *Snow-hut*,..a hut built of snow. **1930** V. Sackville-West *Edwardians* i. 28 He had been marooned.. somewhere near the South Pole in a snow-hut. **1844** *Civ. Eng. & Arch. Jrnl.* VII. 332/2 If the latter freezes, the result is '*snow-ice', which is of no value. **1882** Geikie *Text-bk. Geol.* II. II. 110 Snow-ice is formed above the snow-line, but may descend in glaciers far below it. **1878** Seeley *Stein* II. 513 Out of what planet have these people dropped into Muscovy's frozen *snowland? **1830** M. O'Brien *Jrnl.* (1968) I. ix. 87 It was dark—as dark as it can be with *snowlight. **1879** Browning *Ivan Ivanovitch* 114 Daylight, bred between Moon-light and snow-light. **1872** C. King *Sierra Nevada* vi. 126 Rosy peaks, with dull, silvery *snow-marblings. **1866** Whittier *Snow-Bound* 96 The sun through dazzling *snow-mist shone. **1870** Bryant *Iliad* XIII. II. 40 Seen from afar, like a *snow-mountain's peak. **1882** *Garden* 7 Jan. 5/2 Alpine flowers..striving to bloom in the *snow-ooze on the Alps. **1909** *Snow-patch [see flora 3 b]. **1979** B. John *World of Ice* 26 (*caption*) The peaks and mountain-sides at this time of year are almost free of snow and ice, and only a few perennial snowpatches remain. *a* **1835** Mrs. Hemans *Chamois Hunter's Love* Poems (1875) 450 Where the *snow-peaks gleam like stars. **1837** J. E. Murray *Summer in Pyrenees* II. 201 *note*, The wreath might terminate..in a *snow-plain. **1807** J. Barlow *Columb.* VI. 161 Hail, sleet and *snow-rack far behind him fly. **1854** H. Miller *Sch. & Schm.* (1858) 13 When..the driving snow-rack cleared up. **1857** Emerson *Poems* 41 *Snow-ridges masked each darling spot. **1884** *Congregationalist* June 493 A *snow river crashing down the sides of the mountain. **1880** Burbidge *Gardens of Sun* i. 9 Here and there the surface is rippled like a *snow-ruck. **1827** Clare *Sheph. Cal.* 85 Like spots of *snow-shine in dark fairy rings. **1887** Swinburne *Poems & Ball.* 3rd Ser. (1897) 3 As the sunshine quenches the snowshine. **1807** Gass *Jrnl.* 181 There were several *snow showers during the day. **1850** E. Bronte *Wuthering H.* ii, The first feathery flakes of a snow-shower. **1841** Whittier *Funeral Tree of the Sokokis* 12 Where the ..*snow-slide left its dusky streak. **1891** E. Roper *By Track & Trail* x. 138 High precipitous mountains..scored with snow-slides. **1774** Goldsm. *Nat. Hist.* (1824) I. 69 *Snow-slips, well known, and greatly dreaded by travellers. **1898** *Speaker* Oct. 410 The snow-slips are very destructive in this narrow valley. **1860** Tyndall *Glac.* I. xiv. 96 Precipitous *snow-slopes, fluted by the descent of..avalanches. **1878** Hooker & Ball *Marocco* 263 We had kept close to one of these long and..narrow snowslopes. **1837** Carlyle *Fr. Rev.* III. III. iv, In the *snow-slush of last winter. **1860** Tyndall *Glac.* I. xiv. 96 Our way lying in part through deep snow-slush. **1775** E. Wild *Jrnl.* 6 Dec. in *Mass. Hist. Soc. Proc.* (1886) II. 287 The weather is attended with *Snow Squalls. **1888** *Nature* 2 Feb. 333 Copeland..was almost completely thwarted by snow-squalls. **1837** Carlyle *Fr. Rev.* I. II. i, There are *Snow-statues raised by the poor in hard winter. **1856** Kane *Arctic Explor.* I. ix. 95 The *snow-streams or gullies that led to a gorge. **1819** L. Richmond in Grimshawe *Memoir* (1828) xiii. 432 Illuminated with *snow-sunshine. **1877** Bryant *Poems, Little People of the Snow* 106 The little maiden..climbed the rounded *snow-swells. **1765** Goldsm. *Trav.* 189 The den where *snow-tracks mark the way. **1844** Mrs. Browning *Drama of Exile* 1708 As the *snow-wind beats blindly on the moorland.

**b.** In the sense of 'used for, or in connexion with, snow', as ***snow-anchor***, ***-board***, ***-boot***, ***buggy***, ***chain***, ***-coat***, ***-fence***, ***-fencing***, ***gallery***, ***gauge***, ***-glasses***, ***-pants***, ***-scoop***, ***scooter***, ***-shed***, ***spectacles***, ***-stake***, ***-suit***, ***tractor***, ***tyre***, ***vehicle***, etc.

**1971** C. Bonington *Annapurna South Face* 248 The 'dead men' were an outstanding success and..gave by far the most reliable..*snow anchor we were able to use on the expedition. **1972** D. Haston *In High Places* xi. 120 Using devious combinations of snow-stakes, 'dead men' (or snow-anchors).., they took two days to come out of those overhangs. **1881** W. P. Buchan *Plumbing* (ed. 3) xi. 70 A style which serves both as a *snow-board and as a preventive of broken chimney cans, loose slates, &c., falling over the roof. **1971** *Country Life* 14 Oct. 964/1 Notices warning of snow-board avalanches had been posted..that very morning. **1773** *Phil. Trans.* LXIII. 225 Each of the three species of Tetras..; it is usually said with us, that they have in winter their *snow-boots. **1856** S. Osborn *M'Clure's Discovery North-West Passage* xii. 160 The heavy falls the men experienced in their thick winter clothing and cloth snow-boots. **1962** A. Lurie *Love & Friendship* I. viii. 142 She came..to ask if she could borrow my snowboots to walk in the snow with. **1970** *Toronto Daily Star* 24 Sept. 16/3 (Advt.), Tamarack snow boots. The new style. **1949** *Sun* (Baltimore) 8 Feb. 15/3 Second Army headquarters..is sending 48 '*snow buggy' operators..to the aid of snow-bound Nebraskans... Their main job will be to drive weasels, the Army's special vehicle for snow-covered terrain. **1965** *Kingston* (Ontario) *Whig-Standard* 27 Dec. 17 (*caption*) Roaring through the snow at speeds..approaching 35 miles-an-hour on the..new snow buggy. **1975** *Islander* (Victoria, B.C.) 9 Feb. 12/1 If you don't have *snow chains, don't even try to get up the steep logging road. **1981** P. Turnbull *Deep & Crisp & Even* i. 8 An ambulance with snow chains drove along the street. **1963** *N.Y. Times* 15 Dec. 18/7 (Advt.), This jaunty..pile-lined '*snowcoat' gets you ready for Winter's worst! **1965** *Harper's Bazaar* Nov. 95 Fir green quilted snowcoat. **1768** *Phil. Trans.* LX. 109 *note*, *Snow-eyes, which..are most excellently contrived for preserving the eyes from the effect of the snow in the spring. **1873** G. M. Grant *Ocean to Ocean* ix. 261 The high mountains..act as natural *snow fences. **1885** *Longman's Mag.* Feb. 423 These cuttings had not been protected.. with snow..fences. **1902** *Nature* 4 Sept. 454 Snow-fences are commonly erected in Canada to check the rate of snow-drifting. **1953** *Canad. Geogr. Jrnl.* XLVI. 68/2 Others made cribs out of *snow fencing and piled the grain in the open fields. **1972** L. Hancock *Sleeping Bag* viii. 181 We dug an extensive salt-water pool and walk-in aviary..then snow-fencing enclosures for the raptorial birds. **1884** Knight *Dict. Mech.* Suppl. 826 **Snow Flanges*,..a bar of iron or steel attached to a car or engine to scrape away snow and ice on the sides..of the rails. **1874** *Snow gallery [see *round timber* s.v. round *a.* 15a]. **1975** D. Bagley *Snow Tiger* xix. 157 They build snow galleries over roads..in Switzerland. The snow goes straight over the top. **1886** *Encycl. Brit.* XX. 257/1 Glaisher's rain and *snow gauge. **1939** *Meteorol. Gloss.* (Met. Office) (ed. 3) 172 In the Hellmann-Fuess snow-gauge the snow is caught in a receiver supported on a balance, the displacement of which is continuously recorded. **1952** E. F. Davies *Illyrian Venture* ii. 32 The snow gauges on the mountain passes, dead tree trunks with marks nailed to them to show the depth of the winter drifts. **1927** E. Hemingway *Men without Women* 162 Around the major's eyes were two white circles where his *snow-glasses had protected his face from the sun on the snow. **1975** E. Hillary *Nothing Venture, Nothing Win* xi. 175 Wilkins.. seemed comparatively unhurt, although his snowglasses had cut his forehead. **1887** *19th Cent.* Nov. 672 Mr. Murdock.. found an Eskimo *snow-goggle. **1893** Earl Dunmore *Pamirs* I. 59 The reflection..off the snow would have been positively blinding had we not been provided with snow goggles. **1844** H. Stephens *Bk. Farm* II. 622 A *snow-harrow or a *snow-plough* will be found a useful implement. **1865** Lubbock *Preh. Times* 401 In the South the men have ..*snow-knives, ice-chisels [etc.]. **1948** T. Onraet *Sixty Below* 100 The ordinary *snow pants and parka are made with the least possible openings. **1962** *N.Y. Post* 9 Oct. 22 (Advt.), Infants' pile snowsuits... Matching, contrasting snowpants. **1978** *Detroit Free Press* 5 Mar. D-1/1 It was still cold and your mother made you put on your coat, hat and mittens, but you could never-mind the 'snow pants' by now. **1875** Wood & Lapham *Waiting for Mail* 36 We found him lying beside the *snow-pole just on the hill. **1901** *Blackw. Mag.* Nov. 688/1 It is then only accessible with dog-sleighs and *snow-raquets. **1856** Kane *Arctic Explor.* II. i. 21 A *snow-saw. **1961** J. W. Anderson *Fur Trader's Story* x. 80, I struck the tent, loaded the toboggan with tent, stove, ..*snow scoop.. and so forth, and set off. **1963** *Engineering* 18 Jan. 79 The manufacturers are now considering adding the snow-scoop to their range of standard attachments. **1964** *Star Weekly* (Toronto) 19 Dec. 13/1 The odd little *snow scooters you see cavorting about..represent the newest phenomenon to revolutionize Canadian sport, family living —and business. **1969** *Daily Colonist* (Victoria, B.C.) 5 Sept. 27/3 Reindeer-tending Lapps of northern Norway use snow scooters to round up strays and transport supplies. **1981** *Times* 14 Dec. 22/8 Four policemen..have been..to North Cape, in Norway, for charity. They reached there on snow scooters. **1864** *N. & Q.* 3rd Ser. VI. 454/1 The Icelanders have their *snow-shades, but a reader has no protection from paper glare. **1868** *Oregon State Jrnl.* 22 Aug. 2/3 The Pacific Railroad advertises for a thousand men to build *snow sheds on the summit. **1875** Knight *Dict. Mech.*, *Snow-shed*, a protection for a railway-track in exposed situations. **1882** Pidgeon *Engineer's Holiday* I. 275 The track is covered by snow-sheds. **1965** E. McCourt *Road across Canada* 177 In Glacier [B.C.] more than half a mile of snowsheds, solidly built of steel and concrete.., guard the most vulnerable spots. **1971** *Daily Tel.* 9 Jan. 9/2 The railway line runs through numerous long snow-sheds in these high lands [in Norway]. These are built over the line to keep it free of snow in winter. **1820** Scoresby *Acc. Arctic Reg.* II. 233 A wooden 'mallet', and '*snow-shovel'. **1854** R. G. Latham *Native Races Russian Emp.* 84 The *skide* (pronounced *she*) is a *snow-skate upwards of six feet long. **1897** *Outing* XXIX. 357/2 For this purpose nothing could be better than the snowshoe and snowskate, or ski, of to-day. **1793** Holcroft tr. *Lavater's Physiog.* xix. 97 The effusions of light from the snow (to guard against which the Esquimaux wear *snow-spectacles). **1901** H. Seebohm *Birds of Siberia* v. 47 The glare of the sunshine on the white snow forced us to wear snow spectacles. **1971** C. Bonington *Annapurna South Face* viii. 95, I pushed in a *snow-stake, but it went in too easily and would almost certainly be pulled out if I fell on it. **1972** Snow-stake [see *snow-anchor* above]. **1942** D. Powell *Time to be Born* i. 37 The red *snow suit her mother had promised. **1962** A. Lurie *Love & Friendship* i. iii. 53 Emmy put Freddy into his snow-suit. **1980** *Daily Tel.* 9 Jan. 1/8 There was no sign of the guerrillas in the rugged terrain, but Russians and their armour, including tanks, were everywhere. Some were in white snow suits. **1886** *Daily News* 28 Dec. 5/7 Yesterday morning the *snow-sweep, drawn by six horses, was got to work early. **1936** *Canad. Geogr. Jrnl.* XII. 34/2 Somebody began to work on the idea of snowmobiles and *snow tractors. **1971** *Country Life* 14 Oct. 964/1 Hardly had the two children been freed when they [*sc.* a rescue team] were on the spot, having covered the ground in a snow-tractor. **1885** *Longman's Mag.* Feb. 425 About nine o'clock the 'snow outfit' steamed in. The *snow-train was made up of six vehicles. **1954** *Sun* (Baltimore) 23 Jan. 8/1 Now it's chains vs. *snow tires, the treachery of the steep hill by the lake and stern telephone calls to warn the little woman off the roads. **1968** 'E. McBain' *Fuzz* xii. 197 The snow..presented no major traffic problems as yet, especially if..one had snow tyres on one's automobile. **1978** *Times* 23 Jan. 12/7 Avis.. had only one car they could rent me and it had no snow tyres or chains. **1968** *Globe & Mail* (Toronto) 3 Feb. 46/3 (*heading*) *Snow vehicles.

**c.** In the sense of 'snow-like, white as snow'.

**1750** tr. *Leonardus' Mirr. Stones* 94 It has a brown or iron colour, sprinkled over with snow spots. **1819** Byron *Juan* II. cxxi, Her small snow feet had slippers, but no stocking. **1879** G. M. Hopkins *Poems* (1967) 80 If a wuthering of his palmy snow-pinions scatter a colossal smile Off him.

**d.** *Cookery.* (Cf. 5 a.)

**1861** Mrs. Beeton *Bk. Househ. Managem.* 747 *Snow eggs*, ..4 eggs, ¾ pint of milk,..sugar..vanilla, lemon-rind. *Ibid.* 864 *Snow cake*...½ lb. of *tous-les-mois*, ¼ lb. of..sugar, ¼ lb. of ..butter, 1 egg,..1 lemon. **1877** *Cassell's Dict. Cookery* 887 Snow Cake... Snow Cheese... Snow Cocoa-nut [etc.]. **1894** *Westm. Gaz.* 30 May 8/2 Recipe for Snow Eggs.

**9.** *Comb.* **a.** With pa. pples. (chiefly with instrumental force), as ***snow-backed***, ***-beaten***, ***-blanched***, ***-blown***, ***-born***, ***-bound***, ***-choked***, ***-cooled***, ***-dazed***, ***-dimmed***, ***-drowned***, ***-fed***, ***-hooded***, ***-packed***, ***-shouldered***, etc., or in parasynthetic combs., as ***snow-bearded***, ***-blanketed***, ***-bowered***, ***-capped***, ***-coloured***, ***-crested***, ***-suited***, etc. Also ***snow-rub***, ***-swathe*** vbs.

**1897** Kipling *Five Nations* (1903) 18 While thick around the homestead Our *snow-backed leaders graze. *c* **1745** Armstrong *Misc.* (1770) I. 150 Thro' the *snow-barricadoed cottage door. **1827** Darley *Sylvia* 7 The *snow-bearded tenant of a wilderness. **1836–48** B. D. Walsh *Aristoph., Clouds* I. iii, On the *snow-beaten peak Of Olympus. **1800** Hurdis *Favourite Village* 118 Isles desolate and horrid, *snow-besprent. **1855** Longf. *Hiaw.* ii. 192 From his *snow-besprinkled tresses. **1945** W. de la Mare *Burning-Glass* 23 The *snow-blanched sunshine. **1971** R. Dentry *Encounter at Kharmel* ix. 151 The *snow-blanketed hills. **1866** Whittier *Snow-Bound* 118 The sun, a *snow-blown traveller, sank From sight. **1879** I. Bird *Lady's Life in Rocky Mountains* vii. 97 From this side rise, *snow-born, the bright St. Vrain, and the Big and Little Thompson. **1930** R. Campbell *Adamastor* 62 Fair siren of the snow-born lake. **1814** Byron in L. Hunt *Autobiogr.* (1850) II. 318, I have been *snow-bound..for nearly a month. **1894** Gladstone *Odes of Horace* II. ix. 20 'Mid snow-bound mountains of the Medes. **1919** W. de la Mare *Flora* 42 Still from the *snow-bowered, link-lit street The muffled hooves of horses beat. **1797** Tweddell *Rem.* xxvii. (1815) 150 All the *snow-capt hills of the canton of Berne. **1879** Wallace *Australasia* xii. 242 Its higher mountains are snow-capped. **1857** Emerson *Poems* 62 Wading in the *snow-choked wood. *c* **1580** in *P. M. Barnard's Catal.* No. 30 (1909) 12 Thy trumpet..and thy *snow colourd swan. **1920** R. Graves *Country Sentiment* 63 Or toys or meat or *snow-cooled drink. **1649** G. Daniel *Trinarch., Hen. IV*, cxxxix, Soe may Thessalia..Envy the still *Snow-Couer'd Rhodope. **1856** Kane *Arctic Explor.* II. xxii. 218 Emerging from the snow-covered roof. **1834** J. Phillips in *Encycl. Metrop.* (1845) VI. 705/2 The *snow-crested Alps. **1860** Tyndall *Glac.* I. xvi. 106 Those glorious mountains,.. snow-crested and star-gemmed. **1603** Drayton *Bar. Wars* VI. lxiv, From the *snow-crown'd Skidos lofty cleeues. **1832** G. Downes *Lett. Cont. Countries* I. 99 This fine chain of snow-crowned Alps. *a* **1918** W. Owen *Poems* (1963) 48 We cringe in holes, back on forgotten dreams, and stare, *snow-dazed, deep into grassier ditches. **1957** Blunden *Poems of Many Years* 295 In *snow-dimmed moonlight. **1854** J. S. C. Abbott *Napoleon* (1855) II. i. 14 The deficiency of accommodation for travelers on those bleak and *snow-drifted heights. **1616** J. Lane *Contn. Sqr.'s T.* VII. 225 A plume of *snowe-drivn white. **1776** *Ann. Reg.* 115 *Snow-drowned fields, obstructed roads. **1978** G. Greene *Human Factor* VI. ii. 322 Outside the silence of the snow-drowned street was so extreme that Castle hesitated to break it. **1808** Scott *Marm.* v. Introd., Our *snow-encircled home. **1596** Fitz-Geffrey *Sir F. Drake* (1881) 76 *Snowe-feath'red swan, the Nestor of the West. **1726–46** Thomson *Winter* 995 A thousand *snow-fed torrents. **1820** Shelley *Prometh. Unb.* I. 120 Rock-embosomed lawns, and snow-fed streams. **1936** R. Campbell *Mithraic Emblems* 31 The lily-scented blood, the snow-fed wine of scarlet stain. **1963** *Times* 6 Feb. (New Zealand Suppl.) p. vii/3 The Rangitata itself—snow-fed and treacherous. **1818** Bucke *Italians* III. ii, The *snow-hair'd sire shall recognize his son. **1880** 'Mark Twain' *Tramp Abroad* xxv. 245 The stately border of *snow-hooded mountain peaks. **1945** W. de la Mare *Burning-Glass* 44 A moth, snow-hooded, delicate past belief. **1866** Whittier *Snow-Bound* 99 Woods of *snow-hung oak. **1808** Scott *Marm.* v. Introd., Carriers' *snow-impeded wains. **1850** Marg. Fuller *Wom. 19th C.* (1862) 312 That..freezing, *snow-laden winter. **1642** H. More *Song of Soul* II. App. 99 *Snow-limb'd, rose-cheek'd. **1855** Tennyson *Maud* I. XVIII. iii, Shadowing the snow-limb'd Eve. **1856** Kane *Arctic Explor.* II. vii. 80 After a walk over a heavy *snow-lined country of thirty miles. **1820** Shelley *Prometheus Unbound* I. 434 Yon huge *snow-loaded cedar. **1798** Miss H. M. Williams *Tour Switzerland* II. App. 292 The modest, *snow-mantled nymphs. **1884** *Manch. Exam.* 2 Sept. 5/1 As the ball..is rolled over the snow-mantled earth. **1593** Nashe *Christ's T.* Wks. (Grosart) IV. 113 His pure *snow-molded soft fleshe. **1973** J. M. White *Garden Game* 188 Teague drove his Mercedes..on to the *snow-packed verge. **1593** Nashe *Christ's T.* Wks. (Grosart) IV. 207 Theyr heads, with theyr..*Snow-resembled siluer curlings. **1839–52** Bailey *Festus* 140 Thine are the *snow-robed mountains circling earth. **1853** Kane *Grinnell Exped.* xxxiv. (1856) 306 The crew have been *snow-rubbing their blankets. **1885** Black *White Heather* iii, A large and fleecy cloud that clung around the *snow-scarred peak. **1921** W. de la Mare *Veil* 59 Snake-haired, *snow-shouldered, pure as flame and dew. **1936** R. Campbell *Mithraic Emblems* 17 Each great snow-shouldered beast. **1898** *Edinb. Rev.* Jan. 55 On the *snow-sprinkled braes of Yarrow. **1961** 'E. Lathen' *Banking on Death* (1962) ix. 71 *Snowsuited toddlers frolicking merrily in the snow. **1971** A. Bailey *In Village* (1972) xix. 189 Snow-suited small children. **1843** Browning *Return of Druses* II, Dost thou *snow-swathe thee kinglier, Lebanon, Than in my dreams? **1804** *Europ. Mag.* XLV. 63/2 While, with *snow-tipp'd feet, The.. waves she sports among. **1883** F. S. Renwick *Betrayed* 36 One snow-tipped..feather graced his hair. **1596** Drayton *Bar. Wars* VI. lxiv, From *snow-topd Skidos frostie cleeues. *c* **1750** Johnson *Ode Winter* 12 The snow topt cot, the frozen rill. **1823** Clissold *Ascent Mt. Blanc* 23 The snow-topped Apennines. **1879** Browning *Ivan Ivanovitch* 33 A village, ..*Snow-whitened everywhere except the middle road. **1606** Sylvester *Du Bartas* II. iv. II. *Magnificence* 1073 O how I love thee, My *Snow-winged Dove! **1729** Savage *Wanderer* I. 55 His Robe *snow-wrought, and hoar'd with Age.

**b.** Objective, etc., with vbl. sbs. and pres. pples., as ***snow-casting***, ***-clearing***, ***-dropping***, etc., or with agent-nouns, as ***snow-blower***, ***-breaker***, ***-clearer***, ***-gatherer***, ***-loader***, ***-melter***, ***-scraper***, ***-shifter***, ***-thrower***, etc.

(*a*) **1542** Udall *Erasm. Apoph.* (1877) 243 The *snowe casting season nowe coming in place. **1894** *Westm. Gaz.* 10 Jan. 5/1 He was in charge of the *snow-clearing party. **1838** Miss Pardoe *River & Desert* II. 44 The majestic tamarind tree overshadowed the *snow-dropping acacia. **1849** J. Forbes *Physician's Holiday* viii. (1850) 75 The waters.. overflowed their banks during the *snow-melting season. **1757** Dyer *Fleece* IV. 466 White Imaus, whose *snow-nodding crags Frighten the realms beneath. **1616** Drumm. of Hawth. *Poems* A iv b, *Snow-passing Iuorie that the Eye delights. **1858** Simmonds *Dict. Trade*, **Snow-sweeping Engine*, a plough or other contrivance for removing snow from railways and common roads. **1892** *Daily News* 21 Nov. 5/5 Matters..have reached such a point that snow-sweeping is the one harvest they hope for.

(*b*) **1955** *Hamilton* (Ontario) *Spectator* 25 Jan. 24/3 Street sweepers, *snow blowers, and other city equipment stored outdoors at the Elgin Street yard. **1964** S. Forbes *Long Hate* (1966) x. 92 'We'll have to shovel, I guess.'.. 'Can't you use the snow blower?' **1978** *Daily Tel.* 1 Feb. 1/7 Extra snow-clearing equipment was being sent to the area and the RAF was bringing in a large snowblower from Switzerland. **1791** *Young's Annals Agric.* XVI. 431 The sheep are often obliged to procure their food by scraping the snow off the ground with their feet..; hence they have obtained the name of *snow-breakers. **1963** *Times* 18 Feb. 4/1 The efforts of dedicated Kingsholm *snow-clearers were rewarded, and the surface was unbelievably good in the circumstances. *Ibid.* 28 Jan. 9/6 Clearing is done by a continuous moving belt operation with a plough in front followed by a specially built *snow loader which digs into drifts with rotating blades and funnels it into a line of waiting lorries. **1856** Kane *Arctic Explor.* I. xxxi. 424 To reduce our effete *snow-melter to its elements. **1974** *Globe & Mail* (Toronto) 12 Feb. 5/3 The combined snow loader and melter was designed by Metro roads department and consultants after testing a small 75-ton snow melter during the past three winters. **1851** in H. Greeley *Recoll. Busy Life* (1868) 559 We met with a bad accident..45 miles from Baltimore, our *snow-scraper catching against some part of the track. **1884** Knight *Dict. Mech.* Suppl. 826/2 Snow Scraper. **1962** *Snow-shifter [see Mack *sb.*[6]]. **1891** C. Roberts *Adrift Amer.* 114 Two snow ploughs, and a gang of 75 *snow shovellers. **1875** Knight *Dict. Mech.* 2231/2 **Snow-sweeper*, a vehicle or apparatus adapted for removing snow from paved streets. **1966** *Wall St. Jrnl.* 28 Dec. 1/4 The power-driven snowblower (or *snowthrower, if you prefer), a gadget with reel-type blades that chew through the snow and push it into a chute, from whence it's blown aside. **1978** *Detroit Free Press* 16 Apr. (Gardening Guide) 6 (Advt.), Attachments include 60-inch rotary mower, 48-inch snow thrower, [etc.].

**c.** With adjs., chiefly in the sense of 'as or like snow', as ***snow-bright***, ***-brilliant***, ***-clear***, ***-cool***, ***-deep***, ***-fair***, ***-proof***, ***-soft***, etc.

**1572** *Bossewell's Armorie* Prelim. Verses, Whose *snow-bright skil by snow procurde the Fates to hast thy fate. **1817** Shelley *Rev. Islam* XII. xli, I saw its marge of snow-bright mountains rear Their peaks aloft. **1853** F. W. Newman *Odes of Horace* 148 The slave Briséis With hue *snowbrilliant. **1925** E. Sitwell et al. *Poor Young People* 15 Or peck Anne's *snow-clear cheek. **1919** R. Graves *Treasure Box* 11 Where Sweetheart, my brown mare,..May loll her leathern tongue In *snow-cool water. **1964** J. Michie tr. *Horace's Odes* I. xii. 41 The snow-cool shoulder Of Haemus. **1799** [A. Young] *Agric. Linc.* 328 Mr. Hyde seldom corn feeds, unless turnips are rotten or *snow deep. **1920** T. S. Eliot *Ara Vos Prec* 25 Buried beneath some snow-deep Alps. **1895** Nutt in Meyer *Voy. Bran* I. 176 *Snowfair the bodies from top to toe. **1818** Keats *Endym.* II. 79 Some *snow-light cadences Melting to silence. **1972** 'M. Yorke' *Silent Witness* ii. 26 A small figure lightly encased in *snow-proof garments. **1978** J. Cowley in *Islands* (N.Z.) Aug. 25 Padded nylon windbreakers and snow-proof pants. **1841** Browning *Pippa Passes* Poems (1905) 166 One flash Of the pale, *snow-pure cheek and black bright tresses. **1596** W. Smith *Chloris* (1877) 8 Tripping vpon the *snowe soft downes I spide Three nimphs. **1625** Milton *Death Fair Infant* 19 Down he descended from his Snow-soft chaire. **1924** E. Sitwell *Sleeping Beauty* xvi. 54 Far from *snow-soft sleep. **1959** E. Pound *Thrones* civ. 92 The small breasts snow-soft over tripod. **1867** Gilfillan *Night* I. 12 With the *Snow-still foot of thought.

**10. a.** Special combs.: **snow-belt** *U.S.* [Belt *sb.* 5 a], a region subject to heavy snowfalls; also *attrib.*; **snow-blanket**, **-blink** (see quots.); † **snow-blossom**, a snowflake; **snow-bones** *dial.* (see quots.); **snow-break**, (*a*) a rush of loose or melting snow; (*b*) a narrow strip of forest serving as a protection against snow; (*c*) the breaking of trees by the weight of snow; an area over which this happens; **snow-bucking** *U.S.*, the action of forcing a railway-train through a snow-drift; **snow bunny** *N. Amer. slang*, an inexperienced (usu. female) skier; a pretty girl who frequents ski slopes; **snow-cone** *U.S.* (see quot. 1969); also *attrib.*; **snow course**, a line along which the depth of snow is periodically sampled at fixed points; **snow-craft**, the art of traversing or dealing with snow in mountaineering; **snow-creep**, the gradual movement of snow down a slope; **snow-cripple**, a tree injured by the weight or pressure of snow; **snow cruiser** *N. Amer.*, a motor vehicle designed to travel over snow; *spec.* (with capital initials) a Canadian proprietary term for a type of motorized toboggan; also *attrib.*; hence **snow-cruising** *vbl. sb.*; also *attrib.*; **snow devil**, a column of snow whirled round by the wind (cf. devil *sb.* 11); **snow-dropper** *Cant*, = snow-gatherer (*Slang Dict.* 1864); **snow-dropping** *Cant*, (see quots.); also as gerund; **snow-eater** *Meteorol.* [tr. G. *schneefresser*], a warm wind, esp. a föhn, that causes rapid melting of snow; † **snow-fire** (see quot.); **snow-foot**, (*a*) an accumulation of snow at the foot of steep Arctic sea-coasts; (*b*) a foot adapted for walking on snow; **snow-gatherer** *Cant* (see quot.); **snow grain** *Meteorol.*, a small, opaque, precipitated ice particle, usu. flattened and less than 1 mm. in diameter, that does not bounce on a hard surface; cf. *snow pellet* below; **snow gun** *U.S.* = *snow-maker*; **snow-hole**, (*a*) a hole or opening in the burner of a pyrites kiln; (*b*) a hole in snow used as a temporary shelter; **snow-house**, (*a*) a house in which snow is preserved in warm weather; (*b*) a house or hut built of snow; **snow job** *slang* (orig. *U.S.*), a concerted attempt at flattery, deception, or persuasion; also *attrib.*; hence **snow-job** *v. trans.*, to do a snow job on (someone); **snow-jobbing** *vbl. sb.*, the performing of a snow job; **snow-limit**, the limit (towards the equator) for the fall of snow at sea-level; **snow machine** *N. Amer.*, a motor vehicle designed to travel over snow; also *attrib.*; **snow-maker** (orig. *U.S.*) a device used for the artificial production of a snow-like precipitate for ski-slopes and the like; also, one who makes snow by the use of such a device; so **snow-making** *vbl. sb.* and *ppl. a.*; **snow-melt**, the melting of fallen snow; also, the water that results; **snow-merchant**, one who deals in snow (for cooling purposes); **snowpack** *U.S.*, lying snow that is compressed and hardened by its own weight; **snow pellet** *Meteorol.*, an opaque precipitated ice particle, usu. a few millimetres in diameter, that will bounce on a hard surface; a soft hailstone; cf. *snow grain* above; **snow plane** *N. Amer.*, a type of snowmobile that is mounted on skis and propelled by an engine-driven propeller; **Snow Queen**, the chief character in a fairy-tale of this name by Hans Christian Andersen, used allusively to designate a cold-hearted woman; also *attrib.*; **snow-raking** *N.Z.* (see quots.); **snow roller**, a cylinder of snow formed by the action of the wind rolling it along; **snow-scape**, a snow scene, a landscape covered with snow; **snow scene**, a landscape covered with snow; **snow-sheen**, = *snow-blink*; **snow-skiing** *vbl. sb.* = SKI-ING *vbl. sb.* 1, opp. to water-skiing; so **snow-ski** *v. intr.*; **snow-skier**; **snow-sleep**, a somnolent condition induced by walking in snow; so ***snow-sleepiness***; **snow-snake(s)** *N. Amer.*, 'an Indian game played with a straight wooden rod having a weighted head resembling that of a snake, this rod being slid over a smooth field of snow or down specially constructed runways; the rod used in this game' (Dict. Canad.); hence **snow-snaking**; **snow-sports**, sports that take place on snow, *spec.* skiing; also *attrib.*; †**snow-stone** (see quot.); **snow-tan**, a tanned complexion produced by exposure to snow; **snow-time**, the time of snow, winter.

**1874** *Los Angeles County Ten Thousand Questions Answered* 11/1 There are two great continental railroad routes within the *snowbelt. **1933** *Amer. City* Sept. 53/1 Old-fashioned winters have not been as prevalent in the snow belt in the last few years as they were ten or twenty years ago. **1967** *Wall St. Jrnl.* 1 Feb. 1/4 Some makers predict snowmobile sales soon will surpass boat sales in snowbelt states. **1981** *Nordic Skiing* Jan. 39/1 Thanks to a 120–140 inch snowbelt location, Temple Mountain offers skiing from early December to mid-April. **1863** D. PAGE *Introd. Text-bk. Phys. Geogr.* 154 In the higher latitudes,.. snow forms a warm covering for the soil (the **snow-blanket*, as it is termed by farmers). *Ibid.*, Within the polar circle, also, the darkness of the long winter is.. diminished by the *snow-sheen* or **snow-blink*. **1676** *Phil. Trans.* XI. 734 As hard .. as to shew a specifical difference betwixt several *Snow-blossoms. *a* **1800** PEGGE *Suppl. Grose*, **Snow-bones*, remnants of snow after a thaw. **1862** C. C. ROBINSON *Dial. Leeds* 416 *Snow-bones*, the patches of snow seen stretching along ridges, in ruts, or in furrows, &c., after a partial thaw. **1837** CARLYLE *Fr. Rev.* I. VII. iv, And so, like *snowbreak from the mountains,.. it storms. **1895** W. R. FISHER tr. *Hess's Forest Protection* 482 The term *snow-break* is used to denote the breakage of stems or branches. **1905** *Terms Forestry* (U.S. Dept. Agric. Bureau Forestry) 21 *Snowbreak.* 1. The breaking of trees by snow. 2. An area on which trees have been broken by snow. 3. Shelterbelt. **1928** R. S. TROUP *Silvicultural Systems* v. 70 Its uneven-aged condition up to the pole stage is considered to be a protection against both snowbreak and sliding snow on steep hill-sides. **1933** *Forestry* VII. 146 In spite of the relatively high elevation there was no indication of snowbreak. **1885** *Longman's Mag.* Feb. 422 '*Snow Bucking' in the Rocky Mountains. **1953** P. C. BERG *Dict. New Words in Eng.* 147/2 **Snow bunny*,.. n. Skiing. A beginner, esp. a girl. **1964** *Star Weekly* (Toronto) 19 Dec. 39/1 December used to be a dull month, but that was before our pretty Canadian snow bunnies.. started brightening up the Canadian snow scene. **1968** *Globe & Mail* (Toronto) 13 Jan. 49/6 'Watching you for only two runs, I can see you're not just a 'snow bunny', Coral!' 'No, I was on the women's ski-team at college.' **1972** P. A. WHITNEY *Snowfire* (1973) vi. 100 Snow bunny.. was a term applied to beginners, usually female, who haunted the slopes. **1969** *Daily Tel.* 6 June 18 A *snowcone is a paper cup of flavoured shaved ice, highly popular among children. **1976** *Billings* (Montana) *Gaz.* 4 July 2-B/4 The Jolly Wagons had competition in those days from a snow-cone vendor driving an identical Cushman which contained only ice and flavored syrups. **1933** *Geogr. Rev.* XXIII. 540 It was only necessary to maintain a series of measurements carefully taken in the same spot each year. These measurements, laid out at definite intervals.., were named '*snow courses'. **1965** R. G. KAZMANN *Mod. Hydrol.* ii. 36 This type of measurement, made at frequent intervals over very elaborately organized snow courses.. is the accepted practical method of measuring solid-state precipitation. **1892** C. T. DENT *Mountaineering* 217 *Snowcraft consists largely in the avoidance of difficulties and dangers. **1902** *Encycl. Brit.* XXXI. 23 It [mountaineering] consists of two main divisions, rock-craft and snow-craft. **1908** *Science* 28 Feb. 339 Small trees are directly broken and abraded by weight of snow or by *snow creep. *Ibid.*, *Snow-cripples possess the spire-form, with flourishing upper shoots, but the lower branches and foliage are dying or dead. **1939** *Sun* (Baltimore) 14 Nov. 11/3 A twenty-seven-ton *snow cruiser .. designed to serve as an igloo on wheels to help the forces inspect vast areas of unexplored ice and snow. **1956** *Canad. Trade Mark 102,409* 13 Jan., Wares: Small engine driven snow remover. Trade Mark: Snow-Cruiser. **1966** *Canad. Geogr. Jrnl.* Sept. 79/3 Outboard Marine makes.. Snow Cruiser.. a small motorized toboggan on rubber tires and skis, a variation of the original snowmobile invented by Armand Bombardier of Quebec ten years ago. **1969** *Sears Catal.* Spring/Summer 14 A tent of this type would be ideal for sportsmen, hunters and Snowcruiser enthusiasts. **1966** *British Columbia Digest* Dec. 10 (Advt.), '67 is the big year for *snow cruising.. and you have 3 fabulous OMC Snow Cruisers to choose from! **1968** *Globe & Mail* (Toronto) 15 Jan. 24/3 (Advt.), Wonderful snow-cruising parklands. **1932** F. S. SMYTHE *Kamet Conquered* xii. 169 From the serene skyline of Meade's Col little '*snow devils' were rising against the deepening green of the evening sky. **1962** W. H. MURRAY *Maelstrom* xiv. 183 Whirling snow-devils came charging across the plateau, driving spiculae in their faces. **1847** G. W. M. REYNOLDS *Mysteries of London* III. xxix. 85/1 A stranger looked like a *snow-dropper. **1963** T. & P. MORRIS *Pentonville* viii. 190 The larcenist who steals feminine underwear from clothes-lines (the 'snowdropper') is often a pathetic object of derision and contempt. **1977** *Western Mail* (Cardiff) 5 Mar. 8/1 A 'snowdropper' is a man who steals women's underwear. **1839** *Slang Dict.* 34 **Snow-dropping*, stealing linen off a hedge. **1882** *Sydney Slang Dict.* 9/2 Dick's a broker and has gone out *snow-dropping*. **1930** [see *cattle-duffing* s.v. CATTLE 9]. **1967** *Telegraph* (Brisbane) 1 Mar. 26/4 Patfield had set out last November to steal sheets, but in the most systematic manner of 'snow dropping' (clothes-line thefts) he had stolen everything he could find. **1972** *Observer* 31 Dec. 3/4 He couldn't resist the temptation to go 'snow dropping' (stealing clothes from lines). **1886** *Science* 12 Mar. 242/2 Warm west winds answering to the 'Chinook' winds occur as far south as southern Colorado, though I have seldom heard the name 'Chinook' applied to them in this region. They are here [*sc.* in Colorado Springs] often called Pacific winds, also '*snow-eaters' and 'zephyrs'. **1933** F. H. CHELEY *Camping Out* 197 It was the Chinook wind... The Indians call it the 'snow eater'. **1967** R. W. FAIRBRIDGE *Encycl. Atmospheric Sci. & Astrogeol.* 1151/2 The rapid melting of the snow caused by the chinook ('Snow-eater') is welcomed because it frees the higher pastures. **1771** J. R. FORSTER tr. *Kalm's Trav.* II. 81 We observed a meteor, commonly called a *snow-fire. [*Note.*] Probably nothing but an Aurora borealis. **1881** tr. *Nordenskiöld's Voy. Vega* I. ii. 75 A steep escarpment.. below which there is formed during the course of the winter an immense snow-drift or so-called '*snow-foot'. **1905** *Westm. Gaz.* 11 Mar. 4/2 This peculiarity of 'snow-feet' is not so well marked as in the reindeer or caribou. **1859** *Slang Dict.* 97 **Snow gatherers*, rogues who steal linen from hedges and lines. **1944** H. R. BYERS *Gen. Meteorol.* vi. 125 Granular snow, *snow grains... White, opaque, snow-like grains, similar to soft hail but more or less flattened or oblong. **1967** R. W. FAIRBRIDGE *Encycl. Atmospheric Sci. & Astrogeol.* 772/1 Snow grains.. neither bounce nor break when hitting the ground. **1971** *Industr. & Engin. Chem.* (*Process Design & Devel.*) Jan. 75/1 To cover a bare ski slope, 10 to 15 commercial *snow guns (nozzles in which water and air are combined, usually at 100 psig) are used. **1974** *Compressed Air* Apr. 9/1 The snow-guns are 'very efficient, inexpensive and can be moved easily'. **1880** J. LOMAS *Alkali Trade* 48 So adjusted.. that.. the tongues of flame just show a decided direction towards the exit, or '*snow' hole. **1953** P. PROVENCHER *I live in Woods* vii. 64 To make a snow hole, dig to a depth of five feet at the foot of a steep incline or cliff. **1965** B. E. FREEMAN tr. *Vandel's Biospeleology* xiii. 195 Nivicoles, the inhabitants of snow-holes. **1978** *Daily Colonist* (Victoria, B.C.) 7 May 7/8 The six men and three women spent.. three nights in snow-holes—man-made snow caves—before reaching.. the summit. **1662** J. DAVIES tr. *Olearius' Voy. Amb.* 303 Having made as much [ice] as they desire, they.. put it up into *Snow-Houses, whereof there are so many at Ispahan. **1827** J. HOLMES *Hist. United Brethren* ii. (ed. 2) 80 The Esquimaux now began to build a snow-house, about thirty paces from the beach. **1881** GEIKIE *Prehistoric Europe* 19 He may even have occupied temporary snow-houses, like those made by the Eskimo. **1943** *Amer. Mercury* Nov. 555 There he tries a **snow job* on her (hands her a line) and if she falls for it she's been *snowed under*. **1953** K. TENNANT *Joyful Condemned* xx. 192 He.. made a bee-line for the red-head. 'Now for the snow job,' Geechi murmured. **1962** 'K. ORVIS' *Damned & Destroyed* xxi. 155 Are you going to snow-job me about finding substitutes? **1966** S. MORROW *Moonlighters* (1967) v. 53 Possibly her scepticism accounted for her success with the teenagers... kids were most apt to trust the adults who were immune to a snow job. **1969** C. BURKE *God is Beautiful, Man* (1970) 52 It's better to say yes or no and mean it—than to give a lot of snow job promises anyway. **1979** D. ROBINSON *Eldorado Network* xliii. 291, I just saw you do another snow job. You were in North Wales.. which is why it sounds so convincing. Nice try, Luis. **1966** *National Observer* (U.S.) 19 Dec. 12/2 Democratic county chairmen hereabouts have, of necessity, worked out a terrific combination of railroading, arm twisting, and *snow jobbing, not necessarily involving consent or persuasion. **1973** *Whig-Standard* (Kingston, Ontario) 14 Jan. 15/7 Roads are not for snowmobiles—the *snow machines and other vehicles using the highways simply do not mix. **1976** *News Miner* (Fairbanks, Alaska) 6 Nov. B17/2 Snow machine driving, in which participants may cross miles of wintry terrain on a weekend outing. **1977** *New Yorker* 4 July 42/1 Their snow machine—Ski-Doo Alpine—rests on the floor below the furs. It goes ten miles an hour on the trail, and the two of them ride it. **1955** *N.Y. Times* 30 Jan. II. 31/4 The *snow makers provided a long-needed answer on how to cope with the snowless situation.. in the Southern Catskills. **1963** *Engineering* 13 Sept. 321/3 Snow-makers mix air and water under pressure and blow the resulting mixture in dense 50 ft arcs. **1965** *Economist* 25 Dec. 1416/1 While the rainmakers have been failing, for a decade or more the snowmakers have been succeeding beyond their wildest dreams and as a result.. more American skiers than ever are assured of at least enough snow to try out the new skis which they have been given for Christmas. **1980** J. KRANTZ *Princess Daisy* xxvi. 461 The snow-making machines had started... The snow-makers continued to cover the path. **1954** *U.S. Pat. 2,676,471* 7 At an ambient temperature of 31°F and less, snow has been made at any pressure from 25 to 200 lbs. per square inch by varying the water pressure to give a *snow making mixture. **1956** *Compressed Air Mag.* LXI. 101/3 Snow-making at Fahnestock consists.. of bringing compressed air and water together at a nozzle that acts in the same manner as a paint spray gun. **1960** *N.Y. Herald-Tribune* 13 Nov. VII. 8/1 Across the country.. dozens of snow-making machines are poised, ready to transform bare hillsides into Alpine paradises. **1976** 'A. CROSS' *Question of Max* i. 8 There is a damn snow-making machine on some blasted ski slope. **1927** *Q. Jrnl. Geol. Soc.* LXXXIII. 167 We arrived just as the spring *snow-melt was finishing. **1941** *Yearbk. Agric. 1941* (U.S.) 560 In cleared areas snow depths are intermediate.. and snow melt is rapid. **1971** W. HILLEN *Blackwater River* ii. 16 Snowmelt starting to run from exposed mountain slopes. **1979** *Field* 17 Oct. 1048/3 So far as rainfall is concerned,.. the total amount of this element.. in meteorological records includes snowmelt. **1705** ADDISON *Italy* Wks. 1721 II. 84 The Banditti.. often put the *Snow-merchants under contribution. **1952** *Trans. Amer. Geophysical Union* XXXIII. 874 The water equivalent of the seasonal *snow pack was observed after individual falls. **1955** *Sci. News Let.* 1 Oct. 214/3 Winter snowpack is the source of 40% of California's streamflow. **1973** R. HAYES *Hungarian Game* xxxvi. 215 Beneath the thin, brittle crust there was an inch of powder before the snowpack. **1935** *Jrnl. Faculty Sci. Hokkaido Imp. Univ.* 2nd Ser. I. 215 The *snow pellet or the graupel.. is one of the modified forms of snow crystal. **1967** R. W. FAIRBRIDGE *Encycl. Atmospheric Sci. & Astrogeol.* 442/2 Small hail, under 5 mm, is officially classified as ice pellets or snow pellets. **1953** R. MOON *This is Saskatchewan* ii. 9 Bob Fudge's manufacturing is not confined to *snow planes. **1967** E. B. NICKERSON *Kayaks to Arctic* xix. 186 He had a snow plane—an enclosed cabin on ski runners shoved along by an aeroplane propeller in the fashion of an Everglades swamp buggy. **1972** T. MCHUGH *Time of Buffalo* xii. 145 We rented two snowplanes for a trip into the snow-bound heartland of Yellowstone Park. **1935** MARSH & JELLETT *Nursing-Home Murder* vi. 75 A very cold fishy sort of lady... A *Snow Queen, in fact. **1974** L. DEIGHTON *Spy Story* xi. 111 She gave me the inscrutable Snow-queen smile. **1977** *N.Y. Rev. Bks.* 27 Oct. 14 Charlotte was a Snow Queen who flirted coldly and shamelessly with her son. **1919** *N.Z. Jrnl. Agric.* 20 Feb. 90 After a heavy snowfall.. send out as many men as can be got together.. to get the sheep on to the sunny faces, where a certain amount of thaw may have taken place... This is what is generally known as '*snow-raking'. **1958** J. PASCOE *N.Z. Sheep-Station* in *People of World* 1st Ser. 19 Then the men must stamp out a trail through the snow—a job called 'snow-raking'—and lead the sheep down to the valley flats. **1866** G. J. SYMONS *British Rainfall, 1865* p. vii, *Snow Rollers... The snow ripples up .., and the ripples breaking into sections, the wind rolls each.. until, just like a.. snow-ball, they rapidly increase in size. **1876** *Meteorol. Mag.* XI. 52 This is the first instance recorded of the formation of 'Snow Rollers' in England. **1959** *Weatherwise* XII. 63/2 The area cleared of snow during the formation of snow rollers is usually V-shaped, accounting for their peculiar shape, which is cylindrical with concave ends. **1886** *Christian Leader* 17 June, Charmed by the beauty of the *snow-scape, with the feathery flakes clinging to the twigs. **1891** ATKINSON *Moorland Par.* 372 The unaccustomed eye is fairly bewildered with the strange pale beauty of the snow-scape. **1836** H. C. ROBINSON *Diary* 15 Jan. (1967) 152, I found a *snow scene quite pleasant in this mountainous country. **1921** R. FRY *Let.* 14 Dec. (1972) II. 518 A stupendous Courbet snow scene. **1978** 'L. BLACK' *Foursome* i. 6 It was incongruous against the background of .. correspondence files.. stacks of catalogues, the snow-scene on the calendar. **1975** *New Yorker* 1 Sept. 28/1 You don't play tennis, you don't *snow-ski, you don't water-ski, you don't ride a bicycle... Albert, we have nothing in common. **1941** *Life* 4 Aug. 55/2 (*caption*) Bending her knees like a *snow skier, Hallie rides over the wake. *Ibid.* 54 Combining aquaplaning and *snow skiing, water-skiing was imported from the Riviera several years ago. **1977** *Chicago Tribune* 2 Oct. XII. 33/3 (Advt.), We're looking for a bright, enthusiastic gal, who knows the retail clothing business, especially snow skiing attire. **1901** *Wide World Mag.* VI. 456/2 He had been overcome by that worst of all enemies to the Australian Alpine traveller—*snow-sleep. **1896** MERRIMAN *Sowers* xxxii, It was quite dark,.. and I had *snow-sleepiness. **1844** *Chambers's Edin. Jrnl.* I. 327 They [*sc.* Cherokee Indians].. in winter amuse themselves with their *snow-snakes, which are long smooth sticks of hard wood.. which they send to an extraordinary distance over the smooth surface of the snow. **1888** *Trans. R. Soc. Canada* VI. II. 44 If this is the game spoken of by other writers as 'Snow-snakes', there is nothing in the [Abenaki] name to so indicate. **1959** E. TUNIS *Indians* 56/2 Snow snake was played by all the northern tribes on a level track made by dragging a log or a boy through the snow. **1973** M. CROWELL *Greener Pastures* 81 The wall photograph.. of Indians playing the venerable game of snow-snake. **1978** *Whig-Standard* (Kingston, Ontario) 11 Feb. A8/1 The snow snake is a smooth, thin stick about 2m long. It is thrown along a crust of smooth, hard snow. The player whose snake slides the farthest is the winner. **1979** *Ibid.* 1 Feb. 9/1 It is called *snow-snaking and the Mohawk Indians have played it for centuries. It is not recognized at the Canada Winter Games but maybe it will some day. [**1905** *Country Life* Dec. 181 (*heading*) Practical side of snow and ice sports.] **1966** *Guardian* 15 Oct. 5/2 (Advt.), *Snowsports. 2 weeks including full-board £29.15.0! **1974** *Country Life* 3/10 Jan. 52/1 (Advt.), *Off-season winter rates*.. for skiers and snow-sports enthusiasts. **1753** *Chambers' Cycl.* Suppl., **Snow-stone*,.. a name given by some to a very beautiful stone found in America; of which the Spaniards are very fond. **1901** *Wide World Mag.* VI. 458/2 Almost unrecognisable from *snow-tan and exposure. **1535** COVERDALE *2 Sam.* xxiii. 20 Benaia.. slewe a lyon at a well in the *snowe tyme. **1844** LD. HOUGHTON *Palm Leaves, Kiosk* II. 17 In the bleak snow-time, when the winds rung shrill.

**b.** In names of animals, insects, etc., as **snow bear**, a buff or brown bear, *Ursus arctos isabellinus*, found in the Himalayan region; **snow-camel**, the Bactrian camel, *Camelus bactrianus*; **snow-fish** (?); **snow-flea**, **-fly**, **-gnat**, **-insect**, one or other of several species of small insects frequenting snow (also *snow-fly*, an artificial fly used in angling); esp. one of the genus *Achorutes*; **snow-leopard**, the ounce; **snow-mouse** (see quots.); **snow-panther**, the ounce; **snow-wolf**, a wolf that lives in snowy regions; the (imitation) fur of this animal; **snow-worm**, a worm frequenting or living among snow; esp. = ICE-WORM a.

**1869** A. A. KINLOCH *Large Game Shooting Thibet & N. West* I. xv. 46 The *Snow Bear varies a good deal in size. **1884** R. A. STERNDALE *Nat. Hist. Mammalia India & Ceylon* 111 The bear of which we have the oldest record is almost the same as our Indian or Snow Bear. **1910** *Blackw. Mag.* Oct. 433/2 One of them..got three really good heads, and two snow-bears, in one day. **1901** KIPLING *Kim* viii. 204 Nor is even a Balkh stallion..of any account in the great Northern deserts beside the *snow-camels I have seen. **1833** MARRYAT *P. Simple* xxix, Not cribbled up like a *snow-fish, chucked out on the ice of the river St. Lawrence. **1850** THOREAU *Jrnl.* 16 Dec. in *Writings* (1906) VIII. 125 The snow everywhere was covered with *snow-fleas like pepper. **1868** *Amer. Naturalist* II. 53 The little insects called snow-fleas..are found in winter at the foot of trees. **1888** COMSTOCK *Introd. Entom.* 61 Our common snow-flea is *Achorutes nivicola*. This is sometimes a pest where maple sugar is made, the insects collecting..in the sap. **1943** B. DAMON *Sense of Humus* 106 Snow fleas..have a disagreeable habit of putting an end to their brief existence by drowning themselves in sap buckets. **1668** CHARLETON *Onomast.* 48 *Oripæ*,..*Snow-Flies. **1867** F. FRANCIS *Angling* x. (1880) 379 There is a singular fly used on the Beauly, which is there termed the Snow Fly. **1879** E. P. WRIGHT *Anim. Life* 491 In America we find that these little creatures [*sc.* spring-tails] are at this day called snow-flies. **1894** *Amateur Gardening* 3 Mar. 422 The insects..are known as the Cabbage Powder Wing or Snow Flies (*Aleyrodes proletella*). **1891** *Cent. Dict.* s.v., *Snow-gnat. *Ibid.*, *Snow-insect. **1866** A. MURRAY *Geog. Distrib. Mammals* 99 The Ounce or *Snow Leopard represents the Leopard in the high regions of Thibet. **1902** T. W. WEBBER *Forests Upper India* vi. 54 Prowling snow leopards, white like the weather-beaten rock. *c* **1880** *Cassell's Nat. Hist.* III. 117 The *Snow Mouse (*Arvicola nivalis*), lives on the Alps and Pyrenees, at elevations of 4,000 feet and upwards. **1891** *Cent. Dict.*, *Snow-mouse*,..a lemming of arctic America which turns white in winter, *Cuniculus torquatus*. **1884** STERNDALE *Mammalia India* 184 The Ounce or *Snow Panther. **1910** W. DE LA MARE *Three Mulla-Mulgars* 192 So brave are these *snow-wolves. **1976** *Sunday Mail* (Glasgow) 28 Nov. 46/1 (Advt.), De luxe heavy pile Silver Mink, Ocelot, Tiger, Snow Wolf, they are beautiful. **1608** TOPSELL *Serpents* 816 Old snow..will look somewhat dun..: and therefore the *snow-worms are of the same hiew. **1835** BURNES *Trav. Bokhara* (ed. 2) III. 209 The most singular phenomenon of nature on Hindoo Koosh appears to be the snow-worm, which is described to resemble the silk-worm in its mature state. **1895** *Cambridge Nat. Hist., Insects* I. 194 The occurrence on snow and glaciers of Insects spoken of as snow-fleas, or snow-worms. **1899** H. G. BRYANT in *Proc. Acad. Nat. Sci. Philadelphia* 134 The snow-worms were first observed a few hundred yards from our first camp. **1916** *Trans. Amer. Microsc. Soc.* XXXV. 102 Nothing definite is known concerning the food of these snow-worms.

**c.** In names of birds, as **snow-cock**, a snow-partridge, snow-pheasant, *Tetraogallus*; **snow-flight**, the snowflake or snow-bunting (*Cent. Dict.* 1891); **snow-fowl**, the snow-bunting; **snow-grouse**, the ptarmigan; † **snow-hammer** [ad. G. *schneeammer*], the snow-finch; † **snow-hen**, the ptarmigan; **snow-lark**, ? the snow-finch; **snow-owl**, the snowy owl; **snow-partridge**, (*a*) the snow-pheasant, *Tetraogallus*; (*b*) a Himalayan gallinaceous bird, *Lerwa nivicola*; **snow-petrel** (see quot. 1905); **snow-pheasant** (see quots.); **snow-pigeon**, a pigeon of Northern India and Tibet, *Columba leuconota*; **snow-quail** *U.S.*, the white-tailed ptarmigan, *Lagopus leucurus*; **snow-sparrow**, any passerine bird of the genus *Junco*. Also SNOW-BIRD, -BUNTING, -FINCH, etc.

*c* **1880** *Cassell's Nat. Hist.* IV. 146 The finest representatives of the Partridge are, undoubtedly, the *Snow Cocks or Snow Partridges. **1897** LYDEKKER, etc. *Conc. Knowl. Nat. Hist.* 232 The snow-cocks, or snow-pheasants.., are the largest of the partridge group. **1813** MONTAGU *Ornith.* Suppl. s.v. *Snow-bunting*, *Snow-fowl. Oat-fowl. **1884** COUES *N. Amer. Birds* 585 *Lagopus*, Ptarmigan. *Snow Grouse. **1888** ROOSEVELT in *Cent. Mag.* XXXVI. 210 Up above the timber line were snow-grouse and huge, hoary-white woodchucks. **1802–3** tr. *Pallas's Trav.* (1812) I. 52 During the whole of our journey..we were accompanied by small flights of *snow-hammers. **1648** HEXHAM II, *Een sneeuw-hoen*,..a *Snowe-hen, or a Shoveler so called because of her w[h]itnesse. **1674** tr. *Scheffer's Hist. Lapland* 138, I call it *Lagopus*.., the Germans..term it *Schnaehuner*, i.e. Snow-hens. **1832** J. BREE *St. Herbert's Isle* 48 There never sings the *snow-lark as she soars. **1811** A. WILSON *Amer. Ornith.* Pref. p. xi, *Snow Owl. The largest of his tribe; white, spotted with small brown spots. **1884** COUES *N. Amer. Birds* 510 *Nyctea*, Snow Owls. **1853** *Zoologist* II. 3861 The great *snow-partridge of Persia. *c* **1880** *Cassell's Nat. Hist.* IV. 146 The Himalayan Snow Partridge (*Tetraogallus himalayensis*). **1895** LYDEKKER *Roy. Nat. Hist.* IV. 406 The snow-partridge (*Lerwa nivicola*), inhabiting the higher Himalayan ranges. **1843** *Zoologist* I. 61 The bird called the *snow petrel by sailors. **1905** E. A. WILSON in Capt. Scott *Voy. 'Discovery'* II. App. II. 483 The Snow petrel (*Pagodroma nivea*) is perhaps the most beautiful of all the Southern petrels;..it is pure white all over. **1884** *Encycl. Brit.* XVII. 341 Among the birds [in Nepal] are the ..*snow pheasant (*Tetraogallus himalayensis*), snow partridge. **1885** *Ibid.* XVIII. 733 The fine Snow-Pheasants, *Crossoptilum*—of..which..there are several species. **1902** T. W. WEBBER *Forests Upper India* xii. 148 A remarkable bird, the snow pheasant or snow cock (*Tetraogallus Tibetanus*). **1891** *Cent. Dict.*, *Snow-pigeon. **1905** E. CANDLER *Unveiling of Lhasa* iii. 59 Another common bird is the snow-pigeon. **1895** W. R. OGILVIE-GRANT *Game Birds* I. 45 In the Rocky Mountain region it is generally known by the very appropriate name of 'White' or '*Snow' Quail. **1884** COUES *N. Amer. Birds* 377 *Junco*, *Snow Sparrows. **1895** *Times* 22 Feb. 3/1 The sight of a snow sparrow, the first of the season.

**d.** In names of plants or fruits, as **snow-apple**, a variety of apple (Ash, 1775); **snow bush**, one or other of various shrubs bearing a profusion of white flowers (*Cent. Dict.*); esp. the small silvery shrub, *Calocephalus brownii*, of the family Compositæ, native to Australia; hence ***snow-bushed*** adj.; **snow-gem**, = next (*Cent. Dict.*); **snow glory**, a hardy garden-plant of the genus *Chionodoxa*; **snow-grass**, one of several coarse grasses of upland regions, esp., in New Zealand, a tussock grass of the genus *Danthonia*; cf. DANTHONIA; also *attrib.*; **snow gum**, a shrub or small tree, *Eucalyptus niphophila*, with white bark and glaucous leaves, native to high regions of New South Wales; **snow lily**, a perennial herb, *Erythronium grandiflorum*, belonging to the family Liliaceæ, native to alpine regions of western North America, and bearing white or yellow flowers; **snow-mould** (see quot.); **snow pea** = MANGE-TOUT; **snow-pear** [G. *schneebirne*], a variety of pear; esp. *Pyrus nivalis*, which comes into season after snow has fallen; **snow plant**, (*a*) a snow-alga; (*b*) a plant of the Sierra Nevada in California, *Sarcodes sanguinea*, (see quot. 1905); **snow-rose**, a species of rhododendron (*Cent. Dict.*); **snow-tree** (see quot.).

**1909** A. E. MACK *Bush Calendar* 12 Where the trees were fewer, '*snow bushes' grew white. **1965** *Austral. Encycl.* III. 158/1 Snow-bush, a dense and intricately branched shrub.. forms large and rounded, white-woolly growths. **1946** DYLAN THOMAS *Deaths & Entrances* 28 And the dancers move On the departed *snowbushed green. **1887** *G. Nicholson's Dict. Gardening* III. 447/2 *Snow Glory, a common name for *Chionodoxa Luciliæ*. **1865** *Reader* No. 151. 575/3 The common *snow-grass (*Schœnus Pauciflorus*). **1875** WOOD & LAPHAM *Waiting for Mail* 31 Tethering my good old horse to a tussock of snow-grass. **1898** MORRIS *Austral Eng.* 425 Snow-Grass, *Poa cæspitosa*,..another name for Wiry-grass. **1902** *Webster's Suppl.*, *Snow grass*,.. a coarse tall grass (*Danthonia Raoulii*) of New Zealand. **1906** T. F. CHEESEMAN *Man. N.Z. Flora* 887 Snow-grass. **1918** F. W. HILGENDORE *Pasture Plants & Pastures N.Z.* ii. 42 Snow Grass (*Danthonia raoulii*).—This is another Tussock, growing 4 to 6 feet high. It has broad leaves shining below, and feathery oat-like heads... Its presence in quantity frequently marks the limit above which it is not safe to carry sheep in winter..as indeed its popular name of Snow Grass would indicate. **1930** L. G. D. ACLAND *Early Canterbury Runs* 1st Ser. vi. 131 When he was first thatching the cob house..he put the top of each bundle of snow-grass outside the bottom of the one above so that all the rain ran inwards. **1968** *N.Z. Listener* 10 May 10/4 The beast, a young stag, had its antlers hopelessly entangled in the tough-rooted snowgrass. **1972** P. NEWTON *Sheep Thief* ii. 18 The roof consisting of bare birch rafters with a thick layer of snow grass thatch. **1928** 'BRENT OF BIN BIN' *Up Country* xiv. 237 The *snow-gums stood like brides in veils of perfumed lace. **1964** D. STEWART in R. Ward *Penguin Bk. Austral. Ballads* 278 Hard to say where he came from—..out of a hollow snowgum Or out of a granite boulder. **1981** *Garden* CVI. 275/1 There are..very large trees of the Tasmanian snow gum at Inverewe in Ross-shire. **1907** S. BROWN *Alpine Flora of Canadian Rocky Mountains* 44 (*heading*) *Erythronium grandiflorum* Pursh. **Snow Lily.* **1936** D. MCCOWAN *Animals Canad. Rockies* xxix. 250 Great quantities of the bulbs of Snow Lilies. **1972** *Islander* (Victoria, B.C.) 2 Apr. 13/3 The snow lily..pops its bright yellow head out as soon as the snow has left the hill-sides. **1855** OGILVIE *Suppl.*, **Snow-mould*, a fungous plant, the *Lanosa nivalis*, which grows beneath snow, on grasses or cereal crops. **1949** *Nature Mag.* XLII. 35/2 The *snow pea ..is commonly listed by all large seed-firms as an edible-podded pea. **1956** 'E. MCBAIN' *Cop Hater* (1958) xx. 172 Chinese vegetables; luscious snow peas, and water chestnuts. **1978** *Times* 17 July 14/3 We had a prolific crop of sugar peas, which the Americans call snow peas. **1860** HOGG *Fruit Manual* 212 *Snow [Pear]. See White Doyenné. **1884** *De Candolle's Orig. Cultivated Pl.* 232 Snow-Pear—*Pyrus nivalis*. This variety of pear is cultivated in Austria, in the north of Italy, and in..France. **1846** LINDLEY *Veg. Kingd.* 15 The red and green *Snow-plants, which have been described as Confervæ, and assigned to the genus Protococcus. **1870** *Old & New* Mar. 349/2 The strange snow-plant..must be passed as a railroad traveller passes all things. **1882** *Garden* 18 Feb. 114/3 The Snow Plant of California with its rich colour. **1905** A. R. WALLACE *My Life* II. xxxi. 161 The strange Snow plants (*Sarcodes sanguinea*) ..with a dense spike of flowers of a blood-red colour. **1940** *Oregon: End of Trail* 20 Deeper in the forest grow the waxy Indian pipe, the blood-red snow plant, and the rare moccasin flower. **1959** MUNZ & KECK *California Flora* 436 Snow Plant. Red fleshy usually pubescent saprophyte. **1899** *Gardening Illustr.* 3 June 181/2 The *Snow-tree (*Ozothamnus rosmarinifolius*).

**snow** (snəʊ), *sb.*² Also 7–8 **snaw.** [ad. Du. *snauw*, *snaauw*, or LG. *snau* (hence Da. and Sw. *snau*, G. *schnau*, *schnaue*, and F. *senau*), of doubtful origin.] A small sailing-vessel resembling a brig, carrying a main and fore mast and a supplementary trysail mast close behind the mainmast; formerly employed as a warship.

*α.* **1676** *Lond. Gaz.* No. 1079/3 Ostend, March 29. On the 25 instant,..appeared off of this Harbour..two Snaws of four Guns each. **1695** LUTTRELL *Brief Rel.* (1857) III. 441, 28 sail of French ships,..and among them 6 or 8 snaws of 8 or 10 guns each. **1710** *Ibid.* VI. 532 A French snaw, with 33 men and 4 guns.

*β.* **1721** S. SEWALL *Diary* 14 Apr., A Letter from Capt. Tuthill,..giving me an account of the Arrival of the Snow Anna. **1763** JANSSEN *Smuggling Laid Open* 263 A Snow of 120 Tons, and 48 Men,..Mounting 12 Carriage Guns, besides Swivels. **1784** COLMAN *Prose on Sev. Occas.* (1787) III. 255 Majestick navies in her harbours ride, Skiffs, snows, and frigates anchor by their side. **1810** CRABBE *Borough* i. 52 Far other craft our prouder river shows, Hoys, pinks and sloops; brigs, brigantines and snows. **1846** A. YOUNG *Naut. Dict.* 50 A Brig bends her boom-sail (or..trysail) to the mainmast, while a Snow bends it to a trysail mast: in other respects these two vessels are alike. **1881** CLARK RUSSELL *Ocean Free Lance* II. iv. 193 The whole ocean..was covered by..brigs, snows, tartans, schooners, pinks.

*attrib.* and *Comb.* **1790** BEATSON *Naval & Milit. Mem.* II. 183 The James & Thomas tender..was attacked by a large snow privateer. **1860** *Merc. Mar. Mag.* VII. 148 She was a two-masted vessel,..and snow-rigged.

**snow** (snəʊ), *v.* Pa. t. and pple. snowed (snəʊd). Forms: *α. Sc.* and *north.* 4–5 **snawe,** 5– **snaw;** 4 **snou-,** 5–7 **snowe** (5 **-yn**), 4– **snow.** *Pa. t.* and *pa. pple.* 4, 8– **snawed,** 9 **snaa'd, snaa't;** 6– **snowed.** *β. Pa. t.* 4 **sneu,** 4– (now *dial.*) **snew,** 6 **snewe.** *Pa. pple.* 5 **snawen,** 9 *dial.* **snawn;** 6 **snowen,** 9 *dial.* **snown, snewn.** [f. SNOW *sb.*¹, taking the place of OE. *sníwan*, SNEW *v.* Cf. MDu. *sneuwen*, *sn(o)uwen* (Du. *sneeuwen*), LG. *sneen*, *schneen*, ON. *snjáva*, *snjóva* (Icel. *snjóa*, Norw. *snjoa*, *snjøa*, etc.; Sw. *snöga*, *snöa*, Da. *sne*). The strong conjugation, formerly common, was no doubt due to the influence of BLOW *v.*¹]

**1.** *intr. it snows*, snow falls. Also occas. with *snow* as subject.

Examples of the strong forms are given under *β*.

*α.* **13..** *K. Alis.* 6450 (Laud MS.), Whan it snoweþ, oiþer rineþ. **1412–20** LYDG. *Chron. Troy* I. 1644 Sche koude make ..to hayle and snowe, And frese also. *c* **1425** *Eng. Voc.* in Wr.-Wülcker 665 *Floctat*, snawes... *Ningit*, snawes. *c* **1440** *Promp. Parv.* 462/1 Snowyn, *ningit*. **1486** *Eng. Misc.* (Surtees, 1890) 57 And ther schall it snaw by craft, to be made of waffrons in maner of snaw. **1530** PALSGR. 724/1 In wynter, whan it snoweth, it is good syttynge by a good fyre. **1592** *Arden of Feversham* v. i, As we went, it snowed al the way. **1638** R. BAKER tr. *Balzac's Lett.* (vol. II) 45 Where it is counted for a wonder, that..it was cold or snowed. **1662** J. DAVIES tr. *Mandelslo's Trav.* 4 Though it were very bad weather, and snow'd all night. **1707** FLOYER *Physic. Pulse-Watch* 322 The Barometer sunk to the bottom, it Rain'd and Snow'd. **1772** T. SMITH *Jrnl.* (1849) 287 Though it has snowed very often this month, there has been no deep snows. **1841** DICKENS *Barn. Rudge* xvi, Glad to hear it rained, or snowed, or blew, or froze. **1864** MRS. CARLYLE *Lett.* III. 237 If it..snows as hard there as here.

*β. c* **1330** R. BRUNNE *Chron. Wace* (Rolls) 13551 Also þikke as snow þen [*v.r.* þat] snew, Or al so hail þat stormes blew. **1525** LD. BERNERS *Froiss.* II. 342 Also it rayned, blewe, & snewe, that it was a mervaylouse yvell wether. *c* **1540** COPLAND *Hye Way to Spyttel Ho.* 99 in Hazl. *E.P.P.* IV. 27 For it had snowen, and frosen very strong. **1586** A. DAY *Eng. Secretary* II. (1625) 80, I had as lieue he told me it snew. **1640** E. DACRES tr. *Machiavelli's Prince* 279 Always and in all seasons, whether it rain'd or snew, he went with his head uncover'd. **1695** WOOD *Life* 30 Jan., On T[uesday] the 29 of Jan. it snew all the day. *a* **1800** PEGGE *Suppl. Grose*, *Snew*, the Preterit of *snow*. York. **1870** VERNEY *Lettice Lisle* 295 It never snew once last winter. **1877** *Holderness Gloss.* 131/2 It's snawn all way here.

**2.** To fall, descend, etc., in the manner of snow. Also *fig.*

*a* **1300** *Cursor M.* 6381 It sneu to þam als it war flur. **1833** TENNYSON *Pal. Art* 139 A hundred winters snow'd upon his breast, From cheek and throat and chin. *c* **1860** F. W. FABER *Hymn*, '*The House of Mourning*' xviii, That unrestful gloom, Where the light snows in. **1894** BARING-GOULD *Queen of Love* I. 153 Away shot the cards,..snowing upon the audience in the front rows.

**3. a.** *trans.* To let fall as snow; to cause to descend in the manner of snow; to shower down.

? *a* **1366** CHAUCER *Rom. Rose* 558 Hir throte al so white of hewe, As snawe on braunche snawed newe. **1587** FLEMING *Contn. Holinshed* III. 1355 It hailed small confects, rained rosewater, and snew an artificiall kind of snow. **1598** SHAKS. *Merry W.* v. v. 22 Let the skie raine Potatoes: let it thunder .., haile kissing Comfits, and snow Eringoes. **1608** CHAPMAN *Dk. Byron* v. iii. 233 As a savage boar..holds his anger up, And snows it forth in foam. **1613** HEYWOOD *Braz. Age* II. ii. Wks. 1874 III. 192 Where the Boare Hath in his fury snow'd his scattered foame. **1827** SCOTT *Chron. Canongate* Introd., The theatrical mechanist, who, when the white paper which represented his shower of snow was exhausted, continued the storm by snowing brown. **1847** TENNYSON *Princ.* I. 60 He..tore the king's letter, snow'd it down. **1876** 'MARK TWAIN' *Tom Sawyer* xvi, A sweep of chilly air passed by,..snowing the flaky ashes broadcast about the fire.

**b.** In figurative use. Also *absol.* (quot. 1751).

*a* **1631** DONNE (J.), 'Till age snow white hairs on thee. **1684** N. LEE *Constantine* II. 15, I'll stay till Age His Snow'd a hundred Winters on my Head. **1751** YOUNG *Nt. Th.* v. 602 Time on this head has snow'd. **1878** *N. Amer. Rev.* CXXVI. 166 'Snowing' old inflation speeches over the Eastern states. **1905** SOLLAS *Age of Earth* iii. 65, [The] Eiffel Tower, snowing post-cards from its summit all over the civilized world.

**4. a.** To strew or cover with or as with snow. Also *transf.*

*c* **1400** MAUNDEV. (Roxb.) xiv. 65 Waters and maracez.. whilk a man may noȝt passe, bot if he hafe riȝt hard frost and þat it be wele snawen abouen. **1635** HEYWOOD *London's Sinus Salutis* 295 Even the Horse,..When the most curb'd, and playing with the bit,..snowes the ground. **1743** FRANCIS tr. *Hor., Odes* IV. xiii. 12 Scar'd at thy Wrinkles,.. And Head snow'd o'er with Grey. **1820** SHELLEY *Hymn Merc.* xciv, Three virgin Sisters, who,..Their heads with flour snowed over white and new, Sit in a vale. **1873** SYMONDS *Greek Poets* x. 312 Cherry trees and apricots snow the grass in spring with a white wealth of April blossoms. **1887** F. ROBINSON *New Religio Medici* 133 The mantle..of the Star of India drapes a coffin whose lid is snowed with flowers.

**b.** *fig.* To deceive or win over with plausible words; to kid, to dupe. Also with *under*. *slang* (orig. and chiefly *U.S.*).

**1943** [see *snow job* s.v. SNOW *sb.*[1] 9a]. **1945** D. DEMPSEY in M. Mayorga *Best One-Act Plays of '44* 18 Give me the lid, Greenberg..who you tryin' to snow, Lou-*i*-siana? **1956** 'E. S. AARONS' *Assignment Treason* (1967) v. 43 Were you snowing me about Hackett doing the clobber job on you? **1963** N. FREELING *Because of Cats* xi. 175, I won't get mad. Just don't snow me with any sob-sister business. **1966** H. WAUGH *Pure Poison* (1967) xiv. 87 Roger'd be alone in a corner with some girl and..looked like he was really snowing them. **1980** *Australian* 9 Dec. 6/5 Mr J. C. Moore (the new minister in charge of the Customs Bureau) has taken the most immediate and active interest in the workings of the bureau. Unfortunately, it is most likely that he also will be snowed by the bureaucrats as has been the case with previous ministers.

**5.** To cause (the hair, etc.) to turn white like snow; to invest with white hair.

**1598** SYLVESTER *Du Bartas* II. ii. III. *Colonies* 761 Thou (tender Mother) will not suffer Age To snow my locks in Forrein Pilgrimage. *a* **1689** MRS. BEHN tr. *Cowley's Plants* C.'s Wks. (Grosart) II. 245 In Youth severe, Before the Winter-Age had snow'd their Hair. **1698** FRYER *Acc. E. India & P.* 275 He is a goodly Reverend Old Man, snowed with Age. **1904** *Westm. Gaz.* 28 Dec. 1/3 Yamagata stays in Tokio,..snowed with seventy years.

**6. a.** With *up*. To block, obstruct, incommode, imprison, etc., with snow. Usu. in pa. pple.

**1815** JANE AUSTEN *Emma* xiii, I was snowed up at a friend's house once for a week. **1862** SALA *Seven Sons* I. v. 95 News came from the country of trains snowed-up. **1873** SMILES *Huguen. France* (1881) I. iv. 67 He wrote..from some remote place where he was snowed up.

*transf.* **1837** CARLYLE *Fr. Rev.* I. IV. i, It is a sheer snowing of pamphlets; like to snow up the Government thoroughfares!

**b.** With *under*: To bury in snow; *fig.* to submerge, overwhelm, overpower, etc. Orig. *U.S.*

**1880** E. KIRKE *Garfield* 32 Democrats vied with Republicans..in snowing him under with congratulations. **1894** *United Service Mag.* Oct. 28 Mercier was snowed under by a majority greater than had ever been known in Canadian history. **1911** WEBSTER s.v., The train was snowed under.

**c.** To drive *out*, take *away*, by means of snow.

**1851** MRS. BROWNING *Casa Guidi Wind.* I. Wks. (1904) 345 [To] prove that all the winters which have snowed Cannot snow out the scent..Of a sincere man's virtues. **1891** W. F. MOULTON *Let.* in *Mem.* (1899) 247 Every lingering fragment of inflection would be blown, snowed, sleeted, rained and sunned away.

**d.** With *in*. To block, imprison with snow. Chiefly *N. Amer.*

**1857** G. F. MCDOUGALL *Eventful Voy. 'Resolute'* xiii. 331 The fore and after parts of the upper deck were now snowed in, to the depth of nine inches on the starboard side. **1887** C. B. GEORGE *40 Yrs. on Rail* ix. 188 My train was snowed in during one of the terrible storms. **1970** *Daily Colonist* (Victoria, B.C.) 1 Jan. 1/3 Picture above taken a year ago as worst blizzard in years blanketed area shows cars snowed-in on King's Road.

**7.** *U.S. slang.* To drug, to dope. Also with advbs. Usu. in pa. pple.

**1927** *Amer. Speech* Dec. 167/2 *Snowed in*, dopey, as if full of cocaine. **1934** R. CHANDLER in *Black Mask* July 70/2 She looked snowed, weaved around funny. **1942** BERREY & VAN DEN BARK *Amer. Thes. Slang* §509/30 *Snowed, snowed in, up* or *under*,..under the influence of cocaine. **1956** H. GOLD *Man who was not with It* xxiii. 222 But I figured on how to get snowed.

**snowball** ('snəʊbɔːl), *sb.* Also 5 **snoweballe**, 6 **snowbal(le**, 7– **snow-ball**; 5 *north.* **snayballe**, 8–9 *Sc.* **snawbaw**, 9 **-ba'**. [f. SNOW *sb.*[1] + BALL *sb.*[1] Cf. WFris. *sniebal*, MDu. *snee(u)-*, *sneubal*, Du. *sneeuwbal*, G. *schneeball*, Da. *snebold*, Sw. *snöboll*, Norw. *snjoball*.]

**1. a.** A ball of snow, esp. one made of a size convenient for throwing by hand.

*c* **1400** *Brut* cxcviii, Meny of þe citee..caste oppon him meny snoweballes, and meny oþer reproues dede him. **1483** *Cath. Angl.* 346/2 Snayballe, *floccus, nivenodium*. *a* **1530** HEYWOOD *Play of Wether* 1011 (Brandl), All my pleasure is in..makynge of snow ballys and throwyng the same. **1598** SHAKS. *Merry W.* III. v. 24 My bellies as cold as if I had swallow'd snowbals. **1657** TRAPP *Comm. Job* xxxviii. 22 We see..what paines they take to rake and scrape together snow to make a Snow-ball. **1677** HORNECK *Gt. Law Consid.* iv. 149 As wise an act, as to hope to be warm by..surrounding thy self with snow-balls. **1768–74** TUCKER *Lt. Nat.* (1834) I. 281 If I take a snow-ball into my hand, I shall be satisfied of its coldness by my sensation. **1789** E. DARWIN *Bot. Gard.* II. (1791) 25 *note*, If a piece of Camphor be immersed in a snow-ball. **1816** BYRON *Swiss Jrnl.* Wks. 180/2, I made a snowball and pelted Hobhouse with it. **1853** KANE *Grinnell Exped.* xxx. (1856) 258 By-and-by the sludge which we passed through..became pancakes and snow-balls. **1878** HUXLEY *Physiogr.* 158 When a schoolboy makes a snowball, he squeezes a handful or two of light snow into a hard compact lump.

**b.** In allusive use (common in the 17th c.). Phr. ***a snowball's chance in hell***: see HELL *sb.* 10b. Also ellipt. as ***a snowball's chance***.

(*a*) **1612** WEBSTER *White Devil* IV. iii. 114 Your good heart gathers like a snow-ball, Now your affection's cold. **1613** PURCHAS *Pilgrimage* (1614) 519 They passed through Fraunce, Germanie, Hungarie, their company (like a snow-ball) encreasing as they went. **1674** *Govt. Tongue* vi. 75 For reports we know like snow balls gather still the farther they roule. **1740** RICHARDSON *Pamela* (1824) I. 163 For they are like a snow-ball, and intend to gather company as they go. **1818** COBBETT *Pol. Reg.* XXXIII. 610 His army, increasing like a snowball. **1845** FORD *Handbk. Spain* I. 43 The Caravan like a snow-ball, increases in bulk as it rolls on.

(*b*) **1622** BACON *Hen. VII* (1876) 35 The rebels took their way toward York,..but their snow-ball did not gather as it went. **1645** PAGITT *Heresiogr.* (1647) 3 Before this snowball grew greater by rolling, Count Mansfield raiseth forces. **1649** MILTON *Eikon.* xix. Wks. 1851 III. 473 Such a Snowball hee might easily gather by rowling through those cold and dark provinces of ignorance and leudness.

(*c*) **1934** *Esquire* Sept. 27 He wouldn't have a snowball's chance with you. **1977** *Amer. Machinist* 1 June 27 There is not a snowball's chance in Haiti of making the deadline on an across-the-board basis. **1979** 'A. HAILEY' *Overload* I. I. 4 'Told 'em there wasn't a snowball's chance,' a woman assistant dispatcher called over.

†**c.** *Sc.* In the fig. phr. ***to cast snowballs***, to be reserved or distant. *Obs.*

**1725** RAMSAY *Gentle Sheph.* IV. i, I trow sae,..lasses will come to at last, Tho' for a while they maun their snaw-baws cast. **1821** LIDDLE *Poems* 236 The lasses a' their snaw-baws cast, For fear we should betray.

**d.** The pastime of snow-balling.

**1708** *Brit. Apollo* No. 55. 3/2 A Game at Snow-ball.

**e.** *transf.* A scheme or project that relies for its growth on a snowball effect (see quots.).

**1892** *Whitehall Rev.* 17 Sept. 7/1 The system of 'Snowballs' is multiplication at a very rapid rate, each giver being obliged to bind himself to find a certain number of others who will not only give, but bind themselves each to find an equal number of contributors on the same terms. **1923** H. C. BAILEY *Mr Fortune's Practice* v. 141 It's just like a snowball... When you want subscriptions and have a snowball where every one has to get some one else to subscribe. **1927** E. F. BENSON *Lucia in London* iii. 70 Will she just pick up acquaintances, and pick up more from them, like one of those charity snowballs?

**f.** In bingo, etc.: a cash prize which accumulates through successive games until it is won.

**1949** S. P. LLEWELLYN *Troopships* 5 Last house... May I remind you, gentlemen, that the snowball is now worth over fourteen pounds? **1960** *Guardian* 2 Dec. 23/5 The British Legion..club..was more or less built on Bingo... The crowds, drawn by a 'snowball' on a lucky number which had reached £16, had been growing..too large. **1971** A. ROSS *Huddersfield Job* 129 The snowball—a sort of continuing competition in which the cash prizes, if not won, are carried forward to swell next week's total. **1976** *Evening Post* (Nottingham) 15 Dec. 13/2 Tote Baseball Nos. 20 & 13 & 6 Three winners. Snowball not won.

**2. a.** *Cookery.* One or other of various dishes or confections intended to resemble a ball of snow in appearance.

**1769** MRS. RAFFALD *Eng. Housekpr.* (1778) 263 To make Snow Balls. Pare five large..apples, make a little good hot paste, and roll your apples in it,..make iceing for them..and ice them all over with it about a quarter of an inch thick. **1854** MARION HARLAND *Alone* xxx, A dozen loaves of cake, and ever so many snow-balls. **1877** *Cassell's Dict. Cookery* 887 Fry the snowballs till they are lightly set.

**b.** One of various cocktails (see quots.).

**1930** *Savoy Cocktail Bk.* 150 Snowball Cocktail. $\frac{1}{6}$ Crème de Violette. $\frac{1}{6}$ White Crème de Menthe. $\frac{1}{6}$ Anisette. $\frac{1}{6}$ Sweet Cream. $\frac{1}{3}$ Dry Gin. **1963** D. A. EMBURY *Fine Art of Mixing Drinks* (ed. 2) 289 Snow Ball. A Silver Fizz with whisky in place of the gin and ginger ale in place of the charged water. **1966** J. DOXAT *Booth's Handbk. Cocktails & Mixed Drinks* xiv. 145 Snowball. Ice cube in tall glass. Generous measure of Advocaat; top with Fizzy Lemonade; decorate with slice of Lemon. **1972** A. DRAPER *Death Penalty* ii. 16 Ben ordered the drinks—a snowball for Jeannie and whisky mac for himself. **1979** R. BARNARD *Posthumous Papers* xvii. 158 She ordered a snowball... 'I'm not used to coming into a pub on my own.'

**c.** *U.S.* and *W. Indies.* An ice-cream; a confection made of shaved or chipped ice covered in syrup, etc.

**1941** J. SMILEY *Hash House Lingo* 51 *Snowball*, dip of vanilla ice cream. **1946** K. DUNHAM *Journey to Accompong* 93 My Maroon neighbors..were lolling around..drinking the penny 'snowball' made from chipped ice with a sweet purple syrup poured over it. **1953** H. P. MORRISON in *Caribbean Anthol. Short Stories* 137 Customers of every age milled round to buy 'snow-ball'—cool crushed ice in cheap glass tumblers with red, yellow or even green syrup oozing slowly through the crystalline mass. **1962** [see MAUBY].

**3.** *slang* or *jocular*. (See quots.)

**1785** GROSE *Dict. Vulgar T.*, *Snowball*, a jeering appellation for a negroe. **1819** MOORE *Tom Crib's Memor.* (ed. 3) 45 *note*, *Lily-whites* (or *Snow-balls*), Negroes. **1842** LOVER *Handy Andy* xlvi, The sweep was passing by, and I called him 'snow-ball'.

**4. a.** The Guelder rose, *Viburnum opulus*, or one of its clusters of white flowers. Also used for other species of *Viburnum*.

**1799** SOUTHEY *Eng. Ecl.* Poet Wks. III. 4 In spring the lilac and the snow-ball flower. **1828** CARR *Craven Gloss.*, *Snow-ball*, the Guelder Rose. **1850** *Beck's Florist* July 171 Here's snowballs, and waxberries, and mock-orange flowers, and lilacs. **1880** BESSEY *Botany* 518 Many species [of *Caprifoliaceæ*] are ornamental—e.g...*Viburnum*, the Snowball. **1948** W. ARNOLD-FORSTER *Shrubs for Milder Counties* iv. 184 *V. Opulus sterile*, the familiar 'Snowball', is ..quite good as a hedge.

**b.** *U.S.* (See quots.)

**1834** AUDUBON *Ornith.* II. 121 The Swamp Snowball, *Hydrangea quercifolia*,..found on the broken sandy banks bordering small watercourses. **1902** *Webster's Suppl.*, *Wild snowball*.., the New Jersey tea (*Ceanothus Americanus*), so called from its clusters of small white flowers. **1909** *Cent. Dict.* Suppl., *Little snowball*, the button-bush, *Cephalanthus occidentalis*.

**5.** *attrib.* and *Comb.* **a.** Miscellaneous, as ***snowball chrysanthemum***, ***cocktail***, ***fight***, ***fritters***, ***-like*** adv., ***vendor***, ***war***.

**1662** HIBBERT *Body Divinity* I. 188 Fame, snow-ball like, *crescit eundo*. **1877** *Cassell's Dict. Cookery* 887 Snowball Fritters. **1890** CHAMPLIN & BOSTWICK *Young Folks' Cycl. Games & Sports* 660/1 *Snowball fights*, contests between two parties armed with snowballs. **1899** *Westm. Gaz.* 6 Jan. 4/1 Giant snowball chrysanthemums. **1901** 'IAN MACLAREN' *Yng. Barbarians* iv, As the snowball war was a serious affair. **1930** Snowball cocktail [see sense 2b above]. **1948** *Sun* (Baltimore) 27 Aug. 24/3 Snowball vendors did a rush business.

**b. snowball bush, tree**, the Guelder rose (cf. 4a).

So WFris. *sniebalbeam*, Du. *sneeuwbalboom*, Sw. *snöbollsbuske*, *-träd*.

**1931** W. N. CLUTE *Common Names Plants* 48 Guelder rose, a common name of the snow-ball bush.., is said to be properly elder rose. **1979** *Seymour* (Indiana) *Daily Tribune* 19 May 1/3 The 'snowball bush' in his side yard is in full bloom. **1760** J. LEE *Introd. Bot.* App. 327 Snowball-tree, *Viburnum*. **1783** *Encycl. Brit.* (ed. 2) X. 8713/2 This tree when in bloom exhibits a singularly fine appearance; the flowers..are collected numerously into large globular umbels round like a ball; hence, it is sometimes called *snowball-trees*. **1856** A. GRAY *Man. Bot.* (1860) 168 The well-known Snow-ball Tree..is a cultivated state, with the whole cyme turned into large sterile flowers. **1902** E. T. COOK *Trees & Shrubs for Eng. Gardens* 443 Snowball tree..is too well known to need description. **1973** A. BONAR *Shrubs & Decorative Trees* III. 86 The snowball tree..is more attractive florally.

**c.** Used to denote increase by a kind of geometrical progression, as ***snowball contribution***, ***effect***, ***letter***, ***prize***, ***system***, etc.

**1897** *Westm. Gaz.* 8 Apr. 7/2 An anonymous 'snowball' contribution has been started. **1899** *Ibid.* 28 Jan. 6/1 The scheme of old-age pensions on the snowball system... They offer magnificent terms to any assurer who gets them ten other assurers,..and so on, like the rolling snowball. **1941** I. L. IDRIESS *Great Boomerang* xxxii. 251 It will not be the amount to be spent that will be considered, but the snowball effect of the resulting benefits. **1963** *Daily Tel.* 23 Jan. 20/8 A 'snowball' prize played for evening after evening at a bingo club is legal, provided the management gives the prize money. **1979** P. NIESEWAND *Member of Club* xviii. 142 Hundreds of families emigrate [from South Africa] every month... Each one has a snowball effect. Other families start thinking: should we leave also?

**snowball** ('snəʊbɔːl), *v.* [f. prec. In sense 2 perh. a back-formation from *snow-balling*: but cf. Fris. *sniebalje*, G. *schneeballen*.]

**1. a.** *intr.* To form balls or masses of snow.

**1684** O. HEYWOOD *Diaries* (1883) III. 343 It fell a considerable snow... I..found it very dangerous way, for it snow-balled on my horses feet.

**b.** *fig.* To increase or grow like a snowball rolled across snow; to accumulate or gather momentum at an ever-increasing rate.

**1929** E. N. NICHOLSON *Study of Birds* 39 Some flocks are freshly formed each day, and recruits can be watched joining the original members at intervals until it snowballs up to its full size. **1934** *Sun* (Baltimore) 9 Nov. 26/7 The [housing] program in Maryland is 'snowballing'. **1967** R. LEHMANN *Swan in Evening* III. 104 The success of those classes delighted and amused her. How polyglot they became and how they snowballed. **1969** *New Yorker* 19 Apr. 94/2 When a man knows what to look for, his value snowballs. **1973** *Lebende Sprachen* XVIII. 69/2 Management must appreciate the extra profit that snow-balls from making use of advanced techniques. **1976** *Ilkeston Advertiser* 10 Dec. 15/4 Anyone is welcome to join in at any time during the day. A coach will ferry people around the circuit and singers usually 'snowball' throughout the day.

**2.** *trans.* To throw a snowball at (a person); to pelt with snowballs. Also *fig.*

**1850** L. SAWYER *Way Sk.* (1926) iii. 46 Our men amused themselves with snowballing each other. **1855** in HYDE CLARKE *Dict.* **1889** *Pall Mall G.* 26 Feb. 2/3 The..Opposition..could do nothing but snowball the other side with Pigott all the evening. **1899** *Westm. Gaz.* 24 Apr. 10/1 To hear the old gentleman tell how he had actually snowballed Keats.

**3.** *intr.* To throw snowballs.

**1852** F. A. BUCK *Let.* 18 Dec. in *Yankee Trader* (1930) 112 At first we snow-balled, the whole town engaging in the sport like school boys. **1860** in WORCESTER. **1866** MISS YONGE *Dove in Eagle's Nest* ix, Christina..had been watching them snowballing in the castle court.

So **'snow,balling** *vbl. sb.*, the action or pastime of making and throwing snowballs; also *fig.* and *ppl. a.*

**1861** F. A. BUCK *Let.* 20 Jan. in *Yankee Trader* (1930) 186 Christmas we had a nice lot of egg nog and cake and snow balling. **1870** ALDRICH *Story of a Bad Boy* xii. 124 Snow-balling at school, skating on the mill-pond,..were sports no less exhilarating. **1887** H. SMART *Cleverly Won* iv. 28 They skated,..and at times even relaxed so far as to fall to snowballing. **1887** *Times* (weekly ed.) 30 Dec. 10/1 The mobbing and snowballing of Mr. Gladstone's party. **1941** *Sun* (Baltimore) 3 Nov. 14/1 The constantly snow-balling defense effort may cut into the everyday things we use in normal civilian existence. **1966** *Word Study* Dec. 4/1 Dubious meaning..starts a snow-balling that soon places the intended meaning beyond retrieval. **1971** *Daily Tel.* 29 Dec. 10 The snowballing success of Alan Ayckbourn's plays abroad..is a constant surprise to him. **1973** *Times* 14 Aug. 3/3 The 'snowballing' technique by which researchers were introduced to one drug taker; who introduced a second and so on. **1977** *N.Y. Times* 16 Jan. IV. 19/3 Mr. Kissinger's pet theory of 'linkage', a kind of snowballing of détente, had to be given up.

**snowberry** ('snəʊ,bɛrɪ). [f. SNOW *sb.*[1] Cf. G. *schneebeere* (Nemnich).] A name given to various plants or shrubs bearing white berries, or to the fruit of these.

When denoting the plant or shrub, freq. used attrib. with *bush* (or *tree*). In the earliest example the identification is doubtful:—**1760** J. Lee *Introd. Bot.* App. 327 Snowberry-bush, *Lonicera.*

**1.** A rubiaceous shrub (*Chiococca racemosa*), native to the West Indies and Florida, cultivated as a greenhouse or hothouse plant.

**1815** J. Smith *Panorama Sci. & Art* II. 678 Hothouse Plants... Snow-berry. **1839** R. Sweet *Hothouse & Greenh. Man.* (ed. 6) 54 *Chiococca racemosa* or Snow-berry-bush, thrives well in a mixture of loam and peat. **1864** Grisebach *Flora Brit. W. Ind.* 787/2 Snowberry, *Chiococca racemosa.*

**2. a.** A caprifoliaceous shrub (*Symphoricarpus racemosus*), native to North America and Mexico, commonly grown in gardens and shrubberies.

(*a*) **1813** T. Jefferson *Let.* 8 Dec. in *Orig. Jrnls. Lewis & Clark Exped.* (1905) VII. 393 We call it the snow-berry bush, no botanical name being yet given to it. **1821** W. P. C. Barton *Flora N. Amer.* I. 69 The late Governor Lewis first brought to this city seeds of the snow-berry bush. **1872** Christina Rossetti *Sing Song* 10 A song-singing thrush, Dead at the foot of a snowberry bush. **1894** Mrs. H. Ward *Marcella* I. 16 The branches of a snowberry tree.

(*b*) **1821** W. P. C. Barton *Flora N. Amer.* I. 69 Snow-berry is a very ornamental shrub. **1857** Henfrey *Bot.* 313 The berries..of *Symphoricarpus*, the Snow-berry of our shrubberies, appear to be harmless. **1882** *Garden* 25 Feb. 134/1 The Snowberry..stands almost alone as the representative of the white fruited section.

**b.** The fruit of this shrub.

**1837** Ht. Martineau *Soc. Amer.* II. 245 Smart mulatto girls, with snow-berries in their hair. **1861** Mrs. Stowe *Pearl of Orr's Island* 7 The cheek was white and bloodless as a snowberry.

**3.** *U.S.* **a.** ***creeping snowberry***, a trailing evergreen plant (*Chiogenes hispidula*) common in bogs and woods.

**1856** Gray *Man. Bot.* (1860) 250 *Chiogenes*, Creeping Snow-berry. **1857** Thoreau *Maine W.* (1894) 125 Creeping snow-berry, painted trillium. **1872** De Vere *Americanisms* 404 The queen of them all is said to be the lovely, creeping snowberry (*Chiogenes hispidula*).

**b.** The wintergreen, checkerberry, or tea-berry.

**1866** *Chambers's Encycl.* VIII. 789/2 The name Snowberry is also given to *Gaultheria serpyllifolia*, a native of the bogs of North America.

**4.** *Austr.* The wax-cluster, *Gaultheria hispida.*

**1880** Mrs. Meredith *Tasmanian Friends & Foes* 11 The 'Snow-berry' or 'Wax cluster' is also called native Arbutus.

**'snow-bird.** Also snow bird, snowbird. [f. snow *sb.*[1] Cf. Du. *sneeuwvogel*, G. *schneevogel.*]

**1.** One or other of various small European or American birds, *esp.* the snow-bunting (*Plectrophanes nivalis*), snow-finch (*Montifringilla nivalis*), or snow-sparrow (*Junco hiemalis*).

In the first group of quotations there is some indication of the precise bird intended.

(*a*) **1688** *Phil. Trans.* XVII. 996 The Snow-bird which I take to be much the same with our Hedge Sparrow; this is so called because it seldom appears about Houses but against Snow or very cold Weather. **1709** J. Lawson *Hist. Carolina* 146 The Snow-Birds are most numerous in the North Parts of America, where there are great Snows... They are like the Stones Smach, or Wheat-Ears. **1750** G. Edwards *Nat. Hist. Birds* III. Pl. 126 The Snow-Bird from Hudson's-Bay. This Bird..agrees exactly in Size and Shape with our great Pyed Mountain-Finch, or Brambling. **1771** J. R. Forster tr. *Kalm's Trav.* II. 81 The Swedes call a species of little birds, *Snofogel*, and the English call it Snow-bird. **1802** Montagu *Ornith.* s.v. *Bunting, Snow*, Snow-bird. Snow-flake. **1810** A. Wilson *Amer. Ornith.* II. 129 Snow-Bird, *Fringilla nivalis. Ibid.* 131 The Snow-bird is six inches long, and nine in extent. **1839** Audubon *Syn. Birds N. Amer.* 106 *Niphæa*, Snow-Bird. *Ibid.* 107 *Niphæa Oregona*, Oregon Snow-Bird. **1853** Kane *Grinnell Exped.* xli. (1856) 379 Crowds of little snow-birds (*Emberiza* and *Plectrophanes*), with white breasts and jetty coverts. **1884** Coues *N. Amer. Birds* 377 *Junco*, Snow Sparrows. Snow-birds. *Ibid., Junco hiemalis*,..Eastern Snow-bird. Black Snow-bird.

(*b*) **1798** Miss H. M. Williams *Tour Switzerland* II. App. 293 Her sledgy-car..O'er the pellucid ice her snow-birds drew. **1820** Scoresby *Acc. Arctic Regions* I. 535 The snow-bird, though so delicate in its appearance, is almost as ravenous as the fulmar. **1841** Bryant *Poems, Winter-Piece* 30 The snow-bird twitter'd on the beechen bough. **1880** W. Newton *Serm. for Boys* (1881) 358 The little snow-birds seem to enjoy it all. **1883** *Cent. Mag.* Sept. 681 From the first nest..to the last, which was that of a snow-bird.

**2.** The ivory gull, *Pagophila eburnea.*

**1831** Rennie *Montagu's Ornith. Dict.* 470 Snow Bird, (*Larus eburneus*). **1843** Yarrell *Brit. Birds* III. 449 *Larus candidus*, The Snow-bird.

**3.** *U.S. slang.* One who sniffs cocaine (cf. snow *sb.*[1] 5 d); *gen.* a drug addict.

**1914** Jackson & Hellyer *Vocab. Criminal Slang* 78 A 'snowbird' is the customary designation of the cocaine habitue. **1923** [see loaded *ppl. a.* 3 b]. **1952** *Sunday Times* 3 Feb. 5/4 Present-day New York is not..a city overrun by 'snowbirds' jabbing needles into their arms. **1963** 'M. Corrigan' *Why do Women—?* xxiii. 175 Don't tell me you never heard that name for a dope addict—a snowbird.

**4.** *U.S. slang.* **a.** (See quots.)

**1905** *N.Y. Even. Post* 20 Nov. 6, 28 per cent. deserted after three months, and were presumably 'snow-birds', that is, men who enlist to get food and clothing during the winter months. **1918** *Sat. Even. Post* 23 Nov. 11/1 They belonged to a shiftless class, the members of which often enlist in the army late in the fall because they want a job for the winter—the boys call them snowbirds. **1930** W. H. Waldron *Old Sergeant's Conferences* vii. 123 A 'Snow bird' is a deserter who surrenders in the fall to get a place to stay through the winter.

**b.** (See quot. 1924.)

**1923** *Nation* 31 Oct. 487 In winter, when building is at a standstill in the North, northern workmen, 'snow birds' or 'white doves' in Negro parlance, flock south. **1924** 'Digit' *Confessions 20th Century Hobo* 12 *Snowbird*, in the Southern States a Northerner who migrates south to avoid the winter. **1962** *Economist* 22 Dec. 1206/1 The Negro, who regularly loses his job to the 'snowbirds' from New York in the winter holiday season. **1979** *United States 1980/81* (Penguin Travel Guides) 243 This figure swells..during the winter months when 'snowbirds' arrive. ('Snowbird' is a tricky term as used in Miami, it refers primarily to tourists escaping the Northeastern freeze.)

**5.** *colloq.* A person who likes snow; a snow-sports enthusiast.

**1928** D. H. Lawrence *Let.* in F. Lawrence *Not I* (1934) 269, I am no snow-bird, I hate the stark and shroudy whitemen, white and black. **1973** *Globe & Mail* (Toronto) 8 Dec. 43/8 No joy yet for snowbirds. Snow enthusiasts will have to wait at least one more week before they can start up their snow-mobile engines or put on their skis.

**'snow-blind,** *a.* Also snowblind. [f. snow *sb.*[1] Cf. Du. *sneeuw-*, G. *schnee-*, Da. *sne-*, Sw. *snöblind.*] Having the eyes or sight affected by exposure to the glare of snow. Also *fig.*

**1748** H. Ellis *Voy. Hudson's Bay* 189 [Indians] frequently become Snow-blind in the Spring of the Year. **1865** *Times* 5 Feb., When the day at length dawned there was a thick fog, and I was rapidly becoming snow-blind. **1896** *Harper's Mag.* 728/2 Every man in the party but myself was more or less severely snow-blind. **1946** Dylan Thomas *Deaths & Entrances* 26 It is a winter's tale That the snow blind twilight ferries over the lakes.

So **snow-blinded** *a.*

**1839–52** Bailey *Festus* 316 As tired wanderer, snow-blinded, sinks And swoons upon the swelling drift.

**snow-blindness.** Also snowblindness. [Cf. prec.] Blindness or defective vision caused by exposure of the eyes to the glare of snow.

**1748** H. Ellis *Voy. Hudson's Bay* 137 This Invention prevents Snow-Blindness, a very grievous and painful Distemper, occasioned by the Action of the Light strongly reflected from the Snow upon the Eyes. **1836** *Uncle Philip's Convers. Whale Fishery* 202 The glare of the snow..gave them what was called the snow blindness. **1862** *Peaks, Passes & Glac.* II. 377 Snow-blindness, which..is not blindness at all, but merely a painful affection of the eyes. **1895** *Westm. Gaz.* 11 Apr. 5/1 There were thirty cases of snowblindness and twenty-six cases of frostbite.

*fig.* **1877** E. R. Conder *Basis Faith* Pref. p. xiii, The snow-blindness of moral insensibility.

**snow-broth.** Also *Sc.* snaw-broo, -bru. [f. snow *sb.*[1]] Melted snow; water produced or obtained by the melting of snow, esp. from natural causes.

α. **1600** Holland *Livy* xxi. xxxvi. 413 They were faine to go upon the bare yce underneath, and in the slabberie snow-broth. **1603** Shaks. *Meas. for M.* i. iv. 58 A man, whose blood Is very snow-broth. **1681** Chetham *Angler's Vade-m.* viii. §2 (1689) 89 In cold, frosty or snowy Weather or where store of Snow-broth is in the River. *a* **1700** B. E. *Dict. Cant. Crew, Snow-broth*, Snow-water. **1845** Judd *Margaret* i. vi, This is none of your snow-broth,..it's warming. **1862** C. C. Robinson *Dial. Leeds* 416 *Snow-broth*,..snow melted in a vessel is so called. **1888** *Pall Mall G.* 7 Apr. 5/1 The bitter east winds of March,..and the almost certain 'snow-broth' in the water.

β. **1787** Burns *Brigs of Ayr* 120 In mony a torrent down the snaw-broo rowes. **1803** *Prize Ess. Highl. Soc.* II. 400 Until the melted snow (snaw bru) is out of the water. **1899** *Westm. Gaz.* 21 Jan. 7/2 Fishing will almost certainly be temporarily stopped on account of the 'snaw-broo'.

**snow-bunting.** [f. snow *sb.*[1]] A fringilline bird, *Plectrophanes nivalis*, widely distributed in Arctic regions.

**1771** Forster *Catal. Anim. N. Amer.* 11 Snow-bunting. *Emberiza Nivalis.* **1783** Latham *Gen. Synop. Birds* II. i. 161 Snow Bunting. Size of the Chaffinch. **1811** A. Wilson *Amer. Ornith.* III. 39 The Snow Bunting derives a considerable part of its food from the seeds of certain aquatic plants. **1843** Yarrell *Brit. Birds* I. 426 The Snow Bunting may be generally considered as only a winter visitor to this country. **1872** Coues *N. Amer. Birds* 29 Titmice, redpoll linnets, snow buntings and other northern *Fringillidæ.*

**snowcat** ('snəʊkæt). orig. *N. Amer.* [Respelling of Sno-cat.] A tracked vehicle designed for travelling over snow (heavier and more rugged than a snowmobile). Cf. Sno-cat.

**1955** *Sun* (Baltimore) 10 Dec. 2/3 Two tractor-treaded snowcats will set out for a point in Byrd Land about 600 miles away. **1960** *Maclean's Mag.* 2 Jan. 15/2 The snow is brushed and groomed between one day's skiing and the next by tread-driven machines called snow cats. **1971** *Country Life* 25 Feb. 436/2 The final requiem to Isaac's services came with the Snowcat, a sort of caterpillar contrivance that could do most things bar swim. **1973** *Observer* (Colour Suppl.) 21 Jan. 35/2 You can..make the magical and distinctly tricky trip by snowcat across Iceland's vast Vatnajokull Glacier.

**Snowcem** ('snəʊsɛm). Also snowcem. [f. snow *sb.*[1] + cem(ent *sb.*] The proprietary name of a cement-based (typically white) paint, used for covering external walls. Hence **'Snowcemmed** *a.*, painted with Snowcem.

**1939** *Trade Marks Jrnl.* 20 Sept. 1301 Snowcem. 608,464. Paints having a base of cement. The Cement Marketing Co. Ltd...—1st Aug. 1939. **1947** *E. African Ann. 1946–7* 120 (Advt.), Building Materials..Snow-crete, Colorcrete and Snowcem. **1966** D. Francis *Flying Finish* i. 13 Its drab walls..badly needed a coat of 'Snowcem'. **1969** R. Blythe *Akenfield* 19 The old farmsteads, snowcemmed and trim, ride high on the hills. **1972** J. Blackburn *Devil Daddy* i. 15 Battersby shamed his neighbours with Snowcemmed walls. **1979** B. Hines *Price of Coal* 25 I've heard they've ordered ten thousand gallons of Snowcem to whitewash the shaft with.

**snow-clad,** *a.* [f. snow *sb.*[1]] Clad or covered with snow.

**1809** Byron *Ch. Har.* i. lx, Oh, thou Parnassus!..soaring snow-clad through thy native sky. **1844** H. H. Wilson *Brit. India* III. 10 Whence it stretched..to snow-clad mountains separating it from China. **1865** *Proc. R. Geogr. Soc.* 16 Mr. Thornton made numerous observations of the snow-clad peak.

*transf.* **1839** Sterling *Poems, Coleridge* 153 With sybil eyes, and brow By age snow-clad, yet bright with summer's glow.

**snow-cold,** *a.* [f. snow *sb.*[1] Cf. OE. *snáwceald*, G. *schneekalt.*] As cold as snow.

**1593** Nashe *Christ's T.* Wks. (Grosart) IV. 67 The Sonne of God hath sought to resolue thy snow-colde hart into water. **1832** Tennyson *Œnone* 140 Over her snow-cold breast and angry cheek. **1844** Louisa S. Costello *Béarn & Pyrenees* II. 88 In its snow-cold water I dipped my travelling-cup. **1855** Bailey *Mystic* (ed. 2) 14 Æternal silence laid her snow-cold hand Upon his lips.

†**snowcrie.** *Obs.*[−1] (Meaning uncertain.)

**1402** *Pol. Poems* (Rolls) II. 111 Not in Goddis gospel, but in Sathanas pistile, wher of sorowe and of snowcrie noon is to seken.

**Snowdon** ('snəʊdən). Forms: (see quots.). [See note.] ***Snowdon herald***, one of the six Scottish heralds. Also *ellipt.*

*Snowdon* was occ. used as a name for Stirling, but Jamieson cites statements that the designation of the herald was derived from 'Snowdoune castle of the county of Rosse': cf. his note on Barbour's *Bruce* (1820) iii. 410 (= iv. 181), and the entry in his Dictionary s.v. *Snawdoune.*

**1450** *Excheq. Rolls Scot.* V. 382 Et per solucionem factam Snawdoun heraldo, equitanti..ad regem Anglie,..x *li.* **1473** *Acc. Ld. High Treas. Scot.* I. 45 Gevin to Snawdone,..passande to Anwic [on] secrete materis of the Kingis, xl*s.* **1568** *Sc. Acts, Jas. VI* (1814) III. 47/2 Johne patersone snadoun herauld. **1592–3** *Exchеq. Rolls Scot.* XXII. 308 To Snawdoun,..Rothissay, Merchimont herauldis, every ane of thame takand in the yeir £20. **1636** *Reg. Privy Council Scot.* VI. 190 James Law, Snadoune herald, charged him to..render his house of Arradoull within fifteen days. **1710** Chamberlayne *Pres. St. Gt. Brit.* ii. 414 There are Six Heralds [in Scotland], Albany, Rothesay, Snadown, Marchmont, Yla, and Ross. **1863** [see Ross *sb.*[1]].

**Snowdonian** (snəʊ'dəʊnɪən), *a.* [f. the place-name *Snowdon* (see def.) + -ian.] Of or pertaining to Snowdon, a lofty mountain in North Wales; relating to, found at or near, Snowdon.

**1820** Shelley *Let. Maria Gisborne* 239 The milk-white Snowdonian Antelope. **1829** H. L. Jones (*title*), Illustrations of the Natural Scenery of the Snowdonian Mountains. **1855** A. Sedgwick *British Palæozoic Rocks* Introd. p. xli. *note*, The Snowdonian fossils were both embedded amongst, and overlaid by, contemporaneous plutonic rocks. **1897** Watts-Dunton *Aylwin* xii. iv, Those Snowdonian spirits which her music was supposed to have evoked from the mountain air.

**snow-drift.** Also snowdrift. [f. snow *sb.*[1] Cf. Norw. dial. *snjodrift, -driv*, ON. *snjódrif*, Sw. *snödrifva*, Da. *snedrive.*]

**1.** A heap or mass of snow driven together, or piled up, by the action of the wind.

*a* **1300** *Cursor M.* 9932 Wit-in þis castel þat sua es tift, þat quitter es þan snau drif [*read* drift, *but the Gött. MS. has* on drift]. **1600** Fairfax *Tasso* xx. cxxxvi, As against the warm'th of Titans fire, Snow drifts consume. **1821** Scott *Kenilw.* xxxv, I would rather keep watch on a snow-drift. **1860** G. A. Spottiswoode *Vac. Tour* 96 We were soon planted in a snow-drift, fifty or sixty yards long, higher than the carriage. **1874** Green *Short Hist.* ii. §4. 72 He..helped with his own hands to clear a road through the snowdrifts.

*transf.* **1864** *Daily Telegr.* 16 July, There are snowdrifts of pearls of great price.

**2.** A driving mass or cloud of snow; snow driven before the wind.

**1836** *Uncle Philip's Convers. Whale Fishery* 200 He..never walked farther from the ships than a mile, for fear of being overtaken by a snow-drift. **1892** J. Lumsden *Sheephead & Trotters* 137 The snawdrift, o'er Soutra, in tempest was blawing.

**snowdrop** ('snəʊdrɒp). Also snow-drop. [f. snow *sb.*[1] Cf. G. *schneetropfen, -tröpfchen, -tröpflein*, Sw. *snödroppe*; also G. *schneeglocke*, Du. *sneeuwklokje*, Da. *sneklokke*, Sw. *snöklocka* 'snow-bell'.]

**1. a.** An early-flowering bulbous plant (*Galanthus nivalis*), having a white pendent flower; also, a flower, bulb, or single plant of this.

**1664** Boyle *Colours* 264 Those purely White Flowers that appear about the end of Winter, and are commonly call'd Snow drops. **1664** Evelyn *Kal. Hort.* 81 December...Flowers in Prime,..Snow flowers or drops, Yucca, &c. **1728–46** Thomson *Spring* 529 Fair-handed Spring..Throws out the snowdrop, and the crocus first. **1763–5** Churchill *Gotham* i. Poems 1767 II. 12 The Snow-drop, who, in habit white and plain Comes on the Herald of fair Flora's train. **1796** Withering *Brit. Pl.* (ed. 3) I. 21 The

Snow-drop, though not frequent in a wild state, is to be found in almost every Garden. **1820** SHELLEY *Sensit. Pl.* I. 13 The snowdrop, and then the violet, Arose from the ground with warm rain wet. **1856** DELAMER *Fl. Garden* (1861) 42 There are single and double snowdrops. **1872** TENNYSON *Last Tourn.* 220 The snowdrop only, flowering thro' the year, Would make the world as blank as winter-tide.

*attrib.* **1811** W. R. SPENCER *Poems* 66 The snow-drop paths of innocence. **1865** ALLINGHAM 50 *Mod. Poems, Vernal Voluntary*, Snowdrop-flow'r, and crocus. **1894** *Daily News* 1 June 8/1 The cold and rather trying purity of snowdrop white.

**b.** *transf.* Applied to a girl.

**1833** T. HOOK *Parson's Dau.* I. vii, Our little snow-drop, as I call her, is the cause. **1884** *Milnor* (Dakota) *Teller* 27 June, A photograph gallery where the boys will gather with their little Dakota snowdrops.

**2.** With distinctive terms, or *attrib.* (see quots.).

**1731** MILLER *Gard. Dict.* s.v. *Narcisso-Leucojum*, Lesser Bulbous-violet or Snow-drop. *Ibid.*, Greater Snow-drop or Bulbous-violet. **1822** *Hortus Anglicus* II. 50 *Anemone sylvestris*, Large white flowered or Snow Drop Anemone. **1848** CRAIG II. s.v. *Snow*, The *placid snowdrop* is the Galanthis plicatus, a native of the Crimea. **1891** *Cent. Dict.* s.v. *Royena, R. lucida*, known as *African snowdrop*, or *African bladder-nut*, is a pretty greenhouse species.

**3.** Used as a name for a variety of wheat or potato.

**1844** C. HILLYARD *Pract. Farm. & Grazing* (ed. 4) 89 The Whittington, and my snowdrop white wheat. **1900** *Daily News* 23 July 2/5 Potatoes: Early Puritans,.. Snowdrops.

**4.** *slang.* An American military policeman; hence, any military policeman.

**1944** *N.Y. Times* 9 Apr. IV. 1/7 'Snowdrops'—the London nickname for white-helmeted American military police—were patroling the sidewalks. **1946** H. NICOLSON *Diary* 30 Apr. (1968) 59 Schacht sits in the witness box.. flanked by two young Americans in white helmets. Every hour, two other snowdrops.. take over from their comrades the white batons of office. **1967** 'A. CORDELL' *Bright Cantonese* ix. 100 Where are you goin'?.. Running to the first Snowdrop you can find? **1978** D. KYLE *Black Camelot* xvii. 270 Special detachments of military police 'snowdrops' went from house to house.

**'snowdrop tree.** [f. prec.]

**1.** The Virginian fringe-tree, *Chionanthus virginica*.

**1731** MILLER *Gard. Dict., Arbor Zeylanica*,.. the Snow-drop Tree... This Tree is very hardy in respect to Cold, standing abroad in the open Air. **1753** *Chambers's Cycl.* Suppl., *Snow-drop-tree*, a very beautiful American tree, which bears the cold of our climate in the open air. *Ibid.*, App., *Snow-drop-tree*, the English name of a genus of trees, called by botanists *chionanthus*. **1760** J. LEE *Introd. Bot.* App. 327. **1866** *Treas. Bot.* 270/2 *Chionanthus*, the Snowdrop tree of North America [etc.].

**2.** A North American styraceous tree or shrub of the genus *Halesia*, bearing clusters of drooping white flowers.

**1813** H. MUHLENBERG *Catal. Plant. Amer.* 46 Silverbell tree, or Four-winged Snow-drop tree. **1823** CRABB *Technol. Dict.* s.v. *Halesia*, Four-winged Halesia, or Snow-drop Tree. **1831** AUDUBON *Ornith. Biog.* I. 123 The Snow-Drop Tree, Silver-Bell Tree, or Wild Olive. **1857** HENFREY *Elem. Bot.* §509 *Halesia tetraptera*, another North American plant, is called the Snowdrop-tree, on account of its numerous white bell-shaped blossoms. **1875** *Encycl. Brit.* II. 320 The snow-drop tree.. is one of the hardiest of North American trees.

**3.** A West Indian tree (see quots.).

**1864** GRISEBACH *Flora Brit. W. Ind.* 787/2 Snowdrop tree, *Hænianthus incrassatus.* **1889** *Cent. Dict.* s.v. *Linociera, L. incrassata* of Jamaica, a large tree with panicles of white flowers, is called *snowdrop-tree*.

**4.** ***African snowdrop tree***, = SNOWDROP 2 (quot. 1891).

**1895** in *Funk's Stand. Dict.*

**snowed** (snəʊd), *ppl. a.* [f. SNOW *sb.*[1] or *v.*]

**1.** Cooled with snow. *rare*$^{-1}$.

**1682** SIR T. BROWNE *Chr. Mor.* II. §1 Nero.. lingring after his snowed water, hardly got down an ordinary cup of *Calda*.

**2.** Covered with snow.

**1854** HOOKER *Himal. Jrnls.* I. 184 The sweep of snowed mountains to the eastward. *Ibid.* II. 60 It.. flowed amongst little snowed mountains.

**3.** ***snowed-up***, blocked, stopped, or covered with snow. Also ***snowed-in*** (see SNOW *v.* 6 d).

**1836** FONBLANQUE *Eng. under 7 Administ.* (1837) III. 302 Not one of the *Standard's* snowed-up sixty has found his way to the House of Commons. **1881** *Times* 19 Jan. 10/2 Passing the night in the snowed-up train. **1882** FLOYER *Unexpl. Baluchistan* 364 The valley.. contained every few miles a snowed-up village. **1904** *N.Y. Even. Post* 5 Feb. 3 The Wabash is devoting all its energies to clearing the line of delayed and snowed-in trains. **1982** N. FREELING *Wolfnight* 128 A winter sun on a snowed-in landscape.

**snowfall** ('snəʊfɔːl). Also snow-fall. [f. SNOW *sb.*[1] Cf. G. *schneefall*, Da. *sneefald*, Sw. *snöfall*, ON. *snæ-, snjófall*.]

**1.** A fall of snow; a quantity of snow falling during a certain time. Also *fig.*

**1821** W. C. WELLS *Ess. Dew* (1866) 42 Immediately after a considerable snowfall had ceased. **1849** D. J. BROWNE *Amer. Poultry Yd.* (1855) 149 During melting snow-falls, turkeys will travel very great distances. **1884** *Manch. Exam.* 11 Oct. 4/6 In various parts of the country.. there was a rather heavy snowfall. **1964** M. A. JOHNSON in *Oceanogr. & Marine Biol.* II. 31 In recent years there has been a fundamental change in our picture of the deep-sea floor; previously conditions were thought to be essentially 'static', with negligible currents and the only variation with time being the steady 'snowfall' of sediment to the sea bed. **1969** MRS. L. B. JOHNSON *White House Diary* 10 Jan. (1970) 762 Dinner became a very snowfall of menu cards being passed around the tables for autographs.

**2.** The amount of snow falling at a particular place.

**1875** CROLL *Climate & T.* 382 The fact.. proves that the snowfall must be great. **1889** F. G. WRIGHT *Ice Age N. Amer.* 13 There is abundance of snow-fall.

**snow-field.** Also snowfield. [f. SNOW *sb.*[1] Cf. G. *schneefeld*, Sw. *snöfält*.] An extensive stretch or expanse of snow.

**1845** S. JUDD *Margaret* I. xvii, The snowfields seemed to bloom with glowing sorrel-flowers. **1856** KANE *Arctic Explor.* II. xxiii. 224 The snow-fields before us to the south. **1871** L. STEPHEN *Playgr. Eur.* (1894) v. 120 The sun had long touched the higher snow-fields.

**snow-finch.** Also snow finch. [f. SNOW *sb.*[1]] A species of mountain-finch. (See also quot. 1839.)

**1783** LATHAM *Gen. Synop. Birds* II. I. 264 Snow Finch.. inhabits various parts of the European continent. **1829** GRIFFITH tr. *Cuvier* VII. 139 The Snow Finch, *Fringilla Nivalis.* **1839** AUDUBON *Ornith. Biog.* V. 68 Oregon Snow-Finch, *Fringilla Oregona.* **1882** *Encycl. Brit.* XIV. 676 The Snow-Finch of the Alps, *M[ontifringilla] nivalis*, so often mistaken by travellers for the Snow-Bunting, *Plectrophanes nivalis.* **1894-5** LYDEKKER *Roy. Nat. Hist.* III. 388 The snow-finches form a small group possessing the characteristic form of the true finches.

**snowflake** ('snəʊfleɪk). Also snow-flake. [f. SNOW *sb.*[1] + FLAKE *sb.*[2]]

**1.** One of the small masses in which snow commonly falls.

**1734** *Cupid & Psyche* 28 Soft as the cygnet's down his wings, And as the falling snowflake fair. **1822** SHELLEY '*We meet not as we parted*' ii, That moment is gone for ever,.. Like a snowflake upon the river. **1847** PRESCOTT *Peru* III. ii. (1850) II. 39 A white cloud of pavilions was seen covering the ground as thick as snow-flakes. **1878** HUXLEY *Physiogr.* 63 The largest snow-flakes fall when the temperature is near the freezing point.

**2.** The snow-bunting. (Cf. SNOW-FLECK.)

**1770** PENNANT *Brit. Zool.* IV. 17 Snow Flake. These birds appear in hard weather on the Cheviot Hills, and in the Highlands of Scotland, in amazing flocks. **1793** *Statist. Acc. Scot.* VII. 547 The snowflake, the rail or corncrake. **1837** DUNN *Ornith. Orkn. & Shetl.* 79 The Snowflake appears regularly in both countries. **1845** *Zoologist* III. 822 In hard winters snowflakes come from the North by thousands. **1872** COUES *N. Amer. Birds* 133 Snow Bunting. Snowflake. In breeding plumage, pure white, the back, wings and tail variegated with black.

**3.** One or other variety of *Leucojum*.

**1798** CURTIS *Fl. Londinensis* II. pl. 72 As it differs very essentially in its fructification from the *Galanthus* we have thought it necessary to give it the new English name of *Snowflake.* **1806** J. GALPINE *Brit. Bot.* 168 *Leucojum æstivum*, summer snow-flake. **1866** *Treas. Bot.* 1067/2 Spring Snowflake, *Erinosma.* **1882** *Garden* 28 Jan. 56/3 The Snowflake.. is in full bloom, but owing to want of sun, has not expanded its flowers. **1899** *Gardening Illustr.* 27 May 167/1 In the earliest spring.. the Spring Snowflake (*L. vernum*) is flowering in southern gardens... Later on comes the taller-growing Summer Snowflake (*L. æstivum*).

**4.** (See quot.) Also *attrib.*

**1882** CAULFEILD & SAWARD *Dict. Needlew.* 452/2 *Snow-flake*, a term employed to denote a particular method of weaving woollen cloths, by which process small knots are thrown upon the face. **1890** *Daily News* 8 Jan. 1/6 A Large Lot.. Snowflake Costumes, all Pure Wool.

**5.** A name for a variety of potato.

**1882** *Daily News* 9 Mar. 2 Potatoes,.. foreign Snow-flakes.

**6.** = *hair-line crack* s.v. HAIR-LINE 7. *U.S.*

**1919** *Bull. Amer. Inst. Mining Engineers* Feb. 183 The appearance of 'snow-flakes' is unmistakable... The white silvery area, which always has the appearance of being of a very coarsely crystalline structure, in the specimen stands out in bold contrast to the darker background, and readily justifies the use of the term 'snow-flakes'. **1925** [see *hair crack* s.v. HAIR *sb.* 10]. **1942** [see *fish-eye* s.v. FISH *sb.*[1] 7].

**7.** *attrib.*, as **snowflake curve** *Math.*, a mathematically conceived curve (see quot. 1975) whose sixfold symmetry is reminiscent of that of a snowflake, of interest because its infinite length bounds a finite area.

**1956** W. G. WALTER *Further Outlook* III. iv. 100 Jim Bursley had explained the snowflake curve to me and we had discussed the projection of such a curve into three dimensions. **1975** *Sci. Amer.* Nov. 144/2 Take the analyst's 'snowflake' curve..., which is made in an elementary way from an equilateral triangle of unit side by replacing the middle third of each side with a 'cape', itself the two jutting equal sides of a triangle a third as large as the original, and so on, repeating indefinitely. **1978** *Ibid.* Apr. 21/2 Among the fractals that exhibit strong regularity the best-known are the Peano curves that completely fill the finite region and the beautiful snowflake curve discovered by the Swedish mathematician Helge von Koch in 1904.

**snow-fleck.** Also snowfleck, snow fleck. [f. SNOW *sb.*[1] Cf. prec. 2.] The snow-bunting, or Lapland bunting.

**1683** A. GARDEN in *Macfarlane's Geogr. Coll.* (S.H.S.) II. 142 In winter there is great abundance of the small bird called the Snowfleck. **1769** G. WHITE *Selborne* xxviii, Your account of the greater brambling, or snow-fleck, is very amusing. **1844** H. STEPHENS *Bk. Farm* I. 304 The fieldfare, ..snowfleck, and other birds of passage. **1873** *Routledge's Young Gentl. Mag.* Feb. 153/1 The Lapland Bunting.., often called the Snow-fleck. **1893** COZENS-HARDY *Broad Norf.* 46 *Snow fleck*, snow bunting.

**snow-flower.** Also snowflower.

†**1.** = SNOWDROP 1. *Obs.*

**1664** EVELYN *Kal. Hort.* 81 December... Flowers in Prime,.. Snow flowers or drops, Yucca, &c.

**2.** (See quot.)

**1836** *Backwoods Canada* 240-1 The hepatica is the first flower of the Canadian spring... [They] call it snow-flower, from its coming so soon after the snow disappears.

**3.** = SNOWDROP TREE 1.

**1862** *Chambers's Encycl.* IV. 527/1 The Common Fringe tree or Snowflower.. has.. very numerous snow-white flowers in panicled racemes. **1866** *Treas. Bot.* 1067/2 Snowflower, *Chionanthus virginica*.

†**snowge**, obs. form of SNUDGE *sb.* 1.

*c* **1570** *Durham Deposit.* (Surtees) 106 Sainge that the said Bartram was a covetous snowge. *Ibid.* 107.

**snow-goose.** Also snow goose. [f. SNOW *sb.*[1] Cf. Flem. *sneeuwgans* (Kilian) wild goose, G. *schneegans* (MHG. *snêgans*) wild goose, snow-goose, pelican.] A northern (American) goose of the genus *Chen*, esp. *C. hyperboreus*, characterized by its pure white plumage.

**1771** FORSTER *Catal. N. Amer. Anim.* 16 Snow Goose, *Anas nivalis.* **1785** PENNANT *Arct. Zool.* II. 549 Snow Goose, *Anser Grandinis*..: head, neck, and body of a snowy whiteness. **1814** A. WILSON *Amer. Ornith.* VIII. 76 Snow Goose, *Anas hyperborea.* **1838** AUDUBON *Ornith.* IV. 562 The geographical range of the Snow Goose is very extensive. **1860** MAYNE REID *Hunter's Feast* xxvii, We had also a pair of Canada geese, a snow-goose, and three brant. **1884** LATHROP *True* x. 113 The snow-goose had already been heard piping in the air, on its southward flight.

**snowily** ('snəʊɪlɪ), *adv.* [f. SNOWY *a.*] In a snowy manner; with or through snow; as snow.

**1852** M. ARNOLD *Youth of Nature* 40 Afar rose the peaks Of Parnassus, snowily clear. **1862** THORNBURY *Life Turner* I. 15 The wig is frizzed and snowily powdered. **1887** BOWEN *Virg., Ecl.* II. 16 Dark though he be of complexion, and thou all snowily fair!

**snowiness** ('snəʊɪnɪs). [f. as prec.] The state or condition of being snowy; whiteness.

**1727** BAILEY (vol. II), *Sleetiness*, Raininess and Snowiness. **1868** M. C. LEA *Photogr.* 210 These last may.. give an effect of snowiness in the high lights. **1894** *Daily News* 1 Sept. 6/5 The cool dining room.. with its glossy snowiness of napery.

**'snowing,** *vbl. sb.* [f. SNOW *v.*] The fact of snow falling; the result of this. Also with *in*, and *fig.*

*a* **1320** *Sir Tristr.* 1355 A brid bri3t þai ches As blod opon snoweing. *a* **1700** EVELYN *Diary* Sept. 1646, Because by the frequent snowing the tracts are continualy fill'd up. **1801** MOORE *Bk. Follies* 21 White as the snowings of that Heaven By which those hours of peace were given. **1837** CARLYLE *Fr. Rev.* I. IV. i, It is a sheer snowing of pamphlets; like to snow up the Government thoroughfares. **1885** *Fortn. Rev.* Feb. 170 Soon the snowfalls become more heavy, and the 'snowing-in' begins. *Ibid.*, The 'snowing-in' period is often supposed to be an extremely objectionable and almost intolerable time.

**snowish** ('snəʊɪʃ), *a.* Also 4-5 snowisse, 5 -ych, 6 -yshe, snawishe, 7 *Sc.* -isch. [f. SNOW *sb.*[1]]

†**1.** Resembling snow in whiteness; snowy, snow-white. *Obs.*

*c* **1374** CHAUCER *Troylus* III. 1250 Her snowisse throte, hir brestis rounde and lyte. **1433** LYDG. *S. Edmund* App. 189 A dowe with snowych fetherys whight. **1500-20** DUNBAR *Poems* xxxvii. 9 This angellis weid wes snawith [*read* -ich] in cullour. **1540** PALSGRAVE *Acolastus* II. ii, O Festyuall daye, worthy a snowyshe lytell stone. **1589** WARNER *Alb. Eng.* IV. xx, Her Snowish necke with blewish Vaines. **1603** *Philotus* lxi, 3our snawisch cheiks lyke quhytest Allabast.

**2.** Characterized by the presence or prevalence of snow; somewhat snowy.

**1566** DRANT *Horace, Sat.* II. vi. H vj b, Though whiskinge wyndes do shaue the earth, and though the snawishe day Be shorte, and sharpe.

†**3.** Covered with snow. *Obs.*$^{-1}$

**1589** FLEMING *Virg. Georg.* IV. 75 Tanais floud all snowish (or all ouerlaid with snow), And grounds at no time void of frosts.

**snowk**, variant of SNOKE *v.*

**'snowless,** *a.* [f. SNOW *sb.*[1] Cf. G. *schneelos*, Da. *snełøs*, Sw. *snölös*, etc.] Free from snow; characterized by the absence of snow.

**1828-32** WEBSTER (citing Tooke). **1860** TYNDALL *Glac.* II. iv. 249 A belt, below which, in summer, snowless valleys and plains would extend. **1884** *Harper's Mag.* LXX. 206 It was a black and snowless winter until late in January. **1887** RUSKIN *Præterita* II. 395 The higher summits by midsummer are snowless.

**snow-like,** *a.* and *adv.* [f. SNOW *sb.*[1]]

**A.** *adj.* Like or resembling snow in colour, appearance, etc.

**1663** S. PATRICK *Parab. Pilgr.* xxxv. (1687) 433 But after their resurrection they were of a pure white snow-like colour. **1694** SALMON *Bate's Dispens.* (1713) 209/1 With a Glass Spoon take off the Snow-like Cream as it arises. **1820** SHELLEY *Prom. Unb.* II. iv. 95 Cities then Were built, and through their snow-like columns flowed The warm winds. **1836-41** BRANDE *Chem.* 526 Another portion is frozen into a white snow-like solid. **1895** SWETTENHAM *Malay Sketches* 126 A motionless drift of snow-like cloud.

**B.** *adv.* In or after the manner of snow.

**1850** MRS. BROWNING *Man's Requirem.* iv, Their lids, that fall Snow-like at first meeting.

**snow-line.** Also snowline. [f. SNOW *sb.*[1] Cf. G. *schneelinie*, Sw. *snölinie*.]

**1.** The general level on mountains, etc., above which the snow never completely disappears; the lower limit of perpetual snow, or (more rarely) of snow at a particular season.

**1835** *Partington's Brit. Cycl., Arts & Sci.* II. 712/2 The snow-line, or plane of perpetual snow, is the elevation at which mountains are covered with perpetual snow. **1845** DARWIN *Voy. Nat.* xi. (1852) 245 As the snow-line is so low in Tierra del Fuego, we might have expected that many of the glaciers would have reached the sea. **1875** CROLL *Climate & T.* ii. 28 If those currents were warm, they would elevate the snow-line above themselves.

*fig.* **1839–52** BAILEY *Festus* 468 My thought of thee Above all passionate fire-peaks and above The sacred snowline of my heart. **1902** *Westm. Gaz.* 20 Dec. 2/2 Mr. Haldane.. viewing men and things from above his snow-line.

**2.** (See quot.)

**1898** MORRIS *Austral Eng.* 425 In pastoralists' language of New Zealand, 'above the snow-line' is land covered by snow in winter, but free in summer.

**snow-man.** Also snowman. [f. SNOW *sb.*[1] Cf. Fris. *snieman*, G. *schneeman*, Da. *snemand*.]

**1. a.** A mass of snow made into the figure of a man. Also *transf.*, a man dressed so as to represent or imitate this.

**1827** CLARE *Sheph. Cal.* 3 Making rude forms of various names, Snow-men, or aught his fancy frames. **1902** *Westm. Gaz.* 26 Sept. 7/2 Six men, dressed in wadding and representing musical snowmen.

*attrib.* and *Comb.* **1902** *Academy* 27 Dec. 712/1 The daylight passed in snowman-making on the meadow.

**b.** *Archæol.* Used *attrib.* and *absol.* to designate a technique of clay-modelling (see quot. 1955) or the figurines so produced.

**1908** S. A. COOK *Relig. Anc. Palestine* iii. 31 Small idols.. in the clumsy 'snow-man' technique. **1955** L. WOOLLEY *Alalakh* viii. 244 The vast majority [of figurines].. were hand-modelled more or less in the round in what is called the 'snow-man' technique, i.e. the clay is pinched into shape with the fingers and details are added by sticking on small pellets of clay, as well as by incision with a blunt stick or.. by dotted lines made with a roulette. **1962** D. HARDEN *Phoenicians.* ii. 42 The site.. has produced remains of the seventh century, including some surprisingly primitive snow-man figurines of clay. **1974** J. CHESTERMAN *Classical Terracotta Figures* ii. 29 A group from Cyprus.., known as 'snowmen', was being produced in relative abundance... I think they are jolly little fellows with their peaked caps, pointed beards and stumpy arms.

**c.** Used *attrib.* and *absol.* to designate a type of pottery figure (see quot. 1957).

**1931** D. MACALISTER in *William Duesbury's London Account Bk. 1751–53* p. xxv, I have illustrated several figures in white porcelain... Certain figures of the 'snow-man' type belong to this class. **1933** *Trans. Eng. Ceramic Circle* I. 46 The 'snow man' bag-piper... Another 'snow man' in white porcelain... He looks like a *poilu*, but may be meant for a Chinaman. **1957** MANKOWICZ & HAGGAR *Encycl. Eng. Pottery & Porcelain* 205/1 *'Snowman' figures*, porcelain figures heavily glazed with a thick, opaque, glassy glaze, obscuring the modelling,.. now known.. to be the production of William Littler of Longton Hall, or of Jenkinson at the same works. **1974** *Encycl. Brit. Micropædia* IX. 303/2 *Snowman porcelain*... Called snowmen because of their thick white enveloping glaze, they include figures of human beings and animals.

**2.** *dial.* The snow-bunting.

**1893** COZENS-HARDY *Broad Norf.* 49.

**3.** ***Abominable Snowman***: see ABOMINABLE *a.* 1 c. Also simply ***snowman***.

**1931** J. CANNAN *Ithuriel's Hour* iv. 131 His gods, to say nothing of hairless Snow Men, and the shades of his ancestors. **1937** *Times* 31 Dec. 8/3 Mr. Smythe says that the snowman superstition is known only to the Tibetan or semi-Tibetan peoples. **1959** *Times* 8 Jan. 13/5 In the case of the famous Himalayan 'snowman' the evidence.. seems to point to the existence of perhaps two unknown species.. of anthropoid ape.

**4.** *U.S. slang.* One who snows (SNOW *v.* 4 b) someone.

**1967** P. MCGIRR *Murder is Absurd* iii. 44 You're a great snow man, Warren. But I'm not in dreamland yet. **1977** *Amer. Speech 1975* L. 66 *Snowman*, male who easily wins the affections of females.

**ˈsnowmanship.** *nonce-wd.* [Cf. ICEMANSHIP.] Skill in traversing snow.

**1869** FRESHFIELD *Central Caucasus & Bashan* vii. 194 We spent a pleasant hour on our lofty perch, and then, by a rapid act of what may be called 'snowmanship', rejoined Paul and Alexis.

**snowmobile** (ˈsnəʊməbiːl). orig. *N. Amer.* Also **snow-mobile, snow mobile, snomobile, Snomobile.** [f. SNOW *sb.* + AUTO)MOBILE *a.* and *sb.*] Any motor vehicle designed for travelling over snow; *spec.* a small, light passenger vehicle supported on runners at the front and a traction chain at the rear. Also *attrib.*

**1931** *Times Lit. Suppl.* 5 Feb. 89/1 The American expedition to the South Pole under.. Admiral Byrd was.. carried out in the grand manner... It had a 'snowmobile'; but this did not travel very far before meeting disaster on the rough surface. **1934** *Canad. Patent Office Rec.* 30 Oct. 2464/1 A snowmobile comprising an automobile having a pair of runners extending in place of the automobile front wheels, beams extending longitudinally of the automobile and rearwardly of the rear axle, a third axle mounted adjacent the rear ends of said beams, wheels forming the sole supporting means for the rear of the snowmobile journalled on said third axle, driving gears mounted on the automobile rear axle in place of the ordinary rear wheels, and traction chains connecting said wheels and driving gears. **1947** *Times* 8 Mar. 5/6 They [*sc.* the Eskimos] have seen.. drums of petrol parachuted to the snowmobiles of the Canadian Army exercise 'Musk-Ox'. **1961** *Times* 24 Apr. 16/6, I can.. watch the teenagers race their stripped down jalopies... There are snow-mobiles and snocats. **1966** *Popular Science* Jan. 117 Snow really flies as this snowmobile owner takes his Larson Eagle on a long, thrilling jump. **1968** *Globe & Mail* (Toronto) 3 Feb. 46/4 (Advt.), Snow mobiles, demonstrator sale. **1969** *Daily Tel.* 11 Mar. 24/8 Organisers of a fox-hunt, mounted on snowmobiles, on a frozen lake in Minnesota have been threatened with police action. **1970** *Toronto Daily Star* 24 Sept. 10/4 (Advt.), Snowmobile suits on sale. **1970** *Nature* 29 Aug. 880/1 It is powered by.. air-cooled engines originally developed for the 'sno-mobiles' now so popular during the Canadian winter. **1972** C. MUDIE *Motor Boats & Boating* 82 The question of how to use your Snomobile in high summer has been met by one manufacturer who markets a float attachment and a modified propeller drive so that the basic unit quickly becomes a lakeside holiday flier. **1977** *New Yorker* 2 May 60/2 Dog teams have largely been replaced by snowmobiles. **1980** *Harpers & Queen* Jan. 79/4 Snowmobiles alone use over 117 million gallons of fuel each year in the United States.

Hence **ˈsnowmobiler**, one who drives or rides upon a snowmobile; **ˈsnowmobiling** *vbl. sb.*, the action or sport of using a snowmobile; **ˈsnowmobilist** = SNOWMOBILER.

**1964** *Star Weekly* (Toronto) 19 Dec. 14/1 We'd like to see a broader approach to snowmobiling as a family-style sport. **1967** *Daily Tel.* 14 Mar. 21/1 This weekend, some 11,000 'snowmobilists' were skimming across the snow-covered Adirondacks at speeds up to 30 mph, twice those on downhill slopes. **1968** *Globe & Mail* (Toronto) 13 Jan. 41/5 Snowmobilers would be well advised to obtain from the Ontario Safety League a copy of the Ten Commandments of Snowmobile Safety. **1977** *Time* 7 Feb. 60/2 The arduous route.. led the snowmobilers along busy, narrow roads, through woods and across ditches. **1981** *Northeast Woods & Waters* Jan. 4/1 Years of driving and snowmobiling have prepared me and I always carry spare parts and tools and we fixed it in a jiffy.

† **ˈSnowns.** *Obs.* (See NOUNS and OD 2.)

**1594** R. WILSON *Coblers Proph.* I. i. 63 Course me, snowns, I would thou durst come out of dore.

**ˌsnow-on-the-ˈmountain.**

**1.** *U.S.* An annual spurge, *Euphorbia marginata*, of the family Euphorbiaceæ, native to the central southern United States, and bearing white bracts.

**1873** *Kansas Mag.* June 502/2 Their miller's-plant, or snow-on-the-mountain, is nothing but our spurge. **1878–80** T. MEEHAN *Native Wild Flowers U.S.* Ser. II. I. 79 This Euphorbia marginata.. is called by the people here 'Snow on the Mountain'. **1918** W. CATHER *My Antonia* IV. iv. 364 Every sunflower stalk and clump of snow-on-the-mountain drew itself up high and pointed. **1966** MRS. L. B. JOHNSON *White House Diary* 27 Aug. (1970) 416 And there is snow-on-the-mountains — everywhere — especially in the meadows.

**2.** One of several low-growing, white-flowered, cruciferous plants, esp. white alyssum, *Arabis alpina*, or *Alyssum maritimum*.

**1882** H. FRIEND *Gloss. Devon. Plant Names* 51 Snow-on-the-Mountain. *Alyssum maritimum*, L. **1886** BRITTEN & HOLLAND *Plant Names* 440 Snow-on-the-mountain. (1) *Arabis alpina*..(also Snow-in-summer)... (2) *Cerastium tomentosum*. **1890** J. D. ROBERTSON *Gloss. Dial. & Archaic Words Gloucestershire* 145 Snow-on-the-mountain. *Arabis alpina*, L. **1933** *Downside Rev.* LI. 523 The 'snow-on-the-mountains' was in full bloom, groups of crocuses were holding out their golden fingers just behind it, and the yellow and white looked like strips of spring sunshine.

**snow-plough,** *sb.* Also **snow plough,** *U.S.* **-plow.** [f. SNOW *sb.*[1] Cf. G. *schneepflug*, Da. *sneplov*, Sw. *snöplog*.] **1.** An implement or machine for clearing away snow from a road, railway track, etc.

A number of the various makes are described in Knight *Dict. Mech.* 2230–1 and *Suppl.* 826.

**1792** BELKNAP *Hist. New-Hampshire* III. 79 When a deep snow has obstructed the roads, they are in some places opened by an instrument called a snow plough. It is made of planks, in a triangular form, with two side boards to turn the snow out on either hand. **1829** D. CONWAY *Journ. Norway*, etc. 148 Immediately after the snow has ceased the snow-plough is used. **1858** SIMMONDS *Dict. Trade, Snow-plough*, a machine for clearing away snow from railway tracks. **1888** LEES & CLUTTERBUCK *B.C. 1887* xxxiv. (1892) 379 The huge snow ploughs (driven sometimes by six or eight locomotives) had been at work.

**2.** *Skiing.* = *double stem* s.v. DOUBLE *a.* A. 6. Also *attrib.*

**1905** RICKMERS & RICHARDSON in D. M. M. C. Somerville et al. *Ski-Running* (ed. 2) 69 Stemming is akin to snow-ploughing, and by some German writers the stemming position is termed the half-snow-plough position. **1922** V. CAULFEILD *Ski-ing Turns* vii. 134 Although it is unsafe for any one but an expert to take the snow-plough position when travelling at all fast, this Snow-plough Christiania can be done at a good deal higher speed than the Pure Snow-plough turn. **1936** [see *double stem* s.v. DOUBLE *a.* A. 6]. **1948** P. LUNN *Ski-ing Primer* xi. 56 The snow-plough.. is not only a useful manœuvre in itself, but is also the basis of the stem turn. **1953** A. WOODBURN tr. *Jacques's Downhill Skiing* I. iii. 79 The snow plough position.. is one of the few that the beginner finds quite natural. **1966** A. N. GOODING *Basic Ski-ing* vi. 37 You first learn how to stop by using the Snowplough Brake. **1978** *Observer* 29 Jan. 35/1 Our instructor starts us on snowplough turns (with the tips of the skis pointing inwards). **1981** *Northeast Woods & Waters* Jan. 27/2 The snowplow, the 'dinking on the ski tips inward to make turns or to stop' is definitely a beginner maneuver.

So **ˈsnow-plough** *v. intr.*, to execute a snow-plough in skiing; **ˈsnow-ploughing** *vbl. sb.*

**1904** D. M. M. C. SOMERVILLE et al. *Ski-Running* 39 The Norwegians call it 'snow-ploughing', but 'stemming' is shorter, and, we think, more expressive. **1928** E. JESSUP *Skis & Ski-ing* ix. 124 Very often it suffices to brake with the skis fairly flat on snow. In such cases, bend your knees inward only slightly... When you 'snowplough' in the foregoing fashion, both of your skis are serving as brakes. **1959** P. MOYES *Dead Men don't Ski* iv. 50 They had learnt, now, to snow-plough—putting the tips of their skis together to slow down or stop. **1961** *Times* 14 Feb. 14/7 The usual portly Frenchman.. who charges along, skis wide apart and braking hard by stemming or 'snowploughing'. **1979** N. SLATER *Falcon* ix. 161 He snow-ploughed down towards her .. snapped off his ski-bindings.

† **snowre,** *v. Obs. rare.* [Of obscure origin.] *intr.* To frown or scowl. So † **snowring** *vbl. sb.* and *ppl. a. Obs.*

*c* **1440** *Alph. Tales* 326 And if þou be wed þou may happen wed a shrew at will be þi maister, and þou bus.. suffer many grete wurd & say nothyng agayn, & hafe a snowryng cowntenance. **1508** *Mayd Emlyn* 177 in Hazl. *E.P.P.* IV. 89 Whan she dothe loure, And begynneth to snowre. **1562** J. HEYWOOD *Prov. & Epigr.* (1867) 210 Small diffrence betweene lowryng and snowryng.

**ˈsnow-shoe,** *sb.* Also **snow shoe, snowshoe.** [f. SNOW *sb.*[1] Cf. G. *schneeschuh*, Sw. *snösko*.]

**1. a.** A kind of foot-gear enabling the wearer to walk on the surface of snow, *esp.* one of a pair of racket-shaped frames of light wood, strung and netted with narrow strips of raw hide, used by the Indians and others in North America.

**1674** JOSSELYN *Two Voy.* 55 A crust upon the snow sufficient to bear a man walking with snow-shoos upon it. **1681** GREW *Museum* IV. iii. 375 A Snow-Shooe, used in Greenland, and some other places. **1707** in *Sewall's Diary* (1879) II. 60 They made her put on Snow Shoes, which to manage, requires more than ordinary agility. **1773** *Hist. Brit. Dom. N. Amer.* II. 59 In winter, when the snow would bear, they put on snow-shoes, which were made like a large tennis-racket, and laced them to their feet with the guts of deer. **1806** PIKE *Sources Mississ.* (1810) 69 Who.. went so fast as to render it difficult, for the men with snow shoes, to keep up with them. **1841** CATLIN *N. Amer. Ind.* (1844) I. xxx. 254 The snow shoes are made in a great many forms,.. of a hoop or hoops, bent around for the frame [etc.]. **1884** DAWSON *Hdbk. Canada* 230 It is quite usual in Montreal for young ladies to walk on snow-shoes [etc.].

**b.** One of a pair of skis.

**1864** DASENT *Jest & Earnest* (1873) II. 185, I can.. ride, swim, glide on snowshoon. **1901** H. SEEBOHM *Birds of Siberia* v. 44 On snow-shoes we got along comfortably... They were about seven feet long and six inches wide.

**2.** *U.S.* The snow-shoe rabbit (see 3).

**1888** LEES & CLUTTERBUCK *B.C. 1887* xxiii. (1892) 261 The Snowshoe.. is the largest kind of alpine hare.

**3.** *attrib.*, as ***snow-shoe excursion, expedition, step, track***, etc.; **snow-shoe disease, evil** (see quot. 1809); **snow-shoe foot,** a foot (in certain animals) adapted for walking on snow; **snowshoe hare,** the North American varying hare, *Lepus americanus*; **snow-shoe rabbit** (see quot. 1889); also = *snowshoe hare* above.

**1760** *Lett. to Hon. Brigadier General* 5 The Snow-Shoes Expeditions of America. **1809** A. HENRY *Trav.* 68, I was now troubled with a disorder, called the snow-shoe evil, proceeding from an unusual strain on the tendons of the leg, occasioned by the weight of the snow-shoe, and brings on inflammation. **1889** *Cent. Dict.* s.v. *Rabbit*, *Snow-shoe rabbit*, that variety of the American varying hare which is found in the Rocky Mountains... It has been described as a distinct species, *Lepus bairdi*. **1894** *Outing* XXIV. 271/2 A scuffling, sliding, snow-shoe step. *Ibid.* 357/1 In a mild climate the snowshoe foot might frequently be a serious drawback. **1921** *Frontier* May 11 In a zig-zag pattern in the snow were the tracks of the snow-shoe hares. **1903** J. LONDON *Call of Wild* 90 Leap by leap, like some pale frost wraith, the snowshoe rabbit flashed on ahead. **1971** W. HILLEN *Blackwater River* iii. 21 Snowshoe rabbits, so called because their large hairy feet serve as snowshoes. **1977** *New Yorker* 9 May 96/2 We kicked at some wolf scat, old as winter. It was woolly and white and filled with the hair of a snowshoe hare.

Hence **ˈsnow-shoe** *v. intr.*, to travel on snow-shoes or skis; **ˈsnow-shoed** *a.*, wearing snow-shoes; also *fig.*; **ˈsnow-shoeing** *vbl. sb.*, the action or practice of travelling on snow-shoes, esp. as an exercise or sport; also *attrib.*; **ˈsnow-shoer,** one who uses, or travels on, snow-shoes.

**1880** C. B. BERRY *The Other Side* 214 As we *snowshoed over Lake Joseph. **1890** HIBBS in *Big Game N. Amer.* 41 The depth of snow.. does not enter into account when snow-shoeing. **1896** *Harper's Mag.* Apr. 726/2 The spectacle of a *snow-shoed Indian chasing the fleetest quadruped on earth. **1946** DYLAN THOMAS *Deaths & Entrances* 30 The singing breaks in the snow shoed villages of wishes. **1867** *Territorial Enterprise* (Virginia City, Nevada) 12 Mar. 3/2 A race for a gold buckle, free to all lady *snow-shoers, was also announced. **1884** DAWSON *Hdbk. Canada* 230 A strong turn-out of snow-shoers.. is a very picturesque sight. **1897** *Outing* XXIX. 360/2 Two fine club-houses.. where snow-shoers have long fraternized. **1884** H. CHADWICK *Sports & Pastimes Amer. Boys* 205 One of the favorite winter sports of the Canadians is *snowshoeing, which is enjoyed to a great extent by the clubs of Montreal, who engage in races and long tramps over the hills on snowshoes. **1885** *Cent. Mag.* XXIX. 523 The vicissitudes of lacrosse, snow-shoeing, and tobogganing. **1887** *Cornhill Mag.* Mar. 267 Which outings are the snowshoeing events of the season.

**snow-storm.** Also snowstorm. [f. SNOW *sb.*[1] Cf. G. *schneesturm*, Sw. *snöstorm*.]

**1.** A storm accompanied by a heavy fall of snow.

**1771** A. G. WINSLOW *Diary* 6 Dec. (1895) 8, I was prevented dining at unkle Joshua's by a snow storm. *a* **1800** PEGGE *Suppl. Grose*, *Snow-storm*, a continued snow so long as it lies on the ground. *North.* **1813** SHELLEY *Q. Mab* VIII. 60 Those wastes of frozen billows that were hurled By everlasting snowstorms round the poles. **1860** TYNDALL *Glac.* I. xxiv. 170, I..climbed amid a heavy snow-storm to the Cleft station. **1878** BROWNING *Poets Croisic* 17 Bidding care Keep outside with the snow-storm.

*fig.* **1869** 'MARK TWAIN' *Innocents Abroad* xiii. 125 A snow-storm of waving handkerchiefs. **1893** F. F. MOORE *I Forbid Banns* (1899) 141 The next day there was a snow-storm, with invitation cards for flakes, on her table. **1896** *Westm. Gaz.* 23 Apr. 7/2 He lived in a snow-storm of letters asking him for money.

**2.** A paperweight or toy in the form of a transparent dome or globe containing a representation of a scene and loose snow-like particles, which, when shaken, creates the appearance of a snow-storm. Also *attrib.*

**1926** 'O. DOUGLAS' *Proper Place* xvii. 149 A round glass globe containing a miniature cottage, which, when shaken, became surrounded with whirling snowflakes. 'It's a snow-storm,' she declared triumphantly. **1931** E. SACKVILLE-WEST *Simpson* II. 144 Salathiel held up a glass globe, inside which was a minute Scotch-baronial castle... He shook the globe and a whirlwind of white flakes swirled up... The Snowstorm jerked downwards in his hand. **1939** C. MORLEY *Kitty Foyle* (1940) xxxii. 332 It's good to have a person call your attention to something you're so used to you almost forgot thinking about it. I mean the glass snowstorm ball. Molly's back in Chicago and I take the glass ball and give it a whirl. **1947** 'D. YATES' *Berry Scene* x. 273 My eye was caught by a snowstorm—one of those little glass balls, with a baby cottage inside. And when you shake it, snow-flakes begin to fall. **1967** M. DRABBLE *Jerusalem the Golden* v. 101 Toys..a tower of bricks, a weather house, a huge pendant snowstorm globe containing a small palace and a small forest. **1975** S. LAUDER *Killing Time on Corvo* ix. 85, I recalled, as a child, staring entranced into Modrinka's snowstorm paper-weight.

**3.** *fig.* An appearance of dense snow on a television or radar screen. Cf. SNOW *sb.*[1] 5 f.

**1948** *Nature* 31 Jan. 167/1 The visual effect was that of a violent snowstorm of the type well known to televiewers due to motor-car ignition interference, but at a very much more intense level. **1974** L. DEIGHTON *Spy Story* xviii. 195 The radar screen was a snowstorm that dashed..in a mad rhythm. **1980** J. B. HILTON *Anathema Stone* i. 16 The television set..produced a snow-storm on every channel.

**snow-water.** Also snow water. [f. SNOW *sb.*[1] Cf. Fris. *sniewetter*, MDu. *snee(u)water* (Du. *sneeuwwater*), MHG. *snêwazzer* (G. *schneewasser*), etc.] Water derived or obtained from melted snow. Also *transf.*

*c* **1175** *Lamb. Hom.* 159 þe ter þet mon schet for his emcristenes sunne is inemned snaw water, for hit melt of þe neche horte swa deð þe snaw to-ȝeines þe sunne. **1434** MISYN *Mending of Life* 122 If I be waschyd with snaw watyr. **1535** COVERDALE *Job* ix. 30 Though I wasshed my self with snowe water. **1599** MINSHEU *Span. Dial.* 18 In Spaine they coole their wine by setting the flagons in snow water. **1620** VENNER *Via Recta* Introd. 10 Snow-waters are grosse and ouer-cold. **1694** *Acc. Sev. Late Voy.* (1711) I. 74 Several streams of Snow-water run down in the Cliffs of the Hills. **1763** MILLS *Pract. Husb.* III. 454 He rejects snow water for the same reason. **1789** W. BUCHAN *Dom. Med.* (1790) 67 The inhabitants of the Peak of Derby..have large tumours or wens on their necks. This disease is generally imputed to the snow water. **1809** A. HENRY *Trav.* 278 We supped on wild beef and snow-water. **1855** *Orr's Circ. Sci., Elem. Chem.* 299 Even rain and snow-water are far from pure. **1903** A. C. P. HAGGARD *Sport. Yarns* 273 The snow water used to come down the Don every afternoon.

**snow-white** ('snəʊhwaɪt), *a.* and *sb.* Forms: (see SNOW *sb.*[1] and WHITE *a.*). [f. SNOW *sb.*[1] Cf. Fris. *sniewit*, MDu. *sne(e)wit* (Du. *sneeuwwit*), MLG. *snewit*, MHG. *snêwîz* (G. *schneeweiss*), ON. *snæ-*, *snjóhvítr* (Sw. *snöhvit*, Da. *snehvid*).]

**A.** *adj.* **1.** White as snow; pure white.

α. *c* **1000** ÆLFRIC in Assmann *Ags. Hom.* iv. 186 Ða ȝesloh hine sona se snawhwita hreofla. *a* **1200** *St. Marher.* 18 The hude snaw hwit swartete as hit snarchte. *c* **1205** LAY. 24521 þreo snau-white culueren. *a* **1225** *Leg. Kath.* 2443 Heo.. strahte forð swiftliche þe snawhwite swire. **1596** DALRYMPLE tr. *Leslie's Hist. Scot.* I. 29 Oxne and Bules snawquhyte with a mane thick. **1791** BURNS *Tam o' Shanter* 154 Snaw-white seventeen hunder linnen!

β. *c* **1200** *Trin. Coll. Hom.* 115 þe engles þe wið þe apostles stoden mid snouwite shrude. *a* **1225** *Ancr. R.* 314 Efter his deaðe, he com one niht.., ine snou hwite cloðes. *c* **1386** CHAUCER *Sec. Nun's T.* 254 Tuo corunes han we, Snow white and Rose reed, that shynen cleere. **1390** GOWER *Conf.* I. 306 That ther he was snow whyt tofore, Evere afterward colblak therfore He was transformed. *c* **1450** *Godstow Reg.* 17 þat we ben cladde in a snow-whyȝt stole. **1582** STANYHURST *Æneis* III. (Arb.) 87 Heere..fowre fayre steeds snow whit I marcked. *c* **1610** *Women Saints* 39 She thought she brought forth a snow-white doue. *a* **1700** EVELYN *Diary* 14 Feb. 1645, With her statue over it in snow-white marble. **1763** *Phil. Trans.* LIV. 97 It has a body like a gnat, snow-white. **1807** THOMSON *Chem.* (ed. 3) II. 277 Camphoric acid thus obtained is in snow-white crystals. **1860** TYNDALL *Glac.* I. iii. 30 Above all rose the snow-white cone of the Ortler. **1877** BLACK *Green Past.* ii, Two snow-white and waxen hyacinths.

*Comb.* **1753** *Chambers's Cycl.* Suppl. s.v. *Linaria*, The snow-white flowered creeping toad flax. *Ibid.* s.v. *Plumeria*, The snow-white-flowered plumeria, with..pointed leaves.

**b.** Clad in robes of pure white. *rare.*

**1847** EMERSON *Poems, Each & All*, Her beauty's best attire Was woven still by the snow-white choir.

**2.** In the specific names of fishes, birds, or moths (see quots.).

**1804** SHAW *Gen. Zool.* V. I. 73 Snow-white Salmon. **1809** *Ibid.* VII. I. 149 Snow-White Falcon. *Ibid.* 240 Snow-white Owl spotted with black. **1832** J. RENNIE *Butterfl. & Moths* 224 The Snow White Spot (*Incurvaria spuria*). *Ibid.* 230 The Snow-white Plume (*Pterophorus niveidactylus*).

**B.** *sb.* **a.** Pure white. **b.** A kind of wool of this colour.

**1890** *Science-Gossip* XXVI. 170 The flowers varied in colour from snow-white to green and white flushed with crimson purple. **1896** *Daily News* 23 Jan. 9/4 Cape and Natal wools meet with good competition, and medium to superior snow-whites..have advanced.

Hence **snow-whiteness.**

**1856** RUSKIN *Mod. Paint.* IV. v. iii. §24. 53 The authority for using snow-whiteness as a type of purity.

**snow-wreath** ('snəʊriːθ). [f. SNOW *sb.*[1]]

**1.** A heap of snow blown together by the wind; a snowdrift.

**1818** SCOTT *Hrt. Midl.* viii, The tenants..were not actually turned out of doors among the snow-wreaths. **1854** J. S. C. ABBOTT *Napoleon* (1855) II. ix. 139 The outer ranks melted like snow-wreaths on the river's brink. **1873** SYMONDS *Grk. Poets* xi. 357 The oxen came Down from the mountain through the snow-wreaths deep.

**2.** As a plant-name (see quot.).

**1901** BAILEY & MILLER *Cycl. Amer. Horticult.* III. 1079 [*Neviusia*] *Alabamensis*, Gray. Snow Wreath.

**snowy** ('snəʊɪ), *a.* and *sb.* Forms: α. 1 **snawiȝ**, 3 **snawi**, 5, *Sc.* 8– **snawy**, 8 **snawie**. β. 6–7 **snowie**, **snowey**, 6– **snowy**. [f. SNOW *sb.*[1] Cf. Fris. *snieich*, MDu. *sneeich*, *sneeuwich* (Du. *sneeuwig*), OS. *snêgig* (MLG. *snêyg*, *snyig*), MHG. *schnêig* (G. *schneeig*), Sw. *snöig*, *snögig*.]

**A.** *adj.* **1.** Of weather, time, etc.: Characterized by the presence or prevalence of snow.

*c* **1000** *Saxon Leechd.* III. 274 Se feorða heafod wind.. blæwð norðan cealde & snawlic [*v.r.* snawiȝ]. **1600** PORY tr. *Leo's Africa* IX. 333 It ouerfloweth not but in rainie and snowie weather. **1635** SWAN *Spec. M.* v. §2 (1643) 155 Your experienced husbandman desireth that the winter may be cold and snowie. **1660** BOYLE *New Exp. Phys. Mech.* xviii. 133 It was a Snowy day. **1701** O. HEYWOOD *Diaries* (1885) IV. 175 This is a snowy morning. **1748** T. SMITH *Jrnl.* (1849) 270 A cold, snowy, uncomfortable month. **1800** CAMPBELL *Ode to Winter* 53 Milder yet thy snowy breezes Pour on yonder tented shores. **1830** CARLYLE *Misc.* (1857) II. 143 Let the weather be sunny or snowy. **1884** E. P. ROE *Nat. Ser. Story* vii, The snowiest day of winter.

**2.** Composed of melted snow; consisting, formed, or made of snow.

α. *a* **1240** *Sawles Warde* in *O.E. Hom.* I. 251 þer is..toðes hechelunge iþe snawi weattres. **1483** *Cath. Angl.* 346/2 Snawy, *niueus*. **1785** BURNS *Addr. to Deil* xii, When thowes dissolve the snawy hoord.

β. **1565** COOPER *Thesaurus*, *Niueus liquor*, snowy water. **1613** PURCHAS *Pilgrimage* (1614) 862 The lower Mountaines ..haue more Giantly ouer-lookers, with Snowie lockes and Cloudie lookes. **1730** BAILEY (fol.), *Sleetiness*,..snowy Rain. **1754** GRAY *Pleasure* 26 The sullen year Saw the snowy whirlwind fly. **1784** COWPER *Task* v. 98 On the flood, Indurated and fixt, the snowy weight Lies undissolv'd. **1818** BYRON *Ch. Har.* IV. clxxxi, As the snowy flake, They melt. **1860** TYNDALL *Glac.* I. xii. 90 The Glacier..thrust through the black pines its snowy tongue.

**3. a.** Covered with snow; abounding in snow.

**1548** ELYOT, *Niualia loca*, snowy places. **1592** *Soliman & Pers.* IV. i. 83 Neck, whiter then the snowie Apenines. **1617** MORYSON *Itin.* I. 98 We continually did see the snowy toppes of those Mountaines. **1638** BRATHWAIT *Barnabees Jrnl.* III. (1818) 137 Thence to Ayscarth, from a mountaine ..cliffs steep and snowy..saw I. *a* **1700** EVELYN *Diary* 2 Nov. 1644, Monte Mantuamiato..peeping above any clowds with its snowy head. **1784** COWPER *Task* v. 7 His slanting ray Slides ineffectual down the snowy vale. **1847** TENNYSON *Princ.* IV. 2 The splendour falls on castle walls And snowy summits old in story. **1871** L. STEPHEN *Playgr. Eur.* ii. (1894) 49 The snowy ranges of California..seem to be unpleasantly bare and chill.

*transf.* **1648** J. BEAUMONT *Psyche* XIII. xlv, That fire of leacherous rage Which burnt ev'n in their cold and snowy age.

**b.** Of the picture on a television screen: affected with snow (SNOW *sb.*[1] 5 f).

**1959** LEVY & FRANKEL *Television Servicing* xiv. 442 The picture may become weak and snowy. **1976** H. KEMELMAN *Wednesday Rabbi got Wet* xxiii. 73 She turned the set on... There was a lot of static, and the picture wavered and became snowy.

**4. a.** Of or resembling the pure white colour of snow; snow-white, niveous.

**1590** SPENSER *F.Q.* I. x. 48 That godly aged Sire, With snowy lockes. *Ibid.* III. i. 38 Which staines his snowy skin with hatefull hew. **1592** SHAKS. *Rom. & Jul.* I. v. 50 So shewes a Snowy Doue trooping with Crowes. **1662** J. DAVIES tr. *Olearius' Voy. Amb.* 16 Many antient Men, venerable for their long snowy beards. **1697** DRYDEN *Virg. Georg.* III. 594 Ev'n though a snowy Ram thou shalt behold. **1725** POPE *Odyss.* XXIV. 93 We then collect thy snowy bones. **1786** BURNS *To Mountain Daisy* v, Thy snawie bosom sun-ward spread. **1833** L. RITCHIE *Wand. by Loire* 21 Towering caps of the snowiest muslin, enriched with lace. **1882** *Garden* 9 Sept. 224/3 A charming little plant..with dense tufts of snowy blooms.

*transf.* **1646** BP. HALL *Poems* 95 There did he loose his snowy Innocence.

**b.** Used to qualify *white* or *whiteness*.

**1785** PENNANT *Arct. Zool.* II. 549 Of a snowy whiteness. **1791** COWPER *Yardley Oak* 128 A splinter'd stump bleach'd to a snowy white. **1838** DICKENS *Nickleby* l, Stained rotten canvas looked a snowy white. **1859** JEPHSON *Brittany* v. 50 That snowy whiteness which I so much admired in the Breton caps. **1883** *Longman's Mag.* July 308 Some Alpine buttercups are snowy-white.

**5. a.** In the specific names of birds or animals (see quots.).

**1829** GRIFFITH tr. *Cuvier* VIII. 557 *Snowy Auk, *Mormon Glacialis*. **1895** *Funk's Stand. Dict.*, **Snowy egret* or *heron*, an entirely white egret (*Ardea candidissima*) ranging from New York to Chile. **1829** GRIFFITH tr. *Cuvier* VI. 44 *Snowy Falcon, *Falco niveus*. **1827** *Ibid.* V. 265 *Lepus Glacialis* (*Snowy Hare). **1785** LATHAM *Gen. Synop. Birds* III. I. 92 *Snowy Heron, *Ardea nivea*. **1813** A. WILSON *Amer. Ornith.* VII. 120 Snowy Heron, *Ardea candidissima*. The Snowy Heron seems particularly fond of the salt marshes during summer. **1872** COUES *N. Amer. Birds* 267 Little White Egret. Snowy Heron... Plumage always entirely white. **1885** *Snowy lemming [see LEMMING 2]. **1781** LATHAM *Gen. Synop. Birds* I. I. 132 *Snowy Owl... The whole plumage is white as snow. **1876** *Nature* XIV. 562/1 The additions to the Zoological Society's Gardens.. include..two Snowy Owls (*Nyctea nivea*). **1895** LYDEKKER *Roy. Nat. Hist.* IV. 162 The great snowy owl (*Nyctea scandiaca*) cannot be confounded with any other member of the order, being the only representative of its genus. **1777** FORSTER *Voy. round World* I. 96 Its colour induced us to call it the *snowy-petrel. **1895** LYDEKKER *Roy. Nat. Hist.* IV. 525 The snowy petrel (*Pagodroma nivea*). **1872** COUES *N. Amer. Birds* 245 *Snowy Plover..; several lateral tail feathers entirely white. **1891** *Cent. Dict.* s.v., Snowy plover, *Ægialites nivosus*, a small ring-plover of the Pacific and Mexican Gulf coasts of the United States.

**b.** In names of flowers, etc.

**1822** *Hortus Anglicus* II. 392 *Tussilago Nivea*. Snowy Colt's-foot. **1889** R. A. R. BENNETT *Marine Aquaria* viii. 71 Snowy Anemone,..*Sagartia nivea*. **1901** *Gardener* 12 Jan. 1047/3 In cultivation the Snowy Crowfoot [*Ranunculus amplexicaulis*] generally blooms in April or May.

**c.** ***snowy pear***, the snow-pear (see SNOW *sb.*[1] 9 d).

**1884** *De Candolle's Orig. Cultivated Pl.* 233 The snowy pears cultivated in France to make the drink called perry have become wild in the woods here and there.

**6.** *Comb.*, as ***snowy-banded***, ***-bosomed***, etc.

*a* **1618** SYLVESTER *Cup of Consolation* 10 Wks. (Grosart) II. 263 Where Snow-winged Victory doth wun. **1648** J. BEAUMONT *Psyche* III. cxviii, Pure and snowy-countnanc'd Linen. **1717** ROWE *Ode for New Year* ii, Snowy-headed Winter leads. **1744** AKENSIDE *Pleas. Imag.* III. 434 On the brink of Ganges waits The snowy-vested seer. **1760** FAWKES tr. *Anacreon, Ode* v. 19 With snowy-bosomed Sappho gay. **1830** HOWITT *Bk. Seasons* (1837) 145 The verdurous, snowy-flowered elder. **1836–48** B. D. WALSH *Aristoph., Clouds* I. iii, Mimas's snowy-capped summit. **1855** TENNYSON *Maud* I. VIII, I heard no longer The snowy-banded..priest intone. **1889** DOYLE *M. Clarke* 227 A great herd of snowy-fleeced sheep.

**B.** *sb.* **a.** *slang.* Linen. **b.** The snowy owl.

**1877** J. W. HORSLEY *Jottings fr. Jail* 6 We used to go and smug snowy (steal linen) that was hung out to dry. **1904** P. FOUNTAIN *Great North-West* xiii. 144 If these are European snowies, the North-West Territory bird is probably a distinct variety. *Ibid.*, The snowy made the feathers fly.

Hence **'snowyish** *a.*, somewhat snowy.

**1821** *Blackw. Mag.* X. 570 It is..rawish—coldish—icyish—snowyish.

**'snozzle,** *v. rare.* [Cf. *nozzle*, variant of NUZZLE *v.*[1]] *intr.* = SNUZZLE *v.* I.

**1881** *Spectator* 3 Dec. 1534 The pig snozzles in the gutter.

**snozzle** ('snɒz(ə)l), *sb.* orig. *U.S. slang.* Anglicized form of SCHNOZZLE. Also *transf.*

**1930** D. RUNYON in *Collier's* 20 Dec. 13/2 He no sooner pokes his snozzle into the joint than a guy by the name of Louie the Lug..jumps up. **1931** *Ibid.* 26 Sept. 9/2, I put the old convincer on him by letting him peer down the snozzle of my John Roscoe. **1959** I. & P. OPIE *Lore & Lang. Schoolch.* ix. 155 Children go in for short sharp words, as ..'snozzle'..for nose. **1968** D. O'GRADY *Bottle of Sandwiches* (1969) iv. 60 The poor Old Girl [*sc.* a truck] was mud from anus to snozzle.

**snub** (snʌb), *sb.*[1] Also 6 **snobbe**, **snubbe**. [f. SNUB *v.*[1] Cf. MSw. and Norw. *snubba* in sense 1; Sw. dial. *snubba* a short-stemmed pipe, short-horned cow.]

**I. 1. a.** An act or instance of snubbing; a remark or action intended to repress or rebuke a person.

**1537** CRANMER in *State Papers Hen. VIII*, I. 562 Although in the meane season you suffre some snubbes..for the same, yet one day He will requite altogether. **1583** BABINGTON *Commandm.* (1590) 209 When euer any snubs and checkes in worde or countenance vndeserued arise. **1598** STOW *Surv.* 470 In which Tragedie London..had now and then a part, and had many a snubbe at the kinges hand. *a* **1688** BUNYAN *Israel's Hope Encouraged* Wks. 1852 I. 589 This word 'let' is sometimes used by way of rebuke and snub. **1748** RICHARDSON *Clarissa* (1811) VIII. 10, I..must have been accustomed to snubs and rebuffs from the affluent. **1861** *Sat. Rev.* 14 Sept. 269 When we endeavour to analyse it, the immediate effect of a snub is to induce a feeling of deprivation and exposure. **1885** *Manch. Exam.* 11 Mar. 5/5 Mr. Gladstone..administered to the most presumptuous member of the House a proper snub.

**b.** *pl.* As *int.*, expressing total indifference or contempt. *slang.*

**1934** *Neuphilologische Mitteilungen* XXXV. 130 Prep-school slang..*snubs* interj. accompanied by making a long nose. **1945** E. WAUGH *Brideshead Revisited* I. vi. 135 Now I shall tell her I have had it straight from a real artist, and snubs to her.

†**2.** A check, stop, stay, hindrance. *Obs.*

**1581** T. LAWSON *Orchett* (MS. Lansd. 208 lf. 142b), Mortimer in all haist pursued yᵉ Saxons, And gaue thame snobbes with his Britons. **1615** W. LAWSON *Country Housew. Garden* (1626) 18 Thriuing without snub he will ouerlay your grafted Stocke much. **1672** P. Henry *Diaries & Lett.* (1882) 248 Exchequer stopt from issuing forth moneyes to pay debts for this year, a snub to trade.

**3.** *U.S.* A sudden check given to a rope or cable in running out; a post or stake enabling this to be done.

**1891** in *Cent. Dict.*

**II. 4.** A snag or stub. *rare*

**1590** Spenser *F.Q.* i. viii. 7 Lifting vp his dreadfull club on hight, All arm'd with ragged snubbes and knottie graine. **1925** W. de la Mare *Broomsticks* 220 Not so much as an ole scrubbin'-brush or a snub of soap.

**5.** *Mech.* ? = snug *sb.*[1] 2. Also *fig.*

**1844** *Civil Eng. & Arch. Jrnl.* VII. 19/2 The swings are attached to the frame by means of snubs.., which are bolted vertically to the lower ends of the swings. **1973** R. D. Symons *Where Wagon Led* p. xiii, A man who cannot put a snub on his temper had better leave horses alone.

†**snub**, *sb.*[2] *Obs.*$^{-1}$ [Cf. snub *v.*[2]] A sob.

**1742** Shenstone *Schoolmistr.* xxiv, He..with snubs profound, and heaving breast,..does declare His grievous wrong.

**snub** (snʌb), *sb.*[3] and *a.* [See snub nose.]

**A.** *sb.* **1.** A snub nose.

**1830** Marryat *Pacha Many T.* xv, As my father's nose was aquiline, and mine is a snub. **1840** Barham *Ingol. Leg.* Ser. ii. *Aunt Fanny* vii, She turn'd up her dear little snub at 'the Man'. **1862** Sala *Seven Sons* I. xi. 266 Her nose between the mild retroussé and the decided snub.

**2.** *Geom.* A snub polyhedron or polytope.

**1948** H. S. M. Coxeter *Regular Polytopes* viii. 151 (*heading*) The snub {3, 4, 3}. **1952** Cundy & Rollett *Math. Models* iii. 94 It can be proved..that..there are only thirteen Archimedean solids, two of which occur in two forms. Those two are the two 'snubs'. **1971** M. J. Wenninger *Polyhedron Models* iii. 179 Great inverted snub icosidodecahedron. This polyhedron is another snub that is simpler in construction than most of the others in this set.

**B.** *adj.* **1.** Of the nose: Short and turned up.

**1844** Dickens *Mart. Chuz.* xvi, That order of nose on which the envy of mankind has bestowed the appellation 'snub'. **1853** Mrs. Gaskell *Cranford* i, Her nose was unformed and snub. **1886** Welldon *Aristotle's Rhet.* 30 The aquiline or snub character of a nose.

**2.** Snub-nosed.

**1883** G. Meredith *Poems of Joy of Earth* 39 The snub kids Upon hindlegs went sportive.

**3.** *Geom.* Used to designate certain symmetrical polyhedra and polytopes; in general, they have no mirror symmetry and occur in enantiomorphic pairs. [tr. L. *sīmus* squashed (Kepler *Harmonices Mundi* (1619) V. ii. xxviii. 62).]

A snub cube has as its faces 6 squares and 32 equilateral triangles; a snub dodecahedron has 12 pentagons and 80 equilateral triangles: they are more nearly spherical than the cube and dodecahedron to which Kepler related them, hence the name.

**1934** *Proc. London Math. Soc.* XXXVIII. 338 We might symbolize such a snub polytope by ringing all the dots in the graph. [*Note*] The word 'snub' is a free translation of Kepler's *simus*. **1952** Cundy & Rollett *Math. Models* iii. 101 (*caption*) Snub cube. *Ibid.* 108 (*caption*) Snub dodecahedron. **1971** M. J. Wenninger *Polyhedron Models* i. 32 The snub dodecahedron. This polyhedron has the same relation to the regular dodecahedron that the snub cube has to the regular hexahedron.

**snub** (snʌb), *v.*[1] Also 4 snube, 5–6 snubbe, 7 snubb. [a. ON. *snubba* (MSw. *snubba*, *snobba*), recorded in sense 1; mod. Norw. and Sw. dial. *snubba*, Da. *snubbe*, have also the sense of cutting short, making stumpy, etc. See also snib *v.*[1]]

**1.** *trans.* To check, reprove, or rebuke in a sharp or cutting manner; in later use, to treat or receive (a person, suggestion, etc.) in a way calculated to repress or mortify.

(*a*) *a* **1340** Hampole *Psalter* lviii. 17 They sal snube [*v.r.* snyb] þaim, þat will not be converted. **1483** *Cath. Angl.* 347/2 To Snubbe. **1570** Levins *Manip.* 181 To Snubbe, *arguere, culpare*. *a* **1610** Babington *Wks.* (1622) 48 We see the great..goodnesse of God,..neuer snubbing any child of his for imperfection of faith. **1676** Etheredge *Man of Mode* iii. ii, Do not you fall on him, Medley, and snub him. Sooth him up in his extravagance! **1727** De Foe *Protestant Monastery* 6 When they see the Son curbing the Father, or the Daughter snubbing the Mother. **1796** Mme. D'Arblay *Camilla* V. 9, I often snub Hal..for fear of his getting out of my hands. **1835** Marryat *J. Faithful* xv, Mr. Turnbull occasionally throwing in a word, and each time snubbed by his wife. **1882** B. D. W. Ramsay *Rough Recoll.* I. viii. 187, I ventured to address him, and was most decidedly snubbed. *fig.* **1620** Sanderson *Serm.* I. 146 The force of natural conscience..will be sometimes snubbing, and stinging, and lashing, and vexing him.

(*b*) **1861** Holme Lee *Warp & Woof* I. 30 Ursula..snubbed it as she would have snubbed any plan that did not originate with herself. **1882** in *R. Geog. Soc. Suppl. Papers* I. i. 117 The stream now..runs in rock-strewn whirls and races which snub any question about its navigability. **1891** *Spectator* 2 May, Nothing could be more foolish than to snub voluntary effort.

**b.** *absol.* To employ snubbing; †to scold.

**1694** Congreve *Double-Dealer* iii. vi, I acquiesce, my Lady, but don't snub so loud. **1787** [see snubbee]. **1861** *Sat. Rev.* 14 Sept. 269 But there need be nothing cruel in the man who snubs. **1907** *Blackw. Mag.* Nov. 678/1 The power to snub is a weapon of defence.

†**c.** To take *up* sharply or severely; to order *about* in a sharp fashion. *Obs.*

**1672** Villiers (Dk. Buckhm.) *Rehearsal* iv. i. (Arb.) 95 A fierce Hero, that frights his Mistriss, snubs up Kings,..and does what he will. **1711** Shaftesbury *Charac.* (1737) III. Misc. v. ii. 271 To censure merely what another Person writes, to twitch, snap, snub up, or banter. *a* **1797** Mary Wollstonecr. *Posth. Wks.* (1798) I. 160 She did not like to go to service, to be snubbed about, after being her own mistress.

**2.** †**a.** To check or restrain (a thing); to prevent from having free course or development. *Obs.*

**1583** Babington *Commandm.* (1590) 251 Euery Christian is to take heede..to snub the course of Sathan at the first. **1592** —— *Notes Genesis* xxxviii. §8. 151 Beware we then euer of discontent, and snubbe it betimes. *a* **1624** Bp. M. Smith *Serm.* 186 Wisedome..snubbeth and crosseth all vnlawfull designes. *a* **1688** Bunyan *Christ a Compl. Saviour* Wks. 1853 I. 217 He is holy, and so will snub their lusts.

**b.** *Naut.* and *U.S.* To check or stop (a rope or cable) suddenly while running out; to stop or bring *up* (a boat, etc.) sharply or suddenly, esp. by passing a rope round a post; to fasten or tie (*up*).

(*a*) **1841** R. H. Dana *Seaman's Man.* 124 *Snub*, to check a rope suddenly. **1867** Smyth *Sailor's Word-bk.*, *Snubbing her*, bringing a ship up suddenly with an anchor. **1887** *Century Mag.* Aug. 483/2 A deck-hand forward to 'snub' her in the locks and take a line to the tow-path.

(*b*) **1888** *Century Mag.* Mar. 660/1 He is taught this by being violently snubbed up..the first two or three times that he feels the noose settle round his neck. **1895** *Outing* XXVII. 224/1, I kept him snubbed up too closely for him to get a start. **1903** A. Adams *Log Cowboy* x. 153 We took a guy line from the wagon and snubbed it to a tree.

**3.** To check the growth of; to shorten; to cut, nip, or break *off*, the end of (a thing). Now *rare.*

**1615** W. Lawson *Country Housew. Garden* (1626) 35 Either snub his top with a nip betwixt your finger and your thumb, or with a sharpe knife. **1641** H. Best *Farm. Bks.* (Surtees) 77 The yeere was (as yett) but younge, and the field indifferent good, and not much snubbed. **1704** Ray *Creation* i. (ed. 4) 96 The Trees..whose Heads and Boughs I have observ'd..to be so snub'd by the Winds, as if their Boughs and Leaves had been par'd or shaven off on that side. **1831** Jane Porter *Sir E. Seaward's Narr.* I. 161, I therefore hung the handkerchief on the branch of a tree, that I snubbed off short for the purpose. **1886** *S.W. Linc. Gloss.* 136 You should ha' putten some salt on, it would ha' snubbed them [*sc.* weeds] anyhow.

**b.** To make snub-nosed or snub.

**1796** *Mod. Gulliver* 186 Get snubb'd i' th' nose—or haply singe our beards. **1845** S. Judd *Margaret* i. xiv, They laughed, and snubbed their noses with their handkerchiefs.

†**4.** To cheat or defraud. *Obs.*

**1694** Echard *Plautus* 93 For th' old Men ha' now open'd a Passage for my Tricks to make Incursions, and snub 'em o' their Mony.

**5.** *intr.* To press bluntly.

**1846** in Thornton *Amer. Gloss.* (1912) s.v., I felt the cold nose of the captain of the band [of sharks] snubbing against my side.

Hence **'snubbable** *a.* (Cf. unsnubbable *a.*)

**1908** L. A. Tollemache *Old & Odd Mem.* 130 So wholesomely snubbable as just to stop short of being bores.

**snub**, *v.*[2] Now *dial.* and *U.S.* [var. of snob *v.*[1]] *intr.* To sob.

**1621** T. Bedford *Sin unto Death* 50 He striveth, strugleth, roareth, sobbeth, snubbeth, and ready he is to burst for anger. **1671** in Skinner. **1880** *Scribner's Mag.* June 300/2, I heerd her a-cryin' an' a-snubbin', all night.

**snub-**, the stem of snub *v.*[1] used in a few combs., as †**snub-devil**, a clergyman (*obs. slang*); **snub-line**, **-post**, *U.S.* a snubbing-line or -post.

**1785** Grose *Dict. Vulg. T.*, *Snub devil*, a parson. **1875** Knight *Dict. Mech.* 2231/2 *Snub-post*, a form of bitt or mooring-post on a raft or canal-boat. **1908** H. Day *King Spruce* xxvi, The snub-line down the steep quarter-mile..made a cut-off that doubled the efficiency of the teams.

**snubbed** (snʌbd), *ppl. a.* [f. snub *v.*[1]]

**1.** Checked, restrained; repressed by snubbing.

**1596** Babington *Brief Conf.* 20 Their snubbed harts would call their snubs to remembrance. **1840** Hood *Up Rhine* 228 The snubbed children of a family are often better than the spoiled ones. **1895** Meredith *Amazing Marriage* xii, O but she was a snubbed young woman last night!

**2. a.** Turned up and flattened at the tip.

**1802** H. Martin *Helen of Glenross* I. 70 Mr. Isaac now saw beyond his nose, (no great distance, by the bye, for it is vulgarly snubbed). **1840** Marryat *Poor Jack* viii, His nose [was] snubbed. **1862** Borrow *Wales* cviii, A broad face, grey eyes, a snubbed nose [etc.].

**b.** Shortened, stumpy.

**1835** J. H. Ingraham *South-West* I. iii. 27 With swallow-tailed sterns, snubbed bows, and black hulls. **1903** *Trans. Inst. Naval Archit.* XLV. 26 Conditions in which you may have the 'snubbed' finish of the curve of areas.

**snubbee.** In 8 snubee. [f. snub *v.*[1]] One who is snubbed.

**1787** H. Walpole *Lett. to C'tess Ossory* II. 298 You tell me too that I snub and sneer; I protest I thought I was the snubee.

**snubber** ('snʌbə(r)). [f. snub *v.*[1]]

**1.** One who administers a snub or snubs.

**1861** *Sat. Rev.* 14 Sept. 269 Either the snubber has authority on his side,..or perhaps we have given way to enthusiasm, and are met by ridicule. **1880** 'Ouida' *Moths* III. 18 The disagreeable snappers and snubbers and snarlers.

**2.** *U.S.* One who snubs a rope or boat; a device for snubbing or checking.

**1853** in Thornton *Amer. Gloss.* (1912) II. 825 A snubber ..snubs the boat when she heaves to on the heel-path shore. **1875** Knight *Dict. Mech.* 2231/2 *Snubber*, a cable-stopper.

**3. a.** A simple form of shock-absorber used esp. in motor vehicles. Freq. *attrib.*

**1921** *Daily Colonist* (Victoria, B.C.) 22 Oct. 10/7 (Advt.), Gabriel snubbers increase the riding comfort of any car. **1928** *Sunday Dispatch* 19 Aug. 8 New snubber plates are fitted on the front springs. **1956** Toboldt & Purvis *Automotive Encycl.* 30d/1 The first so called 'shock absorbers' were simple rebound absorbers or snubbers. **1961** *Aeroplane* C. 429/1 The second-stage rotor blades have been fitted with 'snubbers' at approximately their mean height. **1970** *Telegraph* (Brisbane) 18 Dec. 8/1 The trouble with our washing machine..was that it needed a new snubber spring. **1973** R. L. Eshleman in Snowdon & Ungar *Isolation of Mech. Vibration, Impact, & Noise* 228 The friction snubber utilizes coulomb friction between a liner material and the snubber wall. **1980** *Truck & Bus Transportation* (Austral.) Jan. 32/3 The snubber consists of an endless circle of chain encased in a solid block of rubber.

**b.** *Electronics.* A circuit intended to suppress voltage spikes.

**1968** *IEEE Trans. Industry & General Applications* IV. 666/2 With properly damped snubber circuits the commutation transient waveshapes are such that the initial *dv/dt* is highest. **1977** *Design Engin.* July 27/1 All thyristor installations normally require a snubber, or dv/dt suppression network consisting of a capacitor and resistor in series across the device.

**c.** A device used to damp pulsations in, or check the flow of, a fluid.

**1972** L. J. Lortie in Blake & Mitchell *Vibration & Acoustic Measurement Handbk.* xxvii. 542 Using the simple snubber (expansion chamber)..which is made of standard piping components, an original pulse amplitude of 100 pressure units may usually be reduced to the order of ten or five units. **1977** *Sci. Amer.* June 46/2 The rate of descent of the piston is predetermined by the setting of the flow snubber in the dividing plate, which admits the water into the lower half of the cylinder.

**snubbiness** ('snʌbɪnɪs). [f. snubby *a.*[2] and *a.*[3]] The character or quality of being snubby.

**1828** *Lights & Shades* II. 183 The snubbiness and obstinate stupidity of the Irish nose. **1865** Mrs. Gaskell *Wives & Daughters* xxviii, At last there came a day when Mrs. Gibson went beyond her usual negative snubbiness, and..was guilty of positive rudeness.

**snubbing** ('snʌbɪŋ), *vbl. sb.* [f. snub *v.*[1]]

**1. a.** The action of checking, repressing, or rebuking, esp. by means of a snub.

**1600** Surflet *Countrie Farme* vi. xxii. 778 At the least by snubbing and checking of naturall heat. **1693** Bampfield *Reply to Wallis* 55 Other snubbing of Sunday..I remember none, but he often calls the Lords Sabbath by a reflecting addition. **1768** Goldsm. *Good-n. Man* iv, I did hear him say, a little snubbing, before marriage, would teach you to bear it the better afterwards. **1861** *Sat. Rev.* 14 Sept. 268 By cultivating the art of snubbing. **1876** F. E. Trollope *Charming Fellow* III. xxv. 302 The kind-hearted little spinster endured a vast amount of snubbing.

*attrib.* **1869** Trollope *He Knew*, etc. xlii. (1878) 231 On that occasion,..being in a snubbing humour, [she] had snubbed him.

**b.** An instance of this.

**1841** J. H. Newman in *Apologia* (1864) 241, I have managed to take out on my side my snubbing's worth. **1857** S. Osborn *Quedah* xii. 153 They got a severe snubbing for doing so. **1896** A. J. C. Hare *Story Life* II. viii. 99, I was more free from family snubbings than I had ever been before.

**2.** *Naut.* and *U.S.* (See snub *v.*[1] 2 b.)

**1846** A. Young *Naut. Dict.* 288 *Snubbing*, checking or easing off a little of a ship's cable or hawser, in order to prevent a sudden jerk when bringing the vessel up, or on other occasions. **1889** A. T. Pask *Eyes Thames* 69 The snubbing of the chain gives a disagreeable jerking which is trying to the system.

**b.** *attrib.*, as ***snubbing-line***, ***-post***.

**1875** Knight *Dict. Mech.* 2231/2 *Snubbing-line*, the line on the bow of a canal-boat [etc.]. **1887** *Sci. Amer.* 21 May 326/2 A stout line is carried forward, and the ends are attached..to snubbing posts. **1888** *Century Mag.* Mar. 655/2 The high, circular horse-corral, with a snubbing-post in the center. **1900** *Engineering Mag.* XIX. 665 The checking of the ship when afloat is done exclusively by snubbing lines.

**3.** The action of reducing or suppressing oscillation; damping.

**1951** C. E. Crede *Vibration & Shock Isolation* iii. 112 (*heading*) Effect of snubbing. **1961** Harris & —— *Shock & Vibration Handbk.* III. xlv. 24 Because car loading can change from trip to trip, practical considerations dictate a compromise both in the selection of load springs and in the design of a snubbing means.

**'snubbing**, *ppl. a.* [f. snub *v.*[1]] Of the nature of a snub; repressing by a snub or snubs.

**1887** [? Miss Ingham] *Poor Nellie* (1888) 120 He hoped Adela had not thought his abrupt departure rude and snubbing. **1900** Eleanor Glyn *Visits Elizabeth* (1906) 20, I was not once agreeable, or anything but stiff and snubbing.

So **'snubbingly** *adv.*, in a snubbing manner.

**1861** Meredith *Evan Harrington* I. xi. 205 The chairman welcomed them a trifle snubbingly. **1883** Miss Broughton *Belinda* i. vi, 'You never do anything but what you wish yourself?' asks Rivers snubbingly.

**snubbish** ('snʌbɪʃ), *a.* [f. snub *a.* and *v.*[1]]

**1.** Somewhat snub.

**1828** *Ann. Reg., Law Cases* 365/2 A short snubbish nose. **1848** H. Rogers *Ess.* (1874) I. vi. 310 His eyes are not so prominent as yours, nor is his nose so snubbish.

**2.** Repressive; inclined to snub.

**1840** HOOD *An Open Question* 146 Have we not had enough To make Religion sad, and sour, and snubbish?

Hence **'snubbishly** *adv.*; **'snubbishness.**

**1840** *New Monthly Mag.* LVIII. 526 Miss Biggs..turned up her snub-nose more snubbishly. **1848** H. ROGERS *Ess.* (1874) I. vi. 310 He has a strong resemblance to you..in the *snubbishness* of his nose.

**'snubby,** *a.*$^{1}$ *rare*$^{-1}$. [f. SNUB *sb.*$^{1}$ 4.] Knotty.

*a***1758** M. MENDEZ *Seasons, Summer* 1 in *Coll. Poems* (1770) II. 233 Beneath yon snubby oak's extended shade.

**snubby** ('snʌbɪ), *a.*$^{2}$ [f. SNUB *a.* Cf. Sw. dial. *snubbug*, *snubbi*, Icel. *snubbóttr* (Norw. *snubbutt*) in same sense.] Somewhat snub; short, stumpy.

(*a*) **1828** *Blackw. Mag.* XXIII. 494 What a snout he turns up to the morning air,..pimpled, snubby, and snorty. **1860** GEO. ELIOT *Mill on Floss* I. 108 Her little straight nose, not at all snubby. **1894** SIR E. SULLIVAN *Woman* 69 If Cleopatra's nose had been..a little more snubby or a little more aquiline.

(*b*) **1854** MISS BAKER *Northampt. Gloss.* s.v., What a snubby point you've got to your pencil. **1865** WHITNEY *Gayworthys* iv, The snubby end of her little freckled nose.

**snubby** ('snʌbɪ), *a.*$^{3}$ [f. SNUB *v.*$^{1}$] Inclined to snub; repressing with snubs.

**1867** E. V. B. in *Cornhill Mag.* (1907) Feb. 196 She would not understand. She was just a little snubby, I thought. **1889** 'F. ANSTEY' *Pariah* I. iii, You were so very snubby to that poor Mr. Chadwick.

**snubnerlik:** see SNOBBERLY *adv. Obs.*

**snub nose.** Also **snub-nose.** [f. SNUB *v.*$^{1}$ 3. Cf. Norw. dial. *snubbnos* (Ross).] A short stumpy nose turned up and flattened at the tip.

**1724** *Lond. Gaz.* No. 6251/3 He is a thick-set Boy, with a snub Nose. **1793** HOLCROFT tr. *Lavater's Physiog.* xvii. 87 [I know] the Russians by the snub nose. **1818** BYRON *Juan* I. clx, With prying snub-nose, and small eyes, he stood, Following Antonia's motions. **1838** BARHAM Ser. I. *Hand of Glory* (1905) 28 The very snore froze, In his very snub nose. **1875** JOWETT *Plato* (ed. 2) IV. 235 He has a snub nose, and projecting eyes.

**'snub-nosed,** *a.* [f. as prec.]

**1. a.** Having a snub nose.

**1725** BAILEY *Erasm. Colloq.* (1878) I. 44 Can you fancy that..Snub-nos'd, Sparrow-mouth'd, Paunch-belly'd Creature? **1758** *Ann. Reg., Poetry* 439 A snub-nos'd dog to fat inclin'd. **1775** SHERIDAN *Duenna* II. ii, I was taught to believe you a little black, snub-nosed fellow. **1833** MARRYAT *P. Simple* (1863) 187 The lieutenant, who was a little snub-nosed man, with a pimply face. **1882** *Macm. Mag.* XLVI. 126 The snub-nosed effigy on his coins.

**b.** In specific names (see quots.).

*c***1880** *Cassell's Nat. Hist.* II. 255 The Short-headed Whale, or Snub-nosed Cachalot. **1884** COUES *N. Amer. Birds* 807 *Simorhynchus cristatellus*,..Snub-nosed Auk. **1891** *Cent. Dict.* s.v. *Simenchelys*, *S. parasiticus*, the only species, is known as the pug-nosed or snub-nosed eel.

**2.** *fig.* Stumpy; short and broad at the front; abbreviated.

**1925** F. SCOTT FITZGERALD *Great Gatsby* i. 9 A snub-nosed motor-boat..bumped the tide offshore. **1961** E. S. GARDNER in *Webster* s.v., A snub-nosed revolver. **1963** *Times* 5 Feb. 7/5 These snub-nosed,..two-stroke machines. **1966** P. O'DONNELL *Sabre-Tooth* x. 137 A Smith & Wesson Centennial, a snub-nosed hammerless revolver. **1978** S. SHELDON *Bloodline* l. 405 Others carried snub-nosed tear gas rifles.

Hence **'snub-,nosedness.**

**1875** JOWETT *Plato* (ed. 2) IV. 228 The snubnosedness of Theaetetus..is characteristic both of him and Socrates.

†**snuch.** *Obs.*$^{-1}$ [Related to *snudge* in the same way as *slutch*, *smutch*, to *sludge*, *smudge*.] = SNUDGE *sb.*

**1579–80** NORTH *Plutarch* (1595) 135 But in the ende..this bribing wretch was forced for to hold a typling booth, most like a clowne or snuch.

**snuck,** chiefly U.S. pa. t. and pple. of SNEAK *v.*

†**'snuddle,** *v. Obs.*$^{-1}$ [perh. an error for *suddle*, but cf. G. *schnudeln* to snotter, *beschnudeln* to befoul, etc.] *trans.* To defile, dirty.

**1661** K. W. *Conf. Charac.* (1860) 87 She's a fine dirty hieroglip[h]ick of her pigsty recreations, snuddled and kennel'd over with the dirty sackcloth of her gloomy harding.

**snudge** (snʌdʒ), *sb.* [Cf. SNUDGE *v.*$^{1}$, and see also SNOWGE, SNUCH.]

**1.** A miser, a mean avaricious person, a niggard; a sneaking or sponging fellow. Now *dial.*

Very common from *c* 1550 to 1610.

**1545** ASCHAM *Toxoph.* I. (Arb.) 28 Thus youre husbandrie me thinke, is more like the life of a couetouse snudge.., then the labour of a good husband. **1553** T. WILSON *Rhet.* (1567) 82 Some riche snudges hauyng greate wealthe, goe with their hose out at heeles. **1608** DEKKER *Work for Armourers* Wks. (Grosart) IV. 160 Those snudges and miserable cormorants that now feede vpon thee. **1677** MIÈGE *Dict.* II. s.v., A Snudging man, or a Snudge, a man that has a curmudging way with him. **1694** MOTTEUX *Rabelais* v. xvi. (1737) 72 The filthy Snudge is..mischievous. **1877–88** in Cheshire and Sheffield glossaries.

*transf.* **1573** G. HARVEY *Letter-bk.* (Camden) 8 He plaid the veri snudg then that had so much lerning and shoud so litle. **1593** —— *Pierce's Super.* Wks. (Grosart) II. 254 Histories are no snudges in matters of note. **1600** DEKKER *Fortunatus* II. ii, O I feare that deitie Hath stolne him hence, that snudge his destinie.

*Comb.* **1576** T. NEWTON tr. *Lemnie's Complex.* 103 b, Who Snudgelike to his frend..Not one poore draught thereof would send. **1606** *Wily Beguiled* in Hazl. *Dodsley* IX. 232, I heard your father say that he would marry you to Peter Plodall, that puck-fist, that snudge-snout.

†**2.** *Cant.* (See quot.) *Obs.* (Cf. SNUDGE *v.*$^{2}$)

**1676** COLES, *Snudg*, one that hides himself in a house to do mischief. *a***1700** B. E. *Dict. Cant. Crew*, *Snudge*, one that lurks under a Bed, to watch an opportunity to Rob the House.

**snudge** (snʌdʒ), *v.*$^{1}$ [Of obscure origin.]

†**1.** *intr.* To be miserly, stingy, or saving. Also with *it*. *Obs.*

*c***1540** COPLAND *Hye Way to Spyttel Ho.* 25 That man that ..euer is bare, hungry and indygent, Scrapynge and snudgynge without any cease. **1573** TUSSER *Husb.* (1878) 139 Good husbandry snudgeth, for fear of a dout. **1611** FLORIO, *Spilorciáre*, to grudge, to snudge, to dodge or play the slouenlie niggard or pinch-pennie. **1611** COTGR. s.v. *Avoine*, To snudge it; or churlishly to eat all his meat all alone.

**2.** To walk in a stooping or meditative attitude. Freq. with *along*. Now *dial.*

**1677** MIÈGE *Dict.* II. s.v., To Snudge about business, *aller d'un air rampant, comme font les grands avares.* **1687** —— *Gt. Fr. Dict.* II. s.v., To Snudge along, or go like an old Snudge, or like one whose Head is full of business. **1828–** in dial. glossaries (Yorks., Northampt., E. Anglia, Surrey, Sussex).

Hence **'snudging** *vbl. sb.* and *ppl. a.*

**1553** T. WILSON *Rhet.* (1580) 145 Snudgyng wittely rebuked. **1577** STANYHURST *Descr. Irel.* in *Holinshed* (1808) VI. 23 Some of his friends, that were snudging penie-fathers, would take him up verie roughlie for..his outragious expenses. **1677** [see SNUDGE *sb.* 1]. **1687** MIÈGE *Gt. Fr. Dict.* II. s.v., A Snudging along, *demarche de Faquin.* **1713** PRIOR in *Bolingbroke's Corresp.* (1798) II. 445, I cannot imagine how you came to know that snudging boy.

**snudge** (snʌdʒ), *v.*$^{2}$ Now *dial.* [Of obscure origin: perh. related to SNUG *v.*] *intr.* To remain snug and quiet; to nestle.

**1633** G. HERBERT *Temple, Giddinesse* iii, Now he will fight it out, and to the warres; Now eat his bread in peace, And snudge in quiet. **1655** VAUGHAN *Silex Scint.* I. (1858) 124 The Age, the present times are not To snudge in, and embrace a cot. **1686** F. SPENCE tr. *Saint Euvremont's Misc.* Pref. C3, Tragedy, like the Aristotelian virtue, is to lie snudging betwixt them both. **1755** JOHNSON, To *snug*, to lie close; to snudge. **1823–** in dial. glossaries (Westm., Yorks., Derby, Suffolk).

†**'snudgery.** *Obs. rare*$^{-1}$. [f. SNUDGE *sb.*] Miserliness.

**1599** NASHE *Lent. Stuffe* 3 Those graybeard huddle-duddles..were stroke with such stinging remorse of their miserable Euclionisme and snudgery.

**snuff** (snʌf), *sb.*$^{1}$ Forms: 4–6 **snoffe,** 5 **snof,** 9 *dial.* **snoff;** 4–7 **snuffe,** 7 **snuf;** 6– **snuff.** [Of obscure origin: G. *schnuppe* (†*snupe*), which agrees in sense, does not correspond phonetically.]

**I. 1. a.** That portion of a wick, etc., which is partly consumed in the course of burning to give light, and in the case of candles requires to be removed at intervals; †a candle-end.

Also *Mining*, a smift (Gresley, 1883): cf. SNOFF.

**1382** WYCLIF *Exod.* xxv. 38 Candelquenchers, and.. where the snoffes ben quenchid. **1398** TREVISA *Barth. De P.R.* XVIII. xxxix. (MS. Bodl.), ȝif a mare..smelleþ þe snoffe of a candel sheo casteþ here foole. *c***1440** *Promp. Parv.* 462/1 Snuffe, of a candel, *muco.* **1530** PALSGR. 272/1 Snoffe of a candell, *mesche, limignon, lumignon.* **1544** PHAER *Regim. Lyfe* (1553) Eiij, Ye must lay to y$^{e}$ nose..assafetida, or the snuffes of candels. **1577–87** HOLINSHED *Chron.* III. 1208/1 Through negligence of a maiden with a candell, the snuffe falling in an hundred pounds weight of gunpowder. *c***1645** HOWELL *Lett.* (1655) IV. xxi. 58 In som this light goes out with an ill-favor'd stench; But others have a save-all to preserve it from making any snuff at all. *a***1687** H. MORE *Cont. Remark. Stories* (1689) 406 Striking the Candle..and afterwards making three Scrapes on the Snuff to put it out. **1687** MIÈGE *Gt. Fr. Dict.* II, Snuff,..bout *de Chandelle.* **1705** ADDISON *Italy, Antiq. near Naples* 230 A Torch, Snuff and all, goes out in a Moment when dipp'd into the Vapour. **1756** *Phil. Trans.* LV. 185 Hence the suffocating nature of air impregnated with burnt grease, as from snuffs of candles, and the like. **1815** J. SMITH *Panorama Sci. & Art* II. 347 On letting it down again, it will be perfectly lighted from the spark of the snuff. **1843** KEIGHTLEY *Notes Virg., Georg.* I. 390 The thick snuff which gathers on the wick [of the lamp]. **1870** E. PEACOCK *Ralf Skirl.* II. 161 A candle with a long snuff burnt on the table.

*collect.* *a***1400–50** *Bk. Curtasye* 829 in *Babees Bk.* Of wax þese candels alle..; þo snof of hom dose a-way With close sesours. *a***1631** DONNE *Sat.* ii. 78 As a thrifty wench.. barrelling the droppings, and the snuffe, Of wasting candles.

*Comb.* **1709** in J. S. Moore *Goods & Chattels of our Forefathers* (1976) 196 Two brasse Snuffers and Snuff panns, one latten hoop for Cakes, a greater Chayr. **1733** LADY G. BAILLIE *Househ. Bk.* (1911) 381, 2 Snuff pans. **1758** FRANKLIN *Lett.* Wks. 1887 III. 8 There are also snuffers, a snuffstand, and extinguisher, of steel. **1963** *Times* 11 May 11/1 Candle-snuffers fitted with snuff pans were being used in Britain by the mid-fifteenth-century.

**b.** In comparisons, used to describe what is faint, feeble, or on the point of extinction.

**1534** MORE *Comf. agst. Trib.* II. Wks. 1172/1, I can not licken my life more metely now than to the snuffe of a candle. **1589** *Pappe with Hatchet* (1844) 36 A wit worn into the socket, twinkling and pinking like the snuffe of a candle. **1631** QUARLES *Samson* viii, The other are but blasts, That faintly blaze like Oyle-forsaken snuffes. **1654** WARREN *Unbelievers* 252 His Arguments should go out like a snuffe of a candle in the socket. **1730** ? SWIFT *Clad all in Brown* Wks. 1755 IV. I. 263 Thy soul, which through thy hide of buff, Scarce glimmers like a dying snuff. **1786** MME. D'ARBLAY *Diary* 6 Oct., All the poor attendants..drop off, one after another, like so many snuffs of candles. **1869** TROLLOPE *He Knew*, etc. lxxxix. (1878) 494 Some said..that she was going out like the snuff of a candle.

**c.** *fig.* or in fig. context (see quots. and cf. prec.).

**1589** *Hay any Work* 39 Why thou vnsauorly snuffe, dost tow thinke that men know not D. Bridges? **1601** SHAKS. *All's Well* I. ii. 59 Let me not liue..After my flame lackes oyle, to be the snuffe Of yonger spirits. **1652** N. CULVERWEL *Lt. Nature* I. xviii. (1661) 166 The Lamp of a Moralist..may go out in a snuff. *a***1680** CHARNOCK *Attrib. God* (1834) II. 525 Were such filthy snuffs fit of themselves to be kindled by.. a gospel beam? **1705** tr. *Bosman's Guinea* 410 The Buffel soon trod out the small remainder of the Snuff of his Life. **1742** YOUNG *Nt. Th.* VIII. 467 How mean that snuff of glory fortune lights, And death puts out!

**d.** Used to denote something of no value.

**1778** MISS BURNEY *Evelina* lxxxii, Who..cares the snuff of a candle? **1887** W. S. GILBERT *Ruddigore* II, You don't care the snuff of a candle.

**2.** The nozzle of a lamp, in which the wick burns.

**1611** COTGR., *Bec de la lampe*, the socket, or snuffe of the lampe. **1797** *Monthly Mag.* III. 507 There is also a little portative lamp, having only one snuff.

†**3.** A heel-tap; a portion of a drink left at the bottom of a cup. *Obs.*

**1592** NASHE *P. Penilesse* Wks. (Grosart) II. 83 Rather keepe a snuffe in the bottome of the glasse to light you to bed withall. **1616** R. C. *Times' Whistle* (1871) 60 Then each must haue his bout And drink vp all; to leave a litle snuffe Is petty treason. **1647** [H. NEVILE] *Parliam. of Ladies* Title-p., Either malice, or want of wit, hightned with snoffes of Ale or stayned Claret. **1673** O. WALKER *Educ.* II. i. 218 Drinking many in the same cup; and many times the snuffs left by the former. **1731–8** SWIFT *Polite Conv.* 163 (*Miss* drinking part of a Glass of Wine). *Neverout.* Pray, let me drink your Snuff.

*fig.* *a***1640** JACKSON *Creed* XI. xix, The devil still labours to glut men.., then he vents his snuffs or refuse upon them.

**II. 4.** †**a.** *to take..in (the) snuff* (or *to snuff*), to take (a matter) amiss, to take offence at, to be annoyed or indignant at, to resent. *Obs.*

The original reference was no doubt to the unpleasant smell proceeding from the smoking snuff of a candle, but there may also have been association with SNUFF *sb.*$^{2}$ or *v.*$^{2}$ The phrase was especially common between 1580 and 1660.

**1560** DAUS *Sleidane's Comm.* 463 A brute went that the Pope toke it in snuffe [L. *indigne tulisse*] that this truce was made. **1570** FOXE *A. & M.* 2281/1 This matter the Justice tooke sore to snuffe, and was very angry. **1579** W. WILKINSON *Confut. Fam. Love* 41 Hee..taketh it greatly in the snuffe, that his stuffe..should be brought to light. **1617** MORYSON *Itin.* III. 28 Englishmen, especially being young and unexperienced, are apt to take all things in snuffe. **1661** PEPYS *Diary* 6 Oct., Mr. Mills.., I expect, should take it in snuffe that my wife did not come to his child's christening the other day. **1716** T. WARD *Eng. Reform.* 129 Pray take it not, you old Cur-mudgeon, So much in snuff and evil dudgeon.

**b.** *to take snuff*, to take offence or umbrage (*at* a thing). *Obs.* exc. *arch.*

In quot. 1821 associated with SNUFF *sb.*$^{3}$ (cf. PEPPER *sb.* 4 b).

**1565** ALLEN *Defence Purg.* xiv. 262 Aërius,..taking snoffe that he could not get a bisshoprike, fell in to the hæresy of Arius. **1597** BEARD *Theatre God's Judgem.* (1612) 195 The yonker taking snuffe thereat, Why (said hee) takest thou thought for me? **1610** HOLLAND *Camden's Brit.* II. 211 Which the Manksmen hearing, tooke such a snuffe and indignation thereat that they sent for Olave. **1640** FULLER *Joseph's Coat* (1867) 51 Let us heed how we take snuff at the simplicity of God's ordinance. **1692** R. L'ESTRANGE *Fables* I. clxxxv. 156 Jupiter took Snuff at the Contempt, and Punish'd him for't. **1725** *New Cant. Dict.* s.v., *To take Snuff*, to take Pet. [**1821** SCOTT *Kenilw.* i, But take no snuff in the nose about it. **1876** G. H. KINGSLEY *Sport & Trav.* (1900) 322 With hearty hoping that North Britons will not take huffe nor snuffe at these kindly criticisms.]

**5.** A fit of indignation; a huff, pet, rage, passion. Used with *a*, *the*, or without article. Now *Sc.*

(*a*) **1592** GREENE *Upst. Courtier* Wks. (Grosart) XI. 279 These were going away in a snuff, for being thus plainly taunted. **1605** SHAKS. *Lear* III. i. 26 Either in snuffes, and packings of the Dukes, Or the hard Reine which both of them hath borne Against the old kinde King. *c***1620** BP. HALL *Contempl., O.T.* XIV. (1628) 1145 Abners duty..not to flye out in a snuffe.

(*b*) **1607** S. COLLINS *Serm.* (1608) 184 Smothering the talent that he lent thee..in snuffe, and pelting discontent. **1609** B. JONSON *Sil. Wom.* IV. v, He went away in snuffe, and I followed him. **1665** PEPYS *Diary* 19 Sept., I find they go up in snuffe to bed without taking any manner of leave of them.

(*c*) **1886** STEVENSON *Kidnapped* iii. 18 Dinnae fly up in the snuff at me. **1898** COBBAN *Angel of Covenant* xi. 124 The mighty high snuff and dudgeon ye gaed aff wi'.

†**6.** *attrib.* Angry, violent. *Obs.*$^{-1}$

**1582** STANYHURST *Æneis* II. (Arb.) 68 Now me the Myrmidones for captiue prisoner hold not, Nor sterne snuff Dolopans.

**7.** Used *attrib.* to designate pornographic photographs or films involving the actual killing of a woman. Cf. SNUFF *v.*$^{1}$ 1 d.

**1975** *Whig-Standard* (Kingston, Ontario) 2 Oct. 3/6 New York City police detective Joseph Horman said..that the 8-millimetre, eight-reel films called 'snuff' or 'slasher' movies had been in tightly controlled distribution for a month. **1975** *Globe & Mail* (Toronto) 20 Nov. 7/4 There are reports of 'snuff films' in the United States, pornographic movies that contain all the usual perversions but culminate with women being mutilated and killed—for real. **1976** *New Musical Express* 31 Jan. 11/3 The 'snuff movie', a kind of ultimate pornography that has at its climax the supposedly unfaked murder of a young woman. **1977** *Daily Colonist* (Victoria, B.C.) 23 July 3/2 Charged with attempted murder in the making of 'snuff' photographic stills. **1978** S. Sheldon *Bloodline* xlii. 360 For the last several years we have been hearing increasing rumors of snuff films, pornographic films in which at the end of the sexual act the victim is murdered on camera. **1981** *Observer* 12 July 39/4 The merchants and devotees of 'snuff porn' require that the masochistic models who pose for it actually die while receiving some hideous sexual punishment. At the actual moment of death the models are photographed in full colour, with very good lighting.

**snuff** (snʌf), *sb.*² Also 6–7 **snuffe.** [f. snuff *v.*² Cf. MDu. and Du. *snuf*, *snof* snuffing, snuffling, cold in the head, scent (of a thing), G. *schnuff* scent, nose, LG. *snüff* nose, snout; also MDu. *snuuf*, *snuyf*, LG. *snûf* snuffing, snuffles.]

**1.** An (*or* the) act of snuffing, esp. as an expression of contempt or disdain.

**1570** Dee *Math. Pref.* 10 Other (perchaunce) with a proud snuffe will disdain this litle. **1593** Abp. Bancroft *Daungerous Positions* iv. iii. 140 These points are..passed ouer with a snuffe, and with great disdaine. **1629** Gaule *Holy Madnesse* 198 Nought but a glance, a puffe, a snuffe, a frown. **1809** Malkin *Gil Blas* iv. viii. ¶9 That hound-like snuff at an ill construction, with which the devil has armed the noses of the most charitable. **1840** Hood *Up Rhine* 178 Ere a horrible reek..Set the dogs on the snuff. **1849** C. Brontë *Shirley* viii, His nostrils emitted a derisive and defiant snuff. **1866** [see snivel *sb.* 4].

**b.** A persistent snuffling; a disease in sheep.

*a* **1585** Montgomerie *Flyting* 308 The snuff and the snoire, the chaud-peece, the chanker. **1902** *Westm. Gaz.* 13 June 10/2 A sheep affected soon becomes thin and languid, and its painful snuffling has led farmers to call the disease 'snuff'.

†**2.** A puff, blast. *Obs.*

**1613** J. Davies (Heref.) *Muse's Tears* Wks. (Grosart) I. 15/1 Then, let Fates Snuffes and Puffes as winds of Grace, Serene the Heauen of your Maiestick Face. **1642** D. Rogers *Naaman* 439 Though it lye long in the moulds by reason of cold snuffes of weather.

**3.** Smell, odour, scent.

**1763** Stukeley *Palæogr. Sacr.* 93 The immortal, the eternal,..wants not the snuff of mortal incense, for his, but for our own sakes. **1844** Hood *The Turtles* 34 All whiffs, and sniffs, and puffs, and snuffs, From metals, minerals, and dyewood stuffs.

**4.** An inhalation, a sniff, *of* something.

**1822** Galt *Sir A. Wylie* lxxv, Take a snuff of caller air on the brow of the hill. **1852** Mrs. Stowe *Uncle Tom's C.* 151 One snuff of anything disagreeable being..sufficient to put an end to all her earthly trials.

**snuff** (snʌf), *sb.*³ [prob. ad. Du. and Flem. *snuf* or *snuif* (WFris. *snuf*) in the same sense, app. an abbreviation of *snuiftabak* (cf. LG. *snuvtobak*, G. *schnupftabak*, for which Swiss dial. has *schnupf*, *schnopf*): cf. prec. and snuff *v.*²]

**1. a.** A preparation of powdered tobacco for inhaling through the nostrils (in the Southern United States, usually taken orally).

The practice of taking snuff appears to have become fashionable about 1680, but prevailed earlier in Ireland and Scotland (see smutchin and sneezing *vbl. sb.* 2 b).

**1683** *Lond. Gaz.* No. 1800/4 James Norcock, Snuffmaker and Perfumer,..sells all sorts of Snuffs, Spanish and Italian. **1703** *Ibid.* No. 3963/3 Tobacco at 2d. per *lb.* Snuff 4d. 2q. per *lb.* **1724** Swift *Reasons agst. Exam. Drugs* Wks. 1755 III. i. 127 The makers of snuff, who..employ by far the greatest number of hands of any manufacture of the kingdom. **1796** Mme. D'Arblay *Camilla* III. 142 She perceived him, a few yards off, taking a pinch of snuff. **1815** Elphinstone *Acc. Caubul* (1842) I. 307 Their snuff is a dry and fine powder like Scotch snuff. **1837** Dickens *Pickw.* ii, He took snuff with everybody. **1849** [see dip *v.* 5]. **1884** F. M. Crawford *Rom. Singer* I. 23 Ercole takes snuff when he is not smoking. **1891** M. E. Ryan *Pagan of Alleghanies* 105 [Does] your deity of the lower world..chew snuff? **1907** *Dialect Notes* III. 230 *Dip (snuff)*, *v.t.*, to smear snuff on the gums with a brush made by chewing the end of a small stick. **1913** [see dip *v.* 5]. **1951** W. Faulkner *Knight's Gambit* 87 We watched him take..a tin of snuff and tilt a measure of it into the lid and then into his lower lip, tapping the final grain from the lid with..deliberation.

*transf.* **1709** *Brit. Apollo* No. 4. 4/2 A Most Excellent Cephalick Water, or Liquid Snuff.

*fig.* **1719** D'Urfey *Pills* V. 90 A Wench..Gave Snuff to me, Out of her Placket box. **1819** Shelley *Peter Bell 3rd* iii. xix. 3 Sometimes the poor are damned indeed To take.. Cobbett's snuff, revenge.

**b.** Any powder used like snuff, esp. for medical purposes; a sternutatory or errhine. *rare.*

**1861** S. Thomson *Wild Fl.* iii. (ed. 4) 306 Of one, the sneeze-wort yarrow (*Achillea ptarmica*), the leaves..are used as a snuff in head affections.

**c.** The colour of snuff. Also *attrib.* or as *adj.*

**1951** [see mustard *sb.* 1 f]. **1974** *Times* 26 Nov. 19/6 Colour combinations..snuff/ice, blue/white.

**2. a.** A pinch of snuff. [So WFlem. *snuuf.*]

**17..** Ramsay *Vision* xxi. Poems 1877 I. 127 Gallus sneerd and tuke a snuff. **1818** Scott *Hrt. Midl.* Prol., I will enrich ..thy nose with a snuff from my mull. **1863** A. H. Charteris *Life Robertson* x. 308 A snuff between his finger and thumb which he had no time to take. **1897** Pryde *Queer Folk Fife* 87 In his excitement he took four or five snuffs consecutively.

**b.** Used to denote something of small value.

**1809** Donaldson *Poems* 72 My memory, man, 's no worth a snuff. **1844** W. Cross *Disruption* xviii, I wadna gie a snuff for ony minister but a parish minister. **1881** W. Walker in Edwards *Mod. Sc. Poets* Ser. iii. 106 They'll care nae a snuff though grim poverty shake ye.

**c.** A pinch, a very small quantity, *of* something.

**1842** J. Aiton *Domest. Econ.* 258 Put a snuff of the carbonate of soda into the broth pot when it first comes to boil. **1883** *Cassell's Bk. Sports & Pastimes* 50 A snuff of sand, or tuft of grass, to give the requisite elevation.

**3.** In colloquial phrases: **a.** ***up to snuff***, knowing, sharp, not easily deceived; up to the required or usual standard, up to scratch. Also *attrib.*

**1811** Poole *Hamlet Trav.* ii. i, He knows well enough The game we're after: Zooks, he's up to snuff. **1823** Egan *Grose's Dict. Vulg. T.* s.v. *Up*, Up to snuff, and a pinch above it. **1848** Dickens *Dombey* xxxi, An up-to-snuff old vagabond. **1879** Howells *L. Aroostook* xxii, You American ladies are so—up to snuff, as you say. **1906** J. London *Let.* 31 May (1966) 204 As usual, your criticisms are right up to snuff. **1931** *Punch* 4 Nov. 495/2 Now Romney painted well enough, And Reynolds too, they say, And Gainsborough's things are up to snuff, And Lawrence had his day. **1943** E. B. White *Let.* 20 Mar. (1976) 239 The Central Park piece.. is up to snuff or better. **1944** R. Lehmann *Ballad & Source* 204 Madame Jardine says you're to go and see her for a few minutes. Only a *few* to-day. She's not quite up to snuff. **1974** S. Ellin *Stronghold* 33 He did not..go as far as some Quakers by convincement and suggest that birthright Quakers are not quite up to snuff. **1982** *N. & Q.* Feb. 83/1 The publisher's rejection of such received proceedings reflects, I suppose, their commitment to a databank, annual slices of which will suffice to bring future editions of their guides up to snuff.

**b.** ***to beat to snuff***, to beat utterly.

**1819** *Blackw. Mag.* V. 638 All other Colleges, thou beat'st to snuff.

**c.** ***in high snuff***, in high feather; elated.

**1840** R. H. Dana *Bef. Mast* xvi, The Sandwich-Islanders rode down, and were in 'high snuff'.

**d.** ***to give*** (one) ***snuff***, to deal sharply or severely with; to punish.

**1890** [R. C. Lehmann] *Harry Fludyer* 30 He rather gave me snuff about my extravagance. **1896** Baden-Powell *Matabele Campaign* vii, Then with eager haste..he dashed up the rocks to 'give the nigger snuff'.

**4.** *attrib.* and *Comb.*, as ***snuff-bottle***, ***-colour***, ***hand***, ***-handkerchief***, ***-mundungus***, ***-rasp***, ***-shop***, ***-spoon***, ***-stain***, ***-stick***, ***-work***; obj. and obj. gen., as ***snuff-grinder***, ***-maker***, ***-manufacturer***, ***-merchant***, ***-taker***, ***-taking***, ***-using***; instrumental and parasynthetic, as ***snuff-clad***, ***-headed***, ***-stained***; similative, as ***snuff-brown***. Also snuff-box, -coloured, etc.

**1850** *Spirit of Times* 16 Mar. 41/3 Did you see..that old *snuff-bottle? **1884** Gilmour *Mongols* 90 After snuff bottles had been exchanged. **1818** Scott *Hrt. Midl.* Prol., A new coat (*snuff-brown, and with metal buttons). **1857** Livingstone *Trav.* xvii. 319 He had on a snuff-brown coat. **1790** Wolcot (P. Pindar) *Elegy to Apollo* Wks. 1812 II. 278 In proud disdain their *snuff-clad noses rise. **1698** *Phil. Trans.* XX. 461 Down of a dark yellowish *Snuff-Colour. **1883** T. Hardy in *Longman's Mag.* July 256 Her dress and that of the children were mostly of faded snuff-colour. **1763** *Brit. Mag.* July 337/1 He next took up salt with the finger and thumb of his *snuff hand. **1695** Motteux tr. *St. Olon's Morocco* 65 His Face muffled up in a *Snuff-Handkerchief, of a dirty hue. [**1711** Swift *Jrnl. to Stella* 4 May, I have been a mighty handkerchief-monger, and have bought abundance of snuff ones since I have left off taking snuff.] **1849** *Zoologist* VII. 2393 The pochard is a '*snuff-headed wigeon'. **1683** *Lond. Gaz.* No. 1800/4 *Snuffmaker and Perfumer. **1764** *Ann. Reg.* 108 A dreadful fire broke out in the workshop of a snuff-maker. **1822** (*title*), The British Perfumer, *Snuff-Manufacturer, and Colourman's Guide. **1818** Scott *Hrt. Midl.* xxxv, My worthy *snuff-merchant. **1678** Butler *Hud.* iii. ii. 1006 After h'ad ministred a Dose Of *Snuff-Mundungus, to his Nose. **1711** Swift *Wks.* (1824) II. 407 A fine *snuff-rasp of ivory. **1859** Fairholt *Tobacco* (1876) 244 A similar snuff-rasp to this. **1767** S. Paterson *Another Trav.* I. 192, I had recruited myself at one of the best *snuff-shops in Bruges. **1802** *Edin. Rev.* I. 109 Doomed to quiet repose in a snuff-shop. **1892** Rider Haggard *Nada* xx. 166 Watching the two of them over the edge of my *snuff-spoon. **1914** Joyce *Dubliners* 13 The red handkerchief,..blackened..with the *snuff-stains of a week. **1791** Wolcot (P. Pindar) *Magpie & Robin* Wks. 1812 II. 473 With *snuff-stain'd neckcloth. **1879** Tourgee *Fool's Err.* (1883) 43 She had a *snuff-stick in her mouth. **1710** *Tatler* No. 141 ¶6 The Whetter is obliged to refresh himself every moment with a liquor, as the *Snuff-taker with a powder. **1857** E. B. Ramsay *Reminisc. Scot. Life & C.* iii, The inveterate snuff-taker. **1775** Ash, **Snuff-taking*, the act or practice of taking snuff. *a* **1797** in *Encycl. Brit.* (ed. 3) XVII. 565 Allowing 16 hours to a snuff-taking day. **1801** Southey *Lett.* (1856) I. 174 As I have written a reasoning defence of snuff-taking. **1813** *Examiner* 17 May 318/1 The reader has heard of his inordinate snuff-takings. **1886** *Pall Mall G.* 10 Aug. 11/3 *Snuff-using..is on the decline. **1812** J. Smyth *Pract. Customs* (1821) 259 No Tobacco Stalks or *Snuff-work allowed to be imported on penalty of forfeiture.

**5.** Special combs.: **snuff-bean**, the tonka-bean, used for scenting snuff; one of these kept in a snuff-box for this purpose; **snuff-dipper** *U.S.* (see quot. 1859); also ***snuff-dipping***; **snuff-gourd**, a bottle gourd, the dried shell of the fruit of *Lagenaria siceraria*, a white-flowered annual vine; = *snuff-box gourd* s.v. snuff-box 3; **snuffman**, a dealer in snuff; **snuff-paper** (in contemptuous use), bank-notes; **snuff-swab** *U.S.* (see quot.).

**1898** in *Eng. Dial. Dict.* s.v., In the corner o' his mull there aye lay buried a scentit *snuff-bean. **1845** T. J. Green *Texian Exped.* x. 137 We believe the most filthy of all practices is that of your..'*snuff-dippers'. **1859** Bartlett *Dict. Amer.* (ed. 2) 424 *Snuff-dipper*, one who makes a practice of chewing snuff. **1896** *Amer. Missionary* Oct. 324 One sister who had been a snuff-dipper for more than twenty years. **1860** E. M. Cowell *Jrnl.* 22 Apr. in M. W. Disher *Cowells in Amer.* (1934) 65 The ladies have a habit.., '*snuff dipping' which is openly practised in the South, and privately indulged in, in the North. **1896** *Amer. Missionary* Oct. 324 The vile habit of snuff-dipping. **1901** Kipling *Kim* iv. 99 The lama dipped deep into his *snuff-gourd. **1921** *United Free Church Missionary Rec.* June 190/2 Her dress consists simply of a ragged apron of goatskin, and a snuff-gourd hung round her neck. **1723** *Lond. Gaz.* No. 6195/7 Abraham Carcas,..*Snuffman. **1852** Savage *R. Medlicott* iii. i, The shop of a snuffman of the present day. **1826** Scott *Mal. Malagr.* iii. 8 The want of gold, to supply the place of that *snuff-paper of yours. **1872** De Vere *Americanisms* 63 The dipping-stick is also called *snuff-swab.

**snuff**, *int. Sc.* = stuff *int.*

**1725** Ramsay *Gentle Sheph.* ii. i, Spin! Snuff!—Gae break your wheel. **1807–10** R. Tannahill *Poems* (1846) 21 Toot, snuff! 'bout news ye needna be sae thrang.

**snuff** (snʌf), *v.*¹ Also 5–6 **snoffe**, 6–7 **snuffe.** [f. snuff *sb.*¹ LG. *snuppen*, G. *schnuppen*, are used as in sense 1.]

**1. a.** *trans.* To free (a candle, wick, etc.) from the snuff, by pinching or cutting this off, or removing it with a special instrument.

*c* **1450** in Aungier *Syon* (1840) 367 To lyghte and quenche the tapers and candles, and snoffe them. **1465** *Mann. & Househ. Exp.* (Roxb.) 492 Item, the same day my master bowt a snoffer to snoffe wyth candeles. **1530** Palsgr. 724/1 Snoffe the candell, I can nat se to write els. **1573** R. Lever in Luckombe *Hist. Print.* (1771) 111 The first lighteth the candle..and the second doth but snuff it. **1652** N. Culverwel *Lt. Nature* i. ii. (1661) 9 Some unskilful ones, while they go about to snuff the Candle,..put it out. **1691** T. Birch *Life Boyle* B.'s Wks. 1772 I. p. cxxxiv, When the candles are newly snuffed and so the light increased. **1753** Hanway *Trav.* iii. xxxiii. (1762) I. 151 In the middle of the room..was one large wax-candle; which they snuffed with scissers. **1793** *Phil. Trans.* LXXXIV. 100 The candle being occasionally snuffed when it appeared to stand in need of it. **1815** J. Smith *Panorama Sci. & Art* II. 316 The candle or lamp..should have a thick wick, which should be snuffed clean. **1841** Dickens *Barn. Rudge* x, John..placed a pair of ..candlesticks on the table, and snuffed the lights they held. **1887** T. A. Trollope *What I remember* I. i. 26 Two tallow candles, requiring to be snuffed by snuffers lying in a little plated tray.

*absol.* **1637** Heywood *Pleas. Dial.* Wks. 1874 VI. 321 To cleare the taper, if you snuffe too deepe, Out goes the light.

**b.** *fig.* To make clearer or brighter; to purge.

**1574** Hellowes *Gueuara's Fam. Ep.* (1577) 355 It shall not be ouermuch..euerie weeke..once or twice to purge and snuffe the soule. **1577** tr. *Bullinger's Decades* (1592) 348 The ministers of Christ must be..throughly snuffed from all affections of the flesh. **1651** Hobbes *Leviath.* i. v. 22 By exact definitions first snuffed, and purged from ambiguity. *a* **1715** Halifax *On C'tess Dowager of **** 5 Mopsa..Sets up for charming, in her fading days; Snuffs her dim eyes to give one parting blow.

**c.** To suppress temporarily. *rare*⁻¹.

**1650** Fuller *Pisgah* i. x. 33 The Babylonish captivity did onely snuffe Judah for seventy years.

**d.** *slang.* = sense 2 d below.

**1973** C. Alverson *Fighting Back* xxv. 129 Wait'll you see what you've got when Speranza finds out that you put Gino in a position to get snuffed. **1976** F. Warner *Killing Time* i. i. 7 They had to sneak over and come back with a prisoner, and most got snuffed themselves. **1978** T. Gifford *Glendower Legacy* (1979) 158 We should have snuffed this little shit when we had the chance.

**2.** With *out*: †**a.** To remove by snuffing. *Obs.*

*c* **1430** *Wycliffite Bible* Exod. xxv. 38 Where tho thingis, that ben snottid [*v.r.* snuffid] out, ben quenchid.

**b.** To extinguish, put out; to cause to go out or disappear from sight.

**1687** Miége *Gt. Fr. Dict.* ii, To snuff out the Candle. **1818** Byron *Juan* xi. lx, 'Tis strange the mind, that fiery particle, Should let itself be snuff'd out by an article. **1841** Dickens *Barn. Rudge* iii, Slight yellow specks, that seemed to be rapidly snuffed out one by one. **1890** *Science-Gossip* XXVI. 271 During these occultations the light of the star is instantaneously snuffed out, as it were, when overtaken by the moon's limb.

**c.** To eclipse, efface, wipe out; to terminate (life).

**1852** Hawker *Diary* (1893) II. 340, I hope to see the Minié snuffed out, no matter by whom. **1873** C. M. Davies *Unorthodox London* I. 46 At first the attempt was made to 'snuff out' 'The Sling and the Stone'. **1874** L. Stephen *Hours in Libr.* (1892) II. v. 149 A silly coxcombry to be.. snuffed out by the worldly cynicism of the new generation. **1929** Hall & Niles *One Man's War* iii. 25 We..knew..that many lives would be snuffed out ere long. **1981** *Telegraph* (Brisbane) 23 Jan. 4/5 A prosecution witness today admitted she was content that the life of the man known as 'Mr Asia' should be snuffed out.

**d.** *slang.* To kill, to murder.

**1932** E. Wallace *When Gangs came to London* xxviii. 285 Eddie would have snuffed out Cora. **1973** *Philadelphia Inquirer* 7 Oct. (Today Suppl.) 12/1 'You're saying you're going to snuff that guy out before you know?'..'The people who are murdered didn't get an equal chance.' **1980** E. Behr *Getting Even* xv. 174 If I cause too much embarrassment, they'll just snuff me out.

**3. a.** *intr.* To die. *slang* or *colloq.* Also const. *out.*

**1865** *Slang Dict.* 239 *Snuff out*, to die. **1895** A. C. Bicknell *Trav. N. Queensland* xxi. 186 The old man was very feeble, and looked like snuffing out before he had completed his story. **1916** C. J. Dennis *Songs of Sentimental Bloke* v. 43 They think she's snuffed, an' plant 'er in 'er tomb.

**b.** With *it*: = prec. *slang.*

**1885** Sims *Rogues & Vagabonds* iv. 21 Josh Heckett isn't going to snuff it just for a crack on the head. **1896** *Daily News* 26 Mar. 6/4, I have the pleasure to inform you that your mother-in-law snuffed it.

**snuff** (snʌf), *v.*[2] Also 6 snoffe, 6–7 snuffe. [prob. ad. MDu. *snoffen, snuffen* to snuffle, etc., corresponding to G. dial. *schnuffen, †schnüffen* (cf. also LG. and MHG. *snûfen*, G. *schnaufen*), either of imitative origin, or related to MDu. *snuven*, etc.: see SNUVE *v.* In sense 8 perhaps directly from SNUFF *sb.*[3]]

**I.** *trans.* **1.** To draw *up* or *in* through the nostrils by the action of inhalation.

**1527** ANDREW *Brunswyke's Distyll. Waters* D iv, The same water snuffed upward in the nose is very good to puryfye the hede. **1555** EDEN *Decades* (Arb.) 101 Snuffinge vp into theyr nosethryls the pouder. **1579** E. K. *Gloss. Spenser's Sheph. Cal.* Feb. 75 *Venteth*, snuffeth in the wind. **1608** D. T. *Ess. Pol. & Mor.* 59b, For euen so likewise may those little Atomies be snuft vp with the ayre. **1632** tr. *Bruel's Praxis Med.* 151 We will make a powder..and snuffe this vp into the nose. **1697** *Phil. Trans.* XIX. 681 The Juice of this Weed being snuft up the Nose, is good to make one sneeze. **1746** BERKELEY *Sec. Let. Tar-water* §15 Tar-water hath been snuffed up the nostrils. **1782** MISS BURNEY *Cecilia* IX. i, Then I take a walk..and snuff in a little fresh country air. **1818** SCOTT *Rob Roy* xxviii, Snuffing up his breath through his nose. **1872** HUXLEY *Physiol.* viii. 197 When we wish to perceive a faint odour more distinctly, we sniff, or snuff up the air.

*fig.* **1629** H. BURTON *Truth's Triumph* 224 These Pontificians..snuffing vp the winde of vaine opinions. **1639** G. DANIEL *Vervic.* 485 Like to those Who put on Sullen lookes, and grumble short, Who Snuffe poore Women vp, with a hot Nose.

**2.** To inhale, draw up, into or through the nostrils.

*to snuff pepper*: see PEPPER *sb.* 4 b.

**1547** BOORDE *Brev. Health* §264 The pouder of Peper.. snuft or blowen into the nose doth make quycke sternutacions. **1615** ROWLANDS *Melancholie Knt.* 13 Snuffe some into your nostrils till you neese. **1642** H. MORE *Song of Soul* III. I. xxix, The nostrills snuff perfumed wind. **1726** POPE *Odyss.* XIX. 508 The pack impatient snuff the tainted gale. **1774** NICHOLLS in *Corresp. w. Gray* (1843) 175 There I snuffed once more the fragrance of that air. **1814** SCOTT *Wav.* xxxviii, The leading Highlander snuffed the wind like a setting spaniel. **1870** MORRIS *Earthly Par.* III. IV. 239 The Persian merchants stood and snuffed the scent Of frankincense.

*fig.* **1844** DISRAELI *Coningsby* IX. vi. 325 They snuffed the factious air, and felt the coming storm.

**b.** To draw *out* by snuffing. *rare*⁻¹.

**1648** HEXHAM II, *Snuyven, ofte snuffen*, to Snuffe out the Snot or Filth out of ones Nose.

†**3.** To clear (the nose) by inhalation. *Obs.*

**1561** HOLLYBUSH *Hom. Apoth.* 3 If he can not snoffe his nose. **1653** URQUHART *Rabelais* I. xx, Master Janotus with his Adherents vowed never to blow or snuffe their noses, until judgement were given.

**4.** To detect, perceive, or anticipate, by inhaling the odour of. Also freq. *fig.*

**1697** DRYDEN *Virg. Georg.* I. 519 The Cow..from afar can find The Change of Heav'n, and snuffs it in the Wind. *a* **1763** SHENSTONE *Elegies* xxii. 82 E'en now the villain snuffs his wonted prey. **1790** P. FRANCIS in *Four C. Eng. Lett.* (1880) 307, I snuff it [i.e. mischief] in the wind. I taste it already. **1810** SOUTHEY *Kehama* VI. i, What if the hungry tiger..Should snuff his banquet nigh? **1830** GEN. P. THOMPSON *Exerc.* (1842) I. 287 The high church and the tories snuff the possibility of another revolutionary war. **1863** W. C. BALDWIN *Afr. Hunting* ii. 41 The old bull snuffed danger in the wind.

**5.** To smell at, examine by smelling.

**1859** BROWN *Rab & Fr.* §11 He [a dog]..snuffed him all over. **1874** BLACKIE *Self Cult.* 29 Like the racing of some little dog about the moor, snuffing everything and catching nothing. **1888** T. FROST *Country Journalist* iii. 34 He observed a dog..snuff the earth at the edge of the swampy ground.

**II.** *intr.* **6.** To draw air, etc., into the nostrils by an effort of inhalation; to do this in order to smell something. Also const. *after, at.*

α. **1530** PALSGR. 724/1, I snoffe, as a man doth, or a horse, *je reniffle*. Herke how he snoffeth. **1535** COVERDALE *Jer.* ii. 23 Like a wilde Asse..that snoffeth and bloweth.

β. *c* **1530** LD. BERNERS *Arth. Lyt. Bryt.* (1814) 163 Than sir Isembarte..snuffed in the nose, and bette togyder his teth. **1553** *Respublica* III. iv. 775 Come the devill, yf hym luste, staring and snuffing. **1614** B. JONSON *Bart. Fair* II. v, Go, snuffe after your brothers bitch. **1672** VILLIERS (Dk. Buckhm.) *Rehearsal* I. (Arb.) 43 So Boar and Sow, when any storm is nigh, Snuff up, and smell it gath'ring in the Skie. *a* **1720** SEWEL *Hist. Quakers* (1795) II. VII. 61 But the bull snuffing, went a little back. *a* **1761** CAWTHORNE *Antiquarians* 265 Quick to his side he flies amain, And peeps, and snuffs, and peeps again. **1826** SCOTT *Woodst.* iii, The good hound ..continued to snuff around Joseph Tomkins's cloak. **1863** W. C. BALDWIN *Afr. Hunting* ix. 389 He elevated head and tail, snuffed, trotted, and snorted. **1879** BEERBOHM *Patagonia* iv. 61, I woke, roused by some horse which..was snuffing at me curiously.

**b.** Const. *up* one's nose.

**1714** in Addison *Lover* No. 10, He will also snuff up his nose and spit it out as he eats. **1741** CHESTERF. *Lett.* 25 July, Tricks such as snuffing up his nose. **1756** C. SMART tr. *Horace, Sat.* II. vii. (1826) II. 161, I am easily seduced by my appetite; I snuff up my nose at a savoury smell.

**7.** To express scorn, disdain, or contempt by snuffing; to sniff. Freq. const. *at* a thing or person. Now *rare* or *Obs.*

(*a*) **1544** PHAER *Bk. Childr.* (1553) A ij, Suche..will doo nothinge but detract and iudge other, snuffing at all that offendeth the noses. **1575** GASCOIGNE *Glasse of Govt.* Wks. 1910 II. 69 That one being ignorant of that others punishment, shall never grudge or snuffe at the same. **1643** *Lismore Papers* Ser. II. (1888) V. 139 Being snuffed at by some great ones, none of the rest wold signe. **1677** GILPIN *Demonol. Sacra* (1867) 107 Satan first presented these services as a wearisome burden, then they snuffed at them.

(*b*) **1567** DRANT *Horace, Ep.* De Arte Poet. A vij, The noble, honorable rytche..will snuffe, and take it peper in the nose. **1579** TOMSON *Calvin's Serm. Tim.* 61/2 Cursssed shall he be, that shal dare to snuffe against his creator. **1607** HIERON *Wks.* I. 332 When the word of God is preached,.. many worldlings begin by and by to snuffe. **1674** BUNYAN *Christ. Behaviour* Wks. 1852 II. 568 It argueth pride when ..thou snuffest and givest way to thy spirit to be peevish. **1809** MALKIN *Gil Blas* XII. vi. (Rtldg.) 431 If any of my acquaintance should snuff or snigger when they call me Don.

**8.** To inhale powdered tobacco; to take snuff.

**1725** RAMSAY *Gentle Sheph.* III. ii. Prol., The auld anes think it best..to..Snuff, crack, and take their rest. **1826** DISRAELI *V. Grey* V. ii, 'Do you snuff?' and here he extended to Vivian a gold box. **1858** E. B. RAMSAY *Reminisc. Scot. Life & Char.* v, I hope you do not let him *snuff* so much as he did. **1881** DU CHAILLU *Land Midnight Sun* II. 92 The men and women snoked and snuffed a great deal.

**snuff,** *v.*[3] *Cant.* [f. SNUFF *sb.*[3] I.] *intr.* To blind (a shopkeeper) with snuff in order to steal.

**1812** J. H. VAUX *Flash Dict.* s.v. *Snuffing.*

**snuff,** *v.*[4] *techn.* [Of obscure origin.] *trans.* To smooth (leather) in the process of currying.

**1897** C. T. DAVIS *Manuf. Leather* 429 The leather is then set out either by machine or hand, and hung to dry, and when dry..is taken down and snuffed with a buffing slicker.

**'snuff-box.** [SNUFF *sb.*[3] I.]

**1. a.** A box for holding snuff, usually small enough to be carried in the pocket.

**1687** MIÉGE *Gt. Fr. Dict.* II, A Snuff-box, *une Tabatiere.* **1707** *Refl. upon Ridicule* 207 The Snuff-boxes she has in Pockets, and the Profusion she makes of Snuff. **1711** 'J. DISTAFF' *Char. Don Sacheverellio* 4, I have heard the Lid of a Beau's Snuff-Box crack in his Pocket. **1786** MME. D'ARBLAY *Diary* 25 July, She had brought the Queen's snuff-box, to be filled with some snuff. **1837** DICKENS *Pickw.* ii, Colonel Bulder and Sir Thomas Clubber exchanged snuff-boxes. **1846** MCCULLOCH *Brit. Empire* (1854) I. 293 Those beautifully jointed and varnished wooden snuff-boxes, long in universal demand. **1882** SERGT. BALLANTINE *Exper.* xxiii. 221 The owner of the snuff-box is the proprietor of the hall.

**b.** ***musical snuff-box***, one fitted with mechanism capable of playing tunes.

**1825** T. HOOK *Sayings* Ser. II. *Passion & Princ.* ix. III. 139 It was actually handed round the room like a musical snuff-box, or any other indifferent trinket. **1852** R. S. SURTEES *Sponge's Sp. Tour* l, The child, who had been wound up like a musical snuff-box, then went off as follows. **1881** *Grove's Dict. Music* III. 542.

**c.** A puff-ball or similar fungus; usually ***devils' snuff-box*** (see DEVIL *sb.* 25 c.).

**1883–** in Hampshire and Somerset glossaries.

**2.** *slang.* The nose.

**1829** P. EGAN *Boxiana* 2nd Ser. II. 251 He came up with a frown..and, without the slightest ceremony, opened with a fillip on the Gipsy's snuff-box. **1853** 'C. BEDE' *Verdant Green* I. xvi, There's a crack on your snuff-box.

**3.** *attrib.* and *Comb.*, as ***snuff-box maker, painting, wright***; **snuff-box bean**, a species of sea-bean used medicinally, or the plant producing this; **snuff-box gourd**, a species of *Lagenaria*.

**1714** *Lond. Gaz.* No. 5268/10 Snuff-box-maker. **1765** H. WALPOLE *Lett.* (1840) V. 68 Snuff-box-wrights, milliners, &c. **1884** *Athenæum* 9 Aug. 183/3 After a trial of snuff-box painting at Mauchline, Leitch came to London. **1884** *De Candolle's Orig. Cultivated Pl.* 245 Other less common varieties have a flattened, very small fruit, like the snuff-box gourd.

Hence **'snuff-boxer**, a seller of snuff-boxes.

*a* **1871** DE MORGAN *Budget Parad.* (1872) 153 Fifty years ago a fashionable snuff-boxer would be under inducement ..to have a stock with very objectionable pictures.

**snuff-coloured,** *a.* [SNUFF *sb.*[3] I.] Of the colour of snuff; brown, brownish.

Cf. *snuff-colour* s.v. SNUFF *sb.*[3] 4.

**1787** LATHAM *Suppl. Gen. Syn. Birds* I. 129 Snuff-coloured Creeper... The head, neck, and back, are of a deep cinnamon, or snuff-colour. **1803** SYD. SMITH *Delphine* Wks. 1859 I. 45 A grave old gentleman, in a peruke and snuff-coloured clothes. **1860** *All Year Round* No. 65. 351 A man in a high and long snuff-coloured coat. **1892** E. REEVES *Homew. Bound* 80 Dressed in deep snuff-coloured trousers and loose blouse or coat.

**snuff-dish.** [SNUFF *sb.*[1] I.] A dish to hold the snuff of candles or lamps; a snuffer-tray.

**1560** BIBLE (Geneva) *Exod.* xxxvii. 23 And he made for it seuen lampes with ye snuffers, & snufdishes thereof of pure gold. **1611** —— *Exod.* xxv. 38 And the tongs thereof, and the snuffe dishes therof shalbe of pure gold. **1667** PEPYS *Diary* 2 Feb., This night comes home my new silver snuffe-dish, which I do give myself for my closet. **1707** *Lond. Gaz.* No. 4379/4 One Pair of Snuffers and Snuff Dish. **1800** MAR. EDGEWORTH *Parent's Assist.* (1831) II. 207, I was hunting for the snuff-dish; as I knew it must be for candles.

**snuffer**[1] ('snʌfə(r)). Also 5–6 snoffer. [f. SNUFF *v.*[1]]

**1. a.** An instrument used for snuffing, or snuffing out, candles, etc. In later use only in plur. form (also ***a pair of snuffers***).

α. **1465** *Mann. & Househ. Exp.* (Roxb.) 492 Item, the same day my master bowt a snoffer to snoffe wyth candeles. **1517–8** *Rec. St. Mary at Hill* (1905) 296 Paid..for Snoffers of plate for to put owte the tapurs. **1535** COVERDALE *Exod.* xxv. 38 Snoffers and out quenchers of pure golde. **1574** *Churchw. Acc. St. Edmund's, Sarum* (Wilts. Rec. Soc.) 82 The makynge of the Snoffer to serve candelles in the churche.

β. **1538** ELYOT, *Emunctorium*, an instrumente [etc.].., a snuffer. **1596** HARINGTON *Metam. Ajax* (1814) 106 Like to the snuffers or extinguishers wherewith we put out a candle. **1656** W. DU GARD tr. *Comenius' Gate Lat. Unl.* 225 The snuffers ready at hand, to snuff the wick ever and anon. **1687** CHERNOCK in *Magd. Coll.* (O.H.S.) 232 Why did you tear the Buttery book with the snuffers? **1747** FRANKLIN *Lett.* Wks. 1887 II. 72 We light candles, just blown out, by drawing a spark among the smoke between the wire and snuffers. **1764** J. FERGUSON *Lect.* iii. 33 To this kind of lever may be reduced several sorts of instruments, such as scissars, pinchers, snuffers. **1860** MAYHEW *Upper Rhine* Introd. 3 Here it is that our eyes are still cheered with the sight of a pair of snuffers. **1885** *Athenæum* 7 Feb. 189 In [Hogarth's] 'Night' the small man..is known by the snuffers hanging at his girdle to be a drawer at a tavern.

*fig.* **1630** LENNARD tr. *Charron's Wisd.* I. Pref. 6 Sounding him to the quick, entring into him with a candle and a snuffer. **1642** HOWELL *For. Trav.* (Arb.) 77 If these Lights grow dim, there is a Trienniall Snuffer for them. **1827** HARE *Guesses* Ser. I. (1873) 10 A critic should be a pair of snuffers. He is oftener an extinguisher.

**b.** *transf.* The finger and thumb as used for clearing or wiping the nose.

**1843** MARRYAT *M. Violet* xxvii, Employing..the pair of snuffers which natural instinct has supplied him with.

**2.** One who snuffs candles. (Cf. CANDLE-SNUFFER 2.)

**1611** COTGR., *Moucheur*, a snyter, wiper, snuffer. **1722–7** BOYER *Dict. Royal* I. s.v. *Moucheur*, The Snuffer, He that snuffs the Candles at the Play-house. **1761** CHURCHILL *Rosciad* Poems 1769 I. 14 Then came..snuffer, sweeper, shifter, soldier, mute. **1762** FOOTE *Orator* I. Wks. 1799 I. 191 What is all this business about here? *Snuffer.* Can't say, Sir. **1814** W. WILSON *Hist. Dissent. Churches* iv. 78 Betty Gray had been a snuffer of candles at the playhouse.

**3.** *attrib.* and *Comb.* (in sense 1), as ***snuffer(s)-box, -dish, -handle, -pan, -stand, -tray; snuffers-maker.***

**1677** *Lond. Gaz.* No. 1260/4 Two large silver Candlesticks, and Snuffer Pan. **1686** *Ibid.* No. 2203/4 A Silver Snuffer-dish and Snuffers chain'd. **1773** *Lond. Chron.* 7 Sept. 248/3 The following articles were assayed and marked;..bottle stands, snuffer pans [etc.]. **1830** GALT *Lawrie T.* II. i. (1849) 42 He took his cigar out of his mouth, ..trimming it on the edge of the snuffer-tray. **1843** *Ainsworth's Mag.* III. 180 Spectacle cases and snuffer-stands. **1844** *Civil Eng. & Arch. Jrnl.* VII. 130 Moulded per gross, like..snuffer-dishes, inkstands, metal buttons, and brads! **1858** SIMMONDS *Dict. Trade, Snuffers'-maker*, a manufacturer of metal snuffers. **1898** G. B. SHAW *Man of Destiny* 203 With a couple of candles alight, and a broad snuffers tray in the other. **1952** B. & T. HUGHES *Three Centuries of Eng. Domestic Silver* v. 82 The upright snuffer stand, with a vertical socket to receive the snuffer box, was a late Charles II innovation. *Ibid.* 84 An immense amount of ingenuity now began to be lavished upon the ornamentation of snuffer handles. **1960** H. HAYWARD *Handbk. Antique Coll.* 260/1 *Snuffer-tray*, oblong or oval tray with or without small feet and scroll and ring handle at side for holding snuffers. **1971** *Country Life* 10 June 1434/1 A snuffers tray inscribed four years after it was made 'In Memory of Mrs. Jane Parsons, Oct. 11th, 1750'.

**snuffer**[2] ('snʌfə(r)). [f. SNUFF *v.*[2]]

**1.** One who snuffs, or who sniffs disdainfully.

*a* **1610** BABINGTON *Wks.* (1622) 102 Let all snuffers and brow-beaters of honest men consider this. **1648** HEXHAM II, *Een Snuyver*, a Snuffer.

†**2.** *slang* or *dial.* In *pl.* The nostrils. *Obs.*

*a* **1658** CLEVELAND *Sing-song* xxvi, Sybill so sweet, Whose Cheeks on each side of her Snuffers did meet, As round and as plump as a Codlin. **1703** THORESBY *Let. to Ray* (E.D.S.), *Snuffers*, for the nose, or nostrils.

**3.** One who takes snuff.

**1882** J. SNODGRASS tr. *Heine's Relig. & Philos. in Germany* II. 89 You know that he [*sc.* Frederick the Great] composed French verses,..was a prodigious snuffer, and believed in nothing but cannon. **1889** GRETTON *Memory's Harkback* 99, I knew an elderly gentleman who was a great snuffer. **1903** R. LAWSON in R. Wallace *Life & Last Leaves* 628 He was an inveterate snuffer.

**4.** *U.S. local.* A porpoise.

**1829** T. C. HALIBURTON *Hist. & Statist. Acct. Nova-Scotia* II. ix. 404 Fish—Whale Species... Snuffer. **1884** GOODE *Nat. Hist. Aquat. Anim.* 14 On the Atlantic coast occurs most abundantly the little Harbor Porpoise, *Phocæna brachycion* Cope, known to the fishermen as 'Puffer', 'Snuffer', 'Snuffing Pig'.

**'snuffiness.** [f. SNUFFY *a.*[2]] The state of being snuffy.

Jamieson *Suppl.* (1825) gives '*Snuffiness*, sulkiness'.

**1834** CARLYLE in Froude *Hist. First 40 Years* (1882) II. 449 A tendency to pot-belly and snuffiness. **1885** *Even. Standard* 14 Nov. (Cassell), There is a snuffiness, a stuffiness, a general seediness about the former. **1891** *Daily News* 20 June 5/5 Pocket-handkerchiefs only came in with snuff, and were of coloured foulard to hide snuffiness.

**snuffing** ('snʌfɪŋ), *vbl. sb.*[1] [f. SNUFF *v.*[1]]

**1. a.** The action of removing the burnt part of a wick from a candle or lamp.

**1591** PERCIVALL *Sp. Dict.*, *Despavesadura*, the snuffing of a candle. **1638** QUARLES *Hieroglyphics* IV. i, Too much snuffing makes a wast. **1657** W. MORICE *Coena quasi Κοινὴ* xxi. 209 If the lights burn dimme, it is a wildness instead of snuffing to put them out. **1763** W. LEWIS *Phil. Comm. Arts* 28 The Lamps require frequent snuffing and smoke much. **1837** P. KEITH *Bot. Lex.* 360 The candle burns with a clear and brilliant flame, and the wick needs no snuffing. **1884** E. YATES *Recoll.* I. 44 Tallow-candles, which required snuffing ..about every quarter of an hour.

*fig.* **1641** MILTON *Reform.* I. Wks. 1851 III. 22 The dim Taper of this Emperours age that had such need of snuffing.

**b.** The burnt part of a wick which is removed with snuffers or otherwise. Also *fig.*

**1574** HELLOWES *Gueuara's Fam. Ep.* (1577) 357 The bason of gold, wherein they should bestow the snuffings of the lampes. **1652** N. CULVERWEL *Lt. Nature* I. xviii. (1661) 164 The snuffings of Nature, and Reason will never make up a Day. **1789** BUCHAN *Dom. Med.* (1790) 155 Many dirty things,..as spiders, cobwebs, snuffings of candles, &c. **1817** BYRON *Beppo* lxxv, These unquench'd snuffings of the midnight taper.

*attrib.* **1687** MIÉGE *Gt. Fr. Dict.* I, *Porte-mouchettes*,..a snuffing pan.

**2.** The action of putting *out* or extinguishing. **1881** *Nation* (N.Y.) XXXII. 442 The snuffing out of the school by a parietary regulation. **1897** *Advance* (Chicago) 29 July 144/1 The great triumph of Parnell, and his sad, inglorious snuffing-out.

**3.** With *out*: dying. **1922** P. A. ROLLINS *Cowboy* iii. 55 His demise was sometimes referred to as his 'snuffing out'..or 'passing in his checks'.

**snuffing** ('snʌfɪŋ), *vbl. sb.*[2] [f. SNUFF *v.*[2]]

**1.** The action of drawing in air through the nose; sniffing, snuffling. **1540** MORYSINE tr. *Vives' Introd. Wysd.* F iij b, What snuffynge of the nose, what grennynge of the tethe. **1609** W. M. *Man in Moon* (1849) 11 He..keepeth such a snuffing and puffing. *a* **1616** BEAUM. & FL. *Custom of Country* IV. iv, You seem to have a snuffing in your head Sir, A parlous snuffing. **1661** EVELYN *Fumifugium* (1825) 225 Is there under heaven such coughing and snuffing to be heard, as in the London churches and assemblies of people? **1860** MAYNE REID *Hunters' Feast* xxii, I heerd now and then the snuffin' o' the bar.

*fig.* **1573** G. HARVEY *Letter-bk.* (Camden) 32 Seeming nether to be ignorant of the contents of them [letters] nor of M. Nuces snuffing at them. *c* **1584** *Robinson's Handful Delights* (Arb.) 35 And do not snuffe though I be plaine,.. For huffing and snuffing deserueth blame.

**b.** *pl.* Mucus collected in this way. *rare*⁻¹. **1598** FLORIO, *Mocci*, the snots or snuffings of ones nose.

**2.** The action or practice of taking snuff. **1691** WOOD *Ath. Oxon.* II. 419 Intoxicated with bibbing, but more with talking, and snuffing with powder. **1830** MARRYAT *King's Own* xxxv, Snuffing's a vile habit,—I wish I could leave it off. **1859** *Habits of Gd. Society* vii. 252 Sneezing brings me to snuffing, which is an obsolete custom, retained only by a few old gentlemen. **1860** TRISTRAM *Grt. Sahara* xii. 203 Hence the prohibition of smoking, snuffing, and coffee.

**snuffing** ('snʌfɪŋ), *ppl. a.* Also 6 snoffyng. [f. SNUFF *v.*[2]] That snuffs, in various senses. *a* **1548** HALL *Chron., Hen. VIII*, 242 He was a man, that.. could not abide the snoffyng pride of some prelates. **1570** FOXE *A. & M.* II. 1360/1 These snuffing Prelates..hee could neuer abyde. *a* **1618** SYLVESTER *Job Triumphant* IV. 590 Canst thou his tongue with steely Crotchets thrill; Or with a Thorn his snuffing Nose, or Guill? **1683** *Lond. Gaz.* No. 1800/4 At the [sign of the] Jessamine-Tree and Snuffing-Gentleman. **1744** E. MOORE *Fables* vi. 90 Fear wings his flight; the marsh he sought, The snuffing dogs are set at fault. **1884** [see SNUFFER[2] 4].

Hence **'snuffingly** *adv.*, in a snuffing manner. **1577** STANYHURST *Descr. Irel.* i. in *Holinshed*, Here percase some snappish carper will..snuffingly snibbe me. **1891** *Harper's Mag.* Jan. 228/1 The dogs..went about with inquisitive, drooping noses..amongst the various gear which they snuffingly recognized.

**'snuffish,** *a.* *rare*⁻¹. [f. SNUFF *v.*[2]] Somewhat snuffy or touchy. **1689** *Pol. Ballads* (1860) II. 11 Commonwealth Wildman is Jack out of office, Sidney and Norfolk are grown very snuffish. **1727** BAILEY (vol. II), *Snuffish*, apt to take Exceptions at.

† **'snuffkin.** *Obs.* Forms: 5 snwf-, 5–7 snuf-, 6 snof-, 6–7 snuft-, 7 snuff(e)kin; also 5–6 -kyn. [Of obscure origin.] A muff. **1483** *Cath. Angl.* 347/2 A Snufkyn [*v.r.* Snwfkyn], *pellicudia, nebrida.* **1598** FLORIO, *Manicone*, a great sleeue, manchon, muffe or snufkin. **1599–1600** in Nichols *Progr. Q. Eliz.* (1805) III. 135 One snofkyn of crymson satten. **1602** *Entert. Harefield* in Lyly's Wks. 1902 I. 500 'Tis sommer, yet a snuffkin to your lott, But t'will be winter one day, doubte you nott. **1611** COTGR., *Bonne grace*,..a snufkin, or Muffe. **1694** MOTTEUX *Rabelais* IV. lii. (1737) 214 The Crepines of their Hoods, their Ruffles, Snuffekins, and Neck-Ruffs, new wash'd, starch'd, and iron'd.

† **snuffle,** var. of (or error for) SNAFFLE *sb.*[1] **1589** R. HARVEY *Pl. Perc.* 12 She will prepare a boisterous snuffle, for such boisterous head-strong Jaddes, as will be wincing.

**snuffle** ('snʌf(ə)l), *sb.* [f. the vb.]

† **1.** Surf or surge. *Obs.*⁻¹ **1630** CAPT. SMITH *Trav. & Adv.* 54 Such a snuffle of the Sea goeth on the shore, ten may better defend than fifty assault.

**2.** An (*or* the) act of snuffling. *a* **1764** LLOYD *Actor* Poet. Wks. 1774 I. 16/3 With shrug, wink, snuffle, and convulsive limb. **1809** MALKIN *Gil Blas* I. xii. ⁋3 What is a prison above-ground, after so brimstone a snuffle as thou hast had of the regions below? **1835** MARRYAT *J. Faithful* iii, It was an intellectual nose... Its snuffle was consequential, and its sneeze oracular. **1865** BARING-GOULD *Werewolves* viii. 126 She hears the tramping of his approaching feet, and the snuffle of his breath.

**3.** *pl.* A stopped condition of the nose, through a cold in the head or otherwise, causing a snuffling sound in the act of respiration. **1770** MRS. DELANY *Life & Corr.* Ser. II. (1861) I. 317 She has at present a little London cold, but her Grace says it is 'only the snuffles'. **1799** M. UNDERWOOD *Dis. Child.* (ed. 4) III. 107 The slightest symptom..is that called the Snuffles, or stoppage of the nose. **1845** DICKENS *Chimes* iv. 139 The nose afflicted with that disordered action of its functions which is generally termed the Snuffles. **1878** BRYANT *Pract. Surg.* II. 6 The snuffles in infancy are very characteristic.

**4.** A nasal tone in the voice. **1820** SCOTT *Monast.* v, With a hypocritical snuffle, and a sly twinkle of his eye. **1830** H. LEE *Mem. Manager* I. ii. 61 His spectacles..being rather too small for him..increased his natural snuffle. **1859** JEPHSON *Brittany* i. 3 The monotonous whine and snuffle of the children in the National School as they read.

*Comb.* **1889** DOYLE *M. Clarke* 94 Half-a-dozen broad-brimmed snuffle-nosed preachers.

**snuffle** ('snʌf(ə)l), *v.* [prob. ad. Du. and Flem. *snuffelen* (also †*snoffelen*), = Fris. *snuffelje*, LG. *snüffeln* (whence G. *schnüffeln, schnuffeln*) in similar senses: see SNUFF *v.*[2] and -LE.]

**I.** *intr.* † **1.** To show dislike or disdain by snuffing; to sniff *at* a thing in contempt. *Obs.* **1583** GREENE *Mamillia* Wks. (Grosart) II. 128 The young colt, at the first breaking, snuffles at the snaffle. **1600** BRETON *Strange Fort. Two Princes* Wks. (Grosart) II. 12/2 The wicked wretch..in a great rage, snuffling at his cold entertainment. **1609** HOLLAND *Amm. Marcell.* XXV. iv. 268 Making a speech on a time to his souldiors all armed, when they snuffled and became unruly. **1662** R. MATHEW *Unl. Alch.* 165, I know nice noses will snuffel at this Oyl as a thing most detestable.

**2.** To draw air into the nostrils in order to smell something; to snuff or smell *at* a thing. *c* **1600** CHALKHILL *Thealma & Cl.* (1683) 12 Their cry soon reacht his ear, And he came snuffling toward them. **1601** WEEVER *Mirr. Mart.* B iij b, I dream'd I wore a garland of greene willow. But snuffling low, I prickt me with a fether. **1825** SCOTT *Talism.* iii, The steeds..neighed and snuffled fondly around their masters. **1861** HUGHES *Tom Brown at Oxf.* iii, [The dog] went trotting about the room, and snuffling at Schloss's legs. **1889** RIDER HAGGARD *Allan's Wife* 278 The oxen..were very restless—they kept snuffling and blowing.

**3.** To speak through the nose; to have a nasal twang.

Sometimes taken as indicating hypocrisy or canting. *c* **1600** DAY *Begg. Bednall Gr.* III. ii, There's an odde fellow snuffels i' the nose that shows a motion about Bishops-gate. **1634** T. JOHNSON tr. *Parey's Chirurg.* XXIII. iv. (1678) 526 They cannot pronounce their words distinctly, but obscurely and snuffling. **1755** SMOLLETT *Quix.* II. III. viii, Would it not have been better..to cut off half their noses, even though they should snuffle in their speech? **1756** *Connoisseur* No. 126 ⁋6 Snuffling through the nose with an harmonious twang. **1848** THACKERAY *Van. Fair* xli, You would have thought it was the Countess's own Roman nose through which she snuffled. **1888** DOUGHTY *Arabia Deserta* I. 154 He snuffled in his holy talk like an honest Roundhead.

**4.** To draw up air or mucus through the nostrils in an audible or noisy manner. *c* **1600** *Tarlton's Jests* (1628) A 4, Who falling vpon his nose, broke it extremely, that euer after he snuffled in the head. **1611** COTGR., *Renifler*, to snuffle, or snifter often. **1707** J. STEVENS tr. *Quevedo's Com. Wks.* (1709) 435 He..was gaul'd and snuffled [Sp. *con mataduras y muermo*] because they had thrown Feathers into his Manger. **1835** *Politeness & Gd.-breeding* 53 Remember never to whisper, or snuffle and laugh. **1857** C. BRONTE *Professor* vii, How he did snuffle, snort, and wheeze! **1898** *Hutchinson's Arch. Surg.* IX. 141 The child, a girl,..at the age of a month began to snuffle.

† **5.** Of the wind: To blow in fitful gusts. *Obs.* **1633** T. JAMES *Voy.* 24 In the after-noone it began to snuffle and blow. **1781** ARCHER in *Naval Chron.* XI. 286 At eleven at night it began to snuffle, with a monstrous heavy appearance.

**II.** *trans.* **6.** To inhale, to clear, to search out or examine, by snuffling. **1599** A. M. tr. *Gabelhouer's Bk. Physicke* 11/2 Mixe all these.., & snuffle heerof a little in your Nose in the Morninges. **1667** DENHAM *Direct. Painter* II. 18 She shed no tears,.. But onely snuffling her Trunk Cartilaginous, From scaling Ladder she began a story. **1871** B. TAYLOR *Faust* (1875) I. xxii. 199 He snuffles all he snuffle can; 'He scents the Jesuits' traces'.

**7.** To utter, say, declare, etc., in a snuffling or nasal tone. **1641** in Nalson *Collect. Affairs State* (1683) II. 809 Those That snuffle their unlearned Zeal in Prose. **1826** SCOTT *Woodst.* xxxiii, 'I profess I do..,' snuffled the corporal. **1837** CARLYLE *Misc.* (1857) IV. 108 Even the old Marquis snuffles approval. **1865** —— *Fredk. Gt.* VII. vi. (1872) II. 321 Seckendorf..snuffled into him suggestions of mercy. **1892** ZANGWILL *Childr. Ghetto* I. 128 The scarecrow who shambled along snuffling 'Old clo'.

**b.** Similarly with *out* or *forth*. **1828** CUNNINGHAM *N.S. Wales* II. 205 On being questioned how he had existed, he snuffled out [etc.]. **1842** LOVER *Handy Andy* iii, She..snuffled forth at the astonished boy, 'Get out o' that, you dirty cur!' **1891** GOSSE *Gossip Libr.* iii. 33 A whining ballad snuffled out in the street at night by some unhappy minstrel.

**snuffler** ('snʌflə(r)). [f. prec. Cf. Du. *snuffelaar*, LG. *snüff(e)ler*, G. *schnüffler, schnuffler*.] One who snuffles or speaks through the nose; one who speaks cantingly. **1642** *Tom Nash his Ghost* Title-p., To the three scurvy Fellowes of the upstart Family of the Snufflers, Rufflers and Shufflers. **18..** T. MOORE *Canonization of St. B-tt-rw-rth* xiii, Call quickly together the whole tribe of Canters,.. Bring Shakers and Snufflers and Jumpers and Ranters. **1861** HUGHES *Tom Brown at Oxf.* xliv, I never was a snuffler; but this sort of life makes one serious. **1879** A. REED *Alice Bridge of Norwich* 211 'Down with canting snufflers!' began to be heard.

**'snuffless,** *a.* [f. SNUFF *sb.*[1] 1.] Of candles: Having no snuff. **1895** *Army & Navy Stores Price List* 10 Dips... Palmer's Snuffless.

**'snuffliness.** [f. SNUFFLY *a.*] The quality of being snuffly. **1862** J. A. SYMONDS *Let.* c 28 Feb. (1967) I. 336 Nothing cd have exceeded the snuffliness of my journey yesterday. I ..did my cold no good. **1873** MISS BROUGHTON *Nancy* II. 14 Speaking..with a snuffliness of tone, engendered by much crying.

**snuffling** ('snʌflɪŋ), *vbl. sb.* [f. SNUFFLE *v.*] The action of the verb, in various senses. **1580** BLUNDEVIL *Horsemanship* IV. iv. 3 b, Lowd snuffling in the nose, and casting out vapors at his nostrils. **1599** DALLAM in *Early Voy. Levant* (Hakluyt Soc.) 29 They made a great noyse with their snufflinge, and, in the ende, went Runing awaye. **1614–8** LATHAM *Falconry* (1633) 138 As you shall see cause, first in the head by snufling or sniting, or any other signes. **1702** BAYNARD *Cold Baths* II. (1709) 383 To speak without snuffling is hardly genteel. **1822** GOOD *Study Med.* (1829) I. 530 The coryza, or snuffling of old age, is precisely analogous to its ptyalism or drivelling. **1861** BUMSTEAD *Ven. Dis.* (1879) 747 The first indication..is the characteristic snuffling.

**snuffling** ('snʌflɪŋ), *ppl. a.* [f. SNUFFLE *v.*]

**1.** That snuffles; drawing air up the nose, or characterized by this. *a* **1586** SIDNEY *Arcadia* II. (1912) 216 A water spaniell.. came downe the river, shewing that he hunted for a duck, & with a snuffling grace. **1735** SOMERVILLE *Chase* I. 324 His Heart Beats quick; his snuffling Nose, his active Tail Attest his Joy. **1760** *Cautions & Adv. Officers of Army* 98 Little Good can be expected from him whose snuffling Nose, unbraced Nerves, and rotten Carcase, denote him fitter for his Grave..than for his Duty. **1800** HURDIS *Favourite Village* 33 What time the snuffling spaniel, as he runs, Pants freely. **1849** ALB. SMITH *Pottleton Legacy* (1854) 64 Little shrews peered with perking snuffling noses.

*fig.* **1869** BROWNING *Ring & Bk.* XI. 1502 Whose swine-like snuffling greed and grunting lust I had to wink at.

**2.** Speaking through the nose; canting, hypocritical, sanctimonious. *c* **1600** DAY *Begg. Bednall Gr.* IV. i, I think this snuffling slave flouts us. **1719** D'URFEY *Pills* (1872) IV. 124 A Pox of all these snuffling Knaves, That do our Sports despise. **1793** [see SNAFFLING *ppl. a.*]. **1820** W. IRVING *Sketch Bk.* (1859) 69 The service was performed by a snuffling well-fed vicar. **1849** MACAULAY *Hist. Eng.* iii. I. 399 The straight-haired, snuffling, whining saints, who christened their children out of the Book of Nehemiah. **1868** BP. WILBERFORCE in R. S. Wilberforce *Life* (1882) III. ix. 271, I have infinitely more sympathy..with his views concerning the Church than with those of the snuffling Puritan clique.

**3.** Coming or uttered through the nose; nasal. Also *fig.* **1819** SCOTT *Ivanhoe* vii, Answered the Prior, in a sort of snuffling tone. **1841** THACKERAY *Sec. Funeral Napoleon* iii, They chanted something in a weak, snuffling..manner. **1871** LOWELL *Study Wind.* (1886) 278 He bewails..in snuffling heroics.

Hence **'snufflingly** *adv.*, in a snuffling manner. **1619** R. WESTE *Bk. Demeanor* 57 in *Babees Bk.*, Nor practize snufflingly to speake. **1837** *New Monthly Mag.* L. 415 James shuffled, and snuffled,..and snufflingly said [etc.].

**snuffly** ('snʌflɪ), *a.* [f. SNUFFLE *v.*] Characterized by snuffling. **1873** MISS BROUGHTON *Nancy* III. 3, I still speak in a subdued and snuffly voice. **1883** —— *Belinda* I. vi, He has the threatenings of a snuffly cold.

**snuff-mill.** [SNUFF *sb.*[3] 1.]

**1.** *Sc.* A snuff-box, snuff-mull. *a* **1689** W. CLELAND *Poems* (1697) 12 (Jam.), Right well mounted of their gear:—With durk, and snap-work, and snuff-mill. **1707** LADY G. BAILLIE *Household Bk.* (1911) 18 For 3 snuf milnes £4. **1715** *Mar's Lament* in *Roxb. Ball.* (1888) VI. 621 Each man unto the spoyl he gat, some got plaids and snuff-mills in their pack. **1835** D. WEBSTER *Rhymes* 27 (E.D.D.), His snuff-mill was the horn o' ram.

**2.** A mill, or machine, for grinding tobacco into snuff. **1758** in *Jedburgh Gazette* (1906) 29 Sept. 3 Snuff and Waulk Miln, [rent] £7:0:0. **1839** URE *Dict. Arts* 1255 The sides of the snuff-mill have sharp ridges from the top to near the bottom. **1875** KNIGHT *Dict. Mech.* 2232/1 The snuff-mills of Holland are on a very large scale, and are impelled by wind.

**snuff-mull.** *Sc.* [See prec. 1, and MULL *sb.*[6]] A snuff-box. **1808** *Monthly Pantheon* I. 598/2 He was..famous for making Highland dirks and snuff mulls. **1827** SCOTT *Two Drovers* i, Some thrust out their snuff-mulls for the parting pinch. **1854** H. MILLER *Sch. & Schm.* v. (1857) 97 A number of curious little articles... Among the rest, Highland snuff-mulls. **1887** MCNEILL *Blawearie* 101 He.. drew his snuff-mull from his waistcoat pocket, gave three vicious taps on the lid of it [etc.].

**snuffy** ('snʌfɪ), *a.*[1] [f. SNUFF *v.*[2] or SNUFF *sb.*[1] 4.]

**1.** Annoyed, displeased; ready to take offence. **1678** MRS. BEHN *Sir Patient Fancy* IV. i, She left me in the very middle on't so snuffy I'll warrant. *a* **1700** B. E. *Dict. Cant. Crew*, *Captious*, Touchy, Snuffy. **1825** JAMIESON *Suppl.*, *Snuffie*, sulky, displeased; often *Snuffie-like*, Clydes[dale]. **1845** S. JUDD *Margaret* I. xiii, Don't be snuffy, Molly, none of your mulligrubs.

**2.** Of cattle or horses: excitable, spirited, wild. **1955** R. HOBSON *Nothing too Good* xviii. 186 Any ball-up or milling around business up in front of the mile-and-a-half line of snuffy range beef could easily cause the critters to split into the spruce. **1964** *Penguin Bk. Austral. Ballads* 131 I'll yard them snuffy cattle in a way that's safe to swear. **1973** R. Symons *Where Wagon Led* vi. xix. 290 When he worked, he worked. Otherwise he played, mostly at breaking-in the snuffy ones.

**snuffy** ('snʌfɪ), *a.*² [f. snuff *sb.*³]

Bailey (1727, vol. II) gives '*Snuffy*,.. dawbed with Snuff', an earlier instance of either 2a or 2b.

**1.** Like, or resembling, snuff or powdered tobacco in colour or substance.

**1789** T. Williams *Min. Kingd.* I. 285 A brownish ferruginous soft soil, of a snuffy appearance. **1860** Sala *Baddington Peerage* i, They were mostly bright yellow, or of that peculiar shade of green known as 'snuffy'. **1872** Coues *N. Amer. Birds* 290 Head snuffy-brown, and no white patch in front of the eye. **1884** *Harper's Mag.* Mar. 522/2 A black or snuffy dust.

**2. a.** Of persons: Given to taking snuff; bearing marks of the habit of snuff-taking.

*c* **1790** A. Wilson *Watty & Meg* Poet. Wks. (*c* 1846) 151 Nasty, gude-for-naething being! O ye snuffy, drucken sow! **1826** Disraeli *V. Grey* iii. vii. 118 A little odd-looking snuffy old man, with a brown scratch wig. **1848** Thackeray *Trav. Lond.* Wks. 1886 XXIV. 349 Dinners where you meet ..a Knight, and a snuffy little old General. **1888** Mrs. H. Ward *R. Elsmere* 309 Two well-known English antiquarians —very learned, very jealous, and very snuffy.

**b.** Of things: Soiled with snuff. Also *fig.*

**1765** Sterne *Tr. Shandy* VIII. 51 A plan.. upon the lower corner of which.. there is still remaining the marks of a snuffy finger and thumb. **1840** Thackeray *Shabby-genteel Story* i, A snuffy shirt-frill, and enormous breast-pin. *a* **1846** B. R. Haydon *Autobiogr.* (1927) iii. xiii. 229 Brighton gay, gambling, dissipated.. Dieppe dark, old, snuffy and picturesque. **1856** Ld. Cockburn *Mem.* i. (1874) 46 His old snuffy black clothes,.. and his thread-bare blue great-coat. **1885** *Harper's Mag.* Mar. 563/2 [She] pulled out a snuffy pocket-handkerchief. **1925** E. Sitwell *Troy Park* 67 Trees periwigged and snuffy.

**3.** 'Tipsy, drunk' (*Slang Dict.* 1864).

**1823** 'J. Bee' *Slang* 162 *Snuffy*—drunk, with a nasal delivery. *Snuffy*—drunk in the feminine application, and applied but seldom to puling fellows. **1891** *Newcastle Even. Chron.* 30 Jan. 4/6 He considered, if a member got 'snuffy', he should go home, and not come there to annoy the meeting.

**snuft**, *sb. dial.* [variant of snuff *sb.*¹] †**a.** (See quot. 1611.) *Obs.* **b.** The snuff of a candle or the like.

**1611** Cotgr., *Camoufflet*, a Snuft, or cold Pie; a smoakie paper held vnder the nose of a slug, or sleeper. **1657** Reeve *God's Plea* 126 The candle doth yet give a glorious light, we are loth to think of the snuft. **1874** Waugh *Chimney Corner* (1879) 146 He went out as quiet as th' snuft o' a candle. **1881-** in dial. glossaries (Lanc., Chesh., Nott., Leic.).

**snuft**, *v. dial.* [var. of snuff *v.*²] *intr.* To smell, sniff.

**1820** Clare *Rural Life* (ed. 3) 107 As snifting and snufting the clodhopper goes. **1854-** in dial. glossaries (Northampt., Leic., Chesh.).

†**snufter**, *sb. Obs.* [Cf. snuft *sb.*] A snuffer.

**1558** *Lanc. Wills* (Chetham) I. 176 On snufter for candelle.

'**snufter**, *v. dial.* [var. of snifter *v.*] *intr.* To sniff, snuff. Hence '**snuftering** *vbl. sb.*

**1611** Cotgr., *Esbrouëment*,.. a snurting, or snuftering with the nose. *Esbrouër des narines*, to snurt, or snufter. **1632** Sherwood, To snuffe, or snufter often, *renifler, ressimer.* **1876-** in dial. glossaries (Northumbld., Yorksh.).

**snuftkin**, variant of snuffkin.

**snug** (snʌg), *sb.*¹ [Of obscure origin: cf. snag *sb.*]

**1.** A rugged projection; a hard knob or knot; a snag. *rare.*

**1665** Bunyan *Holy City* xv. (1669) 107 There shall be a smooth Face upon the whole Earth, all Snugs, and Hubs, and Hills.. shall now be took away. *a* **1800** *Devon Gloss.* in Halliw. s.v. *Snag*, A snagg, *vel* snugg, a hard wooden ball, commonly some gnurre, knobb, or knott of a tree, which they [boys] make use of at the play of bandy instead of a ball. **1808** Jamieson, *Snugs*, small branches lopped off from a tree.

**2.** *techn.* A projection or ridge cast on a plate, bolt, etc., in order to keep something in position, prevent rotation, or for some similar purpose.

**1843** *Civil Eng. & Arch. Jrnl.* VI. 138/2 Instead of the flanges there are 'snugs' on the tumbler between the chains to keep them on. **1844** H. Stephens *Bk. Farm* II. 214 On the top bar of the frames there are two strong snugs.. cast, sufficient to resist the pressure of the rollers. **1887** D. A. Low *Machine Draw.* (1892) 17 The snug fits into a short groove cut in the side of the hole.

*attrib.* *c* **1850** *Rudim. Nav.* (Weale) 134 *Deck nails*.. have snug heads.

**snug** (snʌg), *sb.*² [f. snug *a.*¹]

**1.** ***the snug***, that which is comfortable, quiet, or private. ***upon the snug***, privately. *rare.*

**1757** S. Foote *Author* i. i. 8 You love the snug, the Chimney-Corner of Life; and retire to this obscure Nook. **1768** *Woman of Honor* I. 187, I escaped from those scenes of tasteless enjoyment.. into the snug of life. **1861** [Mrs. M. A. Paul] *Two Cosmos* i. iv, A bye thing [*sc.* a prize-fight] got up upon the snug at Kilburn Wells.

**2.** *dial.* or *slang.* The bar-parlour of an inn or public-house; = snuggery 1 b. Also ***snug bar.***

**1838** *Actors by Daylight* I. 84 Act-drop.. the signal for the stage-manager to run in from the snug, and bully everybody. **1864** Brierley *Layrock* xiii, Who would have followed him into the snug. **1890** *Eastern Morn. News* (Hull) 16 Apr. 4/9 Charged with having wilfully broken a window in the snug of the Shepherdess Inn. **1894-** in dial. glossaries and texts (Northumbld., Cumbld., Lanc., Warw.). **1903** Somerville & 'Ross' *All on Irish Shore* 226 'Don't be afraid,' said our hostess reassuringly, 'he'll never see ye—sure I have him safe back in the snug!' **1956** J. M. Mogey *Family & Neighbourhood* 105 Solitary women drinkers prefer the snug in a larger public-house. **1967** *Punch* 17 May 736/3 Old women's gossip in the snug-bar.. at 'The Garibaldi'. **1977** *Ibid.* 31 Aug.-6 Sept. 331/2 Angus Beakley's cart-horse went berserk and crashed into the snug of *The Flat Pig And Hat.*

**b.** One of the compartments in the taproom of an old-fashioned inn.

**1860** Dickens *Uncommercial Traveller* (1861) v. 63 Across the room, a series of open pews for Jack.. at the other end, a larger pew.. entitled *snug*, and reserved for mates. **1891** *Scottish Leader* 18 Sept. 5 He came out of one of the 'snugs' or boxes.

**snug** (snʌg), *a.*¹ and *adv.* Also 6-7 **snugg.** [Of doubtful origin; first recorded as a nautical term. In later use app. associated with the early senses of snug *v.*, but it is possible that there is no original connexion between the two.

There is resemblance in form, and some correspondence in sense, to LG. *snügger* (*snigger*), *snögger* slender, smooth, clean, dainty, smart, etc., older Du. *snuggher, snoggher* (Kilian), slender, slim, active (Du. *snugger* lively, sprightly), but evidence of connexion is wanting. Cf. also Sw. *snygg*, Da. *snyg*, neat, tidy, etc., which may be from LG.; but Da. dial. *snøg*, Sw. dial. *snögg* (*snägg*), Norw. dial. *snøgg* (*snegg*) represent ON. *snøggr* (Icel. *snöggur*) short, short-haired, sudden, quick, etc., which is app. represented in English by snog *a.*]

**A.** *adj.* **1.** *Naut.* **a.** Of a ship or her parts: Trim, neat, compact; adequately or properly prepared for, or protected from, bad weather.

*c* **1595** Capt. Wyatt *R. Dudley's Voy. W. Ind.* (Hakluyt Soc.) 58 A verie fine snugg long shipp, having on each side vi. portes open, beside her chase and her sterne peeces. *a* **1642** Sir W. Monson *Naval Tracts* iii. (1704) 358 She will overtop a lower and snug Ship. **1711** W. Sutherland *Ship-build. Assist.* 50 The streighter and snuger the Sheer lies, the less Wind is held to hinder the Motion of the Ship. **1799** *Naval Chron.* II. 304 The stern is.. plain, and snug, without much carving. **1840** R. H. Dana *Bef. Mast* ii. 3 Soon all was snug aloft, and we were again allowed to go below. **1882** Nares *Seamanship* (ed. 6) 46 It would not form so snug a lashing. **1883** *Harper's Mag.* Aug. 447/2 She will be.. snug for any gale.

*fig.* **1848** Dickens *Dombey* iv, The shop seemed almost to become a snug sea-going, ship-shape concern.

**b.** In phrase ***to make snug.***

**1697** Dampier *Voy.* (1699) 380 Captain Read.. ordered the Carpenters to cut down our Quarter Deck to make the Ship snug and the fitter for Sailing. **1719** De Foe *Crusoe* i. (Globe) 9 [To] make everything snug and close, that the Ship might ride as easy as possible. **1726** Shelvocke *Voy. round World* (1757) 70 To ease our bows, and make everything as snug as possible. **1830** Marryat *King's Own* li, We'll make her all snug... Furl the fore and mizen-topsail. **1851** Kitto *Daily Bible Illustr.* lii. iv. (1867) 445 Their next care was to make the ship 'snug', by lowering the sail, and bringing down upon deck her spars and rigging. **1897** Mary Kingsley *W. Africa* 385 We let go the anchor, make all snug and go ashore.

**c.** *transf.* Of persons or things: Neat, trim. Now *Obs.* or *dial.*

**1714** Steele *Lover* No. 15, There was seated just before her a pretty snug Academick. **1725** Ramsay *Gentle Sheph.* i. ii, He kames his hair, indeed, and gaes right snug. **1756** *Connoisseur* No. 126 ¶5 Flowers of rhetoric, injudiciously scattered over a sermon, are as disgusting in his discourse, as the snug wig and scented white handkerchief in his dress. **1789** Gouv. Morris in Sparks *Life & Writ.* (1832) II. 90 Sometimes an orator closes with a good snug resolution which is carried with a huzza.

**d.** Close-fitting; tight.

**1838** in Holloway *Prov. Dict.* **1895** *Westm. Gaz.* 13 Aug. 7/2 The corsage of the gown should not be too snug, but it should be shapely and 'tailor made' to the last degree.

**2. a.** In a state of ease, comfort, or quiet enjoyment. Chiefly pred., and freq. with *in* (a place).

**1630** J. Lane *Contn. Sqr.'s T.* vi. 5 (Ashm. MS.), Now Chaunticleere.. the poise of his clockes watch at twoe gann sterr,.. Yet snugg binn they in cabins. **1706-** [see b]. **1783** Cowper *Lett.* Wks. (1876) 144 There is hardly to be found on Earth I suppose so snug a creature as an Englishman by his fire-side in winter. **1798** Southey *Pious Painter* ii. xi, Released from his prison,.. The Painter is snug in his bed. **1812** H. & J. Smith *Horace in London* 173 Tho' all the while my proper self Is snug at home, My pen shall roam. **1859** W. Collins *Q. of Hearts* (1875) 50, I made a blazing fire.. and sat down to tea, as snug and comfortable as possible. **1891** E. Peacock *N. Brendon* I. 131 He found.. the Colonel's groom making the animals snug for the night.

**b.** In phrases of comparison (see quots.).

**1706** E. Ward *Wooden World Diss.* (1708) 58 He sits as snug as a Bee in a Box, making his Honey. **1769** *Stratford Jubilee* ii. i, If she [a rich widow] has the mopus's, I'll have her, as snug as a bug in a rug. **1809** Malkin *Gil Blas* x. x. ¶23 You will be as snug there as a bug in a blanket. **1833** T. Hook *Love & Pride* vi, You might sit as snug as a bug in a rug. **1886** F. T. Elworthy *W. Somerset Word-bk.* 691 'So snug's a bug in a rug' is the common superlative expression. **1934** J. Buchan *Free Fishers* xiii. 211 Jem hung up his hat and ever since has been as snug as a flea in a blanket. **1936** D. Powell *Turn, Magic Wheel* i. 93 The fetish of permanency, the snug-as-a-bug-in-a-rug fetish. **1974** P. Dickinson *Poison Oracle* ii. 42 You just wait here, snug as a bug in a rug, learning it all second hand.

**c.** With *lie* vb. Also, securely caught or imprisoned. (Cf. 6.)

**1687** Miége *Gt. Fr. Dict.* ii. s.v., To lie snug in a Bed. **1781** Cowper *Anti-Thelyphth.* 79 On southern banks the ruminating sheep Lay snug and warm. **1796** Nelson 1 Aug. in Nicolas *Disp.* (1845) II. 224 This blockade is complete, and we lay very snug in the North Road. **1848** Thackeray *Van. Fair* xii, While Becky Sharp was on her own wing in the country.. Amelia lay snug in her home of Russell Square. **1879** Browning *Martin Relph* 51 Safe in the trap would they now lie snug, had treachery made no sign.

**3. a.** Of places, buildings, etc.: Comfortable and warm, cosy; esp. combining comfort with neatness and compactness.

*c* **1718** Prior *The Ladle* 68 A Country Farm, Where all was snug, and clean, and warm. **1784** Cowper *Task* i. 513 Then snug enclosures in the shelter'd vale.. Delight us. **1806** Beresford *Miseries Hum. Life* iii. vii, Your snug warm bed. **1841** Dickens *Barn. Rudge* ii, Those inside had risen from their snug seats, and were making room in the snuggest corner for the honest locksmith. **1885** Miss Braddon *Wyllard's Weird* i, Heathcote inherited a snug little estate near Bodmin. **1898** J. A. Gibbs *Cotswold Village* 141, I know no.. snugger hostelry than the Swan.

**b.** *Comb.*, as ***snug-box, -chair, -parlour.***

**1702** Farquhar *Twin-Rivals* iv. i, Presently enters Mr. Moabite, followed by a snug-chair, the windows close drawn. **1768** *Woman of Honor* III. 76 That neat snug-box of mine in Surry. **1817** Keatinge *Trav.* II. 5 The snug-parlour travellers of the critic.

**c.** Of climate: Agreeable, pleasant, genial.

**1888** *Harper's Mag.* Mar. 562/1 Duluth has a cool, salubrious summer and a snug winter climate.

**4. a.** Enabling one to live in comfort and comparative ease.

**1735** Fielding *Mod. Husb.* ii. v, Have you no friend that could favor you with some comfortable snug employment, of a thousand or fifteen hundred per annum? **1780** *Mirror* No. 78, Looking out for some snug office, or reversion, to which my interest with several powerful friends might recommend me. **1822** Hazlitt *Table-t.* Ser. ii. iv. (1869) 97 A few hundreds a year are something snug and comfortable. **1867** *Routledge's Ev. Boy's Ann.* 79 A good snug business they've got.

*transf.* **1807** Syd. Smith *Lett. Catholics* (1808) 130 An endless series of snug expectations and cruel disappointments. **1814** Scott *Wav.* v, The snug probability of succeeding to his father's office.

**b.** Moderately well-to-do; comfortably off; 'warm'. Chiefly *Irish dial.*

**1802** Mar. Edgeworth *Moral T.* (1816) I. xv. 121 He was a very cautious snug man, and he did not choose to interfere. **1828** Croker *Leg. S. Irel.* II. 222 Tim himself would have been snug enough sometimes but that he loved the drop. **1842** Lover *Handy Andy* viii, You're a snug man, Mat; you ought to be able to give a husband a trifle with them. **1900** E. Phillpotts *Sons of Morning* iii. iii, 'Twenty pounds ban't much.'.. 'Not to your faither, as he be a snug man enough by accounts.'

**c.** Fairly large or substantial.

**1833** Ht. Martineau *Vanderput & S.* iv. 65, I shipped a snug package of velvets, which certain great folks are at this moment wearing. **1848** Thackeray *Vanity Fair* xl, Having a snug legacy from Miss Crawley. **1873** B. Harte *Fiddletown* 40 This gentleman had made a snug fortune during the felicitous prevalence of a severe epidemic.

**5. a.** Marked or characterized by ease or comfort; comfortable, cosy.

(*a*) **1766** [Anstey] *Bath Guide* xiii. 16 No Lady in London is half so expert At a snug private Party, her Friends to divert. **1781** Han. More in Roberts *Mem.* (1835) I. 210, I was on Monday night at a very snug little party... We had a snug day. **1824** Irving *Tales Trav.* I. 185 They did occasionally give snug dinners to three or four literary men at a time. **1827** Scott *Chron. Canongate* i, The club-room, and the snug hand at whist. **1849** Thackeray *Pendennis* xxxvii, He liked snug dinners of all things in the world.

(*b*) **1813** *Examiner* 15 Feb. 102/2 Denmark and Sweden.. had kept themselves in a very snug neutrality. **1844** Dickens *Mart. Chuz.* xlvi, A sort of snug and comfortable penitence.

†**b.** *Cant.* (See quot.) *Obs.*

**1725** *New Cant. Dict.* s.v., *All's snug*, all's quiet; used by Villains, when every thing is silent, and they hear no body stir to oppose their intended Rogueries.

**c.** Of a borough: Close. (See borough 3 c.) *rare.*

**1844** P. Harwood *Hist. Irish Rebell.* 41 *note*, The other boroughs, which were close or snug, sent the remainder.

**6. a.** In concealment or hiding; out of sight or observation. Chiefly with *lie* vb. (Cf. 2 c.)

**1687** tr. *Sallust* (1692) 185 The Numidians kept themselves and their Horses snug within the Trees and Bushes. **1697** Dryden *Virg. Past.* iii. 24 Did I not see you, Rascal, did I not? Where you lay snug to snap young Damon's Goats? **1733** Swift *On Poetry* Wks. 1755 IV. i. 187 Be sure at Will's, the following day, [To] Lie snug, and hear what criticks say. **1797** F. Reynolds *The Will* iii. i, When a man is in debt, the Capital is the place to lie snug in! **1809** Malkin *Gil Blas* v. i. ¶4 A hue and cry was raised.., but I lay snug, and they missed me. **1815** Scott *Guy M.* xxxiii, But you must remain snug at the Point of Warroch till I come to see you. **1862** Borrow *Wales* lxxxii, Lying snug in cave by day and going out at night to rob.

†**b.** Marked or characterized by privacy, secrecy, or concealment; private, secret. *Obs.*

**1710** Swift *Lett.* (1767) III. 37 Methinks when I write plain.. all the world can see us. A bad scrawl is so snug. **1766** *Life of Quin* i. 7 James had.. carried on what he thought a very snug intrigue with Mrs. L.

**c.** ***to keep*** (..) ***snug***, to keep quiet, to refrain from talking about or alluding to (something). Now *dial.*

**1778** Mme. D'Arblay *Diary* 26 Aug., My conduct has been as uniform in trying to keep snug as my words. **1796** —— *Lett.* 10 July, He,.. laughingly, said, 'So you keep it quite snug'. **1856** Lever *Martins of Cro' M.* 508, I take it for granted that he'll be as glad of a settlement that keeps all 'snug', as ourselves. **1877** *N.W. Linc. Gloss.* 231/2 Doctors an' lawyers is beholden to keep things snug, folks tells 'em.

**7.** Used as an interjection asking for or commanding secrecy, esp. in phrase *snug's the word*.

**1700** CONGREVE *Way of World* I. ii, If throats are to be cut, let swords clash! snug's the word, I shrug and am silent. **1748** FOOTE *Knights* I. Wks. 1799 I. 65 You could give us a little news if you would; come now!—snug!—nobody by! **1809–12** MAR. EDGEWORTH *Vivian* viii, There's a man who could tell you more than any of us, if he would; but snug's the word with Wicksted. **1842** LOVER *Handy Andy* xxi, Whisht,.. not a word... Good-bye, you'll hear more about it to-morrow—snug's the word.

**B.** *adv.* Snugly.

**1674** N. FAIRFAX *Bulk & Selv.* 128, I take the seed.. to be a cluster of bubbles wryed up snug. **1766** [ANSTEY] *Bath Guide* vi. 27 So they hoisted her down just as safe.. And as snug as a Hod'mandod rides in his shell. **1768** GOLDSM. *Good-n. Man* Epil., He eyes the centre, where his friends sit snug. **1831** *Lincoln Herald* 9 Sept. 3/6 It is calculated to button across snug up to the neck. **1853** KANE *Grinnell Exped.* xxix. (1856) 252 The provisions and stores of all sorts are packed snug. **1884** PAE *Eustace* 34 To see you succeed in getting your son and my nephew put snug into the estate.

**†snug,** *a.*[2] *Obs.* [Cf. SNUG *sb.*[1]] ? Snub.

**1626** B. JONSON *Staple of News* III. ii, It is an Automa,.. With a snug nose, and has a nimble taile.

**snug** (snʌg), *v.* [Of obscure origin: in later use associated with, and partly f., SNUG *a.*[1]]

**1. a.** *intr.* Of persons (or animals): To lie or nestle closely or comfortably, esp. in bed; to snuggle. Now *rare* or *dial.* (Cf. SNUDGE *v.*[2])

**1583** GOLDING *Calvin on Deut.* lxvii. 411 In stead of setting forward we retire backe, or els sit snugging stil in our owne slothfulnesse. *a* **1586** SIDNEY *Arcadia* I. (1622) 84 Betwixt them two the peeper tooke his nest, Where snuging well he well appear'd content. **1616** J. LANE *Contn. Sqr.'s T.* vi. 5 While snugginge they in cabbins lay each one. **1692** R. L'ESTRANGE *Fables* (1694) 61 The loving couple lay snugging together. **1824** LAMB *Lett.* (1888) II. 118 Let 'em all snug together, Hebrews and Proselytes of the gate.

*transf.* and *fig.* **1648** J. BEAUMONT *Psyche* II. vi, The Summer Clouds, snugging in laps of Flowers. **1648** HERRICK *Hesper.*, *Upon Roses*, Under a Lawne.. Some ruffled Roses nestling were: And snugging there, they seem'd to lye As in a flowrie Nunnery. **1674** N. FAIRFAX *Bulk & Selv.* 86 The pieces of a body.. are only clapt together at their little smoothnesses as close as they can snug. **1978** T. L. SMITH *Money War* (1979) I. 74 Folding bipod which snugs under the barrel when not in use; large winter trigger.

**b.** With *to* or *into*.

**1674** N. FAIRFAX *Bulk & Selvedge of the World* 110 [An atom] so snugs to another, as not to be in another. **1687** MIÈGE *Gt. Fr. Dict.* II, To snug to his Bed-fellow. **1828–32** WEBSTER s.v., A child snugs to its mother or nurse. **1888** EDMONDSTON & SAXBY *Home Naturalist* 85 After she and Wildie had snugged into bed.

**c.** *U.S.* With *up*.

**1868** M. M. POMEROY *Nonsense* xxvi. 248 She 'snugged up' toward us as gently as a juvenile dove. **1873** J. H. BEADLE *Undeveloped West* v. 106 He used to complain that I 'snugged up' altogether too much.

**2.** With *down*: To nestle, settle down; to make oneself snug or comfortable.

**1603** DEKKER & CHETTLE *Grisill* 100 Then this eye lookes vp, yet downe I snug againe. **1898** *Westm. Gaz.* 4 Mar. 3/1 They turn into the Home for Asiatics, and snug down till Mr. Johnston.. gets them a ship. **1904** 'E. NESBIT' *Phœnix & Carpet* ii. 26 'I'm a baby bear!' said the Lamb, snugging down.

**3.** *trans.* **a.** To place or put snugly, neatly, or comfortably.

**1754** GOLDSM. in Forster *Life* (1871) I. 437 Every woman carries in her hand a stove with coals in it, which, when she sits, she snugs under her petticoats.

**b.** *U.S. slang.* 'To conceal from the owner, to purloin' (Bartlett).

*a* **1859** in Bartlett *Dict. Amer.* (ed. 2) 424 I'd stuff watches, drop pocket-books,.. but I'd never condescend to snug dogs.

**4.** *refl.* To make (oneself) comfortable, secure, or safe (cf. quots.); to bring (oneself) *into* something comfortable.

**1795** *Gazette of the U.S.* (Phila.) 7 March (Thornton), [He will] keep up his credit and character, till he has snugged himself into a good estate. **1822** MRS. E. NATHAN *Langreath* I. 5 His steward, who has snugged himself pretty well by robbing his master and oppressing the poor. **1856** *Leisure Hour* 28 Aug. 559/1 We hear voices and steps just outside, but snug ourselves in the security of our retreat.

**5. a.** To make snug, comfortable, or tidy; to set nicely in order. Freq. with *up* or *down*.

(*a*) **1787** BURNS *Brigs of Ayr* 27 Potatoe-bings are snugged up frae skaith Of coming Winter's biting, frosty breath. **1836** HALIBURTON *Clockm.* Ser. I. xxxv, What the dickens was them two great rolls o' canvass for, I seed snugg'd up and tied to your crupper? *Ibid.* xxxvii, Whenever you see a place all snugged up.., depend on it the folks are of the right kind. **1888** *Cent. Mag.* Aug. 617/2 The tent was shut, and everything snugged up. **1892** LOWNDES *Camping Sketches* I. 44 We snugged things down quite elegantly, in expectation of visitors.

*absol.* **1885** *Field* 19 Dec. 870/3 We snugged up for the night.

(*b*) **1890** CLARK RUSSELL *Marriage at Sea* iv, I snugged her in rugs. **1897** *Advance* (Chicago) 18 Mar. 342/1 They have become an 'Army of Occupation', with huts snugged for winter.

**b.** To put or stow *away* snugly.

**1859** H. W. BEECHER *Life Thoughts* Ser. II. 55 He knows very well where it is snugged away. **1880** L. WALLACE *Ben-Hur* 516 He beheld Esther,.. a small figure snugged away under her father's lap-robe. **1897** *Daily News* 21 June 4/5 You are comfortably snugged away under a wide-spreading arch.

**6.** *Naut.* **a.** To make (a ship, etc.) snug or trim, esp. by lashing or stowing movables, furling or reducing sails, lowering topmasts, etc., in preparation for bad weather; to furl (a sail).

**1881** *Daily Telegr.* 28 Jan., Bit by bit the canvas was snugged until the brig had nothing on her but her lower maintopsail [etc.]. **1881** CLARK RUSSELL *Ocean Free Lance* II. 177 The men were employed in snugging the decks. **1890** —— *Ocean Trag.* I. ix. 189 They had snugged the 'Bride' to very small canvas.

**b.** Similarly with *down*. Also *absol.* and *transf.*

**1893** *Westm. Gaz.* 28 Feb. 10/3 Having hove in their trawl they were all forward.. snugging the vessel down, as they were threatened with more wind. **1899** 'Q.' (Quiller Couch) *Ship of Stars* xxiv, [Taffy] gave the order to snug down and man the cradle for shore. **1918** KIPLING *Land & Sea Tales* (1923) 116 They snugged her down. I don't know how one snugs down an aeroplane.

**snugger** ('snʌgə(r)). [f. prec.: cf. SNUGGING *vbl. sb.* 1.] A device by which cordage is made smooth and uniform.

**1875** KNIGHT *Dict. Mech.* 2192/1 The cordage.. is drawn slowly between closely pressing reciprocating *rubbers* and *snuggers*.

**snuggery** ('snʌgərɪ). Also 9 -erie. [f. SNUG *a.*[1] + -ERY.]

**1. a.** A cosy or comfortable room, esp. one of small size, into which a person retires for seclusion or quiet; a bachelor's den.

**1812** M. EDGEWORTH *Tales of Fashionable Life* V. 268 Let me establish you comfortably in this, which I call my sanctuary—my *snuggery*. **1815** *Zeluca* I. 171 You must come and dine, and.. play whist in a snuggerie with Lady Whitelock. **1825** LOCKHART in Smiles *Mem. J. Murray* (1891) II. xxvii. 229 Habits which render it difficult for me to do any serious work out of my own snuggery. **1853** R. S. SURTEES *Sponge's Sp. Tour* xlii. 230 Each particular apartment.. down to the smallest bachelor snuggery, was replete with elegance and comfort. **1892** BARING-GOULD *Trag. Caesars* I. 192 On the top of the house was a snuggery, into which he retired when he wanted to be entirely alone.

*attrib.* **1857** HUGHES *Tom Brown* II. viii, Tom.. soon managed to place on the snuggery table better materials for a meal. **1898** W. WHITE *Jrnls.* 72 An attempt to make a Cambridge snuggery affair of it.

**b.** *spec.* The bar-parlour of an inn or public-house; = SNUG *sb.*[2] 2.

**1829** P. EGAN *Boxiana* 2nd Ser. II. 206 Shelton, on Friday evening after the fight, made his *bow* to the *Daffy Club*, at the Castle Tavern, Holborn: and, in the *snuggery*, Tom received the £100 stakes, as the reward of his victory. **1837** DICKENS *Pickw.* x, There's these here painted tops in the snuggery inside the bar. **1847** ALB. SMITH *Adv. Chr. Tadpole* xxix. (1879) 259 The bar did not differ from others of its class,.. but the snuggery behind was remarkable.

**2. a.** A snug, comfortable, or cosy house or dwelling.

**1833** T. HOOK *Parson's Dau.* I. i, It [the cottage] was one of the prettiest things imaginable: its interior was a perfect snuggery. **1847** W. IRVING *Life & Lett.* (1866) III. 402 Converting what was once rather a make-shift little mansion into one of the most complete snuggeries in the country. **1893** LADY BURTON *Life Burton* I. 440 The Diplomats have snuggeries here [i.e. Petropolis], and form a pleasant society.

**b.** A snug place, position, feature, etc.

**1850** *Lit. Gazette* 16 Nov. 849/2 The zeal of your modern squire, ensconced in his curtained snuggery of a pew. **1863** HAWTHORNE *Our Old Home* (1883) I. 254 A friend had given us his suburban residence, with all its conveniences, elegancies, and snuggeries. **1867** E. YATES *Forlorn Hope* viii, Lady Muriel rose from the soft snuggery of her cushioned chair. **1953** DYLAN THOMAS *Under Milk Wood* (1954) 2 It is night neddying among the snuggeries of babies.

**3.** A snug company or party. *rare.*

**1831** *Lincoln Herald* 1 July 4/5 Let not this snuggery of literary dunderheads imagine that they are all ambushed. **1958** [see DO-GOOD].

**4.** An easy comfortable position or post; a sinecure. *rare.*

**1839** *Blackw. Mag.* XLV. 767 Another puts his bastard son into a splendid snuggery for life. **1855** TROLLOPE *Warden* iii, Here was a nice man to be initiated into the comfortable arcana of ecclesiastical snuggeries.

**snugging** ('snʌgɪŋ), *vbl. sb.* [f. SNUG *v.*]

**1.** *techn.* The operation of rubbing down a rope in order to give it a smooth finish.

**1875** KNIGHT *Dict. Mech.* 2192/1 The size is flour-paste mixed with other ingredients, and the operation on the rope is called *snugging*, *slicking*, or *finishing*.

**2.** *Naut.* The action of making snug or trim. Also with *up*.

**1886** R. C. LESLIE *Sea Painter's Log* 61 The washing out and snugging-up of a boat at her moorings for the night. **1886** *Pall Mall G.* 14 Sept. 4/3 With a sloop no corresponding order could have been given which would have led to such smart snugging of canvas.

**'snugging,** *ppl. a. rare*[−1]. [f. as prec.] Snug, quiet, sheltered.

**1701** SEDLEY *Happy Pair* Wks. 1722 I. 23 He slily flies to copses, where he finds The snugging woods secure from blasts and winds.

**snuggish** ('snʌgɪʃ), *a.* [f. SNUG *a.*[1]] Somewhat snug; rather comfortable.

**1818** *Blackw. Mag.* III. 404 We had chanced ourselves to cram Into a snuggish treckschuit. **1863** SALA *Capt. Dangerous* II. vii. 233, I accompanied him to the 'Admiral Benbow', a snuggish little hostelry. **1866** CARLYLE *E. Irving* in *Remin.* (1881) II. 260 The Irvings had a dim but snuggish house.

**'snuggle,** *sb. rare.* [f. next.] An act of snuggling; also with *down*. Also, a group of persons or things which are snuggled together.

**1901** 'R. CONNOR' *Man from Glengarry* xx. 328 'You are sure you are comfortable?' 'Quite,' she replied, with a cosy little snuggle down among the cushions. *a* **1910** 'MARK TWAIN' *Autobiogr.* (1924) I. 103 In the early cold mornings a snuggle of children.. occupying the hearthstone. **1935** E. BOWEN *House in Paris* II. i. 87 A snuggle of gothic villas. **1966** J. S. COX *Illustr. Dict. Hairdressing & Wigmaking* p. ix, Words which, when used in conjunction with the word *curls*, are indicative of either the quantity,.. or arrangement of a *group of curls*:.. Ruffle, Snuggle, Soufflé.

**snuggle** ('snʌg(ə)l), *v.* [Cf. SNUG *v.* and -LE.]

**1.** *intr.* Of persons, esp. children: To lie snug or close, esp. for warmth or comfort; to settle down cosily or comfortably; to get or press close to a person, esp. as a mark of affection; to nestle.

**1687** MIÈGE *Gt. Fr. Dict.* II, To Snuggle, or to snuggle together, *se serrer dans un lit.* **1727** BAILEY (vol. II), *To Snuggle*, to lie close together; to embrace one another in Bed. **1823** E. MOOR *Suffolk Words*, *Snuggle*, to lie snug in bed —or to get close together in bad weather. **1850** THACKERAY *Pendennis* lviii, She coaxed and snuggled and smiled. **1854** —— *Newcomes* i, We were friends in a minute—young Newcome snuggling by my side. **1865** DICKENS *Mut. Fr.* I. iii, I snuggled under a little shawl, and it was warm there.

*fig.* **1879** 'E. GARRETT' *Ho. by Works* I. 25 It was a wealthy household,.. where virtue.. snuggled in broad cloth and satin.

**b.** To nestle *close* or near *to* a person or thing.

**1845** S. JUDD *Margaret* I. xiv, Children snuggled to their parents. **1884** *Ordnance Gaz. Scotl.* II. 394 A collie snuggles to his foot. **1900** R. J. MUIR *Myst. Muncraig* xxi. 260 'Don't say that,' moaned the girl, snuggling close.

**c.** With *up* or *down*. Also, to curl up snugly or comfortably.

(*a*) **1840** HALIBURTON *Letter Bag* i. 11, [I] unbooted, unstayed, and snuggled up like a kitten, in bed. **1879** G. MEREDITH *Egoist* xlii, He.. dashed downstairs into the drawing-room, where he snuggled up and dropped asleep. **1880** *19th Cent.* Sept. 451 That is the time to appreciate the comfort of a warm weather-proof house, to snuggle up in your blanket [etc.].

(*b*) **1879** STEVENSON *Trav. Cevennes* 61, [I] put my revolver ready to my hand, and snuggled well down among the sheepskins. **1886** MISS MULOCK *King Arthur* viii. 311 When the old birds are flown we must snuggle down in the empty nest.

**2.** *transf.* Of buildings, etc.: To lie in a sheltered or snug situation; to nestle.

**1862** H. MARRYAT *Year in Sweden* II. 301 Under these bastions snuggle small wood tenements. **1892** *Black & White* 26 Nov. 614/1 The towns.. snuggle among foliage. **1898** BARING-GOULD *Old Eng. Home* i. 18 In a dip in the land,.. snuggling into the folds of the down,.. lies this lovely old house.

**3.** *trans.* To clasp or draw (a person, etc.) to one closely or affectionately; to hug or cuddle.

**1775** ASH, *Snuggle*, to receive into the bosom, to receive into a snug place. **1823** E. MOOR *Suffolk Words* s.v., A nurse hugging a child warmly and kindly, would be said to snuggle it. **1874** CHRISTINA ROSSETTI *Poems*, *Speaking Likenesses* 92 She snuggled it tenderly to her.

**b.** To wrap *in* some warm garment, etc. Also with *up*.

**1867** ALGER *Solitudes Nat. & Man* III. 169 To lie amid the clover..; or, snuggled in furs, to trudge [etc.]. **1893** *Advance* (Chicago) 30 Nov., Little boys whom doting mammas have snuggled up in leggings, mittens and mufflers.

**c.** To push or press, to place or settle, (the head, etc.) in a snug or affectionate manner.

**1883** *Harper's Mag.* Dec. 94/1 He.. patted the little hand snuggled in upon his arm. **1899** DOYLE *Duet* [xiv.] 185 She snuggled her head up against his knee.

**d.** To fit or push closely *into* something.

**1902** *Temple Bar* May 578 As he snuggled the weapon into the groove of the parapet.

**4.** *refl.* To settle or nestle (oneself) *in* a place snugly or comfortably.

**1876** W. WHITE *Holidays in Tyrol* x. 82 Nests erected on poles in which the watchers snuggle themselves.

**'snuggle-pup.** *U.S. slang.* ? *Obs.* Also -pupper, -puppy. [f. SNUGGLE *v.* + PUP *sb.*[1] 2b.] An attractive young girl.

**1922** [see *jazz queen* s.v. JAZZ *sb.* 5]. **1925** LINDSEY & EVANS *Revolt Mod. Youth* v. 58 We go to parties with these young crumpet munchers and snuggle pups. **1933** *Forum & Century* (N.Y.) Dec. 367/2, I glimmed him with a snuggle-puppy.

**snuggler** ('snʌglə(r)). [f. SNUGGLE *v.* + -ER[1].] One who snuggles.

**1887** E. B. CUSTER *Tenting on Plains* xii. 379 It finally dawned upon us that the little horse was a constitutional snuggler. **1939** JOYCE *Finnegans Wake* 548, I chained her chastemate to grippe fiuming snugglers.

**snuggly** ('snʌglɪ), *a. colloq.* [f. SNUGGLE *v.* + -Y[1].] Characterized by or inviting snuggling; snug, close-fitting. Also redupl. as *snuggly-wuggly*.

**1928** A. HUXLEY *Point Counter Point* xvi. 287 Such a dear snuggly-wuggly, lovey-dovey little chap. **1966** R. H. RIMMER *Harrad Experiment* 36 It's [*sc.* sexual intercourse is] going to be nice and snuggly, and lots of fun. **1976** *National Observer* (U.S.) 28 Aug. 15/4 (Advt.), Our own grown-up version of the classic favorite for children. The snuggly fashion that will make any 'big kid' a beautiful baby all over again. Deliciously tantalizing on *her*, and..ruggedly good-looking on *him*.

**'snugify**, *v.* [f. SNUG *a.*[1]] *trans.* To make snug or comfortable.

**1796** LAMB in Talfourd *Life & Lett.* ii. (1840) 12, I devoutly wish that Fortune..may..throw you into London,..and there snugify you for life.

**snugly** ('snʌglɪ), *adv.* [f. SNUG *a.*[1]] In a snug or comfortable manner; cosily, comfortably.

**1611** *Tarlton's Jests* (1844) p. xl, Being thus under saile, going so snugly downe, it made us all so merry. **1732** J. WHALEY *Poems* 180 You,..the reigning Toast, may snuggly err, secure from Harm. **1799** CAMPBELL *The Harper* 15 How snugly we slept in my old coat of gray. **1815** SCOTT *Guy M.* liii, Even in winter it was a sheltered and snugly sequestered spot. **1852** MRS. STOWE *Uncle Tom's C.* xiii. 117 She found herself snugly tucked up on the bed with a blanket over her. **1890** 'R. BOLDREWOOD' *Col. Reformer* (1891) 220 He..professed himself to be snugly lodged.

**b.** Neatly, trimly; closely, securely.

**1800** *Naval Chron.* IV. 134 These balls..might be stopped up snugly to the beams. **1901** *J. Black's Carp. & Build.* 68 A..piece of heavy galvanized sheet iron is fitted into the groove with white lead, and then the parts are brought snugly together.

**snugness** ('snʌgnɪs). [f. as prec.]

**1.** The state, condition, or quality of being snug or comfortable; cosiness. Also *personif.*

**1766** GOLDSM. *Vicar W.* iv, My house..was covered with thatch, which gave it an air of great snugness. **1766** COWPER *Wks.* (1837) XV. 11, I rejoice with you in the snugness of your situation. *c* **1790** WARTON *Phaeton & One-horse Chair* 70 O'er me soft Snugness spreads her wings. **1809** PINKNEY *Trav. France* 179 The fields..are so small as to give them a peculiar air of snugness. **1850** HAWTHORNE *Scarlet Letter* Introd. (1879) 12 All the softness and snugness of an eiderdown pillow. **1873** HAMERTON *Intell. Life* XII. iii. 447 There is a well-known objection to extensive views as wanting in snugness and comfort.

†**2.** Secrecy, reticence. *Obs.*

**1778** MME. D'ARBLAY *Diary* Sept., Had I been allowed to preserve the snugness I had planned, I need not have concerned myself at all about its fate.

**3.** Neatness, trimness; compactness, closeness.

**1799** [A. YOUNG] *Agric. Linc.* 325 Though the Lincoln had the thicker pelt, and more wool, the thickness and snugness of frame of the Leicester made amends. **1802** *Naval Chron.* VII. 178 She..has all the snugness on the water of a large frigate.

**snum** (snʌm), *v.* *U.S. colloq.* Alteration of *swear*, esp. in *I snum* as exclamation. Also as *sb.* in *by snum!* (*obs.*). Cf. VUM *v.*, *sb.*

**1825** J. NEAL *Brother Jonathan* II. 315 By snum; but you're a precious fellow! **1839** *Yale Lit. Mag.* IV. 357 I snum, 'tain't the thing for me. **1904** J. C. LINCOLN *Cap'n Eri* i. 4, I ain't quite a fool yit, Eri Hedge. I guess I know—well, I snum! I forgot that upper vest pocket! **1916** H. L. WILSON *Somewhere in Red Gap* viii. 333 Now, I snum! Here she's two-thirty! **1951** *Publ. Amer. Dial. Soc.* xv. 67 *I snum!*, exclamation of amazement.

†**snur**, *v.* *Obs.*[−1] In 6 snurre. [Imitative, or ad. MLG. *snurren* (hence Da. *snurre*, Sw. and Norw. *snurra*), MHG. *snurren* (G. *schnurren*).] *intr.* To snort.

**1523** SKELTON *Garl. Laurel* 1472 Apollo that whirllid vp his chare, That made sum to snurre and snuf in the wynde.

**snurge** (snɜːdʒ), *sb. slang.* [Cf. SNEAK *sb.*] **a.** In schools, an informer, a tell-tale. **b.** One who curries favour, a toady; generally, an obnoxious person.

**1933** M. HODGE *Wind & Rain* (1934) I. i. 19 He's probably only a kid. He may be a perfect little snurge...for all you know. **1955** M. GILBERT *Sky High* ii. 29 He's such a little snurge... He's so bogus. **1955** *People* (Austral.) 13 July 47/4 She was going to cut off my allowance. But do you know, it was that out-and-out snurge that pleaded for me? **1956** C. P. SNOW *Homecomings* xliv. 308 He had got on a good deal better as a snurge than he would have done as a malcontent.

**snurl**, *sb. dial.* Also 9 snirl, snerl, etc. [Cf. WFlem. *snorrelen* to snuffle or snort.]

†**1.** (See quot.) *Obs.*[−0]

**1674** RAY *S. & E.C. Words* 77 *A Snurle*, a Pose or Cold in the head... Suff. [Hence in Coles, Kersey, Bailey, etc.]

**2.** A nostril.

**1691** RAY *N.C. Words* 137 *Snurles*, Nostrils. **1876-** in northern glossaries.

**snurl**, *v. dial.* Also 9 snirl, snerl. [Cf. SNARL *v.*[1]]

Some other senses in northern dial. and Sc. are recorded in the *Eng. Dial. Dict.*

**1.** *trans.* To ruffle or disturb.

**1719** RAMSAY *3rd Answ. Hamilton* vii, When northern blasts the ocean snurl.

**2.** To turn *up* (the nose) in disdain.

*a* **1833** R. ANDERSON *Cumb. Ballads* (1881) 138 She snurl'd up her neb. **1873** in *Swaledale Gloss.* 24/1.

**snurp**, *v.* [app. the same as the mod. dial. *snurp* (more commonly *snirp*, *snerp*), of Scand. origin: cf. Norw. dial. *snurpa*, *snyrpa* to draw together in wrinkles.] *intr.* To become shrivelled or wrinkled.

*c* **1300** *Old Age* vii. in *E.E.P.* (1862) 149, I snurpe, i snobbe, i sneipe on snovte.

**snurt**, *v.* Now *north.* and *Sc.* Also 5 snvrtyn, 6, 8 *dial.* snourt, 6 snowrt. [prob. imitative.]

**1.** *intr.* To snort; †to sneer; to snore.

*c* **1440** *Promp. Parv.* 462/1 Snvrtyn, or frowne wythe þe nese for scorne or schrewdenesse, *nario.* **1549** COVERDALE, etc. *Erasm. Par. Thess.* 7 That we watche in the dayelight and not lye snourtyng in darkenesse. **1551** *Dr. Haddon's Exhort.* in Furnivall *Ballads fr. MSS.* I. 325 Yet snowrteste thow, & sleapeste sownd. **1611** COTGR., *Brouffer*, to snurt, or snifter with the nose, like a horse. **1790** MRS. WHEELER *Westmld. Dial.* (1821) App. 2 They [fish] snourt when they com out oth girt dub like thunner. **1887** DARLINGTON *Folk Sp. S. Cheshire*, *Snurt*, to snort; but used only of a horse.

†**2.** *trans.* To eject or cast *out* with a snort or clearing of the nose. *Obs. rare.*

**1600** *Minte of Deformities* (Halliw.), One snurts tobacco, as his nose were made A perfum'd jakes for all scurrilities. **1610** MARKHAM *Masterpiece* II. xxii. 256 Giue him liberty to hold downe his head, and to snurt out the filthy matter.

Hence **'snurter**, a snorer; **'snurting** *vbl. sb.* and *ppl. a.*

**1549** COVERDALE, etc. *Erasm. Par. 1 Peter* II. 12 So as he that is the more watchefull, maye rayse vp the drowsye snourtour. **1567** DRANT *Horace, Ep.* I. xiv. E v, Swetely by the husshing brookes to take a snurting nap. **1611** COTGR., *Esbrouëment*,..a snurting, or snuftering with the nose. **1891** *Sheffield Gloss.* Suppl. 54 A man who was blowing through his tobacco pipe said that 'it made a snurting noise'.

†**snush**, *sb. Obs.* [perh. imitative of a sneezing sound, but cf. Da. and Sw. *snus*. See also *snish* SNEESH *sb.*]

**1.** Snuff. (Freq. *c* 1680–1700.)

**1671** CROWNE *Juliana* III. 33 Some snush would purge your simple brain. **1698** *Phil. Trans.* XX. 7 He had Snush on his Hand, as if just ready to take it. **1700** FARQUHAR *Constant Couple* II, [Stage direction] Throws snush into his eye. **1716** M. DAVIES *Athen. Brit.* III. Diss. Drama 31 To see six or seven Spanish and Italian Priestly Converts..Carrying of Snush, like Jews, from Door to Door. **1767** MESTON *Poems* (ed. 6) 82 Bedaub'd with soot, and snush and bubblings. **1825** JAMIESON *Suppl.*, *Snush*, snuff; a term still used by old people; Aberd[een].

**2.** A pinch, or small quantity, of snuff.

**1703** M. MARTIN *Desc. Western Islands* 14 They will tug at the Oar all day long upon Bread and Water, and a snush of Tobacco.

**3.** *attrib.*, as ***snush-box***, ***-tobacco***.

**1682** *Lond. Gaz.* No. 1757/4 A round Gold Snush-box. **1691** tr. *Emilianne's Observ. Journ. Naples* 204 The Gentlemen that Travell'd with me, having presented them with a Paper of Bononia Snush-Tobacco. **1702** T. MORER *Short Acc. Scotl.* 20 They are fond of Tobacco, but more from the Snush-Box than pipe. **1709** PRIOR *Cupid & Ganymede* 13 A Snush-Box, set with bleeding Hearts, Rubies, all pierc'd with Diamond Darts.

†**snush**, *v. Obs. rare.* [Cf. prec.] *trans.* To snuff, snuff *up* (tobacco); to take as snuff.

**1703** M. MARTIN *Desc. Western Islands* 40 She took a Quill with which she ordinarily snushed her Tobacco. *a* **1704** T. BROWN *Wks.* (1720) 126 Then filling his short Pipe, he blows a Blast, And does the burning Weed to Ashes wast, Which, when its cool, he snushes up his Nose.

†**snute**. *Obs.* In 7 snewtte, snut(t)e, snuyt. [ad. Du. *snuit* or Flem. *snuite*, *snute*: cf. SNOUTING[2].] (See quots. 1651.)

**1649** *Rec. Merchant. Adv. Newcastle* (Surtees) I. 157 A little hempe, snute and sope. **1651** *Ibid.* 174 Snutte, a comodity made out of flax. *Ibid.*, In which manufacture there are these 3 partes, that is, the flax.., the snewtte which is the combeings of the tow which was heckled of the flax. **1663** *Ibid.* 59 Tow or snute the c weight, iij d.

†**snut-nose**. *Obs.* [Cf. SNAT-NOSED *a.*] A snub-nose. Also †**snut-nosed** *a.*, snub-nosed. *Obs.*

**1603** HOLLAND *Plutarch's Mor.* 666 If men be jested at, for that they be long-nosed.., or otherwise have short snut-noses. **1706** PHILLIPS (ed. Kersey) s.v. *Silo*, An Ape-Nosed or Snut Nosed Fellow.

†**'snuttering**, *vbl. sb. Obs.*[−1] [Imitative: cf. SNATTER *v.*] Chattering.

*a* **1693** *Urquhart's Rabelais* III. xiii. 107 The..snarling of Messens, rantling of Rats,..snuttering of Monkies.

†**snuve**, *v. Obs.*[−1] [= WFris. *snuve*, MDu. *snuven*, *snuyven* (Du. *snuiven*), LG. *snuven*, MHG. *snuben* (G. *schnauben*), etc., in similar senses.] *trans.* To snuff or sniff.

*c* **1200** *Trin. Coll. Hom.* 191 Þe werse..secheð..at te nose ȝif it beoð open to snuuende unluuede breð.

**'snuzzle**, *v.* Now *dial.* Also 8 snuzle. [? variant of NUZZLE *v.*[1] Cf. SNOOZLE *v.*]

**1.** *intr.* **a.** Of swine: To rout *about* with the snout or nose.

**1737** BRACKEN *Farriery Impr.* (1757) II. 130 Swine will thrive best when they have the Opportunity of..snuzling about, and picking up the Oats, &c.

**b.** Of a dog: To sniff or poke with the nose.

**1861** HUGHES *Tom Brown at Oxford* iii, A way he [a dog] had of going 'snuzzling' about the calves of strangers.

**2.** *dial.* Of persons, esp. children: To nuzzle, snuggle, or settle down comfortably.

**1781** J. HUTTON *Tour to Caves* (ed. 2) Gloss. 96 *Snuzzle*, to hide the face in the bosom as children. [Hence in Grose (1790), Holloway, etc.] **1869-** in dial. glossaries, etc. (Yks., Lanc., Chesh., Nott.).

**sny** (snaɪ), *sb. Shipbuilding.* [Cf. SNYING *vbl. sb.*] (See quots. 1846 and 1875.)

**a. 1711** W. SUTHERLAND *Shipbuild. Assist.* 54 In working up a round Buttock of a Ship, the lower Edge of the Planks will have a sudden Sny aft. **1846** A. YOUNG *Naut. Dict.* 288 In shipbuilding, a plank is said to have sny, when its edge has an upward curve.

**b.** *c* **1850** *Rudim. Nav.* (Weale) 149 The great sny occasioned in full bows..is..to be prevented by introducing steelers. **1875** KNIGHT *Dict. Mech.* 2232/1 *Sny*, ..the trend of the lines of a ship upward from amidship toward the bow and the stern.

†**sny**, *v.*[1] *Obs.*[−1] In 5 snyȝe. [Of obscure origin.] *intr.* To move, proceed.

*a* **1400-50** *Alexander* 4095 Þan snyȝes þar, out of þat snyth hill.., A burly best.

**sny** (snaɪ), *v.*[2] Now *dial.* Forms: 7 snithe, 9 snive; 7, 9 snie, 8–9 sny, 9 snye; 7, 9 snee. [Of obscure origin.] *intr.* To abound, swarm, teem, be infested, *with* something.

**1674** RAY *N.C. Words* 44 To *Snee* or *snie*, to abound or swarm. He *snies* with Lice, he swarms with them. **1675** V. ALSOP *Anti-sozzo* 503 Certainly never did man so snithe with prejudices against Truth. *c* **1746** J. COLLIER (Tim Bobbin) *View Lanc. Dial.* Gloss., *Snye*, to swarm. **1849** HOWITT *Year Bk. Country* 242/32 The villages in the forest sny with children. **1882** *Echo* 16 Jan. 4/1 The place literally 'snives' with rabbits. **1897** J. PRIOR *Ripple & Flood* xix, The watter snies wi' fish.

**snye** (snaɪ). *Canad.* and *local U.S.* Also snie, sny. [ad. Canad. Fr. *chenail*, Fr. *chenal* CHANNEL *sb.*[1]] A side-channel, esp. one creating an island.

**1819** W. KEYES *Diary* 17 Apr. in *Wisconsin Mag. Hist.* (1920) III. 457 Evening, anchor a little above the upper snie (or channel) that leads to the Mississippi. **1826** *Kingston* (Ontario) *Chron.* 3 Nov. 2/5 We are also busy forming a channel through the rapids, for the sake of the raftsmen—this is done by building two strong dams, and deepening what is called a *dry snie*. **1829** J. MACTAGGART *Three Years in Canada* I. 136 At this place, there are numbers of islands formed by snies winding round the Falls. **1886** in *Alberta Hist. Rev.* (1971) Summer 16/2 And from there to the snye which is a short cut into Fort Resolution. **1893** 'MARK TWAIN' in *St. Nicholas* Nov. 24/2 Ef we..slips acrost de river to-night arter de moon's gone down, en kills dat sick fam'ly dat's over on the Sny. **1908** C. MAIR *Through Mackenzie Basin* 40 Much of [the tracking]..is in the water, wading up 'snies', or tortuous shallow channels.. floundering in gumbo slides. **1921** *Beaver* Aug.–Sept. 15/1 The Imperial Oil Company narrowly escaped the loss of their machines, which were lying on the snye at the back of the Fort awaiting favorable weather. **1948** *Canad. Geogr. Jrnl.* Mar. 150/2 The word *snye*, *sny* or *snie* has been used for many years to describe a channel behind an island, with slack current or partly dried, or some such similar feature. **1967** E. B. NICKERSON *Kayaks to Arctic* ii. 17 There is a snye for float planes. **1969** E. W. MORSE *Fur Trade Canoe Routes* II. v. 57 The brigades shot the Allumette Rapids in their main (north) channel, the 'Timber Snye', where a safe canoe course passes.

**snye** (to cut): see SNICK OR SNEE.

**snying** ('snaɪɪŋ), *vbl. sb. Shipbuilding.* [Of obscure origin: cf. SNY *sb.*, and dial. *sny*, *snigh* to turn up the nose.] (See quots.)

**1711** W. SUTHERLAND *Shipbuild. Assist.* 47 As much as possible keep your Work from extream Snying or Cambering. *Ibid.* 164 *Snying*, an arching upwards, where the Middle of the Plank appears higher than the Ends. **1815** BURNEY *Falconer's Mar. Dict.* 488/1 *Snying*, among ship-wrights, a term used for a circular plank, edgeways, to work in the bows of the ship.

So **'snying** *ppl. a.*, having an upward curve or sny.

**1711** W. SUTHERLAND *Shipbuild. Assist.* 47 You will likewise be obliged to have snying (or crooked) Planks. **1736** PEGGE *Kenticisms* (E.D.S.) 48 A stick or bat of timber is said to be a snying piece, when it bends or is somewhat curved. *c* **1850** *Rudim. Nav.* (Weale) 149 *Snying*, a term applied to planks when their edges round or curve upwards. *Ibid.* 152 Its use is to take out the snying edge.

**snythe**, obs. variant of SNATH, scythe-pole.

**snyth-hill**: see SNIDDLE.

**so** (səʊ), *adv.* and *conj.* Forms: (see below). [Common Teut.: OE. *swa*, *swā* (also *swǣ*, *swē*, etc.), = OFris. *sa*, *so* (Fris. *sa*, *so*, *sô*, *sü*, etc.), MDu. *so*, *soo*, *soe* (Du. *zoo*), OS. *sô* (MLG. *so*, LG. *so*, *sou*), OHG. *sô*, *suo* (MHG. *sô*, *sâ*, G. *so*), ON. *svá* (Icel. *svo*, †*so*, Norw. and Da. *saa*, Sw. *så*), Goth. *swa* (also *swē*). The precise relation of some of these forms to each other, and the ultimate origin of the stem, are uncertain.

In OE. frequently strengthened by a preceding *eall* (*all*): for the subsequent history of this see ALSO and AS.]

**A.** Illustration of forms.

**1.** *α.* 1 suae, suæ (suoæ), swæ.

*c* **725** *Corpus Gl.* (Hessels) Q 18 *Quantisper*, suae suiðe. **805** *Charter* in *O.E. Texts* 442 Suæ hueðer hiora suæ leng lifes. *c* **888** K. ÆLFRED *Boeth.* xxxiv. §9 Swæ me ðincð. *c* **950** *Lindisf. Gosp.* Matt. xiii. 32 Suoæ þæt fleȝendo heofnes cymes.

*β.* 1 sue, suue, 1, 3 swe.

*c* **700** CÆDMON *Hymn* 3 Sue he uundra ȝihuaes..or astelidæ. *c* **825** *Vesp. Psalter* ii. 9 Swe swe fet lames. *c* **875** *Erfurt Gloss.*, *Quacumque*, suue suidae. **971** *Blickl. Hom.* 23 Swe we nu ȝeearnian willaþ. *c* **1205** LAY. 29805 And swe he dude seoððe.

*γ.* 1–3 se (2 sæ).

*c* **831** *Charter* in *O.E. Texts* 446 Suelc mon se ðet lond hebbe. **1154** *O.E. Chron.* (Laud MS.) an. 1137, War sæ me tilede. *Ibid.* an. 1140, Ware se he com. *a* **1225** *Leg. Kath.* 49 Se wide se þet lond wes.

**2.** (Only *OE.*, *north.*, and *Sc.*) *α.* 1–7 swa (5 swaa), 1, 4–7 sua, 4 squa; 6 sway, suay, swae.

*Beowulf* 29 Swa he selfa bæd. *c* **950** *Lindisf. Gosp.* Matt. v. 31 Sua hua forletas wif his. *c* **1200** ORMIN Ded. 107 Þatt he't write swa. *c* **1325** *Metr. Hom.* 6 That it be sua. *c* **1375** *Cursor M.* 522 (Fairf.), Squa ys þe firmament. *a* **1400** *Syr Perc.* 524, I rede at it be swaa! *c* **1470** HENRY *Wallace* I. 250 Thai left him swa. **1537** *Registr. Aberdon.* (Maitl. Cl.) I. 413 And sway to continue. **1539** *Lib. Officialis Sti. Andree* (Abbotsford Cl.) 85 Suay þat þe said mareage cum nocht to effect. **1596** DALRYMPLE tr. *Leslie's Hist. Scot.* I. 274 Sua sal ʒe find na place. **1597** MONTGOMERIE *Cherrie & Slae* (ed. 2) 502 Thou sal sie it swae. *a* **1670** SPALDING *Troub. Chas. I* (Spalding Cl.) I. 88 Right sua Caithness, Sutherland [etc.]. **1678** SIR G. MACKENZIE *Crim. Laws Scot.* I. xxi. ii. (1699) 111 In swa far as he came.

*β.* 5–7, 9 **sa,** 6 **saa.**

*a* **1400–50** *Alexander* 259 Sa clere a witt & sa clene. **1513** DOUGLAS *Æneid* I. i. 16 Sa feill dangeris. **1596** DALRYMPLE tr. *Leslie's Hist. Scot.* II. 104 Althoch neuir saa Just. **1673** *Yorkshire Dial.* 4 (E.D.S.), Thou stayes sa lang. **1801** *Lonsdale Dial.* 4 (E.D.S.), I sat up sa lang yesternete. **1887** HALL CAINE *Son of Hagar* I. i, The..days you crack on sa often.

*γ.* 5–6 **say,** 7– **sae;** 6, 9 **sea,** 7 **seay;** 6, 9 **see,** 9 **seea.**

**14..** *Sc. Leg. Saints* xviii. (*Mary Egypt*) 290 Lyand say one athyr syd. **1533** GAU *Richt Vay* 102 Say greit faith. *c* **1566** *Merie Tales of Skelton* S.'s Wks. 1843 I. p. lviii, In gewd faith, saith the Kendallman, do see. **1583** *Leg. Bp. St. Androis* 899 Threttie pundis he conqueist sea. *c* **1620** A. HUME *Brit. Tongue* 17 Sae soft a mynt. **1684** *Yorkshire Dial.* 15 (E.D.S.), What need thou be seay flaid? **1728** RAMSAY *Anacreontic on Love* 12, I thought it sae. **1785** BURNS *2nd Ep. Lapraik* vii, Sae I've begun to scrawl. **1808** J. STAGG *Misc. Poems* 143 Suld ye..be sea daft. **1818** SCOTT *Hrt. Midl.* xvi, Do sae, minister—do sae.

**3.** *α.* 2–3 **swo,** 3 **suo,** 4 **zuo.**

*a* **1200** *Vices & Virtues* 33 Swo he mai me folȝin. *c* **1275** *Passion our Lord* 543 in *O.E. Misc.*, Iesus crist þet suo aros. **1340** *Ayenb.* 1 Zuo by hit.

*β.* 3– **so,** 4–6 **soo,** 5–7 **soe;** *dial.* 8–9 **soa, zo,** 9 **soo, zoo, zaw,** etc.

*a* **1240** in *O.E. Hom.* I. 203 Nere þe heorte so cold. *a* **1300** *Cursor M.* 16762 + 41 Mony grete clerkez..Seghen þe son fare soo. **1387** TREVISA *Higden* (Rolls) VII. 43 þat his broþer ..was so i-slawe. *a* **1400–50** *Alexander* 4772 þat þai suld wax soo. *c* **1420** *Avow. Arth.* xxiv, Is hit soe? **1482** *Cely Papers* (Camden) 131, Y would nott a wreten so. **1557** *Cal. Anc. Rec. Dublin* (1889) 463 The fynes..soo by hym not executed. **1683** *Col. Rec. Pennsylv.* I. 71 Which was soe done. **1746** *Exmoor Scolding* 195 (E.D.S.), And more an zo. **1785** W. HUTTON *Bran New Wark* 421 (E.D.S.), Soa far fra loving the man. **1867** ROCK *Jim an' Nell* xcv, Zo let us muve along.

**B.** Signification.

**I. 1.** In the way or manner described, indicated, or suggested; in that style or fashion.

Contextually the sense may be 'in the same way', 'by that means', etc. For the elliptic phrase *so please you*, etc., see PLEASE *v.* 3 c.

*c* **888** K. ÆLFRED *Boeth.* v. §3 ðelefst ðu þæt..auht godes swa ȝeweorðan mæȝe butan þæ m wyrhtan. *c* **1200** ORMIN Ded. 44 Icc hafe sett her..maniȝ word þe rime swa to fillenn. *a* **1250** *Prov. Ælfred* 350 So me may þane loþe lengust lede. *a* **1300** *Cursor M.* 19005 Fra dede to lijf nu resin es he,..Raisd sua wid godds might. *c* **1386** CHAUCER *Prologue* 102 A Yeman had he, and servantes nomo At that tyme, for him luste ride soo. *a* **1450** *Mirk's Festial* 26 A well yn Rome of watyr turned ynto oyle and ran soo all þat day. **1563** *Homilies* II. *Right Use Ch.* I. (1859) 154 His heavenly grace, wherewith he..endueth his people so there assembled. **1580** in W. H. Hale *Prec. Causes of Office* (1841) 85 They had in their church a godly interlude..Dominus monuit that herafter they do not so prophane their churche. **1643** DENHAM *Cooper's Hill* 202 For so our Children, thus our Friends, we love. **1725** POPE *Odyss.* IV. 159 So moves.. The silver-shafted goddess of the chace! **1780** *Mirror* No. 106, A person, engaged in the ordinary business of life,.. and, while so engaged [etc.]. **1840** THACKERAY *Shabby-genteel Story* viii, There was the woman at Pau; and that girl ..at Vienna. He went on just so about them all. **1874** T. HARDY *Far fr. Mad. Crowd* xx, 'You don't hold the shears right, miss... Incline the edge so,' he said.

**2. a.** With the verbs *do, say, think,* etc., latterly assuming the function of an object and passing into the sense of 'that'.

Placed either after or before the verb; but the latter order is now only literary and archaic, as in the phrase *so to do* (after quot. 1552).

(*a*) *c* **825** *Vesp. Psalter* cxlvii. 20 Ne dyde swe ylcre cneorisse. *c* **1000** *Ags. Gosp.* John xviii. 22 Andswarast ðu swa? *c* **1055** *Byrhtferth's Handboc* in *Anglia* VIII. 301 Do eall swa be eallum þam oðrum. *c* **1205** LAY. 2348 Ah ne dude he nawiht swo. *a* **1300** *Cursor M.* 13056 Qui sais þou sua? **1362** LANGL. *P. Pl.* A. II. 90 þe Tixt telleþ not so. *a* **1400** *Minor Poems fr. Vernon MS.* xxiii. 224 Offreþ þe lombes of Innocensye, For he comaundet so. *c* **1450** in Aungier *Hist. Syon* (1840) 251, I haue not in mende that I seyd so or dyd so. *a* **1536** *Songs, Carols,* etc. (E.E.T.S.) 21 Pesse, dere son, tell me not soo. **1611** BIBLE *Isaiah* xx. 2 And he did so, walking naked. **1697** J. LEWIS *Mem. Dk. Glocester* (1789) 24 When the Princess asked him, who taught him so? he said, Lewis. **1794** MRS. RADCLIFFE *Myst. Udolpho* xxxviii, 'I must believe so, sir,' replied Emily. **1818** SCOTT *Hrt. Midl.* xxiii, It was now the presiding Judge's turn to address the jury. He did so briefly and distinctly. *a* **1834** COLERIDGE *Confess. Enq. Spirit* iii. (1840) 37, I cannot doubt that they think so. **1892** *Law Times Rep.* LXVII. 252/1 If this had not been true, the pilot would have taken very good care to tell us so.

(*b*) *a* **1122** *O.E. Chron.* (Laud MS.) an. 656, Ða seonde se kyning æfter þone abbode, þet he æuestlice scolde to him cumon, & he swa dyde. *a* **1275** *Prov. Ælfred* 292 ȝif he for-swunken swoti wuere, swo hie ne þochte. *a* **1300** *Cursor M.* 4933 Sa þai me tald. **1422** tr. *Secreta Secret., Priv. Priv.* 123 Yf ye So do, ye may haue hoppe [etc.]. **1496** *Cov. Leet Book* 572 þat they may be compelled so to do. **1535** COVERDALE *Judith* vi. 17 He tolde them..how Holofernes people wolde haue slayne him for so sayenge. **1552** *Bk. Common Prayer, Morning Prayer,* Yet oughte we most chiefly so to doe, when [etc.]. **1660** SHARROCK *Vegetables* 16 You must not sow them too thick, for so doing hath lost many a peck of seed. **1816** SCOTT *Bl. Dwarf* xiv, So exclaimed Ellieslaw. **1844** DISRAELI *Coningsby* V. iii, So saying, the secretary effected his escape. **1888** BRYCE *Amer. Commonw.* I. xxxiv. 521 Some State legislatures have affected so to do.

**b.** With auxiliary verbs in elliptic use (requiring the addition of *do* or *to do*). Sometimes emphasizing a previous statement (quot. 1777).

*Beowulf* 797 Ðær hie meahton swa. *a* **1310** in Wright *Lyric P.* xv. 49 Me thunketh myn herte breketh a tuo; Suete God, whi shal hit swo? *a* **1400** *Isumbras* 57 In ȝouthe I maye bothe ryde and goo, When I ame alde I may nott so. *a* **1425** *Cursor M.* 9342 (Trin.), Kyngis anoynt ȝe haue to-fore; So shul ȝe þenne no more. *c* **1475** *Babees Bk.* 127 Now must I telle in shorte, for I muste so [*i.e.* in brief], Youre observaunce that ye shalle done. **1607** SHAKS. *Cor.* II. iii. 262 *Brut[us].* Repaire to th' Capitoll. *All.* We will so. **1777** SHERIDAN *Trip Scarb.* III. iv, It's well I have a husband a-coming, or ecod I'd marry the baker, I would so. **1860** RUSKIN *Unto this Last* iv. §81 All England may, if it so chooses, become one manufacturing town. **1871** R. ELLIS *Catullus* lxi. 97 Forth, fair bride, to the people, if So it likes you.

**c.** In this way; thus; as follows.

*a* **1250** *Prov. Ælfred* 405 For so seyde Salomon, þe wise: 'þe mon þat her wel deþ' [etc.]. *c* **1340** HAMPOLE *Pr. Consc.* I. 480 For when it es born it cryes swa: If it be man it says 'a. a' [etc.]. *c* **1440** *Promp. Parv.* 462 So, or on thys wyse, ..*sic, siccine.* **1611** BIBLE *Isaiah* xviii. 4 For so the Lord sayd vnto me; I will take my rest [etc.]. **1848** THACKERAY *Van. Fair* vi, How Amelia trembled as she opened it! So it ran —[etc.].

**3. a.** Used as predicate with the verb *be.*

In literary use still placed before the verb for emphasis, or in archaic phrases, as *so be it* (formerly used as a rendering of AMEN).

(*a*) *Beowulf* 1471 Ne wæs þæm oðrum swa. *c* **888** K. ÆLFRED *Boeth.* xxxvi. §7 Ac ðeah hi his nu næfre ne ȝe-lefen, ðeah hit is swa. *a* **1000** *Rel. Ant.* I. 35 Ic ȝe-lyfe on..þat ece lif. Sy it swa. **1338** R. BRUNNE *Chron.* (1810) 55, I praye God, if it were so, I strangle of þis brede. *a* **1400–50** *Alexander* 179 Sen it is sett to be soo, & slipe it ne may. **1530** PALSGR. 586 I holde you a noble it is nat so. **1611** BIBLE *Judges* vi. 38 If the deaw be on the fleece onely... And it was so. **1697** COLLIER *Ess. Mor. Subj.* I. (1703) 164 You argue from fact to necessity; 'Tis so, therefore it must be so. **1756** BURKE *Vind. Nat. Soc.* Wks. I. 27 It is always so; but was here emphatically so. **1821** SCOTT *Kenilw.* xviii, If this be all so, is it not reasonable [etc.]. **1862** MISS BRADDON *Lady Audley* xxxiii, I pray that it may be so, but I cannot think that it is so—I cannot even hope that it is so. **1880** 'MARK TWAIN' *Tramp Abroad* xxvii. 246 No! Is that so?

(*b*) *c* **1000** ÆLFRIC *Exod.* x. 11 Hit ne mæȝ na swa beon. **1340** *Ayenb.* 1 Ich bidde þe hit by my sseld..al to mi lyues ende, zuo by hit. *c* **1375** *Cursor M.* 1148 (Fairf.), For if I walde for-gif hit þe, hit nys noȝt worþi so to be. *c* **1375** *Sc. Leg. Saints* ii. (*Paul*) 1015 Gif it swa be, we mon all obey till his lare. **1535** COVERDALE *Judith* xiii. 15 That thou mayest se that it so is, beholde, this is yᵉ heade of Holofernes. **1536** *Primer Salisb. Use* 48 As it..euer shalbe. So be it. **1599** PORTER *Angry Wom. Abingt.* (Percy Soc.) 8 And his men be good fellowes, so it is. **1682** BUNYAN *Holy War* Wks. 1768 II. 7 No reason being annexed, but so I will have it, so it shall be. **1812** CRABBE *Tales* xviii, If he On aught determined, so it was to be. **1833** T. HOOK *Parson's Dau.* I. ix, How the conversation took that particular turn, I do not presume to know—so it was.

**b.** With auxiliary verbs in elliptic use (requiring the addition of *(to) be, (to) have it,* etc.).

*Beowulf* 2091 He mec þær on innan..ȝedon wolde..: hyt ne mihte swa. *c* **1205** LAY. 131 Mid wintre he wes bi-weaued; Swo hit wolde godd. *c* **1440** *Alph. Tales* 83 And Saynt Petur wolde nevur so, it myght nevur com samen agayn. *c* **1489** CAXTON *Sonnes of Aymon* xvii. 392 Ye saye well,..and I am soo contente. **1594** GREENE & LODGE *Looking Gl.* G.'s Wks. (Rtldg.) 130 You are a welcome guest, if so you please. **1701** J. NORRIS *Ideal World* I. ii. 95 We need but..., instead of *I affirm so if so*, say *If so I affirm so*. **1731** POPE *Let. to Hill* 15 Feb., I am very desirous to leave out that note if you like so.

**c.** Followed by a clause introduced by *that.*

*a* **1300** *Cursor M.* 11725 Quer it es sua, yee wat it noght, þat handes mine þis tre has wroght. *c* **1400** *Beryn* 3569 Sith þat it so is, That of the first pleyntyff wee have sikirnes. *a* **1450** *Le Morte Arth.* 2517 The knyghtis..said..that so them thought That syr mordred the sekereste was. **1538** STARKEY *England* I. i. 10 Though hyt be so that man abusyth the..company of man. **1663** S. PATRICK *Parab. Pilgr.* (1687) 474 Yet so it was, that one day he seriously told his Friend. **1711** STEELE *Spect.* No. 144 ¶1 Yet so it is, that People can bear any Quality in the World better than Beauty. **1763** J. BROWN *Poetry & Music* v. 61 How came it so to pass, that the first Race of Men were..of a stronger Turn to Poetry?

**d.** In clauses of supposition (sometimes with omission of *that*). *by so (that)*: see BY *prep.* 23 d.

**13..** in Horstman *Hampole's Wks.* (1896) I. 169 If so be þat þo haf les schame with þi foule herte þen with þi foule body. **1390** GOWER *Conf.* I. 48 That can I do wel, Be so my lif therto wol laste. *c* **1482** in *Cal. Proc. Chanc. Q. Eliz.* II. (1830) Pref. 64 If it hadde be soo that the forsaide John Ferrers hadde not made feithfull promyse. **1495–1611** [see IF *conj.* 8 f]. **1638** BRATHWAIT *Barnabees Jrnl.* (1818) 193 Thus love I thee, so be thou loue me. **1665–1861** [see IF *conj.* 8 f].

**4. a.** Representing a word or phrase already employed: Of that nature or description; of or in that condition, etc.

*c* **1000** ÆLFRIC *Saints' Lives* II. xxix. 52 Paulus..ȝemette ænne blindne mann, se wæ s ȝeboren swa. *c* **1440** *Alph. Tales* 85 A preste þat trowid he was a passand gude synger, not-with-stondyng he was not so. **1563** *Homilies* II. *Fasting* I. (1859) 284 Which works..are called good works, and are so indeed. **1573** TUSSER *Husb.* (1878) 128 Some come, some go, This life is so. *a* **1640** MASSINGER *Old Law* IV. ii, He's merry As if he had no such charge: one with that care Could never be so. **1664** H. MORE *Myst. Iniq.* II. II. i. 338 If the Devil be a Beast, that which makes him so is the wickedness of his nature. **1737** POPE *Hor. Epist.* I. vi. 2 To make men happy, and to keep them so. **1842** BORROW *Bible in Spain* vii, He was half intoxicated, and soon became three parts so. **1885** *Law Reports* 15 Q.B.D. 316 The catch..was worn away, and probably had been so for months.

**b.** With verbs of thinking, considering, etc.: To be such, as such.

*a* **1300** *Cursor M.* 27573 Man es..prode for halines, And lates oft lightly o þaa Men þat er noght funden sua. **1609** BIBLE (Douay) 1 *Macc.* x. *comm.*, It was not in the kings powre to make Jonathas highpriest, but..the king..did so account him. **1644** VICARS *God in Mount* 195 They taking us to be their friends, and wee them so too. **1710** STEELE *Tatler* No. 126 ¶1 Her Attractions would indeed be irresistible, but that she thinks them so. **1784** J. POTTER *Virtuous Villagers* II. 179 Though I am afraid it is not always considered so. **1847** C. BRONTË *J. Eyre* ii, 'Silence! This violence is all most repulsive;' and so, no doubt, she felt it. **1896** *Law Times* C. 358/1 R. became a lunatic, and was so found by inquisition.

**c.** As object after *have.*

**1658** *Whole Duty Man* iii. 52 The first is the having a mean and low opinion of our selves, the second is the being content that others should have so of us. **1662** STILLINGFLEET *Orig. Sacræ* II. iii. §4 Whether the person.. hath divine authority for what he saith. What ground can I have to believe that he hath so?

**d.** With *call, name,* etc.: By that name or designation. (Cf. 6.)

**1608** SHAKS. *Per.* III. iii. 13 My..babe Marina, Whom, for she was borne at sea, I haue named so. **1617** COLLINS *Def. Bp. Ely* To Rdr. p. ix, Hee maruells that the Papists should be so called [sc. *novitii*]. **1659** PEARSON *Creed* (1839) 446 The ..Scriptures..term him plainly and expressly so. **1728** SWIFT *Gulliver* I. viii, My son Johnny, named so after his uncle. **1803** WORDSW. *Blind Highland Boy* 11 A Highland Boy!—why call him so? **1859** HADLEY *Ess.* x. (1873) 194 This mode of 'futurizing' (if we may so call it).

**5.** In various elliptic uses:

†**a.** = Yes. *Obs.*⁻¹

*a* **1425** *Cursor M.* 13560 (Trin.), Somme seide nay & somme so.

**b.** After adverbs and conjunctions, as ***how so? not so, if so,*** etc.

*a* **1300** [see HOW *adv.* 17]. **1526** TINDALE *Luke* i. 60 Not soo, but he shalbe called Jhon. **1579** FULKE *Heskins' Parl.* 155 This hath nothing lesse then that. Why so? **1579** SPENSER *Sheph. Cal.* May 312 If Foxes bene so crafty, as so. *a* **1593** MARLOWE *Edw. II*, v. ii, That Edmund laid a plot To set his brother free, no more but so. **1676** ETHEREDGE *Man of Mode* I. i, *Dor.* I am glad he pitcht upon Loveit. *Bell.* How so? **1819** SCOTT *Ivanhoe* xxviii, He will not die unless we abandon him; and if so, we are indeed answerable for his blood. **1842** TENNYSON *Lady Clare* xi, 'Nay now,..keep the secret all ye can.' She said, 'Not so'. **1871** R. ELLIS *Catullus* lxxxv. 1 Half I hate, half love. How so? one haply requireth. **1896** GUY BOOTHBY *Dr. Nikola* i, 'I know China as well as any living Englishman.' 'Quite so.'

**c.** As an introductory particle. Also *so, so.*

This and the two following uses are common in Shakespeare's plays.

**1593** SHAKS. *Lucr.* 330 So so, quoth he; these lets attend the time. **1602** *How to choose Gd. Wife* in Hazl. *Dodsley* IX. 55 So, let me see: my apron. **1605** *1st Pt. Jeronimo* I. i. 77 So, so, Andrea must be sent imbassador? **1741** RICHARDSON *Pamela* III. 251 And I say..So, my good Friends!—I am glad to see you. **1775** SHERIDAN *Rivals* II. ii, So, so, ma'am! I humbly beg pardon.

**d.** As an expression of approval, or a direction to do something in a particular manner. Also in phr. ***so best.***

(*a*) **1598** SHAKS. *Merry W.* III. i. 109 Giue me thy hand (Celestiall) so. **1627** CAPT. SMITH *Seaman's Gram.* ix. 38 Steare steady & keep your course, so, you go wel. **1649** LOVELACE *Poems* (1864) 112 Where now one *so so* spatters, t'other: *no!* **1669** STURMY *Mariner's Mag.* I. ii. 18 So, thus, keep her thus. **1821** SCOTT *Kenilw.* xxiii, Walk through the apartment... So; feel you not now that you are possessed of the full use of your limbs? **1833** T. HOOK *Parson's Dau.* II. i, Here, let me just turn that curl—there, so. **1867** SMYTH *Sailor's Word-bk.* 637 *So!*, an order to desist temporarily from hauling upon a rope, when it has come to its right position.

(*b*) **1851** MRS. BROWNING *Casa Guidi Wind.* II. Wks. (1904) 372 Shaking Austria's yoke He shattered his own hand and heart. 'So best'. **1860** *Trans. Philol. Soc.* LXI. 164 It is to be an omnium-gatherum, and if this be practicable, so best.

†**e.** = Let it be so; it is well. *Obs.*

**1591** SHAKS. *Two Gentl.* II. i. 137 If it please you, so: if not: why so. **1611** —— *Cymb.* II. iii. 16 If you can penetrate her with your fingering, so.

**f.** With ellipse of 'says' or 'writes'.

**1613** F. T. *Suppl. Discussion of Barlowe's Answer* 220 So he; doubting as you see, of the truth of his witnesses. **1685** STILLINGFL. *Orig. Brit.* i. 9 So Bale; but Pits places him ten years later.

**g.** Ellipt. for *is that so?* expressing (*a*) recognition or realization of a fact or (*b*) questioning or dismissal of a statement (cf. *so what,* sense 10 c below).

**1803** G. COLMAN *John Bull* I. 7 *Peregrine.* Is your house far from the sea-shore? *Mrs. Brulgruddery.* About three miles, Sir. *Peregrine.* So! I have been wandering about since day-break. **1886** *Liverpool Even. Express* 9 Jan. 3/4 'Oh, Mr. Blobbs, you can form no idea of the terrible dream I had last night.'.. 'So?' remarked Mr. Blobbs, continuing the perusal of the morning paper. **1903** FARMER & HENLEY *Slang* VI. 289/1 'The King returns to town to-day' 'So?' **1973** H. NIELSEN *Severed Key* i. 6 'Small craft warnings are out.' 'So?' Simon queried. **1977** W. TUTE *Cairo Sleeper* vii. 122 'You will see whenever Major Masri decides you should see,' the officer said curtly... 'So!' she said to herself. **1978** A. MORICE *Murder by Proxy* i. 13 'He's an estate agent.'.. 'So?' 'So nothing.'

**h.** Used to add emphasis to a statement contradicting a negative assertion made by the previous speaker. *dial.* or *colloq.* (chiefly *U.S.*).

**1913** *Dialect Notes* IV. 55 *So, adj.*, used sometimes as 'too' and 'just the same' are used to intensify an assertion in reply to an expression of scepticism. 'You don't know anything about it!' 'I do *so*!' **1931** *Amer. Speech* VII. 20 *So*, emphatic in absolute use. 'I was—so!' **1937** L. B. Murphy *Social Behavior & Child Personality* ii. 62 Eunice, 'I don't.' Anne, 'You do so.' **1951** N. M. Gunn *Well at World's End* xiv. 101 'You don't like butter!' she cried. 'I do so like butter!' 'You don't! You don't!'.. 'I do so!' he yelled. **1953** K. Tennant *Joyful Condemned* xii. 103 'How old are you?' 'Eighteen.' 'Eighteen, my fat aunt.'.. 'I am so eighteen.' **1979** G. Swarthout *Skeletons* 28 'I've published nineteen!' 'You haven't.' 'I have so.'

**6.** In combinations: **a.** With past (or present) pples., as ***so-caused***, ***-formed***, ***-named***, ***-titled***, etc., ***so-seeming***.

See also so-called, -styled, -termed.

*c* **1430** Hoccleve *Minor Poems* 124 If so-causid seeknesse on me fil As dide on the. **1467–8** *Rolls of Parlt.* V. 629/2 The which soo named brode sette Clothes. **1598** Shaks. *Merry W.* iii. ii. 41, I will.. plucke the borrowed vaile of modestie from the so-seeming Mist[ress] Page. **1602** W. Watson *Decacord.* 181 The so authorized deprives the authorizer of his superioritie over him. **1621** G. Sandys *Ovid's Met.* vii. (1626) 135 Whom now the so-instructed sisters led Into his chamber. **1815** *Ann. Reg., Hist.* 63 Forbidding all his subjects to pay taxes.. to the so-titled imperial government. **1830** Herschel *Study Nat. Phil.* iii. iv. 304 The multiplication of so-considered elementary bodies. **1883** *Nature* XXVII. 326 The so-formed super-phosphate.

**b.** With vbl. sbs., as ***so-doing***, ***-saying***.

**1509** in *Mem. Hen. VII* (Rolls) 444 Farnando Duke and the do[ctor] de Puebla had byn dysstroyed for theyre so doyngys. **1803** tr. *P. Le Brun's Mons. Botte* I. 110 What! asleep yet, sluggard!.. And with so saying, pinched his ear. *a* **1834** Coleridge *Confess. Enq. Spirit* iii. (1840) 37 Because the so thinking supersedes the necessity of all after-thought.

**c.** *Sc.* With advs., as ***so-like***, ***-wise***. Cf. so-gate(s.

**1533** Gau *Richt Vay* 104 To cal thayme selff.. successours of the apostlis, o say lik? say lik? **1556** Lauder *Tractate* 428 Salyke sic Pryde pertenis to trew teaching. **1819** Tennant *Papistry Storm'd* (1827) 158 Sae-wyse the Papists.. Did scatter aff.

**7.** As *adj.* **a.** (See quot. 1867.) **so-fashion** *adv.*, in this or that manner. *U.S. dial.*

**1867** J. F. Dimock *Giraldus Cambrensis' Opera* V. 431 Perhaps it was something like the modern Scotch plaid, wrapped round the body; the so use of which is certainly very ancient. **1890** *Dialect Notes* I. 23 *So fashion*, meaning *so, in that way*. Is this known all over New England? **1903** G. S. Wasson *Cap'n Simeon's Store* v. 86 It don't look right for nobody.. to take and hang on to them tormented ole witch-bridles so-fashion! **1913** R. Frost in *Poetry & Drama* Dec. 415 I'll knock so-fashion and peep round the door When I come back, so you'll know who it is.

†**b.** *slang.* Homosexual. *Obs.*

**1937** in Partridge *Dict. Slang.* **1963** C. Mackenzie *Life & Times* II. 254 'I've come to the conclusion,' he told me, 'that I'm not really "so" at all. I much prefer girls.' At this date [*sc.* 1899] the cant word among homosexuals for their proclivities was 'so'. That seems to have vanished completely from current cant. **1968** J. R. Ackerley *My Father & Myself* xvi. 192 A young 'so' man, picked up by Arthur in a Hyde Park urinal. **1973** *Daily Tel.* (Colour Suppl.) 23 Feb. 51/4 Wilde used to call him 'the architect of the moon'. Rothenstein, Beerbohm,.. and Epstein were his more predictable friends, as he was not.. at all 'gay', as it is now called, or, as it was then called, 'so'.

**II.** Placed at the beginning of a clause with continuative force, and freq. preceded by *and*.

**8.** Used to confirm or strengthen a previous statement.

(*a*) **1154** *O.E. Chron.* (Laud MS.) an. 1135, Men.. sæden ðæt micel þing sculde cumen herefter; sua dide. *c* **1330** *Arth. & Merl.* (Kölbing) 9817 Þe clerk Merlin.. dede hem liȝt,.. So þai dede & blisse made. *c* **1374** Chaucer *Troylus* ii. 1284 'Lo, yond he rit!' Quod she, 'ye, so he dooth'. **1526** Skelton *Magnyf.* 798 Abyde, syr, quod he! mary, so I do. **1590** Shaks. *Com. Err.* v. i. 58 *Ab.* You should for that haue reprehended him. *Adr.* Why so I did. **1611** Bible *Ezra* iv. 24. **1653** Walton *Angler* ii, Now have at him with Killbuck, for he vents again. *Venator.* Marry! so he does. **1757** Foote *Author* i. Wks. 1799 I. 142 You had better hold your chattering, so you had. **1898** Watts-Dunton *Aylwin* iv. iii, My father's birthday? Why, so it is!

(*b*) *c* **1440** *Alph. Tales* 256 He bad þis whik man lay þe dead man ouerthwarte befor hym..; and so he did. **1510** *Sel. Cas. Star Chamber* (Selden) II. 72 Intendyng.. to have drowned the same Shipp, and so hadd doon hadd nott the mariners.. made great.. defence. **1602** in Morris *Troubles Cath. Foref.* (1872) i. iv. 192 My abode at this present is, and so hath been for some years, altogether in London. **1864** Browning *J. Lee's Wife* iv. i, You wanted my love—is that much true? And so I did, love, so I do.

**9.** Denoting similarity or parallelism in some respect between two facts, actions, etc.

(*a*) *c* **888** Ælfred *Boeth.* xxv, Swa doð eac wudufuȝlas. *a* **1200** *Moral Ode* 146 Ful wombe mei lihtliche speken of hunger.. swa mei of pine þe ne cnauð hu þe scal a ilesten. *a* **1250** *Prov. Ælfred* 308 Mony appel is bryht wiþ-vte, and bitter wiþ-inne; So is mony wymmon [etc.]. *c* **1350** *Childhood Jesus* 91 in Horstm. *Altengl. Leg.* (1878) 102/2 'Certes, me thrystyt wonder sore.' 'Certes,' seyt Josep, 'so do I'. *c* **1430** Lydg. *Minor Poems* (Percy Soc.) 24 The sonne chaungith, so doth the pale mone. **1601** R. Johnson *Kingd. & Commw.* (1603) 213 So again was Cyrus by Tomiris, who slue him and all his host. **1671** Milton *Samson* Pref., For so in Physic, things of melancholic hue and quality are us'd against melancholy. **1721** Ramsay *Prospect of Plenty* 7 Sae, th' heedless heir.. Lets ilka sneaking fellow take a pluck. **1842** Browning *Pied Piper* ix, The Mayor looked blue; So did the Corporation too. **1890** *Law Times* LXXXIX. 165/1 If the lienors may insure, so may the owners of the injured ship and cargo.

(*b*) *a* **890** *Charter* in *O.E. Texts* 452 In þissum life ondwardum, & eac swa in þæm towardan life. *a* **1225** *Ancr. R.* 130 Auh Dauid wende þider.. & so deð þe gode ancre. *c* **1400** *Laud Troy Bk.* 11395 He sclow oure kyng Archilogus,.. And so he did kyng Archomene. **1470–85** Malory *Arthur* ix. vi. 348 Thenne was sir Bryan ful gladde and soo was his lady & alle his knyghtes. *a* **1586** Sidney *Ps.* v. ii, Thou.. in endles hatred hast The murd'rous man, and soe the fraudulent. **1646** Sir T. Browne *Pseud. Ep.* iii. xv. 142 Leeches will move both waies; and so will most of those animals, whose bodies consist of round and annulary fibers. **1786** Burns *Ded. to G. Hamilton* 7 When I'm tir'd—and sae are ye, Wi' monie a fulsome, sinfu' lie. **1842** Tennyson *Dora* 26 But in my time a father's word was law, And so it shall be now for me. **1884** *Longman's Mag.* Mar. 492 All other branches of athletic sport.. have their ruling bodies, and so has cycling.

**10. a.** For that reason, on that account, accordingly, consequently, therefore.

The causative force is sometimes very slight, the use approximating to that in b.

(*a*) *c* **1250** *Old Kentish Serm.* in *O.E. Misc.* 32 Hise deciples hedde gret drede of þise tempeste, so hi a-wakede hine. *c* **1374** Chaucer *Troylus* v. 1233 Fayn he wolde dye, So on a day he leyde him doun to slepe. *c* **1420** Lydg. *Assembly of Gods* 434 So forthe yn he went & spake wordys fell. **1563** *Homilies* ii. *Sacrament* i. (1859) 440 So then, as of necessity we must be our selves partakers of this Table [etc.]. **1616** J. Lane *Contn. Sqr.'s T.* vi. 334 What all pleasures dothe containe is greater, so is pleasures soveraigne. **1713** Swift *Cadenus & Vanessa* Wks. 1755 III. ii. 31 The cry'r was order'd to dismiss The court, so made his last O yes! **1821** Scott *Pirate* i, A shelter.. is all I seek for. So name your rent. **1896** Guy Boothby *Dr. Nikola* v, We leave at daybreak for Pekin, so I will wish you good-bye now.

(*b*) *a* **1200** *Vices & Virtues* 35 Karitas is heiȝest and betst of ðese þrie, and swo hie is ouer alle oðre. **1297** R. Glouc. (Rolls) 2091 Maximian was suþþe aslawe,.. & so þei ssrewe robeours abbe hor wille an stounde. *a* **1390** *Wycliffite Bible* (1850) II. 738 And so alle the salmys of Dauid ben maad in noumbre of an hundrid and fifti. *c* **1440** *Alph. Tales* 164 He had not money enogh to pay for þaim; & so he frustid hym. **1549** in *Rep. Hist. MSS. Comm.* Var. Coll. (1907) IV. 282 Quere yf this be not againste the profitt of the common people, and so voide. **1604** *3rd Rep. Hist. MSS. Comm.* 11/1 All these Bills had the royal assent, and so were enacted. *c* **1680** Beveridge *Serm.* (1729) II. 566 He must love God with all his heart and soul, and so above all things in the world. **1818** Byron *Juan* i. v, But then they shone not on the poet's page, And so have been forgotten. **1888** *Law Times* LXXXV. 133/1 A mortgagor's tenant is emphatically a person interested in the equity of redemption, and so entitled to redeem.

**b.** (*a*) As an introductory particle, without a preceding statement (but freq. implying one).

**1710** Swift *Jrnl. to Stella* 21 Sept., So you have got into Presto's lodgings; very fine, truly! **1777** Sheridan *Sch. Scandal* ii. iii, Well—so one of my nephews is a wild rogue, hey? **1809** Byron in R. C. Dallas *Corr. of B.* (1825) I. 95 So Lord G* is married to a rustic! Well done! **1881** Jowett *Thucyd.* I. 42 And so we have met at last, but with what difficulty!

(*b*) [Reflecting Yiddish idioms.] Without implication of a preceding statement, or with concessive force: = well then, in that case, very well; also (introducing interrogative clauses) with adversative force: = but then, anyway.

**1950** B. Malamud in *Partisan Rev.* XVII. 666 Miriam returned after 11.30... 'So where did you go?' Feld asked pleasantly. **1952** M. Pei *Story of English* 182 The adverb *so* at the beginning of a sentence ('So I'll pay for it!'), probably of Yiddish origin, occurs frequently in conversation. **1960** 'E. McBain' *Give Boys Great Big Hand* i. 4 'I warn you.. I ain't got no wine.' 'So who wants wine?' **1977** F. Branston *Up & Coming Man* v. 49 'How much profit..?' 'Impossible to do more than make a wild guess.' 'So make a wild guess.'

**c.** ***so what?***: a retort made to an assertion, implying that the problem expressed has no immediate interest or obvious solution. Also as *attrib. phr.* orig. *U.S.*

**1934** M. H. Weseen *Dict. Amer. Slang* 399 So what?—What of it? What does it matter?.. What does that have to do with the matter? Your remark has no bearing or significance. **1935** F. Baldwin *Innocent Bystander* v. 83 'He has a wife,' said the girl gloomily. 'So what?' asked Angela carelessly. **1938** C. Landery (*title*) So what? a young man's odyssey. **1949** *Hansard Commons* 21 Nov. 104 That is unfortunate and disappointing but, to use an American expression, 'So what?' **1953** in *Shorter Oxf. Eng. Dict.* (1955). Add., The tragedy of the 'So what?' generation. **1960** M. A. Sindall *Matey* xiii. 177 She suddenly yawned and flung the magazine on to the seat. 'So what!' she murmured. **1968** C. Watson *Charity ends at Home* x. 126 No, the fact is that Henny and I got along as well as most. Not around each other's necks all the time, but so what? **1970** T. Hilton *Pre-Raphaelites* viii. 201 Burne-Jones pushed art so far away from this world that our reactions to some of his paintings are of a merely so-what kind.

**11.** Denoting sequence, freq. without implication of manner, and hence passing into: Then, thereupon, thereafter, subsequently.

(*a*) *c* **1300** *Havelok* 2858 Thanne he hauede sikernesse Taken.., so dide he calle þe erl of Cestre. **1393** Langl. *P. Pl.* C. viii. 232 So [*earlier texts* þenne] shalt þow come to a court. *c* **1450** Holland *Howlat* 794 Sa come the Ruke. *c* **1614** Sir W. Mure *Dido & Æneas* Wks. (S.T.S.) I. 72 Achates only he his convoy makes, Swa journey taks where fortune guides the way. **1697** J. Lewis *Mem. Dk. Glocester* (1789) 29 The Princess thought it high time to have him taught to walk regularly, so by degrees to dance.

(*b*) **1470–85** Malory *Arthur* ii. v. 82 Balyn hyt hym thorugh the sheld, and the hauberk perysshed, & so percyd thurgh his body. **1517** Torkington *Pilgr.* (1884) 2 The thursday I went to Seynt Denys.., and so retornyd a gayne the same nyght to Parys. **1585** T. Washington tr. *Nicholay's Voy.* i. vi. 4 b, The Ambassadour shewed hym his commission, and so tooke his leaue of him. **1620** E. Blount *Horæ Subs.* 349 But for a tast and so away. **1715** *Maryland Laws* vi. (1723) 20 Stakes.. with Numbers 1, 2, 3, 4, and so to an Hundred. **1821** Scott *Pirate* ii, Thence by a whaling vessel to Lerwick, and so to Jarlshof. **1892** A. J. Butler tr. *Memoirs Marbot* I. iii. 17 Then we marched out as we had come in, to the drum, and so to bed.

†**12.** Following on conditional clauses: Then.

*a* **1536** Tindale *Doct. Treat.* (Parker Soc.) 433 If thou believe not.., so is it impossible that [etc.]. **1567** *Gude & Godlie B.* (S.T.S.) 18 Will thow thy sinfull lyfe confes,.. Sa ar ȝe worthie, small and greit.

**III.** To that extent; in that degree.

For *ever so*, *never so*, in emphatic use, see ever *adv.* 9 b, c, and never *adv.* 4.

**13. a.** With adjs. or advs. (or equivalent phrases), in negative and interrogative clauses. ***not so*** preceding an adj., in the sense 'not very, none too——': see not *adv.* and *sb.* C 2 d.

(*a*) *c* **888** K. Ælfred *Boeth.* v. §3 Ne ȝelyfe ic no þæt hit ȝeweorþan meahte swa endebyrdlice. *c* **975** *Rushw. Gosp.* Matt. viii. 10 Swa micel ȝeleafa ne ȝemotte ic in Israhele. *c* **1205** Lay. 600 Nes castel nan swa strong. **1297** R. Glouc. (Rolls) 7551 Þer nas prince in al þe world of so noble fame. **1338** R. Brunne *Chron.* (1810) 54 In suilk apparaille dight, þat so riche armes was neuer sene with sight. *c* **1400** *Laud Troy Bk.* 15509 In al this world is non silke, So noble werk, ne so riche. **1501** *Plumpton Corr.* 157, I was never so werie & soferd of my life, since I was borne. **1578** Lyte *Dodoens* 22 The great Bistorte hath long leaves like Patience, but smaller, and not so smothe or playne. **1646** Fuller *Wounded Consc.* (1841) 335 A meaner man, of whose spirituality the patient hath not so high.. conceits. **1746** Francis tr. *Horace, Epist.* ii. i. 46 They neither wrestle, sing, or paint so well. **1797** Godwin *Enquirer* i. vi. 38 Men were no longer shut up in so narrow boundaries. **1803–5** Wordsw. *Solitary Reaper* 13 A voice so thrilling ne'er was heard. **1849** Macaulay *Hist. Eng.* vi. II. 89 The Cavaliers.. were by no means disposed to revive an institution so odious.

(*b*) *c* **900** tr. *Baeda's Hist.* v. ix. (1890) 410 Forhwon seȝdes ðu Æcgbrihte swa ȝemeleaslice & swa wlæclice þa ðing..? *c* **1386** Chaucer *Can. Yeom. Prol. & T.* 340 And if a man wol aske hem prively Why they been clothed so unthriftily [etc.]. **14..** *26 Pol. Poems* xxvi. 24, I.. asked who had.. brought her in so drowpyng chere. **1445** in *Anglia* XXVIII. 281 Is his worship of so litel peys? **1598** Marston *Sco. Villanie* iii. ix, Why lookes neat Curusall so simpringly? **1611** Bible *John* xiv. 9 Haue I bin so long time with you? **1690** Locke *Hum. Und.* iii. v. §9 The reason why I take so particular notice of this. **1735** Berkeley *Querist* §215 Whence is it that Barbs and Arabs are so good horses? **1780** *Mirror* No. 95, She.. asked me, with her usual good-humour, what made me look so grave? **1850** Newman *Difficulties Anglicans* i. v, What am I to say in answer to conduct so preposterous?

**b.** Followed by a relative clause or equivalent complement. (Cf. 24.)

Rarely when the antecedent clause is affirmative.

**1581** in Allen *Martyrdom Campion* (1908) 17 Is it possible to find xii so wicked.. men in this citye.. that will finde us guiltie togeather of this one crime? **1593** Shaks. *Lucrece* 853 No perfection is so absolute, That some impurity doth not pollute. **1601** —— *Jul. C.* i. ii. 316 Who so firme, that cannot be seduc'd? **1610** —— *Temp.* v. 269 A Witch.. so strong That could controle the Moone. **1611** Bible *Job* xli. 10 None is so fierce that dare stirre him vp. **1753** L. M. tr. *Du Boscq's Accompl. Woman* 26 There is no design so black, which Ambition scruples to conceive. **1780** *Mirror* No. 92, There is nothing so absurd or extravagant, which riches.. will not tempt him to commit. **1821** Scott *Kenilw.* viii, He.. came not thither so private but what he was espied by one who told me.

**14. a.** In affirmative clauses, tending to become a mere intensive without comparative force, and sometimes emphasized in speaking and writing.

(*a*) *Beowulf* 347 Ȝif he us ȝeunnan wile, þæt we hine swa godne gretan moton. *c* **888** K. Ælfred *Boeth.* xxxv. §3 Nu ðu þæt swa openlice onȝiten hæfst, ne ðearfe ic nu.. ymb ðæt swincan. *a* **1225** *Leg. Kath.* 171 Þe wrecches þet ha seh swa wraðe werkes wurchen. **1297** R. Glouc. (Rolls) 590 Þat king lotrin.. dude al his wille, vor he lokede so rowe. **1340** Hampole *Pr. Consc.* 4073 Þe empire, þat was swa myghty, Es now destruyed a grete party. **1390** Gower *Conf.* III. 1 This vice, which so out of rule Hath sette ous alle, is cleped Gule. **1412** *26 Pol. Poems* xi. 50 God dede þe make, Put soule of resoun in flesche so frele. **1503** Hawes *Examp. Virt.* xii. 238 Amonge the floures so swete of ayre. **1626** W. Sclater *Exp. 2 Thess.* (1629) 297 The bones of so dogged Contentions. **1678** Dryden *All for Love* iii. i, I fear'd he loved her:.. For 'twere impossible that two, so one, Should not have lov'd the same. **1741** Richardson *Pamela* III. 168 My Face.. was hid in my Bosom, and I looked so silly! **1820** Keats *Lamia* i. 183 To see herself escap'd from so sore ills. **1839–52** Bailey *Festus* 208 The Norman! so noble, and stately and tall. **1882** Floyer *Unexpl. Baluchistan* 302 The absence of ruined buildings, which so invariably form the major part of a Persian town.

(*b*) **1837** Dickens *Pickw.* iv, My dear brother is *so* good. **1853** Mrs. Gaskell *Cranford* i, A man is *so* in the way in the house. **1875** E. FitzGerald *Lett.* (1889) I. 369, I am *so* glad (as the Gushingtons say) that you like the Carlyle.

**b.** Preceded by *a*, *the*, *this*, etc., or possessive pronouns. Now rare except in combs.

*c* **1205** Lay. 3812 Þu eært a swa hende gome. **13..** in Horstm. *Altengl. Leg.* (1875) 75 Of a so ȝong þing. **1340** *Ayenb.* 100 To by zone to ane zuo greate emperur. **1535** Joye *Apol. Tindale* 19 Nothinge performing his so large promyses. **1545** Brinklow *Compl.* 18 Ye may set to reforme thes so wicked lawes. **1629** Gaule *Holy Madnesse* 329 You may see your face in his so transparant cheeks. **1667** Marvell *Corr.* Wks. (Grosart) II. 81 The reason of our so long silence. *a* **1700** Evelyn *Diary* June 1645, Divers statues.., amongst which is the so celebrated Eve. **1865** Ruskin *Sesame* ii. §57 The one weakness of his so mighty love. **1887** Hall Caine *Deemster* xxxix, The so heavy burden thou bearest.

**c.** With adj. and singular sb., in cases similar to next, but without *a*. Now *rare*.

**1297** R. Glouc. (Rolls) 1490 Vor he was so god kniȝt & al so so noble king, He bed vor to ȝiue him is doȝter in spousing. *c* **1400** Maundev. (1839) vi. 66 Thei seyn, that thei scholde not entre in to so holy Place. *c* **1425** Lydg. *Assembly of Gods* 1417 Syth they so long tyme haue made me so madde. **1557** North *Gueuara's Diall Pr.* 110 In the time of so great and excellent philosopher. **1814** Scott *Let.* in *Lockhart* (1837) III. ix. 292 So short time have I been absent. **1867** Ruskin *Time & Tide* ix. §40 In so apparently desultory manner.

**d.** With adj. followed by *a*. †Sometimes preceded by *this*.

(*a*) **13..** *Gaw. & Gr. Knt.* 1538 Gret is þe gode gle,..þat .. ȝe wolde..pyne yow with so pouer a mon. **1412–20** Lydg. *Chron. Troy* IV. 1855 Hector, þat was so noble a knyȝt. **1548** Hall *Chron., Rich. III*, 56b, Yf we dye so glorious a death in so good a quarell. **1624** Quarles *Sion's Sonn.* viii. 4 To kisse the lips of so, so faire a Bride. **1780** *Mirror* No. 95, I thought I had never beheld so interesting an object. *a* **1845** Barham *Ingol. Leg.* Ser. III. *Brothers Birchington* lxvi, So barefaced a blunder. **1902** Gairdner *Hist. Eng. Ch. 16th Cent.* viii. (1903) 140 So insulting a message was clearly out of the question.

(*b*) **1611** Bible *1 Kings* iii. 9 Who is able to iudge this thy so great a people? **1632** Hayward tr. *Biondi's Eromena* 169 Of such as were privy to this so important a secret. *a* **1700** Evelyn *Diary* 22 Apr. 1694, How this so young a gentleman..could live in such an expensive manner. **1736** Butler *Anal.* II. vii, This so remarkable an Establishment.

†**e.** With *a* or *an* inserted before the adj. (cf. SUCH *a*.). Also ***so very a***. *Obs.*

**1569** J. Sanford tr. *Agrippa's Van. Artes* 66b, The feeble definition of so an approved philosopher. **1614** Selden *Titles Honor* 148 Vpon so an apparant diminution of the peoples libertie. **1657** Fuller *Notes Jonah* i. 5 So an unnatural sin was atheism. **1664** Pepys *Diary* 10 Jan., We are all glad, so very a known rogue he was.

†**f.** With *a* inserted between the two parts of a combination. *Obs.*

**1595** Shaks. *John* IV. ii. 27 Putting on so new a fashion'd robe. **1631** Massinger *Believe as You list* II. i, Was there ever So sweete a temperd Roman? **1682** A. Mudie *Pres. St. Scotl.* Ep. Ded. A iiij b, The constitutions of so well a Governed Kingdom. **1756** Toldervy *Hist. 2 Orphans* III. 173 So jealous a pated fellow.

**g.** With an adj. of size or quantity, with the implication of an accompanying gesture: = as—as this. Esp. in phr. ***when I (he,*** etc.) ***was so high***, when I (etc.) was a small child. Hence ***so-high*** adj. Cf. THAT *dem. adv.* b, quot. 1870.

**1876** Geo. Eliot *Dan. Der.* IV. VII. liii. 89 'You would have me love what I have from the time I was so high'—here she held her left hand a yard from the floor. **1899** Kipling *Stalky & Co.* 226 'Do 'ee lov' me, Mary?' 'Iss—fai! Talled 'ee zo since yeou was zo high!' **1916** A. Huxley *Let.* *c* 12 July (1969) 105 Vassall..seems..to have known me when I was 'so high'. **1963** 'B. Graeme' *Almost without Murder* xiv. 157 As a so-high kid I had 'liked' ice cream.

**15.** With verbs. Now usually intensive.

*c* **1375** *Sc. Leg. Saints* xlviii. (*Juliana*) 245 For þe desert þat þu can ma to god, þat þe a-wansit sa. *a* **1425** *Cursor M.* 5290 (Trin.), He haþ delyuered me of my woo, And put me to welþe, no mon so. **1579** Spenser *Sheph. Cal.* Aug. 15 What payne doth thee so appall? **1615** G. Sandys *Trav.* 1 Celebrated for quarries of excellent marble, which do so adorne the Venetian palaces. **1626** T. H[awkins] *Caussin's Holy Crt.* 436, I cannot so harden my hart, but that it may be softned. **1833** Ht. Martineau *Manch. Strike* i. 2 O father, my knees have been aching so all day. **1849** [Eastwick] *Dry Leaves* 22 The waves, which..did in this place so confound and toss about the triremes of Alexander. **1884** C. Gibbon *Fancy Free* xiv, I held back because I loved you so.

†**16.** Equally; to the same extent. *Obs.*$^{-1}$

**1697** Dampier *Voy.* (1729) I. 228 The Tree or Shrub that bears it is like the Prickle-Pear-Tree, about 5 foot high, and so prickly.

**IV.** Introducing one or both of two clauses expressing comparison or correspondence.

†**17. a.** In the way that; as much as; as. *Obs.*

***soon so***, as soon as: see SOON *adv.*

*Beowulf* 490 Site nu to symle,..swa þin sefa hwette. *c* **888** K. Ælfred *Boeth.* xxxix. §12 He..swincð þonne ymb þæt swa he swiðost mæȝ. **971** *Blickl. Hom.* 19 Cleopian we nu in eȝlum mode.., swa se blinda dyde. *a* **1122** *O.E. Chron.* (Laud MS.) an. 1016, Se here..sloȝon & bærndon..swa heora ȝewuna wæs. *a* **1275** *Prov. Ælfred* 608 Sone min so dere, do so ich þe lere. **13..** *K. Alis.* 6260 (W.), A folk..Al blak so cole-brond. *c* **1380** *Sir Ferumb.* 5383 Gweynes fleȝ forþ so wynd and rayn.

†**b.** After numerals: As. *Obs.*

In OE. also in other forms of expression.

*a* **1000** in Thorpe *Laws* I. 190 Syx swa micel. *c* **1330**–*c* **1420** [see TEN C]. **1587** Mascal *Govt. Cattle, Sheepe* (1627) 203 Others with twise so great a stocke.

†**c.** As if. *Obs.*

*a* **900** Cynewulf *Crist* 850 Nu is þon ȝelicost, swa we on laguflode..ceolum liðan. **971** *Blickl. Hom.* 205 And þa fotlastas wæron swutole..on þæm stane, swa hie on wexe wæron aðyde. *c* **1250** *Owl & Night.* 142 Heo song so lude.., Ryht so me grulde schille harpe. *c* **1275** *Passion Our Lord* 542 in *O.E. Misc.* 52 Hi vellen so hi were ded. *c* **1300** *Havelok* 594 Also lith was it þer-inne, So þer brenden cerges inne.

†**d.** After relative pronouns or advs.: So ever.

In OE., and very early ME., the pronoun or adverb was preceded as well as followed by *swa*.

*c* **1175** *Lamb. Hom.* 145 Hwa se wile cume efter me. **1340** Hampole *Pr. Consc.* III. 2595 In what state swa he be þan. *c* **1350** *Will. Palerne* 2565 What man so vs metes, may vs sone knowe. *c* **1400** *Cursor M.* 28788 (Cott. Galba), Whether so askes more rightwisly, Sall be herd of god. *c* **1425** Lydg. *Assembly of Gods* 1406 Dredde shalt thow be, wher so thow become. *c* **1440** *Alph. Tales* 34 Promysyng hym to do what þing so he commanddid hym. **1559** *Mirr. Mag.* (1563) B iv, Whom so they take they slay. *a* **1593** Marlowe *Edw. II*, I. i, Commaund What so thy mind affectes.

†**18.** ***so..so.* a.** = So..as (see 20). *Obs.*

In OE. also *swa swa* without intervening words, and sometimes *swa..swa swa*.

*c* **888** K. Ælfred *Boeth.* xxxix. §4 Swa hit is swa þu sæȝst. **971** *Blickl. Hom.* 137 Hit wæs þa swa leoht swa se merȝenlica steorra. *a* **1240** *Ureisun* in *O.E. Hom.* I. 193 Heo beoð so read so rose, so hwit so þe lilie. **1297** R. Glouc. (Rolls) 5369 Þat londfolc to him com so þikke so it miȝte go. *c* **1330** R. Brunne *Chron. Wace* (Rolls) 6827 Þe arewes come so þykke so reyn. **1393** Langl. *P. Pl.* C. XIV. 188 Ich see noone so ofte sorfeten, Soþliche so mankynde.

†**b.** = As..so (see 22). *Obs.*

In OE. also *swa swa..swa*.

*c* **825** *Vesp. Psalter* cii. 13 Swe mildsað feder bearnum, swe mildsiende bið dryhten ondredendum hine. **971** *Blickl. Hom.* 9 Swa se hyhtenda ȝigant, swa Drihten on middanȝearde bliðe wunode. *a* **1175** *Lamb. Hom.* 39 Swa se þu forȝeuest..swa þin drihten forȝeueð þe þine misdede. **13..** *K. Alis.* (Laud MS.) 2210 So on þe shyngel liþe þe haile, Euery kniȝth so lijþ on oþer. [**1667** Milton *P.L.* VII. 288 So high as heav'd the tumid Hills, so low Down sunk a hollow bottom.]

†**c.** With comparatives: The..the. *Obs.*

*c* **888** K. Ælfred *Boeth.* vii. §4 Swa him mon mare selð, swa hine ma lyst. **971** *Blickl. Hom.* 15 Swa hie him swyþor styrdon, swa he hludor cleopode. *a* **1225** *Ancr. R.* 182 So þe sicnesse is more, se þe goldsmið is bisegure. *a* **1240** *Lofsong* in *O.E. Hom.* I. 215 Þet hit ontende me..in þine luue, so lengre so more. *a* **1400** *Minor Poems fr. Vernon MS.* xxix. v. 47 Hym þouȝte euere so leng so wors.

**19.** In adjurations or asseverations.

*So* has here the sense of 'in that way' or 'to that extent', the complementary clause being omitted. The two usual types are here illustrated separately. For *so help* see also S'ELP, S'HELP, and SWELP.

(*a*) *Beowulf* 435 Ic þæt þonne forhicȝe, swa me Hiȝelac sie ..modes bliðe, þæt [etc.]. *c* **1175** *Lamb. Hom.* 33 Swa me helpe drihten. *c* **1205** Lay. 3041 Iheren ich wlle,..sua þe helpe Appolin, hu deore þe beo lif min. **1382** Wyclif *Exod.* x. 10 So the Lord be with ȝow, what maner thanne Y shal leeue ȝow? *c* **1386** Chaucer *Merch. T.* 931 This schal ben doon.., So wisly God my soule bringe in blisse! [See also SAVE *v.* 2b.] *c* **1440** Lovelich *Merlin* 12034, I wolde, so god me spede, that pes purchaced were betwixen vs two. **1480** in Gross *Gild Merch.* II. 71 Soo god yow help and holydome. **1508** [see HELP *v.* 1c]. **1565** Cooper *Thesaurus* s.v. *Ita*, So god saue me. **1603** Knolles *Hist. Turks* (1621) 572 So helpe me great Mahomet it shall not so be. **1828** Scott *F.M. Perth* xxviii, This seat..I claim as my right—so prosper me God and St. Barr! **1868** [see HELP *v.* 1c].

(*b*) *a* **1300**–*c* **1386** [see THEE *v.*[1] 1b]. *c* **1400** [see THRIVE *v.* B. 2]. *c* **1400** *Gamelyn* 515 And I wil kepe þe dore, so ever here I masse. *c* **1420** *Liber Cocorum* (1862) 6 Þis seȝe I preved, so have I blys. *c* **1475** *Rauf Coilȝear* 53 'Sa mot I thrife,' said the King, 'I speir for nane ill'. *c* **1500** Medwall *Nature* 753 (Brandl), The scald capper sware sythyche [= so thee ich] That yt cost hym euen as myche. *a* **1553** Udall *Royster D.* III. v. (Arb.) 56 The selfe same that I wrote out of, so mote I go. **1598** [see THEE *v.*[1] 1b].

**20. a.** ***so..as, so as***, in such or the same way, manner, etc., as.

*a* **1225** *Leg. Kath.* 1055 Unweoten, þe weneð þet hit beo swa as hit on ehe bereð ham. *a* **1300** *E.E. Psalter* i. 3 Al his liue swa sal it be, Als it fares bi a tre. **1390** Gower *Conf.* Prol. I. 5, I thenke forto touche also The world..So as I can, so as I mai. *c* **1440** *Alph. Tales* 85 Þis preste askid hur whi sho wepud so as sho did. *c* **1489** Caxton *Sonnes of Aymon* iv. 119 Soo well clothed & arrayed, as I have tolde you above. **1535** Coverdale *Gen.* xviii. 5 Do euen so as thou hast spoken. **1554** *Act 1 & 2 Phil. & Mary* c. 8 §52 Hereditaments, so to be amortized as is aforesaid. **1593** Shaks. *Lucr.* 1811 He with the Romans was esteemed so As silly-jeering idiots are with kings. **1611** Bible *Ps.* lxiii. 2 To see thy power and thy glory, so as I haue seen thee in the Sanctuary. **1681** Flavel *Meth. Grace* xxix. 496 They must so walk, as he walked. **1797** *Encycl. Brit.* (ed. 3) XVII. 407/1 Lay the bend mould upon it, so as may best answer the round.

†**b.** In adjurations. *Obs.*

*c* **1386** Chaucer *Clerk's T.* 493 Sche to the sergeant preyde, So as he was a worthy gentilman, That [etc.]. **1390** Gower *Conf.* I. 310, I..beseche Unto the mihti Cupido,.. So as he is of love a godd [etc.]. **1463** in *Somerset Medieval Wills* (1901) 197, I charged ham so as they will answere afore God.

†**c.** With *as* = *as if*. *Obs.*

**1596** Spenser *F.Q.* v. viii. 5 So ran they all, as they had bene at bace.

**21.** ***so..as***, to the same extent, in the same degree, as:

**a.** In negative or interrogative clauses.

*a* **1225** *Ancr. R.* 150 Þenne nis hit to nout so god ase to þe fure of helle. **1362** Langl. *P. Pl.* A. VIII. 167 Bote trustene to Trienals..Is not so syker for þe soule, sertes, as do-wel. *c* **1386** Chaucer *Merch. T.* 45 Who is so trewe and eek so ententyf To kepe him..as is his make? **1581** Allen *Apol.* 121 Death and dungeons be not so terrible things..as they seeme. **1596** Spenser *F.Q.* VI. iii. 1 For a man by nothing is so well bewrayd As by his manners. **1646** in *Verney Mem.* (1907) I. 343 Women were never soe usefull as now. **1670** Dryden *Conq. Granada* I. II. i, His victories we scarce could keep in view, Or polish them so fast as he rough-drew. **1763** C. Johnston *Reverie* I. 260 This is not so strange or ingrateful as it may appear. **1779** *Mirror* No. 58, Emilia, who now observed that her husband was nowhere so happy as in the country. **1842** Tennyson *Morte d' Arthur* 156, I never saw..So great a miracle as yonder hilt. **1849** Macaulay *Hist. Eng.* v. I. 667 Never..had the condition of the Puritans been so deplorable as at that time.

**b.** In affirmative clauses: As..as. Now *arch.* or *dial.* (except in such phrases as *so far as*, *so much as*: see 35b, etc.).

***so long as***: see LONG *adv.* 1b. †***so soon as***: see SOON *adv.*

**1390** Gower *Conf.* I. 154 So seker as I have a lif, Thou scholdest thanne be my wif. *c* **1460** Fortescue *Abs. & Lim. Mon.* (1885) 128 A prince double so myghty as was thair old prince. **1535** Coverdale *2 Sam.* xix. 32 Barsillai was very olde, so good as foure score yeare olde. *c* **1550** R. Bieston *Bayte Fortune* A vj b, Smockes as snow so white. **1621** Bp. Mountagu *Diatribæ* 252 The one is become so old as the other. **1690** Locke *Hum. Und.* I. ii. §14 This Way of arguing is so frivolous, as the Supposition of itself is false. *c* **1790** Imison *Sch. Arts* I. 303 This planet being but a fifth part so big as the earth. **1818** Scott *Rob Roy* xiv, Although I readily gave my uncle the advantage of my pen..so often as he desired to correspond with a neighbour. **1876** Pearse *Daniel Quorm* 155 'Tis a'most so good for ourselves as 'tis for those we try to save.

**c.** Preceding the citation of a special example or instance.

**1582** N. Lichefield tr. *Castanheda's Conq. E. Ind.* 123 So small a kingdome as that is of Portingale. **1664** Marvell *Corr.* Wks. (Grosart) II. 167 Seeing upon so extraordinary occasions as these, the boldest eloquence would lose its speech. **1779** *Mirror* No. 63, It was impossible that a girl so amiable as Emily Hargrave could fail to attract attention. **1820** Keats *Hyperion* II. 321 Have I rous'd Your spleens with so few simple words as these? **1861** Pattison *Ess.* (1889) I. 37 The interest excited in England by events passing in so distant a quarter as Moravia. **1878** T. Hardy *Ret. Native* VI. iii. (1890) 399, I am not fit for town life—so very rural and silly as I always have been.

**d.** With *as* taking the place of an object to the following verb.

**1555** J. Proctor *Hist. Wyat's Rebellion* 37 It is so straunge a case as the world neuer saw. **1629** Drayton in *Sir. J. Beaumont's Bosworth Field* 14 So lasting Pillars to prop up thy Praise, As time shall hardly shake. **1676** Dryden *State of Innocence* IV. i, Is our Perfection of so frail a Make, As ev'ry Plot can undermine or shake?

†**e.** With a comparative: So much. *Obs.*$^{-1}$

**1726** Leoni *Alberti's Archit.* II. 46 Their Arch may come ..so lower as you think fit.

**22.** ***as..so***: **a.** Denoting more or less exact correspondence, similarity, or proportion.

Ormin has *all swa summ..swa* in this use.

*a* **1300** *Cursor M.* 17465 Als þai war for-boght sua þai did. *c* **1340** Hampole *Pr. Consc.* 32 Als he was ay God in trinite Swa be es, and ay God sal be. *a* **1400–50** *Alexander* 14 For as þaire wittis ere with-in, so þer will folowis. *a* **1533** Ld. Berners *Huon* lxvii. 232 Such as the mayster was so was the seruuant. **1553** T. Wilson *Rhet.* Prol. (1580) A v b, As it was, so it is, and so be it still hereafter. **1611** Bible *Prov.* xxiii. 7 For as he thinketh in his heart, so is he. **1711** Addison *Spect.* No. 47 ¶7 In proportion as there are more Follies discovered, so there is more Laughter raised. **1821** Keats *Lamia* I. 260 Even as thou vanishest so shall I die. **1830** Tennyson *Poet* xiv, And as the lightning to the thunder..So was their meaning to her words. **1887** Morris *Odyssey* XI. 586 For as often as stooped the elder when he longed for the water sweet So often it waned.

**b.** Denoting a simple parallelism between two different acts, concepts, etc., and sometimes approaching the sense of 'not only..but (also)'.

*c* **1340** Hampole *Prose Tr.* 2 Als ded slaas all, Swa lufe ouer-comes all. **1563** *Homilies* II. *Sacrament* I. (1859) 439 As of old time God decreed.., so our loving Saviour hath ordained [etc.]. **1588** A. King tr. *Canisius' Catech.* 67 As it vald be verray lang, sa is it verray hard. **1619** in W. Foster *Eng. Factories India* (1906) I. 79 As itt is an unsupportable wrong, soe itt inthralleth us to many other inconveniences. **1677** Marvell *Corr.* Wks. (Grosart) II. 549 As he loved not to make work, so not to leave it imperfect. **1766** Goldsm. *Vicar* iv, As we rose with the sun, so we never pursued our labours after it was gone down. **1831** Loudon *Encycl. Agric.* §6009 As the planters differ in the number of hills.., so are they no less capricious as to the manner of placing them. **1881** Jowett *Thucyd.* I. 45 As in the arts, so also in politics, the new must always prevail over the old.

**V. 23.** ***so that*** (also ***so*** alone), denoting result or logical consequence; also sometimes = 'in order that'.

In the revived use of *so* alone, orig. *U.S.*

(*a*) *Beowulf* 1508 Bær þa seo brimwylf..hringa þengel to hofe sinum, swa he ne mihte no..wæpna ȝewealdan. **1377** Langl. *P. Pl.* B. XIII. 64 Thanne seide I to my-self, so Pacience it herde. **1851** H. Melville *Moby Dick* III. 564 Take your leg off from the crown of the anchor here, though, so I can pass the rope. **1902** E. L. Banks *Autobiogr. Newspaper Girl* xii. 143 One of the books in front of mine was six shillings. I bought it so mine would show. **1913** [see sense 7a above]. **1949** W. Rogers *Autobiogr.* 44 The reason they leave some of our boys over there..is so they can get mail that was sent to them during the war. **1951** C. P. Snow *Masters* i. 3 Shovelling coal up the back of the chimney, throwing it on so it would burn for hours. **1968** *Los Angeles Times* 3 Mar. E6/3 The main reason Gender is back in the classroom is so he can converse in the many languages he knows. **1977** A. Thwaite *Portion for Foxes* 28, I shall make it simple so you understand.

(*b*) *c* **888** K. Ælfred *Boeth.* i, He ȝehet Romanum his freondscipe, swa þæt hi mostan heora ealdrihta wyrðe beon. *c* **950** *Lindisf. Gosp.* Matt. xv. 31 [He] ȝelecnade hea.., sua þæt ðreatas wundradun. *c* **1200** Ormin Ded. 293 Swa þatt he mannkinn wel inoh Off helle mihhte lesenn. *c* **1300** *Havelok* 216 Þe king..dede him sore swinge,..So þat þe blod ran of his fleys. **1340** *Ayenb.* 53 Þe ilke..wylleþ hyealde hire fole uelaȝredes, zuo þet hi ne conne ne hi ne moȝe healde mesure. *c* **1440** *Alph. Tales* 65 Such weddur þat stroyed all þe vynys, ..so at þer wyne had nowder colour nor savor. **1548** Hall *Chron., Hen. IV*, 28b, [They] had conveighed their shippes in to the havens, so that he could not fight with them on the sea. **1600** Pory tr. *Leo's Africa* VI. 280 Of..flesh heere is great scarcitie, so that they are constrained to eate camels flesh onely. **1670** *12th Rep. Hist. MSS. Comm.* App. V. 21 The under pettycoatt very richly laced.., so that 50 or 60 pounds [is] but an ordinary price. *c* **1760** Challoner in E. Burton *Life* (1909) II. xxiv. 28 We will spend our evenings ..at our own lodgings, so that we may be found. **1820** Scott *Monast.* xiv, So that Mary Avenel..was regarded with a mysterious awe. **1886** Stevenson *Kidnapped* xiv, The turf roof of it had fallen entirely in; so that the hut was of no use to me.

**24.** *so..that*, in such a way, to such an extent, that: **a.** With adjs. and advs., or equivalent phrases.

*a***900** CYNEWULF *Crist* 323 Hio..ece stondað..swa beclysed þæt nænig oþer..hy æfre ma eft onluceð. *a***1240** *Ureisun* in *O.E. Hom.* I. 183 [Thou art] swo leoflic and swa lufsum þet te engles a biholdeþ þe. **1297** R. GLOUC. (Rolls) 2207 þe romeins beþ anud of hor trauail so sore..þat hii nolleþ come here nanmore. *c***1340** HAMPOLE *Pr. Consc.* 324 Swilk men er ay swa unstedfast, þat na drede may with þam last. *c***1450** *Merlin* ii. 37 The water maketh so grete bruyt that all that is made a-boven it moste nede falle. **1523** FITZHERB. *Husb.* §151 Theyr cotes be so syde, that they be fayne to tucke them vp whan they ryde. **1574** HELLOWES *Gueuara's Fam. Ep.* (1584) 165 You aske me histories so straunge.., that my wits may not in anye wise but neede goe on Pilgrimage. **1625** PURCHAS *Pilgrims* II. 1138 The wind..came with so great gales, that it raised the sands of the coast very high. **1749** FIELDING *Tom Jones* VI. iii, The Squire was so delighted with this conduct of his daughter, that he scarce eat any dinner. **1802** MAR. EDGEWORTH *Moral Tales* (1816) I. iv. 21 So ill that she could hardly speak. **1862** MISS BRADDON *Lady Audley* viii, He sat so long in this attitude, that Robert turned round at last.

**b.** With verbs.

In verse (more rarely in prose) sometimes placed after the verb, and immediately followed by *that*, but separated from it by a pause.

(*a*) *c***950** *Lindisf. Gosp.* John iii. 16 Suæ..lufade god ðone middangeard þætte sunu his ancende ʒesalde [etc.]. *c***1320** *Cast. of Love* 1523 God leeue vs here so ende, þat we ben worþi to heuene wende. *c***1386** CHAUCER *Prol.* 32 So hadde I spoken with hem..That I was of here felawschipe anon. **1411** *Rolls of Parlt.* III. 651/1 The same Loord the Roos schall so doon to hem, that they schall tellen hem wel payed. **1480** *Cov. Leet Bk.* 437 To so direct that your said Oratours haue all þat..shall accorde with right. *a***1592** GREENE *Alphonsus* I. i, Now a days so irksome idless' sleights..have witch'd each students mind, That death it is [etc.]. **1641** J. JACKSON *True Evang. T.* ii. 130 The example doth so suite the Text, that I could not pretermit it here. **1667** MILTON *P.L.* II. 719 So frownd the mighty Combatants, that Hell Grew darker. **1735** JOHNSON *Lobo's Abyssinia, Descr.* v. 75 This Answer and the Present so provok'd Mahomet..that [etc.]. **1883** *Harper's Mag.* Nov. 905/2 To so cut down his power..that he would be inclined [etc.].

(*b*) *a***1175** *Cott. Hom.* in *O.E. Hom.* I. 231 þa be-fel hit swa þat him a þance befell. *c***1250** *Gen. & Ex.* 3503 Wurð ðin fader and moder so, ðat ðu hem drede and helpe do. *a***1300** *Cursor M.* 7509, I..scok þam be þe berdes sua þat i þair chafftes raue in tua. **1390** GOWER *Conf.* I. 12 Whil the lawe is reuled so That clerkes to the werre entende. **1535** COVERDALE *2 Chron.* iv. 4 It stode so vpon the bullockes, that thre were turned towarde the north [etc.]. *c***1600** SHAKS. *Sonn.* lxxi, I loue you so That I in your sweet thoughts would be forgot, If [etc.]. **1697** *Protestant Mercury* No. 189, A Porter's Wife..Beat her Husband so, that she forced him to leap over a Balconey.

†**c.** Expressing a contrast: Although..yet.

**1633** BP. HALL *Hard Texts, Isaiah* xlii. 2 Yet so shall he be gracious to the penitently dejected, that he shall not beare with the obstinate sinner.

**d.** With *but* (= that..not).

**1842** MACAULAY *Horatius* xviii, There was no heart so bold, But sore it ached.

**25. a.** With omission of *that*, = sense 24.

*a***1310** in Wright *Spec. Lyric P.* 74 Thou art so god a mon, Thi love y ʒyrne also y con. *c***1330** *Arth. & Merl.* 3458 (Kölbing), A dint he ʒaf him so hard, þe launce ran þe brini þurch. *c***1440** *Contin. Brut* II. 583 Caleis was so ferd of you, þey shitte neuer a gate. **15..** *Christ's Kirk* ii. in *Bann. MS.* 283 Thay wer so nyss..Thay squeilit lyk ony gaitis. **1646** SIR T. BROWNE *Pseud. Ep.* II. vi, A plant, so unlike a Rose, it hath been mistaken..for Amomum. **1697** DRYDEN *Virg. Georg.* III. 308 He..treads so light, he scarcely prints the Plains. **1742** YOUNG *Nt. Th.* III. 135 So man is made, nought ministers delight But what his glowing passions can engage. **1818** BYRON *Mazeppa* xviii, Once so near me he alit, I could have smote. **1859** GEO. ELIOT *A. Bede* xiii, Hetty was blushing so, she didn't know whether she was happy or miserable.

**b.** With the *so*-clause placed after that stating the consequence or result.

*a***1225** *Ancr. R.* 222 He bihalt on oðre þet he ne mei nones weis makien vuele iðoncked, so lufful & so reouðful is hire heorte. *c***1340** HAMPOLE *Pr. Consc.* 2317 Out of witte þan þai shuld men flay, Swa orrible and swa foul er þai. *a***1400** *Minor Poems fr. Vernon MS.* xliii. 104 His herte þoruʒ-out his syde He ʒiueþ vs, he is so fre! **14..** HOCCLEVE *Minor Poems* xvi. 4, I may nat deliure hem by no weye, So me werreyeth coynes scarsetee. *c***1500** *Melusine* vi. 28 Raymondin..herd ne saw nought, so sore was hys wit troubled. **1535** COVERDALE *2 Sam.* iii. 11 Then coulde he not answere him one worde agayne, he feared him so. **1626** SIR E. CECIL in *J. Glanville's Voy. Cadiz* (Camden) p. xliii, The shipp had sunke in the sea, she proved so leakie. **1681** DRYDEN *Abs. & Achit.* 813 Friends he has few, so high the madness grows. **1787** BURNS *Halloween* iv, A runt was like a sow-tail, Sae bow't that night. **1822** SCOTT *Nigel* x, Habits ..to young men are like threads of silk, so lightly are they worn, so soon broken. **1867** AUGUSTA WILSON *Vashti* xvii, The azure mantle..seemed to melt in air, so dim were its graceful outlines.

**26. a.** *so* (*that*), in limiting sense: On condition that, provided that, so long as, if only. Cf. 30.

(*a*) *c***1000** *Apollonius of Tyre* (Thorpe) 20 Nim nu lareow appolloni, swa hit þe ne mislicyʒe. *c***1375** *Cursor M.* 5991 (Fairf.), To-morne þe fleys sal be þe fra, so þou be-gyle vs na mare. *c***1386** CHAUCER *H. Fame* I. 423 He had y-swore to hire..That so she saved hym hys lyfe, He wolde haue take hir to hys wife. *c***1460** *Towneley Myst.* xx. 587 All my couandys holden shall be. So I haue felyship me abowte. **1523** FITZHERB. *Husb.* §43 Butter and swynes grease..are good, soo they be not salte. **1613** JACKSON *Creed* II. 453 The proofe were good, so it could be proued. **1658** SIR T. BROWNE *Hydriot.* §2 (1736) 18 Ulysses cared not how meanly he lived, so he might find a noble Tomb after Death. **1710** STEELE *Tatler* No. 208 ¶4 It is no Matter how dirty a Bag it is conveyed to him in,..so the Money is good. **1750** JOHNSON *Rambler* No. 81 ¶2 Which duty ought to be most esteemed, we may continue to debate..; so all be diligently performed. **1812** CARY *Dante, Purg.* IX. 22 So but the suppliant at my feet implore. **1816** BYRON *Ch. Har.* I. xiii. *song*, I'll swiftly go..; Nor care what land thou bear'st me to, So not again to mine.

(*b*) *c***1000** ÆLFRIC *Numb.* xxii. 20 Far mid him, swa þæt [L. *ita duntaxat ut*] þu do, þæt ic þe bebeode. *c***1320** *Cast. Love* 1042 Al þis wyde world I chul ʒeuen þe, So þat þou bouwe and honoure me. **1362** LANGL. *P. Pl.* A. IV. 89, I forʒiue him þat gult.., So þat ʒe assented beo. *c***1425** *Eng. Conq. Irel.* (1896) 8 Oft þe prince hym profred to delyuer hym out of prison, so þat he wold be his helppe to werry vpon þe kynge. *c***1489** CAXTON *Blanchardyn* xlviii. 188 Yf nedes I shal dey, I were..wel content soo that it were in the absence of her. *a***1533** LD. BERNERS *Huon* lviii. 202, I offer to make you amendes..so that ye wyl ayde me. **1583** STUBBES *Anat. Abus.* (1882) II. 85 You condemne not funerall sermons then, so that they be good. **1652** J. WRIGHT tr. *Camus' Nat. Paradox* IX. 211 Writing I am well contented to permit; So that I see your Letter. **1755** *Monitor* No. 8, Let us not regard by what name it shall be called, so that it be carried on vigorously. **1802** MAR. EDGEWORTH *Moral T.* (1816) I. xix. 154 To M. it was..indifferent who was found guilty, so that he could recover his money. **1859** TENNYSON *Marriage Geraint* 304 So that ye do not serve me sparrow-hawks For supper, I will enter.

**b.** In the event that, in case that. *rare.*

*c***1000** *Charter* in Thorpe *Dipl. Angl. Sax.* (1865) 202 He him þet land forbead, swa he æniges brucan wolde. **1872** TENNYSON *Gar. & Lyn.* 268 But, so thou dread to swear, Pass not beneath this gateway.

**VI.** †**27.** *so as*, although. *Obs.*

*c***1300** *Havelok* 337 þat hire haued in sorwe brouth, So as she ne misdede nouth!

**28. a.** *so*.., or *so..as*, *so as*, followed by an infinitive denoting result or consequence.

The omission of *as* is now regarded as irregular.

(*a*) *c***1395** *Plowman's Tale* I. 373 Peter was never so great a fole To leve his key with such a lorell. *c***1407** LYDG. *Reson & Sens.* 943 The Ryvers..so myghty and so large To bere a gret ship or a barge. *c***1450** *Merlin* i. 6 How shulde I be so hardy to do as ye telle me. **1526** TINDALE N.T. *Prol.*, Who ys so blynde to axe why lyght shulde be shewed to them that walke in dercknes. **1579** GOSSON *Sch. Abuse* (Arb.) 65, I am not so childishe to take euery bushe for a monster. **1658** ROWLEY, FORD, etc. *Witch of Edmonton* II. i, If you'll be so kind to ka me one good turn I'll be so courteous to kob you another. **1709** SWIFT *Vind. Bickerstaff* Wks. 1755 II. I. 171 He hath been indeed so wise to make no objections against the truth of my predictions. **1767** WILKES *Corr. w. Friends* (1805) III. 223 Be so good to continue to favour me with your letters. **1803** MARY CHARLTON *Wife & Mistress* IV. 161 She enquired if Mrs. Aubrey had been so kind to procure the child a new wardrobe.

(*b*) **1445** in *Anglia* XXVIII. 271 Nevir the[e] she so diseasyd as oonys..To folowe her wille. **1558** KENNEDY *Comp. Treat.* in *Misc. Wodrow Soc.* (1844) 97 That I..durst be sua baulde, as to attempt sua heych ane purpose. **1648** HEYLIN *Relat. & Observ.* I. 78 Whosoever shall dare to be so good a Patriot as to oppose their Tyranny. **1697** DRYDEN *Virg. Georg.* II. 747 A crop so plenteous, as the land to load. **1711** STEELE *Spect.* No. 53 ¶7, I hope you will not be so apparently partial to the Women, as to let them go wholly unobserved. **1779** *Mirror* No. 17, Our shop was so well frequented, as to require the constant attendance of both of us. **1828** DUPPA *Trav. Italy*, etc. 98 The others were so broken into small fragments as to be useless. **1885** *Law Times Rep.* LIII. 785/1 It is impossible to say that any one case is so in point as to carry this case.

(*c*) *c***1680** BEVERIDGE *Serm.* (1729) II. 283 They all run, but not so as to obtain. **1736** *Gentl. Mag.* VI. 716/1, I think it impossible to amend it..so as to make it a Bill fit for being passed. **1853** *Zoologist* II. 3724 Dismounting and hobbling the horse so as to allow him to feed. **1896** *Law Times* C. 488/1 To repair the drain so as to abate the nuisance complained of.

**b.** With infinitive preceded by a sb. *rare.*

**1709** SWIFT *Merlin's Prediction* Wks. 1755 II. I. 177 The river Thames frozen twice in one year, so as men to walk on it.

**c.** With pa. pples. (*to have* being omitted).

**1790** BURNS *Tam o' Shanter* 17 Hadst thou but been sae wise, As ta'en thy ain wife Kate's advice! **1797** in C. Kegan Paul *W. Godwin* (1876) I. 237 You might have been so good as told me a few more particulars.

**29. a.** *so as*, in such a way that, so that. Now *dial.*

**1523** LD. BERNERS tr. *Froissart* I. xiii. 13 The quene..dyd gyue great Jewelles to eche of them,..so as they all helde them selfe ryght well content. **1609** in *Buccleuch MSS.* (Hist. MSS. Comm.) 82, I understood of the infection lately come to some houses there adjoining, so as I forbear to go thither. *c***1651** in Morris *Troubles Cath. Foref.* (1872) I. vi. 304 This summer we also whited the church and choir,..so as our Monastery was made very handsome. **1751** R. PALTOCK *P. Wilkins* (1884) II. 217 So as the great and small shall be under mutual obligations to each other. **1817** H. T. COLEBROOKE *Algebra*, etc. Notes & Illustr. p. lxxvii, Then you desire to complete your square so as it shall amount to one whole square. **1905** *Longman's Mag.* Apr. 541 So as he could go and see his sweetheart.

**b.** *so..as*, in similar use, with the subject of the second clause either expressed, or implied in the previous context.

(*a*) **1548** WISHART *Conf. Faith* in *Misc. Wodrow Soc.* (1844) 13 We attribute so free wyll to man as we,..wyllynge to do good, fele experience of euyll. **1581** SIDNEY *Apol. Poetrie* (Arb.) 50 The words..beeing so set, as one word cannot be lost. **1608** E. GRIMSTONE *Hist. France* 702 The Emperour..so terrifies the Pope, as hee abandons his vassall Octauio. **1654** *Burton's Diary* (1828) I. 42 This sounded so plausibly in every man's ear, as it was soon embraced. **1738** *Gentl. Mag.* VIII. 327/2 They had Guards so posted, as they were not to be surprized.

(*b*) **1611** SIR W. MURE *Wks.* (S.T.S.) I. 9 Greedie to behold So rair perfectioune as cannot be told. **1678** WALTON *Life Sanderson* 11 Changes those cares into so mutual joys, as makes them become [etc.]. **1779** FORREST *Voy. N. Guinea* 66 With so heavy rain, as penetrated the new roof of the vessel. **1784** MISS CARTER *Lett. to Miss Talbot* IV. 341 My wretched head has been so thoroughly uncomfortable.., as rendered me quite unfit for writing.

**c.** *so..as that*, *so as that*, = prec. (*a*).

**1583** STOCKER *Civ. Warres Lowe C.* I. 1 b, The officers went so neere the consciences of men, as that they spared not to torment pore miserable soules. **1634** MILTON *Comus* 366, I do not think my sister so to seek, Or so unprincipl'd in vertues book,..As that [etc.]. *a***1700** EVELYN *Diary* 22 Mar. 1675, 2 distinct keeles crampt together.., so as that a violent streame ran betweene. *a***1774** GOLDSM. *Surv. Exp. Philos.* (1776) I. 55 When both flames have approached so near as that they join. **1817** H. T. COLEBROOKE *Algebra*, etc. 258 Here the least square quantity must be so devised, as that the second may be an integer.

**30.** *so as*, provided that, etc. Cf. 26.

**1585** T. WASHINGTON tr. *Nicholay's Voy.* IV. i. 114 b, To be preferred vnto the gouernment.., so as they had passed their time..without reprehension. **1598** GRENEWEY *Tacitus, Ann.* III. i. (1622) 64 Which was to him..honourable, so as there were a meane vsed. **1635** R. N. tr. *Camden's Hist. Eliz.* II. 136 Henry Percy offered..to free the Queene of Scots out of prison so as Grange and Carre..would receive her at the borders. **1807** E. S. BARRETT *Rising Sun* I. 127, I care not how you come by them, so as they are ready to supply my wants. **1853** DICKENS *Bleak Ho.* xxvi, He could play 'em a tune on any sort of pot you please, so as it was iron or block tin.

**VII.** In various phrases.

*so to say*: see SAY *v.*[1] 11. *so to speak*: see SPEAK *v.*

†**31.** *than so*, than that. *Obs.*

*a***1425** *Cursor M.* 23568 (Trin.), Mony þingis may we do þat better were vndone þen so. **1525** LD. BERNERS tr. *Froissart* II. 754 Kyng Henry was more gentyll than so; for he had some pytie on hym. **1593** SHAKS. *3 Hen. VI*, III. iii. 104 Lord Aubrey Vere Was done to death, and more then so, my Father. **1677** W. HUGHES *Man of Sin* II. v. 96 'Tis reasonable to suppose, that the Sacrament may be celebrating in more places than so, at once. *a***1716** BLACKALL *Wks.* (1723) I. 213 If it be not more than so, it will not be such an Obedience as God will accept.

**32.** †**a.** *and so*, = next. *Obs. rare.*

*a***1400-50** *Alexander* 1565 Sum with sensours & so with silueryn cheynes. *Ibid.* 2551 If þai were sary & so, na selly me thingke. **1602** [see 33 a].

**b.** *and so on*, used as an abbreviating phrase to avoid further description or the enumeration of further details.

*and so forth*: see FORTH *adv.* 9 b. *and so forward*: see FORWARD *adv.* 1.

**1724** WELSTED *Epist.*, etc. 123 Till, in time, the English we now speak is become as obsolete and unintelligible as that of Chaucer, and so on. **1837** P. KEITH *Bot. Lex.* 258 An incipient stem,..which in the following year is augmented in height as before, and so on in succession as long as the plant grows. **1847** *Howitt's Jrnl.* II. 201/2 While the East London Water Company is supplying an impure water at 5*l.* 12*s.*, and so on, per house. **1899** *Allbutt's Syst. Med.* VIII. 488 There may be high fever,..nausea, vomitings, smart diarrhœa and so on.

**33.** *or so*: **a.** Or something of that kind; or the like.

**1588** SHAKS. *L.L.L.* II. 212 *Ber.* Is she wedded, or no? *Boy.* To her will sir, or so. **1602** —— *Ham.* V. ii. 157 Girdle, Hangers or so [*Qq.* and so]. **1663** BUTLER *Hud.* I. i. 49 He..therefore bore it not about; Unless on Holy-days, or so. **1706** E. WARD *Wooden World Diss.* (1708) 44 Some-times he pores upon a Pack of Cards, or so. **1794** MRS. RADCLIFFE *Myst. Udolpho* xxxi, I used to think nothing on earth could fluster them, unless, indeed, it was a ghost, or so. **1818** BYRON *Juan* Ded. iii, And then you overstrain yourself, or so. **1842** TENNYSON *Day-dream, Revival* iv, My joints are somewhat stiff or so.

**b.** Or about that amount or number; or thereabout.

**1598** SHAKS. *Merry W.* II. i. 50 For an eternall moment, or so. **1601** —— *Twel. N.* III. ii. 59 Some two thousand strong, or so. **1814** SCOTT *Diary* 17 Aug. in *Lockhart* (1837) III. vi. 207 A King's ship about eighteen guns or so. **1861** HUGHES *Tom Brown at Oxf.* III. ii. 35 He returned in an hour or so. **1885** *Manch. Exam.* 10 July 5/3 A Sunday or so ago.

**34. a.** *so or so*, after this or that manner; this or that. Also with *many* (cf. 37 e).

*c***1449** PECOCK *Repr.* III. 350 For that so or so or so (and in noon other wise) it is writun in storie or cronicle. **1570** GOOGE *Pop. Kingd.* (1880) I. 3 b, For no man dare demaunde of him, why dost thou so or so. **1687** SETTLE *Refl. Dryden's Plays* 85 I'le die a thousand deaths before I'le do so or so. **1749** RICHARDSON in Mrs. Barbauld *Corr.* (1804) IV. 291 From her air and..her face, he sets her down in his mind as *so or so*. **1784** *Phil. Trans.* LXXIV. 189 A clock, of such a construction, kept or altered its rate *so or so*. **1835** T. MITCHELL *Aristoph. Acharn.* 307 *note*, Wine..is said..to bear or admit so or so many portions of water.

†**b.** *neither* (also *nothing*) *so nor so*, neither the one nor the other; neither this (way) nor that; not at all the fact or case. *Obs.*

**1583** STUBBES *Anat. Abus.* (1882) II. 34 They persuade the buier it is good, and that it is woorth the money, whereas indeed it is nothing so, nor so. **1584** R. SCOT *Discov. Witchcr.* VI. i. 90 Making you beleeve a thing which is neither so nor so. **1610** A. COOKE *Pope Joan* 12 As though that Temple had had a spire steeple like ours; which is neither so, nor so. **1611** COTGR., *Rien rien*, no no, neither so nor so. **1682** T. FLATMAN *Heraclitus Ridens* No. 73 (1713) II. 198 *Earn.* Most of 'em are said to have either a Competency, or another Trade.. *Jest.* This is neither so nor so.

**VIII.** With various adjs. and advs. of quantity, number, etc.

**35.** *so far*, in literal and transferred senses (see FAR *adv.* 6 and FAR-FORTH *adv.* 2): **a.** Without correlative word or clause.

*a***1300** *Cursor M.* 2253 Now we haue vs sped sa ferr, Vr wil may he noght vs merr. **1390** GOWER *Conf.* II. 33 Yit so fer cowthe I nevere finde Man that .. Me cowthe teche such an art. **1535** Coverdale *Ps.* cii. 12 Loke how wyde the east is from the west, so farre hath he set oure synnes from vs. **1611** Bible *Ps.* xxii. 1 Why art thou so far from helping me? **1696** *A. Telfair's New Confut. Sadd.* Pref. A 2 Having once gone so far, they will easily be induced to believe, that there's no Resurrection at all. **1754** Hume *Hist. Eng.* (1812) I. App. I. 198 He [the King] was even, so far, on a level with the people. *a* **1797** H. Howard in *3rd Rep. Hist. MSS. Comm.* 433/2 Every place given to an Englishman is so far a loss to the people. **1821** Scott *Kenilw.* xxvii, Will you so far trust me? **1832** Greville *Mem.* 27 Mar. (1874) II. 273, I have no doubt that all the ultras will be deeply mortified .. at the success so far of 'the Waverers'. **1892** *Speaker* 3 Sept. 288/1 Nothing has, so far, been allowed to transpire as to its name and contents.

*Comb.* **1880** *Nature* XXI. 407 This so-far improved feature of temperature.

**b.** Followed by *as*, with various constructions.

Examples of the literal sense are placed under (*b*).

(*a*) [*a* **1300** *Cursor M.* 16386 Sacles es he sa feir se sum i can (= so far as I can see).] **1485** *Sc. Acts, Jas. III* (1814) II. 172 Þe Custumaris at þair comptis making .. to be dischargit of safer as þai deliuer to þe said wardan & changeour. **1565** Stapleton tr. *Staphylus' Apol.* 148 Some are .. courtly protestants, which admit Luther so farre as them list. **1723** Sir R. Blackmore *Hist. Conspiracy* Pref. A 8 b, Some .. only advanced so far as to excite Popular Jealousies. **1742** Ld. Hardwicke in *Johnson's Debates* (1787) II. 161 The law .. is however to be so far fixed, as that every man may know his own condition. **1779** *Mirror* No. 14, I had actually gone so far as to write three introductory sentences. **1801** *Farmer's Mag.* Jan. 39 So far as I can now recollect. **1859** Geo. Eliot *A. Bede* xviii, Who played the part of steward so far as it was not performed by old Mr. Donnithorne him-self. **1876** Gladstone *Glean.* (1879) II. 313 So far as we can gather, a sober estimate prevails.

(*b*) **1513** Douglas *Æneid* VI. iii. 83 Sa fer before Achates and Enee As thai mycht weil behald thaim with thair E. **1675** in *Rep. Hist. MSS. Comm.* Var. Coll. IV. 247 Cleanseing the shallowes in the river so farre as Crane Bridge. **1806** Surr *Winter in Lond.* I. 76 Have you in your rambles, ever reached so far as the Park, Edward? **1898** E. P. Evans *Evol. Ethics* vi. 216 He sees clearly so far as his lantern casts its rays.

**c.** In the phrase ***in so far as*** (see in *prep.* 39).

**1546** *Reg. Privy Council Scot.* I. 31 In safer as concernis the said Williamys awine part. **1581** Burne in *Cath. Tractates* (S.T.S.) 140 In safar as thay confes Christ to be the sone of the leuing God. **1672** *Justiciary Rec.* (S.H.S.) 117 The complainer was no Magistrate in swa far as he had not taken the Declaration. **1780** *Mirror* No. 96, In so far as my improvement was concerned, they spared no expence. **1846** H. W. Torrens *Rem. Milit. Hist.* 11 The hieroglyphic inscriptions .., in so far as their characters have been decyphered. **1876** L. Stephen *Hist. Eng. Th. 18th C.* II. 418 Wesley .. differs from Warburton and his like in so far as God is regarded as an active administrator.

**d.** Followed by *that*.

*c* **1489** Caxton *Sonnes of Aymon* ii. 60 Sith that it is soo ferre come that ye wyll not here vs, we shall kepe owr peas. **1542** Udall *Erasm. Apoph.* II. (1877) 259 One of the accusers .. had gone so ferre, that he spake moche what these wordes folowing. **1711** Addison *Spect.* No. 5 ¶3 This strange Dialogue awakened my Curiosity so far, that I immediately bought the Opera. **1845** Stephen *Comm. Laws Eng.* II. 577 It is also so far a source of strength .. that it gives [etc.].

**e.** ***so far from***, used to give emphasis to a different statement following. Also with *that*.

(*a*) **1547** *Homilies* (1859) 112 David was so far from rejoicing at these news, that .. forthwith he rent his clothes. **1677** Miége *Dict.* II. s.v. *Far*, I am so far from loving her, that I hate her. **1736** Ainsworth *Eng.-Lat. Dict.* I. s.v., They were so far from selling, that they bought. **1868** J. H. Blunt *Ref. Ch. Eng.* I. 479 So far was it from doing so that it caused a rapid under-current of reaction.

(*b*) **1779** *Mirror* No. 33, Which, so far from being inconsistent .., is the most probable means of accomplishing it. **1813** Milner in *Suppl. Mem. Eng. Cath.* 305 As to .. the Bible, the Catholic Church, so far from locking that up, requires her Pastors to study the whole of it. **1870** Ruskin *Arrows of the Chace* II. 225 So far from wishing to give votes to women, I would fain take them away from most men.

**f.** In the phr. ***so far, so good***, used to express satisfaction with matters up to a certain point.

**1721** J. Kelly *Scottish Proverbs* 300 *So far, so good.* So much is done to good purpose. **1754** Richardson *Sir Charles Grandison* V. x. 56 'So far, so good,' said aunt Eleanor. **1809** Malkin *Gil Blas* VI. i. ¶11 So far, so good! said the worshipful commissioner; we have only to proceed in our examination. *a* **1843** Southey *Doctor* ccxxxix. (1848) 650 So far so good, but this once influential writer makes an erroneous conclusion. **1875** Ruskin *Fors Clav.* lxi. 11 So far, so good, Nature and facts are beginning to assert themselves.

**36. so long**: (see long *adv.* 1 b, 1 c).

**37. so many. a.** Such a (large) number (of).

*attrib.* *c* **888** K. Ælfred *Boeth.* xxxiii. §2 Þonne hi .. heora God on swa moniȝe dælas todælað, þonne [etc.]. *c* **1230** *Hali Meid.* 8 [It] deð hire in to drechunge, .. & to se monie earmden. **13..** *St. Augustin* 1731 in Horstmann *Altengl. Leg.* (1878) 91 Þer weore laft so mani Signes of wax, .. þat seint Austines chapel [etc.]. **1508** Dunbar *Poems* vii. 66 Thow suld be hye renownit, That did so mony victoryse opteyn. **1577** *St. Aug. Manual* (Longman) 110 How shall it be capable of so many and so great ioyes? **1639** Burton *Will* in *Anat. Mel.* (1893) I. p. xxx, Because there be soe many casualties to which our life is subjecte. *a* **1648** Ld. Herbert *Hen. VIII* (1683) 257 Peradventure lying among so many his Writings and old Letters. **1780** *Mirror* No. 104, It is .. a melancholy circumstance .. to find so many noble palaces deserted by their illustrious owners. **1820** Keats *St. Agnes* xxxviii, Here will I take my rest After so many hours of toil and quest. **1878** Swinburne *To Victor Hugo* xv, Hast thou seen time, who hast seen so many things?

*absol.* *c* **897** K. Ælfred tr. *Gregory's Past. C.* xxviii. 191 Buton he .. sua moniȝe ȝecierre sua he mæsð mæȝe. *c* **1375** *Sc. Leg. Saints* ii. (*Paul*) 162 Þe folk .. þat saw .. he gerte but resone sa mony sla, Raisit in hym sedicione. *c* **1450** Holland *Howlat* 237 Confess cleir can I nocht .. The maner, nor the multitud, so mony thar was. **1573** Tusser *Husb.* (1878) 8 Loiterers I kept so meanie, both Philip, Hob, and Cheanie. **1719** De Foe *Crusoe* II. (Globe) 360 We are not so many of us, here is Room enough for us all. **1812** Crabbe *Tales* ii. 142 Believe it .. glorious to prevail, And stand in safety where so many fail.

**b.** *so* (or *as*) ***many* .., *so many***, used to express equality in numbers. (See also how *adv.* 14 c.)

*c* **950** *Lindisf. Gosp.* Prol. Matt. 1 Swæ moniȝ aron bissena .. swa moniȝe boec. *a* **1548** Hall *Chron., Hen. IV*, 12 b, Verifiynge the olde Prouerbe, so many heades, so many wittes. *a* **1633** J. Austin *Medit.* (1635) 149 So many men, so many minds (saies the proverb): but here they were of one accord. **1718** Ozell tr. *Tournefort's Voy.* II. 181 When a Bassa is in march, so many robbers taken, so many heads off in an instant. **1735** Berkeley *Free-think. in Mathemat.* §44 As many men, so many minds.

**c.** Followed by *as* (†or the relative *that*).

**1340–70** *Alisaunder* 441 Þat by strength of her strife þei straught to foote All so many as his menne mighten areche. *c* **1400** *Brut* ccxxvii. 299 Ȝet were þey threfold so meny of hem as of Englisshe men. **1489** *Acta Dom. Conc.* (1839) 131 Samony of the .. cuschingis, weschale, and seruiotis, as aucht to be deliuerit. **1549** *Compl. Scotl.* 163 Sa mony of ȝou that ar defensabil men sal pas in propir person in battel. **1597** Jas. VI in *3rd Rep. Hist. MSS. Comm.* 422/2 Sa mony as are yet in hands sal be distributit. **1621** Bp. Mountagu *Diatribæ* 426 In this passage there are so many particulars obseruable concerning tithing, as there bee words in the same. **1685** *Caldwell P.* (Maitl. Cl.) I. 150 A man .. gives notice .. by so many windings of his horn as there are horse-men coming. **1735** Johnson *Lobo's Abyssinia, Descr.* x. 98 Every Man being allowed so many Wives as he hath hundreds of Cows. **1825** Scott *Talism.* xxviii, Had I not brought up unexpectedly so many Arabs as rendered the scheme abortive.

*Comb.* **1665** J. Webb *Stone-Heng* (1725) 15 To be a so-many-sided Figure as there are Segments wanting.

**d.** As many; an equal number (of). Freq. in vaguer sense, a number (pack, etc.) of.

(*a*) **1563–4** *Reg. Privy Council Scot.* I. 263 Thai and samony of thair freindis being present. **1568** Grafton *Chron.* II. 43 Hauing with him onely ten horsemen, with so many Archers on horsebacke. **1613** Shaks. *Hen. VIII*, v. iv. 79 We are but men; and what so many may doe, .. we haue done. **1678** Wanley *Wond. Lit. World* v. i. §97. 468/1 In twenty eight Battels he became Master of so many Kingdoms.

(*b*) **1600** Pory tr. *Leo's Africa* IX. 348 The ostriches wander vp and downe .. in orderly troupes, so that a far off a man would take them to be so many horsemen. **1631** Gouge *God's Arrows* v. §11. 422 A few couragious men to great armies of cowards, are as so many Lyons to whole heards of deere. **1711** Addison *Spect.* No. 50 ¶3 Pillars that stand like the Trunks of so many Trees. **1839** Thackeray *Fatal Boots* Oct., The carriage, the house in town, the West India fortune, were only so many lies which I had blindly believed. **1885** *Manch. Exam.* 20 May 5/1 They turned upon him like so many curs let loose.

**e.** Used to denote an unspecified number.

**1533** Gau *Richt Vay* 3 That thay .. suld haiff sa mony thousand zeris of pardone. **1611** Cotgr. s.v. *Chete*, The ship is so many foot deepe in hold. **1631** Gouge *God's Arrows* I. §29. 44 Papists .. going barefoot so many miles. **1780** *Mirror* No. 87, Creeping on his knees up the steps of St. Peter's so many times a day.

**38. so mickle**, = next. (See also insameikle.)

*c* **888** K. Ælfred *Boeth.* i, Þa hit ða ȝelomp þæt se arwyrða wæs on swa micelre nearanesse. **971** *Blickl. Hom.* 25 Nu he swa mycel for ure lufan ȝeþrowode. *c* **1175** *Lamb. Hom.* 31 Ne mahtic ȝelden swa muchel swa ic habbe idon to herme. *a* **1200** *Moral Ode* 357 in *Trin. Coll. Hom.*, He haueð sswo muchel þat he ne bit no more. *c* **1340** Hampole *Pr. Consc.* 6013 Swa mykel folk com never togyder .. sythen þe werld bygan. **14..** *26 Pol. Poems* xxvi. 217 Hym was nat lefte so mekyll a clothe Hys naked body for to hele. **1503** in Littlejohn *Aberd. Sheriff Crt.* (1904) 48 The said corn was samekle of waile in tyme of the spoliacioun therof. **1581** Hamilton *Cath. Traictise* Ep. 2 Not samekle for the present calameteis .., as for [etc.]. **1609** [see mickle B. 1 c]. **1820** Scott *Monast.* Introd. Ep., There were few folk kend sae muckle about the Abbey.

**39. so much.** (See also for-, insomuch.)

* *adj.* **a.** So great, extensive, or abundant; so large a quantity or number of, etc.

*a* **1225** *Leg. Kath.* 1345 Godes sune, þet se muche godlec cudde us alle on eorðe. **13..** *K. Alis.* 1032 (W.), Alle the innes of the toun Haddyn litel foisoun, .. So muche people with hire was. *c* **1380** Wyclif *Sel. Wks.* III. 431 Siche signes drawen fro love of Crist þo þat setten so meche trist in hem. *c* **1400** Love *Bonavent. Mirr.* (1908) 49 Thowh there was so moche nede, I fynde no mynde of furres or pilches. *a* **1529** Skelton *Sp. Parrot* 443 So myche newe makyng, .. So myche translacion in to Englyshe confused. **1613** Shaks. *Hen. VIII*, I. i. 167 This last costly Treaty .., That swallowed so much treasure. **1651** Howell *Venice* 31 Seeing the English buy so much Currans. **1780** *Mirror* No. 110, A performance, the reception of which was liable to so much uncertainty. **1812** Crabbe *Tales* v. 178 That so much beauty .. Raised strong emotions in the poet's mind. **1884** W. S. B. McLaren *Spinning* (ed. 2) 28 Some soda is often put into .. potash soaps just because it will hold so much water.

**b.** So largely possessed *of* something.

**1509** Hawes *Past. Pleas.* III. (Percy Soc.) 15 The fayre tower so muche of ryches Was all about sexangled. **1549–62** Sternhold & H. *Ps.* lxxxvi. 10 For why? thou art so much of might.

**c.** An equal sum or amount of (something).

**1557** in Marsden *Sel. Pl. Crt. Admiralty* (Selden Soc.) II. 72, I .. do owe unto John Levytt .. for so moche redy money of him resayved .. the some of fyfty pownds. **1695** Telfair *New Confut. Sadd.* (1696) 3 He took up the Threshold, found the Tooth, and threw it into the Fire, where it burnt like so much Tallow. **1857** Ruskin *Pol. Econ. Art* ii. §90 Whenever you buy a copy, you buy so much misunderstanding of the original. **1885** Mrs. Lynn Linton *C. Kirkland* I. 219 Even my languages .. were merely so much literary furniture.

** *adv.* **d.** Followed by *the* and a comparative (and sometimes with *by* preceding): To that extent, in that degree.

*a* **1225** *Leg. Kath.* 413 And swa muche þe swiðere þet he bihet to medin ham mid swiðe heh mede. *c* **1425** *Eng. Conq. Irel.* (1896) 6 He .. soiourned thar a whill; & so mych the blethelier, for þer com oft shippes theder. **1560** Daus tr. *Sleidane's Comm.* 216 b, He was brent in a small fire, that hys torment might be so mutch the greater. **1579** Lyly *Euphues* (Arb.) 179 By how much the more thou excellest others in honours, by so much the more thou oughtest to exceed them in honestie. **1611** Bible *Mark* vii. 36 The more hee charged them, so much the more a great deale they published it. **1691** T. H[ale] *Acc. New Invent.* 95 It is so much the worse, by how much it deviates from Equality. **1741** Challoner *Mem. Missionary Priests* Pref. (1803) A 2 Which appeared .., by so much the more wanting, by how much the less [etc.]. **1796** H. Hunter tr. *St.-Pierre's Stud. Nat.* (1799) I. 574 Others frequently concur to this end so much the better, the more that they seem to deviate from it. **1908** R. Bagot *A. Cuthbert* vii. 77 If the lady remained at Syracuse for a day or two, so much the better.

**e.** To such an extent; in such a degree.

**1388** Wyclif *Eccl.* ii. 13 And Y siȝ, that wisdom ȝede so mych bifor foli, as miche as liȝt is dyuerse fro derknessis. **1519** *Interlude Four Elements* in Hazlitt *Dodsley* I. 22, I marvel greatly, That ever ye would use the company So mich of such a knave. **1580** in Allen *Martyrdom Campion* (1908) 26 Rage man or devil never so much. **1692** *E. Walker's tr. Epictetus' Mor.* (1737) To Mr. E. W. on his Transl., Nor is your Author had in less esteem Than that great Man so much admir'd by him. **1742** Ld. Percival in *Johnson's Debates* (1787) II. 265 In so much a better manner than I thought my-self able to do. **1768–74** A. Tucker *Lt. Nat.* (1834) I. 59 How much we desire an absent positive good, so much we are in pain for it. **1831** Scott *Cast. Dang.* ii, But wherefore .. so much displeased but now at my young friend Charles? **1859** Geo. Eliot *A. Bede* xxxvi, Villages, and market-towns—all so much alike to her indifferent eyes.

*Comb.* **1664** Pepys *Diary* 1 Jan., Saw the so much cried-up play of 'Henry the Eighth'. **1734** tr. *Rollin's Anc. Hist.* I. II. vi. (1841) I. 45 These so-much-boasted politicians. **1848** Dickens *Dombey* xxxi, The so-much-to-be-astonished chicken. **1860** E. Falkener *Dædalus* Introd. 2 The so-much-talked-of trabeated ceilings of the ancients.

*** *sb.* **f.** An equal amount; as much.

*c* **1400** *Laud Troy Bk.* 3440 Thei prayed him alle that viage to take, To do so moche for her sake. *c* **1400** *Brut* civ. 105 If ȝe so miche .. haue y-wonne, an C. tymes so miche .. ȝe hauen loste. **1589** *Pappe w. Hatchet* in Lyly's Wks. 1902 III. 407 This is a good settled speech, a Diuine might haue seemd to haue said so much. *c* **1643** Ld. Herbert *Autobiog.* (1824) 32, I never saw him angry .., and have heard so much of him for many years before. *a* **1679** Hobbes *Rhet.* I. vii. 14 More, is so much, and somewhat besides. **1780** *Mirror* No. 94, I cannot say so much for his acquaintance C. D. **1810** Crabbe *Borough* ii. 55 *note*, I would answer, that I understand so much. **1848** Thackeray *Van. Fair* xxxi, He kissed her hand. Except when she was married, he had not done so much for years before.

**g.** A certain unspecified amount, sum, etc.

**1382** Wyclif *Acts* v. 8 Womman, seye to me, if ȝe solden the feeld for so moche? And she seide, Ȝhe, so moche. **1583** Stubbes *Anat. Abus.* (1882) II. 23 That such a thing cost them so much, and so much, and it is woorth this much and that much. **1656** Earl Monm. tr. *Boccalini's Pol. Touchstone* (1674) 269 This .. behaviour .. is as so much of the best Sugar for you Italians, and as so much of the bitterest Poyson for the Spanish Nation. **1696** *Caldwell P.* (Maitl. Cl.) I. 171 They have .. soe much a day for their pocket money. **1737** *Gentl. Mag.* VII. 552/1 They have nothing to do but to work them off as fast as They can, at so much a thousand. **1844** Mrs. Browning *Cry of the Human* v, Each soul is worth so much on 'Change. **1884** W. C. Smith *Kildrostan* 88 Life is lost, By so much, when you lose a perfect sense.

**h.** Thus much, thus far. (Used to sum up or dismiss a matter.)

**1588** Shaks. *L.L.L.* I. i. 240 So much for the time When. **1662** Stillingfl. *Orig. Sacræ* III. ii. §10 And so much for this second Hypothesis. **1707** J. Stevens tr. *Quevedo's Com. Wks.* (1709) 350 So much for that; do you take me Sir. **1794** Scott *Let.* in *Lockhart* (1837) I. vii. 220 So much for public news. **1840** *P. Parley's Ann.* 364 So much for the love of slaughter! **1891** T. Hardy *Tess* (1900) 11/1 So much for Norman blood unaided by Victorian lucre.

**i.** Such an amount, quantity, etc.

See also ever *adv.* 9 b, 9 c, and never *adv.* 4.

**1606** G. Woodcocke *Hist. Ivstine* xxv. 93 There was so much of merit in him. **1711** Addison *Spect.* No. 120 ¶1 Sir Roger is very often merry with me upon my passing so much of my Time among his Poultry. **1732–8** Swift *Polite Conv.* 131 (Footman fills him a Bumper.) Why do you fill so much? **1816** Shelley *Mt. Blanc* 117 So much of life and joy is lost. **1850** Tennyson *In Mem.* lxxiii, So many worlds, so much to do, So little done.

**40. so much as, that**, etc. **a.** With *as* (or †*so*), in ordinary comparative use.

*adj.* *c* **1275** Lay. 25351 Folk þar com wel sone .., so moche so þar neuere hear [= ere] no man ne gadere[de]. *a* **1400–50** *Alexander* 1249 The multitude was so much as menys vs þe writtez. **1568** Grafton *Chron.* II. 18 Somuch grownd as might receyue .. his poore Carkas. **1599** Shaks. *Much Ado* II. iii. 263 *Bene.* You take pleasure then in the message. *Beat.* Yea iust so much as you may take vpon a kniues point. **1668** Wilkins *Real Char.* 339 The other Affix .. is not of so much use or necessity as the rest. **1821** Scott *Kenilw.* xxxix, Take so much leisure as to peruse this letter. **1865** Ruskin *Sesame* ii. §80 Of half so much importance as [etc.].

*sb.* *a* **1400–50** *Alexander* 3306, I .. Has noȝt o maistri so meche as miȝt of my-selfe. *c* **1420** *Sir Amadace* (Camden) l, He wold gif hom .. so muche .. As any lord wold. *c* **1530** Ld. Berners *Arth. Lyt. Bryt.* 330 Often times it fortuned that a man can not attayne to do so muche as he would do. **1559** *Boke Presidentes* 9 That ye will do so muche as .. to present A. B. to the same. **1613** Purchas *Pilgrimage* (1614) 18 Others account so much to Paradise as those foure Riuers doe water. **1678** BUTLER *Hud.* III. ii. 1214 'Tis most true None bring him in so much as you. **1875** M. PATTISON *Casaubon* 522 Casaubon knew of his own age so much as the average of educated men know. **1886** C. E. PASCOE *London of To-day* i. (ed. 3) 24 The poorest memory .. will retain so much as that.

*adv.* *c* **1425** *Eng. Conq. Irel.* (1896) 16 He hatede nothynge so mych as that me shold spek of his stalwardnes. *c* **1449** PECOCK *Repr.* I. iii. 13 A man schulde loue .. his neiȝbore as him silf, thouȝ not so miche as him silf. **1530** PALSGR. 567/1, I gave hym counsayle to the contrarye so moche as lay in me. **1595** in *Cath. Rec. Soc. Publ.* V. 336 All the way he prayed, .. so much as he might. **1634** SIR T. HAWKINS *Pol. Observ.* 13 To these turmoyles, so much weighty as they were new, crosse omens of predictions were added. **1712** STEELE *Spect.* No. 466 ¶3 With a Design to please no one so much as her Father. **1780** *Mirror* No. 79, Not so much by the class of people .. as by the kind of sentiments. **1831** SCOTT *Ct. Rob.* xviii, Her attendant .. kept herself modestly in the background, so much so as hardly to be distinguished.

**b.** Used to emphasize a negation.

*a* **1425** *Cursor M.* 16960 (Trin.), He þat neuer synne dud, ne so muche as hit þouȝt. **1576** FLEMING *Panopl. Epist.* 197 Not so muche as putting pen to paper. *c* **1643** LD. HERBERT *Autobiog.* (1824) 124 Without giving me so much as the least warning. **1697** DAMPIER *Voy.* I. 144 There was not so much as a Meal of Victuals left for them. **1713** STEELE *Englishman* No. 40, I do not remember to have seen any small Birds, nor so much as a Crow or Magpye. **1782** MISS BURNEY *Cecilia* VIII. viii, I should not expect any lady would so much as look at him. **1854** MRS. OLIPHANT *Magdalen Hepburn* II. 51 The priest's *benedicite* was not accompanied by so much as a glance. **1887** BIRRELL *Obiter Dicta* Ser. II. 151 [He] never so much as attained to a seat in the Cabinet.

**c.** With *that*, denoting result or consequence.

*c* **1412** HOCCLEVE *De Reg. Princ.* 1794 Lordes han for to done So mych for hem-self, þat my mateere Out of hir mynde slippith away soone. *c* **1489** CAXTON *Sonnes of Aymon* iv. 119 Soo moche abode the foure sones of Aymon, that the nyghte came. **1595** in *Cath. Rec. Soc. Publ.* V. 290 He .. was so muche greeved that .. he went presently to Confession. *c* **1670** WOOD *Life* (O.H.S.) I. 45 This yeare he had the small pox so much that he was for a time blinded with them. **1766** GOLDSM. *Vicar* iii, My attention was so much taken up .. that I scarce looked forward. **1811** BYRON in R. C. Dallas *Corr. of Byron* (1825) II. 26, I feel myself so much a citizen of the world, that [etc.]. **1850** THACKERAY *Pendennis* xvi, So much so, that one afternoon .. she .. shook hands with him.

**d.** Followed by infinitive without *as*.

**1607** TOURNEUR *Rev. Trag.* I. i, I had so much wit to keepe my thoughts Vp in their built houses. **1874** SWINBURNE *Bothwell* II. ix, Though I have not so much grace To bind again this people fast to God.

**so**, var. SOE; obs. infin. and pa. t. pl. of SEE *v.*

**so.**, abbrev. of SOUTH.

**soader**, obs. f. SOLDER *sb.* and *v.*

**soak** (səʊk), *sb.* Also 6–7, 9 *dial.*, soke. [f. the vb.]

**1. a.** The condition or process of being or becoming soaked; a spell of soaking. Chiefly in the phr. *in soak*: cf. A-SOAK *adv.*

**1598** FLORIO, *Abombare*, .. to steepe or lay in soke. **1687** MIÉGE *Gt. Fr. Dict.* II. s.v. *Soke*, You need give it but one good Soke. **1771** LUCKOMBE *Hist. Print.* 350 He also lays the Ball Leathers in soak to supple them. **1787** JEFFERSON *Writ.* (1859) II. 283, I am not without hopes that a good rod is in soak for Prussia. **1887** BROWN *Doctor* 47 Fixin the die, very slow in the soak, .. But takin the colour through and through!

**b.** A liquid used for maceration; a steep.

**1850** ALLEN *Amer. Farm Book* ii. 48 As a soak or steep for seeds .. there is no doubt of their possessing some value.

**c.** A vat in which hides are macerated.

**1876** tr. *Schultz' Leather Manuf.* 17 Before any portion is put into the soaks. **1897** C. T. DAVIS *Manuf. Leather* vi. 80 Dry salted hides, kips, etc, .. are generally put into a pit of water kept for the purpose, called a soak.

**d.** A heavy saturating rain.

**1891** *Daily News* 20 Aug. 5/1 The long steady soak that finds out the weak spot .. in canvas.

**2.** A percolation of water; water which has oozed through or out of the ground, strata, etc.

**1707** MORTIMER *Husb.* (1721) II. 191 In dry Ground that is not annoyed with any Spring or soak of Water. **1821** COBBETT *Rural Rides* (1885) I. 4 A sort of river; .. the water proceeding from the soak of the higher ground on both sides. **1838** SIMMS *Public Wks. Gt. Brit.* 19 Springs, soaks, or streams of water. **1883** *Specif. Alnwick & Cornhill Rlwy.* 22 Wherever springs, soaks, or streams appear and issue from the face of the slopes.

**b.** *spec.* in Lincolnshire. (Cf. SOCK *sb.*[3] 2.) Also *attrib.*

**1799** [A. YOUNG] *Agric. Linc.* 15 The sock or soak among the silt is sometimes brackish. *Ibid.* 235 Through all the fens of Lincolnshire we hear much of the soak, .. the subterranean water which is found .. usually but a very few feet below the surface. *c* **1818** BRITTON *Lincolnshire* 557 The sea water .., unable to pass by the drains, rises on the surface, and is known by the name of soak. **1851** *Jrnl. R. Agric. Soc.* XII. I. 285 Upon digging down into the sharp silt the soak oozes from the side of the hole.

**c.** *dial.* A piece of marshy, swampy ground.

**1839** SIR G. C. LEWIS *Gloss. Heref.* s.v., A 'green soak', or 'a warm soak', is a small spot of marshy ground in which a spring rises. **1849** J. LLOYD *Eng. Country Gentleman* 6 Where the soak its emerald fringe displays. **1851** STERNBERG *Northampt. Dial.*, *Soke*, a patch of marshy land.

**d.** *Austr.* A depression holding moisture after rain; a damp spot where water may be obtained.

**1894** *Westm. Gaz.* 30 Oct. 4/2 A prospecting party comes along to one of the clay-pans or soaks. **1899** *Times* 24 Feb. 13/1 The rock holes and soaks on which the lives of themselves and their animals depended.

**3.** A heavy drinker; a tippler.

**1820** CLARE *Poems Rural Life* (ed. 3) 93 And hearty soaks oft hand the bottle round. **1889** *Lisbon* (Dakota) *Star* 15 Feb. 2/5, I think I'll corral a lot of chronic old soaks, .. and experiment with them.

**4.** A prolonged draught or drinking-bout.

**1851** STERNBERG *Northampt. Dial.*, *Soke*, .. a long draught. 'A good soke.' **1855** C. G. PARSONS *Inside View Slavery* iv. 51 When the Southron intends to have a 'soak', he takes the bottle to his bed-side.

**soak** (səʊk), *v.* Forms: 1 socian, 4–8 soke, 6–7 soake, 7– soak. Also *pa. pple.* 6–7 soken, 8–9 soaken. [OE. *socian*, f. the weak grade of the stem represented by *súcan* to SUCK, = WFlem. *soken* and *zoken* (De Bo).

The following are examples of the strong pa. pple. (see also SOAKEN *ppl. a.*):—**1586** BRIGHT *Melanch.* xiv. 72 Whose braines are soken. **1597** J. KING *On Jonas* (1618) 176 Dirt soken with blood. **1633** P. FLETCHER *Poet. Misc.* Ps. cxxxvii, Our heart-strings broken, Throats drown'd, and soken With tears. **1793** SMEATON *Edystone L.* §196 So that the pores might be thoroughly soaken with water. **1886** J. ASHBY-STERRY *Lazy Minstrel* 126 Shiny is each mackintosh, Each hat and coat well soaken.]

**I.** *intr.* **1. a.** To lie immersed in a liquid for a considerable time, so as to be saturated or permeated with it; to become thoroughly wet or soft in this manner.

*c* **1000** *Sax. Leechd.* II. 240 Dweorȝe dwostlan weorp on weallende wæter, læt socian on lange. *Ibid.* 252 Asete þonne on hate sunnan .. þæt hit sipiȝe & socige.

*c* **1440** [see SOAKING *vbl. sb.* 1]. **1674** BREVINT *Saul at Endor* 314 The other water which did cure the Palsie, when the little Image of Montague .. had soakt in it. **1687** MIÉGE *Gt. Fr. Dict.* s.v., To lay a Thing a-soking. **1707** *Curios. in Husb. & Gard.* 313 The Sea, in which they soak every Tide. **1833** RENNIE *Alph. Angling* 68 Before using them let them soak about half an hour in water. **1853** SOYER *Pantroph.* 160 As soon as the goose was killed, the liver was put to soak in milk and honey. **1889** *Science-Gossip* XXV. 234 A spoonful of water in which a clove of garlic has soaked for half an hour.

**b.** *transf.* and *fig.*

*a* **1510** DOUGLAS *K. Hart* I. xx, Ryse, fresch Delyte, lat nocht this mater soke. **1687** MIÉGE *Gt. Fr. Dict.* I. s.v. *Mitonner*, This Potage must be kept soaking upon a Chafing-dish, or the like. **1711** ADDISON *Spect.* No. 65 ¶8 Because it is Vulgar to Lye and Soak together, we have each of us our several Settle-Bed. *a* **1791** WESLEY *Serm.* xcviii. (1825) II. 475 By *soaking* (as it is emphatically called) so long between warm sheets, the flesh .. becomes soft and flabby. **1874** J. W. LONG *Amer. Wild-fowl* viii. 142 Now, put these little hints 'to soak', as they say out here.

**c.** To allow moisture to percolate. *rare*$^{-1}$.

**1688** *Phil. Trans.* XVII. 981 It being Sandy Land, soaks and drains admirably well.

**d.** Of metal: to become heated uniformly throughout its mass.

**1843** HOLTZAPFFEL *Turning* I. 241 The work .. should be allowed ample time to get hot, or as it is called, to 'soak'. **1939** J. DEARDEN *Iron & Steel To-day* x. 134 Here the ingots are allowed to 'soak' until they are the same heat all through, and then they are rolled.

**2. a.** To percolate; to penetrate by saturation or infiltration; to ooze. Also with *in*, *through*, etc.

*c* **1440** *Promp. Parv.* 463/2 Sokyn yn, as lycure yn dyuerse þyngys, or drynkyn yn. **1573** TUSSER *Husb.* (1878) 47 For weede and the water so soketh and sucks, that [etc.]. **1587** GASCOIGNE *Flowers*, etc. Wks. 1907 I. 116 [Floods of tears] Whose fountaine .. soketh so, that all my face is styll on flowe. **1607** TOPSELL *Four-f. Beasts* (1658) 188 When the rain descended, it filled the horns, and soked to the root of the Vine. **1657** AUSTEN *Fruit Trees* I. 64 A Barrow full of Rotten Muck, .. the fatnesse whereof will soke in among the roots. **1697** DRYDEN *Virg. Georg.* III. 677 If Sweat remains Unwash'd, and soaks into the empty Veins. **1726** LEONI *Alberti's Archit.* I. 74/2 The Structure .. may .. be rotted by the moisture lying continually soaking upon it. **1776** G. SEMPLE *Building in Water* 42 The Pit .. quite free from Water, except some small Quantity that soaked from the Bed of the River. **1815** SCOTT *Guy M.* xxiii, A narrow channel, through which soaked, rather than flowed, a small stagnant stream. **1884** *Law Times Rep.* LI. 229/2 The water .. soaked under the wall and wetted the mud below it.

**b.** *fig.*

**1583** GOLDING *Calvin on Deut.* xiii. 14 b, God will make them to soke away like water. **1599** BRETON *Miseries of Mamillia* Wks. (Grosart) II. 36/1 Sorrow sokes long ere it slayes. **1642** D. ROGERS *Naaman* 3 The grace of that spirit .. might soke and sinke into the soules of men. **1675** J. SMITH *Christian Religion's Appeal* II. 6 To repel the thought of future Judgment, from soaking into the Spirits. **1881** *Times* 21 May 11/4 The controversialists have separated to give time for them to soak into the minds .. of nations.

†**c.** Of currents: To flow slowly. *Obs.*

**1699** DAMPIER *Voy.* II. III. viii. 103 The Sea-Breezes and the Currents, that soak down between Africa and Brazil.

**d.** With cognate obj.: To make (way) by percolation.

**1815** SCOTT *Guy M.* xxviii, The rivulet beneath .. soaked its way obscurely through wreaths of snow. **1883** STEVENSON *Treas. Isl.* xiv, The nearest of the little rivers soaked its way into the anchorage.

**e.** *transf.* Of heat: to penetrate *through* the mass of an ingot until it is at a uniform temperature.

**1902** *Encycl. Brit.* XXIX. 587/1 Bringing such an ingot .. to the rolling temperature is not really an operation of heating, .. but one of equalizing the temperature, by allowing the internal excess of heat to 'soak' through the mass. **1970** F. SIMONS *Dict. Ferrous Metals* 191 *Soaked steel*, steel heated in a furnace and held at the chosen temperature sufficiently long for the heat to have 'soaked' right through to the centre of the mass, which is only then uniformly heated.

**3.** To drink immoderately; to saturate oneself with liquor.

**1687** A. LOVELL tr. *Thevenot's Trav.* I. 78 You keep soaking in Taverns, and come and make such Complaints to me. **1766** GOLDSM. *Vicar* xxi, You do nothing but soak with the guests all day long, whereas .. I never touch a drop. **1828** RUDDIMAN *Sc. Parish* (1889) 69 The sodger gentry .. sit soaking and drinking. **1883** *19th Cent.* Oct. 594 The shambling and scrofulous shirk whom you may find any night soaking at the pothouse.

**II.** *trans.* **4. a.** Of liquid or moisture: To permeate thoroughly; to saturate with wet. Freq. in passive.

(*a*) *a* **1340**, *c* **1440** [see *fig.* below]. **1544** PHAER *Bk. Childr.* (1553) S iij b, Stepe it in suffycyent rosewater, tyll it bee wel soked. **1577** HARRISON *England* II. vi. (1877) I. 156 The .. barleie .. is steeped in a cesterne .. vntill it be throughlie soked. **1601** HOLLAND *Pliny* I. 567 The ground standeth not drenched and soked with water. **1671** MILTON *Samson* 1726 Let us go find the body where it lies Sok't in his enemies blood. **1748** *Anson's Voy.* II. iv. 219 Several of her casks had rotted, and her bags were soaked through. **1796** H. HUNTER tr. *St.-Pierre's Stud. Nat.* (1799) II. 334 The herbage and the trees are soaked in water. **1876** BRISTOWE *Th. & Pract. Med.* (1878) 280 Not when the marshy ground is thoroughly soaked, but when, after it has been thus soaked [etc.].

(*b*) **1697** DRYDEN *Virg. Georg.* IV. 187 Where .. deep Galesus soaks the yellow Sands. **1784** COWPER *Task* I. 215 When Winter soaks the fields. **1800** tr. *Legrange's Chem.* II. 303 The quantity .. should be sufficient to soak the grain. **1899** *Allbutt's Syst. Med.* VIII. 730 Hyperidrosis .. soaking the boots and stockings with a stinking material.

**b.** *fig.*

*a* **1340** HAMPOLE *Psalter* iii. 5, I am soked in my synne. *c* **1440** *Generydes* 234 The kyng .. was febyll and sokyd with sekenesse. **1600** BRETON *Daffodils & Primroses* Wks. (Grosart) I. 14/1 My tree of true delight is sokde with sorrow. **1630** J. PRESTON *Serm.* 30 Soaked and surfetted with pleasures. **1902** B. GRUNDY *Thames Camp* 88, I am literally soaked in sunshine.

**5. a.** To lay or place in, to wet with, a liquid so as to produce thorough saturation; to steep.

*a* **1425** tr. *Arderne's Treat. Fistula*, etc. 40 It availeþ mich þat þe yuel or sore be wele fomented or soked wiþ vinegre and watre. *c* **1440** *Promp. Parv.* 463/2 Sokyn yn lycure .. to be made softe. **1558** WARDE tr. *Alexis' Secr.* 39 b, Beate the Saffron in poulder, stiepe, and soke it. **1652** J. MAINE tr. *Donne's Epigr.* 94 The ground .. Her Temples now steept in sea-water sokes. **1659** H. MORE *Immort. Soul* III. vii. §8 It is not unlikely, but that they soak their Vehicles in some vaporous or glutinous moisture or other. **1707** MORTIMER *Husb.* 52 If you put Wormwood into the Brine you soak your Corn in. **1771** LUCKOMBE *Hist. Print.* 350 The purpose of soaking them is only to supple them. **1831** DAVIES *Mat. Med.* 260 It is .. covered over with lint, which is afterwards soaked with the same caustic liquid. **1892** *Photogr. Ann.* II. 443 It consists in soaking the positive or negative on glass in a special solution.

*absol.* **1892** *Photogr. Ann.* II. 49 If you must soak, be sure to go over the face of the plate with a wet pledget.

**b.** *fig.*

**1648** G. DANIEL *Eclog* iii. 193 You soake your soules, and by too large a flood. **1879** GEO. ELIOT *Theo. Such* x. 183 We soak our children in habits of contempt. **1895** ZANGWILL *Master* 439 He must soak himself in Paris and forget her.

**c.** *refl.* with reference to excessive drinking.

**1818** SCOTT *Rob Roy* xii, Habitual topers .. acquire the power of soaking themselves with a quantity of liquor [etc.]. **1891** E. ROPER *By Track & Trail* xvii. 256 Even .. where people can get what they choose to drink, they do not soak themselves in beer.

**6. a.** To bake (bread, etc.) thoroughly. Also *fig.*

**1686** GOAD *Celest. Bodies* I. vi. 22 The One baketh, the Other as it were soketh (that I may use Pastery Terms) the Fruits of the Season. **1741** *Compl. Fam.-Piece* I. ii. 133 A Haunch of 12 Pounds Weight will take up three full Hours to be well soaked. *a* **1825** FORBY *Voc. E. Anglia*, *Soak*, to bake thoroughly. It is particularly applied to bread. **1872** DE VERE *Americanisms* 548 Bread .. is said 'to be well soaked', if it is dry and thoroughly well baked.

**b.** To maintain (metal or ceramics) at a constant temperature for a period to ensure that they are uniformly heated.

**1925** *Jrnl. Iron & Steel Inst.* CXII. 491 The ingots should be stripped, soaked, and forged before reaching the temperature of the critical range. **1956** A. K. OSBORNE *Encycl. Iron & Steel Industry* 392/1 The pit was for soaking the ingots or permitting the heat contained in the still molten steel in its interior to penetrate to the outer portions until the temperature of the entire ingot was reasonably uniform. **1966** *McGraw-Hill Encycl. Sci. & Technol.* VII. 346/1 In this type of kiln the cycle of setting ware in the kiln, heating up, 'soaking' or holding at peak temperature for some time, cooling and removing or 'drawing' the ware is repeated for each batch.

**7.** *colloq.* or *slang.* **a.** *to soak one's clay* (or †*face*), to drink (heavily).

**1704** in W. S. Perry *Hist. Coll. Am. Col. Ch.* I. 180 Sober and meek under disgrace, .. Now he's advanced he soaks his face. **1770** *Gentl. Mag.* XL. 559 He is said to .. [have] Soaked his face. **1837** BARHAM *Ingol. Leg.* Ser. I. *Look at the Clock* iv, Mr. David Pryce had been soaking his clay.

**b.** To ply with liquor. Also in passive.

**1822** J. BANIM *O'Hara Tales*, *Peggy Nowlan*, Well? you pumped him? and soaked him? **1884** *Pall Mall G.* 1 Aug. 4/1 He was .. so drunk he could not stand. His friend .. was also pretty well soaked.

**c.** To spend (money) in drink.

**1903** *Daily Chron.* 31 Aug. 3/4 When you meet him give him sixpence... He will soak it, of course, but that is long past mending.

**d.** To put (something) in pawn.

**1882** SALA *Amer. Revis.* (1885) 382 'Soak my gems,' and 'Walker my diamonds'.

**e.** *U.S. slang.* To punish, beat, pummel, strike hard, etc.; to criticize harshly, to 'knock'; *to* *soak it to* (one) = *to sock it to* (one) (see SOCK *v.*[2] 1 c).

**1892** *Columbus* (Ohio) *Even. Dispatch* 29 July 1/4 To-day's Washington Post 'soaks' it to the Southern Democrats in the House who were so rallied in 1885 in their support of the bill making an appropriation to the New Orleans Exposition, but are now opposed to a similar appropriation for the World's Fair. **1896** *Columbus* (Ohio) *Dispatch* 29 July 1 Embezzlers Soaked. The Fines and Sentences Given the Pittsburgh Defaulters. **1896** S. CRANE *George's Mother* xiii. 152 At the gang's corner, they asked: 'Who soaked yeh, Fidsey?' **1904** G. H. LORIMER *Old Gorgon Graham* 18 The unspeakable Turk hadn't been soaked hard enough to suit him [*sc.* an Armenian]. **1908** —— *Jack Spurlock* ii. 44 Yes, he done it! Soak it to him good! *Ibid.* vi. 107 My troubles came at me from all sides, and soaked it to me till my conscience fairly ached. **1915** H. L. WILSON *Ruggles of Red Gap* (1917) xii. 210 If he gets fancy with you, soak him again. You done it once. **1920** WODEHOUSE *Coming of Bill* II. xiv. 239 Soak it to him, kid. **1925** H. L. FOSTER *Trop. Tramp Tourists* iii. 21, I found that we had on board..the man whose newspaper soaked my last book. **1936** [see BUTTON *sb.* 5 g].

**f.** *slang* (orig. *U.S.*). To impose upon (a person, etc.) by an extortionate charge or price; to charge or tax heavily; to borrow or extort money from; to cost a high price. Freq. const. *for* or with indirect object expressing a sum of money. Hence **soak-the-rich**, *attrib. phr.* applied to a policy of progressive taxation (PROGRESSIVE *a.* 3 f); also in similar phrases, as ***soak-the-poor***, etc.

(*a*) **1895** *N.Y. Dramatic News* 23 Nov. 2/2 This little scheme sometimes..enables the photographer to 'soak' them. **1904** *Newspaperdom* 21 Apr. 8 When a local merchant asks you to give his business a friendly notice, soak him 10 or 15 cents a line. **1915** WODEHOUSE *Something Fresh* ii. 37 Especially after poor old Percy had just got soaked for such a pile of money. **1932** D. L. SAYERS *Have his Carcase* xiii. 164 Poor, but not mercenary or dishonest, since he refused to soak Mrs. W. **1936** N. COWARD *To-night at 8.30* II. 60 She soaked her old man plenty, I'm sure—before he took to soaking himself! **1949** [see BRASS *v.*[1] 2]. **1958** *Times* 17 Mar. 12/6, I hope the Court-Leet soaked the Air Ministry, and I expect it did, for these Berkshire men knew their own value. **1966** 'L. LANE' *ABZ of Scouse* 101 Can I soak yer fer a coupler bob? **1971** *Farmers Weekly* 19 Mar. 42/3 If you think this is a soak-the-housewives review, nobody knows more about soaking the housewives than you. **1977** *Time* 21 Nov. 59/2 Then add the investment in sophisticated equipment: a single stainless-steel 1,000-gal. vat can soak the vintner for some $6,000.

(*b*) **1935** J. WARBURG *Hell Bent for Election* 72 He [*sc.* F. D. Roosevelt] thought he was being 'clever' when he tried to steal Huey Long's thunder by suddenly coming out with his 'soak the rich' tax message. **1935** H. L. ICKES in *Lit. Digest* 14 Dec. 6/3 Soak the Rich (Antonym, Soak the Poor)—Newspaperese for a system of taxation founded upon the absurd and revolutionary theory that a man should be assessed taxes in proportion to his ability to pay. **1949** A. CHRISTIE *Crooked House* i. 8 No Soak-the-rich taxes would have any effect on him. He'd just soak the soakers. **1959** *Economist* 7 Feb. 498/1 The Democratic cry that this is a 'soak-the-poor' Budget. **1970** *Wall St. Jrnl.* 29 Apr. 1/5 Soak-the-sinner tax policy remains a stand-by... Taxes on alcoholic beverages and on cigarets have been the most frequent targets for increases. **1972** *Listener* 28 Dec. 898/3 Advocates of populist soak-the-rich policies.

**III. 8. a.** To draw *out*, cause to ooze *out*, by means of soaking.

*c* **1430** *Two Cookery-bks.* 25 Take howhys of Vele, & ley hem on water to soke out þe blode. **1725** *Fam. Dict.* s.v. *Clear-Starching*, Lay it in a dry Cloth to soak out the Sudds. **1733** W. ELLIS *Chiltern & Vale Farm.* 114 Put half the Planks into Water, two or three Weeks, to soak out their Sap. **1892** *Photogr. Ann.* II. 179 The bichromate of potash is next soaked out by immersion in water for about four hours.

**b.** To draw or suck *out*.

**1577** B. GOOGE *Heresbach's Husb.* I. (1586) 22 b, Sowe it with lighter seede, that soketh out lesse the substance of the ground. **1626** BACON *Nat. Hist.* §346 As well by Strengthning the Spirits, as by Soaking out the loose Moisture. **1846** LANDOR *Imag. Conv.* I. 88 The people you describe to me soak out all the juices of our dialect.

†**c.** To drain, exhaust, impoverish. Also *to soak dry* or *up*. *Obs.*

**1577** tr. *Bullinger's Decades* (1592) 165 And sucks & sokes the marow bones vntill they feeble waxe. **1579** LYLY *Euphues* (Arb.) 35 Whereby they might..soake his pursse to reape commoditie. **1605** *1st Part Ieronimo* I. iii, His bounty amongst souldiers sokes him dry. **1626** BACON *Nat. Hist.* §480 All Plants that doe draw much Nourishment from the Earth, and so soake the Earth, and exhaust it. **1661** *Sir Harry Vane's Politicks* 9 It fares with those..as it doth with Gaming Houses, where the Box soaks the Gamesters. **1687** MIÉGE *Gt. Fr. Dict.* II, To soke (or drain) ones Pockets, *épuiser les Poches*. *Ibid.*, A Woman that sokes up a Man, ..*qui épuise un Homme*.

**d.** To allow to drain or ooze *away*.

*a* **1764** LLOYD *Poet. Professors* Wks. 1774 I. 34 Fellows! who've soak'd away their knowledge, In sleepy residence at college.

**9. a.** To allow to sink in; to absorb; to take in by absorption.

**1553** *Short Catech.* in *Lit. & Doc. Edw. VI* (1844) 518 He ought..[to] endeavour himself to hear and soak into his mind the word of the Lord. **1577–87** HOLINSHED *Chron.* I. 16/2 Rather we follow the spider in soking the poison, than in imitating the bee by sucking the honie. **1771** LUCKOMBE *Hist. Print.* 33 The paper..was sleeked..; and this kept it from soaking the ink. **1796** KIRWAN *Elem. Min.* (ed. 2) II. 33 Losing the water soaked by its Crystals.

**b.** With *up*.

*c* **1550** [? G. WALKER] *Detect. Dice-Play* D ij b, Sone after y[t] this likor was..dried, & soked vp in the boies face. **1588** KYD *Househ. Phil.* 187 Wks. (1901) 244 They soke up the superfluous humours of the earth. **1663** BOYLE *Usef. Exp. Nat. Philos.* II. i. 22 Plants..dried..betwixt sheets of paper, which help to soak up the superfluous moisture. **1799** G. SMITH *Laboratory* I. 35 When dry, throw it into the composition,..and stir it about, till it has soaked it up. **1854** LOWELL *Fireside Trav.* (1864) 286 One great mountain that soaked up all the rose of sunset.

**c.** To drink, imbibe, esp. to excess.

**1697** DAMPIER *Voy.* (1729) I. 419 The Men come home fat with soaking this Liquor. **1865** *Reader* No. 117. 339/3 The quantity of port soaked there.

**d.** *pass.* with *in*: to be imbued with, to be profoundly acquainted with (a subject of study).

**1937** *Ann. Reg. 1936* 56 It was generally agreed that the best speeches were made more or less extempore by speakers who were 'soaked' in their subject. *a* **1960** E. M. FORSTER *Maurice* (1971) I. i. 4 Mr Ducie would smile, for he was soaked in evolution.

†**10.** To cause to sink in. *Obs.*[−1]

**1599** SANDYS *Europæ Spec.* (1632) 28 They cast about gently to soake and settle them in mens..consciences.

**IV. 11.** *Comb.*, as *soak-dike*, *-ditch*, *-drain*; †**soakpit** = SOAKAWAY (*obs.*); **soakway** [WAY *adv.*] = SOAKAWAY.

**1970** S. J. HALLAM in C. W. Phillips *Fenland in Roman Times* 23 Settlers clung tenaciously to these rich soils, and we can read from the air the story of their constant efforts to cope with deteriorating drainage: silting, the digging of soak-dykes, renewed silting, re-digging. *Ibid.* 33 The modern soak ditches take the drainage from the field ditches and discharge it into the main channel at regulated points; the Roman soak ditches must have had a similar function. **1963** *Times* 1 Feb. 13/7 The southern fringes of the planned settlement went first; water courses were provided with parallel soak-drains, which in their turn proved inadequate. **1970** P. SALWAY in C. W. Phillips *Fenland in Roman Times* 18 On the silts, continued occupation must have depended on keeping the system of soak-drains in operation. These drains imply sluices to let the water drain out of field and settlement ditches into the main watercourses at low tide and to prevent or control river water entering the ditches at high tide. **1898** E. C. S. MOORE *Sanitary Engin.* i. 5 If made in porous soils so that the liquid soaks away they are called soak-pits; they are dangerous to neighbouring wells. **1956** C. D. PIGOTT in D. L. Linton *Sheffield* 83 Now only *Sphagnum recurvum* is at all frequent and this is no doubt due to its occupation of the wettest soakways which are avoided by sheep. **1978** *Jrnl. R. Soc. Arts* CXXVI. 438/2 These latter [*sc.* rain water channels]..empty into soak-ways at the base of the building.

**soakage** ('səʊkɪdʒ). [f. prec. + -AGE.]

**1. a.** Liquid which has filtered or oozed out.

**1766** *Compl. Farmer* s.v. *Turnep* 7 P 3/2 Water which happens to be the soakage of a dung-yard. **1799** [A. YOUNG] *Agric. Linc.* 244 He could, by taking the whole soakage of the hill, produce a river capable of turning a considerable mill. **1847** *Jrnl. R. Agric. Soc.* VIII. I. 118 They have to throw out the great soakage of water from the rivers Welland and Glen. **1884** *Daily News* 24 Sept. 3/4 The water in it gets contaminated by soakage from the gutter.

*attrib.* **1799** [A. YOUNG] *Agric. Linc.* 284 A soakage drain on each side of it.

**b.** *Austral.* A soak, a waterhole.

**1898** *Geogr. Jrnl.* XI. 261 A small pool of water, evidently a soakage from the surrounding country. **1898** MORRIS *Austral Eng.*, *Soak*, or *Soakage*, a Western and Central Australian term.

**2.** Liquid or moisture absorbed.

**1830** M. DONOVAN *Dom. Econ.* I. 205 The original twenty gallons come off less by the soakage.

**3.** The process of percolating or soaking through. Also *attrib.*, in *Austral.* and *N.Z.* use.

**1867** BAKER *Nile Trib.* v. 102 The escape of the rainfall was by simple soakage. **1888** MISS BRADDON *Fatal Three* I. v, I'm afraid there may have been soakage from that manure-heap into the well. **1904** A. ST. H. GIBBONS *Africa* I. ii. 25 In so thirsty a country as Africa evaporation and soakage must be very considerable. **1921** H. GUTHRIE-SMITH *Tutira* xx. 196 These surface swellings are the result of a blocked soakage system. **1936** I. L. IDRIESS *Cattle King* iv. 30 Often you can dig in a dry creek-bed and obtain soakage water if you dig in the right place. **1937** E. HILL *Great Austral. Loneliness* vi. 53 At the crude soakage wells provided, he [*sc.* a white man] camps in the evenings.

**4.** The fact of lying in soak.

**1855** OGILVIE *Suppl.*, *Soakage*, act of soaking; state of being soaked. **1863** *Possibilities of Creation* 188 His flesh, converted into a species of spermaceti..by long soakage in running water.

**5.** *Electr.* The residual charge of a cable or condenser (*Cent. Dict.* Suppl., citing Houston).

**soakaway** ('səʊkəweɪ). Also **soak-away**. [f. SOAK *v.* + AWAY *adv.*] A pit, usu. filled with hard-core, into which water or other liquids may flow and from which they may percolate slowly into the surrounding subsoil.

**1916** H. G. WELLS *Mr. Britling* II. iv. 331 Every now and then someone stumbles into a soakaway for rain-water. **1928** *Daily Express* 31 May 5/3 Be sure to find out if your kitchen sink drains to a 'soak-away'. If it does, you must not let much water go down it, but throw out washing-up water and suchlike on the garden. **1951** *Archit. Rev.* CIX. 291 The drainage system..consists of a series of septic tanks for soil drains and soakaways for stormwater. **1976** *Sunday Times* (Lagos) 26 Sept. 4/3 He says he can as well repair blocked soak-aways or any job a qualified plumber can do.

**soaked** ('səʊkt), *ppl. a.* [f. SOAK *v.* + -ED[1].]

**1.** *transf.* Dull, lacking in animation.

**1600** *Hosp. Incurable Fooles* 19 Melancholike persons of this kinde, haue pale faces, soaked and hollow eies.

**2.** Steeped, macerated; saturated, drenched.

Also as second element in *rain-*, *water-soaked*, etc.

**1829** *Chapters Phys. Sci.* 197 If there be brought into contact two wetted or soaked bodies. **1841** DICKENS *Barn. Rudge* viii, Is it soaked gunpowder, or blazing oil? **1879** PROCTOR *Pleas. Ways Sc.* xvii. 368 The soaked slopes of great hills give way.

**3.** Intoxicated. Freq. as second element of a *Comb.*

Some of these quotations may be regarded as examples of SOAK *v.* 7 b.

**1737** *Pennsylvania Gaz.* 6–13 Jan. 2/2 He carries too much Sail, Stew'd, Stubb'd, Soak'd, Soft. **1899**, **1908** [see *gin-soaked* adj. s.v. GIN *sb.*[2] 2 b]. **1939** JOYCE *Finnegans Wake* I. 85 The prisoner, soaked in methylated, appeared in dry dock. *a* **1953** E. O'NEILL *Touch of Poet* (1957) IV. 158 Like a rum-soaked trooper, brawling before a brothel on a Saturday night.

†**'soaken**, *v. Obs.* In 6–7 **soken**. [f. SOAK *v.* + -EN[5].] *trans.* To soak.

**1577** FRAMPTON *Joyful News* I. (1596) 20 They leaue it so vntill the water bee sokened into it. **1580** —— *Dial. Yron & Steele* 155 When it is well sokened. **1632** J. HAYWARD tr. *Biondi's Eromena* 36 The pith of bread sokened in Spanish wine.

**soaken** ('səʊk(ə)n), *ppl. a.* [f. SOAK *v.*] Soaked, saturated; intoxicated.

**1651** MANTON *Exp. James* iv. 16 The soaken Adulterer [can boast] of so many acts of uncleanness. **1846** LANDOR *Exam. Shaks.* Wks. 1853 II. 299/2 He spake as bigly and fiercely as a soaken yeoman at an election feast. **1898** *Daily News* 10 Sept. 4/7 Bits of soaken drapery.

**soaker** ('səʊkə(r)). Also 6–8 **soker** (6 **sooker** ?). [f. SOAK *v.* + -ER[1].]

†**1.** A drainer, exhauster. *Obs.*

**1577** B. GOOGE *Heresbach's Husb.* I. (1586) 40 It is a great soker of the grounde. **1610** FOLKINGHAM *Art Surv.* I. x. 31 Wheate, Barley, Woade,..are great impairers and soakers of the soyle. **1629** MASSINGER *Picture* III. iv, I found By sad experience there is no such soaker As a young spongy wife. **1641** DAY *Parliament of Bees* x, He's a male polecat; a mere heart-blood soaker.

**2.** An immoderate drinker; a drunkard. Cf. 3 b.

**1593** *Bacchus Bountie* in *Harl. Misc.* (1809) II. 265 The greatest soakers shal be least controulde. **1652** *Charac. Low Countries* 60 The Dutchman would still be the perfectest soker. **1679** WOOD *Life* (O.H.S.) II. 460 The black pot men carried it for Perot, a thorough paced soaker. **1770** *Ann. Reg.* II. 240 'Tis Soakers like me..That enable you Brewers to ride in your Coaches. **1837** BARHAM *Ingol. Leg.* Ser. I. *Look at the Clock* iv, Amusing himself..With a couple more soakers, Thoroughbred smokers. **1897** *Allbutt's Syst. Med.* II. 865 In the case of a soaker on the verge of delirium tremens.

*fig.* **1593** NASHE *Four Lett. Conf.* Wks. (Grosart) II. 242 A scholler in nothing but the scum of schollership, a stale soker at Tullies Offices. **1665** BRATHWAIT *Comment. Two Tales* (1901) 52, I know you for a notable Soaker; you cannot endure a Sharer. **1700** CONGREVE *Way of World* IV. ii, The sun's..an honest soaker; he has a cellar at your Antipodes.

**3.** *old soaker*: **a.** An old hand at anything; an old stager.

Perh. originally with allusion to drinking (cf. b and 2), but this does not appear in the quotations.

**1589** R. HARVEY *Plain Perc.* (1590) 9 An olde sooker, that caries such Pottical verses of the State of Flanders, in a linnen bag. **1593** G. HARVEY *Pierce's Super.* Wks. (Grosart) II. 295 He was an old soaker indeede: and had more witt in his hoary head, then six hundred of these floorishing greene heads. **1614** MERITON *Christian Mans Assuring-house* 35 A young sinner is easily converted; but olde soakers are hardly reclaimed. *c* **1670** NEWCOME *Diary* (1885) 142 These old soakers with their Record's Arithmetic.

**b.** An old hand at drinking; a regular toper.

**1665** PEPYS *Diary* 15 Feb., A very good dinner among the old sokers. **1670** EACHARD *Cont. Clergy* 31 A task..that would much better fit some old soker at Parnassus, than his sipping unexperienc'd bibbership! *a* **1700** B. E. *Dict. Cant. Crew*, *An old Soker*, a true Pitcher-man. **1829** SCOTT *Anne of G.* xix, Some quiet old soakers, who were already beginning to think of the reckoning. **1863** *Mortons of Bardom* I. 177 Thus assailed, the old soaker was compelled to withdraw.

**4. a.** One who soaks something.

**1611** COTGR., *Trempeur*, a dipper; wetter, moistener; soaker, steeper.

**b.** A drenching rain.

**1789** J. BYNG *Jrnl.* 29 May in *Torrington Diaries* (1938) IV. 95 An approaching Storm made me pull up near the Grey Hound Inn; and well I did, for it came down a Soaker. **1839** HOOD *To St. Swithin* v, Mother of all the Family of Rainers! Saint of the Soakers! **1857** A. MAYHEW *Paved with Gold* II. v, The rain came down in streams of water... 'Here's a soaker!' thought the young Bohemian.

**c.** A soaking pit.

**1928** *Jrnl. Iron & Steel Inst.* CXVII. 201 The heated soakers are fired by blast-furnace gas. **1959** *Ibid.* CXCIII. 368/2 The soaking pit used was an electric soaker with a single trough coke resistor. **1976** *Steel USSR* VI. 194/2 The holding period from the end of casting to charging into the soakers was maintained constant as far as possible.

**5.** A sheet of lead used in roofing to keep out heavy rains.

**1895** *Jrnl. R. Inst. Brit. Archit.* Mar. 351 Hips should have hip-tiles and not soakers.

**soak-hole.** [f. SOAK *v.*] **a.** *Austral.* An enclosed place in a stream, used for sheep-washing. **b.** A hole into or from which water, etc., soaks or drains away.

**1881** A. C. GRANT *Bush Life in Queensland* I. 82 Parallel poles..forming square soak-holes. *Ibid.*, A stage was built, from which the sheep could be allowed to slide easily into the water of the first soak-hole. **1883** *Almondbury Gloss.* 124 The holes where it [*sc.* liquid manure] collects in the yard are called *soak-hoils*.

**soaking** ('səʊkɪŋ), *vbl. sb.* [f. SOAK *v.*]

**1. a.** The action of the vb. in various senses.

*c* **1440** *Promp. Parv.* 463/2 Sokynge, or longe lyynge in lycure, *infusio, inbibitura.* **1576** FLEMING *Panopl. Epist.* 442 These beautifull shapes..not consuming by the soaking of sicknesse. **1611** COTGR., *Trempement,* a..steeping, soaking. **1683** TRYON *Way to Health* 288 This soaking so long in your Bed, weakens all the Members. **1722** DE FOE *Col. Jack* ii, If we were catched, we run the risk of being ducked or pumped, which we call soaking. **1770** H. ST. JOHN in Jesse *Selwyn & Contemp.* (1844) III. 3 The servants were half dead with the soaking and fatigue. **1810** *Sporting Mag.* XXXV. 307 The company got a complete soaking from the inclemency of the weather. **1881** ABNEY *Photogr.* 122 Long soaking of the..emulsion is greatly detrimental.

**b.** *pl.* Liquid which has soaked through.

**1846** BAXTER *Libr. Pract. Agric.* (ed. 4) II. 39 By pumping back the soakings the soluble salts are preserved.

**2.** In iron-working: A special process by which the heat of an ingot is equally distributed through the mass, in order to fit it for rolling. Also, a similar process in which ingots of other metals or ceramic objects are brought to a uniform temperature in a furnace or kiln.

**1884** GREENWOOD *Steel & Iron* 383 Comparatively little heat escapes during the process of soaking. **1926** *Jrnl. Iron & Steel Inst.* CXIII. 648 A cooling curve taken of the 0·48 carbon steel after heating up to 1000°C., and cooled immediately without soaking, gave the ferrite point at the normal temperature. **1964** H. HODGES *Artifacts* i. 39 The early stages of firing [of pottery] are thus slow..; the temperature is allowed to rise slowly by stages, each rise being followed by a period at which a steady temperature is maintained for a time, a process known as soaking. **1966** *McGraw-Hill Encycl. Sci. & Technol.* VI. 379/1 If the alloy is heated to a temperature not far below its freezing temperature and held at that temperature for a long time, interdiffusion of the alloy constituents will tend to eliminate segregation. Such homogenization treatment is frequently called soaking.

**3.** *attrib.*, as (sense 1) *soaking solution, tub, vat*; (sense 2) *soaking operation, pit*; †**soaking club**, a drinking club.

**1690** LOCKE *Hum. Und.* II. xxi. §35 The tickling of his palate with a glass of wine, or the idle chat of a soaking club. **1853** *Nicholson's Operat. Mech.* (ed. 4) 408 Other trays..are to be piled or placed upon this,..until the soaking-tubs or boilers are sufficiently filled. **1882** GJERS in *Iron & Steel Institute* 568 During the soaking operation, a quantity of gas exudes from the ingot. *Ibid.*, Some of this heat..is lost by radiation before the ingot enters into the soaking pit. **1886** C. SCOTT *Sheep-Farming* 134 For this purpose a soaking vat has to be put up. **1890** *Anthony's Photogr. Bulletin* III. 29 The second amendment relates to the soaking solution. **1913** *Jrnl. Iron & Steel Inst.* LXXXVII. I. 67 With a view to having a regular sequence of hot ingots delivered to Gjers soaking-pits, whilst the centre of the ingot was still liquid,.. a central casting-pit was substituted, designed on the Bessemer principle. **1962** *Gloss. Terms Glass Ind.* (*B.S.I.*) 12 *Soaking pit,* a conditioning furnace used to bring glass in open pots to a uniform temperature for castings. **1976** *Steel USSR* VI. 196/2 The duration of holding in the soaking pits for 13–18 t ingots from the end of casting to the start of stripping must not exceed 1 h 10 min.

**soaking** ('səʊkɪŋ), *ppl. a.* [f. SOAK *v.*]

†**1.** Taking in moisture, absorbent; *fig.*, drawing to oneself, tending to drain or exhaust. *Obs.*

*c* **1440** *Promp. Parv.* 463/2 Sokynge grownde, as sondy grownde and other lyke. **1528** TINDALE *Obed. Chr. Man* 159 b, A sokynge consumcion, where in a man complayneth of feblenes and fayntynes. **1575** CHURCHYARD *Chippes* (1817) 186 But loe my skill,..For soaking soores, a soueraigne salue could finde. **1593** Q. ELIZ. *Boeth.* II. metr. iv. 30 [He] Shuns soking Sandes. **1611** SHAKS. *Wint. T.* I. ii. 224 Thy Conceit is soaking, will draw in More then the common Blocks.

†**b.** *transf.* Of persons. *Obs.*

**1565** COOPER, *Barathrum,*..a soking or wasting queane. **1584** LODGE *Alarum* B ij, They finde out..some olde soaking vndermining Solicitour.

†**c.** *soaking doe*, 'a barren doe, that going over the year is fat, when other does have fawns' (Halliwell). *Obs.*

**1588** *Presentment* in *Essex Rev.* XV. (1906) 64 A soaken doe found hurt cominge out of the Purliewe.

**2.** †**a.** Of a fire: Slow. *Obs.* (Cf. SOAK *v.* 6.)

*c* **1450** *Douce MS.* 55 fol. 129 Rost hym with sokynne fyre. *c* **1467** *Noble Bk. Cookry* (1882) 67 Rost hym long with a soking fyere. **1615** MARKHAM *Eng. Housew.* (1660) 73 Then spit it and rost it by a soaking fire.

**b.** *Printing.* (See quots.)

**1683** MOXON *Mech. Exerc., Printing* xxiv. ¶5 A long or a Soaking or Easie Pull, is when the Form feels the force of the Spindle by degrees, till the Bar comes almost to the hither Cheek of the Press. **1888** JACOBI *Printers' Vocab.* 128 *Soaking pull,* a long and easy pull over of the bar-handle of a printing press.

**3.** Percolating; sinking in; flowing slowly.

**1577** HANMER *Anc. Eccl. Hist., Euseb.* I. iii, A certain soaking slumber of drunkenness. **1648** J. BEAUMONT *Psyche* xx. lx, The heav'nly Dew Into Earth's thirsty mouth drops soaking Joy. **1699** DAMPIER *Voy.* II. III. 102 To the East of Cape Roman..you meet only a soaking faint Current.

**4.** Drenching; wetting thoroughly.

**1641** BEST *Farm. Bks.* (Surtees) 59 A good soakinge shower aboute the latter ende of September. **1664** EVELYN *Kal. Hort.* (1729) 193 Rub Moss off your Trees after a soaking Rain. **1753** *Scots Mag.* XV. 76/2 Though drench'd his..hide with soaking rain. **1806** J. BERESFORD *Miseries Hum. Life* II. xiv, A soaking torrent of rain. **1894** HALL CAINE *Manxman* v. vi, The rain was coming down in a soaking drizzle. *transf.* **1863** W. C. BALDWIN *Afr. Hunting* i. 11 The..cause of many a miserable soaking night to myself and others.

**5.** Saturated, drenched.

**1864** ABP. TAIT in *Reminisc. Lady Wake* (1909) xxiv. 280 It was voted dangerous for any one to fall asleep in our soaking state. **1879** ATCHERLEY *Trip to Boërland* 260, I.. stripped off my soaking clothes. **1882** 'OUIDA' *Maremma* I. 181 When the suns of August sucked up the venom from the emerald soaking swamp.

**6.** Quasi-*adv.*, in ***soaking wet***.

**1847** C. BRONTË *J. Eyre* v, All underfoot was still soaking wet with the floods of yesterday. **1863** W. C. BALDWIN *Afr. Hunting* iii. 94 Three miserable soaking-wet days.

**soakingly** ('səʊkɪŋlɪ), *adv.* [f. prec.]

†**1.** Slowly, gently, gradually. *Obs.*

*c* **1386** CHAUCER *Melib.* ¶51 Ye shul geten hem with-outen greet desir, by good leyser, sekyngly [*v.r.* sokyngly] and nat ouer hastily. **1434** MISYN *Mending Life* 119 þo all we may not gedir our hartis to-gidyr as we wold, ȝit may we not leef, bot sokandly stody we to grawe, þat at þe last Ihesu criste may stabil vs. *c* **1440** *Promp. Parv.* 463/2 Sokyngly, *idem quod* esyly. **1542** UDALL *Erasm. Apoph.* (1877) 309 A mannes enemies in battaill, are to be ouercomed..sokingly one pece after an other. **1555** WATREMAN *Fardle Facions* I. ii. 30 The heate of thaier sokyngly warmeth the cold ground. **1683** MOXON *Mech. Exerc., Printing* xxiv. ¶5 This is also call'd a Soft Pull; because it comes Soft and Soakingly and easily down.

†**b.** On or with a slow fire. *Obs.*

*c* **1450** *Two Cookery-bks.* 72 Lete hit boile sokingly on a faire charcole til hit be ynogh. *c* **1467** *Noble Bk. Cookry* (1882) 36 Rost it sokingly. **1530** PALSGR. 595/1 It is rosted sokyngly, *il est cuit,* or *rosty tout a loysir.* **1598** *Epulario* B iv, Let it bake sokingly in the ouen till it be throughly baked. **1638** SHIRLEY *Mart. Soldier* IV. ii, Oh! the Generall Belizarius for my money;..hee will roast soakingly within and without.

**2.** So as to saturate or drench.

In the 16th cent. quots. sense 1 may be implied.

**1540** R. JONAS tr. *Roesslin's Byrth Mankynde* I. iv. 19 Then with a sponge or other cloth dypped in the fore-sayde bathe, let her sokyngly washe her feet. **1579** LANGHAM *Gard. Health* (1633) 521 The broth of Rapes is good for the same purpose, [the heels] being washed and bathed therein sokingly. **1842** DICKENS *Amer. Notes* (1850) 100/2 The driving rain, which now poured down more soakingly than ever.

**b.** *fig.* Deeply, profoundly.

**1593** G. HARVEY *Pierce's Super.* Wks. (Grosart) II. 63 You ..may closely sitt, or sokingly ly at your bookes. **1647** TRAPP *Comm. Jas.* iv. 9 Savouringly and soakingly, with a deep and down right sorrow.

**soak-mill**, var. of *soke-mill*: see SOKE *sb.*[1] 4.

**soal(e, soall**, obs. forms of SOLE *sb.* and *v.*

**soam** (səʊm). *Sc.* and *north.* Forms: α. 5 soym(e, 5 somme, 6 so(l)me, 8– soam. β. 5–7 sowme, 6 soume, sovme, 8 sowm. [prob. a. OF. *some, somme, soume, saume* (med.L. *sauma, sagma*: see SEAM *sb.*[2]) pack-saddle, horse-load; but the difference in the sense is not accounted for by the existing evidence.]

**1.** A rope or chain, attaching a draught-horse or other animal to a wagon, plough, etc.; a trace-rope. Also *attrib.* in *soam-chain*.

α. **1375** BARBOUR *Bruce* x. 180 Hastyly He suld stryk with the ax in twa The hede-soyme. *Ibid.* 233 He..hewit in twa the soym in hy. *c* **1459** *Reg. Aberbrothoc* (Bann. Cl.) II. 108 Owr bailye..straik the sommys in twa and hewyt the plwche. **1535** STEWART *Cron. Scot.* I. 171 Thair wapynis ..[they] maid thame all in somes to thair pleuche. **1582** *Wills & Inv. N.C.* (Surtees, 1860) 46, ij plewes..with socke and culter, viij draught yokes, viij somes. **1765** A. DICKSON *Treat. Agric.* (ed. 2) 255 The soam of the pair immediately before the hindmost must be fixed..to the beam. **1799** J. ROBERTSON *Agric. Perth* 103 That inconvenience is prevented in the plough by using a long chain (provincially a soam). **1844** H. STEPHENS *Book of Farm* I. 626 The leading horses are thus yoked by a second set of common swing-trees to the end of the soam. *Ibid.*, The middle horse pulling by the soam-chain.

β. **1404** *Durh. Acc. Rolls* (Surtees) 398, ij cultris,..iij plogherbandis, viij sowmes. **1451** *Durh. Depos.* (Surtees) 30, iij crokes, j sowme. **1513** *Acc. Ld. High Treas. Scot.* IV. 513 For xx stane of towis to be soumes for the gunnys. **1572** *Wills & Inv. N.C.* (Surtees, 1835) 350, ix sowmes, iiij plewes, iij cowters. **1662** in Pitcairn *Crim. Trials* III. 603 Paddokis did draw the plewgh, as oxen; qwickens wer sowmes. **1752** *Rec. Elgin* (New Spalding Cl.) I. 465 Sowms, thramels, rigwoodies,..and all other..work of..straw, bent or rushes.

**2.** *Coal-mining.* (See quots.)

**1789** BRAND *Hist. Newcastle* II. 681 In low seams, [the coals are drawn] on trams, pulled by two small cords, called soams, by a boy. **1851** GREENWELL *Coal-trade Terms, Northumb. & Durh.* 30 A little boy, who performs his part by pulling the tub by a couple of ropes or traces..called *soams.* **1883** GRESLEY *Gloss. Coal-m.* 229 *Soams,* a pair of cords about three feet in length, by which foals and half marrows pull tubs along the roads.

**Soamin** ('səʊəmɪn). *Pharm.* Also **soamin.** [f. SO(DIUM + AMIN(O-.] A proprietary term for sodium *p*-aminophenylarsonate (= ATOXYL), formerly used to treat skin diseases.

**1908** *Trade Marks Jrnl.* 13 May 763/2 *Soamin*... Chemical substances prepared for use in Medicine and Pharmacy. Henry Solomon Wellcome, trading as Burroughs, Wellcome and Co.,..London EC.; Manufacturing Chemist. **1909** *Official Gaz.* (U.S. Patent Office) 19 Jan. 759/2 Henry Solomon Wellcome, London, England. Filed Nov. 2, 1908. *Soamin*... Sodium Para-amino-phenylarsonates. **1918** J. H. PARSONS *Dis. Eye* (ed. 3) xvii. 354 Arsenic is specially liable to cause optic atrophy, usually total, when administered in the form of trivalent benzol-ring compounds such as atoxyl or soamin. **1920** J. M. H. MCLEOD *Dis. Skin* vi. 111 Arylarsonate Group, which consists of atoxyl or soamin, arsacetin, and orsudan, was at one time much in favour but has fallen into disuse recently.

'**soaming**, *ppl. a.* ? error for *sowning*, sounding.

**1642** H. MORE *Song of Soul* III. ii. 31 A dead glasse.. shapes as they passe As well may see; Lutes heare each soaming diapase.

**so-and-so**, *sb.*, *a.*, and *adv.* Also **so and so, soandso.**

**A.** *sb.* **1.** An indefinite phrase (= 'such a thing, person, number,' etc.) used in place of a more lengthy statement, or as a substitute for an expression or name not exactly remembered or not requiring to be explicitly stated.

(*a*) **1596** SPENSER *F.Q.* IV. vii. 2 So whylome didst thou to faire Florimel; And so and so to noble Britomart. **1727** DE FOE *Syst. Magic* I. iv. (1840) 108 A deep sleep shall come upon you, and you shall dream so and so. **1740** CHEYNE *Regimen* 330 That..he must trust or believe..so and so, and do so and so in consequence. **1831** SCOTT *Ct. Robt.* xxix, If you persevere in your uncivil intention, I will do so and so. **1880** MUIRHEAD tr. *Rules of Ulpian* xxiv. §18 To that man.. let my heir give so-and-so.

(*b*) **1833** M. SCOTT *Tom Cringle* ii, What's his name of this, and so-and-so of t'other. **1855** THACKERAY *Newcomes* lviii, His London Agents were Messrs. So-and-so. **1883** 'ANNIE THOMAS' *Mod. Housewife* 88 I've left most of them for the next time; but the So-and-so's..will be here.

(*c*) **1833** M. SCOTT *Tom Cringle* i, In the year one thousand eight hundred and so and so. **1861** T. A. TROLLOPE *La Beata* I. i. 2 Number so-and-so in such-and-such a street. **1866** RUSKIN *Crown Wild Olive* (1873) 46 Divine service will be 'performed'..at so-and-so o'clock.

**2.** Used *euphem.* as a term of abuse for a person (occas. a thing). Also, with weakened force, as a term of affection.

**1897** W. S. MAUGHAM *Liza of Lambeth* iii. 42 'You little so-and-so!' said Liza, somewhat inelegantly, making a dash at him. **1931** D. L. SAYERS *Five Red Herrings* xii. 132 Some rigmarole about always finding the so-and-so hanging round his place and he wanted to have it out with him. **1943** *Lafayette Alumnus* (Lafayette College, Easton, Pa.) Nov. 5/1 Hiya, Joe, you old so-and-so, haven't seen you since that time, etc., etc. **1945** *Penguin New Writing* XXVI. 55, I told 'em all that but they wouldn't listen, the ignorant soandsos. **1956** B. GOOLDEN *At Foot of Hills* vi. 124 'He felt he oughtn't to leave his work.' 'Poor old so-and-so.' **1958** 'A. BRIDGE' *Portuguese Escape* i. 13 The Countess is a hard-baked, publicity-minded old So-and-so, with about as much consideration for other people as a sack of dried beans! **1968** K. WEATHERLY *Roo Shooter* 107 It's not much good you staying out if some other so-and-so is going to work it, is there? **1973** *Times* 28 Nov. 13/5 The set [of an opera] is an absolute so-and-so to walk about on. **1977** B. PYM *Quartet in Autumn* i. 9 'Hoping to get off early, lazy little so-and-so,' said Norman.

**B.** *adj.* **1.** Paltry, worthless; indifferent; poor in health or circumstances; so-so. Now *dial.*

**1655–6** DESBOROUGH in *Thurloe Papers* IV. 396, I.. acquainted him that such of his brethren..were so and so, and desired him..to advise them tacitly to resign. **1756** TOLDERVY *Hist. 2 Orphans* I. 119 You see..that I am your best friend still, though to be sure you are but so and so. *Ibid.* 131 You know the Doctor died but so and so, as to circumstances. **1883** *Almondbury Gloss.* 124 *So and so,* used for so so, paltry, feeble.

**2.** *euphem.* as a term of abuse.

**1929** E. WALLACE *Kennedy the Con Man* iv. in *Red Aces* 173 'That's what we pay rates and taxes for, and no so-and-so policemen in sight!' He did not say 'so-and-so', but Mr. Reeder thought his profanity was excusable. **1942** B. HIMES *Lunching at Ritzmore* in *Black on Black* (1973) 177 You would..resume your discussions..on defense..or the F.B.I., or the 'so and so' owners of Lockheed, or that (unprintable) Aimee Semple McPherson. **1959** *Listener* 30 July 186/2 Some [clients] are good, some are indifferent, some are a so-and-so nuisance.

**C.** *adv.* **1.** To a certain number or degree.

**1631** GOUGE *God's Arrows* I. xxix. 44 Papists..mumbling over so and so many times the Creed.

**2.** In a certain manner or way.

**1653** W. RAMESEY *Astrol. Restored* To Rdr. 12 Thinking he might have improved it so and so, much better. **1678** CUDWORTH *Intell. Syst.* 420 Vertue and Vice are nothing else but the Soul so and so affected or modified. **1726** BUTLER *Serm. Rolls Chap.* vii. 133 Things were so and so circumstantiated. **1736** —— *Anal.* I. ii, Forewarning us.. that if we act so and so, we shall have such enjoyments.

**3.** With only moderate prosperity, success, etc.

**1844** BALLANTINE *Deanhaugh* ii. 41 'How's the coal trade gaun on?' 'Just so and so.'

**4.** As a mere intensive.

**1959** 'A. FRASER' *High Tension* v. 60 'Why can't Hugh help then? Or won't he?' 'Not so-and-so likely.'

**Soanean** ('səʊnɪən), *a.* [f. the name of Sir John *Soane* (see below) + -AN.] Of, pertaining to, or characteristic of Sir John Soane (1753–1837), British architect, or the buildings designed by him. Also **Soa'nesque** [-ESQUE], '**Soanic** [-IC], *adjs.*

**1842** *Penny Cycl.* XXII. 168/2 He thought proper to limit the time of the 'Soanean Museum' being opened to the public to two days in each week for three months in the year. **1945** E. WAUGH *Brideshead Revisited* I. iv. 72 It was an aesthetic education to live within those walls, to wander from room to room, from the Soanesque library to the Chinese drawing-room. **1948** *Archit. Rev.* CIV. 64/1 An extravagant blend of Soanic abstraction and Italian *grotesquerie.* **1974** SHERWOOD & PEVSNER *Oxfordshire* 815 A doorway with Soanean incised decoration.

**soap** (səʊp), *sb.* Forms: α. 1–2, 4–5 **sape**, *Sc.* 5–6, 9 **saip**, 9 **saep**; 5 **sepe**, 9 *north.* **seeap**, **syep**. β. 3–8 **sope**, 5 **swope**, **shope**, **soope**, 5, 7 **soppe**, 6 **sopp**, **soopp**, **souppe**. γ. 6–7 **soape**, 7– **soap**. [A word widely represented in the European languages. Within the Teutonic group the forms are OE. *sápe*, OFris. type *sêpe (WFris. *sjippe*, EFris. *sêpe*, NFris. *sîp*), MDu. *seepe* (Du. *zeep*), MLG. and LG. *sêpe* (hence Da. *sæbe*), OHG. *seifa*, *seipha* (MHG. *seiffe*, *saiffe*, etc., G. *seife*); the ON. and Icel. *sápa* (Norw. *saapa*, Sw. *såpa*) is app. from OE. The early Teut. **saipōn-* is the source on the one hand of Finnish *saip(p)io*, *saip(p)ua*, Lapp. *saipo*, and on the other of L. *sāpo* (first mentioned by Pliny), whence It. *sapone*, F. *savon*, Sp. *jabon*, Pg. *sabão*, Roum. *sapun*, *sapon*, etc. Whether the word is of purely Teut. origin is doubtful; its occurrence in some of the Tartar languages may indicate that it was introduced by early trade from the East.]

**I. 1. a.** A substance formed by the combination of certain oils and fats with alkaline bases, and used for washing or cleansing purposes. Now usu. distinguished from DETERGENT *sb.*; soap is prepared from natural oils and fats and is precipitated by the ions (notably calcium) present in hard water.

α. *c* **1000** *Sax. Leechd.* II. 76 Meng wiþ sote, sealt, teoro, ..eald sape. *Ibid.* 124 Lyþre mid sapan. *c* **1050** *Voc.* in Wr.-Wülcker 439 *Lumentum*, sape. **1371** in *York Minster Fabric Rolls* (Surtees) 9 Et in sape empto 6*d.* *c* **1400** *Pol. Poems* (Rolls) I. 265 Somme can with a pound of sape Gete him a kyrtelle and a cape. **1455** in *Charters*, etc. *Edinb.* (1871) 80 Wyne, sape, irne, lynnyn clayth. **1500–20** DUNBAR *Poems* liv. 9 Scho schynes lyk ony saip. **1552** ABP. HAMILTON *Catech.* (1884) 23 Suppoise thow wesche the self with saip. **1813** PICKEN *Poems* II. 79 Nor saip nor water e'er it fan'. **1876** ROBINSON *Whitby Gloss.* 165/1 *Seeap*, soap.

β. *a* **1225** *Ancr. R.* 66 More noise he makeð to ȝeien his sope, þen a riche mercer al his deorewurðe ware. **1297** R. GLOUC. (Rolls) 143 Sope aboute couentre & ire at gloucestre. **1339–40** *Ely Sacr. Rolls* II. 92 In sope empt. pro lotura albarum. *c* **1449** PECOCK *Repr.* I. xx. 127 Of bathing and of waisching with oyl and swope. **1499** *Cov. Corpus Chr. Plays* (1902) 89 Paid for shope and gresse to the whyles j.d. **1515** *Sel. Cases Star Chamb.* (Selden) II. 99 He bought Soopp, Tarre, Irne,..and Retailled the same. **1561** T. NORTON *Calvin's Inst.* IV. 158 As though oyle coulde not be wyped awaye..with sope. **1600** PORY tr. *Leo's Africa* II. 47 They make no sope in all the countrey, but..use to wash with lee made of ashes. **1673** RAY *Journ. Low C.* 156 Heer is also made Sope not inferiour for goodness to that of Castile.

γ. **1687** A. LOVELL tr. *Thevenot's Trav.* II. 45 Most part of them would not take Money, but onely Soap, or Tobacco, and chiefly Soap. **1756–7** tr. *Keysler's Trav.* (1760) III. 249 Bologna is likewise celebrated for essences,..soap, and snuff. **1839** DICKENS *Nickleby* vii, You'll always find a little bit of soap in the kitchen window. **1884** KNIGHT *Dict. Mech.* Suppl. 827/1 The blocks of rough soap are first cut into thin shavings. **1940** J. H. WIGNER *Soap Manufacture* i. 20 In the textile trades soap is largely used for removing the natural impurities from the fibre and detergent properties are the main consideration. **1966** *McGraw-Hill Encycl. Sci. & Technol.* XII. 393/1 In ordinary usage the term soap specifies an alkali metal or substituted ammonium salt of a straight-chain carboxylic acid 10–18 carbon atoms in length, and the name detergent is given to synthetic materials of similar structure. **1972** *Materials & Technol.* V. x. 295 In synthetic anionic detergents, the main weaknesses associated with the traditional carboxylate soaps, namely, precipitation in hard water and decomposition in acidic solutions, are avoided by the use of other hydrophilic groups in place of the carboxylate group.

*Prov.* **1592** LODGE *Euphues Shadow* G 3, Who washeth the Asses eares, looseth both his Sope and his labour. **1860** HUGHES *Tom Brown at Oxf.* xxiii, 'Twas waste of soap to lather an ass.

**b.** *fig.*

*c* **1175** *Lamb. Hom.* 53 Monie of þas wimmen..smurieð heom mid blanchet þet is þes deofles sape. **1377** LANGL. *P. Pl.* B. XIV. 6 With þe sope of sykenesse þat seketh wonder depe. **1725** BAILEY *Erasm. Colloq.* 570 Such as by the Lather of Tears, and Soap of Repentance,..have washed away their Pollutions. **1840** HOOD *Kilmansegg, Christening* x, Washing his hands with invisible soap, In imperceptible water.

**c.** In the slang phrase, ***how are you off for soap?***

The early examples afford no clue as to the origin of the expression, and their date is against the view that the sense of 'money' (see below) was intended.

**1834** MARRYAT *P. Simple* iv, A young lady..looked at me very hard and said, 'Well, Reefer, how are you off for soap?' **1837** THACKERAY *Ravenswing* viii. **1886** BARING-GOULD *Crt. Royal* I. ii. 20 They..put their heads into his shop, and asked how he was off for soap.

**d.** *slang.* Flattery. Cf. SOFT SOAP *sb.* 2.

**1854** D. G. ROSSETTI *Let.* 11 May (1965) I. 193, I heard from MacCrae who offers £50 for the water-colour, with all manner of soap and sawder into the bargain. **1859** in *Slang Dict.* 98. **1876** DIPROSE *Laugh & Learn* (Farmer), Flattery is the confectionery of the world. In polite society it goes by the name of soap. **1957** W. FAULKNER *Town* (1958) x. 149 'The pattern,' Uncle Gavin said. 'First the soap, then the threat, then the bribe.'

**e.** *U.S. slang.* Money; now esp. that used in bribery.

**1860** M. O'CONNOR *Lines to Rich Young Lady* iii. (Funk & W.), If thy father hath 'the soap', Do not wash your hands of me. **1892** *Nation* 24 Nov. 385/3 This, combined with more or less 'soap', was undoubtedly instrumental in causing his defeat.

**f.** ***no soap***: an announcement of refusal of a request or offer, failure in an attempt, etc.; 'nothing doing'. *slang* (orig. and chiefly *U.S.*).

**1926** MAINES & GRANT *Wise-Crack Dict.* 11/2 *No soap*, can't talk business. **1929** E. WILSON *I thought of Daisy* iii. 153 If he tries to cut in on you, don't letum—I'll just tellum, no soap! **1932** J. T. FARRELL *Young Lonigan* vi. 216 Studs said he'd take a dozen or two when Nate brought them around. Nate tried to collect in advance; but Studs was no soap for that. **1939** W. FAULKNER *Wild Palms* 42, I told him. Not that I was to meet you at a hotel. I just said, suppose I did. And he still said no soap. **1948** A. N. KEITH *Three came Home* iii. 72 We would..call across... 'No-soap!' or 'Not to-night!' **1957** J. KEROUAC *On Road* (1958) I. xiii. 86 Terry and I tried to find work at the drive-ins. It was no soap anywhere. **1977** 'E. CRISPIN' *Glimpses of Moon* vi. 93 'The police tried to trace the handkerchief, I take it?' 'They did, but no soap.'

**g.** ***not to know*** (someone) ***from a bar of soap***: not to have the slightest acquaintance with. *Austral. colloq.*

**1938** *Smith's Weekly* 26 Nov. 23 (*caption*), I don't know you from a bar of soap. **1943** K. TENNANT *Ride on Stranger* xxv. 319 'Why doesn't she marry the child's father?'.. 'It's my belief she doesn't know him from a bar of soap.' **1970** J. CLEARY *Helga's Web* vii. 130 I've never met any of his—interests. Certainly not this girl. I dunno her from a bar of soap.

**h.** = SOAP OPERA 1 a.

**1943** *N.Y. Times Mag.* 28 Mar. 19 Within these specifications, there is a deal of shrewd craftsmanship in the preparation of the 'soaps'. **1958** *New Statesman* 12 Apr. 455/3 Pay-TV will lure whatever is good in television now and leave those who cannot afford to pay for programmes stuck with an unvaried diet of soap and corn. **1969** A. ARENT *Laying on of Hands* vi. 46, I was one of five writers doing a daytime soap. One script a week. **1974** *Anderson* (S. Carolina) *Independent* 20 Apr. 5A/2 Agnes..had landed a job dialoging soaps for well-known television writer Irna Phillips. **1978** *Amer. Poetry Rev.* July/Aug. 19/3 If you turn on day-time T.V. you will see most of his actors playing rather similar roles in the soaps.

**2. a.** With distinguishing terms, denoting a particular make or kind of soap, as ***alkaline***, ***arsenical***, ***ball***, ***black***, ***hard soap***, etc.; also ***soap of Alicant***, ***lime***, ***soda***, etc.

See also CASTILE, SOFT SOAP, and *curd*, *lead*, *marine*, *resin* or *rosin*, *soda*, *Spanish soap*.

**1703** *Art's Improv.* I. 49 You may mix with your Gluten, either Milk, or Soap of *Alicant. **1842** *Penny Cycl.* XXII. 171/1 White soda soap..in a less pure state,..is called Alicant, Venice, or Spanish soap. **1786** *Phil. Trans.* LXXVI. 156 Then evaporating it, [I] obtained a true *alkaline soap. **1863** W. C. BALDWIN *Afr. Hunting* iii. 73, I ..regretted much that I had no *arsenical soap to preserve the skin. **1728** CHAMBERS *Cycl.* s.v., *Ball-Soap, commonly used in the North, is made with Lyes from Ashes, and Tallow. *c* **1425** tr. *Arderne's Treat. Fistula*, etc. 40 Ane oyntement made of *blakke sope and poudre of bole. **1618** BRETON *Courtier & Countryman* Wks. (Grosart) II. 14/2 Tell her we haue blacke Sope enough already. **1704** *Dict. Rust.*, etc. (1726) s.v., For black Soap, 'tis made with strong Lye..and Whale or Fish-Oil, commonly called Train-Oil. **1753** *Chambers' Cycl.* Suppl. s.v. *Brick*, Some also mention ..*brick-soap, made in oblong pieces. **1882** FLOR. NIGHTINGALE in *Quain's Dict. Med.* 1046 Wash hands and nails carefully with *carbolic soap. **1704** *Dict. Rust.*, etc. (1726) s.v., Soft soap, such as are the *common soap, so called, and black soap. *c* **1840** *Encycl. Metrop.* (1845) VIII. 434/1 Common soap is composed of any kind of oil..with fixed alkali. **1612** tr. *Benvenuto's Passenger* I. i. 23 *French sope to scouer my hands. **1611** BIBLE *Malachi* iii. 2 Like a refiners fire, and like *fullers sope. **1638** *Penit. Conf.* (1657) 346 Whose dresse..is so much..as no Fullers sope can cleanse. *c* **1840** *Encycl. Metrop.* (1845) VIII. 435 [Soft] soap from oleaginous seeds, called *green soaps. **14..** in *Walter of Henley's Husb.* 49 Medell it with *harde sope or tarre. **1600** PORY tr. *Leo's Africa* III. 195 The inhabitants make great store of liquid sope, for they know not how to make hard sope. **1704** *Dict. Rust.*, etc. (1726) s.v., The other hard soap is made in the same manner. **1813** SIR H. DAVY *Agric. Chem.* (1814) 102 Fixed oil, in combination with soda, forms the finest kind of hard soap. **1839** URE *Dict. Arts* 1142 According to the practice of the United Kingdom, six or seven days are required to complete the formation of a pan of hard soap. **1884** W. S. B. MᶜLAREN *Spinning* (ed. 2) 28 The lime..unites with the oil and tallow, forming what is called an insoluble *lime soap. **1839** URE *Dict. Arts* 1143 Soda which contains sulphurets is preferred for making the *mottled or *marbled soap. **1704** *Dict. Rust.*, etc. (1726) s.v., That known by the name of *perfumed Soap. *c* **1865** LETHEBY in *Circ. Sci.* I. 329/2 The compounds of fatty acids with potash are called *potash-soaps. **1839** URE *Dict. Arts* 1149 The *scented soap..speedily consolidates. **1611–2** *Shuttleworths' Acc.* (Chetham Soc.) 198 Twoe pound of *swete sope. *c* **1425** tr. *Arderne's Treat. Fistula*, etc. 76 Of which forseid [things] *white sope may euer more be necessary to a leche. **1539** ELYOT *Castle Helthe* 58 They be somtyme made..of white sope. **1725** *Family Dict.* s.v., To make White Soap, take Two Hundred Pounds of Black Salt-wort [etc.]. **1815** J. SMITH *Panorama Sci. & Art* II. 812 The finest white soap grated small. **1839** URE *Dict. Arts* 1144 Of *yellow or rosin soap.

**b.** ***soap of glass***, or ***glassmaker's soap*** (see quots.).

**1815** J. SMITH *Panorama Sci. & Art* II. 409 A mineral, called the soap of glass,..is the oxide of a peculiar metal called manganese. **1895** *Bloxam's Chem.* (ed. 8) 481 Manganese dioxide (glassmaker's soap) is often added as an oxidising agent.

**c.** ***rock soap***, a variety of bole.

**1883** *Encycl. Brit.* XVI. 425 Magnesian Silicates... Bole. Earthy, in nests and veins... Stolpenite, Rock Soap, Plinthite..are varieties.

**3.** With *a* and pl. A kind of soap.

**1562** TURNER *Herbal* II. (1568) 113 The wild rape.. serueth for scouring oyntmentes and sopes. **1661** LOVELL *Hist. Anim. & Min.* 115 It's used also in powders, sopes,.. and suffumigations. **1712** tr. *Pomet's Hist. Drugs* I. 158 This Soap is very scarce in France. **1744** BERKELEY *Siris* §58 Common soaps are compositions of lixivial salt and oil. **1806** *Culina* 175 The yolk of an egg..is a natural soap, and in all jaundice cases, no food is equal to it. **1811** A. T. THOMSON *Lond. Disp.* (1818) p. lx, Soaps are hydrates, water being always present in them as a constituent. **1842** BISCHOFF *Wool Manuf.* II. 84 It would bring to this country the manufacture of fine soaps.

**II. 4.** *attrib.* **a.** In misc. use, as ***soap bath***, ***-bell*** (Sc.), ***business***, ***-factory***, ***-film***, ***-froth***, ***-lather***, ***-pad***, ***-pipe***, ***-tablet***, etc.

**1843** R. J. GRAVES *Syst. Clin. Med.* xxvii. 339 *Soap baths ..always constituted the first steps of treatment in every form of eruption. **1720** RAMSAY *Rise & Fall of Stocks* 24 As little bairns frae winnocks hy Drap down *saip bells. **1862** G. WILSON *Religio Chem.* 19 A soap-bell sails through it with impunity. **1635** LAUD *Diary* Wks. 1853 III. 223 The *soap business was..settled again upon the new corporation. **1861** *Eng. Cycl., Arts & Sci.* VII. 636 Some of the *soap-factories of the present day. **1924** R. M. OGDEN tr. *Koffka's Growth of Mind* iii. 105 A *soap-film is produced upon a wire-frame..and upon it a little noose of thread is cast in whatever form it may take. **1976** *Sci. Amer.* July 93/3 The area-minimizing principle alone is sufficient to account for the overall geometry of soap films and soap bubbles. **1837** CARLYLE *Fr. Rev.* III. v. iii, But Towns are not built of *soap-froth. **1771** SMOLLETT *Humph. Cl.* I. 238 His face frothed up to the eyes with soap lather. **1832** CARLYLE *Misc.* (1857) III. 48 With artificial fictitious soap-lather. **1820** J. CLELAND *Rise & Progr. Glasgow* 87 An Act was made for encouraging *Soap manufactories. **1842** *Penny Cycl.* XXII. 170/1 The *Soap Manufacture is one of considerable importance. **1958** *Listener* 16 Oct. 627/1 Scour round the inside with a steel wool *soap-pad. **1956** S. BECKETT *Malone Dies* (1958) 21, I remember the *soap-pipe with which, as a child, I used to blow bubbles. **1866** *Treas. Bot.* 952/2 Saponine, a vegetable *soap-principle. **1880** J. DUNBAR *Pract. Paper-maker* 54 *Soap size, made and used in the interior of Russia. **1920** D. H. LAWRENCE *Lost Girl* iv. 52 Happiness is a sort of *soap-tablet—he won't be happy till he gets it. **1799** *Hull Advertiser* 28 Dec. 2/3 Ten casks *soap tallow. **1842** *Penny Cycl.* XXII. 170 *Soap Trade. **1887** *Encycl. Brit.* XXII. 204/2 In England the soap trade did not exist till the 16th century. **1839** URE *Dict. Arts* 577 The roasted *soap-waste was then withdrawn. **1558** WARDE tr. *Alexis' Secr.* 41 Mingle it with the saied *Sope water. **1847** W. C. L. MARTIN *Ox* 155/1 Injections..of soap-water and oil.

**b.** In the names of apparatus used in making soap, as ***soap-cauldron***, ***copper***, ***kettle***, ***mill***, etc.

**1558** WARDE tr. *Alexis' Secr.* 19 b, It shall be good to set the saied cawdron..as *Sope cawdrons be set. **1790** in *Essex Rev.* (1906) XV. 87 The sugar-houses and soap-cauldrons. **1863** in Richardson & Watts *Chem. Technol.* I. 680 Any alkali..which may be introduced into the *soap copper. **1873** WEALE *Dict. Arch.* s.v., **Soap-engine*, a machine upon which the slabs of soap are piled to be cross-cut into bars. **1857** MILLER *Elem. Chem., Org.* vi. §1. 372 It is then cleansed or transferred to the *soap frames to cool. **1875** KNIGHT *Dict. Mech.* 660/2 *Curb*,..an inclined circular plate around the margin of a *soap or salt kettle. **1839** URE *Dict. Arts* 1145 The *soap-pans used in the United Kingdom are made of cast iron.

**c.** In the sense of 'used for holding soap', as ***soap basket***, ***-case***, ***chest***, ***dish***, ***tray***.

**1926–7** *Army & Navy Stores Catal.* 122 Wire sponge and *soap basket. For hanging on bath, etc.—1/-. **1975** *New Yorker* 17 Nov. 145/1 We found an assortment of brass soap baskets to hook over the side of the tub. **1844** G. DODD *Textile Manuf.* iii. 53 In all such machines, whether called 'dye-becks', '*soap-becks', or others. **1875** KNIGHT *Dict. Mech.* 260/1 A soap-beck contains soap-suds. **1895** MEREDITH *Amazing Marriage* viii, He came back bearing his metal *soap-case. **1837** CARLYLE *Fr. Rev.* III. III. i, Likewise coffee-chests, *soap-chests. **1837** DICKENS *Pickw.* xlii, An old cracked basin, ewer and *soap-dish. **1851** MAYHEW *London Lab.* I. 368/1 A green and white chamber service.., with *soap trays and brush trays.

**d.** (in sense 1 h), ***soap fan***, ***land***, ***star***, ***watcher***.

**1976** *National Observer* (U.S.) 10 July 16/2 Real soap fans have a dozen or so fan magazines, newspapers, and newsletters. **1948** Soapland: see SOAP OPERA 1 a. **1977** *Guardian Weekly* 17 Apr. 18/1 People who resent the behaviour of a character she plays don't walk up and slap her, as has happened to more than one American soap star. **1978** *Times* 29 Aug. 1/8 The dedicated soap watcher..can switch channels for a solid five hours..until, at 4.30 p.m... soap-land is closed for another day.

**5.** *Comb.* **a.** With nouns denoting persons, as ***soap-grinder***, ***-monger***, ***-patentee***, ***-projector***, ***-seller***, etc., or in names of appliances, as ***soap-cutter***, ***-holder***, ***-saver***. Also SOAP-BOILER, -MAKER.

(*a*) **14..** *Nom.* in Wr.-Wülcker 687 *Hic smigmator*, a sop-seler. **1549** BALE in Cheeke *Hurt of Sedition* (1641) Pref. a iv b, Some they sold to the Grociers and Sope-sellers. **1646** (*title*), A Looking-Glasse for Sope-Patentees... making discovery of a new Project..propounded (by the Sope-Projectors) to the Parliament. **1648** GAGE *West Ind.* Table, The Sope-houses at Lambeth, with the Sope Patentee belonging to them. **1756** C. LUCAS *Ess. Waters* III. 337 Let the sope-mongers learn not to counteract their boasted agent. **1815** J. SMITH *Panorama Sci. & Art* II. 456 Lime is used by the soap-manufacturer to render soda caustic. **1881** *Instr. Census Clerks* (1885) 77 Dry Soap Grinder. Soap Trimmer.

(*b*) **1833** LOUDON *Encycl. Archit.* §631 Space for soap-holders, brush-trays, &c. **1884** KNIGHT *Dict. Mech.* Suppl. 827/1 *Soap Cutter*, an apparatus for caking or barring soap. **1919** T. Eaton & Co. *Catal.* Spring & Summer 366/4 Wire soap saver 7 c. **1973** *Listener* 25 Jan. 117/2 The soap-saver ..was made like a diffuser-spoon, but bigger, with a basket of open wire-mesh.

**b.** With vbl. sbs., as ***soap-barring***, ***-cutting***, etc. Chiefly in attrib. use.

**1851** *Catal. Gt. Exhibition* p. c, Soap-cutting Machine. **1875** Knight *Dict. Mech.* 2232/2 Soap Barring and Caking Machine. *Ibid.* 2233/1 Soap-crutching Machine. **1899** *Daily News* 23 May 10/2 Soap Stamping and Packing Departments.

**c.** Similative, as ***soap-like***, ***-smooth*** adjs.

**1858** Mayne *Expos. Lex.* 1169/1 The offensive soap-like substance. **1866** *Treas. Bot.* 952/2 Trees.. possessing soap-like properties. **1949** E. Pound *Pisan Cantos* lxxvi. 45 By the soap-smooth stone posts.

**d.** Instrumental, as ***soap-filled*** adj.

**1970** *Which?* May 149/2 The cheapest soap-filled pads cost nearly 2d each.

**6. a.** Special combs.: **soap-ball**, a piece of soap formed as a ball, now esp. by the admixture of starch; **soap-cerate** (see quots.); † **soap-earth**, soapstone; **soap extract**, **-fat**, **-fish** (see quots.); **soap flakes** *pl.*, soap in the form of thin flakes for washing clothes, etc.; **soap-house**, a soap-boiler's premises; **soap leaf**, a leaf of soap (see LEAF *sb.*[1] 10 b); **soap-lees**, spent soap-lye; **soap-liniment** (see quots.); **soap-lock** *U.S.*, a lock of hair made smooth by the application of soap; hence, one who wears such, a low fellow, a rough or rowdy; **soap-lye**, a caustic alkaline lye obtained by running water upon alternate layers of soda ash and quicklime, and used in soap-making; **soapman** *Sc.*, a soap-maker; **soap plaster**, a healing-plaster chiefly composed of soap; **soap powder** (see quot. s.v. *soap extract*); also *loosely*, detergent in the form of a powder; † **soap-scale**, a kind of clay (see quot.); **soap-stock, soapstock**, a crude, partially saponified mixture of fatty acids formed as a by-product in the refining of natural fats; **soap-test** (see quot.); **soap-work(s**, a soap-manufactory.

**1601** Holland *Pliny* II. 420 Those *sope balls that are to polish the skin and to rid it from wrinkles. **1829** Scott *Doom of Devorgoil* III. ii, My soap-ball is of the mild alkali made. **1852** Royle *Man. Mat. Med.* (ed. 2) 540 *Ceratum Saponis Compositum.* Compound *Soap Cerate. *a* **1860** Wood & Bache *Dispensatory U.S.* (1865) 1044 Soap-cerate.. is used in scrofulous swellings and other instances of chronic external inflammation. **1876** Harley *Royle's Man. Mat. Med.* (ed. 6) 243 *Soap Cerate Plaster.* This is a mixture of lead, soap, and the acetates of lead and soda. **1696** *Phil. Trans.* XIX. 228 There is a considerable natural curiosity in the Neighbourhood of Smyrna, called by the Franks *Soap-Earth. **1758** Borlase *Nat. Hist. Cornw.* 70 Near Smyrna there is a fine whitish soap-earth. **1887** *Encycl. Brit.* XXII. 204/1 'Soap powders' and '*soap extracts' are simply preparations of alkalis. **1879** Webster *Suppl.*, **Soap-fat*, the refuse of kitchens, used in making soap. **1876** Goode *Fishes of Bermudas* 60 A '*Soap-fish' also occurs, probably either *Rhypticus saponaceus*.. or *Promicropterus maculatus.* **1926–7** *Army & Navy Stores Catal.* 38/2 *Soap Flakes—lb., -/8. **1933** 'G. Orwell' *Down & Out in Paris & London* xii. 91 There are no soap-flakes, only the treacly soft soap. **1967** N. Freeling *Strike out where not Applicable* 137 It was a little like a copywriter presenting an advertising campaign to a soapflakes manufacturer. **1648** Gage *West. Ind.* 5 Of the *Sope-houses at Lambeth. **1687** Miége *Gt. Fr. Dict.* I, *Savonnerie*,.. a Sope-house, a Place where Soap is made. **1810** *Sporting Mag.* XXXV. 80 The corner of the soap house. **1854** *Hull Improv. Act* 33 Any candle-house.. or soap-house. **1909** *Cent. Dict.* Suppl., *Soap-leaf. **1925** [see LEAF *sb.* 10 b]. **1978** *Times* 4 Nov. 24/5 Good presents for adults: a book of soap leaves. **1746** Langrish *Exper. upon Brutes* 19 Injecting too great a quantity of *Soap-lees. **1789** Buchan *Domest. Med.* (1790) 327 The caustic alkali, or soap-lees, is the medicine chiefly in vogue at present for the stone. **1842** *Penny Cycl.* XXII. 169/1 The nuisance of soap-lees waggons passing through London. **1852** Royle *Man. Mat. Med.* (ed. 2) 540 *Linimentum Saponis...* *Soap Liniment... Stimulant Embrocation. A vehicle for Opium, &c. **1864** *Chambers's Encycl.* VI. 141/2 *Soap Liniment*, or *Opodeldoc*, the constituents of which are soap, camphor, and spirits of rosemary. **1840** *Picayune* (New Orleans) 30 Aug. 2/2 Howard.. is described as.. wearing moustaches and *soap-locks. **1842** 'Uncle Sam' *Peculiarities* I. 119 You are an incendiary, a robber by profession, a soap-lock and a loafer. **1848** Bartlett *Dict. Amer.* 319 *Soap-lock*, a lock of hair made to lie smooth by soaping it. Hence also.. a Rowdy or Loafer. **1854** Marion Harland *Alone* xvi, Shaking.. at the prospect of.. the loss of your soap-locks. **1864** T. L. Nichols *40 Yrs. Amer. Life* I. 173 A German Jew, with.. soaplocks that would have astonished the Bowery in the palmiest days of soaplockism. **1774** T. Percival *Ess.* (1776) III. 144 The *soap ley is so caustic.. that it can be taken only in the smallest quantity. **1857** Miller *Elem. Chem., Org.* viii. 547 It is digested in an imperfect soap ley. **1883** R. Haldane *Workshop Rec.* Ser. II. 311/1 The.. production of crude glycerine from spent soap-lyes. **1813** Picken *Poems* II. 79 In vain was fill'd the *saipman's pan. **1789** *Med. Comment.* II. 344 The.. applications were changed for a *soap plaister. **1876** Harley *Royle's Man. Mat. Med.* (ed. 6) 243 Soap Plaster. **1865** H. Mayhew *Shops & Companies of London* 199/1, I can always make quick work of *my* washing by using 'Harper Twelvetrees' Glycerine *Soap-Powder', and it makes the clothes beautifully clean and white. **1964** M. Drabble *Garrick Year* xii. 193 Putting in my second instalment of soap-powder. **1970** G. Greer *Female Eunuch* 325 Some of the mark-up on soap powders.. could be avoided. **1704** *Dict. Rust.* (1726) s.v. *Clay*, Cowshot-Clay, or the *Soap-scale lying in Coal-mines. **1895** J. Lewkowitsch tr. *Benedikt's Chem. Analysis of Oils, Fats, Waxes* xii. 632 (*heading*) Examination of the fatty matter ('*soap stock'). **1924** Myddleton & Barry *Fats* iii. 35 The recovery of oil from the soap-stock depends for its commercial success upon the ruling prices of the edible oil. **1972** *Materials & Technol.* V. x. 279 [In soap-making] use is also made of by-product fatty materials such as soapstocks and curd oils. **1861** *Eng. Cycl., Arts & Sci.* VII. 637 **Soap-test*, a solution of white curd soap in proof spirit; it is used in ascertaining the amount of hardness of waters. **1649** *Sc. Acts, Chas. II* (1872) VI. II. 300/2 The preiudice whilk the decay of the *Sopeworkis has occasioned to the kingdome. **1695** *Ibid., Will. III* (1822) IX. 491/2 The said Robert Douglas his Soap work. **1839** Ure *Dict. Arts* 1143 Great waste of alkali.. in many soap-works.

**b.** Forming names of plants or trees, or their products: **soap-apple** (see quots.); **soap-bark**, a vegetable principle obtained from certain trees, as the *Quillaja Saponaria* of Chile, the common soapwort, *Saponaria officinalis*, and allied species, and used as a substitute for soap; saponin; **soap-bulb**, the soap-plant; **soap-fruit**, = SOAPBERRY 1; **soap-gentian** *U.S.*, soapwort gentian; **soap-nut**, = SOAPBERRY; also *attrib.*; **soap-plant** *U.S.*, an American liliaceous plant, *Chlorogalum pomeridianum*, used as a detersive; also, the soapberry; **soap-pod** (see quots.); **soap-root** (see quot. 1866); **soap-tree**, one or other of various species of trees or plants (see later quots.), of which the roots, leaves, or fruits yield a substitute for soap; also *attrib.*; **soap-weed**, †(*a*) the soapwort, *Saponaria officinalis*; (*b*) a North American plant (see quots. 1884, 1890); **soapwood**, the timber-tree or shrub *Clethra tinifolia*, native to the West Indies; also, a North American plant (see quot. 1771).

**1760** J. Lee *Introd. Bot.* App. 327 *Soap Apple, *Sapindus.* **1864** Webster, *Soap-plant*, one of several plants used in the place of soap, as the *Phalangium pomeridianum*, a Californian plant... It is called also *soap-apple* and *soap-tree.* **1861** *Eng. Cycl., Arts & Sci.* VII. 636 A substance called **soap bark* was brought to Europe from some tropical country in 1859. **1866** *Treas. Bot.* 952/2 Its bark, called Quillai or Soap-bark, is rough and dark coloured. **1883** R. Haldane *Workshop Rec.* Ser. II. 139/1 An article.. is brushed with a cold decoction of soap-bark. **1874** *Treas. Bot.* Suppl. 1279/2 *Chlorogalum pomeridianum...* The bulbous root, when rubbed in water, makes a lather..: hence it is known as the *Soap-bulb. **1666** J. Davies tr. *Rochefort's Caribby Isles* 48 One fruit.. about the bigness of a small Plumb.. is commonly called the *Soap-fruit. **1845–50** Mrs. Lincoln *Lect. Bot.* App. 105 *Gentiana saponaria*,.. *Soap gentian. **1858** Simmonds *Dict. Trade*, **Soap-nut*, a name for the seed of the *Mimosa abstergens.* **1866** *Treas. Bot.* 5/2 The pods of *Acacia concinna* are used in India like those of the soap-nut for washing the head. **1884** *Encycl. Brit.* XVII. 665/1 Soap nuts are the fruits of various species of *Sapindus*, especially *S. Saponaria*, natives of tropical regions. **1847** Ruxton *Adv. Mexico* xxv. 222 A barren rolling prairie.. covered with the palmilla or *soap-plant. **1859** Bartlett *Dict. Amer.* (ed. 2) 425 Soap-plant (*Chlorogalum pomeridianum*), a plant common in California and New Mexico. **1891** *Cent. Dict.* s.v., *Indian soap-plant*,.. the soapberry *Sapindus acuminatus*, and.. the *Chlorogalum.* **1866** *Treas. Bot.* 1068/1 **Soap-pods*, the Chinese name of the pods of several species of *Cæsalpinia.* **1891** *Cent. Dict.*, *Soapnut*,.. the fruit of .. *Acacia concinna...* Also [called] *soap-pod.* **1846** Lindley *Veg. Kingd.* 497 *Vaccaria vulgaris*.. contains Saponine, as also does the Egyptian *Soap-root. **1866** *Chambers's Encycl.* VIII. 793/1 The Egyptian Soap-root (*Gypsophila struthium*), and the Spanish Soap-root (*G. Hispanica*),.. have been employed for washing from time immemorial. **1666** J. Davies tr. *Rochefort's Caribby Isles* 48 There are two sorts of Trees.. called the *Soap-trees from the vertue they have to whiten clothes. **1756** P. Browne *Jamaica* 206 The Soap Tree [*Sapindus*]... The seed vessels of this plant are very detersive and acrid. **1859** *All Year Round* No. 32. 127 In Chili there is a soap-tree called *Quillaya saponaria.* **1607** Topsell *Four-f. Beasts* (1658) 503 New shorn wool which is very soft, and not trimmed with *sope-weed. **1884** *Encycl. Brit.* XVII. 401 *Y[ucca] filamentosa*, commonly called amole or soap-weed. **1890** Gunter *Miss Nobody* iv, Bare of everything.. but gemma grasses, soap weed, and small cacti. **1732** *Phil. Trans.* XXXVII. 450 *Soap-wood. The Bark and Leaves of this Tree being bruised and mixed with Water produce a Lather. **1771** R. F. Forster *Flora Amer. Sept.* 17 Soapwood, *Rhexia virginica.* **1864** Grisebach *Flora Brit. W. Ind.* 787/2 Soapwood, *Clethra tinifolia.*

**soap** (səʊp), *v.* Also 7 sope, 9 *Sc.* saip, saep. [f. SOAP *sb.* Cf. WFris. *sjipje*, Du. *zeepen*, G. *seifen*, Da. *sæbe*, Sw. *såpa.*]

**1.** *trans.* To rub, smear, lather, or treat in some special way with soap. Also with *up.*

**1585** T. Washington tr. *Nicholay's Voy.* II. xxi. 58 b, After that hee hath well soaped and rubbed your bodie.. wyth a purse of Stammin,.. he washeth you with very cleare water. **1611** Cotgr., *Savonné*, soped, or washed in sope. **1677** *Compl. Servant-Maid* 65 If there be any dirty places soap them a little, then take a little hard brush and soap it well [etc.]. **1725** *Fam. Dict.* s.v. *Clear-Starching*, Take your Lace and roll it.., and between every Roll soap it with Soap. **1771** Mrs. Haywood *New Present for Maid* 265 They [cambrics, etc.] should be.. well soaped. *Ibid.*, Linen soaped as above.. will be freed of all stains. **1802** Colman *Poor Gent.* I. i, Answer me,.. Who have [= has] soap'd up and flower'd your numskull after such a fashion? **1860** Rawlinson *Herodotus* IX. cx. IV. 473 This is the only day in all the year on which the king soaps his head. **1875** F. J. Bird *Dyer's Hand-bk.* 50 The pieces.. are finally washed and soaped.

**2.** *slang.* To address with smooth or flattering words; to flatter.

**1853** 'C. Bede' *Verdant Green* I. x, The tailor and robe-maker.. visibly 'soaped' our hero in what is understood to be the shop-sense of the word. **1865** Dickens *Dr. Marigold* i, These Dear Jacks soap the people shameful, but we Cheap Jacks don't.

**b.** With *over*: (see quot.).

**1857** *Slang Dict.* 19 *Soaped him over*, humbugged him.

**soap**, dial. form of SWOP *v.*

**soap and water.** [SOAP *sb.*] The commonest method of washing, used in phrases referring to standards of personal cleanliness. Also *attrib.*

**1837** H. Martineau *Society in Amer.* II. III. ii. 151 The demand of society for fresh air and soap and water has considerably increased. **1861** Geo. Eliot *Silas Marner* xiv. 243 A great ceremony with soap and water, from which baby came out in new beauty. **1907** G. B. Shaw *Major Barbara* in *John Bull's Other Island* 168 Trans-figured men and women carry their gospel through a transfigured world.. practising what the world will let them practise, including soap and water, color and music. **1922** E. O'Neill *Hairy Ape* iv. 37 Their faces and bodies shine from a soap and water scrubbing. **1961** L. Mumford *City in History* xv. 469 The spread of the soap-and-water habit might well account for the lowering of infant mortality rates. **1973** A. MacVicar *Painted Doll Affair* iii. 39 She was an enthusiast for soap and water, as her schoolgirl complexion showed.

Hence **soap-and-water** *v. trans.*

**1848** Dickens *Dombey* xxxi, By-the-bye, she'll soap-and-water that 'ere tablet presently. **1883** *Pall Mall G.* 27 Oct. 2/1 So soap-and-watering the infant Gargantua as to fit him for a Sunday school.

† **soap-ashes.** *Obs.* [SOAP *sb.* Cf. Du. *zeepaschen*, G. *seifenasche.*] Ashes of certain kinds of wood used in forming a lye in soap-making.

*c* **1515** *Interlude of Four Elements* (Percy Soc.) 30 Pyche, and tarre, and sope asshys. **1557–71** A. Jenkinson *Voy. & Trav.* (Hakl. Soc.) II. 208 Sope ashes are not here in such request that they will acquite the Chardges. **1624** Capt. Smith *Virginia* II. 25 Of Ash and Elme they make sope Ashes. **1651** French *Distill.* vi. 194 Boyle it in a Lixivium made of sope-ashes. **1733** W. Ellis *Chiltern & Vale Farm.* 392 The great goodness there is in these Soap-ashes and all others. **1794** T. Davis *Agric. Wilts* 132 In the neighbourhood of towns, soap-ashes are frequently.. used as a manure. **1837** R. Ellis *Laws & Regul. Customs* III. 401 Soap Ashes are synonymous with Wood Ashes.

**soapberry** (ˈsəʊpbɛrɪ). Also **soap-berry, soap berry.** [SOAP *sb.*]

**1.** The fruit or nut of various species of *Sapindus* (esp. *S. Saponaria*), or of *Acacia concinna*, used in certain countries as a substitute for soap; a soap-nut.

**1693** *Phil. Trans.* XVII. 621 The Sope-Berry, which is properly a Plumm, or between Nut and Plumm. **1819** *Pantologia* X, *Saponaria nucula*,.. soap berries. A spherical fruit, about the size of a cherry. **1858** Mayne *Expos. Lex.* 118/2 *Bermuda Berry*, common name for the soap-nut, or soap-berry produced by the *Sapindus saponaria.*

**2. a.** One or other of the trees bearing this fruit.

**1716** *Petiveriana* I. 222 Soap-berry,.. *Arbor Saponaria.* **1760** J. Lee *Introd. Bot.* App. 327 Soap Berry, *Sapindus.* **1871** Kingsley *At Last* xi, There is a young one fruiting finely in the Botanic Garden at Port of Spain.., a cousin of the Matapalos and of the Soap-berries. **1874** Stewart & Brandis *Flora N. West India* 108 *S[apindus] Saponaria*,.. the West Indian Soapberry, is grown in the West Indies.

**c.** *N. Amer.* A deciduous shrub, *Shepherdia canadensis*, of the family Elæagnaceæ, native to North America, and bearing small yellow flowers followed by edible red berries; also, the berries of this shrub; = *buffalo-berry* s.v. BUFFALO 5.

**1904** A. G. Morice *Hist. N. Interior Brit. Columbia* 61 The soap-berries were ripening. **1923** *Beaver* Dec. 104 In Central British Columbia it [*sc.* Indian ice cream] was made by working to a lather the dried soap berry. **1957** J. R. & I. M. Christie *Story Okanagan Falls* 42 Soap-berry.. bears its gay red-currant-like berries now only for the birds to enjoy. **1963** *Beaver* Autumn 40/1 The interior fresh-water Indians.. readily gave soapberries, kinninnick leaves and bark for smoking.

**3.** *attrib.*, as ***soapberry family***, ***tree.***

**1725** Sloane *Jamaica* II. 132 Sope-berry Tree. **1753** *Chambers' Cycl.* Suppl. s.v. *Sapindus*, There is only one known species of this genus,.. the soapberry tree. **1819** *Pantologia* X, *Sapindus rigidus*, ash-leaved soap-berry tree. .. A native of the West Indies and America. **1847** Darlington *Amer. Weeds*, etc. (1860) 87 *Sapindaceæ.* Soap-berry Family... Fruit capsular or berry-like. **1866** Veness *El Dorado* xi. 119 The root, bark, and seed covering of the huruwassa or soap berry tree is an admirable substitute for soap.

**soap-boiler.** [SOAP *sb.* Cf. Du. *zeepzieder*, G. *seifensieder.*]

**1.** One who boils (the ingredients of) soap; a soap-maker, soap-manufacturer.

**1594** Plat *Jewell-ho.* 77 A wise, wealthie, and ancient Sopeboyler, dwelling without Algate. **1651** French *Distill.* iii. 80 Quench them in the strongest *Lixivium* that Sope-boylers use. **1661** Evelyn *Fumifugium* (1825) 220 Brewers, diers,.. salt and sope-boylers, and some other private trades. **1712** Addison *Spect.* No. 488 ¶ 1, I have a Letter from a Soap-boiler, who condoles with me [etc.]. **1752** Foote *Taste* II, A Bristol farthing, coin'd by a soap-boiler to pay his journeymen, in the scarcity of cash. **1838** Lytton *Alice* VI. iv, The whisper spread among bankers and brewers and soap-boilers and other rich people. **1879** *Cassell's Techn. Educ.* I. 331/2 There is an increasing demand for it [*sc.* caustic soda] on the part of bleachers and soap boilers.

*transf.* **1877** Bagehot *Biogr. Stud.* (1881) 316 Some of the middle-aged men of business, the 'soap-boilers', as the London world disrespectfully calls them.

**b.** In collocations (cf. SOAPER 1 c).

**1707** Mortimer *Husb.* (1721) I. 291 Take Soap-boylers Liquor or Lee which is very sharp and strong. **1815** J. Smith *Panorama Sci. & Art* II. 451 The common bottle-glass is..made with..soap-boiler's waste ashes. **1834-6** *Encycl. Metrop.* (1845) VIII. 475/2 Green Bottle Glass..is commonly made of soap-boiler's waste and sand.

**2.** A pot used for boiling soap; a soap-pan.

**1863** W. C. BALDWIN *Afr. Hunting* vi. 152 The only utensil we could hit upon..to cook him in was a soap-boiler. **1875** KNIGHT *Dict. Mech.* 2233/1 A soap-boiler having a large pipe which receives the vapors rising from the kettle.

**soap-boiling,** *vbl. sb.* [SOAP *sb.*] The business, occupation, or process of boiling soap.

**1634** in Rymer *Fœdera* (1732) XIX. 507 The said Trade of Soap-making or Soap-boiling. **1714** MANDEVILLE *Fab. Bees* (1733) II. 152 Soap-boiling, grain-dying, and other trades and mysteries. **1780** *Phil. Trans.* LXX. 351 Perhaps the addition of this caustic substance would increase its..value, when employed in soap-boiling and other arts. **1834-6** *Encycl. Metrop.* (1845) VIII. 435/1 The first portion..is of course the strongest, and is reserved for the last operation of soap-boiling. **1887** *Encycl. Brit.* XXII. 203/1 The process of soap-boiling is carried out in large iron boilers.

*attrib.* **1884** KNIGHT *Dict. Mech.* Suppl. 827/1 The interior of a soap boiling kettle.

**ˈsoap-box.** [f. SOAP *sb.* + BOX *sb.*$^2$] **a.** A box for holding soap; orig. and still occas., a small receptacle for a ball or bar of soap; later *esp.* a wooden case in which soap is or may be packed, traditionally used as a makeshift stand for a speaker; hence used *fig.* and allusively.

**1660** *Act 12 Chas. II*, c. 4 Sched. s.v. *Boxes*, Soap-boxes the Shock, containing three-score boxes. **1834** *Chambers's Edin. Jrnl.* III. 143/3 A soap-box! A thing with a lid which is found on almost every wash-stand in Great Britain. **1862** *Catal. Internat. Exhib., Brit.* II. No. 6130, Sponge tray, soap boxes, and brush trays. **1907** J. LONDON *Road* 211, I get up on a soap-box to trot out the particular economic bees that buzz in my bonnet. **1912** *Town Topics* 16 Nov. 3/4 The days when a couple of..clerks on inverted soap boxes..were his staff. **1926-7** *Army & Navy Stores Catal.* 104/3 Soap box. Useful for travellers—each 1/6. **1928** *Observer* 1 Apr. 21/4 To use the language of Australian politics, 'Soapbox must be met by soapbox.' **1933** E. O'NEILL *Days without End* I. 32 If you knew what a burden he made my life for years with his preaching. Letter upon letter—each with a soap box inclosed, so to speak. **1943** K. TENNANT *Ride on Stranger* xxiii. 295 She made no answer to this outburst which, she felt, was only old Shanno blowing off steam... 'Back to your soap box,' she said briefly. **1945** N. MITFORD *Pursuit of Love* xiii. 97 She became an out-and-out Communist..preaching her new-found doctrine..from a soap-box in Hyde Park. **1948** M. LASKI *Tory Heaven* xi. 153 At his feet, a wax-faced baby moaned incessantly in a soap-box. **1960** H. HAYWARD *Antique Coll.* 260/1 *Soap-box*, spherical box of silver, pewter or brass for soap-ball, standing on moulded base with screw-on or hinged pierced or plain cover. **1968** *Daily Tel.* (Colour Suppl.) 13 Dec. 19/2, I look upon my wealth, and now the House of Lords, as useful soap boxes. **1977** *Time* 14 Nov. 59/3 The primary U.S. condition for rejoining is that the I.L.O. get off its political soapbox.

**b.** *attrib.* (chiefly with reference to public speaking from a soap-box); **soap-box cart**, a child's cart made from a soap-box; so **soap-box derby** [DERBY 1 d].

**1918** *National Geographic* July 8/1 (*caption*) The soap-box orator and his auditors. **1924** *Telephone Topics* XVIII. 262 (*heading*) Public address system supersedes soap box oratory. **1927** T. C. PEASE *United States* 546 The choice of party candidates by manipulation of party conventions and soap-box primaries. **1933** DYLAN THOMAS *Let.* Sept. (1966) 21 You must excuse my slight soap-box attitude. **1942** E. WAUGH *Put out More Flags* i. 72 Soap-box orators screaming their envy of the rich. **1950** *Manch. Guardian Weekly* 4 May 3/2 The 'Soap Box Derby' is an American festival rather more important to some..youngsters than the Fourth of July. **1960** *Times* 1 Mar. 13/1 The theatrical appeal of her soap-box oratory. **1977** J. VAN DE WETERING *Death of Hawker* xiii. 119, I like inventing. I was always making soap box carts when I was a child.

Hence (U.S.) **soap-box** *v. intr.*, to speak from or as from a soap-box; **soap-boxer**, one who speaks from a soap-box; **soap-boxing** *vbl. sb.*

**1913** *Industrial Worker* (Spokane, Washington) 10 Apr. 4/1 They do want all the publicity that can be given them by the press, by the locals, soap-boxers, and by individual conversation. **1919** U. SINCLAIR *Jimmie Higgins* iv. 42 If he could have an assistant..the soap-boxing could go on every night. **1926** E. O'NEILL *Great God Brown* I. iii. 41 When you got to love to live it's hard to love living. I better join the A.F. of L. and soap-box for the eight-hour night! **1972** *Village Voice* (N.Y.) 1 June 78/3 He's been a soap boxer for the IWW (actually he sang and his brother spoke).

**soap-bubble.** [SOAP *sb.*] An iridescent bubble composed of a thin film of soap and water.

**1800** M. EDGEWORTH *Parent's Assistant* (ed. 3) V. 100 Two other little children..came to him to beg, that he would blow some soap bubbles for them. **1815** J. SMITH *Panorama Sci. & Art* II. 351 By means of the bladder and pipe for filling soap-bubbles with hydrogen. **1830** HERSCHEL *Study Nat. Phil.* 252 Very thin films, either of a liquid (such as a soap-bubble), or of air. **1872** RUSKIN *Eagle's Nest* §131 Can you explain the frame of a soap-bubble?

*fig.* **1828** EMERSON in *Life* (1888) II. 44 The talk has been mere soap-bubbles. **1861** BOYD *Recreat. Country Parson* Ser. II. 195, I have heard men, who spoke in large soap-bubbles.

**soaped** (səʊpt), *ppl. a.* [f. SOAP *sb.* or *v.*]

**1.** Impregnated with soap; soapy. *rare.*

**1729** *Phil. Trans.* XXXVI. 12 Bubbles of soaped Water. *Ibid.* 13 The Tenacity of common Water is very small when compared to that of soaped Water.

**2.** Smeared, covered, washed, etc., with soap.

**1805** *Med. Jrnl.* XIV. 139 The body was well rubbed with soaped flannel. **1825** SCOTT *Jrnl.* 8 Dec., Hunting a pig with a soap'd tail. **1850** CARLYLE *Latter-d. Pamph.* v. (1872) 161 If you can climb a soaped pole. **1890** CLARK RUSSELL *Marriage at Sea* xx, He looked highly soaped and polished.

**ˈsoapen,** *v.* [f. SOAP *sb.* + -EN$^5$.] *trans.* To smear or rub with soap. Hence **ˈsoapened** *ppl. a.*

**1732** FIELDING *Cov. Garden Trag.* I. ix, With my own hands I'll wash thy soapen'd shirt.

**soaper** (ˈsəʊpə(r)). Forms: 3, 5 **sopare**, 4, 7 **soper**, 5 **sopere**, 6– **soaper**. [f. SOAP *sb.* Cf. Du. *zeeper* soap-boiler.]

**1.** †**a.** One who sells soap. *Obs.* **b.** A soap-boiler, soap-maker. Now *Hist.*

*c* **1225** *Ancr. R.* 152 A sopare, þet ne bereð buten sope & nelden, remð & ȝeieð lude & heie þet he bereð. **1393** LANGL. *P. Pl.* C. VI. 72 Sopers and here sones for seluer han be knyghtes. **14..** *Lat.-Eng. Voc.* in Wr.-Wülcker 612 *Smigmator*, a sopere. *c* **1440** *Promp. Parv.* 465/1 Sopare, marchaunt.., *saponarius.* **1591** PERCIVALL *Sp. Dict.*, *Xabonero*, a soaper, *Saponarius.* **1632** in Rymer *Fœdera* (1732) XIX. 381 Divers Persons in..the Society of Sopers within the Citty of Westminster. **1641** *Short Relation conc. Soap-Business* 12 The white soape made by the Soapers of Westminster spoyled and burnt the Linnen. **1805** R. W. DICKSON *Pract. Agric.* I. 247 The waste of soapers..may be made use of in the same way. **1825** JAMIESON *Suppl.*, *Soaper*, a soap-boiler; Aberd[een]. **1828** D'ISRAELI *Chas. I*, II. i. 21 It was urged that barrels of the new soap had been sophisticated by the malice of the old soapers.

*attrib.* **1839** URE *Dict. Arts* 594 [For making] Green window glass, or broad glass... 10 pounds of soaper salts [etc.].

**c.** In collocations, as ***soaper's ashes, liquor, lye, waste.*** (Cf. SOAP-BOILER 1 b.)

**1725** *Family Dict.* s.v. *Blood-running Itch*, Others wash the Horse once or twice in Soaper's Liquor. **1766** *Museum Rusticum* VI. 309 To make a trial..betwixt these ashes..and soapers waste. **1793** *Trans. Soc. Arts* V. 48 Seed steeped in Soaper's ashes. **1817-8** COBBETT *Resid. U.S.* (1822) 76, I see people go with their wagons five miles for soaper's ashes; that is to say, spent ashes. **1879** *Cassell's Techn. Educ.* I. 331/2 The remaining liquor..is commonly called soaper's lye.

**d.** A manufacturer of soap.

**1965** *Economist* 16 Oct. 303/2 Denied any real difference to exploit, the soapers have not even got an expanding market to sell in. **1979** *Jrnl. R. Soc. Arts* Dec. 60/1 The glassmakers and soapers responded to the growing shortage of domestic potash in several ways. **1982** *Shell Technol.* No. 3. 6/2 Manufacturing the surfactant molecules known as detergent active matter falls, normally, into the domain of the chemicals industry. Combining this active matter with the other constituents of a modern synthetic detergent and marketing the finished product is the concern of 'soapers'.

**2.** *techn.* (See quot.)

**1909** *Cent. Dict.* Suppl., *Soaper*, in calico-printing, a machine in which the cloth is washed with soap.

**3.** = SOAP OPERA 1 a. *N. Amer. colloq.*

**1946** *Time* 26 Aug. 56/3 The result: *Pepper Young's Family*, one of radio's most popular soapers. **1972** *Daily Colonist* (Victoria, B.C.) 4 Feb. 2/1 The CBC soaper Whiteoaks of Jalna rates only slightly higher than a documentary on the mating habits of the tsetse fly. **1981** *TV Picture Life* Mar. 6/1 Daytime soapers were dealing with sex and violence far more explicitly than their night-time brothers for quite a while.

**soapery** (ˈsəʊpərɪ). Also 7-8 **soaperie.** [f. SOAP *sb.* Cf. Du. *zeeperij.*] A soap manufactory.

**1674** in J. Cleland *Rise & Progr. Glasgow* (1820) 88 [The premises, for the Soap manufacture, at that time termed the] Soaperie. **1721** WODROW *Hist. Suff. Ch. Scot.* (1830) II. 387/2 The soaperie there [at Glasgow] was guarded, and closely searched for arms and ammunition. **1775** ASH, *Soapery*, the place where soap is made. **1840** *Evid. Hull Docks Comm.* 15 A very large soapery and sugar-refinery. **1886** *Bradford Observer* 6 Mar., To assist..in Working a Soapery on the newest lines, with specialities.

**soapie** (ˈsəʊpɪ). *colloq.* [f. SOAP *sb.* + -IE.] = SOAP OPERA 1 a.

**1964** F. POHL in *Galaxy* Oct. 190/2 You had a nervous breakdown..space cafard, as they call it on the soapies. **1978** *N.Y. Times* 30 Mar. C21/6 Movie: 'Daughters Courageous'... A soapie, granted. And dated. But pleasantly cheerful.

**ˈsoapily,** *adv.* [f. SOAPY *a.*] In a soft or easy manner; smoothly. Also in sense 4 of SOAPY *adj.*

**1833** M. SCOTT *Tom Cringle* xix, [The snake] continuing all the while..to glide soapily along. **1976** A. E. LINDOP in H. Watson *Winter's Crimes 8* 200 Soapily he would say, 'Darling, don't worry.' **1979** *Sci. Amer.* Jan. 26/1 The breakdown of the insulator may have many causes from the death of the maintaining cells to the appearance of a detergentlike metabolite capable of soapily cleaning off the invaluable lipid layers.

**ˈsoapine.** [f. SOAP *sb.* + -INE$^5$.] A kind of powder, used as a substitute for soap.

**1883** R. HALDANE *Workshop Rec.* Ser. II. 33/1 Wash in clean water with 'soapine' in a bath of pottery or clay.

**ˈsoapiness.** [f. SOAPY *a.*] The quality of being soapy, or covered with soap.

**1727** BAILEY (vol. II), *Sopiness*, a being dawbed with Sope. **1855** *Orr's Circ. Sci., Elem. Chem.* 424 Magnesian minerals are characterized by giving the impression of soapiness when touched.

**ˈsoaping,** *vbl. sb.* [f. SOAP *v.*] The action or process of smearing, rubbing, or washing with soap. Also in fig. context.

**1556** in *Shropsh. Parish Doc.* (1903) 57 For sopyng of clothys, vi$^{d}$. **1706** STEVENS *Sp.-Eng. Dict.*, *Enxabonadúra*, sopeing of Linnen. **1823** J. BADCOCK *Domest. Amusem.* 150 'Bristol soap'..by its hardness enables the good wives..to perform the act of soaping more perseveringly. **1834** *Tait's Mag.* I. 726/1 Some spot where Pleasure's tail was free from soaping, And all might seize it fast who felt inclin'd. **1879** C. MARVIN *Our Public Offices* 23 A vast amount of soaping and towelling was then called into action to remove the grime.

*attrib.* **1646** *Looking-Glass for Sope-Patentees* (title-p.), A new Project..to monopolize the Soping-mystery. **1876** *Encycl. Brit.* IV. 688/2 After washing out of the dye-beck the goods [*sc.* calicoes] are passed into a soaping beck.

†**ˈsoapish,** *a. Obs.*$^{-0}$ Somewhat soapy.

**1648** HEXHAM II, *Zeepachtigh*, Soapish.

**ˈsoapist.** [f. SOAP *sb.*] A soap-manufacturer.

**1893** L. KILLEEN *Soldiers at Sea* 29 The eminent *soapists*, whose speciality may be unrivalled in fresh water.

**soapless** (ˈsəʊplɪs), *a.* [f. SOAP *sb.*]

**a.** Lacking soap; *esp.* unwashed, dirty.

**1825** T. HOOK *Sayings* Ser. II. *Passion & Princ.* vi, The washing-stand [was] soapless. **1828** LYTTON *Pelham* II. xii. 120 The offered hand of his new friend..was of a marvellous dingy and soapless aspect. **1858** GEO. ELIOT in Cross *Life* (1885) II. 16 Something more piteous almost than soapless poverty. **1906** [see CANDLELESS *a.*].

**b.** Of shampoo, detergent, etc.: not containing soap.

**1936** *Chemist & Druggist* CXXIV. 56/2 The alternative to sulphonated lorol [*sic*] for soapless shampoos is saponin. **1959** *Which?* Nov. 152/2 All the liquid and cream shampoos, since they are all based on very similar soapless detergents, would clean the hair effectively in hard or soft water. **1966** J. S. COX *Illustr. Dict. Hairdressing & Wigmaking* 140/1 Sulphonated vegetable oils are also used in another type of soapless detergent.

**soap-maker.** [SOAP *sb.*] One who makes soap; a soap-boiler.

**1483** *Cath. Angl.* 318/1 A Sape maker.., *saponarius.* **1558** WARDE tr. *Alexis' Secr.* 41 Take Sope makers water, and boyle it vntill it..become as it were an oyntment. **1597** A. M. tr. *Guillemeau's Fr. Chirurg.* 41 b/1 Take Sope-makers lye, two pounde, Vitriol three ownces. **1634** in Rymer *Fœdera* (1732) XIX. 506 That no Soap-maker whatsoever presume to put any Soap to sale, which shall not be so marked. **1652** (*title*), The Soapmakers Complaint for the Losse of their Trade by Reason of a double excise. **1780** *Westm. Mag.* Suppl. 730/1 John Shand, Coldbath-fields, soap-maker. **1839** URE *Dict. Arts* 1142 Three such boils may be given in..one day's work, by an active soap-maker. **1861** *Eng. Cycl., Arts & Sci.* VII. 636 The carbonic acid is driven off for the soap-maker's purposes.

So **soap-making** *vbl. sb.*

**1603** STOW *Surv.* 253, I haue not read or heard of Sope making in this Cittie till within this fourescore yeares. **1634** in Rymer *Fœdera* (1732) XIX. 507 Other persons..who..have set up a Trade of Soap making as for themselves. **1857** MILLER *Elem. Chem., Org.* vi. §1. 359 It is this [mucilaginous oil] which is chiefly employed in soap-making.

**soapolallie** (ˈsəʊpəʊlælɪ). *N. Amer.* Also **soapol(l)ali(e), soopolallie, sopelalee,** etc. [f. SOAP *sb.* + Chinook Jargon *olallie* berry.] **1.** A thick drink made from crushed soapberries. Cf. SOAPBERRY 2 c.

**1895** *Canad. Mag.* Aug. 344/1 We were fortunate enough to see some Indians eating 'soapolali'. **1944** C. BARBEAU *Mountain Cloud* 199 Here are the stems of blackberries and the wild fruit of the hills that gives sopelalee. **1966** *Islander* (Victoria, B.C.) 27 Feb. 6/2 There was [at the potlatch] also a great deal of oolachan-grease and soapollalie.

**2.** = SOAPBERRY 2 c. Also *attrib.*

**1937** T. STANWELL-FLETCHER *Jrnl.* 23 Sept. in *Driftwood Valley* (1946) 33 On drier, more open ridges..are..dense thickets of small Shepherdia, or soopolallie, bushes. **1953** A. F. FLUKE *Kwakiutl* 21 The berries of the 'soopolally' bush..were dried and stored whole. **1957** J. R. & I. M. CHRISTIE *Story of Okanagan Falls* 42 One little shrub, the Indians' 'soopolallie'..bears its gay red currant-like berries now only for the birds to enjoy. **1976** T. WALKER *Spatsizi* xii. 139 The soap olallie leaves were a darker green, and the fruit larger.

**soap opera.** *colloq.* (orig. *U.S.*). [f. SOAP *sb.* + OPERA.

So called because some of the early sponsors of the programmes were soap manufacturers. For the use of *opera*, cf. *horse opera* s.v. HORSE sb. 27 a.]

**1. a.** A radio or television serial dealing esp. with domestic situations and freq. characterized by melodrama and sentimentality; this type of serial considered as a genre.

[**1938** *Christian Cent.* 24 Aug. 1011/1 These fifteen-minute tragedies..I call the 'soap tragedies'..because it is by the grace of soap I am allowed to shed tears for these characters who suffer so much from life.] **1939** *Newsweek* 13 Nov. 44/2 Transcontinental Network bubbled up out of the 'soap operas'. **1948** *Time* 11 Oct. 40/3 *The Beast in Me* also includes such matter as Humorist Thurber's grimly unhumorous 'Soapland' (studies in contemporary soap opera). **1953** M. DICKENS *No More Meadows* iv. 180 More and more soap operas had hit the air to sell detergents and deodorants and headache pills. **1978** J. IRVING *World according to Garp* xvi. 321 Hoping that the visceral reality of Garp's language..somehow rescued the book from sheer soap opera. **1980** *Times Lit. Suppl.* 24 Oct. 1210/5 Some advertising campaigns [on ITV] have become mini soap-operas.

**b.** *transf.* and *fig.*

**1944** R. CHANDLER *Lady in Lake* v. 36, I haven't heard a word from Muriel in the whole month... I don't have any idea at all where's she's at. With some other guy maybe. I hope he treats her better than I did... Thanks for listening to the soap opera. **1958** *Spectator* 19 Sept. 369/2 Eugene O'Neill's wordy autobiographical play is an endlessly tragic soap-opera, a sort of Mrs. Dale's Diarrhœa. **1962** [see HUFF *sb.* 1]. **1971** 'A. BURGESS' *MF* ii. 25 The act of robbery..near 39th Street... This was daily soap-opera of the streets.

**2.** *attrib.*

**1942** W. STEGNER *Mormon Country* 347 They deal with impressionable virgins caught in the net of polygamy and agonizing worse than any soap-opera heroine through endless difficulties. **1951** M. McLUHAN *Mech. Bride* (1967) 157/1 Soap-opera serials are short on action, long on situations. **1958** *Punch* 9 July 59/2 The revival of 'The Royalty' (BBC) is the latest development in the soap-opera world, on a Channel that has no soap to sell. **1978** S. BRILL *Teamsters* ix. 349 Most of the soap-opera intrigue of innuendo and in-fighting was not terribly subtle.

Hence **soap-ope'ratic, -ope'ratical** *adjs.*, of or characteristic of a soap opera.

**1963** *New Yorker* 1 June 66 'The L-Shaped Room'... A sentimental piece of work, but so justly and successfully sentimental that it nearly always avoids seeming soap-operatic. **1975** *Country Life* 20 Mar. 742/3 A few weeks ago the BBC concluded a soap-operatical version of the loves of Georges Sand. **1979** *Boston Globe* 18 May 39 From her soap-operatic point of view, Watergate was not a national tragedy but rather was the personal pathos of a woman with nothing to give a husband in need.

**soap-rock.** *Min.* [SOAP *sb.*] Steatite; magnesian clay.

**1746** HILL *Theophr.* (1774) 242 The Steatites of the Soap Rock of Cornwall. **1758** BORLASE *Nat. Hist. Cornw.* 66 The most curious of all our clays in Cornwall, is the steatites near the Lizherd, generally called the Soap-rock. **1815** J. SMITH *Panorama Sci. & Art* II. 465 Steatites, or soap-rock, is generally of a greenish colour. **1825** J. NICHOLSON *Operat. Mechanic* 456 The magnesia has obtained the name of soap-rock, and a marked variety of it steatite.

**soap-stone** ('səʊpstəʊn). *Min.* Also **soap stone, soapstone.** [SOAP *sb.* Cf. G. *seif(en)stein.*] A massive variety of talc, of which various kinds are found in several countries, having a smooth greasy feel, and used for various economical or ornamental purposes (occas. as a soap); soap-rock, steatite; also loosely applied to certain soft clays, etc.

**1681** GREW *Musæum* III. I. vi. 321 Soap-Stone, *Steatites*; ..seeming like hard Suet, greasie to the touch. **1778** W. PRYCE *Min. Cornub.* 31 Steatites or Soap Stone, which is in such plenty. **1799** WELD *Trav. N. Amer.* 385 A stone of a very soft texture, called the soap stone, is very commonly found in the back parts of North America. **1837** DANA *Min.* 261 The soapstone..at Lizard Point, Cornwall, when first extracted, may be kneaded like dough. **1850** LYELL *2nd Visit U.S.* II. 50 At Centreport these unctuous marls or calcareous clays [of the chalk formation] are called by the people soap-stone. **1850** ANSTED *Elem. Geol., Min.*, etc. 195 *Saponite*, Piotine, Kerolite, Soapstone (not Steatite). **1851** *Catal. Gt. Exhib.* 1422/1 Chinese figures of soapstone. **1883** GRESLEY *Gloss. Coal-m.* 229 *Soapstone*, a variety of fireclay, sometimes applied to Bind.

*attrib.* **1875** KNIGHT *Dict. Mech.* 2201/1 Soapstone pencils, made from a peculiar stone found near Castleton, Vt. **1883** *Cent. Mag.* XXVI. 596/2 The hearth of an open soap-stone stove. **1884** *Pall Mall G.* 24 July 12/1 Works of art in Foochow soap-stone ware.

**b.** A slab or piece of this, fashioned for some special purpose.

**1890** *Cent. Mag.* XL. 531 He..fished up a disused soap-stone.., put it on the stove.., and stood erect..till the soap-stone was warm.

**soap-sud.** *rare.* [Back-formation from next.] = SOAP-SUDS. Chiefly in attrib. use.

**1727** BOYER *Dict. Royal* I. s.v. *Eau, Eau de Savonnage*, soap-sud. *Ibid.* s.v. *Savonnage.* **1802** *Spirit Public Jrnls.* VI. 278 Your air-balloon sunk to soap-sud bubbles, when compared to it [*sc.* an eclipse]. **1823** J. BADCOCK *Dom. Amusem.* 74 The common soap-sud bubbles of children.

Hence **'soap-suddy** *a.*

**1831** *Blackw. Mag.* XXIX. 1007 The soap-suddy waves in a wash-hand basin. **1850** S. LAING *Obs. Europ. People* xiii. 331 Its water is of a milky, greenish, or soap-suddy hue.

**soap-suds.** Also **soapsuds.** [SOAP *sb.*] Water impregnated with dissolved soap, *esp.* water in which clothes have been washed.

**1611** COTGR., *Savonné*,..frothie like sope-suds, or a lather of sope. **1616** SURFL. & MARKH. *Country Farme* 162 For the speedie growing of hearbes,..there is nothing in the world better..than Sope suds. *a* **1700** EVELYN *Diary* 15 Apr. 1652, It has been..spoil'd by washing it ignorantly with soap-suds. **1707** MORTIMER *Husb.* (1721) I. 120 The moistning of them [*sc.* dry ashes] with..Soap-suds will add mightily to their strength. **1771** MRS. HAYWOOD *New Present for Maid* 256 Silver-plate ought to be washed with soap-suds. **1848** DICKENS *Dombey* ix, A widow-lady, with her sleeves rolled up..and her arms frothy with soap-suds. **1884** KNIGHT *Dict. Mech.* Suppl. 879/2 Make a strong soapsuds, using hot water.

Hence **'soap-sudsy** *a.* (Cf. SOAP-SUDDY.)

**1854** LOWELL *Jrnl. in Italy* Prose Wks. 1890 I. 215 A scanty rill of soapsudsy liquid.

**soapwort** ('səʊpwɜːt). Forms: 6 **sopewurt, -woort,** 7 **-worte (-worth),** 6–8 **-wort,** 7– **soapwort.** [f. SOAP *sb.*, perh. after Du. *zeepkruid* or G. *seifenkraut*, in later G. also *seifenwurz(el.)*]

**1.** One or other of the herbaceous plants belonging to the genus *Saponaria*, which yield a saponaceous principle; esp. the common species, *S. officinalis*; also, the genus itself.

**1548** TURNER *Names Herbes* 66 *Radicula*,..if we had it here,..myghte be called in english sopewurt or skowrwurt. **1597** GERARDE *Herbal* II. cviii. 359 The stalkes of Sope-woort are slipperie. **1629** PARKINSON *Parad.* 352 The ordinary Sopeworte or Bruiseworte with single flowers is often planted in Gardens. **1671** SALMON *Syn. Med.* III. xxii. 428 Soapwort..heals Cuts,..helps the Stone and Dropsie. *a* **1689** MRS. BEHN tr. *Cowley's Plants* C.'s Wks. 1711 III. 374 Soap-wort, tho' coarse thy Name, thou dost excel In Form and art enrich'd with fragrant Smell. **1731** MILLER *Gard. Dict.* s.v. *Lychnis*, The Double Sopewort is a Plant of no great Beauty. **1800** *Med. Jrnl.* III. 365 She was farther directed to apply clysters prepared with soap wort. **1866** *Treas. Bot.* 952/2 Saponine,..found likewise in plants belonging to the cloveworts, soapworts, and a few other orders.

**b.** As a moth-name (see quot.).

**1832** J. RENNIE *Consp. Butterfl. & Moths* 69 The Soap Wort (*Hadena Saponariæ*..) appears the middle of July..; feeds on the Saponaria officinalis and other plants.

**2.** *U.S.* (See quots.)

**1845–50** MRS. LINCOLN *Lect. Bot.* App. 162 *Saponaria vaccaria*, field soap-wort. **1858** SIMMONDS *Dict. Trade*, *Soap-wort*, the root of *Vaccaria vulgaris*, which, like the aril of the soap-berry, contains saponine.

**3.** Any plant of the order *Sapindaceæ.*

**1846** LINDLEY *Veg. Kingd.* 383 A very general character of the Soapworts is to have their embryo either curved, or twisted spirally. **1876** HARLEY *Royle's Mat. Med.* 707 Soapworts..are well illustrated in the horse-chestnut.

**4.** *attrib.*, as ***soapwort family, order*; soapwort gentian,** †(*a*) = sense 1; (*b*) *U.S.*, a variety of gentian.

**1578** LYTE *Dodoens* III. 334 *Alisma siue Saponaria*, Sope-wort Gentian. **1846–50** A. WOOD *Class-bk. Bot.* 453 *Gentiana saponaria*, Soapwort Gentian. **1849** BALFOUR *Man. Bot.* 381 *Sapindaceæ*, the Soapwort Family. **1861** BENTLEY *Man. Bot.* 481 *Sapindaceæ.*—The Soapwort Order.

**soapy** ('səʊpɪ), *a.* Also 7–8 **sopy,** 9 *Sc.* **saipy.** [f. SOAP *sb.* + -Y. Cf. WFris. *sjippich*, G. *seifig.*]

**1.** Smeared with soap; covered with soap-suds or lather.

**1610** G. FLETCHER *Christ's Vict.* II. lix, Such watry orbicles young boyes doe blowe Out from their sopy shells. *a* **1635** RANDOLPH *Conceited Pedlar* Wks. 1875 I. 47 And were't not better to embrace this pretty shambles for beauty ..than to tumble our soapy laundresses? **1747–96** MRS. GLASSE *Cookery* xiii. 188 Take great care the bag or cloth be very clean, not soapy. **1840** DICKENS *Old C. Shop* vii, The door was opened, but nothing came in except a soapy arm.

*transf.* **1778** PRYCE *Min. Cornub.* Gloss., *Soapy Heads*, the joints of stones, smeared with a saponaceous slippery soil.

**2.** Impregnated with soap; containing soap in solution.

**1721** BAILEY, *Suds*, the soapy Liquor in which Clothes are washed. **1826** S. COOPER *First Lines Surg.* (ed. 5) 23 The caustic fixed alkalies, triturated with pus, combine with it into a soapy fluid. **1882** *Garden* 21 Jan. 48/3 The leaves ought to be carefully sponged over with soapy water.

**3.** Of the nature of soap; having the soft or greasy feel of soap; soap-like.

*a* **1722** LISLE *Husb.* (1757) 26 Their chalk is of a fat soapy kind, and they call it marle. **1799** [A. YOUNG] *Agric. Linc.* 10 They have rich loams, soapy and tenacious. **1815** J. SMITH *Panorama Sci. & Art* II. 465 Talc..is soft and soapy to the touch. **1857** MILLER *Elem. Chem.*, *Org.* xii. §1. 686 Oleophosphoric Acid,..in combination with soda,..forms a soapy compound.

**4. a.** Of appearance, feel, etc.: Resembling that of soap; suggestive of soap.

**1732** ARBUTHNOT *Rules of Diet* in *Aliments* 301 Such Substances as are of a soapy Nature. **1803** *Med. Jrnl.* IX. 493 When boiled in it a long time it gives it a soapy appearance. **1838** T. THOMSON *Chem. Org. Bodies* 38 Most of them have a slightly soapy feel. **1843** *Penny Cycl.* XXVI. 261/1 Lustre soapy. Feel greasy. **1852** C. W. HOSKYNS *Talpa* i. (1854) 2 A suspicious kind of sound..which I may describe by the word 'soapy'.

**b.** Having a taste of soap.

**1892** WALSH *Tea* 87 The lower grades are frequently 'soapy' or 'mousey' in flavor.

**5.** *slang.* **a.** Ingratiating, suave, unctuous.

**1854** E. TWISLETON *Let.* 22 June (1928) xi. 202 The Bishop of Oxford I never do like..his manner, when Lords are in presence, richly merits his popular sobriquet of 'Soapy Sam'. **1865** *Pall Mall G.* 28 Oct. 5 But why..do people call him [Bp. Wilberforce] Soapy Sam? **1910** *Blackw. Mag.* Feb. 182/2 He had once been famous for his soapy manners.

**b.** Of fits: Simulated by chewing soap.

**1886** *Daily News* 13 Dec. 5/4 He is known professionally as the 'King of the Soapy Fits Trick'.

**6.** Of style, tone, etc.: smooth, bland, sickly, sentimental.

**1889** G. B. SHAW in *Star* 12 Aug. 3/4 Miss Nettie Carpenter played Svendsen's Romance for Violin, and played it very well, though her tone is just a little soapy—if I may be permitted to use such an expression. **1926** C. CONNOLLY *Let.* 1 June in *Romantic Friendship* (1975) 139 Benson's style is pretty soapy. **1973** *Publishers Weekly* 17 Sept. 59/3 Romance, which gets a bit soapy at times.

**7.** *Comb.*, as ***soapy-looking, -mannered, -tailed.***

*a* **1845** BARHAM *Ingol. Leg.* Ser. III. *Wedding Day* (1905) 435 Don't interfere with their soapy-tail'd pigs. **1853** URE *Dict. Arts*, etc. (ed. 4) II. 458 Soapy-looking compounds with resins and wax. **1890** *Pall Mall G.* 8 Apr. 6/3 The solemn soapy-mannered 'dispenser'.

**soar,** obs. form of SORE.

**soar** (sɔə(r)), *sb.* Also 7 **soare.** [f. SOAR *v.*, perh. partly after F. *essor.*]

In Beaum. & Fletcher's *Bonduca* IV. iv. the second folio (1679) has 'fearless of your bloody soars'; but the reading of the first folio (1647) is 'fears', evidently a misprint for 'sears', i.e. claws.

**1.** The altitude attained in soaring; range of flight upwards. Also *fig.*

**1596** *Edw. III*, II. i, Fly it a pitch aboue the soare of praise. **1667** MILTON *P.L.* v. 270 Within soare Of Towring Eagles. **1792** S. ROGERS *Pleas. Mem.* I. 361 That eye so finely wrought Beyond the search of sense, the soar of thought. **1804** J. GRAHAME *Sabbath* (1839) 22/1 A splendid cloud appeared..; then hovering, floats, High as the soar of eagle. **1892** *Pall Mall G.* 26 May 7/1 It requires the highest soar of fancy to imagine [etc.].

**2.** The act of soaring or rising high.

**1817** COLERIDGE *Satyrane's Lett.* ii. in *Biog. Lit.* (1882) 252 A liberated bird..who now after his first soar of freedom poises himself in the upper air. **1820** SCOTT *Abbot* xv, It is ill whistling for a hawk when she is once on the soar. **1870** ROSSETTI *Poems, Ho. Life* iv, Just when at that swallow's soar Your neck turned so.

*transf.* **1825** BEDDOES *Poems, To Bryan Procter* 166 Wings upraise thee long In the unvacillating soar of song. **1854** LOWELL *Fireside Trav.* (1864) 321 There is none of the spring and soar which one may see even in the Lombard churches. **1890** SAINTSBURY *Elizab. Lit.* iv. 102 A little later we meet with that towering soar of verse which is also peculiar to the period.

**soar** (sɔə(r)), *v.* Forms: 4–5, 7 **sore,** 5–6 **sowre,** 5–7 **soore** (6 *Sc.* **soir**), 6–7 **soare,** 6– **soar.** [ad. F. *essorer* (= It. *sorare*) to fly up, to soar, repr. a pop. Lat. **exaurare*, f. *aura* air.]

**I.** *intr.* **1. a.** Of birds: To fly or mount upwards; to ascend to a towering height; also loosely, to sail or skim at a great height. Occas. with *up.*

*c* **1384** CHAUCER *Ho. Fame* I. 499 Faste be the sonne, as hye As kenne myght I with myn ye, Me thought I sawgh an Egle sore. *c* **1400** MAUNDEV. (Roxb.) vii. 25 When þai see þat fewle sore in þe aer. **1486** *Bk. St. Albans, Hawking* b ij, Hit may happyn that she will sowre so hegh in to the Eyre, that ye shall Nether se hir nor fynde hir. **1530** PALSGR. 725/1, I soore, as an hauke dothe. **1587** *Mirr. Mag., Sabrina* vi, What birde can flye, and soare, if stormes doe rage. **1688** HOLME *Armory* II. xi. 229/2 He beareth Argent, an Eagle volant in bend, (soaring, or flying a loft). **1697** DRYDEN *Virg. Georg.* I. 500 Watchful Herons..mounting upward with erected Flight, Gain on the Skies, and soar above the Sight. **1788** V. KNOX *Winter Even.* xxv. (1790) I. 208 It is not till the wings have acquired strength and agility, that it..dares to soar undauntedly in the fields of air. **1830** HERSCHEL *Study Nat. Philos.* 84 A flight of Condors soaring in circles in a particular spot. **1867** LADY HERBERT *Cradle L.* viii. 217 Here and there eagles and hawks soared above their heads.

**b.** *transf.* Of persons, etc. Chiefly *poet.* or *rhet.*

*c* **1374** CHAUCER *Troylus* I. 670, I have no cause, I wote wele, to sore, As doth an hawk. ? **1593** MARLOWE *Edw. II*, v. i, For such outragious passions cloye my soule, As..often am I sowring vp to heauen. **1602** MARSTON *Antonio's Rev.* III. i. 105 O, in what orbe thy mightie spirit soares. **1743** C. WESLEY *Hymn, 'Christ the Lord'* v, Soar we now where Christ has led. **1792** S. ROGERS *Pleas. Mem.* I. 77 How oft.. We..Soar'd in the swing,..Thro' sister elms. **1849** MACAULAY *Hist. Eng.* vii. II. 265 It was said..that James had furnished the wings with which his brother had soared to a higher region. **1875** MANNING *Mission H. Ghost* xii. 343 We believe ourselves to have wings, and to be soaring into heights of the spiritual life.

**c.** In various *fig.* and *transf.* uses.

**1605** *1st Pt. Jeronimo* II. vi, By that argument you firmly proue honor to sore aboue the pitch of loue. **1648** J. BEAUMONT *Psyche* XXIV. ccxii, Oft she resolved..to wait Heav'n's leisure, till her Heart might thither sore. *a* **1735** LD. LANSDOWNE *On Unnatural Flights in Poetry* 23 Rash hyperboles that soar so high. **1754** SHERLOCK *Disc.* (1759) I. i. 50 It soars above the reach of Human Reason. **1820** SCOTT *Monast.* xiii, On the present occasion..the wrath of good Dame Elspeth soared higher than usual.

**d.** To fly *away.*

**1581** PETTIE *Guazzo's Civ. Conv.* III. (1586) 136 Ther is no man such a Niasse, but that continuall..repulses wil make him soare away.

**e.** To hover *about* a place. Also, of fish: To remain at the surface of the water.

**1592** KYD *Sol. & Pers.* II. ii, My ship shall be..blowne with sighs; So will I soare about the Turkish land, Vntill [etc.]. **1653** WALTON *Angler* 53 The Chubs..will presently rise up to the top again, and lie there soaring till some shadow affrights them again.

**f.** *Aeronaut.* Of an aircraft or its pilot: to fly without the aid of an engine, esp. for an extended period without significant loss of altitude.

**1893** O. CHANUTE in *Amer. Engineer & Railroad Jrnl.* Feb. 85/2 M. de Sanderval..is to be commended for having made an earnest if unsuccessful effort to learn how to soar in a wind like a bird. **1903** W. WRIGHT in *Jrnl. Western Soc. Engineers* VIII. 402 On trial we found that the machine would soar on the side of a hill having a slope of about 7 degrees. *Ibid.* 407 It would be easy to soar in front of any hill of suitable slope, whenever the wind blew with sufficient force to furnish support. **1931** V. W. PAGÉ *ABC of Gliding* vii. 159 An expert in Germany recently soared for a distance of 42 miles. **1940** L. B. BARRINGER *Flight without Power* xii. 218 After being checked out in two-seaters, they are allowed to soar in single-seaters. **1976** D. PIGGOTT *Gliding* (ed. 4) viii. 49 In general, it is not wise to attempt to soar by circling if you are below 500 feet.

**2.** *fig.* To mount, ascend, or rise to a higher or more exalted level in some respect.

The separate groups of quotations illustrate the main variations of usage.

(*a*) **1593** SHAKS. *Rich. II*, I. i. 109 How high a pitch his resolution soares! **1647** COWLEY *Mistr., Vain Love*, Desires, which whilst so high they soar, Are Proud as that I lov'd before. **1811** SHELLEY *Love* 14 Each energy of soul surviving More vivid, soars above. **1863** MISS BRADDON *Eleanor's Victory* II. iii. 41, I don't believe that young lady's soul ever soars above laces and ribbons. **1891** E. PEACOCK *N. Brendon* I. 181 His ambition did not soar high.

(*b*) **1601** BARLOW *Serm. Paules Crosse* 30 He soared in his highest pitch of fauour with her Maiestie. **1622** in Foster *Eng. Factories Ind.* (1908) II. 147 They are nowe aloft and soare in pride. **1663** S. PATRICK *Parab. Pilgr.* (1687) 211 It will depress and thrust you down below others, while you seem to be..soaring to a pitch far above them. **1728** YOUNG *Love Fame* I. 157 When men of infamy to grandeur soar. **1757** JOHNSON *Idler* No. 33 ¶26 From whence they soared to the most elevated heights of literary fame. **1818** SCOTT *Hrt. Midl.* xlviii, The feeling of pique..at seeing Effie..soar suddenly so high above her in life.

(*c*) **1615** BRATHWAIT *Strappado* (1878) 173, I should desire ..To take an Eagles wing and soare farre higher, Then hitherto my weake Muse could attaine. **1663** S. PATRICK *Parab. Pilgr.* (1687) 146 As they think him an Orator who mounts and soars aloft (as they call it) in high-flowen words. **1732** POPE *Ess. Man* I. 91 Hope humbly then; with trembling pinions soar. **1784** COWPER *Task* v. 723 To be divinely free, To soar, and to anticipate the skies. **1816** SHELLEY *Dæmon* I. 206 Then has thy rapt imagination soared Where..The temple of the mightiest Daemon stands. **1870** EMERSON *Soc. & Sol., Courage* Wks. (Bohn) III. 112 Poetry and eloquence catch the hint, and soar to a pitch unknown before.

**3. a.** Of inanimate objects: To ascend, rise up to a height. Also *transf.*

**1697** DRYDEN *Æneid* VIII. 558 The boiling waters roar; And smoky flames through fuming tunnels soar. *a* **1721** SHEFFIELD (Dk. Buckhm.) *Wks.* (1753) I. 12 The sigh which sent forth that..word, Up tow'rds the heavens like a bright meteor soar'd. **1812** BYRON *Ch. Har.* II. iii, Till man shall learn Vainly his incense soars, his victim bleeds.

**b.** Of a mountain, building, etc.: To rise majestically or imposingly to a great altitude. Also with *up*.

**1812** BYRON *Ch. Har.* I. lx, Oh, thou Parnassus! whom I now survey,..soaring snow-clad through thy native sky. **1858** LYTTON *What will He do?* I. iv, At the rear of the palace soars up the old Abbey. **1871** FREEMAN *Norm. Conq.* IV. xviii. 154 Soaring over the city and the intervening valley, rose the height of Penhow.

**c.** Of an amount, price, etc.: to rise or increase rapidly. Hence, of a commodity: to increase rapidly in price.

**1929** T. WOLFE *Look Homeward, Angel* xv. 196 She realized that in a very short time land values would soar beyond her present means. **1965** *New Statesman* 30 Apr. 672/3 The improvement..cannot be more than a stopgap whilst numbers continue to soar. **1978** I. B. SINGER *Shosha* i. 12 The price of meat soared. **1979** *Tucson* (Arizona) *Citizen* 20 Sept. 1 A/4 Gold soared to another record of $380 at London's five major bullion firms.

**II.** *trans.* **4.** To exalt. *rare.*

**1595** BARNFIELD *Poems, Sonnet to T. T.* iv, So those rare Sonnets, where wits ripe doth lie,..doe soare thy fame to skie.

**5.** To perform or accomplish (a flight) by rising high. Freq. in fig. context.

**1659** FULLER *App. Inj. Innoc.* I. 21 Here he soareth so high a flight I cannot follow him. **1745** ELIZA HEYWOOD *Female Spect.* (1748) IV. 71 A person of weak intellects, in attempting to soar too high a flight, not seldom shares the fate of Icarus. **1806** H. SIDDONS *Maid, Wife, & Widow* I. Pref. p. xvii, Here we behold the muse of satire soaring the flights of an eagle.

**6.** To attain or reach (a height) by upward flight; to fly up through (the air, etc.). Also *fig.*

**1667** MILTON *P.L.* VII. 421 They summ'd thir Penns, and soaring th' air sublime With clang despis'd the ground. **1742** YOUNG *Nt. Th.* IV. 612 Of lavish love, stupendous heights to soar. **1765** BEATTIE *To Churchill* 34 He soars Pindaric heights, and sails the waste of Heaven.

**7.** To cause to soar.

**1661** J. HEATH in J. W. Draper *Cent. Broadside Elegies* (1928) No. 43 A Cherubs wing hath soar'd him to this Hight. **1930** R. CAMPBELL *Adamastor* 88 Partaking the strain of the heavenward pride That soars me away from the earth I deride. **1978** A. WELCH *Book of Airports* ii. 28/1 Soaring the glider all the way back to where you started from is both exciting and satisfying. **1982** *Sci. Amer.* July 60/1 With the engine off the craft can be soared like a hang glider.

**soarable** (ˈsɔːrəb(ə)l), *a.* [f. SOAR *v.* + -ABLE.] Suitable for soaring flight. Hence **soaraˈbility**, a soarable condition.

**1922** *Nature* 17 June 799/1 When the air at the level of the fin-ray was 'soarable', as shown by the behavior of dragon-flies. **1922** *Flight* XIV. 620/2 How machines will fare.. remains to be seen. The southern slopes are not nearly so steep, and the extent to which they give soar-ability is at present a matter for speculation. **1961** *Aeroplane & Astronautics* CI. 163/2 The second day..suffered from clamp in the middle but produced soarable periods at either end. *Ibid.*, Nobody went away in the morning soarability, because the post-frontal sky, when it came in late afternoon, should theoretically have been worth waiting for.

**soarage**, variant of SORAGE *Obs.*

**soarant**, *a. Her.* = SOARING *ppl. a.* 2.

**1828** BERRY *Encycl. Her.*, *Soarant, Soaring*, or *Towering*, that is, flying aloft.

**soaraway** (ˈsɔːrəweɪ), *a.* [f. SOAR *v.* + AWAY *adv.*] Soaring, making rapid or impressive progress.

**1977** *Zigzag* Aug. 6/1 All the great American pop styles rolled into one but fueled with the energy of the super soaraway seventies. **1978** *Oxford Jrnl.* 6 Jan. 1/1 The team which has made the Journal a soaraway success. **1982** *Observer* 26 Sept. 9/4 He'll soon be writing for Britain's best and liveliest soaraway Sunday newspaper.

**soard, soare**, obs. forms of SWARD, SORE.

**soarer** (ˈsɔːrə(r)). [f. SOAR *v.*]

**1.** One who or that which soars, in various senses.

**1852** LYTTON *My Novel* XII. xii, Noiseless soarers into gloomy air out of Stygian deeps. **1895** *Advance* (Chicago) 19 Dec. 902/3 Though in eloquence a high soarer, in thought he digs deep. **1900** W. WRIGHT in M. W. McFarland *Papers W. & O. Wright* (1953) I. 34 Hawks are better soarers than buzzards. **1910** *Times* 18 May 14/5 The albatross is pre-eminently the gliding soarer of the bird kingdom. **1978** *Sci. Amer.* July 102/1 Those master soarers, the great albatrosses.

**2.** An aircraft designed for soaring.

**1909** *Flight* 20 Feb. 110/1 For a machine heavier-than-air, the true distinctive expression should decidedly be, 'flying machine', comprising 'flyers', 'gliders', 'soarers', &c. **1931** V. W. PAGÉ *ABC of Gliding* viii. 164 The primary training or school machines..are gliders rather than soarers. **1941** S. P. JOHNSTON *Horizons Unlimited* 30 Sailplanes or soarers are simply light and efficient gliders that may be made to take advantage of up currents of air to attain altitudes far above their launching points.

**soaring** (ˈsɔːrɪŋ), *vbl. sb.* [f. SOAR *v.*]

**1. a.** The action of the verb SOAR. Also *transf.*

**1575** TURBERV. *Faulconrie* 198 They [*sc.* hawks] flee up aloft upon pleasure which with us falconers is called soring. *c* **1630** *Roxb. Ball.* (1888) VI. 455 Holow! my Fancie, holow! ..stay at home with me! leave off thy lofty soaring. **1651** DAVENANT *Gondibert* III. v. 26 Thy love's high soaring cannot be a crime. **1722–7** BOYER *Dict. Royal* I, *Essor*,.. flight, or soaring up. **1856** EMERSON *Eng. Traits, Literature* Wks. (Bohn) II. 105 The union of Saxon precision and oriental soaring, of which Shakespeare is the perfect example. **1880** JEFFERIES *Great Est.* 132 This soaring and wheeling [of jackdaws] is evidently done for recreation.

**b.** *Aeronaut.* Gliding; now *esp.* gliding for extended periods without significant loss of altitude. Freq. *attrib.*

[**1864** *Leisure Hour* 21 May 328/1 The sciences of aerostation and meteorology must progress together as wedded sciences... The effect of a mutual reaction upon each other we are unable to conjecture, further than to anticipate..more than probable extension of the properties and simple soaring power of the balloon.] **1893** *Amer. Engineer & Railroad Jrnl.* LXVII. 396/1 It seems now reasonably possible for designers of soaring machines..to experiment with their apparatus without further search for some hidden secret. **1894** O. CHANUTE *Progr. Flying Machines* p. iv, Aeroplanes for soaring flight. **1896** [see GLIDING *vbl. sb.* 2]. **1903** W. WRIGHT in *Jrnl. Western Soc. Engineers* VIII. 401 In principle Soaring is exactly equivalent to gliding, the practical difference being that in one case the wind moves with an upward trend against a motionless surface, while in the other the surface moves with a downward trend against motionless air. **1931** V. W. PAGÉ *ABC of Gliding* p. vii, Soaring machines or sailplanes are usually monoplanes with a higher aspect ratio than found in the training planes. **1931** P. & M. WHITE *Gliding & Soaring* xviii. 145 Soaring differs from gliding in that the ship, instead of losing altitude, either pursues a level course or gains height. **1952** F. GREEN *ABC of Gliding* 90 Ridge soaring depends basically on the wind. **1958** D. PIGGOTT *Gliding* xviii. 118 Many glider pilots become anxious to start cross-country flying as soon as they have made one or two soaring flights. **1974** *Sci. Amer.* Aug. 14/2 His memberships ..reflect several of his outside interests, which he lists as 'camping, canoeing, gliding and soaring and gardening'. **1979** *Yale Alumni Mag.* Apr. (Suppl.) cn 20/1 He is fully recovered..and still believes that soaring is a great sport.

**2.** An instance of this. Also *fig.* and *transf.*

**1611** COTGR., *Essort*,..a soaring, mounting,..high-rising. **1648** HEXHAM II, *Een Opstijginge*, an Ascention, a Mounting, or a Soaring up. **1762** D. WEBB *Beauties Poetry* 14 The soarings and stoops of the Eagle. **1786** PARR *Educ.* 2 (Todd), Proverbs were ambitiously seized by the lyric and by the epic muse in..their sublimest soarings. **1805** WORDSW. *Waggoner* IV. 80 As if the warbler lost in light Reproved his soarings of the night. **1890** CLARK RUSSELL *Ocean Tragedy* I. vi. 127 These irrational soarings of spirits.

**soaring** (ˈsɔːrɪŋ), *ppl. a.* [f. SOAR *v.*]

**1.** *fig.* Rising to a great height, high pitch, etc.; egregious; ambitious, aspiring; sublime.

(*a*) **1607** SHAKS. *Cor.* II. i. 270 When his soaring Insolence Shall teach the People. **1665** BOYLE *Occas. Refl.* IV. xiii. (1848) 248 To make a Rise to their soaring flight of a Tower, whose Top should reach unto Heaven. **1687** tr. *Sallust* (1692) 33 Of soaring and egregious parts. **1814** SCOTT *Wav.* lix, The same soaring and ardent spirit, for whom the whole earth seemed too narrow. **1848** W. H. KELLY tr. *L. Blanc's Hist. Ten Y.* I. 552 A bold and soaring mind. **1879** STANLEY *Manzoni's Hymn for Whitsunday*, The New World's soaring wants. **1889** *Spectator* 9 Nov. 633/1 This soaring insolence of these Christian young men.

(*b*) **1695** J. EDWARDS *Perfect. H. Script.* 418 This Evangelist..is more sublime and soaring than the rest. **1847** EMERSON *Repres. Men, Montaigne* Wks. (Bohn) I. 351 In the heart of each maiden,..in the soul of the soaring saint, this chasm is found.

**2.** Rising high by means of actual flight; flying high in the air. Also *fig.* and *Her.*

This sense occurs earlier in the comb. *high-soaring*.

**1683** TRYON *Way to Health* xix. (1697) 415 The soaring Wing of a Devout Meditation. **1828** [see SOARANT]. **1868** CUSSANS *Her.* (1893) 95 Soaring, or Volant: Flying. **1871** WHYTE MELVILLE *Sarchedon* I. 4 Those specks on the upper sky widened into huge soaring vultures. **1893** *Westm. Gaz.* 15 Sept. 7/2 The wing-area of soaring birds varies from one to above two square feet per pound of weight.

*transf.* **1891** *Science-Gossip* XXVII. 90 In reference to the soaring flight of birds.

**3.** Of imposing altitude; lofty, towering.

**1687** tr. *Sallust* (1692) 71 They who being arriv'd to large Command, live in the soaring height of Greatness. **1818** BYRON *Ch. Har.* IV. lxxiii, I have seen the soaring Jungfrau rear Her never-trodden snow.

**b.** *Arch.* Rising lightly or gracefully to a considerable height; characterized by loftiness and gracefulness.

**1849** RUSKIN *Seven Lamps* iii. §xxiv. 92 The soaring arches and kingly crowning of the gates of Abbeville. **1849** FREEMAN *Archit.* 6 The solemn massiveness of the Romanesque Cathedral, the soaring majesty of its Gothic successor. **1884** *Cent. Mag.* Mar. 682/1 For them no soaring nave and dimly lighted clearstory.

Hence ˈ**soaringly** *adv.*

**1817** BYRON *Manfred* I. i. 95 Their summits to heaven Shoot soaringly forth. **1844** *Blackw. Mag.* LV. 102 How gallantly the water-jets curve soaringly!

**soather**, obs. form of SOLDER *sb.*

**soave** (soˈave), *adv. Mus.* [It.] As a direction to the performer: softly, gently, with delicacy and tenderness. Also **soaveˈmente**.

**1740** J. GRASSINEAU *Mus. Dict.* 228 *Soave*, or *Soavement*, sweetly or agreeably. **1876** STAINER & BARRETT *Dict. Mus. Terms* 399/2 *Soave, Soavemente* (*It.*), agreeably, delicately, gently, softly, sweetly. **1959** *Collins Mus. Encycl.* 609/2 *Soave*,..in a smooth and gentle manner.

**Soave** (soˈave), *sb.* The name of a town in northern Italy, used *attrib.* and *absol.* to designate a dry white wine made there.

**1935** SCHOONMAKER & MARVEL *Compl. Wine Bk.* v. 130 The most widely sold and the best white wine of Veneto is the dry Soave. **1960** *Spectator* 15 July 114 *Soave* in Italian means 'suave' in English, but the wine gets its name..after the battlemented little town of Soave... It is a white wine, very dry indeed as Italian wines go, with a refreshing acidity. **1969** R. AIRTH *Snatch!* ix. 90 We had a bottle of Soave Bolla, chilled, with the lobster. **1975** *Observer* (Colour Suppl.) 3 Aug. 12/2 Soave, a light dry white from Italy, is getting into more and more shops. It comes from around Verona.

**Soay** (ˈsəʊə). Also **Soa**. The name of an island in the Western Isles, used *absol.* or *attrib.* to designate a small, brownish, short-tailed sheep, *Ovis aries*, belonging to a variety once restricted to the island.

**1906** J. G. MILLAIS *Mammals Gt. Brit.* III. 210 The history of the Soay sheep is unknown. **1912** R. LYDEKKER *Sheep & its Cousins* iv. 59 These small and half-wild Soa sheep belong to a group of breeds, or sub-breeds, which are widely distributed over Northern Europe. **1922** *Nature* 6 May 595/1 It will be gathered that the primitive sheep of Europe was of the Soay type. **1949** E. COXHEAD *Wind in West* vi. 161 A chap..on a wee island north of Skye who's experimenting with the Soay sheep. **1970** *Observer* 26 Apr. (Colour Suppl.) 35/2 The unusually leggy sheep..is a Soay. **1974** R. N. CAMPBELL in P. A. Jewell *Island Survivors* ii. 28 The Soay sheep..is the most primitive domestic form in Europe. *Ibid.* 31 The flocks..of Soays on Soay were left behind. **1979** *Vole* Feb. 45/2 The sheep that are used are Soays, small, brown, attractive animals. A few years ago this very ancient breed faced extinction. Today its future is assured.

**sob** (sɒb), *sb.*[1] Also 4–6 **sobbe**, 8–9 *Sc.* **sab**. [f. SOB *v.*[1]]

**1. a.** An act of sobbing; a convulsive catching of the breath under the influence of grief.

*c* **1374** CHAUCER *Troylus* IV. 375 Among hise sobbes and his sykes sore. **1530** PALSGR. 272/1 Sobbe that cometh in wepynge, *sanglovt*. **1563** SACKVILLE *Induct. Mirr. Mag.* lxxiii. The syghes, the sobbes, the diepe and deadly groane. **1583** W. HUNNIS (*title*), Seuen Sobs of a Sorrowfull Soule for Sinne. **1621** T. WILLIAMSON tr. *Goulart's Wise Vieillard* 46 The rich mans reuenewes are serued in with bitter sops and sobs to. **1712–4** POPE *Rape Lock* iv. 84 There she collects the force of female lungs, Sighs, sobs, and passions. **1798** COLERIDGE *Anc. Mar.* VI. xv, And I with sobs did pray. **1821** SHELLEY *Ginevra* 181 Some melted into tears without a sob. **1863** GEO. ELIOT *Romola* x, Her eyes had been swelling with tears again, and she ended with a sob.

**b.** A similar act or sound expressive of pain or exertion; an utterance resembling a sob.

*c* **1480** HENRYSON *Pract. Medicyne* 55 Sevin sobbis of ane selche. **1784** COWPER *Task* III. 328 Detested sport,..That feeds upon the sobs..Of harmless nature. **1793** WORDSW. *Evening Walk* 443 The tremulous sob of the complaining owl. **1810** SCOTT *Lady of Lake* II. xxv, Right up Ben-Lomond could he press, And not a sob his toil confess.

†**c.** An act, on the part of a horse, of recovering its wind after exertion; an opportunity allowed to it of doing this; hence *fig.*, a rest or respite. Chiefly in the phr. *to give..a sob. Obs.*

**1590** SHAKS. *Com. Err.* IV. iii. 25 The man sir, that when gentlemen are tired giues them a sob, and rests them. **1593** G. MARKHAM *Disc. Horsem.* iii. I, If your Horse..cannot runne long with a winde, but if he want staies or sobbes. **1607** —— *Cavelarice* III. i. 8 These staies and recouerings of wind in the horse, my maisters, the northerne riders call Sobs. **1624** W. BROWNE *Brown's 50 Years' Practice* F 2, Euer yeeld willingly to your hand whensoeuer you see occasion to take him up to giue him a sobe, for that horse I hold to bee perfectly and truly mouthed. *a* **1658** CLEVELAND *To his Hermaphrodite* 44 But was he dead? Did not his Soul.. break up House, like an expensive Lord, That gives his Purse a Sob, and lives at Board?

**2.** *transf.* A sound resembling that of a sob.

**1765** *Compl. Maltster & Brewer* 68 The first filling should not be until the sobs are quite down at the bung. **1820** HOGG *Sheph. Cal.* vii, Goodnight to a' younger brothers, puffings o' love vows, and sabs o' wind! **1881** *Grove's Dict. Music* III. 190 That species of musical sob produced by the repercussion of a prolonged note before the final cadence. **1897** WATTS-DUNTON *Coming of Love* (1899) 9 With sea-sobs warning of the awakened wind.

**3.** *Comb.*, as *sob-broken*, *-like* adjs.

**1816** J. WILSON *City of Plague* Poems 1825 I. 197 Sob-broken words of prayer! *a* **1850** ROSSETTI *Dante & Circle* I. (1874) 72 A voice so sob-broken, So feeble with the agony of tears. **1857** DUFFERIN *Lett. High Lat.* (ed. 3) 93 Wilson's sob-like snores shook..the canvas walls. **1895** *Cent. Mag.* Aug. 571/2 It was..occasionally making a sob-like sound.

**b.** *colloq.* (orig. *U.S.*) with reference to sentimental appeals to the emotions, as ***sob act***, ***-raiser***, ***-reporter***, ***-singer***, ***-song***, ***specialist***, *squad*, *-talk*, *tune*; **sob brother**, *U.S. colloq.*, a sentimental man; **sob sister**, a female journalist who writes sentimental reports or articles; a writer of sob stories; hence in various *transf.* uses, *esp.*: an actress who plays pathetic roles; a sentimental, impractical person, a do-gooder; a journalist who gives advice on readers' problems; **sob story**, a report or article designed to make a sentimental appeal to the emotions; *transf.* a narrative of one's misfortunes, a 'hard luck story'; **sob-stuff**, speech or writing which makes a sentimental appeal to the emotions; also *attrib.*

*a* **1953** E. O'Neill *Long Day's Journey into Night* (1956) iv. 157 He's been putting on the old sob act for you, eh? **1914** J. London *Let.* 23 Sept. (1966) 430 All I can say is that he is a weak-brother, a sob-brother. **1917** S. Graham *Priest of Ideal* xxix. 278 Our great sob-raiser who persistently pleads in the *Primer* for all causes which obviously evoke pity and rage. **1929** *McGraw-Hill Book Notes* 11 Feb., The story in that announcement.. looked too much like the efforts of a newspaper sob-reporter. **1955** *Star* (Johannesburg) 10 Oct. 8/2 Should a squad of police be seconded.. to guard the American 'sob singer' Johnnie Ray? **1912** *Sat. Even. Post* (N.Y.) 7 Dec. 9/3 Of the Daily Blatt's seven sob sisters six had husbands; and of the six it was more or less pure coincidence that five were supported by their wives. **1922** *Opportunities in Motion Picture Ind.* (Photoplay Research Soc.) 5 Some sob-sisters have gratified their ambition to play comedy, and have played it well. **1927** *Sat. Even. Post* (N.Y.) 24 Dec. 62/3 The sob sisters and the sob brothers.. who didn't raise their boys to be soldiers. **1936** Wodehouse *Laughing Gas* xviii. 196 It's one of the things the sob-sisters are sure to write up. **1939** *Sun* (Baltimore) 21 Feb. 9/8 Forecasting opposition to his plan by 'sob-sisters' Goodwin said 'it wouldn't do any harm to give these sob-sisters a couple of wallops too'. **1963** J. Mitford *Amer. Way Death* x. 153 Mrs. St. Johns is best known as one of the original sob sisters, a Hearst reporter in her youth. **1967** *Boston Herald* 8 May 19/5 Now that Svetlana has become America's newest millionaire glamor girl sob-sister, American interest in peeking or looking through the iron curtain is at a new all-time high. **1972** *Listener* 20 July 72/3 Sob sisters, those ladies who advise the unhappy about their problems. **1927** *New Republic* 12 Oct. 211/1 He has possibly scored some moderate hits: in 'Manhattan Mary', 'Broadway', 'The Five Step'.., a curiously constructed sob-song called 'Memories', and the title-piece. **1964** J. P. Clark *Three Plays* 114 So you turn your broad back Upon me and will continue with your sob-songs? **1931** *Kansas City* (Missouri) *Star* 3 Nov. 22/5 It is gratifying.. that the sob specialists can find practically nothing.. to be sorry about. **1912** G. M. Hyde *Newspaper Reporting* 236 The search for human interest material is a modification of the 'sob squad' work of the sensational papers, on more delicate lines. **1913** *Writer's Mag.* Nov. 174/2, I wrote the 'sob' story of 'the City that Turned Down Santa'. **1923** C. E. Montague *Fiery Particles* 177 Thomas Curtayne, the greatest of Irishmen, was to be buried in homely state... Here was a sob-story, manifestly. **1949** *Los Angeles Times* 15 June ii. 4/4 How anyone could heed such a sob story is beyond me. **1979** N. Hynd *False Flags* xxi. 188 'Sometimes a man tries to do too much'.. 'I'm familiar with the old sob story.' **1982** A. Mather *Impetuous Masquerade* xi. 170 And give him some sob-story? **1918** H. C. Witwer in *Collier's* 11 May 15/2 Well, Joe, we gotta lot of new songs over here now, besides 'Where Do We Go From Here?' which same is our favourite and a lot more of the old stand-bys, which runs more to the sob stuff. **1922** C. Sidgwick *Victorian* xxvi. 193 When the girls talked sobstuff at school I always told them I meant to marry a millionaire. **1929** D. H. Lawrence *Pansies* 128 A sickly people will slay us If we touch the sob-stuff crown of such martyrs. **1937** A. Christie *Murder in Mews* ix. 223 Of course I'm sorry. I don't indulge in sob-stuff. But I shall miss him. **1978** N. Marsh *Grave Mistake* iii. 90 He puts on a bit of an act like a guide doing his sob-stuff over Mary Queen of Scots in Edinburgh Castle. **1946** Koestler *Thieves in Night* 219 'That's so much sob-talk,' said Matthews. **1926** E. O'Neill *Great God Brown* ii. i. 46 I love those rotten old sob tunes.

**sob** (sɒb), *sb.*[2] *slang.* [prob. altered form of sov.] A pound.

**1970** G. F. Newman *Sir, You Bastard* iii. 113 Two hundred sobs was a small piece of fifty grand. **1973** 'K. Royce' *Spider Underground* v. 79 Norman could have back his fifty sobs; when I failed I didn't want compensation.

**sob** (sɒb), *v.*[1] Forms: 2 **sobben** (5 **sobbyn**), 4–6 **sobbe** (4 **zobbe**), 5–7 *Sc.* **sobe**, 6– **sob** (7 **sobb**); 8–9 *Sc.* **sab**. [app. of imitative origin: cf. WFris. *sobje*, Du. dial. *sabben* to suck.]

**1. a.** *intr.* To catch the breath in a convulsive manner as the result of violent emotion, esp. grief; to weep in this fashion.

*a* **1200** *Vices & Virtues* 57 Ðe gastliche mann.. lihtliche wepð oðer sobbeð, oðerhwile mid bitere teares, oðerhwile mid wel swete teares. **1340** [see sobbing *vbl. sb.*]. **1377** Langl. *P. Pl.* B. xiv. 326 He.. Swowed and sobbed and syked ful ofte. **1390** Gower *Conf.* II. 319 Sche fond non amendement To syghen or to sobbe more. **1420–22** Lydg. *Thebes* iii. 3380 He can not but sighe, sobbe, and wepe. **1470–85** Malory *Arthur* xviii. ii. 726 She sobbed and wepte a grete whyle. **1530** Palsgr. 724/1 The poore boye sobbed, as his herte shulde brust. **1588** Shaks. *Tit. A.* iii. i. 137 See how my wretched sister sobs and weeps. **1599** —— *Much Ado* ii. iii. 153 Then downe vpon her knees she falls, weepes, sobs, beates her heart. **1611** Cotgr., *Sanglotter*,.. to sob often. **1648** Hexham ii, *Snoffen*,.. to Sigh, or to Sob. **1727** Gay *Begg. Opera* i. xiii, *Polly.* The Boy thus, when his Sparrow's flown,.. Whines, whimpers, sobs and cries. **1786** Burns *Tam Samson* ii, Kilmarnock lang may grunt an' grane, An' sigh an' sab [*v.r.* sob], an' greet her lane. **1820** W. Irving *Sketch Bk.* I. 225 He sank on his knees.. and sobbed like a child. **1852** Thackeray *Esmond* i. ix, Both waved a farewell to him, and little Frank sobbed to leave him. **1891** E. Peacock *N. Brendon* II. 84 Narcissa sobbed with joy and love.

*fig.* **1821** Shelley *Adonais* xiv. 9 The wild Winds flew round, sobbing in their dismay.

**b.** To make a sound resembling sobbing.

**1676** Mace *Musick's Mon.* 170 Cause Them to Sobb, by Slacking your Stopping Hand, so soon as They are Struck. **1721** Kelly *Scot. Prov.* 76 Saugh will sob [in burning] if it was sommer sawn. **1785** Burns *Halloween* x, In loving bleeze they sweetly join, Till white in ase they're sobbin. **1847** T. Brown *Modern Farriery* 410 If he dances about.., sobbing, and drawing his breath quickly, this will be found an indication of his being a whistler, or piper. **1852** *Zoologist* X. 3427 'Sobbing' up and down, as we say of sperm whales. **1879** Farrar *St. Paul* (1883) 49 The thunder.. sobbing far away among the distant hills. **1893** *Tablet* 27 May 819 The great Soul Bell of St. Swithun's was sobbing in the winter wind for the death of the bishop.

**2. a.** To break or burst with sobbing.

**1614** Earl Stirling *Domesday* i. Poems (1637) 100 Heaven (clad with darknesse) mourn'd, th' earth sob'd asunder.

**b.** *refl.* To bring (oneself) *into* a certain state, or *to sleep*, with sobbing.

**1658** *Verney Mem.* (1907) II. 138 If you yourselfe were of such a humour that you should.. sigh and sobb and pout yourselfe into a sicknesse.

**1825** Scott *Betrothed* Concl., Eveline wept,.. she prayed —and, finally, sobbed herself to sleep, like an infant. **1851** Mrs. Browning *Casa Guidi Wind.* ii. 398 On starving homes! where many a lip Has sobbed itself asleep. **1877** Mrs. Forrester *Mignon* I. 191 The child could sob herself to sleep on her father's breast.

**3.** *trans.* **a.** To send *out*, bring *up*, etc., by sobbing or with sobs.

**1718** Pope *Iliad* xvi. 419 He sobs his soul out in a gush of blood. **1748** Richardson *Clarissa* (1811) V. 209 He sob'd up his grief. **1795** Southey *Joan of Arc* v. 162 Then did I.. almost sob my very soul away. **1867** Augusta Wilson *Vashti* xiii, Here.. you will live while there is breath in my body,—unless you wish to make me sob it out and die the sooner.

**b.** To utter with sobs. Usually with *out*.

**1782** Miss Burney *Cecilia* v. x, It was not without the utmost difficulty that she could sob out the cause of this fresh sorrow. **1861** C. M. Yonge *Young Step-mother* iv. 42 'Things didn't use to be stupid when Ned was there!' sobbed Gilbert. **1862** Miss Braddon *Lady Audley* xxxv, 'May God soften this blow for you,' sobbed the young man. **1879** Froude *Cæsar* xxii. 391 Sobbing out their entreaties on their knees.

Hence **sobbed** *ppl. a.*; **'sobber**, one who sobs.

**1894** A. Morrison *Mean Streets* 267 His bright, strenuous eyes were on the sobbers. **1895** W. Platt *Women* 98 Her sobbed thanks washed it as they fell upon it.

**sob**, *v.*[2] Now *dial.* and *U.S.* [Of obscure origin.] *trans.* To soak, saturate, sop. (Usually in pa. pple.)

**1625** Markham *Inrich. Weald Kent* 7 A purer flowre then that which is sobbed in wet. **1658** Evelyn *Fr. Gard.* (1675) 267 When the tree being sobb'd and wet, swells the wood, and loosens the fruit. **1679** —— *Sylva* (ed. 3) 178 As the Rain sobs it too much. **1692** *Rector's Bk. Clayworth* (1910) 98 The meadows were so sobb'd, that it cost 15s to make the way.. passable. **1725** *Family Dict.* s.v. *Sallet*, Let them be rather discreetly sprinkled, than over-much sobb'd with Spring-Water. **1854** Miss Baker *Northampt. Gloss.*, *Sob*, to soak, to sop. *a* **1859** in Bartlett *Dict. Amer.* (ed. 2) 425 The high lands are sobbed and boggy. **1887** *Kentish Gloss.* 154 The cloth.. is all sobbed with the wet.

Hence **sobbed** *ppl. a.*; **'sobbing** *vbl. sb.* and *ppl. a.*

**1664** Evelyn *Sylva* 69 Moss is to be rubb'd.. off.. with a piece of Hair-cloth after a sobbing Rain. **1670** *Ibid.* (ed. 2) 164 For which the best cure is, the plentiful sobbing it in water. **1690** Pepys *Mem. Royal Navy* 72 Rendred black by its long sobbing in water. **1693** Evelyn *De la Quint. Compl. Gard.* 31 Lest the Sob'd Leaves, shut up wet, should soon become foul and squalid.

†**sob**, *v.*[3] *dial. Obs.* [Of obscure origin.] *trans.* To frighten, scare.

In Milton *Ref. Engl.* i. 20 the correct reading is *fob*.

**1671** Skinner *Etymol. Ling. Angl.* s.v., To Sob one, (i.e.) *dialecto Linc. Perterrefacere, Confundere.*

‖**soba** ('sɒba). [Jap.] A type of noodle that is made from buckwheat and is a popular Japanese food. Also *attrib.*

**1896** *Far East* 20 Dec. 33/1 A strange custom of eating *Soba* (a kind of vermicelli made of buckwheat) on the last day of December prevails among a large class of people. **1928** K. Yamato *Shoji* vi. 90 We were presented with bowls of vermicelli, or *soba*. **1936** K. Tezuka *Jap. Food* 25 Sometimes *udon*.. or *soba* (buckwheat noodles) are used in place of boiled rice. **1965** W. Swaan *Jap. Lantern* i. 6 Bowls of steaming *soba*, a type of Chinese noodle dearly beloved by the Japanese. **1971** *Ashmolean Mus. Rep. of Visitors 1970* 54 Soba cup, blue and white decoration of bamboos, probably Arita ware.

Hence **sobaya** (so'baja), in Japan, a shop or restaurant which serves *soba*.

**1958** *Japan* (Unesco) (1964) 727/1 The term *sobaya* is used in eastern Japan for vendors and shops that sell *udon* and *soba*. **1960** B. Leach *Potter in Japan* vi. 132 We made our way to a Sobaya (buckwheat macaroni restaurant) and ate 'Zaru Soba'.

**sobbing** ('sɒbɪŋ), *vbl. sb.* [f. sob *v.*[1] + -ing[1].] The action of giving vent to sobs; the sound produced by this. Also freq. in *pl.*

*sing. c* **1300** *Havelok* 234 Þer was sobbing, siking, and sor. **1340** *Ayenb.* 211 Saint gregorie zaiþ þet zoþliche bidde god is biter zobbinge of uorþenchinge. *c* **1400** *Destr. Troy* 3615 Þerfore sobbyng & sorow ses at þis tyme. *c* **1475** Henryson *Orpheus & Eurydice* (B) 151 Thar was na solace mycht his sobbing cess. **1526** Skelton *Magnyf.* 1877, I pray the,.. let be thy sobbynge. **1582** Stanyhurst *Æneis* ii. (Arb.) 68 In vayne with sobbing was oft that od eccho repeated. **1603** Knolles *Hist. Turks* (1638) 46 Andronicus.. comming vnto his presence.. with sobbing and teares. **1697** Dryden *Virg. Georg.* iii. 755 He deeply groans With patient Sobbing. **1774** Goldsm. *Nat. Hist.* (1824) I. 211 Sobbing is the sigh still more invigorated. **1835** T. Mitchell *Aristoph. Acharn.* 629 *note*, The act of sobbing follows that of weeping and tearing the hair. **1876** M. Foster *Physiol.* ii. ii. (1879) 356 In sobbing a series of.. convulsive inspirations follow each other slowly, the glottis being closed earlier than in the case of hiccough.

*transf.* **1607** Topsell *Four-f. Beasts* (1658) 339 The sobbing in the stomach, called the 'hicket'.

*pl. c* **1440** *Jacob's Well* (1897) 12 He hadde swyche sorwe, syȝhynges, & sobbynges in þe throte. **1630** Drumm. of Hawth. *Flowers of Sion* 26 The hoarse Sobbings of the widow'd Doue. **1711** Addison *Spect.* No. 164 ¶5 His Voice, which was broke with Sighs and Sobbings. **1760–72** H. Brooke *Fool of Qual.* (1809) II. 102, I heard the bitter sobbings of the servants. **1836** E. Howard *R. Reefer* x, I.. felt all happiness amidst my sobbings.

**sobbing** ('sɒbɪŋ), *ppl. a.* [f. sob *v.*[1] + -ing[2].]

**1.** Uttering, giving vent to, sobs. Also, of the voice: Broken by sobs.

*a* **1200** *Vices & Virtues* 85 Þohtes of soðe bereusinge, ðe makieð ðe herte sari and sobbiende. **1451** Capgrave *Life St. Aug.* 22 With ful sobbyng voys uttirryng all þese wordes. *a* **1586** Sidney *Ps.* vi. vii, God hath heard the weeping sobbing voice Of my complayning. **1600** Shaks. *A. Y. L.* ii. i. 66 Weeping and commenting Vpon the sobbing Deere. **1820** Shelley *Prometh. Unb.* i. 455 Some struck and sobbing fawn. **1865** Dickens *Mut. Fr.* iii. i, With a sobbing gaslight in the counting-house window. **1895** *Westm. Gaz.* 14 May 2/2 There were sobbing sides amongst the best when we reached the foot of the Pass.

**2.** Of the nature of a sob or sobs.

**1871** *Standard* 23 Jan., She gave a sobbing sigh, and fell.. insensible. **1894** A. Robertson *Nuggets* 209 A low sobbing sound caught my ear.

**sobbingly** ('sɒbɪŋlɪ), *adv.* [f. prec. + -ly[2].] In a sobbing manner; with sobs.

**1565** Cooper *Thesaurus* s.v. *Interruptus*, To speake sobbingly. **1570** J. Phillip in Farr *Sel. Poet. Eliz.* II. 527 They.. sobbingly did shewe by sighes Their straunge tormenting paynes. **1611** Speed *Hist. Grt. Brit.* ix. xxii. (1632) 1123 [He] sobbingly desired them to be content. **1831** *Blackw. Mag.* XXX. 717 He answered, sobbingly, 'My boy has only done his duty'. **1884** J. Parker *Apost. Life* III. 21 His heart arose to tell what it was then able only sobbingly to say.

**sobby** ('sɒbɪ), *a.* Now *dial.* and *U.S.* [f. sob *v.*[2]] Soaked; saturated with moisture; soppy.

**1611** Cotgr. s.v. *Evieux*, Sobbie earth, soyle full of springs. **1615** Crooke *Body of Man* 66 The sobby and waterish places of the body. **1720** Welton *Suffer. Son of God* II. xv. 398 Lying upon the cold and Sobby Ground. **1847** in *N. Amer. Rev.* Jan. 191 Sent in their wet and sobby condition to New York. **1854** Miss Baker *Northampt. Gloss.* s.v. *Sob*, The land is very sobby. **1887** *Scribner's Mag.* I. 416/2 The sobby earth of the graveyard.

**so being**, *conj.* Chiefly *Sc.* Also 6 **sa beand**, 9 **saebein**; 8 **saebeins**, 8–9 **-biens**, 9 **-bins**. [Elliptic for *it so being that*: see so *adv.* 3 d.]

**1.** = sobeit 1.

**1559** *Caldwell Papers* (Maitl. Cl.) I. 75 For ony occasione bygane or for to come, sa beand yᵉ samyn promoif nocht of hir self. **1637** Rutherford *Lett.* (1862) I. 226 We wᵈ all buy Christ, so being we might make price ourselves. **1870** J. K. Hunter *Life Studies Char.* 231 He would make her a lady, so-being she would join the teetotal society.

**2.** Seeing that; since.

**1680** H. More *Apocal. Apoc.* 263 As the Dragon persecuted the Womans Seed,.. so being he could not hinder her going into the Wilderness. **1725** Ramsay *Gentle Sheph.* i. i, Wha can help Misluck, Saebeins she be sic a thrawin-gabet Chuck? Yonder's a Craig. **1805** M'Indoe *Million of Potatoes* iv, But saebins this is auld term-day, The rent nae doubt ye'll gar us pay.

**sobeit** (səʊ'biːɪt), *conj.* and *sb.* [Originally three words *so be it* (and still sometimes so written): see so *adv.* 3 d, and cf. albeit, howbeit.]

**1.** *conj.* Provided that; if; if only.

**1583** Golding *Calvin on Deut.* cli. 38 b, Yet doeth hee not lay them to our Charge, sobeit that wee mislike of them. **1647** N. Bacon *Disc. Govt. Eng.* i. lix. (1739) 109 They might have anything, sobeit they would suffer him to enjoy his Crown. **1839** Longf. *Hyperion* ii. ix, The heart of his friend cared little whither he went, so be it he were not too much alone.

**2.** *sb.* The exclamation 'So be it' (= let it be so).

**1609** *Ev. Woman in Hum.* i. i. in Bullen *O. Pl.* IV, Thou answerest me an houre after.. like to a Sexton with a Sobeit or Amen.

**sober** ('səʊbə(r)), *a.* Forms: 4–6 **sobre**, **sobur** (6 *Sc.* **sobor**), 5 *Sc.* **sobyre**, **-ire**, 5–6 *Sc.* **sobyr**, **-ir**, 4– **sober**. [a. OF. *sobre* (so mod.F., = It., Sp., Pg. *sobrio*), ad. L. *sōbrius*, which expresses the opposite of *ēbrius* drunk: the ulterior etym. is doubtful. The French word is also the source of MDu. and Du., MLG. and LG. *sober*.]

Various senses of the word tend to pass into or involve each other, and it is frequently difficult to decide which of these was principally intended by the writer.

**I. 1. a.** Moderate, temperate, avoiding excess, in respect of the use of food and drink; not given to the indulgence of appetite.

1338 R. BRUNNE *Chron.* (1810) 311 Of Arthure men say.. he was..sobre & honest. 1340 *Ayenb.* 221 Sobre ine mete and ine drinke. 1390 GOWER *Conf.* I. 11 Thurgh hem that thanne weren goode And sobre and chaste. *c* 1440 *Gesta Rom.* II. xxii. (Add. MS.), That we be sobre in mete and drynk, that we mowe come to everlastyng mede. 1530 PALSGR. 324/2 Sobre of meate and drinke, *sobre.* 1606 CHAPMAN *Gentl. Usher* iii, Shees as discreete a dame As any in these countries, and as sober, But for this onely humour of the cup. 1677 HORNECK *Gt. Law Consid.* v. (1704) 246 How the sober nation many times conquers the more debauched and vicious.

**b.** Of diet, etc.: Moderate, temperate; characterized by the absence of excess or indulgence.

1382 WYCLIF *Ecclus.* xxxi. 37 Helthe is of soule and of body, sobre drink. 1538 STARKEY *England* II. ii. 179 You schal see veray few of sobur and temperat dyat, but they haue helthy and welthy bodys. 1551 T. WILSON *Logike* (1580) 35 Sober diet is good. 1629 HINDE *J. Bruen* (1641) x. 33 And many other such naturall helpes may we use for our sober refreshing and delight. 1743 FRANCIS tr. *Hor., Odes* I. xx. 4 The Vintage of the Sabine Grape, But yet in sober Cups, shall crown the Feast. 1797–1805 S. & HT. LEE *Canterb. T.* I. 365 The sober cheer of which you have already partaken.

**c.** Similarly of conduct, inclination, etc.

1509 FISHER *Funeral Serm. C'tess Richmond* Wks. (1876) 293 Her sobre temperaunce in metes & drynkes. 1590 SPENSER *F.Q.* II. ix. 1 Of all Gods workes.. There is no one more faire and excellent Then is mans body.. Whiles it is kept in sober gouernment. 1746 FRANCIS tr. *Hor., Sat.* II. iii. 8 When Saturn's jovial Feast Seem'd too luxuriant to your sober Taste, Hither you fled.

**2. a.** Not addicted to the use of strong drink; habitually temperate in, or abstaining from, the use of alcoholic liquor; abstemious.

1382 WYCLIF *Titus* ii. 2 That olde men be sobre, chast. *c* 1386 CHAUCER *Merch. T.* 1533 Men moste enquere.. Wher she be wys, or sobre, or dronkelewe. 1474 CAXTON *Chesse* II. i. (1883) 21 That the dronken men shold be punysshyd And the sobre men preysed. 1706 E. WARD *Wooden World Diss.* (1708) 39 He reckons a sober Chaplain in the Navy, to be a down-right Nonconformist. 1729 LAW *Serious Call* ii. (1732) 27 When she feels this intention she will find it as possible to act up to it, as to be strictly sober and chaste. 1815 ELPHINSTONE *Acc. Caubul* (1842) II. 39 They are a sober people, and have none of the vices of the Eusofzyes. 1890 BESANT *Demoniac* v. 50 A sober man himself, even a total abstainer.

*transf.* 1590 SIR J. SMYTH *Disc. Conc. Weapons* Ded. 13 Archerie, which is the soberest exercise of all others to auoide drunkennes and other euills.

**b.** Of things: Not intoxicating.

*a* 1795 COWPER *Moralizer Corrected* 10 The sober cordial of sweet air.

**3. a.** Free from the influence of intoxicating liquor; not intoxicated; not drunk. Also *fig.*

1387 TREVISA *Higden* (Rolls) III. 443, I appele..from Alisaundre þe dronke to Alisaundre þe sobre. 1387–8 T. USK *Test. Love* III. viii. (Skeat) l. 48 Right as whan any person taketh willing to be sobre, and throweth that away, willing to be dronke. 1560 DAUS tr. *Sleidane's Comm.* 339 Thou sobre [L. *sobrius*] hast medled not only with thy Nece, but also with thy Sister and daughter. 1596 SHAKS. *Merch. V.* I. ii. 93 Very vildely in the morning when hee is sober, and most vildely in the afternoone when hee is drunke. *a* 1637 B. JONSON *Goodwife's Ale* in *Athenæum* (1904) 1 Oct., You easily may guesse I am not quite Growne sober yett by these poore lines I wright. 1691 HARTCLIFFE *Virtues* 73 They thought, their Counsels might want Vigour, when they were sober, as well as Caution, when they had drank. 1782 MISS BURNEY *Cecilia* VIII. i, 'What little dog, Sir?' cried Delville, who now began to conclude he was not sober. 1828 SCOTT *F.M. Perth* xv, He is as sober as sleep can make him, after a deep drink. 1885 *Christ. World* 15 Jan. 38/5 The Heathen Chinee..is generally civil and always sober.

*fig.* 1390 GOWER *Conf.* III. 16 Than schalt thou have a lusti drauhte And waxe of lovedrunke sobre.

*transf.* 1548 UDALL, etc. *Erasm. Par. Acts* ii. 10 This was the sobre fulnesse of swete wine. 1831 SCOTT *Cast. Dang.* v, The sober hours of the morning.

†**b.** Fasting. *Obs.*⁻¹

1535 COVERDALE *Dan.* vi. 18 The kynge wente in to his palace, and kepte him sober all night, so that there was no table spred before him.

**II. 4. a.** Of demeanour, speech, etc.: Grave, serious, solemn; indicating or implying a serious mind or purpose.

13.. *E.E. Allit. P.* A. 532 He..sayde to hem with sobre soun, 'Wy stonde ȝe ydel þise dayez longe?' 1390 GOWER *Conf.* III. 64 Sche him axeth..Fro whenne he cam, and what he wolde, And he with sobre wordes tolde. *c* 1400 *Pilgr. Sowle* v. x. (Caxton) 1483) 101 Pacyence come pryckyng with a sobre chere and hitte Ire in the helme. *c* 1450 in Aungier *Syon* (1840) 320 Ther songe schal be sadde, sober, ande symple withe out brekyng of notes, and gay relesynge. 1514 BARCLAY *Cyt. & Uplondyshman* (Percy Soc.) 16 Tell forthe thy sentence, And I shall here the with sobre pacyence. *a* 1548 HALL *Chron., Edw. IV*, 40 To do his message..bothe with a bolde countenaunce, and a sober demeanure. 1600 SHAKS. *A.Y.L.* v. ii. 76 *Orl.* Speak'st thou in sober meanings? *Ros.* By my life I do. 1633 P. FLETCHER *Purple Isl.* XI. ix, The Islands King with sober countenance Aggrates the Knights, who thus his right defended. 1697 DRYDEN *Æneid* I. 219 He sooths with sober words their angry mood.

**b.** In the phrases ***in sober earnest*** or †***sadness.***

Skelton *Magnyf.* 682 uses *Sober Sadnesse* as a name.

1593 [see SADNESS 2 b]. 1615 BEDWELL *Moham. Impost.* III. §108, I say..in sober sadnes, that thou and all such..ought to obserue it well. 1667 POOLE *Dial. between Protest. & Papist* (1735) 181 In sober Sadness, it is enough to make any serious Christian abhor your Church. 1819 J. KEATS *Let.* 21 Sept. (1931) II. 426 Isabella is what I should call..'A weak-sided Poem' with an amusing sober-sadness about it. 1836 PUSEY in Liddon *Life* (1893) I. xviii. 425 In sober earnest, I wish that we could have given you more time to think about it. 1865 TYLOR *Early Hist. Man.* i. 8, I have been startled by hearing it..urged in sober earnest very far outside the range of savage life.

**5. a.** Quiet or sedate in demeanour; of grave, dignified, or discreet deportment; serious or staid in character or conduct.

1362 LANGL. *P. Pl.* A. XI. 121 Þenne schaltou seo Sobre And Symple-of-speche. *c* 1393 CHAUCER *Gentilesse* 9 Truwe of his worde, sobur, pitous, and fre. *c* 1400 *Destr. Troy* 3791 Ulexes..was..Sad of his semblaundes, sober of chere. *c* 1470 HENRY *Wallace* III. 308 Perseys war trew,..Sobyr in pes, and cruell in battaill. 1509 HAWES *Past. Pleas.* XVI. (Percy Soc.) 75 Be ye pacyent and sobre in mode. 1553 T. WILSON *Rhet.* 66 A yonge chylde as sober as a man of fiftye yeres. 1596 SHAKS. *Merch. V.* III. ii. 78 What damned error, but some sober brow Will blesse it? 1632 MILTON *Penseroso* 32 Com pensive Nun, devout and pure, Sober, stedfast, and demure. 1693 tr. *Blancard's Phys. Dict.* (ed. 2), *Medicus*, a Physician, a Man highly skilful in the art of Physick, modest, sober and courteous. 1722 DE FOE *Relig. Courtsh.* I. ii. (1840) 43, I would have been the soberest, gravest, young fellow, that ever you saw in your life. 1783 CRABBE *Village* II. 13 Some of the sermon talk, a sober crowd. 1833 HT. MARTINEAU *Brooke Farm* ix. 109 So sober in her manner, that no one set about guessing whom she would marry. 1849 MACAULAY *Hist. Eng.* vii. II. 253 Sober people predicted that a girl of so little..delicacy would not easily find a husband.

**b.** Of bearing, movement, etc.: Showing no trace of haste, impatience, or the like.

*c* 1350 *Will. Palerne* 4988 Semblant made he sobur so as it him paide, but..in hert it liked him wel ille. *c* 1375 *Sc. Leg. Saints* xix. (*Christopher*) 361 Cristofore þan of sobyre wil rase, & sad þame sone till: 'frendis, tell me quhat ȝe seke!' 1597 SHAKS. *2 Hen. IV*, IV. iii. 86 Our Newes shall goe before vs,..And wee with sober speede will follow you. 1697 DRYDEN *Virg. Georg.* II. 380 Legions..move to meet their Foes with sober Pace. 1814 SCOTT *Lord of Isles* VI. xvi, Pacing back his sober way, Slowly he gain'd his own array.

**6. a.** Of natural forces (†animals), etc.: Quiet, gentle, peaceful.

1398 TREVISA *Barth. De P.R.* XVIII. xcix. (Bodl. MS.), Whan he is tyed to a fige tree he leueþ al his fersenes & is sodenlich sobre. *c* 1400 *Destr. Troy* 2009 The se wex sober ..., Stormes were stille. *c* 1440 *Pallad. on Husb.* I. 1031 A sobur brook amydde or ellis a welle. *c* 1500 *Lancelot* 2477 The soft dew one fra the hewyne doune valis..And throw the sobir and the mwst hwmouris Vp nurisit ar the erbis. 1596 DALRYMPLE tr. *Leslie's Hist. Scot.* II. 242 Thay sayled with a sober and safte wind. *a* 1605 MONTGOMERIE *Cherrie & Slae* 43 (Wreittoun), The aire was sober, soft and sweet. 1662 CHANDLER *Van Helmont's Oriat.* 117 Sober rains are great with young of dew. *a* 1700 B. E. *Dict. Cant. Crew*, *Scotch mist*, a Sober, soaking Rain. 1821 CLARE *Vill. Minstr.* I. 14 As sober evening sweetly siles along.

**b.** Of actions: Free from harshness or violence.

1455 in *Charters*, etc. *Edinb.* (1871) 81 He salbe arrestit in sobir maner as said is. 1456 SIR G. HAYE *Law Arms* (S.T.S.) 185 He salbe content of thair sobir and gracious governaunce. *a* 1548 HALL *Chron., Hen. VIII*, 19 Thei by sobre meanes and gentle exhortation brought all the souldiers to the campe.

**7. a.** Of living, etc.: Characterized by temperance, moderation, or seriousness.

1552 *Bk. Com. Prayer, Gen. Conf.*, A godly, righteous, and sobre lyfe. 1565–6 *Reg. Privy Council Scot.* I. 418 Sanctandrois, quhair he wes in sobir and quiet maner, belevand to haif levit at Goddis peace. *a* 1629 HINDE *J. Bruen* iii. 10 Sober and single dancing of men apart. 1726 DE FOE *Hist. Devil* I. ix. (1840) 102 He led a very religious and sober life. 1781 COWPER *Hope* 129 Men..Live to no sober purpose, and contend That their Creator had no serious end. 1810 CRABBE *Borough* xi. 186 A pious friend, who with the ancient dame At sober cribbage takes an evening game. 1825 SCOTT *Talism.* vii, The dog..looked as if he were ashamed that anything should have moved him to depart so far out of his sober self-control.

**b.** Of a book: Serious, moral.

1844 MRS. HOUSTON *Yacht Voy. Texas* I. 48 Reading their Prayer Books, or some sober book from the ship's library.

**8. a.** Of a temperate or moderate disposition; not readily excited or carried away; of a calm, dispassionate judgement.

1564 *Brief Exam.* 7* The sagest and sobrest in this common wealth..conceyue a better opinion of them. 1662 STILLINGFL. *Orig. Sacræ* III. iv. §13 It is the constant acknowledgement of all sober inquirers into the original of the Greeks. 1685 WOOD *Life* 12 Aug., The phanatiques (nay, some sober men) thinke that this army..is to bring in popery. 1718 *Free-thinker* No. 77, His very Attempts..are sufficient to make sober Men dread the fatal Consequences. 1776 ADAM SMITH *W.N.* II. iv. (1869) I. 360 Sober people.. would not venture into the competition. 1834 H. MILLER *Scenes & Leg.* xi. (1857) 157 The many soberer dreamers who were led to interpret amiss a surer word of prophecy. 1860 FARRAR *Orig. Lang.* ii. 38 Some of the most profound and sober intellects in Europe. *a* 1862 BUCKLE *Civiliz.* (1873) III. v. 392 The sober and patient spirit of the English intellect.

**b.** Not desirous of great things or high estate; humble, unambitious.

1659 HAMMOND *On Ps.* xxxix. 7. 210 Fit to be the matter of a sober mans ambition. 1750 GRAY *Elegy* 74 Far from the madding crowd's ignoble strife, Their sober wishes never learn'd to stray. 1790 BURNS *Ballad Dumfries Election* 132 The Robin in the hedge descends, And sober chirps securely.

**9. a.** Of colour, dress, etc.: Subdued in tone; not glaring, gay, or showy; neutral-tinted.

1596 SHAKS. *Tam. Shr.* I. ii. 132 Now shal my friend.. offer me disguis'd in sober robes..as a schoole-master. 1603 KNOLLES *Hist. Turks* (1621) 832 Hungarians..attired in long sober garments of very fine purple cloth. 1667 MILTON *P.L.* IV. 599 Twilight gray Had in her sober Liverie all things clad. 1781 COWPER *Charity* 262 Ev'ning in her sober vest Drew the grey curtain of the fading west. 1794 MRS. RADCLIFFE *Myst. Udolpho* i, Till the shadows of twilight melted its various features into one tint of sober gray. 1856 STANLEY *Sinai & Pal.* ii. 139 This contrast between the brilliant colours of the flowers and the sober hue of the rest of the landscape. 1885 SWAINSON *Prov. Names Birds* 195 The sober tints of its feathers in winter.

*transf.* 1814 *Sporting Mag.* XLIII. 258 His palet is sober and clean, his pencil animated.

**b.** Unexciting or uneventful; dull.

1838 PRESCOTT *Ferd. & Isab.* I. Pref. p. xiv, The many sober hours I have passed in wading through black-letter tomes. 1860 HAWTHORNE *Marble Faun* (1879) II. xii. 127 That life of sober week days.

**10. a.** Free from extravagance or excess.

1607 SHAKS. *Timon* III. v. 21 With such sober and vnnoted passion He did behooue his anger ere 'twas spent. 1794 BURKE *Duration of Parliaments* Wks. II. 484 So was Rome destroyed by the disorders of continual elections, though those of Rome were sober disorders. 1852 TENNYSON *Ode Wellington* 164 That sober freedom out of which there springs Our loyal passion for our temperate kings. 1856 MACAULAY *Goldsm., Misc. Writ.* (1882) 303/2 The mirth of the 'Goodnatured Man' was sober when compared with the rich drollery of 'She Stoops to Conquer'.

**b.** Moderate, sensible; free from exaggeration; not fanciful or imaginative.

1619 GORGES tr. *Bacon's De Sap. Vet.* 141 We must therefore with a sober and humble iudgement distinguish betweene humanitie and diuinitie. 1674 BREVINT *Saul at Endor* 115 They who will speak at a soberer rate, compare the Virgin to the Moon. 1771 FLETCHER *Checks* Wks. 1795 II. 260 An expression which may be used in a sober, gospel sense of the words. 1781 COWPER *Conversat.* 65 Ev'n when sober truth prevails throughout, They swear it, till affirmance breeds a doubt. 1825 HORNE *Introd. Script.* (ed. 5) II. App. VI. 788 The notes..give a *sober* but practical and evangelical exposition of the allegory. 1889 JESSOPP *Coming of Friars* iv. 169 How much or how little of sober fact there may be in those thrilling incidents..it is impossible to say.

**11.** Guided by sound reason; sane, rational:

†**a.** Of persons. *Obs.*

1638 R. BAKER tr. *Balzac's Lett.* (vol. II) 24 They have painted mee..a mad man amongst the sober. 1657 R. CARPENTER *Astrol.* Ded., In a Bedlam-house the mad People have their sober Keepers. 1690 LOCKE *Hum. Und.* II. xxvii. (1695) 186 Humane Laws not punishing the Mad Man for the Sober Man's Actions. 1786 BOSWELL *Jrnl. Tour Hebrides* (ed. 3) 213 Mad all his life, at least not sober.

**b.** Of the mind, discourse, etc.

1651 HOBBES *Leviath.* I. viii. 36 If some man in Bedlam should entertaine you with sober discourse. 1672 SIR T. BROWNE *Let. Friend* §22 [They are] content to think they dye in good understanding, and in their sober senses. 1729 BUTLER *Serm.* Wks. 1874 II. 86 He was..in a state of mind sober enough to consider death and his last end. 1842 LOVER *Handy Andy* xliv, While the people in their sober senses..were taken in, the old lunatic..could look down and see [etc.].

**III. 12. a.** Of things: Small, insignificant, slight; paltry, trifling, poor. Chiefly *Sc.* ? *Obs.*

*c* 1440 *Alph. Tales* 228 He wrote vnto hym & said at he had done hym a litle sober trispas. 1523 *State Papers, Hen. VIII* (1836) IV. 24 To breke the Chauncellour..fro the Governour, whiche Your Grace think wold bee doone with a sober thing. *a* 1578 LINDESAY (Pitscottie) *Chron. Scot.* (S.T.S.) I. 35 Sober goodis and geir with peace and concord growis ay mair and mair to great substance. 1602 CAMPION *Art Eng. Poesie* 27 He..only makes Th' earth his sober Inne, but still heau'n his home. 1629 SIR W. MURE *True Crucifixe* 2340 His greatest wealth a sober seamelesse coate. 1643 MILTON *Divorce* II. xvi, When they cannot reap the sobrest ends of being together in any tolerable sort. 1796 *Statist. Acc. Scotl.* XVII. 343 It requires the utmost exertion of his industry..to..afford a maintenance, *very sober indeed*, to his family.

†**b.** Moderate or few in number. *Obs.*

1513 MORE *Rich. III* (1883) 15 The Queenes frendes.. broughte the Kynge vppe..with a sober coumpanye. 1548 W. PATTEN *Exped. Scotl.* E vij, We..ar here now but with a sobre cumpenie. [*Margin.*] Sober, is the proper terme whearby the Scottes doo signifie smal, litle, easy, or slender. 1581 *Reg. Privy Council Scot.* III. 420 Thair being sober nowmer of personis thairon.

**13.** *Sc.* Of persons: †**a.** Of low degree; humble, mean; of little importance or dignity. *Obs.*

1533 BELLENDEN *Livy* IV. xvi. (S.T.S.) II. 107, I am bot ane sobir knicht of romane armye. 1565 *Extr. Burgh Rec. Aberd.* (1844) I. 361 Of euery mariage, xviij d. of honest or reche folkis, and xij d. of sobir folkis. *a* 1578 LINDESAY (Pitscottie) *Chron. Scot.* (S.T.S.) I. 87 The iniurieis done to ony of them or the soberest of theme.

**b.** Of little use or worth.

1808 JAMIESON s.v., *A sober servant*, a very indifferent one.

**c.** In poor health; not very well.

1808 JAMIESON s.v., *Very sober*, ailing a good deal. 1882– in *Eng. Dial. Dict.*

**IV. 14.** *Comb.*, chiefly parasynthetic, as ***sober-blooded, -clad, -coloured, -disposed, -hued, -living, -looking, -spoken***, etc.; also ***sober-like, -sad, -wise.***

1597 SHAKS. *2 Hen. IV*, IV. iii. 94 This same young *sober-blooded Boy doth not loue me. 1892 T. WRIGHT *Blue Firedrake* i, A replica of his own starched, sober-minded and *sober-clad self. 1851 BORROW *Lavengro* I. xxv. 317 They were dressed in *sober-coloured habiliments. 1892 'MARK TWAIN' *Amer. Claimant* xvi. 168 He drops into the stoodio as sober-colored as anything you ever see. 1775 S. J. PRATT *Liberal Opin.* xiv. (1783) I. 125 To the great annoyance of many *sober disposed people of the parish. 1867 AUGUSTA WILSON *Vashti* xxxiv, To-day all *sober-hued reflections were exorcised. 1592 WYRLEY *Armorie* 117 He..backe his fighters drue Full *soberlike rash perils to eschue. 1960 *Times* 4 Mar. 13/7 There is a hard-working, *sober-living, self-respecting section among them. *a* 1817 JANE AUSTEN *Northanger Abbey* (1818) I. xi. 183 The morrow brought a very *sober looking morning. 1863

HAWTHORNE *Our Old Home* 77 A *sober-paced pedestrian. **1593** SHAKS. *Lucr.* 1542 So *sober-sad, so weary, and so mild. *c* **1614** SYLVESTER *Micro-cosm.* 374 If sober-sad, Merry Greeks mee Meacok call. **1647** CROMWELL in Stainer *Sp.* (1901) 44 Every *sober-spirited man. **1934** W. S. CHURCHILL *Marlborough* II. xiv. 304 These were very unusual expressions for the *sober-spoken and matter-of-fact Marlborough. **1592** SHAKS. *Rom. & Jul.* III. ii. 11 Come ciuill night, Thou *sober suted Matron all in blacke. **1727–46** THOMSON *Summer* 746 The sober-suited songstress trills her lay. **1842** TENNYSON *You ask me Why* 6 It is the land..That sober-suited Freedom chose. **1850** W. COLLINS *Antonina* iv, The *sober-tinted trees. *a* **1591** H. SMITH *Wks.* (1866) I. 471 He..teacheth them here not to be over-wise, but *sober-wise. *a* **1618** SYLVESTER *Little Bartas* 1053 Wks. (Grosart) II. 94 Sound is the soule, which resteth (sober-wise) Content in Thee.

**sober** ('səʊbə(r)), *v.* Forms: 4–6 sobre, 4– sober (5 soberyn), 4 sobur (5 sobor), 4–5 sobir (5 sobyr). [f. SOBER *a.* Cf. late L. *sōbriāre* to make sober, OF. *sobrier* to live soberly.]

**I.** *trans.* **1. a.** To reduce to a quiet or gentle condition; to appease, pacify.

*c* **1375** *Sc. Leg. Saints* x. (*Matthew*) 443 [He] gat be-for þam þat ware wrathe, & sobryt þam. *c* **1430** LYDG. *Min. Poems* (Percy Soc.) 206 Sobre and appeese suche folk as falle in furye. *c* **1440** *Alph. Tales* 193 Sho sayd: 'Dere Son! Meng þi rightwusnes with mercie!'.. And þan hur Son was soberd & sayd [etc.]. **1483** *Cath. Angl.* 347/2 To Sobyr, *mitigare, placare.* **1535** STEWART *Cron. Scot.* II. 341 With Pecht and Saxone first he hes maid peice, All outwart weir to sober and gar ceiss.

**b.** To moderate, quieten (one's feelings), by the exercise of self-control. Also *refl.*

**1390** GOWER *Conf.* III. 332 With that he sobreth his corage And put awey his hevy chiere. *c* **1400** *Destr. Troy* 3379 Ses now of sorowe, sobur þi chere. *c* **1430** *Syr Gener.* (Roxb.) 7626 Sobre youre hert, ma dame, I you besech. **1530** PALSGR. 724/1, I sober my selfe, I asswage myn anger.

**c.** *refl.* To keep (oneself) temperate.

**1530** PALSGR. 724/2 He can sober hym selfe in his dyete the best that ever I sawe.

**2. a.** To render grave or serious.

**1726** POPE *Odyss.* XXI. 322 They..sent him sober'd home, with better wit. **1823** RUTTER *Fonthill* 40 Sobered almost into a religious feeling, by the oratory and its concomitants. **1854** THOREAU *Walden* xv. (1863) 299 Sobered into silence by the mystery. **1888** BRYCE *Amer. Commw.* III. lxxxvii. 161 Citizens who have been born to power..are sobered by their privileges.

**b.** To render less glaring or conspicuous.

**1843** RUSKIN *Arrows of Chace* (1880) I. 6 Your critic has not allowed for the effect of time on its blues. They are now, indeed, sobered and brought down.

**3.** To make sober; to free from intoxication.

**1709** POPE *Ess. Crit.* 218 Shallow draughts intoxicate the brain, And drinking largely sobers us again. **1743** FRANCIS tr. *Horace, Odes* I. xxxvii. 19 Her, with Egyptian Wine inspir'd,..Augustus sober'd into Tears. **1865** *Pall Mall G.* 23 Oct. 9 Bread and cheese and vinegar to sober A. B.

**4.** To bring *down* to a sober condition in some respect.

**1838** T. MITCHELL *Aristoph. Clouds* 99 We shall not be surprised to find this fanciful system sobered down into the following observation. **1853** KANE *Grinnell Exp.* xxxiii. (1856) 284 Her light mingles so with the twilight of the sun that the stars are quite sobered down. **1877** O. W. HOLMES *How not to settle it* 18 At times when..solemn speeches sober down a dinner.

**II.** *intr.* **5.** To become sober, in various senses. Also with *off* and *up*. Hence as *attrib. phr.*

**1820** SCOTT *Monast.* iv, That was very natural;..but ye hae sobered since that. **1879** G. MACDONALD *P. Faber* II. i. 6 The colour sobered, but the glory grew. **1884** [see SOBERING *vbl. sb.*]. **1891** TUCKLEY *Under the Queen* 244 This gives the topers time to sober off after the heavy siege of the night before. **1901** *Daily Colonist* (Victoria, B.C.) 2 Nov. 5/2 The police yesterday gathered in an Indian woman who was rolling along in the street in a drunken condition with a baby in her arms. She was released as soon as she had sobered up. **1938** E. WAUGH *Scoop* III. ii. 284 'Aunt Agnes and I very much fear that he has taken too much.'.. 'Oh, he'll sober up,' said Uncle Theodore, from deep experience. **1963** AUDEN *Dyer's Hand* 261 When he [*sc.* Cassio] sobers up, his regret is..that he has lost his reputation. **1967** *Listener* 23 Nov. 669/3 The National Federation of Licensed Victuallers announced that they're to back the search for a sober-up pill—an alcohol antidote.

**6.** To settle or quieten *down* in some respect.

**1825** SCOTT *Betrothed* Concl., The ecstasy of delight sobered down into a sort of tranquil wonder. **1844** DICKENS *Mart. Chuz.* viii, Merry is a little giddy, but she'll sober down in time. **1886** *Field* 4 Sept. 349/1 Many a horse who will sober down if struck severely once only, will get furious if the punishment is repeated.

Hence **'sobered** *ppl. a.*; **'soberer**; **'sobering** *vbl. sb.* and *ppl. a.*; also with *down.*

**1794** SOUTHEY *Botany Bay Ecl., Frederic* 60 The hollow howl..Comes with no terror to the *sober'd sense. **1843** RUSKIN *Mod. Paint.* I. 109 Such a sobered high light. **1883** *Harper's Mag.* July 212/2 Breathless hung the sobered throng On the magic of the song. *a* **1849** MANGAN *Poems* (1859) 80 Soother and *soberer of the spirit's fever. *a* **1510** DOUGLAS *K. Hart* 238 His wound to wesche, in *sobering of his sair. **1884** *Pall Mall G.* 1 Aug. 3/3 An enterprising American has initiated a new system of what is called ..'sobering-up'. **1816** JANE AUSTEN *Emma* II. ii. 24 The *sobering suggestions of her own good understanding. *a* **1817** —— *Persuasion* (1818) III. vii. 141 These were words which could not but dwell with her... They were of sobering tendency. **1831** *Society* I. 286 The cogitations of the Countess had not been without their sobering effect on her temper. **1855** MACAULAY *Hist. Eng.* xii. III. 146 Tidings of a very sobering nature had just reached him. **1975** B. MEYRICK *Behind Light* xiv. 183 The sobering-down item of community hymn singing.

**Soberano** (sobe'rano). [Sp., lit. 'sovereign'.] A Spanish brandy; also, a drink of this.

**1963** 'D. CORY' *Hammerhead* iv. 59 He called the barman over and ordered a Soberano. *Ibid.* vii. 109 Downing three fingers of cognac, more exactly Soberano. **1969** R. V. BESTE *Next Time I'll pay my own Fare* vii. 88 Gage opted for..a 'Soberano' which he found to be the least syrupy of the Spanish brandies. **1974** R. JEFFRIES *Mistakenly in Mallorca* xxii. 199 He..went through to the larder for a bottle of Soberano and three glasses... Back on the patio, he poured out three brandies.

**soberize** ('səʊbəraɪz), *v.* [f. SOBER *a.* + -IZE.]

**1.** *trans.* To make sober, in various senses. Also *absol.*

**1706** E. WARD *Hud. Rediv.* (1707) II. VII. 16 Nor is the Cant of Moderation Design'd to soberize the Nation. **1748** RICHARDSON *Clarissa* (1811) IV. xxxvi. 245 The instant I beheld her I was soberized into awe and reverence. **1798** ANNA SEWARD *Lett.* (1811) V. 176 The ensuing stanza, though soberized, is very good. **1819** CRABBE *Tales of Hall* vi. 387, I was thankful for the moral sight, That soberized the vast and wild delight. **1867** *Morning Star* 12 Mar., Much soberised in mind, most of them have returned to Cork.

**2.** *intr.* To become sober.

**1831** *Fraser's Mag.* III. 67 He..emptied his bottle,.. sowed his wild oats,..soberized.

Hence **'soberized, 'soberizing** *ppl. adjs.*

**1840** LADY BURY *Hist. of a Flirt* viii, A quiet soberized look. **1860** MISS F. R. HAVERGAL *Autobiogr.* in *Life* (1880) 88 A soberizing thoughtful time.

**soberly** ('səʊbəlɪ), *adv.* Also 4 sobreliche, -lyche, 5 sobirliche; 4–6 soburly (4 -li), sobirly (6 -lie), soberlie (6 -lye), etc. [f. SOBER *a.* + -LY². Cf. MDu. *soberlike* (Du. *-lijk*), MLG. *soberliken.*] In a sober manner, in various senses of the adj.

**1.** Gravely, seriously, quietly; without any sign of excitement, impatience, or other strong feeling.

(*a*) **13..** *E.E. Allit. P.* A. 256 Soberly after þenne con ho say. *c* **1386** CHAUCER *Frankl. T.* 857 This Philosophre sobrely answerde. *c* **1400** *Destr. Troy* 248 When Pelleus his proses hade..soburly said with a sad wille. *c* **1440** *Alph. Tales* 24 On þe morn..he com vnto þis Crasippus & tolde hym soberlie of his anger. **1535** STEWART *Cron. Scot.* I. 544 The man that had the hound in cuir..Than soberlie askit agane the hound. *a* **1548** HALL *Chron., Edw. IV*, 45 The kyng of England..aunswered to his wordes so soberly, so grauely, and so princely. **1632** LITHGOW *Trav.* III. 80 [He asked me] where was my money? to whom I soberly answered, I had no more then he saw.

(*b*) **1382** WYCLIF *Gen.* xxxii. 22 Whanne sobirly [L. *mature*] he was arysun. *c* **1386** CHAUCER *Shipman's T.* 255 Daun Johan sobrely This chapman took on-part, and privele Sayd him thus. *c* **1425** LYDG. *Assembly of Gods* 802 With countenaunce demure he roode full soburly. **1456** SIR G. HAYE *Law Arms* (S.T.S.) 186 Thai maid offer to passe sobirly and curtaisly. **1508** DUNBAR *Gold. Targe* 130 Ladyes to dance full sobirly assayit. **1595** *Locrine* IV. ii, My wife soberly sate rocking my little babie. **1606** SHAKS. *Ant. & Cl.* I. v. 48 So he nodded, And soberly did mount an Arme-gaunt Steede. **1707** MORTIMER *Husb.* (1721) I. 206 By being acquainted with their Keeper, and being soberly handled, you may with ease remove them from one Pasture to another. **1820** KEATS *Isabella* xx, Then the tale Shall move on soberly, as it is meet. **1884** *Manch. Exam.* 21 Nov. 5/3 To keep the debate soberly within narrow channels.

(*c*) **1589** *Pappe w. Hatchet* (1844) 35 If thou wilt deale soberlie without scoffes, thou shalt be answered grauely without iests. **1594** T. B. *La Primaud. Fr. Acad.* II. 519 This is a matter then of which wee must speake very soberly, and with great reuerence of God. **1684** B. HALE *Pref. Contempl. State Man* p. iii, I have soberly consider'd these Holy and Devout Contemplations. **1689** LOCKE *Govt.* II. ii, As he soberly judges the case to require. **1781** COWPER *Conversat.* 667 That disease, when soberly defin'd, Is the false fire of an o'erheated mind. **1832** HT. MARTINEAU *Life in Wilds* i. 7 That they would deliberate soberly. **1841** *Nonconformist* I. 2 It becomes dissenters..soberly to set about it.

**b.** In all seriousness; with full conviction.

**1579** W. WILKINSON *Confut. Fam. Love* 16, H. N. affirmeth very soberly as it seemeth that the Elders of his broode are illuminated. **1695** KENNETT *Par. Antiq.* ix. 61 Agreeable to the faith of that age, miracles were soberly reported of him.

**c.** Without extravagance or excess.

**1849** MACAULAY *Hist. Eng.* ii. I. 231 The cruelties of Mary's reign..which were neither accurately nor soberly related in the popular martyrologies. **1861** LD. BROUGHAM *Brit. Const.* IX. 119 But these rights [of public meeting] must be soberly and moderately exercised.

**2.** With moderation in respect of natural appetites; temperately.

**1340** *Ayenb.* 248 Hire uor to wyne and habbe, me ssel libbe sobreliche ine þise wordle. *c* **1400** MAUNDEV. (Roxb.) xxxii. 144 Þai liffe so temperately and so soberly in meet and drink. *c* **1430** *Pilgr. Lyf Manhode* I. xix. (1869) 14 Ye muste ete and drinke more sobirliche than other folk. **1538** STARKEY *England* I. ii. 33 Yf men wold gouerne themselfe soburly by temperat dyat, then physycyonys were not to be requyryd. **1600** NASHE *Summer's Last Will* 278 The silly beasts..will rather fall soberly to those thistles..then they will offer to breake their bounds. **1717** POPE *Iliad* IX. 290 Then each..His thirst and hunger soberly repress'd. **1882** *Med. Temp. Jrnl.* 146 They were..as soberly disposed a body of young men as one would wish to see.

**3.** In a poor, humble, or simple manner. ? *Obs.*

**1387** TREVISA *Higden* (Rolls) IV. 79 Þe childe..seide þat he couþe lyve soberliche, and þat lasse cost wolde doo his nede. **1533** BELLENDEN *Livy* Prol. (S.T.S.) I. 2, I will assay How sobirly begouth þe romane blude. ? *a* **1550** *Freiris Berwik* 226 in *Dunbar's Poems* (1893) 293 [That we] Sobirly our selffis dois sustene.

†**4.** Quietly, gently, in respect of motion.

**1477** NORTON *Ordin. Alch.* v. in Ashm. (1652) 85 Whereby Water maie soberly flowe, For violent Fluxes be perilous as nowe. **1660** F. BROOKE tr. *Le Blanc's Trav.* 251 This branch of Tacassin..towards Amina..runs soberly enough.

**5.** Not brightly or garishly.

**1820** W. IRVING *Sketch Bk.* I. 263 It was soberly lighted by a row of Gothic windows.

**sober-minded,** *a.* [SOBER *a.* 14.]

**1.** Of a sober mind; temperate; self-controlled; rational; sensible. Also *absol.*

**1534** TINDALE *Titus* ii. 4 To make the younge wemen sobremynded. *Ibid.* 6 Yonge men lykwyse exhorte that they be sobre mynded. **1642** MILTON *Apol. Smect.* Wks. 1851 III. 279 To teach and convince the rationall and sober-minded. **1766** FORDYCE *Serm. Yng. Women* (1767) I. iii. 110 Women well-bred and sober-minded at the same time. **1838** *Penny Cycl.* XII. 306/1 The views of some of the modern and more sober-minded zoologists. **1876** BANCROFT *Hist. U.S.* III. xvi. 493 'We will die upon the place first,' declared even the sober-minded.

**2.** Characterized by soberness of mind.

**1815** SCOTT *Guy M.* xlvii, Her words..were..too vehement and extravagant for sober-minded communication. **1870** L'ESTRANGE *Life Miss Mitford* I. v. 162 A purpose which, I think, was extremely soberminded and praiseworthy.

Hence **sober-mindedness,** sobriety of mind; prudent self-control, moderation.

**1767** PORTEUS *Serm. bef. Univ. Cambr.* 5 July 7 To induce habits of modesty, humility, temperance, frugality, obedience; in one word, *Sober-mindedness.* **1849** MACAULAY *Hist. Eng.* i. I. 137 A despotism, moderated only by..the sobermindedness [**1858** sobriety], and the magnanimity of the despot. **1875** FARRAR *Seekers after God* II. i. 198 Now sober-mindedness invites us.

†**sobermood.** *Obs.* [f. SOBER *a.* + MOOD *sb.*] Sober-mindedness; sobriety of demeanour.

**1553** GRIMALDE *Cicero's Offices* III. (1558) 165 b, Semelinesse, measurekeping, sobermode, stayednesse, and temperaunce. **1561** T. HOBY tr. *Castiglione's Courtyer* ii. (1900) 112 Fearcenesse seemeth the greater whan it is accompanied with sobermoode. **1593** G. HARVEY *Pierce's Super.* Wks. (Grosart) II. 295 He had..such a sober moode, as might ripen the greenest witt.

**soberness** ('səʊbənɪs). [f. SOBER *a.* + -NESS.] The state or character of being sober; sobriety:

**a.** In respect of the appetites.

*a* **1300** *Cursor M.* 27408 Gains glotory [is assigned] soburnes o mete. *c* **1386** CHAUCER *Pars. T.* ¶ 834 Sobrenesse also, that restreyneth the outrage of drinke. **14..** *Tundale's Vis.* 1869 Thay..kepte hir bodyes ay fre From lechery in chastite, And thay loved soburnes ay. **1509** BARCLAY *Shyp of Folys* (1570) 258 By sobernes subduing their sensualitie. **1530** TINDALE *Answ. More* 8 The soberness and chastising of the members. **1706** PHILLIPS (ed. Kersey), *Sobriety* or *Soberness*, a Vertue by which one abstains from eating and drinking more than is requisite. **1780** *Mirror* No. 73, Habits of virtue and soberness. **1861** RUFFINI *Dr. Antonio* ii, Owing to the care and proverbial soberness of the postilions.

**b.** In respect of demeanour, actions, etc.

*c* **1375** *Sc. Leg. Saints* x. (*Matthew*) 444 [He] sobryt þam.. vith softnes & vith sobrenes. **1382** WYCLIF *Rom.* xii. 3 To not sauere..more than it behoueth for to kunne, but for to kunne to sobrenesse. **1463** G. ASHBY *Prisoner's Refl.* 302 With humylyte and sobURnes. *c* **1470** *Rauf Coilyear* 525 Lat se how we may disseuer with sobernes aneuch. **1528** MORE *Dyaloge* III. Wks. 233/2 Ye hole byble was long before his dayes..with deuocion & sobrenes wel and reuerently red. *a* **1548** HALL *Chron., Hen. V*, 1 Turnyng insolencie and wyldnes into grauitie and sobernes. **1648** FAIRFAX, etc. *Remonstrance* 6 In all humblenesse and sobernesse of minde. **1784** COWPER *Task* II. 480 He would not stoop To conquer those by jocular exploits, Whom truth and soberness assail'd in vain. **1825** COBBETT *Rural Rides* 232, I..stood still,.. looking, in silent soberness, into the window.

†**sobersault.** *Obs.* In 6 soubersawte, 7 sobresault, sobersalt. [ad. F. *soubresaut*, †*-sault*, ad. Prov. *sobresaut*, = Sp. *sobresalto*, f. L. *suprā* above + *saltus* leap.] A somersault.

*c* **1530** LD. BERNERS *Arth. Lyt. Bryt.* (1814) 248 Than came forth juglers..& tomblers wyth theyr soubersawtes. **1611** COTGR., *Soubresault*, a Sobresault, or Summer sault. *a* **1625** FLETCHER *Woman's Prize* III. ii, What a sobersalt When the chaire fell she fetchd, with her heels upward.

**sobersides** ('səʊbəˌsaɪdz). [f. SOBER *a.*] A sedate, serious-minded person. Also *transf.*

**1705** HICKERINGILL *Priest-cr.* IV. Wks. 1716 III. 225 And he said—Nay; or, no, no, Sober-sides, no. **1779** J. WEDGWOOD *Let.* 25 Feb. (1965) 229, I am sorry you have been again out of luck with a horse; but do not despair. I have got a *sober sides* on trial for a week past. **1824** MACTAGGART *Gallovid. Encycl.* 430 *Sobersides*, a creature of sober habits. **1846** MRS. GORE *Engl. Charac.* (1852) 85 The mamma naturally takes part with the Sobersides who has so much sympathy with her rheumatism. **1857** DUFFERIN *Lett. High Lat.* (ed. 3) 221 Innumerable sea-birds sat in the crevices... There was one old sober-sides with whom I passed a good ten minutes tête-à-tête. **1878** SPURGEON *Serm.* XXIV. 252 They say, 'Oh, you old sobersides, how grave you are!'

Hence **'sober-sided** *a.*

**1847** MRS. GORE *Castles in Air* x, After that sober-sided fellow..filled him with qualms that ruined his digestion. **1880** G. W. CABLE *Grandissimes* i. 4 Honoré in mask? he is too sober-sided to do such a thing. **1892** [see CHORAL *a.*[1] 2 c]. **1950** *Psychiatry* Feb. 8/2 A sober-sided, meticulous investigator. **1970** N. ARMSTRONG et al. *First on Moon* ii. 41

The Apollo news center at Cape Kenendy issued a sobersided 'status report'.

†'**soberty.** *Obs.* Forms: 4 sobretee, 4-5 **-te**, **sober-**, **sobirte** (5 **sobirtee**). [a. OF. *sobreté*, *soberté*: see SOBER *a.* and -TY.] Sobriety.

**1303** R. BRUNNE *Handl. Synne* 5972 þou..madest hym drunk,..And he solde hys þyng to þe More þan he wulde yn soberte. **1340** *Ayenb.* 248 Sobrete is a traw wel precious. **1377** LANGL. *P. Pl.* B. XIII. 217 þanne had pacience.. Sobrete, and symple speche and sothfaste byleue. *c* **1430** *Pilgr. Lyf Manhode* I. cxx. (1869) 62 Sobirtee it hatteth in this cuntre, and also ouer see. **1483** CAXTON *Cato* b vj b, Thus sobrete chaseth the deuyl fro the man.

**sobful** ('sɒbfʊl), *a.* *rare.* [f. SOB *sb.* or *v.*[1] + -FUL.] Full of sobs, given to sobbing; provocative of sobs.

**1921** W. J. TURNER *Music & Life* 8 The composer of the most sobful ballad that ever made a drunkard weep. **1924** *Blackw. Mag.* Nov. 692/2 He was not really in a very sobful mood.

**sobole.** Anglicized form of next. *rare*$^{-0}$.

**1866** *Treas. Bot.* 1068/1.

‖**soboles** ('sɒbɒli:z). *Bot.* Also as pl. [L. *sobolēs*, *subolēs*, f. *sub* under + **olēre* to grow.]

†**1.** A shoot, a sprout. *Obs.*

*a* **1722** LISLE *Husb.* (1757) 138, I..observed a new pearly brood of soboles at the root of the said winter-shoot. *Ibid.* 245 Through the center of which tufts the new soboles are formed, and issue out.

**2.** A creeping underground stem.

**1832** LINDLEY *Introd. Bot.* 55 The Creeping stem ..(*soboles*). [*Ibid.* 56 The term soboles is applied by Link and De Candolle to the sucker of trees and shrubs.] **1858** A. IRVINE *Handbk. Brit. Plants* 7 The soboles is entirely underground, producing roots at one end, and leaves at the other.

**sobo'liferous,** *a.* *Bot.* [ad. mod.L. *soboliferus*: see prec. and -FEROUS.] Bearing shoots.

**1753** *Chambers' Cycl.* Suppl. s.v. *Aloe*, The soboliferous American Aloe. **1857** A. GRAY *First Less. Bot.* 231 *Soboliferous*, bearing shoots from near the ground. **1879** —— *Struct. Bot.* Gloss. 433 *Soboliferous*, bearing vigorous lithe shoots.

‖**sobornost** (so'bornost). *Theol.* [a. Russ. *sobórnost'* conciliarism, catholicity.] A unity of persons in a loving fellowship in which each member retains freedom and integrity without excessive individualism.

**1935** O. F. CLARKE tr. *Berdyaev's Freedom & Spirit* iii. 91 The revelation of the Trinity is, however, not that of a heavenly monarchy..but that of heavenly love, the divine *sobornost*. **1962** *Listener* 30 Aug. 317/1 How are we to achieve what Berdyaeff would call a valid *sobornost*—a really felt community? **1976** N. V. RIASANOVSKY *Parting of Ways* iv. 177 Khomiakov's concept of *sobornost*, an association in love, freedom, and truth of believers. **1977** *Church Times* 21 Jan. 13/3 *Sobornost* furthermore provides a further incentive to Roman Catholic officialdom not to regard Church unity too exclusively from a juridical point of view.

‖**Sobralia** (səʊ'breɪlɪə). *Bot.* [f. the name of the Spanish physician and botanist, F. M. *Sobral*.] A genus of orchids; a plant belonging to this genus.

**1866** *Treas. Bot.* 1068/1 *Sobralia*, one of the genera of orchids of the tribe *Vanillidæ*. **1882** *Garden* 9 Dec. 508/3 The Sobralias are Central American Orchids.

**Sobranie** (sə'brɑːnɪ). [Proprietary name: cf. next.] A kind of tobacco or a cigarette made from it. Also *Balkan Sobranie*, and *attrib.*

**1899** *Tobacco* 1 Mar. p. lxvi/2 Register of specialities... cigarettes... Balkan Sobranie—Robt. Lewis, 20, St. James St., Lon., S.W. **1923** *Trade Marks Jrnl.* 19 Sept. 1969 *Sobraine* [sic]... Cigarettes. Isaiah Redstone..cigarette manufacturer. *Ibid.* 19 Dec. 2707 The Balkan Sobranie... Cigarettes. **1927** D. L. SAYERS *Unnatural Death* iii. 31 Lord Peter wriggled into the window seat, lit a Sobranie and clasped his hands about his knees. **1955** N. FITZGERALD *House is Falling* xi. 188 When three Sobranies had been lighted, Lake continued. **1966** L. SOUTHWORTH *Felon in Disguise* vii. 116, I will leave it at the tobacconists... All you have to do is to..ask for the pound tin of Balkan Sobranie you ordered. **1966** 'A. YORK' *Eliminator* iii. 49 She put the pistol away in her bedside drawer and lit a Balkan Sobranie. **1977** *Punch* 31 Aug.–6 Sept. 355/1 Insouciant Senior Lecturers smoked Sobranie.

**Sobranye** (sə'brɑːn(ɪ)jeɪ). Also **Sobraniye**, **-je**, **Subranie.** [ad. Bulg. *săbránie* assembly; cf. Russ. *sobránie* and quot. 1902.] The parliament or national assembly of Bulgaria.

**1894** E. DICEY *Peasant State* xv. 142 There are..three Estates in Bulgaria: the Crown, the Ministers, and the Sobranje. **1902** *Encycl. Brit.* XXVI. 448/2 The national representation is embodied in the Sobranye, or ordinary assembly (Bulgarian, *Sŭbranĭ e*, the Russian form *Sobranye* being usually employed by foreign writers), and the Grand Sobranye, which is convoked in extraordinary circumstances. **1923** G. BUCHANAN *My Mission to Russia* I. ii. 22 In spite, however, of his declaring the elections invalid, the Grand Sobranje met and occupied itself with the difficult task of finding a prince willing to accept the thorny crown which Prince Alexander had laid down. **1957** *Times* 21 Dec. 5/4 Some 4,500,000 to five million Bulgarians will go through the motions of 'electing' a new Sobranye. **1974** J. ROTHSCHILD *East Central Europe between Two World Wars* vii. 334 The Peasantists won 85 seats in the Sŭbranie, the unicameral national legislature.

‖**sobre-vest.** *rare.* [ad. Sp. *sobrevesta.*] An upper coat without sleeves.

**1847** PRESCOTT *Peru* IV. ii. II. 107 The colour of the sobrevest on his armour. *Ibid.* vi. 211 He had made himself conspicuous by a rich sobrevest of white velvet over his armour.

**sobriety** (səʊ'braɪɪtɪ). Also 5-7 **sobrietie**, 6 **sobritie** (?). [ad. F. *sobriété* (= It. *sobrietà*, Sp. *sobriedad*, Pg. *sobriedade*), or L. *sōbrietas*, f. *sōbrius* SOBER *a.*]

**1.** The quality of being sober or moderate in the indulgence of appetite; *spec.* moderation in the use of strong drink.

**1401** *Pol. Poems* (Rolls) II. 32 The freer beleeveth.. chastitie, meeknesse, and sobrietie. **1531** ELYOT *Gov.* III. xxii. (1880) II. 336 The auncient temperaunce and moderation in diete, called sobrietie, or, in a more general terme, frugalite. **1553** T. WILSON *Rhet.* 19 b, Sobrietie is a bridelyng by discrecion the wilfulnesse of desire. **1607** ROWLANDS *Earl of Warw.* 69 Unto licentious life they teach us run, And with sobriety associate never. **1655** S. ASHE *Fun. Serm. Gataker* 32 Let the sad consequences of Noah his intemperance give caution for sobriety unto all ancient persons whatsoever. **1781** COWPER *Conversat.* 807 Sobriety, perhaps, may now be found, Where once intoxication press'd the ground. **1836** THIRLWALL *Greece* II. xiv. 205 Sobriety was not one of the Persian virtues. **1861** GEO. ELIOT *S. Marner* iii, The voice of the good angel, inviting to industry, sobriety, and peace.

**2.** Moderation in any respect; avoidance of excess or extravagance.

**1582** N. T. (Rheims) *Romans* xii. 3 Not to be more wise then behoueth.., but to be wise vnto sobrietie. **1653** BINNING *Serm.* (1845) 646 There is also sobriety in the affections, when they are moderate. *a* **1716** BLACKALL *Wks.* (1723) I. 80 Thoughts evil in themselves, are such as..are contrary to Sobriety. **1779** *Mirror* No. 25, The sobriety of manners which home exhibited. **1794** SULLIVAN *View Nat.* II. 358 Some have imputed this to the sobriety and simplicity of living. **1852** THACKERAY *Esmond* I. ii, Misfortune had not taught those exiles sobriety of life. **1884** *19th Cent.* Mar. 406 Sobriety of dress must be enforced.

**b.** In *pl.* Sober qualities.

**1826** LAMB *Elia* Ser. II. *Sanity true Genius*, The other to the wildest dreams gives the sobrieties of every-day occurrences.

**3.** Staidness, gravity, seriousness; soundness or saneness of judgement, etc.

*a* **1548** HALL *Chron., Rich. III*, 55 b, Of suche sobrietie that it coulde never be judged whyther he ware more dull then quicke in speakynge. **1589** GREENE *Menaphon* (Arb.) 46 Curteous country Swaines shake off this sobrietie. **1647** N. BACON *Disc. Govt. Eng.* I. i. (1739) 1 Others of more sobriety account them no better than Lords. **1675** BAXTER *Catholic Theol.* II. ii. 33 Now whether any man should deny all our Religion,..let sobriety be judge. **1774** REYNOLDS *Disc.* vi. (1876) 384 To bring us entirely to reason and sobriety, let it be observed [etc.]. **1790** BURKE *Fr. Rev.* 60 To secure any degree of sobriety in the propositions made by the leaders in any publick assembly. **1841** SPALDING *Italy & It. Isl.* II. 366 He was quite unapproached in that delicacy of feeling and sobriety of judgment, which he added to his learning and invention. **1879** GREEN *Readings fr. Eng. Hist.* x. 48 He could trust his good sense and wise sobriety of mind.

‖**sobriquet** ('səʊbrɪkeɪ, ‖sɔbrikɛ), *sb.* See also SOUBRIQUET. [F., of uncertain origin.] An epithet, a nickname.

**1646** BUCK *Rich. III*, I. 4 It is controverted amongst the Antiquaries and Heralds, which Earle of Anjou first bare the Sirname and Sobriquet of Plantagenest, or Plantagenet. **1655** FULLER *Ch. Hist.* III. xii. 30 This name was one of the Sobriquets, or penitential nick-names. **1757** STUKELEY *Acc. Rich. of Cirencester* 8 Most of the names then were what we call sobriquets, travelling names,..what we call nick-names. **1807** G. CHALMERS *Caledonia* I. II. vi. 298 The Chronicle.. gives him the sobriquet of *Annuine*. **1860** ADLER *Prov. Poet.* xvi. 364 In his verses he never designated her but by a species of poetic sobriquet. **1875** W. MCILWRAITH *Guide Wigtownshire* 57 Because of this reprehensible state of the town, Whithorn got a not very complimentary sobriquet.

Hence '**sobriquet** *v. trans.*, to nickname. Also **sobri'quetical** *a.*, of or pertaining to sobriquets.

**1842** *Tait's Mag.* IX. 683 He has been sobriquetted by.. Tom Moore, as the Rev. Murtagh O'Mulligan. **1875** LOWER *Eng. Surnames* (ed. 4) II. 23 Surnames, geographical, topographical,..sobriquetical,..and historical.

**soc** (sɒk). Now *Hist.* Also 3, 5-7 **sok**, 7 *Sc.* **sock.** [var. of SOKE[1].]

**1.** A right of local jurisdiction: (see SAC[1]).

**1228** *Mem. Ripon* (Surtees) I. 52 Sok, sak, tol, tem. *a* **1272** *Rolls Parlt.* IV. 55/1 Entre diverses autres fraunchises, Sok & Sak, Thol & Theam. *c* **1450** *Godstow Reg.* 535 With tol and team, sok and sake,..and all other customes. *c* **1460** *Oseney Reg.* 9 Of sake and soc, tol and teme. **1609** SKENE *Reg. Maj.* 177 Power to hald their courts, with sock, sack, pitt, and gallous. *c* **1657** SIR W. MURE *Hist. Ho. Rowallane* Wks. (S.T.S.) II. 241 Holding in cheife of the crowne infeft cum furca et fossa, sock et sack [etc.]. **1671** F. PHILIPPS *Reg. Necess.* 175 All that had Soc a liberty of distributive Justice in their Lands or Territories, and Sac..a power to fine or punish such as were found guilty. **1749** *Hist. Windsor* 121 That they should enjoy all their lands with the liberties of Soc and Sac [etc.]. **1861** PEARSON *Early & Mid. Ages* 180 It may be questioned if this applied to any landowner who had soc of his own. **1874** STUBBS *Const. Hist.* I. v. 103 The hereditary owners of sac and soc in the territory.

**2.** = SOKE[1] 2. *rare.*

**1728** CHAMBERS *Cycl.* s.v., *Soc*,..the Shire, Circuit, or Territory wherein such Power is exercised by him indued with such Jurisdiction. **1824** MANDER Title-p., The Derbyshire Miner's Glossary; or Explanation of the Technical Terms of the Miners, used..within the Soc or Wapentake of Wirksworth.

**soc.** (sɒk), abbrev. of SOCIETY 8 and 10.

**1890** BARRÈRE & LELAND *Dict. Slang* II. 274 *Soc* (printers), this is an abbreviation of the word 'Society'. To be a member of the *Soc.* (compositors'), hence not a 'rat'. **1903** FARMER & HENLEY *Slang* VI. 291/2 *Non-Soc-man*, a *rat*.., a blackleg, a non-Union-man. **1980** 'J. MARCUS' *Marsh Blood* v. 73 The overwhelming number of the Art Soc.'s members were amateurs.

**socade,** variant of SUCCADE.

**socage** ('sɒkɪdʒ). Now *Hist.* Also 4-6 **sokage**, 6 **socadge**, 6- **soccage.** [a. AF. *socage*, *sokage* (Anglo-Lat. *socagium*), f. *soc* SOC + -AGE.

By early writers (Bracton, etc.) supposed to be derived from *soc* plough: see Coke *Inst.* (1628) II. v. §117. The view now generally accepted is that the original distinctive feature of socage was attendance at the court held by the superior in virtue of his right of *soc*.]

**1.** The tenure of land by certain determinate services other than knight-service.

α. *a* **1325** *MS. Rawl. B. 520* lf. 41 þoru suuche dede sokage is ibore out in to fre tenement. **1485** *Rolls of Parlt.* VI. 324/1 [She] entred into the same Meses, Landes and Tenements, in the right of the same David her Son, as his Gardyne in Socage. *a* **1500** *Brome Book* 155 þan must ȝe enquere be what seruyce he helde of this lordscheppe, whether he hylde be skwage or be sokage. **1596** SPENSER *St. Irel.* Wks. (Globe) 674/1 By what services he holdeth his land, whether in cheif or in socadge, or in knightes service. **1628** COKE *On Litt.* 86 Euery tenure which is not tenure in chiualrie is a tenure in socage. **1661** J. STEPHENS *Procurations* 47 As the Tenants in Socage after the said change paid their rents yearly to the Lord. **1766** BLACKSTONE *Comm.* II. 79 Socage, in it's most general and extensive signification, seems to denote a tenure by any certain and determinate service. **1845** POLSON *Eng. Law* in *Encycl. Metrop.* II. 824/1 The guardianship of a minor inheriting an estate in lands of the tenure of socage, devolves on the next of kin, on whom the inheritance cannot possibly descend. **1875** K. E. DIGBY *Real Prop.* i. ii. §3. 47 There can be little doubt that tenure in socage is the successor of the alodial proprietorship of early times.

β. **1538** *Sel. Cases Star Chamber* (Selden Soc.) II. 67 Thomas Knyght..Surrenderyth into the lord hands in Soccage..a mese. **1562** *Richmond. Wills* (Surtees) 151 Hereditaments holden in soccage or of the nature of socage tenure. **1638** COTTON *Tower Rec.* 14 For no man will buy quillets but in soccage. **1700** TYRRELL *Hist. Eng.* II. 815 Nor will We have the Wardship..of the Fee-Farm, Soccage, or Burgage. **1761** HUME *Hist. Eng.* I. xi. 239 He also holds lands of the crown by soccage or any other tenure.

*fig.* **1658** CULPEPPER *Astrol. Judgem. Dis.* 190 Dame Nature..holds by tenure by Soccage of Almighty God. **1834** TAYLOR *Philip van Artevelde* II. v. ii, If he be not the devil's feudatory He holds in soccage of a fiend that is.

**b.** With distinguishing epithets, esp. ***free*** or ***common*** (also ***free and common***) ***socage***, the ordinary form of this tenure.

**1570-6** LAMBARDE *Peramb. Kent* (1826) 486 There be two sortes of Socage, the one Free, the other Base..: the Free Socage descending to the eldest alone. **1609** SKENE *Reg. Maj.* 31 Als meikill of his lands, halden in frie soccage; as the samine sonne will get..be reason of succession. **1671** F. PHILIPPS *Reg. Necess.* 167 Before that late unhappy conversion of those Tenures into free and common socage. **1764** T. HUTCHINSON *Hist. Mass.* v. (1765) 447 They held their lands, as of the manor,..in free and common socage. **1796** MORSE *Amer. Geogr.* I. 148 All lands in Upper Canada are to be granted hereafter in free and common soccage. **1832** C. M. GOODRIDGE *Voy. S. Seas* 255 Land thus disposed of without purchase, is to be..held in f[r]ee and common socage. **1874** GREEN *Short Hist.* ix. 607 The conversion of lands held till then in chivalry into lands held in common socage.

**c.** An estate held in socage. *rare.*

**1464** *Rolls of Parlt.* V. 521/2 In the Maners,.. Tounes, Wapentaches and Socage of Wyrkesworth. **1768** *Ann. Reg., Hist. Europe* 78*/2 At a certain small reserved rent..viz. 50*l*. per ann. for the soccage of Carlisle.

**d.** A payment made to the superior by one holding land in socage. *rare.*

**1859** C. BARKER *Associative Principle* i. 26 The rents and soccage of two mills were applied to the purchase of sheep-skins. **1883** *Cent. Mag.* Aug. 545/1 The payment of free socage came, in time, to be attended with some ceremony.

**2.** *attrib.*, as ***socage freehold***, ***land***, ***roll***, ***service***, ***tenant***, ***tenure***.

**1467** in *Eng. Gilds* (1870) 376 The charter of the seid cite, with the ij. Socage Rollez, shullen be putt in the comyn cofour. *a* **1500** *Brome Bk.* 155 And althow it be sokage lond, ȝet þe eyur [= heir] schall pay a releffe and do his sewte. **1562** Socage tenure [see 1 β]. **1628** COKE *On Litt.* 121 He may deuise by his Will all his Socage Lands. *a* **1658** CLEVELAND *Rustic Rampant* Wks. (1687) 442 Considering the Incertainty of things under that Iron Socage Tenure. **1741** T. ROBINSON *Gavelkind* i. 3 Under this Term were comprehended all Socage Services. **1747** CARTE *Hist. Eng.* I. 423 The taillages that the king had it in his power to levy upon the soccage tenants in his own demesnes. **1818** HALLAM *Mid. Ages* (1872) I. 203 Many of them rather answer to our socage freeholds. **1890** *Athenæum* 4 Jan. 12/2 Owners of land held in England by socage tenure.

**socager** ('sɒkɪdʒə(r)). Now *Hist.* Also 7- **soccager**, 8 **sockager.** [f. prec.] One holding land by socage tenure.

**1647** N. BACON *Disc. Govt. Eng.* I. lxx. (1739) 187 Of these Socagers did arise..the body of English Footmen in their Armies. **1653** *Customes of Soke of Kirton-in-Lindsey, Linc.* (MS.), Upon paine of every forreyner so intruding ten pounds, and every Soccager Five pounds. **1728** CHAMBERS *Cycl.* s.v. *Soc*, Liberty of holding a Court of his Sock-men or Sockagers, that is, his Tenants, whose Tenure is hence called Socage. **1812** G. CHALMERS *Dom. Econ. Gt. Brit.* 4 The barons, the free tenants, the free soccagers, together with the villains, and the slaves. **1874** STUBBS *Const. Hist.* I. vii. 193 He was easily tempted to become a socager, paying rent or gavel, instead of a free..man-at-arms.

**'so-called**, *ppl. a.* Also so called and as one word.

**1. a.** In predicative use (properly without hyphen): Called or designated by that name.

**1657** HOWELL *Londinop.* 304 This Company of the Haberdashers, or Hurrers, of old time so-called. **1696** PHILLIPS, *Rubrick*, a name given to a Book of the Civil Law, so called because the Heads of the Chapters were written in red Letters. **1753** CHALLONER *Cath. Chr. Instr.* 181 The Cluniacenses, so called from their first Abbey of Cluny in France. **1831** SCOTT *Ct. Robt.* xix, He would find him at the Philosopher's Gardens, so called, as belonging to the sage Agelastes. **1847** HALLIW., *Patrick's Purgatory*.. Its entire history is to be found in Mr. Wright's work so called. **1863** A. C. RAMSAY *Phys. Geogr.* 69 The Coralline Crag, so-called because it contains a large number of corals.

**b.** Qualified by *properly*.

**1665** GLANVIL *Scepsis Sci.* v, The Soul is the sole Percipient, which alone hath animadversion and sense properly so called. **1790** [see PROPERLY 2]. **1827** COLERIDGE *Table Talk* 24 June, I do not think there is any jealousy, properly so called, in the character of Othello. **1860** RUSKIN *Mod. Paint.* VI. vi. §4 V. 43 A root, properly so called, is a fibre..which secretes certain elements from the earth.

**2.** In attributive use (hyphened): Called or designated by this name or term, but not properly entitled to it or correctly described by it. Also *loosely* or *catachr.* as a term of abuse.

More recently, and now quite commonly (esp. in technical contexts), used merely to call attention to the description, without implication of incorrectness, as in (*b*). Cf. Du. *zoogenaamd*, *-genoemd*, *-gezeid*, G. *sogenannt*.

(*a*) **1837** CARLYLE *Fr. Rev.* II. I. ii, The Right Side.. persists..in considering..all these so-called Decrees as mere temporary whims. **1862** MILLER *Elem. Chem., Org.* (ed. 2) i. §2. 39 The so-called elementary bodies being really compounds of at least two atoms of the true element. **1884** PENNINGTON *Wiclif* vi. 193 Their so-called poverty is nothing else but a diabolical lie. **1888** O. WILDE in *Woman's World* I. 134/2 'This so-called nineteenth century'—as an impassioned young orator once termed it, after a contemptuous diatribe against the evils of modern civilisation. **1960** C. S. LEWIS *Studies in Words* ix. 226 Rose Macaulay noticed a tendency to prefix 'so called' to almost any adjective when it was used of those the speaker hated; the final absurdity being reached when people referred to the Germans as 'these so-called Germans'. **1980** W. SAFIRE in *N.Y. Times Mag.* 13 Jan. 6/1 Examples of sneer words are 'self-proclaimed', 'would-be', 'purported' and that Soviet favorite, 'so-called'.

(*b*) **1886** C. E. PASCOE *Lond. of To-day* xl. (ed. 3) 341 The leading so-called linendrapers of the metropolis. *a* **1961** in WEBSTER, s.v., His heavy working schedule did not keep the student out of so-called campus politics. **1962** R. CARSON *Silent Spring* viii. 86 The so-called Dutch elm disease entered the United States from Europe about 1930. **1966** G. GREENE *Comedians* I. ii. 46 New buildings..built for an international exhibition in so-called modern style. **1968** *Physics Bull.* Nov. 373/1 The socalled Schrödinger representation. **1977** C. SAGAN *Dragons of Eden* ii. 41 Many spinal-cord neurons seem to have about 10,000 synapses, and the so-called Purkinje cells of the cerebellum may have still more. **1979** P. NIHALANI et al. *Indian & Brit. English* I. 164 A number of so-called transformational grammarians are to attend the teachers' conference at Krishnapur next week.

**soccated**, obs. var. of SOCKETED.

**soccer** ('sɒkə(r)). *colloq.* Also socca, socker. [f. *Assoc.*, short for *Association.* Cf. RUGGER[2].] The game of football as played under Association rules. Also *attrib.* and *Comb.* Hence **'soccerite**, a player of soccer.

**1889** E. C. DOWSON *Let.* 21 Feb. (1967) 38, I absolutely decline to see socca' matches. **1891** *Lock to Lock Times* 24 Oct. 13/2 A sterling player, and has the best interest of the 'socker' game at heart. **1894** *Westm. Gaz.* 11 Jan. 7/1 The rival attractions of 'rugger' and 'socker'. **1895** *19th Cent.* Nov. 862 When the boat-race, sports, and 'soccer' are in most men's minds. **1899** *New Cent. Rev.* V. 118 A Methodist minister—who..doffed the Socker jersey. **1916** BLANCROFT & PULVEMACHER *Handbk. Athletic Games* (1922) 429 Soccer football, as it is called in America, is the English Association Football. **1924** H. DE SELINCOURT *Cricket Match* iv. 83 However any sane person could prefer soccer to cricket the good little Horace totally failed to comprehend. **1935** *Punch* 24 Apr. 476/2 No one more thoroughly qualified to write the history of 'soccer'..can be imagined. **1945** *Gen* 13 Jan. 30/1 Many Soccerites..took to Rugby. **1951** R. CAMPBELL *Light on Dark Horse* 69 My father had founded the Technical College, a 'soccerite' school. **1951** *Sport* 7–13 Jan. 9/1 We had the F.A. scheme to bring the big professional clubs and the soccer-playing schools into closer contact. **1971** L. KOPPETT *N.Y. Times Guide Spectator Sports* xii. 193 All you need to play soccer is a ball, a field and players. **1976** *Field* 18 Nov. 989/2 They roar around, fighting and frolicking beneath like soccer hooligans. **1978** P. MARSH et al. *Rules of Disorder* iv. 97 The soccer terraces offer..a chance to escape from the dreariness of the weekday world.

**soccotrine**, var. of SOCOTRINE.

**soccour**, obs. f. SUCCOUR.

**socdollager**, var. of SOCKDOLAGER.

**soch(e**, obs. ff. SUCH *a.*

**sochete**, var. of SUGET *v.* (subject) *Obs.*

‖**socia.** *Obs. rare.* [L. *socia*, fem. of *socius* companion.] A female friend or companion.

**1797** MRS. A. M. BENNETT *Beggar Girl* (1813) I. 25 The two socias went to the theatre. *Ibid.* IV. 52 Miss was now the most elegant entertainer, except only her socia, Mrs. Bawsky.

**sociability** (səʊʃə'bɪlɪtɪ). Also 5 ? socibbilitee. [f. next + -ITY. Cf. F. *sociabilité*, Sp. *sociabilidad*, Pg. *-idade*.]

**1.** The character or quality of being sociable; friendly disposition or intercourse.

*a* **1475** ASHBY *Poems* (1899) ii. 270 He shall appere false and sedicious, Be al quaint socibbilitees and labour. **1581** MULCASTER *Positions* xxxvii. (1887) 152 Doth he not shew forth an euident sociabilitie and liklyhood, that he will be very well to be liued withall? **1594** PARSONS *Confer. Success.* I. i. 3 Sociability or inclination to liue togeather in company. **1738** WARBURTON *Div. Legat.* II. vi. I. 275 Such then was the Root and Foundation of this Sociability of Religion in the ancient World, so much envied by our modern Infidels. **1786** MME. D'ARBLAY *Diary* 12 Aug., We were flung, by this means, into a style of sociability we might else never have arrived at. **1812** HENRY *Camp. agst. Quebec* 134 Civil wars which extinguish the sociabilities of mankind. **1880** FLO. MARRYAT *Fair-Haired Alda* II. v. 82 They were wofully disappointed by the results of their intended sociability.

**2.** *Ecol.* The extent to which the plants of a species are found in proximity to one another. [The sense is due to Braun-Blanquet and Pavillard, who used F. *sociabilité* (*Vocabulaire de Sociologie végétale* (1922) 3).]

**1922** *Jrnl. Ecol.* X. 246 Where the French terms are practically identical with the English equivalents..they are simply translated... La Sociabilité (Soziabilität, Geselligkeit): disposition of individuals in the interior of an association. Five grades of sociability are expressed as follows. **1932** FULLER & CONARD tr. *Braun-Blanquet's Plant Sociol.* iii. 36 Gregariousness or 'sociability' expresses a space relationship of individual plants, answering the question, how are the individuals or shoots of a species grouped? **1961** HANSON & CHURCHILL *Plant Community* iii. 97 Species that spread only by seed may also show a high degree of sociability, especially in the early stages of succession, as in abandoned fields where certain annual weeds may become very dense. **1973** P. A. COLINVAUX *Introd. Ecol.* v. 65 *Zea mays*..had a cover abundance rating of only '3' since, although the commonest plant, it by no means covered nearly all the ground as it must to rate a '5', and a sociability of '1', earned because it was evenly spaced and thus the extreme loner.

**sociable** ('səʊʃəb(ə)l), *a.* and *sb.* [a. F. *sociable* (= Sp. *sociable*, It. *-abile*, Pg. *-avel*), or ad. L. *sociābilis*, f. *sociāre* to unite, associate: see -ABLE.]

**A.** *adj.* **1. a.** Naturally inclined or disposed to be in company with others of the same species.

**1553** T. WILSON *Rhet.* (1580) 56 Euery societie or companiyng together is delitfull,..for asmuche as Nature hath ordeined vs to be sociable, frendly, and louyng together. **1607** TOPSELL *Four-f. Beasts* (1658) 459 It is a very sociable creature, for they do live together in herds above a thousand in a flock. **1672** TEMPLE *Ess. Govt.* Wks. 1720 I. 99 What it is that makes some Creatures sociable, and others live and range more alone, or in smaller Companies. **1707** HOPE *New Method Fencing* 5 Man being a sociable Creature designed not only for himself, but for..the Community wherein he lives. **1711** ADDISON *Spect.* No. 9 ¶1 Man is said to be a Sociable Animal.

**b.** In names of birds (see quots. and cf. SOCIAL 6 c).

**1801** LATHAM *Syn.* Suppl. II. 192 Sociable Grosbeak.—Size of a bulfinch;..general colour..rufous brown. **1829** GRIFFITH tr. *Cuvier* VI. 163 The Sociable Vulture, or Oricou. **1864–5** WOOD *Homes w. Hands* xxii. (1868) 416 Sociable Weaver Bird is a native of Southern Africa. **1875** *Encycl. Brit.* III. 772 The Sociable Grosbeak of South Africa. *c* **1880** *Cassell's Nat. Hist.* III. 257 The Sociable Vulture (*Otogyps auricularis*). **1908** *Zoologist* Apr. 122 The Sociable Plovers and other rare birds which showed themselves in Kent.

**2. a.** Inclined to seek and enjoy the company of others; disposed to be friendly or affable in company; willing to converse in a pleasant manner.

**1573** G. HARVEY *Letter-bk.* (Camden) 5 This is he that accuseth me of not being sociable, him self so sociable as you se. **1602** F. HERIN *Anat.* 9 The true Phisition is sociable, and readie to communicate. **1656** DUCHESS NEWCASTLE *True Relation* in *Life* (1886) 287, I durst neither look up with my eyes, nor speak, nor be any way sociable. **1706** E. WARD *Wooden World Diss.* (1708) 91 He e'en..turn'd a sociable Sot, like the rest of his Brethren. **1771** FRANKLIN *Autobiog.* Wks. 1840 I. 54 We had a sociable company in the cabin. **1824** SYD. SMITH *America* Wks. 1859 II. 47/1 The great inconvenience..is one which more sociable travellers must feel less acutely. **1893** K. L. BATES *Eng. Relig. Drama* 223 Pity, Contemplation, and Perseverance, sociable old worthies.

*transf.* and *fig.* **1638** SIR T. HERBERT *Trav.* (ed. 2) 181 Nicanor..made a vaine attempt to bring the Euxin and this sea into one, to make it sociable and navigable. *a* **1716** SOUTH *Serm.* (1744) XI. 8 This sociable evil [*sc.* the body], this treacherous Companion, is the enticer and betrayer to all sin. **1852** HAWTHORNE *Wonder-Bk.* (1868) 142 That sociablest of flowers, the little Houstonia.

**b.** Const. *to* a person or thing. *rare.*

**1610** SHAKS. *Temp.* v. 63 Mine eyes ev'n sociable to the shew of thine Fall fellowly drops. **1751** EARL ORRERY *Remarks Swift* (1752) 3 He was sociable only to particular friends, and to them only at particular hours.

**3. a.** Characterized by, pertaining to, contact, intercourse, or companionship with others, esp. in a friendly or pleasant manner.

**1573** G. HARVEY *Letter-bk.* (Camden) 8 These ar ther sociable and fellouli delings. **1594** T. B. *La Primaud. Fr. Acad.* II. 404 The ciuil and sociable nature, in which God hath created them. **1641** J. JACKSON *True Evang. T.* I. 6 Sweet and calme and sociable manners and conversation. **1661** A. BROME *Songs & Poems* 86 A sociable life and free. **1695** KENNETT *Par. Antiq.* ix. 56 This was a sociable practise of that age. **1781** COWPER *Let. to J. Hill* 9 Dec., Comfortably situated by a good fire, and just entering on a sociable conversation. **1841** ELPHINSTONE *Hist. Ind.* II. 99 He had often similar moments of enjoyment, thanks to his sociable habits. **1898** *Atlantic Monthly* Apr. 506/1 The harvesting of potatoes was a sociable toil.

†**b.** *sociable coach*: (cf. SOCIABLE *sb.* 2 a). *Obs.*

**1673** WYCHERLEY *Gentl. Dancing Master* v. i, I will have.. a large, sociable, well painted Coach. **1772** *Town & Co. Mag.* 17 In high spirits Maria stepped into Mrs. Benwell's sociable coach.

†**c.** Of or pertaining to society; social. *Obs.*

**1680** C. NESSE *Church Hist.* 39 Peter explains his two sociable duties, Fear God, Honour the King. **1705** ATTERBURY *Serm.* (1726) I. x. 351 Pressing Men to exercise those Graces which adorn the Sociable State.

†**4. a.** Capable of being combined or joined together. *Obs.*

**1594** HOOKER *Eccl. Pol.* (1676) I. 74 Another Law there is, which toucheth them as they are sociable parts united into one body. **1674** GREW *Anat. Pl., Disc. Mixture* (1682) 231 To render all Bodies Sociable or Mingleable. **1679** NEWTON in Rigaud *Corr. Sci. Men* II. 413 There is a certain secret principle in nature, by which liquors are sociable to some things and unsociable to others.

†**b.** Capable of being made a companion *for* others. *Obs.*

**1608** BRETON *Divine Consid.* Wks. (Grosart) II. 22/1 God ..made him like vnto himselfe.., amiable in his sight, sociable for his Angells, and coheire with his blessed Sonne.

**5.** *Math.* Designating a cycle of three or more integers such that each is the sum of the factors of the previous one; cf. PERFECT *a.* B. 8. [The sense is due to P. Poulet, who used F. *sociable* (*L'Intermédiaire des Mathématiciens* (1918) XXV. 101).]

**1970** *Math. Computation* XXIV. 428 Until now only two groups of sociable numbers were known, respectively of order 5 and 28... I have made an exhaustive search for sociable groups of order $t \leq 10$ of which the lesser number is smaller than $6.10^7$. This search has yielded 9 new groups, ..all of order 4. **1972** C. S. OGILVY *Tomorrow's Math* (ed. 2) v. 113 The numbers 12496→14288→15472→14536→14264→12496 form what has been called a sociable chain of 5 links... The sum of factors of 12496 is 14288, the sum of factors of 14288 is 15472, and so on around the chain.

**B.** *sb.* **1.** †**a.** A social being. *Obs.*

*a* **1613** OVERBURY *A Wife*, etc. (1638) 103 One that Nature made a sociable,..and a crazed disposition hath altered.

**b.** A sociable person. *rare.*

**1927** A. HUXLEY *Proper Studies* 190 The ratio of solitaries to sociables will remain much as it is.

**2. a.** An open, four-wheeled carriage having two seats facing each other and a box-seat for the driver. (Cf. SOCIABLE *a.* 3 b.)

**1780** *Pennsylvania Jrnl. & Weekly Advertiser* 15 Mar. 4/1 Wanted to exchange, a neat sulkey, almost new, for a sociable or handy one horse chair, equally good. **1794** W. FELTON *Anc. & Mod. Carriages* (1801) II. 87 A Sociable is a phaeton with a double or treble body, and is so called from the number of persons it is meant to carry at one time. **1825–9** MRS. SHERWOOD *Lady of Manor* III. 122 The sociable and the travelling-carriage were driven up to the door. **1878** *Rep. Carriages Paris Exhib.* (ed. C. Saunderson, 1879) 8 This shape is becoming very fashionable in Paris, not only in Broughams, but also in Landaus, Victorias, and Sociables.

**b.** A tricycle having two seats side by side.

**1882** *Knowledge* No. 19. 398/1 Great improvements have been made recently in double tricycles, or, as they are generally called, Sociables. **1888** *Pall Mall G.* 2 Feb. 5/1 For years..we ploughed along on sociables with a young lady at our side.

**c.** 'A kind of couch with a curved S-shaped back, for two persons who sit partially facing each other' (Knight *Dict. Mech.* 1875).

**1851** C. CIST *Sketches & Statistics of Cincinnati in 1851* 202 Dressing bureaus, sociables, and *vis-à-vis* are sure to catch the visitor's eye, and to open the visitor's purse. **1872** *Atlantic Monthly* May 544 She was lying on a little sociable or sofa, as he entered. **1930** V. SACKVILLE-WEST *Edwardians* iii. 133 In the centre of the room stood a sociable..on which two persons might sit, facing one another, but properly divided by the arm and wriggle of the S. **1959** *Times* 8 Aug. 9/4, I would venture to claim for something like the double sofa of the illustration the honour of representing the ideals of this whole decade... The seats revolve so that the two occupants—there is ample space for broad backs and expansive crinolines—have room for manoeuvre. It was called a 'sociable'. **1961** L. G. G. RAMSEY *Connoisseur New Guide Antique Eng. Furnit.* 120 The variant known as the 'sociable', 'conversation sofa', or 'tête-à-tête', with the two ends facing each other on the lines of the French 'causeuse' ..was popular for a short time during the 1840's, but seems to have already gone out of favour by the mid-1850's.

**3.** *U.S.* An informal evening party; *esp.* a social church meeting. (Cf. SOCIAL *sb.* 2.)

**1826** LONGF. *Life* (1891) I. vi. 74, I..went with them to a little 'sociable' in the evening, where we had dancing. **1888** T. W. HIGGINSON *Women & Men* 31 She manages the book club and the church sociable. **1895** SARAH M. H. GARDNER *Quaker Idyls* vi. 129 Some of their friends had proposed to have a series of 'sociables'.

Hence **'sociablist**, one who rides a double tricycle.

**1883** *Cyclists Tour. Club Gaz.* Sept. 343/1 Two sociablists pedalling independently.

**sociableness** ('səʊʃəb(ə)lnɪs). [f. prec. + -NESS.] The character or quality of being sociable, in the various senses of the word; sociability.

**1592** MORYSON *Let.* in *Itin.* (1617) I. 36 To which custome gentlemen for sociablenes have submitted themselves. **1613** SIR A. SHERLEY *Trav. Persia* 116 Which will giue an entrance to a kind of sociablenesse, and that will proceed.. to a mutuall friendship. **1653** MORE *Antid. Ath.* II. iv. §3

The two main Properties of Man being Contemplation and Sociableness or love of Converse. **1724** DE FOE *Tour Gt. Brit.* I. iii. 25 Abundance of Gentry being in the Neighbourhood, it adds to the Sociableness of the Place. **1727** [see SOCIALNESS]. **1825** COCKBURN *Mem.* (1856) 195 An absolute passion, indulgence in which gratified..his jovial sociableness. **1855** MACAULAY *Hist. Eng.* vii. III. 50 But of this sociableness William was entirely destitute.

**sociably** ('səʊʃəblɪ), *adv.* [f. as prec.: see -LY².] In a sociable manner; with sociability.

**1573** HARVEY *Lett.-bk.* (Camden) 6 How sociablely he hath delt bi me. **1605** BACON *Adv. Learn.* I. vii. §2 Beasts and birds..stood all sociably together. **1651** HOBBES *Leviath.* II. xvii. 86 Certain living creatures, as Bees, and Ants, live sociably one with another. **1755** *World* (1772) III. 294 [They] spend their evenings very sociably together. **1878** GLADSTONE *Primer of Homer* 111 Wine was sociably enjoyed, but drunkenness was abhorred.

**social** ('səʊʃəl), *a.* and *sb.* Also 6 *Sc.* **sociale**, 7 **sociall**. [a. F. *social*, *-ale* (14th cent. in Godef.; = Sp., Pg. *social*, It. *sociale*), or ad. L. *sociālis*, f. *socius* friend, companion, associate.]

**A.** *adj.* †**1.** Capable of being associated or united *to* others. *Obs.*⁻¹

**1562** WINȜET *Last Blast Tromp.* Wks. (S.T.S.) I. 45 The proude schismatikis and obstinat heretikis, na wayis sociale to the companie of Christiane Catholiks.

†**2.** Associated, allied, combined. *Obs.*

**1620** T. GRANGER *Div. Logike* 20 The former is called the Sole, solitary,..absolute Cause: the latter sociall Causes. **1645** HAMMOND *View Infallib.* 64 'Tis strange you should couple them together as so sociall things which are so distant and separable. **1686** PLOT *Staffordsh.* ii. 80 There may be subjoyned another social cause that may contribute not a little to the elevating Water above its own Level.

**3. a.** Of war: Occurring or taking place between allies or confederates. *rare.*

**1665** MANLEY *Grotius' Low C. Wars* 1, I Intend to Discourse the most famous Warre of our Times, and which may not improperly be called Sociall, or a Warre of Confederates. **1700** SOUTHERNE *Fate of Capua* I. i, Is there a worthier than a social war?

**b.** *spec.* (with *the*). In Roman Hist., the war between Rome and the Italian allies, 90–89 B.C. In Greek Hist., the war between the Athenians and their confederates, 357–355 B.C.

(*a*) **1765** BLACKSTONE *Comm.* I. 159 When, after the social war, all the burghers of Italy were admitted free citizens of Rome. **1842** W. C. TAYLOR *Anc. Hist.* xv. §6 (ed. 3) 436 A much more dangerous war, called the Marsic, the Social, or the Italic, was provoked by the injustice with which the Romans treated their Italian allies.

(*b*) **1788** LEMPRIERE *Class. Dict.*, *Chabrias*, an Athenian general,..killed in the Social war. **1808** MITFORD *Hist. Greece* IV. xxxvi. 267 The War between the Athenians and their Allies, called the Confederate or Social War. **1838** THIRLWALL *Greece* V. xliii. 259 Philip seems to have kept aloof from the Social War.

**4. a.** Marked or characterized by mutual intercourse, friendliness, or geniality; enjoyed, taken, spent, etc., in company with others, esp. with those of a similar class or kindred interests.

***social evening***, an evening meeting of a club, society, etc., of the nature of an entertainment; and evening on which this is held; similarly ***social tea***.

**1667** MILTON *P.L.* VIII. 429 Thou in thy secresie although alone, Best with thy self accompanied, seek'st not Social communication. **1746** FRANCIS tr. *Hor., Sat.* II. vi. 157 While thus we spend the social Night. **1785** BOSWELL *Jrnl. Tour Hebr.* 142 His benevolent, gay, social intercourse. **1794** MRS. RADCLIFFE *Myst. Udolpho* xxxvi, The spacious fire-places, where no mark of social cheer remained. **1810** SIR A. BOSWELL *Edinb.* Poems (1871) 50 When met to drink a social cup of tea. **1848** DICKENS *Dombey* v, Mrs. Chick and Miss Tox were enjoying a social evening. **1857** —— *Little Dorrit* II. xiv. 441 He took pains, on all social occasions, to draw Mr Sparkler out. **1864** —— *Lett.* (1880) II. 214 They want social rest and social recreation for themselves and their families. **1877** *Independent* 8 Feb. 4/3 The social event of the season! **1887** [see VISIT *sb* 1 a]. **1896** W. JAMES *Mem. & Stud.* (1911) i. 3 On this social occasion it has seemed that what Agassiz stood for in the way of character and influence is the more fitting to commemorate. **1899** J. LONDON *Let.* 17 Apr. (1966) 28 So you grow a-weary of the social whirl. **1911** G. STRATTON-PORTER *Harvester* xvi. 342 Wait until afternoon, and pretend you are making a social call. **1915** F. M. HUEFFER *Good Soldier* III. iv. 178 He would dine and pass the evening..at social functions of one kind or another. **1926** Social tea [see *bridge roll* s.v. BRIDGE *sb.*² c]. **1943** G. GREENE *Ministry of Fear* III. ii. 193 Haven't we met—?.. On one of the doctor's social evenings. **1946** L. P. HARTLEY *Sixth Heaven* iii. 67 We saw him chattering away... He loves the social round. **1958** A. HUXLEY *Let.* 20 Oct. (1969) 855, I have been revolving in the social whirl—seeing everybody. **1959** B. BERNARDI *Mugwe, Failing Prophet* i. 6 Social intercourse between the main section of the Tharaka and the Thagichu has never been broken off. **1976** *Eastern Even. News* (Norwich) 9 Dec. 12/7 Patients of St. Andrews Hospital, Thorpe, enjoyed a social evening in the Octagon Centre at the hospital. **1977** P. SCOTT *Staying On* (1978) xiii. 204 In all the years they'd known one another they had never exchanged social visits. **1980** *Jewish Chron.* 4 Jan. 9/3 Brighton and Hove Emunah held a social tea at the Talmud Torah hall of Hove Hebrew Congregation.

†**b.** Expressive of or proceeding from sympathy; sympathetic. *Obs.*

**1726** POPE *Odyss.* XVI. 236 The prince..Hung round his neck, while tears his cheek bedew; Nor less the father pour'd a social flood! **1745** COLLINS *Ode Death Col. Ross* x, Where'er from time thou court'st relief, The Muse shall still, with social grief, Her gentlest promise keep.

**c.** Of, relating to, or connected with fashionable or leisured society (cf. SOCIETY 3 c). See also *social column*, *social register*, sense 12 below.

**1873** TROLLOPE *Eustace Diamonds* III. lxxviii. 331 The police..had..succeeded in sending two scoundrels out of the social world, probably for life. **1894** *Harper's New Monthly Mag.* Oct. 697/2 But who looked so far from their faces, so certain to reveal the types of all styles of the beauty of our theatrical and social queens? **1896** M. CORELLI *Thelma* II. II. ii. 137 In the social world, Fashion, the capricious deity, must be followed. **1903** A. BENNETT *Truth about Author* vi. 80 The editor was enchanted with my social paragraphs. **1911** M. CORELLI *Life Everlasting* xi. 237 It was supposed then..that as I found myself the possessor of an income of between five and six thousand a year, I would naturally..enter upon what is called a social career. **1925** *Ladies' Home Jrnl.* Apr. 163/3 After you married Jack Hollsworth you went into a sort of social eclipse and almost kept out of things entirely. **1930** G. B. SHAW *Apple Cart* I. 39 The King's displeasure is still a sentence of social death within range of St James's Palace. **1938** L. BEMELMANS *Life Class* II. v. 164 Their committee selected their dates..at the beginning of the season, but late enough to give them some knowledge of the social calendar. **1977** G. SCOTT *Hot Pursuit* v. 51 Little country towns where the social calendar revolved gently around race meetings and the seasons.

**5.** †**a.** United by some common tie. *Obs.*

**1717** POPE *Iliad* XI. 339 The social shades the same dark journey go. **1718** *Ibid.* XVI. 1022 Patroclus yields to fear, Retires for succour to his social train.

**b.** Inclined or disposed to friendly intercourse or converse; sociable.

**1729** POPE *On General Withers* 8 Withers, adieu! yet not with thee remove Thy Martial spirit, or thy Social love! **1776** PAINE *Com. Sense* (1791) 55 A few able and social sailors will soon instruct a sufficient number of active land-men in the common work of a ship. **1797–1805** S. & HT. LEE *Canterb. T.* II. 339 Sir Edward was wandering, without one social bosom to confide a thought to, through..Sicily. **1816** JANE AUSTEN *Emma* ii, His own friendly and social disposition. **1849** MACAULAY *Hist. Eng.* ii. I. 168 Charles came forth from that school with social habits, with polite and engaging manners. **1878** MISS BRADDON *Eleanor's Victory* ii, He was very happy and social.

**c.** Consisting or composed of persons associated together in, or for the purpose of, friendly intercourse.

**1792** N. WEBSTER in E. E. Ford *Notes on Life of N. Webster* (1912) I. 363 A number of Gentlemen meet at my house for the purpose of forming a social Club. **1817** COLERIDGE *Biographia Literaria* II. xxii. 136 In the social circles of private life we often find a striking use of the latter put a stop to the general flow of conversation. **1843** MILL *Logic* II. IV. v. 264 The accident that one of the words was used and not the other on a particular occasion or in a particular social circle. **1849** MACAULAY *Hist. Eng.* vii. II. 234 The contest went on in both Houses of Parliament, in every constituent body, in every social circle. **1866** *Month* IV. 54 The social body at Balliol was strengthened between 1830 and 1840 by three important additions. **1872** B. JERROLD *London* xix. 155 The [Covent Garden] piazzas..where a few noteworthy social clubs still linger. **1892** *Photogr. Ann.* II. 652 The club is strictly a 'social' one. **1935** *Burlington Mag.* Apr. 161/2 All social circles allied to the Court. **1966** J. CLEARY *High Commissioner* ix. 185 He..belonged to none of the social clubs. He played golf..at a public course. **1977** *Evening Post* (Nottingham) 24 Jan. 7/6 But the couple who lived there escaped with their lives—because just two hours earlier a neighbour had persuaded them to go with him to a local social club.

**d.** Of a room, a building, etc.: used for friendly intercourse or association. See also *social centre*, sense 12 below.

**1889** KIPLING *From Sea to Sea* (1899) I. xxii. 426 The ladies' saloon..according to American custom, was labelled 'Social Hall'. **1975** C. POTOK *In Beginning* (1976) iv. 234 After the service we all went to the social hall downstairs and there was wine and whiskey and cake.

**6. a.** Living, or disposed to live, in companies or communities; desirous of enjoying the society or companionship of others.

**1722** WOLLASTON *Relig. Nat.* vii. 145 Man is a Social creature: that is, a single man, or family, cannot subsist, or not well, alone out of all Society. **1744** HARRIS *Three Treat.* (1841) 62 Let this then be remembered,..that man by nature is truly a social animal. **1842** *Boston Quarterly Rev.* 184 Man is a social Being. **1853** TRENCH *Proverbs* 127 Man not being merely accidentally gregarious, but essentially social. **1875** JOWETT *Plato* (ed. 2) IV. 279 In the use of the senses, as in his whole nature, man is a social being. **1966** G. N. LEECH *Eng. in Advertising* i. 3 Yet the study of language can be regarded as central to man's study of himself, whether as an individual or as a social being.

**b.** *Zool.* Living together in more or less organized communities; belonging to a community of this kind.

**1831** *Insect Miscellanies* 412/1 Social leaf-mining caterpillars... Social wasps. **1840** tr. *Cuvier's Anim. Kingd.* 599 The Apiariæ are either solitary or social in their habits. *Ibid.* 602 The terminal subgenus of Social Bees. **1859** DARWIN *Orig. Spec.* iv. (1860) 87 In social animals it [i.e. natural selection] will adapt the structure of each individual for the benefit of the community. **1874** CARPENTER *Ment. Phys.* I. ii. (1879) 57 Bees, Wasps, Ants, and other Social Insects.

*transf.* **1864–5** WOOD *Homes w. Hands* xxi. (1879) 411 We now come to the Social Habitations and give precedence to those which are constructed by Mammalia.

**c.** In specific names (see quots. and cf. SOCIABLE *a.* 1 b). ***social whale*** = ***pilot whale*** s.v. PILOT *sb.* 8.

**1781** PENNANT *Quad.* II. 459 The Social Rat..inhabits the Caspian desert. **1801** SHAW *Gen. Zool.* II. I. 93 The Social Mouse is a native of the Caspian deserts. **1850** R. G. CUMMING *Hunter's Life S. Africa* (1902) 57/2 Many of them [trees] were inhabited by whole colonies of the social grosbeak. **1865** H. D. THOREAU *Cape Cod* vii. 130 In the summer and fall sometimes, hundreds of blackfish (the Social Whale..)..are driven ashore. **1869** *Galaxy* Aug. 173 The social-sparrow, *alias* 'hair-bird',..is the smallest of the sparrows. **1884** GOODE *Nat. Hist. Aquat. Anim.* 11 *Globicephalus svineval*,..also called Black Whale, Social Whale.

**d.** *Bot.* Of plants: Growing in a wild state in patches or masses with other members of the same species, esp. so as to cover a large area.

**1834** MRS. SOMERVILLE *Connex. Physical Sci.* xxvii. 274 Very few social plants, such as grasses and heaths that cover large tracts of lands, are to be found between the tropics. **1855** MISS PRATT *Flower. Pl.* III. 268 One of the plants which the botanist terms *social* because never found growing singly, but always in numbers.

**e.** Of ascidians, etc.: Compound.

**1860** *Chambers's Encycl.* I. 466/2 In some kinds (Social Ascidians), the peduncles of a number of individuals are connected by a tubular stem. **1877** HUXLEY *Anat. Inv. Anim.* x. 610 In the compound or social *Tunicata*, many ascidiozooids..are united by a common test.

**7. a.** Pertaining, relating, or due to, connected with, etc., society as a natural or ordinary condition of human life.

In this use, *social* enters into a very large number of collocations, many of which have the quality of set phrases, but have not gained specialized meanings; examples are: ***social background, barrier, capacity, climate, code, consciousness, contact, context, duty, fabric, grace, group, hierarchy, justice, mix, morality, phenomenon, prejudice, problem, question, reason, scale, sympathy, usefulness, virtue, welfare.***

**1695** LOCKE *Some Thoughts concerning Educ.* (ed. 3) 191 Careful guard ought to be kept over them [*sc.* children]; and every least slip in this great social vertue taken notice of and rectified. *a* **1704** —— *Conduct of Understanding* (1754) 164 We should love our neighbour as ourselves, is such a fundamental truth for the regulating human society, that, I think, by that alone, one might without difficulty, determine all the cases and doubts in social morality. **1729** BUTLER *Serm.* Wks. 1874 II. 16 The nature of man considered in his ..social capacity leads him to a right behaviour in society. **1751** JOHNSON *Rambler* No. 180 ¶5 He that devotes himself to retired study naturally sinks from omission to forgetfulness of social duties. **1796** H. HUNTER tr. *St.-Pierre's Stud. Nat.* (1799) II. 411 The social reason quickly recals him to personal interest. **1801** M. EDGEWORTH *Belinda* (1833) I. xvi. 135 His social prejudices were such as ..to supply the place of the power and habit of reasoning. **1814** M. BIRKBECK *Journey through France* 22 The labouring class here is certainly much higher, on the social scale, than with us. **1833** J. S. MILL in *Monthly Repos.* VII. 801 The St. Simonians are, just now, the only association of public writers existing in the world who systematically stir up from the foundation all the great social questions. **1842** COMBE *Digestion* Pref. p. xviii, The degree to which its morbid derangements undermine health, happiness, and social usefulness. **1843** Social phenomenon [see HISTORICAL *a.* (*sb.*) 2 c]. *a* **1854** J. S. MILL *Draft Autobiogr.* (1961) 173 The social problem of the future we considered to be, how to unite the greatest individual liberty of action with an equal ownership of all in the raw material of the globe & an equal participation of all in the benefits of combined labour. **1856** GEO. ELIOT in *Westm. Rev.* X. 70 The study of at least one social group—namely, the factory operatives. **1857** *Edin. Rev.* CVI. 223 Goethe's early experiences at first led him to view the whole social fabric with contempt. **1858** TROLLOPE *Dr. Thorne* I. i. 2 Its social graces, and the general air of clanship which pervades it [*sc.* Barsetshire]. **1859** THACKERAY *Virginians* II. xxxiii. 266 To marry without a competence is..a crime against our social codes. **1861** J. S. MILL in *Fraser's Mag.* Dec. 672/1 This is the highest abstract standard of social and distributive justice. **1863** *Home & Foreign Rev.* Oct. 546 The multiplicity of her characters,..the richness of her social backgrounds. **1864** Social hierarchy [see HIERARCHY 4]. **1869** MILL *Subj. Women* iv. 163 Self-respect, self-help, and self-control..are the essential conditions both of individual prosperity and of social virtue. **1871** A. C. FRASER *Life of Berkeley* ii. 88 He was shocked by the tone of social morality, which so appallingly greeted him on his return. **1872** MORLEY *Voltaire* (1886) 10 Pale unshapen embryos of social sympathy. **1876** H. SPENCER *Princ. Sociol.* I. III. ii. 629 After welfare of the social group and welfare of progeny, comes welfare of parents. **1887** J. BASCOM *Sociol.* i. 9 But, with fitting modifications, they shape also the social contact of diverse ranks. **1892** Social welfare [see WELFARE *sb.* 1]. **1897** *Amer. Jrnl. Sociol.* Nov. 343 As we say in sociological language, there was a very low degree of social consciousness. **1901** W. JAMES *Mem. & Stud.* (1911) vii. 150 There are social prejudices which scientific men themselves obey. **1901** *Amer. Jrnl. Sociol.* Nov. 399 He makes a better home and moves upward in the social scale, perhaps, faster than the immigrant from any other country. **1902** Social justice [see ENVIRONMENTAL *a.*]. **1911** M. CORELLI *Life Everlasting* ix. 210 He doesn't fit into any accepted social code at all. **1927** B. RUSSELL *Outl. Philos.* ii. 27 Knowledge ..as a social phenomenon..is something displayed in bodily movements. **1935** H. EDIB *Clown & his Daughter* xxv. 137 The shadow of a social barrier was added to the damnable shadow of separation! **1935** T. S. ELIOT *Murder in Cathedral* ii. 80 There are times when violence is the only way in which social justice can be secured. **1938** L. MACNEICE *I crossed Minch* ix. 130 A mind must be conditioned by education and social context. **1940** *Economist* 5 Oct. 428/1 More than two decades of extremely divergent developments in contrasting social climates had to be undone. **1947** *Mind* LVI. 327 If we speak of 'social problems', that is something different. **1955** T. WILLIAMS in S. J. Kunitz *20th Cent. Authors* Suppl. I. 1088/1 In St. Louis we suddenly discovered there were two kinds of people, the rich and the poor, and that we belonged more to the latter... It was the beginning of the social-consciousness which I think has marked most of my writing. **1964** M. ARGYLE *Psychol. & Social Probl.* xvi. 199 In limited spheres advice is also given by social scientists,..on the social welfare of the old, young, and poor. **1966** G. N. LEECH *Eng. in Advertising* v. 49 Slang and familiar forms of language.. help..to fix the identity and social background of the speaker. **1967** Social mix [see MIX *sb.*² 1 a]. **1970** *Guardian* 3 June 8/6 The Arts Council and its affiliated agencies..are seen as a vital part of the social fabric for which society must be responsible. **1970** F. C. Weffort in I. L. Horowitz *Masses in Lat. Amer.* xi. 391 It legalized the 'social question'; that is, it formally recognised that the masses have a right to express their aspirations. **1978** *Bookseller* 17 June 3186/3 A school with only 170 children, a high percentage of whom have severe social problems. **1981** G. Priestland *Priestland's Progress* ii. 34 The compilers of the gospels had other things on their minds than..Jewish social problems. **1982** *Times* 14 June 9/5 The bribery, abuse of privilege, and indifference to social welfare on his own [*sc.* the Labour Party] side.

**b.** Of life, conditions, institutions, etc.

**1736** Butler *Anal.* I. i. 28 When we go out of this World, we may pass into..a new State of Life and Action... And this new State may naturally be a social one. **1765** Akenside *Pleas. Imag.* II. 82 Science herself: on whom the wants and cares Of social life depend. **1830** J. S. Mill *Let.* 9 Feb. in *Wks.* (1963) XII. 48 Those parts of our social institutions and policy which at present oppose improvement. **1861** J. S. Mill *Utilit.* iii. 46 The social state is..so natural, so necessary, and so habitual to man. **1868** T. Rogers *Pol. Econ.* xiv. 183 The condition of social life is that different persons should be engaged in different pursuits. **1887** J. Payn *Holiday Tasks* 123 If people would only say what they really think concerning this and that..social life would be much more interesting. **1949** M. Fortes *Social Structure* 55 The British House of Commons is a familiar instance of growth in social institutions and organization. **1957** *Practical Wireless* XXXIII. 727/2 (Advt.), You get a welcome break from the usual routine, with sports, games and a great social life. **1974** in *Wertheim's Evolution & Revolution* 91 In looking for the structural features of social life we look first for the existence of social groups of all kinds.

**c.** Of rank, position, etc., or of persons in respect of these.

**1835** H. Reeve tr. *de Tocqueville's Democracy in Amer.* II. ix. 256 The Anglo-Americans settled in the New World in a state of social equality. **1840** *Ibid.* IV. III. xii. 106 They have allowed the social inferiority of woman to subsist. **1840** J. S. Mill in *Westm. Rev.* Mar. 262 The demoralizing effect of great inequalities in wealth and social rank. **1849** Lyell *2nd Visit U.S.* II. 316 Enjoying..an equality of social rank. **1863** W. C. Baldwin *Afr. Hunting* vii. 273 Albert Smith.. says that the colonies are only refuges for destitute social suicides. **1869** Freeman *Norm. Conq.* III. 78 The rulers of other European states were ready to receive him as their social peer. *a* **1876** H. Martineau *Autobiogr.* (1877) (ed. 3) I. 297 Norwich..has now no claims to social superiority. **1885** W. Harris *Hist. Radical Party* xvii. 429 Whigs and Conservatives alike desired..conditions and limitations which should preserve power to the same social class which had now the control of so many of the constituencies. **1888** E. Bellamy *Looking Backward* xi. 164 Who are willing to be domestic servants..where all are social equals? Our ladies found it hard enough to find such even when there was little pretense of social equality. **1917** N. Douglas *South Wind* xxxix. 453 Her home broken up; her child a bastard; herself and Meadows—social outcasts. **1925** *New Yorker* 11 July 6/1 The fact that Davis is a social outcast because of his want of faith..wouldn't cut any ice. **1928** Mrs. Belloc Lowndes *Diary* 20 Feb. (1971) 113 One of Curzon's most unfortunate peculiarities was his rudeness to those whom he considered his social inferiors. **1934** M. V. Hughes *London Child of Seventies* xiii. 159 One must never suppose that any other people whatsoever are one's social superiors. **1944** L. P. Hartley *Shrimp & Anemone* xiv. 200 The social superiority of the South over all parts of England. **1948** 'G. Orwell' in *Observer* 28 Nov. 4/4 The social misfit..should learn to be contented in his own station. **1958** J. K. Galbraith *Affluent Society* vi. 55 In the central tradition of economic theory, the existence of social classes—of capitalists, middle class, and proletarians—was only surreptitiously conceded. **1964** T. B. Bottomore *Elites & Society* i. 23 S. F. Nadel..emphasizes 'social superiority' as the distinguishing feature of an elite. **1967** A. L. Lloyd *Folk Song in Eng.* ii. 86 The medieval peasant..his illiteracy, his social inferiority. **1970** N. A. Victoria in I. L. Horowitz *Masses in Lat. Amer.* xv. 549 Among the remaining social classes, the split was reflected in general skepticism. **1973** *Listener* 28 June 863/2 The Industrial Revolution..became in time a social revolution and established that social equality on which we all depend.

**d.** *social evil*, prostitution. Also *attrib.* and *transf.* (quot. 1865).

**1857** (*title*), Great Social Evil—Prostitution, the greatest of our Social Evils. **1863** *Sat. Rev.* 626/1 The nauseous category of social-evil literature. **1865** *Slang Dict.* 239 *Social evil*, a name beginning to be applied to street-walkers in consequence of the articles in the newspapers being so headed. **1901** *Contemp. Rev.* Mar. 323 Those slums have become a pandemonium of drunkenness and the social evil.

**e.** *Social Sciences.* Pertaining or due to the interrelations resulting from an individual's association with others or connected with the functions and structures necessary to membership of a group or society. Also *transf.* in *Zool.*

There is no rigid demarcation between this sense and the primary meaning of 7 a and b; the examples given illustrate some of the uses commonly found among writers on the social sciences.

**1840** J. S. Mill in *Edin. Rev.* Oct. 5 By Democracy M. de Tocqueville understands equality of conditions; the absence of all aristocracy, whether constituted by political privileges, or by superiority in individual importance and social power. **1843** Social organism [see dynamics 1 b]. **1852** J. S. Mill in *Westm. Rev.* II. 380 Attention is due to those opinions and feelings,..not as matter of history, but as social forces in present being. **1861** —— *Repr. Govt.* iii. 68 Where this school of public spirit does not exist, scarcely any sense is entertained that private persons, in no eminent social situation, owe any duties to society, except to obey the laws and submit to the government. **1876** H. Spencer *Princ. Sociol.* I. II. iii. 487 That social integration that results from the clustering of clusters, is joined with augmentation of the number contained by each cluster. **1877** G. H. Lewes *Problems* III. 5 A new factor, namely, the social factor. **1878** W. James *Let.* 25 Nov. in R. B. Perry *Tht. & Char. of W. James* (1935) II. 35 Their only weakness would lie in the fact of their social environment not recognizing this as the ultimate interest. **1890** —— *Princ. Psychol.* I. x. 293 A man's Social Self is the recognition which he gets from his mates. **1904** —— *Mem. & Stud.* (1911) vi. 138 It would never occur to a reader of his [*sc.* Spencer's] pages that a social force proper might be anything that acted as a stimulus of social change. **1905** A. W. Small *Gen. Sociol.* xxvii. 381 It is the factor which is essential in the end, to economize and co-ordinate all the details of social adjustment. **1920** Thomas & Znaniecki *Polish Peasant* IV. p. xii, Many individuals.. consider the social isolation and relatively low cultural level of the peasant communities an undesirable phenomenon. **1934** C. W. Morris in G. H. Mead *Mind, Self & Soc.* p. xvi, Though not used by Mead, the term 'social behaviorism' may serve to characterize the relation of Mead's position to that of John B. Watson. **1936** M. Sherif *Psychol. of Social Norms* 3 We shall consider customs, traditions, standards, rules, values, fashions, and all other criteria of conduct which are standardized as a consequence of the contact of individuals, as specific cases of 'social norms'. **1936** *Amer. Jrnl. Orthopsychiatry* VI. 416 (*title*) Trends in social therapy. **1941** Miller & Dollard (*title*) Social learning and imitation. **1941** *Mind* L. 396 Boodin's reflections on society and the social behaviour of men have, obviously, been deeply influenced by these two special sorts of experiences. **1944** *Mind* LIII. 351 It is said to be evident 'on evolutionary grounds' that the individual is 'higher than the state or the social organism'. **1945** E. Mayo *Social Problems of Industrial Civilization* i. 13 Social skill shows itself as a capacity to receive communications from others, and to respond to the attitudes and ideas of others in such fashion as to promote congenial participation in a common task. **1949** M. Mead *Male & Female* i. 10 None of these powers —to kill individuals, to destroy the social integration of groups..are new. **1951** Gerth & Bramstedt tr. *Mannheim's Freedom, Power & Democratic Planning* i. 6 By social techniques I refer to all methods of influencing human behavior so that it fits into the prevailing patterns of social interaction and organization. **1959** W. F. Leopold in J. A. Fishman *Readings Sociol. of Lang.* (1968) 349 The colloquial standard [speech] of an individual has several layers suitable for a variety of social situations. **1964** M. Argyle *Psychol. & Social Probl.* viii. 108 Social factors are of considerable importance in job satisfaction, according to a number of early studies. **1975** E. O. Wilson *Sociobiol.* II. vii. 160/1 Although the development of 'social behavior' has not been analyzed in these animals, the visible responses are.. elementary and stereotyped. **1978** D. Gryll s *Guardians & Angels* i. 31 Traherne..blames the social environment instead of original sin.

**8.** *Psychol.* (See quots.)

**1785** Reid *Intell. Powers* 73 The social as well as the solitary operations of the mind. **1788** —— *Active Powers* v. vi. 664, I call those operations social which necessarily imply social intercourse.

**9.** Concerned with, interested in, the constitution of society and the problems presented by this: **a.** Of persons.

**1833** J. S. Mill in *Monthly Repos.* VII. 269 An error which many..of our social reformers, habitually fall into. **1841** C. Bray *Philos. Necessity* II. 467 A thorough Social Reformer. **1851** Mayhew *Lond. Lab.* II. 242/1 One of the most difficult topics that the social philosopher can deal with. **1859** G. A. Sala *Twice Round Clock* 36, I am glad to observe, for the edification of social economists. **1885** W. Harris *Hist. Radical Party* vii. 120 Some immediate remedy such as the Spencean and other social theorists had to offer. **1898** *Daily News* 12 Oct. 4/4 The Church had always been social and humanitarian. **1919** Branford & Geddes *Coming Polity* (ed. 2) III. i. 223 Compound these three insurgent types of social critic..and you have the disorders of Revolution. **1926** B. Webb *My Apprenticeship* v. 217 In comparison with the preceding generation of social researchers, I suggest that his [*sc.* Charles Booth's] method of analysis constitutes..the first sign-post directing the student on one of the main ways to discovery. **1931** *Times Lit. Suppl.* 22 Oct. 809/2 Like the work of so many of the 'social' novelists of his period, it is to a large extent a sort of narrative journalism of contemporary events. **1941** J. S. Huxley *Uniqueness of Man* xi. 251 Our social planners would undoubtedly benefit from a study of the evolution of individuality in animals. **1949** M. Fortes *Social Structure* p. ix, Their theme was the comparative study of human society by the methods of the natural sciences, and the difference between such studies and those of social philosophers. **1970** R. A. H. Robinson *Origins of Franco's Spain* v. 224 In the terminology of European Catholic thought, the Spanish Monarchists of the 1930s were social-romantics, the *Cedistas* social-reformists. **1970** *Guardian* 7 Aug. 10/5 [Notting Hill's] over-exposure is the result of the number of social agencies and sheer do-gooders that have moved into the area.

**b.** Of sciences, theories, etc.

**1828** J. S. Mill in *Westm. Rev.* IX. 257 In political and social philosophy his [*sc.* Sir Walter Scott's] principles are all summed up in the orthodox one, that whatever is English is best. **1835** H. Reeve tr. *de Tocqueville's Democracy in America* I. ii. 23 The..main ideas which constitute the basis of the social theory of the United States. **1836** J. S. Mill in *Westm. Rev.* XXVI. 11 *Laws* of society, or laws of human nature in the social state..form the subject of a branch of science which may be aptly designated from the title of *social economy*; somewhat less happily by that of *speculative politics*, or the *science* of politics, as contra-distinguished from the art. **1837** —— in *Ibid.* XXVIII. 100 These men raised the cry of social reform. **1841** C. Bray *Philos. Necessity* II. 404 Social Reform. **1845** Polson *Eng. Law* in *Encycl. Metrop.* II. 802/1 Social Economy.—Laws which directly consult the health, wealth, convenience or comfort of the public, may properly be referred to this head. **1887** B. Webb *My Apprenticeship* (1926) 418 Seeking justification in social research. **1899** *Amer. Jrnl. Sociol.* May 765 But they have all come by experience to discover that the social ethics of Christianity can indeed supply a moral basis of a general kind for social work and social politics. **1901** *Ibid.* Jan. 472 We have a social technology—a system of conscious and purposeful organization of persons in which every actual, natural social organization finds its true place, and all factors ..cooperate to realize an increasing aggregate and better proportions of the 'health, wealth, beauty, knowledge, sociability, and rightness' desires. **1914** G. B. Shaw *Dark Lady of Sonnets* 129 Our plays of poverty and squalor..will then be..read only by historical students of social pathology. **1914** *New Republic* 14 Nov. 28/2 The author believes that one way to write best sellers is to write filth. This is not as it should be. These two propositions, taken together, are social criticism. **1920** W. R. Sorley *Hist. Eng. Philos.* xii. 265 Maurice's..work, both in social reform and in religion, derived stimulus and direction from philosophical ideas. **1931** *Proc. Nat. Conf. Social Work 1930* 448 Social planning suggests activity on the part of groups in making planning effective in action. **1937** L. C. Knights in *Scrutiny* VI. 137 It is just possible to claim that Restoration comedy contains 'social criticism' in its handling of 'the vulgar'. **1949** *Mind* LVIII. 383 'Social theory' is the general study of the whole field of social phenomena. **1957** P. Coveney *Poor Monkey* iv. 54 The social novel of Disraeli, Mrs. Gaskell, and Kingsley..represents something essential to the literary consciousness of the age. **1964** M. Argyle *Psychol. & Social Probl.* xvi. 202 Another objection to social planning is that it is felt to increase the power of the state and restrict individual freedom. **1976** *Listener* 3 June 705/3 A different style of thought in social philosophy.. post-Marxist critique. **1979** A. Easson *Elizabeth Gaskell* ii. 61 *Mary Barton* and *North and South* are often spoken of in the context of social fiction. **1980** *Times* 9 Jan. 10/3 The British tradition of politically committed social research.

**c.** Of activities, etc., carried out (esp. by government agencies) to improve the condition of society or for the benefit of society as a whole.

**1964** *Times Rev. Industry & Technol.* Jan. 65/3 The large backlog in 'social' investments—schools, hospitals, public and private housing. **1965** B. Pearce tr. *Preobrazhensky's New Economics* 222 Where the tractor is acquired by society as a whole it will facilitate the transition to the social cultivation of the land throughout the countryside. **1973** *Listener* 1 Mar. 287/2 Love of the poor needs social legislation to stiffen it up. **1977** *Spare Rib* Jan. 25/1 Legislation is ineffectual while cuts in social spending continue.

**10.** ***social chauvinism***, a communist term for the attitude or action of a socialist party which supports the non-socialist government of its country in the prosecution of a war; so ***social chauvinist*** sb. and adj.; ***social democracy***, (the advocacy of) a socialist system achieved by democratic means (formerly also a general term for socialism and communism); ***social democrat***, a member of a political party having socialistic views; also applied *spec.* to a member of the communist party in Russia and elsewhere; now applied chiefly to one who advocates the achievement of socialism by democratic means; *esp.* in the U.K., a member of the Social Democratic Party; hence ***social democratic*** adj., now *esp.* in the U.K. designating a party founded in March 1981 by a group of former Labour MPs; also in extended use; ***social fascist***, term used by communists for a member of any other left-wing party (implying the identity of non-communist socialism with fascism); hence ***social fascism***; ***social-imperialism***, a term used at one time in China (and occas. elsewhere) for policies held to conceal imperialist aims beneath a socialist veneer; hence ***social imperialist***; ***social revolutionary*** adj., advocating or supporting social revolution (applied *spec.* to a former political party in Russia); also as *sb.*

**1976** H. T. Willetts tr. *A. Solzhenitsyn's Lenin in Zurich* 256 'The development of the international socialist movement', he [*sc.* Lenin] wrote, 'is moving slowly..but definitely in the direction of "a break" with opportunism and social chauvinism.' **1957** R. N. Carew Hunt *Guide to Communist Jargon* xliv. 147 The social chauvinists are the socialist leaders who were supporting their bourgeois governments in prosecuting the war as one of national defence. **1974** J. White tr. *Poulantzas's Fascism & Dictatorship* IV. ii. 185 It was during this same period, mainly after 1930, that the *social-chauvinist* side of KPD policy grew decisively. **1888** G. B. Shaw in *Fabian Essays in Socialism* (1889) 183 What then does a gradual transition to Social Democracy mean specifically? It means the gradual extension of the franchise; and the transfer of rent and interest to the State. **1928** [see centrist b]. **1947** *Vogue* May 104/3 Sweden represents the best way of existence a flourishing social-democracy has yet found. **1974** J. White tr. *Poulantzas's Fascism & Dictatorship* IV. i. 151 Social democracy, except sometimes in revolutionary periods, has in principle a permanent mass basis in a capitalist formation. **1981** *Times* 10 Mar. 1/6 Mr Jenkins said that 'well before Easter' the Council for Social Democracy would have been turned into the Social Democrat Party. **1877** *St. James's Gaz.* 7 Mar. (Cassell), This long period of activity has enabled the Social Democrats to found no fewer than twenty-five clubs in London. **1881** Social democrat [see proletariate, -at 2 a]. **1899** *Daily News* 19 July 5/5 The Clericals did not shrink from concluding a regular pact with the Social Democrats. **1918** [see minimalist 1]. **1947** *Partisan Rev.* XIV. 312 Barea was one of those gray murky middle-class Social Democrats who made of his adherence a means of avoiding rather than of engaging in political thought. **1965** *New Statesman* 14 May 753/2 A preference for the Social Democrat stronghold [*sc.* Berlin] over the Christian Democrat capital [*sc.* Bonn]. **1974** tr. *Sniečkus's Soviet Lithuania* 13 During the revolution, increasing numbers of Lithuanian Social-Democrats urged that their party unite with the Russian Social-Democratic Labour Party. **1981** *Times* 26 Mar. 14/8 We have gained the sympathy of a quarter of Britain's voters, and between a third and two-fifths if Social Democrats fight together with Liberals. **1870** *Times* 10 Oct. 3/2 General von Falkenstein has issued the following order:—'The prohibition to hold social Democratic meetings is rescinded.' **1887** [see

INTERNATIONAL *a.* 1 b]. **1893** W. C. ROBINSON tr. *Ten Brink's Hist. Eng. Lit.* II. IV. 24 Many influences . . worked together to produce that social-democratic rising. **1966** I. DEUTSCHER in *Marxism in Our Time* (1972) 36 Trotsky . . represents the Marxist school of thought in its purity, as it existed before its debasement by the social-democratic and Stalinist orthodoxies. **1975** *Times Lit. Suppl.* 23 May 563/4 Recommendations which ranged from orthodox socialist models to moderately social-democratic solutions. **1981** *Guardian* 26 Mar. 4/8 The Social Democratic Party will be launched today. **1981** *Times* 12 Dec. 7/1 It is essential . . to divine in good time which of the two mutually exclusive positions on the subject [of snow] will be taken by each person one meets. As far as snow is concerned, there is no middle ground, no Social Democratic stance. **1941** 'G. ORWELL' in V. Gollancz *Betrayal of Left* 210 All orthodox Communists were committed to the belief that 'Social-fascism' (i.e. Socialism) was the real enemy of the workers. **1974** J. WHITE tr. *Poulantzas's Fascism & Dictatorship* IV. i. 149 It was no accident that the theory of social fascism was unfailingly accompanied by the identification of fascism with the other forms of bourgeois State. *a* **1937** J. BELL in *Essays, Poems & Lett.* (1938) II. 294 'The adversary.' He takes the form of an enthusiastic member of the Young Communist League and he bellows incessantly. That I am a social-democratic, social-fascist, weak-kneed traitor. That I am a bourgeois intellectual. **1961** [see FASCIST *sb.* and *a.*]. **1975** *Guardian* 19 Mar. 2/3 Their [*sc.* the Portuguese Maoists'] stated philosophy is that the Armed Forces movement, the Communist Party, and other left-wing groups are 'Social Fascists'. **1965** tr. *Lenin's Tasks of Third International* in *Coll. Works* XXIX. 502 'Fabian imperialism' and 'social-imperialism' are one and the same thing: socialism in words, imperialism in deeds. **1971** Social imperialism [see REVISIONIST *a.*]. **1978** HUA KUO-FENG in *Peking Rev.* 10 Mar. 35/2 The people's struggle against them, and in particular against Soviet social-imperialism, is on a higher upsurge than ever. **1974** *China Reconstructs* July 4/1 The Soviet revisionist social-imperialists bill Confucius as 'the most holy sage and foremost teacher of China.' **1907** Social revolutionary [see INTEGRALIST *sb.*]. **1918** [see MINIMALIST 1]. **1931** E. WILSON *Axel's Castle* viii. 270 He [*sc.* Rimbaud] had flamed up, at the fall of the Second Empire, with social-revolutionary idealism. **1978** *Listener* 17 Aug. 206/2 Lenin proposed that the land should be given to the peasants. The indignant social revolutionaries shouted out, 'But that's our programme . . and you have opposed it.'

**11.** *Comb.* with other adjs., as ***social-conscious, -cultural, -economic, -emotional, -ethical, -minded, -philosophical, -political, -relational, -religious, -situational.***

**1856** GEO. ELIOT in *Westm. Rev.* X. 68 The views at which he has arrived . ., he sums up in the term—*social-political-conservatism.* **1890** GROSS *Gild Merch.* I. 163 At Barnstaple . . the Gild Merchant seems to have been transformed into a social-religious gild. **1899** *Daily News* 21 June 4/3 Parliament is at last tired of social-political experiments. **1919** M. BEER *Hist. Brit. Socialism* I. I. v. 71 A serious contribution to social-economic speculation. **1932** *Addresses & Proc. Nat. Educ. Assoc. of U.S.* LXX. 231 It has been thought that social-economic planning in the United States would break down our democratic form of government. **1939** A. HUXLEY *After Many a Summer* II. v. 229 For these . . 'normality' in sexual behaviour would be quite different from what it was for the more social-minded. **1940** K. MANNHEIM *Ideology & Utopia* 35 The discovery of the social-situational roots of thought at first, therefore, took the form of unmasking. **1942** C. HIMES *Black on Black* (1973) 183 His social-conscious protestations of hurt had leapt the bounds of amateur sincerity. **1951** PARSONS & SHILS *Toward General Theory of Action* I. i. 18 Fundamentals of behavior psychology . . primary viscerogenic and possibly social-relational needs, cognition and learning. **1956** J. KLEIN *Study of Groups* viii. 118 Social-emotional behaviour. **1960** C. S. LEWIS *Studies in Words* i. 22 Thus from the very first the social-ethical meaning, merely by existing, is bound to separate itself from the status-meaning. **1970** A. G. FRANK in I. L. Horowitz *Masses in Lat. Amer.* vi. 220 There are undoubtedly differences in . . various social-cultural indices between the self-built and the other two types of low-income urban settlements. **1977** A. GIDDENS *Stud. in Social & Polit. Theory* viii. 291 Durkheim . . was very critical of some features of Comte's social-philosophical writings.

**12.** Special collocations. **social action**, deliberate action that results in the restructuring of institutions or a change in the conditions of life in a society; **social anthropology**, the study of (esp. primitive) peoples comparatively through their kinship systems, associations, institutions, culture, etc., and the forces that affect their social systems; hence **social anthropological** *a.*, **social anthropologist**; **social benefit**, (*a*) a benefit to society resulting from technological innovation and the like; (*b*) a benefit (BENEFIT *sb.* 4 d) payable under a system of social security; **social butterfly**, a person who flits from one social entertainment to another or is chiefly occupied with social activities, a socialite; **social case-work, case-worker** = CASE-WORK, CASE-WORKER; **social causation**, the causation of human actions by social factors, or their analysis in these terms; **social centre**, any place in which people gather for communal activities, recreations, etc., *esp.* a building designed for this purpose; **social change**, change in the customs, institutions, or culture of a society brought about by some new, esp. technological or ideological, element; **social character** (see quots.); **social climber**, one who seeks to advance himself socially, esp. by gaining acceptance in fashionable society; hence (as back-formations) **social climb** *sb.* and *v. intr.*, **social climbing** *vbl. sb.* and *ppl. a.*; **social column**, a column in a newspaper or magazine that reports the activities of members of fashionable or leisured society; hence **social columnist**; **social compact** = *social contract*, below; **social conscience**, a conscience that is sensitive to or preoccupied with the problems and injustices of society; **social contract**, (*a*) the mutual agreement which, according to Rousseau's *Contrat social* (1762), forms the basis of human society; (*b*) *transf.*, a mutual agreement between specific groups or elements within a society; **social control**, control of the individual by the social group to which he belongs; control by government, on behalf of society as a whole, of particular sectors of society; **social cost**, the cost to society in terms of effort, ill-health, inconvenience, etc., of some enterprise or innovation; **social cycle** (see quot. 1963); **social Darwinism** *Sociol.*, the Darwinian theory of evolution extended and applied to various aspects of the concept of social progress; hence **social Darwinist** *sb.* and *a.*; **social deprivation**, deprivation of social interaction or of the ordinary benefits of social life; **social dialectology**, the study of the dialects spoken by particular social groups; hence **social dialectologist**; **social differentiation**, the process whereby a group or community becomes separate or distinct; the process whereby the different roles and functions of individuals become institutionalized; **social disease**, any social evil such as poverty, starvation, etc.; *spec. U.S.*, venereal disease (orig. a euphemism); **social disorganization** (see quot. 1920); **social distance** *Social Psychol.*, (*a*) the degree of remoteness that a member of one social group would like to exist or feels to exist between himself and the members of another, expressed (for example) in terms of the relationships to which he would admit them; (*b*) the physical distance between individuals that they find acceptable in social contexts; **social document**, a literary work embodying an authentic and informative description of the social conditions of its time; also *transf.*; **social drinking** *vbl. sb.*, the drinking of alcoholic liquor as a stimulus to, or an accompaniment of, social intercourse; hence as *ppl. a.* and (as back-formations) **social drink** *sb.*, **social drinker**; **social dynamics**, (the branch of sociology treating of) the forces at work in social change; **social engineering** orig. *U.S.*, the application of sociological principles to specific social problems; hence **social engineer**, a specialist in this field; **social evolution**: see EVOLUTION 9; **social fact**, something originating in the institutions or culture of a society which affects the behaviour or attitudes of the individual member of that society; **social geography** (see quot. 1929); hence **social geographer**; **social gospel**, an understanding of the gospel as having especially a social application; used esp. with reference to many U.S. churchmen of the late nineteenth and early twentieth centuries who advocated social reform through the Christian gospel; also *gen.*, a message of salvation for society; **social history**, (*a*) the history of social behaviour or of society (the usual sense); (*b*) the background and circumstances of a social worker's client; hence (in sense (*a*)) **social historian, social-historical** *a.*; **social inquiry report** (see quot. 1967); **social insurance**, the insurance of the citizen against loss of income through sickness, unemployment, etc., with the participation of the government and the employer; also in extended use and *attrib.*; **social lie**, an untrue statement designed to facilitate social relations; hence **social liar**; **social medicine** (see quot. 1925); **social mobility** = MOBILITY[1] 1 c; **social mobilization** *Sociol.*, (see quot. 1961); **social morphology**, (the study of) the various forms of social structure and the changes that take place within them or govern them; **social order**, (*a*) orderliness within society, absence of disorder and unrest; (*b*) the way in which society is organized at a given time, the constituted social system; **social organization**: see ORGANIZATION 2 c; **social ownership** *Socialism*, a form of collective ownership in which the organization and control of an enterprise is shared; esp. ownership and control of an industry, company, etc., by those who work in it (see quot. 1984) or else by the community at large; **social position**: see POSITION *sb.* 9 b; **social process**, a pattern that can be discerned in the way a society coheres and adapts to change over a period of years; **social psychiatry**, the branch of mental health concerned with the social causes and social consequences of mental illness and with the various social methods which may be used to treat such illness; hence **social psychiatric** *a.*, **social psychiatrist**; **social psychology**, the study of human behaviour as it is affected by social factors; hence **social-psychological** *a.*, **social psychologist**; cf. *collective psychology* s.v. COLLECTIVE *a.* 2 d; **social realism**, realism in art and literature that has a specifically social or political content or message; sometimes applied *spec.* to a movement in U.S. art in the 1930s; also *attrib.*; hence **social realist** *sb.* and *a.*, **social realistic** *a.*; **social reality**, a conception of what exists that is affected by the customs and beliefs of the group; **social register** orig. *U.S.*, a register or directory of those who are socially prominent; *transf.*, a union black list; also *attrib.* or as *adj.*; **social releaser** = RELEASER c; **social revolution**, a revolution in the structure and nature of society; *spec.* that anticipated or fostered by socialists and communists (cf. *social revolutionary a.* and *sb.*, sense 10 above); **social role** = RÔLE 2; **social secretary**, a secretary whose function it is to make arrangements for the social activities of a person or society; **social space** *Sociol.*, the 'space', in terms of the difference in social position or individual freedom of action, that is felt to exist between one person and another; **social statics** *Sociol.*, the study of the organization and structure of a stable society or social group; **social status**: see STATUS 3; **social stratification**, the division of society into strata based on social position or class; **social strata, stratum**: see STRATUM 6; **social structure**, the established set of customs, relationships, institutions, etc., of which a social system is composed; hence **social structural** *a.*; **social studies**, an inclusive term for various aspects or branches of the study of human society; **social survey**, a comprehensive and detailed examination of some aspect of the social life, history, problems, etc., of a particular locality; **social system**, a set of interdependent relationships, customs, institutions, etc., that constitute a society; **social table** (see quot. 1952); **social unit**, an individual considered as one of the separate parts of which a society or group is composed; a community or group considered as having a separate identity within a larger whole; **social wage** (see quot. 1975); also *transf.*; **social will**, a term for the desires regarding the affairs of a society or group expressed by its members in general.

**1853** H. MARTINEAU tr. *Comte's Positive Philos.* II. viii. 246 Its distinctive social action . . was well represented by the noble Fabricius. **1873** H. SPENCER *Study of Sociol.* i. 2 Minds in which the conceptions of social actions are thus rudimentary, are also minds ready to harbour wild hopes of benefits to be achieved by administrative agencies. **1937** T. PARSONS (*title*) The structure of social action. **1951** R. FIRTH *Elements of Social Organization* i. 33 No social action, no element of culture, can be adequately studied or defined in isolation. **1953** in S. Tax et al. *Appraisal of Anthropology Today* xiii. 220/2 The outline . . does not vary much from subjects . . considered to be in the cultural/social-anthropological field. **1927** OGBURN & GOLDENWEISER *Social Sciences* ii. 11 Then there are the social anthropologists who make economic activity the basis of social anthropology. **1896** *Academy* 18 Jan. 49/1 Dr. Steinmetz . . found processes of moral, political, and religious development so intricately entwined, that his researches had to spread far over the field of social anthropology. **1908** J. G. FRAZER *Psyche's Task* (1913) 159 (*heading*) The scope of social anthropology, an Inaugural Lecture. **1975** M. BRADBURY *History Man* ix. 147, I worked in social anthropology with him . . he's certainly not a racist. **1872** GEO. ELIOT *Middlemarch* III. lvi. 241 Your neatly-carved argument for a social benefit which they [*sc.* rustics] do *not* feel. **1963** *Listener* 23 May 855/1 Dr Beesley . . and I have attempted a so-called social-benefit study or, as it is sometimes called, a cost-benefit analysis, of the London Victoria line. **1963** J. R. SARGENT in M. Shanks *Lessons of Public Enterprise* xv. 250 A balancing of social benefits against social costs. **1972** *Guardian* 30 Dec. 4/1 From Monday every citizen of the nine nations . . is entitled to the same pay and . . social benefits . . as fellow Europeans. **1910** A. E. HOUSMAN *Let.* 4 Mar. (1971) 108 People are asking me out a great deal too often . . I am not a social butterfly. **1938** D. DU MAURIER *Rebecca* ix. 117 A social butterfly, very modern and plastered with paint. **1975** D. RAMSAY *Descent into Dark* i. 15 To be a social butterfly and make my wife happy. **1917** M. E. RICHMOND *Social Diagnosis* 5 The methods and aims of social case work were or should be the same in every type of service. *Ibid.*, The ground which all social case workers could occupy in common. **1896** F. H. GIDDINGS *Princ. Sociol.* i. 20 Thus the cycle of social causation begins and ends in the physical process. **1937** R. M. MACIVER *Society* xxvi. 476 In social causation there is a logical order of relationship between the factors that we do not find in physical causation. 1964 GOULD & KOLB *Dict. Social Sciences* 647/1 There has been much discussion about the relationship between ideas of social causation and the problem of the freedom of the individual will. 1901 *Amer. Jrnl. Sociol.* Sept. 206 Is there not room for the school..in providing accessible and agreeable social centers? 1922 L. MUMFORD in H. Stearns *Civilization in U.S.* 6 The social centre and the community centre, which in a singularly hard and consciously beatific way have sought to organize fellowship and mutual aid.., are products of the last decade. 1937 *Discovery* Feb. 47/1 Social amelioration through a special milk scheme, a special housing scheme, and the encouragement of camps and social centres. 1978 J. ANDERSON *Angel of Death* v. 42 The main saloon..was the social centre of the yacht. 1836 J. S. MILL in *London & Westm. Rev.* Jan. 28 The main thing which social changes can do for the..higher classes..is gradually to put an end to every kind of unearned distinction. 1856 A. C. FRASER *Ess. Philos.* i. 11 The most memorable religious and social change which the world has witnessed since the introduction of Christianity. 1952 GERTH & MARTINDALE in *Weber's Ancient Judaism* p. xviii, A second sociological issue of concern to Weber is the examination of social changes due to territorial organization and urbanization. 1942 E. FROMM *Fear of Freedom* 239 The social character comprises only a selection of traits, the essential nucleus of the character structure of most members of a group which has developed as the result of the basic experiences and mode of life common to that group. 1961 R. H. WILLIAMS *Long Revol.* I. iii. 79 The 'social character' is a selective response to experience, a learned system of feeling and acting, in a majority of the community into which the child is born. 1975 G. HOWELL *In Vogue* 151/2 Sweaters appear... Their social climb touches its peak..over a grandly outsize evening skirt. 1962 *Sunday Express* 21 Jan. 1/3 Allegations that I was social-climbing among royalty. 1926 S. LEWIS *Mantrap* viii. 95 You sniveling little social climber! 1941 A. CHRISTIE *Evil under Sun* ix. 178 There are many of your English idioms that describe him. The rough diamond! The self-made man! The social climber! 1973 *Black World* Mar. 21 Whatever the shortcomings of our early literary efforts, they ought not be considered in the main as the reprehensible fumblings of middle-class social-climbers. 1924 W. HOLTBY *Crowded Street* xxxviii. 294 The careful tact of years of social climbing. 1927 P. SOROKIN *Social Mobility* vii. 133 There are two types of vertical mobility: ..*social climbing* and *social sinking*. 1938 AUDEN & ISHERWOOD *On Frontier* III. ii. 107 A social-climbing wife and a playboy son. 1960 *Twentieth Century* Dec. 588 A political thriller about a middle-aged reporter who learns of a major scandal involving a Minister of the Crown... Good pictures of the social-climbing Minister,..and various Fleet Street characters. 1978 *Trans. Yorks. Dial. Soc.* LXXVIII. 12 He takes the opportunity to castigate the creeping hypocrisy and social climbing which had always called forth his most bitter satire. 1936 'R. WEST' *Thinking Reed* vii. 223 A crowded paragraph in the social column of the Paris New York *Herald*. 1952 M. ALLINGHAM *Tiger in Smoke* i. 9 Every social column in the country had announced that she was about to marry him. 1976 'R. MACDONALD' *Blue Hammer* ix. 43, I don't intend to write a social column for the rest of my life. 1976 M. GREEN *Children of Sun* vi. 209 Hannen Swaffer was the first social columnist who knew from inside the world he wrote about. 1793, etc. Social compact [see COMPACT *sb.*[1] 1 b]. 1974 *Times* 26 Feb. 12/3 Mr Wilson has sought to defend this rubbish by arguing that a great new 'social compact' with the unions will be achieved, by the terms of which they will agree to forgo wage-increases in return for all the splendidly socialist things Mr Wilson's Government will be doing. 1883 B. POTTER *Let.* July in *Lett. Sidney & Beatrice Webb* (1978) I. 16 So ends the London Season! and I shall return with clear social conscience to my dowdy dress. 1888 G. B. SHAW in *Fabian Essays in Socialism* (1889) 185 The value of Trade Unionism in awakening the social conscience of the skilled workers. 1925 A. HUXLEY *Those Barren Leaves* I. iii. 35 When our dividends came rolling in..we did, it is true, feel almost a twinge of social conscience. 1978 *Architectural Design* 5 June 311/3 Public libraries and art galleries were built by..millionaires with a social conscience. 1849-50 ALISON *Hist. Europe* I. iii. §90. 351 Rousseau's dreams on the social contract. 1967 B. R. WILLIAMS *New Social Contract* 4 In a modern industrial nation..the individual and the community enter in effect into a Social Contract, by which the group as a whole agrees to dedicate a certain part of its total assets..to the provision of benefits for its members. 1972 *Times* 3 Oct. 1/1 'We say that what Britain needs is a new social contract,' Mr Callaghan said. 1974 *Socialist Worker* 23 Nov. 3/4 The last week has seen two massive holes punched through the Social Contract. First by the Rolls-Royce workers in getting their £8 a week rise, then [etc.]. 1977 *Guardian Weekly* 11 Sept. 5/5 The greatest strength of our unarmed police force lies ..in its social contract with the public. 1859 MILL *Liberty* i. 14 The practical question, where to place the limit—how to make the fitting adjustment between individual independence and social control—is a subject on which nearly everything remains to be done. 1896 E. A. ROSS in *Amer. Jrnl. Sociol.* Mar. 519 By Social Control, on the other hand, I mean that ascendancy over the aims and acts of the individual which is exercised on behalf of the group. 1898 F. H. GIDDINGS *Elem. Sociol.* xix. 217 Social control, manifesting itself in the authoritative organization of society as the state, and acting through the organs of government, is sovereignty. 1913 L. T. HOBHOUSE *Devel. & Purpose* p. xvii, A new demand for the extension of collective responsibility and the social control of industrial life. 1951 N. ANNAN *Leslie Stephen* vii. 218 The field of what is now called social control. How do law, custom, religion and moral codes govern men's actions? 1972 *Guardian* 29 Mar. 14/3 By closing its doors relatively early, the public transport system is an effective measure of social control over non-car owners. 1901 *Amer. Jrnl. Sociol.* July 137 For marginal social cost always equals marginal social utility. 1927 G. D. H. COLE *Econ. System* vii. 62 Social cost simply cannot be measured in terms of money, but only in the last resort in terms of human effort and destruction of natural resources. 1977 *N.Y. Rev. Bks.* 31 Mar. 21/2 Rehabilitation [of housing]..has proved to be cheaper in social costs. 1961 *B.S.I. News* Nov. 11/2 The new regulations..also lay down requirements about the lights to be carried on four-wheeled 'social cycles', now common in holiday areas. 1963 *Daily Tel.* 8 July 11/8 A young woman holidaymaker riding a 'social-cycle' was killed... The cycles are often seen at seaside resorts. They are like tricycles with two people sitting beside each other on a bench. 1887 *Mind* XII. 627 There can be no 'social Darwinism'. Social progress is not essentially the result of a struggle, but of intelligence. 1972 P. B. MEDAWAR *Hope of Progress* 71 Social Darwinism in the form expounded by Haeckel provided a theoretical justification for the great biological crimes of Fascism. 1907 *Amer. Jrnl. Sociol.* XII. 709 The great writers on race-struggles never use the term 'social Darwinism' but a number of sociologists have called them 'social Darwinists'. 1945 R. HOFSTADTER *Social Darwinism in Amer. Thought* ii. 25 In applying evolution to society, Spencer, and after him the Social Darwinists, were simply doing poetic justice to its origins. 1981 J. SUTHERLAND *Bestsellers* iv. 57 There is no room for..cosiness in Hailey's social-Darwinist universe. 1958 *Jrnl. Abnormal & Social Psychol.* LVI. 49 (*title*) The effect of brief social deprivation on behaviors for a social re-inforcer. 1979 W. J. FISHMAN *Streets of E. London* 52/2 The social deprivation inherent in East End life. 1977 *Publ. Amer. Dial. Soc.* 1974 LXI/LXII. 4 Social dialectologists in recent years have made numerous attempts to describe the speech of black Americans. 1981 *Amer. Speech* LVI. 104 Social dialectologists..have also neglected important work of the area linguists. 1970 *Jrnl. Eng. Linguistics* IV. 46 (*title*) Social dialectology in America: a critical survey. *Ibid.*, Although..Mencken..and others had discussed American social dialects, the systematic study of the sociology of American English really began in the late 1920's. 1976 *General Linguistics* XVI. 32 *Rustic* is an example of social dialectology at its thoroughly honest best. 1872 H. SPENCER in *Contemp. Rev.* XX. 317 The primary social differentiation which we have noted between the regulative part and the operative part, is presently followed by a distinction.. between the internal arrangements of the two parts. 1903 L. F. WARD *Pure Sociol.* II. x. 202, I propose to use..the sufficiently vague..term *race*..for all the different kinds of social groups that were formed during the process of social differentiation. 1926 C. C. NORTH *Social Differentiation* i. 5 It is essential to any proper understanding of social differentiation that some effort be made to distinguish between the biological and the social in the sources or causes of social distinctions. 1971 F. R. ALLEN *Socio-Cultural Dynamics* iii. 72 Social differentiation as a major view of change. 1891 T. H. HUXLEY (*title*) Social diseases and worse remedies. 1907 *Amer. Jrnl. Sociol.* July 20 (*title*) Prophylaxis of social diseases. 1945 G. ENDORE *Methinks the Lady* vii. 138 What rights? Overtime pay, maybe? Union hours? Sure. Social security, maybe? Or social diseases? 1970 *Guardian* 28 Apr. 10/1 Hard drugs addiction..is a contagious social disease. 1978 R. LUDLUM *Holcroft Covenant* xxvii. 314 She was probably an ODESSA agent and you've come down with a social disease, as planned. 1920 THOMAS & ZNANIECKI *Polish Peasant* IV. i. 2 The question of social disorganization. We can define the latter briefly as a decrease of the influence of existing social rules of behavior upon individual members of the group. 1958 M. ARGYLE *Relig. Behaviour* xi. 136 The evidence showing how the level of mental disorder increases with social disorganization. 1924 R. E. PARK in *Jrnl. Appl. Sociol.* VIII. 344 Prejudice is ..a sort of spontaneous conservation which tends to preserve the social order and the social distances upon which that order rests. 1948 M. SHERIF *Outl. Social Psychol.* xiv. 341 The *average*..member of a group exhibits the degree of prejudice toward the member of another group prescribed by the social distance scale of his group. 1955 G. SIRCOM tr. *Hediger's Psychol. & Behaviour Captive Animals* vi. 83 According to its species, each individual keeps at a greater or lesser distance from its group; that is, the group shows specific social distance. 1960 *Jrnl. Abnormal & Social Psychol.* LXI. 110/1 Bogardus'..ordinal scale of social distance in which a subject indicated zero social distance by stating that he was willing to marry a member of a particular ethnic group, and maximum social distance by stating that he would exclude such a person from the country. 1966 E. T. HALL *Hidden Dimension* x. 115 Desks in the offices of important people are large enough to hold visitors at the far phase of social distance. 1978 P. BAILEY *Leisure & Class in Victorian Eng.* iv. 105 The middle classes were acutely concerned to reinforce, not reduce, social distance. 1921 Social document [see SHOT *sb.*[1] 7 g(a)]. 1937 S. JAMESON in *Fact* May 87/1 Several times on the road to Wigan pier George Orwell stops to give us his frank opinion of socialists as he has met them... In the first part of the book he has provided a social document as vivid, bitter, and telling as one could have asked. 1959 I. & P. OPIE *Lore & Lang. Schoolch.* p. v, This pioneer work and social document of first importance is..something of a curiosity. 1974 *Country Life* 30 May 1339/3 This painting of the *Lawn at Goodwood* 1886..has been purchased by the Goodwood Trust for 7,000 gn. I find it a decided non-event in the world of art, but a social document of real importance. 1976 *New Yorker* 12 Jan. 47/2 He's been boozing. And I don't mean he's just had a 'social' drink or two. 1969 in Halpert & Story *Christmas Mumming in Newfoundland* 84 Deep Harbour fishermen have traditionally celebrated Christmas by group visiting, whether as mummers or as 'social drinkers'. 1977 E. LEONARD *Unknown Man* xiv. 120 I wasn't an alcoholic. I was a heavy social drinker. 1901 B. S. ROWNTREE *Poverty* 316 This [public] house is evidently one where 'social' drinking is carried on. 1958 KELLER & SEELEY *Alcohol Lang.* 22 *Social drinking*. 1. Moderate drinking on social occasions. 2. Drinking to comply with the expectation of companions. 3. Drinking in a way and within the limits accepted by a cultural group. 1969 in Halpert & Story *Christmas Mumming in Newfoundland* 82 At night throngs of 'social-drinking' men threading their way along the narrow footpaths sing between visits. 1843 Social dynamics [see DYNAMICS 1 b]. 1938 B. RUSSELL *Power* i. 11 The laws of social dynamics are laws which can only be stated in terms of power, not in terms of this or that form of power. 1974 *Howard Jrnl.* XIV. 97 Over-crowding and..the introduction of strangers into the resident group, or other alterations in the social dynamics. 1900 W. H. TOLMAN *Industrial Betterment* II. 81 'Of course you are too busy.. and..need someone on your staff whose sole business will be the planning and direction of movements to improve industrial conditions; in other words you need a social engineer.' Social engineering is a new profession. 1980 *Gazette* (Montreal) 22 Mar. 109/2 Woodward and Armstrong..revile the efforts of President and Congress to appoint Supreme Court judges who will not act as left-of-center social engineers. 1899 *Social Engineering* Sept. 18 The following subjects were adopted for A Course of Lectures on Modern Social Problems... Social Engineering a New Profession. 1919 M. BEER *Hist. Brit. Socialism* II. xiv. 287 The Fabian Society appears to form an institute for social engineering. 1945 K. R. POPPER *Open Society* I. ix. 138 The Platonic approach..can be called *Utopian engineering*, as opposed to that kind of social engineering.. which may be described by the name of *piecemeal engineering*. 1980 *Jrnl. R. Soc. Arts* May 351/2 A sort of extension of Architecture..as a vast subject in its own right with a powerful social-engineering content. 1843 J. S. MILL *Logic* II. IV. v. 273 There is hardly a single name, expressive of any moral or social fact calculated to call forth strong affections.., which does not carry with it..a connotation of those strong affections. 1887 MOORE & AVELING tr. *Marx's Capital* I. i. 44 The mutual exchangeability of all kinds of useful private labour is an established social fact. 1938 SOLOVAY & MUELLER tr. *Durkheim's Rules Sociol. Method* p. liii, We gave a definition of social facts as ways of acting or thinking with the peculiar characteristic of exercising a coercive influence on individual consciousnesses. 1977 P. LASLETT *Family Life* 2 History stands as much in need of a theory of itself as of any other form of generalization about social facts. 1929 P. GEDDES in *Sociol. Rev.* XXI. 7 It is a commonplace to every social geographer, that of all forms of rural development over Europe, it is the forest which most definitely thrives and prospers under collective ownership. 1980 *Verbatim* Autumn 1/1 Social geographers are aware of this, of course; it is interesting to find concurrent evidence from a linguistic survey. 1907 G. W. HOKE in *Geogr. Jrnl.* XXIX. 67 In addition to the physiographical group of factors which are by common consent held to be fundamental, the sociological factors are no less fundamental to social geography. 1929 HUNTINGTON & CARLSON *Environmental Basis of Social Geogr.* i. 5 Social geography examines it [*sc.* the relationship between man and his environment] from the point of view of man and his activities, that is, the social aspect. 1886 C. O. BROWN *Talks on Labor Troubles* i. 9 These views..are being read as a new social gospel by hundreds of thousands of people. 1890 *Dawn* II. Suppl. 1 In man's relation to man, Jesus Christ preached a *social* gospel; accordingly, in those relations, his disciples must be socialists. 1917 W. RAUSCHENBUSCH *Theol. for Social Gospel* i. 1 We have a social gospel. We need a systematic theology large enough to match it. *Ibid.* 2 The social gospel has become orthodox. *Ibid.* xix. 279 The social gospel is the voice of prophecy in modern life. 1958 M. ARGYLE *Relig. Behaviour* v. 45 A small college at which it seems that a modernistic and social gospel was widely held among the staff. 1969 A. RICHARDSON *Dict. Christian Theol.* 313/2 The christology of the social gospel focuses on the way the divine life of Christ can get control of human society. *Ibid.*, There were other conspicuous leaders of the social gospel. 1912 A. CONAN DOYLE in *Strand Mag.* Dec. 603/1 There are few social historians of those days who have not told of the long and fierce struggle between..Sir Charles Tregellis and Lord Barrymore. 1973 *Listener* 25 Oct. 571/1 Social historians must do the best they can with such evidence as they have. 1897 *Library Jrnl.* Mar. 139 'Colonial Days in old New York'..is really of the social historical order rather than a book of travel. 1937 *Burlington Mag.* June 310/1 The historical section..is sketchy..and its lack of concentration results in an apparent insufficiency of social-historical facts to explain stylistic changes. 1977 A. WILSON *Strange Ride of R. Kipling* vii. 342, I prefer..a social-historical description of long generations of Evangelical belief ending in post-Darwinian doubt. 1856 G. ROBERTS *Social Hist. of People of Southern Counties of England in Past Centuries* p. v, Researches..disclosed many particulars of the former condition of our countrymen... These have been made available for the express correction of a very general ignorance of our Social History that prevails. 1877 L. H. MORGAN *Ancient Society* II. i. 50 It represents a striking phase of the ancient social history of our race. 1950 MCDOUGALL & CORMACK in C. Morris *Social Casework in Great Britain* ii. 40 The social history..is the essential basis of constructive help. It does not follow from this that.. every client's story must be fully investigated. 1970 D. C. GIBBONS *Delinquent Behaviour* iii. 48 The social history document prepared by the probation officer..looms large in the disposition of the case. 1976 W. GÉRIN *Elizabeth Gaskell* xiv. 152 From the point of view of social history, *North and South* is but a poor successor to the realities of *Mary Barton*. 1967 *Act Eliz. II* c.80 §57 A court of any prescribed class shall before passing on any person a sentence to which the rules apply consider a social inquiry report, that is to say a report about him and his circumstances, made by a probation officer or any other person authorised to do so by the rules. 1977 *Grimsby Even. Tel.* 27 May 13/1 The case had been adjourned for social inquiry and psychiatric reports. 1909 C. R. HENDERSON *Ann. Amer. Acad. Pol. & Social Sci.* Mar. 265 It is time..to adopt some such description as 'social insurance' to cover the methods of guaranteeing income to wage earners and their families in case of sickness, accident, invalidism, feebleness of old age, death of the breadwinner and unemployment. *Ibid.* 270 No voluntary system of social insurance can be economically administered, save upon a foundation of compulsory insurance. 1922 S. A. QUEEN *Social Work in Light of Hist.* xii. 209 The ideal purpose of social insurance is to prevent, and finally to eradicate poverty and the consequent need of relief by meeting the problem at its origin. 1970 *Internat. & Compar. Law Quarterly* 4th Ser. XIX. II. 301 The District Court of Kiel held that payments from a social insurance authority had to be set off against the child's right to maintenance against his father's heirs. 1977 *Times* 10 Sept. 2/6 Research in this field is..a piece of social insurance. 1976 R. HARRIS *Three Candles for Dark* iv. 27 I'm not a liar, or not a real one. A social liar, maybe, like everyone else. 1941 AUDEN *New Year Letter* III. 64 And yet although the social lie Looks double to the dreamer's eye. 1969 M. DRABBLE *Waterfall* 94 She might have invented the information as a social lie (a felicitous duplicity). 1971 W. TUTE *Tarnham Connection* vii. 135 [He] said he was expected back home, which Mado knew to be a social lie. 1919 *Lancet* 24 May 921/1 (*heading*) Social medicine in Vienna. 1925 F. L. DUNHAM *Approach to Social Medicine* i. 14 A need arises in welfare work for a field of preventive science to which social science, psychology, psychiatry and various other departments shall contribute... It may be called *Social Medicine*. 1977 *Lancet* 24 & 31 Dec. 1336/1 What has been the contribution of social medicine to social policy in general and to health-services policy in particular. 1925 P. SOROKIN in *Social Forces* May 635/2 We used to think that in the United States 'social mobility' was greatest. **1954** D. V. Glass (*title*) Social mobility in Britain. **1978** *Listener* 26 Jan. 107/2 The patterns of social mobility over the past generation. **1953** K. W. Deutsch *Nationalism & Social Communication* vi. 114 If there is economic growth, social communication will probably spread and social mobilization will progress. **1961** —— in *Amer. Pol. Sci. Rev.* Sept. 493/1 Social mobilization is a name given to an overall process of change, which happens to substantial parts of the population in countries which are moving from traditional to modern ways of life. **1905** E. A. Ross *Foundations Sociol.* viii. 182 The term..social morphology..will describe, not only human relations and groupings, but also their mutations in the course of time. **1960** *Amer. Sociol. Rev.* XXV. 193/2 Durkheim proposed the examination and comparison of languages..in order to find 'the manner in which social representations adhere to and repel one another', and how any such 'social morphology' is to be explained. **1797** *Encycl. Brit.* XVII. 570/2 Though social order is no longer unknown nor unobserved, yet the form of government is still extremely simple. **1817** Cobbett *Wks.* XXXII. 109 The old charge, that we are seeking to produce riot and confusion, and to destroy 'Social Order'! **1853** H. Martineau tr. *Comte's Positive Philos.* II. vi. i. 6 A polity that could not hold its ground before the natural progress of intelligence and of society can never again serve as a basis of social order. **1909** H. G. Wells *Ann Veronica* vi. 129, I know that our social order is dreadful enough..and sacrifices all that is best and most beautiful in life. **1920** B. Russell *Pract. & Theory Bolshevism* i. ii. 28 He [*sc.* the Communist] is..aiming at the creation of a new social order. **1955** M. Gluckman *Custom & Conflict in Africa* i. 17 What emerges, I think, is that if there are sufficient conflicts of loyalties at work, settlement will be achieved..and social order maintained. **1977** P. Laslett *Family Life* i. 46 The traditional social order on our continent. **1950** *Proc. Co-operative Party Annual Conf.* 47 The purpose of Socialism is to strengthen and expand the various forms of Social ownership and control, of which the Co-operative Movement is an outstanding example. **1961** *Encounter* May 63/1 Of the alternative forms of social ownership, the Co-operative Movement is potentially the most attractive. **1984** *Economist* 29 Sept. 16/2 'Social ownership', a concept embracing co-operatives, worker buy-outs, profit-sharing and municipally-owned competitive enterprises. **1986** *Times* 19 July 2/1 He [*sc.* Nigel Lawson] said Labour knew nationalization was unpopular which is why it had produced the phrase 'social ownership' but that would fool no one. **1835** H. Reeve tr. *de Tocqueville's Democracy in Amer.* II. x. 429 If republican principles are to perish in America, they can only yield after a laborious social process. **1887** [see process *sb.* 5b]. **1947** Henderson & Parsons tr. *Weber's Theory of Social & Econ. Organization* i. 96 Charisma..is thus the bearer of many dynamic tendencies of social processes. **1974** tr. *Wertheim's Evolution & Revolution* 164 The aim of this study is to deal with revolutions as social processes. **1966** G. Tannenbaum in S. Arieti *Amer. Handbk. Psychiatry* xxxv. 577/1 The social psychiatric model is based on public health principles rather than on the traditional clinical prototype. **1964** *Observer* 23 Aug. 1/1 The social psychiatrists..believe that the answers to mental health can only be found by..studying the patient in relation to the groups he moves in. **1924** *Amer. Jrnl. Psychiatry* LXXXI. 149 The Round Table Conferences.. were well attended..36 formed the group which discussed problems of social psychiatry. **1958** D. McK. Rioch in *Symposium on Preventive & Social Psychiatry 1957* p. iv, The last two sessions..are devoted to organizational, therapeutic and other clinical developments of social psychiatry in recent years. **1976** B. H. Kaplan et al. (*title*) Further explorations in social psychiatry. **1909** W. M. Urban *Valuation* i. 2 A collection of social-psychological monographs. **1978** *Language* LIV. 160 It is more surprising ..that he does not refer to the rich social-psychological literature on language attitudes. **1899** *Amer. Jrnl. Sociol.* Mar. 661 To the social psychologist, however, it is evident that economic crises are phenomena that lie wholly within the psychical process of group-life. **1972** M. Argyle *Social Psychol. of Work* i. 3 There are a number of very important social problems in industry today which fall into the sphere of the social psychologist. **1891** E. A. Ross *Let.* 13 Dec. in *Amer. Sociol. Rev.* (1938) III. 364 Do we not need an *Origin of Species* in the dawn of Esthetic and Social Psychology? **1927** *Mod. Philology* Nov. 213 Or, we may study the group, observing every act of a given type... This is social psychology. **1964** Gould & Kolb *Dict. Soc. Sciences* 663/1 Only psychology and sociology include social psychology as part of their explicit subject-matter. **1977** R. Holland *Self & Social Context* v. 167 On the other side of psychology stands sociology, sharing with psychology the field of social psychology, since there are sociologically trained and psychologically trained social psychologists. **1937** L. Cheskin in *Education* Nov. 186/2 Current art..expresses mainly group action, mass movement, class struggle, not individual characters. The artists of today seek to express mainly social realism, not organic realism or naturalism. **1940** C. Connolly in *Horizon* Feb. 70 The flight of Auden and Isherwood..is also a symptom of the failure of social realism as an aesthetic doctrine. **1959** *Times Lit. Suppl.* 6 Nov. p. xxix/4 The collapse of social realism from its heyday during the 1930s... Generally to-day..American art is aloof and bent on wrestling with private problems. Even Ben Shahn, the outstanding social realist of twenty years ago, has come to prefer the expression of emotion through symbolism of his own devising from which political satire is absent. **1972** *Sat. Rev.* (U.S.) 27 May 14/3 The dismal social-realism caricatures that passed for art in the Thirties. **1940** Social realist [see *communist-inspired* s.v. communist 3b]. **1956** *New Yorker* 14 Jan. 71/1 Perhaps the only really native Italian schools..are the one called Spazialismo..and a social-realist one. **1959** [see *social realism* above]. **1976** *Listener* 19 Aug. 218/3 Twenty years ago, the most modern artists in England were called the 'kitchen-sink school'... John Berger wrote social realist reviews of their exhibitions. **1960** *Guardian* 18 Oct. 5/5 The group has..a distinct social realistic bias. **1859** D. Masson *Brit. Novelists* iv. 308 It may be that the representation of social reality is..the proper business of the Novel. **1887** Moore & Aveling tr. *Marx's Capital* I. i. 15 The value of commodities has a purely social reality. **1949** W. L. Warner in M. Fortes *Social Structure* 4 Agreement among the informants assures the status analyst that the social class sytem derived from their statements is.. an ever present..social reality. **1978** *Language* LIV. 449 It may be noted that O's social realities of the West German job market refer more to the over-employment of the 1960's than to the under-employment of the 1970's. **1889** (*title*) Social Register, New York. **1945** *Seafarers' Log* 6 July 6/4 The crew recommended that the 'advantages' of the social register be extended to William Chance and J. D. Bell, both trip carders. **1949** *Sat. Even. Post* 15 Oct. 142/3 The student body..has a heavy sprinkling of millionaires' sons and Social Register families. **1981** *Newsweek* 20 July 24 Martha von Bulow was pure Social Register, born into wealth, educated in the best private schools, and married for a time to an Austrian prince. **1953** N. Tinbergen *Herring Gull's World* ii. 13 Colour can act as a 'social releaser' by releasing a response in another individual just as a call often does. **1962** *Listener* 9 Aug. 207/2 In such tribes we see something very like social releasers. **1831** J. S. Mill *Ess.* (1962) 20 There must be a moral and social revolution,..which shall leave to no man one fraction of unearned distinction or unearned importance. **1890** W. Booth *In Darkest England* i. ix. 80 The Socialist tells me that the great Social Revolution is looming large on the horizon. **1910** H. G. Wells *New Machiavelli* (1911) i. iv. 121 The social revolution and the triumph of the Proletariat after the class war. **1941** *Time* 19 May 98/1 World War II is a social revolution, but not the kind of social revolution almost everybody thinks it is. **1974** tr. *Wertheim's Evolution & Revolution* 173 However, true social revolutions in earlier times showed a religious component as well. **1928** *Psychol. Abstr.* 889 Social role of language. **1949** [see rôle 2]. **1977** Social role [see *role set* s.v. rôle 4]. **1905** E. Wharton *House of Mirth* ii. viii. 417 Carry promised to find somebody who wants a kind of social secretary—you know she makes a speciality of the helpless rich. **1949** 'J. Tey' *Brat Farrar* xxii. 195 She moved him on from one group to another as expertly as a social secretary. **1978** 'J. Horbury' *Diplomatic Affair* i. iv. 43 'Never neglect *placement* if you wish to rise.' .. 'By the time you rise to the point where it matters, some charming social secretary will worry about it for you.' **1925** P. Sorokin *Sociol. of Revol.* xii. 250 Some of their members in two or three years cover an enormous distance in 'social space': from ordinary lawyers,..workers, peasants,..etc., they become persons..occupying high posts. **1927** —— *Social Mobility* i. 3 Persons near each other in geometrical space—*e.g.*, a king and his servant..—are often separated by the greatest distance in social space. **1961** J. N. Findlay *Values & Intentions* ix. 398 The first encounter with social space is normally that of a being without formed views, abilities or values, with a range of beings surpassingly mature,..decided, powerful and in general benign. **1977** T. M. Kando *Social Interaction* xi. 260/1 The study of space becomes truly interesting when it is conceived of as social space. **1843** Social statics [see dynamics 1b]. **1851** H. Spencer (*title*) Social statics. **1958** A. R. Radcliffe-Brown *Meth. in Social Anthropol.* i. v. 128 For social anthropology the task is to formulate and validate statements about the conditions of existence of social systems (laws of social statics) and the regularities that are observable in social change (laws of social dynamics). **1927** P. Sorokin *Social Mobility* ii. 11 Social stratification means the differentiation of a given population into hierarchically superposed classes. **1979** G. Ritzer et al. *Sociol.* ix. 238 Their contention that because social stratification is universal, it must be a functional necessity. **1972** P. Laslett *Household & Family* 58 In the relations of children to servants we may..find.. important and revealing social structural differences. **1835** H. Reeve tr. *de Tocqueville's Democracy in Amer.* I. v. 69 The Constitution of the United States..consists of two distinct social structures, connected, and..encased one within the other. **1872** H. Spencer in *Contemp. Rev.* XX. 311 Social influences which..facilitate further aggregation with consequent further complexity of social structure. **1949** M. Fortes *Social Structure* p. xiii, The study of kinship systems and..the concept of social structure. **1968** Jacobson & Schoepf tr. *Lévi-Strauss's Structural Anthropol.* I. xv. 277 Studies in social structure have to do with the formal aspects of social phenomena. *a* **1854** Mill *Early Draft Autobiogr.* (1961) 108 The social studies of myself and several of my companions assumed a shape which contributed very much to my mental development. **1926** B. Webb *My Apprenticeship* v. 217 A subtle combination of quantitative and qualitative analysis is a necessary factor in social studies. **1938** S. Chase *Tyranny of Words* vii. 78 The social studies are..backward compared to the physical sciences. **1977** *Lancashire Life* Nov. 136/3 In some schools R.E. is lumped together with history and geography and called Humanities or Social Studies. **1927** *Amer. Jrnl. Sociol.* XXXIII. 424 (*title*) The social survey of Tyneside: an English regional social survey. **1948** [see participant *sb.* 1]. **1956** *B.B.C. Handbk. 1957* 106 Two major enquiries by this section, both making use of social-survey methods. **1979** J. MacKenzie *Victorian Courtship* iii. 40 Mary Booth..welcomed the help Beatrice [Potter] proposed to give her husband in his ambitious social survey. **1782** 'J. H. St. John de Crèvecœur' *Lett. from Amer. Farmer* iii. 50 New laws, a new mode of living, a new social system. **1853** H. Martineau tr. *Comte's Positive Philos.* II. vi. i. 11 The passage from one social system to another can never be continuous and direct. **1917** Kipling *Diversity of Creatures* 335, I cannot think it right that any human being should exercise mastery over others in the merciless fashion our tom-fool social system permits. **1951** E. E. Evans-Pritchard *Social Anthropol.* i. 11 The social anthropologist studies societies as wholes. He studies their oecologies, their economics.., their technologies, their arts, *etc.* as parts of general social systems. **1971** P. Worsthorne *Socialist Myth* vii. 143 Socialism has a conception of the role of government which can only be realized in a social system that exalts authority. **1797** in J. Gloag *Short Dict. Furniture* (1969) 626 A Gentleman's social table. **1952** *Ibid.* 436 *Social table*, a small, kidney-shaped table with four legs, and a revolving, cylindrical receptacle for wine bottles, supported on a pillar-and-claw stand, which fitted into the concave curve of the table... It allowed two or three people to sit with their wine near a fire. **1962** 'M. Innes' *Connoisseur's Case* xvi. 190 A gentleman's social table by Hepplewhite. **1873** H. Spencer *Study of Sociol.* xv. 372 No one doubts that the spendthrift or the gambler..is inferior as a social unit. *a* **1899** [see *super-organism* s.v. super- 6b]. **1907** W. James *Pragmatism* vi. 232 Must my thoughts dwell night and day on my personal sins and blemishes..or may I sink and ignore them in order to be a decent social unit? **1939** Auden in *I Believe* (1940) 26 Recent technical advances, such as cheap electrical power, are making smaller social units more of a practical possibility than they seemed fifty years ago. **1978** *Country Life* 17 Aug. 467/1 The family as a social unit. **1969** *Daily Tel.* (Colour Suppl.) 14 Mar. 5/1 Wage rises might have been slightly checked but 'the social wage' has gone up steadily... 'The social wage', in plain English, means Government hand-outs, the exact opposite of a wage. **1971** *Guardian* 7 July 12/4 The real social wage of many low-paid workers has been adversely affected. **1975** M. Thatcher in *Let Children Grow Tall* (1977) 18 People..complain that government takes too much of their incomes for what is now called the 'Social Wage'—the estimated annual value of the services provided out of public funds for each individual. **1977** *Daily News* (Perth, Austral.) 19 Jan. 8/1 If, on becoming a mother, every woman became entitled to a social wage of $100 a week, tax free, then this might achieve a great deal in terms of righting the lot of some women. **1892** L. F. Ward *Let.* 17 Mar. in *Amer. Sociol. Rev.* (1938) June 371 (*heading*) The social will. **1911** J. Ward *Realm of Ends* vi. 118 Is there in any exact sense a social spirit, a social will, a social end, a social conscience? **1942** R. G. Collingwood *New Leviathan* xxi. 152 There is always a discrepancy between the social will and its products.

**B.** *sb.* †**1.** A companion, associate. *Obs. rare.*

**1632** Lithgow *Trav.* x. 426 O Socials! we're not ignorant of losses.

**2.** A social gathering or party, esp. one held by members of a club or association.

**1870** *Mainland Guardian* (New Westminster, Brit. Columbia) 8 Jan. 3/4 A very pleasant Social was given by the ladies and friends in our new mission church on Christmas day. **1876** E. W. Clark *Life Japan* 124 The women..keep their tongues going as briskly during the tea-picking as their sisters of other climes..do at their tea-drinking socials. **1893** *The Month* Aug. 157 The social given by the ladies of the Altar Society was a grand success.

**3.** *ellipt.* for social security 1a or b. *colloq.*

**1981** *Times* 20 May 3/8 I'm getting two wages, one from prison, and one from the social. **1983** J. Wainwright *Their Evil Ways* 17 They were both 'on the social'. *Ibid.* 26 She applied for extra 'social'. She was..sure she was *entitled* to some extra.

**Social Credit.** [f. social *a.* + credit *sb.*]

**1.** A political theory advocated by C. H. Douglas (see Douglas[3]), according to which the supposed chronic deficiency in the purchasing power of consumers was to be remedied through a reduction of prices by means of subsidies to producers or through the giving of additional money to consumers; occas. also, a subsidy under this system. Also short for *Social Credit Party* or *League*.

**1920** A. R. Orage in C. H. Douglas *Credit-Power & Democracy* 166 The effect is inherent in the separation of Real Credit from Financial Credit—Social Credit, that is to say, from Financial Credit privately controlled. **1922** C. H. Douglas *Labour Party & Social Credit* 17 It is an important Report, not..as advancing any valid..criticism of the principles or details of Social Credit. **1935** *Calgary Typo News* 15 Mar. 1/1 We wonder..what is the policy of The Albertan? Liberal, Social Credit or Independent? **1936** S. E. Thomas *This Social Credit Business* 16 If the A + B Theorem is sound, what is the necessity for 'National Dividends' *as well as* Social Credits to retailers? **1944** G. B. Shaw *Everybody's Political What's What?* xi. 84 The apostles of Social Credit once actually persuaded a Canadian legislature to budget on its imaginary riches. **1966** R. S. Milne *Political Parties in New Zealand* iii. 78 *Potentially*, therefore, the Democrats, Democratic Labour, and Social Credit were 'national' parties. **1974** E. McGirr *Murderous Journey* 127 Ricardo's political grin.. calculated to warm the cockles of any voter way back to Douglas Social Credit.

**2.** *attrib.* and *Comb.*, as ***Social Credit analysis***, ***group***, ***leader***, etc.; **Social Credit League**, (*a*) *Canad.*, an organization outside party politics corresponding to the Social Credit Party; (*b*) *N.Z.* (also ***Social Credit Political League***), a political party advocating Social Credit; **Social Credit Party** *Canad.*, a political party whose policies are based on the theory of Social Credit.

**1922** C. H. Douglas *Labour Party & Social Credit* 26 This article successfully avoided any mention or indication of the Social Credit Proposals. *Ibid.* 29 The Social Credit Movement..is in sharp opposition to the official Labour Party and High Finance jointly. **1931** V. A. Demant *This Unemployment* vi. 121 The *Social Credit* analysis of C. H. Douglas, costing expert for the Government during the War. **1934** T. S. Eliot *Rock* i. 12 Ain't you ever 'eard me speak o' the principles of Social Credit Reform? **1935** *Economist* 29 June 1474/1 A Social Credit scheme for Alberta under which he promised to guarantee every adult inhabitant of the Province $25 per week. **1958** *Maclean's Mag.* 10 May 97/4 When the two factions separated Wicks and Savage took the name and formed the Social Credit League. **1958** *Time* (Canadian ed.) 15 Sept. 16/3 The leader of the badly mauled Social Credit party. **1961** *Canada Month* Nov. 11/3 The B.C. Social Credit League offered alternative solutions to his problem. **1965** *Oxf. N.Z. Encyl.* 277/2 Two splinter parties, the Social Credit League and the Communist Party, have contested seats in elections, but neither has ever secured a seat in the House of Representatives. **1966** *Encycl. N.Z.* II. 812/1 In May 1953, the New Zealand Social Credit Political League was formed. **1966** 'H. MacDiarmid' *Company I've Kept* iv. 106 Douglas's Social Credit system (or a partial form of it) was tried out by Alberta, Canada, in the inter-war years. **1967** *Canad. Ann. Rev. 1966* 5 Both the NDP and the small Social Credit group indicated that they were willing to co-operate with the government. **1968** *Globe & Mail* (Toronto) 17 Feb. 8/1 The national Social Credit Party could drive forward to counteract its 'inaccurate image'. **1968** *Landfall* XXII. 365 The men armed with Social Credit conversation for the interval. **1969** *N.Z. News* 5 Nov. 8/5 The Social Credit Leader, Mr. Cracknell, may have all too often been dismissed as something of a political lightweight.

Hence **Social Crediter, Social Creditor**, an advocate of Social Credit; also occas. **Social Creditist** (cf. CREDITISTE).

**1938** *Social Crediter* 17 Sept. 2/1 What I (a Social Crediter) should say to that, is that I don't know whether Sir Oswald agrees with me or not. **1953** M. LOWRY *Sel. Lett.* (1967) 337 The Social Crediters fell, after having made some demonstrations of power. **1963** *Daily Tel.* 31 Oct. 14/2 The Social Creditists, appealing mainly to Quebec nationalism, could muster only 27 votes against 210. **1965** *Economist* 13 Nov. 713/1 In the new [Canadian] house there will still be nine Creditistes attached to Mr Caouette, and five Social Crediters of the Thompson variety. **1976** H. WILSON *Governance of Britain* viii. 161 In past times, not recently, they were told, the number of committed Henry Georgeites, or Douglas Social Creditors, might have put forward similar claims.

**socialism** ('səʊʃəlɪz(ə)m). [a. F. *socialisme* (1832), or independently f. SOCIAL *a.* + -ISM. See also next.

The early history of the word is somewhat obscure. The first use of F. *socialisme* appears to have been in the *Globe* of 13 Feb. 1832, where it was employed in contrast to *personnalité*. In its modern sense it is variously claimed for Leroux or Reybaud, writing within three or four years after this. A different account, assigning the priority of this use to England, is given in the *Encycl. Brit.* (1887) XXII. 205; according to this the word originated in 1835 in the discussions of a society founded by Robert Owen.]

**1.** A theory or policy of social organization which aims at or advocates the ownership and control of the means of production, capital, land, property, etc., by the community as a whole, and their administration or distribution in the interests of all.

Freq. with initial capital.

***Christian socialism***, a doctrine or theory, promulgated about 1850 by F. D. Maurice, C. Kingsley, T. Hughes, and others, advocating a form of socialism on a Christian basis.

**1837** *Leeds Times* 12 Aug. 5/1 *Socialism.*—Messrs. Fleming and Rigby.—On Monday evening..these two gentlemen attended [*sic*] an audience..on the topics of the real nature of man. **1839** J. MATHER (*title*), Socialism Exposed: or 'The Book of the New Moral World' Examined. *Ibid.* App. 22 To explain and expose what Robert Owen's Socialism is. **1840** *Quart. Rev.* Dec. 180 The two great demons in morals and politics, Socialism and Chartism. **1850** *Daily News* 13 Mar. 5/2 The infection of ..'Christian Socialism' is spreading to Whitehall. **1863** FAWCETT *Polit. Econ.* II. i. 181 Socialism, as first propounded by Owen and Fourier, proposed that a society living together should share all the wealth produced. **1881** STEVENSON *Virg. Puerisque* 89, I do not greatly pride myself on having outlived my belief in the fairy tales of Socialism.

**2.** A state of society in which things are held or used in common.

**1879** H. GEORGE *Progr. & Pov.* VI. i. (1881) 188 We have passed out of the socialism of the tribal state.

**socialist** ('səʊʃəlɪst). [Cf. prec. and F. *socialiste* (Reybaud, 1835).]

**1. a.** One who advocates or believes in the theory of socialism; an adherent or supporter of socialism.

**1827** *Co-operative Magazine* Nov. 509 The chief question ..between the modern,..Political Economists, and the Communionists or Socialists, is whether it is more beneficial that this capital should be individual or in common. **1833** *Poor Man's Guardian* 24 Aug. 275/2 [Letter signed] A Socialist. **1833** *The Crisis* 31 Aug. 276/1 The Socialist, who preaches of community of goods, abolition of crime, of punishment, of magistrates, and of marriage. **1853** W. JERDAN *Autobiog.* III. xix. 289 He was..a Socialist in the best sense of the term. **1889** SHAW *Fabian Ess. Socialism* 182 The young Socialist is apt to be catastrophic in his views.

**b.** *Comb.*, as ***socialist-controlled, -dominated, -ridden***.

**1929** *Times* 16 Aug. 11/3 Mr. Moore, the Leader of the Opposition, appealed to the people of this Socialist-ridden State on a promise to substitute for Socialism 'private effort and enterprise'. **1976** N. O'SULLIVAN *Conservatism* v. 124 Whenever important bills were opposed by the House of Lords, he suggested, there might be an appeal, in the form of a mass referendum, over the heads of a socialist-dominated House of Commons to the people. **1976** *Southern Even. Echo* (Southampton) 1 Nov. 3/3 There are many Socialist-controlled local authorities on which the dominant group doesn't give the opposition any places on any committees.

**2.** *attrib.* or as *adj.* Of or pertaining to socialists; socialistic: **a.** Of persons.

**1839** J. MATHER *Socialism Exposed* 23 A socialist lecturer expressed his ideas of God. **1856** GEO. ELIOT *Ess.* (1884) 114 The Socialist party. **1887** *St. James's Gaz.* 8 Feb. (Cassell), The torchlight Socialist procession.

**b.** Of ideas, theories, etc.

**1848** W. E. FORSTER in Reid *Life* (1888) I. vii. 246 The worst of all Socialist plans I have seen is that all have within them..a damning desire to shirk work. **1850** MACAULAY in Trevelyan *Life* (1883) II. 284 The poem is to the last degree Jacobinical, indeed Socialist. **1861** *Illustr. Lond. N.* 17 Aug. 152/1 Working classes..declare their adhesion to the socialist idea.

**c.** In *Combs.* used *attrib.* or as *adj.*, as ***socialist-chauvinist, -feminist, -rebel, -revolutionary, -workman***.

**1919** A. SIRNIS tr. *Lenin's Collapse of Second International* x. 65 This group, the only one which had performed systematic work amongst the masses..turned Socialist-Chauvinist. **1921** D. H. LAWRENCE *Sea & Sardinia* ii. 76 He immediately put on the socialist-workman indignation. **1952** E. HOBSBAWM in *Granta* 15 Nov. 10/2 The Radical age of the 1820s and 1830s, and the mixed socialist-rebel age which overlapped the first world war. **1976** H. T. WILLETTS tr. *Solzhenitsyn's Lenin in Zurich* 253 The Socialist-Revolutionary Party was born at the end of 1901 out of the merging of the Populist groups. **1976** *Women's Report* Sept./Oct. 17/1 They would like feedback from the last issue, articles from individuals and groups giving a socialist-feminist analysis of activities.

**socialistic** (səʊʃə'lɪstɪk), *a.* [f. prec. + -IC.]

**1.** Of or pertaining to, characteristic of, socialism; in accordance with the theory of socialism.

(*a*) **1848** *N.Y. Tribune* 25 Apr. (Bartlett *App.*), That we have..profoundly rejoiced in the Revolution itself, and more especially in its socialistic aspects and tendencies. **1863** H. SPENCER *Ess.* II. 238 And similarly with countless socialistic schemes. **1863** FAWCETT *Pol. Econ.* II. i. 104 Various socialistic experiments were made by Robert Owen. (*b*) **1858** *Sat. Rev.* VI. 639 An elaborate system of socialistic order. **1882** FROUDE in *Fortn. Rev.* CCXXIX. 744 Socialistic equality is pretty and becoming in Utopia. **1894** *Forum* Mar. 101 In any socialistic state there will be one set of positions which will offer chances of wealth.

**2.** Advocating or favouring socialism.

**1864** *Athenæum* 12 Mar. 366/2 Fernando Garrido.. celebrated as a socialistic republican. **1880** MCCARTHY *Own Times* III. 233 Chevalier,..who from having been a member of the socialistic sect..had come to be a practical politician.

Hence **socia'listically** *adv.*

**1887** *Co-operative News* July 657 An amount of saving which even socialistically disposed workmen ought not to disregard. **1892** *Pall Mall G.* 30 Mar. 6/2 The miners are.. in no wise socialistically inclined, he considered.

**socialist realism.** [tr. Russ. *sotsialistícheskiĭ realízm.*] The official theory of art and literature of the Soviet Communist party, according to which the artist's or writer's work should reflect and commend the life and ideals of socialist society. Also *attrib.*

**1934** M. EASTMAN *Artists in Uniform* (rev. ed.) I. ii. 16 The present creative method in proletarian art and literature..is 'Socialist Realism'. *Ibid.* 17 Socialist Realism means seeing all reality as a development toward socialism. **1940** GRAVES & HODGE *Long Week-End* xxiii. 402 The hope that fact-finding would bring to fruition the theory of socialist realism. **1967** G. STEINER *Lang. & Silence* 390 Her recent novels betray the contortions of a genuine artist trying to come to terms with the grey half-truths of 'socialist realism'. **1978** *Jrnl. R. Soc. Arts* Dec. 64/2 In 1934 the term 'socialist realism' came into current use, and architecture suffered from various interpretations of it.

Hence **socialist-realist** *sb.* and *a.*

**1935** G. STRUVE *Soviet Russ. Literature* xiv. 247 It is difficult to say why Sholokhov's *Upturned Soil* should be regarded as a work of a Socialist Realist and not of a realist *tout court.* **1945** H. READ *Coat of Many Colours* vi. 27 The 'socialist-realists' in Russia, who believe that the function of art is primarily to further the cause of socialism. **1958** *Listener* 6 Nov. 727/2 The whole fabric of the so-called 'socialist-realist' architectural philosophy [in the U.S.S.R.], which was actually pseudo-classical, has collapsed. **1964** *Ann. Reg.* 1963 229 He [*sc.* Mr Gomulka]..announced that socialist-realist art would receive special support. **1977** V. S. PRITCHETT *Gentle Barbarian* xiii. 218 The crude, black and white, schematic works of the Socialist Realists of our time.

**socialite** ('səʊʃəlaɪt). *colloq.* (orig. *U.S.*). [f. SOCIAL *a.* and *sb.* + -ITE[1].] A person who is prominent in fashionable society; one who is fond of social activities and entertainments. Also *attrib.*

**1928** *Time* 31 Dec. 30/3 Splendorous as hostess & socialite was Princess Clara in both Germany and England. **1937** D. B. WYNDHAM LEWIS in L. Russell *Press Gang!* 249 *Eric Daintee*, wealthy lissom Mayfair filmamateur, socialite, dressdesigner, surrealist. **1938** E. LYONS *Assignment in Utopia* II. xiv. 226 The main body of amateur sociologists,.. earnest probers, socialite thrill-hunters, and miscellaneous neurotics did not take possession [of Moscow] until the following years. **1944** R. MANVELL *Film* II. vi. 139, I do not think a working girl should take her standards from a socialite. **1956** J. C. MASTERMAN *Case of Four Friends* vii. 125 A rather irresponsible *bon viveur* or socialite (as the young call them). **1960** *Harper's Bazaar* July 19/1 Private citizens in the socialite belt even distribute matches bearing their own monograms. **1978** J. KRANTZ *Scruples* iii. 79 At *Vogue* there are something like twenty-one editors of varying degrees of importance, including those stationed in Paris, Rome, and Madrid who are socialites first, editors second. **1980** *Times Lit. Suppl.* 12 Sept. 1000/4 Although a professional naturalist.., he [*sc.* Victor Jacquemont] was by nature something of a dilettante and very much a socialite.

**sociality** (səʊʃɪ'ælɪtɪ). [ad. F. *socialité* (It. *socialità*) or L. *sociālitas*: see SOCIAL *a.* and -ITY.]

**1. a.** The state or quality of being social; social intercourse or companionship with one's fellows, or the enjoyment of this.

*a* **1649** in *N. & Q.* Ser. I. X. 357 Socialitie becometh the person of the gravest man, soe as he neglect not the due consideration of time, place, and persons. **1658** PHILLIPS, *Sociality*, fellowship, company. **1748** HARTLEY *Observ. Man* I. iv. §1. 420 The Pleasures of Sociality and Mirth. **1775** MME. D'ARBLAY *Early Diary* (1889) II. 94 The Dean is a man of drollery, good humour, and sociality. **1823** SCOTT *Quentin D.* vii, The good Lord kissed the wine-cup by way of parenthesis, remarking, that sociality became Scottish gentlemen. *a* **1881** A. BARRATT *Phys. Metempiric* Pref. p. ix, It was thought that at Oxford he gave many hours to whist and innocent sociality.

**b.** With *pl.* A social act or function.

**1825** LAMB *Elia* II. *Wedding*, In the participated socialities of the little community, I lay down for a brief while my solitary bachelorship. **1861** GEIKIE *Mem. E. Forbes* xiv. 498 Another winter passed pleasantly away. Not, however, without its socialities, its soirées and dinners. **1891** *Blackw. Mag.* CL. 358/2 The socialities of life..require for their satisfactory working a certain amount of ignorance.

**c.** Contrasted with *sociability*: Social intercourse in its formal or conventional aspect.

**1871** MRS. H. WOOD *Red Court Farm* ix. 128 Conscious of his own deficiency on the score of sociality, (not sociability) and fashion. **1897** *Westm. Gaz.* 13 Feb. 2/3 She must be content with the 'sociality'. One hopes it will not degenerate into 'sociability'.

**2.** The action or fact on the part of individuals of forming a society or of associating together; the disposition, impulse, or tendency to do this.

(*a*) **1775** G. WHITE *Selborne* lxvi, There is a wonderful spirit of sociality in the brute creation. **1834** MCMURTRIE *Cuvier's Anim. Kingd.* 429 This is precisely the case with the burrowing wasps..; their sociality is of no higher order than that which exists amongst the inhabitants of the same street. **1932** S. ZUCKERMAN *Soc. Life Monkeys & Apes* xvii. 291 The monkey's sociality. **1966** R. M. LOCKLEY *Grey Seal, Common Seal* ix. 125 The puzzling feature of the sociality of the Farne grey seals is that they continue to crowd together to nurse their pups on certain of the islets only. **1978** *Sci. Amer.* Sept. 139/1 The order also includes many nonsocial species, and the surprising fact is that sociality has originated on a number of separate occasions among the bees, the ants and the wasps.

(*b*) **1839** I. TAYLOR *Theory Another Life* (1847) II. 22 The basis of..communion or sociality among intelligent orders. **1847** GROTE *Greece* II. ix. III. 16 That regulated sociality which required the control of individual passion from every one. **1899** FISKE *Through Nature to God* II. ix. 105 As soon as sociality became established, and Nature's supreme end became the maintenance of the clan organization.

**3.** Companionship or fellowship *in* or *with* some thing or person.

**1806** J. BERESFORD *Miseries Hum. Life* I. 5 My only remaining solace,—that of sociality in sorrow and complaint. **1831** I. TAYLOR in Edwards *Freedom Will* Pref. p. xxxvii, Fatalism..takes its place along with the truths of other exact sciences and should maintain sociality with them. **1863** J. G. MURPHY *Comm., Gen.* xxv. 1–11, Wedlock and the Sabbath, the fountain-heads of sociality with man and God.

**socialization** (ˌsəʊʃəlaɪ'zeɪʃən). [f. next.]

**1.** The action or fact of socializing or establishing upon a socialistic basis.

**1884** W. MORRIS in *Justice* 31 May 2/1 The socialisation of labour which ought to have been a blessing to the community has been turned into a curse by the appropriation of the products of its labour by individuals..; the result of which to the workers has been a dire slavery, of which long hours of labour,..and complete repulsiveness in the work itself have been the greatest evils. **1886** *Pall Mall G.* 22 Sept. 11/2 The socialization of the means and instruments for the creation of wealth by the workers. **1896** *Westm. Gaz.* 18 Sept. 2/2 No one could now be found to deny the possibility..of the socialisation of some services. **1957** *Ann. Reg.* 1956 311 The Chinese People's Republic remained largely preoccupied with the drive for greater industrialization and for the 'socialization' of agriculture. **1965** B. PEARCE tr. *Preobrazhensky's New Economics* 6 The socialization of industry means by its very essence a transference of responsibility in economic leadership to science, to an extent quite unknown in capitalist economics. **1977** D. M. SMITH *Human Geogr.* xii. 359 The effective socialization of production under capitalism..stands in supreme contradiction with private appropriation.

**2.** *Social Sciences.* The process of forming associations or of adapting oneself to them; esp. the process whereby an individual acquires the modifications of behaviour and the values necessary for the stability of the social group of which he is or becomes a member. Also *attrib.*, esp. in ***socialization process***.

**1841** *London Phalanx* 6 Nov. 505/1 Fourier in his analysis of universal movement in society..forms a scale of seven degrees or periods of general progress between..*Edenism*, or the primitive state of humanity..and..*Socialization*, or complete simple association. **1895** G. SIMMEL in *Ann. Amer. Acad. Pol. Sci.* VI. III. 417 The investigation of the forces, forms and development of socialization, of co-operation, of association of individuals, should be the single object of sociology as a special science. **1924** F. H. ALLPORT *Soc. Psychol.* xiv. 378 It is..possible that the evils mentioned are not *necessary* accompaniments of contemporary civilization or of the socialization of mankind. **1924** E. S. BOGARDUS *Fundamentals Soc. Psychol.* xx. 235 The best way to understand the socialization process is to consider the experiences of persons who have..a broad social vision and understanding. **1951** *Mind* LX. 288 This process of 'socialisation'—to use the standard term—produces..the 'personality' of the individual. **1953** WHITING & CHILD *Child Training & Personality* xi. 247 A relatively unimportant role in the total socialization process. **1964** M. ARGYLE *Psychol. & Social Prob.* v. 72 The socialization factor [in reducing the crime rate] is already being manipulated to some extent by placing children from very bad homes in foster homes. **1965** G. P. MURDOCK *Ess.* 44 The processes by which it [*sc.* culture]..is transmitted from one generation to the next (education and socialization). **1980** in N. Warren *Stud. in Cross-Cultural Psychol.* II. v. 215 We know relatively little about an area I shall label 'intellectual socialization'.

**socialize** ('səʊʃəlaɪz), *v.* [f. SOCIAL *a.* + -IZE.]

**1.** *trans.* To render social; to make fit for living in society, esp. in *Social Sciences.* Also, to transmit to an individual the cultural values and standards of behaviour of the social group of which he is regarded as a member.

**1828** [see SOCIALIZING *ppl. a.*]. **1836** LYTTON *Athens* (1837) I. 382 Pisistratus refined the taste and socialized the habits of the citizens. **1846** GROTE *Greece* (1862) II. 566 Socialising and improving the people. **1899** *Allbutt's Syst. Med.* VIII.

254 He [the wrongdoer] is imperfectly socialised. **1932** M. GABAIN tr. *Piaget's Moral Judgment of Child* iv. 350 This assumption gains force if..social constraint does not really suffice to 'socialize' the child but accentuates its egocentrism. **1957** O. R. MCGREGOR *Divorce in Eng.* iii. 79 With horrifying overcrowding..the family could not be a stable, ongoing concern. Children were brutally socialised. **1971** *Mod. Law Rev.* XXXIV. VI. 643 New lawyers are.. informally 'socialised', taught the norms and behaviour patterns which are the basis of a stable legal profession. **1976** *National Observer* (U.S.) 31 July 1/2 She is convinced..that women traditionally have failed to excel physically because they were socialized to think they could not.

**2.** To render socialistic in nature; to establish or develop according to the theories or principles of socialism. Also in extended uses: to administer or organize with social aims in view (rather than predominantly for profit); to finance with public funds; to bring under public control. Also *absol.*

**1846** WORCESTER, *Socialize*,..to regulate or conform to the principles of the Socialists. **1889** SHAW *Fabian Ess. Socialism* 50 It is the municipalities who have done most to 'socialize' our industrial life. **1894** *Daily News* 4 June 7/1 They would 'socialise', as they term it, all the instruments of production, such as mines, factories, railways, and so forth. **1920** M. BEER *Hist. Brit. Socialism* II. III. ix. 181 Maurice's main idea was to socialise the Christian and to Christianise the socialist. **1920** *Westm. Gaz.* 2 Dec. 6/1 The Fehrenbach Cabinet is being increasingly pressed to Socialise, and first of all to Socialise coal. **1926** J. M. KEYNES *End of Laissez-Faire* iv. 42 One of the most interesting and unnoticed developments of recent decades has been the tendency of big enterprise to socialise itself. **1938** *Sun* (Baltimore) 15 June 2/3 Discussions as to what the medical association and the Government might do about 'socializing' or financing with public funds the medical treatment of economically submerged individuals. **1948** *News Chron.* 20 Sept. 3/3 In fact, we have to socialise men's minds—without destroying their individuality and enterprise—as well as socialising the physical assets. **1975** J. DE BRES tr. *Mandel's Late Capitalism* vii. 233 Within the company labour is directly socialized in the sense that the overall plan of the company ..directly determines the output of the various factories, workshops and conveyor belts. **1976** *Ilkeston Advertiser* 10 Dec. 20/3 It could do this by compulsory purchase, saying that it was merely 'socialising' the land by buying it at current use value and preventing a capitalist developer from doing the same, and then re-selling the land at a profit.

**3.** *intr.* To be sociable, participate in social activities. Freq. const. *with*. orig. *U.S.*

**1895** in *Funk's Stand. Dict.* **1900** *Dialect Notes* II. 62 *Socialize*,..to talk with one of the opposite sex. **1934** *Amer. Speech* IX. 76 Did you socialize much in Atlantic City?.. I am not going to socialize much this winter. **1939** JOYCE *Finnegans Wake* (1964) iii. 498 After plenty of his fresh stout and his good balls of malt,..socializing and communicanting in the deification of his members. **1959** V. PACKARD *Status Seekers* xii. 167 Trying to socialize across class barriers can be a strain. **1966** J. PEARL *Crucifixion of Pete McCabe* ii. 21 McCabe could socialize with any of his three neighbours. **1970** *Daily Tel.* 25 Feb. 15/3, I prefer to socialise outside the team but wouldn't go out with any man who was shattered by my job. **1978** *Detroit Free Press* 5 Mar. 6/2 They're hard to spot because they don't like to sit around in trees and socialize with other birds.

Hence **'socializing** *vbl. sb.*

**1904** *Sat. Rev.* 19 Mar. 353 The preliminary necessary to the complete socialising of the state. **1944** J. S. HUXLEY *On Living in Revolution* 21 This humanizing and socializing of sectional groups is one way in which the new social order will differ from the old. **1959** V. PACKARD *Status Seekers* xii. 168 Status is attached to the act of socializing. **1965** B. PEARCE tr. *Preobrazhensky's New Economics* 76 The whole system of regulation of the economy cannot but be affected by the socializing of industry and transport. **1970** *Globe & Mail* (Toronto) 28 Sept. 13/2 Having no brothers or sisters to toughen her, socializing is probably bewildering. **1976** BOTHAM & DONNELLY *Valentino* vi. 45 Lunchtime socialising..brought him into contact with members of a motion picture company.

**'socialized**, *ppl. a.* [f. SOCIALIZE *v.* + -ED[2].] That has been rendered social or socialist. ***socialized medicine***: a system of medical care that is financed and administered by the state.

**1848** HAMILTON *Sabbath* i. 11 Divine worship, among socialised men, requires social agreement. **1887** *Pall Mall G.* 17 Oct. 2/2 The second part..takes place several years later in a rural commune of Socialized England. **1892** G. B. SHAW *Fabian Soc.* (Fabian Tract No. 41) 20 Thousands of thoroughly Socialized Radicals..who would have resisted Socialism fiercely if it had been forced on them. **1935** *Sun* (Baltimore) 16 Feb. 9/1 Traditionally hostile to socialized medical care, the organized medical profession will decide tomorrow whether to temper its stand to the trend of the day toward State control. **1936** J. M. KEYNES *Gen. Theory Employment, Interest & Money* v. xix. 267 Except in a socialised community where wage-policy is settled by decree, there is no means of securing uniform wage reductions for every class of labour. **1939** *Time* 30 Jan. 52/2 Although socialized medicine would certainly limit a patient's free choice of a physician, few people today are free to choose their doctors. **1949** KOESTLER *Insight & Outlook* xiv. 195 The listing together of such different phenomena as, for example, optical projective illusions, hypnosis, and socialized behaviour as manifestations of 'self-transcendence' is arbitrary. **1949** *Sun* (Baltimore) 15 June 12/3 For instance, at this moment the socialized railways of Britain face labor unrest of great intensity, the basic quarrel being over wages. **1964** R. BRADDON *Year Angry Rabbit* ix. 82 'Goddam,' muttered the American sourly, 'why can't you Australians have Socialized Medicine like the Limies?' **1973** *Sci. Amer.* Jan. 33/1 One [*sc.* primate] in particular—the chimpanzee—not only cooperates in the work of the chase but also engages in a remarkably socialized distribution of the prey after the kill. **1976** *Howard Jrnl.* XV. I. 51 The juvenile courts dispensed unchallenged what the Americans call socialized justice. (Socialized simply means individualized civil justice which focuses upon social conditions. It has no party political connotations.) **1977** *Lancet* 17 Sept. 596/1 Why socialised medicine should so often be equated with socialist medicine I fail to understand.

**socializee** (ˌsəʊʃəlaɪˈziː). [f. SOCIALIZE *v.* + -EE[1].] One who is being socialized (in sense 1 of the vb.)

**1952** T. PARSONS *Social System* vi. 209 Thus not only the socializing agents *but the socializee* must be conceived as acting in roles. **1975** *Jrnl. Politics* XXXVII. 83 Yet socialization within the family is not simply a two-generation phenomenon, for the parents themselves were once the socializees instead of the socializers.

**socializer** (ˈsəʊʃəlaɪzə(r)). [f. SOCIALIZE *v.* + -ER[1].] **1.** One who socializes an industry, an economy, or the like. Cf. SOCIALIZE *v.* 2.

**1947** [see DECARTEL(L)IZATION].

**2.** One who or that which makes a person social or sociable; that which induces a sociable atmosphere.

**1974** H. L. FOSTER *Ribbin', Jivin', & Playin' Dozens* iv. 162 The right language at the proper time can serve as a socializer, a relaxing agent, and a positive catalyst to enhance communication. **1975** [see prec.]. **1976** *Word 1971* XXVII. 476 They are *socializers* which function as the verbal oil to ease friction in communication... A's phrase 'How are you?' is a socializer; A does not usually expect to learn B's physiological or psychological problems. **1981** *Underground Grammarian* Oct. 4/1 Our educationists are socializers with political intentions.

**3.** One who likes to participate in social activities.

**1977** J. ANDERSON *Appearance of Evil* iv. 21 She was the quietest member of the family, was less of a socializer than Victor. **1978** G. A. SHEEHAN *Running & Being* ii. 29 His 'good life' is quite different from that of an aggressive football player and the relaxed socializer.

**'socializing**, *ppl. a.* [f. SOCIALIZE *v.*] That socializes or renders social. Also, that revels in participating in social activities.

**1828** *Q. Rev.* XXXVIII. 211 The socialising and humanising effects of a liberal commerce with other nations. **1841** *Tait's Mag.* VIII. 562 The socializing philosophist will change the congregation of battling devils..into a conclave of serenest gods. **1890** H. H. ELLIS *Criminal* vi. 260 Whatever educative and socialising influences the prison may possess. **1965** F. L. UTLEY in Bessinger & Creed *Medieval & Linguistic Stud.* 308 A multiple martyr, to a fretful socializing wife, to the chthonic Mother, to the Judas Wilkes, to and for the Nation. **1980** *London Mag.* July 81/2 Mostly he [*sc.* Somerset Maugham] dealt in types, such as the rich bitch, the honest whore, the socializing snob.

**socially** (ˈsəʊʃəlɪ), *adv.* [f. SOCIAL *a.*]

†**1.** *Sc.* In company. *Obs.*$^{-1}$

**1505** *Extr. Aberd. Reg.* (1844) I. 432 Thai sale..pass tua and ij togidr socialie.

†**2.** As a member of a body or society. (Opposed to *severally*.) *Obs. rare.*

**1642** BRIDGE *Wound. Consc. Cured* 31 The subjects are considered two waies: Socially [and] Severally. **1647** DIGGES *Unlawf. Taking Arms* iv. 88 Which are the acts of them not as single men, but as united bodies, and considered.. socially, not severally.

**3.** In a social manner; sociably.

*a* **1763** SHENSTONE *Ess.* Wks. 1777 II. 215 If the selfish passion of the rest preponderate, it would be self-destructive in a few individuals to be over-socially disposed. **1810** J. FOSTER in *Life & Corr.* (1846) I. 421 We read socially a great deal. **1850** R. G. CUMMING *Hunter's Life S. Africa* (1902) 57/2 These remarkable birds..construct their nests and live socially together under one common roof. **1891** E. KINGLAKE *Austral. at Home* 91 They are young barristers, doctors, or solicitors, sons of..socially minded stock and share brokers.

**4.** In respect of, with regard to, society. Freq. regarded as forming a *Comb.* with a following *adj.* or *ppl. adj.*

**1871** SMILES *Charac.* ii. (1876) 59 The result has been socially disastrous. **1876** *Encycl. Brit.* V. 696/2 The influence of Christianity was making itself felt morally, socially, and politically. **1890** W. H. DAWSON *Unearned Increment* iv. 47 The socially-created value of land. **1909** *Daily Chron.* 3 Nov. 1/1 The Budget taxes one form of 'socially-created wealth'. **1937** L. CHESKIN in *Education* Nov. 186/2 They are socially conscious, they study their society and interpret it, each in his own manner. **1951** M. MCLUHAN *Mech. Bride* (1967) 51/1 Panic enters the socially spotlighted host or hostess. **1955** *Sci. News Let.* 22 Jan. 56/1 Staphylococcus germs that are common even on 'socially clean' hands. **1961** D. JENKINS *Equality & Excellence* vi. 130 The great public schools and socially-privileged private schools. **1964** L. WOOLF *Beginning Again* III. 232 Socially it was the prehistoric era in which one still had servants living in one's house. **1964** *Language* XL. 92 A leading predecessor in socially-oriented thought. **1970** *Daily Tel.* 26 Nov. 9/3 One such smoker said: 'The claustrophobic atmosphere makes pot-smoking socially acceptable.' **1976** *Times* 20 Aug. 4/3 (*caption*) Socially deprived pupils from a West Berlin school. *Ibid.* 4/4 The Government is..deciding to spend £50,000 on job schemes for socially disadvantaged people. **1977** *Daily Tel.* 13 Oct. 10/4 In the past it has been opposed to any 'head counts' of this kind. They were considered socially divisive.

**'socialness.** [f. SOCIAL *a.*] Social quality or character; = SOCIALITY 1.

**1727** BAILEY (vol. II), *Sociableness, Socialness*, social Temper, Fitness for Conversation. **1843** *Proc. Berw. Nat. Club* II. 41 There is a certainty..that the disposition to society and socialness, innate to humanity,..will have fair play. **1901** *Expositor* June 426 Sin is selfishness, and morality is socialness.

**'socialry.** *U.S.* [f. SOCIAL *a.* + -RY.] Social organization.

**1896** A. SMALL *Let.* 22 May in *Social Forces* (1932) Mar. 313/1 'Socialry' has an archaic sight sound & sense which will hardly get itself naturalized in modern society, and as to his division of the factors of life in society with 'economics' & 'socialry'—it is a classification of things that he [*sc.* F. H. Giddings] hasn't begun to correlate in his own thinking. **1902** *Science* 14 Feb. 249/1 In the analogy with primitive socialry.

**social science.** [SOCIAL *a.* 9 b.] The scientific study of the structure and functions of society; any discipline that attempts to study human society, either as a whole or in part, in a systematic way. Also *attrib.*

[**1785** J. ADAMS *Let.* 10 Sept. in *Works* (1854) IX. 540 The social science will never be much improved, until the people unanimously know and consider themselves as the fountain of power. **1791** D.-J. GARAT *Let. à M. Condorcet* 82 Ces vérités..qu'il etoit important de découvrir, de rendre incontestables, sont les premières données de la science sociale, mais elles ne sont point la science.] **1811** tr. *Destutt de Tracy's Commentary Montesquieu's Spirit of Laws* 4, I have no other ambition..than to contribute my effort to the progress of social science, the most important of all to the happiness of man, and that which must necessarily be the last to reach perfection, because it is the product and the result of all the other sciences. **1821** J. BENTHAM *Let.* 21 Apr. in J. H. Burns *J. Bentham & Univ. Coll.* (1962) 8 The minds of the ruling few in their growing state should be turned towards the science so aptly stiled by you *the social science* —that science, in the progress of which the allied powers of tyranny, corruption, and delusion have so long..beheld their final downfall. **1846** LEWES *Biogr. Hist. Philos.* IV. 249 The conception of a social science is due to M. Comte. **1849** *Southern Lit. Messenger* XV. 77/2 On the Importance of the Social Sciences in the present day. **1874** SAYCE *Compar. Philol.* vi. 239 Our linguistic researches will be bounded by the limits of social science and social archæology. **1908** W. MCDOUGALL *Introd. Social Psychol.* p. vii, I hope that the book may be of service to students of all the social sciences. **1949** M. MEAD *Male & Female* 435 The relationship between our social-science skills and our world. **1966** G. N. LEECH *Eng. in Advertising* i. 3 Linguistics..has so far been the least influential of the major social sciences. **1969** *Times* 7 Jan. 8/6 Students reading social science were more sceptical than either the arts students or the scientists. **1971** *New Scientist* 18 Mar. 591/1 It seems more difficult to present a programme of viable-looking research in the social sciences than in the natural sciences. **1977** A. GIDDENS *Stud. in Social & Polit. Theory* ix. 306 Such a view is founded upon an erroneous idea of the relation between lay and social-science concepts.

Hence **social scientific** *a.*, **social scientist**.

**1875** R. J. WRIGHT *Principia; or, Basis of Social Sci.* p. v, *As to Spencer*; we admit he is *the* King of the Social Scientists. **1882** W. JAMES *Let.* 2 Nov. (1920) I. 211 As for Prague, *veni, vidi, vici.* I went there with much trepidation to do my social-scientific duty. **1920** J. M. WILLIAMS *Foundations of Social Sci.* p. xiii, The trend of thought of the psychological social scientists signifies an aim to arrive at truer assumptions, and to keep an open mind toward the psychological, as well as the other aspects of those assumptions. **1971** *Nature* 25 June 538/1 Why do social scientists, particularly American social scientists, murder the English language? **1977** J. M. JOHNSON in Douglas & Johnson *Existential Sociol.* v. 166 Investigations of..social scientific situations.

**social security.** [SOCIAL *a.* 7.]

**1. a.** A system whereby the state provides financial assistance for those citizens whose income is inadequate or non-existent owing to disability, unemployment, old age, etc.

**1908** [see sense 2 below]. **1933** *Old Age Security Herald* June 1/1 Transformed in the *American Association for Social Security*, the organization [*sc.* the American Association for Old Age Security] will continue to function. **1936** A. EPSTEIN *Insecurity* (rev. ed.) p. vi, The Act bars the realization of the relief promised by social insurance even though the law is presented under the glittering title of 'Social Security'. **1941** *Atlantic Charter* (Messages of Presidents, U.S.) (1943) 5 They desire to bring about the fullest collaboration between all nations in the economic field, with the object of securing for all improved labour standards, economic advancement and social security. **1942** *Times* (Weekly ed.) 2 Dec. 2/1 Social security as envisaged in this report is a plan to secure to each citizen an income adequate to satisfy a national minimum standard. *Ibid.*, As regards unification, Sir William Beveridge suggests that there should be a Ministry of Social Security. **1959** G. SLATTER *Gun in My Hand* 44 What in hell are ya doin in Christchurch anyway? Bludgin on the social security, I spose. **1969** N. W. PIRIE *Food Resources* i. 31 The Ministry of Social Security..found that there are now a million children at or below the poverty line [in the U.K.]. *a* **1974** R. CROSSMAN *Diaries* (1975) I. 23 For years I've been a specialist on social security and I know enough about it.

**b.** The money paid out under this system.

**1959** in J. Reid *Kiwi Laughs* (1961) 217 'Use your brains,' said Father Christmas testily. 'When you get to my age you have to live on social security. There's not much over to buy racing cars for every kid that wants one.' **1971** *Sunday Times* (Colour Suppl.) 5 Dec. 28 He has seven of his children to support on social security and family allowances. **1975** J. SYMONS *Three Pipe Problem* xv. 140 And you draw social security? **1976** *National Observer* (U.S.) 2 Oct. 7/2 Ethel.. takes in tourists to complement her Social Security.

**2.** *attrib.*, as ***social-security benefit, legislation, policy***, etc.

**1908** W. S. CHURCHILL *Let.* 4 Jan. in R. S. Churchill *Winston S. Churchill* (1969) II. Compan. II. 759 If we were able to underpin the whole existing social security apparatus with a foundation of comparatively low-grade state safeguards, we should in the result obtain something that would combine the greatest merits both of the English & the German systems. **1935** *N.Y. Times* 15 Aug. 1/4 The Social

Security Bill, providing a broad program of unemployment insurance and old-age pensions.. became law today. **1936** *U.S. Statutes* XLIX. 635 There is hereby established a Social Security Board.. to be composed of three members to be appointed by the President. **1940** *Economist* 31 Aug. 282/1 The old social security tax and the new national security tax. **1941** J. S. Huxley *Uniqueness of Man* p. ix, Subsidized housing, free milk, social security legislation, health insurance, free education..—these are all symptoms of the change. **1942** *Rep. Commissioners Insurance & Allied Services from Organisations* App. G. 35 in *Parl. Papers 1942–3* (Cmd. 6405) VI. 419 Post-war social policy should aim at establishing a *national Plimsoll line* of goods and services for all citizens... Such a social security policy grants the citizens new opportunities and freedoms. **1962** *Listener* 26 July 130/1 Poor people in Mexico City who can attend a social-security clinic. **1964** W. Markfield *To Early Grave* vii. 131 He spread out.. his army discharge papers, his social security card and a B'nai B'rith newsletter. **1966** N. Freeling *Dresden Green* i. 16 Chemists' bills and a social security number. **1969** *Times* 13 Jan. 11/2 £250m. available for higher social security benefits in the very low income range. **1972** *Accountant* 21 Sept. 347/1 The social security structure of individual countries depends heavily on their political climate. *a* **1974** R. Crossman *Diaries* (1976) II. 587 As chairman of the Pensions Committee I just had to get down to thinking what to do about social security payments after devaluation. **1976** W. Trevor *Children of Dynmouth* iii. 80 She was tired of listening to Mrs Slewy complaining about the social security man. **1976** *Ilkeston Advertiser* 10 Dec. 2/2 The Social Security 'scroungers', some of whom deliberately swindle the tax-payers to the extent of £10 million per year. **1978** S. Sheldon *Bloodline* xxxix. 347 People were on record if they had a Social Security number, an insurance policy, a driver's license or a bank account.

**social service.** [social *a.* 7.]

**1.** Service to society or to one's fellow-men, esp. as exhibited in work on behalf of the poor, the underprivileged, etc.

**1851** J. S. Mill *Lett.* (1910) I. 169 Scientific inquiry into the production and distribution of wealth, as a branch of social service. **1890** W. James *Princ. Psychol.* I. xiv. 599 The other social affections, *Benevolence*, *Conscientiousness*, *Ambition*, etc., arise in like manner by the transfer of the bodily pleasure experienced as a reward for social service. **1921** R. H. Tawney *Acquisitive Society* x. 219 If medical officers of health, directors of education, and directors of the Co-operative Wholesale be assumed to be quite uninfluenced by any consciousness of social service. **1926** E. Hemingway *Sun also Rises* ix. 85 'I rather thought it would be good for him.' 'You might take up social service.' 'Don't be nasty.' **1977** R. L. Wolff *Gains & Losses* vii. 404 Sublimation of doubt in sex, social service among the poor as a substitute for faith.. we shall encounter them again and again in.. novels of doubt.

**2.** With *a* and *pl.* A service supplied for the benefit of the community, esp. any of those provided by the central or local government, such as education, medical treatment, social welfare, etc.

**1933** J. Buchan *Prince of Captivity* ii. iii. 230 He is not prepared to go back on our social services... All parties go on sluicing out.. new benefits from the public funds. **1941** 'R. West' *Black Lamb & Grey Falcon* II. 506 This Cockney taxi-driver would be.. able to rely on an amplitude of social services in any emergency. **1945** *Ann. Reg. 1944* i. 82 The basic principle that compensation of workmen for industrial injury should be made a public social service. **1959** *Times Lit. Suppl.* 10 Apr. 203/2 Not even the welfare state and social services, and certainly not the nationalized industries, are now viewed by the mass of adult Britons as immaculate, brought down from Sinai. **1976** *Times* 22 July 16/1 There is more demand to cut taxes than to expand social services.

**3.** *attrib.* **a.** *sing.* (senses 1 and 2), as ***social-service cut, work***, etc.

**1900** J. P. Smyth (*title*) Social service ideals. **1911** J. B. Haldane *Social Workers' Guide* 127/1 Diocesan Social Service Committees. **1921** *Daily Colonist* (Victoria, B.C.) 8 Apr. 9/4 Mrs. Hallam, secretary of the Social Service Committee, requested that Miss Thompson, now acting for the organization as a social worker, be recognized as a woman police officer. **1929** Hughes & Stuenkel (*title*) The Social Service Exchange in Chicago. **1932** *Bombay Chron.* 20 Dec. 5 The work of the Social Service League has been good all round. **1937** M. Hillis *Orchids on your Budget* iii. 57 She also does the marketing by car, does social-service work in it once a week. **1956** F. Lafitte in A. Pryce-Jones *New Outl. Mod. Knowl.* 574 Britain's heavy heritage of obsolescent social-service buildings. *a* **1974** R. Crossman *Diaries* (1976) II. 444 He made an immensely demagogic speech saying that we'd spent more on social services than the Tories in their last three years, denying there was any question of social-service cuts. **1975** *Language for Life* (Dept. Educ. & Sci.) xix. 279 They include the Social Service Departments, Youth Service Departments, probation officers, and officers of the L.E.A. Careers Service.

**b.** *pl.* (sense 2), as ***social services department***, etc.

**1973** *Guardian* 30 May 9/2 Croydon's social services department is setting up a special training programme for new foster parents. **1974** *Times* 13 Nov. 16/2 The whole social services structure leads to good fieldworkers being lost to the management side. *Ibid.*, Management training in the social services field is possible. **1976** *Derbyshire Times* (Peak ed.) 3 Sept. 1/1 The party was from a Social Services home in Wartsones Road, Wolverhampton.

**'socialty.** *rare*$^{-1}$. [f. social *a.*] Sociality.

**1848** Bailey *Festus* (ed. 3) 210 Others [held].. that war and socialty Were equal evils.

**social work.** [social *a.* 7.] Work of benefit to those in need of help, esp. professional or voluntary service of a specialized nature concerned with community welfare and family or social problems arising mainly from poverty, mental or physical handicap, maladjustment, delinquency, etc. Also (with hyphen) *attrib.*

**1890** *Girl's Own Paper* 27 Dec. 197/3 'Stump oratory' may safely be regarded as quite beyond the limits of a woman's social work. **1892** S. M. Lindsay in *Annals Amer. Acad. Pol. & Social Sci.* Nov. 76 The growth of the Krupp cast steel works and the motives of the firm in their social work. **1908** *Busy Man's Mag.* Jan. 88/1 Few who read Mrs. Humphrey Ward's interesting books know of her social work in London. **1914** *Lancet* 31 Jan. 345/2 (*heading*) The sixth international congress of social work and service. **1931** *Economist* 10 Jan. 57/1 For in spite of the very considerable development which organised social work has attained in the United States.. it is not capable of shouldering the responsibility of caring for the wreckage of a major industrial depression. **1964** *New Statesman* 10 Apr. 581/1 An experienced social work teacher from Canada. **1975** *Listener* 14 Aug. 212/1 By the use of social-work skills, probation officers seek to help the offender cope. **1979** G. Wagner *Barnardo* xvii. 299 No teacher training colleges or social work courses existed. **1980** *Times Lit. Suppl.* 28 Nov. 1347/1 Notwithstanding the vagueness of its aims, social work became sanctified as a discrete discipline under the Social Services Act of 1970.

Hence **social worker**, one who undertakes social work, esp. someone professionally trained.

**1904** *Ann. Reg. Univ. Chicago* 245 A training center for social workers. **1912** F. G. D'Aeth in H. Bosanquet *Social Conditions in Provincial Towns* iv. 50 A Local Committee of Social Welfare.. consists of clergy, ministers, and social workers. **1931** *Economist* 10 Jan. 57/1 Social workers in the United States are meeting an unusually 'hard winter' with feelings almost of despair. **1955** Earl Winterton *Fifty Tumultuous Years* 117 Few, if any, of the social workers of today are old enough to remember conditions then. **1964** [see almoner[1] 4]. **1975** *New Yorker* 11 Aug. 27/1 Ma says her social worker will not permit her to move her furniture until the rent is paid for August. **1977** B. Pym *Quartet in Autumn* xxii. 201 A real bossy social-worker type.

†**'sociate,** *sb. Obs.* Also 5–7 sociat. [ad. L. *sociāt-us*: see next.] An associate or colleague; a companion or comrade. Also *transf.*

α. *c* **1450** *Hist. & Art. Masonry* 130 The.. Alderman of the Towne in wyche the congregacions ys holden schall be felaw and sociat to the master of the congregacions. **1582** Stanyhurst *Æneis* ii. (Arb.) 56 Deere sociats,.. Now let vs on forward. **1621** Brathwait *Nat. Embassie* (1877) 109 Wisdome will haue sociats to frequent her. **1638** —— *Barnabees Jrnl.* i. (1818) 39 Night and day with sociats many Drunk I ale both thick and clammy.

β. **1523** *North Co. Wills* (Surtees) 116 To the two sociates with the prior of Horneby. **1588** Parke tr. *Mendoza's Hist. China* 53 He had two sociates for to helpe him. **1640** Yorke *Union Hon., Battles* 58 Wyat and his sociates being greatly encouraged by this new supply. **1706** De Foe *Jure Divino* xi. 260 At this One Blow, the mighty Sociates fell. **1719** —— *Crusoe* ii. (Globe) 376 The three new Sociates began, it seems, to be weary of the.. life they led. **1788** Sir B. Boothby *Elegy* 7 in *Sorrows* (1796) 41 Beloved retreat..; Sociate of joy, when Love and Hope were young.

**'sociate,** *pa. pple.* and *ppl. a. Obs.* exc. *arch.* Also 6 sociat, socyate. [ad. L. *sociāt-us*, pa. pple. of *sociāre*.]

**1.** *pa. pple.* Associated *with* or *to* some thing or person; joined or united *together*.

α. **1501** Douglas *Pal. Hon.* i. xvi, Tell me this wonder, How that ȝe wretchit catiues.. Ar sociat with this court souerane? **1526** *Pilgr. Perf.* (W. de W. 1531) 152 The actyue lyfe is yᵉ lyfe wherby we be sociat and knytte in charite and loue to our neyghbour.

β. **1509** Barclay *Shyp of Folys* (1570) 127 In him is iustice with pitie sociate. **1534** Whitinton *Pullyes Offices* i. (1540) 70 Eloquence wynneth and accompanyeth those with whome we be famylier socyate. **1895** F. Thompson *Sister Songs* 60 But you must be Bound and sociate to me.

†**2.** *ppl. a.* Associated, joint. *Obs.*$^{-1}$

**1706** De Foe *Jure Divino* ii. 11 Belus and Nimrod,.. Who made the patriarchal power comply, And sociate Rule submit to Monarchy.

†**'sociate,** *v. Obs.* [f. L. *sociāt-*, ppl. stem of *sociāre* to unite, combine, etc., f. *socius* companion.]

**1.** *trans.* To associate, join, or unite together; to form into a society or association.

*a* **1578** Lindesay (Pitscottie) *Chron. Scot.* (S.T.S.) I. 112 Of him quhome he persewit maist cruellie,.. sociatit witht the commone enemeis of the realme. **1648–9** *Eikon Bas.* 90 That Government being necessary for the Churches well-being when multiplied and sociated. **1654** Gayton *Pleas. Notes* iv. viii. 220 O let thy loines so fruitfull be To sociate all Monarchy.

**2.** *intr.* To associate, mix, or keep company *with* others.

**1635** Shelford *Five Disc.* ii. 58 One sort will not sociate with the rest of their neighbours in the house of God. **1684** Bunyan *Pilgr.* ii. 44 They seem.. above all others to desire to sociate with, and to be in their Company. **1719** De Foe *Crusoe* ii. (Globe) 359 They would be very willing to assist and sociate with them.

**b.** To combine or league *together*. *rare.*

**1688** Holme *Armoury* iii. 203/2 A Gild or Fraternity of Brothers and Sisters.. are a kind of Religious Laity that Societ [*sic*] together.

**sociation** (səʊʃɪ'eɪʃən, səʊsɪ-). [ad. late L. *sociātio* (cf. older F. *sociation*), or f. sociate *v.* after *association*.]

†**1.** Association, conjunction, union. *Obs. rare.*

**1681** H. More in Glanvil *Sadducismus* Postscr. i. (1726) 12 In vertue of either an express or implicit Sociation or Confederacy with some Evil Spirit. *a* **1716** South *Serm.* (1744) XI. 6 Upon the sociation of the soul with the body.

**2.** *Ecol.* = society 12.

**1930** *Svensk Bot. Tidskrift* XXIV. 492 The most elementary units in the series of phytocoenoses, or the sociations, have until now been studied nearly only by the Scandinavian School of Ecologists (= Phytosociologists). Until 1928 they were called 'associations', but in order to facilitate an international agreement, Scandinavian ecologists have now agreed to accept this term in its Middle-European sense, following Rübel's proposition to apply the new term 'sociation' to the earlier Scandinavian 'associations' (or 'micro-associations'). **1936** *Jrnl. Ecol.* XXIV. 276 It is here proposed to call the aspect society a *sociation* and the layer society a *lamiation*, while the corresponding seral terms would be *socies* and *lamies*. **1973** P. A. Colinvaux *Introd. Ecol.* v. 67 (*caption*) Hypothetical species area curve as used by the Uppsala school for determining both the number of species in the sociation and the minimum area of that sociation.

**sociative** ('səʊʃɪətɪv), *a. Gram.* [ad. F. *sociatif*, *-ive*: see sociate *v.* and -ive.] Denoting or expressing association.

**1871** Kennedy *Public Sch. Lat. Gram.* 437 From this habit of connexion by Relatives, appears to have arisen the use of *quod* before many Conjunctions as a merely Sociative Particle. **1888** —— *Revised Lat. Primer* §232 This [the Ablative of Association] includes the uses of an old case called the Sociative Case, expressing the circumstances associated with the Subject or the action of the Sentence.

*absol.* **1886** *Trans. Amer. Philol. Assoc.* XVII. 79 The pure dative, the locative, and the instrumental (including the sociative).

†**'socie,** *v. Obs.* Also 5 socy-. [ad. OF. *socier*, ad. L. *sociāre*: see sociate *v.*] *trans.* To associate, ally, or join (a person or persons) *to* (another or others), esp. for some common purpose.

**1387** Trevisa *Higden* (Rolls) II. 267 Hym slowh Cyrus i-socied to his eme Darius. *Ibid.* VIII. 333 Þere he [king Edward] socied to hym þe emperour Bevarrus. *c* **1425** *St. Mary of Oignies* ii. vii. in *Anglia* VIII. 170/1 Vnwhile receyued worshypfully of þe senate of holy apostils, operewhile socyed to setes of aungels. **1447** Bokenham *Scyntys* (Roxb.) 98 To Coleyn ful fast he gau hym hye And socyid hym to that holy cumpanye.

**b.** To join or bind (things) *together*.

**1398** Trevisa *Barth. De P.R.* xix. cxxxi. (1495) 941 All the lymmes of the body ben socied togyder by vertue of Armenye.

**socies** ('səʊʃiːz). *Ecol.* [mod.L., f. society after *species* (cf. associes).] The term answering to society 12 in analyses of immature plant communities.

**1916** F. E. Clements *Plant Succession* vii. 138 The socies bears exactly the same relation to consocies and associes that the society does to consociation and association... The term socies comes from the root *seq-* (*sec-*, *soc-*), *follow*. **1926** [see associes]. **1929** *Ecology* X. 133 Each group of seasonals plus the constantly present predominants make up a socies, that is a seasonal subdivision or aspect-phase of the presocies. **1964** [see associes].

‖**sociétaire** (sɔsjetɛr). [Fr., f. *société* society.] An actor who is a full member of the Comédie Française, Paris, and thereby has a share in its management and profits.

**1881** W. H. Rideing *Dramatic Notes, 1880–81* xii. 67 Of the three parts in which London audiences have now seen her [*sc.* Mme Modjeska], this of the gifted and passionate *sociétaire* of the Comédie Française [*sc.* Sarah Bernhardt] illustrates most fully the measure of her genius. **1901** *Scotsman* 16 Apr. 8/7 The vexed question of the distribution of rôles among sociétaires and pensionnaires—full members of the company and salaried aspirants. **1909** Beerbohm in *Sat. Rev.* 30 Oct. 529/1 He, too, has schooled himself in the traditions of the Gaiety, and is a worthy sociétaire. **1923** G. Arthur *Sarah Bernhardt* iv. 66 To the Directors of the Français the *Sociétaires* ranked only by seniority. **1959** *Times* 23 Feb. 12/2 If we had a National Theatre properly based and founded, all of us could be Sociétaires as in the Comédie-Française and be called upon when required.

**so'cietal,** *a.* [f. societ-y + -al[1].] Societary; social. Hence **so'cietally** *adv.*

**1898** *Catal. Yale Univ. 1898–9* 204 A study of the evolution of the institutions of the democratic republic, of the societal organization, and of the history of the money of account. **1903** A. G. Keller *Queries in Ethnography* 55 The Societal System. **1907** [see mores 1]. **1956** *Kenyon Rev.* XVIII. 411 Trager and Smith's results are amazingly coherent, both practically and societally. **1959** *Sunday Times* 22 Nov. 16/4 His [*sc.* Kipling's] passion.. for the values of what D. H. Lawrence (borrowing the revolting word from Dr. Trigant Burrow) called 'societal man'. **1964** [see egocentric *a.*]. **1973** *Black World* Mar. 28 Educational systems are constructed to socialize individuals to perform societally defined and necessitated tasks. **1976** *Times Lit. Suppl.* 19 Nov. 1449/1 Leading educators believe that the schools must keep pace with broad societal changes. **1979** 'A. Hailey' *Overload* iv. vii. 328 The Sequoia Club has been something we all needed—part of our societal system of checks and balances.

**societarian** (səʊsaɪɪ'tɛərɪən), *a.* and *sb.* [f. society, after other words in *-arian*. Cf. F. *sociétaire*.]

**A.** *adj.* Societary; socialistic.

**1822** Lamb *Elia* i. *Compl. Decay of Beggars*, The all-sweeping besom of societarian reformation. *Ibid.*, The.. caprice of any fellow-creature, or set of fellow-creatures, parochial or societarian. *a* **1849** H. Coleridge *Ess.* (1851) II. 19 He could have no sympathy with utilitarian liberaux or societarian philanthropists. **1900** *Speaker* 3 Feb. 476 The return to Greek societarian ideas is now a commonplace.

**B.** *sb.* **1.** One who believes in or advocates some form of socialism; a socialist.

**1842** *Nonconformist* II. 809 Your communitarians, or societarians of modern days. *a* **1866** J. GROTE *Exam. Utilit. Philos.* iv. (1870) 62, I should myself be inclined rather to call Mr. Mill a societarian, if we must have new and sectarian words, than an utilitarian.

**2.** One who moves in or is a member of fashionable society.

**1891** *Boston* (Mass.) *Jrnl.* 2 Jan. 2/3 'Societarians' is a new term for the fashionable four hundred. **1893** *Cornh. Mag.* Sept. 246 Second to none in that varied knowledge required nowadays of the successful societarian.

Hence **socie'tarianism.**

*a* **1866** J. GROTE *Exam. Utilit. Philos.* iv. (1870) 71 What I have called his [Mill's] 'societarianism' would have been superfluous.

†**so'cietary,** *sb. Obs.*⁻¹ [Cf. next.] An associate.

**1652** URQUHART *Jewel* Wks. (1834) 258 These four eminent Scots I have put together, because they were societaries by the name of Jesus, vulgarly called Jesuits.

**societary** (səʊ'saɪɪtərɪ), *a.* [f. SOCIET-Y + -ARY.] Of, pertaining to, concerned or dealing with, society or social conditions; social.

**1847** *Tait's Mag.* XIV. 267 Small farms would also be a return to something like Patriarchalism, a past societary state. **1885** L. OLIPHANT *Sympneumata* 187 It should not be matter for surprise that just and truer order has so lately begun to show itself on the field of societary life. **1886** T. FROST *Country Journalist* v. (1888) 57 Men.. disposed to study societary science.

**so'cietified,** *ppl. a. rare.* [f. SOCIETY + -FY + -ED[1].] Of or made fitting for cultured or fashionable society.

**1934** in WEBSTER. **1936** E. M. FORSTER *Abinger Harvest* 108 The societified lady and the obscure maniac are in a sense the same person.

**so'cietism.** [f. SOCIET-Y + -ISM.] Combination in a society or societies.

**1894** *Daily News* 26 Dec. 3/6 It was a real grievance which hatched secret societism in Ireland. **1896** *Bibliotheca Sacra* July 545 As the perversion of individualism is anarchism, so would the perversion of societism appear to be socialism or collectivism.

**societology** (səʊsaɪɪ'tɒlədʒɪ). *U.S. rare.* [f. SOCIET(Y + -OLOGY.] The study of human society; sociology.

**1895** *Catal. Yale Univ.* 1895–6 62 In connection with this is a course of lectures on systematic sociology (Societology). This course is strictly academical.. and does not take up topics popularly classed under 'social science'. **1915** *Nation* (N.Y.) 14 Oct. 467 He has made a real contribution to the study of society, and has demonstrated (what some of us had begun to doubt) that there is such a subject as sociology—or at least societology. **1924** C. M. CASE *Outlines Introductory Sociol.* p. xxxvi, It [*sc.* sociology] probably *should* be, and more than probably will *not* be, known as 'societology'.

**society** (səʊ'saɪɪtɪ). Also 6 societe(e, societye, 6–7 -tie, 7 socyetye, sosiety. [ad. OF. *societe* (mod.F. *société*, = It. *società*, Sp. *sociedad*, Pg. *sociedade*), ad. L. *societas*, f. *socius* companion, etc.]

**I. 1. a.** Association with one's fellow men, esp. in a friendly or intimate manner; companionship or fellowship. Also rarely of animals (quot. 1774).

**1531** ELYOT *Gov.* (1834) 173 Society, without which man's life is unpleasant and full of anguish. **1581** W. STAFFORD *Exam. Compl.* ii. (1876) 49 To the intent men may knowe that they haue neede one of anothers helpe, and thereby loue and societie to growe among all men the more. **1621** in Foster *Eng. Factories Ind.* (1906) 305 Till now wee have not had to doe with them in matter of moment, but in frendly sosiety. **1658** T. WALL *Charact. Enemies Ch.* 59 It is separation.. that makes them void of Christian society, and common Morality. **1736** BUTLER *Anal.* I. v. 121 Want of everything of this kind.. would render a man as uncapable of Society, as want of language would. **1774** GOLDSM. *Nat. Hist.* (1776) V. 153 As Nature has formed the rapacious class for war, so she seems equally to have fitted these for peace, rest, and society. **1861** MILL *Utilit.* iii. 47 Society between equals can only exist on the understanding that the interests of all are to be regarded equally.

**b.** With possessive pronoun or genitive.

**1588** SHAKS. *L.L.L.* IV. ii. 166, I do dine to day at the fathers of a certaine Pupill of mine... I beseech your Societie. **1663** S. PATRICK *Parab. Pilgr.* (1687) 35 It is a thousand to one but they will find the means.. to insinuate themselves into their society again. **1779** *Mirror* No. 64, I had fancied that.. the want of their society had deprived us of the ease and gaiety of discourse. **1828** SCOTT *F.M. Perth* xxxii, Forced on each other's society, the two desolate women became companions, if not friends. **1868** FREEMAN *Norm. Conq.* (1877) II. 473 A holy anchorite, who had been for forty years cut off from the society of men.

**c.** Association or intercourse *with* or *between* persons, etc. Also *fig.*

**1563** FOXE *A. & M.* 973/2 The societie betwixt Christ & vs, is promised to them that take bread and wyne. *c* **1610** *Women Saints* 11 There was such friendship, societie, and familiarity betweene the Religious of that contrie and England, that [etc.]. **1662** STILLINGFL. *Orig. Sacræ* III. ii. §5 An Island, where he may have no society with mankind. **1690** LOCKE *Govt.* II. ii. Wks. 1727 II. 162 One of those wild savage Beasts, with whom Men can have no Society nor Security. **1803** M. CUTLER in *Life*, etc. (1888) II. 119 The members who are there are not willing to acknowledge they have any society with him. **1831** SCOTT *Cast. Dang.* xvii, You will.. best fulfil the intentions of those by whose orders you act, by holding no society with me whatever, otherwise than is necessary.

**d.** With *a* and pl. An instance of association or companionship with others. *rare.*

**1598** SHAKS. *Merry W.* III. iv. 9 Other barres he layes before me, My Riots past, my wilde Societies. **1780** *Mirror* No. 71. Renouncing a society in which the secret admonitions of his heart frequently told him he could not continue.

**e.** *concr.* Persons with whom one has, or may have, companionship or intercourse. Also *transf.* of plants. †In early use also with poss. pronouns or article.

In some instances the abstract sense is also implied.

**1605** SHAKS. *Macb.* III. iv. 3 Our selfe will mingle with Society, And play the humble Host. **1613** PURCHAS *Pilgrimage* (1614) 411 None are so readie to blame men therein as their Societie. **1696** *Caldwell P.* (Maitland Cl.) I. 171, I lodged.. att the 2 pigeons, where I had a most desyreable societie. **1719** DE FOE *Crusoe* I. 292 Having now Society enough, and our Number being sufficient to put us out of Fear of the Savages. **1759** MILLS tr. *Duhamel's Husb.* II. ii. (1762) 260 Wheat and other plants love society. **1816** JANE AUSTEN *Emma* iii, Mr. Woodhouse was fond of society. .. He liked very much to have his friends come and see him. **1853** READE *Chr. Johnstone* 256 They have plenty of society, real society. **1872** RUSKIN *Fors Clav.* 14 For all society he had two friends.

**2.** The state or condition of living in association, company, or intercourse with others of the same species; the system or mode of life adopted by a body of individuals for the purpose of harmonious co-existence or for mutual benefit, defence, etc.: **a.** In reference to man.

**1553** T. WILSON *Rhet.* (1580) A vj b, Long it was ere that manne knewe hymself,.. so that all thynges waxed sauage, the yearth vntilled, societie neglected. **1599** *Mirrour of Policie* 120 Societie is an assemblie and consent of many in one. **1642** CHARLES I *Declaration* 12 Aug. 23 Against the Laws of Society and civill Conversation. **1650** BULWER *Anthropomet* 172 A due reverence in the first place towards God.., then towards Society wherein we live. **1744** HARRIS *Three Treat.* (1841) 62 We are fitted with powers and dispositions which have only relation to society, and which, out of society, can nowhere else be exercised. **1782** V. KNOX *Ess.* xvi. (1819) I. 93 Is not this system [Christianity], whether well or ill founded, friendly to society? **1835** I. TAYLOR *Spir. Despot.* ii. 58 The inestimable advantages of living in society are unavoidably burdened with some partial evils. *a* **1862** BUCKLE *Misc. Wks.* I. 5 In the earliest stages of society there are many arts, but no sciences.

**b.** In reference to certain animals, insects, etc.

**1794** S. WILLIAMS *Hist. Vermont* (1809) I. 114 The society of beavers seems to be regulated and governed, altogether by natural dispositions, and laws. **1826** SAMOUELLE *Direct. Collect. Insects & Crust.* 39 Wasps, like bees, live in society. **1834** M'MURTRIE *Cuvier's Anim. Kingd.* 390 Its larva lives on the same trees, and frequently in society.

**3. a.** The aggregate of persons living together in a more or less ordered community.

**1639** N. N. tr. *Du Bosq's Compl. Woman* I. 17 Where as then was no other sinne in society then lying, a genuine playnesse.. were enough. **1678** CUDWORTH *Intell. Syst.* I. iv. 431 In doing one action after another, tending to a Common Good, or the good of Humane Society. **1749** LADY LUXBOROUGH *Let. to Shenstone* 24 June, You may be busied to the benefit of society without stirring from your seat. **1782** PRIESTLEY *Corrupt. Chr.* I. I. 5 In few cases has the peace of society been so much disturbed. **1841** *Nonconformist* I. 281 The principles by which the aristocracy have gained.. their Sindbad seat on the shoulders of society. **1873** HAMERTON *Intell. Life* VI. i. 195 Society has only one law, and that is custom.

**b.** With defining or limiting adj.; esp. *good society* (cf. next).

**1779** *Mirror* No. 13, The varied objects which present themselves in cultivated society. **1816** J. SCOTT *Vis. Paris* (ed. 5) 151 The wars of the period.. repressed to a most deplorable degree, what is properly understood by *good society*. **1859** THACKERAY *Virgin.* xliii, There were masquerades and ridottos frequented by all the fine Society. **1893** KATE SANBORN *Truthf. Woman S. California* 40 In regard to society, I find that the 'best society' is much the same all over the civilized world.

**c.** The aggregate of leisured, cultured, or fashionable persons regarded as forming a distinct class or body in a community; *esp.* those persons collectively who are recognized as taking part in fashionable life, social functions, entertainments, etc. Also with *a* and *the.*

(*a*) **1823** BYRON *Juan* XIII. xcv, Society is now one polish'd horde, Form'd of two mighty tribes, the *Bores* and *Bored.* **1846** MRS. GORE *Engl. Char.* 15 The press gossips for society, because society makes no secret of its love of gossiping. **1856** MERIVALE *Rom. Emp.* xli. (1871) V. 124 Ovid is eminently the poet of society. **1893** GRANT ALLEN *Scallywag* I. 6 Who *is* Mr. Gascoyne, and who *is* Mr. Thistleton?.. Are they in society?

(*b*) **1840** THACKERAY *Barber Cox* Feb., The paragraphs in the papers about Mr. Coxe Coxe.. had an effect in a wonderfully short space of time, and we began to get a very pretty society about us. **1842** LOVER *Handy Andy* xxi, Intelligence and courtesy in the one sex, and gentleness and natural grace in the other, making a society not to be ridiculed in the mass.

(*c*) **1848** THACKERAY *Van. Fair* lxii, The performance over, the young fellows lounged about the lobbies, and we saw the society take its departure.

**d.** Personified.

**1784** COWPER *Task* IV. 498 Till at last Society.. Shakes her encumber'd lap, and casts them out. **1831** CARLYLE *Sart. Res.* I. vi, A huge.. Apron, wherein Society works (uneasily enough). **1877** 'RITA' *Vivienne* I. i, Society shrugged its shoulders. **1879** *Daily Telegr.* 15 May, He sinks, smiling, into the arms of Society, and Society.. eats him up.

**e.** *alternative society*: the aggregate of (predominantly young) persons whose cultural values and habits of association purport to represent a preferable and cogent alternative to those of the established social order. Usu. with definite article.

**1969** *It* 13–25 June 21/3 Brother Simon Tugwell is planning a 3-day talk-in on the alternative society. **1971** *Guardian* 16 Mar. 10/4 American cities seem full of young people wanting to 'drop out'—but what do they drop into? It is called 'The Alternative Society' and it is already becoming a vogue term. **1971** *Times Lit. Suppl.* 31 Dec. 1621/5 Sorel, like Nietzsche, preached the need for a new civilization of makers and doers, what is now called a counter-culture or an alternative society. **1975** D. LODGE *Changing Places* v. 164 A middle-aged parasite on the alternative society.

**II.** †**4. a.** The fact or condition of taking part with others or another in some thing or action; participation. *Obs.*

**1534** MORE *Treat. Passion* Wks. 1333/1 The societie of al saintes in the mistical body of Christ. **1560** DAUS tr. *Sleidane's Comm.* 126 For the kynges societie and conjunction.. they yelde him harty thankes. *Ibid.* 218 Who hath perswaded the bisshop of Rome and the French king to the Societie of this war. **1613** PURCHAS *Pilgrimage* IV. iii. I. 298 Pacorus being received into Societie of the Kingdome with his father. **1758** *Ann. Reg.* 16 The Prussians,.. inspired by a society of danger with their King,.. totally defeated the Austrians.

†**b.** A sharing or use in common. *Obs.*⁻¹

**1699** TEMPLE *Hist. Eng.* 14 One Custom there was among the Britains which seems peculiar to themselves,.. which was a Society of Wives among certain numbers, and by common consent.

†**5.** The fact or condition of being connected or related; connexion, relationship; union or alliance; affinity. *Obs.*

**a.** Const. *with* or *between* (some thing or person).

(*a*) **1541** R. COPLAND *Galyen's Terap.* 2 B iv, The sayd indication hath no maner of societe with the cause prymytyfe. **1561** DAUS *Bullinger on Apoc.* (1573) 193 He hath the number of the name of the beast, which hath a societie wyth the beast, which societie that number bewrayeth or sheweth. **1610** BARROUGH *Meth. Physick* III. xxv. (1639) 143 The veine in the right arme.. having society with the veine which is called Vena cava. **1707** *Curios. in Husb. & Gard.* 231 The universal Spirit is Water,.. the Society of the Water with the Sun produces Animals, Vegetables and Minerals.

(*b*) **1601** HOLLAND *Pliny* I. 5 There is not.. so great societie betweene heauen and vs, as [etc.]. **1620** VENNER *Via Recta* 110 There is so great societie betwixt it and the heart.

†**b.** Const. *of* or *in* (something).

**1562** COOPER *Answ. Priv. Masse* (1850) 130 You allege a perpetual society of the body and blood, which ye call *Concomitantiam.* **1610** HOLLAND *Camden's Brit.* 16 If no writer had recorded, that we Englishmen are descended from Germanes,.. the society of their tongues would easily confirme the same. **1646** SIR T. BROWNE *Pseud. Ep.* II. i. (1650) 43 This is a fallacy of Æquivocation, from a society in name inferring an Identity in nature. **1668** CULPEPPER & COLE *Barthol. Anat.* II. iii. 90 The Consent of Vicinity makes nothing to the purpose,.. nor society in the same Office. **1771** *Ann. Reg.* II. 25/2 By long society in party, the sentiments of these men in politics had come to be the same.

†**6. a.** The state or condition of being politically confederated or allied; confederation. *Obs.*

*a* **1548** HALL *Chron., Hen. VII*, 25 b, To exhorte and requyre the kynge of Englande, to entre hys company and societee in armes. **1579** J. STUBBES *Gaping Gulf* B vij b, Absoluing our neyghbour kinges of any auncient leage or late oth of societie. **1623** BINGHAM *Hist. Xenophon* 87 You haue now an opportunitie presented vnto you.. by entring into societie of war with vs, to be reuenged. **1665** MANLEY *Low C. Wars* 974 Many Kings, Princes, and Nations, began to respect the Society and Alliance of Holland.

†**b.** A political alliance, league, or compact.

**1600** HOLLAND *Livy* XXIII. 472 A league and societie was concluded betweene Philip the King of the Macedonians and Anniball. **1606** —— *Suetonius* 8 Hee entred likewise into a Societie with them both, vpon this contract, That [etc.].

†**7. a.** Partnership or combination in or with respect to business or some commercial transaction.

**1569** *Reg. Privy Council Scot.* I. 681 The said Johnne enterit in societie with the said abbot. **1574** *Ibid.* II. 513 Not keping societie in the furthering and furnissing of money.. as the partinaris.. sall appoint. **1592** WEST *1st Pt. Symbol.* §26 Societie is a contract by consent about a thing to be had and used in common on both sides. **1650** *Bounds Publ. Obed.* (ed. 2) 10 Partner-ship or Society (as the Civill Law cals it).

†**b.** Co-operation; assistance. *Obs.*⁻¹

**1586** W. WEBBE *Eng. Poetrie* (Arb.) 34 As for him which .. is addicted without society, by his continuall laboure, to profit this nation.

**III. 8. a.** A number of persons associated together by some common interest or purpose, united by a common vow, holding the same belief or opinion, following the same trade or profession, etc.; an association.

*a* **1548** HALL *Chron., Hen. VII*, 28 b, The societe of saynct George vulgarely called the order of the garter. **1581** ALLEN *Apol.* 29 b, The Seminarie of the Romane Clergie, and other Colleges of the most famous Societie of the name of Iesus. **1612** WOODALL *Surg. Mate* Pref., Wks. (1653) 12 It hath divers wayes brought advantage and good to the whole Societie of Surgeons. **1637** *Decree of Star Chamb. conc. Printing* ¶9 The Company or Society of Stationers. *a* **1720** SEWEL *Hist. Quakers* (1795) I. p. xii, Others of the same Society have not looked upon this as a pattern to imitate.

**1741** WESLEY *Wks.* (1872) I. 301, I read over the names of the United Society. **1783** in Beatson *Pol. Index* (1788) II. 292 A Society or Brotherhood, to be called Knights of the illustrious Order of St. Patrick. **1832** SCOTT *Redgauntlet* let. vii. *note*, An old lady of the Society of Friends. **1867** RUSKIN *Time & Tide* i. §3 All bankers should be members of a great national body, answerable as a society for all deposits. **1877** MOZLEY *Univ. Serm.* iv. 77 The Church is undoubtedly in its design a spiritual society, but it is also a society of this world as well.

**b.** A corporate body of persons having a definite place of residence.

**1588–9** *Act 31 Eliz.* c. 6 §1 Colledges, Churches Collegiat, Churches Cathedrall, Scoles, Hospitalls, Halles, and other like Societies. **1647** CLARENDON *Hist. Reb.* I. §96 In the Society of the Inner Temple, his son made a notable progress. **1849** MACAULAY *Hist. Eng.* vi. II. 98 A society of Benedictine monks was lodged in Saint James's Palace. *Ibid.* viii. 285 The society consisted of a president, of forty fellows, of thirty scholars [etc.].

**9. a.** A collection of individuals composing a community or living under the same organization or government.

*a* **1577** SIR T. SMITH *Commw. Eng.* I. x. (1584) 10 A common wealth is called a society or common doing of a multitude of free men. **1639** HEYWOOD *London's Peaceable Est.* Wks. 1874 V. 358 Greeneland, Muscovy, and Turkey, of which three noble societies you are at this present governour. **1690** LOCKE *Govt.* II. vii. Wks. 1727 II. 182 No Political Society can be, nor subsist without having in itself the Power to preserve the Property..of all those of that Society. **1770** LANGHORNE *Plutarch* (1851) I. 395/2 Every society has more to apprehend from its needy members than from the rich. **1805** WORDSW. *Prelude* XI. 394 There is One great society alone on earth: The noble Living and the noble Dead. **1872** MORLEY *Voltaire* (1886) 3 The Calvinism which in so many important societies displaced it [Catholicism].

**b.** In more limited sense: A company; a small party. Now *rare* or *Obs.*

**1590** SIR J. SMYTH *Disc. Weapons* 16 b, Harquebuziers.. being..aduanced and retired with some societies, or *Cameradas* of loose shot, are of good effect. **1607** SHAKS. *Timon* IV. iii. 21 Therefore be abhorr'd, All Feasts, Societies, and Throngs of men. **1637** MILTON *Lycidas* 179 There entertain him all the Saints above, In solemn troops, and sweet Societies. **1662** J. DAVIES tr. *Olearius' Voy. Amb.* 203 We..entred into a little society among our selves, and.. went all together in a Company. **1725** DE FOE *Voy. r. World* 50 This was not a Business that admitted giving them [i.e. mutineers] Time to club and Cabal together, and form other Societies or Combinations. **1777** W. DALRYMPLE *Trav. Spain & Portugal* xv, The company..making little societies of conversation till towards eleven o'clock.

*fig.* **1594** *Selimus* (Temple Cl.) 1984 We will have hog's cheek, and a dish of tripes, and a society of puddings..: a society of puddings? did you mark that well-used metaphor?

**c.** *Zool.* A group of animals of the same species organized in a co-operative manner.

**1902** *Encycl. Brit.* XXIX. 503/2 Perhaps the most remarkable fact as regards the higher societies of insects is that though the individuals composing a community are the offspring of one mother..yet they do not resemble their parents. **1925** A. D. IMMS *Gen. Textbk. Entomol.* 522 In certain species of the order [Hymenoptera] the individuals have acquired the habit of living together in great societies, as in the case of the ants. **1964** V. B. WIGGLESWORTH *Life of Insects* xiv. 237 All insect societies are overgrown families. **1971** E. O. WILSON *Insect Societies* ii. 6/2 Bird flocks, wolf packs, locust swarms, and groups of communally nesting bees are good examples of elementary societies.

**10. a.** A number of persons united together for the purpose of promoting some branch of study or research by means of meetings, publications, etc.

**1665** *Phil. Trans.* I. 16 Printed with Licence, By John Martyn, and James Allestry, Printers to the Royal Society. *a* **1680** BUTLER *Rem.* (1759) I. 1 A Learn'd Society of late.. Agree'd upon a Summer's Night To search the Moon by her own light. **1763** *Museum Rust.* I. 71 A Letter..from a Member of the Society for encouraging Arts, &c. **1796** H. HUNTER tr. *St.-Pierre's Stud. Nat.* (1799) III. 731 A Society of intelligent Englishmen was formed at London.., the object of which was to prosecute scientific research. **1827** SCOTT *Chron. Canongate* ii, An edition, limited according to the rules of that erudite Society [*sc.* the Bannatyne Club]. **1844** MAITLAND *Dark Ages* 386 At the time when this suggestion was made, the English Historical Society was just being formed. **1900** L. HUXLEY *Life Huxley* (1903) II. i. 4 He became President of the Geological Society in 1872.

**b.** A number of persons meeting together, esp. for the purpose of discussion or debate, conviviality or sociability.

**1673** *Humours Town* 52 You take a wrong notion of our Societies from them; here we have always a numerous Club. **1759** JOHNSON *Idler* No. 48 ¶9 He always runs to a disputing society. **1777** COWPER *Lett.* Wks. (1876) 36 He did not belong to our Thursday society. **1848** THACKERAY *Van. Fair* xlvi, He never would sit down before Sedley at the club even, nor would he have that gentleman's character abused by any member of the society. **1898** *Daily Telegr.* 6 Jan. 9/6 The association for debating all unforbidden subjects which ..was known as 'The Society'.

**c.** *U.S.* = CONGREGATION *sb.* 7.

**1828–32** WEBSTER s.v., In Connecticut, a number of families united and incorporated for the purpose of supporting public worship, is called an ecclesiastical society. **1889** MARY E. WILKINS *A Far-away Melody* (1891) 257 More people went into the Baptist Church, whose Society was much the larger of the two. **1898** *Westm. Gaz.* 4 Nov. 4/2 The unit of the sect [the Methodists] is 'the Society' —composed practically of the communicants attending a particular church.

**d.** A commercial company or association.

**1890** *Daily News* 13 Nov. 7/1 The Investors Protection Society... The society was formed to protect investors and others by advising generally free of charge.

†**11.** A meeting or gathering. *Obs.*

**1712** in W. S. Perry *Hist. Coll. Am. Col. Ch.* I. 192, I can't attend the Society as I would very gladly do. **1741–3** WESLEY *Extr. Jrnl.* (1749) 18 At the society which follow'd, many cried after God.

**12.** *Ecol.* A community of plants within a mature consociation characterized by one or more subdominant species.

**1899** *Bot. Gaz.* XXVII. 111 A plant society is defined as a group of plants living together in a common habitat and subjected to similar life conditions. The term is taken to be the English equivalent of Warming's *Plantesamfund*, translated into the German as *Pflanzenverein*. **1905** F. E. CLEMENTS *Res. Methods in Ecol.* 296 For these areas controlled by principal species, but changing from aspect to aspect, the term *society* is proposed. **1916** —— *Plant Succession* vii. 130 The society is a community characterized by a subdominant or sometimes by two or more subdominants... The society comes next below the consociation in rank, but it is not necessarily a division of it, for the same society may extend through or recur in two or more consociations, *i.e.*, throughout the entire association. **1932** FULLER & CONARD tr. *Braun-Blanquet's Plant Sociol.* xiii. 306 The..'societies' of Clements and Weaver are based entirely upon the dominance of certain species; they are, thus, quite incapable of replacing our association in any system of classification. **1932** *Ecology* XIII. 118 A single pair of terms, society and socies (developmental), has been quite generally applied to subordinate assemblages within associes and associations. **1952** P. W. RICHARDS *Tropical Rain Forest* xi. 259 *Shorea curtesii*..dominates small societies on steep slopes in the hill rain forests of the Malay Peninsula.

**IV. 13.** *attrib.* and *Comb.* **a.** With reference to religious bodies, as ***society-communion, meeting, men, people, -room***, etc.

**1685** W. SMITH in *Biogr. Presbyt.* (1827) II. 83 [They would] rejoice with all such as are joined in this Society-Communion. **1721** WODROW *Hist. Suff. Ch. Scotl.* (1831) IV. 462/2 This year [1688], I find..that the society people made a large collection of money for the relief of several of their number. **1725** P. WALKER in *Biogr. Presbyt.* (1827) I. 160 The..keeping up of Society-meetings for Prayer and Conference. **1744** WESLEY *Wks.* (1872) VIII. 38 The enlarging the society-room to near thrice its first bigness. **1828** IRVING *Last Days* 37 These texts of Scripture..will enable you to confute a whole platform of society orators. **1870** BURTON *Hist. Scot.* VII. 529 The Sanquharians took also the name of 'Society men', as being distributed in 'select societies united in general correspondence'.

**b.** With reference to cultured or fashionable society, as ***society journal, lodging, man, paper***, etc.

**1693** WOOD *Life* 15 June, Peter Wood,..put aside, as 'twas then said, because he was too precise and religious and therefore not fit to make a societie man. **1722** DE FOE *Col. Jack* i, He began to have clothes on his back, to leave the ash-hole, having gotten a society lodging. **1825** C. WESTMACOTT *Eng. Spy* I. 106 Society Whigs and society Tories. **1848** THACKERAY *Van. Fair* li, 'The best' foreigners (as the phrase is in our noble and admirable society slang). **1868** SALA *Lamb's Wks.* I. p. xlii, Hook, with whom society-seeking was a vocation and a passion. **1875** MRS. STOWE *We & Our Neighbours* 205 My sisters..are society girls in the best sense. **1880** J. C. HARRIS *Uncle Remus* viii. 203 'The old man's mind is wandering,' said the society editor. **1882** J. D. McCABE *N.Y. by Sunlight & Gaslight* 228 An engagement ..is promptly announced in one of the 'Society journals'. *c* **1884** (*title*) A society beauty. **1885** *Church Times* 12 June 151 As one of the 'Society' papers suggested in its disgraceful cartoon. **1886** *Fortn. Rev.* Apr. 501 If society-haunting afforded the necessary relaxation. **1888** *St. Louis* (Missouri) *Globe-Democrat* 29 Apr. 22/2 The brainy paragraphs thrown off by one society reporter. **1891** *Girl's Own Paper* 21 Mar. 385/1, I..said I was tired of society life, and..liked nursing better than anything. **1893** 'S. GRAND' *Heavenly Twins* I. xv. 109 You would not counsel a son of yours to marry a society woman of the same character as Major Colquehoun. **1895** T. K. GAVON *Fancy Notions by a Yankee Notion Clerk* 28 Already we have cattle kings, coal barons, merchant princes and society queens. **1910** E. M. FORSTER *Howards End* iii. 19 She did not..pretend that nothing had happened, as a competent society hostess would have done. **1910** CHESTERTON *G. B. Shaw* 152 A pleasant society lady, Lady Cicely Waynefleet. **1911** G. S. PORTER *Harvester* xx. 508 He scanned the society columns of the papers. **1924** GALSWORTHY *White Monkey* I. ix. 73 A society painter and his wife. **1947** 'N. BLAKE' *Minute for Murder* ii. 32 He had been a society photographer before the war. **1949** H. MACLENNAN *Precipice* I. 144 A picture I saw of her in the society page of *The New York Times*. **1950** *New Yorker* 8 Apr. 76/3 Hearst's society columnist, Cholly Knickerbocker. **1950** E. H. GOMBRICH *Story of Art* xxiii. 349 Vandyke had established a standard of society portraits. **1955** L. FEATHER *Encycl. of Jazz* x. 347 *Society band*,..band that plays innocuous commercial dance music. **1956** C. COCKBURN *In Time of Trouble* xvii. 228 The secretary was away attending some society wedding. **1957** D. PIPER *Eng. Face* viii. 199 Behind almost all society portraiture before Reynolds there is a basic, and dead, symmetry. **1959** G. D. PAINTER *Marcel Proust* I. vii. 85 In the name 'Le Gandare' Proust alludes to the society portraitist La Gandara. *Ibid.* xi. 181 A little bird..informed the society columnist of *Le Gaulois*. **1976** C. STORR *Unnatural Fathers* iii. 36 He had had a long liaison with a society beauty. **1977** *Time* 26 Sept. 36/1 The society columns buzzed regularly for years with accounts of their parties and travels aboard an assortment of yachts.

**c.** With reference to societies instituted for special purposes, as ***society goods, man, membership, room, secretary***, etc.; **society hand, house** (see quots. 1888).

**1765–8** ERSKINE *Inst. Law Scot.* III. iii. §27 He is..intitled, upon the division of the society-goods, to..a share. **1861** MAYHEW *Lond. Lab.* III. 221 The Cabinet-makers.. consist, like all other operatives, of two distinct classes, that is to say, of society and non-society men. **1888** JACOBI *Printers' Vocab.* 128 *Society hands*, those belonging to and working under the rules of a trade society. *Ibid.*, *Society houses*, establishments conforming to the rules and paying the recognized scale price for work. **1892** *Photogr. Ann.* II. 809 Society rooms, available upon production of a society membership ticket, or an introduction from a society secretary.

Hence **so'cietyish, so'cietyless** *adjs.*

**1788** MME. D'ARBLAY *Diary* 23 Oct., Societyless, and bookless, and viewless as I am. **1863** WILBERFORCE *Sp. Missions* (1874) 4 The tendency of all that is to cultivate party feeling within the Church..and so by degrees to become one-sided, or what I may call societyish.

**Socinian** (səʊ'sɪnɪən), *sb.* and *a.* [ad. mod.L. *Socinian-us*, f. *Socinus*, Latinized form of the Italian surname *Soz(z)ini*. Cf. F. *Socinien.*]

**A.** *sb.* One of a sect founded by Lælius and Faustus Socinus, two Italian theologians of the 16th century, who denied the divinity of Christ.

**1645** E. PAGITT *Heresiogr.* Ep. Ded. (ed. 2) B 3, We have also Socinians, who teach that Christ dyed not to satisfie for our sins. **1651** BAXTER *Inf. Bapt.* 177 The Socinians say that ..the Doctrine of the Trinity is of Antichrist. **1673** MILTON *True Relig.* Wks. 1851 V. 410 The Arian and Socinian are charg'd to dispute against the Trinity. **1733** NEAL *Hist. Purit.* II. 99 He died a professed Socinian. **1810** CRABBE *Borough* iv. 258 True Independents: while they Calvin hate, They heed as little what Socinians state. **1866** LIDDON *Bampton Lect.* I. (1875) 15 Socinians..assert that Jesus Christ is merely man.

*Comb.* **1698** F. B. *Free but Modest Censure* 31 It is very invidious to go a Socinian-hunting.

**B.** *adj.* Pertaining to the Socinians or their creed.

**1694** (*title*), A Brief Account of the Socinian Trinity. *a* **1704** T. BROWN *Dial. Dead* Wks. 1711 IV. 70 All the Socinian Treatises that stole into the World. **1794** HURD *Life Bp. Warburton* 119 Next to infidels professed, there was no set of writers he treated with less ceremony, than the Socinian. **1842** *Penny Cycl.* XXII. 119/2 This measure.. was followed by the abolition of the two remaining Socinian schools. **1865** PUSEY *Truth Ch. Eng.* 13 The infidel or Socinian press in England.

**So'cinianism.** [f. prec. + -ISM. So F. *Socinianisme.*] The doctrines or special views of the Socinians.

**1643** F. CHEYNELL (*title*), Rise, Growth, and Danger of Socinianisme. **1645** E. PAGITT *Heresiogr.* (ed. 2) 123 For Socinianisme is a compound of many pernicious and antiquitated heresies. **1733** NEAL *Hist. Purit.* II. 375 The Convocation..had condemned Socinianism in general. **1819** BELSHAM *Parr's Wks.* (1828) VIII. 155 It differed almost as much from Socinianism as it did from Athanasianism itself. **1865** PUSEY *Truth Ch. Eng.* 11 The Rationalism in Germany, the Socinianism of Geneva.

**So,cinia'nistic,** *a.* [f. SOCINIAN *sb.* or *a.*] Of a Socinian character.

**1884** *Advance* (Chicago) 14 Feb., An icy Socinianistic form of theism.

**So'cinianize,** *v.* [f. SOCINIAN *sb.* or *a.*]

**1.** *intr.* To adopt or express Socinian views.

**1671** GUMBLE *Life Monck* Pref. 7 He that doth not Socinianize in denying the Christian Religion.

**2.** *trans.* To imbue with Socinian doctrines; to make conformable to Socinianism.

**1695** LOCKE *Vind. Reas. Christ* 13 He would no doubt have found them *all over Socinianized*. *a* **1704** T. BROWN *Two Oxford Scholars* Wks. 1730 I. 4 If I am ever so little.. Socinianis'd. **1797** *Monthly Rev.* XXIII. 560 Who are supposed to reject the Old and to socinianize the New Testament. **1842** *Blackw. Mag.* LI. 166 This made the clandestine plan to Socinianize the church more easy.

Hence **So'cinianized, So'cinianizing** *ppl. adjs.*

**1652** SPARKE *Prim. Devot.* (1663) 393 Socinianized grand-children of Arrius. **1655** J. OWEN *Vind. Evang.* Wks. 1853 XII. 194 The rest of the Socinianizing Arminians. **1793** *Monthly Rev.* XII. 82 The Socinianizing divines, who are the majority. **1851** W. H. GOOLD in *J. Owen's Wks.* II. 276 A confused mass of Socinianized Arminianism.

†**'Socinism.** *Obs.*$^{-1}$ = SOCINIANISM.

**1645** E. PAGITT *Heresiogr.* (ed. 2) 122 Socinisme or Socin[i]anisme hath its name from Lælius Socinus.

**socio-** ('səʊʃɪəʊ, 'səʊsɪəʊ), combining form (on Greek analogies) of L. *socius* companion, associate, etc.

†**1.** Denoting 'fellow-'. *Obs.*$^{-1}$

**1656** *New Almanac* (ed. 2) 7 His socio-forger.

**2.** Used as the first element in a number of hybrid formations (suggested by SOCIOLOGY) having reference to the constitution, study, etc., of society, as **socio'centric** *a.*, tending to focus one's interest on the community or one's own group; hence **socio'centrism**; **soci'ocracy**, government by society as a whole; **'sociocrat**, one who believes in sociocracy; **socio'cratic** *a.*, pertaining to, of the nature of, sociocracy; **sociody'namic** *a.*, tending to produce change in a society or group; hence **sociody'namics** *sb. pl.*; **socioe'cology**, the study of the interactions both among the members of a species and between them and their environment; so **socioeco'logic, -eco'logical** *adjs.*; **soci'ogeny**, the origin and development of society; hence **socio'genic, soci'ogenous** *adjs.*, originating in society or social interaction; **'sociogram** *Sociol.*, a diagrammatic representation of the ratings for popularity, leadership, etc., that members of a small group give each other; a sociometric diagram; **soci'ography**, an empirical method of sociological analysis that makes use of both quantitative and qualitative data; such an analysis; hence **socio'graphic** *a.*; **'sociogroup** *Sociol.*, a group of people who associate for some reason or purpose other than personal preference; **soci'olatry**, the service of society; **socio'medical** *a.*, of or pertaining to the relations between medicine and society; **socio'nomic**, relating to the environmental conditions affecting the formation and development of social groups, esp. as *socionomic sex ratio*, the ratio of females to males in relatively stable social groups; hence **socio'nomics** (*rare*); **soci'ophagous** *a.*, preying upon society or certain parts of it; **socio'static** *a.*, tending to preserve a balance in society.

Various other formations, as *sociogenetic*, *-nomy*, have also been recently used or suggested (*N.E.D.*).

**1881** L. F. WARD in *Trans. Anthrop. Soc. Washington* (1882) I. 97 Those in consequence of which social progress tends to defeat itself—*anti-*sociocentric facts.* **1930** [see CEREBROCENTRIC *a.*]. **1970** J. D. CAUTE *Fanon* iv. 49 There was the Fanon who condemned such insularity as egocentric and sociocentric. **1947** G. MURPHY *Personality* xv. 386 Side by side with egocentrism there was *sociocentrism. **1858** R. CONGREVE tr. *Comte's Catal. Pos. Relig.* xiii. 401 Feudalism combined both.., so as to constitute an anticipation of the final *sociocracy. **1887** *Pall Mall G.* 15 June 3 An idea which in its germ, sociocracy borrows from theocracy. **1887** *Women's Union Jrnl.* 15 Dec. 94 A School of *Sociocrats which held that Communism was impossible because gradations of rank were indestructible. **1887** *Macm. Mag.* Aug. 318 This method of succession, named by Comte *sociocratic heredity. **1934** J. L. MORENO *Who shall Survive?* vii. 74 This demonstrates what we may call the process of slowing down of interest, the cooling off of emotional expansiveness, the *sociodynamic decline of interest. **1977** R. HOLLAND *Self & Social Context* vii. 221 The hypothesis that there are psychodynamic and sociodynamic processes at work even in this relatively 'self-conscious' area of knowledge production. **1978** *Nature* 18 May 184/2 The number of administrators in an organisation expands irresistibly in response to the first law of *sociodynamics. **1972** *Biol. Abstr.* LIV. 6370/2 Geographic vegetational zones are given, as are vegetational stages. *Socioecologic groups are described. **1961** *Ibid.* XXXVI. 5947/1 (*heading*) A *socio-ecological study of pastured domestic rabbits in Mae-sima. **1973** W. P. J. DITTUS in R. H. Tuttle *Socioecol. & Psychol. Primates* 149 Its net reproductive rate is attuned to the availability of food, and is regulated through socioecological mechanisms. **1972** *Biol. Abstr.* LIV. Index 3830/1 *Socio ecology. **1975** L. L. & D. J. KLEIN in R. H. Tuttle *Socioecol. & Psychol. Primates* 83 A dietary factor..that is generally over looked in discussion of primate socioecology, was the degree to which specific primates are able to utilize..varied substances in any single day. **1979** *Nature* 8 Feb. 433/3 The main aims are to study the socio-ecology of the lesser-known species such as the slow loris and the pig-tailed macaque. **1969** ZIGLER & CHILD in Lindzey & Aronson *Handbk. Social Psychol.* III. xxiv. 484 Two main types of interpretations have been employed to explain the cross-cultural findings, the *sociogenic and the psychogenic. **1978** *Language* LIV. 228 His separation of cultures, making sociogenic interaction impossible. **1941** W. DENNIS in *Genetic Psychol. Monographs* XXIII. 187 Prior to the second year of life *sociogenous responses, those which are learned through the intercession of other persons, are few. **1967** C. L. MARKMANN tr. *Fanon's Black Skin, White Masks* (1968) 13 Besides phylogeny and ontogeny stands sociogeny. **1933** J. L. MORENO in *Proc. Amer. Assoc. Mental Deficiency* 236 To visualize how each individual is affected by the maze of attractions and repulsions coming from any individual or going out from any individual of a group we mapped these relations graphically into a **sociogram.* **1972** M. ARGYLE *Social Psychol. of Work* vi. 109 The choices may be plotted to form a sociogram, and this can show the affective structure of a group very clearly. **1954** *Encounter* Dec. 55/1 A *sociographic study attempts to relate all the data concerning a given locality in a meaningful way. **1881** O. T. MASON in *Ann. Rep. Smithsonian Inst.* (1883) 501 Observing and descriptive stage..*sociography. **1940** C. P. LOOMIS *Tönnies's Fundamental Concepts Sociol.* p. xxiv, (*heading*) Empirical sociology or sociography. **1966** *Listener* 12 May 677/1 We do not yet have a sociography of English Catholicism. **1968** *Internat. Encycl. Social Sci.* XV. 49/1 To this he [*sc.* Tönnies]..opposed his own notion of 'sociography', in which systematic observation, case studies, and other qualitative methods were included, together with statistics. **1950** H. H. JENNINGS *Leadership & Isolation* (ed. 2) xiii. 276 This collective, more or less formalized setting, where concerns must be shared and obligations held in common..might appropriately be called ..the *sociogroup. **1956** J. KLEIN *Study of Groups* 179 In sociometric theory a sociogroup is based on preferences involving work in the group. **1858** *Brit. Quart. Rev.* LVI. 441 This is an essential feature of Positivist *sociolatry. **1867** *Contemp. Rev.* VI. 400 The system of sociolatry, which is..to furnish to later generations a complete and permanent religion. **1934** WEBSTER, *Sociomedical. **1961** *Lancet* 2 Sept. 549/1 Euthanasia..is more than a sociomedical problem. **1977** *Time* 10 Jan. 41/1 The flourishing condom market is only one sign of a growing sociomedical phenomenon in the U.S.: a back-to-basics movement in birth control. **1902** J. M. BALDWIN *Social & Ethical Interpretations* (ed. 3) 3 The *Biogenetic* method is valuable mainly in investigating the **socionomic* forces (those which condition or limit social change, but are not themselves social in their character). **1935** *Jrnl. Mammology* XVI. 176 As yet..it is impossible to ascertain the central grouping tendencies and the characteristic socionomic sex ratio (ratio of males to females living within groups). **1976** *Nature* 12 Feb. 459/1 Most body weights..do not take into account interspecies differences in socionomic sex ratio. **1902** J. M. BALDWIN *Social & Ethical Interpretations* (ed. 3) xi. 484 *Socionomics—the science of the relation of social life to its environment, including other social groups. **1892** SPENCER *Princ. Ethics* I. §192. 472 In *sociophagous nations like ours, not much pleasure is caused by contemplating the cessation of conquests. **1895** *Atlantic Monthly* Feb. 195 In a society where the *socio-static press is always at work.

**3.** Used in comb. with adjs., in the sense 'social and..', and in comb. with advbs., in the sense 'socially and..': ***socio-critical***, ***-cultural***, ***-culturally***, ***-demographic***, ***-educational***, ***-emotional***, ***-environmental***, ***-geographic***, ***-geographical***, ***-historical***, ***-industrial***, ***-literary***, ***-official***, ***-political***, ***-politically***, ***-psychological***, ***-psychologically***, ***-regional***, ***-religious***, ***-scientific***, ***-sexual***, ***-technic*** (hence ***socio-technics*** sb. pl.), ***-technical***.

**1963** *Cambr. Rev.* 4 May 401/1 The Leitmotiv of the '*socio-critical' movement [in literature] is 'human destiny and national destiny'. **1929** H. SCHREUDER *Pejorative Sense Devel. in English* II. vi. 65 (*heading*) The *socio-cultural group. **1958** *New Biol.* XXVI. 123 In discussing human potentiality it is not useful to dissociate socio-cultural from biological factors. **1978** *Language* LIV. 188 Linguistics consists partly in an investigation of certain aspects of human socio-cultural behavior. **1980** *Times Lit. Suppl.* 19 Sept. 1044/4 For various socio-cultural reasons, the short story has always occupied a more central place in Australian fiction than in European literatures. **1968** C. A. DOXIADIS *Betw. Dystopia & Utopia* 66 We are not in a position yet to define how far he [*sc.* man] is adjustable either biologically or *socio-culturally. **1972** *Bankers Mag.* Winter 68/2 *Socio-demographic characteristics of the population such as age, sex, income, occupation, race, [etc.]. **1961** *Times* 16 Sept. 9/3 There is here an old *socio-educational dispute in a new context. **1974** *Times Lit. Suppl.* 31 May 580/5 While the mother's strategies correlate with the cognitive development of the child..this correlation is totally unrelated to social class—which effectively deflates some hoary socio-educational myths. **1973** *Word 1966* XXII. 112 Interaction situations, with men preponderantly performing the task role, and women, the *socioemotional. **1969** *Punch* 22 Jan. p. vi/2 *Socio-environmental pressures on me had taken an entirely different turn: I had been seduced by advertising. **1962** in H. O. Beecheno *Introd. Business Stud.* p. iii, A condensed survey of the historical background of our present economy..and the more basic *socio-geographic factors. **1945** *Archit. Rev.* XCVII. 70/1 The *socio-geographical differentiation in our own cities is simple and peaceful compared with that of a newer country like the United States. **1949** *Sci. Amer.* Oct. 53/3 Their philosophical ideas stem from the same *socio-historical conditions of our epoch. **1965** *English Studies* XLVI. 390 Melville embodies the concept of revolt in specific socio-historical frames. **1909** W. H. TOLMAN *Social Engineering* xii. 366 A new profession necessitated by the complexity of *socio-industrial relations. **1891** KIPLING *City Dreadf. N.* 86 They are spared all *socio-official worry. **1933** A. PARRY *Garrets & Pretenders* p. ix, Since Bohemianism is pre-eminently a *socio-literary phenomenon, the periods of its rise and decay coincided fairly well throughout the world. **1980** *Times Lit. Suppl.* 7 Nov. 1249/2 He [*sc.* Edmund Wilson] acquired half a dozen languages that served as socio-literary tools. **1884** *Pall Mall G.* 16 Feb. 2/1 The political or *socio-political questions of the day. **1968** *New Left Rev.* Jan.–Feb. 63 Germany did not merely invent the *ersatz* industrially, it produced it *socio-politically as well. **1899** *Amer. Jrnl. Sociol.* IV. 661 Such a theory can be developed only along *socio-psychological lines. **1970** *Nature* 19 Dec. 1136/1 Too little work has been done on the socio-psychological aspects of spaceflight. **1971** J. J. SHAPIRO tr. *Habermas's Toward Rational Society* ii. 30 Insensitivity to what in more naive times philosphers called 'the good life' can only be broken through today under the *socio-psychologically exceptional conditions of university study. **1964** M. A. K. HALLIDAY et al. *Linguistic Sci.* iv. 86 Our dialects and accents are no longer simply regional: they are regional and social, or '*socio-regional'. **1871** *Aldine* Jan. 18/2 It is a prime merit of such writers as Mr. Keeler and Bret Harte to give a rousing nudge to the saintly self-complacency of our *socio-religious 'priggishness'. **1889** *Spectator* 26 Oct., The socio-religious life of Scotland. **1891** *Nation* 3 Sept. 182 The current *socio-scientific use of *environment* is first found in Carlyle (1827). **1932** S. ZUCKERMAN *Soc. Life Monkeys & Apes* xiv. 215 Facts concerning sub-human primate *socio-sexual responses. **1931** *Sociotechnic [see NUTTERY 3]. **1937** *Burlington Mag.* Nov. 246/1 The concreteness with which *socio-technical problems are realized. **1975** *Times Lit. Suppl.* 28 Feb. 229/3 P. G. Herbst's *Socio-technical Design*..explores the interaction between the social and technical parts of industrial, educational and scientific organizations. **1976** A. CHERNS (*title*) *Sociotechnics. *Ibid.* p. ix, Sociotechnics..is ..a quest for a methodology of bringing the knowledge and concepts of the social sciences to bear on human and social issues.

**sociobiological** (ˌsəʊʃɪəʊbaɪəʊ'lɒdʒɪkəl, ˌsəʊsɪəʊ-), *a.* [f. SOCIO- + BIOLOGICAL *a.*] Of or pertaining to sociobiology. Hence **ˌsociobio'logically** *adv.*

**1921** HANNAY & COLLINGWOOD tr. *Ruggiero's Mod. Philos.* v. 185 Espinas was one of the first to apply the socio-biological method to the treatment of social questions. According to him the instinct of sociability is found in all grades of being, and is shared by animals and men alike. **1948** *Amer. Scientist* XXXVI. 567 We may regard the mechanism, for sociobiological purposes, as given. **1978** M. S. GREGORY et al. *Sociobiology & Human Nature* 3 Pure sociobiological theory, being independent of human biology, does not imply by itself that human social behavior is determined by genes. **1980** *Nature* 24 Apr. 682/1 Sociobiologically sophisticated readers.

**sociobiology** (ˌsəʊʃɪəʊbaɪ'ɒlɒdʒɪ, ˌsəʊsɪəʊ-). [f. SOCIO- + BIOLOGY.] The study of the biological, esp. the ecological and evolutionary, bases of social behaviour.

**1946** J. P. SCOTT in *Minutes Conf. Genetics & Social Behaviour* 5 The central objective of the scientific method is the development of generalizations which are as nearly true as possible... The zoologists and psychologists who work with animals can do their part to help extend these generalizations by working toward the development of comparative sociology, or perhaps it may be called psychobiology or sociobiology. **1948** C. F. HOCKETT in *Amer. Scientist* XXXVI. 564 Since there is no generally accepted word for just what we mean, we can, for the purposes of the present discussion, coin one. On the analogy of *biophysics* we shall speak of *sociobiology*. **1950** J. P. SCOTT in *Ann. N.Y. Acad. Sci.* LI. 1004 An interdisciplinary science which lies between the fields of biology (particularly ecology and physiology) and psychology and sociology. Many names have been given to it, but perhaps the best and most descriptive is 'sociobiology'. **1975** E. O. WILSON *Sociobiology* i. 4/1 Sociobiology is defined as the systematic study of the biological basis of all social behaviour. **1976** *Ann. Rev. Microbiol.* XXX. 236 One of the most exciting aspects of this new field of sociobiology is the chemical control of behavioral responses. **1979** *Nature* 2 Aug. 427/1 The widespread identification of 'sociobiology' with a school of thought is an undeniable fact of current biological sociology.

Hence **ˌsociobi'ologist**, one who studies sociobiology.

**1975** *Times* 29 Dec. 5/1 Interest is growing in the theories of sociobiologists who seek to prove that most human social behaviour has genetic origins. **1980** *Daily Tel.* 10 Mar. 12/8 Sociobiologists hope their theory of behaviour, which seems at present to apply only to individuals, can be expanded into a science which could analyse humanity as a whole.

**'sociodrama.** *Sociol.* Also with hyphen. [f. SOCIO- + DRAMA.] An improvised play acted by or for those involved in a situation of social tension in order to portray different perceptions of the same situation and represent objectively what each experiences in his or her role; a form of psychiatric treatment based on this type of play. Hence **sociodra'matic** *a.*, **socio'dramatist**, someone directing a sociodrama.

**1943** J. L. MORENO in *Sociometry* VI. 331 Sociodrama which deals with inter-group relations and with collective ideologies. *Ibid.* 438 Let us consider first two broad fields of application of sociodramatic procedures. **1952** W. J. H. SPROTT *Social Psychol.* ii. 36 The 'spontaneity training', from which the so-called 'Socio-drama' has been developed. **1958** —— *Human Groups* 188 The elaborate technique of training for foremanship, often employing the socio-drama technique in which foremen take the part of workers and act out a scene. **1964** *Telegraph* (Brisbane) 17 June 8 No one knew what to expect when Jean Jacques Lebel staged his 'sociodramatic event' the other night. **1972** H. J. EYSENCK *Psychology is about People* i. 16 The psychiatrist asks, Is psychotherapy better than sociodrama? **1979** GLASSNER & FREEDMAN *Clinical Sociol.* xiv. 326 In important respects all of the sociodramatic procedures are forms of spontaneity training. *Ibid.*, It is important to distinguish the sociodramatist's view of spontaneity from some others.

**ˌsocio-eco'nomic**, *a.* Also as one word. [f. SOCIO- + ECONOMIC *a.*] That derives from both social and economic factors; that combines both factors to provide an indication of a person's or a group's effective social situation, esp. as ***socio-economic class***, ***status***.

**1883** L. F. WARD *Dynamic Sociol.* I. vii. 525 It is not from an anthropological or ethnological stand-point that our treatise proceeds but rather from a strictly sociological or socio-economic one. **1937** L. B. MURPHY *Social Behaviour & Child Personality* i. 32 Although the socio-economic status was important..it was by no means directly correlated with the educational stimulus which the children received. **1949** M. MEAD in M. Fortes *Social Structure* 18 An account of Arapesh socio-economic life. **1966** BEREITER & ENGELMANN *Teaching Disadvantaged Children* i. 3 Studies of three- to five-year old children from lower socio-economic backgrounds have shown them to be retarded..in every intellectual ability. **1972** *Jrnl. Social Psychol.* LXXXVI. 207 The subjects were required to be from the same socioeconomic class, in this case the middle class. **1978** P. A. COWAN *Piaget: with Feeling* xii. 310 There are studies which compare infants and..children who differ in socioeconomic status.

Hence **socio-eco'nomically** *adv.*

**1955** *Social Problems* July 98 The strong influence of abortion law is seen in the refusal of hospitals to grant socio-economically indicated abortions. **1977** *Lancet* 30 Apr. 955/2 In socioeconomically advanced West Germany the vaccine is specifically recommended for infants with chronic diseases of the heart.

**sociolect** ('səʊsɪəʊlɛkt, 'səʊʃɪəʊ-). [f. SOCIO- + -LECT.] A variety of a language that is characteristic of the social background or status of its user. Also *attrib.* Hence **socio'lectal** *a.*

**1972** [see -LECT]. **1976** *Archivum Linguisticum* VII. 158 Here the functional shift from dialect to sociolect indicators is of particular interest. In fact, dialectal, sociolectal, and stylistic varieties will perhaps be the first 'partial features' which lend themselves to a more ambitious attempt at establishing a complex network of linguistic and social functional co-variation. **1978** *Language* LIV. 227 The book contains 491 pages, written in a highly academic sociolect of German which makes rich use of embedding devices, some sentences being over a page long. **1980** *English World-Wide* I. I. 129 A collection of twelve articles on a variety of sociolectal and dialectal phenomena in British English.

**sociolinguistic** (ˌsəʊsɪəʊlɪŋ'gwɪstɪk, ˌsəʊʃɪəʊ-), *a.* and *sb.* Also **socio-linguistic**. [f. SOCIO- + LINGUISTIC *a.* and *sb.*]

**A.** *adj.* Of or pertaining to the study of language in its social context.

**1949** E. A. NIDA *Morphology* (ed. 2) vi. 152 The reactions of language-users to the sociolinguistic environment. **1952** *Word* VIII. III. 261 Therefore we may expect to come across socio-linguistic situations which we may hesitate to class in one or another of our four categories. **1959** *Amer. Speech* XXXIV. 118 Enumerating these sounds without giving clear indications of all the pertinent sociolinguistic facts can be dangerous. **1964** L. Kaiser in D. Abercombie et al. *Daniel Jones* 102 Ladefoged has discerned three kinds of information: linguistic, sociolinguistic, and personal. **1971** J. Spencer *Eng. Lang. W. Afr.* 7 Before we can understand the processes of stabilisation and change in the English of West Africa, we need a great deal more sociolinguistic evidence. **1978** *Verbatim* Feb. 10/1 Dillard organizes his work around 'sociolinguistic domains' and stresses the importance of discourse over sentence as the primary carrier of meaning.

**B.** *sb. pl.* (usu. const. as *sing.*). The study of language in relation to social factors. Also *attrib.*

**1939** T. C. Hodson in *Man in India* XIX. 94 (*title*) Socio-linguistics in India. **1951** E. Haugen in *Language* XXVII. 213 If semantics should be an undesirable term, there is always 'ethno-linguistics' or perhaps 'socio-linguistics'. **1951** *Directory of American Scholars* 1061/2 Currie, Prof. Haver C(ecil)... History of American thought; socio-linguistics. **1952** H. C. Currie in *Southern Speech Jrnl.* XVIII. 1. 28 This field is here designated *socio-linguistics*. *Ibid.* 36 The present projection of socio-linguistics proposes a fresh start toward researches into the social significance of language in all respects. **1964** *9th Internat. Congress Linguistics 1962* 1129 Those of us who work in the interdisciplinary area of 'socio-linguistics' may feel that we are here at this Congress on sufferance. **1967** *Language* XLIII. 586, I find that sociolinguistics connotes a branch of linguistics or, at best, a neutralization of the fruitful distinction between sociological linguistics and sociology of language. **1979** *London Rev. Bks.* 25 Oct. 4/3 (Advt.), Shows how social psychological theories and methods can increase the explanatory power of sociolinguistics. **1980** *English World-Wide* I. 179 Sociolinguistics intends to produce a linguistic description as its end result, although it uses social facts and methods to arrive at this end.

Hence **socio-ˈlinguist**, a student of or specialist in sociolinguistics; **ˌsociolinˈguistically** *adv.*

**1960** *Amer. Anthropologist* LXVI. 86 Sociolinguists study verbal behavior in terms of the relations between the setting, the participants, the topic, the functions of the interaction, the form, and the values held by the participants about each of these. **1968** W. A. Stewart in J. A. Fishman *Readings in Sociol. of Lang.* 539 [Pidgins] and [Creoles] usually function sociolinguistically as special kinds of dialects of their lexical-source languages. **1972** J. L. Dillard *Black English* v. 193 Men's dialects and languages as well as women's dialects and languages are well known to the sociolinguist. **1973** *Archivum Linguisticum* IV. 70 The following would seem most likely to be sociolinguistically of significance. **1979** *Amer. Speech 1976* LI. 118 Perhaps,..through the combined efforts of dialectologists, sociolinguists, and other observers of language, a more accurate picture will emerge.

**sociologese** (ˌsəʊsɪɒləˈdʒiːz, ˌsəʊʃɪɒ-). [f. SOCIOLOG(Y + -ESE.] A derogatory term used to describe the style of writing supposedly typical of sociologists; a style which is over-complicated or jargonistic and abstruse. Also *attrib.*

**1963** *Times Lit. Suppl.* 29 Mar. 211/1 They are written.. not in Sociologese. **1965** E. Gowers *Fowler's Mod. Eng. Usage* (ed. 2) 570/1 Sociologese, like Commercialese and Officialese, deserves an article to itself. **1969** R. Blackburn in Cockburn & Blackburn *Student Power* 184 The notion of structural contradiction emerges in Sociologese as 'lack of fit' between, for example, the economy and the 'core institutional framework'. **1973** *Times* 8 Nov. 16/3 His first chapter or two is marred by heavy sociologese. **1977** *New Statesman* 1 July 16/3 So, it's 'thwokk', is it? What a pity.. for Mick Shepherd..that he was unable to find a better acoustic whizz-word than this in his dictionary of fifth-rate sociologese clichés. **1982** *Times Lit. Suppl.* 26 Mar. 356/5 *The Culture of Consent* contains, perhaps, too much sociologese for some tastes.

**sociologic** (səʊʃɪəʊˈlɒdʒɪk, səʊsɪ-), *a.* [ad. F. *sociologique*: see prec. 2 and SOCIOLOGY.] Of or pertaining to sociology; concerned or connected with the organization, condition, or study of society. So **socioˈlogical** *a.*; hence **socioˈlogically** *adv.* **sociˈologist**, a student of sociology; one who is interested in social problems. **sociˈologize** *v. intr.*, to make a study of social questions; also *trans.*, to render sociological in character; to study from the standpoint of sociology; hence **sociˈologizing** *ppl. a.* and *vbl. sb.* **ˈsociologue**, a sociologist.

**1861** *Westm. Rev.* Apr. 313 The discovery and verification of *sociologic laws. **1883** *Cent. Mag.* June 312/2 The antagonism felt toward the Indian seems to result..from his sociologic status which differs so widely from our own. **1885** F. Harrison *Choice of Bks.* (1886) 221 There is a..parallel between organic development in sociologic and in biologic types. **1843** Mill *Logic* II. vi. x. 585 There are two kinds of *sociological inquiry. **1865** —— *Comte* 75 The peculiarly complicated nature of sociological studies. **1867** Lewes *Hist. Philos.* (ed. 3) II. 594 It embraced cosmical, but excluded sociological speculations. **1881** *Athenæum* Mar. 363 To throw some light on early Hebrew life by treating it *sociologically. **1884** *Academy* 10 May 326/3 Sociologically he is right in insisting on this distinction. **1843** *Blackw. Mag.* LIII. 399 Presuming these to be decided in a manner favourable to the project of our *Sociologist. **1870** Lowell *Study Wind.* 59 But moralists, sociologists,..have slowly convinced me, that my beggarly sympathies were a sin against society. **1881** Stevenson *Virg. Puerisque* 242 We walk the streets to make romances and to *sociologise. **1971** *New Society* 7 Jan. 24/2 How many sociologists are there in Britain? We do not know, for the profession has not seriously sociologised itself. **1924** *Amer. Jrnl. Sociol.* XXX. 302 (*title*) The *sociologizing movement within political science. **1960** *20th Cent.* May 443 The 'sociologizing' of these disciplines [*sc.* economics and politics] in America.. has increased their current vitality. **1980** *Times Lit. Suppl.* 26 Sept. 1073/3 *The People's Choice* of 1944 is central to the beneficial sociologizing of more than one sector of the political science with which we now live. **1892** *Sat. Rev.* 23 July 106/2 The peasant who has found his *sociologue has to wait yet for his observer.

**sociologism** (səʊsɪˈɒlədʒɪz(ə)m, səʊʃɪˈɒ-). [f. SOCIOLOG(Y + -ISM.] The tendency to ascribe a sociological basis to other disciplines. Hence **socioloˈgistic** *a.*

**1945** K. R. Popper *Open Society* II. xxiii. 202 This theory of Hegel's..is sometimes called 'historicism'... The sociology of knowledge or 'sociologism' is obviously very closely related to or nearly identical with it. *Ibid.* 205 If scientific objectivity were founded, as the sociologistic theory of knowledge naïvely assumes, upon the individual scientist's impartiality,..we should have to say good-bye to it. **1958** W. Stark *Sociology of Knowledge* 331 We have to reject 'sociologism' (a pendant to psychologism). **1964** I. L. Horowitz *New Sociology* 17 The recent work in some quarters, ostensibly critical of excessive sociologism, seems to point precisely in the direction of the self-liquidation of sociology. **1965** E. E. Evans-Pritchard *Theories Primitive Relig.* iii. 70 But, masterly though it was, its conclusions are an unconvincing piece of sociologistic metaphysics. **1977** *Language* LIII. 398 The fact that the autonomy principle underlies K's attack on Doroszewski is shown by the following remark on Saussure's alleged sociologism. **1978** E. A. Tiryakian in Bottomore & Nisbet *Hist. Sociol. Anal.* vi. 212 Durkheim's 'sociologism' in this respect amounts to no less than an epistemological revolution.

**sociology** (səʊʃɪˈɒlədʒɪ, səʊsɪ-). [ad. F. *sociologie* (Comte): see SOCIO- 2 and -LOGY.]

**1. a.** The science or study of the origin, history, and constitution of human society; social science. Also, the study of social organization and institutions and of collective behaviour and interaction, including the individual's relationship to the group; also *attrib.*

**1843** *Blackw. Mag.* LIII. 397 These are to constitute a new science, to be called Social Ethics, or Sociology. **1851** *Fraser's Mag.* XLIV. 452 The new science of sociology, as it is barbarously termed. **1873** Spencer *Stud. Sociol.* iii. 59 Sociology has to recognize truths of social development, structure and function. **1897** L. F. Ward *Social Philos.* i. iv. 66 The nature of this being, man, whose associative habits form the chief subject of sociology. **1927** P. Sorokin *Social Mobility* p. ix, Speculative sociology is passing over. An objective, factual, behavioristic, and quantitative sociology is..superseding it. **1932** S. & B. Webb *Meth. of Social Study* i. 3 Sociology is concerned not with the individual man, regarded as a living organism.., but with relations among men. **1951** Spaulding & Simpson tr. E. Durkheim (*title*) Suicide. A study in sociology. **1965** Howard & Weaver tr. *Aron's Main Currents in Sociolog. Thought* 8 Sociology may be said to be characterized by two specific aims which account for its nature. On the one hand, sociology lays claim to objective and scientific knowledge. On the other, what it claims to know objectively and scientifically is some vaguely defined thing we call society or societies or social phenomena. **1977** R. Holland *Self & Social Context* ix. 260 A college would rather fall below its intake targets and lose revenue than take in sociology students. **1980** *Daily Tel.* 17 Apr. 10/8 He told me that he taught sociology and I told him straight that hogwash was not one of my subjects.

**b.** The application of sociological concepts and analysis to the social context of other disciplines or fields; a particular sociological system.

**1916** E. Ehrlich in *Harvard Law Rev.* XXIX. 582 Mr. Justice Holmes has suggested a criticism of my book on the sociology of law..in that he finds therein no reference to Montesquieu. **1928** P. Sorokin *Contemp. Sociological Theories* i. 40 It will be more convenient to discuss his [*sc.* Weber's] sociology in the chapters on the sociology of religion. **1936** Wirth & Shils tr. *Mannheim's Ideology & Utopia* ii. 69 The simple theory of ideology develops into the sociology of knowledge. **1947** J. Wach (*title*) Sociology of religion. **1965** Howard & Weaver tr. *Aron's Main Currents in Sociological Thought* 7 The specialized sociologies—the sociology of science, the sociology of language, the sociology of art, the sociology of literature—are attempts to explain the evolution of human phenomena in relation to the social milieu. **1978** *Amer. N. & Q.* Feb. 92/1 The first volume.. contains seven essays on the sociology of reading. **1980** *English World-Wide* I. 179 The sociology of language..uses linguistic information as a means of describing social phenomena.

**2.** The study of plant or animal communities. Cf. PHYTOSOCIOLOGY.

**1932** Fuller & Conard tr. *Braun-Blanquet's Plant Sociol.* 1 We may divide all biology into (1) idiobiology: the science of individual organisms; and (2) sociology: the science of organic communities. The latter is divided into the social science of man (sociology in the usual sense), zoosociology, and phytosociology or plant sociology. **1932** S. Zuckerman *Social Life Monkeys & Apes* i. 9 Mammalian sociology has developed without any real regard for questions concerning the validity of anecdotal and anthropomorphic evidence. **1953** D. A. Bannerman *Birds Brit. Isles* I. 35 We are learning more and more regarding what may be termed the sociology of birds. **1960** N. Polunin *Introd. Plant Geogr.* iii. 92 Plant sociology, where considerations of life-forms may help in the description of the structure of the communities.

**sociometric** (səʊsɪəʊˈmɛtrɪk, səʊʃɪəʊ-), *a. Sociol.* and *Social Psychol.* [f. SOCIO- + -METRIC.] Connected with or pertaining to sociometry or the assessment of relationships in groups. Hence **socioˈmetrically** *adv.*; **socioˈmetrics** *sb. pl.* = SOCIOMETRY.

**1933** J. L. Moreno in *Proc. Amer. Assoc. on Mental Deficiency* 224 An instrument to measure the amount of organization shown by social groups is called the sociometric test. **1943** —— in *Sociometry* VI. 316 How a community can be sociometrically tested. **1952** *Personnel Psychol.* V. 178 (*heading*) Sociometrically selected work teams increase production. **1956** C. W. Valentine *Normal Child* xi. 189 The 'sociometric' technique is flexible. **1964** D. F. Dowd in I. L. Horowitz *New Sociol.* 61 A mindless procession that moves from sociology to sociometrics. **1978** P. Marsh et al. *Rules of Disorder* iv. 86 Simply by looking at who meets whom and in what order we can begin to get some idea of the sociometric structure of the football fan culture.

**sociometry** (səʊsɪˈɒmɪtrɪ, səʊʃɪˈɒ-). *Sociol.* and *Social Psychol.* [f. SOCIO- + -METRY.] The qualitative and quantitative analysis of the structure of groups, esp. through charting the relationships that exist between the members of small groups. Hence **sociˈometrist**.

**1908** W. de Morgan *Somehow Good* xi. 99 'I suppose you'd admit there *are* such things as social distinctions?' Sally wouldn't admit anything whatever. If sociometry was to be a science, it must be worked out without axioms or postulates. **1933** J. L. Moreno in *Proc. Amer. Assoc. on Mental Deficiency* 224 The mathematical study of psychological properties of populations, the experimental technique of and the results obtained by the application of quantitative and qualitative methods is called sociometry. **1937** *Sociometry* I. 219 The sociometrist has the task of breaking down..the misunderstandings and fears..in the group he is facing. **1956** J. Klein *Study of Groups* 180 The insistence of the sociometrist that the two kinds of criterion must be presented simultaneously now begins to sound suspicious. **1962** K. M. Evans (*title*) Sociometry and education. **1976** *Times Lit. Suppl.* 26 Mar. 343/2 Mr Lucas deserves a loud cheer for writing a whole informative chapter on the way members of groups affect each other in communities without once using that dreadful word, beloved of educational theories, sociometry.

**sociopath** (ˈsəʊsɪəʊpæθ, ˈsəʊʃɪəʊ-). *Psychol.* [f. SOCIO-, after PSYCHOPATH.] Someone with a personality disorder manifesting itself chiefly in anti-social attitudes and behaviour. Hence **socioˈpathic** *a.*; **sociˈopathy**.

**1930** G. E. Partridge in *Amer. Jrnl. Psychiatry* X. 55 A conspicuous number who..may justly be termed 'sociopathic'. *Ibid.*, We may use the term 'sociopathy' to mean anything deviated or pathological in social relations. *Ibid.* 56 We may exclude from the class of essential sociopaths those whose inadequacy is primarily related to physical weakness, fear, hypersensitiveness, shyness and self-blame. **1940** Hinsie & Schatzky *Psychiatric Dict.* 493/1 *Sociopathy*, this term has generally been used to designate an abnormal or pathological mental attitude toward the environment. **1962** L. Yablonsky *Violent Gang* (1967) xii. 216 The violent-gang structure recruits its participants from the more sociopathic youths living in the disorganized-slum community. **1968** *Listener* 26 Sept. 408/1 In America 'psychopathy' has been replaced by 'sociopathy'. **1976** Smythies & Corbett *Psychiatry* iii. 29 Many sociopaths come from appalling backgrounds or from genetically afflicted families.

‖**socius** (ˈsəʊʃɪəs). [L.]

**1.** An associate or colleague.

**1701** in *Cath. Rec. Soc. Publ.* VII. 106 We were invited to Mr. Ingram's Defension of his Philosophie, & were presented with his & his Socius' Thesis. **1877** J. Morris *Troubles Cath. Forefathers* 3rd Ser. 116 During this time he was Socius to Father Henry Garnet, Vice-Prefect of the English Mission.

**2.** A comrade, companion.

**1859** Sala *Gaslight & D.* xxv. 294 General friend, socius, and adviser of the artists.

**3.** *Philos.* Applied to God, as the 'Great Companion' of man.

**1890** W. James *Princ. Psychol.* I. x. 316 The impulse to pray is a necessary consequence of the fact that whilst the innermost of the empirical selves of a man is a self of the *social* sort, it yet can find its only adequate *socius* in an ideal world. **1917** A. S. Pringle-Pattison *Idea of God* xv. 297 The idea of a divine *socius* has been one of the most abiding inspirations of religious experience.

**4.** The individual person, considered as the unit of human society; the social self.

**1895** J. M. Baldwin *Mental Devel. Child & Race* xi. 338 Both *ego* and *alter* are thus essentially social; each is a *socius*, and each is an imitative creation. **1898** F. H. Giddings *Elements of Sociol.* 10 What, now, is the unit of investigation in Sociology?... In its simplest form society exists whenever an individual has a companion or associate. The socius, then, is the unit of any social group or society. **1912** C. A. Ellwood *Sociol. in Psychol. Aspects* ii. 21 The *socius*, or associated individual,..the unit out of which all the simpler social groups are composed. **1963** S. Koch *Psychol.* VI. p.v, (*title*) Investigations of man as socius: their place in psychology and the social sciences.

**sock** (sɒk), *sb.*[1] Forms: 1 socc, 4–7 socke, 7– sock (7 socque); 4–6 **sokke**, 5–6 **sok** (5 soke). Pl. also sox (see as main entry). [OE. *socc*, ad. L. *soccus* a light low-heeled shoe or slipper: of the same origin are OHG. *soch*, *soc* (MHG. *soc*, *socke*, G. *socke*, *socken*), MLG. *socke*, MDu. *socke*, *soc* (Du. *zok*, WFris. *sok*), OIcel. *sokkr* (Icel. *sokkur*, Norw. *sokk*, Sw. *sock*, Da. *sokke*). Also F. *soque* (1611).]

**1. a.** A covering for the foot, of the nature of a light shoe, slipper, or pump. Now *rare* or *Obs.*

*c* **725** *Corpus Gloss.* S 394 *Soccus*, socc, slebescoh. *a* **1030** *Rule St. Benet* (Logeman) 92 *Pedules et caligas*, soccas & hosan. *c* **1440** *Promp. Parv.* 400/2 Pynsone, sokke, *pedipomita*. **1451** Capgrave *Life St. Gilbert* 99 A peyre of old sokkys, or pinsones, whech our maystir had often wered. **1565** Cooper *Thesaurus*, *Calcearium*, a shoe, pinson, or socke. *Ibid.*, *Calceo*,..to put on shoes, sockes or pinsons.

**1613** PURCHAS *Pilgrimage* (1614) 621 Not being permitted to weare shooes, but in stead thereof vse sockes made of Rushes. **1663** WATERHOUSE *Fortescutus Illustr.* 430 A Shooe like a slipper with an heel, which we call a Sock. **1687** A. LOVELL tr. *Thevenot's Trav.* I. 30 Their Stockins are of Cloth the length of the leg, the feet whereof are socks of yellow or red Leather..sewed to the Stockins. **1799** *Monthly Rev.* XXX. 487 They have all very small feet, from inclosing them as tight as possible in socks of morocco leather. **1855** MACAULAY *Hist. Eng.* xiii. III. 360 The few [Highlanders] who were so luxurious as to wear rude socks of untanned hide.

†**b.** [After It. *zoccollo.*] A sandal, patten, or clog. *Obs. rare.*

**1691** tr. *Emilianne's Frauds Rom. Monks* (ed. 3) 131 A large Convent of Religious,..called by the Italians, *Soccelanti*, because of the wooden Socks they were instead of Shoes. **1696** PHILLIPS (ed. 5), *Socque*, a kind of Sandal, or wooden Patin for the Feet, worn by the begging Friers.

**2. a.** A short stocking covering the foot and usually reaching to the calf of the leg; half-hose; also, = *ankle sock.*

**1327** *Pol. Songs* (Camden) 330 Hii weren sockes in here shon, and felted botes above. *c* **1460** J. RUSSELL *Bk. Nurture* 961 His shon, sokkis, & hosyn, to draw of be ye bolde. **1464** *Mann. & Househ. Exp.* (Roxb.) 481 Payd fore ij. payr shoes and ij. payr sokkes, xvj.d. **1531** *Acc. Ld. High Treas. Scotl.* (1905) VI. 19 Ane elne small canves to be the King ane pair of sokkis. **1599** A. M. tr. *Gabelhouer's Bk. Physicke* 192/2 You must..put on a clean payer of sockes. **1621** BURTON *Anat. Mel.* I. iii. I. ii. (1651) 184 One pulled off his socks, another made ready his bed. **1682** DRYDEN *Medal* Ep. to Whigs, Even Protestant Socks are bought up among you, out of veneration to the name. **1753** HANWAY *Trav.* III. I. (1762) I. 228 They use..socks of wool, which reach over the ankles. **1768** *Phil. Trans.* LX. 122 Two or three pair of woollen socks, which we have on our feet.

*attrib.* and *Comb.* **1883** *Daily News* 17 Sept. 2/3 In the sock department..there are complaints of want of business. **1899** *Ibid.* 27 Dec. 8/3 His tailoring and his sock-darning.

*Phr. c* **1520** SKELTON *Magnyf.* 1362 Trymme at her tayle, or a man can turne a socke. **1538** BALE *Three Laws* iii, They may go turn a sock.

(*b*) Slang and colloq. phrases: ***in one's socks***, as a condition of measurement of stature; = *in one's stockings* s.v. STOCKING *sb.* 5 a (cf. *in one's shoes* s.v. SHOE *sb.* 2 c); ***to knock the socks off*** (someone), and varr. (*U.S.*): to beat thoroughly, to trounce; similarly ***to rot the socks off***; ***to pull one's socks up***: to make an effort, to pull oneself together; ***to put a sock in it***: to stop speaking or making a noise, to shut up; to 'stop it'; usu. in *imp.*; ***old socks*** (orig. *N. Amer.*): a familiar form of address.

**1835** DICKENS *Sk. Boz* (1836) II. 2 He..stood four feet six inches and three-quarters in his socks. **1842** BISCHOFF *Wool Manuf.* II. 311 The socks which the women there knit. **1913** T. H. S. ESCOTT *Anthony Trollope* x. 191 Those who knew Anthony Trollope in the flesh saw in him one who, at his prime, had stood some six feet in his socks. **1927** in C. J. Finger *Frontier Ballads* 69 This Floyd stood six feet in his socks and passed for mighty fly. **1977** *Horse & Hound* 14 Jan. 40/3 (Advt.), 11 hands in his socks... Smart, free-moving pony.

**1845** C. BEECHER *Let.* in M. Rugoff *Beechers* (1981) xi. 212 'Beecher you must put in your best licks today!' 'You must knock the socks off those Old School folks!' And so they stood by to see me fight. **1964** J. PORTER *Dover One* vi. 65 This thick, fruity beverage..was guaranteed by one revolting old boozer as being strong enough to rot the socks off you. **1979** *Arizona Daily Star* 22 July D3/1 'Trucks have been beating our socks off,' said..a spokesman for the Atchison, Topeka & Santa Fe Railway in Chicago. 'But now we have a chance to get some of the business back.'

**1893** H. F. MCCLELLAND *Jack & Beanstalk* 31 Pull up your socks! I'll see naught goes wrong with you. **1906** *Daily Mail* 14 Feb. 6/6 The 'smart set' have got hold of another neat expression. 'You must pull your socks up' is the latest form of saying 'Never mind', or 'Pull yourself together'. **1914** 'BARTIMEUS' *Naval Occasions* xi. 78 Pull your socks up, Ah Chee, an' think of something. **1936** M. KENNEDY *Together & Apart* IV. 294 There's hope for you if you pull your socks up. **1976** *Southern Even. Echo* (Southampton) 11 Nov. 17/5 The dismissal was unfair because Mr. Collier had not been given adequate warning and a chance 'to pull his socks up' before dismissal.

**1919** *Athenæum* 8 Aug. 729/2 The expression 'Put a sock in it', meaning 'Leave off talking, singing or shouting'. **1930** J. B. PRIESTLEY *Good Companions* I. vi. 232 Two or three members of his audience laughed, but a young man in a green cloth cap was very annoyed. 'Oh, put a sock in it,' he said to the ripe gentleman, who immediately and very loudly asked him what he meant by it. **1933** M. LOWRY *Ultramarine* vi. 243 Aw, put a sock in it. Well, I'm going to sleep, chaps, and if you wake me again, the fellow that does it I'll slip him thirteen inches of saltpetre. **1944** 'N. SHUTE' *Pastoral* v. 107 'For Christ's sake put a sock in it,' he had said..'and tell them I want an ambulance down here.' **1978** A. PRICE *'44 Vintage* vi. 69 He..drew his finger across his throat, grinning horribly. 'Put a sock in it, Taf,' said Sergeant Purvis sharply.

**1925** T. DREISER *Amer. Tragedy* I. II. iii. 185 Gee, it's good to have a look at you, old socks! **1934** H. G. RADCLIFFE in *Passing Show* 27 Jan. 5/4 Hey, Morrison, old socks. How's things! **1950** R. MOORE *Candlemas Bay* 19 Ninety.. pounds, Jebby, old socks.

**b.** ***white sock***, a white portion on the leg of a horse, extending half-way up to the knee.

**1893** M. H. HAYES *Points of Horse* xx. (1897) 222 'White stocking'..might be reserved for one that comes up as high as the knee or hock; while that of a 'white sock' might be used to signify the marking when it is shorter.

**c.** *colloq.* A sock used as a receptacle for storing one's money; hence, a store of money. Cf. STOCKING *sb.* 2 a.

**1930** WODEHOUSE *Very Good, Jeeves!* x. 263 Her name was Maudie and he loved her dearly, but the family would have none of it. They dug down into the sock and paid her off. **1949** H. MACLENNAN *Precipice* III. 248 Once we've got enough put away in the sock I'm going to..go back to M.I.T. **1951** CUSACK & JAMES *Come in Spinner* 54 He just can't adjust himself to not having the best. And that's what marriage without a sock in the bank would mean. **1956** B. HOLIDAY *Lady sings Blues* (1973) x. 95, I opened Café Society as an unknown; I left two years later as a star. But you couldn't tell the difference from what I had in my sock.

**d.** *N.Z.* (See quot. 1965.)

**1955** G. BOWEN *Wool Away!* iii. 45 Many sheepowners do not like socks taken off, as it puts hair in the wool. **1965** *N.Z. Listener* 26 Feb. 15/2 *Socks*, wool between the knee and the foot. In some sheds and competitions the instruction 'leave the socks on' means not to shear this wool, which usually contains a proportion of hair.

**3.** *spec.* A light shoe worn by comic actors on the ancient Greek and Roman stage; hence used allusively to denote comedy or the comic muse. ***sock and buskin***, comedy and tragedy, the drama or theatrical profession as a whole.

**1597** BP. HALL *Sat.* I. i. 19 Trumpet,..and socks, and buskins fine, I them bequeath, whose statues [etc.]. **1626** MASSINGER *Roman Actor* I. i, The Greeks, to whom we owe the first invention Both of the buskined scene and humble sock. **1682** DRYDEN *Mac-Fl.* 80 Great Fletcher never treads in buskins here, Nor greater Jonson dares in socks appear. **1746** COLLINS *The Manners* iv, The Comick Sock that binds thy feet! **1783** COWPER *Valediction* 34 To live by buskin, sock, and raree-show. **1809** MALKIN *Gil Blas* III. xi. ¶1 Gentlemen of the sock and buskin are not on the best possible terms with the church. **1817** BYRON *Beppo* xxxi, He was a critic upon operas, too, And knew all niceties of the sock and buskin.

†**4.** (See quot.) *Obs.*$^{-0}$

**1611** COTGR., *Socque*, a socke or sole of durt, or earth, cleauing to the bottome of the foot in a cloggie way, or in a moist & clayie soyle.

**5.** *techn.* (See quots.)

**1851** *Mech. Mag.* 22 Mar. 239 A method of making the 'socks' or uppers of boots. *Ibid.*, The sock is made of knitted material, with an elastic band at top. **1851** *Catal. Gt. Exhib.* 520/1 Varieties of socks for shoes, of cork and gutta percha covered with lamb skin. **1858** SIMMONDS *Dict. Trade*, *Sock*, ..an inner warm sole for a shoe.

**6.** *attrib.* and *Comb.*, as **sock foot** *U.S.* = STOCKING-FOOT c.; hence **sock-footed** *a.*; **sock-suspender** = SUSPENDER 4 b. See also sense 2.

**1934** *Jrnl. Amer. Folk-Lore* XLVII. 52 No boots could he find. He was about to..go to his wedding in his sock feet, when a Voice told him to crawl out from under the bed. **1935** Z. N. HURSTON *Mules & Men* I. viii. 177 Pull off yo' shoes and set in yo' sock feet. **1981** *Nordic Skiing* Jan. 34/2 Chairback is for the making of memories...unforgettable skiing, bone-easing hot shower and sauna, a fine dinner, a tumbler of mulled wine, sock-footed by your woodstove. **1912** E. C. BENTLEY *Trent's last Case* iii. 36 He had on a complete outfit of underclothing, studs in his shirt, sock-suspenders. **1922** WODEHOUSE *Jill the Reckless* xviii. 268 Give me your share of the show for three dollars in cash and I'll throw in a pair of sock-suspenders and an Ingersoll. **1978** S. WILSON *Dealer's Move* ix. 185 One of his trousers had been dragged up to his knee... He was wearing sock suspenders.

**sock** (sɒk), *sb.*[2] *north.* and *Sc.* Forms: 5 sokk(e, 5–6 sok, 5–7 soke; 6 sucke, socke, 7– sock. [a. OF. *soc* (12th cent.; so mod.F.), commonly regarded as of Celtic origin.]

**1.** A ploughshare.

**1404** *Durh. Acc. Rolls* (Surtees) 398, ij aratra cum ij sokkis. **1405–6** *Ibid.* 222 Pro j sok et ploghschoue. **1483** *Cath. Angl.* 348/2 A Sokk of a plughe,..*vomer vel vomis.* **1513** DOUGLAS *Æneid* VII. xi. 79 Al instrumentis of pleuch graith,..As culturis, sokis, and the sovmis gret. **1559** *Wills & Inv. N.C.* (Surtees, 1835) I. 170 A kowter, a soke. **1570** LEVINS *Manip.* 185/1 Ye Sucke of a plow. **1691** RAY *N.C. Words* (ed. 2), A *Sock* or *Plough-sock*, a Plough-share. **1745** tr. *Columella's Husb.* II. i, When such leaves..are..turned over with the sock, and mixed with the lower ground. **1765** A. DICKSON *Treat. Agric.* II. (ed. 2) 236 The plough thus set right by the way of fitting on the sock, will be heavy to draw. **1814** SCOTT *Diary* 6 August in Lockhart, An old-fashioned Zetland plough..had..a coulter, but no sock. **1844** H. STEPHENS *Book Farm* I. 411 The share or sock..is fitted upon a prolongation of the sole-bar of the body-frame. **1890** *Proc. Soc. Antiquaries* 9 Jan. 30 A lad, whilst ploughing,..found the bronze bell wedged on to the 'sock' of the plough.

**b.** *attrib.*, as ***sock-guard***, ***-iron***, ***-plate***.

**1371** *Fabric Rolls York Minster* (Surtees) 7 Et in..j sokeiren, j pari belowes,..emptis. **1844** H. STEPHENS *Book Farm* I. 415 The share is always formed from a plate forged for the express purpose at the iron-mills, and known in the trade by the term *sock-plate.* **1893** in *Eng. Dial. Dict.* s.v, These were wood plews,..an' hed a sock-guard to prevent t' sock comin' off.

**2.** ***sock and scythe***, used to denote ploughing and mowing. Also *attrib.* with *land.*

**1597** SKENE *De Verb. Sign.* M vj b, *Hvsbandland.* conteinis commonlie 6. aikers of sok & syith lande: That is of sik land as may be tilled by ane pleuch, or may be mawed with ane syith. **1824** MACTAGGART *Gallovid. Encycl.* 26, I was fit for baith sock and sythe. *Ibid.* 412 At sock or scythe they hae nae match.

**sock**, *sb.*[3] Now *dial.* Also 1 soc, 4 sok. [OE. *soc* (also *ȝesoc*), f. the weak grade of *sūcan* to suck, = MDu. *soc*, *zoc* suck (Kilian *sock*, WFris. *sok*, the suck of water in the wake of a ship).]

†**1.** Suck (given to a child). *Obs.*

*c* **1000** ÆLFRIC *Gen.* xxi. 8 On þone dæȝ þe man þæt cild fram soce Sarra ateah. **13..** *E.E. Allit. P.* C. 391 Sesez childer of her sok. **1382** WYCLIF *Isaiah* xi. 8 [The child] that shal be taken awei fro sok, or wenyd.

**2.** *dial.* Wet or moisture collecting in, or percolating through, soil. (Cf. SOAK *sb.* 2 b.)

**1799** [A. YOUNG] *Agric. Lincoln.* 15 The sock or soak among the silt is sometimes brackish. *c* **1818** BRITTON *Lincolnshire* 560 Entering the fens, it leaves a portion of its waters and sludge or sock. *a* **1825** FORBY *Voc. E. Anglia*, *Sock*, the superficial moisture of land not properly drained off. **1851** *Jrnl. R. Agric. Soc.* XII. II. 293 Throughout all the marshes and many of the fens are found those subterranean currents called the soak or sock. *Ibid.* 305 A sock-dyke or drain.

**b.** The drainage of a dunghill; liquid manure.

**1790** W. H. MARSHALL *Rur. Econ. Midl.* II. 442 *Sock*, the drainage of a farm yard: hence *Sock-pit*, the receptacle of such drainage. **1896** in *Eng. Dial. Dict.*, There was no sock above the outlet.

**sock** (sɒk), *sb.*[4] *slang.* [Cf. SOCK *v.*[2]]

**1.** A blow; a beating. Chiefly in phr. ***to give*** (one) ***sock(s***, to give a sound thrashing or beating. Also in phr. ***a sock in the eye*** (also *fig.*).

*a* **1700** B. E. *Dict. Cant. Crew* s.v. *Tip*, *Tip the Culls a Sock, for they are sawcy*, Knock down the Men for resisting. **1864** *Slang Dict.* 240 'Give him Sock,' i.e. thrash him well. **1897** *Westm. Gaz.* 30 Nov. 2/2 Hope we give these brutes socks; they are plugging us all round now. **1972** WODEHOUSE *Pearls, Girls, & Monty Bodkin* vi. 87 He's asked you to lunch in the hope of talking you into giving me the sock in the eye on which his heart is set. **1974** —— *Aunts aren't Gentlemen* xiv. 119, I knew that her name would be mud. I still wasn't sure she couldn't even be jugged, and what a sock in the eye that would give Uncle Tom's digestion. **1979** *Woman & Home* June 154/2 The return to tradition; a sock in the eye for the mechanisation that was creating unemployment.

**2.** *U.S. slang.* A strong impact, emphasis, a 'kick'.

**1936** *Swing Music* Mar. 10/1, I used to get a terrific sock out of Rappolo riding high on his clarinet. **1937** B. GOODMAN *This Thing called Swing* 9 *Sock*, emphasis, usually referring to the last chorus. **1950** *Audio Engin.* Sept. 14/3 More low middles increase the *Punch* until the program is *solid*, and has *sock.* **1972** *Publishers' Weekly* 21 Aug. 15/1 (Advt.), Here's solid history with the sock of unforgettable fiction. **1979** *Arizona Daily Star* 22 July C3/2, I figure we have enough speed and sock in our lineup to score runs.

**3.** *attrib.* and *Comb.*, as **sock chorus** *Jazz* (see quot. 1936); **sock cymbal** *Jazz* = HIGH HAT, HIGH-HAT 3; also *attrib.*

**1936** *Delineator* Nov. 49/2 *Sock chorus*, last chorus of an arrangement. **1937** *Metronome* Mar. 31/1 The full sock chorus..hits you between the eyes. **1956** E. HUNTER *Second Ending* iv. 69 They rode into the sock chorus like a storm cloud of marauders. **1936** Sock cymbal [see OFF-BEAT *a.* 1]. **1949** L. FEATHER *Inside Be-bop* III. 80 Kenny originally played the old Jo Jones sock cymbal style. **1972** *Jazz & Blues* Sept. 7/3 You wouldn't play your sock cymbal the same as your ride cymbal.

**sock**, *sb.*[5] *Eton slang.* [Of obscure origin.] Eatables of various kinds, especially dainties.

**1825** C. WESTMACOTT *Eng. Spy* I. 39 Then, after holidays, Tom..gives sock so graciously, that he is the very life of dame ——'s party. **1866** *Routledge's Every Boy's Ann.* 310 Sellers of 'sock', that is, eatables,—sweet mixtures generally. **1881** in Pascoe *Every-day Life*, etc. 25 The consumption of 'sock' too in school was considerable.

*attrib.* **1866** *Routledge's Every Boy's Ann.* 194 There's my old sock-shop.

**sock**, *sb.*[6] [? ellipt. for SOCK-LAMB.] A pet child or young animal.

**1837** BARHAM *Ingol. Leg.* Ser. I. *Spectre of Tappington* (1905) 24 Master Neddy is 'grandpapa's darling', and Mary Anne mamma's particular 'Sock'. **1869** *N. & Q.* 4th Ser. III. 500 You know you are a little sock!

**sock**, *sb.*[7] *slang.* [Of obscure origin: the senses have prob. no connexion with each other.]

†**1.** ? A small coin. (Cf. RAG *sb.*[1] 2 c.) *Obs.*$^{-1}$

**1688** SHADWELL *Sqr. Alsatia* I. i, I went up to the Gaming Ordinary and lost all my Ready; they left me not a rag or sock.

†**2.** A pocket. *Obs.*

*a* **1700** in B. E. *Dict. Cant. Crew.*

**3.** Credit, 'tick'.

**1874** *Slang Dict.* 301 He gets goods on sock, while I pay ready.

**sock**, *sb.*[8] *rare*$^{-1}$. Abbrev. of SOCKET *sb.*

**1803** H. K. WHITE *Gondoline* lxv, The eyes were starting from their socks, The mouth it ghastly grinn'd.

†**sock**, *v.*[1] *Obs.* [Of obscure origin.] *trans.* To sew (a corpse) *in* or *into* a shroud. Also with *up.*

**1584** R. SCOT *Discov. Witchcr.* III. ii. (1886) 33 They which socke the corps. *Ibid.* VI. vii. 99 Needels wherewith dead bodies are sowne or sockt into their sheetes. *a* **1627** MIDDLETON *Witch* I. ii, The same needles..That sews and socks up dead men in their sheets. **1643** *Sussex Arch. Coll.* XX. 105 Paid more for a sheet to socke her in, 2*s.* 8½*d.*, and for laying her forthe and socking of her, 2*s.* 2½*d.*

Hence †**socking-sheet**, a winding-sheet.

**1691** WOOD *Ath. Oxon.* I. 60 It was his custom..every night to hang his shroud and socking or burial-sheet at his beds feet.

**sock**, *v.*[2] *slang.* [Of obscure origin.]

**1.** *trans.* **a.** (*a*) To beat, strike hard, hit. (*b*) *fig.* (*U.S.*) To give a hard blow to; *esp.* to take large sums of money from (someone).

(*a*) *a* **1700** B. E. *Dict. Cant. Crew*, *Sock*, to Beat... *I'll Sock ye*, I'll Drub ye tightly. **1870** R. B. MANSFIELD *School-Life at Winchester College* 234 *Sock*, to hit hard at Cricket. **1890** KIPLING *Barrack-room Ball., Oonts* 15 We socks 'im with a stretcher-pole. **1896** NEWNHAM-DAVIS *Three Men & a God* 30 'Sock 'em, Blackie!' said W. Smith. 'Sock the swine!' echoed his brother. **1916** [see GAS *sb.*[2]]. **1926** *Variety*

29 Dec. 5/3 No craving for expression motivated me when I hung up the finger glove and sliding pads in favor of socking a typewriter. **1933** G. B. Shaw *Political Madhouse in America* 21 Why do you applaud these screen heroes who, when they are not kissing the heroine, are socking jaws? It is a criminal offence to sock a citizen in the jaw. **1982** B. Chatwin *On Black Hill* xiv. 67 The porter had socked him on the jaw, and he now lay, face down on the paving.

(*b*) **1939** J. Steinbeck *Grapes of Wrath* xvi. 248 Find out how much they gonna sock ya for the lessons. **1941** B. Schulberg *What makes Sammy Run!* x. 191 When a moving picture is right, it socks the eye and the ear and the solar plexus. **1943** *Sun* (Baltimore) 8 Nov. 1/2 Cost rises are so precipitate..that one Congressman..suggested 'we're being socked everywhere in foreign countries.' **1973** J. Cleary *Ransom* ii. 44, I don't know what sort of demands they're making. If they're socking the Mayor..the price is gonna be high—he's a very rich man. **1978** *Detroit Free Press* 5 Mar. A.8/1 The township socked the company with a building permit violation.

**b.** *U.S.* (See quot.)

**1848** Bartlett *Dict. Amer.* 320 *To Sock*, to press by a hard blow a man's hat over his head and face. Used in Rhode Island.

**c.** To drive or thrust *in* or *in*(*to*) something. orig. and chiefly *U.S.*

**1843** *Spirit of Times* 15 July 234/1 About one hundred yards from home, Spicer pulled Beppo out, and 'socked in' his spurs. **1845** T. J. Green *Texian Exped.* xvii. 321 The corporal 'socked' it [*sc.* a shoe-maker's awl] in the thick of his back. **1878** J. H. Beadle *Western Wilds* ii. 37 The very next day they put me in jail—socked me right in with them two Hodges. **1892** Kipling *Barrack-room Ball., Cells* 30 'Strewth, but I socked it them hard! **1898** *Westm. Gaz.* 19 Nov. 2/1, I wouldn't have had those fangs socked into me for all the gold mines in these United States.

(*b*) In phrases. *to sock it to* (one): to strike, deal a blow to (that person); to 'give it' to (one). Hence *fig.*; freq. in imp., as catch-phrase *sock it to me* (*them*, etc.)*!*, used to express encouragement, sexual invitation, etc. Also in sb. phr. *sock-it-to-me*, a loud and violent style of music; a piece of such music. orig. and chiefly *U.S.*

**1877** Bartlett *Dict. Americanisms* (ed. 4) 623 Two loafers are fighting; one of the crowd cries out, '*Sock* it to him.' **1883** 'Mark Twain' *Life on Mississippi* xliii. 438 A rich man won't have anything but your very best; and you can..pile it on and sock it to him. **1889** —— *Connecticut Yankee* xxxiii. 422 'Well, observe the difference: you pay eight cents and four mills, we pay only eight cents.' I prepared, now, to sock it to him. I said: 'Look here.., what's become of your high wages you were bragging so about, a few minutes ago?'—and I looked around on the company with placid satisfaction. **1901** *Cent. Mag.* May 124 We shall sock it to them, we shall indeed. **1927** O. W. Holmes in *Holmes-Laski Lett.* (1953) II. 975, I have heard an English judge sock it to the jury in a murder case. **1963** B. J. Chute *Shift to Right* 153 There was a shriek from the panting Trenton stands: 'Yea, Rusty. Sock it to 'em.' **1968** *Tel.* (Brisbane) 15 June 2/3 'Sock it to me' is a catch-phrase which is sweeping America... It's all due to Judy Carne,..who cheekily used the phrase in a weekly comedy show called 'Laugh In'. **1969** R. Lowell *Notebook* 137 The little girl's bedroom, perfect with posters: 'Do not enter,' and 'Sock it to me, Baby.' **1969** *Times* 19 July 9/6 The black American phrase 'sock it to me' (with an obscene connotation). **1969** *Times* 29 July 1/3 If President Nixon is going to 'sock it' to anyone, the likeliest recipient is the South Vietnamese government. **1970** S. Sheldon *Naked Face* (1971) ii. 16 She reached between his legs and stroked him, whispering, 'Go, baby. Sock it to me.' **1970** *Melody Maker* 11 July 19/7 It's good to hear Pickett getting away from the sock-it-to-me and into gentler songs. **1971** *West Indian World* 12 Nov. 14/3 Back to the sock-it-to-me's with Jesse James's 'Don't Nobody Want to Get Married'.. which storms breathlessly along complete with hard-hitting bass and wow-wow guitars. **1977** *New Yorker* 2 May 34/2, I can't afford a second divorce. Daphne would really sock it to me. **1978** *Railway Age* 25 Dec. 25/2 Does all this boil down to some kind of accounting legerdemain that, in the end, will be socking it to the taxpayers?

**d.** *Jazz.* To perform (music) in a swinging manner. Freq. in phr. *to sock it* (*out*).

**1927** *Melody Maker* July 697 Sock out your last chorus on that, my friends. **1933** [see get *v.* 70l]. **1935** *Vanity Fair* XLV. 71/3 Hot artists or bands that can put across their licks successfully are '*senders*';..they can '*sock it*'. **1955** Shapiro & Hentoff *Hear me talkin' to Ya* vii. 79 'Blow it, kid. Sock it out,' Tig and Jones kept shouting, until I finally loosened up and did tricks with that slide that I probably never did before or since. **1968** *Radio Times* 28 Nov. 47/1 He's spent his evenings singing in pubs..'socking' out the rhythm and blues. **1976** *New Yorker* 12 Jan. 37 (*caption*) From the top—'Watermelon Man'. Let's sock it out and give Mrs. Ritterhouse a chance to really cook.

**2.** *intr.* To strike out, deliver blows; to pitch *into* one.

**1856** *Lyrics in War Time, Orphan's Song*, I scolded and I socked, But it minded not a whit. **1864** *Slang Dict.* 240 'Sock into him,' i.e. give him a good drubbing.

Hence '**socking** *vbl. sb.*

**1978** *N.Y. Times* 30 Mar. D 17/2 Harrelson played no part in all the socking because the Mets stopped scoring after four innings and the Phillies after five, and he didn't get into the game until the seventh.

**sock,** *v.*[3] *Eton slang.* [f. sock *sb.*[5]] **a.** *trans.* To treat (one) to sock; to present or give (something) to one. **b.** *intr.* To buy or consume sock.

**1842** *Eton Bureau* 162 Sock means prog, but when you sock a boy anything, he eats it, and you pay for it... I was asked by A—— to sock him a verse the other day, and I had to sock him a construe of his lesson too. **1850** *N. & Q.* 1st Ser. II. 44/2 That a schoolfellow would 'sock him', i.e. treat him to sock at the pastry cooks. **1883** Brinsley-Richards *Seven Years Eton* v. 38 We Eton fellows, great and small, 'socked' prodigiously. **1889** *Macm. Mag.* Nov. 65 My governor socked me a book.

**sock,** *v.*[4] *south-w. dial.* [Imitative.] *intr.* To sigh.

**1863** Barnes *Dorset Gl.*, *Sock*, to sigh with a loudish sound. **1886** T. Hardy *Mayor Casterbr.* II. xviii. 243 She pined and pined, and socked and sighed.

**sock,** *v.*[5] [f. sock *sb.*[1] 2.]

**1.** *trans.* To provide with socks; to put socks on (one).

**1897** Gunter *Ballyho Bey* xx. 231 How beautifully Irene has socked my feet! **1902** Barrie *Little White Bird* xi. 107 She had trouble in socking him every morning.

**2.** *colloq.* (orig. *U.S.*). To put (money) aside as savings. Also with *away*.

**1942** Berrey & Van den Bark *Amer. Thes. Slang* §376/5 *Save*...sock one's money away. **1951** Cusack & James *Come in Spinner* 297, I bet he's socked a pretty packet away. **1962** E. Lucia *Klondike Kate* iii. 97 Instead of gambling a fortune away at the wheels..[Kitty] was wisely socking it into the bank. **1963** C. D. Simak *They walked like Men* ix. 53 They've been busy for the last week scooping it in. People come in loaded and are socking it away. **1971** *Maclean's Mag.* Sept. 11/2 Now they seem to believe that a buck earned is a buck to be socked away. **1978** R. Doliner *On the Edge* v. 84 He's got to have money... How much you figure he socked away?

**3.** *N. Amer.* Of fog, cloud, etc.: to close *in*, to enshroud.

**1950** Webster Add. Sock in. **1953** Berrey & Van den Bark *Amer. Thes. Slang* (1954) §761/2 *Socked in*, ceiling zero. **1955** *Sci. News Let.* 26 Feb. 136 Man-made ice-fog that 'socks in' Arctic airfields can now be licked by a new device developed by the Armour Research Foundation, Chicago. **1969** *Daily Tel.* 21 May 1/6 All of Europe, the Soviet Union,..are socked in cloud cover. **1975** *High Times* Dec. 70/3 Pilots..are often completely socked in by fog and haze. **1976** C. Egleton *State Visit* iii. 25 Wednesday is always a busy day... As long as the airfield isn't socked in.

**sockdolager** (sɒk'dɒlədʒə(r)). *U.S. slang.* Also slock-, slog-, sog-, soc-, -doloer, -dollager, and sock dologer, -doliger. [prob. a fanciful formation.]

**1.** A heavy or knock-down blow; a finisher. Also *fig.*

**1830** *Virginia Literary Museum* I. 479 *Sock dologer*, a decisive blow. **1836** Haliburton *Clockm.* I. xl, I'll give you a sockdologer in the ear with my foot. **1838** *Ibid.* II. xix, I felt my fingers itch to give him a slock-dolager under the ear. *a* **1859** in Bartlett *Dict. Amer.* (ed. 2) 425, I gave the fellow a socdolager over his head with the barrel of my gun. **1892** Gunter *Miss Dividends* (1893) 36 'Yes,—I—reckon it will be a—sockdolager!' mutters her father's friend.

**2.** A form of fish-hook (see quot.).

**1848** Bartlett *Dict. Amer.* 319 *Socdolager*, a patent fish-hook, having two hooks which close upon each other by means of a spring as soon as the fish bites.

**3.** Something exceptional in any respect; esp. a large fish.

**1838** J. F. Cooper *Home as Found* II. 72 There is but one 'sogdollager' in the universe, and that is in Lake Oswego. **1842** *Knickerbocker* XIX. 223 This seemed to be a 'socdoliger' (which translated into Latin, means a ne plus ultra). **1869** Lowell *To Mr. J. Bartlett* 5 Fit for..The Pope himself to see in dream Before his lenten vision gleam, He lies there, the sogdologer. **1884** 'Mark Twain' *Huck. Finn* xx. 192 The thunder would go rumbling and grumbling away,..and then *rip* comes another flash and another sockdologer. **1894** *Blackw. Mag.* Feb. 229 The pleasant remembrance of the capture of a real socdologer.

**socked,** *ppl. a.* [f. sock *sb.*[1]] Wearing socks. In quot. 1788 *fig.*

**1788** *Trifler* No. 2. 21 The buskin'd and sock'd inhabitants of Drury-lane and Covent-garden. **1918** W. J. Locke *Rough Road* xxiii. 293 Her thoughts winged themselves back to an afternoon, remote almost as her socked and sashed childhood. **1937** L. Durrell *Panic Spring* vii. 116 Her brown socked legs stretched out under the dashboard. **1976** 'J. Ross' *I know what it's like to Die* i. 7 Five feet and eight inches..in his socked feet.

**socker,** var. of soccer.

**sockeroo** (ˌsɒkəˈruː). *slang* (orig. *U.S.*). [f. sock *sb.*[4] + -eroo.] Something with an overwhelming impact, a 'smash'.

**1942** *Time* 9 Nov. 77/2 The act was an old-fashioned Hippodrome sockeroo. **1943** *Sat. Rev. Lit.* 18 Dec. 16/3 This program..was a boff, a wham, a sockeroo. **1964** *Spectator* 7 Feb. 178 This latest box-office sockeroo also provides a modest example of the industry's throat-cutting activities. **1977** *Daily Tel.* 22 Apr. 13 The Royal Court's new régime opens with a great loud sockeroo of a play, a thumping American drama of a divided family, rich in purple prose and loaded with gutsy symbolism.

**socket** ('sɒkɪt), *sb.* Forms: 4–6 soket, 5–6 sokett(e, 6 sokkat, sowket; 6 sockat, -itte, 6–7 -ett(e, 7 soacket, socquet, 6– socket. [a. AF. *soket*, dim. of *soc* ploughshare, sock *sb.*[2]]

†**1.** A lance- or spear-head having a form resembling that of a ploughshare. *Obs.*

[*a* **1260** Matth. Paris *Chron. Majora* (Rolls) V. 319 Ferrum remansit in vulnere; quod tamen excisum.. inventum est in mucrone acutissimum instar pugionis,..et brevem formam habens vomeris, unde vulgariter vomerulus vocatur, Gallice soket.]

**13..** *K. Alis.* 4415 (Laud MS.), He took in honde a rede pensel Wiþ a soket of broun stel. *c* **1330** *Arth. & Merl.* 7189 (Kölbing), Gaheriet mett þe douke Fannel Wiþ a launce, þe soket of stiel. *c* **1430** *Syr Gener.* (Roxb.) 9645 His tronchon stikked fast With the soket in mid the shelde. **1502** *Acc. Ld. High Treas. Scot.* II. 352 To Henry, lorymar, for sockatis and dyamandis to the speris, xiiij s. **1535** Stewart *Cron. Scot.* II. 687 Than with the speir..He hit the king richt in at the e, The scharpe sokkat syne throw his heid is gone.

**2. a.** A hollow part or piece, usually of a cylindrical form, constructed to receive some part or thing fitting into it.

**1448** in *Archæol. Jrnl.* LI. 121 Item .j. soket argenteum deauratum pro cruce argentea. *Ibid.* 122, .j. parvum soket. **1483** Caxton *Gold. Leg.* 167 b/1 Another pyece wherin the sokette or morteys was maad that the body of the crosse stood in. **1523** Fitzherb. *Husb.* §21 A wedynge-hoke with a socket set vpon a lyttel staffe of a yarde longe. **1585** T. Washington tr. *Nicholay's Voy.* III. iii. 73 b, A socket of siluer & guilt.., within the top of which socket they set.. plumes of feathers. **1667** *Phil. Trans.* II. 567 Into the Socket of that Iron is put a Staffe. **1699** Dampier *Voy.* II. II. 97 This Iron is fastned by a Socket to a Pole about 14 or 15 Foot long. **1748** *Anson's Voy.* III. v. 341 The heel of the yard is always lodged in one of the sockets. **1820** Scoresby *Acc. Arctic Reg.* II. 223 The harpoon..consists of three conjoined parts, called the 'socket', 'shank', and 'mouth'. **1840** *Civil Eng. & Arch. Jrnl.* III. 349/1 The paddle-beams ..pass the sides of the vessel through what may be called sockets. **1892** *Photogr. Ann.* II. 354 The camera is fitted with..sockets for use on a tripod.

*fig.* **1589** R. Harvey *Pl. Perc.* (1590) 13 A vaine of lauish iangling, that hath made thy palate rise out of socket. **1601** Dent *Pathw. Heaven* 52 The most part [of men] run beyond their bounds, and leape quite out of their sockets.

**b.** *techn.* (See quots.)

**1883** Gresley *Gloss. Coal-m.* 229 *Socket*, the innermost end of a shot hole not blown away after firing. **1884** Knight *Dict. Mech.* Suppl. 827/1 *Socket*, a tool used in well boring to recover and lift rods out of the well.

**c.** An object in which the terminals of an electricity supply are inside holes made to receive the pins of a plug; *spec.* one that is fixed to a wall.

**1885** C. J. Wharton tr. *Hospitalier's Domestic Electr.* vii. 113 The whole [lamp-holder] is fitted to a wooden socket C, which may be screwed into an ordinary chandelier or in place of a gas burner. **1892** [see plug *sb.* 1 c]. **1914** S. C. Batstone *Electric-Light Fitting* vi. 127 The wires come into the socket from behind the skirting. **1938** J. W. Sims *Electr. Installations* 155 Apparatus requiring not more than 50 watts may be supplied from..one 15-amp socket. **1955** N. W. Kay *Mod. Building Encycl.* 637/1 The fuse can be renewed only when the plug-head is withdrawn from the socket. **1977** F. Hall *Building Services & Equipment* II. v. 35/2 The sockets will only accept plugs for 110V, single-phase, 50Hz supply.

**d.** *Golf.* That part of the head of a club into which the shaft is fitted; a shot made off the socket.

**1887** W. G. Simpson *Art of Golf* I. iv. 22 Irons and cleeks ..have sockets instead of necks. **1922** C. Leitch *Golf* 98 There is no bad shot in golf which flurries a player so much as a shot off the socket. **1927** *Daily Express* 12 Feb. 3/7 In the down stroke, the left hand and arm get ahead of the right, and that causes either a socket or a 'push out'. **1963** J. Jacobs *Golf* 78 The socket is simply explained—the club head is being brought down further away from the body than it should be.

**3. a.** The part of a candlestick or chandelier in which the candle is placed.

*c* **1440** *Promp. Parv.* 463/1 Soket, of a candylstykke or oþer lyke, *alorica*. **1477–9** *Rec. St. Mary at Hill* (1905) 81 Payd to Thomas Goldsmyth for the mendyng of..the soket of a siluer candilstike. **1537** *N. Co. Wills* (Surtees) 146, iiij candelstickes with double sowkettes. **1552** Huloet s.v. *Candle beame*, Sockettes to set candels vpon. **1626** Bacon *Sylva* §31 Take a small Waxe Candle, and putt it in a Socket, of Brasse, or Iron. *a* **1701** Maundrell *Journ. Jerus.* (1732) 27 A small lighted wax Taper, a hole in the Cake serving for a Socket. **1760–2** Goldsm. *Cit. W.* xlvi, The candles were burnt to the socket. **1832** Brewster *Nat. Magic* xiii. 325 The candle was burned out in the socket of the candlestick, which stood by her. **1855** Macaulay *Hist. Eng.* xv. III. 521 From dawn till the candles had burned down to their sockets.

**b.** *fig.* or in fig. context.

**1589** *Pappe w. Hatchet* (1844) 36 With a wit worn into the socket, twinkling and pinking like the snuffe of a candle. **1633** Ld. Brooke *Cælica* lxxxvii. 235 When as mans life..In soacket of his earthly lanthorne burnes. **1655** *Nicholas P.* (Camden) II. 323 My smale talent, being now burnt downe to the very socquet. **1756** *Pol. Ballads* (1860) II. 331 In thy arms let me die, And my glory burn clear in the socket. **1827** Scott *Chron. Canongate* i, The light of life..was trembling in the socket. **1862** Goulburn *Pers. Relig.* IV. xii. (1873) 354 Love began to burn a little low in the socket.

*Comb.* **1593** G. Harvey *Pierce's Super.* Wks. (Grosart) II. 119 His socket-worne inuention.

**4.** †**a.** In allusive use. *Obs.*

*c* **1450** *Mankind* 140 in *Macro Plays*, Yf ȝe wyll putt yowur nose in hys wyffis sokett, ȝe xall haue xl[ty] days of pardon. **1638** Brathwait *Barnabees Jrnl.* III. (1818) 109.

**b.** = Socket-money (see 7 c).

**1818** R. Jamieson in *Burt's Lett.* I. 194 *note*, [If they happen to see any kind of freedom between them,..they.. demand the *bulling-siller*.] This tax in England is called *socket*. **1889** Marcroft *Ups & Downs* 10 At the same stir it was arranged for the footings and sockets to come in.

**5.** *Anat.* A hollow or cavity in which some part or articulation (as a tooth, eye, bone, etc.) is inserted.

(*a*) **1601** Holland *Pliny* xxv. xiii. I. 239 Both of them.. serve in a collution to strengthen and keepe them [teeth] fast in their sockets. **1728** Chambers *Cycl.* s.v. *Teeth*, In Men, the ordinary Number of Teeth is 32,..all fix'd in peculiar Sockets. **1774** Goldsm. *Nat. Hist.* (1776) VI. 212 Its root enters into the socket above a foot and an half. In a skull.. at Hamburgh there are two teeth. **1859** J. Tomes *Dental Surg.* 4 The sockets for the first temporary molars.

(*b*) **1615** Crooke *Body of Man* 546 The Membrane of their eye is very hard, and beside they stand deepe in their

sockets. **1668** CULPEPPER & COLE *Barthol. Anat.* IV. vi. 341 To constitute the upper part of the Eye-hole or Socket. **1782** MISS BURNEY *Cecilia* VII. iii, Fixed in mute wonder,..her eyes almost bursting from their sockets. **1843** ABDY *Water Cure* 26 The eyes deep in the socket and feeble. **1890** W. P. BALL *Are Effects of Use & Disuse inherited?* 72 In one species of ant..the sockets have disappeared as well as the eyes.
(*c*) **1664** POWER *Exp. Philos.* I. 27 Below the eyes was two crook'd horns, which..was fasten'd in two sockets at the roots. **1774** GOLDSM. *Nat. Hist.* (1776) V. 20 The quill thus deprived continues in its socket for some months. **1826** KIRBY & SP. *Entomol.* III. xxxiii. 384 The socket..in which the leg is planted. **1837** DICKENS *Pickw.* v, His arms being nearly pulled out of their sockets. **1882** PITMAN *Mission Life Greece & Pal.* 212 The little knob on the end of the hip-bone, which works in a socket in the corresponding bone.

**6.** Applied to parts of plants.

**1657** S. PURCHAS *Pol. Flying-Ins.* 68 Bees gather of all things that have flowers in a hose or socket. **1713** WARDER *True Amazon* 16 Many [flowers]..being kept in their Socket a long time, that should have blown. *a* **1722** LISLE *Husb.* (1757) 138 They, being grown thick and strong, open the socket of the said outward leaf. **1868** *U.S. Rep. Comm. Agric.* (1869) 262 The atocha grass..is not cut like ordinary grass, but is pulled up from its socket.

**7.** *attrib.* and *Comb.* **a.** Attrib. in sense 2, as ***socket-bar, -bit, -castor, -chisel***, etc.; **socket outlet**, a socket (sense 2 c) fixed to a wall and connected to an electricity supply; cf. OUTLET *sb.* 1 e, POINT *sb.*[1] A. 19 e; **socket set**, a number of sockets for use with a socket wrench; **socket wrench**, a wrench equipped with a set of detachable sockets of different sizes.

Many examples of this type occur in modern technical use, and are recorded in special dictionaries.

**1883** GRESLEY *Gloss. Coal-m.* 229 *Socket Bar [a hollow conical-headed iron rod for extricating boring rods from bore holes]. **1532** *Lett. & P. Hen. VIII*, V. 447 A ground auger made with a *socket bit steeled. **1858** SIMMONDS *Dict. Trade*, **Socket-castor*, a metal castor which moves in a socket. **1679** MOXON *Mech. Exerc.* VII. 123 *Socket Chissels ..have their Shank made with an hollow Socket at its top. **1842** GWILT *Archit.* Gloss., *Socket Chisel*, a strong tool used by carpenters for mortising, and worked with a mallet. **1895** *Model Steam Eng.* 38 The *socket end of the rod must have a screw formed on it. **1858** GREENER *Gunnery* 401 The price paid for the *socket joint alone. **1895** *Arnold & Sons' Catal. Surg. Instrum.* 789 *Socket Leg, for amputation above knee, with wooden socket. **1934** *Two-Pole & Earthing-Pin Plugs & Socket-Outlets* (Brit. Standards Inst.) 6 When the plug and the *socket-outlet are in complete engagement no live parts shall be accessible. **1977** *Jrnl. R. Soc. Arts* CXXV. 119/2 There will probably be more storage space [in today's new house] and almost certainly more socket outlets. **1869** RANKINE *Machine & Hand-tools* Pl. O 3, The bearing plate of the jointed *socket-piece. **1858** SIMMONDS *Dict. Trade*, **Socket-pipe*, a pipe worked in a socket. **1847** WEBSTER, **Socket-pole*, a pole armed with an iron socket, and used to propel boats, &c. [**1918** A. L. DYKE *Automobile & Gasoline Engine Encycl.* 613/2 (*caption*) No. 12 combination socket wrench set.] **1935** *Gen. Catal. Tools & Supplies* (Buck & Hickman Ltd.) 270/2 'Ratchet handle' *socket sets. **1976** *Star* (Sheffield) 29 Nov. 5/5 Hinds pleaded guilty to stealing an electric drill and a 52-piece socket set. **1893** *Spons' Mechanics' Own Book* (ed. 4) 80 The stems and handles of *socket spanners are made..separate from the socket portions. **1887** J. R. ALLEN *Early Chr. Symbolism* 134 The head and part of the shaft..have been re-erected in the old *socket-stone. **1869** RANKINE *Machine & Hand-tools* Pl. N 1, The longitudinal liberty of the spindle..in its *socket tube. **1905** W. ROGERS *Pumps & Hydraulics* II. 344 An interchangeable *socket wrench is shown in Fig. 629. **1921** *Car* 31 Mar. 313/2 (Advt.), Your car will be kept in perfect tune if a socket wrench set is in your kit. **1977** *New Yorker* 9 May 34/3 Bicycling accessories for every contingency:.. monkey wrenches, socket wrenches, wrench holders.

**b.** In sense 5, as ***socket-leaf, -leaved; socket-eyed*** adj.

*c* **1711** PETIVER *Gazophyl.* ix. §85 Its Stalks red-spotted and socket-leaved. *Ibid.* §86 Yellow Cape Dragon-Orchis, with broad, pointed Socket-leaves. **1964** F. WARNER *Early Poems* 76 Laws That rule this meaningless and cancered globe In socket-eyed, gigantic merriment. **1975** *New Yorker* 26 May 104/1 Raskolnikov..is played by Georgi Taratorkin, a socket-eyed figure ransacked by self-inquiry and staring at us out of a very lonely desert.

**c.** ***socket-money***. (See quots. and 3 b.) *slang.*

*a* **1700** B. E. *Dict. Cant. Crew*, *Socket-money*, Demanded and Spent upon Marriage. **1772** T. BRYDGES *Homer Trav.* 127 We must likewise come upon ye, By way of costs, for socket-money. **1785** GROSE *Dict. Vulgar T.*, *Socket money*, a whore's fee, or hire, also money paid for a treat, by a married man caught in an intrigue. **1865** *Slang Dict.* 240 *Socket-money*, money extorted by threats of exposure.

Hence **'socketful**; **'socketless** *a.*

**1833** *Fraser's Mag.* VII. 720 The eyes have long been rayless, socketless. **1867** GILFILLAN *Night* III. 53 A socketless and fiercely blazing eye. **1872** B. STEWART *Physics* 30 Water exactly equal in bulk to the brass cylinder (that is to say, a socketful).

**socket**, variant of SUCKET.

**socket** ('sɒkɪt), *v.* Also 7 soccate. [f. SOCKET *sb.*]

**1.** *trans.* To place in, or fit with, a socket.

**1533** *Lett. & P. Hen. VIII*, VI. 642 For mendyng and sockettyng newe Cressytts. **1665** J. WEBB *Stone-Heng* (1725) 214 A Pair of Shears composed of two Masts, socketted or mortaised into a Plank. **1761** *Phil. Trans.* LV. 248 They must be socketed before he can examine [etc.]. **1823** SIR C. BELL in *Phil. Trans.* CXIII. 173 In creatures where the eye is socketed in a cup of cartilage and cannot retract. **1869** RANKINE *Machine & Hand-tools* Pl. P 5, These dies..are.. socketed into the resisting head. **1888** *Athenæum* 16 June 764/3 Five stone bases socketed for wooden uprights.

**2.** *Golf.* To strike (the ball) inadvertently off the socket or heel of a club; to make (a shot) in this way. Also *absol.* Cf. SHANK *v.* 4.

**1911** C. LEITCH *Golf for Girls* 87 If you socket and don't want to, here's the cure. Keep your left elbow close to your side. **1920** *Isis* 27 Oct. 9/1 He socketed a couple of iron shots into the gorse. **1927** *Daily Express* 31 Jan. 8/2 A mashie that persists in socketing the ball. **1961** F. C. AVIS *Sportsman's Gloss.* 210/2 *Socket*, to hit the ball with the shank of the club; also known as Shank.

Hence **'socketer**, one who sockets the ball.

**1912** *New Bk. Golf* 341 Even the most confirmed socketer will find that with such a club socketing is a sheer impossibility. **1952** H. LONGHURST *Golf Mixture* 113 Frostick, of St George's Hill, tells the socketer to keep his head down.

**socketed** ('sɒkɪtɪd), *ppl. a.* [f. SOCKET *sb.* or *v.*]

**1.** Fitted with or placed in a socket.

**1649** in *Archaeol.* X. 404 Two whyte marble colums or pillers, soccated in two foote stepps of black marble. **1713** WARDER *True Amazons* 8 His Tongue being not long enough to reach the Honey out of the socketed Flowers. **1853** RUSKIN *Stones Ven.* III. App. x. 246 So that the socketed arrangement is not seen. **1871** *Archaeol.* XLIII. 446 Two celts, one at least socketed, were found at Hagbourn,..with a socketed spear-head of bronze. **1877** ROSENTHAL *Muscles & Nerves* 95 All these tensions must combine to press together the socketed parts.

**2.** *Golf.* Of a ball or shot: that has been played off the socket.

**1911** C. LEITCH *Golf for Girls* 86 At the finish of a socketted shot. **1963** P. CAMPBELL *How to become Scratch Golfer* v. 57 Tom's contribution is a socketed recovery shot out of the bushes.

**'socketing**, *vbl. sb.* [f. SOCKET *v.*]

**1.** Placing in, or fitting with, a socket.

**1806** SIR C. BELL *Anat. & Phil. Expression* (1872) 41 The socketing of the long canine teeth. **1833** —— *Hand* (1834) 88 The socketing of the teeth in the jaws.

**2.** *Golf.* The action of hitting the ball off the socket.

**1911** C. LEITCH *Golf for Girls* 86 Socketting, that is, hitting the ball off the socket, or shank, as some call it, of the club. **1959** D. REES *Dai Rees on Golf* xxx. 126 Socketing is something which strikes suddenly, like a poisonous adder.

**sockette** (sɒ'kɛt). [f. SOCK *sb.*[1] + -ETTE.] A short sock.

**1950** *Landfall* IV. 309 Tanned legs with neat navy sockettes. **1976** *Times* 26 Mar. 10/4 Sales of hosiery (which includes tights and sockettes etc) run at around 620,000,000 pairs a year.

**sockeye** ('sɒkaɪ). Also **sock-eye, suck-eye, sawkeye**, etc. [ad. Amer. Indian *sukai* 'fish of fishes', the native name on the Fraser River.] The blueback salmon or nerka.

**1887** GOODE *Amer. Fishes* 481 On Frazer River, where this species is the most important Salmon, it is known as the 'Suk-kegh', 'Saw-quai' or 'Suck-eye'. **1891** E. ROPER *By Track & Trail* xxi. 304 It was the 'Sock-eye' salmon which was running then. **1903** *Eng. Illustr. Mag.* XXVIII. 128 The sockeyes which only weigh from five to eight pounds apiece.

**socking** ('sɒkɪŋ), *adv.* and *ppl. a. slang.* [? f. SOCK *v.*[2]: see also B below.] **A.** *adv.* As an intensive, esp. qualifying *big* or *great*: very.

**1896** *Dialect Notes* I. 425 That was a socking big fish. **1942** *Tee Emm* (Air Ministry) II. 67 A socking great Wellington has just gate-crashed the range. **1951** J. B. PRIESTLEY *Festival at Farbridge* III. iii. 548 A teeny drink before lunch, and it turned out to be a socking great double gin and Dubonnet. **1958** M. DICKENS *Man Overboard* viii. 122 A socking great button-hole. **1976** D. FRANCIS *In Frame* iv. 65 A brooch I had..with a socking big diamond in the middle.

**B.** *ppl. a.* A euphemistic substitute for FUCKING *ppl. a.*

**1941** *Penguin New Writing* X. 114 That socking kid's playing a game with me. **1945** S. J. BAKER *Austral. Lang.* xiv. 257 *Socker* and *socking*, as synonyms for an old English vulgarism widely current in this country, are recent inventions.

**'sock-lamb.** [? f. SOCK *sb.*[3]] A lamb brought up by hand; a pet-lamb. Also *transf.*

**1838** HOLLOWAY *Prov. Dict.*, *A sock-lamb*, a lamb brought up by hand and domesticated. **1880** MRS. R. O'REILLY *Stories* III. 299 A sock lamb was nibbling the short grass. **1903** A. AUSTIN *Flodden Field* III, All Ford hath, And all that is within it, save it be That sock-lamb, Margery.

**sockle**, obs. form of SUCKLE.

**sockless** ('sɒklɪs), *a.* [f. SOCK *sb.*[1] + -LESS.] Without socks; wearing no socks.

**1607** BEAUM. & FL. *Woman Hater* I. iii, You shall see many legs too;..one pair, the feet of which, were in times past, sockless. **1651** *Loves of Hero & Leander*, etc. (1653) 53 Whose arm-pits, and whose sockless toes, Are not as sweet as amber. **1970** P. DICKINSON *Seals* vii. 145 His bruised feet slipping sockless in the unfamiliar boots. **1981** *Daily Tel.* 20 Feb. 17/1 Going sockless is the preferred style, 'to give the beachside look that is so desirable'.

**socko** ('sɒkəʊ), *int.*, *a.*, *sb. slang* (orig. and chiefly *U.S.*). [f. SOCK *sb.*[4] + -O[2].] **A.** *int.* An interjection imitative of the sound of a violent blow.

**1924** *Dialect Notes* V. 258 *Sock-o* (blow). **1931** E. LINKLATER *Juan in Amer.* II. i. 63 He hung a lullaby on the Frog's chin—socko! **1936** WODEHOUSE *Laughing Gas* xxi. 226 And then, as she stood there with the love-light shining in her eyes...socko! **1966** L. COHEN *Beautiful Losers* I. 71 We're fat, F.—— Smack! Wham! Pow!—— Fat.—— Socko! Sok! Bash!

**B.** *adj.* Stunningly effective or successful, 'knock-out'.

**1939** J. B. PRIESTLEY *Johnson over Jordan* II. 67 And now, friends, a new novelty act, the first time here, and I know it will be a socko number. **1942** *Photoplay & Movie Mirror* Mar. 6/3 Van Heflin..almost steals the show—and he must be good to rob Taylor of one iota of glory, Bob's that socko. **1960** *Sales Managem.* 6 May 96/1 Automated manufacture, sock-o selling and all-out advertising. **1961** *John o' London's* 14 Dec. 664/2 The religious plays which are at the moment filling our theatres, religion being Socko box office these days. **1972** T. P. MCMAHON *Issue of Bishop's Blood* vii. 83 The blue of the incense rising to the white gold of the altar ..the soaring voices of the seventy or so nuns..provided a socko finish. **1981** *Underground Grammarian* Feb. 3/1 Their latest brochure starts *right off* with this absolutely socko bit of dialog: 'What is cooperative education? In it's simplist [*sic*] definition, it is learning by doing.'

**C.** *sb.* orig. *U.S.* A success, a 'hit'.

**1937** *Amer. Speech* XII. 317/2 *Socko*, a success. **1942** BERREY & VAN DEN BARK *Amer. Thes. Slang* §591/1 *Successful show hit*...socker,..socko, sock show. **1973** WODEHOUSE *Bachelors Anonymous* iii. 23 Triumph or disaster, socko or flop, he went on forever like one of those permanent officials at the Foreign Office.

**socky** ('sɒkɪ), *a. dial.* [f. SOCK *sb.*[3] 2.] Wet, moist, soppy.

*a* **1825–66** in E. Anglian and Linc. glossaries.

**socle** ('sɒk(ə)l, ‖sɔkl). Also 8 **zocle, soccle.** [a. F. *socle*, ad. It. *zoccolo* (also a clog or patten), repr. L. *socculus*, dim. of *soccus* SOCK *sb.*[1] So G. *sockel* (†*socle, zocle*).]

**1.** A low plain block or plinth serving as a pedestal to a statue, column, vase, etc.; also, a plain plinth forming a foundation for a wall.

**1704** HARRIS *Lex. Techn.* I, *Zocle* is a square member in Architecture,..which serves to support a Pillar [etc.]. **1726** LEONI *Alberti's Archit.* I. 39/1 The first Ground-work of your Wall, and the Soccles, which are call'd Foundations too. **1728** CHAMBERS *Cycl.* s.v. *Pedestal*, In the Base are a Plinth for a Socle, over that a Tore carved. **1797** T. HOLCROFT tr. *Stolberg's Trav.* III. lxxxviii. (ed. 2) 455 The pillars stand upon socles. **1843** *Civil Eng. & Arch. Jrnl.* VI. 229/1 An order of square pillars..raised not on a stylobate but merely a socle. **1880** *Nature* XXI. 265 A high round pedestal formed by the foaming sea-water, like the socle of a monument.

**2.** 'One of the ridges or elevations which support the tentacles and sense-bodies of some worms' (*Cent. Dict.* 1891).

**socle**, obs. form of SUCKLE *v.*

**socman** ('sɒkmən). Also 6 **sok-**, 7–9 **sock-**. [ad. Anglo-Lat. *socmannus*, var. of *sokemannus* SOKEMAN.] One who holds land in socage.

α. **1579** *Termes de la Ley* 171 b, Sokmans are the tenants in auncient demesne, that held their lands in Socage. **1651** G. W. tr. *Cowel's Inst.* 94 These were stiled the Kings free Sockmans. **1738** *Hist. View Crt. Exchequer* ii. 19 These Demesne Lands belonging to the Sockmen or Plowmen. **1843** CARLYLE *Past & Pres.* I. ix, The very sockmen with their chubby infants.

β. **1670** T. BLOUNT *Law-Dict.* s.v., The Tenants in ancient Demean seem most properly to be called Socmans. **1747** CARTE *Hist. Eng.* I. 436 How many freemen, socmen, villains,..were in each town, and manor. **1761** HUME *Hist. Eng.* I. App. I. 97 The socmen, who were tenants that could not be removed at pleasure. **1865** KINGSLEY *Herew.* xx, 'You are our lord,' shouted the socmen or tenants.

Hence **'socmanry**, = SOKEMANRY.

**1818** in TODD.

†**socome, socon(e**, irreg. ff. SOKEN. *Obs.*

**1523** FITZHERB. *Bk. Surv.* 9 b, To the cornemilnes.. belongeth Socone, that is to saye, custome of the tenauntes to grynde their corne at the lordes mylne. That maner of gryndyng is called loue Socone, and the lordes tenauntes be called bonde socon. **1607** J. NORDEN *Surv. Dial.* III. 109 The tenants..are bound to grind their corne at the Lords mill: and that kind of custome is called Socome. **1656** BLOUNT *Glossogr.* s.v., There is Bond-socome,..and Love-Socome. [Hence in Phillips, Bailey, etc.]

†**socord**, *sb.* and *a. Obs.*$^{-0}$ [ad. L. *socordia* and *socord-, socors.*] (See quots.)

**1656** BLOUNT *Glossogr.*, *Socord*, luskishness, slothfulness, negligence, idleness, sottishness. **1658** PHILLIPS, *Socord*, sluggish, idle, slothfull.

**socorour**, obs. form of SUCCOURER.

**socotrine** ('sɒkətrɪn, 'səʊkətraɪn), *a.* Forms: α. 5–7 **cicotrine** (7 **cica-**), 6 **cycotryne**. β. 8 **succotorine**, 8–9 **succotrine, socotorine, soccotrine**, 9– **socotrine**. [f. *Socotra* or *Socotora*, the name of an island in the Indian Ocean, close to Africa and Arabia. The early forms represent med.L. *cic-*, *cycotrinus*, whence also obs. F. *cicotrin* (Cotgr.).]

**1.** ***socotrine aloes***, a drug prepared from the juice of the *Aloe socotrina* (or *perryi*), and originally obtained from the island of Socotra.

α. *a* **1425** tr. *Arderne's Treat. Fistula* 90 Medle puluis of aloes cicotrine, mirre, sanguis draconis. **1545** RAYNALD *Womans Bk.* 131 The powder of aloes cycotrine. **1579** LANGHAM *Gard. Health* (1633) 19 Mixe powder of Aloes Cicatrine with iuice of Colworts. **1602** DEKKER *Satirom.* I ij b, Tis not like thy Aloe Cicatrine tongue, bitter.

β. **1704** J. HARRIS *Lex. Techn.* I, *Succotrine Aloes*, is the finest sort that comes from the Island Succotra [etc.]. **1778** *Encycl. Brit.* (ed. 2) I. 263/2 Socotorine aloes. **1799** UNDERWOOD *Dis. Child.* (ed. 4) I. 57, I would rather advise a recourse to clysters..made of succotorine aloes. **1811** A. T. THOMSON *Lond. Disp.* (1818) 20 The real Socotrine aloes, which are now scarce in the market. *Ibid.*, The real Socotrine extract has a peculiar..odour. **1831** DAVIES *Mat. Med.* 356 The socotorine aloes is obtained by cutting the leaves at their base, and keeping them in a vase with the cut side downwards. **1871** GARROD *Mat. Med.* (ed. 3) 339

Socotrine Aloes occurs in reddish-brown masses, opaque or translucent at the edges.

**2.** *socotrine aloe*, the plant yielding the drug.

**1778** *Encycl. Brit.* (ed. 2) I. 262/2 The *vera* or socotorine aloe, hath long, narrow, succulent leaves. **1852** JOHNSON *Cottage Gard. Dict.* 26/2.

**socour, -owr(e**, obs. ff. SUCCOUR *sb.* and *v.*

**Socratean** (sɒkrəˈtiːən), *a. rare.* [See -AN.] Pertaining to or resembling the celebrated Greek philosopher Socrates or his way of life; Socratic.

**1930** BELLOC *Richelieu* I. vi. 114 Father Joseph was short, bullet-headed, of a vivacious Socratean ugliness. **1976** *S. Wales Echo* 26 Nov. 5/1 It's hardly the kind of job that Plato would have relished—and there's nothing Socratean about filling in a VAT return.

**Socratic** (səʊˈkrætɪk), *a.* and *sb.* Also 7 -ick. [ad. L. *Sōcraticus*, ad. Gr. Σωκρατικός, f. Σωκράτης Socrates. So F. *Socratique.*]

**A.** *adj.* Of or pertaining to, characteristic of, Socrates the Athenian philosopher, or his philosophy, methods, character, etc.

*a* **1637** B. JONSON *Horace, Art Paint.* 442 Thy matter first to know, Which the Socratic writings best can show. **1655** STANLEY *Hist. Philos.* (1687) III. 120 Simon.. is reported the first that used the Socratick Discourses. **1741** WATTS *Improv. Mind* I. ix. §19 By questions aptly proposed in the Socratic method. *Ibid.* x. §14 But there are three sorts of disputation,..which are distinguished by these three names, namely, socratic, forensic, and academic. **1778** BURNABY in Sparks *Corr. Amer. Revol.* (1853) II. 103 As philosophical and Socratic as ever. **1847** EMERSON *Repres. Men, Plato* Wks. (Bohn) I. 307 Plato's fame does not stand on a syllogism, or on any masterpieces of the Socratic reasoning. **1874** MAHAFFY *Social Life Greece* x. 294 A marked feature in the Socratic society.

**B.** *sb.* A follower of Socrates.

**1678** CUDWORTH *Intell. Syst.* 408 To Plato we might here joyn Xenophon, because he was his Equal, and a Socratick too. **1875** JEVONS *Money* 197 Aeschines the Socratic. **1886** *Athenæum* 21 Aug. 230/2 The practical agreement of Plato and Aristotle, the two Socratics, on the main problems of ethics.

**So'cratical**, *a.* [f. L. *Sōcratic-us* (see prec.) + -AL[1].] = SOCRATIC *a.*

**1581** MULCASTER *Positions* xiv. (1887) 67 Our children which be no Socraticall saintes. *c* **1618** MORYSON *Itin.* IV. 305 Yet envious readers more obserue the spotts of errours blotted out, then Socraticall sentences newely added. **1641** 'SMECTYMNUUS' *Answ.* xvi. 207 And why doth he..like a Socraticall disputant put off the question with question? **1711** BUDGELL *Spect.* No. 197 ¶13 This has made some approve the Socratical Way of Reasoning. **1753** HANWAY *Trav.* II. xviii. (1762) I. 80 This old man was remarkable for his socratical look.

Hence **So'cratically** *adv.*

**1641** 'SMECTYMNUUS' *Answ.* xiii. 154 This is to answer Socratically, and in answering not to answer. **1678** CUDWORTH *Intell. Syst.* 421 They disputed Socratically after this manner. **1686** GOODMAN *Wint. Ev. Conf.* III. (1705) 60 Treated Socratically and gentilely. **1751** HARRIS *Hermes* I. xi. (1765) 209 'Twas Socratically reasoned..; 'twas Demosthenically spoken. **1896** *Sunday Sch. Jrnl.* Mar. 140 He did this not by any statement of his own, but Socratically.

**So'craticism.** [f. SOCRATIC + -ISM.] The philosophy of Socrates or some aspect of this. Also **'Socratism** (Todd, 1818).

**1878** *Encycl. Brit.* VIII. 579/1 The ultimate views of these two one-sided Socraticisms.

**'Socratist.** *rare.* A Socratic.

**1554** T. MARTIN *Marr. Priests* Ij b, The socratistes said it was better..that al things shuld be in common. **1610** HEALEY *St. Aug. Citie of God* IX. iv. 324 He replied as Aristippus the Socratist did upon the like case. *Ibid.* 730 Both famous Socratists. **1866** MILL in *Edin. Rev.* CXXIII. 337 There are..two complete Plato's in Plato—the Sokratist and the Dogmatist.

**Socratize** (ˈsɒkrətaɪz), *v.* [See -IZE.] *intr.* To philosophize or live after the manner of Socrates.

**1847** tr. *Cesare Cantù's Ref. Europe* I. 23 He passes the day in drinking, making love, and socratizing. **1875** BROWNING *Aristoph. Apol.* 352 Men used to let their hair grow long, To fast, be dirty, and just Socratize.

**socre, socure**, obs. forms of SUCCOUR *v.*

**Socred** (ˈsəʊkrɛd). Abbrev. of SOCIAL CREDIT, SOCIAL CREDITER.

**1955** *Pictou* (Nova Scotia) *Advocate* 24 Feb. 1/1 The addition of the British Columbia Socreds has given them just the monkey glands they needed to restore them! **1962** *Canada Month* Feb. 21/2 Social Credit has been badly damaged by the highhanded methods of B.C.'s Socred government. **1970** J. BLACKBURN *Land of Promise* xv. 191 It was a landslide for the Socreds, the name soon applied to members of the Social Credit Party. **1975** *Australasian Express* 24 Oct. 10/2 (*heading*) Socred fields more women.

**sod** (sɒd), *sb.*[1] Also 5–6 sodde, 7–8 (9 *dial.*) sodd. [app. ad. MDu. *sode, soode* (Du. *zode*) or MLG. *sode* (*sade*; LG. *sode, sudde*), = OFris. *sâtha, sâda* (WFris. *sead, saed, sâdde*), of doubtful origin.

Connexion with SEETHE *v.* has been conjectured, on the supposition that the word may orig. have denoted turf used as fuel, but there is no clear evidence of this.]

**1. a.** A piece or slice of earth together with the grass growing on it, usually square or oblong in shape and of moderate thickness, cut out or pared off from the surface of grass land; a turf. Also const. *of* (grass, turf, etc.).

*c* **1420** *Liber Cocorum* (1862) 6 Yf þy dysshe metes dere ben to salt, Kerve a grene sod..þou schalt, And kover þy pot with þo gresse done. **1483** *Cath. Angl.* 348/1 A Sodde, *vbi* A turfe. **1497–8** *Durh. Acc. Rolls* (Surtees) 100 Pro cariag. xxiiij plaustr. de lez Soddez..usque Westorchard. **1550** BALE *Eng. Votaries* II. 57 b, His owne clergye wold scarsely suffer hym to be buryed..vnder tyrfes or soddes of the grasse. **1577** HOLINSHED *Chron., Hist. Eng.* IV. x. I. 61 She ..mounted vp into an high placeraysed vp of turfe and soddes. *c* **1618** MORYSON *Itin.* IV. 335 Old writers witness that..for a monument they only raysed a turffe or greene Sodd of the earth. **1697** DRYDEN *Æneid* VIII. 237 On sods of turf he set the soldiers round. **1703** THORESBY *Let. to Ray* (E.D.S.) s.v., A turf is thin and round, or oval..; a sod, thick and square, or oblong mostly. **1817** WOLFE *Burial Sir J. Moore* ii, We buried him darkly at dead of night, The sods with our bayonets turning. **1865** SWINBURNE *Poems & Ball., Dolores* 350 Her temple of branches and sods. **1884** *Times* (weekly ed.) 12 Sept. 2/4 Yesterday the first sod was turned of the new school-room.

**b.** *collect.* as a material.

**1826** HOOD *Irish Schoolm.* xii, His tears shall make his turfy seat More sodden, tho' already made of sod. **1827** SCOTT *Highl. Widow* i, The walls of sod, or *divot*, as the Scotch call it, were not four feet high.

**c.** *Sc.* A piece of turf used for fuel; a peat.

**1825** JAMIESON *Suppl.*, *Sod*, a species of earthen fuel, used for the back of a fire on the hearth. **1871** W. ALEXANDER *Johnny Gibb* (1873) 66 [They] had availed themselves of 'a het sod' to light their pipes. **1897** D. BUTLER *Church & Par. Abernethy* v. 78 A lighted sod from the priest's house.

**d.** *dial.* and *Mining.* (See quots.)

**1854** MISS BAKER *Northampt. Gloss.*, *Sods*, square pieces of clay for draining, cut from ploughed land instead of turf. **1881** *Leic. Gloss.*, *Sod*, a clod: not necessarily turf. **1883** GRESLEY *Gloss. Coal-m.* 229 *Sods*, clay beneath coal seams.

**2.** *Sc.* and *north.* In *pl.*, two pieces of turf used as a substitute for a saddle or pack-saddle. Hence, a rough kind of saddle made of cloth, canvas, etc., and stuffed with straw. Freq. ***a pair of sods.***

*a* **1586** R. MAITLAND in Pinkerton *Anc. Sc. Poems* (1786) 322 For thai, that had gude hors and geir, Hes skantlie now ane crukit meir: And for thair sadils thai have soddis. **1681** S. COLVIL *Whigs Supplic.* (1751) 27 He had a lady Del To-Bose, Who never budged from his side; Upon a pair of sodds astride. **1707** LADY GRISELL BAILLIE *Househ. Bk.* (1911) 20 For a pair sods to Doctor S[t] Clairs lady, £1. 16. 0. **1787** GROSE *Prov. Gloss.*, *Sods*, a canvas pack-saddle stuffed with straw. **1822** BEWICK *Mem.* 24, I buckled him [a dog] up in a pair of old 'sods' which covered him beyond both head and tail. **1886** W. BROCKIE *Leg. & Superst.* 39 (Heslop), To get her safely mounted behind him on a well girt pillion or sodds.

**3. a.** The surface of the ground, esp. when turfy or grass-covered; the sward. Freq. *poet.* or *rhet.* Also *N. Amer.*, more generally, soil which is grass-covered; sward which has never been cultivated; the surface of a lawn.

(*a*) **1729** T. COOKE *Tales*, etc. 89 Here be my Dwelling on this native Sod. **1771** SMOLLETT *Humph. Cl.* (1815) 255 If I had but one fair trust with him upon the sod, I'd give him lave to brag all the rest of his life! **1797** GODWIN *Enquirer* I. xiv. 121 He bounds over the sod. **1820** SHELLEY *Question* 13 Tender bluebells, at whose birth The sod scarce heaved. **1833** TENNYSON *Pal. Art* 261 Mouldering with the dull earth's mouldering sod. **1878** *Masque of Poets* 12 A homely product of the common sod.

(*b*) **1745** *Season. Advice Protestants* 17 The strong Sod on the Earth, made so by various Composts. **1810** E. D. CLARKE *Trav. Russia* (1839) 42/1 A..desolate plain, covered only by a thin sod, on which herds of cattle were grazing. **1838** LD. CLEMENTS *Poverty Irel.* 25 It consists, simply, in taking one or two crops of potatoes from the ley, or grass sod.

(*c*) **1968** *Globe & Mail* (Toronto) 17 Feb. 47/1 (Advt.), 1st class sandy land with substantial buildings. This irrigated land would produce excellent sod. **1976** *National Observer* (U.S.) 12 June 5/2 Some Postal Service employes also think that 'a lot of people don't want us to cross their lawns, tear up yards, and stomp holes in the sod.' **1976** *Billings* (Montana) *Gaz.* 5 July 9-C/1 (Advt.), 761 Acres cropland; 600 Acres former cropland, grassed; 800 Acres sod to break.

**b.** Phr. ***under the sod***: dead and buried; ***to put under the sod***: to kill. *colloq.* and *dial.*

**1847** TROLLOPE *Macdermots* III. vii. 286 I've heard the boys say that he would be undher the sod that day six months. *Ibid.* 288 A lot of boys swore together..to put him undher the sod. **1894** H. PEASE *Mark o' Deil* I. 19 'Fear-nowt Charlie,' who wes put under the sod, poor chap, a year come Michaelmas. **1972** K. BONFIGLIOLI *Don't point that Thing* xviii. 159 Happiness is..being alive and wonderful-for-his-age when old so-and-so is under the sod.

**c.** (*a*) The Turf. *Obs.* (*b*) The surface of a cockpit (sense 1); the institution, practice, or action of cock-fighting, the cock-fighting world.

**1755** *Mem. Capt. P. Drake* II. xvi. 265 She had run on the Sodd several Years, had won some Plates of small Value [etc.]. **1812** *Sporting Mag.* XL. 161 He flourished at the gaming-house, and blazed on the sod. **1814** W. SKETCHLEY *Cocker* p. iii, The author having been attached to the sod at a very early period of life..he flatters himself that..his attempt at writing 'The Cocker' will be found to contain.. instruction. **1840** D. P. BLAINE *Encycl. Rural Sports* IX. i. 1208 His chief opponent was Potter, who was feeder for that veteran sportsman, the Earl of Derby, whose attachment for the sod continued unwearied. **1912** W. GILBEY *Sport in Olden Time* 41 So closely was the grass-covered pit associated with the sport, that 'the sod' bore to cocking the same significance as 'the turf' bears to racing. **1977** *Verbatim* Feb. 1/1 Although the cockpit is as remote from the lives of most of us as a brontosaurus wallow, our language has been richly endowed by The Sod, and few of us get through a single day without recourse to at least one phrase from the lexicon of cocking.

**4.** *dial.* **a.** The spot of ground on which one stands.

**1691** RAY *N.C. Words* (ed. 2) 67, I will dye upon the Sod; *i.e.* in the place where I am. **1828** CARR *Craven Gloss.* s.v., I wish I may nivver stir of 't sod.

**b.** ***the* (*old*) *sod***, one's native district or country; *spec.*, Ireland.

**1812** P. EGAN *Boxiana* I. 315 O'Donnel..was a native of Ireland, who left the *sod* at a very early period of his life. **1863** MRS. TOOGOOD *Spec. Yorks. Dial.* (MS.), He does not like to leave the old sod after having lived there so long. **1891** E. ROPER *By Track & Trail* ii. 25 And did ye see ould Ireland lately?.. And how's the poor ould sod? **1892** W. G. LYTTLE *Life in Ballycuddy* 12 (E.D.D.), A'll niver lee the auld sod again. **1939** JOYCE *Finnegans Wake* 19 To say too us to be every tim, nick and larry of us, sons of the sod. *Ibid.* 194 Dry yanks will visit old sod. *a* **1953** E. O'NEILL *Long Day's Journey into Night* (1956) II. ii. 80 Then before his father can react to this insult to the Old Sod, he adds dryly, [etc.]. **1955** J. P. DONLEAVY *Ginger Man* v. 35 I'll give you the jug to remember me when I'm gone from the ould sod, sacked in with some lovely French doll.

**5.** *attrib.* and *Comb.* **a.** Attrib., in the sense 'made, formed, built, or consisting of sods', as ***sod bank, cabin, -cloth, crop, -drain, ground, -house, -hut, -kiln, land***, etc.; also in other uses, as ***sod-draining, -plough, spade***; **sod widow** (see quot. 1946); **sod-worm** (see quot.).

**1799** [A. YOUNG] *Agric. Lincoln.* 383 *Sod banks cost, thirty-five years ago, 1*s.* 2*d.* a rood of seven yards. **1932** W. FAULKNER *Light in August* xi. 232 He found the *sod cabin. **1905** *Sod-cloth [see MUDWALLING *vbl. sb.*]. **1956** C. EVANS *On Climbing* viii. 128 Round the bottom of the tent, on the outside, a foot-wide strip of cloth should run, the 'sod-cloth', on which stones and snow can be put to anchor the tent. **1848** *Rep. U.S. Comm. Patents 1847* 539 This gave a *sod crop without tending of thirty to forty bushels per acre. **1950** *Jrnl. Illinois State Hist. Soc.* Spring 37 They learned to plant a 'sod crop' by cutting upturned furrows with an ax, then dropping in a few kernels of corn. **1844** H. STEPHENS *Book Farm* I. 603 If the turf is tough, so much the better for the durability of the *sod-drain. *Ibid.*, An imperfect form of wedge-draining is practised in some parts of England on strong clay soils, under the name of *sod-draining. **1839** W. SEWALL *Diary* 23 Aug. (1930) 207/1 Broke up the *sod ground in the prairie up the hollow for a yard in which to make brick. **1932** *Randolph Enterprise* (Elkins, W.Va.) 4 Feb. 4/2 Sod ground is about all ploughed and some stubble ground also. **1832** *Bubwith Inclosure Act* 38 A certain cottage or *sod-house. **1937** J. ISE (*title*) Sod-house days. Letters from a Kansas homesteader, 1877–78. **1948** B. SUNDKLER *Bantu Prophets* vi. 183 On the door of the sod house used as a church there is painted a green and white cross. **1977** *Westworld* (Vancouver, B.C.) May–June 6/2 There certainly was nothing like a sod house for being cool in summer and warm in winter. **1869** *Harper's Monthly* June 25/1 A warmer abode than the *sod hut..he will never have. **1896** HOWELLS *Impress. & Exp.* 146 The dugouts or sod-huts of the settlers on the great plains. **1930** L. G. D. ACLAND *Early Canterbury Runs* 1st Ser. ii. 13 Ford built a six-roomed wooden cottage to replace the original sod hut. **1972** *Science* 19 May 747/2 While others were planning fancy facilities, Herzberg's helpers built a sod-hut similar to those used as homes by the early settlers of Saskatchewan. **1806** FORSYTH *Beauties Scotl.* IV. 265 From these..*sod-kilns, perhaps, were copied the shallowness and width of the present stone-kilns. **1856** *Rep. U.S. Comm. Patents 1855*: *Agric.* 262 They were mostly sown upon *sod-land. **1946** *Sun* (Baltimore) 11 Nov. 2/1 Anderson cautioned growers of wheat and flax not to break up sod or grass lands which are not adapted to continued cultivation and which would create erosion hazards in the future. **1875** KNIGHT *Dict. Mech.* 2238/1 **Sod-plow*, a plow long in the share and mold-board, adapted to cut and overturn sod. **1843–52** R. BURN *Techn. Dict.* I, *Revêtement en gazons*,..*sod revetment. **1879** *Cassell's Techn. Educ.* III. 120 Sod revetments form a neat-looking slope. **1793** WORDSW. *Descr. Sketches* 21 For him *sod-seats the cottage-door adorn. *a* **1835** HOGG *Tales, Wool-gatherer* (1866) 72 Jane had sat down on the sod-seat. **1619** S. ATKINSON *Gold Mynes Scotl.* (Bann. Cl.) 1 To use the arte of delving with the *sodd spade. **1649** W. G. *Surv. Newcastle upon Tine* 2 Picts, who brake downe the *Sodd Wall. **1776** LESLY in Young *Tour Irel.* (1780) I. *209 The sod walls, about 10 or 12 inches thick. **1927** *Amer. Speech* II. 278 **Sod* (widow), husband dead. **1946** G. STIMPSON *Bk. about Thousand Things* 349 A grass widow's husband was alive while a *sod widow*'s husband was under the sod. **1973** *Raleigh* (N.C.) *News & Observer* 12 Mar. 34/2 Last but not least is our large number of widows (sod). There are 70. **1834–47** J. S. MACAULAY *Field Fortif.* (1851) 225 The earth above the pebbles is to be retained by a revetment of *sod-work. **1891** *Cent. Dict.*, **Sod-worm*, the larva of certain pyralid moths, as *Crambus exsiccatus*, which destroys the roots of grass and corn.

**b.** Objective, with agent-nouns and vbl. sbs., as ***sod-builder, -cutter, -soaker; sod-burning, -cutting***, etc.

**1796** W. H. MARSHALL *W. England* II. 32 Sodburning the more loamy soils..would be a ready means of meliorating the herbage. **1843–52** R. BURN *Techn. Dict.* I, *Trousse-pas*, sod-cutter's spade. *Ibid.* II. s.v., Sod-builder. *Ibid.* II. s.v., Sod-cutter, *écobue*. **1890** *Science-Gossip* XXVI. 99 If the grass and other sod-forming plants assert themselves. **1892** *Daily News* 7 Jan. 3/3 The sod-cutting ceremony of tomorrow. **1903** Sod-soaker [see *gully-washer* s.v. GULLY *sb.*[1] 4]. **1953** *Manch. Guardian Weekly* 18 June 3/1 'Oh Lord, send us a sod-soaker and not a gully-drencher.' The prayer of the prairie farmer is specific.

(*b*) Special comb. **sod planting** *Agric.*, the sowing of seed in unploughed ground, herbicides being used to kill or control any existing vegetation; so **sod-plant** *v. trans.*, **sod-planted** *ppl. a.*

**1965** *Proc. Southern Weed Control Conf.* XVIII. 146 A second screening test was conducted in 1963 in connection with a new sod planting research program. The aim.. was to develop a high producing summer grain or silage crop grown in a chemically controlled perennial sod which would return to productive pasture in the fall, winter and spring, maintaining a protective mulch cover at all times. **1967** *Agronomy Jrnl.* LIX. 549/1 Removal of the rye immediately before sod-planting corn in the stubble lowered yields as compared to mulched crops. *Ibid.* 548/1 Inclusion of the winter legumes.. did not increase sod-planted corn yields. *Ibid.* 550/1 The moisture conserving aspect of sod planting is most pronounced for droughts of short duration. **1978** *McGraw-Hill Yearbk. Sci. & Technol.* 78/2 Various reduced tillage systems are referred to as direct drilling, minimum tillage, no-tillage, sod planting,.. depending upon the operations used, the crops grown, and the locale.

**c.** With pa. pples., as ***sod-built, -roofed.***

**1805–6** WORDSWORTH *Prelude* (1959) VIII. 613 The Woodman languish'd Within his sod-built cabin. **1814** SCOTT *Lord of Isles* III. i, The rye-grass shakes not on the sod-built fold. **1891** E. ROPER *By Track & Trail* iii. 37 Groups of ruined shanties, sod-roofed, bark-roofed, covered anyhow.

**sod** (sɒd), *pa. pple., ppl. a.*, and *sb.*[2] Forms: 3–4 i-sode, 4–5 sode, 5–7 sodde, 6– sod. [Pa. pple. of SEETHE *v.* Cf. SODDEN *pa. pple.*, etc.]

†**1. a.** Of food, liquor, etc.: Boiled; prepared by boiling. *Obs.*

*pred.* **1297** R. GLOUC. (Rolls) 9164 þe bones hii bere Wel iselt & isode to þe abbeye of redinge. **13..** *Seuyn Sag.* 1574 (W.), Barli-water, that was i-sode. **1422** tr. *Secreta Secret., Priv. Priv.* 246 Flesh y-rostid, wych is more hottyr than.. sode in watyr. **1588** PARKE tr. *Mendoza's Hist. China* 309 Eating of those bodies which they had slaine, some sodde and some roasted. **1621** BURTON *Anat. Mel.* I. ii. II. i. (1651) 70 Beer, if it be.. over strong, or not sod,.. frets and gauls. *attrib.* *c* **1386** CHAUCER *Parson's T.* ⁋827 So thise shrewes ne holden hem nat apayed of roosted flessh and sode flessh. **1390** GOWER *Conf.* II. 270 Sche let do sowe The lond with sode whete aboute. *c* **1430** *Two Cookery-bks.* 42 Nym sode Porke & chese. **1528** PAYNELL *Salerne's Regim.* Q iij, Sodde peres releue the stomake greued. **1598** LODGE *Looking Gl. for Lond. & Eng.* B iv, Whay, curds, creame, sod milke, raw-milke. **1611** CORYAT *Crudities* 373 Rost and sodde meates. **1658** ROWLAND tr. *Moufet's Theat. Ins.* 898 Wool wet in sod or sweet wine.

†**b.** ***twice sod,*** stale, unpalatable. *Obs.*

**1598** B. JONSON *Ev. Man in Hum.* IV. x, Is meat twice sod to you, sir? **1608** CHAPMAN *Byron's Consp.* IV. i. 114 You make all state before Vtterly obsolete; all to come, twice sod. **1610** [see COLEWORT 4]. **1641** J. JACKSON *True Evang. T.* ii. 130 The example doth so suite the Text, that I could not pretermit it here, though it be mentioned before: neither is it 'coleworts twice sod'.

†**c.** Of persons: Sodden, soaked, or steeped *in* liquor. *Obs.*

**1613** BEAUM. & FL. *Captain* IV. ii, All the rest.. are in *Limbo patrum*, Where they lye sod in sack.

**2. a.** Of bread: Sodden. Also as *sb.*: a damper (DAMPER 6) that has not risen. *Austral.*

**1836** *Penny Cycl.* V. 373/1 So that no part of the dough may form a sod or ill-raised bread. **1900–10** in G. A. Wilkes *Dict. Austral. Colloquialisms* (1978) 309/1. **1931** I. L. IDRIESS *Lasseter's Last Ride* v. 36 He made dampers so light that they were in danger of blowing away [and].. had not baked one 'sod' during the entire trip. **1957** R. S. PORTEOUS *Brigalow* 206 His dampers were leaden sods. **1975** X. HERBERT *Poor Fellow my Country* xvi. 838, I want to cook our own damper, too.. don't want one of their sods.

**b.** ***sod oil*** (see quots.).

**1883** R. HALDANE *Workshop Rec.* Ser. II. 367/2 The oil pressed out of the fermented skins is known as 'sod oil'. **1885** A. WATT *Leather Manuf.* xxvii. 341 'Sod oil,' a greasy matter obtained in the treatment of sheep-skins.

†**3.** As *sb.* Boiled meat. *Obs.*

**1548** ELYOT, *Acapna thysia*,.. spoken of a simple feast, wherein is neither bake, roste nor sodde. **1558** WARDE tr. *Alexis' Secr.* 33 b, You maye gyue hym roste and sodde with pottage of *Amylum.* **1600** ROWLAND *Lett. Humours Blood* iii. 9 Not that hee'le cloy him there with rost or sod. *a* **1618** SYLVESTER *Maiden's Blush* 218 While hee is set-up with his Sod and Roast.

**sod** (sɒd), *sb.*[3] [Short for SODOMITE.]

**1.** One who practises or commits sodomy. *coarse slang.*

*c* **1855** *Yokel's Preceptor* 6 It is not long since, in the neighbourhood of Charing Cross, they posted bills in the windows of several respectable public houses, cautioning the public to 'Beware of Sods!' **1859** G. W. MATSELL *Vocabulum* 83 *Sod*, a worn-out debauchee, whom excess of indulgence has rendered unnatural. **1934** V. WOOLF *Let.* 24 Jan. (1979) V. 273, I am writing about sodomy at the moment and wish I could discuss the matter with you; how far can one say openly what is the relation of a woman and a sod? **1949** WYNDHAM LEWIS *Let.* ?8 Mar. (1963) 484 When you come to write your book, its scene our day to day life, I should put in the sods. Sartre has shown what a superb figure of comedy a homo can be. **1968** S. JAMESON *White Crow* xxxiv. 291 Homosexuals are always getting themselves assaulted. You read that some respectable middle-aged bachelor has been beaten insensible on the stairway of his Mayfair flat, and invariably it turns out that he was a sod.

**2. a.** Used as a vulgar term of abuse for (usu.) a male person. Also with weakened force, as the equivalent of 'fellow', 'chap', freq. affectionately or in commiseration; ***odds and sods:*** see ODDS *sb.* 7 b.

**1818** *Sessions* 17 June 283/2 As he passed me he said the other was a b—y s—d. **1931** K. O'BRIEN *Without my Cloak* III. xi. 380 That auld sod of a husband making her black and blue every night of his filthy life. **1931** W. V. TILSLEY *Other Ranks* 12 Lucky sods, getting this far and then going back. **1942** G. KERSH *Nine Lives Bill Nelson* x. 61 There are plenty of sods in this battalion that get their pleasure by exercising their two-penny-ha'penny authority. **1942** T. RATTIGAN *Flare Path* III. 164 Johnny, you old sod! Is it really you? **1957** I. MURDOCH *Sandcastle* xiii. 210 He thought to himself, what a sod I am, what a poor confused sod. **1958** 'E. O'CONNER' *Steak for Breakfast* 28 Good on yer, Martha, yer old sod! **1963** T. PARKER *Unknown Citizen* i. 40 Don't you call me a daft sod, you daft sod. **1968** J. BRAINE *Crying Game* i. 18 It's time he was dead... If you want to destroy the sod, Frank, I'll give you absolutely all the dirt. **1969** D. WALLACE *Turtle* xiv. 148 That's a shame, the poor little dawg, but if that was moine I'd hev that put down. That can't help but make no end o' work, the poor little sod. **1974** N. FREELING *Dressing of Diamond* 201 Yes, now I remember him, cheeky young sod. **1978** *Globe & Mail* (Toronto) 16 Aug. 31/7 And when they do, these lucky sods will forget years of fish-fib training and head pell mell for shore, seeking, of all things, the truth.

**b.** Something difficult; a great nuisance. *slang.*

**1936** 'G. ORWELL' *Keep Aspidistra Flying* i. 11 'Bare' is a sod to 'rhyme'; however, there's always 'air'. **1950** C. MACINNES *To Victor Spoils* I. 84 It'd be a sod if they got through to the Meuse. **1971** V. CANNING *Firecrest* i. 3 At least.. he'd seen them come back, though it was a sod he'd missed them going off. **1977** [see SATIN *sb.* (and *a.*) 6 b].

**c.** ***sod-all,*** nothing, no. Cf. ALL A. 8 f. *slang.*

**1958** K. AMIS *I like it Here* i. 12 There's been sod-all since. **1961** I. JEFFERIES *It wasn't Me!* iii. 39 When I was at that pharmaceutical firm.. I did sod-all for months on end. **1972** J. WAINWRIGHT *Requiem for Loser* viii. 167 Like the concert hall... A bit of a stage—and sod-all else. **1978** 'K. BLAKE' *Where Jungle Ends* iii. 37 Here he was in this cold chill room, and two maniacs sitting playing cards at the table and taking sod-all notice of him.

**d.** ***not to give a sod*** = ***not to give a damn*** s.v. DAMN *sb.* 2. *slang.*

**1961** B. ALDISS *Primal Urge* i. 29 Nobody gave a sod. Euphoria had its high tide. **1973** D. STOREY *Temporary Life* v. ii. 224, I don't give a sod for any of them, Phil.

**e.** ***Sod's Law*** = ***Murphy's law*** s.v. MURPHY[2] 3.

**1970** *New Statesman* 9 Oct. 460/1 Sod's Law.. is the force in nature which causes it to rain mostly at weekends, which makes you get flu when you are on holiday, and which makes the phone ring just as you've got into the bath. **1978** *New Scientist* 7 Sept. 744/1 The great unshakeable list of interdisciplinary laws—Sod's Law, Newton's Fourth Law of Motion, the Inverse Midas Touch and their kin. **1980** *SLR Camera* July 56/2 Even if you're using a masking frame this can easily over-balance. According to Sod's Law, that's going to happen when you're halfway through exposing a sheet of 20 × 16in colour paper costing the best part of £1·30.

**sod** (sɒd), *v.*[1] [f. SOD *sb.*[1] Cf. MDu. *soden, zoden*, LG. *soden, söden*, to make sods, lay with sods.] *trans.* To cover or build up, to provide or lay, with sods or turfs; to turf.

**1653** BLITHE *Eng. Improver Impr.* (ed. 3) 55 One good substantiall Dike, well turfed (or sodded, as the Fen-men call it). **1693** EVELYN *De la Quint. Compl. Gard.* I. 42 Those Terraces must be supported.. by some Banks that shall be sodded on purpose, to make them the more solid and lasting. **1704** *Dict. Rust.* (1726) s.v. *Brick*, To sod, is to cover the Bricks. **1799** [A. YOUNG] *Agric. Lincoln.* 159 Bind the femble into sheaves or beats. Cart it to dykes, sod it. **1839** HOOD *Storm at Hastings* xxix, We snatch'd up the corse thus thrown, Intending, Christian-like, to sod and turf it. **1889** *Harper's Mag.* Sept. 558/2 The slope was sodded and terraced with rows of seats.

**b.** Const. *down, over, up.*

**1763** *Museum Rust.* I. 368 A sorry mound of sods, with some bushes sodded down on top, to keep out sheep. **1821** CLARE *Vill. Minstr.* II. 81 Made up of mud and stones and sodded o'er. **1870** *Daily News* 12 Nov., The.. earthwork, so completely constructed as to have been sodded up with turf.

**sod,** *v.*[2] Now *dial.* [f. SOD *pa. pple.*]

**1.** *intr.* To become sodden or soaked; to stick *together* through wetness.

**1642** D. ROGERS *Naaman* 3 The tree which hath long lien sodding in the ditch. **1644** PLATTES in *Hartlib's Legacy* (1655) 218 If Sand, whence comes its clamminess and aptness to sod together? *a* **1722** LISLE *Husb.* (1757) 246 If the hay made of it sods a little in the wet,.. it becomes tasteless.

**2.** *trans.* To soak with wet.

**1895** A. PATTERSON *Man & Nat. on the Broads* 125 Work on the land where wet grass an' rubbidge sod (soak) yer trowsers below.

**sod,** *v.*[3] *slang.* [f. SOD *sb.*[3]]

**1.** *trans.* = DAMN *v.* 5.

**1904** *Eng. Dial. Dict.* V. 605/2 Phr. *sod him*, may mischief befall him. *w. Yks.* Sod him, he can go to ——. **1942** G. KERSH *Nine Lives Bill Nelson* i. 3 Well, sod the Drill Pig. **1945** *Penguin New Writing* XXIII. 51 Sod that, chummie. **1953** P. SCOTT *Alien Sky* I. viii. 131 At seven-fifteen they had to go out to dinner. Sod it. **1958** —— *Mark of Warrior* II. 131 'Look, you'd better go sick.'.. 'Sod you, Bob. I wouldn't miss it for the world.' **1967** J. WAIN *Smaller Sky* 170 'He'll come out,' said Swarthmore. 'And if he doesn't, we'll sit where we are and you'll get paid for a full day's work, with overtime if necessary, and you won't have to do a stroke.' 'I'd rather be at home,' said the chief cameraman, 'and sod the overtime. I'm definitely sickening for something.' **1971** B. W. ALDISS *Soldier Erect* 209 Quite a road! Sod me! I'll say it is! **1977** *Chainsaw* Sept./Oct. 3/2 Sod it! There goes my banner headline.

**2.** *intr.* With *off:* to go away, depart. Also = ***get away*** s.v. GET *v.* 61 b, and *fig.* Usu. in imp.

**1960** J. SYMONS *Progress of Crime* xv. 92 Now sod off and get your identification parade done. **1968** *Listener* 14 Nov. 650/3 It's good to learn what Mr Reed said to the vicar who complained that boys had damaged a valuable rose tree: 'I told him to sod off.' **1971** F. FORSYTH *Day of Jackal* xx. 335 The policeman asked for papers. The Jackal giggled seductively... 'Sod off,' said the policeman and withdrew. **1976** P. CAVE *High Flying Birds* ii. 16 'Sod off,' I said, 'How can you call a glider a vehicle?' **1977** *Observer* 4 Sept. 14/2, I am simply waiting for the day when I can say 'sod off' to your institution. **1978** I. MURDOCH *Sea* 168 That's right, sod off just when.. the light of understanding has dawned. .. Oh all right, sod off then!

**sod,** obs. pa. t. of SEETHE *v.*

**soda**[1] ('səʊdə). [a. med.L. *soda* (It. and Pg. *soda*, Sp. *soda, sosa*, F. *soude*, †*soulde, soulte*), of unknown origin.]

**1. a.** An alkaline substance obtained originally from the ashes of certain marine or other salt-impregnated plants, esp. species of *Salsola*, and now manufactured artificially from common salt, or occurring in a mineral state as a deposit, esp. in certain lakes, or in solution in the water of such lakes (natron); used largely in commerce, esp. in the manufacture of glass and soap; soda-ash; sodium carbonate ($Na_2CO_3$).

Freq. used as a synonym of sodium in the names of various compounds of the element, as *muriate, nitrate, sulphate*, etc., *of soda.*

**1558** WARDE *Alexis' Secr.* I. IV. 78 Take an vnce of Soda (whiche is asshes made of grasse, whereof glassemakers doo vse to make their Cristall). **1678** R. R[USSELL] tr. *Geber* IV. iv. 245 True Salt-Alkali is made of Zoza (or Soda) dissolved. **1693** tr. *Blancard's Phys. Dict.* (ed. 2), *Soda*, the Ashes of the Herb Kali Burnt, whereof Glass is made. **1767** *Phil. Trans.* LVII. 480 The fossil [alkali] or mineral, called likewise soda and natrum. **1796** KIRWAN *Elem. Min.* (ed. 2) II. 19 Soda affects it but slightly. **1839** URE *Dict. Arts* 1150 Carbonate of Soda.. is the soda of commerce in various states, either crystallized, in lumps, or in a crude powder called soda-ash. **1870** YEATS *Nat. Hist. Comm.* 249 A large proportion of the plants growing on sea-coasts contain soda, whilst inland plants contain potash.

*fig.* **1823** BYRON *Juan* X. lxxiii, Half-solved into these sodas or magnesias, Which form that bitter draught, the human species.

**b.** Sodium bicarbonate, used largely for domestic purposes; baking or cooking soda.

**1851–4** *Tomlinson's Cycl. Usef. Arts* I. 183/1 Mix the soda perfectly with the flour. **1893** *Westm. Gaz.* 21 Apr. 5/2 A half cwt. of soda could be bought for 3*s.*

**c.** ***caustic soda,*** sodium hydroxide or hydrate (NaOH). Cf. CAUSTIC *a.* 1 c.

**1839** URE *Dict. Arts* 132 A ley of caustic soda. *Ibid.*, Caustic soda ley. *Ibid.* 1150 Caustic soda is a white brittle mass,.. having a most corrosive taste and action upon animal matters. **1871** GARROD *Mat. Med.* (ed. 3) 132 Liquor Sodæ, above described, contains caustic soda.

†**2.** The prickly saltwort, *Salsola kali.* = KALI[1] 1.

**1658** tr. *Porta's Nat. Magick* VI. i. 178 The herb Kali or Saltwort is commonly called Soda.

**3.** *Chem.* Sodium oxide ($Na_2O$).

**1826** HENRY *Elem. Chem.* I. 557 The next oxide of sodium is soda. **1856** MILLER *Elem. Chem., Inorg.* 743 Oxide of Sodium, or Soda (NaO), forms the basis of the important series of salts of soda. **1868** WATTS *Dict. Chem., Soda:* This term, in scientific language, is applied to the anhydrous protoxide of sodium ($Na^2O$).

**4. a.** Soda-water.

**1834** J. R. PLANCHÉ *Olympic Revels* in *Extravaganzas* (1879) I. 47 Make him sit down—give him some hock and soda. **1842** LOVER *Handy Andy* i, Bang went the bottle of soda. **1864** SALA *Quite Alone* I. xiv. 220 Keep him on his soda-and-B. That won't do him any harm. **1897** SURG.-CAPT. HUGHES *Medit. Fever* v. 210 An occasional whiskey with water or soda.. is useful.

**b.** A glass or drink of soda-water; also, an ice-cream soda.

**1933** E. O'NEILL *Ah Wilderness!* II. 58 Ever drink anything besides sodas? **1962** A. LURIE *Love & Friendship* viii. 145 Vanilla sodas with strawberry ice-cream. **1973** 'E. MCBAIN' *Hail to Chief* vi. 94 Toy.. put the straws between her lips, and busied herself with the soda.

**5.** *Faro.* In full ***soda card.*** (See quot. 1975.) Phr. ***from soda (card) to hock:*** see HOCK *sb.*[6] b.

**1845** J. H. GREENE *Exposure of Arts & Miseries Gambling* (ed. 2) 135 The top card, when the deal is first commenced, is called the *deal card*; this card neither wins nor loses, and on that account is sometimes called the *soda card.* **1975** *Way to Play* 206/2 The exposed top card is called the 'soda'. It is ignored for betting.

**6.** *Austral. slang.* Something easy to accomplish, a simple task; a 'pushover'.

**1930** V. PALMER *Passage* I. i. 22 'Just one more guess.'.. 'Umph, that's a soda! Must be the old doctor.' *Ibid.* x. 83 They're getting ready for the long dive now, and it ought to be a soda for you. If I hadn't rheumatics down the back of my leg, I'd give it a fly myself. **1943** G. H. JOHNSTON *New Guinea Diary* IV. 136 'The Middle East was a soda beside this,' one of them told me. **1955** A. MARSHALL *I can jump Puddles* 108 Swipe him on the knuckles if you can. If he's like his old man he's a soda. **1966** H. PORTER *Paper Chase* 74 The job, for which I have no really specialized training, is nevertheless a soda.

**7.** *attrib.* and *Comb.*

**a.** Misc., chiefly in sense 1, as ***soda-bath, -compound, -crystals, -lime, pan*** [PAN *sb.*[1] 5 a], ***plain, -salt, soap,*** etc.; ***soda-carbonate, muriate, tartrate***; in *Photogr.* for hyposulphite of soda, as ***soda developer, development, -pyro, -solution,*** etc.; ***soda-chapped*** adj.; **soda-acid,** used *attrib.* to designate a fire extinguisher containing sulphuric acid and sodium bicarbonate (or sometimes the carbonate), which are mixed just before use to provide the gas for expelling the water; **soda-ash,** the sodium carbonate of commerce, = SODA[1] 1; **soda cellulose,** a form of cellulose heavily impregnated with soda, produced by the action of caustic soda on wood-pulp esp. in the manufacture of paper or rayon; **soda glass**, glass containing a high proportion of soda; sometimes = *soda-lime glass*; **soda lake**, a natron lake; **soda-lime glass**, the standard form of glass in everyday use, manufactured essentially from silica, soda, and lime; **soda-lye** (see quot. 1867); **soda-paper, -prairie**, (see quots.); **soda process**, a method of pulping wood by boiling with caustic soda; **soda pulp**, woodpulp made by the soda process; **soda waste** (see quots.).

**1928** R. NORTHWOOD *Fire Extinguishment & Fire Alarm Syst.* xxi. 185 (*caption*) Method of recharging 'The Conquest' *soda-acid extinguisher. **1966** *McGraw-Hill Encycl. Sci. & Technol.* V. 279/1 In the small first-aid water fire extinguishers, a propellant must be provided. Usually this is carbon dioxide, which is either generated when needed (the soda-acid extinguisher) or stored in a cartridge. **1839** *Soda-ash [see 1]. **1884** W. S. B. MCLAREN *Spinning* (ed. 2) 29 Soda crystals, or soda-ash,..are carbonates of soda. **1865** PRINCESS ALICE *Mem.* (1884) 99, I am taking warm *soda-baths in the morning. **1839** URE *Dict. Arts* 1151 The crystals of *soda-carbonate..are now made altogether by the decomposition of sea salt. **1890** *Jrnl. Soc. Chem. Industry* 28 Feb. 225/1 Their production is estimated at 30,000 tons sulphite (wet) and 9,000 *soda cellulose (dry). **1948** J. T. MARSH *Textile Sci.* ii. 19 Sheets of pulp are converted into soda-cellulose by steeping in caustic soda solution. **1973** *Materials & Technol.* VI. iv. 306 The swollen, and still further purified 'soda cellulose' so formed, is broken down into 'crumbs', and these are then transferred to reactor vessels. **1922** JOYCE *Ulysses* 59 *Sodachapped hands. **1845** DAY tr. *Simon's Anim. Chem.* I. 182 Hence the albumen in the blood cannot exist as a *soda-compound (albuminate of soda). **1839** URE *Dict. Arts* 1155 Our commercial *soda crystals are composed of—1 atom of carbonic acid, 1 atom of soda, and 10 atoms of water. **1892** *Photogr. Ann.* II. 89 The *soda developer tends to give softer images. **1890** *Anthony's Photogr. Bulletin* III. 65 *Soda development is apt to give a yellow image. **1864** *Reader* 24 Sept. 387 Such a light is the monochromatic *soda-flame. **1897** A. HARTSHORNE *Old English Glasses* 39 Venetian *soda-glass is much lighter than that made in the Low Countries with potash. **1947** J. C. RICH *Materials & Methods of Sculpture* xi. 329 Sodium carbonate, calcium carbonate, and sand yield a soft or 'soda glass'. **1965** PHILLIPS & WILLIAMS *Inorg. Chem.* I. xiv. 553 Soda glass is conveniently worked at a lower temperature than borosilicate glass. **1839** URE *Dict. Arts* 1155 There are several *soda lakes in Mexico. **1937** *Discovery* Feb. 58/1 A new exhibit presented by the Magadi Soda Lake Co...at the Imperial Institute..illustrates..the exploitation of one of the most remarkable natural soda lakes in the world. **1976** K. THACKERAY *Crownbird* ix. 199 The road..ran steeply down beside a soda lake... The soda was firm near the edge. **1839** URE *Dict. Arts* 132 Avoid lime,..but use it freely after one or two *soda leys. **1867** BLOXAM *Chem.* 266 Soda lye, employed in the manufacture of hard soap, is a solution of hydrate of soda. *Ibid.* 572 A weak soda-ley. **1862** MILLER *Elem. Chem., Org.* i. §1 (ed. 2) 19 A portion of this alkalized lime, or *soda-lime as it is frequently termed. **1917** A. B. SEARLE in G. Martin *Industr. & Manufacturing Chem.* (*Inorg.*) II. 245 For soda-lime glasses the mean coefficient of expansion lies between 0·000023 and 0·000027 per 1°C. **1955** E. B. SHAND *Glass Engin. Handbk.* i. 2/1 Soda-lime glasses are commonly used for bottles, jars, window sheet and plate glass, electric lamp bulbs, and ophthalmic (sight-correcting) lenses. **1971** *Materials & Technol.* II. vi. 340 Soda-lime glasses in commercial use have devitrification temperatures in the region of 900 to 1000°C. **1804** *Phil. Trans.* XCIV. 427 The *soda-muriate of palladium is a deliquescent salt. **1976** K. THACKERAY *Crownbird* v. 82 The plane was flying..over one end of an enormous soda pan. **1875** KNIGHT *Dict. Mech.* 2236/1 **Soda-paper*, a paper made by saturating filtering paper with carbonate of soda. **1793** T. BEDDOES *Calculus* p. x, His experience of the good effects of *soda pills, in cases of biliary concretion. **1946** D. C. PEATTIE *Road of Naturalist* i. 20 You find mariposas all over the West; they change height, change shape and colour, as you trace them from the mountains of Colorado, over the Utah *soda plains. **1859** BARTLETT *Dict. Amer.* (ed. 2) 426 **Soda-prairie*, a plain covered with an efflorescence of soda, elsewhere called natron. **1885** *Encycl. Brit.* XVIII. 226/1 The pulp produced by all those processes is of excellent quality; and, according to the statements of the patentees, it can be prepared at a cost greatly lower than by the *soda process. **1907** *Jrnl. Soc. Chem. Industry* 15 June 561/2 In the period of 1865 to 1875 a large number of mills were erected throughout Canada and the United States, for the cooking of wood by the soda process. **1967** V. STRAUSS *Printing Industry* viii. 532/2 The soda process..has lower yields than the sulfate process..and the recovery of caustic soda is costly. For these and other reasons the soda process is losing ground fast to the sulfate process. **1893** *Jrnl. Soc. Chem. Industry* 30 Sept. 793/2 The product of 1892 included only 12,500 tons of *soda pulp, the remaining 137,500 tons being produced by the sulphite process. **1962** F. T. DAY *Introd. Paper* ii. 20 Deciduous or broad-leafed trees such as the poplar are used in the production of soda pulp. **1889** *Anthony's Photogr. Bulletin* II. 391, I worked always with *soda-pyro. **1836–41** BRANDE *Chem.* (ed. 5) 716 When magnesia is precipitated by excess of carbonate of soda, a portion of the triple *soda-salt is retained. **1834–6** *Encycl. Metrop.* (1845) VIII. 434/1 Common salt..hardens and renders it equal to the *soda soaps. **1884** W. S. B. MCLAREN *Spinning* (ed. 2) 28 Soda soaps are hard, potash soaps are soft. **1809** *Phil. Trans.* XCIX. 327 These parts..certainly afforded no *soda-tartrate of potash. **1849** D. CAMPBELL *Inorg. Chem.* 115 Water dissolves out the soda salts, leaving the insoluble oxisulphide of calcium, known as *soda waste.

**b.** Connected or dealing with sodium carbonate or its manufacture, as ***soda-apparatus***, ***-furnace***, ***industry***, ***-making***, ***manufacture***, etc. Also with agent-nouns, as ***soda-furnacer***, ***maker***.

(*a*) **1839** URE *Dict. Arts* 1151 Soda Manufacture. *Ibid.* 1152 The draught of a soda-furnace must be very sharp. *Ibid.* 1153 In some soda-works, where the decomposing furnace is very large. **1853** *Ure's Dict. Arts* II. 683 The whole process of soda-making. **1875** KNIGHT *Dict. Mech.* 2234/1 Soda-apparatus. **1884** GILMOUR *Mongols* 169 Particularly fatal is this rough road to the wooden axles of the soda carts.

(*b*) **1839** URE *Dict. Arts* 1153 The dexterous management of this transposition characterizes a good soda-furnacer. **1853** *Ure's Dict. Arts* II. 682 Having..obtained a quantity of sulphate of soda, the soda maker now proceeds to his next operation.

**c.** With the names of minerals and rocks containing soda, as ***soda alum***, ***-chabazite***, ***-copperas***, ***-feldspar***, ***-lime-feldspar***, ***-nitre***, ***-saltpetre***, ***-spodumene*** (see quots.) Also ***soda-granitic*** adj.

Many of these terms are now obsolete.

**1837** DANA *Min.* 170 Solfatarite, *alumen volcanicum*. *Soda Alum. **1876** HARLEY *Royle's Mat. Med.* 192 Soda alum and ammonia alum are formed by replacing the equivalent of potash with one of soda or ammonia. **1968** I. KOSTOV *Mineral.* 494 As 'alums' are denoted the following double sulphates:..Soda alum $NaAl(SO_4)_2.12H_2O$. **1935** *Amer. Mineralogist* XX. 58 The high percentage of soda.. justifies the classification of the mineral as *soda-alunite in the broad sense. **1913** *Soda-amphibole [see IMERINITE]. **1931** *Mineral. Mag.* XXII. 453 The brown augite has in places fringes of a green *soda-augite. **1836** T. THOMSON *Min., Geol.*, etc. I. 335 Combinations of the common calcareous-chabasite and the *soda-chabasite of Berzelius. **1844** DANA *Mineral.* 226 A *Soda Copperas has been analyzed by Scheerer. **1868** WATTS *Dict. Chem.*, *Soda copperas*, a sodio-ferric sulphate found in the alum-slate of Modum in Norway. **1863** DANA *Man. Geol.* 56 Albite or *Soda-feldspar. **1889** *Soda-felsite [see KERATOPHYRE]. **1965** G. J. WILLIAMS *Econ. Geol. N.Z.* xi. 167/1 Watters *et al.* (1961) noticed fergusonite in small water-worn grains from a restricted locality in the Canaan area where the Separation Point *soda-granite invades Paleozoic marbles. **1845** DARWIN *Voy. Nat.* xv. 320 Mountain masses of a peculiar white *soda-granitic rock. **1867** *Ure's Dict. Arts* (ed. 6) II. 269 *Soda-lime-felspar (often containing potash); labradorite. **1896** CHESTER *Dict. Min.*, **Soda-nitre*, nitrate of sodium, found as a mineral. **1966** *McGraw-Hill Encycl. Sci. & Technol.* XII. 407/2 Soda niter is by far the most abundant of the nitrate minerals. **1926** *Proc. U.S. Nat. Mus.* LXVIII. Art. 17. 4 It may be chemically classed as a *soda-rhyolite, but none of the calculated normative minerals of rhyolite are found in its mode. **1913** *Soda-richterite [see IMERINITE]. **1848** *Knapp's Chem. Technol.* I. 344 The more common salts of nitric acid..are distinguished from each other by the addition of the name of the base as:..*soda-saltpetre (cubic nitre). **1850** ANSTED *Elem. Geol., Min.*, etc. 193 *Oligoclase*, *Soda-spodumene, a mineral having the same relation to spodumene that albite has to true felspar.

**8.** Made with, or containing, sodium bicarbonate, as ***soda-biscuit***, ***-bread***, ***-cake***, ***-cocktail***, ***-cracker***, ***-fritter***, ***-mint***, ***-powder***, ***-scone***, etc.

**1830** *Albany Jrnl.* 25 Aug. 3/5 Fresh *Soda Biscuit, just received from Treadwell's Bakery. **1891** *Cent. Dict.*, *Soda-biscuit*, a biscuit raised with soda. **1850** N. KINGSLEY *Diary* 3 Aug. (1914) 134 They raised some bread with it, which he said was the best *soda bread ever tasted. **1884** MRS. RIDDELL *Berna Boyle* xiii, The soda bread was rising to a satisfactory thickness. **1846** *Jewish Manual* vii. 155 (*heading*) A *soda cake. **1894** LYTTLE *Betsy Gray* iii. 22 Potato cake, pancakes, soda-cake, and other manufactures. **1818** *N.Y. Herald* 2 July 4/1 We have the Fourth of July thrown in with ..its exhilarating associations so conducive of headaches and *soda cocktails. **1863** *Harper's Mag.* Feb. 313/1 This repast, whatever its name might be, consisted of perhaps half a pound of *soda crackers, two red herrings, and one red apple. **1873** B. HARTE *Fiddletown* 53 Like an enormous japanned soda-cracker. **1837** M. R. WALKER *Diary* in C. M. Drury *Elkanah & Mary Walker* (1940) iii. 91 In the morning baked soda biscuit and fried *soda fritters. **1891** *Cent. Dict.*, **Soda-mint*, a mixture containing sodium bicarbonate and spear-mint. **1895** *Montgomery Ward Catal.* Spring & Summer 261/2 Soda Mint tablets, for sour stomach, colic, flatulency, etc. **1897** *Allbutt's Syst. Med.* III. 741 Bismuth lozenges, soda-mint tablets. **1928** D. L. SAYERS *Unpleasantness at Bellona Club* xv. 170 Suppose.. somebody had dropped a poisoned pill into his usual bottle of soda-mints. **1975** C. MOTT-RADCLYFFE *Foreign Body in Eye* iv. 77 Joyce Britten-Jones asked me one evening whether I had any soda-mints. **1820** *Columbian Centinel* 1 July 3/6 Maynard & Noyes continue to prepare *Soda Powders, of superior quality. **1843** MILL *Logic* I. III. xiii. 575 The old but not undisputed empirical generalization that soda powders weaken the human system. **1856** MRS. CARLYLE *Lett.* II. 291, I..had taken a sip or two of tea and bitten into my *soda-scone.

**9.** Used for, that dispenses, or containing, soda-water, as ***soda bottle***, ***-clerk*** (hence ***-clerking*** vbl. sb.), ***-siphon***, ***-straw***, ***tumbler***, etc. **soda-counter**, the counter of a soda fountain; any counter or bar where soft drinks, ice cream, etc., are sold; **soda-fountain** (also †**-font, -fount**) orig. *U.S.*, (*a*) (see quot. 1875); (*b*) an apparatus for supplying ice-cream sodas, sundaes, etc.; a counter or an establishment of which this is a feature; **soda-jerk, -jerker** [JERK *v.*[1] 7], one who mixes and sells soft drinks, etc., at a soda-fountain; **soda-pop**, flavoured soda-water.

**1824** BYRON *Juan* XVI. ix, Like a soda bottle when its spray Has sparkled. **1941** N. COWARD *Australia Visited* III. 16 That initial contact with the ordinary people [of New York] —the soda clerks, the cops, the struggling young theatre people. **1925** T. DREISER *Amer. Tragedy* I. II. iii. 180 He had wandered on..dishwashing in a restaurant, soda-clerking in a small outlying drug-store. **1846** *Dollar Newspaper* (Philadelphia) 19 Aug. 4/2 He..went up to the soda counter, and 'reckoned they'd take a little whisky'. **1939** A. HUXLEY *After Many a Summer* I. x. 135 Virginia was at the soda-counter, pensively eating a chocolate-and-banana split. **1976** J. LEE *Ninth Man* 31 A customer took a stool at the soda fountain... Dietrich..forced himself to..move.. to the soda counter. **1848** *Knickerbocker* XXXI. 40 They had not a theatre, nor an oyster-saloon, nor a soda-font. **1848** in N. E. Eliason *Tarheel Talk* (1956) 296 My soda fount cost me in ninety dollars. **1908** *Home Herald* (Chicago) 13 May, Here is the popular soda-fount drink known as Coca-Cola. **1824** *Independent Chron.* (Boston) 9 Oct. 3/3 This luxury in a hot and dusty season, together with an ever-flowing Soda Fountain,..he flatters himself will ensure a continuance of public patronage. **1875** KNIGHT *Dict. Mech.* 2235/1 *Soda-fountain*, a vessel for containing soda-water or water charged with carbonic-acid gas under high pressure, and provided with pipes and valves for drawing it off as required. **1876** *Napa* (California) *Reg.* 29 July 4/2 A Woodward avenue drug-store hired a new soda-fountain boy the other day. **1918** G. FRANKAU *One of Them* (1923) II. xv. 108, I loved thy daughters, daintiest as dowdiest; Cadby's tea'd Halls as Fuller's soda-fountain. **1955** R. BLESH *Shining Trumpets* (ed. 3) x. 232 A New Orleans Rhythm Kings' disc, playing in a soda fountain, gave these schoolboys the incentive. **1977** *New Yorker* 6 June 50/2 Afterward, at the soda fountain, they went over the day's movies. **1922** *Collier's* 17 June 4/1 You can tell a big-league head soda jerk by the way he picks up a glass, but the acid test is what kind of chocolate sirup he can make. **1958** *Daily Herald* 24 Mar. 3/7 This bustling little man never forgot his early years when he worked as a fairground barber and soda jerk. **1978** J. UPDIKE *Coup* (1979) iv. 132 The counter-boy, ingloriously dubbed the soda jerk... These 'soda jerks', I came to understand, were recruited from the adolescent ranks of the 'townies'. **1883** G. W. PECK *Groceryman & Peck's Bad Boy* 137 A sensitive soda jerker.. feels that it is worse than three card monte. **1932** WODEHOUSE *Louder & Funnier* 48 He..is now a soda-jerker in a small town in Kansas. **1959** N. MAILER *Advts. for Myself* (1961) 35 The soda jerker..from some outside compulsion had been forced to grow a beard. **1863** W. WHITMAN *Daybks. & Notebks.* (1978) III. 655 The continual soda-pop-like burstings of members calling 'Mr. Speaker! Mr. Speaker!' **1963** *Listener* 14 Feb. 301/3 The man who drove the soda-pop lorry. **1977** *Time* 11 Apr. 5/1 Were a visitor from another planet to read about the saccharin ban, he would conclude that earthlings' basic nutritional needs required large amounts of soda pop, jelly and chewing gum. **1926** *Daily Colonist* (Victoria, B.C.) 4 July 6/1 (Advt.), Warm Weather Supplies. Ice Cream Pails. Soda Straws. Lily Drinking Cups. **1911** *Ibid.* 21 Apr. 6/6 (Advt.), Soda Syphon Holder. This is a handsome silver plated stand into which the syphon fits. **1963** W. SOYINKA *Lion & Jewel* 24 The foreman..unpacks the usual box of bush comforts—soda siphon, whisky bottle and geometric sandwiches.

†**soda**[2]. *Obs.* [a. med.L. *soda*, ad. Arab. *ṣodāʿ*, f. *ṣadaʿ* to split.] Headache.

*c* **1540** BOORDE *Boke for to Lerne* C iij b, The fallyng sycknes called..Appoplesia, Soda. **1590** BARROUGH *Meth. Physick* I. i. (1639) 1 That there are onely three sundry paines in the head: wherof the one is called of the Greeks κεφαλαλγία..; the barbarous sort of Physitians call it Soda. **1661** LOVELL *Hist. Anim. & Min.* 97 It helpeth the soda (that is an old head ach)... With saffron and a little camphire it helps the cold soda. **1693** tr. *Blancard's Phys. Dict.* (ed. 2), *Soda*, the same with *Cephalalgia*.

‖**soda**[3]. *Obs. rare.* [mod.L. *soda*, ad. G. *sod* (*sode*), MLG. *sode*, Du. *zode*, Fris. *soad*(*e*, related to SEETHE *v.*] A form of indigestion; heart-burn.

Never actually adopted in English use.

**1693** tr. *Blancard's Phys. Dict.* (ed. 2), *Soda*, the same with *Ardor ventriculi* [= Heart-burning]. **1753** *Chambers' Cycl.* Suppl., *Soda*,..an uneasy and troublesome sensation of heat about the orifice of the stomach.

**soda'cetic**, *a. Chem.* [f. SOD-A[1] or SOD-IUM + ACETIC *a.*] (See quot.)

**1867** BLOXAM *Chem.* 569 A crystalline mass of sodacetic ether, or acetic ether in which one atom of the hydrogen has been displaced by sodium.

**sodaic** (səʊ'deɪɪk), *a.* [f. SODA[1] + -IC. So F. *sodaïque.*] Containing soda or sodium bicarbonate.

**1834** COOPER *Good's Study Med.* (ed. 4) I. 248 The common sodaic powders, and the effervescing saline draught, are often relished by the patient. **1839** URE *Dict. Arts* 424 The most familiar example [of effervescence] is afforded in the solution of sodaic powders. **1853** *Fraser's Mag.* XLVIII. 480 Some occasion in which he had suspended the use of its sodaic waters at table for champagne.

**sodain(e, -ly**, obs. forms of SUDDEN, -LY.

**sodainty**, variant of SUDDENTY.

†**sodaite**. *Min. Obs.* [f. SODA[1] + -ITE[1] 2 b.] A variety of nephelite or wernerite.

*c* **1830** *Encycl. Metrop.* (1845) VI. 489/2 *Elaolite.* Fettstein. Lythrodes. Sodaite. **1846** *Penny Cycl.* Suppl. II. 305/1 Ekebergite (Sodaite) does not occur crystallized.

**sodalist** ('səʊdəlɪst). [f. SODAL-ITY: see -IST 4.] A member of a Roman Catholic sodality or religious fraternity.

**1794** in *Mem. Stonyhurst Coll.* (1881) 40 No meeting of Sodalists. **1889** *Tablet* 14 Dec. 946 The handsome chapel where the Sodalists are now enabled to hold their services.

**sodalite** ('səʊdəlaɪt). *Min.* [f. SODA[1] + -LITE.] A vitreous, transparent or translucent silicate of aluminium and sodium containing sodium chloride, usually of a greenish blue colour and occurring in certain igneous rocks.

**1810** THOMSON in *Roy. Soc. Edin.* (1812) VI. 387 A Chemical Analysis of Sodalite, a new Mineral from

Greenland. *Ibid.*, The mineral to which I have given the name of Sodalite. **1837** DANA *Min.* 281 Sodalite includes the white and light green crystallized varieties of this species. **1888** RUTLEY *Rock-Forming Min.* 115 Sodalite mostly occurs in rocks of a syenitic character.

†**soda'litious**, *a. Obs.*$^{-0}$ Also -icious. [f. L. *sodalicius*.] (See quots.)

**1656** BLOUNT *Glossogr.*, *Sodalicious*,..belonging to sodality or Fellowship. **1730** BAILEY (fol.), *Sodalitious*, of, or pertaining to Society.

**sodality** (səʊˈdælɪtɪ). [a. F. *sodalité* or ad. L. *sodālitas*, *-itātem* fellowship, brotherhood, fraternity, f. *sodālis* mate, fellow, boon-companion.]

**1.** Association or confederation *with* others; brotherhood, companionship, fellowship.

**1600** W. WATSON *Decacordon* (1602) 168 A participation, ..combination, or sodalitie with the Iesuits to ouerthrow our countrie. **1609** BIBLE (Douay) *Eccl.* iv. *comm.*, If the Father, the Sonne, and the Holie Ghost come withal, this sodalitie is not soone broken. **1655–60** STANLEY *Hist. Philos.* (1687) 389/1 Of Friendship there are four kinds: Sodality, Affinity, Hospitality, Erotick. **1865** *Reader* 7 Oct. 392/2 That literary social sodality by which France had been distinguished for nearly a century. **1888** *Chambers's Jrnl.* 7 Jan. 2 Massinger's claim to the sodality of the craft..might perhaps be considered as of the genuine order.

**2.** In the Roman Catholic Church, a religious guild or brotherhood established for purposes of devotion or mutual help or action; the body of persons forming such a society.

(*a*) **1600** W. WATSON *Decacordon* (1602) 25 [The secular priests] sought no establishing of houses, Colledges, sodalities, societies, or corporations. **1629** WADSWORTH *Pilgr.* iii. 18 The priuiledge of this sodality is that they haue graces, rosaries,..and hallowed graines from his holinesse. **1664** H. MORE *Myst. Iniq.* xx. 76 By being incorporated into this or that holy Sodality or Fraternity. **1716** M. DAVIES *Athen. Brit.* I. 77 The Jansenistical-Romanists..have but very little to do with those little offices, or Sodalities, with their Indulgences. **1832** *Archaeol.* XXIV. 134 The monks of St. Swithin's..and those of New Minster had a sodality among themselves. **1893** J. FAHEY *Hist. Kilmacduagh* 443 The extension of religious sodalities in the several parishes of his diocese.

*attrib.* **1881** *Mem. Stonyhurst Coll.* 41 *note*, The body of the martyr..now lies under the altar of the Sodality Chapel.

(*b*) **1628** in Foley *Rec. Eng. Prov. S.J.* I. i. 114 The Sodalitie of the Chapelet of Our Lady. **1667** in *Cath. Rec. Soc. Publ.* III. 63 He was admitted into the sodality of our B: Lady. **1846** J. MORRIS in Pollen *Life* (1896) ii. 45, I should like very much to be enrolled in your Sodality of the Living Rosary. **1889** *Tablet* 14 Dec. 946 The Sodality of the Immaculate Conception.

**b.** A chapel set apart for or used by a religious sodality.

**1667** in *Cath. Rec. Soc. Publ.* III. 66 He [was] obserued when he thought himself to be alone in the sodality to sprinkle..water vppon the grauestones. **1679** *Trial of White, & other Jesuits* 11 To preach in the Sodality of the English Seminary. **1725** R. PLOWDEN in Foley *Rec. Eng. Prov. S.J.* VII. Introd. p. xl, With much ado, we saved the Church, the Sodality, and that wing where the kitchen is.

**3.** A society, association, or fraternity of any kind.

**1633** *Parthenia Sacra* 180 Sodalities of al sorts & conditions whatsoeuer either Secular or Ecclesiastical. **1699** R. L'ESTRANGE *Erasm. Colloq.* (1725) 262 To see with what Tenderness the Seraphick Sodality wash'd the Body. **1737** L. CLARKE *Hist. Bible* VIII. 572 Others hold, that they were called Herodians, because they constituted a Sodality erected in the Honour of Herod. **1805** MURPHY *Tacitus* I. 184 To create this new sodality the names of the most eminent citizens..were drawn by lot. **1855** MOTLEY *Dutch Rep.* Introd. xiv. (1866) 46 There were also military sodalities of musketeers, crossbowmen, archers, swordsmen, in every town.

**sodamide** (ˈsəʊdəmaɪd). *Chem.* [f. SOD-A$^1$ + AMIDE.] A substance, usually of a greenish colour, formed by treating sodium with gaseous ammonia (cf. quots.).

**1838** T. THOMSON *Chem. Org. Bodies* 7 Sodamide and mercuramide are amidets of sodium and mercury. **1867** BLOXAM *Chem.* 551 When potassium and sodium were heated in gaseous ammonia, hydrogen was evolved, and potassamide and sodamide were produced.

**sodamite**, obs. form of SODOMITE.

**sodan**, obs. f. SOLDAN.

**sodan(le, -ly**, etc., obs. ff. SUDDEN(LY.

**sodar** (ˈsəʊdɑː(r)). [f. SO(UND *sb.*$^3$ + RA)DAR.] A system for investigating the state of the atmosphere, which works on the principle of radar but uses ultrasonic sound waves instead of microwaves.

**1955** M. REIFER *Dict. New Words* 192/2 *Sodar*,..an instrument for detecting weather conditions by recording on an oscilloscope.. the reflected sound waves which have been projected directly overhead. **1974** *Globe & Mail* (Toronto) 1 June 5/1 These new instruments, called lidar.. and sodar.., could be used for things like tracing and identifying particles in the atmosphere..and detecting dangerous wind patterns and turbulence around airport runways. **1976** *McGraw-Hill Yearbk. Sci. & Technol.* 402/2 The active network includes not only the standard pilot balloons and radiosondes with which meteorologists customarily measure wind, temperature, and humidity aloft, but also weather radars.., lidars..and sodars.

**sodar**, obs. f. SOLDER *sb.*$^1$

**sodary**, obs. f. SUDARY.

**soda-water.** Also **soda water**. [f. SODA$^1$ + WATER *sb.*]

**1. a.** Water containing a solution of sodium bicarbonate, or, more generally, charged under pressure with carbon dioxide (carbonic acid gas), strongly effervescent, and used as a beverage or stimulant. Cf. SODA$^1$ 4.

**1802** W. SAUNDERS in *Med. & Phys. Jrnl.* VIII. 492 The gaseous alkaline water commonly called soda water has long been used in this country. **1855** *Orr's Circ. Sci., Elem. Chem.* 385 Much of the so-called soda-water found in commerce is totally devoid of soda or other alkali. **1879** L. STEPHEN *Hours in Libr.* III. 194 The maudlin meditation of a fast young man over his morning's soda-water.

**b.** *attrib.*, as ***soda-water apparatus***, ***-bottle***, ***fountain***, ***manufacturer***, ***-room***, etc.

**1813** E. GERRY JR. *Diary* 4 July (1927) 168 We had not gone far, before the girls ordered the charioteer to stop at the soda water room. **1822** *Sunday Times* 20 Oct. 2/4 William Clarke..soda-water and ginger-beer manufacturer. **1825** T. HOOK *Sayings* Ser. II. *Passion & Princ.* vi, Patent soda-water manufactories. **1839** URE *Dict. Arts* 1156 Improved soda-water apparatus. **1852** DICKENS *Bleak Ho.* (1853) v. 35 Ginger-beer and soda-water bottles. **1858** SIMMONDS *Dict. Trade*, *Soda-water-bottle*, a strong oval-shaped glass bottle, the cork of which is secured by twine and wire to confine the aerated water. *Ibid.*, *Soda-water manufacturer*, a maker and bottler of soda-water. **1862** *Catal. Internat. Exhib., Brit.* II. No. 6246, Patent soda-water machines. **1884** KNIGHT *Dict. Mech.* Suppl. 828/1 Soda-water Fountain.

**2.** Water containing a solution of sodium carbonate for cooling or wetting metal-working tools.

**1891** in *Cent. Dict.* **1895** in *Funk's Stand. Dict.*

**sodayne, -ly**, etc., obs. ff. SUDDEN(LY.

**'sodbuster.** *western N. Amer.* [f. SOD *sb.*$^1$ + BUSTER.] A term, chiefly opprobrious, for a farmer, farmworker, or homesteader in a cattle-grazing region, esp. one who ploughs virgin grassland. Hence **'sodbusting** *vbl. sb.*, ploughing virgin grassland; farming.

**1922** R. STEAD *Neighbours* 126 Between your fine words I figger that you pick up a dollar now an' again by tottin' these tenderfoot sod-busters out over the bald-headed. **1927** C. SANDBURG *Amer. Songbag* 89 Its tune was familiar to the lonely 'sodbuster'. **1958** H. B. ALLEN in *Publ. Amer. Dialect Soc.* xxx. 11 The persistence of *sodbuster* and *soddy* as not necessarily opprobrious designations of the new settlers [in North Dakota]. **1965** G. SHEPHERD *West of Yesterday* x. 72 We owned cows and found that ranching was more attractive than sodbusting. **1970** [see NESTER 2]. **1972** G. BEINE *Land of Coyote* 85 (*heading*) Sod busting a new field. **1979** *Guardian* 24 Mar. 12/1 The conflicts between sodbusters and cattle-men.

**sod corn.** *western N. Amer.* [f. SOD *sb.*$^1$ + CORN *sb.*$^1$] **a.** Corn or maize planted in ploughed up grassland. **b.** Whisky made from sod corn. In full, ***sod-corn whisky***.

**1835** P. SHIRREFF *Tour* xxiv. 248 Indian corn is dropped into every third furrow..and covered with the next cut turf. This crop receives no farther cultivation of any kind, is termed sod corn, and said to yield fifty bushels per acre. **1838** *Bytown* (Ottawa) *Gaz.* 19 Sept. 1/3 The sod corn does not make up more than half a crop, and is..stacked for fodder stock. **1857** E. F. BEADLE *Diary* 2 Aug. (1923) 73 Found the family enjoying themselves over their 'Sod corn whiskey'. **1878** [see BARE-FOOTED *a.* c]. **1913** W. CATHER *O Pioneers!* 27 John Bergson says to his boys, 'Try to break a little more land each year; sod corn is good for fodder.' **1927** K. EUBANK *Horse & Buggy Days* 94 They..ate their dinners,..munching cheese,..which helped along on its onward course by a tumbler or so of sod corn, made in a moonshine still especially for the occasion. **1940** L. I. WILDER *Long Winter* iii. 29 He cut and shocked the sod corn.

**sodded** (ˈsɒdɪd), *ppl. a.*$^1$ [f. SOD *sb.*$^1$ or *v.*$^1$] Covered or laid with, constructed or built of, sods.

**1652** COTTERELL tr. *Calprenède's Cassandra* III. II. (1676) 262 Roxana sat down upon a green sodded bank. **1816** COLERIDGE *Lay Serm.* Introd. p. xxii, Like an aged mourner on the sodded grave of an only one. **1871** *Daily News* 11 Sept., A sodded kitchen [= stove] built and used by a couple of officers..is quite a marvel of versatility.

**'sodded**, *ppl. a.*$^2$ *rare.* [Cf. SOD *ppl. a.* and *v.*$^2$] Sodden, soaked.

**1627** FELTHAM *Resolves* II. xxix, Moorish grounds..are usually boggy and rotten, or of so cold and sodded a temper; as [etc.].

**sodden** (ˈsɒd(ə)n), *pa. pple.*, *ppl. a.*, and *sb.* Forms: α. 4–5 **soþen** (4 **soþin, soiþen**); 4–5 **sothen** (4 **soothen**, 5 **sothyn**). β. 4–5 **sodyn**, 5 **sodun**, **sooden**, 5–6 **soden** (5 **-one**, 6 **-yng**, *Sc.* **-in**); 5– **sodden** (*Sc.* 5–6 **soddyn**, 6 **-in**). [Strong pa. pple. of SEETHE *v.* Cf. SOD *pa. pple.*, etc.]

**1.** Boiled; cooked or prepared by boiling. Now *rare* or *Obs.*

*pred.* a **1300** *Cursor M.* 13373 Þe folk þat dai ful fair was fedd, O bred and flexs bath soþen and bredd. **1382** WYCLIF *Numb.* vi. 19 A shuldre sothen [*v.rr.* sodden, sooden, sodyn, soothen, **1388** sodun] of the wether. c **1400** MAUNDEV. (1839) xix. 208 Thei bryngen..mete alle soden. **1483** CAXTON *Gold. Leg.* 67 Thenne abygail hyed her & toke..v weders sothen. **1570** H. LLOYD *Treas. Health* M v, Lay a hoole egge wel sodden and the shel pylled of. **1600** ROWLAND *Lett. Humours Blood* i. 7 Beere he protestes is sodden and refin'd. **1626** BACON *Sylva* §385 It were good therefore to try it..with Milk Sodden.

*attrib.* **1382** WYCLIF *1 Sam.* ii. 15, I shal not take..sothen [**1388** sodun] flesh, but rawe. c **1400** *Three Kings Cologne* 94 Þis bawme is cleped rawe bawme and the toper is callid soden bawme. **1513** *Bk. Keruynge* in *Babees Bk.* (1868) 274 On that daye he shall serue..soden egges with grene sauce. **1578** LYTE *Dodoens* 217 Dronken in sodden wine it preserveth from dronkennesse. **1645** PAGITT *Heresiogr.* (1662) 9 They were fain to eat Dogs, Cats, Rats, sodden Leather. **1697** DRYDEN *Virg. Georg.* IV. 386 Mix it with thicken'd Juice of sodden Wines. **1780** *Encycl. Brit.* (ed. 2) V. 3571/1 The snails were fed with bran and sodden wine. **1829** BROCKETT *N.C. Gloss.* (ed. 2), *Sodden-wheat*, furmety. **1846** BAXTER *Libr. Pract. Agric.* (ed. 4) I. 455 These, with bran mashes, sodden oats, and exercise, will generally effect a cure.

*transf.* **1606** SHAKS. *Tr. & Cr.* III. i. 44 *Pa.* My businesse seethes. *Ser.* Sodden businesse, there's a stewed phrase indeede.

†**b.** In the proverbial phrase ***coleworts twice*** (etc.) ***sodden***: (see COLEWORT 4).

c **1568** [see COLEWORT 4]. **1579** W. WILKINSON *Confut. Fam. Love* 55 b, The fourth crime..is coalewortes more than tenne times sodden. **1608** HIERON *Answ. Popish Plot* (ed. 2) To Rdr., To redoe things once done, or to oppresse mens stomachs with twise sodden Coleworts, as the prouerb is. **1614** BRADSHAW *Unreasonableness Separation* 83 Some of his own cole-worts, not twice, but twenty times sodden.

**2.** Of persons, their features, etc.: Having the appearance of, or resembling, that which has been soaked or steeped in water; rendered dull, stupid, or expressionless, esp. owing to drunkenness or indulgence in intoxicants; pale and flaccid.

**1599** B. JONSON *Cynthia's Rev.* IV. v, By Hercules, I scorne him, as I doe the sodden Nymph,..his mistris Arete. **1608** SHAKS. *Pericles* IV. ii. 21 The stuff we have, a strong wind will blow it to pieces, they are so pitifully sodden. **1611** BEAUM. & FL. *Knt. Burning Pestle* V. i, Now you with the sodden face, keep in there.

**1841** LYTTON *Nt. & Morn.* I. vi, His complexion was pale and sodden. **1850** KINGSLEY *A. Locke* xxxv, Gaunt, ragged, sodden, blear-eyed, drivelling, the worn-out gin-drinker stood. **1896** HOWELLS *Impress. & Exp.* 74 The soddenest *habitué* of the place brightened.

**b.** Characterized by heaviness, dullness, or want of vivacity.

**1851** RUSKIN *Stones Ven.* III. 86 The peculiar sodden and sensual cunning..seen so often in the countenances of the worst Romish priests. **1870** MORRIS *Earthly Par.* III. IV. 49 All Into dull sodden life did fall.

**3.** Of food: Heavy, doughy; spoiled through over-boiling or imperfect baking.

a **1800** PEGGE *Suppl. Grose*, *Sodden*, over-boiled. North. **1862** MILLER *Elem. Chem.*, *Org.* (ed. 2) ii. §5. 143 Bread prepared from such flour is sticky, heavy, and sodden.

**4.** Saturated or soaked with water or moisture.

**1820** KEATS *Hyperion* I. 17 Upon the sodden ground His old right hand lay nerveless. **1856** DELAMER *Fl. Gard.* (1861) 164 Don't work the ground when it is sodden, muddy, or rendered sticky by a recent frost. **1873** G. C. DAVIES *Mount. & Mere* xvi. 137 The cold water was numbing his limbs and his sodden clothes were dragging him down. **1894** *Daily News* 5 June 3/5 The ground..was in such a terribly sodden condition that cricket was entirely out of the question.

**b.** Const. *in* or *with*. Also *fig.*

**1833** I. TAYLOR *Fanat.* i. 6 Men..with hands sodden in blood. **1860** SMILES *Self-Help* xi. 285 Nothing can be more hurtful to a youth than to have his soul sodden with pleasure. **1870** F. R. WILSON *Ch. Lindisf.* 104 Fungi abound, and the pavement is sodden with damp. **1904** *Field* 6 Feb. 226/2 The ground was so sodden with wet that it was quite unfit to ride over.

**5.** *Comb.*, as ***sodden-faced***, ***-headed***, ***-witted*** adjs.

Also as second element in *brandy-*, *gin-*, *whisky-sodden*, etc.

**1589** *Hay any Work* 25 You sodden headed Asse you, the most part of that law is abrogated. **1606** SHAKS. *Tr. & Cr.* II. i. 47 Thou sodden-witted Lord! thou hast no more braine then I haue in mine elbows. **1753** RICHARDSON *Grandison* (1781) I. 218 The sliest, sodden-faced creature I ever saw.

†**6.** As *sb.* Boiled meat. *Obs.*

c **1375** *Cursor M.* 13373 (Fairf.), Þat folk þat day fulle faire was fed wiþ soiþen & roste & wilde bred. **1456** SIR G. HAYE *Law Arms* (S.T.S.) 78 The tane lufis soddyn, the tothir rost. c **1460** *Towneley Myst.* xii. 224, I haue here in my mayll, sothen and rost.

†**'sodden**, *a. Obs.*$^{-1}$ [f. SOD *sb.*$^1$] Built of sods.

**1639** in *Crt. & Times Chas. I* (1848) II. 285 Belfort (nothing like the name either in strength or beauty, it being the most miserably beggarly sodden town, or town of sods, that ever was made in an afternoon of loam and sticks.

**'sodden** (ˈsɒd(ə)n), *v.* [f. SODDEN *ppl. a.*]

**1.** *trans.* To make sodden; to soak in, or saturate with, water.

**1812** *Ann. Reg.*, *Chron.* 502 The ground becomes compressed and soddened (to use an antiquated term) by the winter rains. **1844** DICKENS *Pict. fr. Italy* (1846) 147 Your pony soddening his girths in water. **1878** *Daily News* 12 June 5 The rains have soddened the earth.

**b.** To render (the faculties) dull or stupid; to deprive of vivacity or freshness.

**1863** COWDEN CLARKE *Shaks. Char.* xvii. 431 His sensuality does not sodden and brutify his faculties, but it quickens their temper and edge. **1883** *Pall Mall G.* 28 Dec. 4/2 His soul has been deadened and soddened by ages of exclusive devotion to the question of bread and cider.

**2.** *intr.* **a.** To become soaked or saturated with water or moisture; to grow soft or rotten in this way.

**1820** BYRON *Mar. Fal.* II. ii. 95 The block may soak their gore; Their heads may sodden in the sun. *a* **1861** WOOLNER *My Beautiful Lady, Tolling Bell* lviii, I wandered wearily.. Through swamps that soddened under stagnant air.

**b.** Of a liquid: To soak *into* something.

**1881** MISS ORMEROD *Injurious Insects* (1890) 345 Dressing ..of some kind which will not sodden into the tree in the heat of the sun.

Hence **'soddened** *ppl. a.*; **'soddening** *vbl. sb.* and *ppl. a.*

**1845** HIRST *Poems* 18 We..laid them in the *soddened ground. **1883** *Knowledge* 3 Aug. 68/1 Soddened fruit enveloped in heavy indigestible pudding paste. **1852** WIGGINS *Embanking* 96 This *soddening, or stagnation of the soil in a watery state. **1890** HUXLEY in *Times* 1 Dec. 13/3 The prostitution of the mind, the soddening of the conscience. **1857** T. MOORE *Handbk. Brit. Ferns* (ed. 3) 28 A *soddening—continued *wetness*, as distinguished from mere dampness, of the soil.

**'soddenly,** *adv.* [f. SODDEN *ppl. a.* + -LY[2].] In a sodden manner; heavily and dully; damply.

**1901** KIPLING *Kim* xv. 390 Kim had reeled to a room with a cot in it, and was dozing soddenly. **1920** *Blackw. Mag.* Apr. 501/2, I slept, fitfully at first, soddenly later. **1939** JOYCE *Finnegans Wake* 514 Or (soddenly) Schott, furtivfired by the riots. **1976** *Church Times* 26 Nov. 5/1, I trudged soddenly along unfamiliar terrain.

**soddenness** ('sɒd(ə)nnɪs). [f. SODDEN *ppl. a.*] Sodden state, quality, or condition.

**1883** H. JAMES *Let.* 25 Nov. (1980) III. 14 Yes, I have read Trollope's autobiography and regard it as one of the most curious and amazing books in all literature, for its density, blockishness and general thickness and soddenness. **1890** *Science* XV. 230/1 The soddenness of improperly boiled or fried foods. **1893** *Westm. Gaz.* 26 Apr. 4/2 The bottom of the uncultivated gardens, where the ground is kept in a chronic state of soddenness.

**sodder,** obs. or dial. f. SOLDER *sb.*[1] and *v.*

**sodding** ('sɒdɪŋ), (*vbl.*) *sb.* [f. SOD *v.*[1]]

**1.** The action of covering, laying, or providing with sods.

**1688** HOLME *Armoury* III. 266/1 *Soding*, is the covering of little shourings and places of shade from Rain, with green Turfs or Grass Sods. **1753** *Chambers' Cycl.* Suppl. s.v., Sodding of brick. **1860** B. TAYLOR in *Life & Lett.* I. xv. 206 We have done something at clearing away rubbish, sodding, and making the surroundings fair to look upon. **1864** ATKINSON *Stanton Grange* 111 The sodding of the roof was beautifully managed.

**2.** Sods or turfs as a material for forming or strengthening embankments, etc.

**1852** WIGGINS *Embanking* 18 But if banks of sand are attempted..the front or facing [should be] guarded with clay, turf, sodding, and stones. **1867** *Jrnl. R. Agric. Soc.* III. II. 664 A good sodding..might be made from the marram.

**3.** *attrib.*, as ***sodding-implement, -mallet, -spade.***

**1875** KNIGHT *Dict. Mech.* 2237/2 *Sodding-implements*, tools for cutting sods and laying them down. **1891** *Cent. Dict.* s.v., Sodding-mallet. *Ibid.*, Sodding-spade.

**'sodding,** *ppl. a.* and *adv. slang.* [f. SOD *v.*[3]] A vague epithet expressing anger or contempt; freq. as a mere intensive.

**1912** D. H. LAWRENCE *Let.* 3 July (1962) I. 134 The miserable sodding rotters..that make up England today. **1929** 'H. GREEN' *Living* iii. 25 'It [*sc.* Australia] am a grand country' 'e said to me, 'this [*sc.* England] be a poor sodding place for a poor bleeder', 'e said. 'I'm for goin'.' **1933** M. LOWRY *Ultramarine* 36, I don't know what you think you're doing idling round this sodding ship. **1950** R. GODDEN *Breath of Air* xix. 235 'That's my sodding business,' said McGinty. **1954** K. AMIS *Lucky Jim* xvii. 168 Cuts his own hair now, you see. Too sodding mean to pay out his one-and-six, that is what it is. My God. **1966** M. WOODHOUSE *Tree Frog* xxi. 155 Hundred and twenty two semiconductors in there, all radiating heat... What are we supposed to do, sodding blow on them? **1968** J. BRAINE *Crying Game* vi. 141 The bastard who was giving me dinner stood me up, and I shall sodding well ring him and tell him I'm going out with someone much nicer. **1976** C. STORR *Unnatural Fathers* ii. 27 My sodding brother got into hospital and then dropped out before his finals. **1980** D. BOGARDE *Gentle Occupation* i. 24 I'll remember this sodding day until the day I die.

**'soddish,** *a.* [f. SOD *sb.*[3]: see -ISH[1].] Awful, 'rotten', terrible.

**1959** W. CAMP *Ruling Passion* xxvii. 237 What a bloody soddish thing to do.

So **'soddishness** [-NESS], behaviour characteristic of a 'sod' (SOD *sb.*[3] 1, 2).

**1938** L. MACNEICE *I crossed Minch* vi. 76 Charles Edward ..sank into chambering and soddishness. **1970** 'D. CRAIG' *Young Men may Die* xvi. 121 Happily there was no opportunity for soddishness about whom I should go with.

**soddite:** see SODDYITE.

**soddy** ('sɒdɪ), *a.* and *sb.* [f. SOD *sb.*[1] + -Y.]

**A.** *adj.* Abounding in sods; consisting or composed of sods; of the nature of a sod.

**1611** COTGR., *Motteux*, cloddie, turfie, soddie. **1778** [W. H. MARSHALL] *Minutes Agric., Observ.* 98 By burying the soddy edge of the Plit, they are now less grassy than the Leys were before plowing. **1846** *Jrnl. R. Agric. Soc.* VII. I. 168 Reduce the soddy texture of the soil.

**B.** *sb.* **1.** A sod-house. *western N. Amer.*

**1877** H. RUEDE *Let.* 24 Apr. in J. Ise *Sod-Louse Days* (1937) 57 Many of the young bachelors..were building their own 'soddies'. **1893** *Pilgrim Missionary* June 8/1 Brother T—— has a large circuit of three churches, and lives in a 'soddy'. **1970** *Islander* (Victoria, B.C.) 29 Nov. 10/4 It was a sort of soddy, the rear dug into a cut-bank.

**2.** One who occupies or who has occupied a sod-house.

**1958** [see SODBUSTER]. **1977** *Westworld* (Vancouver, B.C.) May-June 6/2, I..received a nicely decorated certificate to the effect that I was a Soddy.

**soddyite** ('sɒdɪaɪt). *Min.* Orig. †**soddite.** [Coined in Fr. as *soddite* (A. Schoep 1922, in *Compt. Rend.* CLXXIV. 1067), f. the name of Frederick *Soddy* (1877–1956), English chemist and physicist: see -ITE[1].] A hydrated uranyl silicate found as yellow orthorhombic crystals.

**1922** *Nature* 13 May 631/2 Soddite, a new radioactive mineral. This is a yellow crystalline mineral found associated with curite from Kasolo (Belgian Congo). **1927** *Mineral. Abstr.* III. 233 Soddyite (= soddite), 12 $UO_3.5SiO_2.14H_2O$. **1937** *Mem. Geol. Survey S. Afr.* No. 31. 108 Soddyite. This mineral occurs as an encrustation on quartz with malachite in the pegmatite at Norrabees. **1965** *Amer. Mineralogist* L. 919 Soddyite..occurs in blocky, fibrous, deep-yellow to yellow-green crystals which vein other uranyl minerals in the matrix.

**sodear,** obs. f. SOLDIER.

**sodein, -eyn(e,** obs. ff. SUDDEN *a.*

**sodekene, -dene,** obs. ff. SUBDEACON, -DEAN.

**soden,** obs. f. SOLDAN, SUDDEN *a.*

**soder,** obs. f. SOLDER *sb.*[1] and *v.*

**sodewe,** obs. f. SUBDUE *v.*

**sodger,** obs. or dial. f. SOLDIER.

**sodian** ('səʊdɪən), *a. Min.* [f. SOD(IUM + -IAN 2.] Of a mineral: having a proportion of a constituent element replaced by sodium.

**1930** W. T. SCHALLER in *Amer. Mineralogist* XV. 572 The adjectival endings thus formed for the names of all the chemical elements are given below... Sodium—sodian. **1951** C. PALACHE et al. *Dana's Syst. Min.* (ed. 7) II. 1022 On the dispersion of sodian and manganoan romeite ('atopite') from Brazil see Rose (1919). **1963** W. A. DEER et al. *Rock-Forming Minerals* II. 113 Titanaugites and sodian augites also have more ferric iron than most other pyroxenes.

**sodic** ('səʊdɪk), *a.* [f. SOD-IUM + -IC. Cf. F. *sodique.*]

**a.** *Chem.* Of, containing, or composed of sodium.

**1859** MAYNE *Expos. Lex.* 1170 The only combination known of sodium with sulphur, or—sodic sulphur. **1869** J. PHILLIPS *Vesuv.* iv. 121 Examining..these hollow canals,.. we find sublimed salts, especially ammoniac and sodic chlorides with free sulphur. **1878** HAMILTON *Nervous Dis.* 329 As regards the variety of bromide, I think the sodic is the most reliable and stable.

**b.** *Geol.* Of a mineral or rock: containing an appreciable or a greater-than-average quantity of sodium, often as compared with calcium or potassium. Also applied to a metamorphic process in which such minerals are formed.

**1902** *Jrnl. Geol.* X. 574 The standard $SO_3$-bearing feldspathoid is therefore considered to be a purely sodic noselite. **1927** S. J. SHAND *Eruptive Rocks* xi. 200 More sodic types are also known, in which both orthoclase and quartz are present. **1952** T. F. W. BARTH *Theoret. Petrol.* 96 Plagioclases of gneisses and of crystalline schists, if zoned, usually show inverse order, that is, sodic core, calcic shell. **1967, 1971** [see POTASSIC *a.* b]. **1978** *Nature* 7 Sept. 23/1 In addition to the phenocrysts appropriate to magmas of intermediate bulk composition, andesite and dacite contain both anomalously calcic and sodic plagioclase.

**sodier,** obs. form of SOLDIER.

**sodio-** ('səʊdɪəʊ), comb. form of SODIUM, denoting the presence of that substance or its salts, as ***sodio-aluminic, -aurous, -hydric, -platinic*** adjs.; ***sodio-salicylate.***

**1868** WATTS *Dict. Chem.* s.v. *Sodium*, Sodium occurs as sodio-aluminic fluoride in cryolite. **1868** *Fownes' Chem.* (ed. 10) 421 A sodio-aurous hyposulphite..is prepared by mixing the concentrated solutions of auric chloride and sodium hyposulphite. *Ibid.* 347 A sodiohydric pyrophosphate has been obtained. **1876** HARLEY *Royle's Mat. Med.* 308 Sodio-platinic chloride..is soluble in water. **1898** *Allbutt's Syst. Med.* V. 991 Theobromine, in the form of the sodio-salicylate (diuretin), may be substituted for caffein.

**sodioure,** obs. form of SOLDIER.

**sodipotassic** (ˌsəʊdɪpə'tæsɪk), *a. Geol.* Also **sodo-** (ˌsəʊdəʊ-). [Blend of SODIC and POTASSIC *adjs.*] Containing both sodium and potassium in appreciable quantities.

In quot. 1902 used to denote a specified compositional range in the classification scheme of Cross, Iddings, Pirsson, and Washington.

**1902** *Jrnl. Geol.* X. 596 The minerals of the sodalite group are only present in the sodic or sodipotassic Sub-rangs of Classes I, II and III. **1927** S. J. SHAND *Eruptive Rocks* ix. 163 A typical example of the Quincy granite gave quartz 33, sodipotassic felspar 55, and ægirine and riebeckite 10 per cent. **1974** T. G. SAHAMA in H. Sørensen *Alkaline Rocks* 98/1 The rocks are mainly potassic to perpotassic, but sodopotassic to sodic varieties are known among the jumillites and fortunites.

**sodium** ('səʊdɪəm). *Chem.* [f. SOD-A[1] + -IUM. Named by Davy (1807).]

**1.** An elementary alkaline metal (isolated by Davy in 1807), forming the basis of SODA, closely resembling potassium in its appearance and properties, and occurring most commonly in the chloride (common salt). Symbol Na (for Natrium).

**1807** DAVY in *Phil. Trans.* (1808) I. 32 Potassium and Sodium are the names by which I have ventured to call the two new substances. **1812** —— *Chem. Philos.* 331, I discovered sodium a few days after I discovered potassium, in the year 1807. **1815** J. SMITH *Panorama Sci. & Art* II. 395 Sodium has a much higher point of fusion than potassium. **1856** MILLER *Elem. Chem., Inorg.* 743 Sodium has a bluish white colour; in appearance and properties it much resembles potassium, but is somewhat more volatile. **1879** PROCTOR *Pleas. Ways Sci.* i. 1 A certain double dark line in the solar spectrum is due to the vapour of sodium in the sun's atmosphere.

**2.** *attrib.* **a.** In the names of chemical compounds or groupings, as ***sodium-alcohol, -amyl, bicarbonate, bromide, carbonate,*** etc.; **sodium Amytal** *Pharm.*, the sodium salt of AMYTAL, used as a sedative and hypnotic; sodium 5-ethyl-5-isopropylbarbiturate, $C_{11}H_{17}N_2O_3Na$; **sodium Pentothal** (see PENTOTHAL).

**1857** MILLER *Elem. Chem., Org.* 150 If iodide of amyl be made to act upon the sodium-alcohol. **1862** *Ibid.* (ed. 2) 222 When sodium-ethyl is formed from zinc-ethyl by the action of sodium. *Ibid.* 225 Sodium-amyl would probably furnish caproate of soda. **1868** *Fownes' Chem.* (ed. 10) 337 Sodium Chloride, when pure, is not deliquescent in moderately-dry air. *Ibid.*, Sodium Hydrate, or Caustic Soda. *Ibid.* 338 Sodium Carbonates. *Ibid.* 345 Sodium Hyposulphite..is now used in considerable quantity for photographic purposes. **1873** RALFE *Phys. Chem.* 105 The potassium and sodium phosphates form three varieties of salts. **1929** *Proc. Soc. Exper. Biol. & Med.* XXVI. 709 Anesthesia has been produced in human beings by the intravenous injection of solutions of the anhydrous sodium amytal. **1937** [see SECONAL]. **1938** [see AMYTAL]. **1955** A. HUXLEY *Genius & Goddess* 9 One escapes into reminiscence as one escapes into gin or sodium amytal.

**b.** Misc., as ***sodium-compound, -flame, vapour*** (freq. *attrib.*); **sodium-amalgam,** a compound of mercury and sodium; **sodium-cooled** *a.*, that employs liquid sodium as a coolant; *spec.* of (*a*) an aero-engine exhaust valve, or (*b*) a nuclear reactor; **sodium pump** *Physiol.*, a pump (PUMP *sb.*[1] 1 e) which operates on sodium ions; **sodium soap,** soda soap.

**1862** MILLER *Elem. Chem., Org.* (ed. 2) 219 The potassium and sodium compounds are more energetic than those of zinc. **1866** W. ODLING *Anim. Chem.* 138 Uric acid, by deoxidation with sodium-amalgam, yields a mixture of xanthine and hypoxanthine. **1871** TYNDALL *Fragm. Sci.* (1879) I. xiv. 391 We send our beam of white light through a sodium flame. **1933** *Discovery* Feb. 50/2 In the construction of sodium vapour lamps this difficulty is overcome by introducing a rare gas into the tube. **1934** *Jrnl. R. Aeronaut. Soc.* XXXVIII. 223 The Americans have attained and even exceeded [500 lbs. per sq. in.]..with a poppet valve (sodium cooled) engine. **1951** *Jrnl. Physiol.* CXIV. 143 An active sodium pump cannot be ruled out on the grounds that it would require more energy than is available from the resting metabolism. **1954** *Sci. Amer.* Dec. 38/3 A sodium-cooled reactor, which can be operated at very high temperatures, has greater thermal efficiency than a water-cooled system. **1956** E. MOLLOY *Automobile Engineer's Ref. Bk.* iii. 242 In engines where exhaust-valve cooling is a serious problem, the sodium-cooled valve has been adopted. **1964** [see PUMP *sb.*[1] 1 e]. **1968** M. S. LIVINGSTON *Particle Physics* iii. 39 A well-known example [of a multiplet] is the sodium D-line doublet which gives the yellow color to the light from a sodium-vapor lamp. **1971** *New Scientist* 11 Mar. 529/1 Rudzinski was mainly concerned about the immense complexity of the sodium-cooled technology. **1974** D. & M. WEBSTER *Compar. Vertebr. Morphol.* ix. 183 Instead of osmotically equilibrating, this imbalance of cations is maintained by the cell membrane's physical characteristics plus an enzyme system, called the sodium pump, which actively removes sodium from inside the cell. **1977** *Time* 15 Aug. 11/3 What worries them in particular is that Super Phénix will produce energy from a sophisticated sodium-cooled reactor eight times more powerful than smaller, water-cooled plants.

**c.** Used *attrib.* and in *Comb.* with reference to (the intense yellow light emitted from) discharge tubes containing sodium vapour, used esp. for street lighting.

**1888** RUTLEY *Rock-forming Min.* 128 The refractive index of quartz..in sodium-light. **1912** *Jrnl. Soc. Chem. Industry* 31 Oct. 1010/2 (*heading*) Polarisation; Sodium lamps for. **1933** *Discovery* Oct. 318/2 The electrical impulses corresponding to the television picture signals are converted into the light variations of a specially designed sodium tube. **1956** R. FULLER *Image of Society* viii. 195 The sodium lamps of the bypass. **1959** *New Statesman* 8 Aug. 152/2 Their fight is often associated with the campaign against concrete lamp-posts, sodium lighting and similar 'outrages' on our towns and cities. **1967** A. J. MARSHALL in L. Deighton *London Dossier* 138 Walking in the sodium-lit Kilburn High Road. **1973** J. MANN *Only Security* x. 132 Thea pressed the whole row of light switches and..the sodium strips flickered into brilliance. **1977** D. HARSENT *Dreams of Dead* 35 Midnight, bruised insomniacs, alive to the growing silence and opening to the sodium glare like flowers.

**d.** Objective, as ***sodium-demanding, -retaining*** adjs.

**1977** J. L. HARPER *Population Biol. Plants* xxi. 655 The life cycle strategy is likely in such a case to be influenced by the optimal allocation of sodium between parents and offspring and between the various sodium-demanding activities. **1977** *Proc. R. Soc. Med.* LXX. 692/1 One of the hypotheses.. has been that these patients fail to escape normally from the sodium-retaining effect of aldosterone.

**'sodless,** *a.* [f. SOD *sb.*[1]] Devoid of, not covered by, sods.

*a* **1847** ELIZA COOK *Poor Man's Grave* i. 12 He.. will not leave the sodless heap.

†**sodlet.** *Obs.* Forms: 4 sowdel-; 4, 6 soud(e)let, 6 sodelet(t, sodlett. [? f. OF. *souder* to solder.] A saddle-bar for a window.

**1332** in J. T. Smith *Antiq. Westminster* (1807) 196 [Nine small bars of iron, called] soudlets, [to hold the glass in the said windows]. **1339-40** *Ely Sacr. Rolls* (1907) II. 96 Item in Sowdelibus faciendis per eundem de vj peciis ferri. *Ibid.* II. 97 In diuersis sowdelibus fact... pro fenestris superioris istoriæ Noui Operis. *Ibid.*, Barris et sowdelibus reparand. **1532-3** in E. Law *Hist. Hampton Court Pal.* (1885) 349 For 295 sodlettes servyng the syde wyndows. *Ibid.* 350, 40 sodletts for the harnessyng of the Greatt Wyndow.

*attrib.* **1533** *MS. Rawl. D.* 776 fol. 175 For xxj Fott off sodlett barres. **1536** *MS. Rawl. D.* 780 fol. 59, xxxij[ti] fote of sodelett barrs spent by the glasyers.

**sodoku** ('sodoku). *Path.* [Jap.] The form of rat-bite fever caused by *Spirillum minus*.

**1926** *Trans. Soc. Tropical Med. & Hygiene* XIX. 183 Apert and his colleagues suggested the use of stovarsol or tréparsol by the mouth in the case of persons who had been exposed to the infection of sodoku. **1955** W. L. JELLISON in T. G. Hull *Dis. transmitted from Animals to Man* (ed. 4) xxvii. 539 The term 'sodoku' is from the Japanese (*so*, a rat, *doku*, poison) and is being resorted to more commonly by American workers to avoid controversy and confusion over the correct application of the term rat-bite fever. Sodoku is primarily an infection of rats, mice, and other rodents. **1970** *Scand. Jrnl. Infectious Dis.* II. 71/1 Two aetiologically different but clinically similar diseases may occur as results of rat-bites: the Japanese Sodoku caused by Spirillum minus, and the bacillary form.

**Sodom** ('sɒdəm). [The name of the early city beside the Dead Sea, the wickedness and destruction of which are recorded in Gen. xviii-xix.

The Hebrew form of the name is *S'dōm*; the Sept. has Σόδομα, the Vulg. *Sodoma*, neut. pl. and fem. sing.]

**1.** An extremely wicked or corrupt place. Freq. coupled with *Gomorrah* (see GOMORR(H)EAN *a.* and *sb.*), the name of the other of the two wicked cities of the plain in Gen. xviii-xix.

**1649** C. WALKER *Relat. & Obs.* II. 257 To the prejudice of our other New States-men, and their New erected Sodomes and Spintries at the Mulbury-garden at S. James's. *a* **1704** T. BROWN *Walk r. London, A Tavern* Wks. 1709 III. III. 3 A Tavern is a little Sodom, where as many Vices are daily practic'd, as ever were known in the great one. **1782** J. BROWN *Nat. & Revealed Relig.* v. iv. 461 How could he dwell in a dead carcase, a Sodom of filthiness? **1862** QUEEN VICTORIA *Let.* 7 June in R. Fulford *Dearest Mama* (1968) 67 It was intended he should come home through Paris stopping only a day in order to have got over his visit to that Sodom and Gomorrah. **1864** TROLLOPE *Can you forgive Her?* I. xxiii. 179, I always regarded the States as a Sodom and Gomorrah, prospering in wickedness. **1899** *Westm. Gaz.* 11 Sept. 8/1 Two, even in this military Sodom, had the courage to proclaim Dreyfus innocent. **1972** I. HAMILTON *Thrill Machine* xv. 63 It wasn't exactly Sodom and Gomorrah—the ladies kept their clothes on. **1974** *Listener* 24 Jan. 121/3 Heliogabalus.. reduced Rome to a kind of post-Christian Sodom and Gomorrah.

**2.** ***Sodom apple.*** **a.** Apple of Sodom (see APPLE *sb.* 3). So †*Sodom-fruit.* Also *U.S.*, the horse-nettle, *Solanum carolinense*.

**1615** BRATHWAIT *Strappado* (1878) 48 See painted Sodom-apples faire to th' eye, But being tutcht they perish instantly. **1654** WHITLOCK *Zootomia* 237 They are Sodome Apples, enduring the Eye, not the Touch. **1706** in PHILLIPS (ed. Kersey). [**1736** J. BANCKS *Young's Last Day* 22 Through life we chase, with fond pursuit, What mocks our hope, like Sodom's fruit.] **1738** M. GREEN *Spleen* 33 And Sodom-fruit our pains deceives. **1855** MRS. GASKELL *North & South* iv, The mocking way in which over-fond wishes are too often fulfilled—Sodom apples as they are. **1905** W. J. ROLFE *Shaks. Sonn.* 19 The ashes to which the Sodom-apples of illicit love are turned in the end.

†**b.** A variety of cider-apple. *Obs.*

**1676** WORLIDGE *Cyder* (1691) 212 The Sodome-apple or Bloudy pippin is a fruit of more than ordinary dark colour.

**3.** ***Sodom egg-plant*** (see quot. and cf. 2 a).

**1842** *Penny Cycl.* XXII. 196/1 *Solanum Sodomeum*, Sodom egg-plant, or apple of Sodom.

†**sodometrous,** *a. Obs. rare.* [f. *sodometry* SODOMITRY.] Sodomitical.

**1550** BALE *Eng. Votaries* II. A ij, The Sodometrous vow of theyr simulate chastity. *Ibid.* E ij, His successours shuld se that hys sodometrouse chastyte were well mainteined.

**'Sodomic,** *a. rare.* [f. SODOM + -IC.] Of or pertaining to Sodom; sodomitic.

*c* **1330** R. BRUNNE *Chron. Wace* (Rolls) 14414 He vsed þe synne Sodomyke. **1338** —— *Chron.* (1810) 320 Usure & symonie, & synne sodomike [F. *sodomien*]. **1893** *The Voice* (N.Y.) 20 Apr., America is to have a revival of the Sodomic civilization under more favorable auspices.

**'sodomist.** *rare.* [f. SODOM + -IST.] A sodomite. Also as *adj.* = SODOMITICAL *a.*

**1891** in *Cent. Dict.* **1948** *Rep. Native Laws Commission 1946-48* (Dept. Native Affairs, South Africa) 38/1 We may quote from a memorandum submitted by.. the Reverend H. P. Junod:—'.. He was the son of one of our Evangelists, and refused to submit to the sodomist suggestions and solicitations of old mine workers.' **1950** M. HAY *Foot of Pride* iv. 95 The inhabitants of Cahors.. joined in the [money-lending] business, and Dante put them in Hell alongside the sodomists.

**sodomite** ('sɒdəmaɪt). Forms: 4, 6- sodomite, 4-6 sodomyt(e, 5 sodomit, -ighte, sodamite, sodam-, sodemyte. [a. OF. *sodomite*, or ad. L. *Sodomīta* (Gr. Σοδομίτης), f. SODOM: see -ITE[1] 1 a. Sense 1 occurs also in OF.]

†**1.** Sodomy. *Obs. rare.*

*a* **1300** *Cursor M.* 27966 Vnkindli sin and sodomite, Austin cals al suilk delite, þat es not tuix womman and man. *c* **1315** SHOREHAM IV. 399 And sodomyt hys senne Aȝens kende y-do.

**2.** One who practises or commits sodomy.

*c* **1380** WYCLIF *Wks.* (1880) 55 þat prelatis.. ben gostly sodomytis worse þan bodily sodomytis of sodom and gomor. *a* **1400** *Apol. Loll.* 55 Are þei not.. werr and abhominabler þan carnal sodomits? **1477** CAXTON *Dictes* 11 b, Bren the Sodomytes and punysshe the men taken in fornicacion. **1508** KENNEDIE *Flyting w. Dunbar* 527 Deuill, dampnit dog, sodomyte insatiable. **1579** TOMSON *Calvin's Serm. Tim.* 231/1 Whores as they are, yea.. vile and shamefull Sodomites, committing suche heinous and abhominable actes, that it is horrible to thinke of. **1632** LITHGOW *Trav.* IX. 409 An open Sodomite, and horrible blasphemer. **1682** SHADWELL *Medal* 42 He boasts of Vice (which he did ne'r commit), Calls himself Whoremaster and Sodomite. **1705** HICKERINGILL *Priest-cr.* II. v. 49 An Adulterer, Simonist, Sodomite, Murtherer, Arrian.

**b.** *attrib.* Sodomitic, sodomitish. *rare.*

**13..** *Seuyn Sages* 1564 (W.), Wimmen he louede swithe lite, And usede sinne sodomighte. **1707** J. STEVENS tr. *Quevedo's Com. Wks.* (1709) 510 That Sodomite Page.

**3.** An inhabitant of Sodom.

**1474** CAXTON *Chesse* III. vi. (1883) 134 The.. vnnaturell synne of lecherye of the sodamites. **1526** *Pilgr. Perf.* (W. de W. 1531) 105 b, Thus lyued y[e] vertuous man Loth amonge the Sodomytes. *a* **1591** H. SMITH *Serm.* (1637) 212 When he fought against the Sodomites, the fire took his part. **1643** CARYL *Expos. Job* I. 1752 The Sodomites were surprized, when destroyed; they expected it not. **1737** WHISTON *Josephus, Antiq.* I. xi, About this time the Sodomites grew proud, on account of their riches and great wealth. **1865** R. MORRIS *Gen. & Ex.* 31 *marg.*, The wicked Sodomites beset Lot's house. **1876** B. MARTIN *Messiah's Kingdom* VI. iii. 331 The unnatural lust of the Sodomites.

Hence †**'sodomiter**, a sodomite; †**'sodomitess**, a woman sodomite. *Obs.*

**1523** COVERDALE tr. *Dulichius' Of the Olde God* R, Arystotle the murtherer, Auerrois the sodomyter, Plato the traytour. **1611** BIBLE *Deut.* xxiii. 17 There shalbe no whore [*marg.* sodomitesse] of the daughters of Israel.

**sodo'mitic,** *a. rare.* [ad. L. *Sodomītic-us*. Cf. F. *sodomitique*.] = next.

**1630** J. TAYLOR (Water P.) *Wks.* III. 137/1 The Pope then caus'd all Priests to leaue their wiues, To leade foule Sodomiticke single liues. **1885** *Cyclop. Sci.* VI. 471 Men and women indulged in unnatural and sodomitic commerce.

**sodomitical** (sɒdə'mɪtɪkəl), *a.* [f. L. *Sodomītic-us* (cf. prec.) + -AL[1].]

**1.** Of persons: Guilty of, committing, or practising sodomy.

**1546** *Supplic. Poore Commons* (E.E.T.S.) 75 The outrageiouse belowing of a sorte of sodomiticall buls. **1550** BALE *Eng. Votaries* I. (1560) 4 b That Sodomiticall swarme or brode of Antichrist. **1605** M. SUTCLIFFE *Brief Exam.* 53 Enemies to all lecherous and Sodomiticall Friars. **1667** *Termes de la Ley* 407 By the Common Law.. sodomiticall persons, and hereticks, should be burnt. **1687** SHADWELL *Tenth Sat. Juvenal* 49 A filthy Sodomitical Schoolmaster.

†**b.** With whom sodomy is committed. *Obs.*

*a* **1555** BRADFORD *Hurt of Hearing Mass* (1558) D j b, So are the hartes of our popishe protestaunts.. hardened.. in that they looke, yea, go backe agayne to theyr sodomiticall minion. **1612** *Trav. Four Englishm.* 83 If they haue no beards at all, they call them (if they be yong).. Sodomiticall boyes. **1634** SIR T. HERBERT *Trav.* 87 Hither sometimes the King repaires, and sees the Sodomiticall Boyes and Wenches dance.

**2.** Of the nature of, characterized by, consisting in, or involving sodomy.

**1550** BALE *Eng. Votaries* II. 21 b, Their sodomytycal chastyte agaynst Gods fre instytucyon. **1588** A. KING tr. *Canisius' Catech.* 149 Quhat is writtin of ye Sodomiticall sinne. **1629** L. O[WEN] *Spec. Jesuiticum* 26 Wherein hee shewed his Sodomiticall affection, and diabolicall desire. **1645** E. PAGITT *Heresiogr.* (1661) 225 Their Idolatries and Sodomitical uncleanness they will defend and maintain. **1700** T. BROWN tr. *Fresny's Amusem.* 31 To carry on a Sodomitical Intrigue. **1762** *Gentl. Mag.* 386 A clergyman.. convicted for a Sodomitical attempt. **1864** tr. *Caspar's Forensic Med.* III. 336 *note*, In regard to the question whether such a sodomitical coitus could have taken place.

†**3.** Of places, institutions, etc.: Polluted or infected by sodomy. *Obs.*

**1550** BALE *Apol.* 19 Than were they allowed for a spyrytuall religion in that Sodomiticall church of Antichrist. **1572** R. T. *Discourse* 39 The Church of Christ is holy Hierusalem: The Popes is adulterous Babylon, and Sodomitical Rome. **1600** O. E. (M. SUTCLIFFE) *Repl. Libel* II. ii. 32 To creepe into a Sodomiticall cloister of monkes. **1632** W. LITHGOW *Trav.* II. 76 If all the Priests.. were thus handled.., what a sea of Sodomiticall irreligious blood would ouerflow the halfe of Europe.

Hence **sodo'mitically** *adv.*; **sodo'miticalness**.

**1601** SIR A. SHERLEY *Trav.* (1863) 41 Which if he wanted hee would hire a boy sodomitically to use. **1677** W. HUGHES *Man of Sin* II. xii. 232 Two Noble youths.. being Sodomitically abused by this Infernal Goat. **1718** PRIDEAUX *Connex. O. & N.T.* II. II. 74 Agathocles, being Sodomitically given, fell in love with a beautiful young Man. **1727** BAILEY (vol. II), *Sodomiticalness*, Guiltiness of Sodomy.

**'Sodomitish,** *a. rare.* [f. SODOMITE + -ISH. Cf. OE. *Sodomitisc*.] Sodomitical; of Sodom.

**1535** COVERDALE *2 Esdras* v. 7 The Sodomitysh see shal cast out his fish. **1546** BALE *Eng. Votaries* I. (1550) 53 Hym haue the Sodomytysh knaues dyffamed in the legende of Cuthbert. **1874** W. JONES *N.T. Illustr.* 181 This century of moral purity as compared with the Sodomitish iniquity that revelled there [*sc.* at Pompeii].

†**'sodomitry.** *Obs.* Forms: α. 6-7 sodomitrie, -itry, 6 -itrye, sodomytrie. β. 6 sodometrye, 6-7 -etrie, -etry. [f. SODOMITE + -RY. Cf. OF. *sodomiterie*.]

**1.** = SODOMY 1. (Common *c* 1540-*c* 1650.)

α. **1530** TINDALE *Answ. More* III. xiii, It.. permitteth to abuse men's wives, and suffereth sodomitry. *a* **1533** FRITH *Answ. More* (1548) C vj b, The shamfull sodomitrye of the Trybe of Beniamin. **1577** VAUTROULLIER *Luther on Ep. Gal.* 229 Simonie,.. voluptuousnes, whoredom, sodomitrie and such other infinite abominations. **1634** SIR T. HERBERT *Trav.* 196 The women are not ashamed here (the better to illure the men from Sodomitry) to goe naked. **1673** R. HEAD *Canting Acad.* K 7 The abominable vice of Sodomitry.

β. **1538** BALE *Three Lawes* Pref. 23 Corrupteth with ydolles, and stynkynge Sodometry. **1585** T. WASHINGTON tr. *Nicholay's Voy.* I. viii. 8 Whoredome, sodometrie, theft, and all other.. vices. **1614** BOYS *Wks.* (1630) 256 If there were no stewes, all the world would be full of adulterie, rape, Sodometrie. **1655** FULLER *Ch. Hist.* III. 19 That the sin of Sodometry.. should be punished with heavy Censures.

**2.** = SODOMY 2.

**1592** TIMME *Eng. Lepers* D iij, All offences, even to murthers, incests, Sodomitries, were taxed. **1606** *Rep. Disc. Supreme Power* 49 The blasphemies, the adulteries, the Sodometries.. of diuers other Bishops of Rome.

**sodomize** ('sɒdəmaɪz), *v.* [f. SODOM(Y + -IZE.] *trans.* (occas. *absol.*) To practise sodomy upon (a man or a woman). Also **'sodomized** *ppl. a.*, **'sodomizing** *vbl. sb.*

**1868** tr. *Index Expurgatorius of Martial* 89 You must give up sodomising and womanising. **1888** [see IRRUMATION]. **1969** P. BARNES *Ruling Class* II. vi. 94 Earl of Gurney: You want two seconds of dripping sin to fertilize sodomized idiots. **1971** K. MILLETT *Sexual Politics* (1972) I. i. 13 Her gratitude at being sodomized is positively astonishing. **1972** *Times Lit. Suppl.* 2 June 622/4 Everything, animate and inanimate, appears to be either sodomizing, sodomized, ejaculating or bleeding. **1980** *Ibid.* 19 Sept. 1020/3 Cassady roughly sodomizing another man in a public lavatory.

**sodomy** ('sɒdəmɪ). Forms: 3-5 sodomye (5 zodomye), 4, 6-7 -ie, 6 -i, 5- sodomy. [a. OF. (also mod.F.) *sodomie*: see SODOM and -Y.]

**1.** An unnatural form of sexual intercourse, esp. that of one male with another.

**1297** R. GLOUC. (Rolls) 9038 Mid þe vile sunne of sodomye yproued hii were echon. **1387** TREVISA *Higden* (Rolls) III. 5 Mempricius.. forsook his wyf at þe laste, and vsede sodomye as a schrewe schulde. *c* **1440** *Jacob's Well* 162 þe xiiij. fote depth is sodomye, þat is, synne aȝens kynde. **1536-40** *Pilgr. Tale* 407 The prophet.. which knew before of there sodomi. **1577** tr. *Bullinger's Decades* (1592) 236 The abhominable sinne of Sodomie.. is plainly forbidden. **1650** BULWER *Anthropomet.* 198 Wicked Sodomy, a sin so hateful to Nature it self that she abhors it. **1727** SWIFT *Poisoning E. Curll* Wks. 1755 III. I. 151 Heaven pardon me for publishing the Trials of sodomy. **1782** J. BROWN *Nat. & Revealed Relig.* I. i. 23 Polygamy must occasion.. sodomy, bestiality, or the like. **1864** tr. *Caspar's Forensic Med.* III. 336 It is no secret that the unnatural connection of men with animals, sodomy in the restricted sense of the word, still sneaks about.

*fig.* **1395** PURVEY *Remonstr.* (1851) 7 Symonie is gostli sodomie and eresie.

**2.** An act or instance of this.

**1593** G. HARVEY *Pierce's Super.* Wks. (Grosart) II. 271 Agrippa detesteth his monstrous veneries, and execrable Sodomies. **1621** BURTON *Anat. Mel.* I. iii. II. iv. (1651) 205 Those rapes,.. Sodomies, buggeries of Monkes and Friers.

**sodopotassic,** var. SODIPOTASSIC *a.*

**sody.** *U.S. dial.* and *colloq.* var. SODA[1] (esp. in sense 4 b).

**1900** *Dialect Notes* I. 241 *Soda*. Always *sôdi* in Kansas City. **1907** J. LONDON *White Fang* I. ii. 14 Swallow a spoonful of sody, an' you'll sweeten up wonderful. **1907** *Dialect Notes* III. 200 *Sody, n.*, soda; either bicarbonate of soda or soda water. 'Have a glass of sody with me?' The normal pronunciation seems affected. **1951** W. FAULKNER *Requiem for Nun* III. 267 She's usually got a bottle of sody pop in the icebox. **1975** B. GARFIELD *Hopscotch* viii. 86 There was even a sody-cracker barrel by the fountain.

**sodyak,** obs. form of ZODIAC.

**sodyour,** obs. form of SOLDIER.

**soe** (səʊ). Now *dial.* Forms: α. 4-5 saa, 5 sa, saae, 4-5, 9 sae, 8 cea (see also SAY *sb.*[3]). β. 4, 7-9 so, 5-6 soo (6 swoo), 5- soe (6 sooe, sowe, 8 sow), 7-8 soa. [a. ON. *sá-r*: see SAY *sb.*[3]] A large tub.

α. **1377-8** *Durh. Acc. Rolls* (Surtees) 387 In uno sae empt. pro vitriario. *c* **1425** in Wr.-Wülcker 662 *Hec tina*, sa. **1459-60** *Durh. Acc. Rolls* (Surtees) 152 Pro j saa pro aqua portanda. **1480-1** *Ibid.* 97, j sae;.. ij saez. **1752** *Rec. Elgin* (1903) I. 446 All tubs, ceas,.. and other cooper work. **1889** ELLIS *Pronunc.* v. 799 [In Orkney] *sae* is a pail or bucket.

β. *c* **1300** *Havelok* 933 He kam to þe welle, water up-drow, And filde þer a michel so. *c* **1440** *Promp. Parv.* 462/1 Soo, or cowl, vessel, *tina*. **1459** in *Ripon Ch. Acts* (Surtees) 86 Tubbes, soes, alepoittes. **1541** *Hist. MSS. Commiss., Rutland MSS.* IV. 352 For one soo to the stable. **1578** *Richmond. Wills & Inv.* (Surtees) 282 A swoo with other smole tryfles. **1580-1** *Reg. St. Michael-le-Belfrey, York* (Surtees) I. 33 [A child] by misfortune drowned in a soo of water. **1611** COTGR., *Tine*, a Stand, open Tub, or Soe. **1679–80** *Fabric Rolls York Minster* (Surtees) 352 The child was drowned in a little water in ye bottom of a soa. **1691** RAY *N.C. Words* (ed. 2) 66 A *So* or *Soa*, a Tub with two Ears to carry on a stang. **1866–** in Linc. glossaries.

**b.** *attrib.* and *Comb.*, as ***soe-ful***, ***-staff***, ***-tree***. (See also SASTANGE.)

**14..** *Nom.* in Wr.-Wülcker 725 *Hoc tinarium*, a so-tre. *c* **1440** *Promp. Parv.* 466/1 Soo tre, or cowl tre, *falanga*. **1611** COTGR., *Tinée*, a Stand-full, or Soe-full. **1613** F. ROBARTES *Revenue Gospel* 49 One cluster thereof is carried between two vpon a soa-staffe. **1653** H. MORE *Antid. Ath.* II. vi. §2 For one Bason-full you may fetch up so many Soe-fulls.

**soebak**, var. SUBAK.

**soeffre**, obs. var. SUFFER *v.*

**soeju**, obs. var. SHOYU.

**soel(l**, obs. ff. SOLE *sb.*$^{2}$, *a.*, and *v.*$^{1}$

**sœmeterie**, obs. f. CEMETERY.

**soerty**, obs. f. SURETY.

**soetkoekie** (sʊtˈkuːkiː). *S. Afr.* Also **zoete-koekie, soet-koekie.** [Afrikaans, lit. 'a little sweet cake', f. Du. *zoet* sweet + *koek* cake + *-ie* dim. suff.] A traditional South African spiced biscuit.

**1910** D. FAIRBRIDGE *That which hath Been* ix. 115 Juffvrouw wanted very bad to help hand zoete-koekies. **1939** 'D. RAME' *Wine of Good Hope* III. iii. 368 They ended their tea and the thin bread and butter and soet-koekies of Grim's ceremony. **1949** L. G. GREEN *In Land of Afternoon* xii. 165, I have heard of a special ginger beer which is brewed during Christmas week and served with soetkoekies. **1973** *Fair Lady* 7 Mar. 23 With visions of my Voortrekker ancestors embarking on hazardous journeys with tinfuls of 'mebos', biltong, and 'soet-koekies', I scratched through my recipe book.

**soever** (səʊˈɛvə(r)), *adv.* Also *poet.* **soe'er.** [See So *adv.* and EVER *adv.* 8 e.]

†**1.** Whenever. *Obs.*$^{-1}$

**1517** TORKINGTON *Pilgr.* (1884) 27 And so ever ony Sarazin comyth by that Sepulcre he cast a stonne ther att.

**2.** Used with generalizing or emphatic force after words or phrases preceded by *how*, *what*, *which*, *whose*, etc. (Cf. HOWSOEVER, etc.)

**1557** NORTH *Gueuara's Diall Pr.* IV. xix. (1568) 170 How great a frend .. so euer hee bee to them.

**1580** CAMPION in Allen *Martyrdom* (1908) 23 The feare of what punishment temporal soever. **1595** SHAKS. *John* IV. iii. 91 Whose tongue so ere speakes false. **1610** HOLLAND *Camden's Brit.* (1637) 569 How great, or how faire soever it hath been. **1671** MILTON *Samson* 1015 Which way soever men refer it. **1701** SWIFT *Contests Nobles & Comm.* v, I conceive it far below the Dignity .. of human Nature .. to be engaged in any Party, the most plausible soever, upon such servile Conditions. **1779** *Mirror* No. 24 What pencil, how animated soever, can equal the glories of the sky at sun-set? **1835** J. H. NEWMAN *Par. Serm.* (1837) I. 267 To all who are perplexed in any way soever. **1885** R. BRIDGES *Eros & Psyche* Aug. xxvii, By which law all things soe'er Are .. held.

**sofa** (ˈsəʊfə). Also 7 **soffa**, 7–9 **sopha**; 8 **sophee, sophy**, 9 *vulg.* **sofy.** [= F. *sofa*, *sopha*, It., Sp., and Pg. *sofa*, ad. Arab. *ṣoffah.*]

**1.** In Eastern countries, a part of the floor raised a foot or two, covered with rich carpets and cushions, and used for sitting upon.

*α.* **1625** PURCHAS *Pilgrims* II. IX. 1581 A Sofa spread with very sumptuous Carpets of Gold, .. vpon which the Grand Signior sitteth. **1682** *Lond. Gaz.* No. 1683/3 The Grand Vizier came thither soon after, and sate down on a Stool placed on the Sofa. **1717** LADY M. W. MONTAGU *Lett.* (1893) I. 284 The next room is a very large one paved with marble, and all round it, raised, two sofas of marble, one above another. **1841** LANE *Arab. Nts.* I. 104 He .. beheld .. a young man sitting on a sofa raised to the height of a cubit from the floor.

*β.* *c* **1637** SIR G. COURTHOP *Mem.* 124 A Sopha, which is a place raised from the floor about a foot to sit on. **1682** WHELER *Journ. Greece* v. 350 Making us sit upon a Sopha, and drink Coffee with him. **1808** PARSONS *Trav. Asia*, etc. ii. 22, I paid a visit to the pasha .. and found him sitting on his sopha.

*transf.* **1768** STERNE *Sent. Journ.*, *The Grace*, The old man and his wife .., placing me betwixt them, sat down upon a sopha of turf by the door.

**2.** A long, stuffed seat with a back and ends or end, used for reclining; a form of lounge or couch.

*α.* **1717** BERKELEY *Tour Italy* Wks. 1871 IV. 530 The bridegroom sits on a very low sort of seat not unlike an oriental sofa. **1784** COWPER *Task* I. 88 Convenience next suggested elbow-chairs, And luxury th' accomplish'd Sofa last. **1812** CRABBE *Tales* v. 530 The splendid sofa, which, though made for rest, He then had thought it freedom to have press'd. **1849** LYELL *2nd Visit U.S.* II. 47 Sofas, rocking chairs, tables, and a stove are placed in this room. **1877** MRS. FORRESTER *Mignon* I. 275 She makes him lie on a sofa near the open window.

*transf.* **1864** E. BURRITT *Walk* 313 A row of flower sofas reaching round the garden.

*β.* **1728** YOUNG *Love of Fame* v. 135 On her sophee she sits, Vouchsafing audience to contending wits. **1753–4** RICHARDSON *Grandison* (1781) V. xxiv. 146, I threw myself on a sopha. **1806** BERESFORD *Miseries Hum. Life* II. xxxiii, After having .. diffused yourself on the sopha. **1832** *Country Houses* II. xii. 10 On a sopha in the green-room.

**3.** *attrib.*, as ***sofa-corner***, ***-cover***, ***-cushion***, etc.

**1797–1805** S. & HT. LEE *Canterb. T.* III. 139 A circular pavilion, elegantly fitted up with cushions and sopha seats. **1805** *Times* 7 Nov. 4/2 Card, sofa, and Pembroke tables. **1807** JANE AUSTEN *Let.* 8 Feb. (1932) I. 49 There will then be the Window-Curtains, sofa-cover, & a carpet to be altered. **1825** T. HOOK *Sayings* Ser. II. *Doubts & F.* v, On the opposite side of the sofa table. **1840** THACKERAY *Shabby-genteel Story* vi, That well-known sofa-corner. **1848** —— *Van. Fair* xxi, It was all I could do to prevent myself from throwing the sofa-cushion at her. *a* **1848** MARRYAT *Valerie* viii, The bottle .. which I had .. left under the sofa-pillow. **1848** MRS. GASKELL *Mary Barton* I. vii. 115 The dead body .. which she was laying out on a board, placed on a sort of sofa-settee. **1861** C. M. YONGE *Young Stepmother* xxiii. 333 She felt the misfortune to the beautiful new sofa-cover as a most serious calamity. **1937** *Burlington Mag.* May 240/1 Attempts to introduce gothic ornament into a sofa-table, a bookcase or a chair. **1968** *Canad. Antiques Collector* Aug. 6/2 (Advt.), Exceptionally fine Rosewood Regency sofa table. **1978–9** *House & Garden* Dec./Jan. 78/2 Striped Welsh flannel chair and sofa covers.

**b.** Objective, as ***sofa-maker***, ***-stuffer***.

**1836** T. HOOK *G. Gurney* (1850) I. iii. 43 My friend, the sofa-maker, never troubled himself to inquire after me. **1859** J. C. ATKINSON *Walks & Talks* (1892) 4 A beard that would have been a small fortune to a sofa-stuffer.

**4.** Special combs., as **sofa-back**, (*a*) an antimacassar; (*b*) the back of a sofa; **sofa-bed, -bedstead**, a piece of furniture so constructed as to form a sofa or bed as required; **sofa-carriage**, a carriage having the seat made like that of a sofa; **sofa-ridden**, confined to a sofa (*nonce-wd.*); †**sofa stall**, a seat in a hall or theatre made like a sofa.

**1878** GEO. ELIOT *Let.* 27 June (1956) VII. 33 The sorrows of those who can afford .. to think of anything better than *sofa-backs. **1880** L. HIGGIN *Handbk. Embroidery* 63 Design for sofa-back cover. **1894** 'MARK TWAIN' in *Century Mag.* Jan. 338/2 Tom .. hoisted a leg over the sofa-back. **1805** *Sofa bed [see *chair-bed* s.v. CHAIR *sb.*$^{1}$ 15]. **1816** REPTON *Landsc. Gard., Fragm. on Theory* (1840) 585 To have dressing-rooms, in which *sofa-beds may .. be used. **1823** DE QUINCEY *Incognito* Wks. 1862 X. 9 Down went the little sofa-bed in a closet. **1891** HARDY *Tess* xxxvii. (1900) 92 She induced him to lie down on his own sofa bed. **1833** LOUDON *Encycl. Archit.* §650 We shall give some Designs .. for *sofa-bedsteads. **1841** THACKERAY *Gt. Hoggarty Diam.* xi, A little dusky sofa-bedstead (woe betide him who has to sleep on it!). **1822–29** GOOD *Study Med.* III. 234 The use of his easy and convenient *sofa-carriage. **1862** *Catal. Internat. Exhib., Brit.* II. No. 5686, Sofa carriages, especially constructed for spinal complaints. **1826** MISS MITFORD *Village* Ser. III. (1863) 496 There she sat, *sofa-ridden. **1862** *Notice Mason Jones' Oration on Garibaldi* 8 Apr., *Sofa Stalls. Four Shillings.

Hence ˈ**sofaed** *ppl. a.*, (*a*) seated as on a sofa; (*b*) furnished with a sofa or sofas. ˈ**sofane** *a.*, pertaining to a sofa (*nonce-wd.*).

**1789** E. DARWIN *Bot. Gard.* II. (1791) 69 Sopha'd on silk, amid her charm-built towers, .. In sullen apathy Papaver nods. **1802** T. CAMPBELL *Let.* 28 Aug. (1849) I. xv. 397 A lord's house, fashionable *strangers*, sofa'd saloons, and winding galleries. **1842** DICKENS *Let.* 3 Jan. (1974) III. 7 A comfortable room, .. well-lighted, sofa'd, mirrored, and so forth. **1860** G. VANDENHOFF *Dramatic Reminiscences* vi. 104 A very good-sized room had been fitted up as my dressing-room, cleaned, carpeted, sofa'd, well lit. **1860** DICKENS *Uncomm. Trav.* vi, A sofa, of incomprehensible form regarded from any sofane point of view. **1934** 'A. BRIDGE' *Ginger Griffin* ii. 22 The Grant-Howards sat in the green-sofa'd saloon.

**Sofar** (ˈsəʊfɑː(r)). Also **SOFAR.** [See quot. 1948.] A system in which the sound waves from an underwater explosion (either artificial or natural) are detected at a number of listening stations so that its position can be fixed; more generally, detection of deep explosions a great distance away.

**1947** *Britannica Bk. of Year* 841/2 An underwater sound system, called 'Sofar' .., made possible the location of air and ship survivors as far as 2,000 mi. from shore. **1948** EWING & WORZEL *Long-Range Sound Transmission* 12 A network of four listening stations is being established in the Pacific by the Navy Department, and the name SOFAR, from the words SOund Fixing And Ranging, has been assigned to the system. **1961** H. H. KOELLE *Handbk. Astronaut. Engin.* XXVIII. 28 The missile must carry a Sofar bomb when a deep-water detection system is used, in order to provide a deep sound source. **1966** *McGraw-Hill Encycl. Sci. & Technol.* XIV. 429/2 Shock waves used in Sofar propagate long distances under water, being refracted by the isothermal layers in the oceans. **1979** *Nature* 20–27 Dec. 820/2 The deep ocean sound channel is used to obtain very long range (typically >2,000 km) acoustic transmission via totally refracted propagation paths (SOFAR propagation).

**Sofee**, variant of SUFI$^{1}$.

**soferand**, obs. form of SOVEREIGN *a.*

**sofett.** *rare*$^{-0}$. [f. SOF-A + -ETT(E.] 'A small sofa' (Webster, 1828–32).

**soffit** (ˈsɒfɪt). *Arch.* Forms: *α.* 7–8 **soffita**, 8 **sofita**; 7 **soffeta**, 8 **sapheta**. *β.* 7 **suffito**, 7–8 **soffito, sofitto**; 8 **soffeto**. *γ.* 8 **schofeet, sopheit, suffete**, 8–9 **sofite, soffite**. *δ.* 8 **sofit**, 8– **soffit** (9 **soffet**); 8–9 **suffit.** [In the *α.* and *β.* forms directly a. It. *soffitta* fem. and *soffitto* masc., f. *sof-* (L. *sub*) under + pa. pple. of *figgere* to fix. The later forms are prob. after F. *soffite.*] The under horizontal face of an architrave or overhanging cornice; the under surface of a lintel, vault, or arch; a ceiling.

*α.* **1613–39** I. JONES in Leoni *Palladio's Archit.* (1742) I. 39 The Soffita of the Corona of the Cornice. *a* **1668** LASSELS *Voy. Italy* (1670) II. 103 The *Soffita* or roof of this Church most richly guilt. **1703** [R. NEVE] *City & C. Purchaser* 236 *Sapheta's*, the Boards over the tops of Windows, opposite to the Window-boards at the bottom. **1703** in *Jrnl. Derby. Archæol. Soc.* III. 33 For carving 16 roses in the Sofitas of the hanging square of the Capitalls.

*β.* **1664** EVELYN tr. *Freart's Archit.* v. 20 Those great Roses of the Sofitto or Eves of the Corona. **1710** J. HARRIS *Lex. Techn.* II, *Sofitto*, is the Italian Term in Architecture, for the Eaves of the Corona of the Capital of a Column. **1776** G. SEMPLE *Building in Water* 67 Five Feet from the Soffeto of the Center Arch. *Ibid.* 107.

*γ.* **1725** W. HALFPENNY *Sound Building* 13 To draw the two different Edges of a Twisted Schofeet. **1739** C. LABELYE *Piers Westm. Bridge* 77 The chamfered Joints in the Suffetes of the Arches. **1751** —— *Westm. Br.* 77 Some of their Stones both in the Fronts and their Sopheits were split. **1755** T. H. CROKER *Orl. Fur.* XLII. lxxvii, The lofty columns .. Which the soffites with gems adorned upheld. **1823** RUTTER *Fonthill* 71 The lower part or soffite of the Oriel is exquisitely finished. **1842** GWILT *Encycl. Archit.* §2285 Backs, elbows, and sofites to windows. *a* **1878** SIR G. SCOTT *Lect. Archit.* (1879) I. 280 A rib dropping down a little from the arched soffite.

*δ.* **1728** CHAMBERS *Cycl.*, *Soffito*, or *Sofit*, in Architecture, any Plafond or Ceiling, form'd of cross Beams, or flying Cornices. **1751** J. STUART in *Lett. Lit. Men* (Camden) 389 The Suffit of the Architrave, and Base of the Pilasters. **1807** HUTTON *Course Math.* (ed. 5) II. 88 The window cills or seats, and the soffits above. **1823** P. NICHOLSON *Pract. Builder* 428 The section of the soffit .. is some part of a circle. **1847** LD. LINDSAY *Christian Art* I. 124 The first cupola and the suffits of the two arches intervening between it and the second. **1883** *Specif. Alnwick & Cornhill Rlwy.* 3 In the arches the soffit is to be pointed with the best Portland cement.

*attrib.* **1833** LOUDON *Encycl. Archit.* §755 The soffit boarding. **1851** RUSKIN *Stones Ven.* I. xxviii. 326 We do not look for the soffit decoration.

**soffraunce**, obs. f. SUFFERANCE.

**soffre, soffri**, obs. ff. SUFFER *v.*

**soffym(e**, obs. ff. SOPHISM.

**Sofi**, obs. var. SOPHY, SUFI$^{1}$.

**sofice**, obs. f. SUFFICE *v.*

**Sofism**, var. of SUFISM.

**so-forth.** *rare*$^{-1}$. [See FORTH *adv.* 9 b.] Such and such a thing.

**1611** SHAKS. *Wint. T.* I. ii. 218 They're here with me already; whisp'ring, rounding: Sicilia is a so-forth.

**sofre, sofry**, obs. forms of SUFFER *v.*

**soft** (sɒft, -ɔː-), *sb.* Also 3, 5 **softe**, 8–9 *Sc.* and *north.* **saft.** [f. the adj.]

**1.** That which is agreeable, pleasant, or easy; comfort, ease. *rare.*

*c* **1250** *Gen. & Ex.* 3647 Đis folc is after softe toȝen, And hauen swinc in weiȝe droȝen. *a* **1300** *Cursor M.* 15564 Bot sal we elles suffre samen, bath soft and sare. *c* **1400** *Rom. Rose* 3446 For though thou love thus evermore, To me is neither softe ne sore. **1677** HORNECK *Gt. Law Consid.* iv. (1704) 112 They are afraid it .. will discompose them in their golden dreams, drive them from their softs and ease.

**2. a.** That which is soft or yielding; the soft part *of* something; softness.

**1593** R. BARNES *Parthenophil* III. 83 O Love's soft hills! .. How much, at your smooth soft, my sense amazed is! *Ibid.* 119, I might work miracles to change again The hard to soft! **1611** FLORIO, *Móllo*, .. the soft or spunginesse of any thing, as of crummes of bread. **1653** R. SANDERS *Physiogn.* 63 All this enclosed space is commonly called the soft of the Thumb. **1674** N. FAIRFAX *Bulk & Selv.* 130 His two fore-feet, which he had thrust so into the soft of her sides, as to make two deep doaks there. **1784** COWPER *Task* III. 417 Nor does he spare the soft And succulent, that feeds its giant growth.

*transf.* **1871** R. ELLIS *Catullus* lxviii. 120 Not to a grand-sire old .., so lovely the grandson One dear daughter alone rears i' the soft of his years.

**b.** *Cant.* Bank notes.

**1821** [see *fancy-piece* s.v. FANCY *sb.* and *a.* B. 2]. **1864** in *Slang Dict.* **1955** *Publ. Amer. Dialect Soc.* XXIV. 115 Paper money is known, in general, as *scratch* or *soft*.

**c.** *pl.* Soft coal; also, soft woollen rags.

**1883** GRESLEY *Gloss. Coal-m.* 229 *Softs*, coals which easily break up. **1894** *Times* 17 Apr. 4/5 The best demand was for nuts, .. but Barnsley softs were again to be had at from 7s. 6d. to 8s.

**d.** *pl.* Soft commodities (see SOFT *a.* 20 b (*b*)).

**1979** *Financial Times* 28 Mar. 37/1 Will 'softs' boom next? **1981** *Times* 5 May 17/2 Softs are less homogeneous in outlook because crop conditions vary so much.

**3.** *Phonetics.* A soft or voiced consonant.

**1846** M. WILLIAMS *Sanscr. Gram.* 10 The soft is changed to its unaspirated hard. **1871** ABBOTT & SEELEY *Eng. Lessons* 43 Aspirates and softs .. are modified in a corresponding manner.

**4.** *U.S. political slang.* **a.** A member of a local party which advocated a 'soft money' or paper currency. **b.** A member of one or other party holding moderate views. Cf. SOFT-SHELL *sb.*

**1847–54** in R. H. Thornton *American Gloss.* (1912) s.v. *Hard.* **1859** BARTLETT *Dict. Amer.* (ed. 2) 426 *Soft-shell democrats*, *Soft-shells*, or *Softs*, the less conservative division of the New York Democrats. **1888** BRYCE *Amer. Commw.* II. II. xlvi. 203 The Hunkers and Barnburners who divided the Democratic party forty years ago, and subsequently passed into the 'Hards' and the 'Softs'.

**5.** A soft, simple, or foolish person; a 'softy'. Chiefly *dial.* or *colloq.*

**1854-** in dial. glossaries and texts (Northampt., Linc., Lanc., Berks., etc.). **1859** GEO. ELIOT *A. Bede* ix, It'll do you no good to sit in a spring-cart o' your own, if you've got a soft to drive you. **1864** E. SARGENT *Peculiar* III. 72 If the world were in the hands of such softs the old machine would be smashed up in universal anarchy.

**6.** *Hist. rare.* A Menshevik.

**1950** E. H. CARR *Bolshevik Revol.* I. ii. 30 But the withdrawal of seven delegates who had voted with the 'softs' .. had the result of shifting the balance of votes in favour of the 'hards'. **1955** H. HODGKINSON *Doubletalk* 17 Lenin's group .. was described as 'Iskraists' .. or 'hards'... Its rivals were 'softs', because it approached the membership problem in the spirit of Martov's 'The more people there are called Party members, the better it will be'.

**soft** (sɒft, -ɔː-), *a.* Forms: α. 1–6 softe (4–5 soffte, 4 zoffte), 4– soft. β. *dial.* and *Sc.* 6–7 safte, 6– saft (9 *dial.* zaft). [OE. *sófte* or *sóft*, var. of the more usual *séfte*, which corresponds to WFris. *sêft*, *seaft*, OHG. *semfti* (*samfti*), *semfte*, MHG. *senfte*, obs. G. *senft*. The form without umlaut (probably due to the influence of the adv.) has parallels in MDu. *soft* (*zoft*), *saft*, and *sacht* (Du. *zacht*), MLG. and LG. *sacht*, MHG. and G. *sanft* (dial. *saft*, *sâft*). The relationships of the stem are doubtful.]

Many of the senses tend to involve or pass into each other, esp. in poetic use.

**I. 1. a.** Producing agreeable or pleasant sensations; characterized by ease and quiet enjoyment; of a calm or placid nature.

*c* **1000** ÆLFRIC *Hom.* (Thorpe) I. 566 Ic softum slæpe me ȝereste, swa swa ðu me forlete. *c* **1175** *Lamb. Hom.* 35 Hit walð me þunchen þet softeste beð [= bath] and þet wunsemeste þet ic efre ibad. *c* **1250** *Gen. & Ex.* 2412 Pharaon bad him wurðen wel in softe reste and seli mel. **1390** GOWER *Conf.* I. 312 It hath be sen and felt ful ofte, The harde time after the softe. *c* **1477** CAXTON *Jason* 45 b, Certes the time must be taken as hit cometh, is hit hard or softe. **1500–20** DUNBAR *Poems* xxxv. 9 For weirines on me ane slummer soft Come. **1590** SPENSER *F.Q.* I. ix. 13 Whiles euery sence the humour sweet embayd, And slombring soft my hart did steale away. **1606** SHAKS. *Ant. & Cl.* II. vii. 114 Till that the conquering Wine hath steep't our sense, In soft and delicate Lethe. **1634** MILTON *Comus* 1001 Where young Adonis oft reposes, Waxing well of his deep wound In slumber soft. **1746** FRANCIS tr. *Horace, Epist.* I. xvi. 21 This pleasing, this delicious soft Retreat In Safety guards me from September's Heat. **1812** BYRON *Ch. Har.* II. lxx, Many a joy could he from Night's soft presence glean. **1865** CONINGTON *Hor., Odes* IV. v. (ed. 3) 112 Sweet Peace, soft Plenty, swell the golden grain.

†**b.** Pleasing *in* (or *of*) taste; free from acidity or sharpness. Also of odour: Not pungent, strong, or heavy. *Obs.*

**1398** TREVISA *Barth. De P.R.* IV. vii. (W. de W. 1495) 89 Blood is swete and softe in taast and in towche. *Ibid.* XVI. xciv. (Bodl. MS.), In some place it is softe in sauoure, and in some place moste salt: and in some place moste bitter. *c* **1400** tr. *Secreta Secret., Gov. Lordsh.* 92 His seed ys reed, his odour softe, of good effect. *c* **1475** HENRYSON *Poems* (S.T.S.) III. 152 With ane brewing caldrun full of hait caill, For it wilbe þe softar and sweittar of þe smak. **1797** *London Art of Cookery* 216 Malt is a wholesome nutritious grain, containing a soft, balsamic, oleaginous essence. **1826** *Art Brewing* (ed. 2) 101 Preserving the sweet flavour of the malt .., and the soft richness.

**c.** Pleasing to the eye; free from ruggedness or asperity. Also of colour, or with reference to this: Not crude or glaring; quiet, subdued.

**1702** POPE *Sappho* 15 Soft scenes of solitude no more can please. **1738** GRAY *Tasso* 67 There the soft emerald smiles of verdant hue. **1784** COWPER *Task* I. 766 We can spare The splendour of your lamps; they but eclipse Our softer satellite. **1815** J. SMITH *Panorama Sci. & Art* II. 770 This mode of engraving .., when carefully executed, has a soft and pleasing effect. **1845** BUDD *Dis. Liver* 228 The tissue of the liver is pale, and .. of a soft buff colour. **1869** TOZER *Highl. Turkey* I. 201 Following its stream .. through softer scenery. **1892** *Photogr. Ann.* II. 718 This [Bromide] Paper is very Rapid, and gives very soft and beautiful results.

**d.** Of a photographic film or paper: producing an image of low contrast.

**1910** W. WALLINGTON *Chats on Photogr.* xiii. 113 The paper may be obtained in a number of speeds .. the slower varieties being more suitable for printing soft negatives. **1937** *Amat. Photogr.* ix. 120 The 'soft' grade has the .. merit of registering tone in dense high-lights without clogging shadows. **1966** D. G. BRANDON *Mod. Techniques Metallogr.* 15 An approximately linear dependence of the blackening is only obtained over a limited range of exposure times, and this range is far greater for 'soft' emulsions than for 'hard' ones. **1979** *SLR Camera* Jan. 59/1 If the photographic image shows a large number of tones between the extremes of light and dark, it is said to have soft gradation.

**e.** Of a lens: having low resolving power. Cf. SOFT-FOCUS *a.*, *sb.*, and *v.*

**1958** M. L. HALL *Newnes' Compl. Amat. Photographer* i. 26 Soft lenses. Some highly complex lenses are said to be 'soft' in definition. **1974** *Publishers' Weekly* 24 June 56/2 'Soft lens' photos well suited indeed to the muted inner dignity of these deeply religious black people. **1978** *SLR Camera* Sept. 37/3 How good is the lens on your camera? Is it a bit soft?

**2. a.** Causing or involving little or no discomfort, hardship, or suffering; easily endured or borne.

*c* **1205** LAY. 16109 Soð ich habbe þe isæid, ah nis þe na þe softre. *c* **1250** *Gen. & Ex.* 2057 Queðer-so it wurðe softe or strong, ðe reching wurð on god bi-long. *c* **1320** *Cast. Love* 957 Mi ȝok is softe i-nowh to weren. *c* **1380** WYCLIF *Sel. Wks.* III. 367 For Crist hymself seys þat his ȝok is soffte, and his charge is light. **1526** *Pilgr. Perf.* (W. de W. 1531) 41 b, He hydeth the ferefull scourge of greuous correccyon, and sheweth vs somtymes the softe rodde of his swete disciplyne. *a* **1661** FULLER *Worthies, Worc.* III. (1661) 169 After ten years soft durance in all plenty, .. enjoying a great temporall Estate left him by his Father, He dyed 1569. **1672** SIR T. BROWNE *Let. Friend* §24. 130 Besides his soft death, the incurable state of his disease might somewhat extenuate your sorrow. **1700** LAW *Council of Trade* (1751) 118 Altho' .. this act be a monopoly, .. yet was it incomparably more soft and easy, than those barbarous monopolies of the Kings, James the V and VI.

**b.** Involving little or no exertion or effort; free from toil or labour. Now chiefly *colloq.*, easy, lazy, idle.

**1639** FULLER *Holy War* II. xl. (1840) 104 They were bred in such soft employments, that they were presently foundered with any hard labour. **1655** *Nicholas Papers* (Camden) II. 267 Iff I did not know how much hee is devoted to his ease and a soft kinde of life. **1690** TEMPLE *Ess. Poetry* Wks. 1720 I. 249 Among the Romans, the last .. Scipio passed the soft Hours of his Life in the Conversation of Terence. **1841** BROWNING *Pippa Passes* 146 A soft and easy life these ladies lead! **1858** CARLYLE *Fredk. Gt.* IX. vii. (1872) III. 128 He led a soft and tranquil life with his Regiment at Ruppin. **1889** *Daily News* 12 Oct. 5/1 People crowd into literature, as into other 'soft' professions, because it is genteel. **1894** *Ibid.* 2 Oct. 6/1 The popular idea that romance is 'a soft job'. **1905** VACHELL *The Hill* viii. 181 You have deliberately taken things easy, because you wanted a soft time of it during the summer term.

**c.** Applied in the Soviet Union and China to a class of railway carriage (esp. a sleeper) having soft, upholstered seats.

**1928** *Cook's Continental Timetable* 15 May 102 Sleeping car of direct communication, soft and hard class. **1949** F. MACLEAN *Eastern Approaches* (1951) I. iii. 39 In the train I found myself in a 'soft' compartment with three senior and somewhat supercilious officers of the Red Army. **1954** KOESTLER *Invisible Writing* v. 61 It entitled me .. to travel in the 'soft class' on trains. **1968** BETHELL & BURG tr. *Solzhenitsyn's Cancer Ward* I. xiv. 228 They found it quite unbearable, of course, to travel in ordinary railway carriages... The Rusanovs now travelled only in reserved compartments or 'soft class'. **1974** *Times* 1 Apr. 15/5 All the railways in Europe, and even those in China, have first and second class, although it may be wrapped up as 'hard' and 'soft' in USSR and China. **1978** G. E. NEWBY *Big Red Train Ride* ii. 22 We now took a closer look at our deluxe, 'soft-class' compartment. **1982** *Brit. Med. Jrnl.* 3 Apr. 1031/1 One end of our 'soft-class' carriage [in China].

**3. a.** Of a sound, the voice, etc.: Low, quiet, subdued; not loud, harsh, or rough. Also, melodious, pleasing to the ear, sweet.

*c* **1250** *Owl & Night.* 6 Þat playd wes stif & starc & strong, Sum hwile softe & lud among. *a* **1300** *Cursor M.* 1030 Þar sune es soft and suet sang, Sune of sautes þat þar singes. **1362** LANGL. *P. Pl.* A. IX. 112 He was .. to loken on ful symple, .. Sad of his semblaunt and of softe speche. *c* **1385** CHAUCER *L.G.W.* 745 *Thisbe*, And with a soun as softe as ony shryfte, They lete here wordis thour the clifte pace. *c* **1400** LYDG. *Pilgr. Sowle* (Caxton) I. xxxvii. (1859) 41 Thenne held they a counceyl so softe and so stylle that I nomore herd for a good space. **1422** tr. *Secreta Secret., Priv. Priv.* 177 He lyght fro his hors and in softe laghynge sayde [etc.]. **1508** DUNBAR *Tua Mariit Wemen* 519 The soft souch of the swyr. **1581** MULCASTER *Positions* xii. (1887) 60 Of loude and soft reading. **1605** SHAKS. *Lear* V. iii. 273 Her voice was euer soft, Gentle, and low, an excellent thing in woman. **1697** DRYDEN *Virg. Past.* v. 128 The soft Whispers of the Southern Wind. **1738** GRAY *Propertius* iii. 2 Whence the soft strain and ever-melting verse? **1779** WARNER in Jesse *Selwyn & Contemp.* (1844) IV. 263, I dealt only in the softest inflexions of voice, though with you .. I should have been angry. **1817** KEATS *I stood tip-toe* 95 The soft rustle of a maiden's gown. **1838** DICKENS *O. Twist* xii, There came a soft tap at the door. **1876** BRISTOWE *Th. & Pract. Med.* (1878) 602 A soft systolic murmur is frequently to be heard.

**b.** *spec.* in *Phonetics.* (Opposed to HARD *a.* 16.)

Jonson and Ainsworth employ the term in the contrary sense to that now usual.

**1636** B. JONSON *Eng. Gram.* iv. Wks. (Rtldg.) 772/2 The more general sound [of *f*] is the softest and expresseth the Greek *φ*. **1668** O. PRICE *Eng. Orthogr.* 24 Except .. the soft, s, in concision, circumcision. *Ibid.*, But, th, makes a softer sound .. in worthy, father. **1736** AINSWORTH *Dict.* II. s.v. *T*, *P* is only a softer *b*, and *b* an harder *p*, .. the harder mute before a vowel passing into the softer before a consonant. **1775–** [see HARD *a.* 16]. **1827** HEARD *Gram. Russian Lang.* 4 There are eleven vowels in the Russian alphabet, which are divided into hard and soft. **1845** *Proc. Philol. Soc.* II. 90, *S* is always hard, the soft sound of this letter being invariably represented by *z*. **1883** I. TAYLOR *Alphabet* II. 128 The Etruscan rejects the soft mutes *b*, *g*, *d*, and retains the aspirated mutes *th*, *kh*, *ph*.

**c.** Of musical instruments: Making or emitting a soft sound.

**1561** T. HOBY tr. *Castiglione's Courtyer* I. (1900) 90 The Cretenses used harpes and other softe instrumentes. **1634** MILTON *Comus* 86 With his soft Pipe, and smooth-dittied Song. **1667** —— *P.L.* I. 551 Anon they move .. to the Dorian mood Of Flutes and soft Recorders. **1746** FRANCIS tr. *Horace, Epist.* II. ii. 82 Thee the softer Lyre Delights. **1794** MRS. RADCLIFFE *Myst. Udolpho* xv, Their voices accompanied by a few soft instruments.

**4. a.** Of weather, seasons, etc.: Free from storms or rough winds; genial, mild, balmy. (Cf. 26.)

*c* **1250** *Gen. & Ex.* 3061 Ðis weder is softe, And ðis king hard. **1362** LANGL. *P. Pl.* A. VII. 181 Vppon softe sonenday .. Hungur hem helede wiþ an hot Cake. *c* **1375** *Cursor M.* 24837 (Fairf.), Þe weder soft in somertide sone be-gan to rugg & ride. *c* **1440** *Promp. Parv.* 58/2 Calme or softe, wythe-owte wynde, *calmus*. *c* **1475** HENRYSON *Poems* (S.T.S.) III. 93 The nicht is soft and dry. *a* **1505** KINGSFORD *Chron. Lond.* (1905) 261 This yere was a wonderfull easy and soft wynter, without stormys or frostes. **1697** DRYDEN *Virg. Georg.* II. 457 In this soft Season, .. In prime of all the Year, and Holy-days of Spring. **1705** ADDISON *Italy* 219 In a soft Air and a delicious Situation. **1822** [M. A. KELTY] *Osmond* III. 107 It was a soft, early summer's morning. **1851** CARLYLE *J. Sterling* I. ii, The climate of Bute is rainy, soft of temperature... In that soft rainy climate [etc.]. **1894** BLACKMORE *Perlycross* 401 It is such a soft spring-day.

**b.** Of the sun, rain, wind, etc.: Shining, falling, or blowing gently; not strong, violent, or boisterous.

**1362** LANGL. *P. Pl.* A. Prol. 1 In a somer sesun whon softe was þe sonne. *c* **1400** *Destr. Troy* 6066 Erly at Morne, When the sun vp soght with his softe beames. **1549** *Compl. Scotl.* vi. (1872) 61 The .. southyn vynd .. generis thondir, cluddis, and smal soft ranis. **1596** DALRYMPLE tr. *Leslie's Hist. Scot.* (S.T.S.) II. 238 [He] prosperouslie landes at Leith .. with a safte winde the xix day of maii. **1648** HEXHAM II, *Een soesinge*, a soft or a gentle Gale. **1781** COWPER *Charity* 127 Soft airs and gentle heavings of the wave Impel the fleet. **1823** F. CLISSOLD *Ascent Mt. Blanc* 22 A soft breath of wind spread its folds, and floated it gently in the air. **1843** MRS. CARLYLE *Lett.* I. 206 The beautifullest soft rain to make all fresh again. **1864** TENNYSON *Aylmer's F.* 454 The soft river-breeze, Which fann'd the gardens.

*fig.* **1837** CARLYLE *Fr. Rev.* II. III. vii, Wild burstings of affection were in this great heart; of fierce lightning, and soft dew of pity.

**c.** Of the sea, streams, etc.: Free from rough waves or turbulence; smooth, calm; running calmly or gently.

*c* **1450** *St. Cuthbert* (Surtees) 626 Þe se was soft, þe wawes were stille. **1543** ASCHAM *Toxoph.* (Arb.) 153 There is no shippe better than Gallies be, in a softe and a caulme sea. **1610** HOLLAND *Camden's Brit.* 223 From thence with a soft streame, and gentle fall, Thone runneth by .. Taunton. **1648** MILTON *Ps.* lxxxvii. 27 In thee fresh brooks, and soft streams glance. **1784** COWPER *Task* IV. 64 Rills of oily eloquence in soft Meanders. **1814** SCOTT *Diary* 2 Sept. in *Lockhart*, We here only feel them as a large but soft swell of the sea. **1863** *Smith's Dict. Bible* III. 1311/2 It [Siloah] is not now, nor was it in the days of Isaiah, anything but a very soft and gentle stream.

**5. a.** Of pace, progression, or movement: Leisurely, easy; slow; not hasty or hurried. Now *arch.*

The adverbial phrase (to go, ride, etc.) *a soft pace* appears very frequently from *c* 1370 to 1560.

*c* **1290** *S. Eng. Leg.* I. 297 He ne made no softe pas, Ake wende him þudere ful hastifliche. *c* **1440** *Promp. Parv.* 462/2 Softe, in mevynge, *lentus*. *Ibid.* 472/1 Stalkynge, or soft and sly goynge, *serptura*. **1511** *Guylforde's Pilgr.* (Camden) 77 We made sayle with right softe spede. **1604** E. G[RIMSTONE] *D'Acosta's Hist. Indies* VI. xxviii. 493 Circles .. wherein the Auntients and Noblemen did sing and daunce with a softe and slowe motion. **1663** S. PATRICK *Parab. Pilgr.* xxvii. (1687) 313 A soft pace goes far. **1687** A. LOVELL tr. *Thevenot's Trav.* I. 164 The Dromedaries have .. a good soft trott, and will travel with ease forty Leagues a day. *a* **1704** T. BROWN *To Belinda* ii. Wks. 1711 IV. 100 Love is all Gentleness and Joy, Smooth are his Looks, and soft his Pace. *a* **1822** SHELLEY *Matilda* 5 With slow, soft steps leaving the mountain's steep. **1871** ROSSETTI *Poems, Dante at Verona* xxi, A lady .. at a soft pace Riding the lists round to the dais.

**b.** Having a smooth easy motion. *rare.*

**1470–85** MALORY *Arthur* X. xxviii. 458 Whanne he vnderstood that Kynge Marke had sente for hym, he mounted vpon a softe ambuler and rode to Kynge Marke. **1667** MILTON *P.L.* VIII. 165 The Earth .. that spinning sleeps On her soft Axle, while she paces Eev'n.

†**c.** Of a journey: Performed leisurely. *Obs.*⁻¹

**1606** HOLLAND *Suetonius* 75 The journeyes that he made were soft and small; so that if hee went from Rome but to Tibur or Præneste, he would make two daies of it.

†**6.** Of a fire: Burning slowly or gently; moderate or gentle in heat or intensity; slow. *Obs.*

Common in the 16th and 17th centuries.

**1400** tr. *Secreta Secret., Gov. Lordsh.* 85 After be it put vpon a softe fyr. *a* **1425** tr. *Arderne's Treat. Fistula*, etc. 31 Seþe þam on a softe fyre vnto þey be made oon body. **1527** ANDREW *Brunswyke's Distyll. Waters* H iij, The fyre must be very softe in the begynnyng. **1577** HARRISON *England* II. vi. (1877) I. 157 The more the barleie be dried (yet must it be doone with soft fire) the better the malt is. **1610** HOLLAND *Camden's Brit.* (1637) 453 Redde fillets of Saffron .. are dried at a soft fire. **1689** LUTTRELL *Brief Rel.* (1857) I. 620 Some French incendiaries .. were adjudg'd to be fastned to a stake, with a soft fire round them. **1718** BP. HUTCHINSON *Witchcraft* ii. (1720) 22 Some others roasted the King's Picture by a soft Fire. **1738** CHAMBERS *Cycl.* s.v. *Balsam of sulphur*, Boiling the two together over a soft fire the space of an hour.

*Prov.* *a* **1536** *Proverbs* in *Songs, Carols*, etc. (E.E.T.S.) 128 A softe fire makith swete malte. **1564** BULLEYN *Dram. Dial.* (E.E.T.S.) 6 Softe fire maketh swete Malte. **1663** BUTLER *Hud.* I. iii. 1251 Soft fire, they say, does make sweet Malt. Good Squire. *Festina lente*, not too fast.

**7.** Of a slope, ascent, etc.: Gentle, gradual.

**1659** W. CHAMBERLAYNE *Pharonnida* II. 147 The stately Mount .. to meet the Vale stole down On soft descents. **1781** COWPER *Retirement* 333 Neither heathy wilds .. Nor soft declivities with tufted hills. **1794** MRS. RADCLIFFE *Myst. Udolpho* xxxvi, The strain .. rose, by soft degrees, till the high organ and the choral sounds swelled into full and solemn harmony. **1819** SCOTT *Ivanhoe* xliii, It occupied the brow of a soft and gentle eminence.

**II. 8. a.** Of persons: Gentle or mild in nature or character; inclined to be merciful, lenient, or considerate in dealing with others; free from harshness, severity, or rigour; compassionate, kind, tender-hearted.

Passing into, or not always clearly distinct from, sense 13.

*a* **1122** *O.E. Chron.* an. 1114 (Laud MS.), He wæs swiðe god & softe man & dyde mycel to gode. **1154** *Ibid.* an. 1137, He milde man was & softe & god. *c* **1200** ORMIN 667 Godess enngell iss full meoc, & milde, & soffte, & bliþe. *c* **1205** LAY. 18775 Þa wes Vðer Pendragun þa softer an his mode. *a* **1225** *Ancr. R.* 304 Abuuen us [will be] þe eorre Demare, vor ase softe as he is her, ase herd he bið þer. *c* **1300** *Havelok* 991 Als he was strong, so was he softe. **1390** GOWER *Conf.* I. 371 Thou schalt be soft in compaignie, Withoute Contek or Folhaste. *c* **1430** *Pilgr. Lyf Manhode* I. xv. (1869) 10 Softe he shulde be that hath it, For of to gret rudeshipe mys befalleth. **1533** BELLENDEN *Livy* I. xi. (S.T.S.) I. 68 Na pepill was sa gracius and soft in pvnissing of þare transgressouris or subdittis as þai wer. **1596** DALRYMPLE tr. *Leslie's Hist. Scot.* (S.T.S.) II. 223 This king..saw that as seueir punisment drewe vicious persounis frome vice; sa to be saft, and ouersie, prouokes thame daylie mair. **1612** T. TAYLOR *Comm. Titus* iii. 2 A soft man is..one that will not be so hard in his dealing, as sometime by strict lawe he might. **1697** DRYDEN *Virg. Georg.* IV. 776 The soft Napæan Race will soon relent Their Anger, and remit the Punishment. **1751** CHESTERF. *Lett.* ccxlv. (1792) III. 125 At the first impulse of passion be silent, till you can be soft. **1844** DICKENS *Mart. Chuz.* xxvii, The law being hard upon us, we're not exactly soft upon B. **1852** THACKERAY *Esmond* I. xiv, He..was very soft and gentle with the children. **1890** 'R. BOLDREWOOD' *Colonial Reformer* (1891) 314 They now began to consider that..Neuchamp had been considerate, or, in their phraseology, 'soft,' to an extent altogether unprecedented.

**b.** Of animals: Gentle, docile; lacking in spirit.

*c* **1200** ORMIN 1312 Forr lamb is sofſte & stille deor, & meoc, & milde. **1398** TREVISA *Barth. De P.R.* XVIII. c. (W. de W. 1495) 846 Whan he [a bull] is tyed vnder a fyg tree he lesyth and leueth all his fyersnesse and is sodenly sobre and softe. [*c* **1515** *Cocke Lorell's B.* 1 She is as softe as a lamme yf one do her meue.] **1891** *Pall Mall G.* 15 Sept. 2/3 An English jockey speaks with contempt of 'a soft brute'; when a toreador..speaks of a soft brute, he says it has 'drunk mud'.

**c.** Gentle *in* speech or looks.

*a* **1300** *Cursor M.* 24078 (Edinb.), Fair he wes and fre,.. Soft in speche. **1400** tr. *Secreta Secret., Gov. Lordsh.* 117 þat man ys..wel dysposyd in kynde, þat..ys..softe yn lokynge. **1422** *Ibid., Priv. Priv.* 139 A kynge sholde be good of Speche and Softe in worde.

†**d.** Quiet; not making a noise. *Obs.*

*a* **1430** *Stans Puer* 55 in *Babees Bk.*, At mete & at soper kepe þee stille & softe. *c* **1440** *Promp. Parv.* 462/2 Softe, or esy wythe owte grete dene,..*tranquillus*. *a* **1536** *Proverbs* in *Songs, Carols*, etc. (E.E.T.S.) 130 Besy in stody be þou, child,..& at bedde, softe & sadde.

**e.** Not rigid or severe; lax, yielding. Cf. 11 b.

*a* **1715** BURNET *Own Time* (1734) II. 29 Lord Ancram said I might be what I pleased, if I would be a little softer in the points of religion. **1718** HICKES & NELSON *Kettlewell* III. 315 Some..think him herein too Rigid:..Others have censured him for being too Soft.

**9. a.** Of disposition, look, etc.: Gentle, mild; indicative of a mild or gentle character.

*c* **1200** ORMIN 1461 ȝiff þin herrte iss arefull, & milde, & sofſte, & nesshe. **1377** LANGL. *P. Pl.* B. VIII. 117 Sadde of his semblaunt and of soft chiere. **1390** GOWER *Conf.* I. 83 For feigned semblant is so softe, Unethes love may be war. **1533** BELLENDEN *Livy* II. xi. (S.T.S.) I. 169 Seruilius.., ane man of mare soft Ingyne, said þe myndis of pepill mycht be mare eselie bowit þan brokin. **1818** SCOTT *Br. Lamm.* x, A flush of less soft expression..resumed predominance when he mentioned how meanly he was provided for the entertainment of his guests. **1849** MACAULAY *Hist. Eng.* V. I. 591 Those soft and pleasing features which had won so many hearts. **1880** 'OUIDA' *Moths* 280 She found his soft, pensive eyes looking at her.

**b.** Of qualities, feelings, etc.: Characterized by gentleness or tenderness.

*c* **1200** ORMIN 2899 Swa þatt te millce nohht ne be To sofſte, ne to nesshe. **1593** SHAKS. *Lucr.* 595 Soft pity enters at an iron gate. **1723** RAMSAY *Fair Assembly* x, Belinda.. strikes with love and saft surprise, Where e'er she turns her een. **1746** HERVEY *Medit.* (1818) 147 A heart susceptible of the softest, most compassionate emotions. **1781** COWPER *Table-T.* 484 If human woes her soft attention claim.

**10.** Of words, language, etc.: **a.** Ingratiating, soothing, bland; tender, sentimental.

*c* **1375** *Sc. Leg. Saints* xlv. (*Christina*) 46 þane hir fadire kissit hir ofte, & gluthryt hir with vordis softe. **1390** GOWER *Conf.* I. 72 He with softe wordes milde Conforteth hire. **1535** COVERDALE *Prov.* v. 3 For the lippes of an harlot are a droppinge hony combe, and hir throte is softer then oyle. **1548** UDALL, etc. *Erasm. Par. Luke* 193 b, Is it not a woorde softer then honey, to saie haill maister? **1608** SHAKS. *Per.* IV. iv. 45 No visor does become black villany So well as soft and tender flattery. **1711** STEELE *Spect.* No. 118 ¶2 The Huntsman..whispered the softest Vows of Fidelity in her Ear, and cried [etc.]. **1773** GOLDSM. *Stoops to Conq.* II, What soft things are you saying to your cousin? **1782** MISS BURNEY *Cecilia* II. iii, Can you conjecture who was making these soft speeches? **1842** LOVER *Handy Andy* xxxiv, The coaxing tones of Bridget's voice, inviting Andy, in the softest words, to go to bed. **1865** TROLLOPE *Belton Est.* ix. 94 He was fond of saying soft things which were intended to have no meaning.

**b.** Free from roughness or harshness; tending to tone down or minimize something unpleasant.

**1388** WYCLIF *Prov.* xv. 1 A soft answere brekith ire. *c* **1446** LYDG. *Two Nightingale Poems* 25 Whan he was brought to examynacioun: A soft Aunswere without rebellioun. *c* **1450** *St. Cuthbert* (Surtees) 350 þe bischope mode was all mesyd, þe whene with soft wordes he plesyd. **1660** WATERHOUSE *Arms & Arm.* 38 'Tis very convenient to use a soft Pen, and to offer probable truth with no dictator-like confidence. **1710** ADDISON *Whig Examiner* No. 5 ¶3 They have stated this case in the softest and most palatable terms it will bear. **1753–4** RICHARDSON *Grandison* III. xxvii. 286 You have soft words for hard meanings. **1838** THIRLWALL *Greece* IV. 161 Ambassadors were sent to Agis, to propose alliance with Sparta—a softer term for subjection. **1869** TROLLOPE *He Knew*, etc. xxxii. (1878) 183 If there was anything in what your wife did to offend you, a soft word from you would have put it all right.

**c.** Expressive of what is tender or peaceful. Also *transf.* of a writer.

*a* **1704** T. BROWN *Praise Drunkenness* Wks. 1730 I. 37 Anacreon was famous for a bottle, as he was soft and pleasing in his poetry. **1712** ADDISON *Spectator* No. 369 ¶19 Some Passages are beautiful by being Sublime, others by being Soft. **1743** FRANCIS tr. *Hor., Odes* I. xvi. 26 Shall the Muse again To softer Numbers tune her melting Strain.

**11. a.** Of actions, means, etc.: Gentle or moderate in character; carried on, performed, etc., without harshness, severity, or violence.

**1495** *Act 11 Hen. VII*, c. 2 Preamble, Of his pitie intending to reduce theym therunto by softer meanes then by such extreme rigour. **1588** KYD *Househ. Phil.* Wks. (1901) 260 To aduise thee..not [to] bring them vp vnder so soft and easie discipline as they become..milke sops. **1607** SHAKS. *Cor.* III. ii. 82 Thou,..being bred in broyles, Hast not the soft way, which..Were fit for thee to vse. **1670** CLARENDON *Contempl. Ps.* Tracts (1727) 605 Since they will not entertain that soft approach of his grace towards their conversion, he hath a rougher remedy to apply. **1742** GRAY *Propertius* I. 3 Still may his Bard in softer fights engage. **1754** —— *Progr. Poesy* 16 The..Frantic Passions hear thy soft controul. **1784** COWPER *Task* III. 510 When the temper'd heat..may afford Soft fomentation, and invite the seed. **1837** CARLYLE *Fr. Rev.* I. v. i, The two fly-wheels whirl in the softest manner. **1888** BRYCE *Amer. Commw.* III. lxxxvii. 161 They are disposed to try soft means at first.

**b.** In comparative use: Less rigid or strict.

**1718** HICKES & NELSON *Kettlewell* III. lxxiv. 388 He had been prevailed upon..to take the New Oath according to the Softer Sense.

**c.** *Pol.* Designating a comparatively moderate or centrist section of a political party, or the section of the political spectrum which lies between the 'hard' or extreme faction and the centre. Chiefly as *soft left*. Contr. with HARD *a.* 12 d.

**1977** *Economist* 1 Oct. 16/1 Unless the party's election rules were changed it would still be unlikely that Labour MPs would turn to Mr Tony Benn as their leader, but the chances of their choosing a 'soft left' candidate would be strong. *Ibid.* 29 Oct. 12/2 To introduce capital punishment ..would merely be a way of pressganging many members of Germany's soft left into the thinning ranks of its hard one. **1980** *Ibid.* 27 Sept. 79/2 Mr. Peter Shore, regarded as moderate-to-soft left, has just made a philosophical pitch to be a serious contender. **1985** *N.Y. Times Mag.* 18 Aug. 8/4 Neo-con Daniel Patrick Moynihan, a soft-right, near-left Democrat, objected years ago to the Communist assumption of such words as people's, democratic, [etc.]. **1986** *Times* 25 Feb. 13/1 In his action against the Militants, Mr. Kinnock has had the support of the soft Left.

**12.** Of the hand, etc.: Touching lightly or gently.

Sense 19 is also implied.

**1650** R. STAPYLTON *Strada's Low-C. Wars* I. 24 An incision pains the less when made by a soft hand. **1667** MILTON *P.L.* IV. 471, I will bring thee where no shadow staies..thy soft imbraces. **1743** FRANCIS tr. *Hor., Odes* I. xxiv. 22 What though you can the Lyre command, And sweep its Tones with softer Hand Than Orpheus. **1820** SHELLEY *Hymn Merc.* xxv, Right through the temple..He went with soft light feet. **1901** *N. Amer. Rev.* Feb. 162 The soft hand of the Americans is not as good as the mailed fist of the Germans.

**III. 13. a.** Yielding readily to emotions of a tender nature; easily affected or moved in this way; impressionable. Also *absol.* of persons.

*c* **1205** LAY. 24220 þer custe uader þene sune,..suster custe suster; þa softere heom wes an heorten. *c* **1489** CAXTON *Sonnes of Aymon* iv. 127 His herte wexed softe, & began to wepe full sore. **1588** SHAKS. *L.L.L.* IV. iii. 337 Loues feeling is more soft and sensible, Then are the tender hornes of.. Snayles. **1713** STEELE *Guardian* No. 17 ¶7 Concerning the Soft disposition and generosity of his master. **1747** *Gentl. Mag.* Apr. 194/1 The soft lamented, and the brave approv'd. **1837** CARLYLE *Fr. Rev.* I. II. i, The soft young heart adopts orphans. **1849** MACAULAY *Hist. Eng.* viii. II. 320 His graceful manners,..his soft heart, his open hand, were universally praised. **1880** MRS. L. B. WALFORD *Troublesome Daughters* I. ix. 187 He found himself quite soft on the subject.

**b.** In figurative expressions, as *to have a soft spot in one's heart*, etc. Hence phr. *to have a soft spot for*, to have a tender regard for, be fond of. (See also 19 c.)

**1679** ALSOP *Melius Inq.* II. viii. 361 A tender-Conscienced Person is one that has a Soft place in's Head. **1753** MISS COLLIER *Art Torment.* II. iii. (1811) 135 The man who has a soft place in his heart. **1857** C. M. YONGE *Dynevor Terrace* I. xi. 160 Jane has a soft spot in her heart, and will not think true love is confined within the rank that keeps a gig. **1885** *Cent. Mag.* XXX. 380/2 [He] had rather a soft spot in his heart for Violet. **1887** *Times* (weekly ed.) 30 Sept. 8/2 Cave ..had got the softer side of some of the doorkeepers of the House of Commons. **1902** [see SPOT *sb.*[1] 10 b]. **1947** K. TENNANT *Lost Haven* i. 24 She always did have a soft spot for him. **1971** *New Scientist* 13 May 400/1 He won a scholarship advertised in New Scientist and has had a soft spot for the magazine ever since.

**c.** *to be soft on* or *upon* (a person), to be in love with; to regard amorously or sentimentally.

**1840** THACKERAY *Barber Cox* Jan., Orlando and my girl, who were mighty soft upon one another. **1860** —— *Lovel* vi, I was not a little soft upon her myself, that's the truth. **1888** 'R. BOLDREWOOD' *Robbery under Arms* II. ix. 157, I always thought she was rather soft on Jim.

**14. a.** Easily influenced or swayed; having little power of resistance to the influence of other persons or things; facile, compliant. Also *absol.* of persons.

*c* **1250** *Owl & Night.* 1350 þah sum wif beo of nesche mode, For wimmen beoþ of softe blode. **1535** COVERDALE *Job* xxiii. 16 For in so moch as he is God, he maketh my herte soft: and seynge that he is Allmightie, he putteth me in feare. **1558** KNOX *First Blast* (Arb.) 24 Womankinde is imprudent and soft, (or flexible),..because she is easelie bowed. **1639** SALTMARSH *Policy* 178 In a businesse of passion and affection be suspitious of yourselfe and company, for in such cases you are most open and soft to advantages. **1648–9** *Eikon Bas.* 116 Divines, (of so soft and servile tempers, as disposed them to so sudden acting and compliance). **1751** JOHNSON *Rambler* No. 162 ¶5 Many..who select for friendship and confidence not..the virtuous, but the soft, the civil, and compliant. **1813** SCOTT *Rokeby* I. xxiv, A heart too soft from early life To hold with fortune needful strife. **1849** MACAULAY *Hist. Eng.* V. I. 543 His soft mind had, as usual, taken an impress from the society which surrounded him.

**b.** Weak, effeminate, unmanly.

**1593** SHAKS. *3 Hen. VI*, II. ii. 57 Cheere vp your spirits, our foes are nye, And this soft courage makes your Followers faint. **1620** E. BLOUNT *Horæ Subsec.* 82 In women, and men of soft and effeminated affections. **1628** HOBBES *Thucydides* (1822) 94 The Lacedemonians..ever looked sourly on soft and loose behaviour. **1663** S. PATRICK *Parab. Pilgr.* (1687) 487 [To] keep our selves above the soft pleasures of the flesh into which we are apt to sink. **1716** POPE *Iliad* VI. 362 Sidonian maids..Whom from soft Sidon youthful Paris bore. **1776** GIBBON *Decl. & F.* xii. (1782) I. 413 He was soft yet cruel; devoted to pleasure, but destitute of taste. **1801** STRUTT *Sports & Past.* Introd. p. xi, Violent exercises.. grew out of fashion.., and the education..became proportionably more soft and delicate. **1872** *Routledge's Ev. Boy's Ann.* 455/1 It looks so soft to say you won't fight.

**c.** Refined, delicate. *rare.*

**1601** SHAKS. *Twel. N.* V. i. 331 For your seruice done him, ..So farre beneath your soft and tender breeding. **1604** —— *Ham.* V. ii. 112 (Q.[2]), An absolute gentleman,..of very soft society, and great showing. **1693** EVELYN *De la Quint. Compl. Gard.* I. 58 They say in a pretty popular manner, that..it is impossible to afford them too much Kindness, which is the soft and sparkish Expression they use in speaking of what we vulgarly call Dung.

†**15.** Lax or slack in duty. *Obs.*[−1]

*c* **1386** CHAUCER *Doctor's T.* 101 Under a schepherd softe and necligent, The wolf hath many a schep and lamb torent.

**16. a.** Of a weakly or delicate constitution; not strong or robust; incapable of much physical endurance or exertion.

[**1596** SHAKS. *Tam. Shr.* V. ii. 165 Why are our bodies soft, and weake, and smooth, Vnapt to toyle and trouble.] **1661** LOVELL *Hist. Anim. & Min.* Isagoge c b, Soft and sedentary men must abstaine from it, it being fit only for porters, ploughmen, and mariners. **1697** DRYDEN *Virg. Georg.* I. 685 There Euphrates her soft Off-spring arms. **1781** COWPER *Anti-Thelyphth.* 177 She, regardless of her softer kind, Seiz'd fast the saddle. **1842** COMBE *Digestion* 294 If the individual..is of a soft, sluggish, lymphatic temperament, which stands in need of a healthy stimulus. **1850** MRS. JAMESON *Leg. Monast. Orders* (1863) 46 In those days the coasts of England were, to the soft Italians, a kind of Siberia for distance and desolation. **1888** 'R. BOLDREWOOD' *Robbery under Arms* I. xi. 135 Our horses had been doing nothing lately, and..had, of course, got fat, and were rather soft.

**b.** *colloq.* (See quot.)

**1898** SIR G. ROBERTSON *Chitral* xxxii. 352 The conviction that our troops were broken in spirit—what in India is expressively called soft.

**17.** *the soft(er) sex*, the female sex.

**1648** J. BEAUMONT *Psyche* XIV. i, The softer sex, attending Him And His still-growing woes with tenderer eyes. **1716** POPE *Iliad* V. 435 The king insults the goddess as she flies: ..'Go, let thy own soft sex employ thy care'. **1724** SWIFT *Acc. Wood's Exec.* Misc. 1735 V. 317 Those of the softer Sex who attended the Ceremony. **1833** RITCHIE *Wand. by Loire* 128 That sex, which men call the softer, will dare the very devil, when occasion calls. **1838** LYTTON *Alice* 157 In addition to those qualities which please the softer sex, Legard was a good whist player.

**18. a.** More or less foolish, silly, or simple; lacking ordinary intelligence or common-sense; easily imposed upon or deceived. Also *dial.* or *colloq.*, mentally deficient, half-witted.

**1621** BURTON *Anat. Mel.* I. ii. III. xv. (1651) 130 Your greatest Students are commonly no better, silly, soft fellows. *Ibid.* IV. iv. 149 He made soft fellows stark noddies, and such as were foolish quite mad. *a* **1700** B. E. *Dict. Cant. Crew*, *Soft*, foolish. **1725** BAILEY *Erasm. Colloq.* 277 This is the only Thing that he's soft in; he's sharp as a Needle in anything else. **1775** MISS BURNEY *Early Diary* (1889) II. 124 He looks very soft, in the most extensive meaning of the word; *c'est à dire*, in temper, person, and head. **1835** MARRYAT *J. Faithful* xxv, A good sort of chap enough, but rather soft in the upper-works. **1867** TROLLOPE *Chron. Barset* I. 12 One of the Grantlys was, to say the least of it, very soft.

**b.** *dial.* Stupefied or muddled with drink.

**1836–** in dial. glossaries and texts (*Eng. Dial. Dict.*).

**c.** *colloq.* Foolishly kind, benevolent, considerate, etc.

**1890** 'R. BOLDREWOOD' *Col. Reformer* (1891) 261 Helping other people along the road of life..a thundering soft thing it is, in a general way. *Ibid.* 315 He..did a soft thing in bringing these chaps here.

**d.** *to be* or *go soft on*: to be or become excessively lenient or partial to.

**1883** 'MARK TWAIN' *Life on Mississippi* xxxiv. 373 If he was soft on the Arkansas mosquitoes, he was hard enough on the mosquitoes of Lake Providence to make up for it. **1911** G. B. SHAW *Shewing-up of Blanco Posnet* 405 Why did He make me go soft on the child if He was going hard on it Himself? **1959** *New Statesman* 30 May 751 Why..were we all 'going soft' on Dulles? **1971** *Guardian* 19 Nov. 13/7 In the eyes of the militants, the Guardian is still 'soft on the rebels'.

**IV. 19. a.** Presenting a yielding surface to the touch; not offering absolute resistance to pressure.

*a* **1240** *Ureisun* in *O.E. Hom.* I. 187 Hwet deþ þenne þi blod isched on þe rode, hwet deþ þenne þe large broc of þi softe side? *c* **1250** *Gen. & Ex.* 335 Ðanne is tis fruit wel swiðe good, fair on siȝðhe and softe on hond. *a* **1300** *Cursor M.* 25491 Iesus, þat wald..suffer..Boffetes on þi soft chin.

?*a* **1366** Chaucer *Rom. Rose* 556 Ther nis a fairer nekke, y-wis, To fele how smothe and softe it is. *c* **1440** *Promp. Parv.* 462/2 Softe and smothe, *lenis, planus.* **1508** Dunbar *Tua Mariit Wemen* 28, I saw thre gay ladeis,.. Quhyt seimlie, and soft, as the sweit lillies. **1599** Shaks. *Hen. V*, ii. iii. 61 Touch her soft mouth, and march. **1637** Bp. Hall *Remedy Prophanenesse* ii. §13. 178 The hand that was at the first soft, and tender, after it hath beene inured to worke, growes brawned, and impenetrable. **1700** Dryden *Ovid's Met., Acis, Polyph. & Galatea* 75 More sleek thy Skin,.. And softer to the touch, than down of Swans. **1741–2** Gray *Agrip.* 95 Knows his soft ear the trumpet's thrilling voice. **1847** Tennyson *Princess* vii. 121 Softer all her shape And rounder seem'd. **1896** tr. *Boas' Text-bk. Zool.* 229 The legs arise.. from the soft, lateral portions of the segment.

**b.** Of the pulse. (Cf. hard *a.* 3.)

**1728** Chambers *Cycl.* s.v. *Pulse*, A hard Pulse signifies, 1. That the Membrane of the Artery is dryer than ordinary:.. 3. That the Arteries are full [etc.]. A soft Pulse denotes the contrary to all these. **1834** *Good's Study Med.* (ed. 4) I. 545 If a pulse be small and soft together, then it must be considered as weak. **1843** R. J. Graves *Syst. Clin. Med.* x. 113 A soft slow pulse.

**c.** fig. ***soft spot***, a weak or vulnerable place. (see also 13 b.)

**1933** [see infiltration 1 e]. **1956** A. L. Rowse *Early Churchills* 239 The French.. withdrew behind their fortifications... Marlborough was all for an assault on these; he had proved and found a soft spot opposite Ramillies. **1958** *Engineering* 21 Mar. 361/1 Even if the country as a whole was in the best of economic health, the local soft spots could not be ignored without serious political repercussions. **1965** H. I. Ansoff *Corporate Strategy* vii. 126 If the problem appears as a minor 'soft spot' in an otherwise healthy product-market position, temporary *ad hoc* arrangement.. may suffice. **1975** *Times Lit. Suppl.* 17 Oct. 1233/3 There is probably much truth in Mr Levison's analysis.., but his obvious sincerity and dedication mask a few soft spots in the argument.

**d.** *Mil.* Of a military vehicle: unarmoured. Of a missile base: vulnerable to a direct nuclear explosion because of its construction or location.

**1944** A. Jacob *Traveller's War* vii. 129 The tanks crunch forward like a battle fleet: our 'soft' vehicles in the middle of the phalanx, with the armoured cars of the Dragoon Guards moving on both flanks. **1948** Partridge *Dict. Forces' Slang 1939–45* 175 *Soft-skinned vehicles; soft stuff*, unarmoured vehicles. (Army.) Both of these terms started as slang; the latter remained unofficial, although it did become colloquial; the former very rapidly became colloquial and then official. **1958** [see hard *a.* (*sb.*) 14 f]. **1961** E. Burgess *Long-Range Ballistic Missiles* vi. 182 All forms of long-range missiles now appear to be developing towards the abandonment of the soft base, but there are.. difficulties associated with the hardening concept. **1972** *Dict. Military & Associated Terms* (U.S. Department of Defense) 275/2 *Soft missile base*, a launching base that is not protected against a nuclear explosion.

**e.** *Physics.* Of a mode of vibration in a crystal lattice: such that its frequency decreases to zero as the temperature of the crystal approaches that of a phase transition.

**1964** *Physical Rev.* CXXXVI. a. 429/1 Cochran proposed a theory which links the cause of ferroelectricity in the perovskites to the existence of a temperature-dependent 'soft' lattice vibrational mode. **1967** *Ibid.* CLVII. 396/1 The energy of this soft mode can be extracted from reflectivity measurements in the infrared region. **1973** G. R. Wilkinson in A. Anderson *Raman Effect* II. xi. 813 A number of 'soft' modes of vibration whose frequencies depend upon temperature have been found.

**20. a.** Of cloth, hair, or similar substances: Of a yielding texture, pleasant to the feel or touch; also, capable of being easily folded or put into a different form; flexible.

*c* **1205** Lay. 22763 Water me brohte.., seoððen claðes soften al of white seolke. **1382** Wyclif *Matt.* xi. 8 Loo! thei that ben clothid with softe thingis [**1388** softe clothis] ben in housis of kyngis. *c* **1385** Chaucer *L.G.W.* 1721 *Lucretia*, This noble wif sat by hire beddys side.. And softe wolle.. she wroughte. **1450–80** tr. *Secreta Secret.* 39 And the heer be fulle and softe, that man is deboner. **1508** Dunbar *Tua Mariit Wemen* 96 Soft and soupill as the silk. **1567** *Gude & Godlie Ball.* (S.T.S.) 196 Preistis, leif ȝour pryde, Ȝour skarlet and ȝour veluote soft. **1615** G. Sandys *Trav.* 15 A white soft Bombast intermixed with seeds. **1725** *Fam. Dict.* s.v. *Hair*, If you would have the Hair grow long and soft. **1784** Cowper *Task* i. 11 Satin smooth, Or velvet soft, or plush with shaggy pile. **1788** —— *Gratitude* 17 These carpets, so soft to the foot. **1879** F. Pollok *Sport Brit. Burmah* I. 234 Leather.. which must be kept soft by oil and elbow grease. **1887** Lowell *Democracy* 34 [To] walk along Piccadilly at the height of the Season in a soft hat.

*fig.* **1780** Cowper *Progr. Err.* 313 Caught in a delicate soft silken net By some lewd earl.

**b.** ***soft wares***, or ***goods***, (*a*) woollen or cotton fabrics, such as cretonne, chintz, lace, muslin, velvet, etc., or articles made of these; also ***soft furnishing***(*s*). (*b*) *Comm.*, designating relatively perishable consumer goods such as clothes, foods, and drugs; *spec.* in the commodity market, used of commodities produced from vegetables, such as textiles, rubber, and foodstuffs.

**1833** *Chambers's Edin. Jrnl.* I. 385/3, I could occasionally hear a detached sentence on politics.. the price of stocks—soft goods. **1851** Mayhew *London Labour* I. 378 The most primitive kind of packmen, or hawkers of soft-wares. **1894** *Westm. Gaz.* 27 Sept. 8/2 Lectures intended for those engaged in the soft goods trade. **1898** *Daily News* 8 Jan. 7/3 A traveller in soft goods for an old-established London firm. **1925** *Daily Tel.* 13 May 20/6 Soft furnishing department. **1927** *Ibid.* 11 May 18/6 Manageress wanted... Must have thorough experience in the sale and scheme side of soft furnishings. **1946** *Sun* (Baltimore) 5 Oct. 2/6 These points stand out with respect to the production of 'soft' consumer goods (clothing, food, drugs and the like). **1961** *Ann. Reg. 1960* 502 The value of retail sales rose by 4 per cent, a higher demand for 'soft' goods more than offsetting the drop in purchases of durable household goods. **1967** E. Short *Embroidery & Fabric Collage* iii. 78 Probably the most useful and versatile object in soft furnishings is the cushion. **1976** L. Deighton *Twinkle, twinkle, Little Spy* xvi. 169 She did nothing except sink lower in the soft furnishings and continue to drink. **1979** *Daily Tel.* 9 Oct. 21 While the metal markets continue their volatile course the 'soft' commodities, with the notable exception of sugar, have largely been untouched by the urge to get out of the dollar and currencies in general.

**c.** *U.S.* Of paper money. (Cf. hard *a.* 2.) Also *attrib.*

**1831** T. L. Peacock *Crotchet Castle* xi, The notes of Touch-andgo and Company, soft cash, are now the exclusive currency of all this vicinity. **1878** *N. Amer. Rev.* CXXVII. 103 A Western Democrat on a soft-money platform. **1893** *Daily News* 16 June 2/3 Mr. Cleveland.. found himself compelled to give the hot-headed partisans of 'soft' money a sharp lesson.

**21.** Of a bed, pillow, etc.: Readily yielding to the weight of the body; into or upon which one sinks or settles down comfortably.

*c* **1250** *Owl & Night.* 644 Mi nest is holeuh & rum amidde, So hit is softest myne bridde. *c* **1275** *Sinners Beware* 284 in *O.E. Misc.*, Ye me fedde.. And leyden in softe bedde þo ic a-mong eu eode. **1340** *Ayenb.* 47 Þe zofte bed cloþes,.. and alle manyere eyse of bodye. **1588** Kyd *Househ. Phil.* Wks. (1901) 284 There in a very soft bed I bequeathed my bones to rest. **1599** Shaks. *Hen. V*, iv. i. 14 A good soft Pillow for that good white Head. **1607** —— *Cor.* v. iii. 53 With no softer Cushion then the Flint I kneele before thee. **1667** Milton *P.L.* iv. 334 As they sat recline On the soft downie Bank. **1781** Cowper *Table-T.* 678 He laid his head in luxury's soft lap. **1784** —— *Task* i. 75 Ingenious fancy.. devis'd The soft settee. **1830** Tennyson *Merman* iii, Soft are the moss-beds under the sea. *c* **1885** Rossetti *Sick Child's Medit.* ii. Poems (1904) 263/2 Thou, O Lord, in pain, hadst no pillow soft.

*transf.* **1450–80** *Secreta Secret.* 29 Thingis that makith the body fatte,.. as wyn that is dowsett,.. and slepe aftir mete, soft liyng, and alle good odoures. **1784** Cowper *Task* i. 82 By soft recumbency of outstretch'd limbs. **1819** Scott *Ivanhoe* ii, If the reverend fathers.. loved good cheer and soft lodging.

**22.** Of ground: **a.** Yielding agreeably to the feet.

*c* **1200** Ormin 9666 Þær shall nu newenn greȝȝþedd beon Full smeþe & soffte weȝȝe. ?*a* **1366** Chaucer *Rom. Rose* 128 The medewe softe, swote, and grene, Beet right on the water-syde. **1815** Shelley *Alastor* 448 Soft mossy lawns Beneath these canopies extend their swells.

**b.** Insufficiently hard; allowing a vehicle, person, etc., to sink in, esp. through excess of wet.

**1523** Fitzherb. *Husb.* §5 On marreis ground and soft ground the other wheles be better. **1765** Dickson *Treat. Agric.* (ed. 2) 73 The pasture of plants is enlarged, both in hard and soft land, by stirring and turning it over. *Ibid.* 74 Soft marshy land, by being frequently ploughed, becomes more firm and solid. **1812** *New Bot. Gard.* I. 98 In soft boggy situations. **1816** Scott *Bl. Dwarf* iii, The bog is no abune knee-deep, and better a saft road as bad company. **1872** 'Idstone' [T. Pearce] *The Dog* vi. 58 When the track was plain upon mud or soft ground.

**c.** Of a fall: Made on a soft substance, or in such a way as to escape injury. In quots. *fig.*

**1587** *Mirr. Mag., Rudacke* x, Who climeth so highe, his fall is not soft. **1837** Carlyle *Fr. Rev.* i. iii. viii, Remains only that the Court.. shall make his fall soft.

**d.** *Astronautics.* Of a landing made by a spacecraft: slow enough for no serious damage to be incurred. Chiefly in soft landing *vbl. sb.*

**1958** *Times* 28 Mar. 10/3 Next (in difficulty) would be a 'soft' (controlled) landing [on the moon] by an unmanned vehicle. **1966** E. Burgess *Assault on Moon* v. 151 A soft lunar landing is the landing of a payload on the Moon with a small shock to that payload. **1975** *Daily Tel.* 11 Aug. 11/4 One vehicle will make a soft touchdown on Mars while the large spacecraft which carried it on its journey will remain in orbit.

**e.** Of a substance: readily magnetized by an ambient magnetic field but retaining no permanent magnetization in the absence of such a field.

**1839** G. Bird *Nat. Philos.* 259 If a bar of soft iron be bent in the shape of the letter U. **1873** J. C. Maxwell *Electr. & Magn.* (1881) II. 44 If the magnetic properties of the iron depend entirely on the magnetic force of the field in which it is placed.. it is called soft iron. **1900** *Jrnl. Iron & Steel Inst.* LVII. 403 The author divides the different varieties of iron and steel into those which are magnetically 'soft' and those which are magnetically 'hard'. **1948** F. Brailsford *Magnetic Materials* iv. 69 The most important source of internal strains in the higher grade soft magnetic materials is that due to the presence of impurities held in solution in the metal. **1976** *Nature* 5 Feb. 381/1 In a few cases large randomly directed magnetically soft components were removed in low alternating fields.

**f.** Of glass: softening at a relatively low temperature when heated.

**1925** Hodkin & Cousen *Textbk. Glass Technol.* vi. 51 A.. vessel of soft soda-lime glass in which water is boiled, will liberate so much alkali in 15 minutes as to make impossible correct titrations with decinormal solutions. **1961** G. R. Choppin *Exper. Nuclear Chem.* viii. 121 Since Pyrex glass contains boron.. it is better to use a soft glass tube to hold the source. **1965** Phillips & Williams *Inorg. Chem.* I. xiv. 545 Soft glasses are made by adding soda to the silica. About 25 per cent soda reduces the viscosity of a glass by a factor of $10^{10}$.

**g.** Of a contact lens: made of a soft, yielding material.

**1964** *Highlights Ophthalm.* VII. 252 (*heading*) The new hydrophilic gel, soft, contact lenses. **1971** *Time* 31 May 46, I intend using the soft lenses on every patient I possibly can. **1978** H. Hamand in M. Ruben *Soft Contact Lenses* viii. 128 The thickness of cornea of a rabbit was found to increase by 20% with 17 h of hard lens wear and about 5% with soft lens.

**23. a.** Of a yielding consistency; composed of, or forming, a substance which may easily be moulded or compressed without disintegration.

*c* **1400** tr. *Secreta Secret., Gov. Lordsh.* 68 And whenne a body ys þicke and drye, softe metys and moyste er goode þerto. *a* **1425** tr. *Arderne's Treat. Fistula*, etc. 60 Blode is norischyng of al membrez, als wele of sadde as of softe. **1474** Caxton *Chesse* iii. v. (1883) 123 For the women ben likened vnto softe waxe or softe ayer. *a* **1536** *Proverbs* in *Songs, Carols*, etc. (E.E.T.S.) 132 Whote wortis make softe crustis. **1567** Maplet *Gr. Forest* 100 b, Whose flesh so soft and morsell sweete in all feastes is the hed. **1667** Milton *P.L.* i. 424 Spirits.. Can either Sex assume, or both; so soft And uncompounded is their Essence pure. **1687** Prior & Halifax *Hind & Panth. Transv.* P.'s Wks. 1892 II. 321 A milk-white mouse.. Fed on soft cheese. **1710** J. Clarke tr. *Rohault's Nat. Philos.* (1729) I. 123 A soft Body, which seems to be of a middle Nature betwixt a hard and a liquid Body. **1774** Goldsm. *Nat. Hist.* (1776) VI. 66 To suppose that they entered the rock while it was yet in a soft state. **1815** J. Smith *Panorama Sci. & Art* II. 415 By exposure to heat, potass becomes soft, and.. melts into a transparent glass. **1860** Tyndall *Glac.* i. vii. 48 The snow.. was moist and soft. **1899** *Allbutt's Syst. Med.* VIII. 581 For the scalp .. a soft ointment.. answers well.

**b.** In more or less specific uses (see quots.).

*soft roe*: see roe[2] 1.

**1601** Holland *Pliny* I. 332 Those in the sea which we call Soft-fishes, although they haue no bloud at all, as namely the Pour-cuttles or Polypes. **1745** P. Thomas *Jrnl. Anson's Voy.* 30 A Copper Oven.. for baking Soft-Bread. *Ibid.* 145 The Officers had always soft Bread new baked, which was much better than the Biscuit. **1856** *N. Brit. Rev.* XXVI. 168 If these be the causes of hard and soft cataract. **1889** *Pall Mall. G.* 28 May 3/1 All 'soft meat birds' are observant. I mean by soft meat—which is a birdcatchers' term—the feeders on grubs and worms and flies, rather than on seeds. **1899** *Daily News* 7 Dec. 11/1 The foggy weather had an effect on the carcases in general, rendering them what is called 'soft'.

**c.** Of a semi-fluid consistency.

**1703** Moxon *Mech. Exerc.* 262 In Summer time use your Morter as soft as you can, but in the Winter time pretty stiff or hard. **1791** *Phil. Trans.* LXXXI. 174 Workman keeps stirring and turning over the metal; in 3 m. it becomes soft and semi-fluid. **1898** Bolas *Glass Blowing* 132 An iron rod called a punty.., on the end of which is a mass of soft glass, is now attached to the elongated bulb.

**d.** Of oil: (see quots.).

**1885** *Encycl. Brit.* XVIII. 242 The several kinds of crude paraffin.. are classed as 'hard scale' or 'soft scale', according to their fusing points and consequent degrees of hardness at ordinary temperatures. **1887** Moloney *Forestry W. Africa* 43 In the trade it [palm-oil] is called 'hard' when it contains a larger proportion of 'stearine', 'soft' when it contains a smaller proportion.

**24. a.** Relatively inferior or deficient in hardness.

**1599** Hakluyt *Voy.* II. i. 253 Where there is a great market kept of Diamants, Rubies, Saphires, and many other soft stones. **1670** Pettus *Fodinæ Reg.* 5 And in these Veins of Metals and Minerals are often found Loadstones,.. Rough pearl and Soft diamond. **1815** J. Smith *Panorama Sci. & Art* I. 4 But if heated and cooled gradually, it becomes nearly as soft as pure iron. **1830** Lyell *Princ. Geol.* I. 216 The carbonates of iron, lime, and manganese are so dissolved, that the rock is rendered soft. **1847** Yeowell *Anc. Brit. Church* xii. 140 A head and face rudely carved in a soft stone. **1872** Raymond *Statist. Mines & Min.* 145 So far the mines have been easily worked, the gangue being as yet comparatively soft.

**b.** In specific uses, as ***soft bast***, ***brass***, ***burr*** (see burr *sb.*[5] 3), ***hammer***, ***metal***, ***paste***, ***porcelain***, ***steel***, ***stuff***. (See also paste *sb.* 3 b, porcelain 1 a note, solder *sb.*[1] 4.)

**1875** Bennett & Dyer tr. *Sachs' Bot.* 101 These cell-formations (cambiform, latticed cells, sieve-tubes) may, in combination with the phloëm-parenchyma in which they are imbedded,.. be included in the term **Soft-bast*, in opposition to the true bast. **1888** Jacobi *Printers' Vocab.* 128 **Soft brass*, brass rule which can be easily manipulated, specially manufactured for fancy work. **1964** S. Crawford *Basic Engin. Processes* i. 16 Hammers with heads made of lead, copper, rubber, or rawhide are known as *soft hammers. The head is usually in the form of a cast tube with a recess at each end to locate the soft inserts. **1977** G. Clark *World Prehistory* (ed. 3) v. 212 The introduction of the soft hammer technique resulted in the production of thinner bifaces. **1869** Rankine *Machine & Hand-tools* 63 **Soft metal*, for the bearings of shafts, consists of 50 parts of tin, 1 of copper, and 5 of antimony. **1848** H. R. Forster *Stowe Catal.* 8 Chantilly Porcelain is a fine kind of '*soft paste'. **1879** Soft paste [see paste *sb.* 3 b]. **1884** Knight *Dict. Mech.* Suppl. 828/2 *Soft Paste*, (Ceramics), a name applied to the material of porcelain, which is semi-hard only. **1819** A. Rees *Cycl.* XXVIII. s.v. *Porcelain*, The porcelain is made of these substances [*sc.* porcelain clay and felspar].. but other materials are employed to give the required transparency at a lower temperature. This has received the name of *soft porcelain. **1839** Ure *Dict. Arts* II. 1025 The manufacture of soft porcelain is longer and more difficult than that of hard. **1859** R. Hunt *Guide Mus. Pract. Geol.* (ed. 2) 92 The English porcelain is, what is called, soft porcelain, and is composed of three elements, Kaolin and Cornish China stone—with bone ashes. **1868** Joynson *Metals* 90 For *soft-steel, less than 1 per cent. [of charcoal] being required. **1827** Fitton in *Zool. Jrnl.* III. 416 The 'soft-stuff' [of the Stonesfield slate-beds], occupying about six inches, consists of yellowish very sandy clay, including thin courses of fibrous transparent gypsum.

**c.** ***soft coal***, (*a*) coal that is easily cleft; (*b*) a coal of low rank, usu. a bituminous or a brown coal.

**1789** J. WILLIAMS *Min. Kingd.* I. 232 Sometimes you can judge pretty near the crop or surface whether it will be a hard or soft coal. **1855** J. PHILLIPS *Man. Geol.* 190 'Soft' coal, where the cleat fissures are numerous and broken by cross cleat.

**1857** J. B. JUKES *Student's Man. Geol.* iv. 133 All these minute varieties are commonly included under four principal heads:—1, Caking coal; 2, Splint or hard coal; 3, Cherry or soft coal, and 4, Cannel or parrot coal. **1903** *Bull. U.S. Geol. Surv.* No. 213. 265 By far the largest part of the coal mined [in the Eastern Interior field] is soft bituminous, making a good steam fuel. **1926** J. ROBERTS *Mining Educator* I. 677/1 American cities where the use of 'soft' or smoky coal is forbidden by law. **1958** I. C. F. STATHAM *Coal Mining Practice* (1960) I. ii. 77 Practically all black coals, such as are worked in British coalfields, show banding of soft bright and hard dull coal.. parallel to the bedding. **1979** *Sci. Amer.* Jan. 28/3 Hard coal (anthracite and the various grades of bituminous coal) and soft coal (brown coal and lignite).

**25. a.** Applied to water, such as rain or river water, which is more or less free from calcium and magnesium salts. (Opposed to HARD *a.* 14 a.)

**1755** *Gentl. Mag.* XXV. 361 Keep this bason constantly filled with soft water. **1805** SAUNDERS *Min. Waters* 3 River Water.. is in general much softer and more free from earthy salts. **1878** RAMSAY *Phys. Geogr.* xxxii. 553 The water from the Welsh mountains is also in great part soft.

**b.** orig. *dial.* and *U.S.* Of beverages (usu. cold fruit drinks and the like): Non-alcoholic, non-spirituous.

**1880** in *Antrim & Down Gloss.* 95. **1894** *Outing* XXIV. 236/2 Each regiment had a 'canteen' of its own, where the men could buy.. soft drinks, beer, cigars, pipes, etc. **1911** *Chambers's Jrnl.* Feb. 111/2 In the matter of 'soft' drinks the chemist or druggist is not in it [in Canada]. **1919** P. B. CLAYTON *Tales Talbot House* 29 The House was always what the Canadians called a 'soft drink' establishment, but no one resented this, lapping up tea or cocoa or Bovril with thanksgiving. **1936** G. B. SHAW *Simpleton of Unexpected Isles* Prol. iii. 27 A feast of fruit and bread and soft drinks is spread on the ground. **1944** AUDEN *For Time Being* (1945) 113 Soft drinks and sandwiches may be had in the inns at reasonable prices. **1960** KOESTLER *Lotus & Robot* I. i. 36 A soft-drink cocktail party in the house of a leading Parsee politician. **1964** I. MURDOCH *Italian Girl* iii. 36 You haven't anything soft, ginger beer? All right, tomato juice. **1966** 'A. HALL' *9th Directive* xii. 116 The sun was hot.. soft-drinks men worked their way through [the crowd]. **1978** R. LUDLUM *Holcroft Covenant* xviii. 203 They had proceeded to a second hotel on the rue Chevalle, where a soft-drink sign provided him with a name for the registry: N. Fresca.

**c.** Of a detergent: biodegradable.

**1963** *New Scientist* 27 June 716/1 A soft detergent is one that is biologically soft; that is, readily oxidised in a modern sewage plant. *Ibid.* 717/1 In most western countries the consumption of soap, which is a soft detergent, remains fairly steady or is falling. **1966** *Economist* 23 July 385/1 Replacing this branched chain with a straight chain makes the detergent 'soft'—that is, easily munchable by the hard-working bugs. **1971** *Daily Tel.* 16 Oct. 10/6 The detergent industry switched over to 'soft', biodegradable detergents.

**26.** Of the weather, a day, etc.: Rainy, wet. Chiefly *Sc.* and *north. dial.*

**1812** SIR J. SINCLAIR *Syst. Husb. Scot.* I. Add. 11 If they [slugs] be attacked when on the surface of the ground, where they are every soft morning in search of food. **1828-** in many dial. glossaries, etc. **1829** SCOTT *Jrnl.* 12 July, The day excessively rainy, or, as we call it, soft. **1874** MRS. OLIPHANT *For Love & Life* (1880) 68 The day was fine, notwithstanding the prophecy of 'saft weather'.

**27. a.** *Electronics.* Of a thermionic valve or discharge tube: (*a*) having had an inert gas introduced into it at the time of manufacture in order to modify or enhance its performance; (*b*) containing gas at low pressure as a result of a leak or of outgassing by component parts. [tr. G. *weich*, used in sense (*a*) by W. C. Röntgen 1897, in *Sitzungsber. d. K. Preuss. Akad. d. Wissensch. zu Berlin* 584.]

**1899** [see HARD *a.* (*sb.*) 17 b]. **1901** *Phil. Trans. R. Soc.* CXCVI. 42 The value of $\lambda$ obtained.. for a much 'softer' bulb was ·001, or about four times the absorption of the bulb employed in these experiments. **1921** *Wireless World* 6 Aug. 288/2 One 'soft' triode will give as much amplification as two 'hard' valves. **1931** [see HARD *a.* (*sb.*) 17 b]. **1932** *Discovery* July 216/1 These hard valves were found to be very much more reliable and uniform in their action than earlier 'soft' valves. **1948** *Electronic Engin.* XX. 384/1 In recent years the soft valve (thyratron) counter has been replaced by the hard valve counter. **1956** G. A. MONTGOMERIE *Digital Calculating Machines* ix. 178 The soft valves are usually beam-switching tubes of the multicathode type.

**1919** R. D. BANGAY *Oscillation Valve* 203 There are several indications which enable one to tell when a valve is going 'soft'. The first is loss of power in the oscillatory circuit. **1929** DUNCAN & DREW *Radio Telegr. & Teleph.* xi. 214 The degree of vacuum in the tube would change and some tubes became soft (having less vacuum) while others became hard (having a higher vacuum, with little or no gas present). **1958** W. F. LOVERING *Radio Communication* viii. 173 A valve in which the vacuum is poor is said to be soft; the presence of a small number of molecules of gas adversely affects the performance.

**b.** *Physics.* Of X-rays and gamma rays: of relatively long wavelength and low penetrating power. Of sub-atomic particles: of relatively low energy.

Orig. so called because soft X-rays are emitted by a soft tube (see prec. sense).

**1901** *Phil. Trans. R. Soc.* CXCVI. 516 The radiation from the barium compound is enormously reduced by the interposition of so thin a screen as an ordinary piece of tinfoil; these 'soft' rays accordingly form much the greater part of the whole. **1925** *Proc. Cambr. Philos. Soc.* XXII. 834 The soft $\gamma$-radiation gave a well-marked spectrum containing two strong lines. **1940** *Nature* 20 July 94/2 The beryllium oxide was tested inside a counter so designed that even very soft particles could be detected. **1950** D. H. WILKINSON *Ionization Chambers & Counters* vi. 160 The use of a proportional counter for counting extremely soft electrons which give very few ion pairs, has been proposed. **1960** *Lebende Sprachen* V. 163/2 The soft X-rays emitted from television screens cause great concern among radiologists. **1978** *Nature* 30 Mar. 396/3 There are several isotopes.. which emit radiation sufficiently soft to be shielded even by the syringe wall but which can be presented in a form such that all the tissues of an animal become labelled a short time after injection.

**28.** Miscellaneous *transf.* and *fig.* uses. **a.** Of facts, information, etc.: insubstantial, impressionistic, imprecise (opp. HARD *a.* 7 b, c). Of a science or its method: not amenable to precise mathematical treatment or to experimental verification or refutation; *esp.* in ***soft science***.

**1923** *Sci. Amer.* Feb. 77/2 Its functions and its limitations are to get the facts from the bottom to the top of the coal industry, both hard and soft. **1966** *Time* 3 June 43 Project SIMILE Director Hall T. Sprague says these games are 'to the soft sciences what a laboratory is to the hard sciences of physics, chemistry and biology'. **1968** *Physics Bull.* Oct. 351/2 One of the striking features of the present time is the penetration of 'hard' methods (quantitative, physical analyses) into subjects which were hitherto 'soft' (descriptive, non-numerical). **1970** *Publishers' Weekly* 8 June 154 Hardscience is science (physics, math, chemistry), softscience is the humanities, sociology in particular. **1972** *Lancet* 25 Nov. 1138/1 Clinical departments.. must learn a new respect for the 'soft' data of sociology. **1976** *National Observer* (U.S.) 10 Apr. 20/5 *All the President's Men* is what reporters call a 'soft' story—breezily entertaining but short on hard facts. **1976** *Times Lit. Suppl.* 25 June 766/2 The soft areas in evolutionary theory, which he sorts into a series of Hegelian opposites: adaptive versus nonadaptive traits, [etc.]. **1980** *Dædalus* Spring 94 One might view these various expressions.. spanning (from the 'hard' end) science, history and anthropology.. to (at the 'soft' end) dreams and personal fantasy. **1982** *Daily Tel.* 23 Apr. 22 Most academic articles in all the sciences (hard and soft) are read by very few people.

**b.** *Comm.* Of markets, commodities, etc.: depressed, characterized by falling prices or excess supply. (Cf. FIRM *a.* 7 a.)

**1930** *Morning Post* 19 Aug. 3/4 Oils were generally soft, while Coppers were far from being buoyant. **1935** *Commercial & Financial Chron.* 7 Sept. 1488/2 Gold mining stocks were soft, and international issues were neglected. **1968** *Globe & Mail* (Toronto) 13 Feb. B1/2 At the end of last year, the fish industry in Newfoundland was reeling from the effects of the extremely soft U.S. market. **1981** *Times* 8 May 26/5 Disappointing trading news also left.. Francis Sumner 1p softer at 9p. **1982** *Times* 6 May 17/1 Britain must cease being the soft market for the so-called developing world and action was needed against countries which blocked imports of British goods by crippling duties while having free access to the United Kingdom.

**c.** *Econ.* Of currency: (see quot. 1949). (Cf. also sense 20 c and *hard currency* (*b*) s.v. HARD *a.* 23 b.)

**1940** *Economist* 6 Apr. 609/1 There are some currencies —the 'soft' currencies, notably the lira and the yen—for which no official rates are fixed. **1949** *Times* 10 Sept. 5/7 Soft currency.. is a relative rather than an absolute term. It means a currency of which other countries (or some other countries) have earned more than they can willingly spend in the country whose currency it is... A soft currency is by definition, non-convertible—*i.e.*, cannot be converted into gold or dollars... A currency may, however, be 'transferable' (within limits) and yet remain a soft currency in relation to some other currencies. **1960** *Economist* 15 Oct. 241/1 The United States now 'sells' abroad each year surplus farm products worth more than $1 billion, taking in exchange soft currencies—as one bureaucrat calls them, 'clam shells, coloured buttons and other forms of local currency'. **1967** A. DIMENT *Dolly Dolly Spy* vii. 97, I had changed some of my hard Swiss francs into soft pesetas. **1980** *Times* 23 May 14/6 Some African countries can only make ends meet in Moscow by smuggling in soft roubles bought abroad... This is categorically forbidden by.. most .. western embassies.

**d.** Designating a kind of technology that uses renewable resources such as wind or solar power and human or animal exertion and is not harmful to the natural environment. Also, of energy employed in or derived from this technology.

**1974** *Harper's Mag.* Apr. 6 The term 'soft technology' was coined amid the British counter-culture in 1970. Technology which is soft is gentle on its surroundings, responds to it, incorporates it, feeds it. A nuclear power-generating station doesn't qualify. A wooden windmill with cloth sails grinding local grain does. **1977** A. LOVINS *Soft Energy Paths* ii. 38, I shall call them 'soft' technologies: a textural description, intended to mean not vague, mushy, speculative, or ephemeral, but rather flexible, resilient, sustainable, and benign. Energy paths dependent on soft technologies.. will be called 'soft' energy paths. **1978** *Dædalus* Summer 188 The Progressives.. have tended to emphasize economics and technology, yet they have been 'soft' technological determinists in a way that maintains.. Rousseau's fascination with the potential.. of human autonomy. **1978** *Internat. Relations Dict.* (U.S. Dept. State Library) 2/1 Other terms used synonymously with appropriate technology are alternative technology, intermediate technology, and soft technology.

**V. 29. a.** Special collocations (see also 23 b, d, and 24 b, c; special combinations, corresponding in formation to those (undefined) under senses 30-32, are also included here). ***softback*** *attrib.* (*U.S.*), (of books) bound in paper or limp covers; ***soft-board*** sb., a relatively soft form of fibreboard (see also sense 32); ***soft cancer***, a cancer in which the affected tissue is soft and yielding; now *rare* or *Obs.*; ***soft chancre***, a venereal disease caused by local infection with *Hæmophilus ducreyi*; chancroid; also, one of the characteristic lesions of this disease; ***soft copy***, a legible but transient presentation of information, as on a VDU screen; information so displayed; ***soft-core*** *attrib.* [after *hard-core* (*pornography*): see *hard core* (*b*) s.v. HARD *a.* 23 b], (of pornography) less obscene than hard-core pornography; also *absol.*; ***soft corn***, plausible speech or language; flattery (Bartlett, 1859); ***soft-cover*** attrib., of, pertaining to, or designating a book bound in a limp or paper cover; also (usu. as two words) *ellipt.* for some such phrase as ***soft-cover edition***; hence ***soft-covered*** adj.; ***soft drug***, a drug that is held to be comparatively non-addictive and safe to use; also *fig.*; ***soft food***, the partly digested food which pigeons regurgitate to feed to their young; = PIGEON'S MILK 1; ***soft-foot*** vb. intr. (*N. Amer.*), to go with quiet footsteps, to tiptoe; ***soft fruit*** = *small fruit* s.v. SMALL *a.* 21; ***soft ground***, a sticky covering of wax mixed with grease for an etching plate; also = next; ***soft ground etching***, a process of print-making using plates covered with a soft ground, producing prints with softened lines resembling chalk or pencil drawings; also, a print produced by this process; ***soft hail***, precipitation of snow pellets (see SNOW *sb.*[1] 9 a); ***soft-horn***, a simple or foolish person (*slang*); ***soft line***, a flexible or conciliatory policy; freq. (with hyphen) *attrib.*; hence ***soft-liner***, ***soft-lining*** adj.; ***soft loan*** orig. *U.S.*, a loan, esp. one to a developing country, made on especially favourable terms; † ***soft meat*** = ***soft food*** above; ***soft money***, (*a*) (see sense 20 c); (*b*) (see quot. 1976); ***soft mouth***, a flatterer, smooth speaker; ***soft-nosed*** adj., (of a bullet) expanding; ***soft option***: see OPTION *sb.* 1; ***soft palate***: see PALATE *sb.* 1 b; ***soft plank*** (see quot.); ***soft porn(ography)***: see PORN, PORNO *sb.* 2, PORNOGRAPHY 2 a; ***soft pull***, in Printing (see quots.); ***soft rock***, a type of rock music which is less strident than hard rock; hence ***soft-rocker***; ***soft rot***, any of various bacterial or fungal diseases of vegetables, fruit, and herbaceous plants in which the tissue becomes soft and pulpy; also, a condition of timber in which a fungus renders it soft and brittle; freq. *attrib.*; ***soft sculpture*** (*Pop Art*, etc.), a form of sculpture in cloth, foam rubber, or other pliable materials; ***soft second*** (*Bowls*) (see quot. 1905); ***soft sell*** orig. *U.S.*, advertising or salesmanship that is subtly persuasive rather than aggressive (opp. *hard sell* s.v. HARD *a.* 22 b); also *transf.*, *fig.*, and *attrib.*; ***soft-sell*** vb. trans.; ***soft-selling*** ppl. adj.; ***soft-shoe*** attrib. (orig. *U.S.*), designating, of, or pertaining to a kind of tap-dance performed in soft-soled shoes without metal taps; also *fig.*; hence as *sb.*, a dance of this kind, and as *vb.*; ***soft-shoulder*** orig. *U.S.* [SHOULDER *sb.* 6 j], an unmetalled strip of land at the side of a road; ***soft silk***, silk from which the gum has been removed; ***soft-skinned*** adj., (*a*) having a soft skin (see sense 31); (*b*) *Mil.*, of a military vehicle, unarmoured (cf. sense 19 d above); ***soft snap*** *U.S.*, an easy, pleasant job; a profitable business or undertaking (*colloq.* or *slang*); ***soft solder***: see SOLDER *sb.*[1] 4 a; ***soft sore*** = *soft chancre* above; ***soft sugar***, moist sugar; ***soft tack***, among sailors, bread as distinct from ship's biscuit (see TACK *sb.*[5]); ***soft tissue***, body tissue other than bone and cartilage; also *attrib.*; ***soft tommy*** (see TOMMY); ***soft-top***, a roof of a motor vehicle that is made of soft material and can be opened; a car so fitted, a convertible; freq. *attrib.*; ***soft touch***: see TOUCH *sb.* 20 c; ***soft toy***, a toy animal stuffed with a soft material; ***soft vat*** (see quot.); ***soft wart***, a small, soft, pedunculated growth of skin occurring most frequently on the neck; ***soft woodlands*** (see quot.).

**1958** B. MALAMUD *Magic Barrel* 141 He had got some of his *softback books read. **1966** *Time* 8 July 60/2 Shimkin and three other men in 1939 founded his Pocket Books, Inc., the world's most voluminous soft-back-book producer. *Ibid.* 60/3 Pocket books will be better able to assure authors of bonuses for softback reprint rights. **1966** C. SWEENEY *Scurrying Bush* v. 68 The sagging *soft-board ceiling. **1976** P. HILL *Hunters* v. 43 The inside wall was partially covered by a large sheet of soft-board pinned to which was a large-scale map. **1804** J. ABERNETHY *Surg. Observ. containing Classification of Tumours* 51 The sarcoma which is.. generally found in the testis, and is distinguished by the name of the *soft cancer of that part. **1834** [see SPONGOID *a.* 1]. **1871** *Med. Times & Gaz.* 20 May 568/1 A soft cancer of the uterus. 1894 R. Quain *Dict. Med.* (new ed.) I. 269/2 Encephaloid, medullary, or soft cancer, so named from its usually brain-like appearance and consistence, is softer and grows more rapidly..than scirrhus. 1961 A. S. MacNalty *Brit. Med. Dict.* 247/2 *Soft cancer*, medullary carcinoma. [1965 I. Macdonald in T. F. Nealon *Managem. Patient with Cancer* xvii. 451 The designation of medullary (soft) is less than ideal, but is not of significance unless it refers to bulky, pseudo-encapsulated tumors.] 1859 C. F. Maunder tr. *Ricord's Lect. Chancre* 9 Numerous examples of the *soft chancre. 1887 H. Raphael tr. *Zeissl's Path. & Treatm. Syphilis* ii. 116 In the female the soft chancre is most frequently met with upon the labia majora and minora. 1917 *Act 7 & 8 Geo. V* c. 21 §4 In this Act the expression 'venereal disease' means syphilis, gonorrhœa, or soft chancre. 1961 R. D. Baker *Essent. Path.* ix. 157 Chancroid (soft chancre), a venereal sore on the genital organs, resembles the chancre of syphilis in location but differs in being the starting point of a purely regional process and never a systemic disease. 1968 *Internat. Solid-State Circuits Conf. Digest Technical Papers* 76/1 This scheme permits one to share the same phone link for both hard and *soft-copy output. 1982 *New Yorker* 17 May 34/2 'Soft copy and hard copy' (words on a television screen and words on a piece of paper in hand). 1966 *N.Y. Times* 25 Sept. D 15/4 The *soft-core pornography of advertisements like 'Have you had any lately?' 1971 *Guardian* 9 Mar. 8/2 The market for pure pornography is insatiable, while soft-core porno is waning in appeal. 1973 *Publishers Weekly* 6 Aug. 67/3 Lots of softcore sex scenes as Bertha finds revenge. 1977 *Time Out* 17–23 June 47/2 Borowczyk's slightest and most commercial offering has provoked wildly different responses: great pagan art or ultimate soft-core? 1979 *Listener* 5 July 21/3 The soft-core entertainment end of the television spectrum. 1834 W. A. Carruthers *Kentuckian in N.Y.* I. 98 He's feeding me on *soft corn, thought I. 1948 *Antioch Rev.* Autumn 161 He was all soft corn.., but you couldn't be sure, not with a man like Malcolm. 1958 *Times* 12 Feb. 9/4 Earnings from *soft-cover rights, movie rights, etc. 1961 *Guardian* 20 Oct. 17/5 Creative fiction will eventually prove itself in soft cover in this mass market. 1965 *Amer. N. & Q.* Sept. 13/1 Olms has also initiated an important new series of 'Paperbacks', soft-cover reprints of important scholarly works. 1975 *Bookseller* 16 Aug. 1306/1 What makes a paperback publisher pay nearly two million dollars for the softcover privilege of a book? 1977 *Time* 17 Jan. 54/2 In 1976 U.S. softcover publishers issued more than 150 historical novels, many of them as paperback originals. 1960 *Times* 15 Oct. 7/4 Now British presses also are producing '*soft-covered' volumes that can cost anything up to a guinea. 1959 *Oxford Mail* 14 Jan. 4/4 Dr. D. C. M. Yardley of Oxford found that of about 50 university users of *soft drugs (mostly marihuana) about 20 were regular takers, and that although the latter were convinced they could give it up at any time, in fact they hardly ever did so without professional help. 1968 *Sunday Mail Mag.* (Brisbane) 7 July 6/1 Some 300,000 people in Britain are estimated to be using some form of 'soft drug' such as marijuana, amphetamines or barbiturates. 1969 *Punch* 12 Mar. 376/2 For most of my life I've thought flattery was only a soft drug. It was nice; but I could take it or leave it. 1976 J. Archer *Not Penny More* i. 11 He was a sly, smart little boy, unloved by the school authorities..for his control of the underground school market in soft drugs and liquor. 1876 R. Fulton *Bk. Pigeons* iv. 39 This '*soft food'..is pumped up by the old ones with a sort of vomiting action. 1969 C. R. Hill *Pigeon Guide* vi. 91 At first, the parents will feed the youngsters on soft food (pigeons' milk). 1939 *Ottawa Jrnl.* 22 July 12/8 He *softfooted to the window and looked inside. 1972 J. Mosher *Adultery* iii. xiv. 133 As he soft footed it through the kitchen, father began to whistle a tune she liked. 1918 W. P. Seabrook *Mod. Fruit Growing* vii. 60 In the case of ..*soft (or bottom) fruit cutting back at once may be done. 1956 H. H. Crane *Fruit* i. 9 If the area is very small, it may be possible to grow only soft fruits. 1981 *Observer* 26 Apr. (Colour Suppl.) 47/3 It's obviously much easier to fit soft fruit into a small garden. 1840 S. Fuller *Let.* 31 Jan. in N. N. Solly *Mem. Life David Cox* (1873) iv. 57 We propose to republish... The plates have been proved, and found to be in good condition, particularly the *soft ground, which I consider as good as ever. 1925 E. S. Lumsden *Art of Etching* xiii. 113 Soft-ground (*vernis mou*) is nearly allied to etching proper. 1965 Zigrosser & Gaehde *Guide Coll. Orig. Prints* iv. 56 A soft ground is prepared from hard ground by the addition of tallow or Vaseline. *Ibid.*, Both linear and textured or tonal effects can be created by soft ground. 1868 P. G. Hamerton *Etching & Etchers* v. xi. 340 In some books on engraving, ordinary etching is called *soft-ground etching, to distinguish it from etching done in a hard ground, by the old masters. This old hard ground now being disused, a modern writer may call common etching hard-ground etching, and reserve the title of soft-ground etching for that to which it is here applied. 1873 N. N. Solly *Mem. Life David Cox* iii. 36 Cox had been employed..to make soft ground etchings on copper from his own drawings. 1914 G. T. Plowman *Etching & Other Graphic Arts* xiii. 111 For soft ground etching melt together lard or tallow and an equal amount of etching ground. 1976 P. Coker *Etching Technique* 70 The principle of soft ground etching is that the ground adheres to anything that is brought into contact with it. 1881 W. Marriott *Hints Meteorol. Observers* 16 International symbols... *Soft hail Δ. 1894 [see graupel]. 1945 F. A. Berry et al. *Handbk. Meteorol.* iii. 257 Soft hail usually accompanies the less severe winter or spring storms. 1970 R. M. Longley *Elem. Meteorol.* iv. 91 At the tops of these clouds pellets of soft hail are formed by the collision of the snowflakes found there. 1837 Haliburton *Clockm.* I. xxxi, I allot..that the blue-noses are the most gullible folks on the face of the airth,—rigular *soft horns, that's a fact. 1865 *Slang Dict.* 240 *Soft-horn*, a simpleton, a donkey. 1966 *Sunday Times* 5 June 4 But Canada, Norway, Denmark and Italy prefer a '*soft' line and want to leave the Council where it is to minimise the rupture with France. 1975 *New Left Rev.* Nov.–Dec. 70 The ambassador..may have been part of the soft-line American faction. 1977 *Time* 30 May 20/2 They scorn labor unions and the Communist Party as soft-line collaborators. 1967 *Economist* 18 Feb. 614/2 Life is made even more difficult for the guerrillas, hard-liners by definition, because of their open conflict with the *soft-liners in the Venezuelan communist party. 1980 *N.Y. Times* 17 Jan. A23 Soft-liners will say that the Huyser mission prevented a bloodbath, with the Iranian Army battling the mobs. 1977 *Time* 28 Mar. 13/2 They accuse it [*sc.* the Communist Party] of betraying the revolution and joining the Establishment with its *soft-lining tacit support of Premier Giulio Andreotti's minority government. 1958 *N.Y. Times* 2 Mar. iv. 5/6 The fund is authorized to make some '*soft loans', that is with long maturity and partly repayable in local currency. 1958 *Washington Post* 8 Oct. A12/2 The..American proposal for a new International Development Association, equipped to make softer loans to supplement the 'bankable' advances of the World Bank, is vitally important. 1965 [see I.D.A. s.v. I III]. 1979 *Financial Times* 11 Sept. 9/1 'Hidden subsidies' to the paper industry provided by most European governments—in the form of tax incentives, soft loans and regional employment schemes—will continue. 1765 *Treat. Pigeons* 22 *Soft meat then is a kind of liquid pap, prepared as it were by instinct by the parents, by a dissolution of the hard grains in their craw. 1822 'B. Moubray' *Pract. Treat. Poultry* (ed. 4) xii. 185 Soft meat is a sort of milky fluid or pap secreted in the craw of pigeons, by the wise providence of nature. 1879 Soft meat [see sick *a.* 1 f]. 1971 *Soft money [see penny 9 l]. 1976 *Daily Tel.* 13 Dec. 8/5 'Soft money' is the research money which charitable foundations give to research workers to sponsor two-year or three-year research projects... Scientists who have depended on soft money are now beginning to worry... As the period of the sponsorship runs out, they are starting to be concerned about where the next money is coming from. 1979 *Bull. Amer. Acad. Arts & Sci.* Mar. 8 Research and teaching units that..tend to live on 'soft money' from grants and contracts. 1882 Blackmore *Christowell* xxxi, Mrs. Tubbs liked them, because they were gentlemen; not such *soft-mouths as you see now. 1898 W. S. Churchill *Let.* 5 Aug. in R. S. Churchill *Winston S. Churchill* (1967) I. Compan. II. 957 My thoughts are more concerned with swords—lances—pistols—& *soft-nosed bullets—than with Bills—Acts & bye elections. 1899 *Westm. Gaz.* 1 July 2/3, 200,000 rounds of ammunition, made up with *soft-nosed bullets. 31 a]. 1922 Joyce *Ulysses* 327 Mark for a softnosed bullet. 1979 J. Blackburn *Sins of Father* xviii. 155 Dumdums; soft-nosed bullets... Banned by the Geneva Convention. 1867 Smyth *Sailor's Word-bk.* s.v. *Soft-Plank*, Picking a *soft plank in the deck, is choosing an easy berth. 1683 Moxon *Mech. Exerc., Printing* §xxiv. ¶5 A long or a Soaking or Easie Pull;..this is also call'd a *Soft Pull; because it comes Soft, and Soakingly and easily down. 1787 *Printer's Gram.* 328 That which causes a Soft Pull is putting in pieces of felt or pasteboard. 1888 Jacobi *Printers' Vocab.* 128 *Soft pull*, an easy pull over of the bar-handle of a printing press. 1969 *Harper's Mag.* Sept. 24 Some *soft-rock groups..have invaded the middle-of-the road market themselves. 1971 *Time* 11 Jan. 40 His songs delve ingeniously into hard and soft rock. 1980 *Washington Star* 31 July C1 Forget the sleek Hollywood production..and try to overlook the soft rock theme. 1977 *Time Out* 21 Jan. 43 (*caption*) David Bedford..who regularly set the classical fraternity wondering if one of their boys is turning irredeemably into a *soft-rocker. 1901 *Ann. Rep. Vermont Agric. Exper. Station* No. 13. 299 A rapid *soft rot of carrots caused by a bacillus (*B. carotovorus*). 1937 F. D. Heald *Introd. Plant Path.* iv. 47 Storage and transportation losses may be heavy..in vegetables such as asparagus,..lettuce, etc. by bacterial soft rots (*Bacillus carotovorus*),..in sweet potatoes by soft rot (*Rhizopus nigricans*). 1961 J. S. Boyce *Forest Path.* (ed. 3) xvi. 356 This type of decay, known as soft rot, is usually in the surface layers of wood in service. 1969 G. N. Agrios *Plant Path.* x. 355 Cruciferous plants and onions,..when infected by soft rot bacteria, almost always give off an offensive sulfurous odor. 1976 B. K. Bakshi *Forest Path* III. 306 Treated wood which may show complete freedom from attack from decay fungi may exhibit soft rot attack. 1969 C. Oldenburg in G. Baro *Claes Oldenburg* 18 Drawing in space required an emphasis on volume. This was stimulated by pieces made as props..for the Ray Gun Theatre performances—which led to the '*soft' sculptures. 1982 L. Kallen *No Lady in House* xiii. 121 Soft Sculpture..large squashy objects made of patterned cloth..artfully shaped into human or animal caricatures. 1905 *Harmsworth Encycl.* II. 884/1 Usually a side [in flat-green bowling] is composed of four players, each with a distinct function... The second has to do as he is told. A captain will play his weakest man here (hence the phrase, the '*soft second'). 1955 *Life* 25 July 21/1 Sometimes they ran into the '*soft sell'—'Sit down, we don't want you to order anything, just get acquainted.' 1961 C. Cockburn *View from West* iii. 24 Dons anxious to 'soft sell' ancient Greek culture to the modern world. 1967 V. S. Naipaul *Mimic Men* III. v. 260 Their soft-sell advertisements in the newspapers. 1970 G. F. Newman *Sir, You Bastard* i. 15 Terry Sneed was a sceptic, no soft sell ever bought him. 1970 *Daily Colonist* (Victoria, B.C.) 26 Sept. 15/4 Now Broadway is lucky to have those masters of the softsell gag and casual comedy. 1978 Ld. Drogheda *Double Harness* vi. 58 He..was a master of convincing overstatement whereas my gift was more for what is known in advertising jargon as soft sell. 1982 *Times* 19 Jan. 18/8 We have abandoned the softsell approach and become very aggressive. 1960 *New Left Rev.* Jan./Feb. 3/1 The 'society of equals' is better than the best *soft-selling consumer-capitalist society. 1927 P. Dunning *Broadway* 9 They were a brother act, a team of *soft-shoe dancers. 1935 D. N. Cropper *Dance Dict.* 76 *Soft-shoe*, generally acknowledge[d] to be dancing of the star type and containing certain ballet steps. Any tap dancing done without metal taps or clogs. 1941 *Life* 25 Aug. 74/2 George Primrose was famed as an exponent of 'soft-shoe' dancing 35 years ago. *Ibid.* 77/1 The misleading phrase 'soft-shoe' was applied to an increasingly popular form of mobile, eccentric step dance in rolling 4–4 time. 1962 J. D. Salinger *Franny & Zooey* 180 Les and Bessie did a lovely soft-shoe on sand swiped by Boo Boo from the urn in the lobby. 1965 P. O'Donnell *Modesty Blaise* xviii. 190 We'll make a soft-shoe job of it if we can... Straight for the diamonds..and away. *Ibid.* 197, I don't want to use the gun, not while there's any chance of keeping this soft-shoe. 1967 M. Stewart *Gabriel Hounds* x. 139 He..beckoned. I *soft-shoed after him. 1975 W. McIlvanney *Docherty* I. xvi. 115 Only a few couples still soft-shoed around the floor. 1981 *Daily Tel.* 27 Jan. 12/6 They [*sc.* Adele and Fred Astaire] rapidly soft-shoed their way to acclaim in musical comedies on Broadway. 1939 *Time* 20 Feb. 28/3 Driving toward his home on the outskirts of Indianapolis..he got off the road on a *soft shoulder. 1978 J. Irving *World according to Garp* xii. 231, I run in the stuff of the soft shoulder, in the hot sand and gravel. 1862 M. Merryweather *Experiences of Factory Life* (ed. 3) iii. 31 In 1847, Messrs. C—— had 195 *soft-silk looms at work in this town. *a*1877 Knight *Dict. Mech.* III. 2180/2 Silken thread..is called..if the natural gum is.. removed, *soft silk*. 1921 C. Salter tr. *Ganswindt's Dyeing Silk* i. 155 The bath temperature must..be modified.. being lukewarm for soft silk and hard silk. 1942 *Hutchinson's Pictorial Hist. of War* 10 June–1 Sept. 129/1 That is the protection of all this paraphernalia of supply and maintenance, all what may be called the '*soft-skinned stuff', from air attack. 1980 *Times* 18 Jan. 14/6 Many of the 'soft-skinned' vehicles [brought into Afghanistan] have been civilian trucks, which is normal Russian practice in wartime. 1841 *Spirit of Times* 9 Oct. 378 One of them, however..suddenly lamed herself, and another..'found a *softer snap,' so they paid forfeit to The Heiress. 1887 Francis *Saddle & Mocassin* xii. 227 I've got a 'soft snap' on —can't miss it. 1884 A. Cooper *Syphilis & Pseudo-Syphilis* iv. 33 There are two principal theories with regard to the relations existing between the hard and the *soft sores. 1940 E. T. Burke *Venereal Dis.* xx. 508 The term 'soft sore' or '*ulcus molle*' should, since they lead to much confusion, be discarded and the term 'chancroid' should be used. 1974 Passmore & Robson *Compan. Med. Stud.* III. xiii. 13/2 Chancroid or soft sore..is a venereal infection with *Haemophilus ducreyi*..causing genital ulceration and enlarged, tender inguinal lymph nodes. 1818 Scott *Br. Lamm.* xxiii, A drap brandy to burn, and a wee pickle *saft sugar. 1892 G. M. Gould *Pocket Med. Dict.* 272 *Soft*, not bony, cartilaginous, etc., as the *soft tissues. 1964 L. Martin *Clinical Endocrinol.* (ed. 4) iii. 113 Soft-tissue radiographs of the limbs. 1977 *Proc. R. Soc. Med.* LXX. 256/2 Advocates of early soft-tissue surgery..have reported successful results in a significant number of patients subjected to this method. 1959 *Motor* 23 Sept. 177/2 First *soft-top model in the so-called compact car size. 1967 *Guardian* 3 Oct. 5/3 The soft top now costs £1,212. 1976 *Milton Keynes Express* 18 June 39/6 (Advt.), L registration Triumph Spitfire yellow, 33,000 miles, hard and soft-tops. 1979 *Tucson* (Ariz.) *Mag.* Mar. 25/1 A removable forward hardtop and a convertible softtop rear window. 1917 E. A. Hickman *Soft Toys & how to make Them* 1 The object of this book is to bring instruction in the art of making stuffed or *soft toys. 1950 *Dryad Handicraft Catal.* 93 Soft toy making. 1964 M. Laski in S. Nowell-Smith *Edwardian England* iv. 203 The named soft toy was now starting its long run of popularity..Golliwog..Teddy Bear..Caesar. 1970 *Guardian* 24 Sept. 11/1 Wendy Boston, pioneers in safe soft toys. 1839 Ure *Dict. Arts* 674 A *soft vat..is that which contains too much copperas. 1887 *Jrnl. Cutaneous & Genito-Urinary Dis.* V. 50 The lesions known by the laity as moles, mothers'-marks..and by the profession as acrochordon, ecphyma mollusciforme,..and among English-speaking physicians sometimes as *soft warts. 1967 Soft wart [see molluscum 1 a]. 1859 Bartlett *Dict. Amer.* (ed. 2) 427 **Soft woodlands*, a term applied, in the British Provinces, to the districts or intervals covered with various species of pine trees.

**b.** In the names of plants or trees, as ***soft brome, grass, maple, rush*** (see quots.). Also ***soft corn***, a variety of maize *Zea mays* var. *amylacea*, whose seeds are rich in soft starch; also, maize containing a high quantity of moisture, making it unlikely to keep well; ***soft maple***, one of several maples with less durable wood, esp. the red maple, *Acer rubrum*, or the silver maple, *A. saccharinum*; also, the timber of these trees; ***soft wheat***, one of several varieties of wheat having a soft grain rich in starch.

1817 W. H. Marshall *Review* V. 489 The *soft brome, smooth stalked meadow, smaller fescue, and yellow oat, are partial to dry soils. 1751 J. Bartram *Observations* 60 Last of all was served a great bowl full of Indian dumplings, of new *soft corn, cut or scraped off the ear. 1868 *Mich. Agric. Rep.* VII. 160 Early frosts made considerable 'soft corn'. 1902 A. S. Hitchcock in L. H. Bailey *Cycl. Amer. Hort.* IV. 2004/2 Brazilian Flour Corn sold by seedsmen is a type of the Soft Corn. 1947 *Chicago Tribune* 23 July 9/4 The state must prepare for a soft corn crop this fall. 1785 Martyn *Rousseau's Bot.* xiii. (1794) 151 Several genera; of which the Holcus or *Soft grass is most likely to come under your observation. 1796 Withering *British Pl.* (ed. 3) II. 135 *Holcus lanatus*,..Meadow Soft-grass... *H. mollis*,.. Creeping Soft-grass. 1845 Lindley *Sch. Bot.* (ed. 2) 143 *Holcus lanatus* (Woolly Soft Grass). 1876 *Encycl. Brit.* IV. 264/2 The natives of Africa also make a beverage from the seed of the spiked or eared soft-grass (*Holcus spicatus*). [1778 J. Carver *Trav. N. Amer.* 496 The Maple. Of this tree there are two sorts, the hard and the soft.] 1806 P. Gass *Jrnl.* 6 Apr. (1807) 195 The timber is mostly of the fir kind, with some..*soft maple. 1810 [see maple tree]. 1855 J. Darby *Bot. S. States* 265 *A[cer] dasycarpum*,..Soft Maple. 1891 E. Roper *By Track & Trail* xv. 220 Against this rose the giant cedars, pines and hemlocks, the soft and vine maples [etc.]. 1948 H. A. Jacobs *We chose Country* 25 We..saw the farm buildings, clustered behind a great row of soft maples. 1969 T. H. Everett *Living Trees of World* xxii. 221/1 The most important American soft maples are the red or swamp maple ..and the silver maple. 1861 Miss Pratt *Flower. Pl.* V. 285 *Juncus effusus* (*Soft Rush)..is a common Rush of marshy lands. 1812, 1843 *Soft wheat [see *hard wheat* s.v. hard *a.* 22]. 1875 *Encycl. Brit.* III. 251/1 In commerce the grain is distinguished as white and red, or as hard and soft wheats. 1944 *Sun* (Baltimore) 5 Jan. 13/5 The Office of Price Administration..boosted the maximum prices for soft wheat. 1973 *Times* 3 Dec. 14/2 Soft wheat is cheaper for us thanks to being in the Community.

**c.** In the names of animals, esp. reptiles or fishes, as ***soft-back***, a soft-shelled turtle of the genus *Trionyx*; ***soft clam*** = long-neck 2 b; ***soft crab***, a crab that has shed its shell and is awaiting the hardening of the new one; ***soft tick***, a tick of the family Argasidæ, lacking a dorsal shield; ***soft-tortoise*** (see quots.).

1859 P. H. Gosse *Lett. Alabama* 99 Another Tortoise of even greater size and equal ferocity is the *Soft-back (*Trionyx ferox*). 1872 De Vere *Americanisms* 388 Another tortoise of greater size and equal ferocity is the Softback (*Trionyx ferox*). 1806 D. Roe *Jrnl.* 27 Feb. (1904) 25 Got

Sum *Soft Clams. **1855** *Knickerbocker* XLVI. 222 Along the strand..these great delicacies, 'soft clams' and sand-crabs may be found. **1884** GOODE *Nat. Hist. Aquat. Anim.* 707 The 'Soft Clam', 'Long Clam', or 'Nanninose' (*Mya arenaria*). **1772** L. CARTER *Jrnl.* 10 Oct. in *William & Mary Coll. Q.* (1906) 1st Ser. XIV. 38 Like the shell of a *soft crab, the body of the crab after the shell is off seems by much too large for the shell. **1805** R. PARKINSON *Tour Amer.* 315 Soft crabs..are reckoned great dainties. **1859** BARTLETT *Dict. Amer.* (ed. 2) 398 Shedder-crab, a crab which has recently cast its shell, also called a Soft Crab. **1884** GOODE *Nat. Hist. Aquat. Anim.* 776 The terms 'Soft Crab', 'Paper-shell', and 'Buckler' denote the different stages of consistency of the shell. **1896** LYDEKKER *Roy. Nat. Hist.* V. 376 Of these two unimportant families, the first is represented solely by the *soft-spines (*Malacanthus*). **1932** R. MATHESON *Med. Entomol.* iii. 40 The family Argasidae contains those ticks which lack a scutum and hence have been called the *soft ticks. **1974** *Nature* 25 Jan. 226/1 This is the first proven example of transmission of a mammalian piroplasm by an Argasid ('soft') tick. **1822** J. PARKINSON *Outl. Oryctol.* 303 The *soft tortoise (*Trionyx*). *c* **1880** *Cassell's Nat. Hist.* IV. 256 The Trionycides. The Mud or Soft Tortoises. **1896** LYDEKKER *Roy. Nat. Hist.* V. 98 The most striking peculiarity of the soft-tortoises is to be found in the nature of their shells.

**30. a.** Used with sbs. to form an attributive (or objective) comb., as *soft-bill, -coal, -foot*, etc.

**1829** GRIFFITH tr. *Cuvier* VIII. 617 *Soft-bill Duck, ..*Anas Melanorhynchos*. **1884** KNIGHT *Dict. Mech.* Suppl. 828/1 **Soft Center Steel*, a composition of iron and steel... Used for safes, plows, etc. **1885** W. D. HOWELLS *Silas Lapham* (1891) II. 57 The *soft-coal fire in the grate. **1598** MARLOWE & CHAPMAN *Hero & Leander* v. 3 Sol, and the *soft-foote Howrs hung on his armes. **1916** D. H. LAWRENCE *Amores* 73 When I carried my mother downstairs ..at the beginning Of her *soft-foot malady. **1959** *Listener* 8 Jan. 60/2 The soft-foot priest. **1916** *Daily Colonist* (Victoria, B.C.) 26 July 5/5 Muckers, sewermen, blacksmiths, *softground workers, and timbermen are specially needed. **1868** *U.S. Rep. Munit. War* 165 A hooped, *soft-steel gun. **1977** P. GEDDES *Hangman* xi. 98 She carried everything she owned in the *soft-top suitcase. **1860** *All Year Round* No. 49. 532 Of the *soft-water-drinking towns already named, Lancaster gets water..from millstone grit. **1893** *Pall Mall G.* 30 Jan. 7/3 The tallest people in Great Britain are to be met with in soft-water districts.

**b.** In comb. with adjs. *rare*.

**1603** J. DAVIES (Heref.) *Microcosmos* Wks. (Grosart) I. 20/2 Yea, smoothlie iest at their soft-silken Happe. **1843** HOLTZAPFFEL *Turning* I. 450 The first solder is called by the pewterers hard-pale, the last soft-pale.

**31.** *Comb.* Forming parasynthetic adjs., as ***soft-balled, -bellied, -brained, -coated, conscienced, -fingered***, etc., and derived *sbs.*, as ***soft-mindedness***.

Only the more important or earlier examples of this type are here illustrated.

*a* **1930** D. H. LAWRENCE *Last Poems* (1932) 42 Kisses of the *soft-balled paws. **1923** —— *Birds, Beasts & Flowers* 113 He..trailed his yellow-brown slackness *soft-bellied down. **1687** MIÈGE *Gt. Fr. Dict.* II. s.v., *Soft-brained, or Soft-pated, *qui est un peu foû*. *a* **1918** W. OWEN *Poems* (1931) 98 Comforted years will sit *soft-chaired In rooms of amber. **1859** GEO. ELIOT *A. Bede* xxxvii, The luxurious nature of a round, *soft-coated pet animal. **1820** KEATS *Ode to Psyche* 4 Pardon that thy secrets should be sung Even into thine own *soft-conched ear. **1607** SHAKS. *Cor.* I. i. 37 Though *soft conscienc'd men can be content to say it was for his Countrey. **1970** *Jrnl. General Psychol.* Apr. 183 The other two paintings were non-representational '*soft-edged' geometric abstractions. **1828** P. CUNNINGHAM *N.S. Wales* (ed. 3) II. 190 Weavers, barbers, and such-like *soft-fingered gentry. **1611** TOURNEUR *Ath. Trag.* II. v, I do not like these phlegmatic smooth-skinned, *soft-fleshed fellows. **1928** D. H. LAWRENCE *Woman who rode Away* 113 If a woman looked pleasant and soft-fleshed..they were ardent and generous. **1848** J. R. LOWELL *Poems* 2nd Ser. 167 The red-oak, *softer-grained yields all for lost. **1966** *Listener* 3 Mar. 329/1 Souzay..is..now able to make his beautiful soft-grained voice cover a wide range of human experience. **1886** C. SCOTT *Sheep-Farming* 195 Dogs..of every size and colour, rough and smooth-coated, *soft and hard haired. **1768–74** TUCKER *Lt. Nat.* (1834) II. 277 *Soft-handed Hope, whose soothing touch makes the possessor easy in himself. **1820** KEATS *Ode to Psyche* 18 Their lips touch'd not, but had not bade adieu, As if disjoined by soft-handed slumber. **1842** I. WILLIAMS *Baptistery* III. xvii. 224 Soft-handed Silence near stands looking calmly on. **1868** G. M. HOPKINS *Jrnls. & Papers* (1959) 175 Beauty of the sycamores here, native to the soil, *soft-horned, and falling apart like ashes. **1847** DISRAELI *Tancred* v. ii, Amiable and brave, trustworthy and *soft-mannered. **1592** *Arden of Feversham* II. ii, Why, this would steale *soft metled cowardice. **1540** COVERDALE *Fruitful Lessons* i, Quiet, mild, *soft-minded, tractable, and meek. **1648** HEXHAM II, *Weeck-zinnigh*, Soft-minded, or Enraged. **1919** E. O'NEILL *Moon of Caribbees* 189 It's soft-minded she is, like I've always told you, an' stupid. **1925** F. SCOTT FITZGERALD *Great Gatsby* vi. 120 The transactions in Montana copper.. found him physically robust but on the verge of *soft-mindedness. **1564** ABP. PARKER *Corr.* (Parker Soc.) 214 A good, *soft-natured gentleman. **1619** FLETCHER *Wild-Goose Chase* I. ii, We'l provide thee some soft-natur'd wench. **1776** MICKLE tr. *Camoens' Lusiad* IV. 6 The dawn..With *soft-paced ray dispels the shades obscene. **1857** MISS WINKWORTH *Tauler's Life & Serm.* 164 A soft-paced horse would be much easier for him to ride. **1848** J. R. LOWELL *Uncoll. Poems* (1950) 59 The *soft palmed tradesman coming home at eve. **1978** *Time* 3 July 1/3 Hooray for higher food prices... The American farm worker and farmer have subsidized the American dinner table long enough... There will be the usual soft-palmed protesters. **1680** C. NEES *Church Hist.* 179 Ahaziah..was a *soft-pated prince and low spirited. **1882** JORDAN & GILBERT *Syn. Fishes N. Amer.* 94 *Physostomi*, (The *Soft-rayed Fishes). **1612** CHAPMAN *Widdow's Tears* v, A Souldier and afraid of a dead man? A *soft-r'ode milk-sop? **1886** KIPLING *Departmental Ditties* (ed. 2) 53 From rockridge to spur Fly the *soft-sandalled feet. **1591** SYLVESTER *Du Bartas* I. iv. 807 Those, that.. chase The *soft-skind Martens, for their precious Cace. **1596** NASHE *Saffron Walden* Wks. (Grosart) III. 111 Making loue to those soft skind soules & sweete Nymphes of Helicon. **1896** tr. *Boas' Text-bk. Zool.* 225 Thin plates separated by large soft-skinned interspaces. **1923** D. H. LAWRENCE *Birds, Beasts & Flowers* 201 Now that in England is silence, where before was a moving of *soft-skirted women. **1933** J. BUCHAN *Prince of Captivity* III. ii. 287 The *soft-soled shoes of the pursuit did not slip. **1530** PALSGR. 324/2 *Softespyrited, *modeste*. **1585–6** LEYCESTER *Corr.* (Camden) 273 The audytors here be so soft-spryted men as I dowbt [etc.]. **1641** MILTON *Animadv.* Wks. 1851 III. 186 Thus much..in favour of the softer spirited Christian. **1631** CHAPMAN *Cæsar & Pompey* v. ii, My *soft-spleen'd seruants ouerrule and curb me. **1805** *Edin. Rev.* VII. 5 The eldest..seems to have been a very *soft-tempered youth. **1878** JOAQUIM MILLER *Songs of Italy* 45 When the stars in the soft-tempered breeze Glowed red. **1820** KEATS *Lamia* II. 261 'Lamia!' he cried—and no *soft-toned reply. *c* **1850** *Arab. Nts.* (Rtldg.) 488 A concert of soft-toned flutes, hautboys, lutes. *a* **1873** LYTTON *Pausanias* 78 It goes hard with my pride..to make equals of this *soft-tongued race. **1976** *Milton Keynes Express* 23 July 39/1 Heavy rain during the day provided a *soft-topped, damp wicket which gave a lot of help to the bowlers. **1847** WEBSTER, **Soft-voiced*, having a soft voice. **1894** 'J. S. WINTER' *Red Coats* 63 The remembrance of a soft-eyed, soft-voiced little woman. **1842** LOUDON *Suburban Hort.* 117 The singing-birds are the best for destroying *soft-winged insects such as moths and butterflies. **1916** JOYCE *Portrait of Artist* iv. 180 It was only amid *soft-worded phrases.. that he dared to conceive of the soul or body of a woman moving with tender life.

**b.** In the specific names of animals, birds, plants, etc.

**1803** SHAW *Gen. Zool.* IV. II. 517 *Soft-backed Labrus, *Labrus Malapteronotus*. **1837** SWAINSON *Classif. Birds* II. iii. II. 16 The soft-backed shrikes, or *Malaconoti*. **1678** RAY tr. *Willughby's Ornith.* III. ii. §1. 362 Wormius his Eider or *soft-feathered Duck. *c* **1711** PETIVER *Gazophyl.* VI. §lviii, Soft-feathered Cape Coralline. **1833** *Proc. Berw. Nat. Club* I. 29 *Hieracium molle*—*Soft-leaved Hawkweed. **1840** HODGSON *Hist. Northumb.* III. II. 361/2 *Byrum carneum*, Soft-leaved Thread-moss. **1872** *Routledge's Ev. Boy's Ann.* June 417/2 The soft-leaved Rose (*Rosa mollis*). **1890** *Science-Gossip* XXVI. 136 The soft-leaved cranesbill (*Geranium molle*). **1801** LATHAM *Gen. Synop. Birds* Suppl. II. 224 *Soft-tailed Flycatcher.

**32.** With vbs., as ***soft-board, -boil, -talk***. See also SOFT-LAND *v.*

**1897** C. T. DAVIS *Manuf. Leather* (ed. 2) xxvii. 417 Then the leather is taken down and soft-boarded and hung up to thoroughly dry. **1884** KNIGHT *Dict. Mech.* Suppl. 828 *Soft-boarding*, boarding or bruising the leather on the flesh-side. **1832** GEN. P. THOMPSON *Exerc.* (1842) II. 327 Now just reflect,—meditate for as long time as would soft-boil an egg. **1903** G. B. SHAW *Let.* 21–2 Dec. (1972) II. 384 Mrs Robertson..would have had to get her brains extracted and her face soft-boiled to play the poor pitiful creature Judith [in *The Devil's Disciple*]. **1970** H. MCLEAVE *Question of Negligence* (1973) xxii. 170 The pressure in number-two boiler room is hardly high enough to soft-boil an egg. **1968** *Daily Progress* (Charlottesville, Va.) 15 Apr. 21/2 Young Gentry used artificial bait and said he also had to soft talk the fish as he pulled him in. **1968** B. MATHER *Springers* x. 100 He asked peevishly when the hell we would be moving—and where? I soft-talked him and said any minute.

**33.** With ppl. adjs., as ***soft-looking***.

**1860** C. M. YONGE *Hopes & Fears* I. ii. 33 Honora thought her the prettiest child she had ever seen..such a soft-looking little creature. **1924** 'R. CROMPTON' *William—the Fourth* vi. 87 He said he'd rather be killed than go to an ole dancing class anyway, with that soft-looking kid.

**soft** (sɒft, -ɔ:-), *adv.* Forms: 1, 3–6 softe (5 soffte, 6 safte), 4– soft. [OE. *sófte*, = OS. *sâfto*, OHG. *sanfto, samfto* (MHG. *sanfte, samfte*, G. *sanft*): see prec.] Softly, in various senses.

**I. 1. a.** In a quiet or peaceful state; in a comfortable or easy manner; on a soft bed, couch, etc.; †luxuriously. Now *poet.* or *arch.*, esp. in *to sleep soft*.

*a* **1000** *Genesis* 179 He..softe swæf. *c* **1000** *Saxon Leechd.* II. 292 Reste [he] hine softe. *c* **1205** LAY. 4004 þer he læi softe &..slepte. *Ibid.* 6346 He wes a wel god mon & softe he wolde libben. **13..** *Cursor M.* 3796 (Gött.), Wele was he gladid of þat sight, Soft him thoght he slep þat nyht. **1398** TREVISA *Barth. De P.R.* VII. lviii. (Bodl. MS.), Þis yuell bredeth in ham þat leue esilich and softe, and trauayleþ butte litel. *c* **1400** *Brut* lxvii. 63 Y shal ȝeue ȝow soche a medecyne þat ȝe shulle swete anone ryȝt, and softe slepe. **1601** SHAKS. *All's W.* IV. iii. 368, I will..sleepe as soft As Captaine shall. **1607** —— *Timon* IV. iii. 206 Thy Flatterers..drinke Wine, lye soft. **1667** MILTON *P.L.* VIII. 254 Soft on the flourie herb I found me laid. **1781** COWPER *Anti-Thelyphth.* 8 Fancy.. laid her soft in Amaranthine flow'rs. **1827** SCOTT *Surg. Dau.* ix, The riches of the East expended that they might sleep soft and wake in magnificence. **1850** MRS. BROWNING *The Sleep* iv, Sleep soft, beloved!

**b.** In soft wrappings, surroundings, etc.

*a* **1400–50** *Alexander* 2401 Þat Iowell..Þat was full sekirly & soft all in silke falden. *c* **1440** *York Myst.* xviii. 196, I pray þe.., happe hym warme, And sette hym softe. **1579** GOSSON *Sch. Abuse* (Arb.) 39 They were smoothly appareled, soft lodged, daintely feasted.

**c.** ellipt. for *soft class* (in travelling by train in China or the U.S.S.R.). Also *transf.*, first-class.

**1939** 'M. INNES' *Stop Press* I. ii. 44 As a matter of fact, he's on the train now. But of course travelling soft. **1976** *Times* 13 Nov. 11/1 Trains in China are made up of classless coaches but you travel *hard* or *soft* according to your position.

**2. a.** In a gentle manner; without harshness, roughness, severity, or violence.

*a* **1000** *Boeth. Metr.* xx. 7 Ðu..ȝesewenlicra softe wealdest scirra ȝesceafta. *c* **1250** *Gen. & Ex.* 3874 An oðer siðe he went is ðoȝt Betre and softere. *a* **1300** *Cursor M.* 58 Wyt chaunce of ded,..þat soft began has endyng smart. **1377** LANGL. *P. Pl.* B. xx. 311 Ther is a surgiene in þis sege þat softe can handle. *c* **1385** CHAUCER *L.G.W.* 2708 *Hypermnestra*, And hym she roggith & a-wakyth softe. **14..** *Sir Beues* (M) 605 With drinke and salffe she helid hym softe.

**b.** Without much force, intensity, or vigour; lightly, gently.

*c* **1430** *Two Cookery-bks.* 17 Stere it soffter an sofftere, tylle it come to-gedere; þan gader it to-gederys with a ladelle or a Skymoure, softe, tille it be round to-gedere. *Ibid.* 22 Wrynge it soft þorw a straynoure. **1742** YOUNG *Nt. Th.* II. 241 Silky-soft Favonius, breathe still softer, or be chid. **1757** GRAY *Bard* 71 Fair laughs the Morn, and soft the Zephyr blows. **1793** WORDSW. *Descr. Sk.* 14 Nature loves to show'r Soft on his wounded heart her healing pow'r. **1833** TENNYSON *Lotos-Eaters* Choric Song i, There is sweet music here that softer falls Than petals from blown roses on the grass. **1891** C. JAMES *Rom. Rigmarole* 175 'I fall soft,' he said.

**3. a.** With gentle movement; unobtrusively; without (much) noise or sound; quietly.

*c* **1205** LAY. 26614 þæs cnihtes siȝen þurh þene wude wunder ane softe. *c* **1290** *S. Eng. Leg.* I. 75 Þis holie Man wende forth a-mong heom alle wel softe. *a* **1300** *Cursor M.* 17288 + 127 For drede þai stynted oft For ferd of þe Iews, and sithen welk ful soft. *c* **1374** CHAUCER *Troylus* III. 1535 He softe into his bed gan for to slynke To slepe longe. **1596** SPENSER *F.Q.* IV. xi. 33 Him follow'd Yar, soft washing Norwitch wall. **1742** COLLINS *Passions* (1807) 141 [Runnels] Dashing soft from rocks around. **1820** KEATS *St. Agnes* xxix, Then by the bed-side..soft he set A table.

**b.** With or at a slow or leisurely pace; not hastily or hurriedly.

**1390** GOWER *Conf.* I. 100 He set hire on his hors tofore And forth he takth his weie softe. *c* **1400** *Laud Troy Bk.* 2982 Polidonias Come afftirward with qwene Eleyne, Rydyng soffte vpon the pleyne. *c* **1460** *Towneley Myst.* XXI. 211 All soft may men go far. **1550** CROWLEY *Last Trump* 895 Thou hast forgotten to go soft, thou art so hasty on thy way. **1748** THOMSON *Cast. Indol.* II. xxi, Or where old Cam soft-paces o'er the lea In pensive mood.

**4.** In a low voice or tone; with a soft, melodious, or pleasing sound; not loudly or harshly.

*c* **1290** *S. Eng. Leg.* I. 232 Þis Monekes beden seint Brendan, þat he softe speke. **1297** R. GLOUC. (Rolls) 9769 Þis godeman sat adoun akne..& wel softe..sede þis orison. **1422** tr. *Secreta Secret., Priv. Priv.* 187 The wys man wenethe he Softe laghyth. **1470–85** MALORY *Arthur* V. v. 167 She..sayd Syre knyghte speke softe, for yonder is a deuyll. *a* **1536** *Songs, Carols*, etc. (E.E.T.S.) 118 Syng softe, I say, leste yowr nose blede. **1590** SPENSER *F.Q.* II. xii. 71 The waters fall with difference discreet, Now soft, now loud. **1603** SHAKS. *Meas. for M.* IV. i. 69 Little haue you to say When you depart from him, but soft and low, Remember now my brother. *a* **1763** SHENSTONE *Nancy of Vale* iii. Wks. 1777 I. 128 When from an hazle's artless bower Soft warbled Strephon's tongue. **1784** COWPER *Task* III. 779 And streams ..Now murm'ring soft, now roaring in cascades. **1820** KEATS *Lamia* II. 199 Soft went the music the soft air along. **1896** HOUSMAN *Shropshire Lad* lii, The wanderer..Halts on the bridge to hearken How soft the poplars sigh.

**†5.** Sweetly, odorously. *Obs.*$^{-1}$

*a* **1300** *Cursor M.* 9357 Sco smelles better þen piment, And wel softer [*Fairf.* soter] hir uestement þan ani recles þat es brent.

**6.** To a slight degree or extent; slightly. *rare*.

**13..** *Minor Poems fr. Vernon MS.* xlix. 371 For muche to bi-hote & ȝiue but softe, Makeþ mon to be chalanged ofte. **1812** *New Bot. Gard.* I. 46 The leaves are spear-shaped, soft waved and entire.

**†7.** *soft and fair(ly)*, softly, gently, leisurely. *Obs.* (Cf. 8 b and FAIR *adv.* 7.)

**1390** GOWER *Conf.* III. 194 Thus have I told thee softe and faire Mi feith. **1530** PALSGR. 842/1 Softe and fayre, *tout bellement*. **1535** COVERDALE *Tobit* xi. 3 Let the husholde with thy wife and yᵉ catell come soft & fayrly after vs. **1565** COOPER *Thes.*, *Cunctanter*, slowly; safte and fayre; leasurely. **1625** PURCHAS *Pilgr.* II. 1104 That the Queen should follow soft and fair. **1638** JUNIUS *Paint. Ancients* 29 The Arts..are in processe of time soft and faire forged by a continuall meditation.

*Prov.* **1681** T. FLATMAN *Heraclitus Ridens* No. 32 (1713) I. 208 Soft and fair goes far in a Day. *a* **1700** B. E. *Dict. Cant. Crew* s.v. *Fair*, Soft and Fair goes far. **1736** AINSWORTH I. s.v., Soft and fair goeth far, *festina lente*.

**8. a.** Used as an exclamation with imperative force, either to enjoin silence or deprecate haste. Freq. preceded by *but*, and sometimes followed by *you*. Now only *arch*.

(*a*) *c* **1550** CHEKE *Matt.* xxvii. 49 And yᵉ resideu said, Soft, let vs se whiyer helias com to save him or no. *c* **1590** MARLOWE *Faustus* ix, Soft, sir; a word with you. **1601** SHAKS. *Twel. N.* I. v. 312 Not too fast: soft, soft. **1611** —— *Wint. T.* IV. iv. 402 Soft, Swaine, a-while, beseech you. *a* **1822** SHELLEY *'Tis midnight now'* 82 Soft, my dearest angel, stay. **1852** M. ARNOLD *Tristram & Iseult* i. 7 Soft —who is that stands by the dying fire?

(*b*) *a* **1566** R. EDWARDS *Damon & Pithias* in Dodsley *O. Pl.* (1754) I. 241 But soft, sirs, I pray you huysh. **1589** [? LYLY] *Pappe w. Hatchet* (1844) 22 But soft, I must now make a graue speach. **1639** N. N. tr. *Du Bosq's Compl. Woman* I. 8 But soft, wee take nothing from Pagans. *a* **1721** SHEFFIELD (Dk. Buckhm.) *Wks.* (1753) I. 179 A night..All black, and terrible! but soft! stand close. **1782** HAN. MORE *Moses* III. 14 No one sees me. But soft, does no one listen! **1820** BYRON *Blues* II. 24 A rabble who know not—But soft, here they come!

(*c*) **1599** *George a Greene* Greene's Wks. (Rtldg.) 256 Nay, soft you, sir! you get no entrance here. **1602** SHAKS. *Ham.* III. i. 88 Soft you now, The faire Ophelia! **1635** MEDE *Wks.* (1672) 836 But soft you there, I like not that Method.

**†b.** So ***soft and fair, soft and peace***. *Obs.*

**1576** GASCOIGNE *Steele Glas* (Arb.) 69 Cruel? nay iust, (yea softe and peace good sir) For Iustice sleepes. **1599** SHAKS. *Much Ado* v. iv. 72 Soft and faire Frier, which is

Beatrice? **1611** COTGR., *Tout beau*, take your leisure, soft and faire, not too fast. **1712** ARBUTHNOT *John Bull* (1727) 63 Soft and fair, gentlemen, quoth I; my mother's my mother.

**II.** *Comb.* **9. a.** With pres. pples. (or advs. from these), as *soft-brushing, -circling, -ebbing*, etc.

Similar examples, but unhyphened, are freq. in 18th cent. poetry.

**1606** SYLVESTER *Du Bartas* II. iv. II. *Magnificence* 701 One, in the fresh shade of an Apple-Tree, Lets hang its Quiver, while soft-pantingly 'T exhales hot Vapour. **1667** MILTON *P.L.* VII. 300 Wave rowling after Wave,.. If steep, with torrent rapture, if through Plaine, Soft-ebbing. **1710** PHILIPS *Pastorals* ii. 6 Their Notes soft-warb'ling to the gladsome Spring. **1726** POPE *Odyss.* XVII. 310 They heard, soft-circling in the sky, Sweet Airs ascend. **1743** FRANCIS tr. *Hor., Odes* III. xi. 18 The Dog of Hell, Immense of Bulk, to Thee soft-soothing fell. **1820** KEATS *Lamia* I. 43 The God .. soft-brushing, in his speed, The taller grasses. **1845** F. W. FABER *Let.* 29 Jan. in R. Chapman *Father Faber* (1961) vi. 103 When I know how miserably sinful and soft-living I have been, I ought never to have stepped out in the way that I have done. **1875** LONGF. *Hanging of Crane* iv. 22 Limpid as planets.. Soft-shining through the summer night. *a* **1918** W. OWEN *Poems* (1963) 103 And through those snows my looks shall be soft-going. **1925** E. SITWELL *Troy Park* 45 Like curd soft-falling. **1944** E. BLUNDEN *Shells by Stream* 49 The cloud soft-flaming past the mountain wall.

**b.** In attributive use.

Freq. in 18th cent. poetry; many examples are given by Jodrell.

**1612** DRAYTON *Poly-olb.* III. 401 As some soft-sliding rill .. Extends itself at length unto a goodly stream. **1648** J. BEAUMONT *Psyche* IV. ccxlv, By the side Of some soft-murmuring Current. **1743** FRANCIS tr. *Hor., Odes* III. xix. 20 The soft-swelling Pipe, and the Hautboy sonorous. **1768–74** TUCKER *Lt. Nat.* (1834) II. 263 Benign, soft-shining goddess! [Hope]. **1791** COLERIDGE *Mathem. Problem* iii, The soft-flowing daughter of fright. **1816** J. WILSON *City of Plague* Poems 1825 I. 299 Sinking down As through soft-yielding waters murmuring round me. **1827** KEBLE *Chr. Year, Visitation Sick*, The light from those soft-smiling eyes. **1829** D. JERROLD *Black-Ey'd Susan* I. i. 13 That pretty piece of soft-speaking womanhood. **1836** MRS. BROWNING *Poet's Vow* II. xiii, The silence left By that soft-throbbing speech. **1888** W. WHITMAN *November Boughs* 33 And who art thou? said I to the soft-falling shower... I am the Poem of Earth, said the voice of the rain. **1892** GUNTER *Miss Dividends* (1893) 13 Here a soft-treading waiter knocks upon the door. **1916** D. H. LAWRENCE *Amores* 24 Soft-sailing waters where fears No longer shake. **1965** F. SARGESON *Memoirs of Peon* iv. 73 The shapely soft-speaking Maori girl .. brought me a plate of sandwiches. **1975** *New Yorker* 5 May 109/1 He hit a great, soft-falling shot seven feet beyond the flag. **1977** *Times* 17 Mar. 18/6 A soft-living Mayfair clientele.

**10. a.** With pa. pples., as *soft-bedded, -extended, -roast(ed)*, etc.

**1558** WARDE tr. *Alexis' Secr.* 26 b, A new laied Egge, soft roste. **1725** POPE *Odyss.* VII. 435 There, soft-extended,.. Ulysses sleeps profound! **1726** *Ibid.* XIX. 119 A seat soft spread with furry spoils prepare. **1742** YOUNG *Nt. Th.* IV. 654 Their distant strain,.. Soft wafted on celestial pity's plume. **1831** CARLYLE *Sart. Res.* II. ix, Not sufficiently honoured,.. soft-bedded, and lovingly cared-for.

**b.** In attributive use. **soft-spun**, loosely twisted in spinning; also *transf.*; opp. *hard-spun* s.v. HARD *adv.* 8 e. See also SOFT-LANDED *ppl. a.*

Other examples are given by Jodrell.

**1597** A. M. tr. *Guillemeau's Fr. Chirurg.* 28/1 We must first let him suppe in a soft-dressed egge. **1648** J. BEAUMONT *Psyche* XX. ccxciii, Those lusty Thoughts which in a soft-lay'd Dream [etc.]. **1649** G. DANIEL *Trinarch., Hen. V*, ccxlviii, Spred the feild ore with Soft-Spun Carcasses. **1682** MRS. BEHN *City Heiress* 8 The stealths of Love, the soft-breath'd murmuring Passion. **1748** THOMSON *Castle Indol.* I. xx, The soft-embodied fays through airy portal stream. **1768** *Phil. Trans.* LX. 122 They have shoes of soft-tanned moose skin. **1825** J. NICHOLSON *Operat. Mech.* 481 This soft and soft-glazed pottery is easily scratched by a knife. *a* **1835** MRS. HEMANS *To the New Born* Poems (1875) 502 Bending o'er thy soft-seal'd eyes. **1869** 'MARK TWAIN' *Innoc. Abr.* xxx. 324 A lace-work of soft-tinted crystals of sulphur. **1893** *Outing* XXII. 123/1 The soft-finished, braided raw-silk line. **1902** W. DE LA MARE *Songs of Childhood* 96 As if it were a perfect jewel in the morning's soft-spun hair. **1906** Soft spun [see *hard spun* s.v. HARD *adv.* 8 e]. **1940** E. BLUNDEN *Poems 1930–40* 193 Choose this soft-tinted willow tree. **1964** H. HODGES *Artifacts* ix. 129 Excessively twisted, or *hard-spun*, yarns may kink.. while *soft-spun* threads may lack tight twist may untwist further.

**11.** With adjs., as *soft-bright, -lucent, -slow*.

**1593** SHAKS. *Lucrece* 1220 Her mistress she doth give demure good-morrow, With soft-slow tongue, true mark of modesty. **1837** CARLYLE *Fr. Rev.* II. I. iv, Light Apollo, so clear, soft-lucent. **1863** LD. HOUGHTON *Sel. fr. Wks.* 216 Disparted all those soft-bright diadems.

†**soft**, *v. Obs.* [f. the adj.]

**1.** *trans.* To render (a person, the heart, etc.) less harsh, severe, or obdurate; to mollify, appease, pacify.

*a* **1225** *Ancr. R.* 244 Eadie bonen softeð & paieð ure Louerd. **1390** GOWER *Conf.* I. 318 Witt and resoun conseilen ofte That I myn herte scholde softe. *c* **1430** *Pilgr. Lyf Manhode* I. lii. (1869) 31 Whan it is fulfilled with olde sinne, and harded, j softe it, and make it weepe. *c* **1477** CAXTON *Jason* 47 b, Ther is no herte of lady so hard but by the vertu of youre requestes muste nedes be softed and molefied. **1533** BELLENDEN *Livy* v. xiii. (S.T.S.) II. 194 The distributioun of þir landis softit.. þe myndis of small pepill. **1594** SPENSER *Amoretti* xxxii, Yet cannot all these flames.. her hart more harde then yron soft awhit.

**b.** Const. *to* and inf.

*c* **1430** *Life St. Kath.* (1884) 90 But anoon porphyry softed þe kepers to consente.

**2.** To allay, abate, or assuage the heat, intensity, or pain of (an injury, sore, etc.). Also with double accusative.

(*a*) *a* **1200** *St. Marher.* 5 Lauerd loke to me, ant haue merci of me, softe me mi sar. *c* **1375** *Sc. Leg. Saints* xxxviii. (*Adrian*) 295 With a faire clath scho clengit þare bilis, & softyt hurtis þat ware sare. **14..** *Siege Jerus.* (E.E.T.S.) 5 Canste þou any.. craft vpon erþe To softe þe grete sore þat sitteþ on my cheke? *c* **1440** *Promp. Parv.* 463/1 Softyn, or esyn of peyne,.. *mitigo, allevio.* **1527** ANDREW *Brunswyke's Distyll. Waters* C iv, It softeth the goute podagra in the fete. (*b*) *c* **1440** *Promp. Parv.* 463/1 Softyn, or comfortyn yn sorowe and mornynge, *delinio.* *c* **1470** *Gol. & Gaw.* 1055 Wes nowthir solace nor sang thair sorow to soft.

**3.** To mitigate or moderate, to lower or reduce the intensity of (a passion, emotion, etc.).

*c* **1400** *Apol. Loll.* 112 Wat þat is offrid in felony in þe sacrifice of God it softiþ not, but steriþ his wraþe. *a* **1470** H. PARKER *Dives & P.* (W. de W. 1496) VI. x. 380 The Iacke is softe & nesshe and by his softenesse.. softeth & feynteth all strokes þat cometh there ayenst. **1533** BELLENDEN *Livy* I. iv. (S.T.S.) I. 30 Providing so þai wald soft þe Indignacioun of þare myndis. *Ibid.* III. xi. 293 His collegis.. set þame þe maist presand way þai mycht to soft his preiss.

**4.** To make (words) plausible or specious.

**1382** WYCLIF *Ps.* liv. 22 Softid ben the woordis of hym vp on oile; and thei ben speris. —— *Prov.* ii. 16 That thou be take awey fro an alien womman, and fro a straunge, that softeth [L. *mollit*] hir woordis.

**5.** To render physically soft. Also in fig. context.

*a* **1400** *Prymer* (1895) 60 Wheþer þou hast not softid me as mylk; and hast cruddid me to-gideres as chese? *c* **1430** *Life St. Kath.* (1884) 52 The erthe also is softed wyth rayn and aȝeynward made hard wyth froost.

**6.** *refl.* To calm or restrain (oneself). *rare*$^{-1}$.

*c* **1480** HENRYSON *Fables, Fox, Wolf & Husbandman* xxiii, Schir,.. we ar at it almaist; Soft ȝow ane lytill, and ȝe sall se it sone.

**7.** *intr.* To become or grow soft in various senses.

*c* **1275** LAY. 12042 þe wind gan a-legge an þat weder softi. *a* **1340** HAMPOLE *Psalter* lxxxiii. 2 My hert softid in swetnes of luf.

Hence †'**softing** *vbl. sb.* and *ppl. a.*

**1398** TREVISA *Barth. De P.R.* XIX. xlvii. (W. de W. 1495) 890 Bi grete drynesse they be made smothyng and softynge. **14..** *Siege Jerus.* (E.E.T.S.) 6 þer is a warlich wif.. þat haþ softyng & salue for eche sore out. **1611** COTGR., *Amollissement*, a softing, mollifying, making tender. *Ibid.*, *Amollissant*, softing, mollifying.

‖**softa** ('sɒftə). Also **sophta**. [Turk. *sōfta*, ad. Pers. *sūḫtah* lighted, set on fire (by the teacher, or by zeal for study).] In Turkey, a Muslim theological student; also generally, a pupil engaged in professional studies at a secondary school.

**1613** PURCHAS *Pilgrimage* (1614) 315 Thus haue we taken a leisurely view of the Turkish Hierarchy from the poore Softi to the courtly Cadilescher and pontifical Mufti. **1880** MENZIES *Turkey Old & New* II. 249 The Softas.. were angry with the Government, and threatened the Sultan with deposition. **1895** *Westm. Gaz.* 3 Oct. 5/1 The Softas, or Mussulman theological students.

**softball** ('sɒftbɔːl, sɔːft-). Also **soft-ball, soft ball**. [f. SOFT *a.* + BALL *sb.*[1]] **1.** *Confectionery.* (As two words or with hyphen.) A soft globule of sugar formed (e.g. by dropping into water) as a means of testing that the mass of sugar being boiled has reached a certain stage; hence used *attrib.* and *absol.* to designate this stage.

**1894** E. SKUSE *Compl. Confectioner* 70 Add the cocoanut slices and allow the whole to boil, for say ten minutes, or until the sugar comes to a soft ball. **1907** J. KIRKLAND *Mod. Baker, Confectioner & Caterer* IV. iv. 13 The *soft-ball* or full-feather degree is tested by making a small bulb of sugar between the fingers while cooling in cold water. **1921** [see PANOCHE 2]. **1980** T. STOBART *Cook's Encycl.* 404/1 Soft ball —116°C (240°F). The sugar clinging to the skimmer will now, when shaken, produce a feathery, downy effect. The syrup is now beginning to thicken and will form a soft ball if a little of it is dropped into cold water.

**2.** orig. *N. Amer.* **a.** A game resembling baseball but played on a smaller field with a larger ball that is pitched underarm.

**1926** *Daily Colonist* (Victoria, B.C.) 2 July 5/3 The remainder of the morning was occupied by the younger members of the party in playing soft ball and other less strenuous games. **1947** J. STEINBECK *Wayward Bus* 54 A big and muscular young woman who taught ice hockey and softball and archery at the university. **1977** F. F. FIXX *Compl. Bk. Running* p. xvi, Someone who all his life had played tennis, touch football and Saturday-afternoon softball shouldn't be thus laid low.

**b.** A ball of the kind used in the game of softball.

**1914** *Vanity Fair* Feb. 49 (*caption*) Soft ball, soft hands and a soft game. **1918** *Playground* Sept. 223 Suffice it to say that *Playground Baseball*.. differs from ordinary baseball in four ways, namely: (1) A big *soft* ball is used [etc.]. **1974** [see *softball throw*, sense c below]. **1975** R. KROETSCH *Badlands* 136 Lumps of ice the size of softballs.

**c.** *attrib.*, as *softball court, field, game, team*; **softball question**, a question that is easy to answer; **softball throw**, an athletic event in which a softball is thrown as far as possible.

**1943** J. S. HUXLEY *TVA* ix. 73 The playground is floodlit to give the adults a soft-ball court after their day's work is over. **1958** J. KEROUAC *On Road* III. i. 180 A softball game was going on under floodlights. **1974** *News & Press* (Darlington, S. Carolina) 25 Apr. 11/1 Beverly Robinson won first-place in the long jump and the softball throw. **1976** *New Society* 28 Oct. 209/3 'Why Switzerland?' may seem the ultimate softball question, its answer to be found behind those discreet name-plates along Zurich's Bahnhofstrasse. **1977** J. CHEEVER *Falconer* 4 There was a softball field where the gallows had stood. **1977** *Sci. Amer.* Nov. 15/2 He has also collaborated with Groth 'on a number of double plays for the physics department softball team'.

**3.** Tactical slow and gentle play in lawn tennis. Also *attrib.* So **soft-balling** *ppl. a.*, **soft-ball** *v. trans.* and *intr.*

**1961** *Times* 18 May 5/2 Not only did Sangster adapt his game to the slow court and a soft-balling opponent. **1962** *Times* 25 Apr. 4/7 It was the Chilean's soft ball game that ruffled his opponent's feathers. *Ibid.* 26 June 4/2 Playing soft ball, and apparently resigned to defeat, he was offered a reprieve by a casual opponent. **1976** *Observer* 2 May 23/2 Miss Mottram, who was being made to run hard and dig deep on the dusty red court to stay in the game, decided to soft-ball her, to slow the pace. **1980** *Amer. Speech* 1976 LI. 294 *Softball*, play slow soft shots.

**soft-billed**, *a. Ornith.* [SOFT *a.* 31.] Having a soft bill. Also in specific names.

*a* **1705** RAY *Synop. Avium* (1713) 68 In *Tenuirostras*, Soft Bil'd Birds.. and *Crassirostras*, Hard Bil'd Birds. **1771** G. WHITE *Selborne* xlii, Many of our soft-billed summer birds of passage. **1785** LATHAM *Gen. Synop. Birds* III. II. 522 Soft-billed Duck.. inhabits New Zealand. **1826** MISS MITFORD *Village* Ser. III. (1863) 97 A soft-billed bird, that requires as much care as a nightingale! **1871** DARWIN *Desc. Man* II. xvi. (1890) 490 Many of the soft-billed birds are songsters.

**soft-board(ing**: see SOFT *a.* 32.

**soft-bodied**, *a. Zool.* [SOFT *a.* 31.] Having a soft body.

**1782** *Encycl. Brit.* (ed. 2) IX. 6617/2 These tender and soft-bodied animals [*sc.* frogs]. **1826** KIRBY & SP. *Entomol.* III. xxxv. 655 In soft-bodied insects they [the legs] seem usually more firm and unbending. **1846** PATTERSON *Zool.* 27 The molluscous or soft-bodied animals, which are known as shell-fish. **1872** H. A. NICHOLSON *Palaeont.* 59 No trace of the past existence of which has yet been obtained, or, from their soft-bodied nature, is ever likely to be.

**soft-boiled**, *a.* [f. *soft-boil* vb. s.v. SOFT *a.* 32.] **1.** Of an egg: boiled but not hard-boiled. Also *transf.*

**1889** *Kipling* in *Macmillan's Mag.* Dec. 153/1 You niver had a head worth a soft-boiled egg. **1906** *Woman's Home Companion* Nov. 5/3, I have plenty of towels and soap and soft-boiled eggs. **1948** W. STEVENS *Let.* 2 Apr. (1967) 582 How good grated Parmesan is on soft-boiled eggs. **1954** —— *Let.* 23 July (1967) 841 The weather has been all sparkle with a hot day and soft-boiled night thrown in now and then. **1975** J. MCCLURE *Snake* iii. 37 His big, soft-boiled eyes, with pouches beneath them like black egg-cups.

**2.** Of a person: mild, easy-going; naïve, impractical; opp. HARD-BOILED *a.* 2.

*a* **1930** D. H. LAWRENCE *Last Poems* (1932) 258 O you hard-boiled conservatives and you soft-boiled liberals Don't you *see* how you make bolshevism inevitable? **1942** E. WAUGH *Put out More Flags* iii. 191 Father's friends were all hard-boiled and rich... And then I met Cedric who was poor and very, very soft-boiled. **1963** *Times* 26 Feb. 16/4 But, say the T.V.A. enthusiasts, there is a psychological stimulus in receiving a rebate as opposed to merely not paying tax from the start. Is the British businessman really so soft-boiled? **1978** D. GRYLLS *Guardians & Angels* iv. 142 Dickens['s].. pantheon is crammed with a soft-boiled array of credulous infantile adults.

**soft centre**. Also **soft-centre**. [f. SOFT *a.* + CENTRE *sb.*]

**1. a.** A soft filling inside a chocolate. Also *attrib.*

[**1930** H. W. BYWATERS *Mod. Methods of Cocoa & Chocolate Manuf.* xxv. 251 During recent years chocolates containing soft creme centres.. have increased in popularity.] **1947** 'G. ORWELL' in *Tribune* 7 Mar. 11/3 The same kind of charm as belongs to a pink geranium or a soft-centre chocolate. **1959** [see CENTRE *sb.* 11 e].

**b.** *transf.* A chocolate with a soft filling.

**1970** H. MCLEAVE *Question of Negligence* (1973) ii. 18 Every time Lord Blye turned nasty.. her consumption of *petit fours* and soft centres soared. **1974** P. HAINES *Tea at Gunter's* xiv. 149 Me.. lying about on the settee eating soft centres, and Mantovani on the radiogram.

**2.** A soft heart, esp. in contrast with a tough exterior; a vulnerable or weak core. Also *attrib.*

**1955** E. BLISHEN *Roaring Boys* IV. 194 The fierceness and roughness of the boys was of the surface... The longer I stayed there, the more aware I became of this soft centre. **1973** M. AMIS *Rachel Papers* 148, I gathered from the female novelists I had been reading.. that the malleable, soft-centre syndrome was no longer considered attractive. **1974** *Bookseller* 20 July 197/1 Most of the publishers I've known have had soft centres. They love to be loved, especially by their authors.

**soft-centred**, *a.* [f. prec.] **1.** Of a person or his attitudes: soft-hearted; of works of literature, art, music, etc.: having a weak, vulnerable, or sentimental core.

**1957** *Times Lit. Suppl.* 8 Nov. 674/4 Like his attack on the Monarchy his attachment to Socialism is essentially emotional and soft-centred. **1960** *Listener* 3 Mar. 425/2 The fact that the catalyst is a woman friend.. does not make the play any less soft-centred. **1963** *Times* 7 Mar. 15/3 Like all nice Cockney Jewish characters, Harryboy is soft-centred. **1973** *Art Internat.* Mar. 57/1 His resulting paintings.. proved to be simply a murky, soft-centered brand of Cubism. **1977** *Broadcast* 10 Oct. 17/2 Michael Arlen.. [was] a writer of immense but somewhat soft-centred sophistication.

**2.** Of a chocolate; having a soft centre.

**1970** C. WOOD '*Terrible Hard*', *says Alice* viii. 110 A soft-centred milk chocolate. **1978** *Times Lit. Suppl.* 21 Apr.

438/3 Diamond Jim Brady..regularly ate a twelve-course dinner..ending with five pounds of soft-centred chocolates.

Hence **soft-'centredness**.

**1967** *Guardian* 10 Apr. 6/6 The critics..began to note..a soft-centredness about Britain, a complacency, a reluctance to scrap and build. **1981** *Economist* 28 Nov. 47/1 A mixture of Saudi soft-centredness, Arab pettiness and Syrian bloody-mindedness has led the Arabs to miss a rare opportunity.

**soften** ('sɒf(ə)n, -ɔː-), *v.* Also 4–5 softne, 5 *Sc.* softine, 9 *Sc.* saften. [f. SOFT *a.* + -EN. Cf. SOFT *v.*]

**I.** *trans.* **1. a.** To mitigate, assuage, or diminish; to render less painful or more easy to bear.

*c* **1385** CHAUCER *L.G.W.* Prol. 50 That blisful sight softneth al my sorwe. *c* **1415** HOCCLEVE *Min. Poems* 62 Let your hy worthynesse Oure indigences softne, & abate! **1708** POPE *Ode St. Cecilia's Day* vii, Music can soften pain to ease. *a* **1715** BURNET *Own Time* (1766) II. 13 It would very much soften those apprehensions. **1822** SCOTT *Peveril* xxxii, His lady, who..shared and softened his imprisonment. **1823** —— *Quentin D.* x, All who had contributed to soften the term of his exile. **1842** LOVER *Handy Andy* xlix, After the lapse of a few days had softened the bitter grief.

*absol.* *c* **1375** *Sc. Leg. Saints* xlii. (*Agatha*) 149 Godis angele..vith dew of hewine ma softine sa, þat þi fyre sal me do na wa. *c* **1400** *Rom. Rose* 1925 It softned heere, and prikkith there.

**b.** Similarly with *off*.

**1790** MME. D'ARBLAY *Diary* Jan., To soften off, by the air, a violent headache, I determined upon walking to Chelsea. **1849** FROUDE *Nemesis of Faith* 224 All that woman's care..could do to soften off her end was done.

†**c.** With personal object: To relieve from pain. *Obs.*⁻¹

?*a* **1400** *Morte Arth.* 2601 This prissonere syr Priamus..Sais that he has saluez salle softene vs bothene.

**2. a.** To render more impressionable or tender; to affect emotionally.

**1435** MISYN *Fire of Love* 102 þe saule softynand þer þou..þi tempyll has ordand. **1667** MILTON *P.L.* XI. 110, I behold them soft'nd and with tears Bewailing thir excess. **1827** SCOTT *Jrnl.* 7 Nov., I..fairly softened myself like an old fool, with recalling old stories till I was fit for nothing but shedding tears. **1874** MOZLEY *Univ. Serm.* ix. (1877) 195 Misfortune, adversity, soften the human heart.

**b.** To enervate, weaken, render effeminate.

**1581** SIDNEY *Apol. Poetrie* (Arb.) 51 Howe.., before Poets did soften vs, we were full of courage, giuen to martiall exercises. **1615** CHAPMAN *Odyss.* XII. 64 The Sirens will so soften with their song..His loose affections. **1670** COTTON *Espernon* I. III. 104 A negligent and voluptuous Prince, whose nature being softned, and unnerv'd by ease [etc.]. **1780** *Mirror* No. 94, Softening too much the mind of a young girl, who has to struggle with the difficulties of life. **1828–32** WEBSTER s.v., Troops softened by luxury.

**c.** To make more gentle, delicate, or refined. Also with *into*.

**1709** STEELE *Tatler* No. 10 ¶2 Every Temper..is to be animated and softned by the Influence of Beauty. **1781** COWPER *Charity* 96 This genial intercourse..softens human rock-work into men. **1831** SINCLAIR *Corr.* II. 370 Attention to music..softens the temper. **1841** ELPHINSTONE *Hist. Ind.* II. 249 This mixture probably softened the manners of the people from the first. **1868** MORRIS *Earthly Par.* I. I. 112 Though some divine thought softened all her face.

**3.** To mollify or appease; to render less harsh or severe.

*c* **1450** *Mirour Saluacioun* (Roxb.) 128 Bot marie softnys his ire als oure best mediatrice. **1593** SHAKS. *Lucr.* 591 All which together..Beat at thy rocky..heart, To soften it. **1603** —— *Meas. for M.* I. v. 70 All hope is gone, Vnlesse you haue the grace by your faire praier To soften Angelo. **1725** DE FOE *Voy. r. World* (1840) 342 To soften them a little, and in some measure to please them. **1780** *Mirror* No. 101, Nor was his resentment softened even by her husband's leaving the army. **1835** THIRLWALL *Greece* I. vi. 199 When the sacrifice was designed to soften the anger of an offended deity. **1849** MACAULAY *Hist. Eng.* v. I. 637 That good prelate used all his influence to soften the gaolers. **1864** BRYCE *Holy Rom. Emp.* xv. (1875) 243 It still appeared possible to soften, if not to overcome, their antagonism.

**4. a.** To make physically soft or softer; to lessen the hardness of (a substance).

**1530** PALSGR. 724/2 It is harde yet, but I shall soften it well ynoughe. **1591** SHAKS. *Two Gentl.* III. ii. 79 Orpheus Lute,..Whose golden touch could soften steele and stones. **1604** —— *Oth.* IV. iii. 47 Her salt teares fell from her, and softned the stones. **1656** *Verney Memoirs* (1907) II. 51, I see the same sunn that softens Wax, hardens clay. **1750** tr. *Leonardus' Mirr. Stones* 227 Sometimes deceivers will soften the amber and put into it some extraneous matter. **1796** H. HUNTER tr. *St.-Pierre's Stud. Nat.* (1799) I. 53 With Fire he..hardens clay, softens iron. **1853** SOYER *Pantroph.* 288 They were first softened in milk and honey.

*absol.* **1610** MARKHAM *Masterp.* II. clxxiii. 484 Armoniacke drieth, cooleth, softneth, and draweth.

**b.** To make (water) soft.

**1771** MRS. HAYWOOD *New Present for Maid* 267 Hard water may be softened by laying chalk in the bottoms of the wells or ponds. **1867** BLOXAM *Chem.* 43 Clark's process for softening waters.

**c.** Usu. with *up*. To reduce the strength of (a defensive position) by bombing or other preliminary attack; also *transf.* Hence *fig.*: to undermine the resistance of (a person). *colloq.* (orig. *U.S.*).

**1940** W. L. SHIRER *Berlin Diary* (1941) 378 Stuka dive-bombers are softening the Allied defense positions, making them ripe for an easy attack. **1942** *Sun* (Baltimore) 3 Feb. 1/5 Japanese air raiders engaged in a grand-scale effort to soften up the stronghold for a final invasion thrust. **1949** F. MACLEAN *Eastern Approaches* III. xv. 490 United States Army Air Force Mustangs had 'softened up' the target. **1950** J. DEMPSEY *Championship Fighting* 89 They will enable you to knock out or at least 'soften up' an opponent. **1951** *Here & Now* (N.Z.) May 8/2 These fellowships are part of the general system of 'softening up' overseas journalists and persuading them to see the advantages of the American way of life. **1952** S. KAUFFMANN *Philanderer* (1953) xii. 193 'You make me feel pretty cruel,' he said... Then in a moment she smiled. 'You said that just to soften me up.' **1962** *Listener* 1 Nov. 706/1 The farming industry is being softened up by the clear indications from ministers that changes are coming in the whole support system, whether or not we go into Europe. **1974** *Daily Tel.* 21 Sept. 15 A man who had told police of goings on in Soho was kidnapped in broad daylight, tied to a chair and softened up to find what he had said. **1980** G. B. TRUDEAU *Tad Overweight*, 'Over there's my Soviet-made Makarov mortar.' 'Mortar? What do you use the mortar for?' 'Deer hunting. I like to soften up an area before I hunt it.'

**5. a.** To modify or tone down; to render less pronounced or prominent.

In certain contexts there is implication of other senses. (*a*) **1670–1** MARVELL *Corr.* Wks. (Grosart) II. 382 The clause that makes them riots is thrown out, and severall other clauses softned. **1712** ADDISON *Spect.* No. 399 ¶5 They..do not see our Faults,..or soften them by their Representations. **1714** POPE *Lett.* Wks. 1736 V. 216, I know you will think fit to soften your expression when you see the passage. **1788** GIBBON *Decl. & F.* lii. V. 422 Their stern enthusiasm was softened by time and prosperity. **1812** CRABBE *Tales* xvii. 153, I in vain had tried To soften crime, that cannot be denied. **1856** FROUDE *Hist. Eng.* (1858) I. 463 The scarcely ambiguous answer was something softened the following day. **1879** —— *Cæsar* xx. 346 Others proposed to send a deputation to soften the harshness of his removal.

(*b*) **1810** CRABBE *Borough* ii. 41 For time has soften'd what was harsh when new, And now the stains are all of sober hue. **1835** W. IRVING *Tour Prairies* 159 There was a smoky haze in the atmosphere.., softening the features of the landscape. **1884** *Manch. Exam.* 1 Sept. 5/4 An awning..softened the light and hid the bare rafters.

**b.** Const. *into* or *to*.

**1753** HOGARTH *Anal. Beauty* vi. 29 Horror is softened into reverence. **1784** COWPER *Task* I. 365 'Tis the primal curse, But soften'd into mercy. **1815** J. SMITH *Panorama Sci. & Art* II. 725 These shades, duly softened into each other, will give the idea of a round body. **1842** BARHAM *Ingol. Leg.* Ser. II. *Lay of St. Cuthbert* iii, And he utters—a word which we'll soften to 'Zooks!'

**c.** With *down* (or *away*).

**1799–1805** WORDSW. *Prelude* XIV. 246 Thou didst soften down This over-sternness. **1809** MALKIN *Gil Blas* XI. iv. ¶3 Throughout my narrative I softened down the passages likely to give umbrage to my patron. **1866** MRS. GASKELL *Wives & Dau.* iv, Mrs. Hamley tried sometimes to..soften away opinions which she fancied were offensive to the doctor. **1869** TOZER *Highl. Turkey* II. 264 Inconsistencies..are modified and softened down.

**6.** To make softer in sound.

For Ainsworth's use see the note to SOFT *a.* 3 b.

**1736** AINSWORTH *Lat. Dict.* II. s.v. *D*, This letter..is a *t* hardned, as *t* is a *d* softned. **1794** MRS. RADCLIFFE *Myst. Udolpho* xxvi, He spoke to her in accents somewhat softened from their usual harshness. **1824** BYRON *Def. Transf.* I. ii, How the soldier's rough strain seems Soften'd by distance to a hymn-like cadence! **1890** *Science-Gossip* XXVI. 17 In our modern word *ditch* the final letter has been softened or weakened.

**II.** *intr.* **7. a.** To become soft or softer in various non-physical senses; *esp.* to become more gentle, tender, or emotional; to grow fainter or less pronounced; *Comm.* to lose firmness.

**1611** SHAKS. *Wint. T.* II. ii. 40 We do not know How he may soften at the sight o' th' Childe. **1722–7** BOYER *Dict. Royal* I, *S'adoucir*,..to soften, to grow soft. **1791** MRS. RADCLIFFE *Rom. Forest* i, The terror of La Motte began to subside, and the grief of Adeline to soften. **1794** —— *Myst. Udolpho* iii, Its savage features gradually softened. **1838** T. MITCHELL *Aristoph. Clouds* 31 The scholar..gradually softens at this submission, and becomes sociable and communicative. **1865** CARLYLE *Fredk. Gt.* XXI. viii. (1872) X. 163 His eyes..softened finely in hearing, or telling, some trait of nobleness. **1877** MRS. OLIPHANT *Makers Flor.* viii. 212 Never was heart so hard but it softened before so much gentleness. **1947** *Kiplinger Washington Let.* (Kiplinger Washington Agency) 5 Apr., Consumers are not buying quite enough to take up all production. Luxury markets began to soften last fall. **1982** *Daily Tel.* 6 July 15 American rates might soften following the publication of reassuring money supply figures on Friday evening. **1982** *Times* 17 Aug. 12 The shares softened 2p to 168p after announcement of the results.

**b.** Const. *into*.

**1730** THOMSON *Hymn* 25 Shade unperceived so softening into shade. **1771** *Junius' Lett.* liv. (1788) 296 By what gentle degrees the furious, persecuting zeal of Mr. Horne has softened into moderation. **1820** L. HUNT *Indicator, Deaths Little Children* 203 The pain that is in it softens into pleasure.

**c.** With *away*, *down*, or *off*.

**1797** MRS. RADCLIFFE *Ital.* xii, The responses softened away in distance. **1833** RITCHIE *Wand. Loire* 122 The rocks soften down on the right, and the village of Bouchemain appears. **1840** DICKENS *Master Humphrey's Clock* (Tauchn.) III. 285 A crowd, which..softened off in a confused heap of faces. **1879** BROWNING *Halbert & Hob* 6 Most wildness by degrees Softens away!

**8.** To become physically soft.

**1626** BACON *Sylva* §840 Many of those Bodies, that will not Melt,..will notwithstanding Soften. **1727** BOYER *Dict. Royal* I, *S'amollir*,..(*perdre sa dureté*), to grow soft, tender or pliant, to soften. **1838** THOMSON *Chem. Org. Bodies* 182 When heated it softens at 302°. **1900** *Jrnl. Soc. Dyers* XVI. 7 The acetate..does not begin to soften below a temperature of 150° C.

**softened** (sɒf(ə)nd, -ɔː-), *ppl. a.* [f. SOFTEN *v.*]

**1.** Made or rendered physically soft or yielding.

**1600** SURFLET *Countrie Farme* 95 Mixing..the powder of a softned bricke in her meate. **1688** BOYLE *Final Causes* IV. 191 To..make a Second Attrition of their already much Softned Aliments. **1830** KNOX *Beclard's Anat.* 340 The softened nervous substance is sometimes at the point of being liquid. **1899** *Allbutt's Syst. Med.* VIII. 871 The softened central area of the tumour.

**b.** Characterized by softening or softness.

**1839–47** *Todd's Cycl. Anat.* III. 720 B, The softened condition of the brain is doubtless due to a similar cause. **1843** R. J. GRAVES *Syst. Clin. Med.* xv. 183 Certain phenomena..indicate a softened state of the heart.

**2.** Rendered soft or softer, in other senses.

**1716** POPE *Iliad* VI. 622 The soften'd chief..dried the falling drops, and thus pursued. **1794** MRS. RADCLIFFE *Myst. Udolpho* xxxii, Then..her softened thoughts returned to Valancourt. *Ibid.* xxxviii, The softened music, floating at a distance, soothed her melancholy mind. **1829** SCOTT *Rob Roy* Introd., A softened account of this anecdote. **1852** MRS. STOWE *Uncle Tom's C.* xxvii, 'Get up, child,' said Miss Ophelia in a softened voice. **1873** SYMONDS *Greek Poets* xii. 404 Its pearly greys and softened greens. **1894** MRS. DYAN *Man's Keeping* (1899) 311 She..saw that new softened look in his eyes.

**softener** ('sɒf(ə)nə(r), -ɔː-). [f. as prec.]

**1.** One who or that which softens, in various senses; a mollifier. Also with *down*.

**1608** HIERON *Wks.* I. 722/1 Whose blood is..the principall softner of the heart. **1611** COTGR., *Mollifieur*, a mollifier, softener. **1668** CHARLETON & P. M. *Ephes. & Cimm. Matrons* 72 You are..the obstacles to honour; the softners of courage. **1743** FRANCIS tr. *Hor., Odes* I. xxxii. 20 Thou Softner of each anxious Care. **1839** DICKENS *Nickleby* viii, One of the best softeners of a hard bed. **1894** H. NESBIT *Bush Girl's Rom.* 27 A true helpmate and softener-down of the rough edges. **1954** A. J. HALL *Stand. Handbk. Textiles* (ed. 4) iv. 265 It is important not to use softeners which reduce the fastness of coloured goods to light. **1973** *Times* 1 June 11/5 It tests the water every night, working its little two-inch square brain-box attached to the softener.

**2.** *spec.* A painting-brush of soft hair.

**1843** *Civil Eng. & Arch. Jrnl.* VI. 305/1 Passing a dry brush, called a 'softener', lightly over it. **1873** E. SPON *Workshop Rec.* Ser. I. 6/2 For shading, camel or sable hair brushes, called Softeners, are generally used.

**'softening**, *vbl. sb.* Also 6 soughtening, 6, 8 softning. [f. as prec.]

**1. a.** The action or process of making or becoming soft, in various senses of the adj. Also with *a* and pl.

**1568** TURNER *Herbal* III. 21 It purgeth..gently by soughtening of the belly. **1580** HOLLYBAND *Treas. Fr. Tong*, *Mollification*, softning. **1611** COTGR., *Attendrissement*, a softening, mollifying. **1719** WATERLAND *Vind. Christ's Div.* 223 After the Disguises and Softenings, and Colourings had been carried on so long. **1744** H. BROOKE *Love & Vanity* 124 O such a pretty knack at painting! And all for soft'ning and for sainting! **1802** D. STEWART *Life & Writ. Robertson* I. 42 To unite in his portraits the truth of nature with the softenings of art. **1853** J. H. NEWMAN *Hist. Sk.* Ser. II. I. iii. 105 When their strength declines..there is no softening, no misgiving. **1892** *Photogr. Ann.* II. 203 After this a general softening (that is to say, the graduating of light into shade). **1919** R. D. BANGAY *Oscillation Valve* 203 Any serious 'softening' of the valve will entirely upset its characteristics and action. **1945** *Electronic Engin.* XVII. 338/3 A high grid leak may very rapidly cause softening of the valve. **1946** *Ann. Reg. 1945* 214 The constant harping on the subject [of Turkish Armenia] in the Soviet Press, accompanied by attacks on the régime in power in Turkey, conveyed the impression that the familiar process of softening would in due course be followed by a formal demand. **1957** *Economist* 30 Nov. 809/1 The recent softening of the markets for petroleum products. **1960** N. MITFORD *Don't tell Alfred* xx. 216 When some softening up on these lines had been delivered the campaign settled down to its real objective. **1968** *Globe & Mail* (Toronto) 13 Jan. B1/2 It was too early to tell whether this marked a reversal of the softening trend in these important loans to businesses. **1977** P. STREVENS *New Orientations Teaching Eng.* ii. 24 The integration of prior 'softening-up' with initial presentation and subsequent consolidation and repetition.

**b.** *Path.*, esp. in ***softening of the brain***.

**1830** R. KNOX *Béclard's Anat.* 340 The softening is a very frequent alteration of a part of the central nervous mass. **1835** *Cycl. Pract. Med.* IV. 5/1 When softening of the brain is accompanied by an increase of bulk. **1843** GRAVES *Syst. Clin. Med.* xv. 184 Softening of the heart exists in typhus fever. **1845** BUDD *Dis. Liver* 74 This state of yellow softening. *Ibid.*, Red softening. **1854** JONES & SIEVEKING *Pathol. Anat.* 250 White softening..is chiefly met with in the parts most remote from the grey matter.

**2.** *spec.* (See quots.)

**1728** CHAMBERS *Cycl.*, *Softening*, in Painting, the mixing and diluting of Colours with the Brush or Pencil. **1881** RAYMOND *Mining Gloss.*, *Softening*, of lead, the removal of antimony and other impurities.

**3.** *attrib.*, as ***softening disease, tool***; **softening iron**, in leather-working, an iron plate upon which the wetted hides of animals are stretched; **softening-machine** (see quot. 1875); **softening works**, works for softening drinking-water.

**1834** COOPER *Good's Study Med.* (ed. 4) I. 368 *note*, In the *ramollissement*, or softening disease, the spleen never becomes so large as when it is indurated. **1839** URE *Dict. Arts* 767 They would not bear working upon the softening iron. *Ibid.*, The softening tool is an iron plate [etc.]. **1875** KNIGHT *Dict. Mech.* 2238/1 *Softening-machine*, (Leather,) a machine..for beating the hides in water to saturate them. **1888** *Daily News* 7 June 6/7 A pumping station and softening works. *Ibid.*, The softening plant.

**b.** With *up*, in sense 4 c of the vb., as ***softening-up period, process, raid, technique, trick***.

**1951** *R.A.F. Rev.* Apr.–Mar. 32/3 They helped to cover Allied bombers on 'softening-up' raids on the European fortress. **1953** L. P. HARTLEY *Go-Between* x. 127 The softening-up process, as we should call it now, which he had put me through had been enough. **1954** J. STEIN *Basic Everyday Encycl.* 558/1 This 'softening-up' technique broke communications, disrupted production, disorganized civilian existence, destroyed the German air force. **1971** B. W. ALDISS *Soldier Erect* 229 After a softening up period, another attack was launched. Our attack! **1976** B. LECOMBER *Dead Weight* viii. 90 Leaving the suspect to stew..is the oldest softening-up trick in the book.

**softening,** *ppl. a.* Also 7–8 softning, 8–9 *Sc.* saftening. [f. as prec.]

**1.** Causing to become soft, tender, etc.

(*a*) *c* **1400** *Lanfranc's Cirurg.* 353 Of mollificatif medicyns or softenyng. **1631** WIDDOWES *Nat. Philos.* 36 His oyle for hot and softning nature helpeth diseases of the brest. **1735** BRACKEN *Gentlem. Pocket Farr.* 11 *note*, You ought to keep the Foot..covered with any softning Poultice. **1760–72** H. BROOKE *Fool of Qual.* (1809) II. 151, I got some softening cream, and spread it over the burn. **1861** PALEY *Æschylus* (ed. 2) *Prometh.* 388 *note*, Reducing a swelling by softening applications.

(*b*) **1643** MILTON *Divorce* viii. Wks. 1851 IV. 39 To unsettle our constancie with timerous and softning suggestions. **1668** DAVENANT *Man's the Master* v. i, [Do you] yet strive, with softning pity, to allay that courage? **1729** LAW *Serious Call* xvii. (1761) 293 We may deceive ourselves..with vain and softening comments upon these words. **1794** E. WILLIAMS *Poems* II. 4 He..blended with her glaring hues The soft'ning tints of Art. **1847** PRESCOTT *Peru* IV. iii. (1850) II. 300 When..time had..thrown its softening veil over the past. **1894** MRS. DYAN *Man's Keeping* II. 126 Under the softening shade of her parasol.

**2.** Becoming soft, gentle, tender, etc.

**1730** THOMSON *Hymn* 5 Wide flush the fields; the softening air is balm. **1853** KANE *Grinnell Exped.* xviii. (1856) 140 With a gradually softening tint. **1865** DICKENS *Mut. Fr.* III. ii, 'I can believe that,' said Miss Abbey, with a softening glance at the little creature. **1898** *Allbutt's Syst. Med.* V. 250 Occasionally the enlarged and softening glands adhere to a contiguous organ.

**soft-eyed,** *a.* [SOFT *a.* 31.] Having soft or gentle eyes; tender-eyed.

**1735** POPE *Prol. Sat.* 286 The verse..That tends to..Give..Innocence a fear, Or from the soft-eyed Virgin steal a tear! **1777** POTTER *Æschylus, Supplicants* 109 Soft-ey'd Humanity dwells here. **1859** LD. LYTTON *Wanderer* (ed. 2) 239 She is meekness itself, my soft-eyed little cousin. **1897** MAMIE DICKENS *My Father as I recall him* 82 The latter, a soft-eyed, gentle, good-tempered St. Bernard.

**soft-finned,** *a. Ichth.* [SOFT *a.* 31.] Having soft fins.

**1774** GOLDSM. *Nat. Hist.* (1824) III. 60 The fish..that have soft or cartilaginous fins, are called Soft-finned Fish. **1851** GOSSE *Nat. Hist., Fishes* 200 The Soft-finned Fishes are, in general, inferior to the Spinous-finned in [etc.]. **1896** LYDEKKER *Roy. Nat. Hist.* V. 395 These spiny-finned eels are an exact analogue of the true soft-finned eels. *Ibid.* 430 The Soft-finned Fishes,—Suborder *Anacanthini*.

**soft-'focus,** *a.* and *sb.* Also soft focus. [f. SOFT *a.* + FOCUS *sb.*] **A.** *adj.* **a.** *Photogr.* Characterized by or producing a deliberate slight lack of clarity and definition in a photograph.

**1917** P. L. ANDERSON *Pictorial Photogr.* ii. 42 It should be noted that the soft-focus lens..has greater apparent depth, both of field and of focus. **1940** A. L. M. SOWERBY *Wall's Dict. Photogr.* (ed. 15) 600 It is generally considered that the most pleasing soft-focus effects are obtained by superposing a diffused image upon a more sharply-defined one, this giving a kind of 'halo' round the lights. **1958** [see sense B]. **1975** *Publishers Weekly* 13 Jan. 58/1 Aided by lovely soft-focus photographs.., Miss Bailey tells the story of a little seedling blown away from its mother tree too soon. **1977** J. HEDGECOE *Photographer's Handbk.* 31 The design of soft focus lenses leaves one pronounced optical error, 'spherical aberration'. This gives halos to highlights and a general softness of outline. **1978** P. THEROUX *Picture Palace* ix. 71 Photographs looked freckled and corpse-like, soft-focus poses that might have been painters' instant fossils.

**b.** *fig.* Diffuse, blurred, unclear, imprecise.

**1961** W. T. JONES *Romantic Syndrome* viii. 227 We might begin..by making a count of soft-focus imagery in the works of various poets. **1965** *Punch* 17 Nov. 712 You will see the advantage of reviewing single instalments. It allows elbow-room to savour the glittering detail. Handle the whole book and you fall back on soft-focus generalities, the tiny individual flavours lost. **1975** *New Yorker* 24 Feb. 127/1 The voice is soft-focus, not keenly projected, but of pleasant quality in the middle ranges. **1979** *Listener* 16 Aug. 214/4 This [play]..was full of winsome Irishness and soft-focus sentimentality.

**B.** *sb.* A deliberate slight lack of clarity and definition in a photograph. Also *fig.*

**1958** P. POLLACK *Picture Hist. Photogr.* xx. 261 Dr. P. H. Emerson held that soft focus corresponded to natural vision and that soft-focus photography was an art superior to all other graphic arts. **1961** W. T. JONES *Romantic Syndrome* viii. 235 Once the critic replaces a vague liking for 'romantic qualities' with a preference for 'soft-focus'..he is much more likely to make an adequate assessment of the work of the poets and painters. **1977** *Practical Photogr.* Jan. 23/4 To suggest that this method of obtaining soft-focus costs 1p is ridiculous.

Hence **soft-'focus** *v. trans.*, **soft-'focused** *ppl. a.* (both *fig.* in the examples).

**1957** *Archit. Rev.* CXXI. 319 The whole effect is to blur and 'soft-focus' the precision-made look which has been one of the chief qualities of the curtain wall. **1977** *New Yorker* 27 June 35/1 Rose did not like to look at them, at their soft-focussed meekly smiling gratitude.

**soft-footed,** *a.* [SOFT *a.* 31.] Having feet which tread softly. In early use *fig.*

**1612** CHAPMAN *Rev. Bussy d'Ambois* v. iii, The black soft-footed hour is now on wing. **1656** COWLEY *Pindar. Odes, 2nd Olympique* viii, Soft-footed Winds..Dance through the perfum'd Air. **1736** AINSWORTH I. s.v., Soft footed, *mollipes*. **1894** *Outing* XXIII. 346/2 The soft-footed maid had just left them. **1947** AUDEN *Age of Anxiety* (1948) ii. 47 In the soft-footed Hours of darkness.

Hence **soft-footedly** *adv.*

**1834** LYTTON *Pilgr. Rhine* xi. (1840) 139 He [the fox] walked very soft-footedly.

**†soft-ȝern,** *a. Obs.* [f. SOFT *sb.* + YEARN *a.*] Desirous of ease or luxury. Also **†soft-ȝerne,** love of ease. *Obs.*

*c* **1200** *Trin. Coll. Hom.* 75 þe softȝerne fedeð hem seluen helle fur to honde and fote. *Ibid.*, Softȝerne and ednesse letteð þe mannes shrifte þe þincheð þat he ne mai þolen hunger ne þirst ne oðer pine.

**†softhead**[1]. *Obs. rare.* In 4 soft-, zofthede, 5 softhed. [f. SOFT *a.* + -HEAD.] Softness; gentleness; delicacy.

*c* **1340** HAMPOLE *Psalter* cxliv. 7 þe mynd of þe haboundaunce of þi softhede þai sall rift. **1340** *Ayenb.* 267 Of alle zofthede and nesshede. *c* **1440** *Jacob's Well* 238 In valeys of lownes be..moysture,..softhed & neschhed.

**soft-head**[2]. [f. SOFT *a.* + HEAD *sb.*[1]] One who has a soft head; hence, in mod. use, a silly or stupid person; a simpleton. (Cf. next.)

**1650** BULWER *Anthropomet.* 22 The Brasilians' Heads..are as hard as the wood that growes in their Country,..and when they will injure any white Man, they call him soft-head. *c* **1872** *Hartley's Yorks. Ditties* Ser. II. 64 Shoo must be a poor little softheead. **1892** MANNING *Pastime Papers* 86 To be treated as dreamers, enthusiasts or soft-heads.

**soft-headed,** *a.* [SOFT *a.* 31.] Weak in intellect; foolish, silly, stupid.

**1667** DRYDEN & DK. NEWCASTLE *Sir M. Mar-all* III. i, Adieu soft-headed Sir Martin. **1721** BAILEY, *Cully*,..a Fool, a soft headed Fellow. **1782** MME. D'ARBLAY *Diary* 4 Nov., This young man is very..good, and soft-hearted; but alas! he is also soft-headed. **1824** SCOTT *St. Ronan's* xxxii, He is a strange, soft-headed, sleepy sort of man. **1884** *Christian World* 21 Feb. 139/4 Large numbers of deluded women and soft-headed men.

Hence **soft-headedness.**

**1862** WHYTE MELVILLE *Inside Bar* iii, Probably he was making a mental computation of my soft-headedness.

**soft-hearted,** *a.* [SOFT *a.* 31.] Having a soft or susceptible heart; tender-hearted.

**1593** SHAKS. *2 Hen. VI*, III. ii. 307 Fye Coward woman, and soft harted wretch. **1602** MARSTON *Ant. & Mel.* I. Wks. 1856 I. 17 Why weepes soft hearted Florisell? **1648** J. BEAUMONT *Psyche* XVIII. ix, Hear then, O all soft-hearted Turtles. **1782** MISS BURNEY *Cecilia* v. x, The soft-hearted Mr. Arnott. **1840** DICKENS *Old C. Shop* xiv, He was only a soft-hearted grateful fellow. **1881** JOWETT *Thucyd.* I. 195 Do not be soft-hearted at the sight of their distress.

Hence **soft-heartedness.**

**1580** HOLLYBAND *Treas. Fr. Tong, Mercy*, pitie, mercie, softhartednesse. **1808** *Edin. Rev.* XII. 273 A sort of soft-heartedness towards the sufferings of individuals. **1874** *Contemp. Rev.* Oct. 711 A reputation for soft-heartedness goes far with the crowd.

**softish** ('sɒftɪʃ, -ɔː-), *a.* [f. SOFT *a.* + -ISH.] Somewhat soft; rather tender.

Also *Sc.* and *north. dial.*, somewhat wet or rainy.

**1589** FLEMING *Virg. Georg.* v. 14 To wind..the limber speares about with softish leaues. **1656** W. DU GARD tr. *Comenius' Gate Lat. Unl.* 29 A round lump, softish, beneath chamfered. **1681** GREW *Musæum* III. I. ii. 268 'Tis softish, and somewhat brown. **1766** J. BARTRAM *Jrnl.* 4 Feb. 60 A softish rock full of sea-shells. **1845** *Encycl. Metrop.* XXV. 309/1 A little hair softish and curling. **1878** HUXLEY *Physiogr.* xvi. 271 A bed of softish limestone.

*transf.* **1736** AINSWORTH I, Softish (silly), *ineptus, stupidus*.

**soft-'land,** *v. Astronautics.* Also softland. [Back-formation from next.] *trans.* and *intr.* To land slowly without serious damage, esp. on another planet or a satellite.

*trans.* **1960** *Aeroplane* XCIX. 540 (*caption*) The Surveyor-type probe..should be capable of soft-landing between 100 and 300 lb. of scientific equipment on the Moon. **1960** *Times Mag.* (Seattle) 29 May 22 The first lunar vehicle may be a small robot to be soft-landed on the moon within the next five years. **1966** *Times* 7 Apr. 9/3 This was to have been the final test flight before the United States attempts to softland a real Surveyor space-craft on the moon. **1967** *New Scientist* 1 June 549/3 The balloon itself was constructed of fine polythene and helium-filled... It was soft-landed and recovered for further use. **1970** *Guardian* 21 Sept. 3/7 Russia today soft-landed its Luna 16 unmanned spacecraft on the moon's barren Sea of Fertility.

*intr.* **1964** *Yearbk. Astron.* 1965 135 The LEM will detach from the orbiting parent and soft-land on the Moon. **1967** *New Scientist* 3 Aug. 242/2 *Surveyor III*, which soft-landed on 20 April this year returned over 6000 TV pictures. **1969** *Daily Tel.* 18 July 1 Reports from Moscow..say that Luna 15 is ready 'to soft-land on the moon today' and collect moon dust. **1975** *Times* 7 Apr. 6/1 A manned Soyuz spacecraft..soft-landed southwest of the western Siberian town of Gorno-Altaysk.

So **soft-'landed** *ppl. a.*; **soft-'lander,** a vehicle that is capable of making or has made a soft landing.

**1958** *Proc. Lunar & Planetary Exploration Colloquium* July 13/1 Would you..talk about the design and weight distribution of this soft-landed payload? **1961** *Aeroplane* C. 510/3 Russia's long-range space programme is said to include sending two spaceships to the Moon by 1967. They would be preceded by unmanned 'soft-landers' depositing supplies and propellants. **1966** *Guardian* 28 Dec. 7/1 Luna-13..is returning more information than any other soft lander, whether Russian or American. **1969** *Nature* 12 July 123/1 Between 1966 and 1968, seven Surveyor softlanders were launched which among other things tested the surface strength [of the moon]. **1971** *Ibid.* 26 Nov. 211/2 Such data will be of value in interpreting the findings of soft-landed spacecraft on other planets. **1977** A. HALLAM *Planet Earth* 20/1 The surface panoramas transmitted back to Earth from the Soviet soft-landers Veneras 9 and 10 show a barren landscape that contains both angular and rounded rocks.

**soft landing,** *vbl. sb. Astronautics.* Also softlanding. [f. SOFT *a.* + LANDING *vbl. sb.*]

**1. a.** A landing of a spacecraft that is slow enough for no serious damage to be incurred. Cf. SOFT *a.* 22 d.

**1958** *Proc. Lunar & Planetary Exploration Colloquium* July 13/1 With a soft landing on the moon one might put down a payload of 225 to 800 pounds, but..only about 10 to 25 percent of this would be usable for instruments. **1959** *Washington Post* 24 Mar. A6/4 He said the first 'soft landing' on the moon and return probably will be made with a multi-stage chemical-fueled vehicle. **1966** *Listener* 24 Mar. 427/1 The main events [of 1966] have been the soft landing on the Moon.., and the progress of the two Venus rockets. **1967** *New Scientist* 25 May 448/2 Each of these craft will consist of..an experimental capsule to enter the Martian atmosphere and..make a soft landing either by parachute or ..by means of retro rockets. **1971** *Guardian* 1 July 1/5 The Soyuz made a normal re-entry and soft landing.

**b.** *fig.*

**1969** *Sci. Jrnl.* Jan. 54/3 Should one bombard with excess energy or attempt..a 'soft landing' where the energy of the incoming particle is just enough to allow it to penetrate the barrier, be captured and form the compound nucleus. **1973** *Newsweek* 17 Sept. 65/2 Even if the President succeeds in pulling in the rampaging economy for a soft landing, of course, the arrival will be nonetheless bumpy for many.

**2.** *attrib.* or as *adj.*

**1960** *Aeroplane* XCIX. 541/2 Mr. Stoller said that in 1962 three Ranger vehicles were planned to rough-land payloads on the surface of the Moon. These will be followed by the soft-landing mission. **1962** [see LANDING-PLACE 1 c]. **1965** *Guardian* 29 Dec. 3/7 The Apollo moon landing programme ..depends on highly sophisticated soft-landing techniques. **1969** *New Scientist* 27 Feb. 439/2 The upshot of the planetary experiments should be to discover more about the suitability of Mars to support life; and to select possible sites for future soft-landing craft.

**softling** ('sɒftlɪŋ, -ɔː-), *sb.* Also 6 **saftlynge.** [f. SOFT *a.* + -LING[1].]

**1.** An effeminate or unmanly person; a weakling.

**1547** *Homilies* I. *Agst. Adultery* (1559) Y j, Nor adulterers, nor saftlynges, nor sodomites. **1576** BP. WOOLTON *Chr. Man.* L 6 b, Effeminate men and softlings cause the stoute man to waxe tender. **1605** SYLVESTER *Du Bartas* II. iii. IV. *Captaines* 983 Ador'd of Flatterers, Of Softlings, Wantons, Braves, and Loyterers. **1605** I. TAYLOR *Restoration of Belief* 40 This Emperor—no softling himself.

**2.** A soft little hand, mouse, etc.

**1817** KEATS *Endym.* IV. 316 This cannot be thy hand, and yet it is; And this is sure thine other softling. **1855** BROWNING *Fra Lippo Lippi* 10 And nip each softling of a wee white mouse.

**3.** *attrib.* Of a soft nature.

**1732** WEBSTED *Wks.* (1797) 198 A softling head! that spleeny whims devour. **1874** D. GRAY *Poet. Wks.* 137 With her softling finger tips She touched my hand.

**softly,** *a.* Now *dial.* and *U.S.* [f. SOFT *a.*]

**1.** Of sound, etc.: Quiet, gentle, soft.

**1576** FLEMING *Panopl. Ep.* 276 Out of the hill ranne a pleasant spring, which made a gentle and softly sounde. **1653** HOLCROFT *Procopius, Gothic Wars* IV. 141 They..heare a softly voice calling them to the businesse. **1859** HAWTHORNE *Fr. & It. Note-bks.* (1872) II. 291 Their decorous and softly steps.

**†2.** Soft; yielding to pressure. *Obs.*

**1589** FLEMING *Virg. Georg.* III. 39 The fole or colt..laies down to rest his softly legs.

**†3.** Of pace: Easy, slow, gentle. *Obs.*

**1572** LAVATER *Ghosts* 59 The image goeth before with a softely pase. **1596** SPENSER *F.Q.* VI. vii. 6 The gentle Prince ..they spyde, Ryding a softly pace. **1633** P. FLETCHER *Purple Isl.* VI. lxxvii, The stealing night with softly pace. **1647** TRAPP *Comm. Epist.* 671 When God came to punish Adam he came slowly,..with a softly pace and still voice.

**†4.** Characterized by gentleness, weakness, simplicity, or effeminacy. *Obs.*

**1606** G. W[OODCOCKE] *Lives Emperors* in *Hist. Ivstine* H h 4 This was a prince of a softly wit. **1643** BAKER *Chron.* (1653) 46 The softly disposition of his son Robert. **1672** MARVELL *Reh. Transp.* I. 83 A Person, as he saith himself, of such a tame and softly humour. **1740–42** RICHARDSON *Pamela* IV. 258 The Viscount, whose softly Character, and his Lady's..respectful Conduct to him, notwithstanding that, are both so well known.

**5.** Of persons: **a.** Slow in action; lacking in energy or enterprise.

**1664** *Verney Memoirs* (1899) IV. 74 Many of them are very slow, and (as we call them) softly persons. **1687** MIÈGE *Gt. Fr. Dict.* II. s.v., A softly man, a Man that lacks to be stirring. **1770** J. ADAMS *Diary* 8 July Wks. 1850 II. 245 The softly people where I lodge..are the opposites of every thing great, spirited, and enterprising. **1869** MRS. STOWE *Oldtown Folks* xxvii, All that softly shiftless class, who..are never to be found with anything in hand at the moment that it is wanted.

**b.** Simple, foolish; soft-headed. Now *dial.*

**1687** MIÈGE *Gt. Fr. Dict.* II. s.v., A softly man, a Nidget, or Ninny. **1715** JANE BARKER *Exilius* I. 101 If woman did not moderate his Rule, He'd be a Tyrant, or a softly Fool. **1883** *Almondbury Gloss.* 124 *Softly*, soft-headed; foolish.

**softly** ('sɒftlɪ, -ɔ:-), *adv.* Forms: α. 3–5 **softeliche** (4 **-lyche**), 4–5 **softliche** (4 **-lich**). β. 4 **softili**, 4–6 **softely** (5 **-lie**); 4 **softli**, 4– **softly** (5 **sofft-**, 6 **soughtly**), 5–6 **softlie** (6 **-lye**); 6 **saftlie**, **saftely**, 8– (*Sc.* and *dial.*) **saftly**. [f. SOFT *a.* + -LY². Cf. Du. *zachtelijk*, G. *sanftlich*, *sänftlich*.]

**1.** Gently, carefully, tenderly; in such a manner as to avoid causing pain or injury; without force or violence; with gentle action.

α. *a* **1225** *Ancr. R.* 368 Ne gropie hire non to softeliche. **13..** *Guy Warw.* (A) 1614 And so he dede sikerliche, & seþþe he was heled softliche. **1362** LANGL. *P. Pl.* A. v. 7, I sat Softeliche a-doun and seide my beo-leeue.

β. *a* **1300** *Cursor M.* 8043 Quen þe kyng come ner þaa tres, ..He drou þam softili vp i-nogh. **1390** GOWER *Conf.* II. 98 Into hire bedd myn herte goth, And softly takth hire in his arm. **1400** tr. *Secreta Secret., Gov. Lordsh.* 85 Sethe hem softly to þe half. *c* **1440** *Gesta Rom.* II. xxiii. (Addit. MS.), The Fadir..had lever slee him softly than he shuld so rente hym self. **1545** RAYNALD *Byrth Mankynde* 65 Then must ye fayre and softely thrust it backe agayne. **1592** *Arden of Feversham* III. vi, Then softly drawes she foorth her handkercher. **1611** BIBLE *Transl. Pref.* ¶13 Who gladly would heale the soare..softly and sleightly. —— *Acts* xxvii. 13 And when the South wind blew softly,..they sailed close by Creete. **1695** LD. PRESTON *Boeth.* III. 151 It is then the Sovereign Good which ruleth all things powerfully, and disposeth them softly. **1784** COWPER *Task* I. 762 The moonbeam, sliding softly in between The sleeping leaves. **1816** J. WILSON *City of Plague* II. ii. 219 How softly on the dreamer's head They lay their..hands. **1841** JAMES *Brigand* xxiv, Meyrand will treat you tenderly and softly.

**2.** With a soft or subdued voice or utterance; in a low or gentle tone.

**13..** *Cursor M.* 5140 (Gött.), Þer cam to him a messager, And tald him softli in his ere. **1362** LANGL. *P. Pl.* A. III. 38 Þenne com þer a Confessour..And seide ful softely in schrift as hit weore. *c* **1430** *Pilgr. Lyf Manhode* I. lxxi. (1869) 41 Serteyn, quod j softeliche, ynowh me lakketh. **1544** *Litany* in *Priv. Prayers* (1851) 570 Such among the people as have books..may read them quietly and softly to themself. **1590** SPENSER *F.Q.* III. ii. 5 Thereat she sighing softly, had no powre To speake a while. **1614** DONNE *Lett.* (1631) 196 One thing I must tell you, but so softly, that I am loath to hear myself. **1687** A. LOVELL tr. *Thevenot's Trav.* I. 49 They that are present say softly, or aloud, if they please [etc.]. **1719** DE FOE *Crusoe* II. (Globe) 447 Some [words] he spoke softly, and I could not well hear, others audibly. **1794** MRS. RADCLIFFE *Myst. Udolpho* xxxviii, Emily sighed softly, and bowed her thanks. **1829** LANDOR *Imag. Conv.* Wks. 1853 I. 574/1, I must come behind your chair and whisper softlier. **1894** H. GARDENER *Unoff. Patriot* 314 They shook hands over the situation and both fell to crying softly.

**3. a.** With a slow, easy, or gentle pace or motion.

**1362** LANGL. *P. Pl.* A. II. 135 On a sysoures backe þat softly trotted. **1393** *Ibid.* C. XVI. 29 We reuerencede reson, and romed forth softeliche. *c* **1450** *St. Cuthbert* (Surtees) 6088 On a staffe he leend, he went forthe softely. **1483** CAXTON *Gold. Leg.* 78 b/2 Late thy famylye come softly after with thy wif. **1531** ELYOT *Gov.* (1534) 92 b, As farre or nyghe the marke is his arowe whanne he goeth softly, as whan he renneth. **1560** BIBLE (Geneva) *Isaiah* viii. 6 This people hathe refused the waters of Shiloah that runne softely. **1603** KNOLLES *Hist. Turks* (1621) 268 Surcharged..with the spoile, he was glad to march softlier. **1654** GAYTON *Pleas. Notes* IV. xxiv. 282 Jaques spurr'd and spurr'd, and switch'd, Ride softlier Jaques, shee beseech'd. **1721** SWIFT *Let. to Stella* 30 Apr., He could easily have overtaken me; for I walked softly on purpose. **1759** R. BROWN *Compl. Farmer* 13 Ride him half an hour softly. **1822** SHELLEY *Faust* I. 75 You give me full permission To lead him softly on my path.

†**b.** In a leisurely manner. *Obs. rare.*

*c* **1440** *Alph. Tales* 186 He began to syng þis antem,..and sang it softlie vnto þe end. **1577** B. GOOGE *Heresbach's Husb.* (1586) 128 b, Looke besides that they be..great feeders, but softly, and not ouerhastily.

**c.** *fair and softly*: see FAIR *adv.* 7, and sense 10 below. (Cf. SOFT *adv.* 7.)

**4. a.** Quietly, silently, noiselessly; lightly.

*c* **1386** CHAUCER *Reeve's T.* 138 Out at the dore he gooth.., Whan þat he saugh his tyme, softely. *a* **1400–50** *Alexander* 698 He..Sylis softely him selfe þe cite with-outen. **1587** TURBERV. *Trag. Tales* (1837) 152 And up they thrust the same [*i.e.* the door], And softly entred in. **1610** SHAKS. *Temp.* IV. i. 194 Pray you tread softly, that the blinde Mole may not heare a foot fall. **1681** GLANVILL *Saduc. Triumph* Pref. F iv b, Therefore not to make much noise to disturb these infallible Huffers.., I softly step by them. **1774** GOLDSM. *Nat. Hist.* (1776) III. 207 When the cat walks, it treads very softly, and without the least noise. **1865** MRS. CARLYLE *Lett.* III. 274 Coming down stairs very softly, for fear of waking me. **1902** R. HICHENS *Londoners* 5 She withdrew from the room as softly as a cat.

**b.** So as to avoid observation or notice; unobtrusively.

**1781** COWPER *Conversat.* 389 We next inquire, but softly and by stealth. **1837** CARLYLE *Fr. Rev.* II. II. vi, Necker sees good..to withdraw softly, almost privily. **1889** *Macm. Mag.* Aug. 253/1, I lay stirless, softly sneaking my right hand to the pistol.

**c.** *softly, softly, catchee monkey* (and varr.): proverbial phr. advocating caution or guile as the best way to achieve an end. Also *ellipt.* as *softly, softly* and (with hyphen) *attrib.*

**1907** G. BENHAM *Cassell's Bk. of Quotations* 849/1 'Softly, softly' caught the monkey.—(Negro.) **1942** N. BALCHIN *Darkness falls from Air* x. 176 Softly catch monkey... That's the answer. **1960** *Times* 1 Oct. 7/2 That colloquial adage —'softly, softly, catchee monkey'. **1962** P. BRICKHILL *Deadline* xiii. 152, I didn't pursue it any further then. Softly, softly, catchee monkey—and I hated that phrase. **1967** *Autocar* 28 Dec. 7/1 Softly, softly is our policy too, but not at such expense in time. **1970** *Sunday Times* 5 July 11 (*heading*) Ulster: end of 'softly, softly'. **1971** E. F. SCHOETERS in B. de Ferranti *Living with Computer* viii. 71 Users are naturally applying a 'softly-softly' approach. **1979** *Now!* 14 Sept. 53/2 Sadat and Begin..are both adopting a 'softly-softly' approach to the Palestinian problem.

**5. a.** In ease or comfort; so as to be soft or comfortable; luxuriously.

*a* **1400** N. T. *Prol.* (Paues) 6 Bote he seiþ þat þis wysdom ne is noȝt y-founde in þe lond of men þat lyfeþ softelyche. *a* **1425** tr. *Arderne's Treat. Fistula*, etc. 58 Etyng and slepyng more swetely or softely. **1565** COOPER *Thesaurus*, *Recubare mollius*, to lie more softely. **1648** HEXHAM II, *Zachtelick slapen*, to sleepe Softly or Quietly. *a* **1715** BURNET *Own Time* (1766) I. 80 They endured great hardships; for those parts were not fit to entertain men that had been accustomed to live softly. **1825** SCOTT *Talism.* vii, His couch was trimmed more softly than his master's. **1871** R. ELLIS *Catullus* lxviii. 5 Whom nor softly to rest love's tender sanctity suffers. **1884** W. C. SMITH *Kildrostan* 75 When You make your nest here.., 'Twere well to feather it softly.

**b.** With or in soft surroundings.

**1567** MAPLET *Greene Forest* 46 It groweth in waterie places and those softlye dighted and banked about. **1837** CARLYLE *Fr. Rev.* I. VII. vi, Beautiful all; softly embosomed; as if in sadness, in the dim moist weather!

†**6.** With quiet resignation. *Obs.*⁻¹

*c* **1400** *Rule St. Benet* (Prose) 45 Sho sal recaiue þe cumandement softelie and wid mekenes.

†**7.** In small quantity. *Obs. rare.*

*c* **1400** *Rule St. Benet* (Verse) 1610 Þarfor es wit..Wine or aile softly to tast.

**8.** Gradually; gently.

**1784** COWPER *Task* III. 629 The shapely knoll, That, softly swell'd and gaily dress'd, appears A flow'ry island. **1835** LYTTON *Rienzi* VI. iii, A high but softly sloping and verdant hill. **1864** LOWELL *Fireside Trav.* 269 Hills which round softly upward to Monte Cavi.

**9.** In a subdued manner.

**1817** SHELLEY *Pr. Athanase* I. 63 A cloud..Through which his soul..Shone, softly burning. **1882** SHARP *Rossetti* iii. 184 Behind..is a figure, also softly aureoled.

**10.** Used interjectionally: = SOFT *adv.* 8.

**1596** SHAKS. *Tam. Shrew* I. ii. 238 Softly my Masters. **1611** —— *Wint. T.* IV. iii. 76 Softly, deere sir: good sir, softly. **1671** MILTON *Samson* 115 Softly a while, Let us not break in upon him. **1797** MRS. RADCLIFFE *Italian* xvi, 'Fair and softly,' replied the officer. **1852** MRS. STOWE *Uncle Tom's C.* xvii, 'Softly, softly; don't thee snap and snarl, friend,' said Phineas.

**11.** *Comb.* **a.** With ppl. adjs., as ***softly-featured***, ***-hinted***, ***-shadowed***, etc.

**1598** SHAKS. *Merry W.* I. iv. 25 A softly-sprighted man, is he not? **1842** TENNYSON *Day-Dream* 89 Glows forth each softly-shadow'd arm. **1844** KINGLAKE *Eothen* xxiv, He sent me a softly-worded message. **1859** DICKENS *T. Two Cities* II. ix, His softly-slippered feet made no noise. **1876** 'OUIDA' *Winter City* ix. 249 Making the trifle the medium of a softly-hinted tenderness. **1922** JOYCE *Ulysses* 342 This..lent to her softly-featured face at whiles a look..that imparted a strange yearning tendency to the beautiful eyes.

**b.** With ppl. adjs. and pres. pples., as ***softly-breathing***, ***-burning***, ***-gliding***, etc.

**1681** DRYDEN *Span. Friar* V. i, I..listned to each softly-treading Step. **1703** ROWE *Fair Penit.* II. i, The sprightly String and softly-breathing Flute. **1725** POPE *Odyss.* XV. 390 The softly-stealing pace of Time. **1818** *Gentl. Mag.* LXXXVIII. 62/1 Thames does, by Oxford, softly-pacing, run. **1864** W. C. BRYANT *Thirty Poems* 38 The softly gliding, bashful stream. **1890** 'R. BOLDREWOOD' *Col. Reformer* (1891) 168 The softly-gliding magical motion. **1907** JOYCE *Chamber Music* p. xv, Eastward the gradual dawn prevails Where softly-burning fires appear. **1918** D. H. LAWRENCE *New Poems* 48 Ah, love, Could I but..remove Its softly-stirring, crimson welling-up Of kisses! **1923** —— *Birds, Beasts & Flowers* 38 Vicious, dark cypresses: Vicious, you supple, brooding, softly-swaying pillars of dark flame. **1924** E. SITWELL *Sleeping Beauty* xvii. 68 To catch the softly-smiling wind.

**c.** With adjs., as ***softly dark***, ***-strong***, ***sweet***.

**1794** MRS. RADCLIFFE *Myst. Udolpho* xv, A single note..That, softly sweet, at distance dies. **1837** CARLYLE *Fr. Rev.* II. v. ii, Parliaments..which..were to follow in softly-strong indissoluble sequence. **1898** H. NEWBOLT *Admirals All* 31 The Norman arch, the chancel softly dark.

**softness** ('sɒftnɪs, -ɔ:-). Forms: 1 **softnys(se**, 4 **softnis**; 2–7 **soft-**, 4–7 **softenesse**, 4, 6 **softe-**, 4–7 **softnes**, 7– **softness**; 6 **saft(e)nesse**, 8– *Sc.* **saftness**. [f. SOFT *a.* + -NESS.] The state or quality of being soft, in various senses.

**I. 1.** Ease, comfort; delicacy, luxury; easy or voluptuous living.

*c* **1000** ÆLFRIC in Assmann *Ags. Hom.* ii. 59 Under Moyses laȝe men moston lybban on maran softnysse ..þonne nu. *a* **1225** *Ancr. R.* 196 Þet flesch put propremen touward swetnesse & touward eise, & touward softnesse. *a* **1340** HAMPOLE *Psalter* iv. 9, I sall slepe..with all softnes. **1451** CAPGRAVE *Life St. Gilbert* xvi. 86 To take hardnesse for softnesse, labour for ese. **1607** SHAKS. *Timon* V. i. 36 A Satyre against the softnesse of Prosperity. **1654** tr. *Scudery's Curia Pol.* 181 If he live in the softness of Plenty, and a peaceful Estate. **1704** HEARNE *Duct. Hist.* (1714) I. 389 He spent the next year in Softness and Luxury. **1766** *Ann. Reg.* II. 10 The French noblesse..spend their lives in indolence, softness, and dissipation.

**2. a.** Mildness, gentleness; tenderness of character or disposition.

*a* **1300** *E.E. Psalter* cxliv. 7 Minde of mighthed of þi softnesse Sal þai rift. **1382** WYCLIF *Ecclus.* xlv. 4 In feith and softenesse of hym [Moyses], he made hym hoely. *c* **1440** *Promp. Parv.* 463/1 Softenesse, or myldenesse, *mansuetudo*, *benignitas*. **1526** TINDALE *Phil.* iv. 5 Lette youre softenes be knowen unto all men. **1563** BP. SANDYS in Strype *Ann. Ref.* (1709) xxxv. 356 My lenity and softness was such, that I was not willing to touch him. **1639** SALTMARSH *Policy* 239 As though it were more out of regard than your owne softnesse. **1667** MILTON *P.L.* IV. 298 For contemplation hee and valour formd, For softness shee and sweet attractive Grace. **1726** POPE *Odyss.* XXIII. 105 To softness lost, to spousal love unknown. **1779** *Mirror* No. 22, Sometimes..I have thought she breathed a softness of soul that tempted me to believe her generous. **1828** SCOTT *F.M. Perth* xviii, Are we to be slain in our own streets for the King's softness of heart? **1837** CARLYLE *Fr. Rev.* III. I. i, With her softness and musical speech. **1867** TROLLOPE *Chron. Barset* II. lxii. 193, I found with him..a softness of heart for which I had not looked.

**b.** A display or instance of gentleness or tenderness; a soft word or speech.

**1382** WYCLIF *Gen.* xxxiv. 3 And hir [*sc.* Dinah] sory he swagide with softnessis. *a* **1637** JONSON *Horace Art Poet.* 326 The free spectators..Were to be staid with softnesses. **1678** OTWAY *Friendship in F.* 10 Whispering his softnesses and making his vowes. **1719** YOUNG *Busiris* I. i, O how unlike the softnesses of love! **1882** MRS. OLIPHANT *Lit. Hist. Eng. 1790–1825*, I. 4 The rude and homely life, in which few softnesses existed.

**3.** Weakness of character or disposition, effeminacy; lack of firmness; timidity, pusillanimity.

**1605** BACON *Adv. Learn.* I. ii. §6 From some weakness of body or softness of spirit. **1651** C. CARTWRIGHT *Cert. Relig.* II. 27 By shunning death, he confesseth his weaknesse (or softnesse) of spirit. **1705** STANHOPE *Paraphr.* II. 247 One great Design is to break the softness of a Nature, too indulgent to Flesh and Blood. **1748** *Anson's Voy.* II. xiv. 288 The timidity and softness of our enemy. **1821** BYRON *Mar. Fal.* II. ii, In Bertram There is a hesitating softness, fatal To enterprise like ours. **1879** G. MACDONALD *Sir Gibbie* xxii, A certain gentle indifference she showed to things considered important, the neighbours attributed to weakness of character, and called *softness*.

**II. 4. a.** The state, quality, or property of being soft to the touch, of yielding to pressure, of lacking hardness, firmness, etc.

*c* **1175** *Lamb. Hom.* 83 Oli haueð huppen him lihtnesse and softnesse and hele. **1398** TREVISA *Barth. De P.R.* V. xxvii. (Bodl. MS.), By smeþenes and softenes and nasschenes of grustel. *c* **1440** *Promp. Parv.* 463/1 Softenesse, or smothenesse, *lenitas*. *Ibid.*, Softenesse, yn towchynge, *mollicies*, *mollicia*. **1545** RAYNALD *Byrth Mankynde* 24 In saftnesse of skyn, and plumpenesse of the body fatter and rounder. **1577** B. GOOGE *Heresbach's Husb.* II. (1586) 67 b, The ripenesse whereof is deemed by..the softnesse of the berrie. **1602** MARSTON *Antonio's Rev.* II. ii, Those now lawne pillowes, on whose tender softnesse [etc.]. **1673–4** GREW *Anat. Pl., Anat. Trunks* (1682) 138 Its Softness, depending on the numerousness..of the Aer-Vessels. **1750** tr. *Leonardus' Mirr. Stones* 39 Hardness or softness in stones proceeds from two causes. **1774** GOLDSM. *Nat. Hist.* (1776) III. 355 All that warmth and softness which are so much valued in the furs of the northern animals. **1851** CARPENTER *Man. Phys.* (ed. 2) 5 In Organized structures, softness (resulting from the large proportion of fluid components) may be considered the distinctive quality. **1863** BATES *Nat. Amazons* II. 56 One would mistake it..for a kitten, from..the softness of its fur.

*transf.* **1877** *Fortn. Rev.* Dec. 846 An adaptation to the hardness of their hearts, or..the softness of their brains.

†**b.** Smoothness, calmness. *Obs.*⁻¹

*c* **1205** LAY. 25549 For þere softnesse [of the sea] Ardur gon to slæpen.

**c.** ***softness of the pulse***, the state when the blood-tension is low, so that the artery feels soft and easily compressible.

*a* **1793** HUNTER *On Blood* II. iii. (1794) 318 Softness is not to be depended on as a mark of health. **1813** J. THOMSON *Lect. Inflam.* 73 A softness and fullness of the pulse. **1822–7** GOOD *Study Med.* (1829) II. 45 Hardness and softness of the pulse, together with..wiriness, are not quite so easily learnt as its fulness and smallness.

**d.** The property or quality (in water, etc.) of being soft.

**1815** J. SMITH *Panorama Sci. & Art* II. 487 All these waters, however, possess the property called softness, that is, they will dissolve soap. **1826** *Art of Brewing* (ed. 2) 34 Beers..attenuated so low as to insure transparency and softness.

**e.** The state or property (of a material or device) of being soft, in extended technical usage.

**1900** *Sci. Trans. R. Dublin Soc.* VII. 121 The addition of 2 to 5½ per cent. of silicon to steel..increases the magnetic softness. **1919** R. D. BANGAY *Oscillation Valve* 204 [A blue glow] is produced by the energy expended by the electrons as they collide with the atoms, and if noticeable is a certain indication of the softness of a valve. **1945** *Electronic Engin.* XVII. 338 The maximum value [of the grid leak resistance] ..is limited by the danger of causing softness to develop in the succeeding valve. **1980** *Sci. Amer.* Apr. 94/3 The magnetic 'softness' and high resistivity of glassy alloys also make them likely candidates for the 'read' and 'write' heads in magnetic tape recorders and magnetic disk memories.

**f.** *Econ.* With reference to commodities, prices, etc.: a state of or tendency towards depression. Cf. SOFT *a.* 28 b.

**1927** *Comm. & Financ. Chron.* 20 Aug. 961/1 When sterling is firmer a stronger tone develops in the entire European list. On the other hand when sterling reacts, softness develops in the rest of the list. **1930** *Economist* 27 Sept. 569/1 Apart from the recent weakness in grain and cotton prices, and softness in the copper market, the commodity price structure seems to be strengthening. **1970** *Globe & Mail* (Toronto) 25 Sept. B5/1 William S. Brewster, chairman, attributes the disappointing results to softness in the economy.

**5.** Freedom from harshness; mellowness.

**1736** *Gentl. Mag.* VI. 351/1 To hear the softness of Italian song. **1772–84** *Cook's Voy.* III. xiii. II. 266 One sung a very agreeable air, with a degree of softness and melody which we could not have expected. **1840** *C. O. Müller's Hist. Lit. Greece* iv. §5 That softness and flexibility [of Homer's language]. **1885** MISS BRADDON *Wyllard's Weird* i. I. 22 She pronounced the last word with peculiar softness.

6. Mildness, balminess.

**1828** DUPPA *Trav. Italy*, etc. 181 The air, though cold, had somewhat of softness in its temperature. **1837** DISRAELI *Venetia* v. x, The softness and the splendour of the morn. **1851** DIXON *W. Penn* xxi. (1872) 182 The climate had the softness of the south of France.

7. Absence of hard or sharp outlines.

**1855** *Orr's Circ. Sci., Inorg. Nat.* 186 The characteristic of this scenery will be softness of outline. **1892** *Photogr. Ann.* II. 711 In collotype work the especial aim.. is to get softness with plenty of detail rather than hardness.

**soft pedal**, *sb.* [f. SOFT *a.* + PEDAL *sb.* 1 b (*b*).] A foot-lever on a pianoforte which softens the tone. Also *fig.* (in senses corresponding to those of the vb.: see next) and (with hyphen) *attrib.*

**1856** M. C. CLARKE *tr. Berlioz' Treat. Mod. Instrumentation & Orchestration* 79 A pedal much less used than that which raises the dampers.. is the soft pedal (or one-string pedal). **1861** [see PEDAL *sb.* 1 b]. **1880** GROVE *Dict. Mus.* II. 723/1 He.. thus produces something of the shifting soft pedal *timbre*. **1911** A. B. REEVE *Poisoned Pen* 255 But can't it be done with the soft pedal? **1936** *Times* 12 Oct. 8/5 Some people thought that the 'soft pedal' should be put on the entertainment factor of a zoo, but he [*sc.* J. S. Huxley] did not agree. **1958** *Times* 8 Oct. 6/1 What this particular play demands from a film director is a certain application of the soft pedal. **1961** *Sunday Express* 23 Apr. 1/2 President de Gaulle—whose soft-pedal policy.. has sparked off this third rebellion. **1973** JUNKIN & ORNADEL *Piano can be Fun* 69/2 Calling the damper pedal the 'loud' pedal neatly distinguishes it from the left foot pedal which is called the 'soft' pedal.

**soft-pedal**, *v.* [f. prec.] *trans.* and *intr.* (freq. const. *on*). To reduce the loudness or volume of (a noise); to reduce in force or effect; to tone down, play down, go easy on.

**1915** R. WAGNER in *Sat. Even. Post* 16 Oct. 15/2 The scene was rehearsed time and again, but always the action looked faked because of the necessity of soft-pedaling such a blow. **1916** G. A. ENGLAND *Pod, Bender & Co.* i. 6 Can that! Soft pedal on that chatter, Ben! **1926** R. H. DAVIS *Over my Left Shoulder* xxix. 204 'Captain Sam heap mad!' replied the Peacemaker, with no effort to soft pedal the announcement. **1927** *Daily Express* 19 July 3/4 Both parties are at present 'soft pedalling' on the world-revolution thesis. **1931** F. F. BOND *Mr. Miller of 'The Times'* 170 The leading educational centres tended to stress the utilitarian studies and soft-pedal those courses which sought merely cultural ends. **1932** K. S. PRICHARD *Kiss on Lips & Other Stories* 20 He soft-pedalled about Rose, and the skinflint of an aunt who threatened to take her away. **1944** AUDEN *Sea & Mirror* in *For Time Being* i. 8 Be frank about our heathen foe, For Rome will be a goner If you soft-pedal the loud beast. **1953** A. UPFIELD *Murder must Wait* v. 47 'We'll get something out of her.' 'You will soft-pedal,' Bony said quietly. **1957** W. H. WHYTE *Organization Man* 52 Out of respect for the sense of the meeting you tend to soft-pedal that which would go against the grain. **1965** *Listener* 27 May 764/1 He must have the drug or endure the sheer agony which the romanticists soft-pedal: high-fever, shivering, fits of vomiting, [etc.]. **1978** R. HILL *Pinch of Snuff* vi. 55 You're noted for soft-pedalling on these squatters.

Hence **soft-'pedalling** *vbl. sb.*

**1952** G. RAVERAT *Period Piece* x. 197 Uncle Lenny was far too judicious to need soft-pedalling. **1979** *New Statesman* 6 July 3/3 The concern of homophile organisations to make homosexuality an acceptable alternative has led to a distinct soft-pedalling on ticklish issues like paedophilia and transvestism.

**soft sawder**: see SAWDER *sb.* and *v.*

**soft-shell.** Also soft shell. [f. SOFT *a.*]

1. *attrib.* In the specific names of animals: Provided with a soft shell; = SOFT-SHELLED 1. **soft-shell clam, crab** = *soft clam, crab* s.v. SOFT *a.* 29 c; **soft-shell turtle**, a freshwater turtle of the genus *Trionyx*.

**1805** J. ORDWAY *Jrnl.* 26 May in *Wisconsin Hist. Coll.* (1916) XXII. 218 Passed 2 creeks.. in one of them saw Soft Shell Turtle. **1818** *Amer. Monthly Mag.* II. 296 Soft shell Clam. These animals.. are excellent eating. **1844** J. E. DEKAY *Zool. N.Y.* VI. 11 During this interval, they are known under the name of Soft-shell Crabs, or Shedders. **1847** *Knickerbocker* XXIX. 494 A battle between a soft-shell turtle.. and a terrier puppy. **1860** MAYNE REID *Hunter's Feast* xii, The 'soft-shell' crabs and small tortoises common in the American waters. **1884** GOODE *Nat. Hist. Aquat. Anim.* 152 The food of the Soft-shell Turtles consists of small fishes, snails, and other small animals. **1887** Soft-shell crab [see DIAMOND-BACK *a.*]. **1891** WEBSTER (1897), *Soft-shell clam*,.. the long clam. **1977** E. LEONARD *Unknown Man No. 89* xx. 202 Softshell crabs, very good fish, steak. **1980** *Washington Post* 27 June (Weekend Suppl.) 36/1 You mustn't rush through the throng, hoagie in one hand, soft-shell crab sandwich in the other.

*transf.* **1883** GOODE *Fish. Indust. U.S.* 51 This Crab is eaten in both the hard and soft shell condition.

2. *attrib.* That adopts or advocates a moderate or temperate course or policy. *U.S.*

**1845** *Knickerbocker* XXVI. 285 The 'Hard and Soft Shell Baptists'. **1859** BARTLETT *Dict. Amer.* (ed. 2) 426 *Soft-shell democrats*,.. the less conservative division of the New York Democrats. **1865** *Pall Mall G.* 12 May 1 The type of what the Americans might call the 'soft-shell' Radicals. **1872** DE VERE *Americanisms* 241 Such are the Soft Shell Baptists, so called on account of their less stern manners and less rigid principles.

3. *ellipt.* a. = SOFT *sb.* 4 b. *U.S.*

**1845** [see HARDSHELL *sb.* 2]. **1853** *N.Y. Tribune* 2 Apr. (Bartlett s.v. *Hard-shell*), The difference between a Hardshell and a Softshell. **1866** *Chambers's Encycl.* VIII. 201/1 The 'Soft Shells' were 'Free-soil' Democrats.

b. A soft-shelled lobster, crab or turtle. *U.S.*

**1830** R. C. SANDS *Writings* (1834) II. 230 The soft-shell of the Red River. **1846** T. B. THORPE *Myst. Backwoods* 156 It is Turtle Lake from its abundance of 'green, amphibious soft-shells'. **1884** GOODE *Nat. Hist. Aquat. Anim.* 783 'Black Lobster,' 'Soft-shell,' 'Berried Lobster.' **1935** Z. N. HURSTON *Mules & Men* I. iii. 79 Ah'm gointer prune a gang of soft-shells (turtles). **1941** *Louisiana* (Writers' Program) 227 'Soft-shells' and 'busters' (shedding crabs from which the old shell is pried off) are coated with cracker meal and fried. **1942** [see HARDSHELL *a.* 1]. **1958** R. CONANT *Field Guide Reptiles & Amphibians* 70 The Florida Softshell lives chiefly in lakes; all the others are river turtles to a large degree.

**soft-shelled**, *a.* [SOFT *a.* 31.]

1. Having a soft shell. Chiefly in specific names of animals; esp. of the soft-shell crab or turtle.

**1611** COTGR., *Harde*, a soft-sheld egge. **1771** *Phil. Trans.* LXI. 267 We call it the soft shelled Turtle. **1796** *Rec. Smithtown, N.Y.* (1898) 129 Any person not an inhabitant.. taking Soft shelled clams within the limits of said Town shall pay six pence for every bushel. **1835** J. J. AUDUBON *Ornith. Biogr.* III. 239 He knows.. how to watch the soft-shelled turtle's crawl. **1856** *Rep. Comm. Patents 1855: Agric.* (U.S.) p. xviii, The 'soft-shelled' almond.. is the variety recently introduced and distributed by this Office. *c* **1880** *Cassell's Nat. Hist.* IV. 256 The other Soft-shelled Tortoise (*Trionyx ferox*).. is a voracious animal. **1883** GOODE in *Fisheries Exhib. Lit.* (1884) V. 15 Soft-shelled clam, *Mya arenaria*. **1884** —— *Nat. Hist. Aquat. Anim.* 152 The species of Soft-shelled Tortoises, *Trionychidæ*. *Ibid.* 776 The common edible Crab or Blue Crab—*Callinectes hastatus*... These 'soft-shelled Crabs' are much esteemed by many. **1948** [see *paper-shelled* adj. s.v. PAPER *sb.* 12]. **1953** G. M. DURRELL *Overloaded Ark* xiii. 223 It was a species known as the Soft-shelled Turtle: the shell is fairly smooth and domed, and it protruded round the edge in a great soft rim.

2. *transf.* (Cf. SOFT-SHELL 2.)

**1890** *Daily News* 4 Feb. 5/3 Dissentient Liberals of the soft-shelled species.

**soft soap**, *sb.* Also soft-soap. [f. SOFT *a.*]

1. a. A smeary, semi-liquid soap, made with potash lye; potash soap.

**1634** in Rymer *Fœdera* (1732) XIX. 567/1 That no soft Soap be sold.. for above three pence the pound. **1641** *Short Relation conc. Soap-Business* 4 To make soft soape with Berilla. **1728** CHAMBERS *Cycl.* s.v. *Soap*, The Soft Soap.. is either White or Green. **1812** SIR H. DAVY *Chem. Philos.* 331 Potassa enters into the composition of soft soap. **1883** *Specif. Alnwick & Cornhill Rlwy.* 11 In drilling the holes no oil is to be used, but only soft soap and water.

b. With pl. A make or kind of this.

**1783** *Encycl. Brit.* (ed. 2) X. 8196/2 In soft or liquid soaps,.. cheaper oils are employed. **1857** MILLER *Elem. Chem., Org.* vi. §2. 371 The base.. of the soft soaps is potash. **1879** *Cassell's Techn. Educ.* I. 357/2 The hard, the soft, and the marine soaps.

2. *slang.* Flattery; blarney; 'soft sawder'. Also *attrib.* orig. *U.S.*

**1830** *Reg. Deb. Congress U.S.* 12 Apr. 774, I will not use the vulgar phrase, and say he has been pouring soft soap down the backs of the New York delegation. **1842** *People's Organ* (St. Louis) 15 Apr. 2/2 The magnificent bombshell, rammed full of pride, aristocracy,.. soft-soap, curiosity, folly, display, nonsense, man-worship and small-talk, was touched off. **1848** BARTLETT *Dict. Amer.* 320 *Soft soap*, flattery; blarney. A vulgar phrase, though much used. **1861** HUGHES *Tom Brown at Oxford* xxxiii, He and I are great chums, and a little soft soap will go a long way with him. **1901** DELANNOY *£19,000*, xxxix, 'You're the most sensible woman I've ever met.' 'None of your soft-soap, now!' **1934** *Sun* (Baltimore) 6 Nov. 2/2 Assailing Governor Lehman for his 'soft soap' manner of campaign, the park commissioner.. renewed his assault on the Lehman banking family. **1961** *Radio Times* 6 Apr. 21/2 'Nobody likes to watch a soft-soap interview. People *want* the facts and they can take them,' says Robin Day. **1977** *Irish Times* 8 June 9/6 The public would not be fooled by this 'crazy parade of soft-soap offers'.

**soft-soap**, *v.* Also soft soap. [f. prec.]

1. *trans.* To flatter, 'soft-sawder'. *slang.*

**1840** [MRS. WHITCHER] *Widow Bedott Papers* xxv. (1883) 114 Ye don't ketch me a slanderin' folks behind ther backs and then soft-soapin' 'em to their faces. **1843** in Bartlett *Dict. Amer.* (1848) 320, I am tired of this system of placemen soft-soaping the people. **1883** A. K. GREEN (Mrs. Rohlfs) *Hand & Ring* xxv, I am not a clumsy fellow at softsoaping a girl.

2. To treat or coat with soft soap.

**1900** *Daily News* 7 Aug. 3/4 Long poles.. plentifully soft-soaped.

Hence **soft-soaper**; **soft-soaping** *vbl. sb.*

**1841** J. T. HEWLETT *Parish Clerk* II. 7 Zach, therefore,.. set up in the soft-soaping and deceiving line of business. **1852** 'MARK TWAIN' in *Hannibal Jrnl.* Sept. 16 He was narrowly watching this soft-soaper of Democratic rascality. **1904** *Blackw. Mag.* May 619/2 There are some soft-soapers who never advance and never aspire.

**soft-soapy**, *a. rare.* [f. SOFT SOAP *sb.* + -Y[1].] Flattering, ingratiating, unctuous.

**1904** J. C. LINCOLN *Cap'n Eri* iii. 36 The thing to do is to be sort of soft-soapy and high-toned.

**soft-solder**, *v.* Also soft-sodder. [f. *soft solder*: see SOLDER *sb.*[1] 4.] 1. *trans.* To unite, mend, etc., with soft solder. Hence **soft-soldered** *ppl. a.*

**1843** HOLTZAPFFEL *Turning* I. 433 Copper, brass and iron are soft-soldered. *Ibid.* 444 It is very essential that all soft-soldered joints should be particularly clean. **1900** HASLUCK *Model Eng. Handybk.* 122 The flue and both ends of the boiler should be brazed in their places, not soft-soldered.

2. = *soft-sawder*, s.v. SAWDER *v.* Cf. SOLDER *sb.*[1] 4 b. *U.S. colloq.*

**1866** C. H. SMITH *Bill Arp, so called: Side Show of Southern Side of War* 159 Wouldn't you think that as a matter of policy they would soft sodder us a little and quit their slanderin? **1905** J. C. LINCOLN *Partners of Tide* vi. 111 He soft-soddered me till I felt slippery all over.

**soft-spoken**, *a.* Also 9 *Sc.* saft-. [f. SOFT *adv.*]

1. Of persons: Having, or speaking with, a soft or gentle voice; plausible, affable.

**1609** B. JONSON *Sil. Wom.* I. ii, One.. who is exceedingly soft-spoken; thrifty of her speech. **1826** MISS MITFORD *Village* Ser. II. (1863) 375 George Gosseltine, a sleek, smooth, silky, soft-spoken person. **1840** DICKENS *Old C. Shop* xix, In gorgeous liveries as soft-spoken servants at gambling booths.

2. Of words: Spoken softly, gently, or affably; persuasive.

**1887** MORRIS *Odyss.* x. 70 So I spake, and with words soft-spoken besought them thereunto.

**software** ('sɒftwɛə(r), -ɔː-). [f. SOFT *a.* + WARE *sb.*[3], after HARDWARE 1 c.] 1. *Computers.* a. The programs and procedures required to enable a computer to perform a specific task, as opposed to the physical components of the system (see also quot. 1961). b. *esp.* The body of system programs, including compilers and library routines, required for the operation of a particular computer and often provided by the manufacturer, as opposed to program material provided by a user for a specific task.

In early use, the word was interpreted widely to include program material written by a user, as well as systems programs, and also occas. the cards and tapes by means of which programs and data are read into the system. Popular usage, as represented by sense 2, is freq. wider in meaning than the current more restrictive technical usage (sense b).

**1960** *Communications Assoc. Computing Machinery* June 381 Nearly every manufacturer is claiming compatibility with all other equipment via such software as COBOL. **1961** *Computer Bull.* June 42 The programming expertise, or 'software', that is at the disposal of the computer user comprises expert advice on all matters of machine code programming, comprehensive libraries of subroutines for all purposes, and the PEGASUS/SIRIUS scientific autocode. **1962** D. S. HALACY *Computers* iii. 54 Punched cards, which fall into the category called computer 'software' are cheap, flexible, and compatible with many types of equipment. **1964** *Observer* 13 Dec. 1/1 The toughest problem was the 'software'—particularly the 'supervisory programme', the complex instructions which enable the machine to handle many tasks simultaneously. **1965** HOLLINGDALE & TOOTILL *Electronic Computers* 192 The cost of developing and making the computer itself (the *hardware*) is matched by the cost of making programming schemes for it (often, regrettably, termed *software*). **1966** *New Scientist* 25 Aug. 433/3 The cost of providing 'software'—the programmes for operating the computer on a wide range of problems—is enormous... The user needs to find the bureau which has the appropriate software for his problems. **1967** COX & GROSE *Organization & Handling Bibl. Rec. by Computer* 1 About three years ago, it became clear.. that the computer software which was provided and maintained by the manufacturers was not suited to some of the problems of handling and processing large files of data. **1969** P. DICKINSON *Pride of Heroes* 187 A rather wet young man who sells software for computers. **1971** B. DE FERRANTI *Living with Computer* 89 *Software*, all computer programs, or that part of a computer system that is not hardware. **1972** *Computer Bull.* XVI. 85/1 In those days [*sc.* 1966] the term 'software' was still thought rather disreputable, and the concept was probably thought rather vague... More recently, 'software' has become more particularised and often seems to refer to what we might call 'system software', that is, excluding any programs written for specific applications... Thus we have 'software packages' and 'application packages', and people who write software consider themselves superior to mere programmers. **1977** K. HEGGSTAD in P. G. J. van Sterkenburg et al. *Lexicologie* 163 The unit price of hardware is going down... On the other hand software costs are rising equally dramatically. **1978** J. MCNEIL *Consultant* i. 30 Hardware is what you can touch—the actual computer, all its peripheral devices... Without software all that is quite useless... Software, computer programs—they're the same thing... My software staff are very strictly monitored.

2. *transf.* and *fig.*

**1963** *Flight International* LXXXIII. 186/1 To get at the total commitment one has to consider the 'software' aspect very closely: for every controller at the scope there may need to be five in the background. **1966** *National Observer* (U.S.) 21 Feb. 8/3 This deal.. is the latest.. in a series of corporate marriages combining.. 'the software and the hardware' of education. **1967** *Punch* 24 May 770/3 This documentary was a refreshing change from most space-age reportage, dealing sympathetically with the families of the astronauts living outside the perimeter fence of the Manned Spacecraft Centre in Texas: the software rather than the hardware. **1969** *Guardian* 29 Mar. 4/8 The 'Talking Page'.. is.. being launched with a mass of matching software—a maths course, a reading course, an English course for immigrants. **1978** *Gramophone* June 136/3 They [*sc.* players for digitally recorded discs] will be usable with normal stereo amplifiers and speakers but, of course, they will be incompatible with existing software (records and cassettes). **1979** *Observer* 11 Nov. 33/2 It was phrased in terms of Israel giving the United States 'software'—a more flexible attitude on the Middle East—in return for 'hardware'—arms and military equipment.

3. Special Combs.: **software engineering**, the professional development, production, and management of system software; so **software engineer**; **software house**, a company that specializes in producing and testing software; also *fig.*

**1969** NAUR & RANDELL *Software Engin.* (NATO) 81 Is it possible to have software engineers in the numbers in which we need them, without formal software engineering education? **1979** JENSEN & TONIES *Software Engin.* 14 The software engineer is not a theoretician as is the computer scientist. **1969** (*title*) Software engineering; report of a conference sponsored by the NATO Science Committee, Garmisch, Germany, 7th to 11th October, 1968. **1973** K. W. MORTON in F. L. Bauer *Adv. Course Software Engin.* i. A. 4 When we sit down at a console to write an Algol program, it is software engineering which determines how easy it is to achieve this end. **1982** I. SOMMERVILLE *Software Engin.* i. 3 Software engineering is now maturing into a fully fledged discipline. **1969** *New Scientist* 6 Nov. 285/1 Today there are just over 2000 software houses throughout the world, mostly in America. **1982** *Listener* 23–30 Dec. 31/1 If the world's wealth is maximised by specialisation, Britain should become its 'software house'.

**soft wood, soft-wood.** Also as one word. [SOFT *a.*]

**1. a.** Wood which is relatively soft or easily cut; esp. coniferous trees or their timber. Also *attrib.*

**1832** *Planting* (L.U.K.) 77 The..discriminating characters of hard and of soft woods. **1857** GRAY *First Less. Bot.* 147 In soft woods, such as White-Pine and Basswood. **1884** BOWER & SCOTT *De Bary's Phaner.* 478 Of the forms of vessels,..the reticulately thickened are present exclusively or principally in succulent soft woods. **1905** *Terms Forestry & Logging* (U.S. Dept. Agric.) 48 Softwood..As applied to trees and logs, needle-leafed, coniferous... Softwood..A needle-leafed, or coniferous, tree. **1914** MOON & BROWN *Elem. Forestry* 218 Many of our hardwoods are much softer in their wood structure than certain conifers or so-called softwoods. **1930** *Observer* 26 Jan. 20/4 Every year in Finland, Sweden and Russia millions of pine trees are felled and shipped to London... The trade name for such timber is softwood. **1968** J. ARNOLD *Shell Bk. Country Crafts* xxxi. 321 Yew, though as hard and heavy as oak, is classified as a soft-wood. **1977** J. L. HARPER *Population Biol. Plants* iv. 94 In some hardwood and softwood forests in Maine the buried seed population diverges remarkably in species composition from that of the vegetation.

**b.** Sap-wood, alburnum.

**1842** LOUDON *Suburban Hort.* 21 In woody stems of several years' growth..the more recent exterior layers are known as soft wood or alburnum.

**2.** A species of the West Indian bully-tree.

**1864** GRISEBACH *Flora Brit. W. Ind.* 787/2 Soft-wood, black, *Myrsine læta.*

**soft-wooded,** *a.* [Cf. prec.] Having relatively soft wood.

**1827** STEUART *Planter's G.* (1828) 41 The soft-wooded Trees, such as the Lime and the Horsechestnut. **1851** *B'ham & Midl. Gardeners' Mag.* Aug. 134 Every description of soft-wooded plant should be tied to sticks as they grow. **1897** MARY KINGSLEY *W. Africa* 91 A forest of soft-wooded plants and palms.

**softy** ('sɒftɪ, -ɔː-), *sb. dial.* or *colloq.* Also softie, *Sc.* safty, saftie. [f. SOFT *a.*] **a.** A weak-minded or silly person; a simpleton, noodle, gull.

**1863** MRS. GASKELL *Sylvia's Lovers* II. 21 She were but a softy after all, for she left off doing her work in a proper manner. **1888** MRS. H. WARD *R. Elsmere* 33 He is a kind of softie. **1897** P. WARUNG *Old Regime* 170 He was a softy then, ..and being afraid of the rest of us, we put upon him.

**b.** A very soft-hearted person.

**1886** *19th Cent.* Jan. 80 The sentimental softy..who loses his heart at seventeen, is a father at eighteen, and at nineteen is the husband of a dirty trollop. **1914** *Maclean's Mag.* July 88/3 'It's cruel,' said Steve... 'You're a softy!' he said. **1964** MRS. L. B. JOHNSON *White House Diary* 16 Jan. (1970) A trip that I fear will not meet with the approval of all the members of our family, but which I—maybe I am a softie —very much want her to have. **1970** 'D. HALLIDAY' *Dolly & Cookie Bird* v. 66 You didn't know Daddy like I did. He was an awful old softie inside.

**c.** One who is considered cowardly, weak, or unmanly; a weakling; an effeminate man.

**1895** *Cent. Mag.* Oct. 943/2 If the well-initiated inmates discover that he is unwilling to enter into all their schemes and customs, they call him a 'sucker' or 'softy', and shun his company. **1912** BEERBOHM *Christmas Garland* 16 There was nothing of the softy about Smithers. **1924** J. M. MURRY *Voyage* xii. 227 'It's no go,' he said. 'I'm not going to bed to-night'. 'But.'.. She didn't know what to say. Was he a softy? Or was she his first? **1960** T. MCLEAN *Kings of Rugby* xi. 204 Mr Jenkins declared that the All Blacks of the morrow were 'softies' for wearing such impedimenta [*sc.* shoulder-pads]. **1975** *Liverpool Echo* (Football ed.) 11 Jan. 8/6 He never lost his temper, but he was no softie. **1979** *Beano* 2 June 20/3 (*caption*) Who did that? No-one to be seen except those softies playing soppy games.

**'softy,** *a. rare. N. Amer.* [f. SOFT *a.* + -Y¹.] Characterized by softness.

**1884** 'MARK TWAIN' *Huck. Finn* xxvii. 272 When the place was packed full, the undertaker he slid around in his black gloves with his softy soothering ways. **1970** *Globe & Mail* (Toronto) 25 Sept. 16/2 (Advt.), Fringed shoulder pouches in softy suede.

**sofyme, sofyr, sofyster, -try, sofysyn,** obs. varr. SOPHISM, SUFFER *v.*, SOPHISTER, -TRY, SUFFICE *v.*

**sog** (sɒg), *sb.*¹ Now *s.w. dial.* Also 6 sogge, 9 zog. [Related to SOG *v.*] A soft or marshy piece of ground; a swamp, bog, quagmire.

**1538** LELAND *Itin.* (1769) V. 86 The Pastures..rottith on the Ground, and maketh Sogges and Quikke More. **1805** W. H. MARSHALL *Rur. Econ. W. Eng.* (ed. 2) I. 398 *Sog*, a quagmire. *a* **1887** JEFFERIES *Field & Hedgerow* (1892) 275 The 'sog' or peaty place where the spring rises.

**sog** (sɒg), *sb.*² *dial.* and *U.S.* Also zog. [Of obscure origin.] A drowsy or lethargic state; a sleep, doze, stupor.

**1874** S. P. FOX *Kingsbridge* (ed. 2) 268 A bit of a zog. **1880** *W. Cornwall Gloss.* 53/1 She is in a sweet sog. **1887** *Scribner's Mag.* II. 738 Ezra..waved a limp hand warningly toward the bedroom-door. 'She's layin' in a sog,' he said.

**sog,** *sb.*³ ? *Obs.* A large whale.

**1839** *Knickerbocker* XIII. 379 He was a most extraordinary fish; or, in the vernacular of Nantucket, 'a genuine old sog', of the first water. **1850** SCORESBY *Cheever's Whalem. Adv.* xii. 164 There she blows! Oh, she's a beauty! A regular old sog! A hundred-barreler! **1851** H. MELVILLE *Moby Dick* II. xxxix. 261 Such a sog! such a sogger! Don't ye love sperm!

**sog** (sɒg), *v.* Now *dial.* Also 9 zog. [Of obscure origin: cf. SOG *sb.*¹ and Norw. dial. *soggjast, søggast*, in sense 1.

The *Promp. Parv.* has the comb. *water-soggon* 'aquosus'.]

**1.** *intr.* **a.** To become soaked, or saturated with wet.

**1538** [see SOGGING *ppl. a.*]. *a* **1722** LISLE *Husb.* (1757) 55 The sword of the ground being turned in when wet, lies there sogging. *Ibid.* 169 Nothing makes peas more subject to open the kids than lying sogging in the wet.

**b.** To sink or soak in. Also with *in.*

**1854** MISS BAKER *Northampt. Gloss.* II. 264 If you don't make the roof pretty steer for thatching, the wet will sog in. **1881** *Leic. Gloss.* 249 The summer wet doon't sog in deep.

**2.** *trans.* To steep, soak, or saturate.

**1854** MISS BAKER *Northampt. Gloss.* II. 264 Shoes are sogged, when they are soaked through with wet and mud. **1888** *Berks. Gloss.* 197 The clo-aths as I hung out to dry be all zogged wi' the raain.

Hence **sogging** *vbl. sb.* and *ppl. a.*

**1538** LELAND *Itin.* (1769) V. 15 After the Trees wer cut doune sogging Yerth and Mosse over-coverid them. **1879** MISS JACKSON *Shropsh. Word-Bk.* 397, I got a pretty soggen [in the thunder-storm]. **1910** M. HEWLETT *Rest Harrow* III. iv, Through the sogging rains of Christmas.

‖**'soga,** *sb. Amer.* [Sp. (also Pg. and It.), of doubtful origin.] A rope of esparto grass or other material. Also *attrib.*

**1860** MAYNE REID *Hunters' Feast* xvii, He is exposed..to the perils of..the creaking 'soga' bridge. **1910** *Blackw. Mag.* June 842/2 Gnawing through the sogas of the horses.

Hence **'soga** *v.*, to tie *up* with a soga or sogas.

**1902** HESKETH PRICHARD *Thro' Heart of Patagonia* xi. 161 The next morning we *sogaed* up the horses and set out.

**SOGAT, Sogat** ('səʊgæt). [Acronym f. the initial letters of *S*ociety *o*f *G*raphical and *A*llied *T*rades.] A trade union now composed of paper-workers, etc. (see below), in the printing industries.

The union was formed in 1966 by the amalgamation of the National Union of Printing, Bookbinding, and Paper Workers and the National Society of Operative Printers and Assistants. In 1972 this union was divided, with the paper workers retaining the acronym SOGAT. In 1982 SOGAT amalgamated with the National Society of Operative Printers Graphical and Media Personnel. The new union was called SOGAT 82.

**1966** *Paperworker* Mar. 3/1 Formation of SOGAT. The Registrar of Friendly Societies informed us today of his approval of the..establishment of the Society of Graphical and Allied Trades (SOGAT). **1967** *SOGAT* Feb. 6/1 Only one year ago the Society of Graphical and Allied Trades, now using the coined name SOGAT, came into being. **1969** *Times* 2 May 1/8 About 500 Sogat members..stopped work ..at the Stationery Office's printing plant. **1971** H. WILSON *Labour Government* xiii. 210 SOGAT rejected a multilateral meeting. **1977** in R. Crossman *Diaries* III. 723 Richard Briginshaw, General Secretary of the National Society of Operative Printers, Graphical and Media Personnel (as SOGAT became) 1951–75. **1982** *Times* 8 Nov. 2/4 Sogat '82 hopes that several hundred trade unionists will demonstrate.

†**sogate,** *adv. Obs.* Forms: α. (*north.* and *Sc.*) 4 squagate, 4–5 suagat, 5 swa-, sagat. β. 4–6 sogate, 5 sogat (-get). [f. So *adv.* + GATE *sb.*² Cf. THUS-GATE *adv.*

In MSS. freq. written as two words, and sometimes hyphened in printed texts.]

In this or that manner; in such wise; so, thus.

α. *a* **1300** *Cursor M.* 2750 Sal þou þine auin sua-gat for-fare? *c* **1325** *Metr. Hom.* 146 Suagat spil mi corn ye maye. *c* **1375** *Sc. Leg. Saints* ix. (*Bartholomew*) 92 Quhene þe kynge ..herd þat þe apostil sagat ferd.

β. **1338** R. BRUNNE *Chron.* (1810) 63 þei said, þat.. Edward..had þam so gate awed. *a* **1352** MINOT *Poems* (ed. Hall) viii. 96 God saue þam þat it so-gat wan. *c* **1400** *Destr. Troy* 5207 A cite in the same lond so gat was cald. **1570** LEVINS *Manip.* 39 Sogate, thus, *sic ita, isto modo.*

†**sogates,** *adv. Obs.* Also 5 swagatis, swagates, sagates. [f. as prec. + -S¹.] = prec.

**13..** *Seuen Sages* 2855 (W.), When that thai had so-gates done. **1375** BARBOUR *Bruce* XIX. 253 And swagatis furthward can thai fair. *a* **1400** *Isumbras* 250 Whenne that thay herde hym swa gates crye. *c* **1400** *Pol. Poems* (Rolls) I. 267 This is a quaynt custome..That frers shal..so gates selle ther song.

†**sogbote.** *Obs.* (? Error for *cogbote*, COG *sb.*¹ 3.)

*c* **1475** *Pict. Voc.* in Wr.-Wülcker 805 *Hec facelus*, a sogbote.

**Sogdian** ('sɒgdɪən), *a.* and *sb.* Also Soghdian, Sughdian. [ad. L. *Sogdiānus*, a. Gr. Σογδιανός, f. O. Persian *Suguda*, later *Sugud*.]

**A.** *adj.* Of or belonging to Sogdiana, an ancient Persian province corresponding to the modern Samarkand and Bokhara in the Uzbek S.S.R. **B.** *sb.* **a.** A native of this province. **b.** The Middle Iranian language of this province. Also *attrib.*

**1553** J. BRENDE tr. *Quintus Curtius' Hist.* VII. sig. Ui, When he had ordred all thinges amonges the Sogdians, he.. remoued into Bactria. **1700** G. BOOTH tr. *Diodorus Siculus' Historical Libr.* 785 How the King led his Army against the Sogdians and Scythians. *Ibid.* 787 How the Sogdian Noblemen being led forth to be put to Death, were unexpectedly preserv'd. **1729** J. ROOKE tr. *Arrian's Hist. of Alexander's Exped.* I. IV. xvi. 24 He then, with part of his army, march'd straight into the country of the Sogdians. *Ibid.*, Spitamenes, at the head of a band of Sogdian exiles, who had fled into Scythia,..attack'd a certain castle in Bactria. **1909** *Indogerm. Forsch.* XXV. 182 The Sughdian rendering of the Syriac version of the Greek. **1923** H. G. WELLS *Outl. Hist.* (rev. ed.) xxx. 295/2 A very considerable literature..in Sogdian and another Aryan language has been discovered. **1947** C. P. SNOW *Light & Dark* I. iv. 47 It was written in an unknown variety of Middle Persian called Early Soghdian. **1954** I. GERSHEVITCH (*title*) Grammar of Manichean Sogdian. **1973** R. L. FOX *Alexander the Great* III. xxii. 309 Heavy drinking is the corollary of survival for a traveller in a Sogdian summer. *Ibid.* 314 By now, Sogdians and Bactrians were serving in Alexander's army.

**sogeare, soger, -ing:** see SOLDIER(ING.

**soget, -ette,** varr. SUGET (subject) *Obs.*

**sogetly:** see SUGETLY *Obs.*

**soggamore,** obs. f. SAGAMORE.

**soggarth** ('sɒgərθ). *Irish.* Also sogarth, saggart. [ad. Ir. *sagart*, OIr. *sacart*, *-ard*, ad. L. *sacerdōs*: see SACERDOTAL *a.*] A priest.

**1836** CARLETON *Fardorougha* xvii. (1848) 246 What if you axe to see the Bodagh's son, the young sogarth. **1851** BORROW *Lavengro* x, To send me to school..that I might be made a saggart of. **1898** R. BUCHANAN *Father Anthony* xviii, Can't the soggarth visit a dying man without being followed and spied upon?

**sogged** (sɒgd), *ppl. a.* [f. SOG *v.* + -ED¹.] Soaked, saturated.

**1860** GOSSE *Rom. Nat. Hist.* i. 15 The unwieldy caddis-worms are lazily dragging about their curiously-built houses over the sogged leaves. **1929** H. WILLIAMSON *Beautiful Yrs.* xxiii. 237 A weary, misty dawn dispelled the phantasms and presented a reality of sogged ground and wet drippings from the trees. **1947** K. TENNANT *Lost Haven* iii. 53 Ground's too cold, everything's too sogged for the feed to grow. **1966** S. HEANEY *Death of Naturalist* 23 For days I sadly hung Round the yard, watching the three sogged remains Turn mealy and crisp as old summer dung.

**soggily** ('sɒgɪlɪ), *adv.* [f. next + -LY².] In a soggy manner.

**1939** AUDEN & ISHERWOOD *Journey to a War* 222 The bastard, I thought soggily, he's sneaking off. **1960** *Times* 1 Nov. 16/4 The result [*sc.* a film]..rather soggily directed by Mr. Peter Brook. **1975** C. WESTON *Susannah Screaming* (1976) xxii. 118 'You can see what happened,' Haynes said soggily, mopping his nose. **1981** M. KENYON *Zigzag* xx. 131 Three slabs of still soggily magnificent date cake.

**soggy** ('sɒgɪ), *a.* orig. *dial.* and *U.S.* Also 9 *dial.* zoggy. [f. SOG *sb.*¹ or *v.*]

In B. Jonson *Ev. Man out of Hum.* III. ii. [viii.] ('this greene and soggie multitude') the correct reading is prob. 'foggie', a common word at that date.

**1.** Of land: Soaked with water or moisture; boggy, swampy, marshy.

*a* **1722** LISLE *Husb.* (1757) 49 If the ground falls small, then it may lie soggy and spungy. **1805** W. H. MARSHALL *Rur. Econ. W. Eng.* (ed. 2) I. 398 *Zoggy*, wet, boggy. **1869** B. TAYLOR *Byeways of Europe* I. 247 The soil..already looked soggy and drenched. **1896** *Godey's Mag.* Apr. 351/2 These country roads are..frost-laden and wet, and soft and soggy.

**2. a.** Saturated with wet; soppy, soaked.

*a* **1852** F. M. WHITCHER *Widow Bedott Papers* (1856) xxix. 375 Oh yes, to be sure it needs sugar, the best o' sugar, too; not this wet, soggy, brown sugar. **1863** B. TAYLOR *H. Thurston* xii. 155 He looked out on..fields of soggy, soaked snow. **1886** *Harper's Mag.* Dec. 98 Crumbly, soggy timber. **1897** KIPLING *Capt. Cour.* 19 All he brought up was a soggy packet of cigarettes. **1964** [see *plastic-macked* s.v. PLASTIC *sb.*³ 5].

**b.** Resulting from, caused by, moistness or wetness.

**1876** DUHRING *Dis. Skin* 126 The skin is observed to be of a whitish or yellowish color, and to have a soggy appearance. **1881** *Harper's Mag.* Oct. 650 Every footstep giving out a soggy wheeze from his old wet boots.

**3.** Of bread: Sodden, heavy.

**1868** WHYMPER *Alaska* v. 61 We varied a diet of soggy bread with a kind of thin paste or soup. **1903** *T.P.'s Weekly* 4 Sept. 436/1 Bread is burnt and soggy.

**4. a.** Of persons: Dull, spiritless.

**1896** *Advance* (Chicago) 16 July 88/1 The Slavs are a passive, gregarious, soggy race. **1911** GALSWORTHY *Patrician* II. xxi. 277 The passers-by..looked soft, soggy, without pride or will.

**b.** Of things, in various *transf.* and *fig.* uses: dull, lifeless, lacking in vigour, sluggish; (of steering) unresponsive.

**1928** [see DAWK *sb.*² b]. **1932** [see BLIMEY *int.*]. **1957** J. BRAINE *Room at Top* xxv. 205 The steering [of a car] was low-geared and more than a trifle soggy. **1965** G. McInnes *Road to Gundagai* v. 79 The poor fellow found the evening hanging pretty soggy on his hands. **1966** Williams & Fleming *Spectrosc. Methods in Org. Chem.* iii. 44 The soggy vibrations of the molecule as a whole give rise to a series of absorption bands at low energy, below 1500 cm.$^{-1}$. **1977** *Gramophone* Dec. 1080/1 The brass fanfares at the start of the finale are hardly of the brightest in sound—but then tuttis show the general orchestral sound to be pretty soggy.

5. Moist, close, sultry.

**1896** Baden-Powell *Matabele Campaign* xix, We rattled along through the bush,.. all the time in deep, soggy heat. **1901** W. Churchill *The Crisis* ii. xiv, The day had been soggy and warm.

Hence ˈ**sogginess**.

**1884** Bourke *Snake Dance of Moquis* xv. 173 The sogginess of the roads made slow marching necessary. **1900** *Westm. Gaz.* 16 Aug. 5/3 The sogginess of the ground.

**sogh**, obs. 2nd sing. ind. pa. t. see *v.*

**soght**, obs. pa. t. and pa. pple. seek *v.*; var. sought *sb. Obs.*

**sogorner**, obs. f. sojourner.

**soh** (səʊ), *int.* [var. of so *adv.* 5 c, or simply of exclamatory origin. Cf. soho *int.* 2 and 3.]

**1.** An exclamation denoting anger, scorn, reproof, surprise, etc., on the part of the speaker.

*a* **1814** *Sixteen & Sixty* i. iv. in *New Brit. Theatre* IV. 391 Soh! niece, I am informed that even the presence of.. Violet is to be dispensed with. **1821** Scott *Kenilw.* xvi, 'Soh!' replied the Queen; 'and what was your right' [etc.]. **1831** —— *Ct. Rob.* xxi, 'Soh!' thought the Emperor, 'this difficulty is over'. **1844** Mrs. Browning *Lady Geraldine's Courtship* Concl. ii, Soh! how still the lady standeth!

**2.** Used in soothing or quieting a restive horse, = Gently! Softly! Easy!

**1820** Scott *Monast.* xv, Be quiet, Benedict, there is a good steed—soh, poor fellow! **1850** W. S. Mayo *Kaloolah* 12 [Saying] 'Soh! whow!' to his restive horses.

**soho** (səʊˈhəʊ), *int.* and *sb.*[1] Forms: α. 4 sohou, 5 sohowe, 5, 7 sohow; 5 so how(e, hoowe, 6 sa how, so-, soa hough. β. 4, 7- so ho (5 hoo), 6-7 sohoe, 7- so-ho, soho. [An AF. hunting call, prob. of purely exclamatory origin.

In the *Master of Game* xxxiv. the simple *howe* also occurs, as well as *he howe, here howe*, and *howe here*. The early examples do not support the suggestion in quot. 14.. that the proper form would be *sa how*.]

**1.** A call used by huntsmen to direct the attention of the dogs or of other hunters to a hare which has been discovered or started, or to encourage them in the chase; hence used as a call to draw the attention of any person, announce a discovery, or the like.

α. **1307** in Bain *Calendar* (1884) II. 539 [On a seal, a hare in her form, with motto] Sohou, Sohou. *c* **1410** *Master of Game* xxxiv. (MS. Digby 182), And þenne he shall sey thryes, so howe, and no more. **14..** *Venery de Twety* in *Reliq. Antiq.* I. 154 Sohow is moche to say as sahow, for because that it is short to say, we say al wey sohow. *c* **1485** *E. Eng. Misc.* (Warton Cl.) 44 The furst mane that me doth fynde, Anon he cryit,—So howe! So hoowe! Lo! he sayth, where syttyt an haare! **1576** Turberv. *Venerie* 177 *Sa how* sayeth one, as soone as he me spies. **1591** Shaks. *Two Gentl.* iii. i. 189 *Lau.* So-hough, Soa hough. *Pro.* What seest thou? *Lau.* Him we goe to finde.

β. **13..** *K. Alis.* 3712 (Laud MS.), So ho! so ho! We ben awroke of dogges two! *c* **1475** *Hunt. Hare* 133 (W.), The yomon rode and cryed: 'So hoo!' And putte the hare vp with his boo. **1486** *Bk. St. Albans* e v b, And then So ho so ho, thries and no mo. **1592** Shaks. *Rom. & Jul.* ii. iv. 136 *Mer.* A baud. So ho. *Rom.* What hast thou found? *Mer.* No Hare sir. **1629** Massinger *Picture* v. i, *Hilario* (holds up a piece of bread). So ho! birds! **1684** Bunyan *Pilgr.* ii. (1900) 279 Mr. Great-heart called after him, saying, Soho, Friend, let us have your Company. **1740-2** Richardson *Pamela* III. 312 He ran to the Window, and.. said Hollo—So-ho—Groom —.. Get me my Horse! **1811** *Sporting Mag.* XXXIX. 142 The hills shall re-echo—Soho! **1822** Shelley *Calderon's Mag. Prodig.* i. 48 Soho! Livia, I come; good sport, Livia, soho! **1859** Dickens *T. Two Cities* i. ii, 'So-ho,' the guard sang out, as loud as he could roar.

**b.** As *sb.*

*a* **1572** *Dk. Norfolk's Laws Coursing* in Markham *Country Contentm.* i. vii. (1664) 43 The hare-finder should give the hare three so-hows before he put her from her Lear. [Hence in Holme and later works.] *c* **1589** *Whip for an Ape* in *Lyly's Wks.* (1902) III. 418 Such sohoes, whoopes and hallowes. **1611** Cotgr., *Reclame*, a Sohoe, or Heylaw; a lowd calling, whooting, or whooping to make a Hawke stoope vnto the Lure. **1834** Thacker *Courser's Comp.* I. 167 The person who finds the hare sitting should give a clear so-ho.

**2.** = soh *int.* 1.

**1825** Scott *Talisman* ix, So ho! a goodly fellowship come to see Richard take his leap in the dark. **1885** Bompas *Frank Buckland's Life* 330 'So ho,' I said, 'my theories are right'.

**3.** = soh *int.* 2. (See also quot. 1833.)

**1832** Lytton *Eugene A.* iii. iii, Soho, Jacobina, soho, gently, girl, gently. **1833** in Youatt *Dog* iii. (1845) 96 When the old dog makes a point, the master calls out, 'Down!' or 'Soho!' and holds up his hand.

**Soho** (ˈsəʊhəʊ, səʊˈhəʊ), *sb.*[2] **a.** The name of a district in the West End of London, noted for its foreign population, prostitutes, and restaurants, and latterly for its night clubs, striptease shows, pornography shops, etc. Freq. *attrib.* of things connected with or characteristic of Soho.

**1818** Keats *Let.* 14 Mar. (1931) I. 127 Then who would go Into dark Soho, And chatter with dack'd hair'd critics. **1890** E. Dowson *Let.* 10 or 11 June (1967) 153 The two artists—with some other artistic & Bohemian types might meet in the early part of the book in a Soho restaurant based on Poland. **1905** Chesterton *Club of Queer Trades* iv. 165 Some dirty Soho restaurant. **1913** W. Whitten *Londoner's London* vi. 140 He had always a nice Soho taste in wine. **1930** W. S. Maugham *Cakes & Ale* i. 12 You drive away wondering whether when he comes he will think you are swanking if you ask him to Claridge's or mean if you suggest Soho. **1937** L. MacNeice in Auden & MacNeice *Lett. from Iceland* 129 To pore on picture catalogues and Soho menus. **1959** *Good Food Guide* 221 There is now a good Soho restaurant in Birmingham with a wide menu properly cooked. It is also resolutely described in Soho French. **1964** *Times Lit. Suppl.* 12 Nov. 1019/4 [Frank] Harris.. wrote about sex in the manner and style of the cheapest Soho trash. **1976** *Listener* 26 Feb. 239/2 Sex was.. a mean.. sleezy, Soho-type thing.

**b.** *Hist.* Used *attrib.* to designate a type of tapestry produced in England after 1685, usu. in Soho.

[**1914** W. G. Thomson *Tapestry Weaving in England* xvii. 139 At Christmas 1685 the arras-workers and tailors employed in the Great Wardrobe changed the scene of their labours to offices in Great Queen Street, Soho, which lies between the northwest corner of Lincoln's Inn Fields and Drury Lane.] **1930** H.-C. Mariller *Eng. Tapestries of Eighteenth Cent.* p. xvii, In the absence of records it would be impossible to say which Soho tapestries were executed in the late seventeenth and which in the eighteenth century. *Ibid.* p. xx, There is no clear line of demarcation between the later Mortlake and the earlier Soho tapestries. **1963** *Times* 18 Jan. 10/6 An anonymous purchaser secured four early-eighteenth-century walnut chairs covered in Soho tapestry, for 450 gns. **1978** *Country Life* 13 Apr. 973/1 The Soho tapestries which now line the room were originally bought.. in 1720.

**soˈho**, *v.* Also so-ho. [f. soho *int.*]

**1.** *intr.* To shout or cry 'soho!' Hence **soˈhoing** *vbl. sb.*

**1599** Porter *Angry Wom. Abingt.* iv. iii, Here's so-ho-ing with a plague! **1824** Miss Mitford *Village* Ser. i. (1863) 186 Even May, the most sagacious of greyhounds,.. would as soon listen to Tom sohoing as to old Tray giving tongue.

**2.** *trans.* To announce the discovery or starting of (a hare) by this shout.

**1834** Thacker *Courser's Comp.* I. 150 When a hare is found sitting, she ought to be so-ho'd. **1887** *Field* 5 Feb. 160/3 A third hare was sohoed near the river-side.

‖**soi-disant** (swadizɑ̃), *a.* [F., f. *soi* oneself + *disant*, pres. pple. of *dire* to say.]

**1.** Of persons: Calling oneself; self-styled, would-be. (Usually with implication of pretence or deception.)

**1752** Chesterf. *Lett.* ccxcii. (1792) II. 339 The pious Æneas, who, like many *soi disant* pious people, does the most flagrant injustice and violence. **1794** Scott *Let.* in *Lockhart* (1837) I. vii. 220 The *people*.. seem to interest themselves very little in the fate of their *soi-disant friends*. **1818** *Art Pres. Feet* Pref. p. x, The difference between the.. skilful practitioner, and the soi-disant corn doctor. **1874** Ld. Lennox *Recoll.* I. 273 My *soi-disant* constituent administered a pretty strong dose of soft-sawder. **1884** *Contemp. Rev.* Oct. 545 Is there any society.. where such a piece of snobbism could be represented as possible in a *soi-disant* gentleman?

**2.** Of things: Said or claimed to be such, without really being so; pretended.

**1845** J. W. Croker *Ess. Fr. Rev.* i. (1857) 4 Circumstances which appear to have influenced his *soi-disant* historical labours. **1860** Ruskin *Unto this Last* i. §1 The modern *soi-disant* science of political economy. **1867** Augusta Wilson *Vashti* xxii, A *soi-disant* 'resignation' that draws honeyed lips to the throne of grace.

**soiet(te**, variants of suget (subject) *Obs.*

**soietable**: see sugetable *Obs.*

**soife.** [Local var. of swarf *sb.*] (See quots.)

**1866** J. Chamberlain in *Birmingham & Midl. Hardware Distr.* 608 The 'soife', or iron cuttings from the nicks and threads of the screws, average about four tons per day. *Ibid.*, This 'soife' is bought up and melted down with other iron.

†**soign**, *sb. north. Obs.* In 4 soigne, soy(g)ne, soyny. [a. OF. *soigne, soine*, etc.: see essoin *sb.* For Sc. examples see sonyie *sb.*] Excuse, esp. for wrong-doing or the like.

*a* **1300** *Cursor M.* 2266 For-þi þat tour hatt babilone, þat schending es wit-outen soyne. *Ibid.* 16395 Quen he [Pilate] sagh þat al his soigne þai tok it al to ill. *Ibid.* 26691 þat þou sa wrei þin aun dede, þat [þou] na soigne [*Fairfax* soyny] be-for þe lede.

†**soign**, *v. Obs.* Forms: 4 soigne, 4-5 soyne (4 soyny, 5 soynyn), 5 sonyon. [Cf. prec. and essoin *v.*] *trans.* To excuse or exculpate for transgression, etc.; to essoin.

*a* **1300** *Cursor M.* 26717 He þat nu him-seluen wreis þan, Vr lauerd-self sal soigne [*Fairfax* soyny] þat man. *Ibid.* 29437 þof þou wit cursd man commun, þou sal be soyned wit resun. *a* **1400-50** *Alexander* 1464 He soyned him be his sorement þat sare him forthinkis. *c* **1440** *Promp. Parv.* 464/2 Sonyon, *idem quod* soynyn.

Hence †ˈ**soigning** *vbl. sb. Obs.*

*a* **1300** *Cursor M.* 28123 Quen þat i to scriueyng yede, I wald oft soyngyng for my lede.

‖**soigné** (swaɲe), *a.* Fem. soignée. [Fr., pa. pple. of *soigner* to take care of, f. *soin* care.] Dressed, adorned, tended, or prepared with great care and attention to detail; well-groomed.

**1821** M. Edgeworth *Let.* 27 Nov. (1971) 281 Which would become me best.. to pin or not to pin it. I think rather *not to pin*. It looks less soignée but then I may lose the frill. **1900** G. Arthur *Let.* 25 July in *Letters from Man of No Importance* (1928) 123 The Boers may not be particularly *soigné* in their habits, but the Japanese who are, use very little soap, and swear by vapour baths. **1907** E. Glyn *Three Weeks* xii. 137 This lady was so intensely *soignée*. **1927** A. E. W. Mason *No Other Tiger* xi. 98 As she stood there in that flood of radiance, *soignée*, polished from head to foot. **1936** *Punch* 24 June 710/2 William Powell is of course William Powell—suave and *soigné* and perfectly poised. **1959** *Good Food Guide* 35 The prices remain fairly high but the cooking is genuinely *soigné*. **1978** J. Gardner *Dancing Dodo* xxxv. 276 The soignée women and immaculate men.. who could afford places like the Hilton.

†**soignous**, *a. Obs. rare.* In 4 soigneus, 5 soygneus, -ous. [a. OF. *soigneus* (mod.F. *soigneux, -euse*), f. *soign* (mod.F. *soin*) care, heed.] Careful, heedful.

**1340** *Ayenb.* 155 [Seneca says] þet of þe parties of þe liue ech þenche and is soigneus, ac of al þe liue to ordayny non ne þencþ ne studeþ.

Hence †**soignously** *adv. Obs. rare.*

*c* **1477** Caxton *Jason* 76 [Apollo] founde under his hede the bille afore said whiche he kepte soygneusly. **1481** —— *Godfrey* cciv. 299 To kepe soygnously and defende the turkes fro thyse two Cytees.

**soik**, obs. Sc. form of suck *v.*

**soil** (sɔɪl), *sb.*[1] Forms: 4-8 **soyle** (5 **soylle**), 5, 7-8 **soyl** (6 *Sc.* **soyll**), 5-7 **soile**, 6- **soil**. [a. AF. *soil, soyl* in sense 2 b (1292-1305), app. representing L. *solium* (whence also OF. *soil, suel*: see soil *sb.*[2]), taken in the sense of L. *solum* (F. *sol*) ground. For Sc. forms see also sulye.]

**I. 1. a.** The earth or ground; the face or surface of the earth.

**13..** *E.E. Allit. P.* B. 1387 Vch a syde [of the city] vpon soyle helde seuen myle. *a* **1400-50** *Alexander* 1252 It was semand to siȝt as all þe soyle trymblid. **1412-20** Lydg. *Chron. Troy* i. 4383 Boþe tour & wal [was] with þe soil made pleyn. *a* **1547** Surrey *Æneid* ii. C iv, I saw.. Neptunus town clene razed from the soil. **1588** Shaks. *L.L.L.* iv. ii. 7 The face of *Terra*, the soyle, the land, the earth. **1632** Lithgow *Trav.* viii. 372 The Countrey voyd of Villages, Riuers, or Cultiuage: but the soyle rich in Bestiall. **1660** Milton *Free Commw.* 18 With the Prophet.. to tell the verie soil it self what God hath determined of Coniah and his seed for ever. **1818** Cruise *Digest* (ed. 2) V. 21 In cases of copyholds, a lord may have a right under the soil of the copyholder. *a* **1838** in Murray's *N. Germ.* 90 The precise spot where his foot first touched the soil. **1851** Borrow *Lavengro* lxxv, I flung myself on the soil, and kissed it.

†**b.** The lower ground, the plain. *Obs.*[−1]

**1594** Nashe *Dido* iii. iii. 976 Æneas, leaue these dumpes, and lets away, Some to the mountaines, some vnto the soyle, You to the valleys.

**2. a.** A piece or stretch of ground; a place or site. Now *rare* or *Obs.*

*c* **1400** *Destr. Troy* 2078 He þat set is full sad on a soile euyn, And pight has his place on a playn ground. **1430-40** Lydg. *Bochas* ii. xiii. (1554) 51 b, A soyle she found ful delectable of sight. **1470** in Aungier *Syon Mon.* (1840) 72 A soyle and a grownde of wode callid Blakeley. **1547** in *Vicary's Anat.* (1888) App. iii. i. 131 The Sightes or Soyles wheruppon the same ij churches Are.. buyldyd. **1576** Fleming *Panopl. Epist.* 205 Hauing forgotten the situation of the soyle where he was resident,.. he fell into a ditche. **1647** Hexham i. (Hunting), The ground or soile where a Deere feeds. **1797** T. Wright *Autobiog.* (1864) 89 If I could purchase a soil anywhere nigh.. he would give me the stones.. to build the house.

†**b.** With poss. pron. or genitive. *Obs.*

**1464** *Rolls of Parlt.* V. 529/1 CC acres of wast of oure soile within the Forest. **1467** in *Eng. Gilds* (1870) 371 That euery man kepe his soyle clene and his pavyment hole. **1480** *Cov. Leet Bk.* 459 þe place of the seid weysshyng ys þe soyle of þe hospitall.

†**c.** An estate or property. *Obs. rare.*

**1575** Churchyard *Chippes* (1817) 138 They went towards Seatton,.. where the lady of that soyle.. presented the keyes.. to the generall.

**3.** A land or country; a region, province, or district. Now *Obs.* or *arch.*

*a* **1400-50** *Alexander* 3161 þe sceptoure & þe soile sesid am [I] of Persy. *a* **1513** Fabyan *Chron.* vii. ccxxxv. (1811) 271 Yᵉ kyng.. gaue yᵉ moytie therof to yᵉ duke of Burgoyn, as chefe lorde of yᵗ soyle. **1577** *St. Augustine's Man.* 26 There the daysunne of righteousnesse.. inlighteneth all the Citizens of the heavenly soyle. **1604** E. G[rimstone] *D'Acosta's Hist. Indies* iv. xiv. 250 There is towardes that place a soile which they call, the Land of Emeraldes. **1667** Milton *P.L.* i. 242 Is this the Region, this the Soil, the Clime,.. That we must change for Heav'n? **1727** Gay *Fables* i. x. 2 The man who with undaunted toils Sails unknown seas, to unknown soils. **1781** Cowper *Expost.* 192 Lords of the conquered soil,.. In peace possessing what they won by war.

**4. a.** The place of one's nativity; one's (native) land or country.

*a* **1400-50** *Alexander* 1724 þe souerayne sire of my soyle þat sittis in my trone. **1553** T. Wilson *Rhet.* 51 His soyle also (where he was borne) geveth him to be an evill man. **1597** Hooker *Eccl. Pol.* v. lxxviii. §1 When hunger caused them to leaue their naturall soyle, and to seeke for sustenance in Egypt. **1632** Lithgow *Trav.* i. 7, I choosed.. to seclude my selfe from my soyle. **1697** Dryden *Virg., Past.* x. 70 You.. To shun my sight, your Native Soil forego, And climb the frozen Alps. **1748** Gray *Alliance* 87 The manners speak the idiom of their soil. **1822** Shelley *Chas. 1st* ii. 211 Your Majesty has ever interposed, In lenity towards your native soil [etc.]. **1838** THIRLWALL *Greece* IV. 155 The outcasts whom the cruel policy..of the Athenians had at various times deprived of their native soils.

†**b.** One's domicile or place of residence. Freq. in *to change one's soil. Obs.*

**1555** WATREMAN *Fardle Facions* I. vi. 91 Because thei cary great droues of catteill with them, they chaunge their soile often. **1577–87** HOLINSHED *Chron.* III. 1066/2 Such as could make shift..changed their soile. **1641** MILTON *Ch. Govt.* Wks. 1851 III. 96 Some of our Prelates in all haste meant to change their soile. **1643** BAKER *Chron., Eliz.* 50 His father, ..being persecuted for a Protestant, changed his Soyl.

**5.** In phrases: **a.** *lord of the soil*, the owner of an estate or domain.

**1593** SHAKS. *2 Hen. VI*, IV. x. 26 Heere's the Lord of the soile come to seize me for a stray. **1818** CRUISE *Digest* (ed. 2) I. 53 A class of people in a condition of downright servitude, belonging..to the lord of the soil.

**b.** *child* (*son*, etc.) *of the soil*, a native of a place or country; also, closely connected with or engaged in the cultivation of the ground.

**1814** SOUTHEY *Roderick* I. 7 A yoke galled..the children of the soil. **1861** PEARSON *Early & Mid. Ages England* i. 1 The sons of the soil, whom invasion had dispossessed of their homes. **1882** KEARY *Outl. Prim. Belief* 105 Some have believed themselves *autochthonous*, or children of the soil! **1891** T. HARDY *Tess* (1900) 133/2 Don't, Angel, be so anxious about a mere child of the soil!

**II. 6. a.** The ground with respect to its composition, quality, etc., or as the source of vegetation.

**13..** *E.E. Allit. P.* B. 1039 Þe clay þat clenges þer-by arn corsyes strong,..& suche is alle þe soyle by þat se halues. *Ibid.* C. 443 Þe whyle God of his grace ded growe of þat soyle þe fayrest bynde hym [*sc.* Jonah] abof þat euer burne wyste. **1412–20** LYDG. *Chron. Troy* I. 2606 Þe bareyn soyl to clothen and amende. **1597** SHAKS. *2 Hen. IV*, IV. iv. 54 Most subiect is the fattest Soyle to Weedes. **1604** E. G[RIMSTONE] *D'Acosta's Hist. Indies* IV. vi. 219 The ground and soile of this mountaine is drie, cold and very vnpleasant. **1697** DRYDEN *Virg. Georg.* I. 71 Goad him..Till the bright Share is bury'd in the Soil. **1726** SWIFT *Gulliver* II. vi, I dwelt long upon the fertility of our soil and the temperature of our climate. **1748** GRAY *Alliance* 6 The soil, tho' fertile, will not teem in vain. **1806** *Gazetteer Scotl.* 101 The soil is excellent, being composed of clay and sand. **1882** GEIKIE *Text-bk. Geol.* II. II. vi. 154 Primarily the character of the soil is determined by that of the subsoil.

**b.** *transf.* and *fig.* (or in fig. context).

**1575** G. W. in *Gascoigne's Wks.* (1907) I. 24 Whereof if some but simple seeme, consider well the soyle. They grew not all at home, some came from forreyne fieldes. *c* **1586** C'TESS PEMBROKE *Ps.* LII. viii, Gods house the soile shall bee My rootes to nourish. **1824** LAMB *Elia* II. *Blakesmoor in H—shire*, These were..the wholesome soil which I was planted in. **1869** TOZER *Highl. Turkey* II. 277 This popular literature is found over the whole face of Europe. Turn the soil where you will, and a plentiful crop at once springs up. **1899** *Allbutt's Syst. Med.* VIII. 858 These agents..in some way make the soil [*sc.* the skin] unsuitable for the growth of the fungus.

**7. a.** Without article: Mould; earth. Usu., but not always, such material as will support the growth of plants, as contrasted with subsoil.

*c* **1440** *Promp. Parv.* 342/1 Moold, or soyle of erthe, *solum, humus.* **1530** PALSGR. 272/1 Soyle of grounde, *terrover.* **1590** SPENSER *F.Q.* III. vi. 31 It sited was in fruitfull soyle of old. **1648** MILTON *Psalm* lxxxi. 23 His hands from pots, and mirie soyle Deliver'd were by me. **1685** TEMPLE *Gardens* Wks. 1720 I. 183 Of all sorts of Soil, the best is that upon a Sandy Gravel. *a* **1701** MAUNDRELL *Journ. Jerus.* (1732) 65 Many beds of excellent soil. **1774** BRYANT *Mythol.* II. 214 When the birds were found to return with their feet stained with soil. **1855** DELAMER *Kitchen Gard.* 2 Though the Flemings have, mostly, everything that can be wished for as to soil. **1880** GEIKIE *Phys. Geog.* iv. 187 The layer of soil on which the plants grow. **1906** E. W. HILGARD *Soils* viii. 120 Universal experience has long ago recognized and established the distinction between soil and subsoil: by which are ordinarily meant, respectively, the portion of the soil-material usually subjected to tillage, and what lies beneath. **1932** G. W. ROBINSON *Soils* i. 2 Soil consists essentially of (a) mineral matter,..(b) organic matter,..(c) soil moisture,..and (d) soil air. **1952** L. M. THOMPSON *Soils & Soil Fertility* i. 3 Soil is the mixture of mineral and organic material at the land surface of the earth that is capable of sustaining plant life. **1976** D. STEILA *Geogr. Soils* 2 Soil serves as an anchorage for plants and as their nutrient reservoir.

**b.** *Engin.* Fragmentary or unconsolidated material occurring naturally at or near the earth's surface, regardless of its suitability for plant life. Cf. REGOLITH.

**1934** L. C. URQUHART *Civil Engin. Handbk.* VIII. 632 The earth consists of various rock formations covered with a mantle of unconsolidated products of rock disintegration, called the regolith or, more commonly, the soil, although agriculturists use the term soil in a somewhat different sense. **1967** A. SINGH *Soil Engin.* i. 1 Soil is considered to include all naturally occurring loose or soft deposit overlying the solid bedrock crust. **1972** C. B. HUNT *Geol. Soils* i. 5 In engineering, 'soil' refers to the ground that can be excavated by earth-moving equipment without blasting.

**c.** Friable or powdery material occurring naturally on another planet.

**1967** *Sci. Amer.* Nov. 43/1 Some of the objects observed on the lunar surface were clodlike clumps of soil. **1970** *Nature* 28 Nov. 795/2 (*caption*) Lunakhod-1 tracks in the lunar soil. **1976** *Daily Tel.* 4 Aug. 10/6 The mechanical digging arm on the Viking I lander was activated again yesterday, scooping up fresh soil to explore for basic life forms on Mars. **1977** J. M. PASACHOFF *Contemporary Astron.* III. xiii. 336 The Venera landers also made measurements of the soil, determining that its chemical composition and density correspond to that of basalt, in common with the Earth, the Moon, and Mars.

**8. a.** With *a* and pl. A particular kind of mould or earth.

**1560** BIBLE (Geneva) *Ezek.* xvii. 8 It was planted in a good soile by great waters, that it shulde..beare frute. **1596** SHAKS. *1 Hen. IV*, I. i. 64 The variation of each soyle, Betwixt that Holmeden, and this Seat of ours. **1604** E. G[RIMSTONE] *D'Acosta's Hist. Indies* II. viii. 99 The rest is a sandie and barren soile. **1626** B. JONSON *Staple of N.* II. iv. (1905) 46 But this is a hungry soile, And must be helpt. **1697** DRYDEN *Virg. Georg.* II. 154 Nor ev'ry plant on ev'ry soil will grow. **1726** LEONI *Alberti's Archit.* II. 109/1 There were as many different sorts of wines, as there were of different soyls wherein the vineyards were planted. **1767** A. YOUNG *Farmer's Lett. to People* 140 On three different soils (very light—rich—and very heavy). **1813** SIR H. DAVY *Agric. Chem.* i. (1814) 12 Soils in all cases consist of a mixture of finely divided earthy matters. **1879** *Cassell's Techn. Educ.* I. 171/1 Sandy and peaty soils and marls are in general deficient in this alkali.

*fig.* **1631** BOLTON *Comf. Affl. Consc.* iv. (1635) 197 There is but one good soile, upon which the seed of the Word falls prosperously. **1781** COWPER *Truth* 363 No soil like poverty for growth divine. **1794** PALEY *Evid.* (1825) II. 352 Infidelity is the hardest soil which the propagators of a new religion can have to work upon. **1870** MAX MÜLLER *Sci. Relig.* (1873) 39 In no religion was there a soil so well prepared.

**b.** *Engin.* A particular kind of fragmentary material (sense 7 b above).

**1913** BLANCHARD & DROWNE *Text-bk. Highway Engin.* vi. 127 Some of the more common soils encountered in highway work are classified as gravel, sand, clay, loam, marl, peat and muck. **1966** *McGraw-Hill Encycl. Sci. & Technol.* XII. 450/1 Soils range from deep-lying geologic deposits to agricultural soils.

**9.** *attrib.* and *Comb.*, as ***soil aggregate, amelioration, bacterium*** (usu. *pl.*), ***-breaker, characteristic, classification, compaction, condition, cover, depletion, development, drainage, -draining, fertility, formation, genesis, geography, geology, layer, management, material, microbiology, micro-organism, mineral, moisture, nutrient, organic matter, organism, particle, population, pore, -pulverizer, restoration, -restorer, sterilization, structure, study, temperature, test, texture***; ***soil-binding, -borne, -building, -depleting, -dwelling, -forming, -inhabiting, -restorative, -supporting*** adjs.; ***soil-testing, -warming*** sbs. and adjs.

**1934** *Discovery* July 198/2 Important chemical properties are indicated by the form of the soil aggregates. **1967** Soil aggregate [see KRILIUM]. **1969** *Gloss. for Landscape Work (B.S.I.)* v. 20 Soil amelioration. **1972** EDWARDS & LOFTY *Biol. Earthworms* vii. 171 (*heading*) Soil amelioration by earthworms. **1900** *Knowledge* 2 July 161/2 In removing from the land his annual crop, the farmer carries off the greater part of the year's supply of potential humus whence the soil looks to be provided with Nitrates—by the action of the soil-bacteria—for the coming season. **1973** R. G. KRUEGER et al. *Introd. Microbiol.* xxx. 743/1 Two groups of aerobic soil bacteria are in large part responsible for the conversion of ammonia to nitrate. Representatives of the *Nitrosomonas* group oxidize ammonia to nitrite; those of the *Nitrobacter* group oxidize nitrite to nitrate. **1913** *Bull. Bureau of Soils U.S. Dept. Agric.* No. 96. 19 This wasteful wash can be checked..by seeding the land to soil-binding grasses. **1943** J. S. HUXLEY *TAV* vi. 42 Protective, soil-binding crops. **1946** *Nature* 9 Nov. 661/2 *Verticillium Malthousei* is the causal fungus; it may be soil-borne, or carried by flies. **1968** *Times* 16 Dec. 7/2 The soil-borne diseases, take-all and eyespot. **1977** J. L. HARPER *Population Biol. Plants* v. 139 It is..not particularly easy to discriminate between direct toxic action of soil chemical conditions and indirect effects due to soil-borne pathogens which are themselves determined in distribution by the chemical conditions. **1889** *Pall Mall G.* 25 June 3/1 The same may be said of harrows and soil-breakers. **1920** W. W. WEIR *Productive Soils* i. 9 Because of the source of soil building materials, the nature of soil formation, [etc.]..all soil can not be the same. **1938, 1962** Soil-building [see *soil-depleting* adj. below]. **1902** P. MCCONNELL *Elem. Agric. Geol.* iv. 122 (*heading*) Soil characteristics. **1954** W. D. THORNBURY *Princ. Geomorphol.* iv. 73 No geomorphologist today is adequately trained who lacks an appreciation of the soil-forming processes and a basic understanding of soil characteristics. **1923** *Soil Sci.* XVI. 95 On the basis of this concept of soils and soil classification, field and laboratory studies of soils in Michigan have been undertaken. **1946** L. D. STAMP *Britain's Struct. & Scenery* xi. 92 The basis of the soil classification used for these maps is a textural one:.. broadly the purpose was to separate sands, light, medium and heavy loams, clays and peats. **1972** J. G. CRUICKSHANK *Soil Geogr.* i. 23 Senior members of the national soil surveys such as G. W. Robinson (1932) and B. W. Avery (1956) have been responsible for soil classifications which developed from the work of soil survey in Britain. **1933** *Engin. News-Record* 31 Aug. 245/2 The basic principles of soil compaction..apply to all types of earthfills and to foundation design. **1971** *Power Farming* Mar. 80/1 (Advt.), The Salo [harrow] produces a fine, level, shallow bed with only one or two tractor passes. Soil compaction is reduced to the minimum. **1905** *Jrnl. Agric. Sci.* I. 78 The clover crop feels the effect of the changed soil conditions to a much greater extent. **1966** Soil condition [see *soil survey*, sense 10 below]. **1964** W. C. PUTNAM *Geology* x. 249/1 Soil cover serves to alleviate the starkness of a rock-dominated landscape. **1938** *Sun* (Baltimore) 14 Sept. 4/8 Payments will be made for keeping within soil-depleting acreage allotments and for attaining soil-building goals. **1962** *Times* 12 Oct. (Stand. Bank Suppl.) p. vii/5 The ability to overcome..problems by applying research findings such as .. soil-building rotations as opposed to soil-depleting rotations and harmful practices such as monoculture. **1925** Soil depletion [see MOSAIC *a.*[1] 6]. **1921** *Proc. 41st Ann. Meeting Soc. Promotion Agric. Sci., 1920* (U.S.) 118 A great deal of fundamental work has been done in Russia. It has been concerned..with the working out of the principles and the formulation of the laws of soil development. **1972** J. G. CRUICKSHANK *Soil Geogr.* ii. 57 The origin of parent materials is not significant for soil development except as an indication of the soil properties that may be expected. **1946** L. D. STAMP *Britain's Struct. & Scenery* xi. 100 The relationship between vegetation cover and soil drainage is far from being sufficiently realised. **1840** J. BUEL *Farmer's Comp.* 101 What we term soil-draining, is most frequently resorted to in swamps and low lands. **1970** GAY & CALABY in Krishna & Weesner *Biol. Termites* II. ix. 440 Soil-dwelling colonies commonly build radiating gallery systems on the soil surface to adjacent grass tussocks. **1901** *Proc. 22nd Ann. Meeting Soc. Promotion Agric. Sci.* (U.S.) 62 The subject of humus in its relation to soil fertility. **1968** R. W. FAIRBRIDGE *Encycl. Geomorphol.* 1235/2 Deposition of fine dust (obvious in the case of thick loess) has occurred in very thin mantles..over broad areas. The latter is a vastly underrated factor in the maintenance of soil fertility in wide regions. **1912** *Bull. Bur. Soils U.S. Dept. Agric.* No. 85. 14 The most important agency of soil formation is moisture. **1963** [see PEDOGENESIS]. **1967** M. J. COE *Ecol. Alpine Zone Mt. Kenya* 69 The processes of soil formation are also very evident. **1902** P. MCCONNELL *Elem. Agric. Geol.* iii. 66 (*heading*) List of the principal soil-forming minerals. **1936** [see PEDOGENESIS]. **1972** J. G. CRUICKSHANK *Soil Geogr.* ii. 34 Climate was regarded as the principal and dominant soil-forming factor for the greater part of the short history of pedological thought. **1927** C. F. MARBUT in tr. *Glinka's Great Soil Groups* p. i, The development of the first and only comprehensive theory of soil genesis. **1946** S. A. WILDE *Forest Soils & Forest Growth* iii. 20 An essential factor of soil genesis, the composition of vegetative cover. **1972** Soil genesis [see PEDOCAL]. **1927** C. F. MARBUT tr. *Glinka's Great Soil Groups* 7 The study of the soil geography of North America has..enforced the recognition of the close relationship between the soil and climatic conditions. **1972** J. G. CRUICKSHANK *Soil Geogr.* i. 30 Pedology is, by this definition, very close to soil geography except that the latter is concerned with all kinds of distributions involving soil, from those of natural genesis to limitations for soil cultivation. **1907** J. R. KILROE (*title*) A description of the soil-geology of Ireland, based upon Geological Survey maps and records. **1972** J. G. CRUICKSHANK *Soil Geogr.* i. 16 A further distinction differentiating soil from weathered rock was subsequently made.., but nevertheless the view of soil science as soil geology prevailed for the rest of the nineteenth century in Western Europe and America. **1939** MELHUS & KENT *Elem. Plant Path.* vii. 97 Mercuric chloride in dilute solution has been used in the control of..certain soil-inhabiting pathogens, etc. **1969** W. L. NUTTING in Krishna & Weesner *Biol. Termites* I. viii. 274 There is even less information on the wood- and soil-inhabiting Hodotermitidae. **1911** *Encycl. Brit.* XXV. 351/2 The general evidence indicates that the specific bacteria of cholera discharges are capable of a much longer existence in the superficial soil layers than was formerly supposed. **1964** W. C. PUTNAM *Geology* x. 249/2 Soil layers and particles may be lifted up by the expansion of freezing water. **1968** Soil layer [see PEDOSPHERE]. **1909** *Bull. Bur. Soils U.S. Dept. Agric.* No. 55. 26 This is borne out by the experience of farmers, who testify as to differences in soil management. **1979** W. L. PRITCHETT *Properties & Managem. Forest Soils* p. v, Significant advances have been made in silviculture, especially in reforestation technology and soil management of short rotation forests for fiber production. **1912** *Bull. Bur. Soils U.S. Dept. Agric.* No. 85. 23 Numerous kinds of rocks or soil material, subjected to the action of many agencies and processes,..have resulted in the formation of many varieties or types of soil. **1971** A. R. JUMIKIS *Foundation Engin.* vii. 179 The soil materials to use for building earth cofferdams are sandy clay and clayey sand. **1925** *Soil Sci.* XIX. 201 Agricultural practice has hardly been modified as a result of the development of soil microbiology. **1972** J. G. CRUICKSHANK *Soil Geogr.* i. 15 We are not concerned with the foundation or the history of soil chemistry, soil physics, soil microbiology, soil mineralogy, and other member parts of soil science, but rather with the inception and growth of pedology within the last century. **1916** *Soil Sci.* I. 99 The study of soil microörganisms has attracted the attention of many investigators. **1972** J. G. CRUICKSHANK *Soil Geogr.* 170 Easily attacked by a wide variety of soil microorganisms are substances like protein, sugars, and pectins. **1913** *Phil. Trans. R. Soc.* B. CCIV. 181 The soil solution may not be of constant concentration, because the soil minerals may not be so similar as is supposed, especially after the application of fertilizers. **1980** *Amateur Gardening* 4 Oct. 23/3 Grass needs potassium.., but it is extraordinarily efficient about extracting it from naturally-occurring soil minerals. **1926** *Phytopathology* XVI. 582 Soil temperature and soil moisture were believed by many writers to be responsible in part for the variation in potato mosaic symptoms. **1980** *Amateur Gardening* 4 Oct. 23/1 Nitrogen..applied in the form of a fertiliser dissolves in the soil moisture and is very rapidly lost. **1926** *Phytopathology* XVI. 583 Some attempt has been made to modify the symptoms of mosaic by varying the soil nutrients. **1915** T. L. LYON et al. *Soils* viii. 126 The source of practically all soil organic matter is plant tissue. **1971** *Gloss. Soil Sci. Terms* (Soil Sci. Soc. Amer.) 17/1 *Soil organic matter*, the organic fraction of the soil; includes plant and animal residues at various stages of decomposition, cells and tissues of soil organisms, and substances synthesized by the soil population. **1979** W. L. PRICHETT *Properties & Managem. Forest Soils* xvi. 290 While soil organic matter can be increased by use of green manure crops and the additions of composts.., such increases are temporary due to the decomposition of these materials by soil organisms. **1901** H. M. WARD *Dis. Plants* xv. 143 Cuttings..stuck into ordinary soil in dirty boxes covered with equally dirty glass, present every chance for infection by soil organisms. **1967** M. J. COE *Ecol. Alpine Zone Mt. Kenya* 70 On account of the low temperature..and the consequent paucity of soil organisms, there is a marked inhibition of the chemical breakdown of parent materials. **1900** R. WARINGTON *Lect. Physical Properties Soil* i. 11 Any group of particles obtained by subsidence will not be entirely of the same size in cases where the soil particles consist of substances having different specific gravities. **1914** [see CRUMB *sb.* 1 c]. **1964** W. C. PUTNAM *Geology* x. 245/1 The C-horizon..is a mixture in varying proportions of altered and unaltered rock fragments and soil particles. **1875** KNIGHT *Dict. Mech.* 2238/2 *Soil-pulverizer*, a machine for breaking clods. **1927** Soil population [see EDAPHON]. **1971** *Gloss. Soil Sci. Terms* (Soil

Sci. Soc. Amer.) 17/1 Soil pores. **1976** *Physics Bull.* Aug. 342/3 Marshall's equation..implies a certain connectivity of soil pores which may not always be justified. **1946** *Nature* 2 Nov. 605/1 A combination of cereal agriculture and tree-fruit crops, with subsidiary pasturage, hunting, and fishing, as an approximately stable regime,..presumes a cycle of soil-restoration. **1962** E. SNOW *Red China Today* (1963) lxvii. 508 Many of these toy dams are already used for local power, irrigation and soil-restorative purposes. **1910** *Chambers's Jrnl.* Aug. 560/1 The new alfalfa..is expected to yield an ideal forage and act as a soil-restorer. **1913** L. C. CORBETT *Garden Farming* ii. 23 Soil sterilization has for its direct object the treatment of soil in such a way as to render it free from injurious enemies. **1923** W. F. BEWLEY *Dis. Glasshouse Plants* viii. 154 The practice of soil sterilization is now an accepted method of increasing the fertility of infertile soils. **1920** W. W. WEIR *Productive Soils* ii. 13 Texture should not be confused with soil 'structure' which means the arrangements of the soil grains..or..the relation of the soil particles to each other. **1954** W. D. THORNBURY *Princ. Geomorphol.* iv. 87 Not all soil structures are.. solifluction features, for downslope movement may be either lacking or of minor importance. **1976** *Physics Bull.* Aug. 343/3 This amount of tillage..can also be harmful to the stability of the soil structure. **1927** C. F. MARBUT tr. *Glinka's Great Soil Groups* 10 Natural exposures..can be utilized as aids to soil study by artificial exposures, such as dry wells,..are better. **1972** Soil study [see *soil profile*, sense 10 below]. **1876** *Nature* 13 Jan. 215/2 Disintegrated rocks form soil-supporting vegetation. **1923** W. F. BEWLEY *Dis. Glasshouse Plants* ii. 37 Investigations upon the *Verticillium* wilt of tomatoes..illustrate the importance of air and soil temperatures in conditioning the progress of disease. **1976** L. F. CURTIS et al. *Soils in Brit. Isles* xii. 221 Another effect of good drainage is that it allows the soil temperature to rise more quickly in the spring. **1926** *Public Roads* VII. 153 (*heading*) Simplified soil tests for subgrades and their physical significance. **1978** FRIEDMAN & SANDERS *Princ. Sedimentol.* xiii. 417/1 It suffices for most engineering purposes to put the samples from a soil-test boring into small jars. **1934** *Proc. Amer. Soc. Testing Materials* XXXIV. II. 693 (*heading*) Subgrade soil testing methods. **1979** S. SMITH *Survivor* vi. 74 A local horticulturist giving a demonstration of soil testing. **1980** *Amateur Gardening* 4 Oct. 23/3 Home soil-testing kits can be purchased at quite reasonable prices at garden centres. **1912** R. L. WATTS *Vegetable Gardening* iii. 25 (*heading*) Soil texture. **1971** *Arable Farmer* Feb. 62/1 Soil texture is an important factor in determining the equilibrium of organic matter level. **1938** C. P. QUARRELL *Intensive Salad Production* vi. 72 Before undertaking any system of electrical soil warming the grower should consult the cable manufacturers. **1954** A. G. L. HELLYER *Encycl. Garden Work* 97/1 Electric soil-warming cables may be buried in the soil.

**b.** *attrib.* in *pl.*

**1925** P. EMERSON *Soil Characteristics* I. 22 The soils student should become acquainted with the common soil-forming minerals and rocks. **1945** P. WORK *Vegetable Production & Marketing* x. 164 See soils textbooks for discussions of the principles and practices of land drainage. **1969** *Civil Engin.* June 43/2 The stratum, our soils consultant recommended, could be used for safe bearing pressures of 1,200 and 1,800 psf, for dead load and total load respectively. **1973** [see PEDOLOGY].

**10.** Special combs.: **soil air**, air present in the soil; **soil amendment**, a substance added to the soil to improve its properties, esp. its physical properties; also, the use of such substances; **soil analysis**, the scientific investigation of the composition and structure of soil or soil samples; **soil association**, a group of soils that are related geographically or topographically, esp. ones derived from a common parent material; **soil auger**, a rotary tool (either powered or operated manually) for boring into or taking samples of soil; **soil bank**, (*a*) land taken out of use for agricultural production (? *temporary*); (*b*) the soil as a continuing store of seeds, pathogens, nutrients, etc.; **soil biology**, the study of soil organisms and their life; **soil-bound** *a.*, (*a*) clagged, clodded (cf. *sole-bound* s.v. SOLE *sb.*[1] 9 b); (*b*) bound or attached to the soil; **soil-cap** *Geol.*, a layer of soil and detritus covering strata or bedrock; **soil catena**: see CATENA c; **soil-cement** *a.* and (also without hyphen) *sb.*, (material) composed of soil or a soil substitute that has been strengthened and stabilized by the admixture of cement; **soil chemistry**, the branch of soil science concerned with the chemical properties and reactions of soil; so **soil chemist**; **soil class**, a group of soils similar to one another in texture or (in mod. use) some other physical property; **soil climate**, the prevailing physical conditions in the soil, esp. as they affect soil organisms and plant life; **soil colloid**, a substance present in the soil as a colloid, i.e. in the form of very small particles; **soil conditioner**, a substance added to the soil to improve its physical characteristics, *esp.* one made synthetically for the purpose; **soil conservation**, the protection and safeguarding of the soil against erosion, loss of fertility, and damage; **soil-creep**, the slow creeping or sliding movement of surface-soil down a slope; **soil deficiency**, an insufficiency in the soil of some substance necessary for the proper growth of plants; **soil erosion**, the removal of soil by the action of wind or running water; **soil exhaustion**, the disappearance of fertility from the soil; **soil extract** (see quot. 1971); **soil group**, a group of soils; *spec.* in *Soil Sci.* (also ***great soil group***), each of the relatively small number of groups into which the world's soils are divided on the basis of their profiles and the climate in which they exist; **soil horizon** = HORIZON *sb.* 5 b; **soil mantle**, the soil as a covering of the underlying rock; **soil map** *U.S.*, a map showing the distribution of various kinds of soil; a map showing the location and nature of the various kinds of soil in a region; so **soil mapping** *vbl. sb.*; **soil mark** *Archæol.*, a trace of a levelled or buried feature indicated by differences in the colour or texture of the soil, usu. on ploughed land; **soil mechanics**, the science concerned with the mechanical properties and behaviour of soil as they affect its use in civil engineering; **soil phase**, each of a number of soils that belong to the same soil type or soil series but differ in some feature such as stoniness, slope, etc.; **soil physics** (see quot. 1976); hence **soil physicist**; **soil-pipe** (see quot.); **soil polygon** = POLYGON *sb.* 2 b; **soil profile** = PROFILE *sb.*[1] 4 d; **soil province**: see PROVINCE 6 d; **soil resistivity**, the electrical resistivity of the soil; usu. *attrib.*; **soil sample**, a sample of soil taken for scientific investigation; **soil sampler**, any device for taking soil samples; so **soil sampling** *vbl. sb.*; **soil science** = PEDOLOGY; so **soil scientist** = PEDOLOGIST; **soil separate**, a separate (sense 6) obtained from soil; **soil series**, a group of soils similar in profile, origin, and other characteristics but varying in the texture of the surface horizon; **soil sickness**, a condition of soil in which it has become unable to support the healthy growth of a crop; so **soil-sick** *a.* (*rare*); **soil solution**, the water present around and between soil particles as a dilute solution of mineral salts; **soil stabilization**, the treatment of soil to give it increased resistance to movement, esp. under load, and erosion; **soil stripe** *Geomorphol.*, one of the low ridges of stony soil which occur in cold environments and form parallel, evenly spaced lines; **soil survey**, a systematic examination and mapping of the different kinds of soil present in a region or on a site; a report of the results so obtained; a body of people engaged in such work; so **soil surveyor**; **soil type**, a particular kind of soil; *spec.* in *Soil Sci.*, a subdivision of a soil series made according to the texture of the surface horizon, and representing the lowest unit in the system of classification; (see also quot. 1928); **soil wash**, the movement of soil by ground water; **soil water**, the water present in soil.

**1920** *Mem. Cornell Univ. Agric. Exper. Station* No. 32. 326 Before seeding, some preliminary studies were made in order to ascertain the best method of obtaining the sample of *soil air for analysis. **1972** J. G. CRUICKSHANK *Soil Geogr.* iii. 81 Differences between the composition of soil air and atmospheric air become greater with depth..provided organisms remain present. **1915** T. L. LYON et al. *Soils* xxiv. 542 Gypsum..was a popular *soil amendment in this country before the common commercial fertilizers were used to any great extent. **1967** *Boston Sunday Globe* 28 Apr. B. 67/4 Whenever the garden has to be in a new housing development, liming is particularly needed and all the other additions of manure, peat and fertilizer. This is now called 'soil amendment' by the more technical. **1978** R. C. OELHAF *Organic Agric.* iii. 37 Many 'organic' soil amendments are now on the market which are mainly crushed rock, selling at prices as high as 200 times the price of the ingredients. **1873** *Amer. Jrnl. Sci.* CVI. 289 In *soil analysis special importance attaches to these finer sediments. **1891** R. WALLACE *Rural Econ. Austral. & N.Z.* x. 169 No analyst, using the ordinary processes for soil analysis, can determine whether or not such infinitesimal amounts [of minerals] as are required by the crop are present or are not present in an available form in a soil. **1946** R. J. C. ATKINSON *Field Archaeol.* ii. 62 Another technique which is becoming increasingly valuable to the excavator is that of soil-analysis. **1939** *Yearbk. Agric. 1938* (U.S. Dept. Agric.) 1163 **Soil association*, group of soils, with or without common characteristics, geographically associated in an individual pattern. **1952** L. M. THOMPSON *Soils & Soil Fertility* vi. 87 The most important grouping of series, in so far as the farmer is concerned, is that of the soil association. **1970** E. M. BRIDGES *World Soils* v. 34/1 The Scottish soil scientists have grouped topographically related soils developed on one geological parent material into a soil association. **1927** E. L. WORTHEN *Farm Soils* vi. 224 A *soil auger, if available, should be used instead of a spade for sampling both surface soil and subsoil. **1975** *Sci. Amer.* May 93/1 The oak-hickory-tulip stand and the bigtooth aspen stand are on coarse, well-drained soil, which is aerated to as great a depth as I can reach with a two-meter soil auger. **1955** *Sun* (Baltimore) 26 Nov. 8/2 '*Soil bank' is the current farm bloc slang for a scheme by which farmers are paid by the Government for taking acreage out of the production of surplus crops. **1958** J. K. GALBRAITH *Affluent Society* xx. 221 Wherever possible euphemisms were employed—as this is written, instead of taking acres out of production they are being put into a soil bank. **1977** J. L. HARPER *Population Biol. Plants* iv. 95 In a sense there is a circular argument here; species which have pioneered the succession are strongly persistent in the soil-bank and so appear as pioneer species in the next succession on the area. Do they persist because they are pioneers or do they become pioneers because they have persisted. **1928** *Proc. & Papers 1st Internat. Congr. Soil Sci.* III. 325 *Soil biology is essentially a science of observation and experimentation. **1967** BURGES & RAW *Soil Biol.* p. vi, One of the stimulating developments in soil biology in recent years has been the general recognition that the soil cannot be studied solely from a chemical, microbiological, botanical or zoological standpoint. **1688** HOLME *Armoury* III. 333/2 *Crust Clung* or **Soil Bound*, is an hard, sticking together of the Earth, that nothing will grow on it. **1814** BYRON *Lara* II. viii, That morning he had freed the soil-bound slaves. *c* **1875** WAUGH *Heather* II. 151 As I get owder, I get more soil-bund. **1882** GEIKIE *Text-bk. Geol.* IV. III. 511 Mere gravitation aided by the downward pressure of sliding detritus or '*soil-cap' suffices to bend over the edges of fissile strata. **1936** *Proc. Highway Res. Board* (U.S.) XVI. 324/2 Tests were conducted to determine the moisture-density relations of the raw soil and the *soil-cement mixtures. *Ibid.* 348/2 Would the mixtures of soil-cement when compacted at optimum moisture to maximum density, maintain these characteristics under natural weathering conditions. **1950** *N.Z. Jrnl. Agric.* May 481/1 Soil cement (silty material mixed with cement)..gives a building material which has a definite structural strength, besides being resistant to the action of water and frost. **1966** R. ASHWORTH *Highway Engin.* ix. 161 By far the greatest proportion of soil-cement construction has been carried out in the U.S.A. **1979** R. J. SALTER *Highway Design & Constr.* i. 28 Soil cement may be formed by the addition of cement to a wide range of materials, including natural soils, chalk, pulverised fuel ash ..and processed granular material. **1927** N. M. COMBER *Introd. Scientific Study Soil* xiii. 130 *Soil chemists and agriculturists frequently speak about soil 'types', and yet the definition of the various types is a matter which presents very considerable difficulty. **1959** J. D. CLARK *Prehist. Southern Africa* ii. 36 It should be possible..to amass information concerning the main vegetation patterns..and for this we need the help of the..soil chemist. **1971** *Power Farming* Mar. 54/1 That handbook..is a chemical engineer's handbook and a 'natural' for all contractor services. Soil chemists have played only a minor role in assembling it. **1927** C. F. MARBUT in tr. *Glinka's Great Soil Groups* p. ii, In the more detailed study of the soil profile, the clearer recognition of the nature of soil horizons, soil structures, soil colors and in the relation of *soil chemistry to the processes of soil development in Nature, this book will be of great suggestive value. **1941** J. S. HUXLEY *Uniqueness of Man* vi. 103 What began as a study of local cattle diseases has turned into a problem of the soil chemistry of grasslands. **1972** J. G. CRUICKSHANK *Soil Geogr.* i. 15 In this discussion we are not concerned with the foundation or the history of soil chemistry, soil physics,..and other member parts of soil science, but rather with the inception and growth of pedology within the last century. **1913** *Bull. Bur. Soils U.S. Dept. Agric.* No. 96. 8 A *soil class..includes all soils having the same texture, such as sands, clays, loam, etc. **1951** *Soil Survey Man.* (U.S. Dept. Agric. Handbk. No. 18) 135 Soil class is observed in the field by feeling the soil with the fingers. **1900** R. WARINGTON *Lect. Physical Properties Soil* p. xii, If seeds are to germinate in a soil,..there must be a suitable *soil climate. **1976** A. YOUNG *Tropical Soils & Soil Survey* i. 7 The factor which directly influences soil-forming processes is soil climate rather than air climate. **1915** *Chem. Abstr.* IX. 1084 R. discusses the importance of *soil colloids for agriculture. **1935** *Nature* 24 Aug. 307/2 Much attention was directed..towards the base-exchange properties of soil colloids, particularly from the mineralogical point of view. **1970** J. A. DAJI *Textbk. Soil Sci.* xiii. 120 Soil colloids are of two kinds: (1) inorganic and (2) organic... The organic colloid..is more commonly known as humus. **1952** *Sci. News Let.* 5 Jan. 8/2 The new *soil conditioner changes the structure of clay making it porous and crumbly. **1976** L. F. CURTIS et al. *Soils in Brit. Isles* xv. 285 Soil conditioners may be applied to add stability. **1978** FRIEDMAN & SANDERS *Princ. Sedimentol.* v. 141/2 Zeolites..are mined from sedimentary deposits for use as fillers in the paper industry; as soil conditioners; [etc.]. **1932** *Yearbk. U.S. Dept. Agric.* 349 The national plan for *soil and water conservation calls for the establishment of experiment stations. **1935** *U.S. Laws, Statutes* XLIX. I. 164 The Secretary of Agriculture shall establish an agency to be known as the 'Soil Conservation Service'. **1944** AUDEN *For Time Being* (1945) 90 The Committees on Fen-Drainage and Soil-Conservation. **1952** W. L. MINER *World of W. Faulkner* ii. 61 Since 1933 the various soil conservation programs..have done much for Lafayette county. **1971** *E. Afr. Standard* (Nairobi) 13 Apr. 2/1 The committee stressed that unlike in the colonial era, farmers in the rural areas should now take great pains in soil conservation. **1897** *Archaeol. Jrnl.* Dec. 374 The *soil-creep is slow and the surface soils are of great antiquity. **1925** J. F. COX *Crop Production & Soil Managem.* vii. 116 (*heading*) The elements of fertility, common *soil deficiencies, and fertilizers carrying nitrogen, phosphorus and potassium. **1935** *Discovery* Oct. 294/1 Non-parasitic diseases of plants, due principally to soil deficiencies. **1896** *Nat. Geogr. Mag.* Nov. 368 (*heading*) The economic aspects of *soil erosion. **1944** J. S. HUXLEY *Living in Revolution* iii. 30 It neglected conservation and amenities: the result was deforestation, soil erosion, the dust bowl. **1980** *Sci. Amer.* Sept. 114/2 Major problems related to land use, soil erosion and water pollution are likely to place further limits on the recovery of these nonconventional oil resources. **1920** W. W. WEIR *Productive Soils* vii. 84 In some instances *soil exhaustion may be attributed largely to the removal, mainly through cropping and leaching, of some one or all of the three named elements. **1934** A. TOYNBEE *Study of Hist.* I. 126 As regards the possibility of soil-exhaustion, an observation of latter-day native agriculture in the area.. seems to show that a repeated clearing and burning-off of the tropical forest..does tend..to exhaust the soil. **1946** J. S. HUXLEY *Unesco* II. 28 It is possible to exploit new agricultural methods in a way that is..disastrous to agriculture itself, by causing soil exhaustion or erosion. **1957** G. E. HUTCHINSON *Treat. Limnol.* I. xvii. 896 The vitamins and accessory growth substances in soils and *soil extracts. **1971** *Gloss. Soil Sci. Terms* (Soil Sci. Soc. Amer.) 15/2 *Soil extract*, the solution separated from a soil suspension or from a soil by filtration, centrifugation, suction, or pressure. **1921** *Soil group [see *soil surveyor* below]. **1927** C. F. MARBUT tr. *Glinka's Great Soil Groups* p.

iii, Some of the great soil groups have not been studied by Russian investigators. **1954** W. D. Thornbury *Princ. Geomorphol.* iv. 76 Mature and old soils in areas that are climatically alike are strikingly similar, and it is possible to classify them in soil groups that developed under similar climatic conditions. **1972** J. G. Cruickshank *Soil Geogr.* iv. 110 There is only limited regional association in the world distribution of type profiles or great soil groups. **1976** A. Young *Tropical Soils & Soil Survey* xiii. 241 Although many of the soil groups [of the FAO classification of 1974] are natural soil types, this is structurally an artificial classification. **1923** *Soil Sci.* XVI. 97 The relative amount of silica in the gray horizon appears to be higher than in the *soil horizons below. **1964** W. C. Putnam *Geology* x. 245/1 The C-horizon is essentially a transitional zone between the true soil horizons above and the unaltered parent material below. **1972** J. G. Cruickshank *Soil Geogr.* iii. 93 All soil horizons have a three-dimensional form, but those that have a clearly visible colour and texture.. are perhaps the most convincing examples. **1961** *Listener* 12 Oct. 559/1 The changes that it [*sc.* soil science] recognizes in *soil mantles and geological solids are termed 'weathering'. **1972** J. G. Cruickshank *Soil Geogr.* i. 28 Although the soil body or soil mantle obviously has a three-dimensional form, it has been represented traditionally by a so-called 'two-dimensional' section or slice called the soil profile. **1898** *Yearbk. U.S. Dept. Agric.* 43 One of the first necessities in the development of a new district or in the improvement of an established district is an accurate *soil map of the locality. **1899** *Yearbook U.S. Dept. Agric.* 345 In 1892 the first soil map, based upon the texture and physical properties of soils, was issued. **1927** N. M. Comber *Introd. Scientific Study Soil* xiii. 132 Two important bases of classification.. have been invoked in the attempts to prepare soil maps of agricultural significance. **1975** J. G. Evans *Environment Early Man Brit. Isles* vi. 138 W. F. Grimes was one of the first archaeologists to appreciate the importance of detailed soil maps in studying the settlement distribution of early man. **1920** W. W. Weir *Productive Soils* ii. 22 (*heading*) *Soil mapping. **1928** *Proc. & Papers 1st Internat. Congr. Soil Sci.* IV. 34 In the soil survey of the United States the term Soil Type has been applied to the unit of soil mapping. **1972** J. G. Cruickshank *Soil Geogr.* i. 24 These men and many others, who have been responsible for selective soil mapping in countries like France.. and Yugoslavia, have a history of soil research behind them going back to the nineteenth century. **1939** G. Clark *Archæol & Society* ii. 38 In chalk regions subjected to heavy ploughing, *soil-marks, especially when seen from the air, preserve the sites of ancient monuments. **1950** *Oxoniensia* XV. 7 The best results of an air-survey of Celtic field-systems may be expected from photographs taken during the winter months... Soil-marks.. will be more evident. **1963** E. S. Wood *Collins Field Guide to Archæol.* III. i. 284 Another type of mark is the soil-mark. When earthworks or barrows are levelled, or when grass is stripped, or on bare (ploughed) land, differences in soil-colour become apparent. **1920** *Engin. News-Record* 30 Sept. 630/1 (*heading*) Research in *soil mechanics. **1965** A. B. Carson *Foundation Constr.* iii. 70/1 Despite the relative youth of the science of soil mechanics, the literature on the subject is extensive, particularly that relating the foundation structure to the.. soil or rock formation upon which it will be built. **1977** A. Hallam *Planet Earth* 104 The engineering geologist works with experts in the related fields of soil mechanics and rock mechanics. [**1928** C. F. Marbut in *Proc. & Papers 1st Internat. Congr. Soil Sci.* IV. 51 *Phase*, a subdivision of the soil type covering departures from the typical soil characteristics, insufficient to justify the establishment of a new type, yet worthy of recognition.] **1939** *Yearbk. Agric. 1938* (U.S. Dept. Agric.) 1174 *Soil phase. **1946** Lutz & Chandler *Forest Soils* xii. 424 Soil phases as currently recognized appear to have more significance for the agriculturist than for the forester. **1972** J. G. Cruickshank *Soil Geogr.* viii. 235 Soil phase.. can only be shown in detail and with precision on maps of 1:10,000 scale or larger. **1937** C. A. Hogentogler et al. *Engin. Properties Soil* p. vii, Publications by the soil scientist, the *soil physicist, the agronomist, the pedologist, and the geologist have been drawn upon. **1976** *Physics Bull.* Aug. 341/2 Soil physicists around the world are researching into an incredibly diverse range of phenomena, of which the diffusion of gases to and from plant roots.. and the breakup of soil by tillage implements are just a few examples. **1900** R. Warington *Lect. Physical Properties Soil* p. xi, The only early investigation on *soil physics is that of Schübler, made more than sixty years ago. **1935** *Nature* 24 Aug. 307/1 In the Soil Physics Section, the main interest centred round problems of soil moisture. **1972** [see *soil chemistry* above]. **1976** *Physics Bull.* Aug. 341/2 Soil physics is the branch of soil science that is concerned with the physical constitution and geometrical structure of soil, with the potentials and movements of water, gases and heat in soil, and with the deformation of soil in response to mechanical stress. *a* **1864** Gesner *Practical Treatise on Coal, Petrol.*, etc. (1865) 27 The driving of the *soil-pipe.. is the first thing done. This pipe is four inches in diameter,.. and driven by a heavy block of wood, as in pile driving. **1927** *Q. Jrnl. Geol. Soc.* LXXXIII. 190 *Soil-polygons are divided into (*a*) 'mud-polygons', containing few or no stones, and (*b*) 'stone-polygons', in which stones are arranged in curious patterns over the surface of the mud. **1963** D. W. & E. E. Humphries tr. *Termier's Erosion & Sedimentation* iv. 86 The periglacial zones are equally rich in detrital material and display phenomena completely comparable with those of hot deserts: loess, reg, soil polygons, 'dreikanters' and dunes. **1967** M. J. Coe *Ecol. Alpine Zone Mt. Kenya* 71 On ridge tops, which are usually scattered with boulders and small stones, soil polygons are particularly common. **1906, 1923** *Soil profile [see profile *sb.* 4d]. **1928** *Forestry* II. 15 A natural basis for the classification of soils.. resulted from a study of what have come to be known as soil profiles, vertical exposures of sections of soil down to the unaltered parent rock. **1954** W. D. Thornbury *Princ. Geomorphol.* iv. 76 A mature soil profile exhibits well-developed horizons. **1972** J. G. Cruickshank *Soil Geogr.* i. 28 Sometimes the soil profile is accepted as the basic unit of soil study. **1940** C. A. Heiland *Geophysical Explor.* x. 646 As an example of the galvanic application of intermediate frequency methods, the *soil resistivity bridge.. is illustrated. **1964** R. F. Ficchi *Electrical Interference* viii. 153 Probably the biggest stumbling block in such analytical calculations is the vaguely defined soil-resistivity measurements. **1967** *Gloss. Terms Gas Industry (B.S.I.)* 68 *Soil resistivity survey*, the determination of the electrical resistivity of the soil at intervals along the route of a main to assist in designing a cathodic protection system. **1902** *Bull. U.S. Fish Commission 1901* XXI. 58 For taking *soil samples an instrument was made after drawings in Delbecque. **1975** *New Yorker* 28 Apr. 112/2 District-level officials are now collecting soil samples, so that in the future they can advise the co-ops on the most productive way to use their land. **1902** *Soil sampler [see sampler *sb.*[2] 2]. **1950** *N.Z. Jrnl. Agric.* June 553/3 Holes may be dug with a spade, sunk with a post-hole borer, or cored with a soil sampler [in order to examine the structure of the soil]. **1927** E. L. Worthern *Farm Soils* 409/1 (Index), *Soil sampling. **1958** J. Blish *Case of Conscience* (1959) iv. 41 We will start a soil-sampling programme. **1960** *Farmer & Stockbreeder* 9 Feb. 97/3 Soil-sampling for ectoparasitic eel-worms may be worth a thought. **1915** *Chem. Abstr.* IX. 1084 (*heading*) The development of *soil science from the earliest attempts to the beginning of the twentieth century. **1916** (*periodical title*) Soil science. **1935** *Nature* 24 Aug. 308/1 The very large number of papers dealing with the practical side of soil science.. emphasised the dominating influence exerted on the development of soil science by modern economic conditions. **1938, 1958** [see pedology]. **1972** *Nature* 28 Jan. 231/2 The most characteristic Russian contribution to science was soil science. **1979** W. L. Pritchett *Properties & Managem. Forest Soils* p. v, Most of the basic principles of soil science apply to forest soils as well as to agricultural soils. **1921** *Proc. 41st Ann. Meeting Soc. Promotion Agric. Sci., 1920* (U.S.) 117 The *soil scientist must be concerned primarily with the accumulation or assimilation of knowledge concerning the soil without reference to the use to be made of that knowledge. **1958** *Times* 1 July (Agric. Suppl.) p. ii/2 The plant breeder and the soil scientist have worked hand in hand; together they are responsible for disproving the gloomy prophecies of increasing world hunger so commonly heard only 10 years ago. **1928** *Proc. & Papers 1st Internat. Congr. Soil Sci.* IV. 54 **Soil separate*, one of the several grain-size groups into which the soil is separated by mechanical analysis. **1951** *Soil Survey Man.* (U.S. Dept. Agric. Handbk. No. 18) 207 (*heading*) Size limits of soil separates from two schemes of analysis. **1972** J. G. Cruickshank *Soil Geogr.* ii. 55 These categories of particle size—sometimes called the soil separates—are mixed in any soil into what is called its texture. **1905** *Field Operations of U.S. Bur. Soils, 1904* 35 Whenever there is a general relationship between these two classes of soils, due either to their geological origin, their method of formation, or their location within an area, a common distinctive locality name is used, and the soils thus grouped together are called a *soil series. **1946** L. D. Stamp *Britain's Struct. & Scenery* xi. 95 Within each soil series there may be a considerable range of texture which is important ecologically. **1972** J. G. Cruickshank *Soil Geogr.* i. 29 A soil series is a composite unit, but being the basic unit of soil mapping it is expected to be predominantly composed of one named soil profile type and confined to one parent material. **1962** *Listener* 25 Jan. 174/2 The ground beyond the filter-bed is what we call *soil-sick. **1934** Webster, *Soil sickness. **1938** *Encycl. Brit. Bk. of Year* 111/1 Among more recent concepts is that of the possibility of beneficial root-excretions, to which the older view ascribed toxic properties and the responsibility for soil-sickness. **1960** *Farmer & Stockbreeder* 9 Feb. 97/1 We have long been familiar with the potato root and sugar-beet eelworm.. but other types are now known to cause 'soil sickness'. **1901** *Bull. Div. Soils U.S. Dept. Agric.* No. 17. 5 *Soil solutions from which plants draw their food are for the most part aqueous solutions of the mineral components of the soil. **1957** G. E. Hutchinson *Treat. Limnol.* I. viii. 556 The over-all composition of soil solutions is in fact very similar to that of average river water. **1973** *Sci. Amer.* May 48/2 Perhaps 5 percent of a plant's dry weight is minerals. Eight elements account for the bulk of this amount... All are normally present in the 'soil solution', as the water of the soil is called, at very low concentrations. **1934** *Proc. Amer. Soc. Testing Materials* XXXIV. II. 737 Investigations along the line suggested by Mr. Housel are also considered in our *soil stabilization work. **1950** *Engineering* 13 Jan. 44/3 They were used in conjunction with processes of soil stabilisation in which the stability of the soil under traffic load is improved by adding clay, sand or gravel. **1969** Capper & Cassie *Mech. Engin. Soils* (ed. 5) xi. 234 An important method of soil stabilization is by the use of resins. **1910** *12th Rep. Michigan Acad. Sci.* 52 A comparison of the Asulkan and Greenland *soil stripes with the great barrancas, suggests that the width of ridge.. is in some way a function of the viscosity of the rock paste. **1954** W. D. Thornbury *Princ. Geomorphol.* iv. 89 Earth stripes or soil stripes are similar to stone stripes except that they have finer textures. **1900** *Yearbk. U.S. Dept. Agric. 1899* 26 A detailed *soil survey has been undertaken of the soils of Maryland. **1924** [see separate *sb.* 6]. **1966** R. Ashworth *Highway Engin.* iii. 49 The soil survey involves an exploration of the soil conditions along the proposed road alignment by means of boreholes or trial pits. **1972** J. G. Cruickshank *Soil Geogr.* i. 23 Some of the later private surveys have.. introduced soil terms and definitions adopted later by the national soil surveys. **1921** *Proc. 41st Ann. Meeting Soc. Promotion Agric. Sci., 1920* (U.S.) 119 Before the *soil surveyor had mapped textural soil units over any considerable area he discovered that these units are not all alike, that they are not ultimate soil units therefore but soil groups. **1902** *Instructions to Field Parties & Descr. Soil Types* (U.S. Bur. of Soils) 15 The selection of a provisional name for each *soil type should be made, and in all correspondence and reports this name should be used when speaking of the type. **1928** *Proc. & Papers 1st Internat. Congr. Soil Sci.* IV. 41 The soil type is a subdivision of the soil series based primarily and almost wholly on the texture of the surface soil... The term Soil Type has been used by some writers with a more inclusive meaning, sometimes to indicate the general characteristics of the soils of a region. **1954** W. D. Thornbury *Princ. Geomorphol.* iv. 78 A common soil series in the middle western states is the Miami series... Included in this series are such soil types as the Miami fine sandy loam, Miami loam, Miami silt loam, and Miami silty clay loam. **1967** M. J. Coe *Ecol. Alpine Zone Mt. Kenya* 71 Soil movement and deformation are of great significance in governing the distribution of soil types and in their effect on vegetation. **1972** J. G. Cruickshank *Soil Geogr.* i. 26 In 1904 the soil series was introduced to include all soil types developed on the same parent material. **1926** *Sci. Amer.* Feb. 97/3 Erosion or *soil wash is impoverishing our sloping farm lands. **1962** Soil wash [see sailab]. **1892** J. M. H. Munro *Soils & Manures* i. 25 What this *soil water contains we may see by examining the water running from the drain-pipes of any arable field when no crop is growing on it. **1921** *Discovery* Feb. 47/1 Plants require moisture, and in taking this up by the root-hairs, they also take up their food, consisting of salts dissolved in the soil water. **1976** *Physics Bull.* Aug. 343/3 One of the main obstacles to progress in the physics of soil water is the lack of quantitative methods for describing adequately the geometrical structure of soil at its various levels of organization.

†**soil**, *sb.*[2] *Obs.* Also 6–7 soyle. [a. OF. *soil*, also *soel*, *suel*, *sueil* (mod.F. *seuil*) sill, threshold:—L. *solium* seat.]

**1.** = sill *sb.*[1] 2, 3.

**1447** *Will of Hen. VI*, in Carter *King's Coll. Chapel* 12 A closette.. unther the soil of the yle windows. **1533** in Bayley *Hist. Tower* App. I. xvii, There ys wrought all the soyles and jawmes of twoo greate wyndowes. **1637** in Willis & Clark *Cambridge* (1886) I. 194 Raysing the 4 chappell windows.. and putting in soyles of freestone. **1663** Gerbier *Counsel* 77 Door cases, the Post.. being six and five Inches head and soyle. **1679** Moxon *Mech. Exerc.* ix. 172 Soils.. are either Ground Sells.. or Window Sells.

*attrib.* **1634** in *Archaeologia* XXXV. 197 In the kitchen.. two soyle bords for wyndowes.

**2.** A lintel of a door or window.

**1519** Horman *Vulg.* 138, I hytte my heede ageynst the soyle or transumpt.

**soil** (sɔɪl), *sb.*[3] Forms: α. 5–7 soyle, 6 soyl(l; 5–7 soile, 6– soil, 7– *dial.* sile. β. 5 soule. [Partly a. OF. **soille*, *souille* (mod.F. *souille*, also dial. *soille*) fem., or *soil*, *souil*, etc. (mod. dial. *souil*, *soui*) masc., verbal sbs. from *souiller* soil *v.*[1]; in part directly from the vb.]

**I.** †**1.** A miry or muddy place used by a wild boar for wallowing in. *Obs.*

So F. *souille*; the phrase 'to take soil' corresponds to F. *prendre souille*. The forms *soueil* and *seulg* occur in OF. in the same sense, and Cotgrave gives *soil*, *soeil*, *sueil*.

*c* **1410** *Master of Game* (MS. Digby 182) v, Whan men hunteth þe boore, communlich þei go to þe soyle and soileth hem in þe drytte. And if þei be hurte, þe soile is hir medicyne. **1576** Turberv. *Venerie* 154 At his departure from the soyl, you may perceiue it where he hath gone..: for he goeth out of the soyle all myerie and dyrtie. **1600** Surflet *Countrie Farme* VII. xxvii. 853 The soile of the wilde bore being long, large, and great, doth note and argue the bore to bee great. **1611** Cotgr., *Se souiller* (of a swine) to take soyle, or wallow in the mire. *Ibid.*, *Sueil*,.. the soyle of a wild Bore; the mire wherein hee commonly walloweth.

**2. a.** A pool or stretch of water, used as a refuge by a hunted deer or other animal. Freq. in the phr. † *to go*, or *come, to soil*; *to take* (†*the*) *soil*.

(*a*) *c* **1410** *Master of Game* (MS. Digby 182) xxxiii, When he.. seeth þat betynge vppe þe ryueres and brokes,.. nor goynge to soyle,.. ne may not helpe. **1470–85** Malory *Arthur* XVIII. xxi. 764 Whan the hynde came to the welle, for hete she wente to soyle. *c* **1535** Fisher *Wks.* (E.E.T.S.) 441 As an harte, whan he is chased,.. coueteth to come vnto the soile. **1576** Turberv. *Venerie* 241 When an Hart or any Deare is forced to the water, we say he goeth to the Soyle. **1861** H. Kingsley *Ravenshoe* xxvi, Looking round him as a buck or stag looks when run to soil.

(*b*) **1572** J. Jones *Bathes Buckstone* 1 b, It is not unlikely that the Stagges or buckes wounded, would take soyle ther. **1576** Turberv. *Venerie* 148 There are some lustie yong houndes which will neuer giue ouer a Goate nor suffer him to take Soyle. **1613** W. Browne *Brit. Past.* I. iv, Fida went.. to seeke the Hinde; And found her taking soyle within a flood. **1735** Somerville *Chase* III. 546 He.. Then takes the Soil, and plunges in the Flood Precipitant. **1810** *Sporting Mag.* XXXV. 87 Previously to his taking soil, he lay down under the same tree. **1844** W. H. Maxwell *Wanderings in Highl. & Isl.* I. iii. 97 Last Tuesday a fox took soil; I swam the river, got the brush [etc.]. **1885** *Field* 4 Apr. 427/1 The hounds working up to their deer, he.. crossed.. to the brook, where he took soil.

(*c*) **1486** *Bk. St. Albans* E vij b, At that oder side of the water iff he vp sterte, Then shall ye call hit the soule of the hert. **1600** Fairfax *Tasso* VI. cix, A chased hinde her course doth bend To seeke by soile to finde some ease or good. **1612** Drayton *Poly-olb.* xiii. 137 The noble, stately deer.. Doth beat the brooks and ponds for sweet refreshing soil. **1633** P. Fletcher *Poet. Misc.* 86 As an hart with sweat and bloud embrued.. thirsts in the soil to be. **1674** N. Cox *Gentl. Recreat.* (1677) I. 78 The last Refuge of a Hart sorely hunted is the Water (which, according to Art, is termed the Soil).

†**b.** In fig. use. *Obs.*

**1592** Lyly *Midas* IV. iii, There was a boy leasht on the single, because when he was imbost, he tooke soyle. **1614** B. Jonson *Bart. Fair* I. iii. (1904) 15 O Sir, ha' you tane soyle, here? it's well, a man may reach you, after 3 houres running, yet! **1647** N. Bacon *Disc. Govt. Eng.* lix. (1651) 178 The King.. singles out the Archbishop, and hunts him to soil at Rome.

**II. 3. a.** Staining or soiling; the fact of being soiled or stained; a stain or discolouring mark.

**1501** *Bury Wills* (Camden) 83 A cloth bougth to saue the sayd tabernacle from soyle. **1572** in Feuillerat *Revels Q. Eliz.* (1908) 409 By the fowlnes bothe of the weye and wether and soyll of the wereres. **1602** Marston *Antonio's Rev.* I. ii, Twere best you.. lay in private till the soile of griefe Were cleard your cheeke. **1679** C. Nesse *Antichrist* Ded., As a dark soil in a well drawn picture. **1726** Leoni *Alberti's Archit.* I. 35 That is always best which,.. laid upon a white Cloth, makes the least Soil. **1793** Smeaton *Edystone L.* §316 *note*, The burning of the lamps was found to produce a greater Soil upon the inside of the glasses, than candles. **1816** Jane Taylor *Contrib. by Q.Q.* (1855) III. 15 This dress is less liable to take a soil than any other material. **1885** *Harper's Mag.* Jan. 318/2 The very garments of a Quaker seem incapable of receiving a soil.

**b.** *spec.* (See quot.)

**1843** HOLTZAPFFEL *Turning* I. 445 Lead works are first smeared or soiled around the intended joints, with a mixture of size and lamp-black, called soil.

**c.** Dirt or discolouring matter on cloth.

**1959** MEREDITH & HEARLE *Physical Methods Investigation Textiles* xiv. 376 Both the soiling of textiles and the removal of dirt from them can be investigated by using soils containing radioactive materials. **1968** E. R. TROTMAN *Textile Scouring & Bleaching* iii. 74 It [*sc.* the material] is then scoured under controlled conditions with the detergent under investigation, and the amount of soil removed is measured. **1975** J. LABARTHE *Elem. Textiles* vii. 325 Soil may be deposited on and be made to cling to some of these fabrics as the result of static electricity.

**4.** *fig.* Moral stain or tarnish.

Frequent from *c* 1600 to 1650. An example of OF. *souille* in a similar use is given by Godefroy.

**1597** SHAKS. *2 Hen. IV*, IV. v. 190 For all the soyle of the Atchieuement goes With me, into the Earth. **1602** MARSTON *Antonio's Rev.* II. iii, If the least soyle of lust smeers my pure love. **1641** MILTON *Reform.* II. Wks. 1851 III. 44 With him shee found the purest, and quietest retreat, as being most remote from soile, and disturbance. **1756** JOHNSON in *Boswell* (Oxf. ed.) I. 203 To wear off by meditation any worldly soil contracted in the week. **1770** FOOTE *Lame Lover* III. Wks. 1799 II. 91 There is not a soul..that can lay the least soil, the least spot, on my virtue. **1858** HAWTHORNE *Fr. & It. Note-bks.* II. 183 Disburdening herself of the soil of worldly frailties, and receiving absolution. **1888** MRS. OLIPHANT *Joyce* I. 174 He was good as an angel or a child—there was no soil in him.

**III.** †**5.** Sexual intercourse. *Obs.*

In quot. 1603 perh. a misuse of SOIL *sb.*$^{4}$: cf. Markham *Caval.* (1607) I. vi. 37 where 'soyle and couering' are mentioned together.

**1555** WATREMAN *Fardle Facions* II. xi. 251 Specially, if he haue been late at the soile with a woman. **1603** FLORIO *Montaigne* II. xv. (1632) 346, I have..put forth an old stalion to soile [F. *au haras*], who before did no sooner see or smell a Mare [etc.].

**IV. 6.** Filth; dirty or refuse matter. Also *fig.*

**1608** A. WILLET *Hexapla Exod.* 626 The lampes were.. clensed from the soile..gathered in the night. **1611** J. DAVIES (Heref.) *Wit's Pilgr.* Wks. (Grosart) II. 32/2 Wee should not then lie soaking in shames Soile. **1688** BUNYAN *Water of Life* Wks. 1855 III. 554 Whatever it be that this water of life washeth not, it is soil and given to the curse. **1691** RAY *N.C. Words, Sile*, filth. [Hence in Bailey, Grose, etc.] **1736** PEGGE *Alph. Kenticisms, Soil*, filth and dirt in corn; as, the seeds of several sorts of weeds, and the like.

**7.** Filth and other matter usually carried off by drains; sewage. In *techn.* use, liquid matter likely to contain excrement. Cf. WASTE *sb.* 12 c.

**1601** R. JOHNSON *Kingd. & Commw.* (1603) 69 Strabo writeth that the Romans excelleth the Grecians in clenlinesse of their citties by reason of their channels to conuay away the soyle. **1730** A. GORDON *Maffei's Amphith.* 360 The Use of these Conduits was..to receive and discharge the Urine and other Soil. **1778** *England's Gazetteer* (ed. 2) s.v. *Bristol*, Gutters that are made under ground for carrying off the soil into the rivers. **1842** GWILT *Encycl. Archit.* §2215 Those [pipes]..for carrying away the soil from a water closet. **1868** A. DAWSON *Rambling Recoll.* 6 The domestic soil was discharged *via* the window. **1928** E. T. SWINSON *Sanitation of Buildings* xiv. 246 Lead pipes used for soil, ventilating, and waste purposes in London must be of *drawn* lead. **1973** H. KING *Do your own Home Plumbing* ix. 87 Many older houses have a two-pipe plumbing system consisting of separate waste and soil services. **1977** E. HALL *Home Plumbing* vii. 57/1 From the point of view of drainage, bidets are regarded as being 'waste', not 'soil' fittings.

**8. a.** Ordure, excrement; the dung of animals used as a compost; manure. Cf. also NIGHT-SOIL.

**1607** TOPSELL *Four-f. Beasts* 106 A good woodman must not stick to gather up the deers excrement or soil. *a* **1639** W. WHATELEY *Prototypes* I. iv. (1640) 30 The profitable sheep is ..beneficial..also for her soyle. **1670** J. SMITH *Eng. Improv. Reviv'd* 12 Great Rains will wash down the Dung or soyl therefrom, and much enrich those grounds it runs into. **1799** J. ROBERTSON *Agric. Perth* 340 To extirpate the heath, by means of water and the droping soil of cattle, especially of sheep. **1817** [R. D. C. BROWN] *Lintoun Green* II. xli. 32 To his waist..'Midst muck and soil. **1823** E. MOOR *Suffolk Words* 350 *Sile*, soil, night soil. **1848** GAVIN *Sanitary Ramb.* 12 The soil, itself, is removed from these [privy-] holes, and is dug into the ground to promote its fertility.

**b.** (See quots.)

**1879** *Good Words* 740/1 Here are carts laden with sifted 'soil', so much like gunpowder... The fine dust or 'soil' is used for manure. **1883** *N. & Q.* 6th Ser. VII. 178/2 *Soil*: this term is used for the fine ashes screened out from the breeze.

**9.** *attrib.* and *Comb.*, as ***soil-carrier***, ***-hole***, ***-man***; **soil-pipe**, a sewage or waste-water pipe; *spec.* (see quot. 1928); **soil-release** *a.*, causing the loosening of dirt from cloth during washing; also as *sb.*, such a substance; **soil-tank** (see quot. 1851).

**1737** J. CHAMBERLAYNE *St. Gt. Brit.* II. 224 King's Privy-kitchen: Vincent Bene, Soil Carrier. **1825** *Beverley Lighting Act* ii. 21 Regulations as to privies and soil-holes. **1810** *Hull Improv. Act* 50 No scavenger or dustman, soilman or other person. **1833** LOUDON *Encycl. Archit.* §490 A basin with a soil pipe. **1876** W. P. BUCHAN *Plumbing* xiv. 90 When soil-pipes and waste-pipes are put up *inside* the house, great care should be taken that they are properly fitted up. **1879** *St. George's Hosp. Rep.* IX. 602 She was living in a house where the soil-pipe of the water-closet was defective. **1928** H. E. BABBITT *Plumbing* ix. 156 A soil pipe is any drainage pipe which carries human excrement... A waste pipe carries waste water which does not include human excrement. **1962** *New Statesman* 21 Dec. 897/3 Any fit man, given a certain amount of practice, can climb a soil pipe up to the first floor. **1978** T. PETTIT *Home Plumbing* x. 53/2 Other waste pipes can be run into the soil pipe by means of a range of solvent-welded bossed fittings. **1969** A. J. HALL *Stand. Handbk. Textiles* (ed. 7) v. 340 To overcome such difficulties..'soil-release' agents have become available. These can be applied to the textile materials..during their production, or immediately before washing. **1969** [see *Oxford cloth* s.v. OXFORD]. **1977** D. S. LYLE *Performance Textiles* v. 219 Soil release finishes permit relatively easy removal of soils (especially oily soils) in laundering. **1851** MAYHEW *Lond. Lab.* (1864) II. 495/2 'Soil-tanks' were the filth receptacles of the larger houses, and sometimes works of solid masonry.

**soil** (sɔɪl), *sb.*$^{4}$ Now *local*. Also 7 soyl(e, soile. [Cf. SOIL *v.*$^{4}$]

†**1.** The feeding of horses on cut green fodder, so as to cause purgation. *Obs.*

**1607** TOPSELL *Four-f. Beasts* (1658) 358 If the Horse go to soil in April, after five days..wash him all over with water. **1607** MARKHAM *Caval.* v. vii. 42 Of the soile, or scowring horses with grasse... I wold haue you onelie to put him to the soyle within the house: that is to say, you shal..feede your horse onely with grasse.

**2.** Fresh-cut meadow-grass or other green fodder.

**1868** *N. & Q.* 4th Ser. II. 30/2 His [a horse's] rack was every morning filled with what was called *soil*, that is,..fresh growing meadow-grass. *Ibid.* 308/2 To grow a crop for soil or soiling.

†**soil**, *sb.*$^{5}$ In 6 soyle. [f. SOIL *v.*$^{2}$] The solution of a problem.

*c* **1600** SHAKS. *Sonn.* lxix. 14 Why thy odor matcheth not thy show, The soyle is this, that thou doest common grow.

†**soil**, *sb.*$^{6}$ *Obs.*$^{-1}$ In 6 soyle. (Obscure.)

Possibly an error for *spoyle*, although this is the rime-word in the second line of the stanza.

**1596** SPENSER *F.Q.* IV. iii. 16 As when two Tygers..cruell battell twixt themselues doe make, Whiles neither lets the other touch the soyle.

**soil**, dial. variant of SILE *sb.*$^{1}$ and $^{3}$.

**soil** (sɔɪl), *v.*$^{1}$ Forms: 3 suilen, 5 suyle, sule; 3–4 soilen, 4–7 soyle, 5–7 soile (5 sole); 6–7 soyl, 7– soil. [ad. OF. *suill(i)er*, *soill(i)er*, etc. (mod.F. *souiller*), = Prov. *sulhar*, app.:—pop. Lat. **suculāre*, f. L. *suculus* or *sucula*, dim. of *sus* pig.]

**I.** *trans.* **1.** To defile or pollute with sin or other moral stain. Also *absol.*

*a* **1225** *Ancr. R.* 84 Oðer speche soileð & fuleð. *Ibid.* 158 Men þet suiled hore lippen mid misliche spechen. **1297** R. GLOUC. (Rolls) 7209 Prustes..mid lechors mod Al isoyled. **1340–70** *Alex. & Dind.* 336 Alle manir þingus þat mihte vs soile wiþ sinne. **1426** LYDG. *De Guil. Pilgr.* 985 Thow art soyled..Off the synne orygynal. **1590** SPENSER *F.Q.* II. vii. 62 My soule was soyld with foule iniquitie. **1835** LYTTON *Rienzi* II. iv, The instruments he must use soil himself:..the times will corrupt the reformer. **1842** MANNING *Serm.* i. (1848) I. 5 The lusts of the flesh soiled his spiritual being.

**2. a.** To make foul or dirty, esp. on the surface; to begrime, stain, tarnish. Also *spec.*, of a child or patient: to make foul by defecation (esp. when involuntary); freq. *absol.* Hence '**soiler**.

**1297** R. GLOUC. (Rolls) 8971 Wanne he þi mouþ cusste þat so villiche isoiled is. *c* **1305** *St. Edmund* in *E.E.P.* (1862) 71 So drie þat no cloþ..noþing isoilled nas. **1377** LANGL. *P. Pl.* B. XIII. 458 Thus haukyn þe actyf man hadde ysoiled his cote. *c* **1450** LOVELICH *Merlin* (E.E.T.S.) 11383 With his swerd on honde, that soyled hit was with hors blood & mennes. **1530** PALSGR. 724/2, I soyle, I fyle a thynge with wearyng so that the glosse of it dothe fade, *je salle*. **1593** SHAKS. *Rich. II*, I. iii. 125 That our kingdomes earth should not be soyld With that deere blood which it hath fostered. **1638** JUNIUS *Paint. Ancients* 229 Much handling soileth things and maketh them lose their brightnesse. **1687** MIÈGE *Gt. Fr. Dict.* II. s.v., To soil (or slur) his Clothes, *salir ses Habits*. **1784** COWPER *Task* IV. 555 The stain Appears a spot upon a vestal's robe, The worse for what it soils. **1815** J. SMITH *Panorama Sci. & Art* II. 360 Instead of it we have an earthy opaque powder which soils the hands. **1892** *Photogr. Ann.* II. 337 At any time the covering gets soiled or damaged, a fresh one can be attached. **1943**, etc. [implied in SOILING *vbl. sb.*$^{1}$ I b]. **1943** *Our Towns* (Women's Group on Public Welfare) iii. 85 The mother of the enuretic and the soiler does not teach her child..control of its natural functions. **1956** *Brit. Med. Jrnl.* 15 Dec. 1390/1 The mother or other adults show no resentment or disgust when the child soils the floor or the body of the person caring for it. *absol.* **1805–17** JAMESON *Char. Min.* 257 When a mineral taken between the fingers, or drawn across another body, leaves some particles, or a trace, it is said to soil or colour. **1821** —— *Man. Min.* 85 It is composed of dull dusty particles, which are feebly cohering. Soils feebly. *a* **1961** in WEBSTER, s.v. $^{1}$*soil*, Patients also showed infantile reactions ..continually wetting and soiling. **1977** *New Society* 17 Feb. 333/1 When she started school she still wet and soiled by day and night.

**b.** *fig.* and in fig. context.

*a* **1623** PEMBLE *Grace & Faith* (1635) 48 This water was much soyled by them with the mudde of many idle fables. **1680** OTWAY *Orphan* II. iv, You have soyl'd this Gem, and taken from its value. **1746** FRANCIS tr. *Horace, Epist.* I. xx. 15 But soon as vulgar Hands thy Beauty soil, The Moth shall batten on the silent Spoil. **1805** SCOTT *Last Minstrel* v. xx, Foul treason's stain, Since he bore arms, ne'er soil'd his coat.

**c.** To treat by smearing.

**1843** HOLTZAPFFEL *Turning* I. 445 Lead works are first smeared or soiled around the intended joints, with a mixture of size and lamp-black, called soil.

**3.** *fig.* **a.** To sully or tarnish; to bring disgrace or discredit upon (a person or thing).

**1593** SHAKS. *Rich. II*, IV. i. 23 Either I must, or haue mine honor soyl'd With th' Attaindor of his sland'rous Lippes. **1596** *Sir T. More* (Malone Soc.) 1220 The good Emperour ..will not soyle his honor with the theft of Englishe spoyle. **1602** MARSTON *Ant. & Mel.* v. Wks. 1856 I. 64, I am come To soyle thy house with an eternall blot. **1678** MARVELL *Corr.* Wks. (Grosart) II. 604 Angel hath so soiled you by representing some very late treating..that it will be difficult to wash off those suggestions. **1837** CARLYLE *Fr. Rev.* I. IV. iv, Black falsehood has ineffaceably soiled her name. **1891** *Spectator* 29 Aug., Subjects that have been much soiled and confused by the host of impostors.

†**b.** To charge (a person) falsely *with* something; to asperse. *Obs.*$^{-1}$

**1642** R. CARPENTER *Experience* I. xviii. 122 They brought in the arme of a dead man, with intention to soyle him with murther and sorcerie.

**4.** *intr.* To become dirty or stained; to take on a stain or tarnish.

**1530** PALSGR. 724/2, I love to weare satten of Bruges, but it wyll soyle anone. **1579** GOSSON *Sch. Abuse* (Arb.) 35 To lifte the Gentlewomens roabes from the grounde, for soyling in the duste. **1882** *Imperial Dict.* IV. 127/2 Silver soils sooner than gold.

**II. 5.** *intr.* and †*refl.* Of a wild boar or deer: To roll or wallow in mud or water.

*c* **1410** *Master of Game* (MS. Digby 182) ii, þenne he will go into þe stanke and shalle soile hym þer. *Ibid.* v, Whan men hunteth þe boore, communlich þei go to þe soyle and soileth hem in þe drytte. **1570** LEVINS *Manip.* 214 To soyle as a sowe, *luto volutare*. **1884** JEFFERIES *Red Deer* vi. 102 A stag generally drinks before entering the cover, and afterwards 'soils', that is, lies down and rolls in the water.

**6.** Of a hunted stag: To take to water or marshy ground; †to swim *down*.

*c* **1410** *Master of Game* (MS. Digby 182) ii, Somtyme he shall soyle downe with þe water halfe a myle or more or he come to londe. *c* **1470** *Hors, Shepe & G.* (Roxb.) 29 Assone as he [a hart] taketh the Riuer, he suleth. *a* **1700** B. E. *Dict. Cant. Crew, Soyl*, when any Deer is hard Hunted, and betakes himself to Swimming in any River. **1847** MARRYAT *Childr. N. Forest* viii, The stag made for a swampy ground ..and stood at bay... 'He has soiled,' said Edward. **1906** *Westm. Gaz.* 4 Oct. 4/3 The pack streamed away..to Chalk Water, where the stag soiled.

**III.** †**7.** To cohabit *with*. (Cf. SOIL *sb.*$^{3}$ 5.) *Obs.*

**1722** STEELE *Conscious Lovers* IV. ii, Such a Husband soils with his Wife for a Month perhaps—then Good b'w'y' Madam—the Show's over.

†**soil**, *v.*$^{2}$ *Obs.* Forms: 4–7 soyle, 5–6 soylle, 6 soyl; 4–7 soile, 4–5 soill, 6 soil, *Sc.* soilȝe. [ad. OF. *soille* pres. subj. or *soil* pres. ind. of *soldre*, *soudre*:—L. *solvĕre* to release, loosen: see ASSOIL *v.*]

**1.** *trans.* To absolve (a person) from sin, etc.; = ASSOIL *v.* I.

*a* **1300** *Cursor M.* 29379 þe man þat has þam for to yeme Mai soill þam and þair mendes deme. ? **13..** *Incestuous Daughter* 127 in Herrig *Archiv* LXXIX. 422 þe prest soylyd hyme of his synnys. **13..** *K. Alis.* 7926 (W.), So God me soile, Thou schalt have Calabre and Poyle. *c* **1400** *Ploughman's T.* in *Pol. Poems* (Rolls) I. 333 Of the bishop he hath powere To soile men or els they been lore. **1530** PALSGR. 724/2, I soyle from synne, *je assouls*.

**2.** To set free *of*, release from, an obligation, etc. Cf. ASSOIL *v.* 3.

**1382** WYCLIF *1 Macc.* x. 33 Eche soule..Y leue wilfully with out money; that alle be soiled of her tributis. **1402** *J. Upland* 427 in *Skeat's Chaucer* VII. 203 Whan ye han assoiled me that I have said,..I shall soill thee of thyne order, and save thee to heven!

**3.** To resolve, clear up, expound, or explain; to answer (a question).

**1382** WYCLIF *Judges* xiv. 12 Y shal purpose to ȝow a dowtous word, the which if ȝe soylen to me [etc.]. **1491** CAXTON *Vitas Patr.* (W. de W. 1495) I. xciii. 127 b/2 Thy questyons ben lyghte to soylle, and lyghte to be answerde. **1533** BELLENDEN *Livy* III. xviii. (S.T.S.) II. 21 To soilȝe this questioun ane law was promulgate in comites centuriat. **1542** UDALL *Erasm. Apoph.* 309, I have not learned to soyle no riedles. **1603** HARSNET *Pop. Impost.* 77 Now a few questions I must soyle, and then I wil proceede to your holy geare. **1611** COTGR., *Souldre*, to..cleere, or soile, a doubt.

**4.** To refute (an argument or objection); to overcome by argument; = ASSOIL *v.* 7.

*c* **1380** WYCLIF *Sel. Wks.* III. 432 Herby Aristotle soyliþ an argument, bi whiche it myȝte seme to folis þat kynde failiþ to man. **1532** MORE *Confut. Tindale* Wks. 660/1 It is impossible..for Tyndall..to soyle the reason and auoyde it. **1567** JEWEL *Def. Apol.* IV. i. 359 To avouche and proue the Truthe: After that to soile the obiections brought againste the Truthe.

†**soil**, *v.*$^{3}$ *Obs.* Also 6–7 soyle, 7 soile, soyl. [f. SOIL *sb.*$^{3}$ 9.] *trans.* To supply or treat (land) with dung or other fertilizing matter; to manure.

**1593** NORDEN *Spec. Brit., M'sex & Herts.* II. 18 About the towne is a kinde of chalke,..a stonie Marle, more fit to make lime then to soyle the grounde. **1610** FOLKINGHAM *Art Surv.* I. x. 24 Brittle and fickle Mould..is best soyled with well rotted horse-dung. **1653** H. COGAN tr. *Pinto's Trav.* xxxi. 123 The distribution of this goodly commodity..to manure their ground, which soyled with it, bears three crops in one year. **1692** SOUTH *Serm.* (1697) I. 395 Just as they Soyl their Ground, not that they love the Dirt, but that they expect a Crop.

**soil** (sɔɪl), *v.*$^{4}$ [? f. SOIL *sb.*$^{3}$ 8.]

**1.** *trans.* To feed (horses, cattle, etc.) on fresh-cut green fodder, originally for the purpose of purging; †to feed up or fatten (fowls).

**1605** [see SOILED *ppl. a.*$^{2}$]. **1611** BEAUM. & FL. *Philaster* v. iii, I'le..send you Brawn and Bacon, and soil you every long vacation a brace of foremen, that at Michaelmas shall come up fat and kicking. **1715** *Lond. Gaz.* No. 5325/1 He designs ..to stay about three Weeks at Perez.., to Soil his Cavalry according to the Customs of the Turks. **1736** PEGGE *Kenticisms* (E.D.S.) s.v., To *soil* horses, is to scour or purge 'em, by giving 'em green meat, as tares, green clover, and the like. **1776** A. YOUNG *Tour Irel.* (1780) I. 172 A few sow clover, which increases, to mow for soiling their cows. **1812** SIR J. SINCLAIR *Syst. Husb. Scot.* I. 352 Milch cows give more milk when soiled than when pastured. **1840** *Penny*

*Cycl.* XXII. 192/2 The great advantage of soiling cattle is the increase of manure of the best quality, which is thereby produced. **1868** *N. & Q.* 4th Ser. II. 308/2 To soil a horse with clover or vetches.

**2.** With *off*: To employ, make use of, as fodder for soiling cattle, etc. ? *Obs.*

**1778** [W. H. MARSHALL] *Minutes Agric., Observ.* 30 This part was soiled-off or plowed-in. **1789** *Trans. Soc. Arts* I. 155 Vetches, which were soiled, or fed off, with sheep.

**soil**, *v.*[5] [f. SOIL *sb.*[1] 7.] *trans.* To earth *up*.

**1844** *Jrnl. R. Agric. Soc.* V. I. 92, I soiled the drills up again.

**soil**, obs. var. SILE *v.*[2]

**'soilage.** Also 6–7 soylage. [f. SOIL *sb.*[3] or *v.*[1] + -AGE.]

†**1.** ? A charge or toll for depositing filth or refuse. *Obs.*

**1593** NORDEN *Spec. Brit., Cornw.* (1728) 98 Salt-ashe, .. a pretye market towne... It hath anchorage and soylage of all straunger ships, and the profit of a passage betwene it and Deuon. [Hence in later topographical works.]

†**2.** Rubbish, dirt, filth; manure. *Obs.*

**1598** STOW *Surv.* iii. (1603) 14 Casting of soylage into the streame. **1631** WEEVER *Anc. Funeral Mon.* 379 Moorish ground; in short space raised, by soilage of the Citie vpon them. **1658** tr. *Porta's Nat. Magic* III. xiv. 93 Apply the Pomegranate-tree roots with this kind of soilage or dunging. **1739** 'R. BULL' tr. *Dedekindus' Grobianus* 49 Your proper Steps from Mire obscene defend; And leave the Dirt and Soilage to your Friend. **1758** BINNELL *Descr. Thames* 166 Where the common Rakers of the City use to repose and lay all their Soilage.

**3.** The act or process of soiling; the condition of being soiled. *U.S. rare.*

**1926** *Publishers' Weekly* 22 May 1679/2 One of the practical problems of retail bookselling is the depreciation of stock due to soilage.

**soil-dish**, variant of SILE-DISH, strainer.

**1796** *Hull Advertiser* 24 Sept. 4/3 When the curd is come .. take it out with a soil-dish altogether.

**soile** (sɔɪl). *Cornish dial.* Also 7–9 soil, 7–8 soyle, 9 soyl. [? An irregular local variation of SEAL *sb.*[1] The variation also occurs in Newfoundland English (see *Dict. Newfoundland Eng.*).] The common seal. Cf. SWILE.

**1602** CAREW *Cornw.* I. 34 b, The Seale or Soyle, is in making and growth, not vnlike a Pigge, vgly faced, and footed like a Moldwarp. **1672** JOSSELYN *New Eng. Rarities* 34 The Soile or Sea Calf, a Creature that brings forth her young ones upon dry land. **1674** RAY *Coll. Words, Fishes* 107 On the Rocks near the Lands end they often find the *Phocæ* (which they call Soils) sleeping. *Ibid.*, They distinguish between Soils and Sieles: the Siele they affirm to be a Fish .. much less then the soile, and not taken upon our Coasts. **1758** BORLASE *Nat. Hist. Cornw.* 284 Among the quadruped reptiles we may reckon the seal or sea-calf, vulgarly called in Cornwall the Soyle. *a* **1863** TREGELLAS *Cornish Tales* (1868) 61 Haling the soils up from the say. **1880** *W. Cornwall Gloss.* 53/1.

**soile**, obs. Sc. form of SOLE *sb.*[1]

**soiled** (sɔɪld), *ppl. a.*[1] Forms: 3 suiled, 6–7 soyled, 7 soild, 6– soiled. [f. SOIL *v.*[1]] Defiled; stained, dirtied. Also *fig. Comb.* **soiled dove** *Austral.* and *N. Amer. slang.*, a prostitute.

*a* **1225** *Ancr. R.* 158 Ich am a man mid suilede lippen. **1530** PALSGR. 324/2 Soyled, *ord.* **1588** KYD *Househ. Phil.* Wks. (1901) 272 In the Kitchin, or other soyled places which may spoile or ray her garments. **1590** SPENSER *F.Q.* II. i. 41 Vpon the soiled gras The dead corse of an armed knight was spred. **1671** MILTON *Samson* 123 In slavish habit, ill-fitted weeds O're worn and soild. **1693** DRYDEN, etc. *Juvenal* xv. (1697) 373 One.. Licks the soil'd Earth, .. While reeking with a mangled Ombite's Blood. **1815** J. SMITH *Panorama Sci. & Art* II. 425 It may be conveniently used for whitening soiled books and prints. **1882** *Sydney Slang Dict.* 8/1 *Soiled doves*, the 'midnight meeting' term for prostitutes and 'gay' ladies generally. **1883** THOMAS *Mod. Housewife* 22 That cracked mirror, spoiled carpet, and soiled sofa. **1929** Soiled dove [see HUSTLER 2 c]. **1962** E. LUCIA *Klondike Kate* iii. 95 The line between the dance-hall girls and those of Lousetown was a thin one.. because the soiled doves from across the river intermingled in the variety halls to pick up customers.

*Comb.* **1897** 'S. GRAND' *Beth Book* xvi. 140 A white sheet filched from the soiled-clothes bag. **1905** M. BARNES-GRUNDY *Vacill. Hazel* 59 A soiled-looking man turned the corner of the lane. **1907** *Yesterday's Shopping* (1969) 325/3 Soiled Linen Bags.. Sack shape. **1939** M. ALLINGHAM *Mr Campion & Others* 181 He's only over here for four days and yet he's brought.. a neat little soiled-linen bag embroidered with his monogram.

**soiled,** *ppl. a.*[2] *rare.* [f. SOIL *v.*[4]] Fed with fresh-cut green fodder.

**1605** SHAKS. *Lear* IV. vi. 124 The Fitchew, nor the soyled Horse goes too't with a more riotous appetite. **1811** *Monthly Mag.* XXXIV. 393/1 The condition of the soiled cattle and milch cows, surprized even those most convinced of the advantage of the system.

**soiled,** *a.* [f. SOIL *sb.*[1]] Having a particular or specified kind of soil.

*c* **1645** HOWELL *Lett.* I. II. xv. (1655) 89 The Province .. is far greater, more populous, better soyld, and more stor'd with Gentry. **1799** [A. YOUNG] *Agric. Linc.* 9 This sinks again into another part of the various soiled vale to the Wolds. **1815** M. BIRKBECK *Journ. thro' France* 68 A surface .. as fruitful as a well-soiled plain.

**soiler**: see SOIL *v.*[1] 2 a, FREE-SOILER.

**soilie**, variant of Sc. SULYE *Obs.*

**'soiliness.** *rare.* [f. SOILY *a.*[1]] The state or condition of being soiled; soiled or dirty matter.

*a* **1626** BACON *Physiol. Rem.* in *Baconiana* (1679) 98 To make proof of the Incorporation of Silver and Tin, .. and to observe .. whether it yield no more soiliness than Silver? **1650** FULLER *Pisgah* II. IV. iv. 70 Whether the Priests .. made use thereof [*sc.* a laver] to discover all soiliness in them before they washed.

†**soiling,** *sb. Obs.*[−0] [app. for *siling*, f. SILE *v.*[1] 2.] (See quot.)

**1573–80** BARET *Alv.*, A *Soiling*, a great opening, or gaping of the earth, as it were a deepnesse without bottome.

**soiling** ('sɔɪlɪŋ), *vbl. sb.*[1] [f. SOIL *v.*[1]]

**1. a.** The action of making or becoming dirty, tarnished, or stained. Also *fig.*

**1580** HOLLYBAND *Treas. Fr. Tong, Salissure*, fouling, soyling. **1612** BRINSLEY *Lud. Lit.* iv. (1627) 29 To keepe their bookes from soyling, or marring under their hands. **1635–56** COWLEY *Davideis* I. 871 Thus Souls live cleanly, and no Soiling fear. **1643** MILTON *Divorce* II. xix, Which .. is rather a soiling then a fulfilling of mariage-rites. **1809** *Naval Chron.* XXII. 277 To remove any soiling it might have received. **1892** *Photogr. Ann.* II. 530 Thus avoiding soiling of the glass.

**b.** Defecation (usu. when caused by incontinence or stress in a patient or child).

**1943** *Our Towns* (Women's Group on Public Welfare) iii. 83 Some evacuated children were guilty of deliberate wetting and soiling. **1960** I. BENNETT *Delinquent & Neurotic Children* iii. 113 Faecal incontinence, and soiling episodes. **1980** *Jrnl. R. Soc. Med.* LXXIII. 217 The affected children themselves are liable to behavioural problems such as temper tantrums, soiling and school refusal.

**2.** *spec.* (See SOIL *v.*[1] 5 and 6.) Also *attrib.*

**1549** COVERDALE, etc. *Erasm. Par. 2 Peter* II. 19 The sowe hath washed .. in vayne, if she by and by after she is washen, returne to the soylinges that she had gone from.

**1856** 'STONEHENGE' *Brit. Rur. Sports* 82/2 The deer's haunt is called his lair; .. where he rolls, his soiling-pool. **1884** JEFFERIES *Red Deer* vi. 102 They have their regular 'soiling-pits'—watery places or shallow ponds. **1899** *Westm. Gaz.* 18 Aug. 3/1 'Soiling,' or taking water, less frequently results in throwing hounds off the scent.

†**'soiling,** *vbl. sb.*[2] *Obs.* [f. SOIL *v.*[2]]

**1.** Assoilment, absolution.

*a* **1300** *Cursor M.* 29535 Gain cursing gode all es be-warr, And if þou wat þou ert þair-in His soilling seke wit-vten blin. *c* **1380** WYCLIF *Wks.* (1880) 481 Whanne þer soyling & þer bynding acordide wiþ god in heuene. *c* **1400** *Apol. Loll.* 67 þerfor þe causis are to be peysid, and þan power of bynding and soiling is to be vsid. **1529** MORE *Suppl. Souls* Wks. 290 Blessing and cursing, cyting, suspending and soyling.

**2.** Solution, explanation, answering.

*c* **1380** WYCLIF *Sel. Wks.* I. 386 þanne he putte in dede soilyng of þis questioun. **1388** —— *Dan.* iv. 3 Thei schulden schewe to me the soilyng of the dreem. *c* **1500** *Three Priests Peblis* in Pinkerton *Sc. Poems* (1792) I. 11 Desyrand for to wit the solyeing Of this questioun, this probleame, and this dout. *c* **1530** L. COX *Rhet.* (1899) 64 Confutacion is the soilynge of suche argumentes as maye be induced agaynste our purpose. **1548** GESTE *Priv. Masse* 113 The soylyng of these two last recited scryptures.

**'soiling,** *vbl. sb.*[3] ? *Obs.* [f. SOIL *v.*[3]]

**1.** The action of treating land with manure or compost; manuring, dunging.

**1607** NORDEN *Surv. Dial.* III. 112 Any Tin-mines, .. Marle, or Chalke-pits, slimie or moorish earth, fit for soyling of land. **1665** *Voy. E. India* 362 Which .. doth so enrich their Land, which they never force .. by Soyling of it. **1696** J. CARY *Ess. Coyn* 28 Well manured Lands, whose plentiful Crops do soon repay the Charge of Soiling laid out on them.

**2.** Manure; droppings of animals.

**1610** FOLKINGHAM *Art Surv.* I. x. 26 Plinie reports that Ashes are in such request for soylings neere vnto Po, that they burne their Horse-dung to make them. **1626** BACON *Natural Hist.* §666 That Powdring [*sc.* dust], when a Shower commeth, maketh a kinde of Soyling to the Tree. **1789** *Trans. Soc. Arts* I. 148 All of these, together with the subsequent soilings of the sheep, left the land in admirable condition.

**'soiling,** *vbl. sb.*[4] [f. SOIL *v.*[4]]

**1.** The action or practice of feeding horses, cows, etc., on fresh-cut green fodder, originally in order to cause purgation.

**1607** TOPSELL *Four-f. Beasts* 330 For this purgation is most necessary for Horsses, which is called soyling, and ought to continue ten daies together, without any other meat. **1770** PENNANT *Brit. Zool.* IV. 48 They [*sc.* Persian horses] are fed with chopped straw, .. and instead of soiling, are fed with new-eared or green barley. **1799** WASHINGTON *Writ.* (1893) XIV. 225 For spring, summer, and autumn, it is expected, that soiling of them on green food .. will enable them to perform their work. **1832** *Scoreby Farm Rep.* 27 in *Husb.* (L.U.K.) III, By the practice of soiling, an arable farm may be made to support as much live stock as a grazing one. **1893** *Times* 11 July 4/1 Oats put in [among rye] promptly would give food for soiling or cutting in the autumn.

*attrib.* **1840** *Penny Cycl.* XXII. 193/1 Those countries where the soiling system is most universally adopted.

**2.** *dial.* (See quot.)

*a* **1825** FORBY *Voc. E. Anglia, Soiling*, the last fattening food given to fowls when they are taken up from the stack or barn-door, and cooped for a few days.

**'soiling,** *vbl. sb.*[5] [f. SOIL *sb.*[1]] The action of covering with soil. Also *techn.* (quot. 1876).

**1794** WEDGE *View Agric. Cheshire* 21 Soiling with the plough is thus performed: .. the ground .. is split, or turned both ways upon the young plants. **1876** *Encycl. Brit.* IV. 280/2 A thin layer of ashes .. is spread over the surface [of the hardened malm in brick-making] (this process being technically called *soiling*).

**soiling** ('sɔɪlɪŋ), *ppl. a.*[1] [f. SOIL *v.*[1]] That stains or soils; polluting, defiling.

**1812** CARY *Dante, Purg.* xxx. 52 To save My undew'd cheeks from blur of soiling tears. **1820** CLARE *Poems Rural Life* (ed. 3) 120 From soiling dew the butter-cup Shuts his golden jewels up. **1876** GEO. ELIOT *Dan. Der.* lxvii, Dreading the soiling inferences of his mind.

†**soiling,** *ppl. a.*[2] *Obs.*[−1] [f. SOIL *v.*[2]] Of the nature of a refutation; confuting.

*c* **1449** PECOCK *Repr.* II. xviii. 255 To make a cleer soiling answere to the xiij[e] argument.

**soill,** obs. Sc. variant of SOLE *v.*[1]

†**soillart.** *Obs.*[−1] [f. SOIL *v.*[1]] A name given to the hare.

**13..** *MS. Digby 86* fol. 168 b, He shal saien on oreisoun In þe worshipe of þe hare .., þe go-bi-dich, þe soillart.

**soille,** obs. Sc. form of SOLE *sb.*[1]

**soilless** ('sɔɪllɪs), *a.*[1] [f. SOIL *sb.*[1]]

**a.** Destitute or devoid of soil or mould.

**1828–32** in WEBSTER (citing Bigsby). **1853** *Jrnl. R. Agric. Soc.* XIV. I. 19 The steep, rugged, and nearly soilless sides and crags of the limestone. **1865** SPRATT *Crete* I. 20 A bared and almost soilless part of the mountain-face. **1971** *Daily Tel.* 2 Oct. 8/3 Put each young plant in a pot of its own .. using .. one of the peat-based soilless mixtures.

**b.** Applied to methods of growing plants without soil. Cf. HYDROPONICS.

**1938** *Sat. Even. Post* 20 Aug. 14/2 Having caught the public imagination, soilless farming has the trappings of another 'bubble'. **1946** *Soil Sci.* LXII. 71 Artificial or soilless cultures have been used very extensively during the last 30 years in plant nutrition studies. **1974** D. HARRIS *Hydroponics* ii. 45 Although called variously 'aggregate culture', 'soil-less culture', 'nutriculture', or 'chemiculture', Dr Gericke's term is so universally used that all forms of growing plants without soil are loosely referred to as 'hydroponics'.

**'soilless,** *a.*[2] [f. SOIL *sb.*[3]] Free from soil or stain.

**1868** GEO. ELIOT *Spanish Gypsy* I. 61 As innocent as opening flowers, .. soilless, beautiful.

†**'soilness,** var. of (or error for) SOILINESS.

*a* **1626** BACON *Physiol. Rem.* in *Baconiana* (1679) 95 It will be sweeter and cleaner than Brass alone, which yieldeth a smell or soilness.

**soil-pipe:** see SOIL *sb.*[1] 10 and SOIL *sb.*[3] 9.

†**soilth.** *Obs.*[−1] [f. SOIL *v.*[1] + -TH[1].] An act or instance of soiling or staining.

**1581** MULCASTER *Posit.* xl. (1887) 225 At home spoiles, soilthes, twentie things, are nothing in the parentes .. eye.

**soilure** ('sɔɪljʊə(r)). Also 4, 7 soylure. [a. OF. *soilleure* (mod.F. *souillure*), f. *soillier* SOIL *v.*[1]]

The currency of the word in the 19th cent. is prob. altogether due to the instance in Shakespeare.

**1.** Soiling, sullying, staining.

**1297** R. GLOUC. (Rolls) 8501 þe bodies hii gaderede & vorbarnde hom echon, .. so þat hii were Wiþoute soylure in clannesse al out maisters þere. **1859** TENNYSON *Elaine* 7 Elaine .. Guarded the sacred shield .., Then fearing rust or soilure fashion'd for it A case of silk. **1893** J. K. INGRAM *De Imitatione* Pref. p. viii, The writing has .. suffered from friction or soilure.

**b.** *fig.* (Common in recent literary use.)

**1606** SHAKS. *Tr. & Cr.* IV. i. 56 He merits well to haue her, that doth seeke her, Not making any scruple of her soylure, With such a hell of paine. **1873** ALICE CARY *Last Poems* 114 Soilure of sin .. Cannot harm thy hand so pure. **1888** G. GISSING *Life's Morning* I. iii. 110 With minds disengaged from anxiety of casual soilure. **1890** W. WATSON *Poems* (1906) I. 29 From soilure of ignoble touch Too grandly free.

**2.** A stain, blot, or blemish.

**1829** LANDOR *Imag. Conv.* Wks. 1846 II. 235 He did not conduct him amid flowers and herbage, where a fall would have only been a soilure to our frail human nature. **1895** ZANGWILL *The Master* III. viii, Why had people besmirched the Creation with soilures of cynicism.

**soily** ('sɔɪlɪ), *a.*[1] Also 6 soilly, 7 soylie. [f. SOIL *sb.*[3] or *v.*[1]]

†**1.** Apt to soil or stain. *Obs.*

**1575** LANEHAM *Lett.* (1871) 40 A substauns .. nether so .. brittl to manure az stone, nor yet so soily in vse. *Ibid.* 50 Fayr alleyz .. with sand, not light or to soft, or soilly by dust, but .. pleasaunt too walk on. **1605** WILLET *Hexapla in Gen.* 215 The goodly outward rine or skinne onely doeth keepe in the filthie soylie embers.

**2.** Of the nature or character of soil or tarnish.

**1631** FULLER *Joseph's Coat, David's Sin* xxxii, So spots of sinne the writer's soule did staine, Whose soylie tincture did therein remaine. *Ibid.*, *David's Repentance* iv, I desire His soylie sinnes with deluges to scoure.

**3.** Soiled, stained, dirty.

**1631** W. B. *Touchstone Gold & Silver Wares* 36 When your Touch-stone is .. foul or soily, it may be taken off, by wetting it. **1748** RICHARDSON *Clarissa* VI. 151 Methinks .. you are a little soily, to what we have seen you. **1771** T. HULL *Sir W. Harrington* (1797) III. 214 White sprigg'd muslin, .. now so soily, and hung in such a manner, .. as made her indeed a strange figure. **1890** *Pall Mall G.* 13 Feb. 2/1 A case .. in which are packed .. three or four damp, hot, and soily figures.

**soily**, *a.*[2] Also 8 soiley. [f. SOIL *sb.*[1]] Of the nature of soil; like that of soil or mould.

**1747** HOOSON *Miner's Dict.* Q 3, Veins Strick into this Rachill..in a confused manner, being throne into Joynts, but they are Soiley. **1878** *Scribner's Mag.* XVI. 684/2 Away they went, mare and man,..with a decided soily aroma following them.

**soilyie**, variant of Sc. SULYE *Obs.*

†**soind**, obs. variant of SCHYND.

**1774** G. GIFFORD in Low *Orkney* (1879) 143 Property transmitted by a Deed called a Soind bill. *Ibid.* 144 The disponer delivered the Soind bill to the purchaser.

**soiour**, obs. f. SOLDIER.

**soiour(e, soiowryn**, varr. SOJOUR *sb.* and *v. Obs.*

**soir**, obs. Sc. f. SOAR *v.*, SORE *a.* and *adv.*

‖**soirée** (sware), *sb.* [F. *soirée* evening, evening party, f. *soir* evening:—L. *sērum* late hour, neut. of *sērus* late.] An evening party, gathering, or social meeting. (See also SWARRY.) ***soirée dansante***: see DANSANT *a.*

**1793** F. BURNEY *Jrnl.* 8 Apr. (1972) II. 58 He asked how my Mother did? I said if he came any *soiree*, he would probably see. **1802** C. WILMOT *Let.* 3 Jan. in T. U. Sadleir *Irish Peer on Continent* (1920) 22 We have had abundant specimens of Plays, Balls, Soirées, Thé's, &c. **1820** LADY GRANVILLE *Lett.* (1894) I. 190, I had a soirée last night. **1836** in Col. Hawker *Diary* (1893) II. 107 We had a regular merry soirée on board, and did not leave till past nine. **1856** MRS. BROWNING *Aur. Leigh* III. 391 For exhibition in my drawing-rooms On zoologic soirées. **1892** *Photogr. Ann.* II. 621 Friends' Photographic Society... A *soirée* is held each winter.

Hence **soirée** *v. trans.*, to entertain at an evening party or parties. Also **soiréean** *a.*, **soiréety** *nonce-words.*

**1826** LADY GRANVILLE *Lett.* (1894) I. 397 It has been hard work to dine and soirée all the people. **1834** JEKYLL *Corr.* (1894) 328 This bustle and the eternity of parliamentary sittings keep London in a state of interest and soiréety. **1853** JERDAN *Autobiogr.* IV. 71 To be in readiness for the reception of the soiréean guests.

**soirn, soit**, obs. Sc. ff. SORN *v.*, SUIT *sb.*

‖**soit** (swa), *int.* [Fr., third pers. sing. pres. subj. of *etre* to be.] So be it.

**1889** E. DOWSON *Let.* 16 Nov. (1967) 116 Your letter greatly cheered me—especially by the hope it held out of a meeting at Philippi. Soit! **1912** T. E. LAWRENCE *Let.* 23 June (1954) 217 It seems the Turks suffered a defeat the other day somewhere: *soit*: it won't hurt Turkey. *a* **1935** —— *Mint* (1955) 141 The R.A.F. claims to order our sitting and standing, our lying down and our going forth. *Soit*: but let its direction be extremely good. **1958** L. DURRELL *Mountolive* iv. 90 Well, *soit!*

‖**soixante-neuf** (swasɑ̃t nœf). [Fr., lit. 'sixty-nine'.] Simultaneous cunnilingus and fellatio. Cf. *sixty-nine* s.v. SIXTY *a.* 2 b.

**1888** P. PERRET *Tableaux Vivants* xiii. 109 In familiar language this divine variant of pleasure is called: *faire soixante neuf* (literally, to do '69'). **1970** E. M. BRECHER *Sex Researchers* iv. 98 By a delicate turn of phrase, van de Velde awards his post-Victorian *nihil obstat* to the practice of *soixante-neuf*. **1973** M. AMIS *Rachel Papers* 53 The other couple were writhing about still, now seemingly poised for a session of fully robed soixante-neuf.

‖**soixantine.** *rare*$^{-1}$. [ad. F. *soixantaine*, f. *soixante* sixty.] A period of sixty days.

**1722** DE FOE *Hist. Plague* (1756) 235 Then a body may be capable to continue infected..not a Quarentine of Days only, but a Soixantine, not only 40 Days but 60 Days or longer.

**'soize**, dial. form of SIZE *sb.*[1]

**sojar**, obs. Sc. variant of SOLDIER *sb.*

**sojer**, dial. or colloq. form of SOLDIER *sb.* and *v.*

**sojett**, variant of SUGET (subject) *Obs.*

†**sojour**, *sb. Obs.* Also 4 soiur, 4–5 soiour(e; 5 surioure. [a. OF. *sojur*, *sujur*, etc. (later *sejor*, *sejour*, mod.F. *séjour* SÉJOUR), shortened form of *sujurn* SOJOURN *sb.*] Sojourn.

**13..** *Sir Beues* 3435 Þanne anon, wiþ oute soiur, A wente to þat emperur. **1338** R. BRUNNE *Chron.* (1810) 274 Þe Scottis þat were with inne..þe Baliol suld þam wynne out of þat soioure. *c* **1375** *Sc. Leg. Saints* xxix. (*Placidas*) 721 In þe sammyne toure, quhare his wif mad surioure. *c* **1400** *Rom. Rose* 4282 The which is shette there in the tour, Fulle longe to holde there sojour. *c* **1430** LYDG. *Min. Poems* (Percy Soc.) 246 Skarsly thre monethys he holdith heer sojour. *c* **1450** *Merlin* xxii. 398 The kynge Ban and the kynge Bohors were nothinge at soiour.

†**sojour**, *v. Obs.* Also 4 soioure, -en, 5 soi(o)wryn. [ad. OF. *sojur-*, shortened stem of *sojurner* SOJOURN *v.*] *intr.* To sojourn.

*c* **1330** *Arth. & Merl.* 7269 (Kölbing), Lete we hem here soiouringe & speke of þe oþer kinge. *c* **1380** WYCLIF *Wks.* (1880) 129 But lordis, & ladies namely, schullen soiouren amongis hem many ȝeris. *a* **1400** *R. Brunne's Chron. Wace* (Rolls) 4183 (Petyt MS.), Long ne wald he soioure ne rest. **1593** BILSON *Govt. Christ's Ch.* 7 Isaac and Jacob sojoured as strangers and peregrines in the land of Canaan.

†**sojourant.** *Obs.*$^{-0}$ = SOJOURNANT.

**1499** *Promp. Parv.* (Pynson) P ij b, Soioraunt.

**sojourn** ('sʌ-, 'sɒ-, 'səʊdʒən), *sb.* Forms: α. 3 surgerun, suriurn, 3–4 suriuren. β. 4 soiorn(e, 4, 7 soiourn(e, 5 soiurne, sojorne, 7– sojourn. γ. *Sc.* 5 su(d)iorne, 6 su(d)georne. [a. OF. *surjurn*, *sujurn*, *sojorn*, etc. (= It. *soggiorno*, Pg. and obs. Sp. *sojorno*), vbl. sb. from *surjurner*, etc.: see SOJOURN *v.*

The stressing *so'journ* occasionally appears in poetry.]

**1.** A temporary stay at a place.

α. *c* **1250** *Gen. & Ex.* 2696 Ðoȝ was him ðat surgerun ful loð. *Ibid.* 3308 He maden siðen, fro elim, Mani suriuren in ðe desert sin.

β. **13..** *Guy Warw.* (A.) 2770 Anon after þe tende day Of her soiourn..Gij is to þe douke y-go. **1375** BARBOUR *Bruce* VII. 385 That he to Carleill than vald ga, And a quhill tharin soiorn ma. *c* **1410** *Master of Game* (MS. Digby 182) xii, In longe soiourne þei leseth her clees and hir feet. **1459** *Rolls of Parlt.* V. 363/1 The seid Prince shuld be in sojorne with the Kyng. **1605** SHAKS. *Lear* I. i. 48 The Princes, France & Burgundy,..Long in our Court haue made their amorous soiourne. **1671** MILTON *P.R.* III. 235 Scarce view'd the Gallilean Towns, And once a year Jerusalem, few days Short sojourn. **1814** WORDSW. *Laodamia* 78 Meekly mourn When I depart, for brief is my sojourn. **1839** THIRLWALL *Greece* VI. lii. 276 Here..he made a sojourn of sixty days. **1867** FREEMAN *Norm. Conq.* (1877) I. 215 The Normans were tired of Lewis's prolonged sojourn.

*fig.* **1804** H. K. WHITE in *Rem.* (1825) 270 Your friend, and fellow-traveller in the Tearful sojourn of life.

γ. **1375** BARBOUR *Bruce* XX. 356 A weill gret sudiorne thair he mad. *c* **1375** *Sc. Leg. Saints* I. (*Katherine*) 4 He..to þe cite was cumyne,..& suiorne mad. **1528** LYNDESAY *Dreme* 359 In tyll ane volt, abone that place of paine, Vnto the quhilk, but sudgeorne, we ascendit.

†**b.** A delay; a digression. *Obs.*

*c* **1330** *Arth. & Merl.* 6977 (Kölbing), Lete we now be þis soiourne & speke we of Oriens wroþ. **1508** DUNBAR *Tua Mariit Wemen* 176 Wes neuer sugeorne wer [= worse] set na on that snaill tyrit.

**2.** A place of temporary stay. Also *fig.*

*c* **1350** *Will. Palerne* 3155 He..wasteþ al my londes, saue onliche in þis cite where soiourne wot i neuer. *a* **1400** *Minor Poems fr. Vernon MS.* xxviii. 23 Heil soiourne þat Godus sone to sent. **1423** JAS. I *Kingis Q.* cxiii, There as hir duelling is and hir soiurne. **1667** MILTON *P.L.* III. 15 Thee I re-visit now.., Escap't the Stygian Pool, though long detain'd In that obscure sojourn. **1768** BEATTIE *Minstr.* I. xxvi, Let those deplore their doom, Whose hope still grovels in this dark sojourn. **1810** SOUTHEY *Kehama* XXII. iv, This gloomy bourne, The dread sojourn Of Guilt and twin-born Punishment and Woe. **1858** RAWLINSON tr. *Herodotus* II. cxxxiii. II. 210 Visiting all the places that he had heard were agreeable sojourns.

**sojourn** ('sʌ-, 'sɒ-, 'səʊdʒən), *v.* Forms: α. 3 soriourni, 6 sourgorne. β. 3–4 soiorni, 4–6 soi-, sojorne (6 -eorne), sui-, sujorn(e; 3 soiourny, 3–7 soi-, sojourne (5 souj-), 4–5 soiurne, 4– sojourn. γ. 4 suggeorne, 5 -eourne, 5–6 sogeourn(e; 5 suggourne, sugiorne; 4 sugerne, 6 suggerne. δ. 5–6 sudiorn(e, 6 sudjourne, sudgeorne; 5–6 sudgern(e. [ad. OF. *surjurner*, *sorjorner*, and *sujurner*, *sojorner*, *-journer* (also *sejorner*, *-journer*, mod.F. *séjourner*) in the same sense. The forms in *su-*, *so-*, like It. *soggiornare*, represent a pop. L. **subdiurnāre* (cf. med.L. *subjornare*, *subjurnare*), f. *diurnum* daily, day; those in *sur-*, *sor-* either represent a form with *super-* (cf. med.L. *superdiurnare*) or have been assimilated to other words with this prefix.]

**1.** *intr.* To make a temporary stay in a place; to remain or reside for a time.

α. *c* **1290** *S. Eng. Leg.* I. 147 To þe grete Abbeie to pountenie forto soriourni þere, he sende þis holi Man. **1513** FABYAN *Chron.* VI. cciv. (1811) 214 Whanne kynge Edmunde hadde a season sourgoyned [*sic*] at London, he than made towarde the Danys.

β. *c* **1290** *S. Eng. Leg.* I. 114 Þe king wende in-to Normandie for-to soiorni þere. *a* **1300** *Cursor M.* 3771 Sco send him son in-til aran,..þar-to suiorn for hir sake. *c* **1340** HAMPOLE *Pr. Consc.* 1374 For als gestes we here soiourne Awhile, til we sal hethen tourne. *c* **1430** LYDG. *Min. Poems* (Percy Soc.) 156 Whan watry Phebus had his purpoos take For a sesoun to sojourne in Aquarye. **1470–85** MALORY *Arthur* IV. xix. 143 They soiourned there a vij nyghte. **1555** EDEN *Decades* (Arb.) 133 Valladoleto where we nowe suiorne. **1582** STANYHURST *Æneis* III. (Arb.) 81 There we dyd al soiourne two dayes. **1641** J. JACKSON *True Evang. T.* iii. 201 All the Papists which inhabited, or sojourned within the said limits. **1732** LEDIARD *Sethos* II. VII. 122 He desir'd leave to sojourn a month. **1781** COWPER *Conversat.* 530 The night, they said, is near, We must not now be parted, sojourn here. **1834** LYTTON *Pompeii* I. ii, Several months ago I was sojourning at Neapolis. **1865** TROLLOPE *Belton Est.* xiv, He was sojourning at an hotel in Bond Street.

*refl.* **1338** R. BRUNNE *Chron.* (1810) 3 The Englis kynges turned, þei mot do nomore, Bot soiorned þam a while in rest at Bangore.

γ. *c* **1325** *Orfeo* 47 Orpheo sugerneth in Crassens, That is a cyte of noble defens. *c* **1400** MAUNDEV. (Roxb.) xxx. 136 Þare he suggeournes when him list. *c* **1440** *Generydes* 572 Lenger ther he thought not to sogeourne. **1530** RASTELL *Bk. Purgat.* II. xx. 4, I was in dyvers cytees..longe tyme abydyng and suggernyng. **1535** COVERDALE *Ezek.* xiv. 7 A straunger, that sogeourneth in Israel.

δ. **1375** BARBOUR *Bruce* XVI. 47 Thai sudiornyt thair dayis thre In gret myrth and in rialte. **1470–85** MALORY *Arthur* V. xii. 182 He..sudgerned there a tyme. **1513** DOUGLAS *Æneid* XIII. xi. 80 Indigites, quhilk is als mekill to say As God induellar at thar sudiornis ay.

**b.** *transf.* or *fig.* of things.

*c* **1366** CHAUCER *A.B.C.* 160 Vn-to þat court þou me aiourne,..þer as þat merci euere shal soiourne. **1587** TURBERV. *Trag. Tales* (1837) 26 Thus divers thoughts did sojourne in his brest. **1593** DRAYTON *Ecl.* vi. 13 Mirth is farre away, Nor may it soiourne with sad discontent. **1796** KIRWAN *Elem. Min.* (ed. 2) I. 206 Iron in its metallic state, sojourning with water always extricates inflammable air.

†**c.** To be a lodger in another's house. *Obs.*

**1573** TUSSER *Husb.* (1878) 19 Once charged with children, or likelie to bee, giue ouer to sudgerne, that thinkest to thee.

†**2.** To make stay; to tarry, delay. *Obs.*

**1377** LANGL. *P. Pl.* B. XVII. 83 Whan I seyȝ þis, I soiourned nouȝte but shope me to renne. **1412–20** LYDG. *Chron. Troy* I. 89, I wil no longer make digressioun, Nor in fables no more as now soiourne. *c* **1477** CAXTON *Jason* 36 b, Hit behoueth no lenger to soiourne, for ye muste go or sende unto him with alle diligence. **1594** *Dr. Faustus* in Thoms *E. Eng. Prose Rom.* (1858) III. 403 Because the matter was as strange as true I have sojourned a little too long in it.

†**3.** *trans.* To lodge; to rest or quarter (horses); to have as a lodger. Also *transf.* *Obs.*

**1390** GOWER *Conf.* III. 41 Whan thei weren thus sojorned,..Nero..The men let come in his presence. *Ibid.* 94 And ek it [i.e. rain] may be so sojorned In sondri places up alofte, That into hail it torneth ofte. ? *a* **1400** *Morte Arth.* 153 For-thi salle thow lenge here,..This seuenyghte in solace, to suggourne ȝour horses. **1424** *Sc. Acts, Jas. I* (1814) II. 4/1 Þe kyng forbiddis þat ony cumpanyis..thig or soiorne hors..on kirkmen. **1631** *Archdeaconry of Essex Minute-bk.* fol. 199 b, Enterteyninge and soiourninge in his howse..a fellowe verie negligent in cominge to divine service. **1690** WOOD *Life* 30 April, [They] are sojourned there by one Thomson for 10*s.* a week each.

†**4.** *intr.* To travel, journey. *Obs.*$^{-1}$

**1608** SIR J. HARRINGTON in *Nugæ Ant.* (1804) I. 381, I did once relate to your Highnesse after what sorte his tacklinge was, wherewithe he did sojourn from my house at the Bathe to Greenwiche Palace.

Hence '**sojourning** *ppl. a.*

**1645** J. BOND *Occasus Occid.* 19 Sarah..the Patriarchesse, who willingly followed her sojourning husband up and downe in strange Countries. *a* **1684** LEIGHTON *Comm. 1 Peter* Wks. (1868) 50 It continues all the time of this sojourning life.

†**sojournant**, *sb.* and *a.* *Obs.* Forms: 5 sojournaunt(e, -nante, soiur-, sojornaunt, 6 sudjournente. [a. OF. *sojournant*, etc., pres. pple. of *sojourner* SOJOURN *v.*]

**A.** *sb.* A sojourner; a visitor or guest.

*c* **1400** *Plowman's Tale* in *Pol. Poems* (Rolls) I. 327 Alas! the devill hath cleane hem blent, Soche one is Sathanas sojournaunt. **1477** *Rolls of Parlt.* VI. 186/2 The abiders and sojournantes of the same [town]. **1478** *Paston Lett.* III. 219 Your doughter of Sweynsthorpp and hyr sojornaunt E. Paston recomandyth hem to yow. **1536** in *Lett. Suppress, Monasteries* (Camden) 140 The gentlemens children and sudjournentes that ther doo lif.

**B.** *adj.* Sojourning; residing for a time.

**1439** in Dugdale *Monasticon* (1823) IV. 553/2 Admitte noone sojournauntes wymment with owte lycence of us. **1546** BALE *Eng. Votaries* I. 63 The Chronycles all agre..that she was no nonne but a wenche soiornaunt in the nondrye.

**sojourner** ('sʌ-, 'sɒ-, 'səʊdʒənə(r)). Forms: 5 sogorner, 5–6 soiorner, 6–7 soiourner, 6– sojourner, 7 sojourno(u)r. [f. SOJOURN *v.* + -ER[1].]

**1.** One who sojourns; a temporary resident.

**14..** *Nom.* in Wr.-Wülcker 689 *Hic perhendinator*, a sogorner. **1483** *Cath. Angl.* 348/2 A soiorner, *perhendinator*. **1535** COVERDALE *Lev.* xxv. 40 As an hyred seruaunte and as a soiourner shal he be with the. **1539** BIBLE (Great) *1 Chron.* xxix. 15 We be but straungers before the, and sogeourners, as were all oure fathers. **1605** BACON *Adv. Learn.* II. To King §1 Queene Elizabeth was a soiourner in the world in respect of her vnmarried life. **1662** *Act 14 Chas. II*, c. xii. §1 A native Householder, Sojourner, Apprentice, or Servant. **1756–7** tr. *Keysler's Trav.* (1760) III. 113 Whoe'er thou art, a native, foreigner, or sojourner. **1836** LANE *Mod. Egypt.* I. vi. 193, I replied that, being merely a sojourner in Egypt, I did not like..to take a wife. **1870** R. ANDERSON *Missions Amer. Board* III. 422 They were residents and not sojourners.

*transf.* **1803** *Med. Jrnl.* IX. 157 The Scarlet Fever and Sore Throat, which has for some time been an unwelcome sojourner in our neighbourhood.

**2.** A guest or lodger; a visitor.

**1608** SHAKS. *Per.* IV. ii. 149 Report what a sojourner we have. **1623** MIDDLETON *Women beware Women* II. ii. 176 We've no strangers, woman, None but my sojourners and I. **1660** BLOUNT *Boscobel* I. 25 Mr. John Huddleston (a sojourner at Mr. Thomas Whitgreaves).

†**b.** A boarder living in a house, school, or college, for the purpose of receiving instruction.

*a* **1629** HINDE *J. Bruen* xxxvi. (1641) 114 [He] was very desirous to place them both as sojourners for a season in this gentlemans house. *c* **1672** WOOD *Life* (O.H.S.) I. 108 Having..obtained a comfortable estate by the great pains he took in pedagogie, and by the many sojournours that he alwaies kept in his house. **1691** —— *Ath. Oxon.* I. 13 He [Grocyn] became a Sojournor in Exeter Coll. **1785** *Gentl. Mag.* LV. I. 13 From thence to Oxford, where he [F. Nicholls] was admitted a commoner (or sojourner) of Exeter College [in 1714].

†**sojourness.** *Obs. rare.* In 6 sojornesse. [f. as prec. + -ESS[1].] A female sojourner.

**1587** TURBERV. *Trag. Tales* (1837) 120 That through three months, this Ladie hath been sojornesse with me.

†**sojourney**, *v.* *Obs. rare.* [Alteration of SOJOURN *v.*, after *journey*.] *intr.* To sojourn.

**1657** W. RAND tr. *Gassendi's Life Peiresc* II. 170 Both of us sojourneyed with him at that very time. **1674** MARSDEN in W. Wilson *Hist. Dissent. Ch.* (1808) II. 466 O my soul, what a sojourneying state hath thy life been.

**sojourning** ('sʌ-, 'sɒ-, 'səʊdʒənɪŋ), *vbl. sb.* [f. SOJOURN *v.* + -ING[1].]

**1.** The action or fact of staying temporarily in a place.

*c* **1290** *S. Eng. Leg.* I. 151 þare he bi-lefde in soiourninge al þe ȝwile þat he wolde. **1375** BARBOUR *Bruce* III. 386 He thocht he to Kyntyr wald ga, And swa lang soiowrnyng thar ma, Till wyntir weddir war away. *c* **1477** CAXTON *Jason* 9 b, Peleus on the morne callid Jason and sayd that their long sojournyng displaisid him. **1528** LYNDESAY *Dreme* 470 This Iupiter, withouttin sudgeornyng, Passis throw all the twelf planetis, full ewin, In ȝeris twelf. **1571** GOLDING *Calvin on Ps.* lxix. 35 Quiete continewance is matched ageinste soieorninge for a tyme. **1611** BIBLE *Gen.* xxviii. 4 The lande wherein thou art a stranger [*marg.* of thy soiournings]. **1701** STANHOPE *St. Augustine's Medit.* III. iv. 251 Let my present sojourning tend ever to thee.

†**b.** A place of temporary stay. *Obs.*$^{-1}$

**13..** *K. Alis.* 5209 (Laud MS.), þennes hij wenten wiþ-outen duellyng, And souȝtten better soiournyng.

**c.** The time of temporary stay.

**1611** BIBLE *Exod.* xii. 40 Now the soiourning of the children of Israel, who dwelt in Egypt, was foure hundred and thirtie yeeres. **1782** V. KNOX *Ess.* cxliv. (1819) III. 131 Unfortunate boy [Chatterton]! poorly wast thou accommodated during thy short sojourning among us. **1825** HORNE *Introd. Script.* (ed. 5) III. II. i. 80 During the sojourning of the Israelites in the wilderness, Moses established [etc.].

†**2.** Delay, respite. *Obs. rare.*

**1375** BARBOUR *Bruce* I. 96 Haid ȝe tane keip how at that king Alwayis, for-owtyn soiournyng, Trawayllyt for to wyn senȝhory. *c* **1400** *Laud Troy Bk.* 6022 Gregeis were fayn of that grauntyng [of truce], For thei hadde nede of soiornyng.

**sojournment** ('sʌ-, 'sɒ-, 'səʊdʒənmənt). [ad. F. *séjournement* (OF. *sojorne-, sujurnement*), after SOJOURN *v.*] The action of sojourning; a temporary stay.

*a* **1700** EVELYN *Diary* 2 May 1644, Tours, where we were design'd for the rest of the time I had resolv'd to stay in France, the sojournment being so agreeable. **1756** AMORY *Buncle* (1770) I. 73 Was it possible for Abraham, during his temporary sojournments among them,..to persuade so many tribes to quit their dialect. **1819** *Metropolis* II. 239 After a sojournment of two months, she continued her route towards Paris. **1853** J. H. NEWMAN *Hist. Sk.* Ser. II. I. i. (1873) 7 A constant motive for them to seek out..places of sojournment elsewhere.

*transf.* **1756** C. LUCAS *Ess. Waters* III. 178 Mercury.. makes a longer sojournment in the body than is generally judged. **1794** R. J. SULIVAN *View Nat.* II. 169 The sea announces every where, its different sojournments.

**sôk**, var. SOUK.

**Soka Gakkai** (soːka gakai). Also Sōkagakkai, Sokagakki. [Jap. f. *so* to create + *ka* value + *Gakkai* (learned) society.] In Japan, a lay religious group whose teachings are based on Buddhism.

**1958** *Jap. Christian Quarterly* Apr. 104 (*title*) Sōka Gakkai, strange Buddhist sect. **1964** *Asia Mag.* 18 Oct. 3/2 'Let us propagate Buddhism with high and bright spirit to save the world! The dynamic society with such a transcendental goal is Sokagakkai—the startling new Japanese society. **1964** *Listener* 24 Dec. 998/2 The Soka Gakkai—a kind of mixture of Moral Rearmament and Goldwater republicanism. **1968** P. S. BUCK *People of Japan* xiv. 174 The Soka Gakkai philosophy is an ancient one based on the only Buddhist sect which was, like Christianity, intolerant of all other religions. **1974** *Encycl. Brit. Micropædia* IX. 328/2 The Sōka-gakkai follows an intensive policy of conversion..which increased its membership within a seven-year period (1951–57) from 3,000 families to 765,000 families.

**sokare**, obs. form of SUCKER.

**soke**[1] (səʊk). Now chiefly *Hist.* Also 4 sok, 6–7 soake, 7–9 soak. [ad. med.L. *soca*, ad. OE. *sócn* SOKEN.]

**1.** A right of local jurisdiction; = SOC I, SOKEN 3.

[*a* **1086** *Domesday Bk.* I. 225 b/2 Gitda tenuit cum saca & soca. *Ibid.* VI. 275/2 Abbas clamat socam huius ville. **1114–8** *Laws Hen. I*, IX. 11 (Liebermann), Soca..alia pertinet baronibus socam et sacam habentibus.]

**1598** STOW *Surv.* 36, I..will and command, that they shall inioy the same well and quietly and honourably with sake and soke [etc.]. **1720** STRYPE *Stow's Surv.* II. 12 My [i.e. King Stephen's] Demains with Sake, and Soke, and Toll, and Theam. **1809** BAWDEN tr. *Domesday Bk.* 460 Half a carucate of land..with sac and soke. **1859** C. BARKER *Associative Principle* i. 27 Manorial privileges, such as soke, stallage, or tolls of markets and fairs.

**2.** A district under a particular jurisdiction; a local division of a minor character.

[*a* **1086** *Domesday Bk.* I. 324 Ad hoc manerium pertinet soca haec. **1147–50** *Reg. de Dunfermelyn* (Bann. Cl.) 8 Donauit..eidem capelle decimas dominiorum suorum in soca de Striuelin. **1200** *Rot. Chart.* (1837) 38/1 Do..decem libratis terre in soka nostra de Eyllesham.]

α. *c* **1350** in *Eng. Gilds* (1870) 350 To don here Offys al-so wel in þe sok as in þe Citee a-fore y-seyd. **1442** *Rolls of Parlt.* V. 58/2 The Maner of Snayth, and the Soke of Snayth, in the Schire of Yorke. **1482** *Ibid.* VI. 200/2 Within the said Cite, the Soke of the same, and the Shere of such or any of them. **1540** *Act 32 Hen. VIII*, c. 15 Dioceses..ben deuided into seuerall riddinges, wapentakes, and sokes. **1627** SPEED *England* xxviii. §7 It [Somersham] is the head of those fiue Townes, of which the Soke is composed. **1679** BLOUNT *Anc. Tenures* 9 Coningsburg in Yorkshire..had twenty eight Towns and hamlets within its soke. **1766** ENTICK *London* IV. 305 Certain burgesses..gave to the..church..all the lands and soke, called..Knighten Guild. **1799** [A. YOUNG] *Agric. Lincoln.* 231 A difference in the rights between the Soke of Bolingbroke and Holland Town, have hitherto protracted the proceeding. **1833** *Rep. Comm. Municipal Corporations* 333 Is it the practice to charge the Soke of Grantham with the maintenance of prisoners? **1873** J. LEWIS *Census 1871*, 174 Lincolnshire..comprises 31 wapentakes, hundreds, liberties and sokes. **1884** *Encycl. Brit.* XVII. 556/2 The liberty or soke of Peterborough.

β. **1591** FLETCHER *Russe Commw.* (Hakl. Soc.) 50 An ordinarie rent of money imposed upon everie soake or hundred within the whole realme. **1613** in *Scott. Hist. Rev.* Oct. (1910) 12 Being about to take a lease of the soake of Horncastle. **1704** *Lond. Gaz.* No. 4067/2 Your Majesty's ancient Borough and Soak of Doncaster.

**3.** (See quot. 1788 and SOKEN 2 b.)

**1609** in *Act 5 Geo. III*, c. 26 Preamble, Suits, sokes, multures, and also all and singular profits. **1638** SLINGSBY *Diary* (1836) 22 Ye Mills were worth a great deal more if they had had ye same soak, which..they had, but now ye soak is bought and sold. **1788** W. H. MARSHALL *Yorksh.* II. 354 *Soke* (vulg. *sooac*), an exclusive privilege claimed by a mill, for grinding all the corn which is used within the manor or township it stands in.

**4.** *attrib.*, as *soke-fee*, *-land*, *-mill*, *-reeve*.

*c* **1290** *Fleta* II. lv. (1647) 119 Quod fieri potest per Soke-reves eorum in hustengo. **1741** T. ROBINSON *Gavelkind* v. 85 A Man seised of Land in Soke-Fee. **1858** HOGG *Shelley* II. x. 345 The proprietor of a large soke-mill. **1882** ELTON *Orig. Eng. Hist.* 192 In some places..there are two kinds of copyhold land, the one called 'Bond-land' and the other 'Soke-land'. **1893** BARING-GOULD *Cheap Jack Zita* II. 46 You send a sack of corn to the soak-mill, and you get back half a sack of flour.

†**soke**[2]. *Obs.*$^{-1}$ = SOCK *sb.*[2] I.

The passage is translated from Littleton (II. v. §119), who says above 'soca idem est quod caruca, s. vn soke ou vn charue'; cf. the note on SOCAGE.

**1661** J. STEPHENS *Procurations* 47 A great part of those Tenants which held of their Lords by Socage, did come with their Sokes (their Ploughs) certain dayes in the year to plough and sow the Demesnes of the Lord.

**soke**, obs. form of SOAK *v.*, SUCK *v.*

**sokel**, obs. form of SUCKLE.

**sokelyng(e**, obs. forms of SUCKLING.

**sokeman** ('səʊkmən). Now *Hist.* Also 6–7 *erron.* -mayn, -main. [a. AF. *sokeman* or ad. Anglo-Lat. *sokemannus* (also *sok-, socke-, sochemannus*), f. the OE. word represented by SOKE[1] and SOKEN + MAN *sb.*[1]] A tenant holding land in socage; a socman.

[*a* **1066** *Laws Edw. Confess.* xii. (Thorpe), Manbote in Danelaȝa, de vilano et socheman xii oras. *a* **1086** *Domesday Bk.* I. 273/2 Ibi apposuit Rex W. sex sochemanos pertinentes at Rapendune. **1235–59** BRACTON II. xxxv. (Rolls) I. 614 Tenentes, qui tenent sockagio, sockemanni dici poterunt. *Ibid.* IV. xxviii. III. 378 Et hujusmodi villani sokmanni, proprie dicuntur glebæ ascriptitii. *c* **1290** BRITTON (1865) II. 13 Ceux sount proprement nos sokemans et privelegez en ceste manere. **1367** in Vinogradoff *Villainage in Eng.* (1892) 116 *note*, Teux services comme gents de petits sokemans fierent en auncien temps. *a* **1399** *Ibid.* 91 *note*, Item sokemanni predicti filias suas non possunt maritare sine licencia domini. **1413** *14 Hen. IV*, f 34 in *Year Book* (1605) Hhh vj, Et auxy il ad diuersitie parenter sokeman de franktenure, et sokeman de base tenure. **1567** FITZHERBERT *Nat. Brev.* 14 Quar les tenantz en auncien demesne sont appelles Sokemans, s. tenantz del carue, anglice, le plough. **1581** KITCHIN *Court Leet* 87 b, Mes est diuersitie enter Sokemaynes de franke tenure, et sokemaines de base tenure.]

**1603** STOW *Surv.* vii. 64 The said Robert [Fitzwalter] ought to haue a sokeman. **1607** NORDEN *Surv. Dial.* III. 100 There is also a copy-hold estate, called ancient demeisne, and the tenants, Sokemains. **1614** SELDEN *Titles Honor* 334 Sokemans were but Tenants in socage. **1749** POTE *Hist. Windsor Castle* 2 Together with fourteen sokemen and their lands. **1766** BLACKSTONE *Comm.* II. 87 The statute 28 Edw. I. c. I. declares, that a free sokeman shall give no relief. **1839** *Penny Cycl.* XIII. 245/2 No one was to be distrained..on account of land which he held in manors of the antient demesne of the crown as a sokeman. **1897** MAITLAND *Domesday Bk.* 142 The sokeman's hide or virgate..is composed of many scattered strips.

**b.** *attrib.* in † *sokeman-mote.*

**13..** *Rotuli Hundredorum* (1818) II. 143/1 Item dicunt quod Ermoldus de Boys..solebat facere sectam ad Boxford ad sockemanemot pro terra Ricardi Serle.

**sokemanry** ('səʊkmənrɪ). Now *Hist.* [ad. AF. *sokemanerie* or Anglo-Lat. *sokemanria*: see prec. and -RY.] The tenure of land by a sokeman; also, the sokemen collectively.

[*c* **1290** BRITTON (1865) II. 11 Sokemaneries sount terres et tenementz, qe ne sount mie tenuz par fee de chevaler, ne par graunt serjaunties, ne par petites, mes par simples services. *a* **1399** in Vinogradoff *Villainage in Eng.* (1892) 116 *note*, Quidam tenentes eiusdem manerii tenent terras et tenementa sua in sokemanria.] **1603** STOW *Surv.* vii. 64 What sokeman he will, so he be of the sokemanrie. **1679** BLOUNT *Anc. Tenures* 119 If any of the Sokemanry shall be impleaded. **1766** BLACKSTONE *Comm.* II. vi. 100 Britton also, from such their freedom, calls..their tenure sokemanries. **1865** NICHOLS *Britton* II. 5 *note*, Burgages and sokemanries are changed for such villenages into free tenure. **1896** PEARMAN *Manor of Bensington* 38 There were about forty four sokemanries.

**soken** ('səʊk(ə)n). Now *Hist.* Forms: 1 (9) socn, 3 socne, sockne, 6 socon(e; 4 so(o)kne, sokene, 5 sokyn, 5- soken. [OE. *sócn*, = ON. and Icel. *sókn* (Norw. *sokn*; Sw. *socken*, Da. *sogn* parish), Goth. *sōkns* search, enquiry (cf. OHG. *sôhni*), f. *sōk-* stem of OE. *sécan*, ON. *sœ́kja*, etc., to SEEK. See also the comb. CHURCH-SOKEN.]

†**1.** An attack or assault. *Obs. rare.*

*Beowulf* 1777 Ic þære socne singales wæȝ modceare micle.

†**2.** Resort to, or visiting of, a place; habitual going or haunting. *Obs.*

*c* **1000** ÆLFRIC *Hom.* II. 508 Ða towende se biscop þæt weofod, and þa dwollican socne mid-ealle adwæscte. *a* **1023** WULFSTAN *Hom.* (1883) 134 We..ure synna..ȝeorne betan mid..ælmessan & mid ciriclicere socne. *c* **1205** LAY. 2365 þat inne swiðe feire stude from socne þes folkes. *c* **1290** *S. Eng. Leg.* I. 261 Heo þouȝte, for heo was so i-knowe,..þe lasse sockne heo hadde [= would have] of hire folie. *c* **1440** *Promp. Parv.* 463/2 Sookne, or custome of hauntynge.., *frequentacio, concursus.*

†**b.** *spec.* Resort of tenants or others to a particular mill to have their corn ground; the right of the mill to such custom. (Cf. SOKE[1] 3.) *Obs.*

*c* **1386** CHAUCER *Reeve's T.* 67 Gret soken hath this meller, out of doute, With whete and malt, of al the lond aboute. **1523** FITZHERB. *Surv.* 9 b, That maner of gryndyng is called loue Socone, and the lordes tenauntes be called bonde socon. **1591** *Knaresborough Wills* (Surtees) I. 175 Dareley mylne, with the soken and suite there to belonginge.

†**3.** Right of prosecution, legal investigation, or jurisdiction. Cf. SOKE[1] I. *Obs.*

*a* **1012** *Laws of Æthelred* III. xi, Nan man naȝe nane socne ofer cynges þeȝen buton cyng sylf. *a* **1066** in Kemble *Codex Dipl.* IV. 200 Swa ðæt nan scyrȝerefe oððe motȝerefe ðar habban æni socne oððe ȝemot buton ðes abbudes aȝen hæse. [**1114–8** *Laws Hen. I*, XIX. 2 (Liebermann), Omnium terrarum, quas rex in dominio suo habet, socnam pariter habet.] **1155** in *Anglia* VII. 220 þæt ic hæbbe heom ȝeunnon ..saca & socne..ofer heore aȝene men.

†**b.** (See quot.) *Obs.*$^{-1}$

**1387** TREVISA *Higden* (Rolls) II. 95 Soka, sute of court, and þerof comeþ Sokene, but Sokene oþerwhile is forto aske lawe in þe gretter court.

**4.** = SOKE[1] 2.

*c* **1030** in *Eng. Hist. Rev.* (1912) Jan. 15 Ðis is seo socn into Scyre-burna, mid folc-rihte. [*c* **1133–54** *Libertas Lond.* 4 Donec custos illius socne, in qua manserit, de recto tenendo uicecomiti defecerit.] **1362** LANGL. *P. Pl.* A. II. 78 Rondulf þe Reue of Rotelondes sokene. **1393** *Ibid.* C. III. 111 Bette þe budele of banneburies sokne. **1465** *Paston Lett.* II. 204 Yt ys told me that ȝong Heydon reysyth mych pepyl in the sokyn. **1485** *Rolls of Parlt.* VI. 284/1 The Castell, Mannor and Lordshipp of Kimbalton, with the Sokyn of the same. **1601** HOLLAND *Pliny* I. 535 About Venice and all that tract, the Willowes serue the turne and none else, by reason that the whole soken standeth so much vpon water. *a* **1670** in Blount *Law Dict.* s.v. *Rime*, In the Countrey hard was we That in our Soken shrews should be. **1861** HOOK *Lives Abps.* I. v. 245 By his right of lord of the socn he could try and execute thieves found upon any of his estates. **1874** STUBBS *Const. Hist.* (1875) I. v. 80 The lord of a soken and patron of hundreds of servants and followers.

**soken**, obs. f. pa. pple. SOAK *v.*; var. SOAKEN *v. Obs.*

**soker**, obs. form of SOAKER.

**sokere, sokerel**, obs. ff. SUCKER, SUCKEREL.

**soket**, obs. f. SOCKET *sb.*; var. SUCKET *Obs.*

**sokey**: see WATER SOKEY.

**sokil blome**: see SUCKLEBLOOM.

**sokkat**, obs. f. SOCKET *sb.*

**sokket**, var. SUCKET *Obs.*

‖**soko** ('səʊkəʊ). [Native African name.] A species of anthropoid ape discovered by Livingstone near Lake Tanganyika.

**1870** LIVINGSTONE *Last Jrnl.* 24 Aug., The soko, if large, would do well to stand for a picture of the Devil. **1875** *Zoologist* X. 4359 The soko is so cunning, and has such sharp eyes, that no one can stalk him in front without being seen. **1898** E. P. EVANS *Evol. Ethics* ix. 343 Some species of monkeys, like the chimpanzees and sokos, get up concerts of their own.

**Sokol** ('sɒkɒl). [Czech, lit. 'falcon'.] A Slav gymnastic society first formed in Prague in 1862 (and disbanded in Czechoslovakia in 1952), bearing the falcon as its ensign, and aiming to promote a communal spirit and physical fitness. Also, (a member of) a club in this society.

**1910** W. S. MONROE *Bohemia* x. 189 The organization of the Sokols in 1862 has undoubtedly been the most forceful factor in the social unification of the Bohemian people. *Ibid.* 194 A great gathering of all the Sokol unions of the world was called at Prague in 1887. **1915** *Scotsman* 10 Feb. 10/1 The gymnastic volunteer organizations ('sokols') which are popular among all the Slav nationalities of Austria. **1920** *Public Opinion* 2 July 17/2 Over 100,000 Sokols have responded to the call and of that number 50,000 have been selected—27,000 men and 23,000 women. **1925** E. I. ROBSON *Wayfarer in Czecho-Slovakia* viii. 126 It is a fine sight to see a really big Sokol exhibition, hundreds of men or girls moving like one. **1941** *Ann. Reg. 1940* 200 The systematic arrest of leading Czechs..teachers, and Sokol workers. **1966** *Inland* (Inland Steel Co., Chicago) Autumn 15/2 In Czech settlements the athletic club might still be a *sokol.* **1978** *Chicago* June 56/2 The program will include folk dancing as well as calisthenics and apparatus work. Sponsored by the Central District of the American Sokol Organization.

**sokour(e**, obs. forms of SUCCOUR *sb.* and *v.*

**sol** (sɒl), *sb.*[1] [L. *sōl* (for earlier **sāol*, **sāwol*), = Gr. ἥλιος (Homeric ἠέλιος, Cretan ἀβέλιος), Skr. *suvar*, Lith. *sáule*, Goth. *sauil*, ON. and Icel. *sól* (Norw., Sw., Da. *sol*), Welsh *haul*.]

**1.** The sun (personified).

Used without article and written with capital S.

*c* **1450** *Treat. Astrol.* (MS. Ashm. 337) 2 Sol is hote & dry but not as mars is. **1592** KYD *Span. Trag.* I. i. 23 Ere Sol had slept three nights in Thetis lap. **1593** PEELE *Poems* Wks. (Rtldg.) 601 More beautiful.. Than Sol himself amid the Planets seven. **1609** *Ev. Woman in Hum.* II. in Bullen *O. Pl.* IV, His smile is like the Meridian Sol Discern'd a dauncing in the burbling brook. **1670** D. DENTON *Brief Desc. New York* (1845) 19 The Vines..doth shelter them from the scorching beams of Sols fiery influence. **1712–4** POPE *Rape Lock* I. 13 Sol thro' white curtains shot a tim'rous ray. **1791** COWPER *Retired Cat* 62 Till Sol, declining in the west, Shall call to supper. **1820** COMBE *Syntax, Consol.* v. (Chandos) 203 In bright Sol's diurnal round, No such delightful place was found. **1837** P. KEITH *Bot. Lex.* 277 Clytie, inconsolable for the loss of the affections of Sol,..is represented as brooding over her griefs in silence and in solitude.

†**2. a.** *Alch.* Gold. *Obs.*

*a* **1386** CHAUCER *Can. Yeom. Prol. & T.* 273 Sol gold is, and Luna silver we threpe. [**1460–70** *Bk. Quintessence* I. (1866) 3 Good gold naturel..is clepid of philosophoris sol in latyn.] **1477** NORTON *Ordin. Alch.* iii. in Ashm. (1652) 41 Sol by it selfe, or Mercury alone, Or Sulphur with them. **1591** SYLVESTER *Du Bartas* I. iv. 400 Pure goldy-locks, Sol, States'-friend, Honor-giver. **1599** T. M[OUFET] *Silkwormes* 45 Zeuxis his painted dogge shal barke and whine When Ioue they turne to Sol or Luna fine. **1606** J. DAVIES (Heref.) *Select Husband* Wks. (Grosart) II. 7/1 Though Beauty then seem Sol, at least as rich, It wil be found but Lune, on Tryalls touch. **1610** B. JONSON *Alch.* II. iii, Bright Sol is in his robe. **1651** [see SOLARY *a.* 2]. **1758** [see JUPITER 2 b].

**b.** *Her.* (In blazoning by planets instead of metals) = OR *sb. Obs.*

**1610** GUILLIM *Heraldry* 83 Hee beareth Luna, on a Chiefe Iupiter, a Cherub displaied, Sol. *a* **1646** J. GREGORY *Posthuma, Assyrian Monarchie* (1650) 235 Emperors and Kings ought to bear Gold in their Arms, and then it might bee thus; The Field is *Sol* a Dove volant proper. **1706** PHILLIPS (ed. Kersey), *Sol*..is taken..in Heraldry for the Gold Colour, in the Coats of Soveraign Princes. **1709** HEARNE *Collect.* 6 Nov., Canterbury bears a Staff in Pale Sol. [**1880** *Encycl. Brit.* XI. 691/2 Or, Yellow, Topaz, Sol.]

**c.** ? The topaz. *Obs.*

**1567** MAPLET *Greene Forest* 21 Sol the Precious stone, is in colour like to the Sunne, and is called Sol, for that it giueth reflexions of Sunne beames.

**sol** (sɒl, səʊl), *sb.*[2] *Mus.* Also 6 soule, 7 soll. [The first syllable of L. *solve*: see GAMUT.] The fifth note of Guido's hexachords, and of the octave in modern solmization; the note G in the natural scale of C major.

*c* **1325** in *Rel. Ant.* I. 292 Sol and ut and la, And that froward file that men clepis fa. *a* **1529** SKELTON *Bouge of Court* 258 Wolde to God, it wolde please you some daye.. to..lerne me to synge, Re, my, fa, sol! **1565** *Kyng Daryus* 739 (Brandl), La, soule, soule, fa, my. **1596** SHAKS. *Tam. Shr.* III. i. 77 D sol re, one Cliffe, two notes haue I. **1626** MIDDLETON *Anything for Quiet Life* v. ii, You shall never talk your voice above the key sol, sol, sol. **1662** PLAYFORD *Skill Music* (1674) 1 Ut and Re are now changed into Sol and La. **1728** CHAMBERS *Cycl.* s.v. *Sol-fa-ing*, From *fa* to *sol* is a Tone; also from *sol* to *la*. **1797** *Encycl. Brit.* (ed. 3) XII. 547/2 From the adjuncts of the mode, that is to say, the modes of its two fifths, which for *ut* are *fa* and *sol*, and *re* and *mi* for *la*. **1842** *Penny Cycl.* XXII. 194/1. **1873** H. C. BANISTER *Music* 32 The lowest note, Sol, or G.

Hence **sol** *v.* (in nonce-use).

**1592** SHAKS. *Rom. & Jul.* IV. v. 121 (Q.[1]), Ile re you, Ile fa you, Ile sol you.

‖**sol** (sɒl), *sb.*[3] Now *Hist.* Also 6 soul. [Older F. *sol* (now *sou* SOU), = Prov. *sol*, Pg. and It. *soldo*, Sp. *sueldo*:—L. *solidum*, acc. of *solidus* (sc. *nummus*) a gold coin.] A former coin and money of account in France and some other countries, equal to the twentieth part of a livre, but varying in actual value at different times and places.

**1583** STOCKER *Civ. Warres Lowe C.* III. 87 A pot of sweete mylke, a groat and an halfe, and a pounde of butter two souls. **1605** B. JONSON *Volpone* IV. ii, This fellow, For six sols more, would plead against his Maker. **1611** CORYAT *Crudities* 250 Every Chiquinie containing eleven Livers and twelve Sols: the Liver is nine pence, the Sol an halfe-penny. **1639** S. DU VERGER tr. *Camus' Admir. Events* 352 He put his hand into his pocket, and thinking to draw out a Sol, which is little more than an English penny,..gave it him. **1748** SMOLLETT *R. Random* xliv, My Pay..amounted to five sols a day. **1789** BURKE *Corr.* (1844) III. 122 A new paper-currency..which is to bear an interest of one sol in the livre. **1809** A. HENRY *Trav.* 54 In this exchange, a pound of beaver-skin is reckoned at sixty sols. [**1873** HALE *In His Name* i. 2 He would relax his hold on the odd sols and deniers as if he had never clung to them.]

†**sol**, *sb.*[4] *Obs.* [Abbreviation of *solution*: see OB *sb.*[1]] The solution of a scholastic problem.

**1588–1678** [see OB *sb.*[1]].

‖**sol** (sol), *sb.*[5] Pl. soles. [Sp. *sol* sun: see SOL *sb.*[1]] A Spanish-American (now Peruvian) silver coin; the Peruvian unit of currency.

**1884** BEDFORD *Sailor's Handbk.* 126 Peruvian Gold: 20 Sol Piece, £3 18 6. *Ibid.*, Peruvian: Soles, £0 3 6. **1894** *Daily News* 20 Dec. 5/2 The United States dollar being substituted for the Central American silver dollar or sol as the standard of value. The value of the sol is about 50 cents. (U.S. currency).

**sol** (sɒl), *sb.*[6] *Physical Chem.* [Orig. a suffix f. the first syllable of *solution* (as in ALCOSOL, HYDROSOL).] **1.** A liquid solution or suspension of a colloid. Cf. GEL *sb.*

**1899**, etc. [see GEL *sb.*]. **1936** W. STILES *Introd. Princ. Plant Physiol.* ii. 16 If the ability to flow is our criterion of the sol state, then protoplasm is usually, but by no means always, a sol; but there are other indicators of the colloidal state such as elasticity, rigidity, and inhibition, and these are gel characteristics. **1940** GLASSTONE *Textbk. Physical Chem.* xiv. 1213 The characteristic colors shown by many sols are related in some degree to the particle size; in the course of coagulation, for example, the color of a gold sol changes from red to violet and then to blue. **1970** AMBROSE & EASTY *Cell Biol.* xv. 479 When two hydrophilic sols carrying opposite charges are mixed, viscous drops known as coacervates often form instead of a continuous liquid phase.

**2.** *Comb.*: **sol-gel**, used *attrib.* with reference to the interconversion of sol and gel.

**1915** W. W. TAYLOR *Chem. Colloids* i. 10 (*heading*) Sol-gel transformation. **1922** *Jrnl. Amer. Chem. Soc.* XLIV. 1313 (*heading*) The sol-gel equilibrium in protein systems. **1951** *New. Biol.* X. 14 These interchanges, the so-called sol-gel transformations, are constantly going on in the amoeba. **1967** *Oceanogr. & Marine Biol.* V. 191 Cytoplasmic movement results from sol-gel reactions within cells.

**sol** (sɒl), *sb.*[7] [f. L. *sōl* sun: cf. SOL *sb.*[1]] A solar day on the planet Mars (24 hours 39 minutes).

**1976** *Times* 22 July 1/8 The squat little lander seemed to get through its first sol (as the Martian day..is called) without any problems. **1977** *Sci. Amer.* Nov. 58/3 The release of gas tapered off soon after the first sol. **1979** *New Yorker* 5 Feb. 41 On sol 8..the craft's sampler arm extended straight out and then dropped to the ground.

†**sol**, *a. Obs.* Also **sole**. [Related to SOLE *v.*[3] Cf. SOLWY *a.*] Soiled, dirty.

*c* **1200** *Trin. Hom.* 57 Sume bereð sole cloð to þe watere forto wasshen it clene. *Ibid.* 163 His alter cloð [is] great and sole, and hire chemise smal & hwit, & te albe sol, & hire smoc hwit. *a* **1225** *Ancr. R.* 324 Wule a weob beon..mid one watere wel ibleched, oðer a sol cloð hwit iwaschen?

**-sol**, an ending [f. L. *solum* floor, ground, soil] used to form the names of different kinds and states of soil, as *lithosol* s.v. LITHO-, PERGELISOL.

‖**sola** (ˈsəʊlə), *sb.* Also solah, and *erron.* SOLAR. [Urdū and Bengālī *solā* = Hindī *sholā*: see SHOLA.] A tall leguminous swamp-plant (*Æschynomena aspera* or *paludosa*) of India; the pith of this employed in making light hats. Used *attrib.* with *hat*, *helmet*, *topee*.

(*a*) **1848** tr. *Hoffmeister's Trav. Ceylon*, etc. vii. 248 With only a shirt and a '*solah*' hat. **1857** LADY CANNING in Hare *Two Noble Lives* (1893) II. 255 [The mounted volunteers] with sola helmets on their heads. **1901** *Daily Chron.* 27 May 4/5 Instead of the uncomfortable regulation helmet they are provided with Sola hats.

(*b*) **1845** STOCQUELER *Handbk. Brit. India* (1854) 92 It will be prudent to wear a sola topee, or hat composed of the soft pulp of a tree. **1872** E. BRADDON *Life India* ii. 20 [Where the trees] pour down richly-scented blossoms upon his sola topee. **1900** *Blackw. Mag.* Apr. 516/1 A solah topi with a green-lined rim.

‖**sola** (ˈsəʊlə), *a.* [L. *sōla*, fem. of *sōlus* SOLUS, and It. *sola*, fem. of *solo* SOLO.]

**1.** Of females: Sole, solitary, alone.

**1753** RICHARDSON *Grandison* (1811) V. xxi. 137 Aunt Nell would not have descended *sola* into her greys, nor Cicely Badger neither, if they might have obtained the men of their choice. **1768** MISS BURNEY *Early Diary* (1889) I. 10, I should be content to love *Sola*—and let *Dueto* be reserved for those who have a proper sense of their superiority. **1825** T. HOOK *Sayings* Ser. II. *Sutherl.* I. 39 James..found the matron *sola*, and evidently prepared for a solemn discussion of the weighty affair.

**2.** *techn.* Of bills: (see quot. 1866).

**1737** W. STEPHENS *Jrnl.* 27 Oct. in *Jrnl. Proc. in Georgia* (1742) I. 5 He brought a small Box with sola Bills for a large Sum. **1750** *Colonial Rec. Georgia* (1906) VI. 323 The last Issue of Sola Bills was not sufficient to defray the Estimate to Michaelmas. **1866** CRUMP *Banking* v. 101 A 'sola' bill of exchange is a single bill, as distinguished from bills drawn in 'sets'.

†**sola**, *int. Obs.* Also **sowla**. [Cf. SOHO *int.* and *hola* HOLLA.] A call or cry to attract attention or notice.

**1588** SHAKS. *L.L.L.* IV. i. 151 Ah heauens, it is most patheticall nit. Sowla, sowla. **1596** —— *Merch. V.* V. i. 43 *Loren.* Who calls? *Clo.* Sola, did you see M. Lorenzo?

†ˈ**solable**, *a. Obs.*[−0] [f. L. *sōlārī* to comfort.]

**1623** COCKERAM I, *Solelable* [sic], which may be comforted.

**solace** (ˈsɒləs), *sb.*[1] Forms: α. 3–6 solas, 5–6 solasse, 6 *Sc.* solaes, soles. β. 4– solace, 4–6 sollace. (See also SOLANCE *sb.*) [a. OF. *solas*, later *soulas* (now dial.), = Prov. *solatz*, Sp. *solaz*, It. *sollazzo*:—L. *sōlācium*, *sōlātium*, f. the stem of *sōlārī* to comfort, console. Cf. MDu. and MLG. *solaes*.]

**1.** Comfort, consolation; alleviation of sorrow, distress, or discomfort.

α. *c* **1290** *S. Eng. Leg.* I. 220 Hidere þou come for ovre solas, and nouȝt suych deol to make. *c* **1300** *Life of Beket*, etc. (Percy Soc.) 138 Vourty dawes he was, In a chaumbre al one withoute eni Solas. *c* **1400** *Rom. Rose* 2789, I shalle yeve thee ..Three other thingis, that gret solas Doith to hem that be in my las. *c* **1440** *Gesta Rom.* v. 13 (Harl. MS.), I pray þe, wepe not, but make me solas and comfort, and chere me. **1530** PALSGR. 272 Solasse, comforte, *solas, recomfort, solace*.

β. **1338** R. BRUNNE *Chron.* (1810) 252 His solace was alle reft, þat scho fro him was gon, Ne no sonne him left. **1382** WYCLIF *Heb.* xiii. 22 Forsothe, britheren, I preie ȝou, that ȝe suffre a word of solace. *c* **1400** MAUNDEV. (Roxb.) Pref. 2 þeroff þai hafe grete solace and comforthe. **1483** CAXTON *Gold. Leg.* 203/2, I am with the and shalle gyue to the the solace of my seruaunt paule. **1575** *Mirr. Mag., Hen. VI*, xvii, The solace of my soule my chiefest pleasure was. **1593** SHAKS. *2 Hen. VI*, II. iii. 21 Sorrow would [have] sollace, and mine Age would ease. **1611** HEYWOOD *Gold. Age* I. i, I'le warre with comfort, be at oddes with solace. **1677** MARVELL *Corr.* Wks. (Grosart) II. 560 You will..have the usual solace of those who goe to law, that your adversary hath been at no lesse charges. **1768–74** TUCKER *Lt. Nat.* (1834) II. 653, I want to lay in a stock of solace which shall not fail me in time of need. **1791** MRS. RADCLIFFE *Rom. Forest* iv, She wept also that she could no longer seek solace in the friendship of Adeline. **1839** JAMES *Louis XIV*, III. 143 Though the relief of reading was allowed as some solace to his overloaded heart. **1879** W. H. DIXON *Royal Windsor* II. xvii. 182 Time brought no solace to her widowed heart.

†**2.** Pleasure, enjoyment, delight; entertainment, recreation, amusement. *Obs.*

α. **1297** R. GLOUC. (Rolls) 370 To honti & to winne is mete & to abbe solas & game. *a* **1320** *Sir Tristrem* 2856 þer was miche solas Of alle maner soun And gle. *c* **1386** CHAUCER *Frankl. T.* 74 He goth to his cuntre,..Wher as he lyveth in blisse and in solas. *c* **1430** LYDG. *Minor Poems* (Percy Soc.) 80 Thus thay songe..This melodious ympne withe grete solas. **1484** CAXTON *Fables of Poge* iv, [Hunting and hawking] ought not to be done ful ofte, but somtyme for to take disporte and solas. **1525** LD. BERNERS *Froiss.* II. clx. 178 b, For he kepte reuyll, daunsyng, and solas: and euery daye it was newe to begyn. **1551** R. ROBINSON tr. *More's Utopia* I. (1895) p. xciv, An yle..Ful fraight with worldly welth, with pleasure and solas.

β. *a* **1340** HAMPOLE *Psalter* lxxvi. 3 He amonestis vs to pass fra erthly solace and ȝern anly delit of heuen. **1377** LANGL. *P. Pl.* B. XVIII. 217 God of his goodnesse..Sette hym in solace & in soueregne myrthe. *c* **1400** *Pilgr. Sowle* IV. i. (Caxton, 1483) 58 Hym nedeth of solace and disport wher with to appesen his herte. **1480** CAXTON *Myrr.* II. iii. 67 This is a place whiche is ful of solace, of playsances and of delices. **1519** *Interlude Four Elements* (Percy Soc.) 45 Let us go to the taverne agayn, And make some mery solace. **1590** SPENSER *F.Q.* II. vi. 3 And therein sate a Ladie fresh and faire, Making sweet solace to her selfe alone. **1615** G. SANDYS *Trav.* 176 Sundry smal turrets are dispersed about, which serue for solace as well as for safe-guard. *a* **1629** HINDE *J. Bruen* xxix. (1641) 90 O how great was his rejoycing, and solace, when..he might rejoyce the soules of Gods people. **1667** MILTON *P.L.* IX. 844 Great joy he promis'd to his thoughts, and new Solace in her return.

**3.** That which gives comfort or consolation, †brings pleasure or enjoyment, etc.

*c* **1290** *Beket* 178 in *S. Eng. Leg.* I. 111 For he scholde hire solas beo, and speke to hire with mouþe. *a* **1340** HAMPOLE *Psalter* xxxvii. 11 In þere twa solaces man ioyes. *c* **1400** MAUNDEV. (Roxb.) xix. 88 He hase forsaken..all þe ricches and solacez of þe werld. *c* **1450** tr. *De Imitatione* II. v. 45 God allone..is þe solace of mannys soule & very gladnes of herte. **1597** HOOKER *Eccl. Pol.* v. lxxvi. §8 All which solaces and comforts of this our vnquiet life it pleaseth God oftentimes to bestow. **1597** BACON *Ess., Of Honour & Reputation* (Arb.) 74 Fauorites, such as exceede not this scantling to bee solace to the Soueraigne. **1667** MILTON *P.L.* IV. 486 To have thee by my side Henceforth an individual solace dear. **1794** MRS. RADCLIFFE *Myst. Udolpho* xxxiv, Tell your lady..that this [picture] has been my companion and only solace in all my misfortunes. **1849** ROBERTSON *Serm.* Ser. I. viii. 125 He had cut himself off from the solaces of life.

**4.** *Printing.* (See quot. 1683.)

**1683** MOXON *Mech. Exerc., Printing* 357 The Penalty for the breach of..these Laws and Customs is in Printers Language called a Solace. **1683** [see SOLACE *v.* 4]. **1888** JACOBI *Printers' Vocab.* 128 *Solace*, a penalty imposed by the chapel for the infringement of any of its rules.

†**5.** *rose of solace*, = ROSA SOLIS 2. *Obs.*[−1]

**1604** *Meet. of Gallants at Ordinary* C j b, To the comforting of his poore heart, he powrde downe a leauen shillings in Rose of Solace.

†**solace**, *sb.*[2] *Obs.* Also 6 sollace. [Of obscure origin.] Some substance used for dressing cloth.

**1552** *Act 5 & 6 Edw. VI*, c. 6 §xiv, Whether the same Clothe or Clothes be well and sufficientlye dressed and pressed withe the colde presse, without puttinge therto flox, solace, chalke, flower, or any other deceiptfull thinge. *c* **1560** *Maldon Liber B.* fol. 56 (MS.), Without puttinge therto flocks, sollace, chalke, flower, heare, or any yearne made of lambes wooll. **1613** MAY *Decl. Est. Clothing* v. 29 Flox of the same coulour..which they can sheare as small as dust, which mixt with solace, they spread vpon the musters, and where the cloth may bee seene.

**solace** (ˈsɒləs), *v.* Forms: 3–4 solaci, -cy, 3– solace, 4–5 solas(e, 5 solais, 6 solles, 8 solless. (See also SOLANCE *v.*) [ad. OF. *solacier*, *solasier*, etc., later *soulacier* (now arch.), f. *solas* SOLACE *sb.*[1] Cf. Sp. *solazar*, It. *sollazzare*, med.L. *solatiari*, *-are*; MDu. *solasen*, *-acen*.]

**1.** *trans.* To cheer, comfort, console; †to entertain or recreate.

**1297** R. GLOUC. (Rolls) 11511 Sir simon de Mountfort out of warde nom Sir edward him to solaci. **13..** *Sir Beues* 711 So him solaste þat mai, þat al is care wente awai. *c* **1380** WYCLIF *Sel. Wks.* II. 226 Crist tauȝte men to suffre..and putte hem in hope þerfore to be solasid of God. *c* **1400** *Destr. Troy* 1620 Mony gaumes were begonnen þe grete for to solas. *Ibid.* 13984 Myche solast hir the sight of hir sone þan, To se the lede vppon lyue, þat ho louet most. *c* **1475** *Harl. Contin. Higden* (Rolls) VIII. 456 Thei destroyede a newe maner made..by that prior..for to solace hym and his breþer þer. **1588** SHAKS. *L.L.L.* IV. iii. 377 We will with some strange pastime solace them. **1706** PHILLIPS (ed. Kersey), To *Solace*, to afford Solace or Comfort. **1790**

COWPER *On My Mother's Picture* 4 Thy own sweet smiles I see, The same that oft in childhood solaced me. **1812** J. WILSON *Isle of Palms* I. 506 And it may be such dreams are given.. To solace them that mourn. **1868** FREEMAN *Norm. Conq.* (1877) II. 86 They were often solaced by the company of wives and children.

*absol.* **1820** SHELLEY *Prometh. Unb.* III. iv. 32 Thy simple talk once solaced, now delights.

**b.** To make (a place) cheerful or pleasant.

**1667** MILTON *P.L.* VII. 434 From Branch to Branch the smaller Birds with song Solac'd the Woods. **1746** J. HERVEY *Medit.* (1818) 186 Ye Birds.. who wake the morn, and solace the groves with your artless lays. **1875** GRINDON *Life* i. 8 The walls of old castles and abbeys, which.. ivy and the faithful wallflower alone have solaced.

**c.** To allay, alleviate, assuage, soothe.

**1667** MILTON *P.L.* VIII. 419 The cause of his desire By conversation with his like to help, Or solace his defects. **1712** BLACKMORE *Creation* v. 60 A Cause Supream,.. Who, when implor'd, might timely Succour give, Solace our Anguish, and our Wants relieve. **1797** MRS. RADCLIFFE *Italian* xvii, Paulo was contented to solace his conscience. **1819** SHELLEY *Cenci* III. i. 311 We sate sad together Solacing our despondency with tears. **1833** TENNYSON *Two Voices* 433 A little hint to solace woe.

**2.** *refl.* To give (oneself) comfort or consolation, †entertainment or amusement.

**1340** *Ayenb.* 213 þer-huile þet ich me solaci an playe, iche ne þenche none manne kuead. *c* **1400** *Destr. Troy* 1752 Siker were to sit and solas vs here. *c* **1470** *Gol. & Gaw.* 217 Thus thay solaist thame selvin, suthly to say. **1568** GRAFTON *Chron.* II. 107 Solacyng himselfe with Musicall instrumentes & songes. **1583** BABINGTON *Commandm.* (1590) 314 We dare solace our selues in soft beddes too long for our constitutions. **1639** FULLER *Holy War* III. xv, Henry king of Ierusalem, as he was walking in his palace to solace himself, fell down.. and brake his neck. **1691** RAY *Creation* II. (1704) 464 With the Thoughts and Expectation whereof he solaces himself. **1746** J. HERVEY *Medit.* (1818) 21 He solaced him-self with the prospect of a long, long series of earthly satisfactions. **1860** MOTLEY *Netherl.* (1868) I. v. 283 Duplessis-Mornay often solaced himself by distant communion with that kindred and sympathizing spirit. **1887** RUSKIN *Præterita* II. 231 He solaced himself by making a careful collection of all the Florentine wild-flowers for me.

†**3.** *intr.* To take comfort or consolation, recreation or enjoyment. *Obs.*

**1340** *Ayenb.* 213 Huet kuead is hit yef ich guo playe and solaci. *c* **1475** *Harl. Contin. Higden* (Rolls) VIII. 447 Thei brente þeire faces with yrne that thei scholde not be knowen, and þat Ynglische men scholde not solace of þeire dethe. **1530** PALSGR. 724/2, I am werye of studyenge, I wyll go solace a lytell. **1592** TIMME *Ten Eng. Lepers* 63 Friends do solace and joy togither in honest and godly mirth. **1618** BOLTON *Florus* (1636) 313 He,.. surprised with the love of Queen Cleopatra, solaced on her bosome. **1673** *Lady's Calling* I. iii. §6 Let him stand naked and hungry, whilst they are solacing with that which would relieve him. **1728** VANBR. & CIBBER *Prov. Husb.* I, She herself is solacing in one continual round of cards and good company.

**4.** *trans.* Of printers: To punish (one) corporally for non-payment of a 'solace'. Also *transf.*

**1683** MOXON *Mech. Exerc., Printing* 357 If the Delinquent.. would not pay his Solace.. they Solac'd him. **1784** B. FRANKLIN in *Ann. Reg., Chron.* (1817) 385 This foolish letter is mere chit-chat between ourselves... If, therefore, you show it to any body,.. I will positively solless you.

Hence ˈ**solaced** *ppl. a.*, comforted, consoled.

**1836** MRS. BROWNING *Poet's Vow* II. ii, The solaced friends.

**solaceful** (ˈsɒləsfʊl), *a. rare.* [f. SOLACE *sb.*[1] + -FUL 1.] Full of solace; pleasant, agreeable.

*a* **1618** SYLVESTER *Job Triumphant* IV. 687 The Lord accepted Job, and staid His Thrall-full State,.. And turned it to Solace-full, from sad. **1884** J. PAYNE *Tales fr. Arabic* I. 225 How joyous and how solaceful was life in them whilere!

**solacement** (ˈsɒləsmənt). [f. SOLACE *sb.*[1] + -MENT. So OF. *sollace-, soulacement.*] Solace, solacing, consolation.

**1721** R. KEITH tr. *T. à Kempis, Solil. Soul* xviii. 253 Being disappointed in thy outward Solacement. **1768–74** TUCKER *Lt. Nat.* (1834) II. 545 Discovering daily new sources of solacement we had not discerned before. **1824** SCOTT *Redgauntlet* (1830) II. xix. 214 That.. was a solacement of his feelings which was not at the moment to be thought of. **1871** CARLYLE in *Mrs. Carlyle's Lett.* I. 370 Rather as in duty bound than with much hope of solacement.

**solacer** (ˈsɒləsə(r)). [f. SOLACE *v.* + -ER[1].] One who, or that which, solaces.

**1611** COTGR., *Consolateur*, a consolator, solacer, comforter. **1803** LAMB *Let. to Coleridge* in *Final Mem.* iv. 225 A pipe and some generous Port, and King Lear.. had their effect as solacers. **1873** MISS BRADDON *Lucius Davoren* I. Prol. i. 7 Tobacco, that sweet solacer of weary hours.

**Solacet** (ˈsɒləsɛt). Also **solacet.** [f. SOL(UBLE *a.* + ACET(ATE.] A proprietary name for any of a range of azo-dyestuffs which contain sulphate ester groups and were formerly much used for direct dyeing of artificial fibres.

**1938** *Times* 11 Jan. 9/5 Another is the 'solacet' range, produced within the last half of 1937, for giving bright fast colours to acetate rayons. **1939** *Trade Marks Jrnl.* 17 May 647/1 *Solacet*... Water soluble dyes for cellulose acetate silk. British Dyestuffs Corporation Limited. **1952** K. VENKATARAMAN *Chem. Synthetic Dyes* I. xxi. 646 The Solacets undergo no chemical change during the dyeing process. **1955** *Official Gaz.* (U.S. Patent Office) 7 June TM 7 *Solacet*... For water soluble dyes for cellulose acetate silk. **1964** E. R. TROTMAN *Dyeing & Chem. Technol. of Textile Fibres* (ed. 3) xxiii. 515 The Solacet dyes.. show little redistribution of colour on continued boiling. **1971** R. L. M. ALLEN *Colour Chem.* vi. 71 In consequence of the development of dispersed dyes with improved dyeing and fastness properties the Solacet range has now been superseded.

**solacing** (ˈsɒləsɪŋ), *vbl. sb.* [f. SOLACE *v.*] The action of the verb in various senses; †the fact of taking enjoyment or recreation.

**13..** *K. Alis.* 6746 (W.), Now rideth Alisaunder,.. with muche syngyng, In gret delit and solasyng. **1382** WYCLIF *1 Cor.* xiv. 3 He.. spekith to men, to edificacioun,.. and comfortynge, or solasynge. **1540–1** ELYOT *Image Gov.* (1549) 81 In this solacyng he hunted the harte. *c* **1560** A. SCOTT *Poems* (S.T.S.) xviii. 43 Adew,.. My mirth and sollesing Of erdly gloir. **1631** N. HUNT (*title*), New Recreations, or The Mindes release and solacing. **1683** MOXON *Mech. Exerc., Printing* 357 The manner of Solacing, thus.

ˈ**solacing,** *ppl. a.* [f. SOLACE *v.*] Conveying solace; consoling.

**1721** R. KEITH tr. *T. à Kempis, Solil. Soul* x. 179 The solacing Joy of the Spirit. **1837** CARLYLE *Fr. Rev.* I. VII. vii, For wrath is contagious, and to pent Bodyguards is so solacing. **1862** H. SPENCER *First Princ.* I. v. §32 (1875) 115 The beliefs.. were highly solacing ones. **1890** *Pall Mall G.* 20 Jan. 6/3 Miss Fowler received these solacing remarks with quiet serenity.

† **soˈlacious,** *a. Obs.* Forms: 5–6 solacius, 5–7 solacious; 5 solacyose, 5–6 -ous, 6 -ouse, *Sc.* -us; 6–7 solatious. [a. OF. *solacieus* (*soulaceus*, etc.), f. *solas* SOLACE *sb.*[1] So Sp. *solazoso.*] Affording or giving solace, in various senses of the sb. (Common *c* 1500–1650.)

**1375** BARBOUR *Bruce* x. 290 In cumpany solacius He wes, and thar-with amorus. *c* **1450** tr. *De Imitatione* III. xxiii. 92 þou allone art hiest,.. þou allone most swete & most solacious. **1451** CAPGR. *Life St. Gilbert* 70 He talked mor þan ete, and with solacious countenauns wold he glade his gestis. *a* **1470** H. PARKER *Dives & Pauper* (W. de W. 1496) III. xvii. 153/1 The holy daye hath ben solacyous.. both for soule and bodye. **1503** HAWES *Examp. Virt.* II. xxvii, For they be so fayre and wounderous That theym to se it is solacyous. **1546** BALE *English Votaries* I. 18b, Women greuouse and solacyouse. **1581** MARBECK *Bk. Notes* 1164 Delicious it is in aduersitie, & solatious in all weaknes. **1611** J. DAVIES (Heref.) *Sco. Folly* xliv, Fountaine of Conceits acute and solacious. **1641** SYMONDS *Serm. Ho. Comm.* ¶3 What can be more solatious to a Christian Spirit? **1675** COCKER *Morals* 41 Old Friends to trust, old Gold to keep, old Wine To drink; are a solacious good old Trine. [**1826** GALT *Lairds* xiii, Such solacious participation in the influences of the season, as he called it.]

Hence † **soˈlaciously** *adv. Obs.*

**1526** SKELTON *Magnyf.* 2395 Prosperyte to hym is gyuen solacyusly to man.

† **solacy.** *Obs.*[-1] [ad. L. *solaci-um*: see SOLACE *sb.*[1]] Solace.

**1533** tr. *Erasm. Comm. Crede* 13 That laboure.. the spyryte doth make dulcete and swete with so many solacyes and coumfortes.

† **solagement.** *Obs.*[-1] [ad. F. *soulagement*, †*sollagement*, f. *soulager* to relieve.] Relief.

**1609** J. DAVIES (Heref.) *Holy Roode* F b, That in the Lab'rinth of his Languishment We may.. find solagement.

**solah,** variant of SOLA *sb.*

† **solaire,** var. (after OF. *solaire*) of *salaire*, obs. f. SALARY *sb.*

**1491** CAXTON *Vitas Patr.* (W. de W. 1495) I. xxxvii. 48 b/2 He wold haue gyuen to the Maronner for his solaire a boke of the gospellis.

‖ **solak.** *rare.* Also 6 sola (?), 7 solach, solaque. [a. Turkish *ṣolāq*. So F. *solak.*] (See quots.)

The identity of the word in the first quot. is doubtful. **1520** *Caxton's Chron. Eng.* VII. 141 b/1 In y[e] iiij yeare of kynge Henryes reygne came y[e] Emperour of Constantynople with many greate solaes [*Brut and Caxton* lordes] & knyghtes. [**1615** G. SANDYS *Trav.* I. 75 The Pretorian footmen called the *Solacchi*, whereof there be in number three hundred.] **1678** PHILLIPS, *Solachs*, those of the Grand Seigniors Foot-guard, who are about three hundred, attending upon him with Bows and Arrows. **1687** A. LOVELL tr. *Thevenot's Trav.* I. 69 The Solaques are also of the Infantry, and are the Grand Signior's.. Life-guard, for they attend the Grand Signior when he goes abroad in the city. **1802** JAMES *Milit. Dict.*, *Solaks*, bowmen or archers belonging to the personal guard of the grand signor.

**solan** (ˈsəʊlən). Forms: α. 5– soland (7 sorland), 6 solande, -end, 7–8 solund. β. 6 solane, 7– solan; 8 sollen. [f. ON. and Icel. *súla* (also Icel. *hafsúla*, Norw. *havsula*) gannet; the second element may be ON. *ǫnd*, *and-* (Norw., Sw., Da. *and*) duck. Originally Sc., but known to English writers from the middle of the 17th cent.]

**1.** The gannet (*Sula bassana*), a large sea-fowl resembling a goose, which frequents a few rocks and small islands of Britain, the Faeroes, Iceland, and Canada.

*c* **1450** HOLLAND *Howlat* 700 The Soland [as] stewart was sent; For he couth fro the firmament Fang the fische deid. **1749** COLLINS *On Popular Superstit.* x, Along the Atlantic rock, undreading climb, And of its eggs despoil the solan's nest. **1808** SCOTT *Marm.* III. iii, The rafters.. Bore wealth of winter cheer; Of sea-fowl dried, and solands store. *a* **1851** MOIR *The Bass Rock* ii, At times the solan's wing.. Brushed near us. **1873** BLACK *Pr. Thule* III. ix. 285 A white solan.. struck the water as he dived.

**2.** *attrib.* with *goose*, = sense 1.

α. **1536** BELLENDEN *Chron. Scot.* ix. (1541) B vj b, In it [the Bass Rock] ar incredible noumer of soland geis;.. And ar sene in na part of Albion, bot in this crag and Ailsay. **1596** DALRYMPLE tr. *Leslie's Hist. Scot.* (S.T.S.) I. 55 The neist Ile named Elza.. abundes in Solend geis, and monie vthiris sey foulis. **1651** CLEVELAND *Poems* 37 A Scot, when from the Gallow-Tree got loose, Drops into Styx, and turns a Solund-Goose. **1678** BUTLER *Hud.* III. II. 655 As Barnacles turn Soland-Geese In th' Islands of the Orcades. **1694** FALLE *Jersey* ii. 73 Here are to be seen the famous Sorland Geese, whose Equivocal Generation.. is received by many amongst Us for Truth. **1710** SIBBALD *Hist. Fife* II. 45 The Fowls which most frequent the Bass, are the *Anseres Bassani* or Soland-Geese. **1768** PENNANT *Brit. Zool.* I. Pref. p. v, The clouds of Soland geese which breed on the Bass island. **1821** *Sporting Mag.* VII. 191 A Soland goose or gannet was shot by a fisherman of Southampton. **1843** YARRELL *Brit. Birds* III. 381 The Gannet, or Soland Goose.

β. **1583** *Reg. Privy Council Scot.* III. 624 To draw and alluir the auld solane geise to the boittis. **1668** CHARLETON *Onomast.* 95 *Anser Bassanus*,.. the Solan Goose. **1698** M. MARTIN *Voy. St. Kilda* (1749) 4 A prodigious number of Solan Geese hatching in their Nests. **1725** *Portland Papers* (Hist. MSS. Comm.) VI. 111 The Bass.. I think has no inhabitants but the Solan geese which breed there. **1816** SCOTT *Antiq.* vi, There was the relishing Solan goose, whose smell is so powerful that he is never cooked within doors. **1863** *Intellect. Obs.* Sept. 118 The Solan Goose is not so numerous upon Ailsa as the puffin.

**solanaceous** (sɒləˈneɪʃəs), *a. Bot.* [f. mod.L. *Solanace-æ*, f. L. *sōlānum* nightshade.] Belonging to the *Solanaceæ*, an order of gamopetalous plants which includes the genera *Solanum, Capsicum, Atropa, Hyoscyamus*, etc.

**1804** *Med. Jrnl.* XII. 519 The fruits of several solanaceous plants, as the pseudocapsicum, and the common capsicum. **1822–7** GOOD *Study Med.* (1829) III. 309 The remark will apply to most of the narcotics, whether of the umbellate or solanaceous order. **1875** *Athenæum* 24 July 123/3 The influence of poisonous solanaceous plants,—especially belladonna,—on certain rodents and marsupials.

**solanal** (səˈleɪnəl), *a.* and *sb. Bot.* [f. L. *sōlānum.*] **a.** *adj.* Of or pertaining to, related to, *Solanum* and other genera according to Lindley's classification. **b.** *sb.* A genus or plant related to *Solanum.*

**1846** LINDLEY *Veg. Kingd.* 615 The Solanal Alliance... Natural Orders of Solanals. *Ibid.* 616 Solanal Exogens.

† **solance,** *sb. Obs.* [Alteration of SOLACE *sb.*[1], after forms in *-ance.*] Solace.

*c* **1375** *Sc. Leg. Saints* xxix. (*Placidas*) 728 As ȝung men wil do for solance, & als to mak þar acquintance. *c* **1400** *Melayne* 357 Ne hope ȝe noghte.. þat ne we sall solance see. *Ibid.* 831 Thay crownnede þe Sowdane.., þat Solance was to seene.

So † **solance** *v. Obs.*

**13..** *Guy Warw.* 4293 Gij bileft in court atte mete, Him to play & solanci. *a* **1400** *Relig. Pieces fr. Thornton MS.* 9 þe third es, to solance [*printed* solauce] thaym þat er sorowefull.

**solander** (səˈlændə(r)). [From the name of the Swedish botanist D. C. *Solander* (1736–1782).] A box made in the form of a book, used for holding botanical specimens, papers, maps, etc.

**1788** COWPER *Let. to Lady Hesketh* 5 July, I shall be as happy in the arrival of my Solander as he whose name it bears, was to arrive once more in England after his circum-navigation. **1877** W. JONES *Inaugural Address London Conference of Librarians* 15 Maps should be placed in Solander cases.

**solander,** obs. form of SALLENDER.

**solandra** (səˈlændrə). [mod.L.: see SOLANDER.] A genus of tropical American shrubs belonging to the *Solanaceæ* (sub-order *Atropeæ*); also, a plant belonging to this genus.

**1797** *Encycl. Brit.* (ed. 3) XVII. 597/1 The genus was first named *Solandra*, in honour of Dr. Solander, by Murray in the 14th edition of the *Systema Vegetabilium*. **1866** *Treas. Bot.* 1179/2 Large tubular flowers, as those of *Bignonia*,.. *Solandra*, &c. **1901** *Blackw. Mag.* Feb. 226/1 A large solandra of great age bearing yellowish trumpet-shaped flowers.

**solania** (səˈleɪnɪə). *Chem.* [f. SOLAN-UM + -IA.] An alkaloid found in the woody nightshade.

**1830** LINDLEY *Nat. Syst. Bot.* 233 The active principle of Solanum Dulcamara is an alkali, called Solania. **1884** *Encycl. Brit.* XVII. 499/2 It [*S. Dulcamara*] owes its medicinal activity to a bitter principle yielding.. the alkaloid 'solania'.

**solanicine** (səˈlænɪsɪn). *Chem.* [f. as prec. + -IC + -INE[5].] (See quot. 1868.)

**1868** WATTS *Dict. Chem.*, *Solanicine*,.. a base produced by the action of hydrochloric acid on solanine. *Ibid.* 345 Solanicine.. may be obtained by slow evaporation of its ethereal solution. **1876** HARLEY *Royle's Mat. Med.* 500 Strong hydrochloric acid converts this into an amorphous basic substance, *solanicine.*

**solanidine** (səˈlænɪdɪn). *Chem.* [Cf. prec.] (See quots.)

**1868** WATTS *Dict. Chem.*, *Solanidine*,.. a base produced.. by the action of acids on solanine... Solanidine dissolves easily in alcohol and in ether. **1868** *Fownes' Chem.* (ed. 10) 682 It [solanine] is resolved by boiling with dilute acids into glucose and solanidine.

**solanine** (ˈsɒlənɪn). *Chem.* Also **solanina, solanin.** [a. F. *solanine* (Desfosses, 1821), f. SOLAN-UM + -INE[5].] A poisonous alkaloid, or a compound containing an alkaloid, found in various plants of the genus *Solanum*.

α. **1838** T. THOMSON *Chem. Org. Bodies* 264 Solanina was discovered by M. Desfosses in the berries of the *solanum nigrum*, and in the fruit of the common potatoe. *Ibid.*, Solanina is a white powder, having a pearly lustre. **1842** *Penny Cycl.* XXII. 195/2 The hydrochlorate and acetate of solanina have a gummy appearance when evaporated to dryness.

β. **1838** T. THOMSON *Chem. Org. Bodies* 841 Baup informs us, that potatoes, after they begin to grow, contain a small quantity of solanin. **1859** FAIRHOLT *Tobacco* (1876) 2 The Potato fruit and leaves give us Solanine. **1899** *Allbutt's Syst. Med.* VII. 91 According to Grasset, solanine diminishes the amount of tremor.

‖**solano** (so'lano). [Sp.:—L. *sōlānus*, f. *sōl* sun.] In Spain, a hot south-easterly wind.

[**1604** E. G[RIMSTONE] *D'Acosta's Hist. Indies* III. ii. 120 The Solanus or Easterne winde is commonly hote and troublesome in Spaine.] **1792** J. TOWNSEND *Journ. thro. Spain* II. 360 Whenever they have the Solano wind, that is, whenever the wind blows from Africa, they become liable to pleurisies. **1834** *Encycl. Metrop.* (1845) XXII. 343 The heat in Summer is very great, and, when the Solano or South wind blows, nearly insupportable. **1881** *Standard* 14 July 5 'Ask no grace in the Solano.' So runs the Spanish proverb.

**solanoid** ('sɒlənɔɪd), *a. Path.* [f. SOLAN-UM + -OID.] (See quot.)

**1851** DUNGLISON *Dict. Med. Sci.* (ed. 4), *Solanoid*, resembling a potato... An epithet applied to a form of cancer, which appears to be intermediate between scirrhus and encephaloid.

‖**solanum** (sə'leɪnəm). [L. *sōlānum* nightshade.] A plant of the nightshade family, or the genus of gamopetalous plants of which this is the type; some amount or preparation of the plant used for medical purposes. Also *fig.*

**1578** LYTE *Dodoens* 447 This *solanum* cooleth..more strongly than the Common Nightshade. **1621** BURTON *Anat. Mel.* II. v. I. vi, Simples, as poppy, nightshade or solanum. *a* **1652** J. SMITH *Sel. Disc.* i. 7 That venemous solanum, that deadly nightshade, that drives its cold poison into the understandings of men. **1768–74** TUCKER *Lt. Nat.* (1834) II. 145 Apothecaries, when dispensing a recipe wherein antimony, solanum, laudanum, or mercury is an ingredient, are extremely careful. **1816** TUCKEY *Narr. Exped. R. Zaire* i. (1818) 22 Some herbaceous plants, particularly a convolvulus,..a solanum, a lotus, an aloe, &c. **1880** C. R. MARKHAM *Peruv. Bark* 123 A dense growth of bright-yellow compositæ, and solanums with a purple flower. **1884** tr. *De Candolle's Orig. Cultivated Pl.* 49 The abundance of tuberous solanums growing in the temperate regions of America,..confirms the fact of an American origin.

*attrib.* **1842** BRANDE *Dict. Sci.*, etc. 1129/1 Some of the Solanum tribes. **1861** BENTLEY *Man. Bot.* 598 *Solanaceæ.*—The Solanum or Potato Order. **1884** tr. *De Candolle's Orig. Cultivated Pl.* 53 The sweet potato belongs to the Convolvulus family, the potato to the Solanum family.

**solapsone** (sə'læpsəʊn). *Pharm.* [f. SOL(UBLE *a.* + *d*)*apsone*, name of a drug of which solapsone is a more soluble derivative (f. *d*i(*p*amino-*p*henyl)sulph*one*).] A white powder given as tablets or by injection of an aqueous solution for the treatment of leprosy; the hydrated tetrasodium salt of di(*p*-3-phenyl-1, 3-disulphopropylamino)phenylsulphone, $C_{30}H_{28}N_2O_{14}S_5Na_4.xH_2O$.

**1952** *Brit. Pharm. Codex* Suppl. 66 Solapsone consists mainly of the tetrasodium salt. **1959** R. G. COCHRANE *Leprosy in Theory & Practice* xvii. 212 The following sulphone drugs are those most commonly employed in the treatment of leprosy: (*a*) the parent sulphone..Dapsone (B.P.)..(*b*) Sulphetrone (Solapsone (B.P.)) administered orally or parenterally; [etc.]. **1974** R. M. KIRK et al. *Surgery* ii. 23 Specific treatment [of leprosy] is with dapsone..or solapsone (Sulphetrone) given orally, or by injection,.. twice weekly. **1977** *Martindale's Extra Pharmacopoeia* (ed. 27) 1505/1 In general, the results with solapsone have not been impressive and it has been superseded by more active drugs.

**solar** ('səʊlə(r)), *a.* and *sb.*[1] [ad. L. *sōlār-is*, f. *sōl* sun. Cf. F. *solaire*, Sp. *solar*, Pg. *solar*, It. *solare*.]

**A.** *adj.* **1. a.** Of or pertaining to the sun, its course, light, heat, etc.

*c* **1450** HOLLAND *Howlat* 31 Under the Cirkill solar thir sauoruss seidis War nurist be dame Natur. **1656** BLOUNT *Glossogr.*, *Solar*, of or belonging to the Sun. **1685** DRYDEN *Thren. August.* xii, Our Isle..lay Out of the Solar walk and Heavens high way. **1732** POPE *Ess. Man* I. 102 His soul, proud Science never taught to stray Far as the solar walk, or milky way. **1754** GRAY *Progress Poesy* 54 In climes beyond the solar road. **1769** [see DISC 4]. **1815** J. SMITH *Panorama Sci. & Art* II. 331 In the solar spectrum..heat and light are not present in correspondent degrees. **1863** NEALE *Anal. Th. & Nat.* 221 Our solar universe subsists, through the opposition of the light-and-heat-receiving circumference to the light-and-heat-imparting centre. **1878** STEWART & TAIT *Unseen Univ.* ii. §73. 85 The spots were unmistakably solar phenomena.

**b.** Of time: Determined by the course of the sun; fixed by observation of the sun.

**1594** BLUNDEVIL *Exerc.* III. I. xlv. (1636) 358 The Month Solar is that space of time which the Sunne spendeth in passing thorow any one of the twelve signes. **1662** STILLINGFL. *Orig. Sacræ* I. v. §1 If years be sometimes Lunar, sometimes Solar. *Ibid.*, The Solar moneths were either naturall..or civill. **1704** J. HARRIS *Lex. Techn.* I. s.v., Solar Cycle. **1725** WATTS *Logic* (1736) 47 A Solar Year of three hundred sixty five Days. **1731–8** SWIFT *Polite Conv.* Introd. 44 To be daily delivered fresh, in every company, for twelve solar Months. **1816** PLAYFAIR *Nat. Phil.* II. 81 The mean interval of time between the sun's passing the meridian one day, and his passing it the next, is called a mean solar day. **1840** *Penny Cycl.* XVII. 450/1 The perpetuity of the solar cycle..is destroyed by the new style. **1855** LARDNER *Mus. Sci. & Art* V. 139 The time of 60 swings will be a mean solar minute, and the time of 3600 will be a mean solar hour. **1868** LOCKYER *Elem. Astron.* §437 The period that elapses between two successive passages through the vernal equinox..is called the solar, or tropical year.

**c.** Indicating time in relation to, or by means of, the sun.

**1728** CHAMBERS *Cycl.* s.v. *Dial*, To use a Solar, as a Lunar-Dial, *i.e.* to find the Hour of the Night by a Sun-Dial. **1829** W. PEARSON *Pract. Astron.* II. 314 Besides two good sidereal clocks, a well furnished observatory ought not to be without a good solar clock. **1875** KNIGHT *Dict. Mech.* 2238/2 *Solar Chronometer*, a sun-dial adapted to show mean instead of solar time. **1900** *Jrnl. Sch. Geog.* (U.S.) Apr. 138 Beginning with the Solar Calendar, which is the simpler.

**d.** Of mechanism, etc.: Operating by means of, or with the aid of, the light or heat of the sun.

**1740** [see MICROSCOPE 1 b]. **1831** BREWSTER *Optics* xli. 346 The solar microscope is nothing more than a magic lantern, the light of the sun being used instead of that of a lamp. **1875** VOGEL *Chem. Light & Photogr.* x. 95 To produce photographic images life size, the magic lantern is not used, but the solar camera. **1875** KNIGHT *Dict. Mech.* 2239/1 Solar Engine. *Ibid.*, Solar Telegraph. **1876** J. ERICSSON *Centennial Exhibition* xlv. 561 The solar engine..is composed of three distinct parts—the engine, the steam-generator, and the mechanism by means of which the..energy of the sun's rays ..is increased. **1877–81** VOYLE & STEVENSON *Milit. Dict.* Suppl. 36/2 During the late campaign in Affghanistan, Solar Telegraphy was much resorted to. **1880** J. P. MAUZEY *U.S. Patent 227,028* 27 Apr. 1, I..have invented a new and Improved Solar Heater. **1884** KNIGHT *Dict. Mech.* Suppl. 828/2 *Solar Boiler*, an apparatus intended to utilize the heat of the sun's rays. **1914** *Metal Worker, Plumber & Steam Fitter* LXXXII. 758/2 Ordinarily a solar heater is mounted upon the roof of the house. **1929** C. G. ABBOT in *Smithsonian Sci. Ser.* II. ix. 222 The solar cooker is a delightful luxury. **1955** E. BURGESS *Frontier to Space* viii. 150 The system envisaged is a solar engine which would intercept a relatively minute portion of the 92,000 calories which each square centimetre of the Sun's surface radiates every minute. **1962** A. SHEPARD in *Into Orbit* 83 There is a solar distiller in the kit which will help you convert salt water into the pint of water you need a day to stay alive. **1967** *Daily Tel.* 30 Jan. 10/6 Cooking food at practically no cost has been achieved by scientists at the Hebrew University by the use of a 'solar cooker'. **1979** *Tucson Mag.* Apr. 62/3 A solar heater costs between $2000 and $2600 to buy and install.

**e.** Concerned with or pertaining to the utilization of the sun's rays as a source of energy.

**1972** *Guardian* 17 Oct. 15/6 Ambitious schemes..are under study—including a huge solar farm on earth feeding heat to power stations. **1979** *Washington Star* 8 May A14/2 The crowd wasn't sure how well it liked *him*, impeccably solar though he is when it comes to energy. **1979** *N.Y. Rev. Bks.* 17 May 15/1 It will take a long time for solar energy to become the dominant source of world energy. It will first be necessary to eliminate inefficiencies in solar technologies. **1979** *Guardian* 6 Sept. 4/4 Solar systems were immediately viable.

**2. a.** *Astrol.* Subject to the influence of the sun; having a nature or character determined by the sun.

**1626** BACON *Sylva* §493 They haue denominated some Herbs Solar and some Lunar. **1647** LILLY *Chr. Astrol.* lxxiv. 424 The benefit he expects..shall be by the King, a Magistrate,..or by a Solar man of noble disposition. **1700** DRYDEN *Fables, Cock & Fox* 652 The cock was pleas'd.., And proud beside, as solar people are. **1845** *The Theologian* II. 41 When well dignified, the solar man is..splendid and sumptuous. **1877** *Encycl. Brit.* VII. 294/1 The solar man is grand and generous, the lunar man unsteadfast.

**b.** Sacred to the sun; connected or associated with the worship of the sun.

**1774** J. BRYANT *Mythol.* II. 66 It was at first only a mark of reference, and betokened a solar animal, specifying the particular Deity to whom it was sacred. **1820** W. TOOKE *Lucian* I. 554 The miracle..which Homer relates of the solar-oxen. **1877** W. R. COOPER *Egypt. Obelisks* ii. (1878) 6 In Ra, according to the solar litanies, were combined all the attributes of power and wisdom. **1906** LOCKYER *Stonehenge* v. 51 The assumption of Stonehenge having been a solar temple.

**c.** Representing or symbolizing the sun.

**1807** J. BARLOW *Columb.* III. 531 Meantime the solar king collects from far His martial bands. **1816** G. S. FABER *Orig. Pagan Idol.* II. 106 The solari-tauric Mithras is therefore evidently the solar man-bull Taschter. **1889** I. TAYLOR *Orig. Aryans* vi. 311 Hence few mythologies are altogether free from the loves of solar heroes and dawn maidens.

**d.** Sprung or descended from the sun.

**1788** SIR W. JONES in *Asiatic Researches* (1790) II. 136 The time, when the Solar and Lunar dynasties are believed to have become extinct. **1841** ELPHINSTONE *Hist. Ind.* I. 259 The lunar race has but forty-eight names in the same period, in which the solar has ninety-five.

†**3. a.** *solar earth, metal*, gold. (Cf. SOL *sb.*[1] 2.)
**b.** *solar metal*, a coloured metal. *Obs.*

**1649** G. DANIEL *Trinarch., Hen. V*, cxxix, Wee..need not feare an Asse's Load Of Solar Earth can force the Gates vnshutt. **1666** J. SMITH *Solomon's Portraiture Old Age* (1752) 92 By the help of fire, and possibly some specific menstruum as a proper key for that solar metal. **1800** tr. *Lagrange's Chem.* I. 352 The alchemists gave the name of Solar Metals to those which are coloured; and that of Lunar to those which are white.

**4. a.** Of light, heat, etc.: Proceeding or emanating from the sun.

**1698** FRYER *Acc. E. India & P.* 242 We had our Skins flead off of those Parts exposed to the Solar Rays. **1726** POPE *Odyss.* XIX. 515 Nor winter's boreal blast,..Nor solar ray, could pierce the shady bower. **1796** KIRWAN *Elem. Min.* (ed. 2) I. 125 By concentrated solar heat. **1829** *Chapters Phys. Sci.* 289 The light derived from such sources differs from the solar light in being accompanied by free radiant caloric. **1871** TYNDALL *Fragm. Sci.* (1879) I. ii. 41 The solution.. offers a means of filtering the solar beam. **1884** *Nature* 3 Jan. 217/2 This heater..contains the acting medium, steam or air, employed to transfer solar energy to the motor. **1939** A. HUXLEY *Many a Summer* I. x. 130 It's a gadget..for making use of solar energy. **1976** *National Observer* (U.S.) 21 Feb. 8/3 He's living in a house heated mostly by solar energy.

**b.** Warmed by the sun; sunny.

**1821** BYRON *Sard.* I. ii. 127 Semiramis..led These our Assyrians to the solar shores Of Ganges.

**5.** Resembling that of the sun; comparable to the sun. Also *fig.*

**1754** YOUNG *Centaur not Fabulous* Wks. 1762 IV. 260 They only have solar or self-born light who live up to the dignity of their nature. **1834** MRS. SOMERVILLE *Connex. Phys. Sci.* xxxvi. 402 Solid bodies of a solar nature. **1839–48** BAILEY *Festus* viii. 87, I saw,..Blazing aghast in solar solitude, A panting shadow. **1861** J. BROWN *Horæ Subs.* Ser. II. 62 He was in this respect a solar man: he drew after him his own firmament of planets.

**6.** In Arabic grammar, the epithet of the class of consonants before which the *l* of the article is assimilated; so called because including *sh*, the initial letter of *shems* 'sun'. Opposed to *lunar*.

**1776** J. RICHARDSON *Arab. Gram.* iii. 8 The dentals and linguals are called solar letters. **1855** DAVIS & DAVIDSON *Arabic Reading Less.* p. xxxii, The influence the solar letters exercise upon the article. **1905** *N. & Q.* 30 Dec. 534/1 One of the fourteen solar letters.

**7.** Special collocations: **solar apex**, the point in space, situated in the constellation Lyra, toward which the sun is moving; the apex of the solar way; **solar battery**, a solar cell, or an assembly of such cells; **solar cell**, a photovoltaic device which converts solar radiation into electrical energy; **solar collector**, a device which absorbs solar radiation as heat or reflects it to a focus; †**solar comet** (see quot. 1704); **solar compass**, (*a*) a magnetic instrument turning under the influence of the sun's rays; (*b*) an instrument used in surveying for easy determination of the meridian; **solar constant** (see CONSTANT B, quots. 1869, 1890); **solar eye**, *fig.* (see quot.); **solar eye-piece**, a device used in observations of the sun to diminish the light and heat of this (Knight, 1875); **solar flare** = FLARE *sb.*[1] 1 b; **solar furnace**, an apparatus in which high temperature reactions are carried out at the focus of a system which concentrates the sun's radiation, usually by reflection; **solar ganglion**, = *solar plexus*; **solar glass**, tinted glass for large windows; **solar house** orig. *U.S.*, a solar-heated house; **solar lamp**, (*a*) an argand lamp; (*b*) a grade of electric lamp; **solar myth**, a myth resulting from a personification of the sun and describing its course or attributes as those of some god or hero; **solar neutrino unit**, a unit used in expressing the detected flux of neutrinos from the sun, equal to $10^{-36}$ neutrino captures per target atom per second; abbrev. *SNU* s.v. S 4 a; **solar oil** (see quot. 1868); **solar paddle**, a large, flat array of solar cells projecting from a spacecraft like a paddle; **solar panel**, a panel designed to absorb the sun's rays for the purpose of generating electricity (by means of solar cells) or heating; **solar phosphorus**, a substance which emits light as the result of exposure to sunlight; **solar pillar** = *sun-pillar* s.v. SUN *sb.*[1] 13; **solar plasma** = *solar wind* below; **solar plexus**, a complex of nerves situated at the pit of the stomach; the epigastric plexus; **solar pond, pool**, a pool or lake of very salty water in which convection is inhibited, allowing considerable heating of the bottom water by solar radiation; **solar power**, power derived more or less directly from solar radiation; **solar print**, a photograph made by sunlight; **solar reflector** (see quot.); **solar sail**, a surface designed to utilize the pressure of solar radiation to provide the propulsive force for a spacecraft to which it is attached; so **solar sailing** *vbl. sb.*; **solar salt**, salt obtained by allowing sea water to evaporate in sunlight; **solar spot**, a sunspot; **solar stearin**, a substance obtained from lard; **solar still**, a still, often portable, in which solar radiation is employed to evaporate salty or impure water and produce fresh water; **solar system**, the sun together with all the planets and other bodies connected with it; **solar tables**, tables by which the position of the sun may be ascertained; **solar wheel**, a wheel in a clock serving to show the apparent daily motion of the sun; **solar wind**, the stream of ions and electrons which constantly emanates from the sun and which permeates the solar system.

**1875** *Encycl. Brit.* II. 819 Whose various determinations of the *solar apex are shown in fig. 52. **1954** *N.Y. Times* 26 Apr. 1/2 A *solar battery, the first of its kind, which converts useful amounts of the sun's radiation directly and efficiently into electricity, has been constructed. **1962** SIMPSON & RICHARDS *Physical Princ. Junction Transistors* iv. 73 Most of the radiation from the sun is in the region of 1·0eV and above so that 'solar batteries' can be made from germanium or silicon. The efficiency of the process is greater when silicon is used and commercial solar batteries (sometimes called 'solar cells') are at present made from this material. **1978** W. PALZ *Solar Electr.* iii. 179 The direct conversion of sunlight into electric power is achieved by means of solar batteries, made up of solar cells. **1955** G. L. PEARSON in *Bell Lab. Rec.* July 241/1 The Bell Solar Battery consists of a number of individual silicon *solar cells. **1962** [see *solar battery* above]. **1967** *New Scientist* 25 May 463/2 The *Mariner IV* solar cell surface.. provided power for the first close photographs of the planet Mars. **1980** *Solar Energy* XXIV. facing p. 1 (*caption*) The world's largest solar cell electric power generation station... The 60kW system consists of nearly 98,000 individual silicon solar cells. **1955** *Trans. Conf. Use of Solar Energy* (Tucson, Ariz.) II. I. vi. 75 For optimum performance a *solar collector should face true south (north in the southern hemisphere). **1976** *Toronto Star* 24 Jan. E1/4 A well-insulated detached house requires about 35,000 kilowatt hours of energy per year to heat it. A solar collector of the size on the Mississauga house would be able to supply about half of the heat needed. **1980** *Solar Energy* XXV. facing p. 1 (*caption*) Giant parabolic dish solar collectors.. have produced efficiencies of 71 per cent at 750°F operating temperature. **1704** J. HARRIS *Lex. Techn.* I, *Argyrocomus*, a Silver-coloured Comet differing very little from the *Solar Comet, except that it is of a brighter Silver colour. **1833** T. BROWN *White's Selborne* 227 *note*, Mr. Mark Watt has invented a very.. interesting instrument, which he calls the heliastron, or *solar compass. **1621** BURTON *Anat. Mel.* III. iv. I. i, We must,.. as Ficinus aduiseth us, get vs *solar eyes, spectacles as they that looke on the Sunne. **1938** *Nature* 17 Sept. 500/2 It would.. scarcely be permissible to deduce from the single observation of Carrington.. that the three phenomena, *solar flare, radio fade-out and.. magnetic disturbance, were associated. **1957** *Practical Wireless* XXXIII. 722/1 Solar flares are shortlived, sudden increases in the intensity of the surface brightness in the neighbourhood of sunspots. **1979** C. KILIAN *Icequake* vii. 120 Your plane's electronics go bonkers now and then when another solar flare hits. **1924** M. E. MOREAU *U.S. Patent 1,479,923* The primary object of the present invention is to provide a new and improved *solar furnace for producing an intense heat to be used for scientific purposes. **1951** *Bull. Amer. Ceramic Soc.* XXX. 163/1 A new and important instrument for high-temperature research is the recently developed solar furnace, which, by using the radiant energy of the sun, is able to produce extremely high temperatures in a small area. **1974** *Encycl. Brit. Micropædia* IX. 330/3 Because of its unique ability to heat materials for long periods without contamination, the solar furnace has become an important tool in high-temperature research. **1979** J. F. KREIDER *Medium & High Temp. Solar Processes* vi. 232 (*caption*) White Sands solar furnace showing the single heliostat on the right, the concentrator on the left, and flux control shutters in the center. **1741** A. MONRO *Anat. Nerves* (ed. 3) 57 This great *Solar Ganglion. **1977** *Whitaker's Almanack 1978* 1058/1 The window wall was designed to contain outer sheets of brown *solar glass. **1978** J. MCNEIL *Consultant* iii. 55 The Waterman building soared in dark grey metal and matching tinted solar glass. **1946** *Fortune Mag.* Apr. 166 *Solar houses will be erected in forty-eight states. **1957** *Economist* 28 Sept. 1027/1 The Massachusetts Institute of Technology is building a series of 'solar houses'. **1976** *Toronto Star* 24 Jan. E1/2 At Provident House, another experimental solar house now being built in King Township, the storage tank contains 60,300 gallons of water. **1841** *Mechanics' Mag.* 16 Jan. 34 The invention of the '*Solar Lamp' is due to Mr. Jeremiah Bynner, of Birmingham, by whom it was patented in 1837. **1887** CAROLINE HAZARD *Mem. J. L. Diman* iii. 54 A bright solar lamp shedding its rays around the room. **1870** G. W. COX *Myth. Aryan Nations* I. iv. 53 Of this vast mass of *solar myths, some have emerged into independent legends, others have furnished the groundwork of whole epics. **1970, 1976** *Solar neutrino unit [see *SNU* s.v. S 4a]. **1980** *McGraw-Hill Yearbk. Sci. & Technol.* 397/1 The low rate, if attributed to solar neutrinos, would correspond to a neutrino capture rate in the tank of 0·41 ± 0·07 per day. To compare this rate to [*sic*] the theory, one expresses the neutrino capture rate in solar neutrino units... The rate corresponds to 2·2 ± 0·4 SNU. **1864** *Intell. Obs.* IV. 91 The more volatile [portion] being set apart as *photogen*, and the less as **solar* oil. **1868** WATTS *Dict. Chem.*, *Solar Oil*, a name applied in commerce chiefly to the heavier portions of petroleum and shale-oil. **1962** *Listener* 29 Nov. 902/1 The probe was first instructed to 'find the Sun'—by means of sun-sensors on the bottom of the vehicle and on the '*solar paddles'. **1968** *New Scientist* 2 May 230/2 An even greater increase in power can be obtained by adding solar paddles to the stabilised platform. **1964** *IEEE Trans. Aerospace* II. 770/1 The *solar panel was set on a surface plate with a piece of frosted glass flush against the end of the panel. **1968** *Times* 16 Oct. 8/8 The spacecraft has large solar panels. **1974** P. DICKINSON *Poison Oracle* i. 13 The roof offered the widest possible expanse to the solar panels that provided much of the energy for the palace's gadgetry. **1976** *Pract. Householder* Nov. (Heating Suppl.) 23/2 The past summer .. produced astonishingly high air temperature and sunshine hours so that reservoir temperature and storage tank levels rose and solar panels heated the water quickly. **1800** HENRY *Epit. Chem.* (1808) 184 They yield a *solar phosphorus, called, from its discoverer, Homberg's phosphorus. **1815** J. SMITH *Panorama Sci. & Art* II. 331 The phenomena of the solar phosphori seem to militate against this idea. **1978** *Sci. Amer.* Apr. 149/1 The *solar pillar, a commoner phenomenon, is a vertical shaft of light extending upward from the sun. **1962** *Listener* 29 Nov. 902/1 The *solar plasma (commonly called 'solar wind'), which consists of low-energy charged particles which continually stream outward from the Sun. **1972** A. HEWISH in C. P. Sonett et al. *Solar Wind* vii. 477 Radio waves traversing the solar plasma are scattered by irregularities of plasma density. **1771** *Encycl. Brit.* I. 254/2 Branches of the *solar or cæliac plexus, formed by the eighth pair and intercostals. **1830** R. KNOX *Béclard's Anat.* 346 The union of the nervus vagus of the right side and the solar plexus. **1872** MIVART *Elem. Anat.* x. (1879) 404 The solar plexus.. behind the stomach. **1961** *Sci. News Let.* 12 Aug. 106/2 Instead of using vast expanses of expensive mirrors, a *solar pond traps heat in shallow water. **1971** *Sci. Amer.* June 127/1 The hot, salty water is selectively withdrawn from the solar ponds and used to drive a generator. **1979** *Nature* 11 Jan. 91/2 A solar pond is a water-filled pond, 1–2 m deep, with a blackened bottom for greater heat absorption and a gradually increasing salt concentration towards the base to eliminate convection, which is the main cause of heat loss. **1960** *Daily Tel.* 18 Aug. 16/2 (*heading*) *Solar pools as rival to nuclear power stations. **1975** *Globe & Mail* (Toronto) 15 Dec. 2/8 Scientists have failed to find a way of releasing the potential energy at the bottom of solar pools where water approaches the boiling point. **1979** *Arizona Daily Star* 5 Aug. (Advt. Section) 20/2 Featuring solar pool, putting green, horse facilities & country atmosphere. [**1908** *Sci. Amer.* 8 Feb. 97/1 (*heading*) A new solar power plant.] **1915** *Jrnl. R. Soc. Arts* LXIII. 564/1 *Solar power was quite within the range of practical matters. **1956** *Sci. Amer.* July 97/2 Any attempt to produce solar power means collecting the energy falling on a large area. **1976** *Times* 26 Mar. (Energy Suppl.) p. vi/4 If an equal number of existing houses were converted, domestic solar power could then substitute for about 4 per cent of Britain's energy needs. **1889** *Anthony's Photogr. Bulletin* II. 281 The two first *solar prints that were made in New York in 1853 or 1854. **1879** *Cassell's Techn. Educ.* II. 275 The *Solar Reflector.. enables us to reflect the solar ray into any piece of apparatus or room, suitably situated. **1960** *Aeroplane* XCIX. 693/1 Another interesting concept which has not yet really undergone feasibility determination is that of the *solar sail. With this device, a space 'ship' may some day be able literally to sail through interplanetary space. **1978** *Listener* 6 July 13/3 The 'solar sail' makes space travel in the inner solar system very cheap. **1960** *Aeroplane* XCIX. 744/1 The subject of *solar-sailing. **1973** C. SAGAN *Cosmic Connection* xxiii. 162 Solar sailing, the use of the pressure of sunlight and of the protons and electrons in the solar wind for tripping through the solar system. **1861** J. S. MUSPRATT *Chem., Theoret., Pract., & Analytical* II. 906/1 This Onondaga *solar or coarse salt is unsurpassed.. in the world. **1950** *Thorpe's Dict. Appl. Chem.* (ed. 4) X. 844/2 Some solar salt-factories produce high-quality table-salt by re-dissolving solar salt in water, purifying the resultant brine, and then evaporating it. **1972** *Times* 16 Oct. 19/7 Ventures ranging from solar salt to uranium. **1704** J. HARRIS *Lex. Techn.* I, **Solar Spots*. See *Spots of the Sun*. **1854** BREWSTER *More Worlds* v. 96 The solar spots, which are now universally admitted to be openings in the luminous stratum. **1882** *Encycl. Brit.* XIV. 312 A solid, glistening, and crystalline residue, known in commerce as '*solar stearin', which is useful in candle making. **1946** W. R. P. DELANO *U.S. Patent 2,413,101* (*heading*) *Solar still with nonfogging window. **1970** *Guardian* 15 Jan. 11/2 At the end of 1969.. the Clan McIlwraith sailed.. for Mombasa, carrying a prefabricated solar still for Aldabra, a lonely coral atoll in the Indian Ocean. **1979** *Solar Energy* XXIII. 271/1 The basin-type pitched roof solar still is the commonest and cheapest. *a* **1704** LOCKE *Elem. Nat. Phil.* iii. (1754) 8 Our *solar system consists of the sun, and the planets, and comets moving about it. **1715** tr. *Gregory's Astron.* (1726) I. 132 The common Centre.. of the Solar System. **1842** *Penny Cycl.* XXII. 197/1 We are now to state the relative dimensions of the Solar System in a rough manner. **1812** WOODHOUSE *Astron.* viii. 55 The *Solar Tables give the Sun's longitude. **1819** *Rees's Cycl.* VIII. 3 U, The remedy we have proposed for the inaccuracy of Mr. Ferguson's *solar and lunar wheels. **1958** *Physical Rev.* CX. 1448/1 The geomagnetic field can be penetrated to a considerable depth by tongues of ionized gas from the *solar wind. **1969** *Times* 22 July (Moon Rep.) p. iii/6 Buzz is erecting the solar wind experiment now. **1977** D. HARSENT *Dreams of Dead* 21 Unimaginable, the solar winds roared through space, putting the earth awry. **1978** PASACHOFF & KUTNER *University Astron.* viii. 227 (*caption*) The solar wind causes the wavy streaming of the tails of comets.

**8.** *Comb.*, as ***solar-charged***, ***-diluvian***, ***-form***, ***-generated***, ***-spotted***, ***-terrestrial*** adjs.; ***solar-microscope*** vb.; **solar-heated** *a.*, heated by means of the sun's rays; equipped with a solar heating system; also **solar-heat** *v. trans.* (also *absol.*); **solar heating**, heating by means of the sun's rays, esp. when utilized for water or space heating; also *attrib.*; **solar-powered** *a.*, using power derived directly from the sun's rays.

**1968** G. M. B. DOBSON *Explor. Atmos.* (ed. 2) xi. 195 The effect of the earth's magnetic field on the solar-charged particles is to deflect them back, away from the earth. **1803** G. S. FABER *Cabiri* I. 249 Ogygi-San is equivalent to the solar-diluvian god. **1789** T. TAYLOR *Proclus* (1792) II. 271 When she proceeds from reason to the object of imagination, she naturally obtains a solar-form body. **1978** *N.Y. Times* 30 Mar. A-14/6 The costs of solar-generated electric power currently did not 'stand up' in comparison with other energy sources. **1952** AYRES & SCARLOTT *Energy Sources—Wealth of World* xv. 208 Houses can be solar-heated completely without fuel when the mean atmospheric transmissivity is above 55 percent. **1977** *National Observer* (U.S.) 8 Jan. 8/4 When solar heating a house, the calculations become more complex. **1979** *Sunset* Apr. 132/1 (Advt.), The *Poolsaver* Automatic Solar Pool Cover solar heats and thermal insulates. By day *Poolsaver* absorbs solar energy. **1950** *Heating & Ventilating Engineer* XXIV. 148/1 The practicability of employing solar-heated air as a source of heat in removing moisture from a dehumidifying agent. **1956** *World Symposium on Applied Solar Energy* 107/2 The first solar-heated house was built in 1939 at M.I.T. as part of the Godfrey L. Cabot Solar Energy Conversion Research Project. **1977** *Time* 24 Jan. 19/1 Carter and Mondale will watch the parade in front of the White House from a 60-ft. solar-heated reviewing stand. **1903** C. H. POPE *Solar Heat* i. 43 Another patent for solar-heating devices was obtained ..from the British Government. **1951** *Archit. Rev.* CIX. 291/1 A limited supply of hot water is provided by solar heating systems on the roof of each ward block. **1958** *Times Rev. Industry* Feb. 94/1 The chief advantage claimed for solar heating, compared with other methods, is that the region of high temperature is localized, and contamination of material, while in the molten state, can thus be avoided. **1968** R. A. LYTTLETON *Mysteries Solar Syst.* v. 175 No serious effects of solar heating could be expected at such a distance from the sun, though some intense local heating on [*sic*] the particles through collisions could occur. **1977** 'E. TREVOR' *Theta Syndrome* iii. 43 David Pryor, a solar heating engineer. *a* **1849** POE *Mrs. Browning* Wks. 1864 III. 403 A nature.. solar microscoped into poetry. **1959** *Time* 26 Oct. 58/2 The satellite is shaped like a gyroscope... It squeals like a bagpipe as it signals from two transmitters—one powered by a chemical battery, the other solar-powered. **1978** *Illustr. London News* Nov. 19/2 The Administration succeeded in gaining agreement for.. conservation measures, including tax relief for householders insulating their homes or for installing solar-powered systems. **1881** *Nature* XVIII. 237 The curve of solar-spotted area. **1946** *Nature* 7 Sept. 329/1 Study of precise solar-terrestrial relationships has been a major Smithsonian activity for many years. **1966** *McGraw-Hill Encycl. Sci. & Technol.* I. 619/2 Solar physics.. overlaps with geophysics in the consideration of solar-terrestrial relationships.

**B.** *sb.*[1] **1.** *Photogr.* A solar print.

**1889** *Anthony's Photogr. Bulletin* II. 281 Each unbeknown to the other was making life size solars for the American Institute Fair.

**2.** A solar lamp.

**1853** M. J. MCINTOSH *Lofty & Lowly* i. 9 The astral lamp —solars were not yet invented— .. throws its rays on cases filled with richly gilded volumes. **1976** H. R. F. KEATING *Filmi, Filmi, Inspector Ghote* iii. 29 We are using a great number of different lights for different purposes in filming, Five-Ks, Two-Ks, Sunspots, Solars, Babies.

**3.** *U.S.* Solar radiation as a source of domestic or industrial energy.

**1976** *National Observer* (U.S.) 17 July 9/2 What one is trying to do is go out and demonstrate for the building industry that solar is here for heating buildings. **1978** *Tucson* (Ariz.) *Mag.* Dec. 77 Passage of the solar tax credits by Congress will result in the rapid growth of solar in Southern Arizona.

**solar**, *sb.*[2] Alteration (after prec.) of SOLA *sb.*

**1859** CORNWALLIS *New World* I. 332 A large Stock of Solar Hats, suitable for Port Curtis. **1859** J. LANG *Wand. India* 183 He was dressed in a pair of large jack-boots, corduroy breeches, a shooting-coat, and a solar helmet. **1879** MRS. A. E. JAMES *Ind. Househ. Managem.* 20 One solar topee pith hat.

**solar(e**, variants of SOLLAR *sb.*[1]

**so'lari-**, combining form of L. *sōlāri-s* SOLAR *a.*

**1803** G. S. FABER *Cabiri* I. 204 The solari-diluvian Noah. *Ibid.* II. 369 The solari-agricultural patriarch. **1816** —— *Orig. Pagan Idol.* II. 106 The solari-tauric Mithras.

**solarimeter** (səʊlə'rɪmɪtə(r)). [f. SOLARI- + -METER.] A device for measuring the total intensity of radiation incident upon a surface.

**1926** L. GORCZYŃSKI in *Monthly Weather Rev.* LIV. 381/2 To these direct-reading instruments, designed for both solar and sky radiation, we propose to give the name of 'Solarimeters' in order to distinguish them from pyrheliometers, which serve generally for radiation intensity of the sun at normal incidence. **1940** *Sci. Abstr.* XLIII. 383 The radiative properties of the snow cover were investigated... Two solarimeters were employed. **1969** MCINTOSH & THOM *Essent. Meteorol.* vii. 105 A solarimeter .. detects both direct and diffuse solar radiation. *Ibid.*, An inverted solarimeter detects the short-wave radiation reflected by the surface.

**solarism** ('səʊlərɪz(ə)m). [f. SOLAR *a.* + -ISM.] The theory of solar myths; excessive use of, or adherence to, this theory.

**1885** GLADSTONE in *19th Cent.* XVIII. 700 Solarism—a system which prides itself above all things on its exhibiting the primitive state of things. **1886** —— *Ibid.* XIX. 21 It is to this monopolising pretension that I seek to apply the name of solarism. **1889** MAX MÜLLER *Nat. Relig.* xiii. 349 Fetishism, totemism, animism, solarism, shumanism.

**solarist** ('səʊlərɪst). [f. SOLAR *a.* + -IST.] One who holds the theory of solar myths, esp. to an excessive degree.

**1885** *Standard* 30 Oct. 3/1 The use made by the solarists of far-fetched etymologies. **1895** MAX MÜLLER *Chips* IV. Pref. p. xiii, I have been represented again and again.. as a Solarist, as teaching that the whole of mythology is solar.

**solarium** (sə'lɛərɪəm). Pl. solaria. [L. *sōlārium*, f. *sōl* sun. Cf. SOLLAR *sb.*[1]]

**1.** A sun-dial.

**1842** *Smith's Dict. Gk. & Rom. Antiq.* 487/2 This solarium being made for a different meridian. *Ibid.*, The number of solaria which have been discovered.. in Italy. **1880** L. WALLACE *Ben-Hur* 142 Lifting his eyes from the solarium set under the aplustre for reference in keeping the course.

**2. a.** A terrace, balcony, or room exposed to the rays of the sun, now *spec.* one used for the purpose of treating illness by means of sun-baths; a sun-parlour. Also *fig.* Chiefly *N. Amer.*

**1891** E. EGGLESTON *Faith Doctor* xxvi. 289 My brother kept a health-lift a few years ago.., and then he had a blue-glass solarium. **1894** *The Voice* (N.Y.) 20 Sept., The solariums on the roofs of the houses of the ancient Greeks and Romans testify to the benefits obtained by them from sun baths. **1904** J. WELLS *Life J. H. Wilson* xvi. 139 The Church was a sort of spiritual solarium. **1911** G. W. JAMES *Grand Canyon* iii. 20 It is called the solarium or sun-parlor. **1968** *Globe & Mail* (Toronto) 17 Feb. 45 (Advt.), Separate dining room with adjoining solarium—both overlook ravine. **1978** *Morecambe Guardian* 14 Mar. 25/1 (Advt.), Large.. working kitchen, frontal solarium, porches [ect.].

**b.** A room equipped with sun-lamps.

**1960** *Playboy* Mar. 70/2 There's a poolside soda fountain, as well as bar, massage rooms, steam cabinets, solaria, and Finnish baths. **1972** *Homes & Gardens* Sept. 20/2 The uncertain perils of the British climate.. have finally induced one of our hotels to install a solarium. **1978** *Cornish*

*Guardian* 27 Apr. 16/3 (Advt.). Heated swimming pool, sauna, solarium.

**solarization** (ˌsəʊləraɪˈzeɪʃən). [f. SOLARIZE *v.* + -ATION.]

**1. a.** *Photogr.* The injurious effect produced by over-exposing a negative to the action of light, resulting in the reversal of the image; a similar effect produced by over-printing sensitized paper, etc. More generally, the progressive reduction in the developable density of an emulsion (corresponding to a progressive darkening of the picture) following initial exposure beyond a certain light intensity.

**1853** R. HUNT *Man. Photogr.* 149, I have been enabled to discover at what degree of intensity of light the effect called Solarization is produced. **1854** HADOW in *Jrnl. Photogr. Soc.* I. 191 My pictures were constantly liable to solarization (or darkening of those parts that ought to be whitish). **1889** *Anthony's Photogr. Bulletin* II. 267 Their entire freedom from halation or solarization. **1948** JAMES & HIGGINS *Fund. of Photogr. Theory* iv. 59 The curve representing developable density as a function of exposure passes through a maximum. If the exposure is increased beyond that which produces the maximum density, a decrease in developable density will occur... This effect is known as solarization. **1956** *Focal Encycl. Photogr.* 1079/1 Strictly speaking, solarization is the reversal of the image on a film or plate by an extreme amount of over-exposure... The term has by this time almost lost its original meaning. Nowadays it is applied..to the technique for producing a partly reversed image by exposing the negative to unsafe light during development—actually, the phenomenon known as the Sabattier effect. **1961** *Jrnl. Photogr. Sci.* IX. 195/1 Solarization..is usually attributed to a reduction in the number of developable grains. **1973** *SPSE Handbk. Photogr. Sci. & Engin.* vi. 427 The addition of halogen acceptors..to the emulsions prevents solarization.

**b.** *Photogr.* = *Sabatier effect* s.v. SABATIER. Also called PSEUDO-SOLARIZATION.

**1937** *Photogr. Jrnl.* LXXVII. 21/1 If the original negative consists of a well-exposed object on an unexposed background, the fogging of the background with the second exposure does not come right up to the edge of the image, but leaves a clear white line... This line was formerly only of academic interest. Recently, however, it has been used as the basis of the so-called 'Solarization Process'. **1939** [see *Sabatier effect* s.v. SABATIER]. **1956** [see sense a above]. **1969** M. J. LANGFORD *Adv. Photogr.* xi. 233 The image exposure relative to solarisation fogging exposure makes decisive changes in tone rendering. **1977** J. HEDGECOE *Photographer's Handbk.* 278 The solarization, below, was produced by the black and white method, but with the solarized positive printed onto color negative film, using a colored light source.

**c.** *Plant Physiol.* [a. G. *solarisation* (A. Ursprung 1913, in *Ber. d. Deut. bot. Ges.* XXXV. 57).] The inhibition of photosynthesis as a result of prolonged exposure to high light intensities.

**1925** W. STILES *Photosynthesis* vii. 97 Solarization appears to have no permanently injurious effect on the activities of the leaf. **1960** B. S. MEYER et al. *Introd. Plant Physiol.* (1963) xi. 219 Solarization effects appear to result principally..from the phenomenon of photo-oxidation, in which leaves consume oxygen in the light, and use it in the oxidation of certain cell constituents. **1974** R. G. S. BIDWELL *Plant Physiol.* vii. 170 Very high light intensity may be damaging to plants—solarization is the photodestruction of chlorophyll by excessive illumination. Shade plants are more susceptible to solarization than are sun plants.

**d.** The alteration of the light transmission characteristics of glass as a result of prolonged exposure to visible or ultraviolet light.

**1928** W. W. COBLENTZ *Let. Circular U.S. Bureau Standards* No. 235 (3rd revision) 4 A sample [of glass] which had been in a hospital window..for a year was found to have a transmission of 25 per cent at 302 mμ... Further exposure to the quartz mercury arc reduced the transmission but little, showing that solarization was complete. **1955** E. B. SHAND *Glass Engin. Handbk.* xvi. 145/2 Mercury-vapor lamps utilize a number of glasses of different properties... Because of their exposure to strong ultra-violet radiations, the glasses must be capable of resisting solarization effects to a large degree. **1972** F. L. HARDING in L. D. Pye et al. *Introd. Glass Sci.* 422 Long term exposure to the ultraviolet radiation in sunlight can result in another type of coloring phenomenon known as solarization. If certain multivalent ions..are present in the glass, their valence can be changed by ionizing radiation.

**2.** (See quot.)

**1882** *Nature* 13 July 246 On the instant after the exposure of the eye to strong light,..—solarisation I will call it.

**solarize** (ˈsəʊləraɪz), *v.* [f. SOLAR *a.* + -IZE. So F. *solariser*.]

**1.** *trans.* To affect or modify by the influence of the sun or the action of its rays; *spec.* in *Photogr.*, to injure by over-exposure to light. More widely, to affect by solarization of any kind.

**1853** C. GOODYEAR *Gum-Elastic* I. vii. 114 Another effect yet more remarkable in the treatment of gum-elastic, is that of the sun's rays upon it. When combined with sulphur, and exposed to the action of the sun..it becomes solarized, or divested of its adhesive quality. **1855** BAILEY *Mystic* 13 Then, solarized, he pressed onwards to the sun. **1892** *Photogr. Ann.* II. 74 An exposure to bright sunlight, sufficient to solarise the [film]. **1950** *Jrnl. Amer. Ceramic Soc.* XXXIII. 257/2 From the general appearance of the glasses that were solarized in the mercury arc it became obvious that the depth of color change was slight. **1966** LACOW & LATHROP *Photo Technol.* xix. 229/2 To solarize a negative the developing process is carried on in a normal manner for about 2/3 to 3/4 of the developing time [etc.].

**2.** *intr.* To be affected by solarization.

**1868** M. C. LEA *Photography* 137 (Cent. Dict.), It is a familiar fact that iodide of silver solarizes very easily. **1906** *Westm. Gaz.* 13 Oct. 14/2 There is a tendency on the part of the paper to solarise when printed by direct sunlight. **1955** E. B. SHAND *Glass Engin. Handbk.* xvii. 159 Some glasses will discolor perceptibly, or 'solarize' when exposed to ultra-violet radiations. **1977** *Jrnl. Photogr. Sci.* XXV. 103/2 The emulsion investigated..was a chlorobromide, halide-exchange emulsion which had a low surface/internal speed ratio and which solarized readily.

Hence **ˈsolarized** *ppl. a.*, **solarizing** *ppl. a.* and *vbl. sb.*

**1853** C. GOODYEAR *Gum-Elastic* I. vii. 112 The use of acid gas in connection with the solarizing process. **1870** *Eng. Mech.* 18 Mar. 661/2, I..find..more than one solarised place. **1882** *Nature* 13 July 246 Portions of the solarised eye that had escaped the solarising action. **1890** PULSFORD *Loyalty to Christ* I. 188 Much in the same way that the solarized atmosphere of our world becomes inbuilt..in the trunk and branches of a tree. **1923** B. D. W. LUFF *Chem. of Rubber* i. 18 Articles made with such a composition, when exposed to the sun's rays, a process termed solarising, were said to lose their adhesive nature. **1969** *Focal Encyl. Photogr.* (rev. ed.) 1415/2 The solarizing exposure itself must also be sufficient. Too little leads to..only a partially solarized image with weak border outlines. **1977** Solarized [see SOLARIZATION 1 b]. **1977** R. HATTERSLEY *Photogr. Printing* ii. 20 It involves exposing a print twice: once in the usual way and once with a solarizing light source after development has gone about halfway.

†**ˈsolarly**, *adv.* *Obs.*$^{-1}$ [Irreg. f. L. *sōl-us* alone.] By itself, without addition.

**1657** TOMLINSON *Renou's Disp.* 392 The Succe of Liquorice is..successfully assumed solarly for the affections of the lungs.

†**ˈsolary**, *a.* *Obs.* [ad. L. *sōlāri-s*: see -ARY[2] and cf. SOLAR *a.*]

The various senses of the sb. *solary* given by Blount *Glossogr.* (1656) are merely copied from Cooper's *Thesaurus* s.v. *Solarium* (two entries). In the second ed. of Sir T. Browne's *Pseud. Ep.* VI. xii. *solary* is a misprint for *salary*.

**1.** Of or belonging to, pertaining to, connected with, the sun.

**1588** J. HARVEY *Disc. Probl.* 117 The euent of the said Solarie defect shal be but according to the quantity of the Eclipse it self. **1602** DOLMAN *La Primaud. Fr. Acad.* (1618) III. 721 So likewise doth the shadow of the earth hinder the moone of the solary illumination. **1646** SIR T. BROWNE *Pseud. Ep.* 345 Beside the solary Iris which God shewed unto Noah, there is another Lunary. **1664** POWER *Exp. Phil.* Pref. 16 The Solary Atoms of light. **1716** M. DAVIES *Athen. Brit.* III. *Diss. Physic* 29 Their Statues were..adorn'd with Solary Rays, and crown'd at last with Celestial Beams.

**b.** Of time: = SOLAR *a.* 1 b.

**1614** RALEIGH *Hist. World* II. iii. §6. 255 Ve Adar was an intercalarie Moneth, added..to make the Solarie and Lunarie yeare agree. **1615** H. CROOKE *Body of Man* 336 That is called a Solarie moneth wherein the Sunne runneth through thirty degrees of the Zodiacke. **1697** PRIDEAUX *Life Mahomet* (1716) 73 The Mahometan Year falling eleven Days short of the Solary.

**c.** (See quot.)

**1651** FRENCH *Distill.* vi. 189 There is found a certaine stone in Bononia, which some call a golden Marcasite, some a Solarie Magnes, that receives light from the sun in the day time, and gives it forth in the dark.

**2.** *Alch.* and *Astrol.* Of the nature of the sun; subject to the influence of the sun.

**1605** TIMME *Quersit.* I. xi. 47 There are starres which haue their most colde and moyst spirites;..others, most hote and drie, as the Solarie, and Martialls. **1643** SIR T. BROWNE *Relig. Med.* I. 114 That mysticall mettle of gold, whose solary and celestiall nature I admire. **1651** FRENCH *Distill.* vi. 189 Crude gold..is by them not only called Solary but Sol..it selfe. **1671** BLAGRAVE *Astrol. Pract. Phys.* 156, I do usually cause the patients to wear a select number of solary herbs gathered at the hour of the Sun.

**3.** Pre-eminent like the sun.

**1651** FRENCH *Distill.* Ded. A iij b, This Art of Alchymie is that Solary art, which is more noble then all the other six arts, and sciences.

**Solaster** (səˈlæstə(r)). *Zool.* [mod.L., f. *sōl* sun + *aster*, Gr. ἀστήρ star.] A genus of starfishes, typical of those having more than five rays; a member of this genus, a sun-star.

**1841** E. FORBES *Brit. Star-fishes* 110 The Solasters are suns in the system of sea-stars. **1842** *Penny Cycl.* XXIII. 17/1 Those which have the body radiated,..comprising the genera *Solaster* and *Pentaster* of De Blainville. **1860** WRAXALL *Life in Sea* ix. 224 The Solasters, or Sun-stars, have only two rows of suckers in each furrow.

†**soˈlation**[1]. *Obs. rare.* [a. OF. *solacion*, *solation*, or ad. L. type **sōlātio*, f. *sōlāri* to console.]

**a.** Rejoicing, joy. **b.** Consolation.

**1483** CAXTON *Gold. Leg.* 436/3 In thys tyme of pasque our moder holy chyrche..maketh Solacyon for the resurrexyon of Jhesu cryste. ?*a* **1500** *Chester Pl.* (E.E.T.S.) I. 21 Now sithe I am thus..set in my solation, a biglie blisse here will I builde. **1757** MRS. GRIFFITH *Lett. Henry & Frances* (1767) II. 10 There are pleasures and solations indulged by Providence to every stage of life.

**solation**[2] (sɒˈleɪʃən). *Physical Chem.* [f. SOL *sb.*[6] + -ATION.] The change of a gel into a sol. So **soˈlate** *v. intr.*, to undergo solation; *trans.*, to convert into a sol.

**1915** [see GELATION[2]]. **1926** *Jrnl. Morphol. & Physiol.* XLI. 351 Locomotion in Amoeba is associated with gelation and solation. **1951** *New Biol.* X. 16 The plasmagel must presumably contract at the hind end, as well as solating. **1958** *Jrnl. Cellular & Compar. Physiol.* LII. 270 The plasmagel system of the intact *Amoeba* undergoes complete solation under suitably high pressure. **1977** *Jrnl. Cell Biol.* LXXIV. 909/1 The gel solated slowly at room temperature after forming. *Ibid.* 921/1 Elevated KCl concentrations that solate the *Dictyostelium* gel.

‖**solatium** (səˈleɪʃɪəm). [L. *sōlātium*, *sōlācium*, related to *sōlārī* to console: cf. SOLACE *sb.*[1]]

**1.** A sum of money, or other compensation, given to a person to make up for loss or inconvenience.

**1817** SCOTT *Fam. Lett.* 27 May, It was a *bonus* or *solatium* paid to them by the gentry, to prevent their rising and righting themselves at the expense of the aristocracy. **1853** W. JERDAN *Autobiog.* III. 81 A weekly solatium was arranged to the extent of the author's own suggestion. **1883** *Pall Mall G.* 1 Oct. 8/2 Another offered by way of a solatium in the hour of his disappointment the vacant trusteeship of a well-known charitable institution.

**2.** *spec.* in *Law.* A sum of money paid, over and above the actual damages, as a solace for injured feelings.

**1832** AUSTIN *Jurispr.* (1879) I. xv. 397 The ground of action being not only indemnification for damage, but also solatium for bereavement. **1863** *Illustr. Lond. News* 1 Aug. 103 [A] traveller for a firm of Staffordshire china merchants obtained £500 damages and £300 solatium at a jury trial.

**solay**, error for SPLAY *v.*

**1726** *Gentl. Angler* 156 Solayed, a Technical Term for a Bream being cut up. **1787** BEST *Angling* (ed. 2) 169 *Solay a bream*, cut him up. **1853** BADHAM *Prose Halieut.* (1854) 343 He gobbets trout,..solays bream, and sides haddock.

‖**Solazzi** (soˈlattsi). [The name of the Italian maker.] *Solazzi juice*, a kind of liquorice.

**1861** BENTLEY *Man. Bot.* 527 Various preparations of liquorice are commonly kept in the shops, and sold under the names of..extract of liquorice, Solazzi juice, &c. **1882** *Encycl. Brit.* XIV. 688/1 The quality best appreciated in the United Kingdom is made in Calabria, and sold under the names of Solazzi and Corigliano juice.

†**sold**, *sb.*[1] *Obs.* Forms: α. 4–5 **soude**, **sowde**, 5 **sood-**, **sowede**; 4–5, *Sc.* 8–9 **soud**, **sowd**. β. 5 **sawd(e**. γ. 5–6 **sould(e**. δ. 5–7 **sold**, 6 **solde**. [a. OF. *soude*, *soulde* (more commonly *soudee*, *souldee*, etc.), = It. and Pg. *soldo*, Sp. *sueldo*:—L. *solidum*, acc. sing. of *solidus*: see SOL *sb.*[3] and SOU. (The mod.F. *solde* is due to Italian influence.) Cf. MDu., MLG., MHG. *solt*, Du., G., Da., Sw. *sold*.]

**1.** Pay (esp. of soldiers), wages, salary.

α. *c* **1330** R. BRUNNE *Chron. Wace* (Rolls) 14234 Payen & Cristen knyght..at soud he held. *c* **1380** WYCLIF *Sel. Wks.* III. 146 Fle covetise of godis, and be payed wiþ ȝoure sowdes. **1440** *Paston Lett.* I. 41 My Lord Tresorer graunted the seid vij. c. marc to my Lord of Norffolk, for the arrerag of hys sowde qwyl he was in Scotland. **1475** *Bk. Noblesse* (Roxb.) 31 That the said chieftein must pay his men of soude ..justly. *a* **1513** FABYAN *Chron.* (1811) 519 For the wage & sowde of the Nauaroys and Englysshemen.

β. **1402** *Pol. Poems* (Rolls) II. 94 These paroche preestes that ministren the sacramentis, for a certen sawd bi ȝeer. *c* **1450** *King Ponthus & Fair Sidone* i. (1897) 1, I schal paye their sawde for thre yer.

γ. **1429** *Wills & Inv. N.C.* (Surtees, 1835) 79 Ilk preest hauyng for his sould by yeer viij mrc'. **1473** EDW. IV in *State P. Hen. VIII*, VI. 8 For contentation of a yerely soulde. **1542** PAGET *Ibid.* IX. 198 He myndeth..to borowe the sould of 20000 men for a yere, if He canne obteyne it. **1550** T. NYCOLLS *Thucidides* 216 To paye the soulde or wages of the sayd armye.

δ. **1438** *Bk. Alexander Gt.* (Bann. Cl.) 61 Serue ȝour soldis of the King. *c* **1470** HENRY *Wallace* II. 209 Thi worthi kyn may nocht the saiff for sold. **1544** HARVEL in *St. Papers Hen. VIII*, IX. 619 For lacke of payment of his solde. **1590** SPENSER *F.Q.* II. ix. 6 Were your will, her sold to entertaine, And numbred be mongst knights of Maydenhed. **1601** BP. W. BARLOW *Defence* 131 Lying in campe under sold and pay, fighting as souldiers. **1630** *R. Johnson's Kingd. & Commw.* 163 Lastly, there is the Sold, or pay of 50000 foot.

**2.** *Sc.* A sum or quantity (orig. of money or gold).

**1513** DOUGLAS *Æneid* III. i. 91 With a grete sold of gold fey Priamus Secretlie vmquhile send this Polidorus..to Polymnestor. **1710** RUDDIMAN *Gloss. Douglas' Æneis* s.v. *Sold*, Scot. *Sowd*, as a sowd of money, *i.e.* a great sum. **1795** *Statist. Acc. Scotl.* XIV. 74 *note*, The tradesmen are paid.. with a certain sum or quantity of victual annually agreed on, called *soud*. **1828** MOIR *Mansie Wauch* ii, A sowd of toddy was swallowed. **1845** STILL *Cottar's Sunday* 172 They wha grip Great souds o' hidden treasure.

†**sold**, *sb.*[2] *Obs.*$^{-0}$ In 5 sowde. [? a. OF. **soude* (Pg. *solda*):—L. *solida*: cf. prec. and SOLD *v.*[2]] Solder.

*c* **1440** *Promp. Parv.* 466/1 Sowde, metel, *consolidum solidarium*.

†**sold**, *sb.*[3] *Obs.*$^{-1}$ In 6 soulde, 6–7 solde. [ad. It. *soldo*: cf. SOLD *sb.*[1] and SOL *sb.*[3]] A sol or small coin.

**1547** BOORDE *Introd. Knowl.* xx. 171 They haue myttes, duccates, & soldes [in Hungary]. *Ibid.* xxxvii. 216 In syluer they haue [in Turkey] Aspers and Souldes; and ther be som Souldes that be brasse. **1599** HAKLUYT *Voy.* II. 108 Their horsemen have onely sixe soldes Venetian a day.

†**sold**, *v.*[1] *Obs.* Forms: α. 4–5 **soud-**, 5 **sowd-**, **sawd-**. β. 5–6 **sould(e**, 6 **sowld-**, **sold-**. [f. SOLD *sb.*[1]: cf. OF. *soud-*, *soldeier*. But perh. partly due

to OF. *soudre, saudre, souldre, soldre*:—L. *solvĕre* to pay.]

**1.** *trans.* To pay; to enlist or retain for service by payment. Also *fig.*

α. c**1386** Chaucer *Prioress's T.* 128 O martir soudit to virginite. **1393** Langl. *P. Pl.* C. xxii. 431 Imparfit is þe pope þat..soudeþ hem þat sleeþ suche as he sholde saue. **1456** Sir G. Haye *Law Arms* (S.T.S.) 53 He fand..grete quantitee of gold.., With the quhilk he sawdit grete nowmer of men of armys. a **1470** Gregory *Chron.* in *Hist. Coll. Citizen Lond.* (Camden) 106 To have men sowdyd withe hym ayenst the Duke of Orleans.

β. **1418** in Riley *Lond. Mem.* (1868) 665 Normandye, þere to be soulded or waged wiþ þe Kyng. **1456** Sir G. Haye *Law Arms* (S.T.S.) 143 [He sent] gold in Almayne for to soulde men of armes, for the space of ane ȝere. **1523** Cromwell in Merriman *Life & Lett.* (1902) I. 37 The harmys whiche we ourselffes showld susteyn in sowldyng of so great an army. **1550** T. Nycolls *Thucidides* 221 b, Who..soulded or waged aboutes three houndred souldyars.

**2.** *intr.* To serve as a paid soldier or mercenary.

**1564** Haward *Eutropius* I. 9 Virginius at that time soulded for honest wages..againste the Latines.

Hence †'**solding** *vbl. sb.*$^{1}$ *Obs.*

**1475** *Bk. Noblesse* 29 For lak of good provisions bothe of artillery and ordenaunce for the werre and soudeyng to be made in dew season. *Ibid.* 83 Whiche..were not usid of custom nothing to pay..to the souding of men of armes.

†**sold**, *v.*$^{2}$ *Obs.* Forms: α. 4 soud-, 4–6 sowd-; 4–5 sawd-. β. 5 sould-, 5–6 sold-. [ad. OF. *souder, sauder, soulder*, = Prov. *soudar, soldar*, Sp. and Pg. *soldar*, It. *sodare*:—L. *solidāre* to make solid or firm, f. *solidus* SOLID *a.*]

**1.** *trans.* To solder; to fasten with solder; to unite (metal) by soldering (†or welding).

c**1350** *Leg. Rood* (1871) 77 Dauid made A serkell al of siluer brade, And bad þat it suld sawded be All obout þe haly thre [= tree]. **1398** Trevisa *Barth. De P.R.* xvi. xciii. (Tollem. MS.), Leed may not be sone sowdid to leed noþer to bras, noþer to yren with oute tyn. c**1425** *Seven Sages* (P.) 2023 Than thay sayen at the laste How the piler stode in bras, And with sowdyng sowdyt faste. **1485** Caxton *Chas. Gt.* 103, xxx arches of marble,..whyche ben soulded wyth leed and cyment. **1506** *Acc. Ld. High Treas. Scot.* III. 330 Item, to..ane man that sowdit ane gwn of the Kingis schip, xiiij s.

**2.** *transf.* To unite firmly or closely; *spec.* in medical use (see SOLDER *v.* 2).

**1388** Wyclif *Acts* iii. 7 And anoon hise leggis and hise feet weren sowdid togidere; and he lippide, and stood. **1398** Trevisa *Barth. De P.R.* vii. xxxi. (Bodl. MS.), The couȝe suffreþ not þe wounde to be closed and isawded. a **1425** tr. *Arderne's Treat. Fistula* 45 She trowed..for to haue souded þe place of þe fynger in whiche þe bone..stode bifore. **1502** Arnolde *Chron.* (1811) 170 Som men late the roete end of the vyne be vncutt..til it be sowded with the chiri tree.

**b.** *intr.* To close or heal. (Cf. SOLDER *v.* 6.)

a **1425** tr. *Arderne's Treat. Fistula* 46, I putte-to vnguentum viride vpon stupes, and þe fynger bigan for to soude. *Ibid.* 84 þe sidez of þe wounde byganne for to soude or conglutinate.

Hence †'**solding** *vbl. sb.*$^{2}$ *Obs.*

**1398** Trevisa *Barth. De P.R.* xvi. xix. (Bodl. MS.), [Glue] haþ vertu of drawinge & sowding. c**1425** [see sense 1 above]. **1447–8** *Durh. Acc. Rolls* (Surtees) 275 Pro..le sowdyng unius olle eree. **1508** *Acc. Ld. High Treas. Scot.* IV. 137 Item, for solding..of the Kingis salt fat, ij s. **1533** *Dunmow Churchw. MSS.* fol. 17 b, To the makyng or sowdyng of the bell.

*attrib.* **1341–2** *Ely Sacr. Rolls* II. 117 In factura..soudinghirnes pro fabricacione vitri. **1399** *Fabric Rolls York Minster* (Surtees) 18 Item ij soudyngirens et j helme ferri.

**sold** (səʊld), *ppl. a.* Also 6 solde, *Sc.* sauld. [pa. pple. of SELL *v.*]

**1.** Disposed of by sale. Also *fig.*

**1535** Coverdale *Deut.* xviii. 8 Besydes that which he hath of the solde good of his fathers. **1591** *Exch. Rolls Scotl.* XXII. 162 Thair is to be deducit the rest restand upoun the comptar at the fute of the sauld victuellis. **1637** Rutherford *Lett.* clxv. (1862) V. 384 Except that Christ's grace hath bought such a sold body, I know not what else any may think of me. **1652** in Miss Hickson *Ireland 17th Cent.* (1884) I. 298 As the examt.'s husband told her when he came home next day, and withal said we were 'a sold people'. **1722** De Foe *Col. Jack* xi, The very same low distressed condition as he was in, I mean a sold servant. **1853** Fairbairn *Typology Scripture* I. 339 The sold, hated, and crucified One. **1862** Thornbury *Life of Turner* I. 271 A volume of sketches of sold pictures.

**2.** Denoting a sale effected.

**1862** *Parthenon* 16 Aug. 497/1 Those pictures which have 'sold' tickets. **1891** *Law Times* XCI. 193/1 There was no clause about arbitration on the sold note sent by the brokers to the plaintiffs.

**3.** *slang.* Tricked, deceived. Cf. SELL *v.* 9.

**1876** 'Mark Twain' *Tom Sawyer* xvii. 147 As the 'sold' congregation trooped out they said they would almost be willing to be made ridiculous again.

**4.** *sold-out.* **a.** *colloq.* Bankrupt; exhausted, 'finished'.

**1859** Hotten *Dict. Slang* 98 *Sold up, or out*, broken down, bankrupt. **1958** F. C. Avis *Boxing Ref. Dict.* 104 *Sold out*: said of a boxer who is nearly exhausted. **1973** *Observer* 3 June 25/6 At the end of last season he was physically and mentally sold out. **1977** *New Yorker* 4 July 24/1 A pool player who was vaguely associated with the big-money barracudas and sold-out types hanging back in the pool-hall shadows.

**b.** That has sold all its stock, seats, etc.

**1903** Kipling *Five Nations* 191 The sold-out shops and the bank And the wet, wide-open town. **1960** *Farmer & Stockbreeder* 8 Mar. 60/1 (*heading*) Sold-out at Bath. All available stand space at the Bath and West Show..has been sold. **1975** *High Times* Dec. 21/1 They..are a soldout attraction wherever they perform. **1976** *Early Music* Oct. 447/2 Bodies whose present idea of an 18th-century orchestra is a group playing Haydn and Mozart badly to a sold-out Festival Hall.

†**soldad(e**, Anglicized forms of next. *Obs.*

**1634** Shirley *Example* iii. i, He's marching up the stairs, with another soldade. *Ibid.* iv. i, I do not like this soldad's embassage. **1652** —— *Doubtful Heir* v. E vij b, This 'tis to deal with Soldades.

‖**soldado** (sɒl'dɑdo). Also 6–7 souldado, 9 *erron.* soldada. [Sp. (and Pg.), = It. *soldato* (whence F. *soldat*), f. *soldo* (Sp. *sueldo*) military pay: see SOLD *sb.*$^{1}$]

**1.** A soldier. Also *attrib.*

**1586** J. Hooker *Hist. Irel.* in *Holinshed* II. 105/2 This roisting Rutterkin wholie then standing on the soldado hoigh. **1592** Greene *Upst. Courtier* Wks. (Grosart) XI. 247 To be terrible like a warrior and a Soldado. **1612** Chapman *Widdowes T.* v. i, [Will] No bootie serue you sir Soldado But my poore sister? **1698** Fryer *Acc. E. India & P.* 142 Seizing it by Force with Three Files of Soldadoes. **1819** Scott *Leg. Montrose* ii, Neither Wallenstein nor Pappenheim..would likely listen to the objurgations of boors or burghers against any commander or soldado. **1840** Hor. Smith *Cromwell* I. 268 Sad-visaged and morose soldadoes in suits of buff tarnished and soiled by service. **1864** Burton *Scot Abr.* II. ii. 136 The otherwise single-minded and honourable soldado.

**2.** The South American heron.

**1852** Th. Ross tr. *Humboldt's Trav.* II. xx. 255 On the summits of those [rocks] situated near the Orinoco, flamingos, soldados, and other fishing birds perch.

**3.** The squirrel-fish (*Holocentrus ascensionis*) of the West Indies, etc. (*Webster's Suppl.* 1902.)

**soldan** ('sɒldən). Now *arch.* or *Hist.* Forms: α. 3–7, 9 soudan (4 -en, -on, 6 -ane), 4–6 sowdan (4 -ane, 5 -on, 6 -en, -own), 6 sowdeyn, 6–7 -aine (7 -ayne). β. 4, 6 saudan (4 -ayn, 6 -ant), 4 sawden, 5–6 sawdon, 6 -ant, -an, sodan, -en. γ. 4, 6–7 souldan (5 -one, 7 -en), 6 sowldan, 7 sauldan, suldan. δ. 4- soldan (6 -ane, 7 -ian). [a. OF. *soudan, sodan, souldan, soldan* (also *-ain, -ant*), = Prov. *soudan, saudan*, Cat. *soldá*, Sp. *soldan*, Pg. *soldão*, It. *soldano* (med.L. *soldanus*), ad. Arab. *sulṭān*: see SULTAN.]

**1.** The supreme ruler of one or other of the great Muslim powers or countries of the Middle Ages; *spec.* the Sultan of Egypt.

The *Soldan* is sometimes contrasted with the (*Great*) *Turk* and with the *Sophy* of Persia.

α. **1297** R. Glouc. (Rolls) 10901 þe soudan somdel uor fere Triwes wiþ him nom. **1338** R. Brunne *Chron.* (1810) 140 Bode com..How þe fals soudan destroied alle þe lond. c**1380** Wyclif *Sel. Wks.* III. 375 þei harmen Cristen men more cruely þen þo Soudon of Sarazenes. c**1440** *Generydes* 3942 The Sowdon went ayeyn to his disporte. **1470–85** Malory *Arthur* v. viii. 174 With hym he fond slayne the Sowdan of Surrey. **1513** More *Rich. III* (1883) 79 In a stage play all the people know right wel that he that playeth the sowdayne is percase a sowter. **1568** Grafton *Chron.* II. 87 Feare of treason..to be wrought betwene Saladine the Soudane and king Richard. **1832** tr. *Sismondi's Ital. Rep.* xi. 257 James, who, with the aid of the soudan of Egypt,..seized the crown from his sister and the duke.

*attrib.* **15..** *Droichis Part of Play* 5 in *Dunbar's Poems* (S.T.S.) 314 A sargeand out of Sowdoun land.

β. **13..** *E.E. Allit. P.* B. 1323 Emperour of alle þe erþe & also þe saudan. **1432–50** tr. *Higden* (Rolls) VI. 43 The Sawden and duke of Turkes, the grete malle of Cristen peple. c**1500** *Melusine* 275 My right redoubted lordes the Sawdants of Barbarye & of Damaske. c**1511** *1st Eng. Bk. Amer.* (Arb.) Introd. 31/2 As the[y] wryte to the Sodan, than gyueth he them that they dyssyre.

γ. **1390** Gower *Conf.* I. 180 Thei gon to Barbarie ayein, And ther the Souldan for hem sente. **1475** *Bk. Noblesse* 11 The souldone of Babiloyne had waged hym to doo it. **1587** Greene *Penelope's Web* Wks. (Grosart) V. 181 That Saladyne the mighty Souldan of Ægipt. **1592** Warner *Alb. Eng.* viii. xliii. 207 Richard..wonne Cyprus, Syria, and Ierusalem, debelling quite the Sowldan from his land. **1630** Brathwait *Eng. Gentlem.* (1641) 364 This is all that Souldan Saladine hath left of all his ensignes. **1632** Lithgow *Trav.* vii. 321 The Mamaluks..were the guard of the Suldans, as the Iannizaries are to the great Turke.

δ. **1390** Gower *Conf.* I. 245 The grete Soldan thanne of Perse. **1432–50** tr. *Higden* (Rolls) VI. 313 The Soldan of Babilony. **1562** Whitehorne *Ord. Souldiers* 38 The Turke by meanes of artillerie, againste the Sophi and the Soldan, hathe had victory. **1594** Greene *Selimus* 566 Wks. (Grosart) XIV. 216 We that haue..stript th' Egyptian soldan of his camp. **1614** Raleigh *Hist. World* ii. 199 He plainely shewes, that the Soldans of Egypt were not Lords of the Countrie. **1667** Milton *P.L.* i. 764 Where Champions bold..at the Soldans chair Defi'd the best of Panim chivalry To mortal combat. **1708** J. Philips *Cyder* ii. 83 The Soldan, as he fled, Oft call'd on Alla. **1742** Hume *Ess. & Treat.* i. iv. (1777) I. 29 The soldan of Egypt, or the Emperor of Rome, might drive his harmless subjects..against their sentiments and inclination. **1849** J. A. Carlyle *Dante, Inf.* v, She held the land which the Soldan rules. **1864** Bryce *Holy Rom. Emp.* xii. (1889) 182 It [a letter] bids the Soldan withdraw at once from the dominions of Rome.

†**b.** The governor of a town. *Obs.*$^{-1}$

**1660** F. Brooke tr. *Le Blanc's Trav.* 16 A little turret..where the treasure belonging to the Soudan or Governour of the Town is kept.

**2.** With *a* and pl. A Muslim ruler; one having the rank of sultan.

α. **13..** *K. Alis.* 1781 (W.), Darie..holdith riche gestnyng, Of dukes, eorles, amiraylis, And of soudans. c**1380** Wyclif *Wks.* (1880) 98 More [harm] þan ony soudon or sarsyn or oþer men of wrong bileue. **1430–40** Lydg. *Bochas* ix. xxii (1554) 29 Mightye princes Soudans twayne. c**1470** *Rauf Coilȝear* 898 Thow slane hes oft,..of my Counsingis, Soudanis and sib men. **1572** Bossewell *Armorie* ii. 108 The malignitie and cruell attemptates of the deuelishe rablement, and wicked sowdanes.

γ, δ. **1390** Gower *Conf.* III. 145 A Soldan whilom was of Perce. **1483** *Cath. Angl.* 348/2 A Soldan, *soldanus*. **1598** Hakluyt *Voy.* I. 55 We saw in the Emperours court..many great Soldanes receiuing no due honour. **1601** R. Johnson *Kingd. & Commw.* 195 Who..made paiment to his souldans and soldiers. **1611** Cotgr., *Sultan*, a Sultan, or Souldan. **1795** Southey *Maid of Orleans* ii. 337 Cæsars and Soldans, Emperors and Kings,..here they were all. **1840** Macaulay *Ess., Ranke's Hist.* (1851) II. 136 He could no longer hope to strike down gigantic soldans. **1884** Tennyson *Becket* iv. ii, I had it from an Arab soldan.

'**soldanate.** [ad. It. *soldanato* (med.L. *soldanatus*): see prec.] The power of the Sultan.

**1878** tr. *Villari's Machiavelli* i. vii. II. 191 There is no longer any difference between the Papacy and the *Soldanate*.

†**soldanel, -ell**, Anglicized forms of next.

**1562** Turner *Herbal* (1568) 72 Brassica marina..may be called in englyshe, soldanell, or see folefot. **1760** J. Lee *Introd. Bot.* App. 327 Soldanel, *Soldanella*. *Ibid.*, Soldanel of the Shops, *Convolvulus*. **1786** J. Abercrombie *Arrangem.* in *Gard. Assist.* 54/2 *Convolvulus*, or bindweed.., (*Soldanella*) or sea soldanel minor.

‖**soldanella** (sɒldə'nɛlə). *Bot.* Also 9 *erron.* soldinella. [mod.L., a. It. *soldanella* of obscure origin; hence also Pg. *soldanella*, F. *soldanelle* (16th cent.). Cf. prec.]

†**1.** A species of convolvulus or bindweed, *Convolvulus soldanella*. *Obs.*

**1579** Langham *Gard. Health* 607 Soldanella purgeth downe all kind of watrish humors. **1597** Gerarde *Herbal* ii. ccxciii. 691 Soldanella hurteth the stomacke, and troubleth the weake and delicate bodies which do receiue it in powder. **1601** Holland *Pliny* II. 51 The sea Colewort (otherwise named Soldanella) of all others purgeth most forcibly. **1676** *Phil. Trans.* II. 629 On the Bay-side, Soldanella or Sea-Scurvygrass [grows] in great plenty. **1697** *Ibid.* XIX. 397 Two Purging Sea Bindweeds, call'd in our Shops Soldanella. **1712** tr. *Pomet's Hist. Drugs* I. 89 Soldanella..is a Species of Bindweed or a small Plant that sends forth slender, winding, reddish Stalks.

**2.** A primulaceous plant of the genus *Soldanella*, native in Alpine districts.

**1629** [see MOONWORT 5]. **1688** Holme *Armoury* ii. 111/2 Mountain Soldanella is a bell-flower..of a fair blew. **1867** *Cornhill Mag.* Jan. 54 Masses of purple primulas, yellow pansies, and delicate little soldinella. **1882** *Garden* 3 June 385/3 Soldanellas in leaf soil..have grown well.

‖**soldanelle.** [Fr. *soldanelle.*] = prec. 2.

**1887** Ruskin *Præterita* II. 190 The ledges of the Salève, all aglow with primrose and soldanelle.

†**soldaness.** *Obs. rare.* In 4–5 sowdones, 7 souldannesse. [f. SOLDAN + -ESS$^{1}$.] A sultaness.

c**1386** Chaucer *Man of Law's T.* 274 This sowdones, whom I thus blame and warry, Let pryvely hire counseil gon his way. **1621** Molle *Camerar. Liv. Lib.* iv. i. 222 The Souldannesse, wife to Amurath the third.

**soldanrie.** *arch.* [f. SOLDAN + -RIE, -RY, perh. after OF. *soudanerie.*] Sultanship.

**1825** Scott *Talism.* xx, You might learn to lay aside this scorn of Soldanrie.

†**soldat.** *Obs.* Also 7 soldatt, soldate. [a. F. *soldat*: see SOLDADO.] A soldier.

α. **1584** Hudson *Du Bartas' Judith* 452 Alarm, soldats, alarme. **1591** Jas. I *Lepanto* 664 There a Chieftaine shrillie cries, And Soldats doth command. **1638** Sir T. Herbert *Trav.* (ed. 2) 127 Within the Castle wall are raisd a hundred houses, stored with men, most part soldatts. **1668** R. L'Estrange *Vis. Quev.* v. (1702) 117 Every little Whore takes upon her to be a great Lady;..every Huff, to be a Soldat.

β. **1652** *Roxb. Ball.* (1891) VII. 479 A Soldate on a bench sleeping. **1662** J. Wilson *Cheats* iv. iv, By the faith of a Soldate, and a man of Arms, I will.

**soldatesque** (sɒldə'tɛsk), *sb.* and *a.* [a. F. *soldatesque* (see prec. and -ESQUE), ad. It. *soldatesco* military, *soldatesca* soldiery.]

†**A.** *sb.* The military. *Obs.*

a **1648** Ld. Herbert *Hen. VIII* (1683) 618 The legates in Trent (now free from the Soldatesque) advised how to delay the time. *Ibid.* 635 The Gentry and Soldatesque of the Kingdom.

**B.** *adj.* Of or pertaining to a soldier; soldier-like, soldierly.

**1840** *Tait's Mag.* VII. 417 There was more fire and genuine soldatesque Burschicosity about this old cavalry officer than in any mad French conscript. **1861** Pearson *Early & Mid. Ages* 31 They were subject only to their own tribunals, and encouraged by these in a soldatesque license against civilians.

‖**solde.** *rare.* [F. *solde*: see SOLD *sb.*$^{1}$] Pay.

**1852** *Tait's Mag.* XIX. 549 The Mansfeld is riding by wood and by wold And his troopers take service that's better than solde. **1879** G. Meredith *Egoist* xix, The fellow may well be a faithful soldier and stick to his post, if he receives promise of such a solde.

**solde** (small coin): see SOLD *sb.*$^{3}$

**soldear**, obs. form of SOLDIER *sb.*

**solder** ('sɒldə(r), 'səʊdə(r)), *sb.*$^{1}$ Forms: α. 4–5 soudur, 5 -ure, -our, sowdur, -owre; 4–5 soudre, 5–6 souder, 5–7 (9 *dial.*) sowder (5 -ere, 6 soweder); 9 *dial.* sowther. *β.* 5 sawdur, -yr, 6 -yer; 5 sawd(e)re, 6 sawder (7 -ter), 6–7 saudre, 7 sauder. *γ.* 6–8 soder (7 soader, sodar), 7– sodder; 6 sother, 7 soather. *δ.* 5 souldour, 6–7 soulder (6 sowl-). *ε.* 7 soldure, 7– solder. [a. OF. *soud-*, *saud-*, *soldure* (cf. It. *saldatura*), f. *souder*, etc., SOLD *v.*²

American dictionaries favour the pron. ('sɑːdə(r) = Brit. 'sɒdə(r)). Smart (1836 and 1840) gives only ('sɔːdə(r)).]

**1.** A fusible metallic alloy used for uniting metal surfaces or parts.

Various kinds are distinguished by specific names, as *hard*, *soft* (see sense 4), *white*, *copper*, *gold*, *silver*, *pewterer's*, *plumber's solder*.

*α.* **1374** *Durh. Acc. Rolls* (Surtees) 581 In stangno emp. pro soudur, vi.*s.* *c* **1400** *York Minster Fabric Rolls* (Surtees) 20 Et in iij dos' tyn emptis pro soudre, viii.*s.* viii.*d.* *c* **1485** *E.E. Misc.* (Warton Cl.) 82 To make sowder of tynne. **1513** DOUGLAS *Æneid* VIII. vii. 140 Thai mydlit and thai mixt this feirful souder. **1547** in J. R. Boyle *Hedon* (1875) App. 137 To the plomer for xxx. lb. of soweder. **1603** *Vestry Bks.* (Surtees) 52 For five pounde and a half of sowder to mende the leads. **1829** BROCKETT *N.C. Gloss.* (ed. 2), *Sowther*, solder.

*β.* **1466** *Mann. & Househ. Exp* (Roxb.) 323 Item, for ij. li. saw[d]ere, xij. d. **1492–3** *Rec. St. Mary at Hill* (1905) 187 For a ll. di. of sawdyr to sowdyr þe same pype, xij d. **1539–40** in *Devon N. & Q.* Oct. (1903) 238 Payed for xv. li. of sawdyer for the worke, v.s. **1566** in Peacock *Eng. Ch. Furniture* (1866) 141 An old crwet whearof was made sawder for the glass windowes. **1602** *Shuttleworths' Acc.* (Chetham) 143 To the plumber, for xx pound of pewter to be sawter, .. xˢ. **1667** PRIMATT *City & C. Builder* 70 Sawder is about eight pence or nine pence a pound.

*γ.* **1575** GASCOIGNE *Wks.* (1587) 308 When cutlers .. hide no crackes with soder nor deceit. **1576** *Act 18 Eliz.* c. 15, No Goldsmith .. shall .. use noe Sother .. more then ys necessarie. **1612** STURTEVANT *Metallica* (1854) 36 All compounded mettles of the same kind, as, Pewters, Belmettles, Sodars. **1637** in *Parish Bks. St. Julians, Shrewsbury* I. 27 (MS.), Received for 9 lbs. of Sodder, 3s. **1660** BOYLE *New Exp. Phys. Mech.* xx. 146 We caus'd a skilful Pewterer .. to close it up .. with Soder. **1726** LEONI *Alberti's Archit.* II. 17b, The cramps .. must be fastened into the sheets with hot sodder. **1750** BLANCKLEY *Naval Expos.* 155 Sodder, used by the Plumber for soddering of Pipes.

*δ.* **1428** *Engl. Misc.* (Surtees) 1 Þat nane of þat crafte wirke any lede amang other metaill, bot yf yt be in souldour. **1530** PALSGR. 725, I sowder a metall with sowlder, *je soulde*. **1574** in Feuillerat *Revels Q. Eliz.* (1908) 242 For Leade and sowlder with woorkmanshipp. **1611** COTGR., *Souldure*, .. the knot of soulder which fastens the lead of a glasse window. **1685** BOYLE *Effects of Motion* viii. 99 A gaping crack, which he was fain to fill up with soulder.

*ε.* **1724** SWIFT *Prometheus* Wks. 1751 III. II. 150 Goldsmiths say, the coarsest stuff Will serve for solder well enough. **1756** LUCAS *Ess. Waters* I. 50 He .. assured himself by .. closing it well with solder. **1812** SIR H. DAVY *Chem. Philos.* 400 Lead is used as an ingredient in various solders. **1843** HOLTZAPFFEL *Turning* I. 432 The solders must be necessarily somewhat more fusible than the metals to be joined. **1873** E. SPON *Workshop Rec.* Ser. I. 364/2 The solder will run into the places which have been touched by the spirit of salt.

**2.** *transf.* Any binding or uniting substance. *rare.*

**1582** STANYHURST *Æneis*, etc. (Arb.) 136 Theare chariots doe trauayle .. By reason of the riuer knit with a frostye soder. **1610** HOLLAND *Camden's Brit.* I. 699 The limestone which is the very soader and binder of all morter.

**3.** *fig.* A quality, principle, etc., which unites in any way; a bond or means of union.

*γ.* **1599** SANDYS *Europæ Spec.* (1632) 45 This [being] the end of strifes particular, this the soder of publike peace. **1638** CHILLINGW. *Relig. Prot.* I. iii. §43. 151, I am at my wits end .. to find some glue, or sodder, .. to tye this antecedent and this consequent together. **1662** HIBBERT *Body Divinity* II. 149 The ground or band of the union, the sodder that knit them together.

*ε.* **1611** SPEED *Hist. Gt. Brit.* IX. xiv. §38. 757/2 Money the Cement and soldure of all such actions, .. vtterly fayles. **1649** G. DANIEL *Trinarch., Hen. IV*, cccxviii, This Prodigie to Sence, when Elements (The Solder of the World) combat themselues. **1742** R. BLAIR *Grave* 89 Friendship! .. Sweetener of life, and solder of society! **1863** TYNDALL *Heat* i. 8 Illustrating a principle which forms the very solder of Nature.

**4.** *soft solder*: **a.** A common kind of solder, usually made from tin and lead.

**1594** PLAT *Jewell-ho.* III. 1 Sodered verie close with safte Soder. **1771** *Encycl. Brit.* III. 616/2 Take silver, five penny-weight; brass, four penny-weight; melt them together for soft solder, which runs soonest. **1823** P. NICHOLSON *Pract. Build.* 406 The solder generally made use of by the plumber is called soft solder. **1843** HOLTZAPFFEL *Turning* I. 434 The soft-solder mostly used, is 2 parts tin and 1 part lead. **1858** GREENER *Gunnery* 207 More than five thousand pairs of barrels made and put together with soft solder only.

**b.** Flattery; = *soft sawder* (see SAWDER *sb.*).

**1845** J. R. PLANCHÉ *Golden Fleece* II. 23 Begone, I charge you, none of your soft solder: Your downy words don't weigh with me a feather. **1848** LOWELL *Biglow P.* Ser. I. Wks. (1884) 226 The people [get] their annooal soft-sodder an' taxes. **1863** READE *Very Hard Cash* xliii, She .. sent in a note explaining who she was, with a bit of soft solder. **1869** *Pall Mall G.* 20 Sept. 3 It is so evident .. that a square-jawed ruffian .. will yield like a cherub to soft-solder and coaxing.

**5.** [From the vb.] An act of soldering.

**1733** CHEYNE *Eng. Malady* I. x. (1734) 97 A Tinker can mend a Hole in a Brass Pot .. by a Soder or Patch.

**6.** *attrib.* and *Comb.*

**1858** SIMMONDS *Dict. Trade, Solder-manufacturer*, a maker of cement for metals. **1873** RICHARDS *Operator's Handbk.* 123 For solder joints the silver solder of jewellers is convenient. **1875–84** KNIGHT *Dict. Mech.* s.v., Solder-casting, -cutter, -cutting, -mold. **1895** *Daily News* 24 Dec. 7/1 A powerful solder-pounding machine. **1964** R. F. FICCHI *Electr. Interference* v. 72 (*caption*) Input and output connections .. are solder-sealed terminals and A-N connector. *Ibid.* x. 193 A third method of connecting bus bars is by bolting two soldercoated bus bars, and applying heat to make a continuous connection. **1965** *Wireless World* Sept. 464/2 This unit .. is available with either solder pins for direct connection .. or with valve base pins.

† **solder**, *sb.*² *Obs.*⁻¹

Perh. for *soldier* in sense 4 of that word.

**1603** SIR C. HEYDON *Jud. Astrol.* vii. 187 That out of wheat there should spring vp darnell, solders, and smuttie geare.

**solder** ('sɒldə(r), 'səʊdə(r)), *v.* Forms: *α.* 5–6 (9 *Sc.*) souder, 5–7 soudre; 5–6 (9 *Sc.*) sowder (5 -yr, 6 sowdr-); 8–9 *north.* and *Sc.* sowther, 9 souther. *β.* 6–7 sauder (6 savdr-), 6–7 (9) sawder (7 sawdr-). *γ.* 5–8 soder (7 sodr-), 7 (9 *dial.*) soader (7 soadr-), 7–8 (9 *dial.*) sodder (7 soddr-); 6–8 (9 *dial.*) sother. *δ.* 6–7 soulder. *ε.* 6– solder (6–7 soldr-). [f. SOLDER *sb.*¹ Cf. SOLD *v.*²]

**1.** *trans.* To unite or fasten by means of a metallic solder. Also with *in*, *on*, *together*, *up*, etc.

*α.* *c* **1420** *Chron. Vilod.* 1447 And alle þe mynyssionys of þat nayle .. Weron soudryd fast aȝayne withouȝt ony fayle. **1492–3** *Rec. St. Mary at Hill* (1905) 187 A ll. di. of sawdyr to sowdyr þe same pype, xij *d.* **1495** *Trevisa's Barth. De P.R.* XVI. xcii. (W. de W.) 584 Leed may not be sone soudryd to leed nother to brasse. **1530** PALSGR. 725/2, I wyll sowder this pipe of leede. **1551** RECORDE *Cast. Knowl.* (1556) 59 These plates .. shoulde haue bothe the endes soudred togither. **1613** M. RIDLEY *Magn. Bodies* 85 As though they were tied, glued, and soudred together. **1816** SCOTT *Antiq.* xxvii, It's best to say ye're an auld tinkler, .. for maybe the gudewife will hae something to souther. **1829** BROCKETT *N.C. Gloss.* (ed. 2), *Sowther*, to solder. **1882** *Jamieson's Sc. Dict.* IV. 352/2 *To sowther, souther*, to solder.

*β.* **1511** [see the *vbl. sb.* 1] **1560–1** in Willis & Clark *Cambridge* (1886) II. 628 For mendinge and sawderinge the cunditte pipe. **1570** LEVINS *Manip.* 78 To Sau[d]er, *conferruminare*. **1605** [see the *vbl. sb.* 1].

*γ.* **1561** EDEN *Arte Nauig.* II. xx. 41b, A .. wyre .. made fast or sothered in it. **1601** DOLMAN *La Primaud. Fr. Acad.* 513 As tin doth soder and join togither broken copper. **1660** BOYLE *New Exp. Phys. Mech.* Proem 11 There was soder'd on to the shank of the Cock .. a Plate of Tin. **1684** R. WALLER *Nat. Exp.* 51 When we had first put it through the Ring M, sodered to a small Iron Rod. **1743** in Willis & Clark *Cambridge* (1886) I. 296 To George the goldsmith .. for sothering on a pece of brass. **1769** *Phil. Trans* LIX. 70, I then soddered the wires of each jar to the rod which connected them.

*δ.* **1535** COVERDALE *Dan.* ii. 43 Like as yron wil not be souldered with a potsherde. **1565** COOPER *Thesaurus*, *Agglutino*, .. to soulder together. **1659** LEAK *Water-wks.* 7 Let the pipe DC be souldered to the bottom passing through it. **1687** A. LOVELL tr. *Thevenot's Trav.* III. 39 Having most exactly bent the Ring, they Soulder the two ends of it together.

*ε.* **1594** NASHE *Unfort. Trav.* 59 Yᵉ tail of the siluer pipe stretcht it selfe into the mouth of a great paire of belowes, where it was close soldered. *a* **1700** EVELYN *Diary* 9 Sept. 1678, A plate of brasse soldered thereon. **1712** J. JAMES tr. *Le Blond's Gardening* 200 To the Conduit-Pipe is soldered an upright Pipe, .. and at the End of this Socket is likewise soldered the Brass-Nut. **1731** MILLER *Gard. Dict.*, *Lupulus* 4 G, This Bed is to be cover'd with large double Tin, solder'd together at each Joint. **1815** J. SMITH *Panorama Sci. & Art* II. 11 The end .. of the stop cock, is soldered or screwed into the end of the tube. **1858** LARDNER *Handbk. Nat. Phil.* 307 In this hole is soldered the mouth of another tin bucket. **1895** *Daily Chron.* 15 Jan. 6/7 One of the difficulties in the use of aluminium has been the trouble of soldering it.

**b.** *transf.* To unite firmly or closely, to cause to adhere strongly, by means of some substance or device.

**1601** HOLLAND *Pliny* II. 594 The mortar .. hath not that binding as it ought, and so the walls built therewith are not sodred accordingly. **1606** SHAKS. *Ant. & Cl.* III. iv. 32 As if the world should cleaue, and that slaine men Should soader vp the Rift. **1664** POWER *Exp. Phil.* I. 5 The Common Fly .. can at pleasure .. sodder and be-glew herself to the plain she walks on. **1839–47** *Todd's Cycl. Anat.* III. 243/2 Instances of the toes soldered together, as in the Horse. **1841** *Penny Cycl.* XXI. 158/1 The parietal bones are early soldered to the occipital.

† **2.** *Med.* To cause (wounds) to close up and become whole; to reunite (tissues or bones). *Obs.*

*α.* **1495** *Trevisa's Barth. De P.R.* XVI. xix. (Caxton) 559 Glewe hath vertue .. to soudre [*Bodl. MS.* soude] woundes and blotches. **1597** A. M. tr. *Guillemeau's Fr. Chirurg.* 23 b/1 The foresayed suture is commonlye healed together the seaventh day, and soudered.

*γ.* **1577** FRAMPTON *Joyful Newes* III. (1596) 94 Put into Sores, it healeth and sodereth them forthwith. **1639** T. DE GRAY *Expert Farrier* 341 The iuyce of salendine will conglutinat and sodder the tongue together being cut or wounded. **1656** RIDGLEY *Pract. Physick* 172 A Plaister of Ivy Gum sodders bones wonderfully. **1733** CHEYNE *Eng. Malady* I. x. (1734) 98 The Fluids .. to soder and repair their Wounds.

*δ.* **1600** SURFLET *Countrie Farme* II. xlii. 262 The leaues thereof are good to conglutinate and soulder together both outward and inward wounds. **1652** CULPEPPER *Eng. Physic.* 35 The juyce put into fresh or green wounds doth quickly 'soulder' up the lips of them together.

*ε.* **1628** FORD *Lover's Mel.* I. ii, As the one patches our tattered clothes, so the other solders our diseased flesh. **1769** *Phil. Trans.* LIX. 395 Inflammation solders up the mouths of these little vessels. *a* **1788** POTT *Chirurg. Wks.* II. 208 With a view to closing or soldering broken lymphatics.

**3.** *fig.* To unite, to cause to adhere, in a close, firm, or intimate manner.

*γ.* **1597** HOOKER *Eccl. Pol.* V. lxxvi. §9, I could easily declare, how all things which are of God, hee hath .. sodered as it were together with the glue of mutuall assistance. **1601** DENT *Pathw. Heaven* 83 These carnall worldlings which are fast sodred to the earth! **1642** D. ROGERS *Naaman* 133 Selfe soders matters of all sorts together. **1675** R. BURTHOGGE *Causa Dei* 39 'Tis .. Soul and Body Soder'd into one Compositum that sins. **1708** SWIFT *Sent. Ch. Eng. Man* Wks. 1751 IV. 66 The Presbyterians, Anabaptists, Independents, and other Sects did all .. unite and sodder up their several schemes to join against the Church.

*δ.* **1607** SHAKS. *Timon* IV. iii. 388 Thou visible God, That souldrest close Impossibilities, And mak'st them kisse. **1638** DRUMM. OF HAWTH. *Irene* Wks. (1711) 166 That Power and Frame, which in a Monarchy hath been joined and souldered together many Ages.

*ε.* **1589** *Pappe w. Hatchet* E iij, To the foure & twentie orders of knaues, thou maist solder the foure and twentie orders of fooles. **1646** J. HALL *Horæ Vac.* 98 Friendship .. of equalls is ever best soldered. **1744** E. MOORE *Fables for Ladies* xxii. 58 And, haply, use that precious metal To solder sexes, like a kettle. **1796** BURKE *Corr.* (1844) IV. 383 We have abdicated the crown of Corsica, which had been newly soldered to the crown of Great Britain. **1827** *Gentl. Mag.* XCVII. II. 62 To permit his Royal Patronage to be soldered on to the Bible-Society. **1862** LYTTON *Strange Story* I. 135, I clamped and soldered dogma to dogma in the links of my tinkered logic.

† **b.** To close or block *up* (the ear). *Obs.*⁻¹

**1648** J. BEAUMONT *Psyche* II. ii, No wretched Adder ever soder'd up His wilful ear with trustier cement.

† **c.** *absol.* To remain obdurately deaf. *Obs.*⁻¹

**1642** D. ROGERS *Naaman* 865 That paddle and adoe which you have made to soder and play the Hypocrite.

**4.** *fig.* To bring or restore to a sound or unimpaired condition; to repair, mend, patch up again.

**1607** HIERON *Wks.* I. 471 The more tender the loue, the more hard to be sodered, when it hath receiued a cracke. *c* **1640** J. SMYTH *Lives Berkeleys* (1883) II. 161 This peace was not so soundly on each part sawdred, but that afterwards it leaked at certaine crannells. **1697** C. LESLIE *Snake in Grass* (ed. 2) 179 Thou .. seek'st to sodder their Leaky Infallibility, that thou may'st Inherit it. **1704** SWIFT *T. Tub* ix, An art to sodder and patch up the flaws and imperfections of nature. **1786** BURNS *Twa Dogs* 216 The Men cast out in party-matches, Then sowther a' in deep debauches. **1818** SCOTT *Hrt. Midl.* xlvii, Under pretence that they have southered sin wi' marriage. **1857** GEN. P. THOMPSON *Audi Alt.* I. iii. 8 Fourteen thousand men are on their way to solder with slaughter what must have been the misdoings of somebody.

**b.** Similarly with *up*.

**1594** NASHE *Terrors of Night* Ep. Ded., Pale penurious beautie, which giues dull Painters store of gold to solder vp their leane dints of deformity. **1607** MARSTON *What You Will* I. i, A rout of crased fortunes, whose crakt states Gape to be sodderd up. **1699** GARTH *Dispensary* II. 20 And some would know the issue of their Cause, And whether Gold can sodder up its flaws. **1748** RICHARDSON *Clarissa* (1811) IV. 58 She must therefore choose to be mine, for the sake of soldering up her reputation. **1816** SCOTT *Antiq.* xxiv, But it was a' sowdered up again some gait, and the bairn was sent awa. **1837** CARLYLE *Fr. Rev.* II. v. i, The sad Varennes business has been soldered up.

**5.** *absol.* To perform the operation of uniting with solder.

**1588** PURFOOTE (*title*), Howe to Gylde, Grane, Sowder, and Vernishe. **1639** T. DE GRAY *Expert Farrier* 35 Handy-worke is to heat the iron well, to sodder well. **1715** tr. *Pancirollus' Rerum Mem.* II. vii. 316 One kind of it [mineral] is called Borax, or Green Earth, which the Goldsmiths solder with. **1771** *Encycl. Brit.* III. 616/2 To solder upon silver, brass, or iron. **1850** CARLYLE *Latter-d. Pamph.* IV. 4 Begin to hammer at it, solder at it, .. it will fall to sherds, as sure as rust is rust. **1875** KNIGHT *Dict. Mech.* 62/2 The Egyptians soldered with lead as long ago as the time of Thothmes.

† **b.** Of substances: To promote or cause close union; to serve as solder. *Obs.*

**1495** *Trevisa's Barth. De P.R.* VII. lix. (Caxton) 275 Medycynes that close and soudre and brede good flesshe. **1612** J. DAVIES (Heref.) *Muse's Sacrifice* Wks. (Grosart) II. 69/1 Surgions Bands doe pinch, to solder so. **1645** CALAMY *Indictment* 7 These are the glew that soders; these are the nerves and sinews that joyne a Kingdome together.

**6.** *intr.* To adhere, unite, grow together. Also *fig.*

**1470–85** MALORY *Arthur* XVII. iv. 695 He took the suerd and sette the pecys to gyders and they soudered as fayr as euer they were to fore. **1597** A. M. tr. *Guillemeau's Fr. Chirurg.* 12/1 They [bones] ioyne, and soulder (as it were) together agayne. *Ibid.* 23/1 If they [split lips] can not souder and ioyn, the one with the other. **1639** T. DE GRAY *Expert Farrier* 322 If the sinew or artery be broken, .. to cause it to soder or joyne againe. **1653** BLITHE *Eng. Improver Impr.* 121 Nor [will] the Turf have fitting time to sodder and work together before the dry weather comes. **1737** RAMSAY *Prov.* (1750) 126 Youth and eild never sowder well. **1776** G. WHITE *Selborne* lxx, The tree in the suffering part was plastered with loam ... If the parts coalesced and soldered together .. the party was cured. **1897–1901** in *Eng. Dial. Dict.*

**b.** Const. *with* (a person or thing).

**1641** MILTON *Prel. Episc.* 22 Wee .. take up there those cast principles which will soone cause us to soder up with them againe. **1647** N. BACON *Disc. Govt. Eng.* xlvii. 125 The Tripple Crown could never solder with the English, nor it with that. *c* **1680** R. MACWARD *Contend.* (1723) 4 Others also, with whom we must likewise souder, have been encouraged to repeat .. the same disloyal Practises.

**ˈsolderable,** *a.* [f. SOLDER *v.* + -ABLE.] Able to be joined by means of solder. So **solderaˈbility,** the property of being solderable.

**1949** *Iron Age* 8 Dec. 96/2 The solderability of electro-deposited lead-tin alloy remains excellent for at least 9 months under normal operating conditions. **1959** *Trans. Inst. Metal Finishing* XXXVI. 203 The solderability of various coatings of tin with lead, zinc, cadmium, and of cadmium and silver has been compared. **1961** WEBSTER, Solderable. **1967** E. R. WELLS in C. R. Martens *Technol. Paints, Varnishes & Lacquers* xiii. 214 The urethane single-package low solids..enamels..had the unique advantage of being solderable without removal from the ends of the wires to be joined. **1976** *Wireless World* Nov. 52/1 The transistor terminal pad was quite easily solderable. **1978** *BSI News* Mar. 7/1 The test methods included in the BS 9760 series cover solderability..of surface conductors.

**ˈsoldered,** *ppl. a.* [f. SOLDER *v.* + -ED[1].]

**1. a.** Joined by means of solder. Also with *up*.

**1599** B. JONSON *Cynthia's Rev.* II. ii, Hee will not depart with the waight of a sodred groat. **1725** *Fam. Dict.* s.v. *Reservatory*, Solder'd Pipes are no other than Sheets of Lead, which they bend and solder together at the Junctures. **1834–47** J. S. MACAULAY *Field Fortif.* (1851) 210 In a well-soldered tin or iron case. **1843** HOLTZAPFFEL *Turning* I. 433 All soldered works should be kept under motionless restraint for a period. **1887** *Encycl. Brit.* XXII. 240/2 Secured in closely fitting soldered-up tinned-iron boxes.

**b.** *soldered dot* (Building), a means of fastening sheet lead to woodwork, consisting of a mass of solder put in a depression in the lead after the latter has been fitted into a corresponding depression in the wood and a screw fixed through the bottom of it.

**1893** J. W. CLARKE *Lect. Plumbing* 70/1 Soldered dots never last for any great length of time and the lead invariably breaks away from them. **1930** P. MANSER *Plumbing & Gasfitting* VII. xxii. 1606 Soldered dots are not quite satisfactory as they hold the lead too rigidly, and where the load on them is heavy the screws work through due to the strain on them. **1966** G. E. EVANS *Pattern under Plough* iii. 51 A circle of plumber's black is painted round the outside of the hollow, partly to confine the soldered dot, and partly to give the whole a neat decorative finish.

**2.** *fig.* and *transf.* Patched up; closely united.

**1623** FLETCHER *Bloody Brother* II. i, A soder'd friendship Piec'd out with promises. **1667** MARVELL *Poems* (Grosart) I. 218 He felt His alt'ring form and soder'd limbs to melt. **1859** DARWIN *Orig. Spec.* xii. (1860) 392 The shrivelled wings under the soldered elytra of many insular beetles. **1887** G. MEREDITH *Ball. & Poems* 19 A rough ill-soldered scar..on his cheek-bone.

**ˈsolderer.** Also 6 soudrer. [f. SOLDER *v.* + -ER[1].] One who solders.

**1530** PALSGR. 273/1 Soudrer of metalles, *sovdevr.* **1611** COTGR., *Souldeur*, a Soulderer. **1881** *Instr. Census Clerks* (1885) 95 Smelter, Solderer. **1896** *Daily News* 6 July 2/6 Strike of Sardine Box Solderers.

**ˈsoldering,** *vbl. sb.* [f. SOLDER *v.*]

**1.** The action of joining or mending with solder.

**1466** *Paston Lett.* II. 268 To the glaser for takyn owte of ii. panys of the wyndows..and sowderyng new of the same, xxd. **1472–3** *Durh. Acc. Rolls* (Surtees) 247 Pro sowderyng unius le gutter plumb. **1495** *Trevisa's Barth. De P.R.* XVI. xix. (Caxton) 559 Glewe hath vertue of drawynge and soudrynge. **1511** *Nottingham Rec.* III. 335 Peid to Thomas Illyngworth for sawderyng of a gutter. **1580** FRAMPTON *Dial. Yron & Steele* 148 b, I doe not speake of the finenesse and delicatenesse that there is in sodering of it. **1605** in W. Kelly *Notices Illustr. Drama* (1865) 246 For sawderinge of other panes of glasse in the Halle. **1658** MANTON *Expos. Jude* 2 Wks. 1871 V. 69 But our reconciliation with God, it is like the soldering of a vessel, which is strongest in the crack. **1728** CHAMBERS *Cycl.* s.v., In the Soldering of all these Metals, they generally use Borax in Powder. **1807** T. THOMSON *Chem.* (ed. 3) II. 566 Its great use is to facilitate the soldering of the more precious metals. **1875** KNIGHT *Dict. Mech.* 2240/1 Soldering was apparently unknown in Greece in the time of Homer.

**b.** With adjs., as *hard, soft*.

**1832** BABBAGE *Econ. Manuf.* xv. (ed. 3) 143 Hard soldering gives a better coat of silver. **1843** HOLTZAPFFEL *Turning* I. 433 In soft-soldering, the binding wire is scarcely ever used. **1879** *Cassell's Techn. Educ.* IV. 350 The one method is called *hard* and the other *soft* soldering.

**2.** The action of uniting or joining closely; an instance of this.

**1550** BALE *Apol.* 17 All the unsounde sowderinges of Alyngtons sophistry, wyll not be found able workmanly to clowte up thys foule broken hole. **1603** HOLLAND *Plutarch's Mor.* 226 The commixture and sodering (as it were) of good will and kinde affection. **1642** D. ROGERS *Naaman* 835 All mixtures of selfe, and soderings against the Word. **1728** *Phil. Trans.* XXXV. 634 To steep them in Clay or Fuller's earth..before you heat them, to prevent their soldering with one another. **1857** PUSEY *Doctr. Real Presence* (1869) I. 104, I assert a real union, yet it is not by conclusion or soldering, but Sacramental.

**3.** Solder; material used for soldering with.

**1648** HEXHAM II, *Loot-metael*, Lead-mettall, or Saudering. *a* **1682** SIR T. BROWNE *Tracts* (1683) 4 Refining, Sodering, Dross, Nitre. **1880** *Daily News* 7 Oct. 6/7 A portion of the metal from the tin or from the soldering had become absorbed by the meat.

**4.** A soldered place or part.

**1889** *Telegr. Jrnl.* XXV. 349 Even the delicate solderings of the ends of these wires to the copper clips were apparently the same as ever.

**5.** *attrib.*, chiefly in the names of tools or apparatus used in soldering, as *soldering iron*. Descriptions of many of these are given by Knight *Dict. Mech.* (1875 and 1884).

**1675** BAXTER *Cath. The.* II. I. 280 A man that is set on a sodering design may palliate any Heresie in the world. **1688** HOLME *Armoury* III. 307/1 These Sodering Irons are only used about Lead Workings. *Ibid.*, Other Soddering Irons there are used by other Trades. **1825** J. NICHOLSON *Operat. Mechanic* 633 It is smoothed and finished by rubbing it about with a red-hot soldering iron. **1843** HOLTZAPFFEL *Turning* I. 446 The soldering-tool is then thin and keen on the edge. **1873** E. SPON *Workshop Rec.* Ser. I. 366/1 See that the soldering iron..is well tinned. **1893** *Spons' Mech. Own Book* (ed. 4) 101 A soldering bit may be made by taking a piece of stout brass wire..about 6 in. long [etc.]. **1900** HASLUCK *Mod. Eng. Handybk.* 139 For soft solders, the best flux is a soldering fluid which may be prepared by saturating hydrochloric acid with zinc.

**ˈsoldering,** *ppl. a.* [f. SOLDER *v.*] That solders or unites.

**1599** BUTTES *Dyets Drie Dinner* To Rdrs., Of a stiffening and soddering nature. **1652** BLITHE *Engl. Improver Impr.* 110 There are some Lands, so Binding, so Tough a Sodering Clay.

**ˈsolderless,** *a.* [f. SOLDER *sb.*[1] + -LESS.] Made without solder; that does not require solder.

**1920** C. T. SCHAEFER *Motor Lorry Design* iii. 43 A solderless copper radiator is obtained,..which..withstands severe vibration without failure. **1957** '*Motor Cycling*' *Workbench Wisdom* 75/2 A particularly neat type of solderless nipple. **1974** *Sci. Amer.* Apr. 79/1 The Logic Lab utilizes a solderless, plug-in connection technique for components and wires.

**†soldery.** *Obs.*[−1] In 6 souldery. [f. SOLD *sb.*[1] + -ERY: cf. OF. *souldoierie*.] Pay, payment.

**1502** *Ord. Crysten Men* (W. de W. 1506) I. iii. 38 As it is wryten and regystred in yᵉ wages and souldery of yᵉ holy kynge of glory.

**soldier** (ˈsəʊldʒə(r)), *sb.* Forms: α. 4 saud-, sawder, 5 sauldyer; 4 sawdour, sawgeoure, 5 saud-, sawdiour, 5–6 sawdyour (5 -yor). β. 4 souder, 5 sowder(e, 6 -eer; 5 soudyre, 5–6 sowdier, 6 soudyer; 5 sowdear, 6 -iar, -yare, soudiar; 4 soudior, 5 -eor, sowdior, -yor(e; 4 soudour, 4–5 soudyour(e, 4–6 soudeour, -iour (4 -ioure), 6 soudgour, 7 soujour; 4 sowedeur, 4–5 sowdeour, -iour, 4–6 -your (5 -yowre). γ. 4–5 souldeour, 4–6 -your, 4, 6–7 -iour (6 sowldiour, soulddour); 6 souldiar, -yar, -yer, 6–8 souldier (6 -iere), 7–8 souldjer, 7 soulder. δ. 5–6 soldiour, 6–7 soldior, 6 soldear, -iar, 6– soldier (6 soiler, 7 soldjere). ε. 4 sodiour, -your, 6 sodioure, -ear, -ier. ζ. 6 sogear, -eour, soygear, soi-, sojour, -ar, 7 sojor, 7– soger, sodger. [a. OF. *soud(i)er, saudier, sodyer, soldier* (also with different ending *soldeier, -oier*, etc.), f. *soude* SOLD *sb.*[1] (cf. med.L. *solidārius*). The obs. forms in *-eo(u)r, -io(u)r*, etc., correspond to the OF. variants *soudiour, souldiour, -eour, soldiour*, etc. Owing to the variation in both stem and termination, and the reduction of the *di* to *j* (*g*), the number of former spellings is unusually large.]

**1. a.** One who serves in an army for pay; one who takes part in military service or warfare; *spec.* one of the ordinary rank and file; a private.

*common soldier*: see COMMON *a.* 12 b. *private soldier*: see PRIVATE *a.* 2 b. *foot-soldier*: see FOOT *sb.* 34 c. *soldier of fortune*: see FORTUNE *sb.* 1 e.

α. *a* **1300** *Cursor M.* 24789 He gadird sauders her and þar, To strenth his castels. **13..** *K. Alis.* 1399 (Laud. MS.), And seuen & tuenty hundreþ sawders, Stronge in felde, vpon destrers. *c* **1440** *Contin. Brut* 538 Caleis..was þat tyme kept with saudiours. *c* **1460** *Towneley Myst.* xxx. 222 Thou art the best sawgeoure that euer had I any. **1465** *Paston Lett.* I. 133 The olde sawdyors of Normaundy. *c* **1489** CAXTON *Sonnes of Aymon* iii. 70, I am a sauldyer with Reynawde. [*c* **1500** *Melusine* 208 Your peple that be come hither to take your wages as sawdoyers.]

β. **13..** *Guy Warw.* 5329 Wiþ þat come anoþer kniȝt..: Douke Otus soudour was he. **1338** R. BRUNNE *Chron.* (1810) 109 Aniowe with þer souders was alle biseged & set. *c* **1350** *Will. Palerne* 3954, I sette ȝou for no soudiour but for souerayn lord. **1387** TREVISA *Higden* (Rolls) IV. 255 In þe secounde fyve ȝere þey hadde silver for to paye knyȝtes and soudeours. **1421** *Rolls of Parlt.* IV. 159/2 The pore liege men and Soudeors in the Town. *c* **1450** *Merlin* xii. 174 Lete vs geder oure kyn and oure frendes and sowderes out of alle londes. **1503** *Act 19 Hen. VII*, c. 12 ¶ 11 Callyng hymself a Sowedyer, Shipman, or Travelyngman. **1526** R. WHYTFORD *Martiloge* (1893) 2 Amonge soudyours that were under the capytane & prynce Licyne. **1535** COVERDALE *2 Sam.* iv. 2 There were two men captaynes ouer the soudyers. **1538** STARKEY *England* I. i. 3 He was..neuer gud capitayne that neuer was soudiar.

γ. **1390** GOWER *Conf.* I. 358 How thei stonde of on acord, The Souldeour forth with the lord. *c* **1400** MAUNDEV. (1839) v. 38 Als moche takethe the Amyralle be him allone, as alle the other Souldyours han undre hym. **1474** CAXTON *Chesse* II. iv. (1883) 49 Whan the souldyours see that they [etc.]. **1530** PALSGR. 273/1 Souldier of a strange lande, *auxiliaire*. **1570–6** LAMBARDE *Peramb. Kent* (1826) 141 He maintained a great number of Souldiours within the Castle. **1625** TUKE *Holy Eucharist* A iij b, How that noble Worthy made them bee Destroyed of his souldjers presentlie. **1640–1** *Kirkcudbright War-Committee's Minute Bk.* (1855) 152 To mak present provisione..for clothes and schooes to thair awn souldiors. **1680** OTWAY *Orphan* II. iii, Young Souldier, you've not only study'd War.

δ. *c* **1450** HOLLAND *Howlat* 641 Soldiouris and sumptermen to thai senȝeouris. *a* **1547** SURREY *Æneid* II. 11 What Myrmidon:..What stern Ulysses waged soldiar? **1557** *Anc. Rec. Dubl.* (1889) 468 Every freman becomyng a soilder. **1590** SIR J. SMYTH *Disc. Weapons* Ded. 16 b, Such Officers..cannot faile to make good soldiers. **1601** SHAKS. *Twel. N.* III. iv. 339 As he is a Gentleman and a Soldiour. **1628–9** DIGBY *Voy. Medit.* (Camden) 16 The gran Hogi (that is secretarie) paying the soldiors. **1728** YOUNG *Love Fame* IV. 254 Of boasting more than of a bomb afraid, A soldier should be modest as a maid. **1752** HUME *Ess. & Treat.* (1777) I. 275 A continual succession of wars makes every citizen a soldier. **1829** SCOTT *Anne of G.* xxxiv, The sight of your lordship..has waked the old soldier in myself. **1869** E. A. PARKES *Pract. Hygiene* (ed. 3) 623 The trade of the soldier is war.

ε. *c* **1400** MAUNDEV. (Roxb.) vi. 20 Pure knyghtes and sodyours selles þaire hernays. **1489** *Barbour's Bruce* v. 205 (Edin.), It wes all to gret perill Sa ner thir sodiouurys to ga. **1529** RASTELL *Pastyme* (1811) 108 And wyth new sodears..gave to Arthur anewe battell. **1556** *Chron. Grey Friars* (Camden) 16 The morrow after there ware sodiers arestyd & prisond. **1570** LEVINS *Manip.* 223 A sodioure, *miles, bellator*.

ζ. **1532** in W. M. Williams *Ann. Founders' Co.* (1867) 214 These be the charges for the fyrst Soygears. **1559** *Peebles Burgh Rec.* (1872) 253 The inqueist ordanis the sojarris and allegit men of weir to depas incontinent of the tovne. **1573** *Satir. Poems Reform.* xxxix. 118 With certane Soiouris of the garysoun. **1640–1** *Kirkcudbright War-Committee's Minute Bk.* (1855) 9 The sogers, both the foote and horss. **1650** Z. BOYD in *Zion's Flowers* (1855) Introd. 48 Divers sojours did sing with us. **17..** RAMSAY *Soger Laddie* ii, My doughty laddie..can as a soger and lover behave. **1782** BURNS *I'll go and be a Sodger* 4 I'm twenty-three, and five-feet-nine,—I'll go and be a sodger! **1838** JAS. GRANT *Sk. London* 219 Hollering aloud that he had been a sodger before, but that he was a gentleman now. **1840** R. H. DANA *Bef. Mast* iv, You're neither man, boy, soger, nor sailor!

**b.** A man of military skill and experience.

**1603** SHAKS. *Meas. for M.* III. ii. 155 Hee shall appeare to the enuious, a Scholler, a Statesman, and a Soldier. **1603** MOUNTJOY in Moryson *Itin.* (1617) II. 284 Howsoever he be no Souldier, yet is [he] well acquainted with the businesse of the warre. **1852** TENNYSON *Ode Dk. Wellington* 131 So great a soldier taught us there, What long-enduring hearts could do. **1862** CARLYLE *Fredk. Gt.* XII. ii. III. 181 There is Count von Roth, Silesian Lutheran, an excellent Soldier.

**c.** A small image of a soldier, intended as a child's toy.

**1878** H. S. LEIGH *Town Garland* 56, I will treat her young brother, methinks, To a boxful of soldiers instead.

**d.** A member of the Salvation Army.

**1876** W. BOOTH *Salvation Soldiery* (1882) 70 Get fixed in your mind the ungainsayable truth that every soldier can do something. **1890** —— *In Darkest England* II. v. 168 Emma Y.—Now a Soldier of the Marylebone Slum Post. **1935** *Chambers's Encycl.* IX. 64/2 In some of the jails there is now a regularly organised corps of Salvation Army soldiers. **1978** *Lochaber News* 31 Mar. 3/2 At the evening service four young soldiers..were enrolled by Major Holstead.

**e.** *to play (at) soldiers*: said of children; also derisively of volunteers.

**1911** in *Conc. Oxford Dict.* s.v. *Soldier*. **1969** I. & P. OPIE *Children's Games* xii. 338 There is a noteworthy difference between playing at 'Soldiers' and playing at 'War' with two opposing sides. *Ibid.*, If they [*sc.* the boys] were playing soldiers, she took it as a warning that it was time for her to arm. **1977** *Daily Mirror* 16 Mar. 10/2 (Advt.), I can tell you that digging a trench in pouring rain when you've had no kip is hardly playing at soldiers.

**f.** A rank-and-file member of the Mafia.

**1963** *Organized Crime & Illicit Traffic in Narcotics* (Comm. Govt. Operations, U.S. Senate) I. 80 Then we had what we call a caporegima which is a lieutenant, and then we have what we call soldiers. **1970** L. SANDERS *Anderson Tapes* lxxii. 218 The organization variably known as Cosa Nostra, Syndicate, Mafia, etc., even has military titles for its members—don for general or colonel, *capo* for major or captain, soldier for men in the ranks, etc. **1974** J. GARDNER *Corner Men* xv. 248 Vescari was coming to him. There were several men around him, the don's soldiers. **1977** *Time* 16 May 35/3 Since then scores of new soldiers have signed up [in the Mafia].

**2.** *fig.* (usually with ref. to spiritual service or warfare). Also const. *to* (a purpose, etc.).

**1340** *Ayenb.* 146 We byeþ alle uelaȝes ine þe ost of oure lhorde and his kniȝtes and his soudeurs. *c* **1500** *Melusine* 149 þey name them self sawdyours of our lord Jeshu criste. **1549** *Bk. Common Prayer, Publ. Bapt.*, To continewe his faythfull soldiour and seruaunt unto thy lyfes ende. **1580** in Allen *Martyrdom Campion* (1908) 25 Very many..being restored to the Church, new soldiers geve up their names. **1608** SHAKS. *Per.* IV. i. 8 Nor let pity..melt thee, but be A soldier to thy purpose. **1611** —— *Cymb.* III. iv. 186 This attempt, I am Souldier too. **1649** BP. REYNOLDS *Hosea* ii. 74 Such an oath have all Christ's Souldiers taken. **1737** CHALLONER *Cath. Chr. Instr.* (1753) 20 To make them Soldiers of Christ, and perfect Christians. **1810** SHELLEY *Tremble Kings* 5 We all are soldiers fit to fight. **1860** WARTER *Sea-board* II. 466 No mean soldier of the Church Militant here on earth.

**b.** *to come the old soldier over one*, to take one in, impose upon one. (See COME *v.* 29.)

**1824** SCOTT *St. Ronan's* xviii, I should think he was coming the old soldier over me, and keeping up his game. **1861** HUGHES *Tom Brown at Oxf.* II. xvii. 331 But you needn't try to come the old soldier over me. I'm not quite such a fool as that.

**c.** *old soldier*: one practised or experienced in a thing, or one who pretends to be so. (See also quot. 1912.) Also *attrib.* Cf. senses 2 b and 2 d.

**1722** [see OLD *a.* 5 b]. **1858** GEO. ELIOT *Lett.* (1954) II. 511 He..will be as much interested as I shall be in knowing about the vicissitudes of Coventry journalism, when any new phase or crisis comes of which you can tell us. He is an old soldier, and cares for battles of that sort. **1912** R. A. FREEMAN *Singing Bone* ii. 119 Poor Pratt was what you'd call an old soldier—sly, you know, sir—and a bit of a sneak. **1949** [see HEAD *sb.*[1] 54]. **1950** N. CARDUS *Second Innings* 93 The umpire (an old soldier) confidentially tells you he could see it all coming.

**d.** *Naut. slang* (orig. and chiefly *U.S.*). A worthless seaman; a loafer, a shirker. Also *old soldier*. Cf. SOLDIER *v.* 1 d.

**1840** R. H. DANA *Two Yrs. before Mast* xvii. 154 The captain called him a 'soger', and promised to 'ride him down'. **1849** [see SOLDIERING *vbl. sb.* 2]. **1850** H. MELVILLE *White Jacket* II. xxx. 205 Off Cape Horn some 'sogers' of sailors will stand cupping, and bleeding, and blistering, before they will budge. **1898** A. J. BOYD *Shellback* ii. 28 Some are good men, some mere 'sojers' (useless as seamen—loafers). **1933** E. P. MITCHELL *Deep Water* xxi. 184, I hear that you have shipped as an A.B. You don't look like one, and if you're a soldier you'll get soldier's jobs and be disrated. **1958** B. HAMILTON *Too Much of Water* vi. 140 He's a bit of an old soldier, but a first-rate seaman, and a hundred per cent reliable at sea.

**e.** ***dead soldier*** (*U.S. slang*): an empty bottle. Cf. (*dead*) ***marine*** s.v. MARINE *sb.* 4 d.

**1917** in *Dialect Notes* IV. 322. **1929** *New Yorker* 9 Feb. 42/3 His aim with a dead soldier was..unerring. **1940** R. CHANDLER *Farewell, my Lovely* v. 33, I held up the dead soldier and shook it. Then I..reached for the pint of bonded bourbon. **1979** R. B. GILLESPIE *Crossword Mystery* ii. 50 There weren't any prints on that bottle... That dead soldier was as clean as a whistle.

**f.** *colloq.* A strip or finger of bread or toast.

**1966** N. FREELING *Dresden Green* I. 73 Potato soup with fried onions and 'soldiers' of fried bread. **1971** J. GRIGSON *Good Things* 120 First dip the asparagus into the butter, then into the runny egg yolk, as if it were a child's bread 'soldier'. **1979** *Woman's Own* 21 Apr. 8/3 Our medical writer.. advises: 'Bread, butter and milk is a good idea, but you can't really beat a boiled egg and "soldiers".'

**3.** *transf.* Used as a name for various animals, fishes, etc.

†**a.** A turtle. *Obs.*

**1608** TOPSELL *Serpents* (1658) 798 This Sea-tortoise.., which the common fisher-men call 'the Soldier', because his back seemeth to be armed and covered with a shield and helmet.

**b.** The soldier-crab or hermit-crab.

**1666** J. DAVIES *Hist. Caribby Isles* 78 There is a kind of Snailes, called by the French *Soldats* that is *Souldiers*, because they have no shells proper and peculiar to themselves. **1697** DAMPIER *Voy.* (1699) 39 Under those Trees we found plenty of Soldiers, that live in Shells,..and have two great Claws like a Crab. **1725** SLOANE *Jamaica* II. 272 This small Lobster or Crab differs in very little from the European Souldjer or Hermit-Crab. **1782** P. H. BRUCE *Mem.* XII. 424 Their shell-fish are conques, perriwinkles, coneys, sogers, wilkes, etc. **1833** M. SCOTT *Tom Cringle* vi, The amphibious little creatures, half crab, half lobster, called soldiers.

†**c.** = *soldier-insect* (see 9).

**1699** WAFER *Voy.* 110 If these Soldiers eat of any of the Manchineel-Apples.., their Flesh becomes..infected with that virulent Juice.

†**d.** A Brazilian fish, of which the native name is *camboatá*. *Obs.*

**1703** DAMPIER *Voy.* (1729) III. I. 416 The River Souldier. It's mail'd somewhat like a Sturgeon, the Meat good; they say it gets on Land to seek for Water when the Rivers are near dry.

**e.** A fighting ant or termite; also *Austr.*, a species of large red ant.

(*a*) **1781** *Phil. Trans.* LXXI. 145 Of every species there are three orders; first, the working insects,..next the fighting ones, or soldiers. **1871** KINGSLEY *At Last* viii, The workers and soldiers, I believe, without exception, are blind. **1898** E. P. EVANS *Evol. Ethics* vi. 210 The soldiers may be undeveloped males, although this is by no means certain. (*b*) **1854** G. H. HAYDON *Australian Emigrant* 59 It was a red ant, upwards of an inch in length—'that's a soldier, and he prods hard too'. **1881** *Chequered Career* 324, I was bitten once by a 'soldier', and for ten minutes was in frightful agony.

**f.** One of several deep-water fishes with reddish skins, esp. one of the genus *Hoplostethus*.

**1846** *Zoologist* IV. 1402 The Red Gurnard, *Trigla cuculus*. This species is frequently called 'soldier'. **1905** HASLOPE *Pract. Sea-Fishing* 97 Small Pollack sometimes acquire a bright red colour, and then are termed 'soldiers' in Cornwall. **1935** 'R. M.' *Trawler* x. 51 By far the most plentiful animals in all the catch were the 'soldiers'. **1953** [see DAGERAAD]. **1971** *Grocott's Mail* (Grahamstown, S. Afr.) 28 May 3 Mrs. E. Birch took both the ladies' awards with a soldier of 0·963 kg, another unusual fish and decidedly a deep sea species. **1974** *Nature* 22 Mar. 306/3 The berycoid fishes comprise a mixture of deepwater 'soldiers', *Hoplostethus*, and other genera.

**g.** *slang.* A red herring.

**1811** *Lexicon-Balatronicum*, *Soldier*, a red herring. **1835** MARRYAT *J. Faithful* x, He returned, bringing half a dozen red herrings. 'Here, Tom, grill these sodgers.' **1883** DAY *Fishes Gt. Brit.* II. 210 A red herring..sailors usually designate..as a sodger, or soldier.

**h.** A red spider; a small red beetle; a ladybird.

**1848** JOHNSTON in *Proc. Berw. Nat. Club* II. VI. 290 This insect is called a Tant in England... Our children call it the Soldier, from its scarlet colour. **1854** MISS BAKER *Northampt. Gloss.*, *Soldier*, the small beetle known to entomologists as the *Cantharis livida*. **1858** KINGSLEY *Misc.* (1859) I. 189 The soldier, the soft-winged reddish beetle which haunts the umbelliferous flowers. **1863** [see SAILOR 3 b].

**i.** *Austr.* (See quot.)

**1898** 'R. BOLDREWOOD' *Rom. Canvas Town* 76 They rode on,..seeing nothing living save..four 'soldiers' or forest kangaroos.

**j.** *U.S.* (See quot.)

**1904** P. FOUNTAIN *Great North-West* xix. 224 A bird known locally [in Ohio] as 'the marshal', and sometimes 'the soldier'... It is a very gaudy woodpecker with a great deal of scarlet in the colour of its plumage.

**4.** *dial.* As a plant-name (see quot.).

See also *fresh-water* and *water soldier*.

**1854** MISS BAKER *Northampt. Gloss.*, *Soldier*, another local name for the field poppy, *Papaver Rhæas*.

**5.** A disease of swine characterized by red patches on the skin. (Cf. *soldier-disease* in 9.)

**1882** F. VACHER *Transmiss. Disease by Food* 4 Erysipelas is far from rare among cattle and swine; and passing under such names as..'soldier' is often counted but a trifling ailment. **1890** *Lancet* 2 Aug. 217/2 A disorder affecting pigs, called..in Ireland 'red soldier', from the red patches that appear on the skin in fatal cases.

**6.** A soldier-line (see 9).

**1865** WILCOCKS *Sea-fisherman* (1875) 82 The tide now began to run considerably stronger, and more length on the lines was requisite: I therefore prepared to 'rig a soldier'.

**7.** In allusion to the resemblance to a line of soldiers on parade. **a.** *Carpentry.* Each of a series of short vertical pieces of wood to which a skirting-board is fixed.

**1927** T. CORKHILL in R. Greenhalgh *Building Educator* II. 817/2 The vertical grounds, or soldiers.., are plugged to the wall about every 3 ft. apart. **1950** M. T. TELLING *Carpentry & Joinery* v. 200 The skirting is fixed with nails to the horizontal ground and to the short vertical grounds called 'soldiers'.

**b.** *Building.* (See quot.) Cf. *soldier arch*, *course*, sense 9 below.

**1929** W. C. HUNTINGTON *Building Constr.* iv. 130 Belt courses and flat arches may be formed of brick[s] set on end with the narrow side exposed. Such bricks are called soldiers.

**c.** *Building.* Each of a series of vertical members of timber or metal used to hold formwork in position or support the lining of an excavation.

**1932** DOWSETT & BARTLE *Practical Formwork & Shuttering* ii. 19 The ribs are held in position by uprights made from 3″ × 6″ material; these uprights—frequently referred to as 'soldiers'—are in turn held by 3″ × 6″ horizontal timbers called 'walings'. **1932** T. CORKHILL *Conc. Building Encycl.* 197 *Soldiers*,..heavy vertical timbers placed across several walings and strutted. This is done in stages, to remove the lower struts for a deep excavation, as the wall is built. **1961** *Engineering* 8 Dec. 739/1 Aluminium 'soldiers' are being used..to support the shuttering for the concrete shields of the reactors. **1970** W. G. NASH *Brickwork Three* viii. 175 When a sufficient depth has been supported in this way the whole system is held back by soldiers which are secured by the permanent struts.

**8.** *attrib.* and *Comb.* **a.** Appositive, as ***soldier-boy***, ***-colonist***, ***-hero***, ***-laddie***, ***-man***, etc.

**1861** in *Rebellion Rec.* (1862) I. III. 91 My hungry *soger-boys shall soon have meat and drink. **1978** J. BARNETT *Head of Force* viii. 72 This was his field. The soldier-boy was out of his depth. **1852** MUNDY *Antipodes* (1857) 196 The attempt to make the *soldier-colonist a landed proprietor. *a* **1892** TENNYSON in *Q. Rev.* Oct. (1897) 524 Our great, simple *soldier-hero Gordon. **17..** RAMSAY *Soger Laddie* i, My *soger laddie is over the sea. [**1786** *Har'st Rig* xcviii, The Grey Breeks next, and then she'll try The Sodger Laddie. **1847** TENNYSON *Princ.* Prol. 86 While the twangling violin Struck up with Soldier-laddie.] **1801** R. L. & MAR. EDGEWORTH *Irish Bulls* (1803) 153 Some of his *soldiermen being of the company. **1893** STEVENSON *Catriona* xxx. 354, I went among soldier-men to their big dinners. **1894** H. SPEIGHT *Nidderdale* 187 The original house of the old *soldier-monks at Ribston. **1823** W. ROBINSON in J. A. Heraud *Voy. & Mem. Midshipman* vi. (1837) 101 In a race we had..against the *soldier-officers.. there was a capsize. **1808** MITFORD *Hist. Greece* xxviii. §ix. III. 549 [Xenophon] the *soldier-philosopher-author. **1912** D. H. LAWRENCE in *Eng. Rev.* Jan. 373 Liliencron is well represented. But this *soldier poet is so straight, so free from the modern artist's hyper-sensitive self-consciousness, that we would have more of him. **1958** BLUNDEN *War Poets 1914–18* i. 13 The number and the activity of the soldier-poets of Britain in the First World War were bewildering. **1830** TENNYSON *To J. M. K.* 2 A latter Luther, and a *soldier-priest. **1852** MUNDY *Antipodes* (1857) 35 The old *soldier-robber remaining doggedly at bay. **1892** T. A. COOK *Old Touraine* I. 10 If there is one thing for which Tours is famous it is for its *soldier-saint. **1871** SWINBURNE *Songs bef. Sunrise, Blessed among Women* 11 A godlike *soldier-saviour. **1794** W. B. STEVENS *Jrnl.* 13 Feb. (1965) 135 Stables has displayed a boisterousness of temper..to his *Soldier-Servant..which I cannot palliate. **1872** *Routledge's Ev. Boy's Ann.* 186/2 An awkward soldier-servant.

**b.** Attributive, as ***soldier-caste***, ***-city***, ***-class***, ***-craft***, etc.

**1847** MRS. KERR tr. *Ranke's Hist. Servia* 455 The immediate domination of the *soldier-caste. **1847** TENNYSON *Princ.* v. 7 Threading the *soldier-city. **1847** MRS. KERR tr. *Ranke's Hist. Servia* 160 There was no *soldier-class in Servia. **1855** S. PALMER in Gilchrist *Life Blake* I. 303 That we heard so much of priestcraft, and so little of *soldiercraft and lawyercraft. **1844** LEVER *T. Burke* II. 163 Even there, again, I but showed my *soldier education. **1814** SCOTT *Lord of Isles* III. v, Then do me but the *soldier grace, This glove upon thy helm to place. *a* **1835** MRS. HEMANS *Burial in the Desert* Poems (1875) 517 With a few brief words of *soldier-love. **1837** CARLYLE *Fr. Rev.* II. II. ii, How these things may act on the rude *soldier-mind. **1921** *Daily Colonist* (Victoria, B.C.) 25 Mar. 1/5 The opening for *soldier settlement of about two townships from the Riding Mountain, Manitoba, reserve, will be held at the Dominion land office in Dauphin, Manitoba, in about two weeks. **1930** W. K. HANCOCK *Australia* vii. 141 It would.. be not altogether unfair to separate soldier settlement from closer settlement, and to consider the former as part of the cost of the war. **1977** *Weekly Times* (Melbourne) 19 Jan. 39/2 The property remained in the Bell family until taken up under Soldier Settlement by Mr J. Smedley after World War 2. **1810** SCOTT *Lady of Lake* VI. ii, At dawn the towers of Stirling rang With *soldier-step and weapon-clang. **1944** S. BELLOW *Dangling Man* 182 I'd murder him, *soldier suit or no soldier suit. **1977** H. FAST *Immigrants* II. 141 If you have to put on that lousy soldier suit to live with yourself, then for Christ's sake become a medic or a clerk or something like that.

**c.** Miscellaneous, as ***soldier-breeder***; ***soldier-hearted***, ***-mad*** adjs.; ***soldier-wise*** adv.

**1599** SHAKS. *Hen. V*, v. ii. 219 Thou must therefore needes proue a good Souldier-breeder. **1824** MEDWIN *Conversat. Byron* II. 206 Lord Byron..became, as one of the letters from the place..expresses it, soldier-mad. **1837** CARLYLE *Fr. Rev.* II. I. xi, They have shouldered, soldier-wise, their shovels and picks. **1848** *Blackw. Mag.* Mar. 353 They were buried soldier-fashion in the same grave. **1849** [W. M. W. CALL] *Reverb.* II. 5 Be thou wise and earnest, good and brave, Soldier-hearted.

**9.** Special combs., as **soldier-ant**, = sense 3 e; **soldier arch** *Building*, a soldier course serving as a lintel; **soldier bean** *N. Amer.*, the mottled kidney-shaped seeds of certain varieties of *Phaseolus vulgaris*; **soldier-beetle**, = sense 3 h; **(old) soldier bird**, an Australian bird, *Myzomela sanguinolenta*, with bright red plumage; **soldier-bug**, a predacious North American bug of the genus *Podisus* of the family Pentatomidæ, esp. *P. maculiventris*, which is yellowish brown and has a spine on the underside of its head; **soldier-bush**, = *soldier-wood*; **soldier course** *Building*, a course of bricks set on end with their narrower long face exposed; **soldier disease**, = sense 5; †**soldierfare**, military service or experience; **soldier-fish** = SQUIRREL 4 and *squirrel-fish* s.v. SQUIRREL 7 b; **soldier fly** orig. *U.S.* [tr. mod.L. *Stratiomys*], an often brightly coloured fly of the family Stratiomyidæ, the larvæ of which damage the roots of certain grasses; †**soldier-insect** (see quot.); **soldier-line** (see quot. and cf. sense 6); †**soldier money**, ? money spent in assisting poor soldiers; **soldier-moth**, **-orchis** (see quots.); **soldier orchid** = *military orchid* s.v. MILITARY *a.* 3 b; **soldier palmer**, an artificial fly used in angling; **soldier-pink** *dial.*, a minnow; **soldier-plant**, **-thighed** *a.*, **-wood** (see quots.); **soldier-termite** = sense 3 e.

**1857** LIVINGSTONE *Trav.* xxvii. 537, I observed many regiments of black *soldier-ants. **1963** SEAKINS & SMITH *Practical Brickwork* xiv. 174 (*caption*) Flexible D.P.C. behind *soldier arch. **1972** S. SMITH *Brickwork* xiv. 73 A method of supporting a soldier arch by means of wire ties built into a concrete lintel at the rear, is shown. [**1931** W. G. MCGREGOR *Field Beans in Canada* 8 In Nova Scotia..four leading varieties..are Navy Ottawa 711, White Marrowfat, Soldier, and Yellow Eye.] **1968** E. R. BUCKLER *Ox Bells & Fireflies* vi. 101 Yellow-eyed *soldier beans to be threshed on the barn floor with the leather-jointed flail. **1855** OGILVIE *Suppl.*, **Soldier-beetle*, a name given to coleopterous insects of the genus Telephorus. **1883** W. SAUNDERS *Insects Inj. Fruits* 185 The larva of the soldier-beetle, *Chauliognathus Americanus*.., is also a useful agent in destroying the curculio. **1857** D. BUNCE *Australas. Rem.* 62 The notes peculiar to the..leather-head or old *soldier bird, added in no small degree to the novelties. **1881** *Encycl. Brit.* XII. 139 The males are recognizable by a gorgeous display of crimson or scarlet, which has caused one species..to be known as the Soldier-bird to Australian colonists. **1868** *Mich. Agric. Rep.* VII. 175 [I] found [them] to be *soldier-bugs, with their long harpoon bills thrust into a fine fat slug. **1946** *Richmond* (Va.) *Times-Dispatch* 4 Feb. 4/1 More than two tons of it [*sc.* an insecticide made from sabadilla] was used this year to kill .. the soldier bugs in Illinois. **1948** DALZELL & TOWNSEND *Masonry Simplified* I. vii. 268 *Soldier courses are used mainly as a water table around a building at the level of the first floor. **1979** *Arizona Daily Star* 1 Apr. (Advt. Section) 22/3 Burnt adobe hacienda with Soldier Course on parapet. **1878** *Typhoid Fever Order* (Privy Council), Typhoid fever of Swine (otherwise called *Soldier disease or red disease). **1579–80** NORTH *Plutarch, Sertorius* (1612) 584 The first time of his *souldierfare was, when the Cimbres and Teutons inuaded Gavle. **1632** HOLLAND *Cyrupædia* 43 Whatsoever by their souldier-fare in this expedition, they shall win. **1882** JORDAN & GILBERT *Syn. Fishes N. Amer.* 517 *Pœcilechthys cæruleus*, Blue Darter; Rainbow Darter; *Soldier-fish. **1905** D. S. JORDAN *Guide to Study of Fishes* II. xv. 253 The *soldier-fishes (*Holocentridæ*) also known as squirrel-fishes..are shore fishes very characteristic of rocky banks in the tropical seas. **1931** J. R. NORMAN *Hist. Fishes* iv. 69 Soldier-fishes..of the coral reefs of tropical seas derive their name from the stout and sharply pointed spines with which the fins are provided. **1961** E. S. HERALD *Living Fishes of World* 157/1 Squirrelfishes or soldier-fishes..tend to hide in crevices and cracks. **1842** T. W. HARRIS *Treat. Insects New England Injurious to Vegetation* 408 Most of the *soldier-flies..are armed with two thorns or sharp spines on the hinder part of the thorax. **1905** V. L. KELLOGG *Amer. Insects* xiii. 329 The soldier-flies, Stratiomyidæ, are unfamiliar insects... Many of the species have bright yellow or green markings, and most of them have the abdomen curiously broad and flattened. **1952** J. CLEGG *Freshwater Life Brit. Isles* xiv. 238 The Soldier-flies are the first of the stouter, short-horned flies to be considered. **1975** *N.Z. Jrnl. Agric.* Sept. 7/1 Infestations of grassgrub and soldier fly.. have the effect of inducing a clover-strong pasture which increases the danger of bloat. **1699** WAFER *Voy.* 110 There is a sort of Insect like a Snail in great plenty among the Samballoe's, which is call'd the *Soldier-Insect.., because of the Colour. **1865** WILCOCKS *Sea-fisherman* (1875) 82 A *soldier-line is one of two-stranded hemp twine, having for a sinker a two-pound Mackerel plummet, and is made fast to a strong flexible stick [etc.]. **1593** *Churchw. Acc. Pittington*, etc. (Surtees) 35 Item given to Roberte Morie for *Soldier monie (as he cald it) the xxiiij of November, xiij d. **1603** *Ibid.* 52 Item given to Thomas Kinge for Souldere monie the last day of March, viij s. viij d. **1882** *Cassell's Nat. Hist.* VI. 67 The *Soldier Moth (*Euschema militaris*) is the commonest. **1934, 1969** *Soldier orchid [see *military orchid* s.v. MILITARY *a.* 3 b]. **1863** PRIOR *Plant-n.*, **Soldier-orchis*, from a fancied resemblance in it to a soldier, *Orchis militaris*. **1839** T. C. HOFLAND *Brit. Angler's Man.* xi. (1841) 164 The house fly and small *soldier palmer. **1867** F. FRANCIS *Angling* vi. (1880) 245 Soldier Palmer. A capital fly in warm weather. **1854** MISS BAKER *Northampt. Gloss.*, **Soldier-pink*, the minnow, called by ichthyologists the *Cyprynus Proxinus*. **1864** GRISEBACH *Flora Brit. W. Ind.* 787/2 *Soldier-plant, *Calliandra purpurea*. **1963** *Soldier-termite [see NASUTE *a.* 3]. **1825** JAMIESON *Suppl.*, **Sodger-thee'd*, having little or no money in one's pocket. [Cf. *soldier's thigh* in 9.] **1823** CRABB *Technol. Dict.* II, **Soldier-wood*,..the *Mimosa purpurea* of Linnæus. **1824** LOUDON *Encycl. Gard.* (ed. 2) 1223/1 Soldier-wood, *inga purpurea*. **1866** *Treas. Bot.* 1071/2 Soldier-wood, *Calliandra purpurea*.

**10. a.** Possessive combs., as **† soldier's bottle**, a bottle of extra size; **† soldier's boy**, a camp-follower; **soldier's breeze** = *soldier's wind*; **† soldier's cloth**, coarse cloth; **soldier's farewell** *slang*, an abusive farewell (cf. *sailor's farewell* s.v. SAILOR 5 c); **soldier's heart**, *Path.*, a diseased state of the heart, characterized by a throbbing sensation in the chest and a difficulty in breathing; = *irritable heart*; **soldiers' home**, a place of stay for soldiers; **† soldier's mawnd**, *slang* (see quots.); **soldier's spots**, *Path.*, a variety of macula; **soldier's supper**, a smoke and a drink of water; **soldier's thigh**, *dial.* (see quot., and cf. *soldier-thighed* in 9); **soldier's wind**, a wind which serves either way.

*a* **1700** B. E. *Dict. Cant. Crew*, **Soldier's-bottle*, a large one. **1731–8** SWIFT *Polite Conv.* 177, I hope, you'll give me a Soldier's Bottle. **1611** COTGR., *Goujat*, a *Souldiors boy... *Goujaterie*, Souldiors boyes, or the young rakehells that follow a Campe. **1894** STEVENSON & OSBOURNE *Ebb-Tide* II. vii. 125 The *Farallone* made a *soldier's breeze of it. **1753** HANWAY *Trav.* II. II. xxvi. 156 The advantage in favour of the British subjects in Russia..is about one third part in the customs of *soldiers cloths. **1909** J. R. WARE *Passing Eng.* 229/1 **Soldier's farewell*, 'Go to bed', with noisy additions. **1936** J. CURTIS *Gilt Kid* viii. 82 'Good-bye. I hope they'll poke you into the Lock Hospital.' 'Soldier's farewell to you.' **1938** F. D. SHARPE *Sharpe of Flying Squad* xviii. 184 As you pass through the door, you'll sometimes hear a raspberry... No one wants to accept responsibility for that soldier's farewell. **1979** *Guardian* 12 Nov. 2/5 One school of thought within ITN..is that..the darling [newsreader] of millions then decided to say a soldier's farewell. **1898** *Allbutt's Syst. Med.* V. 851 **Soldier's heart.*—I venture to give this name to a disease well-known to physicians in the army. **1967** *Punch* 29 Mar. 458/3 World War One produced, besides Trench Foot, a syndrome called *Soldier's Heart, caused by great anxiety coupled with severe physical strain. **1971** Soldier's heart [see IRRITABLE *a.* 2 b]. **1860** MRS. GASKELL *Let.* 10 Dec. (1966) 640 This autumn [I]..helped Florence Nightingale ..in establishing a *Soldier's [*sic*] Home in Gibraltar where they can have cheap refreshments, can read, play games, write letters, &c. **1866** J. C. GREG *Life in Army* xxvi. 224 The idea of a Soldiers' Home is, I believe, original with the American people... It is said to have been first instituted in the city of Baltimore in 1861. **1900** *Congress. Rec.* 19 Jan. 1001/1 Part of his [*sc.* the veteran's] meager pension [is] confiscated at Soldiers' Homes. *a* **1700** B. E. *Dict. Cant. Crew*, **Souldiers-Mawn'd*, a Counterfeit Sore or Wound in the Left Arm. **1785** GROSE *Dict. Vulgar T.*, *Soldiers mawnd*, a pretended soldier, begging with a counterfeit wound. **1873** *Dunglison's Dict. Med. Sci.*, *Soldier's spots, *Maculæ albæ*. **1893** J. A. BARRY *Steve Brown's Bunyip* 31 A bite o' rotten bread for breakfus, ditto for dinner, an' a *soldier's supper. **1841** HARTSHORNE *Salop. Ant.* Gloss., **Soldier's thigh*, a slang term for an empty pocket. **1833** MARRYAT *P. Simple* xvi, The wind was what is called at sea a *soldier's wind, that is, blowing so that the ships could lie either way, so as to run out or into the harbour. **1893** H. M. DOUGHTY *Wherry in Wendish Lands* 312 Thence down the Schwielow See, with a light soldier's wind, we crept contentedly to past the Gänse horn.

**b.** In various plant-names, as **soldier's cap, cullion, herb, tea, weed, woundwort, yarrow**.

**1854** MISS BAKER *Northampt. Gloss.*, **Soldier's caps*, the flowers of the monkshood. **1597** GERARDE *Herbal* I. ci. 166 *Souldiers Cullions hath many leaues spred vpon the ground, but lesser than the Souldiers Satyrion. **1760** J. LEE *Introd. Bot.* App. 327 Soldier's Cullions, *Orchis*. **1601** HOLLAND *Pliny* II. 204 The herb which they cal Militaris [*marg.* The *soulders hearbe]. **1611** FLORIO, *Herba militare*, the souldiers hearbe. **1893** *Dunglison's Dict. Med. Sci.*, *Matico*, *Soldier's tea or herb; South American herb, order Piperaceæ. **1851** DUNGLISON *Ibid.* (ed. 4), *Soldier's weed [1893 wood], *Matico*. **1866** *Sowerby's Eng. Bot.* V. 58 It [yarrow] was formerly esteemed as a vulnerary, and its old names of '*soldier's wound-wort' and 'knight's milfoil' bear witness to this. **1578** LYTE *Dodoens* 143 The second is called ..in English..*Souldiers yerrow. **1597** GERARDE *Herbal* II. cclxxxv. 677 *Militaris aquatica*, and *Militaris Aizoides*, or Soldiers Yarrow.

**soldier** ('səʊldʒə(r)), *v.* Also 7 souldiour, 8–9 *Sc.* and *dial.* sodger, 9 soger, sojer. [f. the sb.]

**1. a.** *intr.* To act or serve as a soldier. Also with *it*.

α. **1647** GENTILIS tr. *Malvezzi's Chiefe Events* 187 If I souldiour it with so great a souldiour. **1815** *Ann. Reg., Chron.* App. 307, I will soldier it with anybody, but I will not go to school. **1825** in Col. Hawker *Diary* (1893) I. 287 Too busy soldiering to think of pheasant shooting. **1867** *Morning Star* 30 Jan., I have soldiered for six months at a stretch on a penny a day. **1889** *Sat. Rev.* 16 Mar. 319/1 They soldier as if their very lives depended on it.

β. **1818** SCOTT *Rob Roy* xviii, Thae papist cattle that hae been sodgering abroad. **1852** J. FRASER *King Jas. V*, III. ii, He..said he would sodger nae mair.

**b.** In phrase *to go (a-)soldiering*.

**1756** H. WALPOLE *Lett.* (1846) III. 229 If you think of conveying them through Moreland, he is gone a soldiering. **1816** SCOTT *Old Mort.* vi, This comes o' letting ye gang a-sodgering for a day. **1845** JAMES *Arrah Neil* vii, It does not do to go soldiering in these times without money in one's pocket. **1896** *Pall Mall Mag.* Dec. 458 It was my mother's name, and good to go soldiering with.

**c.** *dial.* To bully; to hector. (Halliwell, 1847.)

**d.** To feign illness, to malinger; to make a mere show of working, to shirk.

**1840** R. H. DANA *Bef. Mast* iv, There is no time to be lost, —no 'sogering', or hanging back then. **1876** C. D. WARNER *Winter on Nile* 248 They stretch out..so far that it needs an opera-glass to discover whether the leaders are pulling or only soldiering. **1890** CLARK RUSSELL *My Shipmate Louise* I. vi. 119 Finding fault with some fellow for 'sogering', as it is called.

**e.** *Mil. slang.* To furbish up accoutrements, etc.

**1885** MRS. J. H. EWING *Story Short Life* 35, I was busy soldiering till too late; so I come in this morning.

**f.** *to soldier on*: to persevere, to carry on doggedly.

**1954** K. AMIS *Lucky Jim* vii. 77 The eeriness.. disconcerted him..but he soldiered pluckily on to his objective. **1959** *Times* 20 Aug. 3/6 Lomax soldiered on and at tea had made 68. **1963** *Times* 21 Feb. 13/2 To give the maximum increase to the new recruits..and to offer a much smaller percentage to men and women who have soldiered on into the thirties and forties is a division hard to justify. **1978** *Jrnl. R. Soc. Med.* LXXI. 648 The alternatives are to let the patient soldier on, or to take the radical approach of abdominoperineal resection.

**2.** *trans.* **a.** ? To drill or train.

**1780** S. J. PRATT *Emma Corbett* (ed. 4) I. 107 Confess, that I am sufficiently soldier'd; for I can hold the pen, and impress the quiet-seeming sentiment.

**b.** To serve *out* one's time as a soldier.

**1873** *Daily News* 21 May 5/6 A man may soldier out his term in the British cavalry [etc.].

**c.** *Austr. slang.* To make temporary use of (another man's horse).

**1891** in *Cent. Dict.*

Hence **'soldiering** *ppl. a.*

**1607** MIDDLETON *The Phœnix* I. ii, Enter the Captain with soldiering fellows. **1795** BURNS '*Fy, let us a*'' x, The wild Scot o' Galloway, Sodgerin gunpowder Blair.

**soldier-crab.** [Cf. SOLDIER *sb.* 3 b.] The hermit-crab.

**1668** CHARLETON *Onomast.* 177 *Cancellus*,..the little Souldier-Crab. **1681** GREW *Musæum* I. v. iv. 121 The Naked-Shrimp, commonly called The Souldier-Crab. **1735** *Phil. Trans.* XXXIX. 115 Others call them Soldier-Crabs, resembling them to Soldiers in Centinels Boxes. **1774** GOLDSM. *Nat. Hist.* (1790) VI. 370 The animal I mean is the Soldier Crab, which has some similitude to the lobster, if divested of its shell. **1819** SAMOUELLE *Entomol. Compend.* 92 Termed indiscriminately Soldier-crabs and Hermit-crabs. **1882** *Cassell's Nat. Hist.* VI. 204 The friendship..between Soldier Crabs and Sea Anemones is very remarkable.

**'soldierdom.** [f. SOLDIER *sb.*] The quality or nature of a soldier.

**1870** *Daily News* 27 Sept., Men whose soldierdom is neither spontaneous nor mercenary. **1888** *Our Corner* Feb. 68 At the base is soldierdom, pure and simple, the merely dominant and fighting man.

**soldieress** ('səʊldʒərɪs). [f. SOLDIER *sb.* + -ESS.] A female soldier.

**1612** *Two Noble K.* I. i, Honour'd Hypolita, Most dreaded Amazonian:..Soldieress. **1864** R. F. BURTON *Dahome* II. 63 In Dahome the soldieresses have two titles.

**'soldierhood.** [f. SOLDIER *sb.* + -HOOD.] The essential qualities of a soldier or soldiery; the condition of being a soldier.

**1846** H. W. TORRENS *Rem. Milit. Hist.* 314 A military power, which has passed from serfdom to national soldierhood. **1861** *Macm. Mag.* III. 325 It was hard indeed to be pre-eminent..amidst that flower of soldierhood. **1883** *Pall Mall G.* 9 Oct. 5/1 He will have come face to face with an almost ideal incarnation of Russian soldierhood.

**soldiering** ('səʊldʒərɪŋ), *vbl. sb.* [f. the vb.]

**1.** The action of serving as a soldier; the state of being a soldier; military service.

**1697** J. LEWIS *Mem. Dk. Glocester* (1789) 59 On a sudden he left off his soldiering, and must needs take to managing a wooden horse. **1722** DE FOE *Col. Jack* (1840) 199 This was my second essay at the trade of soldiering. **1806** *Ann. Rev.* IV. 244 The resistance of the quakers to soldiering and to tythes. **1857** SHERARD OSBORN *Quedah* xvii. 227 He could handle a musket with all the innate love of soldiering of an Irishman. **1884** *Truth* 13 Mar. 372/1 His trade was soldiering, and..he has distinguished himself in his profession.

*attrib.* **1643** [ANGIER] *Lanc. Vall. Achor* 11 God kept up the Soldiering spirit, by Prayers and Psalms. **1884** *Pall Mall G.* 14 Aug. 4/2 Setting down his soldiering experiences with his old corps. **1888** HENTY *Cornet of Horse* xvi. 161, I think this soldiering life makes one restless.

**2.** Malingering, shirking.

**1840** R. H. DANA *Two Yrs. before Mast* xii. 91 '*Sogering*' was the order of the day. **1849** H. MELVILLE *Redburn* I. xii. 118 Sailors were always bitter against any thing like *sogering* ..though this Jackson was a notorious old *soger* the whole voyage. **1894** *Forum* (N.Y.) June 504 There could be no 'sojering'. Inattention and neglect were at the expense of the worker.

**soldierize** ('səʊldʒəraɪz), *v.* Also 6 souldiour-, 7 souldierize, 9 *Sc.* sodgerise. [f. SOLDIER *sb.* + -IZE.]

**1.** *intr.* To serve as a soldier. Also with *it*.

**1593** NASHE *Christ's T.* (1613) 93 What Gentleman hath been cast away at Sea, or disasterly souldiouriz'd it by Land, but they [usurers] haue enforst him thereunto. **1611** COTGR., *Militer*, to warre, goe a warfaring..; to souldierize it. **1708** *Brit. Apollo* No. 77. 2/1 We do..think it lawful for you to Soldierize. **1836** J. MAYNE *Siller Gun* iv, Marching wi' drums and fifes for ever—A' sodgerising!

**2.** *trans.* To make into a soldier.

**1611** COTGR., *Soldatisé*, souldierized, made a souldier. **1798** ANNA SEWARD *Lett.* (1811) V. 143 The male youth and middle life of England are, you know, all soldierized and gone to camps and coasts. **1843** J. J. GURNEY *Mem.* (1854) II. 369 All the male inhabitants are for a time soldierized when young.

**3.** To alter after the manner of soldiers.

**1891** S. MOSTYN *Curatica* 130 The dog, Fidèle by name —soldierized into the Fiddler—had come to my cousin from a brother officer.

**'soldierlike**, *a.* and *adv.* Also 6 souldiour-, -ior-, 6–7 -ier, -yer-; 6 soldior-, -iar-, 7 -jere-. [f. SOLDIER *sb.*]

**A.** *adj.* **1.** Having the character or bearing of a soldier. (Cf. SOLDIERLY *a.* 2.)

**1542** UDALL *Apophthegms* (1877) 53 One of the passingers, a grosse carle, and soldiarlike feloe. *a* **1586** SIDNEY *Apol. Poet.* (Arb.) 46 Which that right Souldier-like Nation thinck the chiefest kindlers of braue courage. **1757** WASHINGTON *Writ.* (1889) I. 468 You are also to be vastly careful..to make them appear always neat and clean, and soldier-like. **1774** in Burke *Corr.* (1844) I. 513 Now every peasant..is erect and soldier-like in his air and gait. **1833** RITCHIE *Wand. Loire* 22 A fine, frank, high-spirited, soldier-like, young fellow. **1884** *Manch. Exam.* 1 Nov. 5/6 They..looked quite soldierlike in their white tunics.

**2.** Appropriate to, worthy of, becoming or befitting, a soldier. (Cf. SOLDIERLY *a.* 1.)

**1553** ASCHAM *Disc. Germany* Wks. (1904) 147 His apparell is souldier like, better knowen by hys fearce doynges then by his gay goyng. **1590** SIR J. SMYTH *Disc. Weapons* 25 Rather vpon fancie than vpon anie souldiourlyke reasons and experience. **1617** COLLINS *Def. Bp. Ely* II. ix. 359 To releeue a souldier..is an act of souldierie, because done for consideration of his souldierlike exploits. **1670** COVEL in *Early Voy. Levant* (Hakl.) 136 Two of our seamen..who made a very soldjere-like retreat. **1711** STEELE *Spect.* No. 136 ¶3 He was the Occasion that the Muscovites kept their Fire in so soldier-like a manner. **1779** *Mirror* No. 11, Officers of the most soldier-like appearance and address. **1813** SOUTHEY *Nelson* vii, A soldier-like and becoming answer. **1837** W. IRVING *Capt. Bonneville* I. 123 As they rode along, they made their wills in soldierlike style. **1872** CUNYNGHAME *Trav. Caucasus* 7 The dress of both officers and men was sensible and soldierlike.

**B.** *adv.* In a manner befitting a soldier.

**1571** GOLDING *Calvin on Ps.* xviii. 38 Althowgh he seeme to speake to souldyerlyke, when he sayeth, he will make none end of slaughter. **1598** BARRET *Theor. Warres* III. i. 35 Hauing done the which, to retire souldier-like, and charge againe. **1631** GOUGE *God's Arrows* v. Ded. 406 Among Souldiers I endeavoured to speake Souldier-like. **1705** I. ROBINS *Hero of the Age* II. vii, How Martially they charge! how Soldier-like they ride! **1706** J. GARDINER *Rapin on Gardens* I. 36 Valiant Halesus..Soldier-like disclos'd his bolder Flame. **1825** SCOTT *Talism.* xxvii, Form yourselves around the ladies soldier-like and firmly. **1881** SWINBURNE *Mary Stuart* I. i. (1899) 29 Why, this rings right Well said, and soldierlike.

**'soldierliness.** [f. next.] The quality of being soldierly.

**1890** *Illustr. Lond. News* 13 Sept. 330/3 Of gentle birth and handsome soldierliness. **1892** PEYTON *Memorabilia Jesus* xv. 418 The action, the chivalry, and the soldierliness of being is the man's.

**soldierly** ('səʊldʒəlɪ), *a.* and *adv.* Also 6–7 souldier-, 7 soldiour-, 8 *Sc.* sogerly. [f. SOLDIER *sb.* + -LY.]

**A.** *adj.* **1.** Becoming or appropriate to, befitting, a soldier or soldiers. (Cf. SOLDIERLIKE *a.* 2.)

**1577** B. GOOGE *Heresbach's Husb.* II. 50 Varro maketh mention of foure kindes of enclosure, the fyrst naturall, the second wylde, the thirde souldierly. [*Ibid.*, The third the Souldiers fortefying.] *a* **1586** SIDNEY *Arcadia* I. vi. ¶2 They had fought rather with beastly furie, then with any souldierly discipline. **1631** CHAPMAN *Cæsar & Pompey* II. 1, Can I hope..to raise my fortunes By creeping up in soldierly degrees? **1665** MANLEY *Grotius' Low C. Wars* 724 They published an answer filled with many souldierly taunts. **1777** ROBERTSON *Hist. Amer.* v. (1778) II. 4 The impetuosity of his temper..mellowed into a cordial soldierly frankness. **1809** MALKIN *Gil Blas* v. i. ¶21 It is not soldierly to shrink from the perils of the field. **1874** GREEN *Short Hist.* iv. §3. 176 The rough soldierly nobleness of his nature breaks out at Falkirk.

**2.** Having the qualities of a soldier. (Cf. SOLDIERLIKE *a.* 1.)

**1610** HOLLAND *Camden's Brit.* I. 450 Some of his kinde souldierly followers founded a Chanterie at Castle Heningham. **1675** TRAHERNE *Chr. Ethics* 325 Little better then a souldierly ruffian. **1763** H. WALPOLE *Lett.* (1891) IV. 68 My nephew..is very soldierly and lively. **1770** BP. FORBES *Jrnl.* (1886) 288 In order to seige, or rather murder, the sogerly Shaw. **1847** C. BRONTE *J. Eyre* xvii, Colonel Dent is a fine soldierly man.

**3.** *Comb.*, as *soldierly-like*, *-looking*.

**1601** in *Sydney Papers* (1746) II. 240 My Lord smootheth over the vncivill Entertainment with..souldiourly-like excuses. **1823** SCOTT *Quentin D.* xvii, A tall, stout, soldierly-looking man.

**B.** *adv.* = SOLDIERLIKE *adv.*

**1585** SIDNEY *Lett.* Misc. Wks. (1829) 309 The companies heer.., whome he had very well and souldierly gou[e]rned. **1611** COTGR., *Soldatesquement*, souldierly, soldier-like. **1650** R. STAPYLTON *Strada's Low C. Wars* x. 8 Never without losse did any army fall off,..though never so skilfully and soldierly. **1886** *St. James' Gaz.* 16 Oct. (Cassell), His warlike daughter smites them hip and thigh, using her sword right soldierly.

**soldiership** ('səʊldʒəʃɪp). [f. SOLDIER *sb.* + -SHIP.] The state or condition of being a soldier; the qualities of a soldier; military experience or skill. Also *fig.* (quot. 1561).

Common *c* 1600 and in the 19th century.

**1561** T. Norton *Calvin's Inst.* IV. 85 There is..most haynous wrong done..if forsakers of monasteries be chosen to the soldiorship of the clergie. **1596** Nashe *Saffron Walden* Wks. (Grosart) III. 153 What his Soldiourship is I cannot iudge. **1605** Shaks. *Macb.* v. iv. 16 Put we on Industrious Souldiership. **1658** *Domestic State Papers* 351 He fears his want of experience in soldiership. **1754** P. H. *Hiberniad* III. 24 A String of Absurdities, relative to the Soldiership of the Irish. **1813** *Examiner* 11 Jan. 17/1 We do not mean to under-value a true spirit of soldiership. **1887** *Spectator* 30 July 1023/2 Soldiership is effectively and systematically taught.

**soldiery** ('səʊldʒərɪ). Forms: *α.* 6 souldiary, 6–7 -iarie; 6–7 souldiourie (7 -ioury, -iorie); 6–7 souldierie, -iery (7 soulgiery), 7 sould(e)rie, -ery. *β.* 6 soldiorie, -iourie, 6–7 -iarie; 7– soldiery. [f. SOLDIER *sb.* + -Y, or ad. OF. *souderie, soud-, souldoierie*, etc.]

**1.** Soldiers collectively; the military; a military class or body.

**1570** Levins *Manip.* 106/2 Soldiourie, *militia.* **1580** Sidney *Let. Q. Eliz.* Misc. Wks. (1829) 245 Of the most popular nation of the world, full of soldiery, and such as used to serve without pay. *a* **1635** Naunton *Fragm. Reg.* (Arb.) 54 The Souldiery..all flockt unto him. **1678** Wanley *Wond. Lit. World* v. ii. §11. 469/2 Leo, a Thracian, elected [Emperor] by the joint consent of Senate and Souldiery. **1745** Wesley *Wks.* (1872) VIII. 173 Do the soldiery walk as those who see themselves on the brink of eternity? **1823** Scott *Quentin D.* xvii, These mercenaries were, of course, a fierce and rapacious soldiery. **1872** E. W. Robertson *Hist. Ess.* Introd. p. xix, The fighting men grew more and more into a soldiery, or a class following the profession of arms for pay.

**2.** Military training; knowledge or science of military matters.

**1579** Digges *Stratiot.* 140 Sundry other principall poyntes of Souldiourie. **1590** Sir J. Smyth *Disc. Weapons* Ded. 13 Vnder the pretence of souldiorie, and warlike Discipline. **1620** J. Ford *Line Life* (1843) 56 That were.. to read a Lecture of souldierie to Hannibal, the most cunningest warriour of his time. *a* **1687** Petty *Pol. Arith.* i. (1690) 17 For Training and Drilling is a small part of Soldiery, in respect of this last mentioned Qualification. **1738** *Gentl. Mag.* VIII. 204/1 If a Genius had attempted to write on such a Subject as Soldiery. **1901** 'Linesman' *Words Eyewitness* iii. (1902) 53 Waiting in the truest spirit of soldiery.

**3.** *attrib.*, as ***soldiery custom, discipline***, etc.

**1598** Barret *Theor. Warres* II. i. 24 To bring our people to more perfection in soldiarie points. **1643** Trapp *Comm. Gen.* xxiv. 9 According to a Souldiery custome in cases of extremity. **1658** Cokaine *Trappolin* I. i, I should never digest the souldiery life. **1682** Sir T. Browne *Chr. Mor.* I. §36 The Heroical vein of Mankind runs much in the Souldiery, and couragious part of the World. **1798** W. Hutton *Family of Hutton* 98 Some soldiery jokes ensued, when our trooper dismounted, and cast a large stone with design to splash her.

**solding (iron)**: see SOLD *v.*[2]

‖**'soldo.** Pl. soldi (also 7 souldyes). [It.:—L. *solidum*: see SOL *sb.*[3]] An Italian coin and money of account, formerly the twentieth part of a lira.

**1599** Hakluyt *Voy.* II. I. 110 You may buy them for 10. *Carchies*, which coine are 4. to a Venetian *Soldo*, which is peny farthing the dozen. **1617** Moryson *Itin.* I. 256 A Pigion for 7 soldi;..one soldo contents a Porter for bringing your victuals from the market. **1636** *Recorde's Ground Arts* 133 A shilling, which is 2 Souldyes, and 20 Souldyes a Lieure of Venice, which is a pound sterling. **1787** Beckford *Italy*, etc. (1805) I. 124 Four soldi a day, when the Duomo was built, were equal to twenty at present. **1841** Browning *Pippa Passes* iv. Poems (1905) 187 Not one *soldo* shall escape me. **1883** tr. *Villari's Machiavelli* II. v. IV. 4 The crowd of Florentines..stripped him of every soldo.

**soldure**, obs. form of SOLDER *sb.*[1]

**sole** (səʊl), *sb.*[1] Forms: 4– sole, 4–5 sool, 4–6 soole (6 solle), 6–7 *Sc.* soille, soile; 4 soul, 6 sowle, 6–7 soale, 6–7 soale, 7–8, 9 *dial.* soal. [a. OF. *sole* (mod.F. *sole* in special senses), = Prov. and Pg. *sola*, Sp. *suela* (cf. It. *soletta*):—pop. and med.L. *sola*, for L. *solea* (whence OF. *suele, seule*, etc.) sandal, shoe. The leading variations of sense appear in OF., and SOLE *sb.*[2] is properly the same word.

A trace of the word appears in OE. in the gloss '*Soleae*, solen' (? for 'solan'), but there is no evidence of continuity. In the other Germanic languages it also occurs in older glosses and later becomes common, as OS. *sola* (pl. *solun*), MLG. *sole, sale* (LG. *soal, saol, sâl*, etc.), MDu. *sole* (*zole*), *sool* (Du. *zool*, Fris. *soal*), OHG. *sola*, MHG. *sole, sol*, rarely *sule, sul* (G. *sohle*); also Da. *saale*, MSw. *sola, sula* (Sw. *såla, sula*), Norw. *sole*, Icel. *sóli*.]

**I. 1. a.** The under surface of the foot; that part of it which normally rests or is placed upon the ground in standing or walking; also, the mark made by this on the ground (quot. *c* 1410).

*c* **1325** *Gloss. W. de Bibbesw.* in Wright *Voc.* 149 *La plaunte*, sole. **1382** Wyclif *Job* xviii. 9 His sole shal ben holde with a grene. —— *Acts* iii. 7 The groundis and plauntis, or solis, of him ben saddid to gidere. *c* **1410** *Master of Game* (MS. Digby 182) xxiv, He knowth hym by þe traces and by his denne and by þe soole. *c* **1532** Du Wes *Introd. Fr.* in *Palsgr.* 903 The soole, *la plante.* **1583** *Leg. Bp. St. Androis* 729 They bring thame farre on ambeling foiles, Bot send thame hame throw on thair soilles. **1590** Spenser *F.Q.* I. x. 9 Most vertuous virgin,..That..Hast wandred through the world now long a day; Yet ceasest not thy wearie soles to lead. **1607** Topsell *Four-f. Beasts* (1658) 95 You would think one of them was the hoof of a Goat, and the other of a Hart, both of them hollow and without soals. **1697** Dryden *Æneid* XI. 1157 By thee protected, with our naked Soles, Thro' Flames unsing'd we march. **1830** R. Knox *Béclard's Anat.* 146 An undulated layer which covers..the double furrowed lines of the dermis, on the palms and soles. **1842** Tennyson *St. S. Stylites* 2 From scalp to sole one slough and crust. **1871** B. Taylor *Faust* (1875) I. xxii. 201 Our shoes are all danced out, we trow, We've but naked soles to run with.

**b.** Freq. with addition *of the* (or *his*, etc.) *foot*.

*c* **1340** Hampole *Pr. Consc.* 1493 Fra þe haterel oboven þe croun..tyl þe sole of þe fot doun. **1387** Trevisa *Higden* (Rolls) IV. 351 For greet knelynge his knees were as þe sooles of his feet. *c* **1440** *Gesta Rom.* xlix. 223 (Harl. MS.), For ther was on him noon helthe, from the toppe of his hede vnto the sole of his fote. **1535** Coverdale *1 Kings* v. 3 Vntyll the Lorde delyuered them vnder the soles of his fete. **1626** Bacon *Sylva* §96 Pigeons bleeding, applyed to the Soales of the Feet, ease the Head. **1686** tr. *Chardin's Coronat. Solyman* 89 For the affront thou hast done me receive a hundred drubs upon the soles of thy feet. **1706–7** Farquhar *Beaux' Strat.* III. i, A little of her Cephalick Plaister to put to the Soals of your Feet. **1809** Malkin *Gil Blas* VII. ii, From the sole of my foot to the crown of my head. **1849** Claridge *Cold Water Cure* 168 Take a shallow foot-bath (only to cover the soles of the foot) for seven to ten minutes.

**c.** *Farriery.* (See quots. 1805, 1831.)

**1610** Markham *Masterp.* II. c. 100 Raze both the quarters of the hoofe..from the cronet vnto the sole of the foote. **1735** Burdon *Pocket Farrier* 79 Never draw a Horse's Soals, on any Pretence whatever. **1798** J. Lawrence *Philos. & Pract. Treat. Horses* II. 233 Nothing to be cut from the soal, binders, or frog, but loose rotten scales. **1805** Boardman *Dict. Veterinary Art* s.v., Sole of a horse, that plate of horn which, encompassing the fleshy sole, covers the whole bottom of the foot. **1831** Youatt *Horse* 285 The Sole..is the under concave and elastic surface of the foot,..extending from the crust to the bars and frog. **1876** Voyle & Stevenson *Milit. Dict.* 393/2.

**d.** *Zool.* The inner or under side of the claw of an animal (cf. quot.).

**1896** tr. *Boas' Text-bk. Zool.* 469 Like Reptiles and Birds, Mammals have cap-shaped claws at the tips of the digits, and here also they are differentiated into two parts, a harder dorsal..wall, and a ventral horny sole,..of looser horn.

**2. a.** The bottom of a boot, shoe, etc.; that part of it upon which the wearer treads (freq. exclusive of the heel); one or other of the pieces of leather or other material of which this is composed (cf. INSOLE and OUT-SOLE). Also, a separate properly-shaped piece of felt or other material placed in the bottom of a boot, shoe, etc.

Also applied to the corresponding part of a stocking or sock: see *stocking-sole*.

*c* **1440** *Promp. Parv.* 463/2 Sole, of a schoo, *solea.* **1530** Palsgr. 272/1 Sole of a shoo, *semelle.* **1548** *Act 2 & 3 Edw. VI*, c. 9 §4 The inner soule of the saide double souled Shoes. **1573** Tusser *Husb.* (1878) 98 A hone and a parer, like sole of a boote. **1602** Shaks. *Ham.* II. ii. 234 On Fortunes Cap, we are not the very Button. *Ham.* Nor the Soales of her Shoo? **1661** Lovell *Hist. Anim. & Min.* 34 The ashes..of an old shooe soale, helps gallings by the shooe. **1720** *Humourist* 84 The same Shoes, with Cork Soals, and square Toes. **1791** Beloe *Herodotus* I. 196 [The] sandals..consisted of one or of more soals, and were fastened with thongs above the foot. **1806** Beresford *Miseries Hum. Life* II. i, The sole of the shoe torn down in walking. **1862** *Catal. Internat. Exhib., Brit.* II. §4977 A hinge in the outer sole, to allow the foot to bend when walking. **1885** *Harper's Mag.* Jan. 280/1 The sole in a machine-made shoe would mean a sole, an inner sole, shank piece.

**b.** With punning allusion to SOUL *sb.*

See also Shaks. *Merch. V.* IV. i. 123; *Rom. & J.* I. iv 15; II. iv. 67, etc.

**1603** Dekker *Wonderfull Yeare* Wks. (Grosart) I. 130 An honest cobler (if at least coblers can be honest that liue altogether amongest wicked soales). **1641** 'Smectymnuus' *Vind. Answ.* xiv. 179 You and they may turn *Fratres Mendicantes*, and go bare foot, if you part with these pairs of soles.

†**c.** A sandal. *Obs. rare.*

**1553** Brende *Q. Curtius* VIII. 53 When their soles [L. *solea*] be taken off, their feet be anointed with sweet odours.

†**d.** *transf.* A thin piece or leaf of iron produced in the manufacture of tin-plate. *Obs.*

**1728** *Phil. Trans.* XXXV. 631 These Leaves are drawn from Bars of Iron, about an Inch square; which being made a little flat, they cut into thin Pieces or Soles (*semelles*).

**II. 3.** †**a.** The foundation of a building; the site of a city, etc. *Obs. rare.*

**1417** *Eng. Misc.* (Surtees) 12 John Hesill sall ga lyne right fra the bak syde of hys post that standys in hys hall hend un to hys sole in thys house that he byggys. *Ibid.*, That Hesyll may hafe rowme thar to lay hys sole, and rayse thys house. *c* **1460** *Towneley Myst.* iii. 391 So wold mo..that I se on this sole of wifis that ar here. **1615** Sandys *Trav.* 127 In the sole, a stone of Porphyr, whereon..she did set our Saviour. *Ibid.* 157 The sole where the New City stood..is now left out of the walls of Jerusalem. **1634** Sir T. Herbert *Trav.* 86 [The mosque is] round built with good white marble five yards high from the sole, the rest is dried bricks.

**b.** The bottom, floor, or hearth of an oven or furnace.

(*a*) **1615** Markham *Eng. Housew.* II. ix, Large Ovens to bake in, the soales thereof, rather of one or two intire stones, than of many bricks. **1847** Halliwell, *Sole*, the floor of an oven. *Linc.* **1876** Page *Adv. Text-bk. Geol.* vii. 136 Leckstones were largely used for the linings and soles of ovens.

(*b*) **1839** Ure *Dict. Arts* 579, *a* is the ash pit vaulted under the sole of the furnace. **1864** *Q. Jrnl. Sci.* I. 493 When it is required to make steel, the coverings of the sole..are omitted. **1884** C. G. W. Lock *Workshop Rec.* Ser. III. 56/1 The sole of the furnace is usually 16 to 24 ft. square.

**c.** *Naut.* (See quots.)

*c* **1850** *Rudim. Navig.* (Weale) 149 *Sole*, a sort of lining to prevent wearing or tearing away the main part to which it may be attached; as to the rudder, bilgeways, &c. **1867** Smyth *Sailor's Word-bk.* s.v., The decks of the cabin and forecastle in some ships, respectively called the cabin and forecastle soles.

**4. a.** = SILL *sb.*[1] 1 and 2. Cf. WINDOW-SOLE. Now *rare.*

**1419–20** *Mem. Ripon* (Surtees) III. 144 Et in ij liminibus de quarcu et ij soles de esch emt. pro ij sperys de novo faciendis in prædicta domo. **1433** *Fabric Rolls York Minster* (Surtees) 53, iij balkes, iiij stanzons, vij bandclogs, iij soles. **1541** in *Proc. Antiq. Scot.* (1860) III. 161 In heicht fra the sollis of the said queir duris..xxxij futtis. **1625** *Burgh Rec. Glasgow* I. 347 The soillis of thair windois being fywe futes abone the flure. **1669** Sturmy *Mariner's Mag.* VII. xxix. 42 A Gally-pot of Fair-water..will set it self level being placed upon the Sole of the Window. **1709** *Phil. Trans.* XXVI. 290 The Water, in some, was as high as the Soles of the Windows. **1844** H. Stephens *Bk. Farm* I. 139 Generally a great number of small articles are thrown on the sole of a work-horse stable window. **1866** Brogden *Prov. Lincs.*, *Sole*,..the seat of a window. **1875** *Encycl. Brit.* II. 473/1 *Sill* or *Sole*.., the horizontal base of a door or window-frame.

**b.** *Naut.* and *Fortif.* (See quots.)

**1769** Falconer *Dict. Marine* (1780), *Sole*, a name sometimes given to the lower side of a gun-port, which however is more properly called the port-sell. **1859** F. A. Griffiths *Artil. Man.* (1862) 248 The sole of the embrazure is the bottom, or space, between the cheeks, or sides. **1879** *Encycl. Brit.* IX. 432 The slope of the bottom of the embrasure, called the 'Sole'.

**c.** *Mining.* (See quots.)

**1839** Ure *Dict. Arts* 843 It may happen that the floor of the gallery shall not be sufficiently firm to afford a sure foundation to the standards; and it may be necessary to make them rest on a horizontal piece called the sole. **1883** Gresley *Gloss. Coal-m.* 229 *Sole*, a piece of timber set underneath a prop.

**d.** A flat tile used as a rest or support for a draining-tile or drain-pipe.

**1843** *Mech. Mag.* XXXIX. 191 Flat tiles, or soles, are formed in nearly the same manner. **1847** Dwyer *Pract. Hydraulic Eng.* 115 When the tiles and soles, or pipe tiles are used in minor drains, each tile should rest equally upon two soles. **1881** *Mechanic* 519 An excellent plan is to lay soles or flat tiles and in these to set half-pipes or bridge-pipes.

**5.** †**a.** The rim of a wheel. *Obs.*[−1]

**1523** Fitzherb. *Husb.* §5 On marreis ground and soft ground the other wheles be better, bycause they be broder on the soule.

**b.** The inner circle of a water-wheel (cf. quot. 1797).

**1673–4** Grew *Anat. Pl., Trunks* (1682) 138 So also the Ladles and Soles of a Mill-wheel are always made of Elm. **1707** Mortimer *Husb.* 332 Elm is a Timber..proper for Water-works, Mills, Soles of Wheels, Pipes, Aquaducts. **1797** *Encycl. Brit.* (ed. 3) XVIII. 903/2 The inner circle..is called the Sole of the wheel, and usually consists of boards nailed to strong wooden rings of compass timber..firmly united with the arms or radii. **1825** J. Nicholson *Operat. Mechanic* 84 Burn's overshot-wheel..forms a large hollow cylinder by its buckets and sole.

**c.** The lower frame-timbers of a wagon, cart, etc. (cf. quots. and SILL *sb.*[1] 1 b).

**1843** *Civil Eng. & Arch. Jrnl.* VI. 265/2 The timber framing which carries the hinge on which the body of the [railway] wagon turns in the act of tipping, is called the 'soles'. **1851** *Coal-Trade Terms Northumb. & Durh.* 49 *Sole*, the part of a chaldron waggon or coal-tub frame to which the bearances for the wheels are attached, and into which the sheths are inserted. **1876** Robinson *Mid-Yks. Gloss.* s.v., The soles of a cart are the middle supporting timbers of the body.

**6. a.** The lower part, bottom, or under surface of anything. Chiefly in more or less specific uses (cf. next).

**1615** Crooke *Body of Man* 629 In Fishes onely the very tippe of the tongue is loose, the rest is fastened downe vnto the Soale of the mouth. **1660** *Markham's Eng. Housew.* II. ii. 72 Put in the soal of a Manchet, a good quantity of sweet butter, and season it with Pepper [etc.]. **1688** Holme *Armoury* III. 289/1 The parts of a Shuttle are,..the Sole, is the Bottom of it, which is smooth shod with Iron Plate. **1769** Falconer *Dict. Marine* (1780), *Fond d'affût*, the sole or bottom of a gun-carriage. **1791** *Selby Bridge Act* 4 The sole of the said bridge..shall not be less than three feet above the ..top of the present artificial or flood banks. **1811** *Acc. Game Curling* 3 The under surface, or sole, as it is called, is polished as nicely as possible, that the stone may move easily along. **1839** Ure *Dict. Arts* 649 The lower piece, or sole of the engine.., is screwed down..to a strong board. **1875** Knight *Dict. Mech.* 1392/2 A block or tray with a flat sole. **1887** *Jamieson's Sc. Dict.* Suppl. 224/1 *Sole*,..the flat bottom of the head of a golf-club.

**b.** *esp.* The under part or surface of a plane-stock, plough, rudder, electrical instrument, etc.

(*a*) **1678** Moxon *Mech. Exerc.* iv. 64 The Iron..will rise above the Sole into the Mouth of the Stock, and consequently not touch the Stuff. *Ibid.* vi. 113 The under-side of a Plain is called the Sole. **1823** P. Nicholson *Pract. Builder* 229 The edge of the iron of a plane is said to be rank-set when it projects considerably below the sole. **1846** Holtzapffel *Turning* II. 499 The sole of a long plane is in a great measure the test of the straightness of the work. **1875** *Carp. & Join.* 26 In the carpenter's plane the sole quickly deteriorates, and must then be planed off true again.

(*b*) **1766** *Museum Rust.* VI. 427 Keep but the sole of the plough level in the ground. **1831** *Sutherland Farm Rep.* 71 in *Husb.* (L.U.K.) III, The ploughing [is] so deep as to leave some of the lime visible below the plough sole. **1831** J. HOLLAND *Manuf. Metal* I. 156 In every plough, not only the parts above named, but the sole or under plate,.. are of iron or cast metal. **1879** *Cassell's Techn. Educ.* I. 290.

(*c*) **1855** *Orr's Circ. Sci., Elem. Chem.* 217 One half of the instrument [i.e. the electrophorus]—to which the term '*sole*' has been given—is now prepared, and it only remains to form the cover. **1866** R. M. FERGUSON *Electr.* 190 The condenser is generally placed in the sole of the instrument [an induction coil], and does not meet the eye.

(*d*) **1867** SMYTH *Sailor's Word-bk.*, *Sole of the Rudder*, a piece of timber attached to its lower part to render it nearly level with the false keel.

**c.** A smooth or flat surface or side.

**1711** W. SUTHERLAND *Shipbuild. Assist.* 164 *Sole of Planks*; the flat Side of them. **1879** *Encycl. Brit.* X. 367 The stones in the boulder-clay..have one or more flat sides or 'soles', are smoothed or polished [etc.].

**7.** †**a.** (See quot.) *Obs.*$^{-1}$

**1610** FOLKINGHAM *Art Surv.* I. iii. 5 The vpper Crust is the Soile or Soale of the Earth.

**b.** The under surface of land or soil; the subsoil. *rare.*

**1683** in *Macfarlane's Geogr. Collect.* (S.H.S.) II. 139 This clay is not so good a sole as the other. **1796** in Robertson *Agric. Perth* (1799) 518 By this means I put the sole of the arable ground, or under surface, as far as I can from the upper surface. **1859** R. F. BURTON *Centr. Afr.* in *Jrnl. Geogr. Soc.* XXIX. 158 Its sole displays quartzose sand, with scatters of granite.

**c.** A (good, etc.) surface or bottom in a field, turf, etc.

**1846** BROCKETT *N.C. Gloss.* (ed. 3) II. 146 If it be smooth and level it is said to have a good sole. **1893** W. FREAM *Youatt's Compl. Grazier* x. i. 898 Crested dogstail grass.. contributes materially to the production of a good 'sole' in the turf of pastures.

**8. a.** *Mining.* The bottom or floor of a vein, level, or working.

**1653** MANLOVE *Customs Lead Mines* 274 Sole of the Rake, Smytham, and many more. **1667** PRIMATT *City & C. Builder* 5 They have the conveniency of driving a drift or sough, from the bottom of the hills to the sole of the Rake. **1747** HOOSON *Miner's Dict.* B iv, The Sole and Roofe, or Skirt. *Ibid.* S iv, When Doorsteds are used, and the Sole of the Drift so soft, that it will not bear the Forks. **1789** J. WILLIAMS *Min. Kingdom* I. 278 The soles of the string were nearly upon a level with the soles of the vein. **1839** URE *Dict. Arts* 981 *Pitcoal*, A platform about 3 feet high is left at the sole. **1886** HOLLAND *Chesh. Gloss.*, *Sole.* Salt-mining term. The bottom of the mine.

**b.** The bottom or lowest part *of* a valley, etc.

**1880** V. L. CAMERON *Future Highway* II. xii. 257 Their tents were pitched as low down as possible, some in the very sole of the valley. **1886** R. F. BURTON *Arab. Nts.* (abr. ed.) III. 410 His men took to flight and fled along the sole of the Wady.

**c.** *dial.* The bottom of a furrow.

**1877** in PEACOCK *N.W. Linc. Gloss.* 232/1.

**d.** *Geol.* The underlying or lowest thrust plane of a thrust.

**1889** H. M. CADELL in *Trans. R. Soc. Edin.* XXXV. 347 This experiment shows that underneath a series of beds, repeated and heaped together by small thrusts, inclined perhaps at considerable angles, there runs..a major thrust or 'sole', inclined at a lower angle, along which the whole mass may have travelled for considerable distances. **1907** J. HORNE in B. N. Peach et al. *Geol. Struct. N.W. Highlands Scotland* xxxii. 464 Owing to..the friction along the unyielding lower plane or 'sole' of the thrust, there was a tendency in the materials to fold over and curve under. **1965** A. HOLMES *Princ. Physical Geol.* (ed. 2) ix. 225 Along the sole of a major thrust severe crushing and grinding of the rocks is to be expected.

**e.** *Geol.* The lowest layer of ice in a glacier, containing rock debris.

**1930** *Amer. Jrnl. Sci.* CCXIX. 13 A rock fragment subjected to the abrasion processes in action on the sole of a glacier. **1952** *Jrnl. Glaciol.* II. 128 This deposit is then pulled along in a continuous manner by the movements of the glacier, thus forming the sole. **1977** A. HALLAM *Planet Earth* 87 In the roofs of these cavities we see the rock-studded glacier sole.

**f.** *Geol.* The under-side of a sedimentary stratum.

**1957**, etc. [see *sole marking*, sense 9 below]. **1972** H. BLATT et al. *Origin Sedimentary Rocks* v. 170 Such structures are normally observed in the field on the sandstone sole. **1972** F. J. PETTIJOHN et al. *Sand & Sandstone* iv. 114 The flute.. preserved as a raised structure or flute cast on the underside or sole of the overlying sand bed.

**III. 9.** *attrib.* and *Comb.* **a.** Simple attrib., as ***sole board(ing, channel, clout, cushion***, etc.; **sole-bar** (also **solebar**) (see quots.); *spec.* a longitudinal member forming part of the under-frame of a railway carriage or wagon; **sole mark, marking** *Geol.*, a feature that is found on the undersurface of sedimentary strata which overlie softer beds, and is the cast of a depression originally formed in the surface of the lower bed; **sole-plate** (also **soleplate**) (see quots.); *spec.* the metal plate forming the base of an electric iron.

**1829** *Glover's Hist. Derby* I. 242 Needham, a London framework-knitter, placed the trucks on the *solebar. **1844** H. STEPHENS *Bk. Farm* I. 414 The sloping edge *d m* represents the enlargement of the sole-bar, on which the share is fitted. **1909** *Cent. Dict.* Suppl., *Sole-bar*, an out-side sill in a railway car. **1930** *Engineering* 24 Jan. 102/2 The main frame..consists of two longitudinals or solebars. **1977** *Modern Railways* Dec. 486/1 Current new stock..has an all-aluminium underframe with the solebars made from continuous extrusions. **1577** *Burgh Rec. Glasgow* I. 67 The said erle furnesand glasbandis, *soil-burdis, lyme, and sand. **1844** H. STEPHENS *Bk. Farm* II. 326 On the inside of the shroud-plates are formed the grooves for securing the ends of the buckets and of the *sole-boarding. **1891** *Cent. Dict.*, **Sole-channel*, in a boot- or shoe-sole, a groove in which the sewing is sunk to protect it from wear. **1821** SCOTT *Pirate* xv, The sock, and the heel, and the *sole-clout of a real steady Scottish pleugh. **1825** JAMIESON *Suppl.*, *Sole-clout*, a thick plate of cast metal attached to that part of the plough which runs on the ground. **1836** *Penny Cycl.* VI. 188/2 The pads or *sole-cushions of the spreading feet [of the camel] are divided into two toes. **1417** in *Eng. Misc.* (Surtees) 11 Fra the *sole end of the frunt before in to the streteward. **1844** H. STEPHENS *Bk. Farm* I. 414 The breadth of the *sole-flange [of a plough] is 2 inches. **1961** J. CHALLINOR *Dict. Geol.* 185/1 *Sole-marks. **1972** J. F. PETTIJOHN et al. *Sand & Sandstone* I. iv. 113 Although they occur in almost all sands, sole marks are particularly abundant in turbidites where they provide the best means of determining current flow. **1978** FRIEDMAN & SANDERS *Princ. Sedimentol.* iv. 110/2 (*caption*) Sole mark assemblage dominated by counterparts of flutes..and transverse scour marks. **1957** P. H. KUENEN in *Jrnl. Geol.* LXV. 231/1 In a number of papers ..mention is made of the occurrence of various types of markings on the sole of the graywackes. The present paper aims at presenting a coherent record of these *sole markings. **1976** R. C. SELLEY *Introd. Sedimentol.* vii. 211 Flutes, grooves and tool marks are three of the commonest sole markings found as interbed sedimentary structures. **1859** *Todd's Cycl. Anat.* V. 531/1 The remarkable dorsal hump, and..the cushion-like *sole-pad of the Dromedary. **1706** STEVENS *Span. Dict.* I, *Soléta*, the *Sole-part of a Stockin. **1869** SIR E. REED *Shipbuild.* iv. 60 In..the screw ships of the Royal Navy.., the *sole-piece is very broad and shallow in wake of the aperture. **1901** BLACK *Scaffolding* 50 The next thing to do is to prepare a sole piece out of 11in. by 4in. which is laid on the firm ground so as to make a little less than a right angle with the inside of the outermost shore. **1741** *Phil. Trans.* XLI. 564 This *Sole-plate answers the Shape of the Foot. **1844** H. STEPHENS *Bk. Farm* II. 310 The sole-plate on which the superstructure of the [crank-] engine is raised. **1875** KNIGHT *Dict. Mech.* 2244/2 *Sole-plate*, the back portion of a water-wheel bucket. **1960** *Housewife* Apr. 86/2 The sole-plate, being extra thin, heats quickly. **1974** *Spartanburg* (S. Carolina) *Herald* 24 Apr. (Sears Advts. Suppl.) 2 Has a 21-vent soleplate. Steams up to 30 minutes at a low setting. **1434** in Rogers *Agric. & Pr.* III. 551/1 [Two] *soolshoon. **1808** JAMIESON, *Soleshoe*, a piece of iron, on what is called the head, or that part of a plough on which the sock, or share, is fixed. **1844** H. STEPHENS *Bk. Farm* I. 408, H is the sole-shoe on which the plough has its principal support. **1593** *Rites & Mon. Ch. Durh.* (Surtees) 23 The said sockett [of a cross] was maid fast with iron and lead to the *sole stone. **1839** URE *Dict. Arts* 1248, f, the sole-stone [of a smelting-furnace], of granite, hewn out basin-shaped. **1884** KNIGHT *Dict. Mech.* Suppl., **Sole Tile*, a flat or bellying tile.., for the bottom of sewers, muffles, or other objects.

**b.** Misc., as ***sole-bound, -shaped; sole-deep, -walking.***

**1610** FOLKINGHAM *Art Surv.* I. viii. 19 Burnt, parched, soale-bound,..and wet spewing grounds. *Ibid.* x. 24 Crust-clung and Soale-bound soyles. **1870** ROLLESTON *Anim. Life* 48 The sole-shaped locomotor disc known as the 'foot'. **1875** KNIGHT *Dict. Mech.* 2243/2 A vertically moving sole-shaped die. **1891** HARDY *Tess* (1900) 105/1 The snow..lay sole-deep upon the floor. **1894** *Pop. Sci. Monthly* June 284 There still exists on this island a singular cat..which is plantigrade (sole-walking).

**c.** Objective, chiefly in names of implements or machines (see quots.).

**1875** KNIGHT *Dict. Mech.* 2242–3 Sole-beating, -channeling, -cutting (etc.) Machine. *Ibid.* 2243 Sole-finishing Tool. *Ibid.* 2244 Sole-shaper. **1885** *Harper's Mag.* Jan. 279/2 The curved outline of the sole is cut by passing the strips beneath two curved sliding or revolving knives in a 'sole-cutting machine'. **1897** *Allbutt's Syst. Med.* II. 933 In 'sole stitching' by American machinery the men are said to have become mercurialised by volatilisation of the metal.

**sole** (səʊl), *sb.*[2] Forms: α. 4– **sole** (5 **soel**). β. 7–8 **soal(e**, 8 **soall**. [a. OF. (also mod.F.) *sole* (= Sp. *suela*), of the same origin as prec., agreeing in sense with L. *solea* (whence Pg. *solha*, It. *sogliola*).]

**1. a.** A common British and European flat-fish (*Solea vulgaris* or *solea*), highly esteemed as food; one or other of the various fishes belonging to the widely-distributed genus *Solea*.

α. **1347** *Durh. Acc. Rolls* (Surtees) 41 In playces, sperling', et soles emp., vj s. x d. **1372** in Riley *Mem. Lond.* (1868) 367 [Certain fish called] Soles. *c* **1450** *Two Cookery Bks.* 103 Sole, boiled, rost, or fryed. Take a sole, and do awey þe hede [etc.]. *c* **1480** *Cely Papers* (Camden) 189 Item whelkes, iiij d. Item iij solys, vij d. *c* **1520** L. ANDREW *Noble Lyfe* III. lxxxv, Solea is the sole, that is a swete fisshe and holsom for seke people. **1555** EDEN *Decades* (Arb.) 300 Dryed fysshe as soles, maydens, playces,..& such other. **1620** VENNER *Via Recta* iv. 72 The Sole verily is to be reckoned among the meats of primest note. **1653** H. COGAN tr. *Pinto's Trav.* xxviii. (1663) 108 It is not possible to deliver the store of fish that is taken in this river, chiefly Soles and Mullets. **1769** PENNANT *Brit. Zool.* III. 190 The sole is found on all our coasts. **1827** SOUTHEY *Devil's Walk* xlviii, Now soles are exceedingly cheap. **1840** *Cuvier's Anim. Kingd.* 324 All the Soles are excellent fishes, and may be had in good condition nearly all the year. **1870** YEATS *Nat. Hist. Comm.* 324 The sole is common on the British coasts, and in season from May to November.

β. **1630** J. TAYLOR (Water P.) *Wks.* I. 117/1 The pide-coat Mackrell, Pilchard, Sprat, and Soale. **1696** *Phil. Trans.* XIX. 350 Here are also good plenty of large Soals, taken in Troul-nets. **1714** GAY *Trivia* II. 294 The jointed Lobster, and unscaly Soale. **1758** JOHNSON *Idler* No. 33 ¶7 Dined alone in my room on a soal. **1797** P. WAKEFIELD *Mental Improv.* (1801) I. 102 A small pectunculus or cockle, is the prey of the soal.

**b.** In collective singular. In quot. 1700 with punning allusion to SOUL *sb.*

**1661** CHILDREY *Brit. Baconica* 18 Soale and Playce (both which follow the tide into the fresh rivers). **1700** T. BROWN tr. *Fresny's Amusem.* 21 An Old Burly Drab, that Screams out the Sale of her Maids and her Sole at the same Instant. **1781** COWPER *Conversat.* 336 Serve him with ven'son, and he chooses fish; With soal—that's just the sort he would not wish. **1899** *Daily News* 15 July 5/1 Sole is dear again, even more than usually so.

**c.** In the names of various dishes, as ***sole bonne femme*** [*bonne femme* s.v. BONNE C]; ***sole (à la) Colbert*** (see quot. 1877); ***sole (à la) meunière*** [MEUNIÈRE *a.* and *adv.*]; ***sole Véronique*** (see quot. 1960).

**1846** A. SOYER *Gastronomic Regenerator* 115 *Sole à la Colbert*,..sole..butter..chopped parsley..chopped tarragon and chervil..lemon juice. *Ibid.*, *Sole à la Meûnière*, ..sole..chopped onions..butter..lemon..cayenne pepper. **1877** E. S. DALLAS *Kettner's Bk. of Table* 136 The sole of Colbert..is a fried sole which after being cooked is boned and then filled with maître d'hôtel butter and with lemon-juice. **1928** D. L. SAYERS *Unpleasantness at Bellona Club* vii. 71 He..had a sole Colbert very well cooked. **1930** R. LEHMANN *Note in Music* v. 205 He..ordered sole *bonne femme*, a mixed grill, salad, trifle, a welsh rarebit. **1960** *Good Housek. Cookery Book* 95/2 *Sole Véronique*,.. sole..mushrooms..wine..cream..grapes..butter. **1966** *Harper's Bazaar* Sept. 87/3 She..does *sole Véronique* with lichees instead of grapes. **1967** G. GREENE *May we borrow your Husband?* 185 For a while the *sole meunière* gave them an excuse not to talk. **1978** F. MULLALLY *Deadly Payoff* xi. 142 The two burly men would..plough through a hearty meal of sea-food, sole *meuniere* and Stilton. **1979** 'L. BLACK' *Penny Murders* iv. 38 Kate..declared she would make it a fish day..a sole. Should it be *Véronique* with white grapes, or *à la Dugléré* [*sic*], cooked in white wine with tomatoes and shallots?

**2.** With distinguishing terms.

See also LEMON *sb.*[2]

**1668** WILKINS *Real Char.* 141 Common Sole. Spotted Sole. **1839** YARRELL *Suppl. Brit. Fishes* 36 The Solenette, or Little Sole. **1840** tr. *Cuvier's Anim. Kingd.* 324 *S. vulgaris*, the Common Sole, is dark-brown on the upper part. **1840** *Penny Cycl.* XVIII. 263/2 Of the subgenus *Monochirus*, one species is found on the British coast, and is known by the names Variegated Sole, Red-backed Flounder, &c. (*M. linguatulus*).

**3.** In American and Australasian use: One or other of various fishes belonging to related genera (esp. *Achirus*) or to the family *Pleuronectidæ*.

**1882** JORDAN & GILBERT *Syn. Fishes N. Amer.* 841 *Achirus.* Soles. **1884** GOODE *Nat. Hist. Aquat. Anim.* 175 The much-prized Sole of Europe, *Solea Vulgaris*, does not occur in the Western Atlantic... Its nearest representative, the American Sole, is found along our coast from Boston. *Ibid.* 182–188. **1898** MORRIS *Austral Eng.* 426. **1903** GOODE & GILL *Amer. Fishes* p. lxviii.

**4.** *attrib.* and *Comb.*, as ***sole fillet, potage, -pritching, -skin; sole-like*** adj.

**1725** *Fam. Dict.* s.v. *Fish Potages*, To prepare a Sole Potage for Fish Days. *Ibid.* s.v. *Sole*, A Dish of Sole Fillets with a Lentil-Cullis. **1834** MEDWIN *Angler in Wales* II. 118 He dwelt with delight on sole-pritching, mackerel-fishing, and cod-fishing. **1859** SALA *Gaslight & D.* x. 120 Dried soleskins wherewith to clear the decoction of the Indian berry. **1881** *Cassell's Nat. Hist.* V. 67 The second sub-order [of *Anacanthini*] consists of the Sole-like division, the Pleuronectoidei.

**sole** (səʊl), *sb.*[3] Now *dial.* Forms: 1 **sal**, 3 **sol**, 4, 6, 9 **sole**, 5 **soole**, 7 **soale**, 9 **soal**, etc. (See also SALE *sb.*[3]) [OE. *sál*, = OS. *sêl* (MLG. and LG. *sêl*, *seil*), MDu. *seel* (Du. *zeel*, Fris. *seel*), OHG. and G. *seil*, ON. *seil*, Goth. **sail* (cf. *insailjan* vb.). Cf. SEAL *sb.*[3] and *v.*[2]]

†**1.** A rope, cord, etc. *Obs.*

*Beowulf* 1906 þa wæs be mæste..seȝl sale fæst. *c* **1000** *Gen.* 372 Me..rideð racentan sal. *c* **1275** *XI Pains of Hell* 162 in *O.E. Misc.* 151 Of heom hi token vnriht mol, For-þi hi drayeþ myd such sol. **1345–6** *Ely Sacr. Rolls* (1907) II. 139 In soles empt. pro dictis Bauderykk.

**2.** *spec.* A rope or cord for tethering or tying up cattle; a wooden collar or yoke used to fasten a cow, etc., in the stall.

*c* **1440** *Promp. Parv.* 463 Soole, beestys teyynge, *trimembrale,..ligaculum.* **1530** PALSGR. 272/2 Sole, a bowe about a beestes necke. **1547** SALESBURY *Welsh Dict.*, *Aerwy*, sole. **1573** TUSSER *Husb.* (1878) 38 Soles, fetters, and shackles, with horselock and pad. **1647** HEXHAM I, A Sole to tye beasts. **1660** *Chirk Castle Acc.* (1908) 93, 3 dozen of soales to tye the cattle. **1826–** in dial. glossaries and texts (N.Cy., Lancs., Chesh., Derby, Shrops., Heref.). **1890** *Glouc. Gloss.*, *Sole*, the noose or loop made of wood attached to one end of the foddering cord, in order to strain the cord up tight.

**sole**, *sb.*[4] *Kent. dial.* ? *Obs.* [OE. *sol* mire, a muddy or miry place (freq. in place-names), = OHG. *sol* (MHG. *sol*, *söl*, G. dial. *sol*, *sohl*).] A pond or pool.

**15..** in Pegge *Kenticisms* (E.D.S.) 48 Besyde the watteringe-sole in thende of Yckhame Streete. **1736** J. LEWIS *Hist. Thanet* (ed. 2) 38 *Soal*, a dirty Pond of standing Water. **1736** PEGGE *Kenticisms* (E.D.S.) 48 *Sole*, a pond, or pool.

**sole**, obs. f. SOUL *sb.*; dial. var. SOWEL, stake.

**sole** (səʊl), *a.* Forms: 4–5 **soul(e**, 5 **sool(l** (**sowle**, **soell**), 5–6 **soole**, 5– **sole**. [a. OF. *soul* (fem. *soule*), *sol* (fem. *sole*), also *sul*, *suel*, *seul* (mod.F. *seul*, *seule*), = Prov. *sol*, Pg. *só*, Sp. and It.

*solo*:—L. *sōlum*, acc. sing. of *sōlus* alone. In later use prob. to some extent directly from Latin.]

**1.** Having no husband or wife; single, unmarried; †celibate. Chiefly in legal use and freq. of women. Now *rare* or *Obs.*

**a.** In predicative use.

The quotations in the first group illustrate the common phrase ***to live sole***.

(*a*) *c* **1386** CHAUCER *Merch. T.* 836 Ne wold he that sche were love ne wyf, But ever lyve as wydow.., Soul as the turtil that lost hath hir make. *c* **1430** LYDG. *Min. Poems* (Percy Soc.) 134 And for it is an impossible To fynde ever suche a wyfe I wil live sowle duryng my lyfe. **1469** *Bury Wills* (Camden) 45 Yf she will leve sowle withowth an husbonde. **1541** BARNES *Wks.* (1573) 311/2, I doe not reprooue that Priestes doth lyue sole. **1570–6** LAMBARDE *Peramb. Kent* (1826) 95 King Edward the Confessor (being otherwise of himself disposed to haue liued sole) tooke unto his wife Edgitha. **1655** FULLER *Ch. Hist.* IX. 163 Indeed Grindal, living, and dying sole, and single, could not be cockering to his own children.

(*b*) **1418** *E.E. Wills* (1882) 34 3if Ionet my wif kepe here soole, withoute husbonde, Twelf-monthe after my decese. **1464** *Rolls of Parlt.* V. 525/2 Eny Gyft or Graunte, by us to hir made while she was soule. **1520** in *Laing Charters* (1899) 82 As longe as she kepeth hirselve sole and wydow. **1548** SOMERSET *Epist. to Scots* Biij b, Yov wil not kepe her sole and vnmaried. **1596** BACON *Max. & Use Com. Law* ix. (1630) 36 The reason is, because shee was once sole. **1726** AYLIFFE *Parergon* 107 Some others are such as a Man cannot make his Wife, though he himself be sole and unmarry'd. **1827** JARMAN *Powell's Devises* II. 289 That her said daughter Martha should pay unto her daughter Mary 30*l.* yearly, while sole and unmarried.

**b.** Attrib., or placed immediately after the sb. ***woman sole***, = *feme-sole* s.v. FEME.

(*a*) **1464** *Rolls of Parlt.* V. 548/2 As if she..were woman soule. **1509–10** *Act 1 Hen. VIII*, c. 18 §2 She [shall] be able ..to sue in her owen name only as a Woman sole. **1628** COKE *On Litt.* 66 If a woman sole shall doe homage. **1642** tr. *Perkins' Prof. Bk.* i. §47. 21 If a woman sole enfeoffe a stranger.

(*b*) **1464** *Rolls of Parlt.* V. 549/1 If she were or had been soule woman at the tyme. **1485** *Ibid.* VI. 285/2 The Countess shall hold..as anie other sole persone not covert of anie Husband. **1558** in Feuillerat *Revels Q. Eliz.* (1908) 7 Albeit he were a sole man without charge of wife or children. **1566** DRANT *Horace, Sat.* II. v. H iij b, Least some shoulde replye..That thou doest good to sole olde men. **1618** J. WILKINSON *Coroners & Sherifes* II. 22 Where any..do make themselues to be beloved of any sole woman, as maide, or widow. **1753–4** RICHARDSON *Grandison* (1781) I. xiv. 84 To what evils..might not I, a sole, an independent young woman, have been exposed?

†**c.** Of life: Pertaining to or involving celibacy.

Common from *c* 1550 to 1590.

**1553** T. WILSON *Rhet.* (1580) 45 These lawes doe declare, how little it is for the common weales aduancement, that.. a Citee should be lesned for loue of sole life. **1579** W. FULKE *Ref. Rastel* 791 He which hath forsaken the profession of sole life, and fallen to..marriage. **1598** BARCKLEY *Felic. Man* v. (1603) 534 Some [men] like a sole life, others thinke it no life without a companion.

**2. a.** Without companions; apart from or unaccompanied by another or others; alone, solitary. Usually predicative.

Common *c* 1400–1450, and freq. with the addition *by himself* or *herself*.

*c* **1400** *Rom. Rose* 3023 He was not soole, for ther was moo; For with hym were other twoo. **1412–20** LYDG. *Chron. Troy* I. 29 The kyng..went allone In-to a wode for to make his mone, Sool by hym silfe. **1474** CAXTON *Chesse* IV. ii. (1883) 168 Whan the kynge hath goon so ferre that alle his men be lost, than he is sole. **1530** PALSGR. 324/2 Sole, alone or solytary, *seul*. **1591** SYLVESTER *Du Bartas* I. i. 77 Shall valiant Scipio Thus himselfe esteem, Never less sole then when he sole doth seem? **1650** HOWELL *Fam. Lett.* II. 121, I am oft times sole, but seldom solitary. **1716** POPE *Iliad* VIII. 250 Sole should he sit, with scarce a God to friend. **1728–46** THOMSON *Spring* 722 All abandon'd to despair, she sings Her sorrows through the night; and on the bough, Sole-sitting [etc.]. **1817** BYRON *Manfred* II. ii. 10, I should be sole in this sweet solitude. **1857** ARNOLD *Rugby Chapel* Wks. (1890) 310 Sole they shall stray.

*attrib.* **1609** BIBLE (Douay) *Baruch* iv. 16 A wicked nation ..which..have led away the beloved of the widow, and made the sole woman [L. *unicam*] desolate of children. **1789** *Triumphs Fortitude* I. 136 As I have none to accuse but myself, so none but myself (sole being as I am) can be involved in its consequences.

†**b.** Separated *from* another. *Obs.*[−1]

*c* **1407** LYDG. *Reson & Sens.* 2703, I abood, Lefte al sool fro my maistresse.

**c.** Of places: Solitary, lonely; secluded.

**1598** YONG *Diana* 43 When I behold The place so sorrowfull and sole. *a* **1618** J. DAVIES (Heref.) *Wit's Pilgr.* Wks. (Grosart) II. 42/1 No State so holie, nor no place so Sole..but is full of Doubt. **1887** SWINBURNE *Locrine* I. ii. 190 There is a bower..still and sole As love could choose for harbourage.

**3. a.** Being, or consisting of, one person only.

***corporation sole***: see CORPORATION 3.

**1399** LANGL. *R. Redeles* I. 62 All was felawis and felawschepe,..No soule persone to punnyshe þe wrongis. **1616** R. C. *Times Whistle* (1871) 58 Although he had noe other company But his sole single selfe to satisfie. **1654** FULLER *Two Serm.* 6 No meere man by his sole selfe without Gods assistance. **1765** BLACKSTONE *Comm.* I. 469 These [two powers] are very unnecessary to a corporation sole. **1861** LD. BROUGHAM *Brit. Const.* xvii. 272 *n.*, Each chapter is a corporation aggregate, and each parson is a corporation sole.

†**b.** ***one sole***, one and no more, one only, a single (person or thing). *Obs.*

*c* **1450** *Merlin* vii. 110 Eche of yow is but oon sole man. **1450–80** tr. *Secreta Secret.* xxvii. 20 Truste thou neuyr in oon sool fisiciane. **1613** W. BROWNE *Brit. Past.* I. i, A jewell, which was never sent To be possest by one sole element. **1626** C. POTTER tr. *Sarpi's Hist. Quarrels* 352 The Ambassador had not..disbursed one sole denier. **1639** N. N. tr. *Du Bosq's Compl. Woman* I. F 4, Is there one sole word in all this worke, to..engender an evill thought?

†**4. a.** In predicative or quasi-advb. use: With no other person or persons; without participator, partner, sharer, etc., in something, esp. in rights, duties, or possessions. *Obs.*

*c* **1450** tr. *De Imitatione* II. viii. 49 Lete ihesu be sool þy derlyng and þy special. **1450** *Rolls of Parlt.* V. 190/1 Eny thyng by us to hym graunted soule, or by us graunted to hym and eny other person or persons joyntly with hym. **1477** *Ibid.* VI. 194/2 Every other persone to whose use the said Duke is sole seised in eny Castelles. **1642** tr. *Perkins' Prof. Bk.* iii. §205. 92 One of the Chapter is sole seised in fee of his owne right of land. **1671** MILTON *P.R.* I. 100, I, when no other durst, sole undertook The dismal expedition.

†**b.** Standing alone; uncontrolled by others.

**1748** RICHARDSON *Clarissa* xiii. I. 74 My father himself could not bear that I should be made Sole, as I may call it, and independent.

**5.** One and only: **a.** Of things.

**1497** BP. ALCOCK *Mons Perfect.* Cj/1 For ye sole ryghtwysnes is in him. **1592** *Sol. & Pers.* II. i, The murtherer will escape Without reueuge, sole salue for such a sore. **1617** MORYSON *Itin.* II. 113 Sir Arthur Chichester had taken the sole Castle held in those parts..by Brian mac Art. **1696** WHISTON *The. Earth* II. (1722) 185 This is the sole way of bringing natural Knowledge to perfection. **1726** SWIFT *Gulliver* IV. xii, But as my sole intention was the public good, I cannot be altogether disappointed. **1798** FERRIAR *Varieties of Man* 223 Those who read for the sole purpose of talking. **1829** LYTTON *Devereux* I. iii, I believe my sole crime was candour. **1862** MILLER *Elem. Chem.*, *Org.* (ed. 2) iii. §3. 177 In this case water and the compound ether are the sole products. **1883** GILMOUR *Mongols* xxiii. 285 He was..the sole support of his father.

**b.** Of persons.

**1513** BRADSHAW *St. Werburge* II. 1506 Athalia.. Commaunded to slee the kynges children all That she myght regne sole princesse imperiall. *a* **1548** HALL *Chron.*, *Hen. VI*, 167 b, Lady Alice, the only child and sole heire of Thomas Montacute. **1596** SPENSER *F.Q.* IV. xii. 30 For death t' adward I ween'd did appertaine To none, but to the seas sole Soueraine. **1647** in *Verney Mem.* (1907) I. 214 In that will my father was left sole executor. **1652** *Nicholas P.* (Camden) 321 L[d] Culpepper design'd by some both in France and Holland to be the K.'s great and sole minister in Holland. **1736** BUTLER *Anal.* II. vii. Wks. 1874 I. 351 The sole author of such a work. **1771** *Junius Lett.* xlviii. (1788) 264 You have..maintained, that the house of commons are the sole judges of their own privileges. **1836** THIRLWALL *Greece* III. 233 Laches, now sole commander, landed a body of the allied troops on the Sicilian coast. **1839** FR. A. KEMBLE *Resid. in Georgia* (1863) 74 The sole manager of these estates. **1892** *Photogr. Ann.* II. 399 Sent to me by Mr. Scholzig, who is their sole agent.

*absol.* **1667** MILTON *P.L.* v. 28 O Sole in whom my thoughts find all repose!

**c.** Singular, unique, unrivalled.

**1398** TREVISA *Barth. De P.R.* XIX. cxvi. (1495) 921 This vnyte [of the Trinity] muste be sole and synguler wythout pere. **1595** SHAKS. *John* IV. iii. 52 This [murder] so sole, and so vnmatcheable. **1667** MILTON *P.L.* v. 272 He seems A Phœnix, gaz'd by all, as that sole Bird When..to Ægyptian Theb's he flies. **1851** MRS. BROWNING *Casa Guidi Wind.* II. 487 The priestly ephod in sole glory swept, When Christ ascended. **1867** HOWELLS *Ital. Journ.* 178 There is a lovely palm-tree, rare, if not sole in that latitude. **1870** DEUTSCH *Rem.* (1874) 193 God is sole of His kind.

†**d.** Placed before a sb., in the sense of 'alone' following it. *Obs. rare.*

*c* **1586** C'TESS PEMBROKE *Ps.* CXIX. iii, Since thy sole edicts containe it, Who search not them how can they gaine it? **1634** SIR T. HAWKINS *Pol. Observ.* 3 That mountaine of fortune which is to be aimed at by sole vertue.

†**6.** Of things, qualities, etc.: Unaccompanied by other things or qualities; standing alone. *Obs.*

(*a*) **1542** BOORDE *Dyetary* x. (1870) 252 Water is not holsome, sole by it selfe. **1562** J. HEYWOOD *Prov. & Epigr.* (1906) 148 Wisdom and folly in thee Is as it were a thing by itself sool.

(*b*) **1590** SWINBURNE *Testaments* 148 When the testator doth not referre his disposition to the sole onelye will of another person,..but to the concreate will, or will ioyned with fact. **1592** WEST *1st Pt. Symbol.* §21 c, Hereupon contracts by consent are defined [as] contracts hauing cause placed in sole consent. **1609** BIBLE (Douay) *Gen.* ii. 17 *comm.*, Neither could it..be better..signified then by a thing sole disobedience is [etc.]. **1622** in *Buccleuch MSS.* (Hist. MSS. Comm.) I. 209 He seeks no other caution or security than the King's sole word.

**7. a.** Of things, rights, duties, etc.: Pertaining or due to, possessed or exercised by, vested in, etc., one person or corporate body to the exclusion of all others; exclusive.

**1597** HOOKER *Eccl. Pol.* V. lvi. §5 Euery of them may haue their sole and seuerall possessions. **1611** KNOLLES *Hist. Turkes* (1638) 167 Vpon any ambitious conceit, or desire of the sole Gouernment. *a* **1661** FULLER *Worthies, Eng.* vi. (1662) 19 This power was sometime sole in a single person and sometimes equally in two together. **1766** BLACKSTONE *Comm.* II. 216 The right of sole succession..was also established with respect to female dignities and titles of honour. **1788** REID *Aristotle's Logic* iv. i. 67 A theory of which he claims the sole invention. **1818** CRUISE *Digest* (ed. 2) I. 486 Where an estate is vested in trustees, for the sole and separate use of a married woman. **1867** RUSKIN *Time & Tide* xxiii. §154 Supreme judges..exercising sole authority in courts of final appeal. **1879** *Athenæum* 6 Sept. 304/3 The present postage system is the sole and undisputed invention of Sir Rowland Hill.

**b.** Similarly of actions.

**1562** *Apol. Priv. Masse* (1850) 9 But you have the other signification of this term private: that is the sole receiving of the sacrament by the priest. **1621** in Elsing *Lords' Deb.* (Camden) App. 153 The priviledge of the sole printing of the Bible. **1651** HOBBES *Leviath.* II. xxii. 119 The End of their Incorporating, is to make their gaine the greater,..by sole buying, and sole selling, both at home, and abroad. **1825** SCOTT *Betrothed* xvii, A good housewife, who..will sometimes even condescend to dress a dish for her husband's sole eating.

**8.** Uniform or unvaried.

**1845** MRS. S. C. HALL *Whiteboy* v. 38 Land..at one time covered with the snowy blossoms of the wild-rush, and at others exhibiting a sole surface of dark brown peat. **1885** MISS GATTY *Juliana H. Ewing* III. 57 He was required to distemper the walls of the drawing-room with a sole colour.

**9.** In quasi-advb. use: Solely.

**1562** J. HEYWOOD *Prov. & Epigr.* (1867) 203 To shew thy thrift soole. **1581** A. HALL *Iliad* II. 31 The burden great, his brother then did beare Sole for his sake in these turmoyles. **1812** CARY *Dante, Parad.* v. 22 Liberty of will; the boon, wherewith All intellectual creatures, and them sole,..[God] hath endow'd. **1820** BYRON *Morg. Mag.* xxv, Think not they lived on locusts sole. **1827** POLLOK *Course T.* VIII, Good and bad..distinguished sole the sons Of men.

**10.** *Comb.* **a.** With vbl. sbs. and pres. pples., as ***sole-being***, ***-speaking***; ***sole-justifying***, ***-lying***, ***-reigning***, ***-ruling***, etc.

**1534** WHITINTON *Tullyes Offices* I. (1540) 71 He wolde flye fro solytarynesse and soole beyng, and wolde seke out a felowe of his study. *c* **1586** C'TESS PEMBROKE *Ps.* XLVII. i, God,..Who high and highlie feared stands, Of all the earth sole-ruling king. **1596** *Edw. III*, II. i, Your progenitour Sole ragning Adam. **1625** B. JONSON *Staple of N.* III. iv, He has the monopoly of sole-speaking. Why, good Sir? you talke all. **1642** J. EATON *Honey-c. Free Justif.* 427 The only soule-saving and sole-saving voice of Christ. **1811** J. P. MALCOLM *Mann. & Cust. London* (ed. 2) II. ii. 20 The true nature of sole-justifying faith. **1831** WORDSW. *To B. R. Haydon* 8 The one Man that laboured to enslave The World, sole-standing high on the bare hill. **1859** G. MEREDITH *R. Feverel* xxi, Two swallows, mates in one nest,..who twittered..to the sole-lying beauty in her bed.

**b.** With pa. pples., etc., as ***sole-begotten***, ***-commissioned***, ***-seated***, ***-thoughted***; also ***sole-happy***, ***-selfly***, ***-sufficient***.

**1591** SYLVESTER *Du Bartas* I. iii. 1123 And Death..Comes very late to his sole-seated Lodge. **1605** *Ibid.* II. iii. I. *Vocation* 1114 Nor as inviron'd,..But rather, as sole-selfly limited, And joyn'd to place. **1606** *Ibid.* iv. II. *Magnificence* 987 Sole-happy Causes of this sumptuous Feast. **1631** *Eng. Primer of Our Lady* 30 Glorie to th' unbegotten Father, And to His sole begotten Son. **1656** R. SIBBS *Conf. Christ & Mary* 71 God is all-sufficient, self-sufficient, sole-sufficient. **1711** SHAFTESB. *Charact.* (1737) III. 340 Is it true..that their excellencys of the present establishment are the sole-commission'd? **1820** KEATS *Eve of St. Agnes* v, These let us wish away, And turn, sole-thoughted, to one Lady there.

**c.** Special combs., as **sole-charge** *attrib. N.Z.*, (*a*) of a teacher: that has sole charge of a school; (*b*) of a school: having only one teacher; also *absol.*; **sole-coloured** *a.*, of a single uniform colour; self coloured; †**sole-sale**, a monopoly; †**sole-talk**, a soliloquy.

**1941** A. CURNOW *Island & Time* 12, I am the sums the sole-charge teachers teach. **1944** H. WILSON *Moonshine* ii. 21 It's [*sc.* the school's] a sole charge. **1955** D. O. W. HALL *Portrait of N.Z.* ix. 171 Small country settlements have their 'sole charge' or single-teacher schools. **1885** MISS GATTY *Juliana H. Ewing* III. 57 The sole-coloured walls well covered with pictures. **1596** BP. W. BARLOW *Three Serm.* ii. 49 The intollerable licenses of Monopoles and Solesales. **1616** T. ROGERS (*title*), Soliloquium Animæ; The sole-talke of the Soule.

**sole**, variant of SOL *a.*, dirty. *Obs.*

**sole** (səʊl), *v.*[1] Also 7 soel, *Sc.* soill; 7–8 soal, *Sc.* soll. [f. SOLE *sb.*[1], perh. through the vbl. sb., which is found earlier. Cf. MDu. *solen* (Du. *zolen*; Fris. *soalje*), LG. *solen*, *salen*, MHG. *solen* (G. *sohlen*, *besohlen*); also Sp. and Pg. *solar*.]

**1.** *trans.* To provide or furnish (a boot, shoe, stocking, etc.) with a sole.

(*a*) **1570** LEVINS *Manip.* 160 To sole, *solum adhibere*. **1580** HOLLYBAND *Treas. Fr. Tong*, *Carreler*, to sole shoes. **1598** *Shuttleworths' Acc.* (Chetham Soc.) 112 Soleinge one pare of shoes, v[d]. **1607** TOPSELL *Four-f. Beasts* (1658) 175 The Scythians make them shooes, and soal them with the backs of Fox and Mise skins. *a* **1680** BUTLER *Rem.* (1759) I. 217 A peripatetic Cobler scorn'd to soal A pair of Shoes of any other School. **1726** SWIFT *Gulliver* IV. x, I soaled my shoes with wood. **1818** SCOTT *Hrt. Midl.* xxix, The deil flay the hide o' it to sole his brogues wi'! **1857** MILLER *Elem. Chem.*, *Org.* vii. §2. 509 [Gutta percha] is employed as a substitute for leather in soling boots and shoes. **1906** SHERRING *Western Tibet* iv. 65 Their shoes..are soled with rope very ingeniously and finely plaited.

*absol.* **1824** SYD. SMITH *Wks.* (1859) II. 45/1 He is at liberty to make a shoe anywhere;..he may sole on the Mississippi,—heel on the Missouri.

(*b*) **1578** in *Archæologia* XXV. 566 Given to a tailor for solinge a payre of stockinges. **1602** SEGAR *Honor, Milit. & Civ.* II. xi. 71 Two others shall put on his blacke nether-stockes soled with leather. **1664** in *Maitland Club Miscell.* (1840) II. 517 For solling his Lordships stockengis.

**b.** To cover with or as with a sole.

**1681** GREW *Musæum* I. vii. ii. 167 The fore-feet are soled each with four little Tufts of Down or short Hair. *Ibid.* 170 His Feet soled with a treble Tuft of a close short..Down.

**c.** To fit the head of a gold-club with a sole.

**1905** *Golf & How to Play it* 11.

**2.** *transf.* To form the base or bottom of.

*a* **1643** CARTWRIGHT *Ordinary* IV. i, My debt-books shall soal Pyes at young Andrew's wedding. **1714** LADY G. BAILLIE *Househ. Bk.* (S.H.S.) 247 For stones to soll the big oven.

**3.** *Golf.* To place the sole of a club on the ground in preparing for a stroke. Also *refl.* and *absol.*

**1909** Vaile *Mod. Golf* 27 Nearly all professionals, when addressing their ball for the put, sole the putter in front of the ball. *Ibid.* 29 The professional soles in front of his ball because [etc.]. *Ibid.*, The driver is made so that it should sole itself when allowed to rest naturally on the ground.

† **sole**, *v.*$^2$ *Obs.* Also 7 **soyle, soal.** [ad. OF. *soler, soller, souler*, var. of *chouler*, etc.: see CHULLE *v.*] *trans.* To throw (a bowl). Also *intr.* of the bowl.

**1638** Wentworth in Carte *Collect. Lett.* (1735) III. 25 The bowl that soyles faire is more probable to run with comeliness and certainty to the mark it is sent. **1658** Bramhall *Schism Guarded* Wks. (1677) 296 'It were strange if he should throw a good cast, who soals his Bowl upon an undersong,' alluding to that ordinary and elegant expression in our English Tongue, 'Soal your Bowl well', that is, be careful to begin your work well. **1679** Coles *Lat. Dict.* I, To sole a bowl, *probe et rite emittere globum.*

† **sole**, *v.*$^3$ *Obs. rare.* [OE. *solian*, = MDu. and MLG. *solen*, OHG. *solôn* (MHG. *solen*): cf. SOL *a.*] *intr.* To become foul or dirty.

*c* **1000** *Reimlied* 67 Searo hwit solaþ, sumur hat colað. *c* **1250** *Owl & Night.* 1276 Nis noht so hot þat hit nacoleþ Ne noht so hwit þat hit ne soleþ.

**sole**, obs. form of SOWL *v.*

‖**solea** ('səʊlɪə). *Eccl.* [Byz. Gr. σολέα, ad. Romanic *solea (cf. It. *soglia*) threshold.] In churches (esp. those of the East), a raised part of the floor in front of a chapel or of the chancel.

**1858** *Ecclesiologist* XIX. 315 The chancel arch [in Shottesbrook church]..is spanned by a high stone screen, outside of which..the prayer-desk stands upon a solea of the width of the screen. **1884** A. J. Butler *Coptic Ch. Egypt* I. iv. 214 In front of all three eastern chapels is a continuous narrow platform or solea.

† '**soleated**, *a.* *Obs.*$^{-0}$ [ad. L. *soleāt-us* wearing sandals.] (See quots.)

**1623** Cockeram I, *Soleated*, shod like a horse, with Iron in his Shooes. **1656** Blount *Glossogr.*, *Soleated*, shod, as horses are, or what wears pattens.

† **solebaiting**, *vbl. sb.* *Obs.* [Alteration of *surbaiting*, after SOLE *sb.*$^1$ and F. *solbature.*] = SURBATING *vbl. sb.*

**1652** H. L'Estrange *Amer. no Jewes* 21 In hot countries people went bare-foot and used to wash their feet for refreshment after surbaiting, or solebaiting, and weariness of travaile.

**solecism** ('sɒləsɪz(ə)m). Forms: α. 6–8 **solœcisme**, 7–9 **solœcism** (7 **solocism**); 6–7 **solæcism(e**, 8 **solaecism**. β. 6–7 **solecisme**, 6– **solecism** (7 **soll-**). [ad. L. *solœcismus*, ad. Gr. σολοικισμός, f. σόλοικος speaking incorrectly, stated by ancient writers to refer to 'the corruption of the Attic dialect among the Athenian colonists at Σόλοι in Cilicia'. So F. *solécisme*, Sp. and It. *solecismo*. The transferred uses of the word also occur in Gr. and L.]

**1.** An impropriety or irregularity in speech or diction; a violation of the rules of grammar or syntax; properly, a faulty concord.

α. **1577** Hanmer *Anc. Eccl. Hist.* (1585) 138 They seeme farre from offending, in any barbarous terme, solœcisme, or ignorant error at all. **1593** Nashe *Foure Lett. Conf.* 70 Sucke out one solœcisme or mishapen English word if thou canst. **1609** Holland *Amm. Marcell.* cjb, A very Solœcisme and incongruitie of Syntaxis. **1699** Bentley *Phal.* 320 All these are gross Solœcisms, the last part of the Sentence not agreeing nor answering to the first; which is the proper definition of a Solœcism. **1702** *Burlesque L'Estrange's Vis. Quevedo* 242 State Aphorismes Cramn'd full with factious Solœcismes. **1839** Brougham *Statesmen Geo. III*, Ser. I. (ed. 2) 72 He certainly spared no pains to eradicate his northern accent, beside being exceedingly careful to avoid provincial solœcisms.

β. **1582** N. T. (Rhem.) Pref. b ij b, They easily take offense of the simple speaches or solecismes. **1588** *Marprel. Epist.* (Arb.) 4 If he did, then he ouersaw many a foule solecisme, many a senceles period. **1660** Jer. Taylor *Ductor* II. iii. rule 14. §34 Solecisms, impure words, and..rude expressions. **1672** Dryden *Defence Epil.* Ess. (ed. Ker) I. 165 Let any man..read diligently the works of Shakespeare and Fletcher, and I dare undertake, that he will find in every page either some solecism of speech, or some notorious flaw in sense. **1717** Wodrow *Corr.* (1843) II. 294, I question much if any of my friends are more sensible of the Scotticisms, yea, solecisms, in my style than I am. **1769** *Junius Lett.* xxvii. (1788) 146 There is something in it, which cannot be..expressed without a solecism in language. **1837** Hallam *Hist. Lit.* I. i. I. 20 We find even early proofs that solecisms of grammar, as well as barbarous phrases.., were very common in Rome itself. **1882** Farrar *Early Chr.* II. 156 The Greek of the Apocalypse is so ungrammatical and so full of solecisms as to be the worst in the entire Greek Testament.

**b.** Without article: Violation of the rules of concord in grammar or syntax; incorrect or ungrammatical speech or diction, or the use of this.

**1583** Fulke *Def. Tr. Script.* i. 47 If the relatiue must alwaies be referred to the antecedent of the same case, to agree with it in case,..there is no Greeke auctor whose workes are extant, but he hath committed Solœcisme. **1603** Holland *Plutarch* Explan. Words, *Solæcisme*, Incongruity of speech, or defect in the purity thereof. **1677** Dryden *Apol. Heroic Poet.* Ess. (ed. Ker) I. 180 A wary man he is in grammar, very nice as to solecism or barbarism. **1699** Bentley *Phal.* 310 Attic, the beloved Dialect of the Sophists,..in which they affected to excell each other, even to Pedantry and Solœcism. **1872** A. Bain *Higher Eng. Gram.* 195 The words employed may be English, but they may be combined in a way that is not English. This is Solecism.

*fig.* **1637** Massinger *Guardian* I. i, Think upon 't, a close friend Or private Mistress, is Court-rhetorick; A Wife, meer rustick Solecism.

**2.** A breach or violation of good manners or etiquette; a blunder or impropriety *in* manners, etc.

(*a*) **1599** *Broughton's Lett.* vi. 19 [It] is surely a solæcisme in manners, and argueth great want of discretion. *a* **1641** Finett *For. Ambass.* (1656) 27 My Lord Walden leaving him at the Court gate and remaining that night (not perhaps without a Solecisme in ceremonie) at Theobalds. **1642** Fuller *Holy & Prof. St.* I. xii. 38 As if she be guilty of casuall incivilities, or solœcismes in manners occasioned by invincible ignorance. **1738** *Gentl. Mag.* VIII. 521/2, I observ'd Prior..whisper somewhat in his Ear, which I suppose was to desire him to rectify that Solecism in Dress. **1778** Miss Burney *Evelina* lxviii, You have committed an outrageous solecism in good manners. **1814** Scott *Wav.* iv, The idea of having committed the slightest solecism in politeness..was agony to him. *a* **1864** Hawthorne *Dr. Grimshawe* xvi. (1891) 208 The cold, unbelieving eye of the Englishman, expectant of solecisms in manners.

(*b*) **1639** Massinger *Unnatural Combat* III. i, He ne'er observed you..take A say of venison or stale fowl by your nose, Which is a solecism at another's table. *a* **1645** Howell *Fam. Lett.* I. I. xl, I should commit a great Solecism, if..I should leave you unsaluted. **1685** in *Verney Mem.* (1904) II. 416, I looke upon it as an ill Omen, that you should committ such a grosse solecisme at your first entrance into the University against your Loving father. **1842** Lever *J. Hinton* v. 33 Who, in the slightest solecism of London manners, could find matter for sarcasm and raillery. **1884** E. Yates *Recoll.* I. 151 In those days smoking in the street was an unpardonable solecism.

**b.** Without article. *rare.*

**1640** Fuller *Abel Rediv.*, *Colet* (1867) I. 116 Solecism he accounted the worst point of slovenry; affecting neatness in his household stuff and clothes. **1642** *Naunton's Fragm. Reg.* 36 For his inside, it may be said, and without solœcisme [1641 offence], that he was his Fathers own sonne.

**3.** An error, incongruity, inconsistency, or impropriety of any kind.

α. **1599** B. Jonson *Cynthia's Rev.* v. ii. [iv], Forgive it now. It was the solæcisme of my starres. **1612** Bacon *Ess.*, *Empire* (Arb.) 300 It is the Solœcisme of power, to thinke to command the ende, and yet not to endure the meane. **1662** Bp. E. Hopkins *Serm. Funerals Hon. A. Grevil* (1663) 18 'Tis as great a solœcisme to think of their graves, as of going to bed at noon day.

β. **1603** Bodley in *Buccleuch MSS.* (Hist. MSS. Comm.) 44 A match..between our Prince and the King of Spain's two years' daughter..is a motion so full of solecisms, as [etc.]. **1753** *De Foe's Tour Gt. Brit.* (ed. 5) I. 266 But tho' exceeding beautiful, yet, I think, to join Roman with Gothic Architecture, is a Solecism. **1792** A. Young *Trav. France* 483 Of all solecisms, none ever equalled Paris demanding that the transport of corn from province to province should be prohibited. **1838** Prescott *Ferd. & Is.* (1846) I. vii. 302 The idea of compelling belief in particular doctrines is a solecism. **1850** Mrs. Jameson *Leg. Monast. Ord.* (1863) 233 Where a fat jovial Franciscan would be a solecism. **1875** Gladstone *Glean.* VI. xviii. 117 What age or country can match the practical solecisms exhibited in the following facts?

**b.** Const. *in* something.

α. **1616** B. Jonson *Epigr.* cxvi, A desperate solœcisme in truth and wit. **1659** C. Simpson *Division-Violist* I. 11 As for Thirds and Sixts,..two, three or more of them, rising or falling together, is no Solæcisme in Musick.

β. **1639** Fuller *Holy War* I. xvi. 23 The Emperours unfurnished their frontiers of garrisons, and laid them open to invasions; a notorious solecisme in policie. **1682** Sir T. Browne *Chr. Mor.* I. §24 To beat down our Foes, and fall down to our Concupiscences, are Solecisms in Moral Schools. **1719** Swift *To Young Clergyman* Wks. 1755 II. II. 11 Stammering, which I take to be one of the worst solecisms in rhetorick. **1741** Middleton *Cicero* II. VIII. 273 Cæsar..committed a dangerous solecism in politics. **1807** *European Mag.* LII. 382/1 To an English dairymaid, the preparation of milk by men would seem a solecism in housewifery. **1824** Miss Mitford *Village* Ser. I. (1866) 68 A terrible solecism in political economy.

**c.** Without article. *rare.*

**1649** Lovelace *Poems* 78 Tis his first Play, twere Solecism 't should goe. **1837** Carlyle *Fr. Rev.* III. II. vi, Their conviction that Louis is a Prisoner of War; and cannot be put to death without injustice, solecism, peril.

Hence **solecismical** *a.* *rare*$^{-0}$.

**1656** Blount *Glossogr.*, *Solecismical*, pertaining to a Solescism, incongruous.

**solecist** ('sɒləsɪst). *rare.* [ad. late L. *solœcista*, = Gr. σολοικιστής.] One who uses solecisms.

**1725** Blackwall *Sacr. Class.* I. ii. §8 Shall a noble writer ..be call'd a solecist and barbarian, for giving a new turn to a word so agreeable to the analogy and genius of the Greek tongue?

**solecistic** (sɒlə'sɪstɪc), *a.* Also **solœcistic(k.** [See prec. and -IC.] Of the nature of or involving solecism: **a.** In speech or diction.

**1806** C. Symmons *Milton* 341 (Jod.), The earliest of these replies, the barbarous and solœcistick style of which [etc.]. **1849** *N. & Q.* I. 149/2 Is it too late to make an effectual stand against the solecistic expression 'Mutual friend'? **1856** W. H. Thompson in Archer Butler *Hist. Anc. Phil.* I. 389 The use of late words, and of solecistic and Latinizing constructions. **1882** Farrar *Early Chr.* II. 296 His solœcistic Greek was sufficient to prove that the language was unfamiliar to him.

**b.** In thought or conduct.

**1865** *Reader* 22 July 87/1 It is rarely that Miss Cobbe distresses fastidiousness by any solecistic ventures in matters of minor import. **1884** *19th Cent.* Jan. 138 Illustrations of the solecistic views which are entertained of those distant parts of the Empire.

**sole'cistical**, *a.* Now *rare* or *Obs.* Also 7 **solœcisticall**, 8–9 **-al.** [See prec. and -ICAL.] Solecistic.

(*a*) **1654** Gayton *Pleas. Notes* IV. xxi. 272 Some long narrative, which was the Apology for the solœcisticall appearances of children. **1837** *Foreign Q. Rev.* XIX. 78 The miserable solecistical conceit of making the chimney-shafts resemble small Doric columns.

(*b*) **1725** Blackwall *Sacr. Class.* (1727) 139 That saying of divine inspiration will be solecistical. **1778** Tyrwhitt *Chaucer's C. Tales* V. 185 According to this hypothesis, the use of these combinations, with respect to the pronouns, is almost always solecistical. **1779** Johnson *L.P.*, *Milton* Wks. 1781 I. 160 Milton..has enforced the charge of a solecism by an expression in itself grossly solecistical. **1818** Hallam *Mid. Ages* II. 300 The nominative Trullo, though solœcistical, is used by ecclesiastical writers in English.

Hence **sole'cistically** *adv.*

**1722** Wollaston *Relig. Nat.* 6 A few scatterd papers, in which I had formerly for my own use set down some of them (briefly, and almost solecistically).

**solecize** ('sɒləsaɪz), *v.* Now *rare* or *Obs.* Also 7, 9 **solecise**, 7 **solœcise, -cize, solæcize.** [ad. Gr. σολοικίζειν, f. σόλοικος: see SOLECISM. So F. *solécíser.*] *intr.* To make use of, or commit, solecisms in language, behaviour, conduct, etc.

(*a*) **1627** W. Sclater *Exp. 2 Thess.* (1629) 225 Absurd fellowes..solecising continually in opinion, speech, action, whole life. **1662** Hibbert *Body of Divinity* I. 207 Men compact of meer incongruities, solecising in all, opinion, speeches and actions.

(*b*) **1655** Stanley *Hist. Philos.* (1687) 30/1 A City, called ..Soleis, whither he brought also some few Athenians, whose Language growing corrupt by that of the Country, they were said to solœcise. **1660** H. More *Myst. Godl.* I. ix. 26 To phansie the Holy Writers to solœcize in their language, when we do not like the sense. **1699** Bentley *Phal.* xii. 320 If these Examples be not sufficient to give Mr. B. some clearer apprehension, what it is to solœcize in the Attic way, it's to no use to add more.

Hence '**solecizer**, '**solecizing** *vbl. sb.*

**1693** J. Edwards *Auth. O. & N. T.* 36 Those persons who dream of solecisms in Holy Scripture are the greatest solecisers themselves. **1895** H. Callan *From Clyde to Jordan* xxvii 283 There is..no solecising even in Soli.

**soled** (səʊld), *ppl. a.* [f. SOLE *sb.*$^1$ or *v.*$^1$] Having a sole or soles (of a specified kind). Chiefly as the second element in various parasynthetic combinations:

**a.** Of boots, shoes, etc. (Cf. SINGLE-SOLED *a.*)

**1480** *Wardr. Acc. Edw. IV* (1830) 118 A pair of shoon double soled,..a pair of shoon single soled. **1541** in *Academy* (1883) 6 Oct. 231/3 For 6 payre of double sollyd showne, 4*s* 6*d*. **1611** Cotgr., *Cothurne*, a fashion of high-soled buskin vsed by the auncient Tragedians. **1756** *Demi-Rep* 35 With twice-sol'd shoes they stamp'd it to the House. **1760** C. Johnston *Chrysal* (1822) III. 154 He sallied out.. in his thick-soled shoes. **1896** *Strand Mag.* XII. 349/1 [The diver's boots] are leaden-soled. **1899** Alice Werner *Captain of Locusts* 237 She put on her flat-soled stuff shoes.

**b.** Of persons or animals.

*a* **1740** Tickell *Fragm. on Hunting* 74 Such be the dog.. thou mean'st to train,..Large leg'd, dry sol'd, and of protended claw.

**c.** Of a water-wheel.

**1834–6** *Encycl. Metrop.* (1845) VIII. 88/2 This wheel.. must..be close boarded, or technically close *soled* round its circumference. **1845** *Ibid.* Index 307/1 Soled wheel.

**Soledon** ('sɒlədən). Also **soledon.** [Blend of SOLUBLE *a.* and *Caledon*, proprietary name of an earlier range of dyes.] A proprietary term for a range of water-soluble vat dyes derived mainly from anthraquinones. Freq. *attrib.*

**1924** *Trade Marks Jrnl.* 24 Dec. 2898 *Soledon*... Dyes and dyestuffs,..Scottish Dyes Ltd. **1929** *Textile Colorist* XLVII. 568/1 Considerable interest has been expressed.. regarding another water-soluble vat dye, Soledon Jade Green. **1938** *Times* 11 Jan. 9/5 A third important recent advance was represented by the 'soledon' colours for cotton fabrics and linens and for rayons. **1952** K. Venkataraman *Synthetic Dyes* II. xxxiv. 1050 About 35 Indigosols and 25 Soledons have been marketed. **1964** *Official Gaz.* (U.S. Patent Office) 22 Dec. TM153 Imperial Chemical Industries Limited... *Soledon*... For dyes and dyestuffs. **1970** *Times* 30 Apr. 12/7 A limited edition of Shaw's works was bound in his [*sc.* J. E. G. Harris's] Soledon jade green cloth. **1971** R. L. M. Allen *Colour Chem.* x. 179 The water-soluble sulphuric ester salts were marketed as Soledon dyes by Scottish Dyes Ltd, and are now produced under the same name by ICI.

**sole-fish.** Now *rare* or *Obs.* = SOLE *sb.*$^2$

**1538** Elyot, *Squatina*, a sole fyshe with a rough skynne. **1591** R. Percival *Sp. Dict.*, *Azedia*, a sole fish, *Soleola*. **1613** Purchas *Pilgrimage* VIII. iv. (1614) 753 The tayle skaled almost of the forme of a Sole-fish. **1708** Wilson *Petronius Arbiter* 78 After which came in a Hare and a Sole-Fish.

**sole-fluke.** *Sc.* ? *Obs.* Also **-fleuk, -flook.** [See FLUKE *sb.*$^1$] The common sole.

**1684–92** Symson in *Macfarlane's Geogr. Collect.* II. (S.H.S.) 80 By this means, they catch Fleuks, sole fleuks, tarbets and severall other fish. *a* **1688** Wallace *Descr. Orkney* (1693) 14 Turbot, Scate, Congir eells, Sole Fleuks. **1710** Sibbald *Hist. Fife* 51 *Buglossus seu Solea*, the Sole flook.

‖**soleil.** [F. *soleil* sun.] A kind of repped woollen fabric.

**1883** *Cassell's Family Mag.* Oct. 696/2, I will begin with the new woollens. There are decided novelties in these... Amazon Soleil is a plain coloured stuff which is repped.

**1896** *Daily News* 27 Mar. 8/7 Orders have been placed for soleil and satin makes.

†**solein**, *a.* and *sb.* *Obs.* Forms: 4, 6 solein(e, 4–6 soleyn(e, 6 solleine; 4 soulein, 5 souleyn; 5 solain, 6 solaine; 5 sulayne, 5–6 solayn(e. [app. a. AF. *solein, *solain, a derivative of *sol* SOLE *a.* Cf. OF. *soltain*, *soutain* (med.L. *solitaneus*). Now represented by SULLEN *a.* (see sense 5).]

A. *adj.* **1.** Unique, singular. *rare.*

*c* **1369** CHAUCER *Dethe Blaunche* 982 Trewly she was to myn eye, The soleyn Fenix of Arabye, For there lyueth never but one. *c* **1460** *Wisdom* 579 in *Macro Plays*, Kynde nobyll of kynrede, me ioy yovyn hase, Ande þat makyt me soleyn. *c* **1475** *Partenay* 6104 So by hym was made and furged again Off Maillers the church, with fresh werke solain.

**b.** Singular, strange, unusual.

**1390** GOWER *Conf.* II. 16 Therof a solein tale I rede, Which I schal telle in remembraunce Upon the sort of loves chaunce. *c* **1475** *Partenay* 5431 Where ye shall finde this solain auenture, Full strang vnto sight of ech creature.

**2.** One and no more; single, sole.

*a* **1400–50** *Alexander* 3805 þis solayne sope if I sup quethire sustene it may þe menbris of þe Messedones & of þe many Persens. **1422** tr. *Secreta Secret.*, *Priv. Priv.* 134 Anothyr yewyth a vyse consail and Sauyth al a roialme, and so may noght do the Souleyn streynth of one man.

**3.** Of places: Lonely, solitary. *rare.*

**1388** WYCLIF *Job* iii. 14 Consuls of erthe, that bilden to hem soleyn places [L. *solitudines*]. **1390** GOWER *Conf.* III. 6 Ofte, whanne I scholde pleie, It makth me drawe out of the weie In soulein place be miselve.

**b.** Of actions: Done in privacy or solitude.

*c* **1475** *Partenay* 4394 Noght-withstandying [he] went to se hir dedes solain.

**4.** Apart from or destitute of a companion or companions; unaccompanied by another or others; all alone; solitary.

*c* **1381** CHAUCER *Parl. Foules* 607 Lat eche of hem ben soleyn al here lyue. *Ibid.* 614 Leue thow soleyn. **1390** GOWER *Conf.* I. 320 Thus fulofte there he sat To muse in his philosophie Solein withoute compaignie. ?*a* **1400** *Morte Arth.* 2592, I gyfe þe grace,.. With-thy thowe say me sothe what thowe here sekes, Thus sengilly and sulayne alle þiselfe one. ?*a* **1412** LYDG. *Two Merchants* 527 He weepith, wayleth soleyn and solitarye. *a* **1542** WYATT *Ps.* cii. 20 in *Anglia* XIX. 437 So made I me the solaine pelycane.

**b.** Of life: Spent in solitude.

*c* **1450** *St. Cuthbert* (Surtees) 2723 His solayn lif he had begonn he vsed forth als he was wonn.

**5.** Averse to society; disinclined to be sociable or friendly; morose, sullen.

For the later history of this sense see SULLEN *a.*

**1399** LANGL. *Rich. Redeles* IV. 66 And some were so soleyne and sad of her wittis, þat er they come to þe clos acombrid þey were. *a* **1400** *Rom. Rose* 3896 He hateth alle trechours, Soleyn folk and envyous. *c* **1440** *Promp. Parv.* 463 Soleyne, of maners, or he þat lovythe no cumpany, *solitarius*. *a* **1529** SKELTON *Sp. Parrot* 304 Addressyng your selfe, lyke a sadde messengere, To ower soleyne seigneour Sadoke. —— *Agst. Comely Coystrowne* 51 It is a solemnpne syre and a solayne. **1597** J. KING *On Jonas* (1618) 282 Philo, mee thinketh, rightly expressed the qualities of these Saturnine, solleine, discontented men.

**b.** *transf.* Of bearing or demeanour.

**1534** MORE *Comf. agst. Tribulacyon* II. Wks. 1200/1 An whole floud of all unhappy mischief, arrogant maner, high solayn solemne port. **1579** SPENSER *Sheph. Cal.* May 213 At last her solein silence she broke, And gan his newe budded beard to stroke.

**6.** Reserved, retiring, modest.

*c* **1450** *Mirour Saluacioun* (Roxb.) 27 Hire speche was lawe and soft, souleyn and fulle discrete.

B. *sb.* **1.** A single or solitary person.

**1377** LANGL. *P. Pl.* B. XII. 205 He sit neither.. wyth maydenes ne with martires, confessoures ne wydwes, But by hym-self as a soleyne, and serued on þe erthe.

**2.** A portion of food for one person.

Perhaps the same as OF. *solain* 'portio monachica (Du Cange, s.v. *solatium*).

*c* **1440** *Promp. Parv.* 463 Soleyne, or a mees of mete for on a-lone, *solinum*.

Hence **soleinty**. *Obs.*

*c* **1400** *Wycliffite Bible, Isaiah* xxiv. 12 Soleyntee (ether desolacioun) is left in the citee, and wretchidnesse schal oppresse the ȝatis. **1420–22** LYDG. *Thebes* I. 259 Thus ful ofte gendred is Envye In folkes hertes, of soleynte and pryde.

**sole-leather.** Also 5 sole-, soollether, 7 soule-, 8 soal-, 9 sole leather. [f. SOLE *sb.*[1] 2 + LEATHER *sb.* Cf. Fris. *soallear*, Du. *zoolleder*, LG. *sol-*, *sålledder*, G. *sohlleder*.]

**1.** Leather of a thick or strong kind used or suitable for the soles of boots, shoes, etc.

**1408** *Litt. Red Bk. Bristol* (1900) II. 103 De faulx quyrs disloialment tannez ou correyez appelles *Solelether* et *ouerlether*. **1408** *Nottingham Rec.* II. 54, iij. pecias de soollether. **1647** N. WARD *Simp. Cobler* 32, I would.. set on the best peece of Soule-leather I have. **1709** *Phil. Trans.* XXVII. 76 Of Substance not unlike to English Bend or Sole-Leather. **1777** *Ibid.* LXVIII. 117 The tanners of this country cannot make soal-leather in less time. **1842** *Penny Cycl.* XXIV. 39/2 The preparation of the thick hides used for sole-leather. **1885** *Harper's Mag.* Jan. 278/1 Sole-leather needs a heavier tannage than upper-leather.

**b.** *attrib.*, as *sole-leather brake*, *case*, *roller*, etc.

**1884** KNIGHT *Dict. Mech.* Suppl. 831 Sole Leather Roller, Stripper. **1892** GREENER *Breech-Loader* 181 Sole-leather cases—that is to say, cases in which best leather is sewn to pine frames,.. do well to carry guns in. **1897** *Outing* XXX. 264/2, I pressed down hard on the sole-leather brake, stopping the reel entirely.

**2.** *Bot.* (See quot.) Also *attrib.*

**1866** *Treas. Bot.* 1071/2 *Sole-leather*, or *Sole-leather Kelp*, a name given to the thicker *Laminariæ*, as *L. digitata*, *bulbosa*, &c., without particular reference to any individual species.

**soleless** ('səʊllɪs), *a.* Also sole-less. [f. SOLE *sb.*[1] + -LESS.] Of boots, shoes, etc.: Having no sole; without soles.

**1790** A. WILSON *Poet. Wks.* (1876) II. 76 Rotten stockings. Soleless trampers. **1848** tr. *Hoffmeister's Trav. Ceylon*, etc. iv. 186 Here, one was limping on with a sole-less shoe. **1855** *Household Wds.* XII. 335 Their shoes are soleless. **1896** BADEN-POWELL *Matabele Campaign* xvi, Umtini.. has made sandals for me to wear over—or at least outside—my soleless shoes.

**solely** ('səʊllɪ), *adv.* Forms: α. 6 sooly, 6–7 solye, solie, 6–8 soly (7 solly, soley). β. 5– solely. [f. SOLE *a.* + -LY[2].]

**1.** As a single person (or thing); without any other as an associate, partner, sharer, etc.; alone; occas., without aid or assistance. (Cf. SOLE *a.* 4.)

α. **1539** ELYOT *Cast. Helthe* 71 That none of the foure complexions haue sooly.. dominion in one man. **1542–3** *Act 34–35 Hen. VIII*, c. 5 §4 Any act or actes lawfully executed in his life by him self solye. **1591** LODGE *Catharos* B iij, Who meanes to sit solie on Olympus, must suffer no climers. **1606** G. W[OODCOCKE] *Lives Emperors* in *Hist. Ivstine* Ll ij, The younger Andronicus gouerned solye. **1622** in Foster *Eng. Factories Ind.* (1908) II. 146 By the Persians turnd outt of all, and they left solly possessors. **1637** *Decree of Star Chamb.* in *Milton's Areop.* (Arb.) 13 Any Copy, book or books,.. which the.. Company of Stationers.. haue the right.. soly to print.

β. **1495** *Act 11 Hen. VII*, c. 52 §1 The landes and tenementis that he held solely or joyntly with other. **1599** SHAKS. *Hen. V*, II. Prol. 4 Now.. Honors thought Reignes solely in the breast of euery man. **1611** KNOLLES *Hist. Turkes* (1638) 243 Solyman shall.. be driuen to leaue Asia, to be again by you solely possessed. **1635** J. HAYWARD tr. *Biondi's Banish'd Virg.* 55 But grant, that they will defend themselves, tell me, will they doe it solely or joyntly? **1746** FRANCIS tr. *Hor.*, *Sat.* I. i. 6 Broken with Toils,.. The Soldier thinks the Merchant solely blest. **1806–31** A. KNOX *Rem.* (1844) I. 61 Those who.. would think themselves solely qualified to mend the Established Church. **1860** MOZLEY *Univ. Serm.* vii. (1877) 151 Is it true that habit, solely and of itself, does produce positive inclination?

†**b.** Apart from or unaccompanied by others; solitarily. *Obs. rare.*

In quot. 1611 passing into adj.

**1582** STANYHURST *Æneis* III. (Arb.) 93 Thus father Æneas soly.. His long dryrye viadge.. chaunted. **1611** SHAKS. *Wint. T.* II. iii. 17 Leaue me solely: goe, See how he fares.

**2.** Only, merely, exclusively; also (contextually), entirely, altogether.

α. **1588** KYD *Househ. Phil.* Wks. (1901) 261 It shall suffise me soly to aduise and counsell that [etc.]. **1594** —— *Cornelia* I. i, Soly through desire of publique rule, Rome and the earth are waxen all as one. **1628** DOUGHTY *Serm. Church-Schismes* 13 Like hote furious spirits abroad, who delight soly in fights and vproares. **1663** SPENCER *Prodigies* (1665) 241 God's Miraculous Works never come forth (like a Jugler's tricks) soly to make men stare and wonder. **1695** WOODWARD *Nat. Hist. Earth* II. 84 The Deluge.. was not solely levelled against Mankind, but principally against the Earth that then was. **1710** PRIDEAUX *Orig. Tithes* iii. 155 The setting out of Tithes, as well as the payment of them, was soly left to the Consciences of men.

β. **1750** tr. *Leonardus' Mirr. Stones* 37 This diversity proceeds solely from the diversity of the substance. **1792** BURKE *Corr.* (1844) III. 387, I cannot say it was written *solely* with a view to the service of that party. I hope its views were more general. **1823** J. MARSHALL *Const. Opin.* (1839) 264 Spain did not rest her title solely on the grant of the Pope. **1855** PRESCOTT *Philip II*, I. v. I. 62 In all his acts he relied solely on himself. **1885** *Manch. Exam.* 21 Feb. 5/3 The questions at issue do not relate solely to Egypt and the Soudan.

†**solembury.** *Obs.*[−0] (See quot.)

**1639** J. SMYTH *Lives Berkeleys* (1885) III. 25 Solemburies, i.e. service berries.

**solemn** ('sɒləm), *a.* (*adv.* and *sb.*). Forms: 4–6 solempne (4 soll-), 6 sol(l)empe; 4–7 solemne, 7 sollemn(e, 6– solemn; 5 solom, 6 sollem, soleme, sol-, sollom(e, 6–7 solemn. See also SOLEMNY *a.* and SOLEN *a.* [a. OF. *solempne*, *solemne* (= Sp. and Pg. *solemne*) or ad. L. *sōl-*, *sollemnis* (later also *sollempnis*), established, appointed, customary, festive, etc.

The formation of the L. word is doubtful; the common variant *sōl-*, *sollennis* (formerly explained as from *sōlus*, *sollus* whole, and *annus* year) is now believed to be due to assimilation, or to association with other adjs. in *-ennis*.]

**1. a.** Associated or connected with religious rites or observances; performed with due ceremony and reverence; having a religious character; sacred.

*a* **1340** HAMPOLE *Psalter, Comm. Cant.* 499 We sall synge oure psalmys, þat is, we sall make solempn þi louyngis. **1340–70** *Alex. & Dind.* 735 ȝit may þer no man.. Wiþ sole[m]pne sacrifice serue hem at onus. **1387** TREVISA *Higden* (Rolls) V. 299 Seint Mammertus.. ordeyned solempne letanyes þat beeþ i-cleped þe Rogaciouns. **1447** BOKENHAM *Seyntys* (Roxb.) 11 It was doon in ful solemne wyse And with many a cerymonye. **1528** CROMWELL in Merriman *Life & Lett.* (1902) I. 319 The seruice daylie doon.. so deuoute, solempne, and full of Armonye. **1599** SANDYS *Europæ Spec.* (1632) 5 The solemnest divine honour which I see in those parts. **1613** PURCHAS *Pilgrimage* (1614) 808 Then came forth the sacrificers, who began the sacrifice of men..: for this was their solemnest festiuall. **1650** FULLER *Pisgah* I. vii. 17 It is answered, that seven was the compleat and solemne number, whereon God him-self emphatically insists. **1667** MILTON *P.L.* I. 390 [They] with cursed things His holy Rites, and solemn Feasts profan'd. **1830** COLERIDGE *Church & State* (ed. 2) 226 During the solemner Sabbaths of the Spirit. **1847** TENNYSON *Princ.* II. 428 At last a solemn grace Concluded, and we sought the gardens.

**b.** *spec.* Of various ecclesiastical ceremonies or services of a special character (see quots.).

**1338** R. BRUNNE *Chron.* (1810) 284 He giffes a solempne cursyng, Tille þo þat þer on liffes. *c* **1515** *Cocke Lorell's B.* 7 A solempne dyryge is songe there, With a grete drynkynge. **1546** *Supplic. Poore Commons* (E.E.T.S.) 69 To this daye, thei vse, on solempne feastes, to folow theyr olde ordinary. **1577** HARRISON *Descr. Brit.* II. i, It happened.. in a Rogation weeke that the clergy goyng in solemne procession [etc.]. **1699** in *Cath. Rec. Soc. Publ.* VII. 54 Father Rector of ye Colledge performed his Jubilee with a Solemn Mass. **1700** *Ibid.* 68 A Solemne Obsequie for Count Colonna of Bornhem. **1753** CHALLONER *Cath. Chr. Instr.* 93 In the high or solemn Mass the Gospel is sung by the Deacon. **1834** K. H. DIGBY *Mores Cath.* v. vii. 188 The festival of the circumcision became solemn in the sixth century. **1866** LEE *Direct. Angl.* (ed. 3) 360 *Solemn Service*, a choral celebration of the Holy Eucharist. **1908** *Ch. Times* 13 Mar. 347/2 Parishioners, friends, and relatives gathered from far and near for the Solemn Requiem.

**2.** Of days or seasons: Marked by the celebration of special observances or rites (esp. of a religious character); distinguished by, or set apart for, special ceremonies.

*c* **1325** *Prose Psalter* cxvii. 25 Stablis þe solempne daie. *c* **1350** *Will. Palerne* 1418 þemperour erded stille in rome at þe ester tide, & for þat solempne sesoun [etc.]. **1387** TREVISA *Higden* (Rolls) VI. 29 He.. forbeed hem mete and drynkenge of wyn but it were in certeyne solempne dayes in þe ȝere. *c* **1400** *Apol. Loll.* 50 þat feyris nor markets had no place in þe kirk in solempne tymis. **1422** tr. *Secreta Secret.*, *Priv. Priv.* 194 In hey festis & solempne dayys. **1533** FRITH *Mirror* (1829) 295 The Jews.. were commanded to keep the seventh day solemn. **1611** BIBLE *Numb.* x. 10 Also in the day of your gladnesse, and in your solemne dayes. **1650** TRAPP *Comm.*, *Exod.* xx. 17 Holie-daies were either quotidian or solemn. *a* **1700** EVELYN *Diary* 23 Apr. 1646, To this there joynes a spacious Hall for sollemn dayes to ballot in.

**3. a.** Performed with, accompanied by, due formality or ceremony; of a formal or ceremonious character.

*c* **1369** CHAUCER *Dethe Blaunche* 302 Eueryche [bird] songe in his wyse The most solempne seruyse. *c* **1386** —— *Squire's T.* 61 This Cambinskan.. halt his feste, so solempne and so riche That in this world ne was ther noon it liche. *c* **1440** *Promp. Parv.* 464/1 Solempne, or feestfulle, *festivus, celeber*. *a* **1529** SKELTON *E. Rummyng* 548 Now truly, to my thynkynge, This is a solempne drinkynge. **1583** MELBANCKE *Philotimus* Ff ij, To morrow next there is solemn hunting in the parke here adioyning. **1610** HOLLAND *Camden's Brit.* 723 A solemne horse running, wherein the horse that outrunneth the rest hath for his prise a little golden bell. **1662** J. DAVIES tr. *Olearius' Voy. Amb.* A ij b, The Accompt of a Solemn Embassy, sent to two of the greatest Princes of Europe and Asia. *a* **1700** EVELYN *Diary* 15 Oct. 1685, Being the King's birth day, there was a solemne ball at Court. **1837** CARLYLE *Fr. Rev.* I. III. iii, Till at length,.. in solemn final session, there bursts forth.. an explosion of eloquence. **1853** J. H. NEWMAN *Hist. Sk.* (1873) II. I. i. 30 They were invited to two solemn banquets.

†**b.** Formal; regular; uniform. *Obs.*

**1639** FULLER *Holy War* IV. ix. (1840) 194 Since which time we find no solemn taking it [the city] by the Turks. *a* **1661** —— *Worthies* (1840) II. 542 Castles.. able to resist (though no solemn siege) a tumultuary incursion. **1668** CULPEPPER & COLE *Barthol. Anat.* I. xvii. 47 Any matter may easily repass .. in the solemn Circulation of the Blood. **1704** *Dict. Rust.* (1726) s.v. *Hot-shoots*, Whereupon they'll continue a glowing, solemn, and constant Fire, for 7 or 8 hours.

†**c.** Customary; carefully observed. *Obs.*[−1]

**1616** B. JONSON *Ev. Man in Humour* Ded. to Camden, So solemne a vice it is with them to vse the authoritie of their ignorance, to the crying downe of Poetry.

†**4. a.** Grand, imposing; sumptuous. *Obs.*

**13..** *E.E. Allit. P.* B. 1171 He sete on Salamones solie, on solemne wyse. *c* **1386** CHAUCER *Man of Lawe's T.* 387 Arryved ben this cristen folk to londe, In Surrie, with a greet solempne route. *c* **1400** *Destr. Troy* 1630 Priam.. a pales gert make Within the Cite full Solempne of a sete riall. **1526** *Pilgr. Perf.* (W. de W. 1531) 142 b, Salomon buylded a solemne temple.. of stones precyous & quadrat or squared. *c* **1586** C'TESS PEMBROKE *Ps.* CX. ii, In solempne robes they glad shall goe. **1589** PUTTENHAM *Eng. Poesie* I. xv. (Arb.) 49 For which purpose also the players garments were made more rich and costly and solemne.

†**b.** Of great dignity or importance. *Obs.*

*c* **1386** CHAUCER *Prol.* 209 Ther was.. A limitour, a ful solempne man. **1387** TREVISA *Higden* (Rolls) I. 3 After solempne and wise writeres of arte. *Ibid.* 95 Babylonia.. was first so solempne þat it conteyned Assyria, Caldea, and Mesopotamia. *c* **1430** LYDG. in *Pol., Rel. & L. Poems* (1866) 28, I fond a lykenesse depict vpon a wal.., The hede of thre fulle solempne and roiall, Intellectus, Memorye, and Resoun. *a* **1513** FABYAN *Chron.* VI. (1811) 183 Ethilstanne.. mette with hym, and his people, at a place called Brymforde, where he had a great and solempne victory. **1596** DALRYMPLE tr. *Leslie's Hist. Scot.* (S.T.S.) I. 230 Thrie Judgement saites to be seperate ane frome another in solemne places.

†**c.** Famous, renowned. *Obs.*

**1387** TREVISA *Higden* (Rolls) II. 421 His temple is solempne in þe ilond Diomedia. **1596** DALRYMPLE tr. *Leslie's Hist. Scot.* (S.T.S.) I. 22 Edinburgh.., quhilke was nocht litle celebrate and solemne.

**5.** Of a formal and serious or deliberate character: a. Of vows or oaths, *spec.* of those made under some religious sanction.

*Solemn League and Covenant*: see COVENANT *sb.* 9 a.

c1315 SHOREHAM I. 1785 Of chastete professioun Hys [= is] solempne by-heste. 13.. *E.E. Allit. P.* C. 239 With sacrafyse vp-set, & solempne vowes. a1450 MYRC 1661 Hym þat brekeþ solempne vow, Or chawnge hyt wole, sende hym forþ now. c1489 CAXTON *Blanchardyn* xlvi. 177 Makyng a grete & a solempne oath. 1559 *Mirr. Mag., Mowbrays Banishment* xi, We all agreed and sware a solempne oth. 1597 HOOKER *Eccl. Pol.* V. lxv. §9 The solemnest vow that wee euer made. 1643 PRYNNE *Sov. Power Parl.* I. (ed. 2) 54 Such faith is to be given to the solemnest Oathes of Kings. 1756-9 A. BUTLER *Lives of Saints, St. Frances,* The Oblates make no solemn vows, only a promise of obedience to the mother-president. 1885 *Month* Nov. 436 The Redemptoristines were approved with solemn vows and are therefore a Religious Order properly so called. 1894 *Ibid.* June 239 According to the Statutes the vows of the choir nuns should be those canonically called 'solemn'.

**b.** Of statements, compacts, documents, etc. Not always clearly distinct from sense 6.

1420 in Ellis *Orig. Lett.* Ser. I. I. 67 And aftirward with a solempne proposicion dennouncede vn to hym thys Pes. c1449 PECOCK *Repr.* I. vi. 31 Alle the trouthis of lawe of kinde..weren writen bifore in thilk solempnest inward book. 1533 MORE *Debell. Salem* v. Wks. 940/1 But then commeth he forthe vppon me..with a very foly & with a solempne lye. 1560 DAUS tr. *Sleidane's Comm.* 257 Therefore we protest..in solemnwyse that we are of this mynd. 1610 HOLLAND *Camden's Brit.* 760 Thomas Musgrave..was by solemne writ of summons called to the Parliament. 1671 MARVELL *Corr.* Wks. (Grosart) II. 385 Our House hath.. made a solemne vote, That aids given by the Commons ought not to be altered. 1702 ADDISON *Dial. Medals* i. Wks. 1766 III. 17 The solemn dissertations that have been made on these weighty subjects! 1741-2 GRAY *Agrip.* I. i, Of mutter'd charms and solemn invocation. 1806 J. BERESFORD *Miseries Hum. Life* II. xviii, The most solemn assurances of the Barometer that there is nothing to fear. 1847 MRS. A. KERR tr. *Ranke's Hist. Servia* 263 A solemn agreement had been entered into; and Russia was entitled to demand its due execution. 1884 *Encycl. Brit.* XVII. 550/2 But neither in England nor in Sicily did official formalism acknowledge even French..as a fit tongue for solemn documents.

**6.** Of a serious, grave, or earnest character:

**a.** Of actions, feelings, etc.

c1449 PECOCK *Repr.* II. viii. 183 If bi the ymagis..schulde be maad eny quyk and feruent and solempne and miche deuout remembraunce. a1548 HALL *Chron., Edw. IV*, 234 He toke of hys cappe, and made a low and solempne obeysance. 1590 GREENE *Never too Late* Wks. (Grosart) VIII. 77 With a solempne conge departing, he went about his busines. 1602 SHAKS. *Ham.* I. ii. 201 A figure like your Father..with sollemne march Goes slow and stately. 1659 HAMMOND *On Ps.* xlviii. 12. 246 Nothing deserving our solemnest meditations. 1705 STANHOPE *Paraphr.* II. 303 Therefore our Zeal, if sincere, will be solemn. 1763 J. BROWN *Poet. & Music* xii. 214 Our parochial Music, in general, is solemn and devout. 1827 SCOTT *Chron. Canongate* i, I shall never forget the solemn tone of expression with which he summed up the incapacities of the paralytic. 1833 TENNYSON *Dream Fair Wom.* lvii, I heard Him, for He spake, and grief became A solemn scorn of ills. 1868 FFOULKES *Church's Creed or Crown's Creed?* 36 There is a solemn document before the world—I may say one of the solemnest.

**b.** Of persons. Also *transf.*

1580-3 GREENE *Mamillia* Wks. (Grosart) II. 239 Be not too sad least he thinke thou art sollempe. 1599 SHAKS. *Hen. V*, IV. i. 318 Where the sad and solemne Priests sing still. 1667 MILTON *P.L.* IV. 648 Silent Night With this her solemn Bird. *Ibid.* XI. 236 Some great Potentate..solemn and sublime, whom not to offend, With reverence I must meet. 1781 COWPER *Conversation* 299 A shallow brain behind a serious mask,..The solemn fop. 1842 LOVER *Handy Andy* xxviii, They were again a reverent flock, and he once more a solemn pastor. 1867 F. H. LUDLOW *Brace of Boys* 265 So confused among the wax-works that he pinched the solemnest showman's legs to see if he was real.

*absol.* 1871 R. ELLIS *Catullus* xxvii. 6 But dull water, avaunt..; seek the sour, the solemn!

**c.** Of the features or looks.

1595 SHAKS. *John* IV. ii. 90 Why do you bend such solemne browes on me? 1761 GRAY *Odin* 76 What Virgins these.. That bend to earth their solemn brow. 1832 BREWSTER *Nat. Magic* iii. 43 Though the eyes were open, the features were solemn and rigid. 1899 MARG. BENSON & GOURLAY *Temple of Mut* i. 11 An Arab girl with solemn eyes.

**7. a.** Fitted to excite serious thoughts or reflections; impressive, awe-inspiring.

c1400 *St. Alexius* (Laud MS.) 867 þe þrid tyme com þe voice Fro hym þat was don on croice wiþ gret solempne liȝth. c1425 *Abraham's Sacr.* 437 in *Bk. of Brome* 68 Lo!..now haue we schowyd Thys solom story to grete and smale. 1522 MORE *De quat. Noviss.* Wks. 84/1 The wind that puffeth vs vp in pride, vpon the solemne sight of worldly worship. 1590 SPENSER *F.Q.* I. viii. 29 There raignd a solemne silence ouer all. 1642 H. MORE *Song Soul* I. III. lxv, In solem silency this vapour rose From this drad Dale. 1719 TICKELL *On the Death of Addison* 15 What awe did the slow solemn knell inspire. 1757 GRAY *Bard* 105 What solemn scenes on Snowdon's height. 1821 SHELLEY *Adonais* xlv, His solemn agony had not Yet faded from him. 1860 TYNDALL *Glac.* I. xviii. 123 The solemn heights of Monte Rosa. 1880 J. F. CLARKE *Self Culture* iii. 75 It becomes vastly more solemn than death.

†**b.** Gloomy, dark, sombre. *Obs.*

1602 SHAKS. *Ham.* I. ii. 78 Customary suites of solemne Blacke. 1616 B. JONSON *Epigr.* I. lxxiii, Your partie-per-pale picture, one halfe drawne In solemne cypres. 1625 BACON *Ess., Adversity* (Arb.) 505 Wee see in Needleworkes and Imbroideries, It is more pleasing, to haue a Liuely Worke, vpon a Sad and Solemne Ground; then to haue a Darke and Melancholy Worke, vpon a Lightsome Ground.

**8.** As *adv.* Solemnly. *rare*$^{-1}$.

1743 FRANCIS tr. *Hor., Sec. Poem* 20 Let the solemn Numbers rise; Solemn sing the Queen of Night.

**9.** As *sb.* Solemnity. *rare*$^{-1}$.

1706 DE FOE *Jure Divino* IV. 81 When subjects..Bind their dissembled homage to the Crown And bend the Solemns of Religion down.

**10.** *Comb.* **a.** Misc., as ***solemn-breathing, -looking, -proud*** adjs., ***solemn-slowly*** adv.

1526 SKELTON *Magnyf.* 1023 Somtyme I syt as I were solempe prowde. 1634 MILTON *Comus* 555 A soft and solemn breathing sound. 1754 GRAY *Progr. Poesy* 14 Parent of sweet and solemn-breathing airs. 1817 LADY MORGAN *France* I. (1818) I. 53 A cold, solemn-looking English sergeant. 1871 G. MACDONALD *Wks. of Fancy & Imag.* ii. 12 Let the bright sails all solemn-slowly pass.

**b.** Parasynthetic, or with pa. pples., as ***solemn-browed, -eyed, -measured, -shaded, -thoughted, -visaged.***

1777 POTTER *Æschylus* (1779) I. 138 For this beneath the solemn-shaded grove Our raptur'd invocations rise. 1838 LD. HOUGHTON *Poems of Many Years* 11 Solemn-measured be your paces. 1842 DICKENS *Amer. Notes* (1850) 151/1 In stiff-necked solemn-visaged piety. 1844 MRS. BROWNING *Lady Geraldine's Courtship* xli, Wordsworth's solemn-thoughted idyl. 1852 MISS MULOCK *Head of Family* vi, A long-limbed, solemn-browed follower of the sciences. 1889 W. B. YEATS *Wanderings of Oisin* 59 Away with us he's going, The solemn-eyed. 1930 M. MEAD *Growing up in New Guinea* ix. 151 A tiny curly grass skirt is fashioned.., and the solemn-eyed baby arrayed in it for a feast day.

†**'solemn,** *v. Obs.* In 5-6 **solemne,** 6 **solemp(n)e.** [f. prec., or ad. OF. *solem(p)ner, -nier.*] *trans.* To solemnize, celebrate.

1483 *Cath. Angl.* 348/2 To Solemne, *solennizare, celebrare.* ?a1500 *Chester Pl.* (Shaks. Soc.) I. 23 To morowe the seventh daye I will solempe [*v.r.* blyn]. 1527 *Lanc. Wills* (Chetham Soc.) I. 34, I will y[t] Sir Iohn Walton occupye and solempne dyvine service at the forsaid Chapell. 1555 EDEN *Decades*, etc. (Arb.) 302 They solemne marriages, and begynne the same with fyre and flynte.

†**solemnacy.** *Obs.*$^{-1}$ In 6 **solempnacie.** [Cf. next and -ACY.] Solemnization.

1591 HORSEY *Trav.* (Hakl. Soc.) 158 The manner and solempnacie of this mariage was so streinge and heathenly.

†**solemnation.** *Obs. rare.* [Cf. SOLEMN *v.*] Solemnization, celebration.

1470-85 MALORY *Arthur* VII. xxxvi. 270 Whan this solemnacion was done, thenne came in the grene knyghte syr Pertylope with thyrtty knyghtes. 1656 EARL MONM. tr. *Boccalini's Advts. fr. Parnass.* 236 The daies solemnation of admittance of the litterati into Parnassus.

**solemncholy** ('sɒləmkəlɪ), *a.* and *sb. pl.* Also **-coly.** [Fancifully f. SOLEMN *a.*, after *melancholy.*] **A.** *adj.* Excessively solemn or serious.

1772 P. V. FITHIAN *Jrnl.* 18 Dec. (1900) 27 Being very *Solemncholly* and somewhat tired, I concluded to stay there all night. 1855 HALIBURTON *Nat. & Hum. Nat.* I. ix. 285 Watch his face as he goes along, slowly and solemncoly through the street. 1863 PYCROFT *Dragons' Teeth* I. 154 With sighs and groans, pale faces, and 'solemncholy' looks. 1894 MELDRUM *Margredel* 67 He's a very solemncholy youth.

**B.** *sb. pl.* A solemn or serious mood. *rare.*

1834 W. A. CARRUTHERS *Kentuckian in New York* I. 214 It drives away the solemncholies, and makes a fellow feel so good-natured, and so comfortable.

†**solemned,** *a. Sc. Obs.* Forms: 5-6 **solempt, -empnit, solemnit** (6 **-yt**), 6 **solemned.** [? f. SOLEMN *v.* + -ED.] Solemn, in various senses.

1423 JAS. I *Kingis Q.* lxxix, Thir peple sawe I stand, With mony a solempt [*so MS.*] contenance. c1450 *Maitl. Club Misc.* III. 203 Ane haly wattyr fat of siluer..for solemnit festis. 1513 DOUGLAS *Æneid* v. ii. 24 Netheles suld I.. exequies, with solempt [*v.r.* solemnyt, solempnit] pomp and fair, Dewlie perform. 1564 KNOX *Bk. Common Order* (1584) C vj, The cutting off..by publicke and solemned sentence, all obstinate and impenitent persons. 1567 *Reg. Privy Council Scot.* I. 542, I faythfullie affirme be my solempnit ayth.

Hence †**solemnedly** *adv. Obs.*

c1375 *Sc. Leg. Saints* xvii. (*Martha*) 202 Al hyre covent.. hyre exequies dewotly did..& solempnitly. 1566 *Acts & Constit. Scotl.* To Rdr., [They] had thair statutis..inrollit, bukit, and solempnitlie red to all the pepill. 1572-3 *Reg. Privy Council Scot.* II. 200 Oure Soverane Lordis Commissioneris..solempnitlie promeist and sweare [etc.].

†**solemnel,** *a. Obs.* Also 5-6 **solempnell(e.** [a. OF. *solempnel, -nal* (F. *solennel*), ad. L. type **sōlemnālis.*] Solemn.

1471 CAXTON *Recuyell* (Sommer) 426/11 Hercules..went to..Salamanque and..he wold make there a solempnell estudye. 1490 —— *Eneydos* xv. 60 An assemble..of metes and of wynes for to kepe a solempnelle feste. 1556 *Aurelio & Isab.* (1608) B iv, The King her father kept her with solemnell keping inclosed. 1600 in *Cath. Tract.* (S.T.S.) 222, I dout not bot your Maiestie sal accomplis this solemnel promesse. 1647 in HEXHAM I. s.v.

**solemness** ('sɒləmnɪs). Also **solemnness.** [f. SOLEMN *a.* + -NESS.] The state or quality of being solemn; solemnity.

1530 PALSGR. 272/2 Solemnesse, *solempnité.* 1561 T. HOBY tr. *Castiglione's Courtyer* IV. (1577) T iv, Pride, wrath, solemnesse and such tiranical fashions as they haue within them. 1642 D. ROGERS *Naaman* 130 When the closnesse, solemnesse,..and necessity of it, is presented to the soule. 1741 RICHARDSON *Pamela* (1824) I. 74 He looked at me with such respect and solemness at parting. 1797-1803 FOSTER in J. E. Ryland *Life & Corr.* (1846) I. 211 Still shades, that dimmed in solemness the lower part of her orb. 1828-32 WEBSTER s.v., The solemness of public worship. 1908 *Nation* Mar. 845/1 He has felt the greater solemnness of a Semitic tongue.

†**solemniation.** *Obs. rare.* [f. L. *sōlemni-s*: cf. SOLEMNATION.] Solemnization.

1603 KNOLLES *Hist. Turks* (1638) 192 For solemniation of the marriage, [Amurath] prepared all things with great magnificence. 1658 CRESHALD *Legacy* 18 Ornaments of Solemniation of the Royall discent.

**solem'nific,** *a. nonce-wd.* [f. SOLEMN *a.* + -(I)FIC.] Affectedly solemn.

1823 BEDDOES *Poems* 225 This speech..begins too designedly in the established form of solemnific invocation.

**solemnify** (sɒ'lɛmnɪfaɪ), *v.* [f. as prec. + -(I)FY.] *trans.* To make solemn. Also *refl.*

1780 J. MAINWARING *Sermons on Several Occasions* p. xxv, Some divines delight to sadden and solemnify their sermons with Scripture passages. 1882 L. C. LILLIE *Prudence* 79 Solemnified by the silent hidden presences. 1885 G. MEREDITH *Diana* III. ix. 164 Mr. Sullivan Smith had solemnified himself to proffer a sober petition.

**so'lemniously** *adv. rare.* Also 6 **solempniouslie.** [f. SOLEMN *a.* + -IOUS: cf. OF. *solemnieus.*] Solemnly.

a1578 LINDESAY (Pitscottie) *Chron. Scot.* (S.T.S.) II. 124 Thaireftir the mariaige was solempniouslie maid. 1910 *Blackw. Mag.* Apr. 607/1 'In the name ov God,' says the Pope, very solemniously, 'what *is* the maning ov all this?'

**solemnity** (sɒ'lɛmnɪtɪ). Forms: 3-4 **solempnete,** 4-5 **-ite(e, -ytee,** 4-6 **-yte,** 4-7 **-itie** (6 **-ytye**); 4 **sollempnete, -ite,** 5 **-itee, -ytee;** 4-5 **solemnete, -ite(e,** 5-6 **-yte,** 6-7 **-itie,** 6- **solemnity.** [a. OF. *solempneté, -ité* (= Sp. *solemnidad*, Pg. *solemnidade*), ad. L. *sōl-, sollem(p)nitas* (postclassical), f. *sōl-, sollem(p)nis* SOLEMN *a.*: see -ITY. The ME. form *solem(p)nete* was app. sometimes stressed on the first syllable: cf. SOLEMNTY.]

**1.** Observance of ceremony or special formality on important occasions: **a.** In the phrases ***with*** or ***in*** (***great***, etc.) ***solemnity.*** Now *rare.*

c1290 *S. Eng. Leg.* I. 169 Heo bureden þat holi bodi hasteliche þere biside With luyte solempnete i-novȝ. 13.. *E.E.Allit. P.* B. 1313 He sesed hem with solemnete, þe souerayn he praysed. 1390 GOWER *Conf.* I. 352 With gret solempnete He was unto his dignete Received, and coroned king. c1400 MAUNDEV. (Roxb.) xxxiv. 153 Þai bere þe body to a hill with grete sollempnytee. 1470-85 MALORY *Arthur* VII. xxxvi. 270 The Bisshop of Caunterbury made the weddyng..with grete solempnyte. a1557 MRS. M. BASSET tr. *More's Treat. Passion* M.'s Wks. 1398 My blessed Martyrs..shal..with woondrefull solempnitie enter into heauen. 1590 SHAKS. *Mids. N.* IV. i. 182 Wee'll hold a feast in great solemnitie. 1611 BIBLE *Transl. Pref.* ⁋2 For bringing backe the Arke of God in solemnitie. 1719 YOUNG *Revenge* v. i, And then, with all the cool solemnity Of public justice, give her to the grave. 1759 ROBERTSON *Hist. Scotl.* Wks. 1813 I. 366 The conference, however, was opened with much solemnity. 1875 *Times* 9 May, The Emperor.. was received with all the solemnity that befits so great a Potentate.

**b.** In general use.

c1340 HAMPOLE *Psalter* cxvii. 26 Makis solempnyte in ȝoure saule. c1380 WYCLIF *Sel. Wks.* II. 124 Þe Jewis calengiden..to have a man ȝovun to hem, for solempnite of þe feeste. c1400 LOVE *Bonavent. Mirr.* (1908) 50 The solempnite and the worthynesse of this feste and this hiȝe day. c1420 *Brut* ccxli. 349 Þe King..welcomed hir.., and made þere alle þe solempnite þat myȝt be do. 1502 *Ord. Crysten Men* (W. de W. 1506) I. ii, Them that be ordeyned of god & of holy churche as well in case of necessyte as of solempnyte. 1553 EDEN *Treat. New. Ind.* (Arb.) 14 The king hereof vseth great pride & solemnitie. 1613 PURCHAS *Pilgr.* (1614) 192 If a female child be borne, there is small solemnitie. 1653 MORE *Antid. Ath.* II. iii. §5 Instead of all this Glory and Solemnity there had been nothing but howlings and shoutings. 1759 ROBERTSON *Hist. Scotl.* VII. Wks. 1813 I. 511 Elizabeth resolved that no circumstance of pomp or solemnity should be wanting. 1821 SHELLEY *Ginevra* 161 The marriage feast and its solemnity Was turned to funeral pomp.

**2.** An occasion of ceremony; an observance or celebration of special importance; a festival or other similar occasion.

a1300 *Cursor M.* 13874 Iesus went him forth.., Til it come a solempnite, He com a-gain in þat cite. 1390 GOWER *Conf.* III. 166 So myhte every man aboute The day of that solempnete His tale telle. c1400 *Brut* Prol. 1 Dioclician þoughte maryen his Doughtres among all þo knyghtys þat tho were at that solempnite. c1425 *Found. St. Bartholomew's* (E.E.T.S.) 47 This childe..was browght to the forsaid chirche yn the solempnyte of the glorious Apostle. a1533 LD. BERNERS *Huon* lxii. 217 Then they went all with the pope to his palays, and there was made the solempnytes of y[e] maryage. 1570-6 LAMBARDE *Peramb. Kent* (1826) 259 King Edwarde the Seconde..held the solemnitie of a whole Christmasse in the house of this Manor. 1617 MORYSON *Itin.* III. 219 Among other solemnities, they roasted an Oxe in the middest of the field for the people. 1673 TEMPLE *Ess. Irel.* Wks. 1720 I. 119 Many..may come, not only as to a publick kind of Solemnity, but as to a great Mart of the best Horses. 1710 PRIDEAUX *Orig. Tithes* ii. 113 Such a multitude of People were fed..during their continuance together at those Solemnities. 1763 J. BROWN *Poet. & Music* §4. 41 Hymns or Odes would be composed, and Sung by their Composers at their festal Solemnities. 1834 K. H. DIGBY *Mores Cath.* v. vii. 218 Assisting on Easter day at the divine office of this great solemnity. 1867 FREEMAN *Norm. Conq.* (1877) I. 426 The king engaged in a remarkable solemnity on the spot which had witnessed his last battle.

†**b.** A ceremonial procession. *Obs.*

**1636** STRODE *Floating Isl.* II. iv, Enter in the midst of the song Amorous ushering the solemnity. **1707** *Lond. Gaz.* No. 4374/1 When the Solemnity came near St. Mark's-Place, the Norton Galley hoisted the Union Colours. **1731** *Gentl. Mag.* I. 441 A Representation of the Solemnity and Procession of the Lord Mayor of London thro' the City.

†**3.** Applied concretely (see quots.). *Obs.*

*c* **1435** *Torr. Portugal* 1591 My two dragons hast thou slan, My solempnite they were. **1449** *Churchw. Acc. St. George's, Stamford* in Nicholls (1797) 133, I bequethe to the seyd Chirch of Seynt George a solempnitie of array for the fest of Corpus Christi.

**4.** † **a.** Proper or regular performance. *Obs.*⁻¹

*c* **1440** *Pallad. on Husb.* IV. 2 At Marches mone, in contrey that is colde, Putacioun hath his solempnite [L. *celebratur*].

**b.** *Law.* Necessary formality, such as is requisite to make an act or document valid.

**1588** in T. Morris *Provosts of Methven* (1875) 72 The solempnitie of the law..[being] obseruit. **1590** SWINBURNE *Testaments* 6 The testament is imperfect in respect of solemnitie, wherein some of the Legall requisites..be wanting. **1665** *Caldwell P.* (Maitl. Cl.) I. 63 Not being sealled be the seall of the partie, quilk was ane essentiall solemnitie of contracts. **1669** CHAMBERLAYNE *Pres. St. Eng.* 158 If she be Plaintiff, the Summons in the Process need not have the solemnity of 15 dayes. **1871** MARKBY *Elem. Law* §171 The contract..should be accompanied by certain solemnities as they are called. **1875** K. E. DIGBY *Real Prop.* x. §1 (1876) 374 No solemnity short of a deed is regarded by our law as sufficient to create a right of this kind.

**5.** The state or character of being solemn or serious; impressiveness; gravity; a solemn utterance or statement.

**1712** ADDISON *Spectator* No. 405 ¶3 That Solemnity of Phrase, which may be drawn from the Sacred Writings. **1741** C. MIDDLETON *Cicero* I. I. 2 A writer, who loves to raise the solemnity of his story by the introduction of something miraculous. **1794** MRS. RADCLIFFE *Myst. Udolpho* xxvii, The solemnity of this silence..subdued her spirits. **1822–7** GOOD *Study Med.* (1829) II. 486 At present, from a knowledge of the circulation of the blood, we can smile at these nugatory solemnities. **1883** FROUDE *Short Stud.* IV. II. i. 164 Subjects which in our fathers' time were approached only with the deepest reverence and solemnity.

† **solemnizate,** *v. Obs.* Forms: 6 **solempnisate, -zate,** *Sc.* **solem(p)nizat.** [f. ppl. stem of med.L. *solem(p)nizare.*] *trans.* To solemnize.

**1538** CRANMER *Misc. Writ.* (Parker Soc.) II. 360 Marriage contracted and solemnisated in lawful age. **1548** UDALL, etc. *Erasm. Par. Matt.* xiv. 80 He dyd solempnisate the day of his birth. **1585** *Rec. Elgin* (Spald. Cl.) 4 That he sall solemnizat the band of matrimonie.

**solemnization** (ˌsɒləmnɪ-, -naɪˈzeɪʃən). Forms: 5 **solempnysacion,** 6 **-yzacion, -izacion, -isacion;** 5 **solemnyzacyoun,** 6 **-izacion,** 6– **-isation, solemnization.** [a. OF. *solem(p)nisation, -ization,* or ad. med.L. *solempnizatio*: see SOLEMNIZE *v.* and -ATION.] The action of solemnizing or celebrating in a ceremonial manner.

**1447** BOKENHAM *Seyntys* (Roxb.) 32 Wych tyme as shuld the solemnyzacyoun Been of that cherche. **1555** WATREMAN *Fardle of Facions* II. xii. 271 He goeth vp to the aultare,..and so procedeth in the Solempnisacion of yᵉ Masse. **1586** in *Cath. Rec. Soc. Publ.* (1911) IX. 167 For the solemnisation of which popish feast we thought these persons would assemble themselves together. **1631** in Ellis *Orig. Lett.* Ser. II. III. 267 On Friday my Lord of Essex..was present at the solemnization of his mothers funeral. **1651** BAXTER *Infant Bapt.* 295 The secondary..Act, and Instrument, being but the Ceremonial solemnization. **1820** *Monthly Rev.* XCI. 501 A solemnization of this kind..would in my judgment..have a happy influence. **1863** H. COX *Instit.* III. iii. 626 Coronation was but a..national solemnization of the descent.

**b.** *spec.* The celebration or performance *of* a marriage.

**1497** BP. ALCOK *Mons Perf.* D iij, The solempnysacion of the maryage of the spouse of heuen. *c* **1535** in Ellis *Orig. Lett.* Ser. II. II. 89 For the solempnisacion of matrimonie betwene you. **1548–9** (Mar.) *Bk. Com. Prayer, Offices* 13 The forme of solemnizacion of matrimonie. **1625** in Ellis *Orig. Lett.* Ser. I. III. 190 The solemnization of the Nuptialls of our King and Queen and the Madam of France. **1748** RICHARDSON *Clarissa* (1811) III. 77 Out came, with great diffidence,..a proposal of speedy solemnization. **1797** MRS. RADCLIFFE *Italian* xiii, To urge an immediate solemnisation of their marriage. **1858** FROUDE *Hist. Eng.* III. xvii. 506 The solemnization of the marriage was extorted from his Majesty against his will.

† **solemnize,** *sb. Obs.*⁻¹ [f. the vb.] Solemnization; solemn rite.

**1590** SPENSER *F.Q.* I. x. 4 Though spousd, yet wanting wedlocks solemnize.

**solemnize** (ˈsɒləmnaɪz), *v.* Forms: 4–6 **solempnise** (5 **-ese, -ish**), 5–6 **-yse, -yze,** 6–7 **solempnize;** 6– **solemnise** (6 **-yse**), **solemnize.** [ad. OF. *solem(p)niser, -izer* (= Sp. and Pg. *solemnizar*), or med.L. *solemnizare*: see SOLEMN *a.* and -IZE. In older verse the stressing *so'lemnize* occasionally appears.]

**1.** *trans.* To dignify or honour by ceremonies; to celebrate or commemorate by special observances or with special formality.

**1382** WYCLIF *1 Esdras* i. 20 There is not solempnisid such a pasch in Irael, fro the times of Samuel. **1460** CAPGR. *Chron.* (Rolls) 66 Hermes wrot a book that Estern day schuld evyr be solempnyzed on a Sunday. **1480** CAXTON *Myrr.* III. x. 155 To solempnise suche dayes as holy chyrche hath ordeyned. **1530** PALSGR. 724/2 The bouchers in London solempnyse saynte Lukes daye above all feestes in the yere. **1597** BEARD *Theatre God's Judgem.* (1612) 272 To the end the better to solemnize his entrie to the crowne, commaunded a sumptuous and pompous banket to be prepared. **1623** LISLE *Ælfric on O. & N. Test.*, Many thousands of Angels solemnised his birth with heavenly songs. **1652** LOVEDAY tr. *Calprenède's Cassandra* I. 22 These two enraged Princes solemniz'd their mutuall fury by the death of so many thousands. **1737** WHISTON *Josephus, Antiq.* XIX. vii. §1 Agrippa was solemnizing his birth-day. **1787** BURNS *Ode Birthday Pr. Chas. Edward* 15 We solemnize this sorrowing natal day, To prove our loyal truth. **1838** THIRLWALL *Greece* xliii. V. 317 The king solemnized his triumph with great magnificence at Dium.

**2.** To celebrate (a marriage) with proper ceremonies and in due form; also, to perform the ceremony of (marriage).

**1426** LYDG. in *Pol. Poems* (Rolls) II. 136 And there in Troys also was solempnesed The mariage, to conferme up the peas. **1491** *Act 7 Hen. VII*, c. 2 §11 So that thoes espousels be solempnysed in Churche, Chapell, or Oratory. **1533–4** *Act 25 Hen. VIII*, c. 12 The mariage, whiche was solempnised betwene his maiestie and..the lady Catherine. **1588** GREENE *Perimedes* Wks. (Grosart) VII. 84 Bradamant ..with great pompe solempnised the Nuptials. **1615** G. SANDYS *Trav.* 66 They buy their wives of their parents, and record the contract before the Cadi, which they after solemnize in this manner. **1657** in *Verney Mem.* (1904) II. 120 The mariage of the Protector's daughter to Warwick's sonne, is forthwith to bee solempnized. **1713** *Guardian* No. 7 ¶3 The immature marriages solemnized in our days. **1797** MRS. RADCLIFFE *Italian* xiii, He found a priest who would solemnize their nuptials. **1847** EMERSON *Poems, Musketaquid* Wks. (Bohn) I. 484 And wide around, the marriage of the plants Is sweetly solemnized. **1886** *Act 49 Vict.* c. 14 §1 No person shall be subject to any proceedings in any court..for solemnizing matrimony between the aforesaid hours.

**b.** To wed ceremonially. *nonce-use.*

**1592** BRETON *Pilgr. Parad.* Wks. (Grosart) I. 20/2 Where sacred mercy first did solempnize The spirite to the fleshe in mariage.

**c.** *absol.* To marry.

**1748** RICHARDSON *Clarissa* (1811) IV. 168 Let the articles be drawn up, and engrossed; and solemnize upon them. **1804** EUGENIA DE ACTON *Tale without Title* I. 112, I am unalterably resolved never to marry any other woman: and ..should I solemnize upon her recovery [etc.].

**3.** To hold, observe, perform, †proclaim, etc., with some amount of ceremony or formality.

**1483** CAXTON *Gold. Leg.* 233/2 Wherfore themperour establisshed..that the counseyl shold be solempnysed at mylane. **1487–8** in *Prymer* (E.E.T.S.) 170 The Banys where solempnishyd & published betwixt Annes Skerne..and Peres Courteys. **1548–9** (May) *Bk. Com. Prayer, Communion* 121 The Minister hauyng alwayes some to communicate with him, may accordingly solempnise so high and holy misteries, with al..due ordre. **1602** WARNER *Alb. Eng.* Prose Addit. 341 There..did [Æneas] solemnize an Anniuersarie at the Tombe of his father. **1603** in Ellis *Orig. Lett.* Ser. I. III. 72 To-morrow..wee doe solemnise the funerails..of her late Majesty. **1641** MILTON *Ch. Govt.* v. Wks. 1851 III. 117 To solemnize some religious monthly meeting different from the Sabbath. **1703** in *Cath. Rec. Soc. Publ.* VII. 149 The Anniversary Service for Henri 4 was Solemnized this Morn. **1821** SCOTT *Kenilw.* xxxiii, The scene of solemnizing some high national festival. **1835** THIRLWALL *Greece* x. I. 427 The Megarian peasantry were compelled to solemnize the obsequies of every Bacchiad. **1897** G. ALLEN *Type-writer Girl* xvii. 189 Dinner solemnised, we withdrew to the comfortable divans of the balcony.

†**4.** To celebrate with praise or commendation; to laud or glorify. *Obs.*

**1514** BARCLAY *Ecloges* iv. (1570) C v b/2 And to what vices that princes moste intende, Those dare these fooles solemnize and commende. *c* **1586** C'TESS PEMBROKE *Ps.* CVIII. i, My hart is bent..God's name to solemnize. *a* **1619** FOTHERBY *Atheom.* II. i. §7 (1622) 184 Vnto the Sunne, whose glorious regiment All dayes solemnize. **1652** LOVEDAY tr. *Calprenède's Cassandra* I. 49 The bravery of the Course was solemnized with a generall Shout. **1687** *Lond. Gaz.* No. 2266/1 We cannot be satisfied..that what Your Majesty hath now done for them, should be more Solemnized, than what You have always done for us.

**5.** To make solemn; to render serious or grave.

**1726** POPE *Odyss.* XVII. 245 Holy horrors solemnize the shade. **1760–72** H. BROOKE *Fool of Qual.* (1809) III. 140 Such an inward awe and veneration..as, for a while, sunk his spirits, and solemnized his features. **1802–12** BENTHAM *Ration. Judic. Evid.* (1827) II. 561 He solemnizes his tone.. and beholds in the air a host of difficulties. **1845** MARTINEAU *Misc.* (1852) 114 A religious ceremonial invested with every beauty that may touch and solemnize their hearts. **1871** MOZLEY *Univ. Serm.* vi. (1876) 131 That remarkable desire ..seems to be innate in all,..the desire to be solemnised. People like being awed.

*absol.* **1865** MOZLEY *Miracles* vii. 133 A supernatural fact ..is a potent influence; it rouses, it solemnizes.

**6.** *intr.* To speak or meditate solemnly.

**1836** *Fraser's Mag.* XIV. 733 [He] had sermonised and solemnised in sepulchral vaults and feudal towers.

Hence **'solemnized** *ppl. a.*

**1641** G. SANDYS *Paraphr. Song Solomon* III. iii. 13 At that solemniz'd Nuptiall Feast.

**'solemnizer.** *rare.* [f. prec.] One who solemnizes or performs a solemn rite.

**1577** HANMER *Anc. Eccl. Hist., Eusebius* x. iv, Setting before our mind the author and solemnizer of this present Feast. *a* **1634** R. CLERKE *Serm.* (1637) 518 The second regard is of the Solemnizer,..Christ himselfe. **1706** STEVENS *Span.-Eng. Dict.* 1, *Solemnizadór*, a Solemnizer.

**'solemnizing,** *vbl. sb.* [f. as prec.] The action of celebrating solemnly or ceremoniously.

**1565** STAPLETON tr. *Bede's Hist. Ch. England* 180 The catholike solemnising and dewe observation of the time of Christes resurrection. **1591** HORSEY *Trav.* (Hakl. Soc.) 171 Great feastings and trumps was at the solempnicinge of this mariage. **1634** BRERETON *Trav.* (Chetham Soc.) 64 It was as long in solemnizing as our marriages. *a* **1714** SHARP *Imit. Christ* iii. Wks. 1754 V. 266 The feast of the dedication, for the solemnizing of which we find our Saviour making a journey to Jerusalem.

**'solemnizing,** *ppl. a.* [f. as prec.] That solemnizes or renders solemn.

**1614** SELDEN *Titles Honor* 137 The Dancers or Singers, and number of the solemnizing Sacrificers. **1807** C. SIMEON in Carus *Life* (1847) 218 This had a sweetly solemnizing effect. **1859** CORNWALLIS *New World* I. 228 No solemnising associations seemed to connect themselves with the.. hallowed ground. **1871** MOZLEY *Univ. Serm.* v. (1876) 105 This judicial character of war..enables it to produce its solemnising type of character.

† **'solemnly,** *a. Obs.*⁻¹ [-LY¹.] Of a solemn or sacred character.

**1482** *Monk of Evesham* (Arb.) 106 Who ys he that wolde not ful gretly sorow to see so feire and so solemly a body to be caste under so grete iniuriis and sore peynys.

**solemnly** (ˈsɒləmlɪ), *adv.* Forms: *α.* 4 **solemplike, -liche;** 4–6 **solemply** (4 **-lie,** 5 **-lye, sollemply**); 4 **solemliche,** 6 **-ly.** *β.* 4 **soll-, solempneliche;** 4–6 **solempnely** (4 **-lie,** 5 **-li**), **solempnly** (6 **-lie**); 5–6 **sollempn(e)ly.** *γ.* 6 **solemnelie,** 6–7 **-ly,** 6– **solemnly.** [f. SOLEMN *a.* + -LY². Cf. OF. *sollempnement*, L. *sollemniter*, MDu. *solem(p)nelic, -lijc.*] In a solemn manner, in various senses of the adj.; ceremoniously, formally; gravely, seriously, etc.

*α.* *a* **1300** *Cursor M.* 6097 In mining sal ye hald þis dai,.. Solemplike wit-in your lai. **1387** TREVISA *Higden* (Rolls) III. 391 To brenne noble bodies whanne þey were dede, and kepe þe askes solempliche in solempne place. *c* **1430** LYDG. *Min. Poems* (Percy Soc.) 19 Solemplye [they] gan him conveye in dede Up into the chirche. **1473** *Rental Bk. Cupar-Angus* (1879) I. 172 The forsad Robert and Thomas ..swur sollemply vpon the haly wangelis. **1535** COVERDALE *Judith* xvi. 26 The daye wherin this victory was gotten, was solemply holden. *a* **1548** HALL *Chron., Hen. IV*, 22 b, The kyng..was by the senate and magestrates solemply receyued. **1565** COOPER *Thes.* s.v. *Celebro*, To bryng solemly to buriynge.

*β.* *a* **1325** *MS. Rawl. B.* 520 lf. 30 b, þat te notes ant te fins ..ben communeliche and sollempneliche i-radde. *c* **1330** R. BRUNNE *Chron. Wace* (Rolls) 15401 He was byried ful solempnely. **1390** GOWER *Conf.* III. 329 The hihe festes of Neptune..Sollempneliche thei besihe. *c* **1449** PECOCK *Repr.* IV. iv. 445 To whom Poul wrote more in quantite and more solempneli and oftir. **1470–85** MALORY *Arthur* VIII. xxxvi. 328 They were wedded and solempnly held theyr maryage. **1513** MORE *Hist. Rich. III*, Wks. 60/1 She was solempnely sworne to say the trouth. **1587** GREENE *Euphues* Wks. (Grosart) VI. 177 Being sollempnly set in a coole Arbour.

*γ.* **1556** ROBINSON *More's Utopia* II. (Arb.) 134 After that warre is ones solemnelie denounced. **1577** B. GOOGE *Heresbach's Husb.* IV. (1586) 170 b, I founde of late..an Owle sitting solemnly in the nest. **1646** SIR T. BROWNE *Pseud. Epid.* 239 Eve..was not solemnly begotten, but suddenly framed. **1671** MILTON *Samson* 1731 To fetch him hence and solemnly attend With silent obsequie. **1716** LADY M. W. MONTAGU *Lett.* I. iii. 12 The thick shade of the trees ..is solemnly delightful. **1766** GOLDSM. *Vicar* i, I solemnly protest I had no hand in it. **1817** SHELLEY *Rev. Islam* v. xli, Solemnly and slow..the wind bore that tumult to and fro. **1855** MACAULAY *Hist. Eng.* xv. III. 507 The right of the people to resist oppression..had been solemnly recognised by the Estates of the realm. **1874** GREEN *Short Hist.* vi. §5. 315 Luther's works were solemnly burnt in St. Paul's.

**solemnness,** variant of SOLEMNESS.

**solemnsides** (ˈsɒləmˌsaɪdz), *a.* and *sb.* [f. SOLEMN *a.* + *-sides* as in SOBERSIDES.] **A.** *adj.* Excessively solemn or serious. **B.** *sb.* An excessively solemn or serious person.

**1922** J. M. BARRIE *Courage* 36 Courage. I do not think it is to be got by your becoming solemnsides before your time. **1957** J. KIRKUP *Only Child* ii. 50 People who are 'solemnsides' cannot account for self-mockery. **1959** I. & P. OPIE *Lore & Lang. Schoolch.* ix. 155 Sobersides, solemnsides.

† **solemnty.** *Obs.* In 4–5 **solempte.** [prob. a reduced form of ME. *'solempnetè.*] Solemnity.

**1303** R. BRUNNE *Handl. Synne* 9632 As a-nouþer chyld shuld ha be þat hade receyuede the solempte. **1382** WYCLIF *Lev.* xxiii. 41 And ȝe shulen halowe the solempte of hym seuen dayes.

† **solemny,** *a.* and *adv. Obs.* In 5 **solempny, -ni.** [f. SOLEMN *a.*] **A.** *adj.* Solemn.

*c* **1420** *Chron. Vilod.* 1797 Bot a solempniere dedicacione for-sothe þer nas In Wylton neuer byfore þat day y-done. **1448–9** METHAM *Wks.* (E.E.T.S.) 51 And euery man that he coude off myrth or pley Schuld schewe yt..this solempny day. *c* **1450** *Godstow Reg.* 489 That the fest of seynt Margarete myght be the more solempnyere and the more devoutly be halowed and honoured.

**B.** *adv.* Solemnly. (Cf. SOLENNY *adv.*)

*c* **1375** *Sc. Leg. Saints* xxvii. (*Machor*) 1207 þare solempni with honoure þai grathit for it a sepulture. *a* **1470** *Contin. Brut* 493 And in euery town by þe way he had solempny his Dirige on þe evyn, & masse on þe morne.

† **solen,** *a.* and *sb.*¹ *Obs.* Also 5 **solenne.** [a. OF. *solenne* (= It. *solenne*), ad. L. *sōl-, sollennis*, var. of *sollemnis* SOLEMN *a.*]

**A.** *adj.* Solemn, in various senses.

**1432–50** tr. *Higden* (Rolls) III. 297 A feste of gandres was made solenne and kepede at Rome in the kalendes of Iune. *c* **1460** *Promp. Parv.* (W.) 421 Solenne, or festful, *festiuus.* **1530** PALSGR. 325/1 Solen, nat cherefull, *pencif.* **1535** STEWART *Cron. Scot.* I. 530 Syne grauit [he] wes in to his graif..with sacrifice solen Of Cristin wyis with mony nobill men. **1570** LEVINS *Manip.* 62 Solen, *solennis*.

**B.** *sb.* ? A formal residence.

**1447** BOKENHAM *Seyntys* (Roxb.) 29 In this seyd cherche was an abbeye, A solenne of munkys whil that it stood.

**solen** ('səʊlən), *sb.*[2] [a. L. *sōlēn*, or Gr. σωλήν, channel, pipe, syringe, shell-fish, etc. So F. *solen*.]

**1.** *Zool.* The razor-fish, *Solen ensis* or *siliqua*.

**1661** R. LOVELL *Anim. & Min.* 240 Solen... The flesh is sweet; they may be eaten fryed or boiled. **1752** HILL *Hist. Anim.* 170 The large, brown, common Solen, called the Razor-shell and Sheath-shell. **1776** MENDES DE COSTA *Elem. Conchol.* 233 Shells with valves, that..are always open and gaping in some part; as chamæ, pinnæ, solens, etc. **1834** MᶜMURTRIE *Cuvier's Anim. Kingd.* 268 In the Solens, properly so called, the shell is cylindrically elongated. **1841–71** T. R. JONES *Anim. Kingd.* 538 The Solen excavates for itself a very deep hole in the sand.

*Comb.* **1839** *Penny Cycl.* XIV. 319 Solen-like Nymphidæ.

**2.** *Surg.* (See quots.)

**1693** tr. *Blancard's Phys. Dict.* (ed. 2), *Solen*, an oblong Instrument which Surgeons use, to contain a broken Member. **1875** KNIGHT *Dict. Mech.* 2244/1 *Solen*,..(*a*) a cradle for a broken limb; (*b*) a tent or tilt of splits or wands to hold the bed-clothes from contact with a broken or sore limb.

Hence (from sense 1) **sole'nacean** *sb.* and *a.*; **sole'naceous** *a.*

**1842** BRANDE *Dict. Sci.*, etc. 1130/1 Solenaceans, *Solenacea*,..the name of a family of Dimiary Bivalve Mollusks, of which the razor shell (*Solen*) is the type. **1850** OGILVIE, *Solenaceous*, relating to the Solenaceans.

**solender**, obs. form of SALLENDER.

**soleness** ('səʊlnɪs). Now *rare*. [f. SOLE *a.*]

†**1.** Solitude; solitariness. *Obs.*

*c* **1449** PECOCK *Repr.* II. xv. 235 Forto haue quietnes and soolnes to preie to God or to a Seint. **1534** WHITINTON *Tullyes Offices* I. (1540) 63 A large house is ofte a reproche to his master, if there be in it soolnesse and no recourse. **1612** J. DAVIES (Heref.) *Muse's Sacr.* Wks. (Grosart) II. 68/2 Solenesse, brings sadnesse; Company, but strife. *a* **1618** SYLVESTER *Monodia* 100 Her selfe to sadnesse and to solenesse taking.

**2.** The state or condition of being sole, alone, or apart.

**1587** GOLDING *De Mornay* vi. 90 The first God..being afore the Beeër, and alone,..yet..abydeth still in the solenesse of his vnitie. **1631** R. BOLTON *Comf. Affl. Consc.* xi. (1635) 274 He is much troubled with solenesse in suffering. *a* **1661** FULLER *Worthies* (1840) I. 39 The laurel importing conquest and sovereignty, and so by consequence soleness in that faculty. **1748** CHESTERF. *Lett.* (1792) II. clx. 74 An advantage which France has;..which is (if I may use the expression) its sole-ness, continuity of riches and power within itself. **1889** *Macm. Mag.* Jan. 205/1 The Greek islander is never coarse, balanced, as he is, with curious soleness, between the barbarian and the gentleman.

**solenette** (səʊl'nɛt, sɒlə'nɛt). Also **solonette.** [Irregularly f. SOLE *sb.*[2] + -(N)ETTE.] The little sole, *Monochirus linguatulus* or *Solea minuta*.

**1839** YARRELL *Suppl. Brit. Fishes* 36 The Solenette, or Little Sole. **1881** *Cassell's Nat. Hist.* V. 73 The Solenette.. attains a length of five inches. **1882** DAY *Fishes Gt. Brit.* II. 45 *Solea parva*... Solonette. **1883** —— *Catal. Internat. Fish. Exhib.* 161 In some small forms, as the Solonette. **1892** *Chambers's Encycl.* IX. 559/2 The Solenette..is the smallest British species.

**'Solenhofen.** [See def.] ***Solenhofen slate*** or ***stone***, a fine-grained variety of limestone, used esp. in lithographic printing, quarried in the upper beds of the Jurassic formation at Solenhofen in Bavaria. So ***Solenhofen bed***.

**1833–4** *Encycl. Metrop.* (1845) VI. 634/1 Solenhofen beds. In the centre of the German Jura..occur beds of white fissile limestone, now universally employed in lithography. **1841** *Penny Cycl.* XXI. 256/1 The Jurassic limestone of Solenhofen, commonly called the Solenhofen slate. **1882** *Encycl. Brit.* XIV. 698/1 The Solenhofen stone, in its chemical decomposition, consists of lime and carbonic acid.

**so'lenial**, *a.* [f. SOLEN-IUM + -IAL.] Of the nature of a canal or pipe.

**1900** G. C. BOURNE in *Trans. Linn. Soc., Zool.* VII. x. 532 Fresh solenial outgrowths of the chief members give rise to new lateral members.

**'solenite.** [a. F. *solénite*: see SOLEN *sb.*[2] and -ITE[1] 2 a.] A fossil razor-fish or solen.

**1828–32** in WEBSTER. **1849** CRAIG, *Solenite*, a fossil Solen, of which Lamarck describes five species as occurring in the neighbourhood of Paris. **1850** OGILVIE s.v., Fragments of solenites are found in the Essex cliffs.

‖**solenium** (sə'liːnɪəm). Pl. solenia. [mod.L., ad. Gr. σωλήνιον, dim. of σωλήν SOLEN *sb.*[2]] (See first quot.)

**1900** G. C. BOURNE in *Trans. Linn. Soc., Zool.* VII. x. 522 The anastomosing canals lined by endoderm which place the zooid cavities in communication have been variously named 'stolons', 'nutritive-canals', 'cœnenchymal tubes', and so on. I propose to call them *solenia*. *Ibid.* 532 The anthostele sends up a solenium.

†**'solenly**, *adv. Obs. rare.* [f. SOLEN *a.* + -LY[2].] Solemnly; ceremoniously.

**1393** LANGL. *P. Pl.* C. IV. 54 In masse and in matyns..we shulleþ synge Solenliche and sothlich as for a sustre of oure ordre. *c* **1400** *Destr. Troy* 8738 There set was full solenly besyde the high aulter, A tabernacle.

†**so'lennial**, *a. Obs.*[−0] [f. L. *solenn-is*: see SOLEN *a.*] Also †**so'lennic** *a.* (See quots.)

**1623** COCKERAM I, *Solennicke*, vsuall once a yeere. **1656** BLOUNT *Glossogr.*, *Solennial*, yearly, used or done every year at a certain time, publick, solemn, accustomed.

†**so'lennit**, var. *solemnit* SOLEMNED *a. Obs.*

**1562** WINȜET *Wks.* (S.T.S.) I. 27 Ane notable cause of thir solennit dayis geuis the said renownit Father Augustine.

†**so'lennity.** *Obs.* Forms: 5 solenite, 5–6 solennite, 6 -itye, 7 -ity. [a. OF. *solennité* (= It. *solennità*), var. of *solemnité* SOLEMNITY.] Solemnity, formal celebration, etc.

*c* **1400** *Laud Troy Bk.* 2753 He wente to that solennite, The temple and that Ioye to se. *c* **1400** *Destr. Troy* 9091 Priam prestly gert ordan A gret solenite. *Ibid.* 9094 With Sacrifice & solenite vnto sere goddes. *c* **1475** *Harl. Contin. Higden* (Rolls) VIII. 446 Within whiche solennite he made iiij erles. **1565** STAPLETON tr. *Bede's Hist. Ch. Eng.* 182 The solennite whereof beginneth in the euening of the xiiij. daye. **1595** in *Cath. Rec. Soc. Publ.* V. 360 Within the Octaves & solennitye of St. Lawrence. **1647** J. TAYLOR *Lib. Proph.* ii. 51 That they should with so great pomp and solennities engage mens perswasions.

So †**solenni'zation** [F. *solennisation*], solemnization. †**'solennize** *v.* [F. *solenniser*, It. *solennizzare*], to solemnize, to perform. †**solenny** *adv.* [cf. SOLEMNY *adv.*], solemnly. *Obs.*

*c* **1450** *Cov. Myst.* (Shaks. Soc.) 71 This is the hyest fest of oure *solennyzacion. *c* **1440** *Pallad. on Husb.* III. 345 And in this mone..Thy graffyng good hit is to *solennize. **1588** GREENE *Perimedes* Wks. (Grosart) VII. 42 The marriage of the Gentlemen was sollenised the next weeke after. **1480** in *10th Rep. Hist. MSS. Comm.* App. V. 315 A Masse of the Holi Goste *solenny sayde and song. **1485** *Ibid.* 319 The Maire..and commynes, bene sworne all and singlerly solenny on the bocke.

**soleno-** (səʊ'liːnəʊ), combining form of Gr. σωλήν channel, pipe, etc., as **so'lenocyte**, one of the cells found in the nephridia of certain polychætan worms; **so'lenodon(t**, one or other of certain insectivorous mammalian rodents native to the West Indies and America, as the agouta, *S. paradoxus*, or the almiqui, *S. cubanus*; **sole'nogyne, soleno'stelic** *a.*, *Bot.* (see quots.); **soleno'stomatous** *a.*, of, belonging to, or resembling the genus *Solenostomus* of lophobranchiate fishes.

Various other examples, as ***solenoconch, solenoglyph, solenopharynx, solenostome***, etc., are recorded in some recent Dicts.

**1902** *Encycl. Brit.* XXXIII. 882 The blind branches are beset with peculiar cells, the *solenocytes. **1840** *Cuvier's Anim. Kingd.* 80 The *Solenodon..resembles a gigantic Shrew, but with coarse fur. **1871** *Cassell's Nat. Hist.* I. 362 The existence of a *Solenodon* in some of the mountainous parts of the island of Cuba. **1896** SCLATER in *Geog. Jrnl.* VII. 288 The affinities of which..seem on the whole to approach the Solenodonts. **1866** *Treas. Bot.* 1071/2 **Solenogyne*, a little Australian perennial herb of the *Compositæ*, now united with *Lagenophora* under the name *L. Solenogyne*. In aspect it is very like our own daisy. **1900** B. D. JACKSON *Gloss. Bot. Terms* 243/1 **Solenostelic*,..having a tubular stele with internal and external phloëm (Jeffrey). **1855** J. PHILLIPS *Man. Geol.* 60 According to the ordinary.. notion of their food, gasteropodous mollusca with shells may be ranked thus:—Holostomatous phytophaga, ..*Solenostomatous zoophaga.

**solenoglyph** (səʊ'liːnəʊglɪf). *Zool.* [ad. F. *solénoglyphe*, mod.L. *Solenoglypha* (A. H. A. Duméril 1853, in *Mém. Acad. Sci.* XXIII. 417), f. SOLENO- + Gr. γλυφή carving.] A venomous snake belonging to a group characterized by extra venom glands and grooved fangs which can be retracted. Also as *adj.* Hence **soleno'glyphous** *a.*, of or pertaining to a snake of this kind.

**1913** G. A. BOULENGER *Snakes of Europe* v. 56 The Proteroglyphs (Cobras, Coral-snakes, Sea-snakes) and the Solenoglyphs (Vipers, Pit-vipers, Rattlesnakes) may be regarded as the diverging extremes in the development of the poison apparatus. **1965** R. & D. MORRIS *Men & Snakes* viii. 177 With the vipers, pit vipers and rattle-snakes, we come to..the Solenoglyphous forms... These are the so-called 'Folding-fang' snakes. **1968** R. D. MARTIN tr. *Wickler's Mimicry in Plants & Animals* xii. 112 The vipers have the most specialised tooth-form,..a longitudinal canal that functions as a poison syringe. This condition is called solenoglyph. **1969** A. BELLAIRS *Life of Reptiles* I. v. 195 If the skull of a poisonous snake is examined, whether it be a proteroglyph or a solenoglyph, it very often appears that there are two fangs in each maxilla, set side by side.

**solenoid** ('sɒlənɔɪd, 'səʊlənɔɪd). [a. F. *solénoïde*, f. Gr. σωλήν: see SOLEN *sb.*[2]]

**1.** *Electr.* An electro-dynamical spiral, formed of a wire with the ends returned parallel to the axis; a series of elementary circuits arranged on this principle.

**1827** J. CUMMING *Man. Electro Dynamics* 240 In the case of a straight solenoïd (an electro-dynamic cylinder) θ is the angle between the axis of the solenoïd and the extremity of the cylinder. **1832** *Handbk. Nat. Philos., Electro-Magnet.* xii. §270 (L.U.K.) 83 Collecting together a great number of similar helices..and uniting them in one mass. Such an arrangement is called by Ampère an Electro-dynamic Solenoid. **1881** *Nature* XXV. 167 The main current is made to pass through a pair of concentric solenoids, and in the annular space between these is hung a solenoid. **1897** CURRY *Theory Electr. & Magnetism* 254 A number of elementary circuits placed at equal distances apart along any line with their planes at right angles to that line is called a solenoid.

**2.** *Med.* A kind of cage for containing a patient during medical treatment.

**1901** *Brit. Med. Jrnl.* No. 2092 Epit. Med. Lit. 19 The subject was seated in a large solenoid or cage, and expired through a gasometer. **1903** *Ibid.* No. 2203. 654 The successful treatment of diphtheria and tetanus within the solenoid.

**3.** *attrib.* and *Comb.*, as ***solenoid-operated*** adj.; **solenoid brake**, a brake actuated by the movement of a core into or out of a solenoid when an electric current is passed through the latter; similarly **solenoid lock**.

**1914** *Machinery* Dec. 328/1 A new automatic solenoid brake for crane, hoist, lift bridge and similar service has recently been developed. **1963** JONES & SCHUBERT *Engin. Encycl.* (ed. 3) 1168 One type of solenoid brake adapted for mill, crane and hoist motors and similar classes of service, is so arranged that the brake mechanism is held in the off or release position by a coil and plunger. **1976** L. DEIGHTON *Twinkle, twinkle Little Spy* iv. 41 The glass door..had an electric solenoid lock. I had to push the override. **1956** *Nature* 14 Jan. 84/2 Two solenoid-operated valves are incorporated in the flow line. **1971** *Jrnl. Gen. Psychol.* LXXXIV. 325 The four match stimuli were presented by the second projector through a solenoid operated shutter which varied exposure duration.

**solenoidal** (sɒl-, səʊlə'nɔɪdəl), *a.* [f. prec. + -AL[1].] Of, pertaining or relating to, a solenoid; of the nature or having the properties of a solenoid. *spec.* of a vector field: having no divergence anywhere, and hence expressible as the curl of another vector field.

**1873** MAXWELL *Electr. & Magn.* I. 21 The distribution of the vector quantity is said to be Solenoidal. **1873** J. C. MAXWELL *Electr. & Magnetism* I. 23 The whole space can be divided into tubes of this kind provided $dX/dx + dY/dy + dZ/dz = 0$, a distribution of a vector quantity consistent with this equation is called a Solenoidal Distribution. **1883** *Encycl. Brit.* XV. 230/2 Solenoidal Magnets..[are] such that the vector I satisfies the solenoidal condition. **1897** CURRY *Theory Electr. & Magnetism* 256 This solenoidal arrangement of the molecular currents. **1909** J. G. COFFIN *Vector Anal.* vi. 154 (*heading*) Separation of a vector point-function W, which has a vector-potential, into solenoidal or rotational and lamellar or irrotational components. **1933** H. PHILLIPS *Vector Anal.* viii. 195 If two vectors satisfy these conditions their difference, being irrotational, solenoidal, piecewise continuous, and zero at infinity, is zero. **1972** A. G. HOWSON *Handbk. Terms Algebra & Anal.* xxxv. 175 A vector field satisfying div **f** = 0, i.e. div **f**(**x**) = 0 for all $\mathbf{x} \in S$, is said to be solenoidal.

Hence **sole'noidally** *adv.*

**1851** *Phil. Trans. R. Soc.* CXLI. 270 The distribution of magnetism in it is said to be solenoidal, and the substance is said to be solenoidally magnetized. **1883** *Encycl. Brit.* XV. 231/1 When a body is solenoidally magnetized. *Ibid.*, The magnetic action of a solenoidally magnetized body.

†**'solent**, *a. Obs.*[−1] [? f. L. *sol-ēre* to be wont.] ? Usual, customary.

**1658** FRANCK *North. Mem.* (1694) p. vi, There the Rocks and the Groves will be our solent Reception, and the Cities and Citadels supply us with Accommodation.

**solepers**, obs. variant of SURPLICE.

**soler**[1] ('səʊlə(r)). [f. SOLE *v.* + -ER[1].] One who soles boots or shoes.

**1884** L. GRONLUND *Co-oper. Commw.* viii. (1886) 173 The operatives in a shoe-factory:..the 'tappers', the 'solers', the 'finishers'. **1902** *Longm. Mag.* Dec. 150 Some were only eyelet-hole makers, others were sole-peggers, or tongue-sewers, or solers and heelers.

†**soler**[2]. *Obs.*[−1] [a. OF. (**soler*) *solier*, f. L. *solium*, perh. by confusion with *soler* SOLLAR *sb.*[1]] A throne.

*a* **1340** HAMPOLE *Ps., Comm. Cant.* 502 þat he sytt wiþ pryncis and hald þe solere of ioy [L. *solium glorie*].

**soler(e**, obs. forms of SOLLAR *sb.*[1]

‖**solera** (so'lera). [Sp.]

**1.** A blend of sherry wine. Also *attrib.*, as ***solera wine***; **solera system** (see quot. 1965).

**1851** REDDING *Mod. Wines* 396 The finest wines come thus into England in cases... Soleras, sixteen years in wood [etc.]. **1876** *From Vineyard to Decanter* 23 In the shippers bodega many soleras are kept, each contained in a given number of butts. **1888** *Encycl. Brit.* XXIV. 607/1 The wines ..are reared for a number of years as *soleras*. **1961** *Times* 16 Jan. 13/5 Sherry is made on the solera system. **1965** A. SICHEL *Penguin Bk. of Wines* III. 227 The solera system is.. a..method of refreshing delicately flavoured old wines still in cask with small quantities of slightly younger wine of the same character in order to keep a continuous stock of mature wine of one type and character always available. **1972** *Times* (Spain Suppl.) 11 May p. iii/2 The sherries are *solera* wines.

**2.** A wine-cask, usu. containing a double butt.

**1863** T. G. SHAW *Wine* 136 Stocks are kept in casks of all sizes, generally double butts, called soleras. *Ibid.* 139 The bungs of the soleras are never driven home.

**'soleret.** *rare.* [ad. med.L. *solarettum*, dim. of *solarium* SOLLAR *sb.*[1]] A small upper room.

**1851** T. H. TURNER *Dom. Archit.* I. v. 217 To make a certain soleret above the gateway there. *Ibid.* iii. 88.

**soleret(te**, variants of SOLLERET.

**†solert**, *a. Obs.* [ad. L. *sōlert-*, stem of *sōlers*, *sollers*, f. *sollus* whole, entire + *ars* art.] Clever, wise; characterized by cleverness.

**1612** COTTA *Disc. Dang. Pract. Phys.* 3 An exact and exquisite disquisition of a sound and solert judgement. **1678** CUDWORTH *Intell. Syst.* I. v. 685 That Man was there-fore the Wisest (or most Solert) of all Animals. *a* **1680** BUTLER *Rem.* (1759) I. 406 Nor is the diligent and solert Dr. less proper for this Administration.

So **†so'lertic** *a. Obs.* Also **†so'lertiousness**, **†solerty** [L. *solertia*], cleverness, ingenuity.

**1623** COCKERAM I, *Solesticke* [sic], craftie. *a* **1649** in *N. & Q.* Ser. I. X. 357 Solertiousnes must be added to the rest, else it will be too dull to meet with every occurrent. **1656** OUGHTRED in Rigaud *Corr. Sci. Men* (1841) I. 90 Which therefore I leave to the solerty of W. J. *a* **1670** HACKET *Abp. Williams* I. (1692) 22 The interpretation of his secret meaning; which abounded to the praise of Mr. Williams's solertiousness.

**†soleship.** *Obs.* [f. SOLE *a.*] The state or fact of being sole or alone in the enjoyment or exercise of a privilege, power, etc.

**1641** SIR E. DERING *Sp. on Relig.* ix. 32 This Bishop.. sublimes it self by assuming a soleship both in Orders and Censures. *Ibid.*, Unless you root out this soleship of Episcopacy. **1643** *Sober Sadnes* 37 The very name of Monarch implies a soleship of Government.

**soletary**, obs. form of SOLITARY *a.*

**sole-tree.** Also 6 soletre, 6–7 soletree, 7 soale-, 7, 9 sole tree. [f. SOLE *sb.*[1] + TREE.] A beam, plank, or piece of timber forming a support, base, or foundation to something.

**1527–8** *Fabric Rolls York Minster* (Surtees) 101 Pro plumbo.. in tegulis, in les fre stone, in evis bordes, severns et j soletre. *c* **1530** *Howden Roll, Ibid.* 354 Owtshot-sparres, sarkynboordes et geists ac soletrees pro thakking. **1632** *Kirton-in-Lindsey Ch. Acc.* in Peacock *N.W. Linc. Gloss.* 232/1 For a peice of wood to make a soale-tree for the seates. **1671** in Holmes *Pontefract Bk. Entries* (1882) 103 Studs for pertitions, soletrees, nayles. **1789** J. WILLIAMS *Min. Kingd.* I. 310 Two door-cheeks, or side-posts,.. a lintel and sole tree. **1833** LOUDON *Encycl. Archit.* §1206 The rise from the channel to the sole-tree.. to be 4 inches. **1877** in Peacock *N.W. Linc. Gloss.* s.v., There'll hev to be a new sole-tree to th' crewyard pump.

**b.** *spec.* in *Mining* (see later quots.).

**1653** MANLOVE *Customs Lead Mines* 258 Stoprice, Yokings, Soletrees, Roach and Ryder. **1747** HOOSON *Miner's Dict.* P iij b, They [small stoce] are composed of two Stoce-blades, two Sole-trees [etc.]..; the Sole-trees and Hang-benches are fastned together with Pins of Wood. **1860** *Eng. & For. Mining Gloss.* (ed. 2) 44 (Derby Terms), *Sole tree*, a piece of wood belonging to stowces to draw ore up from the mine.

‖**soleus** (səʊ'liːəs, 'səʊlɪəs). *Anat.* Also 8 solæus. [mod.L., f. L. *solea* SOLE *sb.*[1]] A muscle of the calf of the leg, situated between the gastrocnemius and the bone. Also *attrib.*

**1676** J. COOKE *Marrow Surg.* 432 These [twin muscles] with *Soleus* are inserted and make the Heels great Tendon. **1704** J. HARRIS *Lex. Techn.* I, *Solæus*, is a Muscle that helps to extend the Foot. **1733** G. DOUGLAS tr. *Winslow's Anat. Expos. Human Body* III. xii. §486 The fleshy Body of the Soleus seems to consist of two Planes of Fibres at least. **1846** BRITTAN tr. *Malgaigne's Man. Oper. Surg.* 145 Divide the attachments of the soleus.. from the tibia. **1854** MAYNE *Expos. Lex.* 367/1 The *Soleus* muscle. **1899** *Allbutt's Syst. Med.* VII. 141 These movements are due to the gastro-cnemius and soleus acting alternately with the antagonistic muscles.

**solewid**, pa. pple. SOLWE *v. Obs.*

**soleyn(e**, variants of SOLEIN *a. Obs.*

**†solf**, *v. Obs.* Also 4–6 solfe (5 solfon), 5 solue, solph-, 6 solff, soulfe; 4 solfye, 5 solfy. See also SOWFF *v.* [ad. OF. (also mod.F.) *solfier* (cf. Sp. *solfear*), f. *sol fa* SOL-FA *sb.*]

**1.** *intr.* = SOL-FA *v.* 1. Also *fig.*

*c* **1330** in *Rel. Ant.* I. 292, I solfe, and singge after,.. I horle at the notes. **1377** LANGL. *P. Pl.* B. v. 423 ȝete can I neither solfe ne synge ne seyntes lyues rede. *c* **1400** *Beryn* 396 He had nede to solue Long or it wer mydnyȝt. *c* **1440** *Promp. Parv.* 464/1 Solfon, *solfo*. *a* **1529** SKELTON *Agst. comely Coystrowne* 23 He solfyth to haute, hys trybyll is to hy. **1542** *St. Papers Hen. VIII* (1849) IX. 238 They are lyke to solfe for yᵗ; for the King chargethe them.. with thinsurrection. **1570** FOXE *A. & M.* (ed. 2) I. 301/2 Their singyng was turned to scoldyng,.. and if in stead of the Organes they had had a drumme, I doubt, but they would haue solfed [**1596** solfaed] by the eares together.

**2.** *trans.* = SOL-FA *v.* 2. Also *fig.*

**1525** BP. CLERK *Let. to Wolsey* (MS. Cott. Vit. B. VII. f. 127), To make the Venetians the more afrayd and to make them to solfe sumwhatt a highar notte. **1553** *Respublica* I. iv. 410 Come on; ye shall Learne to solfe Reformacion, Sing on nowe, Re. **1582** STANYHURST *Æneis* I. (Arb.) 21 [Æneas] This kyrye sad solfing, thee northern bluster aproching Thee sayls tears tag rag.

Hence **†'solfing** *vbl. sb. Obs.*

*c* **1440** *Promp. Parv.* 464/1 Solfynge, *solfacio*. *c* **1500** in *Grose's Antiq. Rep.* (1809) IV. 409 For thy sophisticall solphynge,.. take it forthe!

**sol-fa** ('sɒlfɑː, 'səʊlfɑː), *sb. Mus.* Also 6 solle fa, 6–9 sol fa, 7–8 solfa. [From the syllables *sol* (SOL *sb.*[2]) and *fa* (FA) of the scale: see GAMUT.]

**1.** The set of syllables 'do (or ut), re, mi, fa, sol, la, si', sung to the respective notes of the major scale; the system of singing notes to these syllables; a musical scale or exercise thus sung. †Occas. in the phr. *to sing sol-fa*. *tonic sol-fa*: see TONIC *a.*

**1548** HOOPER *Declar. Commandm.* viii. 134 Souche as syng solle fa, and can do nothyng lesse then the thing that apertainithe to there offyce. **1580** LYLY *Euphues* (Arb.) 213 As froward as the Musition, who being entreated, will scarse sing sol fa, but not desired, straine aboue Ela. **1602** BRETON *Wonders Worth Hearing* Wks. (Grosart) II. 7/2 My Hostesse .. began with a note about Ela to sing them.. a solfa. **1644** MILTON *Areop.* (Arb.) 64 A Harmony and a Catena.. out of which, as out of an alphabet or sol fa,.. a little book-craft.. might furnish him unspeakably. **1714** GAY *What d'ye call it* II. iv, I might have learnt Accounts, and sung Sol-fa. **1730** *Treat. Harmony* 63 We must give the same solfa to the Notes defining the Leaps. **1840** BARHAM *Ingol. Leg.* Ser. II. (1905) 353 We'll have nobody give us *sol fa* but He! **1887** DOWDEN *Life Shelley* II. vii. 309 Claire had her singing-master, and got on prosperously with her *sol fa's*.

*fig.* **1579** LYLY *Euphues* (Arb.) 93 If thou haddest learned .. the first noat of Descant, thou wouldest haue kept thy *Sol. Fa.* [= complaint] to thy selfe.

**2.** *attrib.*, as *sol-fa man*, *notation*.

**1676** *Poor Robin's Intell.* 15–22 Aug. 1/1 He contracts with an able Sol-fa-man to teach him.. the rudiments of song. **1890** W. J. GORDON *Foundry* 82 Hymns.. in which the music is given in the sol-fa notation.

So **†sol-fa-re.** *Obs.*[−1]

**1600** DEKKER *Old Fortunatus* v. ii, There's more music in this, than all the gamut airs, and sol fa res in the world.

**sol-fa** ('sɒlfɑː, 'səʊlfɑː), *v. Mus.* Also 6 sole-fay, 6–7 sol fa, 6–9 solfa. [See prec.]

**1.** *trans.* To sing (a tune, air, etc.) to the sol-fa syllables. Also *fig.*

**1568** V. SKINNER tr. *Montanus' Inquisit.* 40 b, He.. shall not be suffered to speake but in a very low note, whereof they themselues will apoint him the tune, and Solfa it before him. **1597** MORLEY *Mus.* III. 156 You shall not find a musicion.. able to *sol fa* it right. **1609** DOULAND *Ornith. Microl.* 15 He that will Solfa any Song, must aboue all things haue an eye to the Tone. **1730** *Treat. Harmony* 65 When we would solfa any Musick that is written in a Transposed key. **1767** *Ann. Reg., Ess.* 198/2, I sol-fa'd them exactly by note, with-out any ornament. **1833** A. CLARKE in J. B. B. Clarke *Life* I. 61 Each tune was at first sol-fa'd, till it was tolerably well learned. **1862** *Catal. Internat. Exhib., Brit.* II. No. 5383, The teacher Sol-fas a short musical phrase while he points to the notes on the Modulator.

**2.** *intr.* To sing in this manner; to use the sol-fa syllables in singing.

**1584** PEELE *Arraignm. Paris* V. i, Music sounds, and the Nymphs within sing or solfa with voices and instruments awhile. **1609** DOULAND *Ornith. Microl.* 14 To solfa.. is to expresse the Syllables and names of the Voyces. **1623** MIDDLETON *More Dissemblers* V. i, Let whoso would *Sol Fa*, I'ld give them my part. **1730** *Treat. Harmony* 64 Solfaing from D to D, we shall find the Sillables to be the same. *Ibid.* 77 The Leading Part and the Answer to it must Solfa alike. **1809** MALKIN *Gil Blas* V. i. ¶7 To all appearance you sol-fa with your whole heart and soul. **1838** W. GARDINER *Music & Friends* II. 807 In the singing-room they were solfaing in every kind of voice. **1881** *Grove's Dict. Music* III. 545.

**†b.** With *it*. *Obs.*[−1]

**1692** L'ESTRANGE *Fables* I. cccxi, His Son follow'd the Corps, Singing. Why Sirrah, says the Father; You should Howle and Wring your Hands,.. and not go Sol-Fa-ing it about like a Mad-man.

Hence **sol-faer**, one who sol-fas; **sol-faist**, an adherent of the (tonic) sol-fa system.

**1609** J. DOULAND *Ornith. Microl.* 15 Euery Solfaer must needs looke, whether the song be regular, or no. **1882** *Athenæum* 24 June 806/2 We think that the Sol-faists have made out a most excellent case in the replies which Mr. Curwen has collected. **1883** *American* VI. 174 The sol-fa-ists are now a power in the musical world.

**sol-faing**, *vbl. sb.* [f. SOL-FA *v.* + -ING[1].] The action or practice of singing to the sol-fa syllables; solmization.

**1549–62** STERNHOLD & H. *Ps.* To Rdr., The knowledge of perfect Solefaying. **1609** J. DOULAND *Ornith. Microl.* 14 Euery Song may be sung by Solfaing, which is for Nouices, that learne to sing. **1667** C. SIMPSON *Compend. Pract. Mus.* 6 That which we call the sol-fa-ing of a Song. **1730** *Treat. Harmony* 64 The Example of the Octave.. to show how true and certain this method of solfaing is. **1797** *Encycl. Brit.* (ed. 3) XII. 506 *note*, From which characters, except in sol-fa'ing, the notes in the diatonic series are generally named. **1818** *Blackw. Mag.* III. 269 The exercises in solmisation or solfaing, as it is more familiarly called. **1875** STAINER & BARRETT *Dict. Mus. Terms* s.v., In the modern method of Sol-faing no distinction is made between tones and semitones.

*attrib.* **1589** NASHE *Martin Marprelate* Wks. (Grosart) I. 151 Quaint Querristers.. first entred with their Solfaing notes.

‖**solfatara** (solfa'tara). Also 8–9 solfatarra, 9 solfa-tara; 8–9 solfaterra, 8 solfa terra. [The name of a sulphurous volcano near Naples, f. It. *solfo* sulphur.] A volcanic vent, from which only sulphurous exhalations and aqueous vapours are emitted, incrusting the edge with sulphur and other minerals.

a. **1777** FORSTER *Voy. round World* II. 296 The earth which covered these solfatarras.. had a greenish tinge. **1802** PINKERTON *Mod. Geogr.* (1811) 663 A kind of solfatara, or vast mass of sulphur, emitting continual smoke. **1843** *Penny Cycl.* XXVII. 748/2 There are several solfataras, or cones of pure sulphur, and mud volcanoes. **1899** E. J. CHAPMAN *Drama Two Lives* 19 Among them shone A solfatara's fiery cone.

*attrib.* **1882** GEIKIE *Text-Bk. Geol.* 209 The dormant or waning condition of a volcano.. is sometimes called the Solfatara phase.

β. **1796** KIRWAN *Elem. Min.* (ed. 2) II. 2 The sulphureous acid exists.. in various solfaterras. **1871** KINGSLEY *At Last* ii, In case of.. any difficulty occurring in obtaining sulphur from Sicily, a supply.. might be obtained from this and the other like Solfaterras of the British Antilles. **1886** GUILLEMARD *Cruise Marchesa* I. 23 Hot springs and solfaterras are found in the neighbourhood of Tamsui.

Hence **solfa'taric** *a.*

**1885** *Academy* 3 Oct. 225 A legacy of former vulcanicity —the lingering relics of solfataric action. **1895** *Physiographic Processes* (Nat. Geogr. Monographs) I. 18 This action of hot waters is known as solfataric action, and solfataric waters are quite common in volcanic regions.

**†solfaterre**, var. *solfaterra*, SOLFATARA.

**1764** GRAINGER *Sugar Cane* II. 392 *note*, Volcanoes are called sulphurs or solfaterres in the West Indies.

‖**solfège** (sɔlfɛʒ). *Mus.* [Fr.] **a.** = SOLFEGGIO *sb.* **b.** (See quot. 1954.) Also *attrib.*

**1912** E. INGHAM in J. W. Harvey *Eurhythmics Jaques-Dalcroze* 52 The solfège lessons are chiefly for ear-training and practical harmony. **1914** M. GIBB *Chassevant Method of Musical Educ.* ii. 19 In the 'First Solfège' there are no dots used, though there are many examples of tied notes. **1921** H. F. RUBINSTEIN tr. *Jaques-Dalcroze's Rhythm, Music & Educ.* v. 78 One of these groups confined itself to studying solfège, the other commenced pianoforte lessons... The solfège students were then initiated into the study of the piano. **1936** *Times Educ. Suppl.* 13 June 218/2 The course [of Eurhythmics] will consist of daily lessons in rhythmic movement and *solfège*. **1954** *Grove's Dict. Mus.* (ed. 5) VII. 877/2 *Solfège*... Although derived from the Italian *solfeggio*, and originally confined to the same meaning, the French word is now much more comprehensive. It stands for the teaching of the rudiments of music, which includes ear-training as an important factor. **1970** W. APEL *Harvard Dict. Mus.* (ed. 2) 786/1 Extensive courses in solfège.. were first introduced in France and Belgium.

‖**solfeggio** (sol'fɛddʒo), *sb.* Pl. **solfeggi**, **solfeggios.** [It., f. *sol-fa* SOL-FA.] An exercise for the voice, in which the sol-fa syllables are employed; †also *transf.*, an exercise for a musical instrument.

**1774** 'J. COLLIER' *Mus. Trav.* Ded. p. iv, Playing his new Solfeggi to the dying groans of the.. Dantziggers. *Ibid.* 28 He was seated opposite to a glass practising some solfeggi on the flute. **1836** R. FURNESS *Astrol.* I. Wks. (1858) 138 For Thor loved music.., Taught the sol-feggio, Aretino's scale. **1844** CALKIN & BUDD *Mus. Catal.* 191 Solfeggios for the Voice, with an Accompaniment for the Piano Forte. **1873** MISS BRADDON *Str. & Pilgr.* I. vii. 83 You can't imagine I could spend half my existence in shrieking solfeggi.

*attrib.* **1867** *Chamb. Encycl.* IX. 480/1 The seven notes of the diatonic scale are represented by the Solfeggio syllables. **1896** HUTCHINSON tr. *Gounod's Reminisc.* 14, I easily held my place, even at that early age, in a Solfeggio class.

Hence **sol'feggio** *v. rare.*

**1831** *Examiner* 708/2 The verses should be spoken, and then the music solfagioed [*sic*].

**solferino** (sɒlfə'riːnəʊ). [f. the place-name *Solferino* in Italy, because discovered shortly after the battle fought there in 1859.] The bright crimson dye-colour rosaniline. Also *attrib.*

*c* **1865** J. WYLDE *Circ. Sci.* I. 420 Aniline.. is.. used in.. dyeing establishments, for affording the colours.. Magenta, Solferino. **1883** *Chamb. Jrnl.* 15 Dec. 797/2 The number of new names given to various varieties of colour, as mauve, magenta, solferino, &c. **1889** GUNTER *That Frenchman* v. 53 Most of these [dresses] are of.. Solferino reds, or Pompadour greens.

**solfre**, obs. form of SULPHUR.

‖**soli**, pl. of SOLO *sb.*[1]

**soli-** ('səʊlɪ), comb. form of L. *sōlus* sole, alone, as in **soli'biblical** *a.*, that relies or depends on the Bible only; also **soli'biblicism**, **soli'biblist.**

**1854** WATERWORTH *Orig. Anglicanism* 99 They maintain the solibiblical system. *Ibid.* 296 In what conclusions do the solibiblists agree? **1909** *Sat. Rev.* 17 Apr. 501/2 In his opposition to solibiblicism.

**solible**, obs. variant of SOLUBLE *a.*

**†so'licit**, *sb. Obs. rare.* Also 7 sollicite. [f. the vb.] An entreaty or solicitation.

**1611** SHAKS. *Cymb.* II. iii. 52 Frame your selfe To orderly solicits [*1st fol.* solicity], and be friended With aptnesse of the season. **1639** N. N. tr. *Du Bosq's Compl. Woman* II. 11 All his sollicites.. not having force enough to shake the resolution of this Lady. *a* **1657** R. LOVEDAY *Lett.* (1663) 51, I remember your frequent sollicites gained a promise from me to compose you a prayer.

**†so'licit**, *a.* Chiefly *Sc. Obs.* Also 6 sol(l)yst, 6–7 solist(e, solicite. [ad. L. *sollicitus* (*sōlicitus*), f. *sollus* whole, entire, + *citus*, pa. pple. of *ciēre* to put in motion. So Sp. and Pg. *solicito*, It. *solli-*, *sollecito*.]

**1.** Characterized by solicitude or care.

**1513** DOUGLAS *Æneid* VIII. vii. 71, I the hecht All maner thing, wyth sollyst diligence. **1644** MAXWELL *Prerog. Chr. Kings* Ep. Ded. p. v, Episcopacie after the most exact and sollicite triall, is onely the crime [etc.].

**2.** Solicitous; anxious; careful. Also const. *for*, *to* (with inf.), etc.

a. **1533** BELLENDEN *Livy* II. i. (S.T.S.) I. 131 Brutus, seand þe pepill solist with þis suspicioun, callit þame to ane concioun. **1549** *Compl. Scot.* vi. 43 Riche kyng amphion vas verray solist to keip his scheip. **1596** DALRYMPLE tr. *Leslie's Hist. Scot.* (S.T.S.) I. 253 He was verie soliste and kairful for his people. **1606** BIRNIE *Kirk-Buriall* (1833) 8 Why then.. are ye solist what befall a senslesse carrion?

*β.* *c* **1535** FISHER *Wks.* (E.E.T.S.) II. 431 Saint Paule.. is veray solicite and carefull, lest the flocke of Christe shalbe corrupted by theyr heresies. **1596** DALRYMPLE tr. *Leslie's Hist. Scot.* (S.T.S.) I. 307 The peple solicit and sair kairful for the state of the cuntrie. *a* **1614** J. MELVILL *Diary* (Wodrow Soc.) 634 We are not solicite neithir cairfull in this mater. **1644** MAXWELL *Prerog. Chr. Kings* 106 Who knoweth not how ambitious, factious, and discontented spirits, are most ingenious and solicite.

Hence †**so'licitness.** *Sc. Obs.*

**1549** *Compl. Scot.* v. 32, I beleue that oure solistnes ande vane opinione vald altir. *Ibid.* xiii. 112 That ȝe gar ȝour solistnes of the deffens of ȝour comont veil preffer the solistnes of ȝour particular veil.

**solicit** (sə'lɪsɪt), *v.* Forms: 5- solicit, 6 solycit (solucyt), solysset, 7 solissit (6-7 *Sc.* solist); 5-8 solicite, 6-7 solycite; 6-8 sollicite (6 -ycite), 7-8 sollicit. [ad. OF. *sol-*, *solliciter* (mod.F. *solliciter*, = Prov. *sollicitar*, Sp. and Pg. *solicitar*, It. *solli-*, *sollecitare*), or ad. L. *sollicitāre* (*sŏl-*), f. *sollicitus*: see prec.]

**I.** *trans.* †**1.** To disturb, disquiet, trouble; to make anxious, fill with concern. *Obs.*

*a* **1450** tr. *De Imitatione* III. l. 121 If it were so wiþ me, mannys drede shuld not so solicite me, ner þe dartes of wordes shuld not meve me. *a* **1513** FABYAN *Chron.* v. (1811) 106 He solycited so the lordes of Burgoyne, that some of them abhorred the crudelitie of that woman. *c* **1611** CHAPMAN *Iliad* XVI. 10 Hath any ill solicited thine ears Befall'n my Myrmidons? **1637-8** in Willis & Clark *Cambridge* (1886) I. 119 They may enjoy all yᵉ ground.. in what manner they please; we desire no way to sollicite them. **1681** DRYDEN *Span. Friar* III. ii, But anxious Fears sollicit my weak Breast. **1719** YOUNG *Revenge* IV. i, How good in you, my lord, whom nations cares Solicit, and a world in arms obeys!

*refl.* *c* **1685** *Great Frost 1683-4* 17 Ye merchants, to Greenland now leave off your sailing, And for your train oyl yourselves never solicite. **1788** *New London Mag.* 533 They ..consider him as one that..never solicits himself about them.

**2. a.** To entreat or petition (a person) for, or to do, something; to urge, importune; to ask earnestly or persistently.

**1530** PALSGR. 725/1, I solycite one, I call upon him to remembre the seute I make to him, *je solicite.* **1548** GESTE *Pr. Masse* 116 He is reverenced and sollicited but as resident in heaven. **1612** in *Fortescue P.* (Camden) 7 *note*, Hee hath soe confirmed mee in the assurance of your..readie assistance uppon all occasions, that I neede not any more solicite you therein. **1655-60** STANLEY *Hist. Philos.* (1687) 3/2 In this privacy of life he was solicited and sent unto by many Princes, whose invitations..he refused. **1719** in Sir J. Picton *L'pool Rec.* (1886) II. 79 The charge of soliciting the Government for the moneys. **1769** ROBERTSON *Chas. V*, v. Wks. 1813 V. 445 Henry had been soliciting the pope for some time, in order to obtain a divorce from Catherine of Aragon, his queen. **1868** GLADSTONE *Juv. Mundi* ii. (1869) 63 The injured priest, Chruses, solicits all the Achaioi, and most of all the two Atridai. *Ibid.*, There is no sign that he solicited the army.

*transf.* **1626** BP. HALL *Contempl.*, *O.T.* XXI. i, Lebanon is now anew solicited for cedar trees.

**b.** Const. *to* with inf., or with *that.*

**1533** BELLENDEN *Livy* II. i. (S.T.S.) I. 129 Brutus solistit þe pepill to mak þare solemne aithis, neuer to suffir ony kingis regne abone þame. **1560** DAUS tr. *Sleidane's Comm.* 302 The cities and townes of Germany are sollicited to accept the Interim. **1656** EARL MONM. tr. *Boccalini's Advts. fr. Parnass.* I. xiii. (1674) 16 [He] did much solicite his Majesty that he might be admitted. **1676** RAY *Corr.* (1848) 123, I have been lately solicited to reprint my Catalogue of English Plants. **1719** YOUNG *Revenge* I. i, Had I known this before,..I had not then solicited your father To add to my distress. **1855** MACAULAY *Hist. Eng.* xiv. III. 411 He had been solicited to accept indulgences which scarcely any other heretic could by any solicitation obtain.

†**c.** *spec.* To beg (an advocate) to attend to a case. *Obs.*⁻¹

**1536** in Strype *Mem. Cranmer* (1694) App. 32 A Proctor must take sufficient instructions of his Clients, and keep every Court-day..; solicite and instruct his Advocates [etc.].

**3.** To incite or move, to induce or persuade, to some act of lawlessness or insubordination. Freq. const. *to* (with sb. or inf.).

**1565** COOPER *Thesaurus* s.v. *Solicito*, To solicite mens mindes and intice them with brybes. **1570-6** LAMBARDE *Peramb. Kent* (1826) 149 This done, he sollicitеth to rebellion the Bishops, Nobilitie, and Commons of the Realme. **1600** HOLLAND *Livy* X. xxi. 366 The Vmbrians.. were moued to revolt; and the Gaules also sollicited with great summes of mony. **1643** BAKER *Chron.*, *Jas. I*, 134 With a purpose to solicite forreign Princes against the King. **1683** *Brit. Spec.* 102 Boadicea..sollicited the Britains..to a Revolt. **1809** CHRISTIAN *Blackstone's Comm.* IV. 221 One Higgins was indicted..for having incited and solicited a servant to steal his master's property. **1835** [see SOLICITATION 2 d].

**4. a.** To incite, draw on, allure, by some specious representation or argument. (Cf. 5 b.)

**1591** SHAKS. *1 Hen. VI*, v. iii. 190 Solicite Henry with her wonderous praise. Bethinke thee on her Vertues [etc.]. **1592** KYD *Sp. Trag.* III. xv. 19 Though I sleepe, Yet is my mood soliciting their soules. **1609** BIBLE (Douay) *Deut.* xxiv. 7 If any man be taken soliciting his brother of the children of Israel, and selling him.., he shal be slaine. [**1773** GRAY *Corr.* (1843) 153 The said Solicitor (who seems to have solicited the house out of their senses).]

**b.** To court or beg the favour of (a woman), *esp.* with immoral intention.

**1591** SHAKS. *Two Gentl.* v. iv. 40 Therefore be gone, sollicit me no more. **1599** —— *Much Ado* II. i. 70 Daughter, remember what I told you, if the Prince doe solicit you in that kinde, you know your answere. **1614** RICH *Honestie of Age* (1844) 48 Perceiving..the other [Julia] againe to be solicited with witlesse and wanton Roysters. **1632** *High Commiss. Cases* (Camden) 310 He sollicited Ellen Coalman the wife of Joseph Coleman to lye with her. **1712** STEELE *Spect.* No. 402 ¶2 That my Mother, the most mercenary of all Women, is gained by this false Friend of my Husband to sollicit me for him.

**c.** To make immoral attempts upon.

**1645** *Ordin. concerning Suspention fr. Lord's Supper* 6 Any that shall solicite the chastity of any person. **1881** *Times* 2 May 6/5 It appeared that..he had attempted to take familiarities with their maid-servant and solicited her chastity.

**d.** Of women: To accost and importune (men) for immoral purposes. More recently, also with a homosexual (or a pimp) as subj. Also *absol.*

**1710** STEELE *Tatler* No. 201 ¶1 There are those [women] who betray the Innocent of their own Sex, and sollicit the Lewd of ours. **1869** E. A. PARKES *Pract. Hygiene* (ed. 3) 498 Means could easily be adopted to prevent soldiers being solicited by women. **1887** *Spectator* 9 July 919/2 She was arrested by a constable, accused of soliciting gentlemen. **1956** *Act 4 & 5 Eliz. II* c. 69 §32 *Solicitation by men.* It is an offence for a man persistently to solicit or importune in a public place for immoral purposes. **1962** *Law Rep.* 13 Mar. 666 The appeal of the appellant..against his conviction.. that he, being a man, persistently solicited in a public place for immoral purposes..contrary to s. 32 of the Sexual Offences Act, 1956. **1983** J. GARDNER *Elephants in Attic* xvii. 153 She was soliciting to cover her air fare.

**5.** Of things: **a.** To affect (a person or thing) by some form of physical influence or attraction. Now *rare.*

(*a*) **1601** HOLLAND *Pliny* XXXI. vii, Not onely we men are sollicited and moved by salt more than by any thing else to our meat. **1668** CULPEPPER & COLE *Barthol. Anat.* I. ii. 26 That the Excrements may be the longer detained,..and that we may not every foot be sollicited to go to stool.

(*b*) **1646** SIR T. BROWNE *Pseud. Ep.* II. v. (1686) 63 Glass commonly excoriates the parts through which it passeth and solicits them unto a continual expulsion. **1676** HOBBES *Iliad* I. 567 Then gently sleep sollicited each eye. **1690** LOCKE *Hum. Und.* II. i. (1695) 43 Sounds and some tangible Qualities fail not to sollicite their proper Senses, and force an entrance to the Mind. **1829** *Chapters Phys. Sci.* 17 Hardness is classed among the properties relative to certain forces soliciting or impelling bodies. **1852** H. ROGERS *Ecl. Faith* (1853) 285 All effects are the result of properties or susceptibilities in one thing, solicited by external contact with those of others.

**b.** To tempt, entice, allure; to attract or draw by enticement, etc. (Cf. 4.)

**1663** S. PATRICK *Parab. Pilgr.* x. (1687) 52 Did they not perpetually ingross your thoughts, and solicite your desires. **1667** MILTON *P.L.* IX. 743 That Fruit, which with desire.. Sollicited her longing eye. **1759** JOHNSON *Idler* No. 89 ¶10 Innumerable delights sollicit our inclinations. **1780** COWPER *Progr. Err.* 39 The world around solicits his desire. **1817** CHALMERS *Astron. Disc.* ii. (1852) 49 He might have met with much to solicit his fancy, and tempt him to some devious speculation. **1868** GLADSTONE *Juv. Mundi* x. (1869) 403 His early youth is not solicited into vice by finding sensual excess in vogue.

†**6.** To endeavor to draw out (a dart, etc.) by the use of gentle force. *Obs.*

**1697** DRYDEN *Æneid* XII. 590 The fam'd physician.. hastens to the wound. With gentle touches he performs his part, This way and that, soliciting the dart. **1718** POPE *Iliad* XIII. 750 But good Agenor gently from the wound The spear sollicits. **1784** COWPER *Task* III. 115 With gentle force soliciting the darts, He drew them forth.

**7.** *Med.* To seek to draw, to induce or bring on, esp. by gentle means.

**1732** ARBUTHNOT *Rules of Diet* in *Aliments*, etc. 376 One ought to solicit the Humours towards that Part. **1776** T. PERCIVAL *Ess.* III. 266 The same remedies are also employed to solicit the gout to the extremities. **1808** *Med. Jrnl.* XIX. 151 He supposed it owing to an inflammatory tendency conveyed..to the intestines; there 'soliciting excretions'. **1822-7** GOOD *Study Med.* (1829) I. 201 Such aperients.. which act..by soliciting the peristaltic motion of the bowels. *Ibid.* IV. 380 But the action of the bowels must only be solicited, and by no means violently excited.

**II. 8.** †**a.** To conduct, manage, or attend to (business, affairs, etc.); to push forward or prosecute. *Obs.*

**1429** [see SOLICITING *vbl. sb.*]. *c* **1477** CAXTON *Jason* 61 b, They cam where as argos the maister patrone solicited the werk..of the ship. **1518** *Sel. Pl. Star Chamb.* (Selden) II. 131 Wyllyam..went to..the Checker..to pay certeyn money and to solysset other materes that he had thear to doo. **1577** HANMER *Eccl. Hist.*, *Eusebius* IX. ii, The author of all which mischiefe was Theotecnus, who solicited the cause, and egged them of Antioch forwards. **1627** *Lisander & Cal.* III. 47 She went unto Paris,..where she imployed a moneth more..in soliciting her husbands affaires. **1647** CLARENDON *Hist. Reb.* III. §93 A Committee was come from the Parliament in Ireland, to sollicite Matters concerning that Kingdom. **1717** STEELE *Epist. Corr.* (1787) I. 186, I am going to Hampton-court, where the King now is, to solicit some matters relating to our commission. **1789** CHARLOTTE SMITH *Ethelinde* (1814) III. 75 To be employed in soliciting and managing the affairs of his son.

**b.** To conduct (a lawsuit, etc.) as a solicitor; to transact or negotiate in the capacity of a lawagent. ? *Obs.*

**1606** *Act 3 Jas. I*, c. vii, That none be suffered to Solicite any Cause or Causes in any of the Courts..but only..men of sufficient and honest disposition. **1671** CLARENDON *Hist. Reb.* IX. §55 One Brabant, an Atturney at Law, (who had heretofore sollicited the great Suit against Sʳ Richard in the Star-Chamber). **1761** *Ann. Reg.* II. 37 A law-suit,..which he solicited so effectually that it was concluded greatly to the ..advantage of the duke. **1839** *Morning Herald* 3 June, The attorney-at-law who solicited the suits.

†**c.** To stir up, instigate (rebellion, etc.). *Obs.*⁻¹

**1600** W. WATSON *Decacordon* (1602) 262 It is now plaine, that they had then plotted in their harts a shamefull rebellion, which they did sollicite.

†**9. a.** To urge or plead (one's suit, cause, etc.).

*a* **1562** G. CAVENDISH *Wolsey* (1893) 188 Then began bothe noble men and other..to make earnest sewte to Mayster Cromwell for to solicite ther causes to my lord, to gett of hyme his confirmacions. **1577** in Ellis *Orig. Lett.* Ser. II. III. 75 Therfore as yow tender his healthe, I pray yow sollicite the matter to my Lord Treasourer. **1601** SHAKS. *Twel. N.* III. i. 120 But would you vndertake another suite I had rather heare you to solicit that Then Musicke from the spheares. *a* **1677** BARROW *Serm.* (1686) I. xxxi. 447 God and Nature therefore within us do solicite the poor-man's case. **1769** GOLDSM. *Hist. Rome* (1786) I. 424 It was in vain that this great man [Cicero] went up and down the city, soliciting his cause in the habit of a suppliant.

†**b.** To urge or press (a matter). *Obs.*

*c* **1610** KEYMOR *Obs. Dutch Fishing* (1664) 2 Since I sollicited this to have 200. Busses built for England, the Hollanders have made 800. new Busses more. *a* **1648** LD. HERBERT *Hen. VIII* (1683) 424 He seemed to receive some satisfaction,..and therefore forbore a while to solicite this point. **1704** HEARNE *Duct. Hist.* (1714) I. 116 Haggai earnestly exhorts the People of God, to the building of the Temple. *Ibid.*, Zechariah..also solicited the re-building of the Temple.

†**c.** To seek or follow diligently. *Obs.*⁻¹

**1658** FRANCK *North. Mem.* (1821) 29 All that sollicit thy paths of peace shall be found in their duty as by wisdom directed.

**10. a.** To request, petition, or sue for (some thing, favour, etc.); to desire or seek by petition.

**1595** DANIEL *Civil Wars* I. lxxxvi, Who faile not to aduise the Duke with speed, Soliciting to what he soone agreed. **1644** MILTON *Areop.* (Arb.) 54 Who make so many journeys to sollicit their licence. **1676** WYCHERLEY *Pl. Dealer* v. i, *Free.* Give you a Ship! why, you will not solicit it. *Man.* If I have not solicited it by my services, I know no other way. *a* **1700** EVELYN *Diary* 27 Oct. 1675, To..solicite supplies from the Lord Treasurer. **1751** JOHNSON *Rambler* No. 157 ¶5 My acquaintance was solicited by innumerable invitations. **1797** MRS. RADCLIFFE *Italian* i, Even if she were not averse to his suit, how could he solicit her hand? **1844** THIRLWALL *Greece* VIII. 325 Nabis..sent Pythagoras to solicit an interview with Flamininus. **1855** BREWSTER *Newton* II. xix. 214 The object..seems to have been to solicit the favour of the Mogul to the English Company.

**b.** To seek after; to try to find, obtain, or acquire.

**1717** POPE *Eloisa to Abelard* 186, I..Repent old pleasures, and solicit new. **1751** JOHNSON *Rambler* No. 149 ¶11 They never suffer her to appear with them in any place where they solicit notice. **1784** COWPER *Task* II. 635 There we..Solicit pleasure, hopeless of success.

**11.** Of things: To call or ask for, to demand (action, attention, etc.).

**1592** KYD *Sp. Trag.* IV. iv. 127 Neuer hath it left my bloody hart, Soliciting remembrance of my vow. **1613** PURCHAS *Pilgrimage* (1614) 508 After our long perambulation of the Asian Continent, the sea inuironing doth sollicite our next endeuours. **1664** POWER *Exp. Philos.* III. 191 All which incomparable Inventions do not only solicite, but..should inflame our endevours to attempt even Impossibilities. **1817** JAS. MILL *Brit. India* v. vii. II. 613 The formation of a new government solicited his attention. *Ibid.* ix. 694 The affairs and government of India solicited the utmost exertions of their abilities.

**III.** *intr.* (See also 4 d.) **12. a.** To make request or petition; to beg or entreat.

**1509** in *Mem. Hen. VII* (Rolls) 432 Notwythstandeyng that I..have solucytyd unto the kynge and unto hys secretary Almasan..that the sayd ambassatur myȝghte be namyd. **1529** LYNDESAY *Compl.* 53 Had I solistit,..My rewarde had nocht bene to craif. **1608** SHAKS. *Per.* II. v. 69 Resolve your angry father, if my tongue Did e'er solicit. **1686** tr. *Chardin's Trav. Persia* 12 They could not then expect that the French should sollicite in their behalf as they had done before. **1748** *Anson's Voy.* III. ix. 395 Whilst they were thus soliciting. **1796** ELIZA HAMILTON *Lett. Hindoo Rajah* (1811) I. 247 Too modest to solicit, and too proud to bear the harshness of repulse. **1837** CARLYLE *Fr. Rev.* I. II. v, Now too behold..American Plenipotentiaries, here in person soliciting.

**b.** Const. *for.*

**1592** KYD *Sp. Trag.* IV. i, All the Saintes doe sit soliciting For vengeance. **1604** SHAKS. *Oth.* v. ii. 28 If you bethinke your selfe of..Grace, Solicite for it straight. *a* **1700** EVELYN *Diary* 9 July 1665, I went to Hampton Court..to solicite for mony. **1769** GOLDSM. *Hist. Rome* (1786) I. 338 Metellus.. was obliged to solicit at Rome for a continuation of his command. **1802** MARIAN MOORE *Lascelles* II. 49 It was Lascelles' excessive delicacy..which made him not solicit for the purse from Serena. **1808** ELEANOR SLEATH *Bristol Heiress* III. 210 She received several messages from young Benson, soliciting for an interview.

**c.** Const. *to* and inf.

**1654-66** EARL ORRERY *Parthen.* (1676) 794, I solicite to be the miserablest of men, to preserve you from being the unjustest. **1710** SWIFT *Lett.* (1767) III. 65, I was soliciting this day, to present the bishop of Clogher Vice-Chancellor. **1775** S. J. PRATT *Liberal Opin.* lvii. (1783) II. 174, I sat by his bed-side, and gently sollicited to learn the cause of this strange disaster. *c* **1800** R. CUMBERLAND *John De Lancaster* (1809) III. 85 Devereux himself solicits to go with me. **1832** SOUTHEY *Hist. Penins. War* III. 98 The accounts.. represented Ferdinand as still soliciting to be adopted by marriage into the family of the tyrant.

**13.** To act or practise as a solicitor.

**1596** NASHE *Saffron Walden* 83 His mother may haue su'd in *forma pauperis*, but he neuer sollicited in form of papers in the Arches in his life. **1681** *Trial of S. Colledge* 5 No body can solicit for any one that is under an Accusation of High-Treason, unless he be assigned so to do by the Court. **1714** *French Bk. Rates* 13 We have appointed a Person to receive all their Petitions, and solicite for them at our Expence.

1724 SWIFT *Drapier's Lett.* i. Wks. 1761 III. 20 We are at a great distance from the King's Court, and have no body there to solicit for us.

†**14.** To petition *against*, to make intercession *for*, a person or thing. *Obs.*

1609 BIBLE (Douay) *1 Macc.* x. 61 There assembled agaynst him pestilent men of Israel, wicked men soliciting against him. 1612 T. TAYLOR *Comm. Titus* ii. 12. 463 Though many things solicite for these lusts,..yet a Christian man must still stand out in the deniall of them. 1697 COLLIER *Ess. Moral Subj.* II. To Rdr., Some Authors (I am sorry it may be said so) seem to solicit for Vice. 1741 MIDDLETON *Cicero* II. xi. 453 What your mother and sister are now soliciting against in favor of the children.

†**so'licitancy.** *Obs. rare.* In 7 soll-. [See prec. and -ANCY.] Soliciting.

1665 BRATHWAIT *Comment Two Tales* 26 Yet, lest Absolon should be numbred among those weak wooers,..he rears his Battery, though with a more easie sollicitancy, than he did at first. *Ibid.* 154 At her Hands, from whose Sollicitancy he had received his Reprieve. 1890 W. JAMES *Princ. Psychol.* II. xxvi. 551 Those persons obey a curiously narrow teleological superstition who think themselves bound to interpret them [*sc.* the impulsions] in every instance as effects of the secret solicitancy of pleasure and repugnancy of pain.

**solicitant** (sə'lɪsɪtənt), *sb.* and *a.* [ad. L. *sōl-, sollicitant-*, pres. pple. stem of *sollicitāre* SOLICIT *v.*]

**A.** *sb.* One who solicits or requests earnestly.

1802–12 BENTHAM *Ration. Judic. Evid.* (1827) I. 603 To..beg his vote and interest in favour of the solicitant or his friend. 1821 *New Monthly Mag.* II. 598 The sight of an English carriage..drew half a dozen fresh solicitants. 1881 *Academy* No. 459. 127 That wider circle to whom he was only known as a solicitant..for contributions to the paper.

**B.** *adj.* That solicits or begs earnestly; making petition or request.

1886 *Daily Telegr.* 8 Jan. (Cassell), The unemployed labour that is chronically solicitant of a job. 1897 WALSH *Hist. Oxford Movement* iv. (1898) 118 The Bulls of the Popes themselves against solicitant priests.

†**solicitate,** *a. Obs.* Also 5–6 sollicitate, 6 *Sc.* solicitat. [ad. L. *sōl-, sollicitātus*, pa. pple. of *sollicitāre* SOLICIT *v.*] Solicitous, anxious, careful; characterized by care or solicitude.

1432–50 tr. *Higden* (Rolls) III. 403 The kynge of Macedony, sollicitate and besy for the succession of þat realme. 1548 WISHART *Conf. Faith* in *Misc. Wodr. Soc.* (1844) 22 A solicitat and thoughtfull charge of the poore. 1555 EDEN *Decades* (Arb.) 133 Nature was not sollicitate to brynge furthe suche greate fluds.

Hence †**solicitateness.** *Obs.*⁻¹

1560 WHITEHORNE *Arte Warre* 28 b, With greater industrie, & more sollicitatenesse.

†**solicitate,** *v. Obs.* Also 6–7 solicitat, sollicitate. [f. ppl. stem of L. *sōl-, sollicitāre.*]

**1.** *trans.* To manage or conduct.

1547 BP. HOOPER *Declar. Christ* v. D iij, To solicitat and do all there affars as a faythfull Embassadour. 1560 WHITEHORNE *Arte Warre* 102 It is conuenient for thee, to sollicitate this worke in soche wise, that..the Diche maie be digged at least, fower or five yardes in depth.

**2.** To excite, stir up, or stimulate.

1568 C. W[ATSON] *Polybius* 50 b, He sent out his most actiue souldiers to solicitate and prouoke his aduersaries that they might come to the hands of the rest. *Ibid.* 87 He also solicitated the Numidians & Libians to rebellion. 1579 TWYNE *Phis. agst. Fortune* I. xxxviii, The tast of the wyne dooth not so much solicitate the appetite. 1650 EARL MONM. tr. *Senault's Man bec. Guilty* 54 She commits so many faults with delight, stays not for being solicitated by the senses.

**3.** To request, entreat, beseech.

1563 FOXE *A. & M.* 1171/1 The Byshop..dyd vrge & solicitate [him], according to his maner of wordes to recant. 1632 LITHGOW *Trav.* x. 430 They solicitat her..to restore them to their health. a1656 USSHER *Ann.* VI. (1658) 176 Having often sollicitated the King..to pay for the Navy.

**4.** *intr.* To take action, make application.

1572 in Turner *Sel. Rec. Oxford* 347 The Towne Clarke shall go to London to solicitate towching the brewer charter.

**solicitation** (səlɪsɪ'teɪʃən). Forms: α. *Sc.* 5–6 solistatioun (6 -acioun), 6–7 -ation, 6 solyst-, sollistatioun. β. 6–7 sollicitac(i)on, 6–8 -ation (6 -atioun); 6 solicitacion, solyssetacion, 7 solissitation, 7– solicitation. [a. OF. *sol-, sollicitation* (mod.F. *sollicitation*, = Sp. *solicitacion*, Pg. *solicitação*, It. *solle-, sollicitazione*), or ad. L. *sōl-, sollicitātio*: see SOLICIT *v.* and -ATION.]

†**1.** Management, transaction, or pursuit of business, legal affairs, etc. *Obs.*

1492 *Acta Dom. Concilii* 250/1 Þe Soume of fiftj merkis..auch to him..for solistatioun of thar errandis þe tyme he wes alderman of þe said toun. 1529 in Burnet *Hist. Ref.* I. II. Rec. xxii. (1679) 54 So as ye may be sure to have of him effectual concurrence and advice in the furtherance and sollicitation of your Charges. 1642 HARCOURT in *Macm. Mag.* XLV. 289, I presume you are now very bussee in the solissitation of my law bussines. 1722 in *Westm. Gaz.* (1906) 27 Aug. 2/3 To undertake the Sollicitation and Management of any Affairs which may come before either House.

**2.** The action of soliciting, or seeking to obtain by earnest request; entreaty, petition, diligent or importunate asking.

α. 1533 BELLENDEN *Livy* I. xv. (S.T.S.) I. 82 Numa havand na cognossance of Rome,..was chosin but ony his solistacioun, and maid king. 1561 *Reg. Privy Council Scot.* I. 160 To the effect oure Soverane Lady be nocht molestit with importunite, solistatioun, and requeist. 1637–50 Row *Hist. Kirk* (Wodrow Soc.) 221 He was upon great moyen and solistation inlarged, but verie shortlie after he departed this life.

β. 1533 BELLENDEN *Livy* v. vi. (S.T.S.) II. 167 Þai þat war movit be requiest or sollicitatioun of tribunys militare. 1588 LAMBARDE *Eiren.* IV. vii. 514 At the sollicitation and by the meanes of some parties grieued. 1622 WILLIAMS in *Fortescue P.* (Camden) 173 By the sollicitacion of Sir Edw. Cooke I forbore..to doe any thing herein. 1697 LUTTRELL *Brief Relat.* (1857) IV. 296 Great sollicitation has been used for the two latter to change their sentence from death to transportation. 1751 JOHNSON *Rambler* No. 160 ¶2 [Patrons] are sometimes corrupted by Avarice, and sometimes cheated by Credulity, sometimes overpowered by resistless Solicitation. 1780 *Mirror* No. 71, After two years solicitation..Antonio gave up all hopes of success. 1836 SIR H. TAYLOR *Statesman* xxiii. 167 A spirit of justice, ears shut against private solicitation, ought to be regarded as essential qualifications..for the office of private secretary. 1883 *Law Rep. 23 Chanc. Div.* 722 At her solicitation the trustee lent the fund to the husband and it was lost.

**b.** With *a* and pl. An instance of this.

1500–20 DUNBAR *Poems* lvii. 2 Be dyuers..operatiounis Men makis in court thair solistationis. 1596 EARL ESSEX in Ellis *Orig. Lett.* 3rd Ser. IV. 131 His sollicitacons and guifts, offered to the rebells of Irland. 1625 in Foster *Eng. Factories Ind.* (1909) III. 59 Our owne peticions, sollicitations, and complaintes. 1671 MILTON *Samson* 488 Spare that proposal, Father, spare the trouble Of that sollicitation. 1769 *Junius Lett.* xxv. (1780) 140 Your solicitations..were renewed under another administration. 1836 J. MARTIN *Discourses* iv. 121 Without one solicitation on the part of the conquered, peace is offered. 1874 GREEN *Short Hist.* ix. 689 In spite of his master's personal solicitations Churchill remained true to Protestantism.

**c.** The action of soliciting a person of the other sex (cf. SOLICIT *v.* 4 b and 4 d).

1604 SHAKS. *Oth.* IV. ii. 202 If she will returne me my Iewels, I will giue ouer my Suit, and repent my vnlawfull solicitation. a1639 T. CAREW *Upon Sickness of E. S.* 19 Shee Who hath preserv'd her spotless chastity From all solicitation. 1681 OTWAY *Soldier's Fort.* III. i, She cannot be free from the insolent Sollicitations of such Fellows as you are, Sir. 1781 MRS. INCHBALD *I'll tell you what* III. ii, He had just seen the most beautiful girl his eyes ever beheld, to whom he had given a look of solicitation. 1848 DICKENS *Dombey* liv, From my marriage day I found my-self exposed ..to such solicitation and pursuit..from one mean villain. 1887 [see SOLICITEE].

**d.** *Law.* (See quot. and SOLICIT *v.* 3.)

1835 TOMLINS *Law Dict.*, *Solicitations.* It is an indictable offence to solicit and incite another to commit a felony.

**3.** The exertion or operation of a physically attracting influence or force.

1626 BACON *Sylva* §836 By Excitation and Solicitation of the Body Putrified, and the Parts thereof, by the Body Ambient. 1833 HERSCHEL *Astron.* viii. 266 Be it pressure from without or the resultant of many pressures or sollicitations of unknown fluids. 1837 WHEWELL *Hist. Induct. Sci.* (1857) II. 67 The 'solicitation of gravity'. 1884 *N. Amer. Rev.* Aug. 115 The solicitations of Jupiter's attractive force are as urgent on a swiftly rushing body as on one at rest.

**4.** The action of some attractive, enticing, or alluring influence.

1676 HALE *Contempl.* II. *Medit. Lord's Prayer* 153 In these the Objects were innocent, and had in themselves no active solicitation to Evil. 1690 LOCKE *Hum. Und.* II. i. §8 Children ..are surrounded with a world of new things, which, by a constant Sollicitation of their Senses, draw the Mind constantly to them. 1712 ARBUTHNOT *John Bull* (1755) 32 She was..a common mercenary prostitute, and that without any sollicitation from nature. 1758 JOHNSON *Idler* No. 25 ¶10 Vicious sollicitations of appetite, if not checked, will grow more importunate. a1820 T. BROWN *Philos. Human Mind* xcviii. IV. 561 The duty that is exercised in resisting the solicitations of evils. 1884 SULLY *Outl. Psychol.* iv. 99 The power of sustained attention grows with the ability to resist distractions and solicitations.

†**5.** Anxiety; solicitude. *Obs.*

1697 CLAYTON *Acc. Virginia* in *Misc. Curiosa* (1708) III. 297 If..their Heards are stray'd from their Plantations, without more sollicitation they go directly to the Rivers to fetch them home again. a1718 W. PENN in *Life* Wks. I. 135 Whom I ever served with a steady Sollicitation. 1725 *Fam. Dict.* s.v. *Water*, This comes so little..into our Diet..that it is not worth much Sollicitation about it.

Hence **solici'tationism.**

1880 W. D. HOWELLS *Undiscovered Country* iii. 52 What I wish now to establish as the central principle of the spiritistic science is the principle of solicitationism.

**so'licited,** *ppl. a.* [f. SOLICIT *v.*] **a.** Approached with solicitation. **b.** Asked or begged for.

1833 J. H. NEWMAN *Arians* III. iv. (1876) 308 The proposed measure..fixed the attention of the solicited Churches rather upon the argument, than upon the Imperial command. 1856 KANE *Arctic Explor.* II. v. 66 Even the stoutest could hardly bear their once solicited allowance of raw meat.

**solicitee.** *rare.* [f. SOLICIT *v.* + -EE¹.] One who is solicited.

1887 *Pall Mall G.* 25 July 4/2 No charge of solicitation is to be taken except when the solicitee is prepared to come forward and prosecute.

†**soliciter.** *Obs.* Forms: α. 5 solyster, 6 solester; *Sc.* 6 sol(l)istar. β. 5 soluciter, 6 sollycyter, solyciter, 6–7 solliciter (6 *Sc.* -ar), 7– soliciter. [f. SOLICIT *v.* + -ER¹.]

**1.** One who conducts or manages affairs on behalf of another; *spec.* = SOLICITOR 3.

α. 1482 *Cely Papers* (Camden) 118 The bylles of xx*s* of the sarpler schall be sent ynto Inglond to the solyster schorttly. 1563 *Reg. Privy Council Scot.* I. 239 For furnessing of procuratouris, sollistaris, and utheris doers for the saidis merchandis. 1585 *Exchequer Rolls Scot.* XXI. 613 The said James, Lord of Doun, comperand be George Mak, his solistar.

β. 1464 *Rolls of Parlt.* V. 530/1 Provided alwey, that this Acte extend not nor be prejudiciall to Richard Fowler, of or for the Office of oure Soluciter. a1548 HALL *Chron., Hen. IV*, 7 b, He by his priuie frendes and soliciters, caused to be enacted [etc.]. 1576 in Feuillerat *Revels Q. Eliz.* (1908) 415 Cowncellors, soliciters, and atturneies. 1616 R. C. *Times' Whistle* (1871) 46 A daw To a solliciter is now become Iustice of peace & coram. c1630 RISDON *Surv. Devon* §39 (1810) 40 Baldwin Mallet, soliciter unto King Henry the eighth.

**2.** One who takes charge *of*, or action *in*, some affair; a promoter or forwarder.

a1530 WOLSEY in Ellis *Orig. Lett.* 1st Ser. II. 5 To be a sollycyter and setter forth of such thyngs as do and shall conserve my said ende. 1533 BELLENDEN *Livy* v. xiii. (S.T.S.) II. 191 The small pepill tuke purpoiss to continew þe same tribunys þat war solistaris of þare lawis. 1631 GOUGE *God's Arrows* v. 406 You who in the name of the rest were Solliciters in this business. 1664 H. MORE *Myst. Iniq.* 72 As if these were the most serious and earnest soliciters of Religion that one can hope to meet withall.

**3.** A petitioner; = SOLICITOR 4.

α. 1500–20 DUNBAR *Poems* lvii, Quod Dumbar aganis the solistaris in court. 1536 *Cal. Anc. Rec. Dublin* (1889) 498 [We] most umblye desyre youre grase to be owre solester to owre prynse. 1587 A. HUME *Epist. Moncreiff* 197 ȝit all sollistars cannot iustice haue.

β. 1537 *State Papers Hen. VIII*, XII. No. 883, Trustyng your mastershyppe wylbe a solyciter to hym for us. 1588 SHAKS. *L.L.L.* II. 29 In that behalfe..we single you, As our best mouing faire soliciter. 1628 WITHER *Brit. Rememb.* I. 1023 Thou wert Soliciter For King Manasses that Idolater. 1668 *Lond. Gaz.* No. 254/2 That the City of Vienna is much disgusted with the..Liberty given to the Jews, and are earnest solliciters for their Banishment.

**b.** *fig.* Of things.

c1585 MONTGOMERIE *Sonn.* lv. 9 My secrete sighis, solisters for my sute. 1617 HIERON *Wks.* II. 114 Such a conscience..will be a perpetuall solliciter, till it hath brought a man before the Lord. 1652 CRASHAW *Carmen Deo Nostro* Wks. (1904) 195 Cymballs of Heav'n, or Humane sphears, Solliciters of Soules or Eares.

†**4.** A suitor (to a woman). *Obs.*

c1590 *Faire Em* IV. iii, Both which shaddowes of my irreuocable affections I haue not sparde to confirme before him..and all other amorous soliciters.

Hence †**so'licitership,** = SOLICITORSHIP 1. *Obs.*

1592 CHETTLE *Kind-harts Dr.* (1841) 49 Hauing scraped vp a few common places, and, by long sollicitership, got in to be an odd atturney.

**soliciting** (sə'lɪsɪtɪŋ), *vbl. sb.* [f. SOLICIT *v.*] The action of the vb., in various senses.

α. 1429 in Rymer *Fœdera* (1710) X. 420/2 My said Lord the Cardinal, that hath take upon him the Soliciting of the said Cause. 1530 PALSGR. 272/2 Solycityng, steryng, *sollicitation.* 1570 DEE *Math. Pref.* aj, He, with humble request, and instant Solliciting, got the best Rules..for ordring of all Companies..of men. 1625 in Foster *Eng. Factories Ind.* (1909) III. 58 His complaints and sollicitings were utterlie rejected. 1662 MARVELL *Corr.* Wks. (Grosart) II. 85 To Mr. Cressel for his soliciting whole through the businesse. 1709 J. JOHNSON *Clergym. Vade M.* II. 6 By worldly or secular employs we are to understand soliciting in law-suits [etc.]. 1760–72 H. BROOKE *Fool of Qual.* (1809) IV. 134 The remaining time was spent in soliciting for me. 1837 CARLYLE *Fr. Rev.* I. I. ii, Not now by violence and murder, but by soliciting and finesse.

β. 1474 *Acc. Ld. High Treas. Scot.* I. 48 To the solisting of the Kingis materis in the Court of Rome. 1500–20 DUNBAR *Poems* ix. 133 Of fals solisting ffor wrang deliuerance At Counsale, Sessioun, and at Parliament. 1678 SIR G. MACKENZIE *Crim. Laws Scot.* II. xxvi. §7 (1699) 267 The being present at a Consultation with the Pursuer, or the solisting for him, are likewise Branches of partial Counsel.

**so'liciting,** *ppl. a.* [f. as prec.] That solicits, in senses of the verb.

1605 SHAKS. *Lear* I. i. 234 A still soliciting eye, and such a tongue,..Hath lost me in your liking. 1704 J. NORRIS *Ideal World* II. vii. 355 The soliciting motion of adjacent or circumambient bodies. 1816 J. SCOTT *Vis. Paris* (ed. 5) 207 These soliciting females are not easily rebuffed. 1829 *Chapters Phys. Sci.* 17 Properties relative to soliciting forces. 1885 W. ROBERTS *Urin. & Renal Dis.* III. xiii. (ed. 4) 647 The column of liquid in the tube..exercising a soliciting force on the contents of the sac.

**so'licitive,** *a. rare.* [f. as prec. Cf. OF. *sollicitif, -ive.*] Solicitant.

1865 *Times* 4 Feb. 5/4 Perambulating the thoroughfares with eyes shut, and hands extended, solicitive of alms.

**solicitor** (sə'lɪsɪtə(r)). Forms: 5–7 sollicitour, 6–7 -or; 5 solicy-, 5–6 solyci-, 6 solysy-, 5–7 solicitour (6 -oure), 6 solisitor, 6– solicitor. [ad. OF. *sol-, solliciteur* (mod.F. *solliciteur*), f. *solliciter* SOLICIT *v.*: see -OR.]

†**1. a.** One who urges, prompts, or instigates. *Obs.*

1412–20 LYDG. *Troy Book* I. 3797 And of þis Iourne chefe solicytour Was Hercules, þe worthi conquerour. 1540–1 ELYOT *Image Gov.* (1556) 56 Solicitours and furtherers of dishonest appetitis. c1555 HARPSFIELD *Divorce Hen. VIII* (Camden) 254 One that was the chief incenser and solicitor of the first divorce. 1600 HOLLAND *Livy* XXIV. xxxv. 533 No bad sollicitor by word of mouth to further & follow the cause. 1722 WOLLASTON *Relig. Nat.* vi. 144 Promoters or instruments of..wickedness; such as..solicitors in vice.

†**b.** A thing serving to instigate, etc. *Obs.*

1594 T. B. *La Primaud. Fr. Acad.* II. 265 Ioy and hope.. were bestowed vpon him to bee spurres and sollicitours to induce him to seeke after God. 1607 *Scholast. Disc. agst. Antichrist* II. vi. 41 It hath been vsed from time to time, as an agent and a sollicitor to arme the people..against their lawfull Lordes. **1699** ATTERBURY *Serm.* vii. (1737) IV. 203 We usually blame the body to an high degree, as..the sollicitor to every evil act, all that defiles the man. **1751** *Affecting Narr. H.M.S. 'Wager'* 104 Extreme Hunger and Thirst which were our Sollicitors at this Time, will prompt one to the most desperate Undertakings.

†**2. a.** One who conducts, negotiates, or transacts matters on behalf of another or others; a representative, agent, or deputy. *Obs.*

*c* **1425** LYDG. *Assemb. Gods* 912 Hooly heremytes, goddes solycitours, Monasteriall monkes [etc.]. *a* **1513** FABYAN *Chron.* v. (1811) 73 The whiche Paterne had ben solicitour for yᵉ Frenshe Kyng in the foresayd matier. **1546** LANGLEY tr. *Pol. Verg. de Invent.* VIII. ii. 145 Pius the II...instituted the new College of Solicitors & Proctors by whose Counsaill and aduise all bulles and grauntes wer made. **1638** R. BAKER tr. *Balzac's Lett.* (vol. II) 35, I come not therefore as his Solicitour but as his bare witnesse. **1655** FULLER *Ch. Hist.* IX. 203 The principall pillars of the Presbyterian party.. applied themselves by their secret solicitors to James King of Scotland. **1702** W. J. tr. *Bruyn's Voy. Levant* lv. 216 Next to him is the Father Sollicitor, who ought to be a Spaniard born. **1741** MIDDLETON *Cicero* (1742) I. v. 388 His principal Agents and Sollicitors at Rome were his Brother Quintus [etc.].

†**b.** *spec.* An official having charge of the King's or Queen's interests. *Obs.*

**1460** *Rolls of Parlt.* V. 388/1 The Sollicitours for the Quene mad leve of C li. **1503** *Ibid.* VI. 536 Thomas Lucas, the Kyngs Solisitor. **1555** *N.C. Wills* (Surtees, 1908) 235 Mr...Cordall, our soveraign Ladie the Quenes Sollicitor. **1608** CHAPMAN *Dk. of Byron* v. ii, Where the King's chief Solicitor hath said There was in France no man that ever liv'd Whose parts were worth my imitation.

**3. a.** One properly qualified and formally admitted to practise as a law-agent in any court; formerly, one practising in a court of equity, as distinguished from an *attorney*.

The rise of solicitors as a class of legal practitioners, and the gradual recognition and definition of their status, are illustrated by the first group of quotations. For the Scottish usage see Bell *Dict. Law Scot.* s.v.

(*a*) *a* **1577** SIR T. SMITH *Commw. Eng.* II. i. (1589) 44 Solicitors are such, as being learned in the lawes, and informed of their masters cause, doe informe and instruct the Counsellors in the same. **1598** BARCKLEY *Felic. Man* (1631) 398 After that sollicitors were suffered in the middest of them all, to be as it were the skum gatherers of suites. **1653** [F. PHILIPS] *Consid. touching Ct. Chancery* 18 Sollicitors (a race of people was not allowed or heard of in the Law about 100 years agoe). **1681** *Trial of S. Colledge* 6, I know not but he may be criminal that brought you those Papers: for we allow no Sollicitors in cases of Treason. **1729** *Act 2 Geo. II*, c. 23 §3 (An Act for the better Regulation of Attornies and Solicitors). No Person..shall be permitted to act as a Solicitor..unless such Person..be admitted and inrolled..in such of the said Courts of Equity, where he shall act as Solicitor. **1765** BLACKSTONE *Comm.* III. 26 To practice in the court of chancery it is also necessary to be admitted a solicitor therein. **1835** *Penny Cycl.* III. 66/1 A solicitor in any court of equity at Westminster may be sworn, admitted, and enrolled an attorney of his Majesty's courts of law. **1843** *Act 6 & 7 Vict.* c. 73 §21 Be it enacted, That..there shall be a Registrar of Attornies and Solicitors. **1873** [see ATTORNEY *sb.*¹ 3].

(*b*) **1584** LODGE *Alarum* B ij, They finde out..some olde soaking vndermining Solicitour. **1654** FULLER *Two Serm.* 76 Let Diligent Attorneyes so faithfully solicite, let painefull Solicitours so honestly Agitate [etc.]. **1679** *Est. Test* 27, I have heard a..famous Lawyer say, he thought he was one of the ablest Solicitors in England. **1721** DE FOE *Moll Flanders* (1722) 262 Had she employ'd a petty Fogging hedge Solicitor,..I should have brought it to but little. **1798** CHARLOTTE SMITH *Yng. Philos.* III. 58 Sir Appulby..found it convenient to suppose I was willing to await his reference to his solicitor. **1837** DICKENS *Pickw.* ii, The solicitors' wives, and the wine-merchant's wife, headed another grade. **1858** LYTTON *What will He do?* II. xii, I will direct my solicitor to take the right steps to do so. **1897** G. ALLEN *Type-writer Girl* ii. 25 He was..obviously wealthy, though 'twas a third-rate solicitor's.

*fig.* **1650** BULWER *Anthropomet*, More fit for one who had deserved to be Attorney Generall to Nature, then for me, the meanest Sollicitor in her Court.

*attrib.* **1896** *Pall Mall G.* 23 Jan. 10/2 Solicitor and client costs will be enforced in all cases.

**b. Solicitor-General**, a law-officer (in England ranking next to the Attorney-General, in Scotland to the Lord-Advocate), who takes the part of the state or crown in suits affecting the public interest.

In the earliest example perhaps with less specific meaning (cf. 2 b above).

**1533–4** *Act 25 Hen. VIII*, c. 16 §2 The Kinges generall attorney, and generall Solicitour, which for the time is. **1647** CLARENDON *Hist. Reb.* I. §96 He was Recorder of London, Solicitor-General, and King's Attorney, before he was forty years of age. **1708** CHAMBERLAYNE *Pres. St. Gt. Brit.* (1710) 576 The Queen's Serjeants at Law...Sollicitor-General, Robert Eyre, Esq. **1747** *Gentl. Mag.* XVII. 116/1 Upon this the sollicitor general was heard in reply. **1812** *Examiner* 14 Dec. 786/1 At which the Solicitor General expressed such anticipating alarm. **1848** W. H. KELLY tr. *L. Blanc's Hist. Ten Y.* II. 321 The solicitor-general, M. Martin du Nord, began to prepare an indictment. **1876** BANCROFT *Hist. U.S.* IV. xlvi. 217 [He] leased his eloquence to the government for the office of solicitor-general.

**c. Official Solicitor** (see quot. 1977).

**1875** *Minutes of Evidence taken by Commissioners appointed to inquire into Administrative Departments of Courts of Justice* 344/1 in *Parl. Papers* (C. 1245) XXX. 163, I hold the office of official solicitor to the Court of Chancery. **1896** *Law Rep. Chancery Div.* I. 368 We have an officer of this Court who is called the Official Solicitor. **1961** [see AD LITEM]. **1977** *Jowitt's Dict. Eng. Law* (ed. 2) II. 1281/2 The Official Solicitor of the Court of Chancery was an officer whose functions consisted of protecting the Suitors Fund... He is now known as the Official Solicitor of the Supreme Court... He acts for persons suffering under a disability; he acts generally as solicitor in cases in which the Chancery Division requires his services as solicitor; he visits persons in custody for contempt.

**4. a.** One who entreats, requests, or petitions; one who solicits or begs favours; a pleader, intercessor, advocate.

**1551** ROBINSON tr. *More's Utopia* (1895) 18 An euell tale well tolde nedeth none other sollicitour. **1635** JACKSON *Creed* VIII. xiv. 165 That hee might bee a faithfull Solicitor to his Almighty Father for aid and succour unto all that are beset with them. **1673** *True Notion Worship of God* 32 It demonstrates the greatest for God in those that are earnest Solicitours at his Throne. **1720** SWIFT *Fates of Clergymen* Wks. 1755 II. II. 26 His sister was..so good a sollicitor, that by her means he was admitted to read prayers in the family. **1752** HUME *Ess. & Treat.* (1777) II. 417 The Lacedemonians..put up their petitions very early in the morning, in order,.. by being the first solicitors, to pre-engage the gods in their favour. **1860** SMILES *Self-Help* x. 279 The passion for salaries and Government employment ..makes a whole people a mere crowd of servile solicitors for place. **1883** LD. ROSEBERY *Speech at Edin.* 21 July, The brazen solicitor who will not take No for an answer.

*transf.* **1670** EACHARD *Cont. Clergy* 110 Besides the devil, he shall have sollicitors enough.

**b.** With possessive pron., etc., denoting the person on whose behalf the solicitation is made.

**1604** SHAKS. *Oth.* III. iii. 27 Therefore be merry Cassio, For thy Solicitor shall rather dye, Then giue thy cause away. **1639** S. DU VERGER tr. *Camus' Admir. Events* 86 When Ctesiphons wicked sollicitors saw their labour lost with Heraclee, they then addressed themselves to the mother. **1734** tr. *Rollin's Rom. Hist.* (1827) 218 Whenever the young lords had any favour to ask of the King, Cyrus was their solicitor.

**c.** *transf.* Of things.

**1579** HARVEY *Letter-bk.* (Camden) 61 Lett this ilfavorid letter suffize for a dutifull solicitor and remembrer in that behaulfe. **1608** D. T. *Ess. Pol. & Mor.* 48 b, The beautie and fairenesse of his eyes..were the principall, and chiefe Solicitors of her affections towards him. **1661** MORGAN *Sph. Gentry* I. v. 56 Beauty, and Harmony.., being prevailing solicitors for the obteining love and affection.

†**5.** One who, or that which, draws on or entices. *Obs.*

**1594** HOOKER *Eccl. Pol.* I. vii. §3 Appetite is the wills sollicitor, and the will is appetites controller. **1639** S. DU VERGER tr. *Camus' Admir. Events* 22 This voyage, whereunto his owne courage was a sufficient sollicitor. **1655** R. YOUNGE *Agst. Drunkards* 18 He that will be drawn to the Tavern or Alehouse by every idle solicitor..is a Drunkard in Solomon's esteem.

†**6.** ? A recruiting officer. *Obs.*—¹

**1698–9** in R. Steele *Tudor & Stuart Procl.* (1910) I. 508/2, 1st Regiment of Foot Guards:..2 quartermasters, a solicitor, a drum-major [etc.].

**7.** *U.S.* One who solicits business orders, advertising, etc.

**1897** *Scribner's Mag.* Oct. 463/2 A small army of solicitors is despatched to a neighborhood to go from house to house telling people about the features of the paper. **1903** E. L. SHUMAN *Practical Journalism* 200 Have as many good solicitors out as necessary and make your rates low enough to invite this form of advertising. **1916** *John Bull* 13 May 10/2 He called himself a grocer's solicitor, meaning a canvasser for orders. **1926** *Publishers' Weekly* 15 May 1589 Why can't he leave it to the judgment of the printers? Or to the advertising solicitor? **1952** S. EISENBERG *How to earn Income selling Products & Services by Phone* i. 4/2 If you can handle the English language..you can be a telephone solicitor. **1976** D. BARNES *Yesterday is Dead* (1977) II. 207 'No Solicitors', a sign on the glass double doors announced.

**so'licitorship.** [f. prec. + -SHIP.]

**1.** The office, duty, or calling of a solicitor.

*c* **1596** SIR R. CECIL in Campbell *Lives Chancellors* (1856) II. xlvii. 315 To arm him with your observations (for the exercise of solicitorship). **1825** LD. COCKBURN *Mem.* (1856) 155 Blair..held to his comfortable solicitorship and to his own way steadily. **1837** *New Monthly Mag.* LI. 284 His sense of the crookedness or cruelty of the trade was added to his sickening of solicitorship.

**2.** The personality of a solicitor.

**1633** MASSINGER *New Way* II. iii, And yet your good solicitorship, and rogue Wellborn, Were brought into her presence!

**solicitous** (sə'lɪsɪtəs), *a.* Also 6–8 sollicitous. [f. L. *sōl-*, *sollicit-us* (see SOLICIT *a.*) + -OUS. Cf. OF. *sol(l)icitoux, -eux.*]

†**1.** Full of care or concern; anxious, apprehensive, disquiet. *Obs.*

**1621** BURTON *Anat. Mel.* I. ii. III. v, Ever suspitious, anxious, sollicitous, they are childishly drooping without reason. **1658** in *Verney Mem.* (1907) II. 78 Good natures are sollicitous when a misapprehension befalls them. **1674** MILTON *P.R.* II. 120 There without sign of boast, or sign of joy, Sollicitous and blank he thus began. **1706** PHILLIPS (ed. Kersey), *Sollicitous*, full of Care and Fear, troubled or much concerned about a thing. **1741** MIDDLETON *Cicero* I. III. 209 They began to be sollicitous.

**2.** Troubled, anxious, or deeply concerned, on some specified account. Const. with preps., as *about*, *for*, *of*, etc.

(*a*) **1570** FOXE *A. & M.* I. 159/2 He willeth him alwaies to be sollicitous for his soule. **1631** GOUGE *God's Arrows* III. Ep. Ded. p. iv, Moses, when he tarried at home, was very sollicitous for his countrimen in the field. **1699** BENTLEY *Phal.* 422 For a bare Error of the Memory I shall not be solicitous. **1748** *Anson's Voy.* III. i. I. 302 The boat was sent away..; and we were not a little solicitous for her return. **1790** BURKE *Fr. Rev.* 11 Sollicitous chiefly for the peace of my own country, but by no means unconcerned for yours. **1810** BENTHAM *Art of Packing* (1821) 50 The solicitor for the smuggler is solicitous for the smuggler, because,..in being solicitous for his client, he is solicitous for him-self. **1845** SARAH AUSTIN tr. *Ranke's Hist. Ref.* II. 315 They deemed that such an one would be more solicitous for their welfare ..than a stranger.

(*b*) **1647** N. BACON *Govt. Eng.* II. xiii. (1739) 71 These foreign Engagements made the King less sollicitous of the point of Prerogative at home. **1706** E. WARD *Wooden World Diss.* (1708) 16 One so sollicitous of other Mens Healths, cannot be unmindful of his own. **1729** BUTLER *Serm.* Wks. 1874 II. 124 Scarce any shew themselves to advantage, who are over solicitous of doing so. **1828** SCOTT *F.M. Perth* xxx, Your Highness will not expect me to be very solicitous of Henry Smith's interest. **1841** EMERSON *Ess.* I. *Prudence*, You are solicitous of the good-will of the meanest person, uneasy at his ill-will.

(*c*) **1658** SIR T. BROWNE *Hydriot.* Introd., The Persian Magi..being only solicitous about their Bones [etc.]. *a* **1683** OWEN *Holy Spirit* (1693) 14 In this condition the best of Men are apt to be solicitous about their Answers. **1709–29** MANDEY *Syst. Math., Astron.* 351 Concerning those, Astronomers are not Sollicitous, by reason of the Smallness. **1887** RUSKIN *Præterita* II. 330 He was undiligent and effectless—chiefly solicitous about his trousers and gloves.

**b.** With dependent clause.

**1639** MASSINGER *Unnatural Combat* III. ii, He found him Solicitous in what shape she should appear. **1647** H. MORE *Poems* Ded., I am not indeed much solicitous, how every particle of these Poems may please you. **1764** GOLDSM. *Hist. Eng. in Lett.* (1772) I. 57 This weak monarch was in no way solicitous who succeeded. **1784** COWPER *Task* IV. 433 Much solicitous how best He may compensate for a day of sloth. **1836** J. GILBERT *Chr. Atonement* ix. (1852) 285 Why so solicitous that we should be reconciled? **1845** SARAH AUSTIN *Ranke's Hist. Ref.* II. 529 The delegates of the States were chiefly solicitous lest they should be attacked by the remnant of the order in Germany.

**3.** Extremely or particularly careful or attentive; taking the utmost heed or care.

**1609** BIBLE (Douay) *Micah* vi. 8 *comm.*, To love mercie, and to walke solicitous with thy God. **1682** SIR T. BROWNE *Chr. Mor.* I. §33 Move circumspectly, not meticulously, and rather carefully sollicitous, than anxiously sollicitudinous. **1789** BENTHAM *Princ. Legisl.* vi. §41 Under a solicitous and attentive government the ordinary preceptor..is but a deputy as it were to the magistrate.

**4.** Anxious, eager, desirous: **a.** With *to* and inf.

**1647** CLARENDON *Hist. Reb.* I. §21 The Prince..was transported with the thought of it, and most impatiently sollicitous to bring it to pass. **1693** J. EDWARDS *Auth. O. & N. Test.* 384 Those learned and pious writers..were not solicitous to go any farther. **1748** *Anson's Voy.* II. ix. (ed. 4) 316 We were very solicitous to get some positive intelligence. **1779** *Mirror* No. 19, These peculiarities serve only..to make her more solicitous to prevent their effects. **1817** JAS. MILL *Brit. India* II. IV. viii. 284 Whose alliance Hyder was solicitous to gain. **1867** D. DUNCAN *Disc.* vii. 146 God is willing, nay, solicitous to confer these blessings.

**b.** With *in* (governing nouns of action).

**1628** LE GRYS *Barclay's Argenis* 274 To the most of them the Kings being so solicitous in this businesse was not pleasing. **1665** WALTON *Life Hooker* 241 All this time he was solicitous in his study. **1774** GOLDSM. *Nat. Hist.* I. xv. (1824) I. 101 While the merchant and the mariner are solicitous in describing currents and soundings.

**5.** Marked or characterized by anxiety, care, or concern: **a.** Of actions, study, etc.

**1563** FOXE *A. & M.* 1260/1 Whose industrie was alwayes sollicitous, not onelye to them of hys owne companye, but also..for other prysoners. **1645** E. REYNOLDS *Serm. Hosea* vi. 64 A symbole, first, of vigilant care and most intent and sollicitous inspection and providence. **1678** CUDWORTH *Intell. Syst.* 443 The Government of some of them is toilsom and sollicitous. **1736** BUTLER *Anal.* II. vi, An attentive, solicitous, perhaps painful exercise of their understanding about it. **1829** I. TAYLOR *Enthus.* ii. (1867) 32 A solicitous dissection of the changing emotions of the religious life. **1863** H. ROGERS *Life J. Howe* i. 14 It is not after the method of a severe logic or a too solicitous philosophy.

**b.** Of cares, thoughts, etc.

**1650** BULWER *Anthropomet.* 242 The sollicitous cares of his mind, which dry his very bones. *a* **1693** URQUHART *Rabelais* III. xvi. 133 He was in this sad quandary and sollicitous pensiveness. *a* **1703** BURKITT *On N.T.* Luke xii. 30 This vexatious care, and solicitous thoughtfulness. **1717** L. HOWEL *Desiderius* (ed. 3) 55 Being the less incumber'd with uneasy Cares and solicitous Vexations.

**c.** Of life or conditions.

**1661** GAUDEN in C. Wordsworth *Documentary Suppl.* (1825) 19, I doe not desire to live long in this distracted and solicitous condition. **1673** TEMPLE *United Prov.* Wks. 1720 I. 25 The Royal Servitude of a sollicitous Life.

**6.** Of features: Suggestive of solicitude or anxiety.

**1868** SWINBURNE *Ess. & Studies* (1875) 362 The features resolute, solicitous, heroic. **1876** GEO. ELIOT *Dan. Der.* xi, It was not possible for a human aspect to be freer from grimace or solicitous wrigglings.

**so'licitously**, *adv.* [f. prec.] In a solicitous manner, in various senses of the adj.

**1614** T. ADAMS *Semper Idem* Wks. (1629) 857 Many parents are solicitously perplexed, how their children shall doe when they are dead. **1674** BOYLE *Excellency Theol.* I. ii. 66 It needs not be solicitously proved. **1733** SWIFT *Apol.* Wks. 1755 IV. I. 213 You..Do now solicitously shun The cooler air, and dazzling sun. **1799** *Monthly Rev.* XXX. 297 They solicitously shun all commerce with Europeans. **1817** J. SCOTT *Paris Revisit.* (ed. 4) 87 The finest faces hung solicitously over it. **1856** S. DAVIDSON *Bibl. Criticism* xlv. 685 Many Slavic words are formed solicitously after the Greek.

**so'licitousness.** [f. SOLICITOUS *a.*] The state or quality of being solicitous; care, concern; anxiety, solicitude.

**1636** *Divine Tragedie lately Acted* 41 Free your selves on that day..from worldly cares and sollicitousnesse. **1670** G. H. *Hist. of Cardinals* II. I. 123 To behold them with such passion and solicitousness endeavouring the good of Christianity. 1709 J. Clarke tr. *Grotius' Chr. Relig.* ii. xiv. (1818) 122 Solicitousness in procuring and preserving riches. 1724 in *Biogr. Presbyt.* (1827) II. 146 He did run fast ..in great Solicitousness of coming short of his Task. 1874 T. Hardy *Far fr. Mad. Crowd* xlvi, This spoliated effort of his new-born solicitousness.

**so'licitress.** ? *Obs.* Also 7 solicitresse, 8 sollicitress. [Cf. next and -ess.]

**1.** A female who solicits or prefers requests.

1631 Mabbe *Celestina* x. 117, I know not..whether thou art now comming with that Solicitresse of my safety? 1654-66 Earl Orrery *Parthen.* (1676) 593 To disoblige his pretended Solicitress. 1788 Charlotte Smith *Emmeline* (1816) III. 116 She prepared to become a solicitress for favours to a statesman.

*fig.* 1710 Shaftesbury *Charact.* (1737) I. *Adv. Author* iii. 312 They are very powerful Sollicitresses. They never seem to importune us; tho they are ever in our eye.

**2.** A female who entices to immorality.

1634 W. Tirwhyt tr. *Balzac'c Lett.* (vol. I) 270 Yet am I credibly informed, that..she is turned Solicitresse to entice others to vice. *a*1639 W. Whateley *Prototypes* iii. xxxix. (1640) 9 If we consider..the person of his solicitresse,.. how great a patterne is he of invincible purity.

**so'licitrix.** Also sollicitrix. [f. solicitor, after forms in *-trix*.]

**1.** = solicitress 2. *rare.*

1611 Cotgr., *Maquerelle*, a (woman) bawd; the solicitrix of lecherie. 1961 L. P. Hartley *Two for River* 48 When accosted I had not, as some men have, a polite formula of refusal ready: I swerved or..walked straight on. But one evening I couldn't, for my solicitrix..planted herself in front of me and blocked my way.

**2.** A female solicitor; = solicitress 1. ? *Obs.*

1637 Nabbes *Microcosm.* v, Bless me! who's this? one of the devil's she-lawyers?.. Pray how long have you been a solicitrix? 1658 in *Verney Mem.* (1907) II. 77 You have a sollicitrix here,..which is my wife. 1700 T. Brown tr. *Fresny's Amusem.* 46 The first Motion he found in himself, was for the Charming Sollicitrix. 1747 *Mem. Nutrebian Crt.* I. 82 The bishop began with saying what an importunate sollicitrix the dutchess had been.

**solicitude** (sə'lɪsɪtju:d). Also 5-6 sol-, 6 sollycytude, 6-8 sollicitude, 6 -ud. [a. OF. *sol-, sollicitude* (mod.F. *sollicitude*, = Sp. *solicitud*, Pg. *solicitude*, It. *solli-, sollecitudine*), or ad. L. *sōl-, sollicitūdo*, f. *sollicitus* solicit *a.*]

**1.** The state of being solicitous or uneasy in mind; disquietude, anxiety; care, concern.

?*a*1412 Lydg. *Two Merchants* 580 So ar we travailed with solicitude. 1528 Paynell *Salerne's Regim.* (1617) 178 Sollicitude, feare, sadnesse, sleepe it drowneth in. *a*1533 Ld. Berners *Gold. Bk. M. Aurel.* (1546) M vij b, Such as are of a delicate bloudde, haue not soo much sollicitude as the rustical people. *a*1631 Donne *Select.* (1840) 169 Lazarus come forth..from your waters..of solicitude. 1684 *Contempl. State of Man* i. i. (1699) 4 What we desire with impatience, being possessed, brings Care and Solicitude. 1737 Whiston *Josephus, Hist.* iii. i. §1 Yet did the disturbance..in his soul plainly appear by the solicitude he was in. 1769 Robertson *Chas. V*, iv. Wks. 1813 V. 413 Bourbon, on his part, was far from being free from solicitude. 1833 I. Taylor *Fanaticism* v. 102 Free from solicitude, because free from wants. 1849 W. Irving *Mahomed* vii. (1853) 36 These, and other causes of solicitude, preyed upon his spirits.

**2.** Anxious, special, or particular care or attention.

*a*1535 More *Treatise Sacr.* Wks. 1266 What diligence can here suffyse vs? What solicitude can we thynke here ynough? agaynste the cummyng of thys almightye king. 1603 Holland *Plutarch's Mor.* 185, I could wish that the sollicitude and care of the elder [brother] savoured rather of a companion..than of a father. 1750 Johnson *Rambler* No. 39 ¶4 That it is not to be envied for its happiness, appears from the solicitude with which it is avoided. 1794 Sullivan *View Nat.* I. Pref. 7 He has endeavoured, with no small degree of solicitude, to engage their generous affections. 1847 Disraeli *Tancred* i. ii, Never had such solicitude been lavished on human being. 1879 Loftie *Ride in Egypt* 173 The antiquities of Egypt have been made subjects of Government solicitude.

**b.** Const. *about, for*, or *to* (with inf.).

*c*1475 Henryson *Poems* (S.T.S.) III. 60 The grete sollicitude..to wyn this warldis gud, Cessis furthwith. 1533 Bellenden *Livy* ii. xxiv. (S.T.S.) I. 229 þe pepill tuke na sollicitude bot alanerlie for sic thingis as mycht erast fortifie þis new law. 1660 R. Coke *Justice Vind.* 11 There is in every man a solicitude how to live, and so to live that his living be not a burden. 1736 Butler *Anal.* i. ii. Wks. 1874 I. 34 There is reason also for the most active thought and solicitude, to secure that interest. 1751 Johnson *Rambler* No. 174 ¶14 This alarm which they spread by their solicitude to escape me. 1837 Lockhart *Scott* II. vii. 256 That lively solicitude about points of antiquarian detail. 1865 Kingsley *Herew.* x, They manifested affectionate solicitude for them.

†**c.** Const. *of. Obs.*

1490 Caxton *Eneydos* xii. 43 Nor wyth hym remayneth nother..care ne solycytude of thy loue. 1540 *Act 32 Hen. VIII*, c. 26 His grace taketh the care and sollicitud therof. 1541 R. Copland *Galyen's Terap.* 2 Dij, He hath sollycytude of all the body. 1651 Hobbes *Leviath.* i. xii. 52 To be in a perpetuall solicitude of the time to come.

**3.** *pl.* Cares, troubles, anxieties, etc.

1490 Caxton *Eneydos* xxvii. 98 Alle werkes & operacyions humayne, with their solicitudes. 1541 R. Copland *Guydon's Quest. Chirurg.* Qiij b, Aske yf he hath had great solycytudes, & chargeable thoughtes. 1664 H. More *Myst. Iniq.* i. xvi. 58 Those hard trialls and disquieting solicitudes that naturally will attempt them. 1750 tr. *Leonardus' Mirror of Stones* p. iv, You may refresh your mind, wearied with perpetual sollicitudes and labours. 1844 Dickens *Mart. Chuz.* xxxii, Mrs. Todgers looked a little worn by cares of gravy and other such solicitudes. 1872 Geo. Eliot *Middlem.* i, To her the destinies of mankind..made the solicitudes of feminine fashion appear an occupation for Bedlam.

†**4.** Solicitation; importunate petition. *Obs.*[−1]

1556 *Aurelio & Isab.* (1608) B iv, Isabell became verye sore in love with him, seing the verye greate sollicitude and requeste that he made unto her.

Hence †**solicitudeness.** *Obs. rare.*

1547 Boorde *Brev. Health* ccliii. 85 b, It may come of solicitudenes or great study occupyenge the memory so much that it is fracted. *Ibid.* cccxxi. 104 Yf it come by great study and solicitudnes.

**solici'tudinous,** *a.* Also 7 soll-. [f. L. *sōl-, sollicitūdin-*, stem of *sollicitūdo* solicitude.]

**1.** Filled with anxiety, care, or concern. *rare.*

1682 Sir T. Browne *Chr. Morals* i. §33 Move circumspectly.., and rather carefully sollicitous than anxiously sollicitudinous.

**2.** Characterized by solicitude or anxiety.

1829 Lytton *Disowned* 19 Which he promised to prepare with the most solicitudinous dispatch. 1900 *Speaker* 7 Apr. 10/2 My enemies have given me this advice in a well-meaning, sneaking, solicitudinous kind of fashion.

**solid** ('sɒlɪd), *sb.*[1] Also 6-7 solide. [f. the adj., or ad. F. *solide*, L. *solidum*.]

**1.** *Geom.* A body or magnitude of three dimensions; one having length, breadth, and thickness.

*solid of revolution*, one formed by the revolution of a plane figure.

1495 *Trevisa's De P.R.* xix. cxxvii. (W. de W.) 928 The Cubus is properly the Solid ylyke longe, brode, and depe. 1570 Billingsley *Euclid* xi. def. 1. 312 A solide or body is that which hath length, breadth, and thicknes. 1571 Digges *Pantom.* iii. Q, Lyke solides are such as are encompassed with superficies that are lyke and of equall number. 1625 N. Carpenter *Geogr. Del.* i. ii. (1635) 36 As wee esteeme of a circle described in a plaine surface, so must we iudge in solids of a Spheare. 1696 Phillips (ed. 5) s.v., All Solids are either Spherical or Elliptical, which have no Sides or Angles; or Prisms, which are contain'd in Plains. 1725 Watts *Logic* i. vi. §8 Geometry divides its Objects into Lines, Surfaces and Solids. 1816 tr. *Lacroix's Diff. & Int. Calculus* 679 To find the differentials of the volumes and curve surfaces of solids of revolution. 1841 *Penny Cycl.* XIX. 364/2 We have thus the five regular solids, and have shown that there can be no others. 1878 Gurney *Crystal.* 41 A solid cannot be bounded by fewer than four planes.

**2. a.** A solid substance or body.

1698 Keill *Exam. Th. Earth* (1734) 195 For it is not so with solids as with fluids, where all range themselves according to their intensive gravities. *a*1722 Lisle *Husb.* (1757) 7 Nor is it to be objected, that by fire these vegetative particles should be destroyed, seeing they are supposed to be solids. 1812 Sir H. Davy *Chem. Philos.* 65 The first class consists of solids, which compose the great known part of the globe. 1844 G. Bird *Urin. Deposits* 62 The quantity of solids in a fluid ounce of the urine. 1882 Minchin *Unipl. Kinematics* 137 Every one easily recognises a broad distinction between a Fluid and a Solid.

*transf.* 1727 Bailey (vol. II), *Semi-vowels*..are distinguished into Solids and Liquids. *Ibid.*, *Solids*,..or solid Letters, are those which are never liquefied.

**b.** *Physiol.* A solid part or constituent of the body. Used in pl.

Freq. in the 18th cent.; now *Obs.* or *rare.*

1704 F. Fuller *Med. Gymn.* (1711) 26, I come now to shew after what manner [exercise] affects the solids. 1769 E. Bancroft *Guiana* 324 Its use..is indispensably necessary in this climate, to corroborate the solids. 1805 *Med. Jrnl.* XIV. 325 Its influence upon the nervous system through.. the balance between the solids and fluids. [*a*1862 Buckle *Civiliz.* (1869) III. 420 All the solids in the human body are either simple or vital.]

**c.** *Building.* A solid mass of masonry or other construction, esp. that between windows or doors; a pier of a bridge.

1736 N. Hawksmoor *Hist. London Bridge* 9 There are also eighteen Solids or Piers of different Dimensions, from thirty-four to twenty-five Feet thick. 1793 Smeaton *Edystone L.* §45 The whole therefore to the height of the store-room floor..having been made with all possible solidity, was denominated the solid. 1840 *Civil Eng. & Arch. Jrnl.* III. 84/1 To obtain the largest possible admission of light, with the smallest obstruction of solids or piers. 1842 Gwilt *Archit.* §2756 The investigation relative to the voids and solids of doors. *Ibid.* Gloss. s.v. *Pier*, A solid between the doors or windows of a building.

**d.** *Printing.* (See quot.)

1888 Jacobi *Printers' Vocab.* 128 *Solids*, the blacker or more solid parts of a woodcut or other illustration.

**3.** *the solid*, the unbroken mass, the main part or body, of something.

1776 Semple *Building in Water* 148 The Tongues and Grooves to be put on with Spikes and stout Oak Pins, or made out of the Solid. 1840 Browning *Sordello* iv. 168 Her hero's car Clove dizzily the solid of the war. 1908 *Westm. Gaz.* 13 Feb. 4/2 The mechanically operated valves are.. actuated by cams turned from the solid.

**4.** *ellipt.* in *pl.* in various senses: **a.** Solid or substantial dishes or food. **b.** *U.S.* Self-coloured cloths or garments. **c.** *Salt-making.* (See quot.) **d.** *Mining.* (See quot.) **e.** *Sc.* Solid qualities or character.

**a.** 1786 J. Woodforde *Diary* 18 July (1926) II. 258, I.. could eat no solids all day long. 1792 A. Young *Trav. France* 217, I am very well served at dinner with many and good dishes, and some of them solids. 1973 *Jrnl. Genetic Psychol.* CXXIII. 103 It can be seen also in Table 4 that infants did not eat solids at two weeks, but did at five weeks. 1977 W. H. Manville *Good-bye* iv. 40 Junior just began eating solids.

**b.** 1883 *Evening Star* (Washington) 31 Oct. 3/6 Solids are all the go this season. Stripes and checks are very dull.

**c.** *c.* 1886 Holland *Cheshire Gloss.*, *Solids*, the solid brickwork about the fires, on which the bars, bearers, and other ironwork rests.

**d.** 1894 Heslop *Northumbld. Gloss.*, *Solids*, in mining, the solid rock as distinguished from soil, moss, drifts, etc.

**e.** 1896 J. Horne *Canny Countryside* xix. 212 That precentor was never again seen in Knockdry. He lacked 'solids'.

**f.** Special Comb.: **solids-not-fat** *Dairying*, the components of milk other than water and fats and other lipids (being largely lactose and proteins); the proportion of such components in a sample of milk; **solids pump**, a machine for forcing lumpy or granular material, or liquid containing it, through a pipe or chamber against the force of gravity.

1874 J. A. Wanklyn *Milk-Analysis* ix. 38 The effect of skimming is to diminish the proportion of fat, and to leave the proportion of 'solids not fat' unaltered. 1930 *Analyst* LV. 543 The resulting curves..do not indicate that the highest proportion of solids-not-fat is contained in the bottom part of the milk. 1960 *Farmer & Stockbreeder* 5 Jan. 99/1 Changes in solids-not-fat were small, and nearly 19 per cent of the tests in Friesian herds and 7 per cent of those in Ayrshire herds were below the legal minimum standard of 8·5 per cent. 1957 T. G. Hicks *Pump Selection & Application* xiv. 313 Solids pumps..are designed to handle solutions containing large percentages of suspended abrasive materials. 1966 *McGraw-Hill Encycl. Sci. & Technol.* XII. 474/2 The solids pump has found its principal application in the operation of oil-shale retorts. Here it is used to feed crushed shale into the bottom of a conical vessel.

**5.** A solid rubber tyre. (No longer current.)

1919 *Brit. Manufacturer* Nov. 38/1, 50,000 pneumatic tyres a week, in addition to solids. 1924 A. W. Judge *Mod. Motor Cars* II. 178 Both ordinary and Giant Solids.

†**solid,** *sb.*[2] *Obs.* Also solide. [ad. L. *solidus* solidus[1].] A weight or value equivalent to that of the Roman solidus.

1601 Holland *Pliny* II. 36 The ordinarie dose is from half an obolus to a Solid.., according to the strength of the patient. 1609 Bible (Douay) *1 Esdr.* viii. 27 Cuppes of gold twentie, which had a thousand solides.

**solid** ('sɒlɪd), *a.* Forms: 4-7 solide (6-7 solude, 7 solede, sollide); 5- solid (7 solyd, sollid). [a. OF. *solide* (mod.F. *solide*, = Sp., Pg., It. *solido*), or ad. L. *solidus*.]

**I. 1. a.** Free from empty spaces, cavities, interstices, etc.; having the interior completely filled in or up. Opposed to *hollow*.

*c*1391 Chaucer *Astrol.* ii. §26 The excellence of the spere solide..shewyth Manifeste the diuerse assenciouns of signes in diuerse places. 1594 T. B. *La Primaud. Fr. Acad.* ii. 85 Hollow things are more fitte to receiue sounds, and to cause them to be heard better, then things that are solide and more thicke. 1604 R. Cawdrey *Table Alph.*, *Solid*, not hollowe, sound, heavie. 1613 Purchas *Pilgr.* (1614) 567 This was hollow, the other solid. 1796 Kirwan *Elem. Min.* (ed. 2) I. 106 That [piece] examined..was a solid rhomboid. 1842 Loudon *Suburban Hort.* 180 In the construction of walls they are generally built solid; but when the wall is formed entirely of brick, a saving of material is obtained.. by building them hollow. 1863 P. Barry *Dockyard Econ.* 277 Mr. Fawcett introduced the highly important improvement of casting the guns solid and boring them. 1881 *Grove's Dict. Music* III. 179 It was played with the hand,..and had seven strings mounted in a solid wooden frame.

**b.** *spec.* in *Bot.* and *Ent.* (see quots.).

(*a*) 1753 *Chambers' Cycl.* Suppl., *Solid root*..expresses the whole root to be one uniform lump of matter. 1776 J. Lee *Introd. Bot.* 378 *Solidus*, solid, without internal Pores. *c*1789 *Encycl. Brit.* (ed. 3) III. 448/1 *Solid*, consisting of solid substance; as the tulip. 1796 Withering *Brit. Plants* (ed. 3) I. 82 *Solid Root*; fleshy and uniform, as that of a Turnep. 1866 *Treas. Bot.* 1072/1 *Solid*, not hollow or furnished with internal cavities of any kind.

(*b*) 1826 Kirby & Sp. *Entomol.* IV. 259 *Solid* (*Solida*). When the interior is full. *Ibid.* 323 *Solid Knob*.. When the knob consists of a single joint, or if of more, exhibits very faint traces of their separation.

**c.** *Typog.* Having no leads between the lines; unleaded; (see also quot. 1888).

1808 Stower *Printers' Gram.* 163 To a solid page, two leads make the usual white after the head. 1839 T. C. Hansard *Print. & Type-Founding* (1841) 89 How many lines of the particular type used there would be in a page of the given size, supposing it were all solid type. 1888 Jacobi *Printers' Vocab.* 128 *Solid matter*, type composed without leads; also applied to type with but few quadrats in.

**d.** Of a wall, etc.: Having no opening or window; unbroken, blank.

1865 J. Fergusson *Hist. Arch.* ii. ii. ii. I. 427 The apse, properly speaking, is a solid semi-cylinder, surmounted by a semi-dome, but always solid below, though generally broken by windows above.

**2.** *Math.* **a.** Of a body or figure: Having three dimensions.

*c*1430 *Art Nombryng* 14 It is clepede a solide body that hathe þer-in..lengthe, brede, and thiknesse. 1706 Phillips (ed. Kersey) s.v. *Curve*, The Conchoid and the Solid Parabola. 1823 H. J. Brooke *Introd. Crystallogr.* 111 Alternate solid angles replaced by tangent planes. 1841 Brewster *Martyrs Science* iii. i. (1856) 172 What have plane figures to do with solid orbits? 1842 *Penny Cycl.* XXII. 206/1 The rules..for measuring different superficial or solid figures will be found under the several heads.

*fig.* 1830 Carlyle *Misc.* (1857) II. 172 Narrative is linear, Action is solid.

†**b.** Of number or measure: = cubic *a. Obs.*

(*a*) *c*1430 *Art Nombryng* 14 The solide nombre or cubike is þat þat comythe of double ledynge of nombre in nombre.

**1570** BILLINGSLEY *Euclid* VII. def. 18. 187 When three numbers multiplyed together yᵉ one into the other, produce any number, the number produced, is called a solide number. **1704** J. HARRIS *Lex. Techn.* I, *Solid Numbers*, are those which arise from the Multiplication of a Plain Number, by any other whatsoever.

(*b*) **1665** BOYLE *Occas. Refl.* IV. i. (1848) 50 Ten thousand millions of Cubick German Leagues, (and consequently above three-score times as many English miles of solid measure). **1667** PRIMATT *City & C. Builder* 165 A Foot solid measure hath seventeen hundred twenty eight square Inches. **1705** ARBUTHNOT *Coins*, etc. ix. (1727) 91 There are in a solid Foot 1728 solid Inches.

**c.** Of, relating, or pertaining to a geometrical solid or solids (†or to cubic numbers).

**1570** BILLINGSLEY *Euclid* I. prop. 12. 22 A solide perpendiculer line is, when the point, from whence the perpendiculer is drawne, is on high, and without the plaine superficies. **1571** DIGGES *Pantom.* II. xiv. Oj, The thirde kynde of Geometrie, where you shall haue rules to measure, not onely the solide, but also the superficiall contents of all maner bodies. **1684** E. HALLEY (*title*), Discourse concerning the number of roots of solid and biquadratical equations. **1704** J. HARRIS *Lex. Techn.* I, *Solid Place*.. is when the Point is in one of the Conick Sections. *Ibid.*, *Solid Problem*.. is one which can't be Geometrically solved, but by the Intersection of a Circle, and a Conick Section. **1733** H. GORE (*title*), Elements of Solid Geometry. **1842** *Penny Cycl.* XXII. 206/1 Solid, superficial, and linear dimensions. **1885** WATSON & BURBURY *Electr. & Magn.* I. 59, *U*, instead of being a single spherical solid harmonic, may be an infinite series of such harmonics.

**3. a.** Of material substances: Of a dense or massive consistency; composed of particles which are firmly and continuously coherent; hard and compact.

*c* **1532** DU WES *Introd. Fr.* in *Palsgr.* 917 Solude, *massif.* **1567** MAPLET *Gr. Forest* 33 It is nothing solide or massie, but much porouse. **1602** SHAKS. *Ham.* I. ii. 129 Oh that this too too solid Flesh would melt, Thaw, and resolue it selfe into a Dew. **1634** SIR T. HERBERT *Trav.* (1638) 179 In place of solyd walls, it is ingirt with liquid moats or trenches. **1715** tr. *Gregory's Astron.* (1726) I. 170 We shall demonstrate.. that each Planet, the nearer it is to the Sun, the solider or more dense it is. **1742** GRAY *Propertius* ii. 30 What wondrous force the solid earth can move. **1815** J. SMITH *Panorama Sci. & Art* II. 299 The separation of a fluid from the solid or undissolved particles which it contains. **1841** *Penny Cycl.* XXI. 177/2 These secretions are exceedingly numerous, and constitute the great bulk of the solid parts of the plant. **1895** *Naturalist* 26 A solid camphor.

*transf.* **1746** FRANCIS tr. *Horace, Epist.* II. i. 272 To think that Asses should in Judgement sit, In solid Deafness, on the Works of Wit. **1847** TENNYSON *Princ.* III. 110, I forced a way Thro' solid opposition crabb'd and gnarl'd. **1887** LECKY *Eng. in 18th C.* V. 338 There will no longer be any obstacle to a solid despotism.

**b.** Solidified; frozen.

**1697** DRYDEN *Virg. Georg.* III. 561 With Axes first they cleave the Wine, and thence By Weight, the solid Portions they dispence. **1786** S. ROGERS *Ode Superstit.* I. iii, O'er solid seas, where Winter reigns. **1879** *Daily Telegr.* 28 June, Having the bowl of solid soup carefully enwrapped in a copy of the *Sunday Times*.

**c.** In the phr. *solid rock*, with reference to the cutting of steps or passages in it.

**1779** J. MOORE *View Soc. Fr.* (1793) I. 231 We entered the largest saline by a passage cut out of the solid rock. **1794** MRS. RADCLIFFE *Myst. Udolpho* lii, We went through a long passage, and down other steps cut in the solid rock. **1838** *Penny Cycl.* XI. 215/1 Two excavations, wrought with extreme labour, in the solid rock, called galleries.

**d.** Of clouds, the atmosphere, etc.: Having the appearance of a solid or unbroken mass; dense, thick, compact. Chiefly *poet.*

**1807** WORDSW. *Poems Indep. & Liberty* II. v, Clouds, lingering yet, extend in solid bars Through the grey west. **1819** SHELLEY *Ode to West Wind* 27 Thy congregated might Of vapours, from whose solid atmosphere Black rain, and fire, and hail will burst. **1841** BROWNING *Pippa Passes* I. 7 Of yonder gap in the solid gray Of the eastern cloud.

**e.** *Astronautics.* Using solid fuel.

**1949** G. P. SUTTON *Rocket Propulsion Elem.* i. 10 Long duration solid rocket units require an excessively heavy and large combustion chamber. **1961** *Flight* LXXX. 650/2 A study of the requirements associated with the transport, handling, checkout, assembly, and launch of extremely large solid boosters. **1967** *Technology Week* 20 Feb. 13/1 The program will cover the design, development and demonstration of a controllable solid propulsion system using integral propulsion. **1979** J. W. CORNELISSE et al. *Rocket Propulsion* ix. 169 Solid rockets find widespread military and civil applications.

**4.** Of states, conditions, etc.: Characterized by solidity or compactness.

**1597** SHAKS. *2 Hen. IV*, III. i. 48 That one might.. see.. the Continent (Wearie of solide firmenesse) melt it selfe Into the Sea. **1665** BOYLE *Occas. Refl.* (1848) 64 The Leaves.. are of a more solid Texture.. than the Blossoms. **1824** SCOTT *Redgauntlet* ch. xix, A little surprised at the solid weight of the distressed fair one. **1868** LOCKYER *Elem. Astron.* §66 Taking water and iron as instances: when both are in a solid state we get ice and hard iron.

**5. a.** Of rain, etc.: Steady, drenching; continuous. Also, of a day: Characterized by rain of this kind.

**1621** in Foster *Eng. Factories Ind.* (1906) 354 There fell (in a sad and sollid shewer without intermission) soe much unexpected rayne. **1847** HELPS *Friends in C.* I. vi. I. 86 To be looking out on a good solid English wet day. **1868** in Huntley *Glouc. Gloss.* 63 A solid rain.

**b.** Of water: Coming in a compact mass.

**1893** *Outing* XXII. 146/2 Her principal fault is that she is wet in a sea-way, though she rarely ships solid water.

**6.** Having the property of occupying a certain amount of space (cf. SOLIDITY 4).

**1690** LOCKE *Hum. Und.* II. v. (1695) 53 Nor is an Adamant one jot more solid than Water. *Ibid.*, Yet it is not that the parts of the Diamond are more solid than those of Water or resist more. **1794** SULIVAN *View Nature* I. 125 Even a particle of water is solid. **1829** *Nat. Philos., Pneumatics* ii. (L.U.K.) 3 The quality in air which we have called impenetrability, is sometimes called solidity, and air is said to be solid.

**II. 7.** Of a strong, firm, or substantial nature or quality; not slight or flimsy: **a.** Of things (or persons), in figurative applications.

**1586** *Reg. Privy Council Scot.* IV. 61 Upon a gude and solide ordour for convocating of the ministerie to General Assembleis thairefitr. **1606** G. WOODCOCK *Hist. Ivstine* xv. 64 This temper had made them sollude, and fitte for anie foundation. **1665** BOYLE *Occas. Refl.* IV. xiii. (1848) 250 The Decrees of Providence are too solid and fixt to have Violence offered them. **1703** EVELYN *Diary* 11 July, All the points of good and solid architecture. **1746** CHESTERF. *Lett.* cv. (1792) I. 288 As he took so much pains for the graces of oratory only, I conclude he took still more for the more solid parts of it. *a* **1770** JORTIN *Serm.* (1771) I. 30 Faith is gone, having no solid support. **1812** *Examiner* 11 May 302/2 The colouring.. is solid without heaviness. **1860** MOTLEY *Netherl.* iv. (1868) I. 101 There was another way of earning something solid. **1876** BANCROFT *Hist. U.S.* III. vi. 370 His desire was for solid and sure places.

**b.** Of structures, buildings, furniture, etc.

**1644** MILTON *Areop.* (Arb.) 64 How goodly.. were such an obedient unanimity as this... Doubtles a stanch and solid peece of framework, as any January could freeze together. **1687** A. LOVELL tr. *Thevenot's Trav.* II. 47 We saw on our right hand two very solid well built houses. *a* **1700** EVELYN *Diary* 2 June 1676, The furniture is very particular for.. porcelain, and other solid and noble moveables. **1870** HOWSON *Metaph. St. Paul* ii. 72 The solid cities of the Greeks and Romans.

**c.** Of food or liquor.

*a* **1700** EVELYN *Diary* 27 Oct. 1685, There were all the dainties.. of the season,.. venison, plaine solid meate, fowle [etc.]. **1700** DRYDEN *Pref. Fables* Ess. (Ker) II. 258 Whole pyramids of sweetmeats for boys and women, but little of solid meat for men. **1711** STEELE *Spectator* No. 43 ¶4 A Bottle or two of good solid Edifying Port, at honest George's, made a Night chearful, and threw off Reserve. **1822–7** GOOD *Study Med.* (1829) I. 210 One substantial meal of solid animal food daily.

**d.** Of cloth, garments, etc.

**1859** *Habits of Gd. Society* iv. 177 For the country, the attire should be tasteful and solid and strong. **1903** *Sat. Rev.* 5 Dec. 697/2 Solid unbleached calico.. wears well.

**e.** *Cards.* (See quot. 1927.)

**1927** M. C. WORK *Contract Bridge* 145 *Solid suit*, one of such length and strength as to be practically sure of winning every trick in that suit. **1959** *Listener* 12 Feb. 309/1 The jump after a forcing opening bid shows a solid suit. **1976** *Country Life* 1 Apr. 846/2 Even when your trump suit is solid, it may still be fatal to touch it too early.

**8. a.** Combined; consolidated; united. *rare.*

**1596** BACON *Max. & Use Com. Law* xxiv. (1630) 94 So if tenant for life the remainder in fee bee, and they ioine in graunting a rent, this is one solid rent out of both their estates. **1818** HALLAM *Mid. Ages* (1872) I. 204 The other acquired unlimited power over a solid kingdom.

**b.** Unanimous, undivided; united in approval or opposition. Orig. *U.S. solid South*, the politically united southern States of America; the unanimous vote of the white electorate in these States for the Democratic party.

**1855** in P. S. Foner *Business & Slavery* (1941) 114 We are now beaten by the solid vote of the City of New York. **1858** S. COLFAX *Let.* in O. J. Hollister *Life Schuyler Colfax* (1887) 137 We have fallen on strange times when the solid South in the House and a score of Northern Democrats dare to vote '*No*' on a resolution approving existing laws against the African slave trade. **1872** *Chicago Tribune* 14 Oct. 1/3 The Democrats are solid for Greeley in this county. **1876** *Harper's Weekly* 26 Aug. 691/2 We must recognize the solid South as the core of the Democratic party... The solid South is the Southern Confederacy seeking domination of the United States through the machinery of the Democratic party. **1884** *Boston* (Mass.) *Jrnl.* 16 Aug., The vote of the solid South. **1890** HENTY *With Lee in Virginia* 84 The North can never hope to force the solid South back into the Union. **1892** *Boston* (Mass.) *Jrnl.* 8 Nov. 4/4 A solid New England vote for protection. **1974** *Socialist Worker* 23 Nov. 16/5 With the exception of a handful of white scabs on one shift all four shifts are solid. **1977** *Chicago Tribune* 2 Oct. II. 2/5 It is possible for the GOP to revitalize itself by becoming the necessary counterweight to the newly reconstituted Solid South.

**c.** Of persons: Regular or steady in attendance, politics, voting, etc. Chiefly *U.S.*

**1880** *Sen. Rep. 46th U.S. Congress 2 Sess.* No. 693. 326 Q. These gentlemen.. are both good Democrats? A. Yes, sir; they are solid Democrats. **1883** KEIGHLEY *Who are you* 90, I escorted her to Sunday School excursions, and was 'solid' at the picnics and bazaars. **1884** *American* IX. 180 He is, therefore, presumed to be solid as a Southern man. **1888** HOWELLS *Annie Kilburn* xviii, I'm solid for Mr. Peck every time.

**d.** orig. *U.S.* Intimately or closely allied, on friendly terms, *with* another.

**1882** G. W. PECK *Peck's Sunshine* 161, I was pretty solid with him. **1888** *Cent. Mag.* Nov. 30 We thus succeeded in making ourselves 'solid with the administration' before we had been in a town or village forty-eight hours. **1895** *Outing* XXVI. 64, I wanted to get solid with him for a time while he lived. **1951** E. PAUL *Springtime in Paris* iv. 80 He.. went back to his native village in the Ain, where there are plenty of unregenerate Pétainists to this day, quite solid with the bishop and the anti-Jewish provincial administration.

**9.** †**a.** Of time: Continuous, consecutive. *rare.*

**1662** STILLINGFL. *Orig. Sacra* I. v. §8 The uncertainty of heathen chronology, when.. implicite years are given out for solid. **1704** HEARNE *Duct. Hist.* (1714) I. 284 They took implicit Years for solid, and placed those Kings in a Succession which were Contemporary with one another.

**b.** Of a day, hour, etc.: Whole, entire, complete. Now *colloq.*

**1718** PRIOR *Solomon* II. 729 Loose and undisciplin'd the Soldier lay; Or lost in Drink, and Game, the solid Day. **1884** *Boston* (Mass.) *Jrnl.* 16 Aug., The Queen kept her seven solid hours fitting on and trying the current fashions. **1890** 'R. BOLDREWOOD' *Col. Reformer* (1891) 420, I walked him up and down, with the rug on, for a solid hour.

**10. a.** Entirely of the same substance or material (as that specified); of (gold, etc., or a legitimate alloy) and nothing else.

The 'material' is not necessarily pure: the implication is of homogeneity rather than purity, so that, e.g., articles made of plate are excluded but not those made of an alloy.

**1710** STEELE *Tatler* No. 179 ¶6 The Wall toward the North is of solid Stone. **1722–7** BOYER *Dict. Royal* II, Solid Gold, *de l'or massif*. **1844** THIRLWALL *Greece* VIII. 63 The assertion that the gilded statues.. were of solid gold. **1847** YEOWELL *Anc. Brit. Church* x. 101 [Severus] determined to build a wall of solid stone. **1874** STUBBS *Const. Hist.* I. xi. 424 They were purchased with solid gold. **1910** *Jrnl. R. Soc. Arts* LVIII. 260/2 There remained a mere film.. like silver foil... That is, I believe, a fair example of the so-called 'solid silver' sold in our swell shops, with the aid of much electric light and many bowing salesmen. **1926** J. P. DE CASTRO *Law & Practice of hall-marking Gold & Silver Wares* I. 138 Though often legitimately used to differentiate between sterling silver and electro-plated silver, the expression 'solid silver' is frequently a much-abused term. **1962** L. S. SASIENI *Optical Dispensing* i. 3 Solid gold is not necessarily pure gold, but is an alloy of pure gold with other metals. The unalloyed pure metal is known as fine gold. *Ibid.*, The colour of solid gold can be varied by altering the proportions and the metals in the alloy. **1970** CHOATE & DE MAY *Creative Gold- & Silversmithing* ii. 10 Any karat gold is called solid gold to distinguish it from gold-filled metals. **1981** *Daily Tel.* 24 Sept. 17 (Advt.), An absolutely perfect solid gold neckchain... These are not seconds or plated gold —but sound 9 carat gold!

*ellipt.* **1879** *Cassell's Techn. Educ.* IV. 308/1 What is termed 'solid', or gold jewellery of the better qualities.

**b.** Of colour: Of the same tone or shade throughout; uniform, self.

**1883** *Evening Star* (Washington) 31 Oct. 3/6 These solid browns, blacks, greens, reds, and, in fact, all these solid colors, are popular. **1885** GOODALE *Physiol. Bot.* 19 Yellow and Orange dyes. Solid yellow. **1894** *Outing* XXIV. 181/1 The outside of the thighs down to the knees are in solid color.

**c.** *U.S.* Of liquor: Neat, undiluted.

**1894** *Outing* XXIV. 49/1 He always took his liquor solid ..; he swallowed down two-thirds of a tumbler of raw Appleton rum.

**11.** Of persons, their constitution, etc.: Strong, healthy, sturdy.

**1741** WATTS *Improv. Mind* I. xvi. (1801) 126 If persons of this make ever devote themselves to science, they should be well assured of a solid and strong constitution of body. **1837** CARLYLE *Fr. Rev.* I. IV. iv, He walks there, with solid step. **1893** COZENS-HARDY *Broad Norf.* 68 'Solid, bor, solid!' meaning in one's usual health.

**III. 12.** Of persons: **a.** Of sound scholarship or sober judgement in matters of learning or speculation.

**1600** B. JONSON *Ev. Man out of Hum.* Q iij b, A right-eyd and solide Reader may perceiue it was not so great a part of the Heauen awry, as they would make it. **1624** GATAKER *Transubst.* 48 Like an ingenuous solide author. **1665** BUNYAN *Holy Citie* (1669) 259 It makes them grave, knowing, solid Guides, and Unfolders of the Mysteries of the Kingdom. **1709** STRYPE *Ann. Ref.* I. 84 This discourse of Guest shewing him to have been a solid and well-read man, I have transcribed from the original. **1847** L. HUNT *Men, Women, & B.* II. xi. 282 He has by this time become a solid student in Butler. **1875** T. HILL *True Order Stud.* 127 The two most solid thinkers upon these subjects.

**b.** Sober-minded, of reliable judgement, in practical matters; steady, sedate, staid.

**1632** LITHGOW *Trav.* II. 71 The solid, and sad man, is not troubled with the floods and ebbes of Fortune. **1670** G. H. *Hist. Cardinals* III. III. 302 He is an excellent person,.. of a good judgement, and solid, but something too resolute. *a* **1691** FOX *Autobiogr.* in *Jrnl.* (ed. Newman) 280, I.. therefore desired none but solid, weighty Friends might be about me. **1724** in Ramsay *Tea-t. Misc.* (1733) I. 36 O! as thou art bony, be solid and cany, And tent a true lover. **1760** J. WOOLMAN *Jrnl.* vii. (1898) 182 The hearts of some Solid Friends appeared to be united to discourage the practice amongst their members. **1837** CARLYLE *Fr. Rev.* I. III. i, Now nothing but a solid phlegmatic M. de Vergennes sits there. **1888** BRYCE *Amer. Commw.* III. xc. 247 Kearney throve because the solid classes despised him.

**c.** *Sc.* Fully possessed of the mental faculties; of sound mind, sane.

**1606** *Sc. Acts, Jas. VI* (1816) IV. 317/1 Scho tuk occasioun be his infirmitie and waik Judgement, he being than nocht so solide as wes necessar for the weill of his estait. **1822** GALT *Provost* xxii, The heads of the town.. no, may be, just so solid at the time as could have been wished. **1825** JAMIESON *Suppl.*, *Solid*, sane..; used in a negative form, as, 'He's no very solid'.

**d.** *U.S.* and *dial.* Financially sound or reliable; possessing capital, property, or means; well-to-do.

**1788** JEFFERSON *Writ* (1859) II. 443, I wish to see the beef-trade with America taken up by solid hands. **1799**, **1863** in Thornton *Amer. Gloss.* *a* **1904** in *Eng. Dial. Dict.* s.v., She's not poor, she's a solid woman.

**13. a.** Of qualities: Well founded or established; of real value or importance; substantial.

Freq. in the 17th and 18th centuries.

*a* 1601 *Pasquil & Kath.* (1878) III. 99 The pressure of my haires..stands at the seruice of your sollide perfections. 1638 JUNIUS *Paint. Ancients* 122 The..solid joy conceived out of the absolutenesse of the worke. 1654 WHITLOCK *Zootomia* 234 We shall see it a Mint of Solid worth, the good it hath..being inestimable. 1709 STEELE *Tatler* No. 29 ¶ 1 Having a very solid Respect for humane Nature. 1753 FIELDING *Amelia* III. xii, The cheerful, solid comfort which a fond couple enjoy in each other's conversation. 1843 R. J. GRAVES *Syst. Clin. Med.* xxii. 265 Many such portions may exist in the lungs together, without the least solid appearance of inflammation in the pulmonary substance. 1869 FREEMAN *Norm. Conq.* (1875) III. 229 He undoubtedly owed William a debt of solid gratitude.

**b.** Of learning or knowledge.

1668 CULPEPPER & COLE *Barthol. Anat.* 372 Those persons of solid Learning. *a* 1700 EVELYN *Diary* 6 Jan. 1692, He dilated on his..solid knowledge in theology. 1711 HEARNE *Collect.* (O.H.S.) III. 145 These two..are really Books of solid Learning. 1781 WARTON *Hist. Eng. Poetry* III. xxx. 211 She was entertained..with splendid banquets and much solid erudition. 1857 MILLER *Elem. Chem., Org.* i. §1. 6 So essential to the reception and advancement of solid philosophical knowledge. 1882 J. H. BLUNT *Ref. Ch. Eng.* II. 125 He was a man of solid learning.

**14. a.** Of arguments, reasons, etc.: Having a sound or substantial foundation; based upon sound principles or indisputable facts.

1615 W. BEDWELL tr. *Moham. Impost.* II. §87 He..will thus go on by way of solid demonstration. *a* 1661 FULLER *Worthies* (1840) III. 25 Having an excellent faculty in the clear and solid interpreting thereof. 1664 J. WEBB *Stone-Heng* (1725) 101 He can raise no solider an Argument against it. 1740 CHEYNE *Regimen* 305 There seems to be something solid, in one Observation Leibnitz makes. 1866 ROGERS *Agric. & Prices* I. xxiii. 603 Too little information..is given of the price of copper..for the purpose of attempting any solid inference as to the rise..in its value. 1894 *Solicitors' Jrnl.* XXXIX. 3/1 If there were no solid defence to the claim, the plaintiff would certainly obtain his order.

**b.** Similarly of writings, discourse, etc.

1676 GLANVILL *Ess. Philos.* v. 27 The Book and Method of Veronius was kindly..approved by..all the Gallick Clergy, as solid. *a* 1700 EVELYN *Diary* (Chandos) 17 Of solid discourse, affable, humble, and in nothing affected. 1709 STRYPE *Ann. Ref.* I. Pref. p. i, For the Church of England..have been written solid Apologies and Vindications. 1734 *Rollin's Anc. Hist.* (1827) I. 60 A very solid treatise. 1881 *Nation* (N.Y.) XXXII. 459 Of the other papers in the number, which is a 'solid' one.

**15.** Marked by, or involving, serious study or intention; not light, frivolous, or merely amusing.

1647 CLARENDON *Hist. Reb.* I. §186 Dr. Bancroft..disposed the clergy to a more solid course of study. 1648 J. BEAUMONT *Psyche* XX. cxl, Scorn light fond Accents, and reserve thine Ear For those which solid Musick's sweets distil. 1700 T. BROWN tr. *Fresny's Amusem.* v. Wks. 1709 III. I. 46 There's as much difference between their Rhimes and solid Verse, as [etc.]. 1736 *Gentl. Mag.* VI. 315/1 The most amiable Genius is That, which, embracing the most solid Arts, excludes not the Polite ones. 1827 SCOTT *Surg. Dau.* Pref., I doubt there is little solid in his studies—poetry and plays,..all nonsense. 1845 W. A. BUTLER in *Serm.* (1849) Mem. p. xxxvii, Romances debauch the taste for solid reading. 1888 BRYCE *Amer. Commw.* III. lxxx. 59 In other countries statesmen or philosophers do..the solid thinking for the bulk of the people.

**16.** Of judgement, etc.: Of a sober, sound, or practical character.

1662 J. DAVIES tr. *Mandelslo's Trav.* 95 The Queen, who was a woman of a solid judgement. 1683 D. A. *Art of Converse* 12 They shall never please solid judgments. 1718 POPE *Iliad* XV. 322 Not more in councils famed for solid sense, Than winning words and heavenly eloquence. 1805 A. KNOX *Rem.* (1834) I. 31 He who is apparently cold in affection may have solider judgment, and steadier resolution. 1825 SCOTT *Betrothed* Introd., The assistance of men of reading and of solid parts. 1868 MILMAN *St. Paul's* iv. 92 Hallam has said, with his usual solid wisdom [etc.].

**17.** Marked or characterized by a high degree of religious fervour or seriousness.

Used esp. by the Society of Friends.

1740 WHITEFIELD in *Life & Jrnls.* (1756) 436 Preached in the Afternoon to about two Thousand, and have not seen a more solid melting..since my Arrival. 1757 WOOLMAN *Jrnl.* iv. (1898) 123 At the twelfth hour the meeting for worship began, which was a solid meeting. 1769 *Ibid.* x. 259 We had some solid Conversation, under which I felt myself bowed in reverence before the Most High.

**18.** Thorough, downright, vigorous, etc. Used with intensive force and freq. strengthened by *good*, *right*, etc.

1830 GALT *Lawrie T.* III. ii. (1849) 87, I never..had a right solid sound sleep in one. 1873 BURTON *Hist. Scot.* V. lvi. 119 England was to strike the one solid blow that was necessary. 1888 STEVENSON *Black Arrow* 112 Swear your innocency with a good solid oath. 1897 MARY KINGSLEY *W. Africa* 294 Feeling sure that for good solid murderous rascality several of my old Fan acquaintances..would take a lot of beating.

**19.** *Austral.* and *N.Z. slang.* Severe, difficult; unfair.

1916 C. J. DENNIS *Moods of Ginger Mick* 155 *Solid*, severe; severely. 1943 N. MARSH *Colour Scheme* ii. 35 You'd think it was royalty. They've been making it pretty solid for everybody down there. Hauling everything out and shifting us all round. 1948 R. PARK *Harp in South* v. 62 After all, Auntie Josie's got all them kids to look after. It must be pretty solid for her with Grandma as well. 1959 E. LAMBERT *Glory thrown In* 66 They'll be solid on him for that, won't they?

**20.** *U.S. slang.* In the language of jazz: excellent, first-rate, 'great'; (see also quot. 1937). Also as *int. solid sender*: see SENDER d.

1935 *Vanity Fair* (N.Y.) Nov. 38/1 He puts a solid man like Joe on suitcase. 1937 *Amer. Speech* XII. 182/2 *Solid*, describes a player whose improvisation indicates that he is en rapport with the rhythm of the band... A band that is solid has a psychic unanimity of feeling. 1943 *N.Y. Times* 9 May II. 5/4 There has [*sic*] been some solid trumpet players who can really send. 1959 'F. NEWTON' *Jazz Scene* xii. 220 The hipster classifies what other people would call good as 'solid' or 'in there'. 1978 W. HJORTSBERG *Falling Angel* (1979) xii. 54 'Park your axe and have a drink.' 'Solid.' He placed his saxophone case carefully on the table.

**IV.** Quasi-*adv.* **21. a.** Solidly, firmly, completely, etc.; certainly, surely.

A number of dial. uses are given in the *Eng. Dial. Dict.*

1651 DAVENANT *Gondibert* II. vi, Glory, too solid great to taste of pride. 1683 MOXON *Mech. Exerc., Printing* xxiv. ¶ 19 White Pages..make the Heap lower in that place, because they clap solider together. 1937 *Amer. Speech* XII. 232/2 'Are you taking Amelia to the Charcoal Dance?' 'I solid am.' 1944 *Richmond* (Va.) *Times-Dispatch* 5 Oct. 6/3 Dowdy [said] he was going to leave, whereupon the Bayer woman said she'd kill him if he did... Dowdy told her that 'You'll solid have to kill me.' 1946 MEZZROW & WOLF *Really Blues* xii. 226 Not looking for trouble but solid ready for it. 1950 L. HUGHES *Simple speaks his Mind* xx. 108 Man, if I had a rocket plane, I would rock off into space and be solid gone. Gone. Real gone! I mean gone!

**b.** In a body or as a whole; unanimously. In phrases with reference to voting, esp. ***to go solid*** (***for*** or ***against*** some thing or person).

(*a*) 1884 *Pall Mall G.* 9 July 3/1 The episcopal vote..was cast solid for the Government. 1884 *Sat. Rev.* 5 July 1/1 The Government majority has not been in the habit of voting solid with Mr. Goschen lately. 1893 *Times* 22 Apr., For a party to vote solid for a measure in which not 10 per cent. of its members believe.

(*b*) 1888 BRYCE *Amer. Commw.* I. x. 131 The party going solid for whomsoever the majority has approved. 1891 *Sat. Rev.* 24 Jan. 91/2 The fleet seems to have gone almost solid against him.

**c.** ***to book solid***: to sell all the tickets of (a theatre, cinema, etc.). Usu. in *pass.* Also *absol.*

1916 *Variety* 27 Oct. 12/1 The Boston opera house is booked solid until March. 1921 *Kinematograph Monthly Rec.* Feb. 4 So many individual exhibitors are refusing to book 'solid'. 1955 M. ALLINGHAM *Beckoning Lady* vii. 105, I told him the show was booked solid. 1967 N. MARSH *Death at Dolphin* ix. 234 We're booked out solid for another four months.

**d.** Of time: consecutively, without a break.

1938 M. ALLINGHAM *Fashion in Shrouds* xx. 379 I've had forty-eight hours solid and I'm no longer intelligent. 1964 L. DEIGHTON *Funeral in Berlin* xlii. 270 He'll be out for eight hours solid.

**22.** In special collocations: ***solid angle*** (*Math.*), †(*a*) a vertex of a three-dimensional body; (*b*) a quantity associated with a vertex or the like in three dimensions, being proportional to the fraction of a sphere centred on it which would subtend it, and conventionally measured in steradians, of which $4\pi$ make up the whole sphere; ***solid balsam***, Balsam of Tolu; ***solid circuit*** (*Electronics*) = ***integrated circuit*** s.v. INTEGRATED *ppl. a.* b; ***solid diffusion***, migration of atoms within the crystal lattice of a solid; *spec.* in *Geol.*, considered as a possible mechanism for a metasomatizing process in rock masses; ***solid dig***, (see quot.); ***solid fuel***, fuel that is solid, rather than liquid or gaseous; *spec.* (*a*) coal, coke, etc., as opposed to oil, gas, or electricity for domestic heating; (*b*) as used in rocketry; freq. *attrib.*; hence ***solid-fuelled*** adj. (esp. of rockets); ***solid geology***, the geological features of a given region specifically excluding superficial deposits such as clay, sand, etc.; opp. *drift*; ***solid injection***, in diesel engines, the use of a mechanical pump to spray fuel into the cylinder at high pressure, without the use of compressed air; = *airless injection*; ***solid key, rib, shoot, shot*** (see quots.); ***solid solution***, a solid phase consisting of two or more substances uniformly mixed in proportions that can be varied; also, the state of being a constituent of such a phase; ***solid stowing*** (*Coal Mining*), the process of filling abandoned workings with solid material, esp. spoil; ***solid system*** (*Electr. Engin.*), a system of cable-laying in which insulated cables are laid in a trough which is then filled with bitumen; ***solid tyre***, a tyre made of solid rubber, with no pneumatic cavity; so ***solid-tyred*** adj., fitted with such tyres. See also BASTION 1, NEWEL[1] 1, SQUARE *sb.*

1704 J. HARRIS *Lex. Techn.* I, **Solid Angle*, is an Angle made by the meeting of three or more Planes, and those joining in a Point. 1798 C. HUTTON *Course in Math.* I. 327 Similar Solids, contained by plane figures, are such as have all their solid angles equal..and are bounded by the same number of similar planes. 1814 P. BARLOW *New Math. & Philos. Dict.* s.v., Solid angles may be computed and compared with each other, as to quantity, by considering the angular point as the centre of a sphere, and the portion of its surface intercepted between the bounding planes as the measure of the angles. 1820 N. J. LARKIN *Introd. Solid Geom.* 5 [The tetrahedron] differs from every other solid, whose faces are all equal, by having a solid angle opposite to each face. 1928 *Bureau Standards Jrnl. Res.* (U.S.) I. 34 The integrals are to be evaluated..over the surface of a hemisphere (solid angle $2\pi$). 1948 *Research* I. 394/2 Substances..similar to a black body radiating in a solid angle of $2\pi$. 1836 *Pharm. R. Coll. Physicians* 5 Tolu Balsam, the *solid Balsam. 1958 *Proc. Internat. Symp. Electronic Components, Malvern, 1957* 4 The increasing tempo of work on solid state physics may result in *solid circuits of another form. 1961 *Solid-State Electronics* II. 20/1 Work on solid circuits was begun in the United Kingdom in 1956... The objective is..the fabrication of working circuits using doping, shaping and other techniques in single crystals of silicon. 1966 *New Scientist* 30 June 846/3 (*caption*) Solid-circuit amplifier. The chip measures 0·075 × 0·075 in and contains 30 resistors and 30 transistors. 1913 *Rep. Brit. Assoc. Adv. Sci. 1912* 367 The question whether true *solid diffusion ever occurs in minerals is very difficult to answer. 1947 *Geol. Mag.* LXXXIV. 218 More recent work has shown that such transformations are most easily explained as a result of solid diffusion. 1965 P. C. BADGLEY *Structural & Tectonic Princ.* ix. 346 The advocates of solid diffusion propose..large-scale granitization of country rocks without the presence of contemporary magmatic granites in the district. 1888 JACOBI *Printers' Vocab.* 128 **Solid dig*, a lean or bad 'take' of copy. 1891 H. J. PHILLIPS *Fuels* 1 Determining the value of a *solid fuel such as coal, coke, or patent fuel. 1936 *Archit. Rev.* LXXX. 45/1 In electric fires, Tudor and Adam surrounds flourished, and some characteristics of the traditional solid-fuel fireplace were introduced into the designs. 1952 E. BURGESS *Rocket Propulsion* ii. 38 Most British war rockets employed cordite, whereas America used ballistite for their solid-fuel rockets. 1960 *Which?* Jan. 7/2 In general..the most economic fuels are solid fuel and oil. 1971 P. J. MCMAHON *Aircraft Propulsion* x. 295 The most important factors which have led to the increase in interest in solid fuel rockets in recent years ..have been concerned with the convenience and ease of storage of the solid propellants. 1979 H. MCLEAVE *Borderline Case* xiv. 145 Who had cached these..boots, solid-fuel heater, and two sleeping bags? 1958 *Economist* 13 Dec. 985/2 Work is likely to continue on the Titan as a reinforcement for the Atlas..until the *solid-fuelled Minuteman is ready some years hence. 1972 *Nature* 21 Apr. 368/3 The decision to use a solid fuelled disposable booster for the proposed space shuttle effectively limits the number of possible launch sites to Cape Kennedy and Vandenberg Air Force Base. 1937 J. S. FLETT *First 100 Yrs. Geol. Survey Gt. Brit.* v. 113 Many maps of north Yorkshire were issued only with '*Solid' geology. 1946 L. D. STAMP *Britain's Structure & Scenery* iv. 30 Following the practice of the Geological Survey in some of their detailed maps, there are to be two maps—one to show the 'solid' geology as it would appear if superficial deposits such as boulder clay, glacial sands and gravels and clay-with-flints..were removed and the other to show the 'drift' geology with all those surface deposits indicated. 1970 *Watsonia* VIII. 171 A map of the 'drift' as well as the solid geology would have been valuable. 1915 A. P. CHALKLEY *Diesel Engines for Land & Marine Work* (ed. 4) iii. 122 *Solid injection is now being employed with a large number of engines installed in British submarines. 1936 [see *cold starting* s.v. COLD *a.* 19]. 1969 J. FLACK et al. *Marine Combustion Practice* II. v. 154 Airless or solid injection superseded the blast system... Mechanically operated injectors have given way in their turn to automatic injectors. 1862 *Catal. Internat. Exhib., Brit.* II. No. 6105, The key is what is called '*solid', that is, that the 'bits' or 'steps' are cut on the solid metal of the 'web'. 1782 MONRO *Compar. Anat.* (ed. 3) 167 The eight upper ribs were formerly classed into pairs, with particular names to each two, to wit, the crooked, the *solid [etc.]. 1842 GWILT *Archit.* Gloss. 1033 **Solid Shoot* [= *Square Shoot*, a wooden trough for discharging water from a building]. 1876 VOYLE & STEVENSON *Milit. Dict.* 393/2 **Solid Shot*, projectiles made of solid iron or steel. 1890 *Jrnl. Chem. Soc.* LVIII. 1044 As instances of *solid solutions, we have isomorphous mixtures and mixed crystals, amorphous solutions, as in the case of the glasses and certain minerals; and then such cases as the solution of hydrogen by palladium and other metals. 1900 *Proc. R. Soc.* LXVII. 109 Silver and copper are each capable of holding a small percentage of the other in solid solution, but..if both metals are present in considerable amounts, the two solidified solutions exist side by side. 1964 H. HODGES *Artifacts* xix. 215 In brasses containing less than 36% zinc a solid solution, the $\alpha$-phase, is formed in which the zinc atoms enter the space lattice of the copper. 1977 A. HALLAM *Planet Earth* 119 Such a series is called a solid solution series, and all members have the same crystalline structure. 1929 *Trans. Inst. Mining Engineers* LXXVI. 258 *Solid stowing of the goaf is universal, and in most cases consists of dry stowing done by hand. 1964 *Times Rev. Industry* Feb. 48/3 The industry in this area has pioneered a method of dealing with subsidence known as 'solid stowing' in which colliery spoil is dampened and blown under pressure into abandoned seams. 1977 DOWN & STOCKS *Environmental Impact of Mining* xii. 313 Solid stowing reduces *a* [*sc.* the 'subsidence factor'] to about 0·4–0·5. 1891 *Electr. Engineer* 30 Jan. 121/2 In the Callender *Solid system the insulated cables are laid in an iron trough and the whole filled in solid with melted bitumen. 1898 [see BUILT *ppl. a.* 1 b]. 1920 *Whittaker's Electr. Engineer's Pocket-bk.* (ed. 4) 352 The B.O.T. raise no objection to the omission of the copper tape on unarmoured cables laid on the solid system; a great deal of such cable is in use without any leakage trouble. 1953 C. C. BARNES *Power Cables* xv. 154 The solid system is more expensive than burying cables direct in the ground and requires a greater measure of skilled supervision and favourable weather conditions... For the above reasons the solid system is seldom used today. 1891 *Bicycling News* 31 Jan. 77/1 Given a *solid tyre..it will be found that about one half of its diameter is available for tractive and cushioning purposes. 1895 G. B. SHAW *Let.* 6 Aug. (1965) I. 540 It would be a bad machine even of its own kind, the art of building for solid tyres being a decaying one. 1946 W. H. CROUSE *Automobile Engin.* xxvii. 572 Solid tires have very limited usage, their use being confined largely to specialized industrial applications. 1891 *Solid-tyred [see PNEUMATIC *sb.* 3 a]. 1963 BIRD & HUTTON-STOTT *Veteran Motor Car* 17 A horizontal-engined, twin-cylinder, chain-driven, solid-tyred 'dog-cart' was in production by the end of the year.

**23.** *Comb.* **a.** Forming parasynthetic adjs., as ***solid-billed, -browed, -coloured, -headed***, etc. Also *solid-fuelled* (see sense 22), *-tyred* (see sense 22).

*c* **1611** CHAPMAN *Iliad* VIII. 323 When to the solid-ported depths of hell his sonne was sent. **1854** *Orr's Circle Sci., Org. Nat.* I. 239 The ruminants of the deer and elk tribes are those which have antlers, or are 'solid-horned'. **1862** *Catal. Internat. Exhib., Brit.* II. No. 6112, Solid-headed pins. **1876** GEO. ELIOT *Dan. Der.* I. i. 13 A gentleman—solid-browed, stiff and German. **1890** *Cent. Mag.* May 50/1 The White and Black Leghorns are solid-colored birds. **1895** LYDEKKER *Roy. Nat. Hist.* IV. 68 The beak of the solid-billed hornbill (*Rhinoplax vigil*) has..a perfectly solid casque.

**b.** With pples., as ***solid-looking***, ***-seeming***, ***-set***; also ***solid-full*** adj.; **solid-drawn** *a.*, made or shaped by deep drawing (see DEEP *a.* IV. c).

**1888** *Lockwood's Dict. Mech. Engin. Terms* 335 The copper piping for feed, bilge, blow-off, and similar purposes in connection with marine engines..are all solid drawn. **1909** F. W. RAYNES *Domestic Sanitary Engin. & Plumbing* vii. 167 Solid drawn lead pipes have many advantages as soil pipes. **1966** A. W. LEWIS *Gloss. Woodworking Terms* 47 Best-quality brass hinges are 'solid drawn' because they are made by the leaf and the tube for the knuckle being drawn out in a long solid strip which is then cut off into lengths. **1887** GOODE, etc. *Fisheries U.S.* v. II. 579 They hove their dredges,..and when they hauled them in, found them solid-full of scallops. **1840** POE in *Graham's Mag.* Dec. 268/1 These were known by their coats and pantaloons of black or brown..with white cravats and waistcoats, broad solid-looking shoes, and thick hose. **1883** HUXLEY *Pract. Biol.* 23 A roundish more solid-looking particle. **1831** CARLYLE *Sart. Res.* I. viii, This so solid-seeming World. **1877** E. R. CONDER *Basis of Faith* ii. 81 The solid-seeming rock is beheld as a flexible..collection of molecules. **1850** TENNYSON *In Mem.* Concl. iv, Like a statue solid-set, And moulded in colossal calm.

**c.** With sbs., forming attributive compounds, as ***solid-colour***, ***-ink***, ***-propellant***, etc. **solid-shot** *U.S.* (see quot. 1949).

**1883** *Stationer & Bookseller* 8 May 35 Solid-ink Fountain Pens. **1884** KNIGHT *Dict. Mech.* Suppl., *Solid Plate Saw*, a circular saw made of a single plate, as distinguished from a segment saw. **1891** *Cent. Dict.*, Solid-color porcelains. **1946** *Jrnl. Brit. Interplanetary Soc.* VI. 45 The missile is driven by a solid-propellant rocket unit. **1961** Solid-propellant [see APOGEE 4]. **1982** *Navy News* Mar. 18/3 The missiles would be accelerated from rest by two solid-propellant boosters. **1935** *Daily Progress* (Charlottesville, Va.) 25 July 1/5 'Solid shot' votes are within the law in primaries as well as in general elections. **1949** *Richmond* (Va.) *Times-Dispatch* 25 Nov. 4/5 Under the 'solid-shot' method a voter casts his ballot for a single candidate when two or more persons are to be elected to the same office. **1897** *Outing* XXX. 350/1 The club won a handsome solid-silver cup at Long Branch. **1906** E. JOHNSTON *Writing and Illuminating* xii. 213 A solid-stem pattern cuts up the ground into small pieces. **1961** *B.S.I. News* July 23/2 Solid-stem calorimeter thermometers.

**Solidago** (sɒlɪ'deɪgəʊ). [med.L. (but with different application: see the note to CONSOUDE).] **a.** A large genus of perennial plants of the N.O. *Compositæ*, the N. American species of which are especially numerous; golden-rod. **b.** A plant of this genus, esp. *S. virgaurea*, a European and British species, formerly in repute for its medicinal properties, now largely cultivated as a garden flower.

**1771** *Encycl. Brit.* III. 617/1. **1858** A. IRVINE *Handbk. Brit. Plants* 524 *Solidago*,..Golden-Rod. A numerous genus, chiefly American, agreeing in habit, foliage, and flowers with *Aster*, only the flowers of the ray are not blue, ..but yellow, and sometimes white. **1883** *Cent. Mag.* Sept. 723/2 No one would have thought of painting pictures of solidagos on plush for a portière.

‖**solidaire** (sɒlɪ'dɛə(r)), *a.* [Fr.] = SOLIDARY *a.* 2.

**1845** MACAULAY *Let.* 1 Mar. (1977) IV. 244, I certainly did suppose that you considered yourself as solidaire for doctrines which the cabinet has repeatedly and emphatically proclaimed. **1877** W. R. ALGER *Life of Edwin Forrest* I. i. 25 When volition put rigidity into his muscles the centre was solidaire with the periphery. **1942** WYNDHAM LEWIS *Let.* 27 Jan. (1963) 316 But one cannot help feeling *solidaire* with the nation to which one belongs. **1962** *Times Lit. Suppl.* 3 Aug. 556/2 They must be made not 'solidaire' (to use M. Neveux's words) in a shared, superior understanding of the plight of the figure on the stage, but made 'solitaire' as they realize that they each, alone, share his fate.

†**solidare.** *Obs.*$^{-1}$ (An irreg. formation on L. *solid-us* SOLIDUS[1]; perh. an error.)

**1607** SHAKS. *Timon* III. i. 46 Thou know'st well enough.. that this is no time to lend money... Here's three Solidares for thee.

**soli'daric**, *a.* [f. SOLIDAR-ITY + -IC. Cf. F. *solidaire*.] Characterized by solidarity or community of interests. So **'solidarism**, a theory of social organization based on solidarity of interests.

**1874** LANGE *Comm. Zephaniah* 28 The solidaric connection of the false Gods with the kingdom of Satan. **1894** *Thinker* VI. 72 The central position of Christ in regard to humanity, and His solidaric fellowship with it as its head. **1906** E. KELLY *Progr. Working Men* II. ii. 113 The main object to be secured will be described as Solidarity; those who want to secure it as Solidarists, and the doctrine itself as Solidarism.

**'soli,darily**, *adv.* [f. SOLIDARY *a.* + -LY[2].] In a solidary manner; with solidarity.

**1870** *Pall Mall G.* 25 Aug. 4 It would not be well to make the French living in Germany responsible for the misdeed, but France herself ought to be made to answer solidarily for it. **1892** *Temple Bar* June 156 It belongs to us..as a community, and we are collectively and—what is the word?—solidarily responsible for its use.

**solidarist** ('sɒlɪdərɪst), *sb.* (and *a.*) [f. SOLIDARITY + -IST.] A believer in or advocate of solidarism. Also *attrib.* or as *adj.* Hence **solida'ristic** a.

**1884** C. POWER *Philistia* I. i. 4 The polyglot crowd of democratic solidarists. **1957** [see PERSONALISM b]. **1968** *Economist* 28 Dec. 27/3 Further evidence of an 'instrumental collectivism' as opposed to a traditional 'solidaristic collectivism'. **1969** P. WORSLEY in Ionescu & Gellner *Populism* 224 These independent commodity-producers.. were not simply 'petty-bourgeois' individualists, as..their solidarist political associations demonstrate. **1974** B. JESSOP *Traditionalism, Conservatism & Brit. Pol. Culture* ii. 32 The distinctive attribute of secular voters is an absence of solidaristic class consciousness rather than commitment to deferential norms.

**solidarity** (sɒlɪ'dærɪtɪ). [ad. F. *solidarité*, f. *solidaire* solid: see SOLIDARY *a.*]

**1. a.** The fact or quality, on the part of communities, etc., of being perfectly united or at one in some respect, esp. in interests, sympathies, or aspirations; *spec.* with reference to the aspirations or actions of trade-union members. Also *attrib.* and *Comb.*

The French origin of the word is freq. referred to during the period of its introduction into English use. Latterly also the English rendering of Polish *Solidarność*, the name of an independent trade-union movement in Poland, registered in September 1980 and officially banned in October 1982.

**1841** H. DOHERTY *False Assoc. & its Remedy* 24 Solidarity, Solidary. Collective responsibility. Collectively responsible. **1848** *People's Press* II. 161/2 Solidarity is a word of French origin, the naturalisation of which, in this country, is desirable. **1848** GALLENGA *Italy* 429 Actuated.. by a feeling of national *solidarity*—to borrow a French word—which induced all of them to run the same risk. **1856** EMERSON *Eng. Traits* v. 103 One secret of their power is their mutual good understanding... They have solidarity, or responsibleness, and trust in each other. **1877** BROCKETT *Cross & Crescent* 157 Each is responsible to the Czar, but they have no sort of solidarity. **1885** *To-day* III. 83 [Strike manifesto] But if, on the contrary, you design this strike as a step toward a final and definite solution of the great labour question, if you would make it the means of teaching the worker the absolute necessity of combination and of unity, if having secured the adoption of Solidarity you will build upon this a superstructure of Education, if you will learn why you are poor, [etc.]. **1962** *Listener* 31 May 935/1 These gangs have group-cohesiveness (in our present jargon) or solidarity (in socialist jargon), but they are against society. **1963** *Daily Tel.* 5 Feb. 10/2 Twice as many countries are attending this conference as were at the Afro-Asian States conference in Bandung in 1955; but the great difference is that those now meeting are merely 'solidarity organisations'. **1968** *Listener* 6 June 713/1 Well before the last election, sociologists were telling us that an increasing number of working-class people were beginning to look at politics instrumentally rather than in terms of class solidarity or ideological allegiance. **1969** *Ibid.* 30 Jan. 131/3 Afro-Asian Peoples Solidarity Committees display predictable signs at air-ports. **1971** I. DEUTSCHER *Marxism in our Time* (1972) v. 109 The perennial conflict between national egoism and international solidarity becomes more and more visible. **1974** *Socialist Worker* 9 Nov. 6/4 The building workers called a solidarity strike. **1977** *Time* 4 July 7/3 In the months since then, Soviet ideologues have opened a campaign to increase 'fidelity to the principles of inter-nationalist solidarity'—party jargon for rallying round Moscow's flag. **1979** *Time* 13 Aug. 12/3 'Solidarity' marchers arrived from Sanandaj, the Kurds' provincial capital. **1980** *Times* 26 Sept. 6/4 The Warsaw daily *Zycie Warszawy* quoted members of the Solidarity free trade union movement as rejecting reforms of the old unions as mere name-changing. **1980** *Economist* 18 Oct. 46/1 Over 20 unions, including Mr Lech Walesa's Gdansk-based Solidarity (an umbrella organisation representing 50 small unions, and claiming a total membership of over 4m), have applied to register with the courts in Warsaw. **1982** *Times* 9 Oct. 1/5 The Polish Parliament..yesterday voted..for a new trade union law that sounds the death knell of Solidarity. *Ibid.*, In broad outline, the bill dissolves all registered trade unions including Solidarity.

*transf.* **1876** FARRAR *Marlb. Serm.* xxxii. (1877) 321 Knowing..that there is a solidarity in the virtues as in the vices. **1881** *Nature* No. 617. 397 When we thus effect a re-classification of elementary bodies, the solidarity at once breaks down.

**b.** Const. *of* (mankind, a race, etc.).

**1852** *Fraser's Mag.* Jan. 28 We have hived up one of his phrases..—the 'solidarity of the peoples!' **1853** TRENCH *Less. Prov.* 29 The 'solidarity' (to use a word which it is in vain to strive against) of all the nations of Christendom. **1884** S. E. DAWSON *Handbk. Canada* 107 The grand idea of the solidarity of England and the English race through-out the world.

*transf.* **1867** M. ARNOLD *Celtic Lit.* 68 The solidarity, to use that convenient French word, of Breton and Welsh poetry. **1876** L. STEPHEN *Hist. Eng. Th. 18th C.* I. 220 Disputing the solidarity of all the writers of Targums.

**c.** Const. *between* or *with* (others). Also *transf.*

(*a*) **1860** MARSH *Lect. Eng. Lang.* 284 The organs of speech act and react upon each other;..there is, to use a word, which if not now English soon will be, a certain solidarity between them all. **1875** STUBBS *Const. Hist.* xvi. II. 310 There was what is called, in modern phrase, solidarity between him and his people. **1898** *Allbutt's Syst. Med.* V. 67 The solidarity existing between all parts of the lung.

(*b*) **1862** GRATTAN *Beaten Paths* II. 378 Would he not have found his best policy..[in] an alliance, if not quite a solidarity, with England? **1865** E. LUCAS in Manning *Ess. Relig. & Lit.* 374 To refuse any solidarity whatever with it. **1884** *L'pool Mercury* 18 Feb. 5/2 The member for Woodstock..here repudiates all solidarity with his leaders.

**2.** Community or perfect coincidence *of* (or *between*) interests.

**1874** LADY HERBERT tr. *Hübner's Ramble* II. ii. (1878) 518 To establish a solidarity between their commercial interests. **1876** *Contemp. Rev.* June 138 The cry was raised as to the solidarity of the Conservative interests. **1890** GROSS *Gild Merch.* I. 97 A compact body emphatically characterized by fraternal solidarity of interests.

**3.** *Civil Law.* A form of obligation involving joint and several responsibilities or rights.

**1875** POSTE *Gaius* III. 396 Correality and Solidarity agree in this, that in both of them every creditor is severally entitled to receive the whole object of the active obligation, and every debtor is bound to discharge the whole object of the passive obligation.

**'solidarize**, *v. rare.* [ad. F. *solidariser*: see prec. and -IZE.] *trans.* or *refl.* To bring to solidarity. Hence **'solidarizing** *ppl. a.*

**1886** *Pictorial World* 8 Apr. 328 An arrangement of solid facts and figures to prove the..solidarising effects of American republican institutions over those of the Britisher. **1888** *Standard* 4 Feb. 5/6 Germany has, in a measure, solidarized herself with Austria, and that solidarity has its charges.

**solidary** ('sɒlɪdərɪ), *a.* [ad. F. *solidaire*: see SOLID *a.* and -ARY.]

**1.** *Civil Law.* Joint and several.

**1818** COLEBROOKE *Obligations* xiv. 149 The solidary obligation can hardly arise, without such an express provision. **1875** POSTE *Gaius* III. 398 Election to sue the principal debtor discharges a Correal surety.., but not a Solidary surety. **1895** *Law Times* XCIX. 465/1 Anyone who has grasped the difference between a correal and a solidary obligation.

**2.** Characterized by or having solidarity or community of interests.

**1841** [see SOLIDARITY 1]. **1848** *Tait's Mag.* XV. 251 Regarding as solidary, or indissolubly connected together, all the members of the great human family. **1867** VISCT. STRANGFORD *Selection* (1869) II. 64 A struggling Christian population, solidary in sentiment and interest with all other Christian populations in Turkey.

**solidate** ('sɒlɪdeɪt), *sb.* Now *Hist.* [ad. med.L. *solidāta* (*terræ*), f. *solid-us* SOLIDUS[1].] A piece of land of the annual value of a solidus or shilling.

**1610** FOLKINGHAM *Art Surv.* II. vii. 58 There be also other quantities of Land taking their denominations from our vsual Coine; as..Obolates, Denariates, Solidates. *Ibid.* 59 Then must the Obolat be ½ Acre, the Denariat an Acre, the Solidat 12. acres. **1845** NICOLAS *Mem. Chaucer* in *C.'s Wks.* I. 31 On the 28th of December 1375 the King granted Chaucer the custody of five 'solidates' of rent in Solys in Kent. **1882** *Proc. Berwick. Nat. Club* IX. 469 Its master held a hundred solidates of land in pure alms.

†**solidate**, *pa. pple. Obs.* [ad. L. *solidāt-us*, pa. pple. of *solidāre*: see next.] Solid, hard.

**1542** BOORDE *Dyetary* xiii. (1870) 268 So be it that the fysshe be softe and not solydat. *Ibid.*

**'solidate**, *v.* Now *rare.* [f. L. *solidāt-*, ppl. stem of *solidāre* to make solid.]

**1.** *trans.* To make solid or firm; to consolidate. Also *fig.*

**1640** C. HARVEY *Synagogue, Church-Porch* viii, Remember that humility Must solidate and keep all close together. **1650** FULLER *Pisgah* IV. iv. 69 Many being much troubled..how so brickle matter [looking-glasses] when broken could be made usefull, and solidated for this service. **1656** COWLEY *Pindar. Odes, Muse* 67 Wks. (Grosart) II. 18 This shining Piece of Ice Which melts so soon away With the Sun's Ray, Thy Verse does solidate and crystallize. **1894** G. M. FENN *In Alpine Valley* i. 65 On either hand it [i.e. snow] had been solidated by pressure.

†**2.** = CONSOLIDATE *v.* 4. *Obs.*

**1657** TOMLINSON *Renou's Disp.* 31 That..which is effectuall in solidating broken bones. **1684** tr. *Bonet's Merc. Compit.* III. 77 It can..solidate the Bones, which we daily see in other fractures.

†**solidation.** *Obs. rare.* [ad. L. *solidātiōn-em*, f. *solidāre*: see prec. Cf. OF. *solidation*.] Consolidation, strengthening, etc.

**1547** BOORDE *Introd. Knowl.* i. (1870) 121 They stande many a hondred yeares, hauyng no reparacion nor no solidacion of morter. **1656** BLOUNT *Glossogr.*, *Solidation*, a making whole or firm, a soldering.

†**solidatively**, *adv. Obs.*$^{-1}$ [f. OF. *solidatif*, *-ive* + -LY[2].] Solidly.

**1541** R. COPLAND *Guydon's Quest.* D ij b, They [i.e. bones] that haue neyther one nor other ben ioyned solidatiuely.

**solid-hoofed**, *a.* [f. SOLID *a.* 23 a.] Having the hoof whole or undivided; solidungulate, soliped; *spec.* as the designation of certain swine.

**1842** PRICHARD *Nat. Hist. Man* 32 There are breeds of solid-hoofed swine in some parts of England. **1848** BUCKLEY *Iliad* 87 Lest the son of Tydeus should drive away thy solid-hoofed steeds. **1864** BOWEN *Logic* vii. 203 Some herbivora are solid-hoofed. *c* **1880** *Cassell's Nat. Hist.* II. 343 The Solid-hoofed Pigs..show a persistent variation from the even-toed type.

So **solid-hooved** *a.*

**1910** THOMPSON *Aristotle's Hist. Anim.* II. 1 There are in Illyria and in Paeonia and elsewhere solid-hooved swine.

**solidifiable** (sə,lɪdɪ'faɪəb(ə)l), *a.* [f. SOLIDIFY *v.* + -ABLE.] That may be solidified; capable of solidification.

**1858** H. SPENCER *Ess.* I. 5 A..deposition of all solidifiable elements contained in the atmosphere. **1876** GROSS *Dis.*

*Urinary Organs* 186 The manner in which a clot of blood.. detains the solidifiable ingredients.

**solidification** (sə,lɪdɪfɪ'keɪʃən). [f. SOLIDIFY *v.* (see -ATION), or a. F. *solidification*.]

**1.** The action or process of solidifying or becoming solid.

**1811** A. T. THOMSON *Lond. Disp.* (1818) p. xxvii, The solidification of the water when it unites with the lime. **1843** R. J. GRAVES *Syst. Clin. Med.* xx. 242 The diseased lung, whose specific gravity has been much increased by solidification. **1880** C. R. MARKHAM *Peruv. Bark* 188 In the cooling and solidification of granite the quartz is the last mineral element to crystallise and become solid.

*transf.* **1875** JOWETT *Plato* (ed. 2) IV. 273 Force [may be conceived] as the materializing or solidification of motion.

**2.** Consolidation, concentration.

**1891** *Cycl. Temp. & Prohib.* 574/2 There was an increasing realization of the value of solidification and discipline.

**so'lidified,** *ppl. a.* [f. SOLIDIFY *v.*] Rendered solid or compact; changed from a liquid to a solid state.

**1831** R. KNOX *Cloquet's Anat.* 96 A very thick and solidified cranium, in which all the holes which commonly give passage to nerves were obliterated. **1848** CARPENTER *Anim. Phys.* 28 The greater part of the animal tissues seems composed of solidified fibrin. **1858** SIMMONDS *Dict. Trade*, *Solidified milk*, concentrated or preserved milk for use at sea. **1889** WELCH *Text Bk. Naval Archit.* i. 7 The solidified water again becomes liquid.

**so'lidifier.** [f. as prec.] That which solidifies; a consolidator.

**1863** DANA *Man. Geol.* 52 Acting as a general cement and solidifier. **1894** DRUMMOND *Ascent of Man* 269 [War] the purifier of societies, the solidifier of states.

**so'lidiform.** *nonce-word.* [f. SOLID *a.*] A solid body.

**1849** POE *Wks.* (1865) II. 396 He informed us all.. about äeriforms, fluidiforms, and solidiforms.

**solidify** (sə'lɪdɪfaɪ), *v.* [ad. F. *solidifier*: see SOLID *a.* and -(I)FY.]

**1.** *trans.* To render solid; to convert into a solid body; to make firm, hard, or compact.

**1799** KIRWAN *Geol. Ess.* 125 In these cases the water seems to be solidified by a loss of great part of its specific heat. **1807** T. THOMSON *Chem.* (ed. 3) II. 625 This powder ..absorbs water very rapidly, and solidifies it. **1854** RONALDS & RICHARDSON *Chem. Technol.* (ed. 2) I. 148 The pressing machine for solidifying the fuel. **1871** B. STEWART *Heat* §84 Although we cannot as yet solidify alcohol.

*fig.* **1858** HAWTHORNE *Fr. & It. Note-bks.* (1872) II. 223 The difficulty of retaining it in the mind and solidifying it into a description. **1866** *Cornh. Mag.* Oct. 413 He could not solidify the prejudices of the mass. **1889** 'MARK TWAIN' *Yankee at Crt. K. Arth.* viii, The tower episode solidified my power.

**b.** *transf.* To concentrate or consolidate.

**1885** *Manch. Wkly. Times* 20 June 5/5 Disraeli.. sought to solidify them into a party. **1885** *Pall Mall G.* 25 Feb. 10/2 Organizing and solidifying the Liberal vote in the new constituency.

**2.** *intr.* To become solid; to change or pass from a liquid or gaseous to a solid state.

**1837** J. T. SMITH tr. *Vicat's Mortars* 40 In the condition of very stiff paste.. they.. solidify more quickly. **1860** TYNDALL *Glac.* II. xxxi. 409 If.. molten [bismuth].. be poured into a bullet-mould it will expand on solidifying. **1878** HUXLEY *Physiogr.* 60 Water solidifies by reduction of temperature.

Hence **so'lidifying** *vbl. sb.* and *ppl. a.*

**1850** GROVE *Corr. Phys. Forces* (ed. 2) 36 The freezing or solidifying point. **1856** *Orr's Circ. Sci., Pract. Chem.* 469 Oil of poppies retards the solidifying effect.

†**so'lidiousness.** *Obs.*$^{-1}$ [f. SOLID *a.*] Solidity.

**1398** TREVISA *Barth. De P.R.* XVI. lxviii. (1495) 575 For colidnesse and solidiousnesse therof [marble].

†**so'lidipede.** *Obs.*$^{-1}$ [ad. L. *solidipēs, -ped-is* whole-hoofed.] = SOLIPED *sb.*

**1661** LOVELL *Hist. Anim. & Min.* Isagoge a iv, Four-footed beasts.. are. I. Solidipedes, having whole hoofes.

So †**soli'dipedous** *a. Obs.*$^{-1}$ = SOLIPEDOUS *a.*

**1712** J. MORTON *Nat. Hist. Northampt.* 454 The Solipidous [*errata* Solidipedous] or Whole-Hoof'd Kind.

**'solidish,** *a.* [f. SOLID *a.*] Somewhat solid.

**1852** CLOUGH *Poems*, etc. (1869) I. 178 We found our way to the house he used to occupy—a solidish red-brick place.

**solidism** ('sɒlɪdɪz(ə)m). *Med.* [f. SOLID *sb.* + -ISM: cf. F. *solidisme*.] The doctrine or theory which refers all diseases to the state of, or to morbid changes in, the solid parts of the body.

**1832** *Edin. Rev.* LV. 468 Sometimes Humorism, sometimes Solidism seems to be favoured. *a* **1862** BUCKLE *Civiliz.* (1869) III. 419 Cullen.. having built up that system of pathology which is known to medical writers as Solidism.

**solidist** ('sɒlɪdɪst). *Med.* [Cf. prec. and -IST. So F. *solidiste*.] One who believes in or holds the doctrine of solidism.

**1842** *Penny Cycl.* XXIII. 400/1 The doctrines of the fluidists.., of the vitalists and solidists. **1876** tr. *Wagner's Gen. Pathol.* 5 Physicians have distinguished themselves as Humoralists or Solidists.

Hence **soli'distic** *a.*, of or pertaining to the solidists or their theory.

**1876** tr. *Wagner's Gen. Pathol.* 517 We nearly always discover that diseases of tissues and organs cause anomalies of the blood (solidistic pathology as opposed to humoralistic pathology). **1889** *Lancet* 30 Nov. 1123 The 'solidistic' notion of the all-pervading influence of the nervous system.

**solidity** (sə'lɪdɪtɪ). Also 6 solidyte, 6–7 soliditie. [ad. F. *solidité* (= It. *solidità*) or L. *soliditāt-em*, f. *solidus* SOLID: see -ITY.]

**1. a.** The quality of being solid or substantial, in various figurative or transferred senses.

**1532** MORE *Confut. Tindale* Wks. 720/2 The trouth of Goddes woorde.. hath his solidyte, substaunce and fastnesse of and in it selfe. *a* **1610** HEALEY *Cebes* (1636) 150 The genius bids them, never give credence unto her, never to imagine any solidity in her bounties. **1647** CLARENDON *Hist. Reb.* I. §166 No Kingdom.. in the solidity.. of the Laws.. was more Secure than England. **1788** JEFFERSON *Writ.* (1859) II. 542 Assure me of the solidity of your recovery. **1804** GOUV. MORRIS in Sparks *Life & Writ.* (1832) III. 213 Prussia has grown up so fast that there is a want of solidity. **1866** SEELEY *Ecce Homo* iv. (ed. 8) 36 Human relations gained a solidity and permanence which they had never before seemed to have. **1871** TYNDALL *Fragm. Sci.* (1879) II. ii. 39 That unsubstantial pageant of the imagination to which the solidity of science is opposed.

**b.** Of persons, in respect of learning, judgement, character, etc.

**1607** TOPSELL *Four-f. Beasts* (1658) 495 Now I know such is the solidity of divers Readers and people, that [etc.]. *a* **1661** FULLER *Worthies* (1840) II. 14 Men resembled him to one of the ships-royal.. called the Swiftsure, such his celerity and solidity in all affairs. **1695** LD. PRESTON *Boethius* IV. pr. i. (1712) 176 These.. things.. may put an end to thy Complaints, and strengthen thee with all Firmness and Solidity. **1723** WODROW *Corr.* (1843) III. 33 The King expressed at that time an uncommon esteem of Mr. Henderson for his learning, piety, and solidity. **1756** MRS. CALDERWOOD in *Coltness Collect.* (Maitl. Cl.) 148 One must admire them for their solidity, industry, and pains-taking in every thing. **1821** RICH *Journ. Persepolis* 12 Sept. in *Babylon & P.* (1839) 268 The Persians are unthinking, perpetually joking, and deficient in solidity. **1869** M<sup></sup>CLAREN *Serm.* Ser. II. vii. 120 Without that armour, there will not be solidity enough in our character.

**c.** Of argument, demonstration, etc.

**1646** SIR T. BROWNE *Pseud. Ep.* I. vi. (1686) 15 Establishing their assertions with great solidity. **1667** POOLE *Dial. betw. Protest. & Papist* (1735) 70 Not for any Solidity of Argument (that had been pedantick). **1677** OWEN *On Justific.* xii. Wks. 1851 III. 263 Such niceties have more of philosophical subtlety than theological solidity in them. **1775** JOHNSON in *Boswell* (Oxf. ed.) I. 560 That the Colonists could with no solidity argue.. that they should not now be taxed. **1826** KENT *Comm.* 19 In cases where the principal jurists agree, the presumption will be very great in favor of the solidity of their maxims. **1865** PUSEY *Truth Eng. Ch.* 136 A remarkable response, objecting to the decree with much solidity and clearness.

**d.** Of judgement.

**1727** BAILEY (vol. II), *Soundness*,.. Solidity of Judgment. **1774** REID *Aristotle's Logic* ii. §2. 28 In proportion to the solidity and accuracy of a man's judgment. **1796** MORSE *Amer. Geogr.* I. 23 Good sense, perspicuity, accuracy, and solidity of judgment. **1882** HINSDALE *Garfield & Educ.* I. 116 Close observation, high analytical.. ability, solidity of judgment.

**2. a.** The quality or condition of being materially solid; compactness and firmness of texture, structure, etc. Also *fig.*

**1603** HOLLAND *Plutarch's Mor.* 1302 A land altogether barren and unfruitfull, by reason of hardnesse and stiffe soliditie. **1615** G. SANDYS *Trav.* 238 Tunnie;.. in taste something resembling flesh, as in colour and soliditie. **1663** S. PATRICK *Parab. Pilgr.* (1687) 381 We may discern between hardness and softness, a middle temperament, which is called solidity and firmness. **1704** NORRIS *Ideal World* II. i. 46 Solidity, according to the vulgar and popular sense of it, wherein it is used for hardness. **1774** GOLDSM. *Nat. Hist.* (1776) VI. 213 They have the solidity of the hardest bone. **1841** T. R. JONES *Anim. Kingd.* 446 A fibro-cartilaginous substance.. fills the interior of each mandible, and thus gives it sufficient solidity for all required purposes. **1842** LOVER *Handy Andy* ix, When they came to take the hay-stack to pieces, the solidity of its centre rather astonished them.

**b.** Of buildings, edifices, etc.

**1662** GERBIER *Principles* Title-p., The three chief Principles of Magnificent Building, *viz.* Solidity, Conveniency, and Ornament. **1790** BURKE *Fr. Rev.* 72 They load the edifice of society, by setting up in the air what the solidity of the structure requires to be on the ground. **1833** RITCHIE *Wand. Loire* 25 The château.. strikes the spectator by its solidity and magnificence. **1867** EMERSON *Lett. & Soc. Aims* Wks. (Bohn) III. 227 Our.. architecture [is] tent-like, when compared with the monumental solidity of mediæval ..remains in Europe and Asia.

**3. a.** *Geom.* The amount of space occupied by a solid body; volume, cubic or solid content.

**1570** DEE *Math. Pref.* a iij b, To vnderstand the Soliditie, and content of any bodily thing. **1642** H. MORE *Song of Soul* II. I. ii. 42 [The soul] finds out Phæbus vast soliditie By his diametre. **1674** JEAKE *Arith.* (1696) 524 If a Right Cylinder have the Diameter 14, and the Height.. as much; then shall the Area of each Base be 154,.. and the Solidity 2156. **1743** EMERSON *Fluxions* 127 To find a Cone of the greatest Solidity under a given convex Surface and Base *b*. **1825** J. NICHOLSON *Operat. Mechanic* 551 Find the solidity of the trench in cubic feet, and divide it by 27. **1834–47** J. S. MACAULAY *Field Fortif.* (1851) 304 The solidity of the frustrum will be equal to the solidity of the whole cone.

**b.** Relative density or mass.

**1698** KEILL *Exam. Th. Earth* (1734) 33 The surfaces of bodies not increasing in the same proportion with their solidities or weights. **1718** QUINCY *Compl. Disp.* 2 Attraction in all Bodies is *cæteris paribus* as their Solidities. **1740** CHEYNE *Regimen* 2 It is probable, that animated Bodies act according to their Solidities.

**c.** The ratio of the area of the blades of a propeller (counting one side only) to the area of the circle they turn in.

**1926** H. GLAUERT *Elements Aerofoil & Airscrew Theory* xvi. 213 This quantity σ represents the ratio of the area of the blade elements to the area of the annulus at the radial distance *r*, and may be termed the solidity of the blade element. **1953** D. O. DOMMASCH *Elem. Propeller & Helicopter Aerodynamics* ii. 61 As far as propeller operation is concerned, increasing solidity has much the same effect as decreasing the aspect ratio of the wing. **1980** *Sci. Amer.* July 114/2 The twin screws of the 31-knot *Queen Elizabeth 2*, each of which absorbs 55,000 h.p., are appreciably smaller, turn much faster and have an even greater solidity than the screws of the largest tankers.

**4. a.** The property of occupying a certain amount of space.

**1690** LOCKE *Hum. Und.* II. iv. (1695) 52 That which thus hinders the approach of two Bodies, when they are moving one towards another, I call Solidity. **1777** PRIESTLEY *Phil. Necess.* 177 A substance that has no properties besides extension and solidity. **1815** J. SMITH *Panorama Sci. & Art* I. 270 The solidity of matter.. expresses that property which every body possesses of not permitting any other body to occupy the same place with it at the same time. **1884** tr. *Lotze's Metaph.* 304 He mentions Lambert's account of Solidity as a necessary property of all material existence.

**b.** Extension in the three dimensions of space.

**1855** BAIN *Senses & Int.* II. ii. §5 It is this dissimilarity of the pictures that is the chief optical sign of solidity or of three dimensions. **1886** SULLY *Handbk. Psychol.* viii. 140 That the eye has little knowledge of solidity.

**5.** A solid thing or body. Also *fig.*

**1602** SHAKS. *Ham.* III. iv. 49 Heauens face doth glow, Yea this solidity and compound masse.. Is thought-sicke. **1665** *Surv. Affaires of Netherlands* 195 Their Apparel was plain, and their Ambition onely upon Realities and Solidities. **1728** R. MORRIS *Ess. Anc. Archit.* 43 It has a greater Force to sustain the Solidity it supports. **1771** LUCKOMBE *Hist. Print.* 324 By convenience is meant a firm solidity to place the end of the Braces against. **1844** HOOD *The Turtles* 36 Fruits, victual, drink, solidities, or slops. **1866** GEO. ELIOT *F. Holt* ix, A man.. owed a great deal more to himself as the mainstay of all those solidities, than to feelings.. quite unsubstantial.

**6.** = SOLIDARITY 3.

**1706** tr. *Dupin's Eccl. Hist. 16th C.* II. IV. ix. 431 *note*, Solidity in the French Law is a joint Obligation entred into by several Creditors, by which every one of the Obligees binds himself to pay what they all owe in Common, upon the default of the rest. **1818** COLEBROOKE *Obligations* xiv. 149 This solidity in respect of creditors is very rare: it is not to be confounded with indivisibility of obligation. *Ibid.*, The effects of solidity towards creditors, when it does occur, are as follow. Each of the creditors, being so for the whole, may consequently demand the whole [etc.].

**solidly** ('sɒlɪdlɪ), *adv.* [f. SOLID *a.* + -LY[2].] In a solid manner.

**1.** So as to be fixed or firm; firmly, securely.

*c* **1611** CHAPMAN *Iliad* XIV. *comm.*, Hector.. standing it so solidly; for without that consideration, the stone could neuer haue recoild so fiercely. *a* **1700** EVELYN *Diary* 20 Nov. 1644, The stone is.. now cracked in many places, but solidly joyn'd. **1868** MORRIS *Earthly Par.* (1870) I. I. 279 Who on the altar fixed it [an image] solidly Against the beating of the winds and waves. **1889** *Anthony's Photogr. Bulletin* II. 403 The hyposulphite of soda is held pretty solidly by the gelatine.

*Comb.* **1861** FLOR. NIGHTINGALE *Nursing* (ed. 2) 42 In the solidly built old houses.

**b.** *transf.* or *fig.* (esp. with *found, establish*).

**1637–50** ROW *Hist. Kirk* (Wodrow Soc.) 332 Learned men finding Paræus's doctrine to be solidlie founded upon the trueth of God. **1673** S. C. *Art of Complaisance* vi. 54 This vertue.. upon which all the commerce of this life might be very solidly establish'd. *a* **1797** WALPOLE *Mem. Geo. II* (1847) I. i. 3 His brother's jealousy was solidly grounded. **1813** SIR R. WILSON *Priv. Diary* (1862) II. 445 Now Switzerland can be solidly linked in the connection of independent nations. **1884** *Kendal Mercury & Times* 31 Oct. 4/7 All this.. will serve only to weld the followers of Mr. Gladstone more solidly together.

**2.** With solid or valid arguments or reasons; on solid or good grounds.

Freq. in the 17th cent.

**1625–8** tr. *Camden's Hist. Elizabeth* III. (1688) 289 Their Books were.. solidly confuted by Learned men. **1651** BAXTER *Inf. Bapt.* 275 Determining it.. most solidly and excellently. **1693** EVELYN *De la Quint. Compl. Gard.* II. 86 The Tast is the only and real Judge to whom it belongs to Judge Solidly, and without appeal, as well of the Maturity, as of the Goodness. **1720** WATERLAND *Eight Serm.* 275 This appears to be only a groundless surmise, as is largely and solidly proved by.. Bp. Bull. **1756** BURKE *Subl. & B.* I. xvi, Aristotle has spoken so much and so solidly upon the force of imitation. **1853** M. KELLY tr. *Gosselin's Power Pope during Mid. Ages* II. 167 *note*, Muratori proves solidly.. the antiquity of these copies. **1878** E. WHITE *Life in Christ* II. xiii. 151 [This] may be solidly inferred from the following premisses.

**3.** In a real as opposed to a superficial or apparent manner; really, thoroughly, truly.

**1625** HART *Arraignm. Ur.* I. ii. 16 Hippocrates.., not superficially, but solidly learned. **1640** LD. DIGBY *Sp. conc. Trienn. Parl.* (1641) 12 Neither the people can be prosperous and secure, nor the King himselfe solidly happy. **1667** in *Cath. Rec. Soc. Publ.* III. 66 This most sweet childe was solidly vertuous. **1747** CHESTERF. *Lett.* (1792) I. cxix. 323, I.. sacrificed a thousand real pleasures to it; and made myself solidly uneasy by it. **1823** JEFFERSON *Writ.* (1830) IV. 367 In this alliance, Louis, now avowedly, and George, secretly but solidly, were of the contracting parties. **1879** H. JAMES *Hawthorne* 32 Hawthorne's countrymen are solidly proud of him.

**4.** Seriously, solemnly; earnestly.

**1632** LITHGOW *Trav.* x. 475 The two Iesuits.. solidly protested, they were sorry from their heart. **1656** EARL

MONM. tr. *Boccalini's Advts. fr. Parnass.* I. lxv. (1674) 83 He heard the Ottoman Emperor speak so solidly of the care which Princes ought to have. **1676** O. HEYWOOD *Diaries* (1883) III. 147 John Butterworth prayed solidly and tenderly. **1788** in T. W. Marsh *Friends in Surrey & Sussex* (1886) vi. 46 [The Friends having] solidly considered the same, are of opinion [etc.]. **1791** BOSWELL *Johnson* (Oxf. ed.) I. 48 He told me what he read *solidly* at Oxford was Greek.

**5.** In a quiet, sedate, or serious way or manner. **1799** in T. W. Marsh *Friends in Surrey & Sussex* (1886) ii. 18 After sitting solidly awhile he stood up and said [etc.]. **1865** *Daily Telegr.* 8 Nov. 4/4 The old complaints were inflammatory; folks lived slowly and solidly.

**6.** In a body; unanimously. Orig. *U.S.* **1865** BRIGHT in *Morn. Star* 14 Mar., I was told by a citizen of New York..that in the United States alone 100,000 Irish votes were given, as he expressed, solidly—that is in one mass—for General M'Clellan. **1868** GRANT DUFF *Pol. Surv.* 133 They [Congress] will vote solidly for repudiation in any form. **1886** *Manch. Exam.* 26 Feb. 5/5 The Roman Catholic and Nationalist elements..being solidly Tory.

**'solidness.** [f. SOLID *a.*] The quality of being solid, in *lit.* and *fig.* senses; solidity.
(*a*) **1600** SURFLET *Countrie Farme* III. lxviii. 591 Grosse peeces [of gold] in respect of their solidnes consume but a verie little. **1620** I. JONES *Stone-Heng* (1725) 50 The Plainness and Solidness of the Tuscan Order. **1650** VENNER *Via Recta* 154 Peare-Wardens, in regard of the solidnesse of their substance, may be longest kept. **1730** BAILEY (fol.), *Substantiality*,..Solidness, Firmness. **1838** DICKENS *Nickelby* xxxiv, 'Here's flesh' cried Squeers, turning the boy about... 'Here's firmness, here's solidness!'
(*b*) **1630** H. LORD *Banians* 95 To settle us in the solidnesse of our owne faith. **1668** H. MORE *Div. Dial.* II. vi. (1713) 108 The fulness and Solidness of the Cause we contend for. **1681** MANTON *Wks.* (1872) VIII. 23 When they excel you.. for solidness and settledness in manners.

**solid state.** [f. SOLID *a.* + STATE *sb.*] **1.** The condition or state of being solid rather than fluid.
**1866** E. ATKINSON tr. *Ganot's Elem. Treat. Physics* (ed. 2) VII. iv. 425 A metallic salt is introduced either in a solid state or in a state of solution. **1908** *Chem. Abstr.* II. 1654 The electrical conductivity of a series of natural silicates was measured in the solid and liquid states. *Ibid.* 2757 (*heading*) The solid state. **1959** *Cambr. Rev.* 6 June 597/1 The section on nuclear magnetic resonance is almost entirely concerned with wide-line studies on the solid state.

**2.** *attrib.* (Usu. with hyphen.) **a.** Concerned with the structure and properties of solids, esp. with their explanation in terms of atomic and nuclear physics; as ***solid-state physics*** (hence ***solid-state physicist***).
**1953** C. KITTEL (*title*) Introduction to solid state physics. **1956** *Electronic Engin.* XXVIII. 63/1 Research in solid-state physics in recent years has yielded much information on the relations between the electrical magnetic and elastic properties of metals. **1964** *New Scientist* 4 June 595 In his studies, the solid-state physicist must have some means of knowing what compounds are likely to be semi-conducting if he makes them. **1973** *Sci. Amer.* Jan. 98/3 Solid-state physics is currently faced with the problem of constructing an effective theory of noncrystalline, amorphous substances. **1974** *BP Shield Internat.* Oct. p. iii/3 He graduated as an applied physicist and subsequently as a solid state physicist. **1975** *Nature* 20 Nov. 274/2, I think that the solid-state theorist will enjoy this part of the monograph particularly.

**b.** (Employing devices) utilizing the electronic properties of solids (as in transistors and other semiconductor devices, in contrast to the partial vacuum of valves). Occas. *absol.*, such devices collectively.
**1959** *Economist* 23 May 769/2 The transistor, best known of the 'solid-state' devices that employ these materials [*sc.* semiconductors], can do most of the jobs of a valve while taking far less space. **1961** *Times* 30 June 9/2 In this system solid-state electronic circuits..will replace conventional devices for interlocking signals and points. **1965** *Wireless World* July 350/2 Marconi's..showed their new solid-state 4½-inch image orthicon. **1968** *Times* 1 Nov. 23/4 In [computer] hardware, solid-state electronic devices have completely transformed the reliability, cost, speed and size of central processors. **1970** *New Scientist* 15 Oct. (Suppl.) 13/2 Solid state radars are required for airborne applications where size and weight are of prime importance. **1971** *Hi-Fi Sound* Feb. 40/1 (Advt.), All silicon solid state circuitry using 20 transistors and 2 diodes provides a full 20 watts r.m.s. output. **1975** G. J. KING *Audio Handbk.* ix. 202 A high-gain solidstate amplifier. **1978** *Broadcast* 5 June 21/2 The system's information is stored in solid state, not (as one might expect) on floppy disc.

**soli'dungular,** *a. rare.* = next.
**1819** W. LAWRENCE *Nat. Hist. Man* II. i. 250 The great troop of solidungular quadrupeds. **1922** JOYCE *Ulysses* 699 Smart phaeton with good working solidungular cob.

**solidungulate** (sɒlɪˈdʌŋgjʊlət), *a.* and *sb.* [f. L. *solid-us* SOLID *a.* + *ungulātus*, f. *ungula* hoof. So F. *solidongulé*.] = SOLIPED *a.* and *sb.*
**1839–47** *Todd's Cycl. Anat.* III. 237/1 The.. solidungulate quadrupeds, as the Horse and Ass. **1842** BRANDE *Dict. Sci.*, etc. 1130/1 *Solidungulates*,..the name of a tribe of Mammals [etc.]. **1863** DANA *Man. Geol.* 529 Of the Solidungulate or Horse family. **1879** tr. *De Quatrefages' Hum. Spec.* 53 Instead of being cloven-footed,..the race becomes solidungulate.
*transf.* **1863** R. F. BURTON *Abeokuta* II. 120 They had been provided with ammunition-boots, but, not having become by habit solidungulate, they could not use them without risking broken legs.

**solidungulous** (sɒlɪˈdʌŋgjʊləs), *a.* [See prec. and -OUS.] = SOLIPED *a.*
**1650** SIR T. BROWNE *Pseud. Ep.* (ed. 2) 88 It is plainly set down by Aristotle, an Horse and all Solidungulous or whole hoofd animals have no gall. **1681** GREW *Musæum* I. II. ii. 33 The Hoof of a Solidungulous Animal. **1712** J. MORTON *Nat. Hist. Northampt.* 444 The Solidungulous, or whole-Hoofed, the Soles of whose Feet are undivided. **1828** STARK *Elem. Nat. Hist.* I. 139 There is a solidungulous variety [of pig], but in which traces of the hoofs may be observed. **1856** R. KNOX tr. *Edwards' Man. Zool.* §397 In the solidungulous animals, the same happens with the fibula and tibia. **1902** *N. & Q.* Ser. IX. IX. 230/1 The cloven hoof may become solidungulous like that of the horse.

‖**solidus**[1] (ˈsɒlɪdəs). Pl. solidi (ˈsɒlɪdaɪ); also 5–7 solidos. [L., a substantival use of *solidus* (sc. *nummus*) SOLID *a.* The form *solidos* is the L. acc. pl.]
**1. a.** A gold coin of the Roman empire, originally worth about 25 denarii. †**b.** A shilling.
**1387** TREVISA *Higden* (Rolls) II. 313 Gentil men hade rynges, and oþere hadde solidy þat were hole and sownde. **1432–50** tr. *Higden* (Rolls) VII. 301 Kynge William toke this yere of every hyde of grownde in Ynglone vj. solidos of silver. **1487** in *Paston Lett.* III. App. 463, I bequeith to the reparacion of the stepull of the saide churche of Saint Albane xx. solidos. **1609** BIBLE (Douay) *1 Chron.* xxix. 7 And they gaue..of gold, fiue thousand talentes, and ten thousand solidos. **1706** PHILLIPS (ed. Kersey), *Solidus*, an entire or whole piece of Gold-Coin, near the Value of our old Noble or Spur-Royal; but it is now taken for a Shilling. **1860** C. R. SMITH in *Archæol. Cant.* III. 38 The solidi of the Eastern Empire were commonly imitated in France under the Merovingian princes. **1885** *Athenæum* 24 Oct. 541/2 Mr. Webster exhibited..a gold solidus of Constantius.

**2.** A sloping line used to separate shillings from pence, as 12/6, in writing fractions, and for other separations of figures and letters; a shilling-mark. Also *attrib.* Cf. OBLIQUE *sb.* 5.
**1891** in *Cent. Dict.* **1898** G. CHRYSTAL *Introd. Algebra* i. (1902) 3 The symbols / (solidus notation) and : (ratio notation) are equivalent to ÷. **1905** F. H. COLLINS *Author & Printer* s.v. **1909** *Athenæum* 27 Mar. 379/1 The last.. have been quick to adopt the use of the solidus or slanting line instead of the horizontal bar in writing fractions. **1923** N. SHAW *Forecasting Weather* i. 35 A solidus (/) such as occurs in the combination 'bc/r' separates weather at the time of observation from the preceding weather, bc/r thus indicating 'fine or fair after rain or drizzle'. **1947** [see NON-LINEAR *a.* b]. **1971** *Archivum Linguisticum* II. 4 Johnson/Jenkinson's 'oblique dash'.., which is otherwise called a 'solidus' or 'virgule'.

‖**'solidus**[2]. [L. *solidus* SOLID *a.* Adopted in this sense in Ger. by H. W. B. Roozeboom 1899, in *Zeitschr. f. phys. Chem.* XXX. 387.] A line or surface in a binary or ternary phase diagram respectively, or a temperature (corresponding to a point on the line or surface), below which a mixture is entirely solid and above which it consists of solid and liquid in equilibrium. Freq. *attrib.*, as ***solidus curve, temperature***, etc.
**1901**, etc. [see LIQUIDUS]. **1903** *Proc. Royal Soc.* 16 June 284 As indicated by the liquidus and solidus curves approximating closely to one another. **1904** WHETHAM *Rec. Devel. Phys. Sci.* iii. 94 Below the curve *a d b*, or 'solidus', the alloy is entirely solid. *Ibid.* 97 Equilibrium curves lying below the solidus. **1933** LIDDELL & DOAN *Princ. Metall.* III. xvi. 501 The solidus plane of the system..lies at a lower temperature than do any of the binary eutectics concerned. **1935** [see HOMOGENIZED *ppl. a.* 1]. **1959** B. CHALMERS *Physical Metall.* iii. 85 For a ternary alloy the liquidus and solidus are surfaces. **1965** G. V. RAYNOR in R. W. Cahn *Physical Metall.* vii. 325 The solidus temperature for a given alloy composition. **1967** A. H. COTTRELL *Introd. Metall.* xv. 230 This gives a phase diagram with a retrograde solidus curve,..with the striking property that alloys of certain compositions..can become completely solid and then melt again on cooling.

†**solie.** *Obs.* Also soly. [ad. L. *solium*.] A seat, throne.
**13..** *E.E. Allit. P.* B. 1171 He sete on Salamones solie, on solemne wyse. *Ibid.* 1678 Fro þe soly of his solempnete, his solace he leues.

**solie,** obs. form of SOLELY *adv.*

†**solier.** *Obs.* Also solyer. [a. OF. *solier*, = AF. *soler* SOLLAR *sb.*[1]] An upper room.
**1483** CAXTON *Gold. Leg.* 28/1 In the solier where y[e] soupper of Jhesu cryst and of his appostles was made. **1491** —— *Vitas Patr.* (W. de W. 1495) I. xlvii. 87 b/2 She wente uppe in to a Solyer wyth her syster Julyan.

†**so'lific,** *a. Obs.*[−1] [ad. L. type **sōlific-us*, f. *sōl* sun: see -FIC.] Impregnated by the sun. So †**so'lificous** *a.* Also †**so'lificate** *v.*, **'solify** *v.*, *trans.* to expose to the sun, to impregnate with solar qualities.
**1559** MORWYNG *Evonym.* 98 To be solificate or made golden, is when we procure the vertue of the sunne; that is golde to be in it. *Ibid.* 99 You shall put it into the quintessence of wine, and set it forth to be solified and sonned in the spring. **1650** ASHMOLE *Chym. Collect.* 119 Let the powder be most subtile with two parts of Solificous Water. **1678** R. RUSSELL tr. *Geber* III. II. II. xvi. 207 And convert it..into true Solifick and Lunifick, according to that for which the Medicine was prepared.

**solificatio** (ˌsəʊlɪfɪˈkɑːtɪəʊ). *nonce-wd.* [An invented Latin word, formed on SOLIFIC *a.*: see -FICATION.] A radiating warmth as of sunshine.
**1941** AUDEN *New Year Letter* III. 74 Who on the lives about you throw A calm solificatio.

**solifidian** (səʊlɪˈfɪdɪən), *sb.* and *a. Theol.* Also 7 solyfidian, solifidean. [f. L. *sōli-*, combining form of *sōl-us* alone + *fidēs* faith.]
**A.** *sb.* One who holds that faith alone, without works, is sufficient for justification.
The doctrine is based on Rom. iii. 28, where Luther rendered πίστει by 'allein durch den Glauben'.
**1596** BELL *Surv. Popery* III. ix. 394 Good works, which you and your solifidians cannot abide. **1638** CHILLINGW. *Relig. Prot.* I. vii. §33. 406, I never knew any Protestant such a soli-fidian, but that he did believe these divine truths. **1660** H. MORE *Myst. Godl.* To Rdr. 25 That all of the Reformed Churches are not Solifidians. **1742–3** *Observ. Methodists* 3 Very Civil indeed, O ye Solifidians. **1812–29** COLERIDGE in *Lit. Rem.* (1838) III. 122 The heroic Solifidian, Martin Luther himself. **1882** FARRAR *Early Chr.* II. 53 The Solifidian—the believer in the possibility of an abstract faith which can show no works as an evidence of its existence.
**B.** *adj.* **1.** Consisting of, pertaining to, the doctrine of justification by faith alone.
**1605** A. WOTTON *Answ. late Popish Articles* 108 The which solifidian portion ouerthroweth flatly true repentance. **1670** C. GATAKER *Harmony Truth* 63 Who.. have by Tongue and by Pen asserted the Solifidian and Fiduciary way of Justification. **1716** M. DAVIES *Athen. Brit.* II. 220 The same execrable Hypothesis..took in also the Solifidian Adiophorism of all Actions, good or bad. *a* **1773** ALBAN BUTLER *Moveable Feasts & F.* (1852) II. 223 He attacked the Solifidian and Antinomian doctrines. **1884** *Sat. Rev.* 3 Mar. 579 More seeking is needed to discover that theory within the sacred records than the solifidian one.
**2.** Of persons, etc.: Accepting or maintaining this doctrine.
**1628** FELTHAM *Resolves* II. xlvii. (1677) 253 A Solifidean-Christian is a Nullifidean-Pagan, and confutes his tongue with his hand. **1871** J. MARTINEAU *Ess. & Addr.* (1891) IV. 152 We cannot join a Solifidian church.

**soli'fidianism.** [f. prec. + -ISM.] The doctrine or tenet of justification by faith alone.
**1628** BP. HALL *Righteous Mammon* 728 To the conuiction of that lewd slander of solifidianisme. **1691–8** NORRIS *Pract. Disc.* (1711) III. 87 The absurd conceits of Anti-nomianism and Solifidianism. **1772** J. FLETCHER *Logica Genev.* 31 So far is our Church from siding with Antinomian solifidianism,.. that she rather leans to the other extreme. **1820** SOUTHEY *Wesley* II. 365 It is a course which enthusiasm naturally takes, wherever..solifidianism is preached. **1871** J. MARTINEAU *Ess. & Addr.* (1891) IV. 149 Sacerdotalism and Solifidianism gaining nothing by their internecine war.

**soliflual** (səˈlɪfl(j)uːəl), *sb.* and *a. Physical Geogr.* [f. SOLIFLU(CTION + -AL.] **A.** *sb.* Material that has moved by solifluction. *rare.* **B.** *adj.* = SOLIFLUCTIONAL *a.*
**1941** *Trans. R. Soc. Edin.* LX. 376 Generally the layers basal to an aggradational series, following production of an erosion scarp, are re-sorted soliflual. **1965** B. T. BUNTING *Geogr. of Soil* xii. 144 Sørensen classified high-arctic soliflual soils into those of inhomogeneous materal..and those of stoneless fines.

**solifluction** (səʊ-, sɒlɪˈflʌkʃən). *Physical Geogr.* Also -fluxion. [f. L. *sol-um* ground, earth + -I- + *fluction*, FLUXION.] **1.** The gradual movement of waterlogged soil or other surface material down a slope, esp. where the subsoil is frozen and acts as a barrier to the percolation of surface water.
**1906** J. G. ANDERSSON in *Jrnl. Geol.* XIV. 96 This process, the slow flowing from higher to lower ground of masses of waste saturated with water.., I propose to name *solifluction*. **1916** T. G. TAYLOR *With Scott* 115 These symmetrical polygons are due to a slow movement of half-frozen soil, which has been noted in polar lands, and is called solifluxion or soil-creep. **1936** *Geogr. Jrnl.* LXXXVII. 449 Solifluction also is known from the Alps, as for instance in the flysch region of the Segnas Pass. **1938** C. F. S. SHARPE *Landslides & Related Phenomena* iii. 35 The definition given by Andersson..does not limit solifluction to cold climates. From the cases he mentions, however, and from subsequent usages by Eakin.., Nichols.., and others, the word solifluction has come to be intimately associated with frost action. **1957** G. E. HUTCHINSON *Treat. Limnol.* I. i. 144 The presence of such ponds can lead to striking solifluction if the pressure of the water on the down-slope wall is great enough. **1965** M. FIELDES et al. in G. J. Williams *Econ. Geol. N.Z.* xx. 364/2 This solifluxion is thought to account for the emplacement of plastic clays occurring at..localities in the Wellington area. **1974** C. TAYLOR *Fieldwork in Medieval Archaeol.* iv. 85 Deep hollows on the faces of chalk scarps in Wessex are usually the result of periglacial action and solifluction.
**2.** *attrib.*
**1946** F. E. ZEUNER *Dating Past* 119 Solifluction deposits ..are a conspicuous feature of sections from the periglacial zone. **1968** C. R. TWIDALE *Geomorphol.* ix. 274 Small solifluction terraces and lobes are typical of slopes in periglacial regions. **1970** R. J. SMALL *Study of Landforms* i. 2 Our knowledge of the vital role of periglaciation..is based almost wholly on analysis..of the distribution and character of solifluxion gravels.
Hence **soli'fluctional** *a.*, pertaining to or produced by solifluction; also (as a back formation) **'solifluted** *a.*, that has moved by solifluction.
**1924** *Geogr. Jrnl.* LXIII. 225 On well-developed solifluctional slopes of mixed material, the different-sized stones move downwards at different rates. **1954** *Sci. News*

XXXIII. 70 On the continent, the task of dating soliflucted material is aided by interbedded sheets of loess. **1956** *Antiquity* XXX. 99 Weathered carboniferous sandstones (whose upper solifluxional levels are in several places separated by multi-coloured clays). **1971** J. N. JENNINGS in Jennings & Mabbutt *Landform Studies from Australia & New Guinea* xii. 271 Their hummockiness and the way they spread out distally with a bulging lower margin are features in favour of an end-moraine rather than a solifluctional origin. **1977** *Antiquaries Jrnl.* LVII. 187 Some sarsens.. could be derived from chalk or Greensand as could the soliflucted spread in the Vale of Pewsey.

**soliform** (ˈsəʊlɪfɔːm), *a.* [ad. L. type **sōliformis* (f. *sōl* sun), after Gr. ἡλιοειδής.] Resembling the sun; sun-like. Also *absol.*

**1678** CUDWORTH *Intell. Syst.* 204 Light, and Sight or the Seeing Faculty, may both of them rightly be said to be Soliform things, or of Kin to the Sun. **1806** KNOX & JEBB *Corresp.* I. 301 Eye never yet beheld the sun, that was not soliform. **1898** G. MEREDITH *Odes Fr. Hist.* 22 That Soliform [*sc.* Napoleon] made featureless beside His brilliancy who neighboured.

**solifuge.** [ad. L. *solifūga*, var. of *sol(i)pūga*: cf. SOLPUGA.] †**1.** (See quot.). *Obs.*$^{-0}$

**1658** PHILLIPS, *Solifuge*, a certain venemous animal, found chiefly in the Silver Mines of Sardinia.

**2.** = SOLPUGID. Also **so'lifugid** (-dʒɪd) [-ID$^{3}$], in the same sense.

**1925** R. W. G. HINGSTON in E. F. Norton *Fight for Everest, 1924* III. 286 Solifugids occur up to 15,000 feet. **1935** *Discovery* Sept. 282/2 The dread of a Spider or a Solifuge is due to the speed of its movement. **1964** J. HILLABY *Journey to Jade Sea* 182 The total bag was one grasshopper, one dead beetle..and a spider-like animal called a solifuge. **1968** R. D. BARNES *Invertebrate Zool.* (ed. 2) xiii. 399/2 Solifugids possess voracious appetites and feed on all types of small animals, including vertebrates.

**solify**, *v.*: see SOLIFIC *a.*

†**soligene**, *a. Obs.*$^{-0}$ [ad. L. *sōligena*, f. *sōl* sun.] (See quot.) Also †**soli'genian** *a.*, †**so'ligenous** *a.* (see quots.). *Obs.*

**1623** COCKERAM I, *Soligene*, begotten of the Sunne. **1634** SIR T. HERBERT *Trav.* (1638) 305 Their yeare is Soli-genian. **1730** BAILEY (fol.), *Soligenous*, begotten of the Sun.

**soli'geniture.** *rare*$^{-1}$. [f. L. *sōli-*, combining form of *sōlus* alone.] = UNIGENITURE.

**1818** G. S. FABER *Horæ Mosaicæ* I. 178 His only Son, who, from his Soligeniture, was in the Punic dialect called Jehud.

**Solignum** (səˈlɪgnəm). Also **solignum.** Proprietary name for a preservative for timber. Hence **so'lignumed** *a.*, treated with this material.

**1900** *Trade Marks Jrnl.* 17 Oct. 1105 *Solignum*... Preparations for the destruction of weeds, vermin, and insects. Major and Co. Ltd. Chemical manufacturers. **1909** *Chambers's Jrnl.* 27 Feb. 204/1 The preparation known as 'solignum'..is a fluid composition, applied..with a brush, possesses great covering capacity, and..improves with age both in appearance and resistant qualities. **1925** *Glasgow Herald* 19 June 8/8 One [way of dealing with white ants] is to keep painting the wood with solignum, and breaking down the trails whenever they appear. **1932** 'DANE' & SIMPSON *Re-enter Sir John* xx. 270 His neat little dressing-room, matchboard, salignumed [*sic*], sham-antique in the film-studio manner. **1969** *Observer* (Colour Suppl.) 12 Jan. 17/3 The walls continue with a cladding of weatherboarding, solignumed black, to the 12-ft level of the eaves.

**soli-ipsiism.** *nonce-wd.* [f. L. *sōlī ipsī* (our-) selves alone. Cf. SOLIPSISM.] Self-conceit.

**1826** C. BUTLER *Vind. of Bk. Rom. Cath. Ch.* 80 All foreigners observe that England possesses her due share of soli-ipsiism.

**solilo'quacious**, *a.* [f. SOLILOQUY *sb.*, after *loquacious.*] Prone to soliloquize.

**1835** MOORE *Mem.* (1856) VII. 70 My companion, according to his usual fashion, very soliloquacious, but saying much, of course, that was interesting to hear.

**soliloquacity** (ˌsɒlɪləˈkwæsɪtɪ). [Blend of SOLI(LOQUY *sb.* and LOQUACITY: cf. SOLILOQUACIOUS *a.*] Soliloquizing at great length.

**1895** *World* 30 Oct. 25/1 As he is soliloquising to this effect (he out-Hamlets Hamlet in soliloquacity), enter a letter from Mexico. **1967** *Time* 31 Mar. 40/3 Stephen's soliloquy on the beach, Bloom's trip to Paddy Dignam's funeral... Molly Bloom's magnificent end-spurt of soliloquacity.

**'soliloque.** *rare.* [a. F. *soliloque* or ad. L. *soliloquium.*] = SOLILOQUY *sb.*

**1697** BURGHOPE *Disc. Relig. Assemb.* 157 Let the devout receiver turn the doctrine of this sacrament into practical soliloques, and spiritual exercises of the mind. **1710** 'J. DISTAFF' *Char. Don Sacheverellio* 9 There is an absolute necessity that he should drop into the following Soliloque. **1864** WEBSTER, *Soliloque*, that which is said in soliloquy; soliloquy.

**so'liloquent**, *a. rare.* [f. SOLILOQUY *sb.*, after forms in *-loquent.*] Speaking in soliloquy. Also **soli'loquial** *a.*, of the nature of soliloquy.

**1836** *Fraser's Mag.* XIII. 346 They are so wrapped in their own soliloquial musings. **1892** *Fun* 14 Sept. 109/1 A tendency to be soliloquent.

**soliloquist** (səˈlɪləkwɪst). [f. SOLILOQUIZE *v.*: see -IST.] One who soliloquizes or talks to himself; a writer of soliloquies.

**1804** *Miniature* (1806) I. 114, I sallied forth..to make my first appearance among this new species of Soliloquists. **1853** *Athenæum* 15 Oct. 1216 As an essayist and soliloquist, ..we find the Jew exceedingly prosy. **1890** BOWDEN tr. *Hettinger's Nat. Relig.* 285 *note*, We regard a soliloquist as slightly crazed.

‖**soli'loquium.** *Obs.* Also 6 *pl.* soliloquyas. [L.] = SOLILOQUY *sb.*

*c* **1597** HARINGTON in *Nugæ Ant.* (1804) I. 189 Some of the elloquent and excellent soliloquyas of St. Awgustin. **1622** MABBE tr. *Aleman's Guzman d'Alf.* 122, I making a large Soliloquium, and meditation to my selfe, went on a good while with the same. **1665** G. WITHER (*title*), Three Private Meditations... The Third, Intituled *Nil Ultra*, is a Soliloquium. **1897** GLADSTONE *Later Gleanings* xiii. (1898) 384 Soliloquium and Postscript. *Ibid.* 395 *note*, The *Soliloquium* was not written until [etc.].

**soliloquize** (səˈlɪləkwaɪz), *v.* [f. SOLILOQU-Y *sb.* + -IZE.]

**1.** *intr.* To engage in soliloquy; to talk to oneself.

**1759** J. G. COOPER *Ver-Vert* II. 29 He could..at a proper time and place Religiously soliloquise. **1820** BYRON *Juan* III. xcvi, Leaving my people to proceed alone, While I soliloquize beyond expression. **1858** BARONESS BUNSEN in Hare *Life* (1879) II. iv. 235 He soliloquises in a manner in which you would tell a story to a child. **1873** BROWNING *Red Cott. Nt.-cap* 120 Thus, mutely might our friend soliloquize.

**2.** *trans.* **a.** To utter in soliloquy.

**1805** EUGENIA DI ACTON *Nuns of Desert* I. 172 Sometimes he..soliloquised a string of barbarous oaths. **1837** CARLYLE *Fr. Rev.* II. i. ix, No scenic individual, with knavish hypocritical views, will take the trouble to soliloquize a scene. **1854** *Fraser's Mag.* L. 72 Balder soliloquises his ambition.

**b.** To address or apostrophize in soliloquy.

**1823** *New Monthly Mag.* VII. 332 When you are soliloquizing the moon.

Hence **so'liloquizer**, one who soliloquizes. Also **so'liloquizing** *vbl. sb.* and *ppl. a.*; **so'liloquizingly** *adv.*

**1802** *Edin. Rev.* I. 118 Prosopopœia is more suited to the narrator of such a state, than to the *soliloquizer. **1884** *Pall Mall G.* 5 Mar. 5/1 One of those..soliloquisers of villainy who are specially favoured by the dramatist. *c* **1822** CAMPBELL *Note to Byron's Heav. & Earth* iii. 931 Too much tedious *soliloquising. **1837** CARLYLE *Fr. Rev.* I. II. viii, If the soliloquizing Barber ask: 'What has your Lordship done to earn all this?' **1870** MISS BRIDGMAN *R. Lynne* I. xii. 184 In a conversational mood, or, more properly speaking, a soliloquising one. **1840** *New Monthly Mag.* LX. 321 'Comforts?' said Tim, *soliloquizingly.

**soliloquy** (səˈlɪləkwɪ), *sb.* Also 7 soliloquie. [ad. L. *sōliloquium* (introduced by St. Augustine), f. *sōli-*, *sōlus* alone + *loqui* to speak.

In the following quot. the reference is to St. Augustine's *Liber Soliloquiorum*: *c* **1380** in Horstm. *Altengl. Leg.* (1878) 91 þat he dispised so riches, [in] þe bok Soliloquijs he bereþ witnes.]

**1.** An instance of talking to or conversing with oneself, or of uttering one's thoughts aloud without addressing any person.

In quot. 1629 stressed on the first and third syllables.

**1604** R. CAWDREY *Table Alph.* (1613), *Soliloquie*, priuate talke. **1629** QUARLES *Argalus & Parthenia* I. Wks. (Grosart) III. 254/1 His pining thoughts, and her projecting feares; His soliloquies, and her secret teares. **1699** GARTH *Dispens.* IV. 53 He finds no respite from his anxious Grief, Then seeks from this Soliloquy relief. **1756–82** J. WARTON *Ess. Pope* I. vi. 297 It is indeed no other than a passionate soliloquy. **1794** MRS. RADCLIFFE *Myst. Udolpho* xxxv, This enthusiastic soliloquy was interrupted by a rustling noise in the hall. **1852** MRS. STOWE *Uncle Tom's C.* xxxiv, She had hurried on through her story with a wild, passionate utterance;..sometimes speaking as in a soliloquy.

**b.** A literary production representing or imitating a discourse of this nature.

**1641** J. S. (*title*), Soliloqvies Theologicall. **1649** MILTON *Eikon.* Wks. 1851 III. 336 As to the Author of these Soliloquies [etc.]. *c* **1675** ROCHESTER *Satyr agst. Mankind* 74 All this we know..From Patrick's Pilgrim, Sibbs Soliloquies. **1718** PRIOR *Solomon* Pref., Wks. 1892 II. 83 The whole poem is a soliloquy: Solomon is the person that speaks. **1770** (*title*), The Soliloquy: a poem, occasioned by a late decision. **1856** R. A. VAUGHAN *Mystics* (1860) II. 5 The mysticism of the West has produced..soliloquies, sermons, and treatises of divinity. **1873** SYMONDS *Grk. Poets* vi. 183 The soliloquies of Hamlet..must have been lost upon the groundlings of Elizabeth's days.

**2.** Without article: The act of talking to oneself; soliloquizing.

*a* **1668** DAVENANT *News from Plymouth* Wks. (1673) 7 You will find it Such a feast of Soliloquy,..As yet you never tasted. **1738** MRS. ROWE (*title*), Devout Exercises of the Heart in Meditation and Soliloquy. **1839** H. REEVE in J. K. Laughton *Mem.* (1898) I. 104 He confounds soliloquy and colloquy.

Hence **so'liloquy** *v.*, to address (oneself) in a soliloquy. *rare*$^{-1}$.

**1757** MRS. GRIFFITH *Lett. Henry & Frances* (1767) III. 106 Upon such an Occasion as this, one should naturally soliloquy themselves thus.

**soli-lunar** (səʊlɪˈluːnɑː(r)), *a.* [f. L. *sōli-*, *sōl* sun + LUNAR *a.* Cf. SOL-LUNAR *a.*] Relating to, or connected with, both sun and moon.

**1686** GOAD *Celest. Bodies* II. i. 129 We find the same Effect 3 times in 4 years, which is not to be found in the Soli-Lunar Opposition. **1831** BREWSTER *Optics* xv. 135 The combination of the simple soli-lunar tides. **1880** *Church Times* XVIII. 855 A great point is made..about soli-lunar cycles.

**soling** (ˈsəʊlɪŋ), *vbl. sb.* Also 5 **solynge**, 6–7 **soll-**, 6 **sowling**; 7 **sooling.** [f. SOLE *sb.*$^{1}$ or *v.*$^{1}$]

**1.** The action of putting soles upon boots or shoes; freq. = resoling.

**1416** *Maldon Court-Rolls* (Bundle 10, no. 6), Propter vampeyeyng et solynge de vn payre de botys, xii*d.* **1547** in J. H. Glover *Kingsthorpiana* (1883) 102 The same day for the solyng of my shoys, v*d.* **1573** in Feuillerat *Revels Q. Eliz.* (1908) 201 The making and solling of vi paier of startopps. **1653** URQUHART *Rabelais* I. viii, For the soling of them were made use of eleven hundred hides.

*attrib.* **1571** in Feuillerat *Revels Q. Eliz.* (1908) 142 For sowling lether. **1629** *Leather* 12 The..strongest, which might..serue both for sooling leather and vpper leather.

**2.** A sole or foundation laid down in the making of roads over boggy or marshy ground.

**1838** *Civil Eng. & Arch. Jrnl.* I. 383/2 Upon this trunking is to be laid a soling, consisting of a mixed mass of prepared earth and gravel. **1843** *Ibid.* VI. 274/1 The soling should not be laid on, until one, and in some cases two seasons, after the grips have been opened.

**3.** *Golf.* (See SOLE *v.*$^{1}$ 3.)

**1909** VAILE *Mod. Golf* 27 Bad soling and ignorance of the principles of proper soling strike at the very root of the game.

†**soli'nomial**, *a. Obs.* [f. L. *sōli-*, *sōlus* alone, after BINOMIAL, etc.] Consisting of one term.

**1690** LEYBOURN *Curs. Math.* 347 Some other Solinomial Rectangle Parallelipipedon.

**solion.** *Electronics. temporary.* [f. SOL(UTION + ION.] An electrochemical device consisting of two or more electrodes sealed in an electrolyte in which a reversible electrochemical reaction is monitored, versions of which are used as amplifiers, integrators, and as pressure transducers which also sense low-frequency sound and changes in temperature or acceleration. Freq. *attrib.*

**1957** *N.Y. Times* 23 June 24/4 It has been nicknamed 'solion', which is short for ions in solution. *Ibid.*, The laboratory [*sc.* the U.S. Naval Ordnance Laboratory] expects that the solion will make possible cheaper, smaller and simpler electronic control systems. **1962** *New Scientist* 2 Aug. 254/1 The solion tetrode..is used as an integrator or as a low-frequency amplifier. **1966** *McGraw-Hill Encycl. Sci. & Technol.* XII. 482/2 The solion diode uses platinum electrodes in an aqueous solution that may be iodine and potassium iodide. *Ibid.* 483/1 The solion pressure transducer..measures fluid flow through an orifice separating two electrolyte chambers.

**soliped** (ˈsɒlɪpɛd), **-pede** (-piːd), *sb.* and *a.* [ad. med. or mod.L. *sōliped-*, *sōlipēs*, f. *sōli-*, *sōlus* alone, only + *pēs* foot, or alteration of L. *solidipēs*. Cf. F. *solipède*. In the pl. the Latin form *solipedes* (səˈlɪpɪdiːz) has also been employed.]

**A.** *sb.* An animal having a whole or uncloven hoof.

α. **1646** SIR T. BROWNE *Pseud. Ep.* III. ii, It is plainly set downe by Aristotle, an Horse and all Solipeds have no gall. *Ibid.* VI. vi, Solipeds of firm-hooft animals as Horses, Asses, Mules, &c. **1835** KIRBY *Hab. & Inst. Anim.* II. 499 The second Sub-order of the Pachyderms, the Solipeds, the well-known equine and asinine tribes. *a* **1843** *Encycl. Metrop.* (1845) VII. 358* In the Ruminators, in the Solipeds, and most Predatory Beasts. **1882** *19th Cent.* No. 61. 477 Glanders, as every one knows, is a highly contagious disorder of solipeds.

β. **1833** SIR C. BELL *Hand* (1834) 52 There must be a wide difference in the bones of his upper extremity from those of the ruminant or solipede. **1880** BASTIAN *Brain* xvi. 263 In Solipedes, Ruminants, and Carnivores, the lateral lobes also begin to surpass the median in size.

**B.** *adj.* Having a whole hoof; solid-hoofed.

**1656** BLOUNT *Glossogr.*, *Soliped*, that hath a whole or sound foot, not cloven or broken; such is that of a Horse. **1835** KIRBY *Hab. & Inst. Anim.* II. 198 A Family..to which he has given the ancient appellation of Soliped or whole hoofed. **1849** *Zoologist* VII. 2345 A hybrid between a soliped and ruminant animal.

So **so'lipedal, so'lipedous** *adjs.*

**1686** PLOT *Staffordsh.* 266 The most memorable accidents I heard of in this Country to have at any time befallen the Solipedous Animals. **1847** WEBSTER, *Solipedous.* **1882** OGILVIE, *Solipedal.*

**so'lipotence.** *rare*$^{-1}$. [f. L. *sōli-*, *sōlus* alone, after *omnipotence*, etc.] Sole power. So **so'lipotent** *a.*

**1855** MISS COBBE *Ess. Intuitive Morals* (1864) 97 *note*, The absolute unity and solipotence of God is a doctrine which even now is but little recognized. *Ibid.* 102 He is not only omnipotent, but solipotent.

**solipsism** (ˈsɒlɪpsɪz(ə)m). *Metaph.* [f. L. *sōl-us* alone + *ipse* self.] The view or theory that self is the only object of real knowledge or the only thing really existent. Also, = EGOISM 1, and in weakened sense.

**1874** A. C. FRASER *Sel. from Berkeley* 47 Ueberweg suggests that Berkeley's reasoning implies that we can know only *our own* notions of what we call *other* spirits—thus leading, by a *reductio ad absurdum*, to Egoism or Solipsism. *a* **1881** A. BARRATT *Phys. Metempiric* (1883) 25 At any rate, Solipsism, if not inconceivable, is in the highest degree incredible. **1884** *Contemp. Rev.* Feb. 294 As long as we confine ourselves to the world given in experience..we must profess solipsism. **1895** *Month* May 27 Under pain of 'solipsism', of being shut up within our own subjectivity. **1978** *Poetry* Aug. 298 The deep underlying motive of Mark Strand's poetry is solipsism or loneliness of the individual imagination.

Hence **solip'sismal** *a.*

**1892** G. M. McCrie *Miss Naden's World-Scheme* 28 The existence of 'other selves', being secondarily inferred, in no way touches the prime fact of solipsismal monism.

**solipsist** ('sɒlɪpsɪst), *sb.* and *a.* [f. as prec.]

**A.** *sb.* One who accepts the theory of solipsism.

**1891** *Cent. Dict.*, *Solipsist*,..one who believes in his own existence only. **1898** *Q. Rev.* Jan. 65 A philosophy..in which, if consistent, we become subjective idealists and solipsists.

**B.** *adj.* Favouring or characterized by solipsism; also in weakened sense.

**1903** A. E. Taylor *Elements of Metaphysics* III. ii. 202 Why..did Berkeley..accept neither the solipsist nor the sceptical conclusion? **1927** V. McNabb *Cath. Ch. & Philos.* iii. 101 His [*sc.* Kant's] own words are ingenuously solipsist! **1972** *Last Whole Earth Catalog* 16/2 Solipsist tyrants, believing that their will, like their eyeballs, could move mountains, have come to believe that it should trample over these small annoying figures in their visual field.

**solipsistic** (sɒlɪp'sɪstɪk), *a.* [f. solipsism + -istic.] = solipsist *a.*

**1885** W. James in *Mind* X. 37 Men who see each other's bodies sharing the same space..will never practically believe in a pluralism of solipsistic worlds. **1894** *The Forum* May 308 They should not be made self-centred and solipsistic at an age when altruism ought to have its golden day. **1952** A. Wilson *Hemlock & After* II. iii. 145 His intense, solipsistic world of personal ambition. **1958** I. Murdoch *Bell* xiv. 184 But now, driven by this fit of solipsistic melancholy one degree more desperate, she felt the need of an act. **1968** A. Storr *Human Aggression* xi. 104 Psychopaths share with the schizophrenic the characteristic of living in a world which is predominantly solipsistic; that is, in which people and events are not valued in and for themselves, but only in so far as they affect the subject. **1971** E. Shorris *Death of Great Spirit* iv. 66 The vision of Western man—seeing himself in the central role—might have been considered solipsistic only two hundred years ago. **1977** *Dædalus* Summer 42 It expanded, not by conflicts and deals with equals, but by short spurts of solipsistic exuberance at the expense of much weaker neighbors.

Hence **solip'sistically** *adv.*

**1898** W. James in R. B. Perry *Tht. & Char. of W. James* (1935) II. 370 Take me solipsistically if you will. My talk is merely a description of my present field of experience. **1923** *Times Lit. Suppl.* 23 Aug. 549/2 There are traits of experience which almost all of us are accustomed to explain solipsistically—our dream-worlds. **1952** *Mind* LXI. 10 We each solipsistically confined ourselves to statements which we may properly claim to know to be true directly. **1981** *Times Lit. Suppl.* 8 May 512/3 The real tramps aren't..made miserable by self-consciousness. For the most part, they seem solipsistically content, boozily quarrelling.

† **soli'sequious**, *a. Obs.* Also solis(s)equous. [f. L. *sōli-*, *sōl* sun + *sequi* to follow.] Following the sun; turning with the sun.

**1650** Charleton tr. *Van Helmont's Paradoxes* 14 The Heliotropian or Solisequous Flowers are wheeled about after the Sun, by a certaine Magnetisme. **1651** Biggs *New Disp.* ¶72 This solissequous perambulation. **1658** Sir T. Browne *Gard. Cyrus* iv, Large lists of solisequious and Sun-following plants.

**solisgise**, obs. form of syllogize *v.*

**solissit**, obs. form of solicit *v.*

† **'solist.** *Astrol. Obs.*[−1] [f. L. *sōl* sun.] One born under the influence of the sun.

**1569** J. Sanford tr. *Agrippa's Van. Artes* 50b, She pronounceth..that man a Martialiste or Solist.

**solist(e**, obs. Sc. variants of solicit.

**solitaire** ('sɒlɪtɛə(r), sɒlɪ'tɛə(r)), *sb.* [a. F. *solitaire*, ad. L. *sōlitārius* solitary *sb.* and *a.*]

**1.** A person who lives in seclusion, solitude, or retirement; a recluse.

**1716** Pope *Lett.* (1735) I. 153 How often..one Evening of your Conversation has spoil'd me for a Solitaire! **1764** H. Walpole *Corr.* (1891) IV. 296 You see I am likely to totter into a solitaire at three-score. **1797** Mrs. A. M. Bennett *Beggar Girl* (1813) II. 111 The graceful solitaire there was already acquainted with the misfortune. **1826** Disraeli *V. Grey* II. x, Oh! you are here, Mr. Grey, acting the solitaire in the park! **1859** Capern *Ballads & Songs* 140 There I could dwell a studious solitaire.

**2.** A precious stone, usually a diamond, set by itself. Also *ellipt.*, a solitaire ring.

*a* **1727** Mrs. Delany *Life & Corr.* (1861) I. 71 To give me the solitaires, which are at last arrived. **1760** Foote *Minor* II, Many an aigrette and solitaire have I sold, to discharge a lady's play-debt. **1832** Marryat *N. Forster* liii, This diamond *solitaire* that's..upon my finger. **1862** *Catal. Internat. Exhib., Brit.* II. No. 6181, Shirt studs, sleeve links, clasps, solitaires. **1886** R. F. Burton *Arab. Nts.* (abr. ed.) I. p. vii, I saw the evening star hanging like a solitaire from the pure front of the western firmament.

*attrib.* **1836** Marryat *Japhet* lviii, A diamond solitaire ring, which I had intended to have left with my other bijouterie. **1840** —— *Olla Podr.* (Rtldg.) 239 The ring..was a splendid solitaire diamond.

**3.** A game which can be played by one person: **a.** One of various kinds of card-games. **b.** A game played on a board with marbles or pegs, which have to be removed by jumping as in draughts.

**1746** H. Walpole *Lett.* (1846) II. 165 Has Miss Harriet found out any more ways at solitaire? **1825** Bentham *Ration. Reward* 209 As the amusement of a minister of state, ..a more suitable one might be found than a game at *solitaire*. **1850** *Bohn's Handbk. Games* (1867) 556 It is, in fact, a sort of *solitaire* for each player in turn. **1891** Gosse *Gossip Libr.* viii. 95 Like the boards on which people play the game of solitaire.

*attrib.* **1851** Mayhew *Lond. Lab.* II. 17, I am moreover told that in the same second-hand calling were boards known as 'solitaire-boards'. **1873** *Routledge's Young Gentl. Mag.* Jan. 118/2 A ball belonging to a solitaire-board.

**4.** A loose neck-tie of black silk or broad ribbon worn by men in the 18th century.

**1731** *Gentl. Mag.* I. 321 We have brought home the French Coifure, the *Robe de Chambre* of the Women, and *Toupé* and *Solitaire* of the Men. **1768–74** Tucker *Lt. Nat.* (1834) II. 596 The beau, almost throttled in a large solitaire, ..was thought to appear most charming. **1805** W. Cooke *Foote* II. 6 He exhibited a full dress suit, bag wig and *solitaire*, sword, muff, rings, &c. *c* **1839** T. Hook *Sayings* Ser. II. *Sutherl.* (Colburn) 15 A gentleman dressed in a peach-coloured velvet coat, with..a *solitaire* round his neck. [**1882** Gosse *Gray* 28 He ties a vast solitaire around his neck.]

**5.** *Ornith.* **a.** A large flightless bird (*Pezophaps solitarius*) formerly existing in the island of Rodriguez. Cf. solitary *sb.* 3.

**1797** *Encycl. Brit.* (ed. 3) VI. 20/1 The solitaire, or solitary dodo, is a large bird. **1863** Dana *Man. Geol.* 578 The Solitaire is another exterminated bird of the same island. **1896** Newton *Dict. Birds* 892 Perhaps no species has had its osteology examined on so great a scale as the Solitaire.

**b.** A Jamaican bird (*Myiodectes solitarius*).

**1847** Gosse *Birds Jamaica* 205 As far as I know, the food of the Solitaire is exclusively berries. **1860** —— *Rom. Nat. Hist.* 18 The lengthened flute-like notes..of the solitaire.

**6.** A solitary beast of chase.

**1900** Pollok & Thom *Sports Burma* iii. 96 Sportsmen following up a wounded solitaire [*sc.* a gaur] have occasionally been killed.

**7.** *attrib.* Intended for one person only.

**1885** *Pall Mall G.* 15 May 4/1 A variety of painted tea sets and solitaire breakfast sets.

† **solitaire, -are**, *a. Obs.* Forms: α. 4 solitare (5 sola-); *Sc.* 5–7 solitare (6 sole-), 6 solitar, soliter(e, solyter. β. 4–5, 7 solitaire, 5 solytayr, 6 solitair. [a. OF. (also mod.F.) *solitaire* or ad. L. *sōlitārius*: see solitary *a.*] Solitary, in various senses.

α. **1382** Wyclif *Ps.* ci. 8, I..am maad as a spare solitare in the rof. *c* **1440** *Alph. Tales* 444 When þai hafe bene awhile in solatare place be þer ane. *c* **1475** Henryson *Poems* (S.T.S.) III. 33 Quhen he saw þis lady solitar. **1530** Lyndesay *Test. Papyngo* 956 Quhow lang, traist ȝe, those ladyis sall remane So solyter, in sic perfectioun? **1533** Bellenden *Livy* I. viii. (S.T.S.) I. 49 Numa frequentit oft tymes in þis wod, solitare and but ony cumpany. *c* **1614** Sir W. Mure *Dido & Æneas* I. 796 How coms't thir costs thow solitare dost range?

β. **1387** Trevisa tr. *Higden* VI. 109 An holy man þat was solitaire. *c* **1450** *Knt. de La Tour* 124 She made a chaumbre solitaire for this holy man. **1483** Caxton *Gold. Leg.* 192/2 He no thynge desyred so moche as for to accomplysshe commaundementes solytayrs. **1549** *Compl. Scot.* Prol. 9 He vas neiuyr les solitair as quhen he aperit to be solitair. **1569** *Reg. Privy Council Scot.* II. 39 He to be solitair, the nobill men..being for the maist part absent. **1647** H. More *Song of Soul* II. App. 93 Ne further may my wary mind assent From one single experience solitaire.

† **solitaneous**, *a. Obs.*[−0] [f. late L. *sōlitāneus*.] (See quot.)

**1656** Blount *Glossogr.*, *Solitaneous*, solitary, single, alone, without company.

**solitarian** (sɒlɪ'tɛərɪən). *rare.* [f. L. *sōlitārius* solitary + -an.] A recluse, a hermit. Also *transf.*

**1655** Moufet & Bennet *Health's Improv.* xviii. 150 There is never seen of them past one at once, which caused the Latins to call them *Merulas*, that is to say the Solitarians or Hermits. **1661** Sir R. Twysden *Beginners Monast. Life* (1698) 8 This Man..gathered together all the dispersed Monks and other Solitarians of Italy.

† **solitariety.** *Obs. rare.* [f. solitary *a.*] Solitariness, soleness.

**1678** Cudworth *Intell. Syst.* I. iv. §11. 184 This idea of God..essentially includes unity and solitariety. *Ibid.* 336 Always remaining in the solitariety of His own unity.

**solitarily** ('sɒlɪtərɪlɪ), *adv.* Forms: 5–6 solytaryly, 6 solytarily, sol(l)itaryly, solitarilie; 5– solitarily. [f. solitary *a.* + -ly[2].] In a solitary manner.

**1.** In solitude; alone; without company.

**1451** Capgrave *Life St. Aug.* 23 Because þat al his desire was for to prey and study solitarily. **1483** Caxton *Gold. Leg.* 423/2 For as moche that I desyre to lede my lyf solytaryly. **1555** Eden *Decades* (Arb.) 215 A secte of men whiche liued solytarily in the desertes. **1588** Greene *Perimedes* 35 As he sollemnly and sollitaryly walked. *c* **1630** Risdon *Surv. of Devon* §329 (1810) 339 St. Ann's Chapel is solitarily situated. **1698** S. Sewall *Diary* 9 Feb., Coach stood by the way here and there and mov'd solitarily. **1833** *Westm. Rev.* XVIII. 324 They drink as they smoke, solitarily, and without any reference to social enjoyment. **1863** Bates *Nat. Amazon* II. 33 Another nearly allied but much larger species ..sometimes excavates its mine solitarily on sand-banks.

**2.** Apart or distinct from others; singly, solely.

*a* **1641** Bp. Mountagu *Acts & Mon.* (1642) 118 That it could not be David solitarily..appeareth to bee plaine. **1651** Hobbes *Leviath.* IV. xliv. 350 To understand..this text, we are not to consider it solitarily, but jointly with the words precedent, and subsequent. **1677** Plot *Oxfordshire* 200 After what concerns women solitarily consider'd,..come we next to treat of things..that concern women and men joyntly. **1875** Whitney *Life Lang.* viii. 151 Phonetic changes are especially likely to be thus general, instead of solitarily individual.

**solitariness** ('sɒlɪtərɪnɪs). Forms: 6 solytarynes(se, solitarynesse, 6–7 -nes, solitarinesse, 6– solitariness (7 -nes). [f. as prec.]

**1.** The state of being solitary or alone; the fact of being or dwelling apart from others.

Very common *c* 1575–1700, and in the 19th cent.

*a* **1533** Ld. Berners *Golden Bk. M. Aurel.* (1546) Dd iv b, Yf thou bee a wydowe of solytarynesse. **1559** Bercher *Nobylytye Wymen* (Roxb.) 129 He refusethe cumpanye, and desyrethe solytarynes. **1617** Moryson *Itin.* III. 228 Christian the Elector..was reputed..to affect solitarinesse, and little to be seene of the people. **1663** Patrick *Parab. Pilgr.* xxix. (1665) 344 There is very great use of Solitariness, especially in the beginnings of a New Life. **1726** S. Willard *Body of Divinity* 892/2 Man is made for society; solitariness, or living alone, being a trespass against humane nature. **1801** Mar. Edgeworth *Angelina* i, With what soul-rending eloquence does my Angelina describe the ..solitariness she experiences in the crowded metropolis! **1894** Baring-Gould *Kitty Alone* II. 106 Kate had felt acutely this solitariness in which she lived.

*personif.* **1601** Sir W. Cornwallis *Ess.* I. ix, Solitarinesse the mother of Contemplation.

**2.** The state or character of being unfrequented, retired, or secluded; absence of life or stir.

**1560** Daus tr. *Sleidane's Comm.* 159b, But when..the Cardinals, whiche he had sent thither, aduertised him that there was great solitarinesse,..he deferreth the day of the Counsell till Easter folowyng. **1579** W. Fulke *Heskins' Parl.* 252 Taking the solitarinesse of the night,..shee fell downe ..before the altare. **1609** W. M. *Man in Moone* (1849) 3 By the solitarinesse of the house I judged it a lodge in a forrest. **1694** Falle *Jersey* i. 26 The solitariness of the Place, and the want of Necessaries,..causing many of them to desert. **1748** Smollett *Rod. Rand.* xli, The solitariness of the field through which they passed. **1840** R. H. Dana *Bef. Mast* xviii. 52 A silence and solitariness which affected everything. Not a human being but ourselves for miles. **1886** W. J. Tucker *E. Europe* 234 The solitariness of the almost deserted avenue, solitariness only occasionally broken in upon by a hired carriage.

*personif.* **1596** *Edw. III*, III. iii. 23 Leauing at our heeles A ..beaten path For sollitarines to progresse in. **1605** A. Warren *Poor Man's Passions* liii, What Solitarines hath there assign'de For such, as her Inhabitants shall be.

† **soli'tariousness.** *Obs.*[−1] = prec.

**1545** Ascham *Toxoph.* (Arb.) 52 Dysinge and cardynge haue ii. Tutours, the one named Solitariousenes, whyche lurketh in holes and corners, the other called Night.

† **soli'tarity.** *Obs. rare.* [f. solitary *a.* Cf. solitariety.]

**1.** Soleness, singleness.

**1803** W. Taylor in *Monthly Mag.* XIV. 490 He may consequentially..maintain the solitarity of his own existence. **1813** —— *Ibid.* XXXV. 427 Consequently, that the probability of success is increased by the solitarity of the candidate.

**2.** Solitude, want of society.

**1811** W. Taylor in Robberds *Mem.* (1843) II. 351, I shall be abandoned at once to solitarity and penury.

† **solitarness.** *Sc. Obs.*[−1] [f. *solitar* solitaire *a.*] Solitariness.

*a* **1578** Lindesay (Pitscottie) *Chron. Scot.* (S.T.S.) I. 163 He was ane that lowit sollitarnes.

**solitary** ('sɒlɪtərɪ), *sb.* Also 5 solitari(e, solytarye. [Substantive use of the adj.]

**1. a.** One who retires into, or lives in, solitude from religious motives; a hermit or recluse.

**1435** Misyn *Fire of Love* 32 The holy solitari forsoith,..an excellent, goldy seet in heuyns he sall take emangis ordyrs of Aungels. *c* **1440** *Alph. Tales* 92, I went vnto a man þat hight Pachonius, þat dwelte in wyldernes a solitarie. **1651** tr. *De-las-Coveras' Don Fenise* 140 He told him..the course of her life untill the time she had retired her selfe into that solitude, at which the solitary much wondred. **1699** Evelyn *Acetaria* (1729) 166 Those ancient and truly pious Solitaries, who..were driven from their Countries and Repose by the Incursions of barbarous Nations. **1753** Challoner *Cath. Chr. Instr.* 178 From these Beginnings the Desarts of Egypt and of Thebais soon were peopled with innumerable Solitaries. **1813** Eustace *Class. Tour* (1821) III. iii. 69 An hermitage, that seems from its situation to be the cell of one of the holy solitaries of times of old. **1864** Kingsley *Rom. & Teut.* 239 The solitaries of the Thebaid found that they became selfish wild beasts, or went mad, if they remained alone. **1868** Freeman *Norm. Conq.* (1877) II. App. 599 Wythmann at last, after a pilgrimage to Jerusalem, died a solitary.

**b.** One who lives by himself in seclusion or retirement; one who avoids, or is deprived of, the society of others.

*a* **1763** Shenstone *Ess.*, *Vision* (1868) 118 The first meditation of a solitary, is the behaviour of men in active life. **1795–1814** Wordsw. *Excursion* VI. 1062, I noted that the Solitary's cheek Confessed the power of nature. **1816** Scott *Bl. Dwarf* xvi, The door opened, and the Solitary stood before her. *a* **1854** H. Reed *Lect. Brit. Poets* vi. (1857) 224 His [Milton's] life..as a student, as a statesman, and as a solitary. **1898** *Westm. Gaz.* 24 Mar. 4/1 Hardy pioneers, solitaries who had lived on far-off creeks.

† **2.** A solitude, lonely place. *Obs.*

**1594** Peele *Battle of Alcazar* II. iii, I will go hunt these cursed solitaries.

† **3.** = solitaire *sb.* 5 a. *Obs. rare.*

**1708** tr. *F. Leguet's Voy. Rodriguez*, etc. (Hakl. Soc.) I. 64 We left the Dates for the Turtles and other Birds, particularly the Solitaries. *Ibid.* 77–80.

**4.** = SOLITAIRE *sb.* 3. Also *attrib.*

**1798** M. & R. L. EDGEWORTH *Pract. Educ.* i. I. 20 At the solitary-board they must..fix their attention solely upon the figure and the pegs before them. **1806** J. BERESFORD *Miseries Hum. Life* XVI. (1807) 94 For want of better employment, playing at Solitary.

**solitary** ('sɒlɪtərɪ), *a.* Also 4–6 solytarie, 5–6 -ary(e; 4–7 solitarie, 5 -arye; 6 soletary. [ad. L. *sōlitārius*, f. *sōlus* alone; hence also It., Sp., Pg. *solitario*, F. *solitaire* (see SOLITAIRE *a.*).]

**1. a.** Quite alone or unaccompanied; destitute or deprived of the society of others.

*a* **1340** HAMPOLE *Psalter* ci. 8, I am made as sparow solitary in þe hous. **1382** WYCLIF *Esther* xiv. 3 My Lord, that art king alone, help me solitarie. ? *a* **1400** *Morte Arth.* 1576, I salle disseuere that sorte,.. And sett theme fulle solytarie. *c* **1407** LYDG. *Reson & Sens.* 3060 So ful I am of discomfort, ..Fro day to day most ful of moone, Solytarye and allone. **1513** BRADSHAW *St. Werburge* I. 2780 Whan she was solytary, and no man there present. **1555** EDEN *Decades* (Arb.) 173 What one of these solytarie wanderers dyd. *c* **1645** HOWELL *Lett.* (1650) II. 121, I am ofttimes sole, but seldom solitary. **1770** GOLDSM. *Des. Vill.* 129 All but yon widow'd solitary thing [is fled]. **1797** WORDSW. *Old Cumberland Beggar* 44 He travels on, a solitary Man; His age has no companion. **1848** THACKERAY *Van. Fair* lii, He did not know how solitary he was until little Rawdon was gone. **1863** GEO. ELIOT *Romola* xiv, He foresaw himself wandering away solitary in pursuit of some unknown fortune.

*absol.* **1560** BIBLE (Geneva) *Psalm* lxviii. 6 God maketh the solitarie to dwell in families. **1872** O. W. HOLMES *Poet Breakf.-t.* ix, When the solitary, whose hearts are shrivelling, are not set in families!

**b.** Keeping apart or aloof from society; avoiding the company of others; living alone.

*c* **1386** CHAUCER *Knt.'s T.* 507 Solitary he was, and euer alone. **1393** LANGL. *P. Pl.* C. XVIII. 7 Þer were suche eremites Solitarie by hem-self and in here selles lyueden. *c* **1420** LYDG. *Assembly of Gods* 923 Contemplatyf peple that desyre to be Solytary seruauntes vnto God alone. *c* **1440** *Alph. Tales* 477, I saw Saynt Theon sparrid in a cell, solitarie, as it was sayd, xxx[ti] yere. **1557** NORTH *Gueuara's Diall Pr.* 384 There are some so solytary that woulde never be visited. **1592** T. NASHE *P. Penilesse* (ed. 2) 9 Some thinke to be counted rare Politicians and Statesmen, by beeing solitary. **1621** BURTON *Anat. Mel.* I. i. I. v. 16 We call any man Melancholy, that is dull,..ill-disposed, solitary. **1667** MILTON *P.L.* VII. 461 Those rare and solitarie, these in flocks Pasturing at once. **1784** COWPER *Task* VI. 948 The solitary saint Walks forth to meditate at even tide. **1875** WHITNEY *Life Lang.* xiv. 286 The solitary man is as speechless as the lower animals.

*transf.* **1727** BAILEY (vol. II), *Solitariness*,..a solitary Humour.

**c.** Standing alone or by itself; not accompanied or paralleled in any way.

*a* **1633** J. AUSTIN *Medit.* (1635) 263 All three are solitarie. The Guide is but one; the Traveller, one; the Way, one. **1667** MILTON *P.L.* VI. 139 Who..with solitarie hand.. Unaided could have finisht thee. **1750** JOHNSON *Rambler* No. 75 ¶1 The result, not of solitary conjecture, but of practice and experience. **1806** BERESFORD *Miseries Hum. Life* I. Introd. 7 In disputation, the argument cumulative..is admitted to be at least as pressing as the argument solitary. **1850** W. R. WILLIAMS *Relig. Progr.* (1854) ii. 40 Unbelief does not dwell alone, a solitary and sterile sin. **1856** EMERSON *Eng. Traits* iv, Any the least and solitariest fact in our natural history.

**d.** With *a*, *one*, etc.: Single; sole.

**1742** GRAY *Spring* 44 Poor moralist! and what art thou? A solitary fly. **1769** *Junius Lett.* xxvii. (1788) 150 He gives but seven solitary lines to the only subject which can deserve his attention. **1802** GOUVR. MORRIS in Sparks *Life & Writ.* (1832) III. 160, I believe it is a solitary instance. **1830** CRUIKSHANK *Man in Black* i, Not a sous have I in the world besides that solitary five franc piece. **1890** *Science Gossip* XXVI. 49 With one solitary exception the nebular hypothesis explains all.

**e.** ***solitary wave***, a travelling, non-dissipative wave which is neither preceded nor followed by another such disturbance.

[**1837** J. S. RUSSELL in *Trans. R. Soc. Edin.* (1840) XIV. 61 This accumulated mass..appeared to roll forward alone along the surface of the quiescent fluid, a large, solitary, progressive wave.] **1838** RUSSELL & ROBISON in *Rep. Brit. Assoc. Adv. Sci. 1837* 418 This wave had been called the great solitary wave of the fluid. **1876** *Phil. Mag.* I. 262 The very different behaviour of solitary waves according as they are positive or negative... In the former case, the wave has a remarkable permanence, being propagated to great distances without much loss. **1899** [see EQUIVOLUMINAL *a.*]. **1952** RUSSELL & MACMILLAN *Waves & Tides* I. ii. 44 The velocity of solitary waves of small height is: √[g(depth of water + wave height)]. **1976** *Nature* 8 Apr. 510/2 Figure 2*a* and *b* shows typical streamline patterns for waves corresponding to solitary waves of elevation (E solitons) and of depression (D solitons).

**2.** Of places: Marked by solitude; remote, unfrequented, secluded, lonely.

*c* **1374** CHAUCER *Boeth.* I. pr. iii. (1868) 10 Whi art þou comen in to þis solitarie place of myn exil. *c* **1393** —— *Envoy to Scogan* 46, I am..Forgete in solitarie wildirnes. **1447** BOKENHAM *Seyntys* (Roxb.) 36 That neythyr I, ner Seynt Felycyte In solytarye place lengere lefth be. *a* **1533** LD. BERNERS *Huon* xxv. 72 She sawe my mother..in a soletary place. *a* **1548** HALL *Chron., Rich. III*, 22 He sodaynly turned into a solitary wood next adioyning. **1610** HOLLAND *Camden's Brit.* 269 On the north side whereof standeth solitarie a very faire Chappell. **1687** T. BROWN *Saints in Uproar* Wks. 1730 I. 81 We retir'd into a wood, and in this wood found out a most solitary cave. **1774** GOLDSM. *Nat. Hist.* (1776) III. 87 They keep chiefly in the most solitary and inaccessible places. **1849** MACAULAY *Hist. Eng.* v. I. 534 They sent an embassy to a solitary retreat on the shores of Lake Leman. **1873** W. BLACK *Pr. Thule* 4 He drove down the hill to the solitary little inn.

**3.** Characterized by the absence of all companionship or society: **a.** Of actions.

**1382** WYCLIF *Ps.* Heading, The boc begynneth of ympnes and solitarie spechis of the profete Dauyd, of Cryst. *c* **1645** HOWELL *Lett.* II. (1892) I. 443, I was upon point of going abroad to steal a solitary walk. **1667** MILTON *P.L.* II. 632 Satan..toward the Gates of Hell Explores his solitary flight. **1714** WHEATLEY *Bk. Com. Prayer* (ed. 2) vi. §29 To prevent the Solitary Masses which had been introduc'd by the Church of Rome. **1785** REID *Intell. Powers* I. viii. 244 Some operations of our minds, from their very nature, are solitary. **1801** STRUTT *Sports & Past.* IV. ii. 281 The solitary game is so denominated because it is played by one person only. **1845** FORD *Handbk. Spain* I. 48 A long solitary ride is hardly to be recommended. **1896** BADEN-POWELL *Matabele Campaign* iv, The value of solitary scouting does not seem to be sufficiently realized among us nowadays.

**b.** Of life or conditions.

**1451** CAPGRAVE *Life St. Aug.* 38 Foloweris of holy faderis whech lyued in solitarie lif. *c* **1491** *Chast. Goddes Chyld.* 42 Uneth there were ony that mighte abyde in solitarye liuynge. **1538** STARKEY *England* II. ii. 189 In the wych..they schold more profyt..then our monkys haue downe in grete processe of tyme in theyr solytary lyfe. **1600** SHAKS. *A.Y.L.* III. ii. 16 In respect that it is solitary, I like it verie well: but in respect that it is priuate, it is a very vild life. **1697** DRYDEN *Æneid* VI. 1038 Him fair Lavinia..Shall breed in groves, to lead a solitary life. **1736** BUTLER *Anal.* I. v. Wks. 1874 I. 95 Nothing which we at present see would lead us to the thought of a solitary unactive state hereafter. **1791** COWPER *Iliad* XI. 98 Seated in solitary pomp. **1817** SIR F. BURDETT in *Parl. Deb.* 1858 It was much worse to stand in hourly danger of solitary confinement at the caprice or malice of a Minister of State. **1845** MCCULLOCH *Acc. Brit. Empire* (1854) II. 501 The ideas which are generally attached to the term 'solitary confinement'.

*Comb.* **1828** CUNNINGHAM *N.S. Wales* II. 298 All jails have solitary-punishment cells.

**c.** *ellipt.* = Solitary confinement.

**1854** DICKENS *Hard Times* v, A. B.,..committed for eighteen months' solitary. **1916** J. BUCHAN *Greenmantle* v. 62 There was nothing the Boche liked so much as an excuse for sending a poor devil to 'solitary'. **1924** W. M. RAINE *Troubled Waters* xxvi. 262 'He's been in solitary for a week,' explained the warden. **1963** M. DUGGAN in C. K. Stead *N.Z. Short Stories* (1966) 101 Bread and water and solitary and take that writ on his eyeballs. **1978** T. ALLBEURY *Lantern Net* xi. 164, I visited prisoners in solitary every other day.

**4.** *Zool.* In names of various insects, birds, etc., which live alone or in pairs only, as ***solitary bee, cuckoo, dodo***, etc.

**1830** *Insect Transformations* 50 A small *solitary bee, (*Chelostoma florisomne*?) not so large as the domestic fly. **1840** *Cuvier's Anim. Kingd.* 599 The Solitary Bees have never more than the two ordinary kinds of individuals, males and females. **1881** *Cassell's Nat. Hist.* V. 367 The Solitary Bees..form the remainder of the family. **1815** STEPHENS in *Shaw's Gen. Zool.* IX. I. 84 *Solitary Cuckow. **1785** LATHAM *Gen. Synop. Birds* III. I. 3 *Solitary Dodo.. is a large bird. **1829** GRIFFITH tr. *Cuvier* VIII. 446 All those monstrous birds called..Dodo, Solitary Dodo, and Nazarene Dodo. **1810** A. WILSON *Amer. Ornith.* II. 143 *Solitary Flycatcher, *Muscicapa solitaria.* **1831** AUDUBON *Ornith. Biog.* I. 147 The Solitary Fly-catcher, or Vireo, *Vireo solitarius.* **1884** COUES *N. Amer. Birds* 333 *Vireo solitarius*,..*Solitary Greenlet. **1787** LATHAM *Suppl. Gen. Syn. Birds* I. 65 *Solitary Parrot. Size of a Starling. **1813** A. WILSON *Amer. Ornith.* VII. 53 *Solitary Sandpiper, *Tringa solitaria.* **1839** AUDUBON *Ornith. Biog.* V. 583 Solitary Sandpiper, *Totanus Chloropygius.* **1843** YARRELL *Brit. Birds* II. 597 *Scolopax major*, *Solitary Snipe. **1887** NEWTON in *Encycl. Brit.* XXII. 202/2 The Double or Solitary Snipe of English sportsmen,..a larger species. **1600** SURFLET *Countrie Farme* VII. lxii. 892 The *solitarie sparrow is by nature giuen to be melancholike. **1678** RAY tr. *Willughby's Ornith.* II. II. i. xviii. 191 The solitary Sparrow..is of the bigness of a Blackbird. **1743** EDWARDS *Nat. Hist. Birds* I. 18. **1872** COUES *N. Amer. Birds* 259 *Solitary Tattler,..a shy, quiet inhabitant of wet woods. **1884** *Ibid.* 639 *Rhyacophilus solitarius*, Solitary Tattler. **1783** LATHAM *Gen. Synop. Birds* II. I. 52 *Solitary Thrush..frequents mountains and rocky places. **1813** MONTAGU *Ornith.* Suppl. s.v., Solitary Thrush, *Turdus solitarius.* [Cf. Rennie's ed. (1831) 56–58.] **1876–82** NEWTON *Yarrell's Brit. Birds* II. 242 *note*, The real 'Solitary Thrush', *Monticola cyanus.* **1831** AUDUBON *Ornith. Biog.* I. 147 The *Solitary..Vireo, *Vireo solitarius.* **1872** COUES *N. Amer. Birds* 121 Blue-headed, or Solitary Vireo. **1830** *Insect Transformations* 54 Their most formidable enemy is a *solitary wasp (*Cerceris ornata*). **1896** LYDEKKER *Roy. Nat. Hist.* VI. 40 Of the typical solitary wasps (*Masaridæ*)..but little is known. **1730** BAILEY (fol.), **Solitary-Worm*, a Worm in the Intestines, or..in the *Pylorus*.

**5.** *Bot.* Of parts or of plants: Growing singly or separately; not forming clusters or masses.

(*a*) **1796** WITHERING *Brit. Pl.* I. 232 Seeds solitary, compressed. *Ibid.* III. 737 Flowers solitary, terminating. **1807** J. E. SMITH *Phys. Bot.* 420 Bearing..flowers in a peculiar spike, which is either solitary or double. **1837** P. KEITH *Bot. Lex.* 30 They [*sc.* the bracts] are solitary, or in pairs, or multiplicate. **1880** BESSEY *Botany* 428 Flowers solitary in the axils of the leaves—e.g., *Vinca*, Solitary Axillary. *Ibid.* 429 Solitary Terminal.

*Comb.* **1866** *Treas. Bot.* 910/1 Solitary-flowered axillary peduncles.

(*b*) **1837** P. KEITH *Bot. Lex.* 159 The mushrooms are found solitary or in small patches. **1842** LOUDON *Suburban Hort.* 45 Plants of this kind are called solitary, while those which grow in immense masses are said to be social.

**6.** Of ascidians: Simple; not compound.

**1843** *Penny Cycl.* XXV. 353/2 This metamorphosis was observed..both in a solitary and compound Ascidian.

**7.** *Anat.* Single, separate; not multiple.

**1899** *Allbutt's Syst. Med.* VI. 796 The 'solitary bundle' or ascending vago-glosso-pharyngeal root. **1905** ROLLESTON *Dis. Liver* 124 Ten solitary abscesses of the liver.

Hence † **'solitary** *v.*, to seclude. *Obs.*

**1581** G. PETTIE tr. *Guazzo's Civ. Conv.* I. (1586) 9 To reape the fruits of those labours, it behoueth him to solitarie himselfe from sinne.

**soliter(e**, variants of SOLITAIRE *a. Obs.*

**soliton** ('sɒlɪtɒn). *Physics.* [f. SOLIT(ARY *a.* + -ON[1].] A solitary wave (see SOLITARY *a.* 1 e); a quantum or quasiparticle propagated in the manner of a solitary wave.

**1965** ZABUSKY & KRUSKAL in *Physical Rev. Lett.* XV. 240/1 Each such 'solitary-wave pulse' or 'soliton' begins to move uniformly at a rate..which is linearly proportional to its amplitude. **1967** *Ibid.* XIX. 1096/1 The solitons exhibit a remarkable stability in that their identity is preserved through nonlinear interactions. This property of solitons.. was discovered numerically and justifies the name suggestive of particles. **1968** *Trans. Amer. Geophysical Union* XLIX. 209/2 Steep waves in shallow water have nonlinear properties similar to those exhibited by interacting 'solitons', nonlinear dispersive wave entities that arise in solutions of the Korteweg-de-Vries..equation. **1976** [see *solitary wave* s.v. SOLITARY *a.* 1 e]. **1979** *Physica Scripta* XX. 306/1 Solitons appear in many fields of our life ranging from classical fluids, solid state and elementary particle physics to biophysics.

† **'solitous**, *a. Obs.*[−1] [irreg. f. L. *sōlit-ārius.*] Solitary, secluded, retired.

*a* **1656** USSHER *Annals* (1658) 802 This year Tiberius lived at Rhodes a banished man, under colour of leading a solitous life.

**solitude** ('sɒlɪtju:d). Also 6 soll-. [a. OF. *solitude* (also mod.F., = Sp. *solitud*, Pg. *solitude*, It. *solitudine*) or ad. L. *sōlitūdo*, f. *sōlus* alone. Not in common use in English until the 17th c.]

In poetry, esp. of the 18th century, freq. more or less personified in senses 1 and 2, or in a blending of these.

**1.** The state of being or living alone; loneliness, seclusion, solitariness (of persons).

*c* **1374** CHAUCER *Compl. Mars* 65 She hath so grete compassion on her knyght, That dwelleth in solitude til she come. **1592** KYD *Sp. Trag.* I. iv, For sollitude best fits my cheereles mood. **1625** BACON *Ess., Friendship* (Arb.) 165 But little doe Men perceiue, what Solitude is, and how farre it extendeth. **1663** S. PATRICK *Parab. Pilgr.* xxix. (1687) 345 As the wise employ their Solitude in pious counsels. **1709** LADY M. W. MONTAGU *Let. to Miss A. Wortley* 8 Aug., Your letters..are the only pleasures of my solitude. **1764** R. BURN *Poor Laws* 199 There can be no more effectual means..than those of solitude and fasting. **1818** BYRON *Ch. Harold* IV. xxxiii, If from society we learn to live, 'Tis solitude should teach us how to die. **1856** VAUGHAN *Mystics* (1860) I. 53 Solitude brings no escape from spiritual danger. **1887** RUSKIN *Præterita* II. 237, I was not, as I used to suppose, born for solitude.

† **b.** The fact of being sole or unique. *Obs. rare.*

**1642** H. MORE *Song of Soul* IV. 20 All the arguments that I have brought For to disprove the souls strange solitude. **1646** SIR T. BROWNE *Pseud. Ep.* 133 Nor will the solitude of the Phœnix allow this denomination, for many there are of that species.

**2.** Loneliness (of places); remoteness from habitations; absence of life or stir.

**1585** T. WASHINGTON tr. *Nicholay's Voy.* IV. x. 121 b, The desart is of greate compasse and Solitude. **1639** MASSINGER *Unnatural Combat* IV. ii, His doors are fast locked up, and solitude Dwells round about them. **1729** LAW *Serious Call* xxi. 419 The solitude of his little Parish is become matter of great comfort to him. **1794** MRS. RADCLIFFE *Myst. Udolpho* xxxi, During several hours, they travelled through regions of profound solitude. **1825** SCOTT *Betrothed* x, A bustle, equally different from the solitude of the early morning, and from the roar and fury of the subsequent engagement. **1849** JAMES *Woodman* i, Then all was stillness and solitude once more. **1873** HAMERTON *Intell. Life* IX. vi. 325 The solitude of the infinite sea.

**3.** A lonely, unfrequented, or uninhabited place.

**1570–6** LAMBARDE *Peramb. Kent* (1826) 192 Being then a meere solitude, and on no part inhabited. **1617** MORYSON *Itin.* III. 125 There be vast solitudes and untilled Desarts on all sides. **1660** F. BROOKE tr. *Le Blanc's Trav.* 184 High Mountaines, and inpenitrable forests, solitudes, and frightfull deserts. **1712** STEELE in *Pope's Wks.* (1757) VII. 180, I am at a solitude, an house between Hampstead and London. **1788** GIBBON *Decl. & F.* xliii. IV. 277 That busy scene was converted into a silent solitude. **1816** BYRON *Ch. Har.* III. cii, A populous solitude of bees and birds. **1854** MILMAN *Lat. Chr.* III. vi. II. 77 Their Solitudes ceased to be solitary. **1873** SYMONDS *Grk. Poets* x. 319 An Italian of the present day avoids ruinous places and solitudes however splendid.

*fig.* **1843** CARLYLE *Past & Pres.* III. xii, Peopling..the unmeasured solitudes of Time!

**4.** A complete absence or lack. *rare.*

**1605** BACON *Adv. Learn.* II. To the King §8 Hence it proceedeth that Princes find a solitude, in regard of able men to serve them. **1821** LAMB *Elia* I. *Old Benchers Inner Temple*, Thomas Coventry.., who made a solitude of children wherever he came.

**solitudi'narian.** [f. L. *sōlitūdin-*, *sōlitūdo*: see prec.] One who seeks solitude; a recluse.

**1691** tr. *Emilianne's Frauds Rom. Monks* (ed. 3) 229 Some very considerable Places, which formerly have been the Retreats of Solitudinarians. **1725** *Portland Papers* VI. (Hist. MSS. Comm.) 138 A situation..so private and retired from common observation, as the greatest solitudinarian can wish for. **1831** *Mirror* 2 July, XVIII. 2 Like all misanthropes and solitudinarians..he [Rousseau] could never bear to be long out of the general gaze. **1880** BERTHA THOMAS *Violin-Player* III. iv. 112 'There goes a solitudinarian,' said one. 'What is he thinking of that he fights so shy of his kind?'

So †**soli'tudinary** *a.*, characterized by living alone; **soli'tudinize** *v. trans.*, to render solitary; **soli'tudinous** *a.*, characterized by solitude.

**1647** N. BACON *Disc. Govt. Eng.* I. xxxiii. (1682) 49 Their Ancestors liked not to dwell in crowds... This *solitudinary custom could not be soon shaken off. **1834** *New Monthly Mag.* XLII. 22 It adorns, refreshes, and, above all else, *solitudinizes, these little lagoons. **1803** S. PEGGE *Anecdotes of Eng. Lang.* 312, *-ous* is a termination which carries weight with it, and might be admitted, as in *multitudinous*, and other similar words in which it has obtained a situation; as,—magnitudin*ous*, gratitudin*ous*, *solitudin*ous*, plenitudin*ous*, &c. **1892** *Harper's Mag.* Feb. 425/1 So packed with people as to make Broadway look desolate and solitudinous by comparison.

**'solity.** *rare*$^{-1}$. [ad. L. *sōlitās*, f. *sōlus* alone.] Soleness.

**1882** CAVE & BANKS tr. *Dorner's Christian Doctrine* 201 The Solity, Unapproachableness, and Incognizability of God.

‖**'solium.** *rare.* [L.] **a.** A throne. (Cf. SOLIE.) **b.** A tub or similar receptacle for water.

*c* **1806** H. K. WHITE *Christiad* I. xii. Wks. 1807 II. 179 High on a solium of the solid wave.. He stood in silence. **1840** HODGSON *Hist. Northumb.* III. II. 319/2 Whether it had any.. cistern or solium for hot water has not been ascertained.

**solivagant** (sə'lɪvəgənt), *a.* and *sb.* [f. L. *sōlivagus*, f. *sōlus* + *vagārī* to wander: see -ANT.]

**A.** *adj.* Wandering about alone; characterized by going alone.

**1641** J. MEDE *Apostasy of Later Times* 142 All that crew of hypocrites, whether solivagant Hermites, or Anchorites,.. or Coenobites. **1656** BLOUNT *Glossogr.*, *Solivagant*,.. that goes here and there alone, and flies company, wandering all alone, solitary. [Hence in Phillips, Bailey, etc.] **1842** *United Service Mag.* II. 5 The solivagant habit.. is principally confined to intercourse with his peers, for he is usually attended by two or three.. pilot-fish.

**B.** *sb.* One who wanders about alone.

**1621** GRANGER *Eccl.* iv. 99 A Description of the impure drudge;.. That is to say, a soliuagant, or solitary vagrant. **1690** C. NESS *Hist. & Myst. O. & N. Test.* I. 297 Jacob seems to be.. a meer soli-vagant, or solitary vagrant. **1899** 'MONKSHOOD' *Kipling* 160 Dick walks out.. and plays the solivagant for about ten years.

So **so'livagous** *a. rare*$^{-0}$.

**1727** BAILEY (vol. II), *Solivagous*, wandring alone, solitary. **1846** WORCESTER (citing *Gentl. Mag.*).

**soljanka**, var. SOLYANKA.

**solk**, obs. form of SILK.

†**soll**, *v. Sc. Obs.* [Cf. SOLWE *v.* and SOWL *v.*] *trans.* To make foul, defile.

*c* **1375** *Sc. Leg. Saints* xvi. (*Magdalene*) 276 þu.. tholis godis servandis spyll.. & þu lyis solland þe in swet. *Ibid.* xix. (*Christopher*) 644 Owt of bordale he brocht twa.. þat.. lange tyme lay sollit in syne. *Ibid.* xxxiv. 105.

**soll**, variant of SOWL *v.*

**sollage**, obs. form of SULLAGE.

**sollar** ('sɒlə(r)), *sb.*[1] Forms: *α.* 1 solor, (1) 4–7 soler, 4–5 (9) solere. *β.* 5– solar (now the usual form in sense 1 a, esp. when used *Hist.*), 5–6 solare. *γ.* 6– soller (7 -or, 9 -ere), 8 saller. *δ.* 6– sollar (6 -are). [OE. *solor*, *soler-*, = OS. *soleri*, OHG. *solâri*, *solêri* (MHG. *solre*, *sölre*, etc., G. *söller*, †*soller*), MDu. *solre* (Du. *zolder*), MLG. *solder* (LG. *solder*, *soller*), ad. L. *sōlāri-um*, f. *sōl* sun. In ME., however, perh. readopted from AF. *soler*, *solair*, = OF. *solier*, Prov. *solier*, *solar*, Pg. *soalheiro*, It. *solaio*.]

**1. a.** An upper room or apartment in a house or other dwelling; in later use esp. a loft, attic, or garret (sometimes used as a granary or store-room). Now *arch.* or *dial.* exc. *Hist.*

Originally one open to the sun or receiving much sunlight. In OE. only *transf.* and *fig.* The confusion with *cellar* which appears in quot. 13.. is found occasionally in other texts down to the 16th cent.

*α.* *c* **897** K. ÆLFRED tr. *Gregory's Past. C.* 23 Oððæt hio fæstlice ȝestonde on ðæm solore ðæs modes. *a* **1000** *Phœnix* 204 þær se wilda fuȝel.. ofer heanne beam hus ȝetimbreð .. & ȝewicað þær sylf in þam solere.

*a* **1300** *Cursor M.* 15208 He þam lent.. A celer [*Fairf.* soler] in at ete. **13..** *Sir Beues* 1532 Nas mete ne drinke before him leid,.. Boute be a kord of a solere. **1388** WYCLIF *Gen.* vi. 16 Thou [Noah] shalt make soleris.. in the schip. *c* **1400** *Laud Troy Bk.* 15374 Paris thanne & his comperes Come walkyng out of here soleres. **1463** *Bury Wills* (Camden) 32 The ij chambrys with the soler above. **1523** LD. BERNERS *Froissart* I. ccxxxii. 322 The women.. entred into the houses, and went vp into the batylmentes and solers, and cast downe.. stones. **1603** STOW *Surv.* (ed. 2) 270 Sheds or shops, with solers ouer them.

*β.* *c* **1450** *Godstow Reg.* 404 The solare and tenement of the forsaid Laurence. **1542** UDALL *Erasm. Apoph.* 240 b, Must I bee fain to walke on yᵉ solares or loftes of my hous? **1598** STOW *Surv.* 237 Two shops, with solars, sellars, and other edifices. **1606** HOLLAND *Sueton.* 147 [He] slily crept forth and conveied himselfe up into a Solar [*marg.* a garret] next adioyning. *a* **1695** A. WOOD *Hist. Univ. Oxford* (1792) I. 359 Stone steps that led to the solar or chamber. **1789** SMYTH tr. *Aldrich's Archit.* (1818) 112 In the roof there are often rooms which we call solars. **1851** T. H. TURNER *Dom. Archit.* I. 86 The principal chamber after the hall was that called the lord's chamber, or some-times the solar. **1868** FREEMAN in Stephens *Life* (1895) I. vi. 412 All.. of this page has been written.. in the solar of the manor-house. **1895** C. R. B. BARRETT *Surrey* iii. 88 The floor of this solar is sustained by massive oak beams.

*γ.* **1530** PALSGR. 272/2 Soller, a lofte, *garnier*. **1559** *Bury Wills* (Camden) 153 A hutche on the soller. **1580** TUSSER *Husb.* (1878) 129 Then dresse it and laie it in soller vp sweete. **1623** *Maldon Documents* (Bundle 167, no. 1), One litle shop with a soller over it. **1674** RAY *S. & E.C. Words* 77 *Soller*, or *Solar*, an upper Chamber or Loft. *a* **1825** FORBY *Voc. E. Anglia*, *Soller*, a loft. **1839** SIR G. C. LEWIS *Gloss. Heref.*, *Soller*, an upper floor.

*δ.* **1530** PALSGR. 272/2 Sollar, a chambre, *solier*. **1548** UDALL, etc. *Erasm. Par. Acts* xx. 68 There were manye candelles in the sollare where as we wer than assembled. **1577** HARRISON *Descr. Brit.* II. xviii, To such an Inne or sollar there I laie my corne. **1601** HOLLAND *Pliny* I. 433 If they be kept in borded sollors or garners, the oile will be.. lesse in quantitie. **1638** RAWLEY tr. *Bacon's Life & Death* (1650) 5 The placing of Garners, on the Tops of Houses,.. is very commodious. Some also make two Sollars; An Upper, and a Lower. And the upper Sollar hath an hole in it; thorow which the Graine continually descendeth. **1819** H. BUSK *Vestriad* III. 817 Drowsy cits, who in their sollars snore. **1886** J. PAYNE tr. *Boccaccio's Decameron* VIII. vii. III. 90 A little uninhabited tower.. that the shepherds climb up .. to a sollar at the top.

**b.** An elevated chamber or loft in a church, in later use *spec.* in a steeple or belfry.

*c* **1305** *St. Kenelm* 340 in *E.E.P.* (1862) 56 Heo sat in seint peteres churche biside þe abbey ȝate In a soler in þe est side, & lokede out þerate. **1516** *Churchw. Acc.* in *Nicholls* (1797) 156 A locke and a keye to the weste dore of the solare within the church. **1533** *Dunmow Churchw. MS.* fol. 18 b, For makyng of the dore in to the ryngyng soller, 3ˢ 8ᵈ. **1561** *Ludlow Churchw. Acc.* (Camden) 105 For ij fealde and a lader that serveth in the steple or soller. **1570** FOXE *A. & M.* (ed. 2) III. 2281/2 You are one of them that.. pulled downe the Rode seller [1596 sollar, 1684 sollor], and all the Saintes. **1754** T. GARDNER *Hist. Dunwich* 156 The Vice or Stairs do not exceed in Height the upper Soller where the Bells hung. *a* **1825** FORBY *Voc. E. Anglia* 315 A belfry.. is sometimes called the bell-*soller*, sometimes simply the *soller*. **1875** *Encycl. Brit.* II. 473/1 *Solar*, *Soller*,.. an elevated chamber in a church from which to watch the lamps burning before the altars. **1906** RAVEN *Bells* 51 The chamber called the solarium, a name still preserved by ringers in their word 'soller'.

†**c.** A story of a house. *Obs.*

**1585** HIGINS tr. *Junius' Nomencl.* 181/2 *Tristega*,.. an house of three sollers. *Ibid.* 211/2 *Contignatio*,.. rearing of an house in sollers or stories. **1600** HOLLAND *Livy* 1379 Plinie calleth it Septisolium, or seven lofts or solars.

†**2.** A place exposed to the sun. *Obs.*

*c* **1440** *Pallad. on Husb.* VI. 176 At Mayes eende a solar is to paue.

**3.** *Cornish mining.* **a.** A platform in a mine, *esp.* one supporting a ladder.

**1778** PRYCE *Min. Cornub.* 326 A Saller, in a Mine, is a stage or gallery of boards for men to stand on and roll away broken stuff in wheel-barrows... In a footway Shaft, the Saller is the floor for a ladder to rest upon. **1855** J. R. LEIFCHILD *Cornwall* 156 At the foot of each ladder is a platform called a 'sollar', with an opening or man-hole leading to the next ladder beneath. **1896** J. HOCKING *Fields of Fair Renown* i. 8 We are working from the twenty-fathom sollar towards the old mine.

**b.** A raised floor under which air is admitted to a working.

**1778** PRYCE *Min. Cornub.* 147 They lay boards on the bottom of the Adit,.. by which contrivance, called a Saller, the boards being hollow underneath, air is conveyed to the workmen. **1875** J. H. COLLINS *Met. Mining* 116 A natural current may often be produced in a long level by means of an 'air-sollar'. To form an air-sollar, the floor of the level.. is laid about 6 inches above the actual bottom of the level.

**4.** *attrib.*, as ***sollar-board***, ***-chamber***, ***-floor***, etc.

**1398** TREVISA *Barth. De P.R.* XVII. clxii. (Bodl. MS.), Bordes and tables.. whan þei beþ isette in soler flores and serueþ alle men þat beþ þerin. **1648** HEXHAM II, *Een Zolderberdt*, a Sollar-plank or board. **1819** SCOTT *Ivanhoe* vi, I thought to have lodged him in the solere chamber.

Hence **'sollar** *v. trans.*, to furnish with a sollar or flooring. Also **'sollaring** (*vbl.*) *sb.*

**1547** in J. R. Boyle *Hedon* (1875) App. 134 For mendynge the sollerynge over the hye altar, ij.d. **1648** HEXHAM II, *Een planckier*, a Sollering with Plankes. *Ibid.*, *Zolderen*, to Sollar, or to Lay with plankes or boards. **1778** PRYCE *Min. Cornub.* 147 To make these matters clear with regard to driving and Sallering an Adit.

**'sollar**, *sb.*[2], dial. var. of SALLOW *sb.* ? *Obs.*

**1733** W. ELLIS *Chiltern & Vale Farm.* 157 At such Distances may be put in Sollar-sets, Ashen-keys, and Hazel-nuts. *Ibid.* 176 The old Saying, Be the Oak ne'er so stout, the Sollar red will wear it out.

**solle**, obs. form of SOUL *sb.*

**solleret** ('sɒlərɛt). *Archæol.* Also soleret, solerette. [a. OF. *soll-*, *soleret*, dim. of *soll-*, *soler*, *souler* (mod.F. *soulier*) shoe.] A shoe composed of steel plates or scales, forming part of a knight's armour in the 14th and 15th centuries.

**1826** MRS. BRAY *De Foix* iii. 72 Upon his feet are seen the long-toed solerette, or pointed shoe (peculiar to the fourteenth century). **1834** PLANCHÉ *Brit. Costume* 138 With sollerets of over-lapping plates for the feet. **1884** *Athenæum* 16 Aug. 217/2 A fine effigy of a knight.. with sollerets constructed of overlapping scales.

†**sollevate**, *v. Obs. rare.* [f. It. *sollevare* (= Sp. and Pg. *solevar*, F. *soulever*):—L. *sublevāre* SUBLEVATE *v.*] *trans.* To raise in tumult.

*a* **1734** NORTH *Examen* I. ii. §162 (1740) 114 Encouragement from the Magistrates.. to sollevate the Rabble. *Ibid.* II. iv. §85. 273 Fitzharris's [plot] was framed .. to blast the King, arm the Faction, sollevate the Mob.

†**sollevation.** *Obs.* [ad. It. *sollevazione* (= Sp. *solevacion*), f. *sollevare*: see prec.] Insurrection.

**1646** J. HOWELL *Lustra Ludov.* 105 Some of the chiefest instruments of this sollevation were cut off by the sword of Justice. *Ibid.* 127 So this dangerous sollevation was quash'd by a high hand of Royall power. **1687** RYCAUT *Hist. Turks* II. 88 The bright Beams of Justice and Government having dissipated the Storms and Fury of popular Sollevations.

**sollicit, -ation**, obs. ff. SOLICIT, -ATION.

**sollicker** ('sɒlɪkə(r)). *Austral. slang.* Also **soliker.** [Of unknown origin.] Something very big, a 'whopper'. Hence **'sollicking** *a.*, 'whopping'.

**1898** R. GRAEME *From England to Back Blocks* 82 Who was it I heard that in cutting-out some cattle on one of the Methvin plains, did come down a soliker and broke his horse's knees? **1899** 'S. RUDD' *On our Selection* 64 He kicked Farmer what he afterwards called 'a sollicker on the tail'. **1939** FRANKLIN & CUSACK *Pioneers on Parade* 168 She gave me a sollicker of a dose out of a blue bottle. **1946** K. TENNANT *Lost Haven* (1947) x. 155 It was a great big sollicking stitch if ever there was one. **1956** P. WHITE *Tree of Man* I. vii. 91 'You can jump down, can't you? You're quite big, you know.' 'Of course he can... He's a sollicker.'

**sollid(ly**, obs. forms of SOLID(LY.

**sol-lunar**, *a.* Also **solunar.** [f. SOL *sb.*[1] + LUNAR *a.*] Due to the conjunction of sun and moon.

**1790** F. BALFOUR (*title*), Treatise on putrid intestinal remitting fevers, in which the laws of the febrile state and sol-lunar influence explain the forms, crises, etc., of fevers. **1805** —— in *Asiatick Researches* VIII. 10 Exacerbations of sol-lunar power in exciting and reiterating paroxysms. **1936** J. A. KNIGHT *Mod. Angler* xviii. 198 It is well to use a descriptive term or word instead of referring to 'inland tides' or 'the conditions which cause tides'. For this purpose the word 'Solunar' has been coined. Solunar.. may be defined as follows: The time at which the conditions which cause ocean tides (*i.e.* the pull of the sun and the moon) pass the longitudinal meridian of any given point is the Solunar period at that point. **1962** E. BRUTON *Dict. Clocks & Watches* 162 '*Solunar' dial*, daily tidal times, as shown on some wrist-chronographs and used in conjunction with 'solunar tables' (J. Alden Knight) to forecast feeding times of fish and game for sportsmen. **1971** *Nature* 31 Dec. 537/2 The phase lag in the incidence of large earthquakes with respect to overhead position of the Sun and Moon is coincident with the imposition of horizontal force in such a direction and sense as to increase accumulated shear strain if this is due to the solunar torque.

**solly**, variant of SELLY *a. Obs.*; obs. f. SOLELY *adv.*

**sollycytude**, obs. form of SOLICITUDE.

**solme**, obs. form of SOAM.

**'solmizate**, *v. Mus.* [f. next, or F. *solmiser*.] **a.** *trans.* To express by solmization. **b.** *intr.* To employ solmization.

**1891** *Cent. Dict.* s.v. *Tonic*, Chromatic tones are solmizated in the usual way.

**solmization** (sɒlmɪ'zeɪʃən). *Mus.* Also **solmisation.** [ad. F. *solmisation*, f. *solmiser*, f. *sol* SOL[2] + *mi* MI *sb.*] The action or practice of solfaing.

**1730** *Treat. Harmony* 59 The Notes, which.. have in Solmisation different Sillables to express them. **1776** HAWKINS *Hist. Music* IV. III. viii. 351 The best musicians.. had found it expedient to reduce the six syllables used in solmisation to four. **1818** *Blackw. Mag.* III. 269 The exercises in solmisation or solfaing, as it is more familiarly called. **1879** *Grove's Dict. Music* I. 369 The solmization system of Guido d'Arrezo. *Ibid.* 734 So long as the compass of a single Hexachord is not exceeded, its Solmization remains immutable.

‖**solo** ('səʊləʊ), *sb.*[1] and *a.* Also 7 sola. Pl. solos (also soli). [It. *solo*:—L. *sōlum*, *sōlus* SOLE *a.* Cf. SOLUS *a.* and SOLA *a.*]

**A.** *sb.* **I. 1. a.** *Mus.* An instance of a song, melody, or other piece of music being rendered or performed by one singer or player; a piece of vocal or instrumental music performed, or intended for performance, by a single person.

**1695** CONGREVE *Love for Love* II. vii, I don't much matter your Sola's or Sonata's, they give me the Spleen. **1710** *Tatler* No. 222 ¶12 There is not a labourer or handicraftman, that in the cool of the evening does not relieve himself with solo's and sonata's! **1742** POPE *Dunciad* IV. 324 With nothing but a Solo in his head. **1844** *Musical World* XIX. 87/3 There was a solo on the cornet-à-piston by König. **1879** *Grove's Dict. Music* I. 306 The word was used for vocal soli of some length. **1890** J. HATTON *By Order of Czar* II. II. xiv. 180 Walter.. led off with the solo, and the chorus followed.

*transf.* **1755** J. HERVEY *Theron & Aspasio* dial. ix. II. 8 A spreading Cascade.. soothed the Air with a Symphony of soft and gurgling sounds... This liquid Instrument still played its Solo: still pursued its busy Way. **1791** GILPIN *Forest Scenery* III. xi. II. 295 The rook has but two, or three notes; and when he attempts a solo, we cannot praise his song. **1860** O. W. HOLMES *E. Venner* iii, Solos on the slate-pencil (making it *screech* on the slate). **1900** F. F. MOORE *Nell Gwyn* viii, There came from the room.. a loud peal of laughter—not a solo, but a duet.

**b.** *fig.* and in fig. context.

**1749** FIELDING *Tom Jones* V. xi, Though the pedagogue chose rather to play *solos* on the human instrument. **1784**

MME. D'ARBLAY *Diary* Oct., I went upstairs as usual, to treat myself with a solo of impatience for the post. **1849** E. FITZGERALD *Lett.* (1889) I. 195 The trees murmur a continuous soft 'chorus to the solo which my soul discourses within'.

**2.** Performance by one singer or player.

**1779** *Mirror* No. 54 ¶11, In the solo or the song, no such deception as the theatrical is pretended. **1797** *Monthly Mag.* III. 466 We here find a trio introduced by four lines solo. **1834** [A. PRINSEP] *Baboo* II. vii. 124 He was obliged to play his flute-parts of the opera, in solo. **1866** ENGEL *Nat. Music* iii. 111 A very usual form of national songs is that in which Solo and Chorus alternate.

**3.** A dance by one person.

**1794** MRS. RADCLIFFE *Myst. Udolpho* xxxviii, Behind stood a boy flourishing a tambourine, and dancing a solo. **1855** *Englishwoman in Russia* 18 Another peasant danced a solo in very good style. **1857** WILKINSON *Egypt. Time of Pharaohs* 28 Sometimes a man danced a *solo* to their sound, and to the clapping of hands.

**4. a.** *attrib.*, as ***solo exhibition, part, -player.***

**1776** BURNEY *Hist. Music* II. iii. (1789) I. 347 Pliny tells us that he was..the first solo-player. **1785** GROSE *Dict. Vulgar T.*, *Solo player*, a miserable performer on any instrument, who always plays alone, because no one will stay in the room to hear him. **1795** MASON *Ch. Music* I. 52 To perform a solo part in the Church Service. **1846** DICKENS *Cricket on Hearth* i, The kettle had had the last of its solo performance. **1859** *Habits of Gd. Society* v. 217 A bass [voice] should be prohibited, I think, from solo exhibitions, unless very good. **1868** *Athenæum* 29 Feb. 330/2 At Mr. H. Leslie's concert the *soli* parts were extremely well sung.

**b.** Special combs.: **solo organ**, a partial organ introduced into a larger one, for producing solo effects; **solo pitch** (see quot. 1875); **solo stop**, an organ stop of special quality or position for the performance of solos; **solo voice** (see quot. 1873).

**1843** *Civil Eng. & Arch. Jrnl.* VI. 108/1 The fourth is the combination or solo organ, upon which..can be played any stop or stops out of the swell or choir, without interfering with their previous arrangement. **1868** *Athenæum* 11 Apr. 533/3 Another new composition for *solo* voices, chorus of men and orchestra. **1873** H. C. BANISTER *Music* 251 The principal voices in an Oratorio or Opera are termed the Solo voices, as distinguished from the chorus. **1875** STAINER & BARRETT *Dict. Mus. Terms*, *Solo pitch*, the tuning of an instrument a little higher than the ordinary pitch in order to obtain brilliancy of tone with a certain amount of ease to the player.

**II.** †**5.** A carriage accommodating only one person. *Obs.* (Cf. B. 2.)

**1787** J. PUGH *Life J. Hanway* II. 120 His [Hanway's] carriage, which was a kind of Solo, from its holding but one person, was ornamented with his motto, 'never despair'.

**III. 6. a.** In card-playing (see quots.).

**1814** C. JONES *Hoyle's Games Improved* 189 The quotient shews the number of fish to be paid to each of the successful players by the other two; or in event of a Solo to be paid him by each of the three others. **1875** W. B. DICK *Mod. Pocket Hoyle* (ed. 7) 144 *Solo*.—This is an announcement to accomplish the same ends as in bidding to play in 'suit', but without the aid of the Scat cards. **1878** H. GIBBS *Ombre* 38 Solo is an engagement on the part of the Ombre to win the game without discard. *Ibid.* 40 If one player has a hand so good as to enable him to venture a Solo. **1898** 'HOFFMANN' *Hoyle's Games Modern.* 143 [In solo whist] he can call a *solo*, which is a declaration to make five of the thirteen tricks without having a partner.

**b.** ***solo whist, heart solo*** (see quots. 1898, 1907); also *ellipt.*

*c* **1875** W. B. DICK *Mod. Pocket Hoyle* (ed. 6) 146 Thus a player announcing Heart Solo (worth six counters), and having in his hand four Matadores, can bid Heart Solo *with* four Matadores, equal to ten counters, [etc.]. **1888** WILKS & PARDON (*title*) How to play solo whist. **1892** ZANGWILL *Childr. Ghetto* I. 124 Solo-whist had not yet come in to drive everything else out. **1898** 'HOFFMANN' *Hoyle's Games Modern.* 142 The objects of Solo Whist are—to make eight tricks out of the thirteen in conjunction with a partner; to make five or nine tricks out of your own hand against the other three players in combination; or to play your own hand so as to avoid taking a trick. **1907** *Hoyle's Games* 360 *Heart Solo*. This is solo for 3 players, reducing the pack to 24 cards by throwing out the 8 of hearts and all the diamonds but the 7. **1972** C. DRUMMOND *Death at Bar* v. 129 They had looked forward to a cosy evening of cocoa and solo with..the other boys.

**7.** Solo flying; a solo flight.

**1911** *Flight* 16 Sept. 805/1 Capt. Watt made a very good solo round Fargo and Stonehenge, landing exceptionally well. **1928** T. E. LAWRENCE *Let.* 20 Jan. (1938) 569 All decent birds hop it when their infants have done their first solo. **1942** R. HILLARY *Last Enemy* iii. 74 The flight immediately following our first solo was an hour's aerobatics. **1976** B. JACKSON *Flameout* iii. 44 'How long to get your license?' 'Thirty-five hours to solo, if you're good.'

**B.** *adj.* **1. a.** Alone; without a companion or partner; *spec.* with reference to flying. (Cf. SOLUS *a.* and SOLA *a.*).

**1712** ARBUTHNOT *John Bull* I. xvii, How Lewis Baboon attempted to play a game solo in clubs. **1760–72** H. BROOKE *Fool of Qual.* (1809) I. 79 Madam..would not be left solo. **1881** W. S. GILBERT *Foggerty's Fairy* III, Lately I've been dancing solo. **1914** H. ROSHER *In R.N.A.S.* (1916) 15 Hope to be flying solo by Thursday or Friday. **1928** *Daily Mail Year Bk.* 24/1 They can obtain the use of a machine in which to fly solo for £1 an hour. **1934** *Sun* (Baltimore) 22 Oct. 2/1 Lieut. M. Hansen,..who is flying solo, left Athens at 9.11 A.M. for Baghdad. **1946** *Happy Landings* July 4/1 The sergeant-pilot..had amassed the considerable sum of two hours solo on Oxfords. **1955** *Times* 24 Aug. 6/4 Eight years later Colonel Lindbergh took 33hr. 30min. in his monoplane to fly solo non-stop from New York to Paris. **1977** 'J. HERRIOT' *Vet in Spin* x. 113 'I said take her up.' 'You mean, on my own?.. Go solo?'

**b.** Acting alone or without assistance (*spec.* in *N.Z.* of single parents).

**1934** *Sun* (Baltimore) 2 Mar. 19/8 The sportsman pilot..is variously designated as 'private', 'solo' and 'student' pilot. **1965** A. BLACKSHAW *Mountaineering* 19 The risks to the inexperienced *solo* rock climber or snow-and-ice climber are very great. **1966** P. O'DONNELL *Sabre-Tooth* vii. 100 She wondered..if an army of mercenaries was being assembled...But no—he was very much a solo man. **1977** *N.Z. Herald* 8 Jan. II. 2/7 So far, the research has shown that few solo mothers are out to skin the welfare state by claiming a domestic purposes benefit and living on boyfriends.

**2.** Made to accommodate one person. (Cf. A. 5.)

**1774** H. FINLAY *Postal Jrnl.* (Brooklyn, 1867) 52, I was in a solo chair, Wills the guide was on horseback, leading a horse to relieve the chair horse. **1927** *Glasgow Herald* 18 Mar. 11 London..has only two 'solo' machines. Its members, nevertheless, contrived to put in a total of 84 hours flying during..January.

**3.** Of musical instruments, or the players of these: Playing or taking the solo part.

**1862** [see EUPHONION]. **1880** GROVE *Dict. Mus.* s.v. *Cornet*, The great organ Solo Cornet comprised either 5, 4, or 3 ranks of pipes. **1897** SHEDLOCK tr. *Riemann's Dict. Mus.* 745/1 Only one violinist (the solo violin, leader) is to play the passage. **1901** *Jedburgh Gazette* 9 Nov. 2 [He] was librarian [of the band] and solo euphonium.

**4.** That is achieved or performed unaccompanied or unassisted.

**1909** *Flight* 18 Sept. 576/2 After making a short 'solo' flight he came down. **1914** *Daily Express* 22 Sept. 7/4 A solo effort by Cantrell, who weaved his way prettily through the defence, brought the winning goal. **1927** *Glasgow Herald* 30 Sept. 11 He has made the longest solo flight so far achieved by an airman. **1940** *Daily Progress* (Charlottesville, Va.) 25 Jan. 9/4 Police claim she admits one solo holdup, made to prove her nerve. **1944** *Ibid.* 12 Sept. 6/6 The trends within medicine which make solo practice no longer..the best..kind of service for the physician or for the patient. **1955** *Times* 22 Aug. 8/5 Lord de L'Isle and Dudley, V.C., Secretary of State for Air,..has logged 13 hours' solo flying. **1974** *Times* 6 Dec. 5/5 (*caption*) The Prince of Wales after making his first solo deck landing of a Royal Navy Wessex helicopter.

**Solo** ('səʊləʊ), *sb.*[2] The name of a river in Java, used *attrib.* with reference to a neanderthaloid fossil hominid, *Homo soloensis*, known from skulls discovered at Ngandong in the valley of the Solo river in 1931.

**1932** *Discovery* Aug. 240/2 A new type of early man..is to be called 'Solo Man' from the name of the river in the Pleistocene gravels of which the skull was found. **1951** *Anthrop. Papers Amer. Mus.* XLIII. 205 (*title*) Morphology of Solo Man. **1973** B. J. WILLIAMS *Evolution & Human Origins* xi. 185/1 The Solo skulls..appear to be more primitive than Neandertal. *Ibid.*, Solo Man tends to have an occipital torus higher on the skull than did the African Neandertals. **1978** B. G. CAMPBELL *W. E. Le Gros Clark's Fossil Evidence for Human Evolution* (ed. 3) iii. 120 The main problem in this connection lies in the status of the Solo population.

**solo** ('səʊləʊ), *v.* [f. SOLO *sb.*[1] and *a.*] **1.** *intr.* To perform an action on one's own; *spec.* (*a*) to perform a vocal or instrumental solo (now usu. in jazz); (*b*) to fly solo; *spec.* to make one's first solo flight; (*c*) *Mountaineering*, to climb without a partner.

**1886** W. BOOTH *Orders & Regul. Salvation Army* III. ii. 96 All cannot solo or speak eloquently. **1917** J. M. GRIDER *War Birds* (1927) 57, I have been flying for three days and Capt. Harrison says I can solo to-morrow if it's calm. **1931** V. W. PAGÉ *ABC of Gliding* 164 In training glider pilots the student usually 'solos' from the very start. **1932** *Daily Progress* (Charlottesville, Va.) 25 Feb. 4/3 The most magnificent bodega was recently ordered to remove its enormous bar and is now trying to solo to prosperity as a restaurant only. **1942** R. HILLARY *Last Enemy* iii. 72 Here for the first time was a machine in which there was no chance of making a dual circuit as a preliminary. I must solo right off. **1956** B. HOLIDAY *Lady sings Blues* (1973) vi. 60 Whenever Basie had an arranger work out something for me, I'd tell him I wanted Lester to solo behind me. **1958** P. GAMMOND *Decca Bk. of Jazz* xx. 249 With Reinhardt and Grappelly soloing over the pulsating guitars—bass rhythm section. **1962** E. SNOW *Red China Today* (1963) xxiv. 183 All the items I have mentioned are primary sinews of a modern industrial civilization, the development of which enables a nation to 'solo' as a major industrial power. **1964** J. E. B. WRIGHT in Murray & Wright *Craft of Climbing* v. 35, I soloed up the Slab Climb. **1971** M. TAK *Truck Talk* 148 *Solo*, 1. to drive a tractor without a trailer... 2. to drive a rig alone when the driver in question is usually part of a two-man operation. **1972** D. HASTON *In High Places* iv. 57 But what to do? Thoughts of soloing down and alerting a rescue party, but that would have meant a major operation. **1977** *National Observer* (U.S.) 1 Jan. 13/3 If the river is easy, it's fun to solo. But on a formidable stream you need a partner.

**2.** *trans.* To perform (a piece of music) as a solo. *rare.*

**1858** *Punch* 8 May 184/2 The sweetness of his oratory would be completely wasted on the air of '*Keemo Kimo*' soloed by the ophicleide.

**3.** *Mountaineering.* To climb (a mountain, etc.) without a partner.

**1962** *Listener* 8 Nov. 758/2 Not that you climb alone; only very talented fanatics or complete fools 'solo' hard routes. **1975** G. MOFFAT *Miss Pink at Edge of World* xiv. 194 Soloing steep rock at Clive's age is just not on.

Hence **'soloing** *vbl. sb.*; also *attrib.*

**1929** *Papers Mich. Acad. Sci., Arts & Lett.* X. 324/2 *Soloing*, flying alone. **1971** C. BONINGTON *Annapurna South Face* 324 Soloing, climbing without the security of a rope. **1973** —— *Next Horizon* v. 90 Dick..was unaccustomed to fast soloing, and eventually they had turned back before even reaching the foot of the climb proper. **1977** *Rolling Stone* 24 Mar. 66/2 His guitar style combines Hendrix-inspired production technique with virtuoso soloing ability.

**Solochrome** ('səʊləkrəʊm). Also solochrome. A proprietary name for a range of synthetic dyestuffs used esp. in chemical analysis in colour tests for various metals, notably aluminium. Usu. *attrib.* in names of particular dyes.

**1924** *Trade Marks Jrnl.* 23 Apr. 910 *Solochrome*... Chemical substances used in dyeing... British Dyestuffs Corporation Limited. **1938** *Analyst* LXIII. 266 A test for aluminium..has been based on the vivid orange-red fluorescence obtained with aqueous alcoholic solutions of Solochrome Red ERS and Solochrome Violet RS. **1960** A. G. E. PEARSE *Histochem.* (ed. 2) xxiv. 693 Other Solochrome dyes give coloured, non-fluorescent complexes with aluminium hydroxide. **1976** *Lancet* 4 Dec. 1209/2 Undecalcified 6μm sections were prepared and stained with toluidine blue, pH 2·8, and solochrome cyanin.

**solod** ('sɒlət). *Soil Science.* Also **soloth**. Pl. (sometimes const. as *sing.*) **solodi, soloti**; also **solods**. [a. Russ. *sólod'*, f. *sol'* salt.] A type of soil derived from a solonetz by leaching of saline or alkaline constituents, having a pale, leached subsurface horizon, and occurring characteristically under grass or shrub vegetation in semi-arid and desert regions.

**1925** S. A. WAKSMAN tr. *K. K. Gedroits's Soil Absorbing Complex & Absorbed Soil Cations* (U.S. Dept. Agric.) 13 The process of forming a new type of soil from an alkali soil as a mother soil leads to secondary soils ('soloti'), which are distinguished from primary podsol soils both in origin and in the properties of the formation. **1933** *Soil Sci.* XXXVI. 181 The solodi profiles of the semiarid short grass plains zone. *Ibid.* 184 (*caption*) A well-developed solodi. **1934** *Ibid.* XXXVIII. 484 After the complete formation of Soloth with the removal of the mobile colloids, the continued growth of the native grasses again changes the soil to that normal for the region. **1953** *Proc. Soil Sci. Soc. Amer.* XVII. 287 Solod soils ordinarily occur in the lowest local position in the landscape, usually a deep depression, while Solonetz and solodized Solonetz soils develop on level areas or in slight depressions. **1963** D. W. & E. E. HUMPHRIES tr. *Termier's Erosion & Sedimentation* xv. 324 The soloti are the degraded alkaline soils derived from solonetz soils by solotization, a process analogous to podsolization. *Ibid.* 325 Solotis are known in the U.S.S.R. and in the western United States. **1974** E. A. FITZPATRICK *Introd. Soil Sci.* vii. 119 Solods can be regarded as leached solonetzes in which the upper horizons are strongly bleached becoming pale grey or white.

Hence **so'lodic** *a.*, being, resembling, or characteristic of a solod; **'solodize** *v. intr.*, to change into a solod; **solodi'zation** (also **solot-**), the formation of a solod by the leaching of salts from a solonetz; **'solodized (solot-)** *ppl. a.*, altered by this process.

**1925** S. A. WAKSMAN tr. *K. K. Gedroits's Soil Absorbing Complex & Absorbed Soil Cations* (U.S. Dept. Agric.) 14 Just as the carbonates of calcium and magnesium protect the soil of forest zone from podsolization, these salts protect alkaline soils from 'solotization'. *Ibid.* 15 The question of the presence of absorbed hydrogen in solotized soils is still not clear. **1932** E. J. RUSSELL *Soil Conditions & Plant Growth* (ed. 6) iv. 269 In this process of solodisation, the percolating water continues to remove sodium and other products of decomposition from the soil complex, replacing the exchangeable sodium by hydrogen, and depositing the products of decomposition lower down. **1934** *Soil Sci.* XXXVIII. 484 As soon as solonetz forms it immediately begins to solotize with the development of a profile approaching the soloth. **1964** *Jrnl. Soil Sci.* XV. 176 The absence of solodized-solonetz from the deep sands is related to the coarser texture of the material of which they are composed. **1968** H. C. T. STACE et al. *Handbk. Austral. Soils* vi. 153 In the solodized solonetz, solodic soils and red-brown earths the topsoil is acid.., but all..contain secondary carbonate in the deeper horizons. **1978** FANIRAN & AREOLA *Essent. Soil Study* viii. 183 Salinization, solonization, and solodization..resulting in the formation of solonchaks, solonetz, and solodic soils respectively.

†**so'lœcal**, *a. Obs.*[−1] [f. L. **solœc-us*, ad. Gr. σόλοικος: see SOLECISM.] Provincially incorrect.

**1716** M. DAVIES *Athen. Brit.* III. 31 That favours much of the old Saxon or even of the Soloecal Dialect.

‖**solœ'cophanes.** *Obs. rare.* [ad. Gr. σολοικοφανής like a solecism.] An apparent solecism.

**1583** FULKE *Def. Tr. Script.* i. 37 It is either a plaine *solœcophanes*.., or a corruption crept out of the margent into the text. *Ibid.* 43 He which vseth *Solœcophanes* in Greeke committeth not a *solœcisme*. **1727** BAILEY (vol. II), *Soloecophanes*,..that which seemeth to be a Solœcism, (or Impropriety of Speech) and is not.

**'solograph.** *rare* [f. SOL *sb.*[1], after *photograph.*] (See quot. 1858).

**1851** C. CIST *Sketches & Statistics of Cincinnati in 1851* 187 Hawkins, in addition to his daguerrotypes, produces what he terms a *solograph* picture. **1858** SIMMONDS *Dict. Trade*, *Solograph*, a name which has been given to some pictures on paper taken by the talbotype or calotype process.

**soloist** ('səʊləʊɪst). [f. SOLO *sb.*[1] and *a.* + -IST.] One who sings or performs a solo or solos.

**1864** *Realm* 20 Apr. 8 The soloist was Signor Sivori, who played Mendelssohn's violin concerto. **1879** *Sat. Mus. Rev.* 6 Sept. 567 The soloists acquitted themselves thoroughly well. **1890** J. HATTON *By Order of Czar* (1891) 328 Presently the soloist paused in his song.

**soloistic** (səʊləʊˈɪstɪk), *a.* [f. SOLOIST + -IC.] Of, pertaining to, containing, or of the nature of, soloists or solo parts. Also *transf.* Hence **soloˈistically** *adv.*

**1947** A. EINSTEIN *Music in Romantic Era* xvi. 285 Three acts..: each one in two parts, the first part 'soloistic', the second always uniting all the figures of the farce, as the tradition of *opera buffa* demanded. **1952** B. ULANOV *Hist. Jazz in Amer.* (1958) xiv. 165 Edward Inge an alto, and Horace Henderson and Don Kirkpatrick on piano were other soloistic assets of the band. **1961** *Times* 9 June 17/1 The cellos are strung out in front of the basses, which..can cause the cello tone to be diffused when the section is used soloistically. **1974** *Daily Tel.* 11 Feb. 10/4 Every member of the choir seems to command a soloistic projection yet the overall sonority is magnificently blended. **1975** *Gramophone* Aug. 316/3 Above all, the position of the solo viola is too soloistic. **1977** *Country Life* 2 June 1494/3 The commitment, enthusiasm, and general lack of soloistic egotism of almost all involved was delightful to observe. **1980** *Early Music* Jan. 19/1 Soloistic music needs a more generous portion of personal sound.

**Solomon** (ˈsɒləmən). Also 6–7 Salomon. [The name of the Jewish king *Solomon* (in older English usage *Salomon*), L. *Solomon*, *Salomon*, Gr. Σολομών, Σαλομών, Σαλωμών, ad. Heb. *Sh'lōmōh*.] One who resembles, or is comparable to, Solomon, esp. in respect of wisdom or justice; a profoundly wise person, a sage; also ironically, a wiseacre.

**1554** MAYLAND in *Hawes' Past. Pleas.* *iij, The famous Prince and seconde Salomon, Kynge Henrye the Seuenth. **1557** *Tottel's Misc.* (Arb.) 168 In sober wit a Salomon. **1624** BEDELL *Lett.* v. 90 Let our Salomon [James I] be Iudge between them. **1656** EARL MONM. tr. *Boccalini's Advts. fr. Parnass.* II. lix. (1674) 212 Command, makes men seem wise Solomons..who..have no more Brains than a Goose. **1678** BUTLER *Hud.* III. *Lady's Answer to Knight* 195 If you all were Solomons, And Wise and Great as he was once. **1773** H. WALPOLE *Lett.* (1857) VI. 42 These Solomons delight to sit to a maker of wax-work. **1829** SCOTT *Anne of G.* xxx, But the old Swiss is a Solomon compared with him. **1889** *Science-Gossip* XXV. 244 It must imply that there was once an exceptionally wise Paramœcium... The existence of such an infusorial Solomon is at least improbable.

**b.** ***British, English,*** or ***Scotch Solomon***, King James VI of Scotland and I of England.

**1814** W. WILSON *Hist. Dissent. Ch.* IV. 123 About the year 1621, our English Solomon then sitting on the throne. *c* **1830** COLERIDGE in *Lit. Rem.* (1838) III. 48 In the slavering times of our Scotch Solomon.

**solomon**, variant of SALMON *sb.*[2] *Obs.*

† **Solomon-gundy**, perversion of SALMAGUNDI.

**1764** [see SALMAGUNDI 1]. **1769** E. RAFFALD *Engl. Housekpr.* (1778) 281 To make a Solomon-Gundy. **1896** 'Q.' (QUILLER COUCH) *Story of Sea* II. xxviii. 571 A savoury dish of solomon-gundy.

**Solomonian** (sɒləˈməʊnɪən), *a.* Also -ean. [f. SOLOMON + -IAN.] Of, pertaining or relating to, characteristic of, King Solomon; Solomonic.

**1747** *Mem. Nutrebian Crt.* II. 121 Pleased with his Solomonean prudence, by this judicious way of discovering the guilty person. **1835** J. B. ROBERTSON tr. *Schlegel's Philos. Hist.* xviii. (1846) 456 The Solomonian traditions connected with the very foundation of the order of Templars. **1861** *Morn. Chron.* 3 Aug., The Colonel..dismissed the case by a Solomonian judgment. **1896** A. J. BUTLER tr. *Ratzel's Hist. Mankind* I. 134 In giving judgment, he needs no great abundance of Solomonian wisdom.

**Solomonic** (sɒləˈmɒnɪk), *a.* Also 8 -ick. [f. as prec. + -IC.]

**1.** Ascribed to, originating with, Solomon.

**1722** G. MACKENZIE *Writers Scots Nation* III. 517 This is a large Print... Upon the Top is the Blessed Virgin... Then follow Seven Columns... In the 5th Column are..the Solomonick; the Noachick Alphabets. **1873** *Our Work in Palestine* ix. (1874) 160 Solomon's Temple, then, was a rectangle... Wilson's Arch would, therefore, be Solomonic. **1883** A. ROBERTS *O.T. Revision* vi. 126 As..the book was written in Greek, the idea of its Solomonic authorship must at once be set aside.

**2.** Characteristic of Solomon; suggestive of the wisdom of Solomon.

**1857** DICKENS *Dorrit* I. xiii, This sentiment, in itself almost Solomonic. **1861** *Sat. Rev.* 30 Nov. 563 That Solomonic wisdom which is better than..silver. **1876** *Tinsley's Mag.* XIX. 6 With a Solomonic shake of her head.

So † **Soloˈmonical** *a. Obs.*

**1530** LYNDESAY *Test. Papyngo* 2 Suppose I had..sapience more than Salamonicall. **157.** BUCHANAN *Let.* in *Wks.* (S.T.S.) 57, I most neidis præfer the rude Scottis wyt of capitane Cocburne to your inglis solomonical sapience.

**Solomon Islander** (ˈsɒləmən ˈaɪləndə(r)). [f. *Solomon Islands* (see below) + -ER[1].] A native or inhabitant of the Solomon Islands in the southwest Pacific.

**1864** in C. M. Yonge *Life John Coleridge Patteson* (1874) II. ix. 96 Two of the Solomon Islanders distinguished themselves by jumping off the foreyard, and diving under the ship. **1911** F. COOMBE *Islands of Enchantment* III. i. 239 Perchance it is as well that the Solomon Islanders had about 300 years in which to forget the first Christian emissaries before the next visited them! **1951** R. FIRTH *Elements of Social Organization* iii. 92 The Solomon Islander is no less sensitive to the appellation of country bumpkin than is his European counterpart. **1968** *World Book Encycl. Australasia* II. 323 In 1896, Solomon Islanders killed five Austrian scientists who were attempting to climb their sacred mountain.

**Solomon's seal.** Also 6–7 Salomon's seal(e. [tr. med.L. *sigillum Solomōnis* (*Salo-*, *Salamōnis*).

The name has been variously explained as referring to the markings seen on a transverse section of the root-stock, or to the round scars left on this by the decay of the stems, or to the use of the root 'to seal and close up green wounds'.]

**1.** A plant, *Polygonatum multiflorum*, the stems of which bear on the upper part broad sessile leaves and drooping green and white flowers.

**1543** TRAHERON tr. *Vigo's Chirurg.* 182 b/2 Of the rootes of salomons seale sodden after the same maner. **1578** LYTE *Dodoens* 102 White roote or Salomons seale is of two sortes. **1629** PARKINSON *Kitchen Garden* I. vii. 472 Salomon's seal, or (as some call it) Ladder to heauen. **1676** *Phil. Trans.* II. 629 There grow wild in the Woods, Plantane of all sorts, Yellow-Dock,..Solomons-seal [etc.]. **1767** ABERCROMBIE *Ev. Man his own Gardener* (1803) 553 Now is also a proper time to..transplant the roots of..Solomon's seal. **1785** MARTYN *Rousseau's Bot.* xviii. (1794) 249 This species is distinguished from Solomon's-seal..by the flowers growing on a scape or naked stalk. **1826** MISS MITFORD *Village* Ser. II. (1863) 410 The pendent drops of the stately Solomon's seal, which hang like waxen tassels under the full and regular leaves. **1857** A. GRAY *First Lessons Bot.* (1866) 42 Some rootstocks are marked with large round scars of a different sort, like those of the Solomon's Seal. **1882** *Proc. Ber. Nat. Club* IX. 462 Celadine and Solomon's seal were cultivated alongside the houses that we passed.

**2.** Applied to various other plants (see quots.).

**1760** J. LEE *Introd. Bot.* App. 327 Solomon's Seal, Pensylvanian, *Uvularia*. **1846–50** A. WOOD *Class-bk. Bot.* 552 *Majanthemum*... *Convallaria bifolia*. Two-leaved Solomon's Seal. *Ibid.*, *Smilacina*... *Convallaria trifoliata*. Three-leaved Solomon's Seal. **1856** A. GRAY *Man. Bot.* (1860) 467 *Smilacina*. False Solomon's Seal. **1898** MORRIS *Austral Eng.* 426 *Solomon's Seal*,..the Tasmanian name for *Drymophila cyanocarpa*,..also called Turquoise Berry.

**Solon** (ˈsəʊlən). [a. L. *Solōn*, Gr. Σόλων, the early Athenian legislator and one of the seven sages of Greece.] A sage; a wiseacre. Also (with small initial) in the *U.S.*, in weakened sense: a legislator, congressman.

**1625** B. JONSON *Staple of N.* II. iii, Your graue great Solons. **1820** SHELLEY *Œd. Tyr.* I. 64 Ask else your royal Solons. **1840** THACKERAY *Jolly Jack*, When village Solons cursed the Lords. **1903** 'O. HENRY' *Art & Bronco* in *Ainslee's* Feb. 59/1 The season of activity and profit that the congregation of the solons bestowed. The boarding houses were corralling the easy dollars of the gamesome lawmakers. **1948** E. POUND *Pisan Cantos* (1949) lxxxiv. 128 Thus the Solons, in Washington. **1959** *New Scientist* 29 Jan. 230/3 Congress was not in session at the time of the AAAS meeting... But the solons are back in the Capitol now. **1976** *National Observer* (U.S.) 21 Aug. 11/2 The great national political community of solons, scribes, police-men, [etc.].

**solonchak** (ˈsɒləntʃæk). *Soil Science.* Also solontschak, etc. [a. Russ. *solonchák* salt marsh, salt lake, f. *sol'* salt.] A type of salty, alkaline soil that has little or no structure, is characteristically pale in colour, and occurs typically under salt-tolerant vegetation in poorly-drained semi-arid or desert regions.

**1925** S. A. WAKSMAN tr. *K. K. Gedroits's Soil Absorbing Complex & Absorbed Soil Cations* (U.S. Dept. Agric.) 9 The stage of formation of a saline soil (solontshak) will in this case always take place before the stage of formation of an alkaline soil (solonetz). **1927** C. F. MARBUT tr. *Glinka's Great Soil Groups of World* 40 There is no word in English carrying the same meaning conveyed by the expression 'alkali soils with definite structure'. To avoid the use of so long a phrase the Russian word Solonetz will be used in the following pages while the word Solontschak will be used for 'alkali soils without pronounced structure'. **1939** *Agric. in 20th Cent.* 177 Where the soil water tended to move upwards, as in parts of the hot, dry countries, and especially where it contained salts in solution, another set of changes took place and the resulting soils were called 'solontchaks'. **1963** D. W. & E. E. HUMPHRIES tr. *Termier's Erosion & Sedimentation* xv. 325 At the research station at Hamadena, the soils are dominantly solonchak, secondarily characterized by being sodic, magnesian and calcic. **1972** J. G. CRUICKSHANK *Soil Geogr.* iv. 145 Where sodium salts exceed 2 per cent of the mineral matter, a salic horizon is produced which may even be a salt crust on the soil surface under extremely dry conditions and high groundwater table. The soil is called a solonchak.

**solonette**, variant of SOLENETTE.

**solonetz** (ˈsɒlənɛts). *Soil Science.* Also -nez, -nietz. [ad. Russ. *solonéts* salt marsh, salt lake, f. *sol'* salt.] A type of alkaline soil that is rich in carbonates, consists characteristically of a hard, dark, columnar subsoil overlain by a thin, friable surface layer, and occurs in conditions similar to those associated with solonchaks but having better drainage.

**1924** S. A. WAKSMAN tr. *K. K. Gedroits's Ultramechanical Composition of Soils* (U.S. Dept. Agric.) 17 These are soils which have been saline with sodium salts (saline soils) and alkaline soils ('solonez' soil) formed from these as a result of removal of the salt. **1925, 1927** [see SOLONCHAK]. **1932** E. J. RUSSELL *Soil Conditions & Plant Growth* (ed. 6) iv. 268 The last stage, when the solonietz has been exposed to prolonged leaching, is the solod of the Russians. **1938** [see PLANOSOL]. **1968** H. C. T. STACE et al. *Handbk. Austral. Soils* vi. 153 The essential features of solonetz are prominent texture differentiation with an abrupt boundary between loamy A horizons and clay B horizons, neutral to alkaline surface soil and strongly alkaline subsoil [etc.]. **1972** J. G. CRUICKSHANK *Soil Geogr.* iv. 127 (*caption*) A solonetz profile in South Australia showing strong prismatic structure in the B horizon.

Hence **soloˈnetzic** *a.*, being, resembling, or characteristic of a solonetz.

**1935** *Soil Sci.* XL. 465 A strongly solonetzic soil from Chongar. **1974** E. C. STACEY *Peace Country Heritage* ii. 74 If the parental material has a high salt content, a hard-pan solonetzic soil will result.

**so long**: see LONG *adv.* 1 c.

**Solonian** (səˈləʊnɪən), *a.* [See SOLON.] Of, pertaining to, connected with, Solon.

**1843** GROTE in *Class. Mus.* I. 8 The mina as weight..was required to weigh 138 Solonian standard drachmæ. *Ibid.*, The Solonian standard. **1846** —— *Hist. Greece* I. xiv. I. 379 About the time of the Solonian legislation at Athens. **1885** G. W. COX *Lives Gk. Statesmen* 27 *marg.*, Solonian law against neutrality in times of sedition. **1896** GREENRIDGE *Handbk. Gk. Const. Hist.* vi. 151 The permanence of these Solonian property-classes is remarkable.

So **Soˈlonic** *a.*, Sonon-like; Solonian; **ˈSolonist**, a wiseacre.

**1607** T. WALKINGTON *Optic Glass* 126 Like pumpion headed Solonists they looke. **1796** *Mod. Gulliver's Trav.* 102 Instead of any Solonic observations, I wrote the following address. **1888** *Encycl. Brit.* XXIV. 488/2 The system [of weights]..called Attic or Solonic.

**solonization** (ˌsɒlənaɪˈzeɪʃən). *Soil Science.* [f. SOLON(ETZ + -IZATION.] The formation of a solonetzic soil by the leaching of salts from a solonchak. So **ˈsolonized** *ppl. a.*

**1934** *Soil Sci.* XXXVIII. 483 This process is called solonization and might be said to consist of desalinization plus alkalinization. **1945** *Ibid.* LIX. 420 The physical and morphological feature is the compactness of the solonized section of the profile. **1948** *Queensland Jrnl. Agric. Sci.* V. 19 These solonized patches are comparatively wide-spread throughout the habitat of 'sandalwood'. **1963** D. W. & E. E. HUMPHRIES tr. *Termier's Erosion & Sedimentation* xv. 324 In a region of saline soils, the areas undergoing solonization become depressions where structural change brings about compaction of the soil.

**soloth**, var. SOLOD.

**solow**, obs. form of SULLOW, plough.

**solp**, variant of SOWP *v.*, SULP *v. Obs.*

‖ **Solpuga** (sɒlˈpjuːgə). Also 8 Sal-. [L. *solpūga* (*salpūga*), also *solipūga*, *solifūga*: cf. SOLIFUGE.]

**1.** A venomous ant or spider mentioned by classical authors.

**1601** HOLLAND *Pliny* VIII. xxix. 212 In Æthyopia..there is a great countrey..dispeopled sometime by Scorpions, and a Kind of Pismires called Solpugae. **1627** MAY *Lucan* IX. 954 Who, small Solpuga, from thy hole would flee? Yet the three sisters giue their power to thee. **1718** ROWE tr. *Lucan* IX. 1418 Or cou'd we the Salpuga's anger dread?

**2.** *Ent.* A genus of tropical or semi-tropical spiders (belonging to the group *Solpugidæ* or *Solifugæ*); a weasel-spider.

**1815** KIRBY & SP. *Entomol.* iv. (1818) I. 126 The bite of one of the centipedes..is less tremendous than that of the *Solpuga*. **1835** KIRBY *Habits & Inst. Anim.* II. xvi. 86 It seems, therefore, almost certain that the ancient and modern Solpuga are synonymous.

**solpugid** (sɒlˈpjuːdʒɪd). *Ent.* [See prec. and -ID[3].] One of the *Solpugidæ*: (see prec. 2).

**1869** A. S. PACKARD *Guide to Study of Insects* 655 Under the term Pedipalpi we would embrace..the Solpugids and Phalangids. **1875** *Encycl. Brit.* II. 281 The Muscular System of Solpugids appears to be very similar to that of other Arachnids. *Ibid.*, Several Solpugids entered the tent-door. **1912** J. H. COMSTOCK *Spider Bk.* i. 34 Most solpugids spend the day under stones or other rubbish..and come forth at night. **1954** BORROR & DELONG *Introd. Study of Insects* xxx. 787 The body of a solpugid is about ½ inch long and is somewhat constricted in the middle, and the chelicerae are very large.

‖ **sols.** *Obs.* Also solz. [older F. *sols*, var. of *sol* SOL *sb.*[3]] A sou.

*a* **1625** FLETCHER *Elder Brother* II. i, They shall not share a Solz of mine between them. **1706** PHILLIPS (ed. Kersey), *Sols* or *Sous*, a French coin that contains 12 Deniers.

† **solsecle.** *Obs.* Also 5 solcecle, -sykelle, sausikel. [a. OF. *solsecle* (*soucicle*, etc.), ad. L. *solsequium*: see next.] The marigold.

*a* **1310** in Wright *Lyric P.* xvi. 53 Heo is solsecle of suetnesse. *Ibid.* v. 26. *a* **1400** *Pistill of Susan* 110 þe sauge, þe solsecle, so semeliche to siht. *c* **1450** *M.E. Med. Bk.* (Heinrich) 124 Take feþerfoye, matfeloun, mogwort, solcecle, scabyouse [etc.].

‖ **solˈsequium.** *Obs.* [L., f. *sōl* sun + *sequī* to follow.] = prec.

[*c* **1425** tr. *Arderne's Treat. Fistula*, etc. 52 Epithimated with þe iuyse of solsequi, i. marigold. *Ibid.*, þe iuyse of solsiquii.] **1540** *Treas. Poore Men* 44 b, For the Palsey. Take ..two handefull of hertestonge, two handefull of Solsequium. *a* **1568** MONTGOMERIE *Misc. Poems* xv. 2 Lyk as the dum Solsequium..Hings doun his head.

So † **solsequy.** *Obs.*[−1]

*a* **1680** T. BROOKS in Spurgeon *Treas. David* xxx. 7 (1871) II. 58 Bowing and inclining the head, as the solsequy and mallow-flowers.

† **solstacion.** *Obs.*[−1] [ad. L. *sōlstitium*, after *station*: cf. SOLSTICION.] Solstice.

*c* **1400** *Destr. Troy* 10637 Sadmen of Syens, þat settyn hom þerto, Solstacion, for sothe, sayn hit to hat.

† **solstead.** *Obs. rare.* [f. L. *sōl-* in *sōlstitium* (see next) + STEAD *sb.* Cf. SUNSTEAD.] Solstice.

**1601** HOLLAND *Pliny* xxvi. v. 245 If it be gathered about the Summer solstead. **1653** W. RAMESEY *Astrol. Restored* 79 Winter [beginning] at the second Solstead.

**solstice** (ˈsɒlstɪs). Also 7 solsticke, solstist. [a. OF. *solstice* (also mod.F.), ad. L. *sōlstitium* SOLSTITIUM.]

**1.** One or other of the two times in the year, midway between the two equinoxes, when the sun, having reached the tropical points, is farthest from the equator and appears to stand still, i.e. about 21st June (the summer solstice) and 22nd December (the winter solstice).

*c* **1250** *Gen. & Ex.* 150 Two ȝeuelengðhes timen her, And two solstices in ðe ȝer. **1432–50** tr. *Higden* (Rolls) I. 201 There is a welle..whiche floethe ouer with watere abowte the solstice of somer. *Ibid.* III. 51 Whiche Olimpias began in the solstice of wynter, when men of Grece begynne theire yere. **1549** *Compl. Scotl.* vi. 50 The tropic of Cancer..is the solstice of symmyr... The circle of capricorne is callit the solstice of vyntir. **1617** MORYSON *Itin.* III. 269 At Lucern twice each yeere they make election of Senators.., namely, about each Solstice of the yeere. **1660** R. COKE *Power & Subj.* 265 As we see in foxes about the brumal Solstice. **1719** DE FOE *Crusoe* I. 214 This being the southern Solstice, for Winter I cannot call it. **1794** R. J. SULIVAN *View Nat.* I. 410 It is at the solstices that we have the lowest tides in the year. **1834** MRS. SOMERVILLE *Connex. Phys. Sci.* xiii. 99 It is estimated from the winter solstice, the middle of the long annual night under the poles. **1847** LONGF. *Evang.* I. iv. 61 When the air is serene in the sultry solstice of summer.

**b.** *spec.* The summer solstice, or the heat of this.

**1643** SIR T. BROWNE *Relig. Med.* I. §32 So when thy absent beames begin t' impart Againe a Solstice on my frozen heart, My winter's ov'r. **1692** WASHINGTON *Milton's Def. People* i. M.'s Wks. 1851 VIII. 21 May the Gods and Goddesses, Damasippus, bless thee with an everlasting Solstice; that thou mayst always be warm. **1855** SINGLETON *Virgil* I. 48 The solstice from the flock Ward off.

**2.** A solstitial point.

**1601** DOLMAN *La Primaud. Fr. Acad.* III. xx. 96 The Solstists or sun-steads and poles of the Zodiacke. **1646** SIR T. BROWNE *Pseud. Ep.* 227 A temperate heat.., which by his approach unto the solstice he intendeth. **1678** HOBBES *Decameron* Wks. 1845 VII. 104 The distance between the equinoctial and the solstice, is not always the same. **1755** B. MARTIN *Mag. Arts & Sci.* 192/3 These two Points are called the Solstices. **1812** WOODHOUSE *Astron.* ix. 65 The interval of time..between two appearances of the Sun in the solstices. **1842** *Penny Cycl.* XXII. 214/1 *Solstices*, the points of the ecliptic which are highest above the equator.

**3.** *fig.* A turning, culminating, or stopping point; a furthest limit; a crisis.

*a* **1631** DONNE *Select.* (1840) 105 A Christian hath no solstice..where he may stand still, and go no further. **1638** WILKINS *New World* xiv. (1707) 114 Arts are not yet come to their Solstice. **1663** HEATH *Flagellum* (1672) 158 This being the Solstice of his Fortunes. **1860** EMERSON *Conduct of Life, Culture* Wks. (Bohn) II. 370 There is in every constitution a certain solstice.

**4.** *transf.* A standing still (*of* the sun).

**1643** SIR T. BROWNE *Relig. Med.* I. §29 The Jewes that can beleeve the supernaturall solstice of the Sunne in the dayes of Joshua.

† **solsticion.** *Obs.*⁻¹ [ad. L. *sōlstitium*: see prec. and cf. SOLSTACION.] Solstice.

*c* **1391** CHAUCER *Astrolabe* I. §17 In this heued of cancer is the grettest declinacioun northward of the sonne, & ther-for is he cleped the Solsticioun of somer.

† **solsticy.** *Obs.* Also 5–6 solsticie. [ad. L. *sōlstitium*.] Solstice. Also *fig.*

**1570** DEE *Math. Pref.* d iij b, The fashion of the heauen, the Æquinox, the Solsticie, and the course of the Sterres. **1602** MARSTON *Antonio's Rev.* I. iii, You arrive even in the solsticie And highest point of sun-shine happinesse. **1620** MIDDLETON & ROWLEY *World Tost at Tennis* Induct., When the high-heated year Is in her solsticy.

**solstitial** (sɒlˈstɪʃəl), *a.* and *sb.* Also 6–7 -tiall, -ciall, 7–9 -cial. [a. F. *solsticial*, †*solstitial*, or ad. L. *sōlstitiāl-is*, f. *sōlstitium*: see SOLSTICE.]

**A.** *adj.* **1.** Of or belonging to, connected with, a solstice or the solstices.

**1559** W. CUNNINGHAM *Cosmogr. Glasse* 35 They are called Colures, of which th'one..is named th'equinoctiall Colure, and th'other..the solstitiall Colure. **1591** NASHE *Prognost.* Wks. (Grosart) II. 164 The Sunne..at his passage vnto the solsticiall estiuall signe Cancer. **1594** BLUNDEVIL *Exerc.* III. I. xxvii. (1636) 336 Now it is found to have passed that point so farre towards the Solsticiall point, as [etc.]. **1601** HOLLAND *Pliny* I. 8 The shadowes of them that dwell Northerly vnder the Solstitiall circle in Summer. **1634** PEACHAM *Compl. Gentl.* vii. 60 The other passeth thorow the Solstitiall points, and is called the Solstitiall Colure. **1755** B. MARTIN *Mag. Arts & Sci.* 192/3 What Distinction is made of these Solstitial Points? **1812–6** PLAYFAIR *Nat. Phil.* II. 121 From observations of the sun's solstitial altitudes. **1845** *Theologian* II. 36 Cancer..is a watery,..solstitial, and exceedingly fruitful sign. **1894** R. A. GREGORY *Elem. Physiogr.* vii. (ed. 4) 141 Each of the solsticial points being midway between the equinoxes.

**2.** Occurring, taking place, etc., at the time of the solstice(s).

*c* **1610** SIR C. HEYDON *Astrol. Disc.* (1650) 14 These four causes are most evident upon the very solstitial days. **1695** *Phil. Trans.* XIX. 15 In order to determine the Proportion of the Gnomon to the Solstitial shade. **1796** PEGGE *Anonym.* (1809) 431 The solstitial rains are here in England extremely beneficial. **1845** *Peter Parley's Ann.* VI. 133 The setting in of the solstitial season. **1853** KANE *Grinnell Exped.* xxxi. (1856) 266 The solstitial day of greatest darkness. **1881** *Nature* XXIII. 609 The solstitial months, namely June and December.

**3.** Of heat, etc.: Characteristic of the summer solstice. Also as an epithet of the sun, etc., in this connexion.

**1642** H. MORE *Song of Soul* II. II. vii, The glorious Sun.. such as he is in his solstitiall noon. **1667** MILTON *P.L.* x. 656 From the South to bring Solstitial summers heat. **1708** J. PHILIPS *Cyder* I. 13 Sirius parched with Heat Solstitial the green herb. **1795** *Gentl. Mag.* 540 Luxuriant foliage opposes the solstitial sun. **1829** WORDSW. *Th. on the Seasons* ii, Less fair is summer riding high In fierce solstitial power. **1868** KINGSLEY *Christmas Day* 37 That day Shall dawn in glory, and solstitial blaze Of full midsummer sun.

**4. a.** Of plants: Coming up at the summer solstice; growing or fading rapidly.

After *solstitialis herba* in Plautus *Pseud.* I. i. 36.

**1654** WHITLOCK *Zootomia* 475 The short Duration of worldly Happinesse, how aptly called the Solstitiall Plant. **1657–61** HEYLIN *Hist. Reform.* Pref. p. i, So many Ordinances..should be as short lived as Jonas' Gourd, or the solstitial herb in Plautus. **1783** *Phil. Trans.* LXXIV. 417 As the two last are solstitial, and rather delicate plants, I wondered the less at their sensibility.

**b.** Of insects, etc.: Appearing about the time of the summer solstice.

**1812** SHAW *Gen. Zool.* VIII. II. 449 The Solstitial Parrakeet is twice described by Buffon, under different divisions of the genus. **1818** KIRBY & SP. *Introd. Entomol.* II. xxiii. 372 The solstitial and common cockchafer appear in the evening—the former generally coming forth at the summer solstice. **1835** KIRBY *Habits & Inst. Anim.* II. xx. 366 About the time of the summer solstice, the solstitial beetle may be seen and heard buzzing in vast numbers over the trees and hedges.

**5.** Connected with the observation of the solstices.

**1834** *Hist. Astron.* (U.K.S.) vi. 32/1 The construction of the astrolabium..was rather more complicated than that of the solstitial or equatorial armillæ. **1883** *Bible Myths* (ed. 2) 439 An astronomical observatory containing..solstitial and equatorial armils,..and other apparatus. **1906** LOCKYER *Stonehenge* iii. 19 We have in Stonehenge a solstitial temple.

†**B.** *sb.* A solstice. *Obs. rare.*

**1561** EDEN *Arte Nauig.* I. xv. 16 These Tropykes are descrybed by the motion of the fyrst moueable with the points of the Solstitials. **1612** HOPTON *Concord. Yeares* (1615) 53 The Summer and Winter Solstitials.

Hence **solˈstitially** *adv.*, towards the solstices.

**1658** SIR T. BROWNE *Gard. Cyrus* iv. 166 That the Leaves of the Olive and some other trees solstitially turn..is scarce expectable in any Climate. **1894** *Athenæum* 21 Apr. 515/3 The temples were oriented solstitially or equinoctially.

**solstitian** (sɒlˈstɪʃən), *a.* Also 7 solstician. [f. L. *sōlstiti-um* + -AN.] Solstitial.

**1614** J. TAYLOR (Water P.) *Nipping Abuses* E 2 b, Sol.. High mounted in his chiefe solstician pride. **1845** *Theologian* II. 37 Capricornus..is an earthy,..moveable,.. solstitian,..quadrupedal sign.

‖**solstitium** (sɒlˈstɪʃ(ɪ)əm). Pl. solstitia. Also 6 solsticium. [L. *sōlstitium* (med.L. also *-sticium*), f. *sōl* sun (SOL *sb.*[1]) + ppl. stem of *sistĕre* to stand still.] = SOLSTICE.

**1515** A. BARCLAY *Egloges* (1570) C v/2 Then shall my songe be dom Like a Nightingale at the solstitium. **1562** TURNER *Herbal* II. (1568) 98 By that token the Husbandmen know that the Solstitium of Sommer is past. **1609** C. BUTLER *Fem. Mon.* (1634) 44 The Æquinoctia and Solstitia, in which the four quarters of the year..take their beginnings. **1630** J. TAYLOR (Water P.) *Wks.* 2 Aaa 6 b/2 Talkes of the Iewish Thalmud, and Cabals, Solstitiums and Equinoctialls. **1884** R. PATON *Scott. Ch.* x. 102 Christmas took the place of the Pagan Saturnalia and Solstitia.

**solubility** (sɒljʊˈbɪlɪtɪ). [f. SOLUBLE *a.* and *sb.* + -ITY. Cf. F. *solubilité*, It. *solubilità*, Sp. *solubilidad*.]

**1.** The quality or property of being soluble.

**1677** GREW *Anat. Pl.* (1682) 297 Even the changes of the weather will somewhat alter the Solubility of the Salts. **1690** LOCKE *Hum. Und.* II. xxxiii. §23 Its peculiar fixedness and solubility in *aqua regia*. **1771** *Phil. Trans.* LXI. 216 The solubility of water in air. **1794** G. ADAMS *Nat. & Exper. Phil.* I. x. 399 The solubility of salt in water. **1811** A. T. THOMSON *Lond. Disp.* (1818) p. xxiii, A compound of little solubility. **1844** G. BIRD *Urin. Deposits* (1857) 207 Sometimes the crystals form very slowly, owing to their solubility in the precipitant. **1898** *Rev. Brit. Pharm.* 28 Solubilities in alcohol, ammonia solution, and ether are given.

**2.** *Bot.* Capability of easy separation into parts.

**1832** LINDLEY *Introd. Bot.* 165 Solubility arises from the presence of certain transverse contractions of a one-celled pericarpium, through which it finally separates into several closed portions. **1861** BENTLEY *Man. Bot.* 310 The separation taking place in these cases has been supposed to be effected by a process called *solubility*.

**3.** Capability of being solved or explained.

**1882** in *Imperial Dict.*

**4.** Special Combs.: **solubility curve** *Chem.*, a curve showing how the solubility of a substance varies with temperature; **solubility product** *Chem.*, the product of the concentrations (*spec.* the activities) of each of the component ions present in a saturated solution of a sparingly soluble salt.

**1892** *Jrnl. Chem. Soc.* LXII. 1384 (*heading*) Solubility curves of pairs of salts. **1933** A. K. GOARD *Physical Chem.* ii. 36 A break in a solubility curve always indicates that the composition of the solid in equilibrium with the saturated solution has changed. **1971** Solubility curve [see INVARIANT *a.* b]. **1899** J. WALKER *Introd. Physical Chem.* xxvi. 307 The solubility product of silver chloride in water is very small, corresponding to the very slight solubility of the salt. **1978** P. W. ATKINS *Physical Chem.* xii. 361 The magnitude of $K_S$, the solubility product, can be predicted from a knowledge of standard electrode potentials.

**solubilization** (ˌsɒljʊbɪlaɪˈzeɪʃən). [f. next + -ATION.] The process of making something (more) soluble.

**1930** *Brit. Chem. Abstr.* B. XLIX. 1061/1 (*heading*) Solubilisation of a perylenetetracarboxylic di-imide dye and dyes produced thereby. **1946** *Industr. & Engin. Chem.* June 642 (*heading*) Solubilization of insoluble organic liquids by detergents. **1977** *Jrnl. Protozool.* XXIV. 17/2 The selective solubilization of protein C permitted us to determine its source.

**solubilize** (ˈsɒljʊbɪlaɪz), *v.* [f. L. *solūbil-is* SOLUBLE *a.* + -IZE.] *trans.* To increase the solubility of; to convert into a soluble form. Also *absol.*

**1926** [implied at SOLUBILIZING *vbl. sb.* below]. **1930** *U.S. Patent 1,776,971* (*title*) Process of solubilizing a perylenetetracarboxylic di-imide dyestuff. **1947** *Jrnl. Soc. Chem. Industry* Jan. 4/2 Free lauryl sulphonic acid solubilises slightly, even in chloroform. **1970** *Jrnl. Neurobiol.* I. 331 The tissue segments were solubilized. **1977** *Nature* 17 Nov. 272/1 After adding hydroxylamine to complex the excess retinal, the rhodopsin was solubilised by adding..octyl glucoside.

So ˈ**solubilized** *ppl. a.*, ˈ**solubilizing** *vbl. sb.*; also ˈ**solubilizable** *a.*, capable of being solubilized.

**1926** *Brit. Pat.* 275,267 3/2 The use of products..as emulsifying agents or solubilising agents for organic solvents. *Ibid.* 280,647 1 (*title*) Manufacture of a solubilised vat dye and process of dyeing therewith. **1949** E. CHAIN in H. W. Florey et al. *Antibiotics* II. xviii. 748 A solubilizing effect of impurities on other salts of benzylpenicillin..was observed. **1955** *Times* 1 July 16/2 The therapeutic advantages of solubilized aspirin are as much appreciated in a compound including phenacetin and codeine as they are in Disprin itself. **1978** *Nature* 6 Apr. p. xxv/3 Bio-Rad introduce a new solubilisable gel for polyacrylamide gel electrophoresis. **1979** *Experientia* XXXV. 280/2 For the various thicknesses of sections, the ratio of radioactivity level of the intact section to that of the solubilized one was expressed in percent.

**solubilizer** (ˈsɒljʊbɪlaɪzə(r)). [f. prec. + -ER[1].] A solubilizing agent.

**1963** *Chem. Abstr.* LIX. 6203 As solubilizers, Tween 20, 60, 80, Carbowax 1500, and Myrj 52 were used. **1979** *Experientia* XXXV. 280/2 The solubilizer..was added to yield the same concentration of scintillator molecules as in the section undergoing solubilization.

**soluble** (ˈsɒljʊb(ə)l), *a.* and *sb.* Also 5–6 solyble, solible, 6 solubil. [a. OF. (also mod.F.) *soluble*, = Sp. *soluble*, Pg. *soluvel*, It. *solubile*, ad. L. *solūbilis*, f. *solvĕre* to loosen, dissolve, etc.]

**A.** *adj.* **1.** *Med.* **a.** Of the bowels, etc.: Free from constipation or costiveness; relaxed. Now *rare* or *Obs.*

*c* **1400** tr. *Secreta Secret.* 87 It [the medicine] shall make þe takere right noght solyble, or ellys ful litell. **1450–80** *Ibid.* 27 And it is good to travayle and to haue thi wombe soluble. **1539** ELYOT *Cast. Helthe* (1541) 25 Dry figges and old make the bodye soluble. **1563** T. GALE *Antidot.* II. 81 Prouided alwayes that the pacient bee kepte soluble. **1620** VENNER *Via Recta* i. 18 It..maketh the body soluble, and therefore sometimes good for such as are wont to be costiue. **1671** SALMON *Syn. Med.* II. lviii. 345 The Cholick if it be gentle, and the Belly soluble, it is easily cured. **1772** *Phil. Trans.* LXII. 457 The belly should be kept soluble with lenitive Electuary, or any other mild purgative. **1843** R. J. GRAVES *Syst. Clin. Med.* xvii. 196 The citrate of soda..tends to keep up a soluble state of the bowels.

†**b.** Laxative; causing looseness of the bowels.

**1502** ARNOLDE *Chron.* (1811) 171 To take drynkes solyble for to purgen the bodi of euyll humors. **1582** HESTER *Secr. Phiorav.* II. xxvii. 104 Give the Pacient..our Potion of Lignum Sanctum, the whiche is soluble and driying, and purgeth the bloud. **1620** VENNER *Via Recta* (1650) 249 They are of an attenuating and soluble faculty. **1704** J. HARRIS *Lex. Techn.* I. s.v., This is the Soluble Tartar. 'Tis accounted a very good Aperitive Medicine.

**2. a.** Capable of being melted or dissolved.

**1432–50** tr. *Higden* (Rolls) I. 319 In Scicille is white salte, ..whiche, beenge soluble [L. *solubilis*] in the fyre, brestethe and brekethe in the water.

**1764** REID *Inquiry* iii. 115 It is probable that everything that affects the taste is, in some degree, soluble in the saliva. **1794** R. J. SULIVAN *View Nat.* I. 306 There results a soap which is soluble in water. **1814** SIR H. DAVY *Agric. Chem.* 273 To make it afford as much soluble matter as possible to the roots of the plant. **1853** W. GREGORY *Inorg. Chem.* 160 Borates..are for the most part insoluble. The alkaline borates alone are soluble. **1878** HUXLEY *Physiogr.* 117 Whatever soluble constituents exist in the air will be absorbed by the rain.

**b.** As a specific epithet with names of substances. ***soluble blue*** (also ***Soluble Blue***), any of a class of water-soluble dyes that are di- and trisulphonic acid derivatives of aniline blue and are now used chiefly in papers and inks. In *Biochem.* applied to those species of RNA now usu. known as *transfer RNA*.

**1836–41** BRANDE *Chem.* (ed. 5) 595 Solution of chlorine, or of the soluble chlorides. *Ibid.*, The soluble nitrate of silver. **1843** R. J. GRAVES *Syst. Clin. Med.* xxv. 321 The soluble mercury of Hahnemann was chiefly employed. **1861** BENTLEY *Man. Bot.* 471 This forms common cocoa, rock cocoa, soluble cocoa, &c. **1862** E. C. NICHOLSON *Brit.*

*Patent 1857* 3 A colourless solution is obtained which, when neutralized.., developes the improved soluble blue dye. **1875** KNIGHT *Dict. Mech.* 2244/2 For much that is valuable in the preparation and application of water-glass or soluble glass, we are indebted to Dr. Johann Fuchs of Munich. **1879** *Jrnl. Chem. Soc.* XXXVI. 418 In preparing the soluble blues, the monosulphonic acids and higher-substituted acids must be of great purity. **1893** T. E. THORPE *Dict. Appl. Chem.* III. 562/1 Perhaps the readiest way of preparing soluble starch is that recommended by Zulkowski.., who finds that starch dissolves in hot glycerin and is converted into the soluble modification. **1899** *Allbutt's Syst. Med.* VII. 684 Intramuscular injections of the soluble mercurial salts. **1952** K. VENKATARAMAN *Chem. Synthetic Dyes* II. xxiii. 723 Sulphonic acids of phenylated Rosanilines, which are old dyes (Nicholson Blue, Soluble Blue, Water Blue, Alkali Blue; CI 703–707) continue to be extensively used. **1958** M. B. HOAGLAND et al. in *Jrnl. Biol. Chem.* CCXXI. 256 Evidence is presented that a soluble ribonucleic acid..binds amino acids in the presence of adenosine triphosphate. **1961** *Nature* 13 May 582/1 The other principal (10–15 per cent) form of RNA in *E. coli* is soluble RNA (now more appropriately called transfer RNA), which functions in the movement of activated amino-acids to the ribosomes. **1964** G. H. HAGGIS et al. *Introd. Molecular Biol.* xii. 306 Because of its special function this RNA is now generally called transfer-RNA, although it is also sometimes referred to as soluble-RNA, or as acceptor-RNA. **1971** R. L. M. ALLEN *Colour Chem.* viii. 115 A marked bathochromic effect is obtained by phenylation of the amino groups in rosanilines. .. These Soluble Blues are now little used for textile coloration, but are applied to leather, paper and..in printing inks. **1973** *Times* 18 Oct. (Brazil Suppl.) p. v/2 Soluble (instant) coffee exports have grown at a remarkable pace. **1974** E. AMBLER *Doctor Frigo* III. 185, I gave her some soluble aspirin and left. **1977** *Whitaker's Almanack 1978* 914/1 The chief exports are cotton, coffee, beef, gold, sugar, cottonseed, bananas, copper and soluble coffee.

**c.** Dissolving, solvent. *rare.*

**1846** G. E. DAY tr. *Simon's Anim. Chem.* II. 358 It differs from it..in its power of resisting the soluble action of a cold solution of potash.

**3.** Capable of being untied or loosed. *rare.*

**1613** T. ADAMS *Heaven & Earth Recon.* 22 If Balaams Asse hath but an audible voyce, and a soluble Purse. **1847** TENNYSON *Princ.* v. 129 More soluble is this knot, By gentleness than war.

†**4.** Plastic, pliable. Also *fig. Obs.*

**1650** TRAPP *Comm. Deut.* ix. 22 Keep our souls humble, supple, and soluble. **1683** MOXON *Mech. Exerc., Printing* xi. ¶23 This Canvass (to make it more soluble) is wet in Water, and the Water well wrung out again.

**5. a.** Capable of being solved or explained; solvable.

*c* **1705** BP. BERKELEY in Fraser *Life* (1871) 422 In physiques I have a vast view of things soluble hereby. **1850** CARLYLE *Latter-d. Pamph.* i. 4 Questions not very soluble at present, were even sages and heroes set to solve them, began everywhere..to be asked. **1877** SPARROW *Serm.* xxi. 280, I refer now to those subjects, which..have more the appearance of soluble questions.

**b.** *Math.* = SOLVABLE *a.* 3 b.

**1902** *Encycl. Brit.* XXIX. 140/1 A group defines uniquely the set of factor-groups that occur in its composition series. .. When the orders of all the factor-groups are primes the group is said to be soluble. **1940** *Trans. Amer. Math. Soc.* XLVII. 393 A group may be termed soluble, if it may be swept out by an ascending (finite or transfinite) chain of normal subgroups such that the quotient groups of its consecutive terms are abelian groups of finite rank. **1972** [see QUOTIENT 1 b].

**6.** Capable of being resolved; reducible.

**1826** SYD. SMITH *Wks.* (1859) II. 98/1 A great deal of compliment to the wisdom of ancestors, and a great degree of alarm at the dreadful spirit of innovation, are soluble into mere jealousy and envy. **1858** O. W. HOLMES *Aut. Breakf. Table* xi. 107 Love is sparingly soluble in the words of men.

**B.** *sb.* A soluble constituent, esp. of a foodstuff.

**1952** *Poultry Sci.* XXXI. 937/1 There was no change in the hatchability of eggs from the hens receiving condensed fish solubles. **1962** M. N. HILL *Sea* I. vi. 305 (*heading*) Solubles. **1972** *Brit. Jrnl. Nutrition* XXVIII. 221 The main growth-promoting effect of fish solubles has been shown to be mediated through the intestinal microflora of the chick.

**'solubleness.** ? *Obs.* Also 6 **soliblenesse, solublenes,** 7 **solublenesse.** [f. prec. + -NESS.] The state, character, or property of being soluble.

**1574** J. JONES *Nat. Beg. Growing & Living Things* 47 It causeth..Solublenes of the Wombe. **1579** —— *Preserv. Body & Soul* I. xv. 27 Hir..soliblenesse and costiuenesse, must be meane. **1620** VENNER *Via Recta* vii. 150 The onely property that they haue is to mollifie the belly, and procure solublenesse. **1655** MOUFET & BENNET *Health's Improv.* (1746) 287 Warming their Stomachs,..procuring Solubleness and Urine.

**solucyt,** obs. variant of SOLICIT *v.*

**solum** ('səʊləm). [L. *solum* ground.] **1.** Soil, ground. (Chiefly *Sc. Law.*)

**1829** in P. Shaw *Reports* VII. 363 A right of absolute.. property in the *solum*. **1894** J. MACINTOSH *Ayrshire Nts.' Entert.* xi. 199 The solum of the old road having been assigned to the respective proprietors. **1905** *Proc. Antiq. Soc. Scotl.* XXXIX. 346 The Abertay Sands..bid fair by and by to enlarge..the solum of this tract of country.

**2.** *Soil Science.* (Pl. **solums, sola.**) The upper part of a soil profile, in which the soil-forming processes predominantly occur; *spec.* the A and B horizons. [Introduced (as G. *solumhorizont* solum horizon) by B. Frosterus 1922, in *Compt. Rend. de la Conf. Extraordinaire* (*IIème Internat.*) *Agropédologique* (1924) 361.]

**1928** *Proc. & Papers 1st Internat. Congr. Soil Sci.* IV. 7 To the soil body has been given definitely the status of a well defined concept by the application to it of a name consisting of a single term, the *Solum*, by Frosterus. **1942** *Technical Bull. U.S. Dept. Agric.* No. 834. 49 All but small quantities or traces [of carbonates] are leached from the solums of all but the Clyde profile. **1956** *Soil Sci.* LXXXII. 451 In the coarser sand fractions (0.5–2mm.) weatherable mineral material such as granite, diorite, and basalt is abundant in all horizons of the sola. **1972** J. G. CRUICKSHANK *Soil Geogr.* ii. 41 The minimum moisture storage in the solum will be equivalent to between 10 and 15 cm water per unit area.

**solunar,** var. SOL-LUNAR *a.*

‖**solus** ('səʊləs), *a.* [L. *sōlus* alone.]

**1.** Of male persons: **a.** Alone, by oneself.

In older use esp. in stage-directions.

**1599** SHAKS. *Hen. V*, II. i. 48 Will you shogge off? I would haue you solus. **1605** *1st Pt. Jeronimo* III. ii, Enter Ieronimo solus. **1676** SHADWELL *Libertine* II, Jacomo *solus.* **1711** ADDISON *Spectator* No. 29 ¶1 The Famous Blunder in an old Play of *Enter a King and two Fidlers Solus.* **1775** SHERIDAN *Rivals* III. ii, Julia's Dressing-room. Faulkland *solus.* **1829** MARRYAT *F. Mildmay* iii, My meals were sent to me, and I took them *solus* on my chest. **1852** MUNDY *Antipodes* (1857) 35 A solvent looking gentleman, solus in a buggy. **1878** H. S. LEIGH *Town Garland* 140 It is only when *solus*, away from the throng, That I've hypochondrical fits.

**b.** ***solus cum sola*** [L.]: alone with an unchaperoned woman; ***solus cum solo*** [lit. 'alone with (oneself) alone']: all on one's own.

**1611** CORYAT *Crudities* 404 They sing merily together, but especially that sweet & most amorous song of *solus cum solâ.* **1700** DRYDEN *Fables* 226 Stretching his Neck, and warbling in his Throat, *Solus cum Sola*, then was all his *Note.* **1742** R. NORTH *Life of Francis North, Ld. Guilford* 242 But he was in the midst of all the court, *solus cum solo*, alone by himself. **1818** LADY MORGAN *Florence Macarthy* II. iv. 202, I shall have the honour to drink your ladyship's health, *solus cum solo.* **1831** [see CHAPERONLESS *a.*]. **1940** H. H. HENSON *Jrnl.* 24 Mar. in *Retrospect* (1950) III. ii. 88 In the afternoon I had tea with Mrs. Carnegie *solus cum sola.*

**2.** Of females: = SOLA *a.* 1.

**1749** JOHNSON *Irene* v. i. *stage-direct.*, Aspasia, solus. **1844** W. IRVING *Life & Lett.* (1866) III. 353 This must be the hardest task, for so young a creature, to have to play the Queen *solus.* **1882** MRS. B. M. CROKER *Proper Pride* I. ii. 13 Mounted on her chestnut pony she would..scour *solus* round the fields.

**3.** Of things. **a.** *Advertising.* Of an advertisement: that stands alone; sometimes, that deals with one item (e.g. one book) only. Also, pertaining to such advertisements. Also *transf.* and *absol.*

**1937** PARTRIDGE *Dict. Slang* 800/1 *Solus*, an advertisement on a page containing no other advertisement. **1952** *Economist* 5 Apr. 18/2 The advertiser would no doubt be charged varying rates equivalent to 'solus position'. **1958** *Times Lit. Suppl.* 5 Dec. 699/1 Within four days of publication *The Middle Age of Mrs. Eliot* had received solus feature reviews in *The Observer, The Sunday Times*, [etc.]. **1974** *Bookseller* 4 May 2154 (Advt.), Massive promotion. 10 giant solus advertisements in the National Press. **1980** *Financial Rev.* (Sydney) 18 Apr. 42/3 Rod Muir's station does have a rate card which concentrates on selling solus spots— 60 seconds to two minutes. Mr Muir thinks radio has lost a lot of its effectiveness with the clutter of 30 second ads.

**b.** *Comm.* Of an outlet for the sale of oil and petrol: that sells the products of one company only. Also, of or pertaining to such an arrangement.

**1957** *Economist* 7 Dec. 836/2 Whether a solus site offering three grades of one brand of petrol provides less choice than a mixed site offering three brands of the same grade is a question for chemists and advertising men to answer. **1958** *Spectator* 11 July 62/3 The Government had struck a blow against monopoly..by banning 'solus' petrol stations from the new motorways. **1965** *Economist* 7 Aug. 542/1 The major companies selling petrol in Britain have been sure for many months now that the Monopolies Commission would not find the 'solus' or 'tied garage' system, in itself, to be against the public interest. **1976** *Drive* Jan.–Feb. 10/1 One of the busiest solus sites (where only one brand of petrol is sold) in the country.

**solute** ('sɒljuːt, sə'l(j)uːt), *sb.* [ad. L. *solūt-um*, or substantival use of next. Cf. OF. *solut* payment.]

†**1.** A sum to be received in payment. *Obs.*$^{-1}$

**1622** MABBE tr. *Aleman's Guzman d'Alf.* II. 149 His Masters..booke of remembrances, wherein hee sets downe his Solutes and his debts, what he is to receiue and what to pay.

**2.** The substance dissolved in a solution.

**1893** F. G. DONNAN in *Nature* 27 Dec. 200/2 Corresponding to the words 'solvent' and 'solution', some word is very badly wanted to express 'the dissolved substance'. The analogous word is evidently 'solute', and it is as short and euphonious as the others. **1904** WHETHAM *Rec. Develop. Phys. Sci.* iv. 115 The nature of the interaction which occurs between the solute and the solvent is unknown. **1908** *Athenæum* 25 July 102/1 The osmotic action which allows the solvent to pass through a semi-permeable wall while retaining the solute. **1978** P. W. ATKINS *Physical Chem.* viii. 216 When a solute is present there is an extra randomness present in the solution that was not present in the pure solvent.

**solute** (sə'l(j)uːt), *ppl. a.* [ad. L. *solūt-us*, pa. pple. of *solvĕre* SOLVE *v.*]

†**1.** Of loose open texture or composition. *Obs.*

*c* **1440** tr. *Pallad. on Husb.* I. 250 Eek cornys best wole thryue In opon lond, solute. *Ibid.* XIII. 33 In lond that is solute..Not depe hem sette. **1653** H. MORE *Antid. Ath.* App. (1662) 183 From the solute Arenosity (as I may so speak) of Air and Fire.

†**2.** Unmarried. *Obs. rare.*

**1554** *MS. Cant. Cathedral Libr.* Reg. N, lf. 166 b, I haue maried one Agnes Staunton, a single or solute woman. *Ibid.* 167 b, One Anne Wescotte, a single and solute woman.

†**3.** Of discourse: Free, loose, discursive. *Obs.*

**1605** BACON *Adv. Learn.* II. xxv. §10 The Interpretations of the Scriptures are of two sorts: Methodical, and Solute, or at large. **1680** MACWARD *Contendings* (1723) 177 Some, whom you mind to hit right or wrong in a solute and lax discourse.

†**4.** Relaxed, free from care. *Obs.*$^{-1}$

**1742** YOUNG *Nt. Th.* II. 585 God of joyous wit, A brow solute, and ever-laughing eye.

**5.** *Bot.* Not adhering; separate.

**1760** J. LEE *Introd. Bot.* III. xvii. (1765) 210 *Solute*, free or loose, in most Plants. **1866** *Treas. Bot.* 1072/2 *Solute*, completely separate from neighbouring parts.

**6.** Dissolved; in a state of solution. Also *fig.*

**1890** W. C. WILKINSON *Classic Fr. Course* v. 61 (Stand.), His maxims are like hard and sharp crystals,..blandly solute and dilute in Montaigne. **1904** WHETHAM *Rec. Develop. Phys. Sci.* iv. 115 A solution may be regarded as containing a number of little systems, each composed of a solute particle surrounded by an atmosphere of solvent.

†**so'lute,** *v. Obs.* [f. L. *solūt-*, ppl. stem of *solvĕre* SOLVE *v.*]

**1.** *trans.* To solve, explain, clear up.

In common use *c* 1545–75.

**1533** MORE *Answ. Poysoned Bk.* Wks. 1092/1 He myght.. haue soluted theyr question. **1551** T. WILSON *Logike* 64 b, Those that be good grammarians..can gaylie well solute such errours as be made by the mistaking of wordes. **1580** FULKE *Confut. Martial* iv. Wks. (Parker Soc.) II. 167 This question (he saith) is not soluted. **1654** [see the *vbl. sb.*].

**b.** To arrange, settle. *rare*$^{-1}$.

**1560** DAUS tr. *Sleidane's Comm.* 145 That if anye controuersie shall happen in this matter, he shall solute and appease the same.

**2.** To dissolve, nullify. *rare*$^{-1}$.

**1550** EDW. VI. *Jrnl.*, etc. (Roxb.) 523 That the King of Englande..with consent of 6 of the ordre may chaung, overthrow,..and solute any thing that is or shalbe made hereafter concerning this ordre.

Hence †**so'luting** *vbl. sb.*

**1534** CRANMER *Misc. Writ.* (Parker Soc.) II. 277 As well for the defence of the nun's revelations, as for the soluting of my reasons. **1581** MARBECK *Bk. Notes* 172 This..serueth to the soluting of manie like kinde of cauillations. **1654** Z. COKE *Logick* 179 Of the loosing or soluting of Fallacies.

†**so'luteness.** *Obs. rare.* [f. SOLUTE *ppl. a.*] Want of solidity.

**1653** H. MORE *Antid. Ath.* App. (1662) 183 That this soluteness makes those Aereal Compages incapable of Personality..and Sensation.

**solution** (sə'l(j)uːʃən), *sb.* Forms: 4–5 **solucioun, -tioun,** 4–6 **solucion(e,** 6 **solucyon(e, solyssion,** 6– **solution.** [a. OF. *solucion, -tion* (mod.F. *solution*, = Sp. *solucion*, It. *soluzione*) or ad. L. *solūtiōn-, solūtio*, f. ppl. stem of *solvĕre* SOLVE *v.*]

**I. 1. a.** The action or process of solving; the state, condition, or fact of being solved.

**1375** BARBOUR *Bruce* I. 259, I leve all the solucioun Till thaim that ar off mar renoun. *c* **1420** LYDG. *Assembly of Gods* 2022 Yef hit had be nomore but for the solucion Of my demaunde and of thys straunge vysyon. **1526** *Pilgr. Perf.* (W. de W. 1531) 255 The solution of a questyon moued of his sayd blessed deth. **1551** T. WILSON *Logike* (1580) 26 b, Thyne argument..needed then no solution at all. **1620** T. GRANGER *Div. Logike* 316 The answering and solution of all his obiections against vs. **1664** POWER *Exp. Philos.* III. 191 The Solutions of all those former Difficulties are reserved for you..to gratifie Posterity withall. **1736** *Gentl. Mag.* VI. 476 The famous Mr. Leibnitz..own'd that the Solutions of such Problems as these..was a very difficult Task. **1784** COWPER *Task* II. 520 Knots worthy of solution, which alone A Deity could solve. **1838** DE MORGAN *Ess. Probab.* 93 The use of the tables at the end of this work, in the solution of complicated questions. **1879** *Cassell's Techn. Educ.* IV. 91/1 A difficult problem of mixed law and fact for solution by the judges.

**b.** A particular instance or method of solving or settling; an explanation, answer, or decision.

**1382** WYCLIF *Dan.* ii. 25 A man..that shal telle to the kyng the soluccioun. **1401** *Polit. Poems* (Rolls) II. 73 And so thes similitudes, with thes soluciones, ben not worthe the devellis dirt. **1432–50** tr. *Higden* (Rolls) III. 99 Daniel the prophete ȝafe a solucion of a vision to Nabugodonosor in Caldea. **1509** HAWES *Past. Pleas.* XXXII. (Percy Soc.) 157 Now have I answered you your question, And I pray you of a lyke solucion. **1596** BP. W. BARLOW *Three Serm.* iii. 126 This may serue for a short solution. **1667** PEPYS *Diary* 1 May, Expecting the solution of the Judges in this point. **1681** HALLYWELL *Melampronoea* Title-p., A Solution of the Chiefest Objections brought against the Being of Witches. **1711** ADDISON *Spect.* No. 21 ¶6 He might have found a better Solution for this Difficulty, than any of those he has made use of. **1774** PENNANT *Tour Scotl. in 1772* 233 This solution of mine is absolutely denied. **1813** SIR H. DAVY *Agric. Chem.* ii. (1814) 33 These facts afford a rational solution of this curious problem. **1854** FROUDE *Short Stud., Spinoza* (1867) 241 Undoubtedly it provides a solution for every difficulty. **1884** J. QUINCY *Figures of Past* 376 These hard names furnish no solution to the problem he presents to us.

**c.** *Med.* The termination or crisis of a disease.

**1851** DUNGLISON *Med. Lex., Solution*, means, also, with many, the termination of a disease:—..a termination accompanied by critical signs;—and with others, again, it is synonymous with crisis.

†**2.** The action of releasing or setting free; deliverance, release. *Obs.*

*a* **1513** FABYAN *Chron.* (1811) 407 He alonely opteyned nat solucion of his othe, but also..was declaryd kynge of Scicill. **1550** BALE *Eng. Votaries* II. 12 Immediately after thys solucyon or settynge at large of Sathan. **1655** STANLEY *Hist. Philos.* (1687) 88/2 As death is the solution of the Soul from the Body. **1659** H. MORE *Immort. Soul* III. xviii, After this solution of the Souls or Spirits of Wicked Men and Dæmons from their Vehicles.

†**3.** The action of paying; a payment. *Obs.*

**1489** *Sc. Acts, Jas. IV* (1814) II. 222/2 Anent the Recuperatioun..of annuale Rentis in burgh, in falt of Solutioun and payment of the annualis. **1526** *Ord. Househ.* (1790) 229 To the intent the decomptants..may take out the Solutions entred into the said Bookes whereby they may strike their Lydgers. **1563-4** *Sarum Churchw. Acc.* (Swayne, 1896) 109 Allowans for suche solucyones. **1623** COCKERAM I, *Solution*, a payment. *a* **1722** SIR J. LAUDER *Decisions* Suppl. (1826) III. 280 It neither being by solution, nor other transaction, importing the consent of the creditor thereto.

**4.** The action of discharging or fulfilling.

**1869** *Austin's Lect. Jurispr.* lv. II. 915 The Roman Lawyers themselves talk of..the *solution* or the *redemption* of obligations.

**II. 5. a.** The action of dissolving, or changing from a solid or gaseous to a liquid state, by means of a fluid or solvent; the state or fact of being so dissolved.

**1390** GOWER *Conf.* II. 86 Ferst of the distillacion, Forth with the congelacion, Solucion, descencion [etc.]. **1471** RIPLEY *Comp. Alch.* II. i. in Ashm. *Theatr.* (1652) 135 Of Solucion now wyll I speke a word or two. **1612** WOODALL *Surg. Mate* Wks. (1653) 274 *Solution*, a principal part of Chymical practice, whereby the incorporation of things coagulated, is dissolved and attenuated. *a* **1665** K. DIGBY *Chym. Secr.* II. 221 Repeat these solutions seven or eight times. **1791** W. HAMILTON tr. *Berthollet's Dyeing* I. 5 The solution of indigo in the sulphuric (vitriolic) acid. **1800** HENRY *Epit. Chem.* (1808) 15 Mechanical agitation facilitates solution. **1870** TYNDALL *Lect. Electr.* 2 The effect in both cases is..the solution of the zinc, and the liberation of the hydrogen gas.

†**b.** The action of fusing, melting, or distilling by means of heat. *Obs. rare.*

*a* **1676** HALE *Prim. Orig. Man.* (1677) 9 They find by their solutions by Fire, some things which they call by these Names, to be that whereinto Bodies are dissolved. **1688** HOLME *Armoury* III. 425/1 *Distillation*, or *Solution*, is an extracting of Liquors by force of heat.

**c.** *transf.* Fusion, combination.

**1820** KEATS *St. Agnes* xxxvi, The rose Blendeth its odour with the violet,—Solution sweet.

**6. a.** A more or less fluid substance produced by the process of solution (see 5); a liquid or semi-liquid preparation obtained by the combination of a solid with a solvent.

**1594** PLAT *Jewell-ho.* III. 60 A good solucion of salt in oile. **1677** GREW *Anat. Pl.* (1682) 297, I put to this Solution of Nitre, two Drachms of Sal Armoniac; which wholly and easily dissolved in the said Solution. **1705** ARBUTHNOT *Coins*, etc. (1727) 326 He commends..a Solution of Opium in Water to foment the Forehead. **1790** *Phil. Trans.* 359 *note*, I have therefore confined the word solution to express the substance dissolved together with its solvent. **1811** A. T. THOMSON *Lond. Disp.* (1818) 469 A solution of lime should be put into the last bottle. **1855** *Orr's Circ. Sci., Elem. Chem.* 13 We..term the liquid which is obtained a solution of salt in water. **1875** DARWIN *Insectiv. Plants* v. 80 Drops of a solution about as thick as milk.

*fig.* **1858** O. W. HOLMES *Aut. Breakf.-t.* iii. 24 Society is a strong solution of books.

**b.** = *rubber solution* s.v. RUBBER *sb.*[1] 14.

**1897** A. C. PEMBERTON *Complete Cyclist* vii. 190 The edges of the cut must be well cleaned and coated with solution. **1930** F. GARDNER *How to repair your Cycle* 20 Spread a thin layer of solution over the part that has been rubbed. **1974** S. TOWNROE *How to mend your Bike* 44 Never put on the patch until the solution has dried.

**7.** A dissolved state or condition. Freq. *state of solution.*

(*a*) **1802** PALEY *Nat. Theol.* xxi. §3 (1819) 333 Keeping things in a state of solution, that is to say, in a state of fluidity. **1837** P. KEITH *Bot. Lex.* 90 Animal or vegetable substances in a state of solution. **1878** HUXLEY *Physiogr.* 115 Certain chemical compounds in a state of solution.

*transf.* **1859** *Habits Gd. Society* v. 211 Their partners appear in a most disagreeable condition of solution.

(*b*) **1802** PLAYFAIR *Illustr. Huttonian Th. Earth* 494 The volume of the water..necessary to hold in solution the materials of this shell. **1856** RUSKIN *Mod. Paint.* IV. v. ix. §4 As they congealed from their fluid state, whether of watery solution or fiery fusion. **1878** HUXLEY *Physiogr.* 202 The water generally holds silica in solution.

*fig.* **1870** LOWELL *Among my Bks.* Ser. I. 297 His [*sc.* Lessing's] was a mind always in solution. **1877** TALMAGE *Serm.* 338 A tear..is agony in solution.

**8.** *attrib.*, as *solution jar, lake, -tub.*

**1867** *Tomlinson's Cycl. Usef. Arts* App. 14/1 The mouth of the solution jar was again closed. **1877** RAYMOND *Statist. Mines & Min.* 393 The liquid which runs out of the solution-tubs runs into tanks.

**b.** *Physical Geogr.* Denoting features and phenomena resulting from the solvent action of water, as ***solution basin, depression, subsidence***, etc.

**1894** *Pop. Sci. Monthly* June 281 In lime-stone countries, solution lakes are not uncommon. **1931** *Jrnl. Geol.* XXXIX. 641 (*heading*) Solution depressions in sandy sediments of the coastal plain in South Carolina. **1934** C. R. LONGWELL et al. *Outl. Physical Geol.* iv. 73 In some regions sinks, caverns, and solution valleys are so numerous that they give rise to a peculiar and characteristic topography with many surface depressions, irregular drainage patterns, and disappearing streams. **1939** A. K. LOBECK *Geomorphol.* iv. 145 Very large sinks or areas of depression are known as solution basins. **1954** *Geol. Mag.* XCI. 225 A lowering of surface by solution subsidence has been proceeding more or less continuously since Triassic times on this high moorland terrain. **1957** E. E. EVANS *Irish Folk Ways* ii. 18 The lowland of which it is the centre is..diversified by occasional low hills, by intricate solution lakes and by glacial eskers. **1977** *Antiquaries Jrnl.* LVII. 189 Three large masses..recovered from red clay-with-flints filling a solution pipe at Aston Rowant (Oxon.).

**III. 9.** ***solution of continuity***: **a.** *Med.* (Also ***of connexion, of unity***.) The separation from each other of normally continuous parts of the body by external or internal causes.

**1541** R. COPLAND *Galyen's Terap.* 2 A ij, We haue sayd that there is a kynde of dysease, that is called solution of contynuyte. *Ibid.*, There be other kyndes of solutions of continuite. **1625** BACON *Ess., Of Vnity in Relig.* (Arb.) 423 As in the Naturall Body, a Wound or Solution of Continuity is worse then a Corrupt Humor. **1656** RIDGLEY *Pract. Physick* 44 This proceeds from solution of continuity of the Veins and Arteries. **1668** CULPEPPER & COLE *Barthol. Anat.* I. xxviii. 67 In which case also it is necessary that there be a Solution of the Connexion of the Neck. **1707** FLOYER *Physic. Pulse-Watch* 101 The organic Diseases, and the solution of Unity, must be known by the Signs of the particular Diseases. **1748** HARTLEY *Observ. Man* I. i. §1. 36 In manifest Solutions of Continuity occasioned by Wounds, Burns, &c. **1818** E. THOMPSON *Cullen's Nosologia Meth.* (1820) 264 *Vulnus*, a recent, bloody solution of continuity in a soft part, by a hard body. **1835-6** *Todd's Cycl. Anat.* I. 794/1 The consequent solution of connection between the various parts of the body.

*ellipt.* **1580** BLUNDEVIL *Horsemanship* T iij b, If such solution or diuision be in a bone, then is it called a fracture. **1612** WOODALL *Surg. Mate* Wks. (1653) 86 The solution of a Veine is known by blood of red colour and thick substance.

**b.** *transf.* and *fig.* A breach, break, or interruption.

**1654** BRAMHALL *Just Vind.* ii. (1661) 14 Schisme is..a solution of continuity in the body Ecclesiastick. **1656** tr. *Hobbes' Elem. Philos.* (1839) 475 Even the hardest things are broken asunder..by solution of their continuity begun in the outermost superficies. **1707** *Curiosities Husb. & Gard.* 77 The Solution of Continuity may hinder the Juice from mounting. **1750** FRANKLIN *Lett.* Wks. 1840 V. 243 If there be the least crack, the minutest solution of continuity in the glass. **1799** E. DU BOIS *Piece Family Biog.* II. 201 Some there are..who, admitting no solution of continuity in their story, deny any place of rest to..the wearied reader. **1819** SCOTT *Leg. Montrose* xxiii, Rents, and open seams,..might presage a similar solution of continuity in your matrimonial happiness. **1863** TYNDALL *Heat* xii. 408 Magnificent gradations of color, one fading into another without solution of continuity. **1886** *Manch. Exam.* 9 Jan. 5/3 There will be no solution of continuity in this important department of public affairs.

**10.** The action of breaking up or separating; dissolution; bringing to an end.

**1655** VAUGHAN *Silex Scint.* L'ENVOY, Frustrate those cancerous, close arts, Which cause solution in all parts, And strike them dumb. **1664** H. MORE *Myst. Iniq.* iii. 6 The Death of Christ upon the Cross was the solution of the Ceremonial Law of Moses. **1689** LOCKE *Civil Govt.* §80 (1694) 225 Easie and frequent Solutions of Conjugal Society. **1899** *Westm. Gaz.* 30 Oct. 2/1 That Boer policy had not for its aim the solution of British supremacy in South Africa.

†**11.** The action of rendering loose or slack. *Obs.*

**1681** tr. *Willis' Remaining Med. Wks.* Vocab., *Solution*, a loosning or weakning, as of the nerves or joynts.

**IV. 12.** Special Combs.: **solution heat treatment** = *solution treatment* below; **solution set** *Math.*, the set of all the solutions of some equation or condition; **solution treatment** *Metallurgy*, a process designed to render an alloy susceptible to age-hardening, by which it is first heated to make a particular constituent enter into solid solution and then quenched; so **solution-treat** *v. trans.*, **solution-treated** *ppl. a.*

**1935** G. E. DOAN *Princ. Physical Metallurgy* vi. 192 This heating and quenching is called the 'solution heat treatment'. **1979** J. NEELY *Pract. Metallurgy & Materials of Industry* xiv. 187/2 Successful heat treatment depends on putting the copper into solid solution and trapping it there. **1959** ALLENDOERFER & OAKLEY *Fund. Math.* vi. 102 Given a universal set $X$ and an equation $F(x) = G(x)$ involving $x$, the set $\{x|F(x) = G(x)\}$ is called the solution set of the given equation. **1963** WEBBER & BROWN *Basic Concepts Math.* viii. 166 The truth set of an equation is often called the solution set, and members of the solution set are called solutions of the equation. **1972** A. G. HOWSON *Handbk. Terms Algebra & Anal.* i. 5 Those objects of a given set which satisfy an open statement form the solution set of the statement relative to that set. Thus the solution set of $x^2 = 2$ relative to the real numbers is the set $\{+\sqrt{2}, -\sqrt{2}\}$. Relative to the rational numbers.., the solution set of $x^2 = 2$ is empty. **1940** J. D. JEVONS *Metall. of Deep Drawing & Pressing* xv. 577 Rolled sheet could be 'solution-treated' to place it in a ductile condition. **1977** R. B. ROSS *Handbk. Metal Treatment & Testing* 207 Components which have been correctly Solution treated and aged are very often joined by [welding]. **1952** *Jrnl. R. Aeronaut. Soc.* LVI. 235/1 With highly tapered spar booms it is advisable to machine in the solution-treated condition in order that any correction.. may be made before precipitation. **1931** *Metallurgist* VII. 12/2 The age hardening..of duralumin and a number of other alloys of similar type requires a previous heat treatment, which is frequently termed the 'solution' treatment. **1970** P. C. VARLEY *Technol. of Aluminium & its Alloys* v. 62 All solution treatment is carried out in forced air circulation furnaces.

Hence **so'lutional** *a.*, pertaining to a solution.

**1903** *Nature* 3 Dec. 103/2 The persistence of the solutional nucleus.

**solution** (səˈl(j)uːʃən), *v.* [f. the sb.] *trans.* To treat with, fasten or secure by, a solution.

**1891** *Pall Mall G.* 15 Oct. 1/3 A further improvement.. will dispense with the need for solutioning the canvas. **1898** *Cycling* 63 They should preferably not be vulcanised but merely solutioned together.

**solutioned** (səˈl(j)uːʃənd), *ppl. a.* [f. SOLUTION *v.* + -ED[1].] Treated or covered with solution.

**1898** G. L. HILLIER *Cycling for Everybody* 81 The solutioned surface should be left alone for some minutes, which allows of the evaporation of the naphtha. **1909** 'R. ANDOM' *On Tour with Troddles* 264 We strengthened the cover with strips of rubber and solutioned canvas.

**solutionist** (səˈl(j)uːʃənɪst). [f. SOLUTION *sb.* + -IST.] One who solves problems or puzzles; *spec.* an expert solver of crossword puzzles.

**1885** *Liverpool Mercury* 24 Oct. 5 A large proportion belong to the party of the Right... M. Paul de Cassagnac calls them 'Solutionists'. **1915** *Competition Prize-Winner* I. 1 Our supporters may rest assured that no solutionist will be permitted to use our advertising space unless..his methods are absolutely fair. **1926** *Weekly Dispatch* 29 Aug. 3/3 The insertion of clues capable of alternative solutions..gives the ordinary reader an equal chance with the professional solutionist. **1930** *Aberdeen Press & Jrnl.* 3 May 8/2 If you are keen on winning one of the big cash prizes..for competition enthusiasts, why not avail yourself of the help of expert solutionists?

**solutionizing** (səˈl(j)uːʃənaɪzɪŋ), *vbl. sb.* [f. SOLUTION *sb.* + -IZE + -ING[1].] The process of forming a solution; *spec.* = *solution treatment* s.v. SOLUTION *sb.* 12. So **so'lutionized** *ppl. a.*

**1950** *Chambers's Jrnl.* Mar. 189/2 A recently evolved solutionising system, which is used in conjunction with an overhead irrigation plant, allows the soluble plant-foods to be added at any desired rate. **1977** R. B. ROSS *Handbk. Metal Treatment & Testing* 206 The hardening of steel, where [solution treatment]..is occasionally referred to as 'Solutionizing' or 'Austenizing'. **1978** *Jrnl. R. Soc. Arts* CXXVI. 690/2 An aluminium alloy containing 6 per cent copper, Hid54, set in a freshly solutionized condition, was proposed as the rivet material.

†**so'lutist.** *Obs.*[−1] [f. as SOLUTE *v.* + -IST.] One who solves of finds solutions.

**1708** *Brit. Apollo* No. 1. 2/2 Say bold Solutists, solve the Doubt.

†**solutive**, *a.* and *sb. Obs.* Also 6-7 solutiue, 7 solitive. [ad. med.L. *solūtīv-us*, f. *solūt-*, ppl. stem of *solvĕre* SOLVE *v.* Cf. F. *solutif, -ive*, Sp., Pg., and It. *solutivo*.]

**A.** *adj.* **1.** Laxative, relaxing. (Common in 17th cent.)

**1564-78** BULLEIN *Dial. agst. Pest.* (1886) 50 The sirup of Roses solutiue. **1576** G. BAKER tr. *Gesner's Jewell of Health* 112 This electuarie may be matched or myxed with any other solutive medicine. **1620** VENNER *Via Recta* vii. 148 Their iuyce is of an abstersiue and solutiue faculty. **1666** BOYLE *Orig. Forms & Qual.* 135 Yet the Seeds of this Solutive Cassia are Astringent. **1721** W. GIBSON *True Meth. Diet. Horses* xi. (1726) 175 Their first Diet must be.. solutive and opening. **1750** tr. *Leonardus' Mirror of Stones* 101 It has a solutive virtue, as skilful Physicians say.

**2.** Capable of releasing or setting free.

**1649** EVELYN *Of Libery & Servitude* iv. Misc. Writ. (1805) 27 This liberty..is so rare because of her solutive faculty from whatsoever..restrains our affections.

**3.** Capable of dissolving.

**1732** *Hist. Litteraria* III. 372 Its solutive power..extends to the dissolving of all Salts.

**B.** *sb.* **1.** A laxative or purgative medicine.

**1605** TIMME *Quersit.* I. xvi. 82 Out of many other such like things may be extracted both meane and violent solutiues. **1612** WOODALL *Surg. Mate* Wks. (1653) 351 Solutives forbidden in the cure of the Plague. **1674** R. GODFREY *Inj. & Ab. Physic* 203 To advise them to..be sure that the Solutive be safe.

**2.** A solvent.

**1712** tr. *Pomet's Hist. Drugs* I. 177 The Mercury.. becomes a Solutive for Minerals.

**solutizer** (ˈsɒljuːtaɪzə(r)). [f. L. *solūt-*, ppl. stem of *solvere* SOLVE *v.* + -IZE + -ER[1].] = SOLUBILIZER.

**1939** *Refiner & Natural Gas Manufacturer* XVIII. 171/2 It was found that the addition of suitable organic solvents or salts ('solutizers') to an aqueous alkaline solution increased the solubility of the resulting solution for mercaptans. **1957** VAN DER HAVE & VERVER *Petroleum & its Products* v. 197 In the so-called solutizer process the extracting medium is an alkaline solution to which substances have been added for promoting the solubility and reducing the hydrolysis of the alkali mercaptides in water. In one form of such a method, the 'solutizers' are the sodium and potassium salts of certain organic acids.

†**solutory**, *sb.* and *a. Obs.* [See SOLUTIVE *a.* and *sb.* and -ORY. So OF. *solutoire*.]

**A.** *sb.* = SOLUTIVE *sb.* 1.

**1561** HOLLYBUSH *Hom. Apoth.* 26 b, If one..were so bounde in hys belly that he could have no sieges, then make him thys solutorye.

**B.** *adj.* Used for dissolving or melting.

**1650** ASHMOLE *Arcanum* (ed. 3) 255 Dissolve it into Water in a solutory Vessell. **1678** R. RUSSELL *Geber* v. vi. 276 The Solutory or Dissolving Furnace.

**Solutrian** (səʊˈl(j)uːtrɪən), **Solutrean** (sɒl(j)uːˈtriːən), *a.* and *sb.* [ad. F. *solutréen* (G. de Mortillet *c* 1867) f. the place-name *Solutré* in France (dep. Saône-et-Loire).] **A.** *adj.* Of or belonging to, characterized by, the special type of flint implements found in a cave at Solutré; belonging to the same period as these.

**1888** T. WILSON in *Smithsonian Rep. U.S. Nat. Museum* 615 It was in the working of the flint to make these objects that the best art of the Solutrian epoch is manifested. *Ibid.*, One of the fine, Solutrian, leaf-shaped implements. **1896** KEANE *Ethnology* 87 *margin*, Solutrian or Second Cave Age. **1904** WINDLE *Rem. Prehistoric Age Eng.* iii. 57 Solutrean objects underlie those of the Madelainean time at Laugerie Haute.

**B.** *sb.* **a.** The Solutrean culture.

**1928** C. DAWSON *Age of Gods* i. 14 The Aurignacian culture of Europe.. was replaced by the sudden intrusion of a new culture—the Solutrean—which originated in Eastern Europe or Asia. **1946** F. E. ZEUNER *Dating the Past* ix. 289 When the loess phase of this glacial phase was at its climax, Solutrian appeared, north of the Alpine mountain chains, and in Spain. **1969** G. CLARK *World Prehistory* (ed. 2) iii. 61 During the time of the late Solutrean and Early Magdalenian the artists ceased to engrave limbs as though they were hanging from their back-bones. **1975** J. G. EVANS *Environment Early Man Brit. Isles* ii. 49 The French Solutrean, an industry of unsurpassed elegance in its flint work.

**b.** A person of the Solutrean period. *rare.*

**1944** H. G. WELLS *'42 to '44* 178 The distribution of the Solutreans gives a range quite in accordance with the ideas of W. H. Riddell.

**solvability** (sɒlvəˈbɪlɪtɪ). [f. next + -ITY. Cf. F. *solvabilité.*]

**1.** Solvency.

**1722-7** BOYER *Dict. Royal* 1, *Solvabilité*, the being solvable or able to pay; solvability. **1861** J. H. BENNET *Shores of Medit.* I. vii. (1875) 200 Catastrophes.. have latterly made all parties more careful as to solvability. **1885** *Illustr. Lond. News* 11 July 30/3 Confidential notes about the solvability of their customers.

**2.** Solubility.

**1868** E. SEYD *Bullion & For. Exchanges* 82 The various degrees of Solvability.. are determined by experience. **1891** *Cent. Dict.* s.v., The solvability of an equation.

**solvable** (ˈsɒlvəb(ə)l), *a.* Also 7 **solvible, solveable.** [f. SOLVE *v.* + -ABLE, or a. F. *solvable.*]

†**1.** Able to pay; solvent. *Obs.*

**1647** FULLER *Good Th. in Worse T.* Pref., Many sufficient merchants, though not solvable for the present, make use of the latter [method]. **1655** —— *Ch. Hist.* IX. 131 Although imprisonment was imposed by law on persons not solvable. **1672** WYCHERLEY *Love in a Wood* III. iv, Widows are commonly so wise as to be sure their men are solvable before they trust 'em. **1773** *Ann. Reg.* 69 He immediately called an assembly of the deputies of the bank, from whom he obtained their consent to assist all the solvable houses.

†**2.** Payable. *Obs. rare.*

**1655** FULLER *Ch. Hist.* VI. 326 Some of those Corrodies.. were solvable out of the Exchequer.

**3. a.** Capable of being solved.

*a* **1676** HALE *Orig. Man.* I. ii. (1677) 56, I do not inquire how or where, because it is not solvible. **1681** COLVIL *Whigs Supplic.* (1751) 48 Solve several questions he can, Scarce solvable by any man. **1710** *Brit. Apollo* No. 7. 2/2 You can answer all Questions solvable or not. **1785** FRANKLIN *Lett.* Wks. 1840 VI. 526, I have rarely met with a case of a smoky chimney, which has not been solvable on these principles. **1879** PROCTOR *Pleas. Ways Sci.* iii. 56 The problem of determining the sun's distance.. had seemed fairly solvable in but one or two ways. **1896** CAYLEY *Coll. Math. Papers* XI. 402 A solvable case of the quintic equation.

**b.** *Math.* Of a group: that may be regarded as the last of a finite series of groups of which the first is trivial, each being a normal subgroup of the next and each of the quotients being Abelian.

**1892** E. NETTO *Theory of Substitutions* xiv. 267 We may carry over the expressions 'transitive', 'primitive' and 'non-primitive', 'simple' and 'compound' from the group to the equation... Conversely, we apply the term 'solvable', which is taken from the theory of equations, also to groups, and speak of solvable groups as those whose equations are solvable. **1898** *Amer. Jrnl. Math.* XX. 277 The necessary and sufficient condition that a group is solvable is that its $a^{th}$ derivative (derived group) is unity. **1929** *Ibid.* LI. 494 The total number of groups of order 72 is 50. Each of these groups is obviously solvable. **1971** D. GORENSTEIN in Powell & Higman *Finite Simple Groups* ii. 66 The celebrated Feit-Thompson theorem that groups of odd order are solvable implies that every nonabelian simple group has even order. **1982** *Sci. Amer.* Apr. 120/3 An equation is solvable by radicals if and only if the Galois group of the equation is a solvable group.

**4.** Capable of being dissolved. Also *absol.*

**1669** W. SIMPSON *Hydrol. Chym.* 13 The solvent and solvable are both one. **1794** G. ADAMS *Nat. & Exper. Phil.* I. xi. 460 From being insoluble in water, it is now not only solvable therein, but so greedy of moisture as [etc.].

**5.** Capable of being resolved *into* something.

**1804-6** SYD. SMITH *Mor. Philos.* (1850) 368 The love of knowledge is solvable into some other passion at its origin.

Hence **'solvableness.**

**1727** BAILEY (vol. II), *Solvableness*, ability to pay.

**solvate** (ˈsɒlveɪt), *sb. Chem.* [f. SOLV(E *v.* + -ATE[1].] A more or less loosely bonded complex formed between a dissolved species and the solvent.

**1905** *Amer. Chem. Jrnl.* XXXIV. 489 The existence of hydrates or solvates (in the case of non-aqueous solvents) in one form or another is an old conception. **1922** A. W. STEWART *Physico-Chem. Themes* 269 Another form of explanation is arrived at by assuming that solvates are formed on the addition of the salt. **1969** T. C. WADDINGTON *Non-Aqueous Solvents* ii. 18 Because of its ability to donate its lone pair of electrons to form a covalent coordinate link, as well as by ion-dipole attraction, ammonia forms many solvates.

**solvate** (sɒlˈveɪt), *v. Chem.* [f. SOLV(E *v.* + -ATE[3].] *trans.* To form a solvate with (a dissolved species). Usu. as **sol'vated** *pa. pple.* and *ppl. a.* Also (*rare*) *intr.*, to undergo solvation. Hence **sol'vating** *ppl. a.*

**1909** *Publ. Carnegie Inst.* No. 110. 104 When a salt of one of these elements is dissolved in a solvent both the molecules of the salt and the ions formed from them become solvated. **1913** H. C. JONES *New Era Chem.* ix. 165 Non electrolytes solvate very slightly. The electrolytes combine with large amounts of the solvent. *Ibid.*, It is the ions which are the chief solvating agents. **1932** PHILBRICK & HOLMYARD *Text Bk. Theoret. & Inorg. Chem.* xi. 312 Hydrogen chloride is a strong acid only in solvents in which it is solvated. **1958** *Proc. Nat. Acad. Sci.* XLIV. 429 Strongly hydrogen-bonding organic solvents have been found to solvate polypeptides and proteins completely. **1968** V. GUTMANN *Coordination Chem. in Non-Aqueous Solutions* ii. 34 With increasing donor properties of the solvent its solvating properties become stronger. **1971** *Nature* 1 Jan. 13/2 The study of the solvated electron has its origins in the work begun by Kraus at the beginning of this century on the blue solutions formed by dissolving alkali metals in liquid ammonia and amines. Electrical conductivity and other measurements have established that the solvated electron is responsible for the blue colour of these solutions. **1976** J. DAINTITH *Dict. Physical Sci.* 4/2 In solution the hydrogen ion, $H^+$, is solvated by water and often considered to be a hydroxonium ion, $H_3O^+$. **1977** *Sci. Amer.* July 95/1 The solvated electrons in an alkali-metal-ammonia solution should behave like unpaired electrons in an atom and hence should make the solutions paramagnetic. *Ibid.* 98/3 The entire complex can then readily be solvated by a polar liquid such as an amine or an ether.

**solvation** (sɒlˈveɪʃən). *Chem.* [f. SOLV(E *v.* + -ATION.] The process of becoming, or state of being, solvated. Freq. *attrib.*

**1909** *Amer. Chem. Jrnl.* XLI. 41 The theory of solvation in solution. **1917** M. H. FISCHER tr. *Ostwald's Introd. Theoret. & Appl. Colloid Chem.* 51 These colloids are characterized by their great hydration or solvation. Their particles have taken up a large amount of the dispersion media. **1936** R. W. GURNEY *Ions in Solution* i. 4 If a free gaseous ion enters a solvent.. energy is liberated. This is known as the Solvation Energy, and has a characteristic value for each ion in each solvent. **1948** *Nature* 31 Jan. 170/1 When the concentration of organic solvent is increased beyond 50 mol. per cent, organic solvent molecules begin to predominate in the medium and eventually replace the aqueous solvation shell. **1967** MARGERISON & EAST *Introd. Polymer Chem.* v. 239 The questions associated with solvation, its extent, the type of chemical bonding, the number of solvent molecules involved,.. are largely unanswerable. **1976** *Nature* 3 June 435/1 Relaxation rates for $^{17}O$ in monosaccharides have been used to study solvation, the revised estimate of the solvation number being 5 ± 1 water molecules for D-glucose and 2·5 ± 1 for D-ribose at 5 °C.

**Solvay** (ˈsɒlveɪ). *Chem.* [The name of Ernest Solvay (1838–1922), Belgian chemist, who developed the process.] *Solvay* (or †*Solvay's*) *process*: a method of making sodium carbonate using brine, ammonia, and carbon dioxide (which is usu. made as part of the process, by calcining limestone); also called *ammonia-soda process*. Hence *Solvay plant*, etc.

**1879** *Sci. Amer. Suppl.* 12 Apr. 2719/3 From these injurious impurities the Solvay soda is almost absolutely free. **1884** *Jrnl. Soc. Chem. Industry* 29 Dec. 633/1 In the Solvay process there have been introduced important improvements. **1888** C. L. BLOXAM *Chem.* (ed. 6) 262 (*heading*) Ammonia soda process, or Solvay's process. **1947** KIRK & OTHMER *Encycl. Chem. Technol.* I. 402 A 500-ton-per-day soda plant requires gas compressors of about 3000 to 4000 horsepower to handle the suction on the kilns and to compress the gas into the Solvay precipitating towers. **1950** *Thorpe's Dict. Appl. Chem.* (ed. 4) X. 835/1 The earliest Solvay plants used solid salt and dissolved it in a recycled alkaline water obtained from the scrubbing of calciner gases. **1966** *McGraw-Hill Encycl. Sci. & Technol.* II. 399/2 Calcium chloride, obtained as a waste product in the Solvay process. **1974** *Encycl. Brit. Micropædia* IX. 320/1 Its anhydrous form, soda ash ($Na_2CO_3$),.. is now manufactured chiefly by the ammonia-soda (Solvay) process.

**solve,** *sb.* [f. next. Malone's alteration of *solye* = *soyle*: see SOIL *sb.*[5]] Solution.

**1780** *Shakspere's Sonn.* (Malone) lxix. 14 The solve is this —that thou dost common grow.

**solve** (sɒlv), *v.* Also 5 **solvyn,** 6–7 **solue.** [ad. L. *solvĕre* to loosen, dissolve. So Sp. and Pg. *solver*, It. *solvere.*]

†**1.** *trans.* To loosen; to break. *Obs.*

*c* **1440** *Alph. Tales* 254 And on þis maner þai war wunt.. for to solve þer faste. *c* **1450** LYDG. *Secrees* 1259 Afftir the sesouns Solve flewm brennyng or moysture.

†**2. a.** To unbind, untie. *Obs.*

*c* **1440** *Promp. Parv.* 464/1 Solvyn, *supra in* onbyyndyn. *c* **1460** *Ibid.* (Winch.) 322 Onbyyndyn, or solvyn, *soluo.* **1616** BULLOKAR *Eng. Exp.*, *Solue*, to vntie. **1658** PHILLIPS, *Solve*, to loosen, or undo.

†**b.** To absolve. *Obs.*[−1]

**1550** BALE *Image Both Ch.* II. xiii. e iij, Without yᵉ blynd bussynges of a papiste, may no synne be solued.

**3.** To explain, clear up, resolve, answer.

*a* **1533** FRITH *Disput. Purgat.* (1829) 122 The second cause .. is not solved of Rastell; but I had solved it before. **1541** R. COPLAND *Guydon's Quest. Chirurg.* Mj, In the fyrste partycle is moued & solued certayne questyons. **1624** GATAKER *Transubst.* 69 Solving all objections gathered out of their obscurer sayings against Catholic doctrine. **1671** MILTON *P.R.* IV. 573 That Theban Monster that propos'd Her riddle, and him, who solv'd it not, devour'd. **1726** SWIFT *Gulliver* III. ii, He was then deep in a problem, and we attended at least an hour before he could solve it. **1777** PRIESTLEY *Matt. & Spir.* (1782) I. xxii. 284 This writer.. suggests another method of solving this difficulty. **1841** BORROW *Zincali* III. ii. II. 119 The following consideration will help to solve this point. **1885** TEMPLE *Relig. & Sci.* v. 147 It leaves questions to be solved some of which have not been solved yet.

*refl.* **1855** KINGSLEY *Lett.* (1878) I. 455 The problem of life .. solves itself so very soon at best by death.

†**b.** = SALVE *v.*[2] 1. *Obs.*

**1621** BURTON *Anat. Mel.* II. ii. 111, He hath coyned 72 Homocentrickes, to solue all app[e]arances. **1757** MRS. GRIFFITH *Lett. Henry & Frances* (1767) I. 200 On account of solving appearances to her nicety.

**c.** *Math.* To find the answer or solution to (a problem, etc.); to work out.

**1737** *Gentl. Mag.* VII. 675 There must be found one Condition more to solve the Question, or to reduce it to only one unknown Quantity. **1806** HUTTON *Course Math.* I. 247 The general method of solving quadratic equations, is by what is called completing the square. **1828** MOORE *Pract. Navig.* 115 How to solve compound courses, or a traverse, has already been shown in Plane Sailing. **1878** GURNEY *Crystallog.* 119 Anyone who can solve a spherical triangle will have no difficulty.

**4.** To clear off; to pay or discharge.

**1558** in Feuillerat *Revels Q. Eliz.* (1908) Table 1, The Bookes solved as the Dischardge thereof maye appeare in the saide Booke. **1624** WHITE *Reply to Fisher* 564 Summes of money.. to be solued to the Publicans of the Ecclesiasticall Roman Tribute. **1866** J. B. ROSE tr. *Ovid's Met.* 219 Minos returned to his Curetan home, And solved his vows. **1874** *Contemp. Rev.* XXIV. 122 Estates in Hertfordshire.. were able to pay £17,509.. towards solving the debt.

**5.** To dissolve, put an end to, settle.

**1667** MILTON *P.L.* VIII. 55 Hee.. would.. solve high dispute With conjugal Caresses. **1701** STEELE *Christian Hero* 91 An Army, whose Swords can make right in Power, and solve controversy in Belief. *a* **1763** SHENSTONE *Elegy* xv. 86 These the sounds that chase unholy strife! Solve envy's charm.

**6.** To dissolve; to melt.

**1662** [see SOLVED]. **1794** G. ADAMS *Nat. & Exper. Phil.* I. x. 399 It will be easily solved in hot water. **1852** *Jrnl. R. Agric. Soc.* XIII. I. 170 The plant (grass) that takes up the material solved takes up the water also. **1880** *Paper & Printing Trades Jrnl.* XXXI. 4 Solve next a small quantity of bichromate of potassa in distilled water.

*fig.* **1839-52** BAILEY *Festus* 23 The electric touch solved both our souls together.

Hence **solved** *ppl. a.*; **'solving** *vbl. sb.* and *ppl. a.*

**1662** J. CHANDLER *Van Helmont's Oriat.* 309 The solved flowre of Sulphur. *Ibid.*, The solved Body of Sulphur it self. **1706** STEVENS *Span.-Eng. Dict.* I, *Solución*,.. the Solving of a Question. **1756** C. LUCAS *Ess. Waters* II. 164 The solvent and solved both concur in producing these effects in the water. **1847** EMERSON *Poems, Threnody*, My servant Death, with solving rite, Pours finite into infinite. **1852** *Jrnl. R. Agric. Soc.* XIII. I. 170 As long as the water is kept in motion it carries its solved substances with it. **1883** FLEMING *Old Violins* 273 Its presence does not injure the solving power of the alcohol. **1895** *Athenæum* 25 May 665/2 The solving of the vexed questions that beset us.

**solvency** (ˈsɒlvənsɪ). [f. SOLVENT *a.*: see -ENCY.] The state of being solvent. Also *attrib.*

**1727** BAILEY (vol. II), *Solvency*, paying. **1730** —— (fol.), *Solvency*, a Paying or Capacity of paying Debts, &c. **1790** BURKE *Fr. Rev.* 338 The debtor prescribing.. the medium of his solvency to the creditor. **1805** *Ann. Rev.* III. 293 The reputation for solvency of one institution. **1844** H. H. WILSON *Brit. India* I. 533 The bills of private merchants, of whose solvency they could not always feel secure. **1863** FAWCETT *Polit. Econ.* III. ii. 432 All those who place confidence in the solvency of a particular banker. **1891** *Pall Mall G.* 21 Sept. 6/2 The last Blue-book of the Friendly Societies.. gives a solvency valuation of 17*s.* in the pound of the three leading temperance benefit societies.

**'solvend.** ? *Obs.* [ad. L. *solvend-um*, neut. gerundive of *solvĕre* SOLVE *v.*] Something to be dissolved.

**1738** *Phil. Trans.* XLI. 108 The Particles of the Solvend having imbibed the Particles of the Menstruum. **1799** KIRWAN *Geol. Ess.* 467 A fluid whose specific affinity to the particles of a solvend is greater than the integrant affinity of the ultimate particles of the solvend to each other. **1867** *Tomlinson's Cycl. Useful Arts* App. 229/2 A saturated solution.. is one in which the adhesion of the solvent and the cohesion of the solvend mutually balance each other.

‖**sol'vendo.** Now *Sc.* [L., dative gerund of *solvĕre* SOLVE *v.*] Solvent.

Modified forms (as *silvendy*), with transference of meaning, also occur in Sc. dialect use.

*a* **1684** LEIGHTON *Expos. Ten Commandm.* Wks. (1868) 492 If God be solvendo, if he be a sufficient debtor. [**1704** J. HARRIS *Lex. Techn.* I, *Solvendo esse*, a Term in Law, signifying that a Man hath wherewith to pay, or is a Person *solvent.*] **1825** JAMIESON *Suppl.*, *Solvendie*,.. sufficient to pay one's debts, solvent, Ang[us]... *Solvendo* is also used, Aberd[een].

**solvent** (ˈsɒlvənt), *a.* and *sb.* [ad. L. *solvent-*, *solvens*, pres. pple. of *solvĕre* SOLVE *v.*]

**A.** *adj.* **1.** Able to pay all one's debts or liabilities.

**1653** H. COGAN tr. *Pinto's Trav.* lxxviii. 315 Certain Chineses, who were not men solvent, but became bankrupts. **1664** *Addit. to Life Mede* M.'s Wks. (1672) p. xxxvi, Mr. Mede began.. to refuse.., and objected, How shall I be able to be solvent in convenient time? **1698**

LUTTRELL *Brief Rel.* (1857) IV. 379 The commons read the bill..for discovery of solvent prisoners estates. **1812** CRABBE *Borough* xxiii. 49 They would be solvent, and deplore a debt. **1846** GROTE *Greece* (1862) II. 312 A solvent man capable of ..fulfilling a contract. **1885** *Law Times Rep.* LIII. 484/1 If the plaintiff in England had been solvent, no security would have been required.

*transf.* **1667** *Ormonde MSS.* in *10th Rep. Hist. MSS. Comm.* App. V. 45 Sir Daniel Bellingham..is..to issue such solvent assignments as they may receive speedy satisfaction. **1674** *Essex Papers* (Camden) I. 183 'Tis probable y[t] most of y[e] solvent Arrears are already gather'd.

*Comb.* **1852** MUNDY *Antipodes* (1857) 35 A solvent looking gentleman, solus in a buggy, is the very thing for a highwayman.

**2.** Dissolving; causing solution.

**1686** PLOT *Staffordsh.* 9 [Lightning] being of a very subtile nature..and solvent of the parts of bodies. **1791** J. JONES in Beddoes *On Calculus* (1793) 32 The extraordinary efficacy of the sal sodæ I had seen in the last case, induced me to try its solvent powers in this. **1807** *Phil. Trans.* XCVII. 146 The excretory ducts of the glands, which secrete the solvent liquor. **1832** BREWSTER *Nat. Magic* xii. 298 The disintegrating and solvent powers of chemical agents. **1878** HUXLEY *Physiogr.* 122 The comparative ease with which limestone yields to the solvent action of water.

*fig.* **1875** MAINE *Hist. Inst.* xi. 329 Among the most powerful solvent influences were certain philosophical theories.

**3.** Helping to solve or explain.

**1872** TULLOCH *Rational Theol.* I. i. 34 The most significant and solvent of all the rational principles enunciated by Arminianism.

**B.** *sb.* **1. a.** A substance (usually a liquid) having the power of dissolving other substances.

**1671** BOYLE *Usef. Nat. Philos.* II. II. 18 By a substitution of burnt Allom for Vitriol,..we made Solvents for Silver, as good as theirs. **1681** tr. *Willis' Rem. Med. Wks.* Vocab., *Solvent*, that which dissolveth or openeth the parts of the matter to be wrought upon. **1756** C. LUCAS *Ess. Waters* I. 159 Water..is found the most universal solvent of the food of man and other animals. **1782** *Phil. Trans.* LXXIII. 51 If formed by solution, they..retain a portion of their solvent or precipitant. **1827** FARADAY *Chem. Manip.* vi. 187 Some of the acids frequently act as mere solvents. **1871** TYNDALL *Fragm. Sci.* (1879) I. ii. 43 The solvent of the iodine is perfectly transparent.

**b.** *fig.* A dissolving or disintegrating influence.

**1841** EMERSON *Ess., Intellect* Wks. (Bohn) I. 143 Silence is a solvent that destroys personality. **1870** E. PEACOCK *Ralf Skirl.* II. 5 Fine phrases which have acted as solvents upon ..unreasoning Whiggism and Toryism. **1886** *Contemp. Rev.* July 72 The great solvent of Indian caste prejudice is Western thought.

**2.** Something which solves, explains, or settles.

**1865** LECKY *Ration.* (1878) I. 292 Those who, perceiving ..yet undefined discoveries,..imagine that they will prove a universal solvent. **1871** R. H. HUTTON *Ess.* (1877) I. 43 How the absence of theistic faith tends..to make philosophy the universal solvent of fact. **1890** 'R. BOLDREWOOD' *Colonial Ref.* (1891) 317 He..was compelled to employ that only universal solvent, a cash payment.

**3.** A laxative; a loosener.

**1815** KIRBY & SP. *Entomol.* (1818) I. 314 Had I addressed you a century ago,..I should have recommended the woodlouse as a solvent and aperient. **1823** LAMB *Elia* Ser. II. Pref., He took it [tobacco], he would say, as a solvent of speech.

**4.** A person able to pay all his debts.

**1825** COBBETT *Rur. Rides* (1853) 354 Every insolvent blames a solvent, that will not lend him money.

**5.** *attrib.* and *Comb.*, as ***solvent abuse, recovery, -sniffing; solvent-thinned*** adj.; **solvent extraction**, the partial removal of a substance from a solution or a mixture of liquids by utilizing its greater solubility in another liquid or its greater permeability through a membrane; so **solvent-extract** *v. trans.*, to purify by means of solvent extraction; also as *sb.*, a fraction extracted from a mixture by this process; a spell of solvent extraction.

**1977** Solvent abuse [see SNIFFING *vbl. sb.*] **1949** *Our Industry* (Anglo-Iranian Oil Co.) (ed. 2) iv. 116 The kerosine fraction may..be solvent extracted by means of liquid sulphur dioxide. **1956** *Nature* 4 Feb. 224/2 When insulin was added to an acidic solvent-extract of liver..the recovery of the insulin varied between 92 and 93 per cent. **1963** A. J. HALL *Textile Sci.* iii. 122 Another system of purifying wool is to solvent extract it with an organic solvent such as trichloroethylene. **1978** *Nature* 23 Mar. 298/2 Subsequent solvent extract in mixer settlers will separate plutonium nitrate solution. **1920** *Chem. Trade Jrnl.* LXVI. 103 Quantities of oil for edible purposes were being produced by solvent extraction processes. **1949** *Our Industry* (Anglo-Iranian Oil Co.) (ed. 2) iv. 119 Solvent extraction processes are to-day used extensively in the petroleum industry for refining light distillates, kerosines and lubricating oils. **1978** *Sci. Amer.* July 97/3 Solvent extraction across membranes has been known at least since 1913, when Fritz Haber and Reinhardt Beutner showed that a thin film of oil could be employed as a membrane in two kinds of extraction process. **1947** KIRK & OTHMER *Encycl. Chem. Technol.* I. 231 Activated carbon is used on a large scale for solvent recovery. **1977** *Lancet* 8 Jan. 82/1 Cardiac arrhythmias,..neuropsychiatric disorders, and hepatorenal failure have all been reported after solvent sniffing. **1960** *McGraw-Hill Encycl. Sci. & Technol.* IX. 493/1 Solvent-thinned paints, which dry essentially by solvent evaporation, rely on a fairly hard resin as the vehicle.

Hence **'solvently** *adv.*

**1872** H. BUSHNELL *Serm. Living Subj.* 437 That personal life-giving spirit that will touch as it were solvently, all the secret bonds and propagative chains of causes.

**solventless** ('sɒlvəntlɪs), *a.* [f. SOLVENT *sb.* + -LESS.] Without a solvent.

**1936** O. W. ESHBACH *Handbk. Engin. Fund.* XII. xxxiii. 70 (*heading*) Solventless varnishes. **1945** *Jrnl. Applied Physics* XVI. 584/2 A thin film of solventless varnish was applied to each sheet. **1970** *Financial Times* 13 Apr. 9/1 A feature of this two-component solventless coating..is that it can be applied cold.

**solver** ('sɒlvə(r)). [f. SOLVE *v.* + -ER[1].] One who solves.

**1719** DE FOE *Crusoe* I. (Globe) 222 A Casuist, or a Solver of Difficulties. **1864** *Athenæum* No. 1920. 217/2 Solver of problems. **1876** *Academy* 30 Sept. 331/1 The lynx-eyed public solvers often detect some simple second solution. **1898** *Month* Nov. 550 The solver of their doubts and difficulties.

‖**solvitur ambulando** ('sɒlvɪtə(r) æmbjuː'lændəʊ). [L. phr., lit. '(the problem) is solved by walking'.] An appeal to practical experience for the solution of a problem or proof of a statement. Also as *sb. phr.* Also in shortened form **ambulando**, by experience; in the course of things.

Originally an allusion to the reported proof by Diogenes the Cynic of the possibility of motion: see Diogenes Laertius VI. 39.

[**1814** *Artis Logicæ Rudimenta. Accessit Solutio Sophismatum* 67 Ineptum est hoc Sophisma 1. Quia solvitur ambulando; quod fecit Diogenes.] **1852** A. H. CLOUGH *Let.* Mar. in *Poems & Prose Remains* (1869) I. 174 It is not.. simply one's business in life to 'envisager' the most remarkable problems of humanity... Still we may be assured that only time can work out any sort of answer to them for us. '*Solvitur ambulando*.' **1863** J. CONINGTON *Horace's Odes* p. xxv, How easily the '*solvitur ambulando*' of an artist like Mr. Tennyson may disturb a whole chain of ingenious reasoning on the possibilities of things. **1863** C. READE *Hard Cash* I. viii. 226 To the à priori reasoners..he replied by building an engine..hooking on eight carriages, and rattling off up an incline. 'Solvitur ambulando,' quoth Stephenson the stout hearted. **1876** W. JAMES in *Nation* 8 June 369/1 The ultimate decision of which side is right and which wrong shall only be reached *ambulando* or at the final integration of things, if at all. **1906** F. W. MAITLAND *L. Stephen* xvii. 366 He knew that he would have to proceed empirically. *Solvitur ambulando*—the motto of the philosophic tramp—had also to be the motto of the editor. **1930** J. LAIRD *Knowl., Belief & Opin.* iv. 103 Perfectly convincing evidence might turn up, so to say, *ambulando*, when we are engaged in something irrelevant. **1934** A. TOYNBEE *Stud. Hist.* III. 182 A modern Western philosopher applies the historic *solvitur ambulando* to the ancient sophism of the Eleatics. **1955** *Times* 30 Aug. 9/2 To what extent and for what purposes is it justifiable to transform personality by surgery, psychological techniques, or the administration of drugs? In so far as matters of this kind have been the subject of conscious policy in the past solvitur ambulando has been the motto. **1957** G. RYLE in C. A. Mace *Brit. Philos. in Mid-Cent.* 256 The assimilation of language to chess reminds us of what we knew *ambulando* all along.

**solvolyse** ('sɒlvəʊlaɪz), *v. Chem.* Also (*U.S.*) **-lyze.** [f. SOLVOLYSIS after *analyse, analysis*, etc.] **a.** *trans.* To bring about the solvolysis of (a solute); usu. in *pass.* **b.** *intr.* To undergo solvolysis.

**1916** *Chem. Abstr.* X. 2349 A table of salts is given which are 'solvolyzed' by $C_6H_6$. **1921** *Jrnl. Physical Chem.* XXV. 550 Lead chromate solvolyzes. **1965** PHILLIPS & WILLIAMS *Inorg. Chem.* I. xv. 569 In sulphuric acid nearly all inorganic salts are solvolysed in the dissolution process. **1974** *Nature* 19 Apr. 671/1 Tosylate..solvolysed in formic acid at 75°C to give an olefin as the major product. **1977** *Lancet* 24–31 Dec. 1298/1 The bile samples are solvolysed (which ensures that bile-acid sulphate esters are included), and individual acids were measured by gas chromatography.

**solvolysis** (sɒl'vɒlɪsɪs). *Chem.* Pl. **-lyses** (-lɪsiːz). [ad. G. *solvolyse* (P. Walden 1910, in *Sammlung chem. und chem.-techn. Vorträge* XV. x. 447), f. *solvens* SOLVENT *sb.*: see -LYSIS.] The decomposition or dissociation of a solute brought about by the action of the solvent.

**1916** *Chem. Abstr.* X. 2349 Most probably other indifferent, *i.e.*, non-ionizing solvents are also capable of dissociating salts into base and acid. This general property of solvents, which is independent of electrolytic dissociation, is designated 'solvolysis' or solvolytic dissociation. **1922** *Jrnl. Physical Chem.* XXVI. 567 The solvolyses were performed simultaneously in porcelain crucibles in an oven at 225°–230°. **1940** L. P. HAMMETT *Physical Org. Chem.* vi. 171 The product of the solvolysis is not completely racemized. **1972** R. A. JACKSON *Mechanism* iv. 56 Solvolysis of the diester 63 has been postulated to involve the intermediate carbonium ion 64.

So **solvo'lytic** *a.*, pertaining to or of the nature of solvolysis; **solvo'lytically** *adv.*

**1916** [see SOLVOLYSIS]. **1931** *Chem. Rev.* VIII. 199 Goldschmidt and Mathiesen..report the solvolytic constants for a variety of bases in ethyl and methyl alcohols. **1965** PHILLIPS & WILLIAMS *Inorg. Chem.* I. xv. 556 Solvolytic reactions are often of synthetic value, but they also severely limit the range of reactions which may be conducted in a particular solvent. **1974** GILL & WILLIS *Pericyclic Reactions* vi. 148 With a monohalogeno carbene a mixture of *endo-* and *exo*-halogenobicycloalkanes is formed, only one of which will usually be solvolytically reactive. **1975** *Nature* 21 Aug. 681/1 Overberger and Podsiadly have demonstrated the importance of polymeric chain aggregation on the rate of solvolytic reaction.

**solvus** ('sɒlvəs). Pl. solvi. [mod.L., f. L. *solvere* to dissolve, after LIQUIDUS, SOLIDUS[2].] A line or surface in a phase diagram delimiting the region of stability of a solid solution.

**1950** *Jrnl. Geol.* LVIII. 499/2 Now we have a means of establishing the position of the unmixing curve or solvus. **1956** *Amer. Mineralogist* XLIII. 877 In Fig. 4 three solvi are shown. **1963** W. A. DEER et al. *Rock-Forming Minerals* II. 127 If the liquidus minimum passes beyond the intersection with the solvus..the calcium-poor phase would cease to crystallize as a separate phase. **1968** R. A. HIGGINS *Engin. Metall.* (ed. 2) I. ix. 170 The only new feature of the system ..is that we have phase boundaries occurring below the solidus, indicating that phase changes can take place in the solid. On the tin-lead thermal-equilibrium diagram..such phase boundaries..are indicated by the lines *BC* and *FG*. A line such as *BC* or *FG* is often termed as [*sic*] solvus. **1975** *Nature* 3 Apr. 406/2 At 1,450°C a further solvus was reported between the pigeonite and a more calcic diopside.

†**solwe**, *v. Obs.* Forms: *pa. pple.* (and *pa. t.*) 4 solwid (sulwed), soluid, solewid, 4–5 solwyd, solowed; 5 *inf.* sol(o)wyn. [Related to older Flem. *soluwen, seulewen*, MHG. *sulwen*, or to OHG. *solagôn, sologôn* (MHG. *solgen*, also *sulgen*): cf. SOL *a.* and SOLE *v.*[3]]

**1.** *trans.* To defile, soil, sully.

*a* **1300** *Cursor M.* 10637 Vr lauerd wil him neuer bede To saul þat solewid es wit sinn. *Ibid.* 22491 Lauerd! how mai we þan þis thole, þat es sua sulwed in vr sin. *c* **1425** *Cast. Persev.* 3421 in *Macro Plays* 179 Man hathe..solwyd hes sovle with synnys seuene. *c* **1440** *Promp. Parv.* 464/1 Solwyn, or fowlyn (*P.* solowyn), *maculo, deturpo. Ibid.*, Solwynge (*P.* solowynge), *deturpacio, sordidacio.*

**2.** *intr.* To become soiled or dirty.

**1303** R. BRUNNE *Handl. Synne* 9152 Heere ne nayles neuer grewe, Ne solowed cloþes, ne turned hewe.

†**solwy**, *a. Obs. rare.* [Related to prec.] Dirty.

*c* **1320** *Sir Tristr.* 1777 Smockes hadde sche and y, And hir was solwy to sen. *Ibid.* 1788. *c* **1325** *Gloss. W. de Bibbesw.* in Wright *Voc.* 171 [E si la nape seyt trop soyle; *glossed*] solwy.

Hence †**'solwiness**, pollution. *Obs.*

*a* **1300** *Cursor M.* 10887 Wit-vten sin or sulwines Sal þou be maiden als þou es. *Ibid.* 29037.

**soly(e**, obs. ff. SOLELY *adv.*

‖**solyanka** (sə'ljankə). Also **soljanka.** [Russ.] A soup made of vegetables and meat or fish.

**1958** W. BICKEL tr. *Hering's Dict. Classical & Mod. Cookery* 113 *Soljanka is riba*, fish soup. **1970** 'J. MORRIS' *Candywine Devel.* xxv. 280 He..heaped the big serving-spoon with *solyanka* from the dish. **1972** M. GLENNY tr. *Solzhenitsyn's August 1914* xlii. 422 'Well, now, young men —what is it to be? *Solyanka*, meatballs, scrambled eggs?' said the old man invitingly.

**solybubbe**, obs. f. SILLABUB.

**solycit(e, solycytude**, obs. ff. SOLICIT *v.*, SOLICITUDE.

**solydyne**, obs. var. CELANDINE.

*c* **1425** *Eng. Voc.* in Wr.-Wülcker 644 *Hec selidonia*, solydyne.

**Soly'mæan**, *a. rare.* [f. L. *Solyma* for *Hierosolyma* Jerusalem.] Of or belonging to Jerusalem.

**1681** DRYDEN *Abs. & Achit.* 513 The Solymæan Rout.. Saw with Disdain an Ethnick Plot begun.

‖**sol y sombra** (sol i 'sombra). [Sp., lit. 'sun and shade'.] A drink of brandy mixed with anisette or gin.

**1930** W. T. BOOTHBY *'Cocktail Bill' Boothby's World Drinks* (rev. ed.) 148 *Sol y Sombra* (*Sun & Shadow*) Brandy (Spanish) ½ jigger Gin ½ jigger. **1966** C. ROUGVIE *Gredos Reckoning* v. 76 'What's that you're drinking?' '*Sol y sombra*: a mixture of anis and brandy.' **1979** D. SERAFIN *Saturday of Glory* 17 A *sol y sombra*, an explosive mixture of brandy and anisette.

**solys(se)t, solys(se)tacion, solyster**, obs. ff. SOLICIT *v.* and *a.*, SOLICITATION, SOLICITER.

‖**soma**[1] ('səʊmə). Also 8 som. [Skr. *sōma*, = Zend *haōma*, Pers. *hōm*: see HOM.]

**1. a.** An intoxicating drink holding a prominent place in Vedic ritual and religion.

The soma was prepared from the juice of a plant which is commonly supposed to have been *Asclepias acida* or *Sarcostemma viminale* (or *acidum*).

**1827** [see sense 2]. **1843** *Penny Cycl.* XXVI. 174/2 The soma, when properly prepared, is a powerful spirit. **1869** T. C. BARKER *Aryan Civiliz.* i. (1871) 3 From the Hindoo he [the fire-god] has the fermented drink called *soma*. **1872** WHITTIER *Brewing of Soma* iv, From tent to tent The Soma's sacred madness went, A storm of drunken joy. **1876** *Encycl. Brit.* IV. 205/2 The soma..must have played an important part in the ancient worship, at least as early as the Indo-Persian period.

*attrib.* **1843** *Penny Cycl.* XXVI. 175/1 What else is this act of drinking the soma-juice but a kind of sacrament? **1874** L. J. TROTTER *Hist. India* I. i. 4 He [Indra] delights in drinking the sacred soma juice. **1876** *Encycl. Brit.* IV. 205 Among the Vaidik rites the soma-sacrifices are the most solemn and complicated. **1895** A. NUTT *Voy. Bran* I. 321 The immortality claimed by the soma devotee.

**b.** In Aldous Huxley's novel *Brave New World*, a narcotic drug which produces euphoria and hallucination, distributed by the state in order to promote content and social harmony. Also *transf.* and *attrib.*

**1932** A. HUXLEY *Brave New World* iii. 66 There is always *soma*, delicious *soma*, half a gramme for a half-holiday, a gramme for a week-end, two grammes for a trip to the gorgeous East, three for a dark eternity on the moon. *Ibid.* v. 95 The *soma* had begun to work. Eyes shone, cheeks were flushed, the inner light of universal benevolence broke out on every face in happy, friendly smiles. *Ibid.* vi. 107 Bernard swallowed four tablets of *soma* at a gulp. *Ibid.* xv. 246 The two Groups.. were served by the Deputy Sub-Bursar with their *soma* ration. **1959** *Times Lit. Suppl.* 27 Feb. 105/2 The forecast [in *Brave New World*] of a pain-killing, pleasure-giving pill called *soma*, at once the perfect substitute for alcohol, opium and benzedrine, has not yet been wholly fulfilled. **1968** 'J. Le Carré' *Small Town in Germany* ix. 155 If I smoked I'd smoke one of your cigars. I could do with a bit of soma just now. **1976** *Interdisciplinary Sci. Rev.* I. 178/1 Suppose there was national agreement on the need for a 'good' psychoactive drug, one which would be as universally used as the ubiquitous *soma* of *Brave New World.*

**2.** *soma plant*, the plant yielding the soma-juice. Also *ellipt.*

**1785** C. Wilkins tr. *Bhăgvăt Gēētā* ix. 80 The followers of the three *Vēds*, who drink the juice of the *Sōm*.. address me. *Ibid.* 143 *Sōm*—is the name of a creeper, the juice of which is commanded to be drank at the conclusion of a sacrifice. **1827** Colebrooke in *Trans. Royal Asiatic Soc.* I. 455 The presenting of expressed juice of the *sóma* plant. **1866** *Treas. Bot.* s.v. *Asclepias*, The bruised stem and leaves of the Soma plant yield a juice [etc.]. **1882** *Cornh. Mag.* June 720 The soma plant, by which Indra conquers Vritra. **1972** R. G. Wasson *Soma* ii. 10 My candidate for the identity of soma is *Amanita muscaria*.., in English the fly-agaric.

‖**soma**[2] ('səʊmə). *Phys.* [a. Gr. σῶμα body.]

**1.** The body of an organism in contrast to the germ-cells. Also *attrib.* in *soma-plasm*. Also *fig.*

**1889** tr. *Weismann's Ess. Heredity*, etc. 122 It is necessary to distinguish between.. the body in its narrower sense (*soma*) and the germ-cells. *Ibid.* 154 The perishable and vulnerable nature of the *soma*. **1902** *Encycl. Brit.* XXIX. 259/2 With Weismann, we suppose the germ-plasm to be different in kind from the general soma-plasm. **1904** *Brit. Med. Jrnl.* 15 Oct. 966 If the mother be addicted to drink, additional damage may be done to the soma during intra-uterine life. **1914** W. R. Inge *Outspoken Ess.* (1919) 238, I can see no other fate in store for the *soma* of Catholicism; the germ-cells of true Christianity live their own life within it.

**2.** *Anat.* The compact portion of a nerve-cell, excluding the axon.

**1947** R. Lorente de Nó in *Jrnl. Cellular & Compar. Physiol.* XXIX. 211 The word 'soma' will be used to denote the body and all the dendritic branches of the neuron. **1970** *Jrnl. Neurobiol.* I. 340 The somas are likely to be the site of protein synthesis. **1974** *Nature* 8 Nov. 155/1 Studies with a few invertebrate preparations have suggested different ionic mechanisms for spike generation in the soma and axon of the same neurone.

**3.** The body in contrast to the mind or the soul. Opp. *psyche.*

**1958** A. Wilson *Middle Age of Mrs Eliot* I. 72 He says that between Else fussing with his soma and me with his psyche, all he really wants is a complete rest and he wishes he were travelling with you. **1969** *Listener* 26 June 881/2 A score of youths and girls intent on exploring each other honestly and sincerely in psyche and soma can't help generating some degree of excitement. **1976** *Lancet* 30 Oct. 946/2 No personal physician, at any time, has been able to operate successfully without using substances, as symbols of healing of the soma and the psyche.

**somaar**, var. Sommer *adv.*

**somæsthetic** (səʊmiːs'θɛtɪk), *a. Physiol.* Also **-esthetic.** [f. Gr. σῶμα body + αἰσθητικ-ός perceptive.] Pertaining to or designating those sensations (as of pressure, pain, or warmth) which can occur anywhere in the body, in contrast to those that depend on highly localized sense organs (as sight, balance, or taste).

**1899** L. F. Barker *Nerv. System* xlvii. 667 The region of the cortex in which the axones of the general sensory conduction path here considered terminate, I have designated as the somæsthetic area of the cortex. [*Note*] I wish to thank Prof. Gildersleeve, of the Johns Hopkins University, for suggesting this term as a suitable English equivalent for Munk's *Körperfühlsphäre*. **1922** R. S. Woodworth *Psychology* iii. 63 There is a large and important area called the 'somesthetic', connected with the body senses generally, i.e., chiefly with the skin and muscle senses... Destruction of any part of this somesthetic area brings loss of the sensations from the corresponding part of the body. **1949** *Psychosomatic Med.* XI. 338/2 The thalamus probably participates in a crude awareness of somesthetic sensations. **1968** Passmore & Robson *Compan. Med. Stud.* I. xxiv. 51/1 The sensory or postcentral gyrus contains areas 1, 2 and 3 which are often considered together as the somaesthetic cortex, receiving sensations from the opposite side of the body. **1972** *Sci. Amer.* Apr. 82/3 The patient cannot name objects held in his left hand because the somesthetic sensations cannot reach the verbal centers in the left hemisphere. **1977** R. K. Davenport in D. M. Rumbaugh *Language Learning by Chimpanzee* iii. 75 In the brain of nonhuman primates as compared with the human brain, the auditory, visual, and somesthetic association areas are relatively independent.

Hence **somæs'thesis**, the somæsthetic senses.

**1928** *Funk's Stand. Dict.*, Somesthesis. **1950** *Ann. Rev. Psychol.* I. 71 (*heading*) Somesthesis and the chemical senses. **1968** [see kinæsthesis]. **1977** H. G. Burger in B. Bernardi *Concept & Dynamics of Culture* 423 It [*sc.* the angular gyrus] lies between the association cortices of three non-limbic sensation modalities: vision, audition, and internal sensibility (somesthesis).

**Somaj**, var. Samaj.

**somal** ('səʊməl), *a.* [f. Gr. σῶμα body, soma[2].]

**1.** Of or pertaining to the body.

**1900** *Proc. Zool. Soc. Lond.* 20 Feb. 134 The slight difference in size between the dermal and somal chiasters.

**2.** Of or pertaining to the soma of a neurone.

**1967** *Jrnl. Neurochem.* XIV. 329 Instead of a somal site of synthesis, an alternative possibility was considered; namely, a local axonal synthesis after entry from Schwann cells or a diffusion of precursor from the soma down into the axon. **1978** *Nature* 27 July 381/1 We compared the values of unit conductances activated by acetylcholine (ACh) applied to the somal membranes with values reported for other molluscan neurones.

**Somali** (səʊ'mɑːlɪ), *sb.* and *a.* Also **Somal, Somauli,** etc. [Native name.] **A.** *sb.* **a.** A Hamitic people, adherents of Islam, living in the Horn of Africa, esp. in the Somali Democratic Republic (Somalia); a member of this people. **b.** The language of this people which belongs to the Cushitic sub-family and existed until recently in spoken form only. **B.** *adj.* Of or pertaining to the Somalis or their country.

**1814** Somauli [see Swahili]. **1842** *Jrnl. R. Geogr. Soc.* XII. 241 There are also smaller kalifas that trade to Amin, Ugadin, and other parts of the Somauli country. **1850** *Trans. Bombay Geogr. Soc.* IX. 129 The country inhabited by the Somal is very extensive. *Ibid.* 130 Since the occupation of Aden by the English, the Somaulies have continued to cross over in considerable numbers. *Ibid.* 136 The article in Somauli is expressed by ka, ki or ga, gi. **1856** R. F. Burton *First Footsteps E. Africa* 89 In the latter sense it is the polite address to a Somali. *Ibid.* 644/2 Tale of a Somal chief. **1878** [see Galla]. **1888** F. L. James *Unknown Horn of Africa* 30 'Hubla' (Somal for 'virgin'). **1921** H. Rayne *Sun, Sand & Somals* 5 The Somali has deeply religious tendencies. **1930** C. G. Seligman *Races of Africa* v. 124 The early history of the Somali is obscure; that they are essentially Hamitic is certain. **1933** [see Cushite *a.* and *sb.*]. **1937** K. Blixen *Out of Africa* II. iv. 137 The immigrant Somalis.. are severe Mohammedans. *Ibid.* III. iii. 188 The circle of Somali women in my household. **1948** D. Diringer *Alphabet* II. iv. 300 This script, called.. 'the Osmanya script'.. has been created recently for the Somali language by 'Isman Yusuf. **1978** *Encounter* Feb. 52/2 It may be that Cubans using Russian weapons saved Ethiopia from defeat by the Somalis in November 1977. **1978** *Language* LIV. 453 The status of Somali (no official orthography; 184, 201) has changed drastically (Romanization adopted).

Hence **So'malian** *a.* = Somali *a.*

**1948** D. Diringer *Alphabet* II. iv. 300 The origin of the Somalian alphabet. **1976** *Guardian* 23 Aug. 7/1 Her father was Christian and disapproved of the general Somalian habit of infibulation. **1981** *Sci. Amer.* Mar. 29/3 The other [skull] found more recently in a fertilizer factory near Mogadishu, where fishermen who had picked it up on a Somalian beach had sent it.

**Soman** ('səʊmən). Also **soman.** [Ger., of unknown origin.] The name of an odourless organophosphorus nerve gas.

**1951** *Acta Physiol. Scandinavica* Suppl. No. 90. 106 (*table*) Pinacoloxy-methyl-phosphoryl-fluoride (soman). **1953** *Proc. R. Soc. Med.* XLVI. 801 We found.. that 3,4 dihydroxyphenylalanine.. and other *o*-dihydroxybenzene derivatives were able to protect both true and pseudo ChE's [*sc.* cholinesterases] against, not only Sarin, but also against Tabun and Soman. **1968** [see Sarin]. **1969** B. Ford *German Secret Weapons* (1970) 109 Soman has the most terrible effects on soldiers: within seconds they would have been reduced to a state of convulsive collapse and death would be relatively certain. **1980** *Sci. Amer.* Apr. 35/3 Soman, first prepared in Germany in 1944, is believed by Western officials to be the standard Russian nerve gas. **1982** *Guardian* 8 Mar. 12/3 The use of Soman and Tabun gases by the Soviet-directed Ethiopians.

†**so'mandric**, *a. Obs.*[−1] [f. Gr. σῶμα body + ἀνδρ-, ἀνήρ man.] Relating to the human body.

**1716** M. Davies *Athen. Brit.* III. *Diss. Physick* 21 The Cause, why Providence.. also has absconded the great Psyc[h]andrick as well as Somandrick Secret of the Chymical Grand Elixir.

**somar**, var. sommer *adv.*

**Somaschan, Somascan** (səʊ'mæskən), *sb.* and *a.* Also **Somaschian.** [f. It. *Somaschi*, pl. of *Somasco* (cf. next), f. *Somasca*, a place lying north-west from Bergamo in Italy.]

**a.** *sb.* A member of a religious order, chiefly engaged in charitable instruction, founded at Somasca by Gerolamo Emiliani about 1530. **b.** *adj.* Of or pertaining to this order.

**1882–3** Schaff *Encycl. Rel. Knowl.* III. 2214 The order of the Somaschians.. in the Roman-Catholic Church. **1882** T. A. Pope tr. *Capecelatro's Life of St. Philip Neri* II. III. x. 153 He.. co-operated in the erecting of a house of Somaschans for orphan boys. **1936** L. Christiani in E. Eyre *European Civilization* IV. II. i. 162 The immense achievements of Capuchins,.. Somascans, and Barnabites. **1940** E. Graf tr. *Pastor's Hist. of Popes* XXX. iv. 177 In 1647 Innocent dissolved the union between the Doctrinarians and the Somaschans.

So **So'maschi** *sb. pl.*

**1883** *Encycl. Brit.* XVI. 716/2 Clerks regular of St Majolus of Pavia, or 'Somaschi'. **1978** D. H. Farmer *Oxford Dict. Saints* 211/1 [St. Jerome Emiliani] founded orphanages, hospitals, and houses for repentant prostitutes. To look after them he also founded a small congregation of clerks regular, called the Somaschi after their place of origin.

†**Somasque.** *Obs.* Also 7 **Somask.** [a. F. *Somasque*, ad. It. *Somasco*, f. *Somasca* (see prec.).] = Somaschan *sb.*

**1686** tr. *Bouhours' St. Ignatius* v. 284 He had made the same Answer some Years before, in reference to the Somasques, and the Theatines. **1693** tr. *Emiliane's Monast. Orders* xviii. 188 The Fathers of the Christian Doctrin.. petition'd to be united to the Somasks. **1706** tr. *Dupin's Eccl. Hist.* II. IV. xi. 450 Jerome Emiliani, a noble Venetian, in the year 1530 founded some Regular Clerks, called Somasques, from the name of the place where they lived.

**somasteroid** (səʊ'mæstərɔɪd), *a.* and *sb. Zool.* Also **Somasteroid.** [ad. mod.L. *Somasteroidea* (W. K. Spencer 1951, in *Phil. Trans. R. Soc.* B. CCXXXV. 87), f. Gr. σῶμα body + mod.L. *Asteroidea*, name of a subclass or class of echinoderms, f. Gr. ἀστεροειδής (see asteroid *a.* and *sb.*) + L. *-ea*, neut. pl. of *-eus* -eous.]

**A.** *adj.* Belonging or pertaining to the subclass or class Somasteroidea, which belongs in the subphylum Asteroidea of star-shaped echinoderms and comprises extinct forms having broad, petal-like arms with a pinnate structure. **B.** *sb.* A somasteroid echinoderm.

**1955** L. H. Hyman *Invertebrates* IV. xv. 700 The arrangement recently adopted by palaeontologists.., according to which asteroids and ophiuroids derive from a common somasteroid.. ancestor.., must be somehow wrong. **1962** D. Nichols *Echinoderms* iii. 40 The fossilized remains of these ossicles have even been found in the earliest asteroids, the Somasteroids. **1963** *Phil. Trans. R. Soc.* B. CCXLVI. 383 The Asterozoa, or star-shaped echinoderms, may be regarded as a natural taxon, comprising the somasteroids, asteroids and ophiuroids. **1964** [see phanerozone *a.* (*sb.*)]. **1979** W. D. Russell-Hunter *Life of Invertebrates* xxxiv. 607 The smallest class, Somasteroidea, which arose in the Ordovician, was never an extensively diversified group, being relegated by many neontologists to the status of a subclass of the Asteroidea. (The living genus, *Platasterias*, is no longer regarded as a somasteroid.)

**Somastic** (sə'mæstɪk). Also **somastic.** [Prob. f. initials of *S*tandard *O*il (see quot. 1930) + mastic *sb.*] A proprietary term in the U.S. for asphalt-based materials used in coating oil pipelines.

**1930** *Official Gaz.* (U.S. Patent Office) 8 July 365/1 Standard Oil Company of California... *Somastic.* For asphalt, asphalt mastic, and pipe coatings. Claims use since May 8, 1930. **1974** *Petroleum Rev.* XXVIII. 634/1 A 40-ft long pipe.. emerges from a somastic coating machine at Bredero Price's mill in Leith. **1976** *Offshore Platforms & Pipelining* 131/1 Field joints in the overbend are coated with flexible somastic.

**somatal** ('səʊmətəl), *a. Zool.* [f. Gr. σῶμα, σώματ- body.] Of or pertaining to the body.

**1875** Blake *Zool.* 243 The animal is chiefly divided into a somatal and a pallial portion.

**soma'talgia.** *rare.* [f. as prec. + Gr. -αλγία, f. ἄλγος pain.] Bodily pain or suffering.

**1607** Walkington *Opt. Glass* Bj, *Somatalgia* and *Psychalgia*, the one the dyscrasie of the body, the other the malady and distemperature of the soule. **1908** G. S. Hall *Adolescence* I. 480 The readiness with which psychalgia passes to somatalgia.

‖**somaten** (soma'ten, səʊ'mɑːtɛn). Pl. **somatenes.** [a. Catalan (and Sp.) *somatén* an alarm bell; an armed body of citizens.] In Catalonia, a body of civilians armed for the protection of a town or district; a member of this body. Hence **so'matenist** [Catalan *somatenista*], a member of a somaten.

**1845** R. Ford *Hand-bk. Spain* I. 493/1 Thus time was given for the *somaten*, or tocsin, to be rung, and the armed peasantry collected... The Catalan *guerrilleros* were called *Somatenes*, from this bell. **1905** R. Thirlmere *Lett. from Catalonia* I. v. 60 In Olot and other Catalan towns they have what they call *El Somaten*, an armed, local, volunteer force —which closes all the highways at the sound of an alarm bell. **1911** *Encycl. Brit.* XVIII. 566/2 *Miquelets*.. were irregular local troops in Catalonia... They were maintained by the several parishes.. and as they had to turn out for duty on sound of the village alarm-bell (*somaten*) they are frequently called *somatenes*. **1928** *Daily Tel.* 29 May 9/5 A member of the 'Somaten' (Militia) to-day succeeded in finding the young man who ran amok with a rifle last Monday... As he refused to surrender the 'Somatenist' fired and killed him. **1929** A. F. G. Bell in E. A. Peers *Spain* 275 A more efficient city-police, together with the Somatenes and the Civil Guard, maintained order throughout Spain.

**somatic** (səʊ'mætɪk), *a.* and *sb.* [ad. Gr. σωματικός, f. σῶμα, σώματ- body. So F. *somatique.*]

**A.** *adj.* **1.** Of or pertaining to the (or a) body; bodily, corporeal, physical.

**1775** Ash, *Somatic*, corporeal, belonging to a body. **1816** Bentham *Chrestomathia* Wks. 1843 VIII. 187 Somatic, or Somatological fictitious entities. **1859** *Sat. Rev.* 10 Dec. 709/1 Those in which somatic and psychical co-efficients are manifestly intermingled. **1884** Blackmore *Tommy Upmore* I. iii. 23 Variant motions and emotions, both somatic and psychical.

**b.** *Anat.* and *Phys.* of parts of the body.

**1859** Huxley *Oceanic Hydrozoa* 26 The diverticulum of the somatic cavity becomes pyriform. **1861** J. R. Greene *Man. Anim. Kingd., Cœlent.* 6 The nutritive, or somatic, fluid occupying the general cavity of the body. **1881** *Jrnl. Microsc. Sci.* Jan. 73 The two layers of the mesoblast, somatic and splanchnic. **1899** *Allbutt's Syst. Med.* VI. 371 The termination of the somatic nerves derived from the segment of the cord.

**c.** *spec.* Pertaining to the soma in contrast to the germ.

**1888** *Nature* 14 June 156/2 In the Metazoa, the germ-cells, instead of remaining single, give rise to the vast number of somatic cells which compose the adult structure. **1896** MRS. ROMANES *Life & Lett. Romanes* 35 It is demonstrated that the somatic tissues of the scion have exercised an effect on the germinal elements of the stock.

**2.** Affecting the body.

**1835–6** J. A. SYMONDS in *Todd's Cycl. Anat.* I. 791 *note*, The writer is indebted to.. Dr. Prichard for the suggestion of *somatic* [instead of *systemic*],.. but he has not had the courage to introduce it into the text. **1839–47** CARPENTER *Ibid.* III. 757/2 Molecular death is not always an immediate consequence of somatic death. **1899** *Allbutt's Syst. Med.* VIII. 425 Hypnotism could do nothing in somatic affections.

**B.** *sb. pl.* Somatology.

**1816** BENTHAM *Chrestomathia* Wks. 1843 VIII. 87 This branch of Art and Science is entitled to the appellation of Coenoscopic Anthropurgics, or Somatics. **1861** *Sat. Rev.* 15 June 621 The Germans retort by accusing their adversaries .. of 'mechanical, soulless somatics (*somatik*)'.

So **so'matical** *a.*, 'corporeal, bodily, substantial' (Bailey, 1727); **so'matically** *adv.*

**1847** tr. *Feuchtersleben's Med. Psychol.* 219 Somatically they [i.e. certain excitements] act at the expense of the brain. **1902** *Pop. Sci. Monthly* Mar. 421 But while the Seri Indians are so well developed somatically,.. they have been no less notorious.. for unparalleled laziness.

**so'matico-**, combining form of Gr. σωματικός SOMATIC *a.*, in ***somatico-hedonistics*** (see quot.).

**1816** BENTHAM *Chrestomathia* Wks. 1843 VIII. 90 Under the name of Somatico-Hedonistics might be collected and comprehended those branches of art and science which, as above, have for their objects those modifications of pleasure, which have the body for their seat.

**'somatism.** *rare.* [f. as next + -ISM.] Materialism.

? *c* **1720** ? DE FOE *Apparition* D.'s Wks. 1841 XIX. 267 To the prevailing of Somatism and the Hobbëan principle in these times. **1955** *Mind* LXIV. 495 Reism as such is not yet somatism, but somatism finds its place in the framework of reism as a particular case. Every soul is a body—this is the thesis of somatism.

**somatist** (ˈsəʊmətɪst). [f. Gr. σῶμα, σώματ- body, SOMA[2] + -IST.]

†**1.** A materialist. *Obs.*

**1676** GLANVILL *Ess. Philos. & Relig.* IV. 33 The name and notion of such Somatists, as are for meer Matter and Motion, and exclude immaterial Beings. **1694** BURTHOGGE *Reason* 201 What will.. [a] meer Somatist say to the Corps-Candles, or Dead Mens Lights, in Wales?

**2.** *attrib.* Pertaining to, connected with, the soma.

**1908** *Outlook* 5 Sept. 298/1 The issue between the somatist or 'mnemic' theory, as presented by Mr. Darwin and the doctrines of Weismannism.

**somatization** (səʊmətaɪˈzeɪʃən). [f. Gr. σῶμα, σώματ- body, SOMA[2] + -IZATION.] The occurrence of bodily symptoms in consequence of or as an expression of mental disorder. Hence **'somatizing** *a.*, pertaining to or exhibiting such symptoms.

**1925** J. S. VAN TESLAAR tr. *Stekel's Peculiarities of Behav.* II. 341 *Somatization*, conversion of emotional states into physical symptoms. **1943** E. & C. PAUL tr. *Stekel's Interpretation of Dreams* I. iii. 25 Cases where the disorder —through somatization—secures bodily expression. **1954** GRINKER & ROBBINS *Psychosomatic Case Bk.* v. 74 In the narrower sense of the word, psychosomatic disturbances are differentiated from those neuroses in which somatization occurs through innervation of the voluntary nervous system. **1966** *McGraw-Hill Encycl. Sci. & Technol.* XII. 501/1 What characterizes the psychosomatic reaction in contrast to the other somatizing patterns is that there is an involvement of specific organs under the control of the autonomic nervous system. **1970** *Psychol. Rep.* XXVII. 756 One aspect of the stress and somatic reaction problem that has not received attention is the relationship between physiological reactions under laboratory-stress conditions and the tendency for individuals to develop somatic complaints under life stresses, as indicated by a personality characteristic of 'somatization'. **1978** *African Jrnl. Med.* VII. 209/2 Somatisation of psychological disorder.. is common in the Nigerian population. **1980** I. G. & B. R. SARASON *Abnormal Psychol.* (ed. 3) viii. 202/1 The complaints of somatizing patients often lead to unnecessary surgery.

**somato-** (ˈsəʊmətəʊ), *a.* Gr. σωματο-, combining form of σῶμα, σώματ- body (see SOMA[2]), used in a number of scientific terms, as **'somatocœl** *Zool.* [a. G. *somatocœl* (K. Heider 1912, in *Verhandl. d. deutsch. zool. Ges.* XXII. 241), f. Gr. κοιλία cavity of the body], each of a pair of cavities in an echinoderm embryo that develop into the main body cavity of the adult; hence **somato'cœlic** *a.*; **'somatocyst**, a sac forming the proximal end of the hydrosoma in oceanic hydrozoa; **somatoge'netic** *a.*, **soma'togenic** *a.* (see quots.); †**soma'tognosy**, somatology; **somato'metric, -'metrical** *adjs.*, of or pertaining to the measurement of the body; hence **soma'to'metrically** *adv.*; **'somatoplasm**, soma-plasm; **'somatopleure** (see quot. 1874); **somato'pleuric** *a.*, of or belonging to the somatopleure; **somato'psychic** *a. Psychol.* [ad. G. *somatopsychisch* (C. Wernicke 1892, in *Path. des Nervensystems* (1893) 166], (*a*) of or pertaining to awareness of one's own body (? *obs.*); (*b*) arising from or pertaining to the effects of bodily illness on the mind; **somato-'sensory** *a. Physiol.* = SOMÆSTHETIC *a.*; **soma'totomy**, anatomy.

Many similar compounds occur in special works or are recorded in dictionaries, as ***somatoblast, -chrome, -derm, -graphy, -phyte, -phytic***, etc.

**1955** L. H. HYMAN *Invertebrates* IV. xv. 692 The inner walls of the *somatocoels meet above and below the intestine to form the primary mesentery. **1962** D. NICHOLS *Echinoderms* x. 120 Almost as soon as the primary coelomic sacs have been formed, they bud off posteriorly another pair of sacs, the somatocoels, later to form the main coelom of the adult body. **1976** *Nature* 20 May 228/1 All this suggests that the new coelomocytes in the general body cavity can have come only from the *somatocoelic epithelium. **1859** HUXLEY *Oceanic Hydrozoa* 31 The *somatocyst is narrow and subcylindrical. **1870** H. A. NICHOLSON *Man. Zool.* 79 The proximal end of the hydrosoma is modified into a peculiar cavity called the somato-cyst. **1905** G. A. REID *Princip. Heredity* i. 6 Acquired characters take origin (as a rule) in the cell-descendants of the germ-cell; that is, they are *somatogenetic in origin. **1889** in *Rep. Brit. Assoc.* 767 He [Weismann] uses the term **somatogenic* to express those characters which first appear in the body itself. **1811–31** BENTHAM *Logic* App. Wks. 1843 VIII. 284 Somatology, *somatognosy, or somatics. **1939** *Ibid.* 11 Nov. 807/1 By what *somatometric method, which is both reliable and convenient of application, is it possible to assess nutritional status? **1951** *Proc. Sect. Sci. Koninkl. Akad Wetensch. Amsterdam* C. LIV. 480 (*heading*) The quantitative expression of resemblance in the somatometric study of relationship. *Ibid.*, *Somatometrical data of different age-groups are not directly comparable. *Ibid.*, Training and interest will mostly induce the anthropologist to restrict himself to the study of properties than can be demonstrated *somatometrically. **1889** tr. *Weismann's Ess. Heredity*, etc. 104 If the germ-plasm and the substance of the body, the *somatoplasm, have always occupied different spheres. **1890** WEISMANN in *Nature* 6 Feb. 320/2 My germ-plasm or idioplasm of the first ontogenetic grade is not modified into the somatoplasm of Prof. Vines. **1874** FOSTER & BALFOUR *Elem. Embryol.* 38 The upper (or outer) leaf of the blastoderm, from its giving rise to the body-walls, is called the *somatopleure. **1888** *Q. Jrnl. Microscopic Sci.* XXVIII. 111 The lower end lies outside the angle.., between the somatopleure and splanchnopleure. **1874** FOSTER & BALFOUR *Elem. Embryol.* 39 The *somato-pleuric investment of the yolk sac. **1900** *Nature* 12 Apr. 560/2 Prior to the formation of the somatopleuric system represented by the cardinal veins, &c. **1902** *Buck's Handbk. Med. Sci.* (rev. ed.) V. 27/1 Consciousness is a function of the associative mechanism and may be considered in its threefold relationship to the outer world, the body and self—allopsychic, *somatopsychic, and autopsychic. **1927** HENDERSON & GILLESPIE *Text-bk. Psychiatry* II. 13 His division of concepts into those of the outside world, of the personality, and of the body—'allopsychic', 'autopsychic', and 'somatopsychic'. **1955** *A.M.A. Arch. Neurol. & Psychiatry* LXXIII. 403/2 With the increasing severity in the lesion and the growing disability of the patient, much may be learned about the somatopsychic problem, i.e., about the manner in which the increasingly morbid process affects the state of mind of the patient and his relation to himself and his environment. **1961** *Guardian* 17 May 8/5 We should not allow a preoccupation with psychosomatic illness.. to blind us to the advances.. in the treatment of somato-psychic disorders. **1978** F. MANN *Acupuncture* (ed. 3) x. 160 Modern medicine might use the word 'psychosomatic' to describe the diseases considered in this section, as they are physical results of uncontrolled emotion; those in the previous section might be given the label 'somatopsychic', being mental diseases resulting from outer or physical causes. **1952** *Federation Proc.* XI. 5/2 Responses from stimulation of arm and leg subdivisions of *somatosensory area I were similar in location but differed in shape. **1975** *Nature* 30 Oct. 738/1 Axons carrying visual, auditory and somatosensory information converge on the tectum and interlace with tectal neurones. **1978** *Sci. Amer.* Sept. 82/2 In the somatosensory area of the cortex the cells in a column respond to the same type of stimulus (pressure, touch, heat, cold) at the same point on the body surface. **1851** DUNGLISON *Dict. Med. Sci.* 797/1 *Somatotomy.

**somatogamy** (səʊməˈtɒgəmɪ). *Biol.* [ad. G. *somatogamie* (O. Renner 1916, in *Biol. Centralbl.* XXXVI. 349): see SOMATO- and -GAMY.] = PSEUDOGAMY b. So **soma'togamous** *a.*

**1949** I. F. & W. D. HENDERSON *Dict. Sci. Terms* (ed. 4) 403/2 *Somatogamy*, pseudogamy; pseudomixis. **1950** W. B. BRIERLEY tr. *Gäumann's Princ. Plant Infection* iii. 20 The nuclear association, initiated by somatogamous fusion, constitutes.. the pre-condition for transition from the saprophytic to the parasitic mode of life. **1962** G. DALLDORF *Fungi & Fungous Diseases* x. 136 In fungi that undergo somatogamy, such as yeasts.

**somatological** (ˌsəʊmətəʊˈlɒdʒɪkəl), *a.* [f. SOMATO- + -LOGICAL. Cf. F. *somatologique*.] Of or pertaining to somatology.

**1816** BENTHAM *Chrestomathia* Wks. 1843 VIII. 149 Linnæus, the father, as he may be termed, of Somatological tactics. **1820** L. HUNT *Indicator* No. 54 (1822) II. 15 *Kubla Khan*.. he calls 'a psychological curiosity'. It is so; but it is also and still more a somatological or bodily one. **1898** HADDON *Study of Man* 438 Instructions for making certain somatological observations.

Hence ˌ**somato'logically** *adv.*

**1888** *Science* 9 Nov. 227/2 Equal to denying that the Basques and the Fins belong somatologically to the white race. *Ibid.* 228/1.

**soma'tologist.** [See next and -LOGIST.] One who studies, or is skilled in, somatology.

**1893** D. G. BRINTON in *Smithsonian Rep.* 594 The constant blending of extreme physical types which the somatologist discovers in the remains from the oldest cemeteries around that great interior sea.

**somatology** (səʊməˈtɒlədʒɪ). [f. SOMATO- + -LOGY, or ad. mod.L. *somatologia* (O. Casmann, 1596). Cf. F. *somatologie* (1762).]

**1.** A treatise or science dealing with the properties of bodies.

**1736** BAILEY (fol.) Pref., *Somatology*,.. a Discourse of Matter or Substance in the General, the Natures and inseparable Properties of Bodies. **1813–21** BENTHAM *Ontology* Wks. 1843 VIII. 195/1 Somatology, the only branch of physics that comes under the cognisance of sense.

**2.** A treatise or science dealing with the human body in some respect.

**1851** DUNGLISON *Dict. Med. Sci.*, *Somatology*, a treatise on the human body. Anatomy. **1868** PORTER *Human Intellect* (1870) §3. 7 Somatology signifies the science of the body only, and is subdivided into anatomy and physiology. **1898** D. G. BRINTON in Haddon *Study of Man* 491 Somatology.—Physical and Experimental Anthropology.

**somatome** (ˈsəʊmətəʊm). [f. SOMA(TO)- + -TOME.] A section or segment of the body.

**1856** GOODSIR in *Edinb. New Philos. Jrnl.* V. 121 To the constituent segment, with its diverging appendages, I apply the term Somatome... The constituent somatomes are invariably arranged in groups.

Hence **soma'tomic** *a.*

**1882** *Trans. Linn. Soc.* II. III. 166 Only where the notochord lingers can any trace of somatomic division be seen.

**somatomedin** (ˌsəʊmətəʊˈmiːdɪn). *Physiol.* [See quot. 1972.] Any of several peptides present in serum which are thought to act as intermediates in the stimulation of growth by growth hormone.

Quots. 1971, 1972 have no author in common.

**1971** J. M. TANNER et al. in *Arch. Dis. Childhood* XLVI. 761/2 A few patients with short stature have the ability to secrete immunoreactive GH..; but their GH fails to stimulate the production of somatomedin, a substance found in the blood, and previously named 'sulphation factor'. **1972** W. H. DAUGHADAY et al. in *Nature* 14 Jan. 107/2 After consideration of many alternatives to the operational terms 'sulphation factor' or 'thymidine factor', we propose the more general term, 'somatomedin'; the prefix, 'somato', connotes both a hormonal relationship to somatotropin and, also, to the soma which is the target tissue of this agent. 'Medin' is included in the name to indicate that it is an intermediary in somatotropin action. **1978** VAN WYK & UNDERWOOD in G. Litwack *Biochem. Actions Hormones* V. iii. 102 It is.. generally agreed that to belong in the somatomedin group of peptides, a substance must fulfil three criteria: its concentration in serum must be growth-hormone dependent, it must possess insulin-like actions in skeletal tissues, and it must promote the incorporation of sulfate into proteoglycans of cartilage. **1978** F. L. STRAND *Physiology* xix. 360/1 Growth hormone, the somatomedins, insulin, and thyroxine have important anabolic effects that promote wound healing.

**somatostatin** (ˌsəʊmətəʊˈstætɪn). *Physiol.* [See quot. 1973.] A peptide secreted in the hypothalamus and elsewhere whose actions include the inhibition of the release of various hormones, esp. from the anterior pituitary.

**1973** P. BRAZEAU et al. in *Science* 5 Jan. 79/3 We propose to name the peptide described here *somatostatin*, from somato(tropin), a pituitary factor affecting statural growth, and stat(in), from the Latin 'to halt, to arrest'. **1976** *Nature* 10 June 511/2 Somatostatin inhibits the release of growth hormone, thyrotropin and prolactin from the pituitary, of glucagon and insulin from the pancreas, and also of gastrin. **1977** *Lancet* 23 July 166/2 Somatostatin, a tetradecapeptide first isolated from the hypothalamus.., has been demonstrated in large quantities in the gastrointestinal tract and pancreas.

Hence ˌ**somatostati'noma** *Path.*, a tumour secreting excessive quantities of somatostatin.

**1977** *Lancet* 26 Mar. 668/1 Measurements of insulin and glucagon responses during a glucose-tolerance test in somatostatinoma patients may help to explain this apparent association. **1978** *Jrnl. R. Soc. Med.* LXXI. 173 This somatostatinoma gave rise to the clinical abnormalities of hypochlorhydria, steatorrhoea, and a diabetic glucose tolerance curve.

**somatotonic** (səʊmətəˈtɒnɪk), *a.* and *sb.* [f. SOMATO- + TONIC *a.*] **A.** *adj.* Designating or characteristic of a type of personality which is extroverted and aggressive, classified by Sheldon as being associated with a mesomorphic physique. **B.** *sb.* One having this type of personality. So **somatotonia** (-ˈtəʊnɪə), somatotonic personality or characteristics.

**1937** [see CEREBROTONIC *a.* and *sb.*]. **1938** H. G. WELLS *Apropos of Dolores* iv. 214 The classification of main human types and temperaments from Hippocrates' down to the cerebrotonics, somatotonics and viscerotonics of today. **1940** W. H. SHELDON *Varieties Human Physique* i. 8 Somatotonia is the motivational pattern dominated by the will to exertion, exercise and vigorous self-expression. It is the drive toward dominance of the functions of the soma. **1950** A. HUXLEY *Let.* 16 Mar. (1969) 621 We are fortunate to-day in possessing, at long last, a genuinely scientific method for describing physique, temperament and their interrelations..—viscerotonia, somatotonia and cerebrotonia for temperament. **1950** —— *Themes & Variations* 28 The viscerotonic and somatotonic extraverts who are at home in the world. **1969** V. DE SOLA PINTO *City that Shone* iii. 68, I suppose that in modern psychological jargon, as a child in those distant Edwardian days, I could be described as an introvert and cerebrotonic living in a world of extroverts, somatotonics and viscerotonics.

**somatotopic** (ˌsəʊmətəʊˈtɒpɪk), *a. Neurol.* [f. SOMATO- + Gr. *τοπικ-ός* in respect to place (see TOPIC *a.* and *sb.*).] Characterized by or being a relationship between the locations of neurones in the central nervous system and in the tissues they serve. Also **somatoˈtopical** *a.*, in the same sense.

**1945** *Federation Proc.* IV. 31/1 Liminal faradic excitation of the cerebellar cortex reveals somatotopic localization in the anterior lobe and lobulus simplex of decerebrate animals. **1958** A. BRODAL *Neurol. Anat.* iii. 42 Here again is an example of a somatotopical arrangement of a fibre system. **1965** *Jrnl. Anat.* XCIX. 761 (*heading*) Correlation between nuclear morphology and somatotopic organization in the ventro-basal complex of the raccoon's thalamus. **1969** TRUEX & CARPENTER *Human Neuroanat.* (ed. 6) xvii. 423/1 In the cat there is evidence that corticopontine fibers arising from the sensorimotor cortex project in a somatotopical manner onto two longitudinally oriented cell columns within the pontine nuclei. **1976** *Nature* 20 May 190/3 Physiologists have revealed a strict somatotopic map of the skin in the spinal cord.

Hence ˌ**somatoˈtopically** *adv.*, in a manner which preserves such a relationship; ˈ**somatotopy** (*rare*), somatotopic relationship.

**1948** A. BRODAL *Neurol. Anat.* vi. 161 They have mapped out the areas giving response when different parts of the skin are stimulated, and established a pattern which mainly corresponds to that gained from study of human cases. The body is represented somatotopically, with a certain overlapping between adjacent dermatomes. **1961** *Lancet* 2 Sept. 546/2 Discriminative sensation travels by the lemniscal pathway and is relayed somatotopically via the thalamus to the cortex. **1976** *Progress in Sci. Culture* (E. Majorana Centre) Spring 48 The analysis of the properties, of these two inputs, in terms of somatotopy, frequency of discharge, sensory modality, timing and interaction between them suggests that integration of the information channelled through the two inputs on the same Purkyně cell is a basic mechanism of cerebellar operation.

**somatotroph** (ˈsəʊmətəʊtrəʊf). *Physiol.* [Back-formation from next.] A cell of the anterior pituitary which synthesizes somatotrophin (growth hormone).

**1968** *Annales de Biologie Animale, Biochimie, Biophysique* VIII. 22 (*heading*) Cytological characteristics of gonadotroph, thyrotroph, corticotroph, somatotroph cells and of prolactin cells in the anterior lobe of the cattle pituitary. **1978** *Jrnl. R. Soc. Med.* LXXI. 434 There are several sera under study where the antibodies react neither with lactotrophs or somatotrophs.

**somatotrophic** (ˌsəʊmətəʊˈtrəʊfɪk), **-tropic** (ˈtrəʊpɪk, -ˈtrɒpɪk), *a. Physiol.* [f. SOMATO- + -TROPHIC, -TROPIC.] Pertaining to or having the property of stimulating body growth; *spec.* applied to the hormone somatotrophin.

**1938** H. L. WIEMAN *Gen. Zool.* (ed. 3) x. 206 The somatotropic hormone is necessary for the normal growth and development of the body. **1952** *Amer. Jrnl. Physiol.* CLXXI. 381 Some of the most striking effects of..cortisone ..are directly opposed to the actions of the 'growth hormone' or somatotrophic hormone (STH). **1960** *Biol. Abstr.* XXXV. 1154/2 The somatotropic activity of the plasma was evaluated. **1977** *Lancet* 23 July 198/1, HG.H. secretion from another somatotrophic adenoma..was inhibited..by bromocriptine.

Hence **somatoˈtrophin**, **-ˈtropin**, a hormone secreted by the anterior pituitary which promotes the release of somatomedin; growth hormone.

**1947** H. SELYE *Textbk. Endocrinol.* iii. 217/2 Denaturation of somatotrophin by treatment with urea does not influence its growth-promoting potency. **1952** *Endocrinol.* LI. 300 Growth hormone (somatotropin) can produce a growth-promoting and diabetogenic response in the developing chick embryo. **1965** LEE & KNOWLES *Animal Hormones* ii. 21 The growth hormone, also referred to as somatotrophin (STH), not only controls the rate of growth, but also the metabolism necessary for this growth. **1973** *Sci. Amer.* Sept. 41/3 (*caption*) Somatotrophin, acting with other hormones, regulates the normal growth of children. **1974** D. & M. WEBSTER *Compar. Vertebr. Morphol.* xiii. 307 The growth hormone, somatotropin, produced by acidophilic cells, is a branched protein with about 200 amino acids.

**somatotype** (ˈsəʊmətəʊtaɪp), *sb.* [f. SOMATO- + TYPE *sb.*[1]] The physique of an individual as expressed numerically in terms of the extent to which it exhibits the characteristics of each of three extremes (the endomorph, mesomorph, and ectomorph).

**1940** W. H. SHELDON *Varieties Human Physique* i. 7 The patterning of the morphological components, as expressed by the three numerals, is called the somatotype of the individual. After examining..4,000 physiques we were able to describe..76 different somatotypes. **1944** A. HUXLEY *Let.* 19 July (1969) 508 From these a good draughtsman could turn out true representations of the various somatotypes. **1971** *Nature* 12 Mar. 113/2 An analysis of the somatotype data showed that there was a tendency for the twelve individuals to fall into two groups: a mesomorphic group (seven cases—wide heavy—typical somatotype 4,5,2) and an ectomorphic group (five cases—tall thin—typical somatotype 3,2,6). **1978** G. A. SHEEHAN *Running & Being* ii. 28, I dug into his [*sc.* Sheldon's] *Atlas of Men* and there I was. Somatotype 235... The number 235 is somatotype shorthand for little or no fat (2); a moderate amount of muscle (3); and a predominance of skin, hair, nervous tissue and thin bones (5). (The limts being one to seven).

**somatotype** (ˈsəʊmətəʊtaɪp), *v.* [f. prec.] *trans.* To assign to a somatotype.

**1940** W. H. SHELDON *Varieties Human Physique* vii. 220, 400 northern Negroes whom we have photographed and somatotyped. **1951** AUDEN *Nones* (1952) 47 Lovers of big numbers go horribly mad, Would have..all of us Well purged, somatotyped, baptised, taught baseball. **1954** W. H. SHELDON *Atlas of Men* 16/2 By the time I had somatotyped the 12,000 men who made up this total series the foundations were well laid.

So ˈ**somatotyping** *vbl. sb.*, the assignation of somatotypes.

**1940** W. H. SHELDON *Varieties Human Physique* i. 8 The criteria and the procedure for somatotyping..provide a practicable, objective method for segregating and classifying the varieties of human physique. **1959** A. HUXLEY *Let.* 15 Oct. (1969) 880 Have you found in your hospital work that somatotyping along Sheldonian lines has helped? **1978** *Nature* 12 Jan. 193/1 Sheldon is the man who invented somatotyping—a classification of variations in human body structure, to which he related variations in temperament, in physical and mental illness, and in patterns of growth and aging.

**sombre** (ˈsɒmbə(r)), *a.* and *sb.* [a. F. *sombre*, of uncertain origin: cf. Sp. and Pg. *sombrio*, f. *sombra* shade. See also SOMBROUS *a.*]

**A.** *adj.* **1.** Of inanimate natural objects and their attributes: Characterized by the presence of gloom or shadow; depressingly dark, dusky, or obscure.

**1760** H. WALPOLE *Lett.* (1845) IV. 85 Painted ceilings, inlaid floors, and unpainted wainscots make every room sombre. **1777** W. DALRYMPLE *Trav. Sp. & Port.* cxxxii, This city..had a sombre and poor appearance. **1792** A. YOUNG *Trav. France* 184 This coast..dark, gloomy, and silent;—a savage sombre air spread over the whole. **1816** SCOTT *Old Mort.* xliii, The first shoot..of the yet unbroken stream, and the deep and sombre abyss into which it was emptied. **1860** MAURY *Phys. Geog.* xv. §674 The sombre skies and changeable weather of our latitudes. **1882** MISS BRADDON *Mt. Royal* vi, The dining-room was sombre and substantial.

**2.** Of persons, their appearance, etc.: Gloomy, lowering, dark and sullen or dejected.

*a* **1767** GRAINGER *Ode Solitude* 52 Late in Hagley you were seen, With blood-shed eyes, and sombre mien. **1823** BYRON *Island* III. vi, Till lifting up again his sombre eye, It glanced on Torquil. **1865** BARING-GOULD *Werewolves* vi. 75 The man..was a sombre ill-looking fellow.

**b.** Of thoughts, feelings, etc.: Melancholy, dismal, darksome.

**1821** JOANNA BAILLIE *Met. Leg.*, *Ghost Fadon* xxii, All Remain'd in sombre mood. **1832** DOWNES *Lett. Contin. Countr.* I. 390 The entire shore is lined with dilapidated edifices, which would, under other circumstances, have awakened sombre reflections. **1877** MRS. OLIPHANT *Makers Florence* xii. (1877) 297 No doubt it cast a gleam of sombre hope upon his confinement.

**3.** Conveying gloomy ideas or suggestions.

**1768** STERNE *Sent. Journ.*, *Hotel at Paris*, Beshrew the sombre pencil! said I vauntingly. *a* **1854** H. REED *Lect. Eng. Lit.* x. (1878) 334 Sombre as the poem at first appears, it works its way on to happy hopes. **1874** L. STEPHEN *Hours Libr.* (1892) II. ii. 56 Such sketches are a pleasant relief to his more sombre portraiture.

**4.** Of colours or colouring: Of a dark shade or tinge; dark, dull.

**1805** WILKES *Mem.* II. 175 The olive-tree..is a sombre brown, when one expects a green. **1835** J. DUNCAN *Beetles* (Nat. Lib.) 186 Those [insects] that derive their nourishment from decomposed vegetables are usually of a sombre hue. **1866** ROGERS *Agric. & Prices* I. xxii. 577 Ecclesiastics and persons of gravity affected sombre colours.

**b.** Of things in respect of colour. (Cf. 1.)

**1829** GRIFFITH tr. *Cuvier* VIII. 315 Sombre Plover, *Charadrius Fuscus.* **1839** G. BIRD *Nat. Philos.* 333 The chloride of silver..becomes of a deep slate colour in the violet, and in the sombre space beyond it. **1851** BRIMLEY *Ess.* 158 He had originally a fine sombre complexion. **1872** YEATS *Techn. Hist. Comm.* 152 A sombre garb was worn by the nuns, and coarse cowls by the friars.

**5.** *Comb.*, as ***sombre-clad***, ***-coloured***, ***-minded***, ***sombre-looking*** adjs.

**1850** LYNCH *Theoph. Trinal* v. 85 Dissatisfied, querulous, sombre-minded persons. **1872** JENKINSON *Guide English Lakes* (1879) 337 A wild and sombre-looking mass of rocks and precipices. **1889** S. J. HICKSON *Naturalist in N. Celebes* 214 The pious and sombre-clad Christian natives. **1899** MACKAIL *W. Morris* II. 191 The vast sombre-coloured crowd.

**B.** *sb.* Sombre character; sombreness. *rare.*

**1795** H. M. WILLIAMS *Lett. France* I. 164 Fonfrede and Ducos relieved the sombre of the piece by the habitual liveliness of their characters. **1811** *Henry & Isabella* I. 285 A deep sombre spread itself over every thing.

**sombre** (ˈsɒmbə(r)), *v.* [f. SOMBRE *a.*]

**1.** *trans.* To make sombre.

**1787** HILDITCH *Rosa* II. 52 Life, like..the iris bow, is beheld glowing in vivid charms, or sombred by gloom. **1807** SIR R. WILSON in *Life* (1862) II. vii. 208 Our entertainment was somewhat sombred by the intelligence. **1825** *Blackw. Mag.* XVII. 44 The midnight moon Looks sombred o'er the forests. **1873** MORLEY *Rousseau* I. 315 One..whose imagination, already sombred by the triumphant cruelty and superstition which raged around him, was suddenly struck with horror.

**2.** *intr.* To become or grow sombre.

**1848** *Tait's Mag.* XV. 422 The picture sombred. **1893** *Temple Bar* XCIX. 43 Day again had sombred into night.

Hence ˈ**sombred**, ˈ**sombring** *ppl. adjs.*

**1849** WHITTIER *Lakeside* 28 This lake..Walled round with sombering pines. **1873** MASSON *Drumm. of Hawth.* xx. 453 The russet and the yellow coming in patches amid the doubly sombred green.

ˈ**sombreish**, *a. rare*[−1]. Somewhat sombre.

*a* **1845** BARHAM *Ingol. Leg.* Ser. III. *Knt. & the Lady* (1905) 471 Her thoughts having taken a sombre-ish train.

**sombrely** (ˈsɒmbəlɪ), *adv.* [f. SOMBRE *a.* + -LY[2].] In a sombre manner.

**1860** LD. LYTTON *Lucile* II. vi. §4. 11 The brass-fronted, ..audible *αυτος* gone sombrely forth. **1868** GEO. ELIOT *Sp. Gipsy* 351 The boats Went sombrely upon the sombre waves. **1876** —— *Dan. Der.* xxx, The place was sombrely in keeping with the black roads.

**sombreness** (ˈsɒmbənɪs). [f. SOMBRE *a.* + -NESS.] The state of being sombre; gloominess; gloom; dullness.

**1847** in WEBSTER. **1866** *Times* 13 June, Mourning so deep ..that not even a speck of white relieved its sombreness. **1866** GEO. ELIOT *F. Holt* (1868) 53 The general air of sombreness and privation. **1887** *Scribner's Mag.* II. 167/1 The sombreness of the bordering houses.

**sombrerite** (sɒmˈbrɪəraɪt). *Min.* [f. *Sombrero*, one of the Antilles islands + -ITE[1] 2 b.] A compound of phosphate of lime and phosphate of alumina, found on the island of Sombrero and other small islands in the West Indies.

**1862** T. L. PHIPSON in *Jrnl. Chem. Soc.* XV. 277 Its composition and properties prove it to be a new species, to which I have given the name sombrerite.

‖**sombrero** (sɒmˈbrɛərəʊ). Also 7 sumbrero, -briero, 8 somerera (?). [Sp. *sombrero* (= Pg. *sombreiro*), f. *sombra* shade.]

†**1.** An Oriental umbrella or parasol. *Obs.*

Purchas and Herbert also use the fuller expression *sombrero de sol.*

**1598** HAKLUYT *Voy.* II. 258 With a great Sombrero or shadow ouer their heads..as broad as a great cart wheele. **1638** SIR T. HERBERT *Trav.* (ed. 2) 316 Some.. hold a Sumbrero or Umbrella in their hands to lenefie the flaming Sun. **1698** FRYER *Acc. E. India & P.* 51 We saw two Sumbrero's (a Mark for some of Quality) held up in the Boat-stern. **1727** A. HAMILTON *New Acc. E. Ind.* I. xxvii. 338 Some lusty Dutch Men to carry their Palenqueens and Somereras or Umbrellas.

**2.** A broad-brimmed hat, usually of felt or some soft material, of a type common in Spain and Spanish America.

**1770** *Gentl. Mag.* XL. 530 A brown cap or silk net, with a large flatted hat called a *sombrero* over it. **1823** SCOTT *Quent. D.* xiv, A slouched overspreading hat, which resembled the sombrero of a Spanish peasant. **1855** THACKERAY *Newcomes* I. 280 In a velvet coat with a sombrero slouched over his face. **1885** LADY BRASSEY *The Trades* 177 It is sometimes called..the hat-palm, the young shoots making excellent sombreros or panamas.

*attrib.* **1891** E. ROPER *By Track & Trail* ix. 134 Their hats were of the sombrero order. **1900** *Times* 29 Jan. 10/3 Graceful Khaki-coloured sombrero hats.

**3.** *Microbiol.* A bacterial plaque in which a ring of partial lysis surrounds a clear central area.

**1971** CUNNINGHAM & SERCARZ in *European Jrnl. Immunol.* I. 414/1 Plaques which were clear in the middle but with a variable concentric zone of partial lysis at the periphery (christened 'sombreros'), were scored as clear. **1975** *Nature* 20 Feb. 639/1 Those which started as sombreros..always grew into larger sombreros.

**somˈbreroed**, *a.* [f. SOMBRERO + -ED[2].] Wearing or covered by a sombrero.

**1899** F. REMINGTON *Sundown Leflare* 51 Sombreroed and moccasined, Sundown pattered along on his roan pinto. **1906** *Out West* Jan. 49 'Oh, no, you never make it. Too mucho arena!' with an emphatic, disapproving shake of sombreroed head. **1912** D. H. LAWRENCE *Let.* 17 Sept. (1962) I. 147 Black sombrero'd Italians. **1966** H. W. YOXALL *Fashion of Life* xii. 120 A sombreroed, bearded, cloaked individual.

**sombrous** (ˈsɒmbrəs), *a.* [f. F. *sombre* SOMBRE *a.* + -OUS. Cf. obs. F. *sombreux*, Sp. and Pg. *sombroso*.] Sombre; of a sombre character or aspect.

**1.** Of inanimate natural objects and their attributes. Cf. SOMBRE *a.* 1.

*c* **1730** BURT *Lett. N. Scotl.* (1822) I. 286 Their..horrid gloom, made yet more sombrous by the shades..they communicate one to another. **1787–9** WORDSW. *Evening Walk* 156 Where..the sombrous pine And yew-tree o'er the silver rocks recline. **1803** *Forest of Hohenelbe* I. 50 The long sombrous avenue that led to the front of the Castle. **1833** M. SCOTT *Tom Cringle* xiv, The fast falling shades of evening were deepened by the sombrous shadow of the immense tree overhead. **1889** P. H. EMERSON *Eng. Idyls* 47 Ghostly loomed the baleful wreck and sombrous beacons of the channel.

*absol.* **1862** D. G. F. MACDONALD *Brit. Columbia* 332 The whole territory..is endowed with savage beauty.., and extremely interesting to the lover of the sombrous.

**2. a.** Of persons, etc. Cf. SOMBRE *a.* 2.

**1792** *Childr. Thespis* 49 When once in a moon Sombrous John condescends..to glad all his friends. **1799** MRS. J. WEST *Tale of Times* II. 36 Smothered discontent often made him meet..inquiries..with the sombrous brow of sorrow. **1802** —— *Infidel Father* I. 136 Though the sombrous air of melancholy never after left his face. **1834** CAMPBELL *Mrs. Siddons* II. viii. 200 Kemble, [acting] on this occasion, was uncommonly sombrous.

**b.** Of thoughts, feelings, etc. Cf. SOMBRE *a.* 2 b.

**1751** WARBURTON *Pope's Wks.* III. 190 A poor despicable superstition, a low sombrous passion. **1771–2** *Ess. fr. Batchelor* (1773) I. 239 His dull sombrous imagination rendered him incapable of varying his ideas on any subject.

**1817** J. EVANS *Excurs. Windsor*, etc. 373 Under these sombrous feelings, even at this early period of life [etc.]. **1834** CAMPBELL *Mrs. Siddons* II. iii. 78 A serious temper, somewhat inclined to be sombrous.

**3.** Of abstract ideas, conditions, etc.

**1750** WARBURTON *Doct. Grace* I. Wks. 1811 VIII. 293 A sparkling luxuriancy of thought, and a sombrous rankness of expression. **1778** WARTON *Hist. Eng. Poetry* III. xxvii. 150 A certain uniform strain of sombrous gravity. **1795** SOUTHEY *To Lycon*, The venom'd juice will.. Lull reason's powers to sombrous sleep. **1820** *Ann. Reg.* II. 724 The future for Spain appears again under a sombrous and disturbed aspect.

**4.** Of colours or colouring. Also *transf.* Cf. SOMBRE *a.* 4.

**1792** S. ROGERS *Pleasures of Mem.* II. 167 Time's sombrous touches soon correct the piece. **1797** T. PARK *Sonn.* 95 Let him in sombrous colours paint her lot. **1802** MRS. J. WEST *Infidel Father* I. p. iii, The episodical characters have a use besides relieving the sombrous hue of the principal personages.

**b.** = SOMBRE *a.* 4b.

**1799** MRS. J. WEST *Tale of Times* I. 212 The messenger.. found the castle attired in the most sombrous weeds of woe.

**5.** *Comb.*, as **sombrous-looking** adj.

**1802** MRS. J. WEST *Infidel Father* II. 302 The Hymeneal Vulcan sometimes sees as sombrous looking suppliants approach his altar.

Hence **'sombrously** *adv.*; **'sombrousness**.

**1796** *Mod. Gulliver's Trav.* 129 He looked very sombrously. **1847** WEBSTER, *Sombrously*, gloomily. *Sombrousness*, state of being sombrous.

**some** (sʌm), *indef. pron.*, *a.*[1], *adv.*, and *sb.*[1] Forms: 1–6, 9 *dial.* **sum** (9 *dial.* **zum**), 3–4 **summ**, 4–5, 6 *Sc.* **sume, summe**; 4 **soumme**, 5 **soume**, 5 (9 *dial.*) **soom**; 3–5, 7, 9 *dial.* **som** (4 **zom**, 7 *dial.* **z'om**), 5 **somm, somp**; 3–6 **somme**, 3– **some** (4, 9 *dial.* **zome**). [Common Teut.: OE. *sum*, = OFris. *sum* (NFris. *som*), MDu. *som*, *zom* (WFlem. *som*, *zom*), OS. *sum* (MLG. *sum*, *som*), OHG. and MHG. *sum* (G. dial. *sum*, *som*, *söm*), ON. *sumr* (Icel. *sumur*, Norw. *sum*; MSw. *sum*, *som*, Sw. *somt* neut., Da. *somme* pl.), Goth. *sums*; the stem is also found in Gr. ἀμο- (as ἀμόθεν from some place) and Skr. *sama* any, every. The word has had greater currency in English than in the other Teutonic languages, in some of which it is now restricted to dialect use, or represented only by derivatives or compounds, as WFris. *sommige*, *somlike*, Du. *sommige* (also *somtiids*, *somwijlen* sometimes), LG. *sömige* (G. dial. *summige*).]

**A.** *indef. pron.*

For *all and some*, *whole and some*, see ALL *a.* 12, WHOLE *a.*

**I.** In singular uses.

**1.** †**a.** One or other of a number of persons; someone, somebody. In later use also in phr. ***some or other***. *Obs.*

(*a*) *Beowulf* 1432 Sumne Geata leod of flanboȝan feores ȝetwæfde. *a* **1000** *Riddles* xv. 15 (Gr.), þonne ic winde sceal sincfaȝ swelȝan of sumes bosme. *a* **1225** *Ancr. R.* 70 Summes kurteisie is noðeleas iturnd hire to vuele. *c* **1290** *S. Eng. Leg.* I. 131 In þis place sum is þat wolde telle þe kinge fore, and maken him mi fo. **1484** CAXTON *Fables of Æsop* v. x, Whan somme good cometh to somme, it ought not to be reffused. **1509** HAWES *Past. Pleas.* XXIII. (Percy Soc.) 107 Upon one hande some hath thombes twayne; And other also somtyme armes thre. *c* **1581** LODGE *Reply Gosson's Sch. Abuse* (Shaks. Soc.) 23, I feare me some will blushe that readeth this, if he be bitten. **1729** G. ADAMS tr. *Sophocl., Antig.* III. i. II. 39 Therefore.. despise he [Antigone], and suffer the Girl to marry some among the Dead.

(*b*) **1631** HEYLIN *Hist. St. George* 113, I wonder some or other hath not resolu'd the doubt. **1664** D. FLEMING in *Extr. St. Papers rel. Friends* (1912) III. 213, I am halfe of opinion, that some or other hath abused him in this Letter. **1682** BUNYAN *Holy War* (1905) 208 Word, by some or other, could not but be carried to the good King Shaddai.

†**b.** Const. *of* (or gen. pl.). Also of things. *Obs.*

*c* **888** K. ÆLFRED *Boeth.* xviii. §2 He cyðde on sumre his boca ðætte þa ȝet Romana nama ne come ofer þa muntas. *c* **1000** *Ags. Gosp.* Matt. xiii. 25 þa com his feonda sum & ofer-seow hit mid coccele. *Ibid.* Mark viii. 28 Sume [secgað] summe of þam witeȝum. *c* **1100** *Twelfth Cent. Hom.* 134 Ȝif nu eower sum,.. smeað hwæt god beo. **1340** *Ayenb.* 15 Vor onneaþe yualþ þet me ne ualþ in-to þe þrote of zome of þe zeue heauedes. **1638** SIR T. HERBERT *Trav.* (ed. 2) 46 The Cutteries.. have six and thirty Casts among themselves, from some of which none of them but is descended. **1656** SANDERSON *Serm.* (1689) 405 All such sins being easily reducible to some of the former three.

**c.** In the phr. ***some of these*** (..) ***days***, some day soon; before very long.

**1831** in Knapp *Life G. Borrow* (1899) I. 142 Young Simpson will be wanting an able assistant some of these days. **1848** NEWMAN *Loss & Gain* I. xiv, 'We shall have you a papist some of these fine days,' said he. **1851** BORROW *Lavengro* lxxiii, I should not be surprised if he were to come back some of these days.

†**2.** ***some..., some***, one..., another. (Cf. 7.)

*c* **888** K. ÆLFRED *Boeth.* xxxiii. §2 þonne lufað sum ðæt, sum elles hwæt. *c* **1000** *Ags. Gosp.* Matt. xxv. 15 He sealde ..sumum twa [pund], sumum an. *a* **1225** *Ancr. R.* 6 Vor sum is strong, sum is unstrong. *c* **1250** *Gen. & Ex.* 834 Sum was king, and sum kumeling. *c* **1386** CHAUCER *Knt.'s T.* 2173 He mot ben deed,.. Som in his bed, som in the depe see. **1390** GOWER *Conf.* III. 14 For som schal singe and som schal syke.

†**3.** With ordinal numbers: One of (or with) a specified number. *Obs.*

For the use of the ordinal cf. G. *selbdritte*, *-vierte*, etc. In OE. the gen. plur. of the cardinal was employed, as *syxa*, *eahta*, *twelfa sum*: for the later history of this see -SOME[2].

*a* **1225** *Juliana* 79 And te sea sencte him on his þrituðe sum ant þer to ȝet fowre. **13..** *Sir Beues* 203 Him self was boute þe ferþe some Toward þat ferd. *c* **1320** *Sir Tristrem* 817 He busked and made him ȝare Hi[m] fiftend som of kniȝt. *c* **1425** [see THIRDSOME].

**4. a.** A certain indeterminate part of something; a portion. (†In early use freq. following a noun or pronoun, or predicative.) Also ***some..., some***.

*c* **900** *O.E. Chron.* (Parker MS.) an. 877, þa.. ȝefor se here on Miercna lond, & hit ȝedældon sum, & sum Ceolwulfe saldon. *c* **1000** *Ags. Gosp.* Luke viii. 5 þa he þæt seow, sum feoll wið þæne weȝ.. And sum feoll ofer þæne stan. *c* **1275** *Prov. Hendyng* 98 Ȝef thou hauest bred & ale,.. þou del hit sum aboute. **1297** R. GLOUC. (Rolls) 98 He hadde þer to Scropssire som & aluendel of warewik ssire. **1387** TREVISA *Higden* (Rolls) I. 151 Amazonia.. is som in Asia, and som in Europa. *c* **1440** *Promp. Parv.* 484/1 Sum, or sumwhat, or a part of a nowmyr or a noþer thynge. **1572** in Feuillerat *Revels Q. Eliz.* (1908) 162 Sum in Bowltes and sum by lb. **1588** KYD *Househ. Phil.* Wks. (1901) 245 Some was roste, some was backt. **1597** SHAKS. *2 Hen. IV*, Epil., Bate me some, and I will pay you some. **1611** BIBLE *Luke* viii. 6 And some fell vpon a rocke, and.. it withered away. **1796** C. MARSHALL *Gardening* xix. (1813) 371 As it is a small flower, pot some.

**b.** Const. *of* (the thing specified).

*c* **1175** *Lamb. Hom.* 133 Sum of þe sede feol an uppe þe stane. **1297** R. GLOUC. (Rolls) 101 Som of gloucestressire & of warewikssire al so. **1560** BIBLE (Geneva) *Lev.* iv. 7 The Priest also shal put some of the blood.. vpon the hornes of yᵉ altar. **1600** SHAKS. *A.Y.L.* IV. iii. 96 Some of my shame, if you will know of me What man I am. **1639** J. SMYTH in *Glouc. Gloss.* (1890) 200 Ga'as zo'm of thuck bread. **1694** CONGREVE *Double Dealer* v. v, Snuff some of my spirit of hartshorn. **1834–6** *Encycl. Metrop.* (1845) VIII. 762/1 In the act of drying, some of the lac is generally brought to the surface. **1872** MORLEY *Voltaire* (1886) 6 Some of it, much of it, has ceased to be alive for us now.

†**c.** (***by***) ***some and some***, by little and little; by degrees; gradually. *Obs.* (Cf. 8b.)

**1398** TREVISA *Barth. De P.R.* XI. i. (Tollem. MS.), Vapoures, þat beþ gaderid sum and sum in þe erþe. *Ibid.* XVII. cxliii. (Bodl. MS.), Whan þe weþye is swiþe olde, þan he faileþ & roteþ somme and somme. **1602** J. RHODES *Answ. Romish Rhyme* 8 Your doctrine.., which did creepe Into the Church, by some and some.

†**d.** ***some and some***, something in return for something. *Obs.*

**1573** GASCOIGNE *Herbes* Wks. 1907 I. 353 Recompence the lyke agayne: For some and some is honest playe. **1583** MELBANCKE *Philotimus* Tj, Thinke some and some is honest play.

**e.** ***to get some***: to have sexual intercourse; to succeed in finding a sexual partner. *U.S. slang.*

**1889** W. H. HERNDON *Let.* 5 Jan. in E. Hertz *Hidden Lincoln* (1940) 233 Speed about 1839–40 was keeping a pretty woman in this city, and Lincoln, desirous to have *a little*, said to Speed: 'Speed, do you know where I can get *some*?' **1971** E. E. LANDY *Underground Dict.* 88 *Get some..*, obtain sexual intercourse with someone. **1978** J. KRANTZ *Scruples* vi. 173 Since his last visit she was getting some, somewhere, he'd bet his life on it.

**f.** ***and then some***: and (plenty) more in addition. *colloq.* (chiefly *U.S.*).

**1908** 'YESLAH' *Tenderfoot in Southern California* ii. 22 It rains in sheets, in blankets, and in comforters, and then some. **1914** D. O. BARNETT *Lett.* (1915) 19, I picked them out with those glasses, and let them have it, and then some! **1931** T. E. LAWRENCE *Let.* 10 June (1938) 724 It.. will be 12 guineas and then some! **1958** J. CANNAN *And be Villain* i. 24, I waited till the train had gone out and then some. **1976** D. CLARK *Dread & Water* ii. 51 People have got to talk... Tell us everything they know and then some.

**II.** In plural senses.

**5. a.** An indefinite or unspecified (but not large) number of persons (or animals); certain persons not named or enumerated. Also ***some or other***.

*Beowulf* 400 Sume þær bidon, heaðoreaf heoldon. *c* **888** K. ÆLFRED *Boeth.* xi. §1 Sume beoð swiðe æþele & widcuðe on heora ȝebyrdum. *c* **950** *Lindisf. Gosp.* John vii. 44 Sumo.. uilnadon ȝegrioppa hine. **1154** *O.E. Chron.* (Laud MS.) an. 1137, Sume hi diden in crucethus. *c* **1175** *Lamb. Hom.* 3 Heo urnen on-ȝein him.. and summe mid ufele þeonke. *c* **1205** LAY. 27376 Heo sculleð beon islaȝene and summe quic iulaȝene. *a* **1250** *Owl & Night.* 1648 Summe of þe scheules makeþ. *a* **1300** *Cursor M.* 14739 Amang þir men.. War sume þat duues boght and sald. **1375** BARBOUR *Bruce* VI. 440 Thai ourtuk sum at the last, And thame forout mercy can sla. *c* **1440** *Pallad. on Husb.* II. 283 Summe hem kepe Thre nyght in molten donge. **1450** *Paston Lett.* I. 125 Soom sey he wrotte moche [thing]. **1579** SPENSER *Sheph. Cal.* Sept. 152 Neuer was Woolfe seene, many nor some. **1601** HOLLAND *Pliny* I. 117 Some there be that think how it was first founded by Amphitus. **1675** H. MORE in R. Ward *Life* (1710) 361, I do not wonder that some or other are now and then so strangely assaulted. **1747** MRS. GLASSE *Cookery* ix. 88 Some love scalded Gooseberries with them. **1816** J. WILSON *City of Plague* II. i, Some, my son, Would bid thee trust in time. **1842** LOUDON *Suburban Hort.* 121 It feeds on worms.. and according to some, on roots. **1878** T. HARDY *Ret. Native* I. iii. (1890) 21, I shouldn't have cared about the man, though some may say he's good-looking.

**b.** Similarly of things.

*c* **975** *Rushw. Gosp.* Matt. xiii. 4 And þa he seow, sume ȝefeollun bi wæȝe & cuomun fuȝlas heofun & frætun. *a* **1225** *Ancr. R.* 28 Uor þe ten hesten þet ich ibroken habbe, summe oðer alle. **1382** WYCLIF *Matt.* xiii. 4 And the while he soweth, sum felden byside the weye. *a* **1400–50** *Alexander* 568 It.. raynes doune stanys,.. And some as hoge as þi hede fra þe heuyn fallis. *c* **1449** PECOCK *Repr.* III. xiv. 371 And so forth of manye othere staryng gouernauncis, semyng summe wijlde woode. **1547** BOORDE *Brev. Health* Pref., Many obscure termes,.. some & fewe beynge Araby wordes. **1588** LAMBARDE *Eirenarcha* IV. xix. 595 There be also certain matters.. appropriated, some to any, and others to some one, of the generall Sessions. **1607** SIR J. HARINGTON in *Nugæ Ant.* (1804) I. 47 Manie bowlts were roved after him, and some spitefullie feather'd.

†**c.** With pronoun or sb. in apposition. (Cf. B. 7b.) *Obs.*

*c* **900** tr. *Baeda's Hist.* IV. vii[i]. 282 þa sumu [*v.r.* sume] woe nu ȝemdon ȝeþeodan in þis user ciriclice stær. *c* **1000** *Ags. Gosp.* John vi. 64 Ac sume ȝe ne ȝelyfað. *a* **1122** *O.E. Chron.* (Laud MS.) an. 1101, Se cyng syððan scipa ut on sæ sende.., ac hi sume æft æt þære neode abruðon. *c* **1275** *Passion Our Lord* 43 in *O.E. Misc.* 38 Summe hi weren wyse, and duden al bi his rede. **1597** SHAKS. *Lover's Compl.* 148 Yet did I not, as some my equals did, Demaund of him. **1606** —— *Tr. & Cr.* IV. v. 190 (Q.[1]), That I haue said to some my standers by.

**d.** In possessive form. Now *rare.*

**1565** COOPER *Thesaurus* s.v. *Capio*, Sommes consciences beganne to pricke them. **1597** BEARD *Theatre God's Judgem.* (1612) 44 Somes lot it was to be torn in pieces. **1653** BP. WEBBE *Pract. Quiet.* 253 Nor may I condemn all.. for somes unquietness. **1675** E. WILSON *Spadacr. Dunelm.* 67, I fear I have spoken Ænigmatically.. to somes understanding. **1823** BYRON *Juan* XIII. xxx, Howsoe'er it shocks some's Self-love, there's safety in a crowd of coxcombs.

**6.** With *of* (persons or things).

*c* **875** in *O.E. Texts* 178 Ðæt he spræc to his liornæra sumum. *c* **950** *Lindisf. Gosp.* Matt. xxviii. 11 Summe of ðæm haldendum cwomun in ða ceastra. *c* **1175** *Lamb. Hom.* 43 Summe of þan monne sare wepeð. *c* **1200** ORMIN 6574 Sume off ure little flocc þatt lefeþþ uppo Criste. *c* **1275** LAY. 12001 Somme of þaie sipes wonde mid þan wedere. **1303** R. BRUNNE *Handl. Synne* 9997 Lo here a tale for of ȝou sum. *c* **1386** CHAUCER *Can. Yeom. Prol.* 193 Somme of hem synke in to the ground. *c* **1449** PECOCK *Repr.* II. viii. 185 God wrouȝte tho myraclis in summe of tho placis more and ofter than in othere placis like. **1470–85** MALORY *Arthur* VIII. xxxiii. 323 Somme of them were sore hurte. **1537** *Thersytes* 99 in Pollard *Mir. Plays* (1890) 129 Some of the giauntes before Noes floud. **1588** KYD *Househ. Phil.* Wks. (1901) 267 A youth who.. doth seme to write and mannedge some of their affaires. **1611** BIBLE *Rom.* xi. 17 If some of the branches bee broken off. **1664** PEPYS *Diary* 19 Mar., I spent the afternoon in paying some of the charges of the burial. **1748** HARTLEY *Observ. Man* I. i. 63 Some or other of those vibrations which are excited in it. **1779** *Mirror* No. 31, Some of our most celebrated historians have committed errors of the first sort. **1823** SCOTT *Quentin D.* xxxiii, Bring that rascal forward, some of you. **1855** MACAULAY *Hist. Eng.* xvi. III. 715 Some of those who opposed the bill. **1891** E. ROPER *By Track & Trail* xv. 217 Higher up.. there are some of the most sublime scenes I have looked on anywhere.

**7. a.** ***some..., some***, = Some..., others. (Cf. 2.) †Formerly also in ***some... than some***, ***some and some***.

(*a*) *c* **888** K. ÆLFRED *Boeth.* xxxiii. §5 Sume beorhtor sume unbyrhtor, swa swa steorran. *c* **1000** *Ags. Gosp.* Mark xii. 5 Sume hi beoton, sume hi of-sloȝon. **1154** *O.E. Chron.* (Laud MS.) an. 1140, Sume helden mid te king & sume mid þemperice. *c* **1200** *Trin. Coll. Hom.* 101 Sume sitteð and sume ligeð and sume we stondeð. *a* **1225** *Leg. Kath.* 37 Summe þurh muchele ȝeouen.., summe þurh fearlac. **13..** *K. Alis.* 2517 (W.), To divers castles he heom sent:.. Some to Libye, some to Rome. *c* **1380** *Sir Ferumb.* 948 Of summe þay smyte of legges & armes, & of sum þe heuedes þay gerde. *a* **1400–50** *Alexander* 1330 All at he slayn fyndez, He makes to grave, some in grete, some in gray marbyll. *c* **1450** HOLLAND *Howlat* 64 Sum will me dulfully dicht, Sum dyng me to deid. **1523** SKELTON *Garl. Laurel* 250 Some whispred, some rownyd, some spake, and some cryde. **1568** GRAFTON *Chron.* II. 8 Some [fled] into Norway, and some into Denmarke, and some into one Countrie, and some into another. **1611** BIBLE *Psalms* xx. 7 Some trust in charets, and some in horses. **1685** TEMPLE *Misc.* II. *Gardens* (1690) 11 Like Rover Shots, some nearer and some further off, but all at great Distance from the Mark. **1750** tr. *Leonardus' Mirr. Stones* 130 For some are gold, some silver, others copper, and others iron. **1837** P. KEITH *Bot. Lex.* 122 Some are annular, some are reticulated, some are dotted, and some akin to spirals. **1855** KINGSLEY *Westw. Ho!* xxv, Some ran; some did not run.

(*b*) *c* **1491** *Chast. Goddes Chyld.* ii. 7 Our lorde withdraweth him fro some more than fro some. **1526** *Inv. Goods Dk. Richmond* in *Camden Misc.* (1855) 19 Item, Counter-points of all sortes, some bygger than some. **1547** *Bk. of Marchauntes* c vj b, My marchants, of whome truely some be wilier than some. **1821** SCOTT *Kenilw.* xli, Some are wiser than some,.. and some are worse than some.

(*c*) **1522** SKELTON *Why not to Court?* 385 But there is some trauarse Bytwene some and some.

**b.** So ***some..., others*** (†***other***).

*c* **950** *Lindisf. Gosp.* Mark xii. 5 Sume ðurscun, oðero æc ofsloȝon. **1382** WYCLIF *Mark* xii. 5 Betynge summe, but sleynge othere. **1588** KYD *Househ. Phil.* Wks. (1901) 262 Some are naturally borne to commande, and others to obey. **1634** SIR T. HERBERT *Trav.* 189 Some have a smacke of Christ, others of Mahomet. **1696** in *13th Rep. Hist. MSS. Comm.* App. VI. 41 By impowering some, and neglecting others. **1746** P. FRANCIS tr. *Horace, Art Poet.* 491 Some Charm when nigh, Others at Distance more delight your Eye. **1852** MISS YONGE *Cameos* (1877) III. iii. 21 The burghers hurried out, some with the straight cross of France, others with the saltire of Burgundy.

†**c.** Also ***some..., other some***. *Obs.*

**1375** BARBOUR *Bruce* I. 52 For sum wald haiff þe Balleoll king;.. And oþir sum nyt all þat cas. **1532** HERVET *Xenophon's Treat. Househ.* (1768) 74 For some haue gret plenty.. and other some haue scantly so moche as they nede. **1585** T. WASHINGTON tr. *Nicholay's Voy.* II. xvi. 50b, Cesternes.., supported some by vaultes, and othersom by ..pillars. **1611** [see OTHER SOME]. **1634** SIR T. HERBERT *Trav.* 141 Some place it in the circle of the Moone,.. other some vnder the Circle of the Moone. **1700** S. L. tr. *Frykes' Voy. E. Ind.* 121 Some of 'em are far better than other some.

†**8. a.** ***some after some***, = next. *Obs.*[−1]

**1598** GRENEWEY *Tacitus, Ann.* IV. xvi. (1622) 115 Comming some after some, and dropping in by companies.

**b.** ***some and some***, a few at a time, gradually. *Obs.* (Cf. 4 c.)

**1686** tr. *Chardin's Trav. Persia* 63 He put my Goods aboard, some and some, as he saw his Opportunity. **1719** De Foe *Crusoe* II. (Globe) 501 They came dropping in, some and some, not in two Bodies, and in Form.., but all in Heaps. **1769** G. White *Selborne* xxiii, Persons who assert that the swallow kind disappear some and some, gradually, as they come.

**B.** *adj.*

**I.** With singular nouns. (See also 9 c.)

†**1. a.** Of persons or places: A certain. *Obs.*

*c* **888** K. Ælfred *Boeth.* i, þa wæs sum consul,..Boetius wæs ȝehaten. **971** *Blickl. Hom.* 15 þa sæt þær sum blind þearfa be ðon weȝe. *c* **1000** *Ags. Gosp.* John xi. 1 Sum seoc man wæs ȝenemned lazarus of bethania. **1382** Wyclif *Luke* i. 5 Ther was sum prest, Zacharie by name, in the dayes of Eroude. *Ibid.* xviii. 2–3 Sum iuge was in sum citee... Forsothe sum widowe was in that citee. *a* **1578** Lindesay (Pitscottie) *Chron. Scot.* (S.T.S.) II. 87 Sum godlie man [*sc.* John Knox] was in the castell.

†**b.** = one *pron.* 2 b. *Obs.*

**1382** Wyclif *Acts* xxv. 19 Thei hadden aȝens hym summe questiouns..of sum Jhesu deed, whom Poul affermyde for to lyue. **1760** T. Hutchinson *Hist. Mass.* i. 86 A *quo warranto* had been brought by some Sir John Banks, attorney-general [etc.].

**2. a.** One or other; an undetermined or unspecified.

*c* **888** K. Ælfred *Boeth.* xxxvii. §2 þæt mon hehð ænne heafodbeaȝ gyldenne æt sumes ærneweȝes ende. *c* **1000** Ælfric *Saints' Lives* xxxi. 651 Martinus..wolde for sumere neode wið hine spræcan. *c* **1200** Ormin 228 Þeȝȝ wisstenn þatt himm wass þatt daȝȝ Summ unncuþ sihhþe shæwedd. *a* **1225** *Leg. Kath.* 811 Scheoteð forð sum word, & let us onswerien. *c* **1250** *Owl & Night.* 1265 Naueþ mon no sikerhede þat he ne may..adrede þat sum vnhap neih him beo. *a* **1300** *Vox & Wolf* 125 in Hazl. *E.P.P.* I. 62 For he thoute, mid soumme ginne, Him self houp [= up] bringe. **1387** Trevisa *Higden* (Rolls) I. 101 þat hul is ful hiȝe, so þat snowe lyeth all wey in som side of þat hille. *c* **1470** Henry *Wallace* II. 391 Thow Scot, abide, I trow thow be sum spy. **1528** Tindale *Obed. Chr. Man* 89 This worde.. representeth allwaye some promise of God. **1581** J. Bell *Haddon's Answ. Osorius* 360 b, They rest their handes upon some staffe shaking and tremblyng. **1634** Milton *Comus* 485 Som neighbour Wood-man, or at worst, Som roaving Robber. **1663** S. Patrick *Parab. Pilgr.* (1687) 171, I believe you are desirous to have some list of these Enemies. **1725** Pope *Odyss.* viii. 180 Some mean sea-farer in pursuit of gain. **1780** *Mirrour* No. 94, Miss Sophia R. therefore keeps me right..or covers my deviations with some apology. **1825** Scott *Talism.* ii, They had even their knights, or some rank analogous. **1867** Trollope *Chron. Barset* I. xxi. 177, I am going to ask him to put his case into some lawyer's hands. **1876** 'Ouida' *Winter City* vi. 128 A triptych of some old fogey of a painter.

**b.** In adverbial expressions of time and place, with or without a preposition.

See also sometime, -where, -while.

(*a*) *c* **893** K. Ælfred *Oros.* i. i. 17 He sæde þæt he æt sumum cirre wolde fandian [etc.]. *c* **1000** Ælfric *Hom.* I. 62 Þa becom se apostol æt sumum sæle to þære byriȝ Pergamum. *c* **1200** *Trin. Coll. Hom.* 185 Ðos feawe word seide ure drihten..at sume sele. *a* **1225** *Ancr. R.* 48 David.. seide et sume time þat heo was etstert him. *c* **1250** *Owl & Night.* 293 At sum syþe herde i telle hw Alured seyde on his spelle. *a* **1300** *Cursor M.* 20981 He was sua stanid on sum dai, Vneths he bar lif a-way. **1382** Wyclif *Heb.* ii. 6 Sum man witnesside in sum place. *a* **1400–50** *Alexander* 204 Suppos-and þaim in sum tyme for sothe to be knawen. *Ibid.* (MS. D.) 755* He..stighillys hym in som stede a stable by hym one. **1616** B. Jonson *Forest* xiii, No lady, but at some time loves her glass.

(*b*) *a* **900** *O.E. Chron.* (Parker MS.) an. 896, þa sume dæȝe rad se cyng up be þære eæ. *a* **1300** *Cursor M.* 13185 Men mai yeitt se sum sted in france [etc.]. **13..** *Seuyn Sag.* (W.) 2936 Bot wele in hert he hoped ay That he sold hir se sum day. *a* **1425** *Cursor M.* 956 (Trin.), I hete to sende hit ȝou sum tide. **1550** *Reg. Privy Council Scot.* I. 88 He hopis sum day to see his sone [etc.]. **1822** Shelley *Chas. 1st* ii. 451 His Grace..expects to enter the New Jerusalem some Palm Sunday in triumph. **1845** Browning *Home Thoughts fr. Abroad* 4 And whoever wakes in England Sees, some morning, unaware [etc.]. **1865** Ruskin *Sesame* i. §13, I see it is true; or if I do not now, I hope I shall, some day.

**c.** With the indefiniteness emphasized by the addition of *or other* (cf. other B. 5 a), *or another*.

**1590** Shaks. *Com. Err.* i. ii. 95 By some deuise or other, The villaine is ore-wrought of all my monie. **1615** W. Bedwell *Arab. Trudg.* K iij, How oft..shal you not meet with some exoticke and strange terme or other? **1697** Dryden *Dedic. Æneis* a iij b, Yet all this while I have been Sailing with some side-wind or other toward the Point I propos'd in the beginning. **1736** *Swift's Lett.* (1768) IV. 171, I received yours some day or other this week. *a* **1774** Goldsm. *Surv. Exp. Philos.* (1776) II. 14 Certain it is that air is impregnated with salts of some kind or another. **1845** Pattison *Ess.* (1889) I. 9 An impulse which will vent itself in some form or other. **1881** Mrs. L. B. Walford *Dick Netherby* xii. 144 He must write some day or other.

**d.** With adjs. used absolutely. *rare.*

**1579** Spenser *Sheph. Cal.* Mar. 74 [I] Might see the mouing of some quicke, Whose shape appeared not. **1725** Ramsay *Gentl. Sheph.* iii. ii, The man's..possest With some nae good.

**e.** In suggestive or euphemistic use.

**1725** Ramsay *Gentl. Sheph.* v. iii, She's baith a slee and a revengfu' bitch, And that my some-place [= posteriors] finds.

†**3.** Used with an indefinite or generalizing force similar to that of the plural (sense 7). *Obs.*

*c* **888** K. Ælfred *Boeth.* xxxiv. §10 Sumes wuda eard bið on dunum. *c* **1000** Ælfric *Hom.* I. 322 Sumum men he forȝifð wisdom and spræce, sumum god inȝehyd, sumum micelne ȝeleafan. **13..** *Cursor M.* 10226 (Gött.), For þan was sum man god dredand. **1375** Barbour *Bruce* ii. 295 Sum man for eryness will trymbill, Quhen he assayit is sodanly. **1481** Caxton *Reynard* xxviii. (Arb.) 68 The ape.. is wyser in clergie than somme preest. **1535** Coverdale *Ecclus.* vi. 9 And there is some frende that turneth to enemyte, and taketh parte agaynst the. *Ibid.* xx. 5 Some man kepeth sylence, and is founde wyse. **1565** Cooper *Thesaurus, Alburnum*, the fatte that is in some tree. **1638** Junius *Paint. Ancients* 103 In some regard they tooke speciall notice of the difference of wits.

**4. a.** A certain (unspecified) amount, part, degree, or extent of (something), freq. implying 'not little, considerable'. †In OE. also with *the*, *his*, etc.

*c* **888** K. Ælfred *Boeth.* xxiv. §4 Nis nan man þætte sumes eacan ne ðyrfe. *c* **893** —— *Oros.* iii. x. 140 He beæftan ȝebad mid sumum þæm fultume. *c* **920** *O.E. Chron.* an. 913. Sum his fultum worhte þa burȝ. *a* **1200** *Moral Ode* 25 in *O.E. Hom.* I. 161 Sendeð sum god bi-foren eow, þe hwile þet ȝe muȝen, to houene. *c* **1275** *XI Pains of Hell* 290 in *O.E. Misc.* 220 Poul knelid adowne..And prayd..Fore þe soulis in hel sum ryst haue þer. **1375** in Horstmann *Altengl. Leg.* (1878) 125/1 Bote rys, & go we eft wiþ mod For to seken vs sum fod. **1393** Langl. *P. Pl.* C. iii. 128 þat god wolde were ydo with-oute som deceite. ? *c* **1440** *Pol., Rel., & L. Poems* (1903) 246 Lord! sende me sum 'amor' sede. **1478** *Paston Lett.* III. 237 He prayth yow to sende hym sum mony. **1562** *Child Marriages* 189 He came thither to get somme threde. **1590** Shaks. *Mids. N.* i. i. 244 When this Haile some heat from Hermia felt. **1650** Earl Monm. tr. *Senault's Man bec. Guilty* 345 These wise men..mought have some cognizance of the truth. **1677** Marvell *Season. Argum.*, etc. Wks. (1776) II. 562 Where he feathered his nest to some purpose. **1711** Steele *Spect.* No. 100 ¶1 He immediately calls for some Posset-drink for him. *Ibid.* No. 106 ¶5 A Person of good Sense and some Learning. **1761–2** Hume *Hist. Eng.* (1806) IV. lxi. 589 Some state was up-held, but with little expense. **1831** Scott *Cast. Dang.* v, His master..had been a man of some reading. **1855** Macaulay *Hist. Eng.* xviii. IV. 191 In the neighbourhood..was some copsewood and some pasture land. **1890** *Law Times Rep.* LXIII. 767/1 There is some variation in the mode in which the custom is stated.

**b.** With partitive terms, as *part*, *degree*, etc.

See also somedeal, -part, -what.

*c* **1400** *Destr. Troy* 13553 Iff ye haue ferkit any fode to þis frith now,..ges me som part. *c* **1470** *Rauf Coilȝear* 56 For I trow..sum part salbe thyne. **1567** Allen *Def. Priesthood* 306 To geue pardon..is to release some parte, or all the enioyned penaunce. **1648** *Hamilton Papers* (Camden) 226 It is beliued that som parte of the caus is from Scotland. **1780** *Mirror* No. 82, But I can venture to assert, with some degree of confidence, that [etc.]. **1826** *Art of Brewing* (ed. 2) 2, I admit this to be correct advice, in some measure. **1870** J. E. T. Rogers *Hist. Glean.* Ser. ii. 7 Some part of its authority was due to its prestige.

**c.** With terms of time or space.

(*a*) *c* **900** tr. *Baeda's Hist.* v. xii. (1890) 432 þa ic sume tid fram ðe ȝewat [etc.]. *c* **1060** *O.E. Chron.* (MS. C) an. 1055, Hiȝ..wendan..ut on Wealas, & þær laȝon sume hwile. *a* **1200** *Moral Ode* 147 in *O.E. Hom.* I. 169 Hefð he ifonded [it] summe stunde, he wolde al seggen oðer. *a* **1225** *Leg. Kath.* 8 Constantin ferde..in to Fronclonde, & wunede summe hwile þear. *c* **1275** in *O.E. Misc.* 89 þo heo stod ful vaste, and seoþþe sume stunde. *c* **1400** *Pilgr. Sowle* (Caxton, 1483) iii. viii. 55 Al be hit that for somtyme theyr lewd lyf displesid to them seluen. *c* **1643** Ld. Herbert *Autobiog.* (1824) 33 He that can forbear speaking for some while, will remit much of his passion. **1658** J. Webb *Cleopatra* viii. i. 147 [He] continued sometime in the designe. **1710** Addison *Spect.* No. 12 ¶1 It was some time before I could settle my self in a House to my likeing. **1747** in E. H. Burton *Life Bp. Challoner* (1909) I. xiv. 223, I sent the lessons some time ago to Paris. **1838** *Proc. Berw. Nat. Club* I. 173 After lying some time among weedy rocks. **1845–6** Trench *Huls. Lect.* Ser. i. i. 13 No doubt for some while the Church did exist with a canon not full formed. **1891** E. Peacock *N. Brendon* I. 315 Basil hesitated for some time.

(*b*) **1594** Plat *Jewell-ho.* 4 An earthern vessel of some receipte. **1610** Shaks. *Temp.* ii. i. 257 'Twixt which Regions There is some space. **1794** Mrs. Radcliffe *Myst. Udolpho* xxxvi, At some distance among these woods stood a pavilion. **1820** Milner *Suppl. Mem. Eng. Cath.* 313 These authors answered the challenge, each of them in a work of some length. **1867** Freeman *Norm. Conq.* (1877) I. App. 765 The old frontier lies some way to the north. **1869** Tozer *Highl. Turkey* I. 10 The town..is a place of some size.

**d.** With adjs., as *little*, *small*, *considerable*, etc.

**1382** Wyclif *Acts* xv. 33 Sothli sum litil tyme maad there, thei weren dismittid..with pees of bretheren. **1592** *Soliman & Pers.* ii. i, I haue some little replie, if neede require. **1602** Shaks. *Ham.* ii. ii. 14 That you vouch-safe your rest heere in our Court Some little time. **1626** in *Rep. Hist. MSS. Comm.* Var. Coll. (1907) IV. 171 The necessitie of useing some small quantitie of bay salt therein. **1716** Church *Philip's War* (1867) II. 53 Several of his men..was gone some considerable time. **1792** *Gentl. Mag.* 13/2 The bridge ..is some little distance from the main street of Duffield. **1825** Scott *Betrothed* xxviii, Suppose him returning some brief time hence. *a* **1834** Coleridge in *Lit. Rem.* (1836) II. 198 Perhaps, the influence of a princess..may be some little excuse for Albany's weakness. **1902** *Encycl. Brit.* XXVIII. 407/1 Fishes..which swim some little distance above the actual sea-bed.

**e.** *U.S.* In predicative use: Of some account; deserving of consideration.

With quot. 1848 cf. the U.S. colloq. phrase *some pumpkins* s.v. pumpkin 2 b.

**1844** *Spirit of Times* 30 Nov. 474/1 Many people have an idea that the 'big mare' will be 'some' in the race. **1848** Ruxton *Life Far West* (1849) 60 She's 'some' now, that is a fact, and the biggest kind of punkin' at that. **1849** in Bartlett *Dict. Amer.* (1859) s.v., Which was admitted by the oldest inhabitant to be 'some' in the way of cold winters. **1876** 'Mark Twain' *Tom Sawyer* i. 8 Smarty! You think you're *some*, now, don't you. **1890** *Dialect Notes* I. 70 To say of a woman that 'she looks *some*', with emphasis on the *some*.., is equivalent to saying that she looks remarkably well.

**f.** Quite a; a remarkable. Used meiotically, often ironically, to suggest that something or someone is worthy of consideration. *some hope(s)!*: see hope *sb.*[1] 4 a. orig. *U.S.*

**1808** J. Mackintosh in R. J. Mackintosh *Mem. Life Sir J. Mackintosh* (1835) I. viii. 448 You know that Bossuet and Arnauld believed their innocence—some authority. **1855** 'Q. K. P. Doesticks' *Doesticks, what he Says* iv. 28 It was 'some' bridge, in fact, a considerable curiosity, and a 'considerable' bridge. **1914** G. Atherton *Perch of Devil* i. 80 They're some geologists, he added with unwilling admiration. *Ibid.* 108 Butte is some education, believe me. **1925** F. Scott Fitzgerald *Great Gatsby* iii. 60 He smiled with jovial condescension, and added 'some sensation!' Whereupon everybody laughed. **1931** Brophy & Partridge *Songs & Slang Brit. Soldier* (ed. 3) 359 *Some hopes!*, it is most unlikely! **1941** W. S. Churchill *Unrelenting Struggle* (1942) 345 When I warned them [*sc.* the French Government] that Britain would fight on alone whatever they did, their Generals told their Prime Minister and his divided Cabinet: 'In three weeks England will have her neck wrung like a chicken.' Some chicken! Some neck! **1958** 'J. Byrom' *Or be he Dead* v. 69 'I gather you have Miss Canning as your assistant sleuth!'.. 'Some hope'..a good secretary always has to be in love with her boss!' **1976** A. Price *War Game* i. 66 'David has us to console him.'.. 'Some consolation!' murmured Frances. **1977** J. Wainwright *Do Nothin' till you hear from Me* x. 176 'Some band,' murmurs Ted—and there is suppressed excitement in his voice. I say, 'Ted—believe me—this is going to *be* some band.'

**5.** ***some other*** (see other *a.* 5 b).

*c* **950** *Lindisf. Gosp.* Luke xvii. 12 Mið-ðy innfoerde sum oðer werc. *c* **1000** Ælfric *Saints' Lives* xxxi. 691 Se ylca sulpicius and sum oðer broðor. *c* **1200** Ormin 7476 þatt teȝȝ ..shollden..farenn ham till here land All wiþþ summ oþerr weȝȝe. **1303** R. Brunne *Handl. Synne* 3470 As yn cherche to synge or rede, Or of sum oþer holy dede. **1362** Langl. *P. Pl.* A. viii. 34 Sette scolers to scole or to sum oþer craft. *c* **1449** Pecock *Repr.* iii. iv. 302 He which is ouerer.. schulde louȝe him silf in sum other maner. **1560** Whitehorne *Ord. Souldiours* (1588) 6 The residue of the men..may be placed some other where. **1596** *Edw. III*, iv. vii, O, that I were some other countryman! **1611** [see other *a.* 5 b]. **1640** tr. *Verdere's Rom. of Rom.* II. 193, I will take the power to love some otherwhere. **1699** R. L'Estrange *Erasm. Colloq.* (1725) 200 He concluded to take some other Priest with him. **1732** [see other *a.* 5 b]. *a* **1845** [see otherwhere c]. **1858** Hawthorne *Ancestral Footstep* (1883) 514 The old Hospitaller must die in his bed, or some other how.

**6.** Followed by *certain* or *one* with limiting force (cf. one B. 7).

**1561**, **1591** [see certain *a.* 7 b]. **1565** Cooper *Thesaurus, Vnus aliquis*, some one man. **1655** Stanley *Hist. Philos.* (1687) 62/1 Respiring Flames at some certain part. **1746** Francis tr. *Horace, Epist.* ii. i. 53 Some certain Point should finish the Debate. *Ibid.* 76 In some one Excellence their Merit lies. **1865** Ruskin *Sesame* ii. §72 She should..follow at least some one path of scientific attainment.

**II.** With plural nouns.

**7. a.** Certain (taken individually).

Also with limiting terms as *certain*, *other*: cf. 5 and 6.

*c* **888** K. Ælfred *Boeth.* xxv, þæt ælc ȝesceaft bið healdon locen wið hire ȝecynde,..buton monnum & sumum englum. *a* **1122** *O.E. Chron.* (Laud MS.) an. 1119, Wæs mycel eorðbifung on suman steodan her on lande. *c* **1200** Ormin 11214 Affterr þatt sume wise menn O lare itt unnderrstanndenn. *c* **1250** *Owl & Night.* 879 Þeyh summe men beon þurhut gode. *a* **1300** *Cursor M.* 19550 þof summen mai baptise Mai naman..Conferming giue, bot biscop hand. **1340** *Ayenb.* 196 Zom uolk byeþ þet onworþeþ þe poure. **1422** tr. *Secreta Secret., Priv. Priv.* 132 Sum Pryncis ther bene, that..takyn atte har talent trew men goodis. *c* **1491** *Chast. Goddes Chyld.* 53 In somm outwarde signes the prophecye of the deuyll may be knowen. **1526** *Pilgr. Perf.* (W. de W. 1531) 6 Some persones..wyll muse or meruayle. **1562** Winȝet *Wks.* (S.T.S.) I. 23 The durris.. wes calket also with sum notes of dishonour. **1596** Shaks. *Rich. III*, i. iv. 125 Some certaine dregges of conscience are yet within mee. **1651** Hobbes *Leviath.* iv. xlvi. 374 Some.. bodies sink naturally downwards. **1696** [C. Leslie] *Snake in Grass* 88, I wou'd advise some Friends to go to the Dancing-School, and learn a more Gentle and Graceful Mien. **1723** Dk. Wharton *True Briton* No. 24. I. 208, I have heard some People very large in their Exclamations against Creeds and Forms of Faith. **1776** *Trial of Nundocomar* 23/1 Some days he has violent purgings, at other times he gets better. **1826** *Art of Brewing* (ed. 2) 15 Some gentlemen, however,.. have studied the subject more particularly. **1855** J. Phillips *Man. Geol.* 498 Oligoclase occurs in some granites. **1867** Ruskin *Time & Tide* i. §3 Every nation is fitted..for some particular employments or manufactures.

†**b.** With article or pronoun accompanying the noun. (Cf. A. 5 c.) *Obs.*

*c* **893** K. Ælfred *Oros.* i. i. 18 þa teð hie brohton sume þæm cyninge. *c* **1000** Ælfric *Hom.* II. 448 Ðe maȝon ȝehyran sume his ðeawes. *c* **1000** *Ags. Gosp.* Matt. ix. 3 Ða cwædon hiȝ sume þa boceras him betwynan. *c* **1120** *O.E. Chron.* an. 1119, Sume þa castelas he mid strengðe ȝenam. *c* **1205** Lay. 12001 Summe þe scipen wunden forð mid þan wederen. **1297** R. Glouc. (Rolls) 2718 So þat some þe messagers to kermerdin come.

**c.** ***some*...(*other*) *some***, some...other(s). †Also with *than*, and ellipt. for *sometimes*.

*c* **888** K. Ælfred *Boeth.* xxxiv. §10 Sumra wyrta..eard bið on dunum,..sumra on merscum, sumra on morum. *c* **1000** Ælfric *Hom.* II. 48 Sume lareowas sindon beteran ðonne sume. **1377** Langl. *P. Pl.* B. xv. 95 Þere somme bowes ben leued and somme bereth none. **1430–40** Lydg. *Bochas* ix. xxxviii. L'Envoi, Some folke appayre, some dothe amende. **1551** [see other some]. **1611** Shaks. *Wint. T.* iii. iii. 20 Sometimes her head on one side, some another. **1651–1875** [see other some].

**8. a.** A certain number of; a few at least.

*a* **1122** *O.E. Chron.* (Laud MS.) an. 1048, Ða he wæs sume mila oððe mare beheonan Dofran, þa dyde he on his byrnan. **1589** Puttenham *Eng. Poesie* (Arb.) 235, I know..Your some sweete smiles, your some, but louely lowrs. **1610** Shaks. *Tempest* i. ii. 145 They hurried vs a-boord a Barke, Bore vs some Leagues to Sea. **1617** Moryson *Itin.* i. 208 Some flaggons of rich wine, some very white bisket, some pruines and raisins. **1726** Shelvocke *Voy. r. World* 30 To dig a small garden to sow some Lettices, and other sort of sallading. **1785** [Mrs. Grant of Laggan] *Lett.* (1807) II. 96

The house has no other inhabitant at present than an old Sybil..and some legions of rooks and daws. **1822** SCOTT *Nigel* x, It costs but..the journey of some brief days. **1842** LOUDON *Suburban Hort.* 95 The middle and hinder ones die after some weeks' struggle for existence. **1887** *Field* 12 Nov. 734/2 Displaying his science by some beautiful casts.

**b.** In adverbial expressions of time.

**1382** WYCLIF *Acts* x. 48 Thanne thei preieden him, that he schulde dwelle with hem summe dayes.

**1602** in Morris *Troubles Cath. Foref.* (1872) I. iv. 192 My abode..hath been for some years..in London. **1661** *12th Rep. Hist. MSS. Comm.* App. V. 6 Gervise Lucas served.. as gentleman of his horse some years. **1709** MANLEY *Secr. Mem.* (1736) I. 175 A comical Adventure happened to her some Nights ago. **1712** STEELE *Spect.* No. 322 ⁋2 Some Years ago it happened that [etc.]. **1821** MOORE *Mem.* (1853) III. 273 Have not been very well these some days past. **1859** GEO. ELIOT *A. Bede* xxix, We shall meet with better feelings some months hence. **1891** E. PEACOCK *N. Brendon* I. 119 He has been here some years.

**c.** With addition of *few*.

**1582** ALLEN *Martyrdom Campion* (1908) 36 This blessed man,..of whose life I thought good to set downe some few lines also. **1626** BACON *Sylva* §470 If some few Pertusions be made in the Pot. **1665** BOYLE *Occas. Refl.* IV. xiv. (1848) 251 We..caught more in some few Minutes than we had taken in a whole hour before. **1820** KEATS *Isabella* xxxiv, For some few gasping moments. **1847** GROTE *Hist. Greece* (1862) III. xxv. 7 They had some few towns.

**9. a.** Used with numbers to indicate an approximate amount or estimate, and passing into an adv. with the sense 'about, nearly, approximately'. Also *U.S.*, following a numeral.

*c* **888** K. ÆLFRED *Boeth.* xxxviii. §1 þa wæron hi sume ten ȝear on þam ȝewinne. *c* **900** *O.E. Chron.* (Parker MS.) an. 896, þær wurdon..sume feower cyninges þegnas ofslæȝene. *c* **1205** LAY. 28983 þa wunede bi-ȝeonde þere Hunbre.. drenches sume sixe. **1567** MAPLET *Gr. Forest* 84b, The floud Ganges hath Eles some 30 Foote long. **1582** in W. H. Turner *Select. Rec. Oxford* (1880) 424 Some three or fower acres of woode. **1632** MASSINGER *Fatal Dowry* II. ii, They skip into my lord's cast skins some twice a year. **1668** DRYDEN *Even. Love* II. i, I have some three hundred pistoles by me. **1787** BURNS *Auld Farmer's Salut.* iv, It's now some nine-an'-twenty year. **1836** MRS. CARLYLE *Lett.* I. 56 We expect John Carlyle in some ten days. **1865** RUSKIN *Sesame* i. §33 This collection..would probably have been some thousand or twelve hundred pounds. **1892** *Photogr. Ann.* II. 648 The club consists of some 40 members. **1968** *Time* 19 Jan. 7/2 Twenty-some years ago, when I was a nurse on the U.S.S. *Hope*. **1971** R. A. CARTER *Manhattan Primitive* (1972) xi. 104 He's thirty years old, with..a master's degree and forty-some hours towards a doctorate. **1980** in S. Terkel *Amer. Dreams* 2 There were sixty-some contestants from all over the place.

**b.** With numerals denoting the time of day.

**1596** SHAKS. *Tam. Shr.* IV. iii. 189, I thinke 'tis now some seuen a clocke. **1848** THACKERAY *Van. Fair* xxxii, At some ten o'clock the clinking of a sabre might have been heard.

**c.** Hence with singular nouns expressing time, distance, amount, etc.

(*a*) **1592** SHAKS. *Rom. & Jul.* V. iii. 257 When I came (some Minute ere the time Of her awaking). **1596** —— *Merch. V.* III. ii. 9, I would detaine you here some month or two. **1822** SOUTHEY *Lett.* (1856) III. 348 A note from Murray some fortnight ago let me know [etc.]. **1875** B. MEADOWS *Clin. Obs.* 20 Face..not so free as some week or two back.

(*b*) **1595** *Drake's Voy.* (Hakl. Soc.) 7 We came to anchor some saker shott from a forte. **1601** R. JOHNSON *Kingd. & Commw.* (1603) 86 Distant from the towne some halfe mile. **1617** MORYSON *Itin.* I. 191 Some halfe musket shot distance. **1857** HUGHES *Tom Brown* I. iii, Which was distant some mile or so from the school. **1883** C. J. WILLS *Mod. Persia* 203 Some mile and a half through the deserted streets.

(*c*) **1846** S. WILBERFORCE *Sp. Missions* (1874) 98 In order that the English people might buy that luxury some penny a pound cheaper.

**III. 10.** With *other*, *one*, *few*, etc., used absolutely in sing. or plur.

(*a*) *c* **950** *Lindisf. Gosp.* Matt. xiii. 4 Sum oðer ȝefeollon neh woeȝ. *Ibid.* Luke ix. 27 Sint sume oðera her stondað ðaðe [etc.]. **1484** CAXTON *Fables of Auian* v, The leche whiche wylle hele somme other, ought fyrste to hele hym self. **1513** DOUGLAS *Æneid* VI. xv. 7 Sum wtheris better can thair causis pleid. **1592** *Soliman & Pers.* IV. ii, I would my maister had left some other to be his agent here. **1603** KNOLLES *Hist. Turks* (1621) 53 Some other in the meane time playing with his nose, and bobbing him in the face. **1760–2** GOLDSM. *Cit. W.* xiv. ⁋3 There is Seneca, and Bolingbroke, and some others.

(*b*) **1546** *Supplic. Poore Commons* (E.E.T.S.) 85 Perhappes some one of vs hathe hylded C. shepe. **1598–9** HAKLUYT *Voy.* II. I. 56 Most rich & precious stones, some one of which is of more value then a whole kingdome. **1886** C. E. PASCOE *Lond. of To-day* xlii. (ed. 3) 366 To admire and covet, if not to buy, some one of its treasures.

(*c*) **1582** ALLEN *Martyrdom Campion* (1908) 16 Meaning by the state..the welfare of some few..upholden by this new religion. **1621** BP. MOUNTAGU *Diatribæ* 526 Vnlesse *some few, & Many* in your language be all one. *a* **1648** LD. HERBERT *Hen. VIII* (1683) 426 The use that may be made of some few, as two or three in euery Shire. **1735** *Gentl. Mag.* Feb. 106/1 Some few were well dress'd. **1875** HELPS *Soc. Press.* ix. 124 We think—at least, some few of us do—that [etc.].

(*d*) **1601** SHAKS. *Jul. C.* I. iii. 122 Some certaine of the Noblest minded Romans. **1607** —— *Cor.* II. iii. 59 Some certaine of your Brethren.

**C.** *adv.* (See also B. 9.)

**1.** With comparatives: A little; slightly; somewhat. Chiefly *Sc.* and *north.*

*a* **1560** ROLLAND *Crt. Venus* I. 662 Quhill time this corps be sum better applyit. **1636** RUTHERFORD *Lett.* (1862) I. 172 My Well-beloved is some kinder..than ordinary. **1667** O. HEYWOOD *Heart-Treas.* xvi. (1825) II. 219, I am rich still, as rich as ever I was, and some richer. **1741** A. MONRO *Anat.* (ed. 3) 207 The superior bulbous Part of this Bone forms some less than the inferior Half of that..Cavity. **1785** BURNS *To W. Simpson* Postscr. xiii, I hope we..ken some better. **1807** P. GASS *Jrnl.* 219 Yesterday we gave him an Indian sweat, and he is some better to day. **1892** HESLOP *Northumbld. Gloss.* 669 She's some better thi day.

**2.** With verbs: **a.** A certain amount; a little.

**1699** O. HEYWOOD *Diaries* (1885) IV. 162 She bled some still. **1821** *Joseph the Book-Man* 17 Joe in his day had travell'd some. **1822** HOGG *Tales & Sk.* (1837) VI. 272 He spoke some to himself likewise, but it was only one short sentence. **1834** J. HALL *Kentucky* II. 40, I hunt some, and snake a little. **1842** DICKENS in Foster *Life* III. iv, He may walk some, perhaps—not much. **1909** *Lady's Realm* Feb. 468/2 He hunted some, and fished some.

**b.** *U.S.* To some extent; in some degree; somewhat.

The variations of American usage are very fully illustrated in Thornton's *Amer. Gloss.* (1912) 827–9.

**1745** J. EMERSON *Jrnl.* 8 Apr. in *Mass. Hist. Soc. Proc.* (1911) XLIV. 74, I read some in Watson. **1785** *Massachusetts Spy* 28 Apr. 2/3 (Advt.), A tall stout looking fellow,..stammers some in his speech. **1817** *Essex Inst. Hist. Coll.* (1866) VIII. 228 The material of which it is built looks some like marble. **1825** in Thornton *Amer. Gloss.* s.v., [You are] on the huffy order, some, to night. **1843** J. G. WHITTIER in Pickard *Life* (1894) I. 281, I think some of attending the great anti-slavery convention. **1863** DICEY *Federal St.* I. 225 It used to amuse me some..to find that the slaveholders wanted more territory [etc.]. **1889** *Anthony's Photogr. Bulletin* II. 206 Having been troubled some of late to get clear results.

**c.** *U.S.* In emphatic use: Very much, very well, etc.

**1866** LOWELL *Biglow P.* Ser. II. *The Courtin'* xiii, Thet night, I tell ye, she looked *some*! **1894** 'G. EGERTON' *Key-note* 9 'How you love young things!' she says. 'Some.'

**d.** *to go some*: to go well or fast; to do well; to work hard. *slang* (orig. *U.S.*).

*a* **1911** D. G. PHILLIPS *Susan Lenox* (1917) II. ii. 24 He had evidently been 'going some' for several days; the sour, worn, haggard face..suggested a moth-eaten jaguar. **1912** J. SANDILANDS *Western Canad. Dict. & Phrase-Bk.* s.v. *Some*, *That's going some* may mean great speed or excellence of workmanship, or it may even be used in reference to the speed at which a person races to his ruin. **1915** WODEHOUSE *Psmith, Journalist* x. 71, I guess we're making a hit. *Cosy Moments* is going some now. **1966** 'J. HACKSTON' *Father clears Out* 173 He had the easy movements of the retriever, and for a big dog could go some. **1973** J. WAINWRIGHT *Touch of Malice* 8 A uniformed inspector..with..less than five years service under his belt. Jesus—that was going some! **1982** H. LIEBERMAN *Night Call* viii. 47 He'd known the girl for two months; for Daughtry that was going some.

**3.** *dial.* and *U.S.* With adjs. (rarely with advs.): Somewhat.

*c* **1780** in *Amer. Speech 1969* (1973) XLIV. 304 Until it gets some darker. **1817** in Thornton *Amer. Gloss.* s.v., His clothes were some bloody. **1839** MARRYAT *Diary Amer.* Ser. I. II. 226 'Are you cold, miss?' said I to a young lady... 'Some,' was the reply. **1851** STERNBERG *Northampt. Dial.* s.v., It war some wet. **1858–61** E. B. RAMSAY *Remin.* (1870) p. xxi, The heat has made your skin some tender. **1913** [see GUN-PLAY]. **1940** W. FAULKNER *Hamlet* I. ii. 31 We had done been feeding it [*sc.* a horse] for two-three days now by forced draft..and it looked some better now than when we had brung it home. **1956** G. E. EVANS *Ask Fellows who cut Hay* xxv. 231 An old worker..turned the handle and tried it with a few roots. Asked what he thought of it he said with conviction: 'It's some stiff, maaster.' **1976** M. MACHLIN *Pipeline* iv. 44 He's going to be some pissed off when he finds out about this.

**D.** *sb.* An unspecified amount, person, thing, etc. *rare.*

**1830** GALT *Lawrie Todd* II. v, I have myself obstinacious objections—a considerable some—against 'em here parley voos. **1850** L. HUNT *Autobiogr.* xxiv. 381 Some whim, some enjoyment,..with a thousand other somes and probabilities.

†**some**, *sb.*[2] *Obs.* [OE. *sóm*, ablaut-variant of the stem *sam-*: see SAME *a.*] Agreement, concord, peace. Usu. coupled with *saught*(*ness*) or *sib.* (Cf. SOME *a.*[2])

*c* **1000** ÆLFRIC *Hom.* II. 198 Ðam dom-bocum þe se Heofenlica Wealdend his folce ȝesette to some, and to sehtnysse. *a* **1011** *Laws Ethelred* vi. 25 (Liebermann), Beo eallum Cristenum mannum sibb and som ȝemæne, and ælc sacu totwæmed. *c* **1205** LAY. 4099 Heo speken þer to sæhte, to sibbe and to some. *c* **1225** *Ancr. R.* 426 þis is o þing,..þet is God leouest—seihnesse & some. *c* **1275** *Holy Church* 15 in *O.E. Misc.*, For hi heolden cristes men myd sib and myd some.

†**some**, *sb.*[3] *Obs. rare.* [a. OF. *some* (mod.F. *somme*) horse-load.] The number of twelve thousand (nails or needles).

The use survives in mod.F. (Littré s.v. *Somme*).

**1539–40** in *Archaeol. Cant.* (1893) XX. 243, 2 'some' of 'sprygg' 10s. **1545** *Rates of Customs* b viij b, Nidels, the some conteinynge xii M., xs. *Ibid.* c iij, Patten nayles the some, iis.

**some**, obs. form of SOAM, SUM *sb.*

**some**, *a.*[1]: see SOME *indef. pron.*

†**some**, *a.*[2] *Obs.* [Reduced form of I-SOME *a.*]

**1.** United, reconciled; at peace, friendly. Chiefly in phr. ***saught and some***. (Cf. SOME *sb.*[2])

*c* **1205** LAY. 9883 þus heo weoren sahte & þus heo weoren some. *c* **1320** *Cast. Love* 520, I chul fleon and neuere come. Bote my sustren ben sauȝt and some. *Ibid.* 552 Maken Ichulle..Pees and Riht cussen and be sauȝt and some. *a* **1400** *Chron. R. Glouc.* (Rolls) 52 Of þe folc of denemarch þat ȝuyt ne buþ nouȝt some.

**2.** Characterized by peacefulness or quiet.

*c* **1400** *Beryn* 3233 And eke of thy condicioune both sofft & some.

**some**, obs. form of SAME *a.*

*a* **1400–50** *Alexander* (D.) 2063 þe some [*v.r.* selfe] sendesman he in þe sale fyndez.

**-some**, *suffix*[1], representing OE. *-sum*, = OFris. *-sum*, related by ablaut to OS. and OHG. *-sam* (G. *-sam*, Du. *-zaam*), ON. *-samr* (Sw. *-sam*, Da. *-som*), Goth. *-sams*, used in OE. to form adjs. from nouns and adjs., as *friðsum* peaceful, *ȝenyhtsum* abundant, *ánsum* whole, *langsum* lasting, rarely from verbs, as *hýrsum*, *héarsum* obedient. A few of the OE. formations survived in early ME., but only two or three are now in use, as *longsome*, *lovesome*, *winsome*. In ME. a number of new examples appear, some of which soon became obsolete, as *beisome*, *folȝsome*, *friendsome*, *lustsome*, *wlatsome*, while others (chiefly dating from the 14th century) have remained current, as *cumbersome*, *fulsome*, *gamesome*, *gladsome*, *handsome*, *lightsome*, *loathsome*, *noisome*, *wholesome*. The early ME. *buhsum*, *buxum* is now represented by *buxom*, in which the suffix is disguised. In the 16th century appear *awesome*, *brightsome*, *darksome*, *healthsome*, *heartsome*, *quarrelsome*, and the unusual formation *timorsome*. Of later date are *adventuresome*, *bothersome*, *fearsome*, *frightsome*, *lonesome*, *plaguesome*, etc., and various nonce-formations as *clipsome*, *cuddlesome*, *dabblesome*, *divertsome*, some of which have a passive, others an active, sense.

**-some**, *suffix*[2], representing OE. *sum* after numerals in the genitive plural: see SOME *indef. pron.* 3. In ME. the inflexion disappeared, and the pronoun was finally treated as a suffix to the numeral, chiefly with the simple numbers from two to ten; for the history of these see TWOSOME, THREESOME, etc. Other examples are rare, and the *some* may be written as a separate word.

In OS. and OFris. *sum* was similarly used with the gen. pl., as OS. *fahora sum* (one of a few), OFris. *twira-*, *thrira-*, *fiuwerasum*, etc.; the latter are still represented by WFris. *tware-*, *trijere-*, *fjouweresom*, etc.

*a* **1300** *Cursor M.* 5233 Quen þai war gedir al to-gedir, Sex and sexti sum o liues þai war. *c* **1400** *Brut* 236 And also he commandede..þat þai shulde bene put in tuenty-some and in hundredsome. *c* **1470** HENRY *Wallace* IX. 440 Off Scottis men thai semblyt hastely Nyne hundyr sum off worthi chewalry.

**-some**, *suffix*[3], later var. of -SUM *suffix*, occurring in a few words, as WHATSOME, WHERESOME, WHOSOME. Cf. SOMEVER.

**-some**, *suffix*[4], f. Gr. σῶμα body; (*a*) used with this sense, as in *ectosome* s.v. ECTO- *trophosome* s.v. TROPHO-; (*b*) used to form words denoting an intracellular particle, as in ACROSOME, CHROMOSOME, LYSOSOME; (*c*) used to repr. *chromosome*, as in DISOME, MONOSOME 1.

**1921** [see *hexasome* s.v. HEXA-].

**somebody** ('sʌmbədɪ), *sb.* Also 6–8 **some body**. [f. SOME *a.*[1] 2 + BODY *sb.* 13.]

**1. a.** A person unknown, indeterminate, or unnamed; someone, some person.

**1303** R. BRUNNE *Handl. Synne* 3785 þou mayst be wroþe, sum body to chastyse, þogh hate nat yn þy herte ryse. **1526** TINDALE *Luke* viii. 46 And Iesus sayd: Someboody touched me. **1592** *Ard. of Feversham* III. v, Soft, Ales, for here comes some body. **1623** in Ellis *Orig. Lett.* Ser. I. III. 149 If wee should goe away without leaving somboddie behynd us. **1710** ADDISON *Tatler* No. 155 ⁋2, I heard some body at a Distance hemming after me. **1779** *Mirror* No. 17, I cannot help expressing my suspicion, that Mrs. Rebecca Prune has got somebody to write her letter. **1841** BROWNING *Pippa Passes* Poems (1905) 173 Take the pipe out of his mouth, somebody. **1891** FREEMAN in W. R. W. Stephens *Life & Lett.* (1895) II. 428 That is just what I want some-body to do to me.

**b.** ***somebody else***, some other person. Cf. *someone else* s.v. SOME ONE, SOMEONE *pron.* (and *sb.*).

The older form of the possessive, *somebody's else*, has now given way to *somebody else's* (see ELSE *adv.* 1 d).

**1648** HEXHAM II, *Yemandt anders*, Some body else. **1655** OWEN *Vindic. Evang.* Wks. 1851 XII. 263 That blood was not Christ's, but somebody's else that He loved. **1716** M. DAVIES *Athen. Brit.* II. 21 The Author of such Legal Formularies, tho' they had been rough-drawn by his Clerk or some Body else. **1718** J. FOX *Wanderer* 86 To heighten their own Vanity, or some Body's else. **1825** J. NEAL *Bro. Jonathan* II. 27 A kind of shadow, which made me feel as if I had seen it, before,..or somebody else, very much like him. **1860** [see ELSE *adv.* 1 d]. **1892** ZANGWILL *Bow Myst.* 109 All the seats were numbered, so that everybody might have the satisfaction of occupying somebody else's.

(*b*) Also with sense 'a rival for the affections' in phr. ***there*** (or ***it***) ***is somebody else***.

**1911** G. B. SHAW *Getting Married* 200 You have never given me a real reason for refusing me yet. I once thought it was somebody else. There were lots of fellows after you. **1935** D. L. SAYERS *Gaudy Night* xii. 260 'I suppose,' he said in a savage tone, 'there's somebody else.' **1946** 'BRAHMS' & 'SIMON' *Trottie True* iii. 37 'I know what it is.' Joe tried to stop himself but he couldn't. 'There's somebody else.'

**c.** With article or pron.

**1724** SWIFT *Drapier's Lett.* Wks. 1755 V. II. 74 Somebody in England empowered a second somebody to write to a third somebody here. **1786** MRS. A. M. BENNETT *Juvenile Indiscr.* V. 30 He was a somebody he was acquainted with. **1802–12** BENTHAM *Ration. Judic. Evid.* (1827) IV. 26 There is a somebody who is responsible for it, and that somebody is he. **1869** DUNKIN *Midn. Sky* p. ii, It has been the earnest desire of the author to be the 'somebody' of Carlyle. **1871** BROWNING *Balaustion* 308 There spoke up a brisk little somebody.

**d.** Used as a substitute for a personal name. Also ***somebody-or(-the)-other***.

**1825** COBBETT *Rur. Rides* (1853) 346 At Send, or Sutton, ..there is a Baron somebody, with a De before his name. **1842** LOVER *Handy Andy* xxxii, Up came an *aide-de-camp*.., telling him that General Somebody ordered him to bring up his guns. **1867** AUGUSTA WILSON *Vashti* xviii, My boy thinks that the opinion of this Professor Von Somebody is oracular in musical matters. **1935** D. L. SAYERS *Gaudy Night* xii. 255 Mr. Somebody-or-the-other had undertaken ..to climb every tree in St. Giles. **1976** 'L. BLACK' *Healthy Way to Die* iii. 29 The two girls..were the Daughters of Lord Somebody-or-other.

**2. a.** A person of some note, consequence, or importance. Freq. with depreciatory or sarcastic force.

*a* **1566** R. EDWARDS *Damon & Pithias* in Dodsley *O. Pl.* (1744) I. 229 Ere you came hyther, poore I was some body, The king delighted in me, now I am but a noddy. **1590** STOCKWOOD *Rules Constit.* 62 Schollers, which thinke themselues som bodie. **1678** MARVELL *Growth Popery* 33 That they may be thought Some-body. **1704** *Pennsylv. Hist. Soc. Mem.* IX. 345 A desire to be somebody..seems to be the rule of his life. **1755** *Mem. Capt. P. Drake* II. iii. 88, I.. hired a handsome Horse and Furniture, that I might look like somebody. **1835** *Court Mag.* VI. 188/2 The woman who fancies herself *somebody*. **1856** EMERSON *Eng. Traits, Manners* Wks. (Bohn) II. 46 You must be somebody; then you may do this or that, as you will.

**b.** With *a* and pl.

**1601** DENT *Pathw. Heaven* 163 We see many, that think themselues some bodies,..which yet will be taken with it. **1647** TRAPP *Expos. Luke* vii. 28 They are somebodies in heaven, whatever men make of them. *a* **1848** MARRYAT *Valerie* x. (1856) 159 People who are somebodies. **1880** MRS. LYNN LINTON *Rebel of Family* ii, Her dress was expensive, and she was evidently a Somebody. **1899** *Educat. Rev.* Oct. 222 Which exasperates somebodies who feel they are treated as nobodies.

**3.** A person whose name is intentionally suppressed; occas., the Devil. ***somebody up there***, God; a supernatural controlling power.

**1606** SHAKS. *Tr. & Cr.* I. i. 45, I would not (as they tearme it) praise it, but I wold some-body had heard her talke yesterday as I did. **1844** DICKENS *Mart. Chuz.* xxxviii, There is a deeper impression of Somebody's Hoof here. **1972** *Dict. Contemp. & Colloq. Usage* 27/3 *Somebody up there loves (hates) me*, an expression attributing one's good or bad luck..upon being in the good or bad graces of an unseen power above. **1975** J. UPDIKE *Month of Sundays* xxx. 225 In the land of my parish, the shortest day of the year is approaching, and somebody's birthday, I think. **1977** R. PERRY *Dead End* i. 9 All I could do was..pray that somebody up there loved me. **1980** *Times* 10 June 10/1 (*heading*) Somebody up there cares for me.

† **somechare**, *adv. Obs.* In 3 sumchere. [f. SOME *a.*[1] + CHARE *sb.*[1]] On one occasion; some time.

*a* **1225** *Juliana* 4 As he sumchere iseh hire utnume feir,.. he felde him iwundet. *c* **1230** *Hali Meid.* 11 þah ha falewi sum chere mid misliche þohtes.

**somed**, variant of SAMED *adv. Obs.*; obs. var. SUMMED *ppl. a.*

ˈ**someday**, *adv.* [f. SOME *a.*[1] 2 + DAY *sb.*] At some future time. Cf. DAY *sb.* 7 b.

Earlier examples of *some day* as a two-word phrase will be found s.v. SOME *a.* 2 b (*b*).

**1898** G. B. SHAW *Candida* I, in *Plays Pleasant* 94 Theyll ave to give you somethink someday, if it's honly to stop yore mouth. **1902** W. B. YEATS *Cathleen ni Hoolihan* 13 220 We might be put in the way of making Patrick a priest someday, and he so good at his books. **1921** G. B. SHAW *Back to Methuselah* v. 221 Something or other must make an end of you someday. **1939** JOYCE *Finnegans Wake* 119 A tea anyway for a tryst someday. **1940** W. FAULKNER *Hamlet* II. i. 110 He could almost see the husband which she would someday have. **1958** [see MURPHY[2] 3]. **1966** *Punch* 24 Aug. 294 Won't someday a three-minute montage provide a more significant aesthetic treat than a sonnet? **1978** *Amer. Poetry Rev.* July/Aug. 31/3 It will clutch at a heart it did not seem to know, and someday die.

**somedeal** (ˈsʌmdiːl), *sb.*, *adv.*, and *a.* Now *arch.* or *dial.* Forms: 1 **sum dæl**, 2 **summ del**, 4 **sum del(l**, 6 *Sc.* **sum deill, deyll**; 1 (*adv.*) **sume daeli, dæle**, 3 **sume dale**, 4–5 **some dele** (5 **som dele, somme del**), 6–7 **some deale**, 6– **some deal**; 1, 3–5 **sumdel** (5 **summedel**, 5, 9 *dial.* **sumdell**), 3–4 **somdel** (4 **zom-**), 5 **so(u)mdell**, 5, 9 *dial.* **somdell**, 4–5 **somedel** (6 **-dell**); 5–6 **sumdele** (6 **-deale**), *Sc.* **-deil(l**; 4 **somdiel**, 5 *Sc.* **-deill**, 5 **-deele**, 5–6 **-dele, -deale**; 4–6 **somedele**, 5–7 **-deale**, 6– **somedeal** (6 **-deall**). [f. OE. *sum* SOME *a.*[1] 4 b + *dǽl* DEAL *sb.*[1] In advb. use partly representing the OE. instrumental forms *sume dǽle*.]

**A.** *sb.* Some part or portion *of* some thing or things; some, somewhat.

*a* **900** *O.E. Chron.* (Parker MS.) an. 785, Iaenbryht ærcebisc. forlet sumne dæl his bisc'domes. **922** in Birch *Cartul. Sax.* II. 313 Ic sylle sumne dæl londes. *a* **1122** *O.E. Chron.* (Laud MS.) Pref., Scotta sum dæl ȝewat of Ybernian on Brittene. *c* **1200** ORMIN 1106 Nu habbe icc shæwedd ȝuw summ del Off þa Judisskenn lakess. *c* **1320** *Cast. Love* 1371 Sumdel ȝe habbeþ i-herd nou riht Of his strengþe and of his miht. **1375** BARBOUR *Bruce* v. 358 Thai..thaim defendit weill, Till of thair men war slane sumdeill. **1502** ATKYNSON tr. *De Imitatione* II. x. (1893) 188 All worldly & bodely plesurs be..mixte with somdele of vnclenes. **1553** GRIMALDE *Cicero's Offices* I. (1558) 10 Somdeale of our birth our contrey, somedeale our parentes,..do claime. **1593** G. HARVEY *Pierce's Super.* Wks. (Grosart) II. 81 Some deale of Selfe-liking. **1896** CROCKETT *Grey Man* x, You have had some deal of that too.

**b.** *dial.* A considerable number *of* people.

**1851** STERNBERG *Dial. & Folk-Lore Northants* 101 'Was there many people at your feast?' 'Ees, theer war some-deal o' folk.'

**B.** *adv.* In some degree or measure; to some extent; somewhat; partly: **a.** In general use.

*c* **725** *Corpus Gloss.* P 4 *Partim*, sumedaeli. **1154** *O.E. Chron.* an. 1137, Nu we willen sæȝen sumdel wat belamp on Stephnes kinges time. *c* **1205** LAY. 1183 Milc wes i þere scale, & win sume dale [*c* **1275** somdel]. *c* **1290** *S. Eng. Leg.* I. 118 A taillage it is, and sumdel with vnriȝte i-take. *c* **1340** *Ayenb.* 268 þaȝ ich zomdel þis onderstonde. *c* **1380** *Sir Ferumb.* 4238 Hym semede þan it was a knyȝt,..And sumdel was agaste. *c* **1440** *Pallad. on Husb.* XIII. 84 Lord,..do me sumdel rise Thy self in hym to se. *a* **1533** FRITH *Answ. More* (1548) O viij b, I doubte not..but that it doth some deal vexe you. **1579** SPENSER *Sheph. Cal.* May 56 Thou lackest somedele their delight. **1650** T. B[AYLEY] *Worcester's Apoph.* Ep. Ded. 1 Some-deale a pretender unto gratitude. **1849** ROCK *Ch. of Fathers* II. 143 *note*, It would seem, that ornament..varied some deal in shape. **1854** MISS BAKER *Northampt. Gloss.*, *Som-dell*, in some measure, somewhat. **1896** BURGESS *Lowra Biglan* 45 They had got into a way of sitting by themselves some deal of late.

**b.** Qualifying a following adj., adv., or pa. pple.

*a* **1225** *Leg. Kath.* 669 Ha wes sumdel offruht & offearet. *c* **1225** *Ancr. R.* 20 Ȝif hit is halidei, buweð sumdel duneward. *c* **1300** *Beket* 95 This Gilbert him huld Somdel stille. *c* **1386** CHAUCER *Prol.* 446 A good Wif was ther.., But sche was somdel deef. *c* **1440** *Partonope* 3120 Hit was nyght and somdele derk. *c* **1450** *Knt. de la Tour* cix. 148 By as moche as she was sumdel abaisshed. **1524** *State P. Hen. VIII* (1836) IV. 210 Her Grace was somedeall busyed to make us a good aunsuer. **1592** R. D. *Hypnerotomachia* 14 The vpper part of a womans head some deale bare. **1605** JONSON *Volpone* v. vi. [x.], I'le not iustifie The other, but he may be some-deale faulty. **1819** TENNANT *Papistry Storm'd* (1827) 69 Though somedeal auld, In spreit yet juvenil and bauld. **1828** SCOTT *F.M. Perth* xvii, Though we know he was somedeal hurt in that matter.

**c.** With comparatives.

*c* **1000** *Sax. Leechd.* I. 144 Seo [wyrt] hæfð sume dæle læssan leaf ðonne docce. *c* **1200** *Trin. Coll. Hom.* 3 Hit lasteð þre wuke fulle and sum del more. *c* **1300** *Havelok* 2950 The feste of his coruning Laste..Fourti dawes, and sumdel mo. ? *a* **1366** CHAUCER *Rom. Rose* 118 From an hille..Cam doun the streme.., And somedele lasse it was than Seyn. *c* **1374** —— *Boeth.* I. pr. v. (1868) 25 For whiche we wile vsen somedel lyȝter medicines. *c* **1450** *Bk. Curtasye* 808 in *Babees Bk.*, I let hit here ouer passe, To make oure talkyng summedelasse. **1565** JEWEL *Reply Harding* Pref. (1611) 7 Yet am I now some deale the more satisfied by these your trauels. **1583** STUBBES *Anat. Abuses* I. (1879) 53 It were some deal more tollerable. **1830** MISS MITFORD *Village* Ser. IV. (1863) 298 The old red coat, some-deal the worse for wear.

†**C.** *adj.* With *a*: A little; some. *Obs.*$^{-1}$

*c* **1340** HAMPOLE *Prose Tr.* (1866) 17 [He] perauenture hase getyn by grace a som-dele ryste and a clerete in concyence.

Hence † **somedeally** *adv. Obs.*

*c* **1400** HYLTON *Scala Perf.* I. xlii. (W. de W. 1494), This traueylle is somdelyche streyte & narrow.

ˈ**somegate**, *adv. Sc.* and *north. dial.* Also **some gate**. [f. SOME *a.*[1] 2 + GATE *sb.*[2]]

**1.** In some place; somewhere.

**1816** SCOTT *Old Mort.* v, Ye maun take shelter somegate for the night. *a* **1835** HOGG *Sound Morality* Tales (1866) 202/2 A great river..that rises somegate i' the Heelands. **1891** BARRIE *Little Minister* ix, We ken they're some gait, but whaur?

**2.** In some way or manner; somehow.

**1816** SCOTT *Old Mort.* iv, They pay ane some gate or other. **1816** [see SOLDER *sb.* 4 b]. **1876** ROBINSON *Whitby Gloss.* 179/2 *Some-geeat*, in some way; somehow.

**somehow** (ˈsʌmhaʊ), *adv.* Also 8 **some how, some-how**. [f. SOME *a.*[1] 2 + HOW *adv.*]

**1.** In some manner or by some means not understood or defined; one way or another; someway.

**1740–2** RICHARDSON *Pamela* III. 237 A Hint that might some-how be improved. **1794** MRS. RADCLIFFE *Myst. Udolpho* xxvi, I trembled when I saw him, for I always was afraid of him, somehow. **1822** BYRON *Juan* VII. xxxv, Somewhere, somehow, there was a fault. **1861** THACKERAY *Four Georges* iii. (1862) 131 The Royal New York Gazette somehow ceased to be published. **1866** G. MACDONALD *Ann. Q. Neighb.* xxvi. (1878) 448 You're very different somehow from what you used to be.

**2.** In the phr. ***somehow or other, or another***.

(*a*) **1664** P. HENRY *Diaries & Lett.* (1882) 158 An Act.. was made ready, but somehow or other was missing. **1719** [see HOW *adv.* 16]. **1780** *Mirror* No. 78, But, somehow or other, our expectations have been always disappointed. **1809** MALKIN *Gil Blas* II. i. ¶5 His hand shook, to be sure; but somehow or other it contrived to do its duty. **1875** JOWETT *Plato* (ed. 2) I. 203 We contrived at last, somehow or other, to agree in a general conclusion.

(*b*) **1775** S. J. PRATT *Liberal Opin.* cxvi. (1783) IV. 91 Some how or another, Green chatted me into tolerable spirits. **1809** SYD. SMITH *Serm.* I. 75 It somehow or another happens, that the time..is that which would otherwise be appropriated to the duties of religion. **1863** READE *Hard Cash* III. 9 You have made a little palace of it, somehow or another. **1880** F. G. LEE *Ch. under Q. Eliz.* II. 143.

† **somekin(s**, *a. Obs.* Forms: α. 3 **summes cunnes, kinnes**, 4 **som skenus**, 5 **skynnes, summe skynes**. β. 3 **sume kunnes**, 4 **sumkin(e)s**, 5 **som kynnes, somkennys, -kyns**. γ. 3 **somme kine**, 5 **som(m)e kynne, som kyn, somkyn**, 4–5 **sumkyn, -kin**. [f. SOME *a.*[1] 2 + KIN *sb.*[1] 6 b.] Some kind of; some; such.

α. *c* **1200** ORMIN 18702 Forr sumess kinness dedess. *c* **1205** LAY. 21765 Of summes cunnes leoden. **13..** *S. Eng. Leg.* (MS. Bodl. 779) in Herrig *Archiv* LXXXII. 323/592 þat he amended here lif in som skenus matere. *c* **1400** *Laud Troy Bk.* 10766 With som qweyntyse, Or scleght, by som skynnes wyse.

β. *a* **1300** *Floriz & Bl.* 415 To fonde mid sume kunnes ginne Hu he miȝte hire awinne. **13..** *Cursor M.* 207 (Gött.), þer suld ȝe here..Of þe tuelue apostlis sumkins ieste. *c* **1386** CHAUCER *Man of Law's T.* 1137 (Ellesm.), Or Ire or talent or som kynnes affray. *c* **1460** *Towneley Myst.* xiii. 708 Thou grauntt vs somkyns gle.

γ. *c* **1275** LAY. 3949 Swiken him aþohte in somme kine wise. *a* **1300** *Cursor M.* 165 þar sal ȝe find sumkyn dedis þat iesus did. **1375** BARBOUR *Bruce* x. 519 To wyn the wall of the castell Throu sumkyn slicht. *a* **1400–50** *Alexander* 2259 (D.), Of some kynne gamez Off were or of wristylyng.

**somen**, variant of SAMEN *adv. Obs.*

**somen**: see SOMNE *v.*[1] and *v.*[2] *Obs.*

**somend**, obs. form of SUMMON *v.*

**somenour, -owre**, obs. forms of SUMMONER.

**somentale**: see SAMENTALE.

**some one, someone** (ˈsʌmwʌn), *pron.* (and *sb.*). [f. SOME *a.*[1] 2 + ONE 24.] Some person, somebody. ***someone else***, used pregnantly to mean 'a rival for the affections'. Cf. *somebody else* s.v. SOMEBODY *sb.* 1 b.

α. *c* **1305** in *E.E.P.* (1862) 114 To a womman he com..þat heo scholde him to sum on teche. **1382** WYCLIF *Mark* ix. 37 We syȝen sum oon for to caste out fendis in thi name. **1430–40** LYDG. *Bochas* III. xvii. (1554) 90 Sum one, Parcas, shal them therof discharge. **1535** COVERDALE *Eccles.* iv. 14 Some one commeth out of preson, & is made a kynge: & another [etc.]. *a* **1586** *Answ. to Cartwright* 14 It is not peculiar to some one, or to some fewe alone. **1667** MILTON *P.L.* VI. 503 Some one intent on mischief. **1691** J. WILSON *Belphegor* IV. ii, Peradventure your own, or some ones else; who knows. **1706** STEVENS *Span. Dict.* I, *Algúno*, some body or some one. **1820** BYRON *Juan* IV. cx, As some one somewhere sings about the sky. **1858** M. ARNOLD *Merope* 876 To the guest-chamber lead him, some one! **1872** RUSKIN *Fors Clav.* xxii. 17 Properly a carver at some one else's feast.

β. **1848** THACKERAY *Van. Fair* xi, 'I have set my heart on Rawdon running away with someone.' 'A rich someone, or a poor someone?' **1872** CALVERLEY *Fly Leaves* (1903) 73 And I think thou wearest Someone-else's hair. **1896** BADEN-POWELL *Matabele Campaign* vii, As though someone had struck me with a hammer. **1914** 'BARTIMEUS' *Naval Occasions* xxv. 261 It had become necessary to tell Selby that she couldn't love him any longer... Further, by her creed, it was only right that she should tell him about Someone Else as well. **1936** J. CURTIS *Gilt Kid* xviii. 178 There's someone on that roof all right. Two someones. **1941** M. ALLINGHAM *Traitor's Purse* xi. 129 'She broke the engagement.'.. 'Why? 'As she seen someone else?' **1977** A. HUNTER *Gently Instrumental* i. 14 Walt half-choked: 'There's—someone else!'.. 'You dirty old queen, that's just what you'd think.' **1978** P. PORTER *Cost of Seriousness* 30 To whom someones in the city must pay homage.

**somepart**, *adv. Sc.* Also 5–6 **sumpart**, 6 **-pert**, 6, 9 **-pairt**. [f. SOME *a.*[1] 4 b + PART *sb.*] Somewhat; to some extent.

**1456** SIR G. HAYE *Law Arms* (S.T.S.) 14 Suppos it be sum part subtile to understand, settis [= set ye] nocht by. **1500–20** DUNBAR *Poems* lxix. 47 It dois my spreit sum part confort. *c* **1550** ROLLAND *Crt. Venus* I. 38 The day was sumpart set with weit. **1581** N. BURNE *Disput.* To Rdr., As to my auin Ansueris.., I haue sumpairt amplifeit and inlargeit thame. **1898** LD. E. HAMILTON *Mawkin* vii. 91 'Twould make the road somepairt easier.

**somepin**, var. SUMP'N.

ˈ**someplace**, *adv.* and *sb. dial.* and *U.S.* Also **some place**. [f. SOME *a.*[1] + PLACE *sb.*]

**A.** *adv.* Somewhere; (at, in, to, etc.) a particular or unspecified place.

**1880** *N. & Q.* 24 Apr. 340/2 'No place' in Devonshire is the usual form of 'nowhere', 'no place else' and 'some place else' being the commonest forms of 'nowhere else' and 'somewhere else'. **1896** *Dial. Notes* I. 425 *Some place*, somewhere. **1922** JOYCE *Ulysses* 639 Lodging some place about the pit of the stomach. **1933** *Punch* 8 Nov. 511/3 Is there no' a nicer toon some place else? **1937** J. STEINBECK *Of Mice & Men* i. 18 Some place I'd find a cave. **1948** H. L. MENCKEN *Amer. Lang.* Suppl. II. 394 The long-awaited grammarian of vulgar American..will have a gaudy time anatomizing such forms as..'It was some place *else*', [*etc.*]. **1959** M. DOLINSKY *There is no Silence* v. 78 She's here someplace. **1966** T. PYNCHON *Crying of Lot 49* iii. 63 Tony Jaguar decided he could surely unload his harvest of bones on some American someplace... He was right. **1978** *Detroit Free Press* 16 Apr. E.7/4 I've always been able to get a room someplace, but this year I'm struggling.

**B.** *sb.* Somewhere; a particular or unspecified place.

**1922** JOYCE *Ulysses* 758 That drunken little barrelly man that bit his tongue off falling down the mens WC drunk in some place or other. **1940** W. FAULKNER *Hamlet* III. ii. 190 There will be some town, some place close where I can live. **1971** B. PATTEN *Irrelevant Song* 37 (*title*) In someplace further on. **1976** *National Observer* (U.S.) 7 Feb. 15/3 Next the Navy tried Texas, where defense-minded Sen. John

Tower said it was a fine idea—for someplace else. **1977** H. Fast *Immigrants* III. 165 His father came to America from someplace in Poland in eighteen sixty-nine.

†**somer.** *Obs.* Also 5 soomeer, summer, 5–7 sommer. [a. OF. *somer, sumer, somier, sommier* SOMMIER[1] (mod.F. *sommier*, = Prov. *saumier*, It. *somiere*):—late L. *sagmārius (equus, caballus)*, f. *sagma* horseload, whence OF. *some, somme* (see SEAM *sb.*[2]).]

**1.** A pack-horse; a sumpter-horse.

Freq. in the 15th cent.

*α.* **13..** *K. Alis.* 827 (Laud MS.), He hote hem charge seuen somers Wiþ riche rede itried golde. *c* **1380** *Sir Ferumb.* 3140, xxiiij. Vytaylers..By-fore hymen dryue þay somers. *c* **1430** *Pilgr. Lyf Manhode* I. cxlvii. (1869) 75 Thou hast.. thin soomeer that after thee shal come bihynde, which shal bere thin armure. **1454** *Acts Privy Counc.* (1835) VI. 213 To the same Maistre Henry ij. karre horses, v. somers, and j. hak. **1523** Ld. Berners *Froiss.* I. cxlv. 174 Some of the englysshmen..wanne somers, cartes, and caryages. **1577** Holinshed *Desc. Brit.* III. i, The ancient use of somers and sumpter horses is in a maner utterlie relinquished.

*β.* **1404** *Durh. Acc. Rolls* (Surtees) 397 In Stabulo, ij. palafridi, j. sommer. *c* **1470** *Love's Bonavent. Mirr.* xiv. (Sherard MS.), Where bene ȝoure..knyghtes,..horses and herneyes, charyotes and summeres. **1568** Grafton *Chron.* II. 283 Some of the Englishmen..wanne Sommers, Cartes and cariages. **1592** Wyrley *Armorie, Ld. Chandos* 88 Foure vittailed sommers going vnto the same We met. **1601** F. Tate *Househ. Ord. Edw. II*, §30 (1876) 19 A serjant herbergeour of sommers and cart horses.

**b.** In collective singular.

*c* **1330** *Arth. & Merl.* 4710 (Kölbing), Þai seiȝen hem com swiþe ner Seuen hundred charged somer, & seuen hundred cartes al so.

**2.** A pack or burden, esp. one which is carried by a pack-horse.

**13..** *K. Alis.* 5109 (Laud MS.), Ten thousande mules the kynges tresours,..berande heuy somers. **1426** Lydg. *De Guil. Pilgr.* 8706, I pray yow..To ordeyne me a somer, Myn harneys ther-in for to karye. **1430–40** —— *Bochas* IV. xxiii. (1554) 120 [To] stuffe their somers with outragious pillage. **1525** Ld. Berners *Froiss.* II. xxiii. 24 b, I am content that ye bere with you as moche as ye may beare in males and somers.

**3.** *attrib.*, as *somer-horse, nag, -saddle.*

**1384–5** *Durh. Acc. Rolls* (Surtees) 133 In uno Somersadell empt. pro hostilar. **1404** *Ibid.* 397, j. haknay sadyll, ij. somersadyll. *c* **1450** *Erle Tolous* 817 Somer-horsys he let go before, And charyettys stuffud wyth store. **1503** *Will of Etton* (Somerset Ho.), A somer bay nag. *a* **1513** Fabyan *Chron.* VII. (1811) 306 Kynge Rycharde..toke yᵉ kynges sommer horse, with parte of his tresoure.

**somer,** obs. form of SUMMER *sb.* and *v.*

**somer,** var. SOMMER *adv.*

**somer castell:** see SUMMER CASTLE.

**som'ers** ('sʌməz), *adv. U.S.* Also **somers.** Repr. colloq. pronunc. of *somewheres.*

**1876** 'Mark Twain' *Tom Sawyer* xxiii. 182 It keeps me in a sweat, constant, so's I want to hide som'ers. **1884** —— *Huck. Finn* xxiv. 241 It's reckoned he left three or four thousand in cash hid up som'ers. **1896** —— in *Harper's Mag.* Aug. 344/2 His aunt Polly wouldn't let him..go traipsing off somers wasting time. **1909** *Dial. Notes* III. 404 *Som'ers*, adv., somewhere. 'He's *som'ers* around.'

**somersault** ('sʌməsɒlt, -ɔː-), *sb.* Forms: *α.* 6– **somersault** (7 **sommer-**), 6–7 **-saut**, 7 **-salt.** *β.* 7–9 **summersault**, 7 **-saut, -salt.** *γ.* 7 **sombersalt, simber salt.** [ad. OF. *sombresaut, -sault*, alteration of *sobresault*: see SOBERSAULT.] A leap or spring in which a person turns heels over head in the air and alights on his feet; esp. such a feat as performed by acrobats or tumblers; a pitchpoll. Hence, a turning over in this fashion; a complete overturn, upset, etc.

*α.* **1530** Palsgr. 272/2 Somersault, a lepe of a tombler, *sobersault.* **1591** Harington *Orl. Fur.* xxxv. lxviii, With her goldelaunce, She made him the backe somersaut to daunce. [*marg.*] Somersaut is a leape that the tomblers vse to cast them selues forward their heeles ouer their head. **1613** Browne *Brit. Past.* I. iii, As when some boy, trying the Somersaut, Stands on his head and feet. **1675** Cotton *Burlesque upon B.* 99 And make thee from the Christal Vault Take such a dainty Somer-sault. **1801** Strutt *Sports & P.* III. v. 207 Turning with the heels over the head in the air, which is called the Somersault. **1860** *All Year Round* No. 70. 480 It took off its hat and turned a somersault at Lambert's feet. **1878** M. Foster *Physiol.* III. vi. ii. 499 In yet another form the animal..tumbles head over heels in a series of somersaults.

*fig.* *a* **1680** Butler *Rem.* (1759) II. 200 He gives his Opinion the Somer-Salt, and turns the wrong Side of it outwards. **1874** Whittier *Anti-Slavery Convention* Prose Wks. 1889 III. 179 Dr. Lord.., then professedly in favor of emancipation, but who afterwards turned a moral somersault.

*β.* **1611** Cotgr., *Soubresault*, a Sobresault, or Summer sault. **1612** Drayton *Poly-olb.* vi. 52 So doth the salmon vaut, And if at first he faile, his second Summersaut He instantlie assaies. **1630** —— *Muses Elizium* (1892) 13 Ore each Hillock it will vault, And nimbly doe the Summer-sault. **1678** Butler *Hud.* III. iii. 699 For which, some do the Summer-sault And ore the Bar, like Tumblers, vault. **1706** Phillips (ed. Kersey), *Summer-Sault*, a Gambol or Feat of Activity shew'd by a Tumbler. **1865** Dickens *Mut. Fr.* I. vii, A Hindoo baby..curved up with his big head tucked under him, as though he would instantly throw a summersault.

*fig.* **1847** Emerson *Repr. Men* i. *Uses of Gt. Men* Wks. (Bohn) I. 280 Foremost among these activities are the summersaults, spells, and resurrections, wrought by the imagination.

*γ.* **1612** Donne *Progr. Soul* xlvii. (1633) 24 That could make love faces, or could doe The valters sombersalts. **1653** Walton *Compl. Angler* 152 About which time of breeding the He and She frog are observed to use divers simber salts.

Hence **'somersault** *v. intr.*, to make or turn a somersault; to turn over and over. **'somersaulter,** one who performs a somersault.

**1850** *Tait's Mag.* XVII. 378/1 Sometimes..the summer-saulter..alights on the wrong element. **1858** R. S. Surtees *Ask Mamma* lii. 235 A pair of white breeches are summer-saulting in the air. **1887** Jefferies *Amaryllis* xiv, Nothing for the folk but Punch, brass bands, and somersaulters. **1887** W. Rye *Norfolk Broads* 69 A most hearty..kick under the jaw, which sent him [a dog] somersaulting into a rose-bush.

**somerset** ('sʌməsɛt), *sb.*[1] Forms: *α.* 6–8 **sommerset,** 7– **somerset.** *β.* 6– **summerset.** [Alteration or corruption of *somersaut*: see prec.] = SOMERSAULT *sb.*

*α.* **1596** Nashe *Saffron Walden* To Rdr., Desiring him to inspire my pen with some of his nimblest Pomados and Sommersets. **1598** Marston *Sco. Villanie* III. xi. 228 His very intellect Is naught but a curuetting Sommerset. **1626** Fletcher *Fair Maid of Inn* IV. i, Now I wil only make him break his neck in doing a sommerset. **1664** Cotton *Scarron.* I. 590 Dance, run, and leap, frisk, and curvett, Tumble, and do the Sommerset. **1727** Gay *Fables* I. xl, The tumbler whirls the flip-flap round, With somersets he shakes the ground. **1778** *Sketches for Tabernacle Frames* 26 He'll.. Throw Somersets, vault, caper, and curvet. **1806** Beresford *Miseries Hum. Life* VII. lxxix, Amusing the company with an involuntary somerset. **1833** Ritchie *Wand. Loire* 233 One of those somersets—head over heels—which are common on the modern stage. **1874** J. S. Blackie *Self-Culture* 16 If there are..expert tumblers in the circus, let him not imagine that their supple somersets are mere idle tricks to amuse children.

*fig.* **1710** *Acc. Death T. Whigg* 2 He fancy'd the World turn'd round with him, and that the Revolution was just about doing the Somerset. **1837** Carlyle *Fr. Rev.* II. IV. ii, Remark..what somersets and contortions a dead Catholicism is making. **1871** Spencer *Princ. Psychol.* VII. vi. (1872) II. 372 After a considerable amount of practice in throwing intellectual somersets.

*β.* **1591** in *Lyly's Wks.* (1902) I. 442 Hee presently did cast himselfe downe, dooing a Summerset from the Ile into the water. **1670** Eachard *Cont. Clergy* (1705) 21 As if they would turn over their heads, and shew you the double Summerset. **1675** [H. Nevile] *Machiavelli's Marr. Belphegor* Wks. 527 He [the devil] only gave him the Summerset once or twice, and shewed him two or three jugling tricks, and vanish'd. **1762** Sterne *Tr. Shandy* v. xxix, Springing into the air with a summerset, he turned him about like a windmill. **1816** Scott *Fam. Lett.* (1894) I. xii. 362 Authors come to be regarded as tumblers, who are expected to go to church in a summerset. **1860** Tyndall *Glac.* I. xvi. 119 The summerset of this iceberg produced a commotion all over the lake. **1865** J. G. Holland *Plain Talk* iii. 101 The boys of the street turning summersets.

Hence **'somerset** *v.* (*a*) *intr.* To somersault. Also with *it.* (*b*) *trans.* To cause (a person) to turn a somersault.

**1599** Nashe *Lenten Stuffe* 37 Then the sly sheepe-biter issued into the midst, and summer setted and fliptflapt it twenty times aboue ground, as light as a feather. **1812** *Sporting Mag.* XL. 132 Alexanders got his body on his hip, and somersetted him over his head. **1853** R. S. Surtees *Sponge's Sp. Tour* liii. 303 A pair of white breeches summerseting in the air with a horse underneath. **1874** Saxe *One-Legged Dancers* iv, He almost somerseted off the door-steps.

*fig.* **1837** Carlyle *Fr. Rev.* II. IV. ii, In such extraordinary manner does dead Catholicism somerset and caper, skilfully galvanized.

**'somerset,** *sb.*[2] Also **summerset.** [f. the name of Lord Fitzroy *Somerset*, Baron Raglan (1788–1855).] Used *attrib.* or *ellipt.* to designate a form of saddle (see quot. 1875).

**1851** *Catal. Grt. Exhib.* 521/2 A quilted summerset saddle. *Ibid.* 522/2 Somerset hunting saddle-tree. **1862** *Catal. Internat. Exhib., Brit.* II. No. 4685, Ladies' saddle and Somerset saddle. **1875** Knight *Dict. Mech.* 2245/1 *Somerset*.., a saddle padded before the knee and behind the thigh.

**Somer'setian,** *a.* and *sb.* [f. the name of *Somerset*, one of the south-western counties of England.] **a.** *adj.* Of or belonging to the county of Somerset. **b.** *sb.* The dialect of this county.

**1612** Drayton *Poly-olb.* iii. 10 The Sommersetian maids. **1825** Jennings *Obs. Dial. W. Eng.* 12 In another line..he calls the cows *kee*; now this is not Somersetian.

**Somervillian** (sʌmə'vɪlɪən), *a.* and *sb.* [f. the name of *Somerville* College (founded as a women's college in 1879 and named after Mary Somerville) + -IAN.] **A.** *adj.* Of or pertaining to Somerville College, Oxford. **B.** *sb.* A member of the college.

**1896** A. D. Godley in *More Echoes from Oxford Mag.* 64 Ye Somervillian students. **1904** R. Bridges *Let.* 26 May (1940) 50 The Somervillians might object. **1922** Byrne & Mansfield *Somerville College 1879–1921* iii. 38 The War Office was granted the use of the Somerville Buildings for the duration of the war..[which] over-shadowed the situation of the young Somervillians. **1934** R. Macaulay *Going Abroad* xxix. 254 The two Somervillians..passed most of the afternoon and evening with the Josefs. **1966** E. H. Jones *Margery Fry* v. 35 'They were beautiful, in their Liberty dresses,' said an old Somervillian..remembering the leaders of College society in the 'nineties. **1976** 'A. Cross' *Question of Max* ix. 113 In 1918 Somervillians were still being housed in..Oriel College.

**somervillite** ('sʌməvɪlaɪt). *Min.* [See quot. 1823.] A variety of melilite from Vesuvius.

**1823** H. J. A. Brooke in *Q. Jrnl. Sci.* XVI. 276 The next mineral I shall have to describe came to me with some other Vesuvian substances, from Dr. Somerville, from which circumstances I have named it Somervillite. **1837** Dana *Min.* 291 Somervillite accompanies black mica and other minerals, in the ancient scoria of Vesuvius. **1869** J. Phillips *Vesuv.* x. 290 *Humboldtilite*—'Mellilite', 'Somervillite', 'Zurlite', &c.—occurs in gray micaceous lava of Somma, and ejected blocks.

†**some-say.** *Obs.*$^{-1}$ [f. SOME *pron.* + SAY *sb.*[4]] A reported saying or statement.

**1589** Nashe *M. Marprelate* Wks. (Grosart) I. 171 Martin Iunior..knoweth the truth.., yet loath to haue it published, ..seeketh to shadowe it, with other some-saies.

**somesthesis, -esthetic** varr. SOMÆSTHESIS, SOMÆSTHETIC *a.*

**somet, someð,** varr. of SAMED *adv. Obs.*

**something** ('sʌmθɪŋ), *sb.*, (*adj.*,) and *adv.* Forms: 1 **sum þing(c), ðing,** 2 **sum ðinc,** 3–5 **sumþing,** 3– 6 **-thing;** 4 **somþing (zom-), -þyng,** 5 **-thyng** (6 **-e**), 7 **somthing;** 6– **something,** 6 **-thyng,** 9 *dial.* **somethin',** etc. [f. SOME *a.*[1] 2 + THING *sb.*[1] 17. Orig., and freq. down to the end of the 16th cent., written as two words.]

**A.** *sb.* **1. a.** Some unspecified or indeterminate thing (material or immaterial).

For *something like* see LIKE *a.* 2 e, 2 f.

*c* **1000** *Ags. Gosp.* Matt. xx. 20 Ða com to him zebedeis bearna modor..sum þingc fram him biddende. *c* **1200** Ormin 3363 Her icc wile shæwenn ȝuw Summ þing to witerr takenn. *a* **1300** *Cursor M.* 11928 Þar Iesus did in his barn-hide Sum-thing þat es of to rede. **1340** *Ayenb.* 33 Huanne..me him hat zomþing þet him þingþ hard, he him excuseþ. **1382** Wyclif *Luke* vii. 40 Symound, I haue sum thing for to seye to thee. **1503** Dunbar *Thistle & Rose* 23 In my honour sum thing thow go wryt. **1594** T. B. *La Primaud. Fr. Acad.* II. 592 To doe some thing without cause. **1601** Shaks. *All's Well* I. iii. 248 There's something in't More then my Fathers skill. **1638** R. Baker tr. *Balzac's Lett.* (vol. II) 91 Yet something must be done for examples sake. **1681** Dryden *Span. Friar* IV. i, Nay, if you will complain, you shall for something. (*Beats him.*) **1779** *Mirror* No. 27, A slip of paper, with something written on it. **1823** Scott *Quentin D.* xxii, He read something in the looks of his soldiers, which even *he* was obliged to respect. **1863** A. Blomfield *Mem. Bp. Blomfield* I. v. 123 His speeches were those of one who had something to say, not of one who had to say something. **1895** Mrs. Croker *Village Tales* (1896) 30 There, to the left, was *something* coming rapidly through the crops!

*Prov. phr.* **1562** J. Heywood *Prov. & Epigr.* (1867) 132 Some thyng is better then nothyng. **1638** Sanderson *Serm.* (1681) II. 97 Something, we say, hath some savour.

*attrib.* **1593** Shaks. *Rich. II*, II. ii. 36 For nothing hath begot my something greefe.

**b.** Used as a substitute for a name or part of one, or other particular, which is not remembered or is immaterial, etc.

**1764** G. Williams in Jesse *Selwyn & Contemp.* (1843) I. 295 Lady Something Grey is here. **1779** C'tess Upper Ossory *Ibid.* IV. 75 Another man has sworn to shoot a Miss Something, *n'importe*, if she did not run away with him from the Opera. **1818** Scott *Br. Lamm.* xvi, 'His name is Craig—Craig—something, is it not?' 'Craigengelt is the fellow's name,' said the Master. **1862** Borrow *Wild Wales* xxxix, I passed by a place called Llan something. **1896** Baden-Powell *Matabele Campaign* i, I..just caught the five something train.

**c.** Some liquor, drink, or food; esp. in phr. *to take something.*

**1778** Miss Burney *Evelina* lxxxii, Lady Louisa..desired to *take something* before we began our rambles. **1779** *Mirror* No. 25, Come in and have a glass of something after your ride. **1857** Hughes *Tom Brown* I. iv, I'll give you a drop of something to keep the cold out.

**d.** Used (with *between*) to denote an intermediate stage or grade.

**1821–30** Ld. Cockburn *Mem.* ii. (1874) 105 He walked with a slow stealthy step—something between a walk and a hirple. **1823** Scott *Quentin D.* xviii, An officer, who, having taken Deacon's orders, held something between a secular and ecclesiastical character.

**e.** Used to denote an undefined or unknown occupation, or a person in respect of this.

*c* **1863** T. Taylor *Ticket-of-Leave Man* II. 32 If Mr. Gibson would only give you employment. He's something in the City. **1874** Burnard *My Time* xv. 130 May I be prompter, or call-boy, or something? **1886** Pascoe *London of To-day* ii. (ed. 3) 37 The restless gentlemen who are 'something in the city', but no one knows what. **1907** E. Gosse *Father & Son* ii. 21 My uncles..earned a comfortable living, E. by teaching, A. as 'something in the City'. **1951** [see SLINKY *a.*]. **1962** [see COMMUTE *v.* 4 b]. **1978** P. Fitzgerald *Bookshop* ii. 20 He was known to drive up to London to work, and to be something in TV. **1979** R. Barnard *Posthumous Papers* iv. 37 He was something in insurance.

**f.** *or something* (colloq.), used to express an indistinct or unknown alternative.

**1814** Jane Austen *Mansfield Park* I. xi. 223 There were generally delays, a bad passage or *something.* **1899** [see MITTAGESSEN]. **1913** 'S. Rohmer' *Mystery of Dr. Fu-Manchu* i. 4 What, are you moved to London or something? **1926** I. Mackay *Blencarrow* v. 49 Yet undoubtedly this man was drunk or ill, or something. **1938** *Chatelaine* Oct. 25/3 *Our* things must have tattle-tale gray or somethin' 'cause they never shine like *this.* **1951** M. Kennedy *Lucy Carmichael* II. iii. 100 'Aren't they engaged or something?' 'I don't know what you mean by *or something*... It's a vulgar, slipshod phrase.' **1958** *N.Z. Listener* 4 July 7/1 Jarden was off the field—had hurt his foot or something—and it seemed that we might be hard up against it. **1969** N. Freeling *Tsing-Boum* viii. 54 She might have a police record or something. **1978** P. Marsh et al. *Rules of Disorder* iii. 69 You have to fight or else people..think you're a bit soft or something.

**g.** Phrases ***something for everybody*** (or ***everyone***), ***something for nothing***. Also used *attrib.*

**1869** P. T. Barnum *Struggles & Triumphs* viii. 132 When people expect to get 'something for nothing' they are sure to be cheated. **1924** G. B. Shaw *Saint Joan* iv. 41 The Jews generally give value. They make you pay; but they deliver the goods. In my experience the men who want something for nothing are invariably Christians. **1938** E. Ambler *Cause for Alarm* vii. 115 A something-for-nothing proposition always has a string to it. **1955** R. Macaulay *Let.* 20 Aug. in *Last Lett. to Friend* (1962) 206, I personally think it all to the good, as giving something for every one, however different their minds, backgrounds, and religious temperaments. **1960** *N.Y. Times Bk. Rev.* 17 Jan. 1 There's something for everybody. **1971** *Engineering* Apr. 129/2 Something-for-everyone entertainment. **1976** *Glasgow Herald* 26 Nov. 6/2 But human nature dictates that most people..are liable to take advantage of an opportunity to get something for nothing.

**2. a.** A certain part, portion, amount, or share (*of* some thing, quality, etc.); freq., a small part or amount, a slight trace.

*c* **1200** *Trin. Coll. Hom.* 157 Dele hit swo, þat ech nedi.. haue sum þing þer-of. *a* **1300** *Cursor M.* 9530 To quam ilkan he gaf sum-thing Of his might. **1388** Wyclif *Joshua* vii. 1 Sum thing of the halewid thing. *c* **1470** Henry *Wallace* v. 482 Off Inglismen ȝhett sum thing spek I will. **1562** Winȝet *Wks.* (S.T.S.) I. 4 Albeit the time be schort, sum-thing of ȝour prais man we speik. **1643** Sir T. Browne *Relig. Med.* I. §12 A set of things that carry in their Front..something of Divinity. **1677** Yarranton *Eng. Improv.* 55, I hope..I may see something of the Improvement..come to pass. **1710** *Tatler* No. 245 ¶2 Her voice loud and shrill,..and something of a Welch accent. **1780** *Mirror* No. 81, There was something of bustle, as well as of sorrow, all over the house. **1815** Scott *Guy M.* xliii, Something of the tone, and manners, and feeling of a gentleman. **1849** Macaulay *Hist. Eng.* iii. I. 319 He has generally seen something of foreign countries. **1874** Green *Short Hist.* viii. §5. 511 The two Fletchers,..in their unreadable allegories, still preserved something of their master's sweetness.

**b.** Const. *of* with adjective. *Obs.* or *arch.*

**1654** Dorothy Osborne *Lett.* (1888) 257 Love, which, sure, has something of divine in it. **1656** Earl Monm. tr. *Boccalini's Advts. fr. Parnass.* 293 As if something of unseemly, or misbecoming had been asked her.

**c.** ***something of a(n)***, to a certain extent or degree a (person or thing of the kind specified).

**1711** Addison *Spect.* No. 106 ¶6 Sir Roger, amidst all his good Qualities, is something of an Humourist. **1780** *Mirror* No. 70, As he was something of a sportsman, my guardians often permitted me to accompany him to the field. **1802** Mar. Edgeworth *Moral T.* (1816) I. 231, I am something of a judge of china myself. **1826** Disraeli *V. Grey* ii. xiii, Dormer, who was..something of an epicure, looked rather annoyed. **1931** R. Campbell *Georgiad* iii. 55 Even the devil dwindles to a duiker, Who prides himself as something of a spiker. **1939** R. G. Collingwood *Autobiogr.* iv. 27, I had become something of a specialist in Aristotle. **1959** *Listener* 17 Dec. 1083/3 It had been, I admit, something of a party. **1978** *Lancashire Life* Sept. 51/1 During the last war he became something of a legend, working incredible hours and doing general and orthopaedic surgery, as well as obstetrics.

**3. a.** Followed by an adjective.

**1382** Wyclif *Acts* xxiii. 20 Thei ben to sekinge sum thing certeynere [L. *aliquid certius*]. **1598** Shaks. *Merry W.* iii. iii. 75 Ther's something extraordinary in thee. **1610** —— *Temp.* iii. iii. 94 I'th name of something holy, Sir, why stand you In this strange stare? **1663** S. Patrick *Parab. Pilgr.* (1687) 81 The desire..of speaking something extraordinary on this occasion. **1737** *Gentl. Mag.* VII. 182/2 The Epigram ..seems to have something Serious and Noble in the Turn. **1779** *Mirror* No. 61, The most eccentric of them all have something venerable about them. **1819** Scott *Leg. Montr.* xii, Something there was cold in his address, and sinister in his look. **1888** *Academy* 14 Apr. 253/3 Within an ace or so of being something very good indeed.

**b.** ***something damp*** or ***short***, a drink; spirits. *slang* or *colloq.*

*c* **1831** Hood in W. Jerdan *Autobiogr.* (1853) IV. 202, I shall never take 'something short' without dedicating it to the same toast. **1865** *Slang Dict.* 240 *Something damp*, a dram, a drink. *a* **1904** in *Eng. Dial. Dict.* s.v., She always had a drop of something short in her tea (Oxf.).

**c.** ***something*** (***good*** or ***special***), a useful racing tip.

**1907** *Racing Expert* 9 July 3 For the benefit of those who care to wait and act upon the best information. 'The Expert' will occasionally wire when he knows Something Special. **1908** *Racing Judge* 6 June 4 Owing to Bank Holiday this Letter will be sent out on Tuesday Evening... Something good at Manchester will be given. **1937** Partridge *Dict. Slang* 800/2 *Something good*, a good racing tip.

**4. a.** In more emphatic use: A thing, fact, person, etc., of some value, consideration, or regard.

***something in the wind***: see wind *sb.*

**1582** N.T. (Rhemish) *Gal.* vi. 3 If any man esteeme him self to be something, whereas he is nothing. **1611** Beaum. & Fl. *King & No King* iii. ii, To set him..in my rowle, the two hundred and thirteenth man, which is something. **1621** T. Williamson tr. *Goulart's Wise Vieillard* 103, I have so spent my dayes, that I account of my selfe, as one that hath serued for some vse, and for something in the world. **1705** Stanhope *Paraphr.* II. 274 So we may not..falsely imagine we are Something, when in Truth we are Nothing. **1739–56** Doddridge *Fam. Expositor* clxx. (1799) II. 419 *Now you say something*, signifies among us, You speak right. **1802** Mar. Edgeworth *Moral T.* (1816) I. xii. 100 If he could even recover five guineas of it, it would be something. **1865** Whewell in Mrs. S. Douglas *Life* (1881) 540, I shall have Kate's sweet dear face there; and that will be something. **1887** Lowell *Democracy* 46 It is something that two great nations have looked at each other kindly through their tears.

**b.** In the phr. ***there's something in it***, etc.

**1681** *Roxb. Ball.* (1884) V. 255 Their being in Print signifies something in't. **1713** Berkeley *Hylas & Phil.* ii. Wks. 1871 I. 309 There is indeed something in what you say. **1719** De Foe *Crusoe* ii. (Globe) 363 There is something in it, I am persuaded from my own Experience. **1818** T. L. Peacock *Nightm. Abbey* xiv. (1891) 127 True, Raven, there is something in that. I will take your advice. **1847** Tennyson *Princ.* v. 202 She can talk; And there is something in it, as you say. *a* **1902** S. Butler *Way of all Flesh* (1903) liv. 249 When Christina pointed out to him that it would be cheap he replied that there was something in that. **1977** B. Pym *Quartet in Autumn* i. 7 'Cheerful, aren't you,' said Edwin, 'but perhaps there's something in it. Four people on the verge of retirement, each one of us living alone.'

**c.** ***to make something of***, to make important or useful; to improve or raise in some way; to succeed in utilizing to some extent.

**1778** Miss Burney *Evelina* xxvi, She told them that she had it in her head to make something of me. **1814** Jane Austen *Mansf. Park* (1851) 85 If the part is trifling she will have more credit in making something of it. **1836** Mrs. Sherwood *H. Milner* iii. xvi. 310 His hopes of making something of the young man. **1870** Rogers *Hist. Gleanings* Ser. ii. 246 Calumny made something of his relations with William Tooke.

**d.** ***something to see*** (or ***look at***): an impressive sight.

**1808** J. Mackintosh in R. J. Mackintosh *Mem. Life Sir J. Mackintosh* (1835) I. ix. 501 It was something to see children clinging round the necks of their fathers, and sons carrying their infirm parents in pursuit of health. **1942** T. Bailey *Pink Camellia* i. 2 In khaki breeches, sitting her horse like a boy, her white shirt open at the throat, she was something to look at. **1957** E. B. White *Let.* June (1976) 440 Martha is really something to see now.

**e.** ***to have*** (***got***) ***something***, to have an idea or attribute of value or worthy of consideration.

**1938** 'E. Queen' *Four of Hearts* iv. 57 Say..the screwball's got something. Only I got a better idea. **1940** G. Greene *Power & Glory* i. ii. 25 'I would take..a hostage.'.. 'You know,' the chief said, 'you've got something there.' **1948** Powys & Bolton *Don't listen, Ladies!* in *Plays of Year* (1949) 586 The Crusaders, gentlemen, they *had* something. The husband ordered his clothes from the blacksmith, and his wife's from the locksmith. **1960** *Times* 14 Sept. 12/6 Yet that girl 'had something', as any visitor to the United States will find out. **1973** L. Cooper *Tea on Sunday* i. 20 'I'm not at all the nice little wife she wanted for you.' 'She may have something there.'

**f.** Used in various phrases expressing admiration, as ***isn't*** (***that, he***, etc.) ***something?***, ***to be really something***; ***quite something***: see quite *adv.* 5 d.

**1958** B. Nichols *Sweet & Twenties* ii. 42 The Ritz Bar, in those days, really was something. **1967** M. Kenyon *Whole Hog* vii. 81 Isn't that something? So if they [*sc.* pigs] don't know you they're like interested? **1969** Widdowson & Halpert in Halpert & Story *Christmas Mumming in Newfoundland* 161 Mummers were really something when I was a boy. If you wasn't afraid of them, you wasn't afraid of nothing when you was four or five. **1973** A. Christie *Postern of Fate* iii. x. 213 Perhaps it's something important... And so if they..tried to get whatever it was—that really would be something! **1977** 'A. York' *Tallant for Trouble* xi. 163 P. C. Abrahams presented arms..decked..out in full-dress white... 'Oh, isn't he something,' Jennie Kamm exclaimed.

**g.** ***to have something going*** (with ***someone***), to have an 'understanding' or an affectionate relationship (with someone).

**1971** V. Canning *Firecrest* iii. 32 It didn't need any semaphore signals to tell her that there was something going between Mrs. Pilch and Major Cranston. **1973** *Philadelphia Inquirer* (Today Suppl.) 7 Oct. 7/2 Is it true that Sammy Davis Jr. has something going with Linda Lovelace. **1977** E. Leonard *Unknown Man No. 89* xx. 200 She smiled..like they had something going.

**5.** With article or demonstrative pronoun, or in plural (= sense 1): **a.** With adj. preceding. Also in phr. ***a little something***: some food or drink; a snack; refreshments. Cf. sense 1 c.

*sing.* **1577** Harrison *England* ii. vi. (1877) I. 163 A little something was allowed in the morning to young children. **1661** Glanvill *Van. Dogm.* 145 A very slender something in a Fable. **1682** Creech *Lucretius* iii. 75 Then we must add a fourth to this frame, A fourth something, but without a name. **1778** Mme. D'Arblay *Diary* 18 June, An inward something which I cannot account for, prepares me to expect a reverse. **1800** Mrs. Hervey *Mourtray Fam.* III. 165 An unaccountable *something* seemed always to prevent their getting further. **1856** Froude *Hist. Eng.* (1858) II. vi. 91 Every monastery..had..its special something, to attract the interest of the people. **1864** Bowen *Logic* iv. 64 It is only an indeterminate something. **1866** Geo. Eliot *Felix Holt* I. xi. 237 Like the shrill biting talk of a vixenish wife, it.. compelled you to 'take a little something' by way of dulling your sensibility. **1926** A. A. Milne *Winnie-the-Pooh* vi. 77 It was..as if somebody inside him were saying, 'Now then, Pooh, time for a little something.'.. So he sat down and took the top off his jar of honey. **1950** J. Cannan *Murder Included* vii. 146, I wonder if a little something could be provided to pacify the inner man? **1958** Wodehouse *Cocktail Time* xix. 159 Butlers always like to keep their strength up with a little something in the middle of the morning. **1977** P. D. James *Death of Expert Witness* iv. iii. 192, I cook a little something for everyone in the evenings.

*pl.* **1642** H. More *Song Soul* ii. i. iv. 2 Bringing hid Noughts into existencie, Or sleeping Somethings into wide day-light. **1728** Pope *Dunciad* i. 54 Here she beholds yᵉ Chaos dark and deep, Where nameless Somethings in their causes sleep. **1894** *Pall Mall Mag.* Dec. 601 Whispering soft Somethings in Italian. **1897** *Atlantic Monthly* LXXIX. 139 The title of a group of miniature essays..devoted to airy somethings.

**b.** Without prec. adj. Also with genitive (cf. 2 a).

In the 16–17th cent. *somethings* is occasionally found in the sense of *some things*.

*sing.* **1587** Golding *De Mornay* i. (1592) 4 Nowe betweene nothing and something, (how little so euer that something can bee) there is an infinite space. **1590** Shaks. *Com. Err.* ii. ii. 52 Marry sir, for this something that you gaue me for nothing. **1776** Mickle tr. *Camoens' Lusiad* Dissert. 160/1 The opposition of it to the arch-angel Michael..carries in it a something which must displease. **1798** Coleridge *Anc. Mar.* iii. i, I saw a something in the Sky, No bigger than my fist. **1807** T. Thomson *Chem.* (ed. 3) II. 37 Experiments..to discover what that *something* is. **1848** Thackeray *Vanity Fair* lvi, The young gentlemen.. might learn a something of every known science. **1894** Parry *Stud. Grt. Composers* 224 They only wanted words at all as a something to excuse their using their voices.

*pl.* **1656** Hobbes *Six Lessons* Wks. 1845 VII. 301 You allow..your own nothings to be somethings. **1737** *Gentl. Mag.* VII. 560/1, I know Hands, in which a Parcel of Nothings would make a finer Appearance than other Peoples Somethings. **1789** Charlotte Smith *Ethelinde* (1814) II. 143 By having written certain somethings which he was assured by his friends were specimens of uncommon and original genius.

**c.** A certain amount of money.

**1827** Scott *Chron. Canongate* vi, He..had enjoyed legacies, and laid by a something of his own, upon which he now enjoys ease with dignity.

**6. a.** ***something or other***, = sense 1 a, b.

(*a*) **1707** *Refl. upon Ridicule* 218 'Tis hard at long run not to drop something or other, that may notifie their Disposition of Mind. **1752** Foote *Taste* ii. Wks. 1799 I. 20 A sort of Queen, or wife, or something or other to somebody. **1873** B. Harte *Fiddletown* 27 He was arrested on suspicion of being something or other. **1897** Flandrau *Harvard Episodes* 337 The piece was a Spanish something or other through which a tambourine shivered at intervals.

(*b*) **1858** Longf. *M. Standish* ii, The battle of something-or-other. **1897** 'H. S. Merriman' *In Kedar's Tents* vi, The guide, Antonio something-or-other.

**b.** ***something else***, (*a*) In suggestive use. (*b*) *slang* (orig. *N. Amer.*), a different matter; an exceptional or extraordinary (person, event, sight, etc.).

**1844** Dickens *M. Chuz.* xliii, More farewells, more something else's; a parting word from Martin. **1909** R. E. Knowles *Attic Guest* 87 But when a lover comes across a couple of states, leaving behind him a big city—and all the girls are sorry to see him go, that's the best of it—that is something else, as we used to say in the South. **1940** W. Faulkner *Hamlet* i. ii. 33 But when cash money starts changing hands, that's something else. **1949** R. Harvey *Curtain Time* 67 Getting the small performer dressed for a public appearance was something else again. **1957** E. Horne in *N.Y. Times Mag.* 18 Aug. 26/3 Something else—A phenomenon so special it defies description. Thus, when asked if the music is great..a cat may reply, 'No, man, not that; it was something else.' **1960** *Melody Maker* 31 Dec. 5/5 *Philly Joe Jones*: Aside from being a fabulous drummer, he could be a great comedian. He has people lying on the floor, he's so funny. Philly's something else. **1968** *Crescendo* Jan. 27/1 The one I rave about more than any other is the band of 1947... That was something else. It was a dream. **1973** R. L. Simon *Big Fix* (1974) vii. 50 Dillworthy was something else again. **1977** *O.D.* No. 3, 12/1 (*caption*) Oh, wow, these guides are..something else man!

**c.** *Comb.*, as ***something-nothing***, etc.

**1817** Coleridge *Biogr. Lit.* (Bohn) 58 In all these cases the real agent is a something-nothing-everything. **1884** Tennyson *Becket* iii. i, *Henry*. What did you ask her? *Rosamund*. Some daily something-nothing.

**7.** As *adj.* Used euphemistically for 'damned' or other expletive.

**1859** F. Francis *Newton Dogvane* (1888) 252 It's the somethingest robbery I ever saw in my life. **1888** Lees & Clutterbuck *B.C. 1887* xxxii, This is the somethinger somethingest railway I ever struck.

**B.** *adv.* In some degree; to some extent; somewhat; rather, a little.

Except as an archaism, this use chiefly survives in constructions which admit of the word being felt as a noun.

**1. a.** Qualifying a verb.

*c* **1275** *Wom. Samaria* 7 in *O.E. Misc.*, Al so he þiderward sumþing neyhleyhte, He sende his apostles by-voren. **1530** Baynton in Palsgr. *Introd.* 12 Our Englyshe tong hath some thyng altred theyr..terminations. **1585** T. Washington tr. *Nicholay's Voy.* i. xxii. 28 We something doubted the gallies of Genua. **1634** Sir T. Herbert *Trav.* 12 Conies.. something resemble a wilde Cat. **1655** Fuller *Ch. Hist.* i. 40 Many are unsetled about him,..these may be something satisfied if [etc.]. **1785** Holcroft *Tales of Castle* I. 128, I shall be something relieved of a load of sorrow which oppressed me. **1802** W. Fowler *Corr.* (1907) 45, I think they may shrink something before they be put in use. **1856** Froude *Hist. Eng.* (1858) I. 463 The scarcely ambiguous answer was something softened the following day.

**b.** Qualifying a prepositional or adverbial expression of place, extent, distance, time, etc.

**1530** Palsgr. 7 Than shall the *o* be sounded almost lyke this diphthonge *ou*, and some thyng in the noose. **1576** in *Reg. Mag. Sig. Scot.* (1886) 753/2 Ane merche stane set and put sumthing bewest the end of the said dyke. **1605** Shaks. *Macb.* iii. i. 133 For 't must be done to Night, And something from the Pallace. **1611** —— *Wint. T.* ii. ii. 55 Please you come something neerer. **1677** Yarranton *Eng. Improv.* 55, I have been something long upon this Theme. **1697** *Lond. Gaz.* No. 3310/4 A brown Gelding something above 14 hands high,..and something thin footed before. **1719** De Foe *Crusoe* i. (Globe) 297 Our Guide being something before us. **1759** Sterne *Tr. Shandy* ii. xvii, His left hand, raised something above his stomach. **1844** Disraeli *Coningsby* iii. iii, He is a man something under thirty. **1849** Ruskin *Seven Lamps* v. §xxii. 158 The whole reaching to something above a man's height. **1896** Guy Boothby *Dr. Nikola* iv. 79 In something under a quarter of an hour we had reached the wharf.

**2. a.** Qualifying an adj.

Freq. in the 17th and 18th centuries. Now *rare* or *dial.* Also in dial. and colloq. use as an intensive with such adjs. as *cruel, frightful*, etc.

*c* **1510** Barclay *Mirr. Gd. Manners* (1570) B iiij, Thou seest diuers wayes oft leading to one place, Thone something open, thother close and shit. **1548** Turner *Names Herbes* (E.D.S.) 55 So hath a nauet a longe roote and somthynge yealowishe. **1617** Moryson *Itin.* I. 181 Who was of stature something tall, and corpulent. **1666** Marvel *Corr.* Wks. (Grosart) II. 194 There is one Bill orderd to be brought in of a something new nature. **1708** Swift *Sacram. Test* Wks. 1755 II. I. 124, I have the misfortune to be something singular in this belief. **1791** Mrs. Inchbald *Next-door Neighbours* III. ii, Sir George is something nervous. **1827** Cooper *Prairie* I. 30 They told us below, we should find settlers something thinnish hereaway. **1851** E. Ruskin *Let.* 25 Nov. in M. Lutyens *Effie in Venice* (1965) II. 218 Nani makes them a great dish of Fish seasoned strongly with Garlic and the smell is something too dreadful if one happens to pass by the door. **1856** Froude *Hist. Eng.* I. 170 Indifferent to the obligations of gratitude, and something careless of the truth. **1856** G. Meredith *Let.* 15 Dec. (1970) I. 38 The *dulness* is something frightful. **1918** C. Mackenzie *Sylvia Scarlett* I. vii. 208 'These paths are something dreadful, Emmie,' said Mrs. Horne, as the three of them scrambled up through the garden. **1932** L. Golding *Magnolia Street* II. ii. 299 The way the razor trembled..now and again was something cruel.

*Comb.* **1602** Shaks. *Ham.* III. i. 181 Haply the Seas..shall expell This something setled matter in his heart. **1608** Chapman *Byron's Consp.* III. ii, Others that with much strictness imitate The something-stooping carriage of my neck. **1842** Tennyson *Will Waterproof* 131 In a court he saw A something-pottle-bodied boy.

†**b.** With *a* or *an* inserted before the adj. *Obs.*

**1588** J. Read tr. *Arcæus' Comp. Meth.* 77 b, Incorporate it so that it may become something an hard Emplaister. **1597** Shaks. *2 Hen. IV*, I. ii. 215, I was borne with a white head, & somthing a round belly. **1615** G. Sandys *Trav.* 12 Having a secure hauen, yet with something a dangerous entrance. **1664** H. More *Myst. Iniq.* xiv. 163 These seem to have something an over-near affinity with..Heresie. **1770** Warburton in W. & Hurd *Lett.* (1809) 455, I have now had something a longer intermission from my pain. **1784** R. Bage *Barham Downs* I. 26 Will you..increase your sister's fortune to make her something a more suitable match?

**c.** Qualifying an adv. of manner. Also with *adj.* used for *adv.* in dial. and colloq. usage.

**1588** Greene *Pandosto* (1843) 27 She began to simper something sweetely. **1611** Shaks. *Wint. T.* IV. iv. 825 Being something gently consider'd, Ile bring you where he is aboord. **1707** *Curios. in Husb. & Gard.* 21 What he calls a Courtier he uses something roughly. **1713** Berkeley *Hylas & Phil.* I, The inferences sound something oddly. **1822** Scott *Nigel* xvii, 'I said Grahame, sir, not Grime,' said Nigel, something shortly. **1859** Dickens *Christmas Stories, Haunted House* i, 'O!' said I, something snappishly. **1898** G. B. Shaw *You never can Tell* in *Plays Pleasant* 211 *Gentleman*: Did you howl? *The Young Lady*: Oh, something awful. **1909** A. Woollcott *Let.* 24 Sept. (1944) 20 She gads around something fierce, as your friend Bert would say. **1915** J. Webster *Dear Enemy* 300 When he was drunk..he smashed the furniture something awful. **1932** R. Lehmann *Invitation to Waltz* I. iii. 58 Her husband drinks something shocking. **1963** W. H. Missildine *Your Inner Child of Past* xv. 221, I was taken into the assembly hall. And beat up something terrible. **1978** D. Clark *Libertines* ii. 41 'I'll put a plaster on that cut for you.'.. 'Thanks, doctor... It does sting something chronic.'

**d.** With a comparative adj. or adv.

**1592** *Soliman & Pers.* v. iv. 130 Yet some thing more contentedly I die For that [etc.]. **1615** G. Sandys *Trav.* 140 This place is something better then desert. **1669** Sturmy *Mariner's Mag.* v. xii. 57 The Stick being something more than the diam. at the Base Ring. **1713** S. Sewall *Diary* 2 Nov. (1879) II. 406 Sam. is something better, yet full of pain. **1735** Johnson *Lobo's Abyssinia, Voy.* ii. 11, I found him in a Straw-Hat something larger than those of his Subjects. **1821** Scott *Kenilw.* xxxi, You have done your duty something more than boldly. **1829** —— *Anne of G.* xv, Because my thoughts came slower, may be, and something duller, than those of other folk. **1886** Stevenson *Kidnapped* x, Now this song..is something less than just to me.

**e.** Followed by *too* and adj. or adv. Now *arch.*

**1610** Shaks. *Temp.* III. i. 58, I prattle Something too wildely. **1668** H. More *Div. Dial.* II. 38 Something too copious a digression. **1671** Shadwell *Humourist* v, It is something too sudden and temerarious. **1709** Mrs. Manley *Secr. Mem.* (1736) III. 46 Something too large a Head. **1720** De Foe *Capt. Singleton* i. (1840) 3 This fell out something too soon. **1821** Scott *Kenilw.* xii, I got something too deep into his secrets. **1831** —— *Cast. Dang.* vi, We have had something too much of this.

†**f.** Followed by *with* and a superlative, = somewhat or rather (soon, often, etc.). *Obs. rare.*

**1631** Massinger *Emperor East* II. i, Shall I become a votary to Hymen Before my youth hath sacrificed to Venus? 'Tis something with the soonest. **1697** South *Serm.* III. 282 Even that perhaps may be something with the oftenest.

**3.** In various miscellaneous constructions.

**1691** Wood *Ath. Oxon.* II. 179 Say and Sele was..averse to the Court ways, something out of pertinaciousness. **1790** in J. Haggard *Rep. Consist. Crt.* (1822) I. 81 Her deposition ..is highly coloured and inflamed,..something in the style really of a French novel. **1842** Borrow *Bible in Spain* xxxvi, It was..built something in the Moorish taste. **1897** *Academy* 9 Jan. 48/1 Something a bore to many, by reason of talking like a book in coat and breeches.

Hence (chiefly as *nonce-words*) ˈ**something** *v. trans.*, used colloq. in pa. pple. as a euphemism for 'damned' or other imprecation, esp. in the phr. *to see* (one) *somethinged first*; hence ˈ**somethinged** *ppl. a.* **somethingean** *a.* (cf. *somethingth* below). †ˈ**somethingish** *adv.*, somewhat. ˈ**somethingth** *a.*, used to supply the place of a number, name, etc., which is not distinctly remembered or is immaterial (cf. quots. and something A. 1 b).

**1859** F. Francis *N. Dogvane* (1888) 108 As for paying for him, tell him I'll see him *somethinged first. **1867** H. Kingsley *Silcote of S.* xli, He said that he would be somethinged if he gave way. **1882** Miss Braddon *Mt. Royal* II. 92 'Self-will be —— somethinged' growled Leonard. **1837** Dickens *Pickw.* xv, Four *something-ean singers in the costume of their country. **1922** E. Wallace *Valley of Ghosts* xiii. 120 You called me..a fool, and a *somethinged fool, almost the first time we met. **1777** *Vanbrugh's Prov. Wife* IV. iii, Why, she really has the air of a sort of a woman a little *somethingish out of the common. **1854** Mrs. Gaskell *Lett.* (1966) 302, I am very poor; which eases my cares wonderfully, see *somethingth satire of Juvenal. **1871** Meredith *H. Richmond* xli, He killed Harry's friend Seneca in the eighty-somethingth year of his age. **1891** Duncan *Amer. Girl in London* 194 The wife of Colonel So-and-so, commanding the somethingth something. **1898** *Academy* 5 Feb. 149/1 There is a new novel from her pen—her fifty-somethingth, we believe.

ˈ**somethingness.** [f. as something *sb.* + -ness.] The fact or state of being something; real or material existence, entity.

**1675** Duffett *Mock Tempest* v. i, The nothingness of the Mouse,..the somethingness, yea the fullness of it. **1760–2** Goldsm. *Cit. World* xiv, What an unusual share of *somethingness* in his whole appearance! **1839–48** Bailey *Festus* xix. 204 A star falls, and we track a cold dark mass Of trembling half-transparent somethingness. **1890** *Universal Rev.* 15 June 247 The stages..have invariably been from a nothingness of ignorant impotence to a little somethingness of highly self-conscious, arduous performance.

**sometime** (ˈsʌmtaɪm), *adv.* (and *a.*). Forms: 3–6 **sometyme**, 6– **sometime**, 4–6 **somtyme**, 4, 6 *Sc.* **-tym**, 4–5, 7 **-time**; 4–6 **sumtyme** (6 **summ-**), 4 **-time**, 5 **-tym**; 4 **sumetime**, 5 **-tyme**. [f. some *a.*[1] + time *sb.* Down to the 16th c. written either as one word or as two; even in later use the distinction between *sometime* and *some time* is not always clear (cf. some *a.*[1] 4 c).]

**1. a.** At one time or another, with the possibility of recurrence or repetition; now and then; occasionally; = sometimes 1.

Common in the 16th and 17th centuries; now *rare* or *Obs.*

**1340** Hampole *Pr. Consc.* 5880 Þarfor maysters som tyme uses þe wand þat has childer to lere. *c* **1375** *Cursor M.* 13185 (Fairf.), Ȝet fallis sum-time in fraunce wodemen atte saint Iones tide atte þe kirke bote to bide. **1400** tr. *Secreta Secret., Gov. Lordsh.* 81 But som-tyme þis Reubarb is venomous. *c* **1440** *Pallad. on Husb.* I. 44 An hid defaut is sumtyme in nature. **1545** Raynald *Byrth Mankynde* 63 Lykewyse somtyme it commeth to passe that the syde of the chylde commeth forwarde. **1592** Timme *Ten Eng. Lepers* M j, They ..grow verie impacient, and some time dispaire of release. **1622** Wither *Philarete* (1633) K 5 b, My heart is sometime heavy, when I smile. **1679** Puller *Moder. Ch. Eng.* (1843) 227 But sometime fear is the beginning of wisdom. **1700** S. L. tr. *Fryke's Voy. E. Ind.* A ij, I am apt to think, a Dedication sometime to be none of the least [troublesome]. **1809** Syd. Smith *Serm.* I. 286 The very name used to denote it, however unjustly it may be, sometime, applied.

†**b.** *sometime... sometime*, used to introduce antithetical words, clauses, etc. Also with *sometimes* in the first or second place. *Obs.*

(*a*) **1297** R. Glouc. (Rolls) 3438 Þus were..þe saxons Some tyme aboue & some (tyme) binеþe. **1390** Gower *Conf.* II. 28 Somtime nay, somtime yee, Somtime he cam, somtime noght. **1451** Capgr. *Life St. Gilbert* 102 He be-gan to pray, sumtyme loud, sumtyme soft, sumtyme saying, sumtyme singing. *c* **1537** De Benese *Meas. Lande* A j, Somtyme the sellers..somtyme yᵉ byers..be greatly deceyued by the meters thereof. **1582** N. Lichefield tr. *Castanheda's Conq. E. Ind.* I. iii. 10 Going in such sort, as sometime he kept the Sea, and sometime droue towards the lande. **1660** H. Bloome *Archit.* A j, *Gutta*, are drops sometime round, sometime in Triangle fashion. **1700** Wallis in *Collect.* (O.H.S.) I. 316 Dr. Keil sometime at Oxford and sometime at Cambridge alternately, hath..gone through a course of Anatomy.

(*b*) **1589** R. Harvey *Pl. Perc.* (1590) 2 Sometime these madcaps be at a fray: sometimes at a feast. **1621** Burton *Anat. Mel.* I. ii. v. iii. 226 This humor..is sometime in the substance of the Braine, sometimes contained in the Membranes.., sometimes in the passages [etc.].

(*c*) **1599** Shaks. *Much Ado* III. iii. 142 Sometimes fashioning them like Pharaoes souldiours.., sometime like god Bels priests.., sometime like the shauen Hercules. **1674** *Govt. Tongue* v. §2. 120 Somtimes a man invents a perfect falsity of another; somtime he that do's not invent it, yet reports it. **1681** R. L'Estrange *Tully's Offices* 129 For sometimes Bodily Goods fall in Competition with the Goods of Fortune: sometime Outward Goods with Those of the Body: and sometime again [etc.].

**c.** With different correlatives.

*a* **1425** *Cursor M.* 7433 (Trin.), Oþerwhile wiþ harpe, sumtyme with song. **1526–1541** [see otherwhiles 2]. **1586** [see otherwile 2]. **1593** Shaks. *3 Hen. VI*, II. v. 9 Sometime, the Flood preuailes; and than the Winde. *a* **1654** Gataker *Parker* in Fuller *Abel Rediv.* (1867) II. 18 He forbare not frequently to preach,..sometime in his own cathedral church, and at other times in the towns and villages abroad. **1720** [see otherwhile 2].

**d.** Passing into adj. Freq. in phr. *a sometime thing*: something which is occasional or transient.

**1935** G. Gershwin (*song-title*) A woman is a sometime thing. **1959** *Times Lit. Suppl.* 6 Nov. p. xxxi/1 Going to the movies still entailed leaving home and paying money, so that ..the movies were a 'sometime thing' and a reward. **1964** 'E. McBain' *Axe* vi. 115 The game..ain't regular, like you said it was. It's a sometime thing, whenever the urge strikes. **1967** *Observer* 19 Nov. 21/2 Money is a sometime thing for Simon Dee, here today and just possibly gone tomorrow. **1969** *Jrnl. Eng. & Gmc. Philol.* LXVIII. 214 Poetic propriety is a sometime thing. **1980** *Newsweek* 17 Nov. 12/2 Political parties are weaker, the Federal bureaucracy has grown unwieldy and party discipline in Congress is a sometime thing.

**2.** †**a.** At a certain time, on a particular occasion, in the past; once. *Obs.*

**1297** R. Glouc. (Rolls) 8958 Some time as þis gode mold in to halle com. **1375** in Horstmann *Altengl. Leg.* (1878) 130/2 Y trowe wel þow desyre to ete sum del Of þe frut of paradys þat þow of ete som tyme. **1422** tr. *Secreta Secret., Priv. Priv.* 195 Well sholdiste thou remember the þat Sum tym the Quen of Inde the send fair yeftis. **1484** Caxton *Fables of Avian* iv, This fable of an asse whiche somtyme fond the skynne of a lyon. **1526** *Pilgr. Perf.* (W. de W. 1531) 3 b, As it was somtyme shewed to Noe in the tyme of the vniuersal flode. **1581** Pettie tr. *Guazzo's Civ. Conv.* III. (1586) 147 b, Like as the Crauish sometime did. Who [etc.]. **1620** *Frier Rush* 1 There was sometime beyond the Sea edified and founded a certaine house. **1653** Baxter *Saints' Rest* III. vi. (1662) 387 Let the power speak, which sometime said, 'Lazarus arise!' **1661** Ussher *Power of Princes* I. (1683) 50 The first Christian Emperour Constantine used this speech sometime unto his Bishops.

†**b.** At one time; in former times, formerly. *Obs.*

The quotations under (*b*) illustrate the usage with the substantive verb.

(*a*) *c* **1330** R. Brunne *Chron. Wace* (Rolls) 6905 Whylom [*v.r.* som tyme] Bretons landes wonnen;..Now ar þey nought so mykel of myght. **1387–8** T. Usk *Test. Love* III. iii. (Skeat) l. 136 Somtyme, er it were white, it might have be nat white. **14..** *Guy Warw.* 4655 Some tyme þou were of grete honowre. *c* **1460** Fortescue *Abs. & Lim. Mon.* (1885) 131 The kyng off Ffraunce myght not sumtyme dyspende off his demaynes..so mich as myght tho the kynge off England. **1535** Coverdale *Wisd.* v. 3 These are they, whom we somtyme had in derision, & iested vpon. **1570–6** Lambarde *Peramb. Kent* (1826) 193 Farley..belonged sometime to the Monks of Christs church in Canterburie. **1600** J. Pory tr. *Leo's Africa* II. 66 It was sometime gouerned by a certaine tyrant. *a* **1700** Evelyn *Diary* 25 July 1678, A worthy..gentleman, with whom my son was sometime bred in Arundel House. **1786–1805** Tooke *Purley* (1829) I. 404 The whole verb *Dure* was some time used commonly in our language.

(*b*) *a* **1400** Maundev. (1839) viii. 98 Also fro Bethanye to Jerico, was somtyme a litylle Cytee. *c* **1440** *Generydes* 2 Of Inde Somtyme ther was a nobyll kyng. **1484** Caxton *Fables of Alfonce* viii, Somtyme was a kynge whiche hadde a fabulatour. **1535** Coverdale *2 Sam.* xx. 18 The comon sayenge was somtyme: Who so wyll axe, let him axe at Abel. **1570–6** Lambarde *Peramb. Kent* (1826) 283 Where was sometime an auncient Church erected by the Romanes.

†**c.** In descriptive clauses introduced by *that.*

**1387** Trevisa *Higden* (Rolls) III. 129 Seleucus, þat was somtyme plegge and prisoner at Rome. *c* **1400** *Destr. Troy* 1729 Our Cite for sothe, þat sum tyme was here, [þai] Brent. **1445** tr. *Claudian* in *Anglia* XXVIII. 269 Be thyn excytyng craftys lefte þat som tyme were wele knowe.

**d.** In similar use with omission or ellipse of relative and verb. Now *arch.*

*a* **1325** *MS. Rawl. B.* 520 lf. 31 b, No3t with stondinde þe statut sume time at Westmunestre..i made. *c* **1375** *Cursor M.* 13563 (Fairf.), þen ansquared he sum time blinde. **1423** *Cal. Letter-bk. 'I'* (1909) 288 Sir Edward, sumtyme Kyng of Ynglond. **1463** *Bury Wills* (Camden) 16 To Raffe Otle sumtyme my man. **1542** Udall *Erasm. Apoph.* 210 b, Asia sometyme the..welthiest countree of the worlde, had.. been spoyled by Alexander. **1600** Holland *Livy* xxxviii. viii. 987 To have mercie and pitie of their nation sometime linked in amitie unto them. **1633** Rutherford *Lett.* (1862) I. 103 The visage of our Nazarites, sometime whiter than snow, is now become blacker than a coal. **1771** *Antiq. Sarisb.* 109 His body lies..under a large marble stone, sometime inlaid with brass. **1794** Bloomfield *Rep.* 14 A Negro Woman, sometime the Property of H., became free. **1852** *Gentl. Mag.* Jan. 9 John Jewel, sometime Bishop of Salisbury.

†**e.** With *of* or genitive, denoting former ownership or proprietary rights. *Obs.*

**1423** *Coventry Leet Bk.* 52 A house with gardyne sumtyme off John Askemare. **1486** *Rec. St. Mary at Hill* (1905) 1 The tenement sumtyme Rauf a Beryes. **1556** *Chron. Grey Friars* (Camden) 48 The church sumtyme the Gray freeres.

**f.** Preceded by a pronoun or article. Passing into *adj.*

**1490** Caxton *Eneydos* vi. 27 Alle the grete tresours..of hir sayd somtyme husbonde sichee. *c* **1585** Montgomerie *Sonn.* iv. 9 Hou..that som tym peirles place..in furious flammis did burne. **1621** Bp. Montagu *Diatribæ* 144 Agreeing with Tremellius, his sometime Colleague. **1637** Rutherford *Lett.* (1862) I. 254, I wonder now of my sometime boldness to chide and quarrel Christ. **1756** *Connoisseur* No. 118 ¶7 The sometime Professor of Astronomy at Gresham College. **1824** Miss Mitford *Village* Ser. I. (1863) 235 Our sometime constable, the tipsiest..of men, is dead. **1889** Swinburne *Study B. Jonson* 103 A sometime student of the secular [poet].

†**3.** *at* or *in sometime*, = 2 b. *Obs.*

Cf. examples with *some time* under some *a.*[1] 2 b (*a*).

**1340** Hampole *Pr. Consc.* 765 Fone men may now fourty yhere pas, And foner fifty als in somtym was. **1552** Elyot, *Aliquoties*, at sometime. **1579** W. Fulke *Conf. Sanders* 541 At sometime, no citie in Italie was so notable as Rome.

**4. a.** At some future time; on a future occasion. Also in phr. *sometime or other.*

*c* **1386** Chaucer *Knt.'s T.* 385 For possible is,..That by som cas, syn fortune is chaungeable, Thow maist to thy desir som tyme atteyne. —— *Man of Law's T.* 12 Parfay, seistow, somtyme he rekene shal. **1500–20** Dunbar *Poems* xv. 42 Suppois the servand be lang vnquit, The lord sumtyme reward will it. **1545** Ascham *Toxoph.* II. (Arb.) 159, I must nedes somtyme tel you of myne owne experience. *a* **1654** Gataker *Whitgift* in Fuller *Abel Rediv.* (1867) II. 199 His lectures..are said to remain yet under hope of seeing sometime further light. **1741** Berkeley *Lett.* Wks. 1871 IV. 268 You may sometime or other come to Bath. **1839–52**

BAILEY *Festus* 136 Thou too and all the stars..Shall sometime range in bliss the spirit-pasturing skies. **1879** HOWELLS *L. Aroostook* (1883) I. 156 'Will you tell me?' 'Yes, sometime.'

**b.** In attrib. use, with preceding pron. or article.

*a* **1641** BP. MONTAGU *Acts & Mon.* (1642) 157 The meanes which he had appointed for their sometime happinesse to come. **1787** ANNA SEWARD *Lett.* (1811) I. 386 Materials whose sometime publication I meditate. **1805** *Ibid.* VI. 241 The sometime resurrection of the body.

**5. a.** At some indefinite or indeterminate point of time; at some time or other.

**1590** SHAKS. *Mids. N.* II. i. 253 There sleepes Tytania, sometime of the night. [**1797** *Encycl. Brit.* (ed. 3) I. 321/1 Some time in May, the rows must be evened.] **1818** COBBETT *Polit. Reg.* XXXIII. 432 This letter was sent off sometime in October. **1832** SOUTHEY *Hist. Penins. War* III. 279 It was sometime in the 11th century. **1864** TENNYSON *Aylmer's F.* 685 Where indeed The roof so lowly but that beam of Heaven Dawn'd sometime thro' the door-way? **1890** 'R. BOLDREWOOD' *Col. Reformer* (1891) 171 Grant made the light, sometime after nightfall.

†**b.** Just now; recently. *Obs.*

**1779** SHERIDAN *St. Patrick's Day* II. ii, I was sometime taken with a sudden giddiness, and Humphrey..ran to my assistance.

**6. a.** With *since*, = some time ago. *rare.*

The use of the compound in place of the two separate words (*some time*) is evidently due to association with sense 5.

*a* **1700** EVELYN *Diary* 13 Apr. 1652, The letter which some-time since I sent to Deane Cosin's proselyted son. **1792** CHARLOTTE SMITH *Desmond* III. 244 The subject was sometime since exhausted between us. **1897** *Daily News* 13 Sept. 7/1 A sometime since completed [railway] line.

**b.** For some time. *rare*$^{-1}$.

**1801** *Lusignan* IV. 177 She answered that she was very well, and had slept better than she had done sometime.

**sometimes** ('sʌmtaɪmz), *adv.* Forms: 6 **somtymes, 6–7 -times;** *Sc.* 6 **sum tymes, 8 -tyms;** 6 **sometymes, 6– sometimes.** [f. SOME *a.*[1] 7 + *times* pl. of TIME *sb.*]

**1. a.** On some occasions; at times; now and then. Cf. SOMETIME 1 a.

**1526** *Pilgr. Perf.* (W. de W. 1531) 41 b, He..sheweth vs somtymes the softe rodde of his swete disciplyne. **1578** GOSSON in *Sch. Abuse* (Arb.) 77 The Poet which sometimes hath trod awry. **1634** SIR T. HERBERT *Trav.* 87 Hither sometimes the King repaires. **1674** BREVINT *Saul at Endor* 213 Just as notable Rogues are hanged and quartered somtimes with their Pardons about their Necks. **1749** SMOLLETT *Gil Blas* XII. xi. (1782) IV. 262 Three famous physicians, who had the reputation of curing their patients sometimes. **1780** *Mirror* No. 105, I mean those little lectures on morality, sometimes known by the name of scandal. **1849** MACAULAY *Hist. Eng.* x. II. 565 Sometimes he spoke so haughtily that the rustics..were provoked into making insolent replies. **1884** R. W. CHURCH *Bacon* iii. 60 He liked ..to generalise in shrewd and sometimes cynical epigrams.

**b.** With a correlative (see quots. and cf. SOMETIME 1 b and c).

(*a*) **1590** SPENSER *F.Q.* II. vi. 3 Sometimes she sung, as loud as larke in aire, Sometimes she laught [etc.]. [**1611** SHAKS. *Wint. T.* III. iii. 20 Sometimes her head on one side, some another.] **1634** SIR T. HERBERT *Trav.* 87 A streame of water, sometimes so broad as the Thames at London, but other sometimes neere dried vp. **1678** BUNYAN *Pilgr.* I. 42 Somtimes sighingly and somtimes comfortably. **1728** LAW *Serious Call* x. (1898) 129 To be sometimes chaste and modest, and sometimes not. **1776** *Trial of Nundocomar* 22/2 Sometimes he wrote the bonds himself in Nagree, sometimes in Bengal, but always signed them with his own hand. **1849** M. ARNOLD *Strayed Reveller* 265 Sometimes a wild-hair'd Mænad; Sometimes a Faun with torches; And sometimes.. the divine, Belov'd Iacchus. **1901** *Cycl. Tour. Club Gaz.* Oct. 389 Running downhill, sometimes with, and sometimes without, a brake.

(*b*) **1600** J. PORY tr. *Leo's Africa* VII. 294 Sometimes he bringeth not home slaues enough to satisfie the merchants: and otherwhiles they are constrained to awaite there a whole yeere. **1674** RAY *Catal. Fishes* 107 Sometimes they kill them by striking them cross the snout with a pole, otherwhiles they shoot them. **1736** AINSWORTH I. s.v., They are sometimes of this opinion, and at other times of another. **1819** SHELLEY *Peter Bell 3rd* II. ii, Sometimes The Devil is a gentleman; At others a bard [etc.]. **1897** [see OTHERWHILES 2].

(*c*) **1602** B. JONSON *Poetaster* II. ii, Sometimes froward, and then frowning, Sometimes sickish, and then swowning. **1667** MILTON *P.L.* VI. 242 Somtimes on firm ground.., then soaring on main wing. **1815** SHELLEY *Alastor* 496 Sometimes it fell Among the moss.. Now on the polished stones It danced.

**c.** Used adjectivally to denote 'occasional'. Cf. SOMETIME *adv.* (and *a.*) 1 d.

*a* **1945** E. R. EDDISON *Mezentian Gate* (1958) I. v. 44 Nor did they find wholesome nor comfortable..his sometimes flashings into unforeknowable violence. **1974** *Publishers Weekly* 11 Feb. 56/3 Brando's sometimes generosity, his idealism. **1977** *Rolling Stone* 13 Jan. 36/2 Srouji confessed her entire FBI history, starting with her role in the Sixties as a sometimes informant.

†**2. a.** = SOMETIME 2 a and 2 b. *Obs.*

Freq. from *c* 1580 to *c* 1650.

**1563** *Homilies* II. *Matrimony* V vvv j b, And S. Peter saith in that same place.., that holy matrones dyd sometymes decke them selues, not with golde and syluer: but in puttynge theyr whole hope in God. **1576** GASCOIGNE *Philomene* Wks. 1910 II. 182 In Athens reignde somtimes, A king of worthy fame. **1627** HAKEWILL *Apol.* (1630) 374 There is at this day to be seene a board belonging sometimes to Tullius Cicero. **1642** D. ROGERS *Naaman* Ep. Ded. 3 The blessed lights of his ministers, who sometimes shined in our Sphere, but now in Glory. **1665** J. WEBB *Stone-Heng* (1725) 157 The Place where Habor..was some-times betrayed, imprisoned, and executed.

†**b.** = SOMETIME 2 d. *Obs.*

Freq. from *c* 1600 to *c* 1650.

**1577** HANMER *Anc. Eccl. Hist., Socrates, Schol.* v. xi, Probus, sometimes a Consul, was chief governour of Italy. **1592** in J. Morris *Troubles Cath. Forefathers* (1877) 37 John Thomas, sometimes Bishop Goldwell's man, died in the Counter. *a* **1619** FOTHERBY *Atheom.* II. vii. §2 (1622) 262 Thebes in Ægypt, and Orchomenus, sometimes two rich and populous Cities, but now reduced. **1650** T. B[AYLEY] *Worcester's Apoph.* 26 An old ruinated, but sometimes a most famous monastery. **1709** STRYPE *Ann. Ref.* I. xxxiv. 340 One Games, sometimes School-Master of the Choristers in Magdalen College.

†**c.** = SOMETIME 2 e. *Obs.*$^{-1}$

**1610** B. JONSON *Alchemist* v. v, The goods, sometimes the Orphanes, that the Brethren Bought with their siluer pence.

†**d.** = SOMETIME 2 f. *Obs.*

**1593** SHAKS. *Rich. II*, I. ii. 54 Farewell old Gaunt, thy sometimes brothers wife..must end her life. *Ibid.* v. v. 75 Leaue To looke vpon my (sometimes Royall) masters face. **1632** LITHGOW *Trav.* II. 70 Sparta, where that sometimes famous Citty of Lacedemon flourished. **1798** CHARLOTTE SMITH *Yng. Philos.* I. 72 Excelled only by her sometimes tutoress.

†**3.** ***at sometimes***, = sense 1. *Obs.*

**1548** ELYOT, *Aliquoties*, at sometymes. **1584** LODGE *Alarum* (Shaks. Soc.) 60 Manye gentlemen..who at sometimes, as well as yourselfe, were destitute of silver. **1626** T. H[AWKINS] tr. *Caussin's Holy Crt.* 384 One should not..omit at some-times to eleuate his hart to God. **1682** BUNYAN *Holy War* (1905) 202 Yea, the Rascal crue, at sometimes would be for destroying of him. **1719** W. WOOD *Surv. Trade* 4 Those mighty Fleets, that have at sometimes, and when rightly governed, rendered her the Terror of the Ocean.

**sometimey** ('sʌm,taɪmɪ), *a. U.S. Black* and *Prison slang.* [f. SOMETIME *adv.* (and *a.*) + -Y[1].] Variable, unstable.

**1946** MEZZROW & WOLFE *Really the Blues* 378 *Sometimey*, unstable, unpredictable, neurotic. **1969** R. PHARR in A. Chapman *New Black Voices* (1972) 62 She's the evilest and sometime-iest woman I ever shacked up with. **1977** *New Yorker* 24 Oct. 114/2 Men who have transferred to Green Haven from more rigorous but more consistent prisons.. say the Green Haven's officers are 'sometimey'.

**sometour**, obs. form of SUMPTER.

**somette**, obs. form of SUMMIT.

†**so'mever**, *adv. Obs.* Also 5 **som euer**, 6 **some ever.** [f. *som(e* SUM *conj.* + EVER *adv.* Cf. WHATSOMEVER, etc.] = SOEVER 2.

*c* **1440** *Alph. Tales* 58 Whatt howr som euer þat a synner forthynkis his syn. **1560** DAUS tr. *Sleidane's Comm.* 60 b, The same can easely destroye you also, what power somever you have. *Ibid.* 418 b, What action some ever any man had. **1621** R. BOLTON *Stat. Irel.* 347 In whose hands or possession somever.

**someway** ('sʌmweɪ), *adv.* Now chiefly *U.S. colloq.* Also **some way.** [f. SOME *a.*[1] + WAY *sb.*]

**1.** In some way or manner; by some means; somehow.

*c* **1450** *Cov. Myst.* (Shaks. Soc.) 40 God wyl be vengyd on us sum way. **1565** COOPER *Thesaurus, Aliqua*,..someway: by some meanes. **1570** LEVINS *Manip.* 197/4 Someway, *aliqua.* **1641** LD. BROOKE *Disc. Nat. Episc.* I. x. 57 b, All someway oppose the whole Law of Christ. **1674** PRIDEAUX *Lett.* (Camden) 19, I will not yet dispair of Williamson's provideing for you some way or other. **1736** *Gentl. Mag.* VI. 598/1 That his Lordship had a Right some-way to interest himself in Affairs of this Nature. **1798** EDGEWORTH *Pract. Educ.* I. 147 They are to..behave in company some way differently from what they behave every day in their own family. **1822–7** GOOD *Study Med.* (1829) I. 291 We shall have to contemplate..the bile as some way or other damaged in its secretion. **1890** *Advance* (Chicago) 27 Feb., We someway think that contentment is to feel no want. **1892** B. POTTER *Jrnl.* 8 Oct. (1966) 278 They are related someway to Neil Gow. **1902** W. B. YEATS *Where there is Nothing* (1903) v. 106, I thought he would have had half Ireland with him by this time with his great preaching, but someway when he preaches to the people, they don't seem to mind him much. **1922** JOYCE *Ulysses* 180 Pity of course: but somehow you can't cotton on to them someway. **1930** W. FAULKNER *As I lay Dying* 115 It's like he had got into the inside of you, someway. **1938** M. K. RAWLINGS *Yearling* xiv. 140, I hate the hawks eatin' the quail, but I don't someway mind the 'coons eatin' the grapes. **1978** *Washington Post* 22 July A8, I keep the windows open and run my box fan. I figure the Lord will take care of me somehow, someway.

**2.** At some distance. In quot. *transf.* of time.

Usually, and more correctly, written as two words: cf. SOME *a.*[1] 4 c (*b*), quot. 1867.

**1859** GEO. ELIOT *A. Bede* iv, But then came the days of sadness, when Adam was someway on in his teens.

**someways** ('sʌmweɪz), *adv.* Now chiefly *dial.* Also 5 **som-**, 7 **somewayes.** [f. as prec., with genitive or plural *-s.*] = prec. 1.

[*a* **1225** *Ancr. R.* 354 Moni wolde sumes weis þolien vlesches herdschipes. *c* **1230** *Hali Meid.* 9 Hit is tah in wedlac summes weis to þolien as men schal after iheren.] *c* **1440** *York Myst.* xx. 37 He is wente som wayes wrang. **1674** N. FAIRFAX *Bulk & Selv.* 2 It might somewayes also be helpful, to the setting right the thoughts of some others. **1895** *Atlantic Monthly* Mar. 362 The parson's got to get his initiation someways. **1905** MCCARTHY *Dryad* 203 He felt that he must obey; he felt that Esclaramonde had someways ensnared him.

**somewhat** ('sʌmhwɒt), *sb.* and *adv.* Forms: α. 3 **sumhwat, -whet** (*Orm.* **summwhatt**), 3–6 **sumwhat** (5 **-whate, -wat(t**, 6 **-whatt**); 4 **sumquat,** 5 **-qwat,** 6 *Sc.* **-quhat;** 3 **somȝwat,** 4–6 **-whatt,** 5–7 **-what;** 4 **somwat,** 5–6 **-watt;** 4– **somewhat.** β. *dial.* 8 **sumet,** 9 **summat, summut, zum'ot,** etc. [f. SOME *a.*[1] + WHAT *pron.* Down to the end of the 16th cent. written either as one word or as two.] = SOMETHING *sb.* and *adv.*

**A.** *sb.* **1. a.** A certain amount, esp. in the way of statement, information, etc. Freq. with *of* (= concerning). Now *arch.*

*c* **1200** ORMIN 958 Summwhatt icc habbe shæwedd ȝuw Till ȝure sawle fode. *a* **1225** *Leg. Kath.* 506 Schaw sumwhet of ham, for hwi ha beon wurðe for to beon iwurðge. *a* **1300** *Cursor M.* 1496 Spek we sumquat of caym kyn. *c* **1374** CHAUCER *Troylus* I. 672 To thi help yet sumwhat can I say. *c* **1400** MAUNDEV. (Roxb.) vii. 27 Now hafe I schortly talde ȝow sum what of bawme. **1509** FISHER *Funeral Serm. C'tess Richmond* Wks. (1876) 293, I wold reherce somwhat of her demeanyng in this behalue. *a* **1586** SIDNEY *Ps.* XXXIV. ii, Joyne with me, Somwhat to speake of his due praise. **1625** BACON *Ess., Of Cunning* (Arb.) 441 It is strange, how long some Men will lie in wait, to speake somewhat, they desire to say. *a* **1715** BURNET *Own Time* (1753) I. 53, I will relate somewhat concerning the Earl of Antrim. **1801** STRUTT *Sports & Past.* IV. ii. 274 Exasperated at somewhat his antagonist had said. **1819** BYRON *Juan* I. vii, Narrating somewhat of Don Juan's father.

**b.** Some (material or immaterial) thing of unspecified nature, amount, etc. Now *arch.* or *dial.*

α. *a* **1225** *Ancr. R.* 44 So doð euer sumhwat þet god muwe þerof awakenen. *c* **1290** *S. Eng. Leg.* I. 54 He it nolde bileue, 3wane ani pouere man him bede, bote he him som-ȝwat ȝeue. **1350** *Will. Palerne* 3722 It bi-tokenes sum-what, treuli, god turne it to gode. **1390** GOWER *Conf.* II. 210 In ech of hem he fint somwhat That pleseth him. *c* **1400** *Pilgr. Sowle* (Caxton, 1483) I. xv. 14 Late myn estate with som what be amendyd. **1484** CAXTON *Æsop* III. xvi, I deye for honger; gyue me somwhat to ete. **1526** TINDALE *2 Cor.* iv. 8 We are in povertie: but not utterly without somwhat. **1568** GRAFTON *Chron.* II. 340 Such as were wicked..made a shewe as though they would do some-what. *a* **1627** MIDDLETON *Witch* III. i, Nothing lives But has a joy in somewhat. **1693** DRYDEN *Love Triumphant* II. i, I know not why, but somewhat prompts me To read this folded page. **1726** SWIFT *Gulliver* I. viii, I observed..somewhat that looked like a boat overturned. **1797–1805** S. & HT. LEE *Cant. Tales* I. 13 He perceived somewhat glitter amid the grass. **1821** SCOTT *Kenilw.* xi, The tools were worth somewhat. **1842** N. HAWTHORNE in *Longfellow's Life* (1891) I. 441, I have been looking to receive somewhat in the shape of a letter..from you. **1855** KINGSLEY *Westw. Ho!* xiv, Some folk say he's not right in his head; or turned miser, or somewhat.

*Prov.* **1542** J. HEYWOOD *Prov.* (1867) 24 Alwaie somwhat is better then nothyng. **1562** —— *Prov. & Epigr.* 152 Boude wands serue for sumwhat.

β. **1790** MRS. WHEELER *Westmld. Dial.* 59 Yaurs may.. seaav sumet agayn they er aud. **1838** JAS. GRANT *Sk. Lond.* 39 There was no lack either of 'summut' to drink or 'summut' to eat. **1839** in Latham *Hdbk. Eng. Lang.* (1860) 148 Presently, zum 'ot..went dump! **1859** GEO. ELIOT *A. Bede* i, A man must learn summat beside Gospel to make them things.

**c.** Followed by an adjective.

**1665** HOOKE *Microgr.* 74 Instead of meeting with what I look'd for, I met with somewhat more admirable. **1681** HOBBES *Rhet.* Pref., May be presumed to contain somewhat excellent. **1721** BRADLEY *Philos. Acc. Wks. Nat.* 4 The parts ..are bound together by somewhat Oleaginous. **1751** ELIZA HEYWOOD *Betsy Thoughtless* I. 3 Miss Betsy, who had.. somewhat extremely engaging in her manner of behaviour. **1836** EMERSON *Nature, Spirit* Wks. (Bohn) II. 166 It is essential to a true theory of nature and of man, that it should contain somewhat progressive. **1850** ROBERTSON *Serm.* 3rd Ser. ix. §1. 125 [They] mistook the sensation for somewhat half divine.

†**d.** ***by somewhat***, by a certain (small) amount.

**1653** RAMESEY *Astrol. Rest.* 61 Yet he is the swifter of the two by somewhat.

**2. a.** With dependent genitive: Some part, portion, amount, etc., *of* something.

**1297** R. GLOUC. (Rolls) 7587 So þat vewe contreies beþ in engelonde, þat monekes nabbeþ of normandie somwat in hor honde. *a* **1300** *Cursor M.* 4739 Len vs sumquat o þi sede, Was neuer ar sua mikel nede. **1330** R. BRUNNE *Chron.* (1810) 22 þer..a noþer chapelle standes, & somwhat of þat tre, þei bond vntille his handes. *c* **1400** TREVISA *Higden* (Rolls) II. 69 (MS. α), In þis citee is somwhat of þat famous wal. *c* **1440** *Wycliffite Bible* Gen. xl. 4 Sumdel [*v.r.* sum whatt] of tyme passide. **1588** KYD *Househ. Phil.* Wks. (1901) 267 It is thought there is somewhat of theyr dooings in his works. **1658** W. SANDERSON *Graphice* 33 Observe to hit the virtues of the Piece, and to refuse the Vices; for all Masters have somewhat of them both. *a* **1677** BARROW *Serm.* Wks. 1716 II. 71 Doth she not every where present spectacles of delight (somewhat of lively picture, somewhat of gay embroidery, somewhat of elegant symmetry). **1761** HUME *Hist. Eng.* III. liii. 147 By quitting somewhat of his royal prerogative. **1779** *Mirror* No. 10, By that too great niceness..they may mingle somewhat of disgust and uneasiness even in the highest and finest pleasures. **1848** THACKERAY *Van. Fair* lxvi, A conversation of which he could not help hearing somewhat. **1876** STEDMAN *Vict. Poets* vi. 232 It must be acknowledged that somewhat of this applies to Tennyson's variations upon Theocritus.

**b.** Const. *of* with a positive adj. Now *rare.*

**1650** EARL MONM. tr. *Senault's Man bec. Guilty* 36 Tis the desire of seeing somewhat of new which draws us forth. **1669** DRYDEN *Tyrannic Love* I. i, Somewhat of mournful, sure, my ears does wound. **1751** ELIZA HEYWOOD *Betsy Thoughtless* I. 12 These words, as it proved, had somewhat of prophetic in them. **1870** N. HAWTHORNE *Eng. Note-bks.* (1879) I. 273 With somewhat of fantastic in the shape of the clock-tower.

**c.** = SOMETHING *sb.* 2 c.

**1841** HELPS *Ess., On Treatment of Suitors* (1842) 110 You will naturally endeavour to give somewhat of a detailed explanation. **1863** MARY HOWITT tr. *F. Bremer's Greece & Greeks* II. 3 It was somewhat of a surprise to me. **1868**

FREEMAN *Norm. Conq.* (1877) II. 88 He was also somewhat of a time-server.

**3. a.** With limiting word or particle, as ***somewhat else, more, over***, etc.

(*a*) **1390** GOWER *Conf.* II. 96 As thogh I hadde lost a Ring Or somwhat elles. ? **1580** LODGE *Reply Gosson's Sch. Abuse* Wks. (Grosart) I. 29 These things are not the chiefest poynts you shote at; thers somewhat els sticketh in your stomak. **1665** J. NORTH in *Extr. State P. rel. Friends* (1912) III. 235, I haue some-what els to ymparte vnto you. **1736** AINSWORTH I. s.v. *Some*, I must talk of somewhat else.

(*b*) **1398** TREVISA *Barth. De P.R.* XIX. cxxv. (1495) 925 The Suparticularis nombre conteyneth in comparison alle the lesse nombre and somwhat ouer. **1626** B. JONSON *Staple of N.* III. ii, You are a Courtier, Sir, or somewhat more. *c* **1643** LD. HERBERT *Autobiog.* (1824) 16, I shall therefore only say somewhat more of my mother.

**b.** ***somewhat between***, = SOMETHING *sb.* 1 d.

**1823** SCOTT *Quentin D.* xxii, His gesture..was noble, and at the same time resigned, somewhat between the bearing of a feudal noble and of a Christian martyr.

**4. a.** A thing, quality, etc., worth considering or regarding; a person of note or importance.

**1382** WYCLIF *Gal.* ii. 6 Forsoth thei that weren seen for to be sumwhat, no thing to me ȝauen to gidere. **1526** TINDALE *Gal.* vi. 3 Iff a man seme to hym silfe that he is somwhat when in dede he is nothynge. **1663** DRYDEN *Wild Gallant* IV. ii, Nay, the fool is a handsome fool, that's somewhat. **1838** LOWELL *Lett.* (1894) I. 32 It were a strange thing indeed if there were not somewhat in such men as Milton, Sidney [etc.]. **1842** TENNYSON *St. Simeon Stylites* 124 They think that I am somewhat... The silly people take me for a saint. **1859** MASSON *Milton* I. 721 The living society of a place is also somewhat.

†**b.** ***of somewhat***, for some purpose. *Obs.*$^{-1}$

*a* **1400** *Sir Perc.* 854 It servede hym of somwhatt The wylde fyre that he gatt.

**5. a.** With *a*, *the*, etc., and pl. A certain undefined or unknown thing, quality, amount, etc.

**1598** R. BERNARD tr. *Terence* (1607) 30 'In the meane season I hope some-what may be done.'.. 'That some-what will prove just nothing.' **1654** WHITLOCK *Zootomia* 210 Pretty Somewhats they would meane, but sure They understand not themselves any more than I do. **1685** *Gracian's Courtier's Orac.* 220 Several men would be great, if they wanted not a somewhat, without which they never attain to the height of perfection. **1795** *Jemima* I. 218 He has a somewhat in his voice..so pleasant. **1806** H. SIDDONS *Maid, Wife, & Widow* II. 247 A habit of delivering his sentiments with a somewhat of more than dictatorial petulance. **1857** J. RAINE *Mem. J. Hodgson* I. 126 Sending to Hodgson a somewhat which he had left behind him.

**b.** With preceding adj.

**1685** *Gracian's Courtier's Orac.* 117 The secret charm, or the unexpressible somewhat; which the French call *Le Je-ne-sai-quoi.* **1710** BERKELEY *Princ. Hum. Knowl.* §80 Matter is an unknown somewhat—neither substance nor accident. **1785** M. CUTLER in *Life*, etc. (1888) II. 229, I now believe, at least, that there is a certain somewhat, which produced a rotary motion in a sword. **1827** COLERIDGE *Table-t.* 30 Aug., Painting is the intermediate somewhat between a thought and a thing. **1855** BROWNING *One Word More* ix, Thus achievement lacks a gracious somewhat.

**c.** Const. *of* or with adj. following.

**1817** KEATINGE *Trav.* I. 272 Still here attaches..a somewhat of disgraceful to the idea of intoxication. **1825** SCOTT *Fam. Lett.* II. 354 They require the atmosphere of a cigar and the amalgam of a *summat* comfortable. *a* **1858** R. A. VAUGHAN *Ess. & Rem.* (1858) I. 50 A somewhat of their spirit of love..he found ever afterwards indispensable to his heart.

**B.** *adv.* In a certain degree or measure; to some (slight or small) extent; slightly, a little; rather.

**1. a.** Qualifying a verb.

*c* **1200** ORMIN 16882 þærþurrh wass sene þatt he þa Summ-whatt bigunnenn haffde To lefenn o þe Laferrd Crist. *c* **1385** CHAUCER *L.G.W.* Prol. 71 (Fairf.), Ye be diligent To forthren me somwhat in my labour. *c* **1410** *Sir Cleges* 147 Jn with hyr he gan goo, And sumwatt mendyd hys chere. *c* **1440** *Partonope* 4915 To her suster dyd she spek And somwhat her hert to her breke. **1526** TINDALE *Acts* xxvi. 28 Sumwhatt thou bryngest me in mynde for to be come christen. **1577–82** BRETON *Flourish upon Fancie* Wks. (Grosart) I. 17/2 These Drugges,..though they sumwhat please the tast, yet make the bosom stinke. **1646** GAULE *Sel. Cas.* 56 Hereupon it hath been somwhat dissented. **1688** HOLME *Armoury* III. 308/1 The short Graver, which turneth up somewhat at the end. **1780** *Mirror* No. 82, Sir George Rodney's success has somewhat lessened their force. **1812** CARY *Dante, Parad.* II. 53 She somewhat smiled. **1877** J. D. CHAMBERS *Divine Worship* 389 The Forms of these ejaculations varied somewhat.

**b.** Qualifying a preposition.

**1492** HEN. VII *Let.* in G. Griffiths *Hist. Tong* (1894) 224 Desiring you that somwhat bifor the said tyme ye wol addresse you unto us. **1600** in Ingleby *Shaks. Cent. Praise* (Shaks. Soc.) 35 Somwhat before the play began. **1735** JOHNSON *Lobo's Abyssinia, Descr.* viii. 91 To drink somewhat beyond the bounds of exact Temperance. **1756** C. LUCAS *Ess. Waters* I. 10 Spirit of nitre consists of somewhat above one fourth of pure acid. **1819** BYRON *Juan* I. i, Sent to the devil somewhat ere his time.

**c.** ***somewhat as***, in much the same way, to some extent, as.

**1872** MORLEY *Voltaire* (1886) 1 We may think of Voltairism in France, somewhat as we think of Catholicism. **1894** CROCKETT *Stickit Minister* 16 It ran or rather hirpled somewhat as follows.

**2. a.** Qualifying an adjective, adverb, or clause.

(*a*) *a* **1300** *Cursor M.* 11054 þat mensking þam bi-tuin, Was sum-quat diuers, als i wene. *c* **1384** CHAUCER *H. Fame* 1097 But for the ryme ys lyght and lewed Yit make hyt sumwhat agreable. *c* **1400** *Lanfranc's Cirurg.* 48 If þat ilke mater be not hard but sumwhat neische. **1466** *Mann. & Househ. Exp.* (Roxb.) 324 For a sadelle sumwhat worne, ij.s. viij.d. *a* **1533** LD. BERNERS *Huon* xliii. 144 His coloure was sum what pale. **1595** in *Cath. Rec. Soc. Publ.* V. 335 His vtterance was somwhat vnready. **1667** DRYDEN & DK. NEWCASTLE *Sir M. Mar-all* V. ii, Would I were hanged if it be not somewhat probable. **1750** tr. *Leonardus' Mirr. Stones* 92 [It] is a stone of a crystal colour, and somewhat obscure. **1780** *Mirror* No. 105, Somewhat a-kin to the lovers of detraction are the offence-takers. **1826** *Art of Brewing* (ed. 2) 15 Their practice is governed by principles somewhat different. **1885** *Manch. Exam.* 12 May 5/2 It would seem.. that the struggle was somewhat indecisive.

(*b*) **1542** BOORDE *Dyetary* iv. (1870) 238 The seller vnder the pantry, sette somwhat abase. **1592** KYD *Murther. I. Brewen* Wks. (1901) 290 When it drew some what late. **1637** MILTON *Lycidas* 17 Begin, and somwhat loudly sweep the string. **1797–1805** S. & HT. LEE *Cant. T.* I. 195 One, who, having somewhat unexpectedly succeeded to the family title. **1851** MRS. BROWNING *Casa Guidi Wind.* II. 478 If..we Are counted somewhat deeply in their debt. **1869** RUSKIN *Q. of Air* i. §32 Somewhat saucily.

(*c*) **1578** *Reg. Privy Council Scot.* III. 35 Mony injurious wordis, sumquhat in contempt of our Soverane Lord. **1608** E. GRIMSTONE *Hist. France* (1611) 457 A cunning woman, and some-what of her fathers humor. **1678** BUNYAN *Pilgr.* I. 27 Now was Christian somwhat in a muse. **1818** SCOTT *Br. Lamm.* ix, The hounds and huntsmen seemed somewhat at a stand. **1828** LYTTON *Pelham* liii, Somewhat of a lugubrious nature. **1833** HT. MARTINEAU *Berkeley* I. iii. 49 Martin looked somewhat at a loss for an answer, till his wife supplied him with one.

**b.** With a comparative adj. or adv.

*c* **1400** MAUNDEV. (Roxb.) xi. 46 It es sumwhat hyer þan oþer placez of þe citee. **1484** CAXTON *Fables of Auian* xxii, I blowe in hit for to haue it somwhat more cold than hit is. **1514** BARCLAY *Cyt. & Uplondyshman* (Percy Soc.) 6 And somwhat wyser be they also than we. **1597** HOOKER *Eccl. Pol.* v. lv. §5 Somewhat more plainly, to shew a true immediate reason..we acknowledge [etc.]. **1600** PORY tr. *Leo's Africa* VI. 275 The men of this place are black, but the women are some-what fairer. **1696** WHISTON *Th. Earth* IV. (1722) 317 The Lower Earthy Strata would be settling somewhat closer together. **1768** *Woman of Honor* III. 233 A range of thirteen chests rather somewhat larger than the common size. **1815** J. SMITH *Panorama Sci. & Art* II. 173 The pan being brought to somewhat more than a red heat. **1866** CARLYLE in *Mrs. C.'s Lett.* III. 255 She..went home somewhat better. **1875** JOWETT *Plato* (ed. 2) I. 359 Tell me .., in somewhat plainer terms, what you mean!

**c.** With *of the* and a superlative adj. or adv.

**1561** T. HOBY tr. *Castiglione's Courtyer* IV. (1577) Y vij b, Not to make wise to abhorre companie and talke, though somewhat of the wantonest. **1622** MABBE tr. *Aleman's Guzman d'Alf.* I. 30, I got mee (though somewhat of the latest) hungry. **1656** HEYLIN *Surv. France* 218 The revenues of this Archbishoprick are somewhat of the meanest. **1818** SCOTT *Br. Lamm.* xvi, Your morning-draught has been somewhat of the strongest.

**d.** With *a* or *an* inserted before the adj. (or sb.) qualified.

**1588** J. READ *Compend. Method.* 69 b, Barriga..receaued a wounde in his brest, with somewhat a long sword. *a* **1646** GREGORY *Posthuma* (1650) 198 This was somwhat a tolerable impietie, for such great Astronomers to adore the Host of Heaven. **1680** R. L'ESTRANGE *Erasm. Colloq.* 79 [He] may vouchsafe his Assistance also unto us, who are some-what a larger Congregation. **1779** JOHNSON *Drake* Wks. 1787 IV. 417 Being obliged by this accident to somewhat a longer residence among the Moors. **1817** WHEWELL in Mrs. S. Douglas *Life* (1881) 25, I must acknowledge myself somewhat an idle correspondent so far as writing goes. **1891** ANNE MOZLEY *Lett. J. H. Newman* I. iii. 103 There were certainly..definite points about him which made him somewhat a difficulty.

**e.** Preceded by an article or pron.

**1779** *Mirror* No. 61, The contempt in which, to a somewhat unreasonable degree, he holds modern refinement. **1820** SCOTT *Monast.* xxi, The cooling my somewhat too much inflamed visage. **1849** MACAULAY *Hist. Eng.* ii. I. 180 Her admonitions were given in a somewhat perfunctory manner.

**f.** Used as *adj.*

**1819** T. MOORE in *Mem.* (1853) II. 250 Lady Frances W. was to have come with them, but, to my somewhat disappointment, she had been called away.

†**3.** ***somewhat...somewhat***, partly...partly.

**1390** GOWER *Conf.* I. 2, I wolde..wryte a bok betwen the tweie, Somewhat of lust, somewhat of lore. *c* **1400** *Pilgr. Sowle* (Caxton) I. xxx. (1859) 34 He is lettid by the wey somwhat by foly of hym self, somwhat by other. *a* **1425** tr. *Arderne's Treat. Fistula*, etc. 38 þai may ete and drynk and go, and somwhat sitte and somwhat slepe. **1552** LATIMER *Serm.* (1607) 301 A king.., which was not their lawfull nor naturall king, but somewhat with craft and subtilty, and somewhat with power had gotten the Crowne.

†**4.** Followed by *with the* and a superlative, = SOMETHING *adv.* 2 f. *Obs. rare.*

**1542** UDALL *Erasm. Apoph.* 252 b, [She] begoonne somewhat with the soonest to have whyte heares in hir hedde. **1583** GOLDING *Calvin on Deut.* Pref. Ep. 2 Such discourse which might peraduenture be somewhat with the longest. **1610** HOLLAND *Camden's Brit.* 215 A small towne this is, standing somewhat with the lowest.

**5.** ***somewhat like***, in various senses (see LIKE *a.* 2 e, f).

**1593** G. HARVEY *Pierce's Super.* Wks. (Grosart) II. 229 Though she were a lustie bounsing rampe somewhat like Gallamilla. **1611** COTGR., *Bellastre*,..passable, so so, somewhat like. *a* **1620** DYKE *Serm.* (1640) 379 If a man will sell a commodity, hee will sell it somewhat like, or hee will keepe it. **1662** J. DAVIES tr. *Olearius' Voy. Amb.* 165 It was somewhat like a Sturgeon, but was much whiter. **1748** RICHARDSON *Clarissa* (1811) VI. 241 Why this is talking somewhat like. **1859** GEO. ELIOT *A. Bede* viii, It's summat-like to see such a man as that i' the desk of a Sunday! **1890** *Science-Gossip* XXVI. 194 This is somewhat like the one examined by Schrötter.

**6.** ***more than somewhat***, very, extremely; very much.

**1930** D. RUNYON in *Collier's* 13 Sept. 7/3, I am now more nervous than somewhat. **1938** D. WHEATLEY *Uncharted Seas* xi. 190, I thought my nerve was pretty good, but this scares me more than somewhat. **1945** *Tee Emm* (Air Ministry) V. 40 Citizens have been known to leave the premises.., being more than somewhat apprehensive of future developments. **1964** WODEHOUSE *Frozen Assets* viii. 143 She said quite a number of things that wounded my sensitive nature more than somewhat. **1974** V. GIELGUD *In such a Night* vii. 67 It burned me up more than somewhat.

†**somewhatly**, *adv. Obs. rare.* Also 5 **sumwhatly, svmqwatly.** [f. as prec. + -LY².] Somewhat; to some (slight) extent.

*c* **1425** *St. Elizabeth of Spalbeck* in *Anglia* VIII. 108 A whyte lynnen garnemente sumwhatly trailynge on þe erthe. *Ibid.* 115 Sumwhatly streight vp towarde the auter. **1483** *Cath. Angl.* 371 Svmqwatly, *aliqualiter, vtrumque.* [*a* **1711** H. LAMP *Autobiog.* iii. (1895) 26, I staid there about six months, learning the English tongue somewhatly.]

**somewhen** (ˈsʌmhwɛn), *adv.* Also 4 **somwanne, sumwhan(ne.** [f. SOME *a.*¹ + WHEN *adv.*] At some (indefinite or unknown) time; sometime or other. Common in 19th cent. Usu. coupled with *somewhere* or *somehow*.

**1297** R. GLOUC. (Rolls) 5212 Of þe batayles of denemarch þat abbeþ ybe in þis londe... Worst hii were, vor oþere somwanne adde ydo [etc.].

**1833** J. S. MILL *Let.* 5 July in *Wks.* (1963) XII. 163, I shall write out my thoughts more at length somewhere, and somewhen, probably soon. **1863** KINGSLEY *Water-Bab.* 349 Some folks can't help hoping..that they may have another chance, to make things fair and even, somewhere, somewhen, somehow. **1875** WHITNEY *Life Lang.* ix. 174 Spoken somewhere and somewhen in the past. **1876** FREEMAN in W. R. W. Stephens *Life & Lett.* II. 134 To tarry with James Allen..till somewhen about next Wednesday. **1920** H. G. WELLS *Outl. History* (rev. ed.) viii. 37/1 Somewhen about 50,000 years ago..appeared *Homo Neanderthalensis.* **1934** J. L. MYRES in E. Eyre *Europ. Civilization* I. 87 Such accommodation between means and ends, resources and wants, is found to have been achieved, somewhen and somehow, [etc.]. **1975** J. C. MASTERMAN *On Chariot Wheel* v. 40, I cherished the belief that somehow and somewhen I should find my way to Oxford.

ˈ**somewhence**, *adv. rare.* [f. SOME *a.*¹ + WHENCE *adv.*] From some (indefinite) place; from somewhere or other.

**1564** MRS. A. BACON tr. *Jewel's Apol.* L iiij, Fearing that the people shoulde..somwhence els seeke a surer meane of their saluation. **1905** *Daily Chron.* 11 Aug. 4/7 That little boy seems to live on his imaginary trudge—somewhence—somewhither!

**somewhere** (ˈsʌmhwɛə(r)), *adv.* and *sb.* Forms: 3 (*Orm.*) **summhwær**, 4 **sumwhare, -whore, -wher(e,** 6 **-whear;** 4 **sumquar(e, -quer,** 5 **-qwhare;** 4 **sum-, somwar;** 4 **some-,** 5 **somwhare;** 4 **sommewhere,** 5–7 **somwhere,** 5– **somewhere.** [f. SOME *a.*¹ + WHERE *adv.* Down to the end of the 16th c. freq. written as two words.]

**A.** *adv.* **1. a.** In or at some place unspecified, indeterminate, or unknown.

*c* **1200** ORMIN 6929 Forr þatt he wass forrdredd tatt teȝȝ Himm sholldenn summhwær hidenn. **1297** R. GLOUC. (Rolls) 4344 King arþure was þer of ywar, & þoȝte.. Wiþ al is poer bi þe wey somwar him kepe. *a* **1310** in Wright *Spec. Lyric P.* xxxix. 110 He hath hewe sum wher a burthen of brere. **1483** *Cath. Angl.* 371/2 Sumqwhare, *alicubi.* **1526** *Pilgr. Perf.* (W. de W. 1531) 106 An holy saynt..serued in many chirches, and some where here in Englande. **1638** JUNIUS *Paint. Ancients* 14 Others..wander up and downe to meet somewhere with a refreshing shade. **1667** MILTON *P.L.* IX. 256 What malicious Foe..somwhere nigh at hand Watches. **1796** MME. D'ARBLAY *Camilla* IV. 390 A paper in her hand-writing, which she had somewhere lost. **1827** SCOTT *Chron. Canongate* Introd., As it was suspected that he was lurking somewhere on the property, his family were closely watched. **1859** GEO. ELIOT *A. Bede* xxii, Arthur must be somewhere in the back rooms. **1878** G. MACDONALD *Ann. Q. Neighb.* xxvi. 448 There's something wrong somewhere.

**b.** With correlative *somewhere* or *otherwhere*.

**1398** TREVISA *Barth. De P.R.* XIII. iv. (Bodl. MS.), In coloure..somewhare he [a river] is clere and somewhare he is dymme. **1630** *R. Johnson's Kingd. & Commw.* 423 Many places lying waste, somewhere for want of water, somewhere for want of manurance, somewhere for abundance of light sand. **1632** LITHGOW *Trav.* x. 493 A Regall Commission.. being some-where obeyed, and other-where suspended.

**c.** ***somewhere else***, in some other place, elsewhere.

*c* **1500** *Communycacyon* (W. de W.) C ij, Man thou must alwaye suffre payne Here for thy synnes or somwhere elles. **1530** PALSGR. 823/1 Some where els, *quelque aultre part.* **1588** SHAKS. *Tit. A.* IV. iii. 40 She is so imploy'd,..with Ioue in heauen, or some where else: So that [etc.]. **1611** COTGR., *Ailleurs*, elsewhere, somewhere else. **1737** *Gentl. Mag.* VII. 603/2 We must therefore look some where else for the Cause of our present Uneasiness.

**d.** ***somewhere or another*** or ***other***.

**1791** CHARLOTTE SMITH *Celestina* (ed. 2) I. 129 Here Daniel, prythee take and stow it somewhere or another. **1799** E. DU BOIS *Piece Family Biog.* I. 59, 'I have heard somewhere or another,' said he, 'that' [etc.]. **1852** C. W. HOSKYNS *Talpa* i. (1854) 2 Somewhere or other in England there is a flat bleak high-lying district, which [etc.].

**e.** ***somewhere in*** (*France*, etc.), phr. orig. used during the war of 1914–18 in referring to some locality in the theatre of war without identifying it (because of the restrictions of censorship); hence, in extended use, somewhere unspecified for reasons of security or because one's stay there is temporary.

**1915** *Illustr. London News* 20 Feb. 233 (*caption*) The War Area as seen by the Airman: 'somewhere in Flanders' photographed from a reconnoitring Aeroplane. *Ibid.* 241 For the moment 'Victoria' looks like 'Somewhere in France'. **1915** *Daily Sketch* 17 Aug. 12/1 None of these soldiers a year ago expected to be snapped one day..—somewhere in Egypt. **1918** *Wireless World* VI. 390 A Wireless Section 'Somewhere in England'. **1939** Joyce *Finnegans Wake* 21 There was a brannewail that same sabboath night of falling angles somewhere in Erio. **1939** *War Illustr.* 14 Oct. 144 From 'Somewhere in England' to 'Somewhere in France': 1939 Echoes the Story of 1914. **1943** J. B. Priestley *Daylight on Saturday* viii. 52 If our lads was fightin' like 'ell somewhere in France, why yer'd see them production figures take a high jump. **1943** *Gramophone* Sept. 63/3 From Mr. Tony Puddy, Somewhere-in-England. **1973** *Jewish Chron.* 9 Feb. 15/2 The girls I visited recently on a training course 'somewhere in Israel' were not all bunched together in one group. **1977** 'J. le Carré' *Honourable Schoolboy* xvii. 400 The Somewhere-in-England sense of makeshift habitation..of every exiled correspondent.

**2.** To some (unspecified or unknown) place. Usually with the verb *go*.
*c* **1403** Clanvowe *Cuckoo & Night.* 112 Now, gode Cukkow! go som-where away. *a* **1548** Hall *Chron., Edw. V*, 9 Is it not likely that she wyll send him somwhere out of the realme? **1590** Shaks. *Com. Err.* ii. i. 5 Perhaps..from the Mart he's somewhere gone to dinner. **1592** Kyd *Sp. Trag.* iii. x, To..carry you obscurely some where els. **1720** De Foe *Capt. Singleton* (1906) 37 We were upon a voyage and no voyage, we were bound somewhere and nowhere. **1780** Warner in Jesse *Selwyn & Contemp.* (1844) IV. 359 Charles is gone out of town somewhere to-day.

**†3.** In some places; here and there. *Obs. rare.*
**1563** Nowell in *Lett. Lit. Men* (Camden) 20 The coopie ..was interlined and sumwhear blotted. **1578** Lyte *Dodoens* v. xxxiii. 593 The Turnep loueth an open place, it is sowen somwhere in vineyardes, as at Huygarden and the Countrie thereaboutes.

**4.** In some part or passage of a book, etc.; in some work or other.
**1634** Sir T. Herbert *Trav.* 74 The Bashaw, in this Itenerary somewhere spoken of. **1732** Berkeley *Alciphr.* ii. §23 A fable, I somewhere met with in the writings of a Swiss philosopher. **1780** *Mirror* No. 102, Lord Chesterfield says somewhere, that, to..act with spirit, is to..act foolishly. **1820** Byron *Juan* iv. cx, As some one somewhere sings about the sky.

**5. a.** At some time *about* or *in* (a certain specified year, date, etc.).
**1839** *Penny Cycl.* XIII. 168/1 He is said to have been born somewhere about A.D. 40. **1859** Ruskin *Two Paths* iii. §91 An old English cottage,..perhaps built somewhere in the Charleses' times. **1891** C. James *Rom. Rigmarole* iv. 32, I woke up out of my nap somewhere about five o'clock.

**b.** ***somewhere about***, approximately.
**1846** Ryland in *Life & Corr. Foster* II. 343 He kept his room somewhere about two months. **1876** Tait *Rec. Adv. Phys. Sci.* vi. 157 The sun's radiation is..somewhere about thirty-fold that of the same area of the furnace of a locomotive.

**B.** *sb.* Some unspecified or indefinite place.
**1647** Cowley *Mistr.* (1669) 22 Then down I laid my Head; and for a while was Dead, And my freed Soul to a strange Somewhere fled. **1718** D'Urfey *Grecian Heroine* v. i, I would fain think now, But that my Spirits, with my Blood, are posting To their new some-where. **1786** Mrs. A. M. Bennett *Juvenile Indiscr.* I. 54 It was a somewhere, a home. **1914** R. Brooke *Let.* 7 Mar. in *Coll. Poems* (1918) p. cxiii, I shall be glad to be back among you all, and tied to somewhere in England. *Ibid. Let.* Mar. p. cxvii, I want somewhere I needn't always be spick and span in, and somewhere I don't have to pay a vast sum. **1928** W. B. Yeats *Tower* 8 And I myself created Hanrahan And drove him drunk or sober through the dawn From somewhere in the neighbouring cottages. **1930** G. B. Shaw *Apple Cart* ii. 69 All their people came from Scotland or Ireland or Wales or Jerusalem or somewhere. **1942** W. Faulkner *Go down, Moses* 139 A big dog, a hound with a strain of mastiff from somewhere. **1958** B. W. Aldiss *Non-Stop* ii. ii. 79 The ship ..has come *from* somewhere and is going *to* somewhere. These somewheres are more important than the ship.

So **'somewheres** *adv.* (*dial.* or *vulg.*)
**1859** Bartlett *Dict. Amer.* (ed. 2) 428 A hundred dollars, or somewheres there along. **1883** Stevenson *Treas. Isl.* xxviii, I know you've got that ship safe somewheres.

**somewhile** ('sʌmhwaɪl), *adv.* Now *rare*. Forms: 2–3 **sum wile**, 3 **sum(e) hwile**, 4 **sumwhyle**, 4–6 **-while**; 4–5 **sumquile**, **-quyle**, 5 **-qwile**; 5 **somwhyle**, 7 **-while**; 5 **some wile**, **somewhyle**, 5–7, 9 **somewhile**. [f. some *a.*[1] + while *sb.*; cf. WFlem. *somwijl*. In early use freq. written as two words.]

**1.** **†a.** At or in some former time; erewhile; formerly. *Obs.*
**1154** *O.E. Chron.* (Laud MS.) an. 1137, Sume ieden on ælmes þe waren sum wile rice-men. *c* **1230** *Hali Meid.* 5 Syon was sum hwile iclepet þe hehe tur of Ierusalem. **13..** *K. Alis.* 1527 (W.), Ther was sum while, over us, A kyng that hette Neptanabus. **13..** *Gaw. & Gr. Knt.* 625 Hit is a syngne þat Salamon set sum-quyle. *a* **1400-50** *Alexander* 2994 Þan was an ymage within..Of Sexeres þat sum-quyle þat cite had to welde. **1591** Spenser *Ruins of Rome* 242 These..Pallaces..were shepheards cottages somewhile. **1654** H. L'Estrange *Chas. I* (1655) 65 That shell which was some-while the continent of so vast treasures of knowledge.

**†b.** ***somewhile since***, some time ago. *Obs.*
**1652** Needham tr. *Selden's Mare Cl.* 115 Nor must wee let it pass, that somwhile since, there were two Constitutions pretended to in France.

**c.** *attrib.*, passing into *adj.* Former, sometime.
**1860** Ainsworth *Ovingdean Grange* 11 Highly dangerous to the spiritual welfare of his somewhile flock. **1888** *N. & Q.* 7th Ser. VI. 19/1 Richard Doyle, somewhile illustrator of *Punch*.

**†2.** On a certain occasion in the past; once; at one time. *Obs. rare.*
*c* **1200** *Trin. Coll. Hom.* 43 We findeð on þe holie boc, þat ure helende..ferde sumwile mid mede ouere water. *a* **1300** *Cursor M.* 4751 Þe caf he cast o corn sumquile In þe flum þat hait þe nile. *c* **1586** C'tess Pembroke *Ps.* xcix. viii, For sinne they somewhile smarted. **1631** Gouge *God's Arrows* iii. §88. 349 The souldiers that came from Newhaven that was somwhile besieged, and after taken by the enemy.

**3.** At some (unspecified) time; at one time or other; at times, sometimes. Also † ***at somewhile***.
*c* **1250** *Owl & Night.* 6 Þat playd wes..starc & strong, Sum hwile softe & lud among. **1390** Gower *Conf.* I. 367, I have herd sein..That thei som while here cause ladden Be merci. **1426** Lydg. *De Guil. Pilgr.* 11427 What ys the cause ..That a swerd burnysshed cler, Somwhyle rusteth? *c* **1456** Pecock *Bk. of Faith* (1909) 252 Peraventure he schal have nede at sumwhile. **1559** *Mirr. Mag.* (1563) A iv, To serue kings in al pointes men must sum while breke rules. **1560** Whitehorne *Arte Warre* 9 b, Some while it hapned, that in one self time there were manie Emperours. **1579** Spenser *Sheph. Cal.* May 126 Tho vnder colour of shepeheards, somewhile There crept in Wolues, ful of fraude and guile. **1628** Gaule *Pract. The.* (1629) 109 An vniuersall King does not onely some-while fore-goe, but some-what resemble the King Eternall. **1629** in Bradford *Plymouth Plant.* (1856) 246 These now sente..must, some while, be chargable to you & us. **1855** J. Nichol in *Mem.* (1896) iii. 130 The 'beautiful vision' with which all lives worth living have been somewhile brightened.

**b.** With correlative *somewhile* or †*other whiles*.
*a* **1240** *Lofsong* in *O.E. Hom.* I. 205 Sumehwile to pleiful, to drupi oðer hwiles. **13..** *Cursor M.* 7433 (Gött.), Sumquile [*v.r.* oþerwhile] wid harpe, sumquile wid sang. *c* **1400** *Pilgr. Sowle* (Caxton) i. xx. (1859) 26 How ofte haue I warned the byfore, Som whyle aperte, som whyle pryuely. **1575** Vautrollier *Luther on Ep. Galat.* 161 In whom is found continually, somewhile the time of the law, and somewhile the time of grace. **1607** Hieron *Wks.* I. 399 It is termed some while, a blessing themselues; some while an encouraging themselues in a wicked purpose.

**4.** For some time.
**1864** Pusey *Daniel* (1876) 302 His grandfather himself must have been somewhile dead.

**'somewhiles**, *adv.* Now *dial.* or *arch.* Forms: 3 **sumehwules**, 6 **sumwhiles**, **somwhyles**, **somewhiles**, **somewhyles**, 6–7, 9 **somewhiles**. [f. as prec. with genitive or plural *-s*. Cf. WFlem. *somwijls*, Du. *somwijlen*.]

**†1.** At some former time; formerly. *Obs.*$^{-1}$
*a* **1225** *Ancr. R.* 276 Bihold, holie men þet weren sumehwules, hwu heo uesten, & hwu heo wakeden.

**2.** On some occasion(s); sometimes.
Freq. in the latter half of the 16th c.
**1528** Tindale *Obed. Chr. Man* 150 b, The very Gods them selves which sell their pardone so good chepe or some whiles geve them frely for glory sake. **1559** *Mirr. Mag.* (1563) A iij, We let hang the true man somwhyles to saue a thefe. **1594** Carew *Huarte's Exam. Wits* x. (1596) 144 The profession of which they haue made choice (though somwhiles vnworthy). **1626** Fenner *Hidden Manna* (1652) B iij, For the Understanding and Will are somewhiles like Simeon and Levi. **1681** R. L'Estrange *Tully's Offices* 131 Without need some whiles of any other Company. *c* **1863** S. S. Jones *Northumbld.*, etc. 129 There was yen o' them it [= that] somewhiles did nae make things sae smooth as they might have been. **1890** D. G. Mitchell *English Lands* II. iii. 107 Among other writers..who went somewhiles to these suppers..was James Howell. **1901** A. J. Davies *Athirt Downs* ii. iv. 72 Takes a deal of following somewhiles, that it do.

**b.** With correlatives, esp. ***somewhiles..., somewhiles***, = sometimes 1 b.
(*a*) **1547** J. Harrison *Exhort. Scottes* c vj b, Britayne was not always..vnder one Kyng.., but was gouerned somwhiles by one, and somwhiles by mo. **1606** G. W[oodcocke] *Hist. Ivstine* iv. 21 The wind..sendeth foorth in many places, some-whiles flashes of fyre, other some-whiles againe most..dangerous vapors. **1612** Davies *Why Ireland*, etc. (1747) 16 Some whiles one prevailing,.. somewhiles the other.
(*b*) *a* **1553** Udall *Royster D.* i. i, Sometime Lewis Loytrer biddeth me come neere; Somewhyles Watkin Waster maketh vs good cheere. **1560** Whitehorne *Arte Warre* 42 b, Some whiles thei fought with the enemies horses, an other while, thei rescued the fotmen. **1565** Allen *Defence Purg.* xv. 272 One while by the praysies of the doctors and antiquitye, and sumwhiles by thabasing of theime ageine.

**†3.** At some time *before*. *Obs.*$^{-1}$
**1657** W. Rand tr. *Gassendi's Life Peiresc* ii. 254 Having some whiles before procured [an]..Edition of his Divine Poems.

**somewhither** ('sʌmhwɪðə(r)), *adv.* Forms: 5–6 **somwhether**, 6 **-whyther**, 7– **somewhither**. [f. some *a.*[1] + whither *adv.*]

**1.** In some direction.
**1398** Trevisa *Barth. De P.R.* iii. xvii. (W. de W.) 61 The syghte is made by lynes that passyth not awaye forth ryght, but blenchyth somwhether asyde of the strayte waye. **1858** Carlyle *Fredk. Gt.* x. i. (1872) II. 575 Twilight, with here and there a transient spark falling somewhither in it. **1905** *Daily News* 2 May 6 But the time comes when the fashion must change somewhither.

**2.** To some place, = somewhere *adv.* 2.
**1530** Palsgr. 823/1 Somwhyther, *quelque part*. ?*c* **1560** *Trag. Rich. II* (1870) 40 Prethee sweete king letts ride somwhether and it be but to showe ourselues. **1588** Shaks. *Tit. A.* iv. i. 11 Some whether would she haue thee goe with her. *c* **1645** Tullie *Siege of Carlisle* (1840) 13 Bidding her convey the money somewhither. **1779** Forrest *Voy. N. Guinea* 290, I found several persons who..seemed to imagine me bound some whither. **1845** Carlyle *Cromwell* (1857) II. 71 The poor young King is much at a loss;—must go somewhither. **1877** W. Black *Green Past.* xxxiv, Like ghosts waiting for Charon to take them somewhither.

**†b.** ***somewhither else***, to some other place; elsewhere. *Obs.*
**1623** in Ellis *Orig. Lett.* Ser. i. III. 125 [They] would faine hope that he was gone somewhither else then to Spaine. **1658** Earl Monm. tr. *Paruta's Wars Cyprus* 24 The latter.. endeavoured, that the Fleet might go some-whither else. **1700** Bp. Lloyd in Aubrey *Brief Lives* (1813) I. 102 We must think of removing you some whither else where you may have a subsistence.

**†'somewho.** *Obs.*$^{-1}$ In 4 **somwho**. [f. some *a.*[1] + who *pron.*] Some one; somebody.
**1390** Gower *Conf.* I. 15 Ofte is sen that mochel slowthe.. Doth mochel harm, whan fyr is uppe, Bot if somwho the flamme stanche.

**somewhy** ('sʌmhwaɪ), *adv. rare.* [f. some *a.*[1] + why *adv.*] For some reason or reasons.
**1858** *Athenæum* 1 May 555 A buxom, shrill, mean, troublesome woman; yet somehow and some*why* not utterly detestable. **1864** Browning *Dram. Pers. Wks.* 1896 I. 610/1 You learn What some one was somewhere, somewhen, somewhy.

**somewise** ('sʌmwaɪz), *adv.* Now *arch.* Also 5 **somwyse**, 6 **sumwise**. [f. some *a.*[1]: see -wise.] In some way or manner; to some extent. In recent use with *in*.
*c* **1440** *Alph. Tales* 293 Becauce he wold somwyse be occupyed ilka day. **1596** Dalrymple tr. *Leslie's Hist. Scot.* II. 105 To cause his subiectis lyue in peace with him, or sum-wise slokne that hett hatred and Jnuie betuene thame. *a* **1677** Barrow *Serm. Upright Walking* Wks. 1687 I. 60 That nothing can be really profitable..to us, which..doth not somewise conduce to our spiritual interest. **1848** D. G. Rossetti *Last Confession* Poems (1870) 67 The father's, brother's love—was changed, I think, in somewise. **1865** Swinburne *Chastelard* ii. i, I thought I was..lying by my lord, and knew In somewise he was well awake.

**somir**, obs. form of summer.

**somital** ('səʊmɪtəl), *a. Zool.* [f. next.] Of or pertaining to a somite; somitic.
**1890** in *Cent. Dict.* s.v. *Metameric*.

**somite** ('səʊmaɪt). *Zool.* [f. Gr. σῶμα body, soma[2] + -ite.] One or other of the more or less distinct segments into which the bodies of many animals are divided.
**1869** Huxley *Introd. Classif. Anim.* 77 The head of a Crustacean, an Arachnid, a Myriapod, or an Insect is composed of six somites. **1875** C. C. Blake *Zool.* 281 The number of segments or somites in the body of insects never exceeds twenty. **1888** Rolleston & Jackson *Anim. Life* 142 The abdomen..is made up of a number of distinct segments or *somites*.

**somitic** (səʊ'mɪtɪk), *a. Zool.* [f. prec. + -ic.] Of or pertaining to, having the form or character of, a somite.
**1888** Huxley & Martin *Pract. Biol.* 243 These septa are metamerically arranged, one for each somitic constriction. *Ibid.* 244 A series of somitic compartments.

**†'somler.** *Obs.* Chiefly *Sc.* Also 6 **summeleir**, **symleir**, **somme-**, **somlier**, **sommler**, **somlar**, **semlar**. [a. F. *sommelier*, f. *somme* pack.] A butler.
**1543** *St. Papers Hen. VIII*, IX. 325 To gyve commaundement that your sommelier at Bordeaulx might be suffred to departe with such wynes as he had provided for Your Majestie. **1566** *Reg. Privy Council Scot.* I. 451 Leonard Baillie, summeleir to oure Soveranis. **1583** *Excheq. Rolls Scot.* XXI. 563 Threttie tunnis of full Burdehous wyne ..at the cheis and contentment of his hienes somleris.

**somlich**: see seemly *a.*

**somma** ('sɒmə). *Physical Geogr.* Also **Somma**. [a. It. (*Monte*) *Somma*, proper name of the feature of this kind associated with Vesuvius.] A remnant of an older volcanic cone which partly or wholly encircles a younger cone; the rim of a caldera. Freq. *attrib.*, as ***somma ring***.
*c* **1910** H. R. Mill *Dict. Geogr. Terms* in L. D. Stamp *Gloss. Geogr. Terms* (1961) 426 *Somma*, originally, the rampart remaining from the old crater of Vesuvius and forming an arc around one side of the new one. The name is sometimes extended to similar formations in other volcanoes. **1917** T. G. Bonney *T. Anderson's Volcanic Studies* 2nd Ser. vii. 39 This [ridge], according to Dr. Anderson, forms a Somma ring within which rises a smaller and a larger crater, both intermittently active. **1940** *Bull. Volcanologique* VI. 217 The older volcanic mass on the eastern side may be a continuation of the Somma. **1944** C. A. Cotton *Volcanoes as Landscape Forms* xi. 167 An example of a large cumulo-dome which has been built within a wide caldera or 'Somma ring' is the Soufrière of Guadeloupe, in the Lesser Antilles. **1975** Fielder & Wilson *Volcanoes of Earth, Moon & Mars* vii. 88/1 The so-called somma-type of nested cone..is named after Mount Somma, a residual portion of the encircling volcanic rim unit which was the precursor of the present, centrally disposed, Vesuvius. **1979** *Nature* 1 Nov. 24/1 It [*sc.* Soufrière volcano, St. Vincent] is a strato-volcano 1,220 m high with an open summit crater 1·6 km in diameter located in the southern part of a 2-km wide somma crater.

**†sommage.** *Obs. rare.* [a. OF. *sommage* (med.L. *summ-*, *sumagium*), f. *somme* pack.] Baggage; baggage-animals.
*c* **1500** *Melusine* 143 And he made to abyde in the valey all the sommage. *Ibid.* 277 The next day..desloged the vanward, and after the grete batayll, & the sommage & syn

the ryergarde. **1502** tr. *Charter Forest* in Arnolde *Chron.* 80 b, For an horse beryng sommage [L. *sumagium*].

**somme**, obs. f. SOAM, SUM *sb.* and *v.*

**sommed**, obs. var. SUMMED *ppl. a.*

‖**sommelier** (sɔmlje). [Fr.: see SOMLER.] A wine waiter.

**1889** *Harper's Mag.* Apr. 698/1 The 'sommelier', or butler, who runs from table to table, laden with bottles, and distributes here and there strange liquids. **1923** E. P. OPPENHEIM *Inevitable Millionaires* xiv. 146 Harold.. making cryptic signs with his fingers which intimated to the sommelier his urgent need of a cocktail. **1955** M. ALLINGHAM *Beckoning Lady* v. 77 He poured the awkward liquid with the skill of a *sommelier*. **1966** *Punch* 20 July 113/2 Although we've still got some cooks to shoot and many sommeliers to educate, our standards have improved beyond all recognition. **1974** *Times* (Wines & Spirits Suppl.) 2 Dec. p. iii/2 An awe-inspiringly stately *sommelier* and long wine lists.. can often discourage the sale of wine.

**sommer** (ˈsɒmə(r)), *adv. S. Afr. colloq.* Also somaar, 9 somar, somer. [a. Afrikaans *somaar, sommer*.] Just, simply, for no specific reason, without further ado.

**1835** T. BOWKER *Jrnl.* 12 May (MS.), Bowkers party gone out on patrole *somer* heard from the third Division, they have been shooting some Kafirs, & taking Cattle & Goats. **1850** R. G. CUMMING *Five Yrs. Hunter's Life S. Afr.* I. 27 The Dutch word *somar*.. is also a word to which I think I could challenge the most learned school-master in the Colony to attach any definite meaning. It is used by both Boers and Hottentots in almost every sentence. **1920** S. BLACK *Dorp* 174 'Ach, Oom Kaspar, can't I go back to look for my pipe and put it somaar in the box?' 'Nay, kerel, they won't let you go again inside the ballot-box.' **1959** *Cape Times* 15 Aug. (Weekend Mag.) 10/6 Too dangerous to sommer leave it like that with a child about the place. **1969** A. FUGARD *Boesman & Lena* 15 Sannie who? Sommer Sannie Somebody. **1975** *Daily Dispatch* (E. London) 13 June 12 My father was a trader, who sold both blankets and ochre, and to my question as to why the tribesmen didn't sommer buy red blankets instead of going through all the trouble of dyeing white blankets with ochre, he replied that this was for hygienic reasons.

**sommer**, var. SOMER *Obs.*; obs. f. SUMMER *sb.* and *v.*

†**so'mmerse**, *v. Obs.* [f. It. *sommerso*, pa. pple. of *sommergere* SUBMERGE *v.*] *trans.* To submerge, overflow.

**1632** LITHGOW *Trav.* I. 14 This second Sodome should be sommerssed by water. *Ibid.* VI. 255 Many Citties, Mansions, and Stations, haue beene sommerssed with water.

†**sommier**[1]. *Obs. rare.* In 5 sommyer. [a. F. *sommier*.] A pack-horse; = SOMER 1.

**1485** CAXTON *Chas. Gt.* 128 They sawe passe by the castel xx sommyers laden wyth vytayl. *Ibid.* 159 That euery man trusse hys gheer vpon the sommyers.

†**sommier**[2]. *Obs.* Also summier. [a. F. *sommier*, or alteration of *sommer* SUMMER *sb.*[2] after this.] A bearing-beam in a building.

**1623** T. GOAD *Dolef. Euen Song* 11 By the breaking asunder of a maine Sommier or Dormer of that floare. **1625** LISLE *Du Bartas, Noe* 181 Mounting here and there.. Into the esparsed pipes o' th' Sommier thorow-bored. **1631** GOUGE *God's Arrows* IV. §15. 399 The maine Summier which crossed the garret was ten inches square.

†**'sommite**[1]. *Min. Obs.* [f. Mt. *Somma* near Naples + -ITE[1] 2 b.] Nephelite.

**1805** R. JAMESON *Min.* II. 565 Sommite... Its colour is greyish-white. **1823** W. PHILLIPS *Min.* (ed. 3) 125 The Sommite usually occurs in grains, or in small regular hexahedral prisms. **1837** DANA *Min.* 291 Nepheline, *Spatum hexagonum*... Sommite.

‖**sommité**[2] (sɔmite). [Fr., lit. 'summit, top, tip'.] A person of great eminence or influence.

**1856** *Sat. Rev.* 19 Apr. 496/1 We observe the name of numerous *sommités* of the architectural profession. **1859** [see COLLECTIONIZE *v.*]. **1900** W. JAMES *Let.* 2 Apr. (1920) II. 121 We must go in for budding genius, if we seek a European. If an American, we can get a *sommité*! **1938** A. HUXLEY *Let.* 12 Apr. (1969) 434, I thought him [*sc.* Dr. Gerald Webb] a most remarkable old man, and they all say he's one of the *sommités* in the matter of TB. **1965** *Punch* 24 Nov. 752/1 A High Table is an institution; it is not merely a collection of what the French used to call *sommités*.

**sommitie**, obs. form of SUMMITY.

**sommon**, obs. form of SUMMON *v.*

**sommonce, sommon(e)s**, obs. ff. SUMMONS *sb.*

**sommonicion**, var. of SUMMONITION.

**somn-**, combining form of L. *somnus*, used in words based on L. *ambulāre* to walk; the oldest of these in English use are *somnambulation, somnambulism*, and *somnambulist*. (For variant, and in some cases earlier, terms see NOCT-.) **som'nambulance**, sleep-walking, somnambulism. **som'nambulant** *a.*, walking in sleep, somnambulic; *sb.*, a somnambulist. **som'nambular** *a.*, of or pertaining to sleep-walking; also *erron.*, connected with, of the nature of, sleep. **som'nambulary** *a.*, = prec. **som'nambulate** *v. intr.*, to walk during sleep; *trans.*, to walk along (a place) while asleep; hence **som'nambulating** ppl. a. **som,nambu'lation** [mod.L. *somnambulatio*], the action or fact of walking in sleep. **som'nambulator**, = next. **som'nambule** [a. F. *somnambule* (1690), Sp. and Pg. *somn-*, Sp. *sonámbulo*, mod.L. *somnambulus, -ambulo*], a somnambulist. **som'nambulency**, sleep-walking, or a fit of this; also *fig.* **som'nambulic** *a.*, of the nature of, pertaining to, etc., somnambulism; walking during sleep; hence **som'nambulically** *adv.* **som'nambulism** [F. *somnambulisme*, Sp. *-ismo*, mod.L. *somnambulismus*], the fact or habit of walking about and performing other actions while asleep; sleep-walking. **som'nambulist**, one who walks, etc., while asleep; also *attrib.* **som,nambu'listic** *a.*, somnambulic; hence **som,nambu'listically** *adv.* **som'nambulize** *v. intr.*, to walk in sleep; *trans.*, to imagine during sleep-walking; also, to put into a sleep-walking state. **som'nambulous** *a.*, somnambulic (Dunglison, 1873).

**1885** *Science* VI. 78 Committees were appointed on.. hypnotism, clairvoyance, and *somnambulance. **1905** *Daily News* 21 Jan. 6 His old habit or infirmity of somnambulance came back to him. **1843** MRS. CARLYLE *Lett. & Mem.* (1883) I. 231 Four such nights might have made a *somnambulant of a much stronger woman than me. **1866** BLACKMORE *Cradock Nowell* xlix, He was listless, passive, somnolent, —somnambulant. **1887** *Sat. Rev.* 15 Jan. 80 To walk in her sleep and to poison herself while in a somnambulant condition. **1830** LYTTON *Paul Clifford* xvi. (1874) 193 The pair.. mounted the stairs, arm-in-arm, in search of *somnambular accommodations. **1860** MRS. BROWNING *Napoleon III in Italy* v, While the palpitating peaks break out Ecstatic from somnambular repose. **1862** LYTTON *Str. Story* 14 An ardent believer of the reality of somnambular clairvoyance. **1827** SUTHERLAND *Tales Pilgr.* 369, I had become a sleep-walker; but whither my *somnambulary adventures had conducted me, was a riddle I had yet to solve. **1833** CARLYLE *Misc.* (1872) V. 127 This inarticulate age which slumbers and *somnambulates. **1840** —— *Diamond Necklace* xiv, His Eminence again somnambulates the Promenade de la Rose. **1873** M. COLLINS *Squire Silchester* II. xiv. 178 The latter, sometimes over-eating themselves, somnambulate. **1876** *Contemp. Rev.* June 126 A *somnambulating philosophy. **1794–6** E. DARWIN *Zoon.* (1801) I. 325 Though in its greatest degree it has been called *somnambulation or sleep-walking, it is totally different from that sleep. **1803** BEDDOES *Hygëia* IX. 130 The lady, whose reverie or somnambulation is described. **1862** G. MACDONALD *D. Elginbrod* III. xvii, The next day she had a bad head-ache. This with her always followed somnambulation. **1822** PRICHARD *Dis. Nervous Syst.* I. 404 Hoffmann cites the case of a *somnambulator, which [etc.]. **1837** J. F. COOPER *Europe* II. 288 A woman, who was subject to the magnetic influence, or who was what is commonly called a *somnambule*. **1850** J. BRAID *Observ. Trance* 30 The same discretion ought also to be extended to the modes of testing somnambules. **1877** SYMONDS *Renaiss. It.* iii. 147 Walking..like a somnambule sustained by an internal dream. **1829** I. TAYLOR *Enthusiasm* i. (1850) 10 The enthusiast passes through life in a sort of happy *somnambulency. **1865** CARLYLE *Fredk. Gt.* XVIII. iii. (1872) VII. 138 For nations have their somnambulencies. **1841** C. MACKAY *Pop. Delusions* III. 366 The patient was thrown into the *somnambulic state. **1862** G. MACDONALD *D. Elginbrod* II. xxxi, A reproduction of some previous somnambulic experience. **1880** HUTH *Life & Writ. Buckle* I. 34 He..woke the landlady whose somnambulic figure.. had just frightened him. **1887** *Sat. Rev.* 11 June 848 When he wakes, he finds that he has *somnambulically made a pen-and-ink sketch. **1797** *Encycl. Brit.* (ed. 3) XVII. 534/2 Subject to that singular affection or disease called **Somnambulism* or sleep-walking. **1820** SHELLEY *Witch Atl.* lxxv, The soldiers..Walked out of quarters in somnambulism. **1899** *Allbutt's Syst. Med.* VIII. 93 In somnambulism..the secondary consciousness takes control of the whole individual. **1794** MARY WOLLSTONECR. *Hist. View Fr. Rev.* I. 275 It was dangerous to awaken a *somnambulist on the brink of a precipice. **1837** BARHAM *Ingol. Leg.* Ser. I. *Spectre of Tappington* (1905) 23 Never again was Lieutenant Seaforth known to act the part of a somnambulist. **1856** FROUDE *Hist. Eng.* I. 308 A revolution had been effected in Europe by a somnambulist peasant girl. **1887** *Encycl. Brit.* XXII. 158/1 Somnambulists have been observed to write letters or reports,..and play upon musical instruments. **1840** DICKENS *Old C. Shop* (1867) 304 A *somnambulistic leave-taking and walking in her sleep. **1845** E. WARBURTON *Crescent & Cross* I. 216 A black little naked urchin sits on the splinter-bar, continually goading his somnambulistic team. **1899** *Allbutt's Syst. Med.* VIII. 167 Very rarely the patient may be also somnambulistic. **1845** E. WARBURTON *Crescent & Cross* II. 289 The slaves glided about silently and *somnambulistically, or stood with folded arms watching for a sign. *a* **1893** SYMONDS in H. F. Brown *Life* (1895) I. 71, I did not doubt that my spirit could somnambulistically travel from the place. **1832** *Figaro in London* 3 March 52/1 When he *somnambulizes upon the stage. *c* **1850** WHITTIER *Tales & Sk., Mag. & Witch Folk* Prose Wks. 1889 I. 400 A 'wise woman' dreamed, or somnambulized, that a large sum of money..lay buried in the centre of the great swamp.

†**som'naical**, *a. Obs.*[−1] [irreg. f. L. *somnus* or *somnium*.] Pertaining to sleep or dreams.

**1655** EMMOT *Northern Blast* 2 Many were the raptures which I dreamed to have, but all was but a Fancy or Somnaical.

†**somne**, *v.*[1] *Obs.* Forms: 1 somniᵹean, somnian, 3 somnien (somni), somnen, sompnen, some(n). [OE. *sǫmnian*, var. of *samnian*: see SAM *v.*[1] and cf. SUMNE *v.*] *trans.* To assemble, gather, collect, unite.

α. *c* **825** *Vesp. Psalter* cxxviii. 7 Of ðæm ne ᵹefylleð..his sceat se ðe reopan somnað. *a* **1000** *Phœnix* 193 þa swetestan [he] somnað & gædrað wyrta wynsume. *c* **1175** *Lamb. Hom.* 135 In halie chirche þer alle cristene men aȝen to beon isomned to gedere. *c* **1205** LAY. 4152 He somenede færd. *Ibid.* 30628 þer heo gunnen somnien scipen uniuoȝen. *a* **1225** *Ancr. R.* 186 Wult tu to-dealen þet God haueð isompned? *a* **1250** *Prov. Ælfred* 34 in *O.E. Misc.*, He ou wolde wyssye..hw ye myhte..eure saule somnen to criste.

β. *c* **1205** LAY. 5122 þa weoren al þas leoden at Lundene isomed. *c* **1275** *Ibid.* 18631 þo hii to-gadere weren alle hi-somed.

†**somne**, *v.*[2] *Obs.* Forms: α. 3 someni, 3–4 someny, 4–5 somene, 5–6 somen. β. 4 somne. [Variant of *somony*, etc., SUMMON *v.*, with weakening and subsequent elision of the second vowel. See also SOMPNE *v.* and SUMNE *v.*] *trans.* To summon.

α. **1297** R. GLOUC. (Rolls) 3764 Is poer he let someny þat ysprad was wel wyde. *Ibid.* 10379 þe pope..alle þe bissops of engelond let someni to rome. *c* **1380** WYCLIF *Wks.* (1880) 357 If þei somene symple men for þis accusing. **1393** LANGL. *P. Pl.* C. XXII. 214 Grace..consailede hym and conscience the comune to someny. **1401** *Pol. Poems* (Rolls) II. 89 ȝe.. somen men and threten hem, bot if thai ȝif ȝou gode.

β. *c* **1300** *Leg. Rood* (1871) 38 þo þe giwes i-somned were, hi hadde schortliche gret fere. *c* **1380** WYCLIF *Wks.* (1880) 250 þei ben hurlid & somnyd fro day to day, fro fer place to ferþere. **1387** TREVISA *Higden* (Rolls) III. 201 Pictagoras.. somnede hym to fore iuges.

Hence †**'somning** *vbl. sb. Obs.*

**1480** CAXTON *Chron. Eng.* ccxii. 108 b, To warne the parties defendauntz thurgh somnyng ayene. **1529–30** *Rec. St. Mary at Hill* 349 Paid to a Somoner for Somenyng of M[r] hiltons, preist, ij d.

†**'somner.** *Obs.* Forms: α. 4 som(e)nour, 5 somenor, 6 sommenor. β. 4 somenere, 4, 6–7 somner. [f. *somene* SOMNE *v.*[2], or a. AF. *somnour*.] An official summoner. Also *transf.*

α. *c* **1320** *Pol. Songs* (Camden) 157 ȝet ther sitteth somenours syexe other sevene. **1377** LANGL. *P. Pl.* B. XV. 128 Sectoures and sudenes, somnoures and her lemmannes. **1474** *Cal. Anc. Rec. Dublin* (1889) 350 Walter Wotlon somenour. **1570** *Wills & Inv. N.C.* (Surtees 1838) 342 John Roddh'm the sommen[r].

β. **1393** LANGL. *P. Pl.* C. III. 59 Sysours and somners, shereyues and here clerkes. *Ibid.* x. 263 Hure salue ys of *supersedeas* in someneres boxes. **1521** *Coventry Leet-Bk.* 672 At suche tymes as they shal-be Reasonably warnyd by the somner. **1563** *Homilies* II. *Of Repentance* III, When the hyghest somner of all, whiche is death, shall come. **1585** T. WASHINGTON tr. *Nicholay's Voy.* III. xviii. 105 [They] haue like vnto Somners, as many brybes as they can carry away. **1608** MIDDLETON *Trick to catch Old One* II. i, They may do anything there, and fear neither beadle nor somner.

**somni-**, combining form of L. *somnus* sleep, occurring in a number of Latin compounds and English adaptations or imitations of these, as *somnifer* somniferous, *somnificus* somnific, etc. (see below).

**somnial** (ˈsɒmnɪəl), *a. rare.* [a. older F. *somnial*, or ad. L. *somniāl-is*, f. *somni-um* dream.] Of or relating to dreams.

*a* **1693** *Urquhart's Rabelais* III. xiv. 120 To presage or foretell an evil..in matter of Somnial Divinations. **1833** COLERIDGE in *Lit. Rem.* (1838) III. 397 The Somnial magic superinduced on..the active powers of the mind.

†**'somniate**, *v. Obs.*[−1] [f. ppl. stem of L. *somniāre*, f. *somnium* dream.]

**1.** *trans.* To dream (something).

**1657** TOMLINSON *Renou's Disp.* 344 Who being too credulous have committed to presse what the imperite somniated.

**2.** To stupefy, make drowsy.

**1719** DE FOE *Vision of Angelic World* 23 More or less doz'd or somniated with the oppression of Vapours..which occasion sleep.

†**somni'ation.** *Obs. rare.* [See prec. and -ATION.] A sleep; a dream.

**1597** A. M. tr. *Guillemeau's Fr. Chirurg.* †iij, Beinge resuscitated..of a profounde..somniation. **1599** —— tr. *Gabelhouer's Bk. Physicke* 40/2 That expelleth all phantasticalle somniationes.

**'somniative**, *a. rare*[−1]. [See SOMNIATE *v.* and -ATIVE.] Relating to, or producing, dreams.

**1827** COLERIDGE in *Lit. Rem.* (1839) IV. 422 A very rare.. conjunction of the somniative faculty..with the voluntary and other powers of the waking state.

†**'somniatory**, *a. Obs. rare.* [See SOMNIATE *v.* and -ORY.] Of or pertaining to dreams or dreaming.

*a* **1693** *Urquhart's Rabelais* III. xiii, For the..unfolding of these somniatory [F. *somniales*] Vaticinations. *Ibid.*, I will to-morrow break my fast betimes after my somniatory exercitations [F. *songeailles*].

**somnicu'losity.** *rare*[−0]. [Cf. next and -ITY.] 'Sleepiness, drowsiness' (Bailey, 1721).

**som'niculous**, *a. rare.* [ad. L. *somniculōs-us*, f. *somnus* sleep. Cf. obs. F. *somniculeux*.]

**a.** Drowsy, sleepy. **b.** Inducing sleep.

**1656** BLOUNT *Glossogr.*, *Somniculous*, negligent, sleepy, drowzy, sluggish; also that makes drowzy or sleepy. **1819** L. HUNT *Indicator* No. 11 (1822) I. 84 Leaving the somniculous squire propped up in the saddle. **1820** *Ibid.* No. 54 (1822) II. 11 The plain is also full of all sorts of somniculous plants.

**somni'facient**, *a.* and *sb.* [f. SOMNI- + pres. pple. of *facĕre* to make.] **a.** *adj.* Somnific. **b.** *sb.* A soporific. (*Cent. Dict.* 1891.)

†**som'niferic.** *Obs.*$^{-1}$ [Cf. next and -IC.] A soporific.
**1694** SALMON *Bate's Dispens.* (1713) 262/2 It is a most certain Somniferick and Sudorifick.

**somniferous** (sɒm'nɪfərəs), *a.* [f. L. *somnifer* (f. *somni-* SOMNI- + *-ferre* to bring) + -OUS. Cf. F. *somnifère*, Sp. and Pg. *somnifero*, It. *sonnifero*.]
**1.** Inducing sleep; soporific.
**1602** DEKKER *Satirom.* Wks. 1873 I. 255 Twas I that ministred to her chaste bloud, A true somniferous potion, which did steale Her thoughts to sleepe. **1633** BROME *Antipodes* II. iv, You slept most part o' th' journey hitherward, The aire was so somniferous. **1663** BOYLE *Usef. Exp. Nat. Philos.* II. App. 345 A safe and moderately somniferous medicine in feavers. **1754** DODSLEY *Agric.* III. 215 The scarlet poppy..Bows his somniferous head, inviting soon To peaceful slumber the disorder'd mind. **1799** UNDERWOOD *Dis. Childr.* (ed. 4) I. 360 If it follow any somniferous disease. **1837** DICKENS *Pickw.* ii, The wine had exerted its somniferous influence. **1876** HARLEY *Royle's Mat. Med.* 764 The effects..of the other somniferous constituents of opium.
**2.** Somnolent, sleepy.
**1798** in *Spirit Public Jrnls.* (1799) II. 400 A most somniferous Earl gave violent symptoms of animation. **1809** IRVING *Knickerb.* (1861) 153 Those fat, somniferous, respectable burghers.
Hence **som'niferously** *adv.*
**1836** *New Monthly Mag.* XLVI. 13 His translations.. were somniferously dull. *a* **1852** MOORE *Corn & Catholics* ix. Poet. Wks. (1872) 392 A row Of Poppies..Stand forth, somniferously flaming! **1865** E. C. CLAYTON *Cruel Fortune* II. 110 By degrees the heat, and the silence,..operated somniferously on Val.

†**som'nifery.** *Obs.*$^{-1}$ [f. as prec. + -Y.] A place of sleep.
**1600** TOURNEUR *Transf. Metam.* (1878) 202 Unlock the rustie latch That leades into the cave's somniferie.

**somnific** (sɒm'nɪfɪk), *a.* [ad. L. *somnificus*: see SOMNI- and -FIC.] Causing sleep; somniferous.
**1721** BAILEY, *Somnifick*, causing sleep. **1727** A. HAMILTON *New Acc. E. Indies* I. xxiii. 278 Others again take somnifick Medicines, and stand by the Pile till they fall on it while asleep. **1775** S. J. PRATT *Liberal Opin.* cxxxvi. (1783) IV. 254 A somnific fit again overtook him,..and, in the next instant, he was snoring in his chair. **1819** MOORE *Diary* VIII. 189, I agree with you that a great part of 'Lara' is very prosy and somnific. **1834** SOUTHEY *Doctor* (1848) 3 The voice, the manner, the matter,..were all alike somnific.

**somnificator.** *rare*$^{-1}$. [Cf. prec. and -ATOR.] One who induces sleep.
**1806** SOUTHEY *Let.* in *Life* (1850) III. 33 The rector, a humdrum somnificator.

**'somnifuge.** *rare*$^{-1}$. [See SOMNI- and -FUGE.] A means of driving away sleep.
**1890** LOWELL *Lett.* (1894) II. x. 460 He [the nightingale] has a bad character among you as a *somnifuge*.

**som'nifugous**, *a.* *rare*$^{-0}$. [Cf. prec.] 'Driving away sleep' (Bailey, 1721).

†**'somnifying**, *ppl. a.* *Obs. rare.* [See SOMNI- and -FY.] Inducing sleep.
**1634** BRERETON *Trav.* (Chetham Soc.) 40 He also discoursed of..hemlock, which he said was of a most venomous, somnifying, stupifying, and intoxicating quality. **1770** CHATTERTON in Masson *Life* II. iii. (1874) 163 This somnifying liquor had made her voice so like the sweet echo of Miss Hill's that..I should absolutely have imagined it hers.

**somnilo'quacious**, *a.* *rare*$^{-0}$. [See SOMNI- and LOQUACIOUS *a.*] 'Talking or apt to talk in sleep' (Bailey, vol. II, 1731). Also **som'niloquence**, = *somniloquy*. **som'niloquent** *a.*, talking in sleep. **som'niloquism**, = *somniloquy*. **som'niloquist**, one who speaks or talks while asleep. **som'niloquize** *v. intr.*, to talk in (or as in) sleep. **som'niloquous** *a.*, 'apt to talk in sleep' (Webster, 1847). **som'niloquy**, the act or habit of speaking during sleep.
**1841** W. C. DENDY *Philos. Mystery* 306 True *somniloquence is often preceded by a cataleptic state. *Ibid.* 304. **1804** COLERIDGE in *Blackw. Mag.* (1882) CXXXI. 123 The Ideatæ are but *somniloquent Ideotæ. **1821** —— *Ibid.* X. 244 The *somniloquism of the prophetesses under the coercion of the Scandinavian enchanters. **1833** —— in *Lit. Rem.* (1838) III. 397 How often the pen becomes the tongue of a systematic dream,—a *somniloquist! **1866** *Cornh. Mag.* Aug. 231 We may even be prompted to the action of the somnambulist, or somniloquist, without waking. *a* **1901** MYERS *Human Personality* (1903) II. 6 The somnambulist, or rather the somniloquist. **1827** COLERIDGE in *Blackw. Mag.* (1882) CXXXI. 119 Is it not melancholy to hear a man like Steffens *somniloquise in such a mystifying cant? **1847** WEBSTER, **Somniloquy*, the talking of one in a state of somnipathy. **1899** *Allbutt's Syst. Med.* VII. 757 Sleep-talking or somniloquy, and sleep-walking or somnambulism, are states in which the whole brain is not asleep.

**som'nipathy.** [See SOMNI- and -PATHY.] 'Sleep from sympathy, or by the process of mesmerism' (Webster, 1847). Also **som'nipathist**, 'a person in a state of somnipathy' (*Ibid.*).

**Somnite**, obs. form of SUNNITE.

**som'nivolency.** *rare*$^{-1}$. [f. SOMNI- + *-volency*, ad. L. *-volentia* will, desire.] An intended soporific. Also **som'nivolent**, one who desires to sleep.
**1748** RICHARDSON *Clarissa* (1811) V. 345 If these somnivolencies (I hate the word opiates on this occasion) have turned her head. **1885** G. MEREDITH *Diana* xvi, The irrational repetition ploughed the minds of those unhappy somnivolents.

**somnolence** ('sɒmnələns). Also 4–6 sompnolence. [a. OF. *sompnolence* (mod.F. *somnolence*, = Sp. *somnolencia*, Pg. *so(m)nolencia*, It. *sonnolenza*), or ad. L. *somnolentia* (med.L. *sompnolencia*), f. *somnolentus*: see SOMNOLENT *a.*] Inclination to sleep; sleepiness, drowsiness.
*c* **1386** CHAUCER *Pars. T.* ¶705 Than comth Sompnolence, þat is sluggy slombryng. **1390** GOWER *Conf.* II. 94 That I no Sompnolence have used. *c* **1425** *Orolog. Sapient.* iii. in *Anglia* X. 349/32 Wolte þou be ouerlayde with sompnolence and ydelnesse. *c* **1475** *Partenay* 4616 Ho-so do slepe..in sompnolence there, Alway perpetuall there abide shall he. **1542** BOORDE *Dyetary* xix. (1870) 279 Onyons doth prouoke a man..to sompnolence.
**1721** in BAILEY. **1841** W. C. DENDY *Philos. Mystery* 367 Somnolence.—Trance.—Catalepsy. **1862** MERIVALE *Rom. Emp.* lxvi. (1865) VIII. 237 The dignified somnolence of an old-fashioned city like Athens. **1866** G. MACDONALD *Ann. Q. Neighb.* ii, The people had dined and the usual somnolence had followed.
*personif.* **1390** GOWER *Conf.* II. 92 Ther is yit on of compaignie, And he is cleped Sompnolence.

**'somnolency.** [See prec. and -ENCY.] = prec.
**1623** COCKERAM I, *Somnolencie*, sleepinesse. **1727** in BAILEY. **1810** BENTHAM *Packing* (1821) 141 Symptoms of somnolency begin to discover themselves. **1859** R. F. BURTON *Centr. Afr.* in *Jrnl. Geogr. Soc.* XXIX. 285 It affects the head, prevents somnolency. **1875** H. C. WOOD *Therap.* (1879) 218 Prolonged nausea, and retching, interrupted only by intervals of dreamy delirious somnolency.

**somnolent** ('sɒmnələnt), *a.* and *sb.* Also 5–6 sompnolent. [a. OF. *sompnolent* (mod.F. *somnolent*), or ad. L. *somnolentus* (med.L. *sompno-*), f. *somnus* sleep.]
**1.** Tending to cause sleepiness or drowsiness; inclining to sleep.
*c* **1475** *Partenay* 5376 Where it behouith to wacche nightes thre Without any sompnolent slepe to be. **1615** G. SANDYS *Trav.* 292 Takes age in ease and sleepe content? Then Baiæ what more somnolent? **1824** DIBDIN *Libr. Comp.* 531 An effect which we seek in vain in the somnolent pages of Lediard. **1855** DICKENS *Dorrit* xix, He was again painfully aware of a somnolent tendency in Frederick. **1882** DE WINDT *Equator* 75 The noise made by the stream..had a very pleasant and somnolent effect.
**b.** Marked by sleepiness or slowness.
**1812** *Q. Rev.* VIII. 64 The translator restricts his somnolent interrogation to Codrus. **1877** WALLACE *Russia* v. 76 And I must do Anton the justice to say that he served me well in his own somnolent fashion.
**2.** Of persons: Inclined to sleep; heavy with sleep; drowsy. Also *transf.*
**1547** BOORDE *Brev. Health* xiii. (1557) B iij b, If the sycke person do vomit & be sompnouent [*sic*] or sleping. **1623** COCKERAM I, *Somnolent*, sleepie. **1625** JACKSON *Creed* v. xvi. Wks. IV. 118 Deriding the somnolent and sluggish gods of the Epicures. **1721** in BAILEY. **1819** SCOTT *Leg. Montrose* v, I am no whit somnolent; I always hear best with my eyes shut. **1837** BARHAM *Ingol. Leg.* Ser. I. *Grey Dolphin* (1905) 45 Fasting and watching had made him more than usually somnolent. **1891** HARDY *Tess* (1900) 15/2 When they had passed the little town of Stourcastle, dumbly somnolent under its thick brown thatch.
**b.** *sb.* A somnolent or sleepy person; one affected with somnolence.
**1841** W. C. DENDY *Philos. Mystery* 373 Like many other somnolents, she was morose and irritable, especially previous to the sleeping-fit.
Hence **'somnolently** *adv.*, in a somnolent manner; sleepily.
**1615** JACKSON *Creed* IV. II. ix. Wks. III. 378, I know none but may have hope to escape so they will not..somnolently put off the evil day. **1827** *Blackw. Mag.* XXII. 384 Alciphron could not possibly have been more somnolently inclined. **1875** M. COLLINS *Sweet & Twenty* II. vi, An inquisitive investigative youth was Charles, who never threw away his time somnolently.

**somno'lescence.** [See next and -ENCE.] The state or condition of being sleepy; inclination to sleep.
**1831** *Fraser's Mag.* III. 102 The power of inducing the pleasurable sensation of somnolescence. **1898** E. YOUNG *Kingdom of Yellow Robe* vi. 116 Mosquitoes whose buzzing and stinging are effective preventatives of somnolescence.

**somnolescent** (sɒmnə'lɛsənt), *a.* [f. SOMNOLENT *a.*: see -ESCENT.] Drowsy, sleepy; inert.
**1845** FORD *Handbk. Spain* II. 725 Somnolescent over business and awake only to intrigue. **1886** *Encycl. Brit.* XX. 201/1 The animal..lies there in a somnolescent state for perhaps hours.

**'somnolism.** *rare.* [f. SOMNOL-ENT *a.* + -ISM.] The state of being in a mesmeric sleep.
**1849** HADDOCK *Somnolism & Psycheism* 19 Other persons of greater susceptibility..proceed quickly into a state of profound sleep,—or, as I propose to call it, Somnolism.

**'somnolize**, *v.* *rare*$^{-1}$. [f. as prec. + -IZE.] *trans.* To make drowsy or sleepy.
**1831** *Fraser's Mag.* III. 451 The same sort of palaver with which the universities have thought fit to somnolize us.

**som'nopathy.** *rare*$^{-0}$. = SOMNIPATHY.
**1851** DUNGLISON *Dict. Med. Sci.*, *Somnopathy*, somnambulism, magnetic.

†**somno'riferous**, *a.* *Obs.* [Erroneous form of SOMNIFEROUS, after *soporiferous*.] Soporific.
**1590** BARROUGH *Meth. Physick* I. xv. (1639) 24 Water wherein..poppy seed hath been sodden, or some somnoriferous compound. *Ibid.* II. x. 88 Sirupes of Poppy, and other somnoriferous medicines.
So **somno'rific** *a.*
**1865** 'ANNIE THOMAS' *On Guard* ii, The first scene opened on a somnorific, sultry summer afternoon in London. **1880** G. A. TOWNSEND *Tales Chesapeake* 196 The somnorific air of the Springs.

†**'somnorine**, *a.* *Obs.*$^{-1}$ [irreg. f. L. *somnus*.] Seen during sleep.
**1637** VENNER *Treat. of Tobacco* in *Via Recta* 347 By reason of the somnorine visions which this fume doth greatly occasion.

**somnour**, variant of SOMNER *Obs.*

**somnunge**, variant of SAMENING *Obs.*

‖**'Somnus.** [L. *somnus* sleep, also personified as a divinity.] The god of sleep.
*a* **1599** PEELE *Sir Clyomon* xxi. Wks. (Rtldg.) 522/2, I creep out of my drowsy den when Somnus hath suppress The head of every valiant heart. **1710** tr. *Quilletus' Callipædia* III. 144 But as she mourn'd, kind *Somnus* gently stole To her soft Eyes, and lull'd her sinking Soul.

**somod**, var. SAMED *adv.* *Obs.*

**Somogyi unit** (sə'məʊgɪ). *Biochem.* [The name of Michael *Somogyi* (1883–1971), Hungarian-born U.S. biochemist who proposed the unit in 1948 (see quot.).] A unit in terms of which the effectiveness of a solution at catalysing the hydrolysis of starch can be stated (see quot. 1948).
[**1948** M. SOMOGYI in *Ann. Surg.* CXXVIII. 676 One unit is that amount of enzyme which hydrolyzes 1 mg. of starch in 1 hour at 37° and pH7 in phosphate buffer, provided that not more than 44% of the starch is hydrolyzed.] **1956** E. KING *Micro-Anal. in Med. Biochem.* (ed. 3) iv. 92 Amylase activity... Somogyi units per 100ml. of plasma. **1961** *Lancet* 12 Aug. 373/1 A new amyloclastic technique which yields results in the equivalent of Somogyi units has been used to measure amylase activity in sera from..patients with diabetes mellitus. **1974** R. M. KIRK et al. *Surgery* vi. 110 The concentration of serum amylase is normally less than 200 Somogyi units.

**somonce**, obs. f. SUMMONS *sb.*

**somonde, somone, somoni, -ony**, obs. varr. SUMMON *v.*

**somoniter**, obs. var. SUMMONITOR.

**somoron**, obs. f. SUMMER *v.*

**somoun, -own**, obs. ff. SUMMON *sb.* and *v.*

**somounce**, obs. f. SUMMONS *sb.*

**sompe**, obs. f. SUMP.

†**sompnary.** *Obs.*$^{-1}$ [ad. med.L. *sompniaria* (sc. *ars*), f. *sompnium*, L. *somnium* dream.] Divination by dreams; oneiromancy.
*a* **1470** H. PARKER *Dives & Pauper* (W. de W.) I. xxxiv. 73/1 To make ony dyuynynge..by songuary or sompnarye.

†**sompne**, *v.* *Obs.* Also 5 sompny. [Variant of SOMNE *v.*$^2$, with insertion of *p* as in *nempne* NEMN *v.*] *trans.* To summon.
**1362** LANGL. *P. Pl.* A. II. 142 Þus sysoures ben sompned þe false to serue. *c* **1380** WYCLIF *Wks.* (1880) 151 He schal be sompned, ponyschid & cursed. *c* **1386** CHAUCER *Friar's T.* 49 (Harl.), Withoute maundement, a lewed man He couthe sompne. **14..** *Lat.-Eng. Voc.* in Wr.-Wülcker 573 *Cito*, to sompny. **1471** in *10th Rep. Hist. MSS. Comm.* App. V. 309 The seriaunt shal sompne ony suche att his house.
Hence †**'sompning** *vbl. sb.* *Obs.*
*c* **1400** *Plowman's Tale* in *Pol. Poems* (Rolls) I. 330 To speake they shull not be so bold, For sompning to the consistorye. *c* **1400** *Brut* Prol. 1 Dioclician anon lete make a sompnyng. **1490–1** [see SOMPNOUR].

†**sompnour.** *Obs.* Also 5–6 sompner(e. [Variant of *somnour* SOMNER: cf. prec.] An official summoner.
*a.* **1377** LANGL. *P. Pl.* B. III. 33 Sisoures and sompnoures, suche men hir preiseth. *c* **1386** CHAUCER *Prol.* 543 Ther was ..A sompnour and a pardoner also. *c* **1400** *Plowman's Tale* in *Pol. Poems* (Rolls) I. 313 They taken to ferme her sompnours. **1490–1** *Rec. St. Mary at Hill* 164 Paide to William Iames, Sompnour, for sompnyng of iij tenauntes that owed monye to the chyrch, x d. **1555** W. WATREMAN *Fardle of Facions* II. xi. 256 Thei haue also certaine spie-

faultes ordinarilye appoincted (muche like to our Sompnours).

*β.* 14.. *Lat.-Eng. Voc.* in Wr.-Wülcker 573 *Citator*, a Sompnere. *c* 1500 *God Speed the Plough* (Skt.) 65 Than cometh the Sompner to haue som rente. *a* 1535 *Frere & Boy* 478 in Hazl. *E.P.P.* III. 80 Thus they departed in that tyde, The offycyall and the sompnere.

**sompter**, obs. form of SUMPTER.

**somptious**, obs. form of SUMPTUOUS.

†**somredness.** *Obs.*⁻¹ [Related to OE. *samrǽd* harmonious, united.] Concord, unity.

*a* 1225 *Ancr. R.* 254 Nimeð nu uorbisne hu god is onnesse of heorte, & somrednesse of luue þet halt þe gode somed.

†**somrune.** *Obs.*⁻¹ [f. OE. *sǫm-*, *sam-* together + *rún* ROUN.] Council, consultation.

*c* 1205 LAY. 5479 Belin & Brenne beie to-sone nomen heom to ræde & to som rune.

**somun, somyn**, variants of SAMEN *adv. Obs.*

**somundare**, obs. form of SUMMONER.

**somyr(e**, obs. forms of SUMMER.

**son** (sʌn), *sb.*[1] Forms: *α.* 1 sunu, 1–2 suna, (1) 2–5 sune, 4 sunn(e, 4–5 sun, 8 *Sc.* sin. *β.* 3–8 sone (4 zone), 4–5 soone, 4, 6 soon, 6 soonne; 5 soun(e; 4–7 sonne, 4– son (6 *dial.* zon, *Sc.* schon, 7 sonn). [Common Teut.: OE. *sunu* (gen. *suna*), = OFris. *sunu*, *sune*, *sone* (EFris. *sûnû*, WFris. *soan*, NFris. *sen*, *sên*, etc.), MDu. *sone*, *zone* (Du. *zoon*), OS. *sunu* (MLG. *sone*, LG. *sone*, *sön*, *sän*, etc.), OHG. *sunu*, *sun* (MHG. *sune*, *sun*, *son*, G. *sohn*), ON. *sunr*, *sonr* (Icel. *sonur*, Norw. and Sw. *son*, Da. *søn*), Goth. *sunus*. Outside of the Teutonic languages similar forms appear in Lith. *sûnus*, OSlav. *synŭ* (Russ. *syn*), Skr. *sūnu* (Zend. *hunu*). The root *su-* is also that of Gr. *υἱός*.

The declension in OE. is variable through confusion of the different cases and the introduction of new forms, as gen. sing. *sunes*, nom. pl. *sunan*, gen. pl. *sunena*. From early ME. the usual possessive and plural forms are those in *-es* or *-s*.

Senses 2–7 represent for the most part Biblical uses of the word, examples of which occur freely in all the English versions of the Scriptures.]

**1. a.** A male child or person in relation to either or to both of his parents. Sometimes said of animals.

See also MOTHER'S SON.

*α.* *Beowulf* 645 Oþ þæt..sunu Healfdenes secean wolde æfenræste. *c* 888 K. ÆLFRED *Boeth.* xxxviii. §1 Þa wæs þær Apollines dohtor Iobes suna. 971 *Blickl. Hom.* 7 Ðu cennest sunu þone þu nemnest Hælend. *c* 1100 *O.E. Chron.* an. 1052 (MS. D), His sunan wæron eorlas & þæs cynges dyrlingas. *c* 1122 *Ibid.* an. 1121 (Laud MS.), Seo wæs Willelme þes cynges sune..to wife forȝyfan. *c* 1200 ORMIN 488 And ta twa prestess wærenn Aaroness suness baþe. *c* 1250 *Gen. & Ex.* 2175 Alle we ben on faderes sunen. *a* 1300 *Cursor M.* 796 Of þat ilk appel bitt þair suns tethe ar eggeid yitt. 13.. *E.E. Allit. P.* B. 298 He had þre þryuen sunez & þay þre wyuez. *c* 1400 *Destr. Troy* 6567 Se ye not the sun of youre sure kyng..turnyt away? 1559 *Mirr. Mag., O. Glendour* vi, How would we mocke the burden bearing mule If he would brag he wer an horses sunne. 1786 BURNS *Halloween* xvi, Our Stibble-rig was Rab M'Graen... He sin gat Eppie Sim wi' wean.

*β.* *a* 1275 *Prov. Ælfred* 574 in *O.E. Misc.* 134 Sone min swo leue, site me nu bisides. *c* 1290 *S. Eng. Leg.* I. 21 Edwyne, is sone, was king i-maud. 1340 *Ayenb.* 48 Ne uorzakeþ nenne ne uader ne broþer ne zone. 1387 TREVISA *Higden* (Rolls) II. 385 Dedalus wiþ his sone Icarus. *c* 1412 HOCCLEVE *De. Reg. Princ.* 2736 A man þat sone was To a conseil, was take in þis trespas. 1473 *Rental Bk. Cupar-Angus* (1879) I. 191 Thome Sowtar forsaid and his thre sonys. 1529 CROMWELL in Merriman *Life & Lett.* (1902) I. 57, I gyue and bequethe to my saide Soon Gregorye A Bason. 1596 BACON *Max. & Use Com. Law* II. (1635) 48 During the minority of his eldest sonn. 1681 DRYDEN *Abs. & Achit.* I. 32 Indulgent David view'd His Youthful Image in his Son renew'd. 1741–2 GRAY *Agrip.* 67 If the son reign, the mother perishes. 1764 GOLDSM. *Hist. Eng. in Lett.* (1772) IV. 39 Lord Colchester, son to the earl of Rivers. 1812 SOUTHEY *Let.* in *Life* (1850) III. 325 His name is Shelley, son to the member for Shoreham. 1857 BORROW *Rom. Rye* xxxix, Soliman..after his death befriended his young son. 1871 SMILES *Charac.* ii. (1876) 46 To inspire her sons' minds with elevating thoughts. 1974 *New Yorker* 29 Apr. 102/2 A son of..a Thoroughbred, and..a quarter-horse brood mare.

*fig.* 1781 COWPER *Heroism* 59 Famine, and pestilence, her first-born son.

**b.** In the phrase *son and heir*. Also *fig.*

1297 R. GLOUC. (Rolls) 9607 In is warde he let do Henri is eldoste sone & is eir al so. 1338 R. BRUNNE *Chron.* (1810) 5 Sorow & site he made.. For his sonne & heyre. 13.. *E.E. Allit. P.* B. 666, I schal..sothely sende to sare a son & an hayre. 1430–40 LYDG. *Bochas* I. viii, Of Phœbus..Poetes write that he was sonne and heire. 1481 *Cov. Leet Bk.* 475 The son & heir of hym that nowe pretendeth to be kyng. 1576 in *Excheq. Rolls Scotl.* XX. 372 Jhone Dromond,.. quhe is schon and air to his fader Jhone Dromond. 1604 DEKKER *Honest Wh.* I. v, As clean as your sons-and-heirs when they ha' spent all. 1833 TENNYSON *Death Old Year* 31 To see him die..His son and heir doth ride post-haste.

**c.** = SON-IN-LAW.

1533 *Test. Ebor.* (Surtees) VI. 38 My said sone Briane Tunstall. 1596 SHAKS. *Tam. Shr.* v. ii. 78 *Bap.* Sonne, Ile be your halfe, Bianca comes.

**2.** *Theol.* The second person of the Trinity. (Cf. 4 a.)

*c* 825 *Vesp. Hymns* viii. 21 Bledsien we feder & sunu & ðone halȝan gast. *a* 900 *Halsuncge* in *Durh. Rit.* (Surtees) 114 Ic eow halsiȝe on fæder naman, and on suna naman. *c* 1175 *Lamb. Hom.* 85 þe feder and þe sune and þe halie gast. 1340 *Ayenb.* 12 þe oþer article belongeþ to þe zone aze to his godhede. 1382 WYCLIF *1 John* ii. 24 3e shulen dwelle in the sone and the fadir. *c* 1420 [see GOD 5 d]. 1500–20 DUNBAR *Poems* xliv. 29 That Sone is Lord, that Sone is King of kingis. 1548 *Bk. Com. Prayer, Athanas. Creed*, The Father is God, the Son is God. *a* 1628 F. GREVIL in Farr *S.P. Eliz.* (1845) I. 108 We seeme more inwardly to knowe the Sonne. 1671 MILTON *P.R.* II. 260 It was the hour of night, when thus the Son Commun'd in silent walk. 1728 CHAMBERS *Cycl.* s.v. *Trinity*, Father, Son, and Holy Spirit. 1817 SHELLEY *Satan broke Loose* 5 The Father and the Son Knew that strife was now begun. 1858 WHITTIER *Trinitas* 56 Father, and Son, and Holy Call; This day thou hast denied them all!

**3. a.** One who is regarded as, or takes the place of, a son. †Also *spec.* at Cambridge, one presented for a degree by the 'father' of his college. †*white son*: see WHITE *a.*

*c* 825 *Vesp. Psalter* ii. 7 Dryhten cwæð to me: Sunu min ðu earð; to deȝe ic cende ðec. *c* 1000 ÆLFRIC *Exod.* ii. 10 And heo hine lufode, & hæfde for sunu hyre. *c* 1000 *Ags. Gosp.* John xix. 26 Þa cwæþ he to his meder: Wif, her ys þin sunu. *c* 1200 *Trin. Coll. Hom.* 19 Alle men ben godes children, for þat he hem alle shop, and ches hem to sunes and to dohtres. *a* 1400 *Relig. Pieces fr. Thornton MS.* 87 His mercy..That.. me, a wreche, his sun walde make. 1567 *Gude & Godlie B.* (S.T.S.) 33 Quhome God ressaifis to his sone and air, Him will he scurge. 1574 M. STOKYS in Peacock *Stat. Cambr.* (1841) App. A. p. x, The Father..shall call fourthe his eldest sone, & animate hym to dispute. 1665 in Wordsworth *Univ. Life 18th C.* (1874) 412 Then the Father calleth up the Answerer, and showeth him his sons. 1718 PRIOR *Solomon* III. 889 Let Thy command Restore, great Father, Thy instructed son. 1799 WORDSW. *The Fountain* 62 And, Matthew, for thy children dead I'll be a son to thee! 1877 BARING-GOULD *Lives Saints* Oct. 305 The child afterwards lived and died in God's service at Ripon, and was called the bishop's son.

**b.** Used as a term of affectionate address to a man or boy by an older person or by one in a superior (esp. ecclesiastical) relation, and as a term of familiar address without implication of affection. Cf. *old son* s.v. OLD *a.* 8 a.

*c* 950 *Lindisf. Gosp.* Matt. ix. 2 La sunu forȝefen biðon ..ðe synno ðina. 1390 GOWER *Conf.* I. 108 Mi Sone, in alle maner wise, Surquiderie is to despise. *c* 1400 tr. *Secreta Secret., Gov. Lordsh.* 49 Soune most glorious, most rightful Emperour. *c* 1440 *Alph. Tales* 196 Þe bisshop sayd; 'Nay, son,..here hase bene a noder emperour of long tyme'. 1534 MORE *Comf. agst. Trib.* II. Wks. 1183/2 The Foxe..charged hym to..lye styll and sleepe lyke a good sonne. 1603 SHAKS. *Meas. for M.* III. i. 161 *Duke.* Son, I haue ouer-heard what hath past between you & your sister. 1820 SCOTT *Monast.* xxv, 'Prove thy strength, my son, in the name of God!' said the preacher. *Ibid.* xxxii, 'Even now, if thou wilt,' said the Sub-Prior,..'come hither, my son, and kneel down'. 1914 G. B. SHAW *Misalliance* 5 *Bentley*:... I should like to wring your damned neck for you. *Johnny* (*with a derisive laugh*): Try it, my son. 1959 E. H. CLEMENTS *High Tension* vii. 121 No good brooding, son. 1967 *Listener* 22 June 807/2 He was then asked to accompany the police to the police-box in order to confirm his identity. He replied, 'Look, son, I am not moving from this spot. If you want me you will have to arrest me.' 1974 S. MARCUS *Minding Store* (1975) ix. 188 Mr. Seeligson said, 'Son, you've done me a great favor. I appreciate all the trouble you've gone to.'

**4.** *Son of God*: **a.** Jesus Christ. (Cf. 2.) Also †*God's son*. Hence *Son-of-godship*.

*c* 950 *Lindisf. Gosp.* Luke xxii. 70 Cuoedon ða alle, ðu..arð sunu godes. *c* 1200 ORMIN 267 Till þatt Godess Sune Crist Himm shollde onn eorþe shæwenn. *c* 1250 *Gen. & Ex.* 403 And ȝet sal godes dere sune In ȝure kin in werlde wunen. *c* 1340 HAMPOLE *Pr. Consc.* 5044 In..archaungel steven, And in þe son of Goddes awen beme. *c* 1400 *Rule St. Benet* (Prose) vii. 12 Als tapostil saide of godis sune. *a* 1529 SKELTON *Prayer to Second Person* 2 O benygne Jesu,..The only Sonne of God by filiacion. 1588 KYD *Househ. Phil.* 449 Wks. (1901) 250 For our worlde was dignified with the presence of the true Sonne of God. 1667 MILTON *P.L.* III. 138 Beyond compare the Son of God was seen Most glorious. 1728 CHAMBERS *Cycl.* s.v., The Son of God Created the World; the Son of God was Incarnate. 1817 W. TAYLOR in *Monthly Mag.* XLIV. 315 This claim to the son-of-godship renders the facts irrefragably certain. 1884 ADDIS & ARNOLD *Cath. Dict.* (1897) 900/1 The ideas..are applied to Christ, and united to the doctrine of his generation as the Son of God before the world was made.

**b.** A divine being; an angel.

1382 WYCLIF *Job* xxxvii. 7 Who dide doun the corner ston of it, whan..alle the sones of God shulden ioȝen? 1560 BIBLE (Geneva) *Job* i. 6 *marg.*, Meaning, the Angels which are called the sonnes of God. 1599 DAVIES *Immort. Soul* VII. ix. (1714) 47 The Angels, Sons of God are nam'd. 1643 CARYL *Expos. Job* I. 37 The Angels..are the Sons of God by temporal Creation. 1671 MILTON *P.R.* I. 368, I came among the Sons of God, when he Gave up unto my hands Uzzean Job. 1784 COWPER *Task* v. 821.

**c.** One spiritually attached to God.

*c* 950 *Lindisf. Gosp.* John i. 12 [He] ȝesalde ðæm mæht suno godes wosa. 1382 WYCLIF *Rom.* viii. 14 Sothli who euere ben lad by the spirit of God, thes ben the sones of God. 1643 CARYL *Expos. Job* I. 1887 That priviledge is assured to the Sons of God (1 John 3. 2) 'We shall see him as he is'. 1667 MILTON *P.L.* XI. 617 That sober Race of Men, whose lives Religious titl'd them the Sons of God.

**5.** *son of man*: **a.** One of the human race; a mortal. Also pl. *sons of men*.

*c* 825 *Vesp. Psalter* viii. 5 Hwet is..sunu monnes forðon ðu neosas hine? *c* 1000 *Ags. Ps.* lxxix. 16 Si þin seo swiðre hand ..ofer mannes sunu. *a* 1300 *E.E. Psalter* iv. 3 Mennes sones, towhen of hert vnmeke? 1382 WYCLIF *Isaiah* li. 12 Who [art] thou, that thou drede of a deadly man, and of the sone of man. 1562 WINȜET *Wks.* (S.T.S.) I. 14 Thow sone of man, the house of Israell is turnit into drosse. *c* 1639 SIR W. MURE *Ps.* cxlvi. 3 Wks. (S.T.S.) II. 226 Trust not in princes, in the sone Of man who can not save. 1671 MILTON *P.R.* I. 237 The Eternal King, who rules All Heaven and Earth, Angels and Sons of men. 1718 PRIOR *Solomon* I. 1 Ye sons of men, with just regard attend. 1837 CARLYLE *Fr. Rev.* II. I. xii, Deciduous Forests that die and are born again, continually, like the sons of men.

**b.** *spec.* Jesus Christ.

*c* 950 *Lindisf. Gosp.* Matt. viii. 20 Sunu..monnes ne hæfis huer heafud..ȝebeȝes. *c* 1275 *Passion our Lord* 172 in *O.E. Misc.* 42 Monnes sune biþ bi-tauht in sunuulle honde. *a* 1300 *Cursor M.* 19439 And man sun þare se i stand, Iesus, bi godd on his righthand. 1382 WYCLIF *Matt.* viii. 20 But mannes sone hath nat wher he reste his heued. 1575 GASCOIGNE *Posies* (1907) 56 The sunne [is like] the Sonne of man. 1865 RUSKIN *Sesame* ii. §95 Shall the stones cry out against you, that they are the only pillows where the Son of Man can lay His head? 1891 FARRAR *Darkn. & Dawn* lv, Then, with hushed voices,..they spoke of the Days of the Son of Man.

**6. a.** A male descendant *of* some person or representative *of* some race.

*c* 950 *Lindisf. Gosp.* Matt. i. 1 Boc cneurise haelendes cristes dauides sunu abrahames sunu. *c* 1375 *Sc. Leg. Saints* xxxvi. (*Baptist*) 63 Mony sonnis of israel..to god, þar lord, turne sal he. *c* 1386 CHAUCER *Sec. Nun's T.* 62 Though that I, unworthy sone of Eve, Be synful. *c* 1450 HOLLAND *Howlat* 577 The Dowglass..Wan wichtly of weir..Fra sonnis of the Saxonis. 1599 SHAKS. *Much Ado* II. i. 66 Adams sonnes are my brethren. 1781 COWPER *Expost.* 124 Such..People and priest, the sons of Israel were. 1830 SCOTT *Monast.* Introd., They have no share in the promise made to the sons of Adam.

**b.** One who inherits the spirit, or displays the character, *of* some person, etc.

*c* 1380 WYCLIF *Wks.* (1880) 268 Þerfore seiþ austyn..þat þou art his soone whoos werkis þou dost. 1382 —— *Judges* xix. 22 Camen men of that cytee, the sones of Belial. *c* 1386 CHAUCER *Pars. T.* ⁋896 Thay were the sones of Belial, that is, the devel. 1508 DUNBAR *Poems* vii. 12 Welcum the soun of Mars of moste curage. 1594 KYD *Cornelia* IV. i. 167 Braue Romaine Souldiers, sterne-borne sons of Mars. 1672 DRYDEN *Defence* Wks. 1883 IV. 240 They can tell a story of Ben Jonson, and, perhaps, have had fancy enough to give a supper in the Apollo, that they might be called his sons. *a* 1700 B. E. *Dict. Cant. Crew*, *Son of Apollo*, a Scholar... [*Son of*] *Venus*, a Lover of Women. [*Son of*] *Mercury*, a Wit. *a* 1700–1785 [see MARS 1].

**c.** A member or adherent of a religious body or order, or a follower of the founder of one.

1416 *Munim. de Melros* (Bann. Cl.) 539 Alle þe Sonnys of oure hali modir þe kirk. 1590 in *Cath. Rec. Soc. Publ.* V. 189 To be ruled by you as an obedient son of the Society. 1610 HOLLAND *Camden's Brit.* (1637) 174 Young knights.. professe themselves Sonnes of the Church. 1630, 1695 [see MOTHER *sb.*[1] 2 c]. 1757 in Morris *Troubles Cath. Foref.* (1872) I. iv. 206 A son of Ignatius, a Priest of the Society of Jesus. 1851 PUGIN *Chancel Screens* 83 More than a hundred sons of S. Benedict.

**d.** *son of* ——: at one time a common formula for the title of a sequel to a book or film; hence used *joc.* to designate a programme, product, institution, etc., that is a derivative *of* its predecessor.

1929 E. R. BURROUGHS (*title*) Son of Tarzan. 1934 *Picturegoer* 23 June 20/3 *Son of Kong*... By no means a second *King Kong* this picture, nevertheless, has some clever technical qualities. 1941 'B. GRAEME' (*title*) Son of Blackshirt. 1965 [see *horror film* s.v. HORROR *sb.* 6]. 1966 'O. MILLS' *Enemies of Bride* iv. 47, I produced a scintillating piece of non-fiction called..*Elizabethan Domestic Drama*... I got a sequel—Son-of-Elizabethan-Domestic-Drama..— into print as well. 1971 R. PETRIE *Thorne in Flesh* iii. 45 We don't want you playing Son of Sexton Blake... You could get hurt. 1976 *Gramophone* Nov. 910/1 The XSV/3000 is recognizably a 'son of' the XUV/4500Q: it has the same slim-line body and lightweight fixing wings. 1979 *Daily Tel.* 29 Mar. 6/3 (*heading*) Cheaper seats likely if 'Son of Concorde' flies. 1981 *Times* 19 Nov. 13/1 President Reagan ..has now formally endorsed..negotiations..on strategic arms reductions (now known as 'Start', son of Salt).

**7. a.** One who is characterized by the presence, possession, influence, use, etc., *of* some quality or thing.

*c* 950 *Lindisf. Gosp.* Luke x. 6 And ȝif ðer sie sunu sibbes, wunað ofer hia sibb iuera. *c* 1386 CHAUCER *Pars. T.* ⁋312 Forther ouer, it maketh hym þat whilom was a son of Ire to be son of grace. *Ibid.* ⁋335 Therfore be we alle born sones of wratthe and of dampnacion perdurable. 1596 SHAKS. *1 Hen. IV*, II. iv. 191 They are villaines, and the sonnes of darknesse. 1604 E. G[RIMSTONE] *D'Acosta's Hist. Indies* v. i. 329 Amongst all the sonnes of pride, he is the king. 1648 PRYNNE *Plea for Lords* 5 They are the Sonnes of Conquest introduced by the Conquerour. 1700 T. BROWN tr. *Fresny's Amusem.* 42 Certain Sons of Parchment, call'd Solicitors and Barristers. 1748 JOHNSON *Van. Hum. Wishes* 250 The fierce Croatian, and the wild Hussar, With all the sons of ravage crowd the war. 1770 J. ADAMS *Diary* 1 July, Wks. 1850 II. 243 Came home and took a pipe after supper with landlord, who is a staunch, zealous son of liberty. 1803 VISCT. STRANGFORD *Poems of Camoens* Notes (1810) 127 Locks of auburn, and eyes of blue, have ever been dear to the sons of song. 1872 DE VERE *Americanisms* 313 *Sons of wax* is neither an uncommon nor an uncomplimentary name for them [boot and shoe makers].

**b.** A person regarded as the product or offspring *of* a certain country or place.

*son of the soil*: see SOIL *sb.*[1] 5 b.

1595 SHAKS. *John* v. ii. 25 We, the sonnes and children of this Isle. 1628 MILTON *Vac. Exerc.* 91 Whether thou be the Son, Of utmost Tweed, or Oose, or gulphie Dun. 1667 —— *P.L.* II. 692 Art thou hee, Who..Drew after him the third part of Heav'ns Sons? 1746 FRANCIS tr. *Horace, Ep.* I. i. 75 Ye Sons of Rome, let Money first be sought. 1764 GOLDSM. *Trav.* 112 Could Nature's bounty satisfy the breast, The sons of Italy were surely blest. 1807 P. GASS *Jrnl.* 235 These good hearted, hospitable..sons of the west. 1842 BORROW *Bible in Spain* xli, They have taught him their language, which he already speaks as well as if he were a son of the prison. 1871 FREEMAN *Norm. Conq.* (1876) IV. 55 The foreign spoiler..insensibly changed into the Son of the soil, into an Englishman.

*transf.* **1712** BLACKMORE *Creation* VI. 272 See, her tall Sons, the Cedar, Oak, and Pine, The fragrant Myrtle, and the juicy Vine.

**c.** In miscellaneous fig. uses.

**1617** FLETCHER *Valentinian* V. ii. *song*, Easie, sweet,..thou son of night, Pass by his troubled senses. **1837** CARLYLE *Fr. Rev.* I. VI. i, As an actually existing Son of Time, look..at what the Time did bring. **1872** MORLEY *Voltaire* (1886) 3 Man, who is a worm, and the son of a worm.

**d.** In terms of abuse or contempt. Also used *ellipt.* for SON OF A BITCH.

See DUNGHILL *sb.* 2, GUN *sb.* 6c, *sea-cook* s.v. SEA *sb.* 23, SHOEMAKER, WHORE.

**1951** W. FAULKNER *Collected Stories* 171 Are you going to sit there and let a black son rape a white woman on the streets of Jefferson?

**e.** ***Son of Heaven*** (†***Heaven's Son***) [tr. Chinese *tiānzǐ*], the Emperor of China; loosely, any Chinese. Cf. CELESTIAL *a.* 4 and *sb.* 2.

**1613** PURCHAS *Pilgrimage* IV. xvi. 369 The King's Title is, *Lord of the world, and Sonne of Heaven.* **1838** GUTZLAFF & REED *China Opened* II. xxvii. 541 To gain such honours as the Mongol princes pay to Heaven's Son, requires a well-stored treasury. **1850** *North-China Herald* 9 Nov. 58/4 One of the common appellations of the Emperors of China has been and still is *T'ien Tsze*, 'the Son of Heaven!' **1923** S. MERWIN *Silk* (1924) 136 It is now my privilege to serve him who is in all but official style the Son of Heaven. **1938** *Foreign Affairs* XVI. 201 A dignity which the 'Sons of Heaven' consider has belonged to them for thousands of years. **1973** J. LEASOR *Mandarin Gold* i. 1 The Emperor, Tao Kuang, the Son of Heaven, who ruled his celestial empire from..Peking, the forbidden city.

**f.** (***horny-handed***) ***son of toil***, a manual labourer. Now often *ironically*.

**1873** *Q. Rev.* CXXXV. 543 The peculiar virtues of the horny-handed sons of toil received a severe shock in 1848, and finally collapsed in 1871. **1902** 'MARK TWAIN' in *N. Amer. Rev.* Apr. 441 A crowd of ten thousand..proud, untamed democrats, horny-handed sons of toil..and fliers of the eagle. **1933** WODEHOUSE *Heavy Weather* xvii. 298 You look like one of those Sons of Toil Buried by Tons of Soil I once saw in a head-line. **1976** *Times* 23 Mar. 19/4 There won't be any room for your actual horny-handed sons of toil in the TUC; there'll be too many sharp-suited managers.

**8. a.** ***son-before-the-father***, a name given to various plants, as the willow-herb, meadow-saffron, coltsfoot, etc., on account of the flowers appearing before the leaves or because of some other peculiarity.

See Britten & Holland *Dict. Engl. Plant-names* 442.

**1578** LYTE *Dodoens* I. li. 74 The second [= red willow herb] is called of some..*Filius ante patrem*, that is to say, the sonne before the father. **1597** GERARDE *Herbal* I. lxxxii. 131 The Latins thought this a fit name for it *Filius ante Patrem*: and we accordingly may call it, the Sonne before the Father. **1688** HOLME *Armoury* II. 65/1 *The Son before the Father*, so called of some Herbalists. **1825** JAMIESON *Suppl.*, *Son-afore-the-father*, Common Coltsfoot. **1869** *N. & Q.* 4th Ser. III. 35/1. *Ibid.* 91/1.

**b.** ***son-of-the-sun***, the frigate-bird.

**1895** LYDEKKER *Roy. Nat. Hist.* IV. 287 The frigate-bird, which has received the title of the Son-of-the-sun, is one of the most swift and active of all pelagic birds.

**9.** *attrib.*, as ***son-spouse***, ***-worship***; ***son-lover***, a son who is his mother's lover.

**1850** THACKERAY *Pendennis* xxxvi, Son-worship amongst mothers. **1897** *Q. Rev.* July 69 The Great Goddess of Asia, attended by her mystic Son-spouse. **1913** D. H. LAWRENCE *Let.* Jan. (1932) 102 The old son-lover was Œdipus.

**son** (səʊn), *sb.*² Also sone. [a. Sp. *son*, lit. 'sound'.] A slow Cuban dance and song in $\frac{2}{4}$ time; ***son Afro-Cubano***, a form of the son influenced by Negro dances.

**1934** S. R. NELSON *All about Jazz* vii. 167 The Son is far more refined than the Rumba, and when properly danced, is plaintively alluring. The Son is always danced in very slow tempo. This Cuban music is particularly characterized by the continual recurrence of singing. **1939** [see MACUMBA]. **1954** *Grove's Dict. Mus.* (ed. 5) III. 215/1 When Afro-Cuban dances penetrated the port towns of Cuba they were assimilated by Spanish-Cuban folk music... The hybrid forms are then designated by such titles as *son afro-cubano*. **1956** M. STEARNS *Story of Jazz* (1957) iii. 26 The Rhumba, Conga, Son Afro-Cubano, Mambo, and Cha-Cha are predominantly African. **1958** E. BORNEMAN in P. Gammond *Decca Bk. Jazz* xxi. 270 The sone itself usually consisted of an eight-bar theme for solo voice, followed by an improvised four-bar tag, called montuno, that was sung in choir and repeated twice. Whereas the themes of the sones were usually lilting tunes of obviously Spanish descent, the montunos were unmistakably African. **1964** W. G. RAFFÉ *Dict. Dance* 469/2 As a ballroom dance, the *Son* remained very popular until about 1950, when the *Mamba* began to supersede every other dance in *Cuba*. **1973** [see *rumba dancer* s.v. RUMBA *sb.* 2].

**son**, obs. form of SOUND *sb.*, SUN *sb.*¹

**son**, *v. rare.* Also 3 sunen. [f. the sb.]

†**1.** *intr.* To conceive a son. *Obs.*

*c* **1250** *Gen. & Ex.* 981 And seide ȝhe sulde sunen wel And timen, and clepen it [I]smael.

**2.** With *it*: To act or behave as a son.

**1731** FIELDING *Covent Gard. Trag.* Proleg. Wks. 1882 IX. 170 If I mistake not, in the scene immediately preceding, Bilkum and she have mothered and sonned it several times.

‖**so-na** ('sona). *Mus.* Also so na. [Chinese *suǒnà*.] A Chinese wind instrument (see quots.)

**1908** *Jrnl. North-China Branch R. Asiatic Soc.* XXXIX. 87 At Peking the *So Na* is regularly made of two sizes... The similarity of sound between *So Na* and *Zourna*, the name of a Persian oboe, is pointed out by M. Mahillon. **1954** *Grove's Dict. Mus.* (ed. 5) II. 236/1 *So-na* (S.W. *so-la*), conical oboe (wrongly, 'clarinet'). Its name connects it with the Persian *surna*... A wooden pipe with 7 + 1 holes terminated at one end by a copper bell and at the other end by a small reed mouthpiece. **1968** tr. *Hsia Hsiang* in Gray & Cavendish *Chinese Communism in Crisis* 165 A number of people regularly used to crowd into a small cave and listen to an old poor peasant playing the *So-na.* **1975** C. P. MACKERRAS *Chinese Theatre in Mod. Times* 23 Reed instruments are not of great significance in Chinese drama. The only one that need be mentioned here is the *so-na*, which has eight finger-holes and a double reed. Though in this way similar to the Western oboe, the *so-na* is rather shrill and piercing in tone.

†'**sonable**, *a. Obs.*⁻⁰ [ad. L. *sonābilis* (Ovid), f. *sonāre* to sound.] (See quots.)

**1623** COCKERAM I, *Sonable*, sounding shrill. **1727** BAILEY (vol. II), *Sonable*, that will easily sound.

†'**sonage.** *Obs.*⁻¹ In 7 sonnage. [f. SON *sb.*¹ + -AGE.] The status of a son; sonship.

**1605** BROUGHTON *Corrupt. Handl. Relig.* 51 Thus Kimchi ..noteth the Scriptures phrase..for sonnage in Kingdome.

**sonagram**, **-graph**, varr. SONOGRAM, SONOGRAPH I.

**sonance** ('səʊnəns). [f. L. *son-āre* to sound + -ANCE.] Sound; the quality of sounding.

**1599** SHAKS. *Hen. V*, IV. ii. 35 Let the Trumpets sound The Tucket Sonuance [*sic*], and the Note to mount. **1608** HEYWOOD *Lucrece* (1638) 178 If he chance to endure our tongues so much, As but to heare their sonance.

**1859** L. F. SIMPSON *Handbk. Dining* iv. 57 When a key-note is struck, a practised ear discerns one or more sonances. **1892** G. HAKE *Mem. 80 Yrs.* 220 He did not look to musical sonance in his metre and his choice of words.

**sonancy** ('səʊnənsɪ). [f. as prec. + -ANCY.] The quality of being sonant.

**1875** WHITNEY *Life Lang.* iv. 59 A column of air emitted by the lungs, impressed with sonancy and variety of pitch by the larynx. **1884** *Amer. Ann. Deaf & Dumb* Oct. 249 The sonants 'soft', or 'flat', or 'weak', especially when the element of sonancy is suppressed.

**sonant** ('səʊnənt), *a.* and *sb.* [ad. L. *sonant-*, *sonans*, pres. pple. of *sonāre* to sound.]

**A.** *adj.* **a.** Uttered with voice or vocal sound; voiced.

**1846** M. WILLIAMS *Sanscr. Gram.* 14 Final *a* is changed to *o* before all sonant consonants. **1875** WHITNEY *Life Lang.* iv. 57 The conversion of a surd into its corresponding sonant sound. **1894** *Nation* LIX. 180/3 Surd explosive sounds are largely in excess of sonant expletives.

**b.** Syllabic; capable of forming a syllable, or constituting the essential element of a syllable.

**1876** [see DIPHTHONG *sb.* a]. **1932** W. L. GRAFF *Language & Languages* 56 The sound that possesses the highest degree of sonority in a syllable is called syllabic or sonant. **1957** C. L. WRENN in *Wiener Beiträge zur Englischen Philologie* LXV. 255 The metrical value of a sonant or vocalic *n* in words like *forbidd'n*..and *heav'n*.

**B.** *sb.* **1.** A sonant articulation or letter.

**1849** J. R. LOGAN in *Jrnl. Ind. Archipel.* III. 229 (*heading*) Surds into sonants differing both in their organic and aspirate classes. **1875** WHITNEY *Life Lang.* iv. 46 We have changed the first *p* into a different but closely kindred sound, its corresponding sonant *b.* **1880** *Athenæum* 2 Oct. 431/2 Why he should find it necessary to turn initial surd consonants wholesale into sonants, it is impossible to say.

**2.** A syllabic sound; now usu., a syllabic consonant.

**1893** *N.E.D.* s.v. *Consonant* sb., The use of the liquids and nasals as vowels or sonants. **1942** K. MALONE in *Mod. Lang. Q.* Mar. 5 Traces of sonant-consonant opposition may be found in English liquids and nasals: thus *Gardner/Gardiner.* **1949** *Trans. Philol. Soc. 1948* 146 Nasals such as *m, n, ŋ* are often sonants—that is to say, have syllabic function.

**3.** A consonant that can be either syllabic or non-syllabic, i.e. a liquid, nasal, or semivowel.

**1933** L. BLOOMFIELD *Language* vii. 121 In most languages there is a third, intermediate group of *sonants*, phonemes which occur in both syllabic and non-syllabic positions. **1976** *Archivum Linguisticum* VII. 93 It [sc. *stød*]..can fall on sonants as well as vowels (for example, [hwal'b], [sdor'g]; *hvalpe, storke*).

Hence **so'nantic** *a.*, of a sonant character; **'sonantizing** *ppl. a.*, converting into a sonant.

**1879** WHITNEY *Sanskr. Gram.* 37 Vowels and semivowels and nasals exercise a sonantizing influence. **1892** *Classical Rev.* May 189/2 The sonantic function of the..nasals.

**sonantal** (səʊ'næntəl), *a. Phonetics.* [f. SONANT *sb.* + -AL¹.] **1.** Syllabic; = SONANT *a.* b.

**1891** A. L. MAYHEW *Synopsis O.E. Phonol.* 36 The Indg. sonantal liquid l. **1897** *N.E.D.* s.v. *Diphthong*, The combination of a sonantal with a consonantal vowel. *Ibid.*, When these sounds [sc. *y* or *w*]..follow the sonantal vowel, the combination is called a 'falling diphthong'.

**2.** That is or contains a sonant (SONANT *sb.* 3). *rare.*

**1976** *Archivum Linguisticum* VII. 93 The discussion is divided into sections dealing with developments before geminates, in 'diphthongal groups' (vowel + sonant), with 'sonantal finals' (sonant preceded by another consonant) and before two consonants.

**sonar** ('səʊnɑː(r)). orig. *U.S.* [f. initial letters of *so*und *na*vigation (*and*) *r*anging, after *radar.*] A system for use under the sea in which the audible or high-frequency sound reflected or emitted by an object in the sea is used to ascertain its position, nature, or speed; (an) apparatus used for this; also in extended use, a system in which the position of an object in air or water is ascertained by reflected ultrasound, e.g. as used by bats and in diagnostic medicine. Freq. *attrib.* Cf. ASDIC (see quot. 1963).

**1946** *U.S. Navy Press Release* 6 Apr. 1 The word 'sonar' was coined from abbreviations for sound, navigation and ranging, and includes various types of underwater sound devices used in detecting submarines and other submerged objects and in obtaining water depths. **1952** [see ASDIC]. **1961** W. N. KELLOGG *Porpoises & Sonar* (1962) iv. 48 The idea that sonar is systematically used by the great whales and porpoises is..a new and intriguing thought. **1963** *Times* 2 Feb. 5/2 In order to conform with NATO practice, the name Asdic..has been superseded by the word Sonar, the Admiralty announced yesterday... In future Asdic ratings will be known as Sonar operators. **1968** M. WOODHOUSE *Rock Baby* xiii. 129 Bats swooped past my head, bouncing their tiny high-pitched sonar echoes off me. **1971** *Hi-Fi Sound* Feb. 63 (Advt.), The photograph shows Ferrograph recorders at work in the Sonar Room aboard the Hunter Killer nuclear-powered Submarine H.M.S. 'Churchill'. **1971** *New Scientist* 3 June 568/1 The standard method of detecting submerged submarines is by sonar, either active or passive. **1973** *Brit. Med. Jrnl.* 6 Oct. 28/1 The 'in utero' crown-rump length of the fetus may be determined by sonar in the first trimester of pregnancy. **1974** *Sci. Amer.* Mar. 120/2 Frequency-modulation sonars..can exploit a Doppler signal to measure speed. **1979** *Ibid.* Feb. 67/1 (Advt.), These unique sonar cameras send out an inaudible sound signal that bounces off the subject and returns to the camera, in milliseconds—and the lens automatically rotates to perfect focus.

**sonata** (sə(ʊ)'nɑːtə, so'nata). Also with pl. ‖**sonate** (so'nate). [It., fem. pa. pple. of *sonare* to sound. Cf. F. *sonate.*]

**1.** †**a.** A musical composition for instruments as opposed to one for voices (a *cantata*). *Obs.* **b.** An instrumental piece of music, usually for the pianoforte, in several (commonly three or four) movements. ***double sonata*** (see quot. 1880).

**1694** PURCELL *Playford's Skill Music* (ed. 12) 116 But if you Compose Sonata's, there one Treble has as much Predominancy as the other. **1713** *Guardian* No. 67, He has made use of Italian Tunes and Sonatas for promoting the Protestant Interest. **1766** ENTICK *London* IV. 447 Several.. songs are performed, with sonatas or concertos between each. **1801** BUSBY *Dict. Mus.* s.v., The Sonata, of whatever kind, generally opens with an Adagio; and..concludes with an Allegro, or a Presto. **1848** DICKENS *Dombey* liii, I have.. gone accurately through the whole of Beethoven's Sonata in B. **1880** STAINER & BARRETT *Dict. Mus. Terms*, *Double sonata*, a sonata for two solo instruments, as pianoforte and violin, or two pianofortes.

*transf.* **1869** *Routledge's Ev. Boy's Ann.* 469 Morton had recommenced another sonata on his nasal organ.

**c.** ***sonata da camera***, a sonata suitable for performance in a room smaller than a concert-hall; ***sonata da chiesa***, a sonata suitable for performance in a church.

[**1789** C. BURNEY *Gen. Hist. Music* (1935) III. ix. 548 Among the most early of these productions may be ranked the *Suonate per Chiesa*, of Legrenzi, published at Venice 1655; *Suonate da Chiesa e camera*, 1656.] **1801** BUSBY *Dict. Mus.* s.v. Sonata, There are several kinds of *Sonatas*. The Italians, however, reduce them principally to two: the *Sonata da Camera*, or *Chamber Sonata*; and the *Sonata de Chiesa*, or *Church Sonata*. **1883** GROVE *Dict. Mus.* III. 556/2 There are twenty-four 'Sonate da Chiesa' for strings, lute, and organ, twenty-four 'Sonate da Camera' for the same instruments, and twelve Solos or sonatas for violin and violoncello, or 'cembalo'. **1938** *Oxf. Compan. Mus.* 879/2 These may be said to close the period of the Sonata da Chiesa or abstract type of the contrapuntal period. Nearly all these composers also wrote works of the Sonata da Camera (or dance) type. **1968** *Listener* 20 June 813/3 The extent to which purely instrumental pieces were demanded during the services seems altogether extraordinary. This was the cradle of the *sonata da chiesa* and the *concerto grosso.* **1974** *Early Music* July 185/2 Adriano Banchieri was so smitten with the aria..that he set it..as a *sonata da camera* for two violins and bass.

**2.** Without article: The class of music represented by sonatas.

**1883** *Grove's Dict. Music* III. 558/2 The domain of Sonata was for a long while almost monopolised by violinists and writers for the violin.

**3.** *attrib.*, as ***sonata face***, ***form***, ***kind***, ***movement***.

**1703** FARQUHAR *Inconstant* II. ii, I see you have a singing face; a heavy dull sonata face. **1873** H. C. BANISTER *Music* 209 In Concertos..the Sonata form is extended. **1874** OUSELEY *Musical Form* 54 The modern binary form is often but inaccurately styled 'the sonata form'. **1883** *Grove's Dict. Music* III. 554/1 Abstract instrumental music of the Sonata kind. **1942** *Ann. Reg. 1941* 295 Mr. T. S. Eliot's new poem, *The Dry Salvages*..had a sonata movement, the recurring theme being the timelessness of experience. **1947** A. EINSTEIN *Music in Romantic Era* xviii. 350 The musical construction of a sonata or a sonata-movement does not follow real or idealized feelings.

Hence **so'natical** *a. rare*⁻¹.

**1797** *Monthly Mag.* III. 227 The symphony of the present day is perfectly sonatical.

**sonatina** (səʊnə'tiːnə). [It., dim. of SONATA.] A short, simple form of sonata.

[**1724** *Short Explic. For. Wds. in Mus. Bks.* 75 *Suonatina*, a Little, Short, Plain, or Easy Sonata.] **1801** BUSBY *Dict. Mus.*, *Sonatina*, a short sonata. **1869** *Pall Mall G.* 1 Oct. 12 Three sonatinas for the pianoforte by Herr Carl Reinecke. **1883** *Grove's Dict. Music* III. 583 Sonatinas form one of the least satisfactory groups of musical products.

So '**sonatine.** [Cf. F. *sonatine.*]

**1875** OUSELEY *Musical Form* v. 38 In the overtures of Italian operas, and in the first movements of short easy sonatines.

**sonation** (səʊ'neɪʃən). *rare.* [f. L. *son-āre* to sound (see -ATION), or ad. med.L. *sonātio* (Albertus Magnus).] The action of sounding; the faculty of producing sound.

**1655** STANLEY *Hist. Philos.* (1687) 382/1 The act of the object, and the act of the sense it self, as Sonation and Audition, are really the same. **1846** SIR W. HAMILTON *Reid's Wks.* Note D, 828 The actual hearing and the actual sounding... Of these the one may be called audition, the other sonation.

**sonce, soncy,** variants of Sc. SONSE, SONSY.

**sond,** var. *shond* SHAND *sb.*; obs. f. SOUND *a.*

**sond(e,** obs. forms of SAND *sb.*[1] and *sb.*[2]

**Sonda(we, -day(e,** obs. forms of SUNDAY.

**sondage** (sõdaʒ). *Archæol.* [a. Fr. *sondage* sounding, borehole.] A deep trench dug to investigate the stratigraphy of a site.

[**1923** *Glasgow Herald* 13 Sept. 9/5 What is taking place in Berlin now is what the French call 'sondage'... The Chancellor is really endeavouring to see how the land lies.] **1930** *Discovery* Aug. 259/1 Against the south angle of the northern harbour a fairly prominent mound invited a sondage, and it proved to conceal a temple more perfectly preserved than any hitherto found in Mesopotamia. **1952** K. M. KENYON *Beginning in Archaeol.* v. 102 The method of *sondage* is sometimes employed, in which a shaft of comparatively limited area is sunk.. with the avowed object of establishing what is the succession of cultures. **1955** L. WOOLLEY *Alalakh* i. 6 In 1948 and 1949 Mr. Sinclair Hood made *sondages* at Tabara al Akrad. **1977** P. BARKER *Techniques Archaeol. Excavation* 76 We have seen that holes dug into extensive layers can be disastrous for their subsequent interpretation, and anyway the information gained by a 'sondage', however small, relates only to the area of the sondage.

**sonde** (sɒnd). [Fr., 'sounding-line, sounding'.] **a.** A radiosonde or similar device that is sent aloft to transmit or record information on conditions in the atmosphere. Orig. only as the second element in Combs. (as *ballon-sonde, ionosonde, radiosonde*, etc.).

**1901** [see BALLON-SONDE]. **1937** [see RADIOSONDE]. **1943** P. A. ANDERSON et al. *Captive Radiosonde & Wired Sonde Techniques* (U.S. Nat. Defense Res. Council Project P.D.R.C.-647, Rep. No. 3) 4 When the sonde is moved to a new altitude, a pause of 10–30 seconds is adequate to establish equilibrium readings on the meters. **1949** *Sci. Progr.* XXXVII. 490 A direct method of sounding may provide information on solar spectra from which data on the atmosphere above the highest level reached by the sonde may be derived. **1969** MCINTOSH & THOM *Essent. Meteorol.* vii. 111 More recently, ozone sondes have been used to measure the vertical distribution of ozone. **1975** *Nature* 1 May 20/2 A seventh aircraft was used to drop sondes from 40,000 feet and obtain additional vertical profiles of wind and temperature.

**b.** An instrument probe for transmitting information about its surroundings underground or under water.

**1952** *Bull. Amer. Assoc. Petroleum Geologists* XXXVI. 310 The application of the limestone sonde log to the determination of the porosity profile of wells. **1962** *Research* XV. 298/1 This deflection increases as the sonde continues to enter the [coal] seam. **1962** [see RE-ENTRY 2 d]. **1975** G. ANDERSON *Coring* vii. 124 The SP log is a measurement of the electrical potential energy in the mud around the sonde as compared with a reference electrode grounded at the surface.

**sonder** ('zɒndə(r)), *a.* and *sb.* *U.S.* [f. G. *sonderklasse* special class.] **A.** *adj.* Of, pertaining to, or designating a class of small racing yachts. **B.** *sb.* A yacht of this class.

**1909** *N.Y. Even. Post* 9 Sept. 3/3 The Sonder yachtsmen, both victors and vanquished, were received by President Taft today. **1913** C. W. ERNST *Letter* (MS.), Our yachtsmen, since 1907, talk of 'sonder-boats', sonder class, sonder race,—meaning certain boats recognised by the International Yacht Racing Union. **1917** *Rudder* Apr. 328/1 Fred M. Hoyt is to have a Marconi rig put upon his sonder boat Skeezix. There are a few sonders left at Marblehead and the innovation will be watched with much interest. **1948** R. DE KERCHOVE *Internat. Maritime Dict.* 695/2 *Sonder*, a class of small yacht originated in Germany, in which the sum of the waterline length, extreme beam, and extreme draft must not be greater than 32 ft.

**sonder,** obs. f. *sooner* (SOON *adv.*), and SUNDER.

**Sonderbund** ('zɒndəbʊnt). [a. G. *Sonderbund* special league, separate association.] A league formed by the R.C. cantons of Switzerland in 1843 and defeated in a civil war in 1847. Also *attrib.*

**1847** G. GROTE *Seven Lett. Politics Switzerland* i. 17 The invasion.. in.. 1844.. by bands of volunteers.. called the Corps Francs—and the separate league of Seven Cantons, called the Sonderbund. **1887** *Encycl. Brit.* XXII. 795/1 The seven Catholic cantons—Uri, Schwyz, Unterwalden, Lucerne, Zug, Freiburg, and Wallis—formed (September 7, 1843) a 'Sonderbund' or separate league... In December 1845 the Sonderbund turned itself into an armed confederation. **1922** E. & C. PAUL tr. *Oechsli's Hist. Switzerland* xxxiv. 386 The Sonderbund war. **1952** E. BONJOUR et al. *Short Hist. Switzerland* x. 262 The founders of this Sonderbund, as it was soon aptly named. **1973** HOWAT & TAYLOR *Dict. World Hist.* 1465/1 The outnumbered Sonderbund expected Austrian and French help, but the swift victory of the Diet's troops under Dufour forestalled its arrival.

**sonder-cloud.** ? *Obs.* [app. f. G. *sonder* separate.] A cirro-cumulus cloud.

**1827** T. FORSTER *Encycl. Nat. Phenomena* 13 Cirrocumulus or Sondercloud is a congeries of small roundish little clouds in close horizontal apposition. **1844** H. STEPHENS *Bk. Farm* I. 246 Why the heap should be called the *stacken-cloud*,.. the curled heap the *sonder-cloud*,.. is by no means obvious. **1862** *Chambers's Encycl.* III. 86/1.

**sondere man:** see SANDESMAN *Obs.*

‖**Sonderkommando** ('zɒndərkɔˌmando). [G. *Sonderkommando* special detachment.] In Nazi Germany, a detachment of prisoners in a concentration camp responsible for the disposal of the dead; also a member of such a detachment. Also *fig.*

**1951** MOYSE & STENHOUSE tr. *Rousset's World Apart* v. 27 The *Sonderkommando*, totally isolated from the world, condemned to live every second of its eternity with tortured and charred bodies. **1960** S. BECKER tr. *Schwarz-Bart's Last of Just* (1961) VIII. 422 The team of *Sonderkommando* responsible for burning the Jews in the crematory ovens. **1976** *Times Lit. Suppl.* 2 July 815/1 A four-legged Sonderkommando who betrays his fellows to starvation. **1979** J. GARDNER *Nostradamus Traitor* xxxv. 165 The womenfolk prepared a great spread of food... 'Enough food to feed the whole of a Sonderkommando.'

**sonderlypes,** var. of SUNDERLEPES *adv. Obs.*

**sondery,** obs. form of SUNDRY.

**sondesman,** variant of SANDESMAN *Obs.*

**sondir(e, sondre,** obs. forms of SUNDER.

**sondrey, -rie, -ry,** obs. forms of SUNDRY.

**sone** (səʊn). [ad. L. *sonus*.] †**1.** Sound. *Obs.*$^{-1}$

**1616** J. LANE *Contn. Sqr.'s T.* IV. p. 45 *note*, Thence bore vp mongst the spheares of musickes tones, whence are derived all harmonious sones.

**2.** A unit of subjective loudness such that the number of sones is proportional to the loudness of a sound: a tone of frequency 1000 Hz and 40 dB above the listener's audibility threshold produces a loudness of one sone.

**1936** S. S. STEVENS in *Psychol. Rev.* XLIII. 416 It is proposed that the unit of the scale be the loudness of 1000 cycle tone 40db above threshold heard with both ears, and that it be called a sone. **1952** *Sci. News Let.* 28 June 411/2 The field studies.. used the 'sone' as a unit of loudness. The decibel.. measures only the intensity of a noise. It is the loudness that is most objectionable to the human ear. **1958** *Times* 18 July 7/6 The sone scale is.. based on the averaged impressions of supposedly normal individuals in identifying the relative loudness of different sounds, *i.e.*, that they are two, three or four times, &c., as loud as a sound of one sone. **1960** *New Scientist* 25 Feb. 454/1 The American Automobile Manufacturers' Association adopted in 1954 a noise specification for new vehicles of 125 sones measured at 50 feet. **1970** [see NOY].

**sone,** var. SOIGN *v.*, SON *sb.*[2]; obs. var. or f. SON, SOON, SOUND, SUN.

**Sone(n)day,** obs. forms of SUNDAY.

**Sonerila** (sɒnə'ri:lə). *Bot.* [ad. Javanese *soneriila*.] A genus of Eastern plants; a variety or plant belonging to this genus.

**1846** LINDLEY *Veget. Kingd.* 732 The Memecylons are ribless, and so is Sonerila. **1866** *Treas. Bot.* 1072/2. **1880** C. R. MARKHAM *Peruv. Bark* 302 The *Osbeckias* and *Sonerilas* represent the melastomaceous plants. **1882** *Garden* 18 Nov. 442/1 The freely produced and really handsome flowers alone render Sonerilas worthy of a place in gardens.

**Soneryl** ('sɒnərɪl). *Pharm.* Also **soneryl.** A proprietary name (orig. French) for butobarbitone (5-butyl-5-ethylbarbituric acid, $C_{10}H_{16}N_2O_3$), given in tablet form as a sedative and hypnotic.

**1923** *Pharmaceutical Jrnl.* LVI. 170/2 An interesting preparation which Messrs. May and Baker are shortly to issue is 'Soneryl'... Compared with veronal, Soneryl is twice as active. **1923** *Official Gaz.* (U.S. Patent Office) 18 Sept. 395/2 Etablissements Poulenc Frères, Paris... *Soneryl*... Claims use since Apr. 18, 1922. **1933** *Trade Marks Jrnl.* 3 May 510/2 *Soneryl*... A derivative of barbituric acid prepared for use in medicine and pharmacy. May and Baker Ltd... Manufacturing chemists. **1948** J. H. BURN *Lect. Notes Pharmacol.* 44 Tablets of Soneryl (butobarbitone) are used to ensure a good night's sleep either for a patient in hospital or for a normal person travelling by night train. **1959** D. DU MAURIER *Breaking Point* 115, I would sleep on it—if I could sleep, which seemed very doubtful. I took two soneryl tablets, and passed out. **1979** L. BROWN *Encounters With Nature* vi. 79 By taking three Soneryl and four aspirin tablets, I suffered through the night in fitful drowsiness.

†**sonet.** *Obs. rare.* [a. OF. *sonet* (*sonnet*), = Prov. *sonet*, f. *son* sound.] Song, melody, music. Also *attrib.*

**13..** *E.E. Allit. P.* B. 1516 Þer was rynging on ryȝt of ryche metalles,.. Clatering of conacles þat kesten þo burdes, As sonet out of sauteray songe als myry. *c* **1440** *Gesta Rom.* xvi. 55 (Harl. MS.), A nyghtingale sat vpon a tre, & made a passing swete sonet-song.

**sonet, sonetteer,** obs. forms of SONNET(TEER.

‖**son et lumière** (sɒn eɪ 'lu:mi:ɛə(r), ‖sɔn e lymjɛr). Also with capital initials. [Fr., lit. 'sound and light'.] **1.** A form of entertainment using recorded sound and lighting effects, usu. presented at night at a historic building and giving a dramatic narrative of its history. Also *attrib.*

**1957** *Times* 1 Aug. 10/1 A dinner party.. on the occasion of the preview of the *Son et Lumière* spectacle. *Ibid.* 13 Aug. 11/1 In the five years since M. Paul Robert-Houdin first introduced the technique at.. Chambord, *son et lumière* has been adopted at.. buildings of historic interest in France. **1959** *Times* 30 June 12/4 Son et lumière performances are being given this week, starting to-night at Greys Court, Henley-on-Thames. **1969** V. ROWE *Loire* 33 At Chambord, in 1952, a new kind of entertainment was born, *son-et-lumière*, a combination of sound and light effects. **1970** N. FLEMING *Czech Point* (1971) xvi. 205, I felt as visible as a statue in a Son et Lumière display. **1977** J. I. M. STEWART *Madonna of Astrolabe* i. 19 A few years ago we had *son et lumière* in aid of some building project.

**2.** *fig.* Writing or behaviour resembling a *son et lumière* presentation, *esp.* in its dramatic qualities.

**1968** *Punch* 16 Oct. 557/3 The effects are produced by a literary *son et lumière*—by liberal direct quotation of anecdotes, poetry, hymns and music, and a series of splendid photographs, rather than words about palaces. **1969** *Listener* 9 Jan. 41/1 Old Mr Seddeby's performance, from 11 o'clock to one daily, as an elder statesman in decline, an illusion which involved a lot of business with a monocle and a cigar-cutter, was pure *son et lumière*. **1978** *Times Lit. Suppl.* 24 Mar. 336/3 It would have been all too easy to end this biography in *son et lumière* and to paint a Tiepolo ceiling on which Forster is floating up to Olympus.

‖**so'netto.** *Obs.*$^{-1}$ [It. *sonetto*.] = SONNET.

**1589** GREENE *Menaphon* (Arb.) 89 Thus Gentlemen haue you heard my verdite in this Sonetto.

**song** (sɒŋ), *sb.* Forms: *α.* 1 sanc, 1– (latterly *Sc.* and *north. dial.*) **sang** (4 zang), 4–5 **sange.** *β.* 1– song, 3–6 songe (4 zonge), 6–7 songue. [Common Teut.: OE. *sang, sǫng*, = OFris. *sang, song* (WFris. *sang*, EFris. *song*, NFris. *sōng*), MDu. *sanc, zanc*, etc. (Du. *zang*), OS. (MLG., LG.) *sang*, OHG. *sanc, sang* (G. *sang*), ON. *sǫngr, sǫngv-* (Icel. *söngur*, Norw. *song*, Sw. *sång*, Da. *sang*), Goth. *saggws*:—OTeut. *sangwaz*, f. the pret. stem of *singwan* SING *v.*[1]]

**1.** The act or art of singing; the result or effect of this, vocal music; that which is sung (in general or collective sense); occas., poetry.

See also PLAIN-SONG.

*α.* *Beowulf* 1063 Þær wæs sang & sweȝ samod ætgædere fore Healfdenes hildewisan. *c* **888** K. ÆLFRED *Boeth.* xxiv. §1 Þa he þa þis leoð asungen hæfde, þa forlet he þone sang. *a* **1300** *Cursor M.* 1030 Þar sune es soft and suet sang. **1340** *Ayenb.* 60 Þe dyeules noriches þet.. doþ ham slepe ine hare zenne be hare uayre zang. *c* **1400** *Laud Troy Bk.* 18127 Thei halpe hit in with mochel sang. *c* **1450** HOLLAND *Howlat* 943 Thar with dame Natur has to the hevin.. Ascendit sone.. with solace and sang. **1786** BURNS *Twa Dogs* 27 After some dog in Highland sang.

*β.* *a* **900** CYNEWULF *Crist* 1649 Ðær is engla song, eadiȝra blis. *c* **950** *Lindisf. Gosp.* Luke xv. 25 Miððy.. [he] ȝeneolecde to huse, ȝeherde huislung & þæt song. *c* **1205** LAY. 30617 Þer wes blisse & muche song. *c* **1275** *Moral Ode* 347 in *O.E. Misc.*, Þer is alre Murehþe mest myd englene songe. *c* **1330** R. BRUNNE *Chron. Wace* (Rolls) 4025 Of song & of mynstrecye Alle men gaf hym þe maystrie. *c* **1440** *Promp. Parv.* 464/2 Songe, *cantus*. *Ibid.*, Songe, of a manne a-lone, *monodia*. **1526** *Pilgr. Perf.* (W. de W. 1531) 7 b, They shall.. here theyr songe & melody. *a* **1548** HALL *Chron., Hen. VIII*, 214 b, And in the toppe was mervailous swete armony both of song and instrument. **1577–87** HOLINSHED *Chron.* I. 122/2 He.. went about in Mercia to teach song. **1667** MILTON *P.L.* III. 29 Smit with the love of sacred song. *Ibid.* IX. 25 This Subject for Heroic Song Pleas'd me. **1791** COWPER *Judgm. Poets* 17 To poets of renown in song, The nymphs referr'd the cause. **1808** SCOTT *Marm.* I. Introd. 271 The mightiest chiefs of British song Scorn'd not such legends to prolong. **1849** MACAULAY *Hist. Eng.* i. I. 30 As eloquence exists before syntax, and song before prosody. **1878** *Masque Poets* 11 Sing! Sing of what? The world is full of song!

**2. a.** A metrical composition adapted for singing, esp. one in rime and having a regular verse-form; occas., a poem.

*α.* *c* **897** K. ÆLFRED tr. *Gregory's Past. C.* 409 Ða singað ðone sang ðe nan mon elles singan ne mæȝ. **971** *Blickl. Hom.* 45 Þa þe on heofenum syndon, hi þingiaþ for þa þe þyssum sange fylȝeaþ. *a* **1200** *Vices & Virtues* 15 Ða aingles of heuene.. sunge ðane derewurðe sang, Gloria in exselsis deo. *a* **1300** *Cursor M.* 23 Sanges sere of selcuth rime, Inglis, frankys, and latine. *c* **1386** CHAUCER *Reeve's T.* 250 Herdtow euere slyk a sang er now? *c* **1400** *Destr. Troy* 3474 Why fare ye thus now, With.. sanges of myrthe. *c* **1440** *York Myst.* xx. 43 Of sorowes sere schal be my sang. **1533** GAU *Richt Vay* 16 Thay that prouokis ony ewil desir.. with sangis or wordis or foul takine. **1596** DALRYMPLE tr. *Leslie's Hist. Scot.* I. 74 To sing sangs of joy and blythnes. **17..** RAMSAY *Address to Town Council* 6 Sweet Edie's funeral-sang. **1785** BURNS *1st Ep. to J. Lapraik* iii, There was ae sang, amang the rest, Aboon them a' it pleas'd me best.

*β.* *c* **825** *Vesp. Psalter* xxxii. 3 Singað him song neowne. *c* **1175** *Lamb. Hom.* 63 Godes songes beoð alle gode; to þere saule heo senden fode. *c* **1205** LAY. 7005 He cuðen al þeos songes, & þat gleo of ilcche londe. *a* **1250** *Owl & Night.* 722 Vor-þi me singþ in holi chirche, An clerkes ginneþ songes wirche. *c* **1320** *Sir Tristr.* 2654 Of ysonde he made a song. **1340** *Ayenb.* 68 Þe holi gost.. makeþ his ychosene zinge ine hare herten þe zuete zonges of heuene. *c* **1425** *Cast. Persev.* 2336 in *Macro Plays* 147, iij mens songys to syngyn lowde. **1470–85** MALORY *Arthur* x. xxxi. 464 The harper had songe his songe to the ende. **1560** DAUS tr. *Sleidane's Comm.* 238 b, Dyverse Songes beesydes accustomed in churches doe instructe us of the benefyte of Chryst. **1598** BARNFIELD *Pecunia* iii, And add some Musique to a merry Songue. **1649** F. ROBERTS *Clavis Bibl.* 384 Songs being choice succinct pieces gratefull to the eare, helpfull to the memory and delightful to the heart. **1667** MILTON *P.L.* I. 13 My adventrous Song. *Ibid.* III. 413 Thy Name Shall be the copious matter of my Song. **1718** *Free-thinker* No. 69. 100 Much of the same Nature with our Song of 'Britons strike Home' &c. **1776** GIBBON *Decl. & F.* x. I. 244 On the faith of ancient songs, the uncertain.. memorials of barbarians. **1820** SHELLEY *To a Skylark* 90 Our sweetest songs are those that tell of saddest thought. **1878** TRELAWNY *Records Shelley*, etc. ix. 109 Inspiring it towards songs and other poetry.

**b.** ***the Song of Solomon, Song of Songs***, one of the books of the Old Testament.

**1382** WYCLIF *Song Sol.* (heading), Heer gynneth the booc that is clepid Songus [*v.r.* Song] of Songis. **1568** *Bishop's Bible* (headline), The songue of Solomon. **1579** FULKE *Heskins' Parl.* 7 He nameth.. the book of Psalmes,.. and the Song of Salomon. **1611** BIBLE *Song Sol.* i. 1 The song of songs, which is Solomons. *Ibid.* (heading), Solomons song. **1781** WARTON *Hist. Eng. Poetry* III. xxxvi. 317 There were numerous versions of Solomon's Song before the year 1600. **1803** GOOD (*title*), Song of Songs: or, Sacred Idyls. Translated from The Original Hebrew. **1856** S. DAVIDSON *Bibl. Criticism* ii. 19 The song of Deborah exhibits such [dialectal] appearances. So does the Song of Solomon.

**c.** *Naut.* (See quot.)

**1867** SMYTH *Sailor's Word-bk.* 638 *Song*, the call of soundings by the leadsman in the channels.

**d.** *Mus.* A musical setting or composition adapted for singing or suggestive of a song. ***song without words***, an instrumental composition in the style of a song (after Mendelssohn's title 'Lieder ohne Worte'); also *transf.*

**1871** S. SMILES *Character* viii. 219 Cheerfulness.. gives harmony of soul, and is a perpetual song without words. **1875** STAINER & BARRETT *Dict. Mus. Terms* s.v., The second subject of a sonata is sometimes called the 'Song'. **1883** *Grove's Dict. Mus.* III. 368/1 The Song, as we know it in his [Schubert's] hands,.. set to no simple Volkslieder, but to long complex poems,.. —such songs were his and his alone. **1883** R. PRENTICE *Musician* II. 95 The second movement [of a Beethoven sonata] is a veritable Song without Words. **1938** *Oxf. Compan. Mus.* 885/1 *Song without words*, a term introduced by Mendelssohn to cover a type of one-movement pianoforte solo, throughout which a well-marked song-like melody progresses, with an accompaniment. **1974** *Encycl. Brit. Macropædia* XI. 902/1 She [*sc.* Fanny Mendelssohn] had herself written some of the *Songs Without Words* attributed to her brother.

**e.** *transf.* A sound as of singing.

**1822** SHELLEY *Triumph Life* 463 That falling stream's Lethean song. **1877** *Daily News* 3 Nov. 6 New troops without a military history, who have never heard the song of an enemy's bullets. **1895** SNAITH *Mistr. Marvin* xii, The song of metal filled the room.

**3.** The musical utterance of certain birds.

In OE. also used of the cry of the sea-gull and eagle.

*a* **1000** *Boeth. Metr.* xiii. 50 Fuᵹelas.. stunað eal geador welwinsum sanc. *c* **1200** ORMIN 7931 Wop wass uss bitacnedd wel þurrh cullfre & turrtle baþe; Forr þeᵹʒre sang iss lic wiþþ wop. *a* **1250** *Owl & Night.* 221 Þu miht mid þine songe afere Alle þat hereþ þine ibere. *c* **1386** CHAUCER *Manciple's T.* 201 To the crowe he stert,.. And made him blak, and raft him al his song. **1484** CAXTON *Fables of Æsop* IV. iv, The goddes.. haue gyuen.. to the nyghtyngale fayr & playsaunt songe. **1551** T. WILSON *Logike* (1580) 80 Self willed folke.. vse ofte the Cuckowes song. **1590** SPENSER *F.Q.* II. vi. 13 No bird, but did her shrill notes sweetly sing; No song but did containe a louely dit. **1667** MILTON *P.L.* v. 41 The night-warbling Bird, that now awake Tunes sweetest his love-labor'd song. **1725** *Fam. Dict.* s.v. *Canary-Bird*, To make a right choice of this Bird, and to know when he has a good Song. **1773** *Phil. Trans.* LXIII. 290 What is called the song of the Canary bird. **1816** TUCKEY *Narr. Exped. R. Zaire* i. (1818) 31 A very small warbler, the only one that appeared to have any song. **1877** JEFFERIES *Gamekeeper at H.* vii. (1890) 169 All the birds whose song makes them valuable.

**4. a.** In various transf. or fig. uses.

The sense 'a subject or theme of song' occurs in several passages of the Wycliffite (see quot. 1382) and later versions of the Bible.

*Beowulf* 787 þara þe.. ᵹehyrdon gryreleoð galan.. siᵹe-leasne sang. *Ibid.* 2447. **1382** WYCLIF *Job* xxx. 9 Now forsothe I am turned in to the song of hem. —— *Lam.* iii. 14. **14..** *Sir Beues* (M.) 1232 For sone thy songe shall be: welawey! **1436** *Pol. Poems* (Rolls) II. 154 At the sowth-west corner Off gonnes he had a song; That anon he left that place. *c* **1440** *Jacob's Well* 155 Þe feend makyth his men to synge þe song of helle, þat is 'allas & welle-away'. **1548** UDALL, etc. *Erasm. Par. Mark* vii. 52 The foresayed songe was songen in vaine to the deafe Phariseis. **1576** FLEMING *Panopl. Epist.* 325 Sing this song to others. **1594** SHAKS. *Rich. III*, IV. iv. 509 Out on ye, Owles, nothing but Songs of Death. **1621** T. WILLIAMSON tr. *Goulart's Wise Vieillard* 76 The ordinarie burthen of their song is, that all the world is naught. **1653** BINNING *Serm.* (1845) 597 Many listen to the Song of Justification, but they will not abide to hear out all the Song. **1707** *Lockhart Papers* (1817) I. 223 He returned it to the clerk.. with this despising and contemning remark, 'Now there's ane end of ane old song'. **1872** A. DE VERE *Legends St. Patrick* 124 Shall I lengthen out my days Toothless,.. Some losel's song?

**b.** In phrases denoting continuance or change in statements, attitude, etc.

**1390** GOWER *Conf.* I. 260 Now schalt thou singe an other song. **1560** DAUS tr. *Sleidane's Comm.* 393 b, It is the self same song, that hath now ben songen many Yeres. **1706** E. WARD *Wooden World Diss.* (1708) 97 It's the same old Song of Stark Love and Kindness, which they have pip'd to each other these many Years. **1786** BURNS *Earnest Cry & Prayer* xv, She'll teach you, wi' a reekan whittle, Anither sang. **1796** *Grose's Dict. Vulgar T.* (ed. 3) s.v., He changed his song; he altered his account or evidence. **1822** SCOTT *Nigel* ii, Let me catch ye in Barford's Park,.. I could gar some of ye sing another sang.

**c.** A fuss or outcry *about* something.

**1843** *Cracks about Kirk* II. 9 Thae convocation chiels that are makin' sic a sang aboot their sufferings. **1863** MRS. RIDDELL *World in Church* II. 157 She had foreborne likewise and no one made a song about it.

**d.** ***a song in one's heart***, a feeling of joy or pleasure.

**1930** L. HART *With a Song in my Heart* 4 With a song in my heart;—I behold your adorable face. **1946** *Hansard Commons* 9 Apr. 1807, I will find, and find with a song in my heart, whatever money is necessary to finance useful and practical proposals for developing these areas. **1978** *Times* 9 Jan. 13/1 Does the lending rate come down? Then every conservative owner-occupier has a song in his heart.

**e.** ***on (full) song***, in good form, performing well. *colloq.*

**1967** *Autocar* 27 Dec. 10/1 The close and even spacing of the ratios.. make it easy to keep the engine 'on full song' during hard driving. **1971** *Daily Tel.* 21 Aug. 16/1 As the table reveals, most of the leading unit trust managers have at least one fund that is 'on song'. **1974** *Observer* 3 Feb. 24/5 Really on song since beating Manchester City in the Cup, Forest won 5–1. **1981** *Radio Times* 11 Apr. 23/2 If you are on song nothing will break your concentration.

**5.** Used to denote a very small or trifling sum, amount, or value, or a thing of little worth or importance. Freq. ***an old*** (also ***a mere***) ***song***. **a.** In the phr. ***for a(n old) song***, for a mere trifle, for little or nothing.

(*a*) **1601** SHAKS. *All's Well* III. ii. 9, I know a man that had this tricke of melancholy hold a goodly Mannor for a song. *a* **1639** W. WHATELEY *Prototypes* II. xxvi. (1640) 25 To have so little esteem of the outward means of salvation, as to part with them for a song as we say. **1707** *Reflex. upon Ridicule* 262 He retrenches the Number of his Servants or their Wages, and would have them serve, as they say, for a Song. **1751** H. WALPOLE *Lett.* (1846) II. 395 The whole-length Vandykes went for a song! **1808** PIKE *Sources Mississ.* I. App. 10 You will perceive that we have obtained about 100000 acres for a song. **1865** DICKENS *Mut. Fr.* III. xiii, I assure you, the things were going for a song. **1890** JESSOPP *Trials Co. Parson* iv. 173 A brief report was published, and may be purchased now for a song.

(*b*) **1650** H. MORE *Observ.* in *Enthus. Tri.* (1656) 78 Truth is not to be had of God Almighty for an old Song. **1658–9** *Burton's Diary* (1828) III. 239 Haply he compounded for an old song. **1705** *Phil. Trans.* XXIV. 1997 An old Book might be bought for an old Song, (as we say). **1796** *Grose's Dict. Vulgar T.* (ed. 3), It was bought for an old song, i.e. very cheap. **1824** BYRON *Juan* XVI. lix, The cost would be a trifle —an 'old song', Set to some thousands. **1889** T. A. TROLLOPE *What I remember* III. 32 They were acquired 'for an old song'.

**b.** In other uses.

**1798** SOTHEBY tr. *Wieland's Oberon* (1826) I. 53 Oh, fly, Sir! or your life's not worth a song! **1854** MARION HARLAND *Alone* xxvi, Some care, some responsibility—that is a mere song, though. **1879** HESBA STRETTON *Needle's Eye* II. 208 It was a pretty place once, but now it's hardly worth an old song.

**6.** ***song and dance.*** **a.** A form of entertainment (*spec.* a vaudeville act) consisting of singing and dancing. Freq. *attrib.* orig. *U.S.*

[**1628** F. DRAKE *World Encompassed* 76 They yet continued their song and dance a reasonable time.] **1872** S. HALE *Let.* 16 Jan. (1918) iii. 78 He did a 'Song and Dance', two, in fact. **1872** *Chicago Tribune* 13 Oct. 5/6 First week of the distinguished song and dance artists. **1895** *N.Y. Dramatic News* 23 Nov. 13/3 The first double song and dance team was comprised of Wash Norton and Ben Cotton. **1940** *Chatelaine* Apr. 36/2, I practiced my song-and-dance act for weeks. **1959** R. LONGRIGG *Wrong Number* iv. 58 So up she pops from hell or wherever, just the time for a bit of song and dance. **1968** *Radio Times* 28 Nov. 53/1 The song-and-dance patter comedian. **1977** *Time Out* 17–23 June 47/2 Pleasant Nilsson-like song 'n' dance numbers.

**b.** *fig.* A rigmarole, an elaborately contrived story or entreaty, a fuss or outcry. Also *attrib.* *colloq.* (orig. *U.S. slang*). Cf. sense 4 c.

**1895** E. W. TOWNSEND *Chimmie Fadden* 6 Den, 'is whiskers gives me a song an' dance. **1900** B. MATTHEWS *Confident To-Morrow* 9 And it ain't a song-and-dance I'm giving you either. **1913** KIPLING *Diversity of Creatures* (1917) 292, I don't see how this song and dance helps us any. **1922** S. LEWIS *Babbitt* xxxii. 375 George, what's this I hear about some song and dance you gave Colonel Snow about not wanting to join the G.C.L.? **1949** *Time* 5 Sept. 2/3 Labor Leader Preble.. was not impressed by 'the song and dance about [Stefan's] mother and sister being persecuted and murdered'. **1958** 'E. DUNDY' *Dud Avocado* III. vi. 266 If only he hadn't felt obliged to make such a song and dance about it. **1967** 'S. WOODS' *And Shame Devil* 118 'Appen tha means well,' he said, his speech suddenly broadened almost out of all recognition, 'and 'appen tha's joost making a song and dance.' **1980** J. DITTON *Copley's Hunch* II. ii. 132 The Prime Minister wants to make a song and dance about it.

**7.** *attrib.* and *Comb.* **a.** Simple attrib., as ***songcraft*** [cf. OE. *sang-*, *songcræft*], ***-feast***, etc.

**1855** LONGF. *Hiaw.* Introd. 109 A half-effaced inscription, Written with little skill of *song-craft. **1880** W. WATSON *Prince's Quest* (1892) 60 Seeing his charmed songcraft of no might Him to ensnare. **1763** J. BROWN *Poetry & Music* iv. 36 While these.. Savages continue in their present unlettered State.., no material Improvements in their *Song-Feasts can arise. **1881** *Blackw. Mag.* April 517 The bleak solitudes of the *Song-land on the Border. **1944** C. DAY LEWIS *Poetry for You* vi. 61 The chief thing which poets took over from the *song-lyric and preserved in the new lyrical poetry was.. 'singleness of mind'. **1884** *Harper's Mag.* March 537/2 Two pieces of *song-music. **1842** *Penny Cycl.* XXII. 429/1 Audible sound, which may possess the distinctions of *song-notes (musical sounds). **1845** BROWNING *Lett.* (1899) I. 17 These scenes and *song-scraps are such mere escapes of my inner power. **1947** A. EINSTEIN *Music in Romantic Era* xiv. 187 With Op. 24, the Heine *song-sequence, he [*sc.* Schumann] began to write lieder. **1930** P. GEDDES et al. (*title*) *Song-sheet and welcomes. **1967** A. L. LLOYD *Folk Song in England* i. 29 The countless Sorrowful Lamentations of hanged men did not become anchored in tradition.. perhaps because the song-sheets bearing these effusions are of late appearance. **1876** G. M. HOPKINS *Poems* (1967) 176 So tiny a trickle of *song-strain. **1845** W. STEVENSON *Church Scotl. Pulpit* I. 84 It is only from the full.. heart that a *song-stream of devotion can freely flow. **1884** JEFFERIES *Life of Fields* 60 The *song-talk of the finches rises and sinks like the tinkle of a waterfall. **1809** E. CUTLER *Diary* 28 Aug. in J. P. Cutler *Life & Times E. Cutler* (1890) v. 98 Very soon a man began to sing a hymn in a familiar *song-tune. **1824** MRS. CAMERON *Marten & his Scholars* viii. 49 John.. began presently to whistle a song-tune. **1967** A. L. LLOYD *Folk Song in England* iii. 139 As feudal society gives way to capitalism.. recitative melodies are replaced by song-tunes. **1885** *Encycl. Brit.* XIX. 273/1 That true *song-warble which we get in the stornelli and rispetti of the Italian peasants.

**b.** Objective, as ***song-composition***, with agent-nouns, as ***song-composer***, ***-enditer***, ***-maker***, ***-singer***, ***-wright***, ***-writer***, or with vbl. sbs. and ppl. adjs., as ***song-singing***, ***-writing***.

**1947** A. EINSTEIN *Music in Romantic Era* xiv. 184 There were no Italian *song-composers. *Ibid.* 191 The procession of musicians who contributed to Romantic *song-composition. **1713** ROWE *Jane Shore* Prol., Those venerable ancient *Song-Enditers Soar'd many a Pitch above our modern Writers. **1787** BURNS *Let. to W. Nicol* 1 June, It's true, she's as poor 's a *sang-maker. **1892** E. REEVES *Homeward Bound* 10 The rich.. harmonies of later songmakers. **1733** *Weekly Reg.* 8 Dec., Clerks of kitchens, *song-singers, horse-racers, valets-de-chambre. **1743** FRANCIS tr. *Horace, Odes* III. x. 18 Thy Husband, who gives up his Heart for a Ditty To a *Song-singing Wench. **1839** D. BLACK *Hist. Brechin* vii. 157 Zealous song-singing ladies. **1848** W. ALLINGHAM *Diary* 26 Sept. (1907) ii. 43 Dine at Peter Kelly's,.. much song-singing afterwards. **1888** R. BUCHANAN *Heir of Linne* ii, Peasants and fishermen enjoyed his gifts of conversation and song-singing. **1892** *Athenæum* 23 July 124/3 He places Herrick above Shakspeare as a *song-wright. **1821** MRS. HEMANS in H. F. Chorley *Mem.* (1837) I. 83 This being my first appearance before the public as a *song-writer. **1885** *Encycl. Brit.* XIX. 273/1 His songs illustrate an infirmity which even the Scottish song-writers share with the English. **1772** J. AIKIN (*title*) Essays on *song-writing. **1809** *Belfast Monthly Mag.* Mar. 164/2, I promise.. method in my handling the theory and practice of song-writing. **1810** J. AIKIN (*title*), Essays on Song-Writing. **1885** *Encycl. Brit.* XIX. 273 Here, indeed, is the crowning difficulty of song-writing. **1947** A. EINSTEIN *Music in Romantic Era* iv. 35 The song-writing Berlin purists.

**c.** Miscellaneous, as ***song-fraught***, ***-like***, ***-rapt***, ***-timed***, ***-tuned***, ***-wild***, ***-worthy*** adjs.

**1855** BAILEY *Mystic* 32 *Song-fraught wavelets lipped with light. **1861** F. W. FABER *Hymn, Nativ. our Lady* i, *Songlike breezes ever blowing. **1885** W. B. YEATS in *Dublin Univ. Rev.* July 137 A wandering *song-rapt bird. *c* **1873** J. ADDIS *Eliz. Echoes* (1879) 94 Circled with Mænads' *song-timed, dance-timed bounds. **1859** LD. LYTTON *Wanderer* (ed. 2) 205 Take from the wall now, my *song-tuned Lyre. **1937** BLUNDEN *Elegy* 15 The flight of one small *song-wild lark Finds heaven. **1855** PATMORE *Angel in Ho.* II. i. Prel. i, More *Song-worthy and heroic things Than.. war.

**8.** Special combs.: **song-ballet**, (*a*) *U.S. dial.*, a ballad; (*b*) a theatrical work combining songs and ballet; **song-box**, the syrinx of a bird; **song-cycle** [cf. G. *liederzyklus*], a series of songs intended to form one musical entity, and having words dealing with related subjects; **song-flight** (a) flight of a characteristic pattern made by a bird as it sings, in a territorial display; **song-form** *Mus.*, a form used in the composition of songs; *spec.* [tr. G. *liedform*] the form of a simple melody with simple accompaniment, or that of a work in three sections of which the third is a repetition of the first; **song-fowl** *poet.* = SONG-BIRD 1; **song-grosbeak**, one or other species of the American genus *Zamelodia*; **song-hit** *colloq.*, a song which is a popular success; **song-motet**, a simple type of motet; **song-muscle** (see quot.); **song-perch**, a place where a bird perches to sing, so as to establish its territory; **song period**, the part of the year during which the birds of a species sing; **song-plugger** orig. *U.S.*, a person employed to popularize songs, esp. by performing them repeatedly; hence **song-plugging** *vbl. sb.*, **song-plug** *v. trans.*, **song-plugged** *ppl. a.*; **song-post** = *song-perch* above; **song stylist**, a singer admired for his or her style; **song-tide**, time of divine service; **song-voice**, the voice as used in the act of singing.

**1915** *Dialect Notes* IV. 190 **Song-ballet*, *n.*, a song or ballad. **1938** *Sun* (Baltimore) 15 June 6/7 Visitors will join the mountaineers to sing their 'song ballets'. **1962** AUDEN *Dyer's Hand* (1963) 484 We have translated.. Brecht's text for the song-ballet *Die sieben Todsünden* with music by Kurt Weill. **1899** J. A. THOMSON *Sci. Life* 187 The bird's song is nothing to the morphologist, except in so far as the anatomy of the syrinx or *song-box is concerned. **1899** *Westm. Gaz.* 3 May 3/3 Two *song-cycles made up his programme yesterday. **1942** E. BLOM *Music in England* x. 168 Arthur Somervell's settings of poems from Tennyson's 'Maud', which have remained among the world's few great song-cycles. **1978** *Listener* 30 Mar. 412/4 A mature song-cycle by Dallapiccola. **1936** NICHOLSON & KOCH *Songs of Wild Birds* 9 *Song-flight is an extra means of making the singer temporarily as conspicuous as possible. **1961** A. J. BERGER *Bird Study* vi. 186 Song, song flights, and other special displays serve an orientation function: they attract a female to the male's territory or to a nest site. **1884** R. PRENTICE *Musician: Grade 3* 4 The simplest *song-form is constructed on two or three sentences only. **1902** H. C. BANISTER *Mus. Anal.* i. 2 There is a term now in vogue to designate the simplest of all plans or forms: 'Song-Form' or 'Aria-Form'. **1946** R. BLESH *Shining Trumpets* (1949) v. 109 The blues are essentially a song form. **1954** *Grove's Dict. Mus.* (ed. 5) VII. 962/2 The term 'song form,' derived from the German, has unfortunately been used by different writers with different significations. The vagueness which results and the fact that the term is not happily chosen gives rise to doubts whether it had not better be entirely abandoned. **1877** G. M. HOPKINS *Poems* (1967) 71 Not that the sweet-fowl, *song-fowl, needs no rest. **1839** AUDUBON *Syn. Birds N. Amer.* 132 *Coccoborus*, *Song-Grosbeak. *Coccoborus cæruleus*, Blue Song-Grosbeak. **1884** COUES *N. Amer. Birds* 389 *Zamelodia ludoviciana*, Rose-breasted Song Grosbeak. *Zamelodia melanocephala*, Black-headed Song Grosbeak. **1914** 'HIGH JINKS, JR.' *Choice Slang* 18 **Song hit*, a popular song. **1918** [see HIT *sb.* 4]. **1959** 'F. NEWTON' *Jazz Scene* 9 *Pop, pop music*, popular entertainment music as typified by the 'song-hit'. **1942** H. HEWITT *Harmonice Musices Odhecaton* vi. 69 A few '*song-motets' find a place in the Odhecaton. **1974** *Early Music* Oct. 219 Some of his [*sc.* Dufay's] most elegant Latin compositions.. are dedicated to the Virgin Mary, and their treble-dominated texture and lyrical charm—they resemble chansons in many ways—explain why they are called song-motets. **1885** NEWTON in *Encycl. Brit.* XVIII. 29 [As] by the action of the syringeal muscles.. the sounds uttered by the Bird are modified, they are properly called the *Song-muscles. **1934** *British Birds* XXVIII. 15 If a male is on his *song perch when his hen quits her eggs, he usually follows her.. to her feeding ground. **1975** I. ROWLEY *Bird Life* v. 61 The kookaburra defends a large area, but in particular a number of song perches. **1908** *British Birds* I. 367 In the middle of the *song-period all the individuals of a species found in any locality sing every day. **1961** A. J. BERGER *Bird Study* vi. 171 Many species have a short song period (post-breeding) after the molt has been completed. **1927** *Daily Express* 22 Sept. 9/3 'Clap Yo' Hands' must have been *song-plugged for ten minutes right off... 'Do-Do-Do' is another song-plugged number. **1923** *N.Y. Times* 7 Oct. IX. 2/1 **Song plugger*, a retiring representative of a song publisher planted in the audience to call for songs, whistle refrains and applaud. **1927** *Melody Maker* May 437/1 Song pluggers are.. vocalists lent by the music publishers to the dance bands just for the nights on which these bands are due to broadcast, and, of course, sing only their employer's numbers. **1976** R. SANDERS in D. Villiers *Next Year in Jerusalem* 208 Gershwin.. embarked upon his musical career at sixteen as a Tin Pan Alley song plugger and composer. **1927** *Melody Maker* May 433 (*heading*), *Song-plugging thro' the ages. **1972** P. BLACK *Biggest Aspidistra* I. iii. 29 The song-plugging wave did not recede until 1948, when the BBC and the publishers managed to draw up an agreement. **1938** *British Birds* XXXI. 320 The habitat was on open grassy ground with stones and sallow bushes as '*song posts'. **1938** *Sun* (Baltimore) 15 June 6/7 Special guests will be.. Miss Florence Clark, of Detroit, noted *song stylist. **1973** *Black Panther* 24 Mar. 7/1 Elaine Brown, community activist.. is also a musician, composer, lyricist and song stylist. **1853** ROCK *Ch. of Fathers* III. II. 14 If wayfaring.. had hindered him from being with his brethren at public *song-tide in the house of God. **1842** *Penny Cycl.* XXII. 431/2 The glottis must be disciplined.., and proceed gradually from the *song-voice to that of speech.

**song**, obs. pa. t. and pa. pple. SING *v.*[1]

**Song**, var. SUNG.

**'song-bird.** [SONG *sb.*]
**1.** A bird having the power of song; a singing-bird. (Cf. SONGSTER 3.)

**1774** GOLDSM. *Nat. Hist.* IV. iii. (1824) II. 338 Of the nightingale and other soft-billed song birds. **1783** *Encycl. Brit.* (ed. 2) X. 8670/1 The deficiency of most other song-birds in that country. **1857** LIVINGSTONE *Trav.* xvii. 325 It is remarkable that so many song-birds abound where there is a general paucity of other animal life. **1873** SYMONDS *Grk. Poets* viii. 235 Like song-birds rejoicing in their flight.

**2.** *transf.* A superb (female) singer.

**1886** C. E. PASCOE *London of To-day* x. (ed. 3) 106 The reigning queens of song.. are hardly overpaid. Such song-birds are exceedingly rare. **1896** *Godey's Mag.* Apr. 412/2 The second of the noted Magyar song-birds within current recollection was Etelka Gerster.

**'song-book.** [SONG *sb.* Cf. MDu. *sanc-, zancboec*, MLG. *sankbôk*, Du. *(ge)zangboek*, G. *gesangbuch*, Sw. *sångbok*, ON. *söngbók*, etc.]
**1.** One of the service-books of the Anglo-Saxon church (see quots. 1853).

*c* **1000** *Canons of Ælfric* xxi. in Thorpe *Laws* II. 350 þæt synd þa halȝan bec, saltere,.. & mæsse boc, sang-boc, & hand boc. *c* **1000** in Kemble *Cod. Diplom.* IV. 275, .II. fulle sangbec and .I. nihtsang. *a* **1700** EVELYN *Diary* 31 Aug. 1654, A vast old song book or service, and some faire manuscripts [at St. John's College, Cambridge]. **1853** ROCK *Ch. of Fathers* III. II. 18 Out of the Antiphoner.. came forth the full song-book or whole service for the canonical hours. *Ibid.* 20 The song-book corresponded with the Salisbury portous and the Roman breviary.

**2.** A book of songs.

**1489** *Acc. Ld. High Treas. Scot.* I. 114 To Wilȝeam Sangstare of Lythqow for a sang bwke he brocht to the King. *a* **1586** SIDNEY *Arcadia* (1622) 372 As if her eyes had beene his song-Booke, he did the message of his minde in singing these verses. **1656** EARL MONM. tr. *Boccalini's Advts. fr. Parnass.* II. xiv. (1674) 157 Apollo.. received his Song-book with.. extraordinary affection. **1683** W. LLOYD in *Lett. Lit. Men* (Camden) 187, I have besides a Welsh Song-book. **1848** DICKENS *Dombey* xlix, The little table where the Captain had arranged the telescope and song-book. **1851** MAYHEW *Lond. Lab.* I. 298/1 The sale of song-books in the streets.. is smaller than it was two years ago.

† **'songer.** *Obs.* [OE. *sangere, sǫngere*, = OHG. *sangari* (MHG. *senger*, G. *sänger*), ON. *sǫngvari* (Sw. *sångare*, Da. *sanger*), MDu. *sanger* (Du. *zanger*), etc.] A church-singer; a psalm-writer.

*c* **900** tr. *Baeda's Hist.* IV. ii. (1890) 258 Buton Iacobe þæm songere bi þæm we beforan ær sægdon. **971** *Blickl. Hom.* 207 Se bisceop þa ðær ȝesette gode sangeras & mæsse-preostas. *c* **1200** *Trin. Coll. Hom.* 117 Alse þe holi songere seið on his loft songe.

**songewarie**: see SONGUARY.

**songfest** ('sɒŋfɛst). orig. and chiefly *N. Amer.* [f. SONG *sb.* + FEST: cf. G. *sängerfest*.] An informal session of group-singing; a festive sing-song.

**1912** J. SANDILANDS *Western Canad. Dict.* 9/1 *Songfest*, a feast of song. **1916** *Dialect Notes* IV. 354 *Songfest*. 'There's to be a *songfest* at the church Friday night.' **1953** *Manch. Guardian Weekly* 12 Nov. 9/1 According to the 'New York Times':.. Their problem has been greatly complicated by the fact that each time they have tried to speak to the prisoners through the camp public address system the P.O.W. bosses have organised song fests, thrown rocks.. or set up a deafening clamour. **1961** 'I. ROSS' *Old Students Never Die* (1963) viii. 109 The image of Jackie and Alison, holding hands and bowing to us after their little songfest. **1979** *Yale Alumni Mag.* Apr. 30/2 Fifty members of the two groups gathered for a gay, impromptu songfest in Pushkin Square.

**songful** ('sɒŋfʊl), *a.* [f. SONG *sb.* + -FUL.] Abounding in song; musical, melodious.

*a* **1400** *Prymer* (1891) 98 Songful weren to me thi riȝtwesnesses in stede of my pilgrimage. **1728** MALLET *Excursion* Wks. 1759 I. 76 So pass the songful hours. **1782** W. STEVENSON *Hymn to Deity* 14 The songful tenants of the air. **1836** *New Monthly Mag.* XLVIII. 150 Thou lov'st the little songful lyre. **1844** MRS. BROWNING *Mourning Mother* 55 Trees.. That rock to songful sound. **1885** S. COX *Exposit.* vii. 86 Why.. should we not enter into it and dwell in a songful security?

Hence **'songfully** *adv.*; **'songfulness** *sb.*

**1850** KINGSLEY *Misc.* (1859) I. 218 An earnest songfulness (to coin a word) which Wordsworth seldom attained. **1880** N. SMYTH *Old Faiths in New Light* vi. (1882) 218 All things give unto us,.. birds of their songfulness; the moon of her silvery light. **1888** *Sat. Rev.* 28 July 108 They crowd into their boats,.. and pull songfully towards the Rais.

**Songhai** (sɒn'gaɪ). Also Songhay, Songhoi, †Sungai. [Native name.] A people of West Africa, living mainly in Niger and Mali; the Nilo-Saharan language of this people. Also *attrib.*

**1738** F. MOORE tr. *Leo the African's Geographical Hist. Afr.* in *Trav. Inland Parts Afr.* II. 28 The Negroes have a good many languages amongst them, of which.. Sungai is spoken in a great many of their kingdoms. **1858** H. BARTH *Travels & Discoveries in North & Central Afr.* IV. lix. 237 All the huts in these Songhay villages consist merely of reeds. *Ibid.* 238 The Songhay in general are among the most inhospitable people I ever met. **1911** *Encycl. Brit.* XXV. 414/1 According to the *Tarik é Sudan*.. the first king of the Songhoi was called Dialliaman (Arabic *Dia min al Jemen*, 'he is come from Yemen')... The Songhoi emigration must have begun towards the middle of the 7th century... The Songhoi language.. is often known as Kissur. **1930** C. G. SELIGMAN *Races of Afr.* iii. 60 Only in 1500, when Melle was captured by the Songhai king, Omar Askia, did the Melestine Empire cease to exist. *Ibid.* 62 The Songhai are moderately tall, with a stature of about 67 inches. **1957** W. M. HAILEY *Afr. Survey 1956* iii. 86 All languages which are known not to be attached to any of the above Units (e.g. Songhai). **1963** [see SAHARAN *sb.*]. **1966** [see NILO-]. **1977** H. GREENE *FSO-1* xviii. 161 The Republic of Mali.. with Bambara and Fulani tribes in the east, the Songhai and the Malinke and the wandering Tuaregs in the west.

**'songish**, *a. nonce-wd.* [f. SONG *sb.* + -ISH.] Of the nature of song or singing.

**1685** DRYDEN *Pref. Alb. & Alban.* Ess. (Ker) I. 271 The other [part of the opera], which, for want of a proper English word, I must call the *songish part*.

**Songish** (sɒŋ'giːʃ), *sb.* Also Songeesh, Songhees, 9 Songhies, Songhish. [Native name.] An American Indian people of Vancouver Island, British Columbia; the language of this people, a dialect of Straits Salish. Also *attrib.*

**1860** [see KLOOCH]. **1862** R. C. MAYNE *Four Years in Brit. Columbia & Vancouver Island* ii. 30 The road ascends a little hill, on the summit of which lies the Indian village of the Songhies. *Ibid.*, This village of the Songhies presents one of the most squalid pictures of dirt and misery it is possible to conceive. **1865** M. MACFIE *Vancouver Island & Brit. Columbia* xvi. 430 The Songhish tribe, resident near Victoria, hold a general merry-making annually in.. October. **1875** H. H. BANCROFT *Native Races of Pacific States* III. xii. 522 The Songhies said the hunter was transformed into a deer. **1911** *Encycl. Brit.* XXIV. 80/1 *Salishan*, the name of a linguistic family of North American Indian tribes, the more important of which [include] the Salish.., Skokomish, Songeesh, Spokan and Tulalip. **1911** [see POTLATCH *v.*]. **1973** L. C. THOMPSON in T. A. Sebeok *Current Trends in Linguistics* X. 1010 The rest of the dialects extend from Lummi.. across to Songish (Lkungen) around modern Victoria, on Vancouver Island, and on northward to include Saanich.

**songket** ('sɒŋkɛt), *a.* Also 9 sungkit. [Malay.] Of cloth: decorated by interweaving short lengths of gold or silver thread into the material. Also *ellipt.* as *sb.*

**1894** N. B. DENNYS *Descr. Dict. Brit. Malaya* 107 Silk *sarongs*.. woven with silk and gold thread are termed *kain sungkit*. **1953** *Exhib. Malayan Arts & Crafts* (Malayan Agri-Horticultural Assoc.), Hand-woven cloths. The other important category of Malay cloths is that of the *kain songket*. **1963**, **1971** [see KAIN]. **1972** M. SHEPPARD *Taman Indera* 100 (*caption*), The gift is a piece of silk *songket* hand woven cloth, folded in the shape of a bird. *Ibid.* 120 The body of a *songket* sarong is silk, of a single plain colour. The decoration is carried out with gold or silver thread... The songket sarong is worn today by Malay men of all levels of society when attending social functions, and it is therefore in constant demand. **1972** *Malay Mail* 27 May 9/7 (Advt.), We are offering a very wide range of genuine Malaysian songket.

‖**songkok** ('sɒŋkɒk). Also 9 songko. [Malay.] A cap worn by Malays, resembling a skull-cap.

**1894** N. B. DENNYS *Descr. Dict. Brit. Malaya* 108 The skull-cap, *kopia* or *songko*, is worn by some. **1960** S. HARVESTER *Chinese Hammer* i. 8 An affable Indonesian official with his black *songkok* tilted at a rakish angle above his chubby face. **1966** D. FORBES *Heart of Malaya* xiv. 193 The bridegroom wears his *songkok*, the round brimless hat. **1977** P. THEROUX *Consul's File* 38 'This is serious,' he said, glowering and putting on his *songkok*.

**songle** ('sɒŋg(ə)l). *dial.* Also 7–9 songal, -all, 9 songow, -o, -a, etc. [Current only in the counties on the Welsh border, but app. corresponding to obs. or dial. G. *sangel, sängel*, dim. of OHG. *sanga* (MHG., MLG., and G. *sange*), MFlem. *sange, sanghe*, WFlem. *zange* (De Bo), in the same sense. The simpler form appears also in Devonshire and Cornwall *sang, zang*.] A handful of gleaned corn. Cf. SINGLE *sb.* 2.

**1674** BLOUNT *Glossogr.* (ed. 4), *Songal*, or *Songle*, so the poor people in Herefordshire call a handful of corn gleaned or leazed. **1700** T. HYDE *Hist. Relig. Persarum* 391 Spicas.. in parvum Fasciculum seu Manipulum (*Angl.* a Songall) colligatas. **1820** WILBRAHAM *Chesh. Gloss.* 61 *Songow, Songal*, gleaned corn. **1850** COLLINS *Gower Dial.* in *Trans. Phil. Soc.* IV. 223 *Songalls*, gleanings: 'to gather songall' is to glean.

*transf.* **1889** *N. & Q.* 7th Ser. VIII. 363/2, I have just this last week obtained a goodly 'songle' of S. Staffordshire words.

**songless** ('sɒŋlɪs), *a.* [f. SONG *sb.* + -LESS.]
**1.** Devoid of song; not singing.

*c* **1805** KIRKE WHITE *Nelsoni Mors* 13 The woods and storied haunts Of my not songless boyhood. **1832** J. BREE *St. Herbert's Isle* 83 The thrush sits songless on the mistle-toe. **1866** MEREDITH *Vittoria* vii, Before he had quitted the court, he had sunk into songless gloom. **1882** 'OUIDA' *Maremma* I. 192 The clear voices burst over the silence of the songless moor.

**2.** *Ornith.* Lacking the power of song.

**1825** WATERTON *Wand. S. Amer.* (1882) 26 Chiefly in the dry Savannas, you see a songless yawariciri still lovelier than the last. *c* **1882** *Cassell's Nat. Hist.* IV. 109 The Mesomyodi, or Songless Birds. **1895** *Atlantic Monthly* Aug. 277 In the cases of the so-called songless birds there is often no attempt.

Hence **'songlessly** *adv.*

*a* **1849** MANGAN *Poems* (1859) 119 If the saunterer-by songlessly pass Through the long grass. **1856** RUSKIN *Mod. Paint.* IV. v. xix. §6 All the while the veritable peasants are kneeling songlessly.

**songlessness** ('sɒŋlɪsnɪs). [f. SONGLESS *a.* + -NESS.] The state or condition of being songless.

**1924** J. R. HARRIS *As pants Hart* viii. 85, I have often deplored the songlessness of the modern Evangelical and Protestant Churches. **1958** *Times* 9 Sept. 10/5 Another very common bird begins now to sing again after a period of songlessness.

**songlet** ('sɒŋlɪt). [f. SONG *sb.*] A little song.

**1831** FR. A. KEMBLE *Rec. Girlhood* (1878) III. 104 Emily gave me two charming Italian songlets. **1861** D. COOK *Paul Foster's Dau.* I. 164 As they.. coo out their gushing little songlets in delicate trills. **1886** *Illustr. Lond. News* 25 Dec. 716/2 In these songs and songlets.. there is.. the scent of flowers.

† **'songly**, *a. Obs.* [f. SONG *sb.* + -LY[1].] Capable of being sung or expressed in song.

*a* **1300** *E.E. Psalter* cxviii. 54 Sanglic [*v.r.* songlic, L. *cantabiles*] to me ware rightwisnesses þine. *c* **1325** *Prose Ps.* cxviii. 54 Þy riȝtinges were songelich to me. **1435** MISYN *Fire of Love* 50 Qwhils he treuly in songly ioy is gladinde. *Ibid.* 78 A songely þoȝt emonge heuenly citesens rynnys.

**'songman.** [SONG *sb.*]
**1.** A man accustomed to sing songs.

**1603** CHETTLE *Eng. Mourn. Garment* D ij b, Thou sweetest song-man of all English swaines, Awake for shame! **1631** BRATHWAIT *Whimzies, Ballad-monger* 18 It would doe a mans heart good to see how twinne-like hee and his song-man couple. **1890** BARING-GOULD *Old Country Life* 260 The old village bard or songman is rapidly becoming.. extinct.

**2.** A man who sings in a church choir.

**1883** *Pall Mall G.* 18 Sept. 4/2 'The Senior Songman'.. is the story of a quiet cathedral singer. **1887** *Ch. Times* 11 Nov. 911/4 This great company of prelates and clergy, readers and songmen, was very striking.

**'songo(w)**, *v. dial.* Also 9 sangow, songa, etc. [f. *songo(w)*, SONGLE *sb.*] *intr.* To glean.

**1688** HOLME *Armoury* III. 73/2 *Gleaning*, or *Leesing*, or *Songoing*, is gathering of the loose Ears of Corn, after Binding and Loading. **1820-** in western dial. glossaries.

**'song-school.** Now *Hist.* [SONG *sb.* Cf. MHG. *sancschule*, Du. *zangschool*, Sw. *sångskola*.] A school specially devoted to the teaching of (ecclesiastical or secular) singing and music. (In early use chiefly *Sc.*) Also *attrib.*

*a.* **1537** *Reg. Aberdon.* (Maitl.) I. 412 Maister of þe sang schuyll of þe cathedrall kyrk. *c* **1550** ROLLAND *Crt. Venus*

Prol. 203 To put this man to Sang Scule, or playing. **1579** *Acts Jas. VI*, F iij b, For Instructioun of the 3outh in the Airt of Musick and singing.. To erect and set vp ane sang Scule. **1612** *Extr. Aberd. Rec.* (1848) II. 314 Patrick Dauidsoun, maister of the sang schuill. **1621** in R. M. Fergusson *Alex. Hume* (1899) 220 Seattis.. meit for the maister of the sang schooll and his bairnis to sit on.

*β.* **1593** *Rites of Durh.* (Surtees, 1903) 62 A song schoole buylded, for to teach vj children for to learne to singe. **1601** F. GODWIN *Bps. of Eng.* 393 Mending his liuing by teaching a song schoole, for he was a great and cunning Musitian. **1733** [HUNTER] *Durham Cathedral* 99 A convenient Room, wherein is established the Song-school. **1802** FOSBROOKE *Brit. Monachism* II. 201 *Song School.* 'This school,' says Davies, 'was built within the church'. **1903** A. F. LEACH *Mem. Beverley Minster* II. p. cv, The Master of the Choristers or Song-School Master.

**'song-smith.** [SONG *sb.*] A composer or maker of songs. Also as a book-title.

**1795** DIBDIN (*title*), The Song Smith; or, Rigmarole Repository. **1854** EMERSON *Lett. & Soc. Aims, Poet. & Imag.* Wks. (Bohn) III. 165 He and his temple-gods were called song-smiths. **1865** SWINBURNE *Chastelard* I. ii. 35 These jangling song-smiths are keen love-mongers, They snap at all meats. **1899** *The Month* April 354 Arnaldo Daniello, the great song-smith of the vulgar tongue.

**'song-sparrow.** [SONG *sb.*] A common North American song-bird of the genus *Melospiza*, esp. *M. fasciata* (or *melodia*) and *cinerea*.

**1810** A. WILSON *Amer. Ornith.* II. 126 The Song Sparrow builds in the ground, under a tuft of grass. **1860** GOSSE *Rom. Nat. Hist.* 7 The song-sparrow is the chief performer in this early concert. **1872** COUES *N. Amer. Birds* 139 The Eastern song sparrow is simply one variety of a bird distributed from Atlantic to Pacific. **1898** *Atlantic Monthly* LXXXII. 496/1 A song-sparrow singing from a dense swampy thicket.

**songster** ('sɒŋstə(r)). Forms: 1 sangystre, -estre, 4 sangester, 5 *Sc.* sangstere, 6 *Sc.* -(i)star; 4, 7– songster (7 -stare). [See SONG *sb.* and -STER. So MDu. *sangster*, Du. *zangster*.]

**1. a.** One who sings, a singer; orig., a female singer, a songstress.

*c* **1000** ÆLFRIC *Gram.* ix. (Z.) 71 *Hic cantor*, þes sangere. *Haec cantrix*, þeos sangystre [*v.r.* sangestre]. *c* **1330** R. BRUNNE *Chron. Wace* (Rolls) 4032 He was þe best.. Of iogelours & of sangesters. **1382** WYCLIF *Ezek.* xxvi. 13 Y shal make the multitude of thi songsters for to reste. **1497** *Acc. Ld. High Treas. Scot.* I. 368 Henrj of Hadingtoune the sangstere. **1534** *Ibid.* VI. 207 To George Contis, sangstar, to by him hois and doublet agane Pasche. **1624** BEDELL *Lett.* iii. 58 The fault of the Italians: though they thinke themselues the onely songsters in the world. *c* **1670** WOOD *Life* (O.H.S.) I. 274 Sylvanus Taylor,.. fellow of All-soules; and violist and songster. **1713** STEELE *Guardian* No. 23 ¶4 Thus.. Corydon tells Alexis that he is the finest Songster of the Country. **1784** COWPER *Task* I. 498 The peasant too,.. Himself a songster, is as gay as he. **1835** JAMES *Gipsy* xi, Will, you are a songster, let us hear your voice.

*attrib.* **1614** J. DAVIES (Heref.) *Ecl. Willy & Wernocke* G iij b, To feed the Songster-swaines with Arts soot-meats.

**b.** *U.S.* (See quot. 1980.)

**1925** ODUM & JOHNSON *Negro & his Songs* i. 1 Anyone hearing him sing day in and day out, together with thousands of others like him, must agree.. with the oft-repeated song claim of the 'musicianer', 'music-physicianer' and 'songster', that 'All don't see me goin' to hear me sing.' Not only does he sing, but he sings much and sings long with richness and variety. **1964** *Amer. Folk Music Occasional* I. 61 And if you describe the artist with accuracy, it will be with his own apt word: songster. The term suggests a musician who is both performer and inventor and harks back to the time when every Southern town had its songster, a man who was virtually in charge of the community's social life. **1968** P. OLIVER *Screening Blues* ii. 82 The 'songster' generation of singers. **1970** —— *Savannah Syncopators* 7 The instrumental techniques and traditions of the blues singers, the songsters, the ragtime banjoists and guitarists. *Ibid.* 86 Many of the older blues singers and songsters recall playing for white functions. **1980** *New Grove Dict. Music & Musicians* XVII. 17/1 *Songster*, a black American musician of the post-Reconstruction era who performed a wide variety of ballads, dance-tunes, reels and minstrel songs, singing to his own banjo or guitar accompaniment.

**2.** A poet; a writer of songs or verse.

**1585** JAS. I *Ess. Poesie* (Arb.) 27 Homer, who a Songster bene, Albeit a beggar. *a* **1637** B. JONSON *Underwoods* lx. Wks. (Rtldg.) 706/2 Silk will draw some sneaking songster thither, It is a rhyming age, and verses swarm At every stall. **1743** *Pol. Ballads* (1860) II. 304 Each party's joke, Each trifling songster's sport. **1848** MARIOTTI *Italy* II. vi. 214 Giusti may be a rival, but no imitator of the French songster [Béranger]. **1872** SPURGEON *Treas. David* Ps. lix. 14 Here verse six is repeated, as if the songster defied his foes.

**3.** A bird that sings; a song-bird.

**1700** DRYDEN *Flower & Leaf* 449 And either Songster holding out their Throats, And folding up their Wings renew'd their Notes. **1730–46** THOMSON *Autumn* 972 Haply some widow'd songster pours his plaint. **1837** M. DONOVAN *Dom. Econ.* II. 143 The Skylark, a superior songster, is much sought after in most countries where it abounds.

*attrib.* **1783** LATHAM *Gen. Synop. Birds* II. I. 59 Songster Thrush.. has a fine song. **1829** GRIFFITH tr. *Cuvier* VI. 394 Songster Thrush,.. *Turdus Cantor*.

**songstress** ('sɒŋstrɪs). [Cf. prec. and -ESS.]

**a.** A female singer; a poetess. **b.** A female singing-bird.

**1703** LUTTRELL *Brief Rel.* (1857) V. 303 A subscription.. for Mrs. Seigniora, the Italian songstresse at the playhouses here. **1727–46** THOMSON *Summer* 746 Through the soft silence of the listening night, The sober-suited songstress trills her lay. **1801** WORDSW. *Cuckoo & Night.* xlvi, I make a vow, That all this May I will thy songstress be. **1834** LYTTON *Pompeii* I. ii, Either in compliment to the music or in compassion to the songstress. **1871** *Athenæum* 8 July 46 This sisterhood of songstresses is closed by.. Joanna Baillie.

**'song-thrush.** [SONG *sb.* Cf. G. *sangdrossel*, Sw. *sångtrast*.] The common thrush (*Turdus musicus*).

**1668** CHARLETON *Onomast.* 83 The Thrush, Song-Thrush, or Throssle, or Mavis. **1678** RAY *Willughby's Ornith.* 188 The Mavis, Throstle, or Song-thrush. **1770** G. WHITE *Selborne* xxxiii, The first that fail and die are the redwing fieldfares, and then the song-thrushes. **1826** *Sporting Mag.* XVII. 227 This species, however, is larger than the blackbird or song thrush. **1843** *Zoologist* I. 104 It chases the cock song-thrush. **1890** *Science-Gossip* XXVI. 45 The blackbird, songthrush and misselthrush.

**†songuary.** *Obs.* Also 4 songewarie. [app. an error for *songnary*, *-arie*, a. AF. *soungnarie*, ad. med.L. **somniaria* (sc. *ars*); cf. med.L. *somniarius* interpreter of dreams.]

Interpretation of dreams.

**1377** LANGL. *P. Pl.* B. VII. 148, I haue no sauoure in songewarie for I se it ofte faille. *Ibid.* 150 To sette sadnesse in songewarie. *a* **1470** H. PARKER *Dives & Pauper* (W. de W. 1496) I. xxxiv. d iij, To make ony dyuynynge therby or by songuary or sompnarye.

**songy** ('sɒŋɪ), *a.* [f. SONG *sb.*] Having the qualities of a song.

**1870** *Pall Mall G.* 24 Dec. 12 Perhaps the most 'songy' of the whole is one which the musician has left unset.

**sonhood** ('sʌnhʊd). [SON *sb.*[1]] The condition or relation of being a son.

**1602** J. DAVIES (Heref.) *Mirum in Modum* Wks. (Grosart) I. 17/1 Fatherhood, breathing, or Spiration, Son-hood, Procession. **1858** CARLYLE *Fredk. Gt.* II. VII. iv. 208 A Royal Young Man; who.. must not, in the name of son-hood, resist. **1889** *Lux Mundi* App. I. 524 The ties which bind men in the relation of brotherhood and sonhood are the noblest.

**sonic** ('sɒnɪk), *a.* [f. L. *son-us* sound + -IC.]

**1. a.** Employing or operated by sound waves; used esp. with reference to devices and techniques which make use of the reflected echo of a sound pulse.

**1923** *Sci. Amer.* May 330/2 Sonic sounding is rendered possible by the fact that sound vibrations, passing through water and striking a solid surface, are returned as an echo to the source from which they originated. **1924** *Telegr. & Telephone Jrnl.* X. 172/2 The United States destroyers *Hull* and *Corry*, equipped with sonic depth sounders.. have been ordered to survey the ocean bed. **1933** *Geogr. Jrnl.* LXXXI. 572 The exploration of the Maldive ridge by sonic sounding should be interesting. **1952** *Chambers's Jrnl.* June 364/2 After the War a sonic gun was actually found in a German laboratory. **1961** *Flight* LXXIX. 249/2 In addition to the display system, the RH-1 was fitted with Ryan APN-97 Doppler and the sonic altimeter. **1965** *Punch* 17 Mar. 390/1 'That thing [*sc.* a torpedo] live?' I asked. 'Very,' said the Lieutenant-Commander, 'but it's only an antiquated sonic-homing job.' **1967** *Jane's Surface Skimmer Systems 1967–68* 94/1 It receives craft motion input from a sonic height sensor in the bow. **1976** B. BOVA *Multiple Man* (1977) i. 11 If anyone tried to fire a shot.. the scanning lasers would pick up the bullet... Sonic janglers would paralyse everyone in the auditorium.

**b.** Of or pertaining to sound or sound waves, esp. within the audible range.

**1936** *Jrnl. Amer. Chem. Soc.* LVIII. 1071/2 In order to avoid any possible sonic action directly on a test reagent. **1939** [see *sonoluminescence* s.v. SONO-]. **1942** *Jrnl. R. Aeronaut. Soc.* XLVI. 83 The guiding intention will be, to avoid.. the formation of sonic waves, and practical elimination of compression shocks, in order to obtain a minimum of the so-called wave-making resistance. **1947** *Aircraft Engin.* XIX. 180/1 The design of the VG-70 experimental monoplane.. was begun as a determined effort in the field of sonic research. **1962** F. I. ORDWAY et al. *Basic Astronautics* viii. 345 Since the flow often speeds up when passing over a body it is possible for sonic flow to exist over parts of a body which is moving at speeds somewhat less than Mach 1. **1969** L. F. YERGES *Sound, Noise, & Vibration Control* I. 1 There is no essential difference between the sonic and vibratory forms of sound energy. **1972** *Observer* (Colour Suppl.) 22 Oct. 53/2 It is this *depth* of sound which stereophony failed to capture, or so the sonic engineers believed when they looked around for their next breakthrough. **1975** *Sci. Amer.* Oct. 135/1 The ultrasonic world is quieter than the sonic, mainly because its sounds are more local. **1977** *Gramophone* Dec. 1016/1 Sonic beauty abounds in *The Triumphs of Oriana*..: 64 minutes of music packed with admirable clarity.. on a single disc.

**2.** Special collocations: ***sonic bang*** = *sonic boom* below; ***sonic barrier*** = *sound barrier* s.v. SOUND *sb.*[3] 8 a; ***sonic boom***, the sudden loud noise heard when the shock wave from an aircraft travelling faster than sound reaches the ears; ***sonic speed, velocity***, the speed at which sound waves travel in a particular medium, esp. air.

**1953** *Sci. News* XXX. 118 Subsequently two sonic bangs were heard of the same intensity with a small time interval apparently the same as that between the vapour puffs. **1955** *Times* 20 June 8/7 As the new fighters showed their considerable paces the programme was punctuated with 'sonic bangs' as the speed of sound was exceeded in dives. *a* **1974** R. CROSSMAN *Diaries* (1976) II. 169 Next came the Minister of Aviation, Mr Mulley, who had put in a request for urgent legislation on sonic bangs. **1946** *Jrnl. R. Aeronaut. Soc.* L. 445/2, I do not imagine for one moment that man will be happy until he has conquered the 'sonic barrier'. **1955** *Sci. News Let.* 24 Sept. 195 (*caption*) By giving the aircraft a 'wasp waist', engineers.. made it slip more smoothly through the sonic barrier. **1952** *Times* 2 Sept. 4/5 Aircraft travelling at about the speed of sound cause a loud bang, which has become known as the 'sonic boom'. **1966** *Guardian* 2 May 8/6 Mr Amery, Minister of Aviation, told Parliament that damage from the Concord's sonic booms would be 'negligible'. **1969** *Times* 17 Nov. 4/7 Their home collapsed after another sonic boom. **1977** *New Yorker* 24 Oct. 36/2, I heard the explosion even inside the manuscript room... It sounded like a sonic boom. **1946** *Jrnl. R. Aeronaut. Soc.* L. 436/1 The problems of aerodynamics at speeds well in excess of that of sound are in some respects much simpler than those quite near the sonic speed. **1950** *Sci. News* XV. Plate 7 (*caption*) This model aeroplane.. was designed to investigate the forces acting on an aircraft reaching sonic speed. **1962** F. I. ORDWAY et al. *Basic Astronautics* viii. 344 At this point the body is moving at sonic speed and transonic conditions exist. **1942** *Jrnl. R. Aeronaut. Soc.* XLVI. 64 The local 'sonic velocity' *a* is then defined by the expression:—$a^2 = dp/d\rho$. **1949** *Jrnl. Appl. Physics* XX. 638/1 A slowly varying pressure change or signal is transmitted through the mixture with a definite critical or 'sonic' velocity.

Hence **'sonically** *adv.*, by means of sound waves; as regards sound.

**1936** *Jrnl. Amer. Chem. Soc.* LVIII. 1070/2 A quantitative study of certain oxidation reactions sonically activated in the audible range. **1959** *Brookhaven Symp. in Biol.* XII. 11 A sonically fragmented sample. **1975** *Gramophone* June 36/1 Sonically the record is obviously to be preferred to Menuhin's earlier recording with Furtwängler. **1981** *Popular Hi-Fi* Mar. 21/2 The Crimson is a better pre-amplifier sonically.

**‖sonica**, *sb.* and *adv.* *rare.* [F., of obscure origin.] **a.** *sb.* In the game of basset, a card having an immediate effect on the game. **b.** *adv.* Promptly, at once.

**1716** POPE *Basset-Table* 51 The Knave won *Sonica*, which I had chose. **1748** LD. CHESTERFIELD *Lett.* II. xxx. Misc. Wks. 1777 II. 330 My prophecy, as you observe, was fulfilled *sonica*.

**sonicate** ('sɒnɪkeɪt), *sb.* and *v.* [f. SONIC *a.* + -ATE, after *filtrate*, *precipitate*.] **A.** *sb.* A sample which has been subjected to ultrasound so as to fragment the macromolecules and membranes in it.

**1958** M. LITT et al. in *Proc. Nat. Acad. Sci.* XLIV. 144 The production of sonicates (degraded samples) covering more than a tenfold range in molecular weight. **1958** NISHIHARA & DOTY in *Ibid.* 412 Eight 30-cc. aliquots of a stock solution.. were exposed to 9-kilocycle sonic waves in a 50-watt Raytheon magnetostriction generator... The samples produced in this way, termed 'sonicates', are listed. **1979** *Nature* 25 Jan. 314/2 (*caption*) Calvaria were washed again, sonicated, and the sonicate ultracentrifuged.

**B.** *v. trans.* To subject to such treatment.

**1960** *Biochem. & Biophys. Res. Communications* III. 471 Tumor mitochondria were sonicated at maximum intensity (1·3 amps) for two 2·5-minute periods. **1974** *Nature* 20 Dec. 655/1 (*caption*) The DNA fragments were prepared by sonicating calf thymus DNA to a molecular weight of 5·4 × 10[5]. **1978** [see below].

Hence **'sonicated** *ppl. a.*; **soni'cation**, treatment with ultrasound; **'sonicator**, an apparatus for treating samples in this way.

**1958** *Proc. Nat. Acad. Sci.* XLIV. 150 The loss in activity due to sonication occurs only as a result of reduction in molecular size below that required for attachment. **1959** *Brookhaven Symp. in Biol.* XII. 11 The variance due to any change in compositional heterogeneity of the sonicated sample, can be obtained. **1964** *Jrnl. Cellular & Compar. Physiol.* LXIV. 153/1 Washed ghosts were sonicated for ten minutes using an MSE 60 W sonicator. **1969** *Nature* 20 Dec. 1164/2 The supernatant contains the polymerase, which may then be assayed simply by adding sonicated calf thymus DNA. **1970** *Sci. Jrnl.* Apr. 42 Cleaning these parts is a major branch of ultraclean technology involving the application of special solvents, the use of 'sonication'—ultrasonic vibration—to jar the dirt loose,.. and many other highly specialized procedures. **1978** *Jrnl. Protozool.* XXV. 492/2 Other aliquots of *E*[*ncephalitozoon*] *cuniculi*.. were sonicated using a Bronson sonicator.

**sonics** ('sɒnɪks), *sb. pl.* [f. SONIC *a.*: see -IC 2.] Sonic techniques and equipment generally or collectively.

**1955** HUETER & BOLT *Sonics* p. v, The multiplicity of concepts and techniques could be designated by the name *sonics*. *Ibid.*, Sonics encompasses the analysis, testing, and processing of materials and products by the use of mechanical vibratory energy. **1974** 'G. BLACK' *Golden Cockatrice* vi. 102 All three corvettes were now almost motionless.. obviously listening on sonics.

**sonifaction** (səʊnɪ'fækʃən). *Zool.* [f. L. *soni-* (see next) + -FACTION.] The production of sound, on the part of insects, by other means than the vocal organs.

**1884–5** *Standard Nat. Hist.* II. 307 A mode of sonifaction.. similar to that where a boy runs along a fence pushing a stick against the pickets. *Ibid.* 366 Sonifaction is not confined to imagos.

**soniferous** (səʊ'nɪfərəs), *a.* [f. L. *soni-*, combining form of *sonus* sound + -FEROUS.] Sound-bearing; conveying or producing sound.

**1713** DERHAM *Phys.-Theol.* IV. iii. 131 The æthereal part thereof, or Soniferous Particles of Bodies. **1855** *Orr's Circ. Sci., Elem. Chem.* 177 The comparative soniferous properties of the gases.

**Sonifier** ('sɒnɪfaɪə(r)). Also sonifer. [f. as SONIC *a.* + -FY + -ER[1].] The proprietary name of a make of sonicator.

**1961** *Official Gaz.* (U.S. Patent Office) 1 Aug. TM 10/1 Branson Instruments, Inc., Stamford, Conn... *Sonifier*. For electrical generators of ultrasonic energy, ultrasonic energy transducers and electrically powered processing systems for the same. First use Oct. 19, 1960. **1963** *Biochim.*

& *Biophys. Acta* LXXI. 232 A suspension of ghosts..was treated with ultrasonic waves generated by a Branson Model S-75 Sonifier for 15 secs. **1965** *Trade Marks Jrnl.* 16 June 809/2 *Sonifier*. 875,310. Ultrasonic apparatus and instruments included in Class 9. Branson Instruments Incorporated..Connecticut, U.S.A.; manufacturers.—8th Feb. 1965. **1980** *European Jrnl. Biochem.* CV. 164/2 Sonication at 4°C with a Branson B-12 sonifier.

**Soninke** (sɒ'niːŋkeɪ). [Native name.] A member of a people living in Mali and Senegal; the people itself; the Mandingo language or dialects spoken by this people. Also *attrib.* Cf. MALINKE.

**1886** *Encycl. Brit.* XXI. 662/2 The Mandingoes.. comprise the Mandingo proper, occupying Manding, and the Malinkés and Soninkés, scattered about Bambuk, Buré, and Fuladugu. **1911** [see MALINKE]. **1939** C. G. SELIGMAN *Races Afr.* (rev. ed.) iii. 61 The Mandingo..constitute one of the most important groups of Senegal and West Sudan.. and include such large and important tribes as the.. Soninke, Malinke, and Vei. **1971** N. LEVTZION in Ajayi & Crowder *Hist. W. Afr.* I. iv. 124 They are united by..their pride in having once been part of the ancient Soninke kingdom of Wagadu. **1974** *Encycl. Brit. Macropædia* XI. 382/2 Soninke and Dogon are also related to Bambara; Dogon includes many dialects.

**son-in-law** ('sʌnɪnlɔː). [SON *sb.*[1] and LAW *sb.*[1] 3 c.]

**1.** A daughter's husband. Also †***son in the law, son by law.*** (Cf. SON-LAW.)

*a.* **13..** *Cursor M.* 7650 (Gött.), Dauid his sone-in-law for to sla. **1375** BARBOUR *Bruce* XVII. 219 Valter, Steward of Scotland, That..sone-in-law wes to the king. *c* **1425** *Eng. Voc.* in Wr.-Wülcker 672 *Hic gener*, sone-in-law. **1530** PALSGR. 272/2 Sonne in lawe, *gendre*. **1573** *Will T. Daye* (Somerset Ho.), My son in lawe Robert Dobledaie. **1600** PORY tr. *Leo's Africa* III. 144 The brides father..sendes great store of daintie dishes vnto his sonne in law. **1639** *Bury Wills* (Camden) 180, I give unto my sonne-in-law..my second best gown. **1700** EVELYN *Diary* 13 Feb., She left my son-in-law..the mansion house of Adscomb. **1743** FRANCIS tr. *Horace, Odes* II. iv. 16 Her Parents..Shall not their Son-in-law disgrace. **1811** MISS MITFORD in L'Estrange *Life* (1870) I. v. 147 How should you like him for a son-in-law? **1813** SOUTHEY *Nelson* I. 87 Josiah, his son-in-law, went with him.

*β.* **1545** *Reg. Privy Council Scot.* I. 12 Johne Buchquhannane son in the law to the said Lord Johne Levingstoun. [**1582** STANYHURST *Æneis* II. (Arb.) 54 Soon to king Priamus by law.]

†**2.** ? A reputed son. *Obs.*

**1591** LODGE *Catharos* B 4 b, How doth the father of your sonne in law?

†**3.** A stepson. *Obs.*

**1618** BOLTON *Florus* IV. xii. (1636) 318 Cæsar throughly quietted all the nations of that tract..by his sonne in law whose mother hee had married, Claudius Drusus. **1731** FIELDING *Mod. Husb.* II. iii, I hope you will pardon an intercession, my dear, for a son-in-law, which I should not be guilty for a son of my own. **1738** tr. *Guazzo's Art Convers.* 21 The step-mother..can't discern the good qualities of her son-in-law.

Hence **son-in-lawship**.

**1886** HARDY *Woodlanders* (1887) II. ix. 163 It immersed him so deeply in son-in-lawship to Melbury.

‖**sonipes.** *rare*[−1]. [L. *sonipēs*, f. *soni-*, *sonus* sound + *pēs* foot.] A horse.

**1639** in T. de Gray *Expert Farrier* Pref. Verses, I understood how first to use the reyne, And menage sonipes.

†**sonizance.** *Obs.*[−1] (Obscure: perh. an error.)

**1589** PEELE *Eclogue Gratulatory* 27 Then give me leave sonizance to make For chivalry and lovely learning's sake!

**sonk**, var. SUNK *sb.* seat, saddle. *Sc.*

'**sonkin.** *rare*[−1]. In 6 sonnekyn. [f. SON *sb.*[1] + -KIN. Cf. MLG. *soneken* (LG. *söneken*, *sönke*), G. *söhnchen*.] A little son.

**1542** UDALL *Erasm. Apoph.* 207 b, All haill my soonne [*marg.* sonnekyn, or litle soonne].

**sonkyn**, obs. form of SUNKEN *ppl. a.*

†**son-law.** *Obs.* = SON-IN-LAW 1.

**1445** in *Anglia* XXVIII. 265 Happy thou art in such prynce which now thi son lawe is. **1509** *Bury Wills* (Camden) 110 John Femnale, my sonlawe. *Ibid.* 113 Thomas Tise my sonlaw.

**sonless** ('sʌnlɪs), *a.* Also 5 soneles, 6 sonnelesse, 7 -less, sonlesse. [f. SON *sb.*[1] + -LESS.] Having no son; destitute of a son or sons.

**1388** WYCLIF *Gen.* xxvii. 45 Whi schal Y be maad soneles of euer eithir sone in o dai? **1588** T. HUGHES *Misfort. Arthur* v. i. (1900) 118 The wofull Fathers hart, That sawe himselfe thus made a Sonnelesse Sire. **1602** MARSTON *Antonio's Rev.* III. i, A sonne, That..doth complot To make her sonlesse. **1610** HEYWOOD *Gold. Age* II. i, Thus melancholy Saturne hath suruiuing Three Noble sonnes..And yet himselfe thinks sonneless. **1753-4** RICHARDSON *Grandison* (1781) I. 291 Many fatherless, brotherless, sonless families. **1832** *Blackw. Mag.* XXXI. 166 The good old king, whom he has made sonless. **1874** GREEN *Short Hist.* (1881) I. 150 No baron if he was sonless could give a husband to his daughter save with his lord's consent.

**sonlike** ('sʌnlaɪk), *a.* Also 6-7 sonnelike. [f. SON *sb.*[1]] Resembling that of a son; filial.

**1583** BABINGTON *Commandm.* 26 There are two kinds of feare of God, one a seruile feare,..another ioyned with loue of God, called a sonnelike feare. **1594** T. B. *La Primaud. Fr. Acad.* II. 503 They judged..that sonlike respect and love were good prickes to drive them forward. **1657** OWEN *Communion* II. x. Wks. 1851 II. 213 This..sonlike freedom of the Spirit in obedience. **1674** BUNYAN *Christ. Behaviour* Wks. 1855 II. 563 All humble and sonlike carriage.

Hence '**sonlikeness**.

**1876** W. BATHGATE *Deep Things of God* vi. 145 This was sonlikeness without one unfilial flaw or frown.

'**sonly**, *a. rare.* Also 5-6 sonnely. [f. SON *sb.*[1] Cf. MDu. *soon-*, *zoonlijc*, MLG. *sonelik*, MHG. *sunlîch* (G. *sohn-*, *söhnlich*).] Sonlike, filial.

*c* **1450** *Myrr. our Ladye* 247 That..sonne of god hauynge sonnely compassyon to hys mother. **1579** B. GOOGE tr. *Mendoza's Prov.* 64 b, The one is called a seruile feare, the other a sonnely feare... The sonnely feare, is a meddlie of feare and loue together. **1903** in *Life Bp. Westcott* I. Pref. p. x, It is an offering of real sonly devotion.

**sonnd**, obs. f. SAND *sb.*[1] and *sb.*[2]

**Sonne** ('sɒnə). *Bacteriol.* The name of Carl Olaf *Sonne* (1882-1948), Danish bacteriologist, used *attrib.* and formerly in the possessive with reference to the Gram-negative bacterium *Shigella sonnei*, which causes a mild form of dysentery in man. [Described by Sonne in 1915 (*Zentralbl. f. Bakteriol.* LXXV. 408, *Zeitschr. f. klin. Med.* LXXXI. 73).]

**1922** *Jrnl. Path. & Bacteriol.* XXV. 393 (*heading*) The Sonne dysentery bacillus in Australia. *Ibid.*, Thjötta.. recovered the Sonne bacillus from cases of dysentery in Norway. *Ibid.* 394 A culture of Sonne's bacillus. **1927** *Jrnl. Hygiene* XXV. 456 So far, none of the cases of Sonne dysentery confirmed bacteriologically have died. **1930** *Jrnl. Infectious Dis.* XXVII. 468 This experiment was repeated with another strain of the Sonne organism with essentially the same results. **1947** *Ann. Rev. Microbiol.* I. 314 Milder cases are more often caused by the Sonne bacillus than by other *Shigellae*. However, it would be erroneous to conclude from this that infections with *Sh. sonnei* are always light. **1972** *Times* 14 Dec. 2/3 Tests were ordered..after an outbreak in the lines of what was believed to have been Sonne dysentery, a mild form of the disease.

**sonne**, obs. f. SON, SUN.

**Sonnee**, variant of SUNNI.

**sonner**, obs. comp. of SOON *adv.*

**sonnet** ('sɒnɪt), *sb.* Also 6-7 sonet (6 *pl.* sonettes). [a. F. *sonnet* (1543), or ad. It. *sonetto* (the source of the F. word), dim. of *suono* sound.]

**1.** A piece of verse (properly expressive of one main idea) consisting of fourteen decasyllabic lines, with rimes arranged according to one or other of certain definite schemes.

In the first quot. perh. including sense 2. In many instances between 1580 and 1650 it is not clear which sense is intended, as the looser use of the word would appear to have been very common.

**1557** (*title*), Songes and Sonettes, written by the..late Earle of Surrey, and other. **1575** GASCOIGNE *Posies* (1907) 471, I can beste allowe to call those Sonets whiche are of fouretene lynes, every line conteyning tenne syllables. **1595** W. P. in *Spenser's Minor P.* (1910) 370 These sweete conceited Sonets, the deede of..maister Edmond Spenser. **1609** (*title*), Shake-speares Sonnets. Neuer before Imprinted. *a* **1631** DONNE *Lett. to Persons of Hon.* (1651) 104 The Spanish proverb informes me, that he is a fool which cannot make one Sonnet, and he is mad which makes two. **1683** SOAME & DRYDEN tr. *Boileau's Art. Poet.* II. 319 A faultless Sonnet, finish'd thus, would be Worth tedious volumes of loose poetry. *a* **1771** GRAY *Metrum* Wks. 1843 V. 249 Sonnets of Fourteen, on Five Rhymes. [*Note.*] This, and the fourth kind, are the true Sonnet of the Italians. **1797** ANNA SEWARD *Lett.* (1811) IV. 326 My design of publishing, this spring, my centenary of sonnets. **1822** HAZLITT *Table-t.* II. ii. 19 The great object of the Sonnet seems to be to express in musical numbers,..with undivided breath, some occasional thought or personal feeling. **1841** D'ISRAELI *Amen. Lit.* (1867) 304 The Earl of Surrey composed the first sonnets in the English language. **1879** B. TAYLOR *Germ. Lit.* 174 Fischart first introduced the Italian sonnet into German literature.

**2.** A short poem or piece of verse; in early use esp. one of a lyrical and amatory character. Now *rare* or *Obs.*

**1563** (*title*), Eglogs, Epytaphes, and Sonettes, newly written by Barnabe Googe. **1575** GASCOIGNE *Posies* (1907) 471 Some thinke that all Poemes (being short) may be called Sonets. *Ibid.* 472 There are Dyzaynes & Syxaines..which some English writers do also terme by the name of Sonettes. **1599** (*title*), Sonnets To sundry notes of Musicke. **1650** J. COTTON *Sing. Psalms* 19 Neither doe drunkards..usually invent Sonnets. *c* **1674** *Roxb. Ball.* (1886) VI. 274 In this Sonnet you may find A fancy that may please your mind. **1719** HAMILTON *Ep. Ramsay* I. 43 Sae I conclude, and end my sonnet. *c* **1820** G. BEATTIE *John of Arnha* (1826) 15 My dowie sonnet Upo' the Horner's guid braid bonnet.

**3.** *attrib.* and *Comb.*, as ***sonnet-book, -fancier, -like*** adj., ***-maker, -making, -thought, -wise*** adv., ***-writer, -writing***; **sonnet-sequence**, a set of sonnets with a common theme or subject.

**1657** COKAYNE *Obstinate Lady* Poems (1659) 312, I should then perhaps a had a *Sonnet-book ere this. **1824** MACAULAY *Misc. Writ.* (1860) I. 86 These *sonnet-fanciers would do well to reflect [etc.]. **1874** G. M. HOPKINS *Jrnls. & Papers* (1959) 259, I looked at some delicate flying shafted ashes—there was one especially of single *sonnet-like inscape. **1691** WOOD *Antiq.* I. *Fasti* 761 He was at this time a pastoral *Sonnet-maker. **1768-74** TUCKER *Lt. Nat.* (1834) II. 147 This thirst of glory..is to be found among fiddlers and sonnet-makers. **1875** TENNYSON *Q. Mary* II. i, No call for sonnet-sorting now, nor for *sonnet-making either. **1881** D. G. ROSSETTI *Ballads & Sonnets* 161 (*title*) The House of Life: a *sonnet-sequence. **1929** WODEHOUSE *Mr. Mulliner Speaking* v. 141 The poet who was spending the summer at the Anglers' Rest had just begun to read us his new sonnet-sequence. **1973** *Listener* 21 June 830/2 Ever since Shakespeare the sonnet-sequence has grouped itself lightly. **1929** BLUNDEN *Near & Far* 59 All that deep-sighing elegy might mourn, Glad lyric hail, and *sonnet-thought adorn. **1588** GREENE *Perimedes* Wks. (Grosart) VII. 88 The yoong Prince..writ him an answer *Sonnet-wise to this effect. *c* **1645** HOWELL *Lett.* I. v. xxii, I send you the inclos'd Verses Sonnet-wise. **1824** in *Spirit Public Jrnls.* (1825) 355 Verses written sonnet wise On London's learned Lord. **1781** WARTON *Hist. Eng. Poetry* III. 483 George Whetstone, a *sonnet-writer of some rank. **1887** *Encycl. Brit.* XXII. 263/1 The crowning difficulty..of the sonnet writer. **1871** D. G. ROSSETTI *Let.* 2 Aug. (1967) III. 964 A little *sonnet-writing gets done. **1899** MISS E. T. FOWLER *Double Thread* ii. 18 He would willingly have instructed Milton in sonnet-writing.

**sonnet** ('sɒnɪt), *v.* [f. prec. Cf. It. *sonettare*.]

**1.** *intr.* To compose sonnets; to sonnetize.

**1589** G. HARVEY *Pierce's Super.* I. (1593) 48 When Elderton began to ballat, Gascoine to sonnet, Turberuile to madrigal. **1597** BP. HALL *Sat.* I. i, Nor list I Sonnet of my Mistresse face. **1621** LADY M. WROTH *Urania* 467 Loue was such a Lord ouer me, as I..sonnetted when hee inspired mee with it. **1658** FRANCK *North. Mem.* (1821) p. xlviii, And in delightful tones sit sonneting. **1875** TENNYSON *Q. Mary* II. i, Come, now, you're sonnetting again.

**2.** *trans.* †**a.** To fill with sonnets. *Obs. rare.*

**1592** NASHE *P. Penilesse* Wks. (Grosart) II. 27 Hee will.. sonnet a whole quire of paper in praise of Lady Swin-snout.

**b.** To celebrate in a sonnet or sonnets.

**1598** MERES *Pallad. Tamia* 280 b, Daniel hath diuinely sonetted the matchlesse beauty of his Delia. **1887** *St. James's Gaz.* 14 Feb. (Cassell), They sonneted her. **1904** TALLENTYRE *Voltaire* I. vi. 83 He sonneted his hostess now.

**c.** With *out*: To utter in sonnets. *rare*[−1].

**1610** G. FLETCHER *Christ's Vict.* II. lxii, The birds sweet notes, to sonnet out their joyes.

**sonnet**: see SENNET[1].

**sonnetary** ('sɒnətərɪ), *a.* [f. SONNET *sb.*] Relating to, expressed in, sonnets.

**1877** *Scribner's Month. Mag.* XV. 211/2 Two of the ten violate Italian sonnetary laws. **1892** *Cent. Mag.* May 144/1 The sonnetary sorrows of a blighted lover!

**sonneteer** (sɒnɪ'tɪə(r)), *sb.* Also 7 sonnettier, 8- sonnetteer. [ad. It. *sonettiere* (f. *sonetto* sonnet), or f. SONNET *sb.* + -EER[1].] A composer of sonnets; freq. in disparaging sense, a minor or indifferent poet.

*α.* **1665** DRYDEN *Indian Emp.* Epil., He first thinks fit no Sonnettier advance His censure, farther than the Song or Dance. **1678** —— *All for Love* Pref. B j b, Our little Sonnettiers who follow them, have too narrow Souls to judge of Poetry. **1753** *Gray's Inn Jrnl.* (1756) I. 307, I..was a Witness to the Mischief which was occasioned by the polite Sonnetteers. **1791** W. GIFFORD *Baviad* 45 And laugh to scorn th' eternal sonnetteer. **1839** HALLAM *Hist. Lit.* II. v. §76 The English sonnetteers deal less in customary epithets. **1872** BLACKIE *Lays Highl.* Introd. 42 In this matter I am neither a speculative reasoner, nor a sentimental sonnetteer.

*β.* **1677** WYCHERLEY *Pl. Dealer* I. i, The Noble Sonneteer wou'd trouble thee no more with his Madrigals. **1711** ADDISON *Spect.* No. 160 ¶1, I have heard many a little Sonneteer called a fine Genius. *a* **1763** SHENSTONE *Economy* III. 109 How shall I sing the various ill that waits The careful sonneteer? **1835** *Edin. Rev.* LX. 359 She is one of the best of the Italian *sonneteers*. **1877** MRS. OLIPHANT *Makers Flor.* i. 14 The elaborate sonnet put forth avowedly to a.. company of answering sonneteers.

*transf.* **1824** MISS MITFORD *Village* Ser. I. (1863) 63 No cuckoos (that ever I should miss that rascally sonneteer!).

Hence **sonne'teeress.** *nonce-word.*

**1822** *Blackw. Mag.* XII. 657 Our songstresses,.. sonneteeresses, or other 'buildresses of the lofty rhyme'.

**sonneteer** (sɒnɪ'tɪə(r)), *v.* Also sonnetteer. [f. SONNETEER *sb.*]

**1.** *refl.* To make (oneself) a sonneteer.

**1822** *Blackw. Mag.* XI. 740 Shelley will henceforth rave only to the moon. Hunt will sonneteer himself.

**2.** *trans.* To celebrate in sonnets.

**1825** *Blackw. Mag.* XVIII. 617 A prima donna.. sonneteered by half the..idlers from Vesuvius to the Alps.

**3.** *intr.* To compose sonnets.

**1841** LEVER *C. O'Malley* xcvi, The man who has been the very veriest flirt with women—sighing, serenading, sonneteering. **1851** MRS. BROWNING *Casa Guidi Wind.* I. 148 Rimers sonneteering in their sleep. **1899** M. HEWLETT *Litt. Novels Italy, Master Cino & Coal* ii, To sonneteer is very well, but a lover..must live.

**sonne'teering**, *vbl. sb.* [f. prec.] The composition of sonnets; the result of this.

**1797-1805** S. & HT. LEE *Canterb. T.* V. 34, I knew that he had touched up some pretty melancholy love-songs and sonneteerings. **1855** KINGSLEY *Westw. Ho!* ii, He had talked over the art of sonneteering with Tasso. **1887** G. SAINTSBURY *Hist. Elizab. Lit.* iv. (1890) 107 The vast outburst of sonneteering which..distinguished the middle of the last decade of the sixteenth century.

*attrib.* **1841** E. FITZGERALD *Lett.* (1889) I. 72 Just when one's sonneteering age is departing. **1885** *Athenæum* 6 June 722/1 William Shakspeare..wrote sonneteering addresses to a young man.

**sonne'teering**, *ppl. a.* [f. as prec.] Composing or producing sonnets.

**1809** BYRON *Bards & Rev.* 925 Let sonneteering Bowles his strains refine. **1824** MACAULAY *Misc. Writ.* (1860) I. 67 Blue-stocking ladies and sonneteering gentlemen. **1870** LOWELL *Among my Bks.* Ser. I. (1873) 368 In the very height of that divine sonneteering love of Laura.

**'sonneter.** *rare*$^{-1}$. = SONNETEER *sb.*
**1687** WINSTANLEY *Lives Eng. Poets* 99 A publish'd Collection of several Odes of the chief Sonneters of that Age.

**sonnetic** (sɒ'nɛtɪk), *a. rare.* [f. SONNET *sb.*] Characterized by, composed of, sonnets.
**1884** *Blackw. Mag.* June 754 What may be called the sonnetic period in Shakespeare's life. *Ibid.* 757 Many of the ideas.. found in his great sonnetic poem.

**'sonneting,** *vbl. sb.* [f. SONNET *sb.* or *v.*]
**1.** The composition of sonnets; the result of this.
**1588** SHAKS. *L.L.L.* IV. iii. 158 None but Minstrels like of Sonnetting. **1597** BP. HALL *Sat.* I. vii, Then poures he forth in patched Sonettings His loue. **1622** WITHER *Philarete* (1633) K ij, Whilst Great Britaines Shepheards sing English in their Sonnetting. **1649** MILTON *Eikon.* 64 He ascribes all vertue to his Wife, in Straines that come almost to Sonnetting. **1885** *Blackw. Mag.* June 790 To the rage for sonneting, so prevalent in his time, Shakespeare makes frequent reference in his plays. **1889** LANG *Lett. Lit.* 151 The soldiers have quite forsworn sonneting.
**2.** Celebration in a sonnet or sonnets.
**1642** MILTON *Apol. Smect.* Wks. 1851 III. 304 Two whole pages.. that praise the Remonstrant even to the soneting of his fresh cheeks, quick eyes,.. and nimble invention.
**3.** Singing, warbling.
*a* **1645** W. BROWNE *Thirsis Praise* Wks. 1869 II. 282 Leavie Groves now mainely ring, With each sweet birds sonnetting.

**'sonnetish,** *a. rare*$^{-1}$. [f. SONNET *sb.*] Suggestive of a sonnet or sonnets.
**1856** *Titan Mag.* Aug. 124/1 There's a peculiar sonnetish appearance in the eyes of persons under such circumstances.

†**'sonnetist.** *Obs. rare*$^{-1}$. [f. as prec.] A sonneteer.
**1597** BP. HALL *Sat.* I. viii, Great Salomon sings in the English Quire, And is become a newfound Sonetist.

**sonnetize** ('sɒnɪtaɪz), *v.* [f. SONNET *sb.*]
**1.** *intr.* To compose a sonnet or sonnets.
**1798** CHARLOTTE SMITH *Yng. Philos.* III. 74 Yours from Upwood.. has tempted me to sonnetize myself. **1821** *New Monthly Mag.* I. 647 They must.. scratch head, bite nail, and sonnettize. **1821** *Blackw. Mag.* VIII. 541 Let green-sick ladies sonnetize with Bowles.
**2.** *trans.* To celebrate in, make the subject of, a sonnet or sonnets.
**1799** SOUTHEY *Eng. Ecl.* Poet. Wks. III. 68 Bruin-Bear! Now could I sonnetize thy piteous plight. **1824** in *Spirit Public Jrnls.* (1825) 232 The Cocknies heretofore have devoted their time to sonnetizing each other.
Hence **'sonnetizing** *vbl. sb.*
**1832** *Fraser's Mag.* VI. 630 [He] has a good ear for sonnetising.

**sonnetry** ('sɒnɪtrɪ). [f. SONNET *sb.* + -RY.] Sonnet-making.
**1594** *Zepheria* Ded., The sweete tun'd accents of your Delian sonnetrie. **1801** in *Spirit Public Jrnls.* V. 103 *note*, Coining is not felony by the law of sonnetry. **1904** *Westm. Gaz.* 15 June 4/2 This essay on Elizabethan sonnetry.

†**sonnette.** *Obs. rare.* Also 4 sonete, 5 sownette. [a. OF. *sonete, sonnette, sonnet* (mod. F. *sonnette*), f. *son* sound.] A bell.
**13..** *E.E. Allit. P.* B. 1415 Notes of pipes, Tymbres & tabornes,.. Symbales & sonetez. **1491** CAXTON *Vitas Patr.* (W. de W. 1495) I. xlv. 77 b/2 By cause that they songe theyr seruyce, they myghte not here those sayde Camellis, ne theyr grete sownettes ne belles. **1494** in *Lett. Rich. III & Hen. VII* (Rolls) I. 394 Their hors richely trapped.., enramplised with sonnettes of siluer.

**sonnetto'mania.** *nonce-wd.* [See -MANIA.] Madness for sonnets. Also **sonnetto'maniac.**
**1821** *New Monthly Mag.* I. 644 Nothing.. is on record as a specific for the sonnettomania. *Ibid.* 648 The sonnettomaniacs would have in me an historian equal to what the Abderites found in Lucian.

**Sonnite,** variant of SUNNITE.

**sonny** ('sʌnɪ). *colloq.* Also sonnie. [f. SON *sb.*[1] + -Y.] **1. a.** A familiar term of address to a boy or to a man younger than the speaker.
**1870** *Routledge's Ev. Boy's Ann.* 688 Yes, my dear sonny, that is exactly what I mean. **1883** STEVENSON *Treas. Isl.* ii, 'Come here, sonny,' says he. **1891** CLARK RUSSELL *Curatica* i, 'Oh!' said my mother, 'just the very thing! Listen, sonnie!'
**b.** A small boy.
**1850** *Knickerbocker* XXXVI. 288 'Pa' returned towards the cars; when 'sonny', quickly drawing his pocket-pistol, took a drink. **1939** JOYCE *Finnegans Wake* 335 How Holispolis went to Parkland with mabby and sammy and sonny and sissy and mop's varlet de shambles. **1967** [see MUMMY *sb.*[2] 2].
**2.** *Comb.* **sonny boy,** from the title of a popular song, a boy; a man younger than the speaker or writer; freq. as a term of address and with disparaging sense; also *attrib.*; **sonny Jim**: see *sunny Jim* s.v. SUNNY *a.* 5 c.
**1928** A. JOLSON et al. *Sonny Boy* (song) 3 Climb upon my knee, Sonny Boy; You are only three, Sonny Boy. **1937** [see OVER-COMPENSATE *v.*]. **1942** *Gen* 15 June 36/2 So you lay off taking the mike out of women, sonny-boys. **1955** W. GADDIS *Recognitions* III. iv. 850 Lie back and don't try to remember everything now, sonny boy. **1956** H. GOLD *Man who was not with It* (1965) x. 79 A sonnyboy trust that I had the right to be helpless. **1970** *Washington Post* 30 Sept. D1/6 When you're the youngest of four children, 'you know, folks call you like you're a sonny boy, and it stuck to me'. **1978** T. ALLBEURY *Lantern Network* xii. 191 What do you want, sonny boy?.. I don't trust you, you English bastard.

**sonny,** obs. form of SUNNY *a.*

**sono-** ('səʊnəʊ), comb. form of L. *sonus* sound: **sono'chemistry,** (the study of) the chemical action of sound waves; so **sono'chemical** *a.*, of or pertaining to sonochemistry; **,sonolumi'nescence** *Chem.*, luminescence excited in a substance by the passage of sound waves through it; hence **,sonolumi'nescent** *a.*; **so'nolysis** *Chem.* [-LYSIS 1], the decomposition by ultrasound of a liquid, esp. water, as a result of the high temperatures generated within the cavities formed; also, the secondary reactions between the unrecombined decomposition products and the liquid itself or compounds dissolved in it; hence **sono'lytic** *a.*; **sono'lytically** *adv.*; (as a back-formation) **'sonolyse** *v. trans.*, to subject to sonolysis; **'sonolysed** *ppl. a.*
**1953** *Jrnl. Acoustical Soc. Amer.* XXV. 655/1 In view of the frequent attributing of sonochemical reactions to the concomitant heating effect, it is curious that higher temperatures give smaller yields. **1966** *New Scientist* 12 May 367/1 (*caption*) It now seems that a substantial part of the 'fixed' nitrogen available to marine plants and animals is due to sonochemical processes in waves. **1953** A. WEISSLER in *Jrnl. Acoustical Soc. Amer.* XXV. 651 (*heading*) Sonochemistry: the production of chemical changes with sound waves. **1958** *New Scientist* 25 Sept. 926/3 These conditions give rise to many remarkable effects which are now being studied such as sonoluminescence, ultrasonic cleaning and sonochemistry. **1966** *Ibid.* 12 May 367/1 It might well be said that an understanding of sonochemistry is the key to the understanding of numerous chemical changes which take place around us in everyday life. **1939** *Jrnl. Amer. Chem. Soc.* LXI. 2392/1 The luminescence which appears when sound waves pass through liquids has been called acoustic or sonic luminescence, for short, sonoluminescence. **1958** Sonoluminescence [see *sonochemistry* above]. **1976** *Jrnl. Acoustical Soc. Amer.* LX. 103/2 The sonoluminescence from a gas dissolved in water is inversely proportional to the thermal conductivity of the gas. **1974** *Ultrasonics* XII. 25/1 Chemical and sonoluminescent effects occur in gaseous (pseudo) cavitation but never in vaporous cavitation. **1964** *Jrnl. Chem. Physics* XL. 608/2 Water and dilute (0·1*M*) sodium formate solutions of different isotopic composition were subjected to sonolysis under argon... Hydrogen peroxide was produced. **1976** *Canad. Jrnl. Chem.* LIV. 1114/1 In aqueous solution.. the lifetime of chemically active radicals produced by sonolysis is larger than the lifetime of the cavitation bubble. **1964** *Jrnl. Chem. Physics* XL. 608/2 In analogy to radiation chemistry of aqueous solutions, 'molecular' and atomic hydrogen are apparently produced under sonolytic conditions. **1966** *New Scientist* 12 May 367/2 Sonolytically induced polymerization may.. compete with chemically induced processes. **1976** *Canad. Jrnl. Chem.* LIV. 1118/2 The mechanism whereby $H_2O_2$ is produced sonolytically has been the subject of some controversy. **1964** *Jrnl. Chem. Physics* XL. 609/1 $DCO_2Na$O·1*M*, 98% D (pH = 5·5), was sonolyzed in $H_2O$. **1964** *Jrnl. Physical Chem.* LXVIII. 1460/1 The analogy between the behaviour of radiolyzed and sonolyzed aqueous solutions has been pointed out in several studies. **1966** *New Scientist* 12 May 366/1 We may thus envisage a sonolysed system as a heterogeneous process wherein small centres of very high temperature exist in transient gas bubbles dispersed in a liquid medium.

**sonobuoy** ('səʊnəʊbɔɪ). Also sono-buoy, Sono-. [f. SONO- + BUOY *sb.*] A buoy equipped to detect underwater sounds and transmit them automatically by radio.
**1945** *Washington Post* 26 Oct. 1/4 The Sonobuoy, a small buoy tossed overboard from plane or ship in the vicinity of a submarine. This device, in use since 1942, gets the sub's location by sound waves and automatically transmits the information to plane or ship by radio. **1950** *Engineering* 29 Sept. 269/3 There is provision for carrying sono-buoys and military stores on the wings. **1969** *New Scientist* 28 Aug. 420/2 Passive detection, that is, listening devices such as sono-buoys, can also be used. **1972** *Sci. Amer.* July 16/3 A hydrophone, dangling from each sonobuoy at a substantial depth, picks up pressure signals that are then relayed by radio to the aircraft. **1973** *Daily Tel.* 24 July 2/7 An RAF Nimrod maritime reconnaissance aircraft will lay Sonobuoys used to detect submarines.

**sonofa, sonofer.** Colloq. shortening of such phrases as SON OF A BITCH, *son of a gun* s.v. GUN *sb.* 6 c, etc. Cf. SON *sb.* 7 d.
**1951** W. SANSOM *Face of Innocence* i. 1 'Why!' Harry said. 'If it isn't you, you old sonofer!' **1968** 'G. BAGBY' *Another Day—Another Death* iii. 45 You wouldn't have found one man around here who hadn't threatened.. this Clancy sonofa.

**son of a bitch.** *slang.* Also son-of-a-bitch, sonofabitch, sonuvabitch, etc. In pl., sons of bitches. [Cf. SON *sb.* 7 d.]
Now more common in the U.S. than elsewhere.
**1. a.** A despicable or hateful man. Also *attrib.* Cf. *S.O.B.* s.v. S. I. 4 a.
[*c* **1330** *Of Arthour & of Merlin* (1973) 333 Abide þou þef malicious! Biche-sone þou drawest amis þou schalt abigge it ywis! **1605** SHAKS. *King Lear* II. ii, One that.. art nothing but the composition of a Knave, Begger, Coward, Pandar, and the Sonne and Heire of a Mungrill Bitch.] **1707** J. SHIRLEY *Triumph of Wit* (ed. 5) 203 There stands Jack Ketch, that Son of a Bitch, that owes us all a grudge. **1744** A. HAMILTON *Itinerarium* (1907) 229 It was the landlord ordering his negroes, with an imperious and exalted voice. In his orders the known term or epithet of *son of a bitch* was often repeated. **1762** L. STERNE *Let.* 8 Apr. in *Times Lit. Suppl.* (1965) 8 Apr. 284/4 Phelps is a son of a Bitch for saying I was worse than when I left You for I am ten, nay 15 per Cent better. **1800** J. SAPPINGTON in T. Jefferson *Notes on Virginia* 52 Logan's brother.. attempted to strike him, saying, 'White man, son of a bitch'. **1823** BYRON *Don Juan* XI. xli. 123 Pray ask of your next neighbour, If he found not this spawn of tax-born riches, Like lap-dogs, the least civil sons of b——s. **1833** [see BITCH *sb.*[1] 2 a]. **1924** M. KENNEDY *Constant Nymph* III. xvi. 217 You think I ought to want to please every son of a bitch who can pay for a sixpenny ticket. **1929** E. POUND *Let.* 1 Feb. (1971) 224 The stinking sons-of-bitches who rot the country. **1939** S. SPENDER tr. *Toller's Pastor Hall* II. 77 Here, you fat-bellied son of a bitch, hand me some of your margarine. **1945** L. SAXON et al. *Gumbo Ya-Ya* iii. 65 The old woman looked at her for a minute, then she said, quiet-like, 'Well, I'm a son of a bitch!' **1951** J. D. SALINGER *Catcher in Rye* iii. 30 Boy, I can't stand that sonuvabitch. **1959** *Times* 25 Sept. 9/1 Hume.. said.. that a Scotland Yard report must have been prepared by 'some son-of-a-bitch inspector who wants to blacken my name'. **1963** R. SEAVER tr. *Beckett's End* in *Writers in Revolt* 357 He went bustling along.. bowing and scraping and flourishing his hat... The insufferable son of a bitch. **1977** I. SHAW *Beggarman, Thief* II. iii. 139 Arrogant Hollywood sonofabitch.
**b.** With weakened force and neutral or friendly overtones: a fellow, a man.
**1951** E. PAUL *Springtime in Paris* xv. 294 'The son of a bitch is crazy,' said, in soft English, but completely without malice or disapproval. **1958** J. CAREW *Wild Coast* ix. 124 He was a drinking, whoring, kindly savage son-of-a-bitch. **1979** 'A. HAILEY' *Overload* III. xiii. 258 Besides, the son-of-a-bitch had guts and was honest.
**2.** Applied to animals, etc., as a term of abuse.
**1771** SMOLLETT *Humph. Cl.* I. 167 Damn the nasty son of a bitch, and them he belongs to! **1954** C. ODETS *Big Knife* in *Famous Plays 1954* 434 Our story is that the dog—a big son of a bitch—yanked the leash and threw her to the floor. **1958** J. KEROUAC *On Road* iv. 24 We been riding this sonofabitch since Des Moines. **1977** *New Yorker* 27 June 78/3, I figured that that grouse wouldn't be a meal for me... I.. went over to the tree, shook it, and yelled, 'Get outa there you son of a bitch.'
**3.** Applied to a woman as a term of abuse. *rare.*
**1936** H. MILLER *Black Spring* 250 He got to working overtime in order to lay aside the little bribe which would make the frigid son of a bitch come across like a nymphomaniac.
**4.** Used as an expletive.
**1953** W. BURROUGHS *Junkie* (1972) ii. 28 'Sonofabitch!' she snarled. 'They can tell when a woman isn't looking for a pickup.' **1957** M. MILLAR *Soft Talkers* iii. 33 Sonuvabitch, I don't get it. What's the matter? What did *I* do?
**5.** Used in comparisons to suggest strength, ferocity, speed, etc.
**1953** W. BURROUGHS *Junkie* (1972) viii. 75, I hit Philly sick as a sonofabitch. **1976** *New Yorker* 15 Mar. 32/3 Well, I hit that bastard with my white fist and ran out of there like a sonuvabitch.
Hence **son-of-a-bitching** *a.*, a general epithet of abuse.
**1930** J. DOS PASSOS *42nd Parallel* I. 101 Every sonofabitchin yellerleg in the State of Nevada. **1941** E. P. O'DONNELL *Great Big Doorstep* vii. 98 Tayo put his bag down, and shed his coat uncertainly. 'Son of a bitchin pole-vaulter,' he muttered. **1960** J. KIRKWOOD *There must be a Pony!* (1961) i. 12 The meanest son-of-a-bitching parrot you could ever run up against. **1979** 'A. HAILEY' *Overload* IV. xiv. 370 'People!' Paulsen exploded. 'Son-of-a-bitching, stupid people!'

**sonogram** ('səʊnəgræm). Also **sonagram.** [f. SONO- + -GRAM.] A graphical representation, produced by a sonograph, of the distribution of sound energy among different frequencies, esp. as a function of time.
**1956** *New Biol.* XX. 71 (*caption*) Sonograms of songs of two male chaffinches from different 'dialect areas'. **1957** *Jrnl. Acoustical Soc. Amer.* XXIX. 108/1 (*caption*) Sonagrams of the words 'tack' 'task' 'tact'.. illustrating the role that transitions and bursts play in the perception of stops. **1969** R. STENUIT *Dolphin* v. 73 Analysis of the sonogram of a conversation shows click exchanges and whistle exchanges. **1978** *Country Life* 28 Dec. 2225/1 By comparing the sonograms differences can be isolated between the call patterns of individual birds. **1980** *Times* 19 Aug. 12/6 Dr Silver used a hydrophone to record the sounds under water and obtained a visual record in the form of a sonogram.

**sonograph** ('səʊnəgrɑːf, -æ-). [f. SONO- + -GRAPH.] **1.** Also **sonagraph** and with capital initial. An instrument which analyses sound into its component frequencies and produces a graphical record of the results.
*Sonagraph* is registered as a proprietary term in the U.S.
**1951** *Official Gaz.* (U.S. Patent Office) 14 Aug. 345/2 Kay Electric Company, Pine Brook, N.J... *Sona-graph*... For instrument which is a sound spectrograph which produces permanent visual records showing distribution of energy vs. both frequency and time. Claims use since October 1948. **1953** J. B. CARROLL *Study of Lang.* vii. 206 The 'visible-speech' machine developed in the Bell Telephone Laboratories.. produces the same type of record as does the Sonagraph, but on a continuous, transitory basis. **1954** *Nature* 13 Mar. 465/1 All this was changed by the invention of the sound spectrograph, now known commercially as the 'Sonograph'. **1956** *New Biol.* XX. 78 The structure of Chaffinch calls has been studied by making recordings on discs or magnetic tapes, and then analysing them on a sound spectrograph, or sonograph. **1976** J. M. BROWNJOHN tr. *Kirst's Time for Payment* v. 108 The Sonograph can pick up voice frequencies and record them. **1979** *New Scientist* 17 May 537/2 The sonagraph acts as a sonic prism.

**2.** An image of a tract of seabed obtained by means of side-scan sonar.

**1970** *Sci. Jrnl.* Dec. 56/2 By 1964 the geological and economic value of obtaining sonographs of the continental shelf and uppermost continental slope was so evident that the National Institute of Oceanography decided to explore the possibility of adapting the same method for examination of the deeper lying ocean floors. **1974** *Nature* 15 Feb. 453/2 Between this trench and the Italian coast alongslope tectonic trends are seen on sonographs. **1976** *Physics Bull.* Sept. 381/3 Figure 1 a..shows a sonograph of a portion of the seabed in the Bristol channel.

**sonomaite** ('sɒnəməaɪt). *Min.* [See quots.] 'Hydrous sulphate of aluminum and magnesium, closely allied to pickeringite' (Chester).

**1876** *Proc. Nat. Sci. Acad. Philadelphia* 263 Mr. E. Goldsmith stated that he had found among other undetermined minerals collected by Prof. F. V. Hayden in Sonoma County, Cal., near the geysers, one for which he proposed the name Sonomaite. *Ibid.* 264 Sonomaite occurs in silky, colorless crystals. **1881** in WATTS *3rd Suppl.*

**sonometer** (səʊ'nɒmɪtə(r)). [f. *sono-* as combining form of L. *sonus* sound + -METER. In sense 1 perh. after F. *sonomètre*.]

**1.** An instrument for determining the number of vibrations made by a sonorous cord.

**1808** *Edinburgh Encycl.* (1830) I. 128/1 Sonometers are instruments intended for determining the relation between the number of undulations which constitute the several notes of music. **1829** *Chapters Phys. Sci.* 273 In the experiments relative to this object, an instrument called a sonometer is made use of. **1873** W. LEES *Acoustics* I. iii. 23. **1889** BRINSMEAD *Hist. Pianoforte* 40 An extremely useful instrument called the monochord or sonometer.

**2.** An instrument for testing the sense of hearing, or the efficacy of treatment for deafness; an audiometer.

**1849** *Pract. Mech. Jrnl.* Sept. 131 A most important instrument for the use of parties under treatment for deafness,..aptly named the sonometer. **1879** [see AUDIOMETER]. **1894** *Daily News* 14 June 6/4 Amongst the illustrations of applied science were an ingenious sonometer... It measures and tests the relative..perception of hearing.

**3.** *Electr.* A telephone attached to an apparatus for testing metals by means of an induction-coil.

**1879** *Daily News* 31 Dec. 5/4 A difference which is at once indicated by a sound in a telephone attached, which is called the sonometer. **1881** *Nature* XXIII. 520 The sonometer is brought into the circuit.

**Sonoran** (sə'nɔərən), *a.* [f. *Sonora*, the name of a state in North-west Mexico + -AN.]

**1.** Of or pertaining to a biogeographical region including desert areas of the south-western United States and central Mexico.

**1880** E. D. COPE in *Proc. Amer. Philos. Soc.* XVIII. 263 This collection..is of interest as serving to fix the extension of the Sonoran fauna to a point further south. **1892** *Proc. Biol. Soc. Washington* VII. 15 The term 'Sonoran Region' has been applied by Cope and others to an important life area which enters the southwestern part of the United States from the table-land of Mexico. **1902** *Nature* 14 Aug. 374/1 It is somewhat regrettable to find that the author is unable to convince himself of the necessity of a Sonoran region. **1937** *Discovery* July 206/1 This sub-region has much in common with the Sonoran sub-region of the Nearctic Region. **1979** *Tucson* (Ariz.) *Mag.* Feb. 79/1 There are more than 350 varieties of live animals and plants of the Sonoran desert on exhibit.

**2.** Of, pertaining to, or characteristic of a grouping of related Indian languages spoken in southern Arizona and northern Mexico.

The nineteenth-century classification of some Uto-Aztecan languages into a Sonoran sub-group is now discarded.

[**1875** H. H. BANCROFT *Native Races of Pacific States* III. 670 Sound-shunting..has..been found by Mr Buschmann in the languages of his Sonora family.] **1891** D. G. BRINTON *Amer. Race* 123 The Sonoran branch [of the Uto-Aztecan stock] begins on the north with the Pimas, who occupied the middle valley of the Gila, and the land south of it quite to the Rio Yaqui. I continue for it the name of *Sonoran* given by Buschmann, although it extended far beyond the bounds of that province. **1909** A. F. CHAMBERLAIN in *Amer. Anthropologist* XI. 535 A number of Shoshonean languages, from Ute to Nahuatl and some of the Sonoran tongues. **1935** B. L. WHORF in *Ibid.* XXXVII. 606 In times past some of us hoped that the stock could be classified in such a way that we could summarize the situation by stating generalized reflexes for sub-groups such as 'Shoshonean', 'Piman', 'Sonoran', from which the reflexes of the individual tongues in these groups could be derived as a second step. The hope is vain. No such groups exist. **1964** S. M. LAMB in *Univ. Calif. Publ. Ling.* XXXIV. 121 Further investigation of the northern Mexican languages, which Brinton had..put into a single group called Sonoran, revealed a high degree of diversity among them. **1977** C. F. & F. M. VOEGELIN in T. A. Sebeok *Native Languages of Americas* I. 482 The traditional major branches of the Uto-Aztecan family (Shoshonean, Sonoran and Aztec).

**sonorant** (sə'nɔərənt). *Phonetics.* [f. SONOR(OUS *a.* + -ANT[1].] A resonant; a sound produced with the vocal tract so positioned that spontaneous voicing is possible; a vowel, a glide, or a liquid or nasal consonant. Also *attrib.* or as *adj.*

**1934** in WEBSTER. **1943** [see RESONANT *a.* 1 b]. **1956** JAKOBSON & HALLE in Saporta & Bastian *Psycholinguistics* (1961) 349/2 It is advantageous to range these two related classes of phonemes under a common heading of sonorants. **1963** [see OBSTRUENT *sb.* c]. **1968** CHOMSKY & HALLE *Sound Pattern Eng.* 302 Vowels, glides, nasal consonants, and liquids are sonorant. **1978** *Language* LIV. 327 Among these are:..; reduction of palatalized sonorants to simple yod, and of *č ǯ* to *s*. **1981** *Publ. Amer. Dial. Soc.* LXVIII. 30 The major sonority distinction is between sonorants (i.e. nasals, liquids and all vocoids) on the one hand and obstruents (stops, affricates and fricatives) on the other.

†**sonore,** *a. Obs.* Also 5 sonowre, 6 sonour. [ad. L. *sonōr-us* (see SONOROUS *a.*), or a. F. *sonore*.] Sonorous.

**1486** *Bk. St. Albans* d iij, Looke also that thay [*sc.* the bells] be sonowre and well sowndyng and shil. *a* **1542** WYATT *Ps.* li. Prol. 9 On sonour cordes his fingers he extendes. **1657** TOMLINSON *Renou's Disp.* 427 It becomes tinalous, hard and sonore.

†**sono'reity.** *Obs.*[−1] [Cf. prec. and -ITY.] A sonorous word.

**1665** SERGEANT in *Digby's Nat. Bodies* *2 An antick weed, patch't up as they shall please Of Vnions, Moods, and Sonoreities.

**sono'rescence.** [f. L. *sonōr-us* SONOROUS *a.*] The conversion of intermittent radiations into sound.

**1881** E. H. COOK in *Philos. Mag.* May 378 In the new phenomena we have again a change from more rapid into less rapid, which is very similar to that which occurs in fluorescence. To the change which takes place in this case, therefore, I venture to propose the term 'Sonorescence'. **1884** A. DANIELL *Princ. Physics* 512 It has been proposed to call the last-mentioned property of hard rubber the sonorescence of that substance.

Hence **sono'rescent** *a.*

**1881** E. H. COOK in *Philos. Mag.* May 378 A body such as hard rubber..would be called a *sonorescent* body, just as sulphate of quinine is a fluorescent body.

**sono'riety.** *rare*[−1]. = SONORITY.

**1837** W. STOKES *Treatm. Dis. Chest* (1882) 278 The lung rapidly regains its sonoriety.

†**sono'riferous,** *a. Obs.*[−1] [f. L. *sonor*, *sonōris* sound + -(I)FEROUS.] Conveying sound; soniferous. Also †**sonoriferously** *adv.*, resoundingly.

*a* **1693** *Urquhart's Rabelais* III. xxiii. 193 Mars..did raise his Voice—horrifically loud, and sonoriferously high. **1730** CHAMBERLAYNE *Relig. Philos.* I. xiii. §3 When the Sonoriferous Air is come into the Cavity of the External Part of the Ear.

**sono'rific,** *a. rare.* [f. L. *sonor* sound + -(I)FIC.] Producing sound; now *spec.* of insects, producing other than vocal sounds (*Cent. Dict.*).

**1725** WATTS *Logick* I. vi. §3 If he should ask me, why a Clock strikes, and points to the Hour, and I should say, it is by an indicating Form and sonorific Quality. **1784** *Phil. Trans.* LXXIV. 215 It may move much faster than sound travels,..and carry on the sonorific vibrations with it.

**sonority** (sə'nɒrɪtɪ). [a. F. *sonorité*, or ad. L. *sonōritas*, f. *sonōr-us*: see -ITY.] The quality of being sonorous: **a.** Of sounds.

**1623** COCKERAM I, *Sonoritie*, shrilnesse, loudnesse. **1864** *Reader* 16 Jan. 86/1 An amount of sonority..ten times as much as the ten first fiddles of the Brussels Conservatoire. **1874** HULLAH *Speaking Voice* 2 We reduce to a minimum the sonority of our vowels. **1883** *Grove's Dict. Music* III. 426 This depression of the first string..is not unfavourable to sonority.

**b.** Of things or places.

**1879** *Grove's Dict. Music* I. 10 The *salle* [of the theatre] is said to be deficient in sonority. **1883** *Harper's Mag.* Nov. 886/2 The sonority of this reservoir is expected materially to re-enforce the volume of tone. **1897** *Trans. Amer. Pediatric Soc.* IX. 19 The sonority of the chest, and the peculiar character of the respiration.

**c.** Of speech or diction.

**1876** *Contemp. Rev.* XXVIII. 240 Milton's proficiency on the organ is hardly to be forgotten in considering the richness and sonority of his language. **1881** *Athenæum* No. 2811. 328/2 The great virtue of the regular sonnet..is a certain sonority. **1883** LD. LYTTON *Life Lytton* II. 100 The fine sonority of the verse in Tamberlain.

**so'noro-**, used as combining form of SONOROUS *a.*, as in ***sonoro-sibilant*** adj.

**1897** *Allbutt's Syst. Med.* II. 241 Scanty sonoro-sibilant rhoncus..is all that can be heard with the stethoscope.

**sono'rosity.** *rare.* [f. next.] = SONORITY.

**1772** NUGENT *Hist. Fr. Gerund* I. 175 This was the way to baptize a work with elegance and sonorosity. **1885** EMILY LAWLESS *Millionaire's Cousin* v. 105 Such a desperate and, to all appearances, perennial flow of sonorosity.

**sonorous** (sə'nɔərəs, 'sɒnərəs), *a.* [f. L. *sonōr-us*, f. *sonor*, *sonōris*, sound: see -OUS.]

**1. a.** Of things: Giving out, or capable of giving out, a sound, esp. of a deep or ringing character.

**1611** COTGR., *Sonoreux*, sonorous, lowd, shrill, roring. **1656** BLOUNT *Glossogr.*, *Sonorous*, loud; making a great noise, shril, roaring. **1667** MILTON *P.L.* I. 540 Sonorous mettal blowing Martial sounds. **1725** POPE *Odyss.* VIII. 214 Sonorous thro' the shaded air it sings. **1748** HARTLEY *Observ. Man* I. iv. §1. 425 The simple Sounds of all uniform sonorous Bodies. **1789** J. WILLIAMS *Min. Kingd.* I. 410 The steel ores are mostly very hard, the masses being frequently sonorous. **1823** SCORESBY *Jrnl.* 44 Washed linen became hard and sonorous. **1864** ENGEL *Mus. Anc. Nat.* 11 Instruments consisting of a series of pieces of sonorous wood. **1881** A. G. BELL *Sound by Radiant Energy* 1 Substances which became sonorous in the condition of thin diaphragms. **1934** G. B. SHAW *Let.* in *Times* 2 Jan. 11/5 An announcer who pronounced decadent and sonorous as dekkadent and sonnerus would provoke Providence to strike him dumb.

**b.** Of places, etc.: Resounding, roaring, noisy.

**1729** G. ADAMS tr. *Sophocl., Antig.* IV. ii. II. 64 Upon famous Parnassus, or the sonorous Shore. **1796** OWEN *Trav. into Europe* II. 425 The river was extremely violent and sonorous. **1841** THOREAU *Lett.* (1865) 6 What with..the lowing of kine, and the crowing of cocks, our Concord life is sonorous enough.

**2. a.** Of sounds: Having a loud, deep, or resonant character.

**1668** WILKINS *Real Char.* III. xii. 367 To the Sonorous letters of this kind, there are three Mutes of affinity. **1691** RAY *N. Co. Words* (ed. 2) 158 That these three last mentioned are simple Letters..appears in that the sound of them (for they are sonorous) may be continued. **1750** tr. *Leonardus' Mirr. Stones* 90 It..makes the voice sonorous. **1791** COWPER *Iliad* x. 162 Nestor, brave Gerenian, with a voice Sonorous. **1825** T. HOOK *Sayings* Ser. II. *Man of Many Fr.* II. 56 Giving his niece one of those sonorous salutes, which..at least sound genuine. **1859** GEO. ELIOT *A. Bede* ii, His own sonorous utterance of the responses. **1879** S. C. BARTLETT *Egypt to Pal.* xi. 241 The first sound that welcomed us was his sonorous bray.

**b.** *Path.* Of sounds heard in auscultation.

**1827** J. FORBES *Laennec's Dis. Chest* (1834) 109 The respiration was strong, and accompanied by a deep sonorous rhonchus. **1853** MARKHAM *Skoda's Auscult.* 276 Bronchial respiration,..or the hissing and sonorous sounds, may be very distinct. **1876** BRISTOWE *Th. & Pract. Med.* (1878) 388 The deeper notes are usually termed 'sonorous', the acuter notes 'sibilant'.

**c.** *Physics.* Of vibrations or waves.

**1839** G. BIRD *Nat. Philos.* 293 In the same manner as sonorous vibrations convey the sensation of sound to the ear. **1863** TYNDALL *Heat* x. 281 The condensation and rarefaction constitute what is called a sonorous pulse or wave. **1879** G. PRESCOTT *Sp. Telephone* 13 The character of each tone depends not merely upon the number of sonorous vibrations, but upon their intensity or amplitude also.

**3. a.** Of language, diction, etc.: Having a full, rich sound; strong and harmonious.

**1693** DRYDEN *Juvenal* Ded. (1726) p. lxxix, His Expressions are Sonorous and more Noble. **1705** ADDISON *Italy* 99 For this reason the Italian Opera..has something beautiful and sonorous in the Expression. **1791** BOSWELL *Johnson* (Oxford ed.) I. 180, I told him, I thought it a very sonorous hexameter. **1842** PRICHARD *Nat. Hist. Man* 374 They had a sonorous and harmonious language, distinct from all others. **1875** JOWETT *Plato* (ed. 2) II. 121 The word has been lately altered and made sonorous.

**b.** Of persons: having a full and rich style or voice.

**1728** POPE *Dunc.* II. 247 But far o'er all, sonorous Blackmore's strain; Walls, steeples, skies, bray back to him again. **1837** CARLYLE *Fr. Rev.* I. v. vi, Santerre, the sonorous Brewer of the Suburb Saint-Antoine.

**so'norously,** *adv.* [f. prec. + -LY[2].] In a sonorous manner.

**1653** H. MORE *Antid. Ath.* III. ix. (1712) 117 Smacking and grunting very sonorously. **1670** G. H. *Hist. Cardinals* II. II. 173 That pure Evangelical River, that purles so sweetly and sonorously in the ears of the Faithful. **1822-7** GOOD *Study Med.* (1829) II. 410 The patient..breathed sonorously, but without stertor. **1865** MRS. WHITNEY *Gayworthys* ix, The voice rang out once again—startlingly—sonorously.

**so'norousness.** [f. as prec. + -NESS.] The character or quality of being sonorous.

*a* **1691** BOYLE *Ess. Intestine Motions of Solids* vii. Wks. 1772 I. 450 Of what age..such instruments..ought to be, to attain their full and best seasoning for sonorousness. **1777** G. FORSTER *Voy. round World* I. 478 We did not find that sonorousness in the Tonga-Tabboo dialect, which is prevalent in that of Taheitee. **1778** W. PRYCE *Min. Cornub.* 46 A small portion of Bismuth increases the brightness, hardness, and sonorousness of Tin. **1835-6** *Todd's Cycl. Anat.* I. 503/1 The peculiar sonorousness which percussion frequently elicits over the left hypochondrium. **1865** GROTE *Plato* I. i. 73 The colour, sonorousness,..&c., of the bodies around us. **1881** *Nature* XXIV. 42 Sonorousness, under the influence of intermittent light, is a property common to all matter.

†**sonous,** *a. Obs.*[−1] [ad. med.L. *sonōsus*, f. L. *sonus* sound.] Sonorous.

*c* **1450** *Mirour Saluacioun* (Roxb.) 119 Above thaire hovse Was herde a voice of a wynde whilk was fulle hoegely sonovse.

‖**sons bouchés** (sɔ̃ buʃe), *sb. pl.* [Fr., lit. 'blocked sounds'.] In horn-playing, notes stopped by the insertion of the hand into the bell of the instrument; a direction indicating this. Also *attrib.* Cf. CUIVRÉ, *a.*

**1907** T. S. WOTTON *Dict. Mus. Terms*, *Sons bouchés*, closed notes on a horn. [**1927** *Grove's Dict. Mus* (ed. 3) II. 666/2 The composer's intentions should be indicated by the placing of a small cross over the note with the word stopped (Fr. *cuivré* or *sons bouchés*).] **1961** R. M. PEGGE in A. Baines *Musical Instruments through Ages* xi. 302 The hand in the bell..serves for a certain type of muting demanded when the part is marked 'stopped', 'sons bouchés', 'gestopft', or 'chiuso'. **1977** *Early Music* July 427/2 When one closes the bell fully and blows hard, the *sons bouchés* notes are a *whole tone* and not a semitone above the next lower harmonic.

**sonse** (sɒns). *Sc.* (and *Ir.*). Also 5-6 sons, 6- sonce. [ad. Gael. *sonas* good fortune, prosperity, etc.] Abundance, plentifulness, plenty; prosperity.

*c* **1300** in *Wyntoun's Orig. Cron.* VII. x. 3623 Qwhen Alexander our kynge was dede,..Away was sons of alle and brede. **1500-20** DUNBAR *Poems* xxv. 61 God and Sanct Jeill heir ȝow convoy..To sonce and seill, solace and joy. **1535**

STEWART *Cron. Scot.* III. 229 Of fugitouris fra sindrie landis fled, Quhilk lytill sons or nane at hame hes hed, Forlane lownis without riches or micht. *a* **1689** CLELAND *Poems* (1697) 59 There's als much vertue, sonce, and pith In Annan, or the Water of Nith,.. Als any water in all Greece. **1830** CARLETON *Traits Irish Peas.* (1843) I. 195 Bad manners to me,.. if sonse or grace can ever come of it. **1892** *Ballymena Obs.* (E.D.D.), Something of good size and value would be said to have some sonce with it.

**b.** In the phr. *sonse fa'*..., expressing a wish for one's prosperity. (Misused by Ramsay.)

**1719** RAMSAY *1st Answ. Hamilton* i, Sonse fa me, witty, wanton Willy, Gin blyth I was na as a filly [etc.]. **1788** PICKEN *Poems* 157 Sonce fa' yer apen, honest heart Whar double guile ne'er hauntet. **1806** R. JAMIESON *Pop. Ballads* I. 352 Sonse fa' Bobbin John; Want an' wae gae by him.

**sonship** (ˈsʌnʃɪp). Also 6–7 sonneship. [f. SON *sb.*[1] + -SHIP. Cf. Du. *zoonschap*, G. *sohnschaft.*] The position, state, or relation of a son; sonhood.

**1587** GOLDING *De Mornay* v. (1592) 52 His begetting or Sonneship (if I may so tearme it) is more inward than all the breedings or begettings which we commonly see. **1612** T. TAYLOR *Comm. Titus* iii. 7 All our right of sonneship is by Christ. **1646** FULLER *Wounded Consc.* (1841) 321 To disclaim our sonship in God. **1670** G. H. *Hist. Cardinals* I. III. 97 The poor Cloyster of which they boast themselves to be Sons, which Son-ship, is oftentimes purchas'd notwithstanding. **1706** STANHOPE *Paraphr.* III. 294 That Sonship was imparted by Adoption. **1719** WATERLAND *Vind. Christ's Div.* 162 All the Christian Writers speak unanimously of a higher, antecedent Sonship. **1850** F. W. ROBERTSON *Serm.* Ser. III. v. (1853) 73 As in baptism he seals the universal Sonship on the individual by name. **1871** H. B. FORMAN *Our Living Poets* 328 The anguish of the father and the exquisite sonship of the youth.

**ˈsonsily,** *adv. Sc.* [f. SONSY *a.*] In a sonsy or substantial manner.

**1730** in Marshall *Hist. Scenes Perthshire* (1880) 199 A big dog appeared to me.. betwixt the Hilltown and Knowhead of Mause,.. and in passing by touched me sonsily on the thigh at my haunch bane.

**Sonsonate** (sɒnsəˈnɑːteɪ). [The name of a city in San Salvador.] In *attrib.* use: (see quots.).

**1858** SIMMONDS *Dict. Trade*, *Sonsonate Balsam*, a name given to two species of balsam of Peru, a black and a white. **1861** BENTLEY *Man. Bot.* 529 Balsam of Peru is known in commerce under the names of Sonsonate or St. Salvador Black Balsam.

**sonsy** (ˈsɒnsɪ), *a.* Orig. *Sc.*, *Ir.*, and *north. dial.* Also 6 sonse, 7– sonsie, 9 sonzy; 8– soncy, 9 soncie; 9 saunsey, -cy. [f. SONSE.

The opposite term is *donsy* DONSIE *a.* (f. *donse, ad. Gael. *donas* bad luck, misfortune).]

**1.** Bringing luck or good fortune; lucky, fortunate.

**1533** BELLENDEN *Livy* I. xiv. (S.T.S.) I. 80 þis wounder apperit be þe Erne,.. discending fra þe maist sonsy parte of hevin, on þe left hand. **1536** —— *Cron. Scot.* (1821) I. 16 To give them the more esperance of permanent and sonse weird. **1575** *St. Andrews Kirk-Sess. Reg.* (1889) 416 Pay desyrit hir gude-man to pas to the coles witht Dauid Robertson, becaus he was ane sonsy man. **1597** JAS. I *Daemonologie* III. ii. 65 Some were so blinded, as to beleeue that their house was all the sonsier, as they called it, that such spirites resorted there. **1633** *Orkney Witch Trial* in *Abbotsford Club Miscell.* 152 The said Marrion.. said that scho had ane sonsie hand. **1681** *Aberd. Sess. Min.* in W. Ross *Aberdour & Inchcolme* xi. (1885) 332 She said that Elspeth was 'not sonsie'. **1721** KELLY *Sc. Prov.* Introd., It is no Sonsie to meet a bare Foot in the Morning. **1726** in Macfarlane *Geog. Coll.* (S.H.S.) I. 212 They say the river is not sonsy nor yet the loch. **1824** MACTAGGART *Gallovid. Encycl.* 384 A bean podd, that holds five beans, and a pea podd, which contains nine peas, are considered to be sonsy. **1880** *Antrim & Down Gloss.* 95 It's not sonsy to do that.

*Comb.* **1684** RENWICK *Serm.* v. (1776) 72 It is never a sonsy-like manifestation that makes proud.

**b.** Sound, sensible; shrewd. *rare.*

*a* **1689** CLELAND *Poems* (1697) 105 It is a good old sonsie saying, That little wit makes meikle straying. **1720** RAMSAY *Wealth* 15 Sonsy sauls wha first contriv'd the way, With project deep our charges to defray.

**2.** Having a thriving, agreeable, or attractive appearance; plump, buxom, comely and pleasant; comfortable-looking, etc.

The various shades of meaning are fully illustrated in the *Eng. Dial. Dict.*

**a.** Of women or girls.

**1725** RAMSAY *Gentle Sheph.* III. ii, I've twa sonsy lasses, young and fair. **1786** BURNS *Inventory* 54 My sonsie, smirking, dear-bought Bess. **1818** SCOTT *Hrt. Midl.* xxxix, Is she a pretty girl?.. her sister does not get beyond a good comely sonsy lass. **1865** *Cornh. Mag.* Mar. 298 A sonsy, blond-haired young Flemish maiden sat there. **1876** MRS. WHITNEY *Sights & Ins.* II. ii. 356 Mother and three daughters, all so fair and sonsy and merry together.

*transf.* **1830** GALT *Lawrie T.* VII. iv. (1849) 320 Her neck and all about her is of that sonsy comeliness which is most to the taste of a man of my age.

**b.** Of the face.

**1786** BURNS *Twa Dogs* 31 His honest, sonsie, baws'nt face Ay gat him friends in ilka place. **1855** [J. D. BURN] *Beggar Boy* (1859) 125 The amiability of his mind was happily reflected in his broad *soncy* face. **1863** TROLLOPE *Rachel Ray* I. 253, I love to look on a young fellow with a sonsy face.

**c.** Of things.

**1816** SCOTT *Antiq.* v, A weel-favoured, sonsy, decent periwig. **1870** *Gd. Words* Feb. 133/2 The men are dressed.. in a warm blouse and trousers of sonsy grey homespun. **1891** V. C. COTES *Two Girls on a Barge* 140 The long wide streets and the sonsy air of the place.

**3.** Of animals: Tractable, manageable.

**1786** BURNS *Auld Farmer's Salut. Mare* v, Ye ne'er was donsie; But hamely, tawie, quiet an' cannie, An' unco sonsie. **1808** JAMIESON s.v., *A sonsie horse*, one that is peaceable.

**sont** (sɒnt), *v. U.S.* Sometimes used to represent *sent* in the written form of Black speech.

**1890** *Dialect Notes* I. 71 *Sont*, sent. Used mainly by negroes. **1893** H. A. SHANDS *Some Peculiarities of Speech in Mississippi* 58 *Sont*.., Negro for *sent*. **1929** W. FAULKNER *Sound & Fury* 337, I sont dat boy up dar half hour ago. **1942** —— *Go down, Moses* 16 'What for?' he said. 'She just sont hit to you,' the nigger said. *Ibid.* 106 Ah went to yo house last night, but you want dar. She sont me.

**sont,** obs. form of SAINT.

**sont,** var. SUNT.

**sontag** (ˈsɒntæg, ‖ˈzɔntak). The name of Henriette *Sontag* (1806–54), German singer, used to designate a type of knitted or crocheted jacket or cape, with long ends which are crossed in front of the body and tied behind, worn by women in the second half of the 19th century.

**1862** *Harper's Mag.* Oct. 607/1 Constant relays of arrivals were successively denuding themselves of 'Clouds', 'Sontags', 'Mariposas', and other dainty feminine wraps. **1863** A. D. WHITNEY *Faith Gartney's Girlhood* xviii. 161 Faith brought quickly, sontag, jacket and cloak. **1900** E. A. DIX *Deacon Bradbury* 45 Did you hear what she said to Mrs Delane about that worsted sontag she brought?

**Sonthal, Sonthali,** varr. SANTAL[2], SANTALI.

**†ˈsontic,** *a. Obs.*$^{-0}$ (See quot.)

**1656** BLOUNT *Glossogr.*, *Sontick*, noysom, hurtful. *Ibid.*, The *Sontick disease*,.. a continual and extream sickness [etc., copying Cooper *Thes.* s.v. *Sonticus*].

**sonties:** see SANTY *Obs.*

**sony,** obs. Sc. variant of SUNNY *a.*

**†sonyie,** *sb. Sc. Obs.* Also 5–6 sonȝe, 6 sounȝie, sunȝie. [var. SOIGN *sb.*]

**1.** Excuse; plea.

**1438** *Bk. Alexander Grt.* (Bann. Club) 24 Quhan he sawe that na man wald ga, In the message bot sonȝe ma. *c* **1480** HENRYSON *Fables, Wolf & Fox* vii, All thy sonȝeis sall not auaill the. **1500–20** DUNBAR *Poems* lxxix. 3 My cumpt, I sall it mak ȝow cleir, But ony circumstance or sonȝie. *a* **1585** POLWART *Flyting w. Montgomerie* 796 Thou will hing but a sunȝie. *c* **1685** R. MACWARD *Contend.* (1723) 93 But I knew, your last sonzie and shift will be, that they admitted.. non-indulged to preach in the pulpits.

**2.** Hesitation; delay.

*c* **1470** HENRY *Wallace* II. 97 Bot for his tre litill sonȝhe he maid. **1500–20** DUNBAR *Poems* xxvi. 72 Mony slute daw and slepy duddroun, Him serwit ay with sounȝie.

**†sonyie,** *v. Sc. Obs.* In 5–6 sonȝe, 6 soinȝe, sounȝe, sonye, swnye, sunyie. [var. SOIGN *v.*] *intr.* To hesitate, delay, refuse. Also *refl.*

*c* **1470** HENRY *Wallace* III. 110 Than graithit thai thaim till harnes hastely, Thar sonȝeit nane of that gud chewalrye. *c* **1500** KENNEDIE *Passion of Christ* 1526 He sonȝeit him, or he wald forthir pas. **1508** DUNBAR *Poems* vii. 31 Withe us to liue,.. Quhilk never sall swnye for thy saik to bleid. **1536** BELLENDEN *Cron. Scot.* (1821) II. 242 Quhy sonye ye, maist vailyeant campionis? quhy pas ye nocht forthwart with gret spreit? **1573** *Satir. Poems Reform.* xxxix. 368 He soinȝeit not to ga him self and se.

**soo,** north. dial. and Sc. var. SOW *sb.* and *v.*

**soar,** obs. f. SOWAR.

**soobah:** see SUBAH.

**soobahdar, -dary,** variants of SUBAHDAR(Y.

**soocey:** see SOOSY.

**†sood**[1], ? irreg. variant of SOOT *sb.*[1]

*c* **1430** *Pol., Rel., & L. Poems* (1903) 211 Al suche sacrificis y forsake, For þei ben to me as sour as sood.

**†sood**[2], Anglicized form of SODA[2]. *Obs.*$^{-1}$

**1547** BOORDE *Brev. Health* lvii. 26 In the head may be many infirmities, as the Apoplexi,.. the Megrym, the Sood.

**sooder,** variant of SUDRA *Anglo-Ind.*

**ˈsoodle,** *v. dial.* [Of obscure origin.] *intr.* To walk in a slow or leisurely manner; to stroll, saunter.

**1821** CLARE *Vill. Minstr.* I. 19 To go so soodling up and down the street. *Ibid.* II. 93 While I as unconcern'd went soodling on. **1854–** in dial. (chiefly midland) glossaries.

Hence **ˈsoodling** *ppl. a.*, that flows or moves slowly; *poet. rare.* **ˈsoodly** *a.*, leisurely, slow; *dial.*

**1821** CLARE *Vill. Minstr.* II. 67 The horse-boy, with a soodly gait, Slow climbs the stile. **1951** AUDEN *Nones* (1952) 39 The baltering torrent Shrunk to a soodling thread.

**Soofee(ism:** see SUFI(ISM.

**soogan,** var. SUGGAN.

**soogee** (ˈsuːdʒiː). Also soogie, soujie, etc. = next.

**1944** *Time* 10 Jan. 4/3 A bucket of 'soujge'. **1945** *Seafarers' Log* 7 Sept. 4/4 The old soogee bucket and paint brush will be working plenty overtime. **1953** J. MASEFIELD *Conway* (rev. ed.) II. 124 The recipe for the liquid used to clean 'holy ground' was one handful of soft soap, one of 'soojie' (soap powder). **1963** M. LOWRY *Ultramarine* iv. 198 Steamflies.. are stealthily prowling over.. the limp bags of caustic soda and soogie.

So as *v. trans.*, to clean (wood and paintwork) with SOOGEE-MOOGEE; **soog(ie)ing** *vbl. sb.*

**1903** A. SONNICHSEN *Deep Sea Vagabonds* iii. 37 There was soodgee-moodgee. Soodgee is a sailor's horror; it means to wash paint-work with a strong solution of soda and water. **1945** *Seafarers' Log* 29 June 12 Soogieing, chipping, painting, etc., shall not be considered an emergency. **1947** *Ibid.* 14 Mar. 5/2 The messhalls were sougeed out, the gallery cleaned. **1950** R. BISSELL *Stretch on River* vii. 75, I was soogeing down the walls in his [*sc.* the captain's] cabin. **1963** M. LOWRY *Ultramarine* v. 217, I had to do a bit of soogeing in the petty officers' washhouse.

**soogee-moogee** (ˈsuːdʒiː,muːdʒiː). *Naut. slang.* Also soogie-moogie, soojee-moojee, souji-mouji, sugi-mugi, etc. and without hyphens. [Origin unknown.] **a.** A mixture containing caustic soda used for cleaning paintwork and woodwork on ships and boats. Also *attrib.*

**1882** D. KEMP *Yacht & Boat Sailing* (ed. 3) 579 *Soojee Moojee*, a caustic composition sold by yacht fitters for cleaning off old paint, varnish, &c. **1894** R. C. LESLIE *Waterbiography* xiii. 248 A certain caustic composition, known to yachtsmen by the mysterious name of 'skewgy-mewgy'. **1900** F. T. BULLEN *Men of Merchant Service* xiii. 120 No tramp second mate can hope to keep his hands out of the paint pot or the soogee-moogee bucket. **1903** [see SOOGEE *v.*]. **1907** M. ROBERTS *Flying Cloud* xxiv. 229 She was as clean as a new pin with sand and canvas and souji-mouji. **1913** A. W. NELSON *Yankee Swanson* 57 He had a good scrubbing down with 'sudje mudje'. **1924** P. BLUNDELL *Confessions of Seaman* xii. 164 With a bucket containing hot soap and soda water—sougi-mougi sailors call it—he ascended ladders in the swaying engine-room and washed paint work. **1934** J. HANLEY in *Spectator* 26 Jan. 131/1 'There are no sailors to-day,' says [Conrad], 'only Sugi-Mugi men'... Mere washers of paint. Deck-hands on modern ships wash and chip paint, morning, noon and night. **1938** W. E. DEXTER *Rope Yarns* 82 In all the sailing ships I was in I never came across a long-handled holystone, or caustic soda, or 'soogy-moogy'. **1939** H. HUGHES *Through Mighty Seas* ii. 36 All hands wallowed in *soogie moogie*. **1962** A. G. COURSE *Dict. Naut. Terms* 182 *Soogee moogee*, a liquid used for cleaning paintwork and woodwork consisting of soda and water or soap and water.

**b.** A cleaning operation which involves the use of soogee-moogee.

**1935** *Sea Breezes* Jan. 60 The equipment, particularly the sails, would be so perfect that my crew wouldn't mind the 'sooje-mooje' such perfection entailed. **1945** *Time* 31 Dec. 96/3 Soon Sailor Slobodkin.. found himself loading cargo, eating slop and doing soogie moogie (scrubbing paint work) with a crew.

**‖soojee** (ˈsuːdʒiː). Also sooji, soojy, -ie, s(o)ujee. [Hindī *sūjī*.] A flour obtained by grinding Indian wheat; a nutritious food prepared from this. **sooji halwa** [HALWA], a kind of dessert made with soojee.

**1810** T. WILLIAMSON *E. Ind. Vade-mecum* II. 136 *Soojy*, (the basis of the bread,) is frequently boiled into 'stir-about' for breakfast. **1843** PEREIRA *Food & Diet* 307 Semolina, Soujee, and Mannacroup, are granular preparations of wheat, deprived of bran. **1844–1853** [see SEMOLETTA]. **1858** SIMMONDS *Dict. Trade*, *Soojee*, Indian wheat, ground but not pulverized; a kind of semolino. **1955** R. P. JHABVALA *To whom she Will* xxi. 157 O she is such a clever girl, kheer she makes,.. and sooji halwa [etc.]. **1971** *Femina* (Bombay) 16 Apr. 57/2 *Sooji Halwa.* 220 gms. sooji (fine semolina); 60 gms. fat; 110 gms. sugar; 30 gms. peanuts; 2 gms. salt.

*attrib.* **1878** *Life in the Mofussil* I. 213 Sujee flour, ground coarse.

**sook**[1] (sʊk). *Austral.* and *N.Z. slang.* Also sookie. [perh. from Eng. dial. *suck*: see *Eng. Dial. Dict.* s.v. *suck* 19, a 'duffer', a stupid fellow.] A stupid or timid person; a coward; a 'softy'.

**1933** N. SCANLAN *Tides of Youth* xv. 155 He looked a big sookie and wouldn't say a word. **1941** BAKER *Dict. Austral. Slang* 69 *Sook*, a coward, a timid person. **1950** 'B. JAMES' *Advancement of Spencer Button* 9 If he nervously declares he can't fight, and shows that he doesn't want to fight, then he is a 'sook' or a 'sissy'. **1970** G. GREER *Female Eunuch* 79 She may be reviled as a cissy, a sook. **1970** P. WHITE *Vivisector* 11 He wasn't a sook. He could run, shout, play, fight, had scabs on his knees, and twice split Billy Abrams's lip, who was two years older. **1975** *Courier-Mail* (Brisbane) 2 Jan. 9/4 The tough specimen might appear as somewhat of a myth by fearing to be different from his mates in case they might think him a bit of a sook.

Hence **ˈsookey, sooky** *adjs.*, cowardly, 'soft', stupid.

**1953** D. CUSACK *Southern Steel* 328 Get along with you: you're getting real sookey. **1964** *Weekly News* (Auckland) 18 Mar. 58/3 The boys say they feel sooky wearing caps. **1970** *N.Z. Listener* 12 Oct. 13/5 Their attitude of tolerant resignation toward the sooky Maoris who are always getting into trouble.

**sook**[2] (suːk). *U.S.* [Origin unknown.] A mature female blue crab, *Callinectes sapidus*, of the eastern coast of the United States.

**1950** *Sun* (Baltimore) 10 Oct. 32/2 'Sooks' are female blue crabs. Their annual migration.. has been under way for a month. **1978** J. A. MICHENER *Chesapeake* 647 He [*sc.* a blue crab] forgot his own preoccupations in order to swim among the grasses, looking for sooks which had been by-passed in the earlier mating periods. These overlooked females, on their way south to spend the winter near the entrance of the bay, where fertile sooks traditionally prepared to lay their eggs, sent out frantic signals to whatever males might be in the vicinity, for this was the final period in which they could be fertilized.

**sook**, obs. or Sc. var. SUCK *sb.* and *v.*

**sook**, var. SOUK.

†**sooke**, obs. variant of SOKE[1].

**1716** M. DAVIES *Athen. Brit.* II. 72 His two tenements in the Sooke in the Town of Lynn in Norfolk.

**sool** (su:l), *v.* Chiefly *Austral.* and *N.Z.* [var. SOWL *v.*[3]] **1.** *trans.* Of a dog, to attack or worry; freq. in command *sool* (*him*, etc.) Also *absol.* and *transf.*

**1890** MRS. C. PRAED *Romance of Station* I. iv. 71 S'ool him, Bleuey! **1896** MRS. K. L. PARKER *Austral. Legendary Tales* 90 She went quickly towards her camp, calling softly, 'Birree gougou', which meant 'Sool 'em, sool 'em', and was the signal for the dogs to come out. **1904** 'S. RUDD' *Sandy's Selection* 60 'Sool 'im, sool 'im!' the girls were shouting, and the blind dog sooled in moderation. **1935** *Bulletin* (Sydney) 6 Feb. 21/2 A pair of these birds will sometimes 'sool' a hare. **1959** A. UPFIELD *Bony & Black Virgin* xv. 135 'Sool 'em, Bluey,' Bony pleaded, and the dog nosed about and finally went down under the scrub by a hole made by the foxes. **1960** B. CRUMP *Good Keen Man* 24 Another young dog would have been better encouragement than a man lumbering about trying to bark like a dog, and noisily skitching and sooling.

**2.** To urge or goad. Freq. with advbs., esp. *on*.

**1898** *Bulletin* (Sydney) 30 Apr. 31/4 The rest of the company came out and 'sooled' on the twelve [arguers]. It was a glorious scrimmage. **1898** E. E. MORRIS *Austral English* 426/2 Sool.., used colloquially—(1) to excite a dog or set him on. **1911** *Chambers's Jrnl.* Mar. 222/2 Don't 'sool' the dogs to an unwise assault. **1911** L. STONE *Jonah* 31 The Push gathered round, grinning from ear to ear, sooling the women on as if they were dogs. **1916** C. J. DENNIS *Moods of Ginger Mick* 39 The bugles East and West sooled on the dawgs o' war. **1921** E. O'FERRALL in Murdoch & Drake-Brockman *Austral. Short Stories* (1951) 158 Served him right if I sooled th' dog on him! **1942** G. CASEY *It's Harder for Girls* 52 'Sool the dogs offer him,' someone called out. **1960** B. CRUMP *Good Keen Man* 23, I ran over and sooled the dog after the trotting sow. **1963** B. PEARSON *Coal Flat* xii. 227 We'll get an Alsatian and sool it outa you. **1970** G. GREER *Female Eunuch* 190 The hero may.. like a lion-tamer sool her on to his enemies. **1977** C. MCCULLOUGH *Thorn Birds* iv. 80 Father Ralph worked like a man in the grip of some obsession, sooling the dogs after unsuspecting bands of sheep.

Hence '**sooler**, one who incites; an agitator.

**1935** H. R. WILLIAMS *Comrades of Great Adventure* 35 Here, as chief 'sooler', he was urging the passing soldiers to patronize the eating-house. **1938** X. HERBERT *Capricornia* viii. 98 Then a war-monger, or Sooler, as such people were called in the locality, made his voice heard in the land. **1963** —— *Disturbing Element* 141 She had been sending white feathers round... She had become what her former comrades of the I.W.W. called a Sooler.

**sool**, obs. f. SOLE *sb.*[1] and *a.*, SOUL *sb.*; dial. var. SOWEL; var. SOWL *v.*

**soold**, obs. pa. t. of SELL *v.*

**soole**, obs. f. SOLE *sb.*[1], etc.; dial. var. SOWEL.

**sooly**, obs. f. SOLELY *adv.*

†**sooly**, *a. Obs.*[−1] ? Close, sultry.

Perh. an error for *sooltry*, but cf. Du. *zoel*, †*soel*.

**1570** FOXE *A. & M.* (ed. 2) II. 1071/2 The soolye heat of y[e] prison, to me is coldnes: the colde wynter to me is a freshe spryng tyme in the Lord.

**soom**, north. and Sc. var. SWIM.

**soome**, obs. var. SUM.

**soom(n)ed**, obs. varr. SUMMED *ppl. a.*

**soon** (su:n), *adv.* Forms: (see below). [OE. *sóna*, = OS. *sâno*, *sâna*, commonly *sân* (MLG. *sân*), OFris. *sôn*, *sân*, OHG. (and MHG.) *sân*, MFlem. *saen* (WFlem. *zaen*, *zaan*); not represented in Scand., and now obs. in most of the Continental dialects.

As OE. *sóna* had the sense of 'at once, immediately', it did not readily admit of comparison, and no comparative or superlative forms are recorded. The appearance of these in early ME. is due to the more extended sense which the word had by that time acquired.]

A. Forms.

**1.** 1 **sona**, 2–6 (7 *Sc.*) **sone** (4 **zone**), 4–7 **soone**; 3–4 **son**, 5 **sonne**; 5– **soon** (9 *dial.* **suon**, **sooin**, **zoon**).

[For illustration see senses 1–9.]

**2.** *north.* and *Sc.* *α.* 4–5 **soyn**, 4–5, 8 **soyne**, 6 **shoin**.

**13..** *Cursor M.* 16762 + 20 (Cott.), He..sayd þis word ful soyn. *Ibid.* 17288 + 82 þe thrid day after soyne. **1434** MISYN *Mending Life* 124 [It] soyne is cast bak. **1489** *Barbour's Bruce* IV. 367 In-to Kentyre soyn cumin ar thai. **1572** *Mem.* in *Buccleuch MSS.* (Hist. MSS. Comm.) I. 23 How shoin perceaved [etc.]. *c* **1746** J. COLLIER (Tim Bobbin) *View Lanc. Dial.* (1860) 3 So soyne this Morning.

*β.* 4 **sun**, 4, 8– **sune**, 5 **swne**, 6 **suin**, 9 **suen**, **seun**.

**13..** *Cursor M.* 987 (Cott.), þai brak þe forbot als sun. *Ibid.* 1388 Seth..sune com til his fader again. *c* **1470** HENRY *Wallace* v. 1090 Thai sall swne tyne ma. **1596** DALRYMPLE tr. *Leslie's Hist. Scot.* II. 416 How suin he [it]..ressauet had. **1792** BURNS '*I do confess thou art sae fair*' 15 Yet sune thou shalt be thrown aside. **1832** W. STEPHENSON *Gateshead Local Poems* 100 This..pair Will suen myek ye knock under. **1894** R. REID *Kirkbride* i, This..body maun sune be dust.

*γ.* 5 **soune**, **sovne**, 6 **soun**, **sown**, **schowne**.

**14..** *Sc. Leg. Saints* xii. (*Matthias*) 228 þat sovne þu ga. *Ibid.* xl. (*Ninian*) 1198 Furth on sown can he fare. **1489** *Barbour's Bruce* I. 566 The endentur..soune schawyt the iniquite. *a* **1578** LINDESAY (Pitscottie) *Chron. Scot.* (S.T.S.) I. 8 Schowne thair fell ane gret varience.

*δ.* 7 **seaun**, 8 **sean**, 9 **seean**, **seen**.

**1684** *Yorks. Dial.* 3 (E.D.S.), Seaun, seaun,..bring my Skeel. **1790** MRS. WHEELER *Westmld. Dial.* 86 Awr Courtship wod sean hae been at an end. **1871** W. ALEXANDER *Johnny Gibb* xxi. 159 They'll seen get their sairin' o' him an's mither tee. **1876** ROBINSON *Whitby Gloss.* 165/1 It may as weel come seean as syne.

**3.** *Compar.* 3 **sonre**, 4 **sonnere**, 4–5 **sonner** (5 **sonder**, **sonnare**); 4 **sennere**, 5 **sannere**, **-ur**, **-yr** (see also SANDER *adv.*); 4 **sun(n)ere**, 4–5 **sunner**, 5 **sunnar**, 6 *Sc.* **schunar**, **suiner**, 8– *Sc.* **suner**; 4 **sonir**, **-ere**, 4–6 **soner**, 5 **sonare**, **-yre**, 6 **sonar**, **-yr**; 6 **soonner**, 6– **sooner**.

[For illustration see senses 10–13. The form *souner(e* which appears in some of the quotations should prob. be *sonner(e*.]

**4.** *Superl.* 3 **sonest**, 5 **-yst**, 6 **-ast**; 4 **sennest**, **sannest**, **sunnest**, 4–5 **sonnest**; 6– **soonest**.

[For illustration see senses 14–16.]

B. Signification.

**I. 1.** Within a short time (after a particular point of time specified or implied), before long, quickly; †(in early use) without delay, forthwith, straightway: **a.** With reference to a definite past or future time.

*c* **825** *Vesp. Psalter* lxix. 4 Sien forcerred sona [L. *statim*] & scomiende. *c* **897** K. ÆLFRED tr. *Gregory's Past. C.* 196 Ac he him sona ondwyrde, & him swiðe stiernlice stierde. **971** *Blickl. Hom.* 15 He þa sona instæpes ᵹeseh, & þa sona wæs Drihtne fylᵹende. *c* **1030** *Rule St. Benet* (Logeman) 40 þane þonne onginð, sona [L. *mox*] ealle mid arwurðnessa arison. **1154** *O.E. Chron.* (Laud MS.) an. 1135, Agenes him risen sona þa ricemen þe wæron swikes. *c* **1250** *Gen. & Ex.* 1221 Abraham rapede him sone in sped for to fulfillen godes reed. *a* **1300** *Cursor M.* 2995 He did to cal habraham son, And said, 'qui has þou þusgat don?' **1340** *Ayenb.* 173 Efterward þe dyaþ..him ssel sterie zone him to ssrive. **1362** LANGL. *P. Pl.* A. III. 48 þenne he asoylede hire soone, and siþ to hire seide [etc.]. *c* **1400** tr. *Secreta Secret., Gov. Lordsh.* 57 Alexander, coueyte noght þinges coruptibles..þat þou most sone forsake. *c* **1475** *Rauf Coilȝear* 142 Sone was the Supper dicht, and the fyre bet. **1513** MORE *Edw. V* (1641) 8 Whose life he looked that ill dyet would soone shorten. **1567** *Satir. Poems Reform.* viii. 31 Cum, sweir þe saikles sone. **1665** SIR T. HERBERT *Trav.* (1677) 176 We found..that the King's good will became soon diverted. **1697** DRYDEN *Virg. Georg.* IV. 776 The soft Napæan Race will soon repent Their Anger. **1766** GOLDSM. *Vicar* iii, The day soon arrived on which we were to disperse. **1796** H. HUNTER tr. *St.-Pierre's Stud. Nat.* (1799) II. 552 We shall soon have..the exhibition of a museum at the Tuilleries. **1831** SCOTT *Ct. Rob.* xxxii, With ..eyes dimmed by the powerful idea of soon parting with the light of day. **1841** *Penny Cycl.* XXI. 173/1 The rout soon became general. **1875** JOWETT *Plato* (ed. 2) I. 495 The voice of fate calls. Soon I must drink the poison.

**b.** In general statements, in which the time reckoned from is indefinite.

*c* **825** *Vesp. Psalter* xxxvi. 20 Feond..dryhtnes sona [L. *mox*] ᵹearade & upahefene biað. **971** *Blickl. Hom.* 21 Ne he hine na ne onstyreþ, syþþan seo unᵹesynelice sawl him of biþ; ac sona he molsnaþ. *a* **1200** *Vices & Virt.* 99 ȝif hie cumeð fram dieule, prudencia hes icnauð sone. *a* **1275** *Prov. Ælfred* 630 in *O.E. Misc.* 136 Buch þe from þi sete, & bide him sone þer-to. *c* **1300** *Havelok* 78 Wo so dede hem wrong or lath,..He dede hem sone to hauen ricth. **1390** GOWER *Conf.* I. 109 So that it proeveth wel therfore, The strengthe of man is sone lore. **1445** in *Anglia* XXVIII. 271 Wherfore thou preventist tyme, and soon thi bowntee shewist. **1450–80** tr. *Secreta Secret.* iv. 7 His Rewme may not stonde longe in prosperite but sone come to distruccioun. **1538** STARKEY *England* I. ii. 47 The body, yf hyt be not strong, sone..ys oppressyd & ouerthrowne. **1593** SHAKS. *Lucr.* 647 Small lights are soon blown out, huge fires abide. **1633** P. FLETCHER *Purple Isl.* IV. xxxii, Fitting his operation, For swallowing soon to fall, and rise for inspiration. **1774** GOLDSM. *Nat. Hist.* (1776) V. 286 This species soon takes to build in artificial cavities. **1812** *New Botanic Gard.* I. 44 They very soon take root. **1855** *Orr's Circ. Sci., Geol.*, etc. 240 This gas..soon mixes with the air around.

*Prov.* **1530** PALSGR. 885/1 Sone hotte sone colde. **1546–** [see RIPE *a.* 1 c]. *c* **1580** JEFFERIE *Bugbears* IV. v. 58 Lyttle sayd, sone amended. **1670** RAY *Prov.* 285 Little said, soon mendit. **1861** MAYHEW *Lond. Lab.* III. 391 Soon got, soon gone.

†**c.** *till soon*, for a short time. *Obs.*

**1526** SKELTON *Magnyf.* 322 Fare you well tyll sone. **1533** J. HEYWOOD *Pardoner & Frere* Plays (1905) 17 Canst not tarry and abide till soon, And read them then when preaching is done? **1592** KYD *Sp. Trag.* IV. i. 192 Farewell till soone.

**2. a.** Followed by *after* (adv.) or *afterwards* (†also *eft*, *efter*, *thereafter*, *sithen*).

In OE. also *eft(er) sóna*: see EFTER-, EFTSOON(S.

*c* **900** *O.E. Chron.* an. 797 (Parker MS.), And þa sona eft ..he meahte ᵹeseon & sprecan. *c* **950** *Lindisf. Gosp.* Mark xiv. 72 And sona efter se hona ᵹesang. *a* **1122** *O.E. Chron.* an. 1101, And þa sona þæræfter wurdon þa heafodmen.. wiðer-ræden toᵹeanes þam cynge. *c* **1200** ORMIN 7256 And sone siþþenn sennde he forþ þatt Kalldewisshe genge. **1297** R. GLOUC. (Rolls) 8277 ȝut sone þer after an oþer com al so. *c* **1340** HAMPOLE *Pr. Consc.* 68 Als yhe sal here aftirward sone. *c* **1450** *Myrr. our Ladye* 30 They shulde..often fynde themselfe better at ease sone after. *c* **1450** *Brut* ccxlii. 359 Sone aftirward riȝt þere he made his ende. **1577** HARRISON *Descr. Brit.* I. xi, Soone after also it taketh in a rillet called the Bure. *a* **1700** EVELYN *Diary* 21 Oct. 1632, I was soone afterwards sent for into Surrey. **1796** MME. D'ARBLAY *Camilla* I. 182 Soon after, Lionel, galloping across the park, hastily dismounted. **1845** NICOLAS *Mem. Chaucer* in *C.'s Wks.* I. 32 Soon after, he was twice paid 40s...for his half yearly Robes. **1875** *Encycl. Brit.* III. 305/1 Soon afterwards a direct charge of plagiarism was made against Balzac.

**b.** Followed by *after* (prep.) with simple object or clause.

*c* **950** *Lindisf. Gosp.* Matt. xxiv. 29 Sona..æfter costunge daᵹana ðara. *a* **1000** *Cædmon's Satan* 630 Sona æfter þæm wordum. *c* **1200** ORMIN 3332 Sone anan affterr þatt he Wass borenn þær to manne. *c* **1400** *Rom. Rose* 3777 Aftir the calme the trouble soune Mote folowe. *c* **1500** *Melusine* v. (1890) 27 And soone aftir that he had kyssed hym, he..lepe vpon his hors. **1590** SPENSER *F.Q.* II. x. 66 Soone after which, three hundred Lordes he slew Of British bloud. **1779** *Mirror* No. 65, Soon after he returned to his native country, he married Lady C——. **1837** LOCKHART *Scott* I. viii. 247 The young kinsman was introduced to her soon after her arrival at Mertoun. **1879** R. MORRIS *Chaucer's Prol.*, etc. (ed. 6) p. xii, Perhaps now, or perhaps soon after the loss of his office.

**3. a.** Early, betimes; before the time specified or referred to is much advanced.

*a* **1300** *Cursor M.* 3045 Sun on þe morn, quen it was dai. ? *a* **1366** CHAUCER *Rom. Rose* 23, I went soon To bedde. *c* **1385** —— *L.G.W.* 1637 *Hypsipyle*, To come sone at nyght Vn-to hire chambir. **1598** SHAKS. *Merry W.* I. iv. 8 We'll haue a posset for 't soone at night. **1616** B. JONSON *Devil an Ass* I. i, As you make your soone at nights relation. **1697** tr. *Trav. C'tess D'Anois* (1706) 45, I rose in effect very soon next Morning. *c* **1746** [see A. 2 *a*]. **1807** WORDSW. '*The world is too much with us*' 1 Late and soon, Getting and spending, we lay waste our powers. **1859** BARTLETT *Dict. Amer.* (ed. 2) 428 *Soon*, at the South this word is frequently used by all classes as a substitute for early... 'I shall be there soon in the evening.'

†**b.** Early in the evening. *Obs.*

Prob. by ellipse for *soon at night*: see prec.

**1619** A. GIL *Logon. Angl.* (1621) 34 *Quikli* citò, *süner*.. citius, *sünest*..citissimè; nam *sün* hodie apud plurimos significat *ad primam vesperam*, olim *citò*. **1674** RAY *N.C. Words* 44 *Soon*, the Evening: *a soon*, at Even. [Hence in later glossaries.]

**c.** At an early stage, date, period, etc.

**1615** W. LAWSON *Country Housew. Gard.* (1626) 37 Soone crookes the tree that good Camrell must bee. **1664** PEPYS *Diary* 31 Aug., My wife has got me some pretty good oysters, which is very soon and the soonest, I think, I ever eat any. **1771** LUCKOMBE *Hist. Printing* 125 The Abby of St. Albans had printing there very soon. **1876** GLADSTONE *Glean.* (1879) II. 300 For his own eye, the ornaments of his Essay on Milton were so soon as in 1843 gaudy and ungraceful.

**4.** In various phrases denoting 'At the very time or moment when, whenever': †**a.** *soon so.* Also with *sum*, and ellipt. without connecting particle.

The reduced forms *son se*, *sons*, occur in the Ormulum. In OE. *sóna þæs* (*þe*) is also found.

(*a*) *c* **897** K. ÆLFRED tr. *Gregory's Past. C.* 431 Sona swa ic anwoc, swa wilnode ic eft wines. **971** *Blickl. Hom.* 37 Sona swa þu ᵹeseo nacodne wædlan, þonne ᵹeᵹyre þu hine. *a* **1122** *O.E. Chron.* an. 1100, Sona swa se eorl Rotbert into Normandiᵹ com. *c* **1200** ORMIN 6450 Sone swa þatt steorrne stod þa kingess wel itt sæȝhenn. *a* **1225** *Leg. Kath.* 476 Sone se ich seh þe leome of þe soðe lare. **1297** R. GLOUC. (Rolls) 5897 He baptised þis aeldred sone so he was ybore. **1377** LANGL. *P. Pl.* B. x. 226 Was neuere gome..Fairer vnderfongen..þan my-self sothly sone so he wist.

(*b*) *c* **1200** ORMIN 821 Sone summ he cuþe ben Himm ane bi himm sellfenn. **13..** *Cursor M.* 11015 (Gött.), Sone sum vr leuedi was mett wid þe angel.

(*c*) *c* **1250** *Gen. & Ex.* 329 Sone ȝe it ðor-of hauen eten, Al ȝe it sulen witent. *c* **1300** *Havelok* 1354 Sone it was day, sone he him cladde.

†**b.** *so soon so.* *Obs.*

*c* **1175** *Lamb. Hom.* 53 Swa sone se hi beoð iturnd awey from heom? *c* **1250** *Owl & Night.* 518 So sone so þu sittest abrode, þu forleost al þine wise. **13..** *Guy Warw.* (A.) 4173 Amorwe, so sone so it was day. **1377** LANGL. *P. Pl.* B. XVII. 63 So sone so þe samaritan hadde siȝte of þis lede.

**c.** *as soon as.* (Now the ordinary use.) Also †*as soon so.*

From the end of the 15th to the middle of the 18th cent. the *as* and *soon* were commonly written together (*assone*, *assoone*, *asoone*, *assoon*). In ME. *alson(e) as* also occurs: see ALSOON *adv.* I.

*c* **1290** *S. Eng. Leg.* I. 225 As sone as we were ymaked, oure maister was so prout. **1393** LANGL. *P. Pl.* C. xx. 63 Ac as sone so þe samaritan hadde sighte of þat syke, He alyghte a-non. *a* **1400** *Theophilus* xxxi, As sone as he herde of þat tiding, He rapede hym wel swithe. **1445** in *Anglia* XXVIII. 277 Thei wrey thin enemyes to þe as sone as þei the see banke touche. **1484** CAXTON *Fables of Æsop* II. xvii, Assone as the wynter shalle come thow shalt deye. **1548** UDALL, etc. *Erasm. Par. Mark* i. (1552) 121 Assone as Jesus was aduertised thereof. **1577** GOOGE tr. *Heresbach's Husb.* §41 As soone as your Rape seede is of,..you may sowe..Branke as they call it. **1607** HIERON *Wks.* I. 259 Andrew, who assoone as hee had found Christ, went to call Peter. **1642** D. ROGERS *Naaman* 90 Asoone as they feele their need. **1654–66** EARL ORRERY *Parthen.* (1676) 629 As soon as ever I understood.. I made him humble retributions. **1710** PRIDEAUX *Orig. Tithes* v. 282 This Law..fell into disuse assoon as made. **1764** T. HUTCHINSON *Hist. Mass.* I. (1765) 58 Assoon as they knew the terms. **1794** MRS. RADCLIFFE *Myst. Udolpho* xxviii, 'Madame Montoni is now dying, sir,' said Emily, as soon as she saw him. **1861** M. PATTISON *Ess.* (1889) I. 42 As soon as the French trade was again opened.

**d.** *so soon as.* In early use sometimes †*al so*, *also soon as.*

*c* **1330** *Assump. Virg.* (B.M. MS.) 157 So sone as sche hadde doun, Newe cloþes sche dide hure apoun. *c* **1380** WYCLIF *Wks.* (1880) 43 þe same freris ben holden to renne to hem also sone as þei may. **1465** *Paston Lett.* I. 132 Al so sone as I come to the Blakheth, the capteyn made the comens to take me. **1560** DAUS tr. *Sleidane's Comm.* 166 b, The Frenche kyng, so sone as he heard therof, kepte a solempne funerall. **1588** PARKE tr. *Mendoza's Hist. China* 359 So soone as their inditement was read, and iudgement giuen. **1637** *3rd Rep. Hist. MSS. Comm.* 75/1 The Dunkirkers, so soon as they made out what I was, took in their flag. **1700** Tyrrell *Hist. Eng.* II. 823 So soon as the Death of King John was..known. **1751** R. Paltock *P. Wilkins* (1884) II. 243 So soon as he was without the territory of the palace. **1818** Colebrooke *Obligations* 14 The article..is sold so soon as the parties have consented. **1882** J. H. Blunt *Ref. Ch. Eng.* II. 8 So soon as the formal consent of Edward had been obtained.

**e.** ***soon as.*** Now *poet., dial.,* and *colloq.*

*c* **1375** *Cursor M.* 8167 (Fairf.), Sone as he þe king had knawen, welcome he saide. **1640** Habington *Edw. IV*, 24 She was repulst by the inhabitants soone as she landed. **1658** Dryden *Cromwell* vii, Nor was his Vertue poison'd, soon as born. **1746** Francis tr. *Horace, Epist.* I. xix. 13 Soon as I spoke, our rival Bards engage. **1801** *Lusignan* II. 85 [She] had hitherto communicated every thought soon as it had birth. **1885–94** R. Bridges *Eros & Psyche* Aug. xxx, The which she knew, soon as she heard the name. **1907** W. P. Ridge *Name of Garland* ii. 33 Get out of my kitchen soon as you can. **1930** J. B. Priestley *Angel Pavement* ii. 91 We want another man for London and district, soon as we can get one. **1930** W. Faulkner *As I lay Dying* 58, I done put supper on and I'll be there soon as I milk. **1940** —— *Hamlet* I. ii. 26 Jody came in last night. I knowed it soon as I saw him.

**f.** ***how soon (as).*** *Sc. Obs.*

**1557** *Peebles Burgh Rec.* (1872) 236 To be deliuerit.. quhowsone he be requirit thairto. **1563** Winȝet *Wks.* (S.T.S.) I. 124 Quhow sone as a sinnar is resauit..to mercy. **1596** Dalrymple tr. *Leslie's Hist. Scot.* I. 25 Bot how sone thay begin to bigg thair nestis, the grettest gun..will nocht scar thame. **1754** [see how *adv.* 14 b].

**5. a.** ***so soon,*** so quickly, so early. Also followed by *as*.

(*a*) *c* **1320** *Sir Tristr.* 86 Þurch min hert..Ywounded haþ he me So sone. **1382** Wyclif *Gal.* i. 6, I wondre, that thus so soone ȝe ben born ouer fro him. **1535** Coverdale *Exod.* ii. 18 How came ye so soone to daie? **1610** Shaks. *Temp.* II. i. 191 What, all so soone asleepe? **1664** Butler *Hud.* II. iii. 1131 Which way came I Through so immense a space so soon? **1772** *Hist. Rochester* 27 Too large a work to be compleated so soon. **1828** Lytton *Pelham* III. iii, If you are going so soon, honour me by accepting my arm.

(*b*) **1671** Milton *P.R.* IV. 332 Where so soon As in our native Language can I find That solace?

†**b.** ***not so soon...(that)*** or ***but (that),*** = no sooner...than (see 13 b). *Obs.*

**1390** Gower *Conf.* I. 171 This word was noght so sone spoke, That his on yhe anon was loke. *c* **1477** Caxton *Jason* 71 b, Appollo had not so sone finysshid these wordes but that alle they..cryed [etc.]. **1549** Cheke *Hurt Sedit.* (1641) 60 The husbandman had not so soone throwne seed in his ground, but steppeth up the enimy. **1585** T. Washington tr. *Nicholay's Voy.* I. vii, Wee were not so soone on land, the knight..did instantly request me [etc.]. *Ibid.* xx, They were not so soone issued, but were cleane spoyled..of the enimies. **1605** Camden *Rem.* (1623) 217 But hee had not so soone spoken the word, but the surging waue dashed him.

**6. a.** Preceded by *over* or *too*.

*c* **1400** *Rom. Rose* 3842 For Shame to longe hath be thee froo; Over soone she was agoo. *c* **1513** Skelton *Agst. Scottes* 130 Vnto the castell of Norram..to sone ye came. **1599** Shaks., etc. *Pass. Pilgr.* 134 Fair creature, kill'd too soon by death's sharp sting! **1617** Sir W. Mure *Misc. Poems* xviii. Wks. (S.T.S.) I. 38 Too sone, (alace!)..Thy pairt is acted on this wordlie stage. **1720** De Foe *Capt. Singleton* i. (1840) 3 This fell out something too soon. **1821** Shelley *Adonais* xxvii, Why didst thou leave the trodden paths of men Too soon? **1870** E. Peacock *Ralf Skirl.* II. 205 It was not a moment too soon. **1902** Skeat *Havelok* p. xvii, A curious instance of *anticipation*, i.e. the too soon writing down of a coming letter.

**b.** Followed by *enough*.

**1545** Ascham *Toxoph.* II. (Arb.) 114 Not layinge before theyr eyes, thys wyse prouerbe: Sone ynough, if wel ynough. **1685** *Gracian's Courtier's Orac.* 56 Soon enough, if well enough, said a Wise Man. **1784** Cowper *Task* II. 622 A man o' th' town dines late, but soon enough, With reasonable forecast and dispatch T' ensure a side-box station at half price.

**7. a.** ***as soon (as),*** as quickly, as early (as).

*a* **1548** Hall *Chron., Edw. IV*, E j b, He and his folowed so quickly after, that they were almost at ye gates as sone as the Ambassadors. **1594** Davies *Orchestra* xli, The Moon..ends her Pavin thirteen times as soon as doth her brother. **1634** Milton *Comus* 1016 From thence [I] can soar as soon To the corners of the Moon. **1667** —— *P.L.* IV. 464, I soon returnd;..it returnd as soon with answering looks. **1691** Norris *Pract. Disc.* 81 But alas, the Mystery of Iniquity began to work assoon as the Mystery of Godliness.

†**b.** ***as soon,*** at once, forthwith. *Obs.* (Cf. alsoon *adv.* 2.)

**1585** Jas. I *Ess. Poesie* (Arb.) 23 He stays assone, and in his mynde doeth cast What way to take.

†**c.** ***as soon..., as soon,*** at one time..., at another; now..., again. *Obs.*

**1581** Pettie tr. *Guazzo's Civ. Conv.* II. (1586) 78 b, As soone with Gentlemen, as soone with the baser sorte, now and then with Princes, now and then with priuate persons. **1647** Trapp *Marrow Gd. Authors* in *Comm. Ep.* 715 Erasmus..was as soon with Protestants, and as soon with Papists, and so was well thought of on neither side.

**8.** ***as soon (as)*: a.** As readily; as willingly. Also *so soon as, just as soon; as soon as look at you*: see look *v.* 1 a.

**1590** Shaks. *Mids. N.* III. ii. 52 Ile beleeue as soone This whole earth may be bord. **1601** —— *Jul. C.* I. ii. 201 Yet.. I do not know the man I should auoyd So soone as that spare Cassius. **1702** Vanbrugh *False Friend* II. i, I'd as soon undertake to keep Portocarero honest. **1775** Sheridan *St. Patr. Day* II. iv, I had as soon recover, notwithstanding. **1777** —— *Sch. Scand.* I. i, For he'll abuse a stranger just as soon as his best friend. **1816** Whewell in Mrs. S. Douglas *Life* (1881) 22, I had as soon be beaten by him as by anybody else. **1825** Scott *Talism.* x, They would march under the banner of Satan as soon. **1913** W. B. Yeats *Hour-Glass* in *Mask* V. 328 I'd as soon listen to dried peas in a bladder as listen to your thoughts. **1930** A. P. Herbert *Water Gipsies* xvii. 254 I'd as soon have stone-ginger any day. **1966** D. Francis *Flying Finish* x. 133 He waved me to join him, which I would just as soon not have done. **1974** C. Hampton *Savages* (1976) vii. 45 Because Chico well He'd cut your head off soon as say good morning. **1974** M. Hebden *Pride of Dolphins* I. iii. 34 I'd just as soon you dropped me..and let me make my own way home.

**b.** With as much reason or probability.

**1591** Shaks. *Two Gentl.* II. vii. 19 Thou wouldst as soone goe kindle fire with snow As seeke to quench the fire of Loue with words. **1670** Eachard *Cont. Clergy* 86 They may assoon expect..consolation from him that lies rack'd with the gout.., as from a divine thus broken..in his fortunes. **1815** Shelley *Alastor* 509 Measureless ocean may declare as soon..as the universe Tell [etc.].

**c.** Used to suggest denial of a statement.

**1590** Shaks. *Com. Err.* IV. i. 98 *Ant. E.* I sent thee for a rope... *Dro. S.* You sent me for a ropes end as soone.

**9.** *Comb.* With ppl. adjs. (and pples.), as ***soon-arriving, -believing, -coming, -descending, -drying,*** etc.; ***soon-choked, -clad, -come, -contented, -dropped, -finished, -forgotten,*** etc. With infin., as ***soon-to-be.***

**a.** **1581** Sidney *Apol. Poetrie* (Arb.) 34 The soone repenting pride of Agamemnon. **1592** Shaks. *Rom. & Jul.* v. i. 60 A dram of poyson, such soone speeding geare. **1593** —— *Rich. II*, I. i. 101 His soone beleeuing aduersaries. **1616** Drumm. of Hawth. *Poems, Thirsis in Dispraise of Beauty* i, Soone-fading Beautie, which of Hues doth rise. **1617** Hieron *Wks.* II. 192 These shallow and soone-drying streames of outward ioy. **1726–46** Thomson *Winter* 50 The sun.., soon-descending, to the long dark night..the prostrate world resigns. **1886** E. G. White *Historical Sketches* 164/2 The end so near, the warning of a soon-coming Judgment yet to be given to all nations, tongues, and peoples. **1930** Auden *Poems* 17 Hear something of that soon-arriving day.

**b.** *c* **1611** Chapman *Iliad* II. 590 These soon-monied wares We drave into Neleius' town. **1611** Cotgr. s.v *Coupe-queuë*, Two short, and soone-done-words. *Ibid.*, *Messe de chasseur*, a short, or soone-said Masse. **1727–46** Thomson *Summer* 63 Rous'd by the cock, the soon clad shepherd leaves His mossy cottage. **1768–74** Tucker *Lt. Nat.* (1834) II. 103 That unaspiring humility, that soon-contented moderation. **1852** M. Arnold *Absence* 10 Each day brings its petty dust Our soon-chok'd souls to fill. **1866** Howells *Venetian Life* xvi. 257 Soon-sated curiosity slides willingly away. **1901** G. B. Shaw *3 Plays for Puritans* p. xviii, An hour's soon-forgotten fuss. **1902** W. B. Yeats *Where there is Nothing* (1903) II. 44 Not the fighting of men in red coats, that formal, soon finished fighting, but the endless battle, the endless battle. **1925** Blunden *Eng. Poems* 18 And hyacinth-eyes beneath soon-dropt lids. *Ibid.* 36 That now, this soon-come spring, goes slow and sere.

**c.** **1961** *Daily Tel.* 30 Aug. 10/2 He wants to appear in Belgrade at the neutralists' conference as the leader at least of a soon-to-be apparently united country. **1975** *Publishers Weekly* 10 Nov. 51/3 Often the dying are 'released' by the knowledge of their soon-to-be end.

**II.** In the comparative form *sooner*.

**10. a.** Within a shorter time; more quickly; with less delay; at an earlier time or date.

*a* **1225** *Ancr. R.* 266 Þreateð þet ȝe wulleð ȝelden up þene castel bute ȝif he sende ou þe sonre help. ? *a* **1366** Chaucer *Rom. Rose* 969 For he may sonner have gladnesse, Hir langour ought to be the lesse. **1382** Wyclif *Isaiah* lviii. 8 Thin helthe sunnere shal springe. **1432** *Rolls of Parlt.* IV. 405/2 In cas that covenable remedie ne be not sunner purveyde. **1587** Q. Elizabeth in Scoones *Four C. Eng. Lett.* (1880) 31 Excuse my not writing sonar. **1678** Cudworth *Intell. Syst.* I. v. 887 The Question, Why the World..was no sooner, but so lately made? **1686** W. Hopkins tr. *Ratramnus* Diss. i. (1688) 20 Written by him, as some guess, about the Year 850, or perhaps sooner. **1780** *Mirror* No. 105, Sometimes it returns a little sooner by royal proclamation. **1818** Cruise *Digest* (ed. 2) I. 481 Sometimes it is to be done sooner, sometimes later. **1886** C. E. Pascoe *Lond. of To-day* xxx. (ed. 3) 271 The House..sits till six, if the 'Orders of the Day' are not sooner disposed of.

**b.** Followed by *than*.

*c* **1290** *S. Eng. Leg.* I. 240 Wel sonere..hom huy come þane huy outward wende. **1362** Langl. *P. Pl.* A. xi. 274 Sonnere hadde he saluacion þanne seint Ion þe baptist. **1382** Wyclif *John* xx. 4 Thilke other disciple ran bifore sunner than Petre. *c* **1450** *Merlin* 43 Yef I wolde, I sholde fynde hym moche sonner than ye. *c* **1489** Caxton *Sonnes of Aymon* xvii. 396 Charlemagn seketh his dommage; and he shall have it soner than he weneth. **1566** Painter *Pal. Pleas.* I. 47 You went soner awaye then love coulde have time to fasten uppon you. **1581** Pettie tr. *Guazzo's Civ. Conv.* III. (1586) 175 b, I pray you come sooner then you did to daie. ? *a* **1639** Carew *Perswasion to Love* Poems (1651) 3 Tis sooner past, tis sooner done Than Summers rain, or Winters Sun. **1718** *Entertainer* No. 40. 275 Judgment may overtake him sooner than he thinks for. **1880** Geikie *Phys. Geog.* ii. 61 Land gets sooner heated by the sun's rays than the sea.

**c.** ***sooner or later,*** at some time or other.

Usu. with reference to the future, and implying the certain happening of the event referred to.

**1577** B. Googe *Heresbach's Husb.* I. (1586) 44 b, The stones, stickes, and suche baggage..are to be throwen out sooner or later. **1660–67** [see later *adv.*]. **1712** Addison *Spect.* No. 289 ⁋4 The dying Man is one whom, sooner or later, we shall certainly resemble. **1797–1805** S. & Ht. Lee *Canterb. T.* II. 427 To keep up..a correspondence in Italy, would sooner or later betray them. **1818** Scott *Hrt. Midl.* li, I have observed, that, sooner or later, they come to an evil end.

**11. a.** More readily or easily. Chiefly with *than*.

(*a*) *a* **1225** *Ancr. R.* 58 Al ȝet þat falleð to hire,..þurh hwat muhte sonre ful luue of aquiken. **1603** Shaks. *Meas. for M.* v. i. 277, I thinke, if you handled her priuately She would sooner confesse. **1606** —— *Tr. & Cr.* II. i. 17, I shal sooner rayle thee into wit and holinesse. **1664** J. Wilson *A. Commenius* I. i, You may sooner hold An angry Lyon, with a clew of thread. **1842** Lover *Handy Andy* ix, If you had a child.., no one should have the majority sooner.

(*b*) **1303** R. Brunne *Handl. Synne* 789 Sunner he takyth for here veniaunce þan for any oþer chaunce. *c* **1380** Wyclif *Contr. Tracts* Sel. Wks. III. 291 Ȝif þei weren opyn trewe men..þei schulden sunere gete pursuyng..þan fatte benefices. *a* **1548** Hall *Chron., Edw. IV*, I v, He thought the Sunne would soner haue fallen from his circle, then that kyng Lewes..would haue dissimuled. **1553** T. Wilson *Rhet.* (1580) 202 Sir Thomas More..can soner bee remembred of me, then worthely praised of any. **1634** Milton *Comus* 323 Courtesie, Which oft is sooner found in lowly sheds.., then in tapstry Halls. **1678** Moxon *Mech. Exerc.* v. §25. 92 Stuff which may be sooner Hewn than Sawn. **1817** Shelley *Lines to Critic* iii, Thy love will move that bigot cold Sooner than me, thy hate.

**b.** More readily as a matter of choice; preferably, rather. Phr. ***(I'd) sooner (it should be) you than me,*** and varr. cf. rather *adv.* 9 f.

**1457** Hardyng *Chron.* i. in *Eng. Hist. Rev.* Oct. (1912) 743 Your Fadir..souner wolde suche thre as Gedyngton Hafe youe [= given] than so forgone that euydence. **1474** Caxton *Chesse* IV. viii. (1883) 184 Certes thou oughtest sonner wille to dye..than [etc.]. **1699** T. Brown in R. L'Estrange *Erasm. Colloq.* (1725) 333, I would sooner swop her to a Tobacco plantation. **1749** Fielding *Tom Jones* II. iii, I would sooner starve than take any reward for betraying your Ladyship. **1801** Eliz. Helme *St. Marg. Cave* I. 236, I would sooner bear my father's name..rather than be lady of this domain. **1864** Trollope *Can you forgive Her?* I. xiv. 108 You are going down to Cheltenham, are you?..I'd sooner it should be you than me; that's all I can say. **1885** Anstey *Tinted Venus* 171 Why, I'd sooner stay in prison all my life! **1905** H. A. Vachell *Hill* iii. 53 Phew-w-w!..I'd sooner it was you than me, Verney. **1937** A. Thirkell *Summer Half* vi. 181 'Good old Mr. Lorimer,' said Swan, 'sooner he than I.' **1973** 'J. Sturrock' *Wicked Way to Die* iii. 35 'Talk to her I must.' He shook his head. 'Sooner you than me.'

**12.** ***the sooner*: a.** the more quickly, speedily, or early.

**1303** R. Brunne *Handl. Synne* 386 But þerof to haue mochyl affyaunce þe may betyde þe sunner a chaunce. **1387** Trevisa *Higden* (Rolls) VII. 121 Bot it be þe sonner opned, it bryngeþ yn deth. *c* **1440** *Generydes* 3101 His entent the souner myght prevayle. *c* **1440** *Gesta Rom.* lxvi. 382 (Add. MS.), That here payne..myght be released the sonyre for his prayere. **1538** Starkey *England* I. i. 26 That your deuyse ..may the sonar optayne hys frute & effect. **1591** Shaks. *1 Hen. VI*, v. i. 15 The sooner to effect, And surer binde this knot of amitie. **1653** in *Verney Memoirs* (1907) I. 461, I rose one hour the sooner. **1719** London & Wise *Compl. Gard.* xxii, Hereby they will the sooner answer the design propos'd. **1831** Scott *Ct. Rob.* iv, The soldiers joyfully mended their pace in order to meet the sooner with the supplies.

**b.** With co-ordinate clause or phrase containing another comparative.

*c* **1375** *Sc. Leg. Saints* xxx. (*Theodora*) 261 Þe sonare þis be done, þe cause sal be þe les. **1387–8** T. Usk *Test. Love* II. xiv. (Skeat) I. 61 Ever the deper thou somtyme wadest, the sonner thou it founde. *c* **1475** *Mankind* 254 in *Macro Plays* 10 Þe sonner þe leuer, & yt be ewyn a-non! **1477** *Paston Lett.* III. 194 The soner the better, in eschewyng of worsse. **1526** *Pilgr. Perf.* (W. de W. 1531) 6 b, The hyer it ascendeth, the sooner it vanyssheth awaye. **1562** Pilkington *Expos. Abdyas* Pref. 9 The faster a man runnes, the sooner he is wery. **1671** Milton *P.R.* III. 179 The happier raign the sooner it begins. **1731** Miller *Gard. Dict.* s.v. *Fagus*, The sooner they are sown the better, after they are fully ripe. **1824** Scott *Pev.* xlvii, The sooner, then, the root feels the axe, the stroke is more welcome. **1837** P. Keith *Bot. Lex.* 169 The sooner a remedy is applied to it the better. **1855** Kingsley *Westw. Ho!* iv, The less said the sooner mended.

**c.** Followed by *as* or *that*.

In quot. 1763 the sense is 'all the more'.

**1763** *Museum Rust.* I. 206 We think..that two pounds at least should be sown, and this the sooner, as it is a cheap seed. **1825** Scott *Talism.* xvii, He shall die, the rather and the sooner that thou dost entreat for him.

**13. a.** ***no sooner,*** not earlier.

**1408** in Rymer *Fœdera* (1709) VIII. 539/1 Aftir the Entree, or the Deth of the forsaid Erle of Douglas,..and no sounere. **1482** *Cely Papers* (Camden) 123 Here was noon passage no sooner, the wynd was so contrary. **1603** Shaks. *Meas. for M.* III. i. 32 For thine owne bowels..Do curse the Gowt..and the Rheume For ending thee no sooner.

**b.** ***no sooner..., but, than,*** or ***when,*** = as soon as; immediately that. (Cf. 5 b.)

(*a*) **1560** Daus tr. *Sleidane's Comm.* 465 b, He had no soner said so, but he was had thence. **1597** Beard *Theatre God's Judgem.* (1612) 146 Which was no sooner in hand, but the chamber began afresh to shake. **1639** Ld. Digby *Lett. conc. Relig.* (1651) 45 St. John no sooner saw him, but he stept back. **1711** Addison *Spect.* No. 123 ⁋5 Florio was no sooner arrived at the great House.., but Eudoxus took him by the Hand. *a* **1774** Goldsm. tr. *Scarron's Com. Romance* (1775) I. 57 She had no sooner made an end of her speech, but she withdrew. **1825** Scott *Talism.* xxi, There has no sooner any one done me good service, but..he cancels his interest in me by some deep injury.

(*b*) **1594** Kyd *Cornelia* II. 76 Like poyson that..No sooner tutcheth then it taints the blood. **1658** Dryden *Stanzas O. Cromwell* xxiii, No sooner was the French-Man's Cause embrac'd, Than the light Monsieur the grave Don outweigh'd. **1723** Dk. Wharton *True Briton* No. 48, But he had no sooner labour'd himself into a tolerable knowledge of the Affairs of it, than he rode triumphant. **1807** Crabbe *Par. Reg.* III. 553 No sooner he began To round and redden, than away he ran. **1850** Browning *Christmas-Eve* xiii, No sooner said than out in the night!

(*c*) **1697** Dryden *Æneid* IX. 143 No sooner had the goddess ceas'd to speak, When, lo! th' obedient ships their halsers break. **1764** Goldsm. *Hist. Eng. in Lett.* (1772) I. 68 No sooner was his back turned, when a new conspiracy was set on foot.

**III.** In the superlative form *soonest*.

**14. a.** Most quickly, readily, etc. Now freq. (orig. *telegraphese*), as soon as possible.

*a* **1225** *Ancr. R.* 392 Al so is..þet crucifix iset ine chirche, ine swuche stude þet me hit sonest iseo. *c* **1380** Wyclif *Wks.*

(1880) 23 For who so may most gold brynge sunnest schal be sped to grete benefices. **1393** LANGL. *P. Pl.* C. XIII. 223 þat þat rapest rypeþ, roteþ most sannest [*v.rr.* sonnest, sennest]. *c* **1400** *Destr. Troy* 1155 So may we sonyst the souerain distrye. *a* **1425** *Cursor M.* 16049 (Trin.), þei biþouȝte hem.. with what þing þei sonnest shulde do him þenne to dye. **1500–20** DUNBAR *Poems* lxvii. 18 Quha maist it servis sall sonast repent. **1584** COGAN *Haven Health* 133 Pertrich of all foules is most soonest digested. **1601** SIR W. CORNWALLIS *Disc. Seneca* (1631) 72 The most profitable and soonest digested knowledge. **1667** MILTON *P.L.* IV. 893 Where thou mightst hope..soonest [to] recompence Dole with delight. **1771** *Encycl. Brit.* III. 616/2 Melt them together for soft solder, which runs soonest. **1777** R. WATSON *Philip II* (1839) 255 Such troops as could be soonest drawn together, were immediately sent off. **1813** SHELLEY *Q. Mab* I. 183 The spirit..may know How soonest to accomplish the great end. **1815** A. CONSTABLE *Let.* 29 Jan. in *J. Constable's Corr.* (1962) I. 113 The picture you request shall be sent per soonest. **1950** C. M. KORNBLUTH in *Mag. of Fantasy & Sci. Fiction* I. 4 They needed a bright and sparkling little news item..'soonest'. **1962** J. HAY in *E. Queen's 16th Mystery Annual* 163 'Bjornsson and whale to proceed soonest to Regensburg and await further orders,' Twentypenny cabled Hawker. **1977** 'E. CRISPIN' *Glimpses of Moon* xiii. 262 Come back to London soonest prepare leave for Libya soonest terrorists blowing up all the oilwells there. **1977** J. DIDION *Book of Common Prayer* II. xiv. 119 I'm getting you together soonest, that's definite.

**b.** Preceded by *the.*

**1471** *Chron. White Rose* (1845) 92 They dispersed..the soonest they could. **1599** SHAKS. *Hen. V,* III. vi. 120 The gentler Gamester is the soonest winner. **1760** R. BROWN *Compl. Farmer* II. 72 It is a grain that will grow in the ear the soonest of any, if wet.

**15.** ***with the soonest***: †**a.** Rather, or very, early. *Obs.* †**b.** As soon as possible. *Obs.* **c.** *dial.* Too soon.

**1542** UDALL *Erasm. Apoph.* 252b, The same Julia begoonne somewhat with the soonest to have whyte heares in hir hedde. *a* **1600** HOOKER *Eccl. Pol.* VII. xiii. §2 His admirable virtues caused him to be bishop with the soonest. **1631** [see SOMETHING *adv.* 2f]. **1662** J. DAVIES tr. *Olearius' Voy. Amb.* 114 That he would, with the soonest, suppress all monopolies. **1709** MRS. MANLEY *Secret Mem.* (1736) II. 179 Then she would be glad to marry him with the soonest. **1828** CARR *Craven Gloss.* s.v., 'Wi't' *soonest,*' too soon.

**16.** ***at (the) soonest***, at the earliest.

**1751** R. PALTOCK *P. Wilkins* (1884) II. 270, I asked him then how long he should be..; he said, 'Three days at soonest'. **1768** WARBURTON in Hurd *Lett.* (1809) 410 At soonest, it will not begin, till after the next long vacation. **1875** JOWETT *Plato* (ed. 2) I. 190 This Dialogue could not have been composed before 390 at the soonest.

**soon** (suːn), *a.* [Attributive use of prec.]

**1.** Taking place, coming about, happening, etc., soon or quickly; early, speedy. Freq. *U.S. dial.* in phr. ***a soon start (in the morning)***.

*a* **1400** *Minor Poems fr. Vernon MS.* xxv. 49 Heil, sone boote þer bale is neih. *a* **1425** tr. *Arderne's Treat. Fistula,* etc. 70, I haue proued þis ful oft tymez for to be most sone helpyng. *a* **1470** *Dives & Pauper* (W. de W. 1496) IX. iv. 352/1 Soone byleuynge of lesynges bryngeth people to moche folye. **1546** LANGLEY tr. *Pol. Verg. de Invent.* II. 105 The olde proverbe is true; that as soone sowing some-time deceaveth, so late sowing is alway naught. **1591** SYLVESTER *Du Bartas* I. vii. 247 His hardned heart Smoothed the passage for their soon-depart. **1621** QUARLES *Div. Poems, Esther* iv, The proiect pleas'd the King, who made an Act To second what was said with soone effect. **1691** T. H[ALE] *Acc. New Invent.* 79 The soon decay I cannot impute to the Lead-sheathing. **1771** LUCKOMBE *Hist. Printing* 350 Having too much wooll in them..will subject them to soon hardening. **1838** HOLLOWAY *Prov. Dict., Soon,*..the soon or early part of the night. **1891** MISS DOWIE *Girl in Karp.* 287 A white mist, thick, in the soon-twilight to be impenetrable. **1913** H. KEPHART *Our Southern Highlanders* xiii. 296 Spell is used in the sense of while..and soon for early ('a soon start in the morning'). **1930** G. B. JOHNSON in B. A. Botkin *Folk-Say* VII. 357 *Soon,* early, quick, alert. 'A soon breakfast', 'a soon man'. **1949** H. HORNSBY *Lonesome Valley* ii. 21 People must have got a soon start, because the place was full up already. **1951** L. CRAIG *Singing Hills* iii. 18 The furrin woman wanted to get a soon start, come morning.

**2.** In comparative: **a.** Earlier; more speedy or expeditious, etc.

*c* **1380** WYCLIF *Sel. Wks.* I. 235 But Crist tolde hem of sounere perils, þat was betere hem to knowe. **1559** *Mirr. Mag.* (1563) D viij, Which that I myght bryng to the sooner ende, To the byshop of Yorke I dyd the mater breake. **1607** in M. H. Peacock *Hist. Wakefield Gram. Sch.* (1892) 67 Unless in the mean tyme..a sooner daie of meetinge be appointed. **1665** J. WEBB *Stone-Heng* (1725) 90 For the sooner Dispatch, and saving of Cost. **1677** PLOT *Oxfordsh.* 110 There are no signs amongst them of sooner or later production. **1771** *Ann. Reg., Chron.* 173/1 From the death, or any sooner determination of the interest therein, of John York, Esq. **1889** STEVENSON *Master Ballantrae* iii, Which would give us safety for the present, and a sooner hope of deliverance.

†**b.** Former, previous. *Obs.*$^{-1}$

**1495** *Trevisa's Barth. De P.R.* XIV. xxxiv. 480 There growe vines and..apples of palmes as token of the sooner [*MS.* raþer] plente.

**3.** In superlative: **a.** Earliest. Also *absol.*

**1591** PARSONS in *Imp. Consid.* (1675) 79 He..cannot..refuse at the soonest opportunity to attempt it. **1631** MASSINGER *Emperor East* I. i, And we, in private, with our soonest leisure Will give them hearing. **1692** BENTLEY *Boyle Lect.* vi. 27 If they think that there may be a Soonest Instant of possible Creation. **1760–72** H. BROOKE *Fool of Qual.* (1809) III. 92, I was therefore up among the soonest.

**b.** Speediest; quickest. Now *dial.*

**1591** *Troub. Raigne K. John* II. (1611) 73 The King entreats your soonest speed To visit him. **1592** KYD *Sp. Trag.* IV. iv. 110 With soonest speed I hasted to the noise. **1606** SHAKS. *Ant. & Cl.* III. iv. 27 Make your soonest hast, So your desires are yours. **1825** JAMIESON *Suppl.* s.v., *The soonest gait,* the nearest road. **1897** in *Eng. Dial. Dict.* s.v., I said that would be [the] safest..or soonest road for us to go.

**soon** (suːn), *sb. rare.* [Substantival use of SOON *a.*] The near future.

**1940** W. FAULKNER *Hamlet* III. i. 166 They are moving not toward a destination in space but a destination in time..; the sleight hand of May shapes them both, not in the immediate, the soon, but in the now.

**soon,** dial. var. of SOUND *sb.* (swoon).

**soond,** dial. f. SOUND *sb.* and *a.*

**soond(e,** obs. varr. SAND *sb.*

**s'oonds,** dial. var. SWOUNDS, ZOUNDS.

Cf. *Gud soons* s.v. GUD.

**1884** *St. James's Gaz.* 20 June 6/1 The farmers [near Ludlow, Shropshire]..use as common exclamations 'Dear Sores' and 'S'oonds'.

**Soonee,** variant of SUNNI.

**sooner**[1] ('suːnə(r)). *U.S. slang.* [f. SOON *adv.*] One who acts prematurely; *esp.* one who endeavoured to get into Government territory in the West before the time appointed for its settlement (chiefly with reference to the settlement of the territory now known as Oklahoma before the official opening of the area to settlers on 22 April 1889). Hence (with capital initial), an Oklahoman. Also *attrib.*; **the Sooner State**, Oklahoma. Hence **'soonerism**, the practice of the unlawful and premature settlement of Oklahoma.

**1890** in *Columbus* (Ohio) *Dispatch* 7 May, Governor Campbell..thinks it altogether too soon to talk of 1892... The Governor is quite right in declining to be regarded as a sooner. **1890** *Congress. Rec.* 17 Jan. 657/2 We have recognized the fact that there are 'sooners' there. **1892** *Law Times* XCIII. 413/1 The settler that gets in surreptitiously..is called a 'Sooner', because he gets there sooner than the rest. **1893** *Philadelphia Daily Inquirer* 21 Aug., The intention and attempt to keep the Sooners off the Cherokee strip..have come to grief. **1894** *Columbus* (Ohio) *Dispatch* 19 Mar., An important case growing out of the 'soonerism' at the Oklahoma opening will be given a hearing. **1904** *N.Y. Even. Post* 13 June 7 White 'sooners'..were trying to rob them [*sc.* Indians] of some of the most valuable mineral deposits on their reservation. **1930** *Sat. Rev. Lit.* (U.S.) 22 Mar. 841/3 She has done excellent reporting, has constructed a ripping yarn, has given us novel incidents, novel characters, a fresh setting, has created a strange new Sooner mythology. **1939** *New Yorker* 14 Oct. 73 Oklahoma uses on its road signs a phrase which I first heard in Kansas and never again except in the Sooner State. **1945** J. L. MARSHALL *Santa Fe* 232 They watched the line through telescopes and, congratulating themselves on their success in checkmating 'Soonerism', figured it would take the first settlers on the fastest horses, about ninety minutes to reach Oklahoma. **1948** *Okla. Cotton Grower* 15 May 2/2 For the Sooner State planter that is perhaps the first major theorem of the business. **1948** [see OKIE]. **1976** *Billings* (Montana) *Gaz.* 30 June 4-E/2 University of Oklahoma quarterback Joe McReynolds was dropped from the Sooners football roster Tuesday.

**sooner**[2]. *slang* (chiefly *Austral.*). [perh. as prec.] An idler, shirker; applied as a term of abuse to an ineffectual or obstructive person, object, etc. Also *attrib.* in ***sooner dog***.

**1892** K. LENTZNER *Dict. Slang-English of Australia* 117 *Sooner,* a weak idler, a lazy good-for-nothing. **1919** E. DYSON *Hello, Soldier!* 31 He slugged a tubby Hun, Then choked a Fritzie with his dukes, 'n' pinched the sooner's gun! **1936** F. CLUNE *Roaming round Darling* xxv. 270 *Onlookers*: Tongue-tied Joe, a sooner dog, a Scotch dog, a dog of all nations, a hungry goat. **1937** PARTRIDGE *Dict. Slang* 801/1 *Sooner dog,* one that would sooner feed than fight. **1948** V. PALMER *Golconda* xix. 159 'The dirty sooners!' he burst out. 'They don't know a man when they find one, those heads down south.' **1969** P. A. SMITH *Folklore of Austral. Railwaymen* 117 This was an old sooner of an engine. She'd had it. On a stiff climb in a tunnel she began to slip.

**Sooney,** obs. form of SUNNI.

**soonish** ('suːnɪʃ), *adv.* Chiefly *colloq.* or *dial.* [f. SOON *adv.* + -ISH.] Somewhat soon.

**1890** S. S. BUCKMAN *John Darke's Sojourn in Cotteswolds & Elsewhere* vii. 58 Good, honest drink..made a man knaow soonish as he wur a-getting nicely forrud. **1894** *N. & Q.* Ser. VIII. V. 143/1 Napoleon seems to have got off soonish from the field.

**'soonly,** *adv.* Also 5 **sonly.** [f. SOON *adv.* + -LY[2].] Soon; quickly; speedily.

In the passage cited by Johnson from H. More the correct reading is *so only* (= if only).

*c* **1475** *Partenay* 4078 By me sonly distroed shall he be. **1654** E. JOHNSON *Wonder-working Provid.* 9 All people, Nations and Languages, who are soonly to submit to Christs Kingdome. **1829** W. TAYLOR *Hist. Surv. Germ. Poet.* II. 70 Hasten, my daughter, she said,..Coffee is soonly enough.

**soonness** ('suːnnɪs). [f. SOON *adv.* + -NESS.] The condition or quality of being soon; speediness, earliness.

**1668** WILKINS *Real Char.* II. xii. §2. 289 The next pair, *soonness* and *lateness,* doth relate to time future. **1727** BAILEY (vol. II), *Earliness,*..soonness in Time. **1864** *N. Brit. Daily Mail* 6 Dec., We went across the Clyde Street ferry, just for soonness. **1869** EADIE *Galatians* Introd. p. xli, What surprised the apostle was the soonness of the defection.

**soons:** see GUD, and cf. S'OONDS.

**soop** (suːp), *v. Sc.* and *north. dial.* Forms: 6 **swowp-, suowp-, swop-, sowp,** 6, 9 **soup,** 6, 9– **soop,** 9 **supe.** [a. ON. *sópa* (Icel. *sópa,* Norw. and Sw. *sopa*), for earlier **swópan,* related to OE. *swápan*: see SWEEP *v.*]

**1.** *trans.* To sweep (a house, etc.).

*c* **1480** [see the *vbl. sb.*]. **1533** BELLENDEN *Livy* III. iii. (S.T.S.) I. 252 The sorowfull moderis fell..to þe ground, sowpand þe templis with þare hare. **1538** LYNDESAY *Supplic. Contempt. Syde Taillis* 30 Quhare euer thay go, it may be sene, How kirk and calsay thay soup clene. **17..** RAMSAY *Wyfe of Auchtermuchty* x, To soup the house he syne began. **1824** SCOTT *St. Ronan's* xxxii, They that had their bread to won wi' ae arm..had mair to do than to soop houses. **1861** E. B. RAMSAY *Remin.* Ser. II. 44, 'I soupit the poupit,' was John's expressive reply.

*absol.* **1862** HISLOP *Prov. Scot.* 136 Let ilka ane soop before their ain door.

**2.** To remove, clear away, by sweeping.

*c* **1480** HENRYSON *Fables, Cock & Jewel* 76 Iowellis ar tynt..apone þe fluyr, & swoppyt furth anone.

**3.** To assist the progress of (a curling-stone) by sweeping the ice in front of it. Also with *up.*

**1805** MCINDOE *Poems* 56 Supe, supe him up, another says. *a* **1822** A. BOSWELL *Poet. Wks.* (1871) 195 Soop the rink, lads, wide enough, The *hog-scores* mak', and mak' ilk *brough.* **1832–53** *Whistle-binkie* Ser. III. 39 He's weel laid on, soop him up, soop him up. **1885** J. STRATHESK *More Bits from Blinkbonny* (ed. 2) xiv. 270 Soop weel when I tell ye. **1891** H. JOHNSTON *Kilmallie* II. 110 The second and third players were 'sooping up', or 'giving heels' to laggard stones. **1963** *Times* 17 Jan. 12/5 Rob Roy's country today echoed not with the war cry of the MacGregors but with strange shouts of 'Yes, yes' and 'Soop, soop' as the great bonspiel of the curling game was staged for only the second time in 37 years.

Hence **'sooping** *vbl. sb.*

*c* **1480** HENRYSON *Fables, Cock & Jewel* 70 He fand a ioly iasp..wes cassyn out in swopyng of þe hous. **1824** SCOTT *St. Ronan's* xxxii, Wi' their sossings and their soopings. **1937** T. HENDERSON *Lockerbie* ix. 57 The ice being keen it required little soopin'. **1976** *Alyn & Deeside Observer* 10 Dec. 5/2 Part of the fun of the game comes in 'sooping'. This is when the players sweep the ice with special brooms in front of a moving stone to help it go further.

**soop,** obs. f. SOUP *sb.*; obs. or dial. var. SUP *sb.*[1] and *v.*[1]; obs. pa. t. SUP *v.*[1]; obs. var. SWOOP.

**sooparee,** variant of SUPARI.

**soope,** obs. var. SUP *sb.*[1] and *v.*, SWOOP *sb.*

**soopie, soopje,** varr. SOPIE.

**soople,** var. SOUPLE *sb.*; dial. var. SUPPLE *a.*

**soopolallie,** var. SOAPOLALLIE.

**soor**[1] (sʊə(r)). *Med.* [Of obscure origin.] A disease of the mouth, = THRUSH[2] 1. Also *attrib.*

**1897** *Allbutt's Syst. Med.* III. 337 Parasitic Stomatitis (Mycotic stomatitis; Thrush, Soor, Muguet). **1905** *Jrnl. Exper. Med.* 4 Feb. 396 The soor fungus appeared in the cultures made from both kidneys.

**soor**[2] (suːə(r)). *Anglo-Indian slang.* [ad. Hindi *sūar* pig, f. Pali *sūkara-,* Prakrit *sūara-, suara-* pig.] A term of abuse for a person: pig, swine.

**1848** J. H. STOCQUELER *Oriental Interpreter,* Soor, soor-ka-butcha, abusive terms of which the Hindostanee language is fertile. *Soor* is a pig, and *soor-ka-butcha* the offspring of a pig. **1864** HOTTEN *Slang Dict.* 240 *Soor,* an abusive term... *Anglo-Indian.* **1919** 'BOYD CABLE' *Old Contemptibles* vi. 92 'Why don't the *soors* come on an' fight it out?' said Corporal Smedley. **1926** *Blackw. Mag.* July 78/1 '*Soors!*' he cursed. 'They won't give me one of their Union Jacks.' **1936** F. RICHARDS *Old-Soldier Sahib* iv. 74 You black soor, when I order you to do a thing I expect it to be done at once.

**soor,** obs. form of SORE *sb.* and *a.*

‖**sooranjee** (sʊə'rændʒiː). Also **-gie.** [ad. Skr. *suraṅgī.*] The root of *Morinda citrifolia*; a dye obtained from this; morindin.

**1848** ANDERSON in *Trans. Roy. Soc. Edin.* (1849) XVI. 438 The colouring matter of sooranjee, to which I give the name of Morindine. **1866** *Treas. Bot.* 286/1 A dye called Soorangie is procured from the root of *Morinda citrifolia.* **1874** CROOKES *Pract. Handbk. Dyeing & Calico-Printing* 392 Cotton..placed in a bath of the ground-up sooranjee.

**soore,** obs. var. SOAR *v.*, SORE *sb., a.,* and *adv.*

**soorma,** variant of SURMA *Anglo-Ind.*

**soort,** obs. f. SORT *sb.*; dial. f. SORT *v.*

‖**'soosy.** ? *Obs.* Also 7 **sussy,** 7–8 **soosey,** 8 **sooza,** 9 **soocey.** [Urdū (Pers.) *sūsī.*] (See quot. 1858.)

**1621** in Foster *Eng. Fact. India* (1906) 338 The 'sussies' are in good forwardness. **1696** OVINGTON *Voy. Suratt* 218 Rich Silks, such as Atlasses, Cuttanees, Sooseys, Culgars. **1724** *Lond. Gaz.* No. 6253/3 A large Parcel of fine Green Teas,..and a few Soozaes. **1725** *Ibid.* No. 6363/2 Pelongs, Ginghams, Sooseys. **1784** in Seton-Karr *Sel. Calcutta Gaz.* (1864) I. 42 Fine cassimeres of different colours; Patna dimty, and striped sooseys. **1858** SIMMONDS *Dict. Trade, Soocey,* a mixed striped fabric of silk and cotton in India.

DOMI MINA
NVS TIO
ILLV MEA